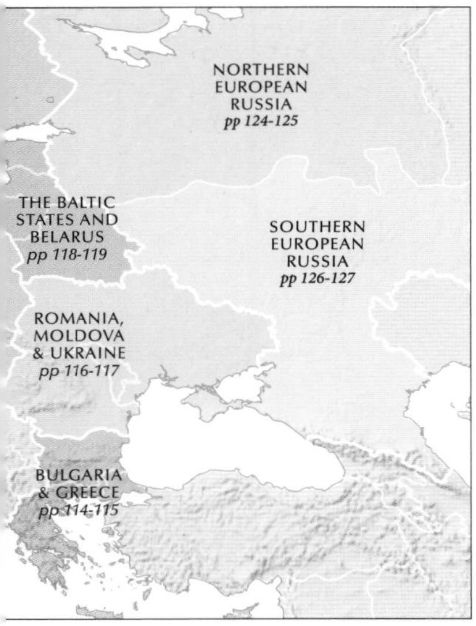
NORTHERN EUROPEAN RUSSIA
pp 124-125
THE BALTIC STATES AND BELARUS
pp 118-119
SOUTHERN EUROPEAN RUSSIA
pp 126-127
ROMANIA, MOLDOVA & UKRAINE
pp 116-117
BULGARIA & GREECE
pp 114-115

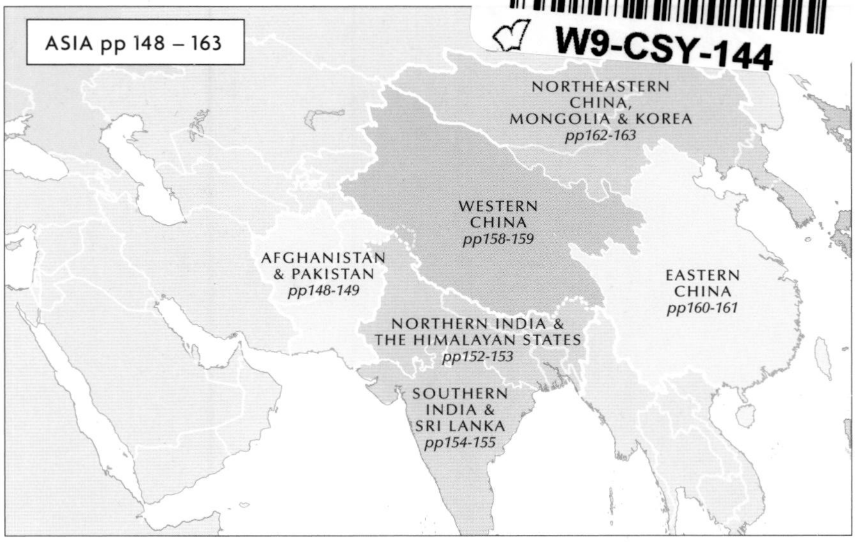
ASIA pp 148 – 163
NORTHEASTERN CHINA, MONGOLIA & KOREA
pp162-163
WESTERN CHINA
pp158-159
AFGHANISTAN & PAKISTAN
pp148-149
EASTERN CHINA
pp160-161
NORTHERN INDIA & THE HIMALAYAN STATES
pp152-153
SOUTHERN INDIA & SRI LANKA
pp154-155

Svalbard
p 92
SCANDINAVIA, FINLAND & ICELAND
pp92-93
THE RUSSIAN FEDERATION
pp122-123
EUROPE
pp 84-127
(also see inset)
KAZAKHSTAN
pp144-145
ASIA
pp 128-173
(also see inset)
TURKEY & THE CAUCASUS
pp136-137
CENTRAL ASIA
pp146-147
JAPAN
pp 164-165
THE MEDITERRANEAN
pp 120-121
Cyprus
p 121
THE NEAR EAST
pp138-139
IRAN & THE GULF STATES
pp142-143
MAINLAND EAST ASIA
pp 156-157
Izu-shoto, Ogasawara-shoto & Kazan-retto
p 165
THE PACIFIC OCEAN
pp 192-193
NORTH AFRICA
pp 74-75
Ryukyu Islands
p 165
Sakishima-shoto
p 165
THE ARABIAN PENINSULA
pp140-141
SOUTH ASIA
pp150-151
Mariana Islands
p 188
Wake Island
p 189
Saipan
p 188
MICRONESIA
pp 188-189
MAINLAND SOUTHEAST ASIA
pp 166-167
Guam
p 188
AFRICA
pp 66-83
Yap
p 188
Chuuk Islands
p 189
Pohnpei
p 189
Marshall Islands
p 189
Babeldaob
p 188
Majuro Atoll
p 189
EAST AFRICA
pp 80-81
Palau
p 188
Micronesia
pp 188-189
Kosrae
p 189
Maldives
p 151
CENTRAL AFRICA
pp 78-79
WESTERN MARITIME SOUTHEAST ASIA
pp 168-169
EASTERN MARITIME SOUTHEAST ASIA
pp 170-171
Nauru
p 189
Tarawa
p 190
Kiribati
p 191
Seychelles
p 172
Tuvalu
p 190
Funafuti Atoll
p 190
Comoro Islands
p 172
THE INDIAN OCEAN
pp 172-173
MELANESIA
pp 186-187
Madagascar
p 172
Mauritius
p 173
Réunion
p 173
AUSTRALASIA & OCEANIA
pp 174-193
SOUTHERN AFRICA
pp 82-83
AUSTRALIA
pp 180-181
SOUTHEAST AUSTRALIA
pp 182-183
NEW ZEALAND
pp 184-185
ANTARCTICA
pp 194-195

WORLD ATLAS

CONCISE

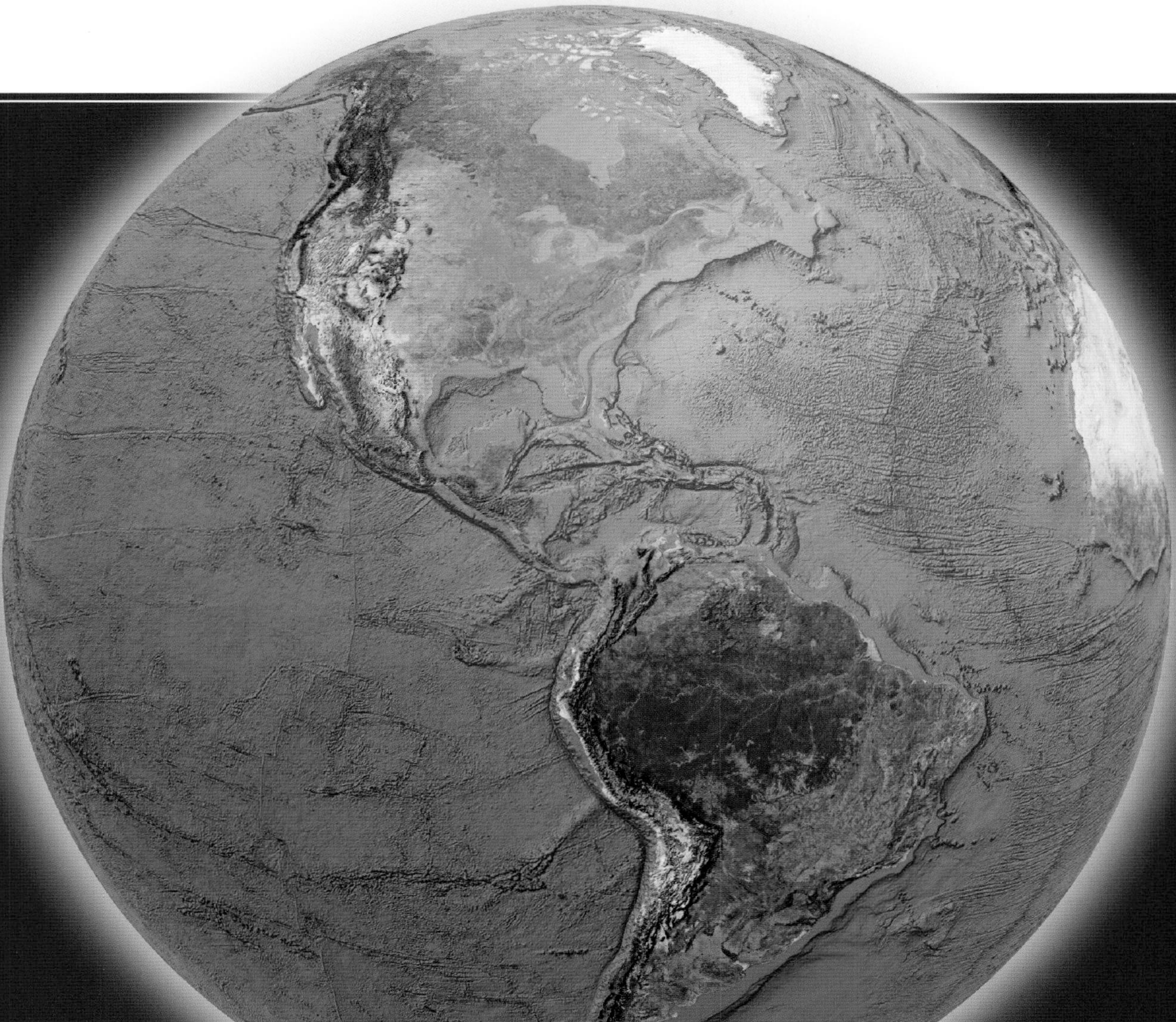

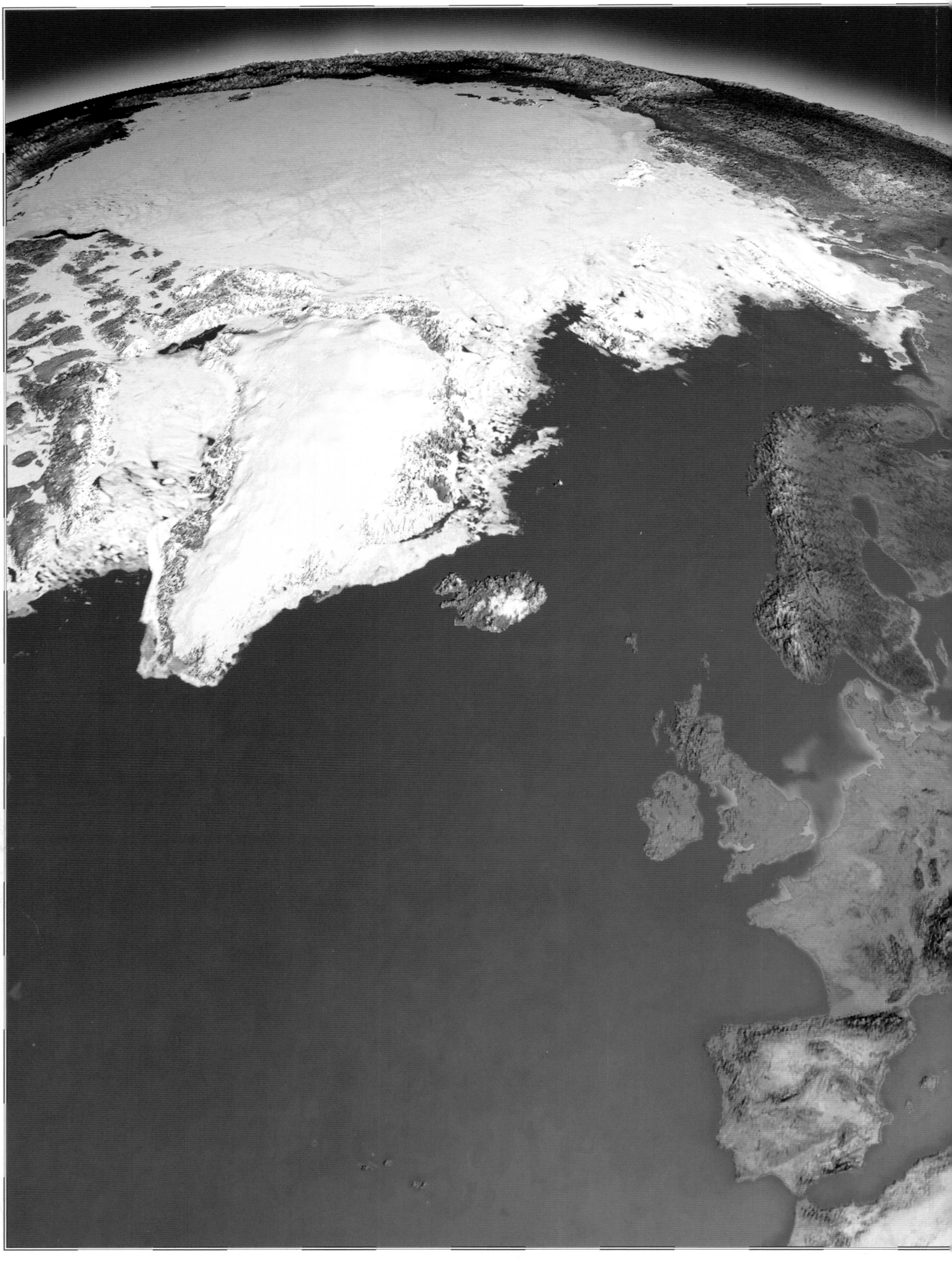

London • New York • Melbourne • Munich • Delhi

WORLD ATLAS

CONCISE

Previously published as *Concise Atlas of the World* and also includes content published in *Reference World Atlas*

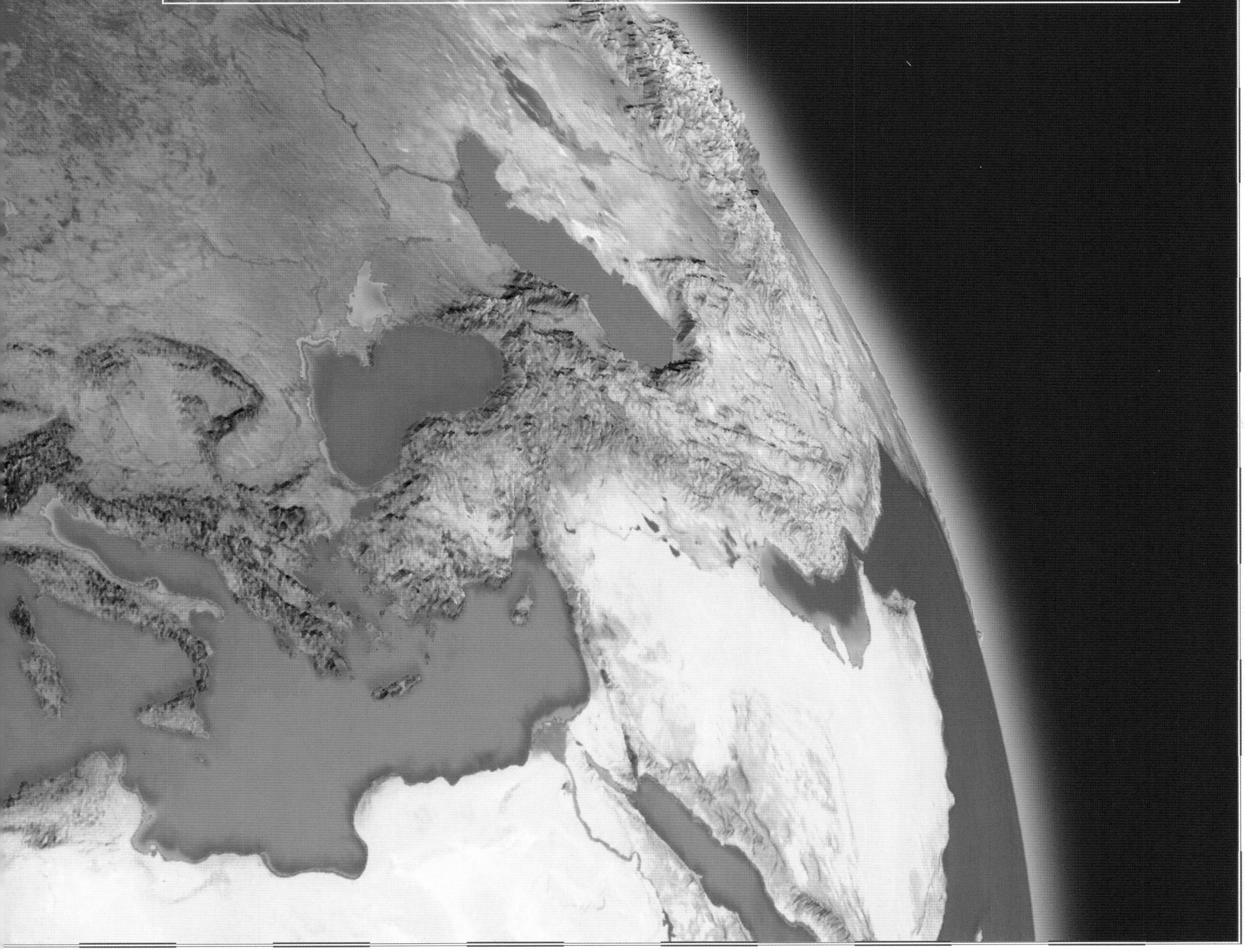

LONDON, NEW YORK, MELBOURNE, MUNICH, DELHI

FOR THE SIXTH EDITION

Publisher Jonathan Metcalf **Art Director** Philip Ormerod **Associate Publisher** Liz Wheeler
Senior Cartographic Editor Simon Mumford **Cartographers** Encompass Graphics Ltd, Brighton, UK **Index database** David Roberts
Jacket Designer Mark Cavanagh **Production Controller** Gemma Sharpe **Production Editor** Rebekah Parsons-King

General Geographical Consultants

Physical Geography Denys Brunsden, Emeritus Professor, Department of Geography, King's College, London
Human Geography Professor J Malcolm Wagstaff, Department of Geography, University of Southampton
Place Names Caroline Burgess, Permanent Committee on Geographical Names, London
Boundaries International Boundaries Research Unit, Mountjoy Research Centre, University of Durham

Digital Mapping Consultants

DK Cartopia developed by George Galfalvi and XMap Ltd, London
Professor Jan-Peter Muller, Department of Photogrammetry and Surveying, University College, London
Cover globes, planets and information on the Solar System provided by Philip Eales and Kevin Tildsley, Planetary Visions Ltd, London

Regional Consultants

North America Dr David Green, Department of Geography, King's College, London • Jim Walsh, Head of Reference, Wessell Library, Tufts University, Medford, Massachussetts
South America Dr David Preston, School of Geography, University of Leeds **Europe** Dr Edward M Yates, formerly of the Department of Geography, King's College, London
Africa Dr Philip Amis, Development Administration Group, University of Birmingham • Dr Ieuan Ll Griffiths, Department of Geography, University of Sussex
Dr Tony Binns, Department of Geography, University of Sussex
Central Asia Dr David Turnock, Department of Geography, University of Leicester **South and East Asia** Dr Jonathan Rigg, Department of Geography, University of Durham
Australasia and Oceania Dr Robert Allison, Department of Geography, University of Durham

Acknowledgments

Digital terrain data created by Eros Data Center, Sioux Falls, South Dakota, USA. Processed by GVS Images Inc, California, USA and Planetary Visions Ltd, London, UK
Cambridge International Reference on Current Affairs (CIRCA), Cambridge, UK • Digitization by Robertson Research International, Swanley, UK • Peter Clark
British Isles maps generated from a dataset supplied by Map Marketing Ltd/European Map Graphics Ltd in combination with DK Cartopia copyright data

DORLING KINDERSLEY CARTOGRAPHY

Editor-in-Chief Andrew Heritage **Managing Cartographer** David Roberts **Senior Cartographic Editor** Roger Bullen
Editorial Direction Louise Cavanagh **Database Manager** Simon Lewis **Art Direction** Chez Picthall

Cartographers
Pamela Alford • James Anderson • Caroline Bowie • Dale Buckton • Tony Chambers • Jan Clark • Bob Croser • Martin Darlison • Damien Demaj • Claire Ellam • Sally Gable
Jeremy Hepworth • Geraldine Horner • Chris Jackson • Christine Johnston • Julia Lunn • Michael Martin • Ed Merritt • James Mills-Hicks • Simon Mumford • John Plumer
John Scott • Ann Stephenson • Gail Townsley • Julie Turner • Sarah Vaughan • Jane Voss • Scott Wallace • Iorwerth Watkins • Bryony Webb • Alan Whitaker • Peter Winfield

Digital Maps Created in DK Cartopia by
Tom Coulson • Thomas Robertshaw
Philip Rowles • Rob Stokes
Managing Editor
Lisa Thomas
Editors
Thomas Heath • Wim Jenkins • Jane Oliver
Siobhan Ryan • Elizabeth Wyse
Editorial Research
Helen Dangerfield • Andrew Rebeiro-Hargrave
Additional Editorial Assistance
Debra Clapson • Robert Damon • Ailsa Heritage
Constance Novis • Jayne Parsons • Chris Whitwell

Placenames Database Team
Natalie Clarkson • Ruth Duxbury • Caroline Falce • John Featherstone • Dan Gardiner
Ciárán Hynes • Margaret Hynes • Helen Rudkin • Margaret Stevenson • Annie Wilson
Senior Managing Art Editor
Philip Lord
Designers
Scott David • Carol Ann Davis • David Douglas • Rhonda Fisher
Karen Gregory • Nicola Liddiard • Paul Williams
Illustrations
Ciárán Hughes • Advanced Illustration, Congleton, UK
Picture Research
Melissa Albany • James Clarke • Anna Lord
Christine Rista • Sarah Moule • Louise Thomas

First American edition, 2001. This revised edition, 2013.

Published in the United States by DK Publishing, 375 Hudson Street, New York, New York 10014

12 13 14 15 16 10 9 8 7 6 5 4 3 2 1

188130 – April 2013

Published in Great Britain by Dorling Kindersley Ltd. A Penguin company.

DK Publishing books are available at special discounts when purchased in bulk for sales promotion, premiums, fundraising, or educational use. For details, contact: DK Publishing Special Markets, 375 Hudson Street, New York, New York 10014 or specialsales@dk.com

A catalog record for this book is avaiable from the Library of Congress

ISBN 978-1-4654-0227-1

Printed and bound in Hong Kong by Hung Hing.

Discover more at **www.dk.com**

Introduction

EVERYTHING YOU NEED TO KNOW ABOUT OUR PLANET TODAY

For many, the outstanding legacy of the twentieth century was the way in which the Earth shrank. In the third millennium, it is increasingly important for us to have a clear vision of the world in which we live. The human population has increased fourfold since 1900. The last scraps of *terra incognita*—the polar regions and ocean depths—have been penetrated and mapped. New regions have been colonized and previously hostile realms claimed for habitation. The growth of air transportation and mass tourism allows many of us to travel further, faster, and more frequently than ever before. In doing so we are given a bird's-eye view of the Earth's surface denied to our forebears.

At the same time, the amount of information about our world has grown enormously. Our multimedia environment hurls uninterrupted streams of data at us, on the printed page, through the airwaves, and across our television, computer, and phone screens; events from all corners of the globe reach us instantaneously and are witnessed as they unfold. Our sense of stability and certainty has been eroded; instead, we are aware that the world is in a constant state of flux and change. Natural disasters, man-made cataclysms, and conflicts between nations remind us daily of the enormity and fragility of our domain. The ongoing threat of international terrorism throws into very stark relief the difficulties that arise when trying to "know" or "understand" our planet and its many cultures.

The current crisis in our "global" culture has made the need greater than ever before for everyone to possess an atlas. DK's **CONCISE** WORLD **ATLAS** has been conceived to meet this need. At its core, like all atlases, it seeks to define where places are located, to describe their main characteristics, and to map them in relation to other places. Every attempt has been made to produce information and maps that are as clear, accurate, and accessible as possible using the latest digital cartographic techniques. In addition, each page of the atlas provides a wealth of further information, bringing the maps to life. Using photographs, diagrams, at-a-glance maps, introductory texts, and captions, the atlas builds up a detailed portrait of those features—cultural, political, economic, and geomorphological—that make each region unique, and which are also the main agents of change.

This sixth edition of the **CONCISE** WORLD **ATLAS** incorporates hundreds of revisions and updates affecting every map and every page, distilling the burgeoning mass of information available through modern technology into an extraordinarily detailed and reliable view of our world.

CONTENTS

Introduction v

Contents .... vi–vii

How to use this Atlas .... viii–ix

THE WORLD

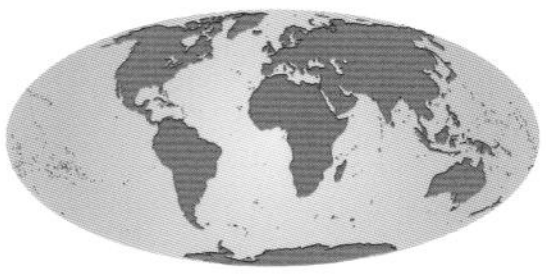

The solar system .... x–xi

The physical world .... xii–xiii

Structure of the Earth .... xiv–xv

Shaping the landscape .... xvi–xvii

The world's oceans .... xviii–xix

The global climate .... xx–xxi

Life on Earth .... xxii–xxiii

Population and settlement .... xxiv–xxv

The economic system .... xxvi–xxvii

The political world .... xxviii–xxix

States and boundaries .... xxx–xxxi

International disputes xxxii

ATLAS OF THE WORLD

North America

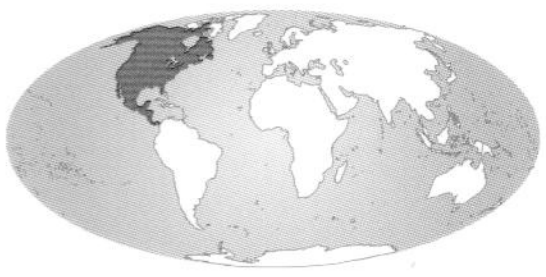

NORTH AMERICA 1

PHYSICAL NORTH AMERICA 2–3

POLITICAL NORTH AMERICA 4–5

NORTH AMERICAN RESOURCES 6–7

Canada 8–9

Canada: Western Provinces 10–11
Alberta, British Columbia, Manitoba, Saskatchewan, Yukon

Canada: Eastern Provinces 12–13
New Brunswick, Newfoundland & Labrador, Nova Scotia, Ontario, Prince Edward Island, Québec, St Pierre & Miquelon

Southeastern Canada 14–15
Southern Ontario, Southern Québec

United States of America 16–17

USA: Northeastern States 18–19
Connecticut, Maine, Massachussetts, New Hampshire, New Jersey, New York, Pennsylvania, Rhode Island, Vermont

USA: Mid-Eastern States 20–21
Delaware, District of Columbia, Kentucky, Maryland, North Carolina, South Carolina, Tennessee, Virginia, West Virginia

USA: Southern States 22–23
Alabama, Florida, Georgia, Louisiana, Mississippi

USA: Texas 24–25

USA: South Midwestern States 26–27
Arkansas, Kansas, Missouri, Oklahoma

USA: Upper Plains States 28–29
Iowa, Minnesota, Nebraska, North Dakota, South Dakota

USA: Great Lakes States 30–31
Illinois, Indiana, Michigan, Ohio, Wisconsin

USA: North Mountain States 32–33
Idaho, Montana, Oregon, Washington, Wyoming

USA: California & Nevada 34–35

USA: South Mountain States 36–37
Arizona, Colorado, New Mexico, Utah

USA: Hawaii & Alaska 38–39

Mexico 40–41

Central America 42–43
Belize, Costa Rica, El Salvador, Guatemala, Honduras, Nicaragua, Panama

The Caribbean 44–45
Anguilla, Antigua & Barbuda, Aruba, Bahamas, Barbados, Bonaire, British Virgin Islands, Cayman Islands, Cuba, Curaçao, Dominica, Dominican Republic, Grenada, Guadeloupe, Haiti, Jamaica, Martinique, Montserrat, Navassa Island, Puerto Rico, St Kitts & Nevis, St Lucia, St Vincent & the Grenadines, Sint Maarten, Trinidad & Tobago, Turks & Caicos Islands, Virgin Islands (US)

South America

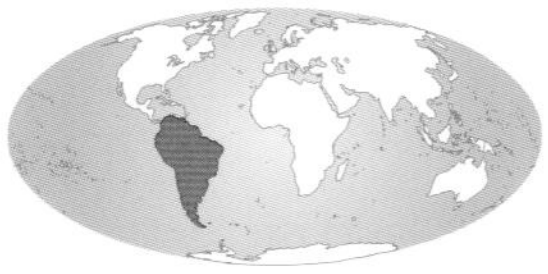

SOUTH AMERICA 46–47

PHYSICAL SOUTH AMERICA 48–49

POLITICAL SOUTH AMERICA 50–51

SOUTH AMERICAN RESOURCES 52–53

Northern South America 54–55
Colombia, French Guiana, Guyana, Suriname, Venezuela

Western South America 56–57
Bolivia, Ecuador, Peru

Brazil 58–59

Eastern South America 60–61
Southeast Brazil, Northeast Argentina, Uruguay

Southern South America 62–63
Argentina, Chile, Paraguay

The Atlantic Ocean 64–65

Africa

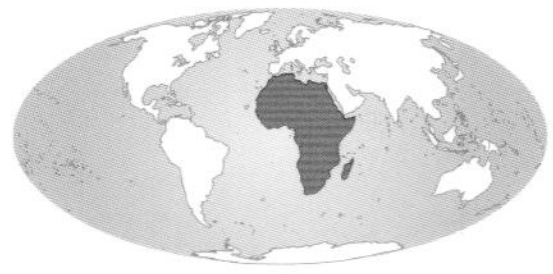

AFRICA 66–67

PHYSICAL AFRICA 68–69

POLITICAL AFRICA 70–71

AFRICAN RESOURCES 72–73

North Africa 74–75
Algeria, Egypt, Libya, Morocco, Tunisia, Western Sahara

West Africa 76–77
Benin, Burkina, Cape Verde, Gambia, Ghana, Guinea, Guinea-Bissau, Ivory Coast, Liberia, Mali, Mauritania, Niger, Nigeria, Senegal, Sierra Leone, Togo

Central Africa 78–79
Cameroon, Central African Republic, Chad, Congo, Dem. Rep. Congo, Equatorial Guinea, Gabon, Sao Tome & Principe

East Africa 80–81
Burundi, Djibouti, Eritrea, Ethiopia, Kenya, Rwanda, Somalia, South Sudan, Sudan, Tanzania, Uganda

Southern Africa 82–83
Angola, Botswana, Lesotho, Malawi, Mozambique, Namibia, South Africa, Swaziland, Zambia, Zimbabwe

Europe

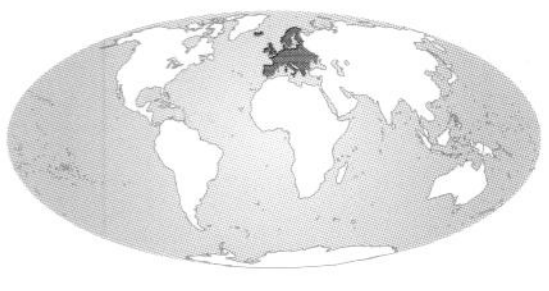

EUROPE 84–85

PHYSICAL EUROPE 86–87

POLITICAL EUROPE 88–89

EUROPEAN RESOURCES 90–91

Scandinavia, Finland & Iceland 92–93
Denmark, Finland, Iceland, Norway, Svalbard, Sweden

Southern Scandinavia 94–95
Denmark, Faeroe Islands, Southern Norway, Southern Sweden

The British Isles 96–97
Channel Islands, Ireland, Isle of Man, United Kingdom

The Low Countries 98–99
Belgium, Luxembourg, Netherlands

Germany 100–101

France 102–103
France, Monaco

The Iberian Peninsula 104–105
Andorra, Gibraltar, Portugal, Spain

The Italian Peninsula 106–107
Italy, San Marino, Vatican City

The Alpine States 108–109
Austria, Liechtenstein, Slovenia, Switzerland

Central Europe 110–111
Czech Republic, Hungary, Poland, Slovakia

Southeast Europe 112–113
Albania, Bosnia & Herzegovina, Croatia, Kosovo, Macedonia, Montenegro, Serbia

Bulgaria & Greece 114–115
(including European Turkey)

Romania, Moldova & Ukraine 116–117

The Baltic States & Belarus 118–119
Belarus, Estonia, Latvia, Lithuania, Kaliningrad

The Mediterranean 120–121

The Russian Federation 122–123

Northern European Russia 124–125

Southern European Russia 126–127

Asia

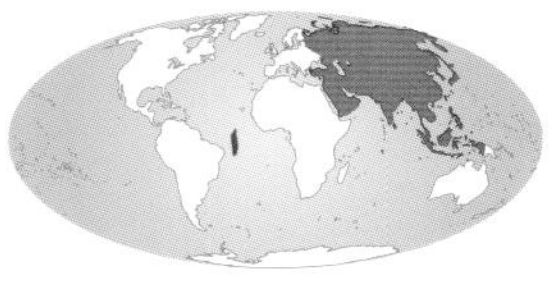

ASIA 128–129

PHYSICAL ASIA 130–131

POLITICAL ASIA 132–133

ASIAN RESOURCES 134–135

Turkey & the Caucasus 136–137
Armenia, Azerbaijan, Georgia, Turkey

The Near East 138–139
Iraq, Israel, Jordan, Lebanon, Syria

The Arabian Peninsula 140–141
Bahrain, Kuwait, Oman, Qatar, Saudi Arabia, United Arab Emirates, Yemen

Iran & the Gulf States 142–143
Bahrain, Iran, Kuwait, Qatar, United Arab Emirates

Kazakhstan 144–145

Central Asia 146–147
Kyrgyzstan, Tajikistan, Turkmenistan, Uzbekistan

Afghanistan & Pakistan 148–149

South Asia 150–151
Bangladesh, Bhutan, India, Maldives, Nepal, Pakistan, Sri Lanka

Northern India & the Himalayan States 152–153
Bangladesh, Bhutan, Nepal, Northern India

Southern India & Sri Lanka 154–155

Mainland East Asia 156–157
China, Mongolia, North Korea, South Korea, Taiwan

Western China 158–159

Eastern China 160–161
Eastern China, Taiwan

Northeastern China, Mongolia & Korea 162–163
Mongolia, Northeastern China, North Korea, South Korea

Japan 164–165

Mainland Southeast Asia 166–167
Cambodia, Laos, Myanmar, Paracel Islands, Thailand, Vietnam

West Maritime Southeast Asia 168–169
Brunei, Indonesia, Malaysia, Singapore

East Maritime Southeast Asia 170–171
East Timor, Indonesia, Philippines

The Indian Ocean 172–173

Australasia & Oceania

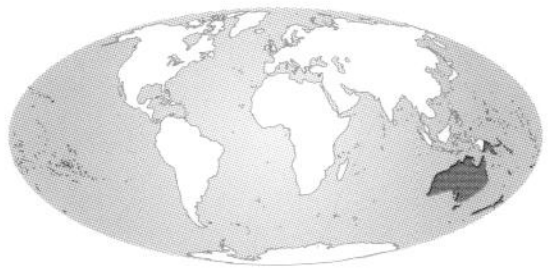

AUSTRALASIA & OCEANIA 174–175

POLITICAL AUSTRALASIA & OCEANIA 176–177

AUSTRALASIAN & OCEANIAN RESOURCES 178–179

Australia 180–181

Southeast Australia 182–183
New South Wales, South Australia, Tasmania, Victoria

New Zealand 184–185

Melanesia 186–187
Fiji, New Caledonia, Papua New Guinea, Solomon Islands, Vanuatu

Micronesia 188–189
Guam, Marshall Islands, Micronesia, Nauru, Northern Mariana Islands, Palau, Wake Island

Polynesia 190–191
Cook Islands, Easter Island, French Polynesia, Kiribati, Niue, Pitcairn Islands, Tokelau, Tuvalu, Wallis & Futuna

The Pacific Ocean 192–193

Antarctica 194–195

The Arctic 196–197

INDEX–GAZETTEER

Geographical comparisons 198–199

Countries of the world including The time zones 200–207

Geographical glossary 208–210

Geographical names 211

Index 212–349

Acknowledgements 350

Key to maps

Regional

Physical features

elevation

- 6000m / 19,686ft
- 4000m / 13,124ft
- 3000m / 9843ft
- 2000m / 6562ft
- 1000m / 3281ft
- 500m / 1640ft
- 250m / 820ft
- 100m / 328ft
- sea level
- below sea level

- elevation above sea level (mountain height)
- volcano
- pass
- elevation below sea level (depression depth)

- sand desert
- lava flow
- coastline
- reef
- atoll

sea depth

- sea level
- -250m / -820ft
- -500m / -1640ft
- -1000m / -3281ft
- -2000m / -6562ft
- -3000m / -9843ft

- seamount / guyot symbol
- undersea spot depth

Drainage features

- main river
- secondary river
- tertiary river
- minor river
- main seasonal river
- secondary seasonal river
- canal
- waterfall
- rapids
- dam
- perennial lake
- seasonal lake
- perennial salt lake
- seasonal salt lake
- reservoir
- salt flat / salt pan
- marsh / salt marsh
- mangrove
- wadi
- spring / well / waterhole / oasis

Ice features

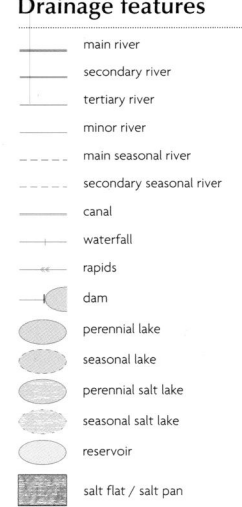

- ice cap / sheet
- ice shelf
- glacier / snowfield
- summer pack ice limit
- winter pack ice limit

Communications

- motorway / highway
- motorway / highway (under construction)
- major road
- minor road
- tunnel (road)
- main railroad
- minor railroad
- tunnel (railroad)
- international airport

Borders

- full international border
- undefined international border
- disputed de facto border
- disputed territorial claim border
- indication of country extent (Pacific only)
- indication of dependent territory extent (Pacific only)
- demarcation/ cease fire line
- autonomous / federal region border
- other 1st order internal administrative border
- 2nd order internal administrative border

Settlements

- built up area

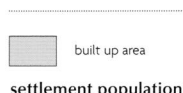

settlement population symbols

- more than 5 million
- 1 million to 5 million
- 500,000 to 1 million
- 100,000 to 500,000
- 50,000 to 100,000
- 10,000 to 50,000
- fewer than 10,000
- country/dependent territory capital city
- autonomous / federal region / other 1st order internal administrative center
- 2nd order internal administrative center

Miscellaneous features

- ancient wall
- site of interest
- scientific station

Graticule features

- lines of latitude and longitude / Equator
- Tropics / Polar circles
- 45° degrees of longitude / latitude

Typographic key

Physical features

landscape features ...	*Namib Desert*
	Massif Central
	ANDES
headland	*Nordkapp*
elevation / volcano / pass	Mount Meru 4556 m
drainage features	*Lake Geneva*
rivers / canals spring / well / waterhole / oasis / waterfall / rapids / dam	*Mekong*
ice features	*Vatnajökull*
sea features..........	*Golfe de Lion*
	Andaman Sea
	INDIAN OCEAN
undersea features ...	*Barracuda Fracture Zone*

Regions

country	ARMENIA
dependent territory with parent state	NIUE (to NZ)
region outside feature area	ANGOLA
autonomous / federal region	MINAS GERAIS
other 1st order internal administrative region	MINSKAYA VOBLASTS'
2nd order internal administrative region	Vaucluse
cultural region	New England

Settlements

capital city	BEIJING
dependent territory capital city	FORT-DE-FRANCE
other settlements ···	Chicago
	Adana
	Tizi Ozou
	Yonezawa
	Farnham

Miscellaneous

sites of interest / miscellaneous	Valley of the Kings
Tropics / Polar circles	*Antarctic Circle*

How to use this Atlas

The atlas is organized by continent, moving eastward from the International Date Line. The opening section describes the world's structure, systems, and its main features. The Atlas of the World which follows, is a continent-by-continent guide to today's world, starting with a comprehensive insight into the physical, political, and economic structure of each continent, followed by integrated mapping and descriptions of each region or country.

The world

The introductory section of the Atlas deals with every aspect of the planet, from physical structure to human geography, providing an overall picture of the world we live in. Complex topics such as the landscape of the Earth, climate, oceans, population, and economic patterns are clearly explained with the aid of maps and diagrams drawn from the latest information.

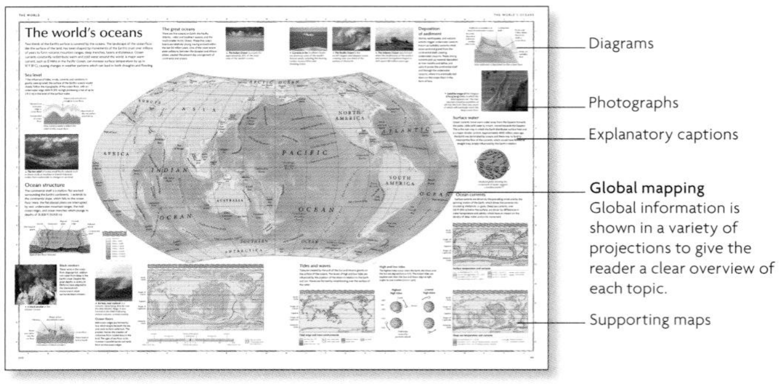
The world's oceans
Diagrams
Photographs
Explanatory captions
Global mapping
Global information is shown in a variety of projections to give the reader a clear overview of each topic.
Supporting maps

The political continent

The political portrait of the continent is a vital reference point for every continental section, showing the position of countries relative to one another, and the relationship between human settlement and geographic location. The complex mosaic of languages spoken in each continent is mapped, as is the effect of communications networks on the pattern of settlement.

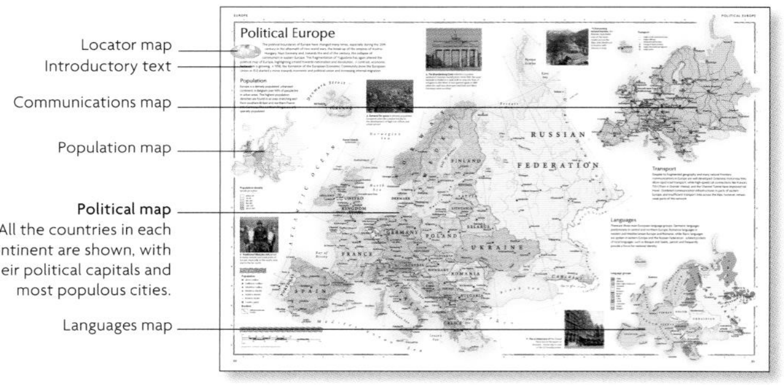
Political Europe
Locator map
Introductory text
Communications map
Population map
Political map
All the countries in each continent are shown, with their political capitals and most populous cities.
Languages map

Continental resources

The Earth's rich natural resources, including oil, gas, minerals, and fertile land, have played a key role in the development of society. These pages show the location of minerals and agricultural resources on each continent, and how they have been instrumental in dictating industrial growth and the varieties of economic activity across the continent.

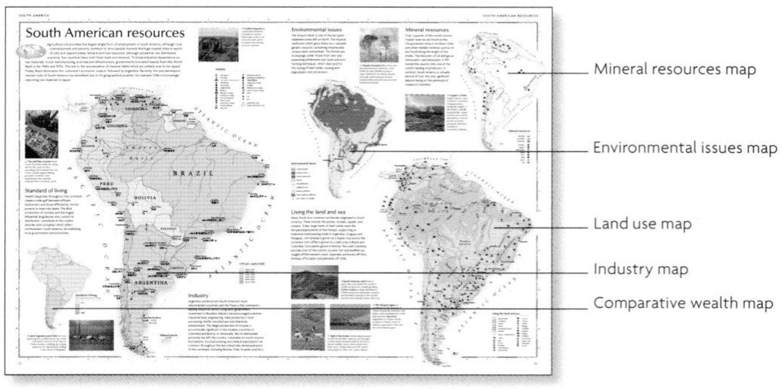
South American resources
Mineral resources map
Environmental issues map
Land use map
Industry map
Comparative wealth map

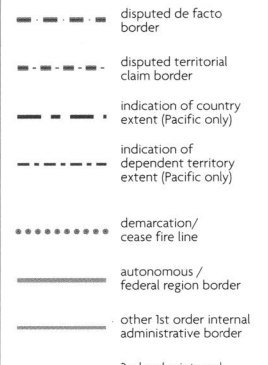

The physical continent

The astonishing variety of landforms, and the dramatic forces that created and continue to shape the landscape, are explained in the continental physical spread. Cross-sections, illustrations, and terrain maps highlight the different parts of the continent, showing how nature's forces have produced the landscapes we see today.

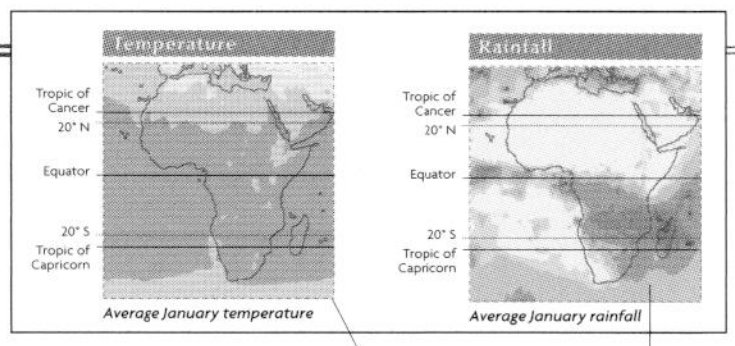
Temperature
Rainfall
Tropic of Cancer
20° N
Equator
20° S
Tropic of Capricorn
Average January temperature
Average January rainfall

Climate charts
Rainfall and temperature charts clearly show the continental patterns of rainfall and temperature.

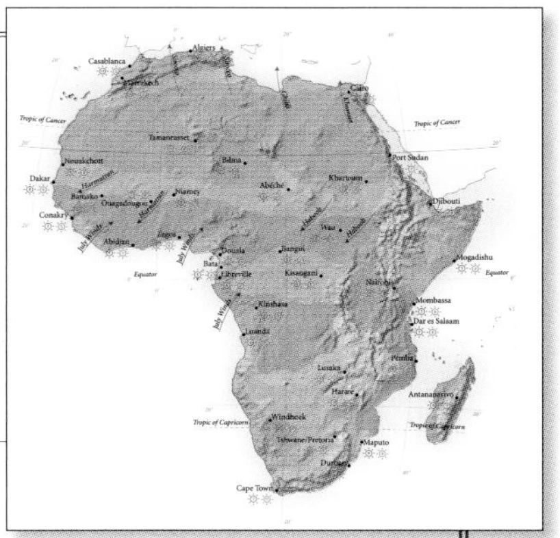

Climate map
Climatic regions vary across each continent. The map displays the differing climatic regions, as well as daily hours of sunshine at selected weather stations.

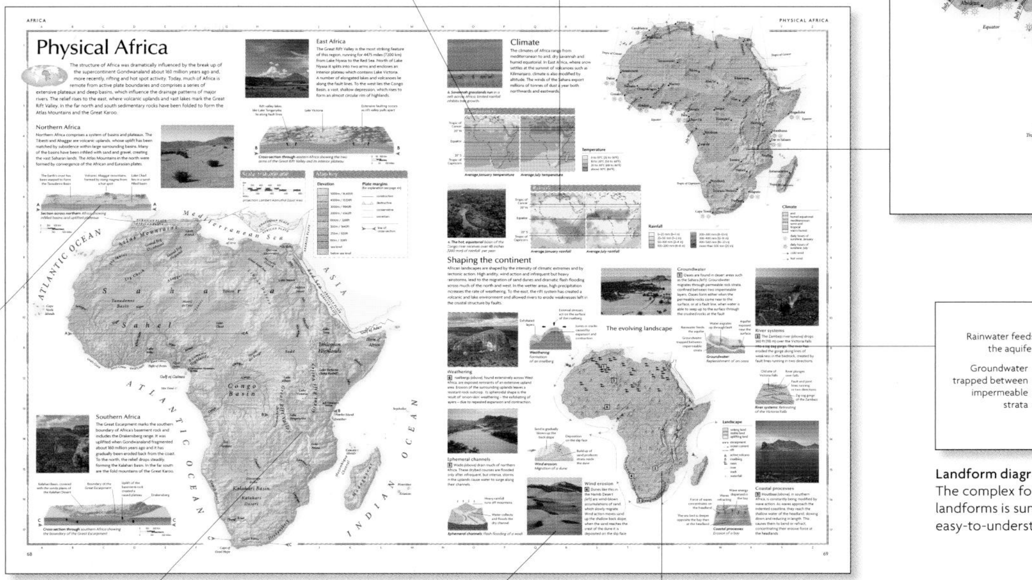
Physical Africa

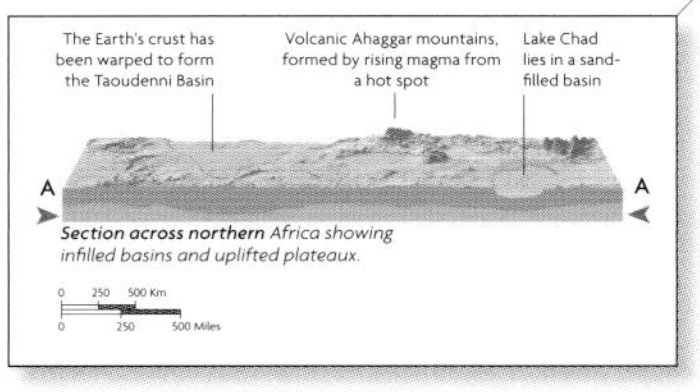
The Earth's crust has been warped to form the Taoudenni Basin
Volcanic Ahaggar mountains, formed by rising magma from a hot spot
Lake Chad lies in a sand-filled basin
A
A
Section across northern Africa showing infilled basins and uplifted plateaux.

Cross-sections
Detailed cross-sections through selected parts of the continent show the underlying geomorphic structure.

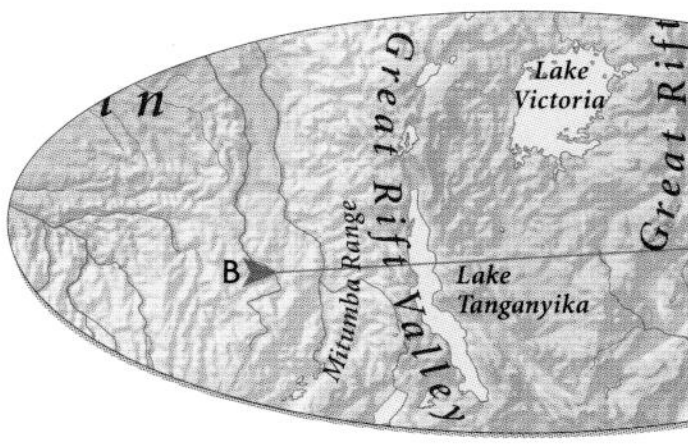
Lake Victoria
Great Rift Valley
Great Rift
Kilimanjaro 5895m
Mitumba Range
Lake Tanganyika
B
B
Pemba Island
Zanzibar

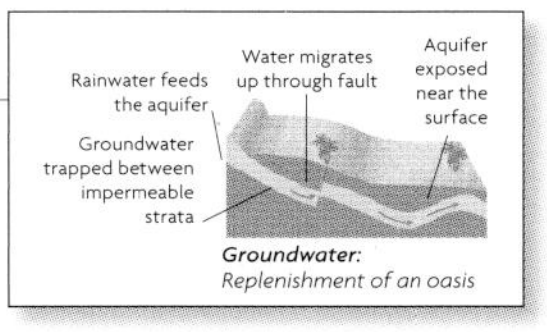
Rainwater feeds the aquifer
Water migrates up through fault
Aquifer exposed near the surface
Groundwater trapped between impermeable strata
Groundwater: Replenishment of an oasis

Landform diagrams
The complex formation of many typical landforms is summarized in these easy-to-understand illustrations.

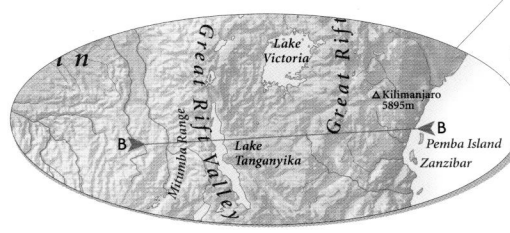

Main physical map
Detailed satellite data has been used to create an accurate and visually striking picture of the surface of the continent.

Photographs
A wide range of beautiful photographs bring the world's regions to life.

Landscape evolution map
The physical shape of each continent is affected by a variety of forces which continually sculpt and modify the landscape. This map shows the major processes which affect different parts of the continent.

Key to transportation symbols
❶ Extent of national paved road network.
❷ Extent of motorways, freeways, or major national highways.
❸ Extent of commercial railroad network.
❹ Extent of inland waterways navigable by commercial craft.

Regional mapping

The main body of the Atlas is a unique regional map set, with detailed information on the terrain, the human geography of the region, and its infrastructure. Around the edge of the map, additional "at-a-glance" maps, give an instant picture of regional industry, land use, and agriculture. The detailed terrain map (shown in perspective), focuses on the main physical features of the region, and is enhanced by annotated illustrations, and photographs of the physical structure.

Transportation network

❶	340,090 miles (544,144 km)	❷	4813 miles (7700 km)
❸	12,872 miles (20,592 km)	❹	2108 miles (3389 km)

New York's commercial success is tied historically to its transportation connections. The Erie Canal, completed in 1825, opened up the Great Lakes and the interior to New York's markets and carried a stream of immigrants into the Midwest.

Transportation network
The differing extent of the transportation network for each region is shown here, along with key facts about the transportation system.

Regional Locator
This small map shows the location of each country in relation to its continent.

Key to main map
A key to the population symbols and land heights accompanies the main map.

World locator
This locates the continent in which the region is found on a small world map.

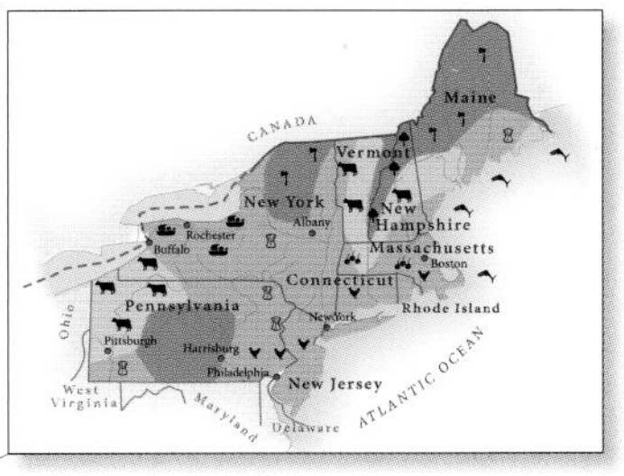
CANADA
Maine
Vermont
New Hampshire
New York
Albany
Rochester
Buffalo
Massachusetts
Boston
Connecticut
Rhode Island
Pennsylvania
Pittsburgh
Harrisburg
Philadelphia
New Jersey
Ohio
West Virginia
Maryland
Delaware
ATLANTIC OCEAN

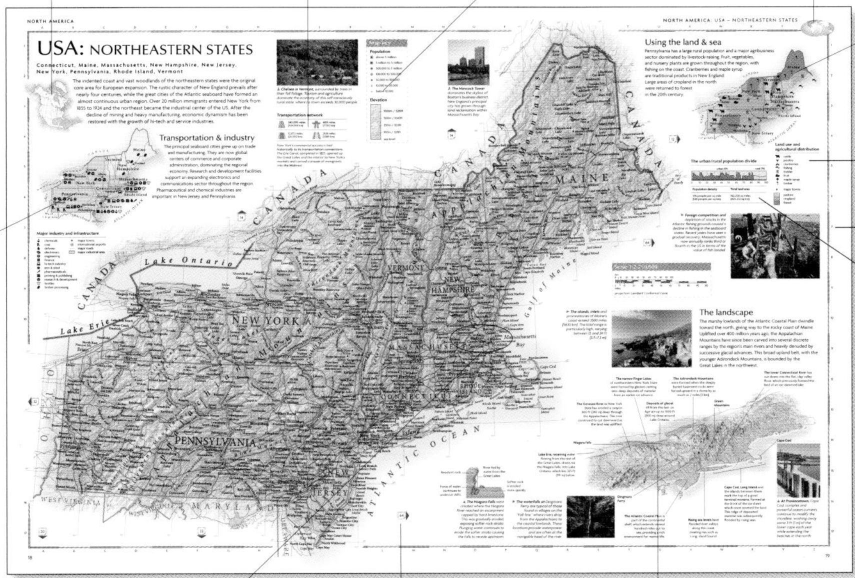
USA: NORTHEASTERN STATES

Land use map
This shows the different types of land use which characterize the region, as well as indicating the principal agricultural activities.

Map keys
Each supporting map has its own key.

Grid reference
The framing grid provides a location reference for each place listed in the Index.

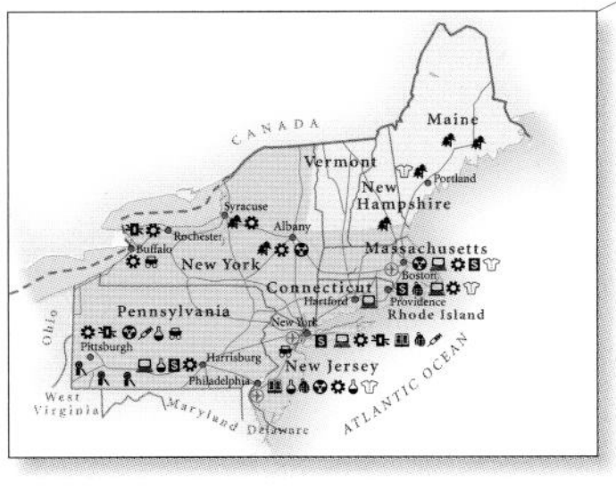
CANADA
Maine
Portland
Vermont
New Hampshire
Syracuse
Albany
Rochester
Buffalo
New York
Massachusetts
Boston
Connecticut
Hartford
Providence
Rhode Island
Pennsylvania
Pittsburgh
Harrisburg
Philadelphia
New Jersey
Ohio
West Virginia
Maryland
Delaware
ATLANTIC OCEAN

Transportation and industry map
The main industrial areas are mapped, and the most important industrial and economic activities of the region are shown .

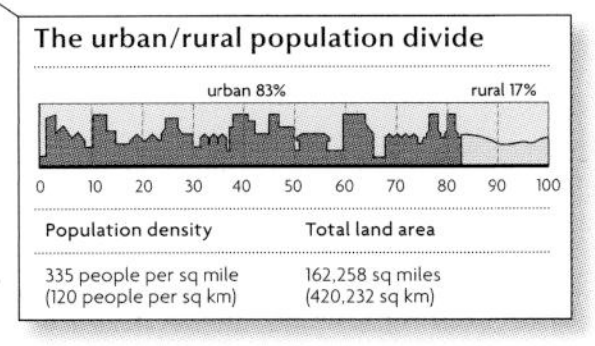
The urban/rural population divide
urban 83%
rural 17%
0 10 20 30 40 50 60 70 80 90 100
Population density
Total land area
335 people per sq mile (120 people per sq km)
162,258 sq miles (420,232 sq km)

Urban/rural population divide
The proportion of people in the region who live in urban and rural areas, as well as the overall population density and land area are clearly shown in these simple graphics.

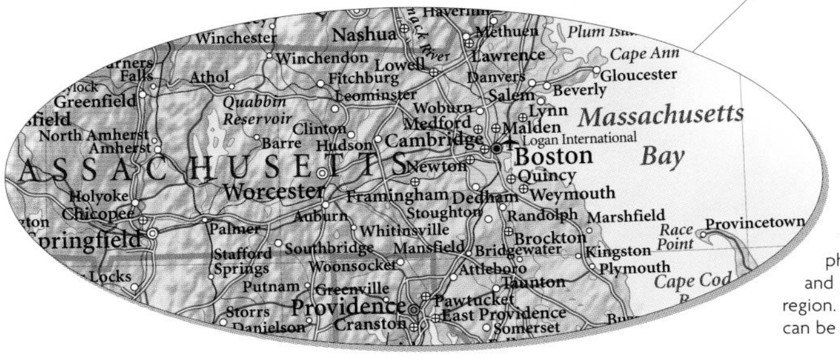
Winchester
Nashua
Methuen
Lawrence
Cape Ann
Gloucester
Athol
Fitchburg
Lowell
Danvers
Beverly
Greenfield
Quabbin Reservoir
Leominster
Salem
Woburn
Lynn
Medford
Malden
Massachusetts Bay
North Amherst
Amherst
Clinton
Barre
Hudson
Cambridge
Logan International
Boston
Quincy
Newton
Weymouth
Worcester
Framingham
Dedham
Holyoke
Chicopee
Springfield
Auburn
Stoughton
Randolph
Marshfield
Palmer
Whitinsville
Brockton
Race Point
Provincetown
Stafford Springs
Southbridge
Woonsocket
Mansfield
Bridgewater
Kingston
Plymouth
Locks
Attleboro
Taunton
Cape Cod
Putnam
Greenville
Pawtucket
Providence
East Providence
Storrs
Danielson
Cranston
Somerset

Continuation symbols
These symbols indicate where adjacent maps can be found.

Main regional map
A wealth of information is displayed on the main map, building up a rich portrait of the interaction between the physical landscape and the human and political geography of each region. The key to the regional maps can be found on page viii.

Landscape map
The computer-generated terrain model accurately portrays an oblique view of the landscape. Annotations highlight the most important geographic features of the region.

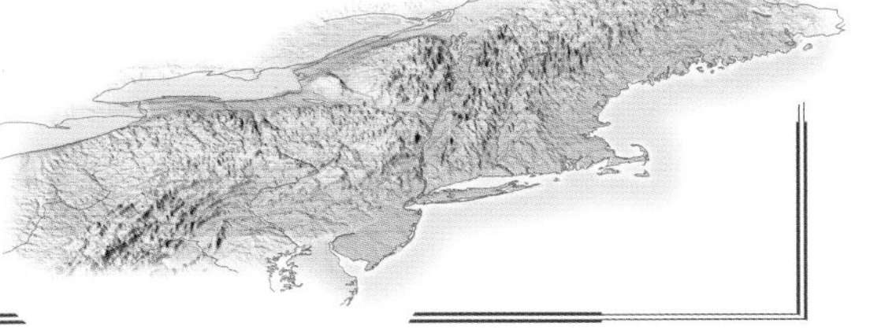

The Solar System

Nine major planets, their satellites, and countless minor planets (asteroids) orbit the Sun to form the Solar System. The Sun, our nearest star, creates energy from nuclear reactions deep within its interior, providing all the light and heat which make life on Earth possible. The Earth is unique in the Solar System in that it supports life: its size, gravitational pull and distance from the Sun have all created the optimum conditions for the evolution of life. The planetary images seen here are composites derived from actual spacecraft images (not shown to scale).

Orbits

All the Solar System's planets and dwarf planets orbit the Sun in the same direction and (apart from Pluto) roughly in the same plane. All the orbits have the shapes of ellipses (stretched circles). However, in most cases, these ellipses are close to being circular: only Pluto and Eris have very elliptical orbits. Orbital period (the time it takes an object to orbit the Sun) increases with distance from the Sun. The more remote objects not only have further to travel with each orbit, they also move more slowly.

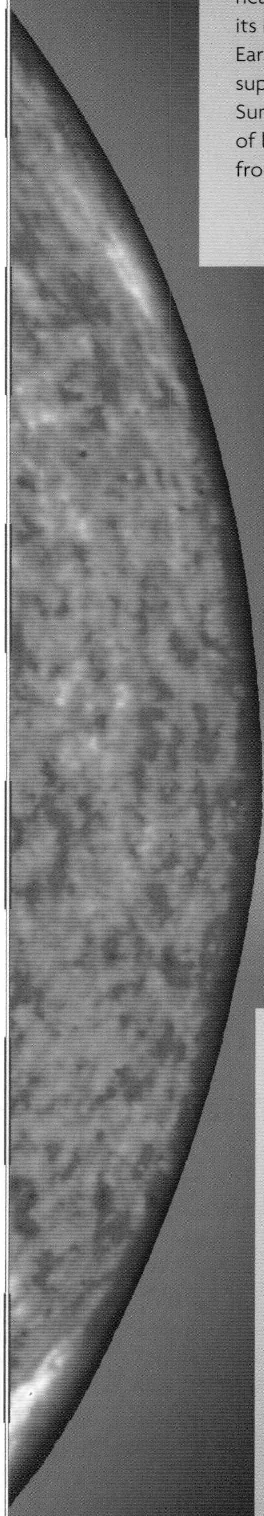

Ceres
(dwarf planet)
Mercury
Venus
Earth
Mars
Jupiter

The Sun

⊖ ***Diameter:*** *864,948 miles (1,392,000 km)*
● ***Mass:*** *1990 million million million million tons*

The Sun was formed when a swirling cloud of dust and gas contracted, pulling matter into its center. When the temperature at the center rose to 1,000,000°C, nuclear fusion – the fusing of hydrogen into helium, creating energy – occurred, releasing a constant stream of heat and light.

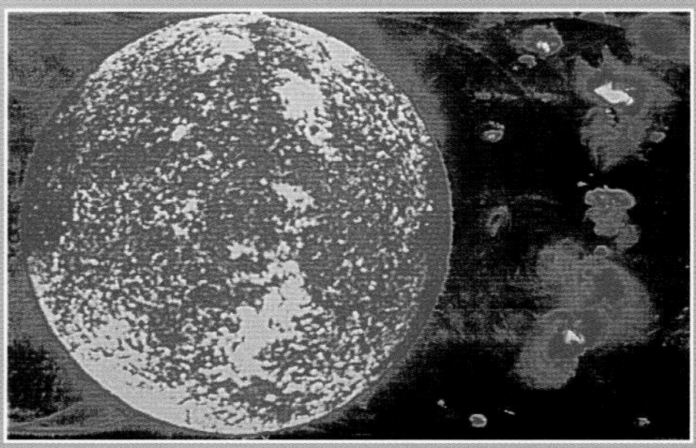

▲ ***Solar flares are*** *sudden bursts of energy from the Sun's surface. They can be 125,000 miles (200,000 km) long.*

The formation of the Solar System

The cloud of dust and gas thrown out by the Sun during its formation cooled to form the Solar System. The smaller planets nearest the Sun are formed of minerals and metals. The outer planets were formed at lower temperatures, and consist of swirling clouds of gases.

Solar eclipse

A solar eclipse occurs when the Moon passes between Earth and the Sun, casting its shadow on Earth's surface. During a total eclipse *(below)*, viewers along a strip of Earth's surface, called the area of totality, see the Sun totally blotted out for a short time, as the umbra (Moon's full shadow) sweeps over them. Outside this area is a larger one, where the Sun appears only partly obscured, as the penumbra (partial shadow) passes over.

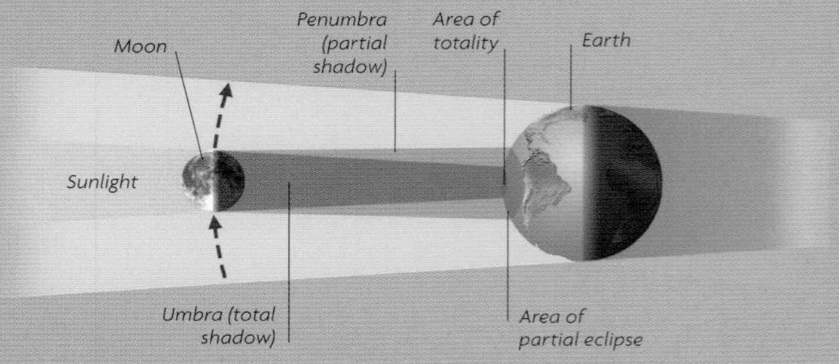
Moon
Penumbra (partial shadow)
Area of totality
Earth
Sunlight
Umbra (total shadow)
Area of partial eclipse

PLANETS									DWARF PLANETS		
	MERCURY	VENUS	EARTH	MARS	JUPITER	SATURN	URANUS	NEPTUNE	CERES	PLUTO	ERIS
DIAMETER	3029 miles (4875 km)	7521 miles (12,104 km)	7928 miles (12,756 km)	4213 miles (6780 km)	88,846 miles (142,984 km)	74,898 miles (120,536 km)	31,763 miles (51,118 km)	30,775 miles (49,528 km)	590 miles (950 km)	1432 miles (2304 km)	1429-1553 miles (2300-2500 km)
AVERAGE DISTANCE FROM THE SUN	36 mill. miles (57.9 mill. km)	67.2 mill. miles (108.2 mill. km)	93 mill. miles (149.6 mill. km)	141.6 mill. miles (227.9 mill. km)	483.6 mill. miles (778.3 mill. km)	889.8 mill. miles (1431 mill. km)	1788 mill. miles (2877 mill. km)	2795 mill. miles (4498 mill. km)	257 mill. miles (414 mill. km)	3675 mill. miles (5915 mill. km)	6344 mill. miles (10,210 mill. km)
ROTATION PERIOD	58.6 days	243 days	23.93 hours	24.62 hours	9.93 hours	10.65 hours	17.24 hours	16.11 hours	9.1 hours	6.38 days	not known
ORBITAL PERIOD	88 days	224.7 days	365.26 days	687 days	11.86 years	29.37 years	84.1 years	164.9 years	4.6 years	248.6 years	557 years
SURFACE TEMPERATURE	-180°C to 430°C (-292°F to 806°F)	480°C (896°F)	-70°C to 55°C (-94°F to 131°F)	-120°C to 25°C (-184°F to 77 °F)	-110°C (-160°F)	-140°C (-220°F)	-200°C (-320°F)	-200°C (-320°F)	-107°C (-161°F)	-230°C (-380°F)	-243°C (-405°F)

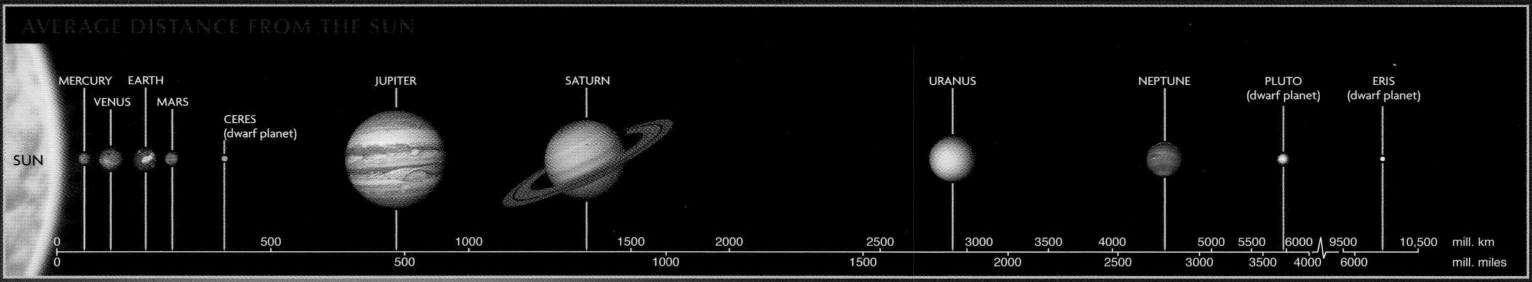
AVERAGE DISTANCE FROM THE SUN
SUN
MERCURY
VENUS
EARTH
MARS
CERES (dwarf planet)
JUPITER
SATURN
URANUS
NEPTUNE
PLUTO (dwarf planet)
ERIS (dwarf planet)
0 500 1000 1500 2000 2500 3000 3500 4000 5000 5500 6000 9500 10,500 mill. km
0 500 1000 1500 2000 2500 3000 3500 4000 6000 mill. miles

Saturn
Uranus
Neptune
Pluto (dwarf planet)
Eris (dwarf planet)

Space Debris

Millions of objects, remnants of planetary formation, circle the Sun in a zone lying between Mars and Jupiter: the asteroid belt. Fragments of asteroids break off to form meteoroids, which can reach the Earth's surface. Comets, composed of ice and dust, originated outside our Solar System. Their elliptical orbit brings them close to the Sun and into the inner Solar System.

▲ ***Meteor Crater** in Arizona is 4200 ft (1300 m) wide and 660 ft (200 m) deep. It was formed over 10,000 years ago.*

Possible and actual meteorite craters

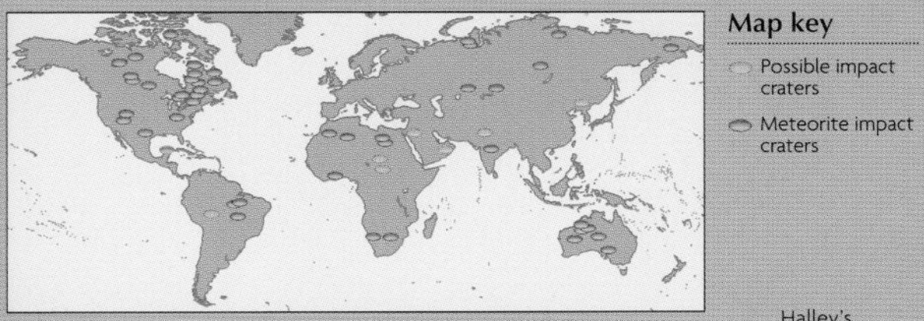
Map key
Possible impact craters
Meteorite impact craters

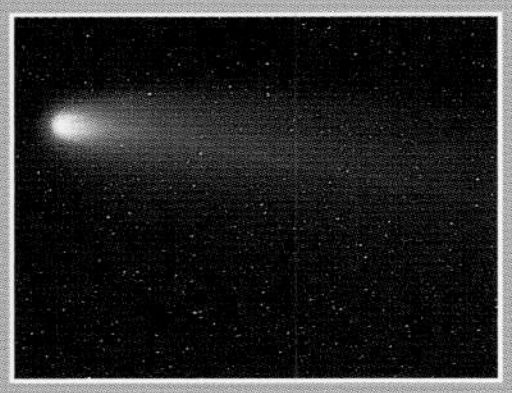

▲ ***The orbit of** Halley's Comet brings it close to the Earth every 76 years. It last visited in 1986.*

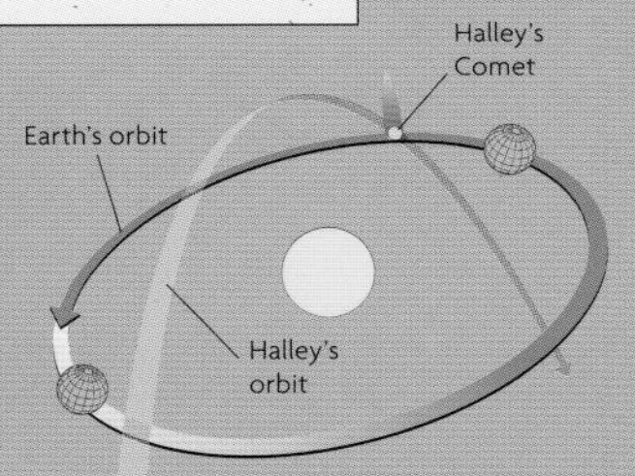
Halley's Comet
Earth's orbit
Halley's orbit

Orbit of Halley's Comet around the Sun

The Earth's Atmosphere

During the early stages of the Earth's formation, ash, lava, carbon dioxide, and water vapor were discharged onto the surface of the planet by constant volcanic eruptions. The water formed the oceans, while carbon dioxide entered the atmosphere or was dissolved in the oceans. Clouds, formed of water droplets, reflected some of the Sun's radiation back into space. The Earth's temperature stabilized and early life forms began to emerge, converting carbon dioxide into life-giving oxygen.

▲ ***It is thought** that the gases that make up the Earth's atmosphere originated deep within the interior, and were released many millions of years ago during intense volcanic actvity, similar to this eruption at Mount St. Helens.*

A B C D E F G H I J K L M

The physical world

The Earth's surface is constantly being transformed: it is uplifted, folded, and faulted by tectonic forces; weathered and eroded by wind, water, and ice. Sometimes change is dramatic, the spectacular results of earthquakes or floods. More often it is a slow process lasting millions of years. A physical map of the world represents a snapshot of the ever-evolving architecture of the Earth. This terrain map shows the whole surface of the Earth, both above and below the sea.

The world in section

These cross-sections around the Earth, one in the northern hemisphere; one straddling the Equator, reveal the limited areas of land above sea level in comparison with the extent of the sea floor. The greater erosive effects of weathering by wind and water limit the upward elevation of land above sea level, while the deep oceans retain their dramatic mountain and trench profiles.

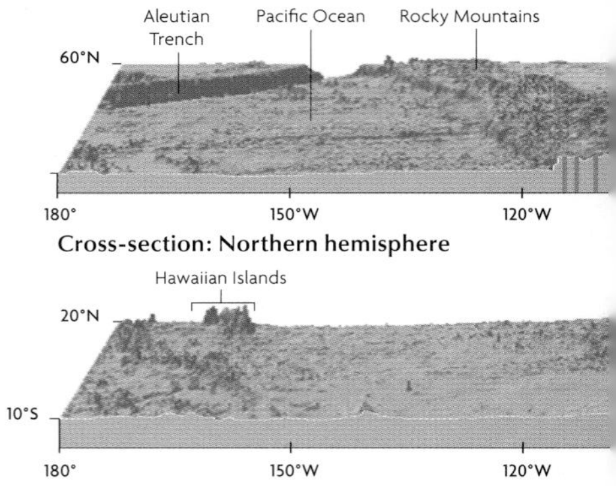

Aleutian Trench
Pacific Ocean
Rocky Mountains
60°N
180°
150°W
120°W
Hawaiian Islands
20°N
10°S
180°
150°W
120°W

Cross-section: Northern hemisphere

Cross-section: Southern hemisphere

Map key

Elevation

- 6000m / 19,686ft
- 4000m / 13,124ft
- 3000m / 9843ft
- 2000m / 6562ft
- 1000m / 3281ft
- 500m / 1640ft
- 250m / 820ft
- 100m / 328ft
- sea level
- below sea level

Sea depth

- sea level
- -250m / -820ft
- -2000m / -6562ft
- -4000m / -13,124ft

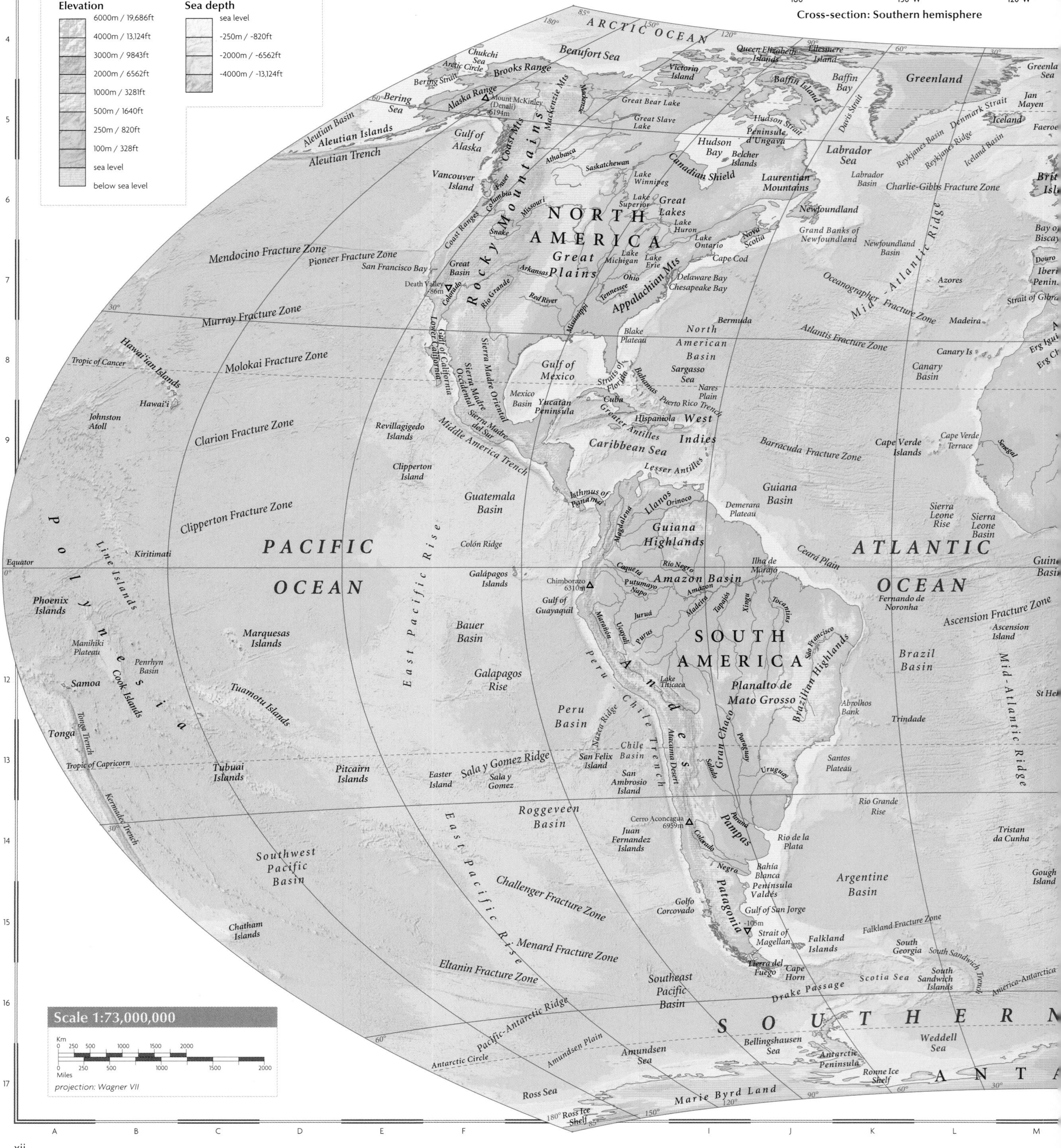

ARCTIC OCEAN
Beaufort Sea
Chukchi Sea
Arctic Circle
Bering Strait
Brooks Range
Alaska Range
Mount McKinley (Denali) 6194m
Bering Sea
Aleutian Basin
Aleutian Islands
Aleutian Trench
Gulf of Alaska
Mackenzie Mts
Victoria Island
Queen Elizabeth Islands
Ellesmere Island
Baffin Island
Baffin Bay
Greenland
Great Bear Lake
Great Slave Lake
Hudson Strait
Peninsule d'Ungava
Davis Strait
Denmark Strait
Iceland
Jan Mayen
Hudson Bay
Belcher Islands
Labrador Sea
Labrador Basin
Reykjanes Basin
Reykjanes Ridge
Iceland Basin
Coast Mts
Rocky Mountains
Athabasca
Saskatchewan
Canadian Shield
Lake Winnipeg
Laurentian Mountains
Charlie-Gibbs Fracture Zone
Vancouver Island
Fraser
Columbia
Missouri
Lake Superior
Great Lakes
Lake Huron
Newfoundland
NORTH AMERICA
Coast Ranges
Snake
Great Plains
Lake Michigan
Lake Erie
Lake Ontario
Nova Scotia
Grand Banks of Newfoundland
Newfoundland Basin
Mendocino Fracture Zone
Pioneer Fracture Zone
San Francisco Bay
Great Basin
Arkansas
Ohio
Cape Cod
Death Valley -86m
Colorado
Rio Grande
Tennessee
Appalachian Mts
Delaware Bay
Chesapeake Bay
Azores
Oceanographer Fracture Zone
Mid-Atlantic Ridge
Red River
Mississippi
Murray Fracture Zone
Bermuda
Madeira
Strait of Gibraltar
Blake Plateau
North American Basin
Atlantis Fracture Zone
Canary Is
Hawai'ian Islands
Tropic of Cancer
Molokai Fracture Zone
Gulf of California
Lower California
Sierra Madre Oriental
Sierra Madre Occidental
Gulf of Mexico
Straits of Florida
Bahamas
Sargasso Sea
Canary Basin
Hawai'i
Mexico Basin
Yucatan Peninsula
Cuba
Nares Plain
Puerto Rico Trench
Sierra Madre del Sur
Greater Antilles
Hispaniola
West Indies
Johnston Atoll
Revillagigedo Islands
Middle America Trench
Caribbean Sea
Clarion Fracture Zone
Barracuda Fracture Zone
Cape Verde Islands
Cape Verde Terrace
Senegal
Lesser Antilles
Clipperton Island
Isthmus of Panama
Llanos
Orinoco
Guiana Basin
Demerara Plateau
Sierra Leone Rise
Sierra Leone Basin
Guatemala Basin
Magdalena
Guiana Highlands
Clipperton Fracture Zone
Polynesia
PACIFIC OCEAN
Colón Ridge
East Pacific Rise
Ceará Plain
ATLANTIC OCEAN
Equator
Line Islands
Kiritimati
Caquetá
Rio Negro
Ilha de Marajó
Guinea Basin
Galápagos Islands
Chimborazo 6310m
Putumayo
Napo
Amazon Basin
Amazon
Tapajós
Xingu
Tocantins
Fernando de Noronha
Phoenix Islands
Gulf of Guayaquil
Juruá
Madeira
Ascension Fracture Zone
Ascension Island
Marquesas Islands
Bauer Basin
Marañón
Ucayali
Purus
SOUTH AMERICA
São Francisco
Brazilian Highlands
Manihiki Plateau
Penrhyn Basin
Peru
Andes
Brazil Basin
Samoa
Cook Islands
Tuamotu Islands
Galapagos Rise
Lake Titicaca
Planalto de Mato Grosso
Abrolhos Bank
St Helena
Trindade
Tonga
Tonga Trench
Peru Basin
Nazca Ridge
Peru Chile Trench
Atacama Desert
Gran Chaco
Paraguay
Salado
Chile Basin
Tropic of Capricorn
Tubuai Islands
Pitcairn Islands
Easter Island
Sala y Gomez Ridge
Sala y Gomez
San Felix Island
San Ambrosio Island
Uruguay
Santos Plateau
Rio Grande Rise
Kermadec Trench
Roggeveen Basin
Cerro Aconcagua 6959m
Paraná
Pampas
Colorado
Rio de la Plata
Tristan da Cunha
Juan Fernandez Islands
Southwest Pacific Basin
Negro
Bahía Blanca
Península Valdés
Argentine Basin
Gough Island
Challenger Fracture Zone
Patagonia
Golfo Corcovado
Gulf of San Jorge
-105m
Chatham Islands
Falkland Fracture Zone
Menard Fracture Zone
Strait of Magellan
Falkland Islands
South Georgia
South Sandwich Trench
Eltanin Fracture Zone
Tierra del Fuego
Cape Horn
Scotia Sea
South Sandwich Islands
America-Antarctica
Southeast Pacific Basin
Drake Passage
Pacific-Antarctic Ridge
SOUTHERN
Weddell Sea
Amundsen Plain
Bellingshausen Sea
Antarctic Circle
Amundsen Sea
Antarctic Peninsula
Ronne Ice Shelf
ANTA
Ross Sea
Marie Byrd Land
Ross Ice Shelf

Scale 1:73,000,000

Km 0 250 500 1000 1500 2000

Miles 0 250 500 1000 1500 2000

projection: Wagner VII

A B C D E F G H I J K L M

N O P Q R S T U V W X Y Z

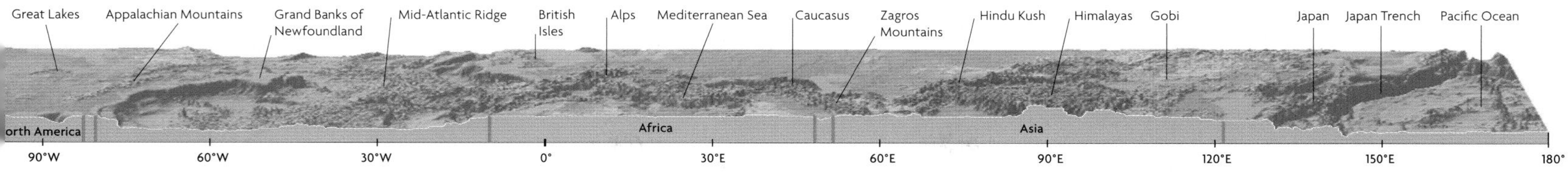

Great Lakes
Appalachian Mountains
Grand Banks of Newfoundland
Mid-Atlantic Ridge
British Isles
Alps
Mediterranean Sea
Caucasus
Zagros Mountains
Hindu Kush
Himalayas
Gobi
Japan
Japan Trench
Pacific Ocean
orth America
Africa
Asia
90°W
60°W
30°W
0°
30°E
60°E
90°E
120°E
150°E
180°

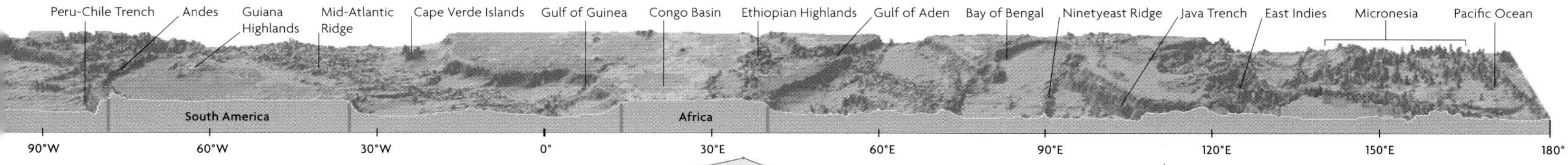

Peru-Chile Trench
Andes
Guiana Highlands
Mid-Atlantic Ridge
Cape Verde Islands
Gulf of Guinea
Congo Basin
Ethiopian Highlands
Gulf of Aden
Bay of Bengal
Ninetyeast Ridge
Java Trench
East Indies
Micronesia
Pacific Ocean
South America
Africa
90°W
60°W
30°W
0°
30°E
60°E
90°E
120°E
150°E
180°

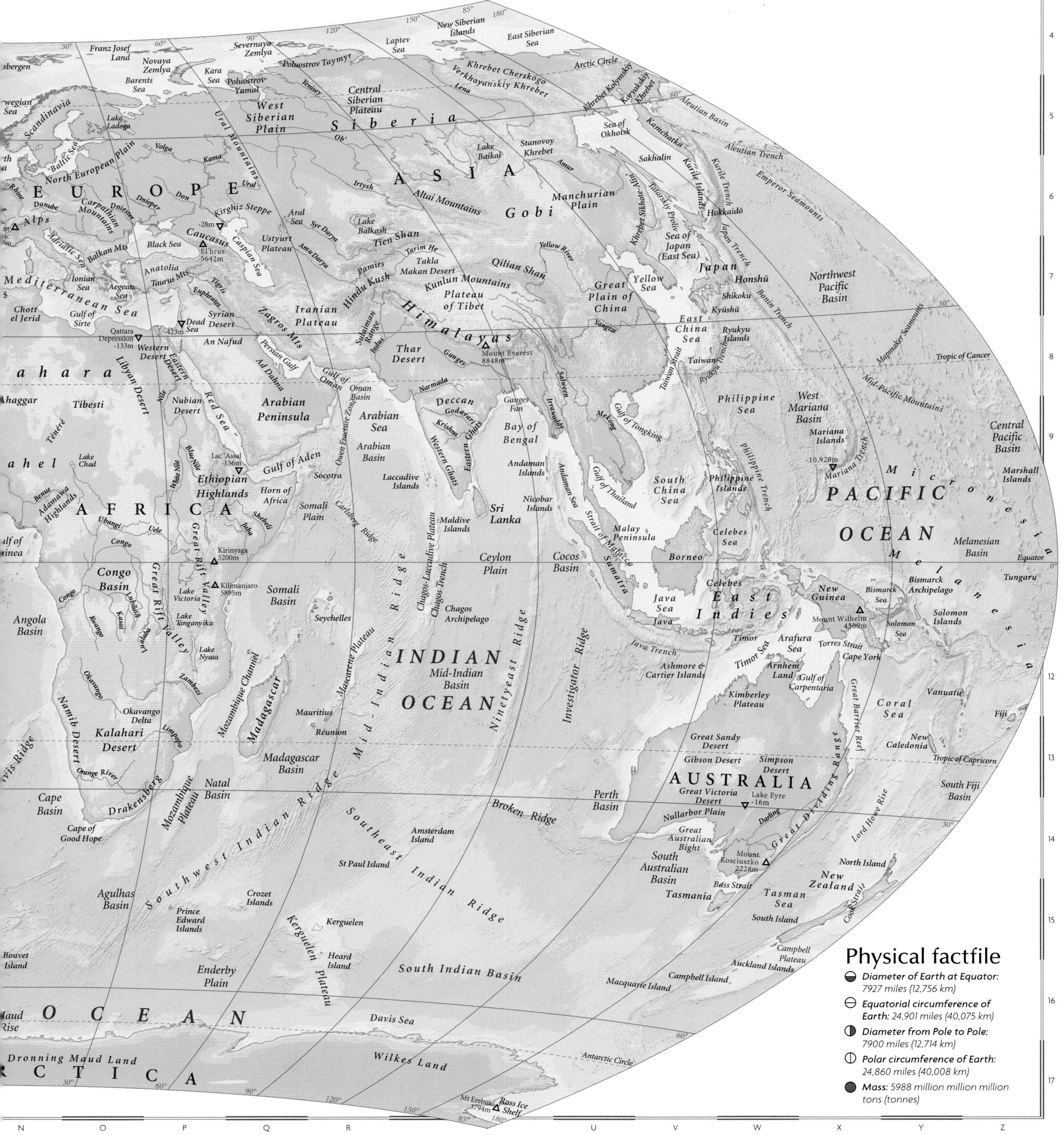

Franz Josef Land
Novaya Zemlya
Barents Sea
Kara Sea
Severnaya Zemlya
Poluostrov Taymyr
Poluostrov Yamal
Laptev Sea
New Siberian Islands
East Siberian Sea
Khrebet Cherskogo
Verkhoyanskiy Khrebet
Lena
Arctic Circle
Yenisey
Central Siberian Plateau
West Siberian Plain
Ural Mountains
Siberia
Ob'
Scandinavia
Norwegian Sea
Lake Ladoga
Baltic Sea
North European Plain
Volga
Kama
Ural
EUROPE
Rhine
Danube
Carpathian Mountains
Dniester
Dnieper
Don
Alps
Adriatic Sea
Balkan Mts
Black Sea
Kirghiz Steppe
-28m
Caucasus
El'brus 5642m
Caspian Sea
Aral Sea
Syr Darya
Amu Darya
Ustyurt Plateau
Lake Balkash
Tien Shan
Irtysh
Altai Mountains
ASIA
Lake Baikal
Stanovoy Khrebet
Amur
Gobi
Manchurian Plain
Sea of Okhotsk
Sakhalin
Khrebet Kolymskiy
Koryakskiy Khrebet
Kamchatka
Aleutian Basin
Aleutian Trench
Emperor Seamounts
Kuril Islands
Kurile Trench
Hokkaidō
Tatarskiy Proliv
Khrebet Sikhote-Alin'
Sea of Japan (East Sea)
Japan Trench
Japan
Honshū
Shikoku
Kyūshū
Bonin Trench
Northwest Pacific Basin
Mediterranean Sea
Ionian Sea
Aegean Sea
Anatolia
Taurus Mts
Tigris
Euphrates
Chott el Jerid
Gulf of Sirte
Syrian Desert
Dead Sea
-423m
Qattara Depression -133m
Western Desert
Eastern Desert
Libyan Desert
Sahara
An Nafud
Zagros Mts
Iranian Plateau
Persian Gulf
Pamirs
Takla Makan Desert
Tarim He
Hindu Kush
Kunlun Mountains
Qilian Shan
Yellow River
Plateau of Tibet
Himalayas
Sulaiman Range
Indus
Thar Desert
Ganges
Mount Everest 8848m
Yangtze
Great Plain of China
Yellow Sea
East China Sea
Ryukyu Islands
Ryukyu Trench
Taiwan
Taiwan Strait
Mapmaker Seamounts
Tropic of Cancer
Mid-Pacific Mountains
Ad Dahna
Gulf of Oman
Oman Basin
Arabian Peninsula
Nubian Desert
Nile
Red Sea
Ahaggar
Tibesti
Ténéré
Sahel
Lake Chad
Blue Nile
White Nile
Lac 'Assal -156m
Gulf of Aden
Ethiopian Highlands
Socotra
Horn of Africa
Owen Fracture Zone
Arabian Sea
Arabian Basin
Narmada
Deccan
Godavari
Krishna
Western Ghats
Eastern Ghats
Ganges Fan
Bay of Bengal
Irrawaddy
Salween
Mekong
Gulf of Tongking
Philippine Sea
Philippine Trench
West Mariana Basin
Mariana Islands
Mariana Trench
-10,920m
Central Pacific Basin
Marshall Islands
Benue
Adamawa Highlands
AFRICA
Ubangi
Uele
Juba
Shebeli
Somali Plain
Carlsberg Ridge
Laccadive Islands
Andaman Islands
Andaman Sea
Nicobar Islands
Sri Lanka
Gulf of Thailand
South China Sea
Philippine Islands
PACIFIC OCEAN
Micronesia
Gulf of Guinea
Congo
Congo Basin
Great Rift Valley
Kirinyaga 5200m
Kilimanjaro 5895m
Lake Victoria
Lake Tanganyika
Lualaba
Kasai
Kwango
Zambezi
Lake Nyasa
Angola Basin
Somali Basin
Seychelles
Maldive Islands
Chagos-Laccadive Plateau
Chagos Trench
Chagos Archipelago
Ceylon Plain
Cocos Basin
Strait of Malacca
Sumatra
Malay Peninsula
Borneo
Celebes Sea
Celebes
Java Sea
Java
East Indies
New Guinea
Mount Wilhelm 4509m
Bismarck Sea
Bismarck Archipelago
Solomon Sea
Solomon Islands
Melanesian Basin
Melanesia
Equator
Tungaru
Okavango
Namib Desert
Okavango Delta
Kalahari Desert
Limpopo
Orange River
Walvis Ridge
Mozambique Channel
Madagascar
Mascarene Plateau
Mauritius
Réunion
Mid-Indian Ridge
INDIAN OCEAN
Mid-Indian Basin
Ninetyeast Ridge
Investigator Ridge
Java Trench
Ashmore & Cartier Islands
Timor
Timor Sea
Arafura Sea
Arnhem Land
Gulf of Carpentaria
Torres Strait
Cape York
Kimberley Plateau
Great Barrier Reef
Coral Sea
Vanuatu
Fiji
New Caledonia
Tropic of Capricorn
Great Sandy Desert
Gibson Desert
Simpson Desert
AUSTRALIA
Great Victoria Desert
Lake Eyre -16m
Great Dividing Range
Darling
Nullarbor Plain
South Fiji Basin
Lord Howe Rise
Cape Basin
Drakensberg
Mozambique Plateau
Natal Basin
Madagascar Basin
Cape of Good Hope
Southwest Indian Ridge
Broken Ridge
Perth Basin
Amsterdam Island
St Paul Island
Southeast Indian Ridge
Great Australian Bight
South Australian Basin
Mount Kosciuszko 2228m
Bass Strait
Tasmania
Tasman Sea
North Island
New Zealand
Cook Strait
South Island
Agulhas Basin
Crozet Islands
Prince Edward Islands
Kerguelen
Kerguelen Plateau
Heard Island
Bouvet Island
Enderby Plain
South Indian Basin
Campbell Plateau
Auckland Islands
Campbell Island
Macquarie Island
Maud Rise
OCEAN
Davis Sea
Antarctic Circle
Dronning Maud Land
Wilkes Land
ANTARCTICA
Mt Erebus 3794m
Ross Ice Shelf
30°
60°
90°
120°
150°
180°
85°

Physical factfile

- *Diameter of Earth at Equator:* 7927 miles (12,756 km)
- *Equatorial circumference of Earth:* 24,901 miles (40,075 km)
- *Diameter from Pole to Pole:* 7900 miles (12,714 km)
- *Polar circumference of Earth:* 24,860 miles (40,008 km)
- *Mass:* 5988 million million million tons (tonnes)

1 2 3 4 5 6 7 8 9 10 11 12 13 14 15 16 17

N O P Q R S T U V W X Y Z

Structure of the Earth

The Earth as it is today is just the latest phase in a constant process of evolution which has occurred over the past 4.5 billion years. The Earth's continents are neither fixed nor stable; over the course of the Earth's history, propelled by currents rising from the intense heat at its center, the great plates on which they lie have moved, collided, joined together, and separated. These processes continue to mold and transform the surface of the Earth, causing earthquakes and volcanic eruptions and creating oceans, mountain ranges, deep ocean trenches, and island chains.

Inside the Earth

The Earth's hot inner core is made up of solid iron, while the outer core is composed of liquid iron and nickel. The mantle nearest the core is viscous, whereas the rocky upper mantle is fairly rigid. The crust is the rocky outer shell of the Earth. Together, the upper mantle and the crust form the lithosphere.

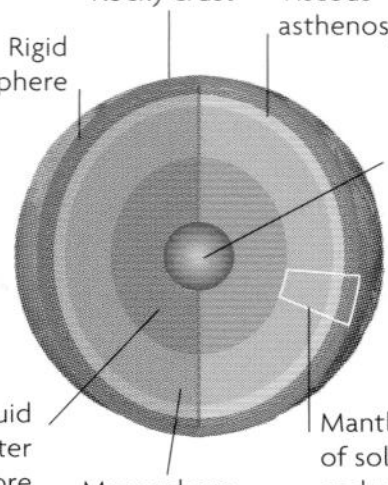
Rocky crust
Viscous asthenosphere
Rigid lithosphere
Inner core of solid iron
Liquid outer core
Mesosphere
Mantle composed of solid rock and magma

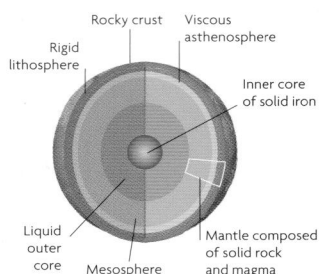

The dynamic Earth

The Earth's crust is made up of eight major (and several minor) rigid continental and oceanic tectonic plates, which fit closely together. The positions of the plates are not static. They are constantly moving relative to one another. The type of movement between plates affects the way in which they alter the structure of the Earth. The oldest parts of the plates, known as shields, are the most stable parts of the Earth and little tectonic activity occurs here.

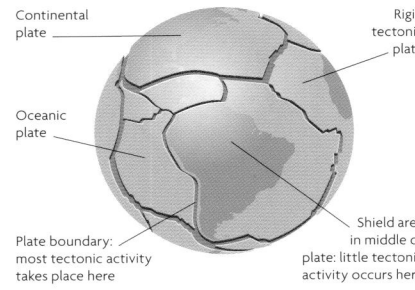

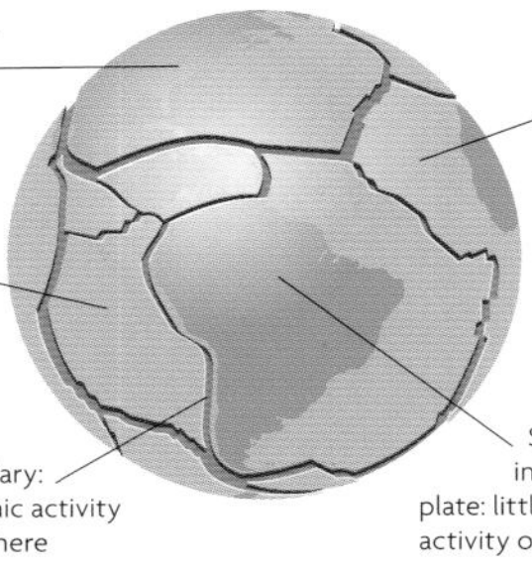
Continental plate
Rigid tectonic plate
Oceanic plate
Plate boundary: most tectonic activity takes place here
Shield area in middle of plate: little tectonic activity occurs here

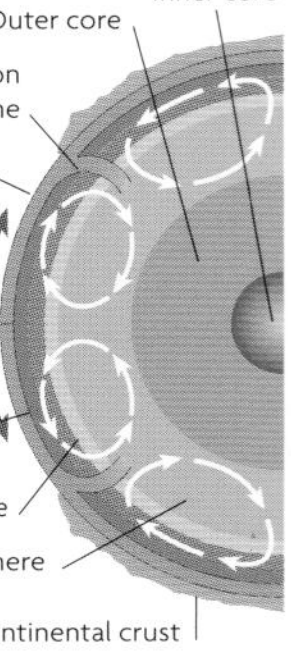
Inner core
Outer core
Subduction zone
Ocean crust
Movement of plate
Mid-ocean ridge
Lithosphere
Asthenosphere
Mesosphere
Continental crust

Convection currents

Deep within the Earth, at its inner core, temperatures may exceed 8,100°F (4,500°C). This heat warms rocks in the mesosphere which rise through the partially molten mantle, displacing cooler rocks just below the solid crust, which sink, and are warmed again by the heat of the mantle. This process is continuous, creating convection currents which form the moving force beneath the Earth's crust.

Plate boundaries

The boundaries between the plates are the areas where most tectonic activity takes place. Three types of movement occur at plate boundaries: the plates can either move toward each other, move apart, or slide past each other. The effect this has on the Earth's structure depends on whether the margin is between two continental plates, two oceanic plates, or an oceanic and continental plate.

▲ ***The Mid-Atlantic Ridge*** *rises above sea level in Iceland, producing geysers and volcanoes.*

Mid-ocean ridges

——— Mid-ocean ridges are formed when two adjacent oceanic plates pull apart, allowing magma to force its way up to the surface, which then cools to form solid rock. Vast amounts of volcanic material are discharged at these mid-ocean ridges which can reach heights of 10,000 ft (3000 m).

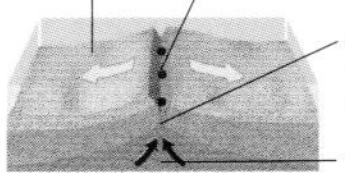
Ocean floor
Earthquake zone
Magma pushed upwards along centre of ridge
Solid mantle

Formation of a mid-ocean ridge

▲ ***Mount Pinatubo*** *is an active volcano, lying on the Pacific "Ring of Fire."*

Ocean plates meeting

△△ Oceanic crust is denser and thinner than continental crust; on average it is 3 miles (5 km) thick, while continental crust averages 18–24 miles (30–40 km). When oceanic plates of similar density meet, the crust is contorted as one plate overrides the other, forming deep sea trenches and volcanic island arcs above sea level.

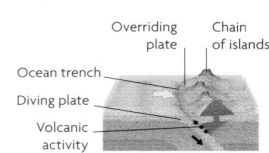

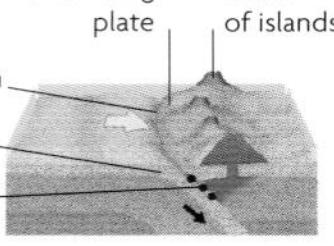
Overriding plate
Chain of islands
Ocean trench
Diving plate
Volcanic activity

Ocean plates meeting to form an island arc

Tectonic activity

- - - - - uncertain plate boundary
▲ volcanic zone
● earthquake zone
● hot spot
rift valley

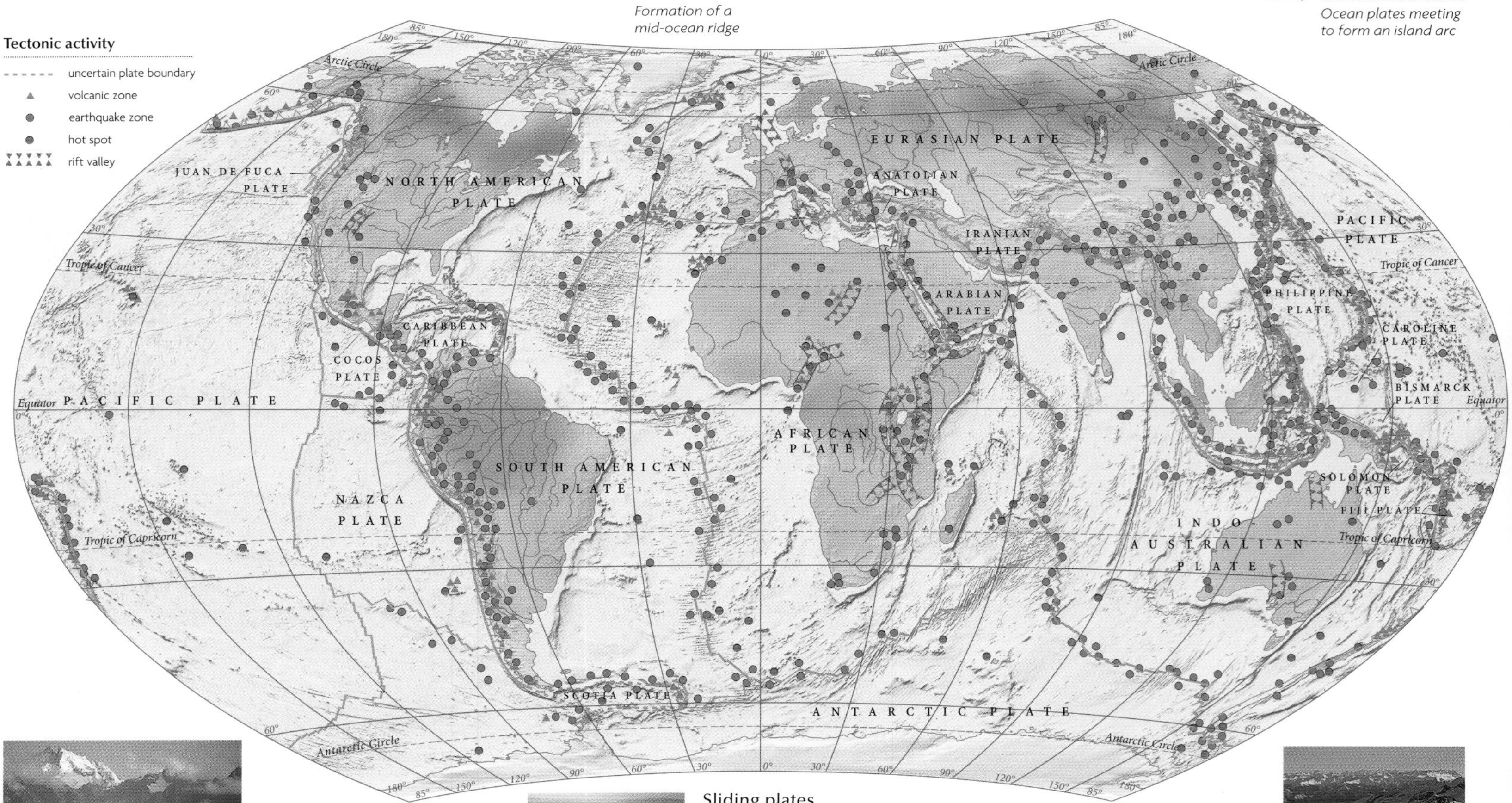
Arctic Circle
JUAN DE FUCA PLATE
NORTH AMERICAN PLATE
EURASIAN PLATE
ANATOLIAN PLATE
IRANIAN PLATE
ARABIAN PLATE
PACIFIC PLATE
PHILIPPINE PLATE
CAROLINE PLATE
BISMARCK PLATE
Tropic of Cancer
CARIBBEAN PLATE
COCOS PLATE
Equator
PACIFIC PLATE
AFRICAN PLATE
SOUTH AMERICAN PLATE
NAZCA PLATE
SOLOMON PLATE
FIJI PLATE
Tropic of Capricorn
INDO AUSTRALIAN PLATE
SCOTIA PLATE
ANTARCTIC PLATE
Antarctic Circle

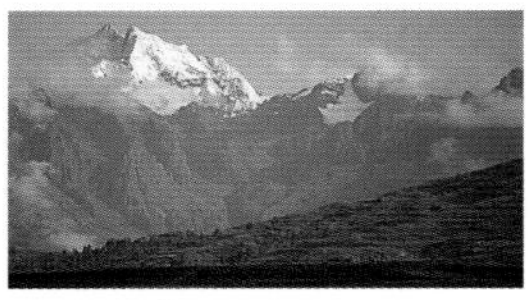

◀ ***The Andean mountain*** *chain is the typical result of the impact of a diving plate.*

Diving plates

△△ When an oceanic and a continental plate meet, the denser oceanic plate is driven underneath the continental plate, which is crumpled by the collision to form mountain ranges. As the ocean plate plunges downward, it heats up, and molten rock (magma) is forced up to the surface.

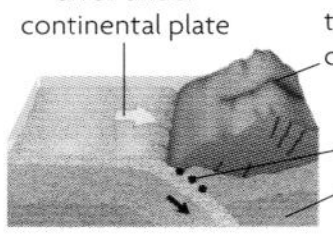
Oceanic plate dives under continental plate
Mountains thrust up by collision
Earthquake zone
Continental plate

Diving plate

▲ ***The deep fracture*** *caused by the sliding plates of the San Andreas Fault can be clearly seen in parts of California.*

Sliding plates

——— When two plates slide past each other, friction is caused along the fault line which divides them. The plates do not move smoothly, and the uneven movement causes earthquakes.

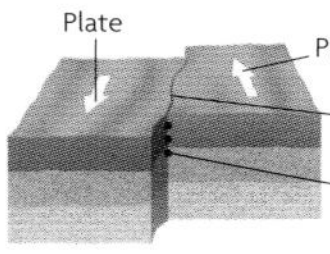
Plate
Plate
Fault line
Earthquake zone

Sliding plates

▶ ***The Alps were*** *formed when the African Plate collided with the Eurasian Plate, about 65 million years ago.*

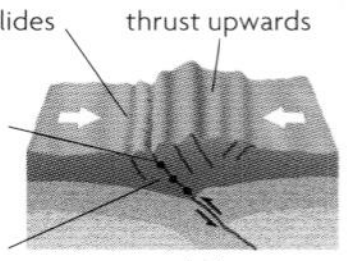
Plate buckles as it collides
Mountains thrust upwards
Earthquake zone
Crust thickens in response to the impact

Continental plates colliding to form a mountain range

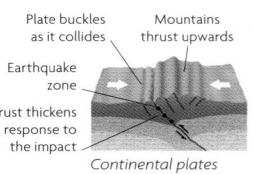

Colliding plates

▲▲▲ When two continental plates collide, great mountain chains are thrust upward as the crust buckles and folds under the force of the impact.

Continental drift

Although the plates which make up the Earth's crust move only a few inches in a year, over the millions of years of the Earth's history, its continents have moved many thousands of miles, to create new continents, oceans, and mountain chains

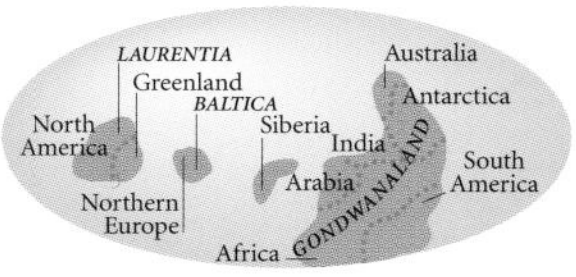
LAURENTIA
Greenland
BALTICA
North America
Siberia
Northern Europe
Arabia
India
Australia
Antarctica
South America
Africa
GONDWANALAND

1: Cambrian period

570–510 million years ago. Most continents are in tropical latitudes. The supercontinent of Gondwanaland reaches the South Pole.

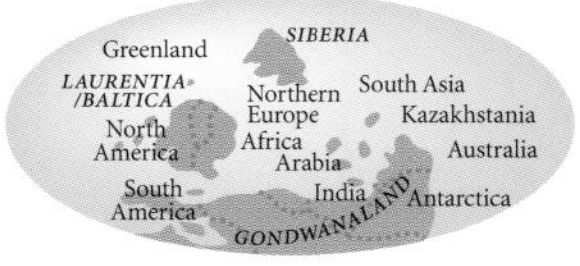
Greenland
SIBERIA
LAURENTIA-/BALTICA
Northern Europe
South Asia
Kazakhstania
North America
Africa
Arabia
Australia
South America
India
Antarctica
GONDWANALAND

2: Devonian period

408–362 million years ago. The continents of Gondwanaland and Laurentia are drifting northward.

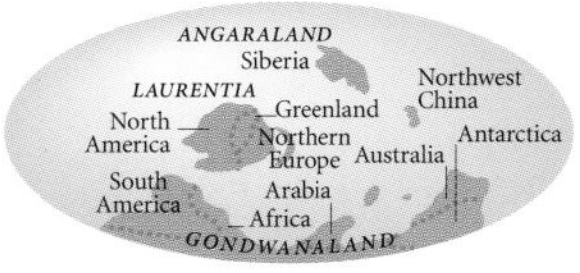
ANGARALAND
Siberia
LAURENTIA
Northwest China
North America
Greenland
Northern Europe
Antarctica
Australia
South America
Arabia
Africa
GONDWANALAND

3: Carboniferous period

362–290 million years ago. The Earth is dominated by three continents; Laurentia, Angaraland, and Gondwanaland.

Greenland
LAURASIA
Siberia
Manchuria
Northern Europe
China
Central Asia
Southeast Asia
North America
Arabia
Africa
India
South America
PANGEA
Australia
Antarctica
GONDWANALAND

4: Triassic period

245–208 million years ago. All three major continents have joined to form the super-continent of Pangea.

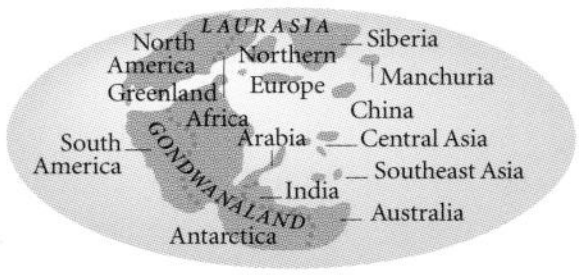
LAURASIA
North America
Greenland
Northern Europe
Siberia
Manchuria
China
South America
Africa
Arabia
Central Asia
Southeast Asia
India
Australia
GONDWANALAND
Antarctica

5: Jurassic period

208–145 million years ago. The super-continent of Pangea begins to break up, causing an overall rise in sea levels.

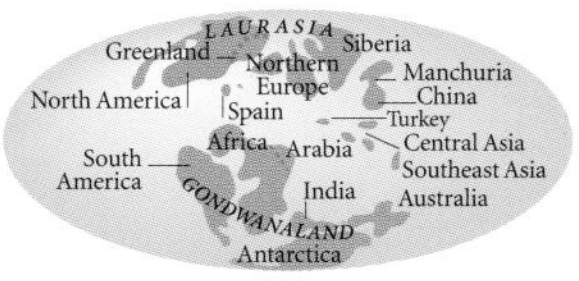
LAURASIA
Greenland
Siberia
Northern Europe
Manchuria
China
North America
Spain
Turkey
Africa
Arabia
Central Asia
Southeast Asia
South America
India
Australia
GONDWANALAND
Antarctica

6: Cretaceous period

145–65 million years ago. Warm, shallow seas cover much of the land: sea levels are about 80 ft (25 m) above present levels.

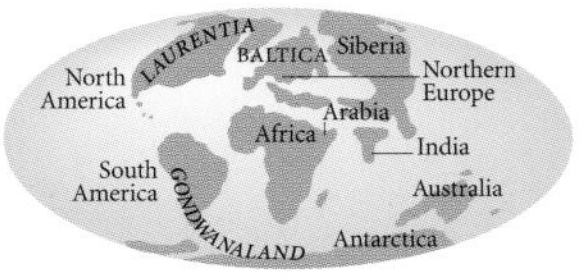
LAURENTIA
BALTICA
Siberia
North America
Northern Europe
Arabia
Africa
India
South America
Australia
GONDWANALAND
Antarctica

7: Tertiary period

65–2 million years ago. Although the world's geography is becoming more recognizable, major events such as the creation of the Himalayan mountain chain, are still to occur during this period.

Continental shields

The centers of the Earth's continents, known as shields, were established between 2500 and 500 million years ago; some contain rocks over three billion years old. They were formed by a series of turbulent events: plate movements, earthquakes, and volcanic eruptions. Since the Pre-Cambrian period, over 570 million years ago, they have experienced little tectonic activity, and today, these flat, low-lying slabs of solidified molten rock form the stable centers of the continents. They are bounded or covered by successive belts of younger sedimentary rock.

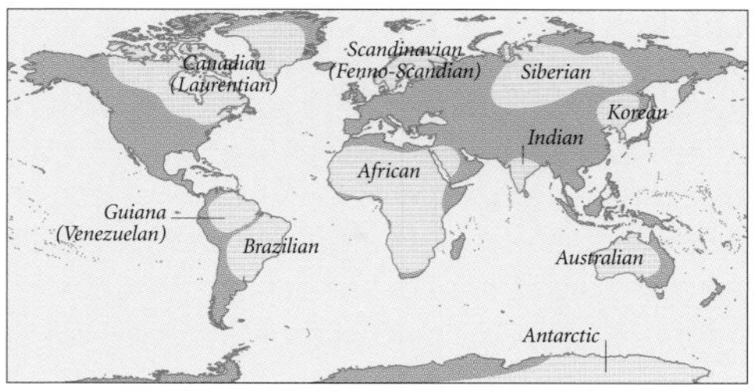
Canadian (Laurentian)
Scandinavian (Fenno-Scandian)
Siberian
Korean
Indian
African
Guiana (Venezuelan)
Brazilian
Australian
Antarctic

The Hawai'ian island chain

A hot spot lying deep beneath the Pacific Ocean pushes a plume of magma from the Earth's mantle up through the Pacific Plate to form volcanic islands. While the hot spot remains stationary, the plate on which the islands sit is moving slowly. A long chain of islands has been created as the plate passes over the hot spot.

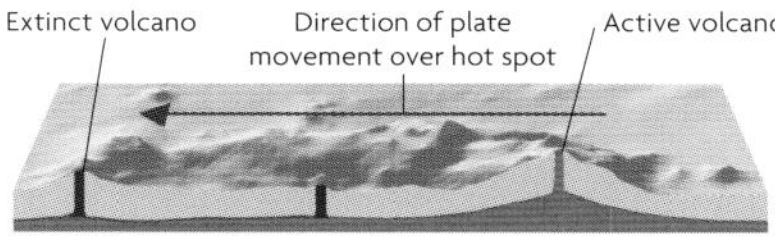
Extinct volcano
Direction of plate movement over hot spot
Active volcano

Cross-section through the Hawai'ian Islands

Evolution of the Hawai'ian Islands

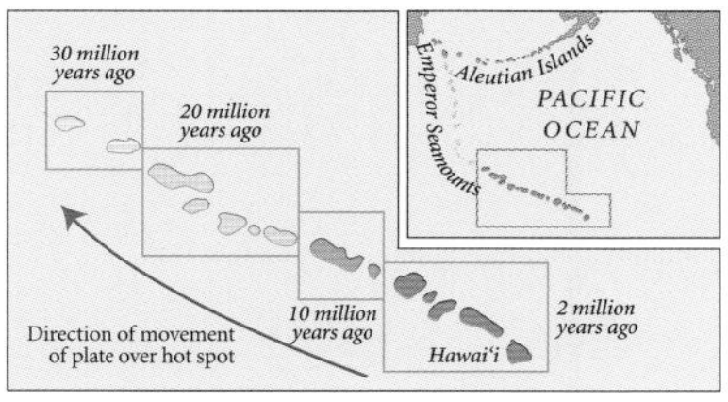
30 million years ago
20 million years ago
10 million years ago
2 million years ago
Hawai'i
Direction of movement of plate over hot spot
Aleutian Islands
Emperor Seamounts
PACIFIC OCEAN

Creation of the Himalayas

Between 10 and 20 million years ago, the Indian subcontinent, part of the ancient continent of Gondwanaland, collided with the continent of Asia. The Indo-Australian Plate continued to move northward, displacing continental crust and uplifting the Himalayas, the world's highest mountain chain.

Movements of India

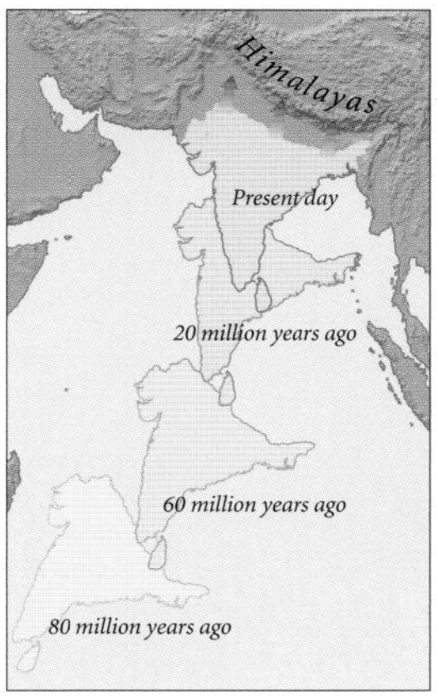
Himalayas
Present day
20 million years ago
60 million years ago
80 million years ago

Force of collision pushes up mountains

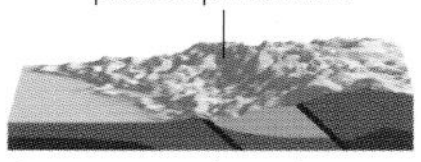

Cross-section through the Himalayas

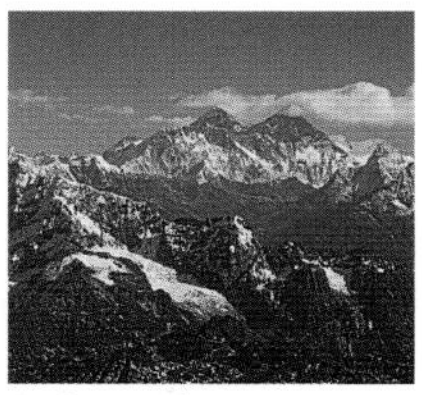

▲ ***The Himalayas were*** *uplifted when the Indian subcontinent collided with Asia.*

The Earth's geology

The Earth's rocks are created in a continual cycle. Exposed rocks are weathered and eroded by wind, water, and chemicals and deposited as sediments. If they pass into the Earth's crust they will be transformed by high temperatures and pressures into metamorphic rocks or they will melt and solidify as igneous rocks.

Sandstone

8 Sandstones are sedimentary rocks formed mainly in deserts, beaches, and deltas. Desert sandstones are formed of grains of quartz which have been well rounded by wind erosion.

▲ ***Rock stacks*** *of desert sandstone, at Bryce Canyon National Park, Utah, US.*

◀ ***Extrusive igneous rocks*** *are formed during volcanic eruptions, as here in Hawai'i.*

Andesite

7 Andesite is an extrusive igneous rock formed from magma which has solidified on the Earth's crust after a volcanic eruption.

▲ ***Gneiss formations in*** *Norway's Jotunheimen Mountains.*

Gneiss

1 Gneiss is a metamorphic rock made at great depth during the formation of mountain chains, when intense heat and pressure transform sedimentary or igneous rocks.

◀ ***Basalt columns at*** *Giant's Causeway, Northern Ireland, UK.*

Basalt

2 Basalt is an igneous rock, formed when small quantities of magma lying close to the Earth's surface cool rapidly.

Limestone

3 Limestone is a sedimentary rock, which is formed mainly from the calcite skeletons of marine animals which have been compressed into rock.

▲ ***Limestone hills, Guilin,*** *China.*

Coral

4 Coral reefs are formed from the skeletons of millions of individual corals.

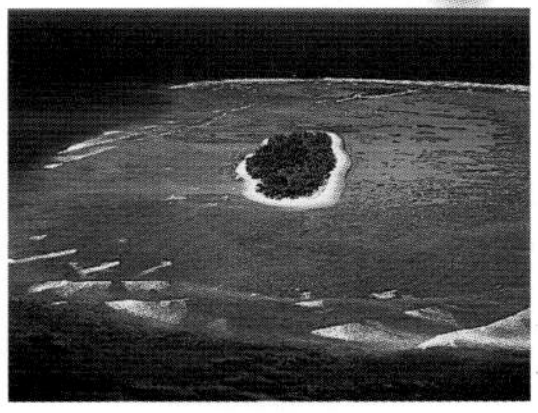

▲ ***Great Barrier Reef,*** *Australia.*

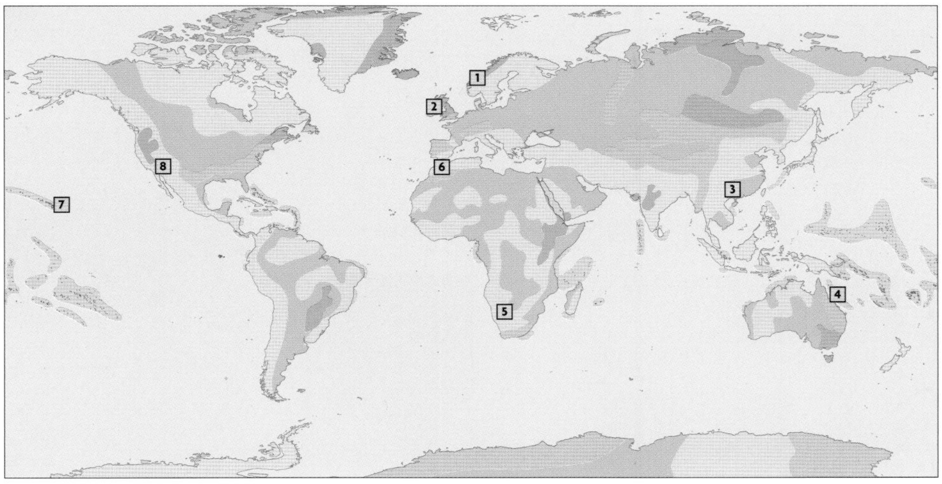
1
2
3
4
5
6
7
8

Geological regions

- continental shield
- sedimentary cover
- coral formation
- igneous rock types

Mountain ranges

- Alpine (new)
- Hercynian (old)
- Caledonian (ancient)

Schist

1 Schist is a metamorphic rock formed during mountain building, when temperature and pressure are comparatively high. Both mudstones and shales reform into schist under these conditions.

▶ ***Schist formations*** *in the Atlas Mountains, northwestern Africa.*

Granite

5 Granite is an intrusive igneous rock formed from magma which has solidified deep within the Earth's crust. The magma cools slowly, producing a coarse-grained rock.

▶ ***Namibia's Namaqualand Plateau*** *is formed of granite.*

Shaping the landscape

The basic material of the Earth's surface is solid rock: valleys, deserts, soil, and sand are all evidence of the powerful agents of weathering, erosion, and deposition which constantly shape and transform the Earth's landscapes. Water, either flowing continually in rivers or seas, or frozen and compacted into solid sheets of ice, has the most clearly visible impact on the Earth's surface. But wind can transport fragments of rock over huge distances and strip away protective layers of vegetation, exposing rock surfaces to the impact of extreme heat and cold.

Coastal water

The world's coastlines are constantly changing; every day, tides deposit, sift and sort sand, and gravel on the shoreline. Over longer periods, powerful wave action erodes cliffs and headlands and carves out bays.

▶ ***A low, wide** sandy beach on South Africa's Cape Peninsula is continually re-shaped by the action of the Atlantic waves.*

▲ ***The sheer chalk** cliffs at Seven Sisters in southern England are constantly under attack from waves.*

Water

Less than 2% of the world's water is on the land, but it is the most powerful agent of landscape change. Water, as rainfall, groundwater, and rivers, can transform landscapes through both erosion and deposition. Eroded material carried by rivers forms the world's most fertile soils.

▲ ***Waterfalls such as** the Iguaçu Falls on the border between Argentina and southern Brazil, erode the underlying rock, causing the falls to retreat.*

Groundwater

In regions where there are porous rocks such as chalk, water is stored underground in large quantities; these reservoirs of water are known as aquifers. Rain percolates through topsoil into the underlying bedrock, creating an underground store of water. The limit of the saturated zone is called the water table.

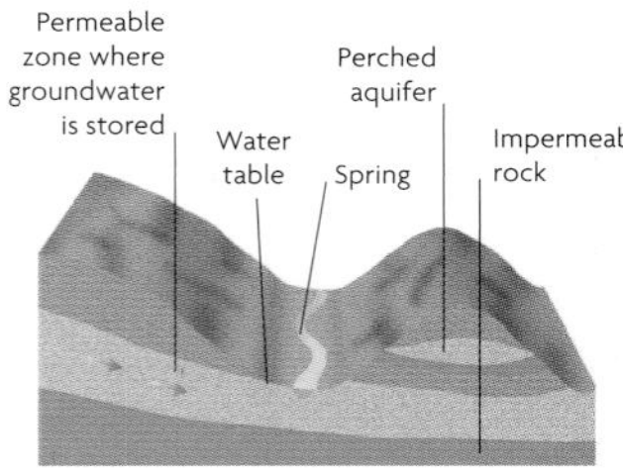
Permeable zone where groundwater is stored
Perched aquifer
Water table
Spring
Impermeable rock

Storage of groundwater in an aquifer

World river systems

drainage basin

World river systems:
Sediment deposited annually per drainage basin

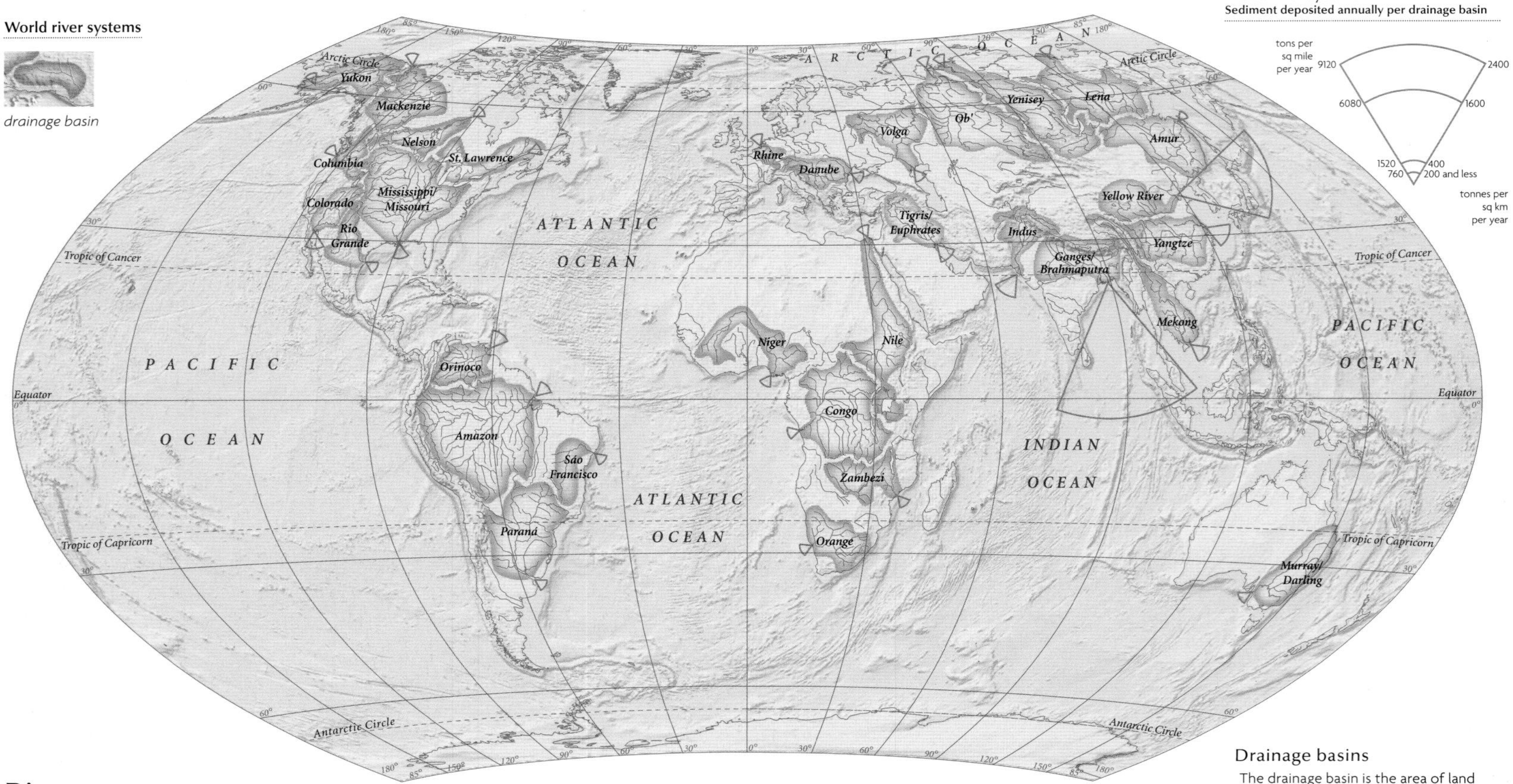
Arctic Circle
Yukon
Mackenzie
Nelson
St. Lawrence
Columbia
Mississippi/ Missouri
Colorado
Rio Grande
Tropic of Cancer
PACIFIC OCEAN
ATLANTIC OCEAN
Orinoco
Amazon
São Francisco
Parana
Equator
Tropic of Capricorn
ARCTIC OCEAN
Rhine
Danube
Volga
Ob'
Yenisey
Lena
Amur
Tigris/ Euphrates
Indus
Ganges/ Brahmaputra
Yellow River
Yangtze
Mekong
Niger
Nile
Congo
Zambezi
Orange
INDIAN OCEAN
Murray/ Darling
Antarctic Circle
tons per sq mile per year
9120
6080
1520
760
2400
1600
400
200 and less
tonnes per sq km per year

Rivers

Rivers erode the land by grinding and dissolving rocks and stones. Most erosion occurs in the river's upper course as it flows through highland areas. Rock fragments are moved along the river bed by fast-flowing water and deposited in areas where the river slows down, such as flat plains, or where the river enters seas or lakes.

River valleys

Over long periods of time rivers erode uplands to form characteristic V-shaped valleys with smooth sides.

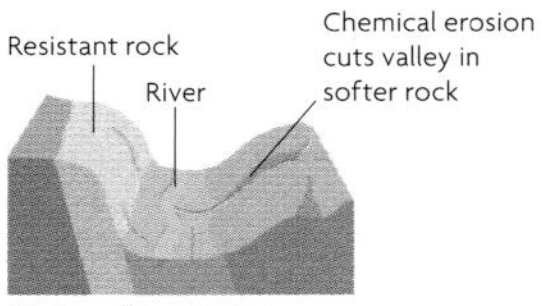
Resistant rock
River
Chemical erosion cuts valley in softer rock

River valley erosion

Deltas

When a river deposits its load of silt and sediment (alluvium) on entering the sea, it may form a delta. As this material accumulates, it chokes the mouth of the river, forcing it to create new channels to reach the sea.

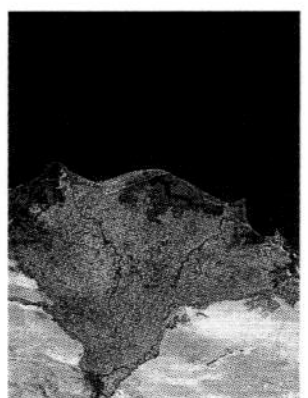

▶ ***The Nile** forms a broad delta as it flows into the Mediterranean.*

Drainage basins

The drainage basin is the area of land drained by a major trunk river and its smaller branch rivers or tributaries. Drainage basins are separated from one another by natural boundaries known as watersheds.

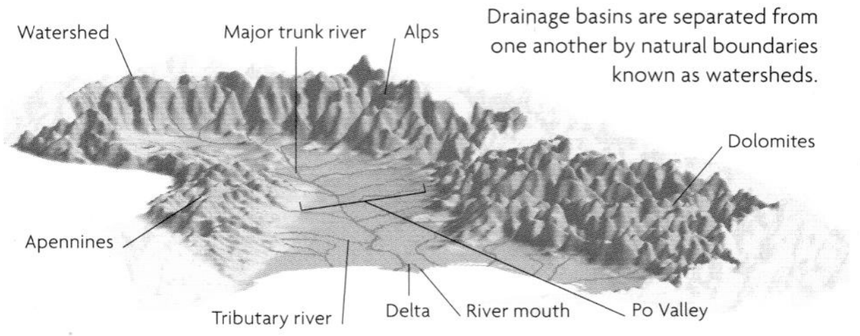
Watershed
Major trunk river
Alps
Dolomites
Apennines
Tributary river
Delta
River mouth
Po Valley

The drainage basin of the Po river, northern Italy.

▲ ***The Mississippi River** forms meanders as it flows across the southern US.*

Meanders

In their lower courses, rivers flow slowly. As they flow across the lowlands, they form looping bends called meanders.

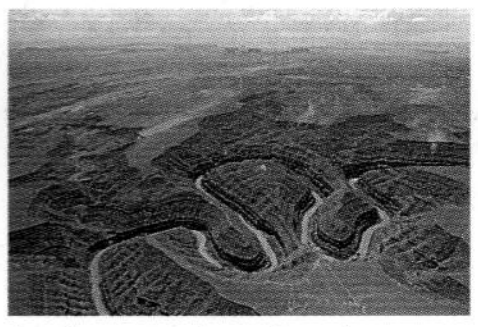

▲ ***The meanders of** Utah's San Juan River have become deeply incised.*

◀ ***Mud is deposited** by China's Yellow River in its lower course.*

Deposition

When rivers have deposited large quantities of fertile alluvium, they are forced to find new channels through the alluvium deposits, creating braided river systems.

Landslides

Heavy rain and associated flooding on slopes can loosen underlying rocks, which crumble, causing the top layers of rock and soil to slip.

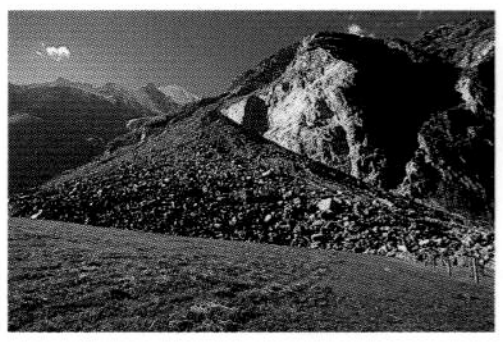

▶ ***A huge landslide** in the Swiss Alps has left massive piles of rocks and pebbles called scree.*

▲ ***A deep gully** in the French Alps caused by the scouring of upper layers of turf.*

Gullies

In areas where soil is thin, rainwater is not effectively absorbed, and may flow overland. The water courses downhill in channels, or gullies, and may lead to rapid erosion of soil.

Ice

During its long history, the Earth has experienced a number of glacial episodes when temperatures were considerably lower than today. During the last Ice Age, 18,000 years ago, ice covered an area three times larger than it does today. Over these periods, the ice has left a remarkable legacy of transformed landscapes.

Glaciers

Glaciers are formed by the compaction of snow into "rivers" of ice. As they move over the landscape, glaciers pick up and carry a load of rocks and boulders which erode the landscape they pass over, and are eventually deposited at the end of the glacier.

▲ ***A massive glacier*** *advancing down a valley in southern Argentina.*

Post-glacial features

When a glacial episode ends, the retreating ice leaves many features. These include depositional ridges called moraines, which may be eroded into low hills known as drumlins; sinuous ridges called eskers; kames, which are rounded hummocks; depressions known as kettle holes; and windblown loess deposits.

Glacial valleys

Glaciers can erode much more powerfully than rivers. They form steep-sided, flat-bottomed valleys with a typical U-shaped profile. Valleys created by tributary glaciers, whose floors have not been eroded to the same depth as the main glacial valley floor, are called hanging valleys

▲ ***The U-shaped profile*** *and piles of morainic debris are characteristic of a valley once filled by a glacier.*

▲ ***A series of*** *hanging valleys high up in the Chilean Andes.*

Past and present world ice-cover and glacial features

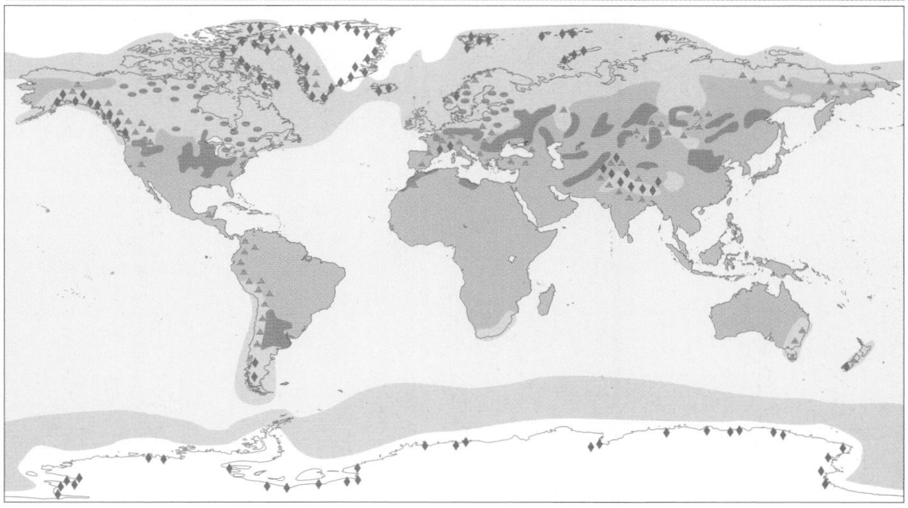

Past and present world ice cover and glacial features

- extent of last Ice Age
- loess deposits
- post-glacial feature
- glacial feature
- present day ice cover
- glacial field

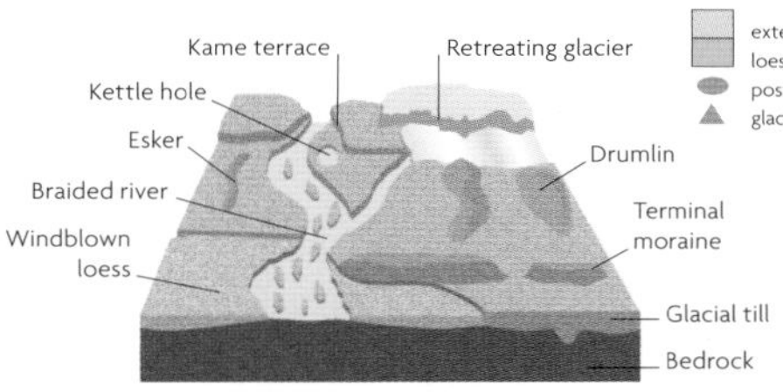
Kame terrace
Retreating glacier
Kettle hole
Esker
Drumlin
Braided river
Terminal moraine
Windblown loess
Glacial till
Bedrock

Post-glacial landscape features

Ice shattering

Water drips into fissures in rocks and freezes, expanding as it does so. The pressure weakens the rock, causing it to crack, and eventually to shatter into polygonal patterns.

▲ ***Irregular polygons show*** *through the sedge-grass tundra in the Yukon, Canada.*

▲ ***The profile of*** *the Matterhorn has been formed by three cirques lying "back-to-back."*

Cirques

Cirques are basin-shaped hollows which mark the head of a glaciated valley. Where neighboring cirques meet, they are divided by sharp rock ridges called arêtes. It is these arêtes which give the Matterhorn its characteristic profile.

Fjords

Fjords are ancient glacial valleys flooded by the sea following the end of a period of glaciation. Beneath the water, the valley floor can be 4000 ft (1300 m) deep.

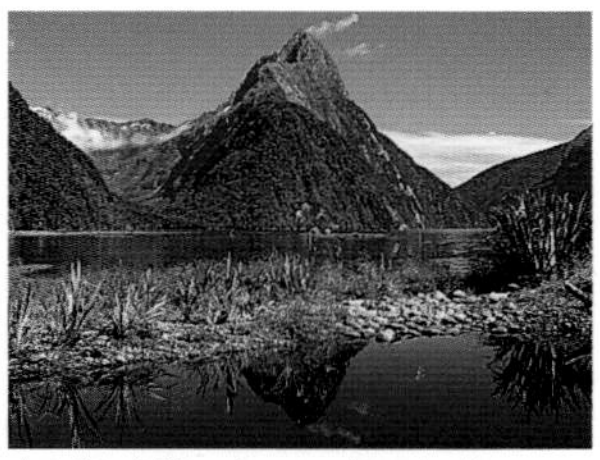

▲ ***A fjord fills*** *a former glacial valley in southern New Zealand.*

Periglaciation

Periglacial areas occur near to the edge of ice sheets. A layer of frozen ground lying just beneath the surface of the land is known as permafrost. When the surface melts in the summer, the water is unable to drain into the frozen ground, and so "creeps" downhill, a process known as solifluction.

Wind

Strong winds can transport rock fragments great distances, especially where there is little vegetation to protect the rock. In desert areas, wind picks up loose, unprotected sand particles, carrying them over great distances. This powerfully abrasive debris is blasted at the surface by the wind, eroding the landscape into dramatic shapes.

Prevailing winds and dust trajectories

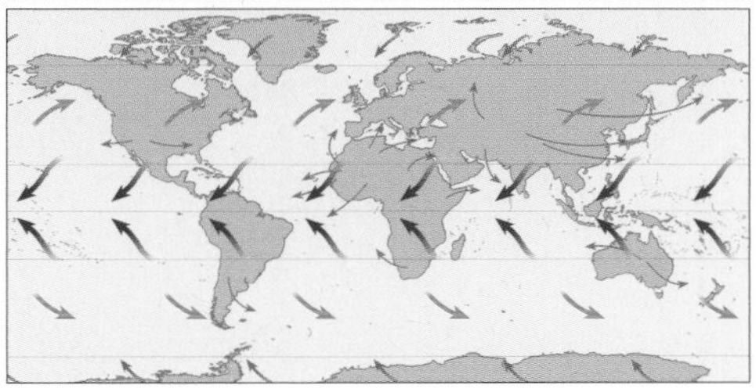

Prevailing winds: northeast trade, southeast trade, westerly, westerly, polar easterly, polar easterly

Dust trajectories: trajectory of aeolian dust

Hot and cold deserts

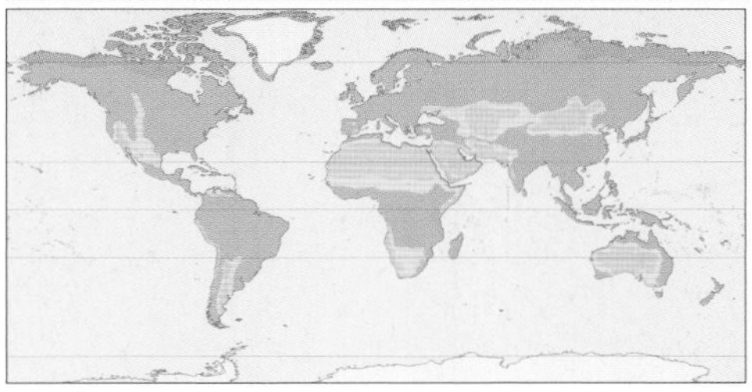

Main desert types: hot arid, semi-arid, cold polar

Temperature

Most of the world's deserts are in the tropics. The cold deserts which occur elsewhere are arid because they are a long way from the rain-giving sea. Rock in deserts is exposed because of lack of vegetation and is susceptible to changes in temperature; extremes of heat and cold can cause both cracks and fissures to appear in the rock.

Deposition

The rocky, stony floors of the world's deserts are swept and scoured by strong winds. The smaller, finer particles of sand are shaped into surface ripples, dunes, or sand mountains, which rise to a height of 650 ft (200 m). Dunes usually form single lines, running perpendicular to the direction of the prevailing wind. These long, straight ridges can extend for over 100 miles (160 km).

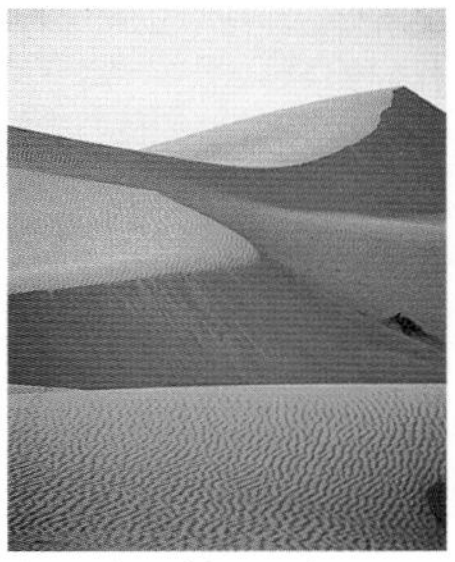

▲ ***Barchan dunes*** *in the Arabian Desert.*

▲ ***Complex dune system*** *in the Sahara.*

Dunes

Dunes are shaped by wind direction and sand supply. Where sand supply is limited, crescent-shaped barchan dunes are formed.

Types of dune

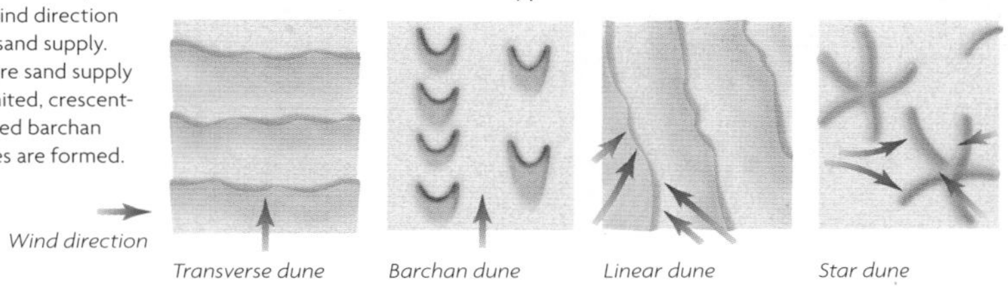
Wind direction
Transverse dune
Barchan dune
Linear dune
Star dune

Heat

Fierce sun can heat the surface of rock, causing it to expand more rapidly than the cooler, underlying layers. This creates tensions which force the rock to crack or break up. In arid regions, the evaporation of water from rock surfaces dissolves certain minerals within the water, causing salt crystals to form in small openings in the rock. The hard crystals force the openings to widen into cracks and fissures.

▲ ***The cracked and*** *parched floor of Death Valley, California. This is one of the hottest deserts on Earth.*

Desert abrasion

Abrasion creates a wide range of desert landforms from faceted pebbles and wind ripples in the sand, to large-scale features such as yardangs (low, streamlined ridges), and scoured desert pavements.

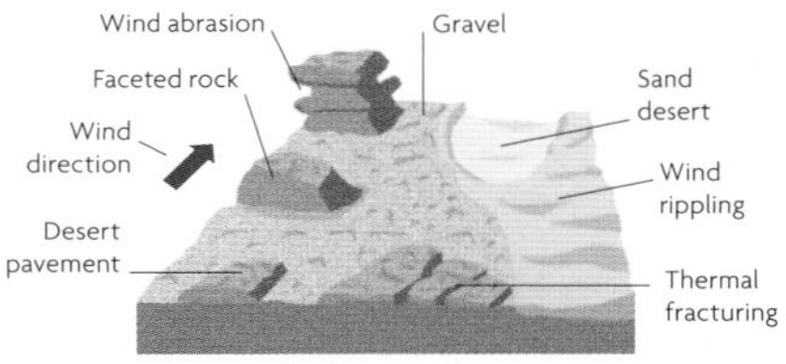
Wind abrasion
Gravel
Faceted rock
Sand desert
Wind direction
Wind rippling
Desert pavement
Thermal fracturing

Features of a desert surface

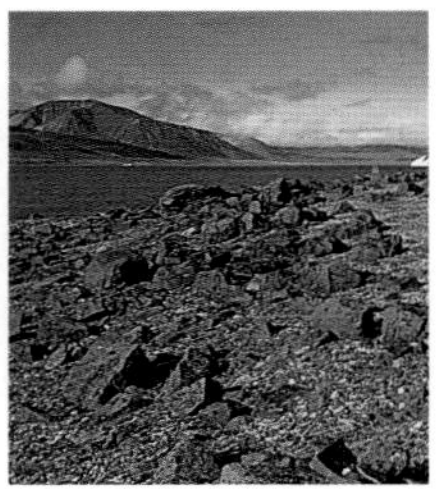

◀ ***This dry valley*** *at Ellesmere Island in the Canadian Arctic is an example of a cold desert. The cracked floor and scoured slopes are features also found in hot deserts.*

The world's oceans

Two-thirds of the Earth's surface is covered by the oceans. The landscape of the ocean floor, like the surface of the land, has been shaped by movements of the Earth's crust over millions of years to form volcanic mountain ranges, deep trenches, basins, and plateaus. Ocean currents constantly redistribute warm and cold water around the world. A major warm current, such as El Niño in the Pacific Ocean, can increase surface temperature by up to 10°F (8°C), causing changes in weather patterns which can lead to both droughts and flooding.

The great oceans

There are five oceans on Earth: the Pacific, Atlantic, Indian, and Southern oceans, and the much smaller Arctic Ocean. These five ocean basins are relatively young, having evolved within the last 80 million years. One of the most recent plate collisions, between the Eurasian and African plates, created the present-day arrangement of continents and oceans.

▲ ***The Indian Ocean*** *accounts for approximately 20% of the total area of the world's oceans.*

Sea level

If the influence of tides, winds, currents, and variations in gravity were ignored, the surface of the Earth's oceans would closely follow the topography of the ocean floor, with an underwater ridge 3000 ft (915 m) high producing a rise of up to 3 ft (1 m) in the level of the surface water.

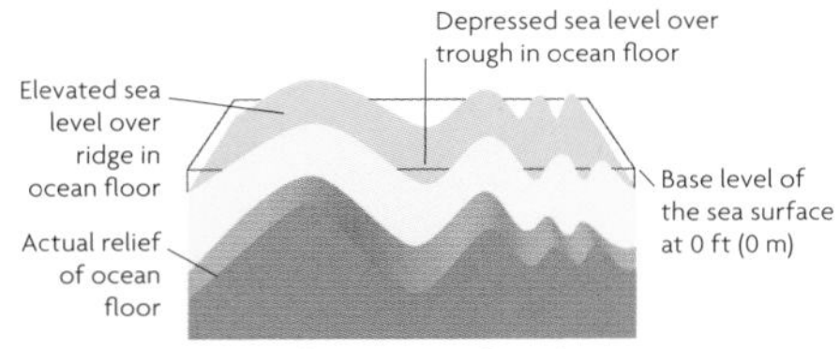

Depressed sea level over trough in ocean floor
Elevated sea level over ridge in ocean floor
Base level of the sea surface at 0 ft (0 m)
Actual relief of ocean floor

How surface waters reflect the relief of the ocean floor

▲ ***The low relief*** *of many small Pacific islands such as these atolls at Huahine in French Polynesia makes them vulnerable to changes in sea level.*

Ocean structure

The continental shelf is a shallow, flat seabed surrounding the Earth's continents. It extends to the continental slope, which falls to the ocean floor. Here, the flat abyssal plains are interrupted by vast, underwater mountain ranges, the mid-ocean ridges, and ocean trenches which plunge to depths of 35,828 ft (10,920 m).

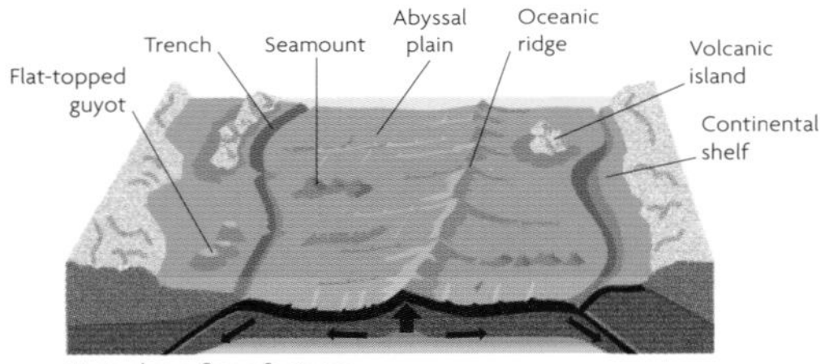

Flat-topped guyot
Trench
Seamount
Abyssal plain
Oceanic ridge
Volcanic island
Continental shelf

Typical sea-floor features

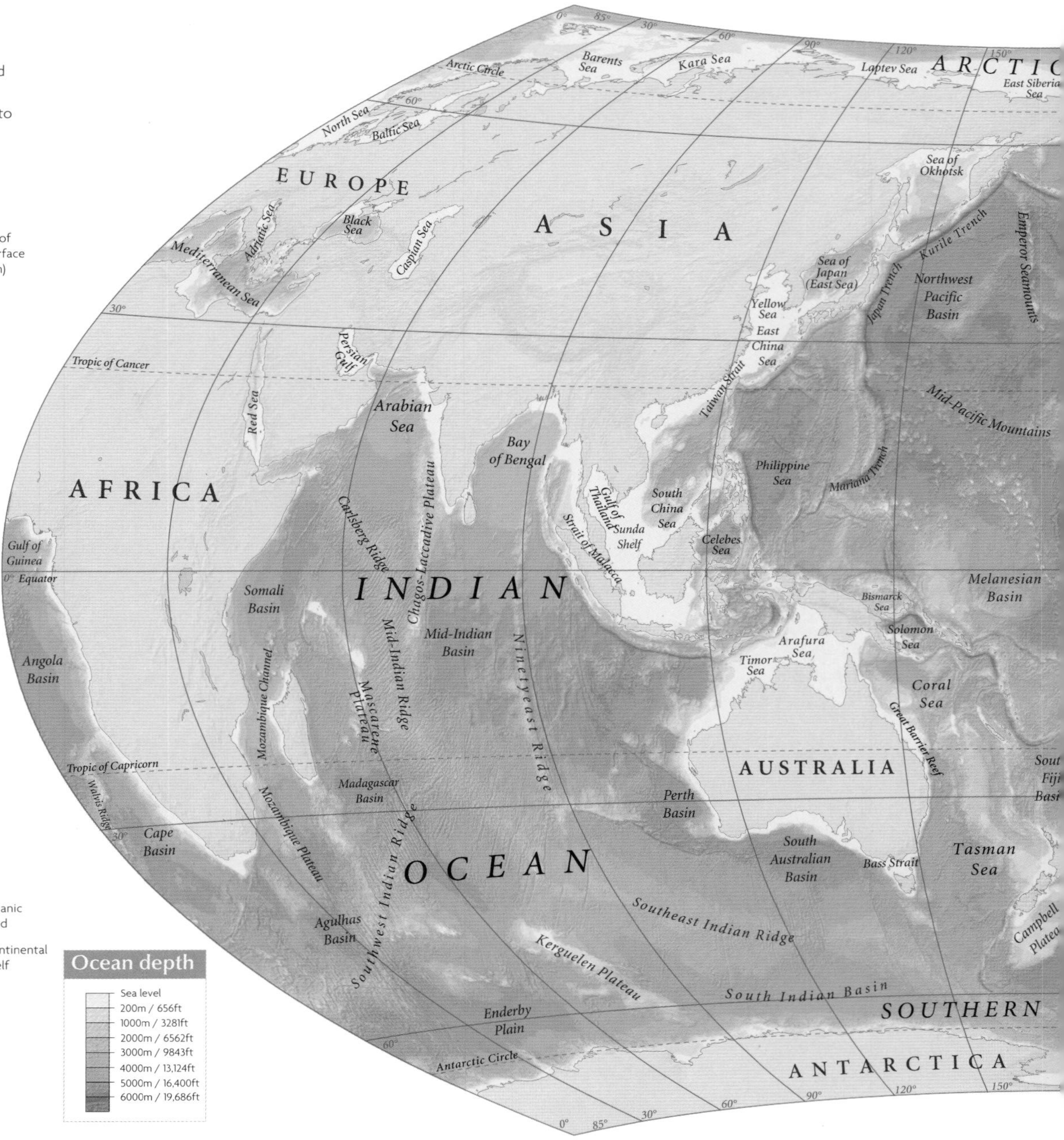

Arctic Circle
Barents Sea
Kara Sea
Laptev Sea
ARCTIC
East Siberian Sea
North Sea
Baltic Sea
EUROPE
Sea of Okhotsk
Black Sea
Caspian Sea
Adriatic Sea
Mediterranean Sea
ASIA
Sea of Japan (East Sea)
Kurile Trench
Japan Trench
Northwest Pacific Basin
Emperor Seamounts
Yellow Sea
East China Sea
Tropic of Cancer
Persian Gulf
Red Sea
Taiwan Strait
Mid-Pacific Mountains
Arabian Sea
Bay of Bengal
Philippine Sea
Mariana Trench
AFRICA
Carlsberg Ridge
Chagos-Laccadive Plateau
Gulf of Thailand
South China Sea
Sunda Shelf
Strait of Malacca
Celebes Sea
Gulf of Guinea
Equator
INDIAN
Somali Basin
Mid-Indian Basin
Mid-Indian Ridge
Ninetyeast Ridge
Bismarck Sea
Solomon Sea
Melanesian Basin
Angola Basin
Mozambique Channel
Mascarene Plateau
Timor Sea
Arafura Sea
Coral Sea
Great Barrier Reef
Tropic of Capricorn
Walvis Ridge
Madagascar Basin
AUSTRALIA
Perth Basin
South Fiji Basin
Cape Basin
Mozambique Plateau
OCEAN
South Australian Basin
Bass Strait
Tasman Sea
Agulhas Basin
Southwest Indian Ridge
Southeast Indian Ridge
Kerguelen Plateau
Campbell Plateau
South Indian Basin
SOUTHERN
Enderby Plain
Antarctic Circle
ANTARCTICA
Ocean depth
Sea level
200m / 656ft
1000m / 3281ft
2000m / 6562ft
3000m / 9843ft
4000m / 13,124ft
5000m / 16,400ft
6000m / 19,686ft

▲ ***A black smoker*** *in the Atlantic Ocean.*

Black smokers

These vents in the ocean floor disgorge hot, sulfur-rich water from deep in the Earth's crust. Despite the great depths, a variety of lifeforms have adapted to the chemical-rich environment which surrounds black smokers.

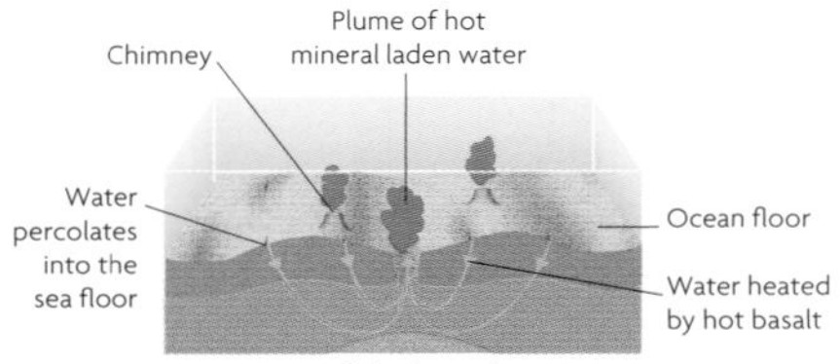

Chimney
Plume of hot mineral laden water
Water percolates into the sea floor
Ocean floor
Water heated by hot basalt

Formation of black smokers

▲ ***Surtsey, near Iceland,*** *is a volcanic island lying directly over the Mid-Atlantic Ridge. It was formed in the 1960s following intense volcanic activity nearby.*

Ocean floors

Mid-ocean ridges are formed by lava which erupts beneath the sea and cools to form solid rock. This process mirrors the creation of volcanoes from cooled lava on the land. The ages of sea floor rocks increase in parallel bands outward from central ocean ridges.

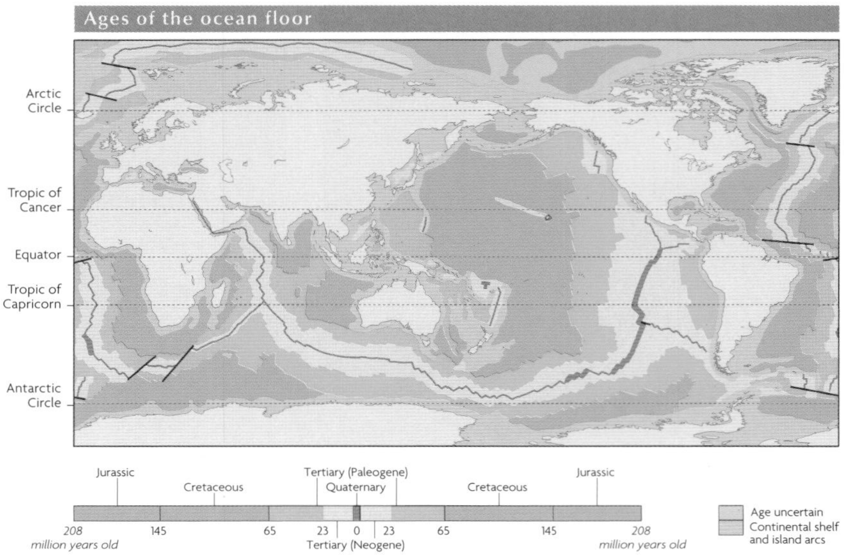

Ages of the ocean floor
Arctic Circle
Tropic of Cancer
Equator
Tropic of Capricorn
Antarctic Circle
Jurassic
Cretaceous
Tertiary (Paleogene)
Quaternary
Cretaceous
Jurassic
208 million years old
145
65
23
0
23
65
145
208 million years old
Tertiary (Neogene)
Age uncertain
Continental shelf and island arcs

▲ **Currents in the** Southern Ocean are driven by some of the world's fiercest winds, including the Roaring Forties, Furious Fifties, and Shrieking Sixties.

▲ **The Pacific Ocean** is the world's largest and deepest ocean, covering over one-third of the surface of the Earth.

▲ **The Atlantic Ocean** was formed when the landmasses of the eastern and western hemispheres began to drift apart 180 million years ago.

Deposition of sediment

Storms, earthquakes, and volcanic activity trigger underwater currents known as turbidity currents which scour sand and gravel from the continental shelf, creating underwater canyons. These strong currents pick up material deposited at river mouths and deltas, and carry it across the continental shelf and through the underwater canyons, where it is eventually laid down on the ocean floor in the form of fans.

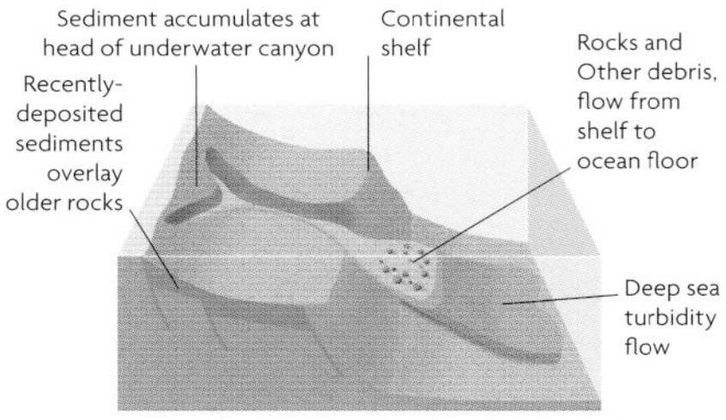
Sediment accumulates at head of underwater canyon
Continental shelf
Rocks and Other debris, flow from shelf to ocean floor
Recently-deposited sediments overlay older rocks
Deep sea turbidity flow

How sediment is deposited on the ocean floor

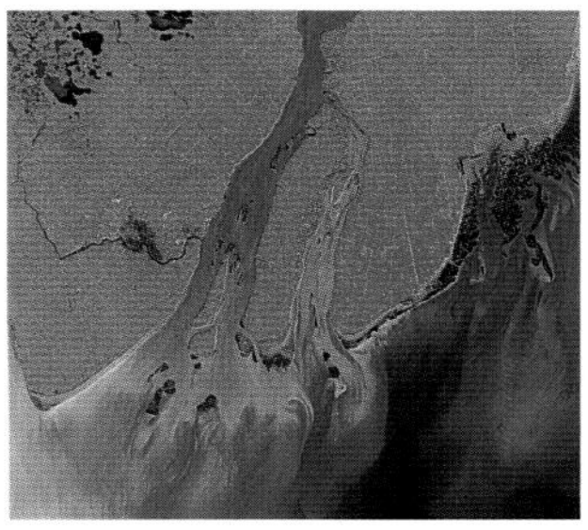

► **Satellite image of** the Yangtze (Chang Jiang) Delta, in which the land appears red. The river deposits immense quantities of silt into the East China Sea, much of which will eventually reach the deep ocean floor.

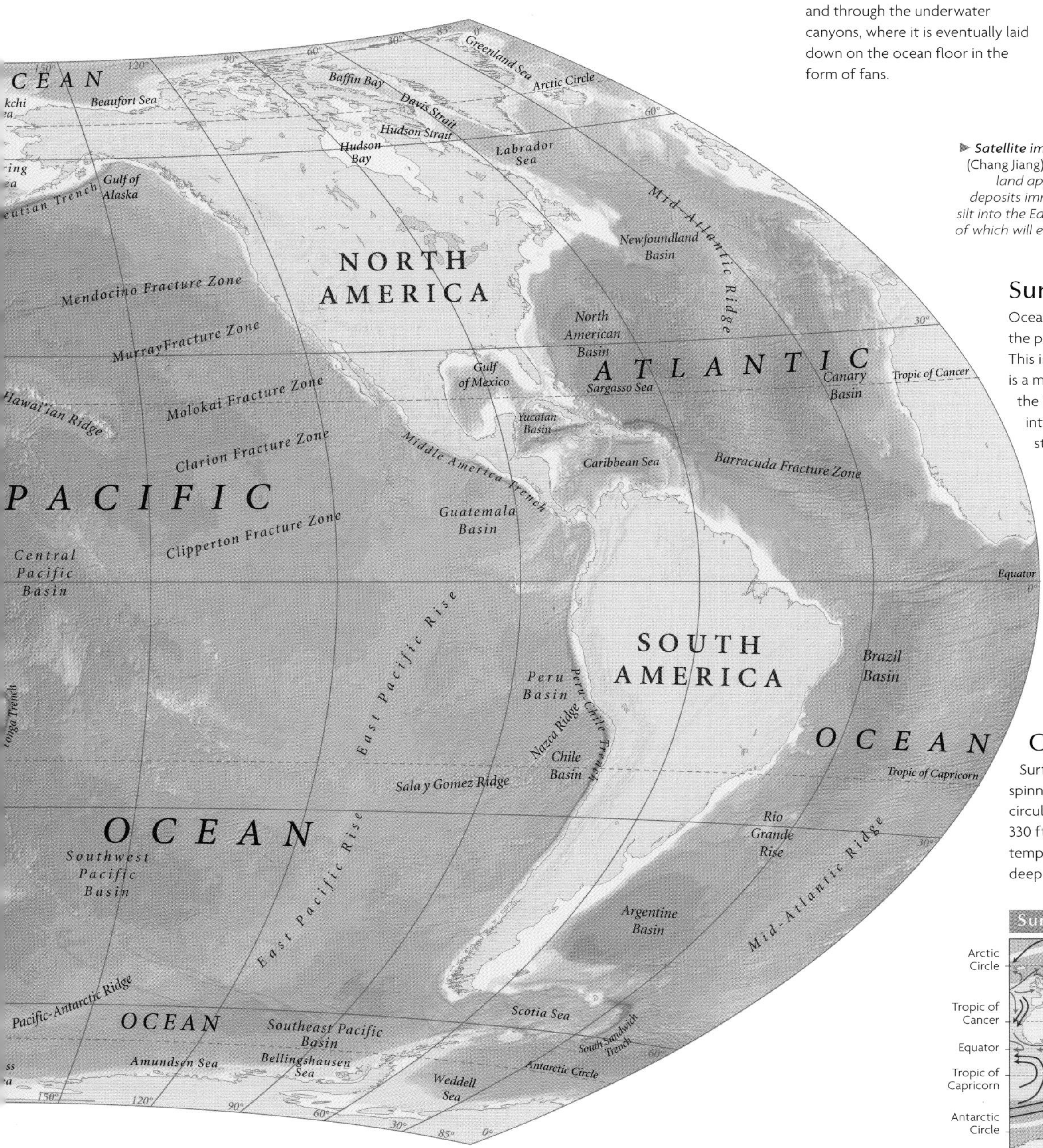
NORTH AMERICA
SOUTH AMERICA
PACIFIC OCEAN
ATLANTIC OCEAN
OCEAN
Greenland Sea
Arctic Circle
Baffin Bay
Davis Strait
Hudson Strait
Hudson Bay
Beaufort Sea
Labrador Sea
Gulf of Alaska
Aleutian Trench
Mid-Atlantic Ridge
Newfoundland Basin
Mendocino Fracture Zone
Murray Fracture Zone
Molokai Fracture Zone
Hawaiian Ridge
Clarion Fracture Zone
Clipperton Fracture Zone
North American Basin
Sargasso Sea
Canary Basin
Tropic of Cancer
Gulf of Mexico
Yucatan Basin
Middle America Trench
Caribbean Sea
Barracuda Fracture Zone
Guatemala Basin
Central Pacific Basin
Equator
East Pacific Rise
Brazil Basin
Peru Basin
Peru-Chile Trench
Nazca Ridge
Chile Basin
Sala y Gomez Ridge
Tropic of Capricorn
Rio Grande Rise
Tonga Trench
Southwest Pacific Basin
Argentine Basin
Mid-Atlantic Ridge
Pacific-Antarctic Ridge
Scotia Sea
South Sandwich Trench
Southeast Pacific Basin
Amundsen Sea
Bellingshausen Sea
Antarctic Circle
Weddell Sea

Surface water

Ocean currents move warm water away from the Equator toward the poles, while cold water is, in turn, moved towards the Equator. This is the main way in which the Earth distributes surface heat and is a major climatic control. Approximately 4000 million years ago, the Earth was dominated by oceans and there was no land to interrupt the flow of the currents, which would have flowed as straight lines, simply influenced by the Earth's rotation.

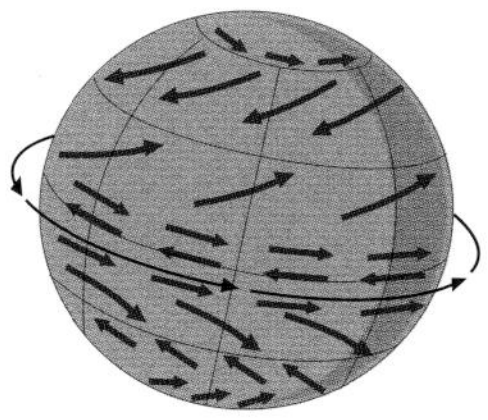

Idealized globe showing the movement of water around a landless Earth.

Ocean currents

Surface currents are driven by the prevailing winds and by the spinning motion of the Earth, which drives the currents into circulating whirlpools,or gyres. Deep sea currents, over 330 ft (100 m) below the surface, are driven by differences in water temperature and salinity, which have an impact on the density of deep water and on its movement.

Surface temperature and currents

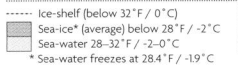

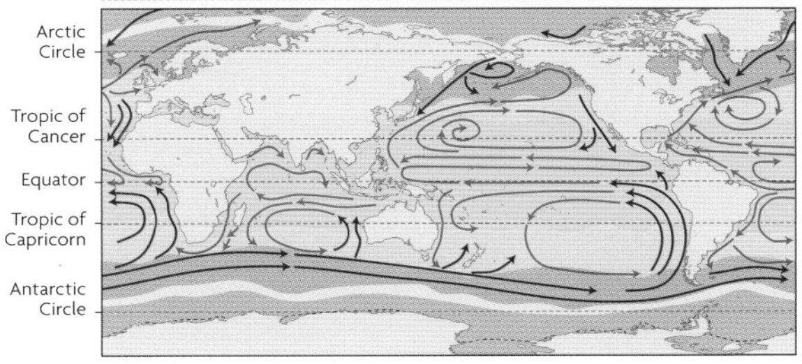
Arctic Circle
Tropic of Cancer
Equator
Tropic of Capricorn
Antarctic Circle

Surface temperature and currents

- Ice-shelf (below 32°F / 0°C)
- Sea-ice* (average) below 28°F / -2°C
- Sea-water 28–32°F / -2–0°C
- 32–50°F / F 0–10°C
- 50–68°F / 10–20°C
- 68–86°F / 20–30°C
- warm current
- cold current

* Sea-water freezes at 28.4°F / -1.9°C

Tides and waves

Tides are created by the pull of the Sun and Moon's gravity on the surface of the oceans. The levels of high and low tides are influenced by the position of the Moon in relation to the Earth and Sun. Waves are formed by wind blowing over the surface of the water.

Tidal range and wave environments

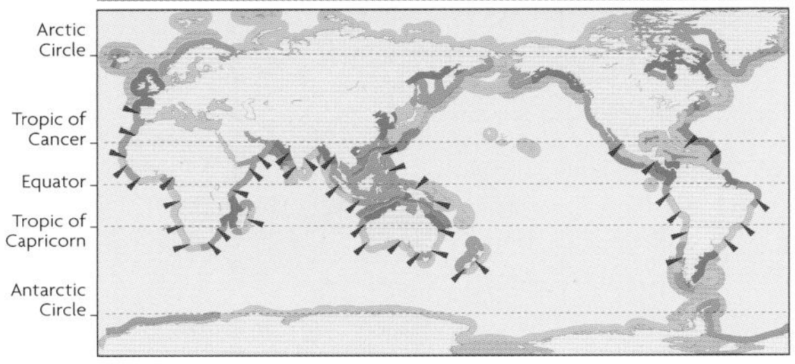
Arctic Circle
Tropic of Cancer
Equator
Tropic of Capricorn
Antarctic Circle

Tidal range and wave environments

- less than 7ft / 2m
- 7–13ft / 2–4m
- greater than 13ft / 4m
- east coast swell
- west coast swell
- tropical cyclone storm wave
- ice-shelf

High and low tides

The highest tides occur when the Earth, the Moon and the Sun are aligned *(below left)*. The lowest tides are experienced when the Sun and Moon align at right angles to one another *(below right)*.

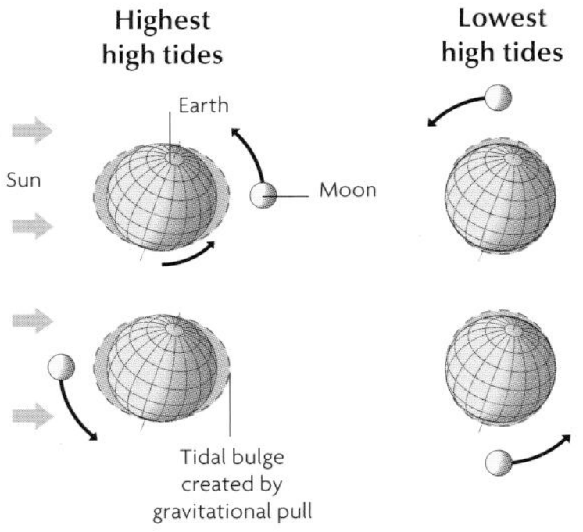
Highest high tides
Lowest high tides
Earth
Sun
Moon
Tidal bulge created by gravitational pull

Deep sea temperature and currents

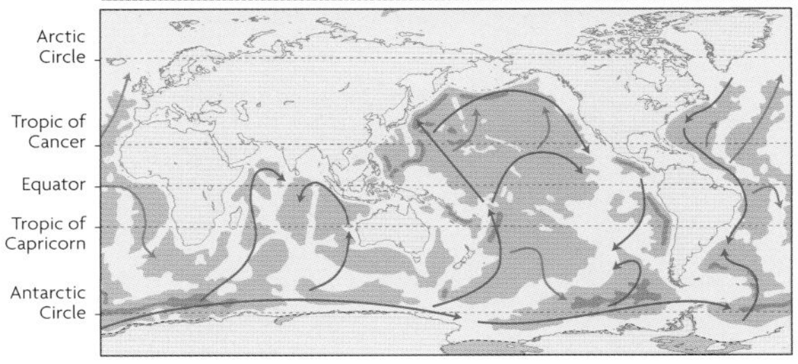
Arctic Circle
Tropic of Cancer
Equator
Tropic of Capricorn
Antarctic Circle

Deep sea temperature and currents

- Ice-shelf (below 32°F / 0°C)
- Sea-water 28–32°F / -2–0°C (below 16,400ft / 5000m)
- Sea-water 32–41°F /0–5°C (below 13,120ft / 4000m)
- Primary currents
- Secondary currents

The global climate

The Earth's climatic types consist of stable patterns of weather conditions averaged out over a long period of time. Different climates are categorized according to particular combinations of temperature and humidity. By contrast, weather consists of short-term fluctuations in wind, temperature, and humidity conditions. Different climates are determined by latitude, altitude, the prevailing wind, and circulation of ocean currents. Longer-term changes in climate, such as global warming or the onset of ice ages, are punctuated by shorter-term events which comprise the day-to-day weather of a region, such as frontal depressions, hurricanes, and blizzards.

The atmosphere, wind and weather

The Earth's atmosphere has been compared to a giant ocean of air which surrounds the planet. Its circulation patterns are similar to the currents in the oceans and are influenced by three factors; the Earth's orbit around the Sun and rotation about its axis, and variations in the amount of heat radiation received from the Sun. If both heat and moisture were not redistributed between the Equator and the poles, large areas of the Earth would be uninhabitable.

◀ ***Heavy fogs,*** *as here in southern England, form as moisture-laden air passes over cold ground.*

Global air circulation

Air does not simply flow from the Equator to the poles, it circulates in giant cells known as Hadley and Ferrel cells. As air warms it expands, becoming less dense and rising; this creates areas of low pressure. As the air rises it cools and condenses, causing heavy rainfall over the tropics and slight snowfall over the poles. This cool air then sinks, forming high pressure belts. At surface level in the tropics these sinking currents are deflected poleward as the westerlies and toward the equator as the trade winds. At the poles they become the polar easterlies.

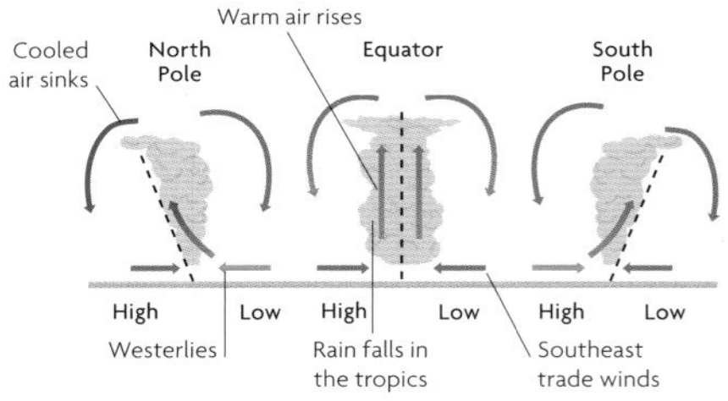

Warm air rises
Cooled air sinks
North Pole
Equator
South Pole
High
Low
High
Low
High
Low
Westerlies
Rain falls in the tropics
Southeast trade winds

▲ ***The Antarctic pack*** *ice expands its area by almost seven times during the winter as temperatures drop and surrounding seas freeze.*

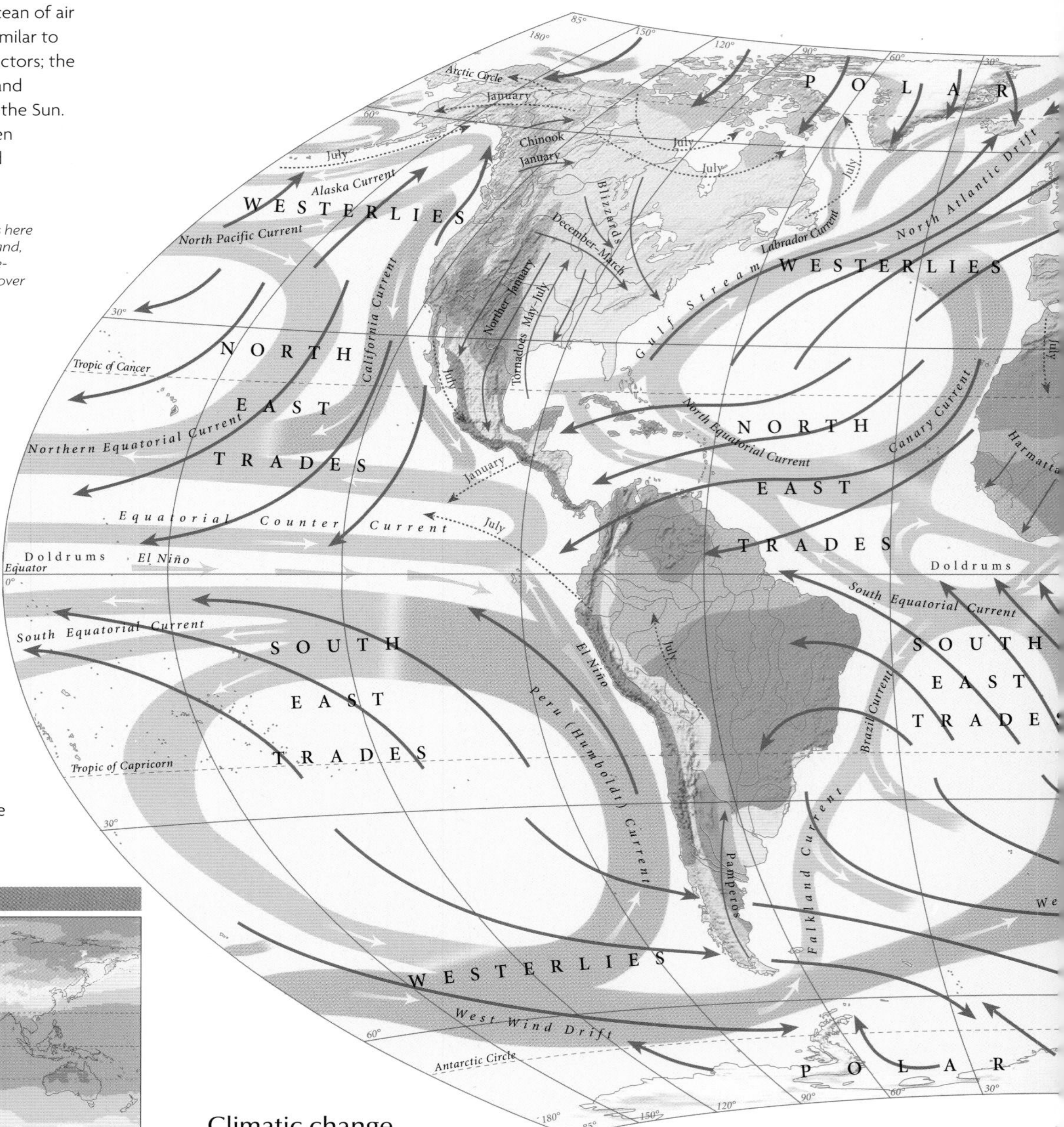

Arctic Circle
January
July
Chinook
Alaska Current
WESTERLIES
North Pacific Current
Blizzards
December–March
Labrador Current
North Atlantic Drift
POLAR
Gulf Stream
Northers January
Tornadoes May–July
California Current
Tropic of Cancer
NORTH EAST TRADES
Northern Equatorial Current
North Equatorial Current
Canary Current
Harmattan
Equatorial Counter Current
Doldrums
El Niño
Equator
South Equatorial Current
SOUTH EAST TRADES
Peru (Humboldt) Current
Brazil Current
Tropic of Capricorn
Falkland Current
Pampero
West Wind Drift
Antarctic Circle

Temperature

The world can be divided into three major climatic zones, stretching like large belts across the latitudes: the tropics which are warm; the cold polar regions and the temperate zones which lie between them. Temperatures across the Earth range from above 86°F (30°C) in the deserts to as low as -70°F (-55°C) at the poles. Temperature is also controlled by altitude; because air becomes cooler and less dense the higher it gets, mountainous regions are typically colder than those areas which are at, or close to, sea level.

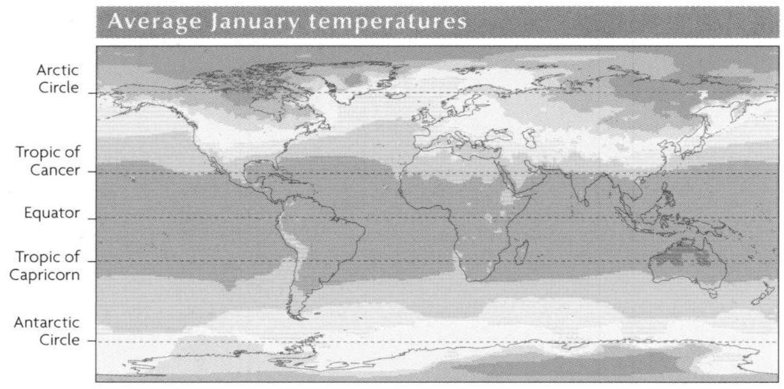

Average January temperatures
Arctic Circle
Tropic of Cancer
Equator
Tropic of Capricorn
Antarctic Circle

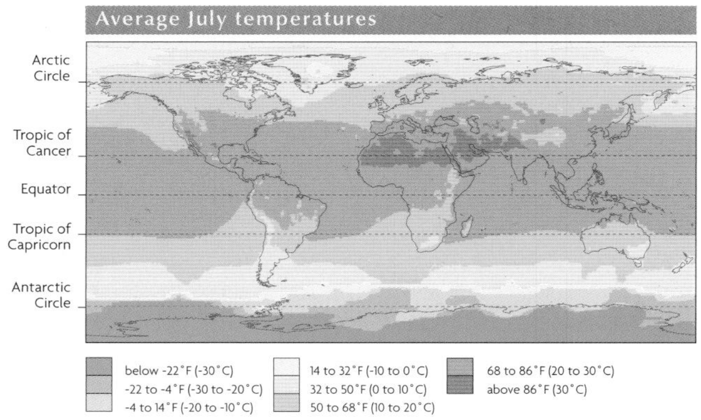

Average July temperatures
Arctic Circle
Tropic of Cancer
Equator
Tropic of Capricorn
Antarctic Circle
below -22°F (-30°C)
-22 to -4°F (-30 to -20°C)
-4 to 14°F (-20 to -10°C)
14 to 32°F (-10 to 0°C)
32 to 50°F (0 to 10°C)
50 to 68°F (10 to 20°C)
68 to 86°F (20 to 30°C)
above 86°F (30°C)

Climatic change

The Earth is currently in a warm phase between ice ages. Warmer temperatures result in higher sea levels as more of the polar ice caps melt. Most of the world's population lives near coasts, so any changes which might cause sea levels to rise, could have a potentially disastrous impact.

▲ ***This ice fair,*** *painted by Pieter Brueghel the Younger in the 17th century, shows the Little Ice Age which peaked around 300 years ago.*

The greenhouse effect

Gases such as carbon dioxide are known as "greenhouse gases" because they allow shortwave solar radiation to enter the Earth's atmosphere, but help to stop longwave radiation from escaping. This traps heat, raising the Earth's temperature. An excess of these gases, such as that which results from the burning of fossil fuels, helps trap more heat and can lead to global warming.

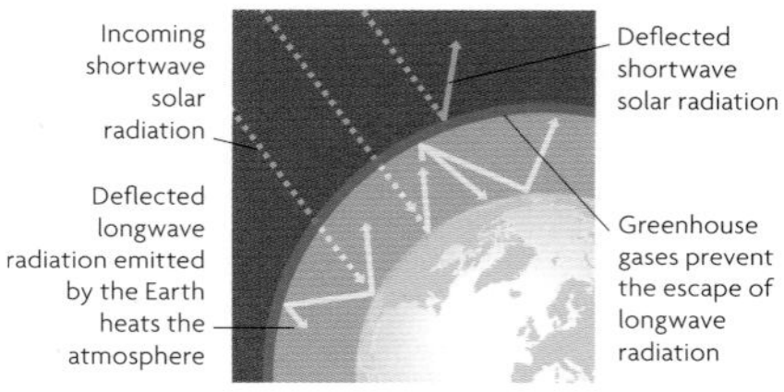

Incoming shortwave solar radiation
Deflected shortwave solar radiation
Deflected longwave radiation emitted by the Earth heats the atmosphere
Greenhouse gases prevent the escape of longwave radiation

◀ *The islands of* the Caribbean, Mexico's Gulf coast and the southeastern US are often hit by hurricanes formed far out in the Atlantic.

Oceanic water circulation

In general, ocean currents parallel the movement of winds across the Earth's surface. Incoming solar energy is greatest at the Equator and least at the poles. So, water in the oceans heats up most at the Equator and flows poleward, cooling as it moves north or south toward the Arctic or Antarctic. The flow is eventually reversed and cold water currents move back toward the Equator. These ocean currents act as a vast system for moving heat from the Equator toward the poles and are a major influence on the distribution of the Earth's climates.

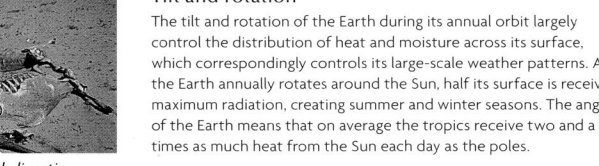

▲ *In marginal climatic* zones years of drought can completely dry out the land and transform grassland to desert.

Tilt and rotation

The tilt and rotation of the Earth during its annual orbit largely control the distribution of heat and moisture across its surface, which correspondingly controls its large-scale weather patterns. As the Earth annually rotates around the Sun, half its surface is receiving maximum radiation, creating summer and winter seasons. The angle of the Earth means that on average the tropics receive two and a half times as much heat from the Sun each day as the poles.

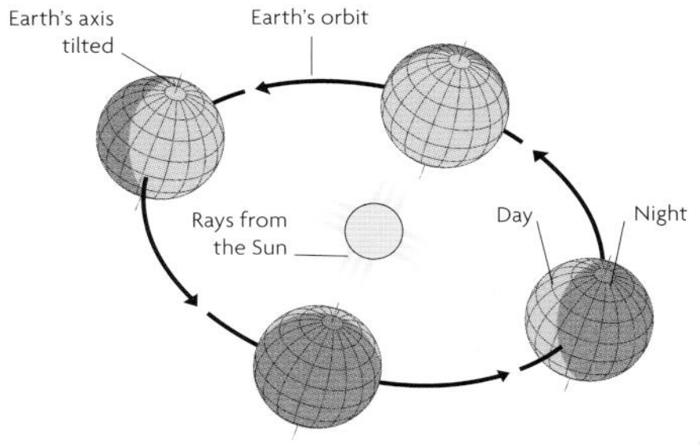

Earth's axis tilted
Earth's orbit
Rays from the Sun
Day
Night

Map key

Climate zones: ice cap; subarctic; tundra; continental; temperate; warm temperate; mediterranean; semi-arid; arid; hot humid; humid equatorial; tropical

Ocean currents: warm; cold

Prevailing winds: warm; cold

Local winds: warm; cold; June seasonal*

* (seasonal winds which can either be warm or cold)

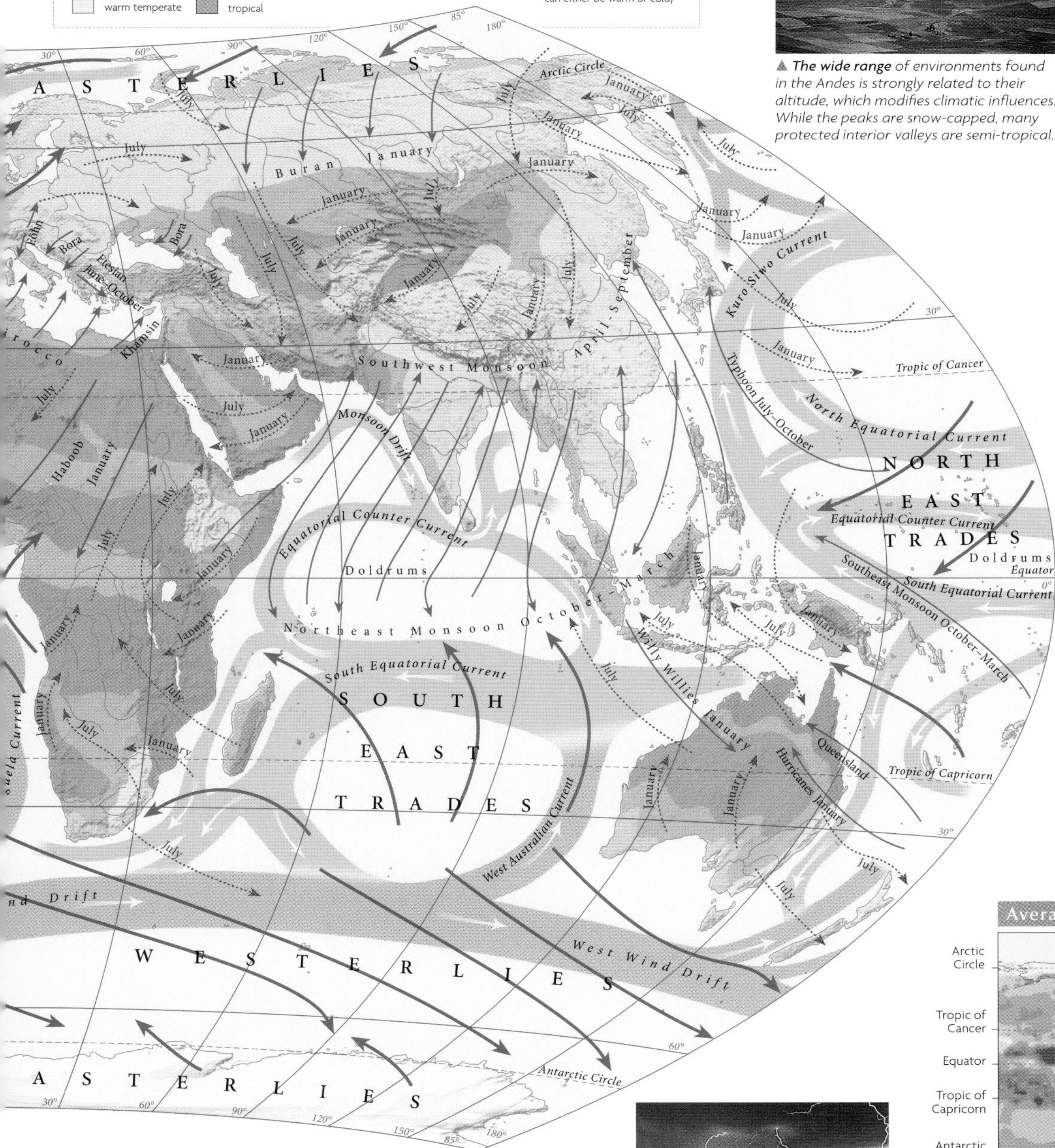

WESTERLIES
Arctic Circle
Buran
Bora
Etesian June–October
Khamsin
Sirocco
Haboob
Monsoon Drift
Southwest Monsoon
April–September
Kuro Siwo Current
Typhoon July–October
Tropic of Cancer
North Equatorial Current
NORTH EAST TRADES
Equatorial Counter Current
Doldrums
Equator
Southeast Monsoon October–March
South Equatorial Current
Northeast Monsoon October–March
SOUTH EAST TRADES
Willy Willies January
Hurricanes January
Queensland
Tropic of Capricorn
West Australian Current
West Wind Drift
Antarctic Circle

▲ *The wide range* of environments found in the Andes is strongly related to their altitude, which modifies climatic influences. While the peaks are snow-capped, many protected interior valleys are semi-tropical.

The Coriolis effect

The rotation of the Earth influences atmospheric circulation by deflecting winds and ocean currents. Winds blowing in the northern hemisphere are deflected to the right and those in the southern hemisphere are deflected to the left, creating large-scale patterns of wind circulation, such as the northeast and southeast trade winds and the westerlies. This effect is greatest at the poles and least at the Equator.

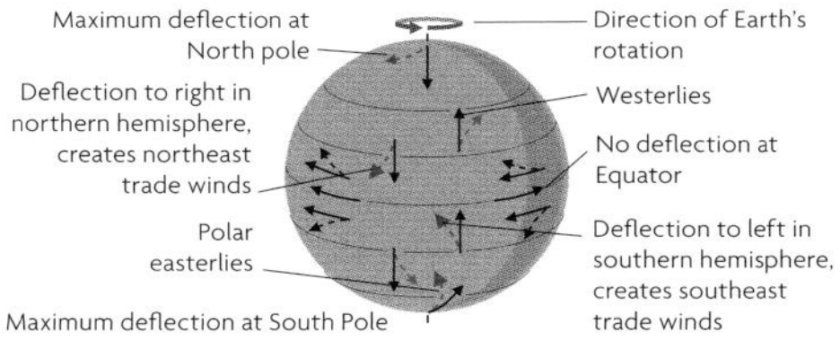

Maximum deflection at North pole
Direction of Earth's rotation
Deflection to right in northern hemisphere, creates northeast trade winds
Westerlies
No deflection at Equator
Polar easterlies
Deflection to left in southern hemisphere, creates southeast trade winds
Maximum deflection at South Pole

Precipitation

When warm air expands, it rises and cools, and the water vapor it carries condenses to form clouds. Heavy, regular rainfall is characteristic of the equatorial region, while the poles are cold and receive only slight snowfall. Tropical regions have marked dry and rainy seasons, while in the temperate regions rainfall is relatively unpredictable.

▲ *Monsoon rains, which* affect southern Asia from May to September, are caused by sea winds blowing across the warm land.

▲ *Heavy tropical rainstorms* occur frequently in Papua New Guinea, often causing soil erosion and landslides in cultivated areas.

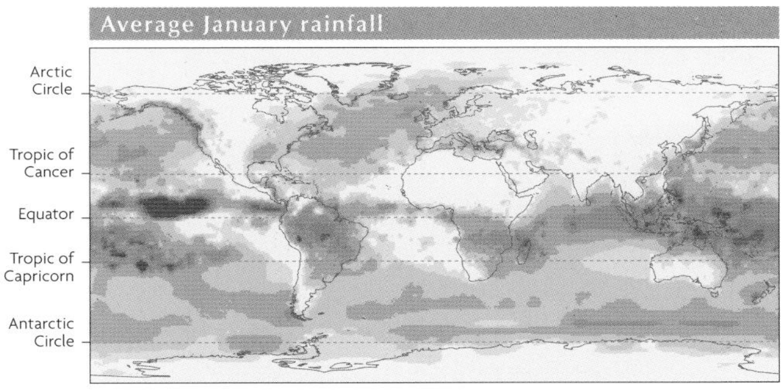

Average January rainfall
Arctic Circle
Tropic of Cancer
Equator
Tropic of Capricorn
Antarctic Circle

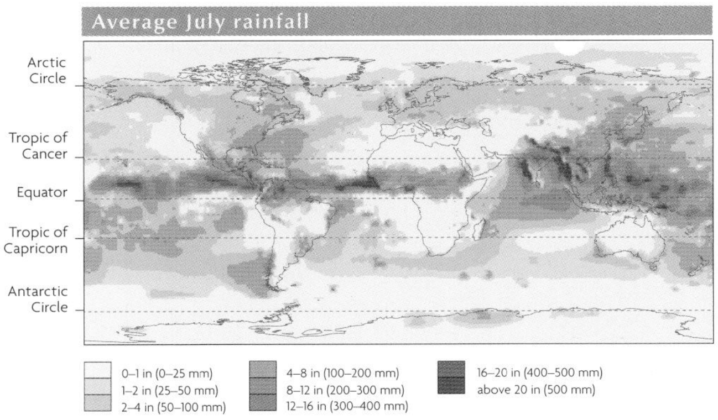

Average July rainfall
Arctic Circle
Tropic of Cancer
Equator
Tropic of Capricorn
Antarctic Circle
0–1 in (0–25 mm)
1–2 in (25–50 mm)
2–4 in (50–100 mm)
4–8 in (100–200 mm)
8–12 in (200–300 mm)
12–16 in (300–400 mm)
16–20 in (400–500 mm)
above 20 in (500 mm)

▲ *The intensity of* some blizzards in Canada and the northern US can give rise to snowdrifts as high as 10 ft (3 m).

▲ *The Atacama Desert* in Chile is one of the driest places on Earth, with an average rainfall of less than 2 inches (50 mm) per year.

▲ *Violent thunderstorms occur* along advancing cold fronts, when cold, dry air masses meet warm, moist air, which rises rapidly, its moisture condensing into thunderclouds. Rain and hail become electrically charged, causing lightning.

The rainshadow effect

When moist air is forced to rise by mountains, it cools and the water vapor falls as precipitation, either as rain or snow. Only the dry, cold air continues over the mountains, leaving inland areas with little or no rain. This is called the rainshadow effect and is one reason for the existence of the Mojave Desert in California, which lies east of the Coast Ranges.

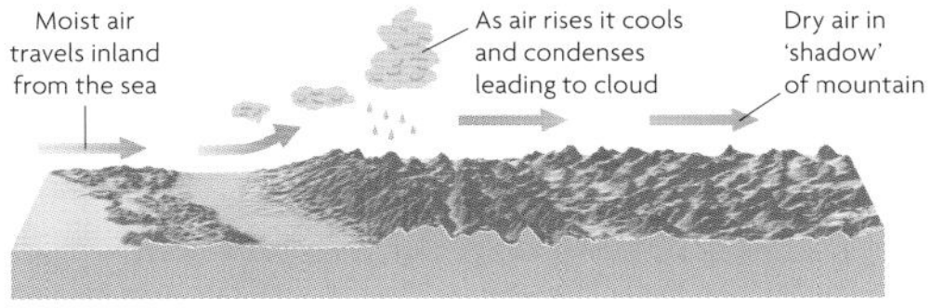

Moist air travels inland from the sea
As air rises it cools and condenses leading to cloud
Dry air in 'shadow' of mountain

The rainshadow effect

Life on Earth

A unique combination of an oxygen-rich atmosphere and plentiful water is the key to life on Earth. Apart from the polar ice caps, there are few areas which have not been colonized by animals or plants over the course of the Earth's history. Plants process sunlight to provide them with their energy, and ultimately all the Earth's animals rely on plants for survival. Because of this reliance, plants are known as primary producers, and the availability of nutrients and temperature of an area is defined as its primary productivity, which affects the quantity and type of animals which are able to live there. This index is affected by climatic factors – cold and aridity restrict the quantity of life, whereas warmth and regular rainfall allow a greater diversity of species.

Biogeographical regions

The Earth can be divided into a series of biogeographical regions, or biomes, ecological communities where certain species of plant and animal coexist within particular climatic conditions. Within these broad classifications, other factors including soil richness, altitude, and human activities such as urbanization, intensive agriculture, and deforestation, affect the local distribution of living species within each biome.

Polar regions

A layer of permanent ice at the Earth's poles covers both seas and land. Very little plant and animal life can exist in these harsh regions.

Tundra

A desolate region, with long, dark freezing winters and short, cold summers. With virtually no soil and large areas of permanently frozen ground known as permafrost, the tundra is largely treeless, though it is briefly clothed by small flowering plants in the summer months.

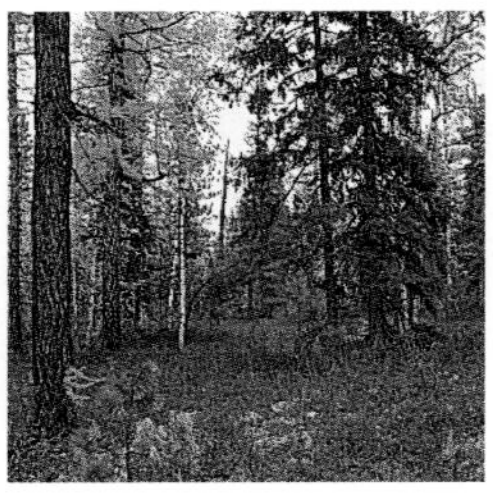

Needleleaf forests

With milder summers than the tundra and less wind,these areas are able to support large forests of coniferous trees.

Broadleaf forests

Much of the northern hemisphere was once covered by deciduous forests, which occurred in areas with marked seasonal variations. Most deciduous forests have been cleared for human settlement.

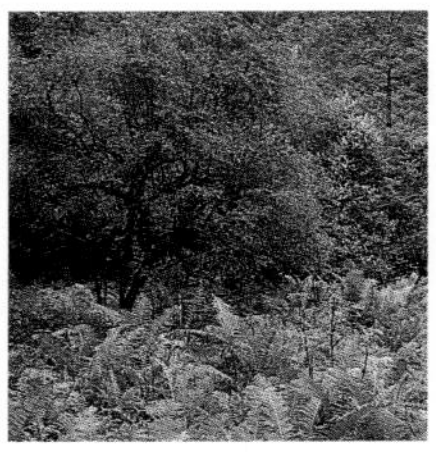

Temperate rain forests

In warmer wetter areas, such as southern China, temperate deciduous forests are replaced by evergreen forest.

Deserts

Deserts are areas with negligible rainfall. Most hot deserts lie within the tropics; cold deserts are dry because of their distance from the moisture-providing sea.

Mediterranean

Hot, dry summers and short winters typify these areas, which were once covered by evergreen shrubs and woodland, but have now been cleared by humans for agriculture.

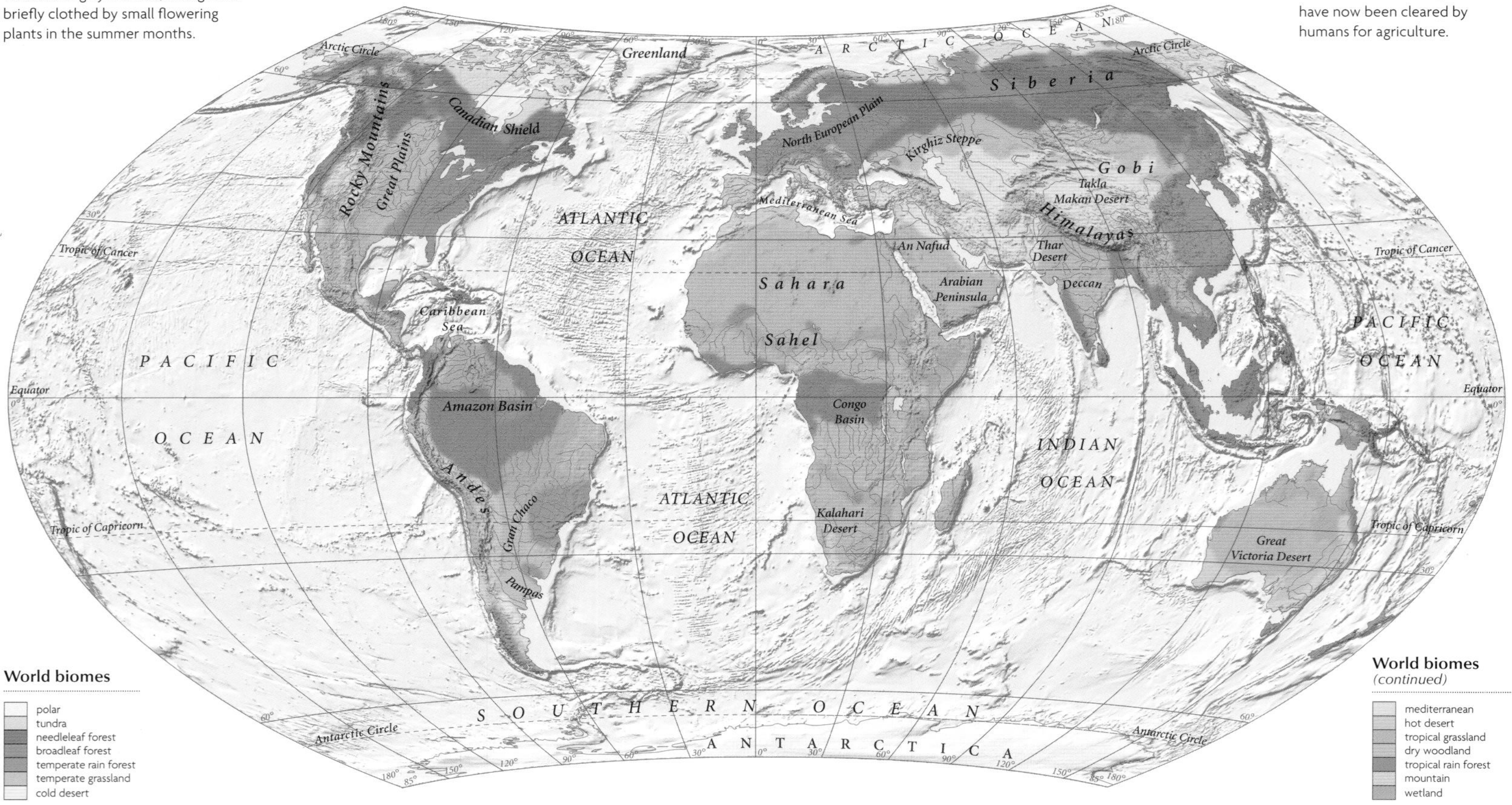
Arctic Circle
Greenland
ARCTIC OCEAN
Siberia
Canadian Shield
Rocky Mountains
Great Plains
North European Plain
Kirghiz Steppe
Gobi
Takla Makan Desert
Himalayas
Mediterranean Sea
ATLANTIC OCEAN
Tropic of Cancer
An Nafud
Thar Desert
Arabian Peninsula
Deccan
Sahara
Caribbean Sea
Sahel
PACIFIC OCEAN
Equator
Amazon Basin
Congo Basin
INDIAN OCEAN
Andes
Gran Chaco
Kalahari Desert
Tropic of Capricorn
Great Victoria Desert
Pampas
SOUTHERN OCEAN
Antarctic Circle
ANTARCTICA

World biomes

- polar
- tundra
- needleleaf forest
- broadleaf forest
- temperate rain forest
- temperate grassland
- cold desert

World biomes *(continued)*

- mediterranean
- hot desert
- tropical grassland
- dry woodland
- tropical rain forest
- mountain
- wetland

Tropical and temperate grasslands

The major grassland areas are found in the centers of the larger continental landmasses. In Africa's tropical savannah regions, seasonal rainfall alternates with drought. Temperate grasslands, also known as steppes and prairies are found in the northern hemisphere, and in South America, where they are known as the pampas.

Dry woodlands

Trees and shrubs, adapted to dry conditions, grow widely spaced from one another, interspersed by savannah grasslands.

Tropical rain forests

Characterized by year-round warmth and high rainfall, tropical rain forests contain the highest diversity of plant and animal species on Earth.

Mountains

Though the lower slopes of mountains may be thickly forested, only ground-hugging shrubs and other vegetation will grow above the tree line which varies according to both altitude and latitude.

Wetlands

Rarely lying above sea level, wetlands are marshes, swamps, and tidal flats. Some, with their moist, fertile soils, are rich feeding grounds for fish and breeding grounds for birds. Others have little soil structure and are too acidic to support much plant and animal life.

Biodiversity

The number of plant and animal species, and the range of genetic diversity within the populations of each species, make up the Earth's biodiversity. The plants and animals which are endemic to a region – that is, those which are found nowhere else in the world – are also important in determining levels of biodiversity. Human settlement and intervention have encroached on many areas of the world once rich in endemic plant and animal species. Increasing international efforts are being made to monitor and conserve the biodiversity of the Earth's remaining wild places.

Animal adaptation

The degree of an animal's adaptability to different climates and conditions is extremely important in ensuring its success as a species. Many animals, particularly the largest mammals, are becoming restricted to ever-smaller regions as human development and modern agricultural practices reduce their natural habitats. In contrast, humans have been responsible – both deliberately and accidentally – for the spread of some of the world's most successful species. Many of these introduced species are now more numerous than the indigenous animal populations.

Polar animals

The frozen wastes of the polar regions are able to support only a small range of species which derive their nutritional requirements from the sea. Animals such as the walrus *(left)* have developed insulating fat, stocky limbs, and double-layered coats to enable them to survive in the freezing conditions.

Desert animals

Many animals which live in the extreme heat and aridity of the deserts are able to survive for days and even months with very little food or water. Their bodies are adapted to lose heat quickly and to store fat and water. The Gila monster *(above)* stores fat in its tail.

Amazon rain forest

The vast Amazon Basin is home to the world's greatest variety of animal species. Animals are adapted to live at many different levels from the treetops to the tangled undergrowth which lies beneath the canopy. The sloth *(below)* hangs upside down in the branches. Its fur grows from its stomach to its back to enable water to run off quickly.

Diversity of animal species

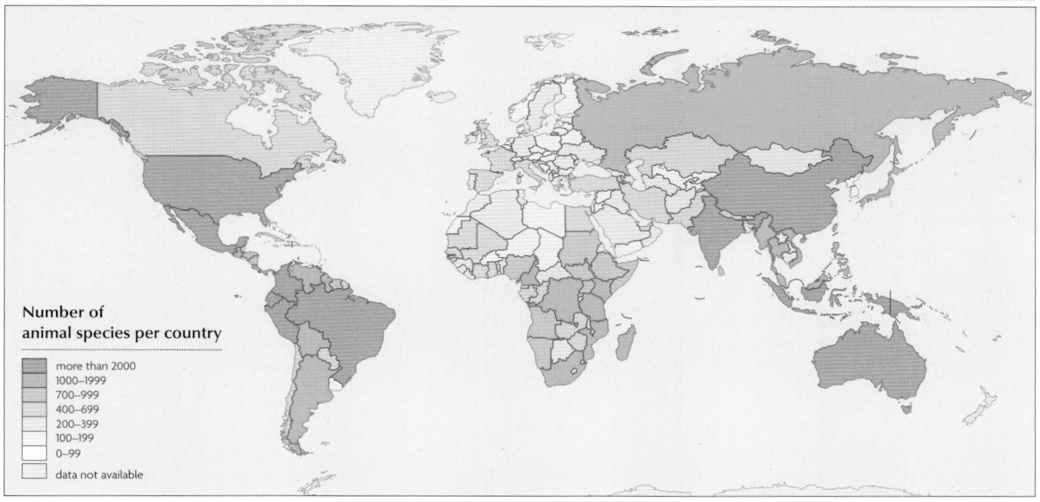
Number of
animal species per country
more than 2000
1000–1999
700–999
400–699
200–399
100–199
0–99
data not available

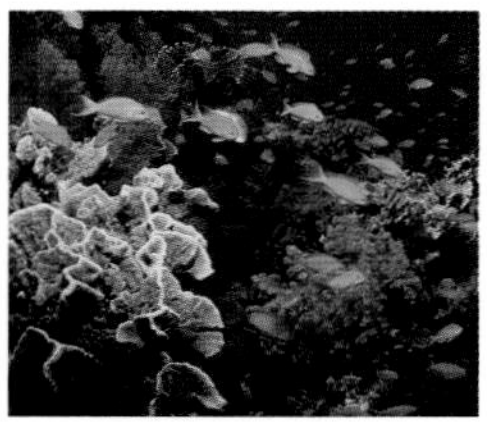

Marine biodiversity

The oceans support a huge variety of different species, from the world's largest mammals like whales and dolphins down to the tiniest plankton. The greatest diversities occur in the warmer seas of continental shelves, where plants are easily able to photosynthesize, and around coral reefs, where complex ecosystems are found. On the ocean floor, nematodes can exist at a depth of more than 10,000 ft (3000 m) below sea level.

High altitudes

Few animals exist in the rarefied atmosphere of the highest mountains. However, birds of prey such as eagles and vultures (*above*), with their superb eyesight can soar as high as 23,000 ft (7000 m) to scan for prey below.

Urban animals

The growth of cities has reduced the amount of habitat available to many species. A number of animals are now moving closer into urban areas to scavenge from the detritus of the modern city (*left*). Rodents, particularly rats and mice, have existed in cities for thousands of years, and many insects, especially moths, quickly develop new coloring to provide them with camouflage.

Endemic species

Isolated areas such as Australia and the island of Madagascar, have the greatest range of endemic species. In Australia, these include marsupials such as the kangaroo (*below*), which carry their young in pouches on their bodies. Destruction of habitat, pollution, hunting, and predators introduced by humans, are threatening this unique biodiversity.

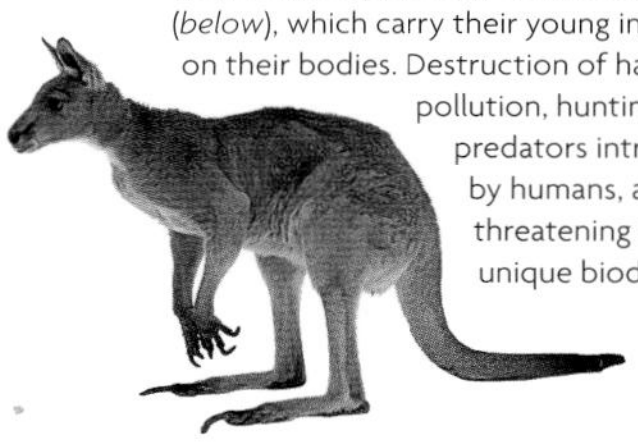

Plant adaptation

Environmental conditions, particularly climate, soil type, and the extent of competition with other organisms, influence the development of plants into a number of distinctive forms. Similar conditions in quite different parts of the world create similar adaptations in the plants, which may then be modified by other, local, factors specific to the region.

Cold conditions

In areas where temperatures rarely rise above freezing, plants such as lichens (*left*) and mosses grow densely, close to the ground.

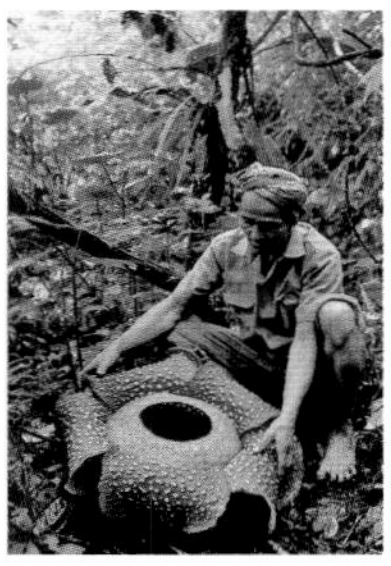

Rain forests

Most of the world's largest and oldest plants are found in rain forests; warmth and heavy rainfall provide ideal conditions for vast plants like the world's largest flower, the rafflesia *(left)*.

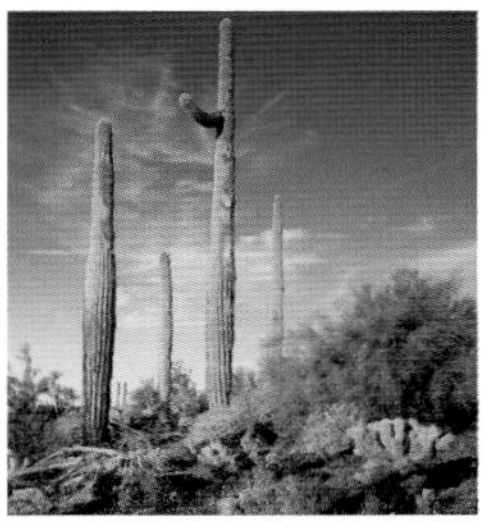

Hot, dry conditions

Arid conditions lead to the development of plants whose surface area has been reduced to a minimum to reduce water loss. In cacti *(above)*, which can survive without water for months, leaves are minimal or not present at all.

Ancient plants

Some of the world's most primitive plants still exist today, including algae, cycads, and many ferns (*above*), reflecting the success with which they have adapted to changing conditions.

Resisting predators

A great variety of plants have developed devices including spines (*above*), poisons, stinging hairs, and an unpleasant taste or smell to deter animal predators.

Diversity of plant species

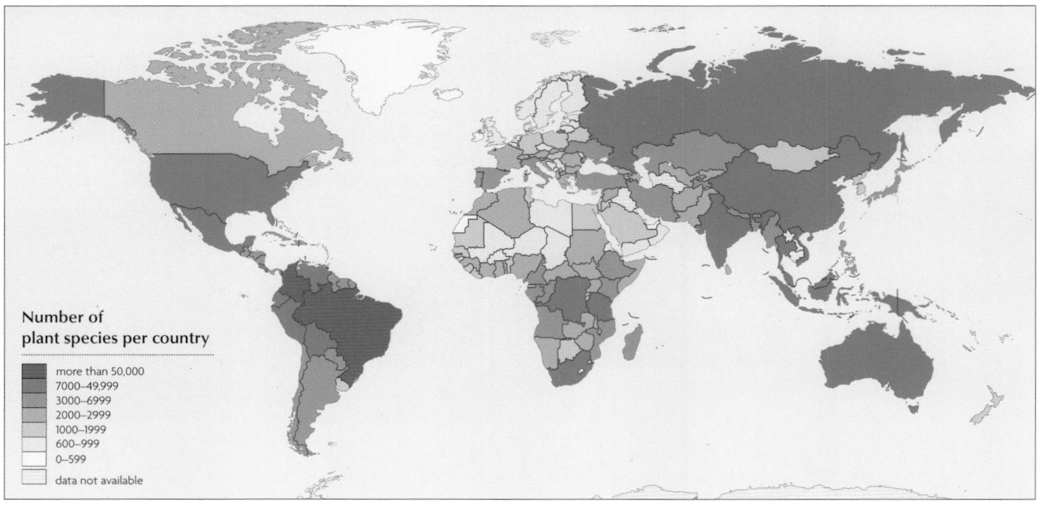
Number of
plant species per country
more than 50,000
7000–49,999
3000–6999
2000–2999
1000–1999
600–999
0–599
data not available

Weeds

Weeds such as bindweed *(above)* are fast-growing, easily dispersed, and tolerant of a number of different environments, enabling them to quickly colonize suitable habitats. They are among the most adaptable of all plants.

Population and settlement

The Earth's population is projected to rise from its current level of about 7 billion to reach some 10.5 billion by 2050. The global distribution of this rapidly growing population is very uneven, and is dictated by climate, terrain, and natural and economic resources. The great majority of the Earth's people live in coastal zones, and along river valleys. Deserts cover over 20% of the Earth's surface, but support less than 5% of the world's population. It is estimated that over half of the world's population live in cities – most of them in Asia – as a result of mass migration from rural areas in search of jobs. Many of these people live in the so-called "megacities," some with populations as great as 40 million.

Patterns of settlement

The past 200 years have seen the most radical shift in world population patterns in recorded history.

Nomadic life

All the world's peoples were hunter-gatherers 10,000 years ago. Today nomads, who live by following available food resources, account for less than 0.0001% of the world's population. They are mainly pastoral herders, moving their livestock from place to place in search of grazing land.

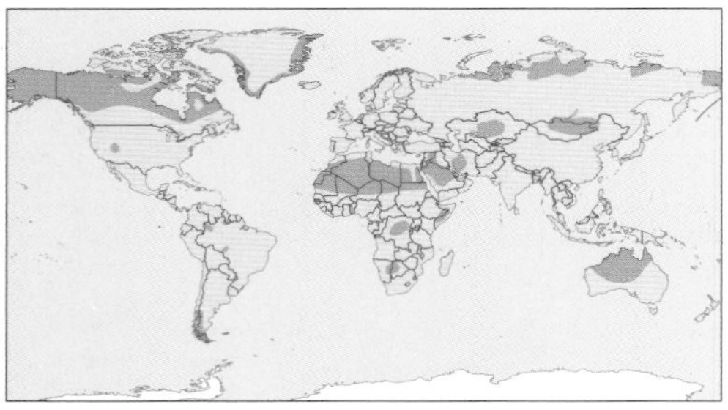

Nomadic population

Nomadic population area

The growth of cities

In 1900 there were only 14 cities in the world with populations of more than a million, mostly in the northern hemisphere. Today, as more and more people in the developing world migrate to towns and cities, there are over 70 cities whose population exceeds 5 million, and around 490 "million-cities."

Million-cities in 1900

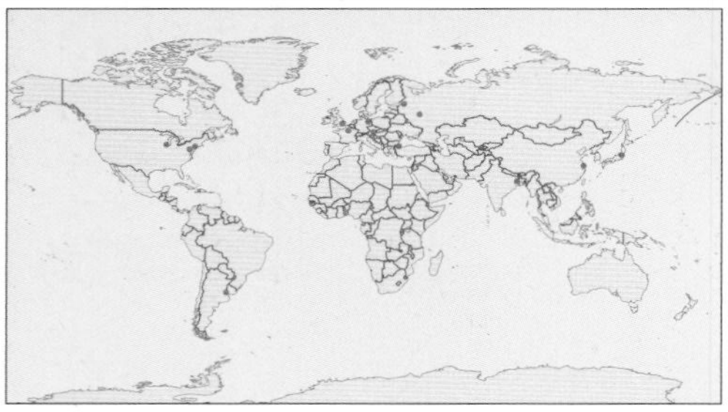

Million-cities in 1900

• Cities over 1 million population

Million-cities in 2005

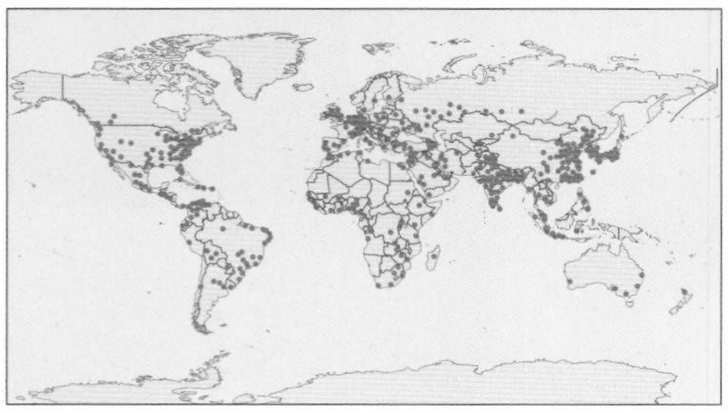

Million-cities in 2005

• Cities over 1 million population

North America

The eastern and western seaboards of the US, with huge expanses of interconnected cities, towns, and suburbs, are vast, densely-populated megalopolises. Central America and the Caribbean also have high population densities. Yet, away from the coasts and in the wildernesses of northern Canada the land is very sparsely settled.

▲ **Vancouver on Canada's** *west coast, grew up as a port city. In recent years it has attracted many Asian immigrants, particularly from the Pacific Rim.*

▲ **North America's central** *plains, the continent's agricultural heartland, are thinly populated and highly productive.*

Europe

With its temperate climate, and rich mineral and natural resources, Europe is generally very densely settled. The continent acts as a magnet for economic migrants from the developing world, and immigration is now widely restricted. Birthrates in Europe are generally low, and in some countries, such as Germany, the populations have stabilized at zero growth, with a fast-growing elderly population.

▲ **Many European cities,** *like Siena, once reflected the "ideal" size for human settlements. Modern technological advances have enabled them to grow far beyond the original walls.*

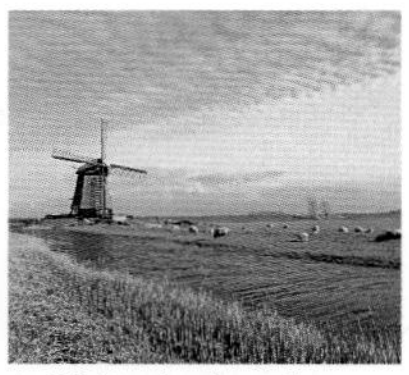

▲ **Within the densely-populated** *Netherlands the reclamation of coastal wetlands is vital to provide much-needed land for agriculture and settlement.*

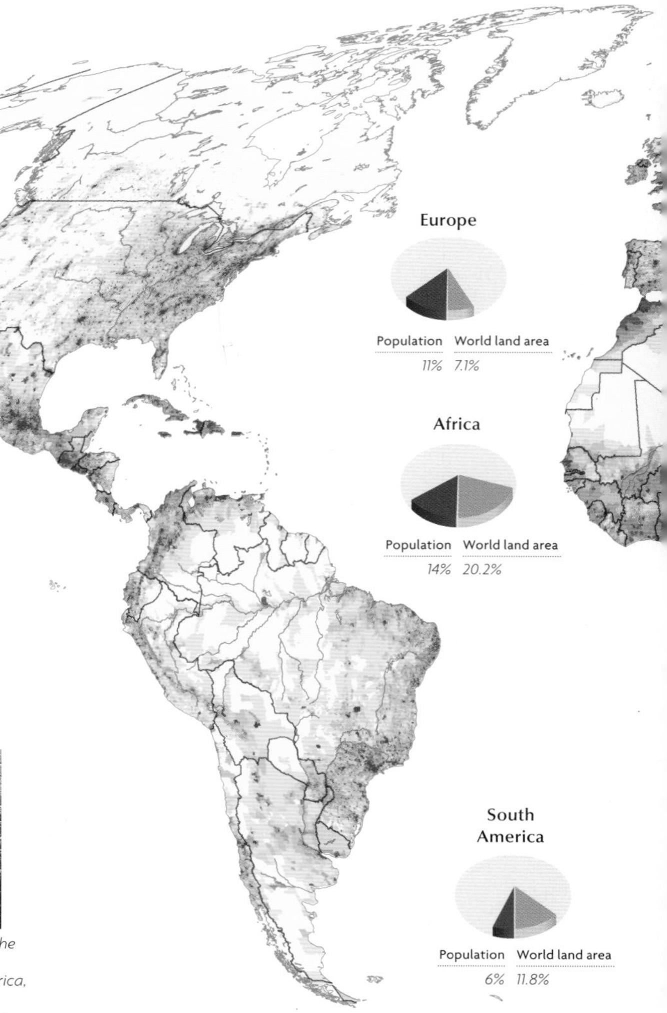
Population density
(inhabitants per sq mile)
520–2600
260–520
130–260
52–130
26–52
13–26
3–13
Fewer than 3
North America
Population 8%
World land area 17%
Europe
Population 11%
World land area 7.1%
Africa
Population 14%
World land area 20.2%
South America
Population 6%
World land area 11.8%

South America

Most settlement in South America is clustered in a narrow belt in coastal zones and in the northern Andes. During the 20th century, cities such as São Paulo and Buenos Aires grew enormously, acting as powerful economic magnets to the rural population. Shantytowns have grown up on the outskirts of many major cities to house these immigrants, often lacking basic amenities.

▲ **Many people in** *western South America live at high altitudes in the Andes, both in cities and in villages such as this one in Bolivia.*

▲ **Venezuela is one** *of the most highly urbanized countries in South America, with nearly 90% of the population living in cities such as Caracas.*

Africa

▲ **Cities such as** *Nairobi (above), Cairo, and Johannesburg have grown rapidly in recent years, although only Cairo has a significant population on a global scale.*

The arid climate of much of Africa means that settlement of the continent is sparse, focusing in coastal areas and fertile regions such as the Nile Valley. Africa still has a high proportion of nomadic agriculturalists, although many are now becoming settled, and the population is predominantly rural.

▲ **Traditional lifestyles and** *homes persist across much of Africa, which has a higher proportion of rural or village-based population than any other continent.*

Asia

Most Asian settlement originally centered around the great river valleys such as the Indus, the Ganges, and the Yangtze. Today, almost 60% of the world's population lives in Asia, many in burgeoning cities – particularly in the economically-buoyant Pacific Rim countries. Even rural population densities are high in many countries; practices such as terracing in Southeast Asia making the most of the available land.

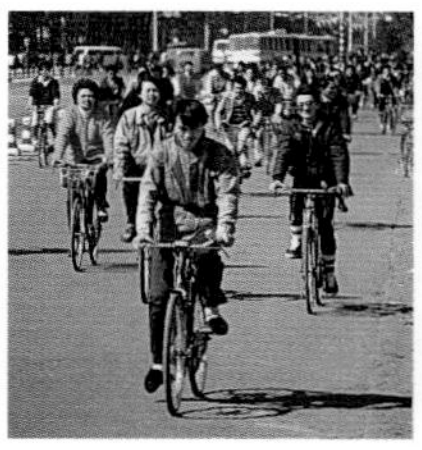

▲ **Many of China's** *cities are now vast urban areas with populations of more than 5 million people.*

▲ **This stilt village** *in Bangladesh is built to resist the regular flooding. Pressure on land, even in rural areas, forces many people to live in marginal areas.*

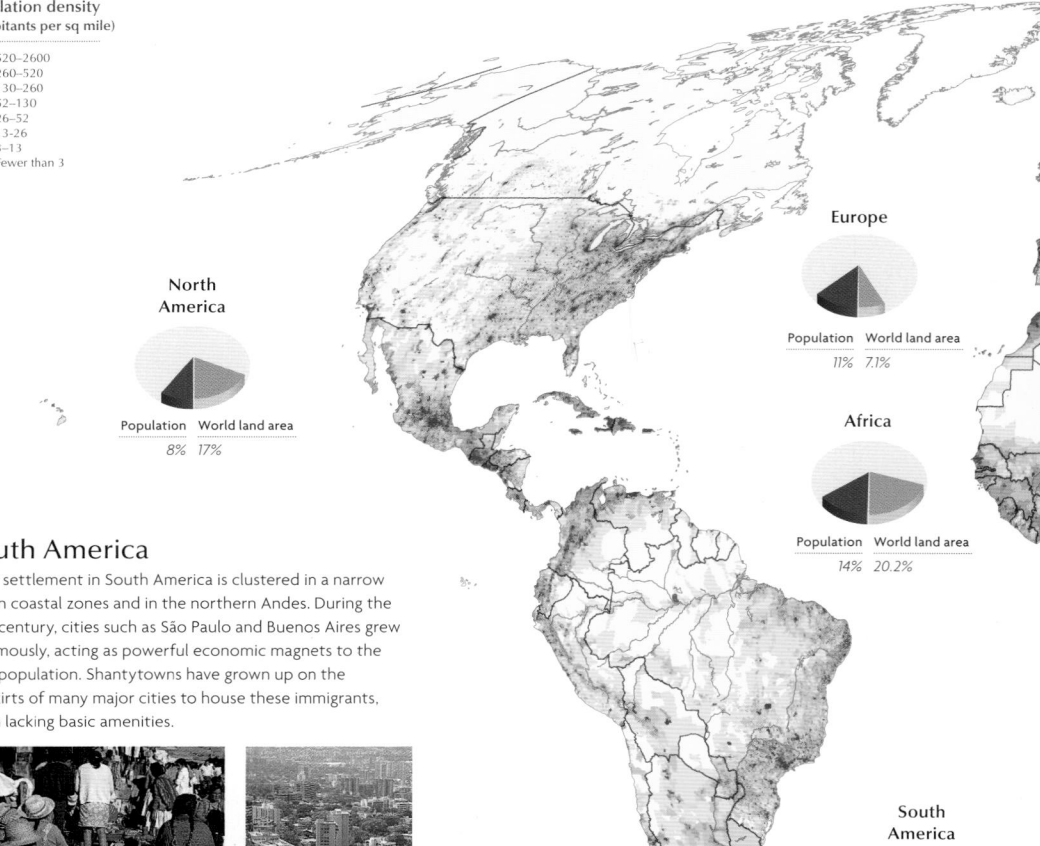

Population structures

Population pyramids are an effective means of showing the age structures of different countries, and highlighting changing trends in population growth and decline. The typical pyramid for a country with a growing, youthful population, is broad-based *(left)*, reflecting a high birthrate and a far larger number of young rather than elderly people. In contrast, countries with populations whose numbers are stabilizing have a more balanced distribution of people in each age band, and may even have lower numbers of people in the youngest age ranges, indicating both a high life expectancy, and that the population is now barely replacing itself *(right)*. The Russian Federation *(center)* is suffering from a declining population, forcing the government to consider a number of measures, including tax incentives and immigration, in an effort to stabilize the population.

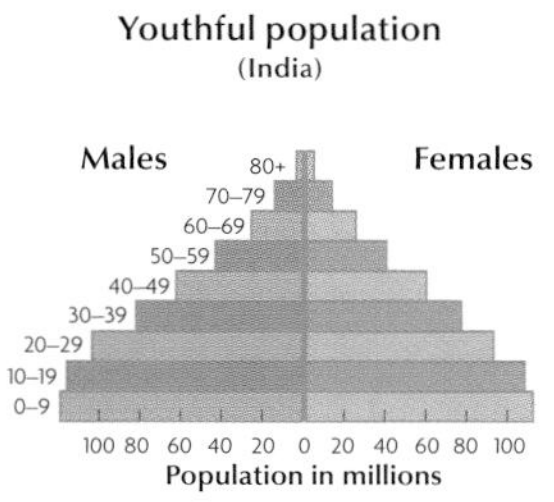
Youthful population
(India)
Males
Females
80+
70–79
60–69
50–59
40–49
30–39
20–29
10–19
0–9
100 80 60 40 20 0 20 40 60 80 100
Population in millions

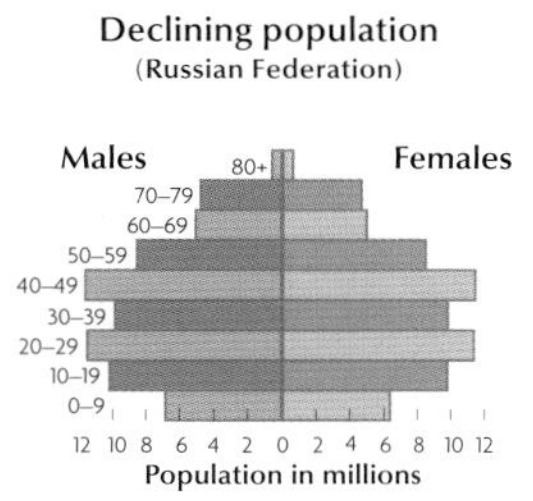
Declining population
(Russian Federation)
Males
Females
80+
70–79
60–69
50–59
40–49
30–39
20–29
10–19
0–9
12 10 8 6 4 2 0 2 4 6 8 10 12
Population in millions

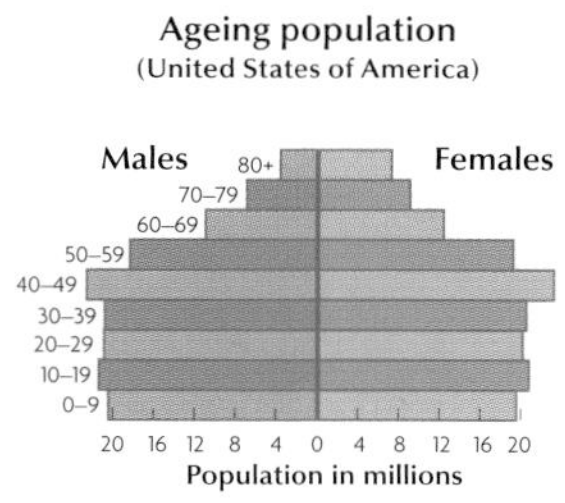
Ageing population
(United States of America)
Males
Females
80+
70–79
60–69
50–59
40–49
30–39
20–29
10–19
0–9
20 16 12 8 4 0 4 8 12 16 20
Population in millions

Population growth

Improvements in food supply and advances in medicine have both played a major role in the remarkable growth in global population, which has increased five-fold over the last 150 years. Food supplies have risen with the mechanization of agriculture and improvements in crop yields. Better nutrition, together with higher standards of public health and sanitation, have led to increased longevity and higher birthrates.

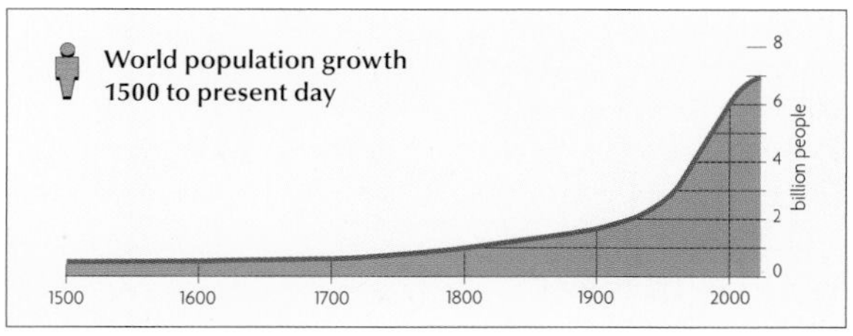
World population growth
1500 to present day
8
6
4
2
0
billion people
1500
1600
1700
1800
1900
2000

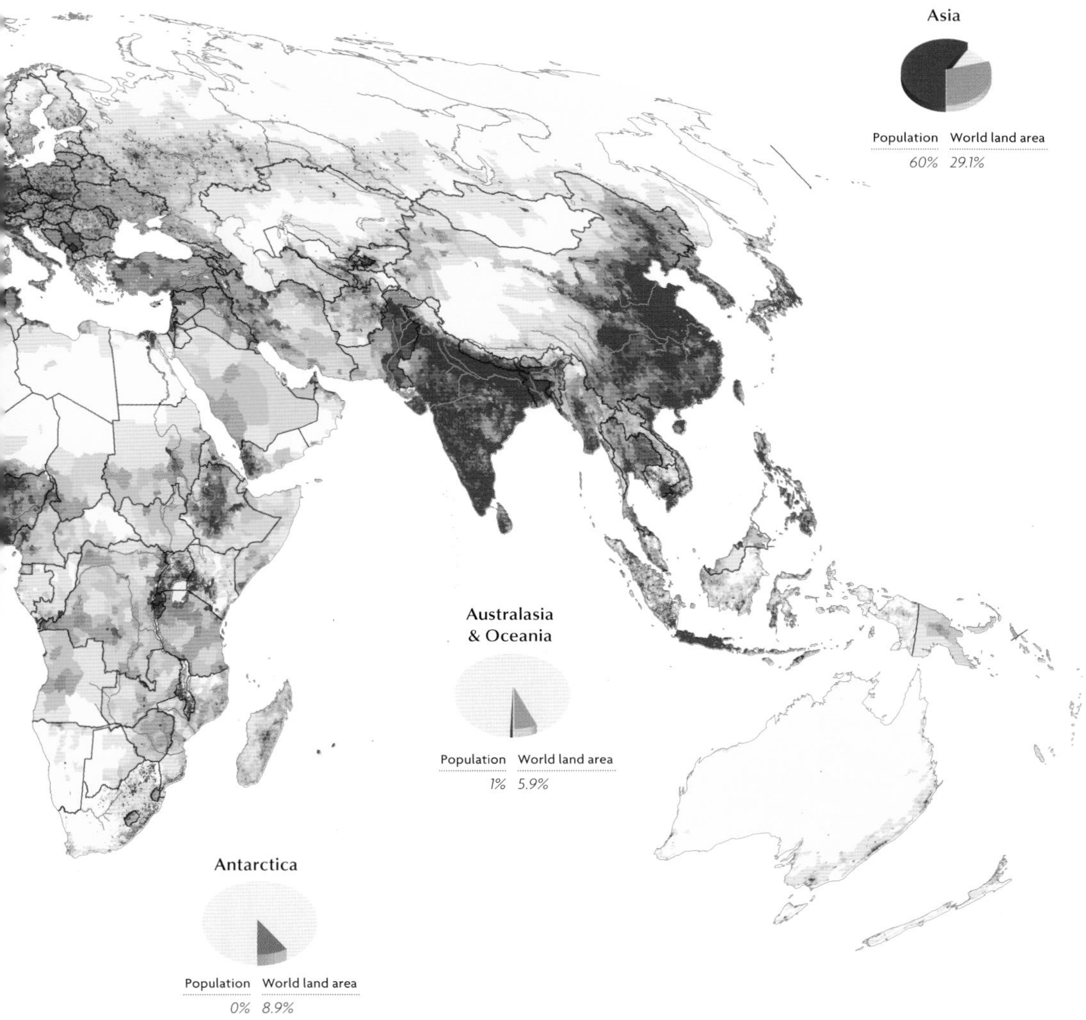
Asia
Population
World land area
60%
29.1%
Australasia
& Oceania
Population
World land area
1%
5.9%
Antarctica
Population
World land area
0%
8.9%

World nutrition

Two-thirds of the world's food supply is consumed by the industrialized nations, many of which have a daily calorific intake far higher than is necessary for their populations to maintain a healthy body weight. In contrast, in the developing world, about 800 million people do not have enough food to meet their basic nutritional needs.

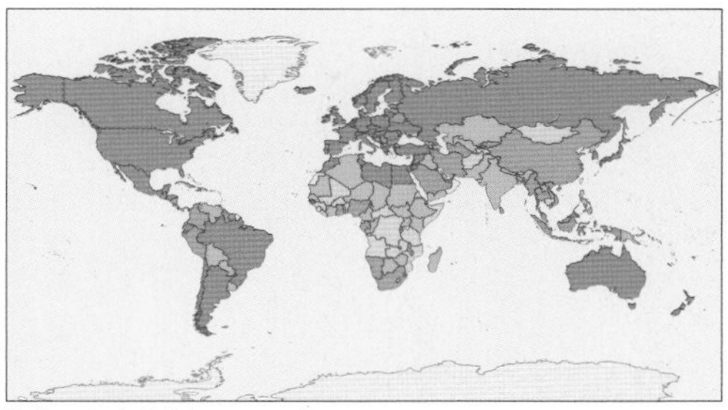

Daily calorie intake per capita

above 3000; 2500–2999; 2000–2499; below 2000; data not available

World life expectancy

Improved public health and living standards have greatly increased life expectancy in the developed world, where people can now expect to live twice as long as they did 100 years ago. In many of the world's poorest nations, inadequate nutrition and disease, means that the average life expectancy still does not exceed 45 years.

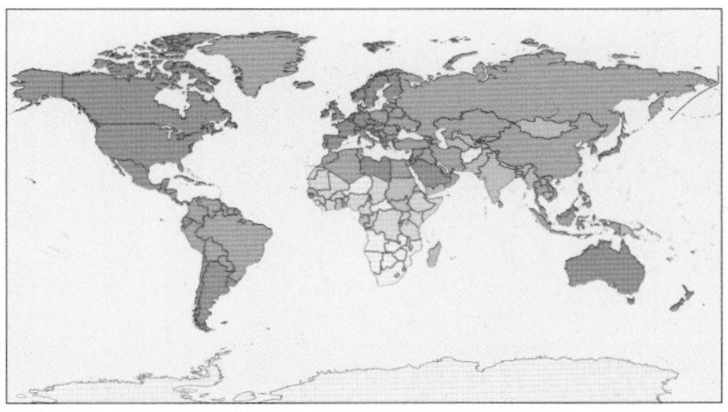

Life expectancy at birth

above 75 years; 65–74 years; 55–64 years; 45–54 years; below 44 years; data not available

Australasia and Oceania

This is the world's most sparsely settled region. The peoples of Australia and New Zealand live mainly in the coastal cities, with only scattered settlements in the arid interior. The Pacific islands can only support limited populations because of their remoteness and lack of resources.

▶ ***Brisbane, on Australia's*** *Gold Coast is the most rapidly expanding city in the country. The great majority of Australia's population lives in cities near the coasts.*

◀ ***The remote highlands*** *of Papua New Guinea are home to a wide variety of peoples, many of whom still subsist by traditional hunting and gathering.*

Average world birth rates

Birthrates are much higher in Africa, Asia, and South America than in Europe and North America. Increased affluence and easy access to contraception are both factors which can lead to a significant decline in a country's birthrate.

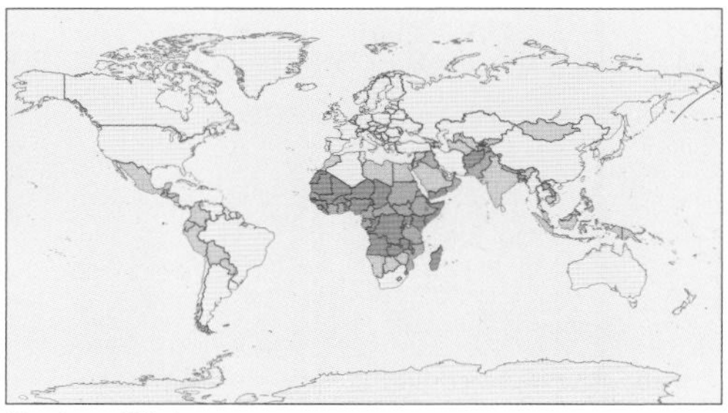

Number of births (per 1000 people)

above 40; 30–39; 20–29; below 20; data not available

World infant mortality

In parts of the developing world infant mortality rates are still high; access to medical services such as immunization, adequate nutrition, and the promotion of breast-feeding have been important in combating infant mortality.

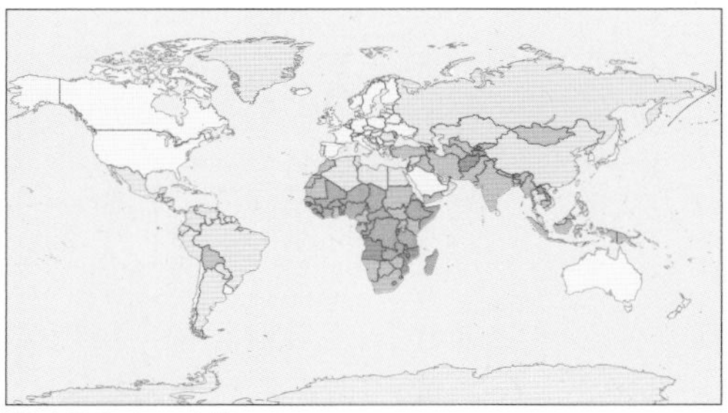

World infant mortality rates (deaths per 1000 live births)

above 125; 75–124; 35–74; 15–34; below 15; data not available

The economic system

The wealthy countries of the developed world, with their aggressive, market-led economies and their access to productive new technologies and international markets, dominate the world economic system. At the other extreme, many of the countries of the developing world are locked in a cycle of national debt, rising populations, and unemployment. In 2008 a major financial crisis swept the world's banking sector leading to a huge downturn in the global economy. Despite this, China overtook Japan in 2010 to become the world's second largest economy.

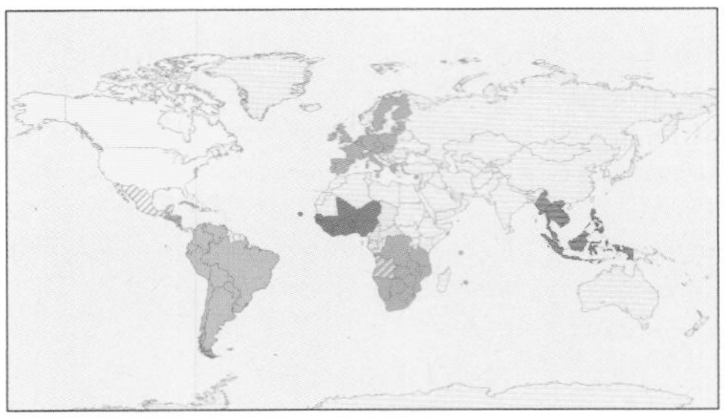

Trade blocs

EU	CACM
NAFTA	SADC
ASEAN	ECOWAS
LAIA	CEEAC

Trade blocs

International trade blocs are formed when groups of countries, often already enjoying close military and political ties, join together to offer mutually preferential terms of trade for both imports and exports. Increasingly, global trade is dominated by three main blocs: the EU, NAFTA, and ASEAN. They are supplanting older trade blocs such as the Commonwealth, a legacy of colonialism.

International trade flows

World trade acts as a stimulus to national economies, encouraging growth. Over the last three decades, as heavy industries have declined, services – banking, insurance, tourism, airlines, and shipping – have taken an increasingly large share of world trade. Manufactured articles now account for nearly two-thirds of world trade; raw materials and food make up less than a quarter of the total.

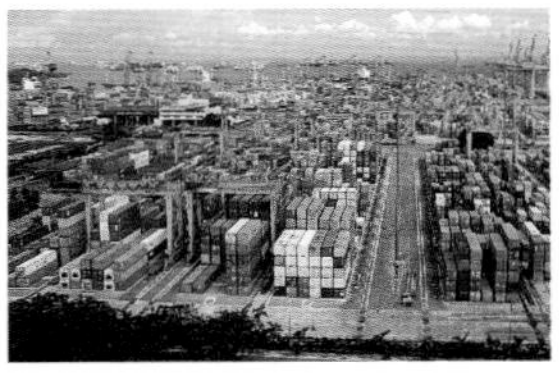

Shipping

Ships carry 80% of international cargo, and extensive container ports, where cargo is stored, are vital links in the international transportation network.

Tentulah Coke!
Coke is it!

Multinationals

Multinational companies are increasingly penetrating inaccessible markets. The reach of many American commodities is now global.

Primary products

Many countries, particularly in the Caribbean and Africa, are still reliant on primary products such as rubber and coffee, which makes them vulnerable to fluctuating prices.

Service industries

Service industries such as banking, tourism and insurance were the fastest-growing industrial sector in the last half of the 20th century. Lloyds of London is the center of the world insurance market.

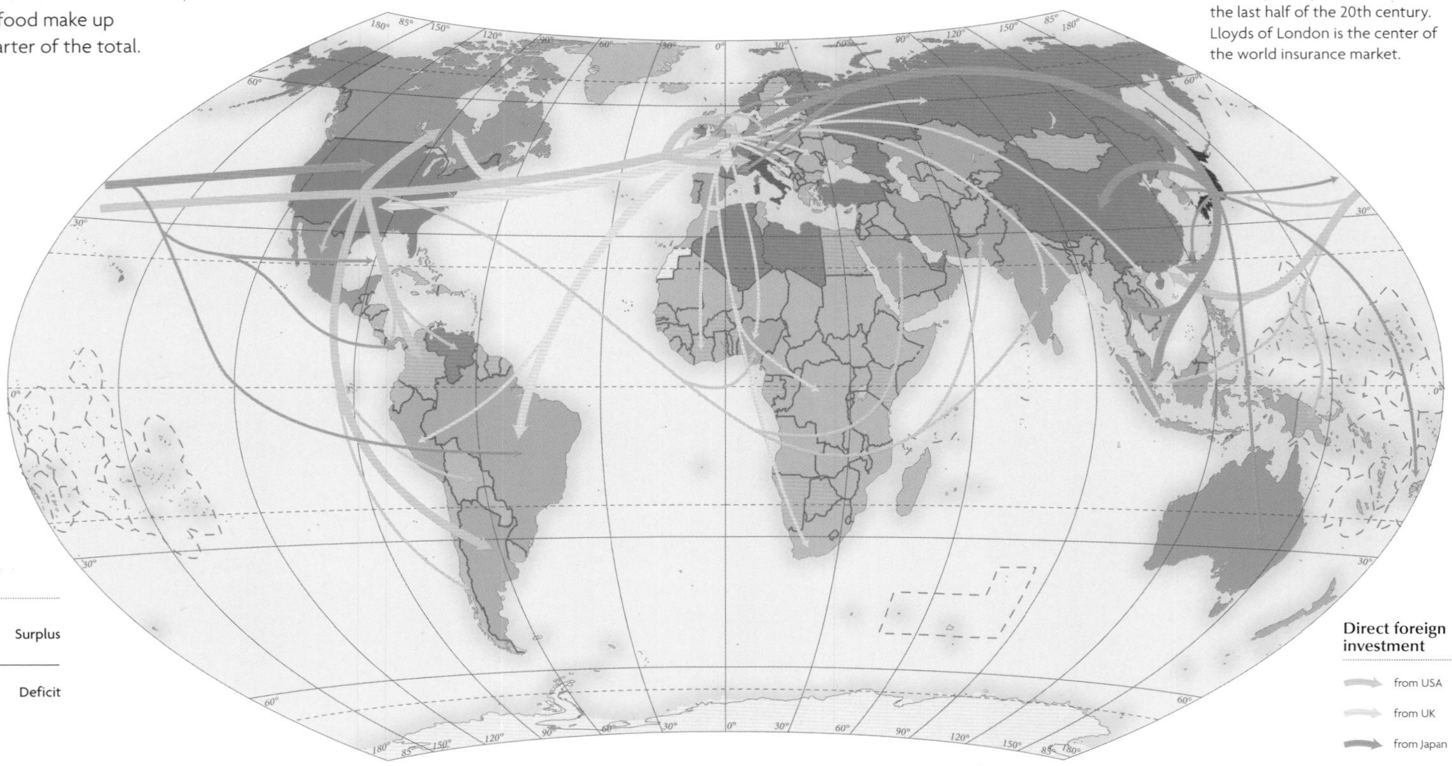

Balance of trade (millions US$)

Surplus: over 30,000; 10,000–29,000; 1000–9999; 0–999

Deficit: 0–999; 1000–9999; 10,000–29,999; over 30,000

data unavailable

Direct foreign investment

from USA

from UK

from Japan

World money markets

The financial world has traditionally been dominated by three major centers – Tokyo, New York, and London, which house the headquarters of stock exchanges, multinational corporations and international banks. Their geographic location means that, at any one time in a 24-hour day, one major market is open for trading in shares, currencies, and commodities. Since the late 1980s, technological advances have enabled transactions between financial centers to occur at ever-greater speed, and new markets have sprung up throughout the world.

Major money markets

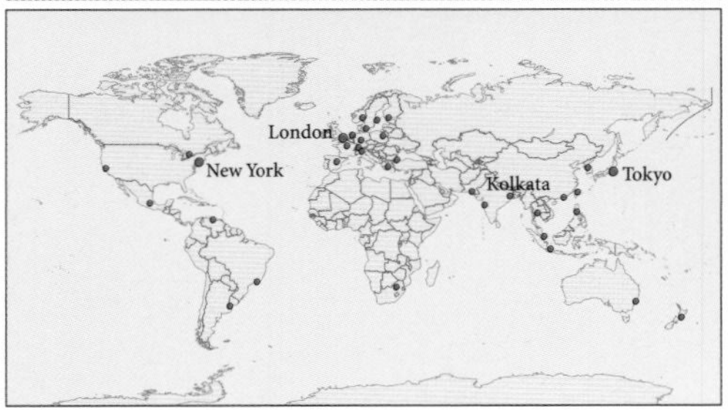
London
New York
Kolkata
Tokyo

Location of major stock markets

● Major stock markets

▲ *The Tokyo Stock Market crashed in 1990, leading to a slow-down in the growth of the world's most powerful economy, and a refocusing on economic policy away from export-led growth and toward the domestic market.*

New stock markets

New stock markets are now opening in many parts of the world, where economies have recently emerged from state controls. In Moscow and Beijing, and several countries in eastern Europe, newly-opened stock exchanges reflect the transition to market-driven economies.

▲ *Dealers at the Kolkata Stock Market. The Indian economy has been opened up to foreign investment and many multinationals now have bases there.*

The developing world

International trade in capital and currency is dominated by the rich nations of the northern hemisphere. In parts of Africa and Asia, where exports of any sort are extremely limited, home-produced commodities are simply sold in local markets.

▲ *Markets have thrived in communist Vietnam since the introduction of a liberal economic policy.*

World wealth disparity

A global assessment of Gross Domestic Product (GDP) by nation reveals great disparities. The developed world, with only a quarter of the world's population, has 80% of the world's manufacturing income. Civil war, conflict, and political instability further undermine the economic self-sufficiency of many of the world's poorest nations.

▲ ***Cities such as*** *Detroit have been badly hit by the decline in heavy industry.*

Urban decay

Although the US still dominates the global economy, it faces deficits in both the federal budget and the balance of trade. Vast discrepancies in personal wealth, high levels of unemployment, and the dismantling of welfare provisions throughout the 1980s have led to severe deprivation in several of the inner cities of North America's industrial heartland.

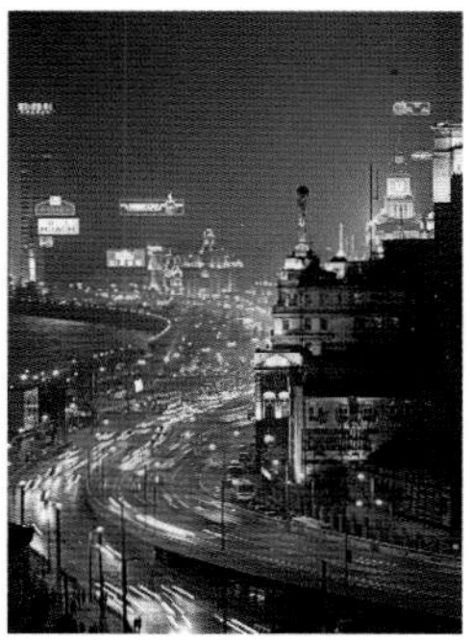

◀ ***Foreign investment has*** *encouraged new infrastructure development in cities like Shanghai.*

Booming cities

Since the 1980s the Chinese government has set up special industrial zones, such as Shanghai, where foreign investment is encouraged through tax incentives. Migrants from rural China pour into these regions in search of work, creating "boomtown" economies.

Urban sprawl

Cities are expanding all over the developing world, attracting economic migrants in search of work and opportunities. In cities such as Rio de Janeiro, housing has not kept pace with the population explosion, and squalid shanty towns *(favelas)* rub shoulders with middle-class housing.

▲ ***The favelas of*** *Rio de Janeiro sprawl over the hills surrounding the city.*

Comparative world wealth

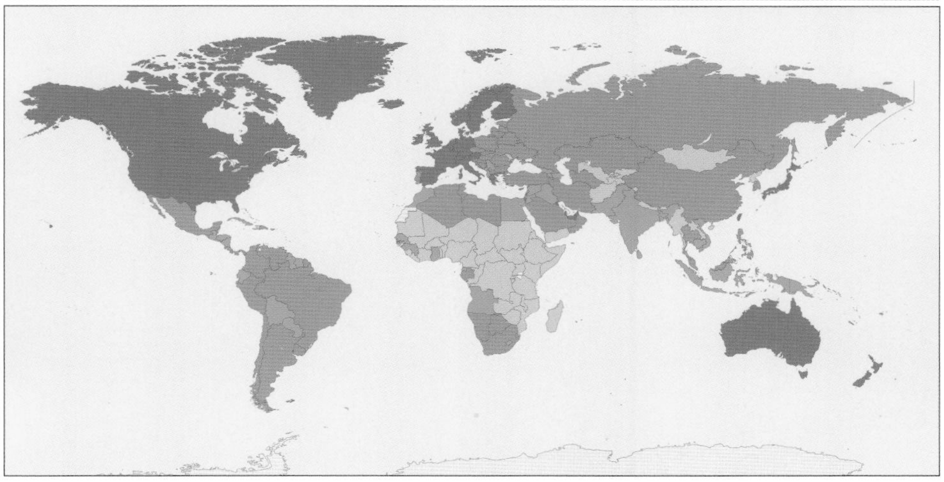

World economies - average GDP per capita (US$)

- above 20,000
- 5000–20,000
- 2000–5000
- below 2000
- data unavailable

Economic "tigers"

The economic "tigers" of the Pacific Rim – China, Singapore, and South Korea – have grown faster than Europe and the US over the last decade. Their export- and service-led economies have benefited from stable government, low labor costs, and foreign investment.

▲ ***Hong Kong, with*** *its fine natural harbour, is one of the most important ports in Asia.*

Agricultural economies

In parts of the developing world, people survive by subsistence farming – only growing enough food for themselves and their families. With no surplus product, they are unable to exchange goods for currency, the only means of escaping the poverty trap. In other countries, farmers have been encouraged to concentrate on growing a single crop for the export market. This reliance on cash crops leaves farmers vulnerable to crop failure and to changes in the market price of the crop.

▲ ***The Ugandan uplands*** *are fertile, but poor infrastructure hampers the export of cash crops.*

▲ ***A shopping arcade*** *in Paris displays a great profusion of luxury goods.*

The affluent West

The capital cities of many countries in the developed world are showcases for consumer goods, reflecting the importance of the service sector, and particularly the retail sector, in the world economy. The idea of shopping as a leisure activity is unique to the western world. Luxury goods and services attract visitors, who in turn generate tourist revenue.

Tourism

In 2004, there were over 940 million tourists worldwide. Tourism is now the world's biggest single industry, employing over 130 million people, though frequently in low-paid unskilled jobs. While tourists are increasingly exploring inaccessible and less-developed regions of the world, the benefits of the industry are not always felt at a local level. There are also worries about the environmental impact of tourism, as the world's last wildernesses increasingly become tourist attractions.

▲ ***Botswana's Okavango Delta*** *is an area rich in wildlife. Tourists go on safaris to the region, but the impact of tourism is controlled.*

Money flows

In 2008 a global financial crisis swept through the world's economic system. The crisis triggered the failure of several major financial institutions and lead to increased borrowing costs known as the "credit crunch". A consequent reduction in economic activity together with rising inflation forced many governments to introduce austerity measures to reduce borrowing and debt, particulary in Europe where massive "bailouts" were needed to keep some European single currency (Euro) countries solvent.

◀ ***In rural Southeast Asia,*** *babies are given medical checks by UNICEF as part of a global aid program sponsored by the UN.*

Tourist arrivals

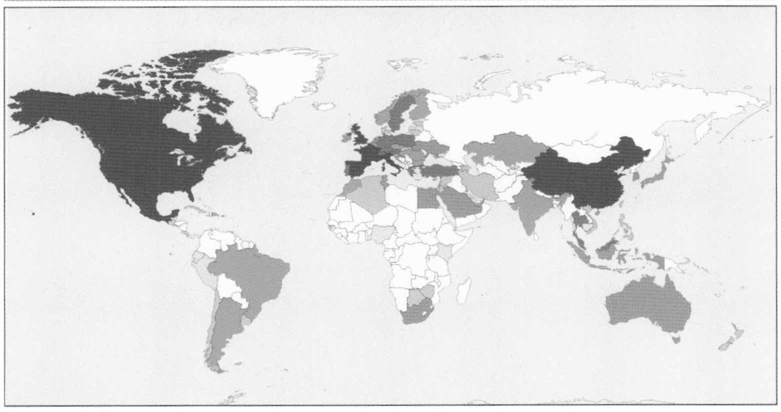

Tourist arrivals

- over 20 million
- 10–20 million
- 5–10 million
- 2.5–5 million
- 1–2.5 million
- 700,000–999,000
- under 700,000
- data unavailable

International debt

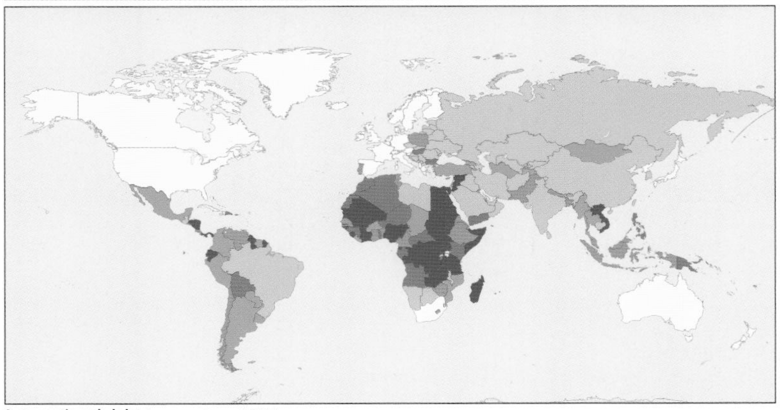

International debt (as percentage of GNI)

- over 100%
- 70–99%
- 50–69%
- 30–49%
- 10–29%
- below 10%
- data unavailable

The political world

There are 196 independent countries in the world today. With the exception of Antarctica, where territorial claims have been deferred by international treaty, every land area of the Earth's surface either belongs to, or is claimed by, one country or another. The largest country in the world is the Russian Federation, the smallest is Vatican City. Some 60 overseas dependent territories remain, administered variously by France, Australia, Denmark, New Zealand, Norway, Portugal, the UK, the US, and the Netherlands.

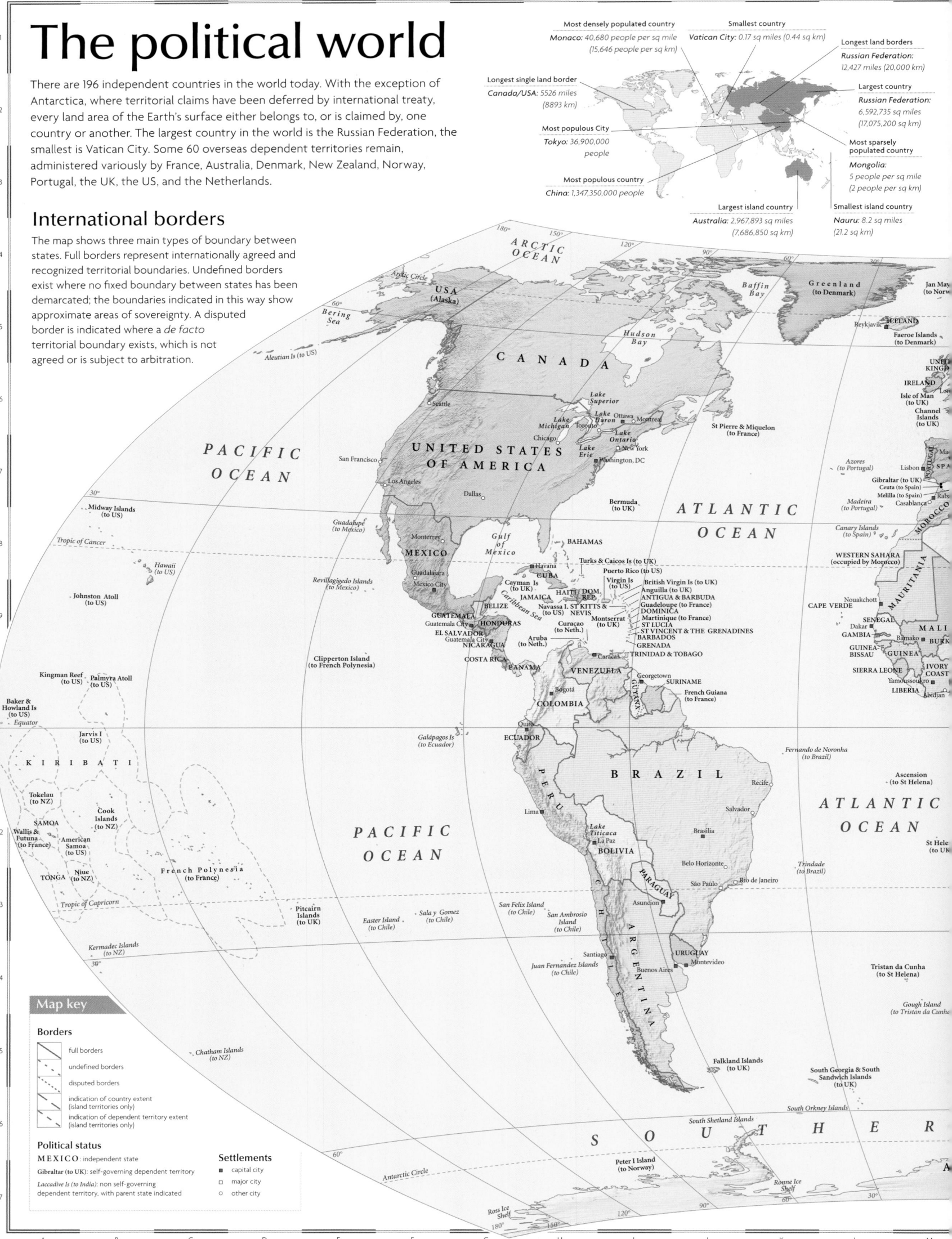

Most densely populated country
Monaco: 40,680 people per sq mile (15,646 people per sq km)
Smallest country
Vatican City: 0.17 sq miles (0.44 sq km)
Longest land borders
Russian Federation: 12,427 miles (20,000 km)
Longest single land border
Canada/USA: 5526 miles (8893 km)
Largest country
Russian Federation: 6,592,735 sq miles (17,075,200 sq km)
Most populous City
Tokyo: 36,900,000 people
Most sparsely populated country
Mongolia: 5 people per sq mile (2 people per sq km)
Most populous country
China: 1,347,350,000 people
Largest island country
Australia: 2,967,893 sq miles (7,686,850 sq km)
Smallest island country
Nauru: 8.2 sq miles (21.2 sq km)

International borders

The map shows three main types of boundary between states. Full borders represent internationally agreed and recognized territorial boundaries. Undefined borders exist where no fixed boundary between states has been demarcated; the boundaries indicated in this way show approximate areas of sovereignty. A disputed border is indicated where a *de facto* territorial boundary exists, which is not agreed or is subject to arbitration.

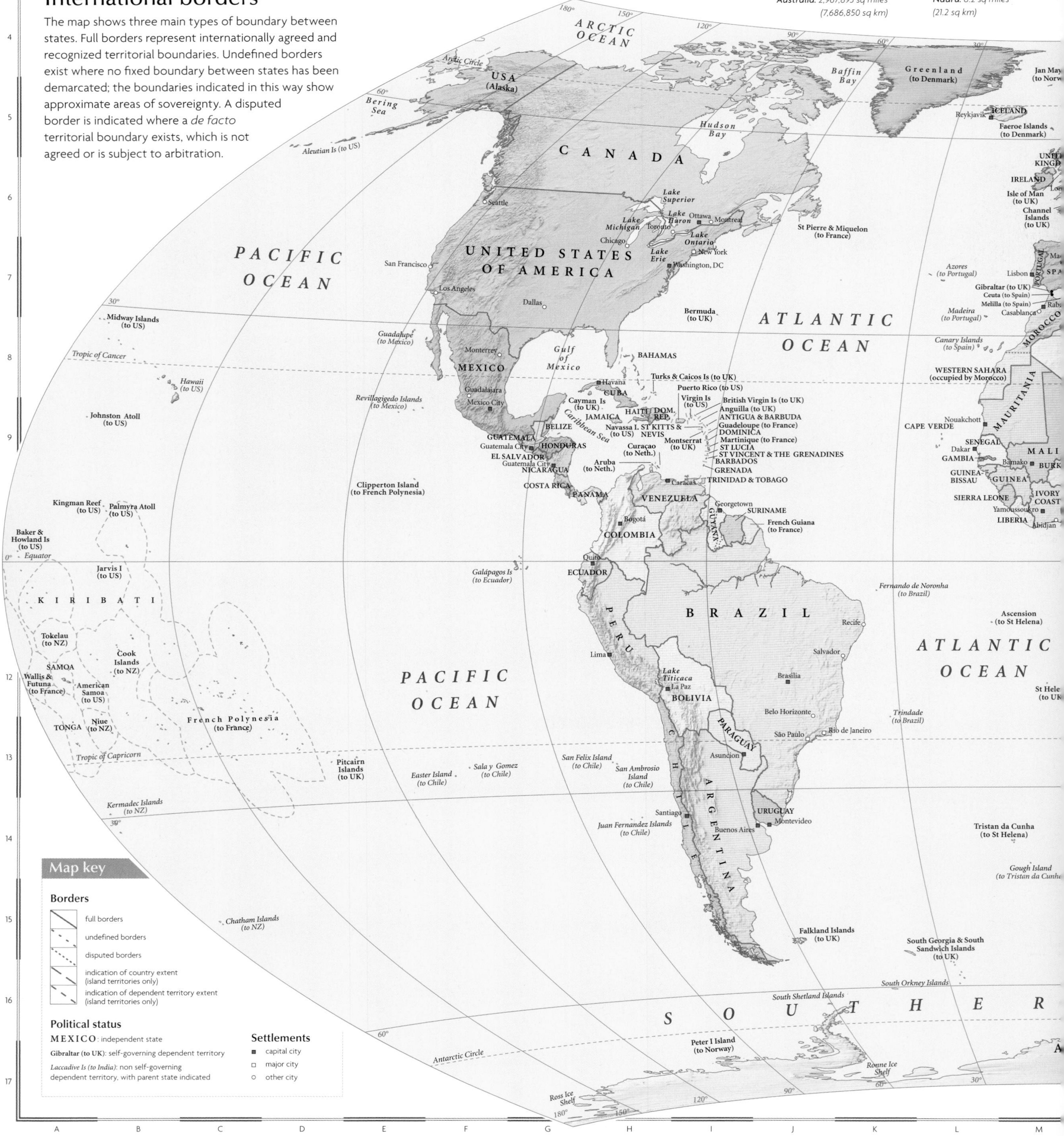

ARCTIC OCEAN
Arctic Circle
Bering Sea
USA (Alaska)
Aleutian Is (to US)
CANADA
Hudson Bay
Baffin Bay
Greenland (to Denmark)
Jan Mayen (to Norway)
ICELAND
Reykjavik
Faeroe Islands (to Denmark)
IRELAND
Isle of Man (to UK)
Channel Islands (to UK)
Seattle
Lake Superior
Lake Michigan
Lake Huron
Lake Ontario
Lake Erie
Ottawa
Montreal
Toronto
Chicago
New York
Washington, DC
St Pierre & Miquelon (to France)
PACIFIC OCEAN
San Francisco
UNITED STATES OF AMERICA
Los Angeles
Dallas
Azores (to Portugal)
Lisbon
Gibraltar (to UK)
Ceuta (to Spain)
Melilla (to Spain)
Casablanca
Madeira (to Portugal)
Midway Islands (to US)
Bermuda (to UK)
ATLANTIC OCEAN
Guadalupe (to Mexico)
Monterrey
Gulf of Mexico
BAHAMAS
Canary Islands (to Spain)
Tropic of Cancer
MEXICO
Havana
Turks & Caicos Is (to UK)
WESTERN SAHARA (occupied by Morocco)
Hawaii (to US)
CUBA
Puerto Rico (to US)
Guadalajara
Revillagigedo Islands (to Mexico)
Mexico City
Cayman Is (to UK)
Virgin Is (to US)
British Virgin Is (to UK)
Anguilla (to UK)
ANTIGUA & BARBUDA
Guadeloupe (to France)
DOMINICA
Martinique (to France)
ST LUCIA
ST VINCENT & THE GRENADINES
BARBADOS
GRENADA
TRINIDAD & TOBAGO
JAMAICA
HAITI
DOM. REP.
Johnston Atoll (to US)
BELIZE
Caribbean Sea
Navassa I. (to US)
ST KITTS & NEVIS
Montserrat (to UK)
Nouakchott
CAPE VERDE
MAURITANIA
GUATEMALA
Guatemala City
HONDURAS
Curaçao (to Neth.)
SENEGAL
Dakar
GAMBIA
MALI
EL SALVADOR
Aruba (to Neth.)
Bamako
NICARAGUA
GUINEA-BISSAU
GUINEA
COSTA RICA
Caracas
Clipperton Island (to French Polynesia)
PANAMA
VENEZUELA
Georgetown
SURINAME
SIERRA LEONE
IVORY COAST
Yamoussoukro
LIBERIA
Abidjan
Kingman Reef (to US)
Palmyra Atoll (to US)
Bogotá
COLOMBIA
GUYANA
French Guiana (to France)
Baker & Howland Is (to US)
Equator
Quito
Jarvis I (to US)
Galápagos Is (to Ecuador)
ECUADOR
Fernando de Noronha (to Brazil)
KIRIBATI
BRAZIL
Recife
Ascension (to St Helena)
Tokelau (to NZ)
PERU
Cook Islands (to NZ)
Lima
Salvador
SAMOA
Wallis & Futuna (to France)
American Samoa (to US)
PACIFIC OCEAN
Lake Titicaca
La Paz
BOLIVIA
Brasília
St Helena (to UK)
Belo Horizonte
Trindade (to Brazil)
French Polynesia (to France)
Niue (to NZ)
TONGA
PARAGUAY
São Paulo
Rio de Janeiro
Tropic of Capricorn
Pitcairn Islands (to UK)
Easter Island (to Chile)
Sala y Gomez (to Chile)
San Felix Island (to Chile)
San Ambrosio Island (to Chile)
Asunción
CHILE
ARGENTINA
URUGUAY
Montevideo
Santiago
Buenos Aires
Kermadec Islands (to NZ)
Juan Fernandez Islands (to Chile)
Tristan da Cunha (to St Helena)
Gough Island (to Tristan da Cunha)
Chatham Islands (to NZ)
Falkland Islands (to UK)
South Georgia & South Sandwich Islands (to UK)
South Orkney Islands
South Shetland Islands
SOUTHERN
Antarctic Circle
Peter I Island (to Norway)
Ronne Ice Shelf
Ross Ice Shelf

Map key

Borders

- full borders
- undefined borders
- disputed borders
- indication of country extent (island territories only)
- indication of dependent territory extent (island territories only)

Political status

MEXICO: independent state

Gibraltar (to UK): self-governing dependent territory

Laccadive Is (to India): non self-governing dependent territory, with parent state indicated

Settlements

- capital city
- major city
- other city

The world in 1914

The early years of the 20th century saw the mainly European colonial empires reaching their greatest extents by 1914. Two world wars inaugurated their disintegration, but even in 1950 there were only 82 independent countries. Since then, over 100 have gained their independence, culminating in the breakup of the Soviet Union and former Yugoslavia in the early 1990s.

Percentage of Earth's land surface controlled by colonial empires in 1914

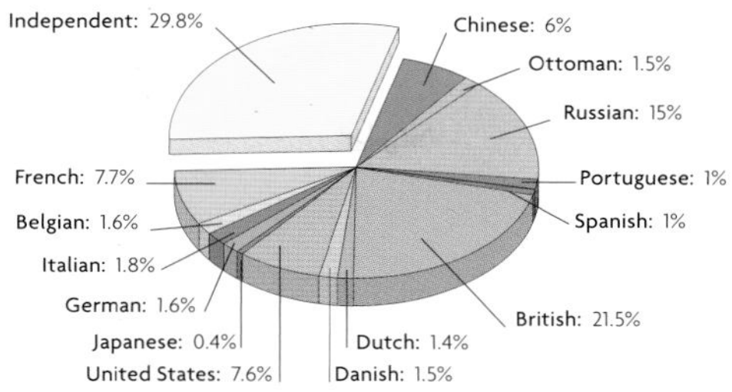
Independent: 29.8%
Chinese: 6%
Ottoman: 1.5%
Russian: 15%
Portuguese: 1%
Spanish: 1%
British: 21.5%
Dutch: 1.4%
Danish: 1.5%
United States: 7.6%
Japanese: 0.4%
German: 1.6%
Italian: 1.8%
Belgian: 1.6%
French: 7.7%

Colonial empires in 1914

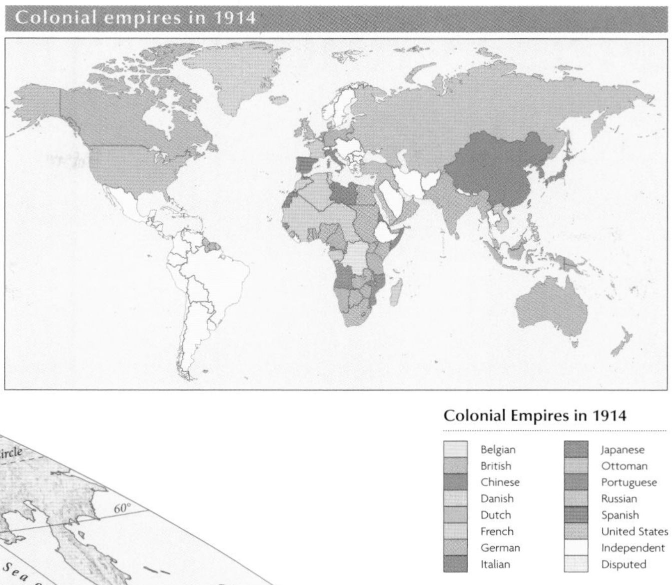
Colonial Empires in 1914
Belgian
British
Chinese
Danish
Dutch
French
German
Italian
Japanese
Ottoman
Portuguese
Russian
Spanish
United States
Independent
Disputed

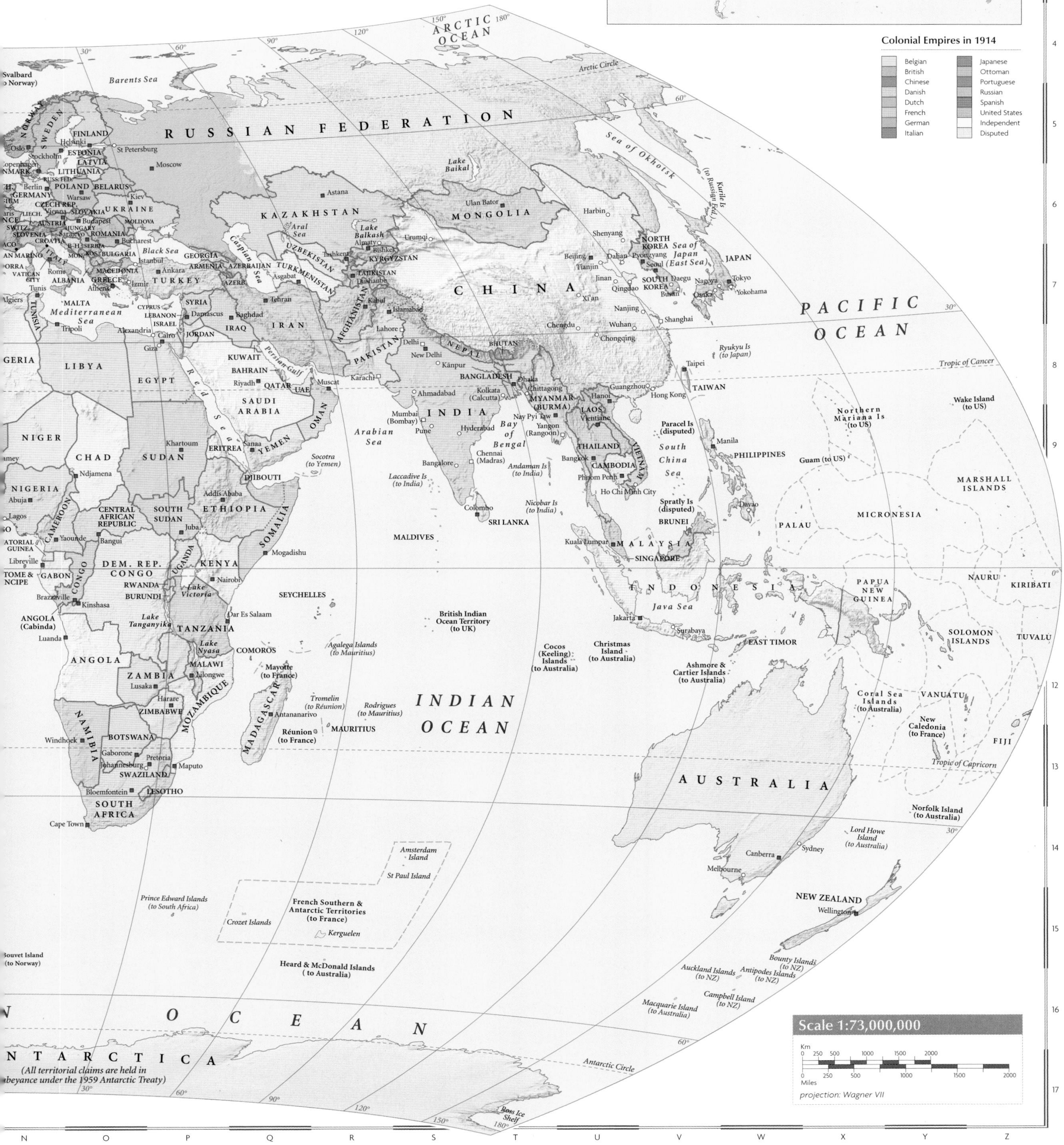
ARCTIC OCEAN
Barents Sea
Arctic Circle
Svalbard (to Norway)
RUSSIAN FEDERATION
FINLAND
Helsinki
St Petersburg
SWEDEN
NORWAY
Oslo
Stockholm
ESTONIA
LATVIA
LITHUANIA
Moscow
RUSS. FED.
POLAND
BELARUS
Berlin
GERMANY
Warsaw
Kiev
CZECH REP.
UKRAINE
Vienna
SLOVAKIA
Budapest
MOLDOVA
AUSTRIA
HUNGARY
SLOVENIA
ROMANIA
CROATIA
Bucharest
SERBIA
BULGARIA
Sofia
Black Sea
GEORGIA
Istanbul
ARMENIA
AZERBAIJAN
Rome
MACEDONIA
Ankara
ALBANIA
GREECE
Athens
Izmir
TURKEY
Tunis
TUNISIA
MALTA
Mediterranean Sea
Tripoli
CYPRUS
LEBANON
SYRIA
Damascus
ISRAEL
Baghdad
IRAQ
Cairo
JORDAN
Alexandria
Giza
Tehran
IRAN
KUWAIT
BAHRAIN
Riyadh
QATAR
UAE
Muscat
OMAN
SAUDI ARABIA
Persian Gulf
Red Sea
LIBYA
EGYPT
NIGER
CHAD
SUDAN
Khartoum
ERITREA
Sanaa
YEMEN
DJIBOUTI
Ndjamena
NIGERIA
Abuja
Lagos
CAMEROON
Yaounde
CENTRAL AFRICAN REPUBLIC
Bangui
SOUTH SUDAN
Juba
ETHIOPIA
Addis Ababa
SOMALIA
Mogadishu
UGANDA
KENYA
Nairobi
GABON
Libreville
CONGO
Brazzaville
Kinshasa
DEM. REP. CONGO
RWANDA
BURUNDI
Lake Victoria
Lake Tanganyika
TANZANIA
Dar Es Salaam
Lake Nyasa
MALAWI
Lilongwe
ANGOLA (Cabinda)
Luanda
ANGOLA
ZAMBIA
Lusaka
Harare
ZIMBABWE
MOZAMBIQUE
NAMIBIA
Windhoek
BOTSWANA
Gaborone
Pretoria
Johannesburg
SWAZILAND
Maputo
Bloemfontein
LESOTHO
SOUTH AFRICA
Cape Town
KAZAKHSTAN
Astana
Aral Sea
Caspian Sea
UZBEKISTAN
TURKMENISTAN
Asgabat
Tashkent
Bishkek
Almaty
Lake Balkash
KYRGYZSTAN
TAJIKISTAN
Dushanbe
AFGHANISTAN
Kabul
Islamabad
PAKISTAN
Lahore
Karachi
Delhi
New Delhi
Kanpur
NEPAL
BHUTAN
BANGLADESH
Dhaka
Chittagong
Kolkata (Calcutta)
Ahmadabad
INDIA
Mumbai (Bombay)
Pune
Hyderabad
Arabian Sea
Bay of Bengal
Chennai (Madras)
Bangalore
Laccadive Is (to India)
Andaman Is (to India)
Nicobar Is (to India)
Colombo
SRI LANKA
MALDIVES
Socotra (to Yemen)
MONGOLIA
Ulan Bator
Lake Baikal
Urumqi
CHINA
Harbin
Shenyang
Beijing
Tianjin
Dalian
Jinan
Qingdao
Xi'an
Nanjing
Shanghai
Wuhan
Chengdu
Chongqing
Guangzhou
Hong Kong
Taipei
TAIWAN
NORTH KOREA
Pyongyang
Seoul
SOUTH KOREA
Daegu
Busan
Sea of Japan (East Sea)
JAPAN
Tokyo
Yokohama
Nagoya
Osaka
Sea of Okhotsk
Kurile Is (to Russian Fed.)
Ryukyu Is (to Japan)
MYANMAR (BURMA)
Nay Pyi Taw
Yangon (Rangoon)
LAOS
Vientiane
Hanoi
THAILAND
Bangkok
CAMBODIA
Phnom Penh
VIETNAM
Ho Chi Minh City
Paracel Is (disputed)
South China Sea
Spratly Is (disputed)
Manila
PHILIPPINES
Davao
BRUNEI
Kuala Lumpur
MALAYSIA
SINGAPORE
INDONESIA
Java Sea
Jakarta
Surabaya
EAST TIMOR
PACIFIC OCEAN
Tropic of Cancer
Northern Mariana Is (to US)
Wake Island (to US)
Guam (to US)
MARSHALL ISLANDS
PALAU
MICRONESIA
PAPUA NEW GUINEA
NAURU
KIRIBATI
SOLOMON ISLANDS
TUVALU
VANUATU
New Caledonia (to France)
FIJI
Tropic of Capricorn
Coral Sea Islands (to Australia)
Norfolk Island (to Australia)
Lord Howe Island (to Australia)
Ashmore & Cartier Islands (to Australia)
Christmas Island (to Australia)
Cocos (Keeling) Islands (to Australia)
AUSTRALIA
Canberra
Sydney
Melbourne
NEW ZEALAND
Wellington
Bounty Islands (to NZ)
Antipodes Islands (to NZ)
Auckland Islands (to NZ)
Campbell Island (to NZ)
Macquarie Island (to Australia)
INDIAN OCEAN
SEYCHELLES
British Indian Ocean Territory (to UK)
COMOROS
Mayotte (to France)
Agalega Islands (to Mauritius)
MADAGASCAR
Antananarivo
Tromelin (to Réunion)
Rodrigues (to Mauritius)
MAURITIUS
Réunion (to France)
Amsterdam Island
St Paul Island
Prince Edward Islands (to South Africa)
French Southern & Antarctic Territories (to France)
Crozet Islands
Kerguelen
Heard & McDonald Islands (to Australia)
Bouvet Island (to Norway)
OCEAN
ANTARCTICA
(All territorial claims are held in abeyance under the 1959 Antarctic Treaty)
Antarctic Circle
Ross Ice Shelf
Scale 1:73,000,000
Km 0 250 500 1000 1500 2000
Miles 0 250 500 1000 1500 2000
projection: Wagner VII

States and boundaries

There are almost 200 sovereign states in the world today; in 1950 there were only 82. Over the last half-century national self-determination has been a driving force for many states with a history of colonialism and oppression. As more borders have been added to the world map, the number of international border disputes has increased.

In many cases, where the impetus toward independence has been religious or ethnic, disputes with minority groups have also caused violent internal conflict. While many newly-formed states have moved peacefully toward independence, successfully establishing government by multiparty democracy, dictatorship by military regime or individual despot is often the result of the internal power-struggles which characterize the early stages in the lives of new nations.

The nature of politics

Democracy is a broad term: it can range from the ideal of multiparty elections and fair representation to, in countries such as Singapore, a thin disguise for single-party rule. In despotic regimes, on the other hand, a single, often personal authority has total power; institutions such as parliament and the military are mere instruments of the dictator.

◀ ***The stars and** stripes of the US flag are a potent symbol of the country's status as a federal democracy.*

The changing world map

Decolonization

In 1950, large areas of the world remained under the control of a handful of European countries *(page xxix)*. The process of decolonization had begun in Asia, where, following the Second World War, much of southern and southeastern Asia sought and achieved self-determination. In the 1960s, a host of African states achieved independence, so that by 1965, most of the larger tracts of the European overseas empires had been substantially eroded. The final major stage in decolonization came with the breakup of the Soviet Union and the Eastern bloc after 1990. The process continues today as the last toeholds of European colonialism, often tiny island nations, press increasingly for independence.

▲ ***Icons of communism,** including statues of former leaders such as Lenin and Stalin, were destroyed when the Soviet bloc was dismantled in 1989, creating several new nations.*

▲ ***Iran has been** one of the modern world's few true theocracies; Islam has an impact on every aspect of political life.*

▲ ***North Korea is** an independent communist republic. Power was transferred directly to Kim Jong-un in 2012 following the death of his father Kim Jong-il.*

New nations 1945–1965

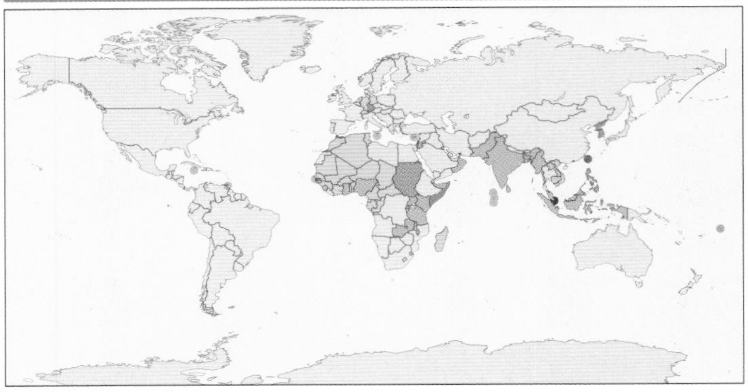

New nations 1965–present

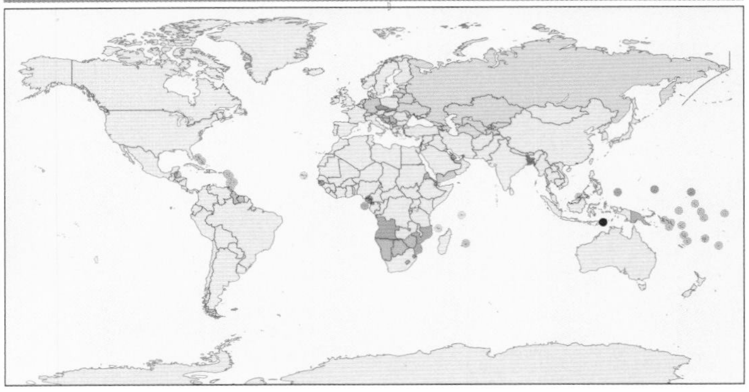

Administration at the time of independence

- Australia
- Aust/NZ/UK
- Belgium
- China
- Czechoslovakia
- Egypt/UK
- Ethiopia
- France
- France/UK
- Indonesia
- Italy
- Japan
- Malaysia
- Netherlands
- New Zealand
- Pakistan
- Portugal
- South Africa
- Spain
- Sudan
- UK
- Unified country
- USA
- USSR
- Yugoslavia

◀ ***Afghanistan** has suffered decades of war and occupation resulting in widespread destruction. The hardline Taliban government were ousted by a US-led coalition in 2001 but efforts to stabilize the country are still continuing over ten years later.*

◀ ***In early 2011,** Egypt underwent a revolution, part of the so called "Arab Spring," which resulted in the ousting of President Hosni Mubarak after nearly 30 years in power.*

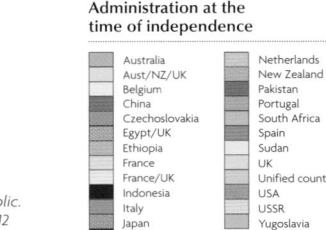

▲ ***In Brunei the** Sultan has ruled by decree since 1962; power is closely tied to the royal family. The Sultan's brothers are responsible for finance and foreign affairs.*

Types of government

- Multiparty democracy for more than 10 yrs
- Multiparty democracy within last 10 yrs
- Single-party government
- Military regime
- Theocracy
- Monarchy
- Non-party system
- Transitional regime
- Current civil unrest

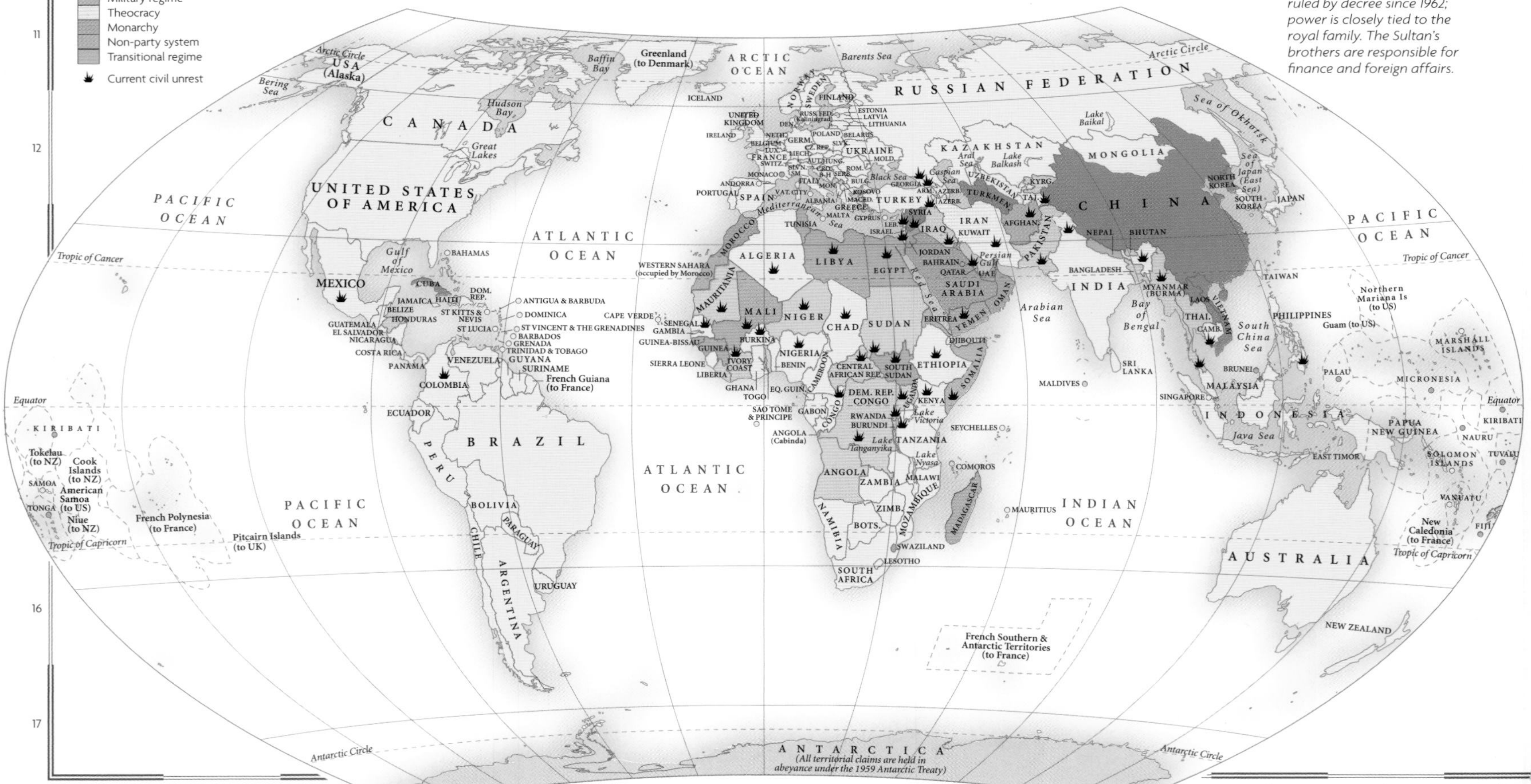
ARCTIC OCEAN
RUSSIAN FEDERATION
CANADA
UNITED STATES OF AMERICA
PACIFIC OCEAN
ATLANTIC OCEAN
INDIAN OCEAN
MEXICO
BRAZIL
ARGENTINA
ALGERIA
LIBYA
EGYPT
SAUDI ARABIA
KAZAKHSTAN
MONGOLIA
CHINA
INDIA
AUSTRALIA
NEW ZEALAND
SOUTH AFRICA
ANTARCTICA
(All territorial claims are held in abeyance under the 1959 Antarctic Treaty)
Greenland (to Denmark)
French Polynesia (to France)
Pitcairn Islands (to UK)
French Southern & Antarctic Territories (to France)
Tropic of Cancer
Tropic of Capricorn
Equator
Arctic Circle
Antarctic Circle

Lines on the map

The determination of international boundaries can use a variety of criteria. Many of the borders between older states follow physical boundaries; some mirror religious and ethnic differences; others are the legacy of complex histories of conflict and colonialism, while others have been imposed by international agreements or arbitration.

Post-colonial borders

When the European colonial empires in Africa were dismantled during the second half of the 20th century, the outlines of the new African states mirrored colonial boundaries. These boundaries had been drawn up by colonial administrators, often based on inadequate geographical knowledge. Such arbitrary boundaries were imposed on people of different languages, racial groups, religions, and customs. This confused legacy often led to civil and international war.

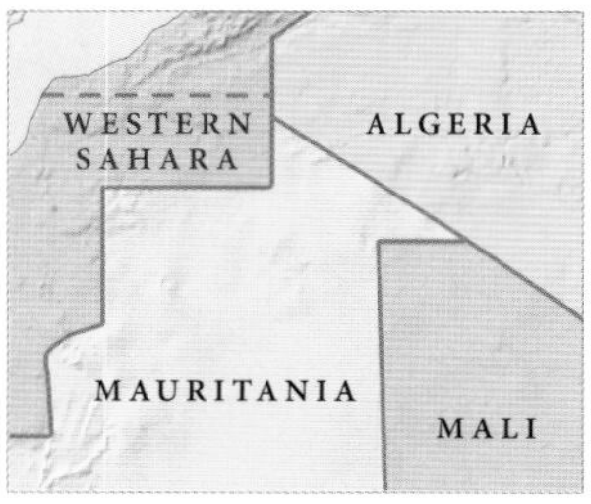
WESTERN SAHARA
ALGERIA
MAURITANIA
MALI

▲ ***The conflict that*** *has plagued many African countries since independence has caused millions of people to become refugees.*

Enclaves

The shifting political map over the course of history has frequently led to anomalous situations. Parts of national territories may become isolated by territorial agreement, forming an enclave. The West German part of the city of Berlin, which until 1989 lay a hundred miles (160km) within East German territory, was a famous example

Baltic Sea
ESTONIA
RUSSIAN FEDERATION
LATVIA
LITHUANIA
RUSS. FED. (Kaliningrad)
BELARUS
POLAND

▲ ***Since the independence*** *of Lithuania and Belarus, the peoples of the Russian enclave of Kaliningrad have become physically isolated.*

Antarctica

When Antarctic exploration began a century ago, seven nations, Australia, Argentina, Britain, Chile, France, New Zealand, and Norway, laid claim to the new territory. In 1961 the Antarctic Treaty, now signed by 45 nations, agreed to hold all territorial claims in abeyance.

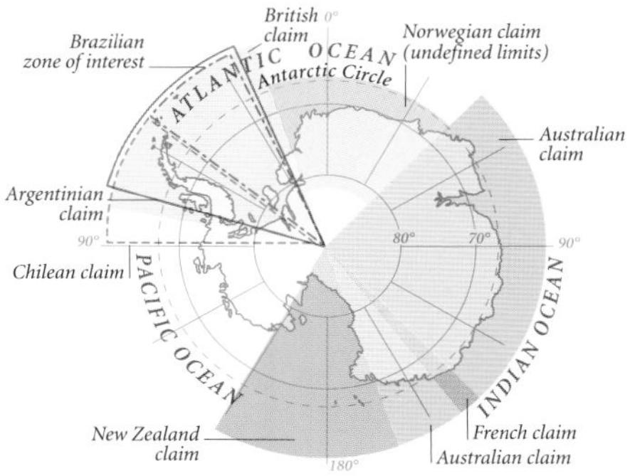
British claim
0°
Brazilian zone of interest
Norwegian claim (undefined limits)
ATLANTIC OCEAN
Antarctic Circle
Australian claim
Argentinian claim
90°
80°
70°
90°
Chilean claim
PACIFIC OCEAN
INDIAN OCEAN
New Zealand claim
180°
French claim
Australian claim

Geometric borders

Straight lines and lines of longitude and latitude have occasionally been used to determine international boundaries; and indeed the world's second longest continuous international boundary, between Canada and the USA follows the 49th Parallel for over one-third of its course. Many Canadian, American, and Australian internal administrative boundaries are similarly determined using a geometric solution.

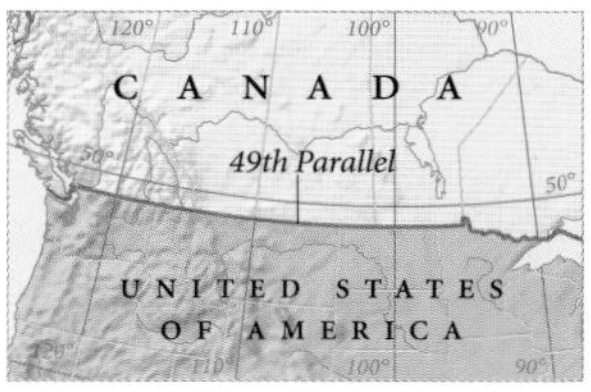
120°
110°
100°
90°
CANADA
49th Parallel
50°
UNITED STATES OF AMERICA

▲ ***Different farming techniques*** *in Canada and the US clearly mark the course of the international boundary in this satellite map.*

World boundaries

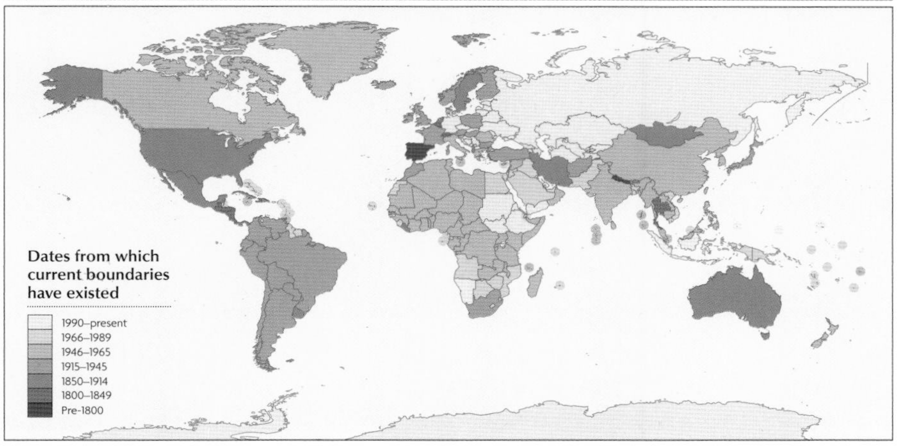
Dates from which current boundaries have existed
1990–present
1966–1989
1946–1965
1915–1945
1850–1914
1800–1849
Pre-1800

Physical borders

Many of the world's countries are divided by physical borders: lakes, rivers, mountains. The demarcation of such boundaries can, however, lead to disputes. Control of waterways, water supplies, and fisheries are frequent causes of international friction.

Lake borders

Countries which lie next to lakes usually fix their borders in the middle of the lake. Unusually the Lake Nyasa border between Malawi and Tanzania runs along Tanzania's shore.

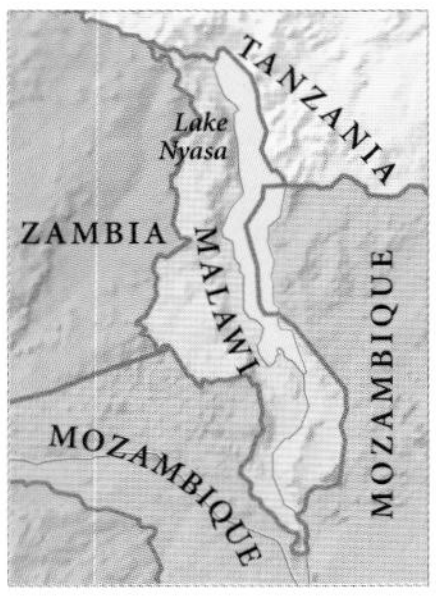
TANZANIA
Lake Nyasa
ZAMBIA
MALAWI
MOZAMBIQUE
MOZAMBIQUE

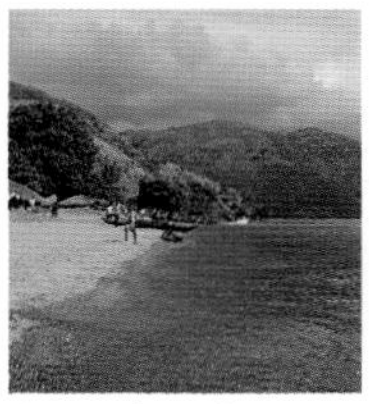

▲ ***Complicated agreements between*** *colonial powers led to the awkward division of Lake Nyasa.*

River borders

Rivers alone account for one-sixth of the world's borders. Many great rivers form boundaries between a number of countries. Changes in a river's course and interruptions of its natural flow can lead to disputes, particularly in areas where water is scarce. The center of the river's course is the nominal boundary line.

GERMANY
Danube
SLOVAKIA
UKRAINE
AUSTRIA
HUNGARY
ROMANIA
CROATIA
Danube
SERBIA
BULGARIA

▲ ***The Danube forms*** *all or part of the border between nine European nations.*

Mountain borders

Mountain ranges form natural barriers and are the basis for many major borders, particularly in Europe and Asia. The watershed is the conventional boundary demarcation line, but its accurate determination is often problematic.

FRANCE
Pyrenees
ANDORRA
SPAIN

▲ ***The Pyrenees form*** *a natural mountain border between France and Spain.*

Shifting boundaries – Poland

Borders between countries can change dramatically over time. The nations of eastern Europe have been particularly affected by changing boundaries. Poland is an example of a country whose boundaries have changed so significantly that it has literally moved around Europe. At the start of the 16th century, Poland was the largest nation in Europe. Between 1772 and 1795, it was absorbed into Prussia, Austria, and Russia, and it effectively ceased to exist. After the First World War, Poland became an independent country once more, but its borders changed again after the Second World War following invasions by both Soviet Russia and Nazi Germany.

Moscow
POLAND
Warsaw
Kiev

▲ ***In 1634, Poland*** *was the largest nation in Europe, its eastern boundary reaching toward Moscow.*

Moscow
RUSSIA
PRUSSIA
Warsaw
Kiev
AUSTRIA

▲ ***From 1772–1795, Poland*** *was gradually partitioned between Austria, Russia, and Prussia. Its eastern boundary receded by over 100 miles (160 km).*

Moscow
POLAND
Warsaw
Kiev

▲ ***Following the First World War,*** *Poland was reinstated as an independent state, but it was less than half the size it had been in 1634.*

Moscow
POLAND
Warsaw
Kiev

▲ ***After the Second World War,*** *the Baltic Sea border was extended westward, but much of the eastern territory was annexed by Russia.*

International disputes

There are more than 60 disputed borders or territories in the world today. Although many of these disputes can be settled by peaceful negotiation, some areas have become a focus for international conflict. Ethnic tensions have been a major source of territorial disagreement throughout history, as has the ownership of, and access to, valuable natural resources. The turmoil of the postcolonial era in many parts of Africa is partly a result of the 19th century "carve-up" of the continent, which created potential for conflict by drawing often arbitrary lines through linguistic and cultural areas.

Jammu and Kashmir

Disputes over Jammu and Kashmir have caused three serious wars between India and Pakistan since 1947. Pakistan wishes to annex the largely Muslim territory, while India refuses to cede any territory or to hold a referendum, and also lays claim to the entire territory. Most international maps show the "line of control" agreed in 1972 as the *de facto* border. In addition, India has territorial disputes with neighboring China. The situation is further complicated by a Kashmiri independence movement, active since the late 1980s.

▲ **Indian army troops** *maintain their positions in the mountainous terrain of northern Kashmir.*

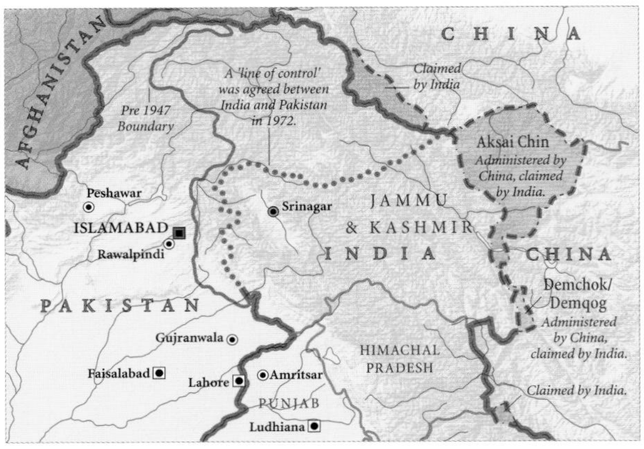

CHINA
AFGHANISTAN
Pre 1947 Boundary
A 'line of control' was agreed between India and Pakistan in 1972.
Claimed by India
Aksai Chin
Administered by China, claimed by India.
Peshawar
ISLAMABAD
Rawalpindi
Srinagar
JAMMU & KASHMIR
INDIA
CHINA
PAKISTAN
Demchok/ Demqog
Administered by China, claimed by India.
Gujranwala
Faisalabad
Lahore
Amritsar
HIMACHAL PRADESH
PUNJAB
Ludhiana
Claimed by India.

North and South Korea

Since 1953, the *de facto* border between North and South Korea has been a cease-fire line which straddles the 38th Parallel and is designated as a demilitarized zone. Both countries have heavy fortifications and troop concentrations behind this zone.

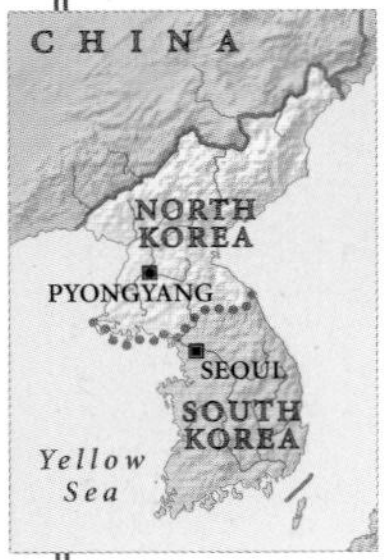

CHINA
NORTH KOREA
PYONGYANG
SEOUL
SOUTH KOREA
Yellow Sea

▲ **Heavy fortifications on** *the border between North and South Korea.*

Cyprus

Cyprus was partitioned in 1974, following an invasion by Turkish troops. The south is now the Greek Cypriot Republic of Cyprus, while the self-proclaimed Turkish Republic of Northern Cyprus is recognized only by Turkey.

FREEDOM FOR CY

▲ *The so-called* **"green line"** *divides Cyprus into Greek and Turkish sectors.*

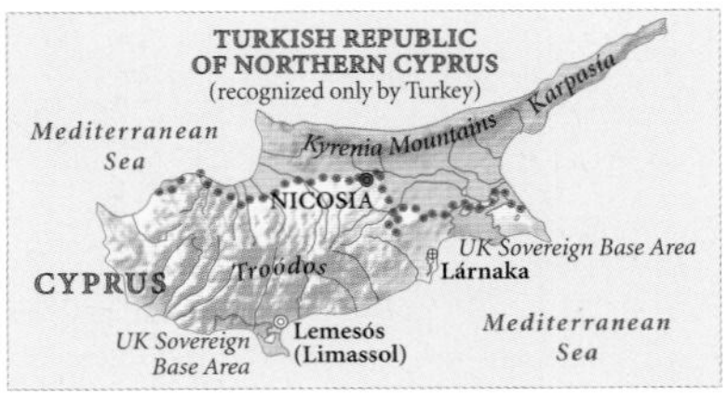

TURKISH REPUBLIC OF NORTHERN CYPRUS
(recognized only by Turkey)
Mediterranean Sea
Karpasia
Kyrenia Mountains
NICOSIA
CYPRUS
Troodos
UK Sovereign Base Area
Lárnaka
UK Sovereign Base Area
Lemesós (Limassol)
Mediterranean Sea

Conflicts and international disputes
UN peacekeeping missions 2002-2012
Major active territorial or border disputes
Countries involved in internal conflict
Active territorial or border disputes and internal conflict
RUSSIAN FEDERATION
Kurile Islands
Chechnya
MOLDOVA
GEORGIA
ARMENIA
AZERB.
TURKEY
SYRIA
CYPRUS
LEBANON
ISRAEL
IRAQ
IRAN
AFGHANISTAN
TAJIKISTAN
PAKISTAN
Aksai Chin
Jammu and Kashmir
CHINA
NORTH KOREA
SOUTH KOREA
Arunachal Pradesh
BHUTAN
INDIA
BANGLADESH
MYANMAR (BURMA)
THAI.
VIETNAM
CAMBODIA
Senkaku Islands
TAIWAN
Paracel Islands
PHILIPPINES
Spratly Islands
MALAYSIA
BRITISH INDIAN OCEAN TERRITORY
EAST TIMOR
CROATIA
B.&H.
KOS.
BULG.
MACEDONIA
SPAIN
Gibraltar
Ceuta
Melilla
MOROCCO
WESTERN SAHARA
ALGERIA
LIBYA
EGYPT
MAURITANIA
MALI
NIGER
CHAD
SUDAN
ERITREA
YEMEN
SENEGAL
BURKINA
NIGERIA
SOUTH SUDAN
ETHIOPIA
SOMALIA
SIERRA LEONE
LIBERIA
IVORY COAST
BENIN
CAMEROON
C.A.R.
DEM. REP. CONGO
UGANDA
KENYA
CONGO
RWANDA
BURUNDI
Cabinda
ANGOLA
ZAMBIA
ZIMBABWE
BOTSWANA
MEXICO
CUBA
Guantanamo Bay
HAITI
BELIZE
VENEZUELA
GUYANA
SURINAME
French Guiana
COLOMBIA
ECUADOR
PERU
BRAZIL
BOLIVIA
CHILE
URUGUAY
ARGENTINA
Falkland Islands

The Falkland Islands

The British dependent territory of the Falkland Islands was invaded by Argentina in 1982, sparking a full-scale war with the UK. Tensions ran high during 2012 in the build up to the thirtieth anniversary of the conflict.

◀ **British warships in** *Falkland Sound during the 1982 war with Argentina.*

Israel

Israel was created in 1948 following the 1947 UN Resolution (147) on Palestine. Until 1979 Israel had no borders, only cease-fire lines from a series of wars in 1948, 1967, and 1973. Treaties with Egypt in 1979 and Jordan in 1994 led to these borders being defined and agreed. Negotiations over Israeli settlements and Palestinian self-government seen little effective progress since 2000.

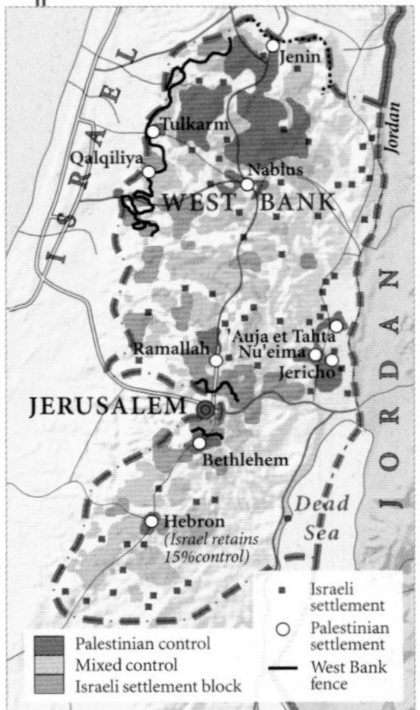

Jenin
ISRAEL
Tulkarm
Qalqiliya
Nablus
WEST BANK
Jordan
Ramallah
Auja et Tahta
Nu'eima
Jericho
JERUSALEM
Bethlehem
JORDAN
Hebron
(Israel retains 15% control)
Dead Sea
Palestinian control
Mixed control
Israeli settlement block
Israeli settlement
Palestinian settlement
West Bank fence

LEBANON
Mediterranean Sea
GOLAN HEIGHTS
SYRIA
WEST BANK
GAZA STRIP
ISRAEL
JORDAN
EGYPT

▲ **Barbed-wire fences surround** *a settlement in the Golan Heights.*

Former Yugoslavia

Following the disintegration in 1991 of the communist state of Yugoslavia, the breakaway states of Croatia and Bosnia and Herzegovina came into conflict with the "parent" state (consisting of Serbia and Montenegro). Warfare focused on ethnic and territorial ambitions in Bosnia. The tenuous Dayton Accord of 1995 sought to recognize the post-1990 borders, whilst providing for ethnic partition and required international peace-keeping troops to maintain the terms of the peace.

CROATIA
Sava
Bihać
Brčko
Banja Luka
Tuzla
Jajce
BOSNIA & HERZEGOVINA
Srebrenica
Drina
Gornji Vakuf
SARAJEVO
Goražde
SERBIA
Split
Mostar
Adriatic Sea
MONTENEGRO
Dubrovnik
Republika Srpska
Federacija Bosna i Hercegovina

▲ **Most claimant states** *have small military garrisons on the Spratly Islands.*

The Spratly Islands

The site of potential oil and natural gas reserves, the Spratly Islands in the South China Sea have been claimed by China, Vietnam, Taiwan, Malaysia, and the Philippines since the Japanese gave up a wartime claim in 1951.

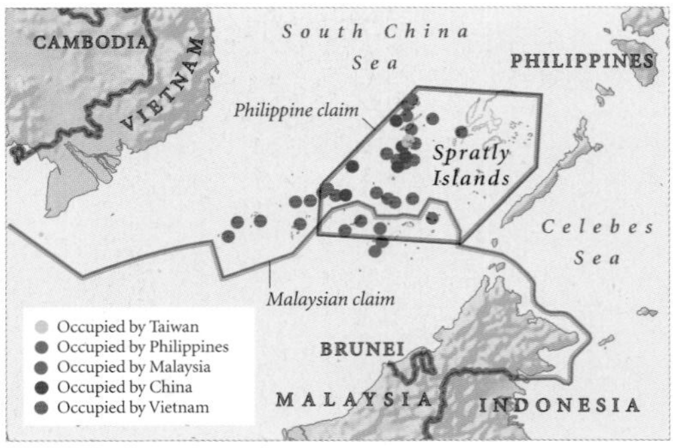

CAMBODIA
VIETNAM
South China Sea
PHILIPPINES
Philippine claim
Spratly Islands
Celebes Sea
Malaysian claim
BRUNEI
MALAYSIA
INDONESIA
Occupied by Taiwan
Occupied by Philippines
Occupied by Malaysia
Occupied by China
Occupied by Vietnam

ATLAS
OF THE WORLD

THE MAPS IN THIS ATLAS ARE ARRANGED CONTINENT BY CONTINENT, STARTING FROM THE INTERNATIONAL DATE LINE, AND MOVING EASTWARD. THE MAPS PROVIDE A UNIQUE VIEW OF TODAY'S WORLD, COMBINING TRADITIONAL CARTOGRAPHIC TECHNIQUES WITH THE LATEST REMOTE-SENSED AND DIGITAL TECHNOLOGY.

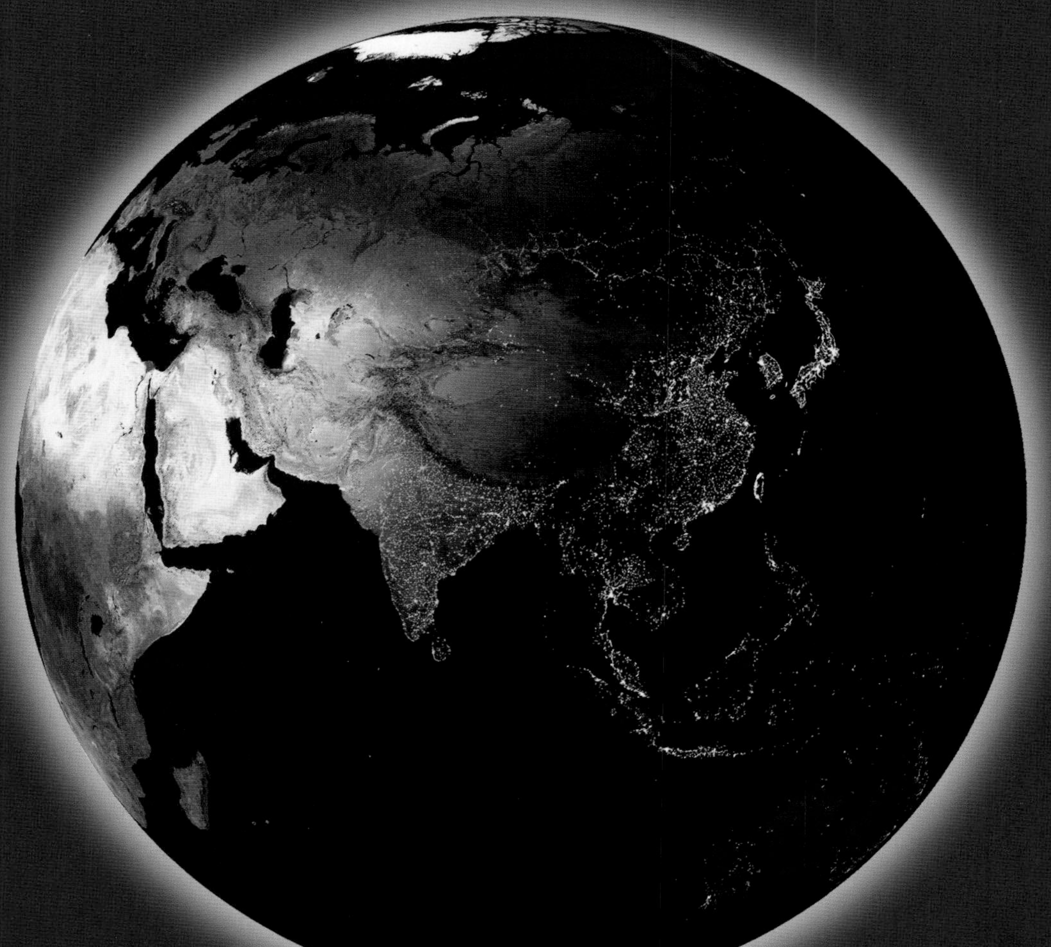

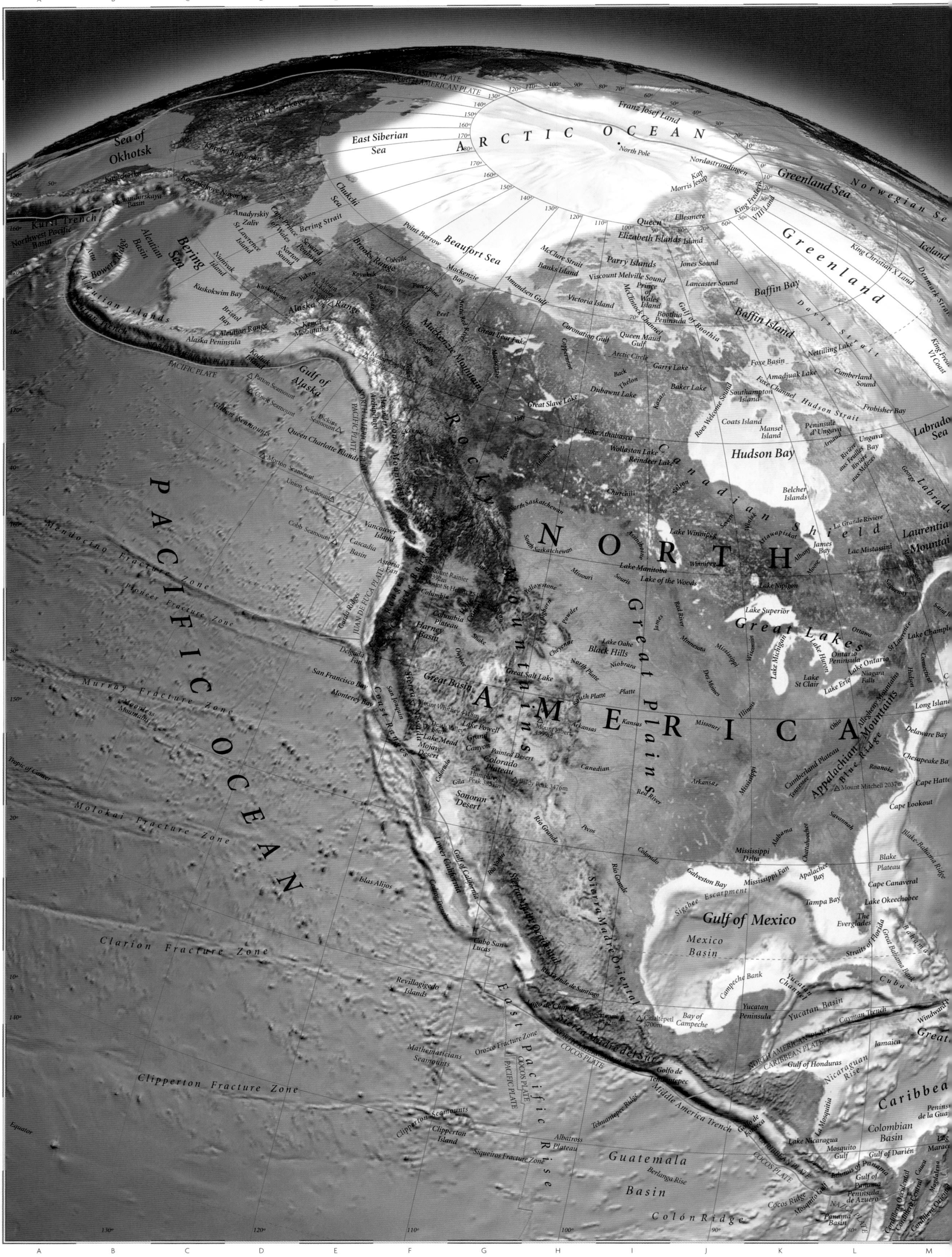

ARCTIC OCEAN
North Pole
Franz Josef Land
East Siberian Sea
Sea of Okhotsk
Chukchi Sea
Bering Strait
Bering Sea
Beaufort Sea
Greenland Sea
Greenland
Baffin Bay
Baffin Island
Davis Strait
Queen Elizabeth Islands
Parry Islands
Banks Island
Victoria Island
Hudson Bay
Hudson Strait
Labrador Sea
Canadian Shield
Great Slave Lake
Great Bear Lake
Lake Athabasca
Lake Winnipeg
NORTH AMERICA
Rocky Mountains
Great Plains
Great Lakes
Lake Superior
Lake Michigan
Lake Huron
Lake Erie
Lake Ontario
Appalachian Mountains
Great Salt Lake
Great Basin
Colorado Plateau
Sonoran Desert
Sierra Madre Occidental
Sierra Madre Oriental
Gulf of Mexico
Mexico Basin
Yucatan Peninsula
Bay of Campeche
Gulf of California
Gulf of Alaska
Alaska Peninsula
Aleutian Islands
Kurtil Trench
Vancouver Island
PACIFIC OCEAN
Mendocino Fracture Zone
Pioneer Fracture Zone
Murray Fracture Zone
Molokai Fracture Zone
Clarion Fracture Zone
Clipperton Fracture Zone
East Pacific Rise
Middle America Trench
Guatemala Basin
Colón Ridge
Caribbean
Colombian Basin
Gulf of Honduras
Cuba

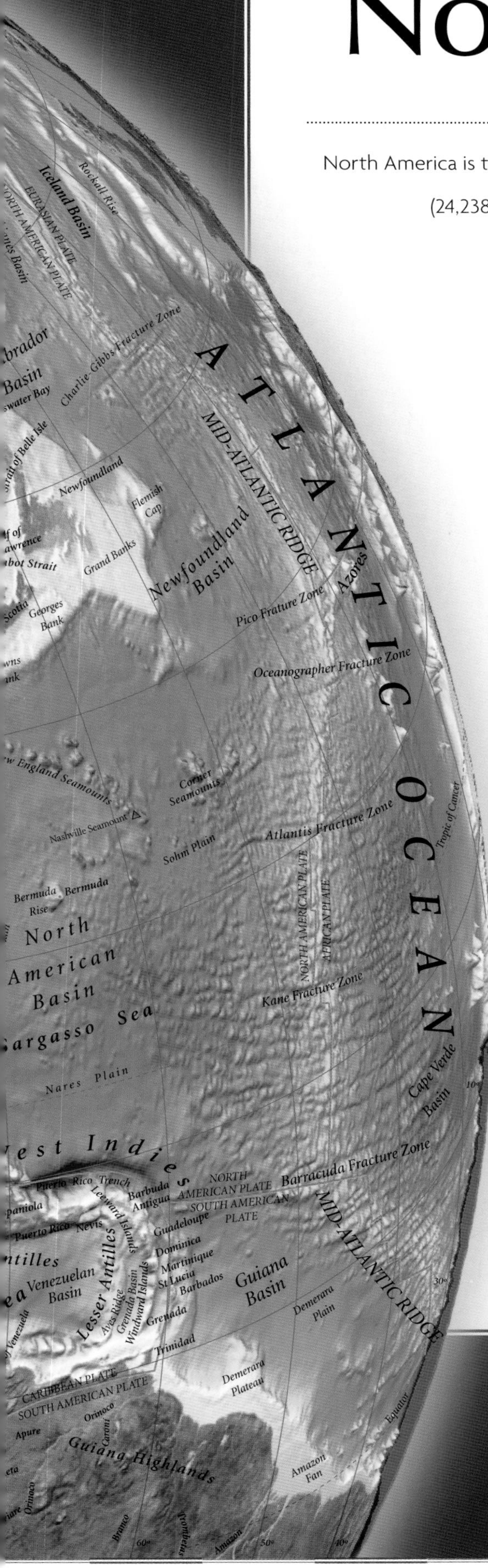
ATLANTIC OCEAN
MID-ATLANTIC RIDGE
Iceland Basin
Rockall Rise
EURASIAN PLATE
NORTH AMERICAN PLATE
Charlie-Gibbs Fracture Zone
Newfoundland
Flemish Cap
Grand Banks
Newfoundland Basin
Georges Bank
Azores
Pico Fracture Zone
Oceanographer Fracture Zone
Corner Seamounts
Nashville Seamount
Sohm Plain
Atlantis Fracture Zone
Tropic of Cancer
Bermuda Rise
Bermuda
North American Basin
NORTH AMERICAN PLATE
AFRICAN PLATE
Kane Fracture Zone
Sargasso Sea
Nares Plain
Cape Verde Basin
Barracuda Fracture Zone
Puerto Rico Trench
Barbuda
Antigua
Guadeloupe
Dominica
Martinique
St Lucia
Barbados
Grenada
Trinidad
Lesser Antilles
Venezuelan Basin
Guiana Basin
Demerara Plain
Demerara Plateau
CARIBBEAN PLATE
SOUTH AMERICAN PLATE
Orinoco
Guiana Highlands
Amazon Fan
Equator

North America

North America is the world's third largest continent with a total area of 9,358,340 sq miles (24,238,000 sq km) including Greenland and the Caribbean islands. It lies wholly within the Northern Hemisphere.

○ ***Greatest extent, North–South:*** *4600 miles / 7400 km*

□ ***Greatest extent, East–West:*** *3500 miles / 5700 km*

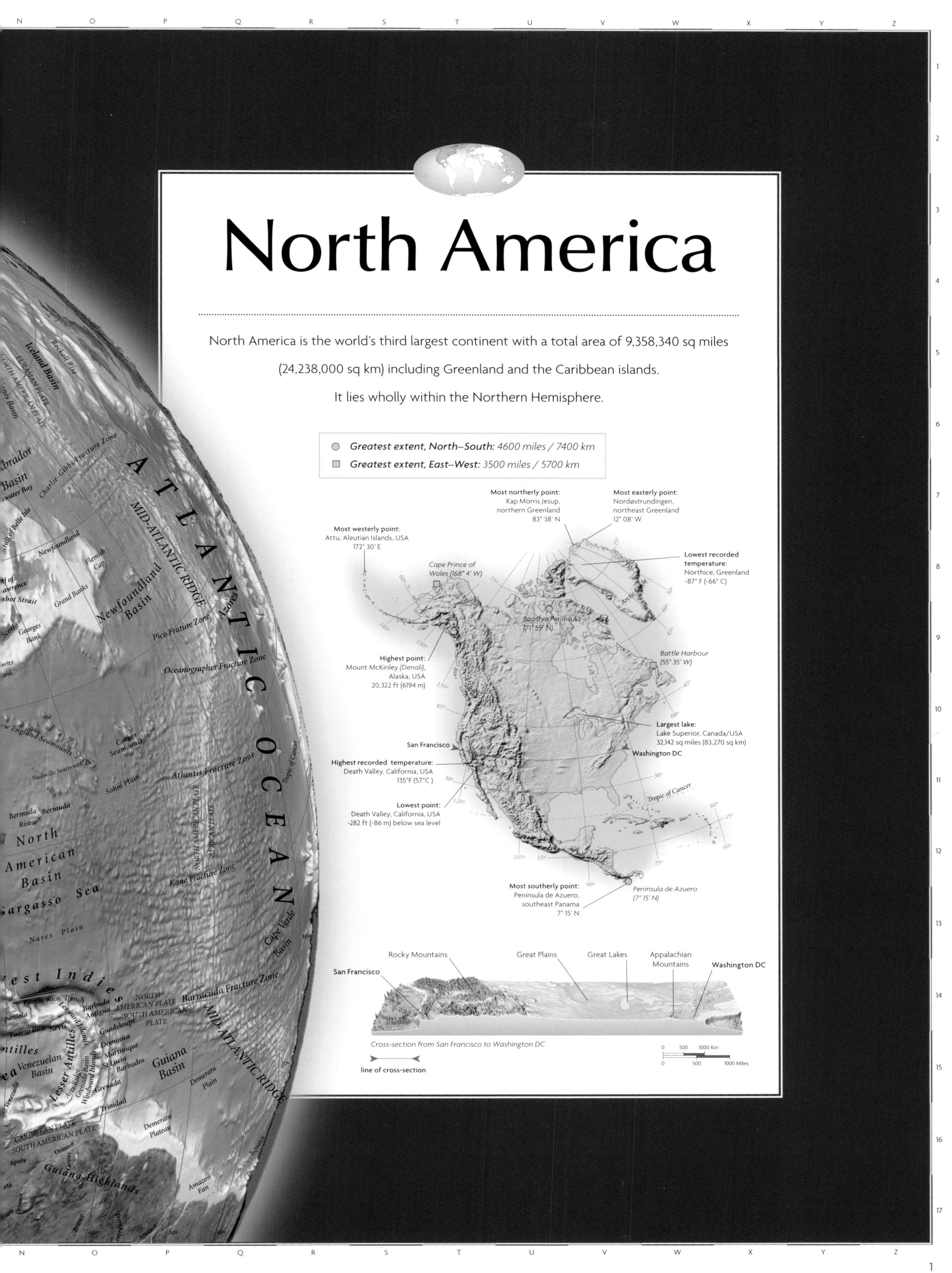

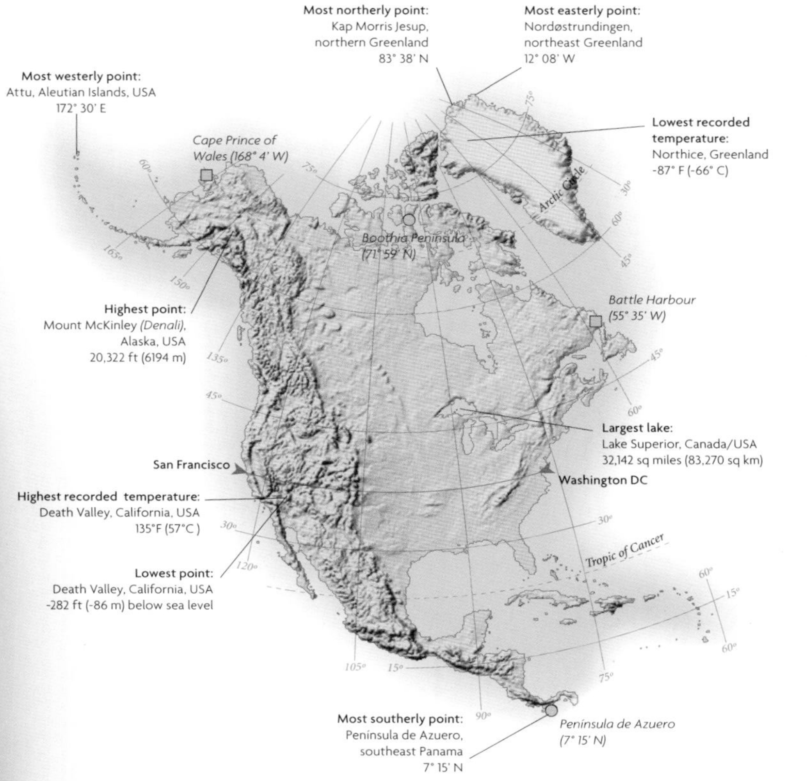
Most northerly point:
Kap Morris Jesup, northern Greenland
83° 38′ N
Most easterly point:
Nordøstrundingen, northeast Greenland
12° 08′ W
Most westerly point:
Attu, Aleutian Islands, USA
172° 30′ E
Cape Prince of Wales (168° 4′ W)
Lowest recorded temperature:
Northice, Greenland
-87° F (-66° C)
Arctic Circle
Boothia Peninsula (71° 59′ N)
Highest point:
Mount McKinley (Denali), Alaska, USA
20,322 ft (6194 m)
Battle Harbour (55° 35′ W)
Largest lake:
Lake Superior, Canada/USA
32,142 sq miles (83,270 sq km)
San Francisco
Washington DC
Highest recorded temperature:
Death Valley, California, USA
135°F (57°C)
Tropic of Cancer
Lowest point:
Death Valley, California, USA
-282 ft (-86 m) below sea level
Most southerly point:
Peninsula de Azuero, southeast Panama
7° 15′ N
Peninsula de Azuero (7° 15′ N)

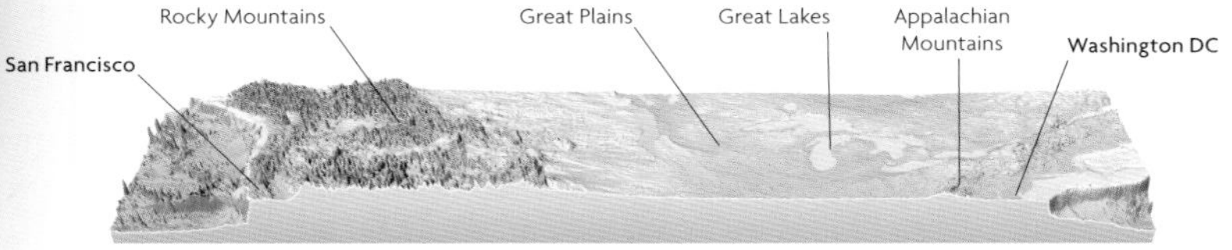
Rocky Mountains
Great Plains
Great Lakes
Appalachian Mountains
San Francisco
Washington DC
0 500 1000 Km
0 500 1000 Miles

Cross-section from San Francisco to Washington DC

line of cross-section

Physical North America

The North American continent can be divided into a number of major structural areas: the Western Cordillera, the Canadian Shield, the Great Plains, and Central Lowlands, and the Appalachians. Other smaller regions include the Gulf Atlantic Coastal Plain which borders the southern coast of North America from the southern Appalachians to the Great Plains. This area includes the expanding Mississippi Delta. A chain of volcanic islands, running in an arc around the margin of the Caribbean Plate, lie to the east of the Gulf of Mexico.

The Western Cordillera

About 80 million years ago the Pacific and North American plates collided, uplifting the Western Cordillera. This consists of the Aleutian, Coast, Cascade, and Sierra Nevada mountains, and the inland Rocky Mountains. These run parallel from the Arctic to Mexico.

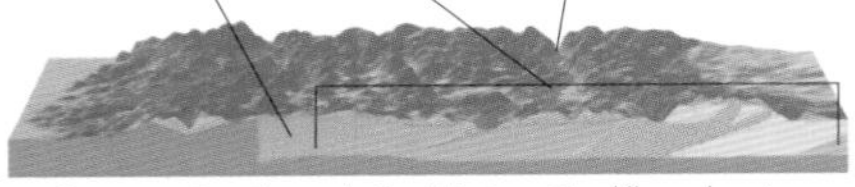

Volcanic rock
Strata have been thrust eastward along fault lines
The Rocky Mountain Trench is the longest linear fault on the continent
B
B
0 50 100 Km
0 50 100 Miles

Cross-section through the Western Cordillera showing direction of mountain building.

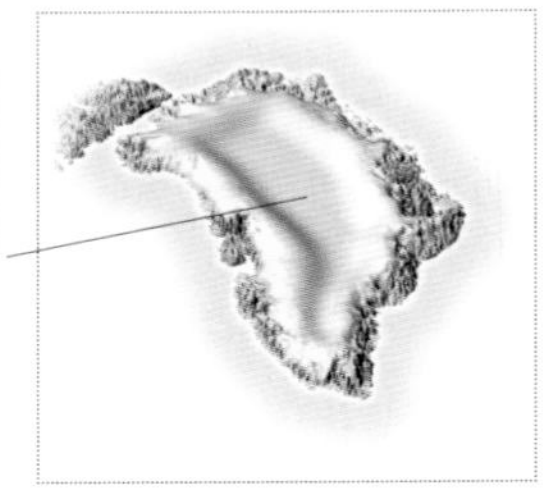

The weight of the ice sheet, 1.8 miles (3 km) thick, has depressed the land to 0.6 miles (1 km) below sea level

▲ *This computer-generated view shows the ice-covered island of Greenland without its ice cap.*

The Canadian Shield

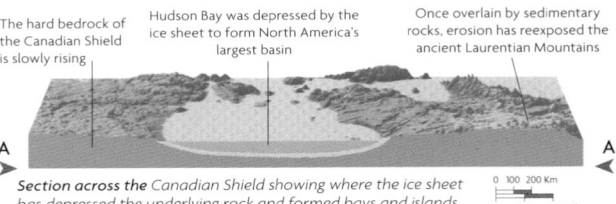

Spanning northern Canada and Greenland, this geologically stable plain forms the heart of the continent, containing rocks more than two billion years old. A long history of weathering and repeated glaciation has scoured the region, leaving flat plains, gentle hummocks, numerous small basins and lakes, and the bays and islands of the Arctic.

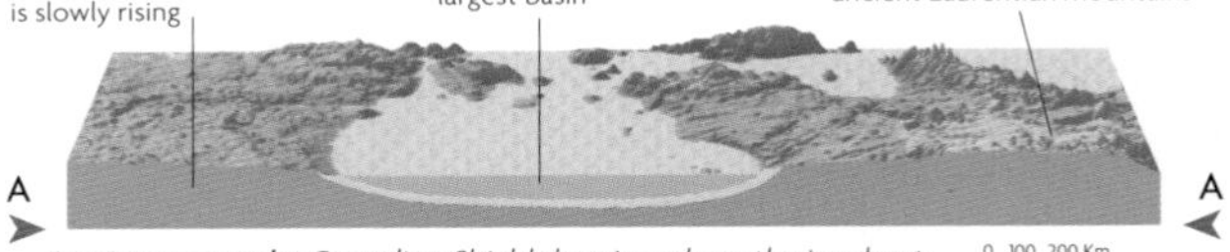

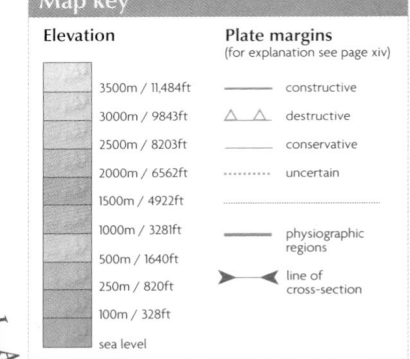

The hard bedrock of the Canadian Shield is slowly rising
Hudson Bay was depressed by the ice sheet to form North America's largest basin
Once overlain by sedimentary rocks, erosion has reexposed the ancient Laurentian Mountains
A
A
0 100 200 Km
0 100 200 Miles

***Section across the** Canadian Shield showing where the ice sheet has depressed the underlying rock and formed bays and islands.*

Map key

Elevation	Plate margins (for explanation see page xiv)
3500m / 11,484ft	constructive
3000m / 9843ft	destructive
2500m / 8203ft	conservative
2000m / 6562ft	uncertain
1500m / 4922ft	
1000m / 3281ft	physiographic regions
500m / 1640ft	line of cross-section
250m / 820ft	
100m / 328ft	
sea level	

Scale 1:42,000,000

Km 0 200 400 600 800 1000

Miles 0 200 400 600 800 1000

projection: Lambert Azimuthal Equal Area

ASIA
Bering Strait
Bering Sea
Aleutian Islands
Aleutian Range
Alaska Range
Mount McKinley 6194m
Brooks Range
Beaufort Sea
Mackenzie Delta
Mackenzie Mountains
Mackenzie
Great Bear Lake
Gulf of Alaska
NORTH AMERICAN PLATE
PACIFIC PLATE
Coast Mountains
WESTERN CORDILLERA
ROCKY MOUNTAINS
Great Slave Lake
Lake Athabasca
Reindeer Lake
CANADIAN SHIELD
CENTRAL LOWLANDS
GREAT PLAINS
JUAN DE FUCA PLATE
Mount Rainier 4392m
Mount St Helens 2549m
Cascade Range
Great Basin
Great Salt Lake
Sierra Nevada
San Joaquin Valley
San Andreas Fault
Death Valley -86m
Grand Canyon
Colorado
Colorado Plateau
Mojave Desert
Sonoran Desert
Lower California
Gulf of California
Sierra Madre Occidental
Sierra Madre Oriental
Rio Grande
Arkansas
Missouri
Mississippi
Ohio
Lake Winnipeg
Lake Manitoba
Lake Superior
Lake Michigan
Lake Huron
Lake Erie
Lake Ontario
Great Lakes
St Lawrence
Appalachian Mountains
APPALACHIANS
Cape Cod
GULF ATLANTIC COASTAL PLAIN
Mississippi Delta
Gulf of Mexico
Yucatan Peninsula
Volcán Pico de Orizaba 5700m
Sierra Madre del Sur
Lake Nicaragua
Isthmus of Panama
Greenland
Baffin Bay
Baffin Island
Davis Strait
Foxe Basin
Hudson Strait
Hudson Bay
Labrador Sea
Labrador
Laurentian Mountains
Newfoundland
Nova Scotia
ATLANTIC OCEAN
PACIFIC OCEAN
West Indies
Greater Antilles
Lesser Antilles
Caribbean Sea
NORTH AMERICAN PLATE
CARIBBEAN PLATE
SOUTH AMERICAN PLATE
SOUTH AMERICA
A
A
B
B
C
C
D
D

The Great Plains & Central Lowlands

Deposits left by retreating glaciers and rivers have made this vast flat area very fertile. In the north this is the result of glaciation, with deposits up to one mile (1.7 km) thick, covering the basement rock. To the south and west, the massive Missouri/Mississippi river system has for centuries deposited silt across the plains, creating broad, flat floodplains and deltas.

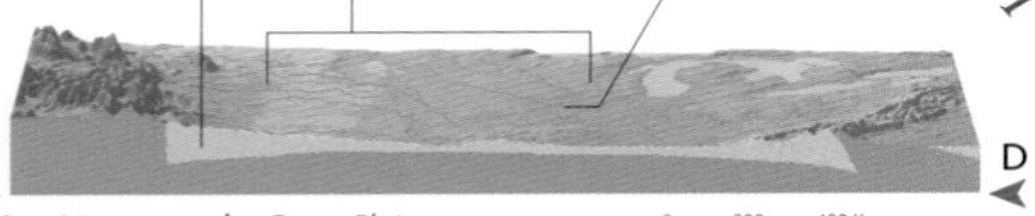

Sedimentary layers overlay domed basement rock
Upland rivers drain south toward the Mississippi Basin
Confluence of the Missouri and Mississippi Rivers
D
D
0 200 400 Km
0 200 400 Miles

***Section across the** Great Plains and Central Lowlands showing river systems and structure.*

The Appalachians

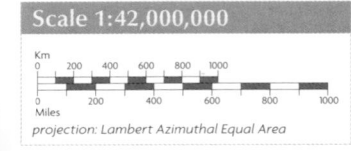

The Appalachian Mountains, uplifted about 400 million years ago, are some of the oldest in the world. They have been lowered and rounded by erosion and now slope gently toward the Atlantic across a broad coastal plain.

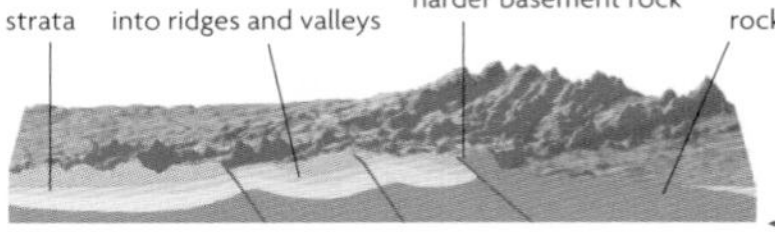

Horizontal strata
Sedimentary strata folded and faulted into ridges and valleys
Softer strata has been crumpled against the harder basement rock
Hard basement rock
C
C
0 25 50 Km
0 25 50 Miles

***Cross-section through the** Appalachians showing the numerous folds, which have subsequently been weathered to create a rounded relief.*

N O P Q R S T U V W X Y Z

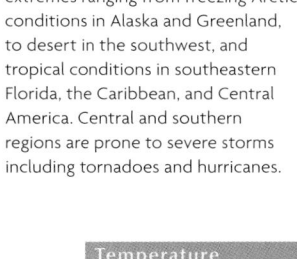

▲ *"Tornado alley" in the Mississippi Valley suffers frequent tornadoes.*

Climate

North America's climate includes extremes ranging from freezing Arctic conditions in Alaska and Greenland, to desert in the southwest, and tropical conditions in southeastern Florida, the Caribbean, and Central America. Central and southern regions are prone to severe storms including tornadoes and hurricanes.

Climate

- ice cap
- tundra
- subarctic
- cool continental
- warm humid
- semiarid
- arid
- humid equatorial
- tropical
- daily hours of sunshine, January
- daily hours of sunshine, July
- direction of hurricanes
- tornado zones

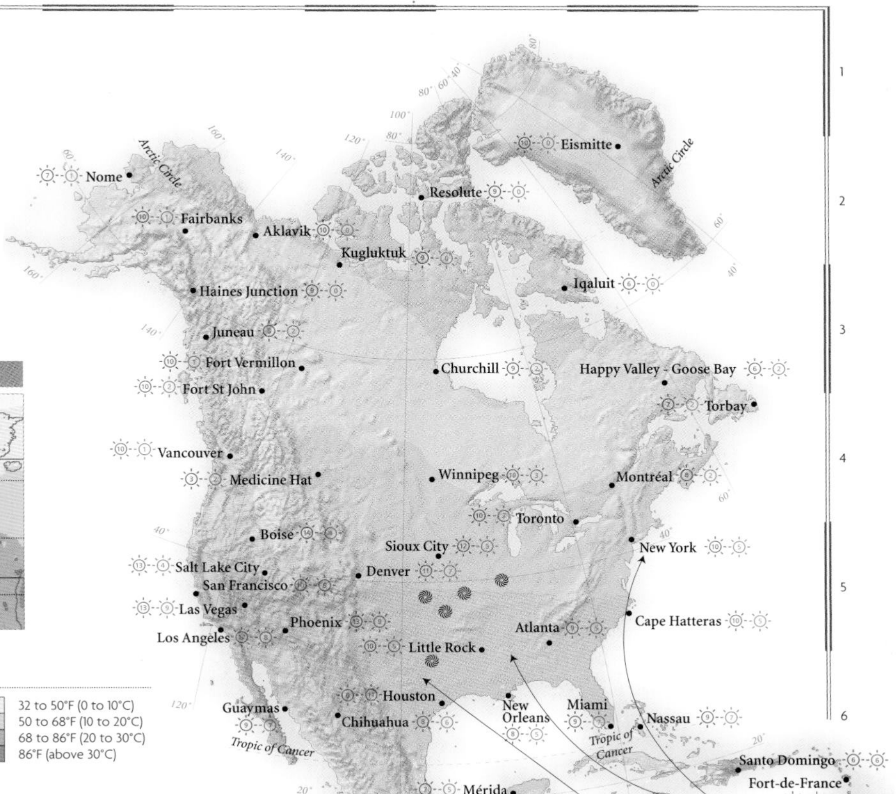

Arctic Circle
Tropic of Cancer
Nome
Fairbanks
Aklavik
Eismitte
Resolute
Kugluktuk
Iqaluit
Haines Junction
Juneau
Fort Vermillon
Fort St John
Churchill
Happy Valley - Goose Bay
Torbay
Vancouver
Medicine Hat
Winnipeg
Montréal
Toronto
Boise
Sioux City
New York
Salt Lake City
San Francisco
Denver
Las Vegas
Phoenix
Atlanta
Cape Hatteras
Los Angeles
Little Rock
Guaymas
Houston
New Orleans
Miami
Nassau
Chihuahua
Santo Domingo
Fort-de-France
Mérida
Kingston
Acapulco
San Salvador
San José

▲ *Much of the southwest is semi-desert; receiving less than 12 inches (300 mm) of rainfall a year.*

Temperature

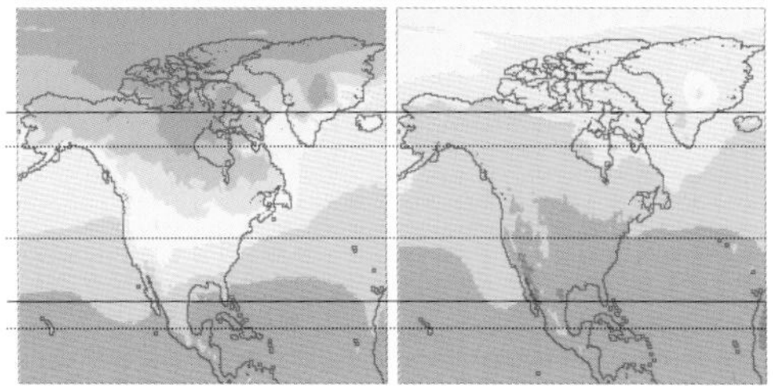

Arctic Circle
60° N
40° N
Tropic of Cancer
20° N

Average January temperature *Average July temperature*

Temperature

- -22°F (below -30°C)
- -22 to -4°F (-30 to -20°C)
- -4 to 14°F (-20 to -10°C)
- 14 to 32°F (-10 to 0°C)
- 32 to 50°F (0 to 10°C)
- 50 to 68°F (10 to 20°C)
- 68 to 86°F (20 to 30°C)
- 86°F (above 30°C)

Rainfall

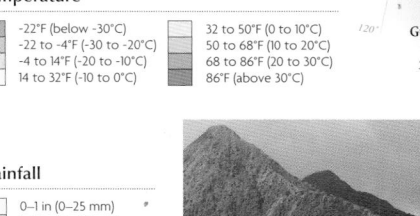

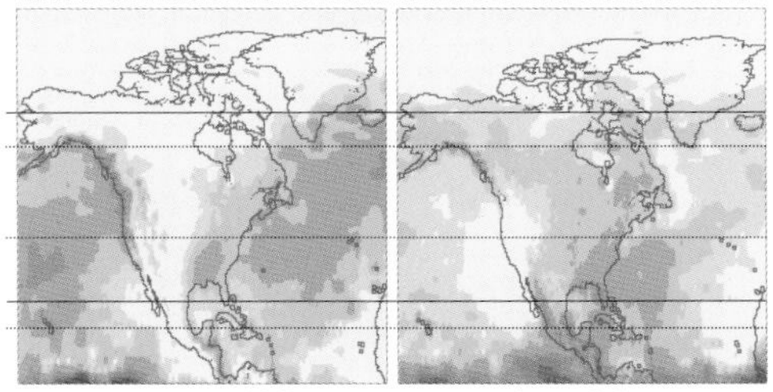

Arctic Circle
60° N
40° N
Tropic of Cancer
20° N

Average January rainfall *Average July rainfall*

Rainfall

- 0–1 in (0–25 mm)
- 1–2 in (25–50 mm)
- 2–4 in (50–100 mm)
- 4–8 in (100–200 mm)
- 8–12 in (200–300 mm)
- 12–16 in (300–400 mm)
- 16–20 in (400–500 mm)
- more than 20 in (500 mm)

◀ ***The lush, green** mountains of the Lesser Antilles receive annual rainfalls of up to 360 inches (9000 mm).*

Shaping the continent

Glacial processes affect much of northern Canada, Greenland, and the Western Cordillera. Along the western coast of North America, Central America, and the Caribbean, underlying plates moving together lead to earthquakes and volcanic eruptions. The vast river systems, fed by mountain streams, constantly erode and deposit material along their paths.

Volcanic activity

1 Mount St. Helens volcano *(right)* in the Cascade Range erupted violently in May 1980, killing 57 people and leveling large areas of forest. The lateral blast filled a valley with debris for 15 miles (25 km).

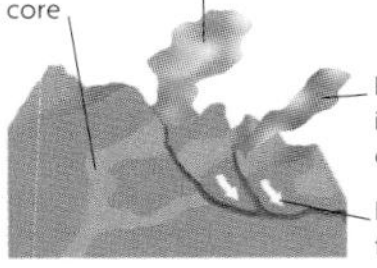

Molten rock at volcano's core
Vertical eruption
Lateral explosion increases extent of damage
Landslide fills valley

***Volcanic activity:** Eruption of Mount St Helens*

Periglaciation

2 The ground in the far north is nearly always frozen: the surface thaws only in summer. This freeze-thaw process produces features such as pingos *(left)*; formed by the freezing of groundwater. With each successive winter ice accumulates producing a mound with a core of ice.

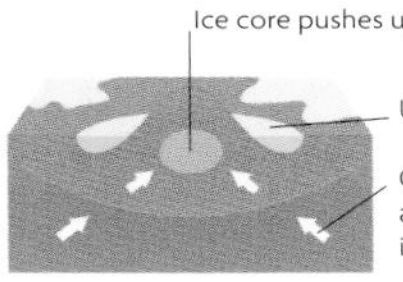

Ice core pushes up ground to form pingo
Unfrozen lake
Groundwater attracted to ice core

***Periglaciation:** Formation of a pingo in the Mackenzie Delta*

Post-glacial lakes

3 A chain of lakes from Great Bear Lake to the Great Lakes *(above)* was created as the ice retreated northward. Glaciers scoured hollows in the softer lowland rock. Glacial deposits at the lip of the hollows, and ridges of harder rock, trapped water to form lakes.

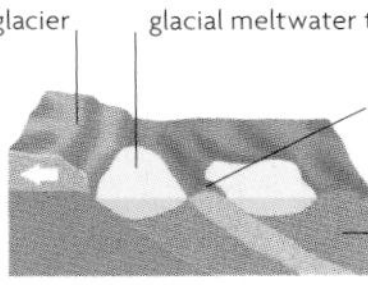

Retreating glacier
Ice-scoured hollow filled with glacial meltwater to form a lake
Harder rock creates a barrier between lakes
Softer lowland rock

***Post-glacial lakes:** Formation of the Great Lakes*

The evolving landscape

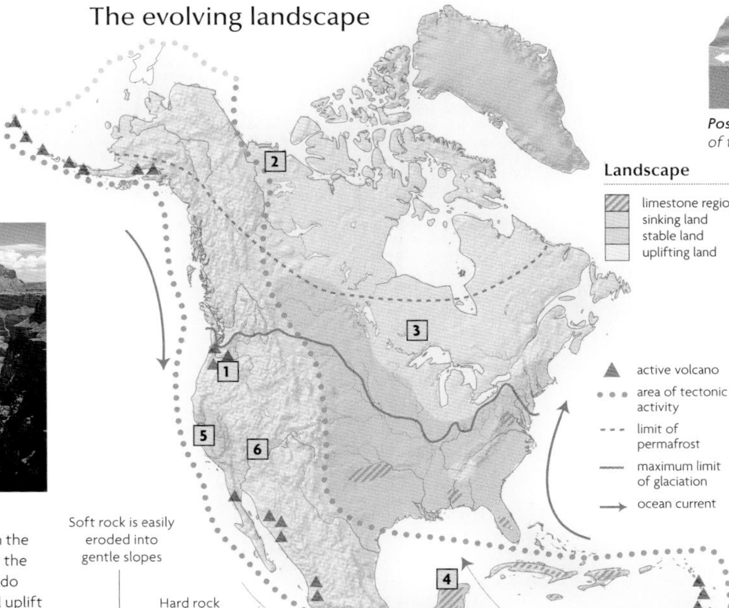

1
2
3
4
5
6

Landscape

- limestone region
- sinking land
- stable land
- uplifting land
- active volcano
- area of tectonic activity
- limit of permafrost
- maximum limit of glaciation
- ocean current

Seismic activity

5 The San Andreas Fault *(above)* places much of the North America's west coast under constant threat from earthquakes. It is caused by the Pacific Plate grinding past the North American Plate at a faster rate, though in the same direction.

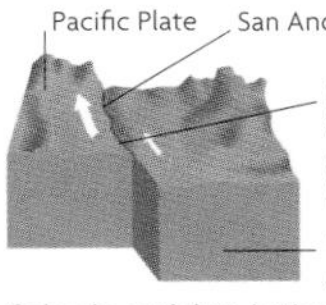

Pacific Plate
San Andreas Fault
Fault is caused by faster movement of Pacific Plate
North American Plate

***Seismic activity:** Action of the San Andreas Fault*

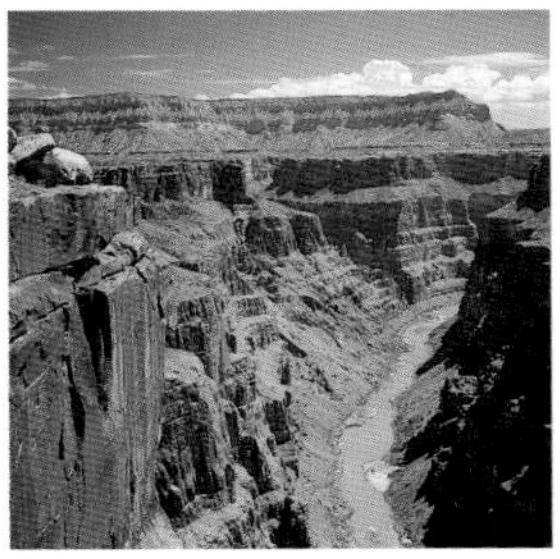

River erosion

6 The Grand Canyon *(above)* in the Colorado Plateau was created by the downward erosion of the Colorado River, combined with the gradual uplift of the plateau, over the past 30 million years. The contours of the canyon formed as the softer rock layers eroded into gentle slopes, and the hard rock layers into cliffs. The depth varies from 3855–6560 ft (1175–2000 m).

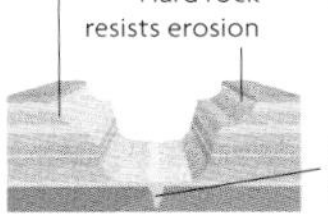

Soft rock is easily eroded into gentle slopes
Hard rock resists erosion
Colorado River cuts down through rock

***River Erosion:** Formation of the Grand Canyon*

Weathering

4 The Yucatan Peninsula is a vast, flat limestone plateau in southern Mexico. Weathering action from both rainwater and underground streams has enlarged fractures in the rock to form caves and hollows, called sinkholes *(above)*.

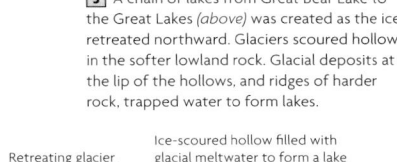

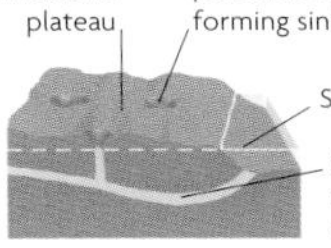

Porous limestone plateau
Rainwater erodes porous rock forming sinkholes
Sea level
Underground stream further erodes rock

***Weathering:** Water erosion on the Yucatan Peninsula*

N O P Q R S T U V W X Y Z

Political North America

Democracy is well established in some parts of the continent but is a recent phenomenon in others. The economically dominant nations of Canada and the US have a long democratic tradition but elsewhere, notably in the countries of Central America, political turmoil has been more common. In Nicaragua and Haiti, harsh dictatorships have only recently been superseded by democratically elected governments. North America's largest countries, Canada, Mexico, and the US have federal state systems, sharing political power between national and state governments. The US has intervened militarily on several occasions in Central America and the Caribbean to protect its strategic interests.

Transportation

In the 19th century, railroads opened up the North American continent. Air transportation is now more common for long distance passenger travel, although railroads are still extensively used for bulk freight transportation. Waterways like the Mississippi River are important for the transportation of bulk materials, and the Panama Canal is a vital link between the Pacific and Atlantic Oceans. In the 20th century, road transportation increased massively, with the introduction of cheap, mass-produced motor cars and extensive highway construction.

◀ *This busy suburban* interchange in Los Angeles is part of the US's Interstate freeway system. Construction of the 55,000 mile (88,500 km) freeway network began in the 1950s, and it now connects most major cities, and carries one-fifth of the US's road traffic.

Dutch Harbor
Fairbanks
Tuktoyaktuk
Anchorage
Skagway
Hay River
Prince Rupert
Prince George
Edmonton
Calgary
Nanaimo
Vancouver
Seattle
Portland
Spokane
Butte
Coos Bay
Winnipeg
Thunder Bay
Duluth
Fargo
Minneapolis
Sault Ste. Marie
Québec
St.John
Halifax
St.John's
Montréal
Albany
Boston
Toronto
Detroit
New York
Newark
Philadelphia
Baltimore
Washington DC
Norfolk
Sioux Falls
Chicago
Toledo
Cheyenne
Omaha
Salt Lake City
Oakland
San Francisco
Denver
Kansas City
Saint Louis
Nashville
Wilmington
Charleston
Los Angeles
Long Beach
San Diego
Phoenix
Albuquerque
Oklahoma City
Memphis
Atlanta
Birmingham
Savannah
Jacksonville
Dallas
El Paso
Mobile
Orlando
Isla Cedros
Chihuahua
San Antonio
Houston
New Orleans
Tampa
Miami
Corpus Christi
Monterrey
Havana
San Juan
Mazatlán
Tampico
Mérida
Kingston
Manzanillo
Toluca
Mexico City
Coatzacoalcos
Salina Cruz
Guatemala City
San Salvador
Corinto
Balboa
Panama Canal
Panama City
Transportation
major roads and highways
major railroads
major canals
international borders
transport intersections
international airports
major ports

▲ *The 40 mile* (65 km) long Panama Canal cuts through the Isthmus of Panama, a narrow strip of land connecting North and South America. Opened in 1914, the canal reduced the journey between the Atlantic and Pacific oceans by almost 8000 nautical miles (14,800 km).

◀ *Low-density housing developments* such as this one on the outskirts of Phoenix, Arizona, reflect the US's abundance of land and a dispersed population, dependent on the car for personal mobility.

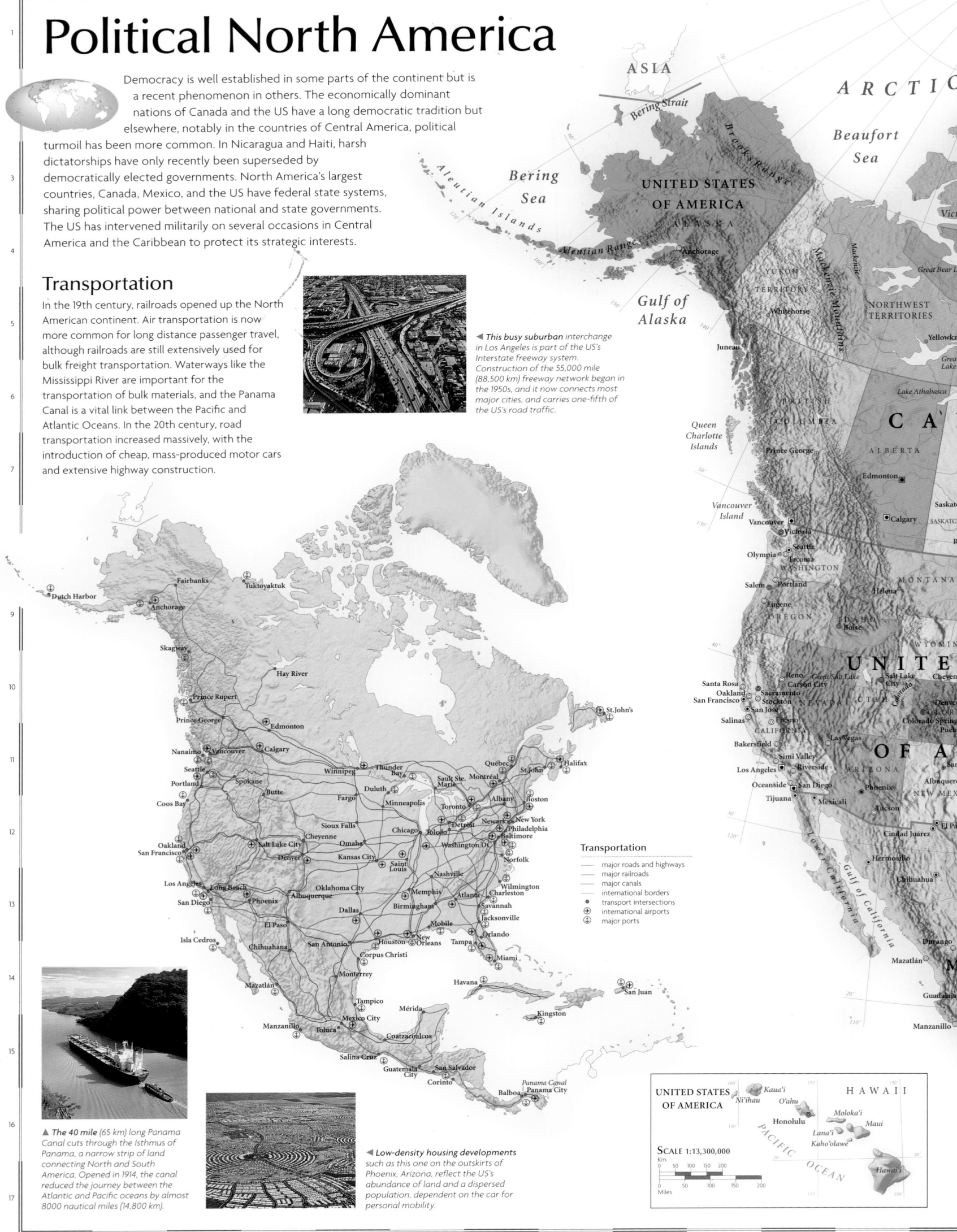

ASIA
Bering Strait
ARCTIC
Beaufort Sea
Brooks Range
Bering Sea
UNITED STATES OF AMERICA
ALASKA
Aleutian Islands
Aleutian Range
Anchorage
Gulf of Alaska
YUKON TERRITORY
Whitehorse
Mackenzie Mountains
Mackenzie
NORTHWEST TERRITORIES
Great Bear Lake
Yellowknife
Great Slave Lake
Juneau
Lake Athabasca
BRITISH COLUMBIA
Queen Charlotte Islands
CAN
ALBERTA
Prince George
Edmonton
Vancouver Island
Vancouver
Victoria
Calgary
Saskatoon
SASKATCHEWAN
Seattle
Olympia
Tacoma
WASHINGTON
MONTANA
Salem
Portland
Helena
Eugene
OREGON
IDAHO
Boise
WYOMING
UNITED
Reno
Great Salt Lake
Salt Lake City
Cheyenne
Santa Rosa
Carson City
Oakland
Sacramento
San Francisco
Stockton
NEVADA
UTAH
Denver
San Jose
Colorado
Colorado Springs
Salinas
Fresno
Pueblo
CALIFORNIA
Bakersfield
Las Vegas
OF AM
Simi Valley
Santa Fe
Los Angeles
Riverside
ARIZONA
Albuquerque
Oceanside
San Diego
Phoenix
NEW MEXICO
Tijuana
Mexicali
Tucson
Ciudad Juárez
El Paso
Lower California
Gulf of California
Hermosillo
Chihuahua
Durango
Mazatlán
Guadalajara
Manzanillo

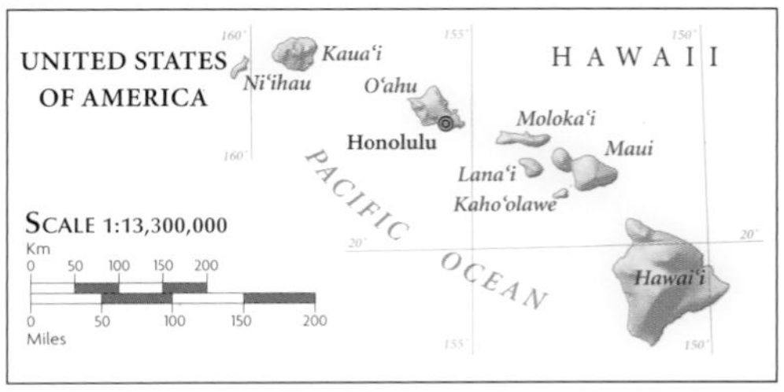
UNITED STATES OF AMERICA
HAWAII
Kaua'i
Ni'ihau
O'ahu
Honolulu
Moloka'i
Maui
Lana'i
Kaho'olawe
Hawai'i
PACIFIC OCEAN
SCALE 1:13,300,000
Km
0 50 100 150 200
0 50 100 150 200
Miles

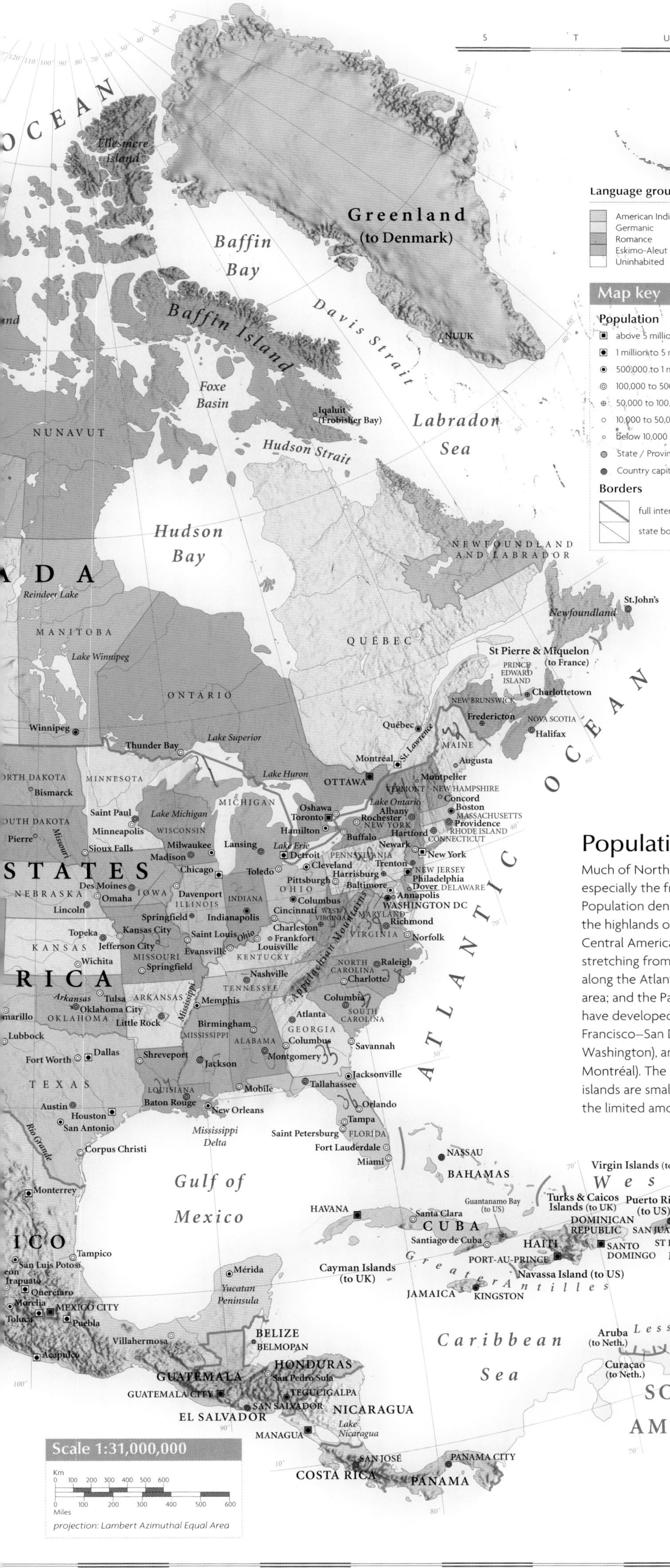
Greenland
(to Denmark)
Baffin Bay
Baffin Island
Davis Strait
NUUK
Ellesmere Island
Foxe Basin
Iqaluit (Frobisher Bay)
Labrador Sea
Hudson Strait
NUNAVUT
Hudson Bay
NEWFOUNDLAND AND LABRADOR
Newfoundland
St.John's
QUÉBEC
MANITOBA
Reindeer Lake
Lake Winnipeg
ONTARIO
Winnipeg
Thunder Bay
Lake Superior
St Pierre & Miquelon (to France)
PRINCE EDWARD ISLAND
Charlottetown
NEW BRUNSWICK
Fredericton
NOVA SCOTIA
Halifax
Québec
Montréal
OTTAWA
MAINE
Augusta
Montpelier
VERMONT
NEW HAMPSHIRE
Concord
Boston
MASSACHUSETTS
Providence
RHODE ISLAND
CONNECTICUT
Hartford
Albany
Rochester
NEW YORK
New York
Buffalo
Newark
Trenton
NEW JERSEY
Philadelphia
Dover
DELAWARE
Annapolis
WASHINGTON DC
Richmond
Norfolk
Raleigh
Charlotte
Columbia
Atlanta
Savannah
Jacksonville
Tallahassee
Orlando
Tampa
Saint Petersburg
Fort Lauderdale
Miami
FLORIDA
Lake Huron
Lake Ontario
Lake Erie
Lake Michigan
Oshawa
Toronto
Hamilton
Detroit
Cleveland
Toledo
Pittsburgh
Harrisburg
Baltimore
PENNSYLVANIA
OHIO
Columbus
Cincinnati
Charleston
Frankfort
Louisville
KENTUCKY
WEST VIRGINIA
VIRGINIA
MARYLAND
Appalachian Mountains
Nashville
TENNESSEE
NORTH CAROLINA
SOUTH CAROLINA
GEORGIA
Columbus
Montgomery
ALABAMA
Birmingham
Mobile
Memphis
MISSISSIPPI
Jackson
LOUISIANA
Baton Rouge
New Orleans
Mississippi Delta
Shreveport
ARKANSAS
Little Rock
Indianapolis
INDIANA
ILLINOIS
Springfield
Chicago
Saint Louis
MISSOURI
Jefferson City
Springfield
Evansville
Kansas City
Topeka
KANSAS
Wichita
Tulsa
Oklahoma City
OKLAHOMA
Arkansas
Amarillo
Lubbock
Fort Worth
Dallas
TEXAS
Austin
Houston
San Antonio
Corpus Christi
Rio Grande
MICHIGAN
Lansing
Milwaukee
Madison
WISCONSIN
Minneapolis
Saint Paul
MINNESOTA
IOWA
Des Moines
Davenport
Omaha
Lincoln
NEBRASKA
Sioux Falls
SOUTH DAKOTA
Pierre
NORTH DAKOTA
Bismarck
Missouri
Ohio
Mississippi
ATLANTIC OCEAN
Gulf of Mexico
Monterrey
Tampico
San Luis Potosí
Irapuato
Querétaro
Morelia
MEXICO CITY
Toluca
Puebla
Acapulco
Villahermosa
Mérida
Yucatan Peninsula
BELIZE
BELMOPAN
HONDURAS
San Pedro Sula
TEGUCIGALPA
GUATEMALA
GUATEMALA CITY
SAN SALVADOR
EL SALVADOR
NICARAGUA
Lake Nicaragua
MANAGUA
SAN JOSÉ
COSTA RICA
PANAMA CITY
PANAMA
NASSAU
BAHAMAS
HAVANA
Santa Clara
CUBA
Guantanamo Bay (to US)
Santiago de Cuba
Cayman Islands (to UK)
JAMAICA
KINGSTON
Greater Antilles
Turks & Caicos Islands (to UK)
HAITI
PORT-AU-PRINCE
Navassa Island (to US)
DOMINICAN REPUBLIC
SANTO DOMINGO
Puerto Rico (to US)
SAN JUAN
Virgin Islands (to US)
British Virgin Islands (to UK)
Anguilla (to UK)
West Indies
ST KITTS & NEVIS
Montserrat (to UK)
ANTIGUA & BARBUDA
Guadeloupe (to France)
DOMINICA
Martinique (to France)
ST LUCIA
BARBADOS
ST VINCENT & THE GRENADINES
GRENADA
TRINIDAD & TOBAGO
PORT-OF-SPAIN
Lesser Antilles
Aruba (to Neth.)
Curaçao (to Neth.)
Bonaire (to Neth.)
Caribbean Sea
SOUTH AMERICA
Map key
Population
above 5 million
1 million to 5 million
500,000 to 1 million
100,000 to 500,000
50,000 to 100,000
10,000 to 50,000
Below 10,000
State / Province capital
Country capital
Borders
full international border
state border
Scale 1:31,000,000
Km
0 100 200 300 400 500 600
0 100 200 300 400 500 600
Miles
projection: Lambert Azimuthal Equal Area

Language groups
American Indian
Germanic
Romance
Eskimo-Aleut
Uninhabited
ESKIMO-ALEUT
ATHABASCAN
ALGONQUIN
FRENCH
ENGLISH
ENGLISH/SPANISH
UTO-AZTECAN
FRENCH/ENGLISH
ENGLISH/SPANISH
ENGLISH
SPANISH
FRENCH
CREOLE
CREOLE
CREOLE
MAYAN
SPANISH

Languages

The three major official languages of North America are of European origin, brought by settlers in the 16th century. In Canada, French and English are spoken; in the US, English is the main language, with large Spanish-speaking areas in the southwest; Mexicans are Spanish-speaking; while the Caribbean islands use French, English, and Spanish as well as the hybrid Creole tongues. In isolated areas, languages of the indigenous peoples still exist, such as Inuit in the far north of the continent.

▲ *Land in northern Canada has been set aside for Inuit reserves, allowing the Inuit and other Native American groups to maintain their traditional practices and culture.*

Population

Much of North America is almost empty, especially the frozen far north. Population densities are highest in the highlands of Mexico and Central America; the coastal plain stretching from the Gulf of Mexico along the Atlantic coast; the Great Lakes area; and the Pacific coast. Large conurbations have developed, notably the San-San (San Francisco–San Diego), Boswash (Boston–Washington), and Main Street (Toronto–Montréal). The populations of the Caribbean islands are small, but settlement is dense, due to the limited amount of land available.

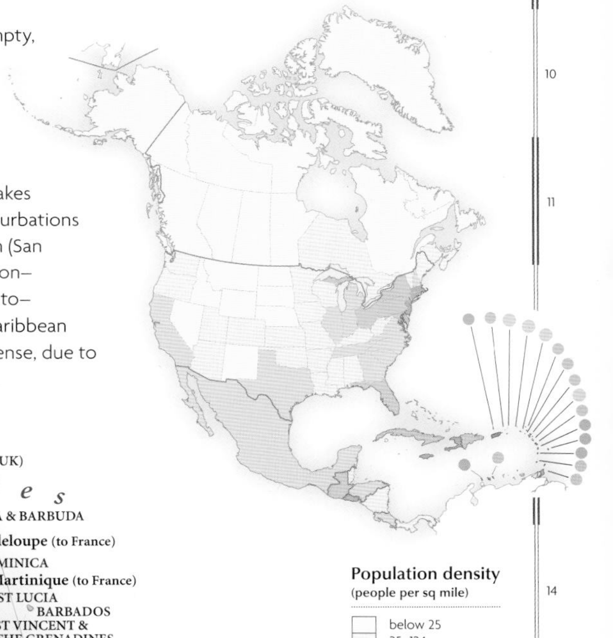
Population density
(people per sq mile)
below 25
25–124
125–259
260–649
650–1300
above 1300

► *Mexico City is one of the world's largest and highest cities. Fresh water supplies are dwindling, while air pollution regularly creates thick smog.*

North American resources

The two northern countries of Canada and the US are richly endowed with natural resources that have helped to fuel economic development. The US is the world's largest economy, although today it is facing stiff competition from the Far East. Mexico has relied on oil revenues but there are hopes that the North American Free Trade Agreement (NAFTA), will encourage trade growth with Canada and the US. The poorer countries of Central America and the Caribbean depend largely on cash crops and tourism.

Industry

The modern, industrialized economies of the US and Canada contrast sharply with those of Mexico, Central America, and the Caribbean. Manufacturing is especially important in the US; vehicle production is concentrated around the Great Lakes, while electronic and hi-tech industries are increasingly found in the western and southern states. Mexico depends on oil exports and assembly work, taking advantage of cheap labor. Many Central American and Caribbean countries rely heavily on agricultural exports.

▲ *After its purchase from Russia in 1867, Alaska's frozen lands were largely ignored by the US. Oil reserves similar in magnitude to those in eastern Texas were discovered in Prudhoe Bay, Alaska in 1968. Freezing temperatures and a fragile environment hamper oil extraction.*

Standard of living

The US and Canada have one of the highest overall standards of living in the world. However, many people still live in poverty, especially in urban ghettos and some rural areas. Central America and the Caribbean are markedly poorer than their wealthier northern neighbors. Haiti is the poorest country in the western hemisphere.

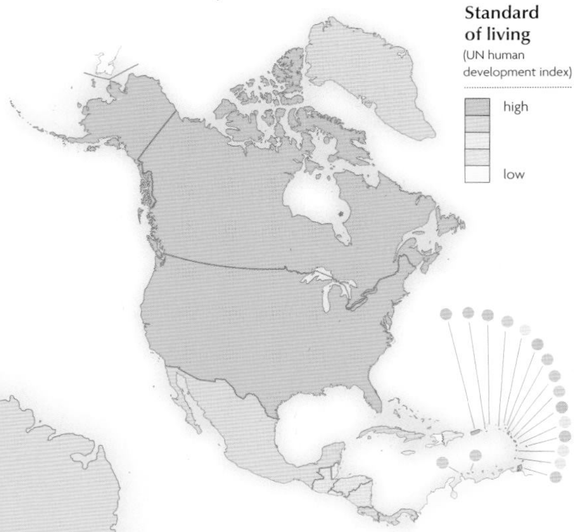
Standard of living
(UN human development index)
high
low

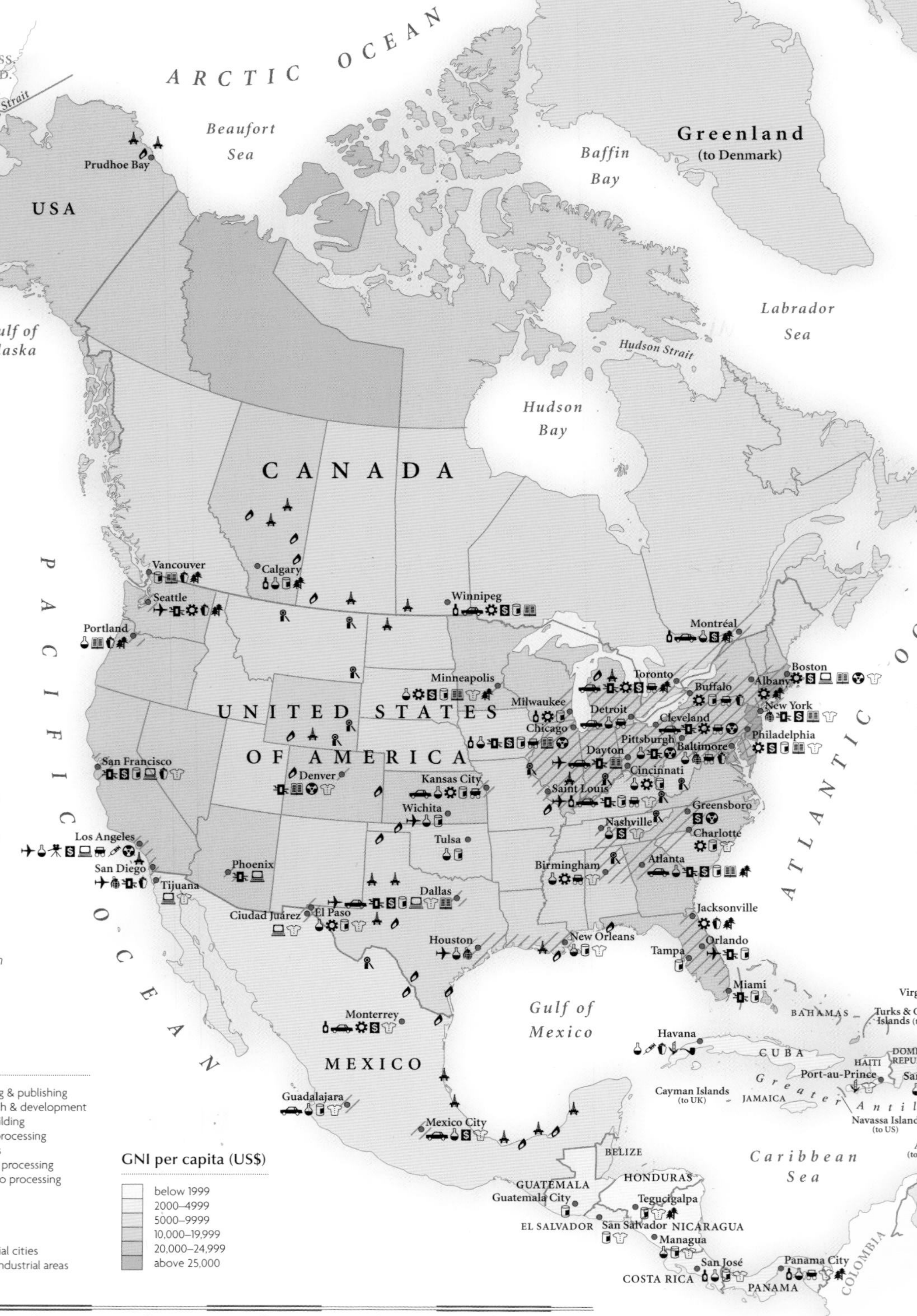
ARCTIC OCEAN
RUSS. FED.
Bering Strait
Bering Sea
Beaufort Sea
Prudhoe Bay
USA
Baffin Bay
Greenland (to Denmark)
Labrador Sea
Hudson Strait
Hudson Bay
Gulf of Alaska
CANADA
PACIFIC OCEAN
ATLANTIC OCEAN
Vancouver
Calgary
Winnipeg
Seattle
Portland
Montréal
Toronto
Boston
Buffalo
Albany
New York
Philadelphia
Minneapolis
Milwaukee
Detroit
Chicago
Cleveland
Pittsburgh
Baltimore
Dayton
Cincinnati
UNITED STATES OF AMERICA
San Francisco
Denver
Kansas City
Saint Louis
Wichita
Nashville
Greensboro
Charlotte
Los Angeles
San Diego
Tijuana
Phoenix
Tulsa
Birmingham
Atlanta
Dallas
Ciudad Juárez
El Paso
Jacksonville
Houston
New Orleans
Orlando
Tampa
Miami
Monterrey
MEXICO
Gulf of Mexico
Havana
CUBA
BAHAMAS
Turks & Caicos Islands (to UK)
Virgin Islands (to US)
British Virgin Islands (to UK)
Anguilla (to UK)
Puerto Rico (to US)
ST KITTS & NEVIS
ANTIGUA & BARBUDA
Montserrat (to UK)
Guadeloupe (to France)
DOMINICA
Martinique (to France)
ST LUCIA
BARBADOS
ST VINCENT & THE GRENADINES
GRENADA
TRINIDAD & TOBAGO
Port-of-Spain
West Indies
HAITI
DOMINICAN REPUBLIC
Port-au-Prince
San Juan
Santo Domingo
Cayman Islands (to UK)
JAMAICA
Greater Antilles
Navassa Island (to US)
Lesser Antilles
Aruba (to Neth.)
Curaçao (to Neth.)
Bonaire (to Neth.)
VENEZUELA
Guadalajara
Mexico City
BELIZE
Caribbean Sea
GUATEMALA
Guatemala City
HONDURAS
Tegucigalpa
EL SALVADOR
San Salvador
NICARAGUA
Managua
San José
COSTA RICA
Panama City
PANAMA
COLOMBIA
Industry
aerospace
brewing
car/vehicle manufacture
chemicals
defense
electronics
engineering
film industry
finance
food processing
hi-tech industry
iron & steel
pharmaceuticals
printing & publishing
research & development
shipbuilding
sugar processing
textiles
timber processing
tobacco processing
coal
oil
gas
industrial cities
major industrial areas
GNI per capita (US$)
below 1999
2000–4999
5000–9999
10,000–19,999
20,000–24,999
above 25,000

▲ *Fish such as cod, flounder, and plaice are caught in the Grand Banks, off the Newfoundland coast, and processed in many North Atlantic coastal settlements.*

▲ *South of San Francisco, "Silicon Valley" is both a national and international center for hi-tech industries, electronic industries, and research institutions.*

▲ *Multinational companies rely on cheap labor and tax benefits to facilitate the assembly of vehicle parts in Mexican factories.*

▲ *The health of the Wall Street stock market in New York is the standard measure of the state of the economy.*

N O P Q R S T U V W X Y Z

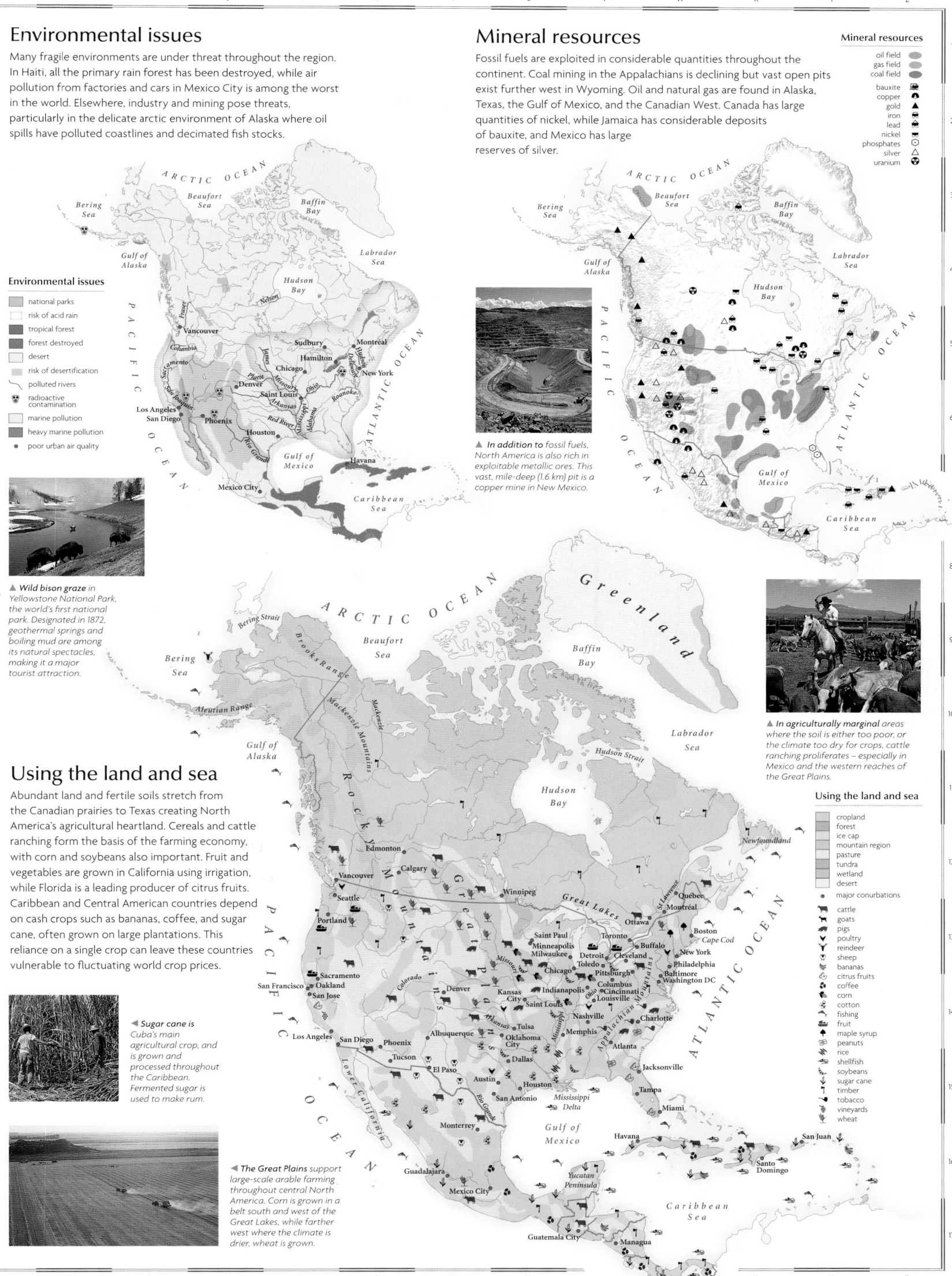

Environmental issues

Many fragile environments are under threat throughout the region. In Haiti, all the primary rain forest has been destroyed, while air pollution from factories and cars in Mexico City is among the worst in the world. Elsewhere, industry and mining pose threats, particularly in the delicate arctic environment of Alaska where oil spills have polluted coastlines and decimated fish stocks.

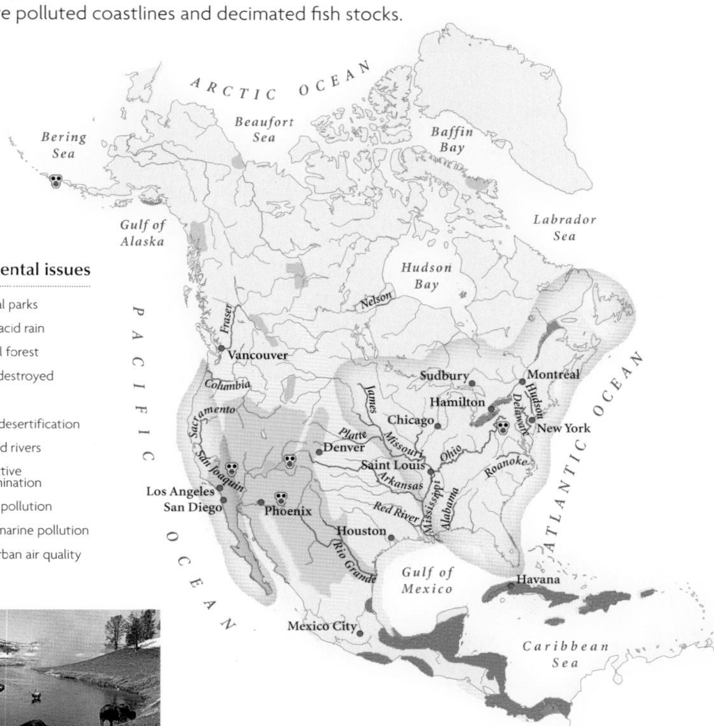
Environmental issues
national parks
risk of acid rain
tropical forest
forest destroyed
desert
risk of desertification
polluted rivers
radioactive contamination
marine pollution
heavy marine pollution
poor urban air quality
ARCTIC OCEAN
Beaufort Sea
Bering Sea
Baffin Bay
Gulf of Alaska
Labrador Sea
Hudson Bay
PACIFIC OCEAN
ATLANTIC OCEAN
Gulf of Mexico
Caribbean Sea
Vancouver
Sudbury
Montreal
Hamilton
Chicago
New York
Denver
Saint Louis
Los Angeles
San Diego
Phoenix
Houston
Havana
Mexico City

▲ *Wild bison graze in Yellowstone National Park, the world's first national park. Designated in 1872, geothermal springs and boiling mud are among its natural spectacles, making it a major tourist attraction.*

Mineral resources

Fossil fuels are exploited in considerable quantities throughout the continent. Coal mining in the Appalachians is declining but vast open pits exist further west in Wyoming. Oil and natural gas are found in Alaska, Texas, the Gulf of Mexico, and the Canadian West. Canada has large quantities of nickel, while Jamaica has considerable deposits of bauxite, and Mexico has large reserves of silver.

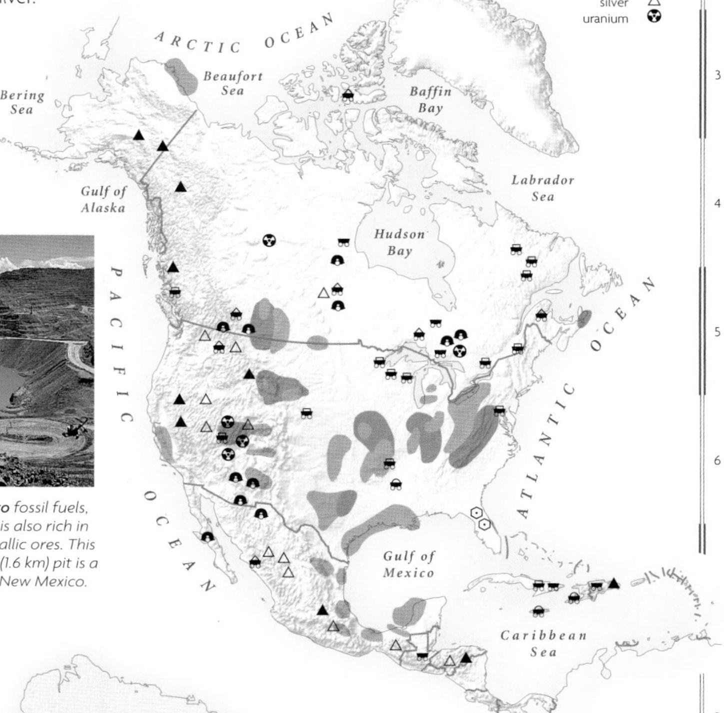
Mineral resources
oil field
gas field
coal field
bauxite
copper
gold
iron
lead
nickel
phosphates
silver
uranium
ARCTIC OCEAN
Beaufort Sea
Bering Sea
Baffin Bay
Gulf of Alaska
Labrador Sea
Hudson Bay
PACIFIC OCEAN
ATLANTIC OCEAN
Gulf of Mexico
Caribbean Sea

▲ *In addition to fossil fuels, North America is also rich in exploitable metallic ores. This vast, mile-deep (1.6 km) pit is a copper mine in New Mexico.*

Using the land and sea

Abundant land and fertile soils stretch from the Canadian prairies to Texas creating North America's agricultural heartland. Cereals and cattle ranching form the basis of the farming economy, with corn and soybeans also important. Fruit and vegetables are grown in California using irrigation, while Florida is a leading producer of citrus fruits. Caribbean and Central American countries depend on cash crops such as bananas, coffee, and sugar cane, often grown on large plantations. This reliance on a single crop can leave these countries vulnerable to fluctuating world crop prices.

▲ *In agriculturally marginal areas where the soil is either too poor, or the climate too dry for crops, cattle ranching proliferates – especially in Mexico and the western reaches of the Great Plains.*

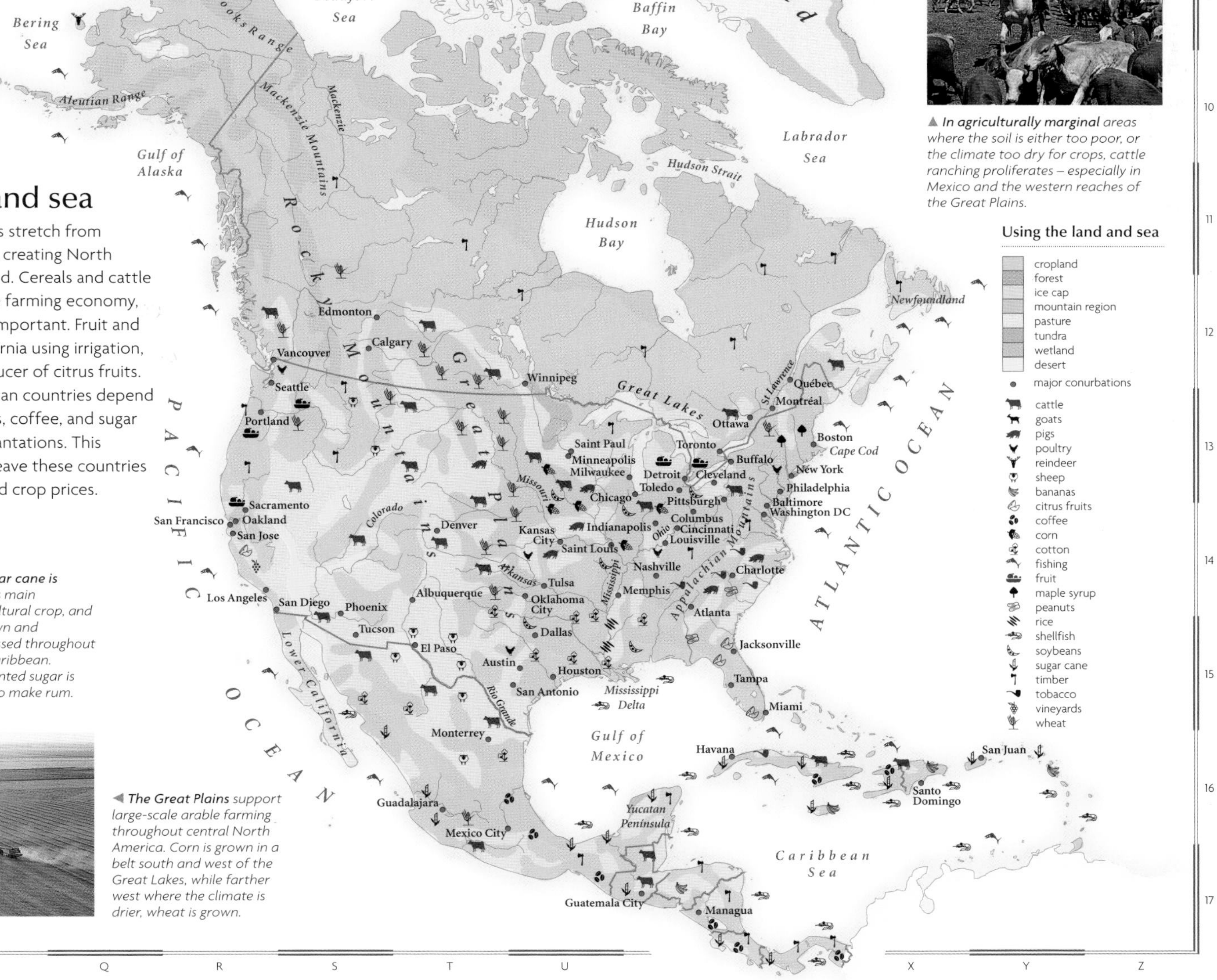
Using the land and sea
cropland
forest
ice cap
mountain region
pasture
tundra
wetland
desert
major conurbations
cattle
goats
pigs
poultry
reindeer
sheep
bananas
citrus fruits
coffee
corn
cotton
fishing
fruit
maple syrup
peanuts
rice
shellfish
soybeans
sugar cane
timber
tobacco
vineyards
wheat
ARCTIC OCEAN
Greenland
Bering Strait
Bering Sea
Beaufort Sea
Baffin Bay
Brooks Range
Aleutian Range
Mackenzie Mountains
Gulf of Alaska
Labrador Sea
Hudson Strait
Hudson Bay
Rocky Mountains
Great Plains
Great Lakes
Newfoundland
PACIFIC OCEAN
ATLANTIC OCEAN
Edmonton
Calgary
Vancouver
Seattle
Portland
Winnipeg
Québec
Montréal
Ottawa
Toronto
Boston
Cape Cod
Buffalo
New York
Saint Paul
Minneapolis
Milwaukee
Detroit
Cleveland
Toledo
Chicago
Pittsburgh
Philadelphia
Baltimore
Washington DC
Columbus
Cincinnati
Louisville
Indianapolis
Sacramento
San Francisco
Oakland
San Jose
Denver
Kansas City
Saint Louis
Nashville
Charlotte
Los Angeles
San Diego
Phoenix
Albuquerque
Tulsa
Oklahoma City
Memphis
Atlanta
Tucson
El Paso
Dallas
Austin
Houston
San Antonio
Jacksonville
Tampa
Miami
Mississippi Delta
Lower California
Monterrey
Gulf of Mexico
Havana
San Juan
Santo Domingo
Yucatan Peninsula
Guadalajara
Mexico City
Caribbean Sea
Guatemala City
Managua

◀ *Sugar cane is Cuba's main agricultural crop, and is grown and processed throughout the Caribbean. Fermented sugar is used to make rum.*

◀ *The Great Plains support large-scale arable farming throughout central North America. Corn is grown in a belt south and west of the Great Lakes, while farther west where the climate is drier, wheat is grown.*

N O P Q R S T U V W X Y Z

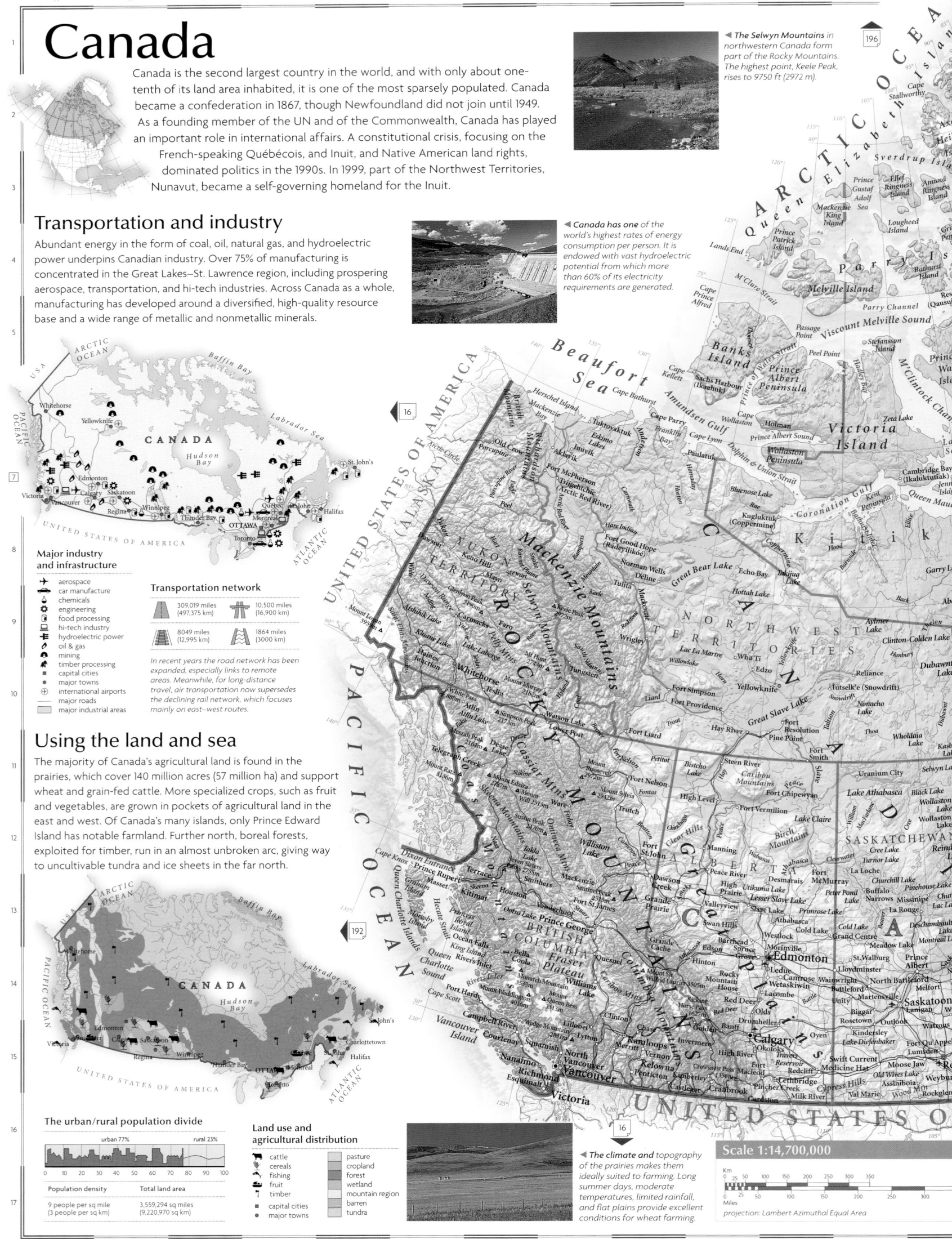

Canada

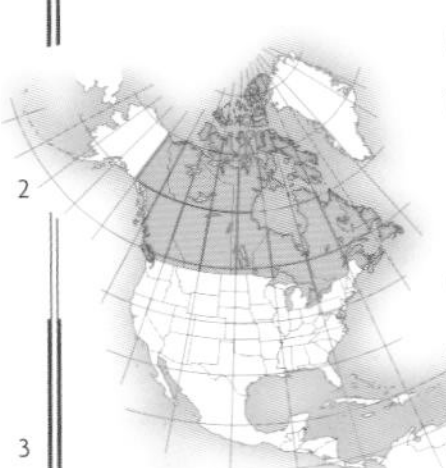

Canada is the second largest country in the world, and with only about one-tenth of its land area inhabited, it is one of the most sparsely populated. Canada became a confederation in 1867, though Newfoundland did not join until 1949. As a founding member of the UN and of the Commonwealth, Canada has played an important role in international affairs. A constitutional crisis, focusing on the French-speaking Québécois, and Inuit, and Native American land rights, dominated politics in the 1990s. In 1999, part of the Northwest Territories, Nunavut, became a self-governing homeland for the Inuit.

The Selwyn Mountains in northwestern Canada form part of the Rocky Mountains. The highest point, Keele Peak, rises to 9750 ft (2972 m).

Transportation and industry

Abundant energy in the form of coal, oil, natural gas, and hydroelectric power underpins Canadian industry. Over 75% of manufacturing is concentrated in the Great Lakes–St. Lawrence region, including prospering aerospace, transportation, and hi-tech industries. Across Canada as a whole, manufacturing has developed around a diversified, high-quality resource base and a wide range of metallic and nonmetallic minerals.

Canada has one of the world's highest rates of energy consumption per person. It is endowed with vast hydroelectric potential from which more than 60% of its electricity requirements are generated.

ARCTIC OCEAN
Baffin Bay
Labrador Sea
USA
PACIFIC OCEAN
Whitehorse
Yellowknife
CANADA
Hudson Bay
St. John's
Edmonton
Calgary
Saskatoon
Victoria
Vancouver
Regina
Winnipeg
Thunder Bay
Quebec
Montreal
Saint John
Halifax
OTTAWA
Toronto
UNITED STATES OF AMERICA
ATLANTIC OCEAN

Major industry and infrastructure

- aerospace
- car manufacture
- chemicals
- engineering
- food processing
- hi-tech industry
- hydroelectric power
- oil & gas
- mining
- timber processing
- capital cities
- major towns
- international airports
- major roads
- major industrial areas

Transportation network

- 309,019 miles (497,375 km)
- 10,500 miles (16,900 km)
- 8049 miles (12,995 km)
- 1864 miles (3000 km)

In recent years the road network has been expanded, especially links to remote areas. Meanwhile, for long-distance travel, air transportation now supersedes the declining rail network, which focuses mainly on east–west routes.

Using the land and sea

The majority of Canada's agricultural land is found in the prairies, which cover 140 million acres (57 million ha) and support wheat and grain-fed cattle. More specialized crops, such as fruit and vegetables, are grown in pockets of agricultural land in the east and west. Of Canada's many islands, only Prince Edward Island has notable farmland. Further north, boreal forests, exploited for timber, run in an almost unbroken arc, giving way to uncultivable tundra and ice sheets in the far north.

ARCTIC OCEAN
Baffin Bay
Labrador Sea
USA
PACIFIC OCEAN
Whitehorse
CANADA
Hudson Bay
Edmonton
Calgary
Saskatoon
Vancouver
Victoria
Regina
Winnipeg
Thunder Bay
OTTAWA
Montreal
Toronto
Saint John
Halifax
Charlottetown
St. John's
UNITED STATES OF AMERICA
ATLANTIC OCEAN

The urban/rural population divide

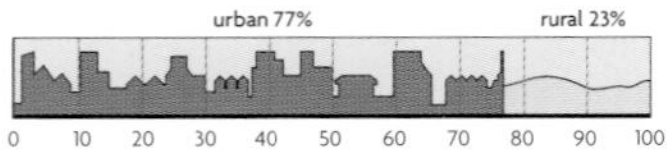
urban 77%
rural 23%
0
10
20
30
40
50
60
70
80
90
100

Population density	Total land area
9 people per sq mile (3 people per sq km)	3,559,294 sq miles (9,220,970 sq km)

Land use and agricultural distribution

- cattle
- cereals
- fishing
- fruit
- timber
- capital cities
- major towns
- pasture
- cropland
- forest
- wetland
- mountain region
- barren
- tundra

The climate and topography of the prairies makes them ideally suited to farming. Long summer days, moderate temperatures, limited rainfall, and flat plains provide excellent conditions for wheat farming.

ARCTIC OCEAN
Queen Elizabeth Islands
Sverdrup Islands
Cape Stallworthy
Prince Gustaf Adolf Sea
Ellef Ringnes Island
Amund Ringness Island
Mackenzie King Island
Lougheed Island
Prince Patrick Island
Lands End
Parry Islands
Bathurst Island
Melville Island
M'Clure Strait
Cape Prince Alfred
Parry Channel
Viscount Melville Sound
Passage Point
Banks Island
Stefansson Island
Prince of Wales Strait
Peel Point
Prince Albert Peninsula
M'Clintock Channel
Beaufort Sea
Cape Kellett
Sachs Harbour (Ikaahuk)
Cape Bathurst
Amundsen Gulf
Cape Parry
Cape Wollaston
Holman
Prince Albert Sound
Victoria Island
Wollaston Peninsula
Cambridge Bay (Ikaluktutiak)
Queen Maud
Coronation Gulf
Kent Peninsula
Dolphin & Union Strait
Herschel Island
Mackenzie Bay
Tuktoyaktuk
Eskimo Lakes
Inuvik
Aklavik
Old Crow
Porcupine
Richardson Mountains
Arctic Circle
Fort McPherson
Tsiigehtchic (Arctic Red River)
Paulatuk
Bluenose Lake
Kugluktuk (Coppermine)
UNITED STATES OF AMERICA (ALASKA)
Hare Indian
Fort Good Hope (Rádeyilikóé)
Norman Wells
Déline
Great Bear Lake
Echo Bay
Takijuq Lake
Hottah Lake
Dawson
YUKON TERRITORY
Keno Hill
Mayo
Stewart
Mackenzie Mountains
Selwyn Mountains
Keele Peak 2972m
Tulita
Wrigley
NORTHWEST TERRITORIES
Aylmer Lake
Clinton-Colden Lake
Dubawnt Lake
Mount Logan 5959m
Kluane Lake
Haines Junction
Carmacks
Faro
Lake Laberge
Whitehorse
Teslin
Mount Murray 2163m
Tungsten
Lac La Martre
Wha Ti
Edzo
Yellowknife
Reliance
Lutselk'e (Snowdrift)
Fort Simpson
Fort Providence
Great Slave Lake
Fort Resolution
Pine Point
Hay River
Fort Smith
White Pass
Atlin
Atlin Lake
Watson Lake
Lower Post
Fort Liard
ROCKY MOUNTAINS
Cassiar Mountains
Coast Mountains
Telegraph Creek
Mount Ratz 3136m
Mount Edziza 2787m
Fort Nelson
Mount Roosevelt 2972m
Caribou Mountains
Uranium City
Lake Athabasca
Fort Chipewyan
High Level
Fort Vermilion
Lake Claire
Birch Mountains
Omineca Mountains
Skeena Mountains
Williston Lake
Dixon Entrance
Prince Rupert
Masset
Graham Island
Queen Charlotte Islands
Hecate Strait
Moresby Island
Terrace
Kitimat
Smithers
Houston
Mackenzie
Fort St. John
Dawson Creek
Grande Prairie
Peace River
Manning
Fort McMurray
ALBERTA
SASKATCHEWAN
Prince George
Quesnel
BRITISH COLUMBIA
Fraser Plateau
Williams Lake
Bella Coola
Queen Charlotte Sound
Port Hardy
Cape Scott
Mount Waddington 4016m
Grande Cache
Edson
Hinton
Edmonton
Red Deer
Lloydminster
North Battleford
Saskatoon
Calgary
Banff
Golden
Kamloops
Vernon
Kelowna
Penticton
Lethbridge
Medicine Hat
Swift Current
Moose Jaw
Cypress Hills
Campbell River
Courtenay
Nanaimo
Vancouver Island
North Vancouver
Vancouver
Richmond
Esquimalt
Victoria
PACIFIC OCEAN
UNITED STATES OF AMERICA
Great Plains
Columbia Mountains
16
192
196

Scale 1:14,700,000

projection: Lambert Azimuthal Equal Area

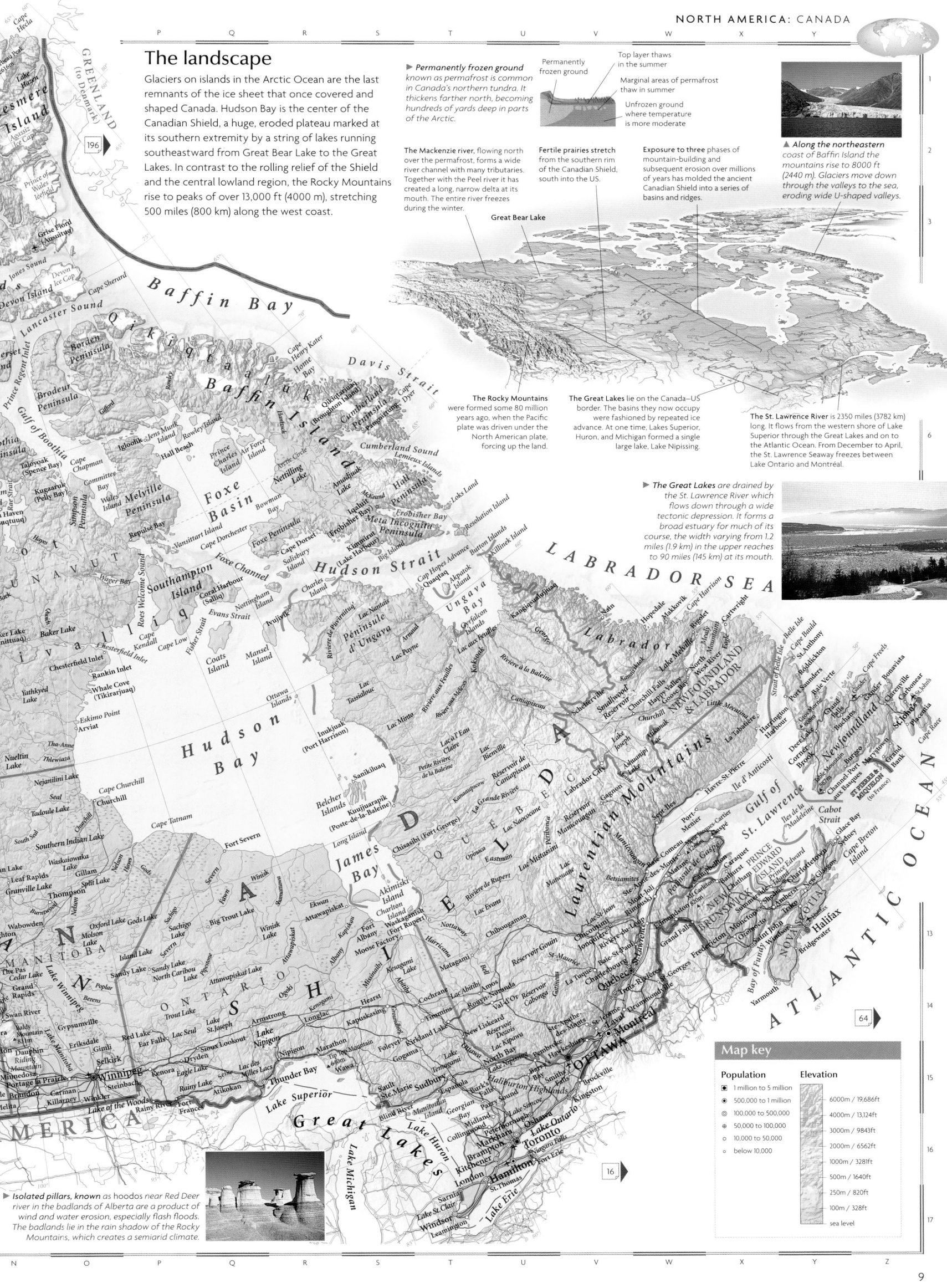

The landscape

Glaciers on islands in the Arctic Ocean are the last remnants of the ice sheet that once covered and shaped Canada. Hudson Bay is the center of the Canadian Shield, a huge, eroded plateau marked at its southern extremity by a string of lakes running southeastward from Great Bear Lake to the Great Lakes. In contrast to the rolling relief of the Shield and the central lowland region, the Rocky Mountains rise to peaks of over 13,000 ft (4000 m), stretching 500 miles (800 km) along the west coast.

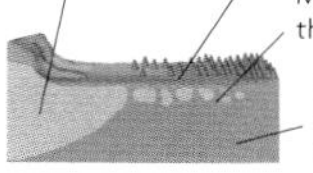

Permanently frozen ground
Top layer thaws in the summer
Marginal areas of permafrost thaw in summer
Unfrozen ground where temperature is more moderate

► ***Permanently frozen ground*** *known as permafrost is common in Canada's northern tundra. It thickens farther north, becoming hundreds of yards deep in parts of the Arctic.*

▲ ***Along the northeastern*** *coast of Baffin Island the mountains rise to 8000 ft (2440 m). Glaciers move down through the valleys to the sea, eroding wide U-shaped valleys.*

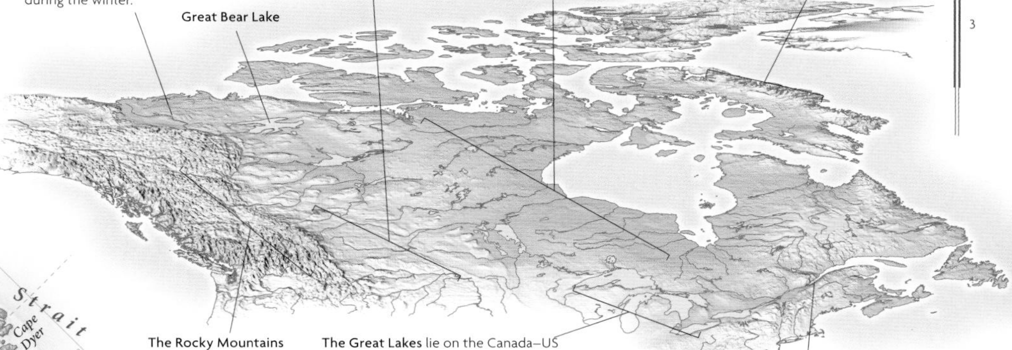

Great Bear Lake

The Mackenzie river, flowing north over the permafrost, forms a wide river channel with many tributaries. Together with the Peel river it has created a long, narrow delta at its mouth. The entire river freezes during the winter.

Fertile prairies stretch from the southern rim of the Canadian Shield, south into the US.

Exposure to three phases of mountain-building and subsequent erosion over millions of years has molded the ancient Canadian Shield into a series of basins and ridges.

The Rocky Mountains were formed some 80 million years ago, when the Pacific plate was driven under the North American plate, forcing up the land.

The Great Lakes lie on the Canada–US border. The basins they now occupy were fashioned by repeated ice advance. At one time, Lakes Superior, Huron, and Michigan formed a single large lake, Lake Nipissing.

The St. Lawrence River is 2350 miles (3782 km) long. It flows from the western shore of Lake Superior through the Great Lakes and on to the Atlantic Ocean. From December to April, the St. Lawrence Seaway freezes between Lake Ontario and Montréal.

► ***The Great Lakes*** *are drained by the St. Lawrence River which flows down through a wide tectonic depression. It forms a broad estuary for much of its course, the width varying from 1.2 miles (1.9 km) in the upper reaches to 90 miles (145 km) at its mouth.*

P Q R S T U V W X Y
N O P Q R S T U V W X Y Z
GREENLAND (to Denmark)
196
Baffin Bay
Qikiqtaaluk
Baffin Island
Davis Strait
Foxe Basin
Cumberland Sound
Hudson Strait
LABRADOR SEA
Ungava Bay
Péninsule d'Ungava
Labrador
NEWFOUNDLAND & LABRADOR
Newfoundland
Hudson Bay
James Bay
Southampton Island
Melville Peninsula
Devon Island
Lancaster Sound
Borden Peninsula
Brodeur Peninsula
Gulf of Boothia
NUNAVUT
MANITOBA
ONTARIO
QUEBEC
CANADIAN SHIELD
Laurentian Mountains
Gulf of St. Lawrence
NEW BRUNSWICK
PRINCE EDWARD ISLAND
NOVA SCOTIA
Cape Breton Island
Halifax
Québec
Montréal
OTTAWA
Toronto
Hamilton
Winnipeg
Thunder Bay
Lake Superior
Lake Huron
Lake Michigan
Lake Ontario
Lake Erie
Great Lakes
Lake Winnipeg
ATLANTIC OCEAN
AMERICA
64
16

Map key

Population

- 1 million to 5 million
- 500,000 to 1 million
- 100,000 to 500,000
- 50,000 to 100,000
- 10,000 to 50,000
- below 10,000

Elevation

- 6000m / 19,686ft
- 4000m / 13,124ft
- 3000m / 9843ft
- 2000m / 6562ft
- 1000m / 3281ft
- 500m / 1640ft
- 250m / 820ft
- 100m / 328ft
- sea level

► ***Isolated pillars, known*** *as hoodoos near Red Deer river in the badlands of Alberta are a product of wind and water erosion, especially flash floods. The badlands lie in the rain shadow of the Rocky Mountains, which creates a semiarid climate.*

Canada: WESTERN PROVINCES

Alberta, British Columbia, Manitoba, Saskatchewan, Yukon Territory

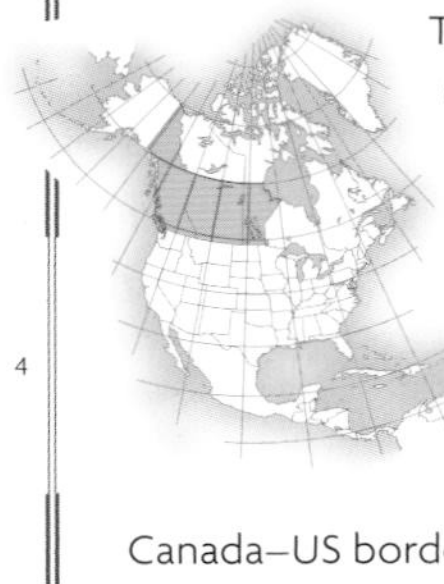

The mountains of the west coast, incorporating British Columbia and the Yukon Territory, descend into the vast, flat prairies of Alberta, Saskatchewan, and Manitoba. The empty lands and fertile soils of the prairie provinces attracted migrants, and the descendants of early European immigrants still make up a large proportion of the population. The mechanization of agriculture has reduced the need for labor, and rural population densities remain low. The majority of the people live within 100 miles (160 km) of the southern Canada–US border, and in British Columbia, one of the leading Canadian provinces in terms of economic wealth. The Yukon Territory, in the far north, remains a relatively unspoiled wilderness, containing large, untapped mineral reserves. This province has a significant population of Native American people, many of whom maintain a traditional lifestyle.

16

Using the land and sea

Wheat farming is the economic mainstay of Alberta, Manitoba, and Saskatchewan, which contain 82% of farmland in Canada. Cattle are also raised on the prairies. Forestry and fishing are the most prominent resource-based industries in British Columbia. Despite the mountainous terrain, fruit and specialized grains can be grown in the Okanagan and Fraser valleys.

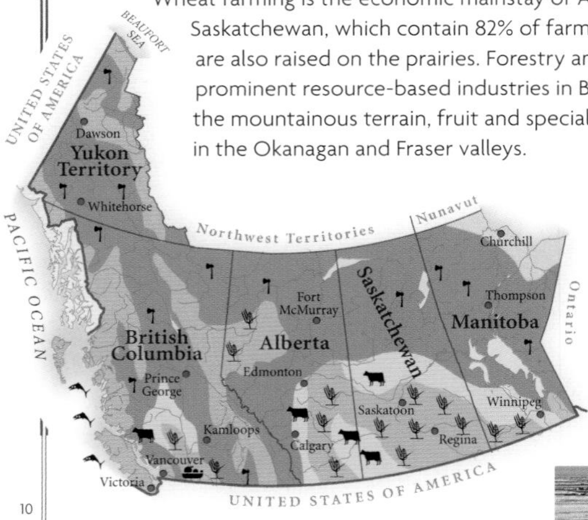
Land use and agricultural distribution
cattle
cereals
fishing
fruit
timber
major towns
pasture
cropland
forest
wetland
barren
tundra
BEAUFORT SEA
UNITED STATES OF AMERICA
Dawson
Yukon Territory
Whitehorse
Northwest Territories
Nunavut
Churchill
Fort McMurray
Saskatchewan
Thompson
Manitoba
Ontario
British Columbia
Alberta
Edmonton
Prince George
Saskatoon
Winnipeg
Kamloops
Regina
Calgary
Vancouver
Victoria
PACIFIC OCEAN
UNITED STATES OF AMERICA

▲ *Large, highly-mechanized and often very specialized farms, requiring huge investment but little labor, characterize modern farming in the prairies.*

The urban/rural population divide

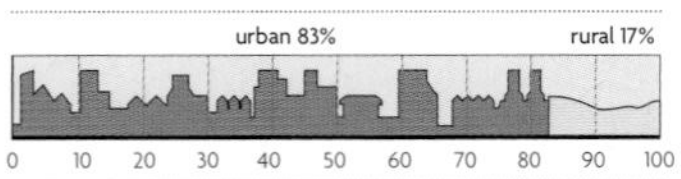
urban 83%
rural 17%
0
10
20
30
40
50
60
70
80
90
100

Population density	Total land area
8 people per sq mile (3 people per sq km)	1,230,547 sq miles (3,187,120 sq km)

Transportation & industry

The western provinces contain a wealth of mineral resources. Alberta holds the bulk of Canada's fossil fuels; the other provinces contain reserves of metallic ores, such as zinc, lead, and silver. Isolation from markets has slowed the development of manufacturing, restricting it to the large cities like Vancouver, Winnipeg, and Calgary. Hydroelectric power is widely exploited, although there is increasing concern about potential ecological damage.

Transportation network

- 82,438 miles (135,145 km)
- 6459 miles (10,401 km)
- 24,041 miles (38,694 km)
- None

The transportation network of the western provinces is dominated by east–west routes that weave through mountain passes and spread across the plains. Access to some northern areas is restricted to air travel.

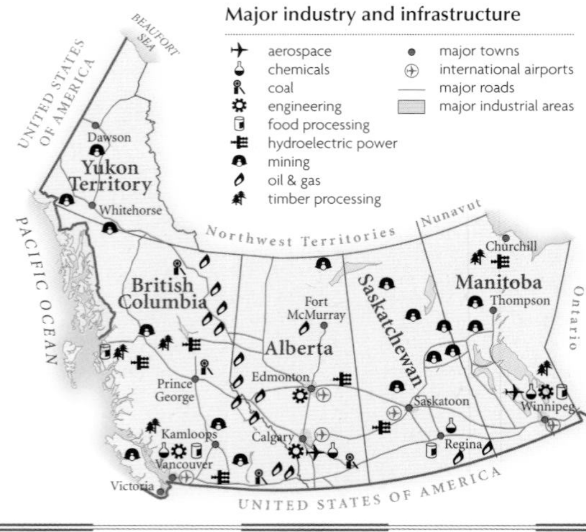
Major industry and infrastructure
aerospace
chemicals
coal
engineering
food processing
hydroelectric power
mining
oil & gas
timber processing
major towns
international airports
major roads
major industrial areas
BEAUFORT SEA
UNITED STATES OF AMERICA
Dawson
Yukon Territory
Whitehorse
Northwest Territories
Nunavut
Churchill
Manitoba
Thompson
British Columbia
Fort McMurray
Saskatchewan
Alberta
Edmonton
Prince George
Saskatoon
Winnipeg
Kamloops
Calgary
Regina
Vancouver
Victoria
PACIFIC OCEAN
Ontario
UNITED STATES OF AMERICA

◀ *Much of the* Yukon Territory *is uninhabited tundra. Industry is based on the extraction of mineral resources, and to a lesser extent, on the scattered forests of the south.*

192

Beaufort Sea
Herschel Island
Mackenzie Bay
British Mountains
UNITED STATES OF AMERICA (ALASKA)
Richardson Mountains
Old Crow
Porcupine
Arctic Circle
Eagle Plain
Peel
Ogilvie
Ogilvie Mountains
YUKON TERRITORY
Mackenzie Mountains
Selwyn Mountains
NORTHWEST TERRITORIES
Dawson
Klondike
Clinton Creek
Glenboyle
Stewart River
Keno Hill
Mayo
Stewart Crossing
Coffee Creek
Pelly
Beaver Creek
Minto
Keele Peak 2972m
Kluane Lake
Carmacks
Faro
Ross River
Pelly Mountains
Burwash Landing
Mount Logan 5959m
Saint Elias Mountains
Seward Glacier
Haines Junction
Lake Laberge
Whitehorse
Johnsons Crossing
Jakes Corner
Carcross
Mount Hunt 2743m
Mount Murray 2162m
Chilkoot Pass 1067m
White Pass 880m
Teslin
Atlin
Simpson Peak 2173m
Upper Liard
Watson Lake
Lower Post
Good Hope Lake
Cassiar
Cassiar Mountains
Nakina
Coal River
Liard River
Muncho Lake
Fort Nelson
Dease Lake
Meszah Peak 2164m
Telegraph Creek
Glenora
Mount Edziza 2787m
Mount Ratz 3136m
Skeena Mountains
Mount Will 2515m
Mount Sylvia 2942m
Prophet River
Trutch
Sikanni Chief
Pink Mountain
PACIFIC OCEAN
ROCKY MOUNTAINS
BRITISH COLUMBIA
Mount Pattullo 2729m
Meziadin Junction
Stewart
Sustut Peak 2470m
Williston Lake
Hudson's Hope
Portland Inlet
Cranberry Junction
Kitwanga
Hazelton
New Hazelton
Takla Lake
Dixon Entrance
Prince Rupert
Terrace
Babine Lake
Mackenzie
Cape Knox
Masset
Graham Island
Port Edward
Kitimat
Houston
Burns Lake
Fort St.James
Port Clements
Queen Charlotte
Queen Charlotte Islands
Hecate Strait
Moresby Island
Sandspit
Banks Island
Princess Royal Island
Kemano
Ootsa Lake
Fraser Lake
Vanderhoof
Prince George
Aristazabal Island
Eutsuk Lake
Ocean Falls
Bella Bella
Hagensborg
Bella Coola
Nazko
Quesnel
Anahim Lake
Fraser Plateau
Williams Lake
Queen Charlotte Sound
Cape St.James
Dawsons Landing
Rivers Inlet
Mount Waddington 4016m
Tatla Lake
100 Mile House
Cape Caution
Queen Charlotte Strait
Cape Scott
Port Hardy
Winter Harbour
Port Alice
Port McNeill
Mount Queen Bess 3313m
Mount Gilbert 3109m
Clinton
Vancouver Island
Gold River
Tahsis
Campbell River
Whistler
Powell River
Pemberton
Nootka Sound
Comox
Courtenay
Strait of Georgia
Squamish
North Vancouver
Vancouver
Burnaby
Port Alberni
Tofino
Ucluelet
Nanaimo
Richmond
Ladysmith
Duncan
Victoria
Esquimalt
Barkley Sound
Strait of Juan de Fuca

▲ *The* Fraser River *valley is a major area of settlement in British Columbia. Railroads cross the Rocky Mountains via this valley.*

▲ *Established in 1907,* Jasper National Park *lies in the heart of the Rocky Mountains. It is noted for its spectacular alpine scenery and contains part of the large Columbia Icefield.*

N O P Q R S T U V W X Y

1 2 3 4 5 6 7 8 9

The landscape

The massive Rocky Mountains form a continental divide between rivers flowing eastward and westward. The interior plains lie east of the mountains, stretching from the Arctic Circle south into the US. Covered with glacial deposits from the last Ice Age, these are interspersed with hilly regions and long, steep escarpments.

Map key

Population

- ◉ 500,000 to 1 million
- ◎ 100,000 to 500,000
- ⊕ 50,000 to 100,000
- ○ 10,000 to 50,000
- ∘ below 10,000

Elevation

- 6000m / 19,686ft
- 4000m / 13,124ft
- 3000m / 9843ft
- 2000m / 6562ft
- 1000m / 3281ft
- 500m / 1640ft
- 250m / 820ft
- 100m / 328ft
- sea level

Scale 1:8,250,000

Km 0 25 50 100 150 200 250

Miles 0 25 50 100 150 200 250

projection: Lambert Conformal Conic

Vegetated island
Bar
River flow is diverted by deposited sediments
Sand flat

▲ ***Braided rivers are** shallow and fast-flowing. The interlaced branches are formed when excess sediments, which can no longer be transported, are deposited. The sediments collect in the river channel forming bars and sand flats. Islands form when the bars are colonized by vegetation.*

▲ ***Across the tundra** of northern Manitoba, widespread permafrost inhibits water from permeating the soil. This causes rivers like the Churchill to flow in many channels, which can be frozen for up to six months during the winter.*

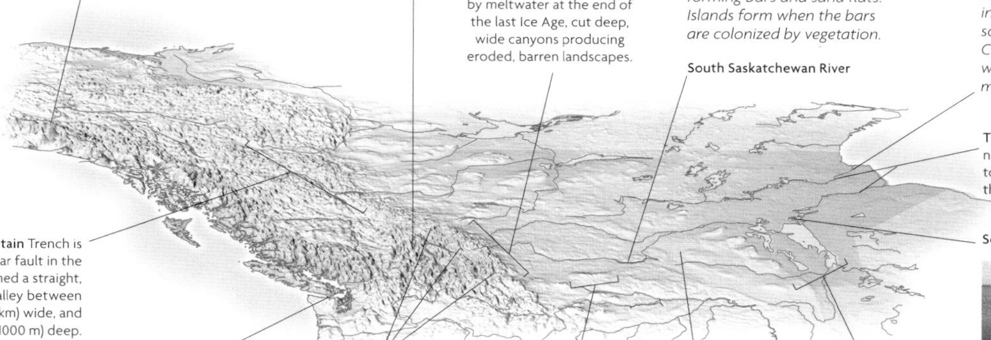

Mount Logan rises 19,551 ft (5959 m). It is the highest peak in Canada.
The Columbia Icefield in the Rocky Mountains is the source of two major rivers, the Athabasca and the North Saskatchewan.
The badlands of Alberta were created when east-flowing rivers, swollen by meltwater at the end of the last Ice Age, cut deep, wide canyons producing eroded, barren landscapes.
South Saskatchewan River
The Nelson and Churchill rivers drain northward across the Canadian Shield to Hudson Bay. The shield covers three-fifths of Saskatchewan.
Setting Lake
The Rocky Mountain Trench is the longest linear fault in the world. It has formed a straight, flat-bottomed valley between 2–9 miles (4–15 km) wide, and up to 3280 ft (1000 m) deep.
Hundreds of islands dot the fjord-indented coast of British Columbia; the largest is Vancouver Island.
Three major passes cut through the Rocky Mountains: Yellowhead, Kicking Horse, and Crowsnest. They are all used as transportation routes through the mountains.
The Cypress Hills rise to 4806 ft (1465 m) above the surrounding plain. Having escaped the last glaciation they contain unique plant and animal life. The silvery lupine, bunchberry, and lodgepole pine all grow in the cool, moist climate of the hills.
The Alberta and Saskatchewan plains bear strong testament to past glaciations. The Assiniboine, Saskatchewan and Qu'Appelle rivers occupy flat-bottomed, steep-sided valleys eroded during the last Ice Age by glacial meltwater.
The lowlands of Manitoba are a basin that once held the vast post-glacial Lake Agassiz, remnants of which include Lake Winnipeg, Lake Winnipegosis, and Lake Manitoba.

▲ ***Ancient granite outcrops,** part of the Canadian Shield, rise above the surface of Setting Lake, which was initially formed by meltwater from the last Ice Age.*

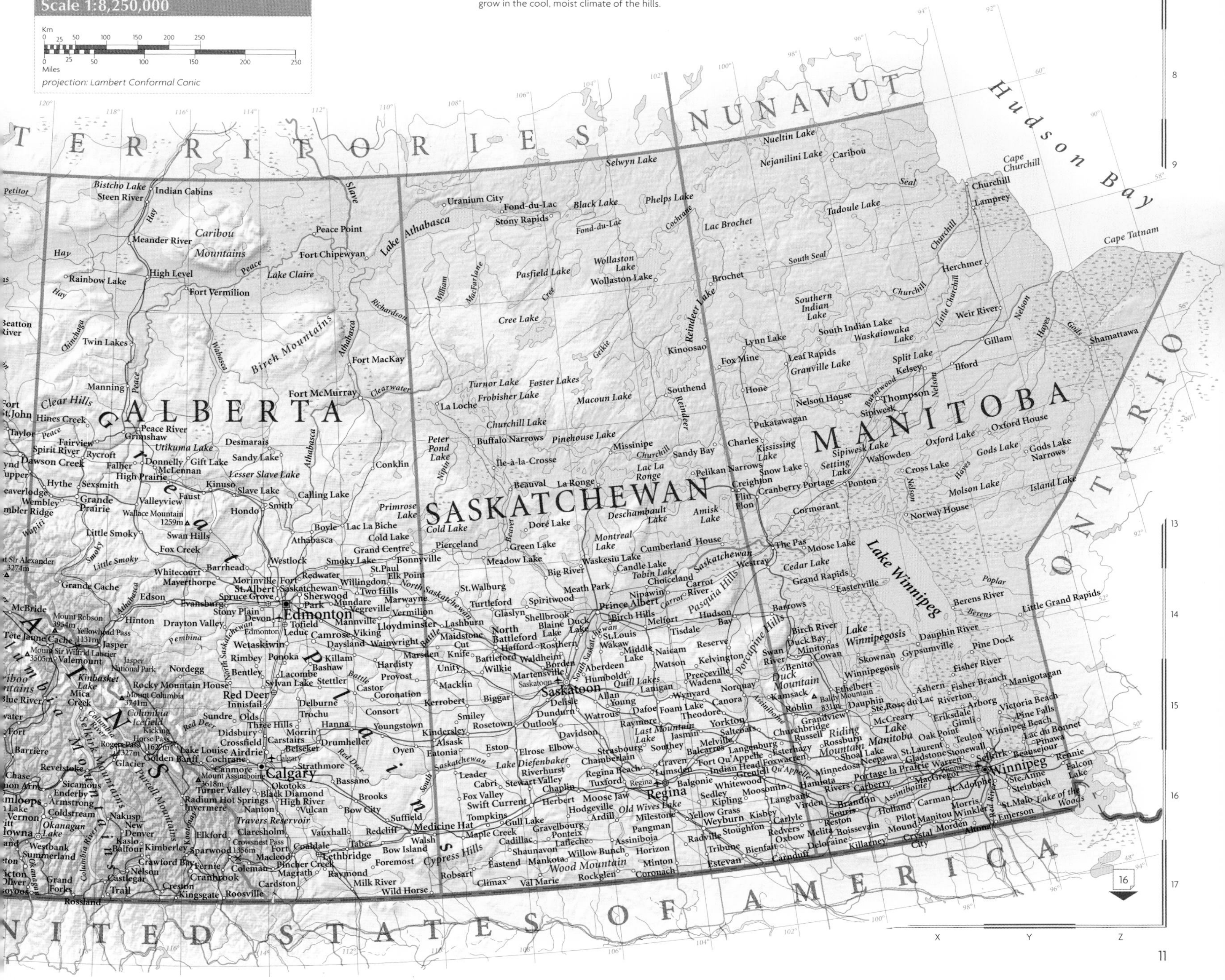

NUNAVUT
TERRITORIES
Hudson Bay
ALBERTA
SASKATCHEWAN
MANITOBA
ONTARIO
UNITED STATES OF AMERICA
Lake Athabasca
Lake Winnipeg
Lake Winnipegosis
Reindeer Lake
Wollaston Lake
Lesser Slave Lake
Cape Churchill
Cape Tatnam
Churchill
Edmonton
Calgary
Saskatoon
Regina
Winnipeg
Red Deer
Lethbridge
Medicine Hat
Prince Albert
Moose Jaw
Brandon
Fort McMurray
Grande Prairie
Thompson
Flin Flon
The Pas
Yorkton
Swift Current
North Battleford
Lloydminster
Dauphin
Portage la Prairie
Steinbach
Selkirk
Cypress Hills
Wood Mountain
Birch Mountains
Caribou Mountains
Porcupine Hills
Pasquia Hills
Duck Mountain
Riding Mountain
16

X Y Z

13 14 15 16 17

Canada: EASTERN PROVINCES

New Brunswick, Newfoundland & Labrador, Nova Scotia, Ontario, Prince Edward Island, Québec, ***St Pierre & Miquelon (to France)***

Colonized by both the English and the French during the 16th century, Canada's eastern provinces are still marked by their dual influences. They contain the last fragment of once-sizeable French territories, the islands of St. Pierre and Miquelon. French remains Canada's second official language and Québec's first language. The population of the eastern provinces is highly concentrated in the south, especially along the border with the US. A recent decline in fishing in the Atlantic provinces has encouraged a steady flow of westerly migration to more prosperous regions. The north, around Hudson Bay, remains snow-covered for most of the year and the indigenous Inuit people make up the bulk of its sparse population.

◀ ***Rocher Percé,** is 290 ft (88 m) high. Lying off the southeastern coast of Québec, it is a sanctuary for sea birds.*

Scale 1:7,750,000

Km 0 25 50 100 150 200
Miles 0 25 50 100 150 200

projection: Lambert Conformal Conic

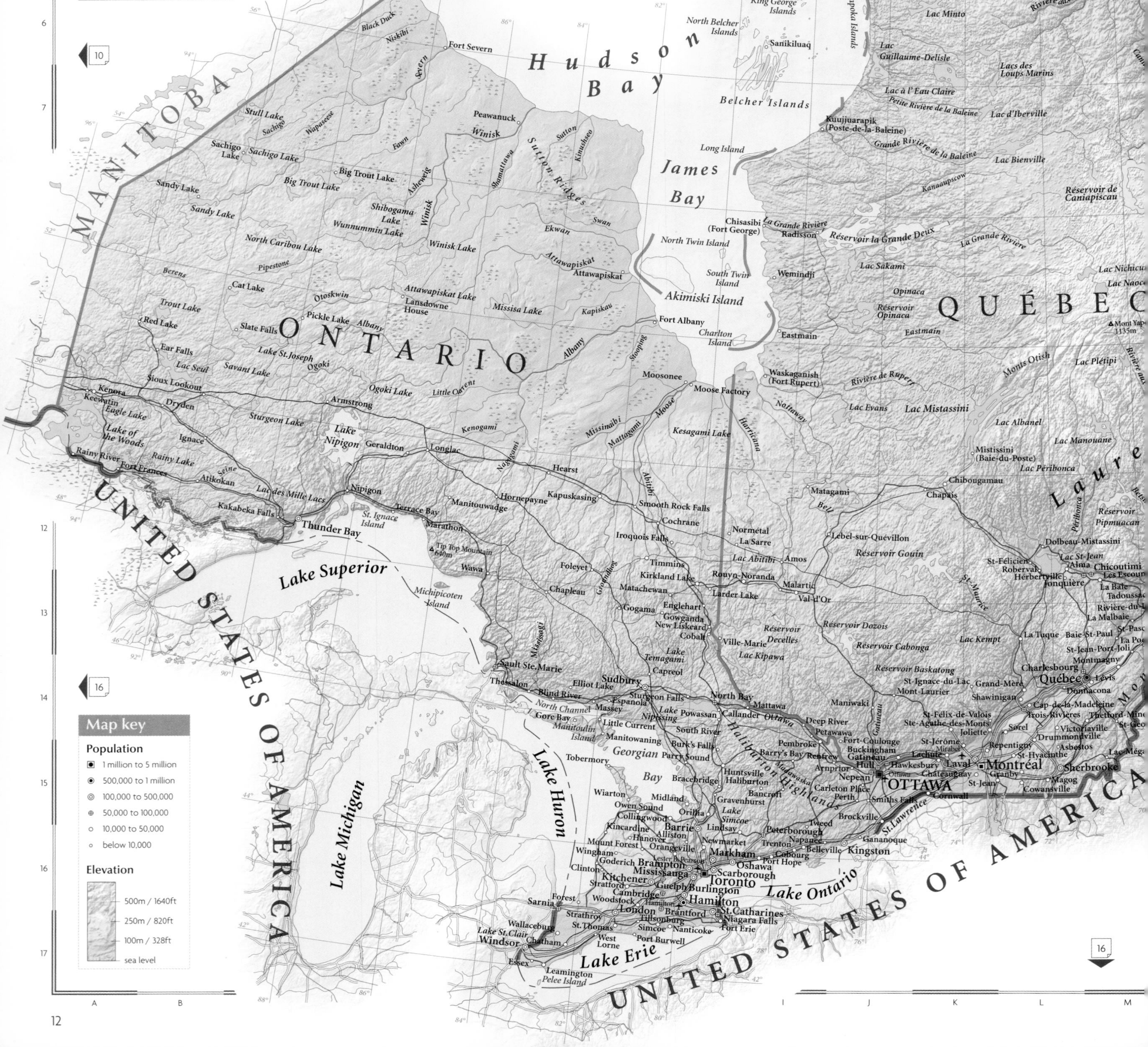

Hudson Bay
James Bay
Hudson Strait
Péninsule d' Ungava
NUNAVUT
MANITOBA
ONTARIO
QUÉBEC
UNITED STATES OF AMERICA
Lake Superior
Lake Michigan
Lake Huron
Georgian Bay
Lake Erie
Lake Ontario
Lake Nipigon
Lake of the Woods
Akimiski Island
Belcher Islands
Mansel Island
Charles Island
Sleeper Islands
King George Islands
North Belcher Islands
Ottawa Islands
Long Island
North Twin Island
South Twin Island
Charlton Island
Manitoulin Island
Michipicoten Island
St. Ignace Island
Ivujivik
Salluit
Déception
Kangiqsujuaq
Quaqtaq
Kangirsuk
Puvirnituq
Inukjuak (Port Harrison)
Sanikiluaq
Kuujjuarapik (Poste-de-la-Baleine)
Chisasibi (Fort George)
Radisson
Wemindji
Eastmain
Waskaganish (Fort Rupert)
Moosonee
Moose Factory
Fort Albany
Attawapiskat
Peawanuck
Fort Severn
Big Trout Lake
Sachigo Lake
Pickle Lake
Lansdowne House
Sioux Lookout
Kenora
Keewatin
Dryden
Armstrong
Geraldton
Longlac
Hearst
Kapuskasing
Hornepayne
Manitouwadge
Nipigon
Terrace Bay
Marathon
Thunder Bay
Wawa
Tip Top Mountain 640m
Atikokan
Fort Frances
Rainy River
Chapleau
Foleyet
Timmins
Cochrane
Smooth Rock Falls
Iroquois Falls
Kirkland Lake
Rouyn-Noranda
Val-d'Or
Amos
La Sarre
Normétal
Matagami
Chapais
Chibougamau
Mistissini (Baie-du-Poste)
Lebel-sur-Quévillon
Sault Ste.Marie
Thessalon
Elliot Lake
Sudbury
North Bay
Mattawa
Espanola
Sturgeon Falls
Parry Sound
Huntsville
Bracebridge
Pembroke
Renfrew
Arnprior
OTTAWA
Hull
Gatineau
Cornwall
Kingston
Belleville
Peterborough
Oshawa
Toronto
Scarborough
Markham
Mississauga
Brampton
Hamilton
Burlington
St.Catharines
Niagara Falls
Guelph
Kitchener
Cambridge
Brantford
London
Sarnia
Windsor
Chatham
Leamington
Pelee Island
Owen Sound
Barrie
Orillia
Montréal
Laval
Québec
Lévis
Trois-Rivières
Sherbrooke
Drummondville
Granby
Saint-Jérôme
Shawinigan
Grand-Mère
La Tuque
Chicoutimi
Jonquière
Alma
Roberval
Dolbeau-Mistassini
Lac Mistassini
Réservoir Gouin
Réservoir Cabonga
Réservoir Baskatong
Réservoir Dozois
Réservoir de Caniapiscau
Réservoir la Grande Deux
Réservoir Opinaca
Réservoir Pipmuacan
Lac Guillaume-Delisle
Lac à l'Eau Claire
Lac Minto
Lac Bienville
Lac Nipigon
Lac Seul
Lake Nipissing
Lake Simcoe
Mont Otish
Monts Otish
Haliburton Highlands
Sutton Ridges

Map key

Population
■ 1 million to 5 million
◉ 500,000 to 1 million
◎ 100,000 to 500,000
⊕ 50,000 to 100,000
○ 10,000 to 50,000
○ below 10,000

Elevation
500m / 1640ft
250m / 820ft
100m / 328ft
sea level

196
8
10
16
16

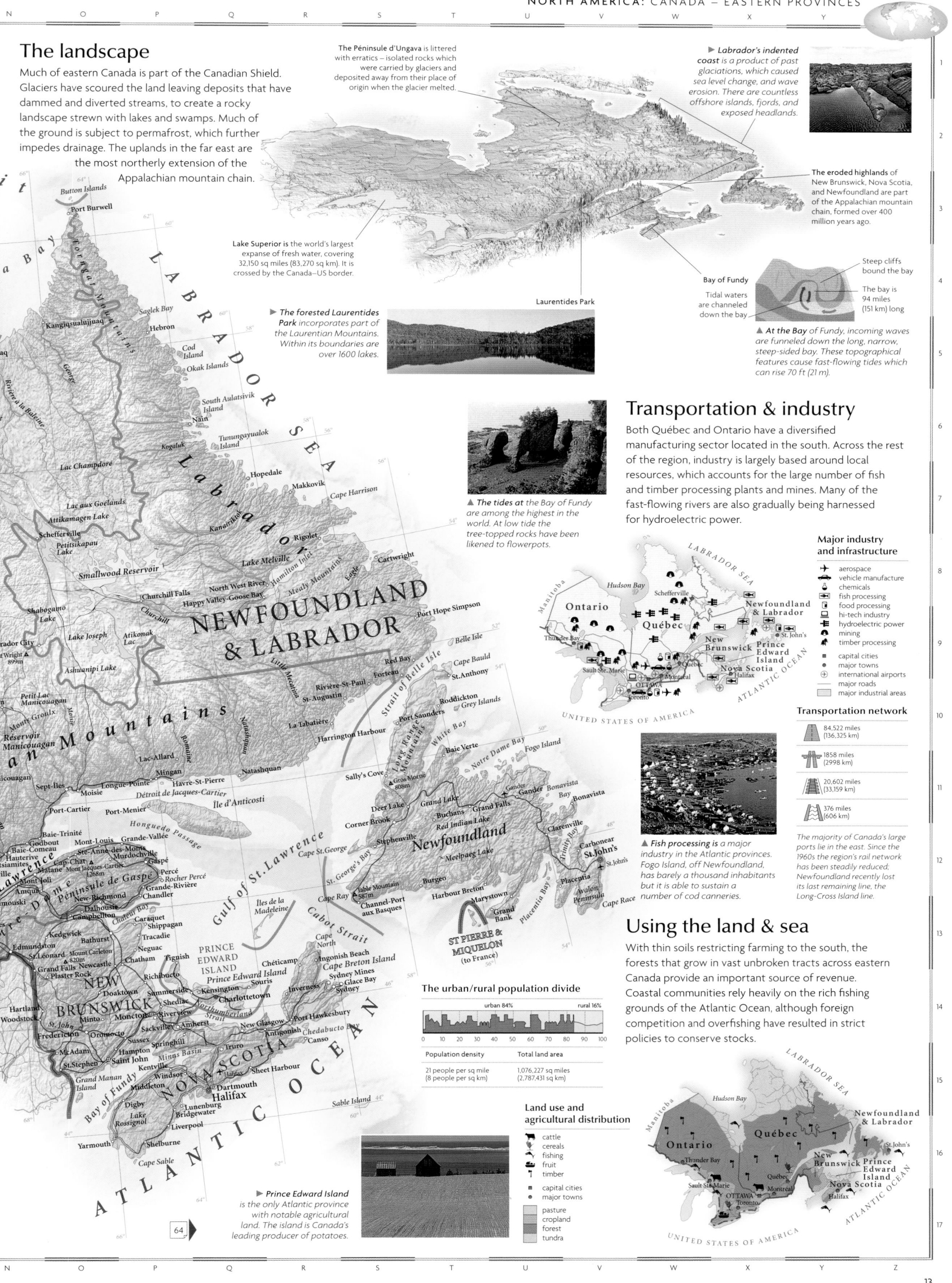

The landscape

Much of eastern Canada is part of the Canadian Shield. Glaciers have scoured the land leaving deposits that have dammed and diverted streams, to create a rocky landscape strewn with lakes and swamps. Much of the ground is subject to permafrost, which further impedes drainage. The uplands in the far east are the most northerly extension of the Appalachian mountain chain.

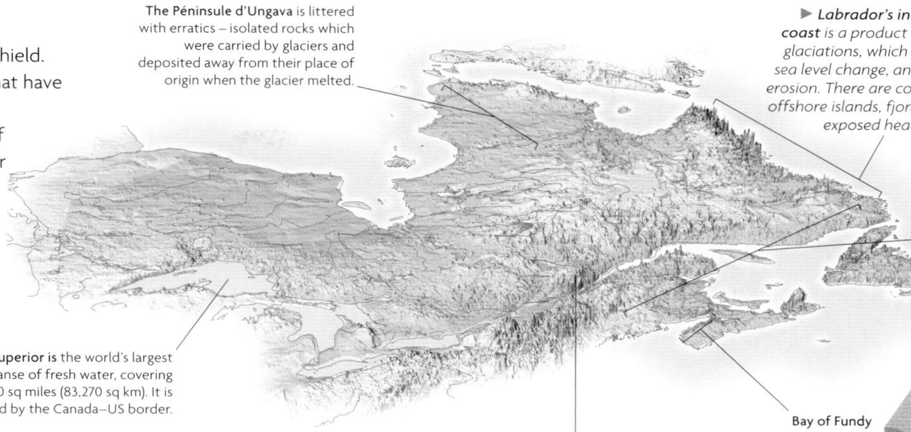
The Péninsule d'Ungava is littered with erratics – isolated rocks which were carried by glaciers and deposited away from their place of origin when the glacier melted.
Lake Superior is the world's largest expanse of fresh water, covering 32,150 sq miles (83,270 sq km). It is crossed by the Canada–US border.
Laurentides Park
Bay of Fundy
The eroded highlands of New Brunswick, Nova Scotia, and Newfoundland are part of the Appalachian mountain chain, formed over 400 million years ago.

▶ *Labrador's indented coast is a product of past glaciations, which caused sea level change, and wave erosion. There are countless offshore islands, fjords, and exposed headlands.*

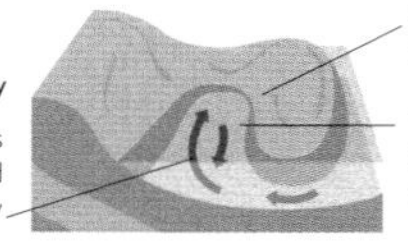
Steep cliffs bound the bay
The bay is 94 miles (151 km) long
Tidal waters are channeled down the bay

▲ *At the Bay of Fundy, incoming waves are funneled down the long, narrow, steep-sided bay. These topographical features cause fast-flowing tides which can rise 70 ft (21 m).*

▶ *The forested Laurentides Park incorporates part of the Laurentian Mountains. Within its boundaries are over 1600 lakes.*

Button Islands
Port Burwell
LABRADOR SEA
Torngat Mountains
Saglek Bay
Hebron
Kangiqsualujjuaq
George
Cod Island
Okak Islands
Rivière à la Baleine
South Aulatsivik Island
Nain
Tunungayualok Island
Kogaluk
Lac Champdore
Labrador
Hopedale
Makkovik
Cape Harrison
Lac aux Goélands
Attikamagen Lake
Schefferville
Petitsikapau Lake
Kanairiktok
Rigolet
Smallwood Reservoir
Lake Melville
Hamilton Inlet
Mealy Mountains
Eagle
Cartwright
Churchill Falls
North West River
Happy Valley-Goose Bay
NEWFOUNDLAND & LABRADOR
Port Hope Simpson
Shabogamo Lake
Churchill
Lake Joseph
Atikonak Lac
Labrador City
Wabush
Mont Wright ▲ 899m
Belle Isle
Cape Bauld
St.Anthony
Red Bay
Forteau
Ashuanipi Lake
Little Mecatina
Rivière-St-Paul
St-Augustin
Strait of Belle Isle
Petit Lac Manicouagan
Monts Groulx
Moisie
Réservoir Manicouagan
Mountains
Natashquan
Romaine
La Tabatière
Roddickton
Grey Islands
Port Saunders
Harrington Harbour
White Bay
Long Range Mountains
Baie Verte
Notre Dame Bay
Fogo Island
Lac-Allard
Mingan
Natashquan
Sally's Cove
Gros Morne 808m
Gander
Bonavista Bay
Bonavista
Manicouagan
Sept-Îles
Moisie
Longue-Pointe
Havre-St-Pierre
Détroit de Jacques-Cartier
Île d'Anticosti
Deer Lake
Grand Lake
Buchans
Grand Falls
Red Indian Lake
Clarenville
Port-Cartier
Port-Menier
Honguedo Passage
Corner Brook
Stephenville
Newfoundland
Trinity Bay
Carbonear
St.John's
Baie-Trinité
Godbout
Baie-Comeau
Mont-Louis
Grande-Vallée
Ste-Anne-des-Monts
Murdochville
Hauterive
Cap-Chat
Mont Jacques-Cartier 1268m
Gaspé
Matane
Mont-Joli
Amqui
Rimouski
Percé
Rocher Percé
Péninsule de Gaspé
Grande-Rivière
Chandler
New-Richmond
Dalhousie
Campbellton
Chaleur Bay
Gulf of St.Lawrence
Cape St.George
St. George's Bay
Table Mountain 587m
Cape Ray
Channel-Port aux Basques
Meelpaeg Lake
Burgeo
Harbour Breton
Marystown
Grand Bank
Placentia Bay
Placentia
Avalon Peninsula
Cape Race
Îles de la Madeleine
Cabot Strait
ST PIERRE & MIQUELON (to France)
Caraquet
Shippagan
Tracadie
Kedgwick
Bathurst
Edmundston
St.Léonard
Mount Carleton 820m
Newcastle
Neguac
Chatham
Tignish
PRINCE EDWARD ISLAND
Prince Edward Island
Chéticamp
Cape North
Ingonish Beach
Cape Breton Island
Sydney Mines
Glace Bay
Sydney
Grand Falls
Plaster Rock
NEW BRUNSWICK
Richibucto
Doaktown
Summerside
Kensington
Souris
Charlottetown
Inverness
Hartland
Woodstock
Shediac
Riverview
Minto
Moncton
Northumberland Strait
St.John
Sackville
Amherst
New Glasgow
Antigonish
Port Hawkesbury
Chedabucto Bay
Canso
Fredericton
Oromocto
Sussex
Springhill
Truro
McAdam
Hampton
Minas Basin
St.Stephen
Saint John
Kentville
NOVA SCOTIA
Sheet Harbour
Grand Manan Island
Bay of Fundy
Windsor
Halifax
Middleton
Dartmouth
Digby
Lunenburg
Bridgewater
Lake Rossignol
Liverpool
Sable Island
Yarmouth
Shelburne
Cape Sable
ATLANTIC OCEAN

64

Transportation & industry

Both Québec and Ontario have a diversified manufacturing sector located in the south. Across the rest of the region, industry is largely based around local resources, which accounts for the large number of fish and timber processing plants and mines. Many of the fast-flowing rivers are also gradually being harnessed for hydroelectric power.

▲ *The tides at the Bay of Fundy are among the highest in the world. At low tide the tree-topped rocks have been likened to flowerpots.*

LABRADOR SEA
Hudson Bay
Manitoba
Ontario
Schefferville
Québec
Newfoundland & Labrador
Thunder Bay
New Brunswick
Prince Edward Island
St. John's
Sault Ste. Marie
Québec
Montréal
Nova Scotia
Halifax
OTTAWA
Toronto
ATLANTIC OCEAN
UNITED STATES OF AMERICA

Major industry and infrastructure

- aerospace
- vehicle manufacture
- chemicals
- fish processing
- food processing
- hi-tech industry
- hydroelectric power
- mining
- timber processing
- capital cities
- major towns
- international airports
- major roads
- major industrial areas

Transportation network

Roads	84,522 miles (136,325 km)
Highways	1858 miles (2998 km)
Railways	20,602 miles (33,159 km)
Waterways	376 miles (606 km)

The majority of Canada's large ports lie in the east. Since the 1960s the region's rail network has been steadily reduced; Newfoundland recently lost its last remaining line, the Long-Cross Island line.

▲ *Fish processing is a major industry in the Atlantic provinces. Fogo Island, off Newfoundland, has barely a thousand inhabitants but it is able to sustain a number of cod canneries.*

Using the land & sea

With thin soils restricting farming to the south, the forests that grow in vast unbroken tracts across eastern Canada provide an important source of revenue. Coastal communities rely heavily on the rich fishing grounds of the Atlantic Ocean, although foreign competition and overfishing have resulted in strict policies to conserve stocks.

The urban/rural population divide

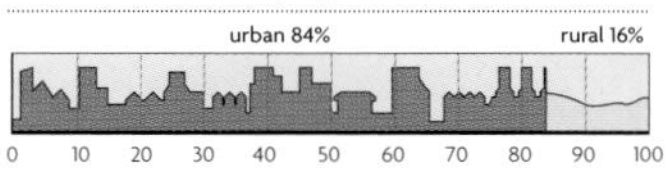
urban 84%
rural 16%
0 10 20 30 40 50 60 70 80 90 100

Population density	Total land area
21 people per sq mile (8 people per sq km)	1,076,227 sq miles (2,787,431 sq km)

▶ *Prince Edward Island is the only Atlantic province with notable agricultural land. The island is Canada's leading producer of potatoes.*

Land use and agricultural distribution

- cattle
- cereals
- fishing
- fruit
- timber
- capital cities
- major towns
- pasture
- cropland
- forest
- tundra

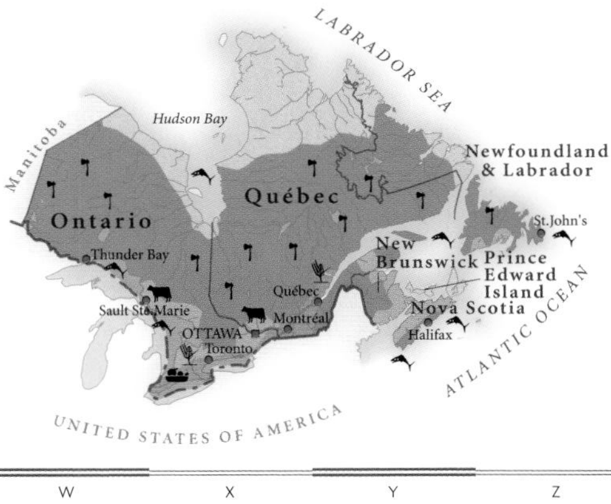
LABRADOR SEA
Hudson Bay
Manitoba
Newfoundland & Labrador
Québec
Ontario
St.John's
Thunder Bay
New Brunswick
Prince Edward Island
Québec
Sault Ste.Marie
Montréal
Nova Scotia
OTTAWA
Toronto
Halifax
ATLANTIC OCEAN
UNITED STATES OF AMERICA

Southeastern Canada

Southern Ontario, Southern Québec

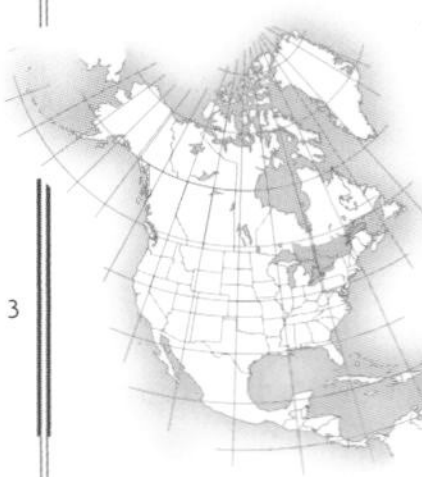

The southern parts of Québec and Ontario form the economic heart of Canada. The two provinces are divided by their language and culture; in Québec, French is the main language, whereas English is spoken in Ontario. Separatist sentiment in Québec has led to a provincial referendum on the question of a sovereignty association with Canada.

The region contains Canada's capital, Ottawa, and its two largest cities: Toronto, the center of commerce, and Montréal, the cultural and administrative heart of French Canada.

▲ ***The port at** Montréal is situated on the St. Lawrence Seaway. A network of 16 locks allows oceangoing vessels access to routes once plied by fur-trappers and early settlers.*

Transportation & industry

The cities of southern Québec and Ontario, and their hinterlands, form the heart of Canadian manufacturing industry. Toronto is Canada's leading financial center, and Ontario's motor and aerospace industries have developed around the city. A major center for nickel mining lies to the north of Toronto. Most of Québec's industry is located in Montréal, the oldest port in North America. Chemicals, paper manufacture, and the construction of transportation equipment are leading industrial activities.

► ***Niagara Falls lies** on the border between Canada and the US. It comprises a system of two falls: American Falls, in New York, is separated from Horseshoe Falls, in Ontario, by Goat Island. Horseshoe Falls, seen here, plunges 184 ft (56 m) and is 2500 ft (762 m) wide.*

Major industry and infrastructure

- car manufacture
- chemicals
- engineering
- finance
- food processing
- hi-tech industry
- mining
- iron & steel
- textiles
- paper industry
- timber processing
- capital cities
- major towns
- international airports
- major roads
- major industrial areas

Sault Ste.Marie
North Bay
Québec
Lake Huron
Ontario
Montréal
OTTAWA
Toronto
Lake Ontario
Lake Erie
UNITED STATES OF AMERICA
New Brunswick
Gaspé

Transportation network

The opening of the St. Lawrence Seaway in 1959 finally allowed oceangoing ships (up to 24,000 tons [tonnes]) access to the interior of Canada, creating a vital trading route.

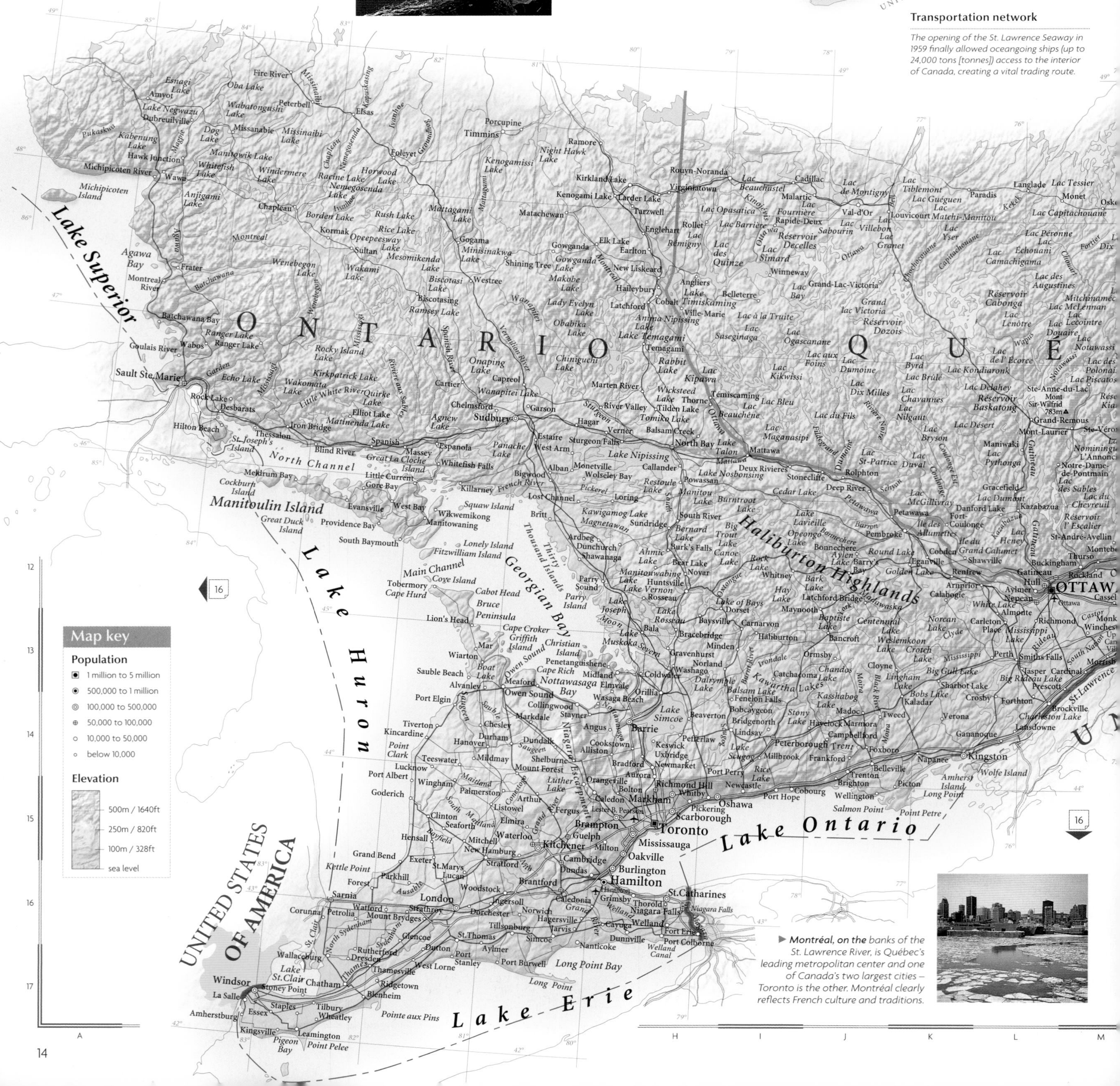

ONTARIO
QUÉBEC
Lake Superior
Lake Huron
Lake Ontario
Lake Erie
Georgian Bay
North Channel
Manitoulin Island
Haliburton Highlands
UNITED STATES OF AMERICA
Sault Ste.Marie
Sudbury
North Bay
Timmins
Kirkland Lake
Rouyn-Noranda
Val-d'Or
Ottawa
Toronto
Hamilton
Kitchener
London
Windsor
Kingston
Barrie
Oshawa
Mississauga
Brampton
Markham
Oakville
Burlington
St.Catharines
Niagara Falls
Guelph
Cambridge
Sarnia
Peterborough
Belleville
Gatineau
Map key
Population
1 million to 5 million
500,000 to 1 million
100,000 to 500,000
50,000 to 100,000
10,000 to 50,000
below 10,000
Elevation
500m / 1640ft
250m / 820ft
100m / 328ft
sea level

16

16

► ***Montréal, on the** banks of the St. Lawrence River, is Québec's leading metropolitan center and one of Canada's two largest cities – Toronto is the other. Montréal clearly reflects French culture and traditions.*

N O P Q R S T U V W X Y

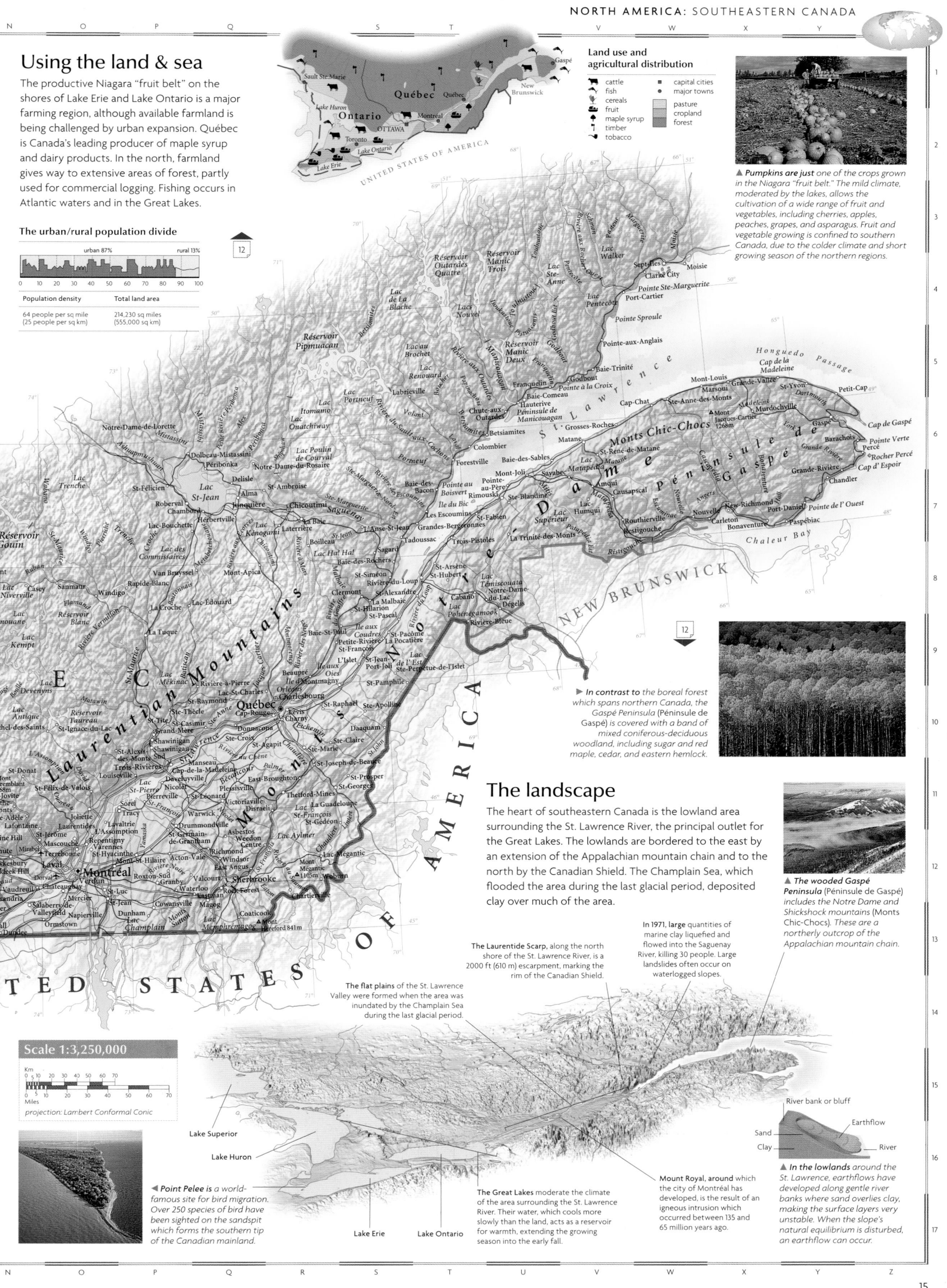

Using the land & sea

The productive Niagara "fruit belt" on the shores of Lake Erie and Lake Ontario is a major farming region, although available farmland is being challenged by urban expansion. Québec is Canada's leading producer of maple syrup and dairy products. In the north, farmland gives way to extensive areas of forest, partly used for commercial logging. Fishing occurs in Atlantic waters and in the Great Lakes.

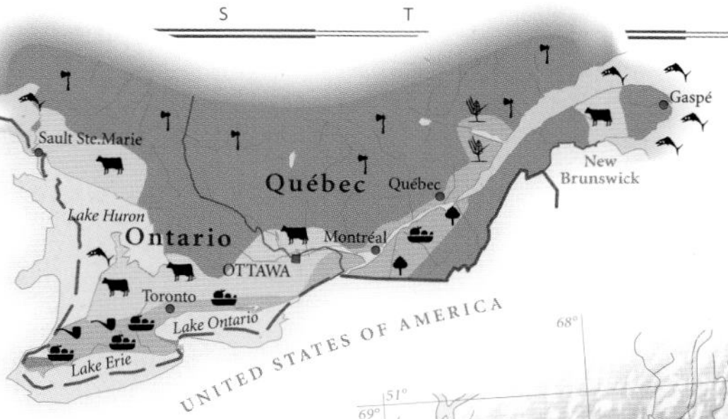
Sault Ste. Marie
Québec
Québec
Gaspé
New Brunswick
Lake Huron
Ontario
Montréal
OTTAWA
Toronto
Lake Ontario
Lake Erie
UNITED STATES OF AMERICA

Land use and agricultural distribution

- cattle
- fish
- cereals
- fruit
- maple syrup
- timber
- tobacco
- capital cities
- major towns
- pasture
- cropland
- forest

▲ ***Pumpkins are just*** *one of the crops grown in the Niagara "fruit belt." The mild climate, moderated by the lakes, allows the cultivation of a wide range of fruit and vegetables, including cherries, apples, peaches, grapes, and asparagus. Fruit and vegetable growing is confined to southern Canada, due to the colder climate and short growing season of the northern regions.*

The urban/rural population divide

urban 87% rural 13%

0 10 20 30 40 50 60 70 80 90 100

Population density	Total land area
64 people per sq mile (25 people per sq km)	214,230 sq miles (555,000 sq km)

12

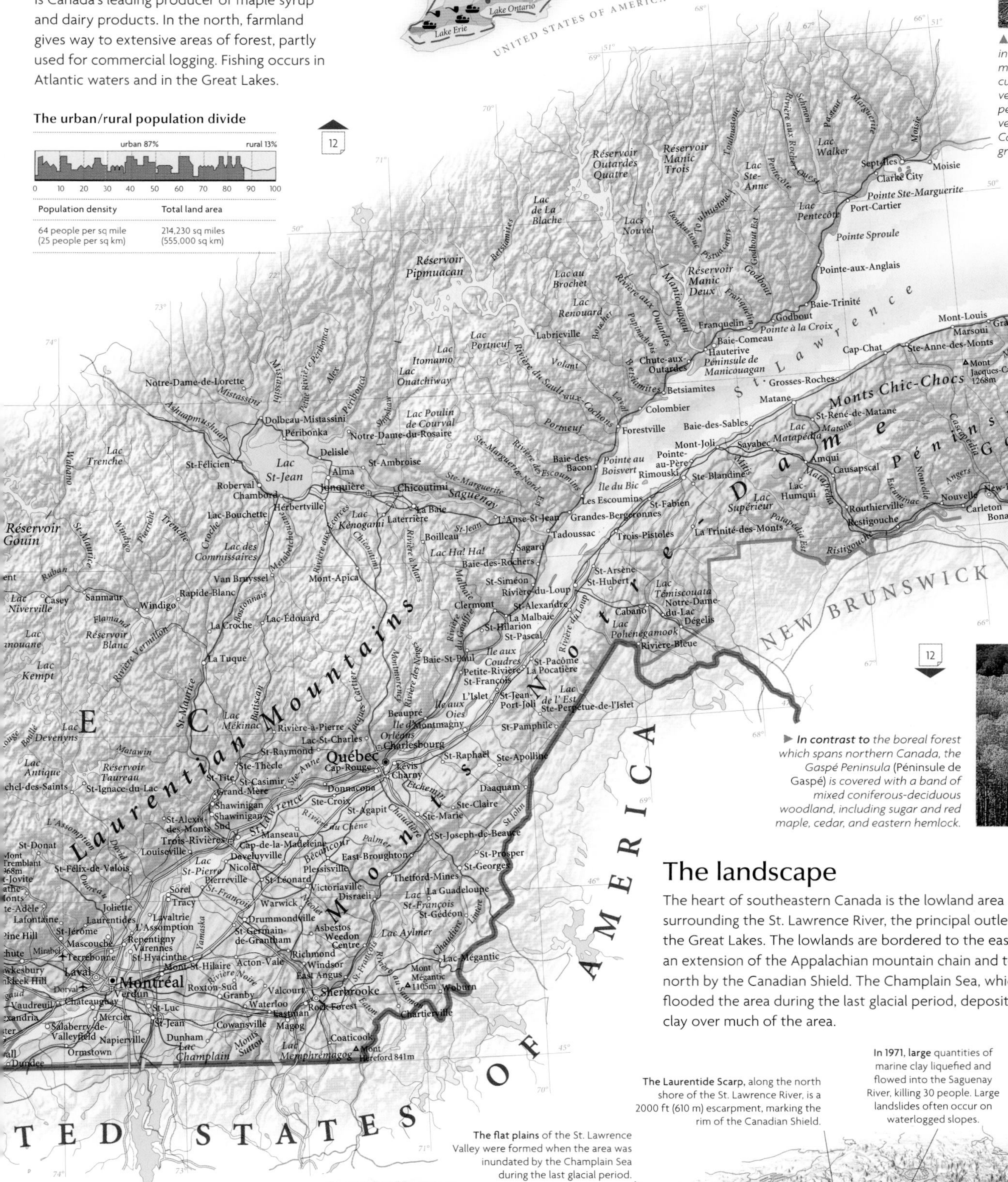
Laurentian Mountains
Monts Notre-Dame
Monts Chic-Chocs
Péninsule de Gaspé
St Lawrence
Honguedo Passage
Chaleur Bay
NEW BRUNSWICK
UNITED STATES OF AMERICA
Québec
Montréal
Sherbrooke
Trois-Rivières
Chicoutimi
Jonquière
Saguenay
Lac St-Jean
Réservoir Pipmuacan
Réservoir Manic Trois
Réservoir Outardes Quatre
Réservoir Manic Deux
Réservoir Gouin
Lac Témiscouata
Baie-Comeau
Sept-Îles
Port-Cartier
Rimouski
Matane
Gaspé
Percé
Mont Jacques-Cartier 1268m
Mont Mégantic 1105m
Mont Hereford 841m
Lac Memphrémagog
Rivière-du-Loup
Tadoussac
Dolbeau-Mistassini
Alma
La Tuque
Shawinigan
Drummondville
Victoriaville
Thetford-Mines
Lévis
Laval
Granby
Saint-Hyacinthe
Lac Champlain
Pointe des Monts

12

► ***In contrast to*** *the boreal forest which spans northern Canada, the Gaspé Peninsula (Péninsule de Gaspé) is covered with a band of mixed coniferous-deciduous woodland, including sugar and red maple, cedar, and eastern hemlock.*

The landscape

The heart of southeastern Canada is the lowland area surrounding the St. Lawrence River, the principal outlet for the Great Lakes. The lowlands are bordered to the east by an extension of the Appalachian mountain chain and to the north by the Canadian Shield. The Champlain Sea, which flooded the area during the last glacial period, deposited clay over much of the area.

▲ ***The wooded Gaspé Peninsula*** *(Péninsule de Gaspé) includes the Notre Dame and Shickshock mountains (Monts Chic-Chocs). These are a northerly outcrop of the Appalachian mountain chain.*

Scale 1:3,250,000

Km 0 5 10 20 30 40 50 60 70

Miles 0 5 10 20 30 40 50 60 70

projection: Lambert Conformal Conic

◄ ***Point Pelee*** *is a world-famous site for bird migration. Over 250 species of bird have been sighted on the sandspit which forms the southern tip of the Canadian mainland.*

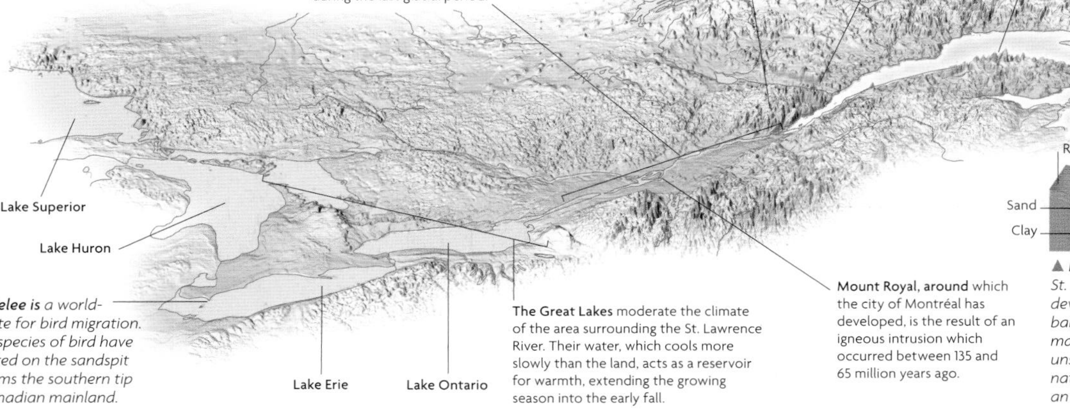
Lake Superior
Lake Huron
Lake Erie
Lake Ontario

The flat plains of the St. Lawrence Valley were formed when the area was inundated by the Champlain Sea during the last glacial period.

The Laurentide Scarp, along the north shore of the St. Lawrence River, is a 2000 ft (610 m) escarpment, marking the rim of the Canadian Shield.

In 1971, large quantities of marine clay liquefied and flowed into the Saguenay River, killing 30 people. Large landslides often occur on waterlogged slopes.

The Great Lakes moderate the climate of the area surrounding the St. Lawrence River. Their water, which cools more slowly than the land, acts as a reservoir for warmth, extending the growing season into the early fall.

Mount Royal, around which the city of Montréal has developed, is the result of an igneous intrusion which occurred between 135 and 65 million years ago.

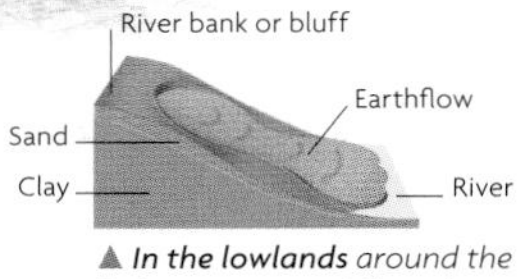
River bank or bluff
Earthflow
Sand
Clay
River

▲ ***In the lowlands*** *around the St. Lawrence, earthflows have developed along gentle river banks where sand overlies clay, making the surface layers very unstable. When the slope's natural equilibrium is disturbed, an earthflow can occur.*

N O P Q R S T U V W X Y Z

The United States of America

COTERMINOUS US (FOR ALASKA AND HAWAII SEE PAGES 38-39)

The US's progression from frontier territory to economic and political superpower has taken less than 200 years. The 48 coterminous states, along with the outlying states of Alaska and Hawaii, are part of a federal union, held together by the guiding principles of the US Constitution, which embodies the ideals of democracy and liberty for all. Abundant fertile land and a rich resource base fueled and sustained US economic development. With the spread of agriculture and the growth of trade and industry came the need for a larger workforce, which was supplied by millions of immigrants, many seeking an escape from poverty and political or religious persecution. Immigration continues today, particularly from Central America and Asia.

▲ *Washington DC was established as the site for the nation's capital in 1790. It is home to the seat of national government, on Capitol Hill, as well as the President's official residence, the White House.*

► *The clear waters of Niagara Falls cascade 190 ft (58 m) into the gorge below. It is one of America's most famous spectacles and a leading tourist attraction. The falls are slowly receding and the gorge may one day stretch from Lake Ontario to Lake Erie.*

▲ *Mount Rainier is a dormant volcano in the Cascade Range, Washington. This 14,090 ft (4392 m) peak is flanked by the most extensive glacier outside Alaska.*

Scale 1:12,700,000
projection: Lambert Azimuthal Equal Area
CANADA
PACIFIC OCEAN
UNITED STATES
MEXICO
ROCKY MOUNTAINS
GREAT PLAINS
WASHINGTON
OREGON
IDAHO
MONTANA
WYOMING
NEVADA
UTAH
COLORADO
CALIFORNIA
ARIZONA
NEW MEXICO
NORTH DAKOTA
SOUTH DAKOTA
NEBRASKA
KANSAS
OKLAHOMA
TEXAS
Seattle
Portland
San Francisco
Los Angeles
San Diego
Las Vegas
Phoenix
Salt Lake City
Denver
Albuquerque
El Paso
Dallas
Houston
San Antonio
Austin
Oklahoma City
Great Salt Lake
Colorado Plateau
Great Basin
8
40
192

Transportation & industry

The US has been the industrial powerhouse of the world since the Second World War, pioneering mass-production and the consumer lifestyle. Initially, heavy engineering and manufacturing in the northeast led the economy. Today, heavy industry has declined and the US economy is driven by service and financial industries, with the most important being defense, hi-tech, and electronics.

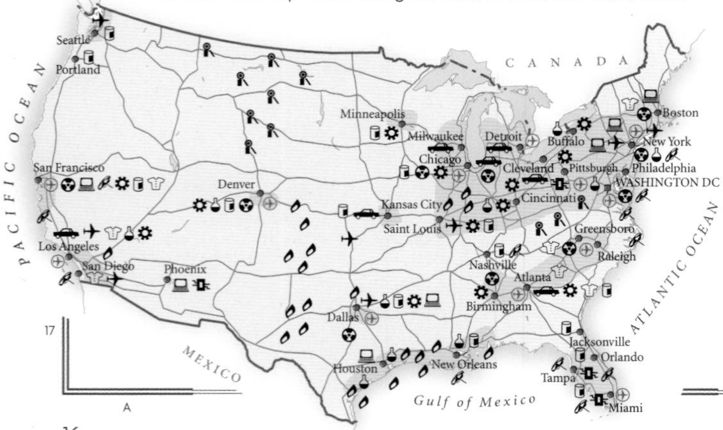
CANADA
PACIFIC OCEAN
ATLANTIC OCEAN
MEXICO
Gulf of Mexico
Seattle
Portland
San Francisco
Los Angeles
San Diego
Phoenix
Denver
Minneapolis
Milwaukee
Chicago
Detroit
Cleveland
Buffalo
Pittsburgh
Philadelphia
New York
Boston
WASHINGTON DC
Kansas City
Saint Louis
Cincinnati
Greensboro
Raleigh
Nashville
Atlanta
Birmingham
Dallas
Houston
New Orleans
Jacksonville
Orlando
Tampa
Miami

Transportation network

3,875,040 miles (6,240,000 km)		52,388 miles (84,361 km)	
148,308 miles (235,238 km)		25,467 miles (41,009 km)	

Transportation in the US is dominated by the car which, with the extensive Interstate Highway system, allows great personal mobility. Today, internal air flights between major cities provide the most rapid cross-country travel.

Major industry and infrastructure

- aerospace
- car manufacture
- chemicals
- coal
- electronics
- engineering
- food processing
- hi-tech industry
- oil & gas
- research & development
- textiles
- tourism
- capital cities
- major towns
- international airports
- major roads
- major industrial areas

The landscape

The high, rugged mountain ranges of the west are about 80 million years old, geologically young compared to the old, eroded, Appalachian mountain chain, which dates from when North America and Europe were joined together as part of the supercontinent Pangaea, 400 million years ago. In contrast, the Great Plains and Mississippi Basin have a low relief and fertile soils.

Mount Rainier
Great Plains
The Great Lakes
Niagara Falls

Death Valley, California, 282 ft (86 m) below sea level, is the lowest point in the western hemisphere, and one of the hottest places on Earth. Temperatures of 135° F (57° C) have been recorded here.

Monument Valley's striking sandstone spires and pillars *(buttes)* have been formed by the action of wind, water, heat, and cold.

The deep gullies of South Dakota's badlands are created by periodic, torrential rainfall, which erodes the soft soils and rocks. Their form has been greatly affected by changes in land use.

Most of the US is drained by the great Mississippi River system. At its mouth, where levées are breached, floodwaters are carried to the swamps through a series of channels. This region is known as the bayou.

Barrier beaches, bars and spits are typical of the Atlantic coast. These sand formations around Cape Hatteras stretch along the coast for 200 miles (320 km).

The Great Smoky Mountains, part of the ancient Appalachian mountain chain, formed a natural barrier to early settlers attempting to penetrate the country's interior.

The Everglades are a vast area of sawgrass swamp covering 4000 sq miles (10,300 sq km) of southern Florida.

◀ *Devils Tower, in Wyoming is a 1280 ft (390 m) intrusion of basalt rock, which cooled to form octagonal pillars. In 1906 it became the first US National Monument.*

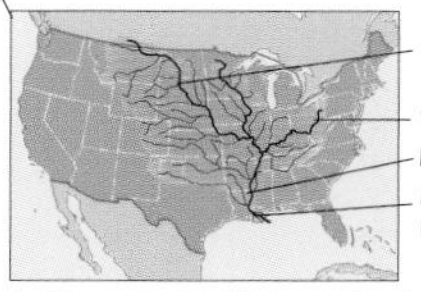
Missouri River
Ohio River
Mississippi River
Mississippi Delta

▲ *The massive drainage basin of the Mississippi covers 1,250,000 sq miles (3,200,000 sq km). It includes all areas drained by the Mississippi and its chief tributaries, the Missouri and Ohio Rivers, and drains the entire region from the Appalachians to the Rockies.*

CANADA
UNITED STATES OF AMERICA
ATLANTIC OCEAN
Gulf of Maine
Lake Superior
Lake Michigan
Lake Huron
Lake Ontario
Lake Erie
Appalachian Mountains
Piedmont
WASHINGTON DC
New York
Boston
Philadelphia
Chicago
Detroit
Atlanta
Miami
New Orleans
Straits of Florida
8
64
64

Map key

Population

- ■ above 5 million
- ▣ 1 million to 5 million
- ◉ 500,000 to 1 million
- ◎ 100,000 to 500,000
- ⊕ 50,000 to 100,000
- ○ 10,000 to 50,000
- ∘ below 10,000

Elevation

- 4000m / 13,124ft
- 3000m / 9843ft
- 2000m / 6562ft
- 1000m / 3281ft
- 500m / 1640ft
- 250m / 820ft
- 100m / 328ft
- sea level

Using the land and sea

Over half of the US is used for agriculture, typified by the large cereal grain farms and cattle ranches of the Great Plains and Midwest prairie regions. Although wheat and corn are still primary crops, a diverse range of fruits and vegetables are grown in the fertile areas, particularly near the east and west coasts. Despite the abundance of cultivable land, inadequate soil management has resulted in a third of the topsoil being lost through wind and water erosion.

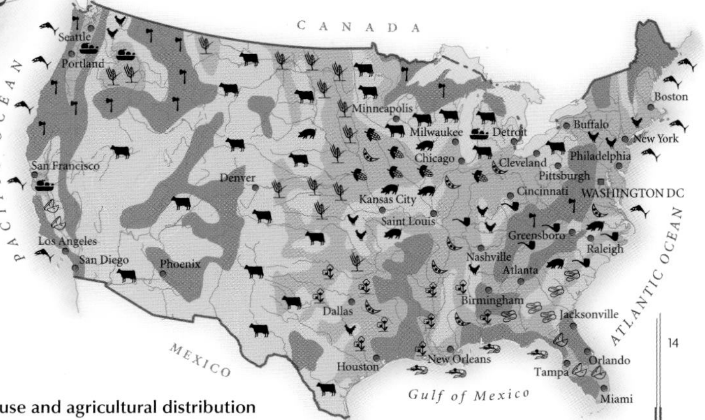
CANADA
PACIFIC OCEAN
ATLANTIC OCEAN
MEXICO
Gulf of Mexico
Seattle
Portland
San Francisco
Los Angeles
San Diego
Phoenix
Denver
Dallas
Houston
New Orleans
Minneapolis
Milwaukee
Detroit
Chicago
Kansas City
Saint Louis
Nashville
Atlanta
Birmingham
Jacksonville
Orlando
Tampa
Miami
Cleveland
Pittsburgh
Cincinnati
Buffalo
Boston
New York
Philadelphia
WASHINGTON DC
Greensboro
Raleigh

Land use and agricultural distribution

- cattle
- pigs
- poultry
- citrus fruits
- cotton
- fishing
- fruit
- corn
- peanuts
- shellfish
- soybeans
- timber
- tobacco
- wheat
- ■ capital cities
- ● major towns
- pasture
- cropland
- forest
- wetland
- desert
- mountain region

The urban/rural population divide

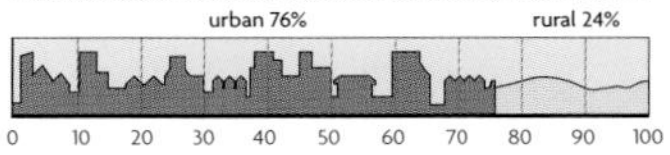
urban 76%
rural 24%
0
10
20
30
40
50
60
70
80
90
100

Population density	Total land area
98 people per sq mile (38 people per sq km)	2,959,045 sq miles (7,663,631 sq km)

▶ *Fakahatchee Strand is part of the extensive subtropical swamps in the Florida Everglades. The swamps support a wide variety of animal life, including many rare birds, fish, alligators, and crocodiles.*

◀ *Farming on the Great Plains and in the Midwest is characterized by large-scale, mechanized wheat farms.*

USA: NORTHEASTERN STATES

Connecticut, Maine, Massachusetts, New Hampshire, New Jersey, New York, Pennsylvania, Rhode Island, Vermont

The indented coast and vast woodlands of the northeastern states were the original core area for European expansion. The rustic character of New England prevails after nearly four centuries, while the great cities of the Atlantic seaboard have formed an almost continuous urban region. Over 20 million immigrants entered New York from 1855 to 1924 and the northeast became the industrial center of the US. After the decline of mining and heavy manufacturing, economic dynamism has been restored with the growth of hi-tech and service industries.

▲ *Chelsea in Vermont, surrounded by trees in their fall foliage. Tourism and agriculture dominate the economy of this self-consciously rural state, where no town exceeds 30,000 people.*

Map key

Population

- above 5 million
- 1 million to 5 million
- 500,000 to 1 million
- 100,000 to 500,000
- 50,000 to 100,000
- 10,000 to 50,000
- below 10,000

Elevation

- 1000m / 3281ft
- 500m / 1640ft
- 250m / 820ft
- 100m / 328ft
- sea level

Transportation network

- 340,090 miles (544,144 km)
- 4813 miles (7700 km)
- 12,872 miles (20,592 km)
- 2108 miles (3389 km)

New York's commercial success is tied historically to its transportation connections. The Erie Canal, completed in 1825, opened up the Great Lakes and the interior to New York's markets and carried a stream of immigrants into the Midwest.

Transportation & industry

The principal seaboard cities grew up on trade and manufacturing. They are now global centers of commerce and corporate administration, dominating the regional economy. Research and development facilities support an expanding electronics and communications sector throughout the region. Pharmaceutical and chemical industries are important in New Jersey and Pennsylvania.

CANADA
Maine
Portland
Vermont
New Hampshire
Syracuse
Albany
Rochester
Buffalo
New York
Massachusetts
Boston
Connecticut
Hartford
Providence
Rhode Island
Pennsylvania
Ohio
Pittsburgh
Harrisburg
New York
New Jersey
Philadelphia
ATLANTIC OCEAN
West Virginia
Maryland
Delaware

Major industry and infrastructure

- chemicals
- coal
- defense
- electronics
- engineering
- finance
- hi-tech industry
- iron & steel
- pharmaceuticals
- printing & publishing
- research & development
- textiles
- timber processing
- major towns
- international airports
- major roads
- major industrial area

CANADA
Lake Ontario
Lake Erie
NEW YORK
PENNSYLVANIA
NEW JERSEY
VERMONT
MASSACHUSETTS
CONNECTICUT
OHIO
WEST VIRGINIA
MARYLAND
DELAWARE
ATLANTIC OCEAN
Long Island
Adirondack Mountains
Catskill Mountains
Appalachian Mountains
Allegheny Plateau
Allegheny Mountains
Blue Mountain
Finger Lakes
Lake Champlain
Saint Lawrence River
Thousand Islands
New York
Philadelphia
Pittsburgh
Buffalo
Rochester
Syracuse
Albany
Binghamton
Utica
Erie
Harrisburg
Allentown
Scranton
Trenton
Newark
Jersey City
Atlantic City
Cape May
Plattsburgh
Burlington
Montpelier
Springfield
Hartford
Bridgeport
Stamford
Yonkers
Paterson
Camden
Lancaster
Reading
York
Altoona
State College
Williamsport
Wilkes Barre
Elmira
Ithaca
Watertown
Oswego
Niagara Falls
Schenectady
Troy
Pittsfield
Kingston
Poughkeepsie
Gettysburg
Chambersburg
Johnstown
Washington
New Castle
Sharon
Meadville
Warren
Bradford
Olean
Jamestown
Dunkirk

14
32
20
22
64

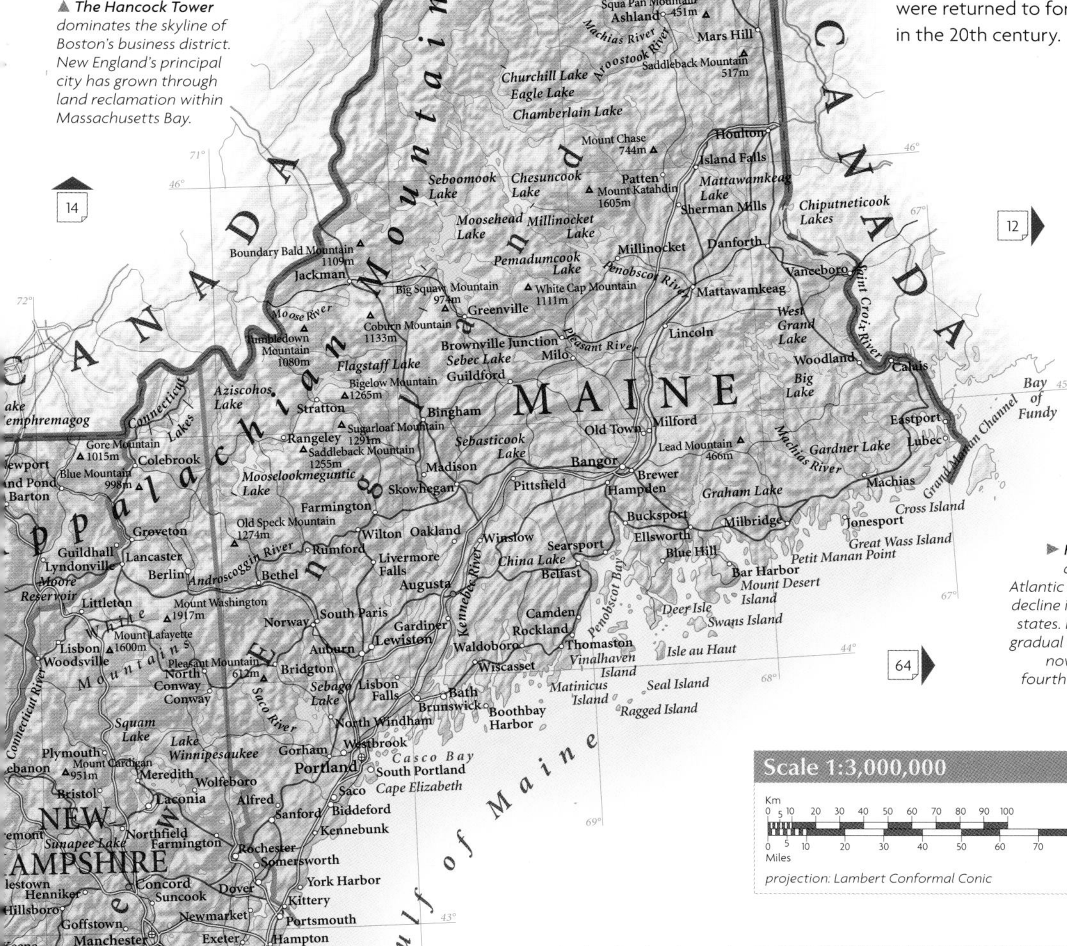

CANADA
MAINE
NEW HAMPSHIRE
MASSACHUSETTS
RHODE ISLAND
Appalachian Mountains
Longfellow Mountains
White Mountains
New England
Gulf of Maine
Bay of Fundy
Grand Manan Channel
Saint John River
Madawaska
Fort Kent
Van Buren
Caribou
Presque Isle
Fort Fairfield
Houlton
Millinocket
Mount Katahdin 1605m
Moosehead Lake
Bangor
Augusta
Portland
Lewiston
Casco Bay
Cape Elizabeth
Biddeford
Portsmouth
Manchester
Concord
Nashua
Lowell
Lawrence
Salem
Boston
Massachusetts Bay
Cape Cod Bay
Cape Cod
Provincetown
Plymouth
Worcester
Providence
Fall River
New Bedford
Buzzards Bay
Nantucket Sound
Martha's Vineyard
Nantucket Island
Block Island
Montauk Point
Mount Washington 1917m
Lake Winnipesaukee
Sebago Lake
Mount Desert Island
Penobscot Bay

14

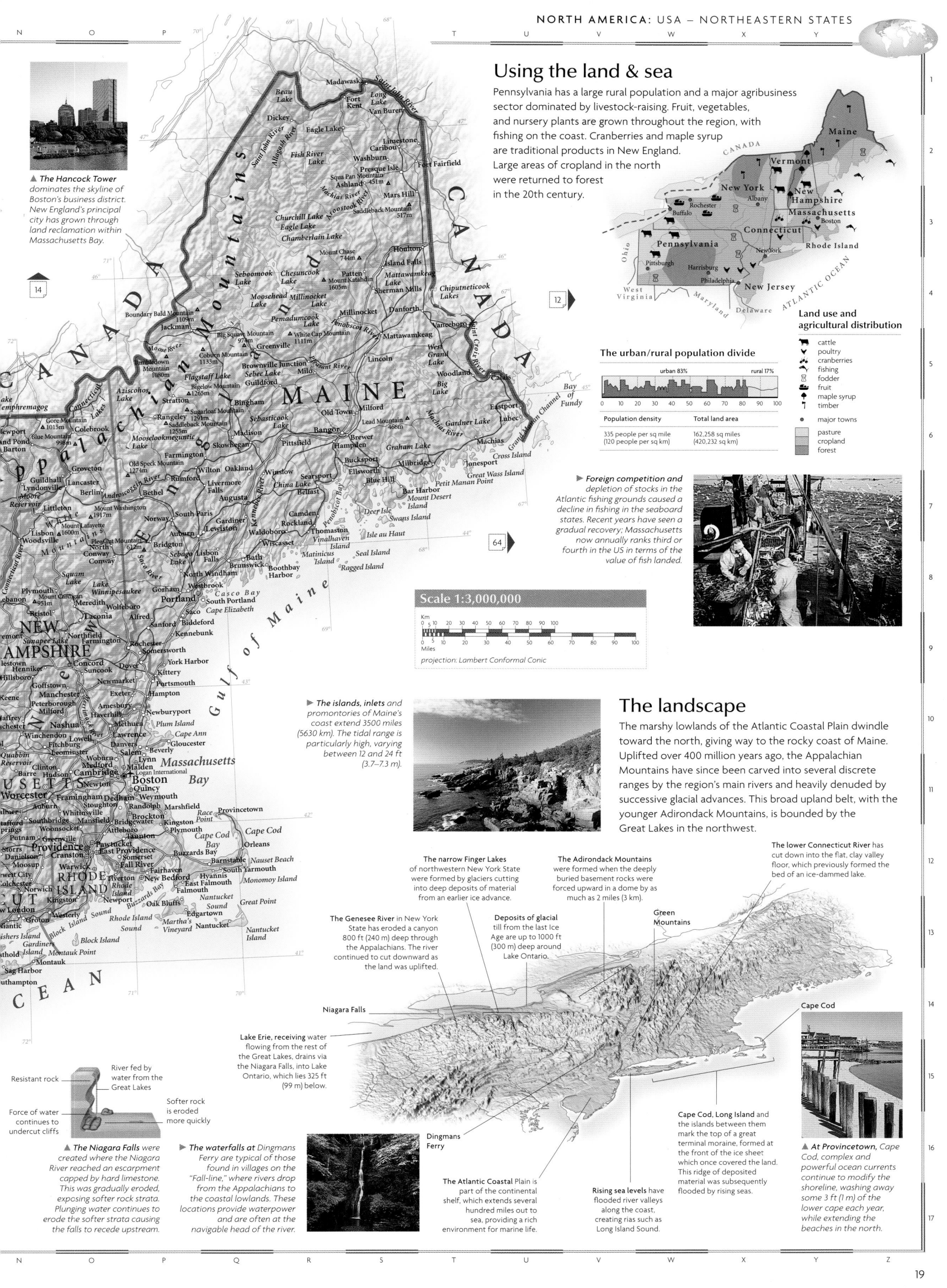

▲ *The Hancock Tower dominates the skyline of Boston's business district. New England's principal city has grown through land reclamation within Massachusetts Bay.*

12

64

Scale 1:3,000,000

Km 0 5 10 20 30 40 50 60 70 80 90 100

Miles 0 5 10 20 30 40 50 60 70 80 90 100

projection: Lambert Conformal Conic

Using the land & sea

Pennsylvania has a large rural population and a major agribusiness sector dominated by livestock-raising. Fruit, vegetables, and nursery plants are grown throughout the region, with fishing on the coast. Cranberries and maple syrup are traditional products in New England. Large areas of cropland in the north were returned to forest in the 20th century.

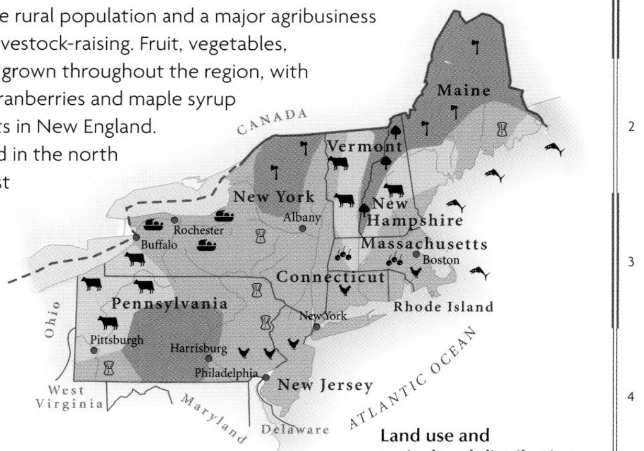

CANADA
Maine
Vermont
New York
New Hampshire
Massachusetts
Connecticut
Rhode Island
Pennsylvania
New Jersey
Delaware
Maryland
West Virginia
Ohio
ATLANTIC OCEAN
Albany
Rochester
Buffalo
Boston
New York
Pittsburgh
Harrisburg
Philadelphia

Land use and agricultural distribution

- cattle
- poultry
- cranberries
- fishing
- fodder
- fruit
- maple syrup
- timber
- major towns
- pasture
- cropland
- forest

The urban/rural population divide

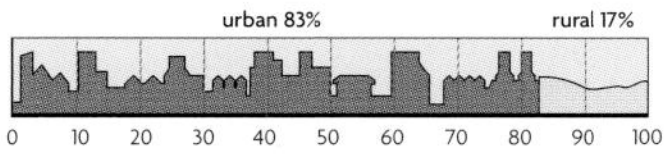

urban 83%
rural 17%
0 10 20 30 40 50 60 70 80 90 100

Population density	Total land area
335 people per sq mile (120 people per sq km)	162,258 sq miles (420,232 sq km)

▶ *Foreign competition and depletion of stocks in the Atlantic fishing grounds caused a decline in fishing in the seaboard states. Recent years have seen a gradual recovery; Massachusetts now annually ranks third or fourth in the US in terms of the value of fish landed.*

▶ *The islands, inlets and promontories of Maine's coast extend 3500 miles (5630 km). The tidal range is particularly high, varying between 12 and 24 ft (3.7–7.3 m).*

The landscape

The marshy lowlands of the Atlantic Coastal Plain dwindle toward the north, giving way to the rocky coast of Maine. Uplifted over 400 million years ago, the Appalachian Mountains have since been carved into several discrete ranges by the region's main rivers and heavily denuded by successive glacial advances. This broad upland belt, with the younger Adirondack Mountains, is bounded by the Great Lakes in the northwest.

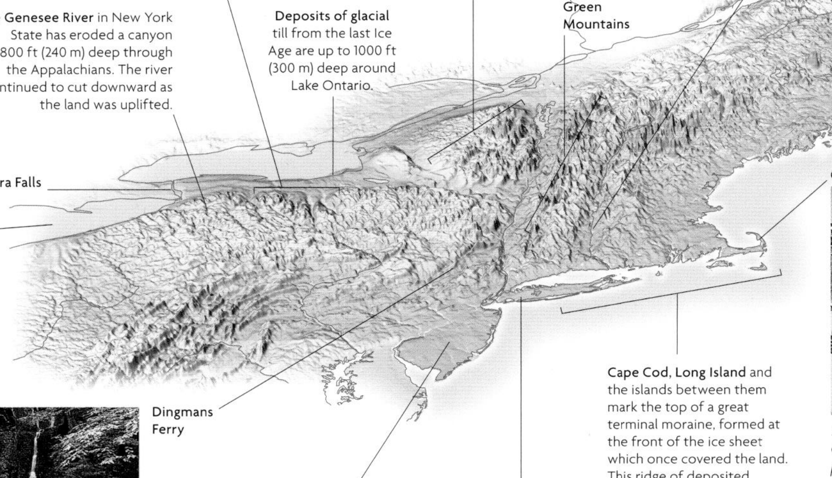

The narrow Finger Lakes of northwestern New York State were formed by glaciers cutting into deep deposits of material from an earlier ice advance.
The Adirondack Mountains were formed when the deeply buried basement rocks were forced upward in a dome by as much as 2 miles (3 km).
The lower Connecticut River has cut down into the flat, clay valley floor, which previously formed the bed of an ice-dammed lake.
The Genesee River in New York State has eroded a canyon 800 ft (240 m) deep through the Appalachians. The river continued to cut downward as the land was uplifted.
Deposits of glacial till from the last Ice Age are up to 1000 ft (300 m) deep around Lake Ontario.
Green Mountains
Niagara Falls
Cape Cod
Lake Erie, receiving water flowing from the rest of the Great Lakes, drains via the Niagara Falls, into Lake Ontario, which lies 325 ft (99 m) below.
Dingmans Ferry
Cape Cod, Long Island and the islands between them mark the top of a great terminal moraine, formed at the front of the ice sheet which once covered the land. This ridge of deposited material was subsequently flooded by rising seas.
The Atlantic Coastal Plain is part of the continental shelf, which extends several hundred miles out to sea, providing a rich environment for marine life.
Rising sea levels have flooded river valleys along the coast, creating rias such as Long Island Sound.

▲ *At Provincetown, Cape Cod, complex and powerful ocean currents continue to modify the shoreline, washing away some 3 ft (1 m) of the lower cape each year, while extending the beaches in the north.*

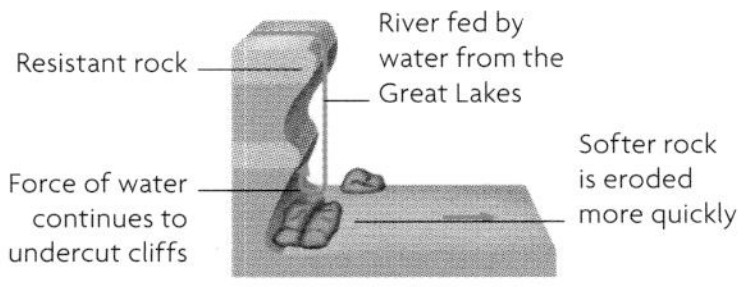

Resistant rock
River fed by water from the Great Lakes
Softer rock is eroded more quickly
Force of water continues to undercut cliffs

▲ *The Niagara Falls were created where the Niagara River reached an escarpment capped by hard limestone. This was gradually eroded, exposing softer rock strata. Plunging water continues to erode the softer strata causing the falls to recede upstream.*

▶ *The waterfalls at Dingmans Ferry are typical of those found in villages on the "Fall-line," where rivers drop from the Appalachians to the coastal lowlands. These locations provide waterpower and are often at the navigable head of the river.*

USA: MID-EASTERN STATES

Delaware, District of Columbia, Kentucky, Maryland, North Carolina, South Carolina, Tennessee, Virginia, West Virginia

Key events in American history took place in this diverse region, which became the front line between the North and the South during the Civil War of the 1860s. Strong regional contrasts exist between the fertile coastal plains, the isolated upcountry of the Appalachian Mountains, and the cotton-growing areas of the Mississippi lowlands to the west. While coal mining, a traditional industry in the Appalachians, has declined in recent years leaving much rural poverty, service industries elsewhere have increased, especially in Washington DC, the nation's capital.

Map key

Population

- 500,000 to 1 million
- 100,000 to 500,000
- 50,000 to 100,000
- 10,000 to 50,000
- below 10,000

Elevation

- 6000m / 19,686ft
- 4000m / 13,124ft
- 3000m / 9843ft
- 2000m / 6562ft
- 1000m / 3281ft
- 500m / 1640ft
- 250m / 820ft
- 100m / 328ft
- sea level

Scale 1:3,250,000

Km 0 5 10 20 30 40 50 60 70 80

Miles 0 5 10 20 30 40 50 60 70 80

projection: Lambert Conformal Conic

▲ *The Bluegrass region of Kentucky centers on the town of Lexington. This exceptionally fertile rolling plain is well known for its thoroughbred horse-breeding ranches.*

Transportation & industry

In the urbanized northeast, manufacturing remains important, alongside a burgeoning service sector. North Carolina is a major center for industrial research and development. Traditional industries include Tennessee whiskey and textiles in South Carolina. The decline of open-pit coal mining in the Appalachians has been hastened by environmental controls, although adventure-tourism is a flourishing new industry.

Major industry and infrastructure

- adventure-tourism
- car manufacture
- coal
- electronics
- engineering
- finance
- food processing
- hi-tech industry
- mining
- research & development
- textiles
- capital cities
- major towns
- international airports
- major roads
- major industrial areas

Pennsylvania
Ohio
Indiana
Illinois
Missouri
Arkansas
Mississippi
Alabama
Georgia
Maryland
Baltimore
WASHINGTON DC
Delaware
Charleston
W.Virginia
Virginia
Richmond
Louisville
Kentucky
Nashville
Memphis
Tennessee
North Carolina
Raleigh
South Carolina
Columbia
ATLANTIC OCEAN

Transportation network

452,218 miles (723,548 km)	5737 miles (8267 km)
18,336 miles (29,503 km)	4404 miles (7081 km)

Tennessee's rivers are part of an important inland bulk transportation network. Memphis connects with New Orleans in the south, and with cities as distant as Minneapolis, Sioux City, Chicago, and Pittsburgh, via the Mississippi and its tributaries.

INDIANA
ILLINOIS
MISSOURI
ARKANSAS
KENTUCKY
TENNESSEE
MISSISSIPPI
ALABAMA
Louisville
Frankfort
Lexington
Covington
Owensboro
Henderson
Paducah
Bowling Green
Clarksville
Nashville
Murfreesboro
Jackson
Memphis
Chattanooga
Cleveland
Ohio River
Mississippi River
Tennessee River
Cumberland River
Kentucky Lake
Lake Barkley

30
26
26
22

The landscape

The eastern tributaries of the Mississippi drain the interior lowlands. The Cumberland Plateau and the parallel ranges of the Appalachians have been successively uplifted and eroded over time, with the eastern side reduced to a series of foothills known as the Piedmont. The broad coastal plain gradually falls away into salt marshes, lagoons, and offshore bars, broken by flooded estuaries along the shores of the Atlantic.

◀ *Farmland on the eastern shores of Chesapeake Bay is sustained by artificial drainage. The area also provides refuge for a variety of waterfowl.*

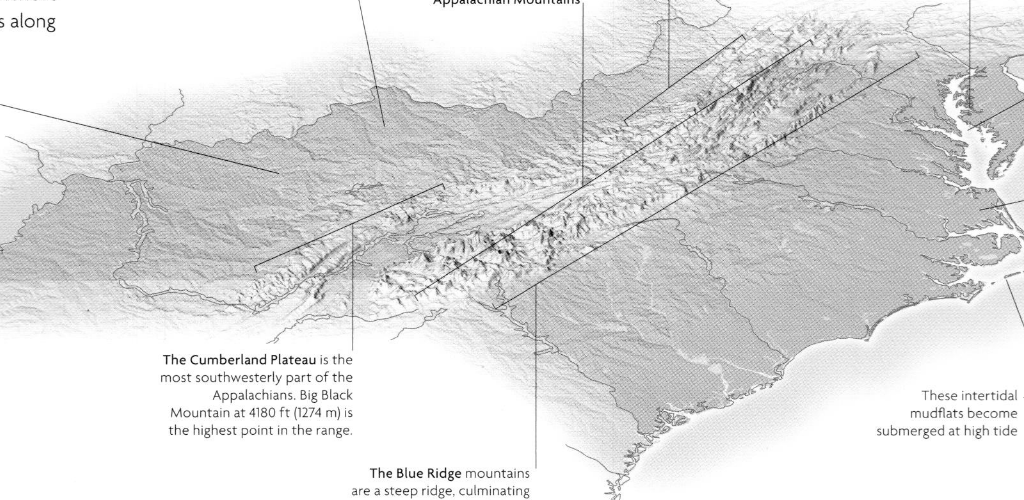

Natural Bridge in eastern Kentucky is an arch 78 ft (26 m) long and 65 ft (20 m) high. It has been shaped from resistant sandstone by gradual weathering processes, which removed the softer rock lying underneath.

The Allegheny Mountains form the northwestern edge of the Appalachian mountain chain. Continuous folding has formed rich seams of bituminous coal.

Appalachian Mountains

The Mammoth Cave is part of an extensive cave system in the limestone region of southwestern Kentucky. It stretches for over 300 miles (485 km) on five different levels and contains three rivers and three lakes.

The Mississippi River and its tributary the Ohio River form the western border of the region.

The Cumberland Plateau is the most southwesterly part of the Appalachians. Big Black Mountain at 4180 ft (1274 m) is the highest point in the range.

The Blue Ridge mountains are a steep ridge, culminating in Mount Mitchell, the highest point in the Appalachians, at 6684 ft (2037 m).

The many inlets of Chesapeake Bay are the flooded tributaries of the main river valley, which have been inundated by rising sea levels.

Salt marshes such as Great Dismal Swamp, develop where the coast is sheltered. Vast areas of such marshland have been reclaimed for farmland and settlement.

Cape Hatteras is the easternmost point of an offshore barrier island, a wave-deposited sand-bar which has become permanent, establishing its own vegetation.

◀ *The Great Smoky Mountains form the western escarpment of the Appalachians. The region is heavily forested, with over 130 species of tree.*

Barrier islands

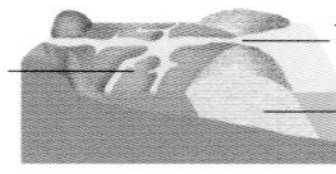

Tidal inlet
Barrier island
These intertidal mudflats become submerged at high tide

▲ *Barrier islands are common along the coasts of North and South Carolina. As sea levels rise, wave action builds up ridges of sand and pebbles parallel to the coast, separated by lagoons or intertidal mud flats, which are flooded at high tide.*

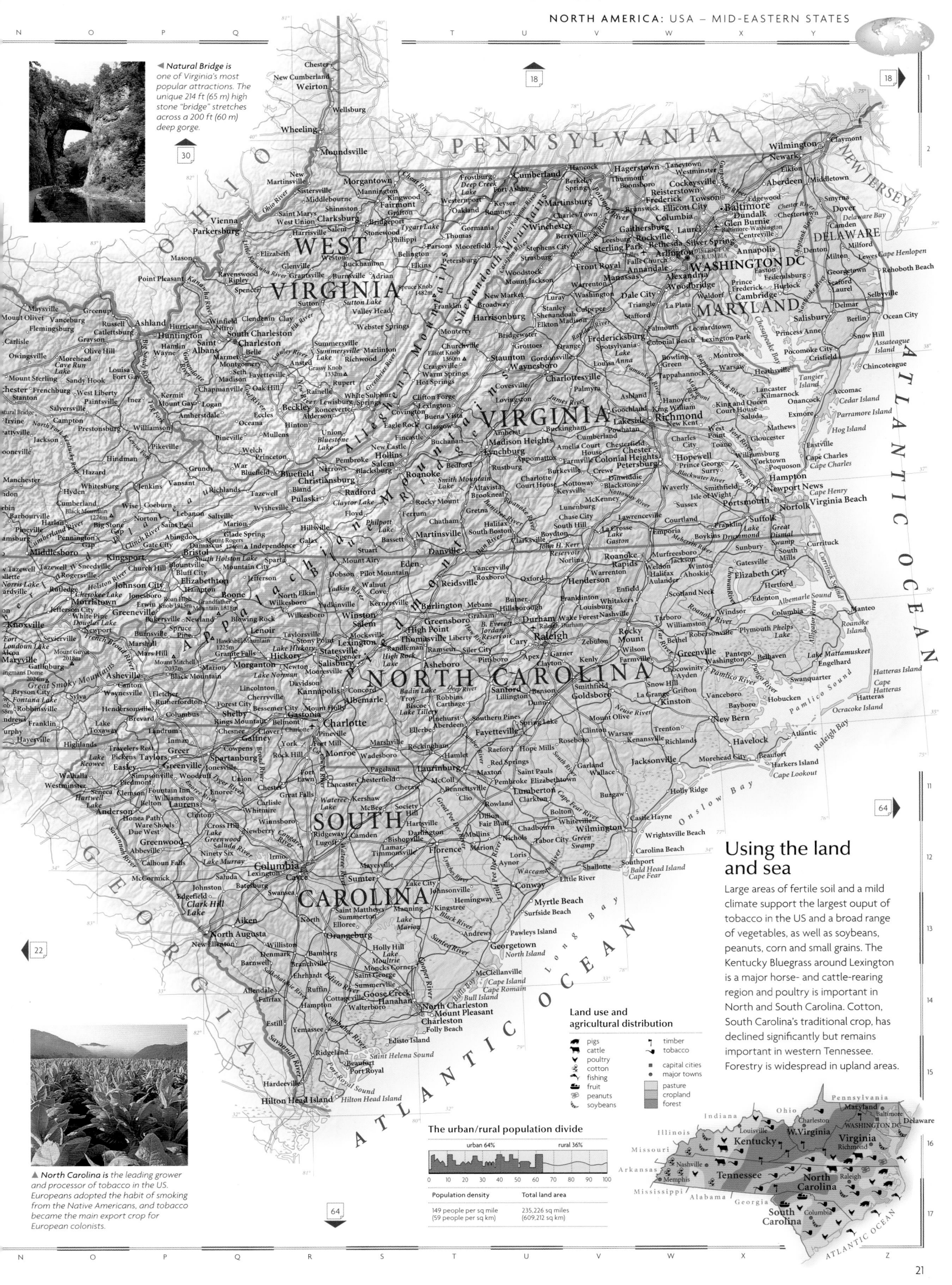

◀ **Natural Bridge** *is one of Virginia's most popular attractions. The unique 214 ft (65 m) high stone "bridge" stretches across a 200 ft (60 m) deep gorge.*

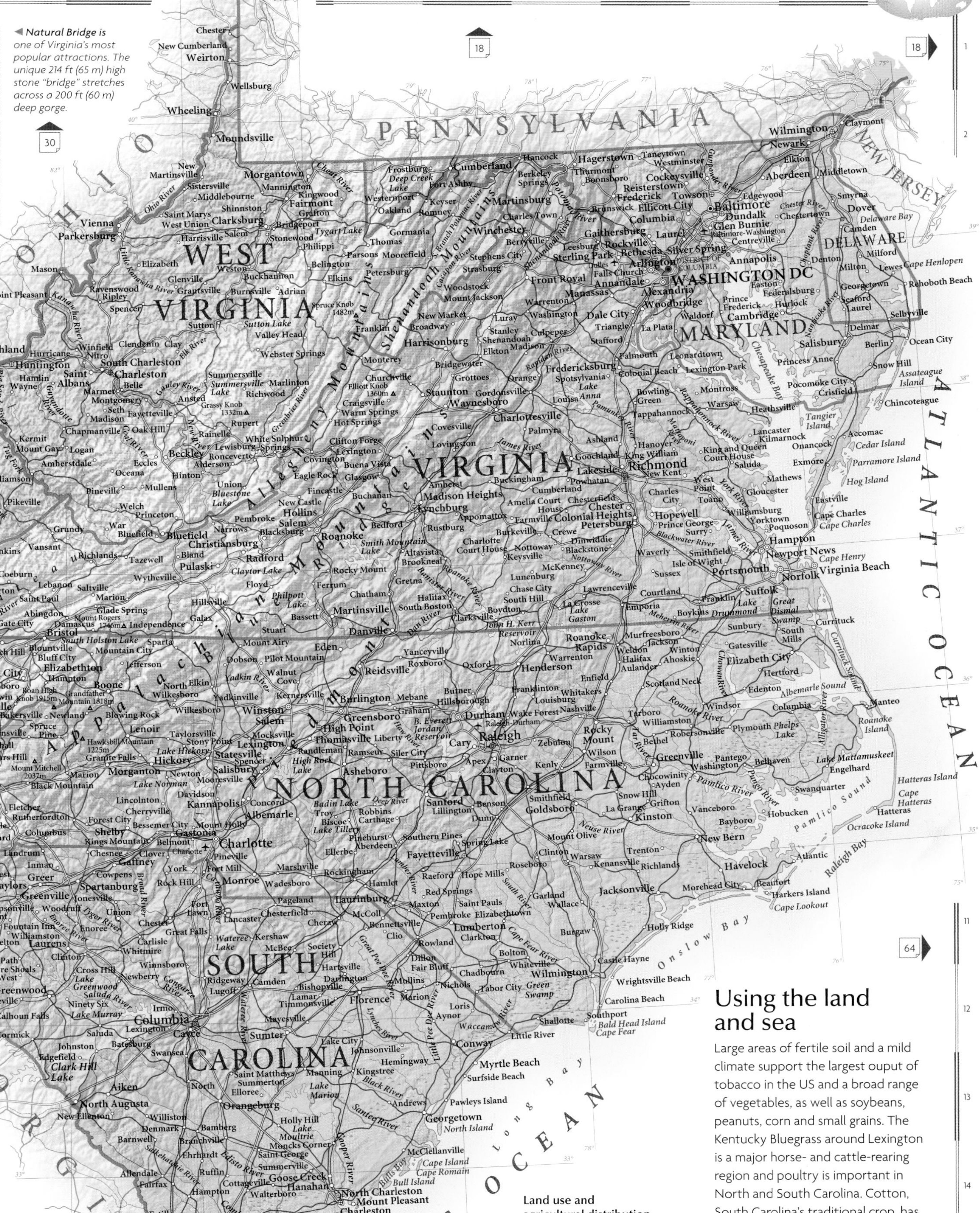

PENNSYLVANIA
OHIO
WEST VIRGINIA
VIRGINIA
MARYLAND
DELAWARE
NEW JERSEY
WASHINGTON DC
NORTH CAROLINA
SOUTH CAROLINA
GEORGIA
ATLANTIC OCEAN
Appalachian Mountains
Allegheny Mountains
Blue Ridge Mountains
Shenandoah Mountains
Great Smoky Mountains
Piedmont
Chesapeake Bay
Pamlico Sound
Albemarle Sound
Onslow Bay
Long Bay
Raleigh Bay
Richmond
Raleigh
Columbia
Baltimore
Charlotte
Norfolk
Virginia Beach
Charleston
Wilmington
Greensboro
Durham
Roanoke
Lynchburg
Knoxville
Asheville
Myrtle Beach
Hilton Head Island

18
30
22
64

Using the land and sea

Large areas of fertile soil and a mild climate support the largest ouput of tobacco in the US and a broad range of vegetables, as well as soybeans, peanuts, corn and small grains. The Kentucky Bluegrass around Lexington is a major horse- and cattle-rearing region and poultry is important in North and South Carolina. Cotton, South Carolina's traditional crop, has declined significantly but remains important in western Tennessee. Forestry is widespread in upland areas.

Land use and agricultural distribution

- pigs
- cattle
- poultry
- cotton
- fishing
- fruit
- peanuts
- soybeans
- timber
- tobacco
- capital cities
- major towns
- pasture
- cropland
- forest

Pennsylvania
Ohio
Indiana
Illinois
Missouri
Arkansas
Mississippi
Alabama
Georgia
Kentucky
W.Virginia
Virginia
Maryland
Delaware
Tennessee
North Carolina
South Carolina
Charleston
Louisville
Nashville
Memphis
Richmond
Raleigh
Columbia
Baltimore
WASHINGTON DC
ATLANTIC OCEAN

The urban/rural population divide

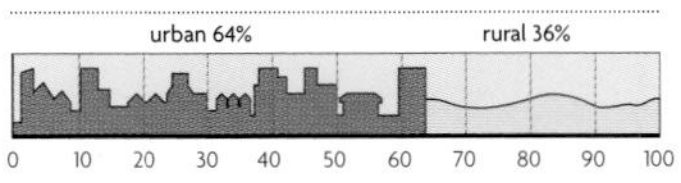

urban 64%
rural 36%
0
10
20
30
40
50
60
70
80
90
100

Population density	Total land area
149 people per sq mile (59 people per sq km)	235,226 sq miles (609,212 sq km)

▲ **North Carolina** *is the leading grower and processor of tobacco in the US. Europeans adopted the habit of smoking from the Native Americans, and tobacco became the main export crop for European colonists.*

USA: SOUTHERN STATES

Alabama, Florida, Georgia, Louisiana, Mississippi

The South has maintained a separate identity and outlook throughout the history of the US. Defeat in the Civil War (1861–65) brought chronic poverty to the former confederate states, while the subsequent liberation of four million slaves began a struggle not resolved until the 1960s, when the Civil Rights movement achieved an end to legal racial segregation. Many parts of the South have experienced rapid change. Tourism and retirement communities, together with agriculture, have fueled growth in Florida, while defense-related industries have boosted the growth of cities such as Miami and Atlanta. Many people retain a strong attachment to their history and culture, evidenced by Creole-speaking Cajuns in Louisiana and Hispanic communities in South Florida.

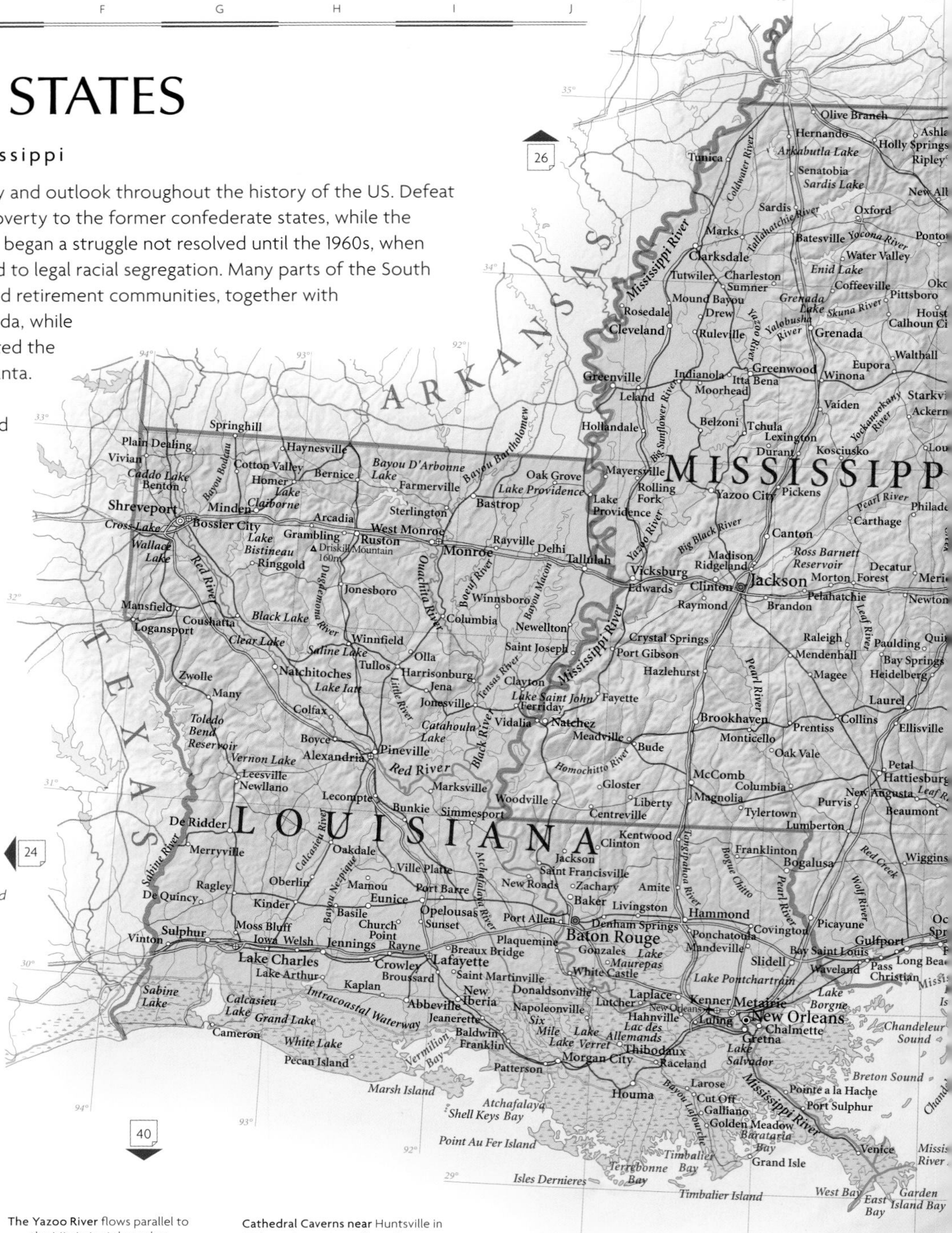

ARKANSAS
MISSISSIPPI
LOUISIANA
TEXAS
Shreveport
Monroe
Jackson
Baton Rouge
New Orleans
Lafayette
Lake Charles
Alexandria
Vicksburg
Lake Pontchartrain
Mississippi River
Red River
Gulfport
Houma

26
24
40

Transportation & industry

Florida's tourist trade is only part of a flourishing service sector, which has swelled the principal cities of the south. Petroleum and mineral extraction has made the Gulf Coast a major industrial region. Traditional textile production remains important in Georgia, while advanced new industries have grown from the NASA Space Program.

Transportation network

- 441,625 miles (706,600 km)
- 5116 miles (8186 km)
- 16,597 miles (26,555 km)
- 6179 miles (9942 km)

Atlanta's Hartsfield International airport is one of the busiest in the world. A dramatic rise in the use of regional air transportation has helped to integrate the major cities of the southern states.

◀ ***The French Quarter** is the traditional cultural center of New Orleans. The city, extensively damaged by Hurricane Katrina in 2005, once thrived on the cotton trade but now relies mainly on tourism and on oil from the Gulf of Mexico.*

Tennessee
N. Carolina
South Carolina
Arkansas
Mississippi
Alabama
Georgia
Louisiana
Florida
Texas
Huntsville
Birmingham
Atlanta
Savannah
Montgomery
Jackson
Baton Rouge
New Orleans
Mobile
Tallahassee
Jacksonville
Daytona Beach
Orlando
Tampa
Melbourne
Miami
Key West
Gulf of Mexico
ATLANTIC OCEAN

Major industry and infrastructure

- aerospace
- car manufacture
- chemicals
- coal
- defense
- electronics
- engineering
- food processing
- oil
- textiles
- tourism
- major towns
- international airports
- major roads
- major industrial areas

▲ ***The cypress swamps** of the Mississippi Delta form in the backswamps behind the levées of the river and in the multitude of subsiding delta basins.*

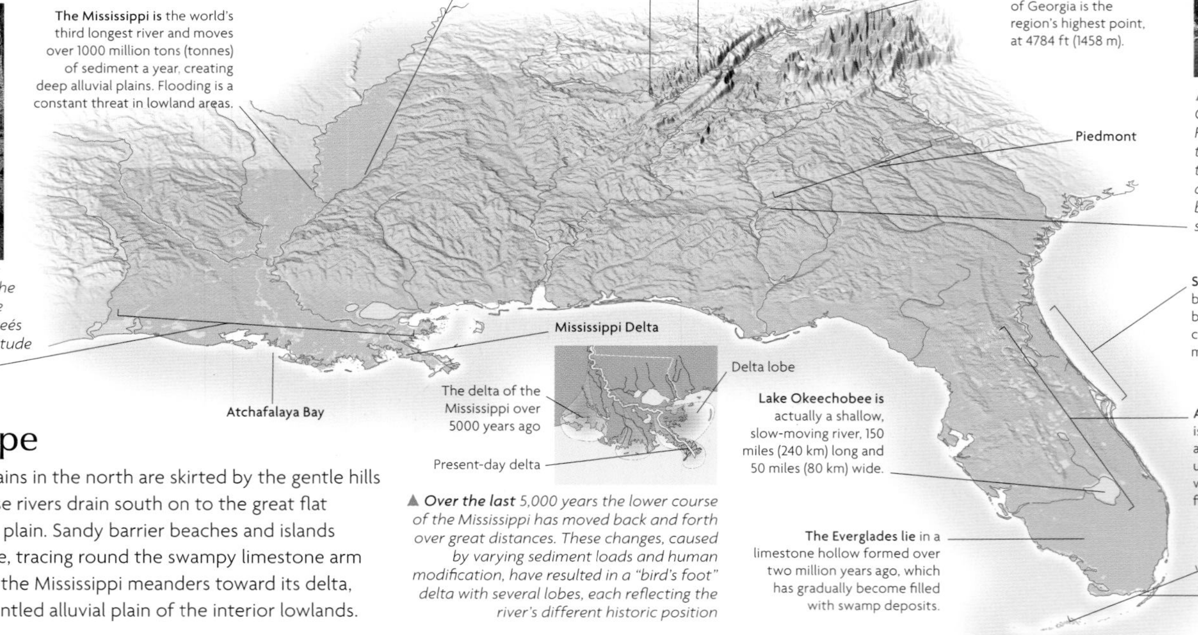

Mississippi Delta
Atchafalaya Bay
Piedmont
Delta lobe
Present-day delta
Florida Keys

The Yazoo River flows parallel to the Mississippi through a common floodplain. The confluence of the rivers is deferred downstream because flood deposition has built the Mississippi channel up above the level of the Yazoo.

Cathedral Caverns near Huntsville in Alabama is a system of vast limestone caves, with a main opening 1000 ft (300 m) high and 150 ft (50 m) wide.

At De Soto Falls, Alabama, the Little River descends into the deepest canyon east of the Mississippi, with sheer cliff walls up to 700 ft (230 m) high.

Brasstown Bald in the Blue Ridge mountains of Georgia is the region's highest point, at 4784 ft (1458 m).

The Mississippi is the world's third longest river and moves over 1000 million tons (tonnes) of sediment a year, creating deep alluvial plains. Flooding is a constant threat in lowland areas.

The delta of the Mississippi over 5000 years ago

▲ ***Over the last** 5,000 years the lower course of the Mississippi has moved back and forth over great distances. These changes, caused by varying sediment loads and human modification, have resulted in a "bird's foot" delta with several lobes, each reflecting the river's different historic position*

Lake Okeechobee is actually a shallow, slow-moving river, 150 miles (240 km) long and 50 miles (80 km) wide.

The Everglades lie in a limestone hollow formed over two million years ago, which has gradually become filled with swamp deposits.

▲ ***In Providence Canyon,** Georgia, the Chattahoochee River has cut straight down through the sandy bedrock, to leave sheer rock faces and pinnacles, which have been smoothed by subsequent weathering.*

Sandbars, deposited by waves breaking offshore, form barrier beaches along much of the coastline, creating sheltered lagoons and salt marshes behind them.

Across Florida the coastal plain is mostly less than 75 ft (25 m) above sea level. The land is underlain by limestone, pitted with hollows which have been filled by over 10,000 lakes.

The landscape

The Blue Ridge mountains in the north are skirted by the gentle hills of the Piedmont, whose rivers drain south on to the great flat expanse of the coastal plain. Sandy barrier beaches and islands dominate the sea shore, tracing round the swampy limestone arm of Florida. In the west, the Mississippi meanders toward its delta, crossing the thickly mantled alluvial plain of the interior lowlands.

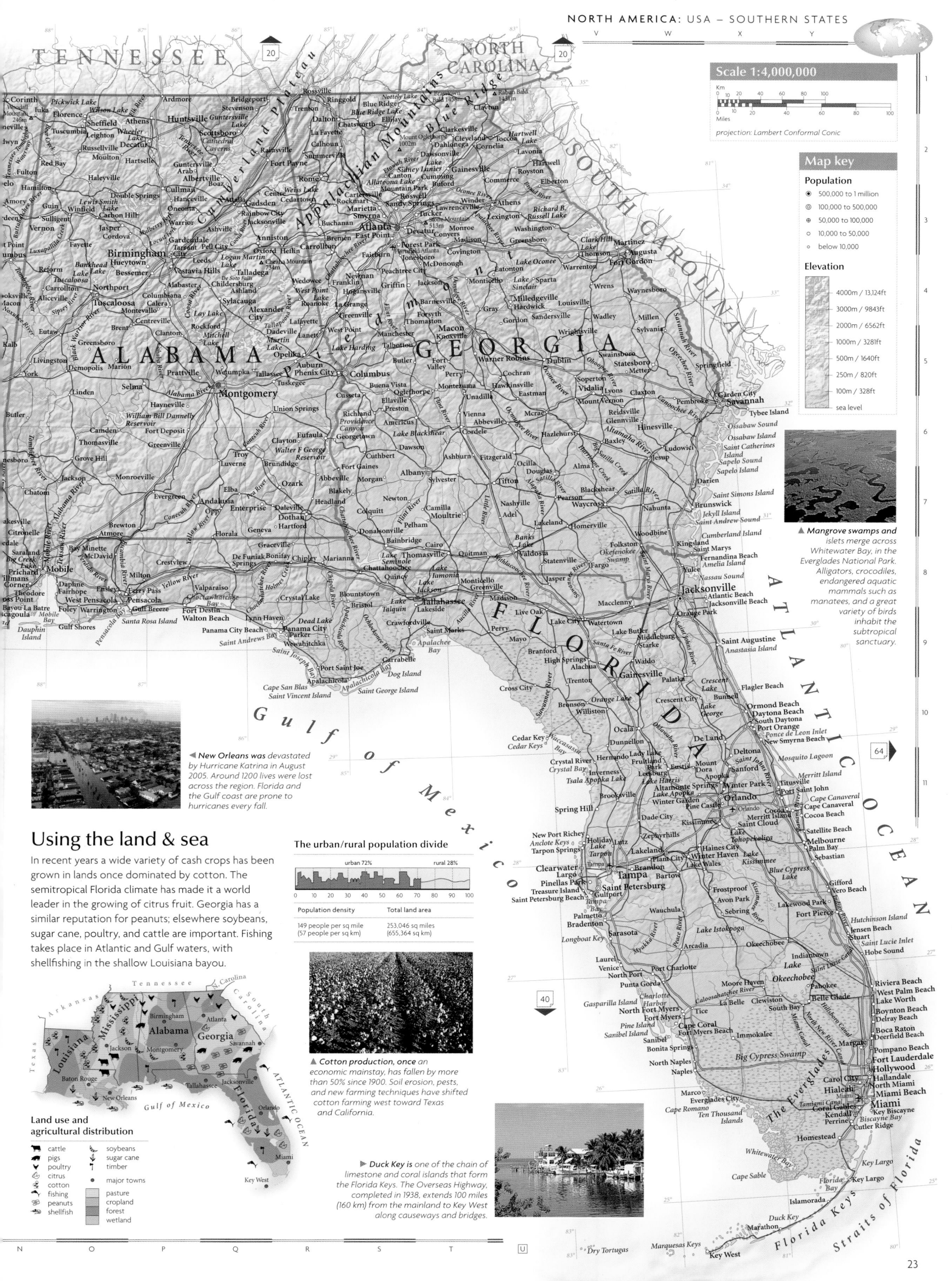

TENNESSEE
NORTH CAROLINA
SOUTH CAROLINA
ALABAMA
GEORGIA
FLORIDA
Cumberland Plateau
Appalachian Mountains
Blue Ridge
Piedmont
Gulf of Mexico
ATLANTIC OCEAN
Straits of Florida
Florida Keys
The Everglades
Birmingham
Montgomery
Atlanta
Tallahassee
Jacksonville
Orlando
Tampa
Saint Petersburg
Miami
Savannah
Augusta
Columbus
Macon
Mobile
Pensacola
Huntsville
Gainesville
Key West
Lake Okeechobee
Big Cypress Swamp
Okefenokee Swamp

Scale 1:4,000,000

projection: Lambert Conformal Conic

Map key

Population

- 500,000 to 1 million
- 100,000 to 500,000
- 50,000 to 100,000
- 10,000 to 50,000
- below 10,000

Elevation

- 4000m / 13,124ft
- 3000m / 9843ft
- 2000m / 6562ft
- 1000m / 3281ft
- 500m / 1640ft
- 250m / 820ft
- 100m / 328ft
- sea level

▲ *Mangrove swamps and islets merge across Whitewater Bay, in the Everglades National Park. Alligators, crocodiles, endangered aquatic mammals such as manatees, and a great variety of birds inhabit the subtropical sanctuary.*

◀ *New Orleans was devastated by Hurricane Katrina in August 2005. Around 1200 lives were lost across the region. Florida and the Gulf coast are prone to hurricanes every fall.*

Using the land & sea

In recent years a wide variety of cash crops has been grown in lands once dominated by cotton. The semitropical Florida climate has made it a world leader in the growing of citrus fruit. Georgia has a similar reputation for peanuts; elsewhere soybeans, sugar cane, poultry, and cattle are important. Fishing takes place in Atlantic and Gulf waters, with shellfishing in the shallow Louisiana bayou.

The urban/rural population divide

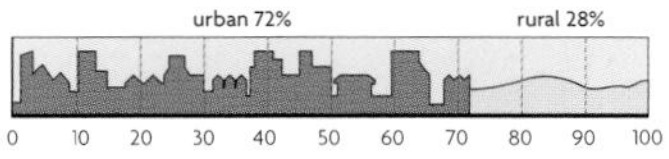
urban 72%
rural 28%
0
10
20
30
40
50
60
70
80
90
100

Population density	Total land area
149 people per sq mile (57 people per sq km)	253,046 sq miles (655,364 sq km)

▲ *Cotton production, once an economic mainstay, has fallen by more than 50% since 1900. Soil erosion, pests, and new farming techniques have shifted cotton farming west toward Texas and California.*

Tennessee
N. Carolina
South Carolina
Arkansas
Texas
Louisiana
Mississippi
Alabama
Georgia
Florida
Birmingham
Atlanta
Jackson
Montgomery
Savannah
Baton Rouge
New Orleans
Tallahassee
Jacksonville
Orlando
Miami
Key West
Gulf of Mexico
ATLANTIC OCEAN

Land use and agricultural distribution

- cattle
- pigs
- poultry
- citrus
- cotton
- fishing
- peanuts
- shellfish
- soybeans
- sugar cane
- timber
- major towns
- pasture
- cropland
- forest
- wetland

▶ *Duck Key is one of the chain of limestone and coral islands that form the Florida Keys. The Overseas Highway, completed in 1938, extends 100 miles (160 km) from the mainland to Key West along causeways and bridges.*

USA: Texas

First explored by Spaniards moving north from Mexico in search of gold, Texas was controlled by Spain and then by Mexico, before becoming an independent republic in 1836, and joining the Union of States in 1845. During the 19th century, many migrants who came to Texas raised cattle on the abundant land; in the 20th century, they were joined by prospectors attracted by the promise of oil riches. Today, although natural resources, especially oil, still form the basis of its wealth, the diversified Texan economy includes thriving hi-tech and financial industries. The major urban centers, home to 80% of the population, lie in the south and east, and include Houston, the "oil-city," and Dallas–Fort Worth. Hispanic influences remain strong, especially in southern and western Texas.

▲ ***Dallas was founded** in 1841 as a prairie trading post and its development was stimulated by the arrival of railroads. Cotton and then oil funded the town's early growth. Today, the modern, high rise skyline of Dallas reflects the city's position as a leading center of banking, insurance, and the petroleum industry in the southwest.*

Using the land

Cotton production and livestock-raising, particularly cattle, dominate farming, although crop failures and the demands of local markets have led to some diversification. Following the introduction of modern farming techniques, cotton production spread out from the east to the plains of western Texas. Cattle ranches are widespread, while sheep and goats are raised on the dry Edwards Plateau.

▲ ***The huge cattle** ranches of Texas developed during the 19th century when land was plentiful and could be acquired cheaply. Today, more cattle and sheep are raised in Texas than in any other state.*

Land use and agricultural distribution

- cattle
- goats
- sheep
- cereals
- cotton
- major towns
- pasture
- cropland
- forest
- barren

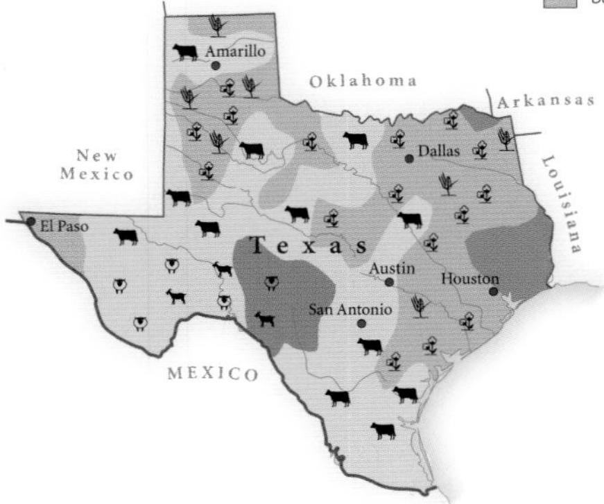

Amarillo
Oklahoma
Arkansas
New Mexico
Dallas
Louisiana
El Paso
Texas
Austin
Houston
San Antonio
MEXICO

The urban/rural population divide

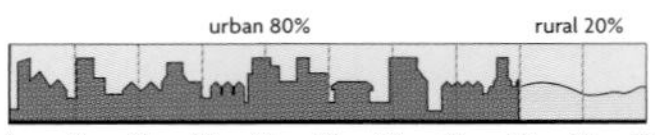

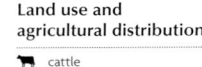

urban 80%
rural 20%
0 10 20 30 40 50 60 70 80 90 100

Population density	Total land area
84 people per sq mile (33 people per sq km)	261,797 sq miles (678,028 sq km)

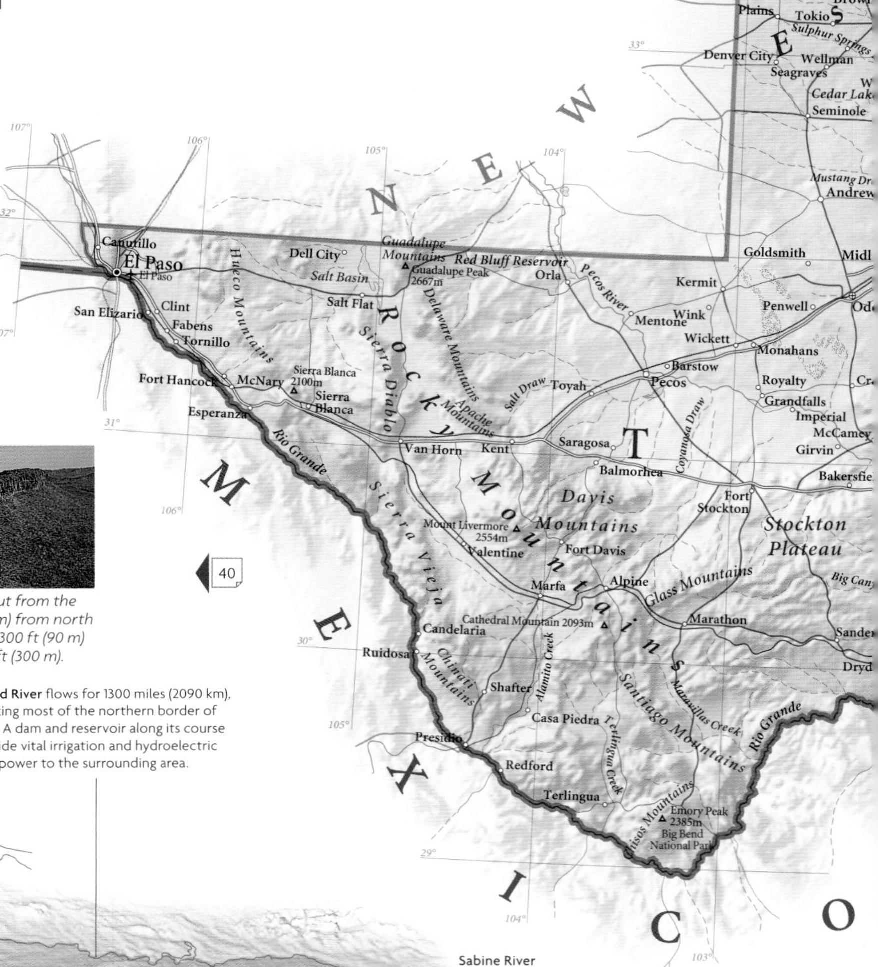

Texline
Dalhart
Hartley
Channing
Canadian River
Adrian
Wildorado
Hereford
Friona
Bovina
Dimmitt
Farwell
Running Water Draw
Springlake
Muleshoe
Earth
Sudan
Amherst
Enochs
Littlefield
Morton
Whiteface
Levelland
Ropes
Sundown
Meadow
Brownfield
Sulphur Draw
Plains
Tokio
Sulphur Springs
Denver City
Wellman
Seagraves
Cedar Lake
Seminole
Mustang Draw
Andrews
NEW MEXICO
MEXICO
Canutillo
El Paso
San Elizario
Clint
Fabens
Tornillo
Fort Hancock
McNary
Esperanza
Rio Grande
Hueco Mountains
Dell City
Salt Basin
Salt Flat
Guadalupe Mountains
Guadalupe Peak 2667m
Red Bluff Reservoir
Orla
Pecos River
Sierra Diablo
Delaware Mountains
Apache Mountains
Sierra Blanca 2100m
Sierra Blanca
Van Horn
Kent
Toyah
Salt Draw
Mentone
Wink
Kermit
Wickett
Pecos
Barstow
Goldsmith
Penwell
Monahans
Royalty
Grandfalls
Imperial
McCamey
Girvin
Saragosa
Balmorhea
Coyanosa Draw
Fort Stockton
Bakersfield
Stockton Plateau
Davis Mountains
Mount Livermore 2554m
Valentine
Fort Davis
Sierra Vieja
Marfa
Alpine
Glass Mountains
Marathon
Candelaria
Cathedral Mountain 2093m
Ruidosa
Chinati Mountains
Alamito Creek
Shafter
Casa Piedra
Terlingua Creek
Santiago Mountains
Maravillas Creek
Presidio
Redford
Terlingua
Chisos Mountains
Emory Peak 2385m
Big Bend National Park
Rocky Mountains

36

40

The landscape

Texas is made up of a series of massive steps descending from the mountains and high plains of the west and northwest to the coastal lowlands in the southeast. Many of the state's borders are delineated by water. The Rio Grande flows from the Rocky Mountains to the Gulf of Mexico, marking the border with Mexico.

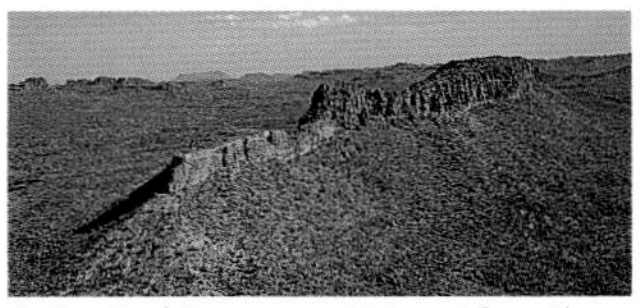

▲ ***Cap Rock Escarpment** juts out from the plains, running 200 miles (320 km) from north to south. Its height varies from 300 ft (90 m) rising to sheer cliffs up to 1000 ft (300 m).*

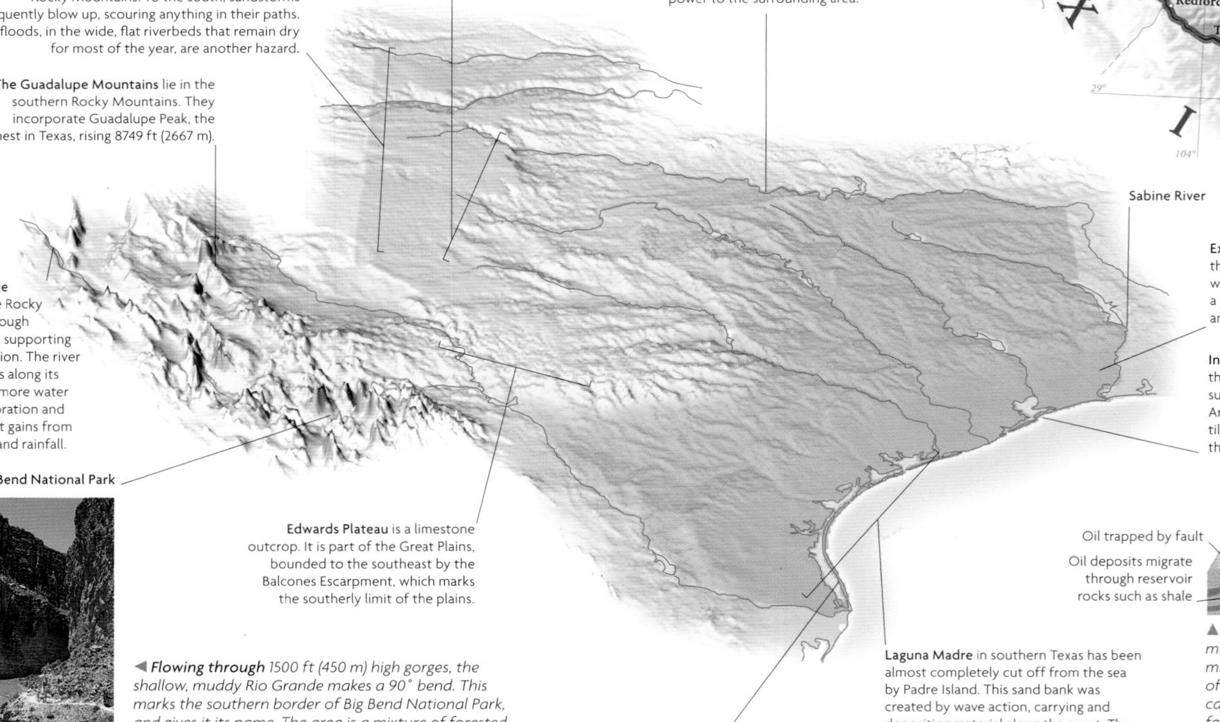

The Llano Estacado or Staked Plain in northern Texas is known for its harsh environment. In the north, freezing winds carrying ice and snow sweep down from the Rocky Mountains. To the south, sandstorms frequently blow up, scouring anything in their paths. Flash floods, in the wide, flat riverbeds that remain dry for most of the year, are another hazard.

The Red River flows for 1300 miles (2090 km), marking most of the northern border of Texas. A dam and reservoir along its course provide vital irrigation and hydroelectric power to the surrounding area.

The Guadalupe Mountains lie in the southern Rocky Mountains. They incorporate Guadalupe Peak, the highest in Texas, rising 8749 ft (2667 m).

Sabine River

Extensive forests of pine and cypress grow in the eastern corner of the coastal lowlands where the average rainfall is 45 inches (1145 mm) a year. This is higher than the rest of the state and over twice the average in the west.

The Rio Grande flows from the Rocky Mountains through semi-arid land, supporting sparse vegetation. The river actually shrinks along its course, losing more water through evaporation and seepage than it gains from its tributaries and rainfall.

In the coastal lowlands of southeastern Texas the Earth's crust is warping, causing the land to subside and allowing the sea to invade. Around Galveston, the rate of downward tilting is 6 inches (15 cm) per year. Erosion of the coast is also exacerbated by hurricanes.

Big Bend National Park

Edwards Plateau is a limestone outcrop. It is part of the Great Plains, bounded to the southeast by the Balcones Escarpment, which marks the southerly limit of the plains.

◀ ***Flowing through** 1500 ft (450 m) high gorges, the shallow, muddy Rio Grande makes a 90° bend. This marks the southern border of Big Bend National Park, and gives it its name. The area is a mixture of forested mountains, deserts, and canyons.*

Padre Island

Laguna Madre in southern Texas has been almost completely cut off from the sea by Padre Island. This sand bank was created by wave action, carrying and depositing material along the coast. The process is known as longshore drift.

Oil deposits

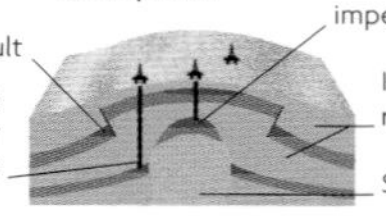

Oil trapped by fault
Oil deposits migrate through reservoir rocks such as shale
Oil accumulates beneath impermeable cap rock
Impermeable rock strata
Salt dome

▲ ***Oil deposits are** found beneath much of Texas. They collect as oil migrates upward through porous layers of rock until it is trapped, either by a cap of rock above a salt dome, or by a fault line which exposes impermeable rock through which the oil cannot rise.*

Transportation & industry

Industry in the 20th century was largely concentrated on the processing of local raw materials, especially oil – deposits were discovered under 65% of the state's area. The technological demands of the oil industry and defense-related institutions, particularly NASA, have stimulated the development of numerous electronics and hi-tech firms which, alongside many national corporate headquarters, are based in Dallas–Fort Worth and Houston.

Major industry and infrastructure

- chemicals
- defense
- engineering
- finance
- food processing
- gas
- hi-tech industry
- mining
- oil
- textiles
- major towns
- international airports
- major roads
- major industrial areas

Transportation network

293,509 miles (496,614 km)	3229 miles (5166 km)
10,681 miles (17,089 km)	845 miles (1359 km)

The sheer size of Texas promoted the development of an extensive road and rail network. The highway system, although well-developed, is concentrated in the east.

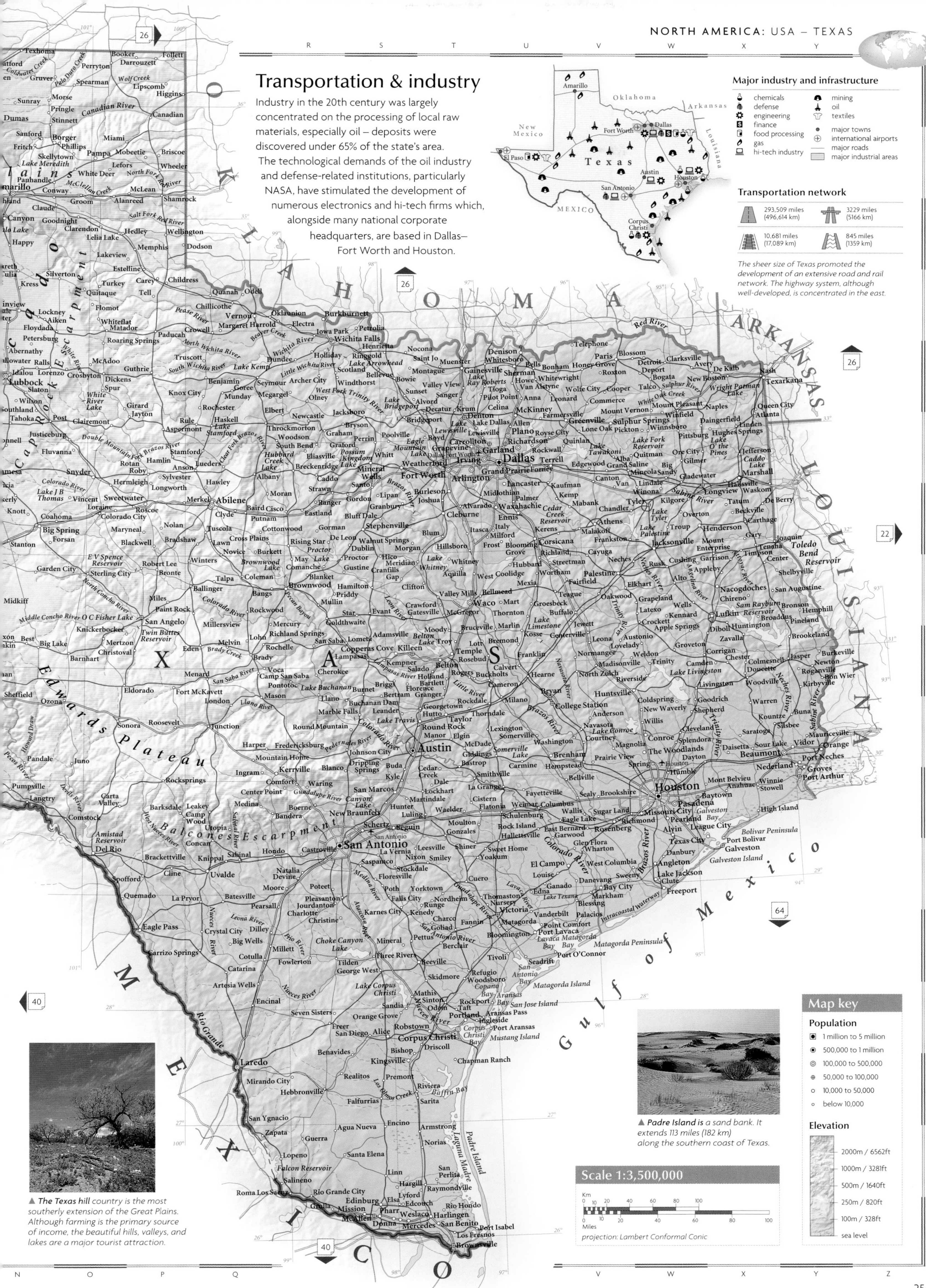

OKLAHOMA
ARKANSAS
LOUISIANA
TEXAS
MEXICO
Gulf of Mexico
Edwards Plateau
Balcones Escarpment
Amarillo
Lubbock
Abilene
San Angelo
Wichita Falls
Fort Worth
Dallas
Arlington
Waco
Austin
San Antonio
Houston
Beaumont
Port Arthur
Galveston
Corpus Christi
Laredo
Brownsville
Tyler
Texarkana
Red River
Rio Grande
Padre Island
Laguna Madre

▲ *The Texas hill country is the most southerly extension of the Great Plains. Although farming is the primary source of income, the beautiful hills, valleys, and lakes are a major tourist attraction.*

▲ *Padre Island is a sand bank. It extends 113 miles (182 km) along the southern coast of Texas.*

Scale 1:3,500,000

Km 0 10 20 40 60 80 100

Miles 0 10 20 40 60 80 100

projection: Lambert Conformal Conic

Map key

Population

- 1 million to 5 million
- 500,000 to 1 million
- 100,000 to 500,000
- 50,000 to 100,000
- 10,000 to 50,000
- below 10,000

Elevation

- 2000m / 6562ft
- 1000m / 3281ft
- 500m / 1640ft
- 250m / 820ft
- 100m / 328ft
- sea level

26 40 22 64

USA: SOUTH MIDWESTERN STATES

Arkansas, Kansas, Missouri, Oklahoma

The expansion of the US focused on this region in the mid-19th century. Settlers spread from the confluence of the Missouri and Mississippi rivers up onto the Great Plains. This treeless expanse, which early explorers had called the Great American Desert was turned into one of the world's richest agricultural regions. But periodic droughts, coupled with overintensive farming, led to the "dustbowl" soil erosion crisis of the 1930s, the abandonment of many farms, and a mass exodus to the west coast. The land has since recovered, although the mechanization of agriculture has led to a decline in the rural population. In recent years, suburban residential development has spread rapidly across the wooded Ozark Plateau in the east of the region.

Transportation & industry

The processing of agricultural products, such as brewing and meatpacking, has been traditionally important in these states. In Kansas and Oklahoma, diversified manufacturing now supplements income from fossil fuels; Wichita has become a world center for aeronautical engineering, an industry which also employs many people in neighboring Missouri.

Nebraska
Iowa
Illinois
Colorado
Kansas
Topeka
Kansas City
Saint Louis
Wichita
Missouri
Kentucky
New Mexico
Tulsa
Oklahoma
Arkansas
Tennessee
Oklahoma City
Little Rock
Mississippi
Texas
Louisiana

Major industry and infrastructure

- aerospace
- engineering
- finance
- food processing
- gas
- mining
- oil
- vehicle manufacture
- major towns
- international airports
- major roads
- major industrial areas

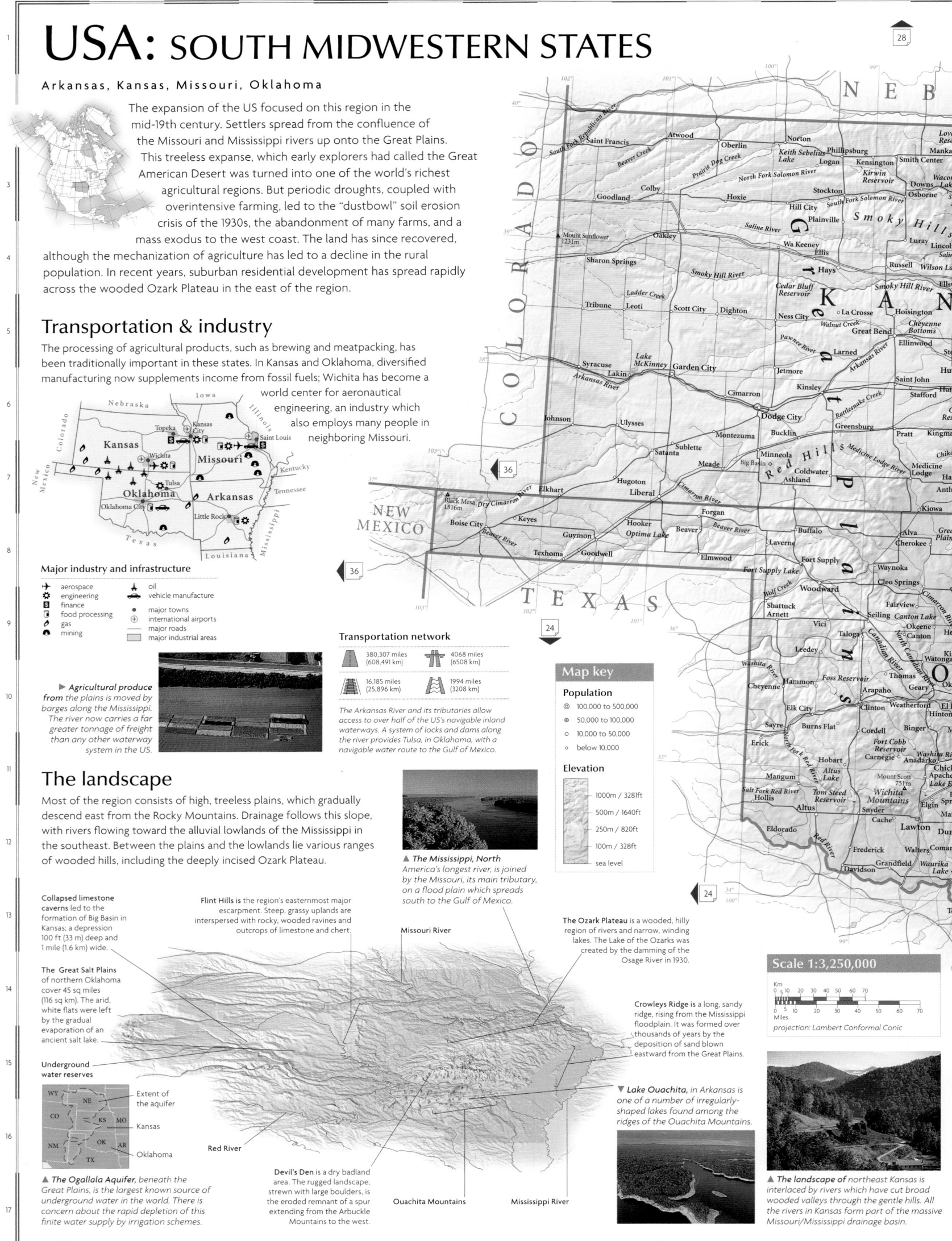

► *Agricultural produce from the plains is moved by barges along the Mississippi. The river now carries a far greater tonnage of freight than any other waterway system in the US.*

Transportation network

380,307 miles (608,491 km)	4068 miles (6508 km)
16,185 miles (25,896 km)	1994 miles (3208 km)

The Arkansas River and its tributaries allow access to over half of the US's navigable inland waterways. A system of locks and dams along the river provides Tulsa, in Oklahoma, with a navigable water route to the Gulf of Mexico.

28
N E B
COLORADO
KANSAS
Great Plains
Smoky Hills
Red Hills
Saint Francis
Atwood
Oberlin
Norton
Phillipsburg
Keith Sebelius Lake
Logan
Kensington
Smith Center
Mankato
Kirwin Reservoir
Downs
Osborne
Goodland
Colby
Hoxie
Stockton
Hill City
Plainville
Mount Sunflower 1231m
Oakley
Wa Keeney
Ellis
Hays
Russell
Wilson Lake
Luray
Lincoln
Sharon Springs
Smoky Hill River
Saline River
Tribune
Leoti
Scott City
Dighton
Ness City
La Crosse
Hoisington
Cheyenne Bottoms
Great Bend
Ellinwood
Larned
Syracuse
Lakin
Lake McKinney
Garden City
Jetmore
Kinsley
Saint John
Stafford
Cimarron
Dodge City
Johnson
Ulysses
Montezuma
Bucklin
Greensburg
Pratt
Kingman
Sublette
Satanta
Meade
Minneola
Big Basin
Coldwater
Ashland
Medicine Lodge
Hugoton
Liberal
Elkhart
36
NEW MEXICO
Black Mesa 1516m
Boise City
Keyes
Guymon
Hooker
Optima Lake
Forgan
Beaver
Buffalo
Alva
Cherokee
Kiowa
Texhoma
Goodwell
Elmwood
Laverne
Fort Supply
Fort Supply Lake
Waynoka
Woodward
Cleo Springs
Fairview
Seiling
Canton Lake
Okeene
Canton
Shattuck
Arnett
Vici
Taloga
Leedey
Watonga
Thomas
Geary
Hammon
Foss Reservoir
Cheyenne
Arapaho
Elk City
Clinton
Weatherford
Burns Flat
Sayre
Cordell
Binger
Erick
Fort Cobb Reservoir
Carnegie
Anadarko
Hobart
Altus Lake
Mangum
Mount Scott 751m
Wichita Mountains
Salt Fork Red River
Hollis
Tom Steed Reservoir
Altus
Snyder
Cache
Lawton
Eldorado
Frederick
Walters
Grandfield
Davidson
TEXAS
24
Red River
Cimarron River
Arkansas River
Canadian River
Washita River
Beaver River
Walnut Creek
Pawnee River
Rattlesnake Creek
Medicine Lodge River
North Fork Red River
Wolf Creek
Ladder Creek
Beaver Creek
Prairie Dog Creek
North Fork Solomon River
South Fork Solomon River
South Fork Republican River
Dry Cimarron River
North Canadian River
Scale 1:3,250,000
projection: Lambert Conformal Conic

Map key

Population

- 100,000 to 500,000
- 50,000 to 100,000
- 10,000 to 50,000
- below 10,000

Elevation

- 1000m / 3281ft
- 500m / 1640ft
- 250m / 820ft
- 100m / 328ft
- sea level

The landscape

Most of the region consists of high, treeless plains, which gradually descend east from the Rocky Mountains. Drainage follows this slope, with rivers flowing toward the alluvial lowlands of the Mississippi in the southeast. Between the plains and the lowlands lie various ranges of wooded hills, including the deeply incised Ozark Plateau.

▲ *The Mississippi, North America's longest river, is joined by the Missouri, its main tributary, on a flood plain which spreads south to the Gulf of Mexico.*

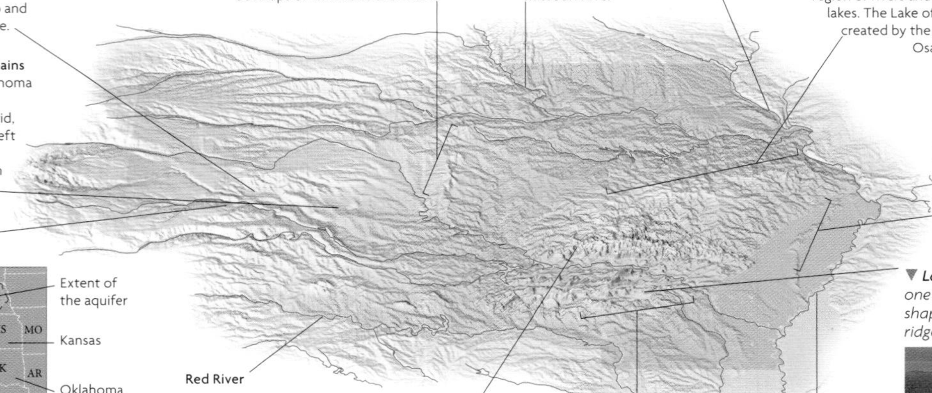

Collapsed limestone caverns led to the formation of Big Basin in Kansas; a depression 100 ft (33 m) deep and 1 mile (1.6 km) wide.

Flint Hills is the region's easternmost major escarpment. Steep, grassy uplands are interspersed with rocky, wooded ravines and outcrops of limestone and chert.

Missouri River

The Ozark Plateau is a wooded, hilly region of rivers and narrow, winding lakes. The Lake of the Ozarks was created by the damming of the Osage River in 1930.

The Great Salt Plains of northern Oklahoma cover 45 sq miles (116 sq km). The arid, white flats were left by the gradual evaporation of an ancient salt lake.

Crowleys Ridge is a long, sandy ridge, rising from the Mississippi floodplain. It was formed over thousands of years by the deposition of sand blown eastward from the Great Plains.

Underground water reserves

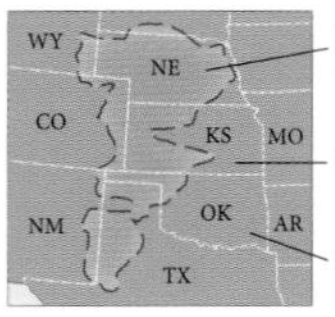
WY
NE
CO
KS
MO
NM
OK
AR
TX
Extent of the aquifer
Kansas
Oklahoma

▲ *The Ogallala Aquifer, beneath the Great Plains, is the largest known source of underground water in the world. There is concern about the rapid depletion of this finite water supply by irrigation schemes.*

Red River

Devil's Den is a dry badland area. The rugged landscape, strewn with large boulders, is the eroded remnant of a spur extending from the Arbuckle Mountains to the west.

Ouachita Mountains

Mississippi River

▼ *Lake Ouachita, in Arkansas is one of a number of irregularly-shaped lakes found among the ridges of the Ouachita Mountains.*

▲ *The landscape of northeast Kansas is interlaced by rivers which have cut broad wooded valleys through the gentle hills. All the rivers in Kansas form part of the massive Missouri/Mississippi drainage basin.*

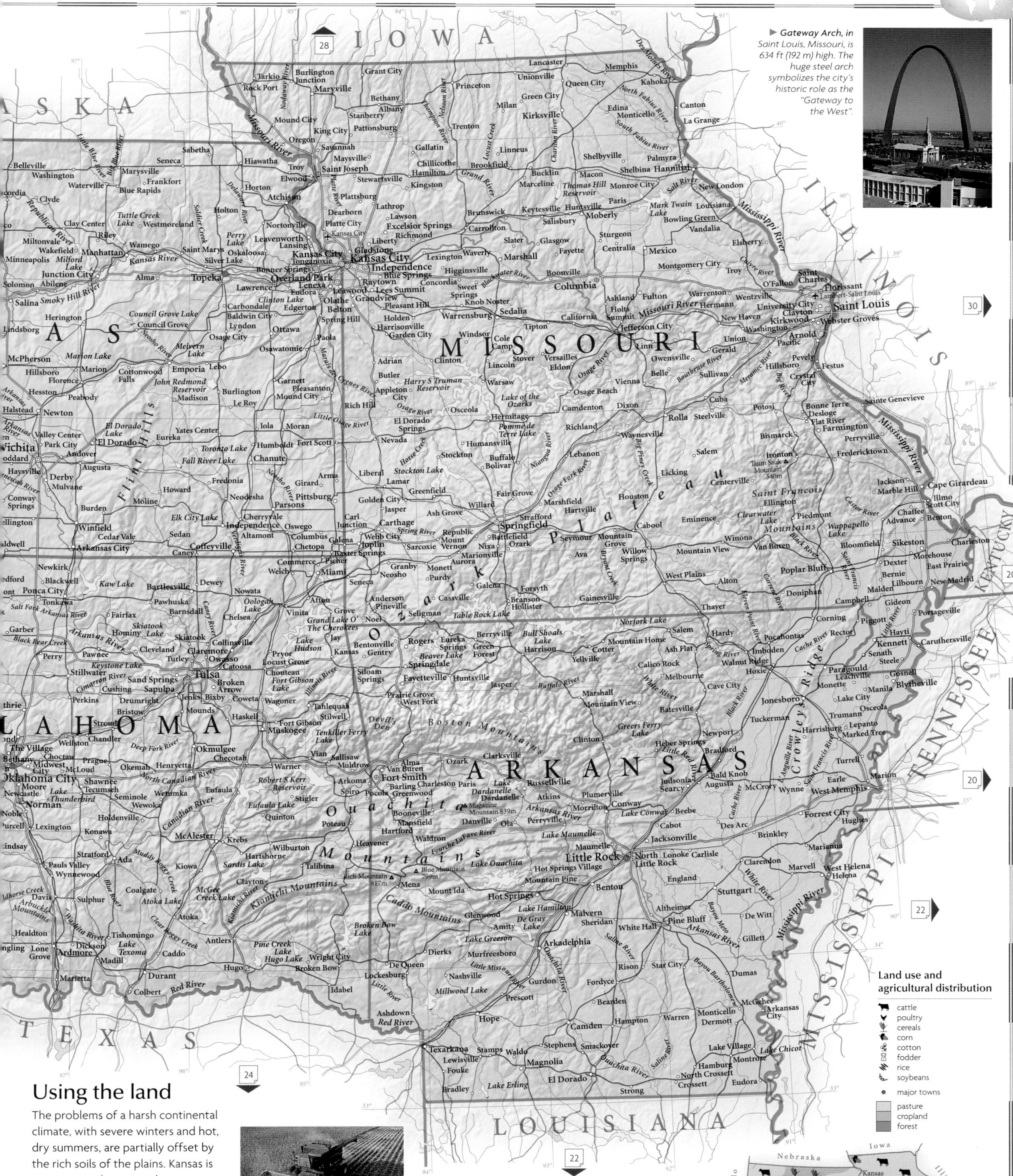
N O P Q R S T U V W X Y
IOWA
28
ILLINOIS
30
KANSAS
MISSOURI
Ozark Plateau
OKLAHOMA
ARKANSAS
Ouachita Mountains
Boston Mountains
Crowley's Ridge
TENNESSEE
KENTUCKY
MISSISSIPPI
TEXAS
LOUISIANA
20
20
22
22
24
Kansas City
Saint Louis
Jefferson City
Springfield
Topeka
Wichita
Tulsa
Oklahoma City
Fort Smith
Little Rock
Mississippi River
Missouri River
Arkansas River
Red River
1 2 3 4 5 6 7 8 9 10 11 12 13 14 15 16 17

▶ *Gateway Arch, in Saint Louis, Missouri, is 634 ft (192 m) high. The huge steel arch symbolizes the city's historic role as the "Gateway to the West".*

Land use and agricultural distribution

- cattle
- poultry
- cereals
- corn
- cotton
- fodder
- rice
- soybeans
- major towns
- pasture
- cropland
- forest

Using the land

The problems of a harsh continental climate, with severe winters and hot, dry summers, are partially offset by the rich soils of the plains. Kansas is a major cereal crop producer, ranking first in US production of wheat and sorghum. Rainfall increases toward the east, favoring the cultivation of soybeans, cotton, and rice, with corn concentrated in Missouri. Huge herds of cattle are raised in Oklahoma, Kansas, and Missouri.

▲ *A combine harvester works the land on the great plains. A hundred years ago this region, also known as the prairies – the French word for pasture – was covered with tall, wild grasses.*

The urban/rural population divide

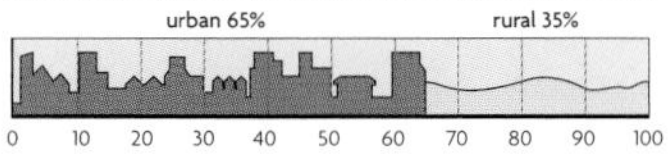
urban 65%
rural 35%
0 10 20 30 40 50 60 70 80 90 100

Population density	Total land area
54 people per sq mile (21 people per sq km)	271,436 sq miles (702,992 sq km)

Nebraska
Iowa
Illinois
Colorado
Kansas City
Topeka
Saint Louis
Kansas
Wichita
Missouri
Kentucky
New Mexico
Tulsa
Tennessee
Oklahoma
Arkansas
Oklahoma City
Little Rock
Mississippi
Texas
Louisiana

USA: UPPER PLAINS STATES

Iowa, Minnesota, Nebraska, North Dakota, South Dakota

Lying at the very heart of the North American continent, much of this region was acquired from France as part of the Louisiana Purchase in 1803. The area was largely bypassed by the early waves of westward migrants. When Europeans did settle, during the 19th century, they displaced the Native Americans who lived on the plains. The settlers planted arable crops and raised cattle on the immensely fertile prairie land, founding an agrarian tradition which flourishes today. Most of this region remains rural; of the five states, only in Minnesota has there been significant diversification away from agriculture and resource-based industries into the hi-tech and service sectors.

Using the land

The popular image of these states as agricultural is entirely justified; prairies stretch uninterrupted across most of the area. Croplands fall into two regions: the wheat belt of the plains, and the corn belt of the central US. Cash crops, such as soybeans, are grown to supplement incomes. Livestock, particularly pigs and cattle, are raised throughout this region.

The urban/rural population divide

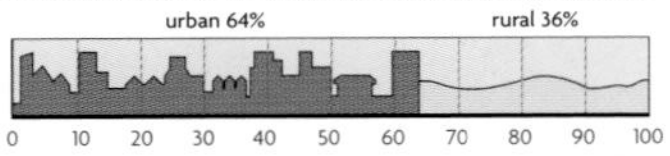
urban 64%
rural 36%
0 10 20 30 40 50 60 70 80 90 100

Population density	Total land area
31 people per sq mile (12 people per sq km)	357,212 sq miles (925,143 sq km)

► ***Dark, fertile prairie*** *soils in the southeast provide Minnesota's most productive farmland. Hot, humid summers create a long growing season for corn cultivation.*

CANADA
North Dakota
Bismarck
Minnesota
Lake Superior
Montana
South Dakota
Pierre
Minneapolis
Saint Paul
Wisconsin
Wyoming
Iowa
Cedar Rapids
Des Moines
Illinois
Nebraska
Omaha
Lincoln
Colorado
Missouri
Kansas

Land use and agricultural distribution

- cattle
- pigs
- corn
- soybeans
- wheat
- major towns
- pasture
- cropland
- forest
- wetland

Transportation & industry

Food processing and the production of farm machinery are supported by the large agricultural sector. Mineral exploitation is also an important activity: gold is mined in the ore-rich Black Hills of South Dakota, and both North Dakota and Nebraska are emerging as major petroleum producers.

Transportation network

504,522 miles (807,235 km)	3422 miles (5475 km)
16,940 miles (27,104 km)	683 miles (1098 km)

Nebraska's central location has made it an important transportation artery for east–west traffic. Minnesota's road network radiates out from the hub of the twin cities, Minneapolis–Saint Paul.

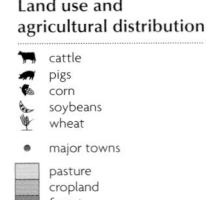

► ***Water erosion along*** *the Little Missouri River has carried away sedimentary deposits, creating rugged landscapes known as badlands.*

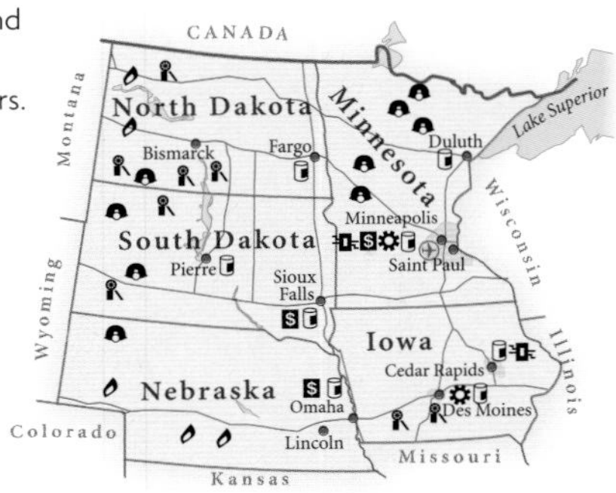
CANADA
North Dakota
Bismarck
Fargo
Duluth
Lake Superior
Minnesota
Montana
Minneapolis
South Dakota
Pierre
Saint Paul
Wisconsin
Sioux Falls
Wyoming
Iowa
Cedar Rapids
Illinois
Nebraska
Omaha
Des Moines
Lincoln
Colorado
Missouri
Kansas

Major industry and infrastructure

- coal
- engineering
- electronics
- finance
- food processing
- oil & gas
- mining
- major towns
- international airports
- major roads
- major industrial areas

The landscape

These states straddle the Great Plains and the lowlands of the central US, with Minnesota lying in a transition zone between the eastern forests and the prairies. The region was shaped by repeated ice advances and retreats, leaving a flat relief, broken only by the numerous lakes and broad river networks that drain the prairies.

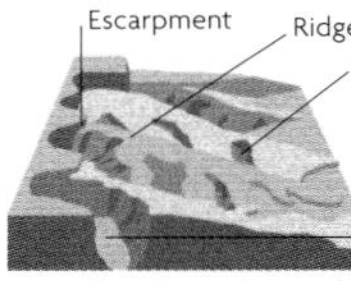
Escarpment
Ridge
In permeable strata hollows are formed by small mudslides
Water flowing into gullies erodes back the escarpment

▲ ***Badlands are formed*** *by stormwater run-off. This flows down the impermeable strata of the escarpment and saturates the permeable strata, leading to mudslides and the formation of gullies.*

▲ ***In the badlands*** *of North and South Dakota, horizontal layers of sandstone have been eroded by rivers, leaving a landscape of narrow gullies, sharp crests and pinnacles.*

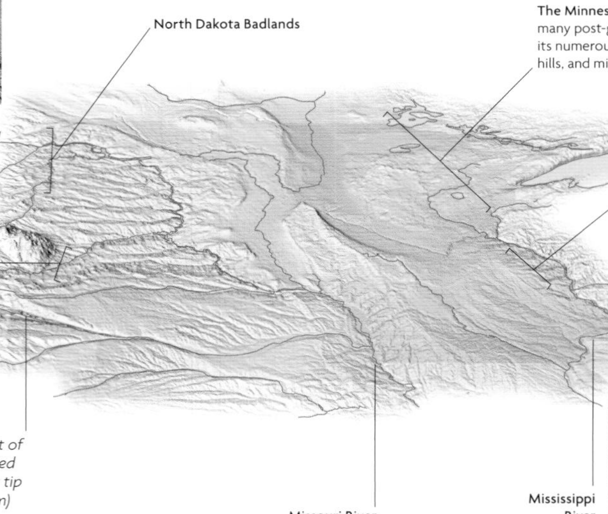
North Dakota Badlands
The Minnesota landscape contains many post-glacial features, including its numerous lakes, boulder-strewn hills, and mineral-rich deposits.
South Dakota Badlands
Although it escaped the last glaciation, the limestone bedrock of southeastern Minnesota has been eroded by surface and subterranean streams, leaving a network of underground caverns and steepsided valleys.
Missouri River
Mississippi River

▲ ***Chimney Rock*** *is a remnant of an ancient land surface, eroded by the North Platte River. The tip of its spire stands 500 ft (150 m) above the plain.*

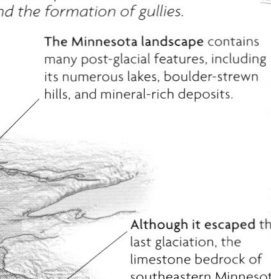

◄ ***In northeastern Iowa,*** *the Mississippi and its tributaries have deeply incised the underlying bedrock creating a hilly terrain, with bluffs standing 300 ft (90 m) above the valley.*

MONTANA
WYOMING
COLORADO
NO
SOUT
NE
Williston
Watford City
Lake Sakakawea
Little Missouri River
Killdeer Mountains
Dickinson
Beach
Sentinel Butte 1045m
Medora
Badlands
Knife River
Heart River
Lake Tschida
White Butte 1069m
Marmarth
Bowman
Hettinger
Lemmon
Buffalo
Belle Fourche
Belle Fourche Reservoir
Spearfish
Lead
Deadwood
Sturgis
Black Hills
Harney Peak 2207m
Mount Rushmore 1745m
Rapid City
Custer
Hermosa
Hot Springs
Angostura Reservoir
Edgemont
Oelrichs
Badlands
Wall
Philip
Kadoka
Interior
Cheyenne River
White River
Pine Ridge
Batesland
Martin
Chadron
Crawford
Harrison
Rushville
Hay Springs
Gordon
Box Butte Reservoir
Niobrara River
Hemingford
Alliance
Scottsbluff
Gering
Mitchell
Morrill
Chimney Rock
Bayard
Bridgeport
Hogback Mountain 1549m
Harrisburg
Kimball
Sidney
Chappell
Ogallala
Lake C. W. McConaughy
North Platte River
South Platte River
Sand Hills
Oshkosh
Arthur
Grant
Imperial
Enders Reservoir
Hayes Center
Benkelman
Swanson Lake
Trenton
32

► *Along the shores of Lake Superior in Minnesota, the average number of frostfree days can be as few as 90, and frosts may occur in any month of the year.*

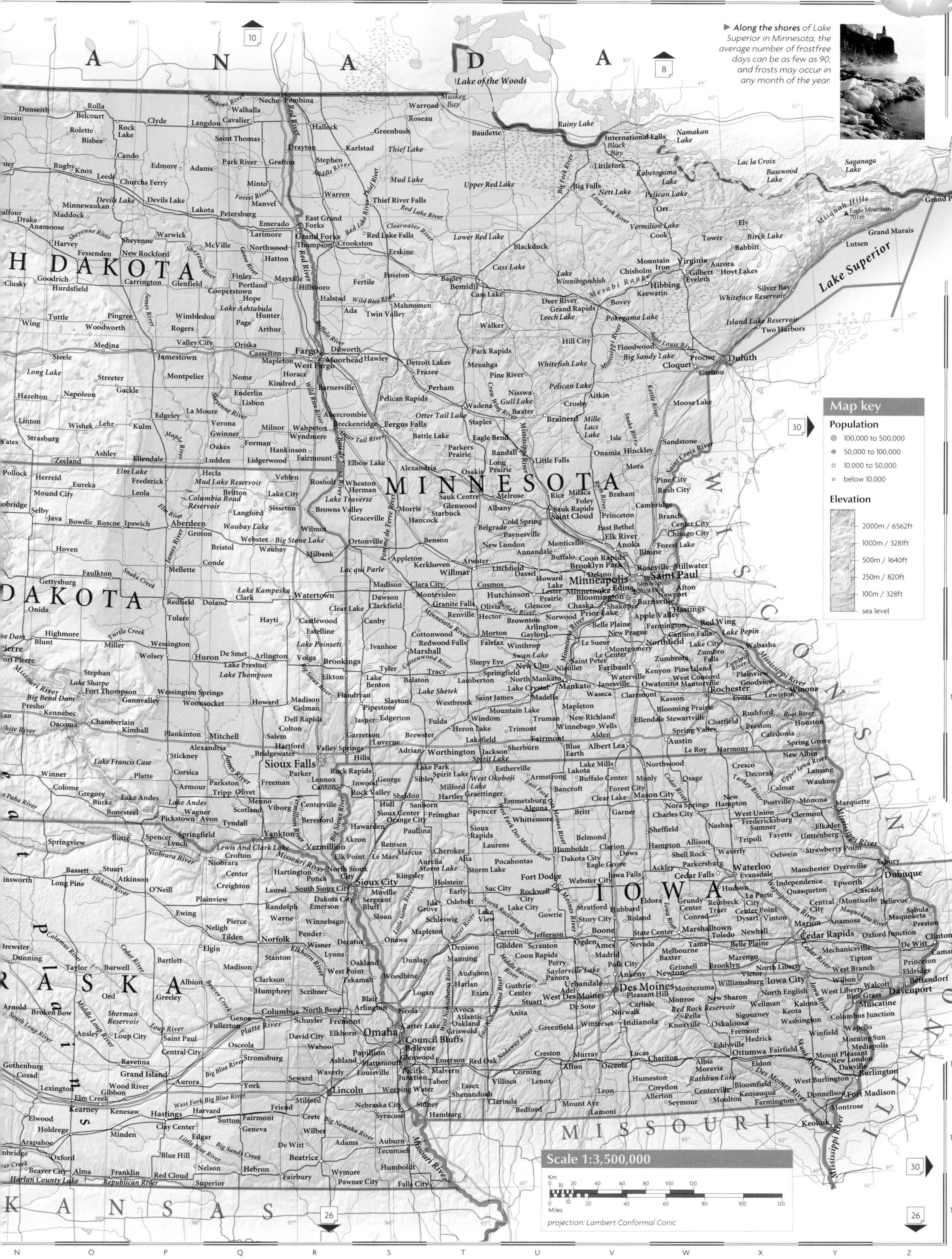
N O P Q R S T U V W X Y Z
1 2 3 4 5 6 7 8 9 10 11 12 13 14 15 16 17
CANADA
NORTH DAKOTA
SOUTH DAKOTA
MINNESOTA
WISCONSIN
IOWA
NEBRASKA
ILLINOIS
MISSOURI
KANSAS
Lake of the Woods
Rainy Lake
Upper Red Lake
Lower Red Lake
Lake Superior
Mesabi Range
Misquah Hills
Eagle Mountain 701m
Red River
Missouri River
Mississippi River
Des Moines River
Minnesota River
Bismarck
Fargo
Moorhead
Grand Forks
Duluth
Minneapolis
Saint Paul
Rochester
Sioux Falls
Sioux City
Omaha
Council Bluffs
Lincoln
Des Moines
Cedar Rapids
Davenport
Dubuque
Waterloo
Map key
Population
100,000 to 500,000
50,000 to 100,000
10,000 to 50,000
below 10,000
Elevation
2000m / 6562ft
1000m / 3281ft
500m / 1640ft
250m / 820ft
100m / 328ft
sea level
Scale 1:3,500,000
Km
0 10 20 40 60 80 100 120
0 10 20 40 60 80 100 120
Miles
projection: Lambert Conformal Conic
10
8
30
26

USA: GREAT LAKES STATES

Illinois, Indiana, Michigan, Ohio, Wisconsin

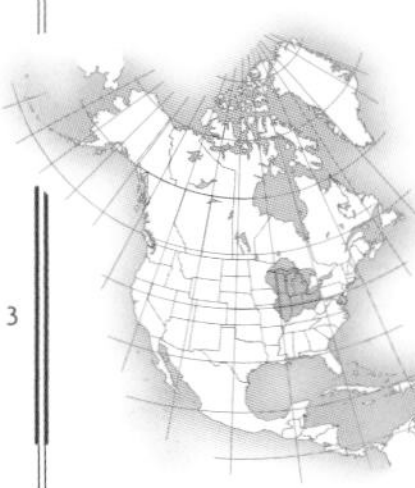

The states bordering the Great Lakes developed rapidly in the second half of the 19th century as a result of improvements in communications: railroads to the west and waterways to the south and east. Fertile land and good links with growing eastern seaboard cities encouraged the development of agriculture and food processing. Migrants from Europe and other parts of the US flooded into the region and for much of the 20th century the region's economy boomed. However, in recent years heavy industry has declined, earning the region the unwanted label the "Rustbelt."

Transportation & industry

Lake Superior
CANADA
Michigan
Minnesota
Wisconsin
Lake Michigan
Lake Huron
Lake Ontario
New York
Lake Erie
Milwaukee
Madison
Chicago
Lansing
Saginaw
Detroit
Toledo
Cleveland
Pennsylvania
Iowa
Peoria
Springfield
Illinois
Indiana
Indianapolis
Ohio
Columbus
Cincinnati
West Virginia
Missouri
Kentucky

The Great Lakes region is the center of the US car industry. Since the early part of the 20th century, its prosperity has been closely linked to the fortunes of automobile manufacturing. Iron and steel production has expanded to meet demand from this industry. In the 1970s, nationwide recession, cheaper foreign competition in the automobile sector, pollution in and around the Great Lakes, and the collapse of the meatpacking industry, centered on Chicago, forced these states to diversify their industrial base. New industries have emerged, notably electronics, service, and finance industries.

Major industry and infrastructure

car manufacture	research & development
coal	textiles
electronics	major towns
engineering	international airports
finance	major roads
food processing	major industrial areas
iron & steel	
oil	

Transportation network

540,682 miles (865,091 km)	6550 miles (10,480 km)
24,928 miles (39,884 km)	2330 miles (3748 km)

Few areas of the US have a comparable system. Chicago is a principal transportation terminus with a dense network of roads, railroads, and Interstate freeways that radiates out from the city.

► ***Ever since Ransom Olds** and Henry Ford started mass-producing automobiles in Detroit early in the 20th century, the city's name has become synonymous with the American automotive industry.*

The landscape

Much of this region shows the impact of glaciation which lasted until about 10,000 years ago, and extended as far south as Illinois and Ohio. Although the relief of the region slopes toward the Great Lakes, because the ice sheets blocked northerly drainage, most of the rivers today flow southward, forming part of the massive Mississippi/Missouri drainage basin.

◄ ***The dunes near** Sleeping Bear Point rise 400 ft (120 m) from the banks of Lake Michigan. They are constantly being resculpted by wind action.*

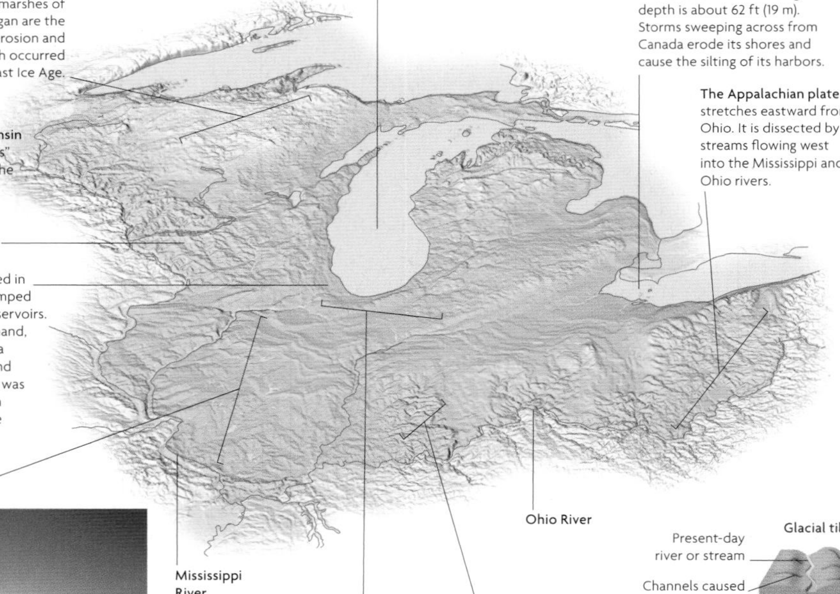

Lake Michigan
Mississippi River
Ohio River
Illinois plains

The many lakes and marshes of Wisconsin and Michigan are the result of glacial erosion and deposition which occurred during the last Ice Age.

Southwestern Wisconsin is known as a "driftless" area. Unlike most of the region, low hills protected it from erosion by the advancing ice sheet.

Most of the water used in northern Illinois is pumped from underground reservoirs. Due to increased demand, many areas now face a water shortage. Around Joliet, the water table was lowered by more than 700 ft (210 m) over the last century.

Lake Erie is the shallowest of the five Great Lakes. Its average depth is about 62 ft (19 m). Storms sweeping across from Canada erode its shores and cause the silting of its harbors.

The Appalachian plateau stretches eastward from Ohio. It is dissected by streams flowing west into the Mississippi and Ohio rivers.

Relic landforms from the last glaciation, such as shallow basins and ridges, cover all but the south of this region. Ridges, known as moraines, up to 300 ft (100 m) high, lie to the south of Lake Michigan.

Unlike the level prairie to the north, southern Indiana is relatively rugged. Limestone in the hills has been dissolved by water, producing features such as sinkholes and underground caves.

▲ *The plains of Illinois are characteristic of drift landscapes, scoured and flattened by glacial erosion and covered with fertile glacial deposits.*

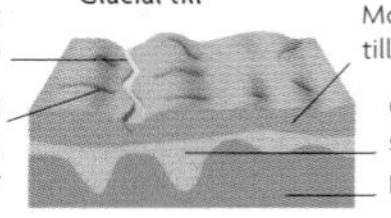

Glacial till
Present-day river or stream
Channels caused by outwash from melting glacier
Most recent till deposits
Older till sheet
Bedrock

▲ *As a result of successive glacial depositions, the total depth of till along the former southern margin of the Laurentide ice sheet can exceed 1300 ft (400 m).*

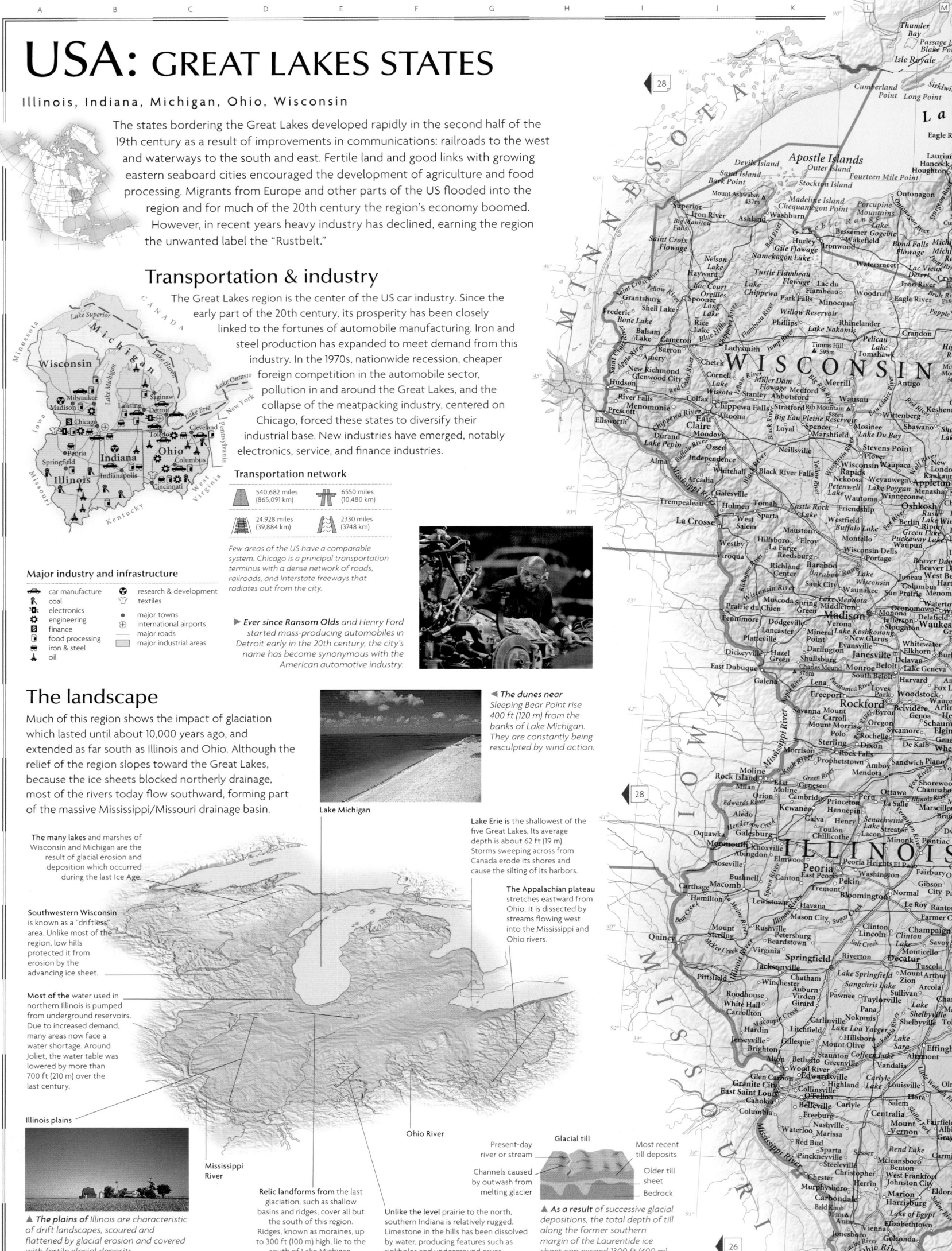

MINNESOTA
WISCONSIN
ILLINOIS
IOWA
MISSOURI
Lake Superior
Apostle Islands
Madison
Milwaukee
La Crosse
Eau Claire
Green Bay
Rockford
Peoria
Springfield
Decatur
Quincy
East Saint Louis
Mississippi River
Ohio River
Cairo

28
28
26

CANADA
MICHIGAN
INDIANA
OHIO
NEW YORK
PENNSYLVANIA
WEST VIRGINIA
KENTUCKY
Lake Huron
Lake Erie
Lake Ontario
Lake Michigan
Georgian Bay
North Channel
Main Channel
Chicago
Detroit
Cleveland
Columbus
Indianapolis
Toledo
Cincinnati
Fort Wayne
Grand Rapids
Lansing
Flint
Saginaw
Dayton
Akron
Youngstown
South Bend
Evansville

8
18
18
20
20

The urban/rural population divide

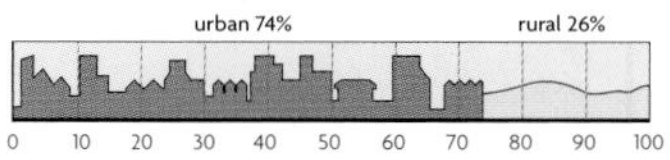
urban 74%
rural 26%
0 10 20 30 40 50 60 70 80 90 100

Population density	Total land area
189 people per sq mile (73 people per sq km)	243,513 sq miles (630,674 sq km)

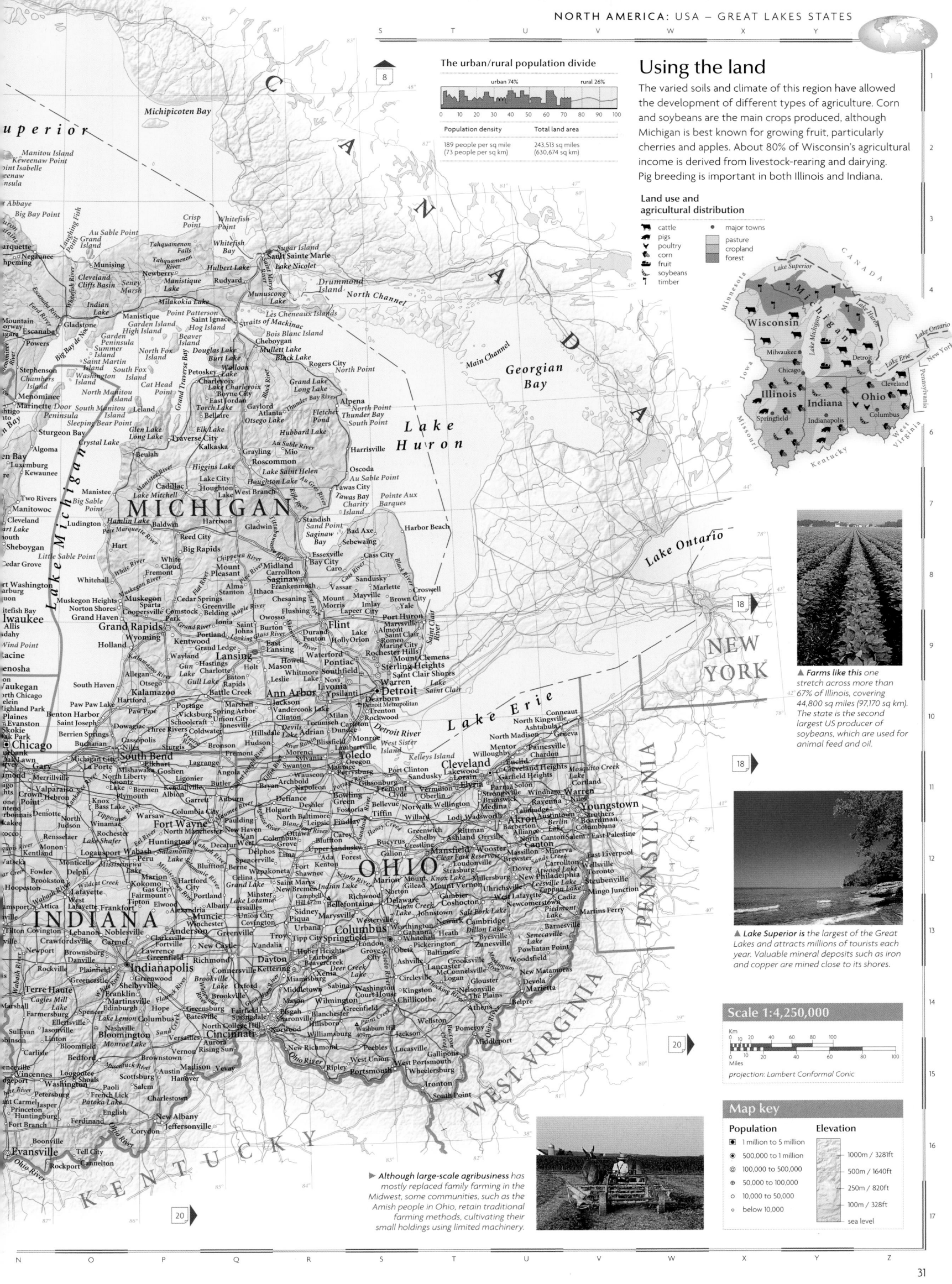

Using the land

The varied soils and climate of this region have allowed the development of different types of agriculture. Corn and soybeans are the main crops produced, although Michigan is best known for growing fruit, particularly cherries and apples. About 80% of Wisconsin's agricultural income is derived from livestock-rearing and dairying. Pig breeding is important in both Illinois and Indiana.

Land use and agricultural distribution

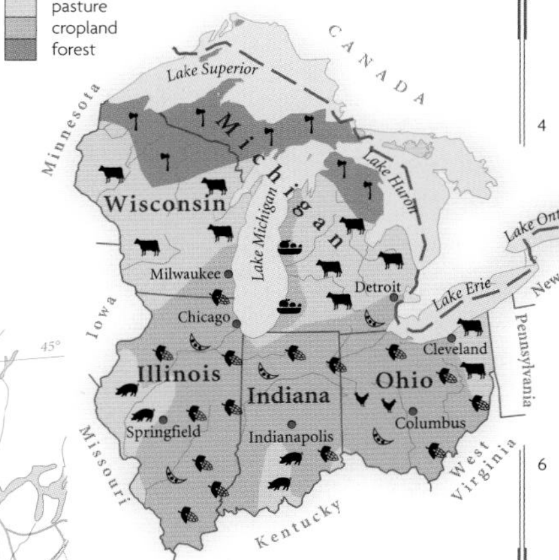
cattle
pigs
poultry
corn
fruit
soybeans
timber
major towns
pasture
cropland
forest
CANADA
Lake Superior
Minnesota
Wisconsin
Michigan
Lake Michigan
Lake Huron
Lake Ontario
Lake Erie
New York
Pennsylvania
Milwaukee
Chicago
Detroit
Cleveland
Illinois
Indiana
Ohio
Springfield
Indianapolis
Columbus
Iowa
Missouri
Kentucky
West Virginia

▲ *Farms like this one stretch across more than 67% of Illinois, covering 44,800 sq miles (97,170 sq km). The state is the second largest US producer of soybeans, which are used for animal feed and oil.*

▲ *Lake Superior is the largest of the Great Lakes and attracts millions of tourists each year. Valuable mineral deposits such as iron and copper are mined close to its shores.*

Scale 1:4,250,000

Km 0 10 20 40 60 80 100
0 10 20 40 60 80 100 Miles

projection: Lambert Conformal Conic

▶ *Although large-scale agribusiness has mostly replaced family farming in the Midwest, some communities, such as the Amish people in Ohio, retain traditional farming methods, cultivating their small holdings using limited machinery.*

Map key

Population

- 1 million to 5 million
- 500,000 to 1 million
- 100,000 to 500,000
- 50,000 to 100,000
- 10,000 to 50,000
- below 10,000

Elevation

- 1000m / 3281ft
- 500m / 1640ft
- 250m / 820ft
- 100m / 328ft
- sea level

USA: NORTH MOUNTAIN STATES

Idaho, Montana, Oregon, Washington, Wyoming

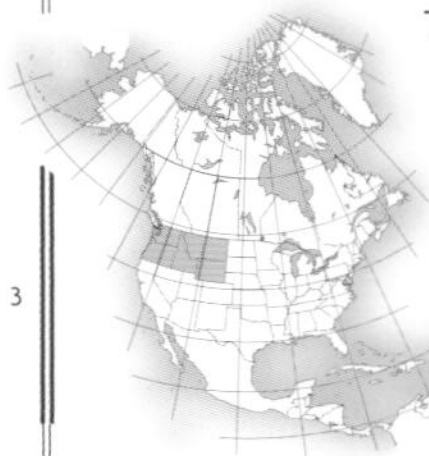

The remoteness of the northwestern states, coupled with the rugged landscape, ensured that this was one of the last areas settled by Europeans in the 19th century. Fur-trappers and gold-prospectors followed the Snake River westward as it wound its way through the Rocky Mountains. The states of the northwest have pioneered many conservationist policies, with the first US National Park opened at Yellowstone in 1872. More recently, the Cascades and Rocky Mountains have become havens for adventure tourism. The mountains still serve to isolate the western seaboard from the rest of the continent. This isolation has encouraged West Coast cities to expand their trade links with countries of the Pacific Rim.

▲ *The Snake River has cut down into the basalt of the Columbia Basin to form Hells Canyon, the deepest in the US, with cliffs up to 7900 ft (2408 m) high.*

Map key

Population

- 500,000 to 1 million
- 100,000 to 500,000
- 50,000 to 100,000
- 10,000 to 50,000
- below 10,000

Elevation

- 4000m / 13,124ft
- 3000m / 9843ft
- 2000m / 6562ft
- 1000m / 3281ft
- 500m / 1640ft
- 250m / 820ft
- 100m / 328ft
- sea level

► ***Fine-textured, volcanic** soils in the hilly Palouse region of eastern Washington are susceptible to erosion.*

Using the land

Wheat farming in the east gives way to cattle ranching as rainfall decreases. Irrigated farming in the Snake River valley produces large yields of potatoes and other vegetables. Dairying and fruit-growing take place in the wet western lowlands between the mountain ranges.

The urban/rural population divide

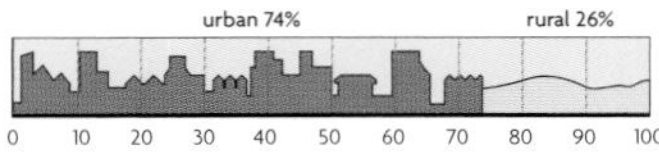

urban 74%
rural 26%
0 10 20 30 40 50 60 70 80 90 100

Population density	Total land area
26 people per sq mile (10 people per sq km)	487,970 sq miles (1,263,716 sq km)

Scale 1:4,250,000

Km 0 10 20 40 60 80 100

Miles 0 10 20 40 60 80 100

projection: Lambert Conformal Conic

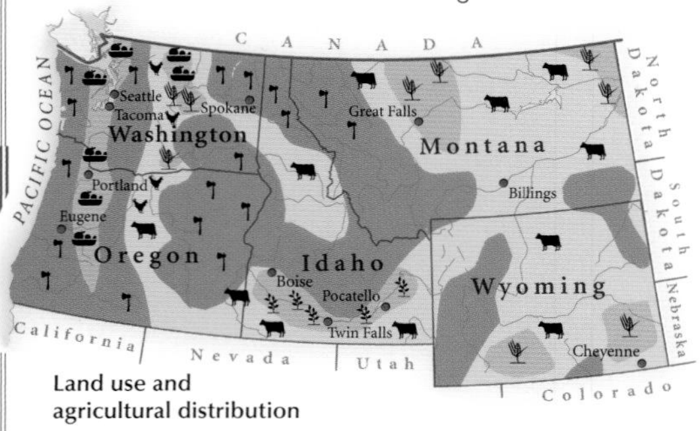

CANADA
PACIFIC OCEAN
Seattle
Tacoma
Spokane
Washington
Great Falls
Montana
Portland
Eugene
Oregon
Billings
Idaho
Boise
Pocatello
Wyoming
Twin Falls
Cheyenne
California
Nevada
Utah
Colorado
North Dakota
South Dakota
Nebraska

Land use and agricultural distribution

- cattle
- poultry
- cereals
- fruit
- potatoes
- timber
- major towns
- pasture
- cropland
- forest

Transportation & industry

Minerals and timber are extremely important in this region. Uranium, precious metals, copper, and coal are all mined, the latter in vast open-cast pits in Wyoming; oil and natural gas are extracted further north. Manufacturing, notably related to the aerospace and electronics industries, is important in western cities.

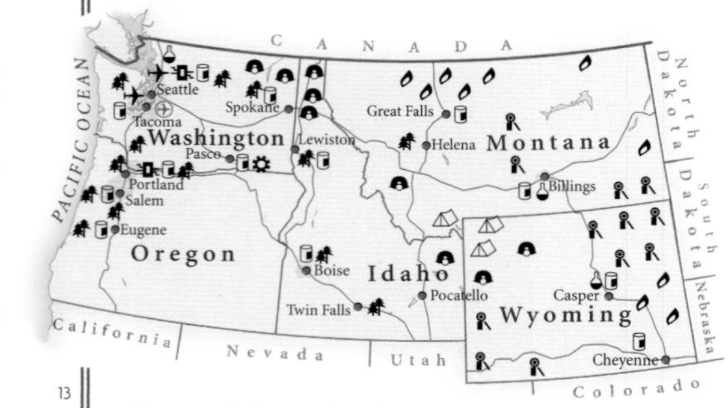

CANADA
PACIFIC OCEAN
Seattle
Tacoma
Spokane
Washington
Lewiston
Pasco
Great Falls
Helena
Montana
Portland
Salem
Eugene
Oregon
Billings
Boise
Idaho
Pocatello
Twin Falls
Casper
Wyoming
Cheyenne
California
Nevada
Utah
Colorado
North Dakota
South Dakota
Nebraska

Transportation network

- 347,857 miles (556,571 km)
- 4200 miles (6720 km)
- 12,354 miles (19,766 km)
- 1108 miles (1782 km)

The Union Pacific Railroad has been in service across Wyoming since 1867. The route through the Rocky Mountains is now shared with the Interstate 80, a major east–west highway.

Major industry and infrastructure

- adventure tourism
- aerospace
- coal
- chemicals
- electronics
- food processing
- mining
- oil & gas
- timber processing
- major towns
- international airports
- major roads
- major industrial areas

WASHINGTON
OREGON
PACIFIC OCEAN
CALIFORNIA
NEVADA
Columbia Basin
Harney Basin
Olympic Mountains
Blue Mountains
Seattle
Tacoma
Spokane
Portland
Salem
Eugene
Olympia
Vancouver
Bellingham
Yakima
Walla Walla
Pendleton
Bend
Medford
Klamath Falls
Columbia River
Snake River
Mount Rainier 4392m
Mount Hood 3424m
Crater Lake

8

192

◄ ***Seattle lies in** one of Puget Sound's many inlets. The city receives oil and other resources from Alaska, and benefits from expanding trade across the Pacific.*

34

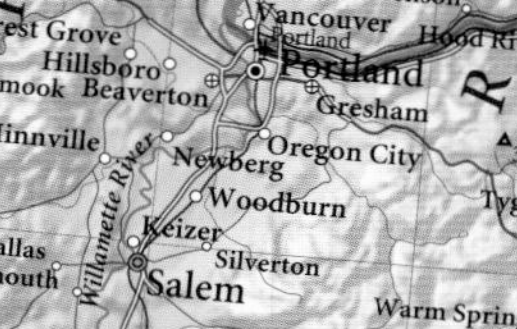

◄ ***Crater Lake, Oregon,** is 6 miles (10 km) wide and 1800 ft (600 m) deep. It marks the site of a volcanic cone, which collapsed after an eruption within the last 7000 years.*

34

The landscape

The Rocky Mountains are flanked by lower parallel ranges, which spread onto the Great Plains in the east and surmount the broad lava plateau which extends westward. The Cascade Range divides the Columbia Basin from the coastlands, where the low areas around Puget Sound are broken by the steep, volcanic Olympic Mountains and the wooded hills of the Coast Ranges.

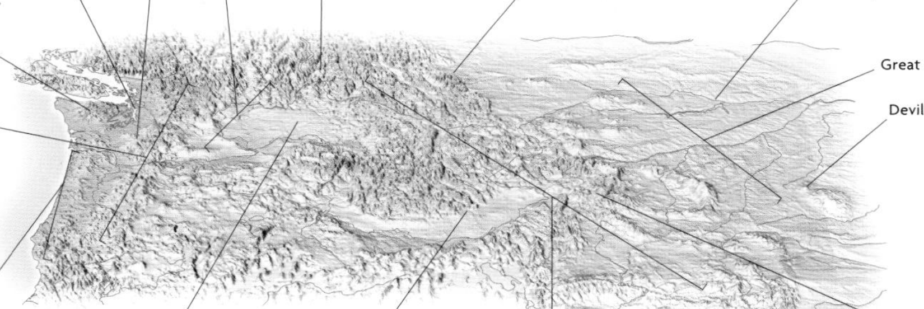
Puget Sound
Columbia Basin
Coast Ranges
Great Plains
Devil's Tower
Rocky Mountains

Glacial valleys on the seaward side of the Olympic Mountains receive about 142 inches (3600 mm) of rain per year, supporting the only true rain forest of the northern hemisphere.

Mount St. Helens erupted in 1980, killing 57 people and devastating a huge area.

Grand Coulee and the lesser *coulées* (ravines) were cut by cataclysmic floods, from the release of an ice-dammed lake, at the end of the last Ice Age.

The Continental Divide, or watershed, crosses the Lewis Range. From here, rivers flow east to Hudson Bay, south to the Gulf of Mexico and west to the Pacific Ocean.

The Cascades are glacially scoured volcanic mountains, the highest of which is Mount Rainier, a dormant volcano at 14,409 ft (4392 m).

The plateaus of the Columbia and Snake rivers represent one of the world's largest accumulations of lava. Over 5 million years ago, successive flows of molten basalt buried the existing land surface by up to 450 ft (150 m).

The contorted rock shapes at "Craters of the Moon" National Monument in Idaho were left 2000 years ago by the sporadic upwelling of viscous lava from fissures in the basalt plateau.

► ***Piney Buttes are** the remnants of an older, higher land surface gradually weathered and eroded into isolated outcrops with flat tops and steep sides.*

▲ ***Water from the** hot springs in Yellowstone National Park deposits minerals as it cools in rock pools. Long periods of deposition have created these rock terraces.*

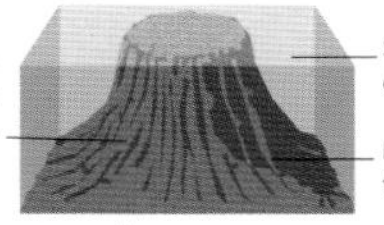
Molten rock cools, forming parallel columns
Surrounding strata eroded away
Molten rock wells up from the Earth's core

▲ ***Devil's Tower in** Wyoming is an igneous intrusion, formed below the Earth's surface. Molten rock intruded through cracks in the overlying strata and cooled. Over time, the softer rock layers have been eroded away, leaving only the tower standing.*

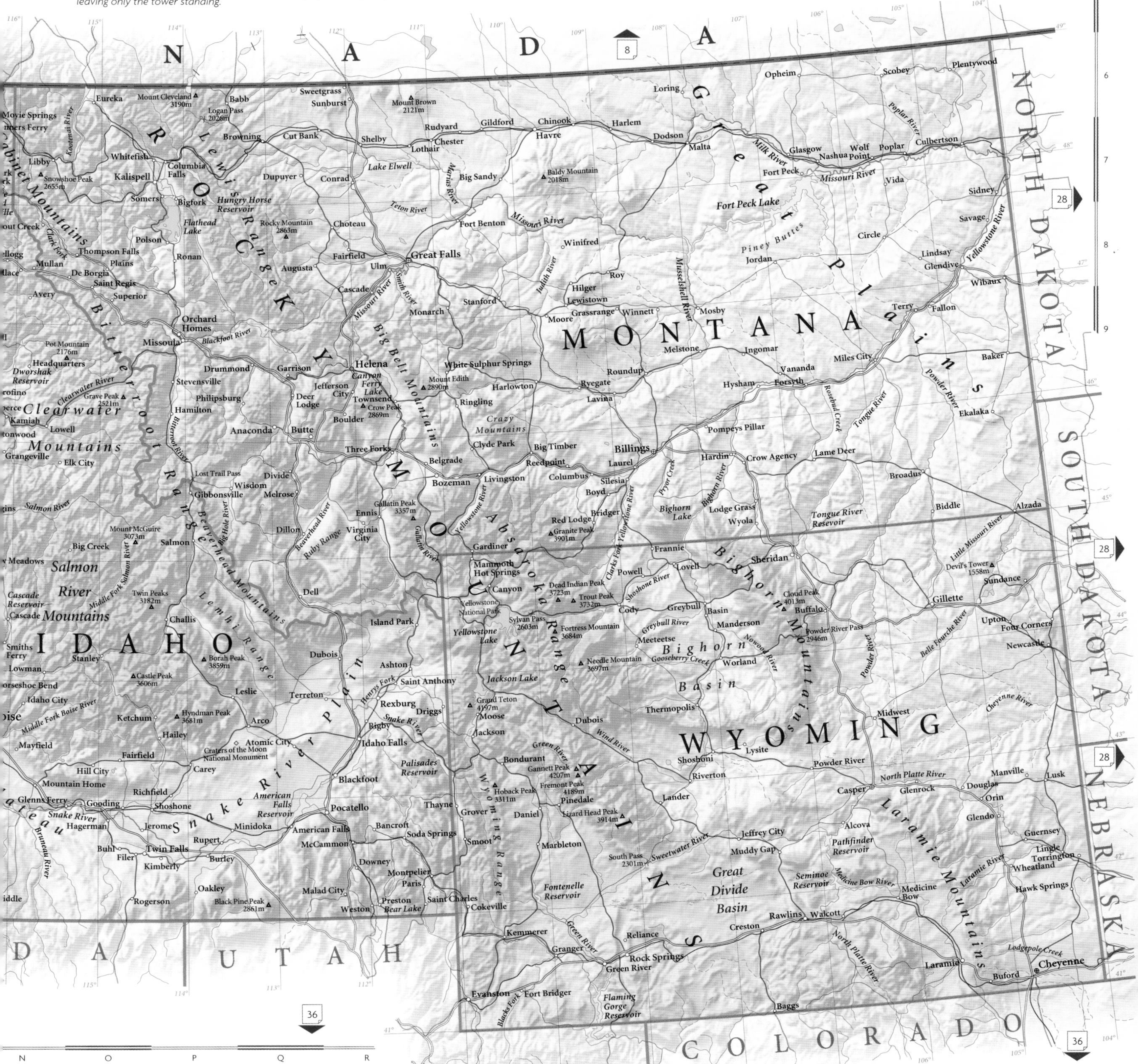
CANADA
NORTH DAKOTA
SOUTH DAKOTA
NEBRASKA
COLORADO
UTAH
IDAHO
MONTANA
WYOMING
ROCKY MOUNTAINS
Great Plains
Lewis Range
Bitterroot Range
Clearwater Mountains
Salmon River Mountains
Lemhi Range
Big Belt Mountains
Absaroka Range
Bighorn Mountains
Bighorn Basin
Wind River Range
Wyoming Range
Laramie Mountains
Great Divide Basin
Snake River Plain
Fort Peck Lake
Piney Buttes
Yellowstone Lake
Great Falls
Helena
Missoula
Billings
Bozeman
Butte
Cheyenne
Casper
Laramie
Rock Springs
Idaho Falls
Pocatello
Twin Falls
Sheridan
Gillette
Devils Tower 1558m
Grand Teton 4197m
Gannett Peak 4207m
Granite Peak 3901m
Borah Peak 3859m
28
36
8

USA: CALIFORNIA & NEVADA

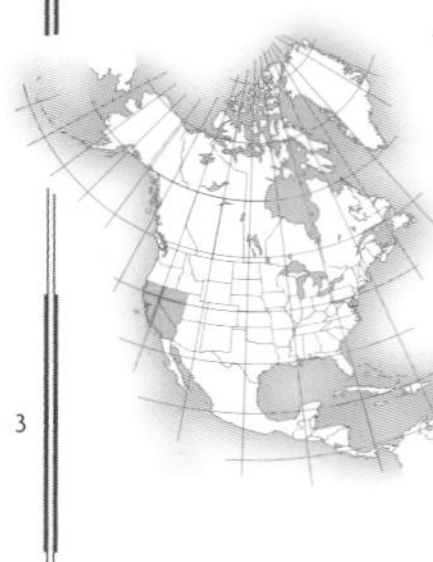

The Gold Rush of 1849 attracted the first major wave of European settlers to the West Coast. The pleasant climate, beautiful scenery, and dynamic economy continue to attract immigrants – despite the ever-present danger of earthquakes – and California has become the US's most populous state. The overwhelmingly urban population is concentrated in the vast conurbations of Los Angeles, San Francisco, and San Diego; new immigrants include people from South Korea, the Philippines, Vietnam, and Mexico. Nevada's arid lands were initially exploited for minerals; in recent years, revenue from mining has been superseded by income from the tourist and gambling centers of Las Vegas and Reno.

Map key

Population
- 1 million to 5 million
- 500,000 to 1 million
- 100,000 to 500,000
- 50,000 to 100,000
- 10,000 to 50,000
- below 10,000

Elevation
- 4000m / 13,124ft
- 3000m / 9843ft
- 2000m / 6562ft
- 1000m / 3281ft
- 500m / 1640ft
- 250m / 820ft
- 100m / 328ft
- sea level

Scale 1:3,250,000

Km 0 5 10 20 30 40 50 60 70 80
Miles 0 5 10 20 30 40 50 60 70 80

projection: Lambert Conformal Conic

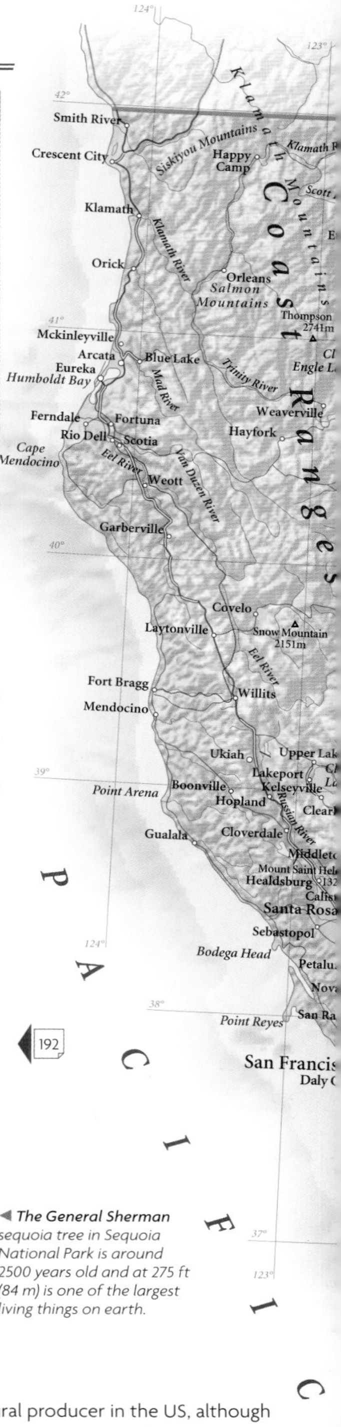
Klamath Mountains
Smith River
Crescent City
Siskiyou Mountains
Happy Camp
Klamath
Klamath River
Orick
Orleans
Salmon Mountains
Coast Ranges
Thompson 2741m
Mckinleyville
Arcata
Blue Lake
Eureka
Humboldt Bay
Trinity River
Weaverville
Ferndale
Fortuna
Rio Dell
Scotia
Hayfork
Cape Mendocino
Eel River
Van Duzen River
Weott
Garberville
Covelo
Laytonville
Snow Mountain 2151m
Fort Bragg
Willits
Mendocino
Ukiah
Boonville
Lakeport
Kelseyville
Point Arena
Hopland
Gualala
Cloverdale
Middletown
Healdsburg
Santa Rosa
Sebastopol
Bodega Head
Point Reyes
San Francisco
PACIFIC

192

Transportation & industry

Nevada's rich mineral reserves ushered in a period of mining wealth which has now been replaced by revenue generated from gambling. California supports a broad set of activities including defense-related industries and research and development facilities. "Silicon Valley," near San Francisco, is a world leading center for micro-electronics, while tourism and the Los Angeles film industry also generate large incomes.

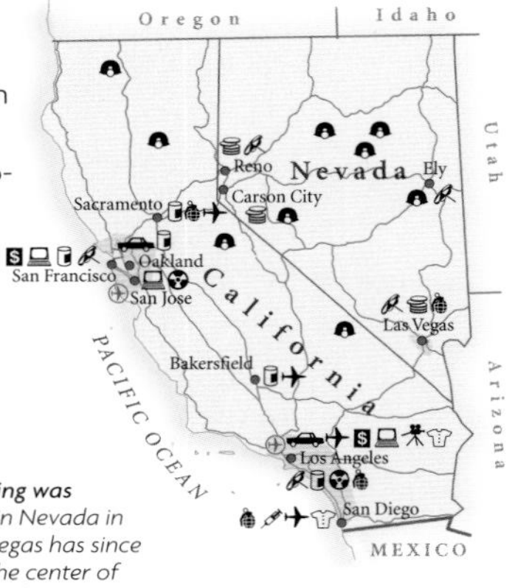
Oregon
Idaho
Utah
Arizona
Nevada
California
Reno
Carson City
Ely
Sacramento
San Francisco
Oakland
San Jose
Las Vegas
Bakersfield
Los Angeles
San Diego
PACIFIC OCEAN
MEXICO

Major industry and infrastructure
- aerospace
- car manufacture
- defense
- film industry
- finance
- food processing
- gambling
- hi-tech industry
- mining
- pharmaceuticals
- research & development
- textiles
- tourism
- major towns
- international airports
- major roads
- major industrial areas

Transportation network

211,459 miles (338,334 km)	2944 miles (4710 km)
7822 miles (12,595 km)	190 miles (360 km)

In California, the motor vehicle is a vital part of daily life, and an extensive freeway system runs throughout the state, cementing its position as the most important mode of transport.

DUNES
OASIS
CASINO

◀ ***Gambling was legalized** in Nevada in 1931. Las Vegas has since become the center of this multimillion dollar industry.*

The landscape

The broad Central Valley divides California's coastal mountains from the Sierra Nevada. The San Andreas Fault, running beneath much of the state, is the site of frequent earth tremors and sometimes more serious earthquakes. East of the Sierra Nevada, the landscape is characterized by the basin and range topography with stony deserts and many salt lakes.

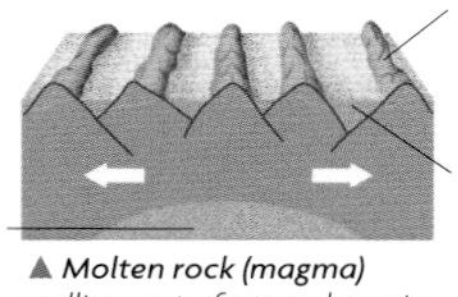
Rising molten rock causes stretching of the Earth's crust
Extensive cracking (faulting) uplifted a series of ridges
As ridges are eroded they fill intervening valleys with sediments

▲ ***Molten rock (magma)** welling up to form a dome in the Earth's interior, causes the brittle surface rocks to stretch and crack. Some areas were uplifted to form mountains (ranges), while others sunk to form flat valleys (basins).*

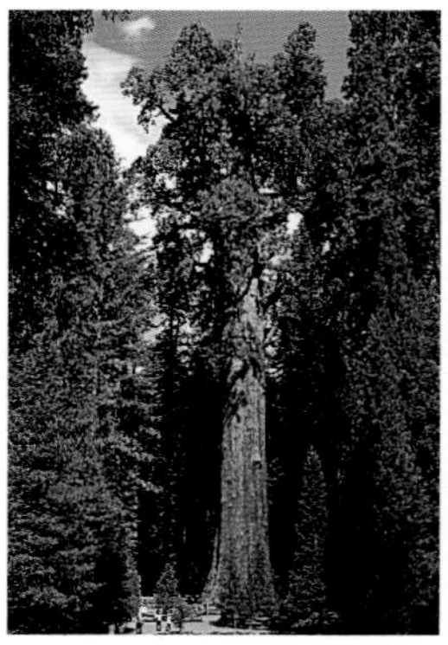

◀ ***The General Sherman** sequoia tree in Sequoia National Park is around 2500 years old and at 275 ft (84 m) is one of the largest living things on earth.*

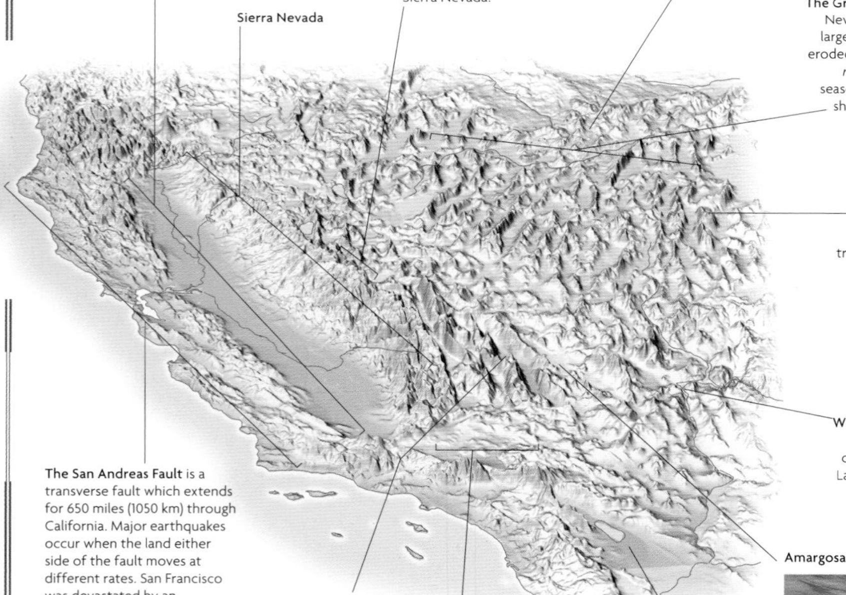
Most of California's agriculture is confined to the fertile and extensively irrigated Central Valley, running between the Coast Ranges and the Sierra Nevada. It incorporates the San Joaquin and Sacramento valleys.
The dramatic granitic rock formations of Half Dome and El Capitan, and the verdant coniferous forests, attract millions of visitors annually to Yosemite National Park in the Sierra Nevada.
Sierra Nevada
The Great Basin dominates most of Nevada's topography containing large open basins, punctuated by eroded features such as *buttes* and *mesas*. River flow tends to be seasonal, dependent upon spring showers and winter snow melt.
Wheeler Peak is home to some of the world's oldest trees, bristlecone pines, which live for up to 5000 years.
When the Hoover Dam across the Colorado River was completed in 1936, it created Lake Mead, one of the largest artificial lakes in the world, extending for 115 miles (285 km) upstream.
The San Andreas Fault is a transverse fault which extends for 650 miles (1050 km) through California. Major earthquakes occur when the land either side of the fault moves at different rates. San Francisco was devastated by an earthquake in 1906.
Death Valley
Amargosa Desert
The sparsely populated Mojave Desert receives less than 8 inches (200 mm) of rainfall a year. It is used extensively for weapons-testing and military purposes.
The Salton Sea was created accidentally between 1905 and 1907 when an irrigation channel from the Colorado River broke out of its banks and formed this salty 300 sq mile (777 sq km), landlocked lake.

▶ ***Named by migrating** settlers in 1849, Death Valley is the driest, hottest place in North America, as well as being the lowest point on land in the western hemisphere, at 282 ft (86 m) below sea level.*

▲ ***The Sierra Nevada** create a "rainshadow," preventing rain from reaching much of Nevada. Pacific air masses, passing over the mountains, are stripped of their moisture.*

Using the land

California is the leading agricultural producer in the US, although low rainfall makes irrigation essential. The long growing season and abundant sunshine allow many crops to be grown in the fertile Central Valley including grapes, citrus fruits, vegetables, and cotton. Almost 17 million acres (6.8 million hectares) of California's forests are used commercially. Nevada's arid climate and poor soil are largely unsuitable for agriculture; 85% of its land is state owned and large areas are used for underground testing of nuclear weapons.

Land use and agricultural distribution
- cattle
- citrus fruits
- fruit
- irrigation
- timber
- vineyards
- major towns
- pasture
- cropland
- forest
- desert

Oregon
Idaho
Utah
Nevada
Reno
Sacramento
San Francisco
California
Las Vegas
Arizona
PACIFIC OCEAN
Los Angeles
San Diego
MEXICO

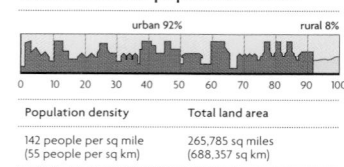

▲ ***Without considerable irrigation,** this fertile valley at Palm Springs would still be part of the Sonoran Desert. California's farmers account for about 80% of the state's total water usage.*

The urban/rural population divide

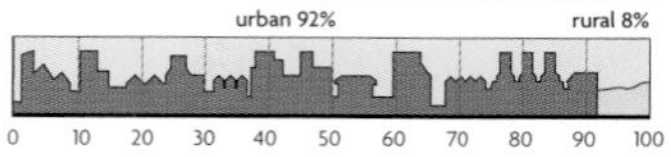
urban 92%
rural 8%
0 10 20 30 40 50 60 70 80 90 100

Population density	Total land area
142 people per sq mile (55 people per sq km)	265,785 sq miles (688,357 sq km)

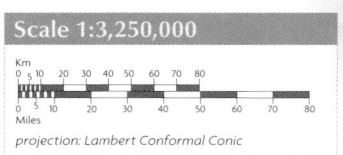

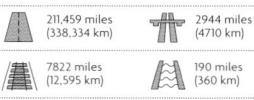

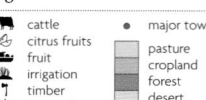

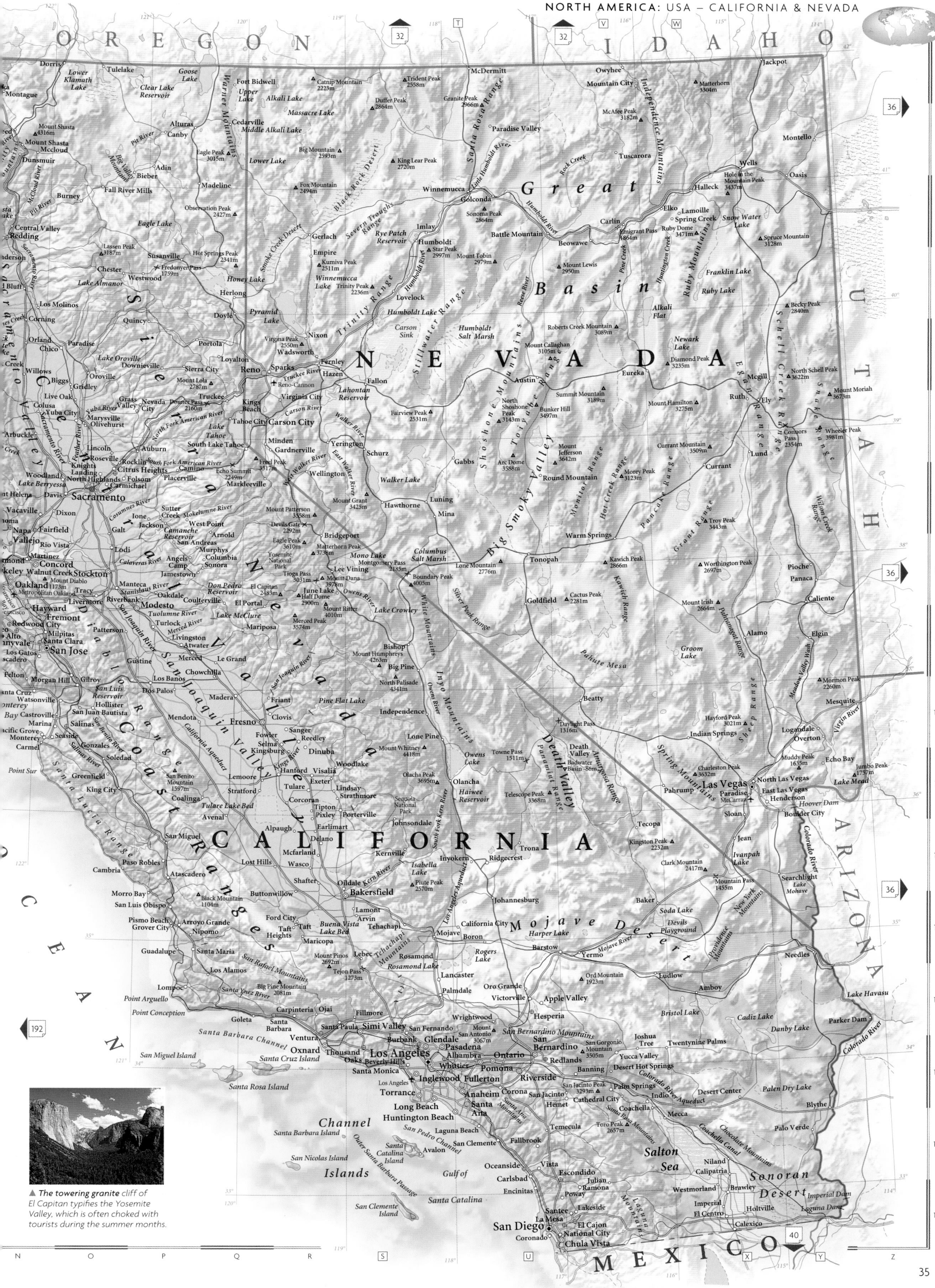

OREGON
IDAHO
UTAH
ARIZONA
MEXICO
NEVADA
CALIFORNIA
Great Basin
OCEAN
Sierra Nevada
Central Valley
San Joaquin Valley
Coast Ranges
Diablo Range
Mojave Desert
Sonoran Desert
Death Valley
Salton Sea
Channel Islands
Lake Tahoe
Mono Lake
Lake Mead
Owens Lake
Santa Barbara Channel
Gulf of Santa Catalina
Reno
Carson City
Las Vegas
Sacramento
San Francisco
Oakland
San Jose
Fresno
Bakersfield
Los Angeles
San Diego
Santa Barbara
Modesto
Stockton
Redding
Winnemucca
Elko
Ely
Tonopah
Hawthorne
Fallon
Henderson
Riverside
San Bernardino
Long Beach
Pasadena
Anaheim
Palm Springs
Barstow
Needles
Blythe
El Centro
Calexico
Mount Shasta 4316m
Mount Whitney 4418m
Boundary Peak 4005m
Wheeler Peak 3981m
Yosemite National Park
Sequoia National Park
Hoover Dam
Parker Dam
Colorado River
Humboldt River
Imperial Dam
Point Conception
Point Arguello
Point Sur
Santa Rosa Island
Santa Cruz Island
San Miguel Island
Santa Catalina Island
San Clemente Island
San Nicolas Island
Santa Barbara Island

▲ **The towering granite** *cliff of El Capitan typifies the Yosemite Valley, which is often choked with tourists during the summer months.*

USA: SOUTH MOUNTAIN STATES

Arizona, Colorado, New Mexico, Utah

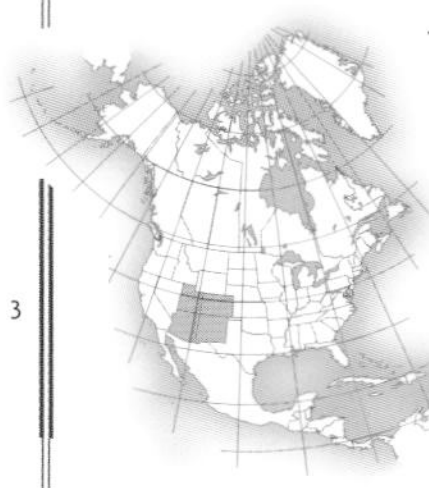

This arid region, characterized by expansive plateaus and spectacular canyons is home to several distinct peoples. The ruins of cliff dwellings built a thousand years ago by the Anasazi people still exist today, and native Americans own one-third of the land in Arizona. Spanish and Mexican conquest and settlement left a hispanic presence which is strongest in New Mexico. The Mormons, who came to the Great Salt Lake seeking religious freedom in 1847, were among the earliest Anglo-American settlers and now make up over 70% of Utah's population. The region's mineral wealth drove rapid development in the 20th century, yet the constraints of a fragile environment, including widespread water shortages, may limit prospects for growth.

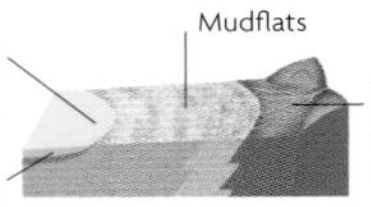
Mudflats
When water evaporates it leaves a salt pan
Lake is fed by seasonal snow melt
Water level of lake varies according to quantity of run-off received from snow melt

▲ *The Great Salt Lake is an ephemeral lake; it can remain dry for extended periods, leaving a pan of evaporated mineral salts in its center.*

The landscape

The arid, rocky expanse of the Colorado Plateau is dissected by immense canyons of the Colorado River. Desert lies to the north and south and branches of the Rocky Mountains run east and west. The Great Salt Lake and Desert lie within the Great Basin, a barren region of parallel mountain ranges that extends into Arizona.

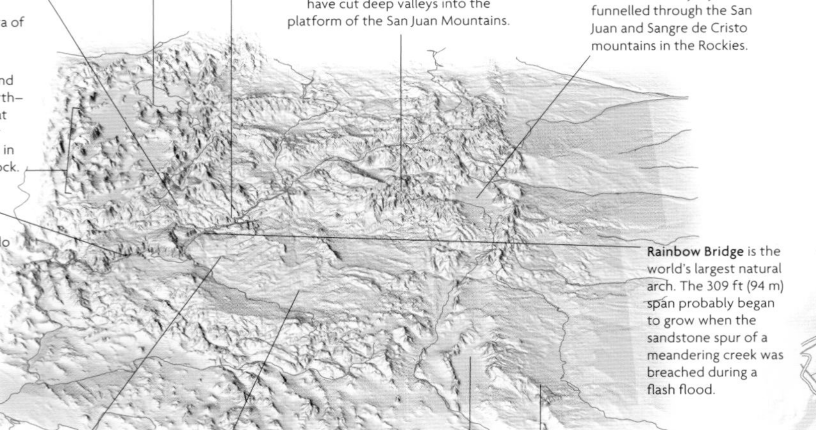
Over 13 million years of weathering has created thousands of spires and pinnacles from the alternating rock strata of Bryce Canyon.
Lake Powell
The Rio Grande has its source in several meltwater streams, which have cut deep valleys into the platform of the San Juan Mountains.
Sand dunes, 600 ft (180 m) high, have been deposited in San Luis Valley, by winds funnelled through the San Juan and Sangre de Cristo mountains in the Rockies.
The parallel basins and ridges, which run north–south along the Great Basin, reflect a major series of block-faults in the underlying bedrock.
Parts of the Grand Canyon, which cuts through the Colorado Plateau,are 16 miles (25 km) wide. The Colorado River has cut down 6262 ft (2000 m), exposing rock strata more than 2 billion years old.
Rainbow Bridge is the world's largest natural arch. The 309 ft (94 m) span probably began to grow when the sandstone spur of a meandering creek was breached during a flash flood.
The striking color effects seen in the Painted Desert come from minerals such as gypsum and haematite, combined with ambient heat and dust.
Petrified Forest
Shifting gypsum sands produce a constantly changing land surface, overwhelming plants and any other obstacles in Tularosa Valley.

► *In the arid landscape of Petrified Forest National Park in Arizona, the grain of prehistoric trees has been preserved as a fossil imprint in the rocks. The bog-preserved trees were gradually turned to stone by seeping mineral-rich water.*

► *The intricate stalactites of Carlsbad Caverns have grown with the seepage of calcium-rich water over the last 100,000 years. The huge caves are home to around 100,000 Mexican freetail bats..*

Transportation & industry

New industries have helped reduce the region's dependence on the extraction of minerals and fossil fuels. Precision manufacture has grown rapidly, particularly in Arizona and Colorado. Salt Lake City and Denver are well-established financial centers and New Mexico, the main US producer of uranium, is a prominent region for nuclear research. Colorado is the most important US center for winter sports.

Transportation network

232,434 miles (373,986 km)	4059 miles (6515 km)
8627 miles (13,881 km)	none

The Colorado Rockies are crossed by 32 mountain passes, some as high as 12,183 ft (3713 m). The Eisenhower Tunnel west of Denver carries Interstate Highway 70 straight through the Continental Divide.

Idaho
Wyoming
Nebraska
Salt Lake City
Denver
Utah
Colorado Springs
Colorado
Kansas
Nevada
Oklahoma
Arizona
Sante Fe
Albuquerque
New Mexico
Texas
California
Phoenix
Tucson
MEXICO

Major industry and infrastructure

- chemicals
- coal
- defense
- finance
- food processing
- hi-tech industry
- oil & gas
- mining
- research & development
- winter sports
- major towns
- international airports
- major roads
- major industrial areas

▲ *Glen Canyon Dam on the Colorado river was completed in 1964. it provides hydroelectric power and irrigation water as part of a long-term federal project to harness the river.*

◄ *The flat tablelands (mesas), and the isolated pinnacles (buttes) which rise from the floor of Monument Valley are the resistant remnants of an earlier land surface, gradually cut back by erosion under arid conditions.*

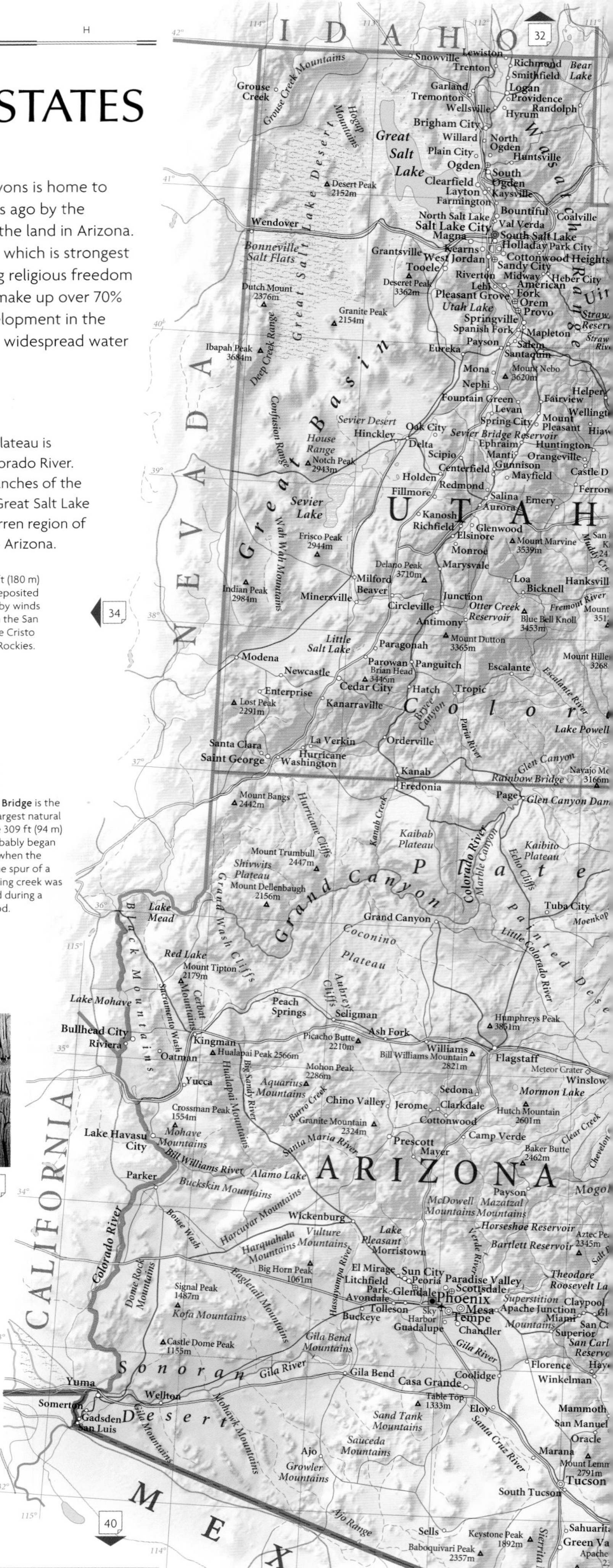
IDAHO
NEVADA
UTAH
ARIZONA
CALIFORNIA
MEXICO
Great Salt Lake
Great Salt Lake Desert
Great Basin
Salt Lake City
Ogden
Provo
Sevier Lake
Colorado Plateau
Grand Canyon
Lake Mead
Lake Powell
Painted Desert
Sonoran Desert
Colorado River
Gila River
Kingman
Flagstaff
Prescott
Phoenix
Mesa
Tempe
Yuma
Tucson
Saint George
Cedar City
Lake Havasu City
Bullhead City
32
34
40

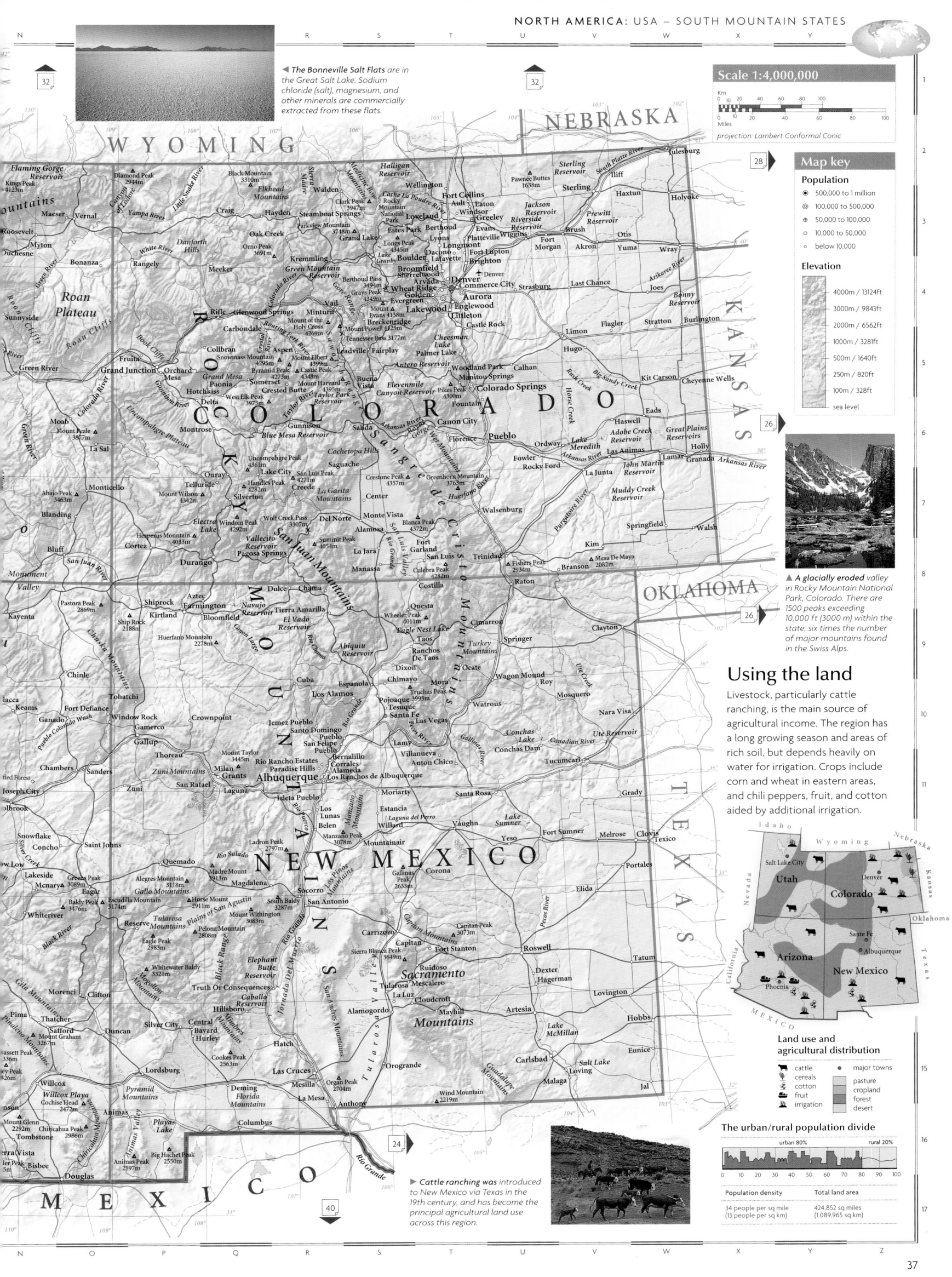

◀ ***The Bonneville Salt Flats*** *are in the Great Salt Lake. Sodium chloride (salt), magnesium, and other minerals are commercially extracted from these flats.*

WYOMING
NEBRASKA
KANSAS
OKLAHOMA
TEXAS
COLORADO
NEW MEXICO
MEXICO
ROCKY MOUNTAINS
Roan Plateau
Flaming Gorge Reservoir
Diamond Peak 2944m
Black Mountain 3310m
Elkhead Mountains
Halligan Reservoir
Sterling Reservoir
Pawnee Buttes 1638m
Julesburg
Sterling
Iliff
Haxtun
Holyoke
Fort Collins
Wellington
Walden
Craig
Hayden
Steamboat Springs
Loveland
Greeley
Estes Park
Jackson Reservoir
Prewitt Reservoir
Brush
Fort Morgan
Akron
Otis
Yuma
Wray
Meeker
Rangely
Kremmling
Boulder
Longmont
Brighton
Denver
Aurora
Lakewood
Littleton
Golden
Wheat Ridge
Arvada
Castle Rock
Strasburg
Last Chance
Joes
Bonny Reservoir
Limon
Flagler
Stratton
Burlington
Hugo
Glenwood Springs
Rifle
Vail
Minturn
Breckenridge
Mount of the Holy Cross 4269m
Mount Evans 4138m
Grays Peak 4349m
Carbondale
Aspen
Leadville
Fairplay
Mount Elbert 4399m
Grand Junction
Fruita
Orchard Mesa
Delta
Paonia
Hotchkiss
Somerset
Crested Butte
Buena Vista
Salida
Gunnison
Montrose
Woodland Park
Manitou Springs
Colorado Springs
Calhan
Kit Carson
Cheyenne Wells
Pikes Peak 4300m
Fountain
Canon City
Florence
Pueblo
Ordway
Eads
Haswell
Adobe Creek Reservoir
Great Plains Reservoirs
Lake Meredith
Fowler
Rocky Ford
La Junta
Las Animas
John Martin Reservoir
Lamar
Granada
Holly
Arkansas River
Moab
Mount Peale 3877m
La Sal
Monticello
Blanding
Bluff
Uncompahgre Peak 4361m
Lake City
Ouray
Telluride
Silverton
Mount Wilson 4342m
Saguache
Creede
Crestone Peak 4357m
Center
Monte Vista
Del Norte
Alamosa
Blanca Peak 4372m
Walsenburg
Springfield
Walsh
Cortez
Durango
Pagosa Springs
La Jara
Fort Garland
San Luis
Manassa
Trinidad
Fishers Peak 2934m
Branson
Kim
Mesa De Maya 2082m
San Juan Mountains
Sangre de Cristo Mountains
Kayenta
Shiprock
Farmington
Aztec
Bloomfield
Kirtland
Dulce
Chama
Tierra Amarilla
El Vado Reservoir
Questa
Wheeler Peak 4011m
Eagle Nest Lake
Taos
Raton
Cimarron
Springer
Clayton
Ranchos De Taos
Abiquiu Reservoir
Dixon
Ocate
Chimayo
Mora
Truchas Peak 3993m
Espanola
Los Alamos
Cuba
Wagon Mound
Roy
Mosquero
Nara Visa
Chinle
Tohatchi
Fort Defiance
Window Rock
Gallup
Crownpoint
Jemez Pueblo
Santa Fe
Las Vegas
Pojoaque
Tesuque
Watrous
Conchas Lake
Conchas Dam
Ute Reservoir
Tucumcari
Thoreau
Zuni
Grants
Milan
Laguna
San Rafael
Mount Taylor 3445m
Rio Rancho Estates
Albuquerque
Bernalillo
Corrales
Alameda
Los Ranchos de Albuquerque
Isleta Pueblo
Los Lunas
Belen
Moriarty
Estancia
Willard
Santa Rosa
Vaughn
Lake Sumner
Fort Sumner
Yeso
Melrose
Clovis
Texico
Grady
Portales
Quemado
Magdalena
Socorro
San Antonio
Ladron Peak 2797m
Gallinas Peak 2633m
Corona
Elida
Reserve
Carrizozo
Capitan
Fort Stanton
Roswell
Dexter
Hagerman
Tatum
Lovington
Hobbs
Truth Or Consequences
Elephant Butte Reservoir
Caballo Reservoir
Hillsboro
Ruidoso
Tularosa
Mescalero
Sacramento Mountains
Cloudcroft
Mayhill
Alamogordo
La Luz
Artesia
Lake McMillan
Eunice
Carlsbad
Loving
Malaga
Jal
Silver City
Bayard
Hurley
Hatch
Las Cruces
Mesilla
La Mesa
Anthony
Orogrande
Deming
Lordsburg
Columbus
Animas
Playas Lake
Clifton
Morenci
Safford
Thatcher
Duncan
Willcox
Douglas
Bisbee
Tombstone
White Sands
Rio Grande

Scale 1:4,000,000

Km 0 10 20 40 60 80 100
Miles 0 10 20 40 60 80 100

projection: Lambert Conformal Conic

Map key

Population

- ◉ 500,000 to 1 million
- ◎ 100,000 to 500,000
- ⊕ 50,000 to 100,000
- ○ 10,000 to 50,000
- ○ below 10,000

Elevation

- 4000m / 13124ft
- 3000m / 9843ft
- 2000m / 6562ft
- 1000m / 3281ft
- 500m / 1640ft
- 250m / 820ft
- 100m / 328ft
- sea level

▲ ***A glacially eroded*** *valley in Rocky Mountain National Park, Colorado. There are 1500 peaks exceeding 10,000 ft (3000 m) within the state, six times the number of major mountains found in the Swiss Alps.*

Using the land

Livestock, particularly cattle ranching, is the main source of agricultural income. The region has a long growing season and areas of rich soil, but depends heavily on water for irrigation. Crops include corn and wheat in eastern areas, and chili peppers, fruit, and cotton aided by additional irrigation.

Idaho
Wyoming
Nebraska
Kansas
Oklahoma
Texas
Mexico
California
Nevada
Utah
Colorado
Arizona
New Mexico
Salt Lake City
Denver
Santa Fe
Albuquerque
Phoenix

Land use and agricultural distribution

- cattle
- cereals
- cotton
- fruit
- irrigation
- ● major towns
- pasture
- cropland
- forest
- desert

The urban/rural population divide

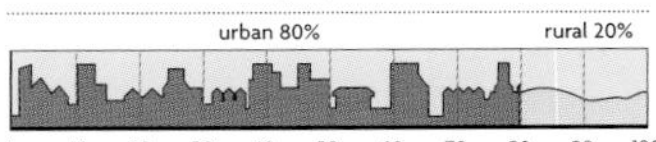

urban 80%
rural 20%
0 10 20 30 40 50 60 70 80 90 100

Population density	Total land area
34 people per sq mile (13 people per sq km)	424,852 sq miles (1,089,965 sq km)

▶ ***Cattle ranching was*** *introduced to New Mexico via Texas in the 19th century, and has become the principal agricultural land use across this region.*

32 32 28 26 26 24 40

USA: HAWAII

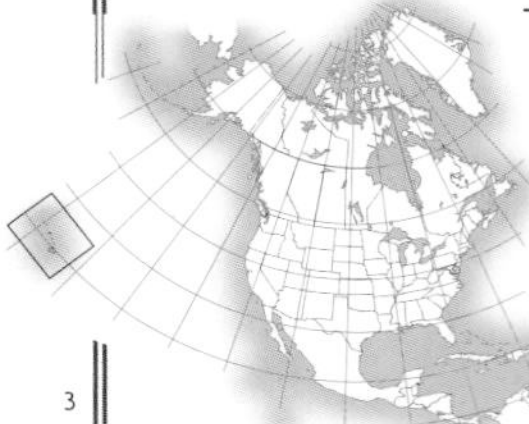

The 122 islands of the Hawai'ian archipelago – which are part of Polynesia – are the peaks of the world's largest volcanoes. They rise approximately 6 miles (9.7 km) from the floor of the Pacific Ocean. The largest, the island of Hawai'i, remains highly active. Hawaii became the US's 50th state in 1959. A tradition of receiving immigrant workers is reflected in the islands' ethnic diversity, with peoples drawn from around the rim of the Pacific. Only 2% of the current population are native Polynesians.

▲ *The island of* Moloka'i *is formed from volcanic rock. Mature sand dunes cover the rocks in coastal areas.*

Transportation & industry

Tourism dominates the economy, with over 90% of the population employed in services. The naval base at Pearl Harbor is also a major source of employment. Industry is concentrated on the island of O'ahu and relies mostly on imported materials, while agricultural produce is processed locally.

Transportation network

4102 miles (6600 km)	43 miles (69 km)
none	none

Hawaii relies on ocean-surface transportation. Honolulu is the main focus of this network, bringing foreign trade and the markets of mainland US to Hawaii's outer islands.

◀ *Haleakala's extinct volcanic crater is the world's largest. The giant caldera, containing many secondary cones, is 2000 ft (600 m) deep and 20 miles (32 km) in circumference.*

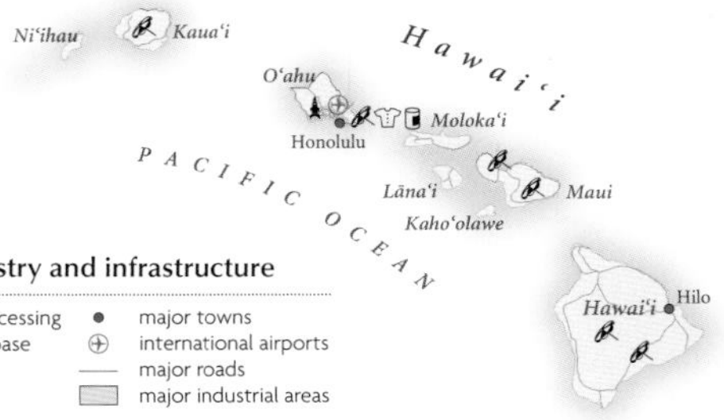

Ni'ihau
Kaua'i
O'ahu
Honolulu
Moloka'i
Hawai'i
PACIFIC OCEAN
Lāna'i
Maui
Kaho'olawe
Hawai'i
Hilo

Major industry and infrastructure

- food processing
- military base
- textiles
- tourism
- major towns
- international airports
- major roads
- major industrial areas

Using the land & sea

The ice-free coastline of Alaska provides access to salmon fisheries and more than 129 million acres (52.2 million ha) of forest. Most of Alaska is uncultivable, and around 90% of food is imported. Barley, hay, and hothouse products are grown around Anchorage, where dairy farming is also concentrated.

The urban/rural population divide

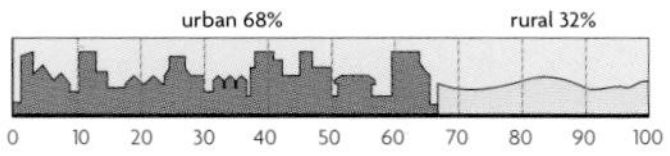

urban 68%
rural 32%
0 10 20 30 40 50 60 70 80 90 100

Population density	Total land area
1 person per sq mile (0.4 people per sq km)	571,951 sq miles (1,481,296 sq km)

◀ *A raft of timber from the Tongass forest is hauled by a tug, bound for the pulp mills of the Alaskan coast between Juneau and Ketchikan.*

Scale 1:4,000,000

Km 0 10 20 40 60 80 100
Miles 0 10 20 40 60 80 100
projection: Lambert Conformal Conic

Map key

Population

- 100,000 to 500,000
- 50,000 to 100,000
- 10,000 to 50,000
- below 10,000

Elevation

- 4000m / 13,124ft
- 3000m / 9843ft
- 2000m / 6562ft
- 1000m / 3281ft
- 500m / 1640ft
- 250m / 820ft
- 100m / 328ft
- sea level

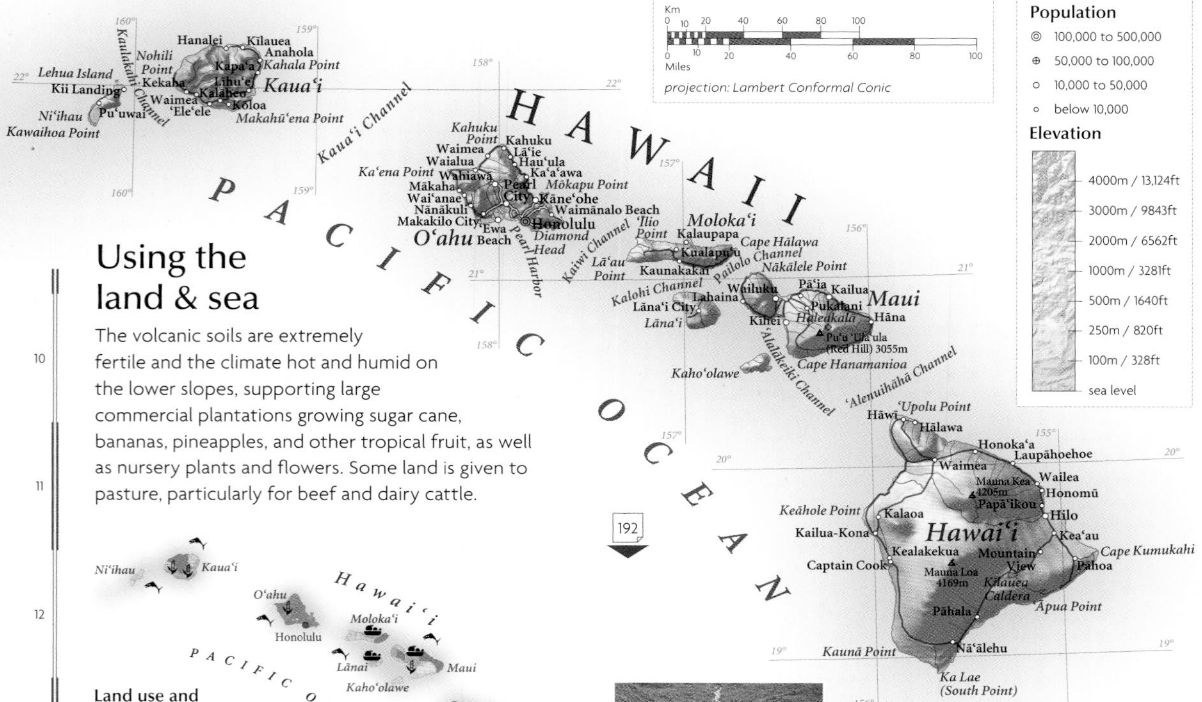

HAWAII
PACIFIC OCEAN
Lehua Island
Kii Landing
Ni'ihau
Pu'uwai
Kawaihoa Point
Kaulakahi Channel
Hanalei
Kīlauea
Anahola
Kapa'a
Kahala Point
Līhu'e
Nohili Point
Kekaha
Waimea
'Ele'ele
Kalaheo
Kōloa
Kaua'i
Makahū'ena Point
Kaua'i Channel
Kahuku Point
Kahuku
Lā'ie
Hau'ula
Ka'a'awa
Ka'ena Point
Waimea
Waialua
Wahiawā
Mōkapu Point
Mākaha
Pearl City
Kāne'ohe
Wai'anae
Nānākuli
Waimānalo Beach
Makakilo City
Ewa Beach
Honolulu
O'ahu
Diamond Head
Pearl Harbor
Kaiwi Channel
Moloka'i
'Ilio Point
Kalaupapa
Cape Hālawa
Kualapu'u
Lā'au Point
Kaunakakai
Pailolo Channel
Nākālele Point
Kalohi Channel
Lahaina
Wailuku
Pā'ia
Kailua
Lāna'i City
Lāna'i
Kīhei
Pukalani
Haleakalā
Maui
Hāna
Pu'u 'Ula'ula (Red Hill) 3055m
Cape Hanamanioa
Kaho'olawe
Alalākeiki Channel
'Alenuihāhā Channel
'Upolu Point
Hāwī
Hālawa
Honoka'a
Laupāhoehoe
Waimea
Mauna Kea 4205m
Wailea
Honomū
Papa'ikou
Hilo
Keāhole Point
Kalaoa
Kailua-Kona
Kea'au
Hawai'i
Kealakekua
Captain Cook
Mountain View
Cape Kumukahi
Pāhoa
Mauna Loa 4169m
Kīlauea Caldera
Pāhala
'Apua Point
Kaunā Point
Nā'ālehu
Ka Lae (South Point)
192

Using the land & sea

The volcanic soils are extremely fertile and the climate hot and humid on the lower slopes, supporting large commercial plantations growing sugar cane, bananas, pineapples, and other tropical fruit, as well as nursery plants and flowers. Some land is given to pasture, particularly for beef and dairy cattle.

Ni'ihau
Kaua'i
O'ahu
Honolulu
Hawai'i
Moloka'i
Lānai
Maui
Kaho'olawe
PACIFIC OCEAN
Hilo
Hawai'i

Land use and agricultural distribution

- cattle
- fishing
- fruit
- sugar cane
- major towns
- pasture
- cropland
- forest
- mountain region

▶ *The island of* Kaua'i *is one of the wettest places in the world, receiving some 450 inches (11,500 mm) of rain a year.*

The urban/rural population divide

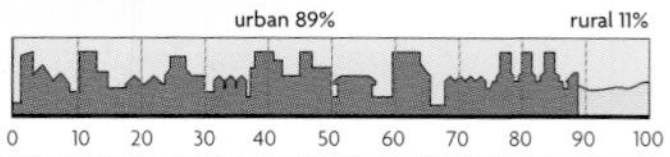

urban 89%
rural 11%
0 10 20 30 40 50 60 70 80 90 100

Population density	Total land area
189 people per sq mile (73 people per sq km)	6,423 sq miles (16,636 sq km)

Cape Lisburne
Wevok
Point Hope
CHUKCHI SEA
Kivalina
Kotzebue Sound
Arctic Circle
RUSSIAN FEDERATION
122
Shishmaref
Bering Strait
Little Diomede Island
Cape Prince of Wales
Wales Mountain 883m
Brooks Mountain
Kougarok Mountain
Brevig Mission
Teller
Port Clarence
Cape Douglas
Cape Rodney
Nome
Solomon
Cape Nome
Northwest Cape
Gambell
Savoonga
Saint Lawrence Island
Southwest Cape
Camp Kulowiye
Northeast Cape
Southeast Cape
BERING SEA
192
Emmonak
Alakanuk
Sheldons Point
Yukon River
Mountain Village
Scammon Bay
Hooper Bay
Chevak
Hall Island
Glory of Russia Cape
Saint Matthew Island
Upright Cape
Pinnacle Island
Hazen Bay
Newtok
Aropuk Lake
Tanunak
Toksook Bay
Nightmute
Cape Mohican
Mekoryuk
Nunivak Island
Etolin Strait
Chefornak
Roberts Mountain 510m
Kipnuk
Kwigillingok
Cape Mendenhall
Kuskokwim Bay
Saint Paul Island
Saint Paul
Pribilof Islands
Saint George Island
Saint George

Map key

Population

- 100,000 to 500,000
- 50,000 to 100,000
- 10,000 to 50,000
- below 10,000

Elevation

- 4000m / 13,124ft
- 3000m / 9843ft
- 2000m / 6562ft
- 1000m / 3281ft
- 500m / 1640ft
- 250m / 820ft
- 100m / 328ft
- sea level

Scale 1:9,000,000

Km 0 25 50 100 150 200 250
Miles 0 25 50 100 150 200 250
projection: Lambert Conformal Conic

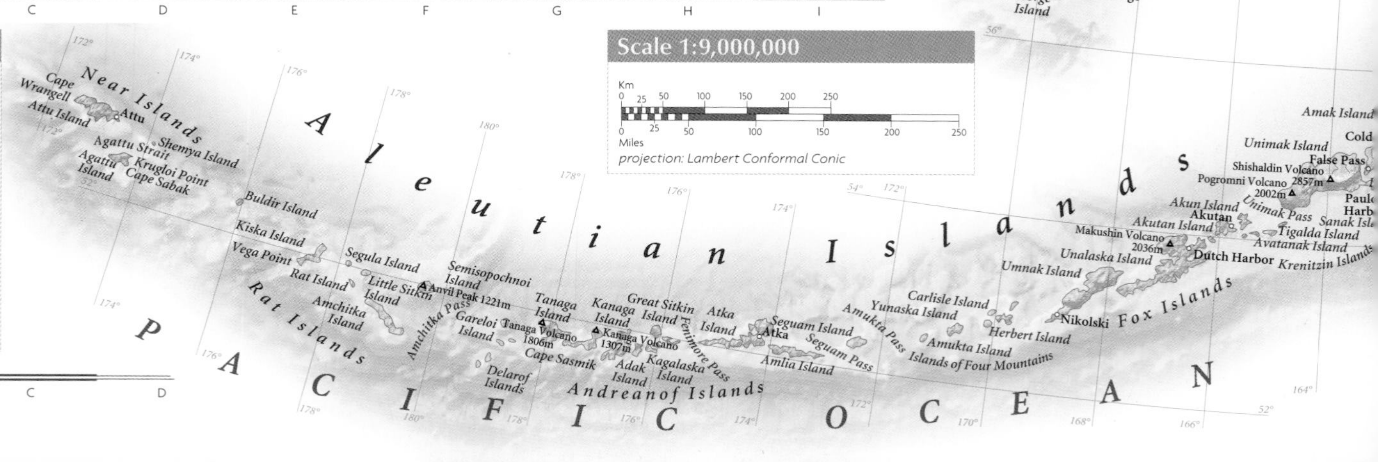

Aleutian Islands
PACIFIC OCEAN
Near Islands
Cape Wrangell
Attu
Attu Island
Shemya Island
Agattu Strait
Agattu Island
Krugloi Point
Cape Sabak
Buldir Island
Kiska Island
Vega Point
Rat Island
Segula Island
Little Sitkin Island
Amchitka Island
Rat Islands
Semisopochnoi Island
Anvil Peak 1221m
Amchitka Pass
Gareloi Island
Tanaga Island
Tanaga Volcano 1806m
Kanaga Island
Kanaga Volcano 1307m
Great Sitkin Island
Adak Island
Cape Sasmik
Kagalaska Island
Delarof Islands
Andreanof Islands
Atka Island
Atka
Fenimore Pass
Seguam Island
Seguam Pass
Amlia Island
Amukta Pass
Yunaska Island
Carlisle Island
Amukta Island
Islands of Four Mountains
Herbert Island
Nikolski
Fox Islands
Umnak Island
Unalaska Island
Makushin Volcano 2036m
Akutan Island
Akutan
Akun Island
Dutch Harbor
Unimak Pass
Tigalda Island
Avatanak Island
Krenitzin Islands
Sanak Islands
Unimak Island
Shishaldin Volcano 2857m
Pogromni Volcano 2002m
False Pass
Amak Island

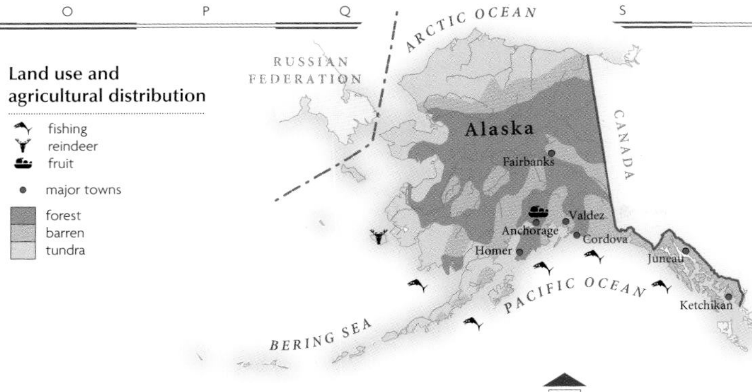
Land use and agricultural distribution
fishing
reindeer
fruit
major towns
forest
barren
tundra
ARCTIC OCEAN
RUSSIAN FEDERATION
CANADA
Alaska
Fairbanks
Anchorage
Valdez
Cordova
Homer
Juneau
Ketchikan
PACIFIC OCEAN
BERING SEA

USA: ALASKA

Almost 650,000 people live in Alaska, a wilderness of ice, forest, mountains, and plains, purchased from Russia in 1867 and twice the size of Texas. The discovery of large oil reserves has brought prosperity to the US's "last frontier," while advancing the need to preserve natural habitats and the traditional livelihoods of indigenous peoples, such as the Aleuts and Inupiaq.

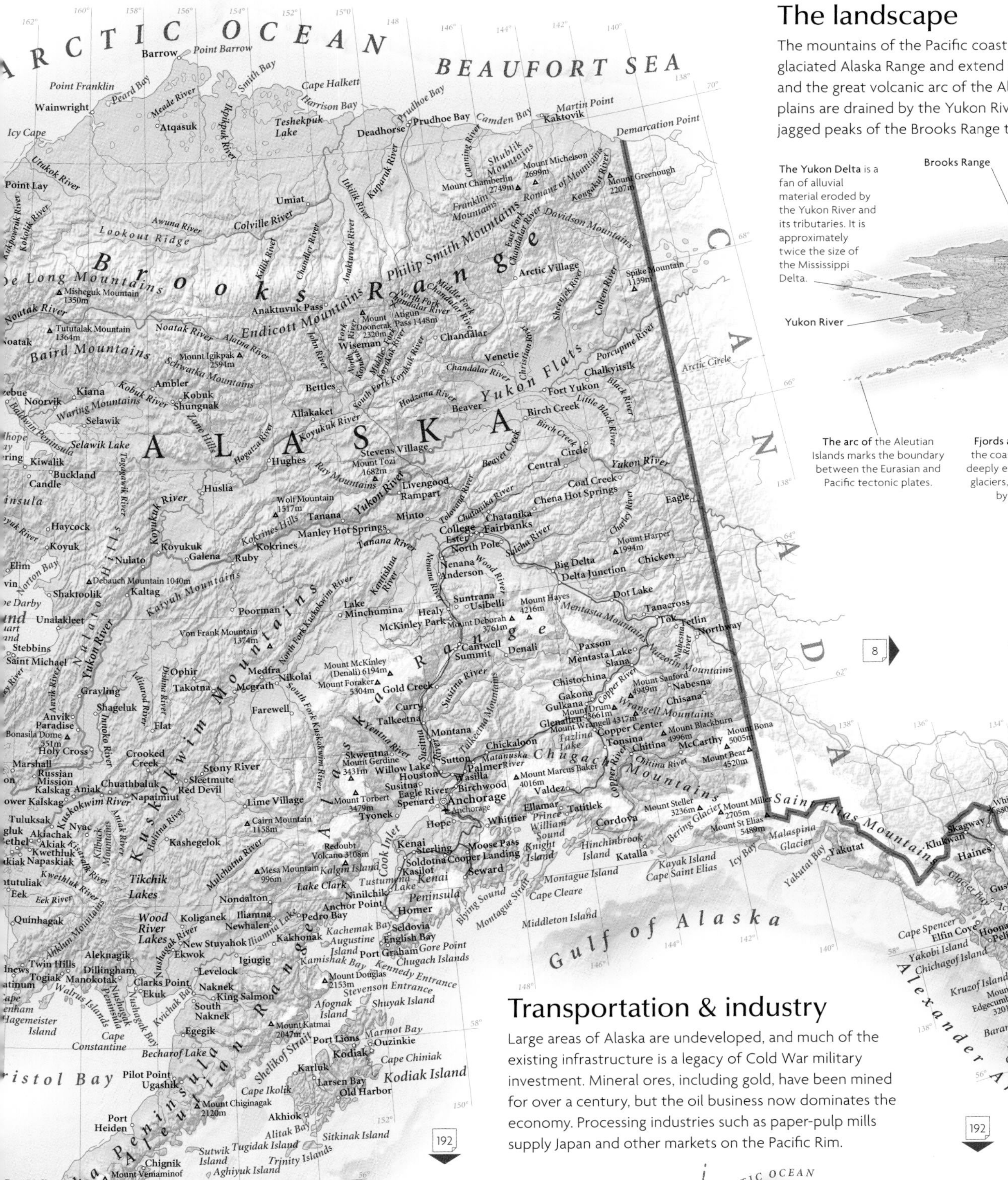
ARCTIC OCEAN
BEAUFORT SEA
A L A S K A
Brooks Range
Alaska Range
Gulf of Alaska
Alexander Archipelago
Bristol Bay
Alaska Peninsula
Aleutian Range
Kodiak Island
C A N A D A

The landscape

The mountains of the Pacific coast culminate in the heavily glaciated Alaska Range and extend west, to the Alaska Peninsula and the great volcanic arc of the Aleutian Islands. The interior plains are drained by the Yukon River and bounded by the bare, jagged peaks of the Brooks Range to the north.

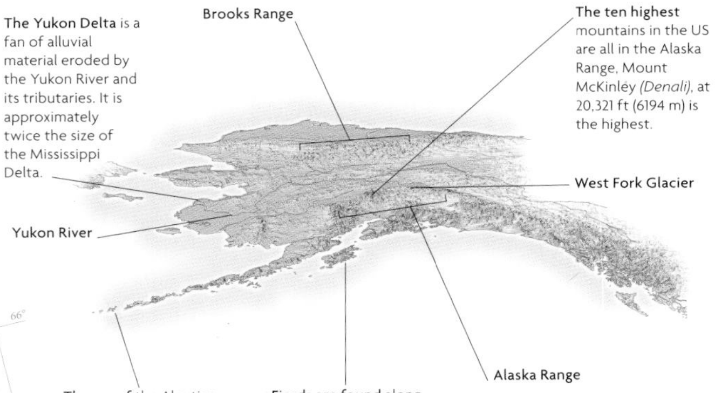
The Yukon Delta is a fan of alluvial material eroded by the Yukon River and its tributaries. It is approximately twice the size of the Mississippi Delta.
Brooks Range
The ten highest mountains in the US are all in the Alaska Range. Mount McKinley (Denali), at 20,321 ft (6194 m) is the highest.
West Fork Glacier
Yukon River
The arc of the Aleutian Islands marks the boundary between the Eurasian and Pacific tectonic plates.
Fjords are found along the coast where valleys, deeply excavated by large glaciers, were inundated by rising seas.
Alaska Range

▲ *By August, the Alaska Range is covered with autumnal tundra vegetation.*

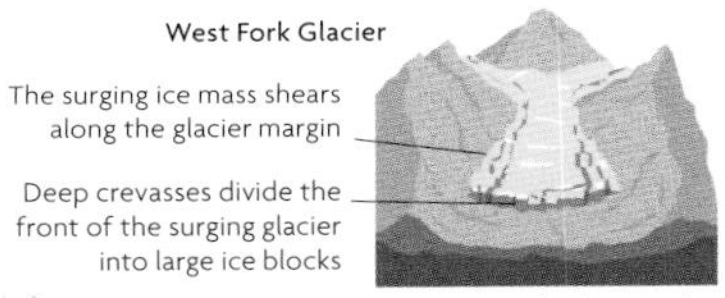
West Fork Glacier
The surging ice mass shears along the glacier margin
Deep crevasses divide the front of the surging glacier into large ice blocks

▲ *Surging glaciers make rapid and dramatic advances, normally after periods of snow accumulation. West Fork Glacier in the Susitna River Basin traveled 2.5 miles (4 km) in 1987.*

Transportation & industry

Large areas of Alaska are undeveloped, and much of the existing infrastructure is a legacy of Cold War military investment. Mineral ores, including gold, have been mined for over a century, but the oil business now dominates the economy. Processing industries such as paper-pulp mills supply Japan and other markets on the Pacific Rim.

Transportation network

13,524 miles (21,760 km)	49 miles (78 km)
482 miles (772 km)	none

Over 40 million gallons (182 million litres) of oil are pumped through the Trans-Alaska Pipeline every day. The oil takes six days to travel the 789 miles (1262 km) from Prudhoe Bay to Valdez.

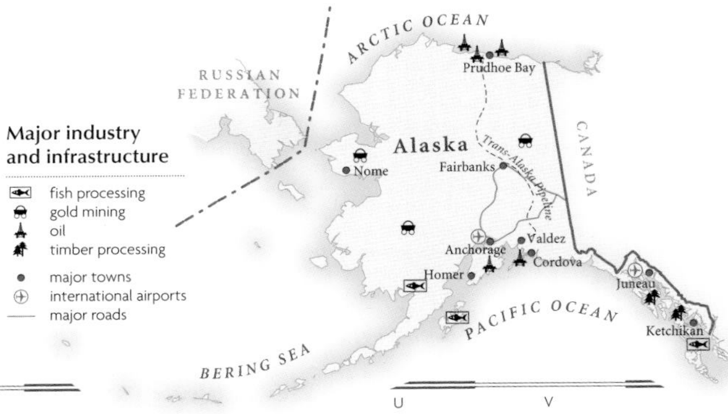
Major industry and infrastructure
fish processing
gold mining
oil
timber processing
major towns
international airports
major roads
ARCTIC OCEAN
Prudhoe Bay
RUSSIAN FEDERATION
CANADA
Alaska
Nome
Fairbanks
Trans-Alaska Pipeline
Anchorage
Valdez
Cordova
Homer
Juneau
Ketchikan
PACIFIC OCEAN
BERING SEA

▲ *The Trans-Alaska Pipeline has carried crude oil from Prudhoe Bay since 1977. The oilfield is the US's largest and is estimated to be equal in size to the biggest oilfields of the Persian Gulf.*

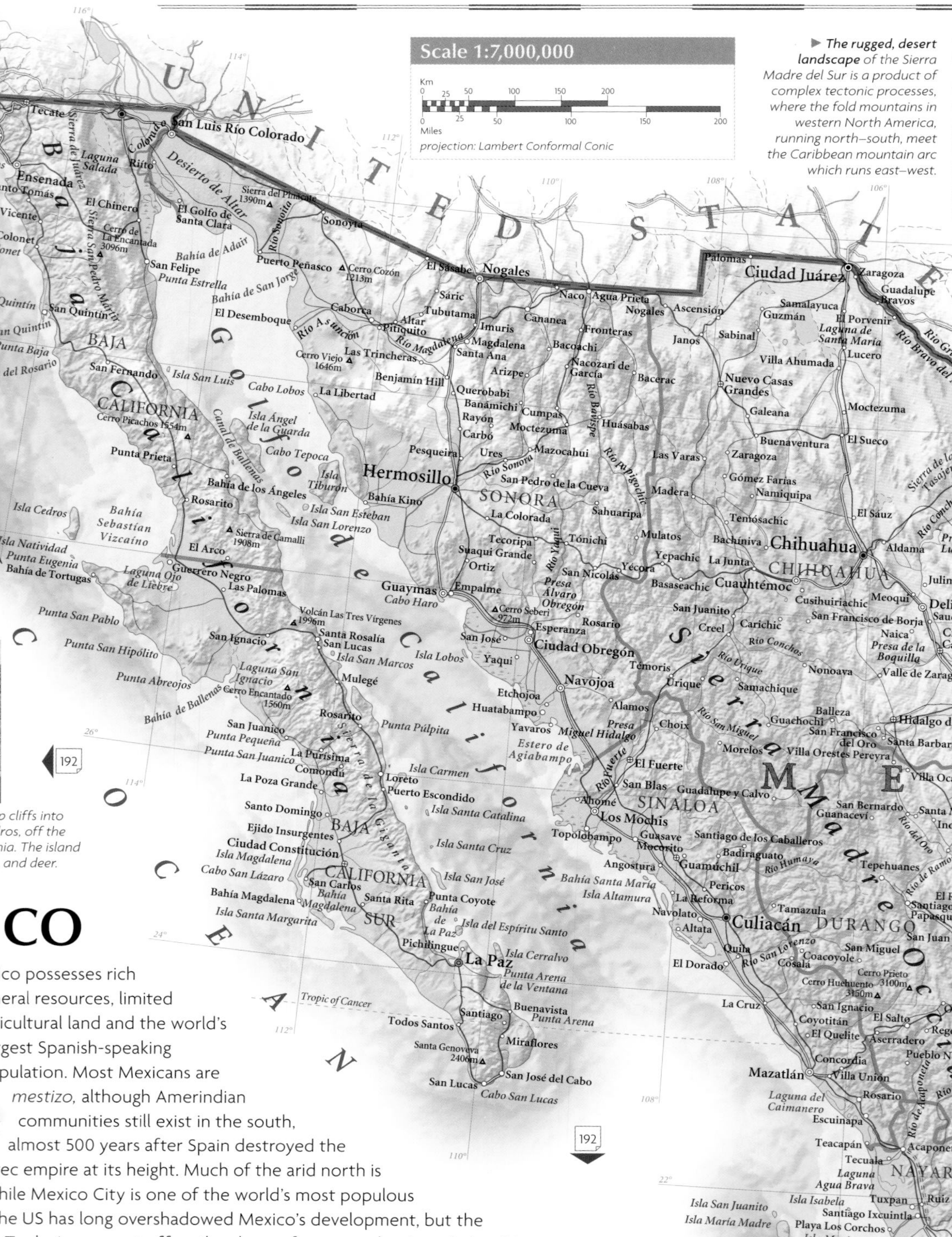

Tijuana
UNITED STATES OF AMERICA
PACIFIC OCEAN
Golfo de California
BAJA CALIFORNIA
BAJA CALIFORNIA SUR
SONORA
CHIHUAHUA
COAHUILA
SINALOA
DURANGO
NAYARIT
ZACATECAS
JALISCO
COLIMA
MICHOACÁN
AGUASCALIENTES
Sierra Madre Occidental
MEXICO
Hermosillo
Chihuahua
Ciudad Juárez
Culiacán
Mazatlán
Durango
Guadalajara
La Paz
Tropic of Cancer

192

16

Scale 1:7,000,000

Km 0 25 50 100 150 200

Miles 0 25 50 100 150 200

projection: Lambert Conformal Conic

► ***The rugged, desert landscape*** *of the Sierra Madre del Sur is a product of complex tectonic processes, where the fold mountains in western North America, running north–south, meet the Caribbean mountain arc which runs east–west.*

▲ ***Wave action has*** *cut steep cliffs into the igneous rocks of Isla Cedros, off the Pacific coast of Baja California. The island is home to sea lions, reptiles, and deer.*

Mexico

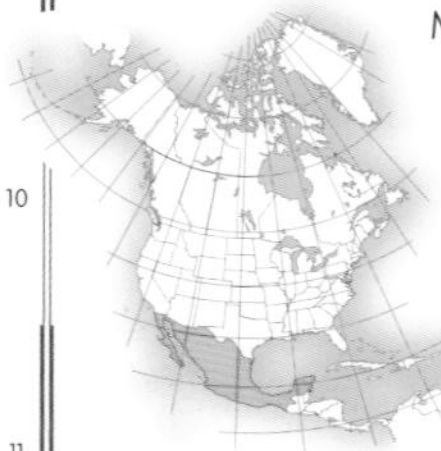

Mexico possesses rich mineral resources, limited agricultural land and the world's largest Spanish-speaking population. Most Mexicans are *mestizo*, although Amerindian communities still exist in the south, almost 500 years after Spain destroyed the Aztec empire at its height. Much of the arid north is sparsely inhabited, while Mexico City is one of the world's most populous cities. Conflict with the US has long overshadowed Mexico's development, but the North American Free Trade Agreement offers the chance for a more benign relationship, which may help to offset Mexico's problems of hyperinflation, foreign debt, unequal wealth distribution, and political instability.

Using the land & sea

Corn occupies much of the cultivated area. Commercial plantations of coffee, sugar, vanilla, and cotton are found along the Gulf coastal plain and in irrigated parts of the arid north, which is otherwise used for extensive ranching. Fishing is important, particularly shellfish for export. A soaring population has created the need for grain imports since 1980.

The urban/rural population divide

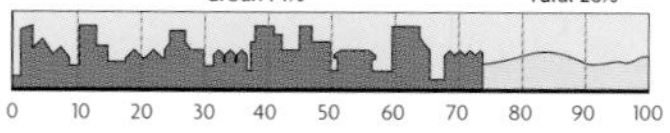

urban 74%
rural 26%
0 10 20 30 40 50 60 70 80 90 100

Population density	Total land area
140 people per sq mile (54 people per sq km)	755,865 sq miles (1,958,200 sq km)

Land use and agricultural distribution

Tijuana
UNITED STATES OF AMERICA
Gulf of California
MEXICO
Monterrey
Gulf of Mexico
Mérida
Guadalajara
MEXICO CITY
PACIFIC OCEAN
Acapulco
BELIZE
GUATEMALA

cattle, coffee, corn, cotton, fishing, shellfish, sugar cane, timber, vanilla

capital cities, major towns

pasture, cropland, forest, desert

► ***Coffee beans spread*** *out to dry in the sun. Coffee, grown mainly on the Gulf coastal plain, is Mexico's most valuable export crop.*

Map key

Mexico: Administrative regions

Ⓓ Distrito Federal

Population	Elevation
above 5 million	4000m / 13,124ft
1 million to 5 million	3000m / 9843ft
500,000 to 1 million	2000m / 6562ft
100,000 to 500,000	1000m / 3281ft
50,000 to 100,000	500m / 1640ft
10,000 to 50,000	250m / 820ft
below 10,000	100m / 328ft
	sea level

192

The landscape

The great central plateau rises gently southward from the Rio Grande, isolated from the coastal plains by the Sierra Madre Oriental and Occidental. The two ranges converge from east and west respectively, culminating in high volcanic peaks around Mexico City. Further ranges of the Sierra Madre rise to the south of the Balsas basin, skirted by the low-lying Isthmus of Tehuantepec *(Istmo de Tehuantepec)* and Yucatan Peninsula.

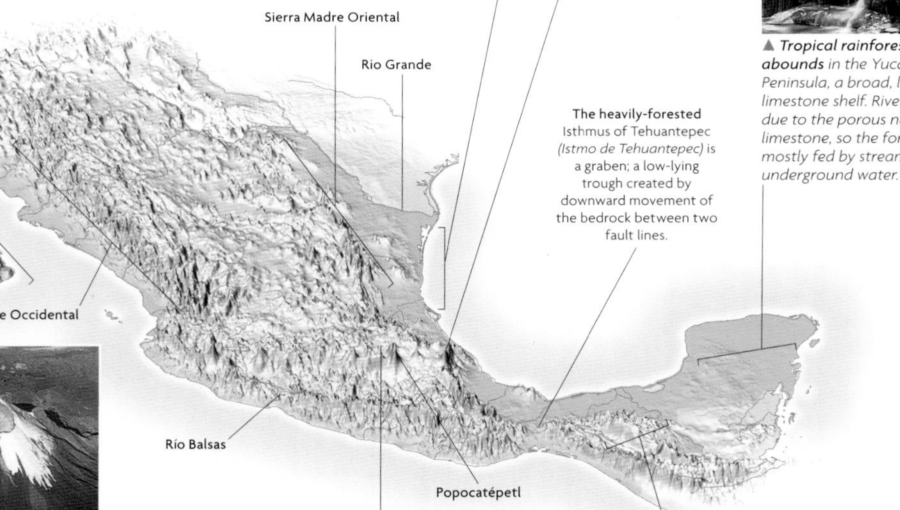

The long, narrow, extremely arid peninsula of Baja (lower) California is an elongated granite block, separated from the mainland by the flooded rift valley of the Gulf of California *(Golfo de California)*.
Wave action has constructed sand bars which shelter lagoons along the shore of the Gulf coastal plain.
The dormant cone of Volcán Pico de Orizaba is, at 18,700 ft (5700 m), the highest peak in Mexico. In North America, only Mount McKinley and Mount Logan are taller.
Sierra Madre Oriental
Rio Grande
The heavily-forested Isthmus of Tehuantepec *(Istmo de Tehuantepec)* is a graben; a low-lying trough created by downward movement of the bedrock between two fault lines.
Sierra Madre Occidental
Río Balsas
Popocatépetl
The unstable, earthquake-prone, upland basin around Mexico City was once a region of shallow lakes. Flood control measures and domestic consumption over the last four centuries have caused the virtual disappearance of this surface water.
The highlands of Chiapas are a series of *horsts*, blocks of land thrust upward between two fault lines. Volcanic cones have developed where lava has flowed out from the faults.

▲ ***Tropical rainforest abounds** in the Yucatan Peninsula, a broad, low limestone shelf. Rivers are rare due to the porous nature of limestone, so the forest is mostly fed by streams and underground water.*

Formation of the Gulf of California

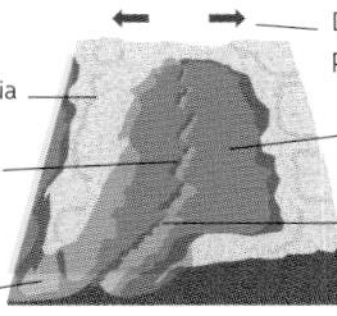

Direction of plate movement
Baja California
Gulf of California
Transform fault
Spreading oceanic ridge
Edge of continental crust

▲ ***The Gulf of** California (Golfo de California) began to open out about 4 million years ago as a result of rifting and plate displacement along transform faults.*

▲ ***Popocatépetl is a** dormant volcano, part of the Pacific "Ring of Fire." The crater is over half a mile (1 km) wide.*

16

Transportation & industry

Oil and gas on the Gulf coast are Mexico's main sources of export income. Metal mining has declined but the country remains a leading global producer of silver. Manufacturing is heavily concentrated around the metropolitan area of Mexico City, while the duty-free movement of goods in the US border region, under the *Maquiladora* (twin plant) scheme, has created new hi-tech and service growth centers.

UNITED STATES OF AMERICA
Tijuana
Ciudad Juárez
Gulf of California
MEXICO
Nuevo Laredo
Matamoros
Monterrey
Durango
San Lucas
Mazatlán
San Luis Potosí
Gulf of Mexico
Tampico
Guadalajara
MEXICO CITY
Mérida
Puebla
Veracruz
Acapulco
Oaxaca
BELIZE
GUATEMALA
PACIFIC OCEAN

Major industry and infrastructure

- brewing
- car manufacture
- chemicals
- electronics
- fish processing
- maquiladoras
- mining
- oil & gas
- textiles
- capital cities
- major towns
- international airports
- major roads
- major industrial areas

▲ ***A stone figure** reclines by the Temple of Warriors, within the Mayan city of Chichén-Itzá. The Maya civilization flourished across the Yucatan Peninsula between 200 and 900 AD.*

Transportation network

- 67,564 miles (108,746 km)
- 3994 miles (6429 km)
- 16,561 miles (26,656 km)
- 1801 miles (2900 km)

Fast, modern highways or autopistas now link Mexico City with Toluca, Puebla and other satellite cities, yet distant centers like Chihuahua are still served by narrow roads and an outdated railroad network.

NUEVO LEÓN
TAMAULIPAS
SAN LUIS POTOSÍ
Sierra Madre Oriental
Monterrey
Matamoros
Nuevo Laredo
Ciudad Victoria
Tampico
Ciudad Madero
San Luis Potosí
Querétaro
Guanajuato
HIDALGO
VERACRUZ-LLAVE
MEXICO
México (MEXICO CITY)
Toluca
Puebla
Cuernavaca
Tlaxcala
PUEBLA
MORELOS
GUERRERO
OAXACA
Oaxaca
Acapulco
Chilpancingo
Veracruz
Xalapa
Bahía de Campeche
Coatzacoalcos
TABASCO
Villahermosa
CHIAPAS
Tuxtla
Tapachula
Istmo de Tehuantepec
Golfo de Tehuantepec
Sierra Madre del Sur
Yucatan Channel
Yucatan Peninsula
YUCATAN
Mérida
Cancún
Campeche
CAMPECHE
QUINTANA ROO
Chetumal
BELIZE
GUATEMALA
PACIFIC OCEAN
Tropic of Cancer

58
42
42

Yucatan Peninsula
MEXICO
BELIZE
BELMOPAN
Belize City
GUATEMALA
CIUDAD DE GUATEMALA (GUATEMALA CITY)
EL SALVADOR
SAN SALVADOR
HONDURAS
TEGUCIGALPA
NICARAGUA
MANAGUA
COSTA RICA
CARIBBEAN
PACIFIC OCEAN
Gulf of Honduras
Lago de Nicaragua
Lago de Managua
Lago Petén Itzá
ISLAS DE LA BAHÍA
Lighthouse Reef
Glovers Reef
Turneffe Islands
Chetumal Bay
Ambergris Cay
San Pedro Sula
La Ceiba
San Miguel
Santa Ana
León
Granada
Chinandega
Golfo de Fonseca
Golfo de Papagayo
Golfo de Nicoya
Puntarenas
Cabo Blanco

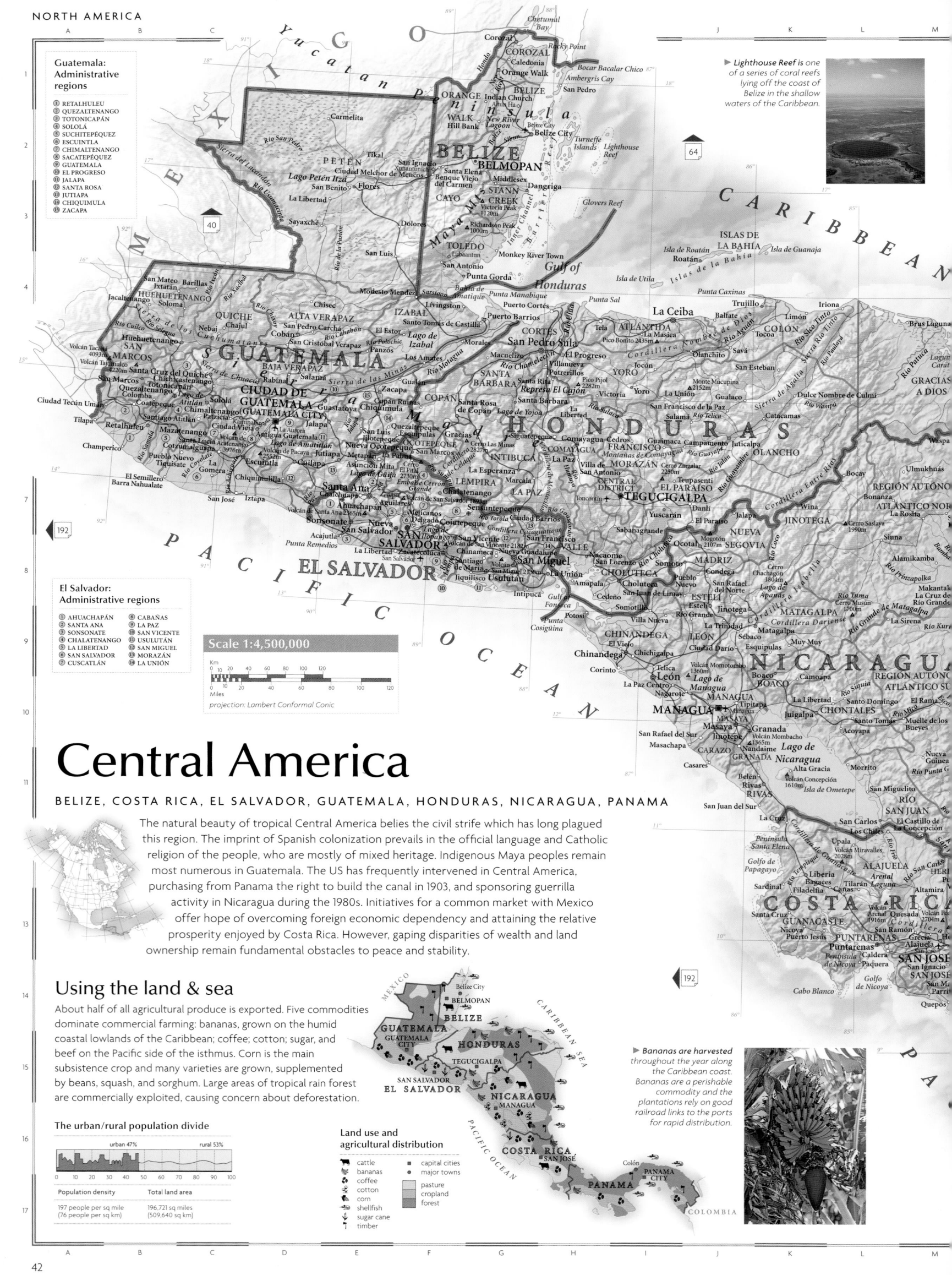

Guatemala: Administrative regions

1. RETALHULEU
2. QUEZALTENANGO
3. TOTONICAPÁN
4. SOLOLÁ
5. SUCHITEPÉQUEZ
6. ESCUINTLA
7. CHIMALTENANGO
8. SACATEPÉQUEZ
9. GUATEMALA
10. EL PROGRESO
11. JALAPA
12. SANTA ROSA
13. JUTIAPA
14. CHIQUIMULA
15. ZACAPA

El Salvador: Administrative regions

1. AHUACHAPÁN
2. SANTA ANA
3. SONSONATE
4. CHALATENANGO
5. LA LIBERTAD
6. SAN SALVADOR
7. CUSCATLÁN
8. CABAÑAS
9. LA PAZ
10. SAN VICENTE
11. USULUTÁN
12. SAN MIGUEL
13. MORAZÁN
14. LA UNIÓN

Scale 1:4,500,000

Km 0 10 20 40 60 80 100 120
Miles 0 10 20 40 60 80 100 120

projection: Lambert Conformal Conic

40
64
192
192

*▶ **Lighthouse Reef** is one of a series of coral reefs lying off the coast of Belize in the shallow waters of the Caribbean.*

Central America

BELIZE, COSTA RICA, EL SALVADOR, GUATEMALA, HONDURAS, NICARAGUA, PANAMA

The natural beauty of tropical Central America belies the civil strife which has long plagued this region. The imprint of Spanish colonization prevails in the official language and Catholic religion of the people, who are mostly of mixed heritage. Indigenous Maya peoples remain most numerous in Guatemala. The US has frequently intervened in Central America, purchasing from Panama the right to build the canal in 1903, and sponsoring guerrilla activity in Nicaragua during the 1980s. Initiatives for a common market with Mexico offer hope of overcoming foreign economic dependency and attaining the relative prosperity enjoyed by Costa Rica. However, gaping disparities of wealth and land ownership remain fundamental obstacles to peace and stability.

Using the land & sea

About half of all agricultural produce is exported. Five commodities dominate commercial farming: bananas, grown on the humid coastal lowlands of the Caribbean; coffee; cotton; sugar, and beef on the Pacific side of the isthmus. Corn is the main subsistence crop and many varieties are grown, supplemented by beans, squash, and sorghum. Large areas of tropical rain forest are commercially exploited, causing concern about deforestation.

The urban/rural population divide

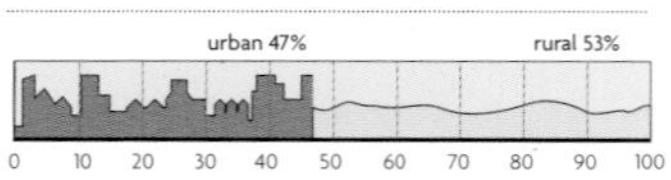
urban 47%
rural 53%
0 10 20 30 40 50 60 70 80 90 100

Population density	Total land area
197 people per sq mile (76 people per sq km)	196,721 sq miles (509,640 sq km)

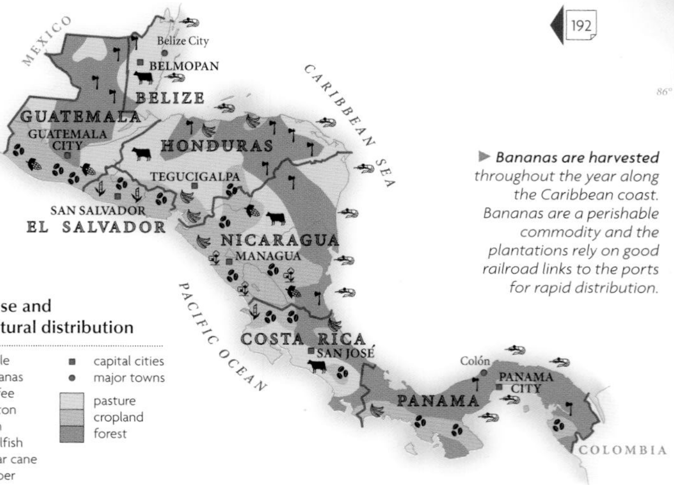
MEXICO
Belize City
BELMOPAN
BELIZE
GUATEMALA
GUATEMALA CITY
HONDURAS
TEGUCIGALPA
SAN SALVADOR
EL SALVADOR
NICARAGUA
MANAGUA
COSTA RICA
SAN JOSÉ
PANAMA
PANAMA CITY
Colón
COLOMBIA
CARIBBEAN SEA
PACIFIC OCEAN

Land use and agricultural distribution

- cattle
- bananas
- coffee
- cotton
- corn
- shellfish
- sugar cane
- timber
- capital cities
- major towns
- pasture
- cropland
- forest

*▶ **Bananas are harvested** throughout the year along the Caribbean coast. Bananas are a perishable commodity and the plantations rely on good railroad links to the ports for rapid distribution.*

The landscape

The Sierra Madre range spreads west from Mexico, between the narrow Pacific coastal plain and the limestone lowland of Petén. Parallel hill ranges sweep across Honduras and extend south, past the Caribbean Mosquito Coast, to lakes Managua and Nicaragua. The Cordillera Central rises to the south, gradually descending to Lake Gatún *(Lago Gatún)*. A highly active volcanic belt runs along the Pacific seaboard from Mexico to Costa Rica.

▲ ***The 990 ft*** *(300 m) deep crater occupied by Lake Atitlán* (Lago de Atitlán) *was created after a volcanic explosion caused the original cone to collapse in on itself. On its shores lie other volcanic cones.*

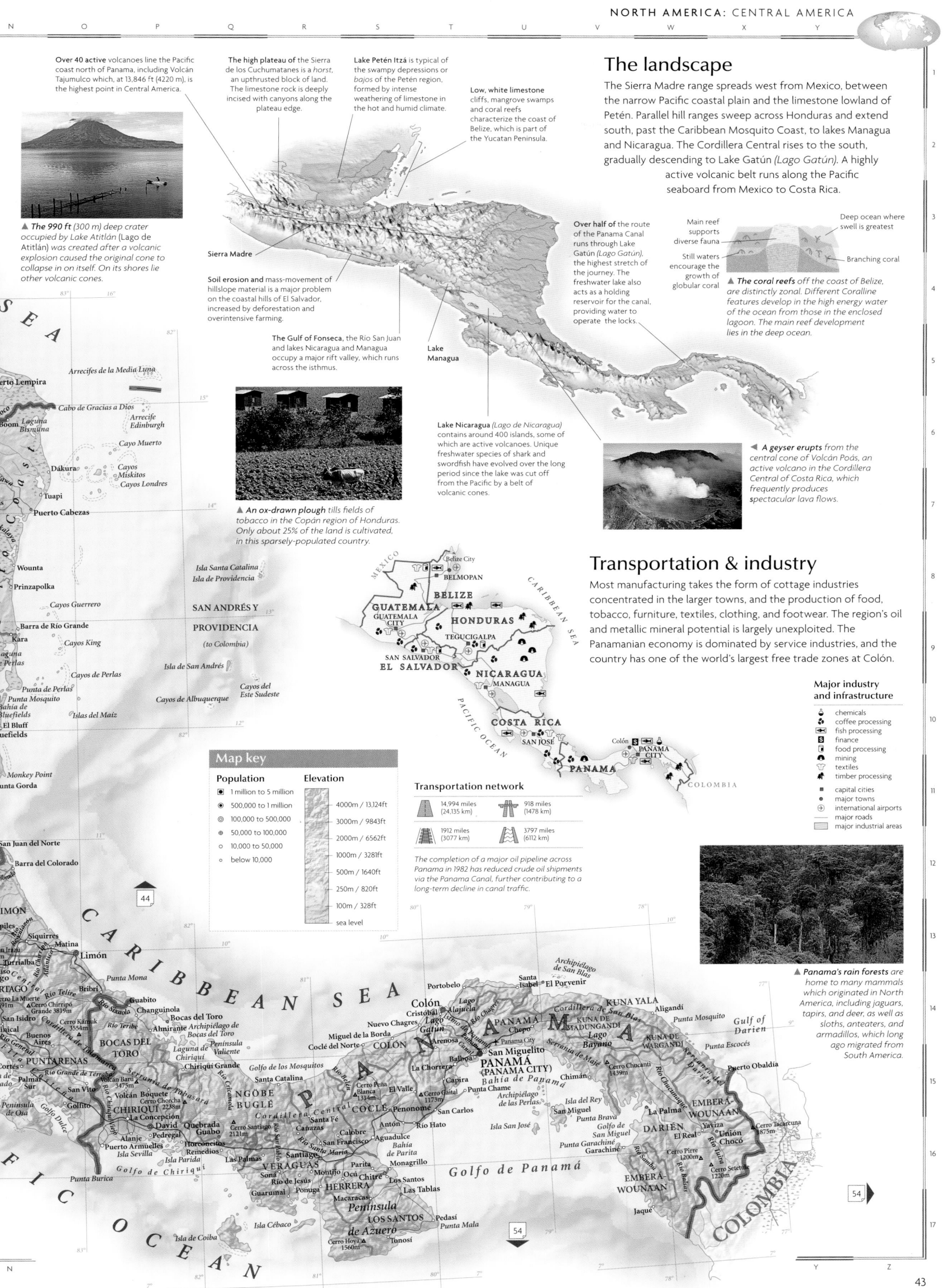

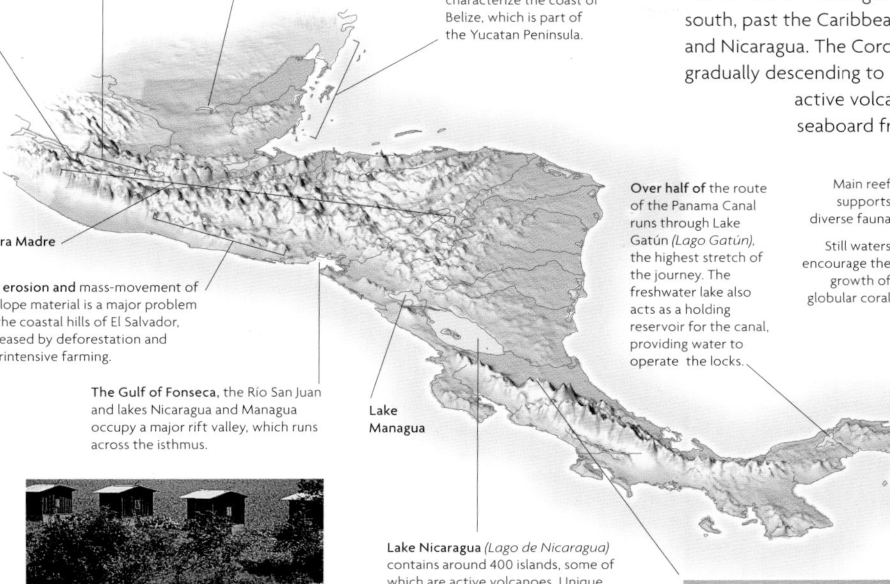

Over 40 active volcanoes line the Pacific coast north of Panama, including Volcán Tajumulco which, at 13,846 ft (4220 m), is the highest point in Central America.
The high plateau of the Sierra de los Cuchumatanes is a *horst*, an upthrusted block of land. The limestone rock is deeply incised with canyons along the plateau edge.
Lake Petén Itzá is typical of the swampy depressions or *bajos* of the Petén region, formed by intense weathering of limestone in the hot and humid climate.
Low, white limestone cliffs, mangrove swamps and coral reefs characterize the coast of Belize, which is part of the Yucatan Peninsula.
Sierra Madre
Soil erosion and mass-movement of hillslope material is a major problem on the coastal hills of El Salvador, increased by deforestation and overintensive farming.
The Gulf of Fonseca, the Río San Juan and lakes Nicaragua and Managua occupy a major rift valley, which runs across the isthmus.
Lake Managua
Lake Nicaragua *(Lago de Nicaragua)* contains around 400 islands, some of which are active volcanoes. Unique freshwater species of shark and swordfish have evolved over the long period since the lake was cut off from the Pacific by a belt of volcanic cones.
Over half of the route of the Panama Canal runs through Lake Gatún *(Lago Gatún)*, the highest stretch of the journey. The freshwater lake also acts as a holding reservoir for the canal, providing water to operate the locks.

Main reef supports diverse fauna
Still waters encourage the growth of globular coral
Deep ocean where swell is greatest
Branching coral

▲ ***The coral reefs*** *off the coast of Belize, are distinctly zonal. Different Coralline features develop in the high energy water of the ocean from those in the enclosed lagoon. The main reef development lies in the deep ocean.*

▲ ***An ox-drawn plough*** *tills fields of tobacco in the Copán region of Honduras. Only about 25% of the land is cultivated, in this sparsely-populated country.*

◀ ***A geyser erupts*** *from the central cone of Volcán Poás, an active volcano in the Cordillera Central of Costa Rica, which frequently produces spectacular lava flows.*

Transportation & industry

Most manufacturing takes the form of cottage industries concentrated in the larger towns, and the production of food, tobacco, furniture, textiles, clothing, and footwear. The region's oil and metallic mineral potential is largely unexploited. The Panamanian economy is dominated by service industries, and the country has one of the world's largest free trade zones at Colón.

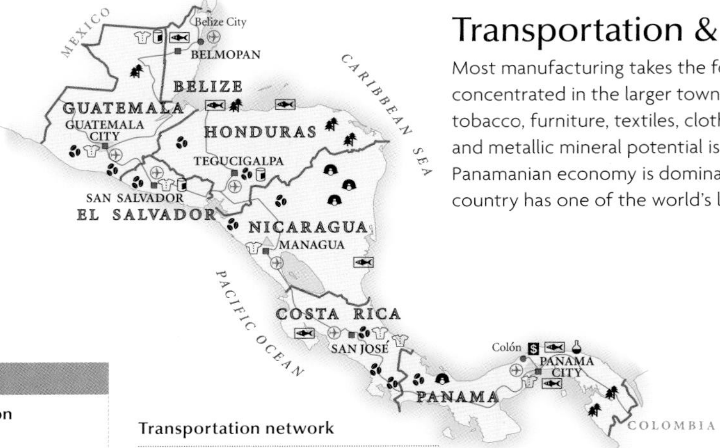

MEXICO
Belize City
BELMOPAN
BELIZE
GUATEMALA
GUATEMALA CITY
HONDURAS
TEGUCIGALPA
SAN SALVADOR
EL SALVADOR
NICARAGUA
MANAGUA
CARIBBEAN SEA
PACIFIC OCEAN
COSTA RICA
SAN JOSÉ
Colón
PANAMA CITY
PANAMA
COLOMBIA

Major industry and infrastructure

- chemicals
- coffee processing
- fish processing
- finance
- food processing
- mining
- textiles
- timber processing
- capital cities
- major towns
- international airports
- major roads
- major industrial areas

Transportation network

14,994 miles (24,135 km)		918 miles (1478 km)	
1912 miles (3077 km)		3797 miles (6112 km)	

The completion of a major oil pipeline across Panama in 1982 has reduced crude oil shipments via the Panama Canal, further contributing to a long-term decline in canal traffic.

▲ ***Panama's rain forests*** *are home to many mammals which originated in North America, including jaguars, tapirs, and deer, as well as sloths, anteaters, and armadillos, which long ago migrated from South America.*

Map key

Population

- 1 million to 5 million
- 500,000 to 1 million
- 100,000 to 500,000
- 50,000 to 100,000
- 10,000 to 50,000
- below 10,000

Elevation

- 4000m / 13,124ft
- 3000m / 9843ft
- 2000m / 6562ft
- 1000m / 3281ft
- 500m / 1640ft
- 250m / 820ft
- 100m / 328ft
- sea level

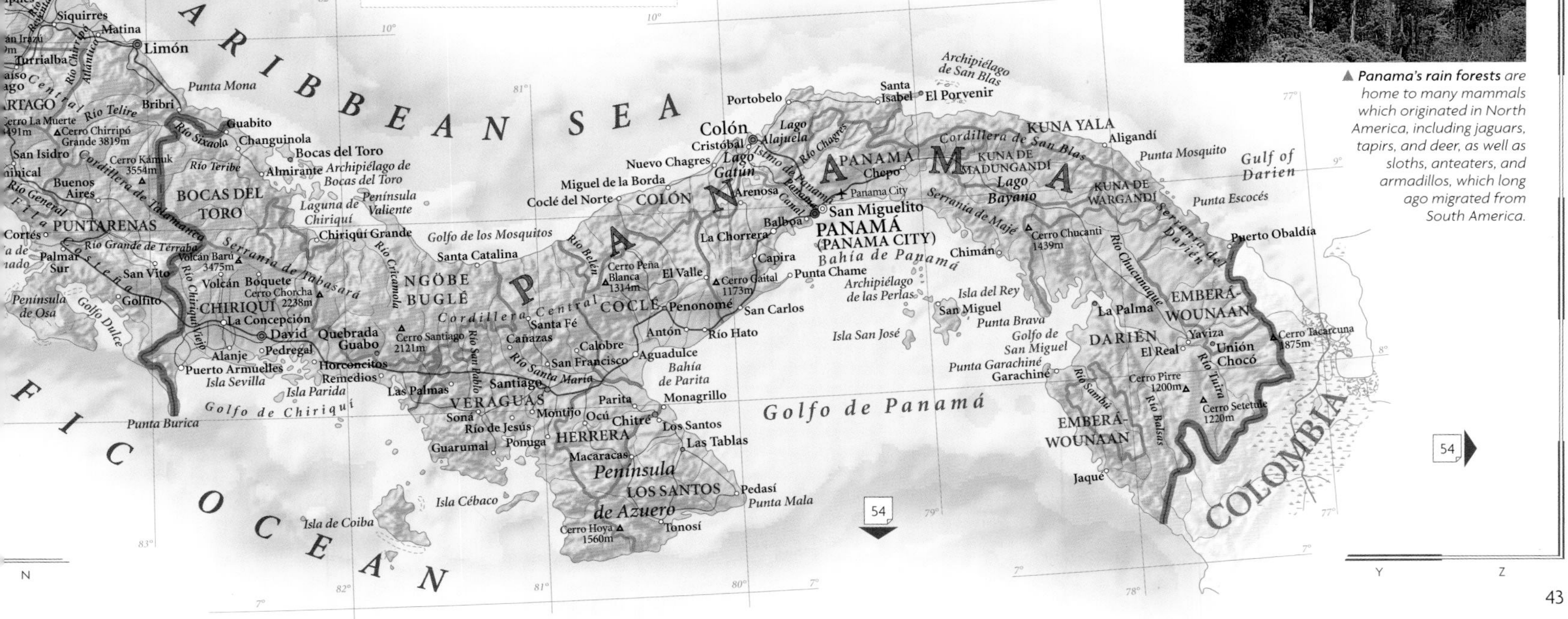

CARIBBEAN SEA
PACIFIC OCEAN
Arrecifes de la Media Luna
Cabo de Gracias a Dios
Arrecife Edinburgh
Laguna Bismuna
Cayo Muerto
Dákura
Cayos Miskitos
Cayos Londres
Tuapi
Puerto Cabezas
Wounta
Prinzapolka
Cayos Guerrero
Isla Santa Catalina
Isla de Providencia
SAN ANDRÉS Y PROVIDENCIA
(to Colombia)
Barra de Río Grande
Kara
Cayos King
Laguna de Perlas
Isla de San Andrés
Cayos de Perlas
Punta de Perlas
Punta Mosquito
Bahía de Bluefields
El Bluff
Islas del Maíz
Cayos del Este Sudeste
Cayos de Albuquerque
Monkey Point
San Juan del Norte
Barra del Colorado
LIMÓN
Siquirres
Matina
Limón
Turrialba
Punta Mona
Río Telire
Bribri
Guabito
Changuinola
Bocas del Toro
Archipiélago de Bocas del Toro
Almirante
BOCAS DEL TORO
Península Valiente
Laguna de Chiriquí
Chiriquí Grande
Cerro Chirripó Grande 3819m
Cerro Kámuk 3554m
San Isidro
Buenos Aires
PUNTARENAS
Río Grande de Térraba
Palmar Sur
San Vito
Golfito
Golfo Dulce
Península de Osa
Volcán Barú 3475m
Volcán Boquete
Cerro Chorcha 2238m
CHIRIQUÍ
La Concepción
David
Quebrada Guabo
Pedregal
Alanje
Puerto Armuelles
Horconcitos
Remedios
Isla Sevilla
Isla Parida
Golfo de Chiriquí
Punta Burica
NGÖBE BUGLÉ
Cerro Santiago 2121m
Las Palmas
Santiago
VERAGUAS
Soná
Río de Jesús
Guarumal
Ponuga
Montijo
Ocú
Isla Cébaco
Isla de Coiba
Golfo de los Mosquitos
Santa Catalina
Cerro Peña Blanca 1314m
Cordillera Central
Santa Fé
Cañazas
San Francisco
COCLÉ
Penonomé
Antón
Aguadulce
Bahía de Parita
Parita
Chitré
Monagrillo
HERRERA
Macaracas
Península de Azuero
LOS SANTOS
Los Santos
Las Tablas
Pedasí
Punta Mala
Tonosí
Cerro Hoya 1560m
Golfo de Panamá
Portobelo
Colón
Cristóbal
Nuevo Chagres
Miguel de la Borda
Coclé del Norte
COLÓN
Lago Gatún
Arenosa
El Valle
Cerro Gaital 1173m
Capira
La Chorrera
Balboa
San Miguelito
PANAMÁ (PANAMA CITY)
PANAMÁ
Chepo
Lago Bayano
Punta Chame
San Carlos
Río Hato
Bahía de Panamá
Chimán
Archipiélago de las Perlas
Isla del Rey
San Miguel
Isla San José
Punta Brava
Golfo de San Miguel
Punta Garachiné
Garachiné
Santa Isabel
El Porvenir
Archipiélago de San Blas
KUNA YALA
Cordillera de San Blas
KUNA DE MADUNGANDI
KUNA DE WARGANDI
Aligandí
Punta Mosquito
Gulf of Darien
Punta Escocés
Serranía de Majé
Cerro Chucantí 1439m
Puerto Obaldía
Serranía del Darién
EMBERÁ-WOUNAAN
La Palma
DARIÉN
Yaviza
Unión Chocó
El Real
Cerro Pirre 1200m
Cerro Setetule 1220m
Cerro Tacarcuna 1875m
Jaqué
COLOMBIA

44
54
54

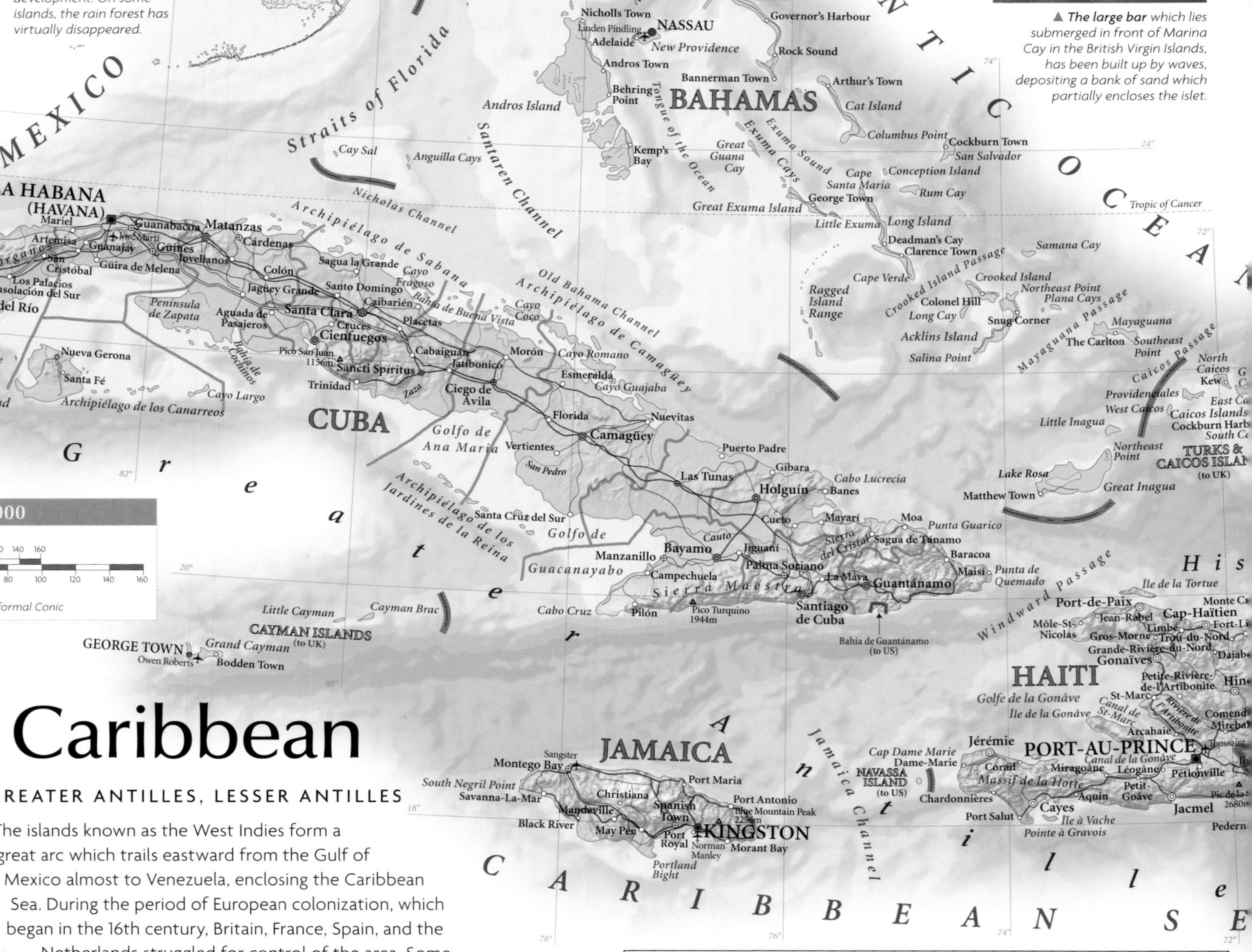

16
UNITED STATES OF AMERICA
64
GULF OF MEXICO
Straits of Florida
ATLANTIC OCEAN
Tropic of Cancer
Great Sale Cay
Little Abaco
Coopers Town
West End Point
West End
Pelican Point
Freeport
Grand Bahama Island
Eight Mile Rock
Marsh Harbour
Great Abaco
Moores Island
Cherokee Sound
Northwest Providence Channel
Southwest Point
Bimini Islands
Berry Islands
Northeast Providence Channel
Current
Eleuthera Island
Nicholls Town
Governor's Harbour
NASSAU
Adelaide
New Providence
Andros Town
Rock Sound
Bannerman Town
Arthur's Town
Behring Point
BAHAMAS
Cat Island
Andros Island
Tongue of the Ocean
Exuma Sound
Columbus Point
Cockburn Town
San Salvador
Kemp's Bay
Great Guana Cay
Exuma Cays
Cape Santa Maria
Conception Island
Rum Cay
George Town
Great Exuma Island
Long Island
Little Exuma
Cay Sal
Anguilla Cays
Santaren Channel
Nicholas Channel
Deadman's Cay
Clarence Town
Samana Cay
Cape Verde
Crooked Island
Crooked Island Passage
Northeast Point
Plana Cays
Ragged Island Range
Colonel Hill
Long Cay
Snug Corner
Acklins Island
Mayaguana Passage
Mayaguana
The Carlton
Southeast Point
Salina Point
LA HABANA (HAVANA)
Mariel
Guanabacoa
Matanzas
Cárdenas
Archipiélago de los Colorados
Artemisa
Guanajay
Güines
Jovellanos
Archipiélago de Sabana
Minas de Matahambre
San Cristóbal
Güira de Melena
Colón
Sagua la Grande
Golfo de Guanahacabibes
Sierra de los Órganos
Los Palacios
Consolación del Sur
Jagüey Grande
Santo Domingo
Cayo Fragoso
Caibarién
Bahía de Buena Vista
Old Bahama Channel
Guane
Pinar del Río
Península de Zapata
Aguada de Pasajeros
Santa Clara
Cabo de San Antonio
Cienfuegos
Placetas
Cayo Coco
Archipiélago de Camagüey
Cabo Corrientes
Cayos de San Felipe
Nueva Gerona
Pico San Juan 1156m
Sancti Spíritus
Cabaiguán
Jatibonico
Morón
Cayo Romano
Santa Fé
Trinidad
Zaza
Ciego de Ávila
Esmeralda
Cayo Guajaba
Yucatan Channel
Isla de la Juventud
Cayo Largo
Archipiélago de los Canarreos
CUBA
Florida
Nuevitas
Camagüey
Golfo de Ana María
Vertientes
Puerto Padre
San Pedro
Gibara
Las Tunas
Cabo Lucrecia
Holguín
Banes
Archipiélago de los Jardines de la Reina
Santa Cruz del Sur
Golfo de Guacanayabo
Cueto
Mayarí
Moa
Punta Guarico
Cauto
Sierra del Cristal
Sagua de Tánamo
Bayamo
Jiguaní
Baracoa
Manzanillo
Palma Soriano
Campechuela
Sierra Maestra
La Maya
Guantánamo
Maisí
Punta de Quemado
Cabo Cruz
Pilón
Pico Turquino 1944m
Santiago de Cuba
Bahía de Guantánamo (to US)
Windward Passage
Little Cayman
Cayman Brac
CAYMAN ISLANDS (to UK)
GEORGE TOWN
Grand Cayman
Owen Roberts
Bodden Town
Great Inagua
Matthew Town
Lake Rosa
Little Inagua
Northeast Point
Caicos Passage
North Caicos
Kew
Providenciales
West Caicos
Caicos Islands
East Caicos
Cockburn Harbour
TURKS & CAICOS ISLANDS (to UK)
Île de la Tortue
Port-de-Paix
Jean-Rabel
Cap-Haïtien
Môle-St-Nicolas
Limbé
Gros-Morne
Trou-du-Nord
Grande-Rivière-du-Nord
Gonaïves
HAITI
Petite-Rivière-de-l'Artibonite
St-Marc
Golfe de la Gonâve
Canal de St-Marc
Île de la Gonâve
Arcahaie
Jérémie
PORT-AU-PRINCE
Cap Dame Marie
Dame-Marie
NAVASSA ISLAND (to US)
Corail
Miragoâne
Canal de la Gonâve
Léogâne
Pétionville
Massif de la Hotte
Petit-Goâve
Chardonnières
Aquin
Cayes
Jacmel
Port Salut
Île à Vache
Pointe à Gravois
JAMAICA
Sangster
Montego Bay
South Negril Point
Savanna-La-Mar
Christiana
Port Maria
Mandeville
Spanish Town
Port Antonio
Blue Mountain Peak 2256m
Black River
May Pen
KINGSTON
Port Royal
Norman Manley
Morant Bay
Portland Bight
Jamaica Channel
Greater Antilles
CARIBBEAN SEA

◄ *The Caribbean's virgin rain forest, seen here in Jamaica, is increasingly at risk from agricultural, industrial and tourist development. On some islands, the rain forest has virtually disappeared.*

▲ ***The large bar** which lies submerged in front of Marina Cay in the British Virgin Islands, has been built up by waves, depositing a bank of sand which partially encloses the islet.*

Scale 1:6,000,000

projection: Lambert Conformal Conic

The Caribbean

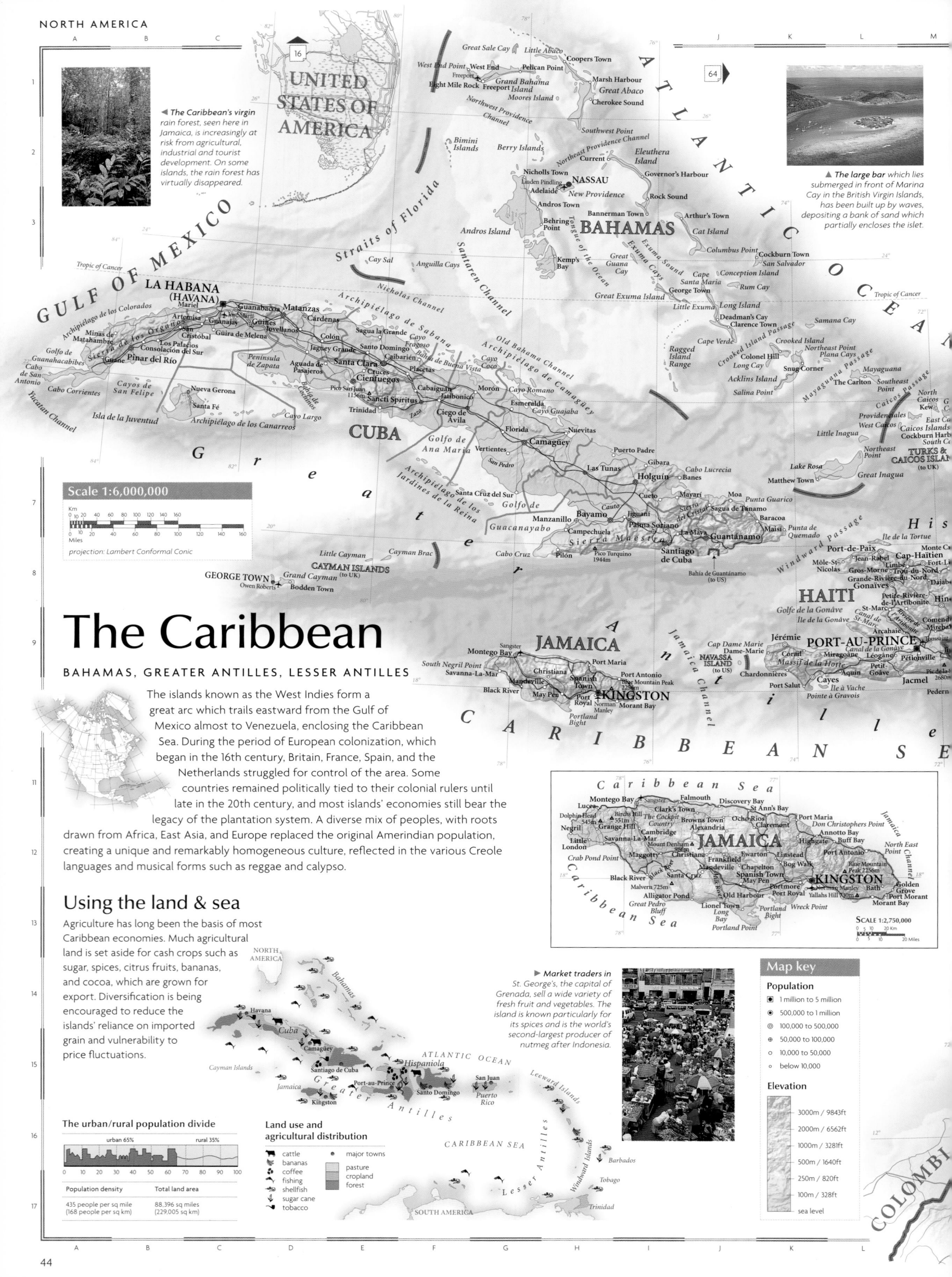

BAHAMAS, GREATER ANTILLES, LESSER ANTILLES

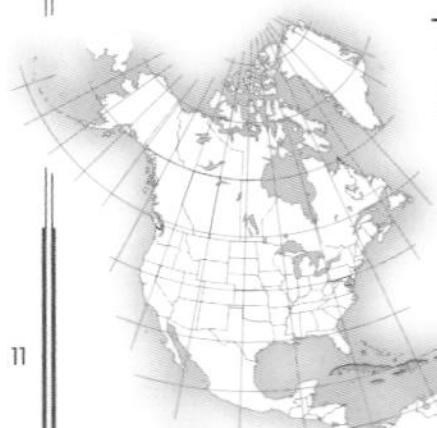

The islands known as the West Indies form a great arc which trails eastward from the Gulf of Mexico almost to Venezuela, enclosing the Caribbean Sea. During the period of European colonization, which began in the 16th century, Britain, France, Spain, and the Netherlands struggled for control of the area. Some countries remained politically tied to their colonial rulers until late in the 20th century, and most islands' economies still bear the legacy of the plantation system. A diverse mix of peoples, with roots drawn from Africa, East Asia, and Europe replaced the original Amerindian population, creating a unique and remarkably homogeneous culture, reflected in the various Creole languages and musical forms such as reggae and calypso.

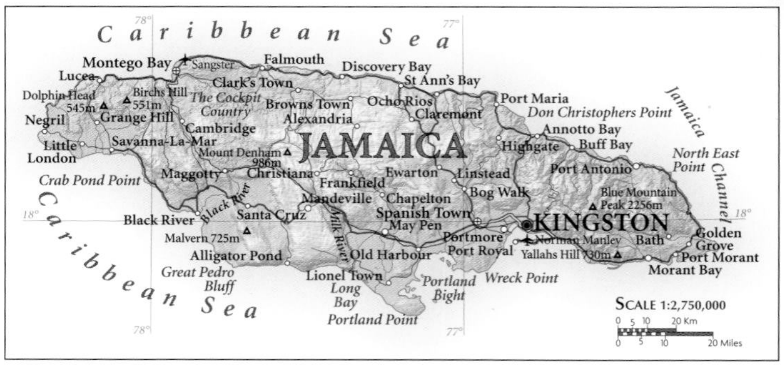

Caribbean Sea
Montego Bay
Sangster
Falmouth
Discovery Bay
Lucea
St Ann's Bay
Clark's Town
Dolphin Head 545m
Birchs Hill 531m
The Cockpit Country
Browns Town
Ocho Rios
Port Maria
Negril
Grange Hill
Claremont
Don Christophers Point
Cambridge
Alexandria
Annotto Bay
Little London
Savanna-La-Mar
Mount Denham 986m
JAMAICA
Highgate
Buff Bay
Maggotty
Christiana
North East Point
Crab Pond Point
Ewarton
Linstead
Port Antonio
Frankfield
Mandeville
Chapelton
Bog Walk
Blue Mountain Peak 2256m
Black River
Santa Cruz
Spanish Town
Jamaica Channel
Black River
May Pen
KINGSTON
Malvern 725m
Milk River
Portmore
Norman Manley
Golden Grove
Alligator Pond
Old Harbour
Port Royal
Yallahs Hill 730m
Bath
Port Morant
Great Pedro Bluff
Lionel Town
Morant Bay
Long Bay
Portland Bight
Wreck Point
Portland Point
Caribbean Sea
SCALE 1:2,750,000

Using the land & sea

Agriculture has long been the basis of most Caribbean economies. Much agricultural land is set aside for cash crops such as sugar, spices, citrus fruits, bananas, and cocoa, which are grown for export. Diversification is being encouraged to reduce the islands' reliance on imported grain and vulnerability to price fluctuations.

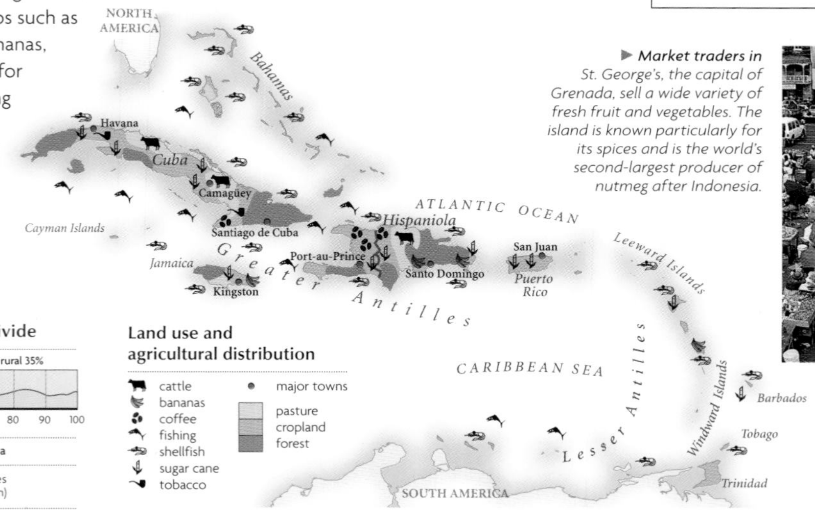

NORTH AMERICA
Bahamas
Havana
Cuba
Camagüey
Cayman Islands
Santiago de Cuba
Hispaniola
ATLANTIC OCEAN
Jamaica
Port-au-Prince
Santo Domingo
San Juan
Puerto Rico
Kingston
Greater Antilles
Leeward Islands
CARIBBEAN SEA
Lesser Antilles
Windward Islands
Barbados
Tobago
Trinidad
SOUTH AMERICA

Land use and agricultural distribution

- cattle
- bananas
- coffee
- fishing
- shellfish
- sugar cane
- tobacco
- major towns
- pasture
- cropland
- forest

The urban/rural population divide

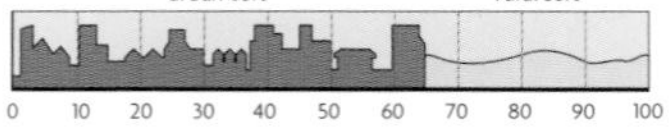

urban 65%
rural 35%
0
10
20
30
40
50
60
70
80
90
100

Population density	Total land area
435 people per sq mile (168 people per sq km)	88,396 sq miles (229,005 sq km)

► ***Market traders in** St. George's, the capital of Grenada, sell a wide variety of fresh fruit and vegetables. The island is known particularly for its spices and is the world's second-largest producer of nutmeg after Indonesia.*

Map key

Population

- 1 million to 5 million
- 500,000 to 1 million
- 100,000 to 500,000
- 50,000 to 100,000
- 10,000 to 50,000
- below 10,000

Elevation

- 3000m / 9843ft
- 2000m / 6562ft
- 1000m / 3281ft
- 500m / 1640ft
- 250m / 820ft
- 100m / 328ft
- sea level

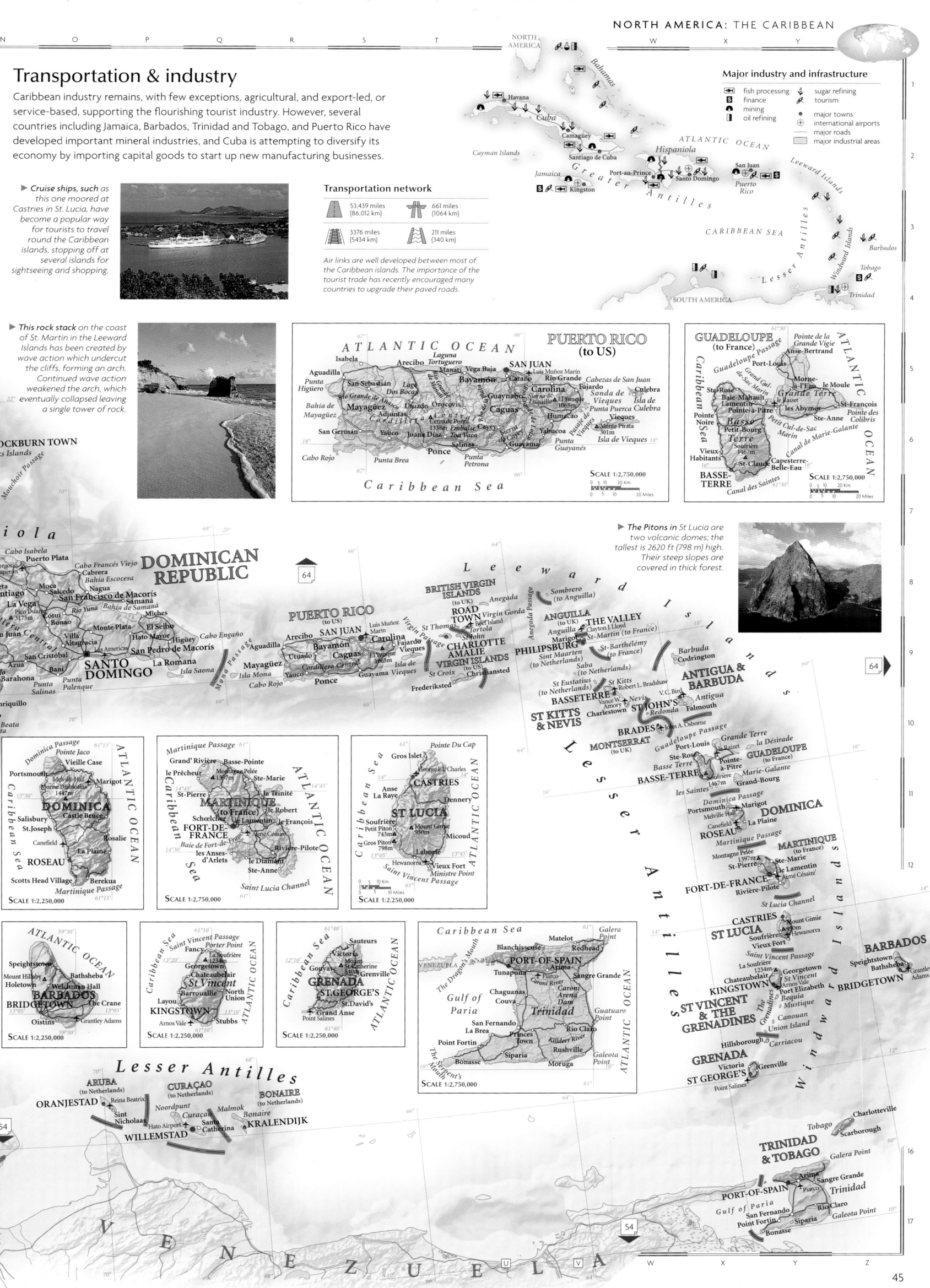

Transportation & industry

Caribbean industry remains, with few exceptions, agricultural, and export-led, or service-based, supporting the flourishing tourist industry. However, several countries including Jamaica, Barbados, Trinidad and Tobago, and Puerto Rico have developed important mineral industries, and Cuba is attempting to diversify its economy by importing capital goods to start up new manufacturing businesses.

► **Cruise ships, such** as this one moored at Castries in St. Lucia, have become a popular way for tourists to travel round the Caribbean islands, stopping off at several islands for sightseeing and shopping.

Transportation network

53,439 miles (86,012 km)	661 miles (1064 km)
3376 miles (5434 km)	211 miles (340 km)

Air links are well developed between most of the Caribbean islands. The importance of the tourist trade has recently encouraged many countries to upgrade their paved roads.

NORTH AMERICA
Major industry and infrastructure
fish processing
finance
mining
oil refining
sugar refining
tourism
major towns
international airports
major roads
major industrial areas
Bahamas
Havana
Cuba
Camagüey
Santiago de Cuba
Cayman Islands
Jamaica
Kingston
Greater Antilles
Hispaniola
Port-au-Prince
Santo Domingo
ATLANTIC OCEAN
San Juan
Puerto Rico
Leeward Islands
CARIBBEAN SEA
Lesser Antilles
Windward Islands
Barbados
Tobago
Trinidad
SOUTH AMERICA

► **This rock stack** on the coast of St. Martin in the Leeward Islands has been created by wave action which undercut the cliffs, forming an arch. Continued wave action weakened the arch, which eventually collapsed leaving a single tower of rock.

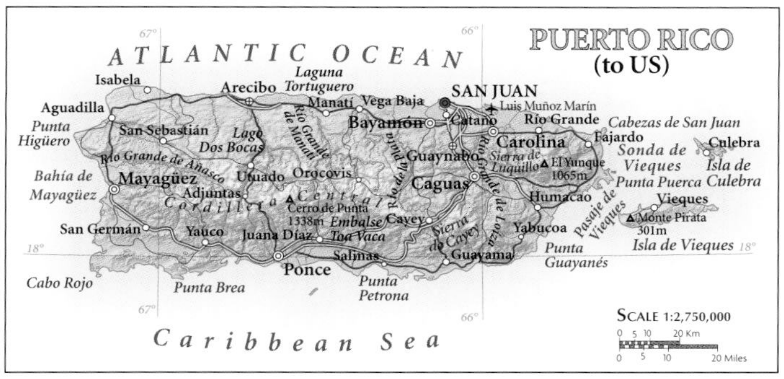
PUERTO RICO
(to US)
ATLANTIC OCEAN
Caribbean Sea
Isabela
Arecibo
Aguadilla
Punta Higüero
Bahía de Mayagüez
Mayagüez
San Germán
Cabo Rojo
Yauco
Juana Díaz
Ponce
Punta Brea
Salinas
Guayama
Punta Petrona
SAN JUAN
Bayamón
Carolina
Caguas
Humacao
Fajardo
Culebra
Isla de Culebra
Vieques
Isla de Vieques
Yabucoa
Punta Guayanés
Cordillera Central
Cerro de Punta 1338m
El Yunque 1065m
Monte Pirata 301m
SCALE 1:2,750,000

GUADELOUPE
(to France)
Caribbean Sea
ATLANTIC OCEAN
Pointe de la Grande Vigie
Anse-Bertrand
Port-Louis
Grande Terre
Le Moule
Morne-à-l'Eau
Ste-Rose
Baie-Mahault
Lamentin
Pointe-à-Pitre
les Abymes
Ste-Anne
St-François
Pointe des Colibris
Pointe Noire
Basse Terre
Petit-Bourg
Soufrière 1467m
Vieux-Habitants
St-Claude
Capesterre-Belle-Eau
BASSE-TERRE
Canal des Saintes
Marie-Galante
SCALE 1:2,750,000

► **The Pitons** in St Lucia are two volcanic domes; the tallest is 2620 ft (798 m) high. Their steep slopes are covered in thick forest.

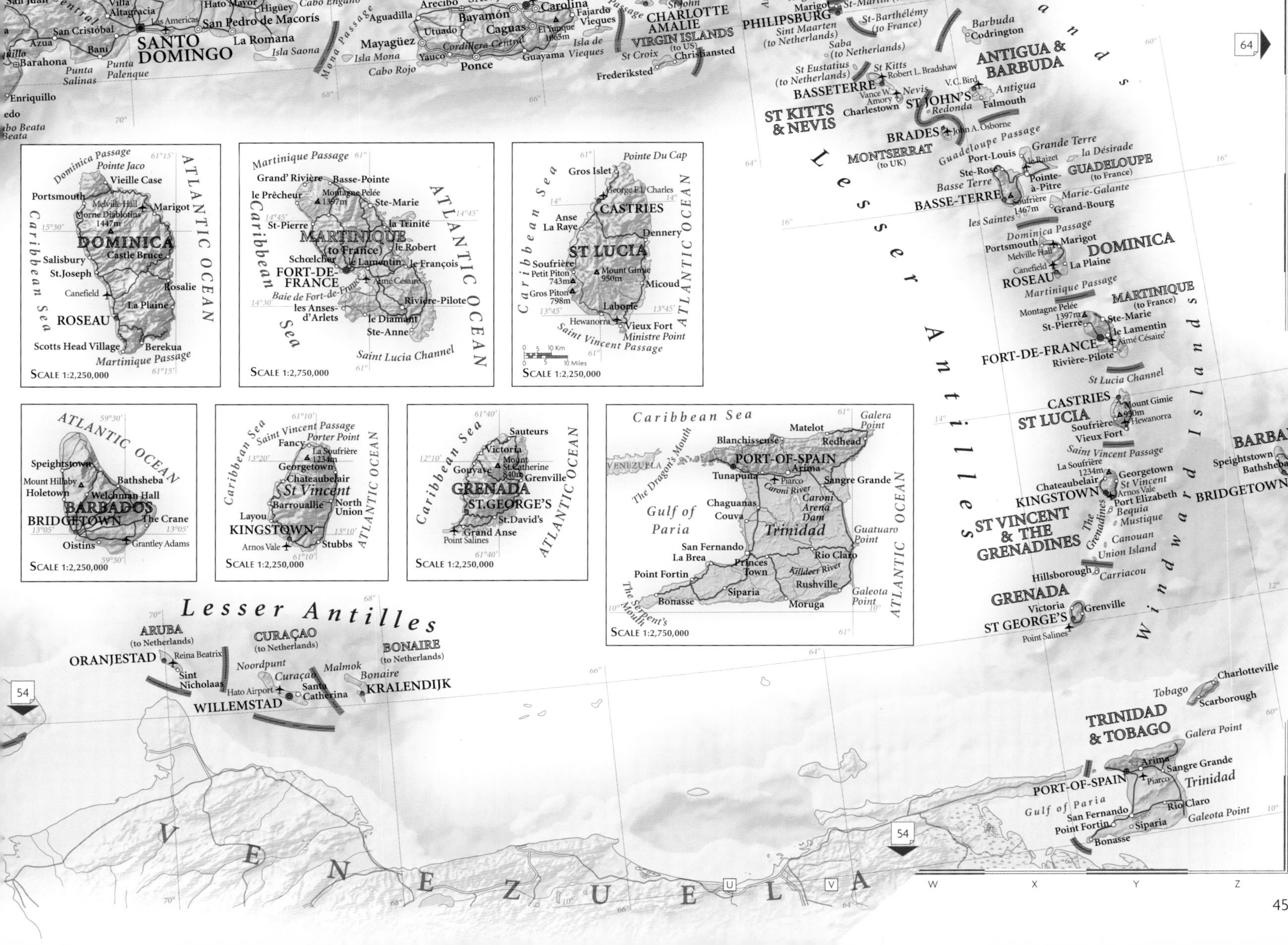
COCKBURN TOWN
Turks Islands
Mouchoir Passage
DOMINICAN REPUBLIC
Cabo Isabela
Puerto Plata
Santiago
La Vega
Pico Duarte 3175m
San Francisco de Macoris
Cabo Francés Viejo
Cabrera
Bahía Escocesa
Nagua
Samaná
Bahía de Samaná
Miches
Monte Plata
El Seibo
Hato Mayor
Higüey
Cabo Engaño
San Pedro de Macoris
La Romana
Isla Saona
SANTO DOMINGO
San Cristóbal
Azua
Barahona
Bani
Punta Salinas
Punta Palenque
Enriquillo
Mona Passage
PUERTO RICO
(to US)
SAN JUAN
Arecibo
Aguadilla
Mayagüez
Isla Mona
Cabo Rojo
Bayamón
Carolina
Caguas
Cordillera Central
Ponce
Yauco
Guayama
Vieques
Fajardo
Leeward Islands
BRITISH VIRGIN ISLANDS
(to UK)
ROAD TOWN
Anegada
Virgin Gorda
St Thomas
St John
CHARLOTTE AMALIE
VIRGIN ISLANDS
(to US)
St Croix
Christiansted
Frederiksted
Anegada Passage
Sombrero
(to Anguilla)
ANGUILLA
(to UK)
THE VALLEY
PHILIPSBURG
Sint Maarten
(to Netherlands)
St-Martin (to France)
St-Barthélémy
(to France)
Saba
(to Netherlands)
St Eustatius
(to Netherlands)
St Kitts
BASSETERRE
Nevis
Charlestown
ST KITTS & NEVIS
Barbuda
Codrington
ANTIGUA & BARBUDA
ST JOHN'S
Antigua
Falmouth
Redonda
BRADES
MONTSERRAT
(to UK)
Guadeloupe Passage
GUADELOUPE
(to France)
Grande Terre
la Désirade
Port-Louis
Ste-Rose
Basse Terre
BASSE-TERRE
Pointe-à-Pitre
Marie-Galante
Grand-Bourg
les Saintes
Lesser Antilles
Dominica Passage
Portsmouth
DOMINICA
Marigot
La Plaine
ROSEAU
Martinique Passage
MARTINIQUE
(to France)
Ste-Marie
St-Pierre
Le Lamentin
FORT-DE-FRANCE
Rivière-Pilote
St Lucia Channel
CASTRIES
ST LUCIA
Soufrière
Vieux Fort
Saint Vincent Passage
Georgetown
St Vincent
KINGSTOWN
ST VINCENT & THE GRENADINES
Bequia
Mustique
Canouan
Union Island
Carriacou
Hillsborough
BARBADOS
Speightstown
Bathsheba
BRIDGETOWN
GRENADA
Grenville
ST GEORGE'S
Point Salines
Windward Islands
Lesser Antilles
ARUBA
(to Netherlands)
ORANJESTAD
CURAÇAO
(to Netherlands)
Curaçao
WILLEMSTAD
BONAIRE
(to Netherlands)
Bonaire
KRALENDIJK
TRINIDAD & TOBAGO
Tobago
Scarborough
Charlotteville
PORT-OF-SPAIN
Arima
Sangre Grande
Trinidad
Rio Claro
Galeota Point
Galera Point
Gulf of Paria
San Fernando
Point Fortin
Siparia
Bonasse
VENEZUELA
DOMINICA
ATLANTIC OCEAN
Caribbean Sea
Dominica Passage
Pointe Jaco
Vieille Case
Portsmouth
Marigot
Morne Diablotins 1447m
Castle Bruce
Salisbury
St.Joseph
Canefield
Rosalie
La Plaine
ROSEAU
Scotts Head Village
Berekua
Martinique Passage
SCALE 1:2,250,000
Martinique Passage
Grand' Rivière
Basse-Pointe
le Prêcheur
Montagne Pelée 1397m
Ste-Marie
la Trinité
St-Pierre
MARTINIQUE
(to France)
le Robert
le Lamentin
le François
FORT-DE-FRANCE
Baie de Fort-de-France
les Anses-d'Arlets
Rivière-Pilote
le Diamant
Ste-Anne
Caribbean Sea
ATLANTIC OCEAN
Saint Lucia Channel
SCALE 1:2,750,000
Pointe Du Cap
Gros Islet
CASTRIES
Anse La Raye
Dennery
ST LUCIA
Soufrière
Petit Piton 743m
Gros Piton 798m
Mount Gimie 950m
Micoud
Laborie
Hewanorra
Vieux Fort
Ministre Point
Saint Vincent Passage
Caribbean Sea
ATLANTIC OCEAN
SCALE 1:2,250,000
ATLANTIC OCEAN
Speightstown
Mount Hillaby
Holetown
Bathsheba
Welchman Hall
BARBADOS
BRIDGETOWN
The Crane
Oistins
Grantley Adams
SCALE 1:2,250,000
Caribbean Sea
Saint Vincent Passage
Porter Point
Fancy
La Soufrière 1234m
Georgetown
Chateaubelair
St Vincent
Barrouallie
North Union
Layou
KINGSTOWN
Arnos Vale
Stubbs
ATLANTIC OCEAN
SCALE 1:2,250,000
Caribbean Sea
Sauteurs
Victoria
Mount St Catherine 840m
Gouyave
Grenville
GRENADA
ST.GEORGE'S
St.David's
Grand Anse
Point Salines
ATLANTIC OCEAN
SCALE 1:2,250,000
Caribbean Sea
Matelot
Galera Point
Blanchisseuse
Redhead
PORT-OF-SPAIN
Arima
Piarco
Tunapuna
Sangre Grande
VENEZUELA
The Dragon's Mouth
Caroni River
Caroni Arena Dam
Gulf of Paria
Chaguanas
Couva
Trinidad
Guatuaro Point
San Fernando
La Brea
Rio Claro
Point Fortin
Princes Town
Rushville
Siparia
Bonasse
Moruga
Galeota Point
The Serpent's Mouth
ATLANTIC OCEAN
SCALE 1:2,750,000

NORT
Rio Grande
Sierra Madre Oriental
Sierra Madre Occidental
Gulf of California
Lower California
Cedros Trench
San Lucas Cape
Lago de Chapala
East Pacific Rise
Tehuantepec Ridge
Union Reefs
Clipperton Seamounts
Clipperton Island
PACIFIC
COCOS PL
NAZCA PL
NAZCA PLATE
PACIFIC PLATE

South America

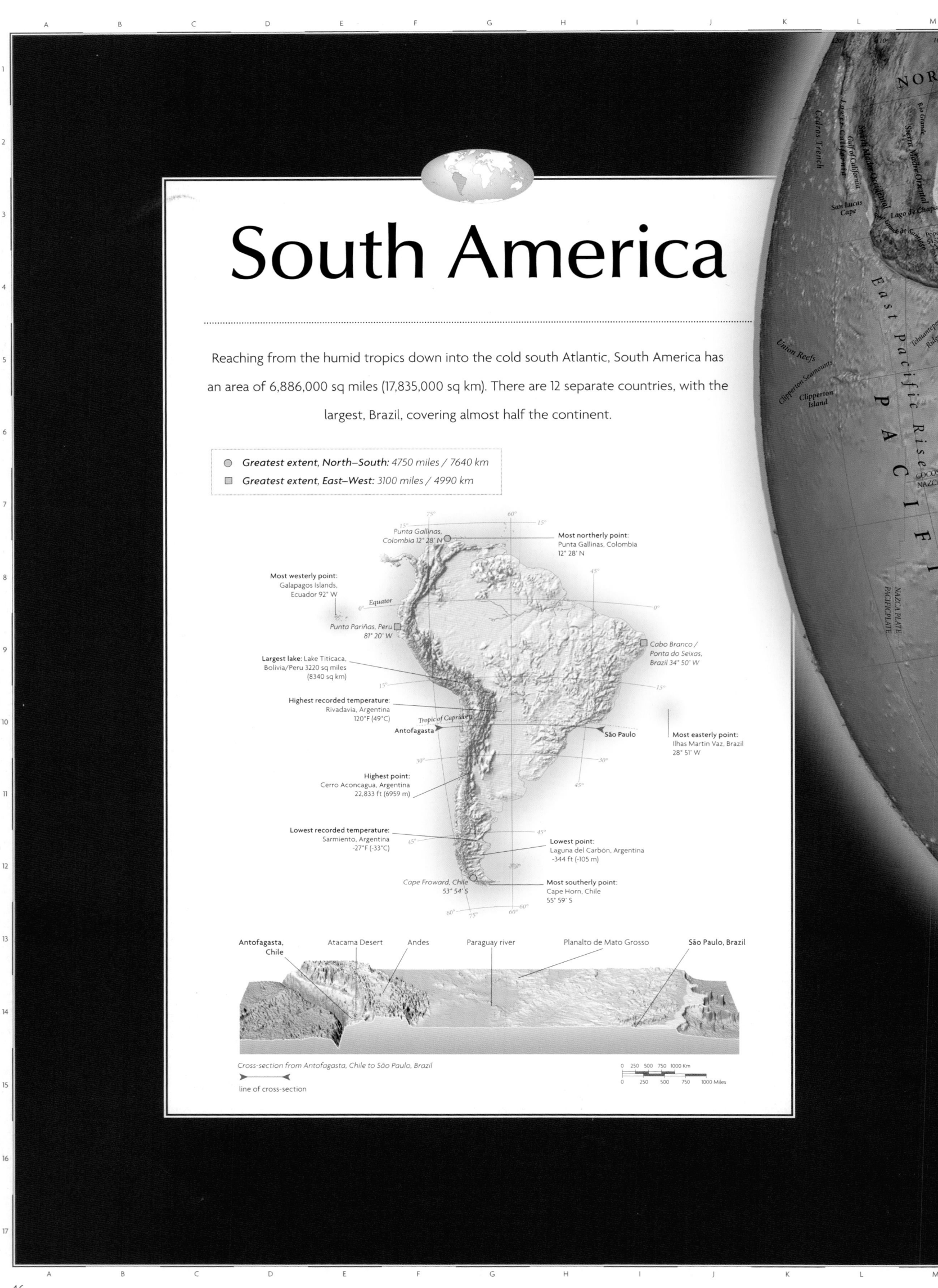

Reaching from the humid tropics down into the cold south Atlantic, South America has an area of 6,886,000 sq miles (17,835,000 sq km). There are 12 separate countries, with the largest, Brazil, covering almost half the continent.

- ○ ***Greatest extent, North–South:*** *4750 miles / 7640 km*
- □ ***Greatest extent, East–West:*** *3100 miles / 4990 km*

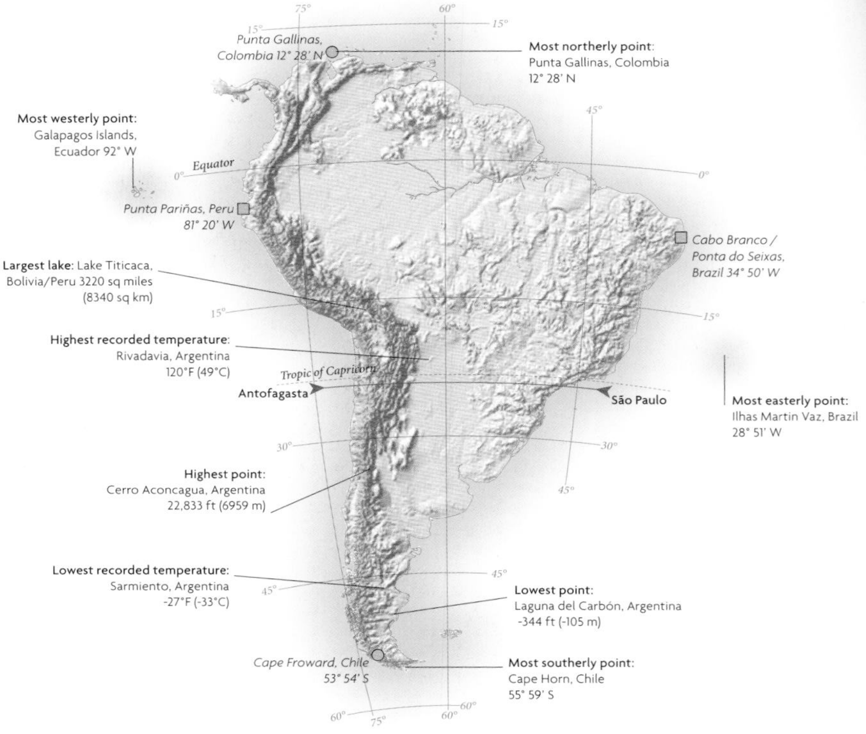
Punta Gallinas, Colombia 12° 28' N
Most northerly point: Punta Gallinas, Colombia 12° 28' N
Most westerly point: Galapagos Islands, Ecuador 92° W
Equator
Punta Pariñas, Peru 81° 20' W
Cabo Branco / Ponta do Seixas, Brazil 34° 50' W
Largest lake: Lake Titicaca, Bolivia/Peru 3220 sq miles (8340 sq km)
Highest recorded temperature: Rivadavia, Argentina 120°F (49°C)
Tropic of Capricorn
Antofagasta
São Paulo
Most easterly point: Ilhas Martin Vaz, Brazil 28° 51' W
Highest point: Cerro Aconcagua, Argentina 22,833 ft (6959 m)
Lowest recorded temperature: Sarmiento, Argentina -27°F (-33°C)
Lowest point: Laguna del Carbón, Argentina -344 ft (-105 m)
Cape Froward, Chile 53° 54' S
Most southerly point: Cape Horn, Chile 55° 59' S

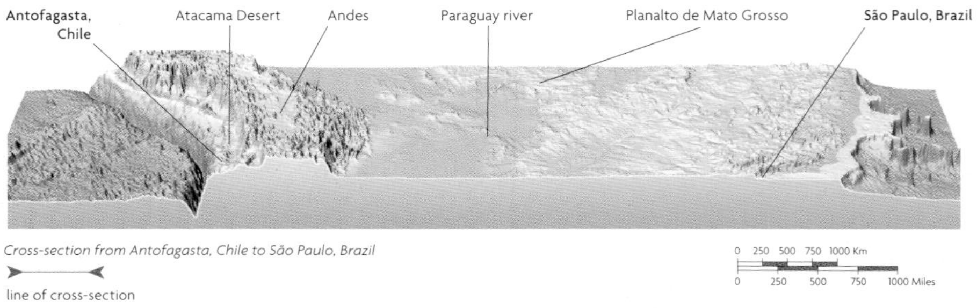
Antofagasta, Chile
Atacama Desert
Andes
Paraguay river
Planalto de Mato Grosso
São Paulo, Brazil
0 250 500 750 1000 Km
0 250 500 750 1000 Miles

Cross-section from Antofagasta, Chile to São Paulo, Brazil

line of cross-section

N O P Q R S T U V W X Y Z
1 2 3 4 5 6 7 8 9 10 11 12 13 14 15 16 17
Sargasso Sea
Nares Plain
Hatteras Plain
Cape Canaveral
Lake Okeechobee
Apalachee Bay
Gulf of Mexico
Straits of Florida
Great Bahama Bank
Bahamas
West Indies
Puerto Rico Trench
Cuba
Greater Antilles
Windward Passage
Hispaniola
Puerto Rico
Leeward Islands
Nevis
Barbuda
Antigua
Guadeloupe
Dominica
Martinique
Saint Lucia
Barbados
Grenada
Tobago
Trinidad
Yucatan Basin
Cayman Trench
Cayman Trough
Jamaica
Gulf of Honduras
Caribbean Sea
Lesser Antilles
Grenada Basin
Windward Islands
Punta Gallinas
Aruba
Bonaire
Curaçao
Isla de Margarita
Península de la Guajira
Gulf of Venezuela
Lake Maracaibo
Cordillera de la Costa
Colombian Basin
Mosquito Coast
Nicaraguan Rise
Lake Nicaragua
Gulf of Fonseca
Mosquito Gulf
Isthmus of Panama
Gulf of Darien
Gulf of Panama
Península de Azuero
Colón Ridge
Panama Basin
Middle America Trench
NORTH AMERICAN PLATE
SOUTH AMERICAN PLATE
CARIBBEAN PLATE
MID-ATLANTIC RIDGE
ATLANTIC OCEAN
Tropic of Cancer
Cape Verde Basin
Cape Verde Islands
Gambia Plain
AFRICAN PLATE
Doldrums Fracture Zone
Demerara Plain
Guiana Basin
Four North Fracture Zone
Saint Paul Fracture Zone
Equator
Ceará Plain
Amazon Fan
Baía de Marajó
Ilha de Marajó
Baía de São Marcos
Atol das Rocas
Fernando de Noronha
Cabo de São Roque
Cabo Branco
Pernambuco Plain
Llanos
Orinoco
Apure
Arauca
Meta
Caura
Caroní
Guiana Highlands
Uraricoera
Essequibo
Courantyne
Maroni
Oyapock
Tumuc-Humac Mountains
Araguari
Serra Parima
Branco
Trombetas
Jari
Paru
Pará de Oeste
Cordillera Occidental
Cordillera Central
Cordillera Oriental
Vichada
Guaviare
Caquetá
Putumayo
Napo
Vaupés
Rio Negro
Jauaperi
Represa Balbina
Amazon Basin
Amazon
Xingu
Tapajós
Japurá
Içá
Jutaí
Purus
Madeira
Canumã
Teles Pires
Juruena
Iriri
SOUTH AMERICA
Represa de Tucuruí
Tocantins
Mearim
Itapicuru
Parnaíba
Serra Grande
Planalto da Borborema
Represa de Itaparica
Represa de Sobradinho
Chapada das Mangabeiras
Serra Geral de Goiás
São Francisco
Chapada Diamantina
Baía de Todos os Santos
Paraguaçu
Brazilian Highlands
Serra do Espinhaço
Brazil Basin
Abrolhos Bank
Trindade Spur
Doce
Tropic of Capricorn
Chimborazo 6310m
Gulf of Guayaquil
Punta Pariñas
Galapagos Islands
Cordillera Real
Marañón
Juruá
Tapauá
Ituxi
Acre
Aripuanã
Roosevelt
Chapada dos Parecis
Serra do Cachimbo
São Manuel
Serra Formosa
Xingu
Serra do Roncador
Mortes
Araguaia
Planalto de Mato Grosso
Ucayali
Urubamba
Madre de Dios
Guaporé
Mamoré
Beni
Rapulo
ANDES
Cordillera Oriental
Cordillera Occidental
SOUTH AMERICAN PLATE
NAZCA PLATE
Lake Titicaca
Yungas
Rio Grande
Lago Poopó
Altiplano
Peru-Chile Trench
Atacama Desert
Paranaíba
Pantanal
Taquari
Paraguay
Aporé
Rio Grande
Serra do Paranapiacaba
Serra da Mantiqueira
Ilha de São Sebastião
Santos Plateau
Serra do Mar
Pilcomayo
Gran Chaco
Represa de Itaipú
Iguaçu
Serra Geral
Paraná
Ilha de São Francisco
Rio Grande Rise
Uruguay
Mesopotamia
Lagoa dos Patos
Embalse de Rio Negro
Rio Negro
Cuchilla Grande
Mirim Lagoon
Río de la Plata
Salado
Dulce
Sierras de Córdoba
Laguna Mar Chiquita
Aconcagua
Pampas
Argentine Basin
Colorado
Río Negro
Bahía Blanca
Neuquén
Limay
Golfo San Matías
Chubut
Argentine Plain
Patagonia
Chico
Gulf of San Jorge
Deseado
Lago Buenos Aires
Golfo Corcovado
Archipiélago de los Chonos
Bahía Grande
Strait of Magellan
Tierra del Fuego
Cape Horn
Falkland Escarpment
Maurice Ewing Bank
Falkland Plateau
Falkland Islands
South Georgia
South Georgia Rise
South Sandwich Trench
South Sandwich Islands
Scotia Ridge
SOUTH AMERICAN PLATE
SCOTIA PLATE
Scotia Sea
ANTARCTIC PLATE
South Shetland Islands
South Shetland Trough
South Orkney Islands
Weddell Sea
ANTARCTICA
Peru Basin
Mendaña Fracture Zone
Nazca Ridge
Chile Basin
Islas de los Desventurados
Sala y Gomez Fracture Zone
Easter Island
Roggeveen Basin
Juan Fernández Islands
East Pacific Rise
NAZCA PLATE
ANTARCTIC PLATE
PACIFIC PLATE
OCEAN

Physical South America

Three major physiographic regions characterize South America. The oldest, the ancient Brazilian Shield and the smaller Guiana and Patagonian shields, form the stable core of the continent. Stretching along the entire west coast are the younger Andean fold mountains with many summits rising to 20,000 ft (6100 m). These two diverse regions are separated by a number of sedimentary basins carrying South America's large river systems to the sea. These include the massive Amazon Basin and the basin of the Gran Chaco.

The Amazon Basin and Guiana Shield

The Amazon river occupies a large depression in the Earth's crust, formed by the uplift of the Andes. It is covered by thick volcanic deposits and layers of alluvium – these have been laid down by the Amazon's many tributaries. To the north is the smaller Guiana Shield.

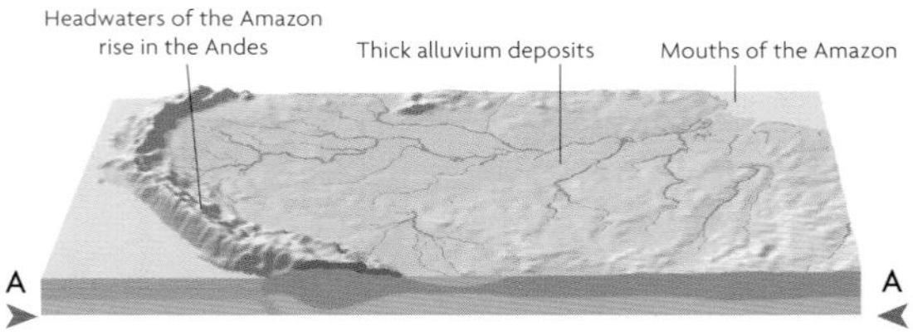
Headwaters of the Amazon rise in the Andes
Thick alluvium deposits
Mouths of the Amazon
A
A
0 500 1000 Km
0 500 1000 Miles

Section across northern South America showing Amazon Basin and its drainage pattern.

Scale 1:30,500,000

Km 0 200 400 600 800
Miles 0 200 400 600 800
projection: Lambert Azimuthal Equal Area

ATLANTIC OCEAN
PACIFIC OCEAN
ATLANTIC OCEAN
Punta Gallinas
Gulf of Venezuela
Lake Maracaibo
Gulf of Darien
Gulf of Panama
COCOS PLATE
NAZCA PLATE
Llanos
Orinoco
Cauca
Magdalena
Cordillera Occidental
Cordillera Central
Cordillera Oriental
Pakaraima Mountains
GUIANA SHIELD
Guiana Highlands
Tumuc-Humac Mountains
Rio Negro
Japurá
Branco
Represa Balbina
Amazon
Ilha de Marajó
Cotopaxi 5897m
Chimborazo 6310m
Cordillera Real
Putumayo
Amazon Basin
Gulf of Guayaquil
Marañón
Juruá
Purus
Madeira
Tapajós
Xingu
Tocantins
Serra dos Carajás
Cabo de São Roque
Punta Negra
SOUTH AMERICAN PLATE
NAZCA PLATE
Ucayali
Nevado Huascarán 6768m
Serra do Cachimbo
Araguaia
Tocantins
Planalto da Borborema
Represa de Sobradinho
BRAZILIAN SHIELD
Chapada dos Parecis
Guaporé
Serra Formosa
Serra do Roncador
Serra Dourada
Planalto de Mato Grosso
São Francisco
Brazilian Highlands
Serra do Espinhaço
SUB ANDEAN SYSTEM
Madre de Dios
Lake Titicaca
Lago Poopó
Altiplano
Pantanal
Serra do Caiapó
Serra de Maracajú
Paraná
Serra da Mantiqueira
Atacama Desert
Pilcomayo
Gran Chaco
Paraguay
Serra Geral
Serra do Mar
Cerro Ojos del Salado 6880m
Andes
Paraná
Mesopotamia
Uruguay
Lagoa dos Patos
Cerro Aconcagua 6959m
Mirim Lagoon
Salado
Pampas
Río de la Plata
NAZCA PLATE
SOUTH AMERICAN PLATE
Colorado
Río Negro
Península Valdés
Isla de Chiloé
Lago Colhué Huapí
Chico
Gulf of San Jorge
Deseado
PATAGONIAN SHIELD
Patagonia
Golfo de Penas
ANTARCTIC PLATE
Bahía Grande
Falkland Islands
Strait of Magellan
Tierra del Fuego
SOUTH AMERICAN PLATE
SCOTIA PLATE
Cape Horn
A
A
B
B
C
C

The Andean Uplands

The Andean Uplands run along the west coast of South America. They are being uplifted as the Nazca Plate is subducted beneath the South American Plate. They contain some of the world's largest volcanoes, such as Cotopaxi, and Lake Titicaca which occupies a dormant site. The far south has many large ice-sheets and a fragmented coastline.

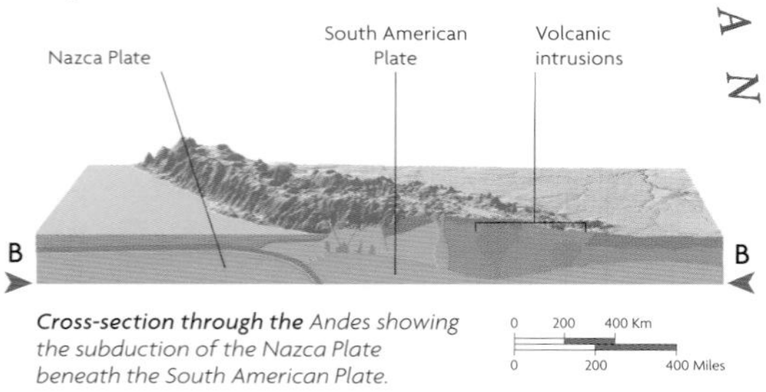
Nazca Plate
South American Plate
Volcanic intrusions
B
B
0 200 400 Km
0 200 400 Miles

Cross-section through the Andes showing the subduction of the Nazca Plate beneath the South American Plate.

Map key

Elevation

- 6000m / 19,686ft
- 4000m / 13,124ft
- 3000m / 9843ft
- 2000m / 6562ft
- 1000m / 3281ft
- 500m / 1640ft
- 250m / 820ft
- 100m / 328ft
- sea level

Plate margins (for explanation see page xiv)

- constructive
- destructive
- conservative
- uncertain
- physiographic regions
- line of cross-section

The Brazilian Shield and Gran Chaco

The immense Brazilian Shield underlies more than one-third of South America. It is pitted with numerous volcanic intrusions, and a large basaltic plateau exists between the Paraná river and the Atlantic Ocean. The flat Gran Chaco lies to the west of the shield, covered by sedimentary deposits eroded from the Andes, and transported by South America's mighty rivers.

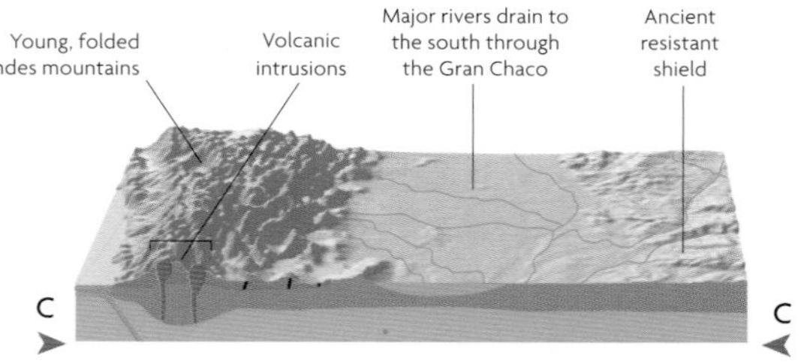
Young, folded Andes mountains
Volcanic intrusions
Major rivers drain to the south through the Gran Chaco
Ancient resistant shield
C
C
0 200 400 Km
0 200 400 Miles

Section across central South America showing the flat basin of the Gran Chaco and the ancient Brazilian Shield.

Climate

The climate of South America is influenced by three principal factors: the seasonal shift of high pressure air masses over the tropics, cold ocean currents along the western coast, affecting temperature and precipitation, and the mountain barrier produced by by the Andes, which creates a rain shadow over much of the south.

▲ ***Mild winters and** cool summers typify the extensive Pampas grasslands of Argentina.*

▲ ***Chile's hyperarid Atacama Desert** is renowned as one of the driest places on Earth.*

Climate

- tundra
- cool continental
- warm humid
- semiarid
- arid
- humid equatorial
- tropical
- daily hours of sunshine, January
- daily hours of sunshine, July
- → cold wind

Maracaibo
Caracas
Georgetown
Cayenne
Bogotá
Equator
Quito
Belém
Manaus
Altos
Recife
Lima
Brasília
La Paz
Santa Cruz
Belo Horizonte
La Quiaca
Tropic of Capricorn
Rio de Janeiro
Antofagasta
Asunción
Córdoba
Porto Alegre
Santiago
Buenos Aires
Montevideo
Concepción
Pamperos
Stanley

Temperature

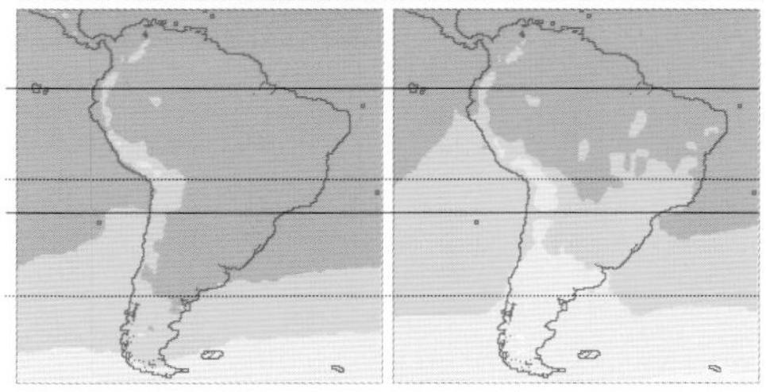
Equator
20° S
Tropic of Capricorn
40° S

Average January temperature *Average July temperature*

Temperature

- below -22°F (-30°C)
- -22 to -4°F (-30 to -20°C)
- -4 to 14°F (-20 to -10°C)
- 14 to 32°F (-10 to 0°C)
- 32 to 50°F (0 to 10°C)
- 50°F to 68°F (10 to 20°C)
- 68 to 86°F (20 to 30°C)
- above 86°F (30°C)

Rainfall

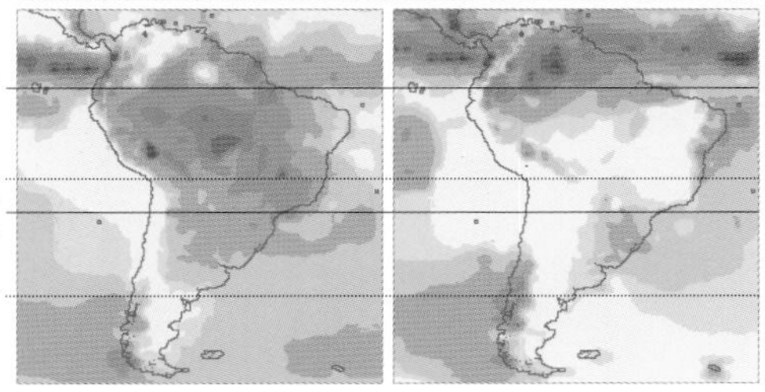
Equator
20° S
Tropic of Capricorn
40° S

Average January rainfall *Average July rainfall*

Rainfall

- 0–1 in (0–25 mm)
- 1–2 in (25–50 mm)
- 2–4 in (50–100 mm)
- 4–8 in (100–200 mm)
- 8–12 in (200–300 mm)
- 12–16 in (300–400 mm)
- 16–20 in (400–500 mm)
- more than 20 in (500 mm)

▲ ***Tropical conditions are** found across over half of South America. When both rainfall and temperatures are high, hot humid rain forests prevail.*

Shaping the continent

South America's active tectonic belt has been extensively folded over millions of years; landslides are still frequent in the mountains. The large river systems that erode the mountains flow across resistant shield areas, depositing sediment. Present-day glaciation affects the distinctive landscape of the far south.

Chemical weathering

1 Table mountains *(left)* are the eroded remnants of an ancient upland. As water percolates along cracks in these high, flat-topped mountains it forms intricate cave systems. Chemical weathering also isolates large blocks which then collapse, accumulating as rockfalls at the foot of scarp slopes.

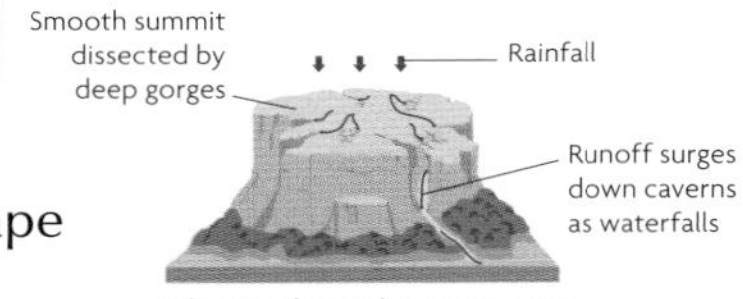
Smooth summit dissected by deep gorges
Rainfall
Runoff surges down caverns as waterfalls

***Chemical weathering:** Erosion of the Guyana Shield*

River systems

2 Along the Amazon *(above)* there is a great variation in rates of erosion. As the headwaters of the Amazon flow from the Andes, they erode and transport vast quantities of sediment, and are known as whitewaters. Across the shield areas erosion rates are very low. These rivers, carrying rotting vegetation, are called blackwaters.

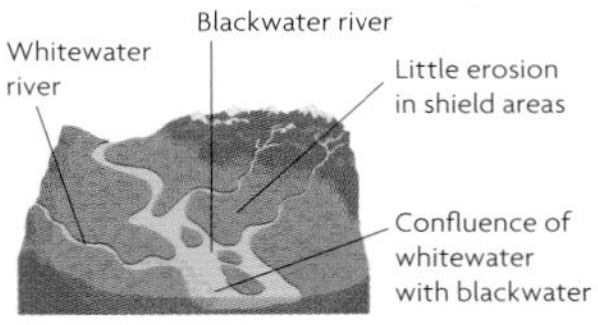
Blackwater river
Whitewater river
Little erosion in shield areas
Confluence of whitewater with blackwater

***River systems:** Suspended sediments in the Amazon*

Mass movement

6 Debris slides are common in the highlands of South America *(left)*. They occur where soil on a slope is saturated by rainwater and therefore less stable. The actual slides are often triggered by earthquakes.

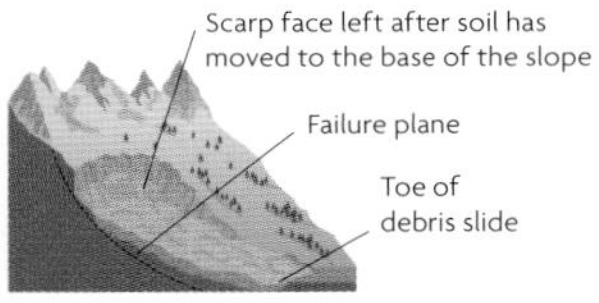
Scarp face left after soil has moved to the base of the slope
Failure plane
Toe of debris slide

***Mass movement:** A section of a debris slide*

The evolving landscape

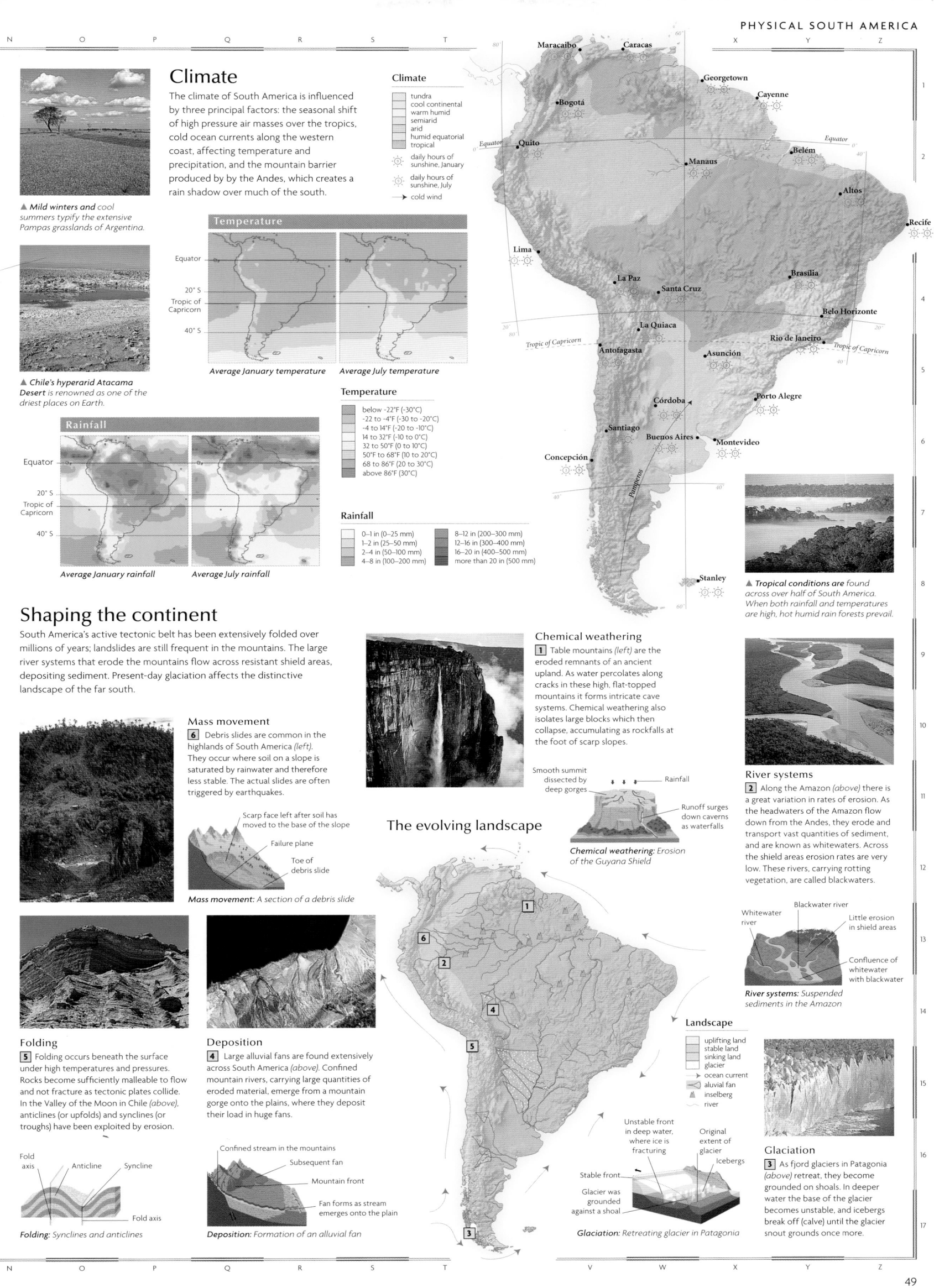

1
6
2
4
5
3

Landscape

- uplifting land
- stable land
- sinking land
- glacier
- ocean current
- aluvial fan
- inselberg
- river

Folding

5 Folding occurs beneath the surface under high temperatures and pressures. Rocks become sufficiently malleable to flow and not fracture as tectonic plates collide. In the Valley of the Moon in Chile *(above)*, anticlines (or upfolds) and synclines (or troughs) have been exploited by erosion.

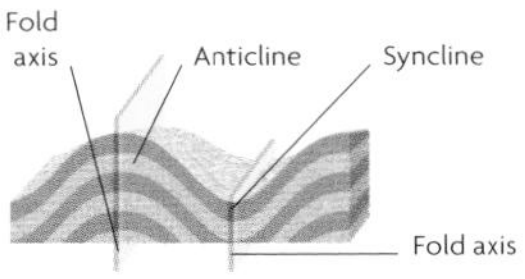
Fold axis
Anticline
Syncline
Fold axis

***Folding:** Synclines and anticlines*

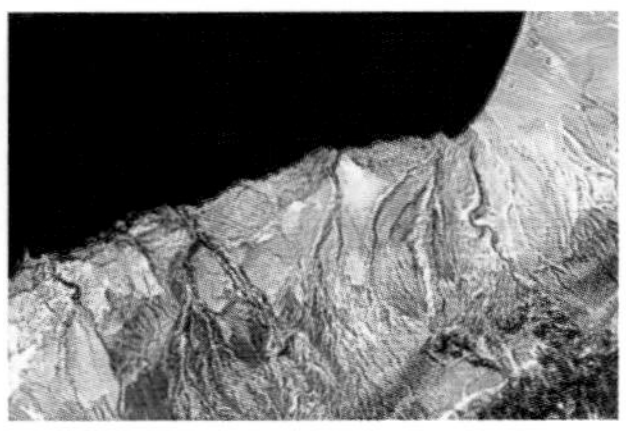

Deposition

4 Large alluvial fans are found extensively across South America *(above)*. Confined mountain rivers, carrying large quantities of eroded material, emerge from a mountain gorge onto the plains, where they deposit their load in huge fans.

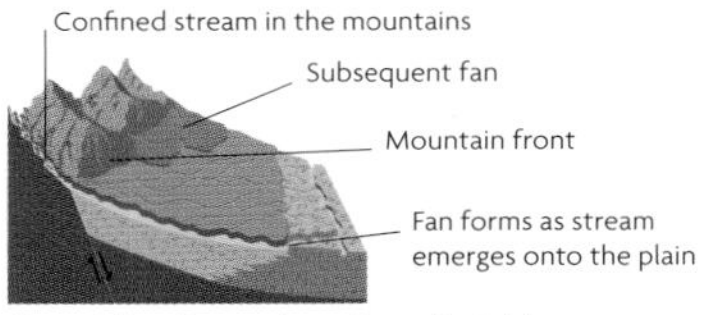
Confined stream in the mountains
Subsequent fan
Mountain front
Fan forms as stream emerges onto the plain

***Deposition:** Formation of an alluvial fan*

Glaciation

3 As fjord glaciers in Patagonia *(above)* retreat, they become grounded on shoals. In deeper water the base of the glacier becomes unstable, and icebergs break off (calve) until the glacier snout grounds once more.

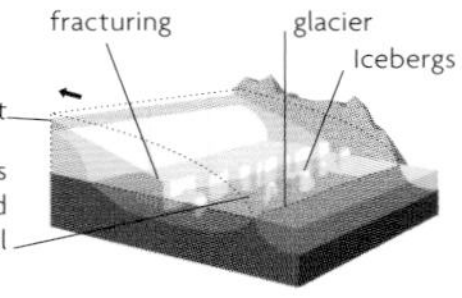
Unstable front in deep water, where ice is fracturing
Original extent of glacier
Icebergs
Stable front
Glacier was grounded against a shoal

***Glaciation:** Retreating glacier in Patagonia*

Political South America

Modern South America's political boundaries have their origins in the territorial endeavors of explorers during the 16th century, who claimed almost the entire continent for Portugal and Spain. The Portuguese land in the east later evolved into the federal state of Brazil, while the Spanish vice-royalties eventually emerged as separate independent nation-states in the early 19th century. South America's growing population has become increasingly urbanized, with the growth of coastal cities into large conurbations like Rio de Janeiro and Buenos Aires. In Brazil, Argentina, Chile, and Uruguay, a succession of military dictatorships has given way to fragile, but strengthening, democracies.

◀ ***Europe retains a** small foothold in South America. Kourou in French Guiana was the site chosen by the European Space Agency to launch the Ariane rocket. As a result of its status as a French overseas department, French Guiana is actually part of the European Union.*

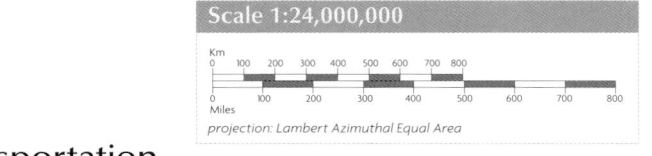

Scale 1:24,000,000

Km 0 100 200 300 400 500 600 700 800

Miles 0 100 200 300 400 500 600 700 800

projection: Lambert Azimuthal Equal Area

Barranquilla
Ciénaga
Cartagena
La Guaira
Maracaibo
Caracas
La Cruz
Cúcuta
San Cristóbal
Bucaramanga
Georgetown
Paramaribo
Cayenne
Bogotá
Buenaventura
Cali
Quito
Guayaquil
Belém
Manaus
Santarém
Trans-Amazon Highway
São Luís
Fortaleza
Teresina
Porto Franco
Humaitá
Trans-Amazon Highway
Porto Velho
Pan-American Highway
Picos
Salgueiro
Recife
Juazeiro
Maceió
Barreiras
Feira de Santana
Aracaju
Callao
Lima
Salvador
Cuiabá
Brasília
La Paz
Goiânia
Arequipa
Santa Cruz
Arica
Belo Horizonte
São José do Rio Preto
Campo Grande
Vitória
Ourinhos
Antofagasta
São Paulo
Rio de Janeiro
Santos
Asunción
Apucarana
Salta
Curitiba
Paranaguá
San Miguel de Tucumán
Pan-American Highway
Resistencia
Santa Maria
Coquimbo
Porto Alegre
Córdoba
Sante Fe
Mendoza
San Luis
Rosario
Rio Grande
Valparaíso
Santiago
Rio Cuarto
Mercedes
Buenos Aires
Montevideo
San Rafael
Talcahuano
Concepción
Mar del Plata
Neuquén
Bahía Blanca
Zapala
Puerto Montt
Comodoro Rivadavia
Punta Arenas
Transportation
major roads and highways
major railroads
international borders
transport intersections
international airports
major ports

Transportation

Most major road and rail routes are confined to the coastal regions by the forbidding natural barriers of the Andes mountains and the Amazon Basin. Few major cross-continental routes exist, although Buenos Aires serves as a transportation center for the main rail links to La Paz and Valparaíso, while the construction of the Trans-Amazon and Pan-American Highways have made direct road travel possible from Recife to Lima and from Puerto Montt up the coast into central America. A new waterway project is proposed to transform the River Paraguay into a major shipping route, although it involves considerable wetland destruction.

▶ ***South America's most** extensive rail network is centered on the Argentinian capital, Buenos Aires.The construction of new rail lines ouward from this important port, allowed the colonization of the Pampas lands for agriculture.*

Languages

Prior to European exploration in the 16th century, a diverse range of indigenous languages were spoken across the continent. With the arrival of Iberian settlers, Spanish became the dominant language, with Portuguese spoken in Brazil, and Native American languages such as Quechua and Guaraní, becoming concentrated in the continental interior. Today this pattern persists, although successive European colonization has led to Dutch being spoken in Suriname, English in Guyana, and French in French Guiana, while in large urban areas, Japanese and Chinese are increasingly common.

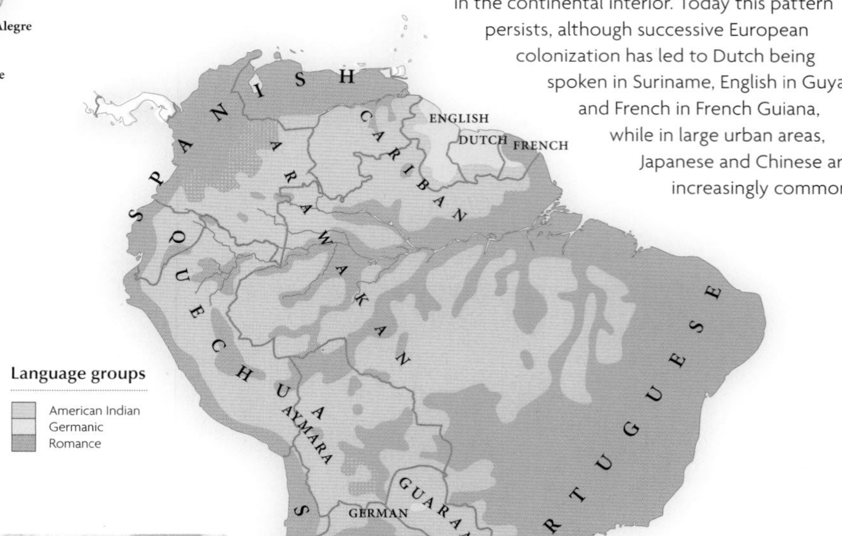
SPANISH
ENGLISH
DUTCH
FRENCH
CARIBAN
ARAWAKAN
QUECHUA
AYMARA
SPANISH
GUARANI
PORTUGUESE
GERMAN
GERMAN
GERMAN
Language groups
American Indian
Germanic
Romance

▶ ***Chile's main port,** Valparaíso, is a vital national shipping center, in addition to playing a key role in the growing trade with Pacific nations. The country's awkward, elongated shape means that sea transportation is frequently used for internal travel and communications in Chile.*

▲ ***Indigenous South American** lifestyles have not been totally submerged by European cultures and languages. The continental interior, and particularly the Amazon Basin, is still home to many different ethnic peoples.*

▶ ***Lima's magnificent** cathedral reflects South America's colonial past with its unmistakably Spanish style. In July 1821, Peru became the last Spanish colony on the mainland to declare independence.*

Caribbean Sea
ATLANTIC OCEAN
PACIFIC OCEAN
Q R S T U V W X Y Z N O P
1 2 3 4 7 8 9 10 11 12 13 15 16 17
Equator
Tropic of Capricorn
PANAMA
Gulf of Panama
Gulf of Darien
Gulf of Venezuela
Santa Marta
Barranquilla
Cartagena
Maracaibo
Valledupar
Cabimas
Lake Maracaibo
Valencia
CARACAS
Maracay
Barquisimeto
Cumaná
TRINIDAD & TOBAGO
Barinas
Monteria
Cúcuta
San Cristóbal
Llanos
Orinoco
Ciudad Guayana
Venezuelan territorial claim
VENEZUELA
GEORGETOWN
Linden
GUYANA
PARAMARIBO
CAYENNE
SURINAME
Surinamese territorial claims
French Guiana (to France)
Guiana Highlands
Bucaramanga
Medellín
Manizales
Pereira
Armenia
BOGOTÁ
Ibagué
Cali
Cauca
Magdalena
COLOMBIA
Rio Negro
Boa Vista
RORAIMA
Branco
AMAPÁ
Macapá
Pasto
Esmeraldas
QUITO
ECUADOR
Ambato
Riobamba
Portoviejo
Guayaquil
Babahoyo
Cuenca
Machala
Caqueta
Putumayo
Japurá
Amazon
Represa Balbina
Amazon Basin
AMAZONAS
Manaus
Santarém
Belém
São Luís
Iquitos
Marañón
Juruá
Purus
Madeira
Tapajós
Xingu
Tocantins
PARÁ
MARANHÃO
Fortaleza
Teresina
CEARÁ
RIO GRANDE DO NORTE
Natal
PARAÍBA
João Pessoa
PERNAMBUCO
Jaboatão
Recife
PIAUÍ
Piura
Chiclayo
Trujillo
PERU
Ucayali
ACRE
Rio Branco
Porto Velho
RONDÔNIA
Araguaia
Palmas
TOCANTINS
Juazeiro
ALAGOAS
Maceió
Represa de Sobradinho
SERGIPE
Aracaju
BRAZIL
BAHIA
Salvador
Callao
LIMA
Huancayo
Cusco
Andes
Madre de Dios
MATO GROSSO
Planalto de Mato Grosso
Cuiabá
BRASÍLIA
DISTRITO FEDERAL
São Francisco
Brazilian Highlands
Goiânia
GOIÁS
MINAS GERAIS
BOLIVIA
Arequipa
Lake Titicaca
LA PAZ
Cochabamba
Oruro
Santa Cruz
SUCRE
Tacna
Arica
Lago Poopó
Iquique
Pilcomayo
Paraguay
PARAGUAY
Campo Grande
MATO GROSSO DO SUL
Belo Horizonte
Vitória
ESPÍRITO SANTO
Ribeirão Preto
SÃO PAULO
Juiz de Fora
Tocopilla
Atacama Desert
San Salvador de Jujuy
Gran Chaco
Paraná
Londrina
Campinas
Osasco
Nova Iguaçu
São Paulo
RIO DE JANEIRO
Niterói
Rio de Janeiro
Sorocaba
Santos
Antofagasta
Salta
ASUNCIÓN
Ciudad del Este
PARANÁ
Curitiba
Formosa
Villarrica
San Miguel de Tucumán
SANTA CATARINA
Florianópolis
Santiago del Estero
Resistencia
Corrientes
Posadas
RIO GRANDE DO SUL
Santa Maria
Porto Alegre
La Rioja
La Serena
Coquimbo
Córdoba
San Juan
Santa Fe
Paraná
Uruguay
Tacuarembó
Melo
Viña del Mar
Valparaíso
SANTIAGO
Mendoza
San Luis
Rosario
URUGUAY
BUENOS AIRES
La Plata
Río de la Plata
MONTEVIDEO
CHILE
ARGENTINA
Linares
Salado
Santa Rosa
Pampas
Concepción
Lota
Neuquén
Colorado
Bahía Blanca
Mar del Plata
Temuco
Río Negro
Valdivia
Puerto Montt
Patagonia
Rawson
Lago Colhué Huapí
Chico
Gulf of San Jorge
Deseado
Golfo de Penas
Bahía Grande
Río Gallegos
Falkland Islands (to UK)
STANLEY
Strait of Magellan
Punta Arenas
Ushuaia
Beagle Channel
Cape Horn
Map key
Population
above 5 million
1 million to 5 million
500,000 to 1 million
100,000 to 500,000
50,000 to 100,000
10,000 to 50,000
below 10,000
Country capital
State capital
Borders
full international border
disputed de facto border
disputed territorial claim border
state border

▶ *In April 1960,* Brazil's government began the move from Rio de Janeiro to Brasília, a futuristic new city built in the sparsely populated interior. Brasília is now the federal capital of Brazil.

▶ *Rapid urbanization was* a feature of most South American countries in the latter half of the 20th century. In many cases, this unchecked growth has led to the development of sprawling slums, lacking adequate water and sewerage facilities.

▲ *Perched high in* the Andes like many of the cities in western South America, La Paz, Bolivia is the world's highest capital city at over 11,500 ft (3500 m).

Population

Almost half of South America's population lives in Brazil but, due to the large uninhabited expanses of the Amazon Basin, its overall population density is much lower than in other countries. During the 20th century the most important population trend was the movement from rural to urban areas, giving rise to great population concentrations in large cities like São Paulo, Rio de Janeiro, Caracas, Lima, Bogotá, and Buenos Aires.

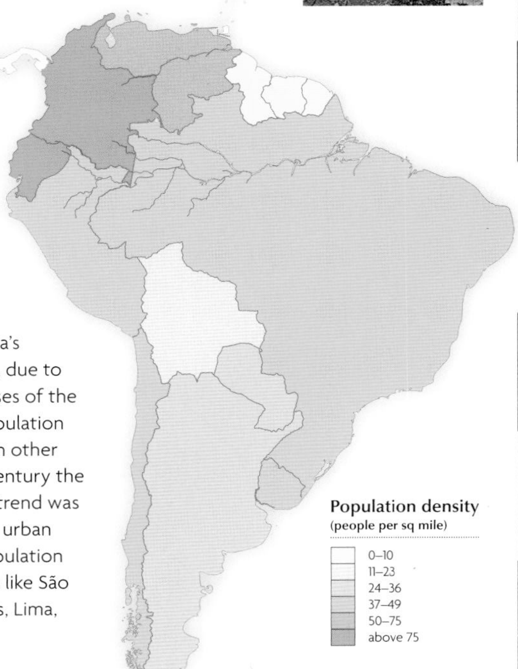
Population density
(people per sq mile)
0–10
11–23
24–36
37–49
50–75
above 75

South American resources

Agriculture still provides the largest single form of employment in South America, although rural unemployment and poverty continue to drive people towards the huge coastal cities in search of jobs and opportunities. Mineral and fuel resources, although substantial, are distributed unevenly; few countries have both fossil fuels and minerals. To break industrial dependence on raw materials, boost manufacturing, and improve infrastructure, governments borrowed heavily from the World Bank in the 1960s and 1970s. This led to the accumulation of massive debts which are unlikely ever to be repaid. Today, Brazil dominates the continent's economic output, followed by Argentina. Recently, the less-developed western side of South America has benefited due to its geographical position; for example Chile is increasingly exporting raw materials to Japan.

◀ *Ciudad Guayana is a planned industrial complex in eastern Venezuela, built as an iron and steel center to exploit the nearby iron ore reserves.*

▲ *The cold Peru Current flows north from the Antarctic along the Pacific coast of Peru, providing rich nutrients for one of the world's largest fishing grounds. However, over exploitation has severely reduced Peru's anchovy catch.*

Industry
aerospace
brewing
car/vehicle manufacture
chemicals
electronics
engineering
finance
fish processing
food processing
hi-tech industry
iron & steel
meat processing
metal refining
narcotics
pharmaceuticals
printing & publishing
shipbuilding
sugar processing
textiles
timber processing
tobacco processing
wine
oil
gas
industrial cities
major industrial areas
Caribbean Sea
ATLANTIC OCEAN
PACIFIC OCEAN
PANAMA
Gulf of Panama
Barranquilla
Cartagena
Maracaibo
Barquisimeto
Caracas
Valencia
Ciudad Guayana
VENEZUELA
Medellín
Bogotá
Cali
COLOMBIA
Georgetown
GUYANA
Paramaribo
SURINAME
French Guiana (to France)
Quito
ECUADOR
Guayaquil
Amazon Basin
Manaus
Belém
Iquitos
Fortaleza
Natal
Recife
Maceió
Salvador
BRAZIL
Chiclayo
Chimbote
PERU
Lima
Cusco
Arequipa
BOLIVIA
La Paz
Santa Cruz
Sucre
Brasília
Arica
Iquique
Chuquicamata
Belo Horizonte
PARAGUAY
Antofagasta
São Paulo
Rio de Janeiro
Asunción
Ciudad del Este
Curitiba
San Miguel de Tucumán
Corrientes
CHILE
Porto Alegre
Córdoba
Santa Fe
Rosario
URUGUAY
Rio Grande
Valparaíso
Mendoza
Santiago
Buenos Aires
Montevideo
Talca
ARGENTINA
Concepción
Bahía Blanca
Neuquén
Valdivia
Comodoro Rivadavia
Gulf of San Jorge
Bahía Grande
Falkland Islands (to UK)
Punta Arenas
Strait of Magellan
Cape Horn
GNI per capita (US$)
below 999
1000–1999
2000–2999
3000–3999
4000–4999
above 5000

Standard of living

Wealth disparities throughout the continent create a wide gulf between affluent landowners and those afflicted by chronic poverty in inner city slums. The illicit production of cocaine, and the hugely influential drug barons who control its distribution, contribute to the violent disorder and corruption which affect northwestern South America, destabilizing local governments and economies.

Standard of living
(UN human development index)
low
high

▶ *Both Argentina and Chile are now exploring the southernmost tip of the continent in search of oil. Here in Punta Arenas, a drilling rig is being prepared for exploratory drilling in the Strait of Magellan.*

Industry

Argentina and Brazil are South America's most industrialized countries and São Paulo is the continent's leading industrial center. Long-term government investment in Brazilian industry has encouraged a diverse industrial base; engineering, steel production, food processing, textile manufacture, and chemicals predominate. The illegal production of cocaine is economically significant in the Andean countries of Colombia and Bolivia. In Venezuela, the oil-dominated economy has left the country vulnerable to world oil price fluctuations. Food processing and mineral exploitation are common throughout the less industrially developed parts of the continent, including Bolivia, Chile, Ecuador, and Peru.

Environmental issues

The Amazon Basin is one of the last great wilderness areas left on Earth. The tropical rain forests which grow there are a valuable genetic resource, containing innumerable unique plants and animals. The forests are increasingly under threat from new and expanding settlements and "slash-and-burn" farming techniques, which clear land for the raising of beef cattle, causing land degradation and soil erosion.

▲ *Clouds of smoke billow from the burning Amazon rainforest. Over 11,500 sq miles (30,000 sq km) of virgin rainforest are being cleared annually, destroying an ancient, irreplaceable, natural resource and biodiverse habitat.*

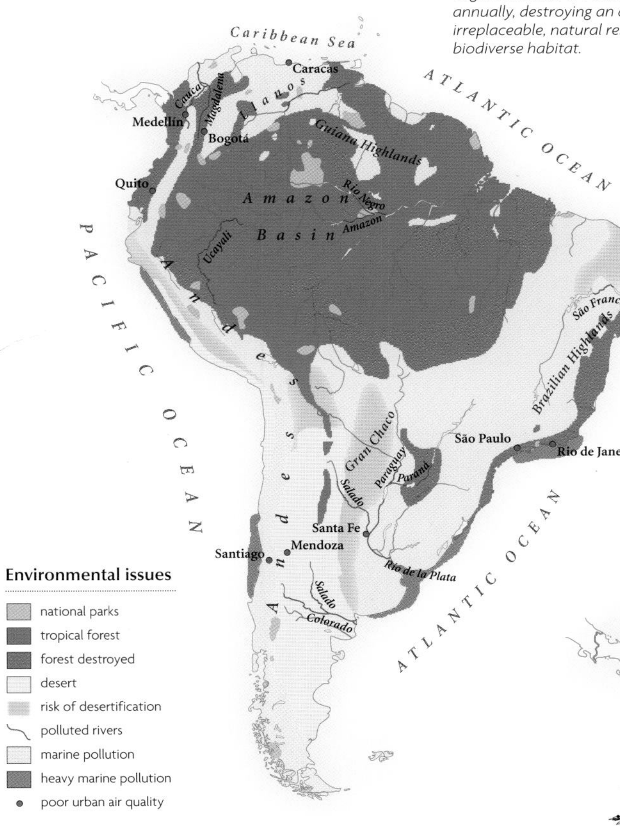
Caribbean Sea
ATLANTIC OCEAN
PACIFIC OCEAN
Caracas
Medellín
Bogotá
Quito
Llanos
Guiana Highlands
Amazon Basin
Rio Negro
Amazon
Ucayali
Andes
São Francisco
Brazilian Highlands
Gran Chaco
Paraguay
Paraná
Salado
São Paulo
Rio de Janeiro
Santa Fe
Mendoza
Santiago
Río de la Plata
Colorado
Environmental issues
national parks
tropical forest
forest destroyed
desert
risk of desertification
polluted rivers
marine pollution
heavy marine pollution
poor urban air quality

Mineral resources

Over a quarter of the world's known copper reserves are found at the Chuquicamata mine in northern Chile, and other metallic minerals such as tin are found along the length of the Andes. The discovery of oil and gas at Venezuela's Lake Maracaibo in 1917 turned the country into one of the world's leading oil producers. In contrast, South America is virtually devoid of coal, the only significant deposit being on the peninsula of Guajira in Colombia.

▲ *Copper is Chile's largest export, most of which is mined at Chuquicamata. Along the length of the Andes, metallic minerals like copper and tin are found in abundance, formed by the excessive pressures and heat involved in mountain-building.*

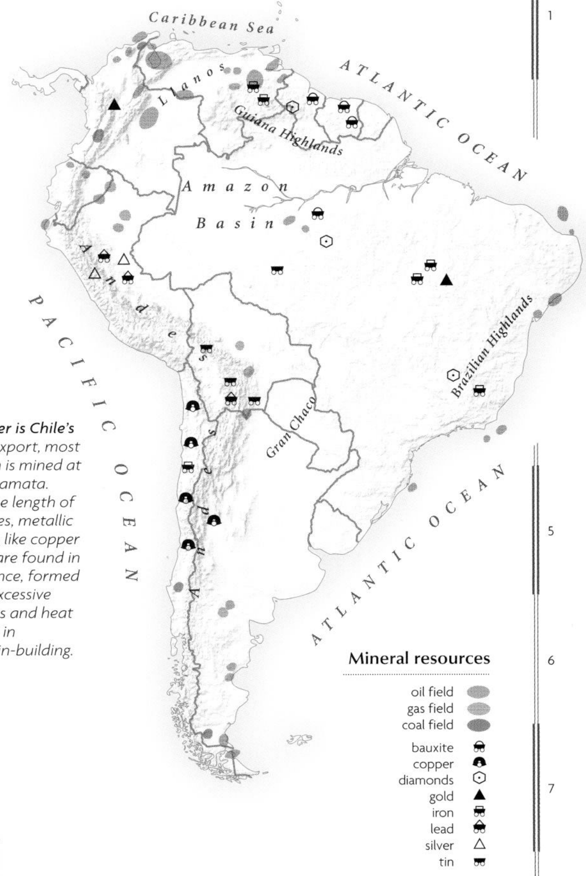
Caribbean Sea
ATLANTIC OCEAN
PACIFIC OCEAN
Llanos
Guiana Highlands
Amazon Basin
Andes
Gran Chaco
Brazilian Highlands
Mineral resources
oil field
gas field
coal field
bauxite
copper
diamonds
gold
iron
lead
silver
tin

Using the land and sea

Many foods now common worldwide originated in South America. These include the potato, tomato, squash, and cassava. Today, large herds of beef cattle roam the temperate grasslands of the Pampas, supporting an extensive meatpacking trade in Argentina, Uruguay and Paraguay. Corn is grown as a staple crop across the continent and coffee is grown as a cash crop in Brazil and Colombia. Coca plants grown in Bolivia, Peru, and Colombia provide most of the world's cocaine. Fish and shellfish are caught off the western coast, especially anchovies off Peru, shrimps off Ecuador and pilchards off Chile.

◀ *South America, and Brazil in particular, now leads the world in coffee production, mainly growing Coffea arabica in large plantations. Coffee beans are harvested, roasted and brewed to produce the world's second most popular drink, after tea.*

◀ *High in the Andes, hardy alpacas graze on the barren land. Alpacas are thought to have been domesticated by the Incas, whose nobility wore robes made from their wool. Today, they are still reared and prized for their soft, warm fleeces.*

◀ *The Pampas region of southeast South America is characterized by extensive, flat plains, and populated by cattle and ranchers (gauchos). Argentina is a major world producer of beef, much of which is exported to the US for use in hamburgers.*

Caribbean Sea
ATLANTIC OCEAN
PACIFIC OCEAN
Barranquilla
Maracaibo
Caracas
Gulf of Darien
Gulf of Panama
Medellín
Bogotá
Cali
Magdalena
Llanos
Orinoco
Guiana Highlands
Rio Negro
Amazon Basin
Putumayo
Amazon
Manaus
Marañón
Gulf of Guayaquil
Juruá
Purus
Madeira
Tapajós
Xingu
Tocantins
Araguaia
Ilha de Marajó
Belém
Fortaleza
Recife
Salvador
Andes
Lima
Planalto de Mato Grosso
Brasília
São Francisco
Brazilian Highlands
Belo Horizonte
Rio de Janeiro
São Paulo
Curitiba
Pilcomayo
Gran Chaco
Paraguay
Paraná
Uruguay
Porto Alegre
Córdoba
Rosario
Santiago
Buenos Aires
Montevideo
Pampas
Colorado
Río Negro
Chico
Gulf of San Jorge
Patagonia
Bahía Grande
Tierra del Fuego
Cape Horn
Using the land and sea
barren land
cropland
desert
forest
mountain region
pasture
major conurbations
cattle
pigs
sheep
bananas
corn
citrus fruits
cocoa
cotton
coffee
fishing
oil palms
peanuts
rubber
shellfish
soybeans
sugar cane
vineyards
wheat

Northern South America

COLOMBIA, GUYANA, SURINAME, VENEZUELA, French Guiana (to France)

Fringed by the Pacific and Atlantic oceans and the Caribbean Sea, South America's northern region has a rich range of natural resources, some exploited for centuries by colonial powers including the Spanish, French, Dutch, and British, others still to be fully explored. The prospects for further economic development in Colombia, Guyana, and Suriname are blighted by drug-related violence and political instability. Venezuela, despite huge incomes from its oil reserves, remains less developed in other industrial sectors. French Guiana is an overseas *département* of France, now seeking greater autonomy. Most of the major population centers, such as Bogotá, have grown up in the temperate conditions of the high Andes or, like Caracas, at strategic points along the Caribbean coast.

▶ *Flowers grown in* Colombia are exported all over the world, and include fine carnations and roses. Here, workers are cutting roses which have been grown in plastic greenhouses.

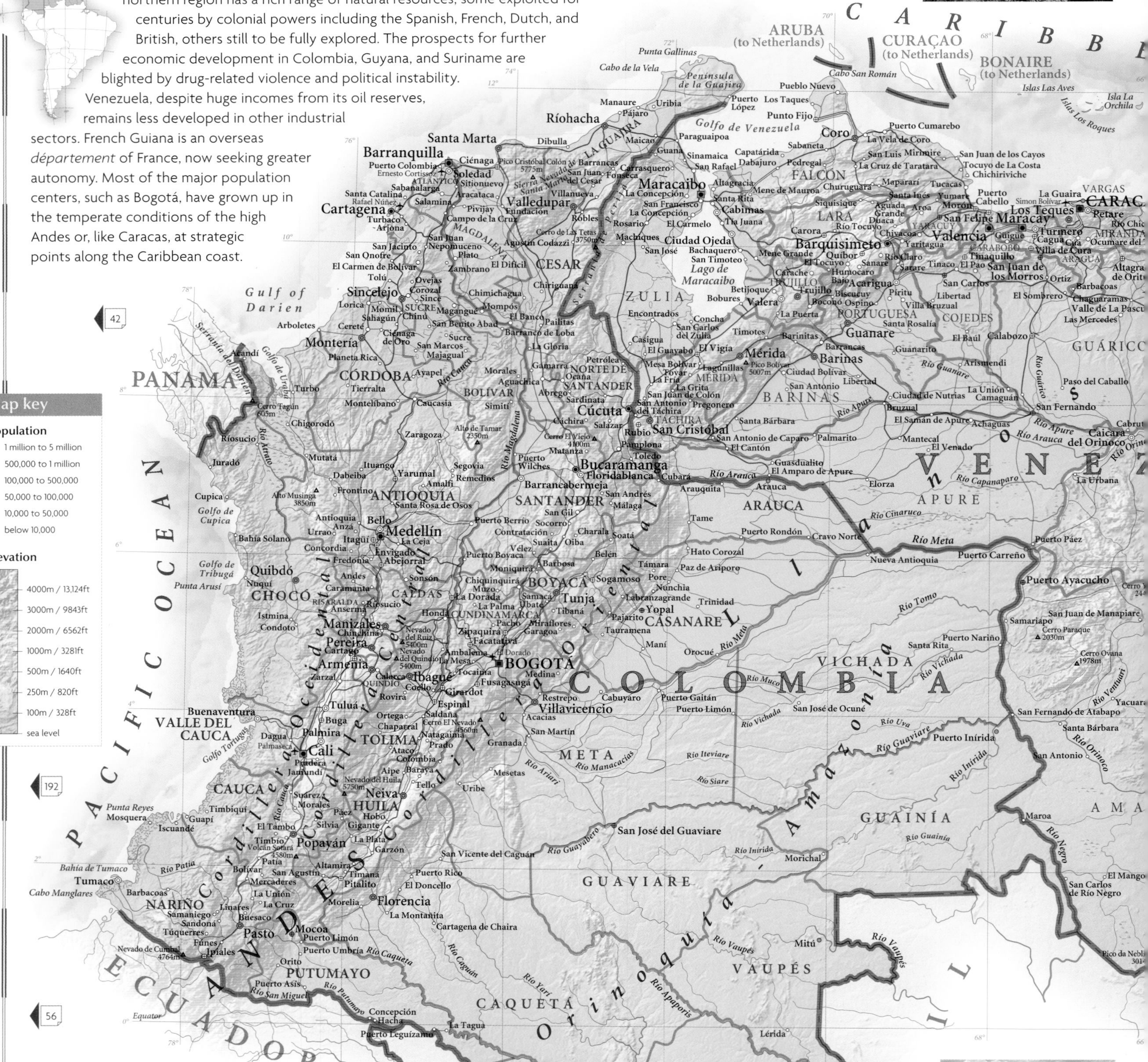

CARIBBEAN
ARUBA (to Netherlands)
CURAÇAO (to Netherlands)
BONAIRE (to Netherlands)
PANAMA
PACIFIC OCEAN
COLOMBIA
VENEZUELA
ECUADOR
PERU
BRAZIL
ANDES
Cordillera Occidental
Cordillera Central
Cordillera Oriental
Llanos
Amazonia
Orinoco
Gulf of Darien
Golfo de Venezuela
Lago de Maracaibo
BOGOTÁ
Medellín
Cali
Barranquilla
Cartagena
Santa Marta
Bucaramanga
Cúcuta
Maracaibo
Valencia
Maracay
Barquisimeto
Mérida
Barinas
Leticia
Map key
Population
1 million to 5 million
500,000 to 1 million
100,000 to 500,000
50,000 to 100,000
10,000 to 50,000
below 10,000
Elevation
4000m / 13,124ft
3000m / 9843ft
2000m / 6562ft
1000m / 3281ft
500m / 1640ft
250m / 820ft
100m / 328ft
sea level
Scale 1:7,250,000
projection: Lambert Azimuthal Equal Area

▲ *Large open squares* like the Plaza de Bolívar in Bogotá are characteristic of many cities founded by the Spanish.

◀ *Scattered farms and* villages have grown up on the gentle slopes of this Colombian river valley, utilizing the fertile soils for farming.

▲ *The Orinoco river* flows from its source in the southern Guiana Highlands to form a broad delta on Venezuela's Atlantic coast. One of its distributary channels opens into a wide bay called the Serpent's Mouth.

Transportation & industry

Many mineral resources are mined in Colombia, including fuels, gold, and precious and semiprecious stones. Revenues from coffee and exports of illegal narcotics are crucial to the economy. Venezuela's major economic activity is the oil industry around Lake Maracaibo *(Lago de Maracaibo)*. Sugar and bauxite are exported from Guyana and Suriname.

Transportation network

(roads)	31,720 miles (51,054 km)
(highways)	3411 miles (5490 km)
(railways)	2448 miles (3940 km)
(waterways)	22,429 miles (36,100 km)

Rivers are an important means of transportation in Colombia; many are extensively navigable. The Pan-American Highway runs through Colombia. In Venezuela, much infrastructure investment is linked to the oil industry.

Caribbean Sea
ATLANTIC OCEAN
PACIFIC OCEAN
Maracaibo
Barranquilla
Valencia
CARACAS
Cumaná
Ciudad Guayana
VENEZUELA
GEORGETOWN
PARAMARIBO
Cayenne
GUYANA
SURINAME
FRENCH GUIANA
Medellín
BOGOTÁ
Cali
COLOMBIA
PANAMA
ECUADOR
PERU
BRAZIL

Major industry and infrastructure

- chemicals
- finance
- food processing
- iron & steel
- narcotics
- mining
- oil
- oil refining
- pharmaceuticals
- textiles
- timber processing
- capital cities
- major towns
- international airports
- major roads
- major industrial areas

▲ ***Vast oil reserves** around Lake Maracaibo* (Lago de Maracaibo) *form the focus of Venezuelan industry. Incomes from oil are used to invest in other industries and in the development of infrastructure.*

Using the land

The Andean basins support cereals and potatoes. Livestock graze at higher altitudes and on the drier tropical grasslands known as the *llanos;* hardy goats are reared in scrubland areas. Grown at higher elevations, coffee is an important cash crop, as is cotton, sugar cane, bananas, citrus fruits, cocoa, and rice, farmed on the Caribbean lowlands. Coca is the most widely grown narcotic plant, with heroin poppies grown in Colombia and marijuana in lowland areas throughout the region.

Caribbean Sea
ATLANTIC OCEAN
PACIFIC OCEAN
PANAMA
Maracaibo
CARACAS
VENEZUELA
GEORGETOWN
PARAMARIBO
CAYENNE
GUYANA
SURINAME
FRENCH GUIANA
Medellín
BOGOTÁ
COLOMBIA
ECUADOR
PERU
BRAZIL

Land use and agricultural distribution

- cattle
- goats
- bananas
- cereals
- coffee
- cotton
- sugar cane
- capital cities
- major towns
- pasture
- cropland
- forest
- wetlands
- mountain region

The urban/rural population divide

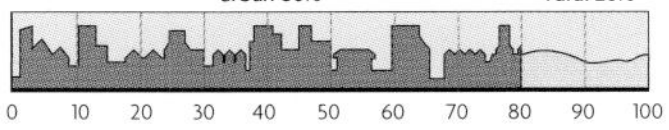

urban 80%
rural 20%
0
10
20
30
40
50
60
70
80
90
100

Population density	Total land area
78 people per sq mile (30 people per sq km)	1,111,317 sq miles (2,879,060 sq km)

SEA
ATLANTIC OCEAN
TRINIDAD & TOBAGO
64
58
Isla Blanquilla
Islas Los Testigos
Isla de Margarita
Juangriego
La Asunción
Pampatar
Porlamar
Boca de Pozo
NUEVA ESPARTA
Punta de Piedras
Carúpano
Río Caribe
Puerto de Hierro
Cumaná
SUCRE
Güiria
Gulf of Paria
Barcelona
Maturín
The Serpent's Mouth
Punta Baja
Pedernales
Tucupita
DELTA AMACURO
MONAGAS
ANZOÁTEGUI
El Tigre
Río Orinoco
Ciudad Guayana
Ciudad Bolívar
Curiapo
Waini Point
Port Kaituma
Charity
Essequibo Islands
GEORGETOWN
Parika
Bartica
Linden
New Amsterdam
Rose Hall
Corriverton
Nieuw Nickerie
Wageningen
Totness
Groningen
Lelydorp
PARAMARIBO
Nieuw Amsterdam
WANICA
COMMEWIJNE
SARAMACCA
CORONIE
NICKERIE
PARA
MAROWIJNE
Albina
St-Laurent-du-Maroni
Mana
Iracoubo
Sinnamary
Îles du Salut
Île du Diable
Centre Spatial Guyanais
Kourou
CAYENNE
Rémire
Matoury
Roura
Cacao
Régina
Ouanary
St-Georges
Camopi
Pointe Béhague
Baie de L'Oyapok
Saül
Maripasoula
FRENCH GUIANA (to France)
SURINAME
SIPALIWINI
Brokopondo
Brownsweg
Apetina
Juliana Top 1230m
Tafelberg 1026m
Hendrik Top 957m
GUYANA
Mount Roraima 2810m
Ayanganna Mountain 2042m
Mahdia
Kaieteur Falls
Kurupukari
Lethem
Kanuku Mountains
Sauriwaunawa
Kuyuwini Landing
Johi Village
Acarai Mountains
Tumuc-Humac Mountains
(Claimed by Suriname)
(Venezuela claims all of Guyana west of Essequibo river)
Pakaraima Mountains
Guiana Highlands
BOLÍVAR
Salto Ángel
Uruyén
Canaima
Santa Elena de Uairén
Gran Sabana
Sierra Parima
Puerto Ayacucho
Río Orinoco
Sierra Tapirapecó
Sierra de Unturán
Equator
BRAZIL
ATLANTIC OCEAN

▲ ***The Sierra Nevada** de Santa Marta is a granite massif which rises sharply from the Caribbean lowlands to snow-covered peaks, the tallest of which is 18,947 ft (5775 m) high.*

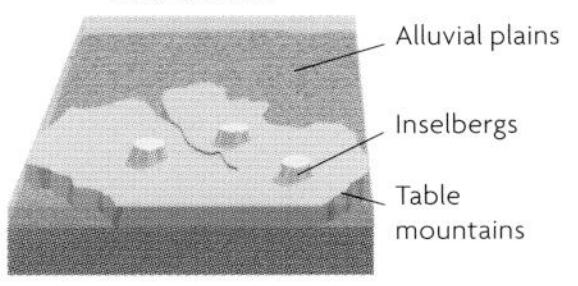

Guiana Shield
Alluvial plains
Inselbergs
Table mountains

▲ ***The Guiana Shield** is one of the oldest land surfaces in the world – probably formed more than 4 billion years ago. Chemical weathering over millions of years has created flat-topped table mountains and large numbers of inselbergs.*

The landscape

At its northernmost reaches, in western Colombia and Venezuela, the great Andean mountain chain splits into three distinct ranges: the Cordillera Oriental, Cordillera Central, and Cordillera Occidental, intercut by a complex series of lesser ranges and basins. The relief becomes lower toward the coast and the interior plains of the northern Amazon Basin, rising again into the tropical hills of the Guiana Highlands.

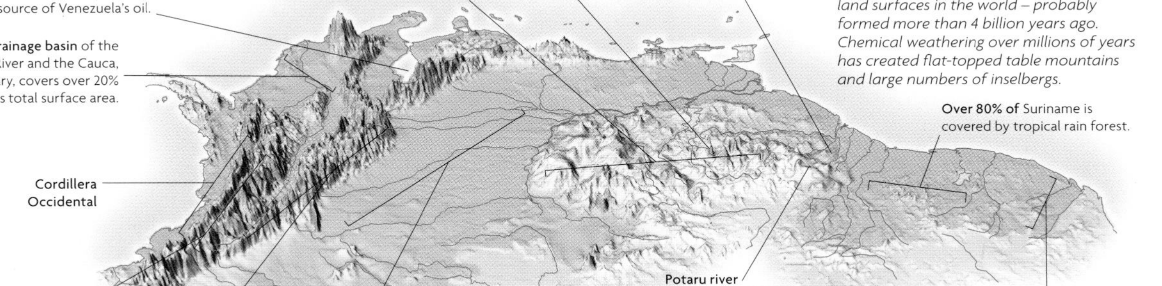

Lake Maracaibo *(Lago de Maracaibo)* is not a true lake but a shallow inlet of the Caribbean Sea. It is the main source of Venezuela's oil.
In the Guiana Highlands, Venezuela's most remote region, the ancient crystalline rocks contain deposits of iron ore, gold, and diamonds.
Angel Falls *(Salto Ángel)*, at 3212 ft (979 m), is the world's highest waterfall.
Igneous intrusions into the crystalline plateau which forms most of central Guyana have led to the formation of the many rapids that characterize Guyana's rivers.
The drainage basin of the Magdalena River and the Cauca, its main tributary, covers over 20% of Colombia's total surface area.
Over 80% of Suriname is covered by tropical rain forest.
Cordillera Occidental
Cordillera Central
Cordillera Oriental
Colombia's eastern lowlands are known locally as *llanos*, meaning grasslands.
Potaru river
Most of the land in French Guiana is low-lying; here, the rocks of the Guiana Highlands have been eroded by rivers flowing toward the sea.

► ***The Potaru river** descends 741 ft (226 m) over a sandstone ledge at the Kaieteur Falls in Guyana.*

Western South America

BOLIVIA, ECUADOR, PERU

The three states of Western South America share a similar geography and recent history. Dominated by the Inca empire until Spanish conquest in the 16th century, they achieved independence from Spain in the early 19th century. The precipitous terrain of the Andes presents severe difficulties for overland transportation and continues to be a barrier to national unity and stability. Although Ecuador is now a relatively stable democracy, the military is highly influential in Peru and Bolivia, while the drug trade and associated corruption discourages external aid and economic progress. Wealth and power are still largely concentrated in the hands of a small elite of families, who attained their position during the Spanish colonial period. Energy resources and political recognition for the indigenous peoples are becoming increasingly important issues, particularly in Bolivia.

▶ *Ecuador's capital city,* *Quito, lies high in the Andes, nestling between snowcapped peaks. At 9350 ft (2850 m), Quito is the second highest capital in the world – La Paz in Bolivia is the highest.*

The landscape

Bolivia, Peru, and Ecuador each possess a high Andean mountain region and an eastern region consisting of tropical lowlands and the Andean slope leading down to them. Toward the south of the region, the mountains widen to form the high plateau of the Altiplano. Peru and Ecuador also have fertile, lowland coastal plains. A wide variety of environments include *selva* (tropical rain forest), *montaña* (mountain forest), and grassland.

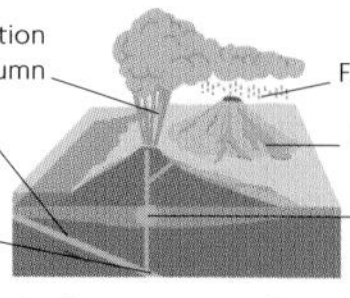
Eruption column
Falling ash
Lava flows
Subduction zone
Magma chamber
Zone of magma generation

▲ ***There are many*** *large and active volcanoes in the Andes. Magma generated in the heart of the volcano erupts in a huge cloud of ash. Ashfall deposits are common throughout the Andes and the rock produced is known as andesite. This is rapidly soaked by heavy rain, causing massive debris flows.*

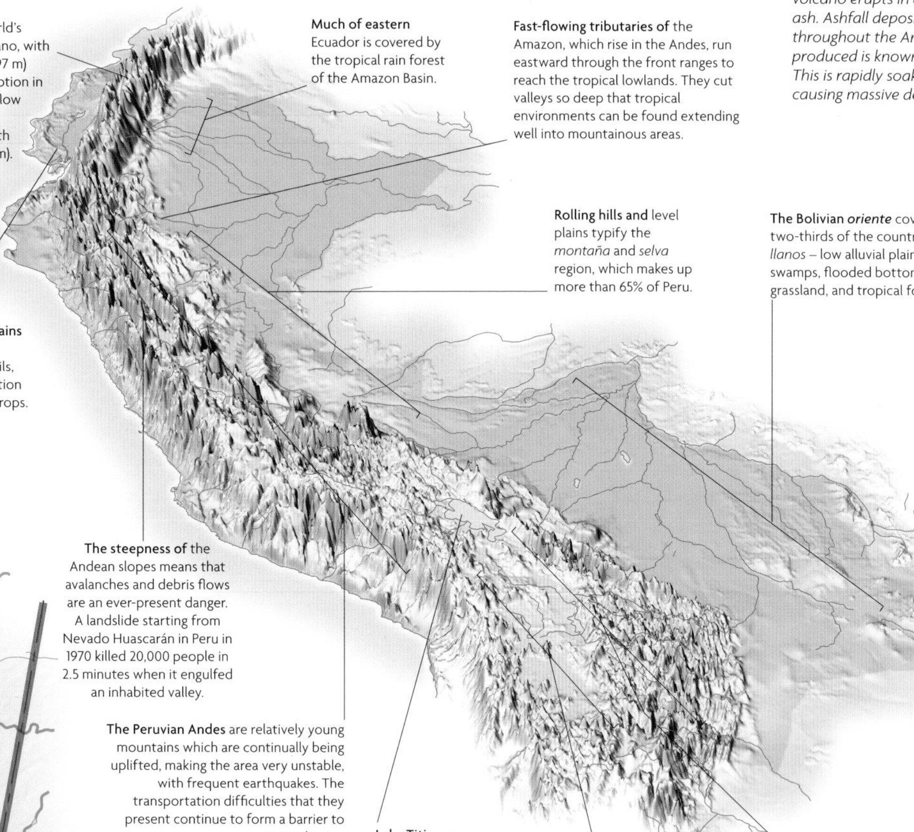

Cotopaxi is the world's highest active volcano, with a peak 19,347 ft (5897 m) high. A massive eruption in 1877 caused a mudflow which destroyed everything in its path for 150 miles (240 km).

Much of eastern Ecuador is covered by the tropical rain forest of the Amazon Basin.

Fast-flowing tributaries of the Amazon, which rise in the Andes, run eastward through the front ranges to reach the tropical lowlands. They cut valleys so deep that tropical environments can be found extending well into mountainous areas.

Rolling hills and level plains typify the *montaña* and *selva* region, which makes up more than 65% of Peru.

The Bolivian ***oriente*** covers more than two-thirds of the country. It includes *llanos* – low alluvial plains, massive swamps, flooded bottomlands, savannah grassland, and tropical forests.

The coastal floodplains are the source of Ecuador's richest soils, enabling the cultivation of a wide range of crops.

The steepness of the Andean slopes means that avalanches and debris flows are an ever-present danger. A landslide starting from Nevado Huascarán in Peru in 1970 killed 20,000 people in 2.5 minutes when it engulfed an inhabited valley.

The Peruvian Andes are relatively young mountains which are continually being uplifted, making the area very unstable, with frequent earthquakes. The transportation difficulties that they present continue to form a barrier to national unity.

The Altiplano is a flat, high plateau lying between the Cordillera Oriental and the Cordillera Occidental at a height of up to 12,500 ft (3800 m). At its margins lie many spurs and alluvial fans.

Lake Titicaca

▲ ***Lake Titicaca, which*** *forms part of the border between Peru and Bolivia, is the largest lake in South America and the highest significant body of water in the world at an altitude of 12,507 ft (3812 m).*

Bolivian Andes

▲ ***Nevado de Illampu*** *and Nevado de Ancohuma, at 21,275 ft (6485 m) and 21,490 ft (6550 m) respectively, form Illampu, the highest mountain in the Bolivian Andes.*

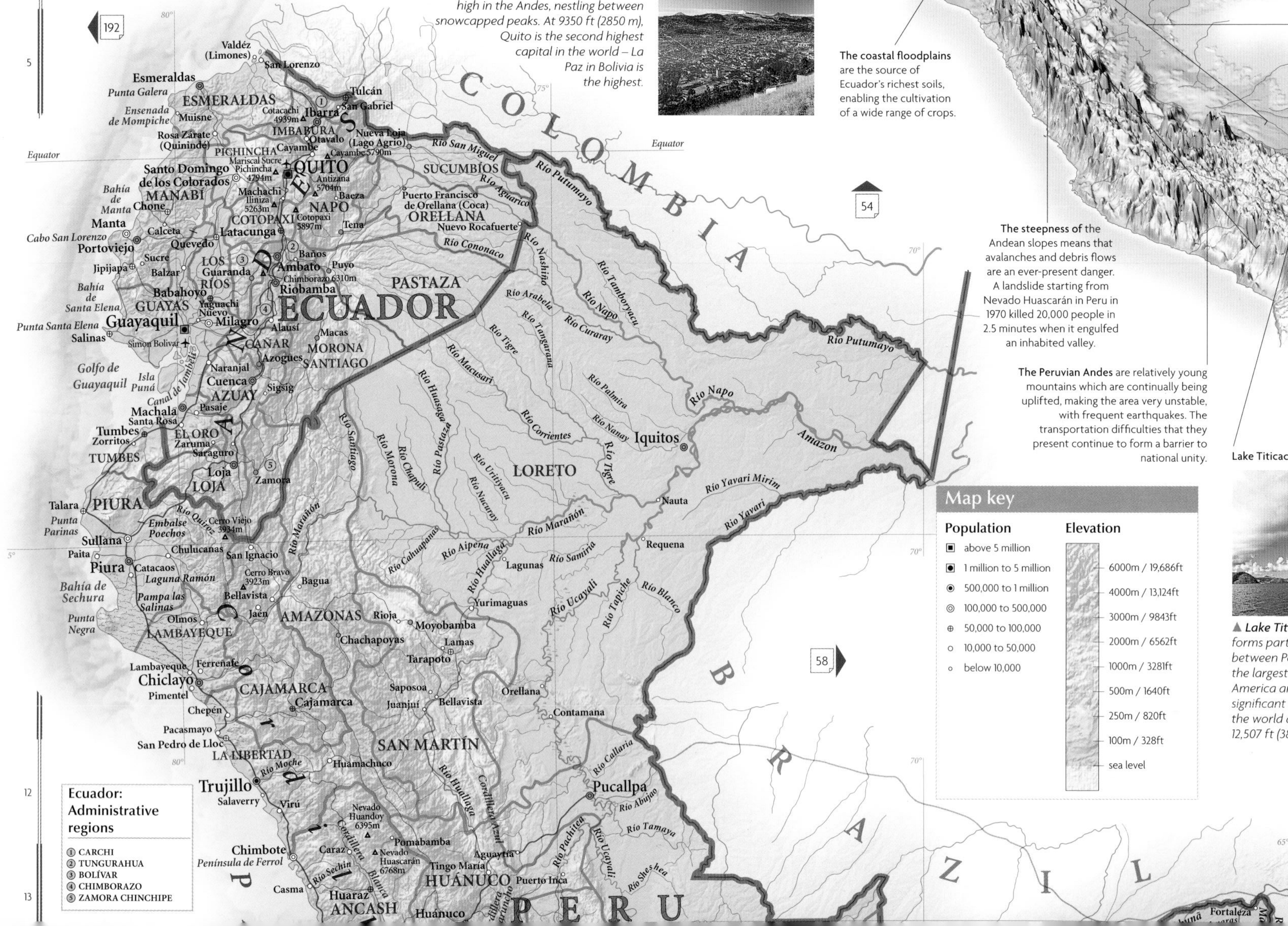
COLOMBIA
ECUADOR
PERU
BRAZIL
QUITO
Guayaquil
Cuenca
Iquitos
Pucallpa
Trujillo
Chiclayo
Piura
Chimbote
LORETO
SAN MARTÍN
AMAZONAS
CAJAMARCA
LA LIBERTAD
PIURA
TUMBES
LAMBAYEQUE
ANCASH
HUÁNUCO
PASTAZA
MORONA SANTIAGO
SUCUMBÍOS
ORELLANA
NAPO
ESMERALDAS
MANABÍ
GUAYAS
LOS RÍOS
EL ORO
LOJA
AZUAY
CAÑAR
PICHINCHA
IMBABURA
COTOPAXI
Amazon
Río Putumayo
Río Napo
Río Marañón
Río Ucayali
Río Huallaga
Río Tigre
Río Yavarí
Equator

192

54

58

Ecuador: Administrative regions

1. CARCHI
2. TUNGURAHUA
3. BOLÍVAR
4. CHIMBORAZO
5. ZAMORA CHINCHIPE

Map key

Population

- above 5 million
- 1 million to 5 million
- 500,000 to 1 million
- 100,000 to 500,000
- 50,000 to 100,000
- 10,000 to 50,000
- below 10,000

Elevation

- 6000m / 19,686ft
- 4000m / 13,124ft
- 3000m / 9843ft
- 2000m / 6562ft
- 1000m / 3281ft
- 500m / 1640ft
- 250m / 820ft
- 100m / 328ft
- sea level

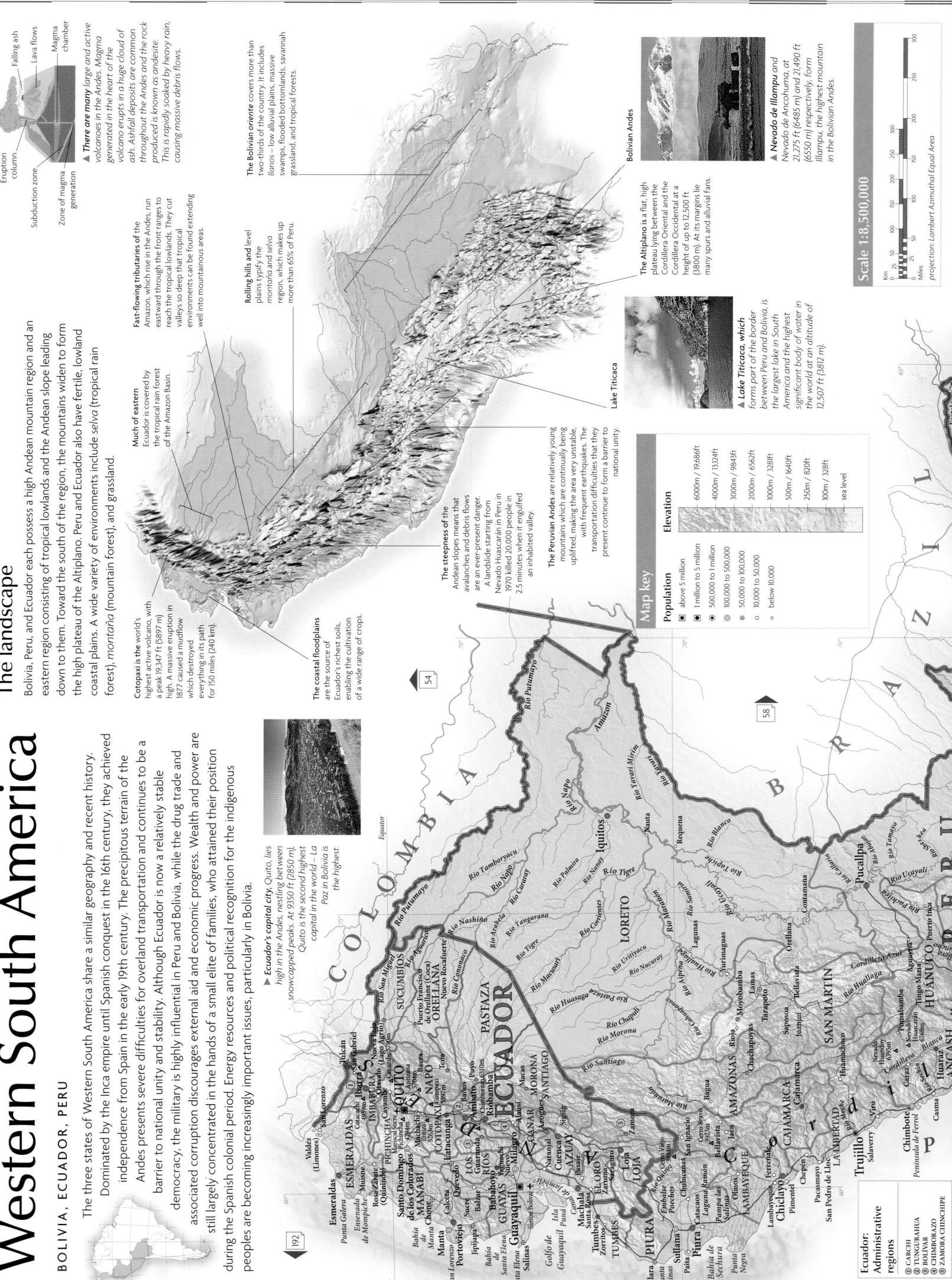

Scale 1:8,500,000

Km 0 25 50 100 150 200 250 300

Miles 0 25 50 100 150 200 250 300

projection: Lambert Azimuthal Equal Area

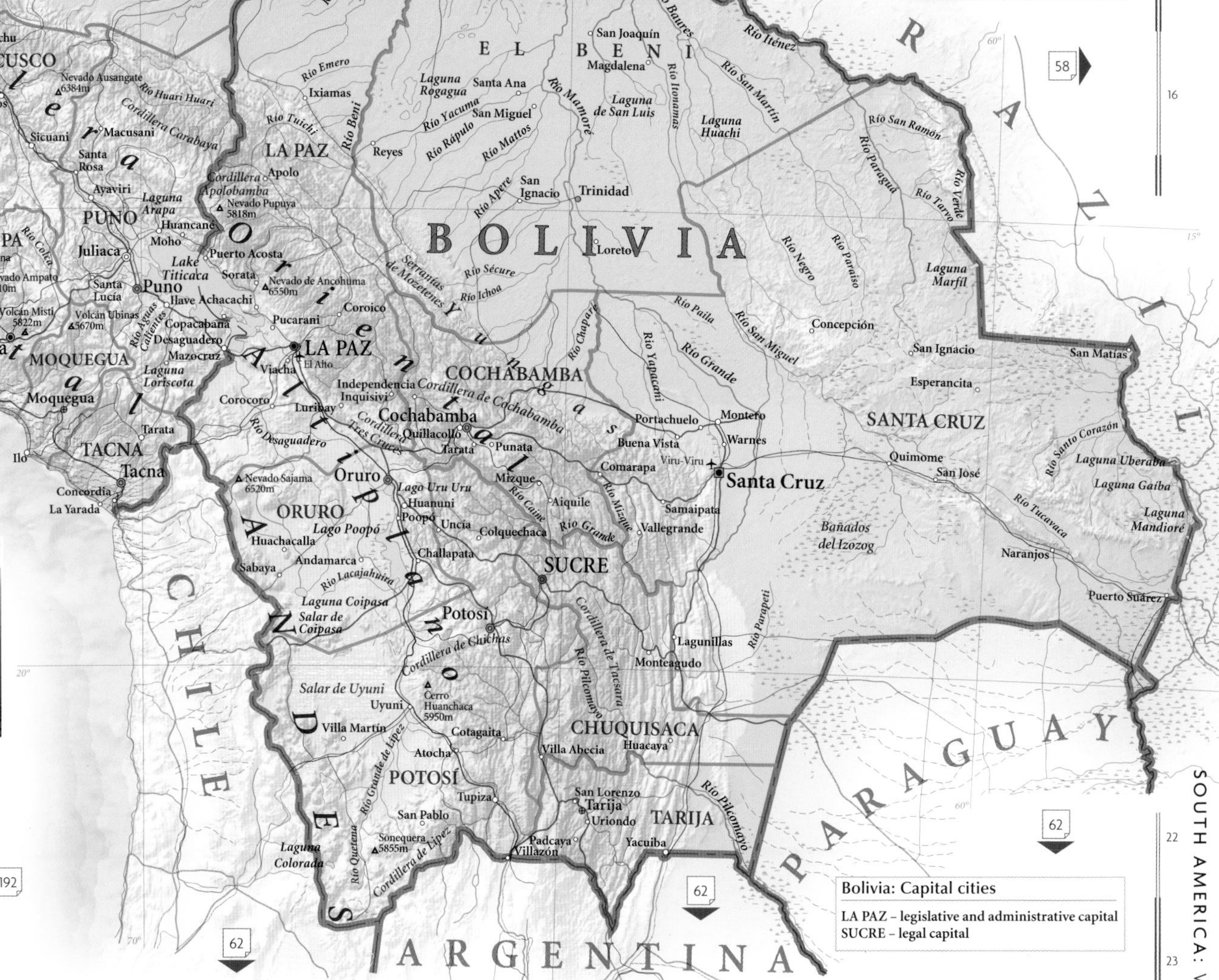
BOLIVIA
BRAZIL
PARAGUAY
ARGENTINA
CHILE
PACIFIC OCEAN
PANDO
BENI
LA PAZ
COCHABAMBA
SANTA CRUZ
ORURO
POTOSÍ
CHUQUISACA
TARIJA
MADRE DE DIOS
CUSCO
PUNO
AREQUIPA
MOQUEGUA
TACNA
APURÍMAC
AYACUCHO
HUANCAVELICA
JUNÍN
ICA
LIMA
LA PAZ
SUCRE
Santa Cruz
Cochabamba
Oruro
Potosí
Tarija
Trinidad
Cobija
Lima
Callao
Cusco
Arequipa
Puno
Tacna
Lake Titicaca
Salar de Uyuni
Machu Picchu
Cordillera Oriental
Altiplano
Andes
Cordillera Occidental
Yungas
58
62
62
62
192
192

▲ **A colony of** marine iguanas basks on the rocks of Isla Fernandina in the Galápagos Islands. Charles Darwin's theory of evolution was inspired by the differences he found between the animal species on neighboring islands in the Galápagos.

Galápagos Islands
(Archipiélago de Colón)
Isla Pinta
Isla Marchena
Isla Genovesa
GALÁPAGOS
(to Ecuador)
Equator
Volcán Wolf 1646m
Volcán Darwin 1280m
Volcán La Cumbra 1463m
Isla Fernandina
Volcán Alcebo 1097m
Isla San Salvador
Isla Pinzón
Isla Santa Cruz
Puerto Ayora
Volcán Santo Tomás 1490m
Isla Santa Fe
Puerto Baquerizo Moreno
Isla San Cristóbal
Isla Isabela
Puerto Villamil
Isla Santa María
Isla Española
PACIFIC OCEAN
(same scale as main map)

◀ **The Galapagos Islands** are mainly composed of lava, with very little vegetation near to the coasts, although the wetter inland slopes are mantled with forest.

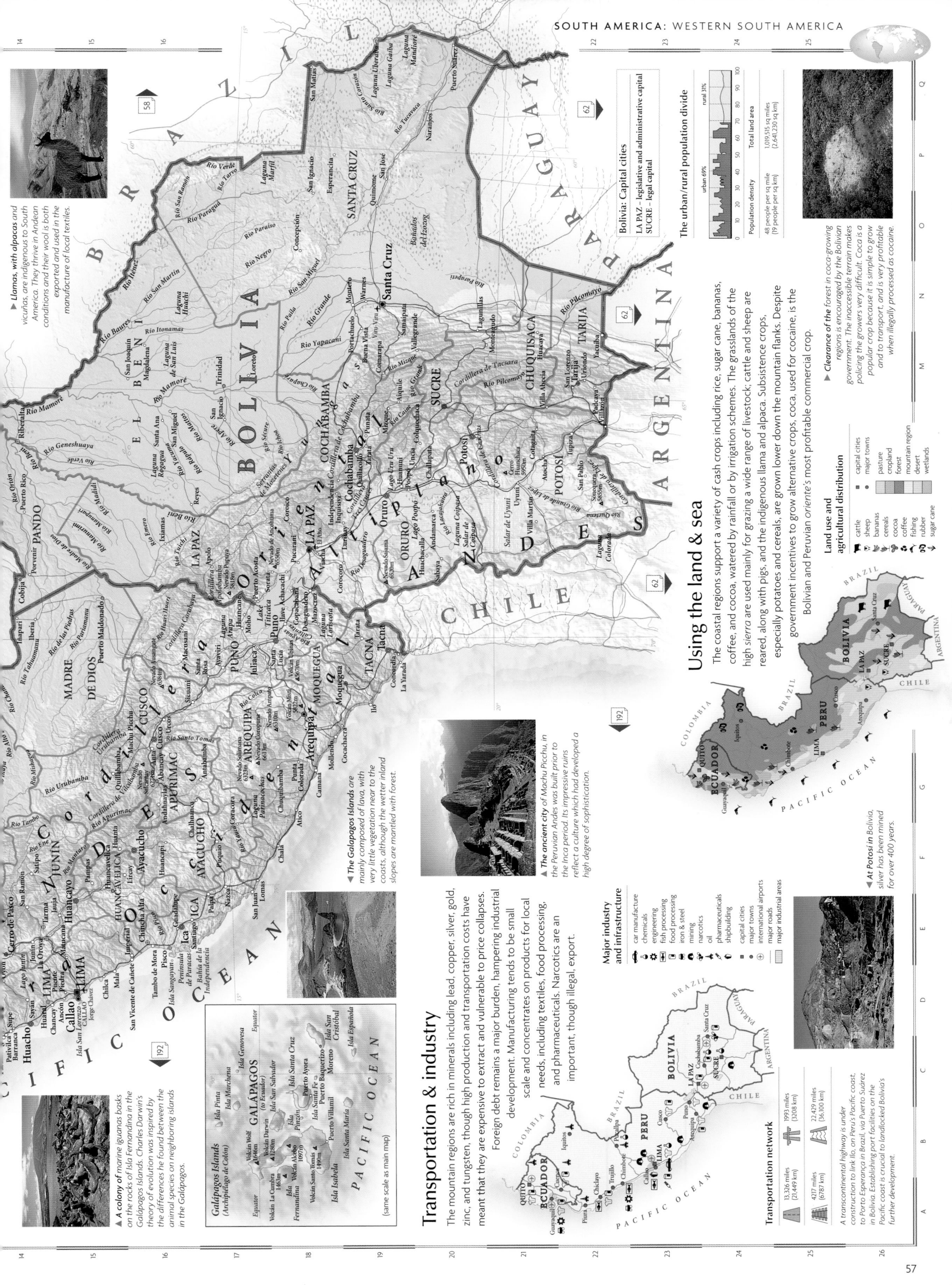

▶ **Llamas, with alpacas** and vicuñas, are indigenous to South America. They thrive in Andean conditions and their wool is both exported and used in the manufacture of local textiles.

Transportation & industry

The mountain regions are rich in minerals including lead, copper, silver, gold, zinc, and tungsten, though high production and transportation costs have meant that they are expensive to extract and vulnerable to price collapses. Foreign debt remains a major burden, hampering industrial development. Manufacturing tends to be small scale and concentrates on products for local needs, including textiles, food processing, and pharmaceuticals. Narcotics are an important, though illegal, export.

▲ **The ancient city** of Machu Picchu, in the Peruvian Andes was built prior to the Inca period. Its impressive ruins reflect a culture which had developed a high degree of sophistication.

COLOMBIA
QUITO
ECUADOR
Guayaquil
Cuenca
Iquitos
Piura
Chiclayo
Trujillo
Chimbote
Pucallpa
BRAZIL
PERU
Callao
LIMA
Cusco
Puno
Arequipa
BOLIVIA
LA PAZ
Cochabamba
SUCRE
Santa Cruz
CHILE
ARGENTINA
PARAGUAY
PACIFIC OCEAN

Major industry and infrastructure

- car manufacture
- chemicals
- engineering
- fish processing
- food processing
- iron & steel
- mining
- narcotics
- oil
- pharmaceuticals
- shipbuilding
- capital cities
- major towns
- international airports
- major roads
- major industrial areas

Transportation network

13,326 miles (21,449 km)	1993 miles (3208 km)
4217 miles (6787 km)	22,429 miles (36,100 km)

A transcontinental highway is under construction to link Ilo, on Peru's Pacific coast, to Porto Esperança in Brazil, via Puerto Suárez in Bolivia. Establishing port facilities on the Pacific coast is crucial to landlocked Bolivia's further development.

◀ **At Potosí in** Bolivia, silver has been mined for over 400 years.

Bolivia: Capital cities

LA PAZ – legislative and administrative capital
SUCRE – legal capital

Using the land & sea

The coastal regions support a variety of cash crops including rice, sugar cane, bananas, coffee, and cocoa, watered by rainfall or by irrigation schemes. The grasslands of the high *sierra* are used mainly for grazing a wide range of livestock; cattle and sheep are reared, along with pigs, and the indigenous llama and alpaca. Subsistence crops, especially potatoes and cereals, are grown lower down the mountain flanks. Despite government incentives to grow alternative crops, coca, used for cocaine, is the Bolivian and Peruvian *oriente's* most profitable commercial crop.

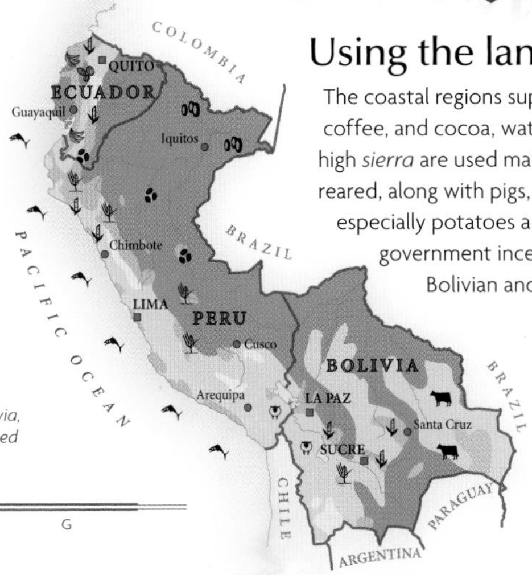
COLOMBIA
QUITO
ECUADOR
Guayaquil
Iquitos
Chimbote
BRAZIL
LIMA
PERU
Cusco
Arequipa
BOLIVIA
LA PAZ
SUCRE
Santa Cruz
CHILE
PARAGUAY
ARGENTINA
PACIFIC OCEAN

Land use and agricultural distribution

- cattle
- sheep
- bananas
- cereals
- cocoa
- coffee
- fishing
- rubber
- sugar cane
- capital cities
- major towns
- pasture
- cropland
- forest
- mountain region
- desert
- wetlands

The urban/rural population divide

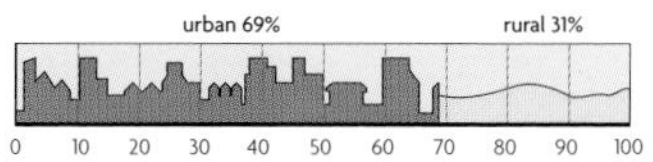
urban 69%
rural 31%
0
10
20
30
40
50
60
70
80
90
100

Population density	Total land area
48 people per sq mile (19 people per sq km)	1,019,515 sq miles (2,641,230 sq km)

▶ **Clearance of the** forest in coca-growing regions is encouraged by the Bolivian government. The inaccessible terrain makes policing the growers very difficult. Coca is a popular crop because it is simple to grow and to transport, and is very profitable when illegally processed as cocaine.

Brazil

Brazil is the largest country in South America, with a population of 191 million – almost half the combined total of the continent. The 26 states which make up the federal republic of Brazil are administered from the purpose-built capital, Brasília. Tropical rain forest, covering more than one-third of the country, contains rich natural resources, but great tracts are sacrificed to agriculture, industry and urban expansion on a daily basis. Most of Brazil's multiethnic population now live in cities, some of which are vast areas of urban sprawl; São Paulo is one of the world's biggest conurbations, with more than 20 million inhabitants. Although prosperity is a reality for some, many people still live in great poverty, and mounting foreign debts continue to damage Brazil's prospects of economic advancement.

Using the land

Brazil has immense natural resources, including minerals and hardwoods, many of which are found in the fragile rain forest. Brazil is the world's leading coffee grower and a major producer of livestock, sugar, and orange juice concentrate. Soybeans for animal feed, particularly for poultry feed, have become the country's most significant crop.

The urban/rural population divide

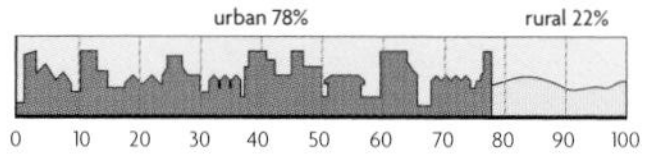

urban 78%
rural 22%
0 10 20 30 40 50 60 70 80 90 100

Population density	Total land area
55 people per sq mile (21 people per sq km)	3,286,472 sq miles (8,511,970 sq km)

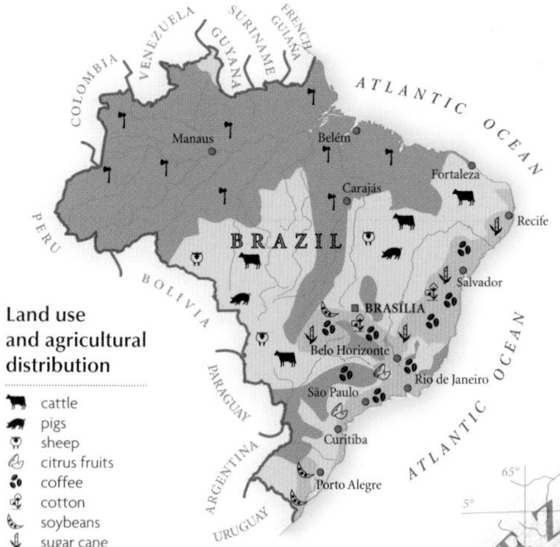

ATLANTIC OCEAN
COLOMBIA
VENEZUELA
GUYANA
SURINAME
FRENCH GUIANA
PERU
BOLIVIA
PARAGUAY
ARGENTINA
URUGUAY
BRAZIL
Manaus
Belém
Fortaleza
Carajás
Recife
Salvador
BRASÍLIA
Belo Horizonte
Rio de Janeiro
São Paulo
Curitiba
Porto Alegre

Land use and agricultural distribution

- cattle
- pigs
- sheep
- citrus fruits
- coffee
- cotton
- soybeans
- sugar cane
- timber
- capital cities
- major towns
- pasture
- cropland
- forest

▶ *The fecundity of parts of Brazil's rain forest results from exceptionally high levels of rainfall and the quantities of silt deposited by the Amazon river system.*

The landscape

The Amazon Basin, containing the largest area of tropical rain forest on Earth, covers nearly half of Brazil. It is bordered by two shield areas: in the south by the Brazilian Highlands, and in the north by the Guiana Highlands. The east coast is dominated by a great escarpment which runs for 1600 miles (2565 km).

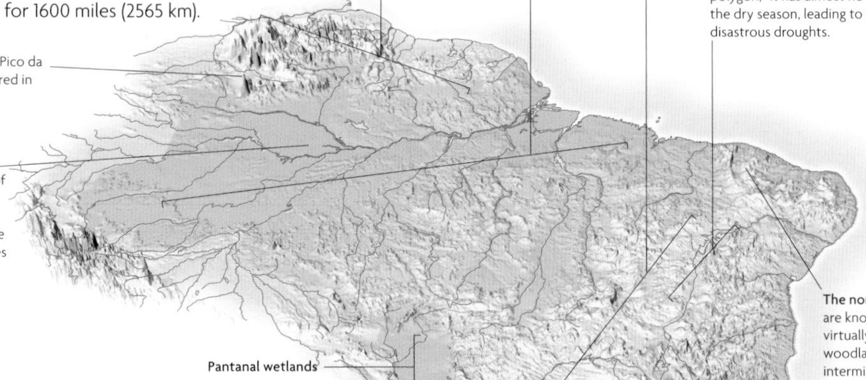

Guiana Highlands
Pantanal wetlands

Brazil's highest mountain is the Pico da Neblina which was only discovered in 1962. It is 9888 ft (3014 m) high.

The floodplains which border the Amazon river are made up of a variety of different features including shallow lakes and swamps, mangrove forests in the tidal delta area, and fertile leveés on river banks and point bars.

The Amazon Basin is the largest river basin in the world. The Amazon river and over a thousand tributaries drain an area of 2,375,000 sq miles (6,150,000 sq km) and carry one-fifth of the world's fresh water out to sea.

The ancient Brazilian Highlands have a varied topography. Their plateaus, hills, and deep valleys are bordered by highly-eroded mountains containing important mineral deposits. They are drained by three great river systems, the Amazon, the Paraguay–Paraná, and the São Francisco.

The São Francisco Basin has a climate unique in Brazil. Known as the "drought polygon," it has almost no rain during the dry season, leading to regular disastrous droughts.

The northeastern scrublands are known as the *caatinga*, a virtually impenetrable thorny woodland, sometimes intermixed with cacti where water is scarce.

The famous Sugar Loaf Mountain (*Pão de Açúcar*) which overlooks Rio de Janeiro is a fine example of a volcanic plug a domed core of solidified lava left after the slopes of the original volcano have eroded away.

Deep natural harbors such as Baia de Guanabara were created where the steep slopes of the Serra da Mantiqueira plunge directly into the ocean.

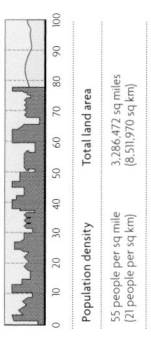

▶ *The Pantanal region in the south of Brazil is an extension of the Gran Chaco plain. The swamps and marshes of this area are renowned for their beauty, and abundant and unique wildlife, including wildfowl and these caimans, a type of crocodile.*

◀ *The Iguaçu river surges over the spectacular Iguaçu Falls (Saltos do Iguaçu) toward the Paraná river. Falls like these are increasingly under pressure from large-scale hydroelectric projects such as that at Itaipú.*

Hillslope gullying

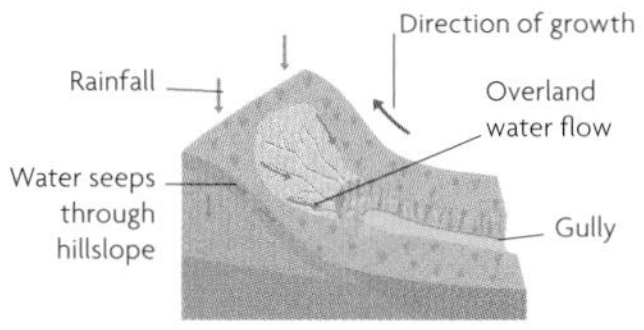

Rainfall
Direction of growth
Overland water flow
Water seeps through hillslope
Gully

◀ *Large-scale gullies are common in Brazil, particularly on hillslopes from which vegetation has been removed. Gullies grow headwards (up the slope), aided by a combination of erosion through water seepage and rainwater runoff.*

Map key

Population	Elevation
above 5 million	3000m / 9843ft
1 million to 5 million	2000m / 6562ft
500,000 to 1 million	1000m / 3281ft
100,000 to 500,000	500m / 1640ft
50,000 to 100,000	250m / 820ft
10,000 to 50,000	100m / 328ft
below 10,000	sea level

54
64
56
COLOMBIA
VENEZUELA
GUYANA
SURINAME
FRENCH GUIANA (to France)
ATLANTIC OCEAN
Guiana Highlands
Amazon Basin
RORAIMA
AMAPÁ
Boa Vista
Macapá
Belém
Manaus
Santarém
São Luís
Mount Roraima 2810m
Pico da Neblina 3014m
Tumuc-Humac Mountains
Pakaraima Mountains
Acaraí Mountains
Serra Parima
Serra do Tapirapecó
Ilha de Marajó
Mouths of the Amazon
Cabo Orange
Oiapoque
Equator

BRAZIL
PERU
BOLIVIA
PARAGUAY
ARGENTINA
URUGUAY
ATLANTIC OCEAN
ACRE
RONDÔNIA
MATO GROSSO
MATO GROSSO DO SUL
TOCANTINS
GOIÁS
DISTRITO FEDERAL
MINAS GERAIS
BAHIA
PIAUÍ
SÃO PAULO
PARANÁ
SANTA CATARINA
RIO GRANDE DO SUL
RIO DE JANEIRO
ESPÍRITO SANTO
PERNAMBUCO
PARAÍBA
ALAGOAS
SERGIPE
RIO GRANDE DO NORTE
Planalto Central
(Brazilian Highlands)
Planalto de Mato Grosso
Pantanal
Serra do Cachimbo
Serra Formosa
Chapada dos Parecis
Chapada Diamantina
Espigão Mestre
Serra Geral
Serra do Mar
Tropic of Capricorn
Brasília
Rio de Janeiro
São Paulo
Belo Horizonte
Salvador
Recife
Natal
Maceió
Aracaju
Vitória
Curitiba
Florianópolis
Porto Alegre
Campo Grande
Cuiabá
Goiânia
Porto Velho
Rio Branco
Palmas do Tocantins
João Pessoa
Campinas
Santos
Niterói
Nova Iguaçu
Pelotas
Rio Grande
Lagoa Mirim
Lagoa Mangueira
Scale 1:14,250,000
projection: Lambert Azimuthal Equal Area

Scale 1:14,250,000

projection: Lambert Azimuthal Equal Area

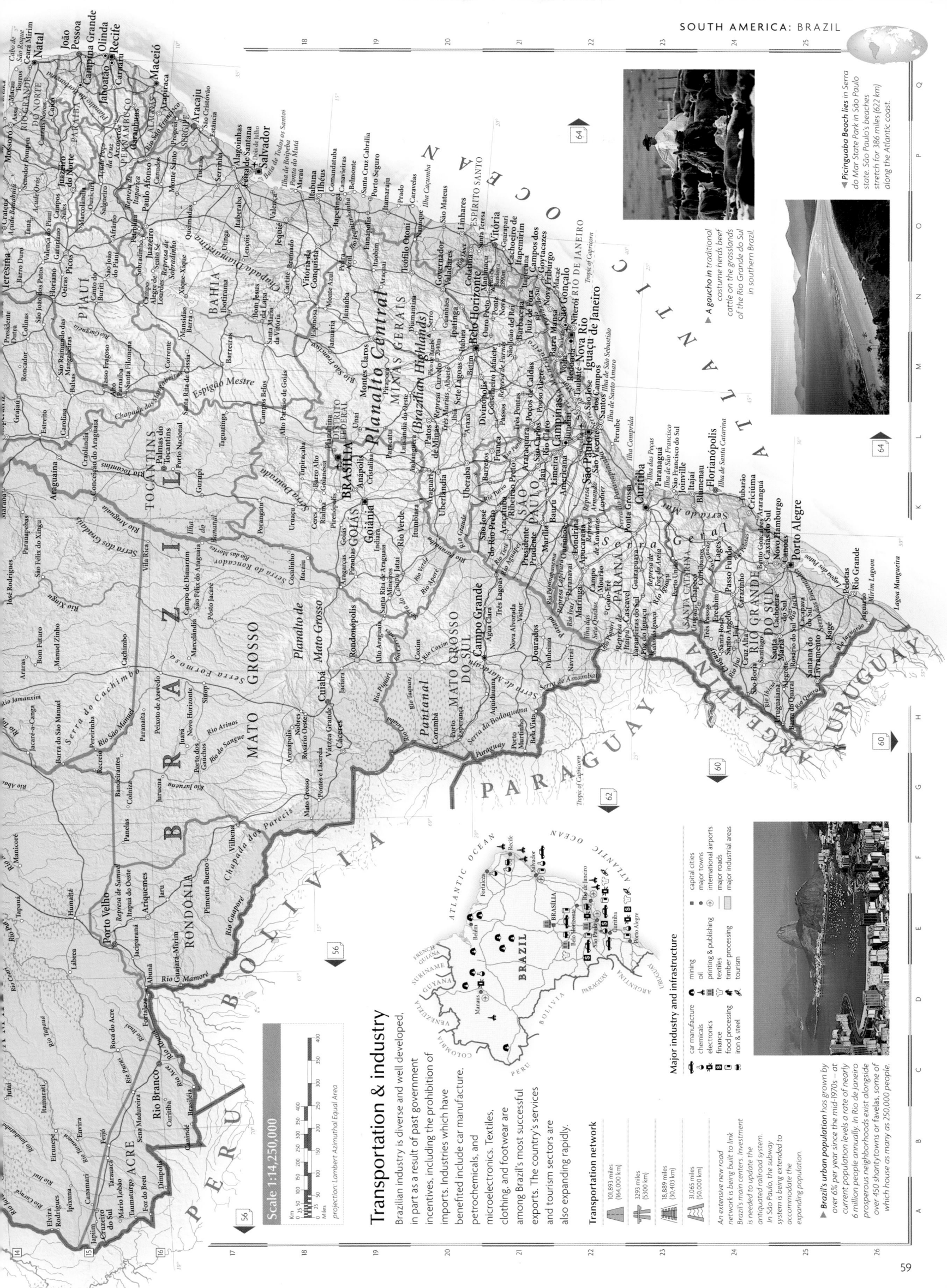

Transportation & industry

Brazilian industry is diverse and well developed, in part as a result of past government incentives, including the prohibition of imports. Industries which have benefited include car manufacture, petrochemicals, and microelectronics. Textiles, clothing, and footwear are among Brazil's most successful exports. The country's services and tourism sectors are also expanding rapidly.

BRAZIL
ATLANTIC OCEAN
COLOMBIA
VENEZUELA
GUYANA
SURINAME
FRENCH GUIANA
PERU
BOLIVIA
PARAGUAY
ARGENTINA
URUGUAY
Manaus
Belém
Fortaleza
Recife
Salvador
BRASÍLIA
Belo Horizonte
Rio de Janeiro
São Paulo
Curitiba
Porto Alegre

Transportation network

101,893 miles (164,000 km)	
3293 miles (5300 km)	
18,889 miles (30,403 km)	
31,065 miles (50,000 km)	

An extensive new road network is being built to link Brazil's main centers. Investment is needed to update the antiquated railroad system. In São Paulo, the subway system is being extended to accommodate the expanding population.

Major industry and infrastructure

- car manufacture
- chemicals
- electronics
- finance
- food processing
- iron & steel
- mining
- oil
- printing & publishing
- textiles
- timber processing
- tourism
- capital cities
- major towns
- international airports
- major roads
- major industrial areas

▶ ***Brazil's urban population*** *has grown by over 6% per year since the mid-1970s – at current population levels a rate of nearly 6 million people annually. In Rio de Janeiro prosperous neighborhoods exist alongside over 450 shantytowns or favelas, some of which house as many as 250,000 people.*

▶ *A **gaucho** in traditional costume herds beef cattle on the grasslands of the Rio Grande do Sul in southern Brazil.*

◀ ***Picinguaba Beach lies*** *in Serra do Mar State Park in São Paulo state. São Paulo's beaches stretch for 386 miles (622 km) along the Atlantic coast.*

Eastern South America

URUGUAY, NORTHEAST ARGENTINA, SOUTHEAST BRAZIL

The vast conurbations of Rio de Janeiro, São Paulo, and Buenos Aires form the core of South America's highly-urbanized eastern region. São Paulo state, with over 40 million inhabitants, is among the world's 20 most powerful economies, and São Paulo is the fastest growing city on the continent. Rio de Janeiro and Buenos Aires, transformed in the last hundred years from port cities to great metropolitan areas each with more than 10 million inhabitants, typify the unstructured growth and wealth disparities of South America's great cities. In Uruguay, over two fifths of the population lives in the capital, Montevideo, which faces Buenos Aires across the Plate River *(Río de la Plata)*. Immigration from the countryside has created severe pressure on the urban infrastructure, particularly on available housing, leading to a profusion of crowded shanty settlements *(favelas* or *barrios)*.

Using the land

Most of Uruguay and the Pampas of northern Argentina are devoted to the rearing of livestock, especially cattle and sheep, which are central to both countries' economies. Soybeans, first produced in Brazil's Rio Grande do Sul, are now more widely grown for large-scale export, as are cereals, sugar cane, and grapes. Subsistence crops, including potatoes, corn and sugar beets, are grown on the remaining arable land.

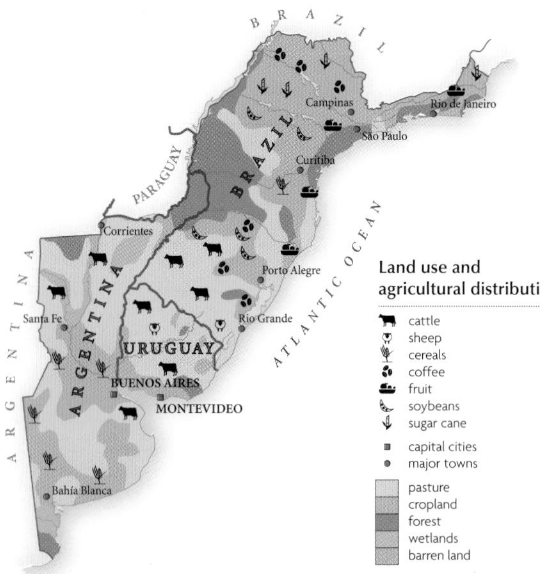
BRAZIL
PARAGUAY
ARGENTINA
URUGUAY
ATLANTIC OCEAN
Rio de Janeiro
São Paulo
Campinas
Curitiba
Corrientes
Porto Alegre
Rio Grande
Santa Fe
BUENOS AIRES
MONTEVIDEO
Bahía Blanca
Land use and agricultural distribution
cattle
sheep
cereals
coffee
fruit
soybeans
sugar cane
capital cities
major towns
pasture
cropland
forest
wetlands
barren land

◀ *The rolling grasslands of Uruguay are ideally suited to the rearing of cattle. Beef is the country's main export commodity, valued at over one billion US dollars in 2006.*

Scale 1:7,000,000

Km 0 25 50 100 150 200

Miles 0 25 50 100 150 200

projection: Lambert Azimuthal Equal Area

▲ ***Soybeans are harvested,*** *pressed, and processed into soycake, which is used as animal feed. The cake is fed mainly to chickens on large-scale factory farms, and the growth in soy production has been an important factor in the expansion of the Brazilian poultry trade.*

Transportation & industry

Southeast Brazil is home to much of the important motor and capital goods industry, largely based around São Paulo; iron and steel production is also concentrated in this region. Uruguay's economy continues to be based mainly on the export of livestock products including meat and leather goods. Buenos Aires is Argentina's chief port, and the region has a varied and sophisticated economic base including service-based industries such as finance and publishing, as well as primary processing.

Map key

Population
- above 5 million
- 1 million to 5 million
- 500,000 to 1 million
- 100,000 to 500,000
- 50,000 to 100,000
- 10,000 to 50,000
- below 10,000

Elevation
- 2000m / 6562ft
- 1000m / 3281ft
- 500m / 1640ft
- 250m / 820ft
- 100m / 328ft
- sea level

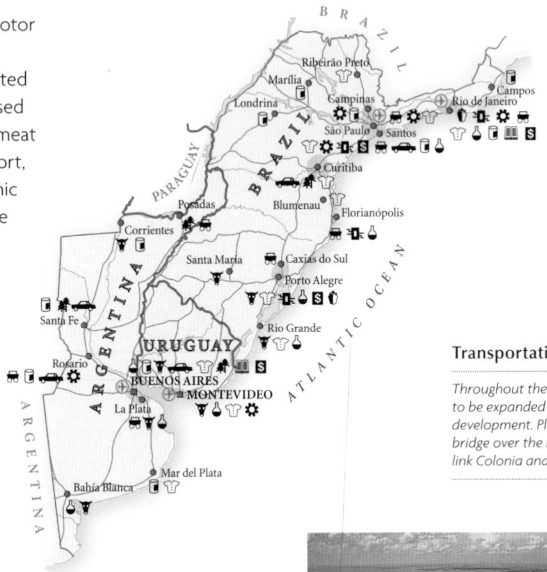
BRAZIL
PARAGUAY
ARGENTINA
URUGUAY
ATLANTIC OCEAN
Ribeirão Preto
Marília
Londrina
Campinas
Rio de Janeiro
Campos
São Paulo
Santos
Curitiba
Posadas
Blumenau
Florianópolis
Corrientes
Santa Maria
Caxias do Sul
Porto Alegre
Rio Grande
Santa Fe
Rosario
BUENOS AIRES
MONTEVIDEO
La Plata
Mar del Plata
Bahía Blanca
Major industry and infrastructure
car manufacture
chemicals
engineering
finance
food processing
iron & steel
meat processing
printing & publishing
shipbuilding
textiles
timber processing
capital cities
major towns
international airports
major roads
major industrial areas

Transportation network

Throughout the region, road networks need to be expanded to cope with urban development. Plans are underway to build a bridge over the Plate River (Río de la Plata) to link Colonia and Buenos Aires.

▲ ***The Itaipú dam*** *on the Paraná river is one of the largest hydroelectric projects in the world, jointly financed by Brazil and Paraguay.*

MINAS GERAIS
MATO GROSSO DO SUL
SÃO PAULO
PARANÁ
PARAGUAY
ESPÍRITO SANTO
RIO DE JANEIRO
São Paulo
Rio de Janeiro
Campinas
Curitiba
Santos
Niterói
São Gonçalo
Nova Iguaçu
Osasco
São Bernardo do Campo
Ribeirão Preto
Sorocaba
Londrina
Maringá
Ponta Grossa
Tropic of Capricorn
Serra do Mar
Serra da Mantiqueira
Serra de Paranapiacaba
OCEAN

58

62

64

▶ *Rio de Janeiro's annual carnival, Mardi Gras, which ushers in the start of Lent, is an extravagant five-day parade through the city, characterized by fantastically decorated floats, exuberant dancing, and samba music.*

The landscape

The southern reaches of the Brazilian Highlands follow the Atlantic coast to form low, rolling hills in the northeast of Uruguay. Much of South America's mid-eastern region and all of Uruguay has a gentle relief with land rarely rising above 300 ft (100 m). Argentina's northeast comprises two main regions: a long, narrow lowland known as Mesopotamia; and part of the Pampas grasslands.

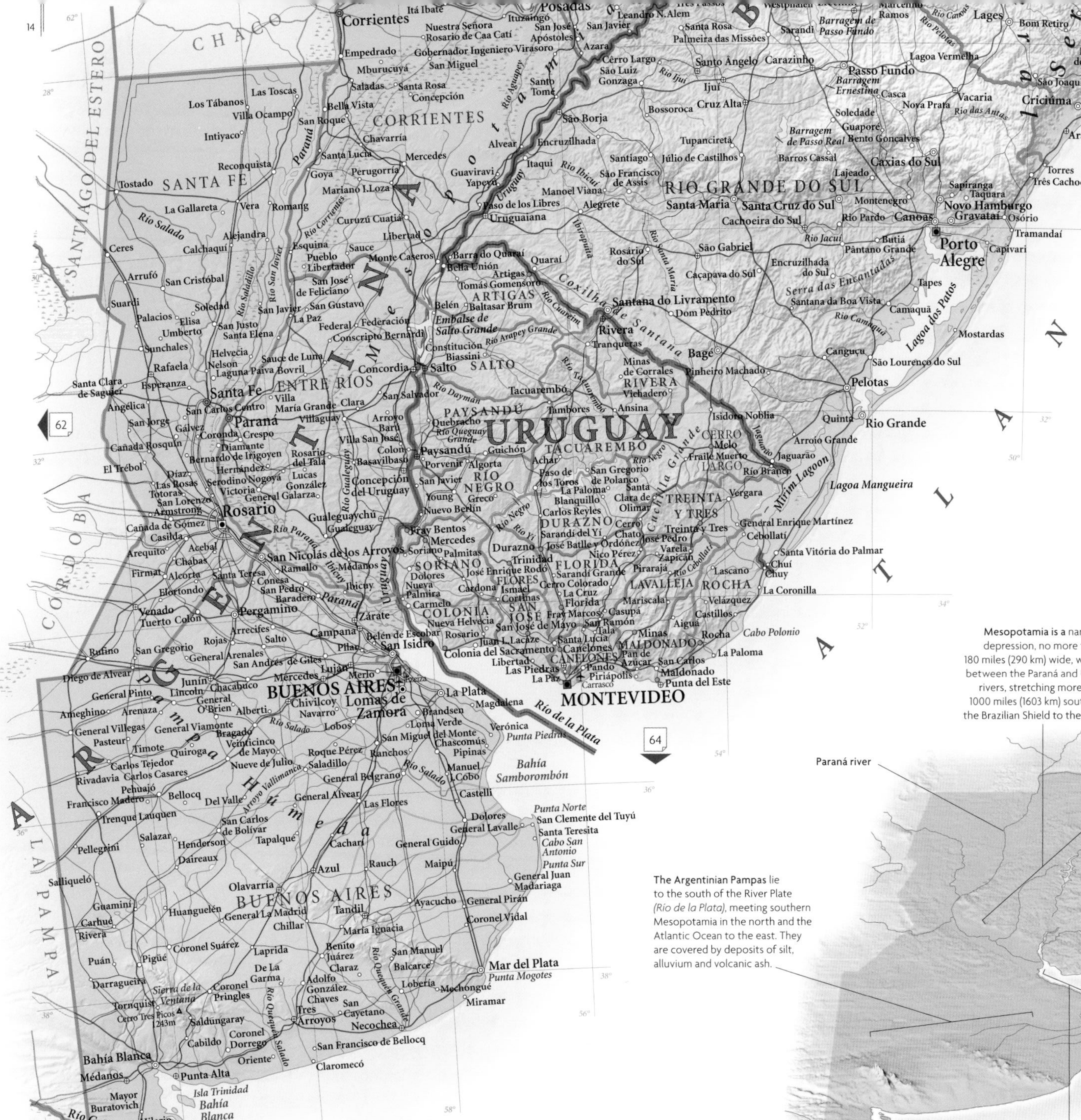

ARGENTINA
URUGUAY
ATLANTIC
BUENOS AIRES
MONTEVIDEO
Rosario
Porto Alegre
Pelotas
Rio Grande
Mar del Plata
Bahía Blanca
Santa Fe
Paraná
Corrientes
Posadas
Florianópolis
RIO GRANDE DO SUL
SANTA FE
CORRIENTES
ENTRE RÍOS
CHACO
SANTIAGO DEL ESTERO
CÓRDOBA
LA PAMPA
RÍO NEGRO
Río de la Plata
Lagoa dos Patos
Lagoa Mirim
Bahía Samborombón
Pampa Húmeda

62
64
64
26

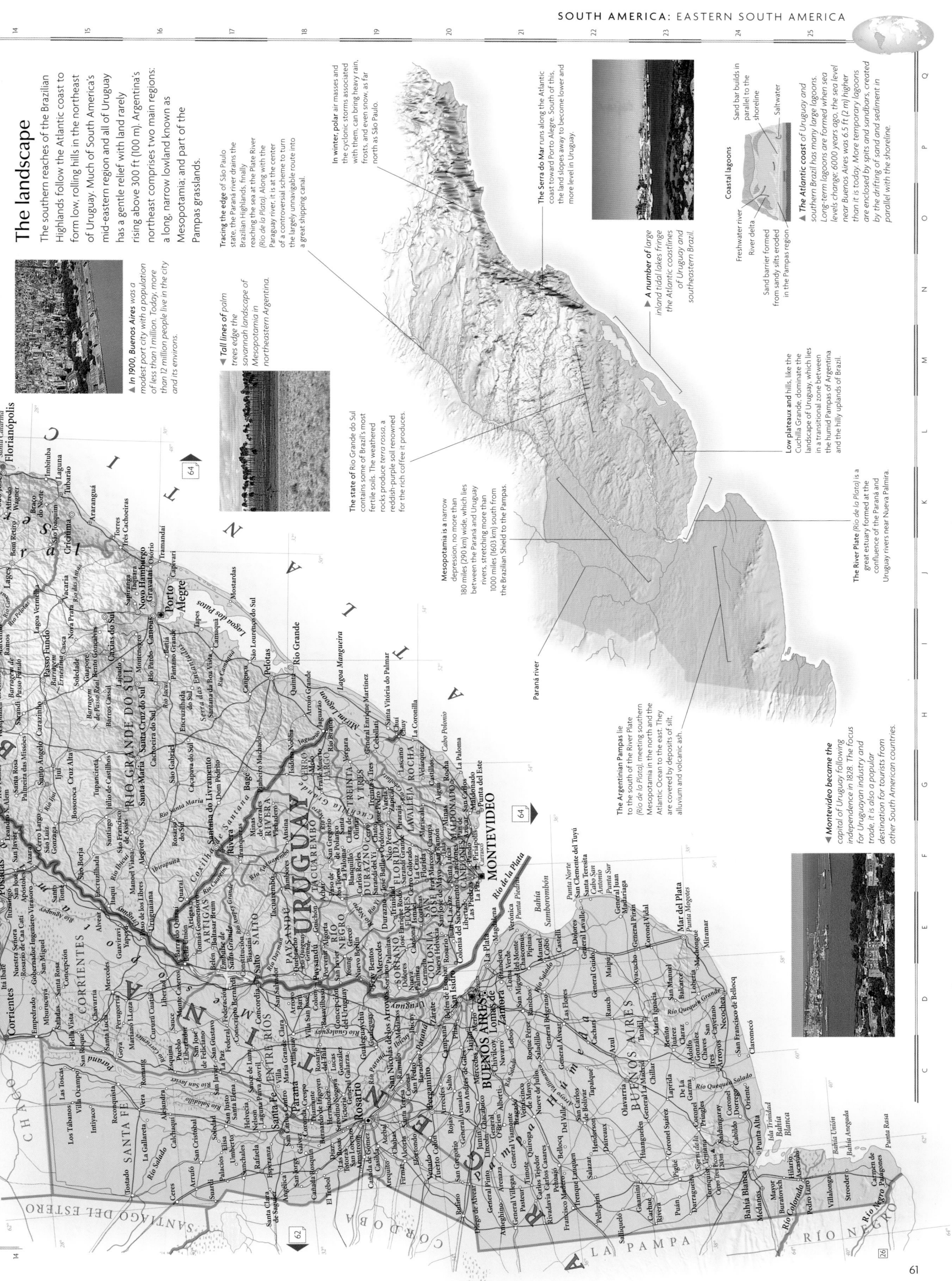

▲ *In 1900, **Buenos Aires** was a modest port city with a population of less than 1 million. Today, more than 12 million people live in the city and its environs.*

◀ ***Tall lines of** palm trees edge the savannah landscape of Mesopotamia in northeastern Argentina.*

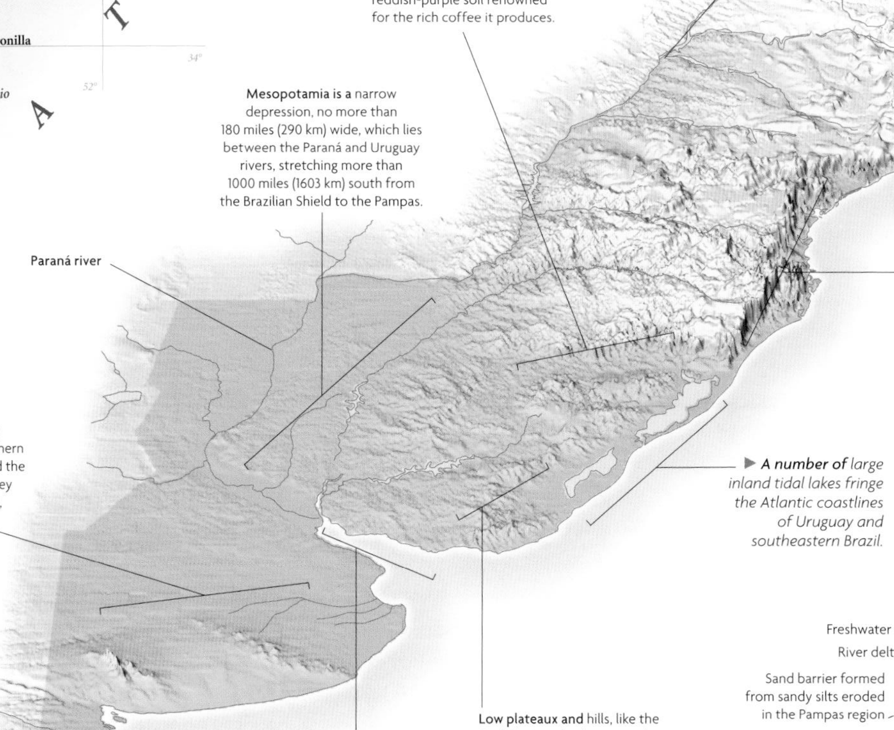

Tracing the edge of São Paulo state, the Paraná river drains the Brazilian Highlands, finally reaching the sea at the Plate River *(Río de la Plata)*. Along with the Paraguay river, it is at the center of a controversial scheme to turn the largely unnavigable route into a great shipping canal.

In winter, polar air masses and the cyclonic storms associated with them, can bring heavy rain, frosts, and even snow, as far north as São Paulo.

The state of Rio Grande do Sul contains some of Brazil's most fertile soils. The weathered rocks produce *terra rossa*, a reddish-purple soil renowned for the rich coffee it produces.

Mesopotamia is a narrow depression, no more than 180 miles (290 km) wide, which lies between the Paraná and Uruguay rivers, stretching more than 1000 miles (1603 km) south from the Brazilian Shield to the Pampas.

Paraná river

The Serra do Mar runs along the Atlantic coast toward Porto Alegre. South of this, the land slopes away to become lower and more level in Uruguay.

The Argentinian Pampas lie to the south of the River Plate *(Río de la Plata)*, meeting southern Mesopotamia in the north and the Atlantic Ocean to the east. They are covered by deposits of silt, alluvium and volcanic ash.

▶ ***A number of** large inland tidal lakes fringe the Atlantic coastlines of Uruguay and southeastern Brazil.*

Low plateaux and hills, like the Cuchilla Grande, dominate the landscape of Uruguay, which lies in a transitional zone between the humid Pampas of Argentina and the hilly uplands of Brazil.

The River Plate *(Río de la Plata)* is a great estuary formed at the confluence of the Paraná and Uruguay rivers near Nueva Palmira.

◀ ***Montevideo** became the capital of Uruguay following independence in 1828. The focus for Uruguayan industry and trade, it is also a popular destination for tourists from other South American countries.*

Coastal lagoons

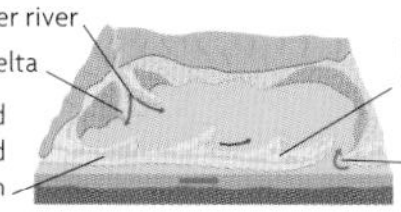

Freshwater river
River delta
Sand barrier formed from sandy silts eroded in the Pampas region
Sand bar builds in parallel to the shoreline
Saltwater

▲ ***The Atlantic coast** of Uruguay and southern Brazil has many large lagoons. Long-term lagoons are formed when sea levels change; 6000 years ago, the sea level near Buenos Aires was 6.5 ft (2 m) higher than it is today. More temporary lagoons are enclosed by spits and sandbars, created by the drifting of sand and sediment in parallel with the shoreline.*

Southern South America

ARGENTINA, CHILE, PARAGUAY

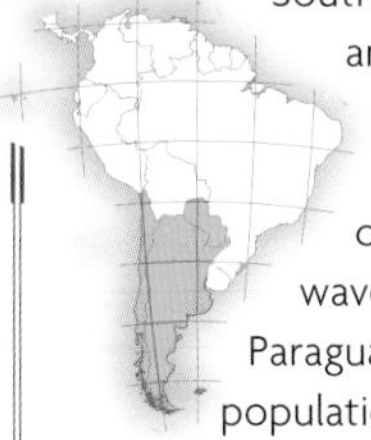

South America's cone-shaped southern region is shared by Argentina and Chile, two overwhelmingly urbanized nations whose populations live mainly in or around the capital cities, Buenos Aires and Santiago. The people are largely *mestizo* or of European origin; in the early 20th century Argentina absorbed waves of new European immigrants, many from Italy and Germany. Paraguay is far less urbanized than its neighbors, with a homogeneous population of mixed Spanish and Guaraní origin, who retain their Indian roots through the Guaraní language. Though most Paraguayans live in the southeast, near Asunción, the indigenous Indians live in the sparsely populated Gran Chaco. The Gran Chaco is also home to some of Argentina's minority indigenous peoples, who otherwise live mainly in Andean regions. Chile's estimated 800,000 Mapauche Indians live almost exclusively in the south.

Transportation & industry

Food processing and agricultural exports remain a fundamental part of Argentina's economy. The growth of manufacturing is regularly hampered by hyper-inflation and massive foreign debts. The world's most important copper producer and one of the top twenty gold producers, Chile also has a thriving wine and grape industry. Most Paraguayan exports involve primary processing, although domestic goods are produced for home markets.

▲ ***Chuquicamata copper mine,*** *lies on a desert plateau near Calama in the Andes of northern Chile. It is the world's largest open-pit copper mine.*

PERU
BOLIVIA
BRAZIL
PARAGUAY
CHILE
ARGENTINA
URUGUAY
ASUNCIÓN
Ciudad del Este
Resistencia
Posadas
Córdoba
Rosario
Mendoza
SANTIAGO
BUENOS AIRES
Arica
Iquique
Antofagasta
Valparaíso
Talca
Concepción
Valdivia
Puerto Montt
Bahía Blanca
Comodoro Rivadavia
Punta Arenas
PACIFIC OCEAN
ATLANTIC OCEAN

Major industry and infrastructure

chemicals		capital cities	
engineering		major towns	
food processing		international airports	
meat processing		major roads	
mining		major industrial areas	
oil			
textiles			
timber processing			

Transportation network

55,062 miles (93,453 km)	3038 miles (4889 km)
26,811 miles (43,153 km)	9180 miles (14,775 km)

Argentina's state transportation system is under-going privatization, though the outmoded rail network requires updating. Paraguay requires foreign investment to upgrade its roads and railroads. Essential internal air routes, especially across the Andes, are well developed in all three countries.

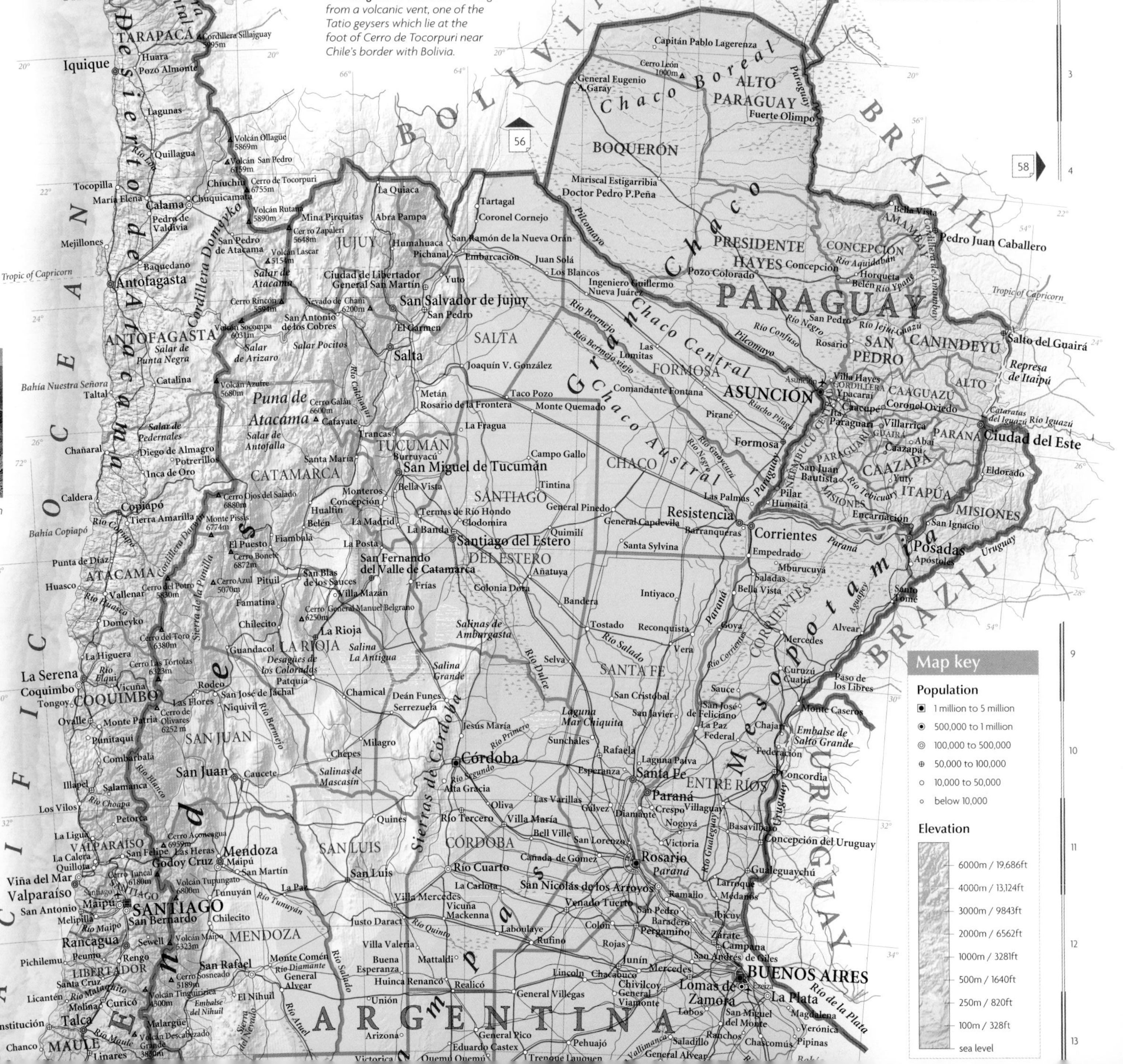
PERU
BOLIVIA
BRAZIL
PARAGUAY
ARGENTINA
URUGUAY
PACIFIC OCEAN
Desierto de Atacama
Gran Chaco
Chaco Boreal
Chaco Central
Chaco Austral
Mesopotamia
Puna de Atacama
Sierras de Córdoba
ASUNCIÓN
BUENOS AIRES
SANTIAGO
Arica
Iquique
Antofagasta
Calama
Copiapó
La Serena
Coquimbo
Valparaíso
Viña del Mar
Rancagua
Talca
San Salvador de Jujuy
Salta
San Miguel de Tucumán
Santiago del Estero
San Fernando del Valle de Catamarca
La Rioja
San Juan
Mendoza
San Luis
Córdoba
Santa Fe
Paraná
Rosario
Resistencia
Corrientes
Formosa
Posadas
Ciudad del Este
Encarnación
Concepción
Pedro Juan Caballero
La Plata
Lomas de Zamora
56
58
Map key
Population
1 million to 5 million
500,000 to 1 million
100,000 to 500,000
50,000 to 100,000
10,000 to 50,000
below 10,000
Elevation
6000m / 19,686ft
4000m / 13,124ft
3000m / 9843ft
2000m / 6562ft
1000m / 3281ft
500m / 1640ft
250m / 820ft
100m / 328ft
sea level

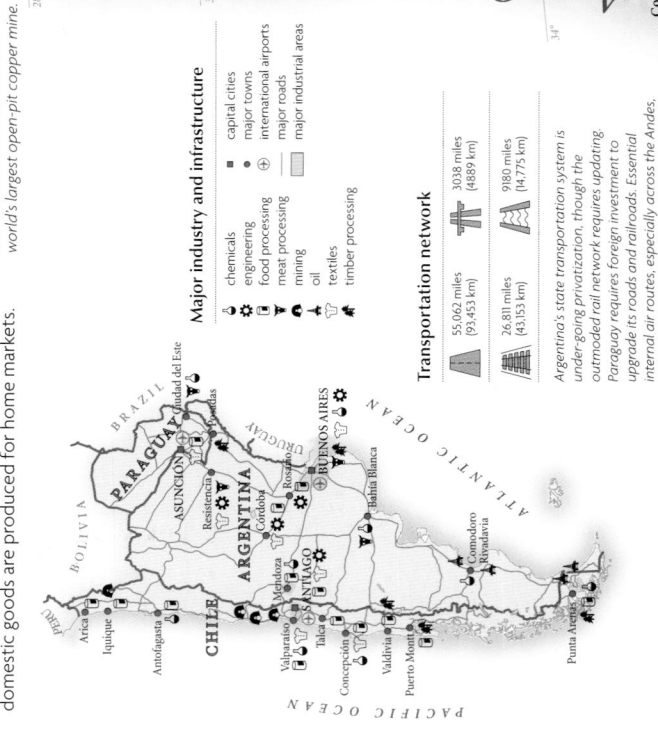

▲ ***Boiling water*** *and steam emerge from a volcanic vent, one of the Tatio geysers which lie at the foot of Cerro de Tocorpuri near Chile's border with Bolivia.*

▶ ***Floodwaters cover*** *the land in the Gran Chaco, partly submerging its vegetation of fan palms and hyacinths.*

The landscape

The Andes run from north to south, forming a precipitous natural border between Chile and Argentina. East of the Andes are the scrublands of the Gran Chaco and the plains of the Pampas, which extend northward toward Paraguay. In the far southwest, Chile's indented Pacific coastline has many features typical of areas which have been affected by glaciation.

▲ *The Atacama Desert* (Desierto de Atacama) *in Chile is one of the driest places on Earth where some areas have never recorded any rain. It contains a number of salt lakes.*

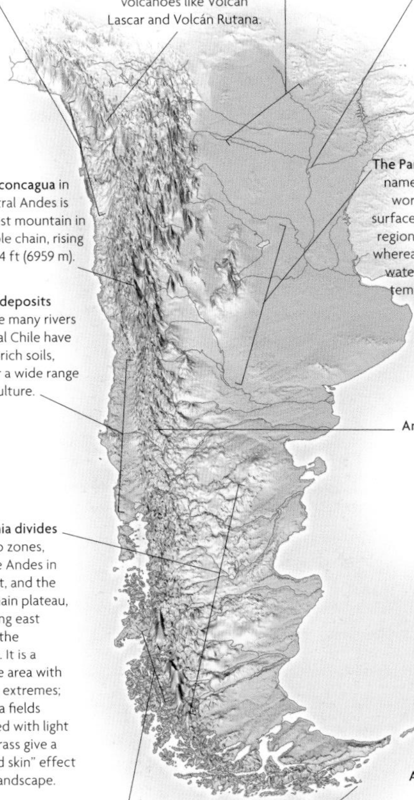

Andes

The Gran Chaco combines poor drainage, extremely hot temperatures and thorn-infested scrub to make it one of South America's most inhospitable regions.

Landlocked Paraguay relies on its river system for access to the sea and to produce hydroelectric power. The most important river system is the Paraguay–Paraná which provides links into neighboring countries including Brazil, Uruguay, and Argentina.

Most of the highest mountains in Chile's northern Andes are volcanoes like Volcán Lascar and Volcán Rutana.

The Pampas derive their name from an Indian word meaning flat surface. The dry western region is largely desert, whereas the east is well-watered, supporting temperate grasses.

Cerro Aconcagua in the central Andes is the tallest mountain in the whole chain, rising to 22,834 ft (6959 m).

Alluvial deposits from the many rivers in central Chile have created rich soils, ideal for a wide range of agriculture.

Patagonia divides into two zones, with the Andes in the west, and the lower main plateau, extending east toward the Atlantic. It is a desolate area with climatic extremes; dark lava fields scattered with light bunchgrass give a "leopard skin" effect to the landscape.

The Patagonian ice sheet is the world's third largest ice field, covering 6560 sq miles (17,000 sq km). Patagonia also contains many typical features from past glaciations. These include glacial lakes, U-shaped valleys, fjords, and deep-cut channels.

Cape Horn is the most southerly point of South America. The severity of the "Roaring Forties" winds makes the Horn one of the world's most treacherous shipping regions.

Argentinian Pampas

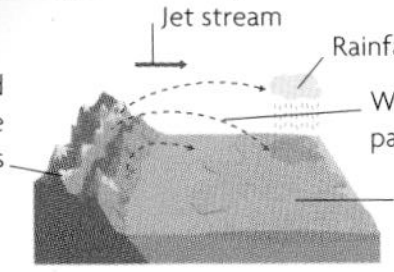

Jet stream
Rainfall
Ice-capped Andes are source of loess
Windblown particles
Thick layer of loess sediments

▲ ***A thick, fertile layer** of loess lies in the basin underlying the Argentinian Pampas. It has been laid down following successive periods of glaciation. The minute loess particles are transported as dust and deposited by a downward air motion, or following rainfall.*

192

CHILE
ARGENTINA
NEUQUÉN
LA PAMPA
RÍO NEGRO
CHUBUT
SANTA CRUZ
ARAUCANÍA
LOS RÍOS
LOS LAGOS
AISÉN
MAGALLANES
Patagonia
ATLANTIC OCEAN
Puerto Montt
Temuco
Valdivia
Osorno
Neuquén
General Roca
Bahía Blanca
Mar del Plata
Viedma
Rawson
Trelew
Comodoro Rivadavia
Puerto Natales
Punta Arenas
Río Gallegos
Ushuaia
Tierra del Fuego
Golfo San Matías
Golfo San Jorge
Bahía Grande
Península Valdés
Isla de Chiloé
Isla Wellington
Archipiélago de los Chonos
Estrecho de Le Maire
Isla de los Estados
Cabo de Hornos (Cape Horn)
Drake Passage
FALKLAND ISLANDS (to UK)
West Falkland
East Falkland
STANLEY

64

▲ ***Great blocks of** ice break away from the jagged blue peaks of these ice mountains to form icebergs off the coast of Patagonia, Argentina's most southerly region.*

Using the land & sea

The rich plains of the Pampas support massive herds of cattle, producing meat, milk, and hides essential to the domestic and export markets of both Argentina and Paraguay. Wheat and fruit are Argentina's other major agricultural products. A wide range of soft fruits, citrus fruits, and more specialized crops such as walnuts, and grapes for wine and the table, are grown in Chile's fertile Central Valley, while the landscape to the south is dominated by forestry, mainly growing commercial radiata pine. Paraguay is self-sufficient in wheat and other staples. Cotton, coffee, tobacco, and oil sources such as soybeans, are the major export crops.

The urban/rural population divide

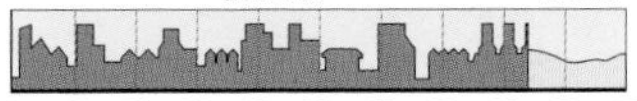

urban 84%
rural 16%
0 10 20 30 40 50 60 70 80 90 100

Population density	Total land area
40 people per sq mile (15 people per sq km)	1,498,757 sq miles (3,882,790 sq km)

Land use and agricultural distribution

cattle, sheep, cereals, fruit, grapes, timber, fishing

capital cities, major towns

pasture, cropland, forest, barren land, mountain region, desert

PERU
BOLIVIA
BRAZIL
PARAGUAY
ASUNCION
URUGUAY
CHILE
ARGENTINA
PACIFIC OCEAN
ATLANTIC OCEAN
Antofagasta
Salta
Posadas
Córdoba
Rosario
Mendoza
SANTIAGO
BUENOS AIRES
Concepción
Valdivia
Bahía Blanca
Punta Arenas

Scale 1:9,750,000

Km 0 25 50 100 150 200
Miles 0 25 50 100 150 200

projection: Lambert Azimuthal Equal Area

▲ ***Charred tree stumps** surround a cattle enclosure on the island of Tierra del Fuego in southern Argentina. Forest clearance to provide grazing land for cattle is of major environmental concern.*

The Atlantic Ocean

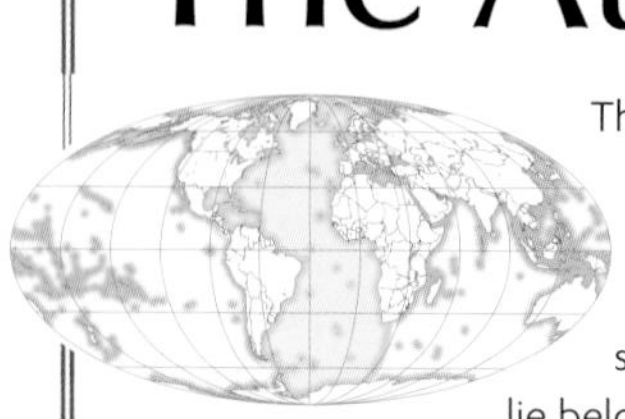

The Atlantic is the youngest of the world's oceans, formed about 180 million years ago when the landmasses of the eastern and western hemispheres separated. Its underwater topography is dominated by the Mid-Atlantic Ridge, a huge mountain system running north to south along the center of the ocean. Although most of the ridge's peaks lie below the sea, some emerge as volcanic islands, like Iceland and the Azores. The Atlantic contains a wealth of resources, including substantial oil and gas reserves and rich fishing grounds. Until the 1950s, the north Atlantic was the world's busiest shipping route; cheaper air transportation and alternative routes have shifted patterns of world trade.

▲ **Surtsey near Iceland,** *lies on the Mid-Atlantic Ridge. The island was formed in 1963 following a volcanic eruption caused by sea-floor spreading.*

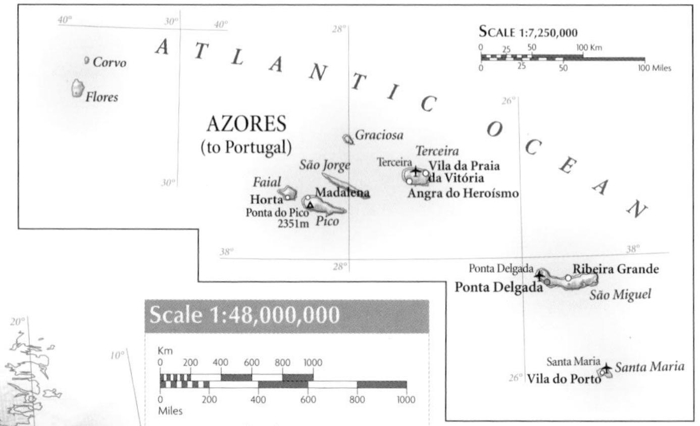

AZORES
(to Portugal)
ATLANTIC OCEAN
SCALE 1:7,250,000
Corvo
Flores
Graciosa
Terceira
São Jorge
Faial
Horta
Madalena
Ponta do Pico 2351m
Pico
Vila da Praia da Vitória
Angra do Heroísmo
Ponta Delgada
Ribeira Grande
São Miguel
Santa Maria
Vila do Porto

Resources

Development of the oil and gas reserves in the Atlantic began in the 1940s around the Gulf of Mexico. Since then other areas have been exploited, including the North Sea, the west coast of Africa and the area east of Newfoundland and Nova Scotia. There is also extensive mining of sand, gravel, and shell deposits by the US and UK. For centuries, the north Atlantic's fishing grounds have been utilized more heavily than other oceans, leading to a serious decline in many fish stocks.

NORTH AMERICA
EUROPE
AFRICA
SOUTH AMERICA
ATLANTIC OCEAN
ANTARCTICA
Reykjavík
Rotterdam
New York
Gibraltar
New Orleans
Sargasso Sea
Caribbean Sea
La Guaira
Cristóbal
Lagos
Rio de Janeiro
Buenos Aires
Cape Town
Scotia Sea
Weddell Sea
Resources (including wildlife)
fish
whales
aggregates
oil & gas
major towns
major ports

▲ *Fishing in the seas around northwestern Europe dates back over 1500 years. The high nutrient content of the seas makes them ideal breeding grounds for many species of fish.*

Scale 1:48,000,000
projection: Mollweide
NORTH AMERICA
CANADA
UNITED STATES OF AMERICA
SOUTH AMERICA
EUROPE
AFRICA
ATLANTIC
Mid-Atlantic Ridge
Greenland (to Denmark)
ICELAND
Labrador Sea
Baffin Bay
Gulf of Mexico
Caribbean Sea
Sargasso Sea
Charlie-Gibbs Fracture Zone
Northwest Atlantic Mid-Ocean Canyon
Newfoundland Basin
Sohm Plain
Nares Plain
Kane Fracture Zone
Atlantis Fracture Zone
Oceanographer Fracture Zone
East Azores Fracture Zone
Barracuda Fracture Zone
Vema Fracture Zone
Doldrums Fracture Zone
Cape Verde Basin
MADEIRA (to Portugal)
ISLAS CANARIAS (CANARY ISLANDS) (to Spain)
BERMUDA (to UK)

▲ *On January 5 1993, the oil tanker Braer ran aground in the Shetland Islands, spilling 83,660 tons (85,000 tonnes) of light crude oil into the ocean, devastating the local marine ecosystem.*

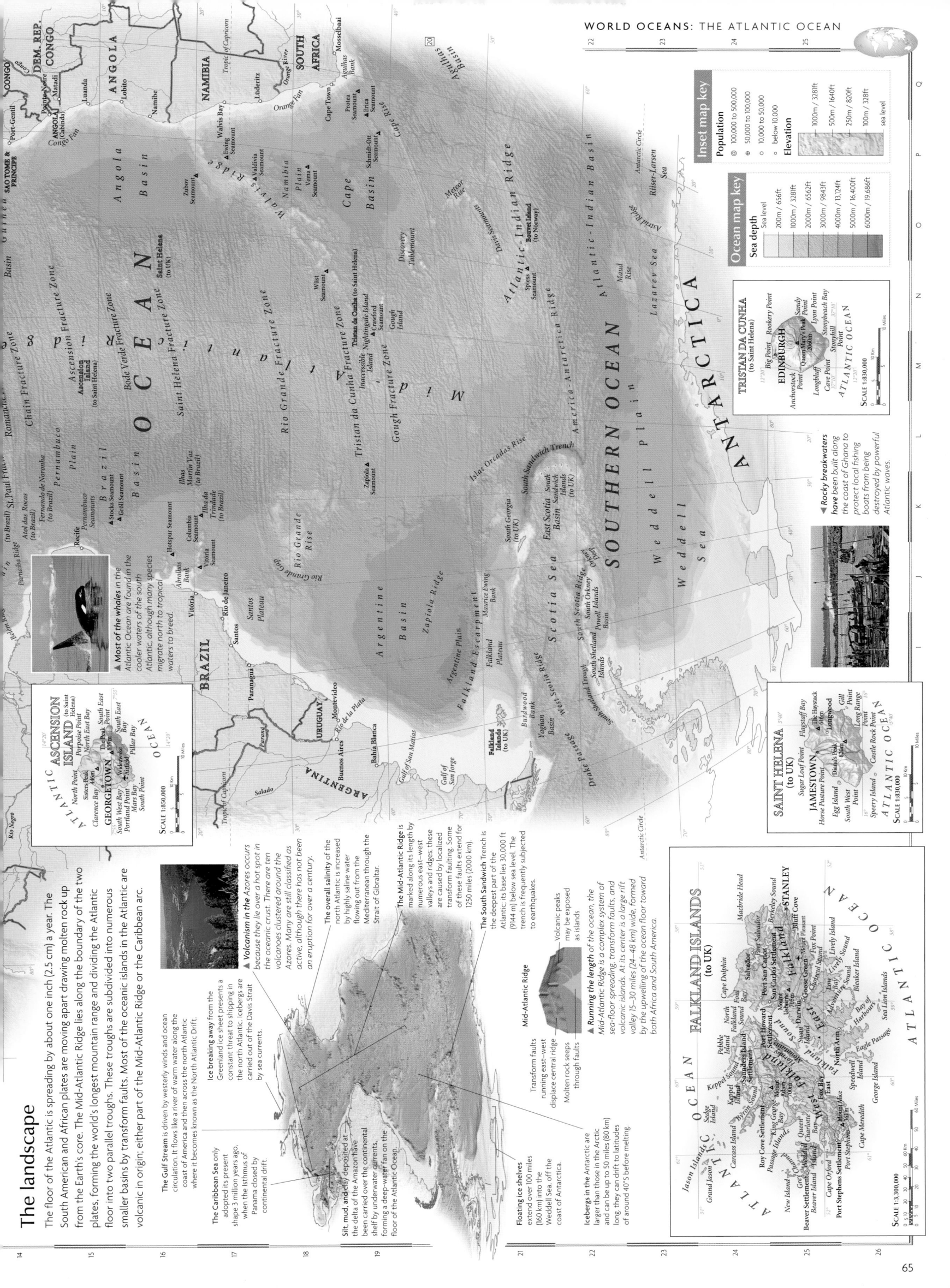

The landscape

The floor of the Atlantic is spreading by about one inch (2.5 cm) a year. The South American and African plates are moving apart drawing molten rock up from the Earth's core. The Mid-Atlantic Ridge lies along the boundary of the two plates, forming the world's longest mountain range and dividing the Atlantic floor into two parallel troughs. These troughs are subdivided into numerous smaller basins by transform faults. Most of the oceanic islands in the Atlantic are volcanic in origin; either part of the Mid-Atlantic Ridge or the Caribbean arc.

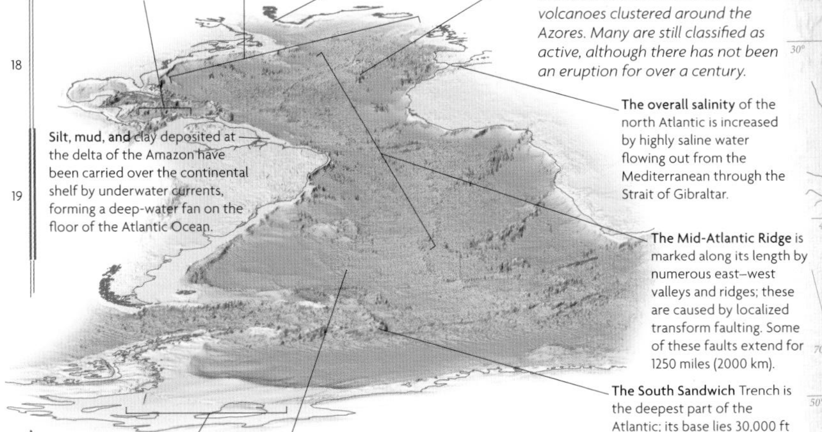

The Gulf Stream is driven by westerly winds and ocean circulation. It flows like a river of warm water along the coast of America and then across the north Atlantic where it becomes known as the North Atlantic Drift.

The Caribbean Sea only adopted its present shape 3 million years ago, when the Isthmus of Panama closed by continental drift.

Ice breaking away from the Greenland ice sheet presents a constant threat to shipping in the north Atlantic. Icebergs are carried out of the Davis Strait by sea currents.

▲ ***Volcanism in the** Azores occurs because they lie over a hot spot in the oceanic crust. There are ten volcanoes clustered around the Azores. Many are still classified as active, although there has not been an eruption for over a century.*

Silt, mud, and clay deposited at the delta of the Amazon have been carried over the continental shelf by underwater currents, forming a deep-water fan on the floor of the Atlantic Ocean.

The overall salinity of the north Atlantic is increased by highly saline water flowing out from the Mediterranean through the Strait of Gibraltar.

The Mid-Atlantic Ridge is marked along its length by numerous east–west valleys and ridges; these are caused by localized transform faulting. Some of these faults extend for 1250 miles (2000 km).

The South Sandwich Trench is the deepest part of the Atlantic; its base lies 30,000 ft (9144 m) below sea level. The trench is frequently subjected to earthquakes.

Floating ice shelves extend over 100 miles (160 km) into the Weddell Sea, off the coast of Antarctica.

Icebergs in the Antarctic are larger than those in the Arctic and can be up to 50 miles (80 km) long. they can drift to latitudes of around 40°S before melting.

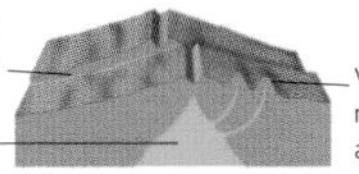
Mid-Atlantic Ridge
Transform faults running east–west displace central ridge
Molten rock seeps through faults
Volcanic peaks may be exposed as islands

▲ ***Running the length** of the ocean, the Mid-Atlantic Ridge is a complex system of sea-floor spreading, transform faults, and volcanic islands. At its center is a large rift valley 15–30 miles (24–48 km) wide, formed by the upwelling of the ocean floor toward both Africa and South America.*

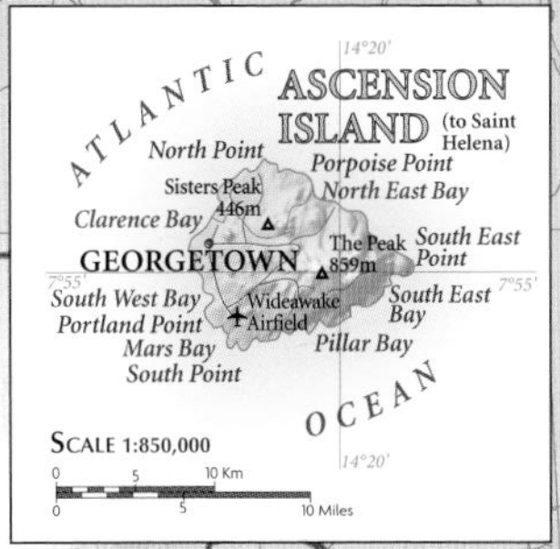
ASCENSION ISLAND (to Saint Helena)
ATLANTIC OCEAN
North Point
Porpoise Point
North East Bay
Sisters Peak 446m
Clarence Bay
GEORGETOWN
The Peak 859m
South East Point
South West Bay
Wideawake Airfield
South East Bay
Portland Point
Mars Bay
Pillar Bay
South Point
SCALE 1:850,000

▲ ***Most of the whales** in the Atlantic Ocean are found in the cooler waters of the south Atlantic, although many species migrate north to tropical waters to breed.*

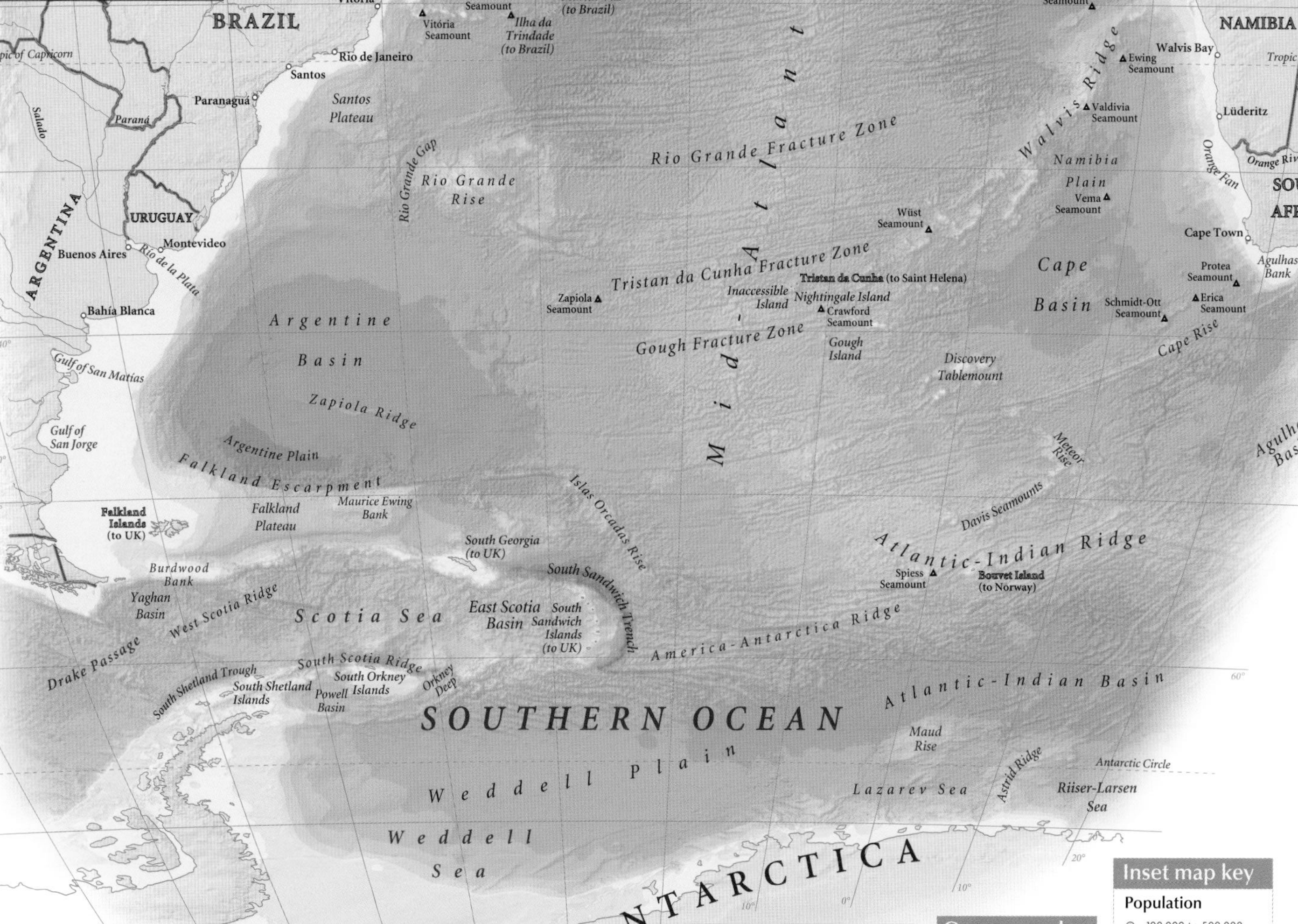
SOUTHERN OCEAN
OCEAN
Mid-Atlantic Ridge
ANTARCTICA
BRAZIL
ARGENTINA
URUGUAY
NAMIBIA
ANGOLA
SOUTH AFRICA
DEM. REP. CONGO
CONGO
SAO TOME & PRINCIPE
Angola Basin
Cape Basin
Brazil Basin
Argentine Basin
Scotia Sea
Weddell Sea
Weddell Plain
Lazarev Sea
Riiser-Larsen Sea
Walvis Ridge
Rio Grande Rise
Rio Grande Fracture Zone
Saint Helena Fracture Zone
Ascension Fracture Zone
Bode Verde Fracture Zone
Tristan da Cunha Fracture Zone
Gough Fracture Zone
Chain Fracture Zone
Atlantic-Indian Ridge
Atlantic-Indian Basin
America-Antarctica Ridge
South Sandwich Trench
Drake Passage
Falkland Escarpment
Falkland Plateau
Santos Plateau
Zapiola Ridge
Argentine Plain
Islas Orcadas Rise
Agulhas Basin
Cape Rise
Meteor Rise
Maud Rise
Saint Helena (to UK)
Bouvet Island (to Norway)
Falkland Islands (to UK)
Antarctic Circle
Tropic of Capricorn

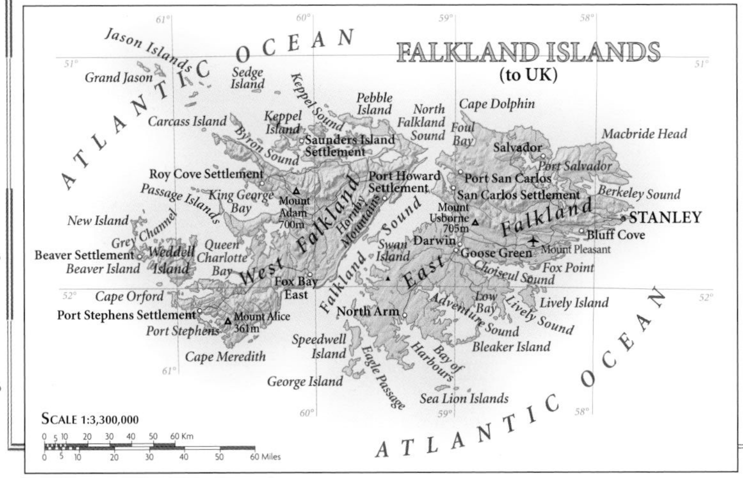
FALKLAND ISLANDS (to UK)
ATLANTIC OCEAN
STANLEY
West Falkland
East Falkland
Falkland Sound
Jason Islands
Grand Jason
Sedge Island
Keppel Island
Pebble Island
Cape Dolphin
Macbride Head
Carcass Island
Saunders Island Settlement
Port Howard Settlement
Port San Carlos
San Carlos Settlement
Port Salvador
Salvador
Berkeley Sound
Roy Cove Settlement
New Island
Beaver Settlement
Beaver Island
Weddell Island
Fox Bay East
Mount Adam 700m
Mount Usborne 705m
Darwin
Goose Green
Bluff Cove
Mount Pleasant
North Arm
Lively Island
Speedwell Island
George Island
Sea Lion Islands
Bleaker Island
Cape Orford
Port Stephens Settlement
Mount Alice 361m
Cape Meredith
SCALE 1:3,300,000

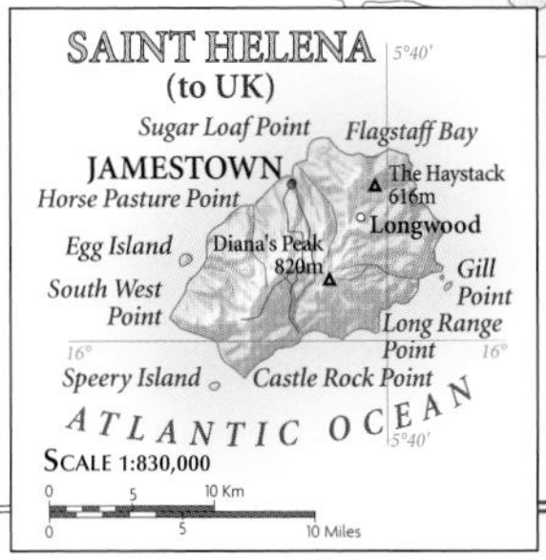
SAINT HELENA (to UK)
JAMESTOWN
Sugar Loaf Point
Flagstaff Bay
Horse Pasture Point
The Haystack 616m
Longwood
Egg Island
Diana's Peak 820m
Gill Point
South West Point
Long Range Point
Speery Island
Castle Rock Point
ATLANTIC OCEAN
SCALE 1:830,000

◀ ***Rocky breakwaters** have been built along the coast of Ghana to protect local fishing boats from being destroyed by powerful Atlantic waves.*

TRISTAN DA CUNHA (to Saint Helena)
Big Point
Rookery Point
EDINBURGH
Anchorstock Point
Queen Mary's Peak 2060m
Sandy Point
Longbluff
Lyon Point
Cave Point
Stonyhill Point
Stonybeach Bay
ATLANTIC OCEAN
SCALE 1:830,000

Ocean map key

Sea depth

- Sea level
- 200m / 656ft
- 1000m / 3281ft
- 2000m / 6562ft
- 3000m / 9843ft
- 4000m / 13,124ft
- 5000m / 16,400ft
- 6000m / 19,686ft

Inset map key

Population

- 100,000 to 500,000
- 50,000 to 100,000
- 10,000 to 50,000
- below 10,000

Elevation

- 1000m / 3281ft
- 500m / 1640ft
- 250m / 820ft
- 100m / 328ft
- sea level

Africa

The world's second largest continent, Africa covers an area of 11,712,434 sq miles (30,355,000 sq km). It has 57 separate countries, including Madagascar, Comoros, Mauritius, and the Seychelles in the Indian Ocean – the highest number of any continent.

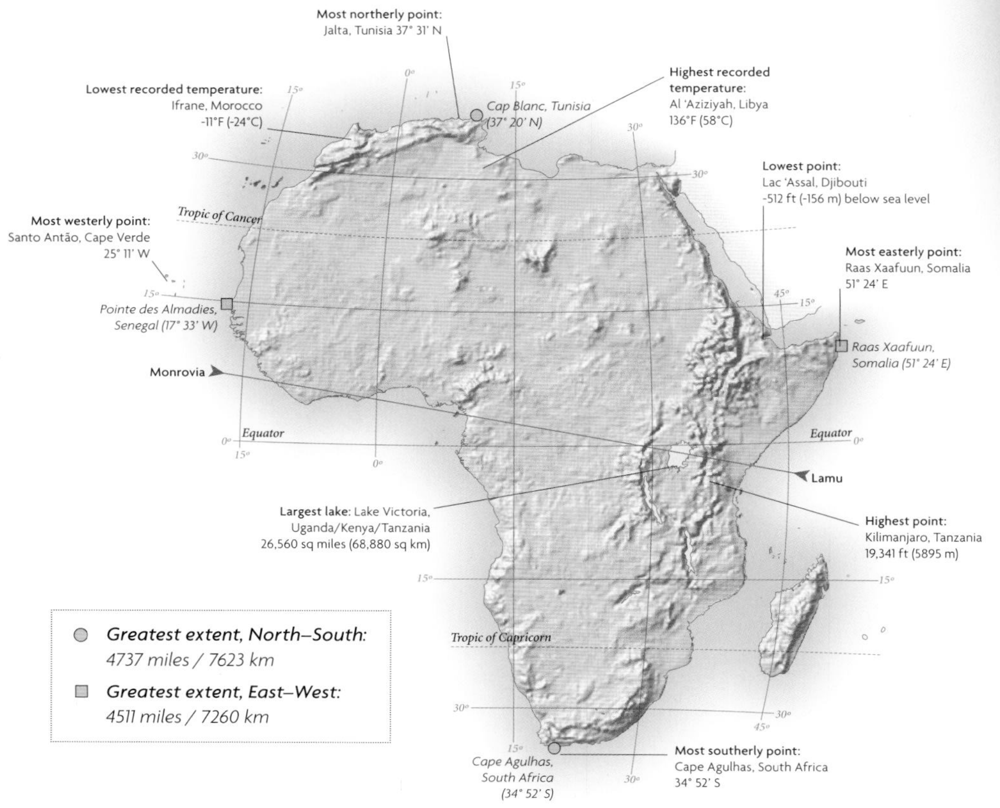

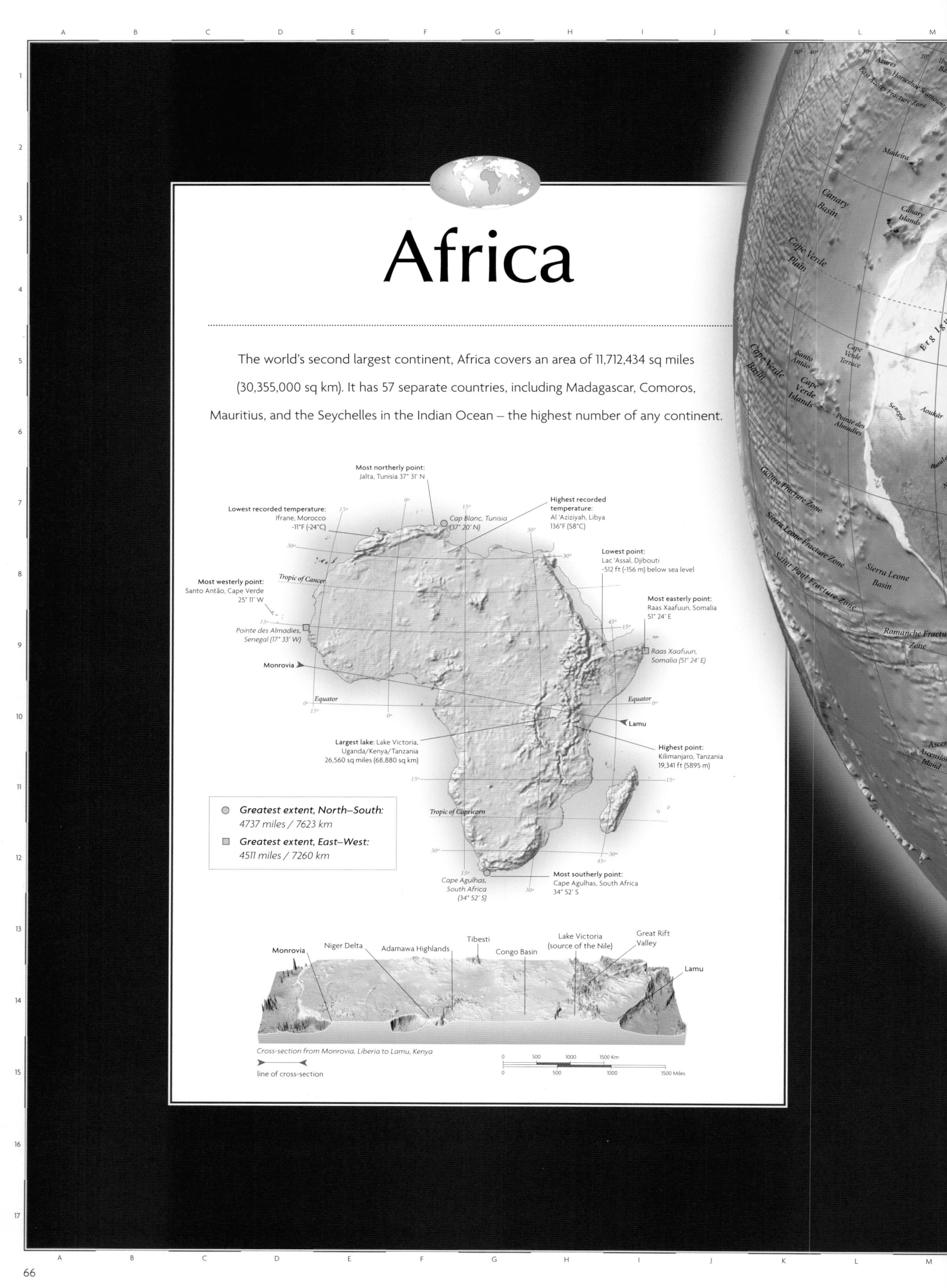

Most northerly point:
Jalta, Tunisia 37° 31' N
Cap Blanc, Tunisia (37° 20' N)
Lowest recorded temperature:
Ifrane, Morocco
-11°F (-24°C)
Highest recorded temperature:
Al 'Aziziyah, Libya
136°F (58°C)
Lowest point:
Lac 'Assal, Djibouti
-512 ft (-156 m) below sea level
Most westerly point:
Santo Antão, Cape Verde
25° 11' W
Pointe des Almadies, Senegal (17° 33' W)
Most easterly point:
Raas Xaafuun, Somalia
51° 24' E
Raas Xaafuun, Somalia (51° 24' E)
Tropic of Cancer
Monrovia
Equator
Lamu
Largest lake: Lake Victoria,
Uganda/Kenya/Tanzania
26,560 sq miles (68,880 sq km)
Highest point:
Kilimanjaro, Tanzania
19,341 ft (5895 m)
Tropic of Capricorn
Cape Agulhas, South Africa (34° 52' S)
Most southerly point:
Cape Agulhas, South Africa
34° 52' S

Greatest extent, North–South: *4737 miles / 7623 km*

Greatest extent, East–West: *4511 miles / 7260 km*

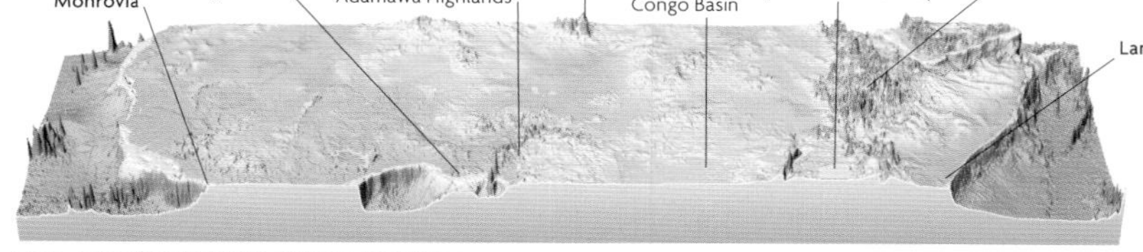

Monrovia
Niger Delta
Adamawa Highlands
Tibesti
Congo Basin
Lake Victoria (source of the Nile)
Great Rift Valley
Lamu
0 500 1000 1500 Km
0 500 1000 1500 Miles

Cross-section from Monrovia, Liberia to Lamu, Kenya

line of cross-section

Azores
Horseshoe Seamounts
East Azores Fracture Zone
Madeira
Canary Basin
Canary Islands
Cape Verde Plain
Cape Verde Terrace
Santo Antão
Cape Verde Basin
Cape Verde Islands
Pointe des Almadies
Senegal
Aoukâr
Guinea Fracture Zone
Sierra Leone Fracture Zone
Saint Paul Fracture Zone
Sierra Leone Basin
Romanche Fracture Zone
Ascension Island

N O P Q R S T U V W X Y Z

1 2 3 4 5 6 7 8 9 10 11 12 13 14 15 16 17

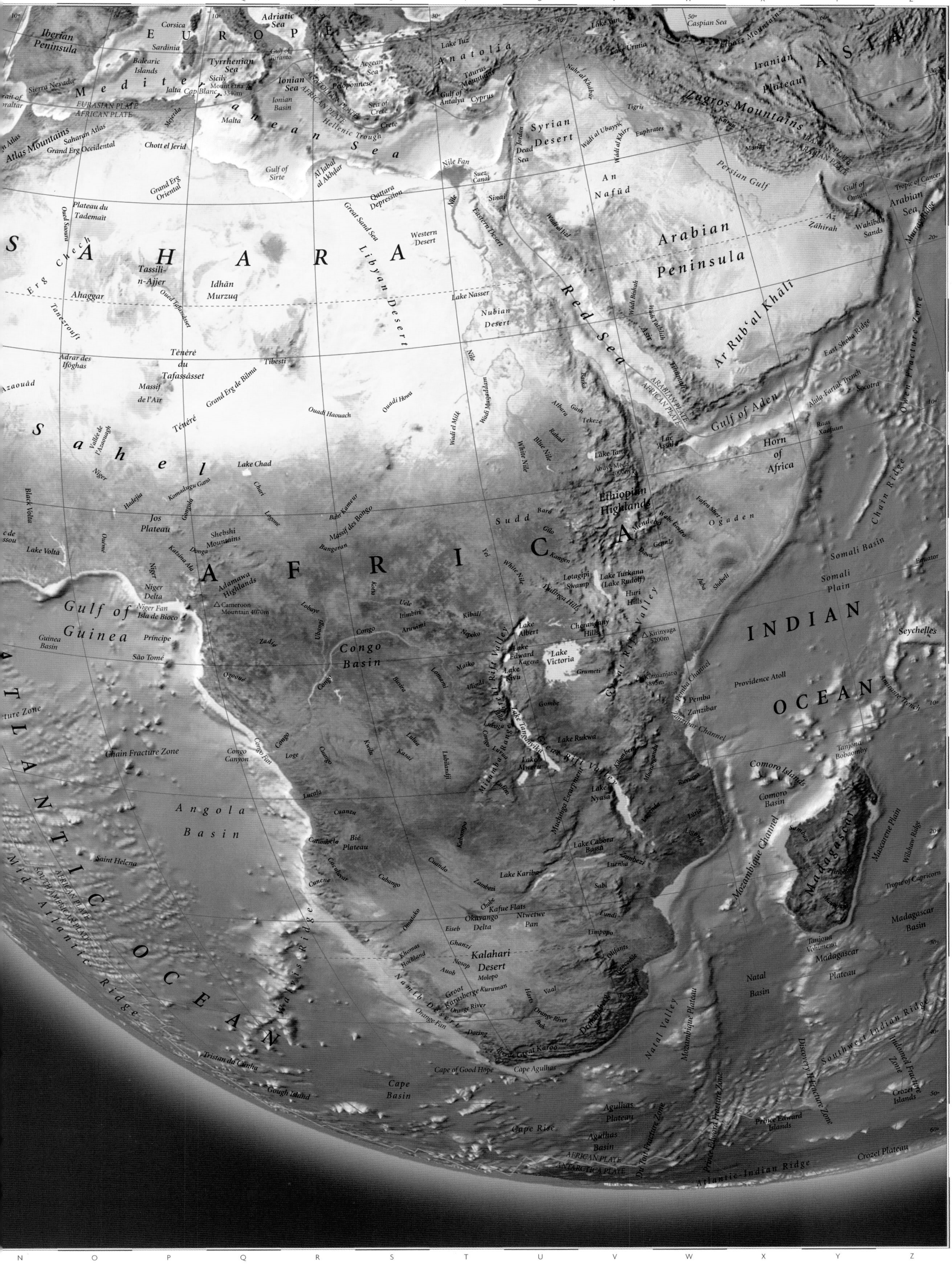

EUROPE
ASIA
AFRICA
SAHARA
Sahel
INDIAN OCEAN
ATLANTIC OCEAN
Iberian Peninsula
Corsica
Sardinia
Balearic Islands
Adriatic Sea
Tyrrhenian Sea
Sicily
Mount Etna 3340m
Malta
Mediterranean Sea
Ionian Sea
Ionian Basin
Gulf of Taranto
Aegean Sea
Peloponnese
Sea of Crete
Crete
Hellenic Trough
Anatolia
Lake Tuz
Taurus Mountains
Gulf of Antalya
Cyprus
Lake Van
Lake Urmia
Caspian Sea
Iranian Plateau
Zagros Mountains
EURASIAN PLATE
AFRICAN PLATE
ANATOLIAN PLATE
IRANIAN PLATE
ARABIAN PLATE
Sierra Nevada
Atlas Mountains
Saharan Atlas
Grand Erg Occidental
Chott el Jerid
Grand Erg Oriental
Gulf of Sirte
Al Jabal al Akhdar
Qattara Depression
Great Sand Sea
Western Desert
Libyan Desert
Nile Fan
Suez Canal
Sinai
Nile
Eastern Desert
Dead Sea
Jordan
Syrian Desert
Tigris
Euphrates
An Nafūd
Persian Gulf
Gulf of Oman
Tropic of Cancer
Arabian Sea
Arabian Peninsula
Red Sea
Ar Rub' al Khālī
Lake Nasser
Nubian Desert
Plateau du Tademaït
Oued Saoura
Erg Chech
Tassili-n-Ajjer
Idhān Murzuq
Ahaggar
Tanezrouft
Adrar des Ifôghas
Ténéré du Tafassâsset
Tibesti
Massif de l'Aïr
Grand Erg de Bilma
Ténéré
Ouadi Haouach
Ouadi Howa
Wadi el Milk
Wadi Muqaddam
Lake Chad
Niger
Komadugu Gana
Chari
Logone
Hadejia
Jos Plateau
Gongola
Black Volta
Lake Volta
Shebshi Mountains
Adamawa Highlands
Niger Delta
Niger Fan
Cameroon Mountain 4070m
Gulf of Guinea
Isla de Bioco
Príncipe
São Tomé
Guinea Basin
Bamingui Bangoran
Massif des Bongo
Sudd
White Nile
Blue Nile
Atbara
Lake Tana
Ethiopian Highlands
Lac Assal
Gulf of Aden
Horn of Africa
Socotra
Ogaden
Lotagipi Swamp
Lake Turkana (Lake Rudolf)
Huri Hills
Ubangi
Uele
Congo
Congo Basin
Lake Albert
Lake Edward
Lake Kivu
Lake Victoria
Kirinyaga 5200m
Kilimanjaro 5895m
Great Rift Valley
Lake Tanganyika
Lake Rukwa
Lake Mweru
Lake Nyasa
Pemba
Zanzibar
Pemba Channel
Zanzibar Channel
Providence Atoll
Seychelles
Somali Basin
Somali Plain
Equator
Chain Ridge
Owen Fracture Zone
East Sheba Ridge
Comoro Islands
Comoro Basin
Mozambique Channel
Madagascar
Mascarene Plain
Tropic of Capricorn
Madagascar Basin
Madagascar Plateau
Chain Fracture Zone
Congo Canyon
Congo Fan
Angola Basin
Bié Plateau
Saint Helena
Mid-Atlantic Ridge
Walvis Ridge
Lake Cabora Bassa
Zambezi
Lake Kariba
Kafue Flats
Okavango Delta
Ntwetwe Pan
Kalahari Desert
Limpopo
Namib Desert
Orange River
Orange Fan
Great Karoo
Drakensberg
Cape of Good Hope
Cape Agulhas
Tristan da Cunha
Gough Island
Cape Basin
Cape Rise
Agulhas Plateau
Agulhas Basin
Natal Valley
Natal Basin
Mozambique Plateau
Prince Edward Islands
Crozet Islands
Crozet Plateau
Southwest Indian Ridge
Atlantic-Indian Ridge
ANTARCTICA PLATE

N O P Q R S T U V W X Y Z

Physical Africa

The structure of Africa was dramatically influenced by the break up of the supercontinent Gondwanaland about 160 million years ago and, more recently, rifting and hot spot activity. Today, much of Africa is remote from active plate boundaries and comprises a series of extensive plateaus and deep basins, which influence the drainage patterns of major rivers. The relief rises to the east, where volcanic uplands and vast lakes mark the Great Rift Valley. In the far north and south sedimentary rocks have been folded to form the Atlas Mountains and the Great Karoo.

Northern Africa

Northern Africa comprises a system of basins and plateaus. The Tibesti and Ahaggar are volcanic uplands, whose uplift has been matched by subsidence within large surrounding basins. Many of the basins have been infilled with sand and gravel, creating the vast Saharan lands. The Atlas Mountains in the north were formed by convergence of the African and Eurasian plates.

The Earth's crust has been warped to form the Taoudenni Basin
Volcanic Ahaggar mountains, formed by rising magma from a hot spot
Lake Chad lies in a sand-filled basin
A
A
0 250 500 Km
0 250 500 Miles

Section across northern *Africa showing infilled basins and uplifted plateaus.*

East Africa

The Great Rift Valley is the most striking feature of this region, running for 4475 miles (7200 km) from Lake Nyasa to the Red Sea. North of Lake Nyasa it splits into two arms and encloses an interior plateau which contains Lake Victoria. A number of elongated lakes and volcanoes lie along the fault lines. To the west lies the Congo Basin, a vast, shallow depression, which rises to form an almost circular rim of highlands.

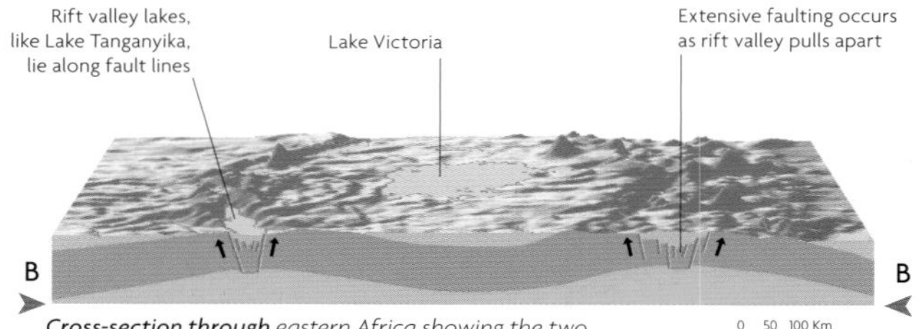
Rift valley lakes, like Lake Tanganyika, lie along fault lines
Lake Victoria
Extensive faulting occurs as rift valley pulls apart
B
B
0 50 100 Km
0 50 100 Miles

Cross-section through *eastern Africa showing the two arms of the Great Rift Valley and its interior plateau.*

Scale 1:40,000,000

Km 0 200 400 600 800

Miles 0 200 400 600 800

projection: Lambert Azimuthal Equal Area

Map key

Elevation

- 5000m / 16,405ft
- 4000m / 13,124ft
- 3000m / 9843ft
- 2000m / 6562ft
- 1000m / 3281ft
- 500m / 1640ft
- 250m / 820ft
- 100m / 328ft
- sea level
- below sea level

Plate margins
(for explanation see page xiv)

- constructive
- destructive
- conservative
- uncertain
- line of cross-section

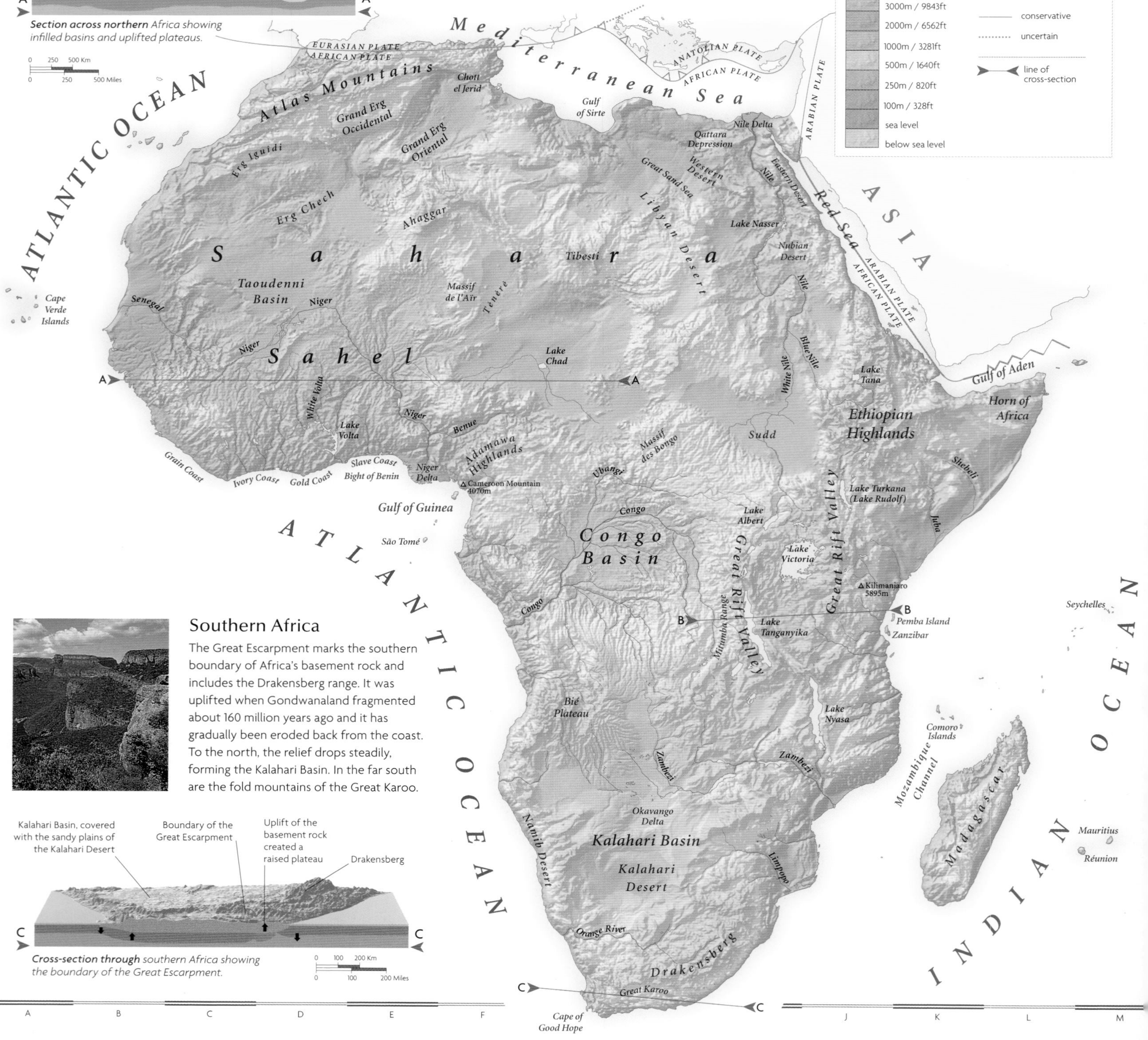
Mediterranean Sea
EURASIAN PLATE
AFRICAN PLATE
ANATOLIAN PLATE
AFRICAN PLATE
ARABIAN PLATE
ATLANTIC OCEAN
Atlas Mountains
Chott el Jerid
Gulf of Sirte
Grand Erg Occidental
Grand Erg Oriental
Erg Iguidi
Erg Chech
Ahaggar
Sahara
Qattara Depression
Nile Delta
Western Desert
Great Sand Sea
Libyan Desert
Eastern Desert
Nile
Lake Nasser
Nubian Desert
Red Sea
ASIA
ARABIAN PLATE
AFRICAN PLATE
Tibesti
Taoudenni Basin
Niger
Massif de l'Aïr
Ténéré
Senegal
Cape Verde Islands
Sahel
Lake Chad
Blue Nile
White Nile
Lake Tana
Gulf of Aden
Horn of Africa
Ethiopian Highlands
White Volta
Lake Volta
Benue
Adamawa Highlands
Massif des Bongo
Sudd
Grain Coast
Ivory Coast
Gold Coast
Slave Coast
Bight of Benin
Niger Delta
Cameroon Mountain 4070m
Gulf of Guinea
São Tomé
Ubangi
Congo
Lake Albert
Lake Turkana (Lake Rudolf)
Shebeli
Juba
Congo Basin
Lake Victoria
Great Rift Valley
Kilimanjaro 5895m
Mitumba Range
Lake Tanganyika
Pemba Island
Zanzibar
Seychelles
INDIAN OCEAN
Bié Plateau
Lake Nyasa
Comoro Islands
Mozambique Channel
Madagascar
Zambezi
Okavango Delta
Kalahari Basin
Kalahari Desert
Namib Desert
Limpopo
Mauritius
Réunion
Orange River
Drakensberg
Great Karoo
Cape of Good Hope

Southern Africa

The Great Escarpment marks the southern boundary of Africa's basement rock and includes the Drakensberg range. It was uplifted when Gondwanaland fragmented about 160 million years ago and it has gradually been eroded back from the coast. To the north, the relief drops steadily, forming the Kalahari Basin. In the far south are the fold mountains of the Great Karoo.

Kalahari Basin, covered with the sandy plains of the Kalahari Desert

Boundary of the Great Escarpment

Uplift of the basement rock created a raised plateau

Drakensberg

Cross-section through *southern Africa showing the boundary of the Great Escarpment.*

▲ **Savannah grasslands run** *in a belt across Africa; limited rainfall inhibits tree growth.*

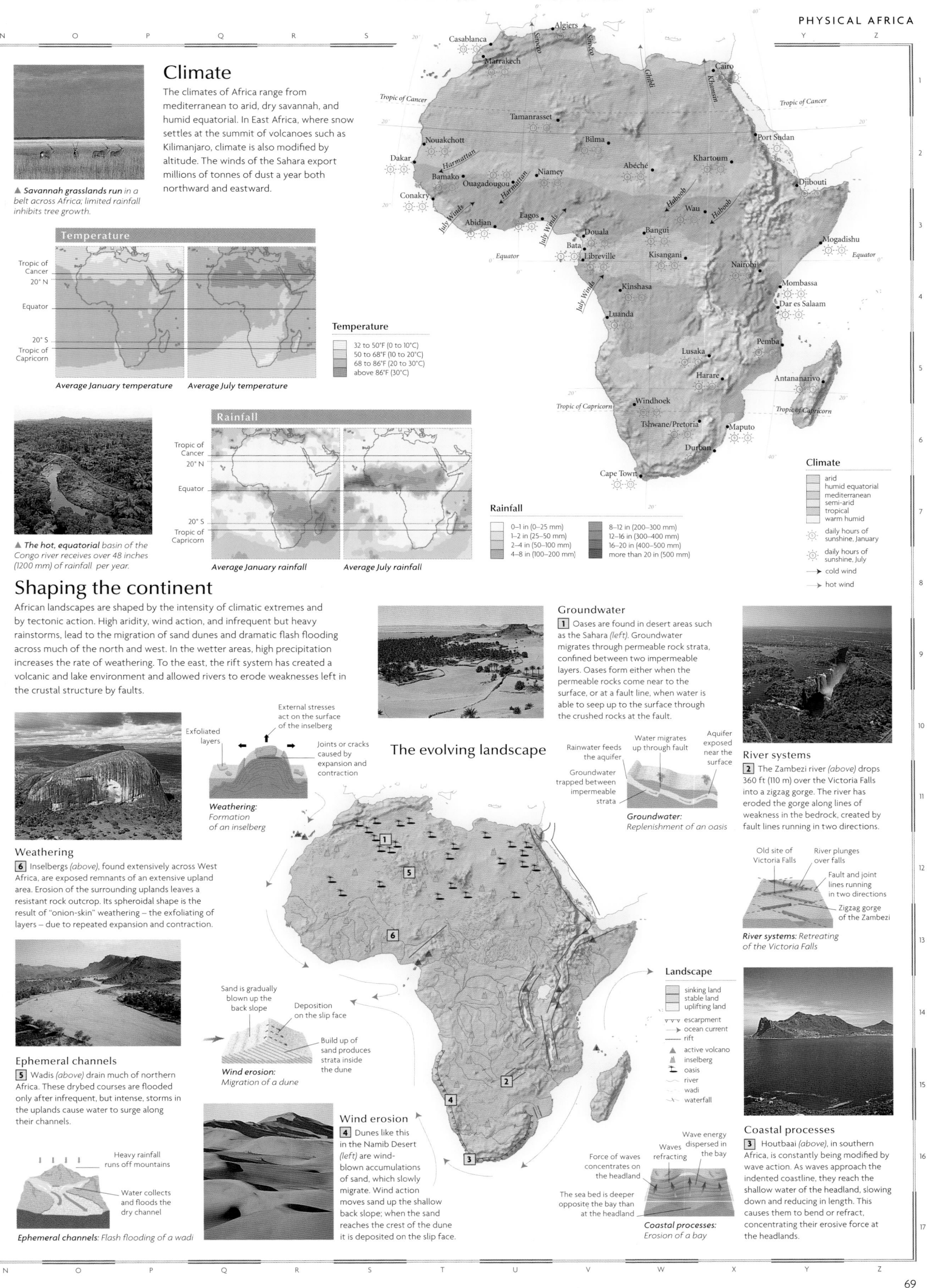

Climate

The climates of Africa range from mediterranean to arid, dry savannah, and humid equatorial. In East Africa, where snow settles at the summit of volcanoes such as Kilimanjaro, climate is also modified by altitude. The winds of the Sahara export millions of tons of dust a year both northward and eastward.

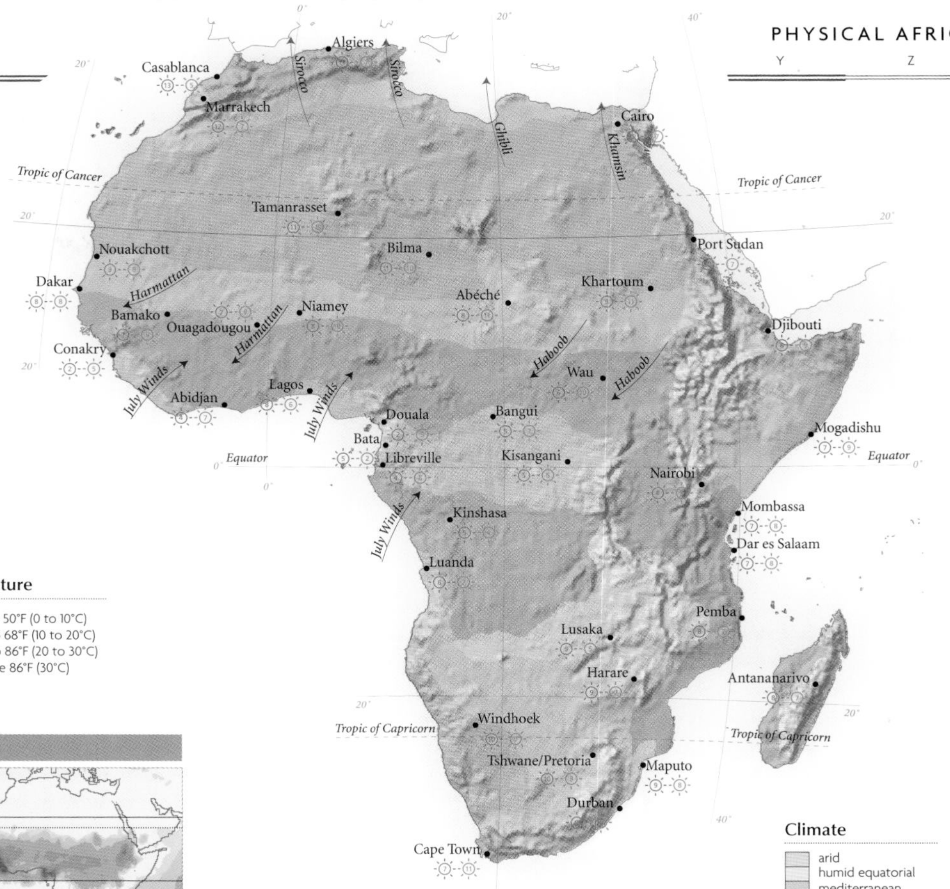
Algiers
Casablanca
Marrakech
Sirocco
Ghibli
Cairo
Khamsin
Tropic of Cancer
Tamanrasset
Nouakchott
Bilma
Port Sudan
Dakar
Harmattan
Abéché
Khartoum
Bamako
Niamey
Ouagadougou
Djibouti
Conakry
Haboob
Wau
July Winds
Abidjan
Lagos
Douala
Bangui
Mogadishu
Bata
Libreville
Kisangani
Equator
Nairobi
Kinshasa
Mombasa
Dar es Salaam
Luanda
Pemba
Lusaka
Harare
Antananarivo
Windhoek
Tropic of Capricorn
Tshwane/Pretoria
Maputo
Durban
Cape Town

Temperature

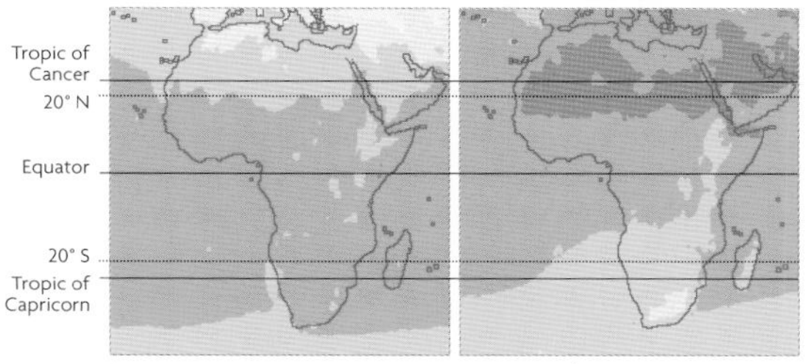
Tropic of Cancer
20° N
Equator
20° S
Tropic of Capricorn
Average January temperature *Average July temperature*

Temperature
- 32 to 50°F (0 to 10°C)
- 50 to 68°F (10 to 20°C)
- 68 to 86°F (20 to 30°C)
- above 86°F (30°C)

▲ **The hot, equatorial** *basin of the Congo river receives over 48 inches (1200 mm) of rainfall per year.*

Rainfall

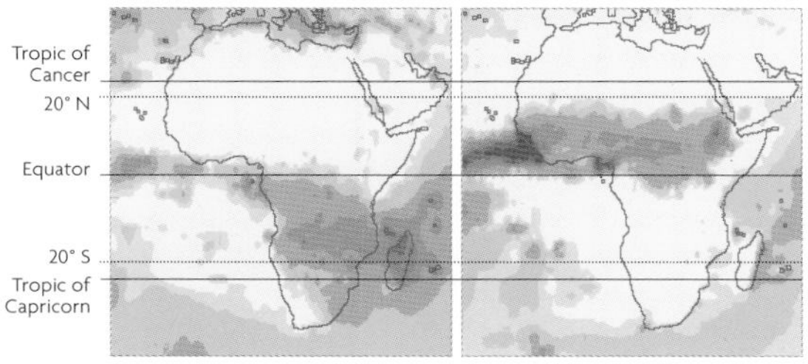
Tropic of Cancer
20° N
Equator
20° S
Tropic of Capricorn
Average January rainfall *Average July rainfall*

Rainfall
- 0–1 in (0–25 mm)
- 1–2 in (25–50 mm)
- 2–4 in (50–100 mm)
- 4–8 in (100–200 mm)
- 8–12 in (200–300 mm)
- 12–16 in (300–400 mm)
- 16–20 in (400–500 mm)
- more than 20 in (500 mm)

Climate
- arid
- humid equatorial
- mediterranean
- semi-arid
- tropical
- warm humid
- daily hours of sunshine, January
- daily hours of sunshine, July
- cold wind
- hot wind

Shaping the continent

African landscapes are shaped by the intensity of climatic extremes and by tectonic action. High aridity, wind action, and infrequent but heavy rainstorms, lead to the migration of sand dunes and dramatic flash flooding across much of the north and west. In the wetter areas, high precipitation increases the rate of weathering. To the east, the rift system has created a volcanic and lake environment and allowed rivers to erode weaknesses left in the crustal structure by faults.

Groundwater

1 Oases are found in desert areas such as the Sahara *(left)*. Groundwater migrates through permeable rock strata, confined between two impermeable layers. Oases form either when the permeable rocks come near to the surface, or at a fault line, when water is able to seep up to the surface through the crushed rocks at the fault.

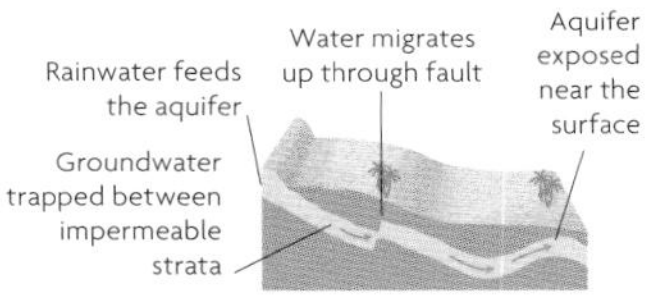
Rainwater feeds the aquifer
Water migrates up through fault
Aquifer exposed near the surface
Groundwater trapped between impermeable strata
Groundwater: *Replenishment of an oasis*

River systems

2 The Zambezi river *(above)* drops 360 ft (110 m) over the Victoria Falls into a zigzag gorge. The river has eroded the gorge along lines of weakness in the bedrock, created by fault lines running in two directions.

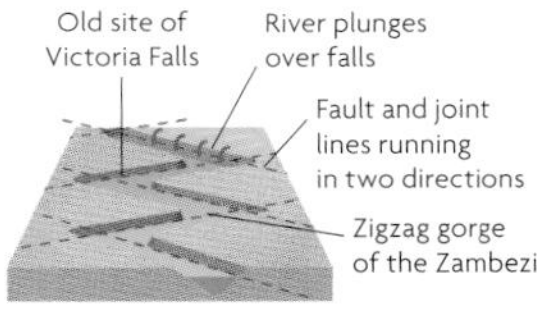
Old site of Victoria Falls
River plunges over falls
Fault and joint lines running in two directions
Zigzag gorge of the Zambezi
River systems: *Retreating of the Victoria Falls*

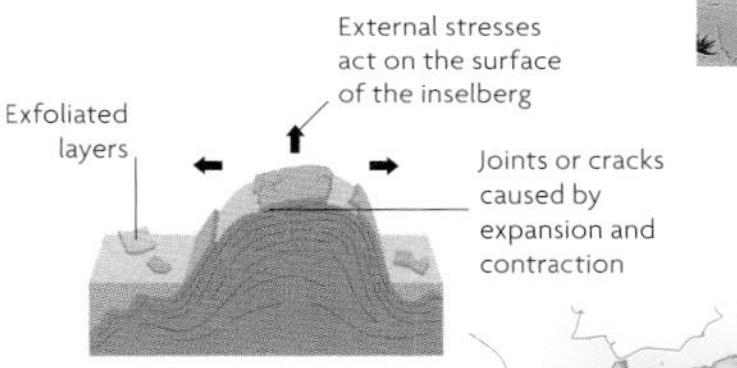
External stresses act on the surface of the inselberg
Exfoliated layers
Joints or cracks caused by expansion and contraction
Weathering: *Formation of an inselberg*

Weathering

6 Inselbergs *(above)*, found extensively across West Africa, are exposed remnants of an extensive upland area. Erosion of the surrounding uplands leaves a resistant rock outcrop. Its spheroidal shape is the result of "onion-skin" weathering – the exfoliating of layers – due to repeated expansion and contraction.

The evolving landscape

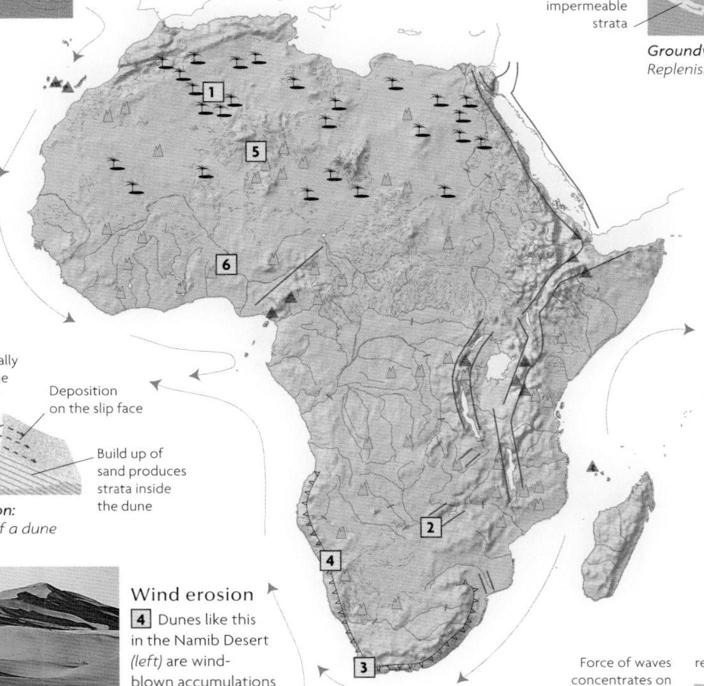
1
2
3
4
5
6

Landscape
- sinking land
- stable land
- uplifting land
- escarpment
- ocean current
- rift
- active volcano
- inselberg
- oasis
- river
- wadi
- waterfall

Ephemeral channels

5 Wadis *(above)* drain much of northern Africa. These drybed courses are flooded only after infrequent, but intense, storms in the uplands cause water to surge along their channels.

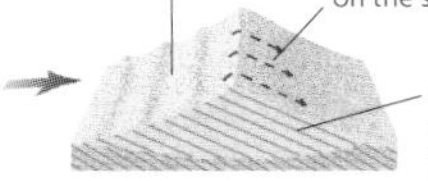
Sand is gradually blown up the back slope
Deposition on the slip face
Build up of sand produces strata inside the dune
Wind erosion: *Migration of a dune*

Coastal processes

3 Houtbaai *(above)*, in southern Africa, is constantly being modified by wave action. As waves approach the indented coastline, they reach the shallow water of the headland, slowing down and reducing in length. This causes them to bend or refract, concentrating their erosive force at the headlands.

Wind erosion

4 Dunes like this in the Namib Desert *(left)* are wind-blown accumulations of sand, which slowly migrate. Wind action moves sand up the shallow back slope; when the sand reaches the crest of the dune it is deposited on the slip face.

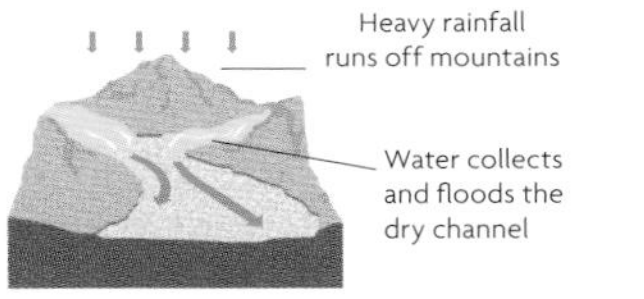
Heavy rainfall runs off mountains
Water collects and floods the dry channel
Ephemeral channels: *Flash flooding of a wadi*

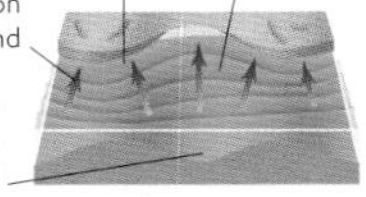
Force of waves concentrates on the headland
Waves refracting
Wave energy dispersed in the bay
The sea bed is deeper opposite the bay than at the headland
Coastal processes: *Erosion of a bay*

Political Africa

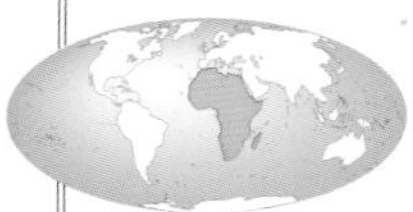

The political map of modern Africa only emerged following the end of the Second World War. Over the next half-century, all of the countries formerly controlled by European powers gained independence from their colonial rulers – only Liberia and Ethiopia were never colonized. The postcolonial era has not been an easy period for many countries, but there have been moves toward multiparty democracy across much of the continent. In South Africa, democratic elections replaced the internationally-condemned apartheid system only in 1994. Other countries have still to find political stability; corruption in government, and ethnic tensions are serious problems. National infrastructures, based on the colonial transportation systems built to exploit Africa's resources, are often inappropriate for independent economic development.

PORTUGA
Madeira
(to Portugal)
Casablan
Safi
Marrake
MOROCC
Agadir
Canary Islands
(to Spain)
LAÂYOUNE
Western
Sahara
(Occupied
by Morocco)
Tropic of Cancer
S
MAURITANI
NOUAKCHOTT
CAPE
VERDE
PRAIA
Senegal
SENEGAL
DAKAR
Kaolack
GAMBIA
BANJUL
BAMAKO
GUINEA-
BISSAU
BISSAU
GUINEA
CONAKRY
Koidu
FREETOWN
SIERRA LEONE
IV
YAMOUSSOUKR
CO
MONROVIA
LIBERIA

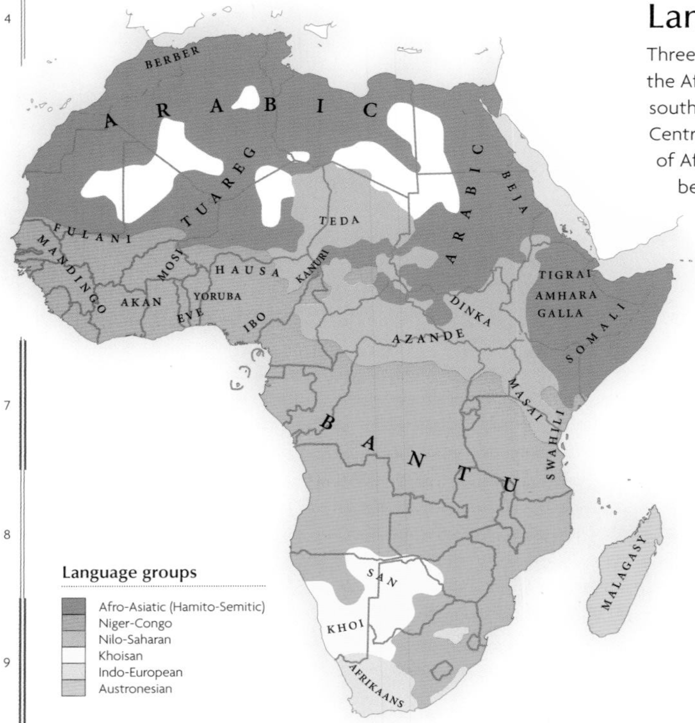
BERBER
A R A B I C
ARABIC
TUAREG
TEDA
BEJA
FULANI
MANDINGO
MOSI
HAUSA
KANURI
AKAN
YORUBA
EWE
IBO
TIGRAI
AMHARA
GALLA
DINKA
SOMALI
AZANDE
MASAI
B A N T U
SWAHILI
SAN
KHOI
AFRIKAANS
MALAGASY
Language groups
Afro-Asiatic (Hamito-Semitic)
Niger-Congo
Nilo-Saharan
Khoisan
Indo-European
Austronesian

Languages

Three major world languages act as *lingua francas* across the African continent: Arabic in North Africa; English in southern and eastern Africa and Nigeria; and French in Central and West Africa, and in Madagascar. A huge number of African languages are spoken as well – over 2000 have been recorded, with more than 400 in Nigeria alone – reflecting the continuing importance of traditional cultures and values. In the north of the continent, the extensive use of Arabic reflects Middle Eastern influences while Bantu languages are widely-spoken across much of southern Africa.

Official African languages

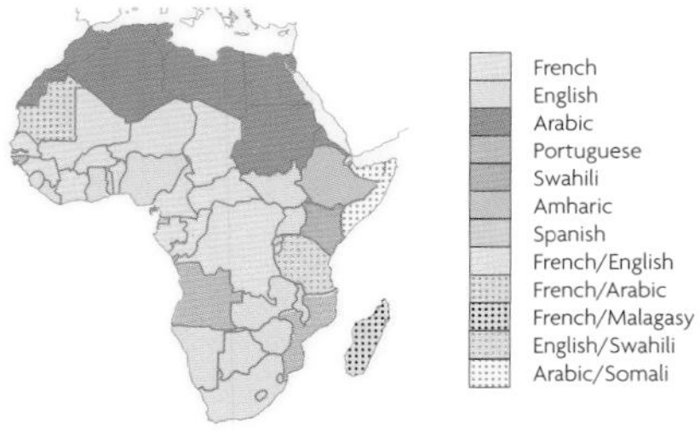
French
English
Arabic
Portuguese
Swahili
Amharic
Spanish
French/English
French/Arabic
French/Malagasy
English/Swahili
Arabic/Somali

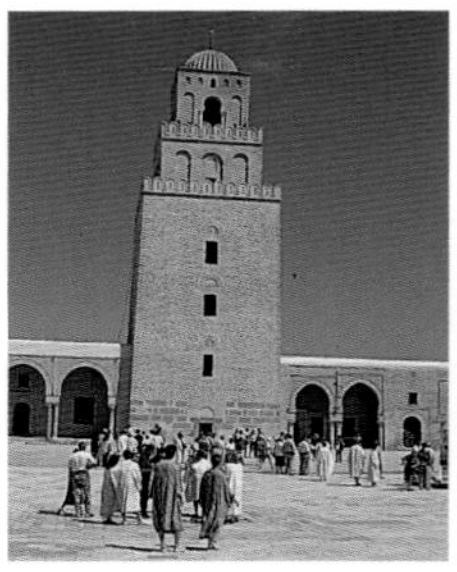

▲ ***Islamic influences are*** *evident throughout North Africa. The Great Mosque at Kairouan, Tunisia, is Africa's holiest Islamic place.*

▲ ***In northeastern Nigeria,*** *people speak Kanuri – a dialect of the Nilo-Saharan language group.*

Transportation

African railroads were built to aid the exploitation of natural resources, and most offer passage only from the interior to the coastal cities, leaving large parts of the continent untouched – five landlocked countries have no railroads at all. The Congo, Nile, and Niger river networks offer limited access to land within the continental interior, but have a number of waterfalls and cataracts which prevent navigation from the sea. Many roads were developed in the 1960s and 1970s, but economic difficulties are making the maintenance and expansion of the networks difficult.

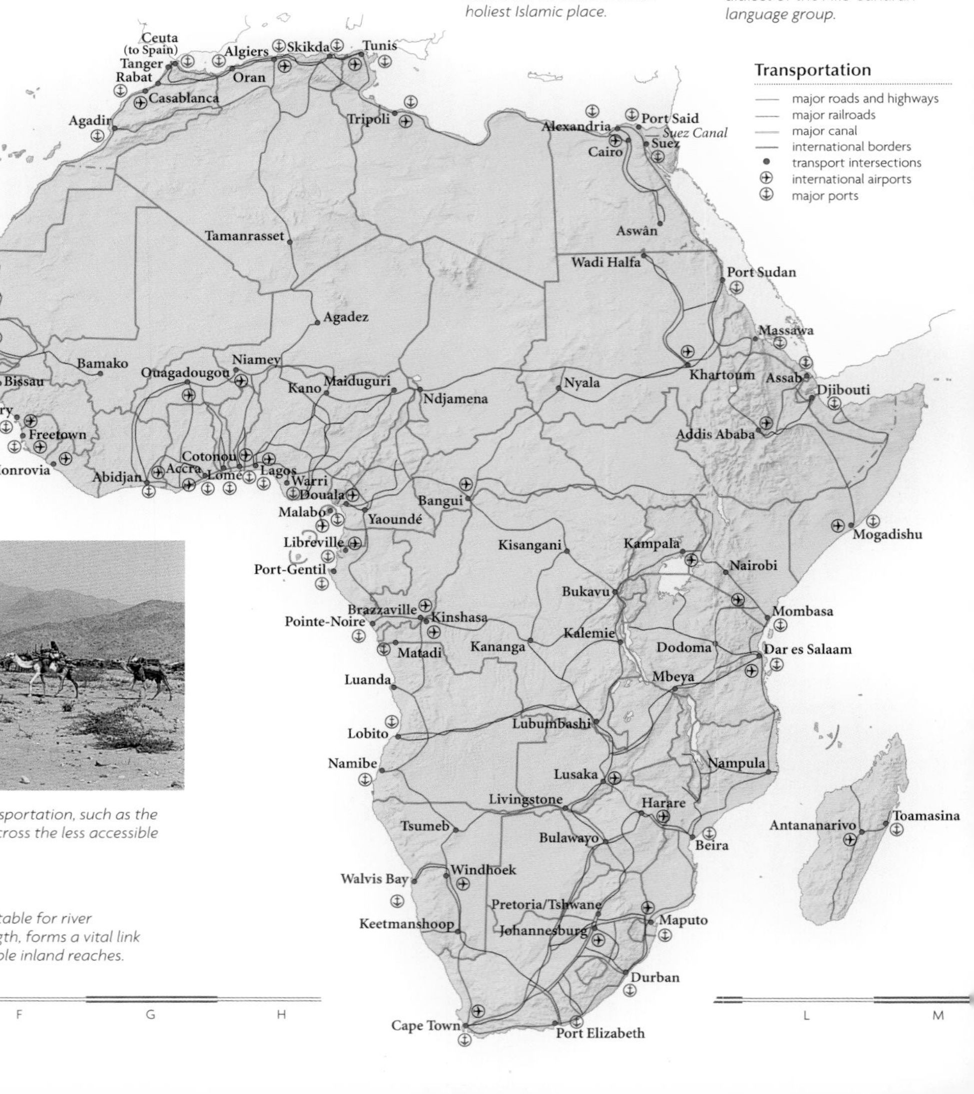
Ceuta
(to Spain)
Tanger
Rabat
Casablanca
Agadir
Algiers
Skikda
Tunis
Oran
Tripoli
Alexandria
Port Said
Suez Canal
Cairo
Suez
Aswân
Wadi Halfa
Port Sudan
Tamanrasset
Nouâdhibou
Nouakchott
Agadez
Dakar
Banjul
Bissau
Bamako
Niamey
Ouagadougou
Kano
Maiduguri
Ndjamena
Nyala
Khartoum
Massawa
Assab
Djibouti
Conakry
Freetown
Monrovia
Abidjan
Accra
Cotonou
Lomé
Lagos
Warri
Douala
Malabo
Yaoundé
Bangui
Addis Ababa
Mogadishu
Libreville
Port-Gentil
Kisangani
Kampala
Nairobi
Bukavu
Brazzaville
Kinshasa
Pointe-Noire
Matadi
Kananga
Kalemie
Mombasa
Dodoma
Dar es Salaam
Luanda
Mbeya
Lobito
Lubumbashi
Namibe
Lusaka
Nampula
Livingstone
Harare
Tsumeb
Bulawayo
Beira
Antananarivo
Toamasina
Walvis Bay
Windhoek
Pretoria/Tshwane
Johannesburg
Maputo
Keetmanshoop
Durban
Cape Town
Port Elizabeth
Transportation
major roads and highways
major railroads
major canal
international borders
transport intersections
international airports
major ports

► ***South Africa has*** *the largest concentration of railroads in Africa. Over 20,000 miles (32,000 km) of routes have been built since 1870.*

▲ ***Traditional means of*** *transportation, such as the camel, are still widely used across the less accessible parts of Africa.*

◄ ***The Congo river,*** *though not suitable for river transportation along its entire length, forms a vital link for people and goods in its navigable inland reaches.*

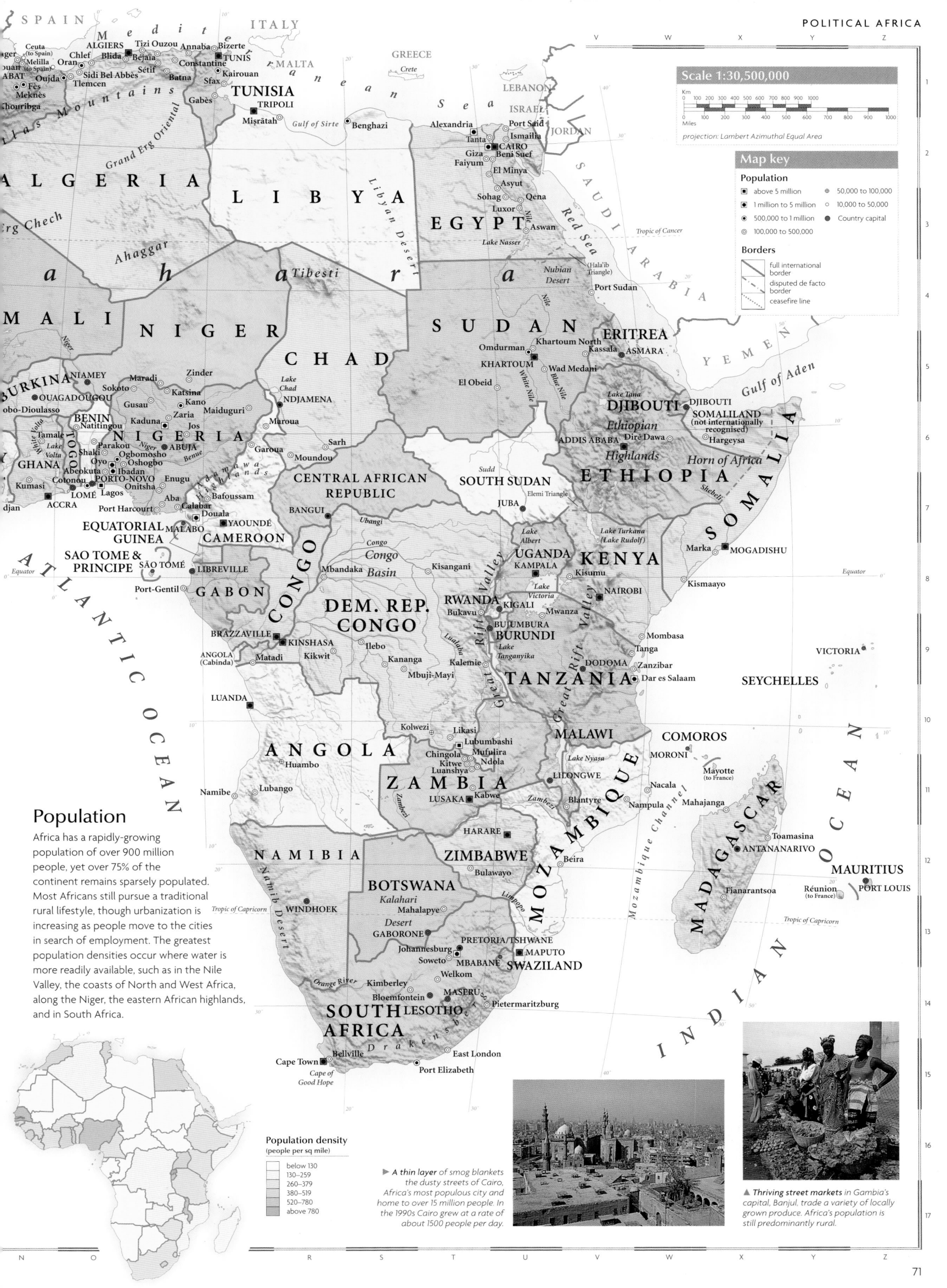

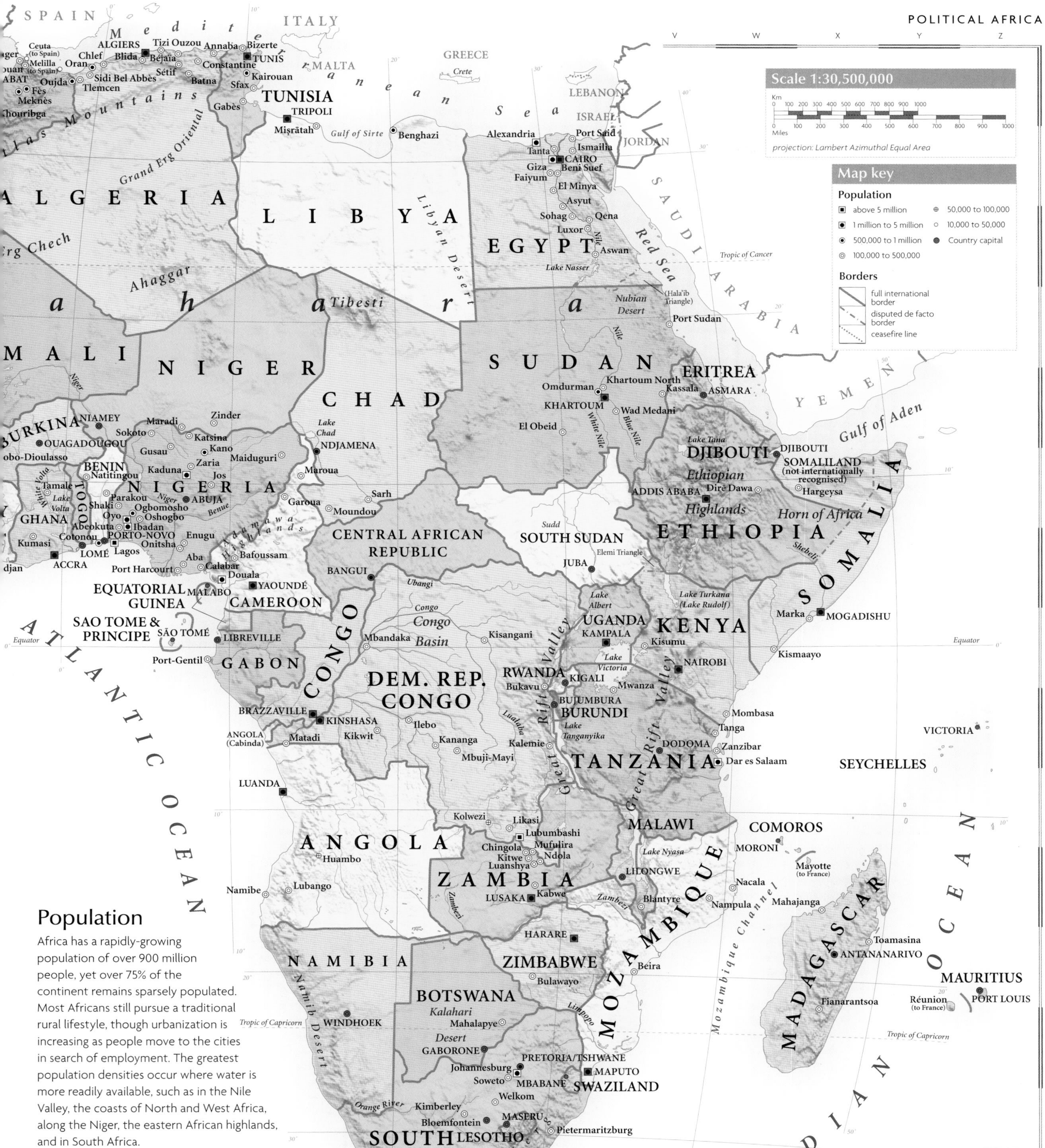
Scale 1:30,500,000
Km
0 100 200 300 400 500 600 700 800 900 1000
Miles
0 100 200 300 400 500 600 700 800 900 1000
projection: Lambert Azimuthal Equal Area
Map key
Population
above 5 million
1 million to 5 million
500,000 to 1 million
100,000 to 500,000
50,000 to 100,000
10,000 to 50,000
Country capital
Borders
full international border
disputed de facto border
ceasefire line
SPAIN
ITALY
GREECE
Crete
MALTA
TUNISIA
TUNIS
TRIPOLI
ALGERIA
ALGIERS
LIBYA
EGYPT
CAIRO
Alexandria
LEBANON
ISRAEL
JORDAN
SAUDI ARABIA
YEMEN
Mediterranean Sea
Gulf of Sirte
Benghazi
Libyan Desert
Red Sea
Lake Nasser
Tropic of Cancer
Sahara
Tibesti
Ahaggar
MALI
NIGER
CHAD
SUDAN
KHARTOUM
ERITREA
ASMARA
DJIBOUTI
SOMALILAND (not internationally recognised)
Gulf of Aden
ETHIOPIA
ADDIS ABABA
Ethiopian Highlands
Horn of Africa
SOMALIA
MOGADISHU
NIAMEY
NDJAMENA
BURKINA
OUAGADOUGOU
BENIN
TOGO
GHANA
ACCRA
LOMÉ
PORTO-NOVO
NIGERIA
ABUJA
Lagos
CENTRAL AFRICAN REPUBLIC
BANGUI
SOUTH SUDAN
JUBA
EQUATORIAL GUINEA
MALABO
CAMEROON
YAOUNDÉ
SAO TOME & PRINCIPE
SÃO TOMÉ
GABON
LIBREVILLE
CONGO
BRAZZAVILLE
DEM. REP. CONGO
KINSHASA
Congo Basin
UGANDA
KAMPALA
KENYA
NAIROBI
Equator
RWANDA
KIGALI
BURUNDI
BUJUMBURA
TANZANIA
DODOMA
Dar es Salaam
Great Rift Valley
VICTORIA
SEYCHELLES
ATLANTIC OCEAN
LUANDA
ANGOLA
ZAMBIA
LUSAKA
MALAWI
LILONGWE
COMOROS
MORONI
Mayotte (to France)
MOZAMBIQUE
MAPUTO
Mozambique Channel
MADAGASCAR
ANTANANARIVO
MAURITIUS
PORT LOUIS
Réunion (to France)
ZIMBABWE
HARARE
NAMIBIA
WINDHOEK
Namib Desert
BOTSWANA
GABORONE
Kalahari Desert
Tropic of Capricorn
PRETORIA/TSHWANE
Johannesburg
MBABANE
SWAZILAND
MASERU
LESOTHO
SOUTH AFRICA
Cape Town
Cape of Good Hope
Drakensberg
Port Elizabeth
East London
INDIAN OCEAN

Population

Africa has a rapidly-growing population of over 900 million people, yet over 75% of the continent remains sparsely populated. Most Africans still pursue a traditional rural lifestyle, though urbanization is increasing as people move to the cities in search of employment. The greatest population densities occur where water is more readily available, such as in the Nile Valley, the coasts of North and West Africa, along the Niger, the eastern African highlands, and in South Africa.

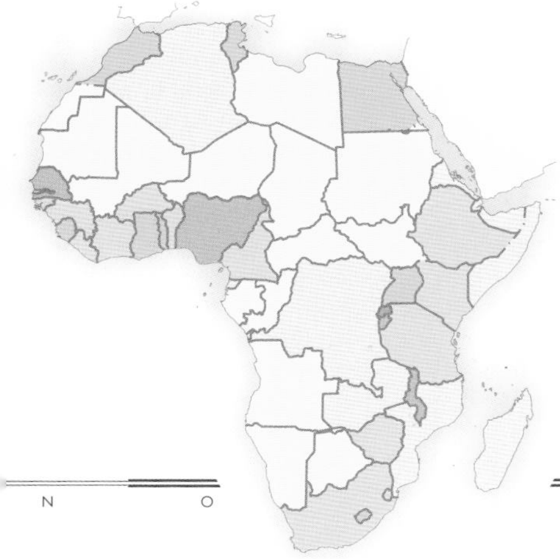

Population density
(people per sq mile)

- below 130
- 130–259
- 260–379
- 380–519
- 520–780
- above 780

▶ **A thin layer** of smog blankets the dusty streets of Cairo, Africa's most populous city and home to over 15 million people. In the 1990s Cairo grew at a rate of about 1500 people per day.

▲ **Thriving street markets** in Gambia's capital, Banjul, trade a variety of locally grown produce. Africa's population is still predominantly rural.

African resources

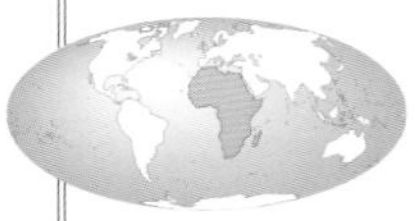

The economies of most African countries are dominated by subsistence and cash crop agriculture, with limited industrialization. Manufacturing is largely confined to South Africa. Many countries depend on a single resource, such as copper or gold, or a cash crop, such as coffee, for export income, which can leave them vulnerable to fluctuations in world commodity prices. In order to diversify their economies and develop a wider industrial base, investment from overseas is being actively sought by many African governments.

Industry

Many African industries concentrate on the extraction and processing of raw materials. These include the oil industry, food processing, mining, and textile production. South Africa accounts for over half of the continent's industrial output with much of the remainder coming from the countries along the northern coast. Over 60% of Africa's workforce is employed in agriculture.

◀ *The unspoiled natural splendor of wildlife reserves, like the Serengeti National Park in Tanzania, attract tourists to Africa from around the globe. The tourist industry in Kenya and Tanzania is particularly well developed, where it accounts for almost 10% of GNI.*

Standard of living

Since the 1960s most countries in Africa have seen significant improvements in life expectancy, healthcare, and education. However, 28 of the 30 most deprived countries in the world are African, and the continent as a whole lies well behind the rest of the world in terms of meeting many basic human needs.

Standard of living
(UN human development index)
high
low

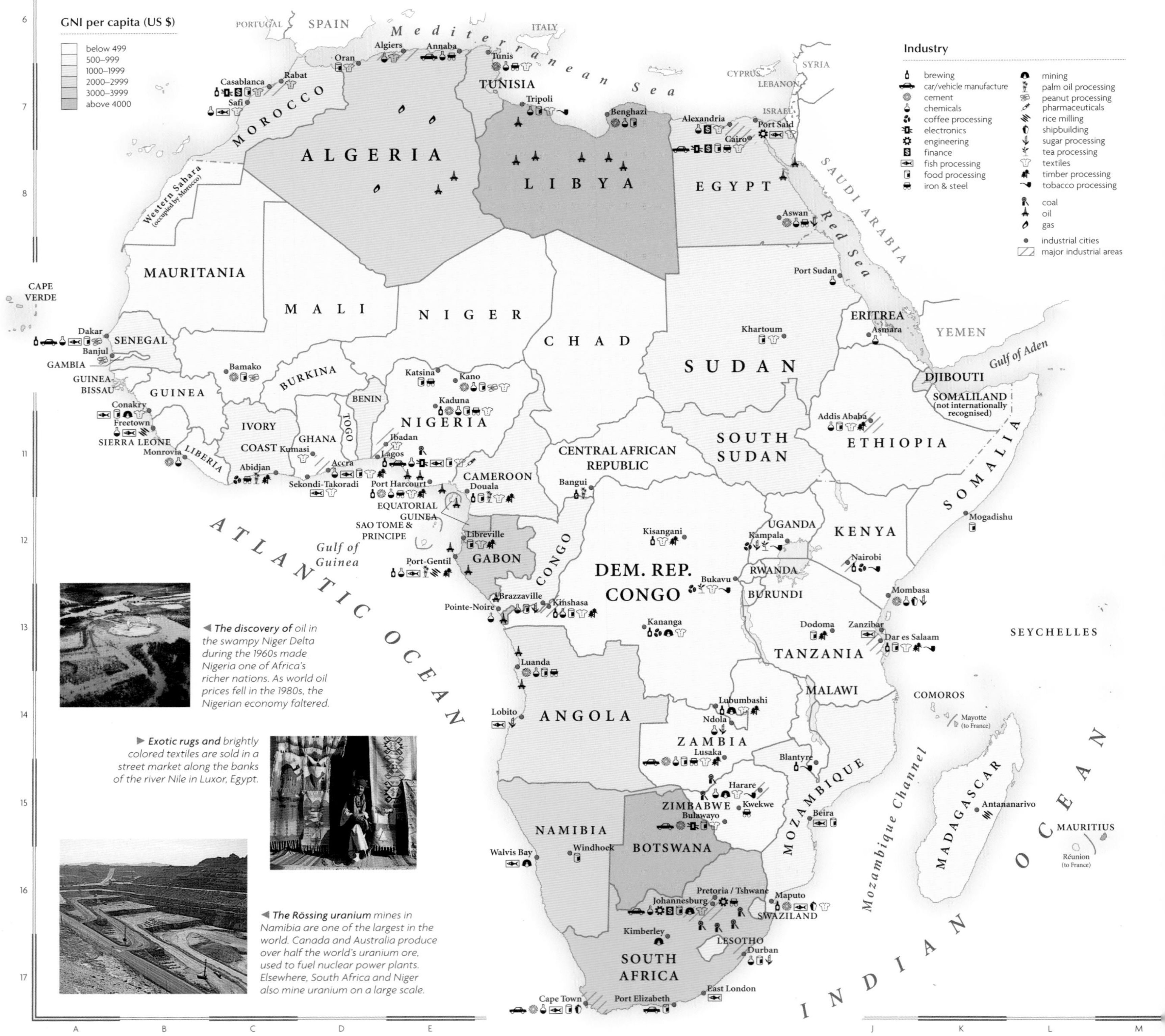

GNI per capita (US $)
below 499
500–999
1000–1999
2000–2999
3000–3999
above 4000
Industry
brewing
car/vehicle manufacture
cement
chemicals
coffee processing
electronics
engineering
finance
fish processing
food processing
iron & steel
mining
palm oil processing
peanut processing
pharmaceuticals
rice milling
shipbuilding
sugar processing
tea processing
textiles
timber processing
tobacco processing
coal
oil
gas
industrial cities
major industrial areas
PORTUGAL
SPAIN
ITALY
Mediterranean Sea
CYPRUS
SYRIA
LEBANON
ISRAEL
SAUDI ARABIA
Red Sea
YEMEN
Gulf of Aden
Algiers
Annaba
Oran
Tunis
TUNISIA
Tripoli
Benghazi
Alexandria
Port Said
Cairo
Casablanca
Rabat
Safi
MOROCCO
ALGERIA
LIBYA
EGYPT
Aswan
Western Sahara (occupied by Morocco)
MAURITANIA
MALI
NIGER
CHAD
SUDAN
Port Sudan
Khartoum
ERITREA
Asmara
DJIBOUTI
SOMALILAND (not internationally recognised)
Addis Ababa
ETHIOPIA
SOMALIA
Mogadishu
CAPE VERDE
Dakar
SENEGAL
Banjul
GAMBIA
GUINEA-BISSAU
GUINEA
Conakry
Freetown
SIERRA LEONE
Monrovia
LIBERIA
Bamako
BURKINA
IVORY COAST
Abidjan
GHANA
Kumasi
Accra
Sekondi-Takoradi
TOGO
BENIN
Katsina
Kano
Kaduna
NIGERIA
Ibadan
Lagos
Port Harcourt
CAMEROON
Douala
EQUATORIAL GUINEA
SAO TOME & PRINCIPE
CENTRAL AFRICAN REPUBLIC
Bangui
SOUTH SUDAN
ATLANTIC OCEAN
Gulf of Guinea
Libreville
GABON
Port-Gentil
CONGO
Brazzaville
Pointe-Noire
Kinshasa
DEM. REP. CONGO
Kisangani
Bukavu
Kananga
UGANDA
Kampala
RWANDA
BURUNDI
KENYA
Nairobi
Mombasa
Dodoma
Zanzibar
Dar es Salaam
TANZANIA
SEYCHELLES
Luanda
Lobito
ANGOLA
Lubumbashi
Ndola
ZAMBIA
Lusaka
MALAWI
Blantyre
COMOROS
Mayotte (to France)
Harare
ZIMBABWE
Bulawayo
Kwekwe
MOZAMBIQUE
Beira
Mozambique Channel
MADAGASCAR
Antananarivo
MAURITIUS
Réunion (to France)
NAMIBIA
Walvis Bay
Windhoek
BOTSWANA
Pretoria / Tshwane
Johannesburg
Maputo
SWAZILAND
Kimberley
LESOTHO
Durban
SOUTH AFRICA
Cape Town
Port Elizabeth
East London
INDIAN OCEAN

◀ *The discovery of oil in the swampy Niger Delta during the 1960s made Nigeria one of Africa's richer nations. As world oil prices fell in the 1980s, the Nigerian economy faltered.*

▶ *Exotic rugs and brightly colored textiles are sold in a street market along the banks of the river Nile in Luxor, Egypt.*

◀ *The Rössing uranium mines in Namibia are one of the largest in the world. Canada and Australia produce over half the world's uranium ore, used to fuel nuclear power plants. Elsewhere, South Africa and Niger also mine uranium on a large scale.*

N O P Q R S T U V W X Y Z

Environmental issues

One of Africa's most serious environmental problems occurs in marginal areas such as the Sahel where scrub and forest clearance, often for cooking fuel, combined with overgrazing, are causing desertification. Game reserves in southern and eastern Africa have helped to preserve many endangered animals, although the needs of growing populations have led to conflict over land use, and poaching is a serious problem.

Environmental issues

- national parks
- tropical forest
- forest destroyed
- desert
- desertification
- polluted rivers
- radioactive contamination
- marine pollution
- heavy marine pollution
- poor urban air quality

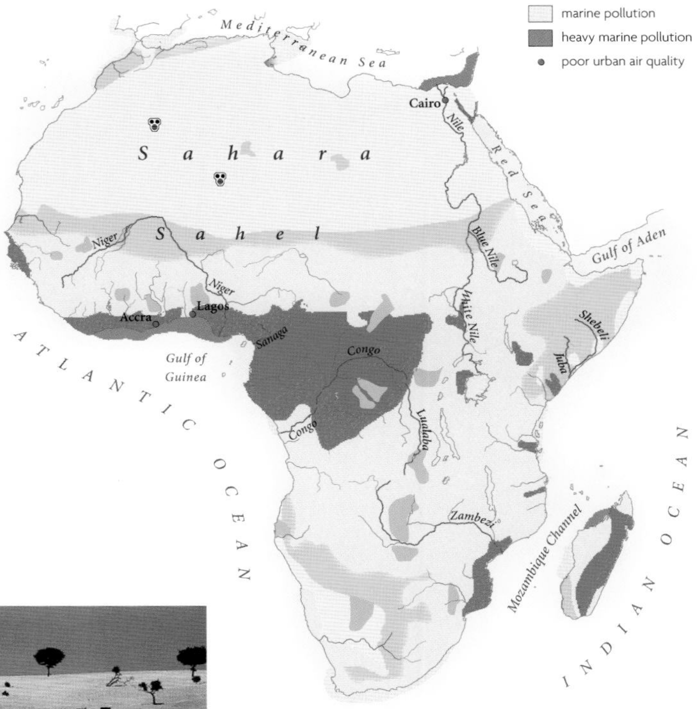
Mediterranean Sea
Cairo
Nile
Red Sea
Sahara
Sahel
Niger
Blue Nile
White Nile
Gulf of Aden
Accra
Lagos
Sanaga
Congo
Shebeli
Juba
Gulf of Guinea
Lualaba
ATLANTIC OCEAN
Zambezi
Mozambique Channel
INDIAN OCEAN

▲ ***The Sahel's delicate*** *natural equilibrium is easily destroyed by the clearing of vegetation, drought, and overgrazing. This causes the Sahara to advance south, engulfing the savannah grasslands.*

Mineral resources

Africa's ancient plateaus contain some of the world's most substantial reserves of precious stones and metals. About 15% of the world's gold is mined in South Africa; Zambia has great copper deposits; and diamonds are mined in Botswana, Dem. Rep. Congo, and South Africa. Oil has brought great economic benefits to Algeria, Libya, and Nigeria.

Mineral resources

- oil field
- gas field
- coal field
- bauxite
- copper
- diamonds
- gold
- iron
- phosphates
- tin
- uranium

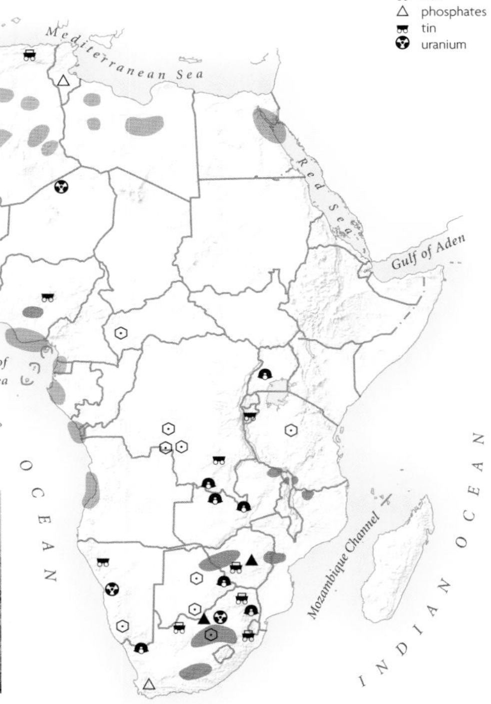
Mediterranean Sea
Red Sea
Gulf of Aden
Gulf of Guinea
ATLANTIC OCEAN
Mozambique Channel
INDIAN OCEAN

▲ ***North and West*** *Africa have large deposits of white phosphate minerals, which are used in making fertilizers. Morocco, Senegal, and Tunisia are among the continent's leading producers.*

▲ ***Workers on a*** *tea plantation gather one of Africa's most important cash crops, providing a valuable source of income. Coffee, rubber, bananas, cotton, and cocoa are also widely grown as cash crops.*

◀ ***Surrounded by desert,*** *the fertile floodplains of the Nile Valley and Delta have been extensively irrigated, farmed, and settled since 3000 BC.*

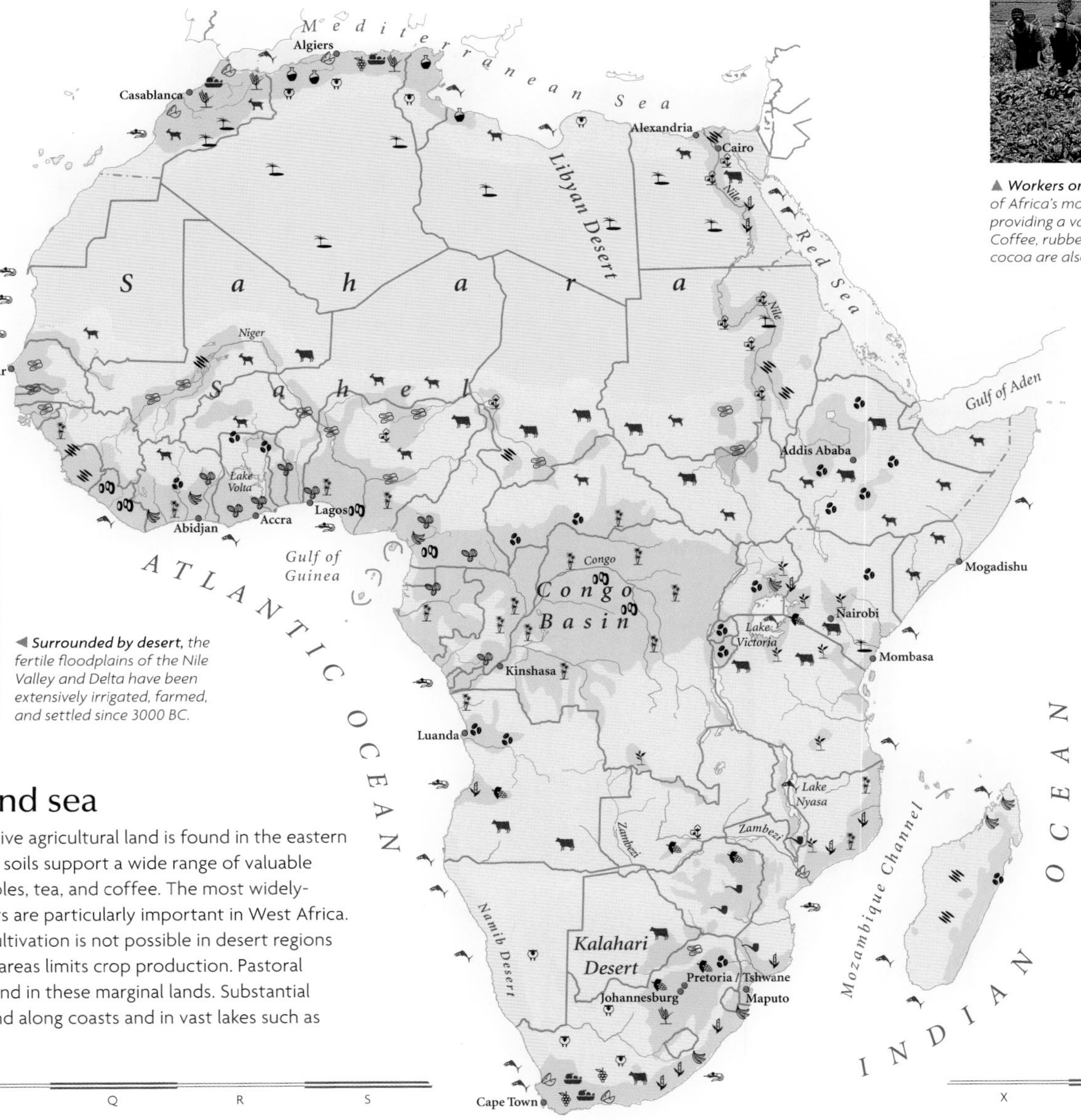
Mediterranean Sea
Algiers
Casablanca
Alexandria
Cairo
Libyan Desert
Nile
Red Sea
Sahara
Niger
Dakar
Sahel
Lake Volta
Abidjan
Accra
Lagos
Addis Ababa
Gulf of Aden
Gulf of Guinea
Congo
Congo Basin
Mogadishu
Lake Victoria
Nairobi
Mombasa
Kinshasa
ATLANTIC OCEAN
Luanda
Lake Nyasa
Zambezi
Mozambique Channel
INDIAN OCEAN
Namib Desert
Kalahari Desert
Pretoria / Tshwane
Johannesburg
Maputo
Cape Town

Using the land and sea

- cropland
- desert
- forest
- pasture
- wetland
- major conurbations
- cattle
- goats
- cereals
- sheep
- bananas
- corn
- citrus fruits
- cocoa
- cotton
- coffee
- dates
- fishing
- fruit
- oil palms
- olives
- peanuts
- rice
- rubber
- shellfish
- sugar cane
- tea
- tobacco
- vineyards
- wheat

Using the land and sea

Some of Africa's most productive agricultural land is found in the eastern volcanic uplands, where fertile soils support a wide range of valuable export crops including vegetables, tea, and coffee. The most widely-grown grain is corn and peanuts are particularly important in West Africa. Without intensive irrigation, cultivation is not possible in desert regions and unreliable rainfall in other areas limits crop production. Pastoral herding is most commonly found in these marginal lands. Substantial local fishing industries are found along coasts and in vast lakes such as Lake Nyasa and Lake Victoria.

N O P Q R S X Y Z

A B C D E F G H I J K L M

North Africa

ALGERIA, EGYPT, LIBYA, MOROCCO, TUNISIA, WESTERN SAHARA

Fringed by the Mediterranean along the northern coast and by the arid Sahara in the south, North Africa reflects the influence of many invaders, both European and, most importantly, Arab, giving the region an almost universal Islamic flavor and a common Arabic language. The countries lying to the west of Egypt are often referred to as the Maghreb, an Arabic term for "west." Today, Morocco and Tunisia exploit their culture and landscape for tourism, while rich oil and gas deposits aid development in Libya and Algeria, despite political turmoil. Egypt, with its fertile, Nile-watered agricultural land and varied industrial base, is the most populous nation.

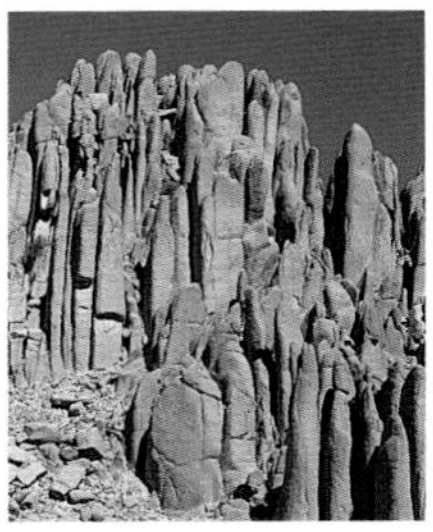

▲ ***These rock piles*** *in Algeria's Ahaggar mountains are the result of weathering caused by extremes of temperature. Great cracks or joints appear in the rocks, which are then worn and smoothed by the wind.*

The landscape

The Atlas Mountains, which extend across much of Morocco, northern Algeria, and Tunisia, are part of the fold mountain system which also runs through much of southern Europe. They recede to the south and east, becoming a steppe landscape before meeting the Sahara desert which covers more than 90% of the region. The sediments of the Sahara overlie an ancient plateau of crystalline rock, some of which is more than four billion years old.

Map key

Population

- ▣ above 5 million
- ◙ 1 million to 5 million
- ◉ 500,000 to 1 million
- ◎ 100,000 to 500,000
- ⊕ 50,000 to 100,000
- ○ 10,000 to 50,000
- ∘ below 10,000

Elevation

- 4000m / 13,124ft
- 3000m / 9843ft
- 2000m / 6562ft
- 1000m / 3281ft
- 500m / 1640ft
- 250m / 820ft
- 100m / 328ft
- sea level

Scale 1:12,250,000

Km 0 25 50 100 150 200 250 300

Miles 0 25 50 100 150 200 250 300

projection: Lambert Azimuthal Equal Area

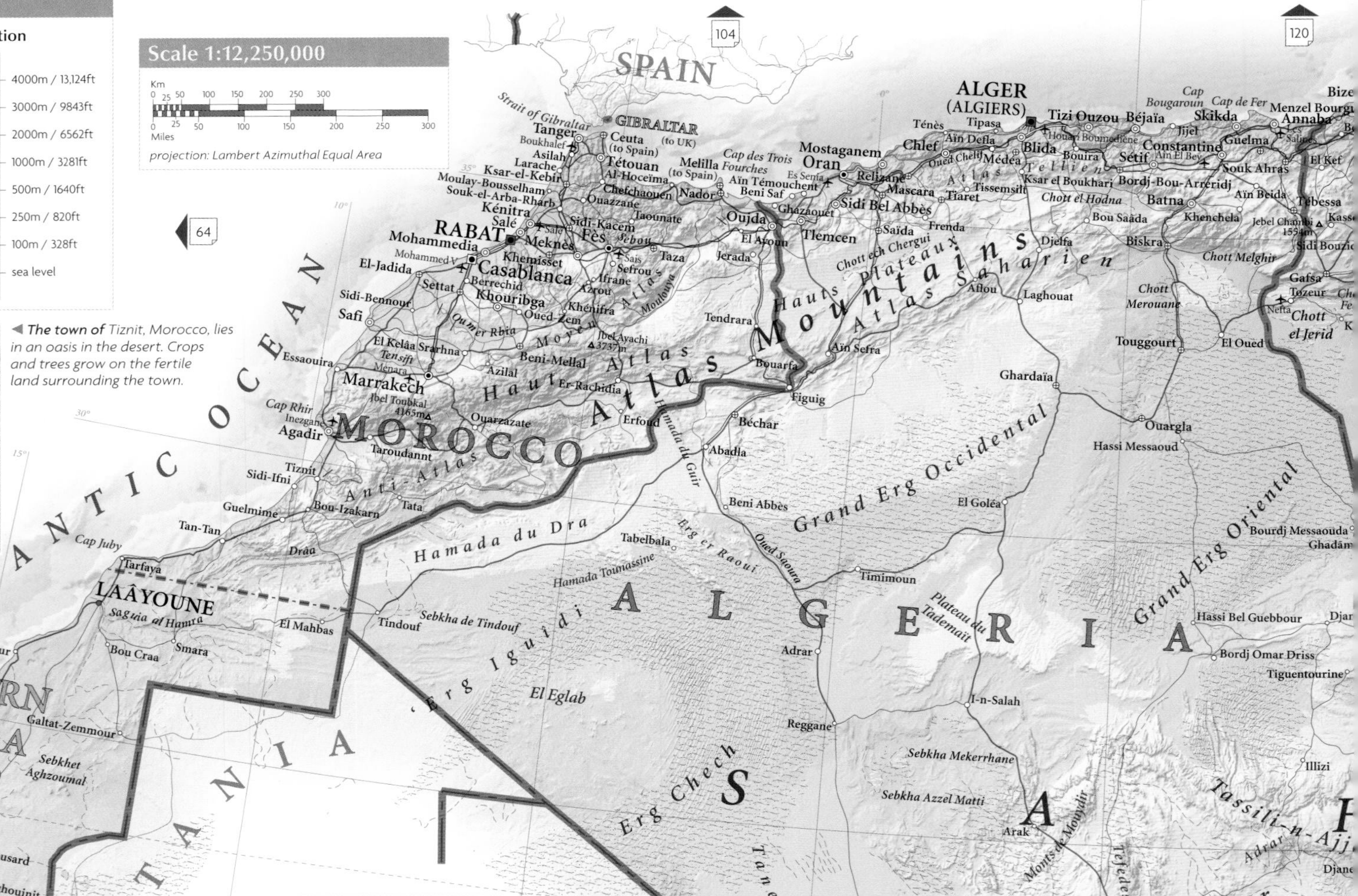

SPAIN
GIBRALTAR (to UK)
Strait of Gibraltar
Tanger
Ceuta (to Spain)
Tétouan
Melilla (to Spain)
Al-Hoceima
Nador
Larache
Ksar-el-Kebir
Chefchaouen
Ouazzane
Souk-el-Arba-Rharb
Kénitra
Salé
RABAT
Meknès
Fès
Mohammedia
Casablanca
Khemisset
El-Jadida
Settat
Berrechid
Khouribga
Sidi-Bennour
Safi
Essaouira
Marrakech
Jbel Toubkal 4165m
Agadir
Taroudannt
Tiznit
Sidi-Ifni
Guelmime
Bou-Izakarn
Tata
Tan-Tan
Cap Juby
Tarfaya
LAÂYOUNE
Smara
Boujdour
Bou Craa
WESTERN SAHARA
(occupied by Morocco)
Ad Dakhla
Tropic of Cancer
Cap Barbas
Aousard
Bir-Gandouz
Techla
Lagouira
MOROCCO
ATLANTIC OCEAN
MAURITANIA
MALI
NIGER
ALGERIA
Haut Atlas
Anti-Atlas
Moyen Atlas
Atlas Mountains
Hamada du Dra
Erg Iguidi
Erg Chech
Tanezrouft
Grand Erg Occidental
Grand Erg Oriental
Hauts Plateaux
Atlas Saharien
Tell Atlas
ALGER (ALGIERS)
Oran
Mostaganem
Tlemcen
Sidi Bel Abbès
Oujda
Chlef
Blida
Médéa
Tizi Ouzou
Béjaïa
Skikda
Annaba
Constantine
Sétif
Batna
Biskra
Tébessa
Djelfa
Laghouat
Aflou
Bechar
Figuig
Abadla
Beni Abbès
Tabelbala
Timimoun
Adrar
Reggane
El Goléa
Ghardaïa
Ouargla
Hassi Messaoud
Touggourt
El Oued
Tindouf
Sebkha de Tindouf
El Eglab
I-n-Salah
Tamanrasset
Ahaggar
Tahat 3003m
Atakor
Silet
Tassili-n-Ajjer
Illizi
Djanet
Bordj Omar Driss
Hassi Bel Guebbour
Bourdj Messaouda
Ghadâmis
I-n-Guezzam
Tassili ta-n-Ahaggar
Plateau du Tademaït
Chott Melghir
Chott el Jerid

◀ ***The town of*** *Tiznit, Morocco, lies in an oasis in the desert. Crops and trees grow on the fertile land surrounding the town.*

▶ ***The Grand Erg Occidental*** *is one of Algeria's great Saharan sand seas. Wind force and direction determines the nature of landforms such as the linear or seif dunes in the foreground.*

104 120 64 76 76

Using the land & sea

Sheltered valleys in the Atlas Mountains, the Nile Valley and Delta, and the Mediterranean coast are the main sources of good farming land. A wide variety of valuable crops including cereals, rice, and cotton, and woods such as cedar and cork, are grown. Typical Mediterranean crops such as olives, figs, dates, and citrus fruits also thrive in these areas. The Nile Valley is particularly fertile, and most of Egypt's population lives close to the river. Elsewhere, irrigation is essential to improve crop yields on the desert margins.

Land use and agricultural distribution

- goats
- sheep
- cereals
- citrus fruits
- cork
- cotton
- dates
- fishing
- olives
- vineyards
- capital cities
- major towns
- pasture
- cropland
- forest
- desert

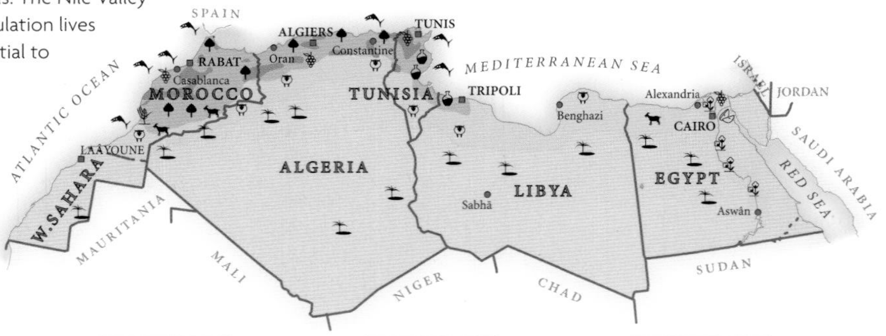

SPAIN
ALGIERS
Oran
Constantine
TUNIS
RABAT
Casablanca
MOROCCO
TUNISIA
TRIPOLI
MEDITERRANEAN SEA
ATLANTIC OCEAN
LAÂYOUNE
W. SAHARA
ALGERIA
Benghazi
Sabhā
LIBYA
Alexandria
CAIRO
EGYPT
Aswān
ISRAEL
JORDAN
SAUDI ARABIA
RED SEA
MAURITANIA
MALI
NIGER
CHAD
SUDAN

The urban/rural population divide

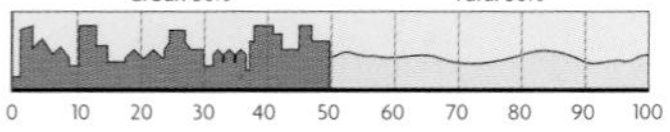

urban 50%
rural 50%
0 10 20 30 40 50 60 70 80 90 100

Population density	Total land area
65 people per sq mile (25 people per sq km)	2,215,020 sq miles (5,738,394 sq km)

▲ ***Many North African*** *nomads, such as the Bedouin, maintain a traditional pastoral lifestyle on the desert fringes, moving their herds of sheep, goats, and camels from place to place – crossing country borders in order to find sufficient grazing land.*

A B C D E F G H I J K L M

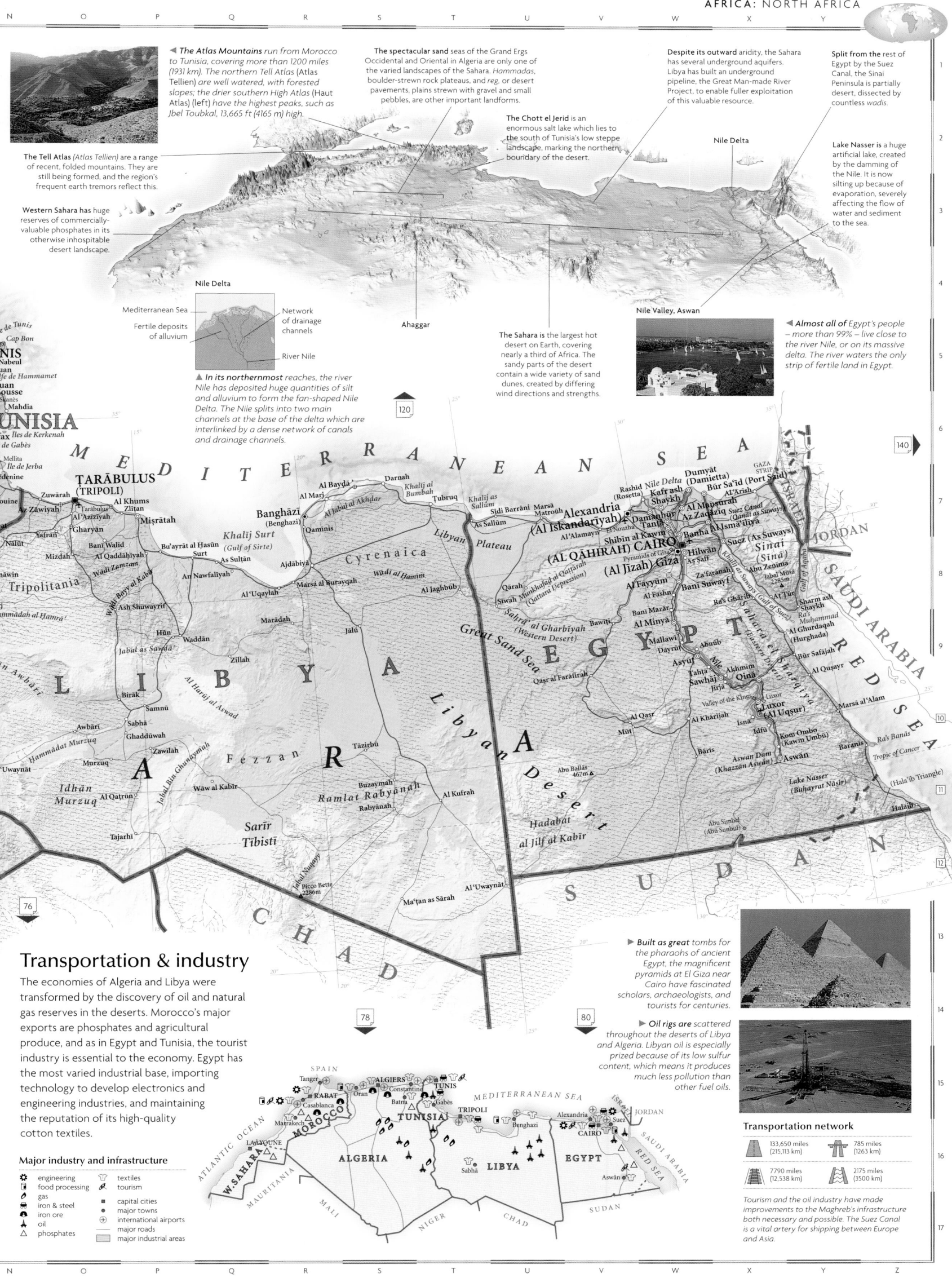

◀ *The Atlas Mountains run from Morocco to Tunisia, covering more than 1200 miles (1931 km). The northern Tell Atlas* (Atlas Tellien) *are well watered, with forested slopes; the drier southern High Atlas* (Haut Atlas) (left) *have the highest peaks, such as Jbel Toubkal, 13,665 ft (4165 m) high.*

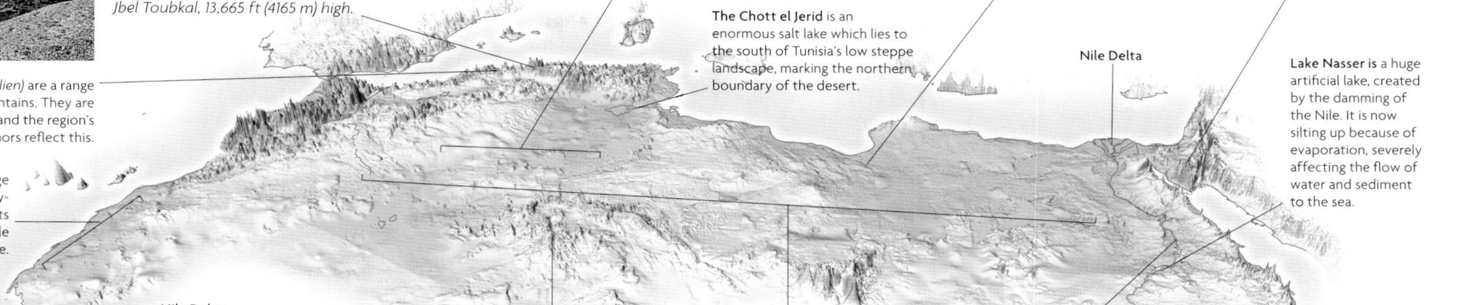

The spectacular sand seas of the Grand Ergs Occidental and Oriental in Algeria are only one of the varied landscapes of the Sahara. *Hammadas*, boulder-strewn rock plateaus, and *reg*, or desert pavements, plains strewn with gravel and small pebbles, are other important landforms.

Despite its outward aridity, the Sahara has several underground aquifers. Libya has built an underground pipeline, the Great Man-made River Project, to enable fuller exploitation of this valuable resource.

Split from the rest of Egypt by the Suez Canal, the Sinai Peninsula is partially desert, dissected by countless *wadis.*

The Chott el Jerid is an enormous salt lake which lies to the south of Tunisia's low steppe landscape, marking the northern boundary of the desert.

The Tell Atlas (*Atlas Tellien*) are a range of recent, folded mountains. They are still being formed, and the region's frequent earth tremors reflect this.

Nile Delta

Lake Nasser is a huge artificial lake, created by the damming of the Nile. It is now silting up because of evaporation, severely affecting the flow of water and sediment to the sea.

Western Sahara has huge reserves of commercially-valuable phosphates in its otherwise inhospitable desert landscape.

Ahaggar

The Sahara is the largest hot desert on Earth, covering nearly a third of Africa. The sandy parts of the desert contain a wide variety of sand dunes, created by differing wind directions and strengths.

Nile Valley, Aswan

Nile Delta

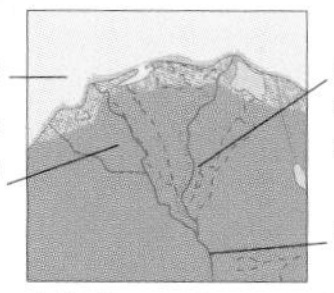

Mediterranean Sea
Fertile deposits of alluvium
Network of drainage channels
River Nile

▲ *In its northernmost reaches, the river Nile has deposited huge quantities of silt and alluvium to form the fan-shaped Nile Delta. The Nile splits into two main channels at the base of the delta which are interlinked by a dense network of canals and drainage channels.*

◀ *Almost all of Egypt's people – more than 99% – live close to the river Nile, or on its massive delta. The river waters the only strip of fertile land in Egypt.*

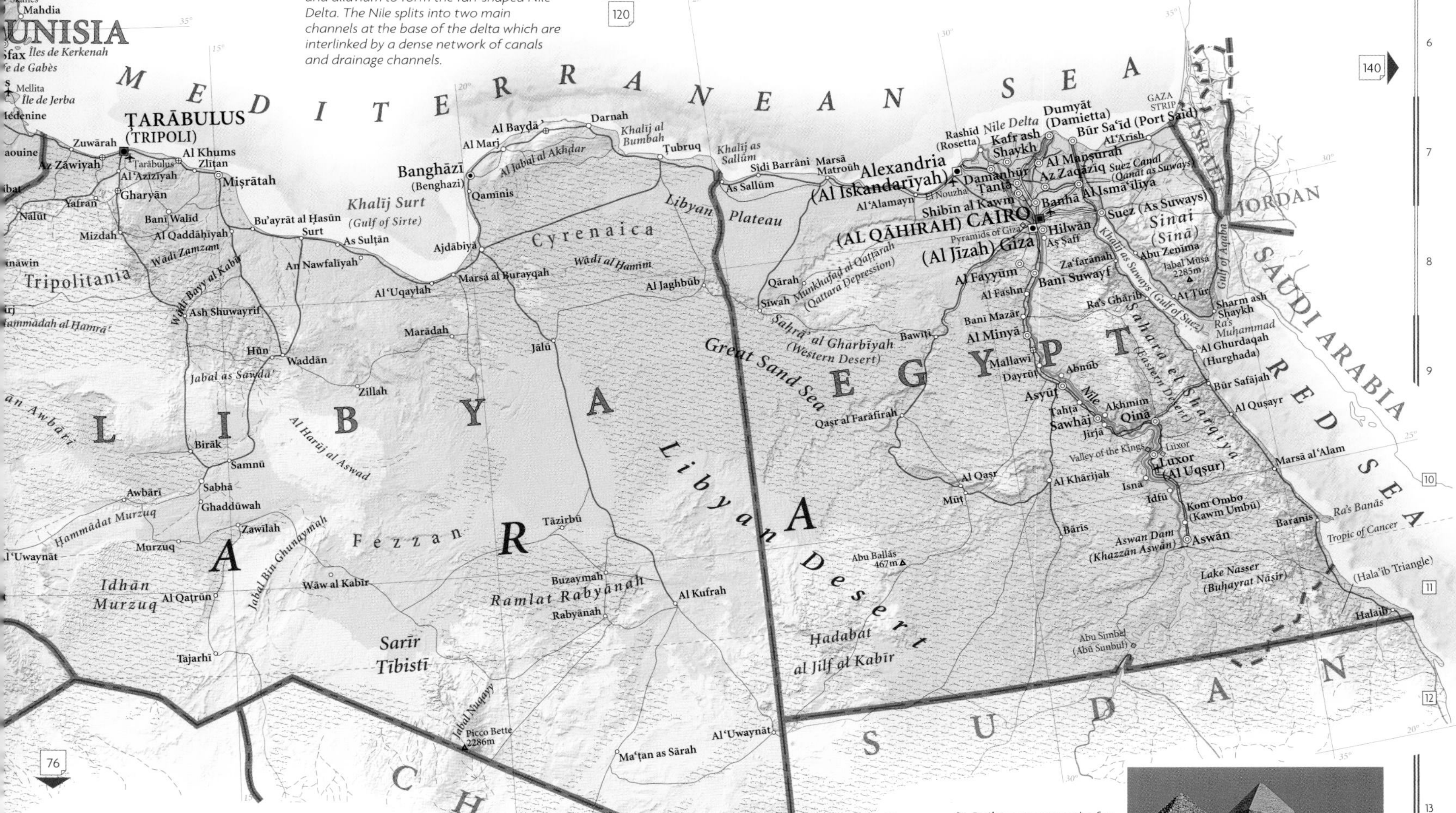

120
140
76
78
80
MEDITERRANEAN SEA
TUNISIA
Golfe de Tunis
Cap Bon
Nabeul
Golfe de Hammamet
Sousse
Mahdia
Sfax
Îles de Kerkenah
Golfe de Gabès
Île de Jerba
Médenine
ṬARĀBULUS (TRIPOLI)
Zuwārah
Az Zāwiyah
Al Khums
Zlīṭan
Miṣrātah
Al 'Azīzīyah
Gharyān
Yafran
Nālūt
Mizdah
Banī Walīd
Al Qaddāḥīyah
Tripolitania
Wādī Zamzam
Wādī Bayy al Kabīr
Ash Shuwayrif
Ḥammādat al Ḥamrā'
Bu'ayrāt al Ḥasūn
Surt
As Sulṭān
Khalīj Surt (Gulf of Sirte)
An Nawfalīyah
Al 'Uqaylah
Banghāzī (Benghazi)
Qamīnis
Ajdābiyā
Al Bayḍā'
Al Marj
Darnah
Khalīj al Bumbah
Tubruq
Jabal al Akhḍar
Cyrenaica
Wādī al Ḥamīm
Marsá al Burayqah
Al Jaghbūb
Marādah
Jālū
Hūn
Waddān
Jabal as Sawdā'
Zillah
LIBYA
Al Harūj al Aswad
Birāk
Samnū
Sabhā
Awbārī
Ghaddūwah
Ḥammādat Murzuq
Zawīlah
Murzuq
Fezzan
Tāzirbū
Wāw al Kabīr
Jabal Bin Ghunaymah
Idhān Murzuq
Al Qaṭrūn
Tajarhī
Buzaymah
Ramlat Rabyānah
Rabyānah
Al Kufrah
Sarīr Tibistī
Jabal Nuqay
Picco Bette 2286m
Ma'ṭan as Sārah
Al 'Uwaynāt
Libyan Desert
Libyan Plateau
Khalīj as Sallūm
As Sallūm
Sīdī Barrānī
Marsá Maṭroūḥ
Alexandria (Al Iskandarīyah)
Al 'Alamayn
El Nouzha
Rashīd (Rosetta)
Nile Delta
Dumyāṭ (Damietta)
Būr Sa'īd (Port Said)
Kafr ash Shaykh
Damanhūr
Ṭanṭā
Al Manṣūrah
Az Zaqāzīq
Al 'Arīsh
Suez Canal (Qanāt as Suways)
Al Ismā'īlīya
Banhā
Shibīn al Kawm
CAIRO (AL QĀHIRAH)
Pyramids of Giza
(Al Jīzah) Giza
Ḥilwān
Aṣ Ṣaff
Suez (As Suways)
Sinai (Sīnā')
Abu Zenīma
Jabal Mūsá 2285m
At Ṭūr
Gulf of Aqaba
Sharm ash Shaykh
Ra's Muḥammad
GAZA STRIP
ISRAEL
JORDAN
SAUDI ARABIA
Qārah
Sīwah
Munkhafaḍ al Qaṭṭārah (Qattara Depression)
Al Fayyūm
Al Fashn
Banī Suwayf
Za'farānah
Khalīj as Suways (Gulf of Suez)
Ra's Ghārib
Bani Mazār
Al Minyā
Bawīṭī
Ṣaḥrā' al Gharbīyah (Western Desert)
Great Sand Sea
EGYPT
Mallawī
Dayrūṭ
Abnūb
Asyūṭ
Nile
Ṭahṭā
Sawhāj
Jirjā
Akhmīm
Qinā
Ṣaḥrā' esh Sharqīya (Eastern Desert)
Al Ghurdaqah (Hurghada)
Būr Safājah
Al Quṣayr
Qaṣr al Farāfirah
Valley of the Kings
Luxor (Al Uqṣur)
Al Kharijah
Al Qaṣr
Mūṭ
Isnā
Idfū
Kom Ombo (Kawm Umbū)
Marsā al 'Alam
Bārīs
Aswan Dam (Khazzān Aswān)
Aswān
Baranīs
Ra's Banās
Tropic of Cancer
RED SEA
Abu Ballās 467m
Lake Nasser (Buḥayrat Nāṣir)
(Halā'ib Triangle)
Ḥalā'ib
Hadabat al Jilf al Kabīr
Abu Simbel (Abū Sunbul)
SUDAN
CHAD

▶ *Built as great tombs for the pharaohs of ancient Egypt, the magnificent pyramids at El Giza near Cairo have fascinated scholars, archaeologists, and tourists for centuries.*

▶ *Oil rigs are scattered throughout the deserts of Libya and Algeria. Libyan oil is especially prized because of its low sulfur content, which means it produces much less pollution than other fuel oils.*

Transportation & industry

The economies of Algeria and Libya were transformed by the discovery of oil and natural gas reserves in the deserts. Morocco's major exports are phosphates and agricultural produce, and as in Egypt and Tunisia, the tourist industry is essential to the economy. Egypt has the most varied industrial base, importing technology to develop electronics and engineering industries, and maintaining the reputation of its high-quality cotton textiles.

Major industry and infrastructure

engineering	textiles
food processing	tourism
gas	capital cities
iron & steel	major towns
iron ore	international airports
oil	major roads
phosphates	major industrial areas

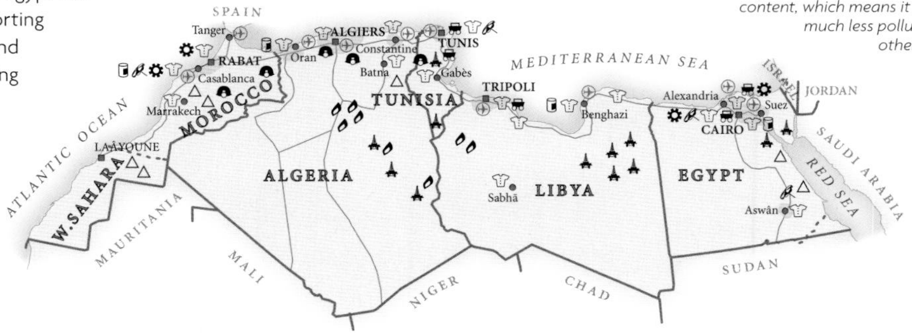

SPAIN
Tanger
RABAT
Casablanca
Marrakech
MOROCCO
ATLANTIC OCEAN
LAAYOUNE
W. SAHARA
MAURITANIA
Oran
ALGIERS
Constantine
Batna
TUNIS
Gabès
TUNISIA
ALGERIA
MALI
NIGER
MEDITERRANEAN SEA
TRIPOLI
Benghazi
Sabhā
LIBYA
CHAD
Alexandria
CAIRO
Suez
ISRAEL
JORDAN
EGYPT
Aswān
RED SEA
SAUDI ARABIA
SUDAN

Transportation network

133,650 miles (215,113 km)	785 miles (1263 km)
7790 miles (12,538 km)	2175 miles (3500 km)

Tourism and the oil industry have made improvements to the Maghreb's infrastructure both necessary and possible. The Suez Canal is a vital artery for shipping between Europe and Asia.

West Africa

BENIN, BURKINA, CAPE VERDE, GAMBIA, GHANA, GUINEA, GUINEA-BISSAU, IVORY COAST, LIBERIA, MALI, MAURITANIA, NIGER, NIGERIA, SENEGAL, SIERRA LEONE, TOGO

▶ *The dry scrub of the Sahel is only suitable for grazing herd animals like these cattle in Mali.*

West Africa is an immensely diverse region, encompassing the desert landscapes and mainly Muslim populations of the southern Saharan countries, and the tropical rain forests of the more humid south, with a great variety of local languages and cultures. The rich natural resources and accessibility of the area were quickly exploited by Europeans; most of the Africans taken by slave traders came from this region, causing serious depopulation. The very different influences of West Africa's leading colonial powers, Britain and France, remain today, reflected in the languages and institutions of the countries they once governed.

Scale 1:10,000,000

Km 0 25 50 100 150 200 250

Miles 0 25 50 100 150 200 250

projection: Lambert Azimuthal Equal Area

Transportation & industry

Abundant natural resources including oil and metallic minerals are found in much of West Africa, although investment is required for their further exploitation. Nigeria experienced an oil boom during the 1970s but subsequent growth has been sporadic. Most industry in other countries has a primary basis, including mining, logging, and food processing.

Transportation network

- 62,154 miles (100,038 km)
- 1037 miles (1669 km)
- 6752 miles (10,867 km)
- 10,192 miles (16,405 km)

The road and rail systems are most developed near the coasts. Some of the landlocked countries remain disadvantaged by the difficulty of access to ports, and their poor road networks.

MOROCCO
W. SAHARA
ALGERIA
LIBYA
MAURITANIA
NOUAKCHOTT
MALI
NIGER
CHAD
DAKAR
SENEGAL
BANJUL
GAMBIA
BISSAU
GUINEA-BISSAU
GUINEA
CONAKRY
BAMAKO
NIAMEY
BURKINA
OUAGADOUGOU
NIGERIA
Kano
ABUJA
SIERRA LEONE
FREETOWN
IVORY COAST
GHANA
TOGO
BENIN
Ibadan
Lagos
ACCRA
MONROVIA
LIBERIA
YAMOUSSOUKRO
LOMÉ
PORTO-NOVO
Port Harcourt
CAMEROON
ATLANTIC OCEAN

Major industry and infrastructure

- chemicals
- cotton spinning
- food processing
- mining
- oil
- palm oil processing
- peanut processing
- textiles
- vehicle manufacture
- capital cities
- major towns
- international airports
- major roads
- major industrial areas

Map key

Population

- Above 5 million
- 1 million to 5 million
- 500,000 to 1 million
- 100,000 to 500,000
- 50,000 to 100,000
- 10,000 to 50,000
- below 10,000

Elevation

- 2000m / 6562ft
- 1000m / 3281ft
- 500m / 1640ft
- 250m / 820ft
- 100m / 328ft
- sea level

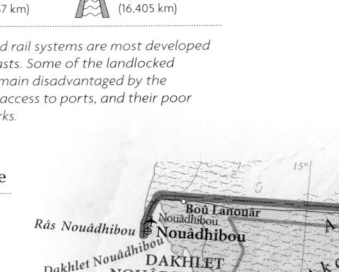

CAPE VERDE
Santo Antão
Pombas
Ilhas de Barlavento
Mindelo
São Vicente
Ribeira Brava
São Nicolau
Pedra Lume
Sal
Boa Vista
João Barrosa
ATLANTIC OCEAN
Tarrafal
Maio
Fogo
São Filipe
Santiago
PRAIA
Ilhas de Sotavento
(same scale as main map)

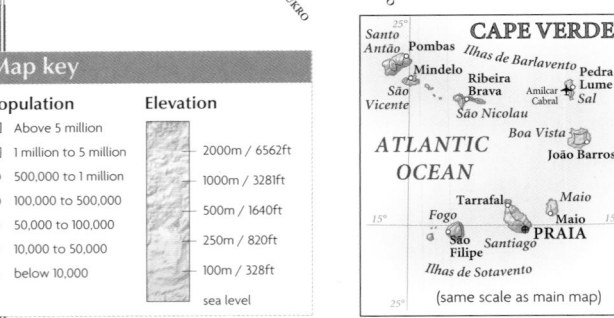

◀ *The southern regions of West Africa still contain great swathes of tropical rainforest, including some of the world's most prized hardwood trees, such as mahogany and iroko.*

Using the land & sea

The humid southern regions are most suitable for cultivation; in these areas, cash crops such as coffee, cotton, cocoa, and rubber are grown in large quantities. Peanuts are grown throughout West Africa. In the north, advancing desertification has made the Sahel increasingly uncultivable, and pastoral farming is more common. Great herds of sheep, cattle, and goats are grazed on the savannah grasses. Fishing is important in coastal and delta areas.

▲ *The Gambia, mainland Africa's smallest country, produces great quantities of peanuts. Winnowing is used to separate the nuts from their stalks.*

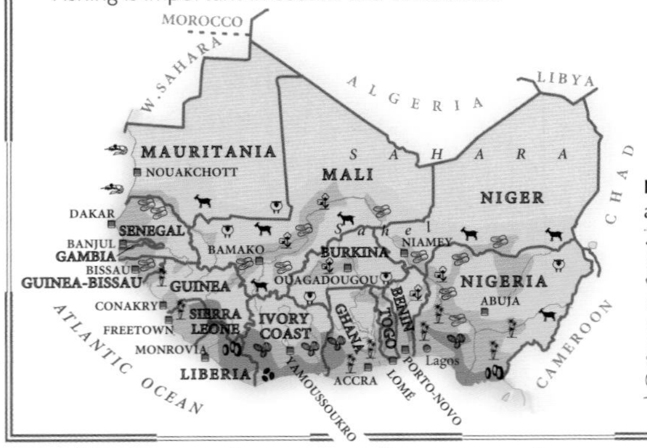
MOROCCO
W. SAHARA
ALGERIA
LIBYA
SAHARA
MAURITANIA
NOUAKCHOTT
MALI
NIGER
CHAD
DAKAR
SENEGAL
BANJUL
GAMBIA
BISSAU
GUINEA-BISSAU
GUINEA
BAMAKO
NIAMEY
BURKINA
OUAGADOUGOU
NIGERIA
ABUJA
CONAKRY
SIERRA LEONE
FREETOWN
IVORY COAST
GHANA
TOGO
BENIN
MONROVIA
LIBERIA
ACCRA
LOMÉ
PORTO-NOVO
Lagos
YAMOUSSOUKRO
CAMEROON
ATLANTIC OCEAN

Land use and agricultural distribution

- goats
- sheep
- cocoa
- coffee
- cotton
- oil palms
- peanuts
- rubber
- shellfish
- capital cities
- major towns
- pasture
- cropland
- forest
- desert

The urban/rural population divide

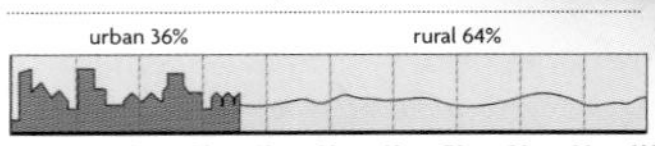
urban 36%
rural 64%
0
10
20
30
40
50
60
70
80
90
100

Population density	Total land area
104 people per sq mile (40 people per sq km)	2,337,137 sq miles (6,054,760 sq km)

WESTERN SAHARA (occupied by Morocco)
TIRIS ZEMMOUR
Tropic of Cancer
MAURITANIA
NOUAKCHOTT
ADRAR
INCHIRI
TAGANT
TRARZA
BRAKNA
ASSABA
GORGOL
HODH EL GHARBI
DAKHLET NOUÂDHIBOU
Nouâdhibou
ATLANTIC OCEAN
SENEGAL
DAKAR
GAMBIA
BANJUL
GUINEA-BISSAU
BISSAU
GUINEA
CONAKRY
SIERRA LEONE
FREETOWN
LIBERIA
MONROVIA
BAMAKO
KAYES
KOULIKORO
SIKASSO
Fouta Djallon
Cap Verga
Arquipélago dos Bijagós
Sherbro Island
Cape Palmas

▲ *Inselbergs, found across the Sahel, are isolated hills, or outcrops, formed where the surrounding plain has eroded away, leaving only the more resistant remnants of the original plateau.*

The dry grasslands of the Sahel border the southern reaches of the Sahara. Overgrazing, drought, and the cutting down of trees for firewood, means that much of the Sahel is turning irrevocably to desert.

▶ ***The Niger river*** *flows for 2600 miles (4181 km) from Fouta Djallon, on the plateau of Guinea, via southern Mali, where it supports rich fish stocks, on through the desert, and finally through Nigeria to the Gulf of Guinea.*

The landscape

There are two major topographical areas in West Africa: the northern deserts are part of the Saharan region which stretches across the whole continent; the grasslands of the Sahel and the southern Guinea coast are part of Africa's central plateau. The landscape is generally low, rarely rising above 1500 ft (457 m) and consists mainly of plains, broken by an occasional high plateau or mountain range.

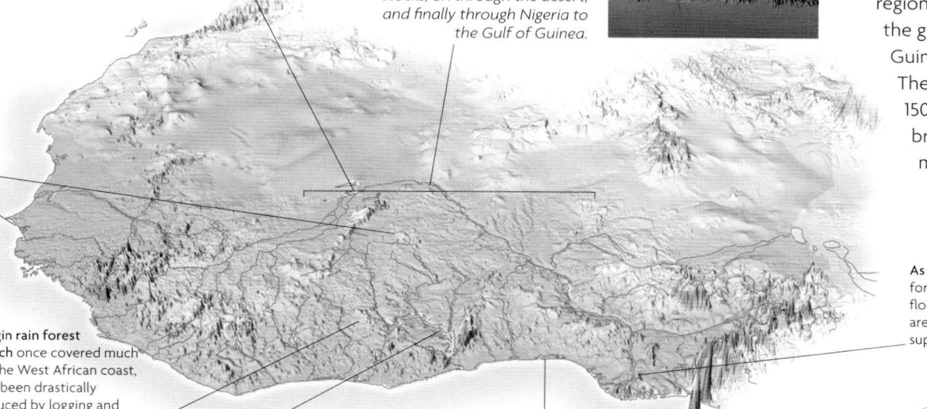

Two types of coastline characterize West Africa. Swampy, muddy coasts, colonized by mangroves occur on river deltas and where ocean currents are weak, like the coast of Senegal. Sandy beaches, with barrier ridges and lagoons, form where currents are stronger.

Virgin rain forest which once covered much of the West African coast, has been drastically reduced by logging and agricultural land clearance.

Lake Volta is an artificial lake, created by the damming of the Volta river. It links the drier northern areas with the coast and is intended to provide fresh water for drinking, fisheries, and irrigation.

As it nears the Gulf of Guinea, the Niger forks into many strands. When the river floods, alluvium is deposited over a wide area. This creates fertile soils, able to support both crops and livestock.

Barrier beaches

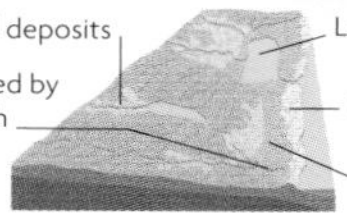

Fluvial deposits
Lagoon
River dammed by barrier beach
Barrier beach
Estuarine deposits

▲ *Along much of the West African coast, barrier beaches have built up and dammed river mouths, forming fluvial and estuarine plains.*

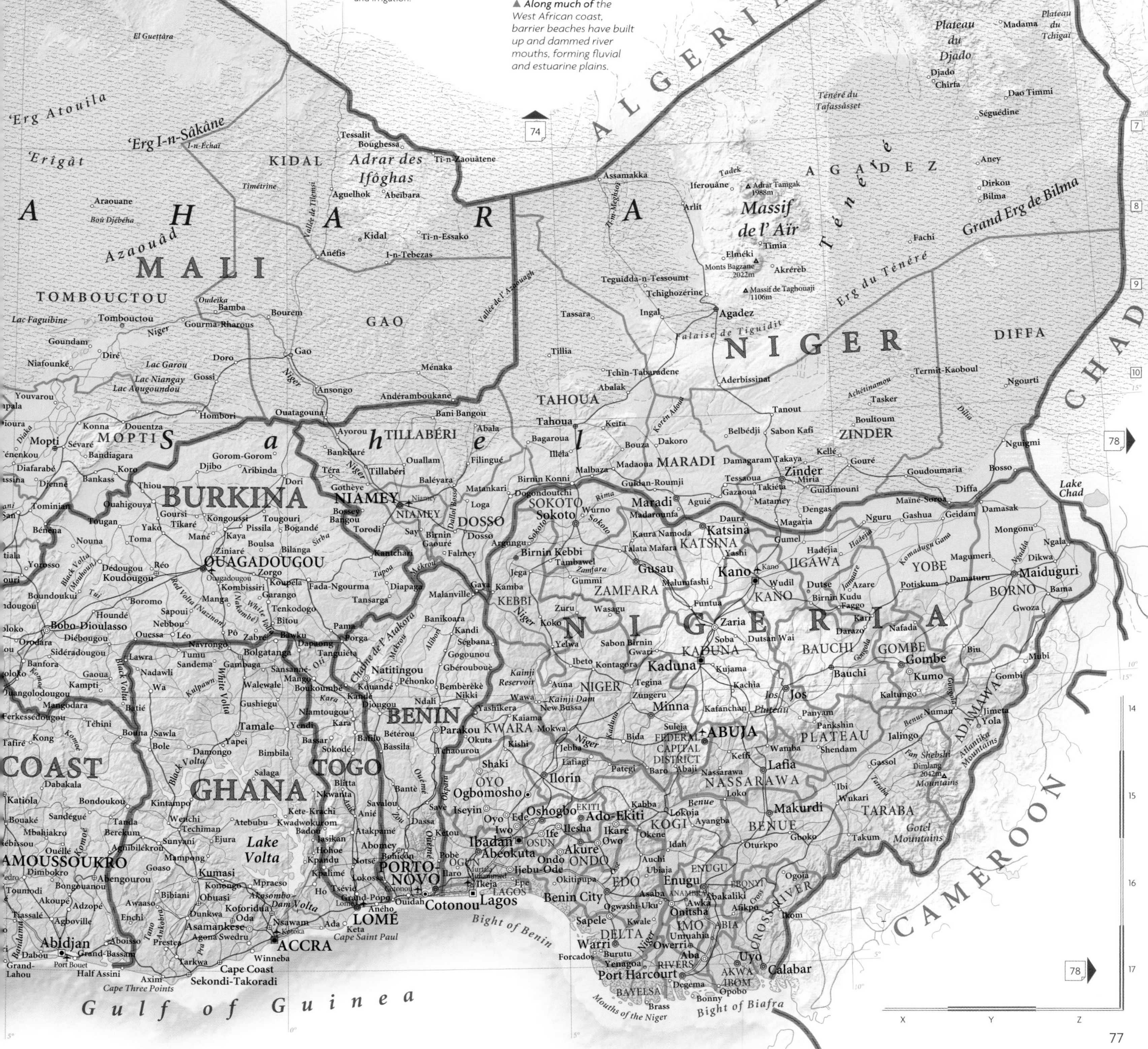

N O P Q R S T U V W X Y
ALGERIA
LIBYA
MALI
NIGER
BURKINA
NIGERIA
BENIN
TOGO
GHANA
COAST
CHAD
CAMEROON
SAHARA
Sahel
Gulf of Guinea
Bight of Benin
Bight of Biafra
Mouths of the Niger
Lake Chad
Lake Volta
Massif de l' Aïr
Ténéré
Grand Erg de Bilma
Erg du Ténéré
Adrar des Ifôghas
Plateau du Djado
Plateau du Manguéni
Tropic of Cancer
AGADEZ
Agadez
TOMBOUCTOU
Tombouctou
KIDAL
Kidal
GAO
Gao
TAHOUA
Tahoua
TILLABÉRI
NIAMEY
Niamey
DOSSO
MARADI
Maradi
ZINDER
Zinder
DIFFA
OUAGADOUGOU
ABUJA
Kano
Kaduna
Jos
Ibadan
Lagos
PORTO-NOVO
Cotonou
LOMÉ
ACCRA
Abidjan
Tamale
Kumasi
Maiduguri
Sokoto
Ilorin
Port Harcourt
Calabar
Benin City
Enugu
Makurdi
74
78

Central Africa

CAMEROON, CENTRAL AFRICAN REPUBLIC, CHAD, CONGO, DEM. REP. CONGO, EQUATORIAL GUINEA, GABON, SAO TOME & PRINCIPE

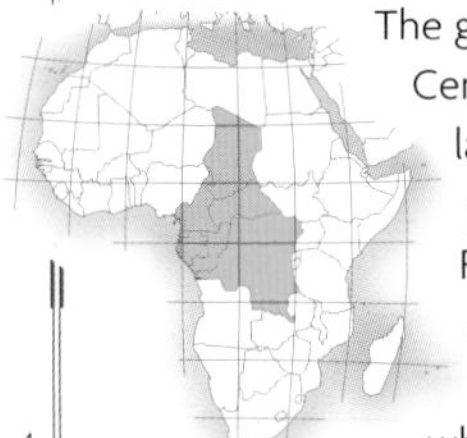

The great rain forest basin of the Congo river embraces most of remote Central Africa. The interior was largely unknown to Europeans until late in the 19th century, when its tribal kingdoms were split – principally between France and Belgium – with Sao Tome and Principe the lone Portuguese territory, and Equatorial Guinea controlled by Spain. Open democracy and regional economic integration are important goals for these nations – several of which have only recently emerged from restrictive regimes – and investment is needed to improve transportation infrastructures. Many of the small, but fast-growing and increasingly urban population, speak French, the regional *lingua franca*, along with several hundred Pygmy, Bantu, and Sudanic dialects.

Transportation & industry

Large reserves of valuable minerals are found in Central Africa: copper, cobalt, zinc, and diamonds are mined in Dem. Rep. Congo and manganese in Gabon. Congo, Cameroon, Gabon, and Equatorial Guinea have oil deposits and oil has also been recently discovered in Chad. Goods such as palm oil and rubber are processed for export.

▲ *The ancient rocks* of Dem. Rep. Congo hold immense and varied mineral reserves. This open pit copper mine is at Kolwezi in the far south.

LIBYA
NIGER
SUDAN
SOUTH SUDAN
CHAD
NDJAMENA
NIGERIA
CAMEROON
CENTRAL AFRICAN REPUBLIC
BANGUI
YAOUNDE
Douala
MALABO
EQ. GUINEA
SAO TOME & PRINCIPE
LIBREVILLE
Port-Gentil
GABON
CONGO
BRAZZAVILLE
KINSHASA
DEM. REP. CONGO
Kisangani
Bukavu
Kananga
Kolwezi
Lubumbashi
UGANDA
RWANDA
BURUNDI
TANZANIA
ZAMBIA
ANGOLA
ANGOLA (CABINDA)
ATLANTIC OCEAN

Major industry and infrastructure

- brewing
- chemicals
- cobalt
- copper
- diamonds
- food processing
- manganese
- oil
- palm oil processing
- textiles
- tin
- capital cities
- major towns
- international airports
- major roads
- major industrial areas

Transportation network

102,747 miles (165,774 km)	37 miles (60 km)
3985 miles (6414 km)	14,110 miles (22,710 km)

The Trans-Gabon railroad, which began operating in 1987, has opened up new sources of timber and manganese. Elsewhere, much investment is needed to update and improve road, rail, and water transportation.

76

The landscape

Lake Chad lies in a desert basin bounded by the volcanic Tibesti mountains in the north, plateaus in the east and, in the south, the broad watershed of the Congo basin. The vast circular depression of the Congo is isolated from the coastal plain by the granite Massif du Chaillu. To the northwest, the volcanoes and fold mountains of the Cameroon Ridge *(Dorsale Camerounaise)* extend as islands into the Gulf of Guinea. The high fold mountains fringing the east of the Congo Basin fall steeply to the lakes of the Great Rift Valley.

◀ *A plug of resistant lava, at the southwestern end of the Cameroon Ridge* (Dorsale Camerounaise), *is all that remains of an eroded volcano.*

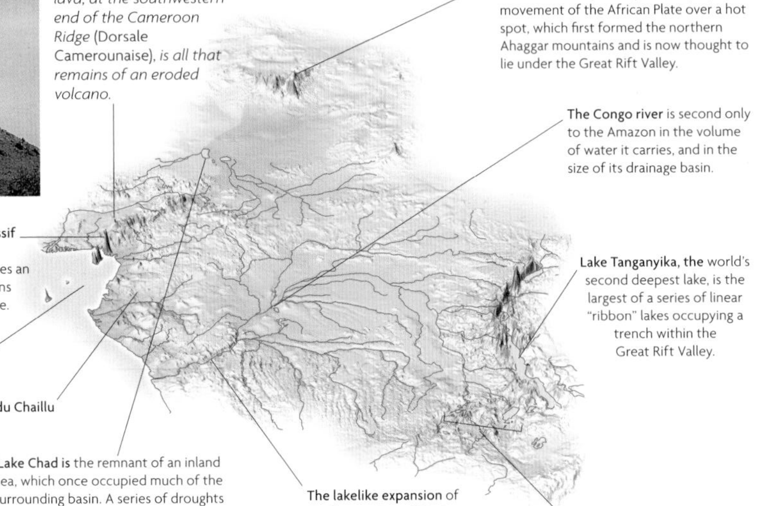

The volcanic massif of Cameroon Mountain occupies an area which remains volcanically active.

Gulf of Guinea

Massif du Chaillu

Lake Chad is the remnant of an inland sea, which once occupied much of the surrounding basin. A series of droughts since the 1970s has reduced the area of this shallow freshwater lake to about 1000 sq miles (2599 sq km).

The lakelike expansion of the Congo river at Stanley Pool is the lowest point of the interior basin, although the river still descends more than 1000 ft (300 m) to reach the sea.

Rich mineral deposits in the "Copper Belt" of Dem. Rep. Congo were formed under intense heat and pressure when the ancient African Shield was uplifted to form the region's mountains.

The Tibesti mountains are the highest in the Sahara. They were pushed up by the movement of the African Plate over a hot spot, which first formed the northern Ahaggar mountains and is now thought to lie under the Great Rift Valley.

The Congo river is second only to the Amazon in the volume of water it carries, and in the size of its drainage basin.

Lake Tanganyika, the world's second deepest lake, is the largest of a series of linear "ribbon" lakes occupying a trench within the Great Rift Valley.

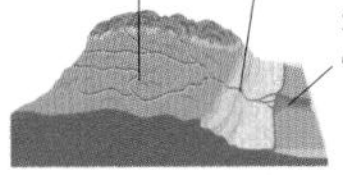
Broad, shallow basin
Waterfalls and cataracts
Submarine canyon

▲ *The Congo river flows sluggishly through the rain forest of the interior basin. Toward the coast, the river drops steeply in a series of waterfalls and cataracts. At this point, the erosional power of the river becomes so great that it has formed a deep submarine canyon offshore.*

▲ *Virgin tropical rain forest covers the Ruwenzori range on the borders of Dem. Rep. Congo and Uganda.*

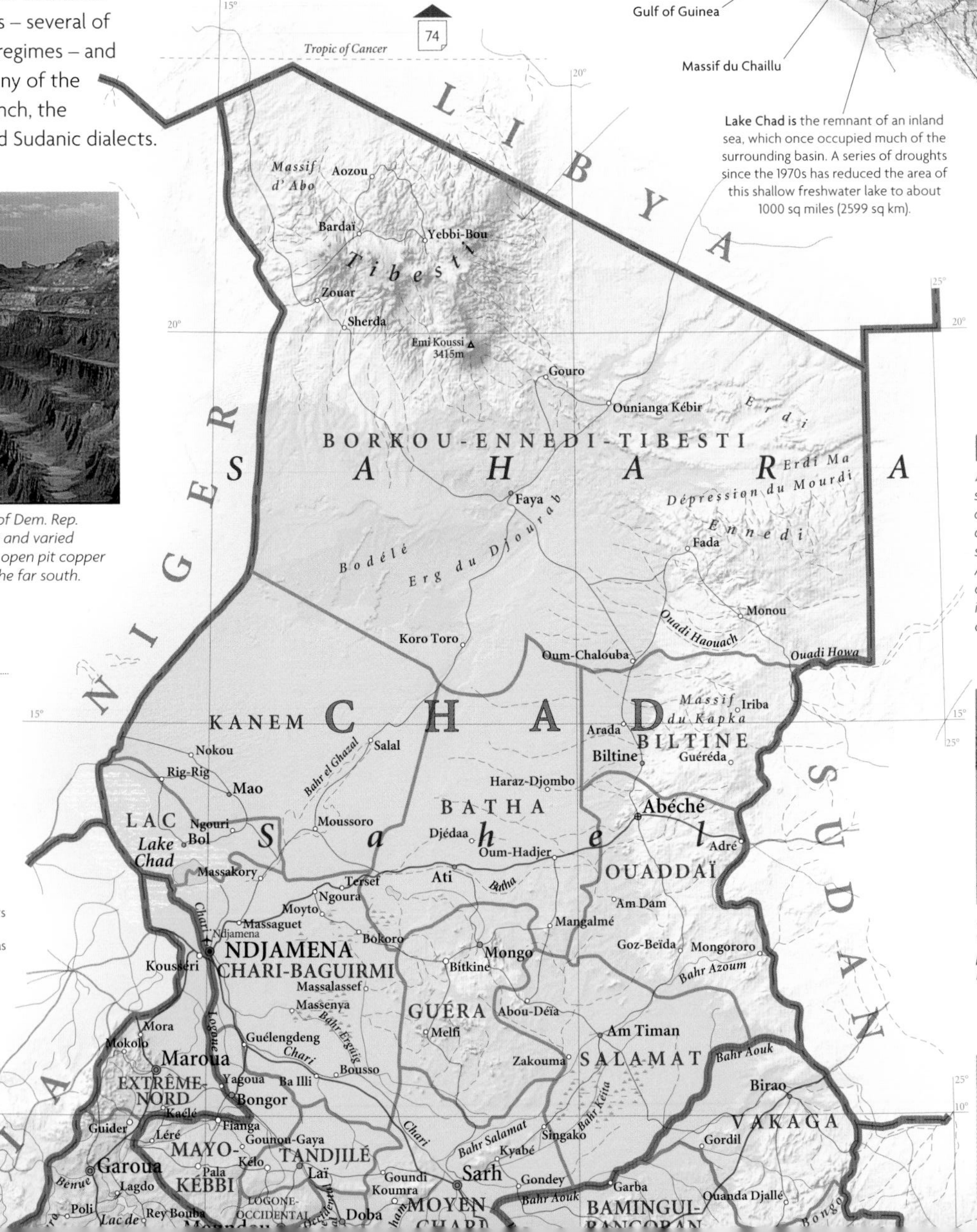
Tropic of Cancer
LIBYA
NIGER
SUDAN
CHAD
SAHARA
BORKOU-ENNEDI-TIBESTI
Tibesti
Massif d'Abo
Aozou
Bardaï
Yebbi-Bou
Zouar
Sherda
Emi Koussi 3415m
Gouro
Ounianga Kébir
Faya
Bodélé
Erg du Djourab
Erdi Ma
Dépression du Mourdi
Ennedi
Fada
Monou
Ouadi Haouach
Ouadi Howa
Oum-Chalouba
Koro Toro
KANEM
Salal
Nokou
Rig-Rig
Mao
LAC
Lake Chad
Ngouri
Bol
Massakory
Moussoro
Sahel
BATHA
Haraz-Djombo
Djédaa
Oum-Hadjer
Ati
Massif du Kapka
Iriba
BILTINE
Arada
Biltine
Guéréda
Abéché
Adré
OUADDAÏ
Am Dam
Mangalmé
Goz-Beïda
Mongororo
Bahr Azoum
Mongo
Bitkine
GUÉRA
Abou-Deïa
Melfi
Am Timan
SALAMAT
Zakouma
Bahr Aouk
Birao
VAKAGA
Gordil
Ouanda Djallé
NDJAMENA
CHARI-BAGUIRMI
Massaguet
Moyto
Ngoura
Bokoro
Tersef
Massalassef
Massenya
Kousséri
Mora
Mokolo
Maroua
EXTRÊME-NORD
Yagoua
Ba Illi
Bongor
Guélengdeng
Bousso
Chari
Fianga
Gounou-Gaya
MAYO-KEBBI
TANDJILÉ
Kélo
Laï
Guider
Léré
Garoua
Pala
Lagdo
Poli
Rey Bouba
Bénoué
LOGONE-OCCIDENTAL
Doba
Goundi
Koumra
Sarh
MOYEN-CHARI
Kyabé
Singako
Bahr Salamat
Gondey
Garba
BAMINGUI-BANGORAN
74

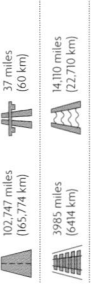

▲ *The vast sandflats surrounding Lake Chad were once covered by water. Changing climatic patterns caused the lake to shrink, and desert now covers much of its previous area.*

Scale 1:10,500,000

Km 0 25 50 100 150 200 250

Miles 0 25 50 100 150 200 250

projection: Lambert Azimuthal Equal Area

Map key

Population

- 1 million to 5 million
- 500,000 to 1 million
- 100,000 to 500,000
- 50,000 to 100,000
- 10,000 to 50,000
- below 10,000

Elevation

- 4000m / 13,124ft
- 3000m / 9843ft
- 2000m / 6562ft
- 1000m / 3281ft
- 500m / 1640ft
- 250m / 820ft
- 100m / 328ft
- sea level

▲ ***The great Congo** river forms part of the border between Congo and Dem. Rep. Congo. The river is fast-flowing, and a series of falls and rapids means that it is only partly navigable.*

CENTRAL AFRICAN REPUBLIC
CAMEROON
EQUATORIAL GUINEA
SAO TOME & PRINCIPE
GABON
CONGO
DEM. REP. CONGO
SOUTH SUDAN
UGANDA
RWANDA
BURUNDI
TANZANIA
ZAMBIA
ANGOLA
ANGOLA (CABINDA)
ATLANTIC OCEAN
Gulf of Guinea
Bight of Biafra
BANGUI
YAOUNDÉ
MALABO
LIBREVILLE
SÃO TOMÉ
BRAZZAVILLE
KINSHASA
Lake Tanganyika
Congo Basin

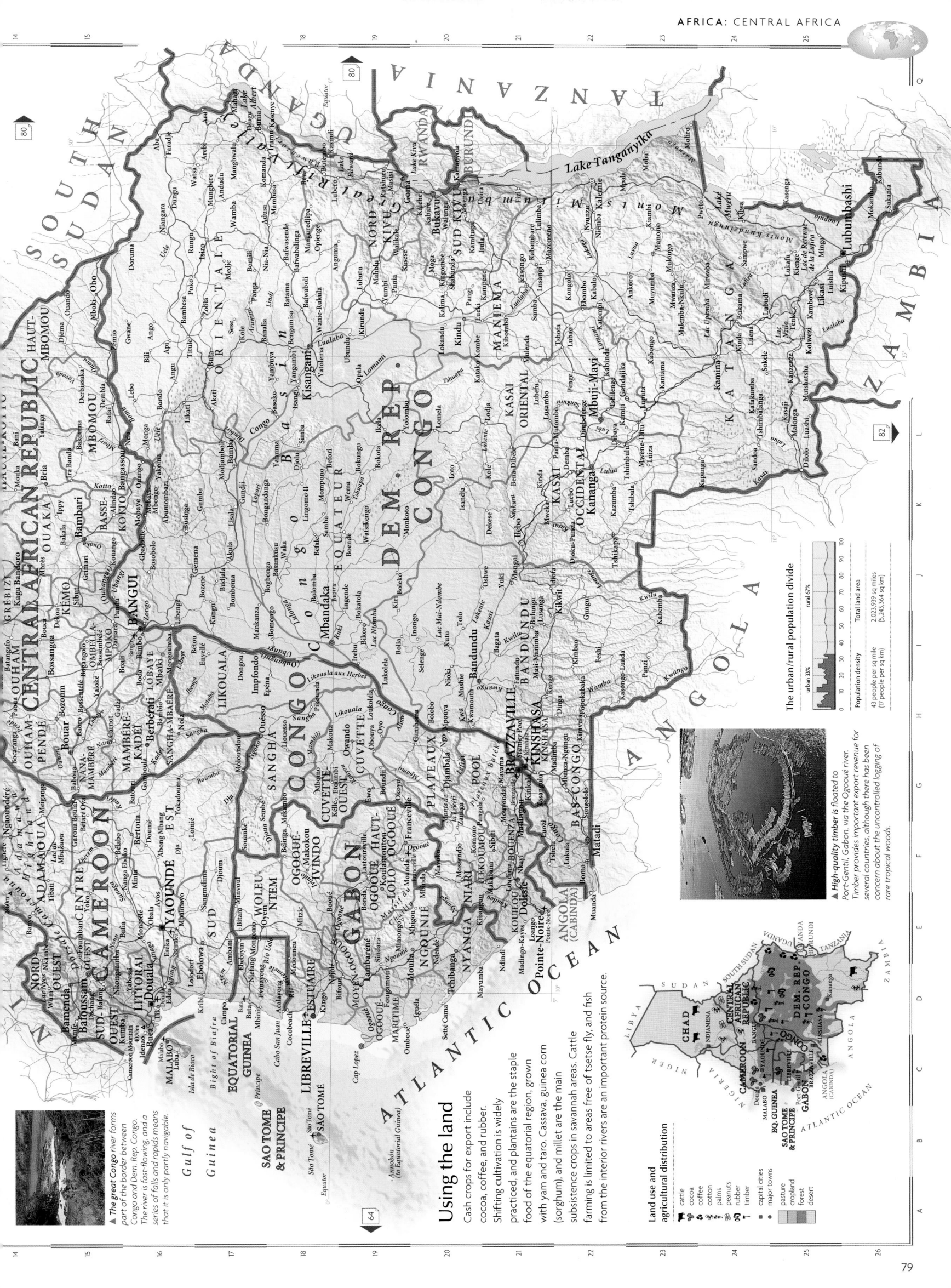

Using the land

Cash crops for export include cocoa, coffee, and rubber. Shifting cultivation is widely practiced, and plantains are the staple food of the equatorial region, grown with yam and taro. Cassava, guinea corn (sorghum), and millet are the main subsistence crops in savannah areas. Cattle farming is limited to areas free of tsetse fly, and fish from the interior rivers are an important protein source.

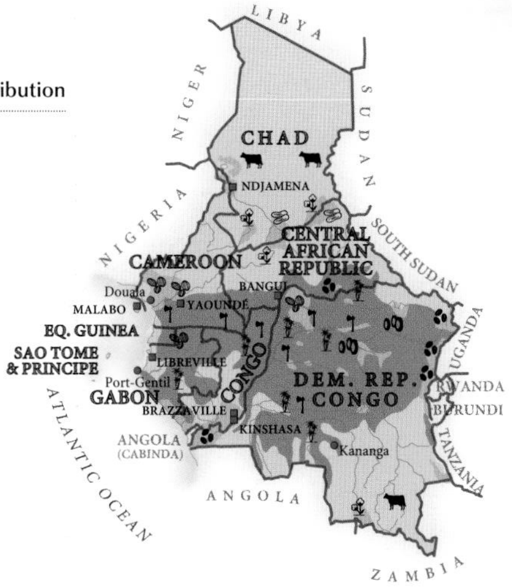

Land use and agricultural distribution
cattle
cocoa
coffee
cotton
palms
peanuts
rubber
timber
capital cities
major towns
pasture
cropland
forest
desert
LIBYA
NIGER
CHAD
SUDAN
NIGERIA
NDJAMENA
CAMEROON
CENTRAL AFRICAN REPUBLIC
SOUTH SUDAN
MALABO
EQ. GUINEA
SAO TOME & PRINCIPE
GABON
CONGO
DEM. REP. CONGO
UGANDA
RWANDA
BURUNDI
TANZANIA
ANGOLA
ANGOLA (CABINDA)
ATLANTIC OCEAN
ZAMBIA
KINSHASA
BRAZZAVILLE
LIBREVILLE
YAOUNDÉ
BANGUI
Kananga

▲ ***High-quality timber is** floated to Port-Gentil, Gabon, via the Ogooué river. Timber provides important export revenue for several countries, although there has been concern about the uncontrolled logging of rare tropical woods.*

The urban/rural population divide

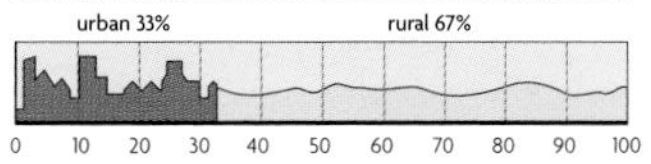

urban 33%
rural 67%
0 10 20 30 40 50 60 70 80 90 100

Population density	Total land area
43 people per sq mile (17 people per sq km)	2,023,939 sq miles (5,243,364 sq km)

East Africa

BURUNDI, DJIBOUTI, ERITREA, ETHIOPIA, KENYA, RWANDA, SOMALIA, SOUTH SUDAN, SUDAN, TANZANIA, UGANDA

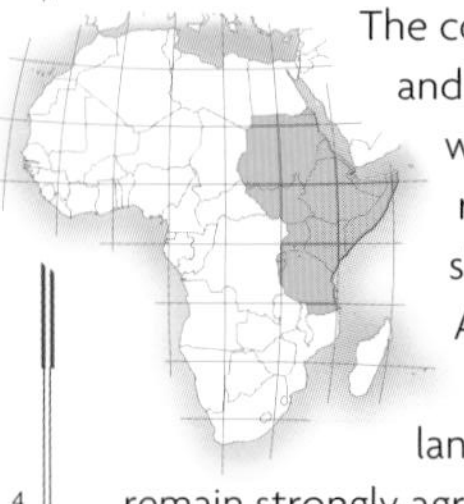

The countries of East Africa divide into two distinct cultural regions. Sudan and the "Horn" nations have been influenced by the Middle East; Ethiopia was the home of one of the earliest Christian civilizations, and Sudan reflects both Muslim and Christian influences. The southern countries share a closer cultural affinity with other sub-Saharan nations. Some of Africa's most densely populated countries lie in this region, and the needs of a growing number of people have put pressure on marginal lands and fragile environments. Although most East African economies remain strongly agricultural, Kenya has developed a varied industrial base.

The landscape

East Africa's most significant landscape feature is the Great Rift Valley, which formed during the most recent phase of continental movement when the rigid basement rocks cracked and buckled. Great blocks of land were raised and lowered, creating huge flat-bottomed valleys and steep escarpments, sometimes covered by volcanic extrusions in highland areas.

◀ ***This dome at** Gonder, in Ethiopia, is a volcanic intrusion, formed when molten rock pushed up the surface of the Earth and then solidified, leaving an outcrop of igneous rock.*

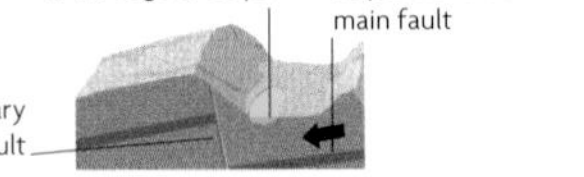
Ephemeral lake forms at far edge of slope
Central block slopes towards main fault
Boundary fault

▲ ***The eastern arm** of the Great Rift Valley is gradually being pulled apart; however the forces on one side are greater than the other causing the land to slope. This affects regional drainage which migrates down the slope.*

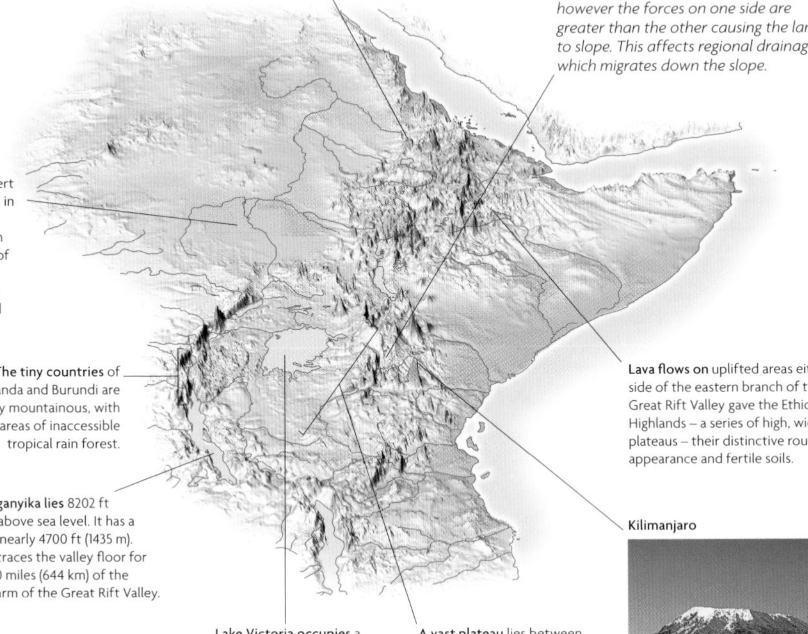

In contrast to the desert conditions that prevail in much of Sudan to the north, annual rainfall in the tropical wetlands of the southern Sudd region in South Sudan, can sometimes exceed 40 inches (1000 mm).

The tiny countries of Rwanda and Burundi are mainly mountainous, with large areas of inaccessible tropical rain forest.

Lake Tanganyika lies 8202 ft (2500 m) above sea level. It has a depth of nearly 4700 ft (1435 m). The lake traces the valley floor for some 400 miles (644 km) of the western arm of the Great Rift Valley.

Lake Victoria occupies a vast basin between the two arms of the Great Rift Valley. It is the world's second largest lake in terms of surface area, extending 26,560 sq miles (68,880 sq km). The lake contains numerous islands and coral reefs.

A vast plateau lies between the eastern and western rift valleys in Kenya, Uganda, and western Tanzania. It has been leveled by long periods of erosion to form a peneplain, but is dotted with inselbergs – outcrops of more resistant rocks.

Lava flows on uplifted areas either side of the eastern branch of the Great Rift Valley gave the Ethiopian Highlands – a series of high, wide plateaus – their distinctive rounded appearance and fertile soils.

Kilimanjaro

▲ ***An extinct volcano,** Kilimanjaro is Africa's highest mountain, rising 19,340 ft (5895 m). Once famed for its snow-capped peak, this has almost competely melted due to changing climatic conditions.*

▶ ***The Kassala region** in eastern Sudan is watered by the Atbara River, an important tributary of the Nile. Most of the population is engaged in agriculture, growing cotton and cereals.*

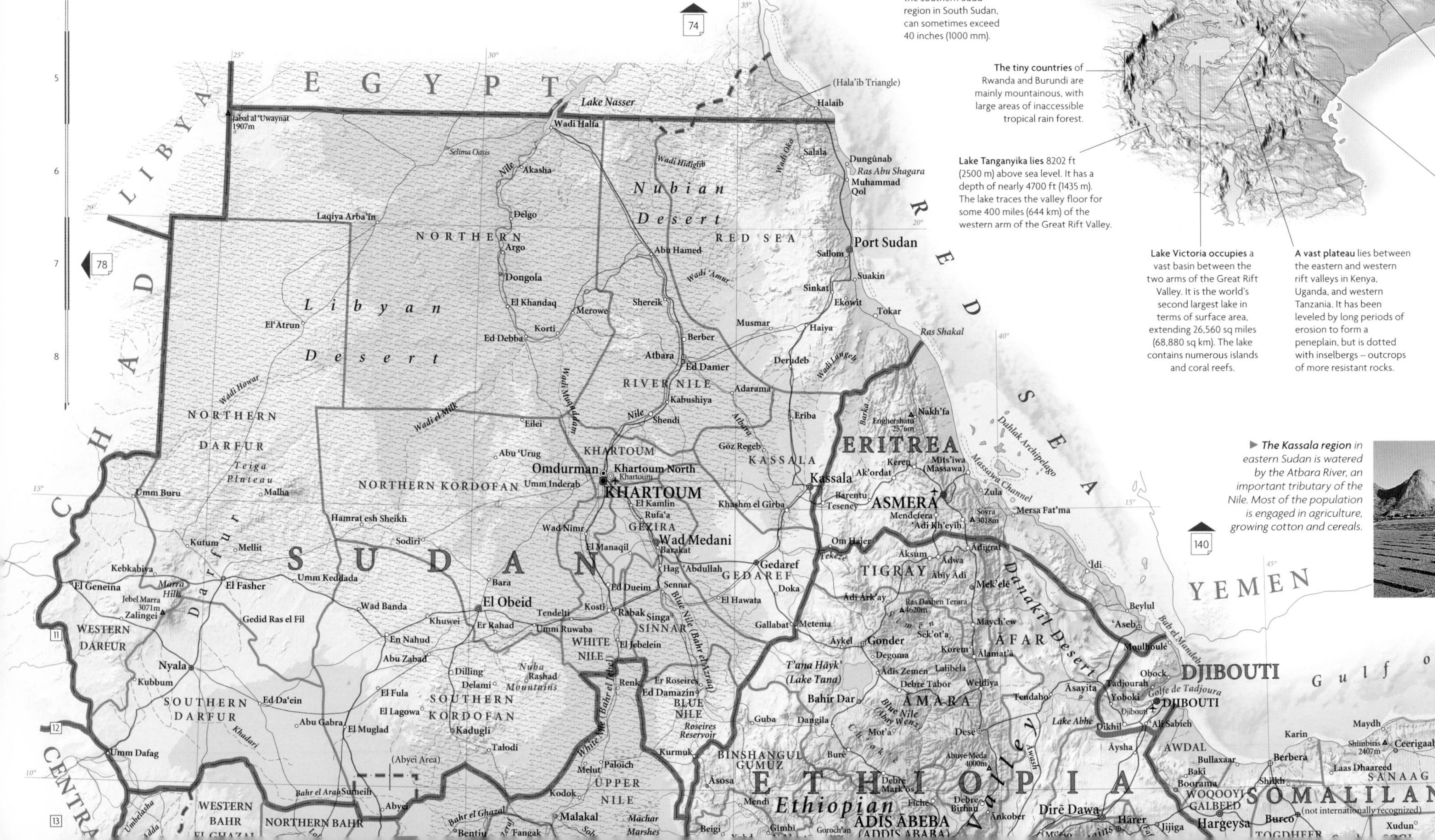
EGYPT
LIBYA
CHAD
SUDAN
ERITREA
ETHIOPIA
DJIBOUTI
YEMEN
SOMALILAND
(not internationally recognized)
RED SEA
Gulf of Aden
Libyan Desert
Nubian Desert
Danakil Desert
Lake Nasser
KHARTOUM
Omdurman
Khartoum North
Port Sudan
Kassala
ASMERA
DJIBOUTI
ADIS ABEBA
(ADDIS ABABA)
Hargeysa
El Obeid
Wad Medani
Gedaref
Atbara
Dongola
Wadi Halfa
Halaib
(Hala'ib Triangle)
NORTHERN
RIVER NILE
RED SEA
KASSALA
KHARTOUM
GEZIRA
GEDAREF
SINNAR
WHITE NILE
BLUE NILE
NORTHERN KORDOFAN
SOUTHERN KORDOFAN
NORTHERN DARFUR
SOUTHERN DARFUR
WESTERN DARFUR
UPPER NILE
TIGRAY
AMARA
AFAR
BINSHANGUL GUMUZ
T'ana Hāyk' (Lake Tana)
Dahlak Archipelago
Massawa Channel
Bab el Mandeb
Golfe de Tadjoura
Ethiopian
74
78
140

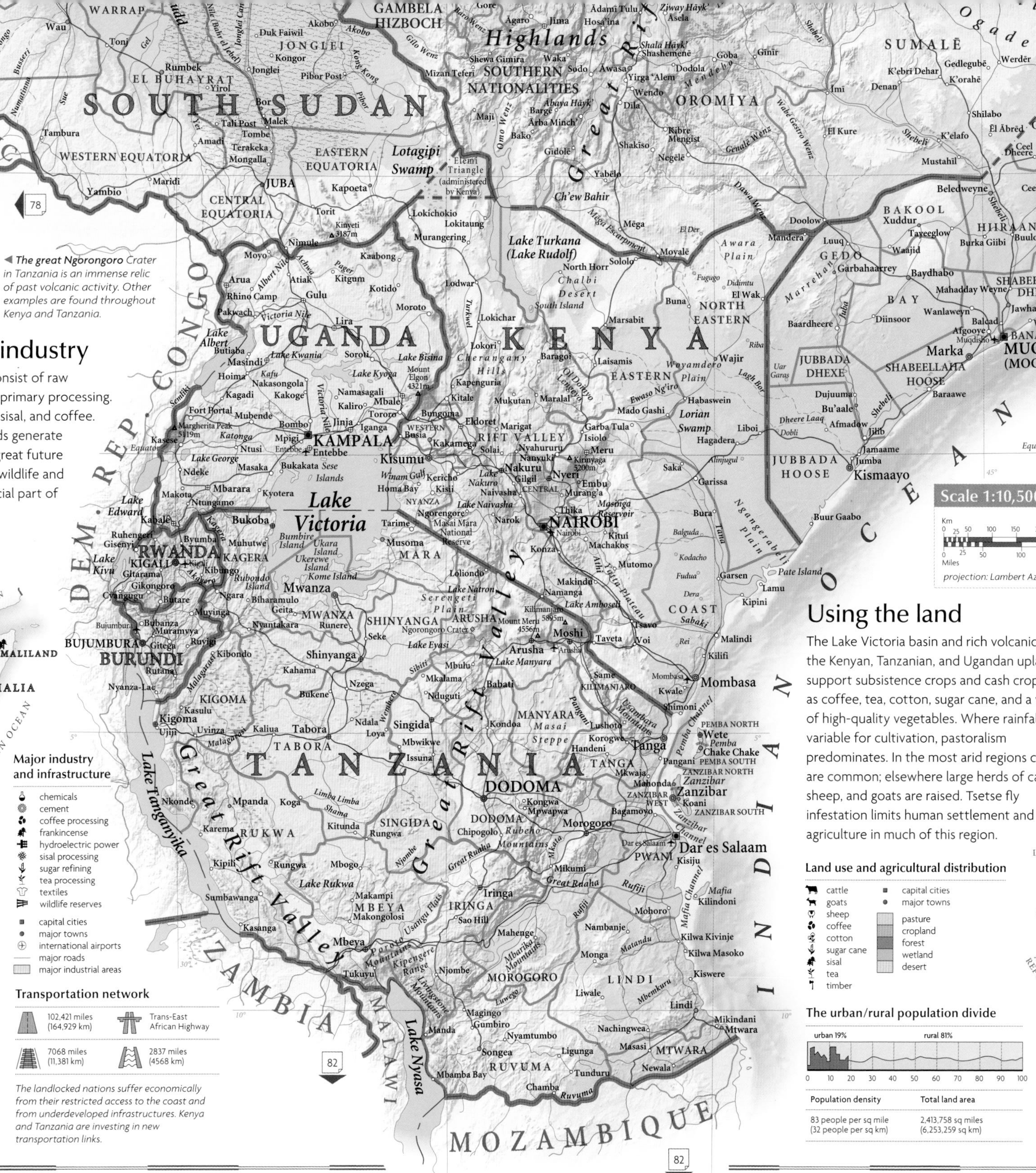
SOUTH SUDAN
UGANDA
KENYA
TANZANIA
SOMALIA
RWANDA
BURUNDI
DEM. REP. CONGO
ZAMBIA
MALAWI
MOZAMBIQUE
CENTRAL AFRICAN REPUBLIC
Lake Victoria
Lake Turkana (Lake Rudolf)
Lake Tanganyika
Lake Nyasa
Great Rift Valley
INDIAN OCEAN
KAMPALA
NAIROBI
DODOMA
KIGALI
BUJUMBURA
JUBA
MUQDISHO (MOGADISHU)
Mombasa
Dar es Salaam
Zanzibar
Kismaayo
Equator

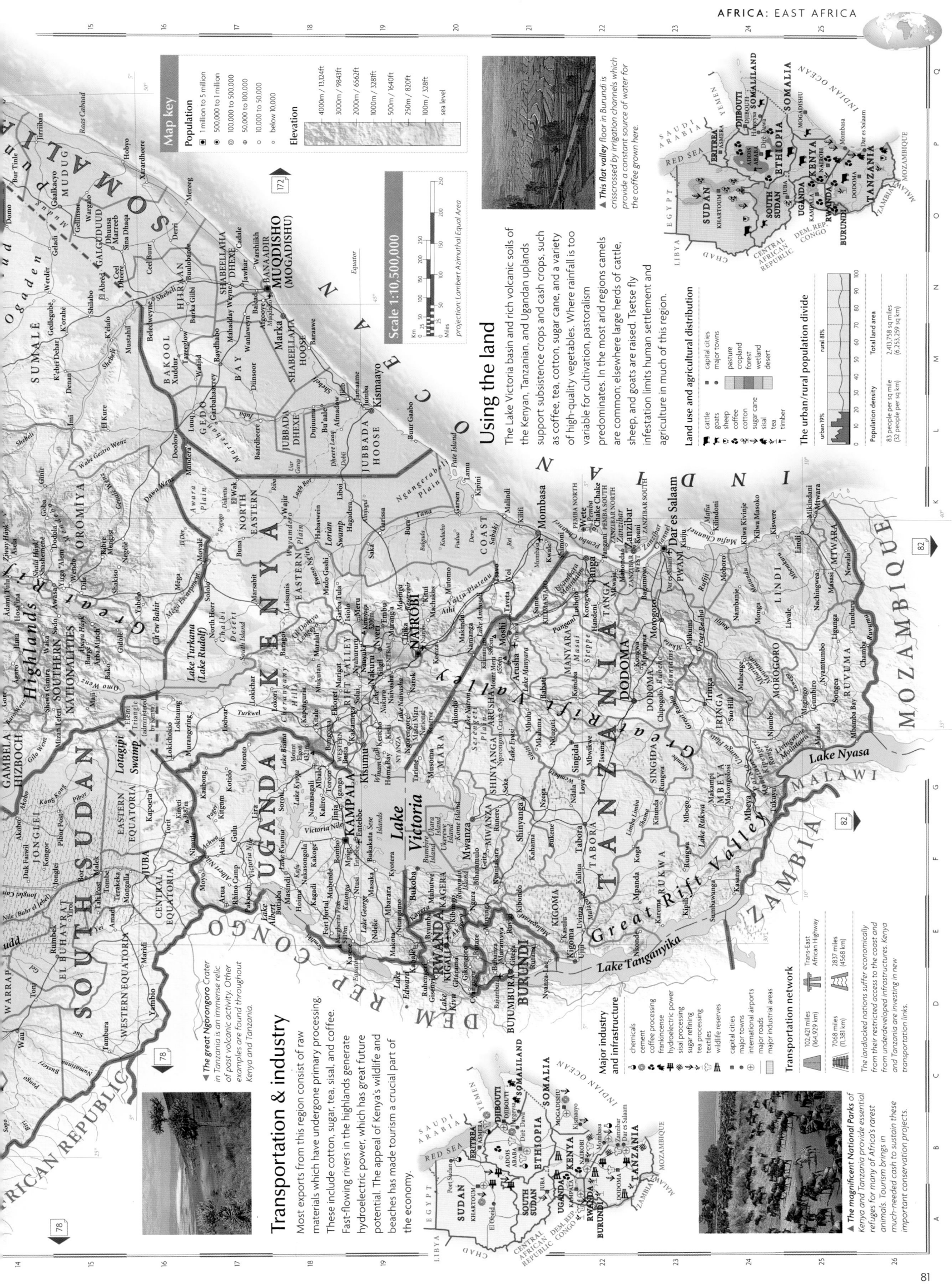

Map key

Population

- 1 million to 5 million
- 500,000 to 1 million
- 100,000 to 500,000
- 50,000 to 100,000
- 10,000 to 50,000
- below 10,000

Elevation

- 4000m / 13,124ft
- 3000m / 9843ft
- 2000m / 6562ft
- 1000m / 3281ft
- 500m / 1640ft
- 250m / 820ft
- 100m / 328ft
- sea level

Scale 1:10,500,000

Km 0 25 50 100 150 200 250
Miles 0 25 50 100 150 200 250

projection: Lambert Azimuthal Equal Area

78
172
82

◀ *The great Ngorongoro Crater in Tanzania is an immense relic of past volcanic activity. Other examples are found throughout Kenya and Tanzania.*

Transportation & industry

Most exports from this region consist of raw materials which have undergone primary processing. These include cotton, sugar, tea, sisal, and coffee. Fast-flowing rivers in the highlands generate hydroelectric power, which has great future potential. The appeal of Kenya's wildlife and beaches has made tourism a crucial part of the economy.

SUDAN
SOUTH SUDAN
ETHIOPIA
SOMALIA
KENYA
UGANDA
RWANDA
BURUNDI
TANZANIA
ERITREA
DJIBOUTI
SOMALILAND
INDIAN OCEAN
RED SEA

Major industry and infrastructure

- chemicals
- cement
- coffee processing
- frankincense
- hydroelectric power
- sisal processing
- sugar refining
- tea processing
- textiles
- wildlife reserves
- capital cities
- major towns
- international airports
- major roads
- major industrial areas

Transportation network

- 102,421 miles (164,929 km)
- 7068 miles (11,381 km)
- Trans-East African Highway
- 2837 miles (4568 km)

The landlocked nations suffer economically from their restricted access to the coast and from underdeveloped infrastructures. Kenya and Tanzania are investing in new transportation links.

▲ *The magnificent National Parks of Kenya and Tanzania provide essential refuges for many of Africa's rarest animals. Tourism brings in much-needed cash to sustain these important conservation projects.*

Using the land

The Lake Victoria basin and rich volcanic soils of the Kenyan, Tanzanian, and Ugandan uplands support subsistence crops and cash crops, such as coffee, tea, cotton, sugar cane, and a variety of high-quality vegetables. Where rainfall is too variable for cultivation, pastoralism predominates. In the most arid regions camels are common; elsewhere large herds of cattle, sheep, and goats are raised. Tsetse fly infestation limits human settlement and agriculture in much of this region.

▲ *This flat valley floor in Burundi is crisscrossed by irrigation channels which provide a constant source of water for the coffee grown here.*

Land use and agricultural distribution

- cattle
- goats
- sheep
- coffee
- cotton
- sugar cane
- sisal
- tea
- timber
- capital cities
- major towns
- pasture
- cropland
- forest
- wetland
- desert

SUDAN
SOUTH SUDAN
ETHIOPIA
SOMALIA
KENYA
UGANDA
RWANDA
BURUNDI
TANZANIA
ERITREA
DJIBOUTI
SOMALILAND
INDIAN OCEAN
RED SEA

The urban/rural population divide

urban 19% — rural 81%

0 10 20 30 40 50 60 70 80 90 100

Population density	Total land area
83 people per sq mile (32 people per sq km)	2,413,758 sq miles (6,253,259 sq km)

Southern Africa

ANGOLA, BOTSWANA, LESOTHO, MALAWI, MOZAMBIQUE, NAMIBIA, SOUTH AFRICA, SWAZILAND, ZAMBIA, ZIMBABWE

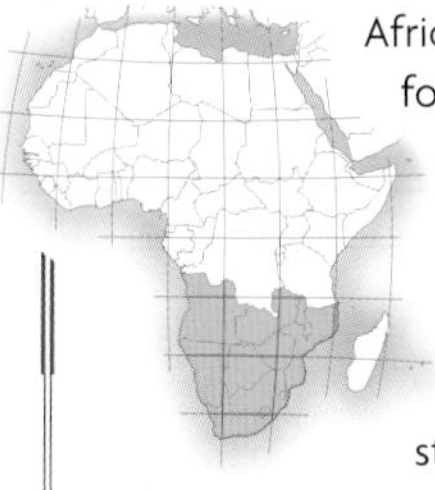

Africa's vast southern plateau has been a contested homeland for disparate peoples for many centuries. The European incursion began with the slave trade and quickened in the 19th century, when the discovery of enormous mineral wealth secured South Africa's regional economic dominance. The struggle against white minority rule led to strife in Namibia, Zimbabwe, and the former Portuguese territories of Angola and Mozambique. South Africa's notorious apartheid laws, which denied basic human rights to more than 75% of the people, led to the state being internationally ostracized until 1994, when the first fully democratic elections inaugurated a new era of racial justice.

Transportation & industry

South Africa, the world's largest exporter of gold, has a varied economy which generates about 75% of the region's income and draws migrant labor from neighboring states. Angola exports petroleum; Botswana and Namibia rely on diamond mining; and Zambia is seeking to diversify its economy to compensate for declining copper reserves.

◀ *Almost all new mining ventures in Zimbabwe are now subject to government control. This mine at Bindura in northeastern Zimbabwe produces nickel, one of the country's top three minerals in terms of economic value*

DEM. REP. CONGO
TANZANIA
LUANDA
Lobito
ANGOLA
ZAMBIA
Ndola
LUSAKA
MALAWI
LILONGWE
Blantyre
HARARE
MOZAMBIQUE
ZIMBABWE
Bulawayo
Beira
NAMIBIA
WINDHOEK
Walvis Bay
BOTSWANA
GABORONE
PRETORIA / TSHWANE
MAPUTO
MBABANE
SWAZILAND
Johannesburg
MASERU
LESOTHO
Durban
S.AFRICA
CAPE TOWN
Port Elizabeth
ATLANTIC OCEAN
INDIAN OCEAN

Major industry and infrastructure

car manufacture	gold	capital cities
coal	oil	major towns
copper	textiles	international airports
diamonds	uranium	major roads
food processing	wildlife reserves	major industrial areas

The landscape

Most of southern Africa rests on a concave plateau comprising the Kalahari basin and a mountainous fringe, skirted by a coastal plain which widens out in Mozambique. The plateau extends north, toward the Planalto de Bié in Angola, the Congo Basin and the lake-filled troughs of the Great Rift Valley. The eastern region is drained by the Zambezi and Limpopo rivers, and the Orange is the major western river.

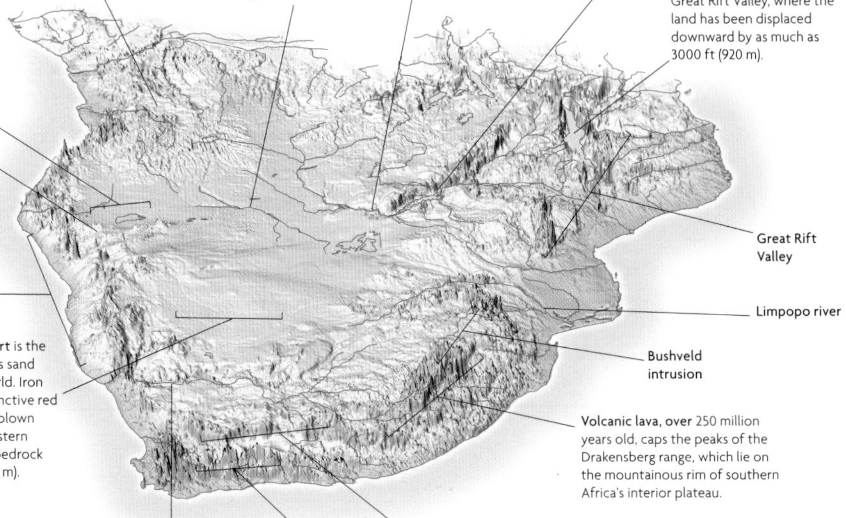
At Victoria Falls, the Zambezi river has cut a spectacular gorge taking advantage of large joints in the basalt, which were first formed as the lava cooled and contracted.
The Okavango/Cubango River flows from the Planalto de Bié to the swamplands of the Okavango Delta, one of the world's largest inland deltas, where it divides into countless distributary channels, feeding out into the desert.
Planalto de Bié
Thousands of years of evaporating water have produced the Etosha Pan, one of the largest salt flats in the world. Lake and river sediments in the area indicate that the region was once less arid.
Khorixas, Namibia
Lake Nyasa occupies one of the deep troughs of the Great Rift Valley, where the land has been displaced downward by as much as 3000 ft (920 m).
Great Rift Valley
Limpopo river
Namib Desert
The Kalahari desert is the largest continuous sand surface in the world. Iron oxide gives a distinctive red color to the windblown sand, which, in eastern areas covers the bedrock by over 200 ft (60 m).
Bushveld intrusion
Volcanic lava, over 250 million years old, caps the peaks of the Drakensberg range, which lie on the mountainous rim of southern Africa's interior plateau.
The Orange River, one of the longest in Africa, rises in Lesotho and is the only major river in the south which flows westward, rather than to the east coast.
The mountains of the Little Karoo are composed of sedimentary rocks which have been substantially folded and faulted.
Broad, flat-topped mountains characterize the Great Karoo, which have been cut from level rock strata under extremely arid conditions.

▶ *The fast-flowing Zambezi river cuts a deep, wide channel as it flows along the Zimbabwe/Zambia border.*

▲ *Finger Rock, near Khorixas, Namibia is a remnant of a former land surface, which has been denuded by erosion over the last 5 million years. These occasional stacks of partially weathered rocks interrupt the plains of the dry southern interior.*

Transportation network

84,213 miles (135,609 km)	746 miles (1202 km)
23,208 miles (37,372 km)	3815 miles (6144 km)

Southern Africa's Cape-gauge rail network is by far the largest in the continent. About two-thirds of the 20,000 mile (32,000 km) system lies within South Africa. Lines such as the Harare–Bulawayo route have become corridors for industrial growth.

▲ *Following a series of droughts, this baobab tree in Zimbabwe now stands alone in a field once filled by sugar cane. The thick trunk and small leaves of the baobab help it to conserve water, enabling it to survive even in drought conditions.*

Bushveld intrusion

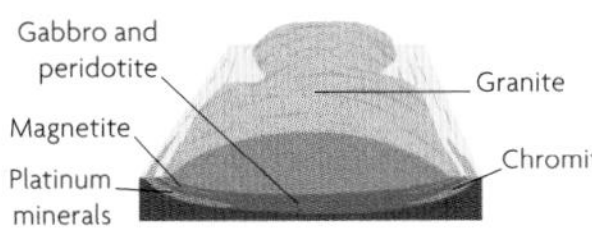
Gabbro and peridotite
Magnetite
Platinum minerals
Granite
Chromite

▲ *The Bushveld intrusion lies on South Africa's high "veld." Molten magma intruded into the Earth's crust creating a saucer-shaped feature, more than 180 miles (300 km) across, containing regular layers of precious minerals, overlain by a dome of granite.*

Scale 1:10,500,000

Km 0 25 50 100 150 200 250 300
Miles 0 25 50 100 150 200 250 300

projection: Lambert Azimuthal Equal Area

Map key

Population

- 1 million to 5 million
- 500,000 to 1 million
- 100,000 to 500,000
- 50,000 to 100,000
- 10,000 to 50,000
- below 10,000

Elevation

- 3000m / 9843ft
- 2000m / 6562ft
- 1000m / 3281ft
- 500m / 1640ft
- 250m / 820ft
- 100m / 328ft
- sea level

South Africa: Capital cities

PRETORIA / TSHWANE – administrative capital
CAPE TOWN – legislative capital
BLOEMFONTEIN – judicial capital

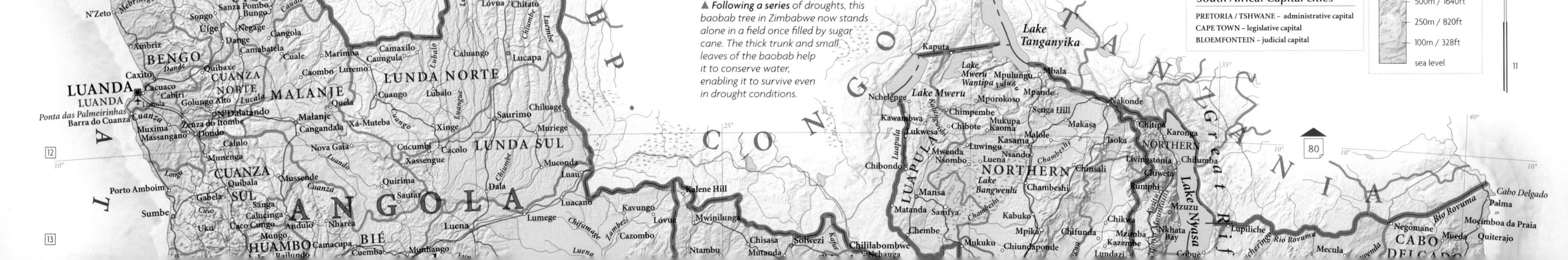
CONGO
CABINDA (To Angola)
Cacongo
Cabinda
Ponta Vermelha
Soyo
ZAIRE
M'Banza Congo
UIGE
BENGO
LUANDA
CUANZA NORTE
MALANJE
LUNDA NORTE
LUNDA SUL
CUANZA SUL
ANGOLA
HUAMBO
BIÉ
Porto Amboim
Sumbe
DEM. REP. CONGO
Lake Tanganyika
Lake Mweru
NORTHERN
LUAPULA
TANZANIA
Lake Nyasa
Great Rift
CABO DELGADO
Mecula
Palma
Mocimboa da Praia
Quiterajo
78
80
78
78
80

ZAMBIA
MALAWI
LILONGWE
LUSAKA
HARARE
ZIMBABWE
MOZAMBIQUE
NAMIBIA
WINDHOEK
BOTSWANA
GABORONE
Kalahari
Desert
SOUTH AFRICA
PRETORIA /TSHWANE
Johannesburg
MAPUTO
MBABANE
SWAZILAND
MASERU
LESOTHO
BLOEMFONTEIN
CAPE TOWN
Port Elizabeth
Durban
Mozambique Channel
INDIAN OCEAN
ATLANTIC OCEAN
Namib Desert
Tropic of Capricorn

172
64

▲ **A wide range** *of crops are grown in South Africa, aided in many areas by irrigation schemes, such as the Orange River Project, which supplement irregular rainfall.*

Using the land

Tea, cotton, sisal, and tobacco are grown commercially in the southeast, with vines and citrus fruits near the southern coast. Coffee is grown in northern Angola. Corn is the main staple crop, grown with cassava, pulses, or potatoes. Poor soils and cyclical drought limit farming to extensive pastoralism in most of Namibia and Botswana.

Land use and agricultural distribution

- cattle
- citrus fruits
- coffee
- corn
- cotton
- tea
- tobacco
- vineyards
- capital cities
- major towns
- pasture
- cropland
- forest
- desert

DEM. REP. CONGO
TANZANIA
LUANDA
ANGOLA
ZAMBIA
LUSAKA
MALAWI
LILONGWE
HARARE
ZIMBABWE
MOZAMBIQUE
NAMIBIA
WINDHOEK
BOTSWANA
GABORONE
PRETORIA / TSHWANE
MAPUTO
MBABANE
SWAZILAND
Johannesburg
MASERU
LESOTHO
S. AFRICA
CAPE TOWN
ATLANTIC OCEAN
INDIAN OCEAN

The urban/rural population divide

urban 39% rural 61%

Population density	Total land area
49 people per sq mile (19 people per sq km)	2,281,596 sq miles (5,910,870 sq km)

▲ **The arid Namib Desert** *stretches along much of the coast of Namibia. Great diamond deposits lie beneath the miles of constantly shifting sand dunes.*

◀ **Table Mountain, with** *its flat top and clothlike folds overlooks the bay at Cape Town, home to South Africa's parliament.*

ARCTIC OCEAN
North Pole
Ellesmere Island
Greenland
King Frederik VIII Land
King Christian X Land
Greenland Sea
Spitsbergen
Franz Josef Land
Ostrov Rudol'fa
Severnaya Zemlya
Laptev Sea
Poluostrov Taymyr
Kara Sea
Mys Flissingskiy
Novaya Zemlya
Barents Sea
Bjørnøya
Barents Trough
North Cape
Nordkinn
Murmansk Rise
Kara Strait
Poluostrov Yamal
Baydaratskaya Guba
Gulf of Ob
Yenisey
West Siberian Plain
Ural Mountains
ASIA
NORTH AMERICAN PLATE
EURASIAN PLATE
Jan Mayen Fracture Zone
Jan Mayen
Jan Mayen Ridge
Kolbeinsey Ridge
Denmark Strait
Arctic Circle
Iceland Plateau
Iceland
Vatnajökull
Bjargtangar
Reykjanes Ridge
Norwegian Sea
Norwegian Basin
Voring Plateau
Tromsøflaket
Fugløya Bank
Vesterålen
Lofoten
Kebnekaise 2117m
Inarijärvi
Torneälven
Luleälven
Kola Peninsula
Ozero Imandra
Ostrov Kolguyev
Poluostrov Kanin
Pechora
White Sea
Timanskiy Kryazh
Mezen'
Onega Bay
Ozero Vygozero
Northern Dvina
Lake Onega
Lake Ladoga
Svir
Ozero Beloye
Rybinsk Reservoir
Sukhona
Yug
Vyatka
Kama
Chusovaya
Gor'kiy Reservoir
Kuybyshev Reservoir
Belaya
Ural
Traena Bank
Scandinavia
Kölen
Umeälven
Oulujoki
Kemijoki
Gulf of Bothnia
Galdhøpiggen 2469m
Ljungan
Ljusnan
Glåma
Åland
Gulf of Finland
Lake Peipus
Msta
Lake Ilmen
Gulf of Riga
Lake Pskov
Vänern
Vättern
Gotland
Baltic Sea
Faeroe-Iceland Ridge
Faeroe Islands
Iceland Basin
Bill Baileys Bank
Faeroe-Shetland Trough
Shetland Islands
Viking Bank
Norwegian Trench
Hatton Ridge
Orkney Islands
Outer Hebrides
Rockall Rise
Ben Nevis 1343m
Grampian Mountains
Feni Ridge
Rockall Trough
North Channel
North Sea
Jutland Bank
Skagerrak
Kattegat
Jutland
Sjælland
Great Fisher Bank
Dogger Bank
British Isles
Ireland
Irish Sea
Pennines
Shannon
Snowdon 1085m
Trent
Britain
Severn
Celtic Sea
St. George's Channel
Bristol Channel
Celtic Shelf
Thames
Land's End
Strait of Dover
English Channel
Channel Islands
Frisian Islands
Porcupine Plain
ATLANTIC OCEAN
Neman
Western Dvina
Moskva
Oka
Sura
Volga Upland
Volga
Kama
Central Russian Upland
Klyaz'ma
Seym
Don
Khoper
North European Plain
Elbe
Oder
Warta
Vistula
Bug
Pripet Marshes
Byerezino
Dnieper
Desna
EUROPE
Harz
Ardennes
Rhine
Meuse
Moselle
Marne
Seine
Dnieper Lowlands
Kiev Reservoir
Kremenchuk Reservoir
Donets
Tsimlyansk Reservoir
Kirghiz Steppe
Yergeni
Manych
Dniester
Podil's'ka Vysochina
Pivdennyy Buh
Carpathian Mountains
Tisza
Siret
Prut
Black Sea Lowland
Sea of Azov
Kuban'
Crimea
Kerch Strait
Black Sea
Danube
Black Forest
Vosges
Lake Constance
Lake Geneva
Loire
Cher
Saône
Massif Central
Mont Blanc 4807m
Lake Garda
Po
Bakony
Lake Balaton
Great Hungarian Plain
Drava
Sava
Transylvanian Alps
Bay of Biscay
Biscay Plain
Charcot Seamounts
Azores-Biscay Rise
Garonne
Dordogne
Lot
Cévennes
Rhône
Theta Gap
Galicia Bank
Iberian Plain
Miño
Cordillera Cantábrica
Iberian Peninsula
Duero
Douro
Aragón
Ebro
Sistema Ibérico
Sistema Central
Pyrenees
Aneto 3404m
Gulf of Lion
Ligurian Sea
Arno
Adriatic Sea
Dinaric Alps
Apennines
Tiber
Corno Grande 2912m
Adriatic Basin
Lake Scutari
Lake Ohrid
Lake Prespa
Balkan Mountains
Maritsa
Rhodope Mountains
Bosporus
Sea of Marmara
EURASIAN PLATE
ANATOLIAN PLATE
Anatolia
Lake Tuz
Taurus Mountains
Gulf of Antalya
Cabo da Roca
Tagus
Tagus Plain
Guadiana
Sierra Morena
Guadalquivir
Júcar
Segura
Gulf of Valencia
Balearic Islands
Corsica
Strait of Bonifacio
Sardinia
Tyrrhenian Sea
Tyrrhenian Basin
Gulf of Taranto
Strait of Otranto
Strait of Messina
Mount Etna 3340m
Sicily
Strait of Sicily
Ionian Sea
Ionian Basin
Malta
Peloponnese
Mirtoan Sea
Aegean Sea
Sea of Crete
Karpathos Strait
Kasos Strait
Gavdo
Rhodes Basin
Cyprus
Cyprus Basin
Gorringe Ridge
Cape Saint Vincent
Horseshoe Seamounts
Ampère Seamount
Punta de Tarifa
Strait of Gibraltar
Alboran Sea
Sistemas Béticos
Sierra Nevada
Algerian Basin
Mediterranean Sea
Oued Chelif
EURASIAN PLATE
AFRICAN PLATE
Tell Atlas
Rif
Sebou
Moulouya
Oum er Rbia
Middle Atlas
Atlas Mountains
High Atlas
Saharan Atlas
Chott el Jerid
Mediterranean Ridge
Levantine Basin
Nile Fan
Suez Canal
Nile
Gulf of Sirte
Seine Plain
Seine Seamount
Madeira
Agadir Canyon
Dacia Seamount
Canary Islands
Grand Erg Occidental
Grand Erg Oriental
Qattara Depression -133m
Western Desert
Libyan Desert
Erg Iguidi
Erg Chech
SAHARA
AFRICA

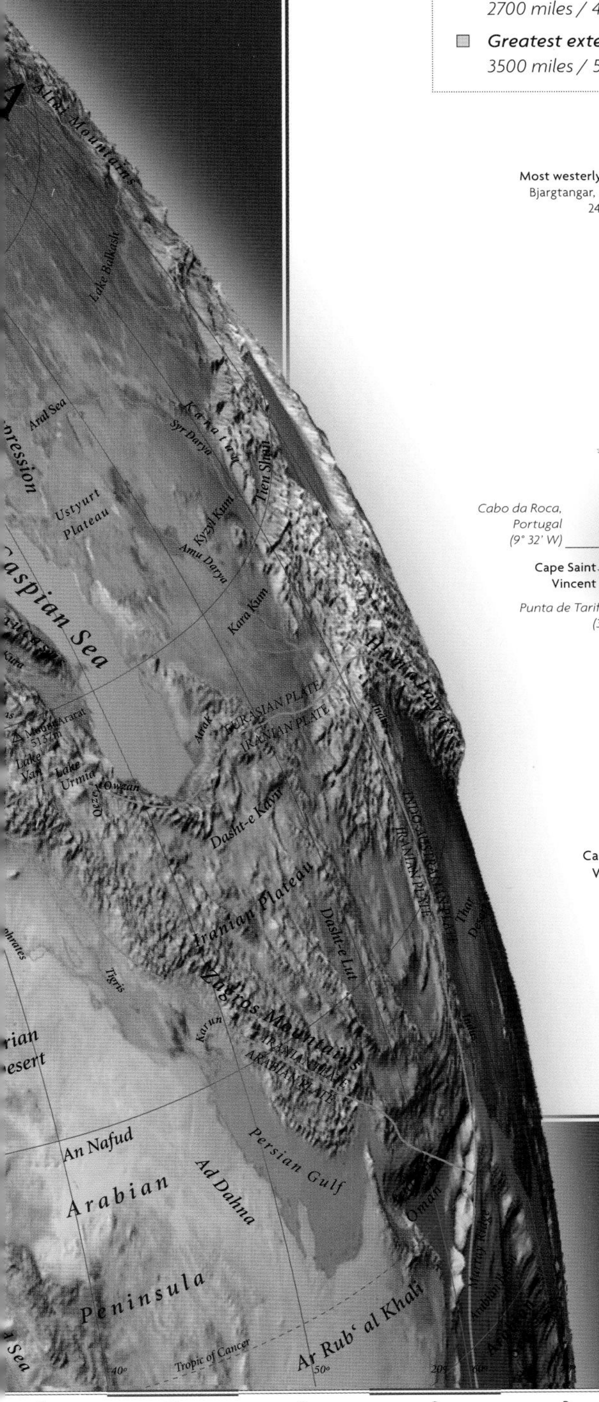
Caspian Sea
Aral Sea
Ustyurt Plateau
Lake Balkhash
Syr Darya
Amu Darya
Kyzyl Kum
Kara Kum
Tien Shan
Dasht-e Kavir
Iranian Plateau
Dasht-e Lut
Zagros Mountains
Tigris
Persian Gulf
An Nafud
Arabian
Ad Dahna
Peninsula
Ar Rub' al Khali
Oman
Tropic of Cancer

Europe

Europe is the world's second smallest continent, covering 4,053,309 sq miles (10,498,000 sq km). It comprises 46 separate countries, including Turkey and the Russian Federation, although the greater parts of these nations lie in Asia.

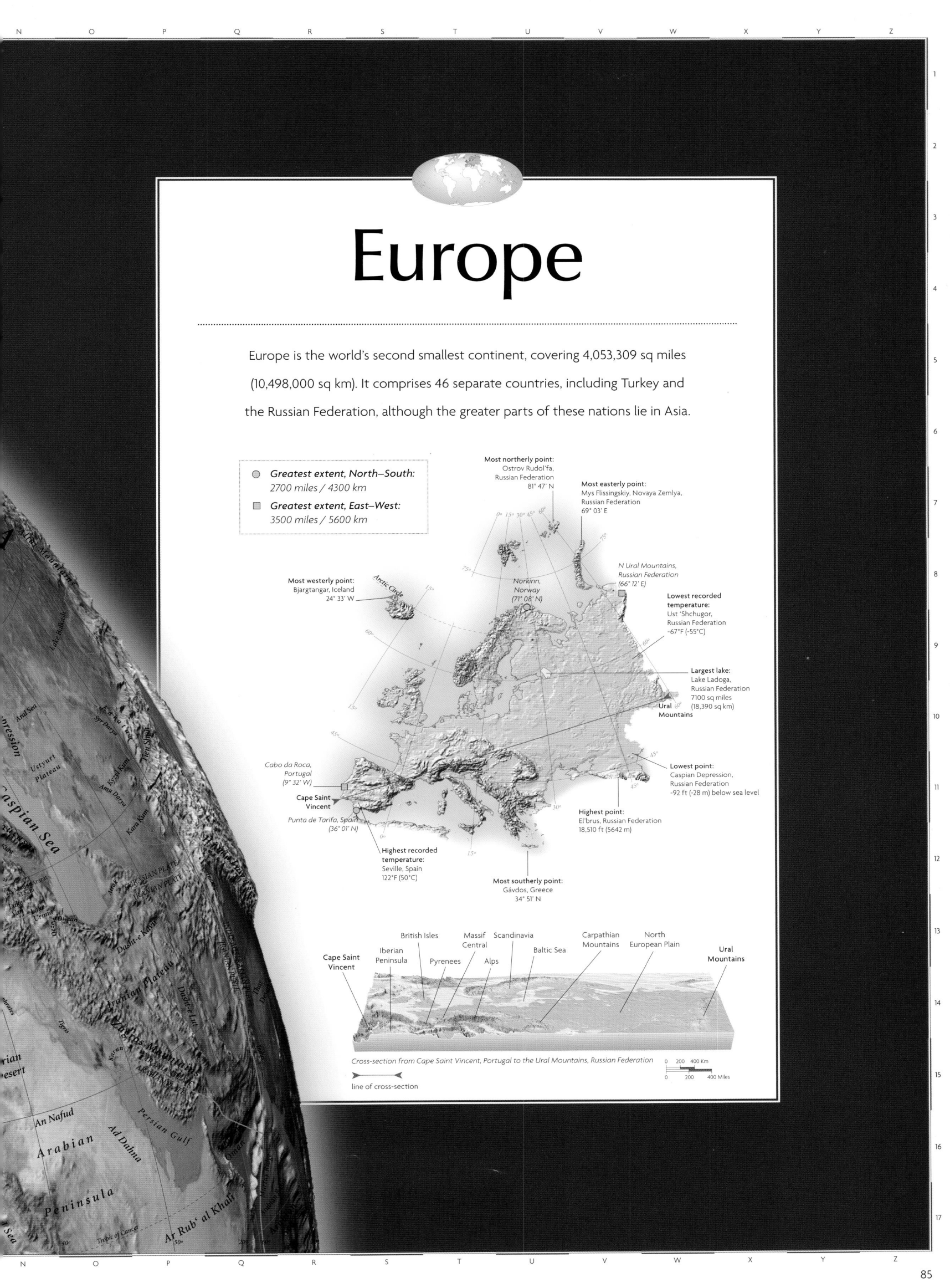

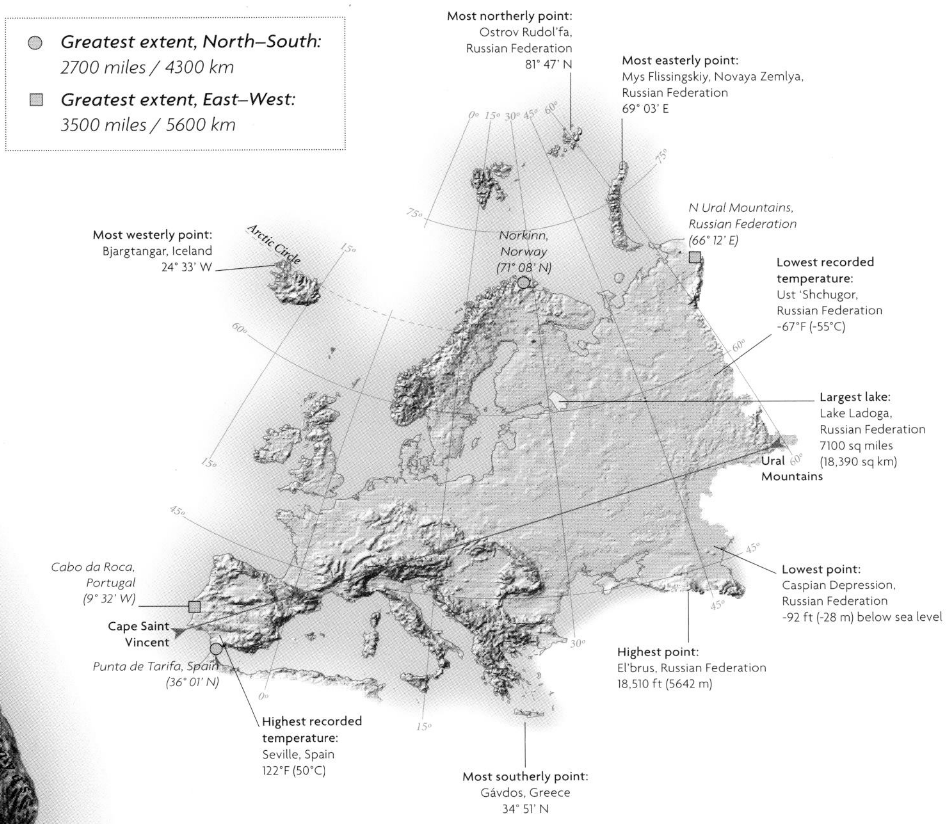
Greatest extent, North–South: 2700 miles / 4300 km
Greatest extent, East–West: 3500 miles / 5600 km
Most northerly point: Ostrov Rudol'fa, Russian Federation 81° 47' N
Most easterly point: Mys Flissingskiy, Novaya Zemlya, Russian Federation 69° 03' E
Most westerly point: Bjargtangar, Iceland 24° 33' W
Arctic Circle
Norkinn, Norway (71° 08' N)
N Ural Mountains, Russian Federation (66° 12' E)
Lowest recorded temperature: Ust 'Shchugor, Russian Federation -67°F (-55°C)
Largest lake: Lake Ladoga, Russian Federation 7100 sq miles (18,390 sq km)
Ural Mountains
Cabo da Roca, Portugal (9° 32' W)
Cape Saint Vincent
Punta de Tarifa, Spain (36° 01' N)
Lowest point: Caspian Depression, Russian Federation -92 ft (-28 m) below sea level
Highest point: El'brus, Russian Federation 18,510 ft (5642 m)
Highest recorded temperature: Seville, Spain 122°F (50°C)
Most southerly point: Gávdos, Greece 34° 51' N

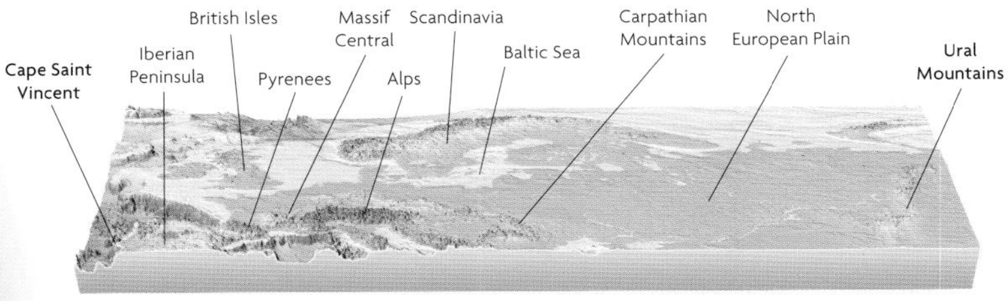
Cape Saint Vincent
Iberian Peninsula
British Isles
Pyrenees
Massif Central
Alps
Scandinavia
Baltic Sea
Carpathian Mountains
North European Plain
Ural Mountains

Cross-section from Cape Saint Vincent, Portugal to the Ural Mountains, Russian Federation

0 200 400 Km
0 200 400 Miles

line of cross-section

Physical Europe

The physical diversity of Europe belies its relatively small size. To the northwest and south it is enclosed by mountains. The older, rounded Atlantic Highlands of Scandinavia and the British Isles lie to the north and the younger, rugged peaks of the Alpine Uplands to the south. In between lies the North European Plain, stretching 2485 miles (4000 km) from The Fens in England to the Ural Mountains in Russia. South of the plain lies a series of gently folded sedimentary rocks separated by ancient plateaus, known as massifs.

The North European Plain

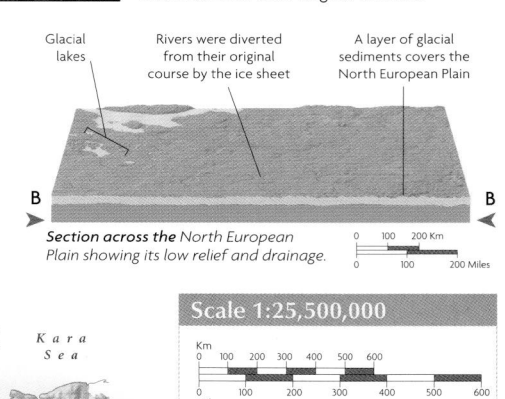

Rising less than 1000 ft (300 m) above sea level, the North European Plain strongly reflects past glaciation. Ridges of both coarse moraine and finer, windblown deposits have accumulated over much of the region. The ice sheet also diverted a number of river channels from their original courses.

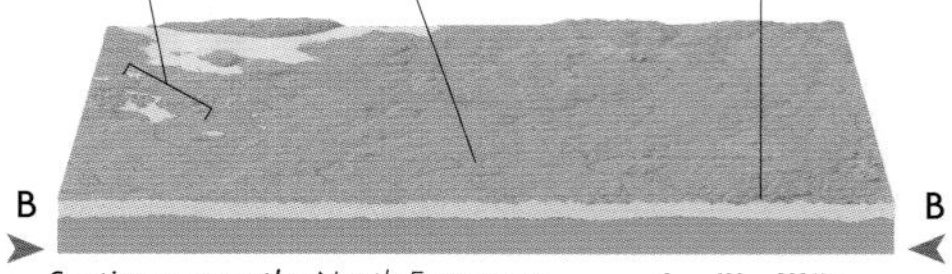
Glacial lakes
Rivers were diverted from their original course by the ice sheet
A layer of glacial sediments covers the North European Plain
B
B
0 100 200 Km
0 100 200 Miles

Section across the North European Plain showing its low relief and drainage.

The Atlantic Highlands

The Atlantic Highlands were formed by compression against the Scandinavian Shield during the Caledonian mountain-building period over 500 million years ago. The highlands were once part of a continuous mountain chain, now divided by the North Sea and a submerged rift valley.

The Atlantic Highlands continue in the British Isles
Rift valley buried by sediments
North Sea
Atlantic Highlands in Norway
Rocks affected by ancient mountain-building
Scandinavian Shield
A
A
0 100 200 Km
0 100 200 Miles

Cross-section through northeastern Europe showing the continuous mountain chain and rift valley system.

Scale 1:25,500,000
Km 0 100 200 300 400 500 600
0 100 200 300 400 500 600 Miles
projection: Lambert Azimuthal Equal Area
Map key
Elevation
4000m / 13,124ft
3000m / 9843ft
2000m / 6562ft
1000m / 3281ft
500m / 1640ft
250m / 820ft
100m / 328ft
sea level
Plate margins
(for explanation see page xiv)
constructive
destructive
conservative
uncertain
physiographic regions
line of cross-section
Novaya Zemlya
Kara Sea
Ostrov Kolguyev
Barents Sea
Kola Peninsula
White Sea
Iceland
NORTH AMERICAN PLATE
EURASIAN PLATE
Norwegian Sea
ATLANTIC HIGHLANDS
Kölen
Faeroe Islands
Shetland Islands
Outer Hebrides
ATLANTIC OCEAN
Gulf of Bothnia
SCANDINAVIAN SHIELD
Northern Dvina
Lake Onega
Lake Ladoga
Ural Mountains
British Isles
Ireland
Shannon
Vänern
Vättern
Gulf of Riga
North Sea
Jutland
Baltic Sea
Britain
The Fens
Thames
English Channel
Western Dvina
NORTH EUROPEAN PLAIN
Central Russian Upland
Volga Uplands
Volga
Elbe
Rhine
Oder
Vistula
Harz
Ardennes
Seine
Loire
PLATEAUX AND LOWLANDS
Danube
Carpathian Mountains
Dnieper
Don
Dniester
Bay of Biscay
Massif Central
Mt Blanc 4807m
Garonne
Rhône
Alps
Great Hungarian Plain
Sea of Azov
Crimea
Caspian Sea
Caucasus
El'brus 5642m
Douro
Iberian Peninsula
Pyrenees
Ebro
ALPINE UPLANDS
Po
Apennines
Dinaric Alps
Adriatic Sea
Balkan Mountains
Black Sea
ASIA
Corsica
Sardinia
Guadalquivir
Balearic Islands
Tyrrhenian Sea
Vesuvius 1171m
EURASIAN PLATE
AFRICAN PLATE
ANATOLIAN PLATE
Mediterranean Sea
Sicily
Etna 3263m
Ionian Sea
Peloponnese
Aegean Sea
Crete

The plateaus and lowlands

The uplifted plateaus or massifs of southern central Europe are the result of long-term erosion, later followed by uplift. They are the source areas of many of the rivers which drain Europe's lowlands. In some of the higher reaches, fractures have enabled igneous rocks from deep in the Earth to reach the surface.

The Alpine Uplands

The collision of the African and European continents, which began about 65 million years ago, folded and then uplifted a series of mountain ranges running across southern Europe and into Asia. Two major lines of folding can be traced: one includes the Pyrenees, the Alps, and the Carpathian Mountains; the other incorporates the Apennines and the Dinaric Alps.

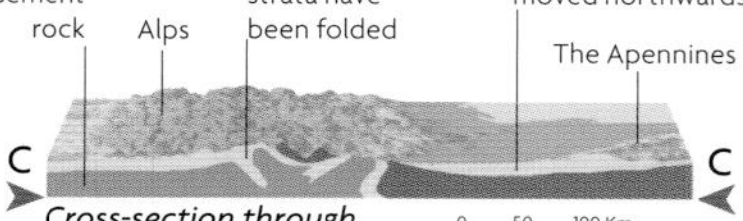
European basement rock
Alps
Weak sedimentary strata have been folded
African Plate moved northwards
The Apennines
C
C
0 50 100 Km
0 50 100 Miles

Cross-section through the Alps showing folding and faulting caused by plate tectonics.

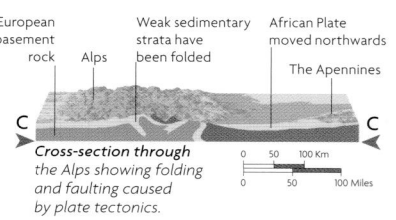

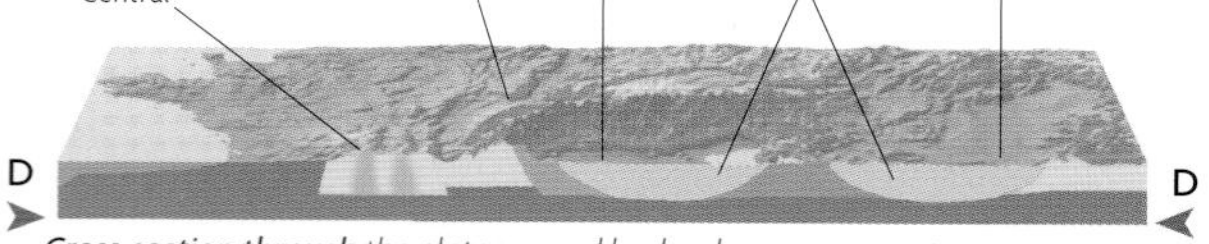
Igneous rocks have intruded into the Massif Central
Older, eroded massifs lie behind the arc of the Alps
Po Valley
Tectonically formed basins
Great Hungarian Plain
D
D
0 100 Km
0 100 Miles

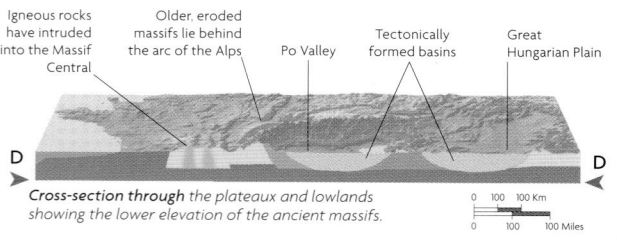

Cross-section through the plateaux and lowlands showing the lower elevation of the ancient massifs.

▲ *Frost grips northern and eastern Europe during the long cold winters. Lakes and rivers frequently freeze.*

Climate

Europe experiences few extremes in either rainfall or temperature, with the exception of the far north and south. Along the west coast, the warm currents of the North Atlantic Drift moderate temperatures. Although east–west air movement is relatively unimpeded by relief, the Alpine Uplands halt the progress of north–south air masses, protecting most of the Mediterranean from cold, north winds.

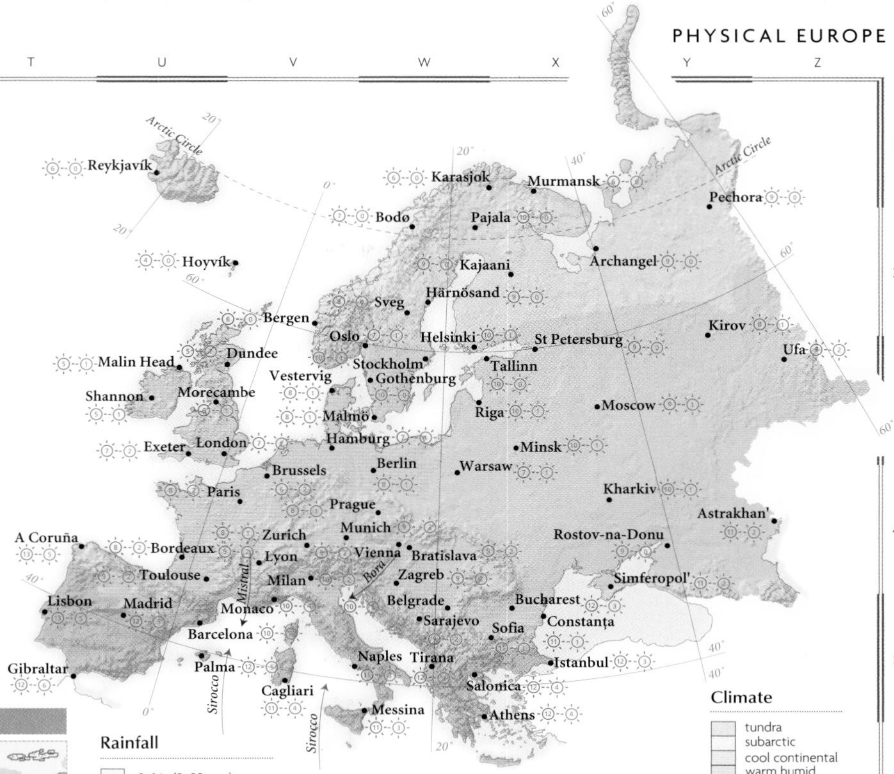
Arctic Circle
Reykjavík
Hoyvík
Bergen
Malin Head
Dundee
Shannon
Morecambe
Exeter
London
Karasjok
Murmansk
Pechora
Bodø
Pajala
Kajaani
Archangel
Härnösand
Sveg
Oslo
Helsinki
St Petersburg
Kirov
Ufa
Vestervig
Stockholm
Gothenburg
Tallinn
Malmö
Riga
Moscow
Hamburg
Berlin
Minsk
Brussels
Warsaw
Paris
Prague
Kharkiv
Munich
Astrakhan'
A Coruña
Bordeaux
Zurich
Vienna
Bratislava
Rostov-na-Donu
Lyon
Toulouse
Milan
Zagreb
Simferopol'
Mistral
Bora
Lisbon
Madrid
Monaco
Belgrade
Bucharest
Sarajevo
Constanța
Sofia
Barcelona
Gibraltar
Palma
Naples
Tirana
Istanbul
Cagliari
Salonica
Messina
Athens
Sirocco

Temperature

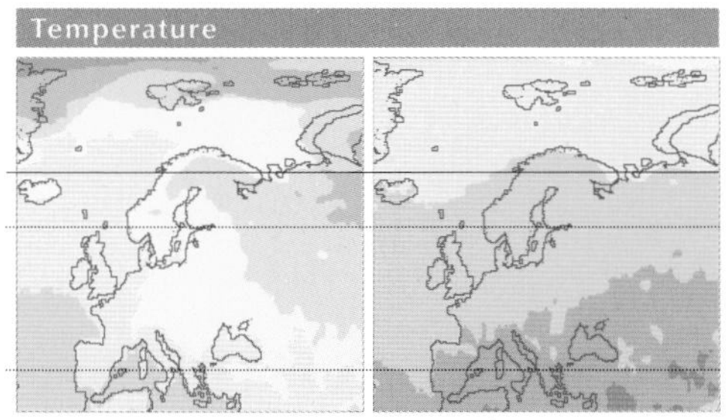
Temperature
Arctic Circle
60° N
40° N

Average January temperature *Average July temperature*

Temperature

- below -22°F (-30°C)
- -22 to -4°F (-30 to -20°C)
- -4 to 14°F (-20 to -10°C)
- 14 to 32°F (-10 to 0°C)
- 32 to 50°F (0 to 10°C)
- 50 to 68°F (10 to 20°C)
- 68 to 86°F (20 to 30°C)
- above 86°F (30°C)

▲ *Mild temperatures and frequent rainfall contribute to the fertile farming land found over much of northwestern Europe.*

Rainfall

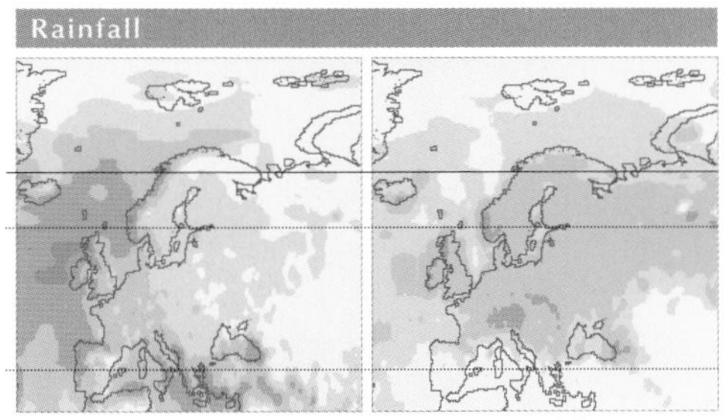
Rainfall
Arctic Circle
60° N
40° N

Average January rainfall *Average July rainfall*

Rainfall

- 0–1 in (0–25 mm)
- 1–2 in (25–50 mm)
- 2–4 in (50–100 mm)
- 4–8 in (100–200 mm)
- 8–12 in (200–300 mm)
- 12–16 in (300–400 mm)
- 16–20 in (400–500 mm)
- more than 20 in (500 mm)

▶ *Dusty Sirocco winds from Africa help create the semiarid scrubland common across the Mediterranean coastlands of southern Europe.*

Climate

- tundra
- subarctic
- cool continental
- warm humid
- mediterranean
- semi-arid
- daily hours of sunshine, January
- daily hours of sunshine, July
- cold wind
- hot wind

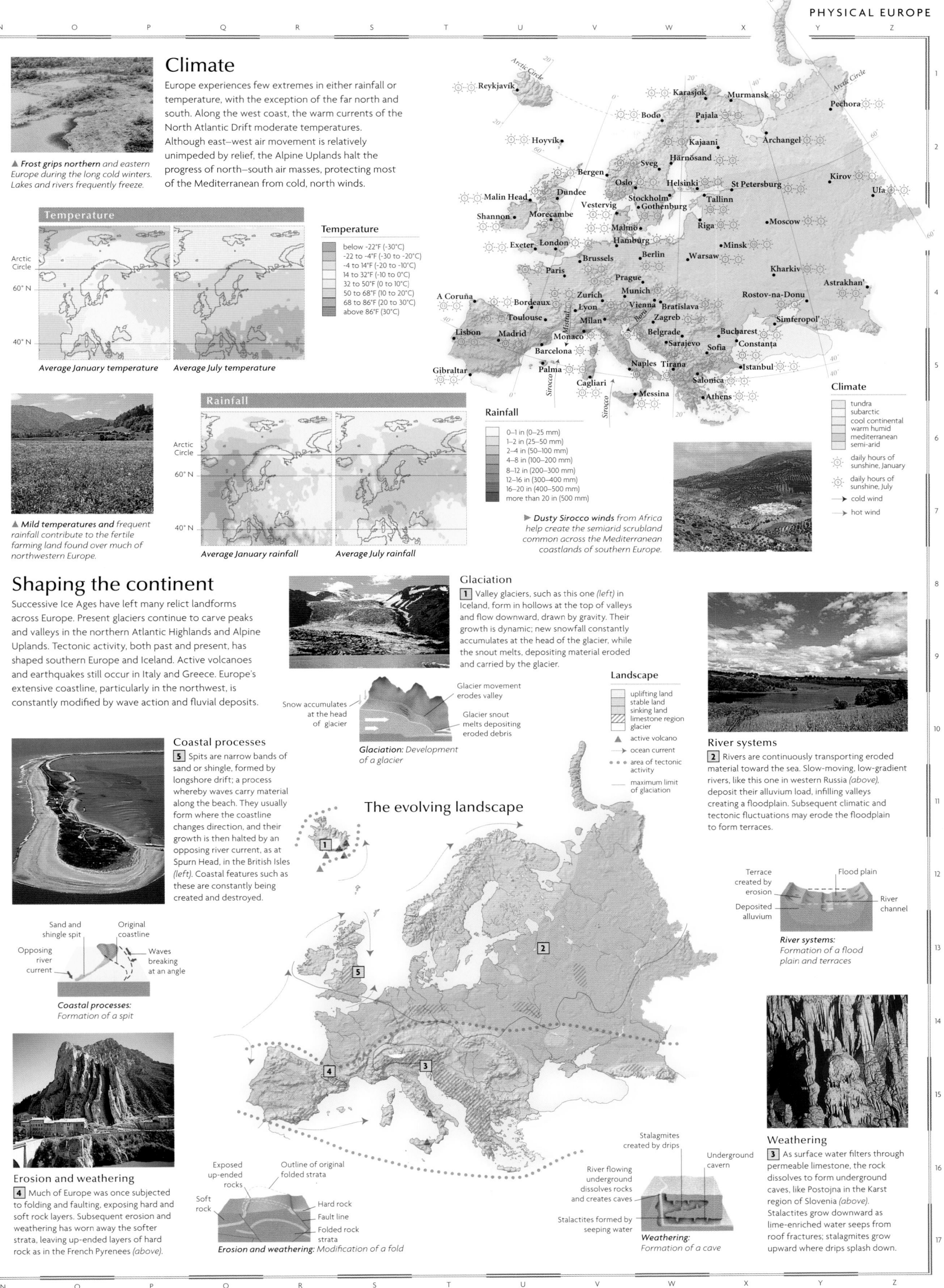

Shaping the continent

Successive Ice Ages have left many relict landforms across Europe. Present glaciers continue to carve peaks and valleys in the northern Atlantic Highlands and Alpine Uplands. Tectonic activity, both past and present, has shaped southern Europe and Iceland. Active volcanoes and earthquakes still occur in Italy and Greece. Europe's extensive coastline, particularly in the northwest, is constantly modified by wave action and fluvial deposits.

Glaciation

1 Valley glaciers, such as this one *(left)* in Iceland, form in hollows at the top of valleys and flow downward, drawn by gravity. Their growth is dynamic; new snowfall constantly accumulates at the head of the glacier, while the snout melts, depositing material eroded and carried by the glacier.

Snow accumulates at the head of glacier
Glacier movement erodes valley
Glacier snout melts depositing eroded debris

***Glaciation:** Development of a glacier*

River systems

2 Rivers are continuously transporting eroded material toward the sea. Slow-moving, low-gradient rivers, like this one in western Russia *(above)*, deposit their alluvium load, infilling valleys creating a floodplain. Subsequent climatic and tectonic fluctuations may erode the floodplain to form terraces.

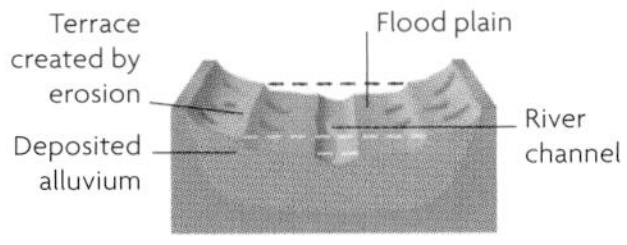
Terrace created by erosion
Flood plain
River channel
Deposited alluvium

***River systems:** Formation of a flood plain and terraces*

Coastal processes

5 Spits are narrow bands of sand or shingle, formed by longshore drift; a process whereby waves carry material along the beach. They usually form where the coastline changes direction, and their growth is then halted by an opposing river current, as at Spurn Head, in the British Isles *(left)*. Coastal features such as these are constantly being created and destroyed.

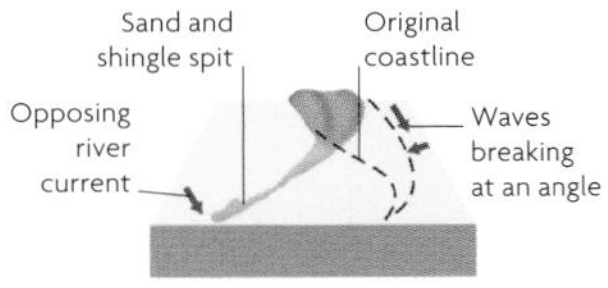
Sand and shingle spit
Original coastline
Opposing river current
Waves breaking at an angle

***Coastal processes:** Formation of a spit*

The evolving landscape

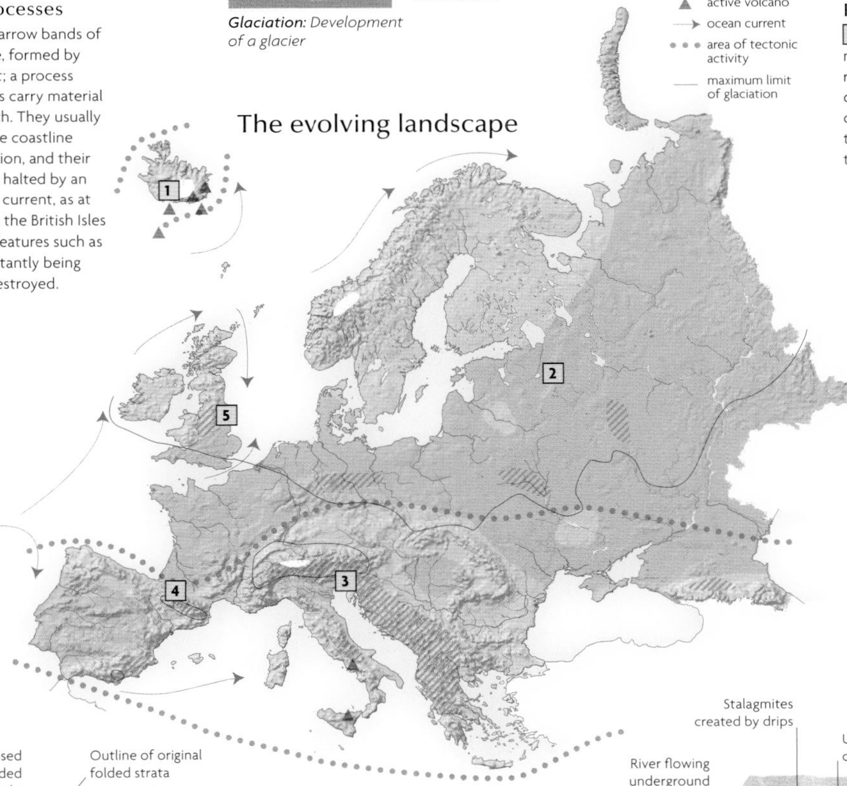
1
2
3
4
5

Landscape

- uplifting land
- stable land
- sinking land
- limestone region
- glacier
- ▲ active volcano
- ocean current
- area of tectonic activity
- maximum limit of glaciation

Erosion and weathering

4 Much of Europe was once subjected to folding and faulting, exposing hard and soft rock layers. Subsequent erosion and weathering has worn away the softer strata, leaving up-ended layers of hard rock as in the French Pyrenees *(above)*.

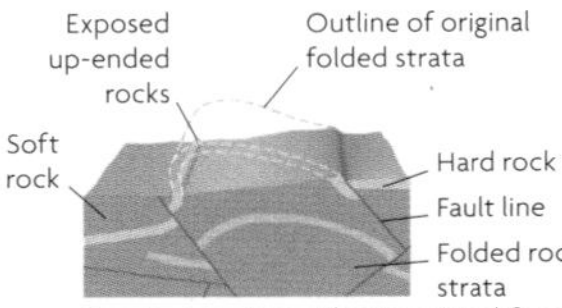
Exposed up-ended rocks
Outline of original folded strata
Soft rock
Hard rock
Fault line
Folded rock strata

***Erosion and weathering:** Modification of a fold*

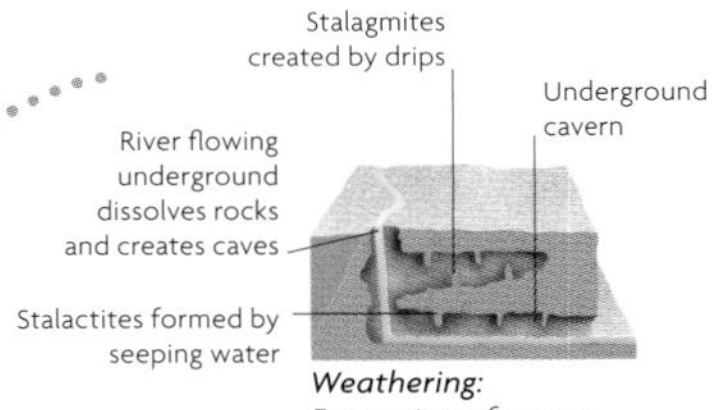
Stalagmites created by drips
Underground cavern
River flowing underground dissolves rocks and creates caves
Stalactites formed by seeping water

***Weathering:** Formation of a cave*

Weathering

3 As surface water filters through permeable limestone, the rock dissolves to form underground caves, like Postojna in the Karst region of Slovenia *(above)*. Stalactites grow downward as lime-enriched water seeps from roof fractures; stalagmites grow upward where drips splash down.

A B C D E F G H I J K L M

Political Europe

The political boundaries of Europe have changed many times, especially during the 20th century in the aftermath of two world wars, the breakup of the empires of Austria-Hungary, Nazi Germany and, toward the end of the century, the collapse of communism in eastern Europe. The fragmentation of Yugoslavia has again altered the political map of Europe, highlighting a trend toward nationalism and devolution. In contrast, economic federalism is growing. In 1958, the formation of the European Economic Community (now the European Union or EU) started a move toward economic and political union and increasing internal migration.

▲ ***The Brandenburg Gate** in Berlin is a potent symbol of German reunification. From 1961, the road beneath it ended in a wall, built to stop the flow of refugees to the West. It was opened again in 1989 when the wall was destroyed and East and West Germany were reunited.*

Population

Europe is a densely populated, urbanized continent; in Belgium over 90% of people live in urban areas. The highest population densities are found in an area stretching east from southern Britain and northern France, into Germany. The northern fringes are only sparsely populated.

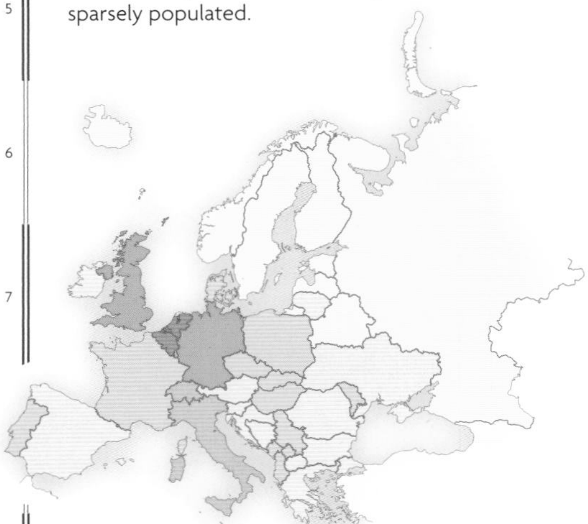

Population density
(people per sq mile)

- below 130
- 130–259
- 260–379
- 380–519
- 520–780
- above 780

▲ ***Demand for space** in densely populated European cities like London has led to the development of high-rise offices and urban sprawl.*

▲ ***Traditional lifestyles still** persist in many remote and rural parts of Europe, especially in the south, east, and in the far north.*

Denmark Strait
Arctic Circle
REYKJAVÍK
ICELAND
Norwegian Sea
Faeroe Islands
(to Denmark)
ATLANTIC OCEAN
Shetland Islands
Orkney Islands
Outer Hebrides
SCOTLAND
Aberdeen
Dundee
Glasgow
Edinburgh
NORTHERN IRELAND
Belfast
IRELAND
DUBLIN
Isle of Man
(to UK)
Newcastle upon Tyne
UNITED KINGDOM
Liverpool
Manchester
Leeds
Sheffield
WALES
Birmingham
ENGLAND
Cardiff
Thames
LONDON
Southampton
North Sea
Channel Islands
(to UK)
English Channel
NORWAY
Trondheim
Bergen
Stavanger
OSLO
Kristiansand
SWEDEN
Gulf of Bothnia
FINLAND
Tampere
Turku
HELSINKI
Åland
Uppsala
Örebro
STOCKHOLM
Vänern
Vättern
Gothenburg
Jönköping
Gotland
Baltic Sea
DENMARK
Aalborg
COPENHAGEN
Odense
Helsingborg
Malmö
Murmansk
St Petersburg
TALLINN
ESTONIA
LATVIA
RIGA
Ventspils
Liepāja
Western Dvina
LITHUANIA
Kaunas
VILNIUS
RUSS. FED.
(Kaliningrad)
Kaliningrad
Gdańsk
Vitsyebsk
MINSK
Babruysk
BELARUS
Homyel'
Brest
AMSTERDAM
NETH.
THE HAGUE
Rotterdam
Groningen
Bremen
Hamburg
Elbe
Nijmegen
Hanover
Oder
BERLIN
Antwerp
BELGIUM
BRUSSELS
Liège
Düsseldorf
Bonn
Rhine
GERMANY
Leipzig
Dresden
Frankfurt am Main
LUXEMBOURG
Bydgoszcz
Vistula
Poznań
Łódź
WARSAW
POLAND
Wrocław
Kraków
PRAGUE
CZECH REPUBLIC
Nuremberg
Stuttgart
Strasbourg
Munich
Salzburg
Danube
VIENNA
SLOVAKIA
BRATISLAVA
Győr
Miskolc
BUDAPEST
HUNGARY
L'viv
UKRAINE
Chernivtsi
Dniester
MOLDOVA
CHIȘINĂU
Cluj-Napoca
ROMANIA
Brașov
BUCHAREST
Constanța
Ruse
Varna
Burgas
BULGARIA
SOFIA
Stara Zagora
Istanbul
le Havre
Seine
Rennes
PARIS
Orléans
St-Nazaire
Nantes
Loire
Bay of Biscay
FRANCE
Limoges
Bordeaux
Lyon
Geneva
BERN
Zurich
SWITZERLAND
Alps
Innsbruck
AUSTRIA
LIECHTENSTEIN
LJUBLJANA
SLOVENIA
Trieste
ZAGREB
CROATIA
Milan
Turin
Verona
Venice
Po
Genoa
Bologna
Florence
SAN MARINO
Pisa
MONACO
Nice
Marseille
Rhône
Toulouse
Pyrenees
ANDORRA LA VELLA
ANDORRA
Bilbao
Ebro
A Coruña
Porto
Duero
Valladolid
PORTUGAL
Tagus
LISBON
Setúbal
MADRID
Zaragoza
SPAIN
Barcelona
Valencia
Seville
Córdoba
Cádiz
Málaga
Murcia
Gibraltar
(to UK)
Ceuta
(to Spain)
Melilla
(to Spain)
Ibiza
Palma
Majorca
Minorca
Balearic Islands
Corsica
Sardinia
Cagliari
ITALY
VATICAN CITY
ROME
Adriatic Sea
Naples
Bari
Tyrrhenian Sea
Cosenza
Palermo
Sicily
Messina
Catania
MALTA
VALLETTA
Mediterranean Sea
Ionian Sea
BOS. & HERZ.
SARAJEVO
Mostar
BELGRADE
SERBIA
MONTENEGRO
PODGORICA
KOSOVO
(disputed)
PRISHTINE
SKOPJE
MACEDONIA
TIRANA
ALBANIA
Salonica
Larisa
GREECE
Aegean Sea
ATHENS
Piraeus
Iráklion
Crete

Map key

Population

- above 5 million
- 1 million to 5 million
- 500,000 to 1 million
- 100,000 to 500,000
- 50,000 to 100,000
- 10,000 to 50,000
- Country capital

Borders

- full international border

Scale 1:17,250,000

Km 0 100 200 300 400 500 600 700

Miles 0 100 200 300 400 500 600 700

projection: Lambert Azimuthal Equal Area

A B C D E F G H I

N O P Q R S T U V W Z
1 2 3 4 5 6 7 8 9 10 11 12 13 14 15 16 17
Novaya Zemlya
Kara Sea
Vorkuta
Arctic Circle
Barents Sea
Ural Mountains
White Sea
Archangel
Northern Dvina
RUSSIAN FEDERATION
Lake Onega
Perm'
Kirov
Vologda
Ufa
Yaroslavl'
Kazan'
Nizhniy Novgorod
Ul'yanovsk
Tol'yatti
Samara
Orenburg
MOSCOW
Tula
Kazakhstan
Saratov
Voronezh
Kharkiv
Volgograd
INE
Dnipropetrovs'k
Donets'k
Volga
Astrakhan'
Rostov-na-Donu
Caspian Sea
Dnieper
Sea of Azov
Stavropol'
Grozny
Simferopol'
Novorossiysk
Caucasus
Georgia
Azerbaijan
Black Sea

Overcoming natural barriers, the Brenner Autobahn, one of the main routes across the Alps, links Innsbruck in Austria with Verona in Italy.

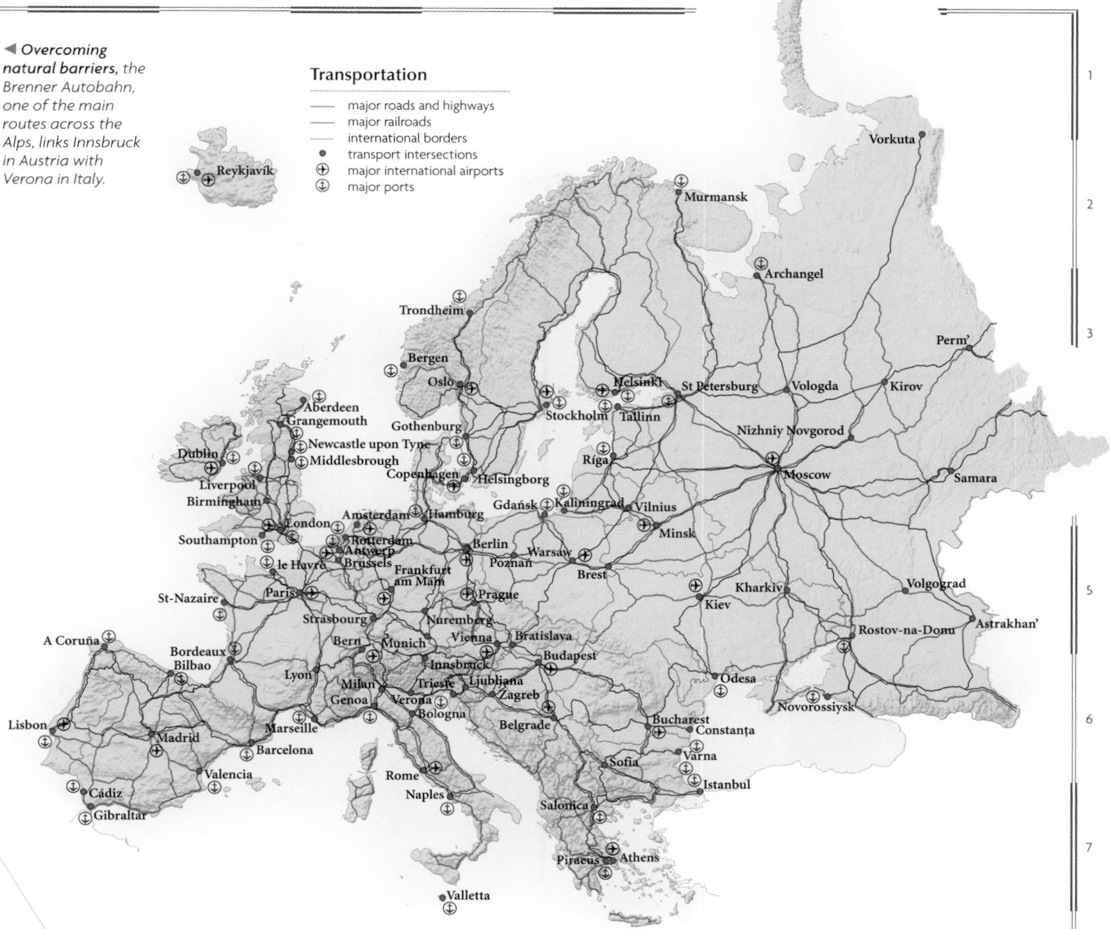

Transportation
major roads and highways
major railroads
international borders
transport intersections
major international airports
major ports
Reykjavík
Murmansk
Vorkuta
Archangel
Trondheim
Bergen
Oslo
Perm'
Helsinki
St Petersburg
Vologda
Kirov
Stockholm
Tallinn
Aberdeen
Grangemouth
Gothenburg
Nizhniy Novgorod
Newcastle upon Tyne
Middlesbrough
Riga
Dublin
Copenhagen
Helsingborg
Moscow
Samara
Liverpool
Birmingham
Gdańsk
Kaliningrad
Vilnius
Minsk
Amsterdam
Hamburg
London
Rotterdam
Antwerp
Southampton
Brussels
Berlin
Poznań
Warsaw
le Havre
Frankfurt am Main
Brest
Kharkiv
Volgograd
St-Nazaire
Paris
Prague
Kiev
Strasbourg
Nuremberg
Astrakhan'
A Coruña
Bern
Munich
Vienna
Bratislava
Rostov-na-Donu
Bordeaux
Bilbao
Budapest
Innsbruck
Lyon
Milan
Trieste
Ljubljana
Odesa
Genoa
Verona
Zagreb
Novorossiysk
Bologna
Lisbon
Marseille
Belgrade
Bucharest
Constanța
Madrid
Barcelona
Varna
Sofia
Valencia
Rome
Istanbul
Naples
Cádiz
Gibraltar
Salonica
Piraeus
Athens
Valletta

Transportation

Despite its fragmented geography and many natural frontiers, communications in Europe are well developed. Extensive highway links allow rapid road transportation. High-speed rail connections like France's TGV *(Train à Grande Vitesse)*, and the Channel Tunnel have improved rail travel. Outdated communication infrastructures in parts of eastern Europe, and insufficient transportation links across the Alps, however, remain weak parts of the network.

Languages

There are three main European language groups: Germanic languages predominate in central and northern Europe; Romance languages in western and Mediterranean Europe and Romania; while Slavic languages are spoken in eastern Europe and the Russian Federation. Isolated pockets of local languages, such as Basque and Gaelic, persist and frequently provide a focus for national identity.

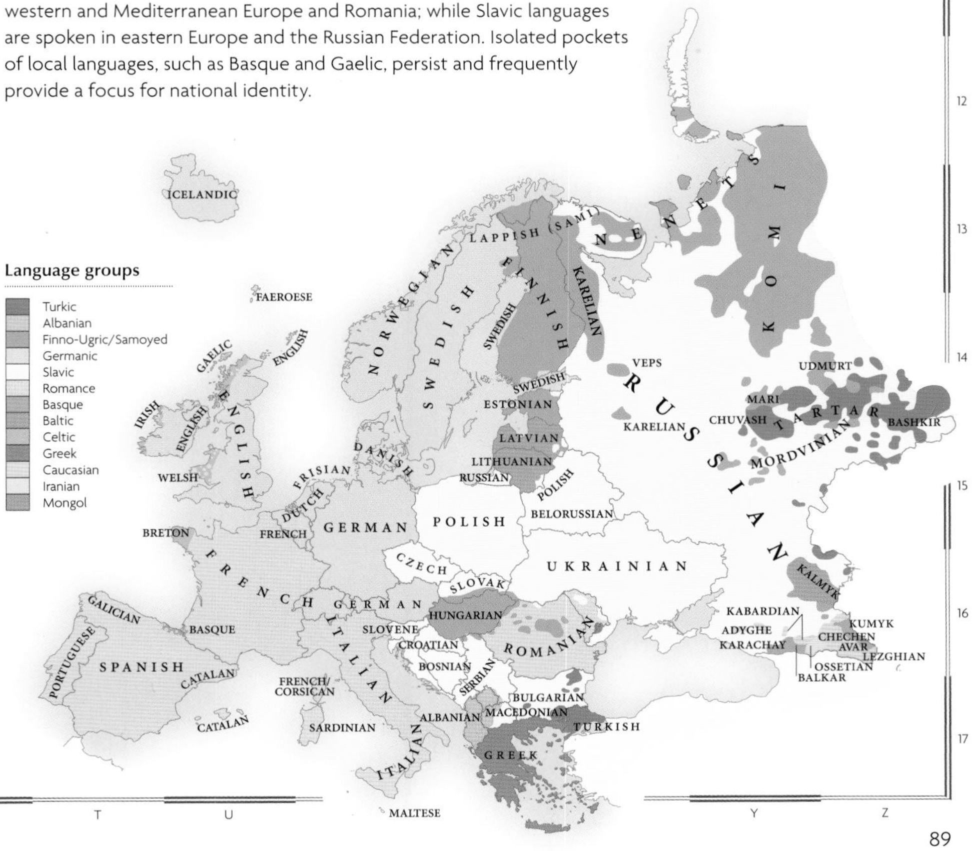

Language groups
Turkic
Albanian
Finno-Ugric/Samoyed
Germanic
Slavic
Romance
Basque
Baltic
Celtic
Greek
Caucasian
Iranian
Mongol
ICELANDIC
FAEROESE
LAPPISH (SAMI)
NENETS
KOMI
NORWEGIAN
SWEDISH
FINNISH
KARELIAN
GAELIC
ENGLISH
IRISH
VEPS
UDMURT
SWEDISH
ESTONIAN
RUSSIAN
KARELIAN
MARI
CHUVASH
TARTAR
BASHKIR
MORDVINIAN
WELSH
DANISH
LATVIAN
LITHUANIAN
RUSSIAN
POLISH
FRISIAN
DUTCH
BELORUSSIAN
BRETON
FRENCH
GERMAN
POLISH
CZECH
SLOVAK
UKRAINIAN
KALMYK
GALICIAN
FRENCH
GERMAN
HUNGARIAN
KABARDIAN
ADYGHE
KARACHAY
KUMYK
CHECHEN
AVAR
LEZGHIAN
OSSETIAN
BALKAR
PORTUGUESE
BASQUE
SLOVENE
CROATIAN
ROMANIAN
SPANISH
CATALAN
ITALIAN
BOSNIAN
SERBIAN
FRENCH/CORSICAN
BULGARIAN
MACEDONIAN
TURKISH
CATALAN
SARDINIAN
ALBANIAN
GREEK
ITALIAN
MALTESE

The architecture of the Grand Place lies at the heart of Brussels – home city to one of the EU headquarters.

European resources

Europe's large tracts of fertile, accessible land, combined with its generally temperate climate, have allowed a greater percentage of land to be used for agricultural purposes than in any other continent. Extensive coal and iron ore deposits were used to create steel and manufacturing industries during the 19th and 20th centuries. Today, although natural resources have been widely exploited, and heavy industry is of declining importance, the growth of hi-tech and service industries has enabled Europe to maintain its wealth.

Standard of living

Living standards in western Europe are among the highest in the world, although there is a growing sector of homeless, jobless people. Eastern Europeans have lower overall standards of living – a legacy of stagnated economies.

Standard of living
(UN human development index)
low
high
data not available

Industry

Europe's wealth was generated by the rise of industry and colonial exploitation during the 19th century. The mining of abundant natural resources made Europe the industrial center of the world. Adaptation has been essential in the changing world economy, and a move to service-based industries has been widespread except in eastern Europe, where heavy industry still dominates.

▲ *Other power sources are becoming more attractive as fossil fuels run out; 16% of Europe's electricity is now provided by hydroelectric power.*

▲ *Countries like Hungary are still struggling to modernize inefficient factories left over from extensive, centrally-planned industrialization during the communist era.*

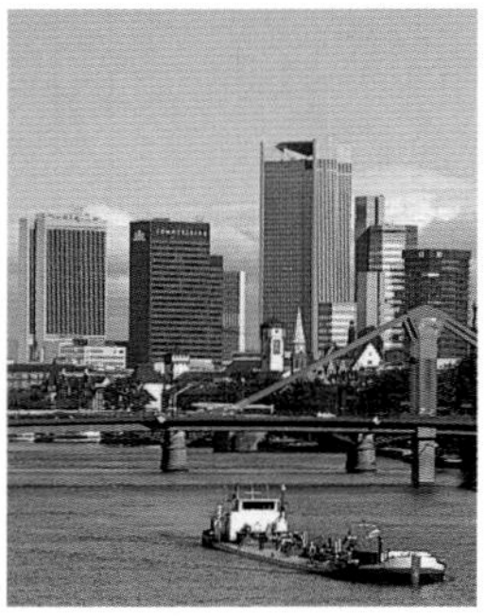

◀ *Frankfurt am Main is an example of a modern service-based city. The skyline is dominated by headquarters from the worlds of banking and commerce.*

▶ *Skiing brings millions of tourists to the slopes each year, which means that even unproductive, marginal land is used to create wealth in the French, Swiss, Italian, and Austrian Alps.*

GNI per capita (US $)
below 1999
2000–4999
5000–9999
10,000–19,999
20,000–24,999
above 25,000
Industry
aerospace
brewing
car/vehicle manufacture
chemicals
defense
electronics
engineering
finance
food processing
hi-tech industry
iron & steel
pharmaceuticals
printing & publishing
shipbuilding
textiles
timber processing
wine
coal
oil
gas
industrial cities
major industrial areas
ATLANTIC OCEAN
Norwegian Sea
North Sea
Barents Sea
Baltic Sea
Gulf of Bothnia
Bay of Biscay
Mediterranean Sea
Tyrrhenian Sea
Adriatic Sea
Ionian Sea
Aegean Sea
Black Sea
Caspian Sea
Balearic Islands
Novaya Zemlya
Ostrov Kolguyev
Faeroe Islands (to Denmark)
ICELAND
IRELAND
UNITED KINGDOM
NORWAY
SWEDEN
FINLAND
DENMARK
ESTONIA
LATVIA
LITHUANIA
RUSS. FED. (Kaliningrad)
BELARUS
POLAND
GERMANY
NETH.
BELG.
LUX.
FRANCE
SWITZ.
LIECH.
AUSTRIA
CZECH REP.
SLOVAKIA
HUNGARY
UKRAINE
MOLDOVA
ROMANIA
SLVN.
CROATIA
BOSNIA & HERZ.
SERBIA
MONT.
KOSOVO
ALBANIA
MACED.
BULGARIA
GREECE
TURKEY
ITALY
SAN MARINO
VATICAN CITY
MONACO
ANDORRA
SPAIN
PORTUGAL
MALTA
MOROCCO
GEORGIA
AZERBAIJAN
KAZAKHSTAN
RUSSIAN FEDERATION
Reykjavík
Trondheim
Bergen
Oslo
Stockholm
Gothenburg
Malmö
Copenhagen
Turku
Helsinki
Tallinn
St Petersburg
Murmansk
Archangel
Riga
Vilnius
Gdańsk
Minsk
Glasgow
Belfast
Newcastle upon Tyne
Isle of Man (to UK)
Dublin
Liverpool
Manchester
Birmingham
Cardiff
London
Channel Islands (to UK)
Amsterdam
Rotterdam
Antwerp
Essen
Brussels
Lille
Liège
Cologne
Hamburg
Berlin
Leipzig
Dresden
Poznań
Łódź
Warsaw
Kraków
Katowice
Prague
Frankfurt am Main
Stuttgart
Munich
Metz
Strasbourg
Rouen
Paris
Nantes
Bordeaux
Lyon
Toulouse
Marseille
Zürich
Linz
Vienna
Bratislava
Budapest
Turin
Milan
Venice
Genoa
Bologna
Zagreb
Rome
Naples
Taranto
Palermo
Sicily
Sardinia
Corsica
Belgrade
Sofia
Ploești
Bucharest
Constanța
Varna
Istanbul
Salonica
Athens
Piraeus
Crete
Kiev
Kharkiv
Dnipropetrovs'k
Kryvyy Rih
Donets'k
Odesa
Rostov-na-Donu
Volgograd
Voronezh
Kursk
Saratov
Samara
Tol'yatti
Kazan'
Ufa
Perm'
Nizhniy Novgorod
Ivanovo
Yaroslavl'
Cherepovets
Moscow
Ryazan'
Tula
A Coruña
Bilbao
Porto
Lisbon
Madrid
Barcelona
Seville
Gibraltar (to UK)
Ceuta (to Spain)
Melilla (to Spain)

Environmental issues
national parks
marine pollution
risk of acid rain
heavy marine pollution
polluted rivers
poor urban air quality
radioactive contamination
Barents Sea
Norwegian Sea
ATLANTIC OCEAN
North Sea
Glasgow
Dublin
Birmingham
London
Brussels
Paris
Frankfurt am Main
Essen
Berlin
Leipzig
Bydgoszcz
Warsaw
Prague
Kraków
St Petersburg
Moscow
Volga
Kiev
Volgograd
Donets'k
Dnipropetrovs'k
Miskolc
Budapest
Zagreb
Milan
Bucharest
Ruse
Black Sea
Caspian Sea
Lisbon
Madrid
Adriatic Sea
Tyrrhenian Sea
Ionian Sea
Athens
Aegean Sea
Mediterranean Sea

Mineral resources

Fossil fuels are Europe's main mineral resource, although fuel demand far outstrips production. Sizeable coal reserves remain in the Donbass in Ukraine, Germany's Ruhr Valley and Poland. Oil and gas reserves are found mainly in the North Sea, the Volga Basin and the Caucasus.

▶ *The valuable oil and gas reserves in the North Sea were first discovered in the early 1960s, and are exploited by the UK, Denmark, Germany, and Norway.*

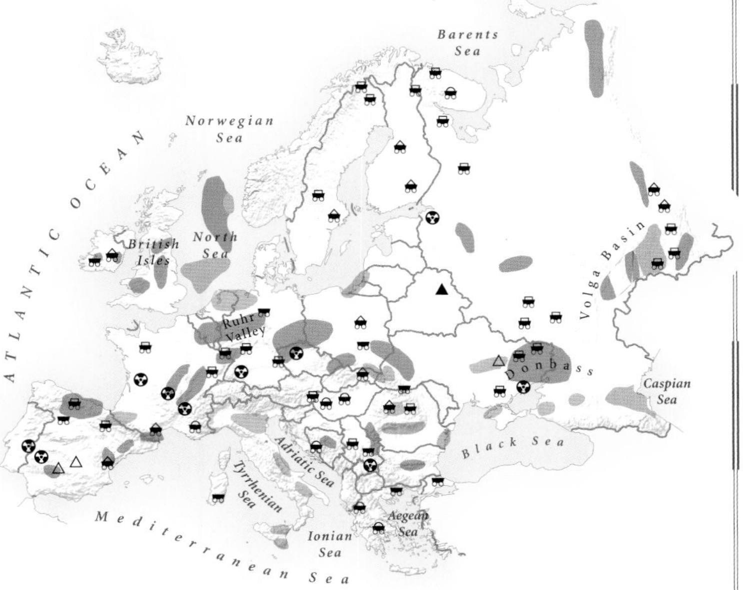
Mineral resources
oil field
gas field
coal field
bauxite
iron
lead
mercury
potassium
uranium
zinc
Barents Sea
Norwegian Sea
ATLANTIC OCEAN
British Isles
North Sea
Ruhr Valley
Volga Basin
Donbass
Caspian Sea
Black Sea
Adriatic Sea
Tyrrhenian Sea
Ionian Sea
Aegean Sea
Mediterranean Sea

Environmental issues

The partially enclosed waters of the Baltic and Mediterranean seas have become heavily polluted, while the Barents Sea is contaminated with spent nuclear fuel from Russia's navy. During the later stages of the 20th Century acid rain caused by unchecked emissions from factories and power stations was actively destroying northern forests. However, since then international efforts to reduce pollution have brought significant improvements in many areas.

▲ *Coniferous forest covers vast swathes of northern Scandinavia and the Russian Federation. Pollutants from other parts of Europe mixing with rainfall are causing defoliation and serious damage to many forests.*

▶ *The Camargue in the Rhône Delta, southern France, is a protected wetland area, famous for its native population of white horses, and unique bird and plant life.*

Using the land and sea

Europe's swelling urban population and the outward expansion of many cities has created acute competition for land. Despite this, European resourcefulness has maximized land potential, and over half of Europe's land is still used for a wide variety of agricultural purposes. Land in northern Europe is used for cattle-rearing, pasture, and arable crops. Toward the Mediterranean, the mild climate allows the growing of grapes for wine; olives, sunflowers, tobacco, and citrus fruits. EU subsidies, however, have resulted in massive overproduction and a land "set-aside" policy has been introduced.

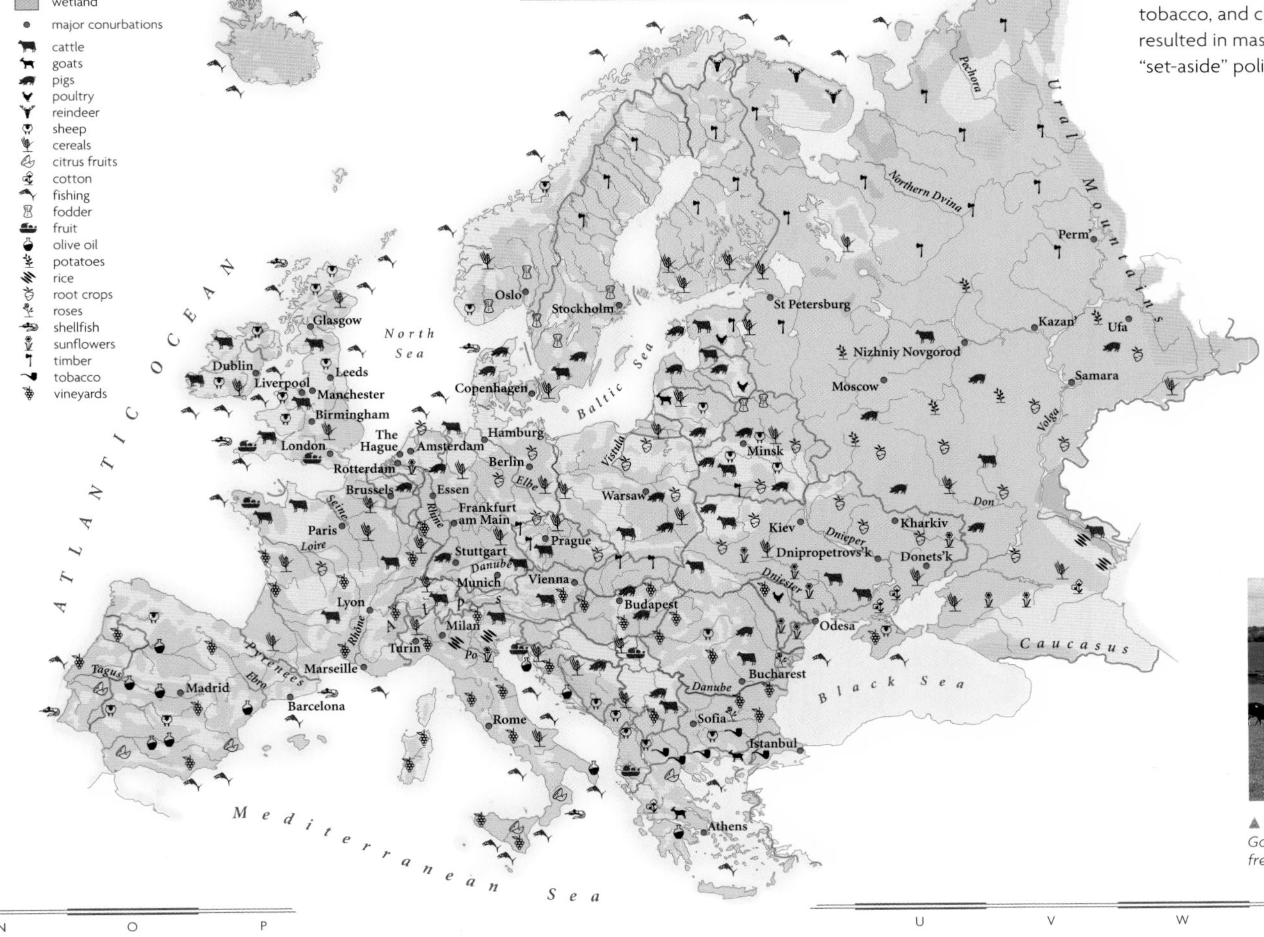
Using the land and sea
cropland
forest
ice cap
mountain region
pasture
tundra
wetland
major conurbations
cattle
goats
pigs
poultry
reindeer
sheep
cereals
citrus fruits
cotton
fishing
fodder
fruit
olive oil
potatoes
rice
root crops
roses
shellfish
sunflowers
timber
tobacco
vineyards
ATLANTIC OCEAN
North Sea
Baltic Sea
Ural Mountains
Black Sea
Caucasus
Mediterranean Sea
Oslo
Stockholm
St Petersburg
Glasgow
Dublin
Leeds
Liverpool
Manchester
Birmingham
Copenhagen
Hamburg
London
The Hague
Amsterdam
Rotterdam
Berlin
Minsk
Brussels
Essen
Warsaw
Paris
Frankfurt am Main
Prague
Kiev
Kharkiv
Dnipropetrovs'k
Donets'k
Stuttgart
Munich
Vienna
Lyon
Milan
Budapest
Odesa
Turin
Marseille
Bucharest
Madrid
Barcelona
Rome
Sofia
Istanbul
Athens
Moscow
Nizhniy Novgorod
Perm'
Kazan'
Ufa
Samara

▲ *Bulgarian roses are one of the many diverse crops grown in Europe. Rose oil, extracted from the petals, is used in perfume making.*

▲ *Lowland pastures are used for dairy farming. Good transportation links and refrigeration allow fresh milk to be distributed throughout Europe.*

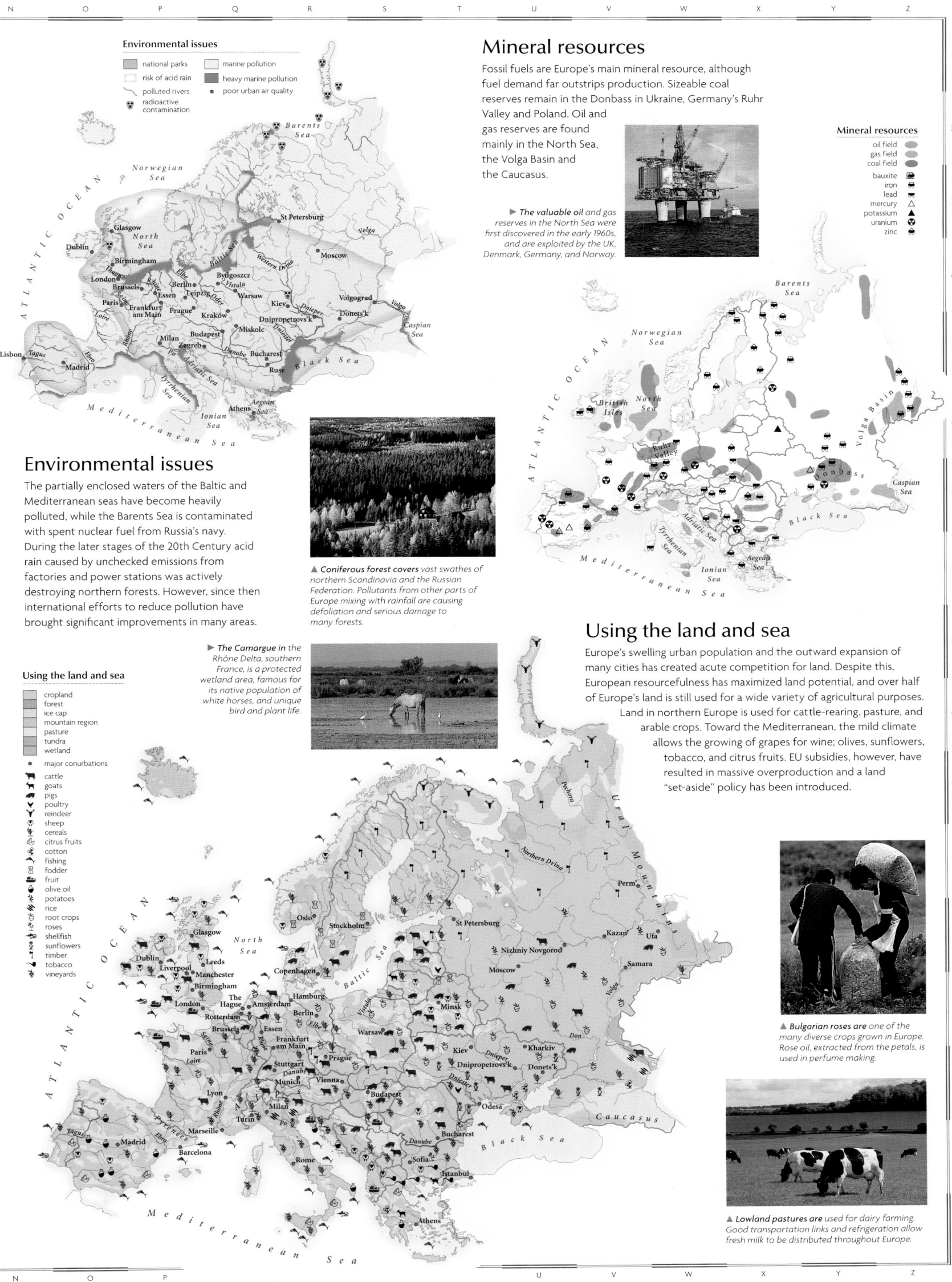

Scandinavia, Finland & Iceland

DENMARK, NORWAY, SWEDEN, FINLAND, ICELAND

Jutting into the Arctic Circle, this northern swath of Europe has some of the continent's harshest environments, but benefits from great reserves of oil, gas, and natural evergreen forests. While most early settlers came from the south, migrants to Finland came from the east, giving it a distinct language and culture. Since the late 19th century, the Scandinavian states have developed strong egalitarian traditions. Today, their welfare benefits systems are among the most extensive in the world, and standards of living are high. The Lapps, or Sami, maintain their traditional lifestyle in the northern regions of Norway, Sweden, and Finland.

The landscape

Glaciers up to 10,000 ft (3000 m) deep covered most of Scandinavia and Finland during the last Ice Age. The effects of glaciation mark the entire landscape, from the mountains to the lowlands, across the tundra landscape of Lapland, and the lake districts of Sweden and Finland.

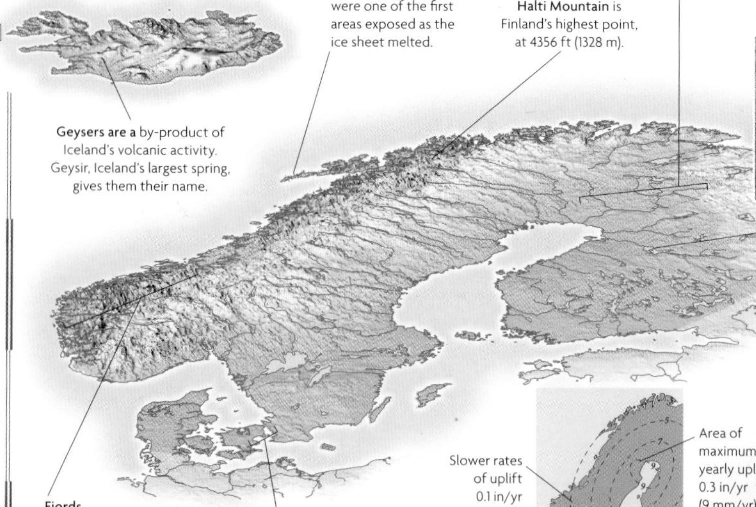

The Lofoten Islands were one of the first areas exposed as the ice sheet melted.

Halti Mountain is Finland's highest point, at 4356 ft (1328 m).

Lapland, north of the Arctic Circle, is an area of undulating fells and plains known as tundra. The subsoil is permanently frozen and therefore impermeable. There are many peat bogs. Pools reappear in the summer when the surface thaws.

Geysers are a by-product of Iceland's volcanic activity. Geysir, Iceland's largest spring, gives them their name.

Oulujärvi

◀ ***Finland's landscape was*** *fashioned by ice action. Glaciers gouged out its distinctive shallow lake basins, such as Oulujärvi, and left debris called moraines in their wake.*

Fjords

▲ ***The fjords on*** *the western coast of Norway were once gentle river valleys. Their deep floors and steep sides were carved out by glaciers during the last Ice Age, and they were later flooded by the sea.*

Sjælland coast

▲ ***On the coast*** *of Sjælland, these cliffs have been eroded by the sea, exposing layers of chalk and limestone.*

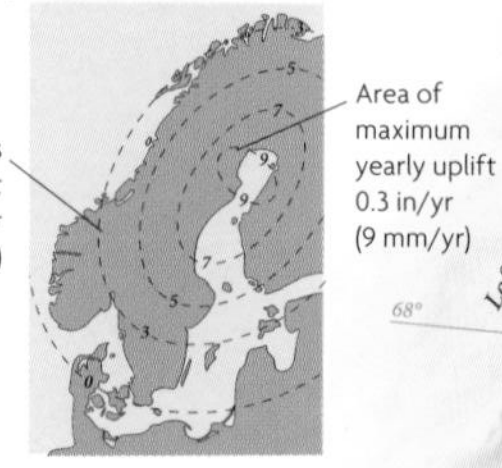

Slower rates of uplift 0.1 in/yr (3 mm/yr)
Area of maximum yearly uplift 0.3 in/yr (9 mm/yr)

▲ ***Scandinavia is still*** *recovering from the last Ice Age, when ice depressed the land by 2000 ft (600 m). This gradual uplift is known as isostatic rebound.*

Denmark Strait
GREENLAND SEA
ATLANTIC OCEAN
ICELAND
REYKJAVÍK
VESTFIRDHIR
NORDHURLAND EYSTRA
NORDHURLAND VESTRA
VESTURLAND
SUDHURLAND
AUSTURLAND
Vatnajökull
Hvannadalshnúkur 2119m

(same scale as main map)

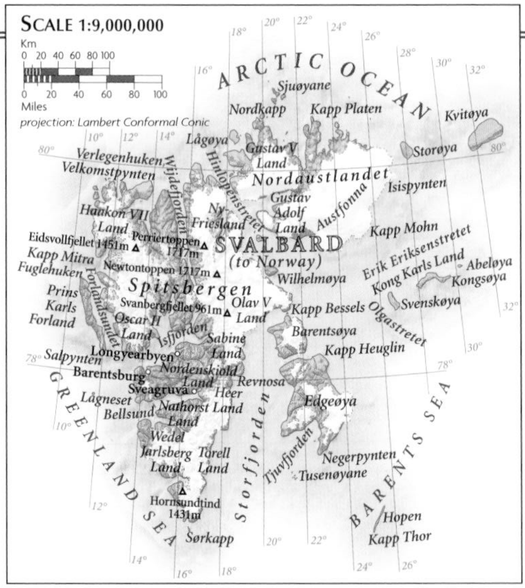

SCALE 1:9,000,000
projection: Lambert Conformal Conic
ARCTIC OCEAN
SVALBARD (to Norway)
Spitsbergen
Nordaustlandet
BARENTS SEA
GREENLAND SEA

Using the land & sea

The cold climate, short growing season, poorly developed soil, steep slopes, and exposure to high winds across northern regions means that most agriculture is concentrated, with the population, in the south. Most of Finland and much of Norway and Sweden are covered by dense forests of pine, spruce, and birch, which supply the timber industries.

Scale 1:5,500,000

Km 0 10 20 40 60 80 100 120 140 160
Miles 0 10 20 40 60 80 100 120 140 160
projection: Lambert Conformal Conic

ARCTIC OCEAN
BARENTS SEA
RUSSIAN FEDERATION
FINNMARK
TROMS
NORDLAND
NORRBOTTEN
LAPPI
Lapland
Nordkapp (North Cape)

122

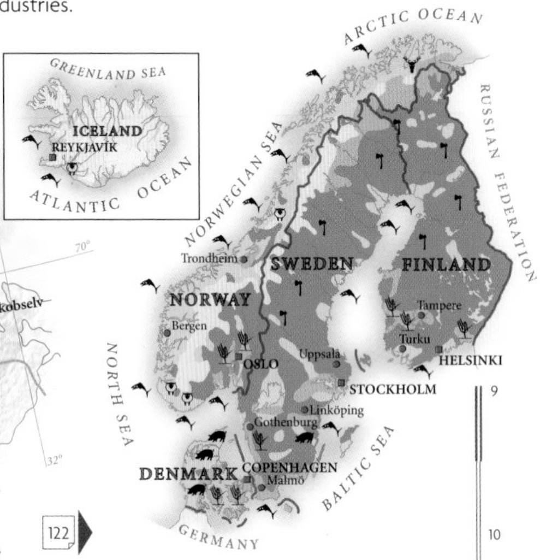

ARCTIC OCEAN
RUSSIAN FEDERATION
NORWEGIAN SEA
NORTH SEA
BALTIC SEA
GREENLAND SEA
ATLANTIC OCEAN
ICELAND
REYKJAVÍK
NORWAY
SWEDEN
FINLAND
DENMARK
GERMANY
OSLO
STOCKHOLM
HELSINKI
COPENHAGEN

Land use and agricultural distribution

fishing, pigs, reindeer, sheep, cereals, timber; capital cities, major towns; pasture, cropland, forest, mountain region, tundra

The urban/rural population divide

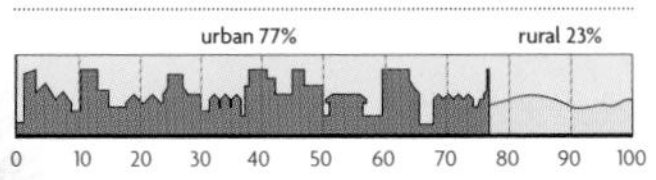

urban 77%
rural 23%
0 10 20 30 40 50 60 70 80 90 100

Population density	Total land area
51 people per sq mile (20 people per sq km)	473,970 sq miles (1,227,610 sq km)

NORWEGIAN SEA
NORWAY
SWEDEN
FINLAND
DENMARK
GERMANY
RUSSIAN FEDERATION
NORTH SEA
BALTIC SEA
Skagerrak
Kattegat
Gulf of Bothnia
Gulf of Finland
OSLO
STOCKHOLM
HELSINKI
KØBENHAVN (COPENHAGEN)
100

▲ **Many Lappish people,** *in addition to traditional reindeer herding, now also make their living from fishing and farming, or working in cities. Tourism provides some with an extra source of income.*

▲ **Sweden is one** *of the world's largest producers of wood and wood-based products. The traditional movement of logs by floating them down rivers has now been largely replaced by the use of trucks.*

Map key

Population

- 1 million to 5 million
- 500,000 to 1 million
- 100,000 to 500,000
- 50,000 to 100,000
- 10,000 to 50,000
- below 10,000

Elevation

- 2000m / 6562ft
- 1000m / 3281ft
- 500m / 1640ft
- 250m / 820ft
- 100m / 328ft
- sea level

Transportation & industry

Norway derives its premier industry, the production of oil and gas, from the North Sea, while Denmark exploits its own oil and gas reserves. Hydroelectric power is a major industry, particularly in Sweden and Iceland. Timber processing remains significant in Finland and Sweden, but metal and engineering industries are increasingly important. In Iceland, fish products are the main source of export earnings.

Transportation network

- 226,735 miles (364,936 km)
- 2042 miles (3286 km)
- 13,704 miles (22,057 km)
- 6,661 miles (10,721 km)

Although roads now reach most areas, the railroads are markedly less developed. Much of the north is not served by rail and must rely on air and sea services for long distance travel and freight transportation.

▶ **The use of** *geothermal power in Iceland began half a century ago. Today geothermal power stations supply 89% of the country's domestic heating requirements.*

GREENLAND SEA
ICELAND
REYKJAVÍK
ATLANTIC OCEAN

Major industry and infrastructure

- car manufacture
- engineering
- fish processing
- hydroelectric power
- nuclear power
- oil & gas
- timber processing
- capital cities
- major towns
- international airports
- major roads
- major industrial areas

ARCTIC OCEAN
NORWEGIAN SEA
RUSSIAN FEDERATION
NORTH SEA
BALTIC SEA
GERMANY
NORWAY
SWEDEN
FINLAND
DENMARK
OSLO
STOCKHOLM
HELSINKI
COPENHAGEN
Trondheim
Bergen
Stavanger
Narvik
Luleå
Umeå
Oulu
Kemi
Rovaniemi
Tampere
Turku
Uppsala
Örebro
Jönköping
Gothenburg
Aalborg
Odense
Malmö

Southern Scandinavia

SOUTHERN NORWAY, SOUTHERN SWEDEN, DENMARK

Scandinavia's economic and political hub is the more habitable and accessible southern region. Many of the area's major cities are on the southern coasts, including Oslo and Stockholm, the capitals of Norway and Sweden. In Denmark, most of the population and the capital, Copenhagen, are located on its many islands. A cultural unity links the three Scandinavian countries. Their main languages, Danish, Swedish, and Norwegian, are mutually intelligible, and they all retain their monarchies, although the parliaments have legislative control.

Using the land

Agriculture in southern Scandinavia is highly mechanized although farms are small. Denmark is the most intensively farmed country and its western pastureland is used mainly for pig farming. Cereal crops including wheat, barley, and oats, predominate in eastern Denmark and in the far south of Sweden. Southern Norway, and Sweden have large tracts of forest which are exploited for logging.

The urban/rural population divide

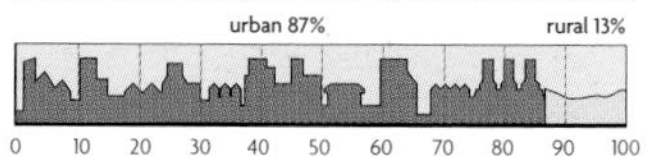
urban 87%
rural 13%
0 10 20 30 40 50 60 70 80 90 100

Population density	Total land area
112 people per sq mile (43 people per sq km)	173,487 sq miles (456,564 sq km)

Land use and agricultural distribution

cattle
pigs
sheep
cereals
fodder
root crops
timber
capital cities
major towns
pasture
cropland
forest
mountain region
NORWEGIAN SEA
Trondheim
NORWAY
Bergen
OSLO
SWEDEN
Uppsala
Örebro
STOCKHOLM
Linköping
Gothenburg
NORTH SEA
Aalborg
DENMARK
COPENHAGEN
Odense
Malmö
BALTIC SEA
GERMANY

▲ In Norway winters are longer and colder inland than in coastal areas, where the warm current of the North Atlantic Drift moderates the climate.

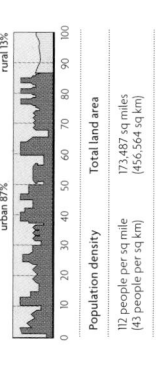

The landscape

Southern Scandinavia, with the exception of Norway, has a flatter terrain than the rest of the region. Denmark and southern Sweden are both extensions of the North European Plain. In this area, because of glacial deposition rather than erosion, the soils are deeper and more fertile.

◀ *In the past, glaciers such as this one in Olden, Norway, were much larger. Today, many are retreating to yield the spectacular glacial scenery.*

▲ *Limestone pillars eroded by the sea dot the coast of Gotland and surrounding islands.*

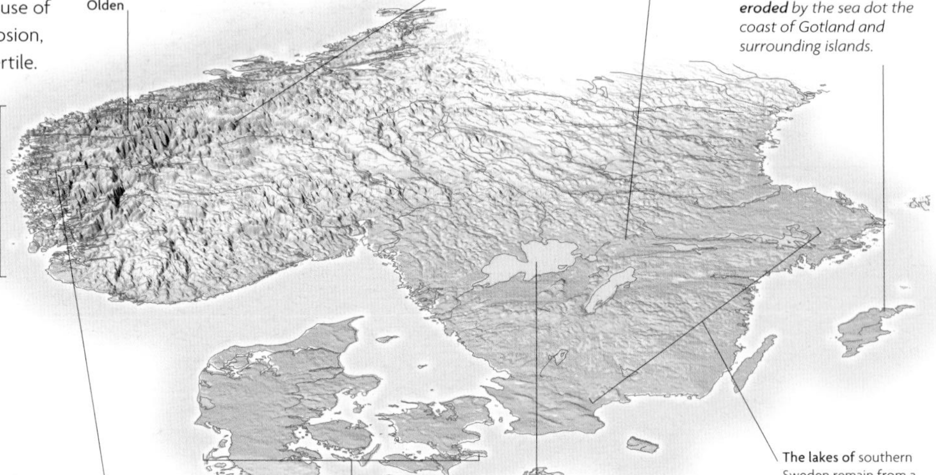
Olden
Sognefjorden

Acid rain, caused by industrial pollution carried north from elsewhere in Europe, harms plant and animal life in Scandinavian forests and lakes. The region's surface rocks lack lime to neutralize the acid, so making the problem more serious.

The peak of Glittertind in the Jotunheimen mountains is 8110 ft (2472 m) high.

Distinctive low ridges, called eskers, are found across southern Sweden. They are formed from sand and gravel deposits left by retreating glaciers.

Denmark's flat and fertile soils are formed on glacial deposits between 100–160 ft (30–50 m) deep.

Vänern in Sweden is the largest lake in Scandinavia. It covers an area of 2080 sq miles (5390 sq km).

The lakes of southern Sweden remain from a period when the land was completely flooded. As the ice which covered the area melted, the land rose, leaving lakes in shallow, ice-scoured depressions. Sweden has over 90,000 lakes.

Sognefjorden

Erosion by glaciers deepened existing river valleys
Sea level
When the ice retreated the valley was flooded by the sea
Old valley floor

▲ *Sognefjorden is the deepest of Norway's many fjords. It drops to 4291 ft (1308 m) below sea level.*

NORWEGIAN SEA
NORD-TRØNDELAG
SØR-TRØNDELAG
MØRE OG ROMSDAL
SOGN OG FJORDANE
OPPLAND
HEDMARK
JÄMTLAND
VÄSTERNORRLAND
GÄVLEBORG
DALARNA
NORWAY
Gulf of Bothnia
Trondheim
Kristiansund
Molde
Ålesund
Lillehammer
Hamar
Elverum
Røros
Storsylen 1762m
Snøhetta 2286m
Glittertind 2472m
Galdhøpiggen 2469m

96
92
92

Scale 1:3,250,000

Km 0 5 10 20 30 40 50 60 70 80 90 100
Miles 0 5 10 20 30 40 50 60 70 80 90 100

projection: Lambert Conformal Conic

Map key

Population
- 1 million to 5 million
- 500,000 to 1 million
- 100,000 to 500,000
- 50,000 to 100,000
- 10,000 to 50,000
- below 10,000

Elevation
- 2000m / 6562ft
- 1000m / 3281ft
- 500m / 1640ft
- 250m / 820ft
- 100m / 328ft

▲ **Shipbuilding in Gothenburg** has declined in recent years as manufacturers in other sectors have come to the fore. One of these is the car firm, Volvo, a major employer in Gothenburg.

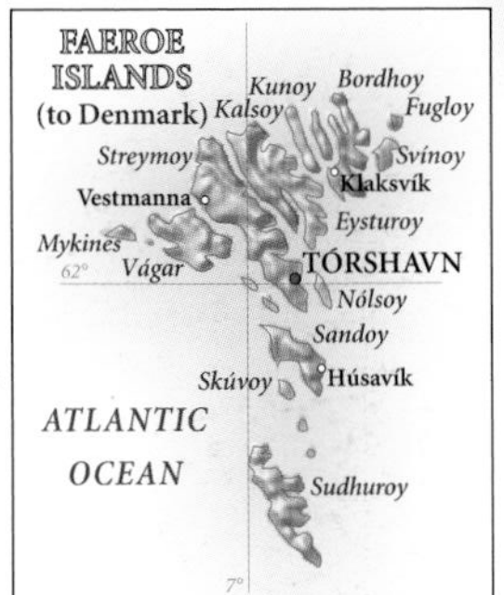
FAEROE ISLANDS (to Denmark)
Kunoy
Bordhoy
Fugloy
Kalsoy
Svinoy
Streymoy
Klaksvík
Vestmanna
Eysturoy
Mykines
Vágar
TÓRSHAVN
Nólsoy
Sandoy
Skúvoy
Húsavík
ATLANTIC OCEAN
Sudhuroy

(same scale as main map)

FINLAND
BUSKERUD
HORDALAND
ROGALAND
TELEMARK
VEST-AGDER
AUST-AGDER
ØSTFOLD
AKERSHUS
OSLO
VÄRMLAND
VÄSTMANLAND
UPPSALA
STOCKHOLM
ÖREBRO
SÖDERMANLAND
VÄSTRA GÖTALAND
ÖSTERGÖTLAND
JÖNKÖPING
KALMAR
HALLAND
KRONOBERG
BLEKINGE
SKÅNE
S W E D E N
Skagerrak
Kattegat
NORTH SEA
BALTIC SEA
Gotland
Öland
Bornholm
NORDJYLLAND
MIDTJYLLAND
SYDDANMARK
SJÆLLAND
KØBENHAVN
Jylland
Sjælland
D E N M A R K
G E R M A N Y
Göteborg (Gothenburg)
Malmö
Aalborg
Århus
Odense
Stavanger
Kristiansand

96
110
100

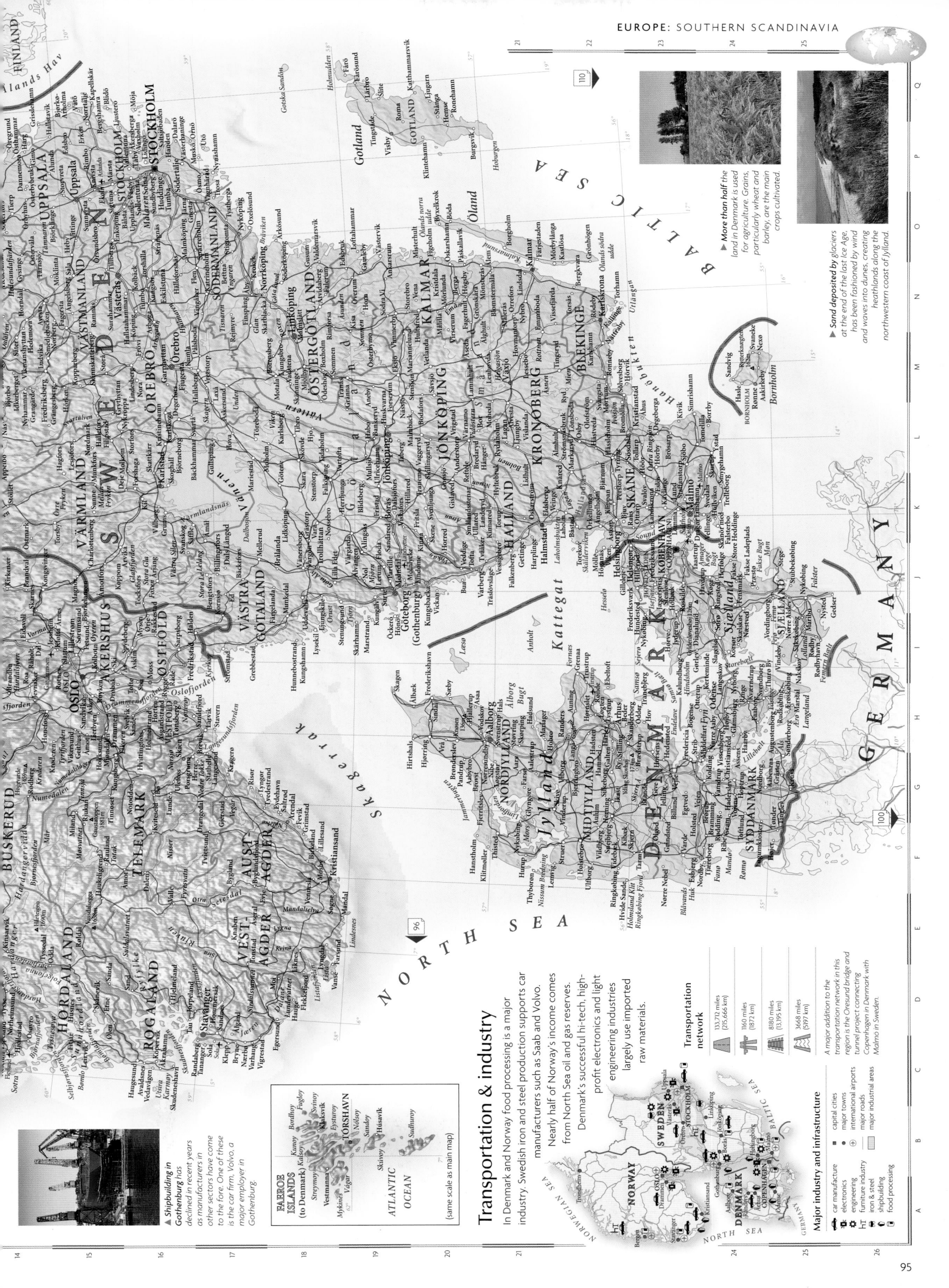

▶ **More than half** the land in Denmark is used for agriculture. Grains, particularly wheat and barley, are the main crops cultivated.

▶ **Sand deposited by** glaciers at the end of the last Ice Age, has been fashioned by wind and waves into dunes, creating heathlands along the northwestern coast of Jylland.

Transportation & industry

In Denmark and Norway food processing is a major industry. Swedish iron and steel production supports car manufacturers such as Saab and Volvo. Nearly half of Norway's income comes from North Sea oil and gas reserves. Denmark's successful hi-tech, high-profit electronics and light engineering industries largely use imported raw materials.

NORWEGIAN SEA
NORTH SEA
BALTIC SEA
GERMANY
NORWAY
SWEDEN
DENMARK
Trondheim
Bergen
Stavanger
Kristiansand
OSLO
Drammen
Västerås
Uppsala
Örebro
STOCKHOLM
Linköping
Jönköping
Borås
Gothenburg
Aalborg
Randers
Århus
Odense
COPENHAGEN
Helsingborg
Malmö

Major industry and infrastructure

- car manufacture
- electronics
- engineering
- furniture industry
- iron & steel
- shipbuilding
- food processing
- capital cities
- major towns
- international airports
- major roads
- major industrial areas

Transportation network

- 133,712 miles (215,666 km)
- 1160 miles (1872 km)
- 8180 miles (13,195 km)
- 3668 miles (5197 km)

A major addition to the transportation network in this region is the Oresund bridge and tunnel project connecting Copenhagen in Denmark with Malmo in Sweden.

The British Isles

UNITED KINGDOM, IRELAND

The British Isles have for centuries played a central role in European and world history. England, Wales, Scotland, and Northern Ireland together form the United Kingdom (UK), while the southern portion of Ireland is an independent country, self-governing since 1921. Although England has tended to be the politically and economically dominant partner in the UK, the Scots, Welsh, and Irish maintain independent cultures, distinct national identities and languages. Southeastern England is the most densely populated part of this crowded region, with over eight million people living in and around the London area.

Transportation & industry

The British Isles' industrial base was founded primarily on coal, iron, and textiles, based largely in the north. Today, the most productive sectors include hi-tech industries clustered mainly in southeastern England, chemicals, finance, and the service sector, particularly tourism.

Major industry and infrastructure

- car manufacture
- chemicals
- engineering
- hi-tech industry
- iron & steel
- tourism
- capital cities
- major towns
- international airports
- major roads
- major industrial areas

ATLANTIC OCEAN
NORTH SEA
English Channel
UNITED KINGDOM
IRELAND
Aberdeen
Dundee
Edinburgh
Glasgow
Newcastle upon Tyne
Belfast
Leeds
Liverpool
Manchester
DUBLIN
Nottingham
Birmingham
Norwich
Cork
Oxford
Cardiff
Bristol
LONDON

Transportation network

285,947 miles (460,240 km)		2023 miles (3578 km)	
11,825 miles (19,032km)		3976 miles (6400 km)	

The UK's congested roads have become a major focus of environmental concern in recent years. No longer an island, the UK was finally linked to continental Europe by the Channel Tunnel in 1994.

◀ **Clew Bay in** *western Ireland, is characteristic of the heavily indented west coast, where deep wide-mouthed bays separate the mountains of Mayo, Donegal, and Kerry as they thrust out into the Atlantic Ocean.*

▲ ***The valley of*** *Glen Coe in the Scottish Highlands is a U-shaped valley, typical of the north and west of the British Isles, where glaciers shaped much of the landscape.*

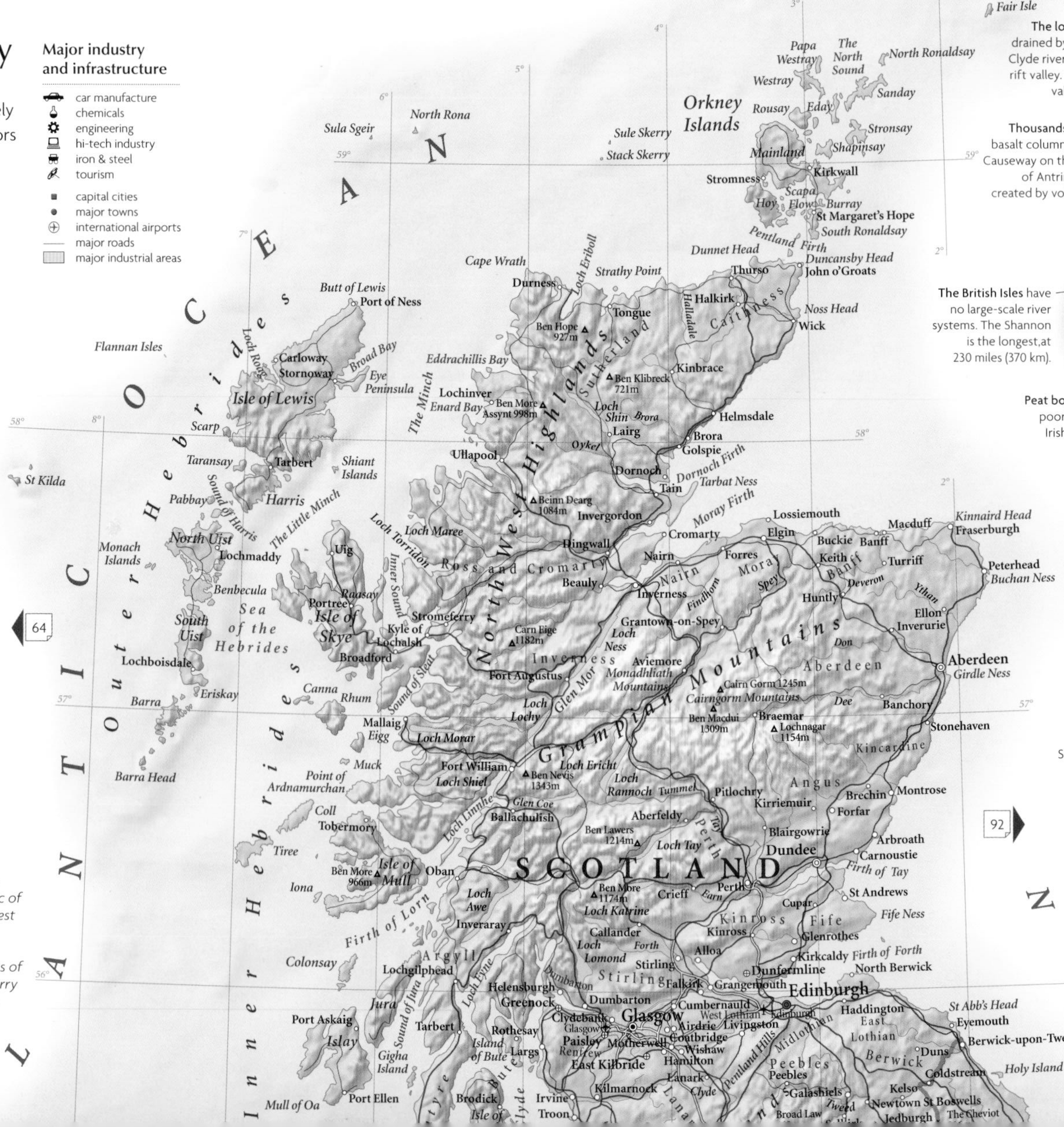

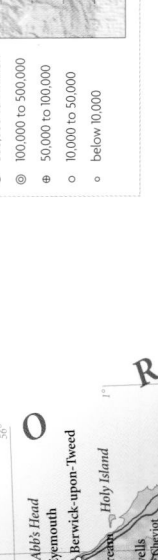

ATLANTIC OCEAN
NORTH SEA
Shetland Islands
Orkney Islands
SCOTLAND
Outer Hebrides
Inner Hebrides
Sea of the Hebrides
North West Highlands
Grampian Mountains
Herma Ness
Unst
Fetlar
Yell
Yell Sound
Sullom Voe
Out Skerries
Whalsay
Hillswick
St Magnus Bay
Papa Stour
Mainland
Lerwick
Bressay
Foula
Scalloway
West Burra
Fitful Head
Sumburgh Head
Fair Isle
North Ronaldsay
Sanday
Stronsay
Shapinsay
Kirkwall
Stromness
Hoy
Scapa Flow
Burray
St Margaret's Hope
South Ronaldsay
Pentland Firth
Duncansby Head
John o'Groats
Dunnet Head
Thurso
Noss Head
Wick
Sula Sgeir
North Rona
Sule Skerry
Stack Skerry
Cape Wrath
Durness
Strathy Point
Tongue
Halkirk
Kinbrace
Helmsdale
Brora
Golspie
Dornoch
Tain
Lairg
Ullapool
Lochinver
Butt of Lewis
Port of Ness
Carloway
Stornoway
Isle of Lewis
Tarbert
Harris
Scarp
Taransay
Pabbay
North Uist
Lochmaddy
Benbecula
South Uist
Lochboisdale
Eriskay
Barra
Barra Head
Flannan Isles
St Kilda
Monach Islands
Shiant Islands
The Minch
The Little Minch
Uig
Portree
Isle of Skye
Broadford
Raasay
Kyle of Lochalsh
Stromeferry
Inner Sound
Canna
Rhum
Eigg
Muck
Mallaig
Coll
Tiree
Tobermory
Isle of Mull
Iona
Oban
Colonsay
Jura
Islay
Port Askaig
Port Ellen
Mull of Oa
Gigha Island
Fort William
Ben Nevis 1343m
Fort Augustus
Inverness
Nairn
Forres
Elgin
Lossiemouth
Buckie
Banff
Macduff
Fraserburgh
Kinnaird Head
Peterhead
Buchan Ness
Turriff
Huntly
Ellon
Inverurie
Aberdeen
Girdle Ness
Banchory
Stonehaven
Braemar
Lochnagar 1154m
Cairn Gorm 1245m
Cairngorm Mountains
Ben Macdui 1309m
Aviemore
Grantown-on-Spey
Pitlochry
Kirriemuir
Forfar
Brechin
Montrose
Arbroath
Carnoustie
Dundee
Firth of Tay
St Andrews
Fife Ness
Perth
Crieff
Cupar
Glenrothes
Kirkcaldy
Firth of Forth
North Berwick
Dunfermline
Edinburgh
Stirling
Falkirk
Grangemouth
Haddington
Dunbar
Livingston
Cumbernauld
Glasgow
Motherwell
Airdrie
Coatbridge
Paisley
Renfrew
Clydebank
Dumbarton
East Kilbride
Hamilton
Wishaw
Lanark
Kilmarnock
Irvine
Troon
Greenock
Helensburgh
Rothesay
Isle of Bute
Largs
Brodick
Inveraray
Lochgilphead
Callander
Loch Lomond
Loch Katrine
Loch Tay
Loch Ness
Loch Rannoch
Loch Ericht
Loch Linnhe
Loch Maree
Loch Torridon
Firth of Lorn
Moray Firth
Dornoch Firth
Cromarty
Invergordon
Tarbat Ness
St Abb's Head
Eyemouth
Berwick-upon-Tweed
Holy Island
Coldstream
Duns
Kelso
Galashiels
Peebles
Jedburgh
Newtown St Boswells
The Cheviot

The landscape

Rugged uplands dominate the landscape of Scotland, Wales, and northern England. All the peaks in the British Isles over 4000 ft (1219 m) lie in highland Scotland. Lowland England rises into several ranges of rolling hills, including the older Mendips, and the Cotswolds and the Chilterns, which were formed at the same time as the Alps in southern Europe.

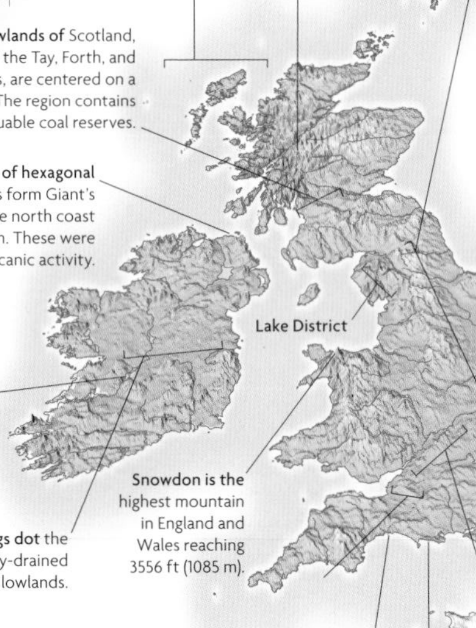

Over 600 islands, mostly uninhabited, lie west and north of the Scottish mainland.
Ben Nevis at 4409 ft (1343 m) is the highest peak in the UK.
The Pennines, sometimes called "the backbone of England," are formed of limestones and grits.
The lowlands of Scotland, drained by the Tay, Forth, and Clyde rivers, are centered on a rift valley. The region contains valuable coal reserves.
Thousands of hexagonal basalt columns form Giant's Causeway on the north coast of Antrim. These were created by volcanic activity.
Lake District
The Fens are a low-lying area reclaimed from the sea.
The British Isles have no large-scale river systems. The Shannon is the longest,at 230 miles (370 km).
Snowdon is the highest mountain in England and Wales reaching 3556 ft (1085 m).
Peat bogs dot the poorly-drained Irish lowlands.
Chiltern Hills
The Cotswold Hills are characterized by a series of limestone ridges overlooking clay vales.
Durdle Door
Black Ven, Lyme Regis

▲ ***Ullswater in the*** *Lake District fills a deep valley formed by glacial erosion.*

◀ ***Dartmoor,*** ***studded with*** *tors, is an exposed part of a vast granite dome, formed when molten rock intruded into the Earth's crust.*

▲ ***Coastal erosion around*** *the British Isles forms striking features such as this limestone arch, Durdle Door in Dorset.*

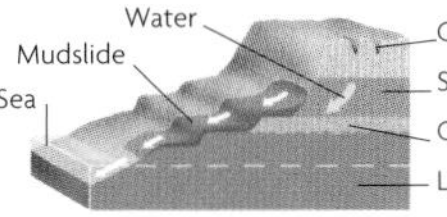

Water
Cracks
Sandstone
Mudslide
Sea
Clay
Limestone

▲ ***Much of the*** *south coast is subject to landslides. Following rain, porous sandstones feed water into the underlying, less permeable clays which then crumble and slide into the sea.*

Map key

Population

- above 5 million
- 1 million to 5 million
- 500,000 to 1 million
- 100,000 to 500,000
- 50,000 to 100,000
- 10,000 to 50,000
- below 10,000

Elevation

- 1000m / 3281ft
- 500m / 1640ft
- 250m / 820ft
- 100m / 328ft
- sea level

64
92

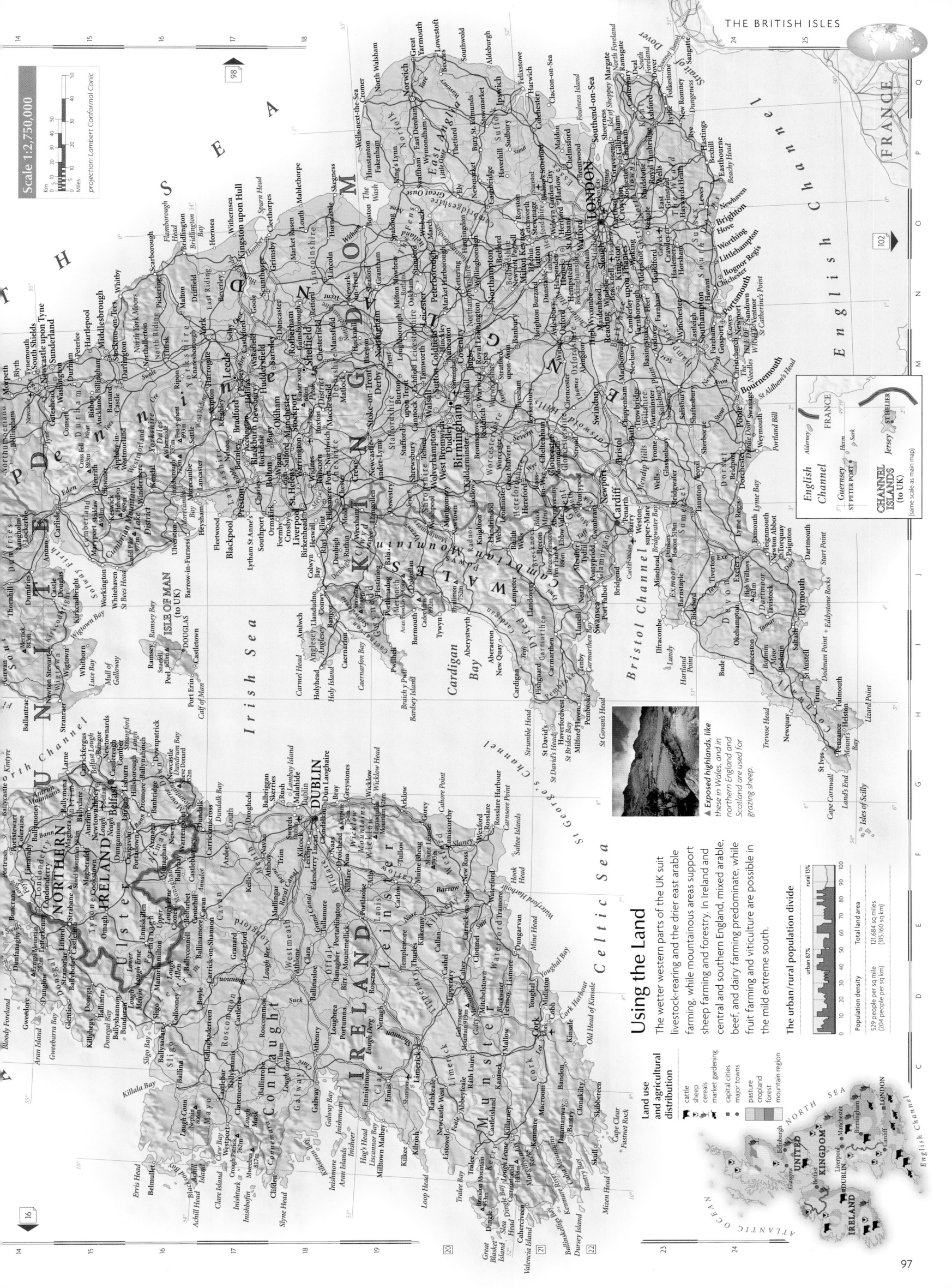

Scale 1:2,750,000
projection: Lambert Conformal Conic
UNITED KINGDOM
IRELAND
NORTHERN IRELAND
FRANCE
Ulster
Connaught
Leinster
Munster
WALES
ENGLAND
NORTH SEA
Irish Sea
Celtic Sea
St George's Channel
English Channel
Bristol Channel
Cardigan Bay
North Channel
Solway Firth
Strait of Dover
ISLE OF MAN (to UK)
DOUGLAS
DUBLIN
LONDON
Pennines
Cambrian Mountains
Isles of Scilly
English Channel
CHANNEL ISLANDS (to UK)
(same scale as main map)
Guernsey
ST PETER PORT
Jersey
ST HELIER
Alderney
Herm
Sark
16
98
102

Using the Land

The wetter western parts of the UK suit livestock-rearing and the drier east arable farming, while mountainous areas support sheep farming and forestry. In Ireland and central and southern England, mixed arable, beef, and dairy farming predominate, while fruit farming and viticulture are possible in the mild extreme south.

▲ *Exposed highlands, like these in Wales, and in northern England and Scotland are used for grazing sheep.*

Land use and agricultural distribution

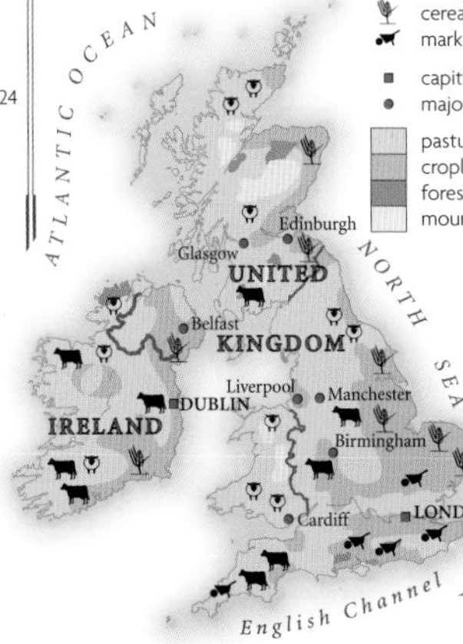
cattle
sheep
cereals
market gardening
capital cities
major towns
pasture
cropland
forest
mountain region
ATLANTIC OCEAN
NORTH SEA
English Channel
UNITED KINGDOM
IRELAND
Edinburgh
Glasgow
Belfast
DUBLIN
Liverpool
Manchester
Birmingham
Cardiff
LONDON

The urban/rural population divide

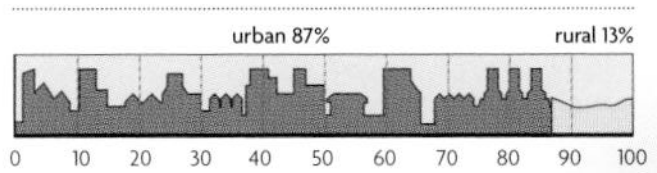
urban 87%
rural 13%
0
10
20
30
40
50
60
70
80
90
100

Population density	Total land area
529 people per sq mile (204 people per sq km)	121,684 sq miles (315,160 sq km)

The Low Countries

BELGIUM, LUXEMBOURG, NETHERLANDS

One of northwestern Europe's strategic crossroads, the Low Countries are united by a common history in which they have often been a battleground in European wars. For over a thousand years they were ruled by foreign powers. Even after they achieved independence, the three countries maintained close links, later forming the world's first totally free labor and goods market, the Benelux Economic Union, which became the core of the European Community (now the European Union or EU). These states have remained at the forefront of wider European cooperation; Brussels, The Hague, and Luxembourg are hosts to major institutions of the EU.

NETHERLANDS
AMSTERDAM
THE HAGUE
Rotterdam
Breda
Utrecht
Enschede
Nijmegen
Eindhoven
Groningen
Antwerp
Bruges
Ghent
Kortrijk
BRUSSELS
BELGIUM
Maastricht
Liège
Charleroi
LUXEMBOURG
LUXEMBOURG
Differdange
NORTH SEA
GERMANY
FRANCE

Major industry and infrastructure

- aerospace
- finance
- engineering
- hi-tech industry
- pharmaceuticals
- textiles
- capital cities
- major towns
- international airports
- major roads
- major industrial areas

Transportation & industry

In the western Netherlands, a massive, sprawling industrialized zone encompasses many new hi-tech and service industries. Belgium's central region has emerged as the country's light manufacturing and services center. Luxembourg city is home to more than 160 banks and the European headquarters of many international companies.

Transportation network

140,588 miles (226,281 km)	2565 miles (4129 km)
4099 miles (6598 km)	4134 miles (6653 km)

The Low Countries hold a key position on the North Sea, containing Europe's two largest ports, Rotterdam and Antwerp, which are connected to a comprehensive system of inland waterways.

The landscape

The main geographical regions of the Netherlands are the northern glacial heathlands, the low-lying lands of the Rhine and Maas/Meuse, the reclaimed polders, and the dune coast and islands. Belgium includes part of the Ardennes, together with the coalfields on its northern flanks, and the fertile Flanders plain.

Schoorl

◀ ***Heathlands, like these** at Schoorl, are found along the coast of the Netherlands. Much of the coast was breached by the sea in the 5th century, creating its distinctive inlets and islands.*

▲ ***One-third of the** Netherlands lies below sea level and flooding is a constant threat. Barrages have been built across the mouths of many rivers to contain floodwaters.*

Dune system
Sea
Polder
Drainage ditch

▲ ***Extensive sand dune** systems along the coast have prevented flooding of the land. Behind the dunes, marshy land is drained to form polders, usable land suitable for agriculture.*

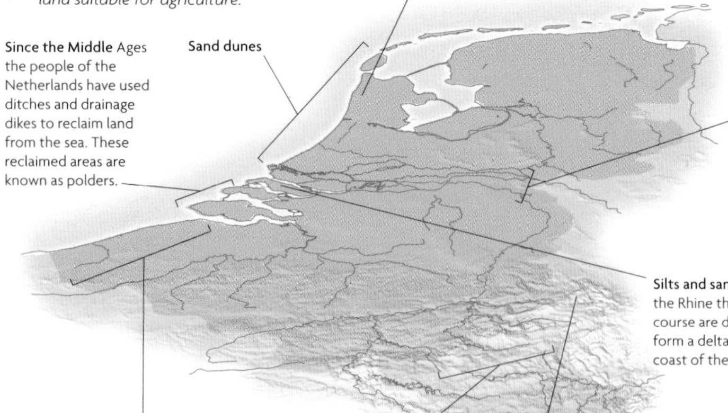

Sand dunes

Since the Middle Ages the people of the Netherlands have used ditches and drainage dikes to reclaim land from the sea. These reclaimed areas are known as polders.

The parallel valleys of the Maas/Meuse and Rhine rivers were created when the Rhine was deflected from its previous course by the ice sheet which formed during the last Ice Age.

Silts and sands eroded by the Rhine throughout its course are deposited to form a delta on the west coast of the Netherlands.

The loess soils of the Flanders Plain in western Belgium provide excellent conditions for arable farming.

Ardennes

▶ ***Uplifted and folded** 220 million years ago, the Ardennes have since been reduced to relatively level plateaus, then sharply incised by rivers such as the Maas/Meuse.*

Hautes Fagnes is the highest part of Belgium. The bogs and streams in this upland region result from high rainfall and low temperatures.

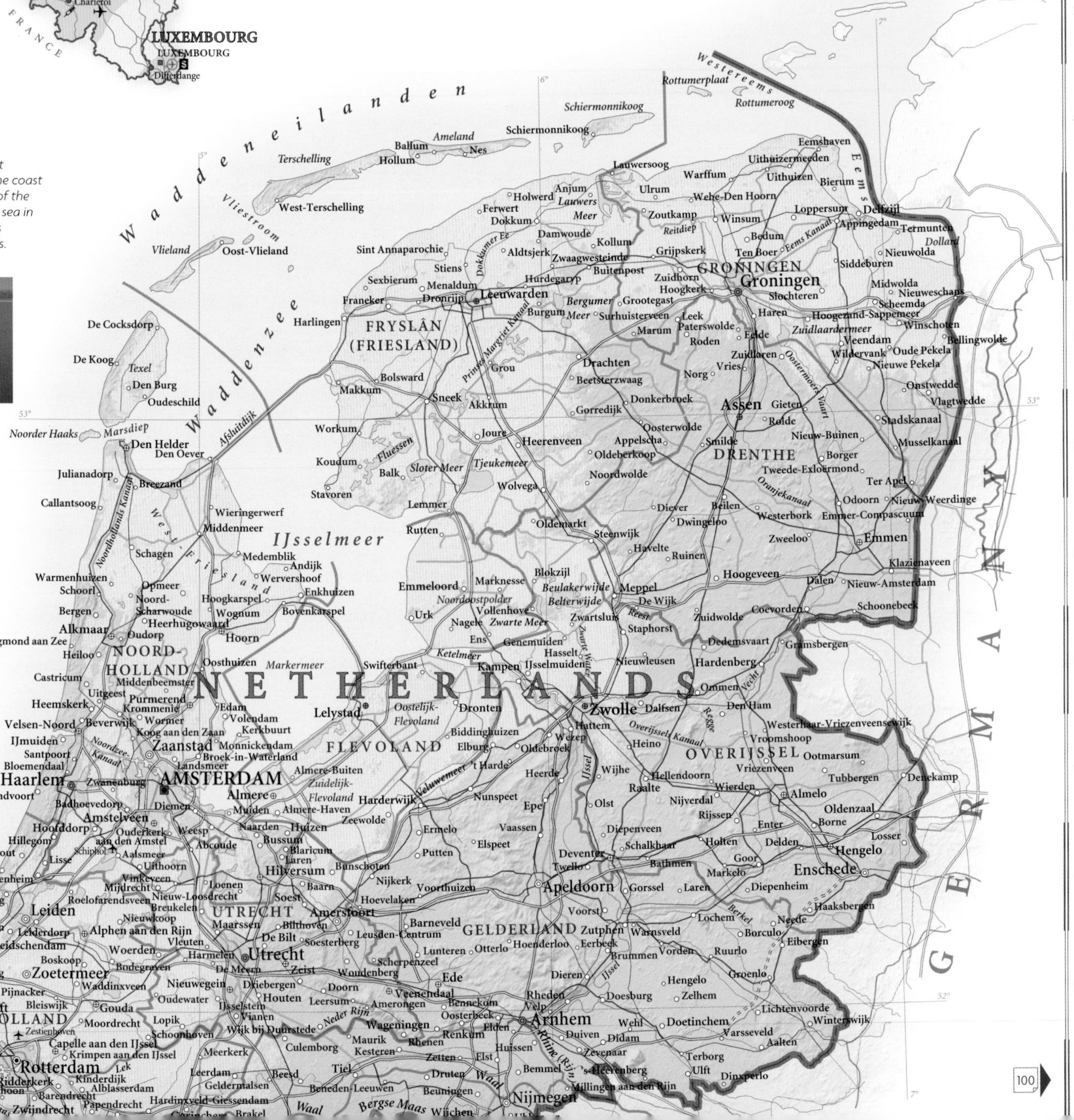
NETHERLANDS
Waddeneilanden
Waddenzee
IJsselmeer
NORTH SEA
GERMANY
GRONINGEN
Groningen
FRYSLÂN (FRIESLAND)
Leeuwarden
DRENTHE
Assen
OVERIJSSEL
Zwolle
FLEVOLAND
Lelystad
NOORD-HOLLAND
AMSTERDAM
Haarlem
UTRECHT
Utrecht
GELDERLAND
Arnhem
ZUID-HOLLAND
'S-GRAVENHAGE (THE HAGUE)
Rotterdam
Texel
Vlieland
Terschelling
Ameland
Schiermonnikoog
Enschede
Apeldoorn
Nijmegen
Emmen
100

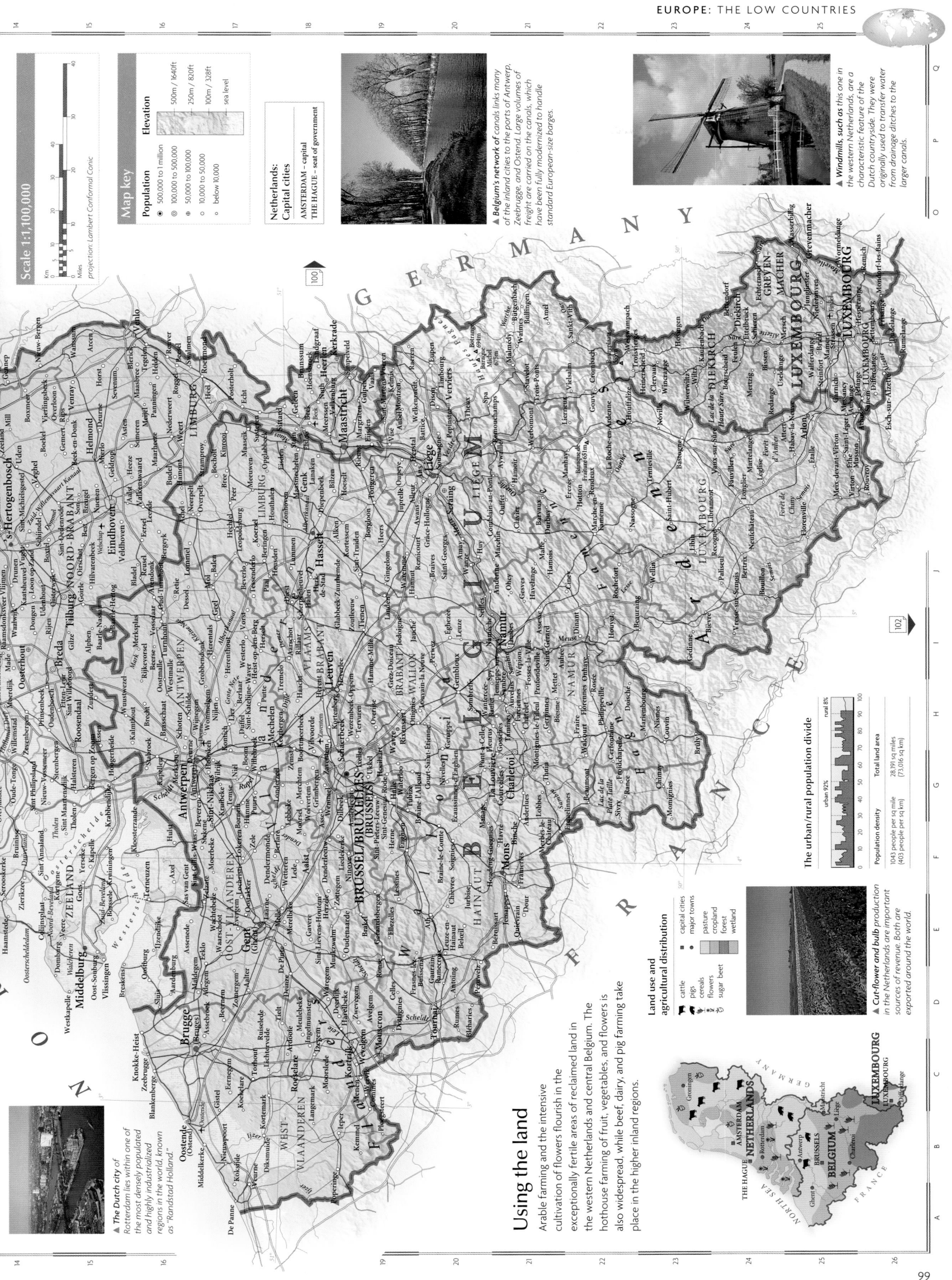

NORTH SEA
GERMANY
FRANCE
BELGIUM
LUXEMBOURG
ZEELAND
NOORD-BRABANT
LIMBURG
WEST-VLAANDEREN
OOST-VLAANDEREN
ANTWERPEN
VLAAMS BRABANT
BRABANT WALLON
HAINAUT
NAMUR
LIEGE
LUXEMBOURG
DIEKIRCH
GREVEN-MACHER
Flanders
Wallonia
Famenne
Ardennes
Fagne
Hautes Fagnes
Middelburg
Vlissingen
Breda
Tilburg
Eindhoven
's-Hertogenbosch
Helmond
Venlo
Roermond
Maastricht
Antwerpen (Antwerp)
Brugge (Bruges)
Gent (Ghent)
Oostende (Ostend)
Kortrijk
Mouscron
Tournai
Mons
Charleroi
Namur
Liège
Verviers
Hasselt
Genk
Leuven
Mechelen
Sint-Niklaas
BRUSSEL/BRUXELLES (BRUSSELS)
Arlon
Esch-sur-Alzette
LUXEMBOURG
Scheldt
Westerschelde
Oosterschelde
Meuse
Sambre
Albertkanaal
100
102

Scale 1:1,100,000

Km 0 5 10 20 30 40

Miles 0 5 10 20 30 40

projection: Lambert Conformal Conic

Map key

Population

- 500,000 to 1 million
- 100,000 to 500,000
- 50,000 to 100,000
- 10,000 to 50,000
- below 10,000

Elevation

- 500m / 1640ft
- 250m / 820ft
- 100m / 328ft
- sea level

Netherlands: Capital cities

AMSTERDAM – capital
THE HAGUE – seat of government

▲ ***The Dutch city*** *of Rotterdam lies within one of the most densely populated and highly industrialized regions in the world, known as "Randstad Holland."*

▲ ***Belgium's network of*** *canals links many of the inland cities to the ports of Antwerp, Zeebrugge, and Ostend. Large volumes of freight are carried on the canals, which have been fully modernized to handle standard European-size barges.*

▲ ***Windmills, such as*** *this one in the western Netherlands, are a characteristic feature of the Dutch countryside. They were originally used to transfer water from drainage ditches to the larger canals.*

Using the land

Arable farming and the intensive cultivation of flowers flourish in the exceptionally fertile areas of reclaimed land in the western Netherlands and central Belgium. The hothouse farming of fruit, vegetables, and flowers is also widespread, while beef, dairy, and pig farming take place in the higher inland regions.

NORTH SEA
GERMANY
FRANCE
Groningen
AMSTERDAM
THE HAGUE
NETHERLANDS
Rotterdam
Antwerp
BRUSSELS
Ghent
Maastricht
BELGIUM
Liège
Charleroi
LUXEMBOURG
LUXEMBOURG
Differdange

Land use and agricultural distribution

- cattle
- pigs
- cereals
- flowers
- sugar beet
- capital cities
- major towns
- pasture
- cropland
- forest
- wetland

▲ ***Cut-flower and bulb*** *production in the Netherlands are important sources of revenue. Both are exported around the world.*

The urban/rural population divide

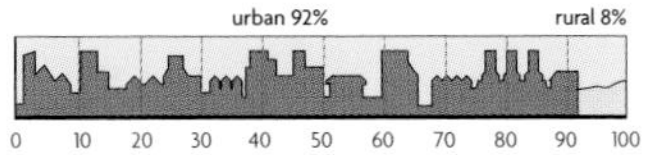

urban 92%
rural 8%
0 10 20 30 40 50 60 70 80 90 100

Population density	Total land area
1043 people per sq mile (403 people per sq km)	28,191 sq miles (73,016 sq km)

Germany

Despite the devastation of its industry and infrastructure during the Second World War and its separation from eastern Germany during the Cold War, West Germany made a rapid recovery in the following generation to become Europe's most formidable economic power. When the Berlin Wall was dismantled in 1989, the two halves of Germany were politically united for the first time in 40 years. Complete social and economic unity remain a longer term goal, as East German industry and society adapt to a free market. Germany has been a key player in the creation of the European Union (EU) and in moves toward a single European currency.

Using the land

Germany has a large, efficient agricultural sector, and produces more than three-quarters of its own food. The major crops grown are cereals and sugar beet on the more fertile soils, and root crops, rye, oats, and fodder on the poorer soils of the northern plains and central uplands. Southern Germany is also a principal producer of high quality wines. Vineyards cover the slopes surrounding the Rhine and its tributaries.

DENMARK
BALTIC SEA
NORTH SEA
POLAND
NETHERLANDS
BELG.
LUX.
FRANCE
SWITZ.
AUSTRIA
CZECH REPUBLIC
GERMANY
Hamburg
Bremen
BERLIN
Essen
Dortmund
Düsseldorf
Cologne
Leipzig
Dresden
Frankfurt am Main
Saarbrücken
Nuremberg
Stuttgart
Munich

Land use and agricultural distribution

- cattle
- pigs
- cereals
- sugar beet
- vineyards
- capital cities
- major towns
- pasture
- cropland
- forest

The urban/rural population divide

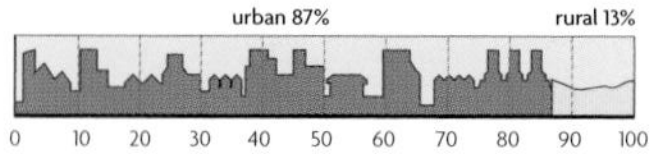
urban 87%
rural 13%
0 10 20 30 40 50 60 70 80 90 100

Population density	Total land area
612 people per sq mile (236 people per sq km)	13,804 sq miles (356,910 sq km)

▲ ***The Moselle river*** *flows through the Rhine State Uplands (*Rheinisches Schiefergebirge*). During a period of uplift, preexisting river meanders were deeply incised, to form its present dramatic contours.*

▶ ***The heathlands of*** *northern Germany are covered by glacial deposits of sandy outwash soil which makes them largely infertile. They support only sheep and solitary trees.*

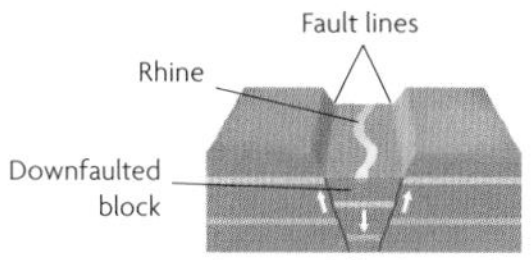
Fault lines
Rhine
Downfaulted block

▲ ***Part of the*** *floor of the Rhine Rift Valley was let down between two parallel faults in the Earth's crust.*

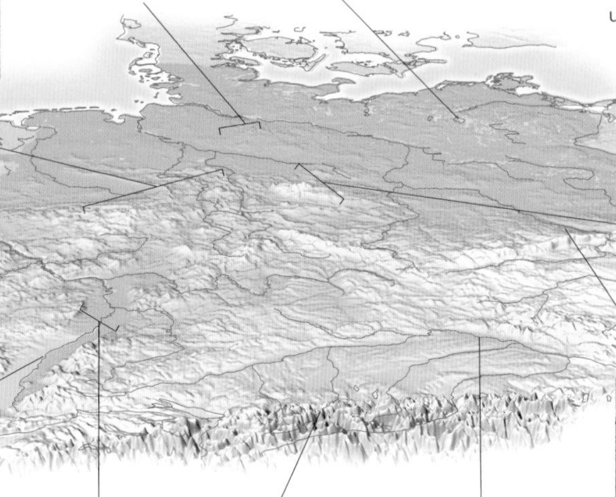
Much of the landscape of northern Germany has been shaped by glaciation. During the last Ice Age, the ice sheet advanced as far the northern slopes of the central uplands.
Lüneburg Heath (*Lüneburger Heide*)
Müritz lake covers 45 sq miles (117 sq km), but is only 108 ft (33 m) deep. It lies in a shallow valley formed by meltwater flowing out from a retreating ice sheet. These valleys are known as *Urstromtäler*.
The Harz Mountains were formed 300 million years ago. They are block-faulted mountains, formed when a section of the Earth's crust was thrust up between two faults.
Elbe river
The Rhine is Germany's principal waterway and one of Europe's longest rivers, flowing 820 miles (1320 km).
Rhine Rift Valley
Zugspitze, the highest peak in Germany at 9719 ft (2962 m), was formed during the Alpine mountain-building period, 30 million years ago.
The Danube rises in the Black Forest (*Schwarzwald*) and flows east, across a wide valley, on its course to the Black Sea.

The landscape

The plains of northern Germany, the volcanic plateaus and mountains of the central uplands, and the Bavarian Alps are the three principal geographic regions in Germany. North to south the land rises steadily from barely 300 ft (90 m) in the plains to 6500 ft (2000 m) in the Bavarian Alps, which are a small but distinct region in the far south.

◀ ***The Elbe flows*** *in wide meanders across the north German plain to the North Sea. At its mouth it is 10 miles (16 km) wide.*

Scale 1:2,500,000

projection: Lambert Conformal Conic

NORTH SEA
BALTIC SEA
DENMARK
POLAND
NETHERLANDS
North Frisian Islands (Nordfriesische Inseln)
Ostfriesische Inseln
Helgoländer Bucht
Kieler Bucht
Mecklenburger Bucht
Pomeranian Bay
SCHLESWIG-HOLSTEIN
MECKLENBURG-VORPOMMERN
NIEDERSACHSEN
BRANDENBURG
BREMEN
HAMBURG
BERLIN
Hamburg
Bremen
Hannover
Kiel
Lübeck
Rostock
Schwerin
Potsdam
Flensburg
Stralsund
Greifswald
Oldenburg
Osnabrück
Bremerhaven
Wilhelmshaven
Cuxhaven
Neubrandenburg
Wolfsburg
Braunschweig
Celle
Lüneburg
Rügen
Usedom
Fehmarn
Helgoland
Elbe
Weser
Ems
Havel
Oder
Müritz
Lüneburger Heide
92
96
98
110

Map key

Population

- ▣ 1 million to 5 million
- ◉ 500,000 to 1 million
- ◎ 100,000 to 500,000
- ⊕ 50,000 to 100,000
- ○ 10,000 to 50,000
- ∘ below 10,000

Elevation

- 2000m / 6562ft
- 1000m / 3281ft
- 500m / 1640ft
- 250m / 820ft
- 100m / 328ft
- sea level

98

Transportation network

- 403,544 miles (649,515 km)
- 7323 miles (11,756 km)
- 22,258 miles (35,868 km)
- 4660 miles (7500 km)

Germany has a complex network of inland waterways. The Rhine and Danube are at the center of a vast canal system which links central and eastern Europe to the north.

GERMANY
BELGIUM
LUXEMBOURG
FRANCE
SWITZERLAND
AUSTRIA
CZECH REPUBLIC
NORDRHEIN-WESTFALEN
RHEINLAND-PFALZ
SAARLAND
HESSEN
THÜRINGEN
SACHSEN
BADEN-WÜRTTEMBERG
BAYERN
Köln (Cologne)
Düsseldorf
Essen
Dortmund
Bonn
Frankfurt am Main
Wiesbaden
Mainz
Stuttgart
Nürnberg (Nuremberg)
München (Munich)
Dresden
Leipzig
Erfurt
Saarbrücken
Lake Constance
Bavarian Alps
Erzgebirge
Schwäbische Alb
Bohemian Forest
Zugspitze 2962m

▲ *The Bavarian Alps straddle the country's southern border at an average height of 6500 ft (2000 m).*

110

102

108

108

Transportation & industry

Today, the main industries which contribute to Germany's economic power are industrial machine building, electronics, chemicals, and car manufacture, including the famous Mercedes and BMW firms. While the introduction of a free market in the east has forced the closure of many less efficient companies there, west German manufacturers have moved in to set up new plants and businesses.

DENMARK
NORTH SEA
BALTIC SEA
NETHERLANDS
POLAND
CZECH REPUBLIC
AUSTRIA
SWITZ.
FRANCE
LUX.
BELG.
GERMANY
Kiel
Rostock
Hamburg
Bremen
BERLIN
Osnabrück
Hannover
Dortmund
Essen
Düsseldorf
Cologne
Leipzig
Dresden
Frankfurt am Main
Saarbrücken
Heidelberg
Nuremberg
Stuttgart
Ingolstadt
Augsburg
Munich

Major industry and infrastructure

- car manufacture
- chemicals
- hi-tech industry
- iron & steel
- mining
- precision engineering
- research & development
- shipbuilding
- capital cities
- major towns
- international airports
- major roads
- major industrial areas

▲ *In the Black Forest* (Schwarzwald), *in southwestern Germany, woodland cloaks sandstone and granite hills, which contain rich mineral springs.*

France

FRANCE, MONACO

Europe's second largest nation and the founder of modern Republican government, France is a major center of culture and fashion, and a leading producer of both agricultural and industrial goods. It has played a leading role in European events for centuries, and remains a key player in the push toward European unity. The Paris Basin is the most highly populated area; Île de France is home to over 11 million people. Large parts of France remain thinly populated, particularly the mountainous Massif Central, Pyrenees, and southern Alps.

◀ *The chalk cliffs of Normandy (Normandie) and southeastern England form part of a single geological region, now divided in two by the English Channel.*

The landscape

France's landscape was fashioned by two phases of mountain-building. The northwestern peninsula, the Massif Central, and the Vosges date from 220 million years ago. The complex folds of the Alps and Pyrenees, the gently-folded Jura, and the low-lying sedimentary areas of the Paris, Garonne, and Rhône basins started to form 65 million years ago.

▲ *The Paris Basin consists of a layered sequence of sedimentary rocks. Fertile soils over much of the area make good agricultural land.*

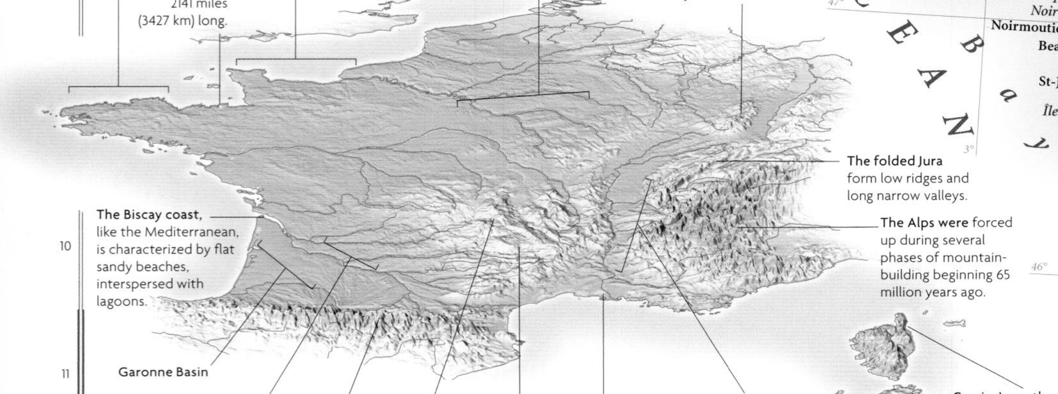

The coast of Brittany (Bretagne) is highly indented where deep valleys in the northwestern peninsula were drowned by the sea.
The Normandy (Normandie) coastline is characterized by high chalk cliffs.
The coastline of France is 2141 miles (3427 km) long.
The gently rounded summits of the Vosges are over 200 million years old.
The folded Jura form low ridges and long narrow valleys.
The Alps were forced up during several phases of mountain-building beginning 65 million years ago.
The Biscay coast, like the Mediterranean, is characterized by flat sandy beaches, interspersed with lagoons.
Garonne Basin
The Dordogne region contains spectacular examples of limestone scenery including caves and gorges.
The Pyrenees form a natural border between France and Spain.
The ancient Massif Central, disturbed by the formation of the Alps, was subject to volcanism that only ceased during the last 10,000 years.
Rhône Basin
Corsica's northeastern peninsula has dramatic cliffs of folded limestone.

◀ *The volcanic landscape of the Auvergne where the cones of its extinct volcanoes have worn away to leave "plugs" of lava.*

Rhône Delta

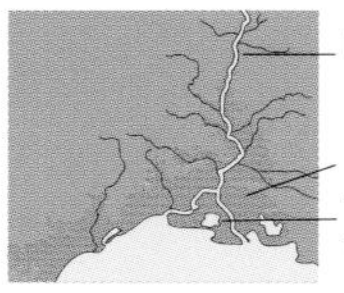

Rhône
Delta plain
The marshes of the Camargue

▲ *Deposition in the Rhône Delta is wave-dominated. Sea currents carry river sediments extending the delta plain westwards.*

Transportation & industry

Today the main French growth industries are hi-tech, including micro-electronics, telecommunications and aerospace. Other important sectors are the nuclear industry, only rivalled in scale by that of the US, car manufacture, dominated by the giants Renault and Peugeot, and a highly diversified tourist industry.

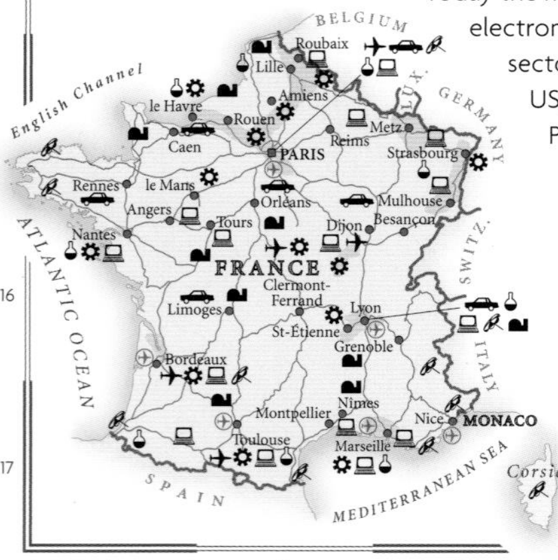

BELGIUM
English Channel
Roubaix
Lille
Amiens
le Havre
Rouen
Caen
Reims
Metz
PARIS
Strasbourg
GERMANY
LUX.
Rennes
le Mans
Orléans
Angers
Mulhouse
Tours
Dijon
Besançon
Nantes
FRANCE
SWITZ.
Clermont-Ferrand
Limoges
Lyon
St-Étienne
Grenoble
ITALY
ATLANTIC OCEAN
Bordeaux
Montpellier
Nîmes
Nice
MONACO
Toulouse
Marseille
MEDITERRANEAN SEA
Corsica
SPAIN

Major industry and infrastructure

- aerospace industry
- car manufacture
- chemicals
- engineering
- hi-tech industry
- nuclear power
- tourism
- capital cities
- major towns
- international airports
- major roads
- major industrial areas

Transportation network

555,473 miles (894,050 km)	7305 miles (11,758 km)
10,399 miles (16,737 km)	1159 miles (1863 km)

The French TGV (Train à Grande Vitesse) leads the world in high-speed train technology, and provides a service which can be faster, door-to-door, than air travel.

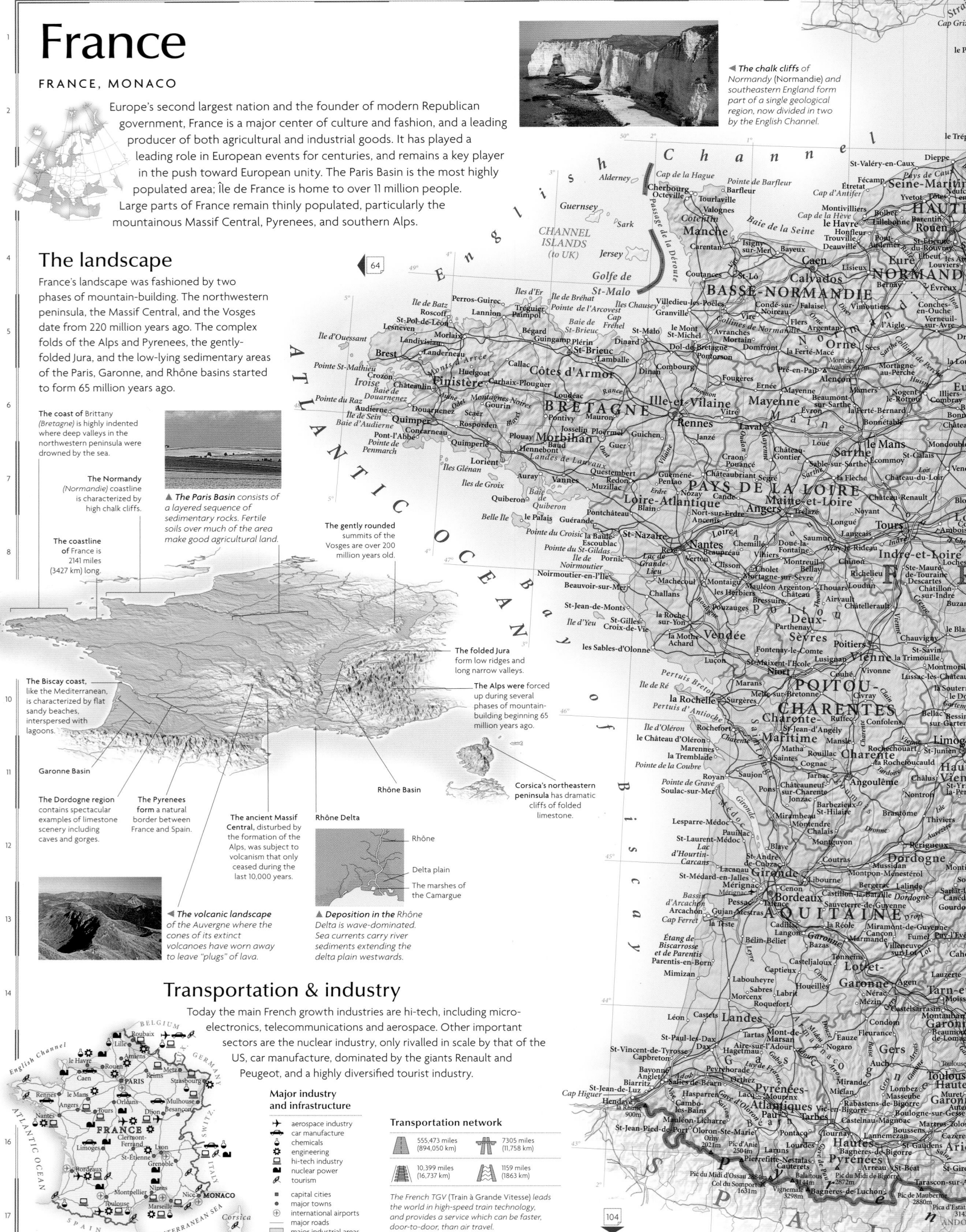

UNITED KINGDOM
English Channel
CHANNEL ISLANDS (to UK)
Guernsey
Jersey
Alderney
Sark
Golfe de St-Malo
BASSE-NORMANDIE
HAUTE-NORMANDIE
BRETAGNE
PAYS DE LA LOIRE
POITOU-CHARENTES
AQUITAINE
ATLANTIC OCEAN
Bay of Biscay
Rennes
Nantes
Brest
Caen
Bordeaux
Angers
Tours
Poitiers
la Rochelle
Le Mans
Landes
Pyrénées-Atlantiques
Hautes-Pyrénées
SPAIN

64

104

North Sea
BELGIUM
GERMANY
LUXEMBOURG
SWITZERLAND
ITALY
MONACO
MEDITERRANEAN SEA
Golfe du Lion
NORD-PAS-DE-CALAIS
PICARDIE
CHAMPAGNE-ARDENNE
ÎLE-DE-FRANCE
LORRAINE
ALSACE
BOURGOGNE
FRANCHE-COMTÉ
AUVERGNE
RHÔNE-ALPES
PROVENCE-ALPES-CÔTE D'AZUR
LANGUEDOC-ROUSSILLON
Massif Central
Jura
Alpes
PARIS
Lyon
Marseille
Strasbourg
98
100
108
106

Scale 1:3,000,000

Km 0 5 10 20 30 40 50 60 70 80
Miles 0 5 10 20 30 40 50 60 70 80
projection: Lambert Conformal Conic

Map key

Population	Elevation
above 5 million	4000m / 13,124ft
1 million to 5 million	3000m / 9843ft
500,000 to 1 million	2000m / 6562ft
100,000 to 500,000	1000m / 3281ft
50,000 to 100,000	500m / 1640ft
10,000 to 50,000	250m / 820ft
below 10,000	100m / 328ft
	sea level

Using the land

France is western Europe's leading agricultural producer, and benefits from high levels of EU subsidy. The variation in climate and soils across the country provides great potential for agriculture and forestry, reflected in the range of products cultivated, including cereals, olives, herbs, and grapes for its famous wines.

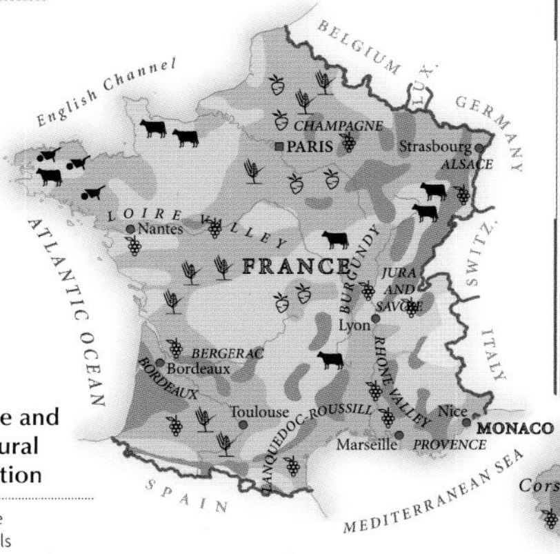
English Channel
BELGIUM
GERMANY
CHAMPAGNE
PARIS
Strasbourg
ALSACE
LOIRE VALLEY
Nantes
FRANCE
BURGUNDY
JURA AND SAVOIE
Lyon
ATLANTIC OCEAN
BERGERAC
Bordeaux
BORDEAUX
Toulouse
LANGUEDOC-ROUSSILLON
RHÔNE VALLEY
Nice
MONACO
Marseille
PROVENCE
SPAIN
MEDITERRANEAN SEA
Corsica
SWITZ.
ITALY

Land use and agricultural distribution

- cattle
- cereals
- market gardening
- sugar beet
- vineyards
- capital cities
- major towns
- pasture
- cropland
- forest
- mountain region

► ***The Romans first** introduced winemaking to France when they occupied the region. Traditional vineyards can be found all over France, producing many of the world's classic wines.*

The urban/rural population divide

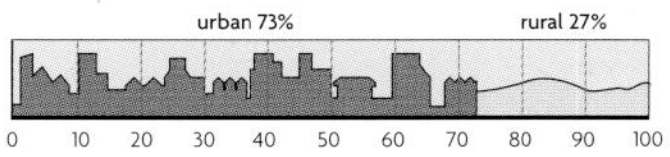
urban 73%
rural 27%
0 10 20 30 40 50 60 70 80 90 100

Population density	Total land area
285 people per sq mile (110 people per sq km)	212,930 sq miles (551,500 sq km)

► ***The rugged hills** and cliffs of Corsica were uplifted when the African and Eurasian plates collided. Frost action during the Ice Age created their present form.*

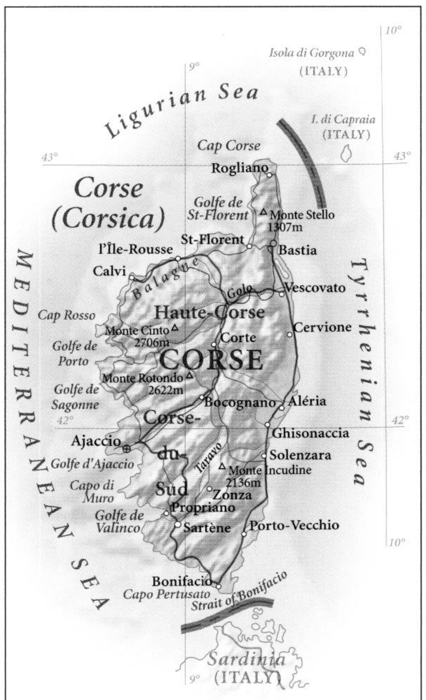
Ligurian Sea
Corse (Corsica)
MEDITERRANEAN SEA
Tyrrhenian Sea
CORSE
Haute-Corse
Corse-du-Sud
Bastia
Ajaccio
Bonifacio
Strait of Bonifacio
Sardinia (ITALY)

(same scale as main map)

◄ ***In the sunny** climate of Southern France olives, vines, peppers, garlic, and lavender now grow in place of the forests that once covered much of the area.*

The Iberian peninsula

ANDORRA, GIBRALTAR, PORTUGAL, SPAIN (Azores, Canary Islands, Madeira on p.64)

The Iberian peninsula is separated from the rest of Europe by the Pyrenees, and at its most southerly point is only 5 miles (8 km) from North Africa. The location of Iberia has been central to its diverse history. The Greeks, Carthaginians, Romans, Visigoths, and most recently the Moors, invaded Iberia at various times. For much of the 20th century, both Spain and Portugal were governed by right-wing dictators. Since the establishment of democratic governments in the mid-1970s, modernization has been rapid and both countries are now among the most popular of European holiday destinations.

Using the land

The principal crops grown in Iberia are cereals, especially wheat and barley. Both countries are major wine producers, most notably of Rioja, sherry, and port. Sheep are kept throughout the region, and citrus fruits thrive on the Mediterranean coast. The successful forest industry in Iberia produces 84% of the world's cork.

▲ ***The steep, terraced** slopes of the Douro Valley in northern Portugal, are used to cultivate vines. The grapes harvested produce Portugal's famous port wine.*

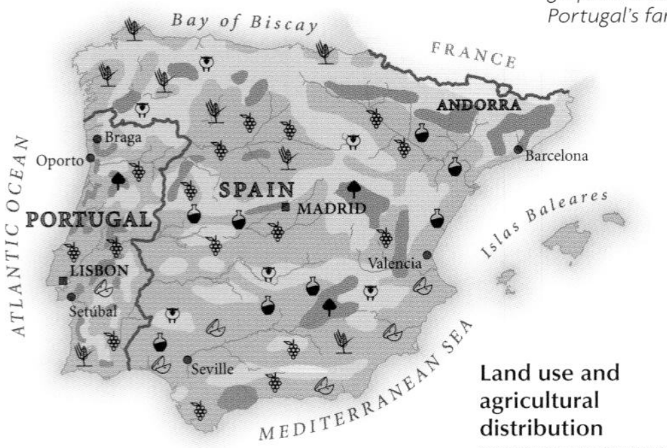
Bay of Biscay
FRANCE
ANDORRA
Barcelona
Braga
Oporto
SPAIN
MADRID
Islas Baleares
PORTUGAL
LISBON
Valencia
Setúbal
Seville
MEDITERRANEAN SEA
ATLANTIC OCEAN

Land use and agricultural distribution

- sheep
- cereals
- citrus fruit
- olives
- vineyards
- cork
- capital cities
- major towns
- pasture
- cropland
- forest
- mountain region

The urban/rural population divide

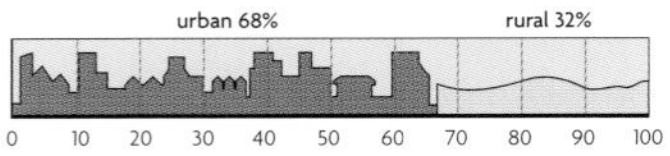
urban 68%
rural 32%
0
10
20
30
40
50
60
70
80
90
100

Population density	Total land area
215 people per sq mile (83 people per sq km)	230,569 sq miles (597,170 sq km)

Transportation & industry

Since the 1970s, the economies of Spain and Portugal have expanded and diversified. In both countries, tourism has outstripped agriculture in economic importance. Spain's resource base is varied, including coal, iron, and the world's largest reserves of mercury. Portugal is a leading producer of tungsten ore.

Bay of Biscay
A Coruña
Gijón
Bilbao
Vitoria-Gasteiz
FRANCE
ANDORRA
Vigo
Braga
Valladolid
Zaragoza
Barcelona
Oporto
Aveiro
PORTUGAL
MADRID
Islas Baleares
Palma
LISBON
SPAIN
Valencia
Setúbal
Alicante
Murcia
Córdoba
Cartagena
Seville
Granada
Huelva
Málaga
MEDITERRANEAN SEA
ATLANTIC OCEAN

Major industry and infrastructure

- car manufacture
- chemicals
- engineering
- fish processing
- mining
- textiles
- tourism
- capital cities
- major towns
- international airports
- major roads
- major industrial areas

Transportation network

241,720 miles (388,990 km)	1552 miles (2529 km)
11,793 miles (18,979 km)	1159 miles (1865 km)

Radiating from Madrid, the road network in Spain dates from the 18th century, but now includes many highways. Portugal's road system has been completely modernized in recent years.

◀ ***The eroded cliffs** of the Algarve in southern Portugal were carved by Atlantic waves. The numerous rocky bays and beaches, and the region's pleasant climate, have made it a popular tourist destination.*

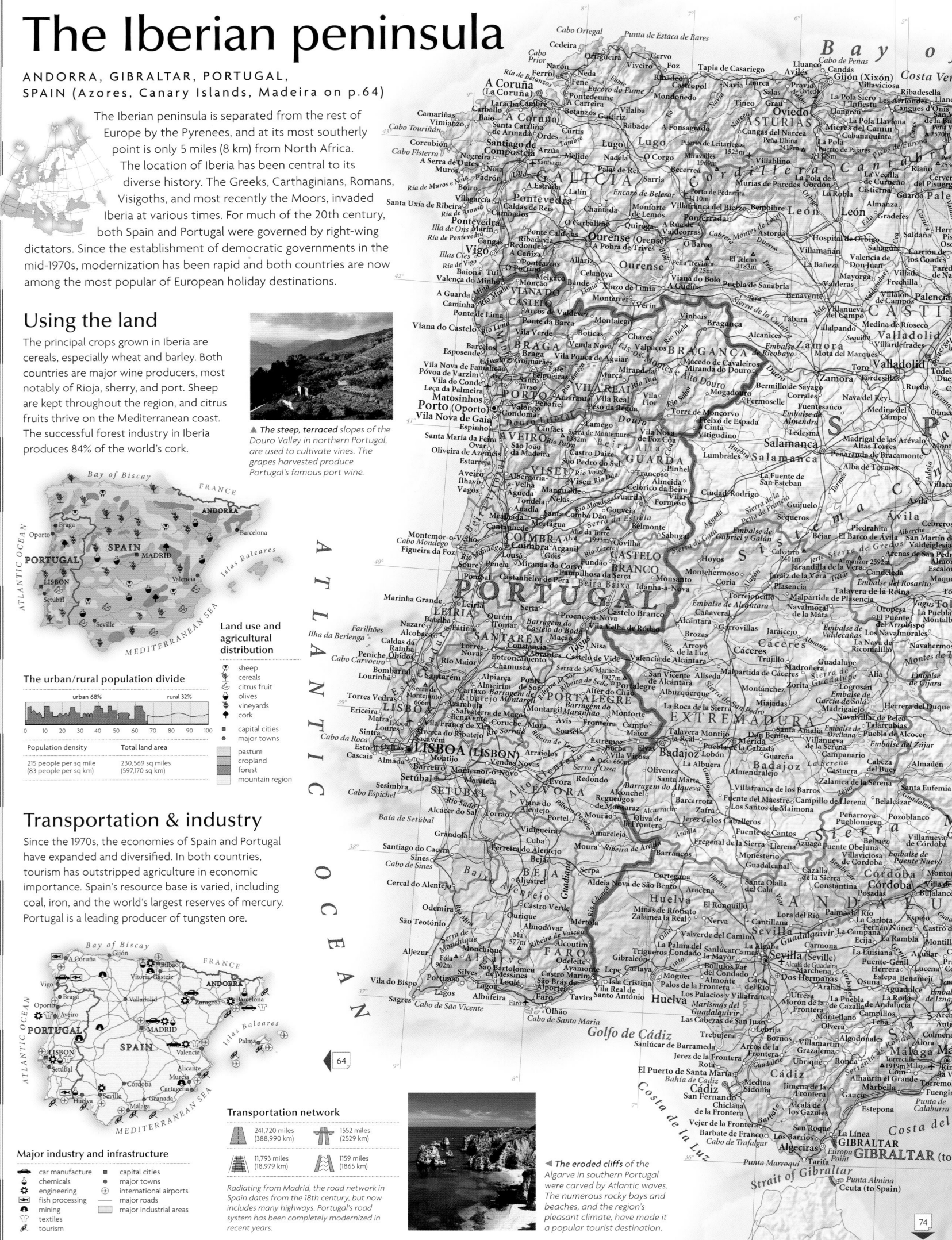

Bay of
Costa Verde
Cabo Ortegal
Punta de Estaca de Bares
A Coruña
(La Coruña)
Ferrol
GALICIA
Lugo
Oviedo
Gijón (Xixón)
ASTURIAS
Cordillera Cantábrica
León
Santiago de Compostela
Pontevedra
Vigo
Ourense (Orense)
Ponferrada
Braga
BRAGANÇA
Bragança
Porto (Oporto)
Vila Nova de Gaia
Zamora
Valladolid
Salamanca
Ávila
Sistema Central
Aveiro
Coimbra
Viseu
GUARDA
CASTELO BRANCO
PORTUGAL
LEIRIA
SANTARÉM
PORTALEGRE
LISBOA (LISBON)
Setúbal
SETÚBAL
ÉVORA
Badajoz
EXTREMADURA
Cáceres
Mérida
BEJA
Beja
FARO
Faro
Huelva
Sevilla (Seville)
Córdoba
Cádiz
Jerez de la Frontera
Algeciras
GIBRALTAR
Strait of Gibraltar
Ceuta (to Spain)
MOROCCO
Golfo de Cádiz
Costa de la Luz
Cabo de São Vicente
ATLANTIC OCEAN
Duero
Douro
Tagus
Guadiana
Guadalquivir
64
74

N O P Q R S T U V W X Y
102
Bay of Biscay
Donostia/San Sebastián
Bilbao
Vitoria-Gasteiz
Pamplona (Iruña)
Logroño
Burgos
Pyrenees
ANDORRA
ANDORRA LA VELLA
CATALUÑA
Lleida
Girona
Barcelona
L'Hospitalet de Llobregat
Tarragona
Costa Brava
Golf de Sant Jordi
Huesca
Zaragoza
ARAGÓN
Teruel
Castelló
Castellón de la Plana
Valencia
Golfo de Valencia
Alicante (Alacant)
Costa Blanca
Murcia
Cartagena
Albacete
CASTILLA-LA MANCHA
Guadalajara
Cuenca
MADRID
Toledo
Jaén
Granada
Almería
Costa del Sol
Alboran Sea
Melilla (to Spain)
MEDITERRANEAN SEA
Islas Baleares (Balearic Islands)
Menorca (Minorca)
Mallorca (Majorca)
Palma
Ibiza
Formentera
1 2 3 4 5 6 10 11 12 13 14 16 17
R S T U V W X Y Z

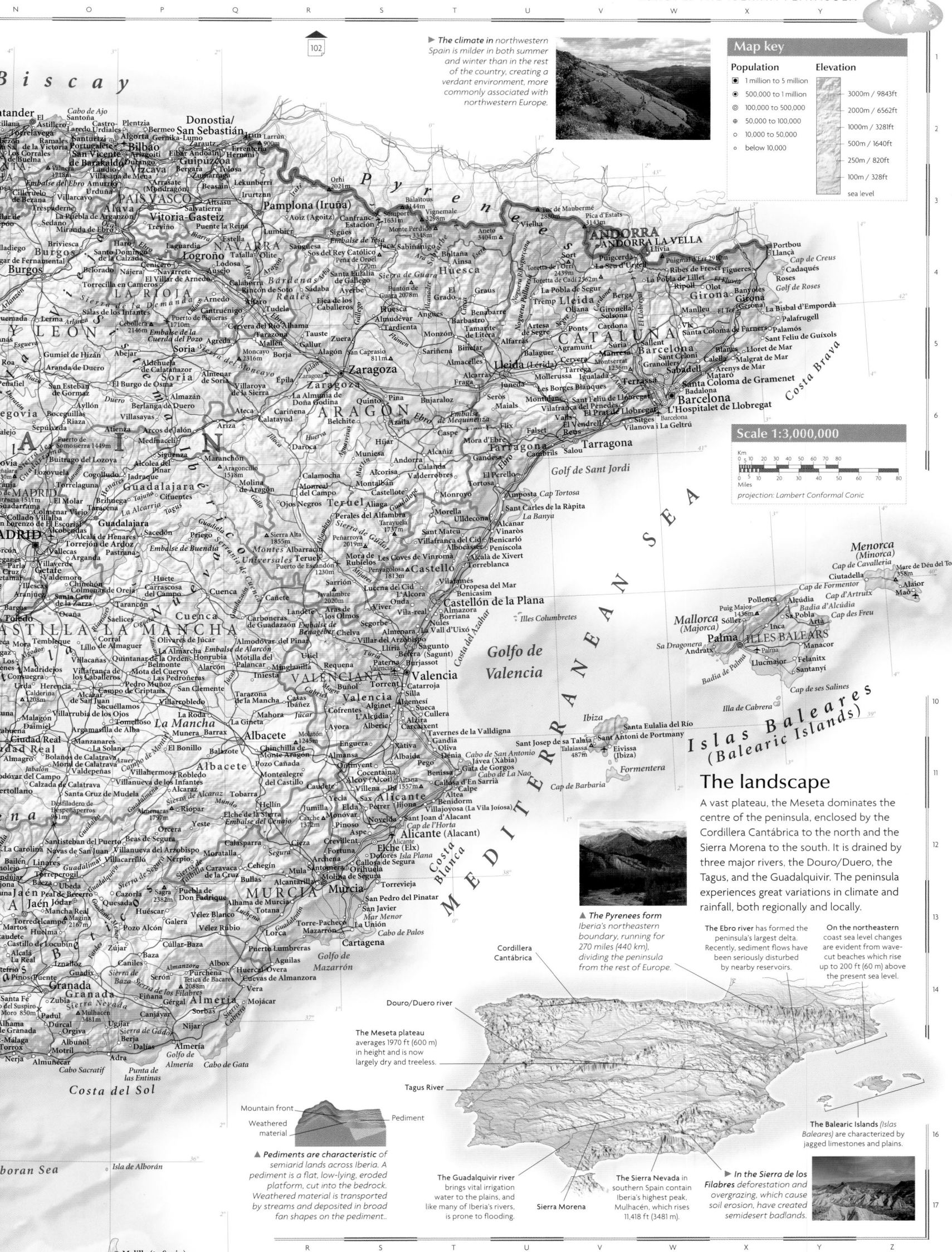

▶ *The climate in northwestern Spain is milder in both summer and winter than in the rest of the country, creating a verdant environment, more commonly associated with northwestern Europe.*

Map key

Population

- 1 million to 5 million
- 500,000 to 1 million
- 100,000 to 500,000
- 50,000 to 100,000
- 10,000 to 50,000
- below 10,000

Elevation

- 3000m / 9843ft
- 2000m / 6562ft
- 1000m / 3281ft
- 500m / 1640ft
- 250m / 820ft
- 100m / 328ft
- sea level

Scale 1:3,000,000

Km 0 5 10 20 30 40 50 60 70 80

Miles 0 5 10 20 30 40 50 60 70 80

projection: Lambert Conformal Conic

The landscape

A vast plateau, the Meseta dominates the centre of the peninsula, enclosed by the Cordillera Cantábrica to the north and the Sierra Morena to the south. It is drained by three major rivers, the Douro/Duero, the Tagus, and the Guadalquivir. The peninsula experiences great variations in climate and rainfall, both regionally and locally.

▲ *The Pyrenees form Iberia's northeastern boundary, running for 270 miles (440 km), dividing the peninsula from the rest of Europe.*

Cordillera Cantábrica
The Ebro river has formed the peninsula's largest delta. Recently, sediment flows have been seriously disturbed by nearby reservoirs.
On the northeastern coast sea level changes are evident from wave-cut beaches which rise up to 200 ft (60 m) above the present sea level.
Douro/Duero river
The Meseta plateau averages 1970 ft (600 m) in height and is now largely dry and treeless.
Tagus River
The Balearic Islands (Islas Baleares) are characterized by jagged limestones and plains.
The Guadalquivir river brings vital irrigation water to the plains, and like many of Iberia's rivers, is prone to flooding.
Sierra Morena
The Sierra Nevada in southern Spain contain Iberia's highest peak, Mulhacén, which rises 11,418 ft (3481 m).

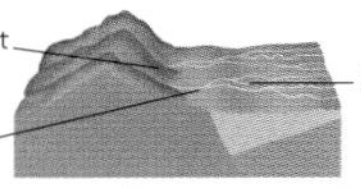
Mountain front
Weathered material
Pediment

▲ *Pediments are characteristic of semiarid lands across Iberia. A pediment is a flat, low-lying, eroded platform, cut into the bedrock. Weathered material is transported by streams and deposited in broad fan shapes on the pediment.*

▶ *In the Sierra de los Filabres deforestation and overgrazing, which cause soil erosion, have created semidesert badlands.*

The Italian peninsula

ITALY, SAN MARINO, VATICAN CITY

The Italian peninsula is a land of great contrasts. Until unification in 1861, Italy was a collection of independent states, whose competitiveness during the Renaissance resulted in the architectural and artistic magnificence of cities such as Rome, Florence, and Venice. The majority of Italy's population and economic activity is concentrated in the north, centered on the sophisticated industrial city of Milan. Southern Italy, the *Mezzogiorno*, has a harsh terrain, and remains far less developed than the north. Attempts to attract industry and investment in the south are frequently deterred by the entrenched network of organized crime and corruption.

The landscape

The mainly mountainous and hilly Italian peninsula took its present form following a collision between the African and Eurasian tectonic plates. The Alps in the northwest rise to a high point of 15,772 ft (4807 m) at Mont Blanc *(Monte Bianco)* on the French border, while the Apennines *(Appennino)* form a rugged backbone, running along the entire length of the country.

▶ *The island of Sardinia is an ancient land mass; an uplifted section of very old igneous rocks. Its rugged mountainous regions provide pasture for sheep and goats, while its valleys support some agriculture.*

▲ ***The Dolomites** (Alpi Dolomitiche) are formed of thick limestones, overlying weaker marine strata. They have distinctive serrated peaks and many massive landslides occur.*

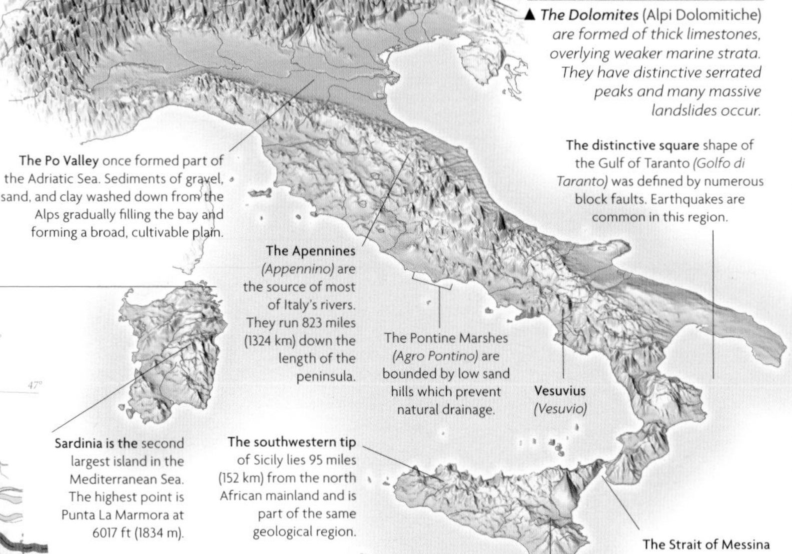

Mont Blanc (Monte Bianco)
Costa Smeralda
Vesuvius (Vesuvio)

The Po Valley once formed part of the Adriatic Sea. Sediments of gravel, sand, and clay washed down from the Alps gradually filling the bay and forming a broad, cultivable plain.

The distinctive square shape of the Gulf of Taranto *(Golfo di Taranto)* was defined by numerous block faults. Earthquakes are common in this region.

The Apennines *(Appennino)* are the source of most of Italy's rivers. They run 823 miles (1324 km) down the length of the peninsula.

The Pontine Marshes *(Agro Pontino)* are bounded by low sand hills which prevent natural drainage.

Sardinia is the second largest island in the Mediterranean Sea. The highest point is Punta La Marmora at 6017 ft (1834 m).

The southwestern tip of Sicily lies 95 miles (152 km) from the north African mainland and is part of the same geological region.

The Strait of Messina *(Stretto di Messina)* is between 2 and 12 miles (3–19 km) wide, and is a rich fishing ground.

Sicily is the largest island in the Mediterranean at 9926 sq miles (25,708 sq km).

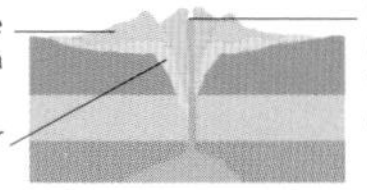

Vesuvius (Vesuvio)
Monte Somma
Old crater
Present-day crater has developed within the old crater of Monte Somma

▲ ***There have been** four volcanoes on the site of Vesuvius since volcanic activity began here more than 10,000 years ago.*

SWITZERLAND
AUSTRIA
SLOVENIA
CROATIA
FRANCE
MONACO
Gulf of Venice
Ligurian Sea
Golfo di Genova
Scale 1:2,750,000
projection: Lambert Conformal Conic

108 108 108 112 120 102 11

Using the land

Italy produces 95% of its own food. The best farming land is in the Po Valley in northern Italy, where soft wheat and rice are grown. Irrigation is essential to agriculture in much of the south. Italy is a major producer and exporter of citrus fruits, olives, tomatoes, and wine.

The urban/rural population divide

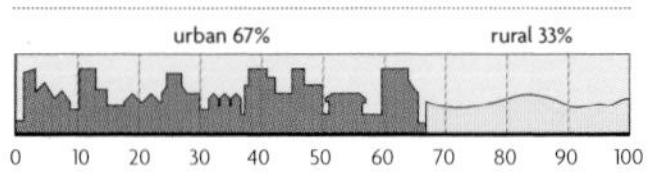

urban 67%
rural 33%
0 10 20 30 40 50 60 70 80 90 100

Population density	Total land area
506 people per sq mile (195 people per sq km)	116,320 sq miles (301,270 sq km)

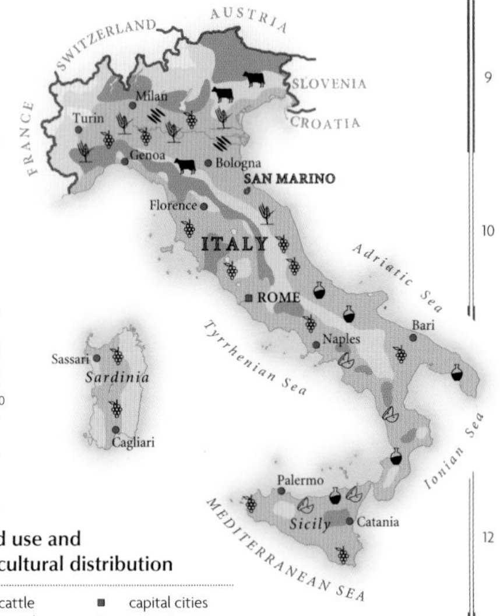

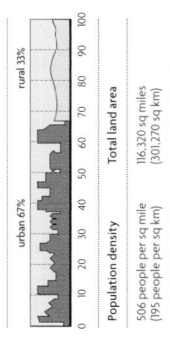

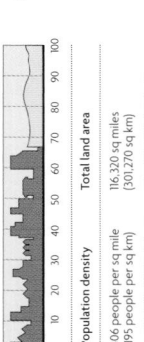

SWITZERLAND
AUSTRIA
SLOVENIA
CROATIA
FRANCE
SAN MARINO
ITALY
ROME
Milan
Turin
Genoa
Bologna
Florence
Naples
Bari
Sassari
Sardinia
Cagliari
Palermo
Sicily
Catania
Adriatic Sea
Tyrrhenian Sea
Ionian Sea
MEDITERRANEAN SEA

Land use and agricultural distribution

cattle, cereals, citrus fruits, olive oil, rice, vineyards, capital cities, major towns, pasture, cropland, forest, mountain region

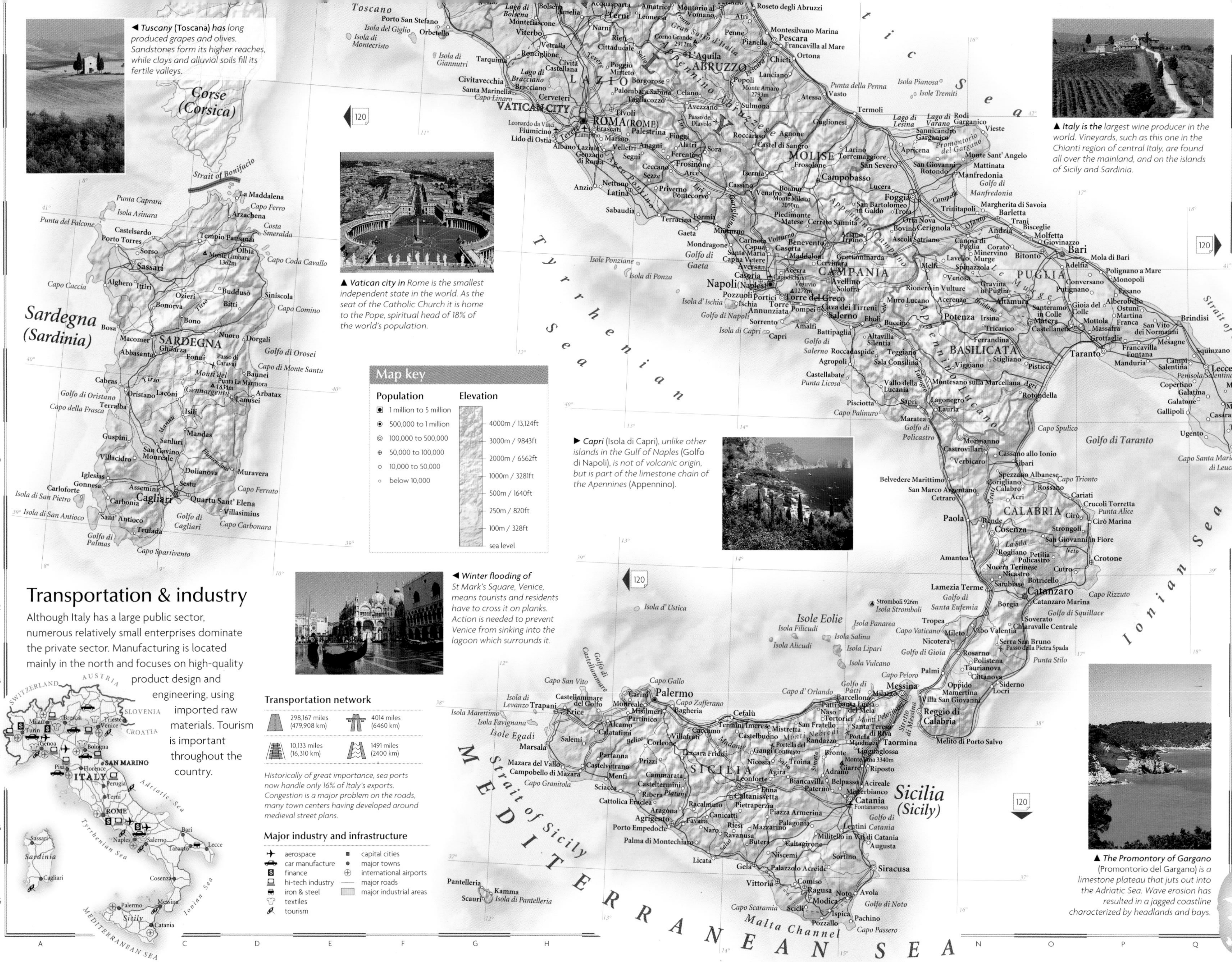
Toscano
Corse (Corsica)
Sardegna (Sardinia)
SARDEGNA
Strait of Bonifacio
LAZIO
ABRUZZO
MOLISE
CAMPANIA
PUGLIA
BASILICATA
CALABRIA
SICILIA
Sicilia (Sicily)
ROMA (ROME)
VATICAN CITY
Napoli
Bari
Taranto
Palermo
Messina
Catania
Cagliari
Adriatic Sea
Tyrrhenian Sea
Ionian Sea
MEDITERRANEAN SEA
Strait of Otranto
Strait of Sicily
Malta Channel
Golfo di Taranto
Isole Eolie
Appennino
120

◀ *Tuscany* (Toscana) *has long produced grapes and olives. Sandstones form its higher reaches, while clays and alluvial soils fill its fertile valleys.*

▲ *Vatican city in* Rome *is the smallest independent state in the world. As the seat of the Catholic Church it is home to the Pope, spiritual head of 18% of the world's population.*

▲ *Italy is the largest wine producer in the world. Vineyards, such as this one in the Chianti region of central Italy, are found all over the mainland, and on the islands of Sicily and Sardinia.*

Map key

Population
- ▣ 1 million to 5 million
- ◉ 500,000 to 1 million
- ◎ 100,000 to 500,000
- ⊕ 50,000 to 100,000
- ○ 10,000 to 50,000
- ◦ below 10,000

Elevation
- 4000m / 13,124ft
- 3000m / 9843ft
- 2000m / 6562ft
- 1000m / 3281ft
- 500m / 1640ft
- 250m / 820ft
- 100m / 328ft
- sea level

▶ *Capri* (Isola di Capri), *unlike other islands in the Gulf of Naples* (Golfo di Napoli), *is not of volcanic origin, but is part of the limestone chain of the Apennines* (Appennino).

◀ *Winter flooding of St Mark's Square, Venice, means tourists and residents have to cross it on planks. Action is needed to prevent Venice from sinking into the lagoon which surrounds it.*

▲ *The Promontory of Gargano* (Promontorio del Gargano) *is a limestone plateau that juts out into the Adriatic Sea. Wave erosion has resulted in a jagged coastline characterized by headlands and bays.*

Transportation & industry

Although Italy has a large public sector, numerous relatively small enterprises dominate the private sector. Manufacturing is located mainly in the north and focuses on high-quality product design and engineering, using imported raw materials. Tourism is important throughout the country.

Transportation network

298,167 miles (479,908 km)	4014 miles (6460 km)
10,133 miles (16,310 km)	1491 miles (2400 km)

Historically of great importance, sea ports now handle only 16% of Italy's exports. Congestion is a major problem on the roads, many town centers having developed around medieval street plans.

Major industry and infrastructure

aerospace	capital cities
car manufacture	major towns
finance	international airports
hi-tech industry	major roads
iron & steel	major industrial areas
textiles	
tourism	

The Alpine states

AUSTRIA, LIECHTENSTEIN, SLOVENIA, SWITZERLAND

The Alpine countries of Austria, Switzerland, Liechtenstein, and Slovenia form a narrow strip across western Europe's geographical core, lying on the main north–south trading routes across the Alps. Switzerland, politically neutral since 1815, is an important international meeting place and houses one of the headquarters of the United Nations, it only became a member in 2002. Austria, once at the heart of the great Habsburg Empire has been a fully independent nation since 1955, and maintains a deserved reputation as an international center of culture. Slovenia declared independence from the former Yugoslavia in 1991 and despite initial economic hardship, is now starting to achieve the prosperity enjoyed by its Alpine neighbors.

Using the land

The Alpine region's mountainous terrain discourages cultivation over much of the land area. The primary agricultural activity is the raising of dairy and beef cattle on the pasture land of the lower mountain slopes. Austria is self-supporting in grains, and crops such as wheat, barley, and grapes are grown on the east Austrian lowlands. Woodlands are more prevalent in the eastern Alps; both Austria and Slovenia have large tracts of forest.

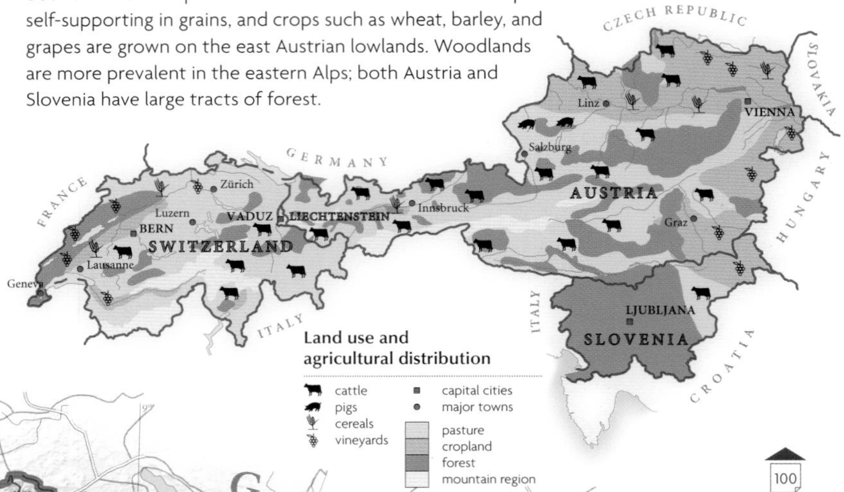
CZECH REPUBLIC
SLOVAKIA
GERMANY
FRANCE
HUNGARY
ITALY
CROATIA
Linz
VIENNA
Salzburg
AUSTRIA
Graz
Zürich
Luzern
VADUZ
LIECHTENSTEIN
Innsbruck
BERN
SWITZERLAND
Lausanne
Geneva
LJUBLJANA
SLOVENIA
Land use and agricultural distribution
cattle
pigs
cereals
vineyards
capital cities
major towns
pasture
cropland
forest
mountain region

◀ *The Matterhorn, on the Swiss-Italian border, is one of the highest mountains in the Alps, at 14,692 ft (4478 m). The term "horn" refers to its distinctive peak, formed by three glaciers eroding hollows, known as cirques, in each of its sides.*

100
102
106
GERMANY
FRANCE
SWITZERLAND
LIECHTENSTEIN
VADUZ
BERN
Basel
Schaffhausen
Lake Constance
Zürich
Luzern
Lausanne
Genève (Geneva)
Lake Geneva (Lac Léman)
Lac de Neuchâtel
Vierwaldstätter See
Berner Alpen
Glarner Alpen
Pennine Alps
Lepontine Alps
Rhaetian Alps
Lago di Lugano
Lake Maggiore
Lugano
Bellinzona
Chur
Innsbruck
Jungfrau 4158m
Eiger 3970m
Finsteraarhorn 4274m
Matterhorn 4478m
Dufour Spitze 4634m
Weisshorn 4505m
Grand Combin 4314m
Great Saint Bernard Pass 2469m
Simplon Pass 2005m
Piz Bernina 4049m
Tödi 3614m
Piz Buin 3312m
JURA
VALAIS
TICINO
GRAUBÜNDEN
FRIBOURG
VAUD
TIROL

▲ *Constricted as it cuts through ridges in the Alps, the Danube meanders across the lowlands, where uplift combined with river erosion has deepened meanders.*

The landscape

The Alps occupy three-fifths of Switzerland, most of southern Austria and the northwest of Slovenia. They were formed by the collision of the African and Eurasian tectonic plates, which began 65 million years ago. Their complex geology is reflected in the differing heights and rock types of the various ranges. The Rhine flows along Liechtenstein's border with Switzerland, creating a broad floodplain in the north and west of Liechtenstein. In the far northeast and east are a number of lowland regions, including the Vienna Basin, Burgenland, and the plain of the Danube. Slovenia's major rivers largely flow across the lower eastern regions; in the west, the rivers flow underground through the limestone Karst region.

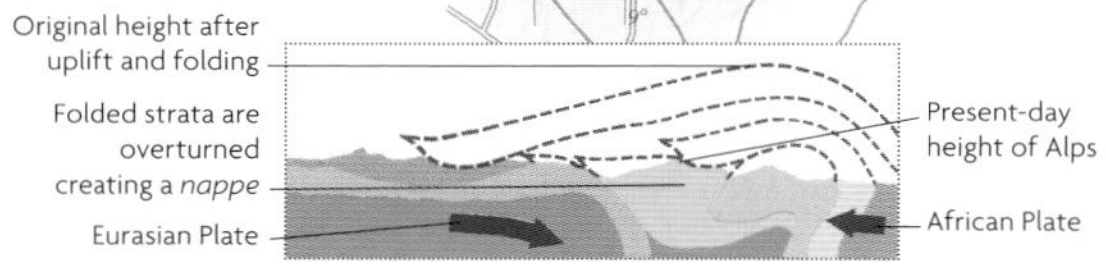
Original height after uplift and folding
Folded strata are overturned creating a *nappe*
Eurasian Plate
Present-day height of Alps
African Plate

▲ *The convergence of the African and Eurasian plates compressed and folded huge masses of rock strata. As the plates continued to move together, the folded strata were overturned, creating complex nappes. Much of the rock strata has since been eroded, resulting in the current topography of the Alps.*

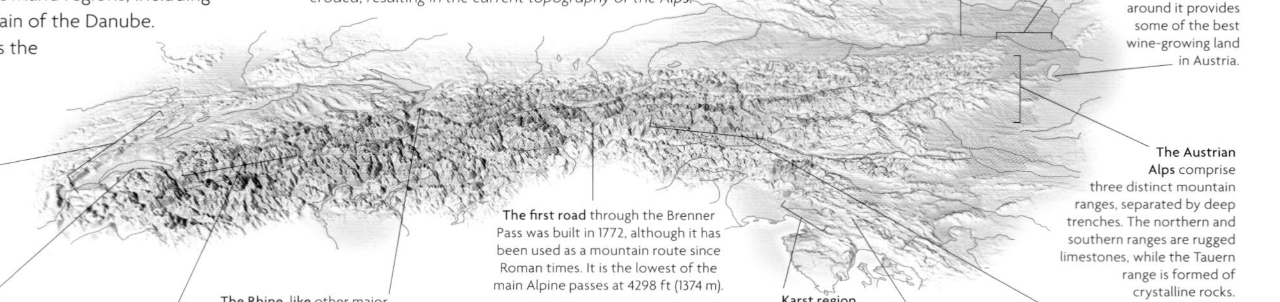
Karst region

The Vienna Basin lies mainly below 390 ft (120 m). It gradually subsided and filled with sediment as the Alps were uplifted.

Neusiedler See straddles the border of Austria and Hungary; the area around it provides some of the best wine-growing land in Austria.

The Austrian Alps comprise three distinct mountain ranges, separated by deep trenches. The northern and southern ranges are rugged limestones, while the Tauern range is formed of crystalline rocks.

The mountains of the Jura form a natural border between Switzerland and France. Their marine limestones date from over 200 million years ago. When the Alps were formed the Jura were folded into a series of parallel ridges and troughs.

The first road through the Brenner Pass was built in 1772, although it has been used as a mountain route since Roman times. It is the lowest of the main Alpine passes at 4298 ft (1374 m).

Tectonic activity has resulted in dramatic changes in land height over very short distances. Lake Geneva, lying at 1221 ft (372 m) is only 43 miles (70 km) away from the 15,772 ft (4807 m) peak of Mont Blanc, on the France–Italy border.

The Bernese Alps *(Berner Alpen)* contain the Aletsch, which at 15 miles (24 km) is the longest Alpine glacier.

The Rhine, like other major Alpine rivers, follows a broad, flat trough between the mountains. Along part of its course, the Rhine forms the boundary between Switzerland and Liechtenstein.

▶ *The deep, blue lakes of the Karst region are part of a drainage network which runs largely underground through this limestone area.*

The limestone cave system at Postojna extends for more than 10 miles (16 km) and includes caverns reaching 125 ft (40 m) in height and width.

The Tauern range in the central Austrian Alps contains the highest mountain in Austria, the towering Grossglockner, rising 12,461 ft (3798 m).

The urban/rural population divide

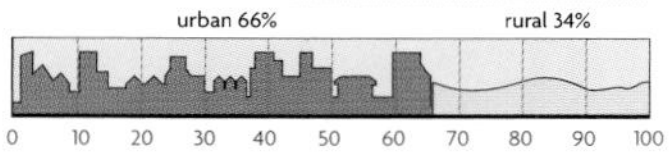
urban 66%
rural 34%
0 10 20 30 40 50 60 70 80 90 100

Population density	Total land area
314 people per sq mile (121 people per sq km)	56,135 sq miles (145,390 sq km)

◀ *In this mountainous region, the flatter, more accessible areas are often used for both cattle grazing and recreation.*

CZECH REPUBLIC
SLOVAKIA
HUNGARY
AUSTRIA
SLOVENIA
CROATIA
GERMANY
ITALY
WIEN (VIENNA)
Linz
Salzburg
Graz
Klagenfurt
Innsbruck
Sankt Pölten
LJUBLJANA
Maribor
Gulf of Trieste
OBERÖSTERREICH
NIEDERÖSTERREICH
STEIERMARK
BURGENLAND
SALZBURG
KÄRNTEN
TIROL
Hohe Tauern
Niedere Tauern
Karawanken
Karnische Alpen
Danube (Donau)
Drava
Sava
Grossglockner 3798m
100
106
110
112

◀ *These converging glaciers are marked by dark lines of moraine. This eroded material is carried by glaciers, and deposited as the ice melts.*

Scale 1:2,000,000

Km 0 5 10 20 30 40 50 60
Miles 0 5 10 20 30 40 50 60

projection: Lambert Conformal Conic

Map key

Population
- 1 million to 5 million
- 500,000 to 1 million
- 100,000 to 500,000
- 50,000 to 100,000
- 10,000 to 50,000
- below 10,000

Elevation
- 4000m / 13,124ft
- 3000m / 9843ft
- 2000m / 6562ft
- 1000m / 3281ft
- 500m / 1640ft
- 250m / 820ft
- 100m / 328ft
- sea level

▶ *The Austrian Tirol contains some of the most spectacular Alpine scenery. Snow cover is a permanent feature in the highest reaches.*

Transportation & industry

All four nations concentrate on high-quality manufacturing and services. Austrian iron and steel production is complemented by construction industries; and Slovenia, traditionally the industrial powerhouse of the western Balkans has increasingly diversified industries. Liechtenstein and Switzerland, lacking raw materials, produce pharmaceuticals and precision instruments, such as watches, and act as international banking centers. The spectacular scenery of the region encourages tourism all year round.

Transportation network

181,107 miles (291,497 km)	2116 miles (3405 km)
6368 miles (10,249 km)	993 miles (1598 km)

Tunnels and passes through the Alps are an important feature of this region. The NEAT project, providing two new high-speed rail links between Basel and Milan, was given approval in 1992.

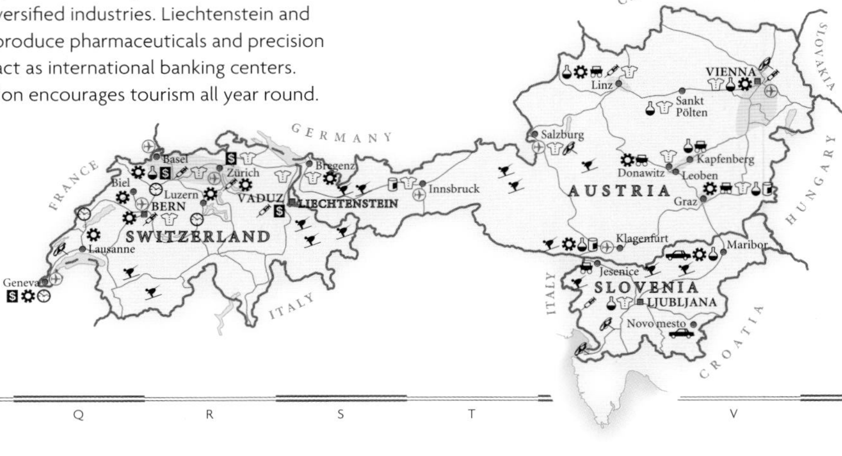
CZECH REPUBLIC
SLOVAKIA
GERMANY
FRANCE
ITALY
HUNGARY
CROATIA
SWITZERLAND
AUSTRIA
SLOVENIA
VIENNA
Linz
Sankt Pölten
Salzburg
Donawitz
Kapfenberg
Leoben
Graz
Klagenfurt
Maribor
Jesenice
LJUBLJANA
Novo mesto
Innsbruck
LIECHTENSTEIN
VADUZ
Bregenz
Zürich
Basel
Biel
Luzern
BERN
Lausanne
Geneva

Major industry and infrastructure
- car manufacture
- chemicals
- engineering
- finance
- food processing
- iron & steel
- pharmaceuticals
- textiles
- tourism
- watch making
- winter sports
- capital cities
- major towns
- international airports
- major roads
- major industrial areas

▲ *The Schönbrunn Palace in Vienna was the summer residence of the Habsburg monarchy. Today, it is a major tourist attraction.*

Central Europe

CZECH REPUBLIC, HUNGARY, POLAND, SLOVAKIA

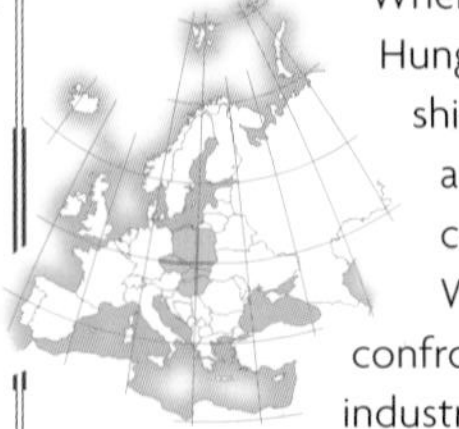

When Slovakia and the Czech Republic became separate countries in 1993, they joined Hungary and Poland in a new role as independent nation states, following centuries of shifting boundaries and imperial strife. This turbulent history bequeathed the region a rich cultural heritage, shared through the works of its many great writers and composers, and celebrated in the vibrant historic capitals of Prague, Budapest, and Warsaw. Having shaken off years of Soviet domination in 1989, these states are confronting the challenge of winning commercial investment to modernize outmoded industries as they integrate their economies with those of the European Union.

The landscape

The forested Carpathian Mountains, uplifted with the Alps, lie southeast of the older Bohemian Massif, which contains the Sudeten and Krusné Hory *(Erzgebirge)* ranges. They divide the fertile plains of the Danube to the south and the Vistula *(Wisla)*, which flows north across vast expanses of glacial deposits into the Baltic Sea.

◀ ***The Berounka river*** *cuts through the precipitous wooded landscape of the Bohemian Massif, banked by a broad floodplain.*

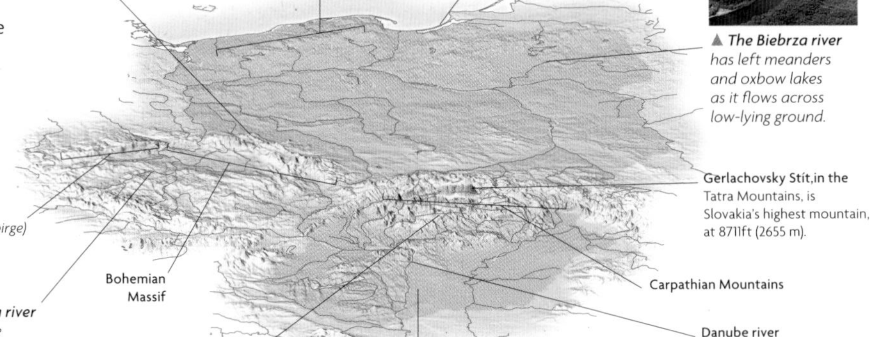

Krusné Hory (Erzgebirge)
Bohemian Massif
Carpathian Mountains
Danube river

Hot mineral springs occur where geothermally heated water wells up through faults and fractures in the rocks of the Sudeten Mountains.

Pomerania is a sandy coastal region of glacially-formed lakes stretching west from the Vistula *(Wisla)*.

Longshore currents moving east along the Baltic coast have built a 40 mile (65 km) spit composed of material from the Vistula *(Wisla)* river.

The Slovak Ore Mountains *(Slovenské Rudohorie)* are noted for their mineral resources, including high-grade iron ore.

The Great Hungarian Plain formed by the floodplain of the Danube is a mixture of steppe and cultivated land, covering nearly half of Hungary's total area.

Gerlachovsky Stít,in the Tatra Mountains, is Slovakia's highest mountain, at 8711ft (2655 m).

▲ ***The Biebrza river*** *has left meanders and oxbow lakes as it flows across low-lying ground.*

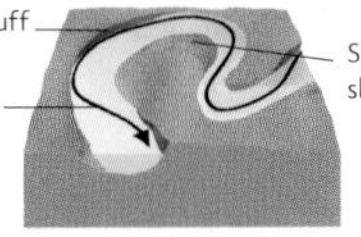

Bluff
Direction of flow
Slip-off slope

▲ ***Meanders form as** rivers flow across plains at a low gradient. A steep cliff or bluff, forms on the outside curve, and a gentler slip-off slope on the inside bend.*

Transportation & industry

Heavy industry has dominated postwar life in Central Europe. Poland has large coal reserves, having inherited the Silesian coalfield from Germany after the Second World War, allowing the export of large quantities of coal, along with other minerals. Hungary specializes in consumer goods and services, while Slovakia's industrial base is still relatively small. The Czech Republic's traditional glassworks and breweries bring some stability to its precarious Soviet-built manufacturing sector.

BALTIC SEA
RUSSIAN FED. (Kaliningrad)
LITHUANIA
BELARUS
UKRAINE
ROMANIA
SERBIA
CROATIA
SLOVENIA
AUSTRIA
GERMANY
Gdańsk
Szczecin
Białystok
WARSAW
Poznań
Łódź
POLAND
Wrocław
Katowice
Kraków
Ostrava
PRAGUE
CZECH REPUBLIC
Brno
SLOVAKIA
BRATISLAVA
Miskolc
Győr
BUDAPEST
HUNGARY
Szeged

Major industry and infrastructure

- car manufacture
- chemicals
- engineering
- food processing
- mining
- shipbuilding
- tourism
- capital cities
- major towns
- international airports
- major roads
- major industrial areas

Transportation network

- 213,997 miles (344,600 km)
- 817 miles (1315 km)
- 27,479 miles (44,249 km)
- 3784 miles (6094 km)

The huge growth of tourism and business has prompted major investment in the transportation infrastructure, with new roadbuilding schemes within and between the main cities of the region.

▲ ***Budapest, the capital** of Hungary, straddles the Danube. It comprises the historic towns of Buda, on the west bank, and Pest, which contains the Parliament Building, seen here on the far bank.*

BALTIC SEA
Pomeranian Bay
Gulf of Danzig
RUSSIAN FEDERATION (Kaliningrad)
LITHUANIA
BELARUS
GERMANY
POLAND
POMORSKIE
ZACHODNIO-POMORSKIE
WARMIŃSKO-MAZURSKIE
PODLASKIE
KUJAWSKO-POMORSKIE
MAZOWIECKIE
WIELKOPOLSKIE
LUBUSKIE
ŁÓDZKIE
LUBELSKIE
Szczecin
Koszalin
Słupsk
Gdynia
Gdańsk
Elbląg
Olsztyn
Białystok
Bydgoszcz
Toruń
Poznań
Płock
WARSZAWA (WARSAW)
Łódź
Kalisz
118

UKRAINE
ROMANIA
SERBIA
CROATIA
SLOVENIA
AUSTRIA
GERMANY
CZECH REPUBLIC
SLOVAKIA
HUNGARY
PRAHA (PRAGUE)
BRATISLAVA
BUDAPEST
Carpathian Mountains
Bohemian Forest
Little Alföld
Great Hungarian Plain
Slovenské rudohorie
Tatra Mountains
Kraków
Wrocław
Katowice
Brno
Ostrava
Košice
Debrecen
Szeged
Pécs
Győr
100
108
112
116

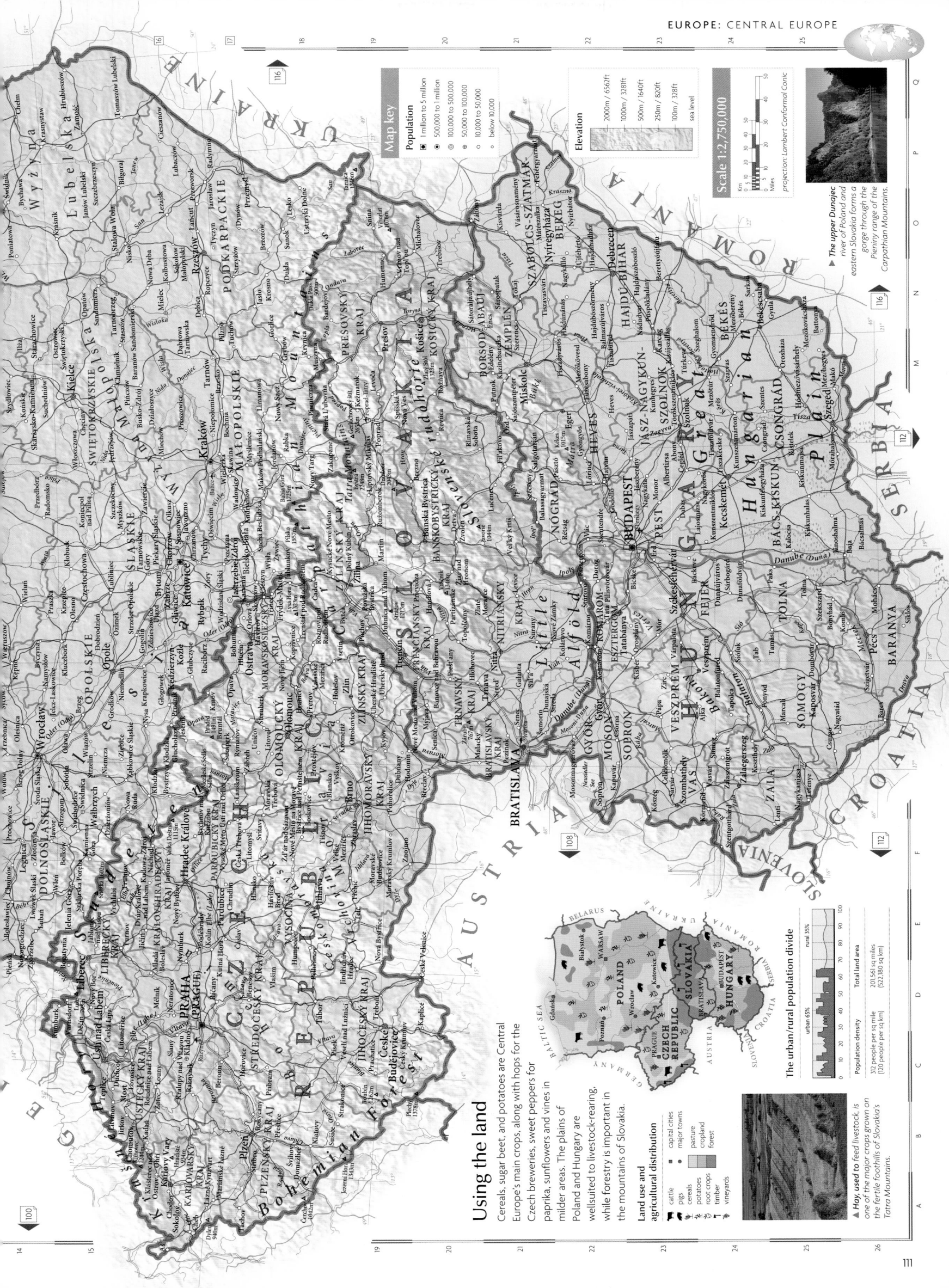

Map key

Population

- 1 million to 5 million
- 500,000 to 1 million
- 100,000 to 500,000
- 50,000 to 100,000
- 10,000 to 50,000
- below 10,000

Elevation

- 2000m / 6562ft
- 1000m / 3281ft
- 500m / 1640ft
- 250m / 820ft
- 100m / 328ft
- sea level

Scale 1:2,750,000

projection: Lambert Conformal Conic

Using the land

Cereals, sugar beet, and potatoes are Central Europe's main crops, along with hops for the Czech breweries, sweet peppers for paprika, sunflowers and vines in milder areas. The plains of Poland and Hungary are wellsuited to livestock-rearing, while forestry is important in the mountains of Slovakia.

Land use and agricultural distribution

- cattle
- pigs
- cereals
- potatoes
- root crops
- timber
- vineyards
- capital cities
- major towns
- pasture
- cropland
- forest

BALTIC SEA
BELARUS
UKRAINE
ROMANIA
SERBIA
CROATIA
SLOVENIA
AUSTRIA
GERMANY
POLAND
CZECH REPUBLIC
SLOVAKIA
HUNGARY
WARSAW
PRAGUE
BRATISLAVA
BUDAPEST
Gdańsk
Białystok
Poznań
Wrocław
Katowice

▲ **Hay, used to** *feed livestock, is one of the major crops grown on the fertile foothills of Slovakia's Tatra Mountains.*

The urban/rural population divide

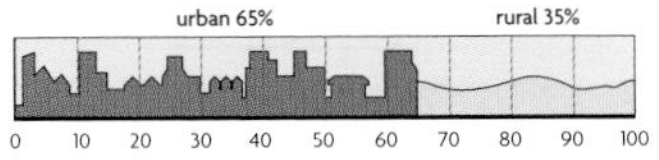
urban 65%
rural 35%
0
10
20
30
40
50
60
70
80
90
100

Population density	Total land area
312 people per sq mile (120 people per sq km)	201,561 sq miles (522,180 sq km)

▶ ***The upper Dunajec*** *river of Poland and eastern Slovakia forms a gorge through the Pieniny range of the Carpathian Mountains.*

Southeast Europe

ALBANIA, BOSNIA & HERZEGOVINA, CROATIA, KOSOVO, MACEDONIA, MONTENEGRO, SERBIA

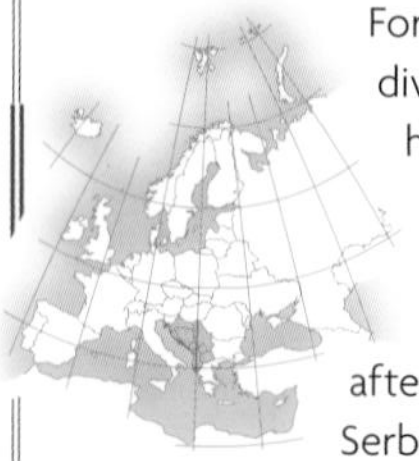

For 46 years the federation of Yugoslavia held together the most diverse ethnic region in Europe, along the picturesque mountain hinterland of the Dalmatian coast. Economic collapse resulted in internal tensions. In the early 1990s, civil war broke out in both Croatia and Bosnia as the ethnic populations struggled to establish their own exclusive territories. Peace was only restored by the UN after NATO launched air strikes in 1995. Montenegro voted to split from Serbia in 2006. More recently, Kosovo controversially declared independence from Serbia in 2008, although this may take some time to be fully recognized. Neighboring Albania is slowly improving its fragile economy but remains one of Europe's poorest nations.

▲ ***Hot, dry summers** and mild winters offer excellent conditions for viticulture in Montenegro. The precipitous Dinaric Alps have kept this region relatively isolated for centuries.*

The landscape

The Tisza, Sava, and Drava Rivers drain the broad northern lowland, meeting the Danube after it crosses the Hungarian border. In the west, the Dinaric Alps divide the Adriatic Sea from the interior. Mainland valleys and elongated islands run parallel to the steep Dalmatian *(Dalmacija)* coastline, following alternating bands of resistant limestone.

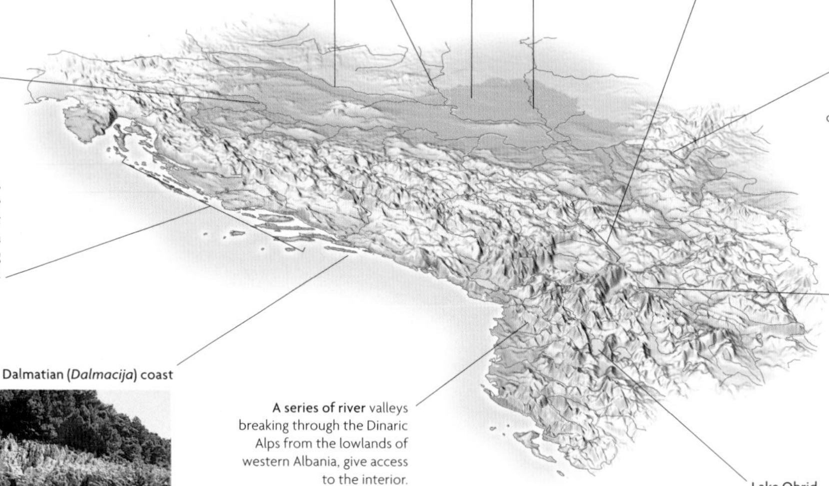
At least 70% of the fresh water in the western Balkans drains eastward into theBlack Sea, mostly via the Danube *(Dunav)*.
The river floodplains of the Pannonian Basin are flanked by terraces of gravel and wind-blown glacial deposits known as loess.
Drava river
Tisza river
Sava river
The elongated islands, promontories and straits of the Dalmatian *(Dalmacija)* coast were formed as the Adriatic Sea rose to flood valleys running parallel to the shore.
Dalmatian (*Dalmacija*) coast
A series of river valleys breaking through the Dinaric Alps from the lowlands of western Albania, give access to the interior.
At Iron Gate *(Derdap)*, on the border with Romania, the Danube narrows and cuts through foothills of the Balkan and Carpathian mountains, forming the deepest gorge in Europe.
A major earthquake at Skopje, Macedonia, in 1963 killed 1000 people. The whole region lies on an active crustal plate margin.
Lake Ohrid

Poljes in the Kosovo region

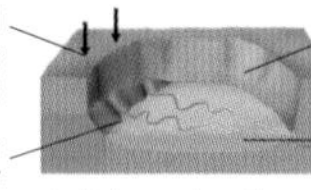
Underground drainage along joints in the rock
Spring at foot of cliff
Sheer limestone walls enclose all sides
Flat *polje* floor

▲ ***Rain and underground** water dissolve limestone along massive vertical joints (cracks). This creates* poljes: *depressions several miles across with steep walls and broad, flat floors.*

▶ ***Limestone cliffs along** the Dalmatian* (Dalmacija) *shoreline are heavily eroded, as salt water dissolves the rock along existing horizontal cracks, or joints. This tends to form a platform of rock at the foot of the cliff.*

▲ ***Lake Ohrid borders** Albania and Macedonia. Ohrid is the deepest lake in the western Balkans, reaching depths of 938 ft (286 m).*

Scale 1:2,750,000

Km 0 5 10 20 30 40 50 60 70
Miles 0 5 10 20 30 40 50 60 70

projection: Lambert Conformal Conic

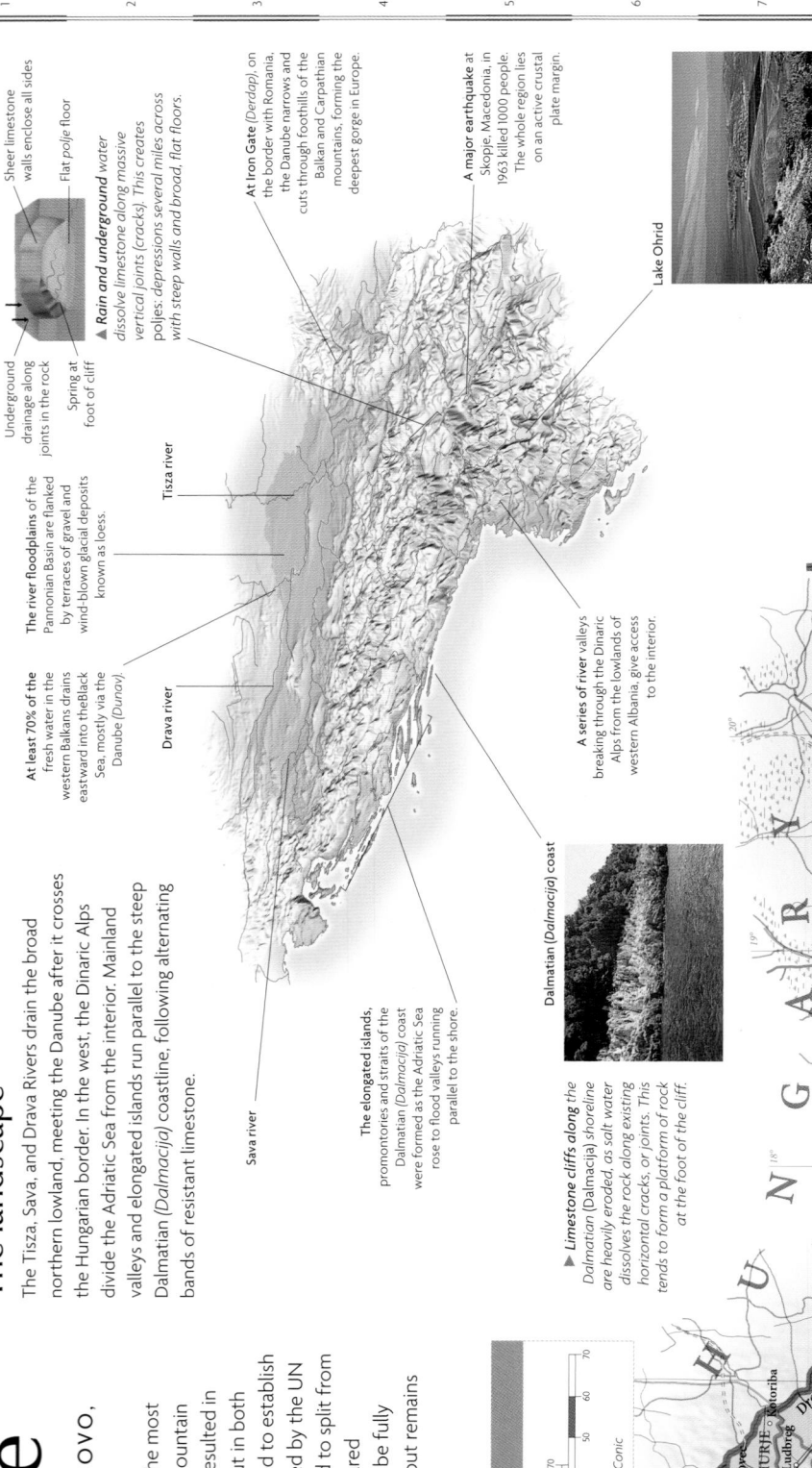

HUNGARY
SLOVENIA
CROATIA
ROMANIA
BOSNIA & HERZEGOVINA
SERBIA
VOJVODINA
ZAGREB
BEOGRAD (BELGRADE)
Novi Sad
Osijek
Rijeka
Zadar
Subotica
Banja Luka
Tuzla
Gulf of Trieste
Sava
Drava
Danube (Dunav)
Tisa
Drina

108
110
116
114
120

◀ ***The historic center*** *of Mostar in southern Bosnia, with its famous 16th-century Turkish bridge, was destroyed by shelling during 1993. The bridge was rebuilt and opened again in 2004.*

MONTENEGRO
PODGORICA
KOSOVO
(Full independence not yet recognized)
PRISHTINË (PRISTINA)
SKOPJE
MACEDONIA
ALBANIA
TIRANË (TIRANA)
SPLIT-DALMACIJA
DUBROVNIK-NERETVA
Split
Dubrovnik
Adriatic Sea
Strait of Otranto
GREECE
BULGARIA
Lake Ohrid
Lake Prespa
Dinaric Alps

114

Transportation & industry

Processing industries based on the region's wealth of mineral reserves predominate in Albania and Macedonia. In other regions, industrial plants have been commandeered, if not destroyed in the war and mineral extraction has severely declined. The fast-flowing rivers found throughout the Dinaric Alps are exploited to generate hydroelectric power.

In February 2008, Kosovo (a UN Protectorate within Serbia since 1999) declared independence. Although recognized by several countries, this decision has proved controversial with other states wary of setting a precedent for separatist groups within their own borders. It is therefore likely to be some time before Kosovo becomes universally recognized.

SLOVENIA
HUNGARY
ROMANIA
BULGARIA
GREECE
CROATIA
BOSNIA & HERZEGOVINA
SERBIA
MONTENEGRO
KOSOVO
MACEDONIA
ALBANIA
ZAGREB
BELGRADE
SARAJEVO
PODGORICA
PRISTINA
SKOPJE
TIRANA
Adriatic Sea

Major industry and infrastructure

- aluminum refining
- car manufacture
- chemicals
- engineering
- food processing
- hydroelectric power
- mining
- shipbuilding
- textiles
- timber processing
- capital cities
- major towns
- international airports
- major roads

Transportation network

46,996 miles (75,642 km)	685 miles (1103 km)
5413 miles (8713 km)	879 miles (1415 km)

The war has resulted in the destruction or disintegration of infrastructure for transportation, communications, and power supply, though this is now in the process of recovery.

▶ ***Industrial processing plants*** *were established throughout Albania by the Hoxha regime, which collapsed in 1992. They remain incongruous among the villages of one of Europe's most conservative rural societies.*

▲ ***The ancient Croatian*** *port of Dubrovnik was one of the former Yugoslavia's most popular tourist resorts and an important point of access to the sea along the Dalmatian (Dalmacija) coast. Shelling of the old city by Serb forces in 1991 provoked international condemnation.*

Using the land

Crops of wheat, maize, sugar beet, vegetables, and fruit are widely grown. The hilly terrain is suited to forestry and livestock farming. The mild, Mediterranean climate of the coastal regions provides ideal conditions for growing vines and olives. Albania's largely agricultural economy has been adversely affected by the recent dismantling of state farms.

SLOVENIA
HUNGARY
ROMANIA
BULGARIA
GREECE
CROATIA
BOSNIA & HERZEGOVINA
SERBIA
MONTENEGRO
KOSOVO
MACEDONIA
ALBANIA
ZAGREB
BELGRADE
SARAJEVO
PODGORICA
PRISTINA
SKOPJE
TIRANA
Adriatic Sea

Land use and agricultural distribution

- pigs
- sheep
- cereals
- fruit
- olives
- sugar beet
- timber
- tobacco
- vineyards
- capital cities
- major towns
- pasture
- cropland
- forest
- mountain region

◀ ***Sweet red peppers*** *are dried in the sun, ready to make paprika. Macedonia's economy is mainly agricultural and its fertile soils support a broad range of crops.*

The urban/rural population divide

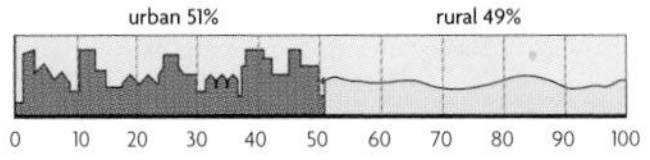

urban 51%
rural 49%
0 10 20 30 40 50 60 70 80 90 100

Population density	Total land area
240 people per sq mile (93 people per sq km)	95,038 sq miles (246,278 sq km)

▶ ***The Tara river*** *is one of Montenegro's major rivers. It flows into the Danube via the Drina and Sava rivers. Along its course the Tara has eroded spectacular gorges up to 3280 ft (1000 m) deep.*

Map key

Population

- 1 million to 5 million
- 500,000 to 1 million
- 100,000 to 500,000
- 50,000 to 100,000
- 10,000 to 50,000
- below 10,000

Elevation

- 2000m / 6562ft
- 1000m / 3281ft
- 500m / 1640ft
- 250m / 820ft
- 100m / 328ft
- sea level

Bulgaria & Greece

Including EUROPEAN TURKEY

Greece is renowned as the original hearth of western civilization. The rugged terrain and numerous islands have profoundly affected its development, creating a strong agricultural and maritime tradition. In the past 50 years, this formerly rural society has rapidly urbanized, with one third of the population now living in the capital, Athens, and in the northern city of Salonica. Bulgaria, dominated for centuries by the Ottoman Turks, became part of the eastern bloc after the Second World War, only slowly emerging from Soviet influence in 1989. Moves toward democracy led to some instability in Bulgaria and Greece, now outweighed by the challenge of integration with the European Union.

Transportation & industry

Soviet investment introduced heavy industry into Bulgaria, and the processing of agricultural produce, such as tobacco, is important throughout the country. Both countries have substantial shipyards and Greece has one of the world's largest merchant fleets. Many small craft workshops, producing textiles and processed foods, are clustered around Greek cities. The service and construction sectors have profited from the successful tourist industry.

ROMANIA
BULGARIA
SOFIA
Pleven
Ruse
Varna
Stara Zagora
Burgas
Plovdiv
SERBIA
MACEDONIA
BLACK SEA
TURKEY
Istanbul
GREECE
Salonica
Larisa
Volos
Aegean Sea
ATHENS
Patra
Corinth
Ionian Sea
Irakleio
MEDITERRANEAN SEA
ALBANIA

112

Major industry and infrastructure

- chemicals
- engineering
- food processing
- shipbuilding
- textiles
- tourism
- capital cities
- major towns
- international airports
- major roads
- major industrial areas

Transportation network

- 103,930 miles (167,630 km)
- 345 miles (557 km)
- 4346 miles (6995 km)
- 294 miles (474 km)

Bulgaria's railroads require investment to revive an outdated infrastructure. In Greece, despite a developing road network, ferry-boats remain the most effective form of transportation in many areas.

▲ ***A towering pinnacle** at Metéora in central Greece is home to the monastery of Roussanou. The 24 rock towers which dominate the plain of Thessaly (Thessalía) are remnants of an old plateau. Long-term weathering along fissures in the rock has worn away the rest of the plateau.*

The landscape

Bulgaria's Balkan mountains divide the Danubian Plain (*Dunavska Ravnina*) and Maritsa Basin, meeting the Black Sea in the east along sandy beaches. The steep Rhodope Mountains form a natural barrier with Greece, while the younger Pindus form a rugged central spine which descends into the Aegean Sea to give a vast archipelago of over 2000 islands, the largest of which is Crete.

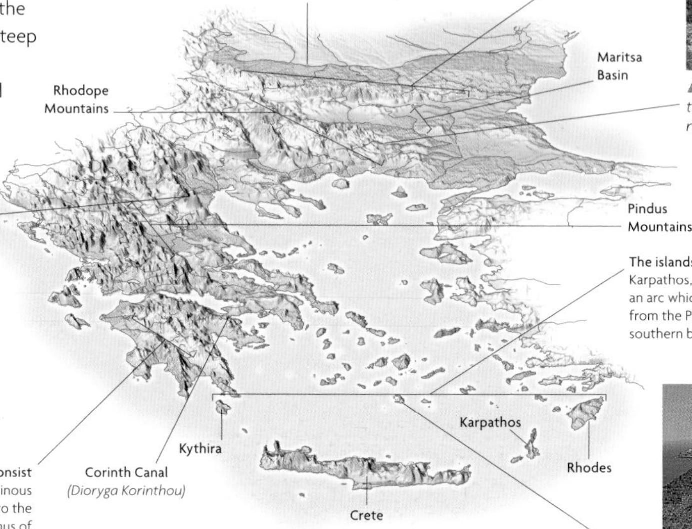
The Danube, Europe's second longest river, forms most of Bulgaria's northern border. The Danubian plain (*Dunavska Ravnina*), extending from the southern bank, is extremely fertile.
Balkan Mountains
Maritsa Basin
Rhodope Mountains
Mount Olympus is the mythical home of the Greek Gods and, at 9570 ft (2917 m), is the highest mountain in Greece.
Pindus Mountains
The islands of Crete, Kythira, Karpathos, and Rhodes are part of an arc which bends southeastward from the Peloponnese, forming the southern boundary of the Aegean.
Karpathos
Rhodes
Kythira
Crete
Corinth Canal (*Dioryga Korinthou*)
The Peloponnese consist of several mountainous peninsulas, linked to the mainland by the Isthmus of Corinth. The Corinth Canal (*Dioryga Korinthou*), built in 1893, cuts through the isthmus, linking the Aegean and Ionian Seas.

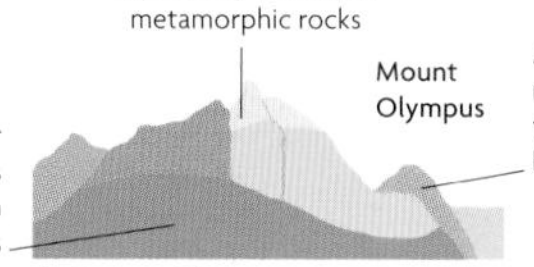
Limestone rocks exposed by erosion of metamorphic rocks
Mount Olympus
Ancient metamorphic rock, formed miles below the surface
Younger limestones created in shallow seas

▲ ***Mount Olympus** is a composite of rocks formed by two major tectonic events. First the older metamorphic rocks were thrust over the limestones, then two million years ago regional warping and subsequent erosion, reexposed the limestone.*

▲ ***The Arda river** cuts through the Rhodope Mountains in rugged, rocky gorges.*

▲ ***Layers of black** volcanic ash still cover the island of Santorini. This volcano last erupted 3500 years ago, but still shows signs of volcanic activity.*

ROMANIA
SERBIA
MACEDONIA
BULGARIA
TURKEY
BLACK SEA
Dunavska Ravnina
Rhodope Mountains
Sofia
Plovdiv
Varna
Burgas
Ruse
Stara Zagora
Istanbul
Edirne
Dobrich
Shumen
Pleven
Vidin
Scale 1:2,750,000
projection: Lambert Conformal Conic

116
112

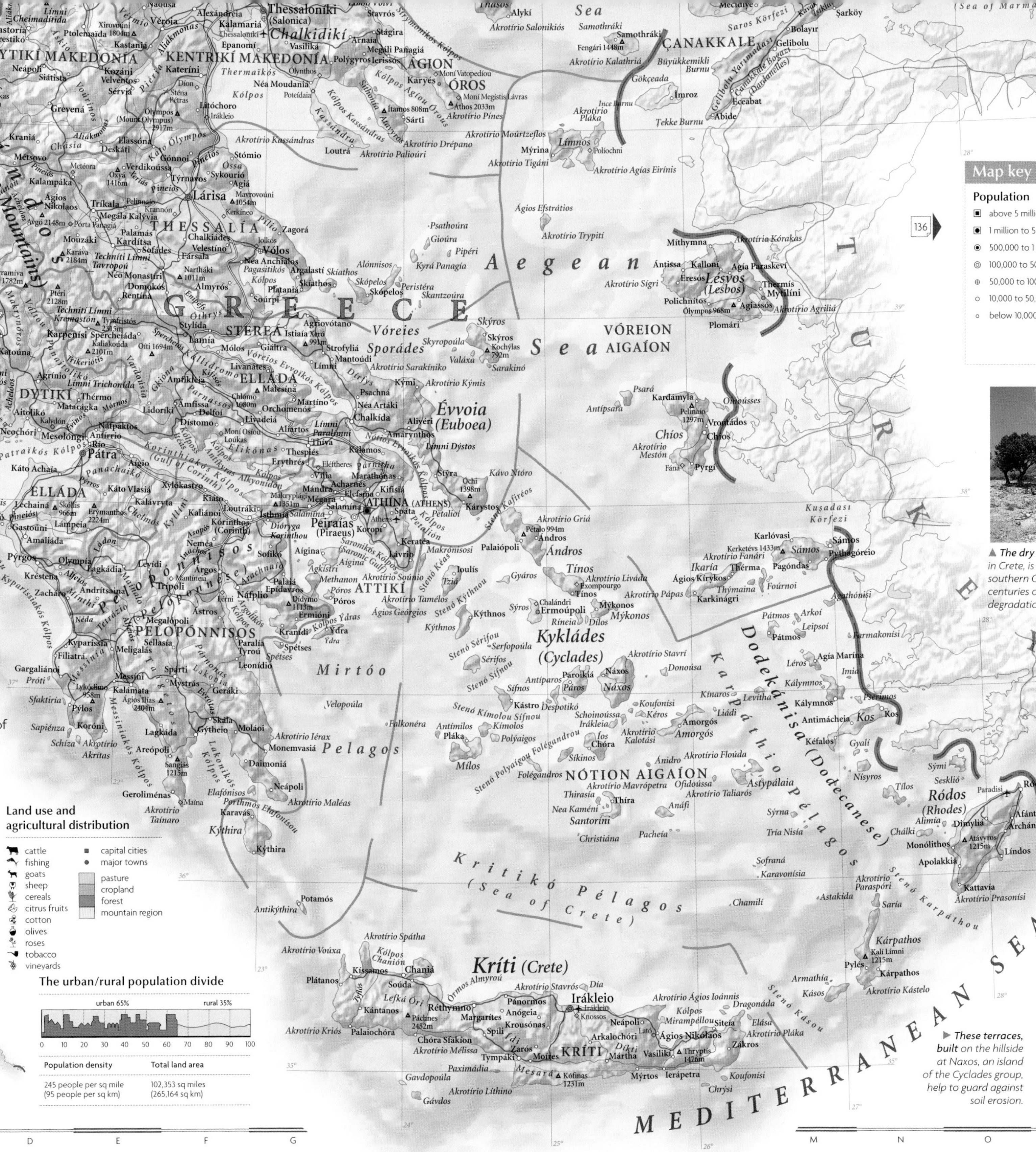
ALBANIA
GREECE
TURKEY
Aegean Sea
Ionian Sea
Ióniа Nisiá (Ionian Islands)
MEDITERRANEAN SEA
Píndos (Pindus Mountains)
Thessaloníki (Salonica)
Athína (Athens)
Peiraiás (Piraeus)
Pátra
Lárisa
Vólos
Irákleio
Kríti (Crete)
Kykládes (Cyclades)
Dodekánisa (Dodecanese)
Ródos (Rhodes)
Évvoia (Euboea)
Pelopónnisos
Kritikó Pélagos (Sea of Crete)
Mirtóo Pelagos
Karpáthio Pélagos
VÓREION AIGAÍON
NÓTION AIGAÍON
ÇANAKKALE
112
136
120
24

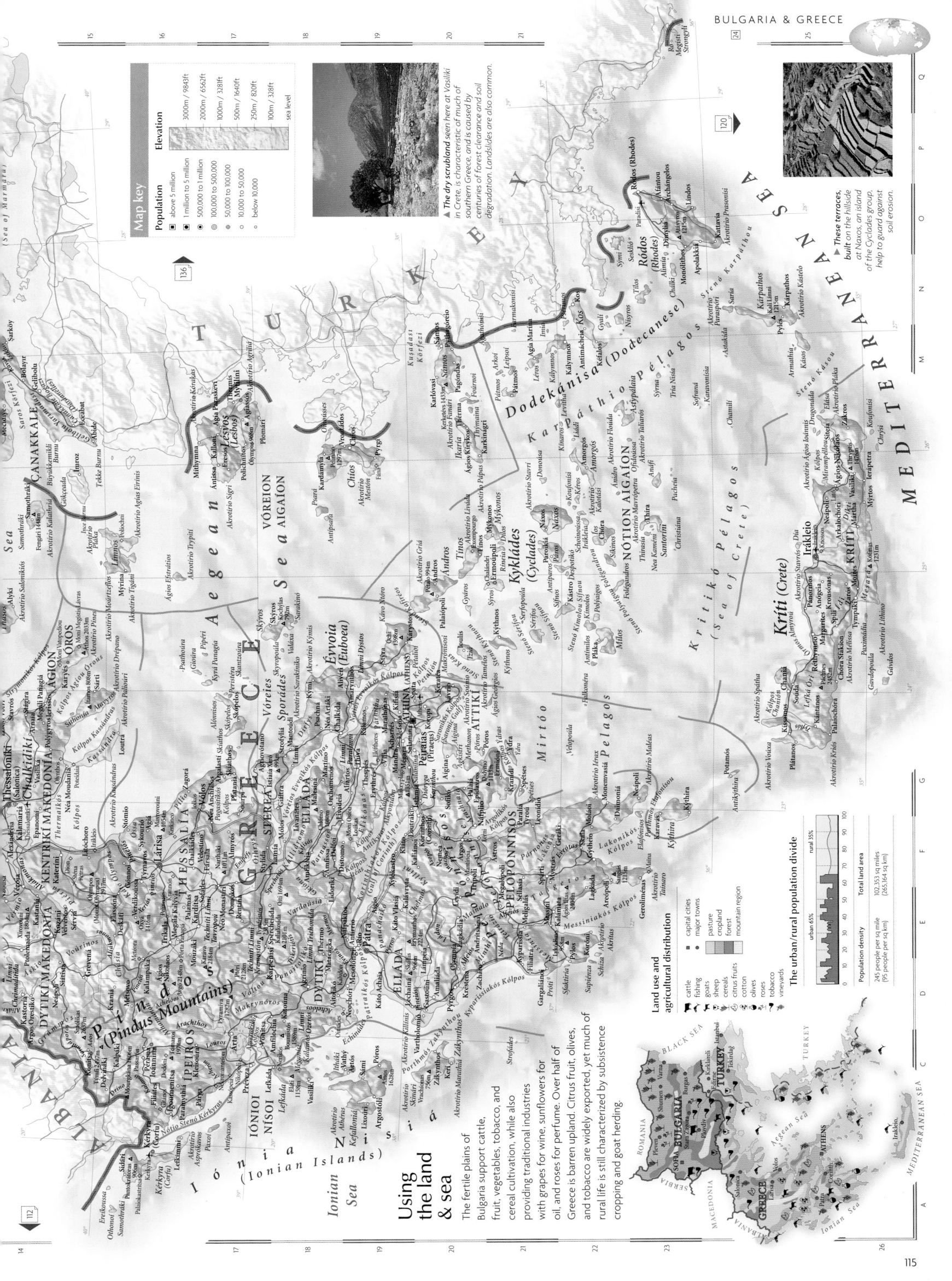

Map key

Population
- above 5 million
- 1 million to 5 million
- 500,000 to 1 million
- 100,000 to 500,000
- 50,000 to 100,000
- 10,000 to 50,000
- below 10,000

Elevation
- 3000m / 9843ft
- 2000m / 6562ft
- 1000m / 3281ft
- 500m / 1640ft
- 250m / 820ft
- 100m / 328ft
- sea level

▲ *The dry scrubland seen here at Vasilikí in Crete, is characteristic of much of southern Greece, and is caused by centuries of forest clearance and soil degradation. Landslides are also common.*

Using the land & sea

The fertile plains of Bulgaria support cattle, fruit, vegetables, tobacco, and cereal cultivation, while also providing traditional industries with grapes for wine, sunflowers for oil, and roses for perfume. Over half of Greece is barren upland. Citrus fruit, olives, and tobacco are widely exported, yet much of rural life is still characterized by subsistence cropping and goat herding.

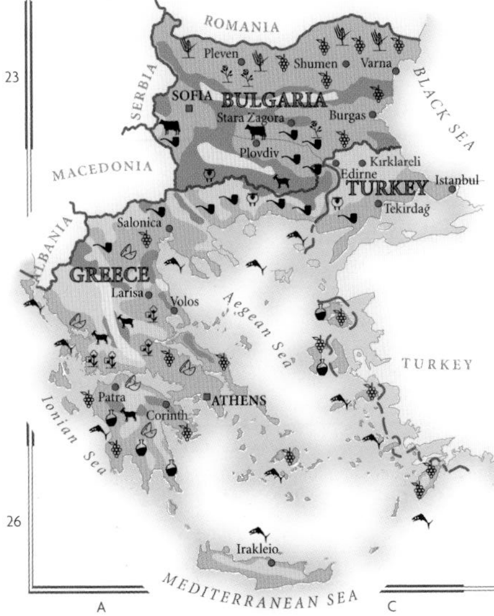
ROMANIA
SERBIA
BLACK SEA
MACEDONIA
ALBANIA
BULGARIA
TURKEY
GREECE
SOFIA
ATHENS
Pleven
Shumen
Varna
Stara Zagora
Burgas
Plovdiv
Kirklareli
Edirne
Istanbul
Tekirdağ
Salonica
Larisa
Volos
Patra
Corinth
Irakleio
Aegean Sea
Ionian Sea
MEDITERRANEAN SEA

Land use and agricultural distribution

- cattle
- fishing
- goats
- sheep
- cereals
- citrus fruits
- cotton
- olives
- roses
- tobacco
- vineyards
- capital cities
- major towns
- pasture
- cropland
- forest
- mountain region

The urban/rural population divide

urban 65% rural 35%

0 10 20 30 40 50 60 70 80 90 100

Population density	Total land area
245 people per sq mile (95 people per sq km)	102,353 sq miles (265,164 sq km)

▶ *These terraces, built on the hillside at Naxos, an island of the Cyclades group, help to guard against soil erosion.*

A B C D E F G H I J K L M

Romania, Moldova & Ukraine

The industrial, social, and cultural make-up of Romania and the former Soviet states of Moldova and Ukraine still bear the imprint of their communist past. As part of the USSR, Ukraine was a leading agricultural, industrial, and energy producer. These industries, like those in Moldova and Romania, are now being reoriented more firmly toward western markets. As a result of shifting borders, and Soviet policy actively encouraging Russian immigration into other Soviet states like Ukraine and Moldova, all three countries now contain large numbers of foreign nationals. Moldovans and Romanians are still close in terms of language and culture, although Moldova is striving to remain an independent nation.

B E L A
Pripet Marshes
VOLYNS'KA OBLAST'
RIVNENS'KA OBLAST'
ZHYTOMYRS'KA
L'VIVS'KA OBLAST'
L'viv
Luts'k
Rivne
Ternopil'
TERNOPIL'S'KA OBLAST'
KHMEL'NYTS'KA
Khmel'nyts'kyy
Podil's'
Ivano-Frankivs'k
IVANO-FRANKIVS'KA
ZAKARPATS'KA OBLAST'
Uzhhorod
Chernivtsi
CHERNIVETS'KA OBLAST'
P O L A N D
S L O V A K I A
H U N G A R Y
S E R B I A
B U L G A R I A
R O M A N I A
Satu Mare
Baia Mare
MARAMUREȘ
Oradea
BIHOR
Cluj-Napoca
CLUJ
Transylvania
Târgu Mureș
MUREȘ
HARGHITA
Suceava
SUCEAVA
Botoșani
BOTOȘANI
Iași
IAȘI
NEAMȚ
Piatra-Neamț
Bacău
BACĂU
Vaslui
VASLUI
Arad
ARAD
Timișoara
TIMIȘ
Alba Iulia
ALBA
Deva
HUNEDOARA
Sibiu
SIBIU
Brașov
BRAȘOV
COVASNA
VRANCEA
Galați
GALAȚI
Brăila
BRĂILA
Buzău
BUZĂU
PRAHOVA
Ploiești
Pitești
ARGEȘ
VÂLCEA
GORJ
Târgu Jiu
CARAȘ-SEVERIN
MEHEDINȚI
Drobeta-Turnu Severin
Craiova
DOLJ
OLT
Slatina
TELEORMAN
GIURGIU
Giurgiu
BUCUREȘTI (BUCHAREST)
IALOMIȚA
CĂLĂRAȘI
Călărași
Danube (Dunărea)
MOL

Using the land

The fertile black soils of Ukraine, often called "the breadbasket of Europe," have enabled the cultivation of a variety of cereals and vegetables, which are widely exported. Romania and Moldova also grow cereals, sunflowers, and vegetables, and are noted for the quality of their wines.

◀ *The fertile lands and tolerant climate of Moldova are ideally suited to growing grapes for wine.*

BELARUS
RUSSIAN FEDERATION
POLAND
SLOVAKIA
HUNGARY
SERBIA
BULGARIA
BLACK SEA
UKRAINE
MOLDOVA
ROMANIA
KIEV
L'viv
Chernivtsi
Dnipropetrovs'k
CHIȘINĂU
Odesa
Timișoara
Brașov
BUCHAREST

Land use and agricultural distribution

- cattle
- pigs
- poultry
- sheep
- cereals
- cotton
- sugar beet
- sunflowers
- vineyards
- capital cities
- major towns
- pasture
- cropland
- forest
- wetland

The urban/rural population divide

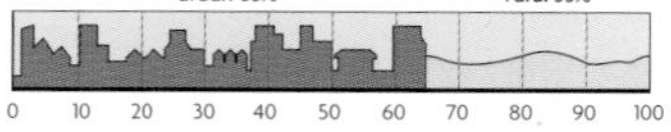

urban 65%
rural 35%
0 10 20 30 40 50 60 70 80 90 100

Population density	Total land area
222 people per sq mile (86 people per sq km)	334,947 sq miles (867,740 sq km)

◀ *Glacial lakes are found throughout the Transylvanian Alps (Carpatii Meridionali), although the mountains no longer have any permanent snow cover.*

Transportation & industry

Heavy industry using local raw materials characterizes much of this region. The industrial heartland of Ukraine, specializing in metal and machine-building industries, is based around its vast mineral reserves in the Donbass region. In Moldova, food processing draws on produce from its agricultural sector. Romanian industry relies both on local raw materials and imported iron, steel, and oil.

BELARUS
RUSSIAN FEDERATION
POLAND
SLOVAKIA
HUNGARY
SERBIA
BULGARIA
BLACK SEA
UKRAINE
MOLDOVA
ROMANIA
KIEV
Luts'k
L'viv
Chernivtsi
Kharkiv
Kremenchuk
Dnipropetrovs'k
Donets'k
Donbass
Kryvyy Rih
Bălți
CHIȘINĂU
Odesa
Simferopol'
Cluj-Napoca
Timișoara
Brașov
Galați
BUCHAREST

Major industry and infrastructure

- car manufacture
- chemicals
- coal
- engineering
- food processing
- mining
- oil & gas
- textiles
- tourism
- capital cities
- major towns
- international airports
- major roads
- major industrial areas

Transportation network

170,707 miles (274,757 km)	1170 miles (1883 km)
21,474 miles (34,563 km)	4130 miles (6647 km)

Increased industrialization has necessitated the upgrading of road and rail networks in all three countries. Modernization has tended to focus only on major cities and industrial areas.

110

110

112

114

▶ *During the 1960s and 1970s, many industries, like this carbon factory, developed using the mineral resources on the flanks of the Transylvanian Alps (Carpatii Meridionali).*

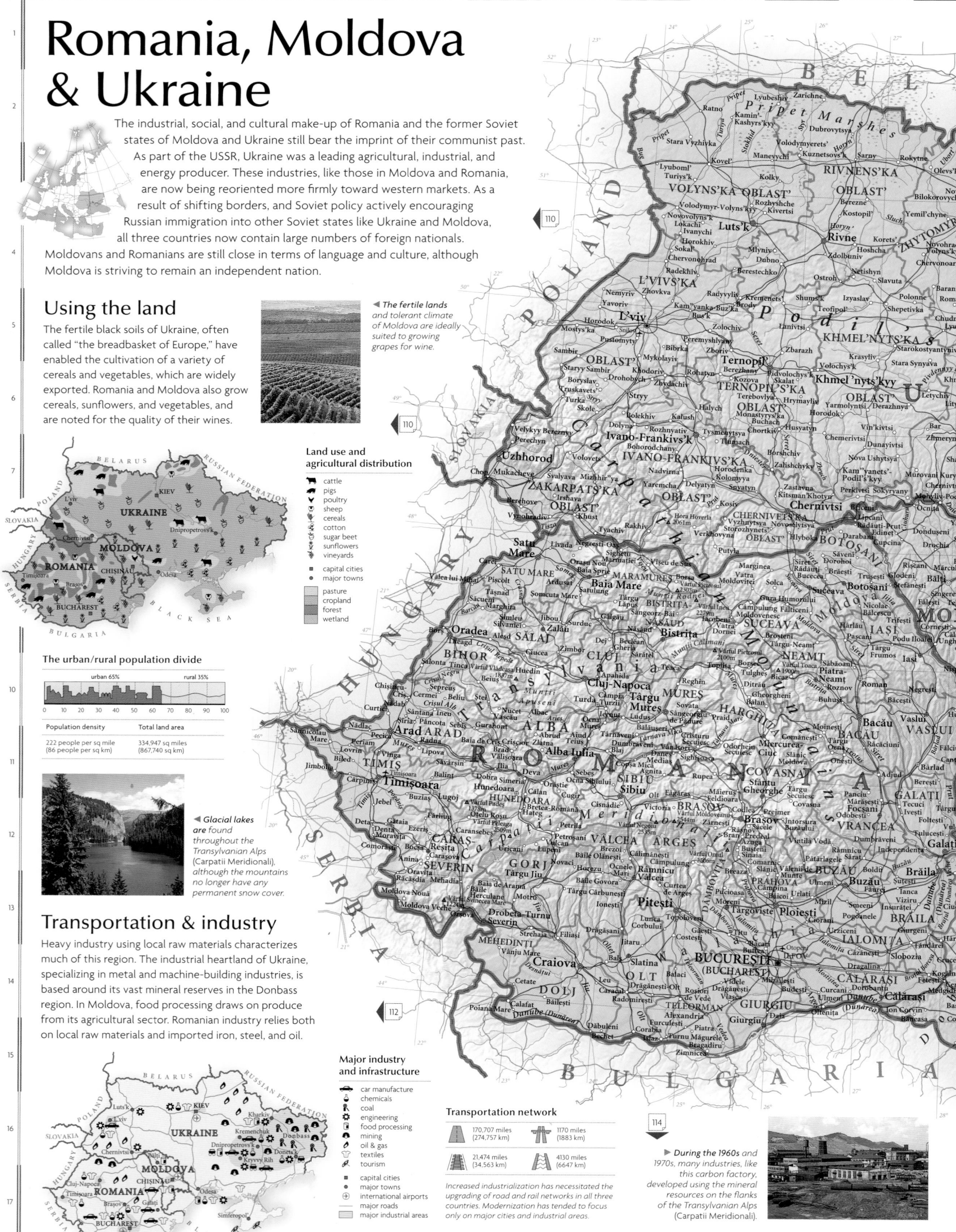

A E F G H I J K L M

N O P Q R S T U V W X Y Z
118
122
126
120
Scale 1:3,500,000
Km
Miles
projection: Lambert Conformal Conic
Map key
Population
1 million to 5 million
500,000 to 1 million
100,000 to 500,000
50,000 to 100,000
10,000 to 50,000
below 10,000
Elevation
2000m / 6562ft
1000m / 3281ft
500m / 1640ft
250m / 820ft
100m / 328ft
sea level
RUSSIAN FEDERATION
UKRAINE
Dniepr Lowland
Black Sea Lowland
Sea of Azov
Gulf of Taganrog
BLACK SEA
Karkinits'ka Zatoka
Kerch Strait
AVTONOMNA RESPUBLIKA KRYM
Kryms'kyy Pivostriv
Kryms'ki Hory
Hora Roman-Kosh 1545m
CHERNIHIVS'KA OBLAST'
SUMS'KA OBLAST'
KYYIVS'KA
POLTAVS'KA OBLAST'
KHARKIVS'KA OBLAST'
LUHANS'KA OBLAST'
DONETS'KA OBLAST'
DNIPROPETROVS'KA OBLAST'
ZAPORIZ'KA OBLAST'
KHERSONS'KA OBLAST'
MYKOLAYIVS'KA OBLAST'
ODES'KA OBLAST'
KIROVOHRADS'KA OBLAST'
CHERKAS'KA OBLAST'
KYYIV (KIEV)
Chernihiv
Sumy
Kharkiv
Poltava
Cherkasy
Kremenchuk
Kirovohrad
Dnipropetrovs'k
Donets'k
Luhans'k
Zaporizhzhya
Kryvyy Rih
Mykolayiv
Kherson
Odesa
Melitopol'
Mariupol'
Berdyans'k
Simferopol'
Sevastopol'
Yalta
Kerch
Yevpatoriya
Zhytomyr
CHIŞINĂU
Tulcea
Constanţa
Hurzuf
Alupka
Mys Sarych
Mys Khersones
Mys Tarkhankut
Mys Kazantyp
Mys Mehanom
Arabats'ka Strilka
Kakhovs'ke Vodoskhovyshche
Kremenchuts'ke Vodoskhovyshche
Kyyivs'ke Vodoskhovyshche
Dnipro
Donets'
Old glaciated valley
Water has eroded a new post-glacial valley

▲ *The Swallow's Nest castle at Yalta is one of many tourist resorts on the Crimean (Krym) coast, dubbed the "Russian Riviera."*

▲ **Balkas are common** *throughout Ukraine. They are large U-shaped valleys, formed during the last Ice Age, which contain narrower, deep valleys. These were incised by a sudden flow of water, following an icemelt.*

The landscape

Vast flat lowlands and gently rolling hills cover most of southeastern Europe. In the southwest, the Carpathian Mountains form a gentle arc. To the south of the Carpathian Mountains lies the Danube Plain, across which the Danube river flows to the Black Sea. To the north and east, the hills of Moldova level out into low plains, running east to the steppes of Ukraine.

▶ ***Divided into crystalline** massifs, the southern arm of the Carpathian Mountains, the Transylvanian Alps* (Carpatii Meridionali)*, extend 170 miles (274 km) across southwestern Romania.*

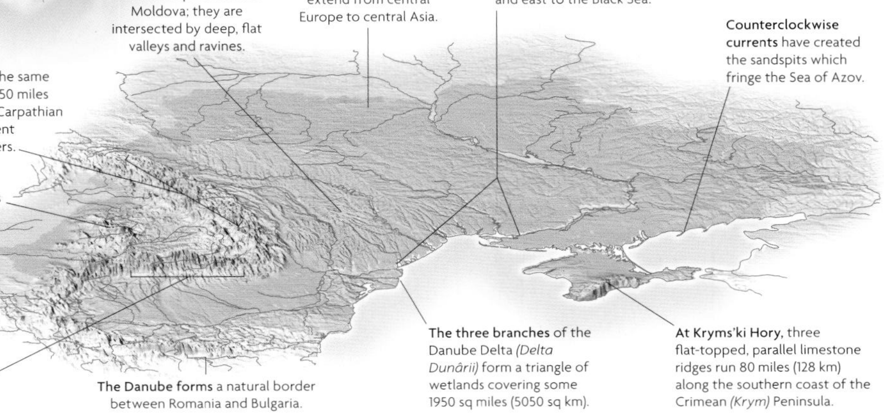
Uplifted and folded at the same time as the Alps, some 250 miles (400 km) of the eastern Carpathian Mountains contain ancient volcanic cones and craters.
The Apuseni Mountains *(Muntii Apuseni)* are rich in mineral deposits, including gold and iron ore.
Transylvanian Alps *(Carpatii Meridionali)*
The Codrii Hills dominate the landscape of central Moldova; they are intersected by deep, flat valleys and ravines.
Steppe landscape covers two-thirds of Ukraine. These flat, treeless grasslands extend from central Europe to central Asia.
Most of the major rivers in southeastern Europe, like the Danube, the Dniester, and Dnieper flow south and east to the Black Sea.
Counterclockwise currents have created the sandspits which fringe the Sea of Azov.
The Danube forms a natural border between Romania and Bulgaria.
The three branches of the Danube Delta *(Delta Dunării)* form a triangle of wetlands covering some 1950 sq miles (5050 sq km).
At Kryms'ki Hory, three flat-topped, parallel limestone ridges run 80 miles (128 km) along the southern coast of the Crimean *(Krym)* Peninsula.

The Baltic states & Belarus

BELARUS, ESTONIA, LATVIA, LITHUANIA, Kaliningrad

Occupying Europe's main corridor to Russia, the four distinct cultures of Estonia, Latvia, Lithuania, and Belarus share a history of struggle for nationhood against the interests of more powerful neighbors. As the first republics to declare their independence from the Soviet Union in 1990–91, the Baltic states of Estonia, Latvia, and Lithuania sought an economic role in the EU, while reaffirming their European cultural roots through the church and a strong musical tradition. Meanwhile, Belarus has shown economic and political allegiance to Russia by joining the Commonwealth of Independent States.

▲ *The seaport of Riga is Latvia's capital and the center of economic and cultural life. With a 32% Russian minority in Latvia, language and the right to national citizenship are key issues.*

Gulf of Finland
Gulf of Riga
BALTIC SEA
Irbe Strait
Narva Bay
Lake Peipus
Lake Pskov
RUSSIAN FEDERATION
RUSSIA
ESTONIA
LATVIA
LITHUANIA
TALLINN
RĪGA
Tartu
Daugavpils
Klaipėda
Šiauliai
Panevėžys
Vitsyebsk
Liepāja
Ventspils
Jūrmala
Jelgava
Saaremaa
Hiiumaa
Vidzeme
Augstiene
Žemaičiu Aukštumas
Western Dvina (Daugava)

122

122

Using the land

Across the four nations cattle and pig farming are widespread, together with diverse arable crops, including flax for making linen, potatoes used to produce vodka, cereals, and other vegetables. Almost a third of the land is forested; demand for timber has increased the importance of forest management.

Land use and agricultural distribution

- cattle
- pigs
- cereals
- flax
- potatoes
- timber
- capital cities
- major towns
- pasture
- cropland
- forest
- wetland

TALLINN
ESTONIA
Tartu
Võru
RIGA
LATVIA
Ventspils
Liepāja
Daugavpils
Šiauliai
LITHUANIA
Kaunas
VILNIUS
Alytus
Vitsyebsk
MINSK
BELARUS
Babruysk
Homyel'
Brest
RUSS.FED.
Kaliningrad
BALTIC SEA
RUSSIAN FEDERATION
POLAND
UKRAINE

The urban/rural population divide

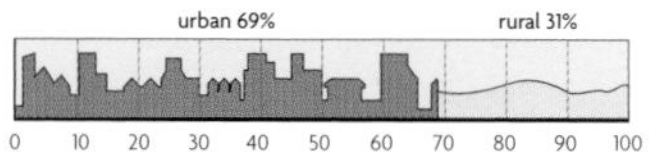
urban 69%
rural 31%
0
10
20
30
40
50
60
70
80
90
100

Population density	Total land area
122 people per sq mile (47 people per sq km)	145,006 sq miles (375,656 sq km)

▶ *A pine forest in northern Belarus. Conifers in the north give way to hardwood forest farther south. Timber mills are supplied with logs floated along the country's many navigable waterways.*

▲ *The Western Dvina river provides hydroelectric power and, during the summer months, access to the Baltic Sea. The lower course of the river freezes from December to April.*

Map key

Population

- 1 million to 5 million
- 500,000 to 1 million
- 100,000 to 500,000
- 50,000 to 100,000
- 10,000 to 50,000
- below 10,000

Elevation

- 250m / 820ft
- 100m / 328ft
- sea level

RUSSIAN FEDERATION
KALININGRADSKAYA OBLAST'
Kaliningrad
POLAND
LITHUANIA
VILNIUS
BELARUS
MINSK
HRODZYENSKAYA VOBLASTS'
MINSKAYA VOBLASTS'
MAHILYOWSKAYA VOBLASTS'
BRESTSKAYA VOBLASTS'
HOMYEL'SKAYA VOBLASTS'
Hrodna
Brest
Babruysk
Mahilyow
Homyel'
Orsha
Pripet Marshes
UKRAINE
Scale 1:2,750,000
projection: Lambert Conformal Conic
110
116

The landscape

Rock-strewn glacial plains meet the Baltic Sea along a coast of cliffs and sandy beaches. Hundreds of islands ranging from tiny, rocky outcrops to the large island of Saaremaa, lie scattered off the Estonian mainland, creating an archipelago. Lakes and marshes in low-lying areas give way to mixed woodland on fertile, undulating ground, with remnants of the primeval forest which once covered most of Europe preserved at Byelavyezhskaya Pushcha in western Belarus.

◀ *Saaremaa is the largest island in the Estonian archipelago. The southeastern parts are flat and fertile, giving way to numerous low hills and ridges toward the northwest.*

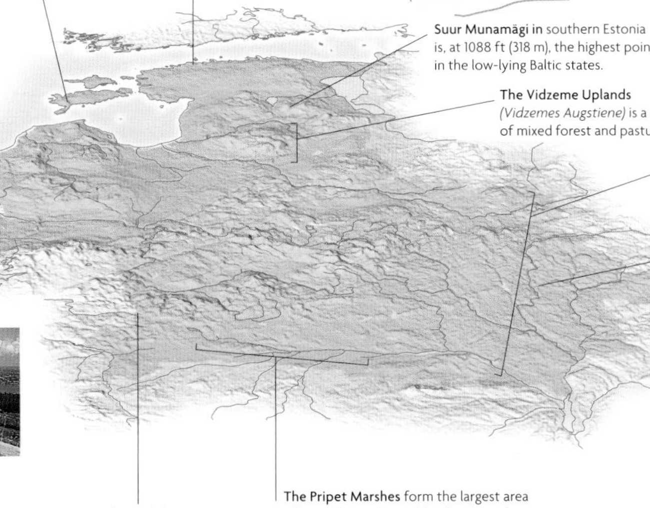
Saaremaa Island
There are many shallow depressions across Estonia. These formed as the ice sheet retreated and water from the melting ice was concentrated into lake basins, which eventually found outlets in the Baltic Sea.
A small delta has formed where the Neman river flows into the protected waters of Courland Lagoon, behind Courland Spit.
Suur Munamägi in southern Estonia is, at 1088 ft (318 m), the highest point in the low-lying Baltic states.
The Vidzeme Uplands (Vidzemes Augstiene) is a region of mixed forest and pasture.
Nuclear fallout from the 1986 Chernobyl (Chornobyl') disaster in Ukraine has contaminated large areas of agricultural land in Belarus.
The Dnieper river is the third longest in Europe and forms the heart of Belarus's drainage system.
Courland Spit
Byelavyezhskaya Pushcha
The Pripet Marshes form the largest area of "unreclaimed" marshland in Europe. They also provide a network of navigable waterways across southern Belarus.

▲ *Courland Spit is one of the largest of its kind on the Baltic coast, created by longshore currents moving eastward.*

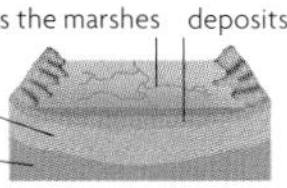
Pripet Marshes
A network of streams and creeks drains across the marshes
Peat deposits
Glacial deposits
Broad tectonic basin

▲ *This large area of marshland lies in a broad tectonic depression, mantled by glacial deposits. Peat deposits have developed below the marshes, which are prone to spring flooding.*

Transportation & industry

Recent economic restructuring has meant modernizing old Soviet industries such as vehicle production and the paper industry, and expanding the light engineering and electronics sectors. There has also been a revival of traditional crafts like carpentry and amber work. Although Estonia has oil shale reserves, the Baltic economies still rely heavily on Russian raw materials and energy.

Transportation network

242,810 miles (391,630 km)	40 miles (64 km)
6830 miles (11,016 km)	376 miles (606 km)

Railroads are being superseded by roads linking the ports with eastern Europe and Russia. A highway connecting the three Baltic capitals with Warsaw has been proposed.

TALLINN
ESTONIA
Tartu
Võru
BALTIC SEA
Ventspils
Liepāja
RIGA
LATVIA
Daugavpils
Šiauliai
LITHUANIA
Kaunas
VILNIUS
RUSS.FED.
Kaliningrad
RUSSIAN FEDERATION
Vitsyebsk
MINSK
Babruysk
Homyel'
BELARUS
Brest
POLAND
UKRAINE

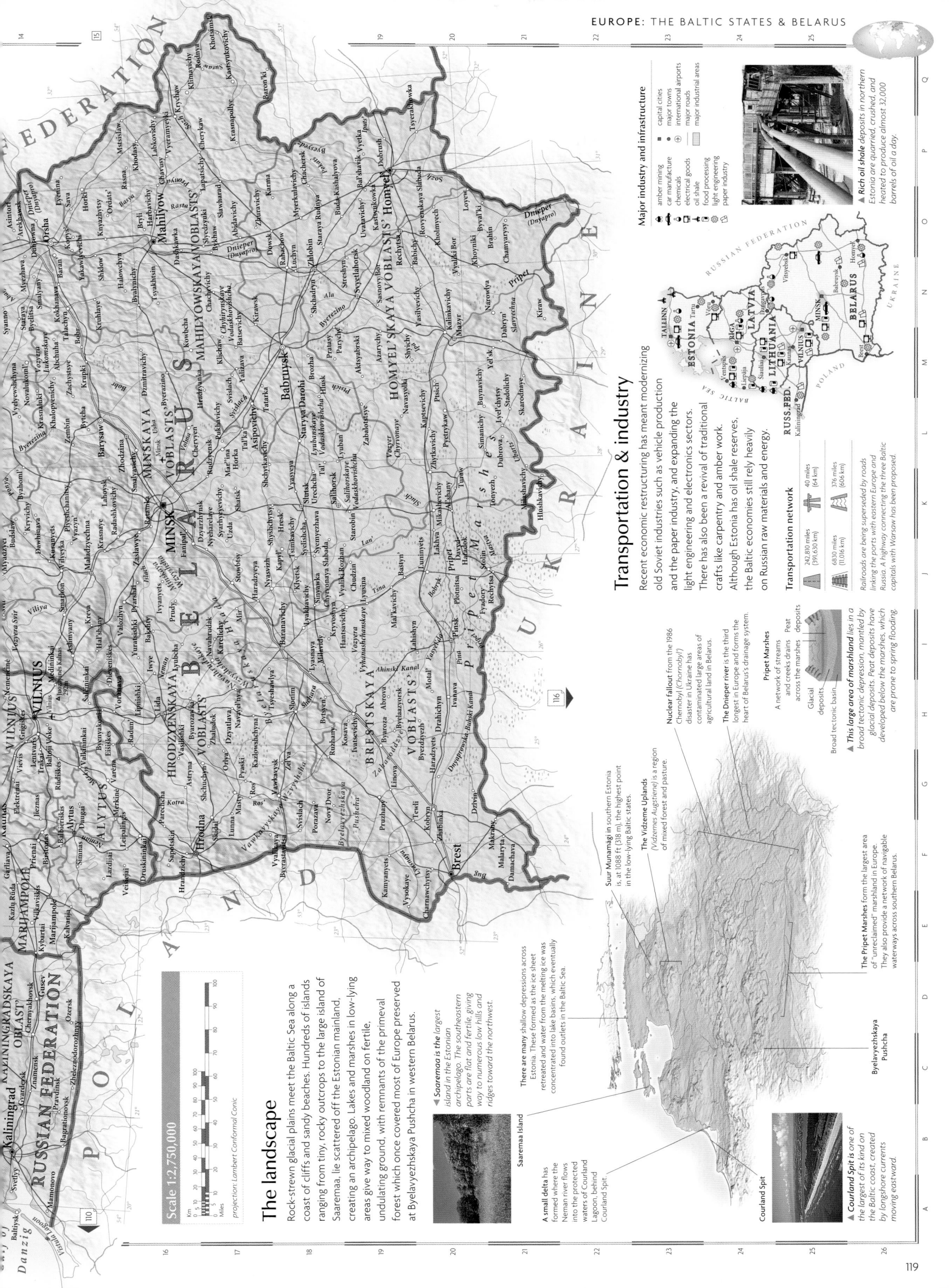

Major industry and infrastructure

- amber mining
- car manufacture
- chemicals
- electrical goods
- oil shale
- food processing
- light engineering
- paper industry
- capital cities
- major towns
- international airports
- major roads
- major industrial areas

▲ *Rich oil shale deposits in northern Estonia are quarried, crushed, and heated to produce almost 32,000 barrels of oil a day.*

The Mediterranean

The Mediterranean Sea stretches over 2500 miles (4000 km) east to west, separating Europe from Africa. At its westernmost point it is connected to the Atlantic Ocean through the Strait of Gibraltar. In the east, the Suez canal, opened in 1869, gives passage to the Indian Ocean. In the northeast, linked by the Sea of Marmara, lies the Black Sea. The Mediterranean is bordered by almost 30 states and territories, and more than 100 million people live on its shores and islands. Throughout history, the Mediterranean has been a focal area for many great empires and civilizations, reflected in the variety of cultures found on its shores. Since the 1960s, development along the southern coast of Europe has expanded rapidly to accommodate increasing numbers of tourists and to enable the exploitation of oil and gas reserves. This has resulted in rising levels of pollution, threatening the future of the sea.

▲ *Monte Carlo is just one of the luxurious resorts scattered along the Riviera, which stretches along the coast from Cannes in France to La Spezia in Italy. The region's mild winters and hot summers have attracted wealthy tourists since the early 19th century.*

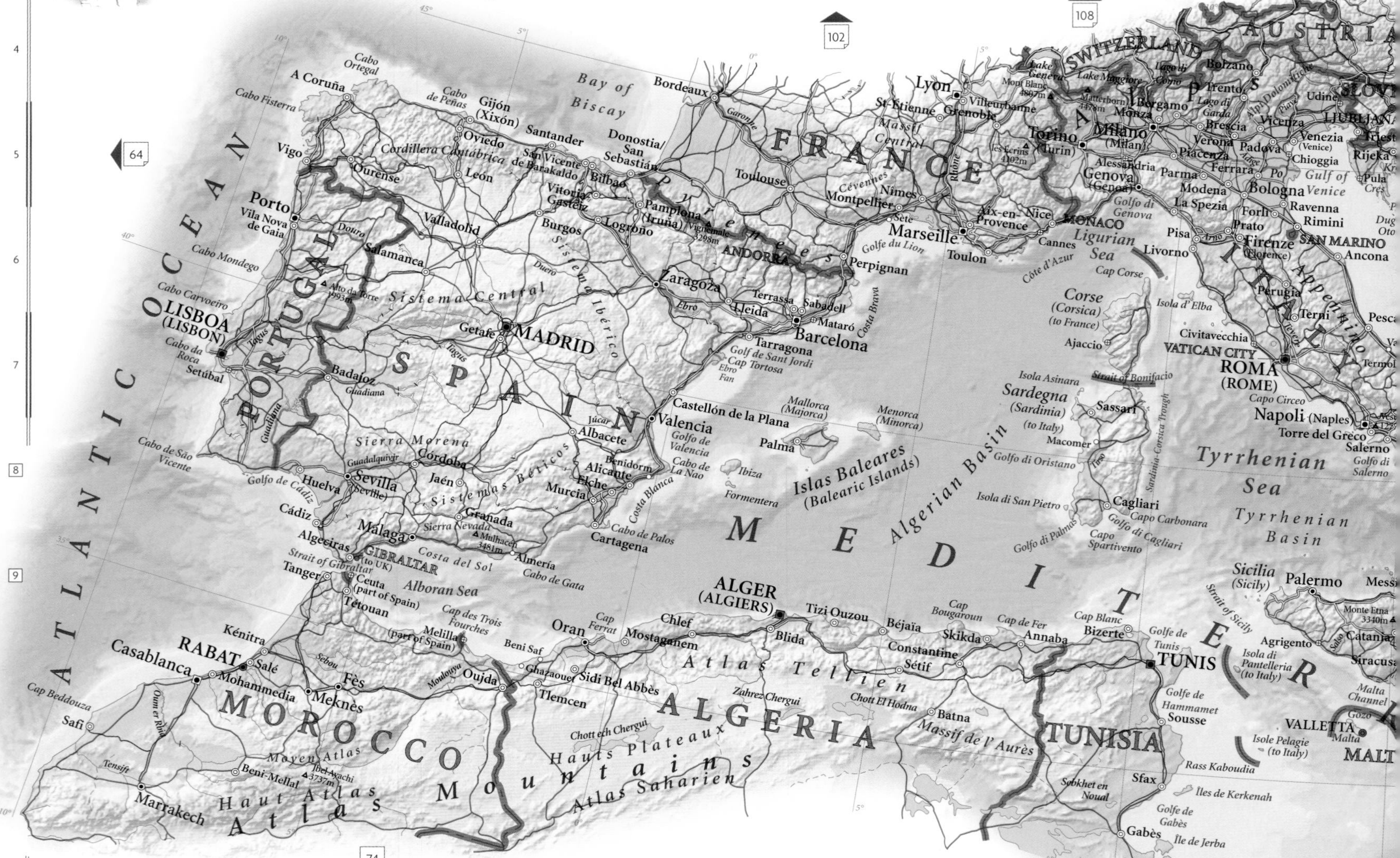

ATLANTIC OCEAN
Bay of Biscay
FRANCE
SPAIN
PORTUGAL
ITALY
SWITZERLAND
AUSTRIA
ANDORRA
MONACO
SAN MARINO
VATICAN CITY
MOROCCO
ALGERIA
TUNISIA
MALTA
MEDITERRANEAN
Algerian Basin
Islas Baleares (Balearic Islands)
Tyrrhenian Sea
Tyrrhenian Basin
Ligurian Sea
Alboran Sea
GIBRALTAR (to UK)
Strait of Gibraltar
LISBOA (LISBON)
MADRID
Barcelona
Valencia
Sevilla
Málaga
Porto
Marseille
Toulouse
Bordeaux
Lyon
Torino (Turin)
Milano (Milan)
Genova (Genoa)
Firenze (Florence)
ROMA (ROME)
Napoli (Naples)
Palermo
Cagliari
Sardegna (Sardinia) (to Italy)
Corse (Corsica) (to France)
Sicilia (Sicily)
ALGER (ALGIERS)
Oran
RABAT
Casablanca
Fès
Marrakech
TUNIS
Sfax
VALLETTA
ṬARĀBULUS (TRIPOLI)
Pyrenees
Sistema Central
Sierra Morena
Atlas Tellien
Hauts Plateaux
Atlas Saharien
Haut Atlas
Moyen Atlas
Atlas Mountains

The landscape

The Mediterranean Sea is almost totally landlocked, joined to the Atlantic Ocean through the Strait of Gibraltar, which is only 8 miles (13 km) wide. Lying on an active plate margin, sea floor movements have formed a variety of basins, troughs, and ridges. A submarine ridge running from Tunisia to the island of Sicily divides the Mediterranean into two distinct basins. The western basin is characterized by broad, smooth abyssal (or ocean) plains. In contrast, the eastern basin is dominated by a large ridge system, running east to west.

The narrow Strait of Gibraltar inhibits water exchange between the Mediterranean Sea and the Atlantic Ocean, producing a high degree of salinity and a low tidal range within the Mediterranean. The lack of tides has encouraged the build-up of pollutants in many semienclosed bays.

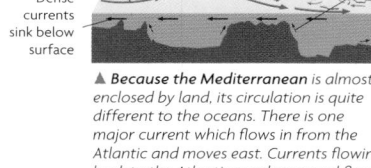

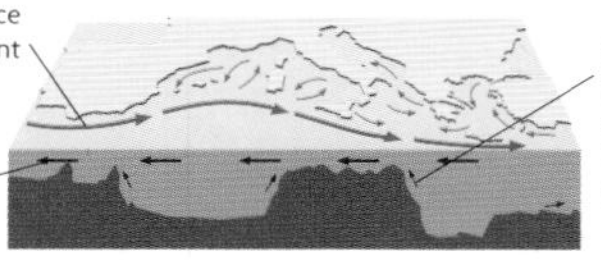

Main surface current
Dense currents sink below surface
Denser, more saline currents flow back to Atlantic

▲ ***Because the Mediterranean** is almost enclosed by land, its circulation is quite different to the oceans. There is one major current which flows in from the Atlantic and moves east. Currents flowing back to the Atlantic are denser and flow below the main current.*

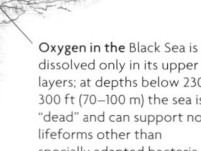

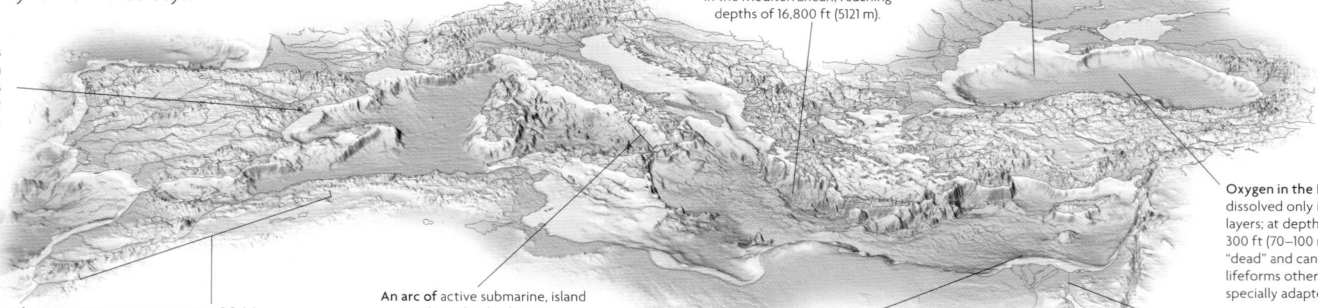

Industrial pollution flowing from the Dnieper and Danube rivers has destroyed a large proportion of the fish population that used to inhabit the upper layers of the Black Sea.
The Ionian Basin is the deepest in the Mediterranean, reaching depths of 16,800 ft (5121 m).
The edge of the Eurasian Plate is edged by a continental shelf. In the Mediterranean Sea this is widest at the Ebro Fan where it extends 60 miles (96 km).
Oxygen in the Black Sea is dissolved only in its upper layers; at depths below 230–300 ft (70–100 m) the sea is "dead" and can support no lifeforms other than specially adapted bacteria.
An arc of active submarine, island and mainland volcanoes, including Etna and Vesuvius, lie in and around southern Italy. The area is also susceptible to earthquakes and landslides.
Nutrient flows into the eastern Mediterranean, and sediment flows to the Nile Delta have been severely lowered by the building of the Aswan Dam across the Nile in Eygpt. This is causing the delta to shrink.
The Suez Canal, opened in 1869, extends 100 miles (160 km) from Port Said to the Gulf of Suez.

◀ ***The Atlas Mountains** are a range of fold mountains that lie in Morocco and Algeria. They run parallel to the Mediterranean, forming a topographical and climatic divide between the Mediterranean coast and the western Sahara.*

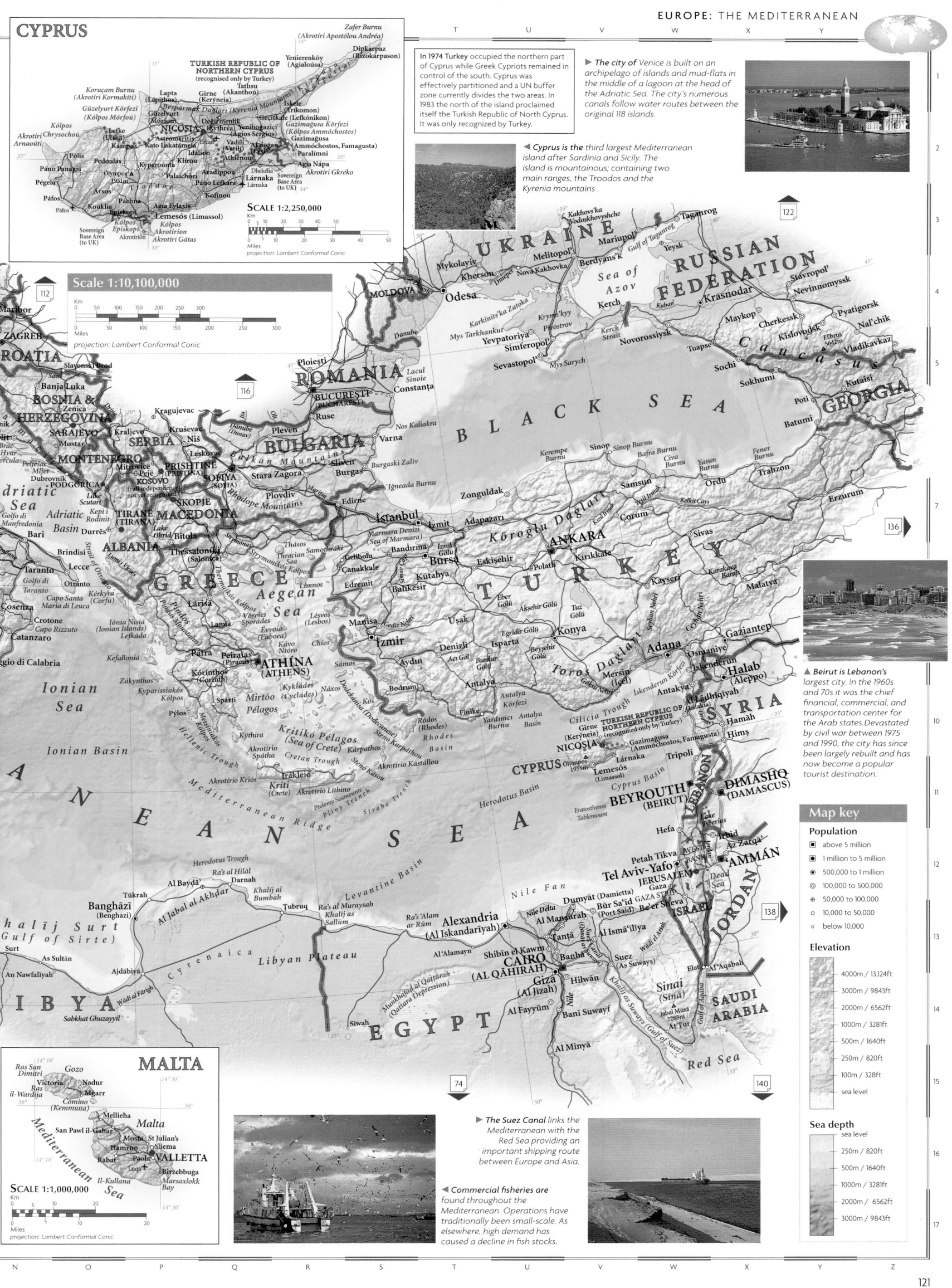

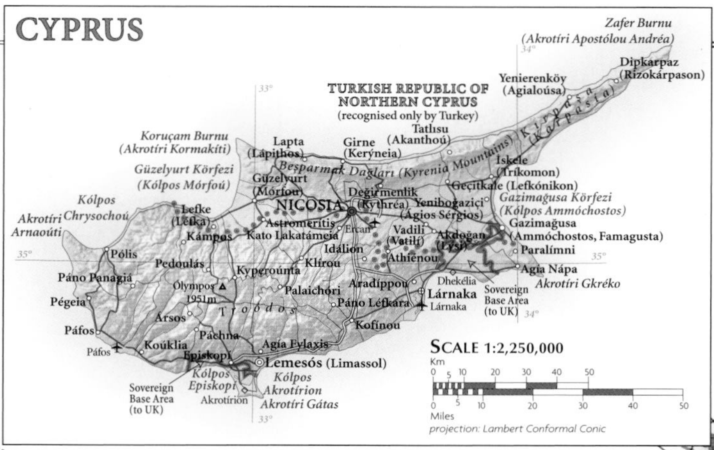
CYPRUS
TURKISH REPUBLIC OF NORTHERN CYPRUS (recognised only by Turkey)
Zafer Burnu (Akrotíri Apostólou Andréa)
Dipkarpaz (Rizokárpason)
Yenierenköy (Agialoúsa)
Tatlısu (Akanthoú)
Koruçam Burnu (Akrotíri Kormakíti)
Güzelyurt Körfezi (Kólpos Mórfou)
Lapta (Lápithos)
Girne (Kerýneia)
Beşparmak Dağları (Kyrenia Mountains)
Iskele (Trikomon)
Geçitkale (Lefkónikon)
Güzelyurt (Mórfou)
Değirmenlik (Kythréa)
Yeniboğaziçi (Agios Sérgios)
NICOSIA
Gazimağusa Körfezi (Kólpos Ammóchostos)
Gazimağusa (Ammóchostos, Famagusta)
Akrotíri Arnaoúti
Kólpos Chrysochoú
Lefke (Léfka)
Kámpos
Astromerítis
Kato Lakatámeia
Vadili (Vatili)
Akdoğan (Lysi)
Athiénou
Idálion
Paralímni
Agía Nápa
Akrotíri Gkréko
Pólis
Pedoulás
Kyperoúnta
Klírou
Pano Panagiá
Olympos 1951m
Palaichóri
Aradippou
Dhekélia Sovereign Base Area (to UK)
Pégeia
Tróodos
Páno Léfkara
Lárnaka
Árzos
Páfos
Páchna
Kofínou
Koúklia
Episkopí
Agia Fylaxis
Lemesós (Limassol)
Kólpos Episkopí
Kólpos Akrotírion
Akrotírion
Akrotíri Gátas
Sovereign Base Area (to UK)
SCALE 1:2,250,000
Km 0 5 10 20 30 40 50
Miles 0 5 10 20 30 40 50
projection: Lambert Conformal Conic

In 1974 Turkey occupied the northern part of Cyprus while Greek Cypriots remained in control of the south. Cyprus was effectively partitioned and a UN buffer zone currently divides the two areas. In 1983 the north of the island proclaimed itself the Turkish Republic of North Cyprus. It was only recognized by Turkey.

► The city of Venice is built on an archipelago of islands and mud-flats in the middle of a lagoon at the head of the Adriatic Sea. The city's numerous canals follow water routes between the original 118 islands.

◄ Cyprus is the third largest Mediterranean island after Sardinia and Sicily. The island is mountainous; containing two main ranges, the Troodos and the Kyrenia mountains.

Scale 1:10,100,000
Km 0 50 100 150 200 250 300
Miles 0 50 100 150 200 250 300
projection: Lambert Conformal Conic
112
116
122
136
138
74
140
UKRAINE
RUSSIAN FEDERATION
MOLDOVA
ROMANIA
BUCUREŞTI (BUCHAREST)
BULGARIA
SERBIA
BOSNIA & HERZEGOVINA
SARAJEVO
MONTENEGRO
PODGORICA
KOSOVO (full independence not yet recognized)
PRISHTINË (PRIŠTINA)
SOFIYA (SOFIA)
SKOPJE
MACEDONIA
ALBANIA
TIRANË (TIRANA)
GREECE
ATHÍNA (ATHENS)
TURKEY
ANKARA
İstanbul
GEORGIA
SYRIA
DIMASHQ (DAMASCUS)
LEBANON
BEYROUTH (BEIRUT)
ISRAEL
JERUSALEM
WEST BANK
Tel Aviv-Yafo
JORDAN
'AMMĀN
EGYPT
CAIRO (AL QĀHIRAH)
Alexandria (Al Iskandarīyah)
LIBYA
SAUDI ARABIA
CYPRUS
NICOSIA
TURKISH REPUBLIC OF NORTHERN CYPRUS (recognized only by Turkey)
BLACK SEA
Sea of Azov
Aegean Sea
Ionian Sea
Adriatic Sea
MEDITERRANEAN SEA
Red Sea
Dead Sea
Caucasus
Balkan Mountains
Rhodope Mountains
Pindus Mountains
Köroğlu Dağları
Toros Dağları
Kritikó Pélagos (Sea of Crete)
Mirtóo Pélagos
Marmara Denizi (Sea of Marmara)
Ionian Basin
Hellenic Trough
Mediterranean Ridge
Herodotus Basin
Herodotus Trough
Levantine Basin
Cyprus Basin
Eratosthenes Tablemount
Nile Fan
Libyan Plateau
Cyrenaica
Khalīj Surt (Gulf of Sirte)
Sinai (Sīnā')
Gulf of Aqaba
Khalīj as Suways (Gulf of Suez)
Munkhafaḍ al Qaṭṭārah (Qattara Depression)
Odesa
Kherson
Mykolayiv
Melitopol'
Mariupol'
Berdyans'k
Taganrog
Yeysk
Krasnodar
Stavropol'
Nevinnomyssk
Pyatigorsk
Nal'chik
Vladikavkaz
El'brus 5642m
Kislovodsk
Cherkessk
Maykop
Novorossiysk
Tuapse
Sochi
Sokhumi
Kutaisi
Poti
Batumi
Kerch
Simferopol'
Sevastopol'
Yevpatoriya
Dnieper
Danube
Ploieşti
Constanţa
Ruse
Varna
Burgas
Pleven
Stara Zagora
Plovdiv
Edirne
Niš
Kruševac
Kragujevac
Kraljevo
Leskovac
Mostar
Zenica
Banja Luka
Slavonski Brod
ZAGREB
Maribor
Dubrovnik
Bari
Brindisi
Taranto
Lecce
Otranto
Cosenza
Crotone
Catanzaro
Durrës
Bitola
Thessaloníki (Salonica)
Lárisa
Lamía
Pátra
Peiraías (Piraeus)
Kórinthos (Corinth)
Spárti
Pýlos
Kefallonía
Zákynthos
Kérkyra (Corfu)
Ionía Nisiá (Ionian Islands)
Lésvos (Lesbos)
Chíos
Sámos
Límnos
Thásos
Samothráki
Kykládes (Cyclades)
Náxos
Dodekanisa (Dodecanese)
Kós
Ródos (Rhodes)
Kárpathos
Kýthira
Irákleio
Kríti (Crete)
Edirne
İzmit
Adapazarı
Bursa
Bandırma
Gelibolu
Çanakkale
Balıkesir
Edremit
Kütahya
Eskişehir
Manisa
İzmir
Aydın
Bodrum
Denizli
Uşak
Isparta
Antalya
Finike
Konya
Polatlı
Kırıkkale
Zonguldak
Sinop
Samsun
Çorum
Ordu
Trabzon
Erzurum
Sivas
Kayseri
Malatya
Gaziantep
Adana
Mersin (İçel)
Osmaniye
İskenderun
Antakya
Halab (Aleppo)
Al Lādhiqīyah (Latakia)
Ḥamāh
Ḥimş
Tripoli
Lárnaka
Lemesós (Limassol)
Olympos 1951m
Gazimağusa (Ammóchostos, Famagusta)
Girne (Kerýneia)
Hefa
Petah Tikva
Gaza
Be'er Sheva
Irbid
Az Zarqā'
Elat
Al 'Aqabah
Jabal Mūsā 2285m
Aţ Ţūr
Suez (As Suways)
Al Ismā'īlīya
Būr Sa'īd (Port Said)
Dumyāţ (Damietta)
Al Manşūrah
Ţanţā
Banhā
Shibīn el Kawm
Gîza (Al Jīzah)
Ḥilwān
Al Fayyūm
Banī Suwayf
Al Minyā
Siwah
Al 'Alamayn
Ra's 'Alam ar Rūm
Ra's al Muraysah
Khalīj as Sallūm
Tubruq
Darnah
Al Bayḍā'
Ţūkrah
Banghāzī (Benghazi)
Ajdābiyā
As Sulţān
An Nawfalīyah
Surt
Sabkhat Ghuzayyil
Wādī al Fārigh

▲ Beirut is Lebanon's largest city. In the 1960s and 70s it was the chief financial, commercial, and transportation center for the Arab states. Devastated by civil war between 1975 and 1990, the city has since been largely rebuilt and has now become a popular tourist destination.

Map key

Population

- above 5 million
- 1 million to 5 million
- 500,000 to 1 million
- 100,000 to 500,000
- 50,000 to 100,000
- 10,000 to 50,000
- below 10,000

Elevation

- 4000m / 13,124ft
- 3000m / 9843ft
- 2000m / 6562ft
- 1000m / 3281ft
- 500m / 1640ft
- 250m / 820ft
- 100m / 328ft
- sea level

Sea depth

- sea level
- 250m / 820ft
- 500m / 1640ft
- 1000m / 3281ft
- 2000m / 6562ft
- 3000m / 9843ft

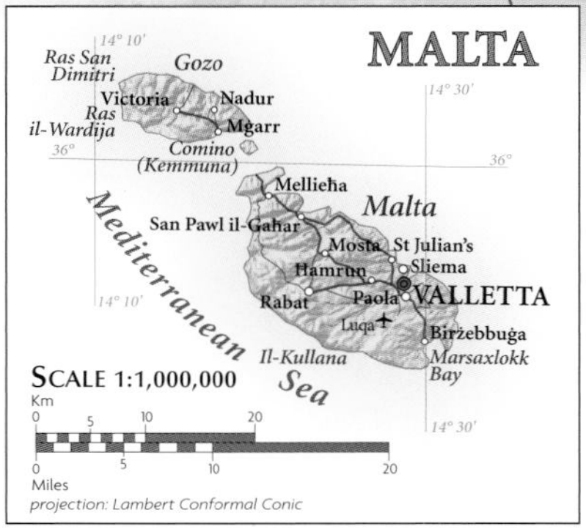
MALTA
Gozo
Ras San Dimitri
Victoria
Nadur
Ras il-Wardija
Mġarr
Comino (Kemmuna)
Mellieħa
Malta
San Pawl il-Baħar
Mosta
St Julian's
Ħamrun
Sliema
VALLETTA
Rabat
Paola
Luqa
Birżebbuġa
Marsaxlokk Bay
Il-Kullana
Mediterranean Sea
SCALE 1:1,000,000
Km 0 5 10 20
Miles 0 5 10 20
projection: Lambert Conformal Conic

► The Suez Canal links the Mediterranean with the Red Sea providing an important shipping route between Europe and Asia.

◄ Commercial fisheries are found throughout the Mediterranean. Operations have traditionally been small-scale. As elsewhere, high demand has caused a decline in fish stocks.

The Russian Federation

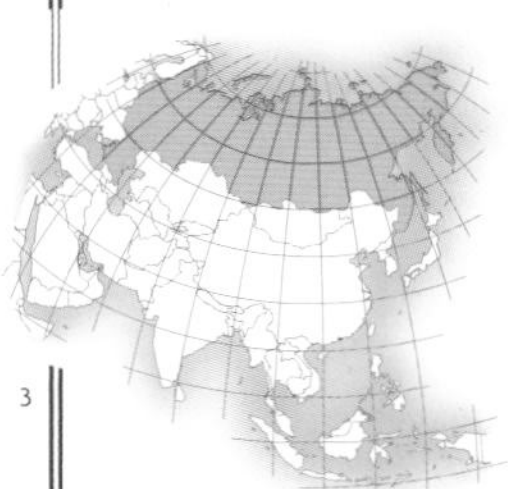

The Cold War era of global relations was concluded in 1991 with the formal dissolution of the Soviet Union. The Russian Federation declared its separate sovereignty from the foundering communist empire following independence declarations from a number of former Soviet republics. As the leading member of the Commonwealth of Independent States, the Russian Federation has a central role in the development of post-Soviet Eurasia. Crossing 11 time zones, the Russian Federation is almost twice the size of the US, and with more than 150 ethnic minorities and 21 autonomous republics, regionalist dissent within its own territory remains a danger.

▶ *Summer beds of moss and lichen scatter a 90% surface cover of ice across the islands of Franz Josef Land (Zemlya Frantsa-Iosifa), the northernmost land in the eastern hemisphere.*

THE RUSSIAN FEDERATION: ADMINISTRATIVE REGIONS

The administrative area names in European Russia have been omitted west of the Ural Mountains. Please refer to pages 124–125 and 126–127 where these areas are shown at a larger scale.

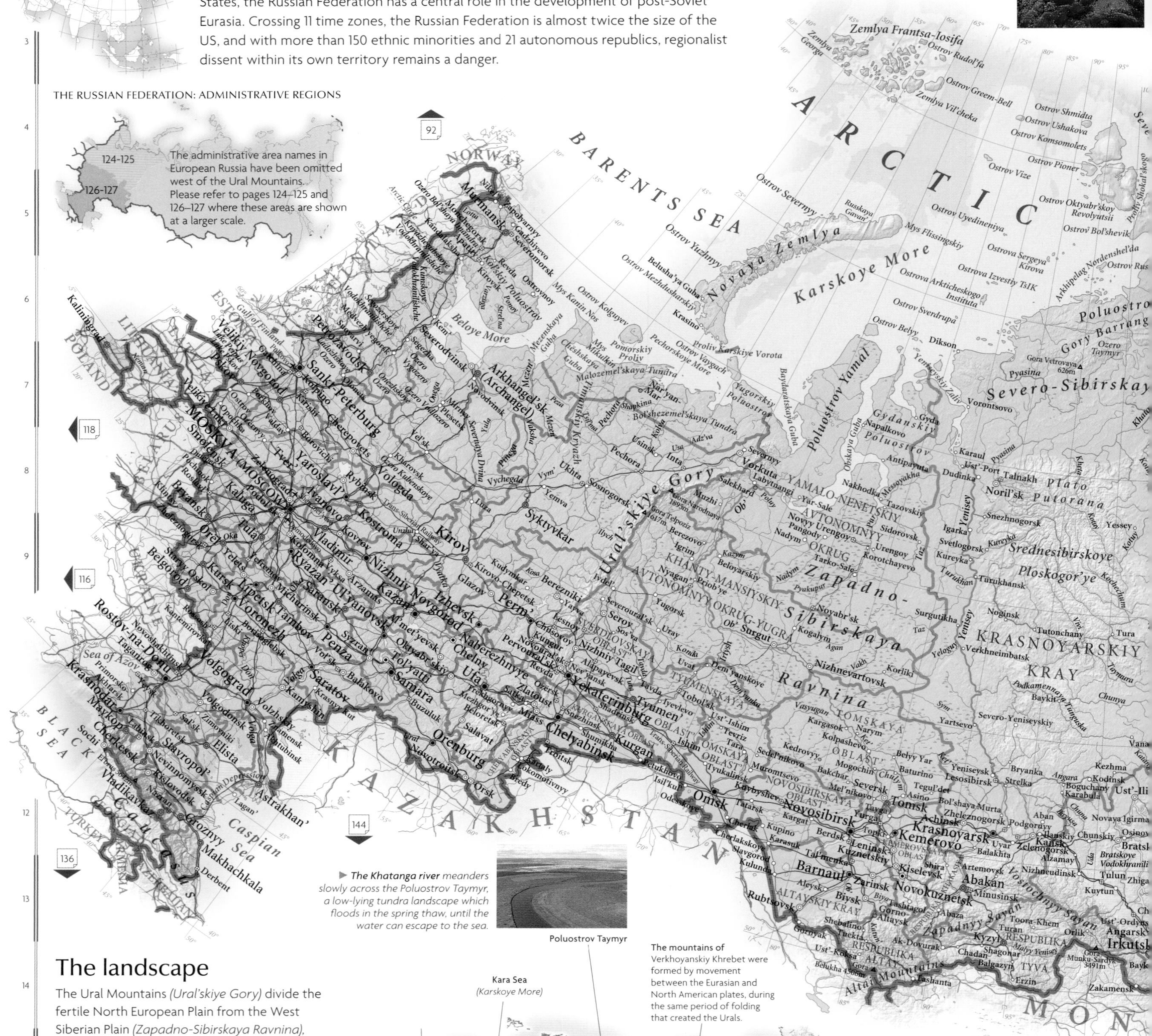

124-125
126-127
92
118
116
136
144
162
BARENTS SEA
ARCTIC
Karskoye More
Beloye More
Caspian Sea
BLACK SEA
Sea of Azov
NORWAY
FINLAND
ESTONIA
LATVIA
LITHUANIA
POLAND
BELARUS
UKRAINE
KAZAKHSTAN
GEORGIA
TURKEY
MON
Zemlya Frantsa-Iosifa
Novaya Zemlya
Severo-Sibirskaya
Poluostrov Yamal
Gydanskiy Poluostrov
Ural'skiye Gory
Zapadno-Sibirskaya Ravnina
Srednesibirskoye Ploskogor'ye
Plato Putorana
KRASNOYARSKIY KRAY
YAMALO-NENETSKIY AVTONOMNYY OKRUG
KHANTY-MANSIYSKIY AVTONOMNYY OKRUG-YUGRA
TOMSKAYA OBLAST'
NOVOSIBIRSKAYA OBLAST'
OMSKAYA OBLAST'
TYUMENSKAYA OBLAST'
SVERDLOVSKAYA OBLAST'
ALTAYSKIY KRAY
RESPUBLIKA ALTAY
RESPUBLIKA TYVA
Kaliningrad
Murmansk
Arkhangel'sk (Archangel)
Sankt-Peterburg
Moskva (Moscow)
Velikiy Novgorod
Pskov
Smolensk
Bryansk
Kaluga
Tula
Orel
Kursk
Belgorod
Voronezh
Lipetsk
Tambov
Ryazan'
Vladimir
Ivanovo
Yaroslavl'
Kostroma
Vologda
Kirov
Nizhniy Novgorod
Kazan'
Izhevsk
Perm'
Ul'yanovsk
Penza
Saratov
Samara
Tol'yatti
Ufa
Orenburg
Volgograd
Rostov-na-Donu
Krasnodar
Stavropol'
Elista
Astrakhan'
Makhachkala
Groznyy
Vladikavkaz
Syktyvkar
Vorkuta
Yekaterinburg
Chelyabinsk
Tyumen'
Kurgan
Omsk
Novosibirsk
Tomsk
Kemerovo
Novokuznetsk
Barnaul
Krasnoyarsk
Abakan
Kyzyl
Irkutsk
Noril'sk
Dudinka
Dikson
Surgut
Nizhnevartovsk
Salekhard
Novyy Urengoy
Caucasus
Altai Mountains

▶ *The Khatanga river meanders slowly across the Poluostrov Taymyr, a low-lying tundra landscape which floods in the spring thaw, until the water can escape to the sea.*

The landscape

The Ural Mountains *(Ural'skiye Gory)* divide the fertile North European Plain from the West Siberian Plain *(Zapadno-Sibirskaya Ravnina)*, the world's largest area of flat ground, crossed by giant rivers flowing north to the Kara Sea *(Karskoye More)*. The land rises to the Central Siberian Plateau *(Srednesibirskoye Ploskogor'ye)* and becomes more mountainous to the southeast. These immense topographic regions intersect with latitudinal vegetation bands. The tundra of the extreme north gives way to a vast area of coniferous woodland, which is known as *taiga*, larger than the Amazon rain forest. This belt turns to mixed forest and then steppe grasslands toward the south.

Poluostrov Taymyr

Kara Sea *(Karskoye More)*

The mountains of Verkhoyanskiy Khrebet were formed by movement between the Eurasian and North American plates, during the same period of folding that created the Urals.

Yukagirskoye Ploskogor'ye is a rolling plain with isolated drumlins, domelike features resulting from glacial deposition.

The Ural Mountains *(Ural'skiye Gory)* extend 1550 miles (2500 km). They were formed over 280 million years ago, folded as the East European and Siberian plates moved closer together.

The Yenisey is one of the world's longest rivers, and also among the most languid, dropping only 500 ft (152 m) over 1200 miles (2000 km).

▶ *Lake Baikal (Ozero Baykal), occupies a rift valley and is the world's deepest lake, over 1 mile (1.6 km) in depth. It is fed by over 300 rivers and drained by just one, the Angara.*

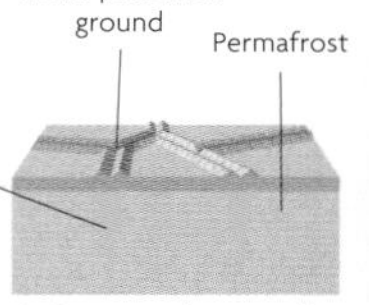

Polygon shapes create patterned ground
Permafrost
Permanent ice wedges up to 16 ft (5 m) deep

▲ *Patterned ground is a permafrost feature found extensively across northern Russia. Seasonal contraction of the permafrost creates polygonal cracks, which are filled by ice wedges.*

N O P Q T U V W X Y

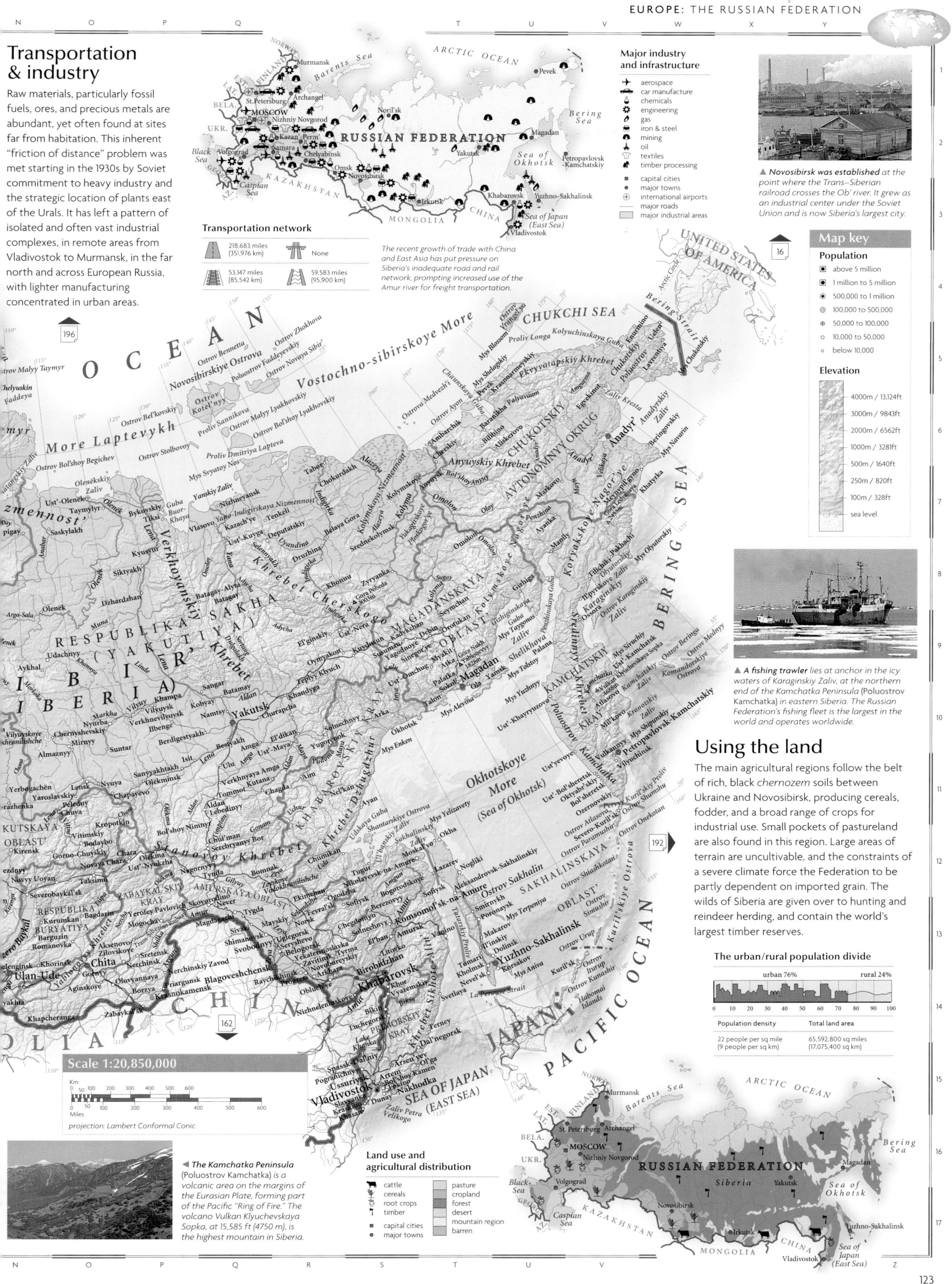

Transportation & industry

Raw materials, particularly fossil fuels, ores, and precious metals are abundant, yet often found at sites far from habitation. This inherent "friction of distance" problem was met starting in the 1930s by Soviet commitment to heavy industry and the strategic location of plants east of the Urals. It has left a pattern of isolated and often vast industrial complexes, in remote areas from Vladivostok to Murmansk, in the far north and across European Russia, with lighter manufacturing concentrated in urban areas.

ARCTIC OCEAN
Barents Sea
Murmansk
Archangel
St. Petersburg
MOSCOW
Nizhniy Novgorod
Kazan'
Perm'
Samara
Volgograd
Chelyabinsk
Omsk
Novosibirsk
Noril'sk
RUSSIAN FEDERATION
Yakutsk
Irkutsk
Pevek
Magadan
Bering Sea
Sea of Okhotsk
Petropavlovsk-Kamchatskiy
Khabarovsk
Yuzhno-Sakhalinsk
Sea of Japan (East Sea)
Vladivostok
BELA.
UKR.
Black Sea
Caspian Sea
KAZAKHSTAN
MONGOLIA
CHINA

Major industry and infrastructure

- aerospace
- car manufacture
- chemicals
- engineering
- gas
- iron & steel
- mining
- oil
- textiles
- timber processing
- capital cities
- major towns
- international airports
- major roads
- major industrial areas

Transportation network

218,683 miles (351,976 km)		None	
53,147 miles (85,542 km)		59,583 miles (95,900 km)	

The recent growth of trade with China and East Asia has put pressure on Siberia's inadequate road and rail network, prompting increased use of the Amur river for freight transportation.

▲ ***Novosibirsk was established*** *at the point where the Trans-Siberian railroad crosses the Ob' river. It grew as an industrial center under the Soviet Union and is now Siberia's largest city.*

16

Map key

Population

- above 5 million
- 1 million to 5 million
- 500,000 to 1 million
- 100,000 to 500,000
- 50,000 to 100,000
- 10,000 to 50,000
- below 10,000

Elevation

- 4000m / 13,124ft
- 3000m / 9843ft
- 2000m / 6562ft
- 1000m / 3281ft
- 500m / 1640ft
- 250m / 820ft
- 100m / 328ft
- sea level

196

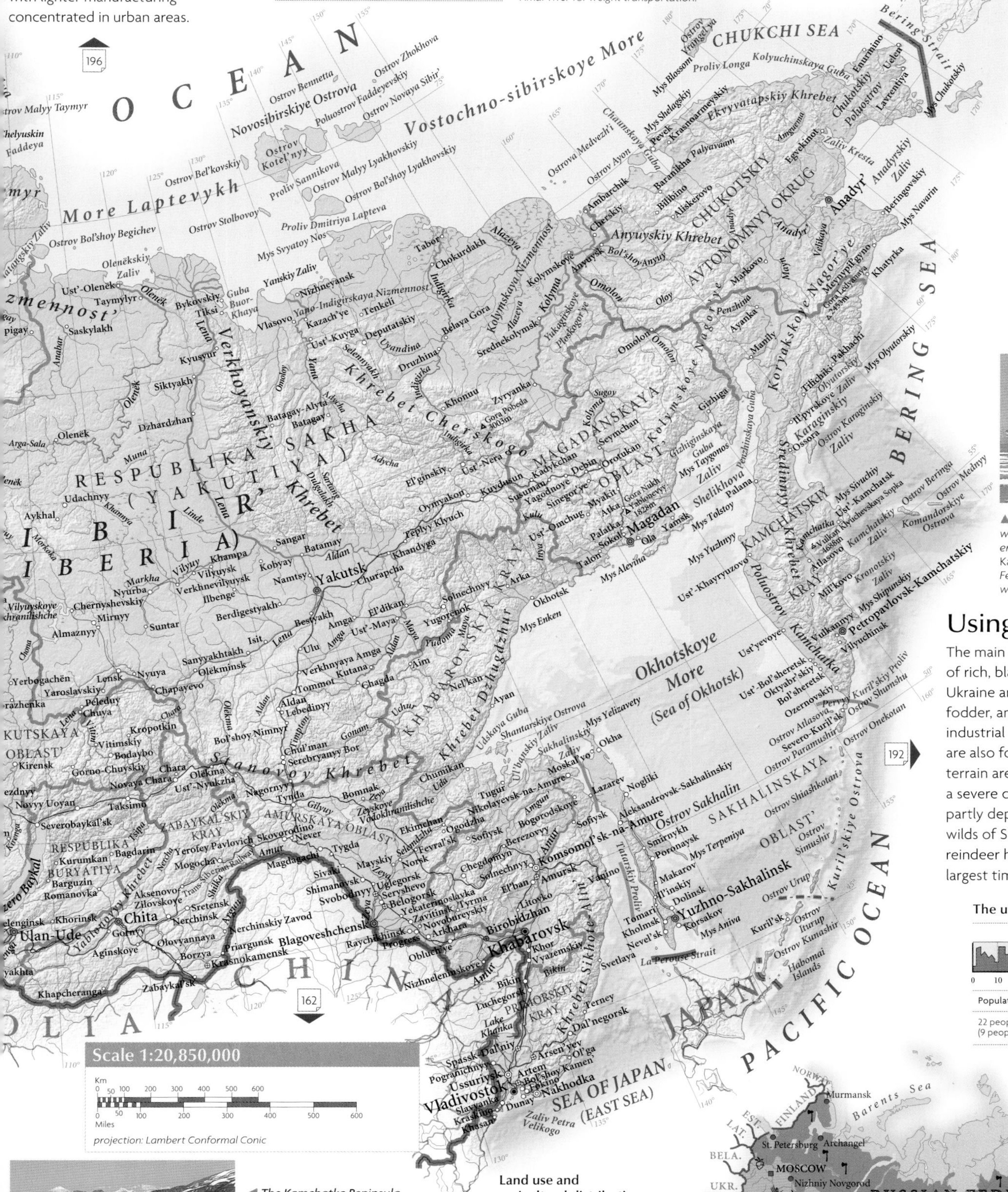
OCEAN
CHUKCHI SEA
UNITED STATES OF AMERICA
Bering Strait
Vostochno-sibirskoye More
More Laptevykh
Novosibirskiye Ostrova
Ostrov Kotel'nyy
CHUKOTSKIY AVTONOMNYY OKRUG
Anadyr'
RESPUBLIKA SAKHA (YAKUTIYA)
Khrebet Cherskogo
Verkhoyanskiy Khrebet
Yakutsk
MAGADANSKAYA OBLAST'
Magadan
BERING SEA
KAMCHATSKIY KRAY
Petropavlovsk-Kamchatskiy
Okhotskoye More (Sea of Okhotsk)
SIBERIA
Stanovoy Khrebet
KHABAROVSKIY KRAY
SAKHALINSKAYA OBLAST'
Yuzhno-Sakhalinsk
Khabarovsk
Chita
Ulan-Ude
Blagoveshchensk
Birobidzhan
PRIMORSKIY KRAY
Vladivostok
Nakhodka
SEA OF JAPAN (EAST SEA)
JAPAN
PACIFIC OCEAN
CHINA
Kuril'skiye Ostrova

192

162

Scale 1:20,850,000

projection: Lambert Conformal Conic

▲ ***A fishing trawler*** *lies at anchor in the icy waters of Karaginskiy Zaliv, at the northern end of the Kamchatka Peninsula (Poluostrov Kamchatka) in eastern Siberia. The Russian Federation's fishing fleet is the largest in the world and operates worldwide.*

Using the land

The main agricultural regions follow the belt of rich, black *chernozem* soils between Ukraine and Novosibirsk, producing cereals, fodder, and a broad range of crops for industrial use. Small pockets of pastureland are also found in this region. Large areas of terrain are uncultivable, and the constraints of a severe climate force the Federation to be partly dependent on imported grain. The wilds of Siberia are given over to hunting and reindeer herding, and contain the world's largest timber reserves.

The urban/rural population divide

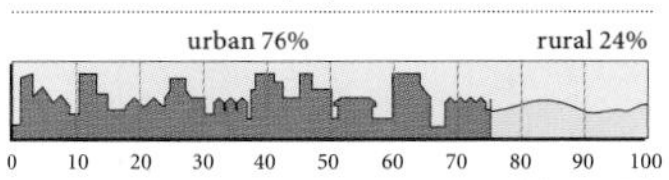
urban 76%
rural 24%
0
10
20
30
40
50
60
70
80
90
100

Population density	Total land area
22 people per sq mile (9 people per sq km)	6,592,800 sq miles (17,075,400 sq km)

◀ ***The Kamchatka Peninsula*** *(Poluostrov Kamchatka) is a volcanic area on the margins of the Eurasian Plate, forming part of the Pacific "Ring of Fire." The volcano Vulkan Klyuchevskaya Sopka, at 15,585 ft (4750 m), is the highest mountain in Siberia.*

Land use and agricultural distribution

- cattle
- cereals
- root crops
- timber
- capital cities
- major towns
- pasture
- cropland
- forest
- desert
- mountain region
- barren

ARCTIC OCEAN
Barents Sea
Murmansk
Archangel
St. Petersburg
MOSCOW
Nizhniy Novgorod
Volgograd
RUSSIAN FEDERATION
Siberia
Yakutsk
Magadan
Bering Sea
Sea of Okhotsk
Novosibirsk
Irkutsk
Yuzhno-Sakhalinsk
Sea of Japan (East Sea)
Vladivostok
BELA.
UKR.
Black Sea
Caspian Sea
KAZAKHSTAN
MONGOLIA
CHINA

N O P Q R S T U V Z

Northern European Russia

Reaching into the Arctic Circle, this region of lakeland, forest and tundra is historically bound to Europe by St Petersburg, the old imperial capital of Tsarist Russia and home to a third of the region's population. Communist rule from Moscow left the north politically marginalized, contributing to the present problems of outmoded industry, poor infrastructure and serious environmental neglect. However, with borders embracing Finland, Norway, the Baltic and the northern sea route to the Atlantic, the region's success in foreign trade is now of prime importance to the Russian economy.

▶ *St. Peter and Paul Fortress is the oldest building in St Petersburg, founded by Peter the Great in 1703 as a modern, European capital for Russia.*

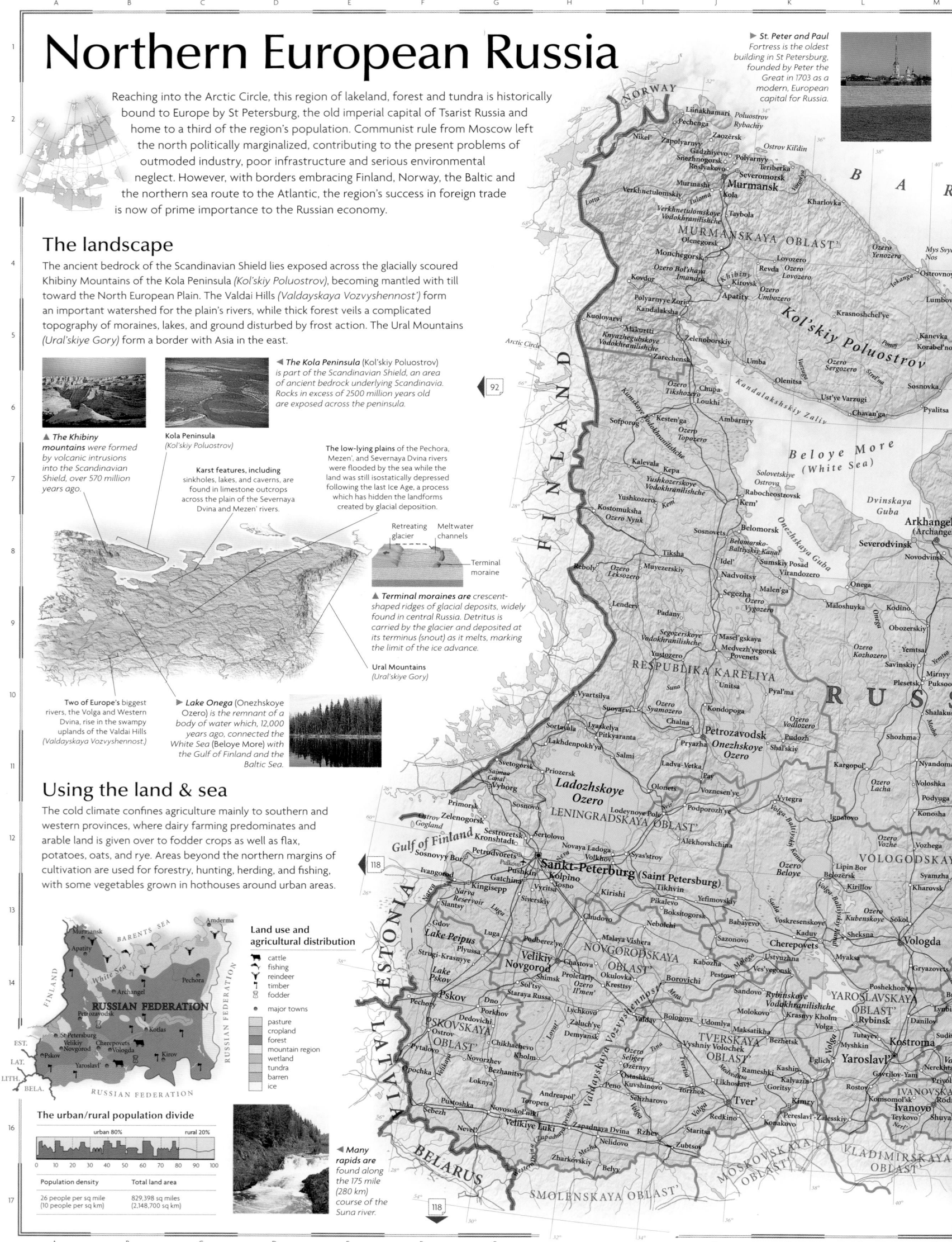

The landscape

The ancient bedrock of the Scandinavian Shield lies exposed across the glacially scoured Khibiny Mountains of the Kola Peninsula *(Kol'skiy Poluostrov)*, becoming mantled with till toward the North European Plain. The Valdai Hills *(Valdayskaya Vozvyshennost')* form an important watershed for the plain's rivers, while thick forest veils a complicated topography of moraines, lakes, and ground disturbed by frost action. The Ural Mountains *(Ural'skiye Gory)* form a border with Asia in the east.

▲ ***The Khibiny mountains** were formed by volcanic intrusions into the Scandinavian Shield, over 570 million years ago.*

Kola Peninsula *(Kol'skiy Poluostrov)*

◀ ***The Kola Peninsula** (Kol'skiy Poluostrov) is part of the Scandinavian Shield, an area of ancient bedrock underlying Scandinavia. Rocks in excess of 2500 million years old are exposed across the peninsula.*

Karst features, including sinkholes, lakes, and caverns, are found in limestone outcrops across the plain of the Severnaya Dvina and Mezen' rivers.
The low-lying plains of the Pechora, Mezen', and Severnaya Dvina rivers were flooded by the sea while the land was still isostatically depressed following the last Ice Age, a process which has hidden the landforms created by glacial deposition.
Ural Mountains *(Ural'skiye Gory)*
Two of Europe's biggest rivers, the Volga and Western Dvina, rise in the swampy uplands of the Valdai Hills *(Valdayskaya Vozvyshennost.)*

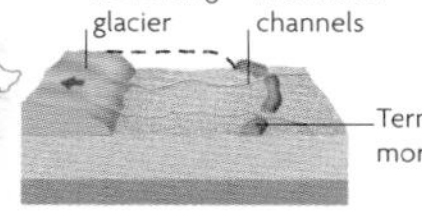

Retreating glacier
Meltwater channels
Terminal moraine

▲ ***Terminal moraines are** crescent-shaped ridges of glacial deposits, widely found in central Russia. Detritus is carried by the glacier and deposited at its terminus (snout) as it melts, marking the limit of the ice advance.*

▶ ***Lake Onega** (Onezhskoye Ozero) is the remnant of a body of water which, 12,000 years ago, connected the White Sea (Beloye More) with the Gulf of Finland and the Baltic Sea.*

Using the land & sea

The cold climate confines agriculture mainly to southern and western provinces, where dairy farming predominates and arable land is given over to fodder crops as well as flax, potatoes, oats, and rye. Areas beyond the northern margins of cultivation are used for forestry, hunting, herding, and fishing, with some vegetables grown in hothouses around urban areas.

Murmansk
Apatity
BARENTS SEA
Amderma
White Sea
Archangel
Pechora
RUSSIAN FEDERATION
Petrozavodsk
Kotlas
St Petersburg
Velikiy Novgorod
Cherepovets
Vologda
Pskov
Kirov
Yaroslavl'
FINLAND
EST.
LAT.
LITH.
BELA.
RUSSIAN FEDERATION
Land use and agricultural distribution
cattle
fishing
reindeer
timber
fodder
major towns
pasture
cropland
forest
mountain region
wetland
tundra
barren
ice

The urban/rural population divide

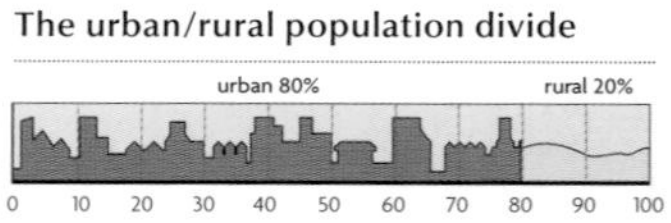

urban 80%
rural 20%
0
10
20
30
40
50
60
70
80
90
100

Population density	Total land area
26 people per sq mile (10 people per sq km)	829,398 sq miles (2,148,700 sq km)

◀ ***Many rapids are** found along the 175 mile (280 km) course of the Suna river.*

NORWAY
FINLAND
ESTONIA
LATVIA
BELARUS
Barents Sea
RUSSIAN FEDERATION
Liinakhamari
Pechenga
Poluostrov Rybachiy
Nikel'
Zapolyarnyy
Zaozërsk
Ostrov Kil'din
Gadzhiyevo
Polyarnyy
Snezhnogorsk
Teriberka
Roslyakovo
Severomorsk
Murmashi
Murmansk
Kola
Verkhnetulomskiy
Kharlovka
Verkhnetulomskoye Vodokhranilishche
Taybola
MURMANSKAYA OBLAST'
Olenegorsk
Monchegorsk
Lovozero
Ozero Bol'shaya Imandra
Khibiny
Revda
Ozero Lovozero
Kovdor
Kirovsk
Apatity
Ozero Umbozero
Polyarnyye Zori
Kandalaksha
Kol'skiy Poluostrov
Krasnoshchel'ye
Kuoloyarvi
Alakurtti
Knyazhegubskoye Vodokhranilishche
Zelenoborskiy
Arctic Circle
Zarechensk
Umba
Olenitsa
Ozero Sergozero
Sosnovka
Kanevka
Ozero Tikshozero
Chupa
Loukhi
Kandalakshskiy Zaliv
Ust'ye Varzugi
Chavan'ga
Pyalitsa
Sofporog
Kesten'ga
Ozero Topozero
Ambarnyy
Beloye More (White Sea)
Kalevala
Kepa
Yushkozerskoye Vodokhranilishche
Solovetskiye Ostrova
Rabocheostrovsk
Kem'
Yushkozero
Kostomuksha
Ozero Nyuk
Dvinskaya Guba
Arkhangel'sk (Archangel)
Severodvinsk
Novodvinsk
Sosnovets
Belomorsk
Onezhskaya Guba
Belomorsko-Baltiyskiy Kanal
Sumskiy Posad
Tiksha
Idel'
Virandozero
Reboly
Ozero Leksozero
Muyezerskiy
Nadvoitsy
Onega
Segezha
Malen'ga
Ozero Vygozero
Lendery
Padany
Maloshuyka
Kodino
Obozerskiy
Segozerskoye Vodokhranilishche
Masel'gskaya
Medvezh'yegorsk
Povenets
Ozero Kozhozero
Yemtsa
Yustozero
Savinskiy
Mirnyy
RESPUBLIKA KARELIYA
Unitsa
Plesetsk
Pyal'ma
Vyartsilya
Suna
Ozero Syamozero
Kondopoga
Ozero Vodlozero
Suoyarvi
Chalna
Sortavala
Lyaskelya
Pitkyaranta
Petrozavodsk
Pudozh
Lakhdenpokh'ya
Pryazha
Onezhskoye Ozero
Shal'skiy
Shozhma
Salmi
Svetogorsk
Priozersk
Ladva-Vetka
Kargopol'
Nyandoma
Saimaa Canal
Vyborg
Ladozhskoye Ozero
Pay
Olonets
Voznesen'ye
Ozero Lacha
Konosha
Primorsk
Sosnovo
Lodeynoye Pole
Svir'
Podporozh'ye
Vytegra
Ostrov Gogland
Zelenogorsk
LENINGRADSKAYA OBLAST'
Ignatovo
Sestroretsk
Kronshtadt
Sertolovo
Alekhovshchina
Ozero Vozhe
Vozhega
Gulf of Finland
Novaya Ladoga
Petrodvorets
Volkhov
Syas'stroy
VOLOGODSKAYA
Sosnovyy Bor
Pulkovo
Sankt-Peterburg (Saint Petersburg)
Lipin Bor
Belozërsk
Ivangorod
Pushkin
Kolpino
Ozero Beloye
Syamzha
Kingisepp
Gatchina
Tosno
Tikhvin
Kirillov
Kharovsk
Narva
Vyritsa
Kirishi
Pikalevo
Yefimovskiy
Narva Reservoir
Slantsy
Siverskiy
Boksitogorsk
Luga
Chudovo
Nebolchi
Babayevo
Voskresenskoye
Ozero Kubenskoye
Sokol
Gdov
Kaduy
Sheksna
Lake Peipus
Luga
Malaya Vishera
Sazonovo
Cherepovets
Vologda
Plyussa
Podberez'ye
NOVGORODSKAYA OBLAST'
Strugi-Krasnyye
Velikiy Novgorod
Chastova
Ustyuzhna
Myaksa
Lake Pskov
Shimsk
Proletariy
Okulovka
Kabozha
Pestovo
Ves'yegonsk
Gryazovets
Sol'tsy
Ozero Il'men'
Krestsy
Borovichi
Pskov
Staraya Russa
Sandovo
Rybinskoye Vodokhranilishche
Poshekhon'ye
Pechory
Dno
Valdayskaya Vozvyshennost'
YAROSLAVSKAYA OBLAST'
Porkhov
Lychkovo
Molokovo
Krasnyy Kholm
Rybinsk
Danilov
Dedovichi
Zaluch'ye
Valday
Bologoye
Udomlya
Maksatikha
Volga
Tutayev
PSKOVSKAYA OBLAST'
Demyansk
Ostrov
TVERSKAYA OBLAST'
Bezhetsk
Myshkin
Kostroma
Pytalovo
Chikhachevo
Ozero Seliger
Vyshniy Volochek
Uglich
Yaroslavl'
Novorzhev
Kholm
Ozërnyy
Rameshki
Kashin
Gavrilov-Yam
Nerekhta
Opochka
Bezhanitsy
Ostashkov
Medvedikha
Kalyazin
Priyolzhsk
Loknya
Kuvshinovo
Likhoslavl'
Goritsy
Rostov
Andreapol'
Torzhok
Selizharovo
Kimry
IVANOVSKAYA
Pustoshka
Toropets
Tver'
Komsomol'sk
Novosokol'niki
Sebezh
Redkino
Ivanovo
Velikiye Luki
Pereslavl'-Zalesskiy
Teykovo
Shuya
Nevel'
Zapadnaya Dvina
Rzhev
Staritsa
Konakovo
Nelidovo
Zubtsov
MOSKOVSKAYA OBLAST'
VLADIMIRSKAYA OBLAST'
Zharkovskiy
Belyy
SMOLENSKAYA OBLAST'

92
118
118

◄ *The Ural Mountains* (Ural'skiye Gory) *form the traditional boundary between Europe and Asia. Elevations rarely exceed 6000 ft (1830 m). The region is extremely barren in the far northern latitudes.*

BARENTS SEA
Ostrov Vaygach
Amderma
Yugorskiy Poluostrov
Khrebet Pay-Khoy
Ostrov Dolgiy
Ostrov Kolguyev
Bugrino
Kanin Nos
Mys Kanin Nos
Pomorskiy Proliv
Tobseda
Pechorskaya Guba
Varandey
Chernaya
Khal'mer-Yu
Nosovaya
NENETSKIY AVTONOMNYY OKRUG
Malozemel'skaya Tundra
Bol'shezemel'skaya Tundra
Nar'yan-Mar
Oksino
Indiga
Shoyna
Poluostrov Kanin
Kanin Kamen'
Mys Mikulkin
Cheshskaya Guba
Chizha
Nizhnyaya Pësha
Velikovisochnoye
Yërmitsa
Khorey-Ver
Promyshlennyy
Severnyy
Komsomol'skiy
Vorkuta
Vorgashor
Mul'da
Yeletskiy
Gora Payyer 1472m
Arctic Circle
Sivomaskinskiy
Abez'
Adz'vavom
Gryada Chernyshëva
Polyarnyy Ural
Ural'skiye Gory
YAMALO-NENETSKIY AVTONOMNYY OKRUG
Timanskiy Kryazh
Kochmes
Inta
Verkhnyaya Inta
Usinsk
Kos'yu
Kozhym
Ostrov Morzhovets
Mezenskaya Guba
Koyda
Kamenka
Mezen'
Khabarikha
ARKHANGEL'SKAYA OBLAST'
Synya
Pechora
Gora Narodnaya 1895m
Gora Sabiya 1497m
Ust'-Tsil'ma
Shchel'yayur
Myla
Kozhva
Izhma
Kadzherom
Irayël'
KHANTY-MANSIYSKIY AVTONOMNYY OKRUG
Kuloy
Leshukonskoye
Pinega
Ust'-Shchuger
Kyrta
Gora Telpoziz 1617m
Chuprovo
Vazhgort
Podcher'ye
Vuktyl
Dutovo
Karpogory
RESPUBLIKA KOMI
Nizhniy Odes
Ukhta
Vodnyy
Yarega
Sosnogorsk
Gora Kozhimiz 1195m
Severnyy Ural
Nyukhcha
Yertom
Koslan
Meshchura
Voyvozh
Nizhnyaya-Omra
Troitsko-Pechorsk
RUSSIAN FEDERATION
Yemva
Pomozdino
Rochegda
Verkhnyaya Toyma
Shenkursk
Mikun'
Yarensk
Chasovo
Zheshart
Storozhevsk
Ust'-Kulom
Myyëldino
Kur'ya
Petretsovo
Ezhva
Syktyvkar
Krasnozatonskiy
Gora Isherim 1331m
Bestuzhevo
Cherevkovo
Rovdino
Krasnoborsk
Kotlas
Koryazhma
Vychegodskiy
Oktyabr'skiy
Kizema
Krasavino
Vizinga
Nyrob
Velikiy Ustyug
Luza
Cherdyn'
Krasnovishersk
Gora Vogul'skiy Kamen' 1066m
Tarnogskiy Gorodok
Nyuksenitsa
Kazhym
Gayny
PERMSKIY KRAY
Podosinovets
Pinyug
Kosa
Solikamsk
Sukhona
Kichmengskiy Gorodok
Lesnoy
Loyno
Usol'ye
Yayva
Oparino
Rudnichnyy
Kochevo
Berezniki
Aleksandrovsk
Severnyye Uvaly
Murashi
Nagorsk
Kirs
Yurla
Kizel
Ugleural'skiy
Gubakha
Imeni Babushkina
Nikol'sk
Pavino
Peskovka
Kudymkar
Chermoz
Kamskoye Vodokhranilishche
Sredniy Ural
Belaya Kholunitsa
Afanas'yevo
Yus'va
Gremyachinsk
Gornozavodsk
Soligalich
Yur'ya
Il'inskiy
Chusovoy
Slobodskoy
Kirovo-Chepetsk
Dobryanka
Chukhloma
Kologriv
Kirov
Omutninsk
Polazna
Krasnokamsk
Lys'va
KOSTROMSKAYA OBLAST'
Orlov
Cheptsa
Perm'
Galich
Manturovo
Vetluzhskiy
Novovyatsk
Zuyevka
Vereshchagino
Kotel'nich
KIROVSKAYA OBLAST'
Nytva
Zvezdnyy
Kyn
Neya
Shar'ya
Leninskoye
Yug
Ocher
Okhansk
Suna
Bogorodskoye
Kungur
Makar'yev
Ostrovskoye
Tuzha
Sovetsk
Nolinsk
Osa
Suksun
Pizhma
Medvedok
Votkinskoye Vodokhranilishche
SVERDLOVSKAYA OBLAST'
Yaransk
UDMURTSKAYA RESPUBLIKA
Yur'yevets
NIZHEGORODSKAYA OBLAST'
Urzhum
Kil'mez'
Chaykovskiy
Chernushka
Puchezh
Gor'kovskoye Vodokhranilishche
Kuyeda
RESPUBLIKA MARIY EL
Malmyzh
Vyatskiye Polyany
Sosnovka
RESPUBLIKA BASHKORTOSTAN
RESPUBLIKA TATARSTAN

Scale 1:6,000,000

Km 0 10 20 40 60 80 100 120 140

0 10 20 40 60 80 100 120 140 Miles

projection: Lambert Conformal Conic

Map key

Population

- 1 million to 5 million
- 500,000 to 1 million
- 100,000 to 500,000
- 50,000 to 100,000
- 10,000 to 50,000
- below 10,000

Elevation

- 1000m / 3281ft
- 500m / 1640ft
- 250m / 820ft
- 100m / 328ft
- sea level

Transportation & industry

The ports of St. Petersburg, Murmansk, and Archangel serve a regional economy led by large-scale resource extraction. Nickel, iron ore, and apatite are mined in the Kola Peninsula *(Kol'skiy Poluostrov)*, and fossil fuels in the Pechora Basin. Paper production is central to Archangel's vast timber industry, while St. Petersburg, drawing on ample labor, has become a major manufacturing center.

Amderma
Murmansk
BARENTS SEA
Apatity
White Sea
Pechora
Archangel
FINLAND
RUSSIAN FEDERATION
Petrozavodsk
Kotlas
St Petersburg
Cherepovets
Vologda
EST.
Velikiy Novgorod
Pskov
LAT.
Kirov
Yaroslavl'
LITH.
BELA.
RUSSIAN FEDERATION

Major industry and infrastructure

- chemicals
- coal
- defense
- engineering
- food processing
- hydroelectric power
- mining
- oil & gas
- textiles
- timber processing
- major towns
- international airports
- major roads
- major industrial areas

Transportation network

- 53,700 miles (85,920 km)
- None
- 10,300 miles (16,572 km)
- 12,500 miles (20,000 km)

Railroads linking remote industrial centers with the region's ports are the principal means of supply, although the impressive system of canals, linking natural waterways, is used for freight haulage during the summer.

► *Ice forces the port at St. Petersburg to close in winter, yet Murmansk, on the Barents Sea, remains open, its waters prevented from freezing by warmer ocean currents extending from the North Atlantic Drift.*

BALTIC SEA
LITHUANIA
POLAND
BELARUS
UKRAINE
Sea of Azov
BLACK SEA
KALININGRADSKAYA OBLAST'
Kaliningrad
Smolensk
SMOLENSKAYA OBLAST'
Bryansk
BRYANSKAYA OBLAST'
MOSKVA (MOSCOW)
MOSKOVSKAYA OBLAST'
TVERSKAYA OBLAST'
Kaluga
KALUZHSKAYA OBLAST'
Tula
Ryazan'
Orel
ORLOVSKAYA OBLAST'
Kursk
KURSKAYA OBLAST'
Belgorod
BELGORODSKAYA OBLAST'
Lipetsk
LIPETSKAYA OBLAST'
Voronezh
VORONEZHSKAYA OBLAST'
ROSTOVSKAYA OBLAST'
Rostov-na-Donu
Taganrog
Shakhty
Novocherkassk
KRASNODARSKIY KRAY
Krasnodar
Novorossiysk
Maykop
Sochi
Vladimir
Stavropol'
Cherkessk
Srednerusskaya Vozvyshennost'
Smolensko-Moskovskaya Vozvyshennost'

118

► *Kaliningrad has been a Russian enclave since 1945. The port is an important center for the Russian Federation's Baltic fishing fleet.*

◄ ***St Basil's Cathedral,*** *completed in 1561, stands in Moscow's Red Square next to the Kremlin; the original fortified stronghold of the city.*

110

Southern European Russia

118

This region, divided from Asia by desert, seas, and mountains, has exerted a powerful influence both east and west since the 13th century. Over 70 years of Communist rule produced a highly urbanized, industrial society dominated by Moscow, which was the capital of the Soviet Union until 1991. Almost two-thirds of the Russian Federation's population live in this core area, with a relatively high per capita share of its wealth. However, the rapid growth of a market economy has caused great social upheaval, with rising crime and political instability.

The landscape

Ancient folds in the deep sedimentary strata of the North European Plain have created a sequence of high and low regions. The Central Russian Upland *(Srednerusskaya Vozvyshennost')* in the west is deeply incised by rivers draining into the lowland of the Oka and Don rivers. In the east the Volga, Europe's longest river, flows south to the Caspian Sea, dividing the Volga Uplands *(Privolzhskaya Vozvyshennost')* from the foothills of the Ural Mountains *(Ural'skiye Gory)*. The Caucasus mountains and the Black Sea form a natural border to the southwest.

▲ ***A plantation of*** *Scots pine helps consolidate the loose sandy soils of the Meshchera Lowland* (Meshcherskaya Nizmennost), *which lies on the bed of an old glacial lake.*

116

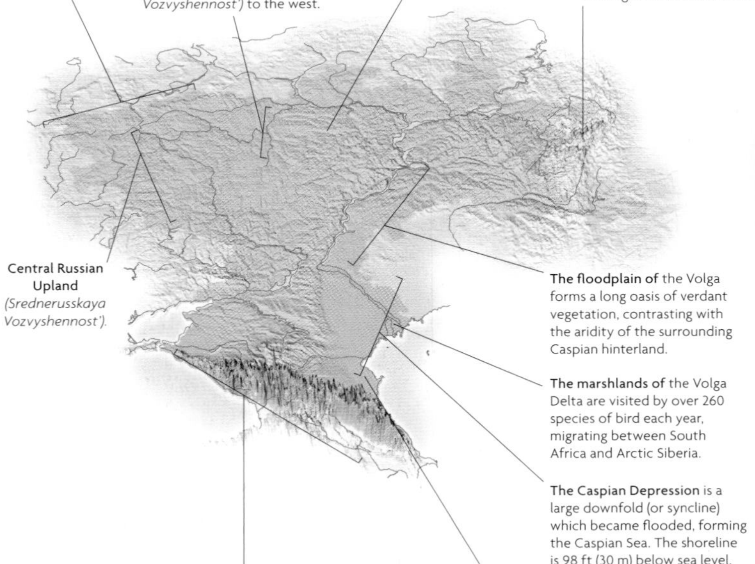

The Smolensk-Moscow Upland *(Smolensko-Moskovskaya Vozvyshennost')* is a series of terminal moraine ridges marking the southern extent of the last glaciation.

Glacial till covers the bedrock to the north of the North European Plain, giving a gentle surface relief.

The lowland of the Oka and Don rivers lies over a broad trough, between the upfolds of the Volga Uplands *(Privolzhskaya Vozvyshennost')* to the east, and the Central Russian Upland *(Srednerusskaya Vozvyshennost')* to the west.

The southern Ural mountains *(Ural'skiye Gory)* consist of several parallel ranges of ancient fold mountains running from north to south.

Central Russian Upland *(Srednerusskaya Vozvyshennost').*

The floodplain of the Volga forms a long oasis of verdant vegetation, contrasting with the aridity of the surrounding Caspian hinterland.

The marshlands of the Volga Delta are visited by over 260 species of bird each year, migrating between South Africa and Arctic Siberia.

The Caspian Depression is a large downfold (or syncline) which became flooded, forming the Caspian Sea. The shoreline is 98 ft (30 m) below sea level.

Drifting sand occupies large areas of the south, forming dunes up to 50 ft (15 m) high.

◄ ***The Caucasus mountains*** *run from the Black Sea to the Caspian Sea. They include El' brus which, at 18,511 ft (5642 m), is the highest point in Europe. It is still uplifting at a rate of 0.4 inches (10 mm) per year.*

Salt dome

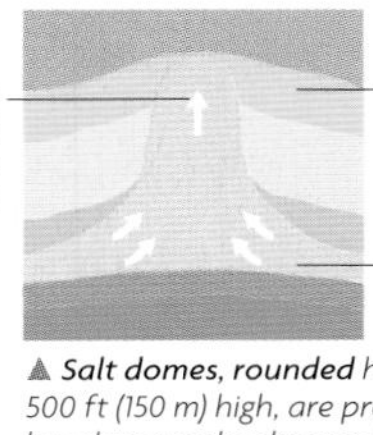
Salt dome is forced up and through the rock strata
Sedimentary strata
Salts are forced upwards by denser overlying strata

▲ ***Salt domes, rounded*** *hills up to 500 ft (150 m) high, are produced as less dense rock salts are displaced under the extreme pressure of denser, overlying strata and forced up toward the surface creating domes. They are widespread in the Caspian Depression.*

Scale 1:6,000,000
Km
Miles
projection: Lambert Conformal Conic
Map key
Population
above 5 million
1 million to 5 million
500,000 to 1 million
100,000 to 500,000
50,000 to 100,000
10,000 to 50,000
below 10,000
Elevation
4000m / 13,124ft
3000m / 9843ft
2000m / 6562ft
1000m / 3281ft
500m / 1640ft
250m / 820ft
100m / 328ft
sea level
RUSSIAN FEDERATION
KAZAKHSTAN
KOSTROMSKAYA OBLAST'
KIROVSKAYA OBLAST'
PERMSKIY
SVERDLOVSKAYA OBLAST'
CHELYABINSKAYA OBLAST'
NIZHEGORODSKAYA OBLAST'
RESPUBLIKA MARIY EL
UDMURTSKAYA RESPUBLIKA
CHUVASHSKAYA RESPUBLIKA
RESPUBLIKA TATARSTAN
RESPUBLIKA BASHKORTOSTAN
RESPUBLIKA MORDOVIYA
UL'YANOVSKAYA OBLAST'
PENZENSKAYA OBLAST'
SAMARSKAYA OBLAST'
ORENBURGSKAYA OBLAST'
SARATOVSKAYA OBLAST'
VOLGOGRADSKAYA OBLAST'
ASTRAKHANSKAYA OBLAST'
RESPUBLIKA KALMYKIYA
STAVROPOL'SKIY KRAY
CHECHENSKAYA RESPUBLIKA
RESPUBLIKA DAGESTAN
GEORGIA
AZERBAIJAN
Caspian Sea
Caspian Depression
Ural'skiye Gory
Nizhniy Novgorod
Kazan'
Samara
Tol'yatti
Ul'yanovsk
Saratov
Volgograd
Astrakhan'
Ufa
Orenburg
Penza
Izhevsk
Cheboksary
Naberezhnyye Chelny
Makhachkala
Groznyy
Elista
Saransk
Orsk
136
144
136

Using the land

In the cold, humid north and in the southern Urals *(Ural'skiye Gory)*, small grains, potatoes, and flax are commonly rotated with legumes which support livestock farming. The rich *chernozem* (or black earth) areas support diverse crops such as sugar beet, hemp, sunflowers, millet, and vegetables. Further south, aridity restricts husbandry to extensive grazing, with intensive fruit and rice cultivation along the oasis of the Volga.

The urban/rural population divide

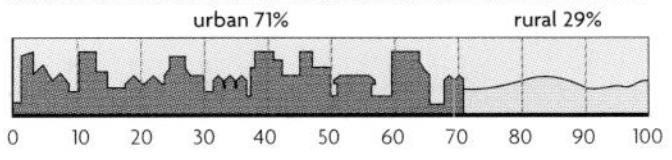
urban 71%
rural 29%
0
10
20
30
40
50
60
70
80
90
100

Population density	Total land area
119 people per sq mile (46 people per sq km)	705,916 sq miles (1,828,800 sq km)

Land use and agricultural distribution

- sheep
- flax
- potatoes
- rice
- sunflowers
- sugar beet
- timber
- capital cities
- major towns
- pasture
- cropland
- forest
- wetland
- mountain region
- tundra

RUSSIAN FEDERATION
MOSCOW
Nizhniy Novgorod
Ufa
Samara
Voronezh
Orsk
RUSSIAN FEDERATION
BELARUS
UKRAINE
KAZAKHSTAN
Rostov-na-Donu
Astrakhan'
Sea of Azov
Caspian Sea
Groznyy
BLACK SEA
GEORGIA
AZERB.

Transportation & industry

Manufacturing is largely based around Moscow and the Volga region, which became a major industrial area during the Second World War. Both Moscow and Nizhniy Novgorod are centers of skilled labor for light manufacturing and engineering. Most of Russia's main chemical plants are located along the Volga, and one of the world's largest car factories was recently opened in Tol'yatti. Processing and machine construction plants use oil, gas, and hydroelectric power from the Volga Basin and metallic minerals from the Urals *(Ural'skiye Gory)* and Kursk.

◄ ***Industrial plants are** massed along the Volga. Environmental stress from decades of unbridled industrial development has prompted widespread concern about pollution levels.*

Transportation network

250,000 miles (402,000 km)	None
28,000 miles (44,800 km)	16,300 miles (26,080 km)

Seventy private and national flag airlines have been created from the reorganization of the state airline Aeroflot, which maintained the world's largest fleet of aircraft during the Soviet era.

Major industry and infrastructure

- aerospace
- car manufacture
- chemicals
- defense
- electronics
- engineering
- gas
- mining
- oil
- textiles
- capital cities
- major towns
- international airports
- major roads
- major industrial areas

RUSSIAN FEDERATION
MOSCOW
Nizhniy Novgorod
Kazan'
Ufa
Tula
Ryazan'
Ul'yanovsk
Bryansk
Penza
Tol'yatti
Kursk
Samara
Voronezh
Saratov
Orsk
Belgorod
RUSSIAN FEDERATION
Volgograd
BELARUS
UKRAINE
KAZAKHSTAN
Rostov-na-Donu
Sea of Azov
Astrakhan'
Stavropol'
Caspian Sea
Groznyy
BLACK SEA
GEORGIA
AZERB.

Asia

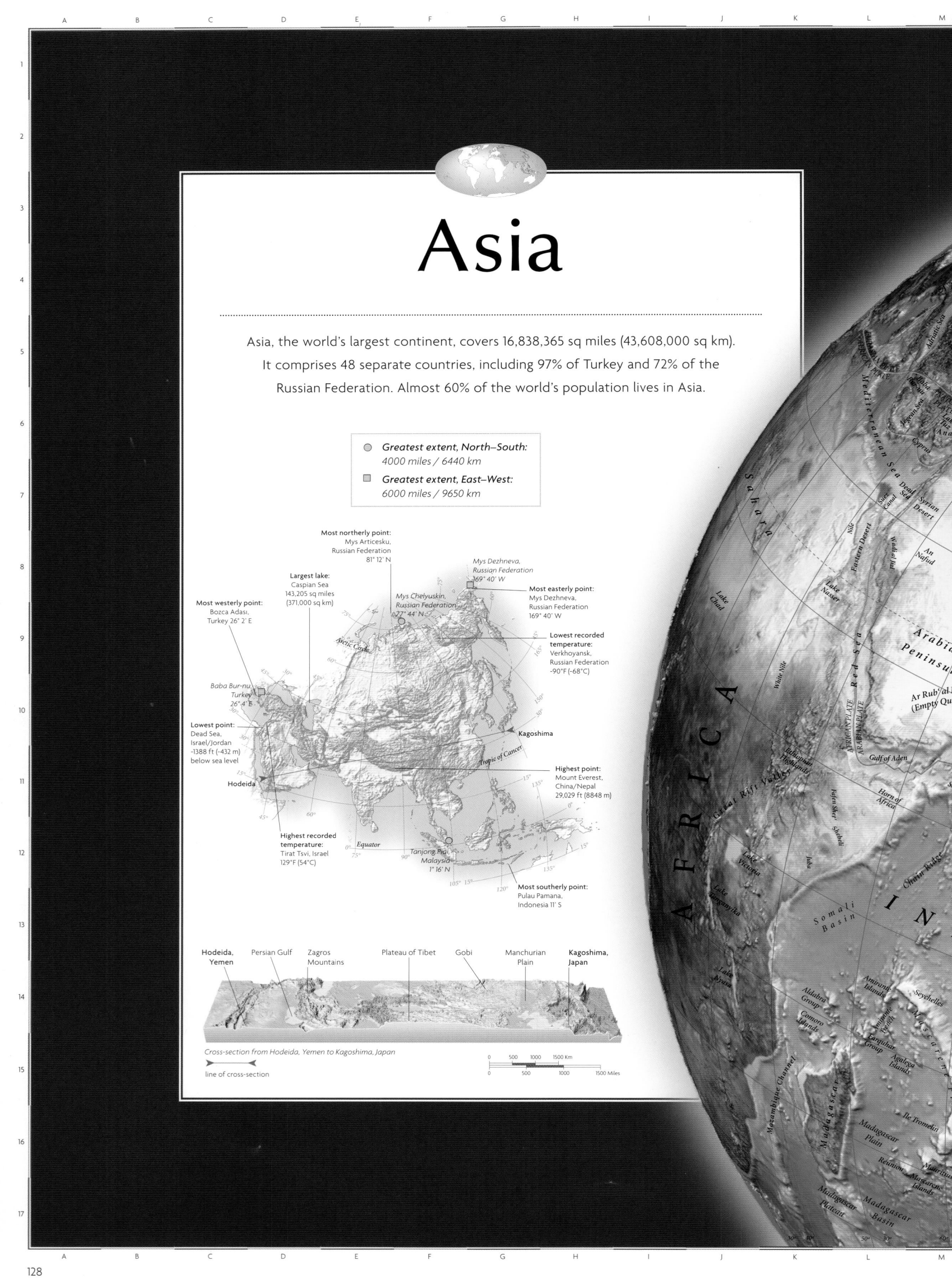

Asia, the world's largest continent, covers 16,838,365 sq miles (43,608,000 sq km). It comprises 48 separate countries, including 97% of Turkey and 72% of the Russian Federation. Almost 60% of the world's population lives in Asia.

○ ***Greatest extent, North–South:*** *4000 miles / 6440 km*

□ ***Greatest extent, East–West:*** *6000 miles / 9650 km*

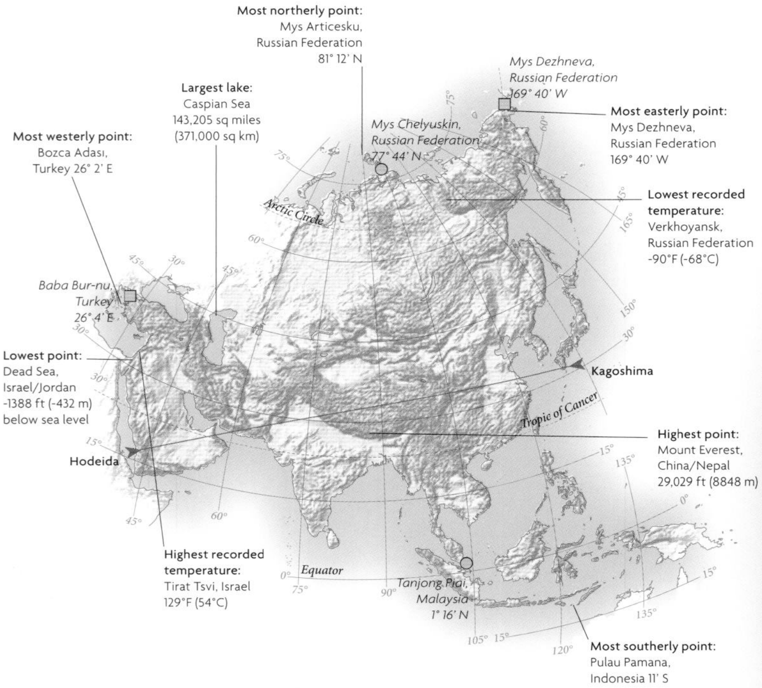

Most northerly point:
Mys Articesku,
Russian Federation
81° 12' N
Largest lake:
Caspian Sea
143,205 sq miles
(371,000 sq km)
Most westerly point:
Bozca Adası,
Turkey 26° 2' E
Mys Dezhneva,
Russian Federation
169° 40' W
Most easterly point:
Mys Dezhneva,
Russian Federation
169° 40' W
Mys Chelyuskin,
Russian Federation
77° 44' N
Lowest recorded
temperature:
Verkhoyansk,
Russian Federation
-90°F (-68°C)
Arctic Circle
Baba Bur-nu,
Turkey
26° 4' E
Lowest point:
Dead Sea,
Israel/Jordan
-1388 ft (-432 m)
below sea level
Kagoshima
Tropic of Cancer
Hodeida
Highest point:
Mount Everest,
China/Nepal
29,029 ft (8848 m)
Highest recorded
temperature:
Tirat Tsvi, Israel
129°F (54°C)
Equator
Tanjong Piai,
Malaysia
1° 16' N
Most southerly point:
Pulau Pamana,
Indonesia 11' S

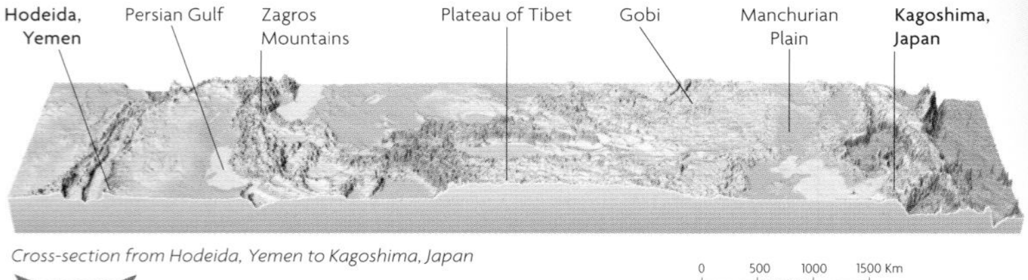

Hodeida,
Yemen
Persian Gulf
Zagros
Mountains
Plateau of Tibet
Gobi
Manchurian
Plain
Kagoshima,
Japan
0 500 1000 1500 Km
0 500 1000 1500 Miles

Cross-section from Hodeida, Yemen to Kagoshima, Japan

line of cross-section

AFRICA
Sahara
Mediterranean Sea
Aegean Sea
Cyprus
Dead Sea
Suez Canal
Syrian Desert
Nile
Eastern Desert
An Nafud
Lake Nasser
Lake Chad
Red Sea
Arabian Peninsula
White Nile
AFRICAN PLATE
ARABIAN PLATE
Gulf of Aden
Ethiopian Highlands
Great Rift Valley
Horn of Africa
Lake Victoria
Lake Tanganyika
Somali Basin
Lake Nyasa
Aldabra Group
Comoro Islands
Amirante Islands
Seychelles
Farquhar Group
Agalega Islands
Mozambique Channel
Madagascar
Île Tromelin
Madagascar Plain
Réunion
Mauritius
Mascarene Islands
Madagascar Plateau
Madagascar Basin

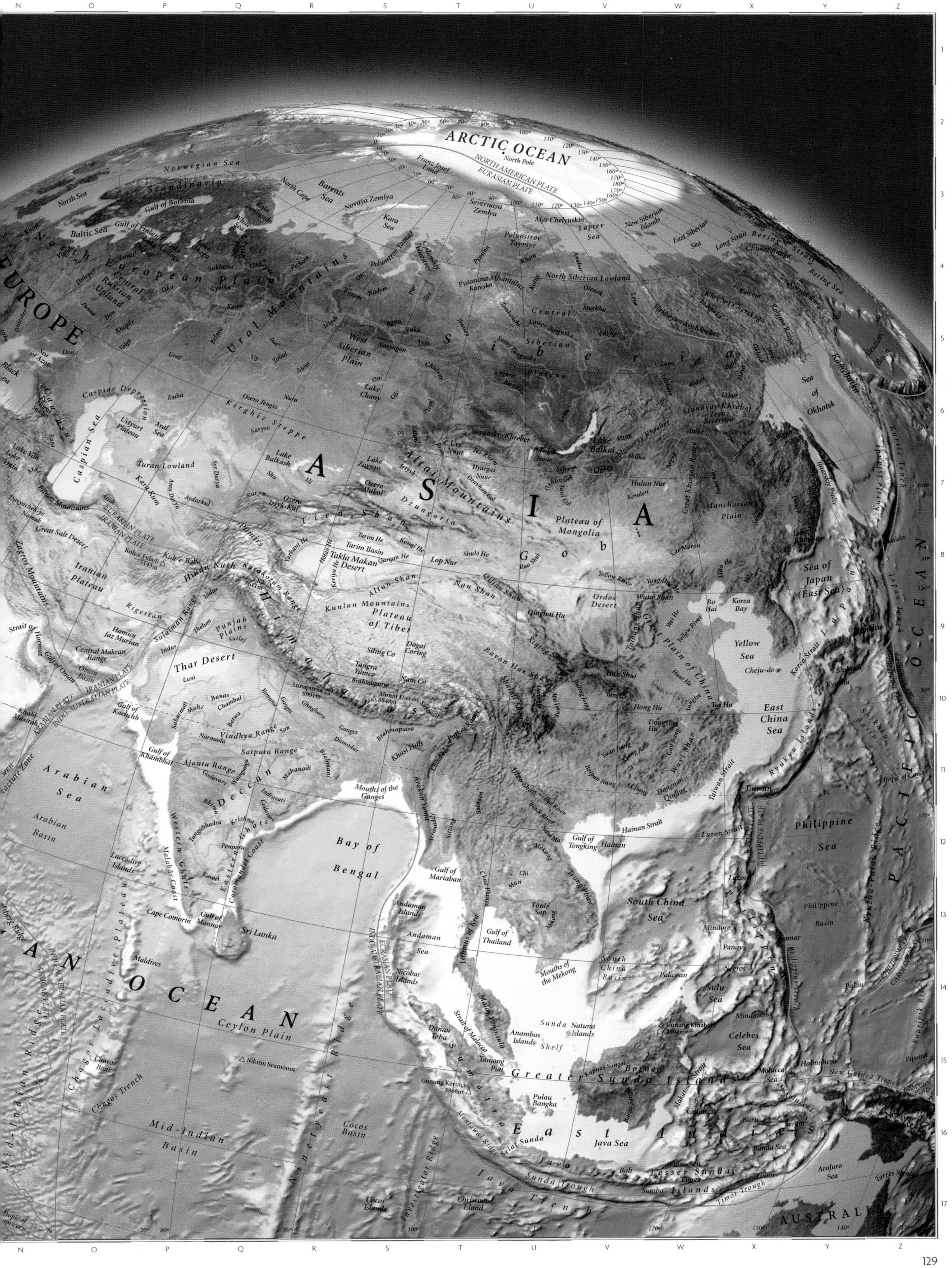
N O P Q R S T U V W X Y Z
1 2 3 4 5 6 7 8 9 10 11 12 13 14 15 16 17
ARCTIC OCEAN
North Pole
NORTH AMERICAN PLATE
EURASIAN PLATE
Franz Josef Land
Norwegian Sea
Scandinavia
North Sea
Gulf of Bothnia
North Cape
Barents Sea
Novaya Zemlya
Kara Sea
Severnaya Zemlya
Mys Chelyuskin
Laptev Sea
New Siberian Islands
East Siberian Sea
Long Strait
Bering Strait
Chukot Range
Bering Sea
Baltic Sea
Gulf of Finland
Lake Ladoga
Lake Onega
White Sea
Kola Peninsula
North European Plain
Central Russian Upland
EUROPE
Ural Mountains
Poluostrov Yamal
Poluostrov Taymyr
North Siberian Lowland
Putorana Mountains
Central Siberian Plateau
Siberia
West Siberian Plain
Verkhoyanskiy Khrebet
Khrebet Cherskogo
Kolyma Range
Koryak Range
Kamchatka
Aleutian Basin
Sea of Okhotsk
Sea of Azov
Black Sea
Caucasus
Caspian Depression
Caspian Sea
Ustyurt Plateau
Aral Sea
Kirghiz Steppe
Lake Chany
Lake Balkhash
Lake Zaysan
Turan Lowland
Kara Kum
Lake Baikal
Sayanskiy Khrebet
Stanovoy Khrebet
Zeya Reservoir
Yablonovyy Khrebet
Altai Mountains
ASIA
Tien Shan
Dzungaria
Plateau of Mongolia
Gobi
Great Khingan Range
Manchurian Plain
Kurile Islands
Kurile Trench
Hokkaido
Sea of Japan (East Sea)
Japan
Japan Trench
PACIFIC OCEAN
Elburz Mountains
Great Salt Desert
EURASIAN PLATE
IRANIAN PLATE
Pamirs
Kuh-e Baba
Hindu Kush
Karakoram Range
K2 8611m
Tarim Basin
Takla Makan Desert
Lop Nur
Zagros Mountains
Iranian Plateau
Rigestan
Altun Shan
Nan Shan
Qilian Shan
Kunlun Mountains
Plateau of Tibet
Qinghai Hu
Ordos Desert
Yellow River
Bo Hai
Korea Bay
Yellow Sea
Cheju-do
Korea Strait
Strait of Hormuz
Gulf of Oman
Hamun Jaz Murian
Central Makran Range
Sulaiman Range
Punjab Plains
Thar Desert
Himalayas
Annapurna 8091m
Mount Everest 8848m
Great Plain of China
Hong Hu
Dongting Hu
East China Sea
Ryukyu Islands
Gulf of Kachchh
ARABIAN PLATE
INDO-AUSTRALIAN PLATE
Vindhya Range
Satpura Range
Gulf of Khambhat
Ajanta Range
Khasi Hills
Arabian Sea
Arabian Basin
Deccan
Mouths of the Ganges
Taiwan Strait
Taiwan
Tropic of Cancer
Philippine Sea
Bay of Bengal
Gulf of Martaban
Gulf of Tongking
Hainan Strait
Hainan
Luzon Strait
Luzon
Lacadive Islands
Western Ghats
Eastern Ghats
Malabar Coast
Coromandel Coast
Cape Comorin
Gulf of Mannar
Sri Lanka
Andaman Islands
Andaman Sea
Gulf of Thailand
Tônlé Sap
South China Sea
Mindoro
Panay
Negros
Palawan
Philippine Basin
Philippine Trench
Maldives
INDIAN OCEAN
Nicobar Islands
Mouths of the Mekong
South China Basin
Sulu Sea
Mindanao
Palau
Ceylon Plain
Malay Peninsula
Strait of Malacca
Sunda Shelf
Natuna Islands
Anambas Islands
Gunung Kinabalu 4094m
Celebes Sea
Chagos Bank
Nikitin Seamount
Chagos Trench
Greater Sunda Islands
Borneo
Moluccas
Halmahera
New Guinea Trench
Equator
Sumatra
Gunung Kerinci 3806m
Pulau Bangka
Ninetyeast Ridge
Mid-Indian Basin
Mid-Indian Ridge
Cocos Basin
East Indies
Java Sea
Celebes
Buru
Seram
Banda Sea
Arafura Sea
Java
Bali
Lesser Sundas
Flores
Sumba Islands
Timor
Timor Trough
Sunda Trough
Java Trench
Investigator Ridge
Cocos Islands
Christmas Island
Tropic of Capricorn
AUSTRALIA
Torres Strait

Physical Asia

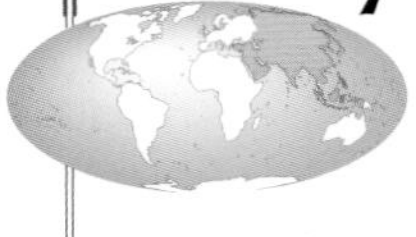

The structure of Asia can be divided into two distinct regions. The landscape of northern Asia consists of old mountain chains, shields, plateaus, and basins, like the Ural Mountains in the west and the Central Siberian Plateau to the east. To the south of this region, are a series of plateaus and basins, including the vast Plateau of Tibet and the Tarim Basin. In contrast, the landscapes of southern Asia are much younger, formed by tectonic activity beginning about 65 million years ago, leading to an almost continuous mountain chain running from Europe, across much of Asia, and culminating in the mighty Himalayan mountain belt, formed when the Indo-Australian Plate collided with the Eurasian Plate. They are still being uplifted today. North of the mountains lies a belt of deserts, including the Gobi and the Takla Makan. In the far south, tectonic activity has formed narrow island arcs, extending over 4000 miles (7000 km). To the west lies the Arabian Shield, once part of the African Plate. As it was rifted apart from Africa, the Arabian Plate collided with the Eurasian Plate, uplifting the Zagros Mountains.

Coastal Lowlands and Island Arcs

The coastal plains that fringe Southeast Asia contain many large delta systems, caused by high levels of rainfall and erosion of the Himalayas, the Plateau of Tibet, and relict loess deposits. To the south is an extensive island archipelago, lying on the drowned Sunda Shelf. Most of these islands are volcanic in origin, caused by the subduction of the Indo-Australian Plate beneath the Eurasian Plate.

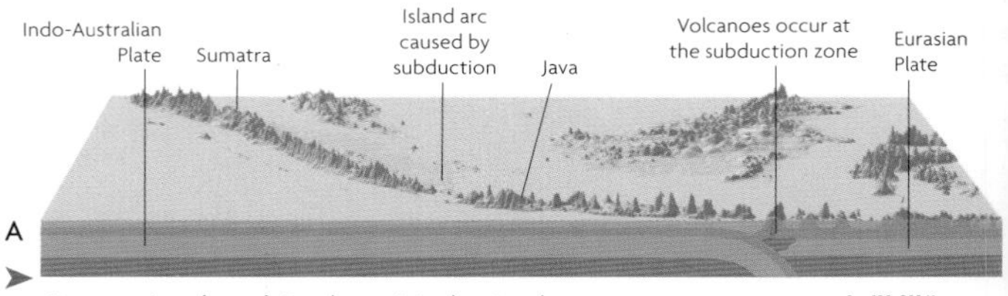
Indo-Australian Plate
Sumatra
Island arc caused by subduction
Java
Volcanoes occur at the subduction zone
Eurasian Plate
A
0 100 200 Km
0 100 200 Miles

***Cross-section through** Southeast Asia showing the subduction zone between the Indo-Australian and Eurasian plates and the island arc.*

The Indian Shield and Himalayan System

The large shield area beneath the Indian subcontinent is between 2.5 and 3.5 billion years old. As the floor of the southern Indian Ocean spread, it pushed the Indian Shield north. This was eventually driven beneath the Plateau of Tibet. This process closed up the ancient Tethys Sea and uplifted the world's highest mountain chain, the Himalayas. Much of the uplifted rock strata was from the seabed of the Tethys Sea, partly accounting for the weakness of the rocks and the high levels of erosion found in the Himalayas.

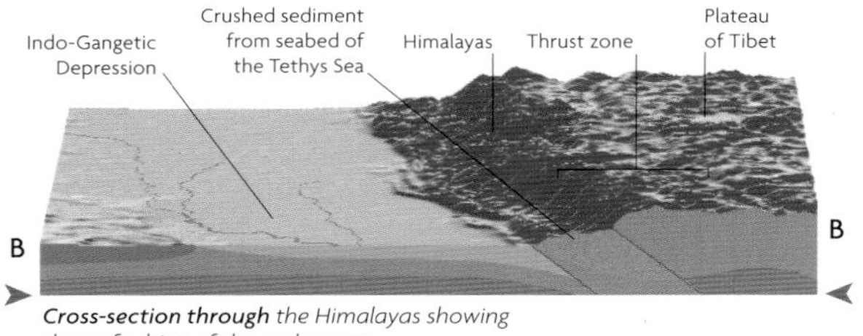
Indo-Gangetic Depression
Crushed sediment from seabed of the Tethys Sea
Himalayas
Thrust zone
Plateau of Tibet
B
B
0 50 100 Km
0 50 100 Miles

***Cross-section through** the Himalayas showing thrust faulting of the rock strata.*

East Asian Plains and Uplands

Several, small, isolated shield areas, such as the Shandong Peninsula, are found in east Asia. Between these stable shield areas, large river systems like the Yangtze and the Yellow River have deposited thick layers of sediment, forming extensive alluvial plains. The largest of these is the Great Plain of China, the relief of which does not rise above 300 ft (100 m).

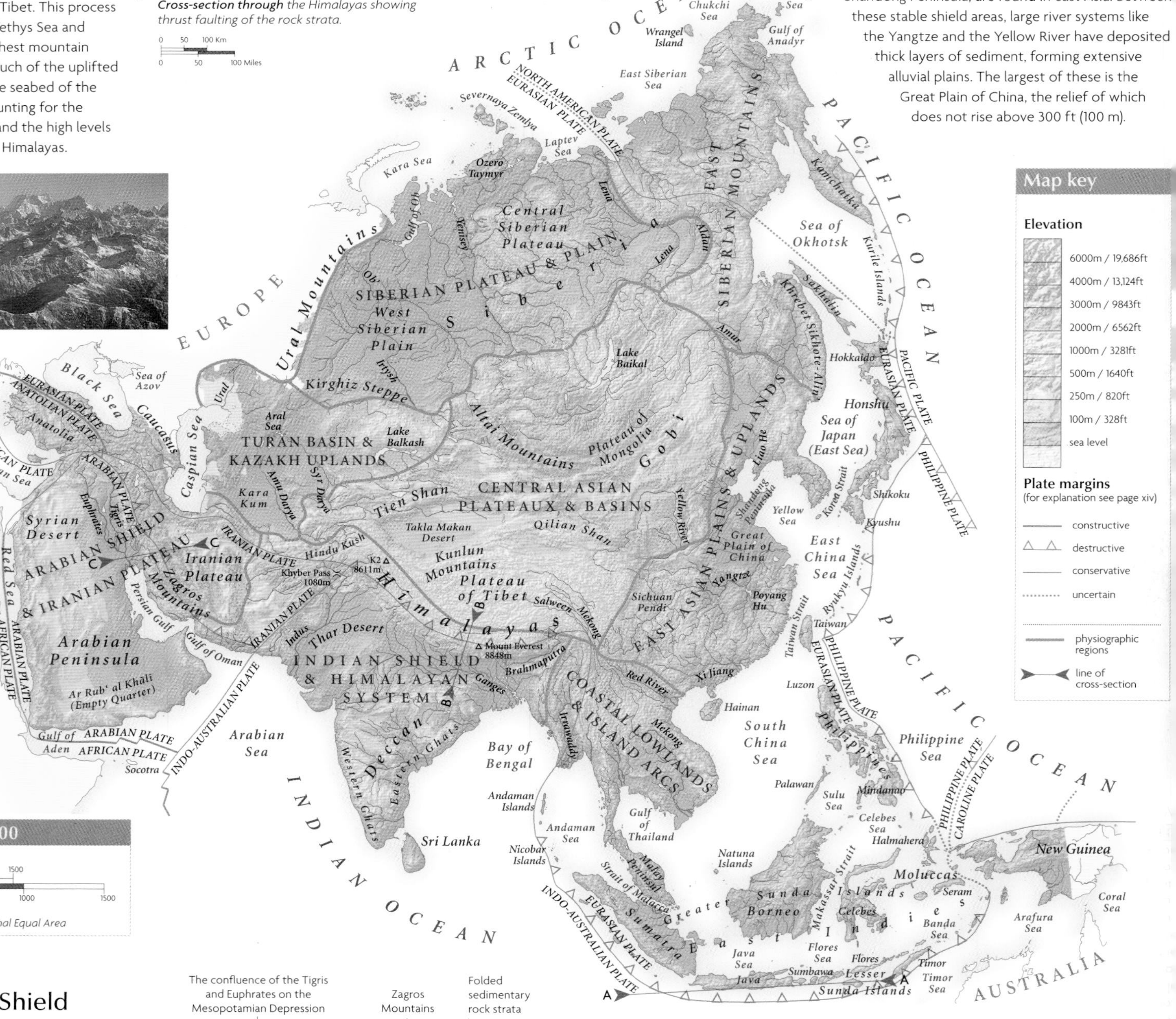
ARCTIC OCEAN
PACIFIC OCEAN
INDIAN OCEAN
EUROPE
AFRICA
AUSTRALIA
Chukchi Sea
Bering Sea
Wrangel Island
Gulf of Anadyr
East Siberian Sea
Severnaya Zemlya
Laptev Sea
Kara Sea
Ozero Taymyr
NORTH AMERICAN PLATE
EURASIAN PLATE
EAST SIBERIAN MOUNTAINS
Kamchatka
Sea of Okhotsk
Kurile Islands
Sakhalin
Khrebet Sikhote-Alin
Central Siberian Plateau
SIBERIAN PLATEAU & PLAINS
Siberia
West Siberian Plain
Ural Mountains
Lena
Aldan
Yenisey
Ob'
Gulf of Ob
Irtysh
Amur
Lake Baikal
Hokkaido
Honshu
Sea of Japan (East Sea)
PACIFIC PLATE
EURASIAN PLATE
PHILIPPINE PLATE
Shikoku
Kyushu
Korea Strait
Black Sea
Sea of Azov
EURASIAN PLATE
ANATOLIAN PLATE
Anatolia
Caucasus
Caspian Sea
Ural
Kirghiz Steppe
Aral Sea
Lake Balkash
TURAN BASIN & KAZAKH UPLANDS
Kara Kum
Amu Darya
Syr Darya
Altai Mountains
Plateau of Mongolia
Gobi
EAST ASIAN PLAINS & UPLANDS
Liao He
Shandong Peninsula
Yellow Sea
Yellow River
Tien Shan
CENTRAL ASIAN PLATEAUX & BASINS
Qilian Shan
Great Plain of China
East China Sea
Ryukyu Islands
Mediterranean Sea
AFRICAN PLATE
ARABIAN PLATE
Syrian Desert
Euphrates
Tigris
ARABIAN SHIELD & IRANIAN PLATEAU
Iranian Plateau
IRANIAN PLATE
Hindu Kush
K2 8611m
Khyber Pass 1080m
Takla Makan Desert
Kunlun Mountains
Plateau of Tibet
Zagros Mountains
Persian Gulf
Red Sea
ARABIAN PLATE
AFRICAN PLATE
Arabian Peninsula
Ar Rub' al Khali (Empty Quarter)
Gulf of Oman
Indus
Thar Desert
Himalayas
Mount Everest 8848m
Brahmaputra
Salween
Mekong
Yangtze
Sichuan Pendi
Poyang Hu
Taiwan Strait
Taiwan
INDIAN SHIELD & HIMALAYAN SYSTEM
Ganges
Red River
Xi Jiang
Hainan
Luzon
Gulf of Aden
ARABIAN PLATE
AFRICAN PLATE
Socotra
INDO-AUSTRALIAN PLATE
Arabian Sea
Deccan
Western Ghats
Eastern Ghats
Bay of Bengal
Irrawaddy
COASTAL LOWLANDS & ISLAND ARCS
Mekong
South China Sea
Philippines
Philippine Sea
PHILIPPINE PLATE
CAROLINE PLATE
Andaman Islands
Andaman Sea
Gulf of Thailand
Palawan
Sulu Sea
Mindanao
Sri Lanka
Nicobar Islands
Malay Peninsula
Strait of Malacca
Natuna Islands
Celebes Sea
Halmahera
New Guinea
Sumatra
Greater Sunda Islands
Borneo
Makassar Strait
Celebes
Moluccas
Seram
Banda Sea
East Indies
Coral Sea
Arafura Sea
Java Sea
Java
Flores Sea
Flores
Sumbawa
Lesser Sunda Islands
Timor
Timor Sea
INDO-AUSTRALIAN PLATE
EURASIAN PLATE
A
A
B
C
C

Map key

Elevation

- 6000m / 19,686ft
- 4000m / 13,124ft
- 3000m / 9843ft
- 2000m / 6562ft
- 1000m / 3281ft
- 500m / 1640ft
- 250m / 820ft
- 100m / 328ft
- sea level

Plate margins
(for explanation see page xiv)

- constructive
- destructive
- conservative
- uncertain
- physiographic regions
- line of cross-section

Scale 1:63,000,000

Km 0 250 500 1000 1500
Miles 0 250 500 1000 1500

projection: Lambert Azimuthal Equal Area

The Arabian Shield and Iranian Plateau

Approximately five million years ago, rifting of the continental crust split the Arabian Plate from the African Plate and flooded the Red Sea. As this rift spread, the Arabian Plate collided with the Eurasian Plate, transforming part of the Tethys seabed into the Zagros Mountains which run northwest-southeast across western Iran.

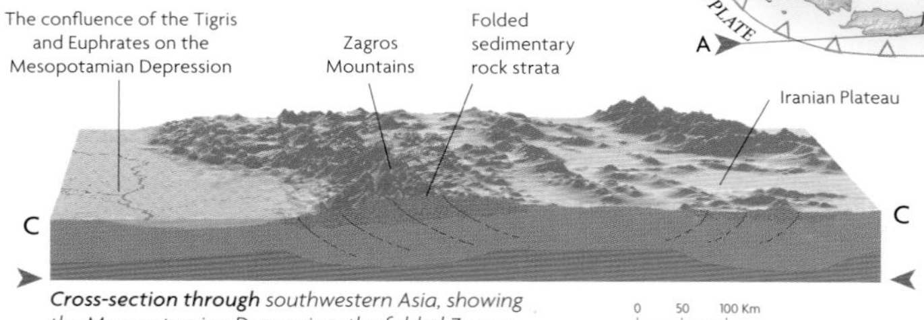
The confluence of the Tigris and Euphrates on the Mesopotamian Depression
Zagros Mountains
Folded sedimentary rock strata
Iranian Plateau
C
C
0 50 100 Km
0 50 100 Miles

***Cross-section through** southwestern Asia, showing the Mesopotamian Depression, the folded Zagros Mountains, and the Iranian Plateau.*

Climate

The climate of Asia exhibits marked differences from region to region, with freezing polar conditions in the north, hot and cold deserts in central regions and subtropical conditions throughout the south. Much of this variation can be attributed to enormous mountain barriers and internal depressions found across the continent. Monsoon winds, which reverse semiannually, cause alternate wet and dry seasons across southern Asia. These air masses moving north from the ocean are stripped of their moisture over the Himalayas causing arid conditions across the Plateau of Tibet. Both the south and east are susceptible to tropical cyclones or typhoons.

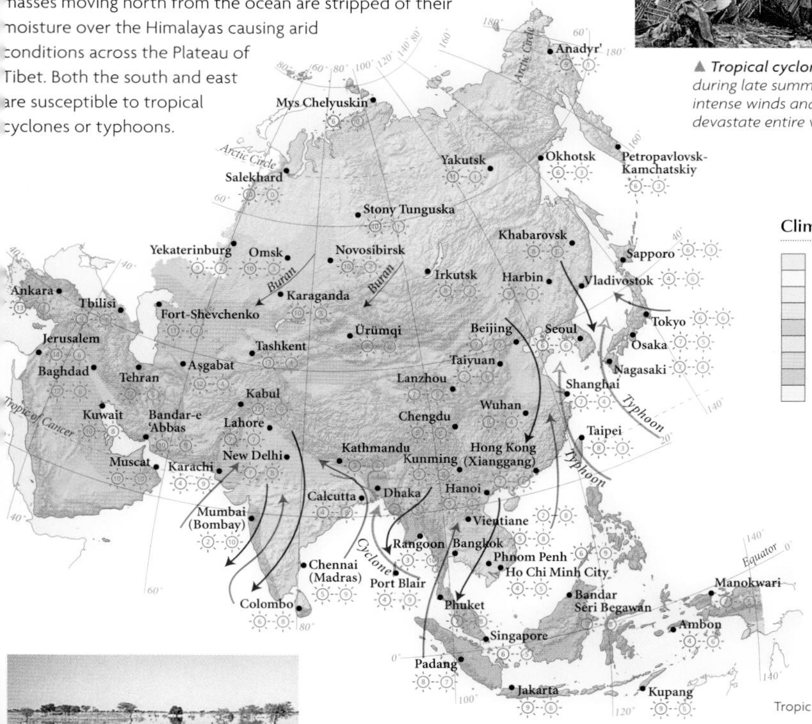
Anadyr'
Mys Chelyuskin
Arctic Circle
Salekhard
Yakutsk
Okhotsk
Petropavlovsk-Kamchatskiy
Stony Tunguska
Khabarovsk
Yekaterinburg
Omsk
Novosibirsk
Irkutsk
Harbin
Sapporo
Vladivostok
Ankara
Tbilisi
Karaganda
Fort-Shevchenko
Ürümqi
Beijing
Seoul
Tokyo
Osaka
Jerusalem
Baghdad
Tehran
Asgabat
Tashkent
Taiyuan
Nagasaki
Lanzhou
Shanghai
Typhoon
Kabul
Kuwait
Bandar-e 'Abbas
Lahore
Chengdu
Wuhan
Taipei
Muscat
Karachi
New Delhi
Kathmandu
Kunming
Hong Kong (Xianggang)
Calcutta
Dhaka
Hanoi
Mumbai (Bombay)
Vientiane
Rangoon
Bangkok
Chennai (Madras)
Cyclone
Port Blair
Phnom Penh
Ho Chi Minh City
Manokwari
Equator
Colombo
Phuket
Bandar Seri Begawan
Ambon
Singapore
Padang
Jakarta
Kupang
Tropic of Cancer

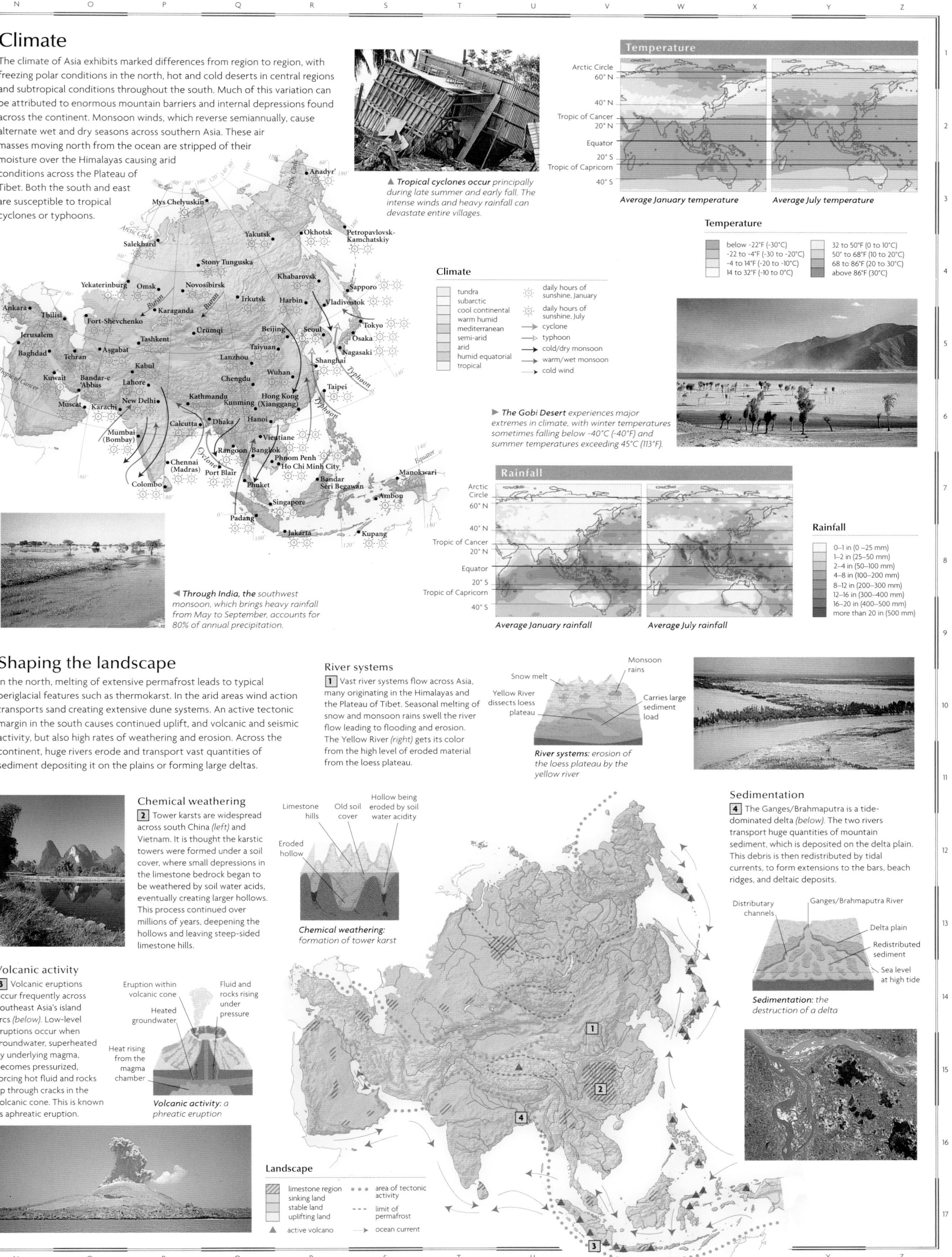

▲ *Tropical cyclones occur principally during late summer and early fall. The intense winds and heavy rainfall can devastate entire villages.*

Temperature

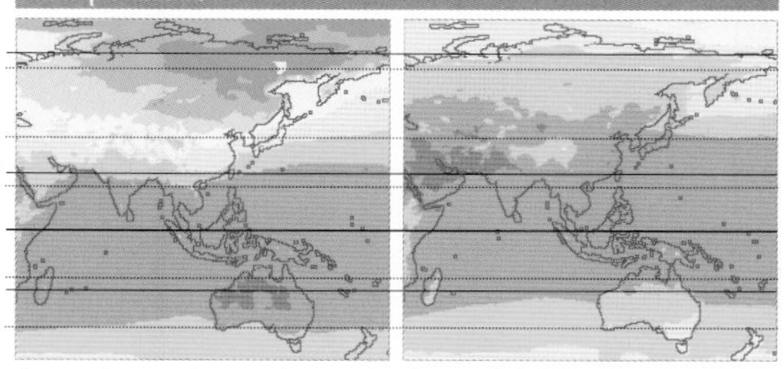
Arctic Circle
60° N
40° N
Tropic of Cancer
20° N
Equator
20° S
Tropic of Capricorn
40° S

Average January temperature *Average July temperature*

Temperature

- below -22°F (-30°C)
- -22 to -4°F (-30 to -20°C)
- -4 to 14°F (-20 to -10°C)
- 14 to 32°F (-10 to 0°C)
- 32 to 50°F (0 to 10°C)
- 50° to 68°F (10 to 20°C)
- 68 to 86°F (20 to 30°C)
- above 86°F (30°C)

Climate

- tundra
- subarctic
- cool continental
- warm humid
- mediterranean
- semi-arid
- arid
- humid equatorial
- tropical
- daily hours of sunshine, January
- daily hours of sunshine, July
- cyclone
- typhoon
- cold/dry monsoon
- warm/wet monsoon
- cold wind

► *The Gobi Desert experiences major extremes in climate, with winter temperatures sometimes falling below -40°C (-40°F) and summer temperatures exceeding 45°C (113°F).*

Rainfall

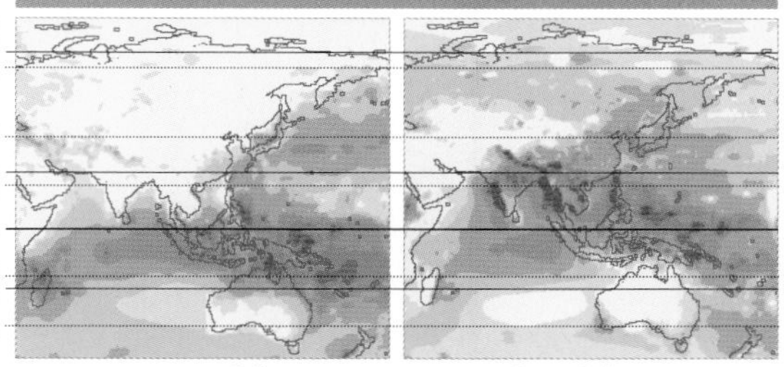
Arctic Circle
60° N
40° N
Tropic of Cancer
20° N
Equator
20° S
Tropic of Capricorn
40° S

Average January rainfall *Average July rainfall*

Rainfall

- 0–1 in (0 –25 mm)
- 1–2 in (25–50 mm)
- 2–4 in (50–100 mm)
- 4–8 in (100–200 mm)
- 8–12 in (200–300 mm)
- 12–16 in (300–400 mm)
- 16–20 in (400–500 mm)
- more than 20 in (500 mm)

◄ *Through India, the southwest monsoon, which brings heavy rainfall from May to September, accounts for 80% of annual precipitation.*

Shaping the landscape

In the north, melting of extensive permafrost leads to typical periglacial features such as thermokarst. In the arid areas wind action transports sand creating extensive dune systems. An active tectonic margin in the south causes continued uplift, and volcanic and seismic activity, but also high rates of weathering and erosion. Across the continent, huge rivers erode and transport vast quantities of sediment depositing it on the plains or forming large deltas.

River systems

1 Vast river systems flow across Asia, many originating in the Himalayas and the Plateau of Tibet. Seasonal melting of snow and monsoon rains swell the river flow leading to flooding and erosion. The Yellow River *(right)* gets its color from the high level of eroded material from the loess plateau.

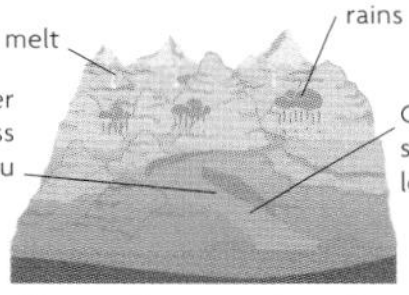
Monsoon rains
Snow melt
Yellow River dissects loess plateau
Carries large sediment load

River systems: erosion of the loess plateau by the yellow river

Chemical weathering

2 Tower karsts are widespread across south China *(left)* and Vietnam. It is thought the karstic towers were formed under a soil cover, where small depressions in the limestone bedrock began to be weathered by soil water acids, eventually creating larger hollows. This process continued over millions of years, deepening the hollows and leaving steep-sided limestone hills.

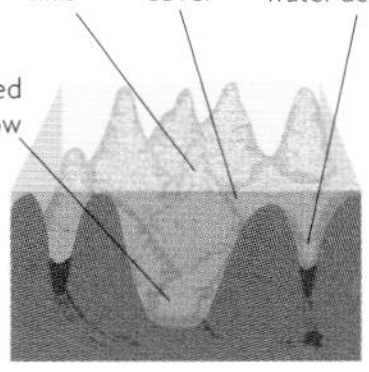
Limestone hills
Old soil cover
Hollow being eroded by soil water acidity
Eroded hollow

Chemical weathering: formation of tower karst

Volcanic activity

3 Volcanic eruptions occur frequently across southeast Asia's island arcs *(below)*. Low-level eruptions occur when groundwater, superheated by underlying magma, becomes pressurized, forcing hot fluid and rocks up through cracks in the volcanic cone. This is known as aphreatic eruption.

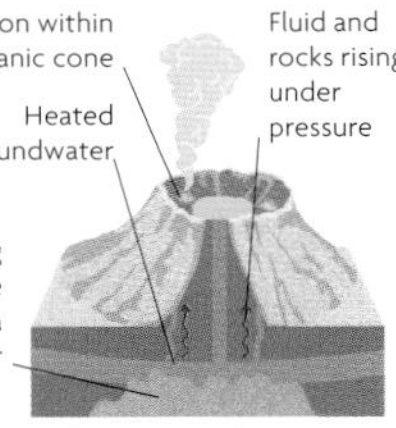
Eruption within volcanic cone
Fluid and rocks rising under pressure
Heated groundwater
Heat rising from the magma chamber

Volcanic activity: a phreatic eruption

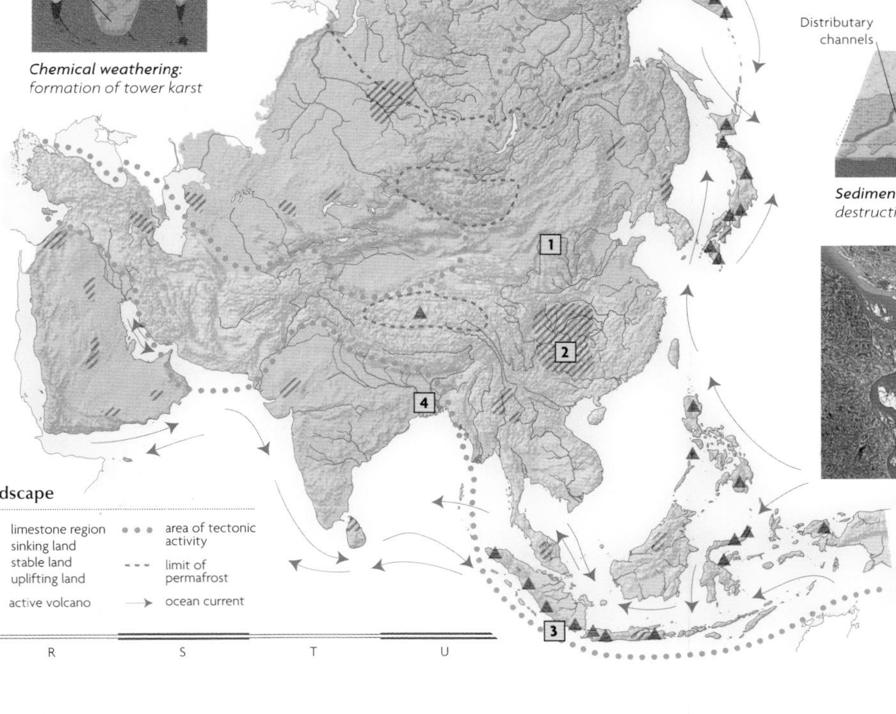
1
2
3
4

Landscape

- limestone region
- sinking land
- stable land
- uplifting land
- active volcano
- area of tectonic activity
- limit of permafrost
- ocean current

Sedimentation

4 The Ganges/Brahmaputra is a tide-dominated delta *(below)*. The two rivers transport huge quantities of mountain sediment, which is deposited on the delta plain. This debris is then redistributed by tidal currents, to form extensions to the bars, beach ridges, and deltaic deposits.

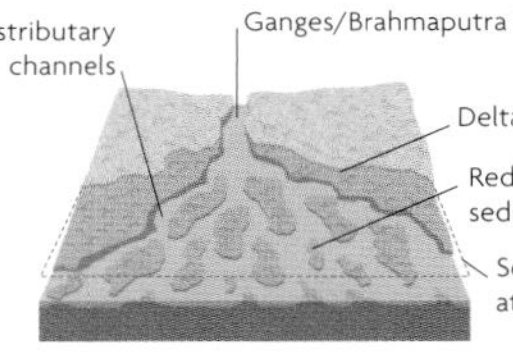
Distributary channels
Ganges/Brahmaputra River
Delta plain
Redistributed sediment
Sea level at high tide

Sedimentation: the destruction of a delta

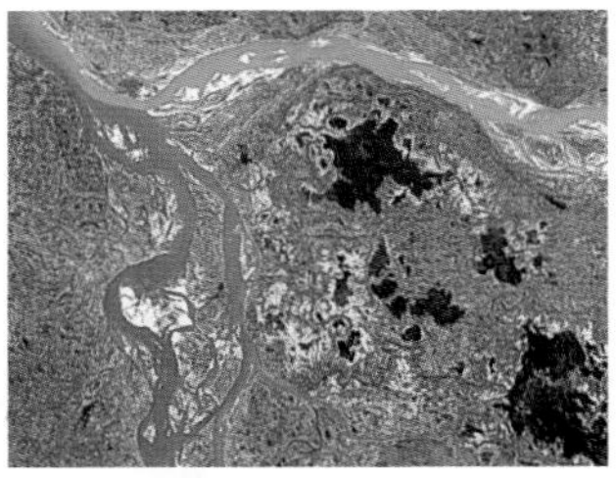

Political Asia

Asia is the world's largest continent, encompassing many different and discrete realms, from the desert Arab lands of the southwest to the subtropical archipelago of Indonesia; from the vast barren wastes of Siberia to the fertile river valleys of China and South Asia, seats of some of the world's most ancient civilizations. The collapse of the Soviet Union has fragmented the north of the continent into the Siberian portion of the Russian Federation, and the new republics of Central Asia. Strong religious traditions heavily influence the politics of South and Southwest Asia. Hindu and Muslim rivalries threaten to upset the political equilibrium in South Asia where India – in terms of population – remains the world's largest democracy. Communist China another population giant, is reasserting its position as a world and political power, while on its doorstep, the economically progressive and dynamic Pacific Rim countries, led by Japan, continue to assert their worldwide economic force.

ARCTIC OCEAN
East Siberian Sea
Laptev Sea
Kara Sea
RUSSIAN FEDERATION
Central Siberian Plateau
West Siberian Plain
Ural Mountains
EUROPE
Yekaterinburg
Chelyabinsk
Omsk
Tomsk
Novosibirsk
Krasnoyarsk
Novokuznetsk
Irkutsk
Yakutsk
Noril'sk
Lake Baikal
ASTANA
KAZAKHSTAN
Karaganda
Semipalatinsk
Zhezkazgan
Aral Sea
Lake Balkash
Balkash
Kyzylorda
Ural'sk
Rudnyy
Aktau
Caspian Sea
Black Sea
Istanbul
ANKARA
TURKEY
Anatolia
Adana
Gaziantep
Sokhumi
GEORGIA
K'ut'aisi
TBILISI
Bat'umi
ARMENIA
YEREVAN
Gäncä
AZERB.
BAKU
Tabriz
CYPRUS
NICOSIA
LEBANON
BEIRUT
Tripoli
Aleppo
SYRIA
DAMASCUS
Haifa
Tel Aviv-Yafo
Gaza
JERUSALEM
AMMAN
ISRAEL
JORDAN
Mosul
Kirkuk
BAGHDAD
IRAQ
An Najaf
Basra
KUWAIT
TEHRAN
Qom
Esfahan
Ahvaz
IRAN
Iranian Plateau
Shiraz
Kerman
Zahedan
Bandar-e 'Abbas
Mashhad
Gorgan
SAUDI ARABIA
RIYADH
Jedda
At Ta'if
MANAMA
BAHRAIN
QATAR
DOHA
ABU DHABI
UAE
Arabian Peninsula
Ar Rub' al Khali (Empty Quarter)
MUSCAT
Ar Rustaq
Sur
OMAN
SANA
YEMEN
Ta'izz
Aden
Gulf of Aden
Socotra (to Yemen)
Red Sea
AFRICA
Arabian Sea
Gulf of Oman
TURKMENISTAN
AŞGABAT
Dasoguz
UZBEKISTAN
TASHKENT
KYRGYZSTAN
BISHKEK
Taraz
Almaty
Karakol
Osh
DUSHANBE
TAJIKISTAN
AFGHANISTAN
KABUL
Herat
Kandahar
Balkh
Qal'eh-ye Now
PAKISTAN
ISLAMABAD
Peshawar
Gujranwala
Faisalabad
Lahore
Multan
Quetta
Larkana
Shikarpur
Karachi
Hyderabad
Srinagar
Jammu
Ludhiana
Delhi
NEW DELHI
Jaipur
Agra
Bareilly
Kanpur
Lucknow
INDIA
Ahmadabad
Vadodara
Surat
Indore
Bhopal
Nagpur
Mumbai (Bombay)
Pune
Solapur
Hyderabad
Vijayawada
Hubli
Bangalore
Mysore
Chennai (Madras)
Coimbatore
Kochi
Thiruvananthapuram
Varanasi
Patna
Jamshedpur
Kolkata (Calcutta)
Bhubaneshwar
NEPAL
KATHMANDU
THIMPHU
BHUTAN
BANGLADESH
DHAKA
Rajshahi
Khulna
Chittagong
Rangpur
Guwahati
SRI LANKA
COLOMBO
SRI JAYEWARDENAPURA KOTTE
Jaffna
INDIAN OCEAN
Bay of Bengal
Andaman Islands (to India)
Nicobar Islands (to India)
Andaman Sea
MYANMAR
Mandalay
NAY PYI TAW
Rangoon
Pegu
Bassein
Prome
Pakokku
Taunggyi
THAILAND
BANGKOK
CAMBODIA
PHNOM PENH
LAOS
VIENTIANE
HANOI
Gulf of Thailand
Kota Bharu
KUALA LUMPUR
PUTRAJAYA
SINGAPORE
Medan
Sumatra
Padang
Palembang
Jambi
Equator
MONGOLIA
ULAN BATOR
Gobi
Erdenet
Choybalsan
Sühbaatar
CHINA
Ürümqi
Tarim He
Takla Makan Desert
Tien Shan
Kunlun Mountains
Plateau of Tibet
Himalayas
Lanzhou
Xi'an
Chengdu
Chongqing
Kunming
Mianyang
Leshan
Baotou
Datong
Taiyuan
(claimed by India)
(line of control)
(administered by China, claimed by India)
(Much of Arunachal Pradesh is claimed by China)
Arctic Circle
Tropic of Cancer

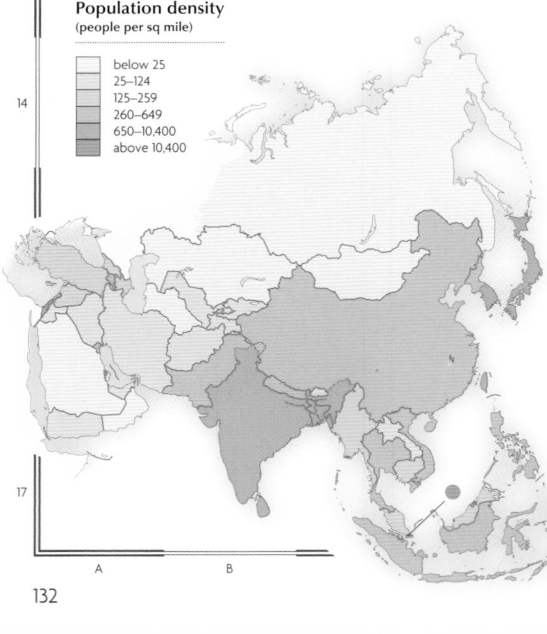
Population density
(people per sq mile)
below 25
25–124
125–259
260–649
650–10,400
above 10,400

Population

Some of the world's most populous and least populous regions are in Asia. The plains of eastern China, the Ganges river plains in India, Japan, and the Indonesian island of Java, all have very high population densities; by contrast parts of Siberia and the Plateau of Tibet are virtually uninhabited. China has the world's greatest population – 20% of the globe's total – while India, with the second largest, is likely to overtake China within 30 years.

◀ *Over 13 million people bustle through Kolkata's maze of crowded, narrow streets. Population densities in India's largest city reach almost 85,000 per sq mile (33,000 per sq km).*

N O P Q R S T U V W X Y Z
1 2 3 4 5 7 8 9 10 11 12 15 16 17
Bering Sea
Anadyr'
Arctic Circle
PACIFIC OCEAN
Kolyma Range
Kamchatka
Magadan
Petropavlovsk-Kamchatskiy
Sea of Okhotsk
Kurile Islands
Sakhalin
Amur
Yuzhno-Sakhalinsk
Khabarovsk
Hokkaido
Sapporo
Qiqihar
Harbin
Changchun
Jilin
Vladivostok
Chongjin
Sea of Japan (East Sea)
Sendai
JAPAN
Liao He
NORTH KOREA
Shenyang
Anshan
Hamhung
Wonsan
TOKYO
Yokohama
Honshu
PYONGYANG
SOUTH KOREA
Kyoto
Nagoya
Dalian
SEOUL
Kobe
Osaka
Tangshan
Incheon
Daegu
Hiroshima
SEJONG CITY
Busan
Kitakyushu
Qingdao
Fukuoka
Kumamoto
Jinan
Yellow Sea
Kagoshima
Xuzhou
Huainan
Nanjing
Shanghai
East China Sea
Hefei
Hangzhou
Ningbo
Wuhan
Jinhua
Ryukyu Islands
Tropic of Cancer
Nanchang
Changsha
Fuzhou
Taiwan Strait
TAIPEI
Hengyang
Taizhong
TAIWAN
Shantou
Tainan
Gaoxiong
Guangzhou
Hong Kong (Xianggang)
Philippine Sea
Tuguegarao
Luzon
Baguio
South China Sea
MANILA
Legazpi City
PHILIPPINES
Bacolod
Cebu
Mindanao
Davao
Zamboanga
General Santos
Equator
Jayapura
BANDAR SERI BEGAWAN
BRUNEI
Manado
New Guinea
Papua (Irian Jaya)
Borneo
Moluccas
Balikpapan
Celebes
Ambon
Pontianak
INDONESIA
Banjarmasin
Makassar
Java Sea
Flores Sea
Flores
DILI
EAST TIMOR
Semarang
Surabaya
Java
Timor
Timor Sea
Malang

Map key

Population

- above 5 million
- 1 million to 5 million
- 500,000 to 1 million
- 100,000 to 500,000
- 50,000 to 100,000
- 10,000 to 50,000
- Country capital

Borders

- full international border
- disputed de facto border
- disputed territorial claim border
- undefined border
- ceasefire line

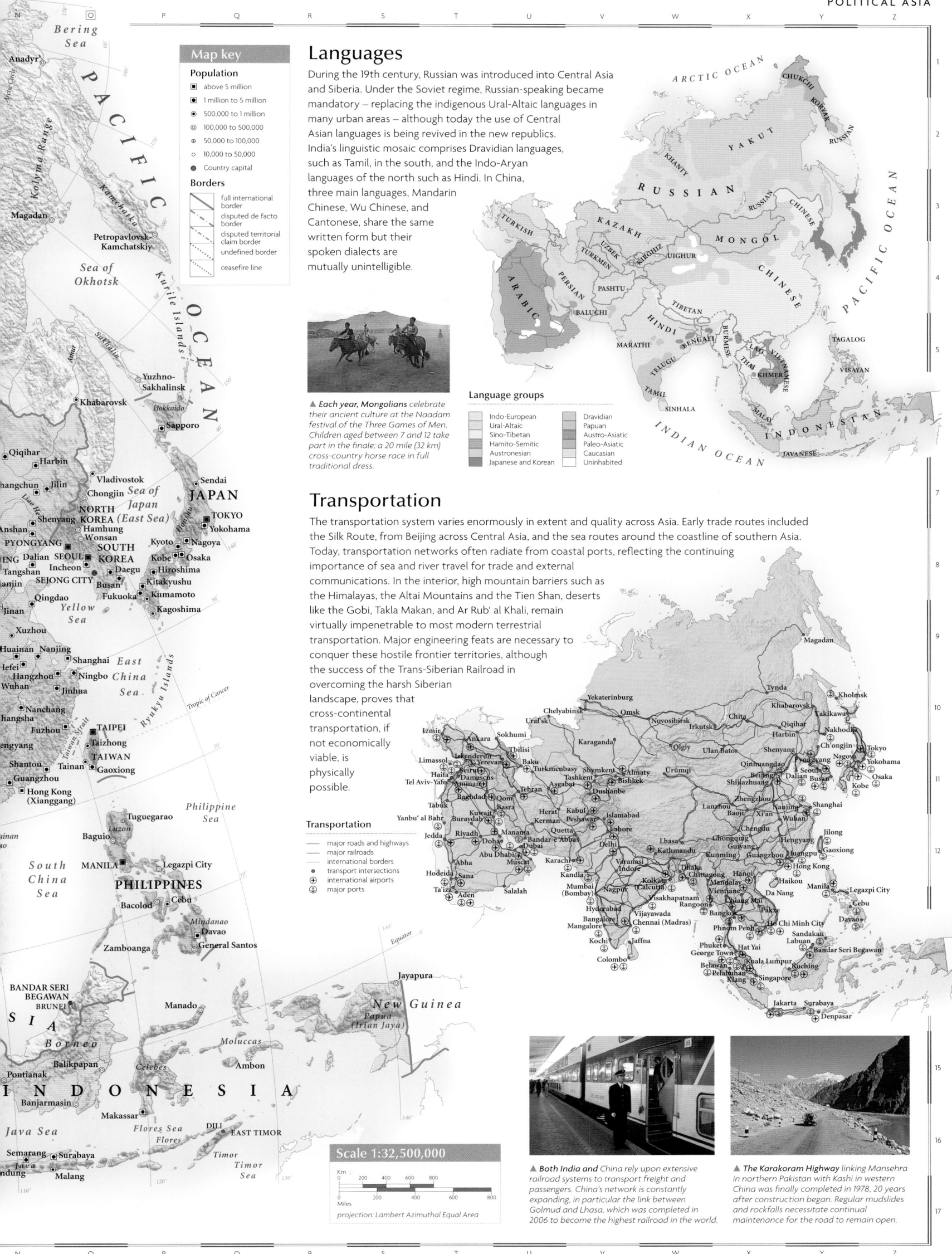

Languages

During the 19th century, Russian was introduced into Central Asia and Siberia. Under the Soviet regime, Russian-speaking became mandatory – replacing the indigenous Ural-Altaic languages in many urban areas – although today the use of Central Asian languages is being revived in the new republics. India's linguistic mosaic comprises Dravidian languages, such as Tamil, in the south, and the Indo-Aryan languages of the north such as Hindi. In China, three main languages, Mandarin Chinese, Wu Chinese, and Cantonese, share the same written form but their spoken dialects are mutually unintelligible.

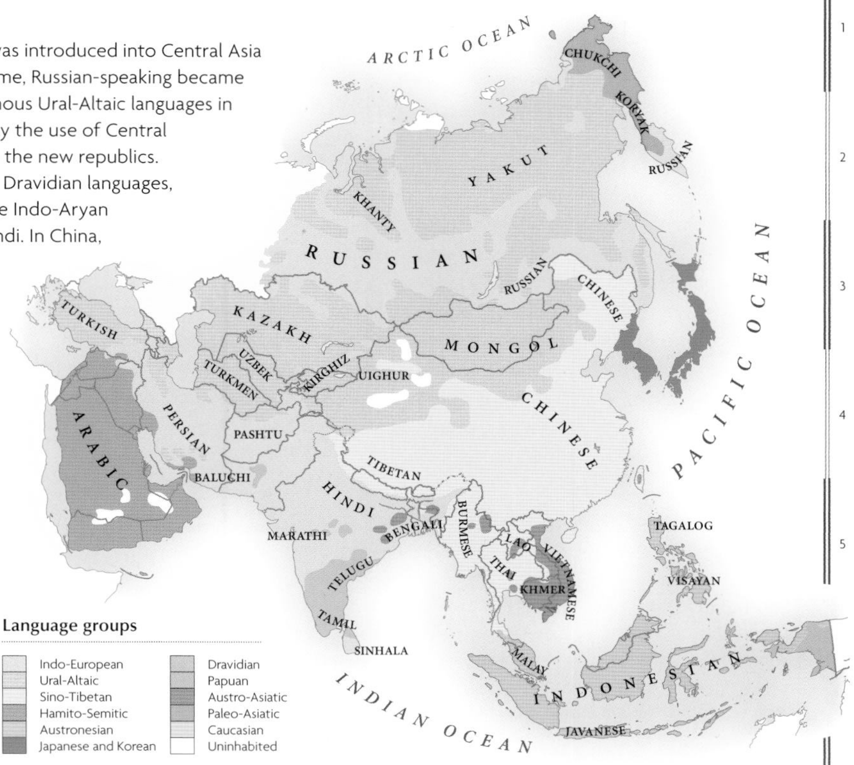

ARCTIC OCEAN
CHUKCHI
KORYAK
RUSSIAN
YAKUT
KHANTY
RUSSIAN
TURKISH
KAZAKH
RUSSIAN
CHINESE
MONGOL
PACIFIC OCEAN
UZBEK
TURKMEN
KIRGHIZ
UIGHUR
ARABIC
PERSIAN
PASHTU
CHINESE
BALUCHI
TIBETAN
HINDI
MARATHI
BENGALI
BURMESE
LAO
TAGALOG
THAI
VIETNAMESE
TELUGU
KHMER
VISAYAN
TAMIL
SINHALA
MALAY
INDONESIAN
INDIAN OCEAN
JAVANESE

▲ ***Each year, Mongolians** celebrate their ancient culture at the Naadam festival of the Three Games of Men. Children aged between 7 and 12 take part in the finale; a 20 mile (32 km) cross-country horse race in full traditional dress.*

Language groups

- Indo-European
- Ural-Altaic
- Sino-Tibetan
- Hamito-Semitic
- Austronesian
- Japanese and Korean
- Dravidian
- Papuan
- Austro-Asiatic
- Paleo-Asiatic
- Caucasian
- Uninhabited

Transportation

The transportation system varies enormously in extent and quality across Asia. Early trade routes included the Silk Route, from Beijing across Central Asia, and the sea routes around the coastline of southern Asia. Today, transportation networks often radiate from coastal ports, reflecting the continuing importance of sea and river travel for trade and external communications. In the interior, high mountain barriers such as the Himalayas, the Altai Mountains and the Tien Shan, deserts like the Gobi, Takla Makan, and Ar Rubʻ al Khali, remain virtually impenetrable to most modern terrestrial transportation. Major engineering feats are necessary to conquer these hostile frontier territories, although the success of the Trans-Siberian Railroad in overcoming the harsh Siberian landscape, proves that cross-continental transportation, if not economically viable, is physically possible.

Magadan
Yekaterinburg
Tynda
Kholmsk
Chelyabinsk
Omsk
Khabarovsk
Ural'sk
Novosibirsk
Irkutsk
Chita
Takikawa
Nakhodka
Izmir
Ankara
Sokhumi
Karaganda
Qiqihar
Harbin
Ch'ongjin
Tokyo
Tbilisi
Qlgiy
Ulan Bator
Shenyang
Limassol
Iskenderun
Yerevan
Pyongyang
Nagoya
Yokohama
Beirut
Baku
Qinhuangdao
Seoul
Osaka
Haifa
Damascus
Turkmenbasy
Shymkent
Almaty
Ürümqi
Beijing
Dalian
Busan
Tel Aviv-Yafo
Amman
Tashkent
Bishkek
Shijiazhuang
Kobe
Asgabat
Dushanbe
Baghdad
Qom
Tehran
Zhengzhou
Tabuk
Basra
Lanzhou
Nanjing
Shanghai
Herat
Kabul
Baoji
Xi'an
Yanbu' al Bahr
Kuwait
Kerman
Peshawar
Islamabad
Wuhan
Buraydah
Chengdu
Jedda
Manama
Quetta
Lahore
Jilong
Riyadh
Bandar-e 'Abbas
Lhasa
Chongqing
Hengyang
Doha
Dubai
Delhi
Kathmandu
Guiyang
Gaoxiong
Abu Dhabi
Kunming
Guangzhou
Huangpu
Abha
Muscat
Karachi
Hong Kong
Varanasi
Dhaka
Hanoi
Hodeida
Kandla
Indore
Chittagong
Haikou
Manila
Sana
Kolkata (Calcutta)
Mandalay
Legazpi City
Ta'izz
Mumbai (Bombay)
Nagpur
Vientiane
Da Nang
Aden
Salalah
Visakhapatnam
Rangoon
Chiang Mai
Cebu
Hyderabad
Pakxe
Vijayawada
Bangkok
Davao
Bangalore
Chennai (Madras)
Phnom Penh
Ho Chi Minh City
Mangalore
Sandakan
Kochi
Jaffna
Labuan
Phuket
Hat Yai
Bandar Seri Begawan
George Town
Colombo
Belawan
Kuala Lumpur
Kuching
Pelabuhan Klang
Singapore
Jakarta
Surabaya
Denpasar

Transportation

- major roads and highways
- major railroads
- international borders
- transport intersections
- international airports
- major ports

Scale 1:32,500,000

Km 0 200 400 600 800

0 200 400 600 800 Miles

projection: Lambert Azimuthal Equal Area

▲ ***Both India and** China rely upon extensive railroad systems to transport freight and passengers. China's network is constantly expanding, in particular the link between Golmud and Lhasa, which was completed in 2006 to become the highest railroad in the world.*

▲ ***The Karakoram Highway** linking Mansehra in northern Pakistan with Kashi in western China was finally completed in 1978, 20 years after construction began. Regular mudslides and rockfalls necessitate continual maintenance for the road to remain open.*

Asian resources

Although agriculture remains the economic mainstay of most Asian countries, the number of people employed in agriculture has steadily declined, as new industries have been developed during the past 30 years. China, Indonesia, Malaysia, Thailand, and Turkey have all experienced far-reaching structural change in their economies, while the breakup of the Soviet Union has created a new economic challenge in the Central Asian republics. The countries of The Persian Gulf illustrate the rapid transformation from rural nomadism to modern, urban society which oil wealth has brought to parts of the continent. Asia's most economically dynamic countries, Japan, Singapore, South Korea, and Taiwan, fringe the Pacific Ocean and are known as the Pacific Rim. In contrast, other Southeast Asian countries like Laos and Cambodia remain both economically and industrially underdeveloped.

Standard of living

Despite Japan's high standards of living, and Southwest Asia's oil-derived wealth, immense disparities exist across the continent. Afghanistan remains one of the world's most underdeveloped nations, as do the mountain states of Nepal and Bhutan. Further rapid population growth is exacerbating poverty and overcrowding in many parts of India and Bangladesh.

Standard of living
(UN human development index)

low

high

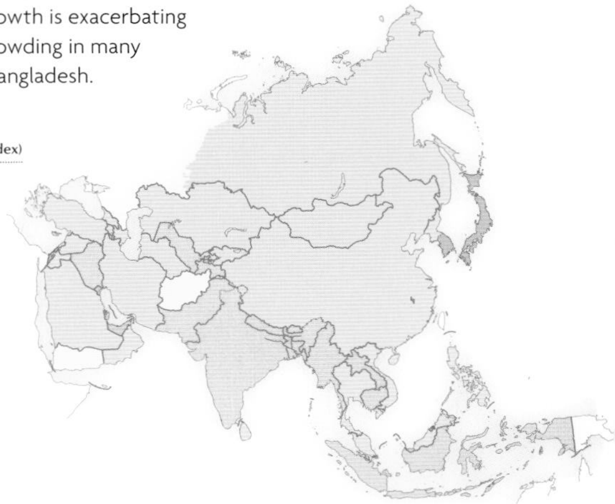

Industry

East Asian industry leads the continent in both productivity and efficiency; electronics, hi-tech industries, car manufacture, and shipbuilding are important. The so-called economic "tigers" of the Pacific Rim are Japan, South Korea, and Taiwan and in recent years China has rediscovered its potential as an economic superpower. Heavy industries such as engineering, chemicals, and steel typify the industrial complexes along the corridor created by the Trans-Siberian Railroad, the Fergana Valley in Central Asia, and also much of the huge industrial plain of east China. The discovery of oil in the Persian Gulf has brought immense wealth to countries that previously relied on subsistence agriculture on marginal desert land.

▲ *On a small island at the southern tip of the Malay Peninsula lies Singapore, one of the Pacific Rim's most vibrant economic centers. Multinational banking and finance form the core of the city's wealth.*

Industry
aerospace
brewing
car/vehicle manufacture
cement
chemicals
electronics
engineering
finance
fish processing
food processing
hi-tech industry
iron & steel
pharmaceuticals
printing & publishing
shipbuilding
sugar processing
tea processing
textiles
timber processing
tobacco processing
coal
oil
gas
industrial cities
major industrial areas
GNI per capita (US$)
below 1999
2000–4999
5000–9999
10,000–19,999
20,000–24,999
above 25,000
ARCTIC OCEAN
PACIFIC OCEAN
INDIAN OCEAN
Sea of Okhotsk
Arabian Sea
South China Sea
Gulf of Aden
Gulf of Oman
Red Sea
Caspian Sea
Aral Sea
Persian Gulf
RUSSIAN FEDERATION
KAZAKHSTAN
MONGOLIA
CHINA
JAPAN
NORTH KOREA
SOUTH KOREA
TURKEY
GEORGIA
ARMENIA
AZERB.
CYPRUS
LEBANON
SYRIA
ISRAEL
JORDAN
IRAQ
IRAN
KUWAIT
SAUDI ARABIA
BAHRAIN
QATAR
UAE
OMAN
YEMEN
TURKMENISTAN
UZBEKISTAN
KYRGYZSTAN
TAJIKISTAN
AFGHANISTAN
PAKISTAN
INDIA
NEPAL
BHUTAN
BANGLADESH
SRI LANKA
MYANMAR
THAILAND
LAOS
VIETNAM
CAMBODIA
PHILIPPINES
TAIWAN
MALAYSIA
BRUNEI
SINGAPORE
INDONESIA
EAST TIMOR
Trans-Siberian Railway
Yakutsk
Yekaterinburg
Chelyabinsk
Magnitogorsk
Omsk
Novosibirsk
Krasnoyarsk
Kemerovo
Novokuznetsk
Bratsk
Irkutsk
Khabarovsk
Vladivostok
Harbin
Karaganda
Ulan Bator
Istanbul
Izmir
Ankara
Tbilisi
Yerevan
Baku
Beirut
Damascus
Tel Aviv-Yafo
Amman
Kirkuk
Baghdad
Tehran
Isfahan
Basra
Kuwait
Ad Damman
Riyadh
Jedda
Abu Dhabi
Dubai
Asgabat
Tashkent
Almaty
Dushanbe
Farghona
Ürümqi
Shenyang
Beijing
Tianjin
Pyongyang
Dalian
Seoul
Busan
Tokyo
Nagoya
Kobe
Qingdao
Jinan
Taiyuan
Zhengzhou
Lanzhou
Nanjing
Shanghai
Xi'an
Wuhan
Chengdu
Chongqing
Taipei
Rawalpindi
Lahore
Delhi
Karachi
Kanpur
Ahmadabad
Indore
Jamshedpur
Dhaka
Chittagong
Kolkata (Calcutta)
Mandalay
Kunming
Guangzhou
Hong Kong
Hanoi
Mumbai (Bombay)
Nagpur
Rangoon
Da Nang
Manila
Bangkok
Bangalore
Chennai (Madras)
Ho Chi Minh City
Kuala Lumpur
Singapore
Jakarta
Surabaya

▲ *Iron and steel, engineering, and shipbuilding typify the heavy industry found in eastern China's industrial cities, especially the nation's leading manufacturing center, Shanghai.*

◀ *Traditional industries are still crucial to many rural economies across Asia. Here, on the Vietnamese coast, salt has been extracted from seawater by evaporation and is being loaded into a van to take to market.*

Environmental issues

The transformation of Uzbekistan by the former Soviet Union into the world's fifth largest producer of cotton led to the diversion of several major rivers for irrigation. Starved of this water, the Aral Sea diminished in volume by over 75% since 1960, irreversibly altering the ecology of the area. Heavy industries in eastern China have polluted coastal waters, rivers, and urban air, while in Myanmar, Malaysia, and Indonesia, ancient hardwood rainforests are felled faster than they can regenerate.

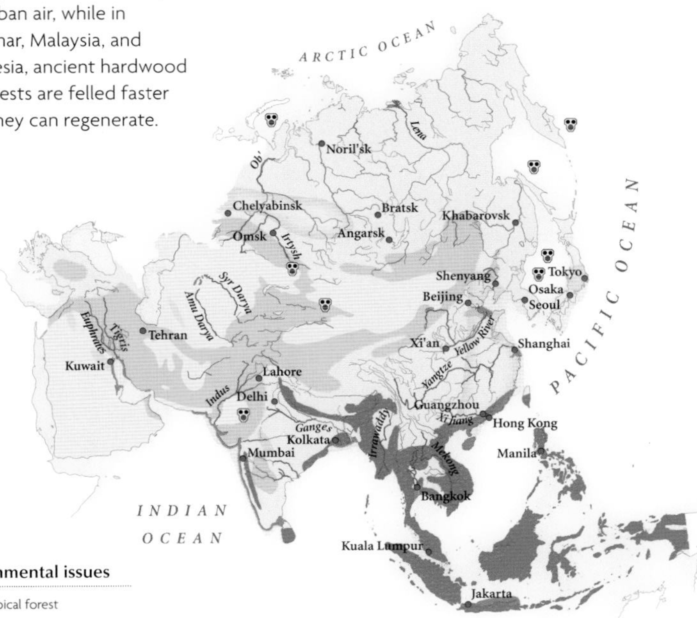
ARCTIC OCEAN
PACIFIC OCEAN
INDIAN OCEAN
Noril'sk
Lena
Ob'
Chelyabinsk
Omsk
Irtysh
Bratsk
Angarsk
Khabarovsk
Shenyang
Beijing
Tokyo
Osaka
Seoul
Syr Darya
Amu Darya
Tehran
Euphrates
Tigris
Kuwait
Xi'an
Yellow River
Shanghai
Yangtze
Lahore
Indus
Delhi
Guangzhou
Xi Jiang
Hong Kong
Ganges
Kolkata
Mumbai
Irrawaddy
Mekong
Manila
Bangkok
Kuala Lumpur
Jakarta

Environmental issues

- tropical forest
- forest destroyed
- desert
- desertification
- acid rain
- polluted rivers
- marine pollution
- heavy marine pollution
- radioactive contamination
- poor urban air quality

▲ *Although Siberia remains a quintessentially frozen, inhospitable wasteland, vast untapped mineral reserves – especially the oil and gas of the West Siberian Plain – have lured industrial development to the area since the 1950s and 1960s.*

Mineral resources

- oil field
- gas field
- coal field
- chromite
- copper
- gold
- iron
- lead
- nickel
- platinum
- tin
- wolfram

Mineral resources

At least 60% of the world's known oil and gas deposits are found in Asia; notably the vast oil fields of the Persian Gulf, and the less-exploited oil and gas fields of the Ob' basin in west Siberia. Immense coal reserves in Siberia and China have been utilized to support large steel industries. Southeast Asia has some of the world's largest deposits of tin, found in a belt running down the Malay Peninsula to Indonesia.

ARCTIC OCEAN
PACIFIC OCEAN
Himalayas
INDIAN OCEAN

◀ *Commercial logging activities in Borneo have placed great stress on the rainforest ecosystem. Government attempts to regulate the timber companies and control illegal logging have only been partially successful.*

Using the land and sea

Vast areas of Asia remain uncultivated as a result of unsuitable climatic and soil conditions. In favourable areas such as river deltas, farming is intensive. Rice is the staple crop of most Asian countries, grown in paddy fields on waterlogged alluvial plains and terraced hillsides, and often irrigated for higher yields. Across the black earth region of the Eurasian steppe in southern Siberia and Kazakhstan, wheat farming is the dominant activity. Cash crops, like tea in Sri Lanka and dates in the Arabian Peninsula, are grown for export, and provide valuable income. The sovereignty of the rich fishing grounds in the South China Sea is disputed by China, Malaysia, Taiwan, the Philippines, and Vietnam, because of potential oil reserves.

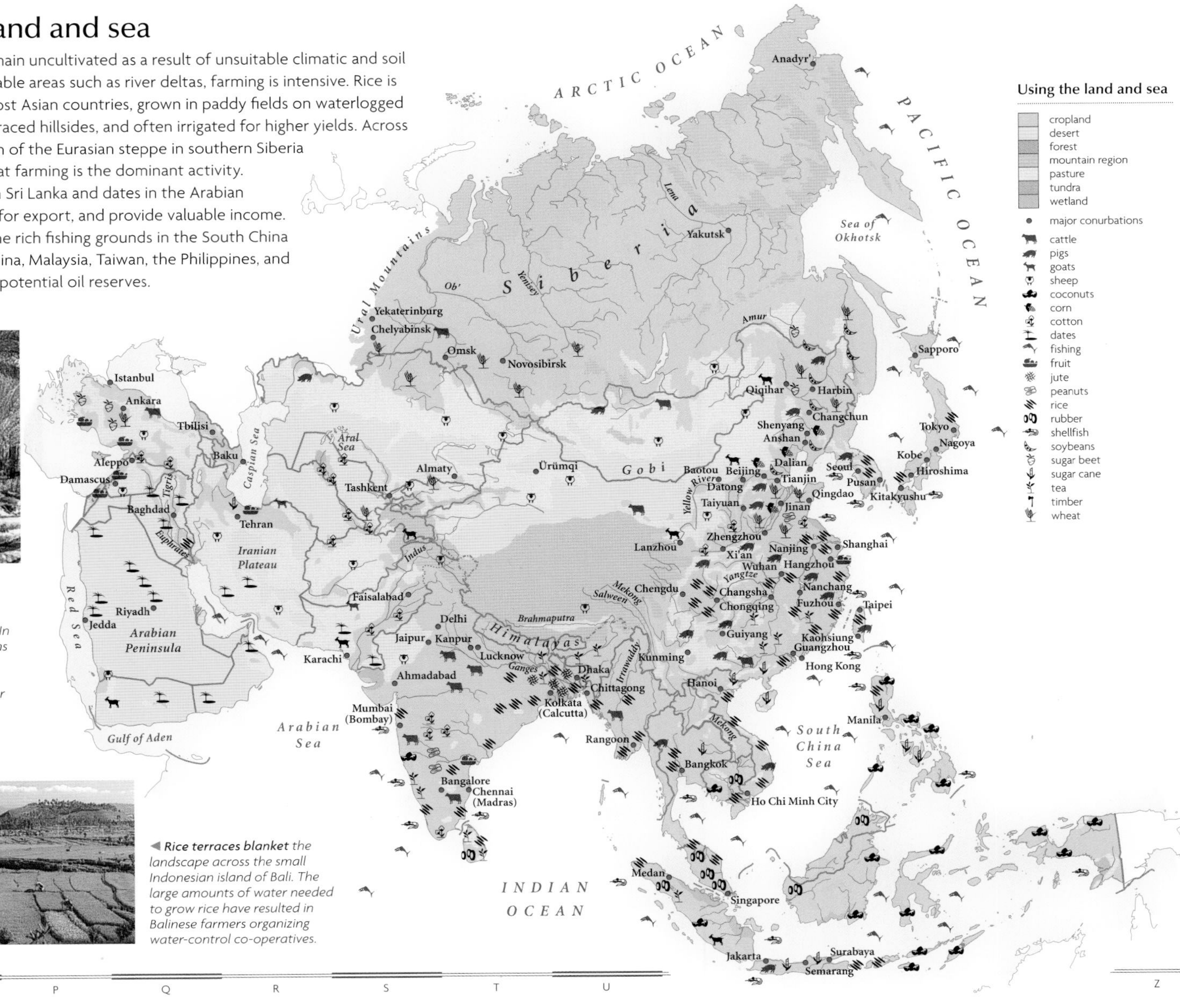
ARCTIC OCEAN
PACIFIC OCEAN
Anadyr'
Siberia
Lena
Yakutsk
Sea of Okhotsk
Ural Mountains
Ob'
Yenisey
Amur
Yekaterinburg
Chelyabinsk
Omsk
Novosibirsk
Sapporo
Istanbul
Ankara
Tbilisi
Baku
Caspian Sea
Aral Sea
Qiqihar
Harbin
Changchun
Shenyang
Anshan
Tokyo
Nagoya
Aleppo
Damascus
Tigris
Baghdad
Euphrates
Tehran
Iranian Plateau
Almaty
Tashkent
Ürümqi
Gobi
Baotou
Beijing
Dalian
Tianjin
Seoul
Pusan
Kobe
Hiroshima
Kitakyushu
Datong
Qingdao
Taiyuan
Jinan
Yellow River
Lanzhou
Zhengzhou
Xi'an
Nanjing
Shanghai
Wuhan
Hangzhou
Indus
Faisalabad
Chengdu
Yangtze
Changsha
Nanchang
Fuzhou
Taipei
Chongqing
Salween
Mekong
Brahmaputra
Himalayas
Red Sea
Riyadh
Jedda
Arabian Peninsula
Delhi
Jaipur
Kanpur
Lucknow
Guiyang
Kaohsiung
Guangzhou
Hong Kong
Kunming
Karachi
Ganges
Dhaka
Irrawaddy
Ahmadabad
Chittagong
Hanoi
Kolkata (Calcutta)
Mumbai (Bombay)
Gulf of Aden
Arabian Sea
Rangoon
Manila
South China Sea
Bangkok
Bangalore
Chennai (Madras)
Ho Chi Minh City
Medan
INDIAN OCEAN
Singapore
Jakarta
Surabaya
Semarang

Using the land and sea

- cropland
- desert
- forest
- mountain region
- pasture
- tundra
- wetland
- major conurbations
- cattle
- pigs
- goats
- sheep
- coconuts
- corn
- cotton
- dates
- fishing
- fruit
- jute
- peanuts
- rice
- rubber
- shellfish
- soybeans
- sugar beet
- sugar cane
- tea
- timber
- wheat

▲ *Date palms have been cultivated in oases throughout the Arabian Peninsula since antiquity. In addition to the fruit, palms are used for timber, fuel, rope, and for making vinegar, syrup and a liquor known as arrack.*

◀ *Rice terraces blanket the landscape across the small Indonesian island of Bali. The large amounts of water needed to grow rice have resulted in Balinese farmers organizing water-control co-operatives.*

Turkey & the Caucasus

ARMENIA, AZERBAIJAN, GEORGIA, TURKEY

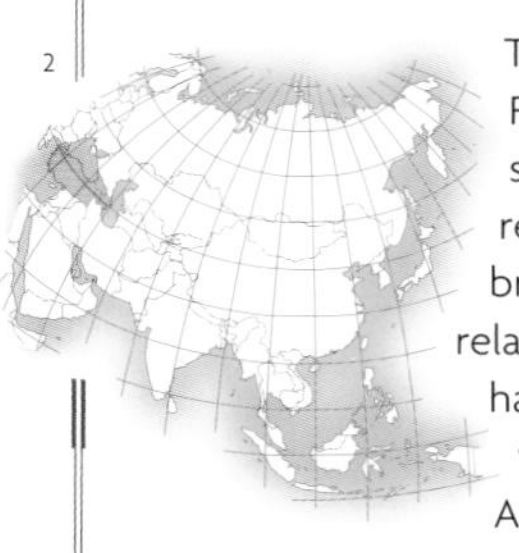

This region occupies the fragmented junction between Europe, Asia, and the Russian Federation. Sunni Islam provides a common identity for the secular state of Turkey, which the revered leader Kemal Atatürk established from the remnants of the Ottoman Empire after the First World War. Turkey has a broad resource base and expanding trade links with Europe, but the east is relatively undeveloped and strife between the state and a large Kurdish minority has yet to be resolved. Georgia is similarly challenged by ethnic separatism, while the Christian state of Armenia and the mainly Muslim and oil-rich Azerbaijan are locked in conflict over the territory of Nagorno-Karabakh.

Using the land & sea

Turkey is largely self-sufficient in food. The irrigated Black Sea coastlands have the world's highest yields of hazelnuts. Tobacco, cotton, sultanas, tea, and figs are the region's main cash crops and a great range of fruit and vegetables are grown. Wine grapes are among the labor-intensive crops which allow full use of limited agricultural land in the Caucasus. Sturgeon fishing is particularly important in Azerbaijan.

RUSSIAN FEDERATION
CASPIAN SEA
BULGARIA
BLACK SEA
GREECE
Istanbul
GEORGIA
TBILISI
ARMENIA
BAKU
AZERBAIJAN
YEREVAN
ANKARA
Samsun
Izmir
Konya
TURKEY
Diyarbakır
IRAN
Antalya
Adana
IRAQ
SYRIA
MEDITERRANEAN SEA

Land use and agricultural distribution

- cattle
- goats
- cotton
- fishing
- fruit
- hazelnuts
- olives
- sugar beet
- tobacco
- vineyards

- capital cities
- major towns

- pasture
- cropland
- forest

The urban/rural population divide

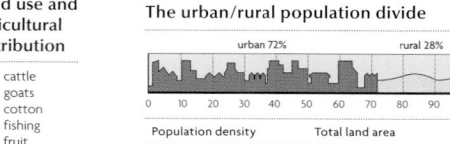

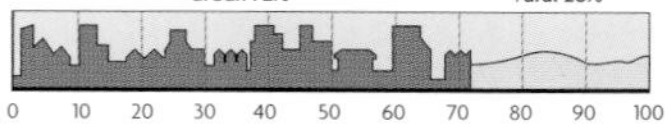
urban 72%
rural 28%
0
10
20
30
40
50
60
70
80
90
100

Population density	Total land area
238 people per sq mile (92 people per sq km)	368,912 sq miles (955,730 sq km)

Transportation & industry

Turkey leads the region's well diversified economy. Petrochemicals, textiles, engineering, and food processing are the main industries. Azerbaijan is able to export oil, while the other states rely heavily on hydroelectric power and imported fuel. Georgia produces precision machinery. War and earthquake damage have devastated Armenia's infrastructure.

▲ *Azerbaijan has substantial oil reserves, located in and around the Caspian Sea. They were some of the earliest oilfields in the world to be exploited.*

RUSSIAN FEDERATION
CASPIAN SEA
BULGARIA
BLACK SEA
GREECE
Istanbul
İzmit
Bursa
Samsun
Kutaisi
GEORGIA
TBILISI
Batumi
ARMENIA
BAKU
YEREVAN
AZERBAIJAN
ANKARA
Sivas
Erzurum
İzmir
TURKEY
Kayseri
Konya
Diyarbakır
IRAN
Antalya
Adana
Gaziantep
İskenderun
IRAQ
SYRIA
MEDITERRANEAN SEA

Major industry and infrastructure

- carpet weaving
- cement
- chemicals
- coal
- engineering
- food processing
- oil
- textiles
- tourism
- vehicle manufacture

- capital cities
- major towns
- international airports
- major roads
- major industrial areas

Transportation network

- 114,867 miles (184,882 km)
- 5778 miles (9300 km)
- 8120 miles (13,069 km)
- 745 miles (1200 km)

Physical and political barriers have severely limited communications between Armenia, Georgia and Azerbaijan. Turkey has a relatively well-developed transportation network.

▲ *For many centuries, Istanbul has held tremendous strategic importance as a crucial gateway between Europe and Asia. Founded by the Greeks as Byzantium, the city became the center of the East Roman Empire and was known as Constantinople to the Romans. From the 15th century onward the city became the center of the great Ottoman Empire.*

BULGARIA
GREECE
BLACK SEA
Edirne
Kırklareli
KIRKLARELİ
Lüleburgaz
TEKİRDAĞ
Tekirdağ
İSTANBUL
İstanbul
Marmara Denizi
(Sea of Marmara)
Çanakkale
ÇANAKKALE
Bursa
BURSA
Zonguldak
ZONGULDAK
Bartın
BARTIN
Karabük
KARABÜK
Kastamonu
KASTAMONU
Sinop
SİNOP
Samsun
SAMSUN
İzmit
KOCAELİ
Adapazarı
SAKARYA
Düzce
DÜZCE
Bolu
BOLU
Çankırı
ÇANKIRI
Çorum
ÇORUM
Amasya
AMASYA
Tokat
TOKAT
Balıkesir
BALIKESİR
Eskişehir
ESKİŞEHİR
ANKARA
Kırıkkale
KIRIKKALE
Yozgat
YOZGAT
Sivas
Aegean Sea
Kütahya
KÜTAHYA
Manisa
MANİSA
İzmir
İZMİR
Uşak
UŞAK
Afyon
AFYON
Kırşehir
KIRŞEHİR
Nevşehir
NEVŞEHİR
Kayseri
KAYSERİ
Aydın
AYDIN
Denizli
DENİZLİ
Isparta
ISPARTA
Burdur
BURDUR
Konya
KONYA
Aksaray
AKSARAY
Niğde
NİĞDE
Kahramanmaraş
KAHRAMANMARAŞ
Muğla
MUĞLA
Antalya
ANTALYA
Karaman
KARAMAN
Mersin (İçel)
İÇEL
Adana
ADANA
Osmaniye
OSMANİYE
Gaziantep
Kilis
KİLİS
Antakya
HATAY
TURKEY
Anatolia
Toros Dağları
Köroğlu Dağları
Küre Dağları
MEDITERRANEAN SEA

114
114
120

The landscape

The deeply eroded hills and salty basins of the Anatolian Plateau are bordered by several mountain ranges along the Black Sea coast, and the limestone Taurus Mountains *(Toros Daglari)* in the south. A lowland trough divides the Caucasus and the Lesser Caucasus, which form a formidable barrier of peaks in the north.

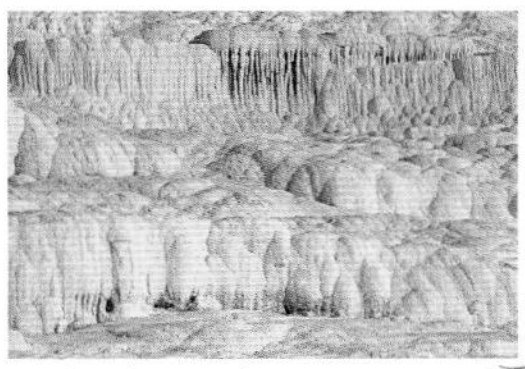

▲ *The white rock terraces at Pamukkale in western Turkey were formed when underground water, heated by volcanic activity, dissolved minerals in the rocks. When the water reached the surface and evaporated the minerals were left behind in these extraordinary formations.*

Limestone weathering in the Anatolian Plateau

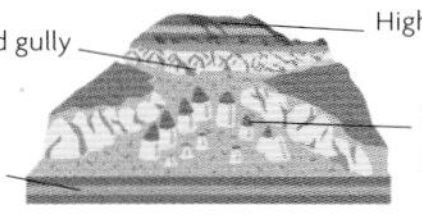

Eroded gully
High plateau
Layers of tephra
Remnant landforms

▲ ***In central Turkey,*** *rainwater has chemically weathered away numerous layers of limestone, leaving isolated outcrops and pinnacles and deep eroded gullies.*

▶ ***The Caucasus are*** *fold mountains, which formed around the same time as the Taurus Mountains (Toros Daglari) around 65 million years ago and have since been modified by volcanic eruptions.*

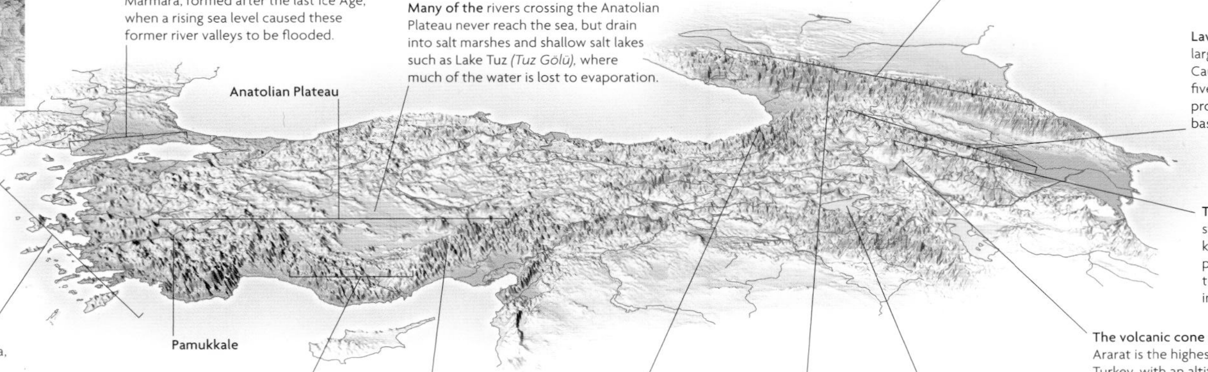

Anatolian Plateau
Pamukkale

The straits of the Bosporus and the Dardanelles, respectively linking the Black and Mediterranean seas with the Sea of Marmara, formed after the last Ice Age, when a rising sea level caused these former river valleys to be flooded.

Many of the rivers crossing the Anatolian Plateau never reach the sea, but drain into salt marshes and shallow salt lakes such as Lake Tuz *(Tuz Gölü)*, where much of the water is lost to evaporation.

Lava has flowed over large areas of the Lesser Caucasus within the last five million years, producing extensive basalt plateaus.

The earthquake that struck Armenia in 1988 killed over 55,000 people and devastated the country's infrastructure.

Long, parallel mountain ranges run from east to west into the Aegean Sea, which has risen since the last Ice Age to form a drowned coastline of numerous islands and extended inlets.

The folded peaks of the Taurus Mountains *(Toros Daglari)* were formed 60–65 million years ago, at the same time as the Alps. The rock is mainly limestone, with deep caves, gorges, and underground rivers.

The Cilician Gates *(Gülek Bogazi)*, a major pass through the Taurus Mountains *(Toros Daglari)*, is the point where streams flow from the interior plateau onto the lowland of Adana.

Thick, temperate forest veils the seaward slopes of the Kaçkar Daglari. The southern slopes, which lie in a rainshadow, are dry and barren.

The granite massif near Surami divides the lowlands of Georgia from the oil-rich basin of Azerbaijan's Kura river, which has built a large delta into the Caspian Sea.

The shallow, saline Lake Van *(Van Gölü)* is the largest lake in Turkey. Dry terraces mark a previous shoreline 181 ft (55 m) above the present water level.

The volcanic cone of Mount Ararat is the highest peak in Turkey, with an altitude of 16,853 ft (5137 m).

▶ ***Since the 6th*** *century BC, the pinnacles and caves of east-central Anatolia have been utilized as dwellings. Many are still inhabited today.*

Map key

Population

- above 5 million
- 1 million to 5 million
- 500,000 to 1 million
- 100,000 to 500,000
- 50,000 to 100,000
- 10,000 to 50,000
- below 10,000

Elevation

- 4000m / 13,124ft
- 3000m / 9843ft
- 2000m / 6562ft
- 1000m / 3281ft
- 500m / 1640ft
- 250m / 820ft
- 100m / 328ft
- sea level

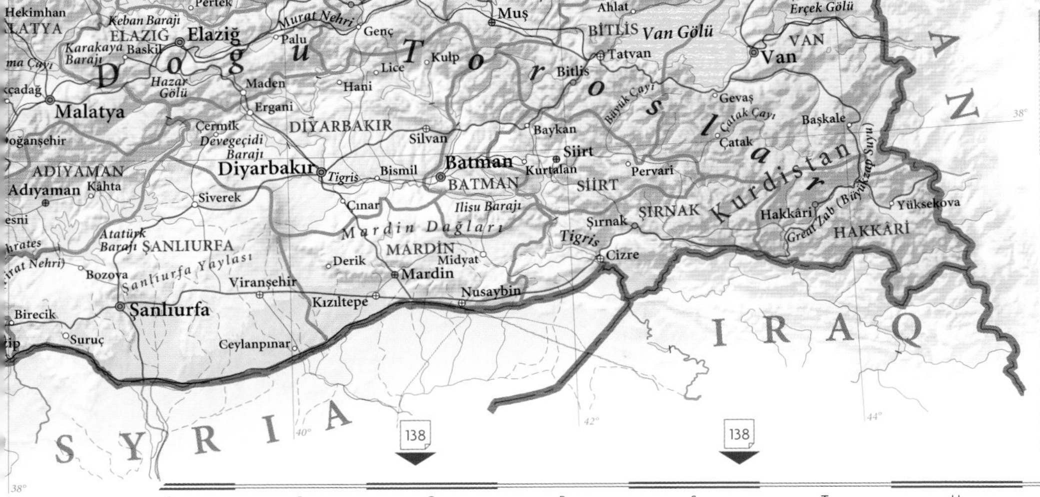

RUSSIAN FEDERATION
GEORGIA
ARMENIA
AZERBAIJAN
IRAN
IRAQ
SYRIA
Caspian Sea
TBILISI
YEREVAN
BAKI (Baku)
Sokhumi
Batumi
Kutaisi
Rustavi
Gyumri
Vanadzor
Gäncä
Sumqayit
Trabzon
Erzurum
Kars
Van
Van Gölü
Diyarbakır
Batman
Malatya
Elazığ
Şanlıurfa
Mardin

122

142

Scale 1:4,500,000

km 0 10 20 40 60 80 100 120

Miles 0 10 20 40 60 80 100 120

projection: Lambert Conformal Conic

▲ ***The fisheries of*** *Azerbaijan are noted for their hauls of sturgeon, and the Caspian Sea accounts for 80% of the world's total catch. However, stocks are now under serious threat due to overfishing.*

▲ ***Traditional steam baths*** *are found throughout the region, and are used for socializing as well as for bathing.*

138 138

The Near East

IRAQ, ISRAEL, JORDAN, LEBANON, SYRIA

Some of the world's oldest civilizations developed in this region – the Fertile Crescent – which is venerated by Jews, Muslims, and Christians, but torn by competing religious, ethnic, and national claims to the land. Turkish Ottoman rule ended with the First World War and the region was divided into areas administered by Britain and France. The UN endorsed calls for a Jewish homeland in what was then Palestine and in 1948 the state of Israel was declared. Hostility towards the Jewish state led to a series of wars with its Arab neighbors. After 2000, attempts to broker peaceful resolutions with both the Palestinian population and with adjacent Arab states were hampered by a revival of Islamic militarism and conflicting international interests in the oil-rich region. This led to an Israeli retrenchment and culminated in a US-led invasion of Iraq in 2003, which toppled the Ba'athist regime of Saddam Hussein in the name of a "war on terror".

136
120
140
TURKEY
SYRIA
LEBANON
ISRAEL
JORDAN
EGYPT
MEDITERRANEAN SEA
Halab (Aleppo)
Al Lādhiqīyah (Latakia)
Hamāh
Ḥimṣ (Homs)
BEYROUTH (BEIRUT)
DIMASHQ (DAMASCUS)
Hefa (Haifa)
Tel Aviv-Yafo
JERUSALEM
AMMAN
Irbid
Az Zarqā'
Be'er Sheva
Al 'Aqabah
Elat
Gulf of Aqaba
Dead Sea
Lake Tiberias (Sea of Galilee)
Gaza Strip
West Bank
Golan Heights
Syrian Desert
Ar Raqqah
Tudmur (Palmyra)
Ma'ān
Al Karak

Using the land & sea

Water scarcity limits cropland to the north and to areas watered principally by the Tigris, Euphrates, and Jordan rivers. In Israel, new irrigation techniques are allowing cultivation in the arid Negev. Wheat is the chief grain and large areas of scrub support livestock herding. Commercial produce includes dates, tobacco, citrus fruits, olives, grapes, and cotton, which is Syria's main export crop. Fishing is still important in the Mediterranean.

The urban/rural population divide

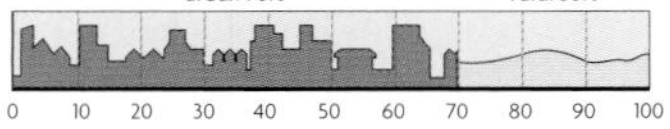

urban 70%
rural 30%
0 10 20 30 40 50 60 70 80 90 100

Population density	Total land area
217 people per sq mile (84 people per sq km)	325,460 sq miles (843,160 sq km)

Land use and agricultural distribution

- sheep
- cereals
- citrus fruits
- cotton
- dates
- fishing
- rice
- tobacco
- capital cities
- major towns
- pasture
- cropland
- wetland
- desert

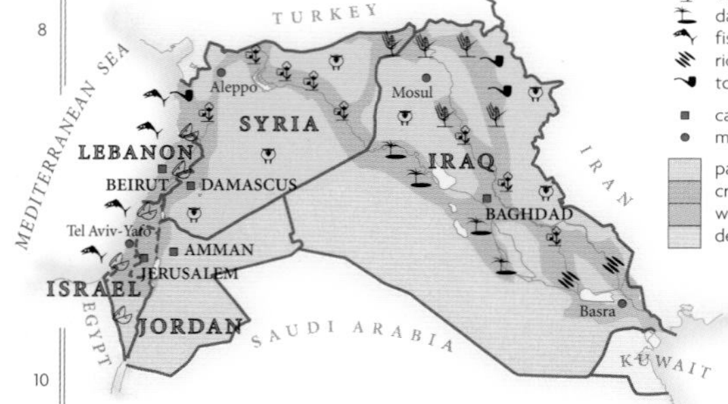

TURKEY
MEDITERRANEAN SEA
Aleppo
SYRIA
Mosul
LEBANON
BEIRUT
DAMASCUS
IRAQ
IRAN
BAGHDAD
Tel Aviv-Yafo
AMMAN
JERUSALEM
ISRAEL
JORDAN
EGYPT
SAUDI ARABIA
Basra
KUWAIT

Transportation & industry

The petrochemical industry is well established, and central to the economies of Syria and Iraq, which was the world's second largest oil exporter before the war with Iran which began in 1980. Lebanon has traditionally been a center for commerce, while Israel has a well-diversified economy with an expanding tourist industry, despite few natural resources.

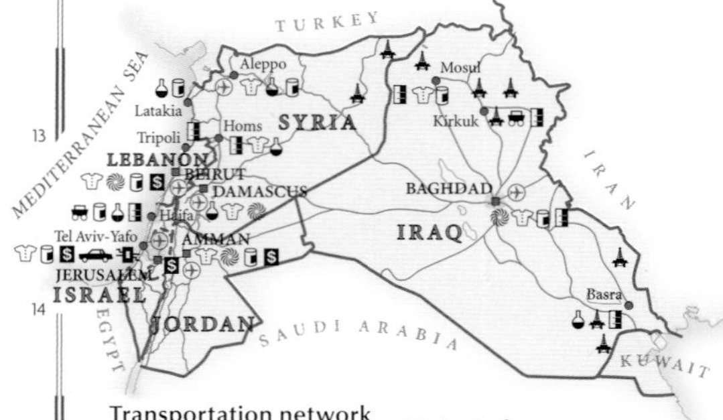

TURKEY
MEDITERRANEAN SEA
Aleppo
Mosul
Latakia
Homs
SYRIA
Kirkuk
LEBANON
BEIRUT
DAMASCUS
Haifa
BAGHDAD
IRAQ
IRAN
Tel Aviv-Yafo
AMMAN
JERUSALEM
ISRAEL
JORDAN
Basra
EGYPT
SAUDI ARABIA
KUWAIT

Transportation network

- 49,859 miles (80,249 km)
- 1365 miles (2197 km)
- 3826 miles (6158 km)
- 1171 miles (1885 km)

Jordan's seaport of Al 'Aqabah is connected to Damascus in Syria by road and rail. This route to the Red Sea provides for large exports of phosphate and trade with states in the Persian Gulf.

Major industry and infrastructure

- car manufacture
- cement
- chemicals
- electronics
- finance
- food processing
- iron & steel
- oil
- oil refining
- textiles
- capital cities
- major towns
- international airports
- major roads
- major industrial areas

▲ *The city of Petra, carved from spectacular rose-colored limestone, lies deep within a canyon in southern Jordan. Revenues from the spice trade funded the construction of the city which was built by the Nabatean people in about 400 BC.*

► *Water and wind erosion over thousands of years have created the Canyon of the Oasis at Ein 'Avdat in the Negev Desert (HaNegev). Extreme diurnal temperature fluctuations, coupled with wind erosion, have caused layers of rock to crack and peel away.*

◄ *The Dome of the Rock in Jerusalem is a magnificent mosque, revered by Muslims. Close by is the Wailing Wall, the city's most sacred Jewish landmark and the Church of the Holy Sepulchre, a famous Christian place of worship.*

The landscape

The Al Jazirah plateau divides the Euphrates and Tigris rivers, which cross the Mesopotamian plain to reach their confluence in the southeast. The rocky Syrian Desert extends west to the northern extremity of the Great Rift Valley, which runs from the mountains of Lebanon to the Gulf of Aqaba. The Jordan river flows south along this trough into the Dead Sea, divided from the Mediterranean coastal plain by a steep-sided plateau.

N O P Q R S T U V W X Y Z
1 2 3 4 5 6 7 8 9 10 11 15 16 17
Kurdistan
IRAN
IRAQ
ARABIA
KUWAIT
Persian Gulf
AL JAZIRAH
AL HASAKAH
NĪNAWÁ
DAHŪK
ARBĪL
AS SULAYMĀNĪYAH
AT TA'MĪM
ŞALĀH AD DĪN
DIYĀLÁ
AL ANBĀR
BĀBIL
KARBALĀ'
WĀSIT
AL QĀDISĪYAH
MAYSĀN
DHĪ QĀR
AN NAJAF
AL MUTHANNÁ
AL BAŞRAH
BAGHDAD
Al Mawşil (Mosul)
Arbīl
Kirkūk
As Sulaymānīyah
Tikrīt
Sāmarrā'
Ba'qūbah
Al Fallūjah
Ar Ramādī
Karbalā'
Al Hillah
An Najaf
Ad Dīwānīyah
Al Kūt
Al 'Amārah
An Nāşirīyah
As Samāwah
Al Başrah (Basra)
Ar Ruţbah
Al Qāmishlī
Al Hasakah
Zākhō
Dahūk
Tigris
Euphrates
Great Zab
Little Zab
Buhayrat ath Tharthār
Buhayrat al Habbānīyah
Hawr al Hammār
Map key
Population
1 million to 5 million
500,000 to 1 million
100,000 to 500,000
50,000 to 100,000
10,000 to 50,000
below 10,000
Elevation
4000m / 13,124ft
3000m / 9843ft
2000m / 6562ft
1000m / 3281ft
500m / 1640ft
250m / 820ft
100m / 328ft
sea level
Scale 1: 3,500,000
Km 0 10 20 40 60 80 100
Miles 0 10 20 40 60 80 100
projection: Lambert Conformal Conic

140

142

142

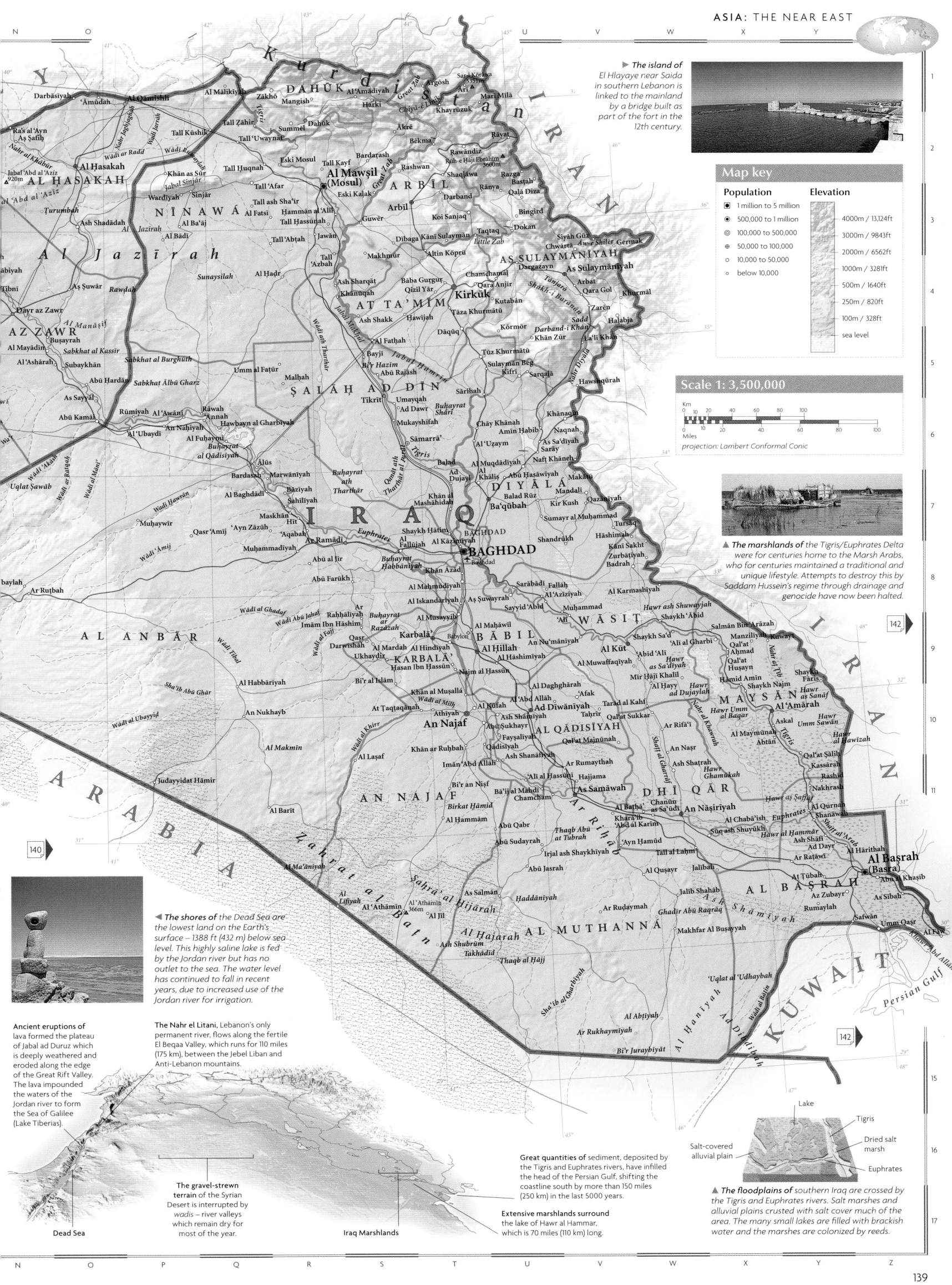

▶ *The island of El Hlayaye near Saida in southern Lebanon is linked to the mainland by a bridge built as part of the fort in the 12th century.*

▲ ***The marshlands of*** *the Tigris/Euphrates Delta were for centuries home to the Marsh Arabs, who for centuries maintained a traditional and unique lifestyle. Attempts to destroy this by Saddam Hussein's regime through drainage and genocide have now been halted.*

◀ ***The shores of*** *the Dead Sea are the lowest land on the Earth's surface – 1388 ft (432 m) below sea level. This highly saline lake is fed by the Jordan river but has no outlet to the sea. The water level has continued to fall in recent years, due to increased use of the Jordan river for irrigation.*

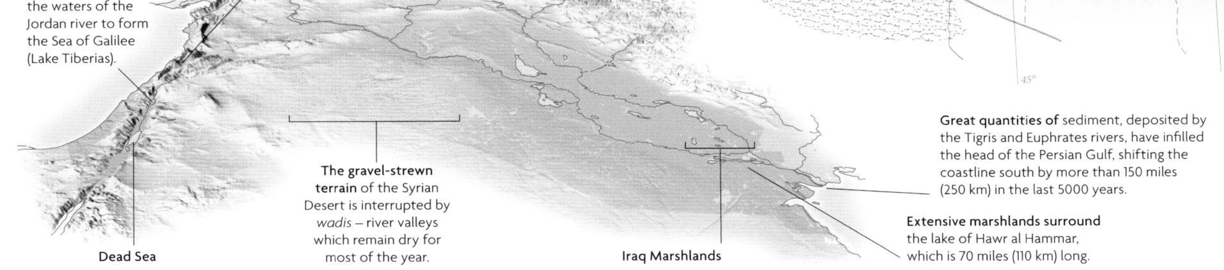
Dead Sea
Iraq Marshlands

Ancient eruptions of lava formed the plateau of Jabal ad Duruz which is deeply weathered and eroded along the edge of the Great Rift Valley. The lava impounded the waters of the Jordan river to form the Sea of Galilee (Lake Tiberias).

The Nahr el Litani, Lebanon's only permanent river, flows along the fertile El Beqaa Valley, which runs for 110 miles (175 km), between the Jebel Liban and Anti-Lebanon mountains.

The gravel-strewn terrain of the Syrian Desert is interrupted by *wadis* – river valleys which remain dry for most of the year.

Great quantities of sediment, deposited by the Tigris and Euphrates rivers, have infilled the head of the Persian Gulf, shifting the coastline south by more than 150 miles (250 km) in the last 5000 years.

Extensive marshlands surround the lake of Hawr al Hammar, which is 70 miles (110 km) long.

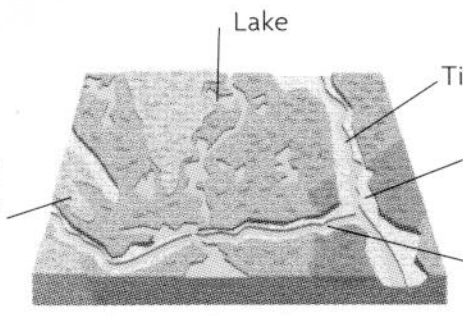
Lake
Tigris
Salt-covered alluvial plain
Dried salt marsh
Euphrates

▲ ***The floodplains of*** *southern Iraq are crossed by the Tigris and Euphrates rivers. Salt marshes and alluvial plains crusted with salt cover much of the area. The many small lakes are filled with brackish water and the marshes are colonized by reeds.*

The Arabian Peninsula

BAHRAIN, KUWAIT, OMAN, QATAR, SAUDI ARABIA, UNITED ARAB EMIRATES (UAE), YEMEN

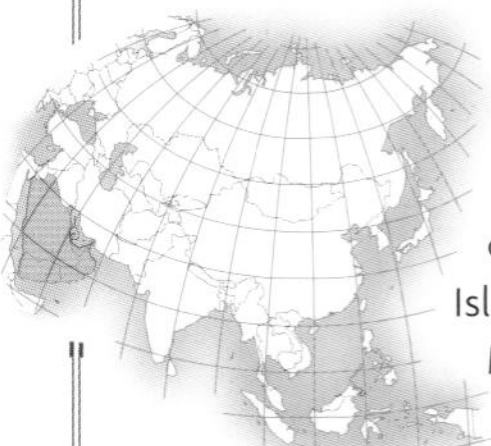

Huge expanses of desert cover much of the Arabian Peninsula, limiting settlement to oases, the mountains along the Red Sea, and coastal belts. The most populous area is the fertile highlands of Yemen. The Islamic faith and Arabic language give the region a cultural and religious unity, and the Saudi city of Mecca *(Makkah)* is Islam's most holy place, visited by over two million pilgrims each year. More than half the world's oil reserves are contained in this region, and the exploitation of oil and gas has brought great wealth, particularly to Saudi Arabia. Yemen and Oman are the least developed of the Arabian states, with large rural populations. Within Saudi Arabia over 86% of the people live in urban areas.

Using the land

Most of the Arabian Peninsula is unsuited to settled agriculture, making irrigation and land reclamation projects essential. The narrow coastal plain and isolated oases, commonly amounting to less than 1% of the land area, are used to cultivate grains, coffee, and exotic fruits. Goats, sheep, and camels are widespread throughout the region.

The urban/rural population divide

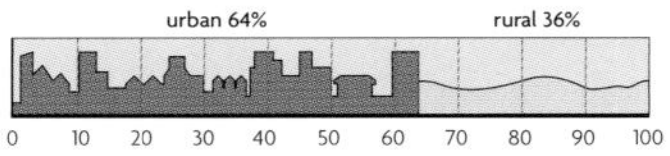
urban 64%
rural 36%
0 10 20 30 40 50 60 70 80 90 100

Population density	Total land area
50 people per sq mile (19 people per sq km)	1,147,856 sq miles (2,973,720 sq km)

Land use and agricultural distribution

goats, sheep, cereals, coffee, dates, fruit; capital cities, major towns; pasture, cropland, desert

IRAQ
JORDAN
ISRAEL
EGYPT
KUWAIT
Persian Gulf
IRAN
BAHRAIN
MANAMA
QATAR
DOHA
Dubai
ABU DHABI
UAE
OMAN
Gulf of Oman
MUSCAT
RIYADH
Medina
Jedda
SAUDI ARABIA
Red Sea
SUDAN
ERITREA
Abha
SANA
YEMEN
Aden
ARABIAN SEA
Socotra (to Yemen)
Gulf of Aden
Bab el Mandeb
DJIBOUTI
SOMALIA
SOMALILAND

◀ *The fertile soils of Yemen have encouraged settlement of almost all of the land from sea level up to the mountains at 10,000 ft (3050 m). In the higher reaches elaborate terraces have been constructed to facilitate crop cultivation.*

The landscape

A plateau more than 2500 ft (760 m) high extends across much of the Arabian Peninsula. The plateau slopes eastward from the massive, rifted escarpment along the coast of the Red Sea, to the shallow waters of the Persian Gulf. The interior is characterized by *cuesta*s and valleys, drained by a system of *wadis*. A crescent of sand and gravel deserts lies to the east.

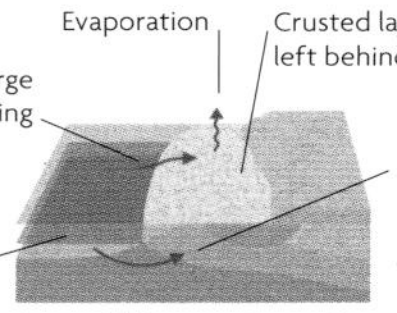
Evaporation
Crusted layer left behind
Storm surge flooding
Normal level of tidal range
Salt wedge penetrates inland water

▲ *A sabkha is a flat, salt-encrusted plain which occurs near the coast just above the high water mark. Flooding by sea water leads to saturation of the land with saline-rich groundwater. As this evaporates, a cracked layer of sand, cemented together with salt, gypsum, and calcium carbonate is left behind.*

The An Nafud Desert is covered with *barchan* dunes varying between 30–100 ft (10–30 m) high. The "horns" of the crescent-shaped dunes reflect the direction in which they are being moved by the wind.

Inselbergs are dotted over a wide area of the Najd Plateau. These resistant remnants of the ancient basement rock are left standing when the softer weathered rock has been worn away.

Few areas in the Arabian Peninsula have rivers flowing through them. Most are drained by ephemeral watercourses called *wadis*.

Across the Najd Plateau the flat relief is broken by *mesas*; steep-sided rock plateaus and *cuestas*; ridges with one steep and one gentle slope.

The Hejaz *(Al Hijaz)* and Asir mountains form part of the same geological region as the highlands of Sudan and Eritrea, to which they were once joined. They were separated when faulting opened the Red Sea, over 50 million years ago.

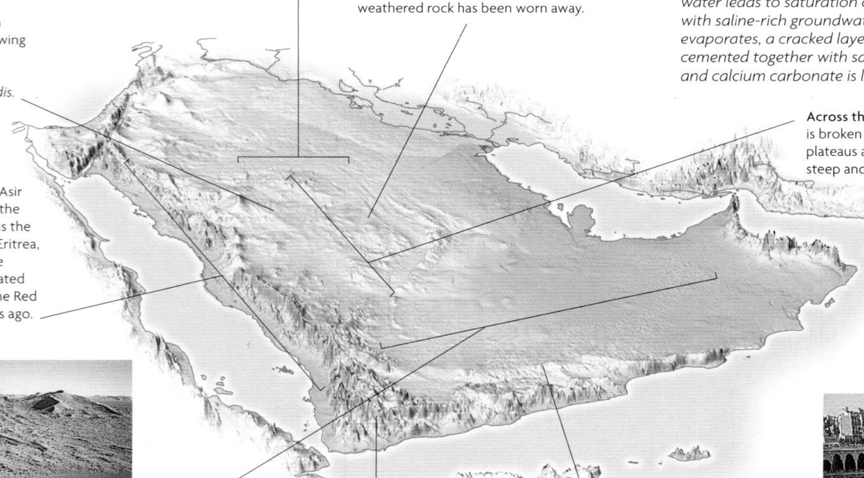

▲ ***Ar Rubʿ al Khali,*** *also known as the Empty Quarter, is the most arid part of the Arabian Peninsula. It is the largest uninterrupted sand desert in the world. Ridges of sand up to 25 miles (40 km) long, run northeast–southwest, giving characteristic linear dunes.*

The Jabal an Nabi Shu'ayb in Yemen is the highest point on the peninsula, rising to 12,336 ft (3760 m).

The Arabian Shield underpins the west of the peninsula. It is a fragment of the ancient continent, Gondwanaland, which was separated by rifting millions of years ago.

◀ ***Every Muslim must*** *make at least one pilgrimage or hajj to Mecca (Makkah), in Saudi Arabia, during their lifetime. The cloth-covered shrine is called the Kaʿbah, and is regarded by Muslims as the most sacred place on Earth.*

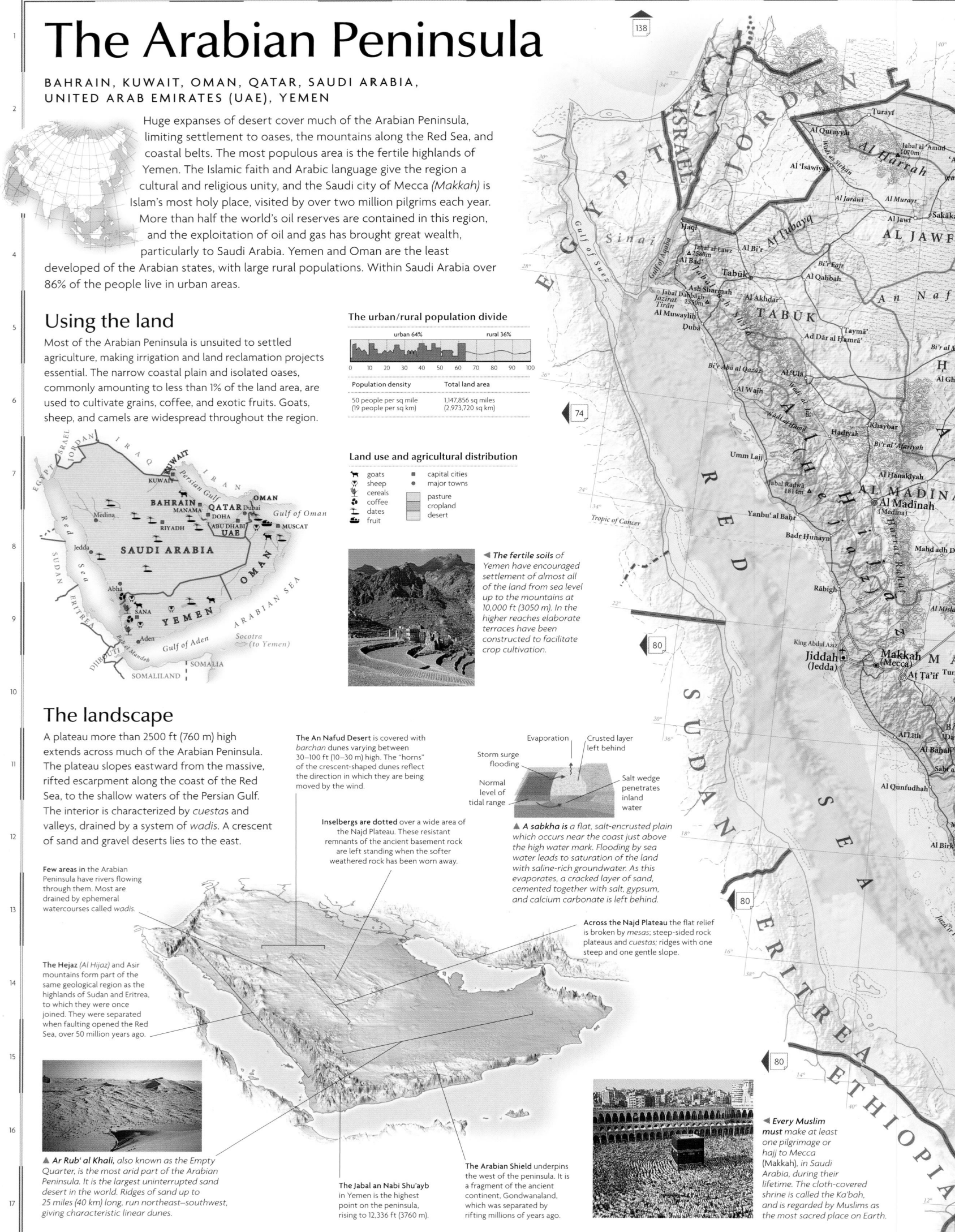

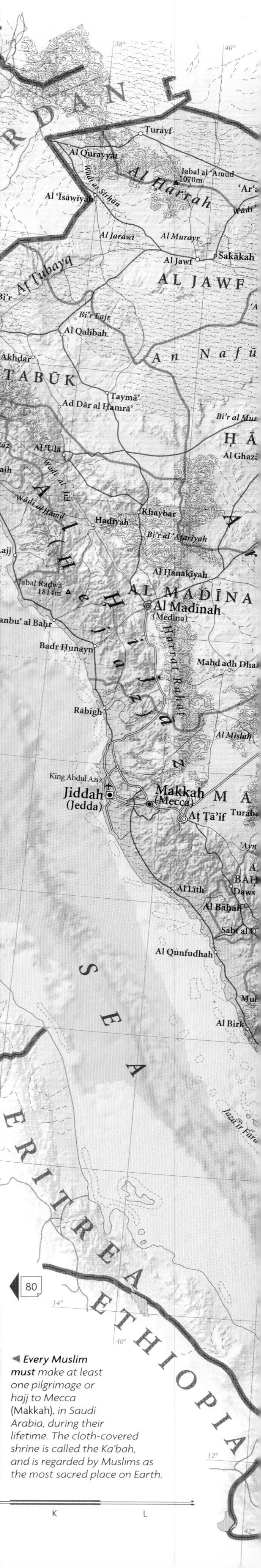
138
ISRAEL
JORDAN
EGYPT
Sinai
Gulf of Suez
Gulf of Aqaba
Turayf
Al Qurayyat
Al Harrah
Al ʿIsawiyah
Al Jarawi
Al Murayr
Sakakah
Al Jawf
AL JAWF
Haql
Al Bi'r
Al Bad'
Tabuk
Al Qalibah
TABUK
Al Akhdar
Al Muwaylih
Duba
Tayma'
An Nafud
Al Wajh
Al ʿUla
Khaybar
Umm Lajj
Al Hanakiyah
AL MADINA
Al Madinah (Medina)
Yanbuʿ al Bahr
Badr Hunayn
Tropic of Cancer
Rabigh
King Abdul Aziz
Jiddah (Jedda)
Makkah (Mecca)
At Ta'if
RED SEA
Al Lith
Al Qunfudhah
SUDAN
ERITREA
ETHIOPIA
74
80

N O P Q R S T U V W X Y

138

◀ *Saudi Arabia contains the world's largest oil reserves, lying mainly along the Persian Gulf coast. Each day the region produces around 10 million barrels of oil. Here, in the desert, excess oil is being burnt off.*

Transportation & industry

The extraction and refining of oil and gas are the major industrial activities in the Arabian Peninsula. The region also has an active construction sector, with many Arab cities reflecting the wealth generated by the oil industry. The service sector is dominated by financial and technical institutions, which, like the construction sector, mainly serve the oil industry. Traditional handicrafts such as carpet-weaving are found in rural areas.

Transportation network

44,832 miles (72,159 km)	673 miles (1083 km)
670 miles (1078 km)	none

Internal surface transportation is poorly developed across the peninsula. Along the coast, commercial routes have developed, but connections between bordering states rely on major airports.

ISRAEL
JORDAN
IRAQ
EGYPT
KUWAIT
Persian Gulf
IRAN
Al Jubayl
Ad Dammam
BAHRAIN
MANAMA
QATAR
DOHA
OMAN
Dubai
ABU DHABI
UAE
Gulf of Oman
MUSCAT
Yanbu' al Bahr
RIYADH
Red Sea
Jedda
SAUDI ARABIA
SUDAN
OMAN
ERITREA
SANA
YEMEN
Al Mukalla
ARABIAN SEA
Aden
Bab el Mandeb
Gulf of Aden
Socotra (to Yemen)
DJIBOUTI
SOMALILAND
SOMALIA

Major industry and infrastructure

cement	capital cities
chemicals	major towns
iron & steel	international airports
oil	major roads
oil refining	major industrial areas
food processing	

142

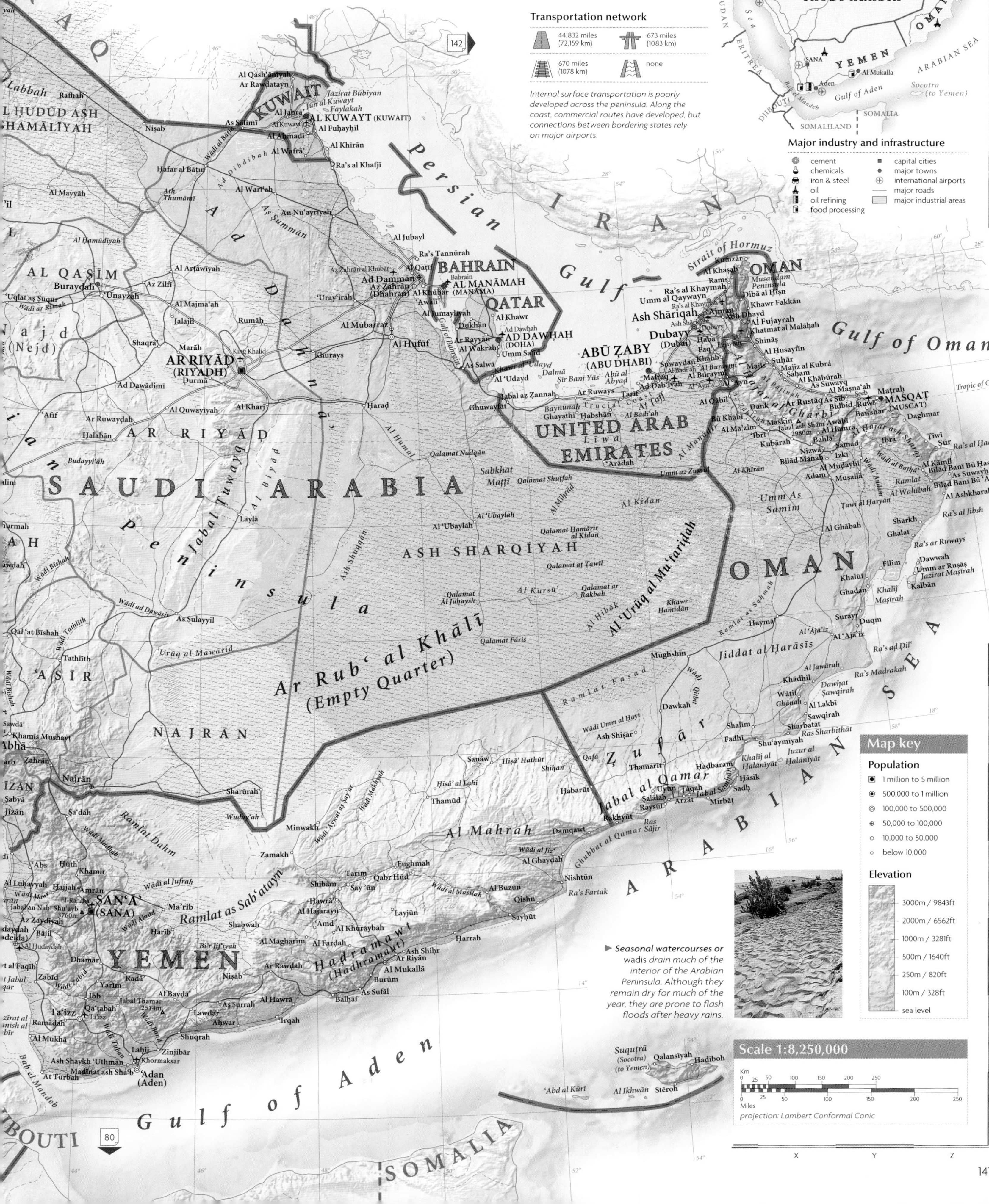

IRAQ
KUWAIT
AL KUWAYT (KUWAIT)
Persian Gulf
IRAN
Strait of Hormuz
BAHRAIN
AL MANĀMAH (MANAMA)
QATAR
AD DAWḤAH (DOHA)
ABŪ ẒABY (ABU DHABI)
Dubayy (Dubai)
UNITED ARAB EMIRATES
OMAN
MASQAṬ (MUSCAT)
Gulf of Oman
Tropic of Cancer
AL QAṢĪM
Najd (Nejd)
AR RIYĀḌ (RIYADH)
AR RIYĀḌ
SAUDI ARABIA
Arabian Peninsula
Ad Dahnā'
ASH SHARQĪYAH
Ar Rub' al Khālī (Empty Quarter)
NAJRĀN
'ASĪR
Ẓufār
Al Mahrah
Ḥaḍramawt (Hadhramaut)
Ramlat as Sab'atayn
YEMEN
ṢAN'Ā' (SANA)
'Adan (Aden)
Gulf of Aden
ARABIAN SEA
Suquṭrā (Socotra) (to Yemen)
DJIBOUTI
SOMALIA
Bab el Mandeb

▶ *Seasonal watercourses or wadis drain much of the interior of the Arabian Peninsula. Although they remain dry for much of the year, they are prone to flash floods after heavy rains.*

Map key

Population

- 1 million to 5 million
- 500,000 to 1 million
- 100,000 to 500,000
- 50,000 to 100,000
- 10,000 to 50,000
- below 10,000

Elevation

- 3000m / 9843ft
- 2000m / 6562ft
- 1000m / 3281ft
- 500m / 1640ft
- 250m / 820ft
- 100m / 328ft
- sea level

Scale 1:8,250,000

Km 0 25 50 100 150 200 250
Miles 0 25 50 100 150 200 250

projection: Lambert Conformal Conic

80

X Y Z

Iran & the Gulf states

136

BAHRAIN, IRAN, KUWAIT, QATAR, UNITED ARAB EMIRATES (UAE)

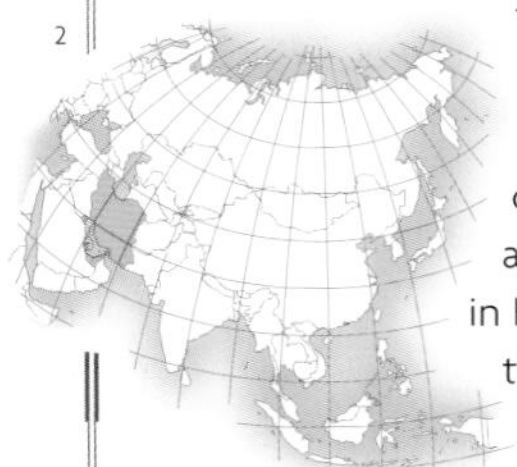

The discovery of oil in the Persian Gulf in the 1930s brought great wealth to the surrounding states. The revenue was largely used to modernize industry and infrastructure, initiating great social change in these formerly agrarian countries. Today, over 90% of the people in the Gulf states live in urban areas, and foreign nationals make up a sizeable proportion of the population in Kuwait, Qatar, and the United Arab Emirates. The importance of control of the oil reserves has led to a number of territorial disputes, including most recently the Iran–Iraq War (1980-88) and the First Gulf War (1991). Islam is practiced almost exclusively throughout the region and two distinct strands are found; Sunni Muslims in Qatar, Kuwait, and UAE, and Shi'a Muslims in Iran and Bahrain. In 1979 Iran became the world's largest theocracy.

138

The landscape

The land rises steeply from the fragmented coastal lowlands bordering the Persian Gulf, to reach Iran's interior plateau, bounded by heavily eroded mountain chains. An unstable plate boundary runs northwest to southeast across Iran causing frequent earthquakes. On the sandy west coast of the Persian Gulf, the relief is generally flat, with patches of salt marsh. Bahrain consists of two groups of islands, which are mostly small and rocky.

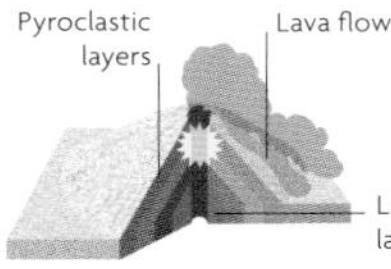

Pyroclastic layers
Lava flow
Lava flow layers

▲ *Qolleh-ye Damavand in the Elburz Mountains is a composite volcano. It comprises layers of lava and pyroclastic fragmentary rocks which accumulate on the slopes of the volcano after being ejected into the air.*

▲ *Marine sediments from deep beneath the ancient Tethys Sea have been uplifted to form the Elburz Mountains, which stretch along the shores of the Caspian Sea, northern Iran.*

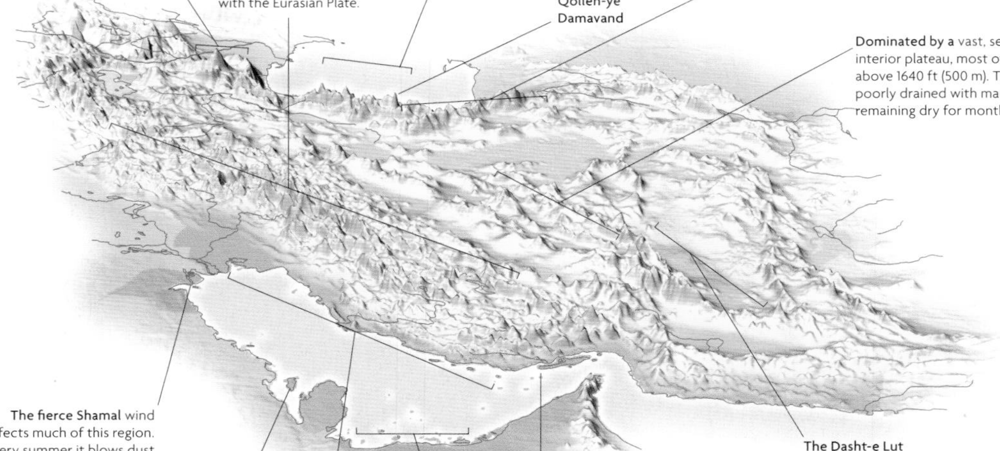

Caspian Sea
Qolleh-ye Damavand
The Dasht-e Lut

Lava and ash from previous volcanic activity covers a 200 mile (320 km) stretch from the border with Azerbaijan to the Caspian Sea.

Iran's two mountain chains, the Zagros and Elburz, were uplifted at the same time as the Alps in Europe, when the African Plate collided with the Eurasian Plate.

Dominated by a vast, semi-arid interior plateau, most of Iran lies above 1640 ft (500 m). The region is poorly drained with many of its basins remaining dry for months at a time.

The fierce Shamal wind affects much of this region. Every summer it blows dust south from the flood plains of the Tigris and Euphrates, reducing visibility to such an extent that Kuwait International Airport is frequently forced to close.

Autumn winds blowing across the Persian Gulf can reach speeds of up to 95 mph (150 kmph) causing severe storms, squalls, and waterspouts.

Prolific springs tapping artesian water make cultivation possible across the north of Bahrain's main island. This provides a sharp contrast to the sandy plains in the south and west.

The oilfields of the Persian Gulf are formed from marine shale deposits lying in sedimentary basins at the margins of the Zagros Mountains.

Numerous islands lie along the southern coast of the Persian Gulf. Some of these are salt domes, created when less dense salts were displaced and forced up to the surface by denser, overlying strata.

◀ *The Dasht-e Lut covers a large portion of eastern Iran with its dry, wind-eroded plain of scattered sandstone pillars and salty depressions. During the summer, temperatures soar, making it one of the world's hottest, driest places.*

140

Using the land & sea

Along the coast of the Caspian Sea, desalinated water allows fruits and vegetables to be produced, although water shortages and desert soils still limit farming. Sheep are the most important livestock raised in Iran and commercial forests cover the northwest of the country. Shrimp stocks were decimated by pollution during the Gulf War, but fishing remains important for domestic and export markets.

ARMENIA
AZERBAIJAN
TURKEY
Tabriz
Caspian Sea
TURKMENISTAN
Mashhad
TEHRAN
IRAQ
IRAN
Esfahan
AFGHANISTAN
Abadan
KUWAIT
KUWAIT
Kerman
Shiraz
PAKISTAN
Persian Gulf
Bandar-e Abbas
SAUDI ARABIA
BAHRAIN
MANAMA
DOHA
QATAR
ABU DHABI
Gulf of Oman
U.A.E.
OMAN

Land use and agricultural distribution

goats	capital cities
sheep	major towns
cereals	pasture
citrus fruits	cropland
cotton	forest
dates	desert
fishing	wetland
timber	

The urban/rural population divide

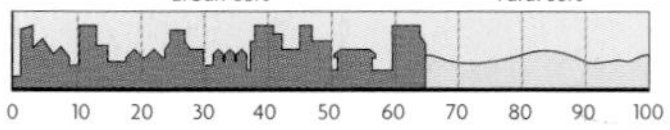

urban 65%
rural 35%
0
10
20
30
40
50
60
70
80
90
100

Population density	Total land area
112 people per sq mile (43 people per sq km)	642,883 sq miles (1,665,500 sq km)

◀ *All of the Gulf states have commercial fishing fleets. Before the discovery of oil, fishing was the region's leading industry.*

◀ *The Kuwait Towers in the center of Kuwait are symbols of the vast wealth oil has brought to the country. Before 1960, the city had only one main street and was surrounded by a mud wall.*

136
ARMENIA
AZERBAIJAN
TURKEY
Mākū
Sīāh Chashmeh
Khvoy
Salmās
Qūshchī
Orūmīyeh
Tabrīz
Marand
Zonūz
Sūfīān
Ahar
Kuhhā-ye Sabalān 4811m
Ardabīl
ĀZARBĀYJĀN-E SHARQĪ
Bostānābad
Hashtrūd
Bonāb
Marāgheh
Mīāneh
Khalkhāl
Rasht
Bandar-e Anzalī
Fowman
Naqadeh
Pīrānshahr
Mahābād
Mīāndowāb
ĀZARBĀYJĀN-E GHARBĪ
Būkān
Zanjān
Soltānīyeh
ZANJĀN
Qazvīn
Abhar
Qeydār
Saqqez
Bāneh
Dīvāndarreh
Bījār
KORDESTĀN
Marīvān
Sanandaj
Qorveh
Pāveh
HAMADĀN
Hamadān
Qasr-e Shīrīn
Sar-e Pol-e Zahāb
Sonqor
Kermānshāh (Bākhtarān)
Kangāvar
Tūysarkān
KERMĀNSHĀH
Eslāmābād-e Gharb
Malāyer
Arāk
Eyvān
Īlām
Borūjerd
LORESTĀN
Khorramābād
Dorūd
Āmirābād
Mehrān
Darreh Shahr
ĪLĀM
Dehlorān
Andīmeshk
Dezfūl
Shūsh
Shūshtar
Masjed Soleymān
Sūsangerd
KHŪZESTĀN
Ahvāz
Khorramshahr
Ābādān
Behbahān
Bandar-e Māhshahr
Omīdīyeh
Shatt al Arab
IRAQ
Al Qash'ānīyah
Ar Rawdatayn
KUWAIT
Jazīrat Būbīyān
Jūn al Kuwayt
Faylakah
Al Jahrā'
AL KUWAYT (KUWAIT)
As Sālimī
Al Aḥmadī
Al Fuḥayḥīl
Aş Şubayḥīyah
Al Khīrān
Al Wafrā'
Persian Gulf
SAUDI ARABIA
AL MANĀMA (MANAMA)
Tropic of Cancer

◀ *Many volcanoes lie in Iran's 1200 mile (1930 km) volcanic belt, including the country's highest peak, the now-extinct Qolleh-ye Damavand at 18,600 ft (5671 m).*

146

▶ *Extensive oil and gas exploitation in the Gulf region has allowed the economic transformation of the Gulf states. Consequently, many of these states have a hugely improved per capita income compared to the 1960's.*

Transportation & industry

Both onshore and offshore oil reserves are exploited throughout the region. Kuwait not only extracts but also refines 80% of its oil. Bahrain has diversified its economy to become the main commercial and financial center in the Persian Gulf. Iran produces a wide range of products: textile mills are widespread and carpet weaving is an important export industry.

Major industry and infrastructure

- carpet manufacture
- chemicals
- finance
- food processing
- oil
- oil refining
- textiles
- capital city
- major towns
- international airports
- major roads
- major industrial areas

Transportation network

63,543 miles (102,274 km)	884 miles (1423 km)
3822 miles (6151 km)	562 miles (904 km)

Major towns and neighboring countries are linked by adequate road networks, although rural areas are less well served. Bahrain is linked to the mainland by a 15 mile (25 km) long causeway.

N O P Q R S T U V W X Y
1 2 3 4 5 6 7 8 9 10 15 16 17
TURKMENISTAN
Caspian Sea
GOLESTĀN
KHORĀSĀN-E SHOMĀLĪ
Koppeh Dāgh
Mashhad
Gorgān
Bojnūrd
Sārī
Bābol
MĀZANDARĀN
TEHRĀN
Semnān
SEMNĀN
Dasht-e Kavīr
KHORĀSĀN-E RAZAVĪ
QOM
Qom
IRAN
EṢFAHĀN
Eṣfahān
YAZD
Yazd
Iranian Plateau
KHORĀSĀN-E JONŪBĪ
Birjand
Dasht-e Lūt
Kermān
KERMĀN
Shīrāz
FĀRS
CHAHĀR MAHALL VA BAKHTĪĀRĪ
Zagros Mountains
Bandar-e Būshehr
BŪSHEHR
HORMOZGĀN
Bandar-e 'Abbās
Zāhedān
SĪSTĀN VA BALŪCHESTĀN
AFGHANISTAN
PAKISTAN
Makran
Makran Coast
Strait of Hormuz
BAHRAIN
QATAR
AD DAWḤAH (DOHA)
OMAN
Dubayy (Dubai)
Ash Shāriqah
ABŪ ẒABY (ABU DHABI)
UNITED ARAB EMIRATES
Trucial Coast
Gulf of Oman
Tropic of Cancer
Scale 1:6,000,000
Km 0 10 20 40 60 80 100 120 140 160 180 200
Miles 0 10 20 40 60 80 100 120 140 160 180 200
projection: Lambert Conformal Conic

148

148

Map key

Population

- above 5 million
- 1 million to 5 million
- 500,000 to 1 million
- 100,000 to 500,000
- 50,000 to 100,000
- 10,000 to 50,000
- below 10,000

Elevation

- 4000m / 13,124ft
- 3000m / 9843ft
- 2000m / 6562ft
- 1000m / 3281ft
- 500m / 1640ft
- 250m / 820ft
- 100m / 328ft
- sea level

Kazakhstan

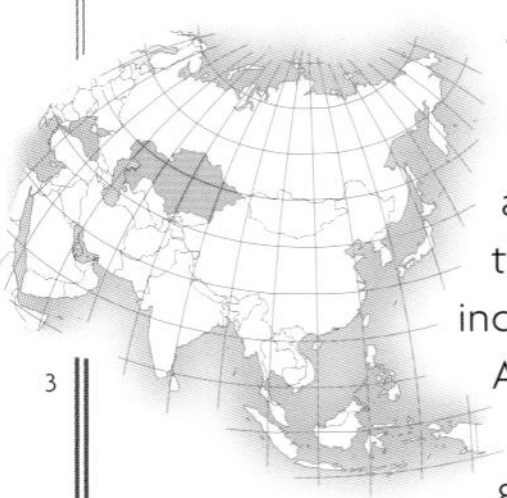

Abundant natural resources lie in the immense steppe grasslands, deserts, and central plateau of the former Soviet republic of Kazakhstan. An intensive program of industrial and agricultural development to exploit these resources during the Soviet era resulted in catastrophic industrial pollution, including fallout from nuclear testing and the shrinkage of the Aral Sea. Since independence, the government has encouraged foreign investment and liberalized the economy to promote growth. The adoption of Kazakh as the national language is intended to encourage a new sense of national identity in a state where living conditions for the majority remain harsh, both in cramped urban centers and impoverished rural areas.

Transportation & industry

The single most important industry in Kazakhstan is mining, based around extensive oil deposits near the Caspian Sea, the world's largest chromium mine, and vast reserves of iron ore. Recent foreign investment has helped to develop industries including food processing and steel manufacture, and to expand the exploitation of mineral resources. The Russian space program is still based at Baykonyr, near Kyzylorda in central Kazakhstan.

RUSSIAN FEDERATION
Petropavlovsk
Pavlodar
Rudnyy
ASTANA
Ural'sk
Aktobe
Temirtau
Karagandy
Semipalatinsk
Ust'Kamenogorsk
Atyrau
KAZAKHSTAN
Zhezkazgan
Aral Sea
Caspian Sea
Aktau
Kyzylorda
Taldykorgan
Almaty
Taraz
Shymkent
UZBEKISTAN
KYRGYZSTAN
CHINA
TURKMENISTAN

Major industry and infrastructure

- chemicals
- engineering
- fish processing
- food processing
- iron & steel
- metallurgy
- mining
- oil
- capital cities
- major towns
- international airports
- major roads
- major industrial areas

Transportation network

- 48,263 miles (77,680 km)
- none
- 8483 miles (13,660 km)
- 3900 miles (2423 km)

Industrial areas in the north and east are well-connected to Russia. Air and rail links with Germany and China have been established through foreign investment. Better access to Baltic ports is being sought.

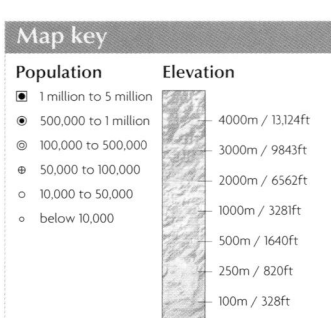

*◄ **An open-pit coal mine** in Kazakhstan. Foreign investment is being actively sought by the Kazakh government in order to fully exploit the potential of the country's rich mineral reserves.*

Using the land & sea

The rearing of large herds of sheep and goats on the steppe grasslands forms the core of Kazakh agriculture. Arable cultivation and cotton-growing in pasture and desert areas was encouraged during the Soviet era, but relative yields are low. The heavy use of fertilizers and the diversion of natural water sources for irrigation has degraded much of the land.

The urban/rural population divide

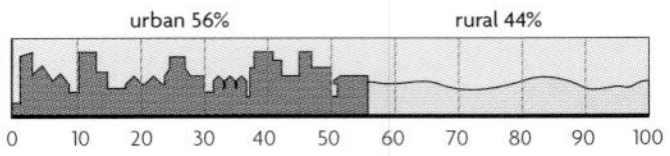

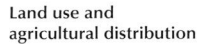

urban 56%
rural 44%
0
10
20
30
40
50
60
70
80
90
100

Population density	Total land area
16 people per sq mile (6 people per sq km)	1,048,878 sq miles (2,717,300 sq km)

Land use and agricultural distribution

- cattle
- goats
- sheep
- cotton
- fishing
- wheat
- capital cities
- major towns
- pasture
- cropland
- forest
- mountain region
- desert

RUSSIAN FEDERATION
Uralsk
Rudnyy
ASTANA
Ust'Kamenogorsk
Semipalatinsk
Karagandy
Atyrau
KAZAKHSTAN
Aral Sea
Caspian Sea
Aktau
Kyzylorda
Taldykorgan
Almaty
Shymkent
UZBEKISTAN
KYRGYZSTA
CHINA
TURKMENISTAN

*◄ **The nomadic peoples** who moved their herds around the steppe grasslands are now largely settled, although echoes of their traditional lifestyle, in particular their superb riding skills, remain.*

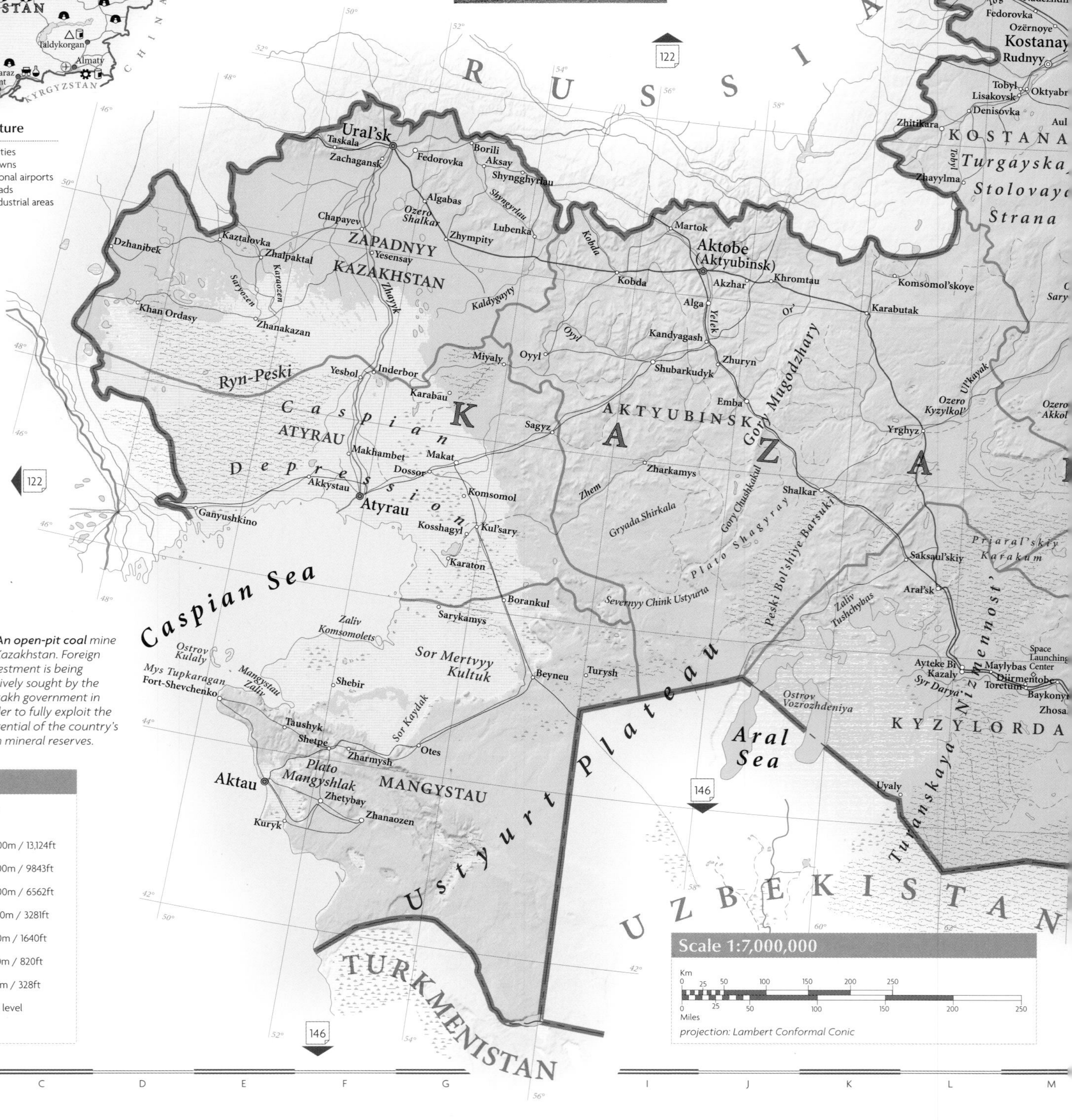

RUSSIA
122
Ural'sk
Taskala
Zachagansk
Fedorovka
Borili
Aksay
Shyngghyrlau
Algabas
Ozero Shalkar
Chapayev
Lubenka
Zhympity
Kaztalovka
Zhalpaktal
Dzhanibek
ZAPADNYY KAZAKHSTAN
Yesensay
Khan Ordasy
Zhanakazan
Martok
Aktobe (Aktyubinsk)
Kobda
Akzhar
Khromtau
Alga
Kandyagash
Zhuryn
Shubarkudyk
Oyyl
Miyaly
Yesbol
Inderbor
Ryn-Peski
Karabau
Caspian Depression
ATYRAU
Makhambet
Makat
Dossor
Akkystau
Atyrau
Ganyushkino
Komsomol
Kosshagyl
Kul'sary
Karaton
Sagyz
AKTYUBINSK
Emba
Gory Mugodzhary
Zharkamys
Zhem
Gryada Shirkala
Plato Shagyray
Peski Bol'shiye Barsuki
Shalkar
Borankul
Severnyy Chink Ustyurta
Caspian Sea
Zaliv Komsomolets
Sarykamys
Sor Mertvyy Kultuk
Ostrov Kulaly
Mys Tupkaragan
Fort-Shevchenko
Mangystau Zaliv
Shebir
Beyneu
Turysh
Taushyk
Shetpe
Zharmysh
Otes
Sor Kaydak
Aktau
Plato Mangyshlak
Zhetybay
Zhanaozen
Kuryk
MANGYSTAU
Ustyurt Plateau
Aral Sea
Ostrov Vozrozhdeniya
146
UZBEKISTAN
TURKMENISTAN
Karabalyk
Fedorovka
Ozërnoye
Kostanay
Rudnyy
Tobyl
Lisakovsk
Denisovka
Zhitikara
KOSTANA
Turgayska
Stolovaya Strana
Zhayylma
Komsomol'skoye
Karabutak
Ozero Kyzylkol'
Yrghyz
Priaral'skiy Karakum
Saksaul'skiy
Aral'sk
Zaliv Tushchybas
Ayteke Bi
Kazaly
Syr Darya
Toretam
Maylybas
Space Launching Center
KYZYLORDA
Uyaly
Turanskaya Nizmennost'
Scale 1:7,000,000
Km
Miles
projection: Lambert Conformal Conic

Map key

Population	Elevation
1 million to 5 million	4000m / 13,124ft
500,000 to 1 million	3000m / 9843ft
100,000 to 500,000	2000m / 6562ft
50,000 to 100,000	1000m / 3281ft
10,000 to 50,000	500m / 1640ft
below 10,000	250m / 820ft
	100m / 328ft
	sea level

N O P Q R S T U V W X Y

The landscape

Stretching more than 1250 miles (2000 km) from the Caspian Sea in the west to China in the east, more than 40% of Kazakhstan is covered by steppe grasslands which give way to barren desert in the south. The land rises eastward towards the mineral-rich central plateau, to form the Altai Mountains.

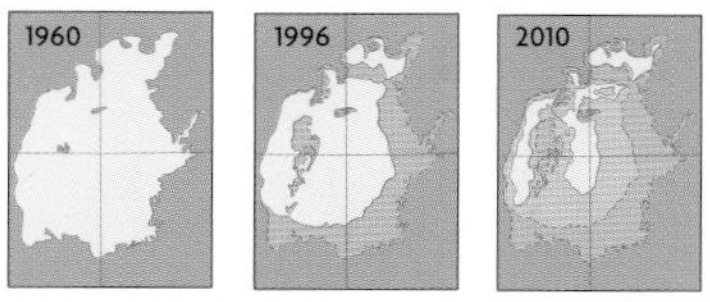
1960
1996
2010

▲ ***Since 1960, the** Aral Sea has shrunk by 75%, become extremely saline, and lost all but five of its once-abundant fish species. Factors in this ecological disaster include the excessive use of fertilizers, defoliants and the diversion of its main source rivers for the irrigation of desert lands.*

The Caspian Sea is the largest body of inland water in the world.

The desert of Peski Bol'shiye Barsuki is mainly sandy, displaying a number of classic dune formations. Groundwater supports a small amount of vegetation.

A large number of salt lakes fill depressions in the rolling uplands of central Kazakhstan.

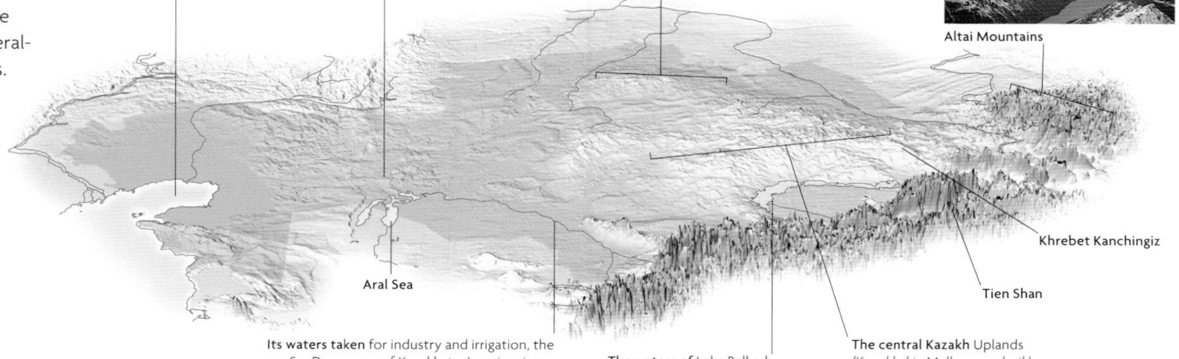
Aral Sea
Altai Mountains
Khrebet Kanchingiz
Tien Shan

Its waters taken for industry and irrigation, the Syr Darya, one of Kazakhstan's major rivers, now barely reaches the Aral Sea which it used to fill. Like many Kazakh rivers it has been heavily polluted with chemicals and its flow has been restricted by up to 60%.

The waters of Lake Balkash *(Ozero Balkash)*, unlike those of the Aral Sea, are still able to support a fishing industry.

The central Kazakh Uplands *(Kazakhskiy Melkosopochnik)* contain much of the country's mineral riches. The landscape is largely flat with occasional rocky outcrops and hillocks.

▶ ***The Altai Mountains** lie on Kazakhstan's eastern borders with China and the Russian Federation. Cold and largely barren, they are the source of many of the rivers which flow across the steppe.*

▶ ***Immense stretches** of steppe grasslands characterize much of the Kazakh landscape. These lowland areas have been used for arable cultivation in recent years, although problems with irrigation have meant that much of the land is being allowed to revert to its natural vegetation and pastoral usage.*

FEDERATION
KAZAKHSTAN
KYRGYZSTAN
CHINA
Petropavlovsk
SEVERNYY KAZAKHSTAN
Kokshetau
AKMOLA
ASTANA
Pavlodar
PAVLODAR
Semey
Ust'-Kamenogorsk
VOSTOCHNYY KAZAKHSTAN
Altai Mountains
Gora Belukha 4506m
Ozero Zaysan
Temirtau
Karagandy
Saryarka
KARAGANDY
Zhezkazgan
Ozero Balkash
Betpakdala
Balkhash
Taldykorgan
ALMATY
Almaty (Alma-Ata)
Pik Khan Tengri 6995m
Tien Shan
Kirghiz Range
ZHAMBYL
Taraz
Peski Moyynkum
YUZHNYY KAZAKHSTAN
Shymkent
Kyzylorda
Syr Darya
Kyzyl Kum
Khrebet Karatau
Ozero Alakol'
Ozero Tengiz
Nuclear Testing Ground

122
122
156
146

▲ ***Rows of pine** trees edge this valley near Almaty. The snow-covered slopes in the background are used for skiing.*

R S T U V W X Y Z

Central Asia

KYRGYZSTAN, TAJIKISTAN, TURKMENISTAN, UZBEKISTAN

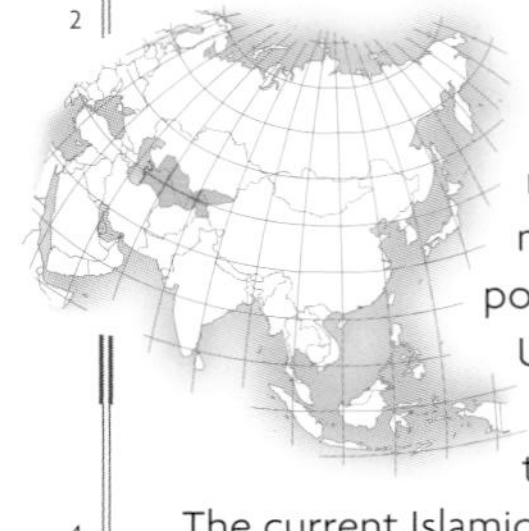

The four republics that declared independence in 1991 were created in the early years of the Soviet Union, promoting ethnic divisions in a region whose common focus, since the 8th century, has been Islam. Traditional rural, nomadic ways of life have survived the Soviet era, while the benefits of modern industry and grand irrigation schemes have resulted in severe pollution in the delicate, arid environment of the steppe, particularly in Uzbekistan. Many ethnic minority groups are scattered among the four republics, with isolated communities in the mountains of Kyrgyzstan.

The current Islamic revival has brought hope of greater regional unity, in spite of religious factionalism which, in 1992, plunged Tajikistan into civil war.

◄ *The desert of* the Kara Kum (Garagum) *occupies over 70% of Turkmenistan; its wind-scoured surface of dune ridges and depressions severely limits human settlement.*

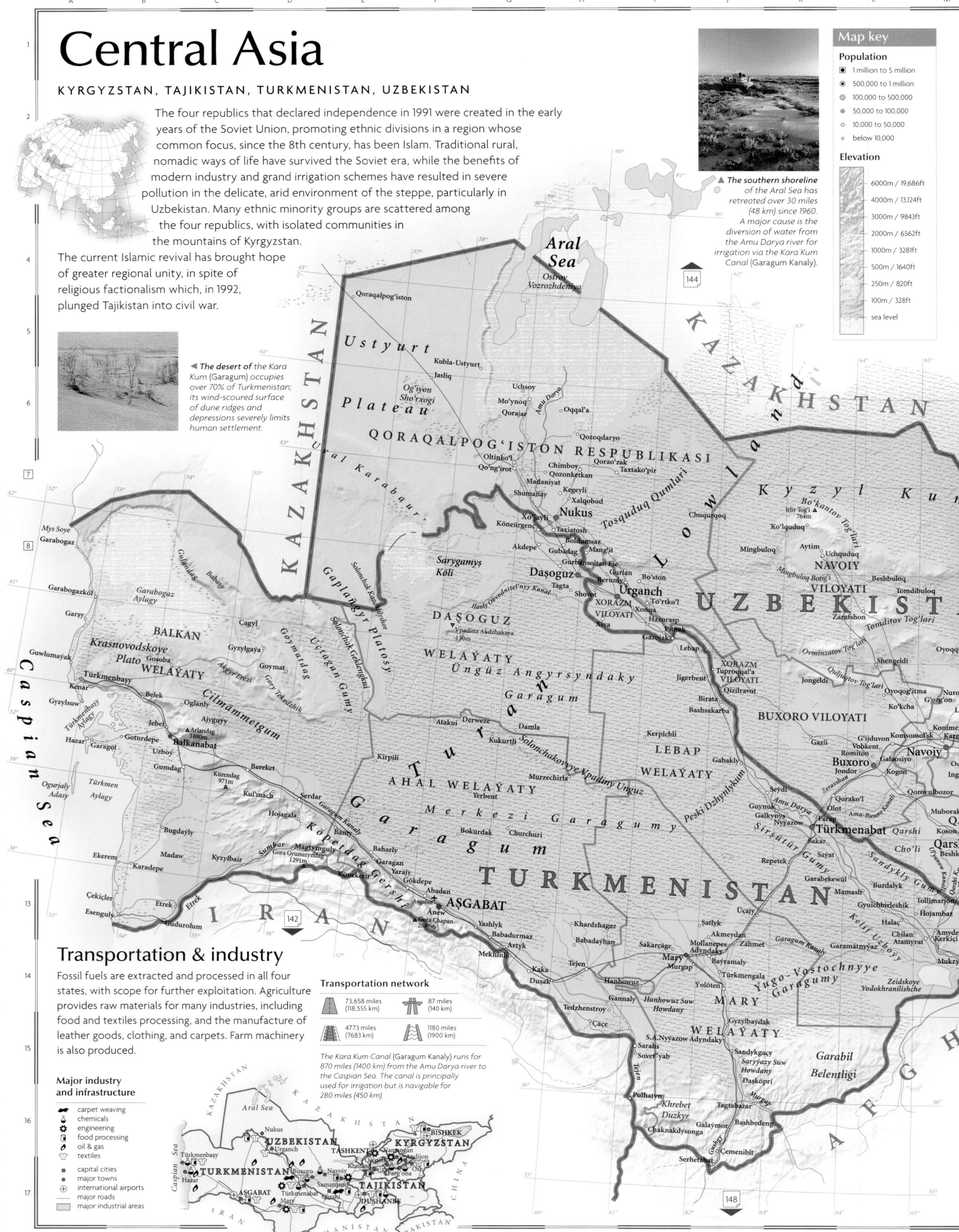

▲ *The southern shoreline of the Aral Sea has retreated over 30 miles (48 km) since 1960. A major cause is the diversion of water from the Amu Darya river for irrigation via the Kara Kum Canal* (Garagum Kanaly).

Map key

Population

- 1 million to 5 million
- 500,000 to 1 million
- 100,000 to 500,000
- 50,000 to 100,000
- 10,000 to 50,000
- below 10,000

Elevation

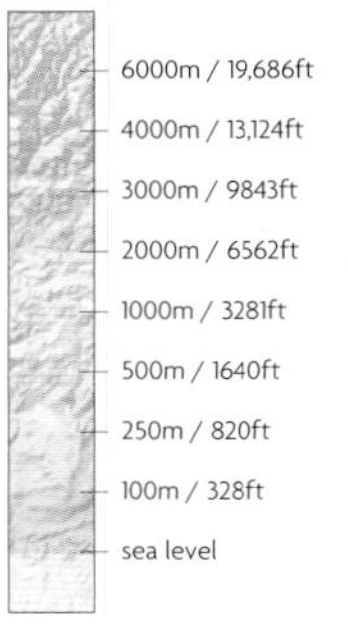

6000m / 19,686ft
4000m / 13,124ft
3000m / 9843ft
2000m / 6562ft
1000m / 3281ft
500m / 1640ft
250m / 820ft
100m / 328ft
sea level

Aral Sea
Ostrov Vozrozhdeniya
KAZAKHSTAN
Ustyurt Plateau
QORAQALPOG'ISTON RESPUBLIKASI
Qoraqalpog'iston
Kubla-Ustyurt
Jasliq
Nukus
Urganch
Daşoguz
Sarygamyş Köli
DAŞOGUZ WELAÝATY
Turan Lowland
Kyzyl Kum
UZBEKISTAN
NAVOIY VILOYATI
BUXORO VILOYATI
Buxoro
Navoiy
Türkmenabat
Qarshi
BALKAN WELAÝATY
Krasnovodskoye Plato
Türkmenbaşy
Balkanabat
Garabogazköl
Caspian Sea
Garagum
Ahal Welaýaty
LEBAP WELAÝATY
Garagum Kanaly
Köpetdag
AŞGABAT
Mary
MARY WELAÝATY
TURKMENISTAN
Serhetabat
Gushgy
IRAN
AFGHANISTAN
Gora Chapan 2889m
Arlandag 1880m
Kürendag 971m
Gora Gyunuzyndag 1291m
Vpadina Akdzhakaya -130m
Amu Darya
Zeidskoye Vodokhranilishche

144
142
148

Transportation & industry

Fossil fuels are extracted and processed in all four states, with scope for further exploitation. Agriculture provides raw materials for many industries, including food and textiles processing, and the manufacture of leather goods, clothing, and carpets. Farm machinery is also produced.

Transportation network

73,658 miles (118,555 km)	87 miles (140 km)
4773 miles (7683 km)	1180 miles (1900 km)

The Kara Kum Canal (Garagum Kanaly) *runs for 870 miles (1400 km) from the Amu Darya river to the Caspian Sea. The canal is principally used for irrigation but is navigable for 280 miles (450 km).*

Major industry and infrastructure

- carpet weaving
- chemicals
- engineering
- food processing
- oil & gas
- textiles
- capital cities
- major towns
- international airports
- major roads
- major industrial areas

KAZAKHSTAN
Aral Sea
Nukus
UZBEKISTAN
Urganch
TASHKENT
BISHKEK
KYRGYZSTAN
Namangan
Andijon
Osh
Farg'ona
Khujand
Navoiy
Samarqand
TAJIKISTAN
DUSHANBE
Qarshi
Türkmenbasy
TURKMENISTAN
Hazar
AŞGABAT
Türkmenabat
Mary
Caspian Sea
IRAN
AFGHANISTAN
PAKISTAN
CHINA

The landscape

The great Tien Shan and Pamir ranges meet in a succession of high mountain chains. These mountains encircle the fertile Fergana Valley and reach west into the desert of the Kyzyl Kum, dividing the Syr Darya and Amu Darya rivers. Sandy steppeland extends to the shores of the Caspian Sea, with the desert of the Kara Kum *(Garagum)* in the south. The Amu Darya drains into the Aral Sea in the north.

The Amu Darya is the only river in Central Asia with a sufficient volume of water to cross the desert of the Kara Kum *(Garagum)* from the Pamirs to the Aral Sea, where it forms a delta largely vegetated by scrub grasses.

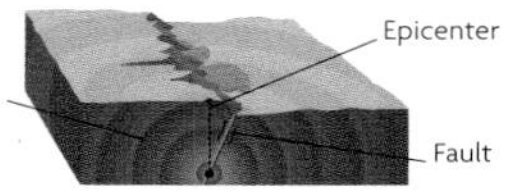
Shock waves travel through ground
Epicenter
Fault

▲ ***In the heavily*** *fractured and faulted mountain region, earthquakes are common, caused by the sudden release of tension along active fault lines.*

◀ ***Bare mountains provide*** *a stark background to the croplands along the Naryn river in Kyrgyzstan. Irrigation is essential for cultivation in this dry region.*

Salt marshes fill many of the depressions in the Ustyurt Plateau, a barren, rocky tableland about 650 ft (200 m) above sea level.

Some of the world's largest deposits of marine salts are found in Garabogaz Aylagy. This shallow, saline gulf has an average depth of only 33 ft (10 m), and a very high evaporation rate, producing the salty deposits.

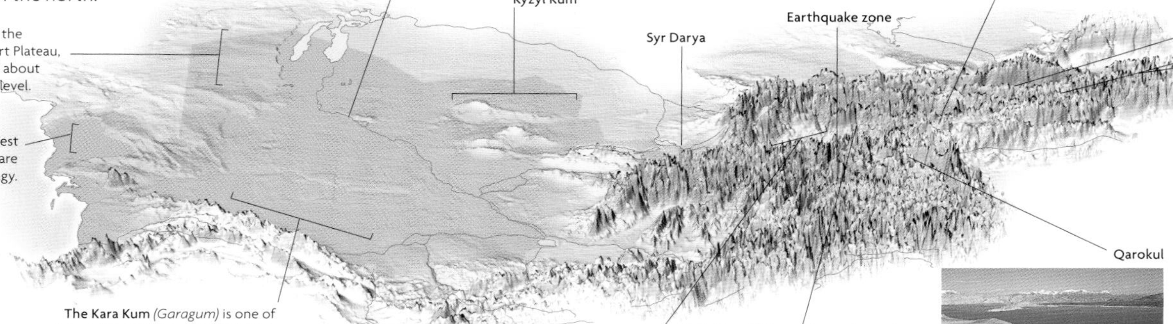
Kyzyl Kum
Earthquake zone
Syr Darya
Naryn river
Tien Shan
Qarokul

Ozero Issyk-Kul' lies at an altitude of 5193 ft (1584 m). The lake remains ice-free throughout the year, due to the slight salinity of the water.

▲ ***The Tien Shan*** *extend from China in the east, reaching heights over 24,400 ft (7439 m) and branching into many parallel ranges in the west.*

The Kara Kum *(Garagum)* is one of the world's largest expanses of sand. Wind action has created a terrain of shifting, crescent-shaped sand dunes known as barchans.

A series of major rock faults has created the Fergana Valley, a deep depression surrounded by high mountains. Water from the Syr Darya river and from underground sources supports intensive agriculture, despite minimal rainfall.

Qullai Ismoili Somoni, was formerly known as Mount Communism, so named because it was the highest point in the the former Soviet Union, rising to 24,590 ft (7495 m).

◀ ***Nestling high in*** *the Pamir range, and fed by glacial meltwater, Qarokul is the largest of the lakes in this region.*

Scale 1:4,750,000

Km 0 10 20 40 60 80 100 120
Miles 0 10 20 40 60 80 100 120

projection: Lambert Conformal Conic

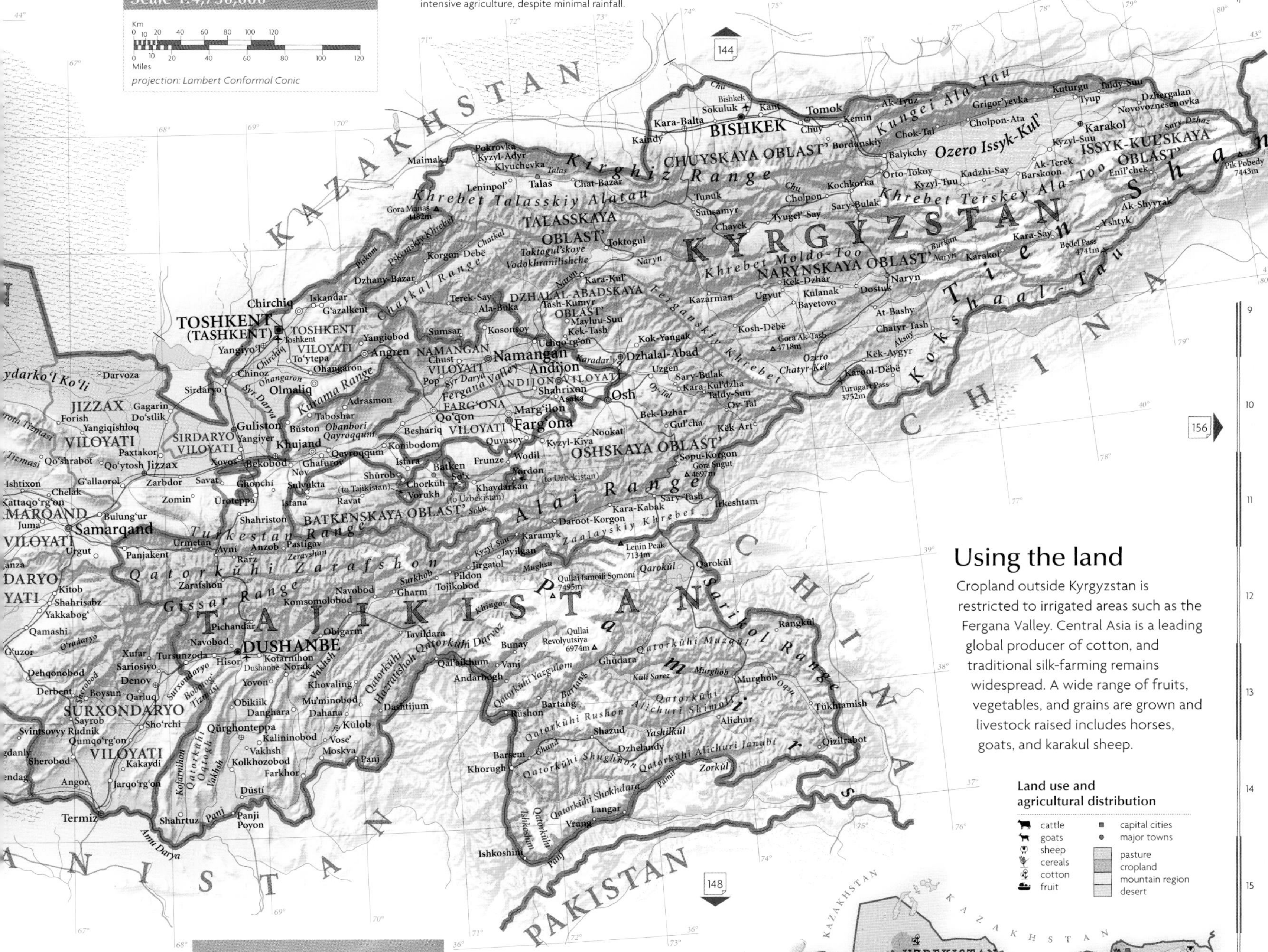
KAZAKHSTAN
KYRGYZSTAN
TAJIKISTAN
CHINA
PAKISTAN
BISHKEK
TOSHKENT (TASHKENT)
DUSHANBE
Samarqand
Namangan
Andijon
Farg'ona
Osh
Khujand
Ozero Issyk-Kul'
Tien Shan
Alai Range
Pamirs
Pik Pobedy 7443m
Qullai Ismoili Somoni 7495m
Lenin Peak 7134m
Qarokul
CHUYSKAYA OBLAST'
TALASSKAYA OBLAST'
DZHALAL-ABADSKAYA OBLAST'
NARYNSKAYA OBLAST'
ISSYK-KUL'SKAYA OBLAST'
OSHSKAYA OBLAST'
BATKENSKAYA OBLAST'
144
148
156

Using the land

Cropland outside Kyrgyzstan is restricted to irrigated areas such as the Fergana Valley. Central Asia is a leading global producer of cotton, and traditional silk-farming remains widespread. A wide range of fruits, vegetables, and grains are grown and livestock raised includes horses, goats, and karakul sheep.

▶ ***Plentiful sunshine,*** *rich soils and massive irrigation schemes have made Uzbekistan the world's fifth largest cotton producer, although water shortages now prevent any further expansion of irrigated land.*

The urban/rural population divide

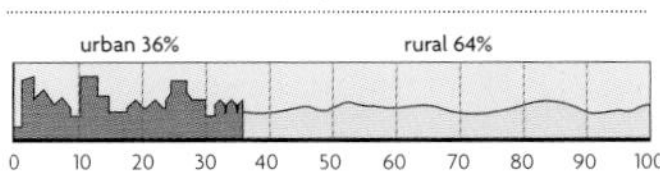
urban 36%
rural 64%
0 10 20 30 40 50 60 70 80 90 100

Population density	Total land area
88 people per sq mile (34 people per sq km)	492,961 sq miles (1,277,100 sq km)

Land use and agricultural distribution

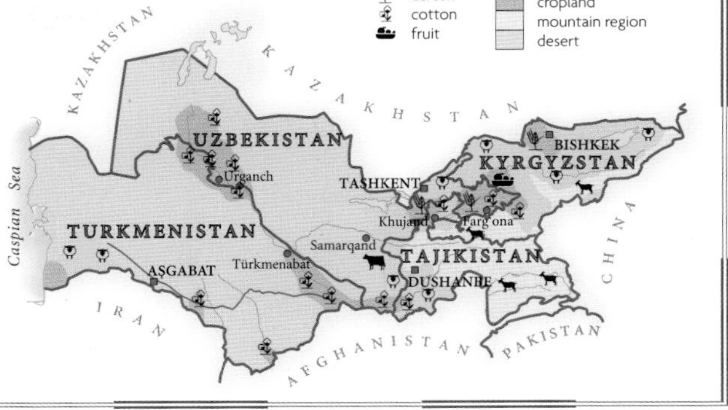
cattle
goats
sheep
cereals
cotton
fruit
capital cities
major towns
pasture
cropland
mountain region
desert
KAZAKHSTAN
UZBEKISTAN
TURKMENISTAN
KYRGYZSTAN
TAJIKISTAN
IRAN
AFGHANISTAN
PAKISTAN
CHINA
Caspian Sea
BISHKEK
TASHKENT
DUSHANBE
AŞGABAT
Urganch
Türkmenabat
Samarqand
Khujand
Farg'ona

Afghanistan & Pakistan

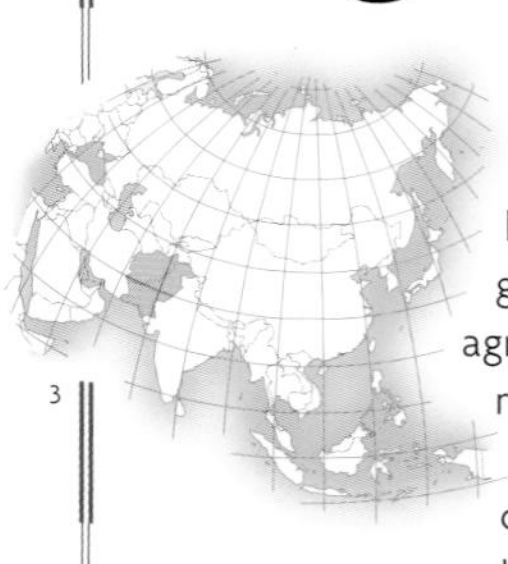

Pakistan was created by the partition of British India in 1947, becoming the western arm of a new Islamic state for Indian Muslims; the eastern sector, in Bengal, seceded to become the separate country of Bangladesh in 1971. Over half of Pakistan's 158 million people live in the Punjab, at the fertile head of the great Indus Basin. The river sustains a national economy based on irrigated agriculture, including cotton for the vital textiles industry. Afghanistan, a mountainous, landlocked country, with an ancient and independent culture, has been wracked by war since 1979. Factional strife escalated into an international conflict in late 2001, as US-led troops ousted the militant and fundamentally Islamist *taliban* regime as part of their "war on terror."

◀ *The town of Bamian lies high inthe Hindu Kush west of Kabul. Between the 2nd and 5th centuries two huge statues of Buddha were carved into the nearby rock,the largest of which stood 125 ft (38 m) high. The statues were destroyed by the taliban regime in March 2001.*

UZBEKISTAN
TAJIKISTAN
TURKMENISTAN
CHINA
IRAN
INDIA
ARABIAN SEA
AFGHANISTAN
PAKISTAN
Mazar-e Sharif
KABUL
Herat
Peshawar
ISLAMABAD
Rawalpindi
Kandahar
Lahore
Faisalabad
Quetta
Multan
Bahawalpur
Sukkur
Karachi
Hyderabad

Transportation & industry

Pakistan is highly dependent on the cotton textiles industry, although diversified manufacture is expanding around cities such as Karachi and Lahore. Afghanistan's limited industry is based mainly on the processing of agricultural raw materials and includes traditional crafts such as carpet weaving.

Major industry and infrastructure

- carpet weaving
- chemicals
- engineering
- finance
- food processing
- iron & steel
- oil & gas
- textiles
- capital cities
- major towns
- international airports
- major roads
- major industrial areas

Transportation network

- 96,154 miles (154,763 km)
- 211 miles (340 km)
- 4852 miles (7814 km)
- 745 miles (1200 km)

The Karakoram Highway was completed after 20 years of construction in 1978. It breaches the Himalayan mountain barrier providing a commercial motor route linking lowland Pakistan and China.

► *The Karakoram Highway is one of the highest major roads in the world. It took over 24,000 workers almost 20 years to complete.*

The landscape

Afghanistan's topography is dominated by the mountains of the Hindu Kush, which spread south and west into numerous mountain spurs. The dry plateau of southwestern Afghanistan extends into Pakistan and the hills which overlook the great Indus Basin. In northern Pakistan the Hindu Kush, Himalayan, and Karakoram ranges meet to form one of the world's highest mountain regions.

◀ *The Hunza river rises in the northern Karakoram Range, running for 120 miles (193 km) before joining the Gilgit river.*

► *The arid Hindu Kush makes much of Afghanistan uninhabitable, with over 50% of the land lying above 6500 ft (2000 m).*

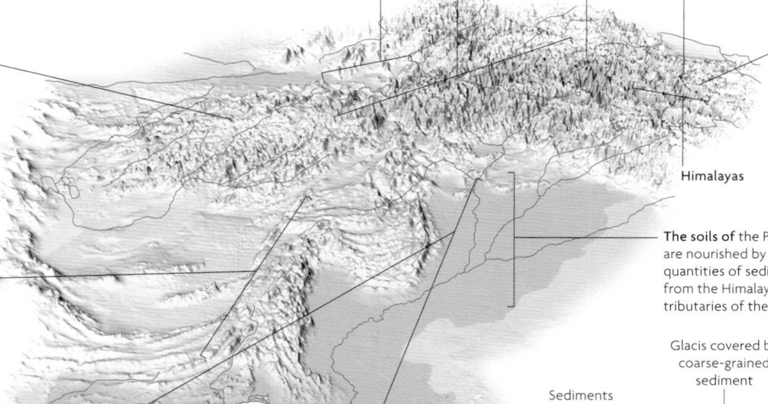

Hunza river
The plains and foothills which extend from the northern slopes of the Hindu Kush are part of the great grassy steppe lands of Central Asia.
Hindu Kush
K2 (Mount Godwin Austen), in the Karakoram Range, is the second highest mountain in the world, at an altitude of 28,251 ft (8611 m).
Frequent earthquakes mean that mountain-building processes are continuing in this region, as the Indo-Australian Plate drifts northward, colliding with the Eurasian Plate.
Some of the largest glaciers outside the polar regions are found in the Karakoram Range, including Siachen Glacier *(Siachen Muztagh)*, which is 40 miles (72 km) long.
Himalayas
Mountain chains running southwest from the Hindu Kush into Pakistan form a barrier to the humid winds which blow from the Indian Ocean, creating arid conditions across southern Afghanistan.
The soils of the Punjab plain are nourished by enormous quantities of sediment, carried from the Himalayas by the five tributaries of the Indus river.
The Indus Basin is part of the Indus-Ganges lowland, a vast depression which has been filled with layers of sediment over the last 50 million years. These deposits are estimated to be over 16,400 ft (5000 m) deep.
The Indus Delta is prone to heavy flooding and high levels of salinity. It remains a largely uncultivated wilderness area.

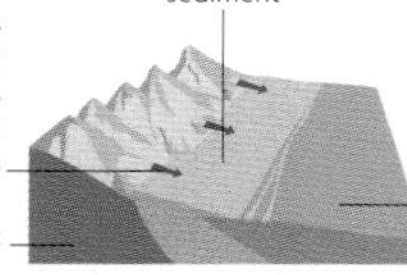

Glacis covered by coarse-grained sediment
Sediments washed down from mountains accumulate on glacis slopes
Bedrock
Fine sediments deposited on salt flats are removed by wind erosion.

▲ *Glacis are gentle, debris-covered slopes which lead into saltflats or deserts. They typically occur at the base of mountains in arid regions such as Afghanistan.*

146
TURKMEN
Kārīz-e Elyās
Towraghoudī
Qarah Bāgh
Kushk
Bālā Murghāb
BĀDGHĪS
Qal'ah-ye Now
Qādis
Eslām Qal'eh
Kūhestān
Dasht-e Hamdam Āb
Zindah Jān
Herāt
Ghōriān
HERĀT
Selseleh-ye Sefīd Kūh
Namakzar
GHŌR
AFGHA
IRAN
Shīndand
Dak
Anār Darah
Dasht-e Bābūs
FARĀH
142
Farāh Rūd
Farāh
Dilārām
Now Zād
Hāmūn-e Şāberi
Dasht-e Khāsh
Hāmūn-e Pūzak
NĪMRŌZ
Gereshk
Lashkar Gāh
Chakhānsūr
Zaranj
Dasht-e Mārgow
Darwēshān
HELMAND
Dīshū
Daryā-ye Helmand
Dasht-e Gowd-e Zereh
Chāgai Hills
Nok Kundi
Yakmach
Dālbandīn
Dasht-i Tāhlāb
Hāmūn-i Māshkel
BAL
Kamarod
Siāhān Range
Tagas
Panjgūr
Central Makran
Ispikān
Mand
Nasīrābād
Kech
Hoshāb
Turbat
Dasht
Suntsar
Jiwani
Gwādar
Gwādar West Bay
Gwādar East Bay
Pasni
Khor Kalamat
Astola Island
Ormāra
Scale 1:5,000,000
Km
Miles
projection: Lambert Conformal Conic

TAJIKISTAN
UZBEKISTAN
CHINA
INDIA
PAKISTAN
Hindu Kush
Karakoram Range
JAMMU & KASHMIR
KHYBER PAKHTUNKHWA
PUNJAB
SINDH
Thar Desert
ARABIAN SEA
Rann of Kachchh
Mouths of the Indus
Toba Kākar Range
Sulaimān Range
Kīrthar Range
Central Brāhui Range
Potwar Plateau
Salt Range
Sind Sagar Doab
KĀBUL
ISLĀMĀBĀD
Rāwalpindi
Peshāwar
Lahore
Faisalābād
Gujrānwāla
Multān
Hyderābād
Karāchi
Quetta
Kandahār
Mazār-e Sharīf
Jalālābād
Bahāwalpur
Sukkur
Sargodha
Sialkot
K2 8611m
Gasherbrum 8068m
Nanga Parbat 8126m
Tirich Mīr 7708m
Khyber Pass 1080m
Karakoram Pass 5568m
(claimed by India)
146
156
150
172
N O P Q R S T U V W X Y Z
1 2 3 4 8 9 10 11 12 13 15 16 17

Map key

Population

- above 5 million
- 1 million to 5 million
- 500,000 to 1 million
- 100,000 to 500,000
- 50,000 to 100,000
- 10,000 to 50,000
- below 10,000

Elevation

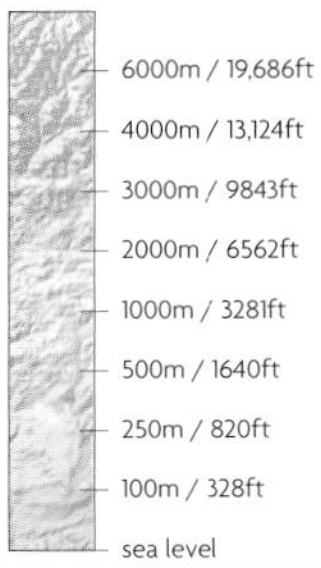
6000m / 19,686ft
4000m / 13,124ft
3000m / 9843ft
2000m / 6562ft
1000m / 3281ft
500m / 1640ft
250m / 820ft
100m / 328ft
sea level

▲ *Fed on meltwater from the snows and glaciers of the Karakoram Range and the Hindu Kush, the Indus is the longest of the rivers which rise in this region. The sophisticated Indus Valley civilization flourished along its banks from 4000 BC, forming one of the world's earliest civilizations.*

Using the land

Massive irrigation schemes and new crop strains have helped to boost Pakistan's wheat, rice, and cotton production in the last 40 years. Wheat is the chief staple of Afghanistan, where cropland is severely limited. Large revenues have been generated by the illegal export of opium poppies and cannabis. Livestock-raising is widespread in both countries.

The urban/rural population divide

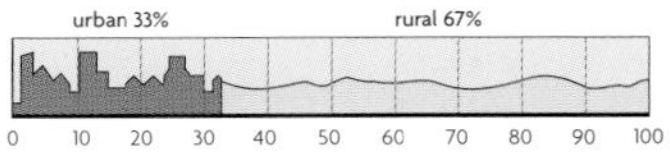
urban 33%
rural 67%
0 10 20 30 40 50 60 70 80 90 100

Population density	Total land area
323 people per sq mile (125 people per sq km)	549,266 sq miles (1,422,970 sq km)

Land use and agricultural distribution

- goats
- sheep
- cereals
- cotton
- dates
- rice
- capital cities
- major towns
- pasture
- cropland
- forest
- mountain region
- desert
- wetland

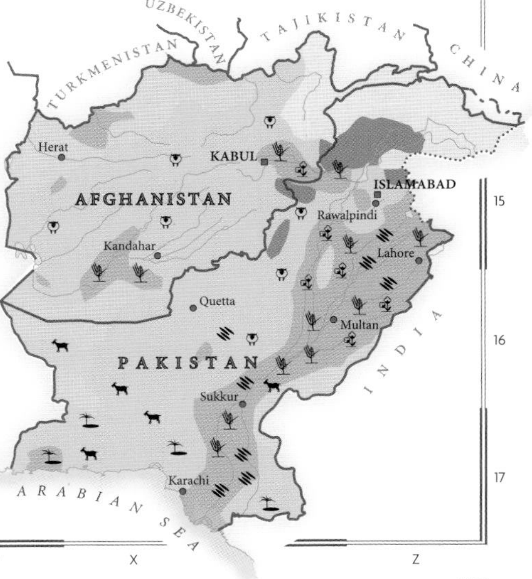
UZBEKISTAN
TAJIKISTAN
TURKMENISTAN
CHINA
IRAN
INDIA
AFGHANISTAN
PAKISTAN
ARABIAN SEA
Herat
KABUL
ISLAMABAD
Rawalpindi
Kandahar
Lahore
Quetta
Multan
Sukkur
Karachi

▲ *Cotton workers in Pakistan pack huge bales of unspun cotton to be washed and processed. The cotton and textile industry is of growing economic importance, producing more than 36 million sq yards (30 million sq m) of woven cloth annually.*

South Asia

BANGLADESH, BHUTAN, INDIA, MALDIVES, NEPAL, PAKISTAN, SRI LANKA

More than one-fifth of the world's population lives in the south Asian subcontinent. Great cultural diversity has come from a long succession of foreign invaders, including Hindu Aryans, Islamic Moguls, and the British, whose empire incorporated the princely states of the Maharajas and extended to the borders of Nepal and Bhutan in the Himalayas. Independent since 1947, India is the world's largest democracy, and at the current rate of growth, may overtake China as the world's most populous country during the 21st century. There are points of tension in the region over claims for independence by the Sikhs in the Indian Punjab and the Tamil separatists in Sri Lanka, and the long-standing dispute with Pakistan over Jammu and Kashmir in the north.

◀ ***The towering Karakoram** and Hindu Kush ranges, formed at the same time as the Himalayas, dominate Pakistan's northern borders. K2 on the border of northern Pakistan is the second highest mountain on Earth, at 28,251 ft (8611 m).*

The landscape

South Asia is effectively isolated from the rest of Asia by desert along the western flank of Pakistan, and a continuous wall of mountains, dominated by the Himalayas, to the north and east. The great basins of the Indus and Ganges separate this mountain fringe from the rolling plateau of the Indian peninsula, which is bordered by a line of coastal hills, the Eastern and Western Ghats.

◀ ***The Indus valley** near Skardu in northern Pakistan has been partially infilled by great quantities of eroded sediment. Most of this is carried from the region's bare slopes by swollen rivers during the spring thaw and mass movement activity.*

The Himalayas are the highest and most extensive mountain system in the world. They were formed when the Indo-Australian Plate collided with the Eurasian Plate about 40 million years ago, thrusting up huge masses of land and creating a "ripple" effect, which formed lesser mountain ranges in Tibet and Southeast Asia. Mount Everest is the world's tallest mountain at 29,029 ft (8848 m).

Almost all of Bangladesh lies in the immense delta formed by the Ganges and the Brahmaputra which merge and flow out into the Bay of Bengal.

The Indus river flows more than 1970 miles (3180 km) from southwestern Tibet to its mouth on the Arabian Sea. It has an estimated catchment area of 450,000 sq miles (1,165,500 sq km).

The coast of western Pakistan is a staircase of folded rock strata caused by successive periods of rapid uplift.

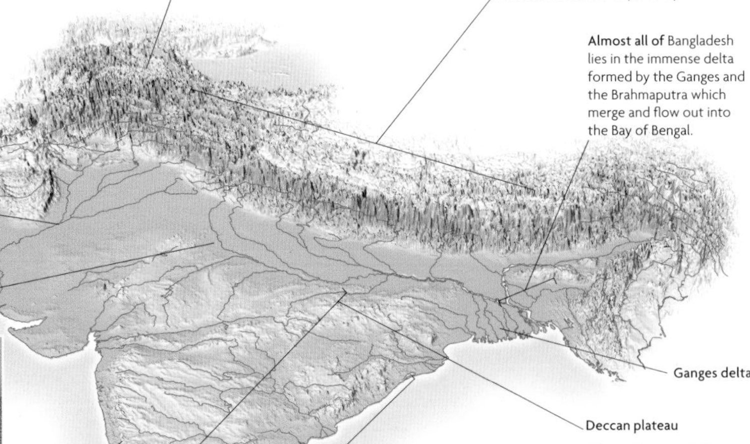

Bharatpur
Ganges delta
Deccan plateau
Eastern Ghats

▲ ***Rivers flowing from** the Himalayas into a broad depression in northern India have formed marshes around Bharatpur. They are now a sanctuary for numerous bird species.*

The Western Ghats are formed by a fault scarp which runs unbroken for more than 930 miles (1500 km). They reach their highest point at the southern Cardamom Hills.

Trivandrum in southern India normally receives the first of the monsoon rains, which are essential to south Asian agriculture and moderate the extreme summer heat. The monsoon then moves northward over a period of about two months.

Coastal deposition has formed many typical features along the western coast of Sri Lanka. These include spits and bars, sometimes enclosing lagoons.

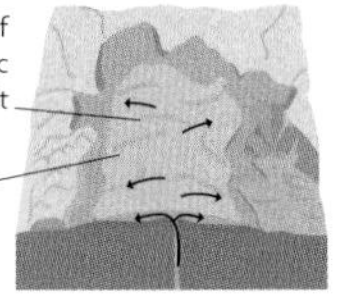

Layers of volcanic basalt
Stepped valleys or 'traps'

▲ ***The Deccan plateau** covers an area of more than 123,553 sq miles (320,000 sq km). It is formed of deep layers of volcanic basalt, reaching thicknesses of more than 9800 ft (3000 m) toward the coast. Distinctive stepped valleys cut in the basalt plateau by rivers are known as "traps."*

146
156
148
156
156
142

AFGHANISTAN
TAJIKISTAN
CHINA
PAKISTAN
IRAN
INDIA
NEPAL
BHUTAN
BANGLADESH
Hindu Kush
Karakoram Range
Toba Kakar Range
Sulaiman Range
Zāskār Range
Thar Desert
Chāgai Hills
Central Makrān Range
Central Brāhui Range
BALUCHISTĀN
KHYBER PAKHTUNKHWA
PUNJAB
SIND
RĀJASTHĀN
HARYĀNA
HIMACHAL PRADESH
UTTARAKHAND
UTTAR PRADESH
JAMMU & KASHMIR
BIHĀR
ASSAM
MEGHALAYA
ARUNACHAL PRADESH
NAGALAND
MANIPUR
SIKKIM
ISLĀMĀBĀD
NEW DELHI
KATHMANDU
THIMPHU
Quetta
Peshāwar
Rāwalpindi
Lahore
Multān
Faisalābād
Hyderābād
Karāchi
Srīnagar
Jammu
Amritsar
Ludhiāna
Chandīgarh
Shimla
Dehra Dūn
Meerut
Delhi
Agra
Jaipur
Jodhpur
Kānpur
Lucknow
Allahābād
Vārānasi
Patna
Gwalior
Kota
Gorakhpur
Guwāhāti
Shillong
Imphāl
Dibrugarh
K2 8611m
Nanga Parbat 8126m
Mount Everest 8848m
Annapurna 8091m
Nanda Devi 7817m
Kula Kangri 7554m
Khyber Pass 1080m
Karakoram Pass 5508m
Aksai Chin (Administered by China, claimed by India)
Demchok/Dêmqog (Administered by China, claimed by India)
(Administered by China, claimed by India)
(Much of Arunāchal Pradesh is claimed by China)
(Claimed by India)
(Line of control)
Tropic of Cancer
Mouths of the Indus
Rann of Kachchh

Map key

Population

- above 5 million
- 1 million to 5 million
- 500,000 to 1 million
- 100,000 to 500,000
- 50,000 to 100,000
- 10,000 to 50,000
- below 10,000

Elevation

- 6000m / 19,686ft
- 4000m / 13,124ft
- 3000m / 9843ft
- 2000m / 6562ft
- 1000m / 3281ft
- 500m / 1640ft
- 250m / 820ft
- 100m / 328ft
- sea level

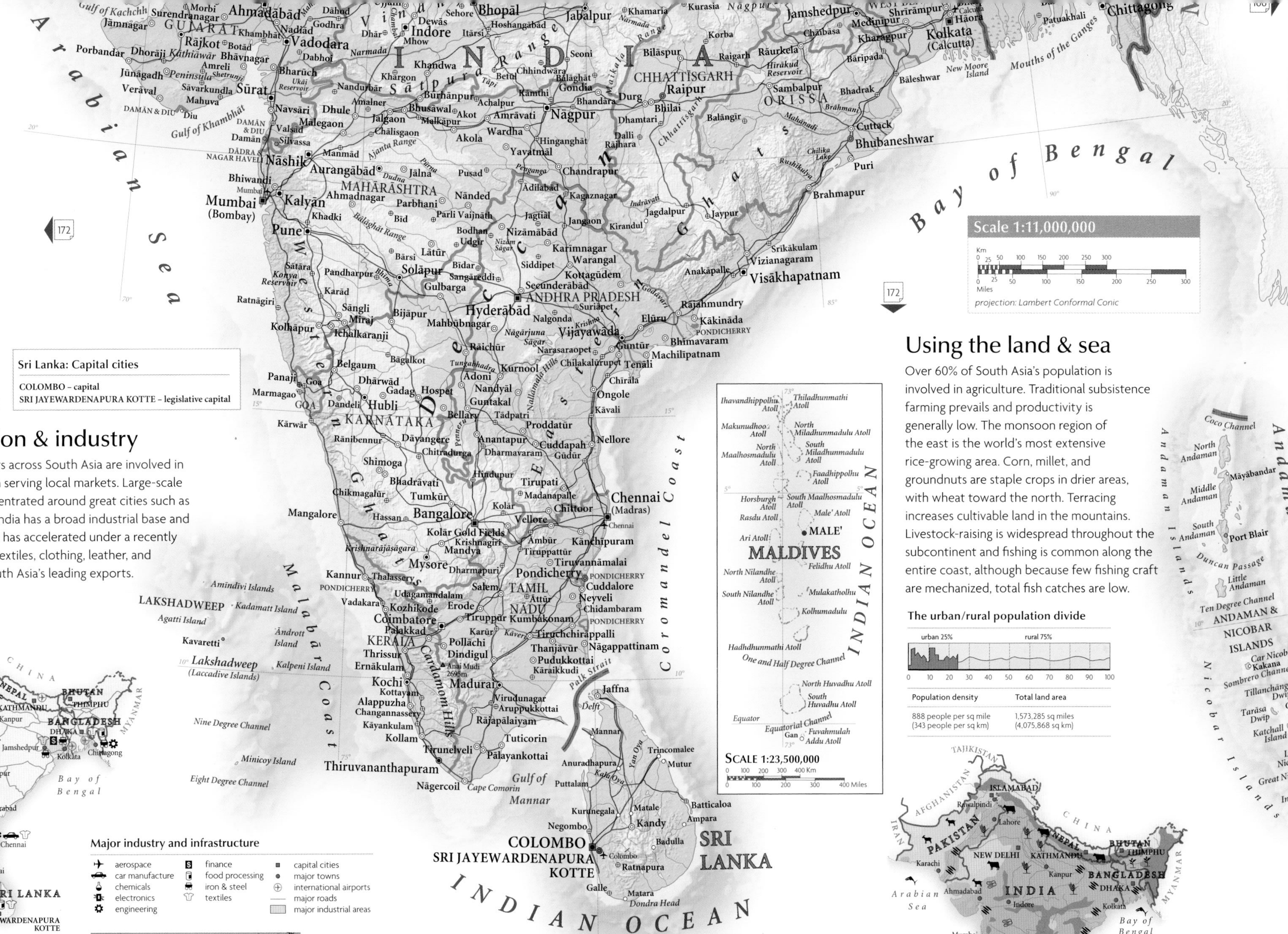
Arabian Sea
Bay of Bengal
INDIAN OCEAN
INDIA
SRI LANKA
MALDIVES
LAKSHADWEEP
ANDAMAN & NICOBAR ISLANDS
Andaman Sea
Malabar Coast
Coromandel Coast
Western Ghats
Eastern Ghats
Deccan
Mumbai (Bombay)
Kolkata (Calcutta)
Chennai (Madras)
Hyderābād
Bangalore
COLOMBO
SRI JAYEWARDENAPURA KOTTE
MALE'
Scale 1:11,000,000
projection: Lambert Conformal Conic
SCALE 1:23,500,000

Sri Lanka: Capital cities

COLOMBO – capital
SRI JAYEWARDENAPURA KOTTE – legislative capital

172

Transportation & industry

Most industrial workers across South Asia are involved in small-scale production serving local markets. Large-scale industry remains concentrated around great cities such as Kolkata and Mumbai. India has a broad industrial base and manufacturing growth has accelerated under a recently liberalized economy. Textiles, clothing, leather, and jewelry are among South Asia's leading exports.

PAKISTAN
INDIA
NEPAL
BHUTAN
BANGLADESH
SRI LANKA
CHINA
Arabian Sea
Bay of Bengal
INDIAN OCEAN

Major industry and infrastructure

- aerospace
- car manufacture
- chemicals
- electronics
- engineering
- finance
- food processing
- iron & steel
- textiles
- capital cities
- major towns
- international airports
- major roads
- major industrial areas

Transportation network

1,068,996 miles (1,720,579 km)	21,015 miles (33,840 km)
46,724 miles (75,204 km)	15,319 miles (24,656 km)

India's railroad network, established under British colonial rule, is the sixth most extensive in the world and continues to play a unique role in integrating the country's disparate regions.

◀ ***Religion and commerce** sit side by side in the Nepalese capital, Kathmandu. Nepal is a Hindu state and these small, highly decorated shrines are commonplace. As in India, cows are venerated, and allowed free rein throughout the city.*

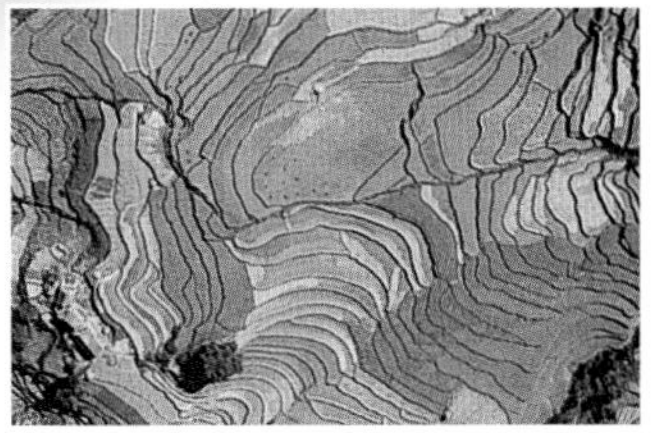

▶ ***Terracing allows steep** hillslopes to be cultivated in Nepal, a country where agricultural land is very limited. Because of poor soil quality, these terraces are often abandoned within a few years.*

172

Using the land & sea

Over 60% of South Asia's population is involved in agriculture. Traditional subsistence farming prevails and productivity is generally low. The monsoon region of the east is the world's most extensive rice-growing area. Corn, millet, and groundnuts are staple crops in drier areas, with wheat toward the north. Terracing increases cultivable land in the mountains. Livestock-raising is widespread throughout the subcontinent and fishing is common along the entire coast, although because few fishing craft are mechanized, total fish catches are low.

The urban/rural population divide

urban 25% | rural 75%

Population density	Total land area
888 people per sq mile (343 people per sq km)	1,573,285 sq miles (4,075,868 sq km)

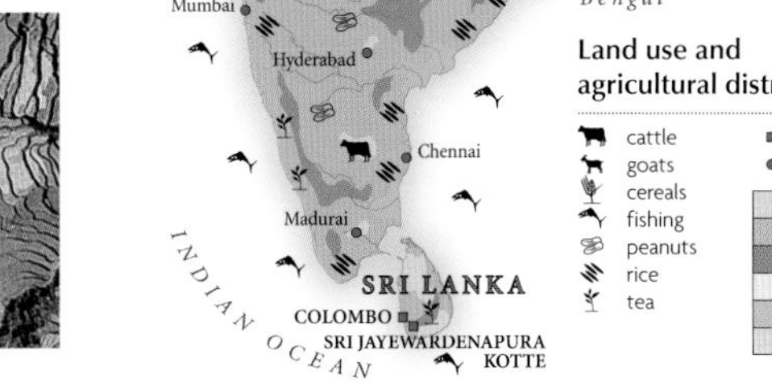
PAKISTAN
INDIA
NEPAL
BHUTAN
BANGLADESH
SRI LANKA
CHINA
Arabian Sea
Bay of Bengal
INDIAN OCEAN

Land use and agricultural distribution

- cattle
- goats
- cereals
- fishing
- peanuts
- rice
- tea
- capital cities
- major towns
- pasture
- cropland
- forest
- mountain region
- wetland
- desert

Northern India & the Himalayan states

BANGLADESH, BHUTAN, NEPAL, Arunachal Pradesh, Assam, Bihar, Chandigarh, Delhi, Haryana, Himachal Pradesh, Jammu & Kashmir, Jharkhand, Manipur, Meghalaya, Mizoram, Nagaland, Punjab, Rajasthan, Sikkim, Tripura, Uttarakhand, Uttar Pradesh, West Bengal

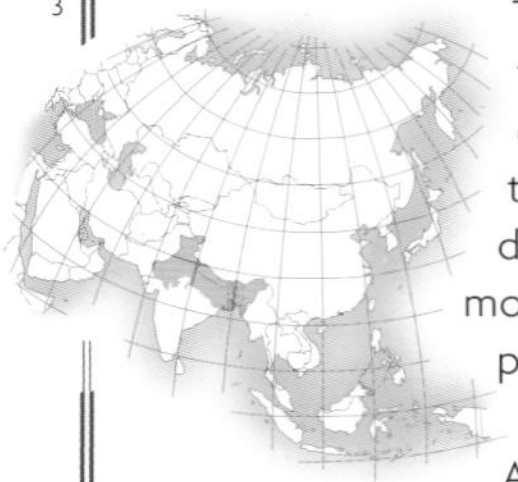

The Ganges and Brahmaputra river basins and the massive mountain barrier of the Himalayas define this region's landscape and have served to reinforce potent cultural and religious differences among its people. Hinduism pervades most aspects of national life and is a growing political force within India, a secular country which also encompasses the center of Sikhism at Amritsar and the world's largest Muslim minority. Nepal is a crowded mountain state, which faces severe ecological problems from deforestation, while the tiny Himalayan Buddhist kingdom of Bhutan is emerging from long-term isolation, to welcome selected visitors. The Muslim state of Bangladesh, formerly East Pakistan, is one of the world's most densely populated countries and one of the poorest, with more than 145 million people living largely on the massive Ganges/Brahmaputra delta. Many Bangladeshis live under threat of repeated, catastrophic floods.

◀ *The Golden Temple in Amritsar, the most sacred shrine of the Sikh religion, was the scene of violent clashes between Sikh separatists and government forces in 1984.*

Scale 1:6,500,000
Km
Miles
projection: Lambert Conformal Conic
AFGHANISTAN
CHINA
PAKISTAN
Thar Desert
JAMMU AND KASHMIR
HIMACHAL PRADESH
PUNJAB
HARYANA
RAJASTHAN
UTTARAKHAND
UTTAR PRADESH
MADHYA PRADESH
GUJARAT
FAR WESTERN
INDIA
Karakoram Range
Ladakh Range
Zaskar Range
Pir Panjal Range
Aravalli Range
Aksai Chin
(Administered by China, claimed by India)
Demchok/Dêmqog
(Administered by China, claimed by India)
(Claimed by India)
(Line of control)
K2 8611m
Nanga Parbat 8126m
Gasherbrum 8068m
Srinagar
Jammu
Amritsar
Ludhiana
Chandigarh
Shimla
Dehra Dūn
Meerut
Ghaziābād
Delhi
NEW DELHI
Farīdābād
Jaipur
Jodhpur
Bīkāner
Ajmer
Kota
Udaipur
Āgra
Lucknow
Kānpur
Allahābād
Bareilly
Jhānsi
Tropic of Cancer
148
154
156

Map key

Population

- ■ 1 million to 5 million
- ◉ 500,000 to 1 million
- ◎ 100,000 to 500,000
- ⊕ 50,000 to 100,000
- ○ 10,000 to 50,000
- ○ below 10,000

Elevation

- 6000m / 19,686ft
- 4000m / 13,124ft
- 3000m / 9843ft
- 2000m / 6562ft
- 1000m / 3281ft
- 500m / 1640ft
- 250m / 820ft
- 100m / 328ft
- sea level

Transportation & industry

Textiles, engineering, chemicals, and electronics are leading industries in north India. The plateau of Chota Nagpur provides ore for iron and steel production in the major industrial region northeast of Kolkata. Bangladesh processes jute and Nepal has a small manufacturing sector based on agricultural produce, while Bhutan's limited industry is concentrated in the southern lowland area.

PAKISTAN
CHINA
NEPAL
BHUTAN
INDIA
BANGLADESH
MYANMAR
BAY OF BENGAL
Srinagar
Amritsar
Ludhiana
Chandigarh
Delhi
NEW DELHI
Jaipur
Jodhpur
Kota
Kanpur
Lucknow
KATHMANDU
THIMPHU
Dibrugarh
Guwahati
DHAKA
Chittagong
Kolkata
Jamshedpur
Ranchi
Dhanbad

Major industry and infrastructure

- adventure tourism
- car manufacture
- chemicals
- coal
- electronics
- engineering
- finance
- food processing
- iron & steel
- jute processing
- oil
- tea processing
- textiles
- capital cities
- major towns
- international airports
- major roads
- major industrial areas

Transportation network

Over 60% of Bangladesh's internal trade is carried by boat. The country has a very disjointed land transportation network, with no bridges over the Brahmaputra and few road crossings on the Ganges river.

The landscape

Most of the region is drained by the Ganges river, which meets the Brahmaputra in Bangladesh to form an immense delta before flowing into the Bay of Bengal. The Himalayas extend eastward over 1500 miles (2400 km), from the parallel ranges running through Jammu and Kashmir. The Thar Desert occupies the southwest.

▶ *The Pir Panjal Range in southwestern Kashmir rises to elevations of 12,500 ft (3810 m). Despite the freezing conditions, settlements and extensive pastures are found above the tree line.*

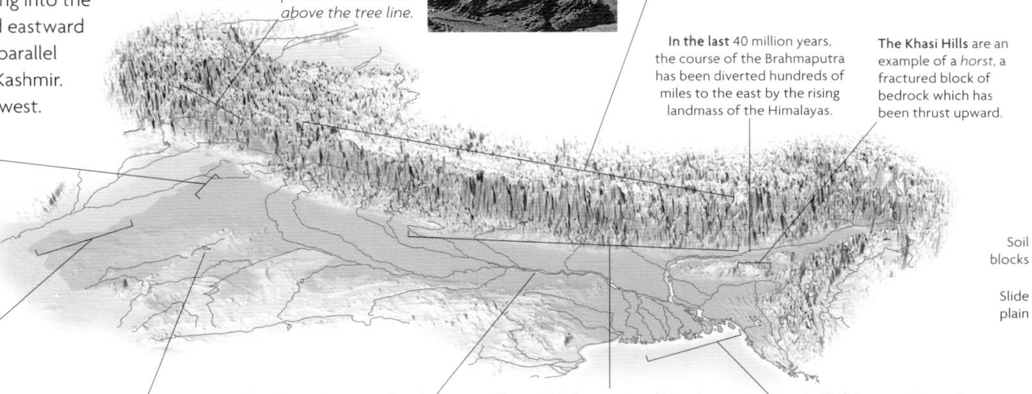

The northern ranges of the Himalayas contain the highest mountains in the world, with average heights of more than 23,000 ft (7000 m) and many peaks higher than 26,000 ft (8000 m).

In the last 40 million years, the course of the Brahmaputra has been diverted hundreds of miles to the east by the rising landmass of the Himalayas.

The Khasi Hills are an example of a *horst*, a fractured block of bedrock which has been thrust upward.

The Indian Punjab lies mainly to the west of the Ganges watershed and its rivers flow into the Indus. Control of this water resource has been a source of great friction with neighboring Pakistan.

The border between India and Pakistan runs through the Thar Desert, an area of sandy seif dunes 50–100 ft (15–30 m) in height. Fossils found in the desert indicate that the dunes, stabilized by vegetation, have been in their current position for about 3000 years.

Sambhar Salt Lake in Rajasthan is India's largest lake. Unlike most of the Himalayan lakes which are glacial in origin – formed in ice-scoured basinsor as the result of depositional damming – it is an ephemeral salt lake filled periodically by flash flooding.

The Ganges river, sacred to the Hindu people, drains a vast lowland area at the base of the Himalayas. The northern plains are covered by sandy deposits, broken by mud banks formed when the river floods.

The rapid deforestation of Himalayan valleys has led to acute soil erosion and increased rates of rainwater runoff, both cited as possible causes of the worsening floods downstream in the Ganges/Brahmaputra delta, although natural rates are high and may be the real cause.

Over half of the great Ganges/Brahmaputra delta floods each year during the monsoon as rivers, swollen by meltwater from the Himalayas and by excess rainwater, break their banks and fertilize the land with nutrient-rich sediment.

▲ ***The summit of*** *Machhapuchhre rises to 22,942 ft (6993 m). It is also known as the "Fish's Tail" because of its distinctive peak.*

Debris slides in the middle Himalayas

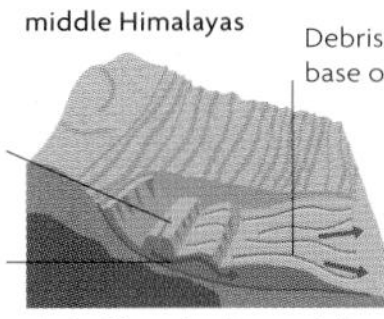
Debris fans at base of slope
Soil blocks
Slide plain

▲ ***Soil loss*** *in the middle Himalayas has largely been attributed to debris slides, where large blocks of soil are mobilized by saturation along a slide plane. Once mobile, the soil slides down the slope, gaining speed and thinning to form a fan at the base of the slope.*

Using the land

Grain production dominates land use. Rice is most widely grown in the east. Irrigation and new crop strains have dramatically increased yields in the Punjab, a major wheat-producing area. River floodplains are intensively farmed and livestock herding is widespread, particularly in Bhutan. Regional crops include jute in Bangladesh, tea in Assam, cardamom in Sikkim, and saffron in Kashmir.

The urban/rural population divide

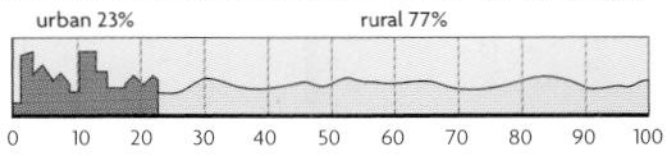
urban 23%
rural 77%
0 10 20 30 40 50 60 70 80 90 100

Population density	Total land area
993 people per sq mile (384 people per sq km)	665,104 sq miles (1,723,068 sq km)

Land use and agricultural distribution

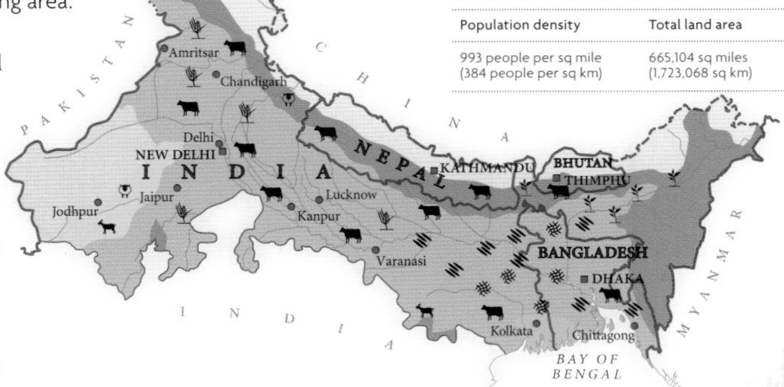
cattle
goats
sheep
cereals
jute
rice
tea
capital cities
major towns
pasture
cropland
forest
mountain region
wetland
desert
PAKISTAN
CHINA
INDIA
NEPAL
BHUTAN
BANGLADESH
MYANMAR
Srinagar
Amritsar
Chandigarh
Delhi
NEW DELHI
Jaipur
Jodhpur
Lucknow
Kanpur
Varanasi
KATHMANDU
THIMPHU
DHAKA
Kolkata
Chittagong
BAY OF BENGAL

▲ ***An adverse climate,*** *steep slopes, and poor soils limit crop cultivation in Bhutan, which is a largely agrarian economy. Rice, corn, and wheat are the main staples, although orchards are being established as the soil and climate suit this type of farming.*

CHINA
NEPAL
INDIA
BHUTAN
BANGLADESH
MYANMAR
SIKKIM
ARUNACHAL PRADESH
ASSAM
MEGHALAYA
NAGALAND
MANIPUR
MIZORAM
TRIPURA
BIHAR
JHARKHAND
WEST BENGAL
ORISSA
CHHATTISGARH
KATHMANDU
THIMPHU
DHAKA
Mount Everest 8848m
Kanchenjunga 8598m
Annapurna 8091m
Dhawalagiri 8167m
Manaslu 8163m
Machhapuchhre 6993m
Lhotse 8516m
Kula Kangri 7554m
Chomo Lhari 7314m
Kangto 7102m
(Much of Arunāchal Pradesh is claimed by China)
Patna
Varanasi
Kolkata (Calcutta)
Chittagong
Khulna
Barisal
Rajshahi
Sylhet
Shillong
Guwahati
Imphal
Agartala
Ranchi
Jamshedpur
Dhanbad
Gaya
Muzaffarpur
Darbhanga
Bhagalpur
Gorakhpur
Darjiling
Gangtok
Pokhara
Biratnagar
Dibrugarh
Kohima
Aizawl
Bay of Bengal
Mouths of the Ganges
Sundarbans
Tropic of Cancer
156
172
166

▲ ***Flooded streets in*** *Dhaka, Bangladesh are a testament to the region's vulnerability to flooding. In 1988 alone, 75% of the country was flooded, leaving thousands of people dead and over 25 million homeless.*

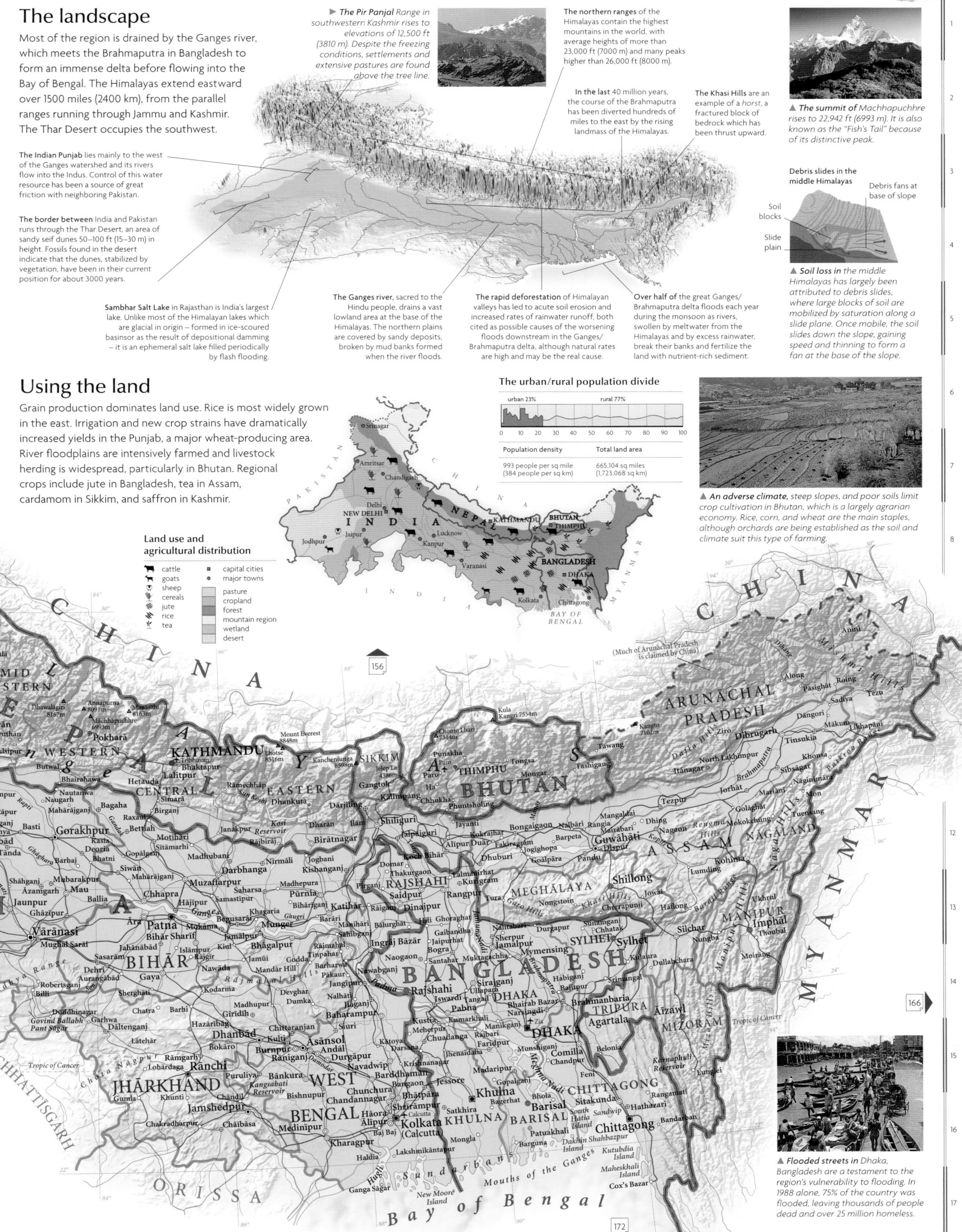

Southern India & Sri Lanka

SRI LANKA, Andhra Pradesh, Chhattisgarh, Dadra & Nagar Haveli, Daman & Diu, Goa, Gujarat, Karnataka, Kerala, Lakshadweep, Madhya Pradesh, Maharashtra, Orissa, Pondicherry, Tamil Nadu

The unique and highly independent southern states reflect the diverse and decentralized nature of India, which has fourteen official languages. The southern half of the peninsula lay beyond the reach of early invaders from the north and retained the distinct and ancient culture of Dravidian peoples such as the Tamils, whose language is spoken in preference to Hindi throughout southern India. The interior plateau of southern India is less densely populated than the coastal lowlands, where the European colonial imprint is strongest. Urban and industrial growth is accelerating, but southern India's vast population remains predominantly rural. The island of Sri Lanka has two distinct cultural groups; the mainly Buddhist Sinhalese majority, and the Tamil minority whose struggle for a homeland in the northeast has led to prolonged civil war.

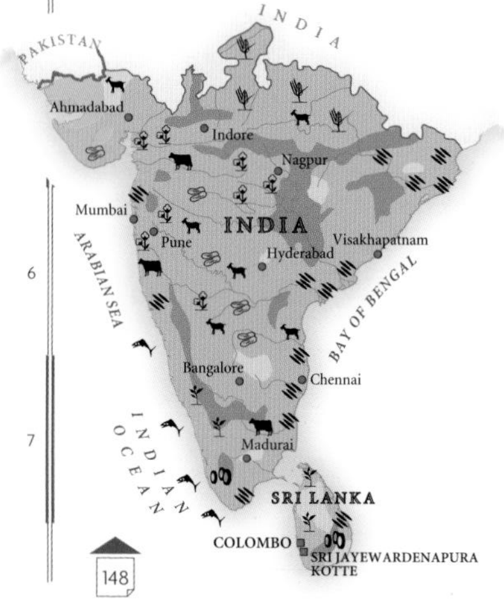
INDIA
PAKISTAN
Ahmadabad
Indore
Nagpur
Mumbai
Pune
Hyderabad
Visakhapatnam
ARABIAN SEA
BAY OF BENGAL
Bangalore
Chennai
INDIAN OCEAN
Madurai
SRI LANKA
COLOMBO
SRI JAYEWARDENAPURA KOTTE
148

Using the land and sea

Rice is the main staple in the east, in Sri Lanka and along the humid Malabar Coast. Peanuts are grown on the Deccan plateau, with wheat, corn, and chickpeas, toward the north. Sri Lanka is a leading exporter of tea, coconuts and rubber. Cotton plantations supply local mills around Nagpur and Mumbai. Fishing supports many communities in Kerala and the Laccadive Islands.

Land use and agricultural distribution

cattle, goats, cereals, cotton, fishing, peanuts, rice, rubber, tea, capital cities, major towns, pasture, cropland, forest, wetland

The urban/rural population divide

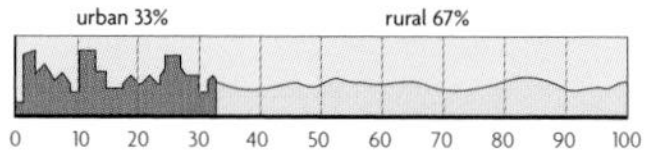
urban 33%
rural 67%
0 10 20 30 40 50 60 70 80 90 100

Population density	Total land area
730 people per sq mile (282 people per sq km)	698,295 sq miles (1,809,054 sq km)

The landscape

The undulating Deccan plateau underlies most of southern India; it slopes gently down toward the east and is largely enclosed by the Ghats coastal hill ranges. The Western Ghats run continuously along the Arabian Sea coast, while the Eastern Ghats are interrupted by rivers which follow the slope of the plateau and flow across broad lowlands into the Bay of Bengal. The plateaus and basins of Sri Lanka's central highlands are surrounded by a broad plain.

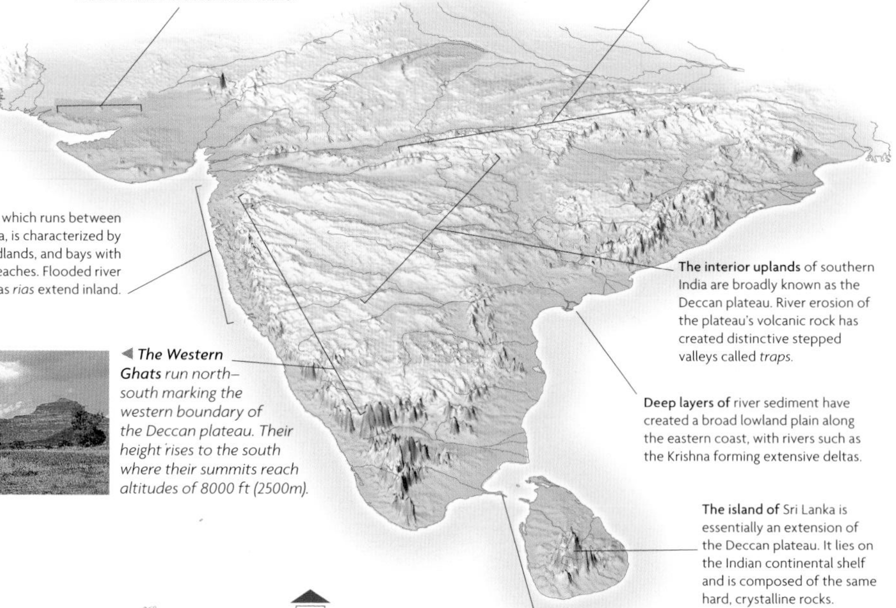

The Rann of Kachchh tidal marshes encircle the low-lying Kachchh peninsula. For several months during the rainy season the water level of the marshes rises and Kachchh becomes an island.

Along the northern boundary of the Deccan plateau, old basement rocks are interspersed with younger sedimentary strata. This creates spectacular scarplands, cut by numerous waterfalls along the softer sedimentary strata.

The Konkan coast, which runs between Daman and Goa, is characterized by rocky headlands, and bays with crescent-shaped beaches. Flooded river valleys known as *rias* extend inland.

The interior uplands of southern India are broadly known as the Deccan plateau. River erosion of the plateau's volcanic rock has created distinctive stepped valleys called *traps*.

Deep layers of river sediment have created a broad lowland plain along the eastern coast, with rivers such as the Krishna forming extensive deltas.

The island of Sri Lanka is essentially an extension of the Deccan plateau. It lies on the Indian continental shelf and is composed of the same hard, crystalline rocks.

◀ ***The Western Ghats** run north–south marking the western boundary of the Deccan plateau. Their height rises to the south where their summits reach altitudes of 8000 ft (2500m).*

Adam's Bridge

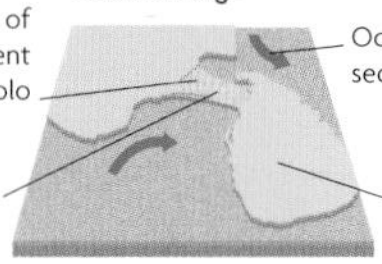
Relict of ancient tombolo
Adam's Bridge
Ocean currents cause sediment build up
Sri Lanka

▲ ***Adam's Bridge (Rama's Bridge)** is a chain of sandy shoals lying about 4 ft (1.2 m) under the sea between India and Sri Lanka. They once formed the world's longest tombolo, or land bridge, before the sea level began to rise several thousand years ago.*

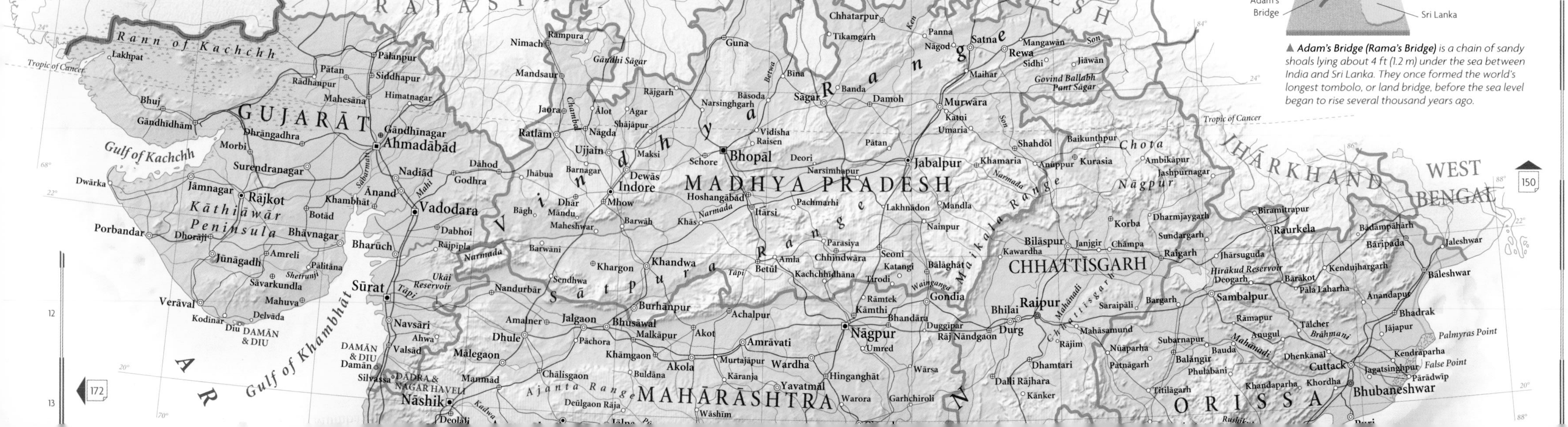
PAKISTAN
RĀJASTHĀN
UTTAR PRADESH
GUJARĀT
MADHYA PRADESH
CHHATTĪSGARH
JHĀRKHAND
WEST BENGAL
MAHĀRĀSHTRA
ORISSA
Rann of Kachchh
Gulf of Kachchh
Gulf of Khambhat
Kāthiāwār Peninsula
Tropic of Cancer
Ahmadābād
Vadodara
Sūrat
Rājkot
Bhopāl
Indore
Jabalpur
Gwalior
Nāgpur
Raipur
Bhubaneshwar
Nāshik
DAMĀN & DIU
DADRA & NAGAR HAVELI
148
150
172

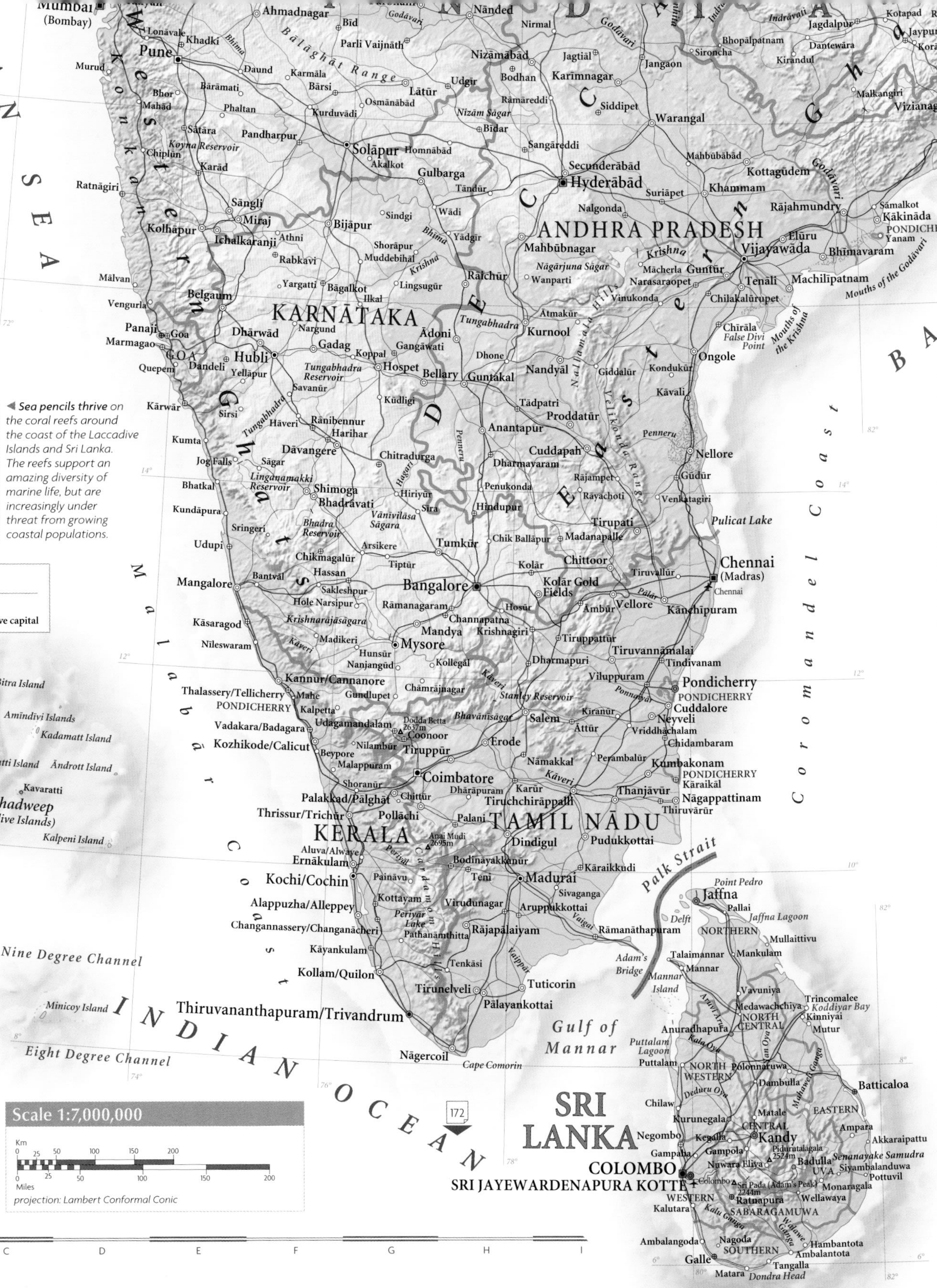

Mumbai (Bombay)
Pune
Ahmadnagar
Nānded
Nizāmābād
Karīmnagar
Warangal
Hyderābād
Secunderābād
Solāpur
Gulbarga
ANDHRA PRADESH
KARNĀTAKA
TAMIL NĀDU
KERALA
GOA
Panaji
Hubli
Belgaum
Dhārwād
Bellary
Kurnool
Vijayawāda
Guntūr
Rājahmundry
Kākināda
Visākhapatnam
Vizianagaram
Nellore
Chennai (Madras)
Pondicherry
Cuddalore
Vellore
Bangalore
Mysore
Mangalore
Kannur/Cannanore
Kozhikode/Calicut
Coimbatore
Thrissur/Trichur
Kochi/Cochin
Alappuzha/Alleppey
Kollam/Quilon
Thiruvananthapuram/Trivandrum
Nāgercoil
Cape Comorin
Madurai
Tiruchchirāppalli
Thanjāvūr
Tirunelveli
Tuticorin
Salem
Erode
Tirupati
Ongole
Western Ghats
Eastern Ghats
Konkan
Malabar Coast
Coromandel Coast
Bālāghāt Range
Deccan
Palk Strait
Gulf of Mannar
Adam's Bridge
BAY OF BENGAL
ARABIAN SEA
INDIAN OCEAN
LAKSHADWEEP
Lakshadweep (Laccadive Islands)
Nine Degree Channel
Eight Degree Channel
Minicoy Island
Kavaratti
SRI LANKA
Jaffna
Trincomalee
Anurādhapura
Batticaloa
Kandy
Kurunegala
Negombo
COLOMBO
SRI JAYEWARDENAPURA KOTTE
Galle
Matara
Hambantota
Dondra Head
Point Pedro
172

Map key

Population

- ▣ above 5 million
- ◼ 1 million to 5 million
- ● 500,000 to 1 million
- ◎ 100,000 to 500,000
- ⊕ 50,000 to 100,000
- ○ 10,000 to 50,000
- ◦ below 10,000

Elevation

- 2000m / 6562ft
- 1000m / 3281ft
- 500m / 1640ft
- 250m / 820ft
- 100m / 328ft
- sea level

◀ ***Sea pencils thrive*** *on the coral reefs around the coast of the Laccadive Islands and Sri Lanka. The reefs support an amazing diversity of marine life, but are increasingly under threat from growing coastal populations.*

Sri Lanka: Capital cities

COLOMBO – capital
SRI JAYEWARDENAPURA KOTTE – legislative capital

▲ ***Local fisheries around*** *Sri Lanka afford great potential. However, many fishermen living on the coastal fringes saw their livelihoods destroyed by the devastating effects of the Asian tsunami in 2004.*

Scale 1:7,000,000

Km 0 25 50 100 150 200
Miles 0 25 50 100 150 200

projection: Lambert Conformal Conic

▲ ***The great triumphal*** *arch of Charminar, built in 1591, epitomizes the fine Islamic architecture which the Moghuls brought from the north to Hyderabad, the capital of Andhra Pradesh.*

Transportation & industry

South India has a broad industrial base, with three leading regions. Around Mumbai, Bangalore, and Ahmadabad, cotton mills and chemical plants make use of cheap hydroelectric power generated in the Western Ghats. Light engineering and textiles are well established to the south and west of Chennai. Sri Lanka's industry is based mainly on the processing of agricultural products.

Major industry and infrastructure

- aerospace
- car manufacture
- chemicals
- electronics
- engineering
- food processing
- iron & steel
- pharmaceuticals
- printing & publishing
- shipbuilding
- tea processing
- textiles
- tobacco processing
- capital cities
- major towns
- international airports
- major roads
- major industrial areas

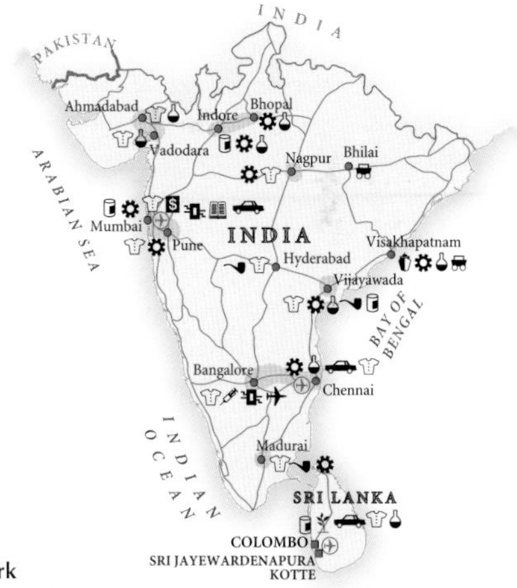

PAKISTAN
INDIA
Ahmadabad
Indore
Bhopal
Vadodara
Nagpur
Bhilai
Mumbai
Pune
Hyderabad
Visakhapatnam
Vijayawada
ARABIAN SEA
BAY OF BENGAL
Bangalore
Chennai
Madurai
INDIAN OCEAN
SRI LANKA
COLOMBO
SRI JAYEWARDENAPURA KOTTE

Transportation network

India's hard-surfaced road network has grown almost tenfold since independence, yet many villages are still only accessible on foot, even in densely populated rural areas.

▶ ***Mumbai is one*** *of the largest and most densely-populated cities in the world. It is the center of India's textile trade and has important finance and commerce sectors.*

Mainland East Asia

CHINA, MONGOLIA, NORTH KOREA, SOUTH KOREA, TAIWAN

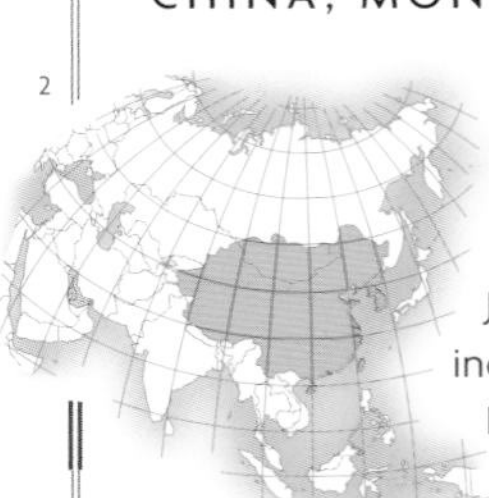

China, the world's most populous nation, has an unbroken cultural history, longer than that of any other country, and is rapidly emerging as a leading world power. When Mao Zedong established Communist rule in 1949, China had become a backward feudal empire, stricken by civil war and over a century of European and Japanese incursions. The closed regime withstood the traumas of rapid industrialization, communal farming, and the brutal purges of the Cultural Revolution but, since the 1980s has introduced economic reforms, led by expanded foreign trade. China's population is heavily concentrated in the east and, despite accelerating urban growth, remains predominantly rural. One cultural group, the Han, make up over 90% of the people, while five "Autonomous Regions" have been established in the south and west for the main ethnic minorities.

◀ *Gansu province, through which the ancient Silk Route passes on its way to the west, is characterized by extensive loess deposits which are terraced and used for crop cultivation.*

KAZAKHSTAN
KYRGYZSTAN
TAJIKISTAN
AFGHANISTAN
INDIA
NEPAL
BHUTAN
MYANMAR
XINJIANG UYGUR ZIZHIQU
Taklimakan Shamo
Tarim Pendi
Tien Shan
Junggar Pendi
Ürümqi
Kunlun Shan
Altun Shan
Qingzang Gaoyuan (Plateau of Tibet)
XIZANG ZIZHIQU (TIBET)
Lhasa
HIMALAYAS
Mount Everest 8848m
Qaidam Pendi
Altai Mountains
HOVD
BAYAN-ÖLGIY
UVS

122
144
146
150
150
150
150
166

Transportation & industry

Large-scale industrial growth has always been a priority of the Communist government. Metals and machine production, chemicals, and engineering are among the leading industries, concentrated in the major cities of the east coast. Textiles and clothing manufacture, the main consumer goods sector, is relatively well dispersed, with a few significant centers such as Shanghai, Beijing, and Hong Kong.

RUSSIAN FEDERATION
KAZAKH.
KYRG.
TAJIK.
PAK.
INDIA
NEPAL
BHUT.
MYANMAR
LAOS
VIET.
ULAN BATOR
MONGOLIA
CHINA
NORTH KOREA
PYONGYANG
SOUTH KOREA
SEOUL
SEJONG CITY
BEIJING
Shenyang
Taiyuan
Lanzhou
Nanjing
Shanghai
Wuhan
Chongqing
Kunming
Guangzhou
Hong Kong
TAIPEI
TAIWAN
Major industry and infrastructure
car manufacture
chemicals
electronics
engineering
finance
food processing
iron & steel
shipbuilding
textiles
capital cities
major towns
international airports
major roads
major industrial areas

Transportation network

829,790 miles (1,335,571 km)	12,740 miles (20,506 km)
43,976 miles (70,780 km)	70,991 miles (114,262 km)

Ever-increasing demand for rail transportation has led to major improvment and expansion of the network, notably the 690 mile (1100 km) link between Golmud and Lhasa opened in 2006.

◀ *Coal is China's most abundant mineral resource. This mine at Fuxin in Liaoning province is used to provide coal for a nearby power station.*

The landscape

The East Asian landmass is arranged in three distinct levels, the highest of which is the Plateau of Tibet in the southwest. The arid uplands of northwestern China form a barren middle step. The main rivers flow eastward from these two platforms to the East China and South China sea coasts, across a broad region of alluvial lowlands and low hills.

◀ *Paektu-san, at 9023 ft (2750 m), is North Korea's highest peak; an extinct volcanic cone now filled by a crater lake.*

▲ *The Plateau of Tibet occupies about a quarter of China's total area. The Yangtze, Mekong, Indus, and Brahmaputra rivers all originate in the south and east of the plateau.*

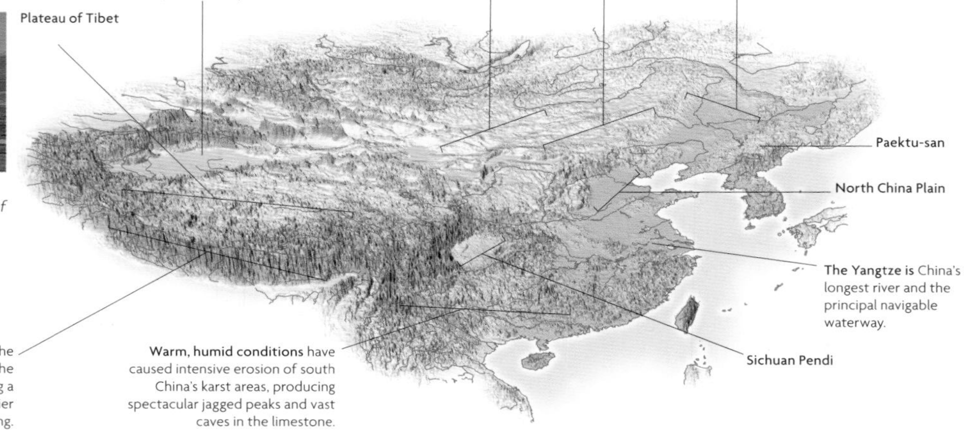

Plateau of Tibet
Tarim Basin (Tarim Pendi)
The Gobi Desert extends across the Nei Mongol Gaoyuan; a vast saucer-shaped upland surrounded by a rim of higher mountains.
The loess plateau of northern China is the world's greatest expanse of loess, a loose soil made up of wind-blown material. The plateau has been heavily eroded by tributaries of the Yellow River.
Shifting sand dunes are found in the arid west of the northeast China Plain, while the eastern part of this great expanse is wet and swampy.
Paektu-san
North China Plain
The Yangtze is China's longest river and the principal navigable waterway.
Sichuan Pendi
The Himalayas extend along the southwestern edge of the Plateau of Tibet, forming a continuous mountain barrier over 1500 miles (2500 km) long.
Warm, humid conditions have caused intensive erosion of south China's karst areas, producing spectacular jagged peaks and vast caves in the limestone.

River-eroded fine soils
Thick blanket of loess

▲ *Because of its very small grain-size, loess has been easily transported and deposited by winds which scour the plains, and in northern China, deposits of loess can be up to 3000 ft (1000 m) thick. Loess-based soils are very fertile, but clearing land for agriculture quickly destabilizes the soil and allows it to be eroded.*

◀ *Although it is over 30 years since his death, the legacy of Chairman Mao Zedong, architect of the Great Proletarian Cultural Revolution, is still very much in evidence across China's landscape. In 1959 Mao launched a 20-year period of industrialization and socioeconomic realignment, rejecting western ideals and social codes.*

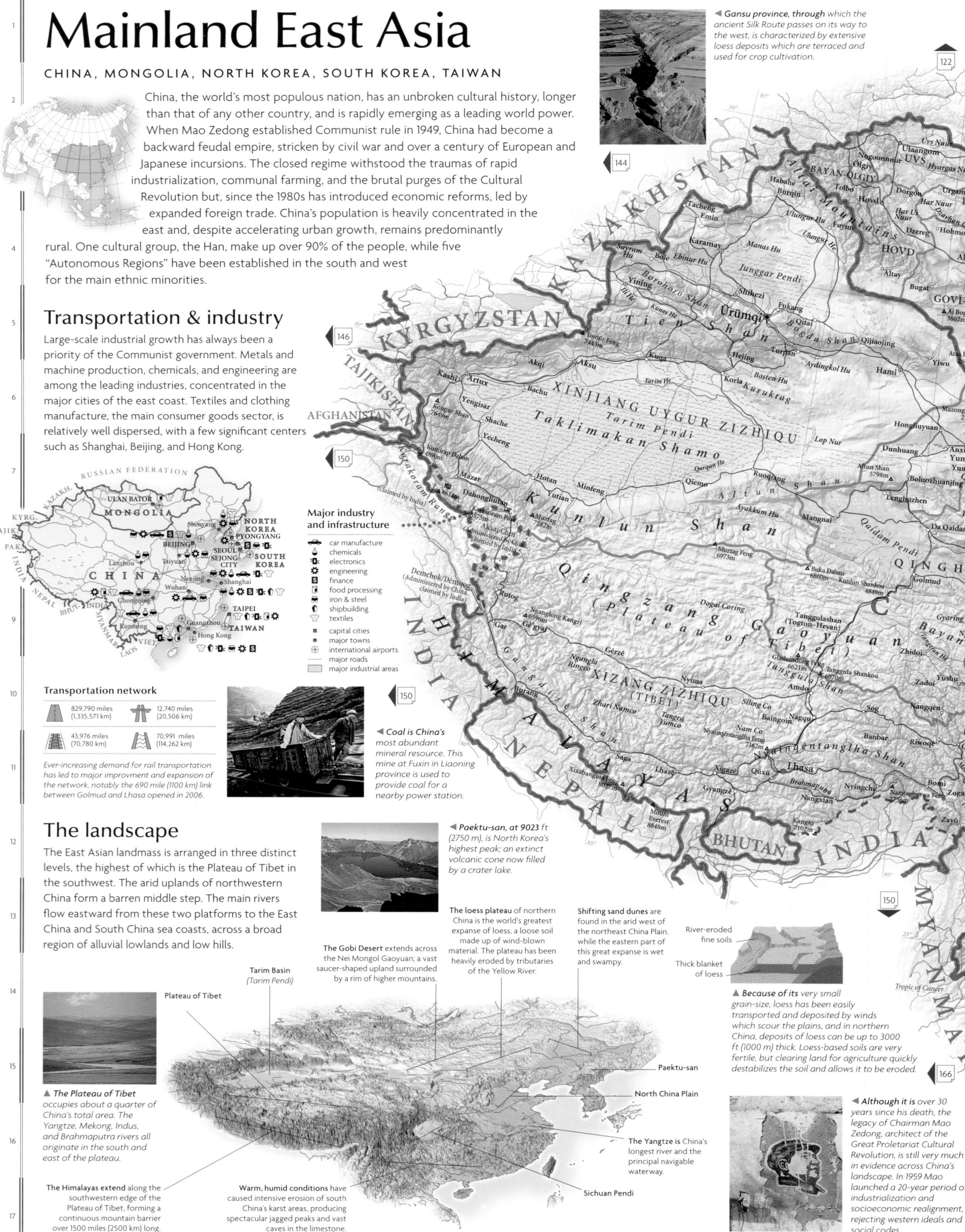

Scale 1:14,000,000
Km
0 25 50 100 150 200 250 300 350 400
Miles
0 25 50 100 150 200 250 300 350 400
projection: Lambert Conformal Conic
Map key
Population
above 5 million
1 million to 5 million
500,000 to 1 million
100,000 to 500,000
50,000 to 100,000
10,000 to 50,000
below 10,000
Elevation
6000m / 19,686ft
4000m / 13,124ft
3000m / 9843ft
2000m / 6562ft
1000m / 3281ft
500m / 1640ft
250m / 820ft
100m / 328ft
sea level
RUSSIAN FEDERATION
MONGOLIA
ULAANBAATAR (ULAN BATOR)
Gobi
NORTH KOREA
P'YŎNGYANG
SOUTH KOREA
SEOUL
SEJONG CITY
SEA OF JAPAN (EAST SEA)
JAPAN
Yellow Sea
Bo Hai
Korea Bay
EAST CHINA SEA
SOUTH CHINA SEA
TAIWAN
TAIPEI (T'AIPEI)
Tropic of Cancer
VIETNAM
LAOS
Gulf of Tongking
HAINAN
BEIJING (PEKING)
Tianjin
Shanghai
SHANGHAI SHI
Chongqing
Guangzhou
Hong Kong (Xianggang)
Macao (Aomen)
Wuhan
Nanjing
Xi'an
Chengdu
Harbin
Shenyang
HEILONGJIANG
JILIN
LIAONING
HEBEI
SHANDONG
SHANXI
HENAN
SHAANXI
JIANGSU
ANHUI
HUBEI
ZHEJIANG
SICHUAN
CHONGQING SHI
HUNAN
JIANGXI
FUJIAN
GUIZHOU
YUNNAN
GUANGXI ZHUANGZU ZIZHIQU
GUANGDONG
NINGXIA
NEI MONGOL ZIZHIQU (INNER MONGOLIA)
Da Hinggan Ling
(China and Taiwan claim all of each other's territory)
122
164
192
166

Using the land & sea

Around 90% of China is unsuitable for cultivation, being either climatically or topographically adverse, or lacking sufficiently fertile soils. Most of the west is used for nomadic herding, while farmland is concentrated in the eastern monsoon region, with rice grown in the tropical and subtropical south. Cereals and soybeans predominate as rainfall and temperatures decline further north.

◀ *The Great Wall of China remains one of the world's largest-ever construction projects, and is so vast that it is visible from space. Sections were added as late as 1640 and it runs for over 4000 miles (6400 km) from the Yellow Sea to Central Asia.*

The urban/rural population divide

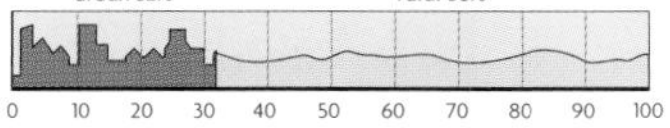

urban 32%
rural 68%
0 10 20 30 40 50 60 70 80 90 100

Population density	Total land area
325 people per sq mile (125 people per sq km)	4,288,672 sq miles (11,110,550 sq km)

Land use and agricultural distribution

pigs
sheep
corn
cotton
fishing
fruit
rice
sugar cane
soybeans
capital cities
major towns
pasture
cropland
forest
mountain region
RUSSIAN FEDERATION
ULAN BATOR
MONGOLIA
KAZAKH.
KYRG.
TAJIK.
PAK.
INDIA
NEPAL
BHUTAN
INDIA
MYANMAR
LAOS
VIET.
Ürümqi
Harbin
NORTH KOREA
PYONGYANG
Shenyang
BEIJING
SEOUL
SEJONG CITY
SOUTH KOREA
CHINA
Lhasa
Wuhan
Shanghai
TAIPEI
TAIWAN
Kunming
Guangzhou

Western China

Gansu, Ningxia, Qinghai, Tibet, Xinjiang

The plateaus and basins of China's dry, desolate western domain are sparsely populated and largely undeveloped, although they have rich mineral reserves; they also form a critical buffer zone for China, in a geographically important and culturally sensitive part of the Asian continent. Across most of the west, the Han Chinese are outnumbered by a range of cultural groups, including the Uygur, the largest group of the various seminomadic Muslim peoples from Central Asia. The remote, inhospitable Plateau of Tibet is the world's coldest and highest plateau. It has been occupied by the Chinese since 1950. Tibet is one of western China's five "Autonomous Regions," but its reclusive Buddhist culture has been systematically undermined by the Chinese government.

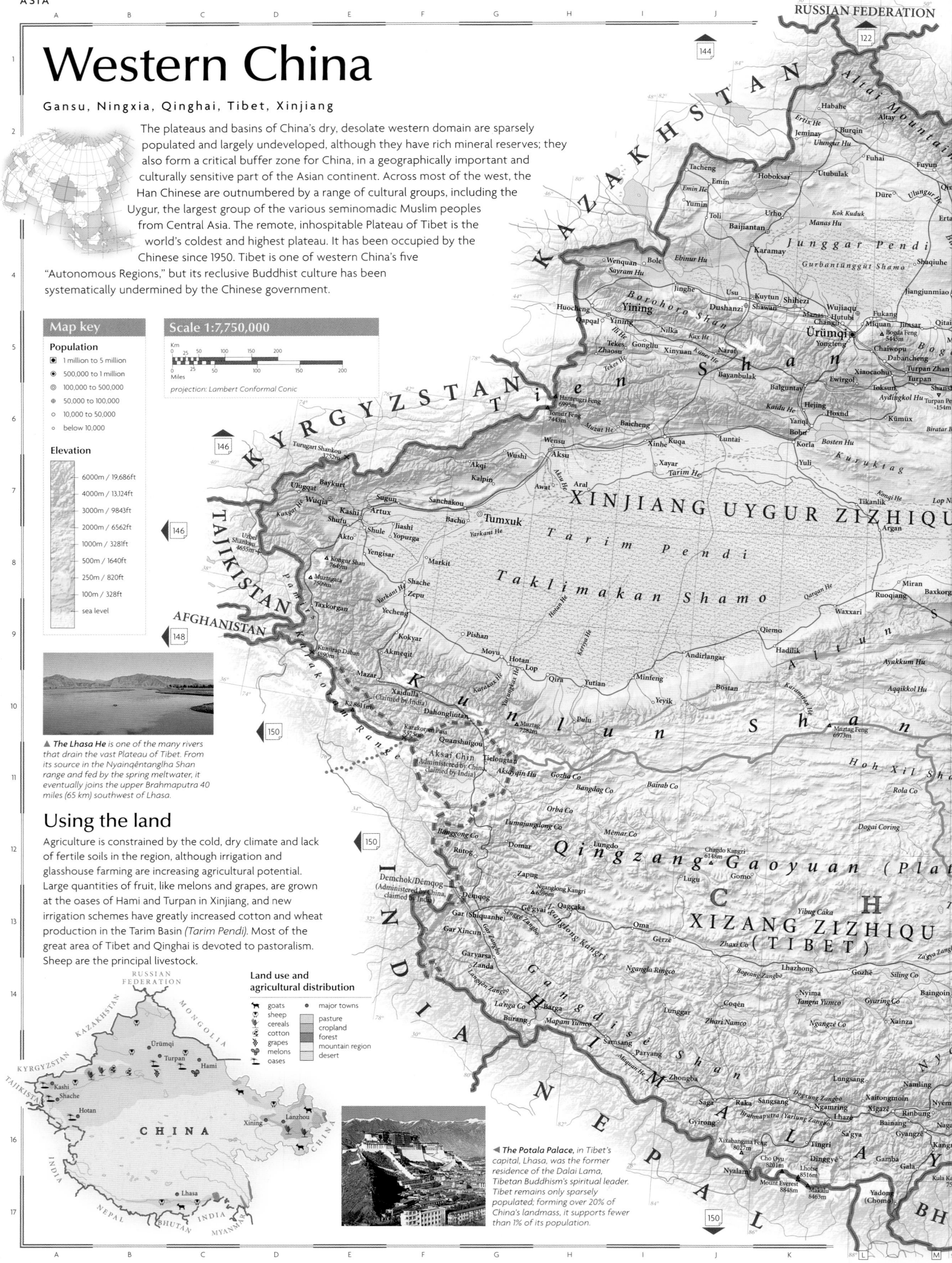

Map key
Population
1 million to 5 million
500,000 to 1 million
100,000 to 500,000
50,000 to 100,000
10,000 to 50,000
below 10,000
Elevation
6000m / 19,686ft
4000m / 13,124ft
3000m / 9843ft
2000m / 6562ft
1000m / 3281ft
500m / 1640ft
250m / 820ft
100m / 328ft
sea level
Scale 1:7,750,000
projection: Lambert Conformal Conic
RUSSIAN FEDERATION
KAZAKHSTAN
KYRGYZSTAN
TAJIKISTAN
AFGHANISTAN
INDIA
NEPAL
XINJIANG UYGUR ZIZHIQU
XIZANG ZIZHIQU (TIBET)
Tarim Pendi
Taklimakan Shamo
Junggar Pendi
Tien Shan
Kunlun Shan
Altun Shan
Qingzang Gaoyuan (Plateau of Tibet)
Gangdise Shan
Karakoram Range
Ürümqi
Yining
Kashi
Hotan
Shache
Aksu
Karamay
Mount Everest 8848m
Aksai Chin (Administered by China, claimed by India)
Demchok/Dêmqog (Administered by China, claimed by India)

▲ *The Lhasa He is one of the many rivers that drain the vast Plateau of Tibet. From its source in the Nyainqêntanglha Shan range and fed by the spring meltwater, it eventually joins the upper Brahmaputra 40 miles (65 km) southwest of Lhasa.*

Using the land

Agriculture is constrained by the cold, dry climate and lack of fertile soils in the region, although irrigation and glasshouse farming are increasing agricultural potential. Large quantities of fruit, like melons and grapes, are grown at the oases of Hami and Turpan in Xinjiang, and new irrigation schemes have greatly increased cotton and wheat production in the Tarim Basin *(Tarim Pendi)*. Most of the great area of Tibet and Qinghai is devoted to pastoralism. Sheep are the principal livestock.

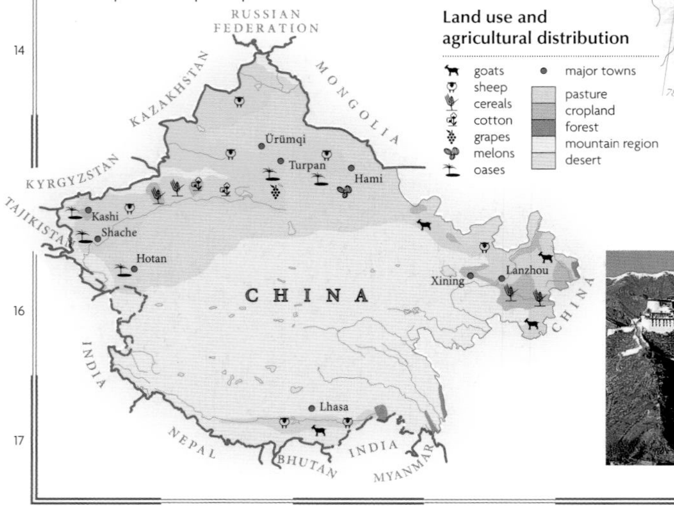
Land use and agricultural distribution
goats
sheep
cereals
cotton
grapes
melons
oases
major towns
pasture
cropland
forest
mountain region
desert
RUSSIAN FEDERATION
KAZAKHSTAN
MONGOLIA
KYRGYZSTAN
TAJIKISTAN
CHINA
INDIA
NEPAL
BHUTAN
MYANMAR
Ürümqi
Turpan
Hami
Kashi
Shache
Hotan
Xining
Lanzhou
Lhasa

◀ *The Potala Palace, in Tibet's capital, Lhasa, was the former residence of the Dalai Lama, Tibetan Buddhism's spiritual leader. Tibet remains only sparsely populated; forming over 20% of China's landmass, it supports fewer than 1% of its population.*

N O P Q R S T U V W X Y
O P Q R S T U V W Z
MONGOLIA
NEI MONGOL ZIZHIQU
GANSU
NINGXIA
QINGHAI
SICHUAN
SHAANXI
INDIA
MYANMAR
YUNNAN
Plateau of Tibet
Barkol Hu
Barkol
Qijiaojing
Yiwu
Hami
Wutongwozi Quan
Naran Sebstein Bulag
Yandun
Shankou
Xingxingxia
Gongpoquan
Mazong Shan 2584m
Hongliuyuan
Xijian Quan
Qiaowan
Anxi
Yumen
Kox Kuduk
Dunhuang
Yumendong
Jiayuguan
Jinta
Jiuquan (Suzhou)
Gaotai
Zhangye (Ganzhou)
Shandan
Linze
Hongwansi
Jinchang
Mingin
Yongchang
Wuwei
Hongliuwan
Boluozhuanjing
Dangchengwan
Altun Shan 5798m
Dangjin Shankou
Suhai Hu
Lenghuzhen
Har Hu
Qilian
Obo
Minle
Changweiliang
Yuka
Da Qaidam
Mangnai
Qaidam Pendi
Bayan Shan 5030m
Delhi
Tianjun
Qinghai Hu
Datong
Huzhu
Xining
Ledu
Haiyan
Huangyuan
Huangzhong
Minhe
Hualong
Gonghe
Ulan
Caka Yanhu
Toson Hu
Dabsan Hu
Bei Hulsan Hu
Ganq
Bolontay
Golmud
Dulan
Guide
Lanzhou
Yongjing
Yuzhong
Baiyin
Jingtai
Zhongwei
Zhongning
Yinchuan
Huinong
Pingluo
Helan
Lingwu
Wuzhong
Yanchi
Tongxin
Liwang
Haiyuan
Jingyuan
Guyuan
Xiji
Longde
Huining
Dingxi
Huanxian
Huachi
Qingcheng
Qingyang (Xifeng)
Pingliang (Kongtong)
Heshui
Ningxian
Zhengning
Huating
Jingchuan
Zhuanglang
Zhangjiachuan
Tongwei
Qin'an
Tianshui
Gangu
Wushan
Longxi
Weiyuan
Lintao
Kangle
Hezheng
Linxia
Xiahe
Hezuo
Lintan
Jone
Minxian
Lixian
Xihe
Huixian
Dangchang
Chengxian
Longnan (Wudu)
Kangxian
Wenxian
Tewo
Zhugqu
Luqu
Maqu
Tongren
Xinghai
Hoika
Tongde
Zêkog
Yêgainnyin
Huashixia
Madoi
Maqên Kangri 6282m
Maqên
Gadê
Darlag
Sogruma
Jigzhi
Baima
Anyêmaqên Shan
Bayan Har Shan
Burhan Budai Shan
Kunlun Shankou 4849m
Hoh Sai Hu
Huiten Nur
Dorgê Co
Wudaoliang
Yagradagzê Shan 5202m
Ngoring Hu
Gyaring Hu
Erdaogou
Tanggulashan (Togton Heyan)
Qumarlêb
Zhidoi
Qingshuihe
Chindu
Yushu
Zaqên
Zadoi
Wenquan
Tanggula Shankou 6070m
Amdo
Nyainrong
Xagquka
Baqên
Dangqên
Sog
Biru
Nagqu
Dêngqên
Dainkognubma
Nanggên
Goinsargoin
Jomda
Riwoqê
Toba
Qamdo
Gonjo
Zhag'yab
Sa'ngain
Banbar
Lhorong
Lhari
Soila
Baxoi
Qumdo
Bomi (Bowo)
Sumzom
Zogang
Markam
Namjagbarwa Feng 7756m
Nyingchi (Bayizhen)
Nyingchi (Pula)
Mainling
Mêdog
Rawu
Gongbo'gyamda
Dongjug
Damxung
Poindo
Lhünzhub
Maizhokunggar
Dagzê
Doilungdêqên
Nêdong
Sangri
Zhanang
Qonggyai
Qusum
Gyaca
Nangxian
Comai
Lhünzê
Qayü
Cona
Kangto 7102m
Zayü
Walung
Nyainqêntanglha Shan
Tanggula Shan
Hengduan Shan
Ningjing Shan
Huang He (Yellow River)
Qilian Shan
Danghe Nanshan
Datong Shan
Bailong Jiang
Xiqing Shan
Wei He
Ruo Shui
Buka Daban 6860m
Hoh Xil Hu
Ulan Ul Hu
Togton He
Gladaindong Feng 6621m
Nam Co
Yarlung Zangbo
Brahmaputra
Salween (Nu Jiang)
Mekong (Lancang Jiang)
Tongtian He
Za Qu
Dam Qu
Qumar He
Beilu He
Qaidam He
Tulagt Ar Gol
Shule He
Hei He
Dahang He
Buh He
Yuka He
Lenglong Ling 4843m
Menyuan
Gulang
Tianzhu
Yongdeng
Tao He
162
160
150
166

The landscape

The Himalayas mark the southwestern edge of the Plateau of Tibet, an extreme mountain wilderness which occupies nearly a quarter of China's total area. A large structural depression, the Qaidam Pendi, lies at its northeastern edge. The Kunlun mountain chain isolates the plateau from the desert to the north, where the Tien Shan range forms a spur between the Tarim Basin *(Tarim Pendi)* and Dzungarian Basin *(Junggar Pendi)*.

Dzungarian Basin *(Junggar Pendi)*
The Tien Shan reach elevations of over 24,419 ft (7435 m) and have permanent ice fields, from which large glaciers extend.
Northwestern China is largely a region of internal drainage. The Tarim He flows only as far as Lop Nur, where its water is lost by evapotranspiration from the lake and land surface.
A vast glacial lake filled much of the Tarim Basin *(Tarim Pendi)* during the last Ice Age. This area is now occupied by the Takla Makan Desert *(Taklimakan Shamo)*. A remnant of the lake, Lop Nur, forms the eastern margin, where it is fed by the Tarim He.
The Turpan Depression *(Turpan Pendi)* is the lowest and hottest place in China. Temperatures can exceed 117°F (47°C) around the lake of Aydingkol Hu, which lies 505 ft (154 m) below sea level.
Sand dunes cover western parts of the the basin of Qaidam Pendi. Strong winds frequently carry the sands east, threatening the agricultural areas around the lake of Qinghai Hu.
Mount Everest is the world's highest peak, at 29,029 ft (8848 m). The summit marks the border between China and Nepal.

▶ ***The Bogda Shan****, an eastward arm of the Tien Shan range, rise high above the Turpan Depression* (Turpan Pendi).

◀ ***The terrain of*** *the Plateau of Tibet consists of mountain peaks and open plateaus, dotted with brackish lakes. These are probably remnants of the Tethys Sea, which covered the area before it was uplifted following the collision of the Indo-Australian and Eurasian plates.*

Tarim Basin *(Tarim Pendi)*

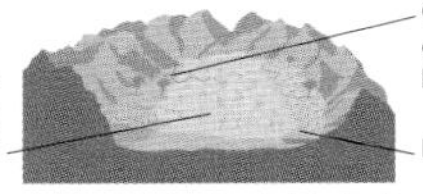
Oases at edge of basin
Barchan sand dunes in Takla Makan Desert *(Taklimakan Shamo)*
Lop Nur

▲ ***The Tarim Basin*** (Tarim Pendi) *has no permanent rivers. Rainfall from the surrounding Plateau of Tibet and Tien Shan ranges drains into the basin's sand and gravel floor.*

▲ ***From its source,*** *high in eastern Qinghai, the Yellow River starts on a 3395 mile (5464 km) journey to the Yellow Sea.*

Transportation & industry

Oil extraction at Yumen and in the Dzungarian and Qaidam basins has led to the growth of the petrochemical industry and a range of heavy manufacturing plants in the cities of Lanzhou and Urumqi. Tibet, and most of Xinjiang, have little industry beyond traditional handicrafts, especially textiles at Hotan and Kashi, located along the ancient Silk Route. Nuclear and space-research testing are carried out at Lop Nur in Xinjiang.

Transportation network

The construction of roads connecting Lhasa in Tibet with Sichuan, Qinghai, and Xinjiang was achieved in the 1950s, in spite of the extreme physical conditions of the Plateau of Tibet.

RUSSIAN FEDERATION
KAZAKHSTAN
MONGOLIA
KYRGYZSTAN
TAJIKISTAN
INDIA
NEPAL
BHUTAN
INDIA
MYANMAR
CHINA
CHINA
Karamay
Shihezi
Ürümqi
Hami
Turpan
Kashi
Shache
Hotan
Yumen
Jiuquan
Yinchuan
Xining
Lanzhou
Lhasa

Major industry and infrastructure

agribusiness	nuclear testing
chemicals	oil
coal	textiles
engineering	major towns
food processing	major roads
iron & steel	major industrial areas

Eastern China

TAIWAN, Anhui, Beijing, Chongqing, Fujian, Guangdong, Guangxi, Guizhou, Hainan, Hebei, Henan, Hubei, Hunan, Jiangsu, Jiangxi, Shaanxi, Shandong, Shanghai, Shanxi, Sichuan, Tianjin, Yunnan, Zhejiang

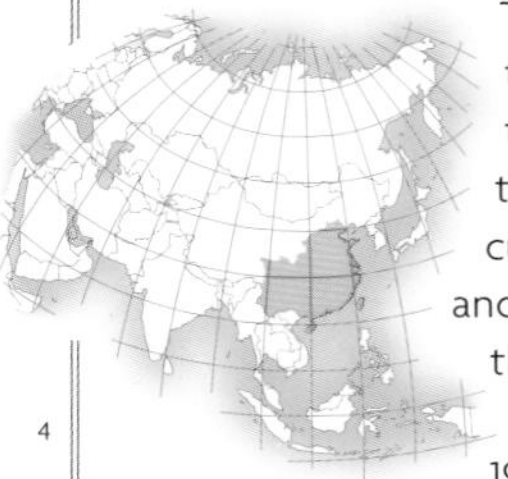

The east is China's heartland. Massive industrial development since 1949 has transformed much of the densely populated rural landscape, in a region still prone to flooding and drought. Over 30 cities have populations of over a million, including the giant metropolis of Shanghai and the capital Beijing, which has been China's cultural and political center since the 13th century. The ethnically diverse southwest and the oil-rich interior provinces of Sichuan and Shaanxi have largely missed out on the remarkable economic growth occurring in designated free-trade areas along the coasts of the South and East China seas. The republic of Taiwan was established in 1949 by Chinese nationalists ousted from the mainland by the victorious Communist forces. Taiwan now has one of the strongest economies in the world but its sovereignty is not recognized by China. Hong Kong provides a major international trade link for China; a 99-year "lease" period of British control was concluded in 1997.

▲ *North of the Qin Ling range in Shaanxi province, is an agriculturally fertile region covered with fine, wind-blown deposits and known as the loess plateau. The loose sediments are vulnerable to water erosion.*

Using the land & sea

This is a region of intensive cultivation. Wheat, millet, sorghum, and cotton are the main crops of the Yellow River basin. South from Sichuan, rice becomes the principal crop, grown with wheat, corn, and cotton along the Yangtze river. Tea is produced in the hills and sugar cane along the coast of the southeast, where flat land is limited. Pigs and poultry are raised in great numbers.

CHINA
BEIJING
Tianjin
Bo Hai
Taiyuan
Qingdao
Yellow Sea
CHINA
Xi'an
Shanghai
Hangzhou
East China Sea
Chengdu
Wuhan
INDIA
CHINA
Fuzhou
TAIPEI
TAIWAN
Kunming
Guangzhou
Hong Kong
MYANMAR
VIETNAM
LAOS
Hainan Dao
South China Sea

Land use and agricultural distribution

- cattle
- pigs
- cereals
- corn
- cotton
- fishing
- peanuts
- rice
- sugar cane
- tea
- capital cities
- major towns
- pasture
- cropland
- forest
- mountain region

▲ *On the hills above the North China Plain, slopes are terraced to utilize the rich loess soils of the Taihang Shan range.*

QINGHAI
GANSU
SICHUAN
Sichuan Pendi
XIZANG ZIZHIQU (TIBET)
Chengdu
Chongqing
CHONGQING SHI
Mianyang
Nanchong
Guang'an
Leshan
Zigong
Yibin
Luzhou
Neijiang
Xi'an
SHAANXI
Qin Ling
Baoji
Xianyang
Hanzhong
Ankang
GUIZHOU
Guiyang
Zunyi
Anshun
Duyun
Kaili
YUNNAN
Kunming
Qujing
Xuanwei
Gejiu
Dali
Baoshan
Simao
Jinghong
GUANGXI ZHUANGZU ZIZHIQU
Nanning
Liuzhou
Laibin
Guilin
Wuzhou
Yulin
Beihai
Qinzhou
Zhanjiang
Haikou
Hainan Dao
HAINAN
Sanya
Gulf of Tongking
MYANMAR
LAOS
VIETNAM
Tropic of Cancer
Three Gorges Dam
Three Gorges Reservoir
Yichang
Dongting Hu

158
158
158
158
162
166
166
166
166

Map key

Population

- above 5 million
- 1 million to 5 million
- 500,000 to 1 million
- 100,000 to 500,000
- 50,000 to 100,000
- 10,000 to 50,000
- below 10,000

Elevation

- 6000m / 19,686ft
- 4000m / 13,124ft
- 3000m / 9843ft
- 2000m / 6562ft
- 1000m / 3281ft
- 500m / 1640ft
- 250m / 820ft
- 100m / 328ft
- sea level

Scale 1:8,500,000

Km 0 25 50 100 150 200 250 300

Miles 0 25 50 100 150 200 250 300

projection: Lambert Conformal Conic

◀ *The former Portuguese territory of Macao, with its colonial architecture, bars and casinos, reverted to Chinese rule in 1999.*

N S T U V W X Y
BEIJING (PEKING)
BEIJING SHI
TIANJIN SHI
HEBEI
SHANDONG
HENAN
JIANGSU
ANHUI
SHANGHAI SHI
ZHEJIANG
JIANGXI
FUJIAN
GUANGDONG
TAIWAN
Bo Hai
Bohai Haixia
Yellow Sea
EAST CHINA SEA
SOUTH CHINA SEA
Taiwan Strait
Shanghai
Nanjing
Hangzhou
Wuhan
Changsha
Nanchang
Fuzhou
Xiamen
TAIPEI (TAIBEI)
Kowloon (Jiulong)
Hong Kong (Xianggang)
Macao (Aomen)
Guangzhou
Qingdao
Jinan
Zhengzhou
Shijiazhuang
Hefei
Senkaku-shotō (claimed by China, Japan and Taiwan)
(China and Taiwan claim all of each other's territory)
Tropic of Cancer
Bashi Channel
162
192
192

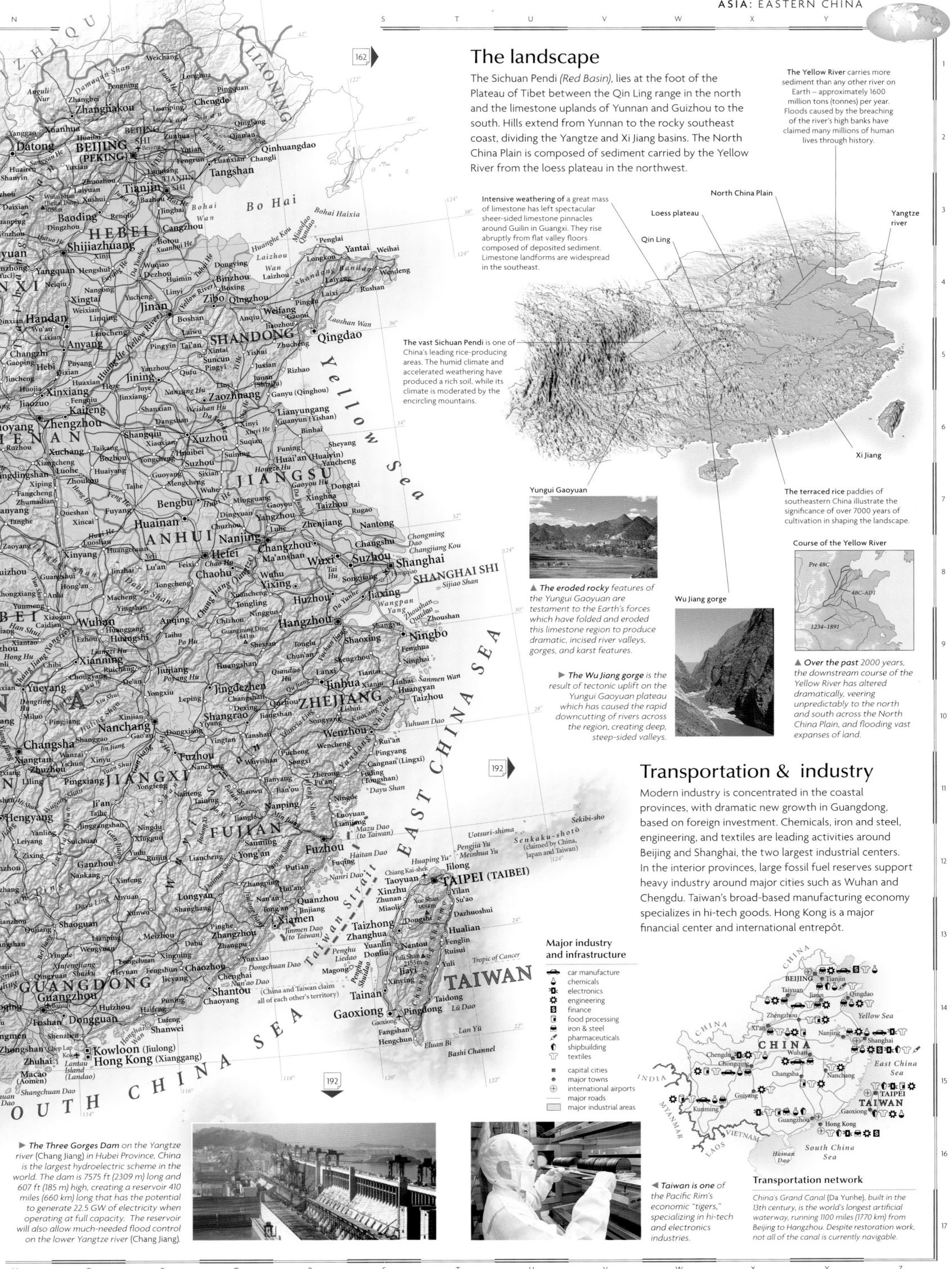

The landscape

The Sichuan Pendi *(Red Basin)*, lies at the foot of the Plateau of Tibet between the Qin Ling range in the north and the limestone uplands of Yunnan and Guizhou to the south. Hills extend from Yunnan to the rocky southeast coast, dividing the Yangtze and Xi Jiang basins. The North China Plain is composed of sediment carried by the Yellow River from the loess plateau in the northwest.

The Yellow River carries more sediment than any other river on Earth – approximately 1600 million tons (tonnes) per year. Floods caused by the breaching of the river's high banks have claimed many millions of human lives through history.

Intensive weathering of a great mass of limestone has left spectacular sheer-sided limestone pinnacles around Guilin in Guangxi. They rise abruptly from flat valley floors composed of deposited sediment. Limestone landforms are widespread in the southeast.

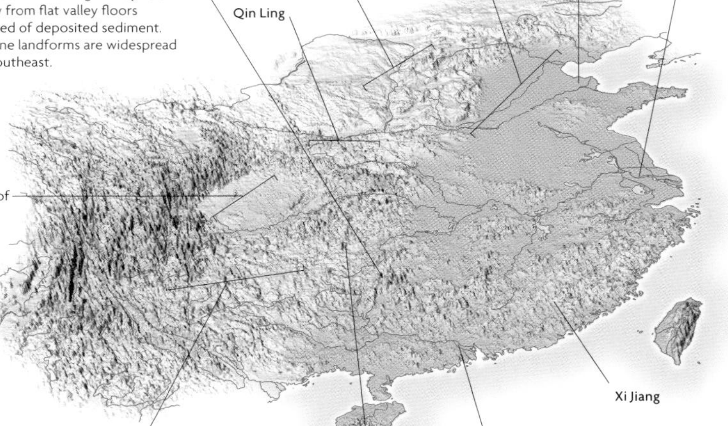

North China Plain
Loess plateau
Qin Ling
Yangtze river
Xi Jiang

The vast Sichuan Pendi is one of China's leading rice-producing areas. The humid climate and accelerated weathering have produced a rich soil, while its climate is moderated by the encircling mountains.

The terraced rice paddies of southeastern China illustrate the significance of over 7000 years of cultivation in shaping the landscape.

Yungui Gaoyuan

▲ ***The eroded rocky** features of the Yungui Gaoyuan are testament to the Earth's forces which have folded and eroded this limestone region to produce dramatic, incised river valleys, gorges, and karst features.*

Wu Jiang gorge

► ***The Wu Jiang gorge** is the result of tectonic uplift on the Yungui Gaoyuan plateau which has caused the rapid downcutting of rivers across the region, creating deep, steep-sided valleys.*

Course of the Yellow River

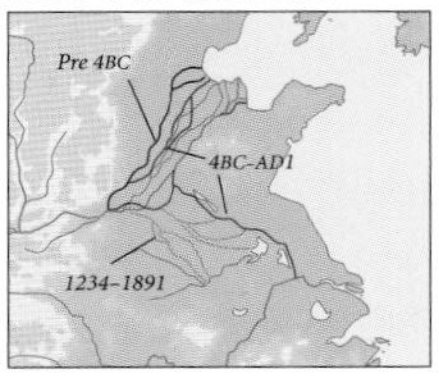

Pre 4BC
4BC-AD1
1234–1891

▲ ***Over the past** 2000 years, the downstream course of the Yellow River has altered dramatically, veering unpredictably to the north and south across the North China Plain, and flooding vast expanses of land.*

Transportation & industry

Modern industry is concentrated in the coastal provinces, with dramatic new growth in Guangdong, based on foreign investment. Chemicals, iron and steel, engineering, and textiles are leading activities around Beijing and Shanghai, the two largest industrial centers. In the interior provinces, large fossil fuel reserves support heavy industry around major cities such as Wuhan and Chengdu. Taiwan's broad-based manufacturing economy specializes in hi-tech goods. Hong Kong is a major financial center and international entrepôt.

Major industry and infrastructure

- car manufacture
- chemicals
- electronics
- engineering
- finance
- food processing
- iron & steel
- pharmaceuticals
- shipbuilding
- textiles
- capital cities
- major towns
- international airports
- major roads
- major industrial areas

CHINA
BEIJING
Tianjin
Taiyuan
Jinan
Qingdao
Zhengzhou
Yellow Sea
Xi'an
Nanjing
Shanghai
CHINA
Wuhan
Chengdu
Chongqing
Changsha
Nanchang
East China Sea
INDIA
Guiyang
TAIPEI
TAIWAN
Kunming
Gaoxiong
Guangzhou
Hong Kong
MYANMAR
VIETNAM
LAOS
Hainan Dao
South China Sea

Transportation network

China's Grand Canal (Da Yunhe), built in the 13th century, is the world's longest artificial waterway, running 1100 miles (1770 km) from Beijing to Hangzhou. Despite restoration work, not all of the canal is currently navigable.

► ***The Three Gorges Dam** on the Yangtze river (Chang Jiang) in Hubei Province, China is the largest hydroelectric scheme in the world. The dam is 7575 ft (2309 m) long and 607 ft (185 m) high, creating a reservoir 410 miles (660 km) long that has the potential to generate 22.5 GW of electricity when operating at full capacity. The reservoir will also allow much-needed flood control on the lower Yangtze river (Chang Jiang).*

◄ ***Taiwan is one** of the Pacific Rim's economic "tigers," specializing in hi-tech and electronics industries.*

Northeastern China, Mongolia & Korea

MONGOLIA, NORTH KOREA, SOUTH KOREA, Heilongjiang, Inner Mongolia, Jilin, Liaoning

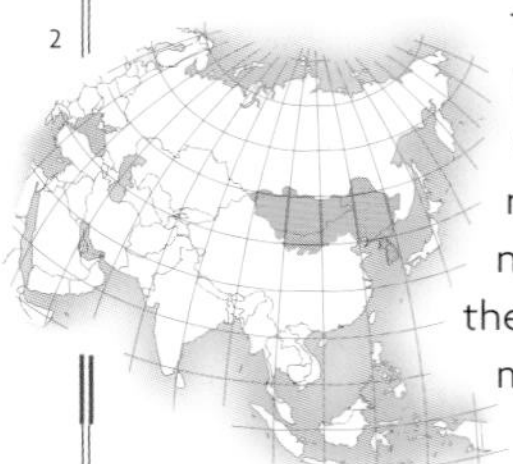

This northerly region has been a domain of shifting borders and competing colonial powers for centuries. Mongolia was the heartland of Chinghiz Khan's vast Mongol empire in the 13th century, while northeastern China was home to the Manchus, China's last ruling dynasty (1644–1911). The mineral and forest wealth of the northeast helped make this China's principal region of heavy industry, although the outdated state factories now face decline. South Korea's state-led market economy has grown dramatically and Seoul is now one of the world's largest cities. The austere communist regime of North Korea has isolated itself from the expanding markets of the Pacific Rim and faces continuing economic stagnation.

▲ *The Eurasian steppe stretches from the mouth of the Danube in Europe, to Mongolia. In Mongolia, nomadic people have lived in felt huts called yurts or gers, for thousands of years.*

Map key

Population

- above 5 million
- 1 million to 5 million
- 500,000 to 1 million
- 100,000 to 500,000
- 50,000 to 100,000
- 10,000 to 50,000
- below 10,000

Elevation

- 4000m / 13,124ft
- 3000m / 9843ft
- 2000m / 6562ft
- 1000m / 3281ft
- 500m / 1640ft
- 250m / 820ft
- 100m / 328ft
- sea level

Scale 1:7,750,000

Km 0 25 50 100 150 200

Miles 0 25 50 100 150 200

projection: Lambert Conformal Conic

RUSSIAN FEDERATION
MONGOLIA
XINJIANG UYGUR ZIZHIQU
GANSU
NINGXIA
BAYAN-ÖLGIY
UVS
HÖVSGÖL
HOVD
DZAVHAN
ARHANGAY
BULGAN
SELENGE
DARHAN UUL
ORHON
TÖV
GOVĬ-ALTAY
BAYANHONGOR
ÖVÖRHANGAY
DUNDGOVĬ
ÖMNÖGOVĬ
ULAANBAATAR (ULAN BATOR)
Altai Mountains
Hangayn Nuruu
Govi Altayn Nuruu
Badain Jaran Shamo
Tengger Shamo
Lang Shan
Uvs Nuur
Hövsgöl Nuur
Ulaangom
Ölgiy
Hovd
Uliastay
Mörön
Erdenet
Darhan
Sühbaatar
Dalandzadgad
Bayanhongor
Altay
Dalain Hob
Bayan Hot
Wuhai (Haibowan)
158
122

The landscape

The great North China Plain is largely enclosed by mountain ranges including the Great and Lesser Khingan Ranges *(Da Hinggan Ling* and *Xiao Hinggan Ling)* in the north, and the Changbai Shan, which extend south into the rugged peninsula of Korea. The broad steppeland plateau of Nei Mongol Gaoyuan borders the southeastern edge of the great cold desert of the Gobi which extends west across the southern reaches of Mongolia. In northwest Mongolia the Altai Mountains and various lesser ranges are interspersed with lakeland basins.

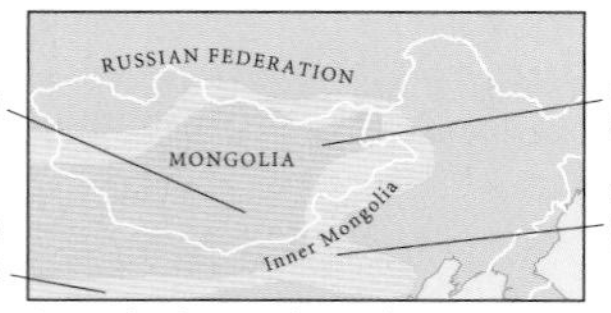

RUSSIAN FEDERATION
MONGOLIA
Inner Mongolia
Gobi
Semiarid zone
Desert zone
Ordos Desert (Mu Us Shadi)

▲ ***Much of Mongolia** and Inner Mongolia is a vast desert area. To the south and east, a semiarid region extends into China proper.*

▲ ***The Gobi desert** stretches from Central Asia, through Mongolia and into China. Bare rock surfaces, rather than sand dunes, typify the cold desert landscape of the Gobi.*

Tributaries of the Amur river follow U-shaped valleys through the Great Khingan Range *(Da Hinggan Ling)*. These were cut by ice-age glaciers between 3 and 10 million years ago.

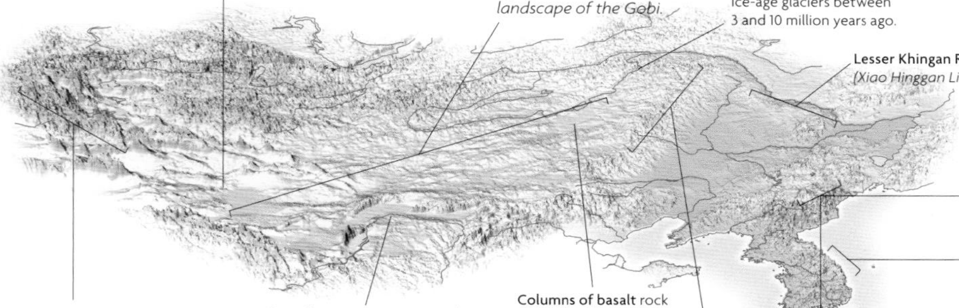

Lesser Khingan Range (Xiao Hinggan Ling)
Changbai Shan
T'aebaek-sanmaek

The Altai Mountains are the highest and longest of the mountain ranges that extend into Mongolia from the northwest. These mountains provide one of the last refuges for the endangered snow leopard.

The Yellow River sweeps north around the Ordos Desert *(Mu Us Shadi)*, bringing water to an otherwise barren region.

Columns of basalt rock protrude in occasional clusters from the flat surface of the eastern Gobi. Their regular, six-sided form was produced when the rock cooled and contracted from its molten state.

Great Khingan Range *(Da Hinggan Ling)*

A crater lake occupies the 9023 ft (2750 m) snowy summit of the extinct volcano Paektu-san, the highest peak in the mountains of the Changbai Shan.

◀ ***The wooded mountain** range of T'aebaek-sanmaek forms the backbone of the Korean peninsula, running north–south along the eastern coastline.*

Transportation & industry

North Korea's centrally-planned economy is strongly oriented toward heavy industry, while South Korea has a broad manufacturing base which includes textiles, steel, electronics, and one of the world's largest shipbuilding industries. Mongolia and Inner Mongolia's great mineral resource potential is largely undeveloped. The heavy industrial region around Shenyang produces iron, steel, chemicals, and cement on a massive scale.

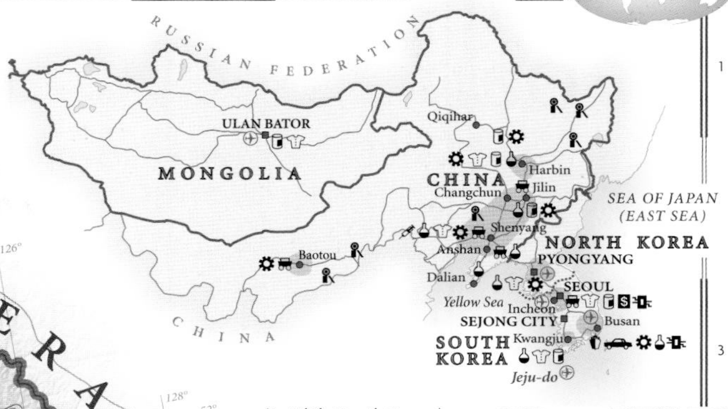
Major industry and infrastructure
car manufacture
chemicals
coal
electronics
engineering
finance
food processing
iron & steel
pharmaceuticals
shipbuilding
textiles
capital cities
major towns
international airports
major roads
major industrial areas
RUSSIAN FEDERATION
MONGOLIA
ULAN BATOR
CHINA
Qiqihar
Harbin
Changchun
Jilin
Shenyang
Baotou
Anshan
Dalian
NORTH KOREA
PYONGYANG
SEA OF JAPAN (EAST SEA)
Yellow Sea
Incheon
SEOUL
SEJONG CITY
SOUTH KOREA
Kwangju
Busan
Jeju-do

▲ *Ulan Bator, the Mongolian capital bears many of the hallmarks of Soviet-style central planning, the result of economic and industrial assistance from the Soviet Union following Mongolian independence in 1921.*

Transportation network

Liaoning has China's most comprehensive railroad network, the legacy of the Japanese occupation of Manchuria in the 20th century. The railroads are used primarily for freight transportation.

► *While North Korea has remained politically and economically isolated from the rest of the world, South Korea has enjoyed immense economic growth. It has benefited considerably from US economic aid in the aftermath of the Korean war of 1950–1953.*

RUSSIAN FEDERATION
MONGOLIA
CHINA
NORTH KOREA
SOUTH KOREA
JAPAN
HEILONGJIANG
JILIN
LIAONING
HEBEI
SHANXI
DORNOD
HENTIY
SÜHBAATAR
Nei Mongol Gaoyuan
Da Hinggan Ling
Xiao Hinggan Ling
Harbin
Changchun
Shenyang
Qiqihar
Daqing
Jilin
Anshan
Fushun
Benxi
Dalian
Dandong
Chifeng
Tongliao
Baotou
Hohhot
Manzhouli
Choybalsan
Ulanhot
Mudanjiang
Jiamusi
P'YŎNGYANG
SEOUL
Incheon
Daejeon
Daegu
Gwangju
Busan
Ulsan
Jeju
Bo Hai
Korea Bay
Liaodong Wan
Yellow Sea
Sea of Japan (East Sea)
Korea Strait
122
160

South Korea: Capital cities

SEOUL – capital
SEJONG CITY – administrative capital

Using the land & sea

Mongolia and Inner Mongolia rely heavily on livestock farming, with only about 1% of the land area cultivated. Northeastern China produces wheat, corn, soybeans, and sugar beet. The cool climate limits the range of crops and large upland areas of the northeast remain forested. Rice is the staple food of North and South Korea. The latter has become a leading ocean-fishing nation.

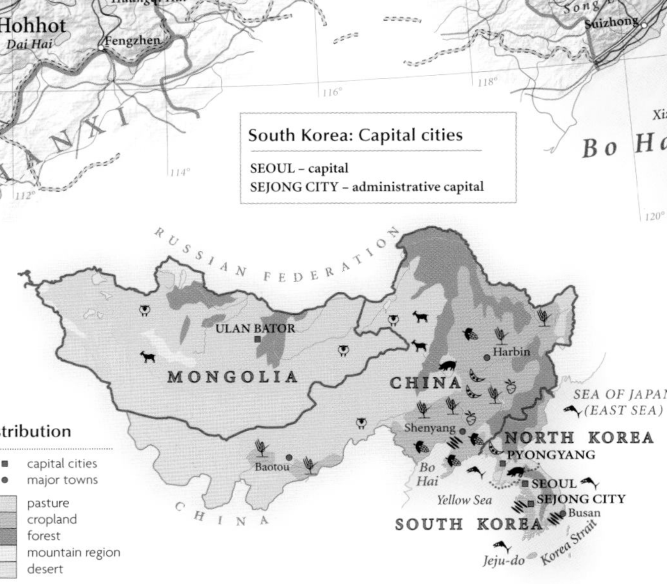
Land use and agricultural distribution
goats
pigs
sheep
corn
fishing
rice
soybeans
sugar beet
wheat
capital cities
major towns
pasture
cropland
forest
mountain region
desert
RUSSIAN FEDERATION
ULAN BATOR
MONGOLIA
CHINA
Harbin
Shenyang
Baotou
NORTH KOREA
PYONGYANG
SEA OF JAPAN (EAST SEA)
Bo Hai
Yellow Sea
SEOUL
SEJONG CITY
Busan
SOUTH KOREA
Jeju-do
Korea Strait

A B C D E F G H I J K L M

Japan

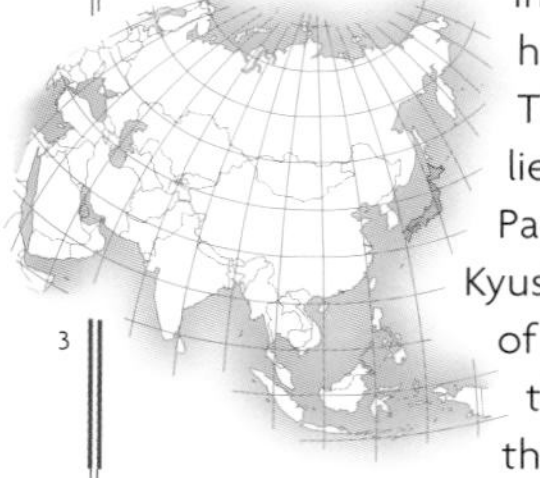

In the years since the end of the Second World War, Japan has become the world's most dynamic industrial nation. The country comprises a string of over 4000 islands which lie in a great northeast to southwest arc in the northwest Pacific. Four major islands: Hokkaido, Honshu, Shikoku, and Kyushu are home to the great majority of Japan's population of 128 million people, although the mountainous terrain of the central region means that most cities are situated on the coast. A densely populated industrial belt stretches along much of Honshu's southern coast, including Japan's crowded capital, Tokyo. Alongside its spectacular economic growth and the increasing westernization of its cities, Japan still maintains a highly individual culture, reflected in its traditional food, formal behavioral codes, unique Shinto religion, and a deep reverence for the emperor.

Using the land & sea

Although only about 11% of Japan is suitable for cultivation, substantial government support, a favorable climate and intensive farming methods enable the country to be virtually self-sufficient in rice productio[n]. Northern Hokkaido, the largest and most productive farming region, has an open terrain and climate similar to that of the American Midwest, and produces over half of Japan's cereal requirements. Farmers are being encouraged to diversify by growing fruit, vegetables, and wheat, as well as raising livestock.

Land use and agricultural distribution

- cattle
- pigs
- fishing
- cereals
- citrus fruits
- fruit
- herbs
- rice
- root crops
- tobacco

- capital cities
- major towns

- pasture
- cropland
- forest

The urban/rural population divide

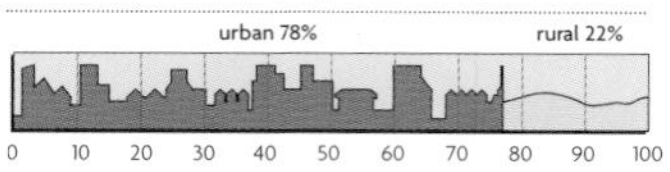

urban 78%
rural 22%
0 10 20 30 40 50 60 70 80 90 100

Population density	Total land area
885 people per sq mile (342 people per sq km)	145,869 sq miles (377,800 sq km)

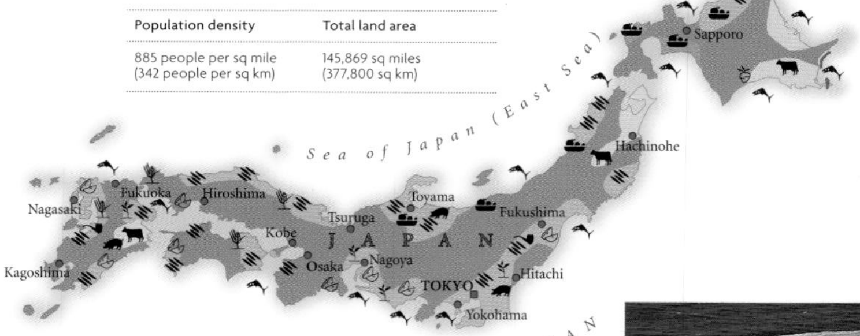

Sapporo
Sea of Japan (East Sea)
Hachinohe
Fukuoka
Hiroshima
Nagasaki
Toyama
Fukushima
Kobe
Tsuruga
JAPAN
Osaka
Nagoya
Kagoshima
Hitachi
TOKYO
Yokohama
PACIFIC OCEAN

► *Cutting terraces maximizes the limited agricultural land, enabling Japan to produce large quantities of rice.*

The landscape

The islands of Japan lie on the Pacific "Ring of Fire," and form a series of clearly defined arcs. The largely mountainous landscape was formed very recently in geological terms. Volcanic eruptions and earthquakes continue to reshape the terrain and shake the country's complex infrastructure. There is no single continuous mountain range; the mountains divide into many small land blocks separated by lowlands and dissected by numerous river valleys.

Sea of Japan (East Sea)
Active volcanic island
Japan Trench (subduction zone)

▲ ***Japan is part** of an arc of volcanic islands, formed by the Pacific Plate diving under the Eurasian Plate. This process generates intense stress which is periodically released as earthquakes.*

◄ ***Mount Fuji is** Japan's highest mountain, rising 12,388 ft (3776 m) above the Kanto Plain in the central region of Honshu. The flat land below is suitable for growing crops such as tea. Like many Japanese mountains, it is revered as a sacred site.*

A number of rivers which emerge from the volcanic parts of northwestern Honshu are so highly acidic that their water is unsuitable for irrigation and consumption.

► ***Trees cling to** the sheer slopes of the waterfalls on the northern island of Hokkaido. The island's climate is similar to that in northern Europe, with long, cold winters and short, warm summers.*

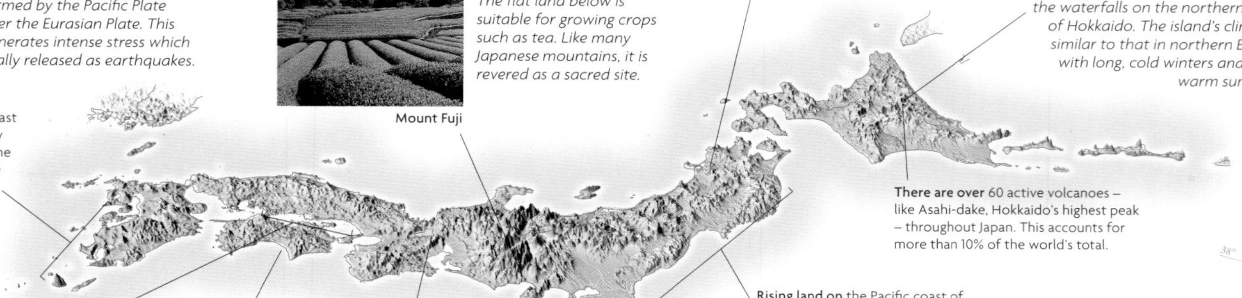

Mount Fuji

In much of Kyushu the coast is subsiding, giving a highly indented coastline. In some places, former hilltops are barely visible above the current sea level.

There are over 60 active volcanoes – like Asahi-dake, Hokkaido's highest peak – throughout Japan. This accounts for more than 10% of the world's total.

The Inland Sea *(Seto-naikai)* has resulted from the depression of faulted blocks which has allowed sea water to invade the region between northern Shikoku and western Honshu.

Strong southeasterly winds blowing onshore during the winter create sand dunes which extend for miles along the eastern coasts.

Biwa-ko is the largest lake in Japan, covering 260 sq miles (673 sq km) in central Honshu. The depression in which it lies was created by recent faulting of the underlying rocks.

Rising land on the Pacific coast of Honshu leads to typical features such as raised beaches, some lying over 1000 ft (300 m) above sea level.

Sea of Japan
JAPAN
Korea Strait
Tsushima
Oki-shotō
Matsue
Tottori
Hiroshima
Kitakyūshū
Fukuoka
Nagasaki
Kumamoto
Kyūshū
Kagoshima
Miyazaki
Ōita
Matsuyama
Shikoku
Kōchi
Tokushima
Takamatsu
Okayama
Kōbe
Ōsaka
Kyōto
Nara
Wakayama
Nagoya
Gifu
Fukui
Kanazawa
Toyama
Shizuoka
Hamamatsu
East China Sea
Philippine Sea
Ōsumi-kaikyō
Tanega-shima
Yaku-shima

157

▼ ***Autumnal trees near** Gifu, on central Honshu, create a spectacular display. Native trees on this island include camphor, pasania, Japanese evergreen oak, camellia, and holly.*

► ***The Kobe earthquake** in January 1995 highlighted Japan's vulnerability to earthquakes, despite technological advances. It shattered much of the infrastructure of this important port. More than 5000 people died as buildings and overhead highways collapsed and fires broke out.*

▲ *The mountain of* O-Akan-dake overlooks lakes and dense forest in the Akan National Park in eastern Hokkaido. The highest mountains lie in the center of the island, with ranges over 6000 ft (1800 m) in the central mountain region.

▲ *A number of* new volcanoes emerged in Japan during the 20th century. They exist alongside older cones like this one in Aso-Kuju National Park on Kyushu, now dormant and grass-covered.

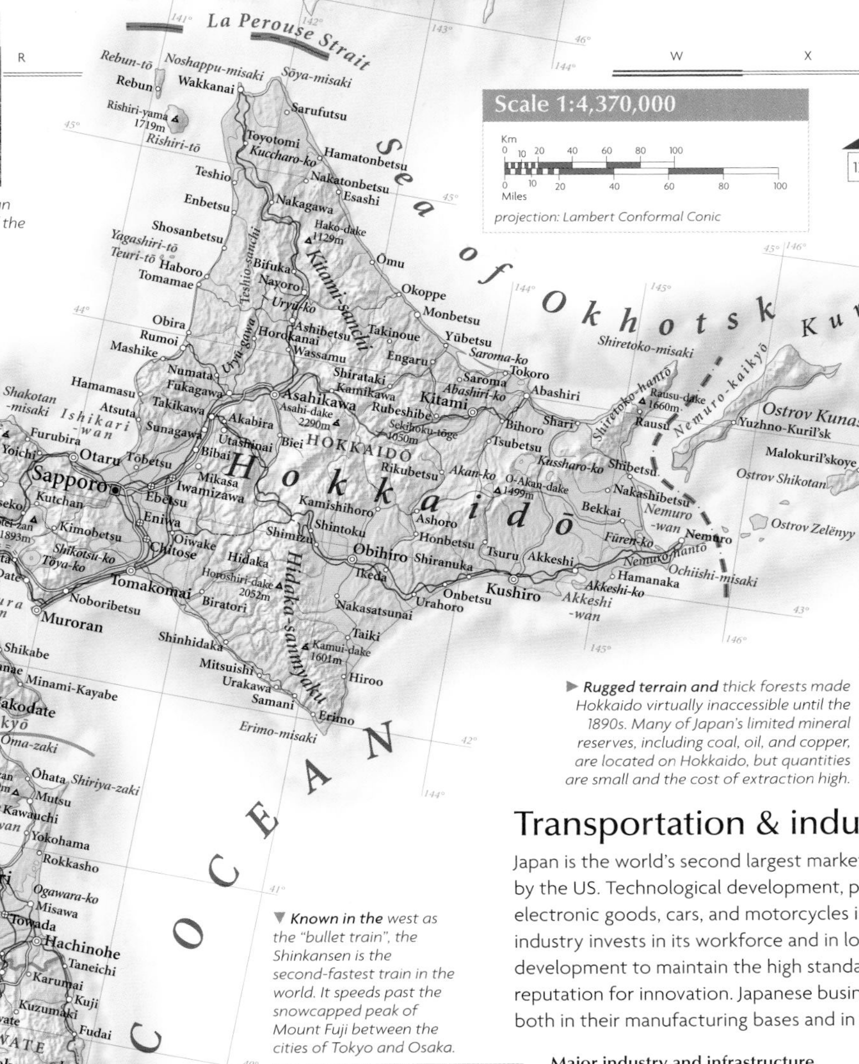

Scale 1:4,370,000
projection: Lambert Conformal Conic
Map key
Population
above 5 million
1 million to 5 million
500,000 to 1 million
100,000 to 500,000
50,000 to 100,000
10,000 to 50,000
below 10,000
Elevation
4000m / 13,124ft
3000m / 9843ft
2000m / 6562ft
1000m / 3281ft
500m / 1640ft
250m / 820ft
100m / 328ft
sea level
La Perouse Strait
Sea of Okhotsk
Kurile Islands
Hokkaidō
Sapporo
Asahikawa
Hakodate
Kushiro
Tsugaru-kaikyō
Aomori
Sendai
Niigata
TOKYO
Yokohama
Chiba
Kawasaki
Honshū
Sea of Japan (East Sea)
PACIFIC OCEAN
Ostrov Iturup
(Administered by Russian Federation, claimed by Japan)
Ostrov Kunashir
Ostrov Shikotan
122
192

► *Rugged terrain and* thick forests made Hokkaido virtually inaccessible until the 1890s. Many of Japan's limited mineral reserves, including coal, oil, and copper, are located on Hokkaido, but quantities are small and the cost of extraction high.

Transportation & industry

Japan is the world's second largest market economy, outranked only by the US. Technological development, particularly of computers, electronic goods, cars, and motorcycles is second to none. Japanese industry invests in its workforce and in long-term research and development to maintain the high standard of its products and a reputation for innovation. Japanese businesses are now global both in their manufacturing bases and in the distribution of goods.

▼ *Known in the* west as the "bullet train", the Shinkansen is the second-fastest train in the world. It speeds past the snowcapped peak of Mount Fuji between the cities of Tokyo and Osaka.

Major industry and infrastructure

- brewing
- car manufacture
- chemicals
- hi-tech industry
- engineering
- finance
- iron & steel
- research & development
- shipbuilding
- textiles
- winter sports
- capital cities
- major towns
- international airports
- major roads
- major industrial areas

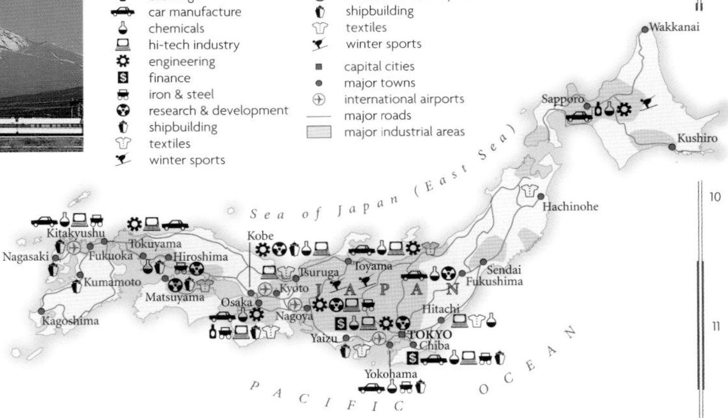
Wakkanai
Sapporo
Kushiro
Sea of Japan (East Sea)
Hachinohe
Kitakyushu
Nagasaki
Fukuoka
Tokuyama
Hiroshima
Kobe
Kumamoto
Matsuyama
Osaka
Kyoto
Tsuruga
Toyama
Nagoya
Sendai
Fukushima
Kagoshima
Hitachi
TOKYO
Chiba
Yaizu
Yokohama
JAPAN
PACIFIC OCEAN

Transportation network

557,978 miles (898,082 km)	4257 miles (6851 km)
12,486 miles (20,096 km)	1099 miles (1770 km)

Japanese road construction traditionally lagged behind that of its extensive and technologically advanced railroad network. The road network's relative lack of development has led to severe urban congestion, although expressways have now been built in some cities.

▲ *On Friday 11* March, 2011 a 9.0 magnitude undersea earthquake 43 miles (70 km) off the coast of Honshu triggered a huge tsunami that devastated the coastal area around Sendai, costing the lives of almost 16,000 people.

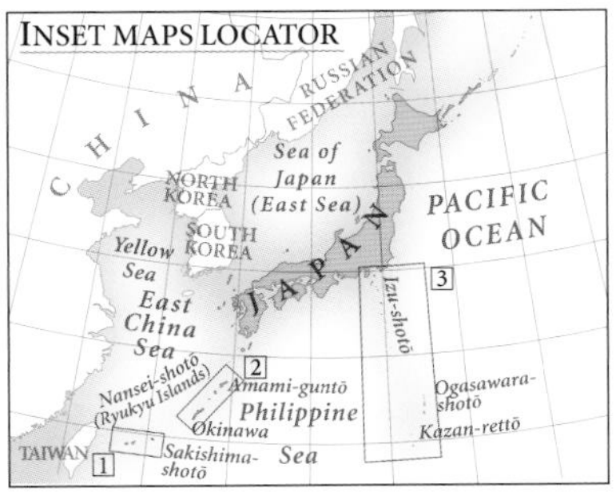
INSET MAPS LOCATOR
CHINA
RUSSIAN FEDERATION
NORTH KOREA
SOUTH KOREA
Sea of Japan (East Sea)
JAPAN
PACIFIC OCEAN
Yellow Sea
East China Sea
TAIWAN
Nansei-shotō (Ryukyu Islands)
Okinawa
Sakishima-shotō
Amami-guntō
Philippine Sea
Izu-shotō
Ogasawara-shotō
Kazan-rettō
1
2
3

East China Sea
Sakishima-shotō
Miyako-shotō
Yaeyama-shotō
OKINAWA
Philippine Sea
Yonaguni
Iriomote-jima
Ishigaki
Hateruma-jima
SCALE 1:4,800,000
1

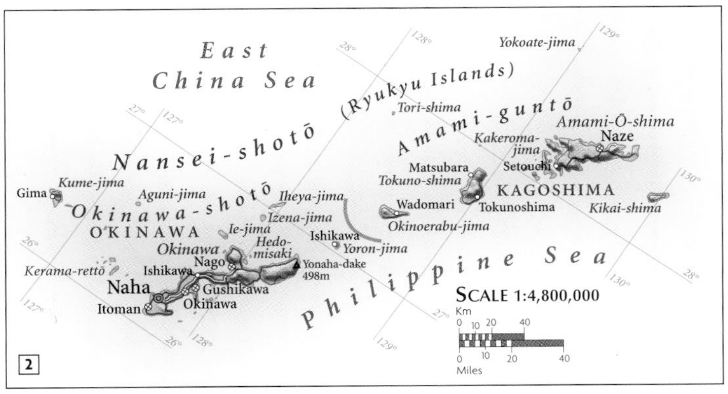
East China Sea
Nansei-shotō (Ryukyu Islands)
Amami-guntō
Okinawa-shotō
OKINAWA
KAGOSHIMA
Amami-Ō-shima
Naze
Naha
Philippine Sea
SCALE 1:4,800,000
2

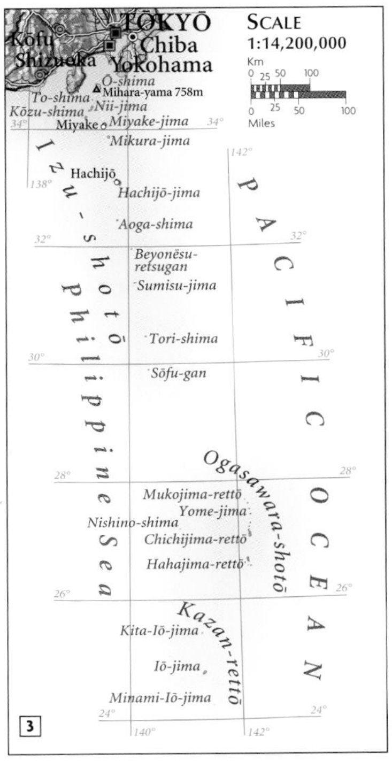
TOKYO
Chiba
Yokohama
Shizuoka
SCALE 1:14,200,000
Izu-shotō
Hachijō-jima
Philippine Sea
PACIFIC OCEAN
Ogasawara-shotō
Kazan-rettō
Iō-jima
Minami-Iō-jima
3

Mainland Southeast Asia

CAMBODIA, LAOS, MYANMAR, THAILAND, VIETNAM

Thickly forested mountains, intercut by the broad valleys of five great rivers characterize the landscape of Southeast Asia's mainland countries. Agriculture remains the main activity for much of the population, which is concentrated in the river flood plains and deltas. Linked ethnic and cultural roots give the region a distinct identity. Most people on the mainland are Theravada Buddhists, and the Philippines is the only predominantly Christian country in Southeast Asia. Foreign intervention began in the 16th century with the opening of the spice trade; Cambodia, Laos and Vietnam were French colonies until the end of the Second World War, Myanmar was under British control. Only Thailand was never colonized. Today, Thailand is poised to play a leading role in the economic development of the Pacific Rim, and Laos and Vietnam have begun to mend the devastation of the Vietnam War, and to develop their economies. With continuing political instability and a shattered infrastructure, Cambodia faces an uncertain future, while Myanmar is seeking investment and the ending of its long isolation from the world community.

▲ ***The Irrawaddy river*** *is Myanmar's vital central artery, watering the ricefields and providing a rich source of fish, as well as an important transport link, particularly for local traffic.*

The landscape

A series of mountain ranges runs north–south through the mainland, formed as the result of the collision between the Eurasian Plate and the Indian subcontinent, which created the Himalayas. They are interspersed by the valleys of a number of great rivers. On their passage to the sea these rivers have deposited sediment, forming huge, fertile flood plains and deltas.

The coastline of the Isthmus of Kra

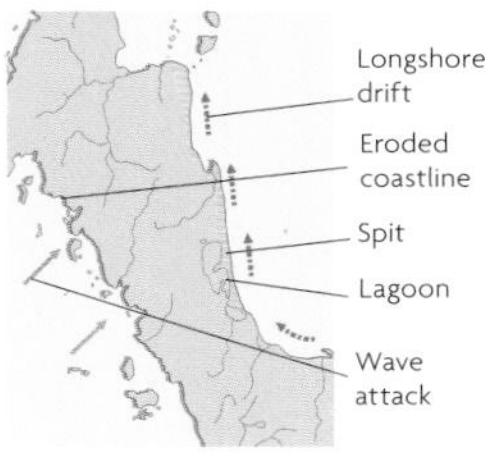

Longshore drift
Eroded coastline
Spit
Lagoon
Wave attack

◀ ***The east and*** *west coasts of the Isthmus of Kra differ greatly. The tectonically uplifting west coast is exposed to the harsh south-westerly monsoon and is heavily eroded. On the east coast, longshore currents produce depositional features such as spits and lagoons.*

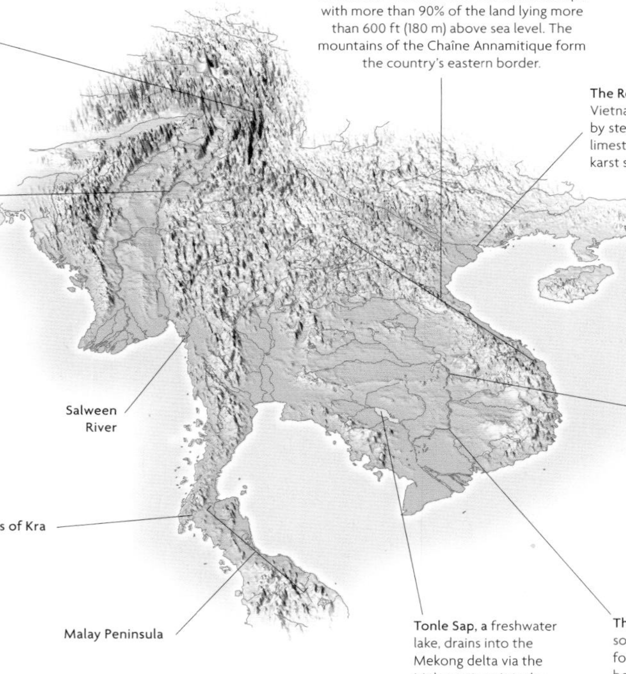

Mountains dominate the Laotian landscape with more than 90% of the land lying more than 600 ft (180 m) above sea level. The mountains of the Chaîne Annamitique form the country's eastern border.
Hkakabo Razi is the highest point in mainland Southeast Asia. It rises 19,300 ft (5885 m) at the border between China and Myanmar.
The Red River delta in northern Vietnam is fringed to the north by steep-sided, round-topped limestone hills, typical of karst scenery.
The Irrawaddy river runs virtually north–south, draining the plains of northern Myanmar. The Irrawaddy delta is the country's main rice-growing area.
Salween River
Isthmus of Kra
Malay Peninsula
Tonle Sap, a freshwater lake, drains into the Mekong delta via the Mekong river. It is the largest lake in Southeast Asia.
The Mekong river flows through southern China and Myanmar, then for much of its length forms the border between Laos and Thailand, flowing through Cambodia before terminating in a vast delta on the southern Vietnamese coast.

▲ ***The coast of*** *the Isthmus of Kra, in southeast Thailand has many small, precipitous islands like these, formed by chemical erosion on limestone, which is weathered along vertical cracks. The humidity of the climate in Southeast Asia increases the rate of weathering.*

◀ ***The fast-flowing waters*** *of the Mekong river cascade over this waterfall in Champasak province in Laos. The force of the water erodes rocks at the base of the fall.*

Using the land and sea

The fertile flood plains of rivers such as the Mekong and Salween, and the humid climate, enable the production of rice throughout the region. Cambodia, Laos, and Myanmar still have substantial forests, producing hardwoods such as teak and rosewood. Cash crops include tropical fruits such as coconuts, bananas and pineapples, rubber, oil palm, sugar cane and the jute substitute, kenaf. Pigs and cattle are the main livestock raised. Large quantities of marine and freshwater fish are caught throughout the region.

▲ ***Commercial logging*** *– still widespread in Myanmar – has now been stopped in Thailand because of over-exploitation of the tropical rainforest.*

The urban/rural population divide

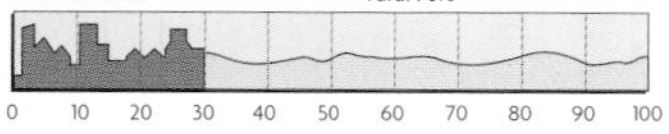

urban 30%
rural 70%
0 10 20 30 40 50 60 70 80 90 100

Population density	Total land area
345 people per sq mile (133 people per sq km)	733,828 sq miles (1,901,110 sq km)

BANGLADESH
INDIA
CHINA
MYANMAR
Mandalay
NAY PYI TAW
HANOI
Gulf of Tongking
Bay of Bengal
VIENTIANE
LAOS
Hue
Rangoon
THAILAND
BANGKOK
VIETNAM
CAMBODIA
Andaman Sea
PHNOM PENH
South China Sea
Gulf of Thailand
Ho Chi Minh City
MALAYSIA

Land use and agricultural distribution

- cattle
- pigs
- bananas
- coconuts
- fishing
- oil palms
- rice
- rubber
- sugar cane
- timber
- capital cities
- major towns
- pasture
- cropland
- forest
- wetland

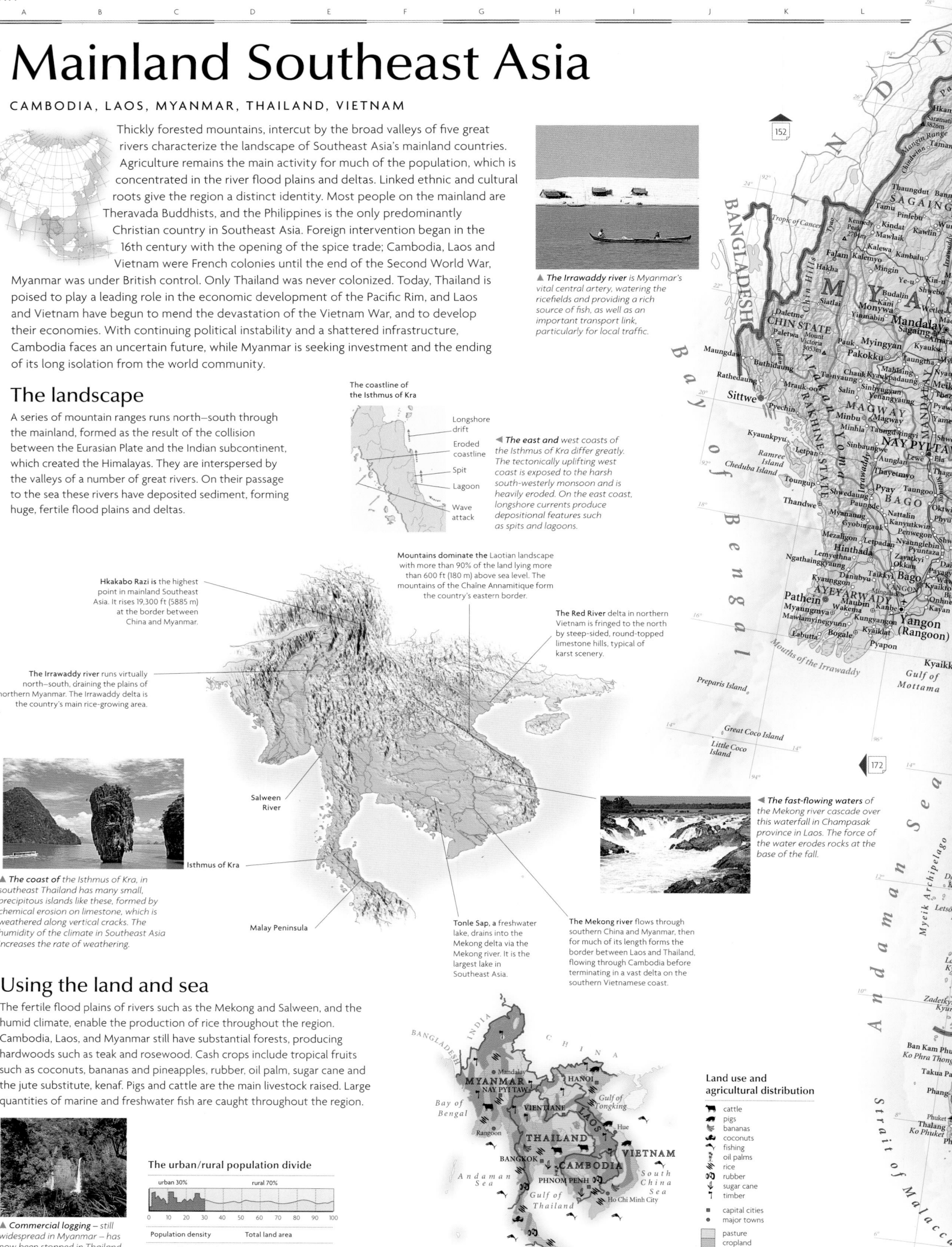

BANGLADESH
Bay of Bengal
Andaman Sea
MYANMAR
SAGAING
CHIN STATE
RAKHINE STATE
MAGWAY
BAGO
AYEYARWADY
YANGON
Hkamti
Saramati 3826m
Tamanthi
Thaungdut
Tamu
Kindat
Kalewa
Kalemyo
Mingin
Falam
Hakha
Tiddim
Mawlaik
Kawlin
Shwebo
Ye-u
Budalin
Monywa
Mandalay
Sagaing
Amarapura
Kyaukse
Paletwa
Mount Victoria 3053m
Pauk
Myingyan
Pakokku
Taungtha
Maungdaw
Buthidaung
Rathedaung
Sittwe
Kyaukpyu
Ramree Island
Cheduba Island
Sinbaungwe
Minbu
Magway
Minhla
NAY PYI TAW
Toungup
Thandwe
Shwedaung
Paungde
Pyay
Taungoo
Nattalin
Kanyutkwin
Penwegon
Letpadan
Hinthada
Ngathainggyaung
Pathein
Myaungmya
Wakema
Maubin
Kungyangon
Mawlamyinegyun
Labutta
Bogale
Kyaiklat
Pyapon
Bago
Yangon (Rangoon)
Mouths of the Irrawaddy
Kyaikkami
Gulf of Mottama
Preparis Island
Great Coco Island
Little Coco Island
Tropic of Cancer
Myeik Archipelago
Ban Kam Phuang
Ko Phra Thong
Takua Pa
Phang-Nga
Phuket
Thalang
Ko Phuket
Strait of Malacca

152
172
168

Transportation & industry

Industrial manufacturing has become increasingly important in Thailand and Vietnam in recent years. The assembling of component-based electrical and electronic goods is becoming more common throughout this region, with foreign companies benefiting from low labour costs and the upgrading of technology. The economies of Myanmar and Cambodia are still based on agricultural produce and the processing of raw materials. Tin is the region's most important metal, and nickel, copper and chromite are also mined, although the quantities produced are not significant on a global scale. Thailand's successful tourist industry is the country's highest earner of foreign exchange.

Transportation network

82,958 miles (133,524 km)
267 miles (430 km)
7500 miles (12,071 km)
28,585 miles (46,008 km)

Transportation development has concentrated on the building of road networks. Water and sea transport remain important, although air links have improved, particularly in Thailand and the Philippines.

CHINA
INDIA
BANGLADESH
MYANMAR
NAY PYI TAW
Mandalay
HANOI
Hai Phong
Gulf of Tongking
Bay of Bengal
Chiang Mai
VIENTIANE
LAOS
Hue
Da Nang
Rangoon
Moulmein
THAILAND
VIETNAM
Andaman Sea
BANGKOK
CAMBODIA
South China Sea
PHNOM PENH
Ho Chi Minh City
Gulf of Thailand
Hat Yai
MALAYSIA

Major industry and infrastructure

- chemicals
- electronics
- engineering
- finance
- food processing
- iron & steel
- oil & gas
- mining
- shipbuilding
- textiles
- timber processing
- capital cities
- major towns
- international airports
- major roads
- major industrial areas

THAILAND
LAOS
VIETNAM
CAMBODIA
CHINA
KRUNG THEP (BANGKOK)
VIANGCHAN (VIENTIANE)
PHNUM PENH (PHNOM PENH)
HANOI
Hai Phong
Đa Năng
Huê
Hô Chi Minh
Gulf of Tongking
Gulf of Thailand
SOUTH CHINA SEA
PARACEL ISLANDS (disputed)
Tropic of Cancer
MALAYSIA

160
160
170
168

▶ *Opium poppies are destroyed under army supervision in Thailand. This action is part of a government-sponsored initiative to reduce the trade in drugs such as heroin, which is derived from these plants. Drug trafficking is a major problem throughout the region; the area is known as the "Golden Triangle", and Laos is the third-largest producer of opium poppies in the world.*

The Paracel Islands are a strategically sensitive island group, disputed by several surrounding countries. The Paracels are claimed by China, Taiwan, and Vietnam, though only China has actually occupied them.

Map key

Population

- above 5 million
- 1 million to 5 million
- 500,000 to 1 million
- 100,000 to 500,000
- 50,000 to 100,000
- 10,000 to 50,000
- below 10,000

Elevation

- 4000m / 13,124ft
- 3000m / 9843ft
- 2000m / 6562ft
- 1000m / 3281ft
- 500m / 1640ft
- 250m / 820ft
- 100m / 328ft
- sea level

Scale 1:8,600,000

Km 0 25 50 100 150 200
Miles 0 25 50 100 150 200

projection: Lambert Conformal Conic

▼ *The city of Hue in central Vietnam was the country's capital under the 13 emperors of the Nguyen dynasty from 1802 to 1945. It is the site of a number of religious monuments, including the Thien-Mu Pagoda.*

Western Maritime Southeast Asia

BRUNEI, INDONESIA, MALAYSIA, SINGAPORE

The world's largest archipelago, Indonesia's myriad islands stretch 3100 miles (5000 km) eastward across the Pacific, from the Malay Peninsula to western New Guinea. Only about 1500 of the 13,677 islands are inhabited and the huge, predominently Muslim population is unevenly distributed, with some two-thirds crowded onto the western islands of Java, Madura, and Bali. The national government is trying to resettle large numbers of people from these islands to other parts of the country to reduce population pressure there. Malaysia, split between the mainland and the east Malaysian states of Sabah and Sarawak on Borneo, has a diverse population, as well as a fast-growing economy, although the pace of its development is still far outstripped by that of Singapore. This small island nation is the financial and commercial capital of Southeast Asia. The Sultanate of Brunei in northern Borneo, one of the world's last princely states, has an extremely high standard of living, based on its oil revenues.

The landscape

Indonesia's western islands are characterized by rugged volcanic mountains cloaked with dense tropical forest, which slope down to coastal plains covered by thick alluvial swamps. The Sunda Shelf, an extension of the Eurasian Plate, lies between Java, Bali, Sumatra, and Borneo. These islands' mountains rise from a base below the sea, and they were once joined together by dry land, which has since been submerged by rising sea levels.

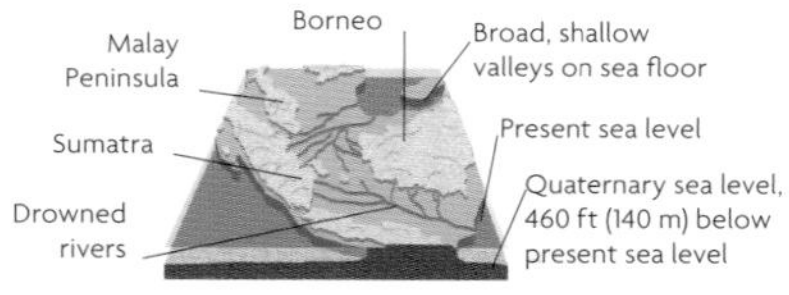
Borneo
Malay Peninsula
Broad, shallow valleys on sea floor
Sumatra
Present sea level
Drowned rivers
Quaternary sea level, 460 ft (140 m) below present sea level

▲ ***The Sunda Shelf** underlies this whole region. It is one of the largest submarine shelves in the world, covering an area of 714,285 sq miles (1,850,000 sq km). During the early Quaternary period, when sea levels were lower, the shelf was exposed.*

◄ ***On January 24**, 2005 a 9.2 magnitude earthquake off the coast of Sumatra triggered a devastating tsunami that was up to 90 ft (30 m) high in places. The death toll was estimated to be around 230,000 people from fourteen different countries around the Indian Ocean.*

Malay Peninsula has a rugged east coast, but the west coast, fronting the Strait of Malacca, has many sheltered beaches and bays. The two coasts are divided by the Banjaran Titiwangsa, which run the length of the peninsula.

Gunung Kinabalu is the highest peak in Malaysia, rising 13,455 ft (4101 m).

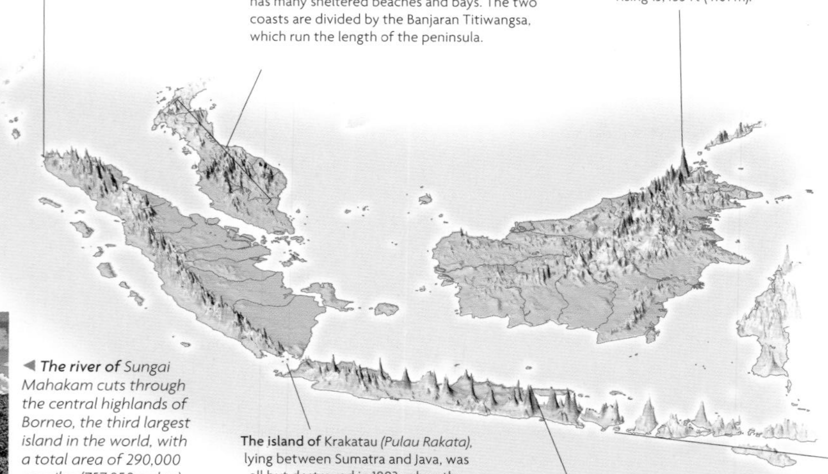
Gunung Semeru

The island of Krakatau *(Pulau Rakata)*, lying between Sumatra and Java, was all but destroyed in 1883, when the volcano erupted. The release of gas and dust into the atmosphere disrupted cloud cover and global weather patterns for several years.

Indonesia has more than 220 volcanoes, most of which are still active. They are strung out along the island arc from Sumatra through the Lesser Sunda Islands, into the Moluccas and Celebes.

◄ ***The river of** Sungai Mahakam cuts through the central highlands of Borneo, the third largest island in the world, with a total area of 290,000 sq miles (757,050 sq km). Although mountainous, Borneo is one of the most stable of the Indonesian islands, with little volcanic activity.*

Transportation & industry

Singapore has a thriving economy based on international trade and finance. Annual trade through the port is among the highest of any in the world. Indonesia's western islands still depend on natural resources, particularly petroleum, gas, and wood, although the economy is rapidly diversifying with manufactured exports including garments, consumer electronics, and footwear. A high-profile aircraft industry has developed in Bandung on Java. Malaysia has a fast-growing and varied manufacturing sector, although oil, gas, and timber remain important resource-based industries.

► ***Ranks of gleaming** skyscrapers, new motorways and infrastructure construction reflect the investment which is pouring into Southeast Asian cities like the Malaysian capital, Kuala Lumpur. Traditional housing and markets still exist amidst the new developments. Many of the city's inhabitants subsist at a level far removed from the prosperity implied by its outward modernity.*

Malaysia: Capital cities
KUALA LUMPUR – capital
PUTRAJAYA – administrative capital

THAILAND
Malay Peninsula
Strait of Malacca
Kota Bharu
Kuala Terengganu
George Town
Pulau Pinang
Ipoh
Kuantan
KUALA LUMPUR
PUTRAJAYA
Seremban
Melaka
Johor Bahru
SINGAPORE
Tanjungpinang
Pekanbaru
Banda Aceh
Medan
ACEH
SUMATERA UTARA
RIAU
Padang
SUMATERA BARAT
JAMBI
Jambi
Palembang
BENGKULU
Bengkulu
Sumatra
Kepulauan Batu
Pulau Siberut
Selat Mentawai
Kepulauan Mentawai
Pulau Enggano
Equator
INDIAN OCEAN

166
172
172

THAILAND
South China Sea
BRUNEI
BANDAR SERI BEGAWAN
George Town
Medan
KUALA LUMPUR
MALAYSIA
PUTRAJAYA
SINGAPORE
Kuching
Celebes Sea
Borneo
Pontianak
Balikpapan
Padang
Sumatra
Palembang
Java Sea
INDIAN OCEAN
INDONESIA
JAKARTA
Bandung
Semarang
Surabaya
Java
Denpasar

Transportation network

- 165,272 miles (266,010 km)
- 958 miles (1,542 km)
- 5,061 miles (8,146 km)
- 18,070 miles (29,084 km)

Singapore's metro system, completed in 1991, is among the most efficient in the world. Malaysia has several fast, modern highways and most roads are paved. Indonesia's many islands make improvement of the shipping infrastructure a priority.

Major industry and infrastructure

- aerospace
- copra processing
- chemicals
- electronics
- engineering
- finance
- food processing
- iron & steel
- oil
- ship building
- timber processing
- textiles
- capital cities
- major towns
- international airports
- major roads
- major industrial areas

Using the land and sea

Rice is the most important arable crop in Indonesia and Malaysia, and both countries manage to meet almost all of their domestic demand. Malaysian rubber accounts for 25% of world production and is the main cash crop, grown on plantations and small farms, along with oil palms and copra. Timber is exported from both Malaysia and Indonesia. Modern agricultural techniques enable Singapore to produce fruits and vegetables despite a shortage of suitable land.

▶ Spiral cuts in the bark of this rubber palm show where it has been tapped. Sophisticated 'cloning' techniques mean that trees which produce consistently high quantities of rubber can be easily reproduced.

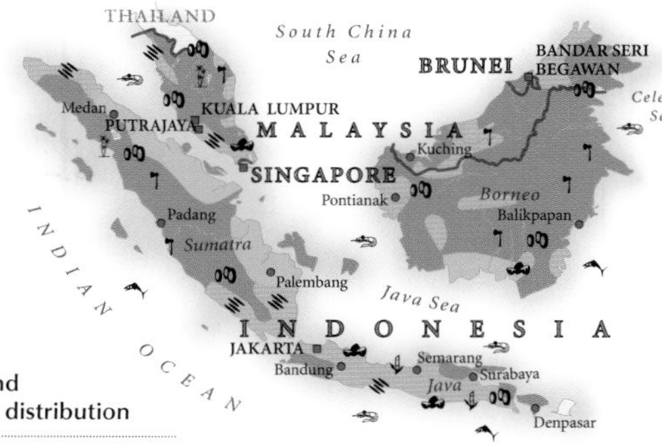
THAILAND
South China Sea
BRUNEI
BANDAR SERI BEGAWAN
Medan
PUTRAJAYA
KUALA LUMPUR
MALAYSIA
Kuching
Celebes Sea
SINGAPORE
Pontianak
Borneo
Balikpapan
Padang
Sumatra
Palembang
Java Sea
INDIAN OCEAN
INDONESIA
JAKARTA
Bandung
Semarang
Surabaya
Java
Denpasar

Land use and agricultural distribution

- coconuts
- fishing
- oil palms
- rice
- rubber
- shellfish
- sugar cane
- timber
- capital cities
- major towns
- pasture
- cropland
- forest
- wetland

The urban/rural population divide

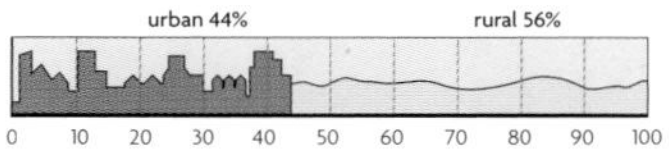
urban 44%
rural 56%
0 10 20 30 40 50 60 70 80 90 100

Population density	Total land area
297 people per sq mile (115 people per sq km)	828,356 sq miles (2,146,000 sq km)

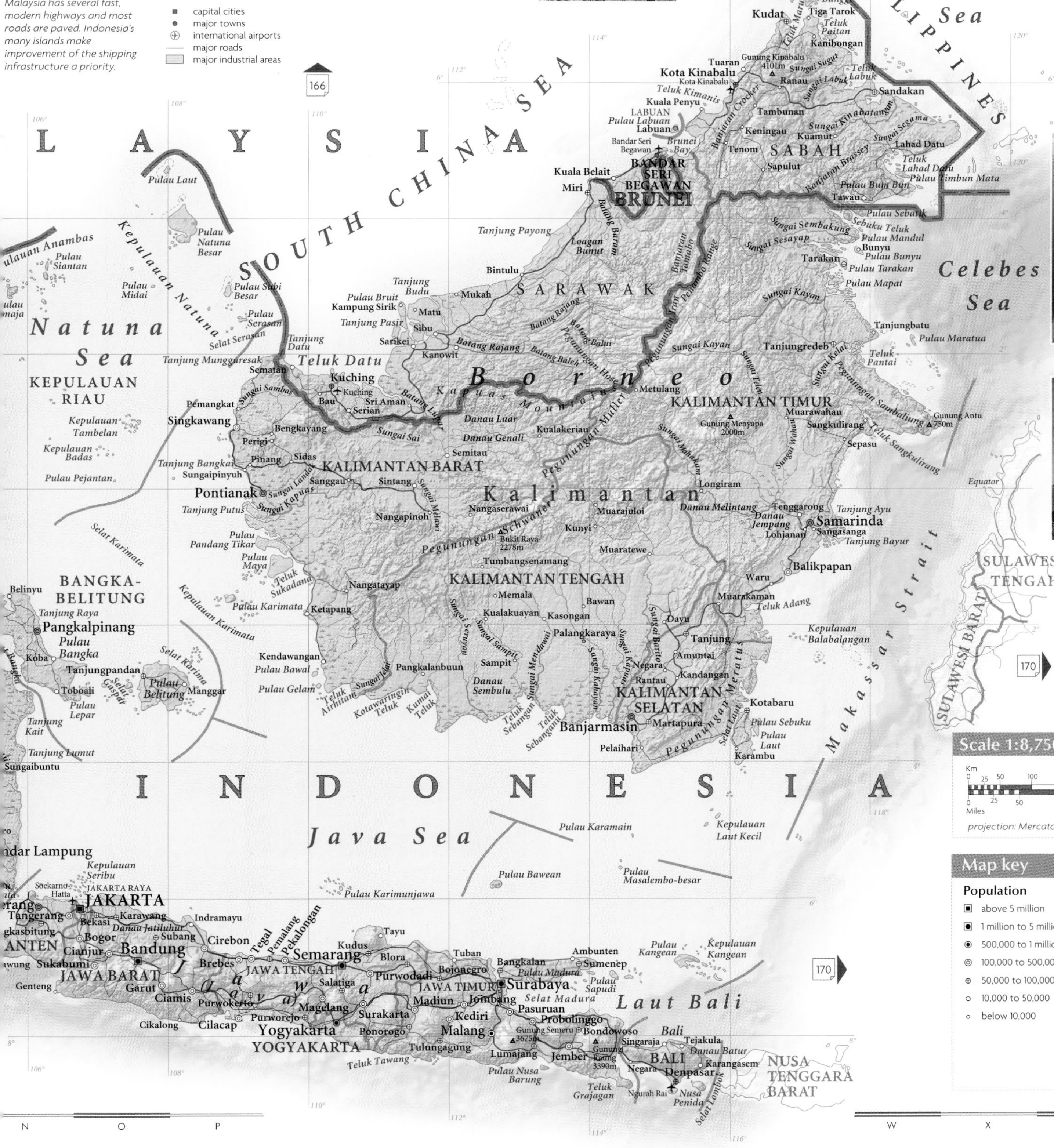
N O P Q R S T U V W X Y
1 2 3 4 5 6 7 8 9 10 11 12 13 14 15 16 17
166
170
PHILIPPINES
Sulu Sea
Balabac Strait
Pulau Balambangan
Pulau Banggi
Kudat
Tiga Tarok
Teluk Paitan
Kanibongan
Gunung Kinabalu 4101m
Tuaran
Kota Kinabalu
Ranau
Teluk Labuk
Sandakan
Teluk Kimanis
Kuala Penyu
LABUAN
Pulau Labuan
Labuan
Tambunan
Keningau
Kuamut
Tenom
SABAH
Lahad Datu
Teluk Lahad Datu
Pulau Timbun Mata
Sapulut
Bandar Seri Begawan
Brunei Bay
BANDAR SERI BEGAWAN
BRUNEI
Kuala Belait
Miri
Pulau Bum Bum
Tawau
Pulau Sebatik
Pulau Mandul
Pulau Bunyu
Tarakan
Pulau Tarakan
Pulau Mapat
Celebes Sea
Tanjungbatu
Pulau Maratua
Tanjungredeb
Teluk Pantai
SOUTH CHINA SEA
MALAYSIA
Pulau Laut
Pulau Natuna Besar
Kepulauan Natuna
Kepulauan Anambas
Pulau Siantan
Pulau Midai
Pulau Subi Besar
Pulau Serasan
Selat Serasan
Natuna Sea
KEPULAUAN RIAU
Tanjung Datu
Teluk Datu
Tanjung Payong
Loagan Bunut
Bintulu
Tanjung Budu
Mukah
SARAWAK
Pulau Bruit
Kampung Sirik
Tanjung Pasir
Matu
Sibu
Sarikei
Kanowit
Batang Rajang
Tanjung Munggaresak
Sematan
Kuching
Bau
Sri Aman
Serian
Borneo
Kapuas Mountains
Metulang
KALIMANTAN TIMUR
Gunung Menyapa 2000m
Muarawahau
Sangkulirang
Gunung Antu 750m
Sepasu
Equator
Pemangkat
Singkawang
Kepulauan Tambelan
Kepulauan Badas
Pulau Pejantan
Bengkayang
Perigi
Pinang
Sidas
Tanjung Bangkai
Sungaipinyuh
KALIMANTAN BARAT
Sanggau
Sintang
Danau Luar
Danau Genali
Semitau
Kualakeriau
Pontianak
Tanjung Putus
Kalimantan
Nangaserawai
Nangapinoh
Muarajuloi
Kunyi
Longiram
Danau Melintang
Tenggarong
Danau Jempang
Lohjanan
Samarinda
Sangasanga
Tanjung Ayu
Tanjung Bayur
Selat Karimata
Pulau Pandang Tikar
Pulau Maya
Teluk Sukadana
Pegunungan Schwaner
Bukit Raya 2278m
Muaratewe
Tumbangsenamang
KALIMANTAN TENGAH
Balikpapan
Waru
Muarakaman
Teluk Adang
Makassar Strait
SULAWESI TENGAH
SULAWESI BARAT
Belinyu
BANGKA-BELITUNG
Tanjung Raya
Pangkalpinang
Pulau Bangka
Koba
Tanjungpandan
Pulau Belitung
Manggar
Tobodi
Pulau Lepar
Tanjung Kait
Tanjung Lumut
Sungaibuntu
Kepulauan Karimata
Pulau Karimata
Ketapang
Nangatayap
Memala
Kualakuayan
Kasongan
Bawan
Palangkaraya
Dayu
Tanjung
Amuntai
Kepulauan Balabalangan
Kendawangan
Pulau Bawal
Pulau Gelam
Teluk Airhitam
Kotawaringin
Teluk Kumai
Pangkalanbuun
Sampit
Danau Sembulu
Teluk Sebangan
Negara
Rantau
Kandangan
KALIMANTAN SELATAN
Martapura
Banjarmasin
Pelaihari
Kotabaru
Pulau Sebuku
Pulau Laut
Karambu
Pegunungan Meratus
INDONESIA
Java Sea
Pulau Karamain
Kepulauan Laut Kecil
Pulau Bawean
Pulau Masalembo-besar
Pulau Karimunjawa
Bandar Lampung
Kepulauan Seribu
JAKARTA RAYA
JAKARTA
Tangerang
Bekasi
Karawang
Indramayu
Danau Jatiluhur
Subang
Cirebon
Bogor
BANTEN
Cianjur
Bandung
Sukabumi
JAWA BARAT
Garut
Ciamis
Genteng
Cikalong
Cilacap
Brebes
Tegal
Pemalang
Pekalongan
Semarang
JAWA TENGAH
Kudus
Tayu
Blora
Salatiga
Purwokerto
Magelang
Purworejo
Yogyakarta
YOGYAKARTA
Surakarta
Ponorogo
Purwodadi
Tuban
Bojonegoro
JAWA TIMUR
Surabaya
Madiun
Jombang
Kediri
Malang
Tulungagung
Bangkalan
Pulau Madura
Ambunten
Sumenep
Pulau Sapudi
Selat Madura
Pasuruan
Probolinggo
Gunung Semeru 3676m
Bondowoso
Lumajang
Jember
Gunung Raung 3390m
Teluk Tawang
Pulau Nusa Barung
Teluk Grajagan
Laut Bali
Pulau Kangean
Kepulauan Kangean
Bali
Singaraja
Tejakula
Danau Batur
Karangasem
BALI
Negara
Denpasar
Ngurah Rai
Nusa Penida
Selat Lombok
NUSA TENGGARA BARAT
N O P W X Y Z

▼ This tiny island near Kota Kinabalu, in Sabah, eastern Malaysia, is a part of a designated national park. Thickly forested, it is surrounded by broad, sandy beaches and shallow inland seas.

▲ The volcano of Gunung Semeru in eastern Java lies on the Pacific "Ring of Fire". It is part of the ancient Tennegger volcano and remains highly active.

Scale 1:8,750,000

Km 0 25 50 100 150 200
Miles 0 25 50 100 150 200

projection: Mercator

Map key

Population

- above 5 million
- 1 million to 5 million
- 500,000 to 1 million
- 100,000 to 500,000
- 50,000 to 100,000
- 10,000 to 50,000
- below 10,000

Elevation

- 4000m / 13,124ft
- 3000m / 9843ft
- 2000m / 6562ft
- 1000m / 3281ft
- 500m / 1640ft
- 250m / 820ft
- 100m / 328ft
- sea level

Eastern Maritime Southeast Asia

EAST TIMOR, INDONESIA, PHILIPPINES

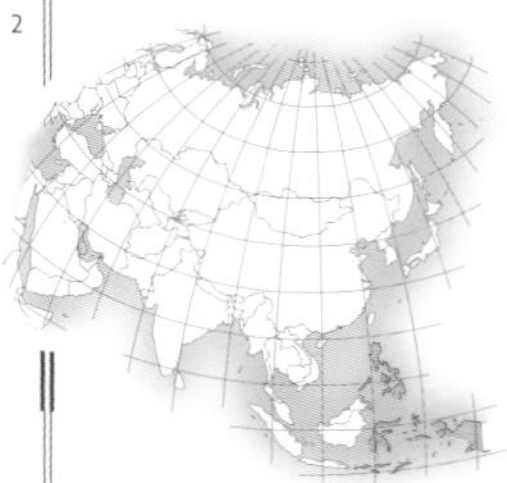

The Philippines takes its name from Philip II of Spain who was king when the islands were colonized during the 16th century. Almost 400 years of Spanish, and later US, rule have left their mark on the country's culture; English is widely spoken and over 90% of the population is Christian. The Philippines' economy is agriculturally based – inadequate infrastructure and electrical power shortages have so far hampered faster industrial growth. Indonesia's eastern islands are less economically developed than the rest of the country. Papua (Irian Jaya), which constitutes the western portion of New Guinea, is one of the world's last great wildernesses. East Timor is the newest independent state in the world, gaining full autonomy in 2002.

▲ ***The traditional boat-shaped** houses of the Toraja people in Sulawesi. Although now Christian, the Toraja still practice the animist traditions and rituals of their ancestors. They are famous for their elaborate funeral ceremonies and burial sites in cliffside caves.*

The landscape

Located on the Pacific "Ring of Fire" the Philippines' 7100 islands are subject to frequent earthquakes and volcanic activity. Their terrain is largely mountainous, with narrow coastal plains and interior valleys and plains. Luzon and Mindanao are by far the largest islands and comprise roughly 66% of the country's area. Indonesia's eastern islands are mountainous and dotted with volcanoes, both active and dormant.

▶ ***Lake Taal on** the Philippines island of Luzon lies within the crater of an immense volcano that erupted twice in the 20th century, first in 1911 and again in 1965, causing the deaths of more than 3200 people.*

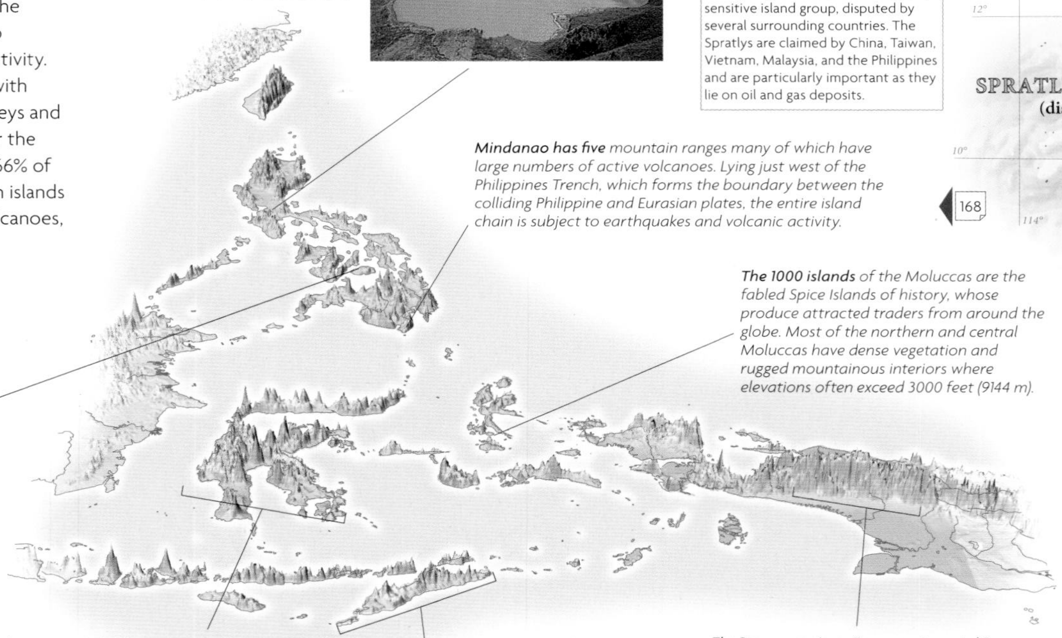

***Mindanao has five** mountain ranges many of which have large numbers of active volcanoes. Lying just west of the Philippines Trench, which forms the boundary between the colliding Philippine and Eurasian plates, the entire island chain is subject to earthquakes and volcanic activity.*

***The 1000 islands** of the Moluccas are the fabled Spice Islands of history, whose produce attracted traders from around the globe. Most of the northern and central Moluccas have dense vegetation and rugged mountainous interiors where elevations often exceed 3000 feet (9144 m).*

The four-pronged island of Celebes is the product of complex tectonic activity which ruptured and then reattached small fragments of the Earth's crust to form the island's many peninsulas.

Coral islands such as Timor in eastern Indonesia show evidence of very recent and dramatic movements of the Earth's plates. Reefs in Timor have risen by as much as 4000 ft (1300 m) in the last million years.

The Pegunungan Jayawijaya range in central Papua (Irian Jaya) contains the world's highest range of limestone mountains, some with peaks more than 16,400 ft (5000 m) high. Heavy rainfall and high temperatures, which promote rapid weathering, have led to the creation of large underground caves and river systems such as the river of Sungai Baliem.

▲ ***Bohol in the** southern Philippines is famous for its so-called "chocolate hills". There are more than 1000 of these regular mounds on the island. The hills are limestone in origin, the smoothed remains of an earlier cycle of erosion. Their brown appearance in the dry season gives them their name.*

The Spratly Islands are a strategically sensitive island group, disputed by several surrounding countries. The Spratlys are claimed by China, Taiwan, Vietnam, Malaysia, and the Philippines and are particularly important as they lie on oil and gas deposits.

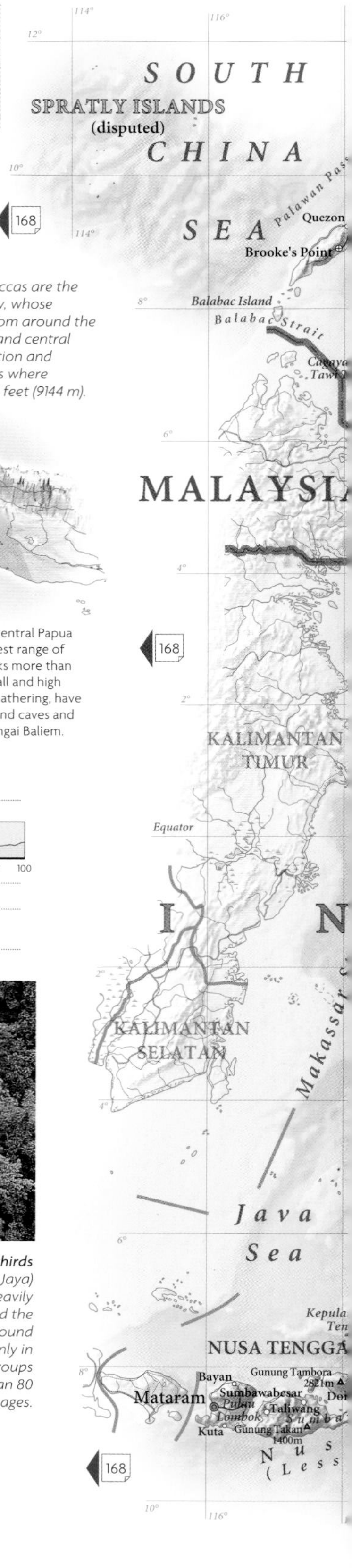
SOUTH CHINA SEA
SPRATLY ISLANDS
(disputed)
168
Palawan Passage
Quezon
Brooke's Point
Balabac Island
Balabac Strait
MALAYSIA
168
KALIMANTAN TIMUR
Equator
KALIMANTAN SELATAN
Makassar
Java Sea
NUSA TENGGARA
Mataram
Bayan
Gunung Tambora 2821m
Sumbawabesar
Lombok
Taliwang
Kuta
168

Using the land and sea

Indonesia's eastern islands are less intensively cultivated than those in the west. Coconuts, coffee and spices such as cloves and nutmeg are the major commercial crops while rice, corn and soybeans are grown for local consumption. The Philippines' rich, fertile soils support year-round production of a wide range of crops. The country is one of the world's largest producers of coconuts and a major exporter of coconut products, including one-third of the world's copra. Although much of the arable land is given over to rice and corn, the main staple food crops, tropical fruits such as bananas, pineapples and mangos, and sugar cane are also grown for export.

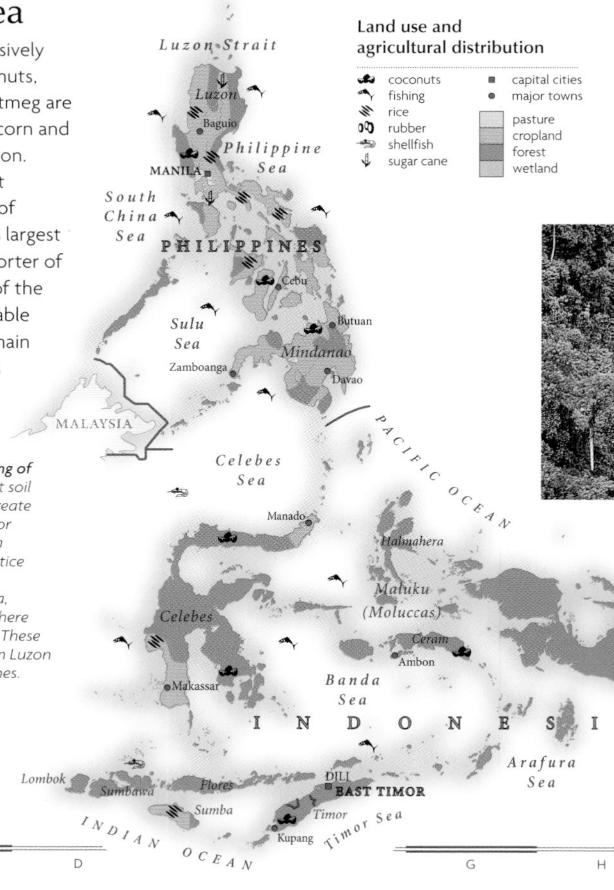
Luzon Strait
Luzon
Baguio
Philippine Sea
MANILA
South China Sea
PHILIPPINES
Cebu
Sulu Sea
Butuan
Mindanao
Zamboanga
Davao
MALAYSIA
PACIFIC OCEAN
Celebes Sea
Manado
Halmahera
Maluku (Moluccas)
Celebes
Ceram
Ambon
Jayapura
Makassar
Banda Sea
New Guinea
PAPUA NEW GUINEA
INDONESIA
Arafura Sea
Lombok
Sumbawa
Flores
Sumba
DILI
EAST TIMOR
Timor
Kupang
Timor Sea
INDIAN OCEAN

Land use and agricultural distribution

- coconuts
- fishing
- rice
- rubber
- shellfish
- sugar cane
- capital cities
- major towns
- pasture
- cropland
- forest
- wetland

The urban/rural population divide

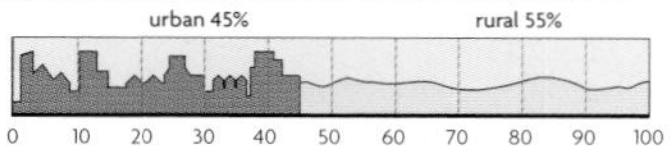
urban 45%
rural 55%
0
10
20
30
40
50
60
70
80
90
100

Population density	Total land area
258 people per sq mile (160 people per sq km)	654,771 sq miles (1,053,755 sq km)

▲ *More than two-thirds of Papua's (Irian Jaya) land area is heavily forested and the population of around 1.5 million live mainly in isolated tribal groups using more than 80 distinct languages.*

◀ ***The terracing of** land to restrict soil erosion and create flat surfaces for agriculture is a common practice throughout Southeast Asia, particularly where land is scarce. These terraces are on Luzon in the Philippines.*

Transportation & industry

The Philippines' economy is primarily a mixture of agriculture and light industry. The manufacturing sector is still developing; many factories are licensees of foreign companies producing finished goods for export. Mining is also important – the country's chromite, nickel, and copper deposits are among the largest in the world. Agriculture is the main activity in eastern Indonesia. Most industry has a primary basis, including logging, food-processing, and mining. Nickel, the most important metal, is produced on Sulawesi, in Papua (Irian Jaya), and in the Moluccas.

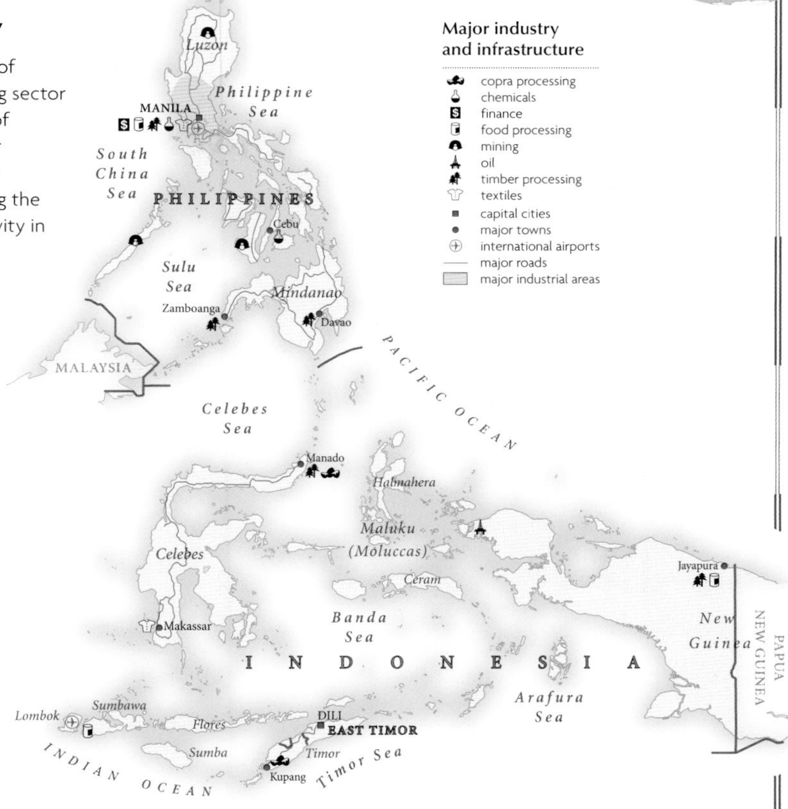
Major industry and infrastructure
copra processing
chemicals
finance
food processing
mining
oil
timber processing
textiles
capital cities
major towns
international airports
major roads
major industrial areas
Luzon Strait
Luzon
MANILA
Philippine Sea
South China Sea
PHILIPPINES
Cebu
Sulu Sea
Zamboanga
Mindanao
Davao
MALAYSIA
PACIFIC OCEAN
Celebes Sea
Manado
Halmahera
Maluku (Moluccas)
Celebes
Ceram
Jayapura
Makassar
Banda Sea
New Guinea
PAPUA NEW GUINEA
INDONESIA
Arafura Sea
Sumbawa
Lombok
Flores
DILI
EAST TIMOR
Sumba
Timor
Kupang
Timor Sea
INDIAN OCEAN

Transportation network

16,652 miles (26,800 km)

None

500 miles (805 km)

8704 miles (14,008 km)

Sulawesi has some good roads, but on Papua (Irian Jaya) and the Moluccas there are few road interconnections between major settled areas. Water and sea transportation remain important although air links have improved in the Philippines.

crissa
EGO

▲ *Manila is the Philippines' chief port and transportation center, and the focus of the country's commercial, industrial, and cultural activities. Much of the city lies below sea level, and it suffers from floods during the rainy summer season.*

Map key

Population

- above 5 million
- 1 million to 5 million
- 500,000 to 1 million
- 100,000 to 500,000
- 50,000 to 100,000
- 10,000 to 50,000
- below 10,000

Elevation

- 4000m / 13,124ft
- 3000m / 9843ft
- 2000m / 6562ft
- 1000m / 3281ft
- 500m / 1640ft
- 250m / 820ft
- 100m / 328ft
- sea level

Scale 1:,11,800,000

Km 0 50 100 200 300 400

Miles 0 50 100 200 300 400

projection: Mercator

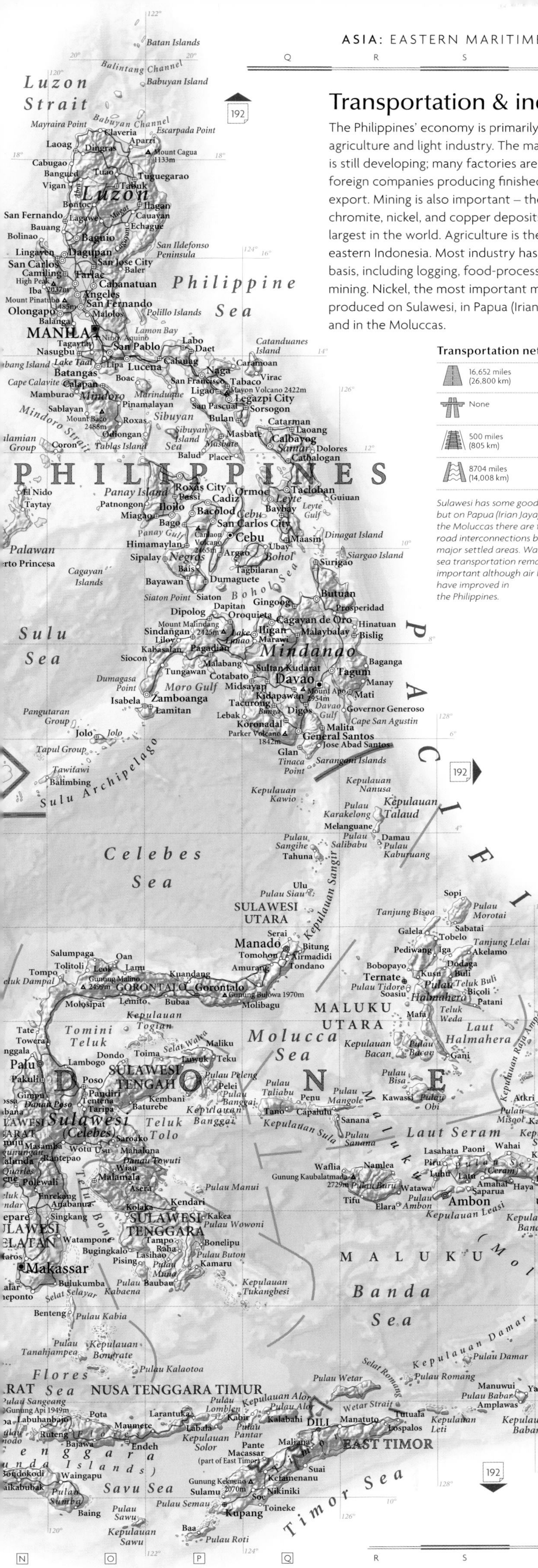
Luzon Strait
Batan Islands
Balintang Channel
Babuyan Island
Babuyan Channel
Luzon
Philippine Sea
MANILA
Sulu Sea
PHILIPPINES
Mindanao
Davao
Zamboanga
Cebu
Celebes Sea
PACIFIC OCEAN
SULAWESI UTARA
Manado
Molucca Sea
MALUKU UTARA
Halmahera
Sulawesi (Celebes)
SULAWESI TENGAH
SULAWESI TENGGARA
Makassar
Laut Seram
Ambon
MALUKU (Moluccas)
Banda Sea
IRIAN JAYA BARAT
PAPUA (IRIAN JAYA)
Jayapura
New Guinea
PAPUA NEW GUINEA
Arafura Sea
NUSA TENGGARA TIMUR
Flores Sea
DILI
EAST TIMOR
Kupang
Timor Sea
Savu Sea
Torres Strait

192
186

The Indian Ocean

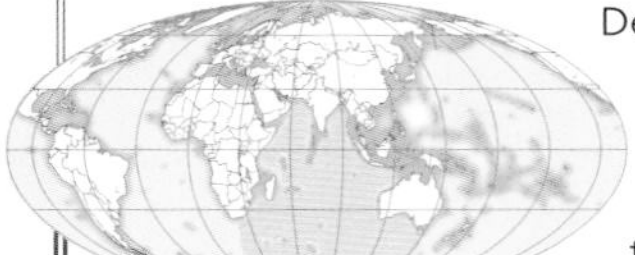

Despite being the smallest of the three major oceans, the evolution of the Indian Ocean was the most complex. The ocean basin was formed during the breakup of the supercontinent Gondwanaland, when the Indian subcontinent moved northeast, Africa moved west, and Australia separated from Antarctica. Like the Pacific Ocean, the warm waters of the Indian Ocean are punctuated by coral atolls and islands. About one-fifth of the world's population – over a billion people – live on its shores. In 2004, over 290,000 died and millions more were left homeless after a tsunami devastated large stretches of the ocean's coastline.

The landscape

The Indian Ocean began forming about 150 million years ago, but in its present form it is relatively young, only about 36 million years old. Along the three subterranean mountain chains of its mid-ocean ridge the seafloor is still spreading. The Indian Ocean has fewer trenches than other oceans and only a narrow continental shelf around most of its surrounding land.

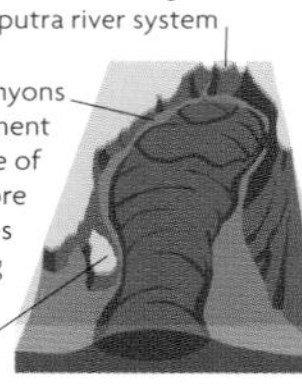

Sediments come from Ganges/ Brahmaputra river system
Submarine canyons transport sediment to fan – some of these are more than 1500 miles (2500 km) long
Sri Lanka

▲ *The Ganges Fan is one of the world's largest submarine accumulations of sediment, extending far beyond Sri Lanka. It is fed by the Ganges/Brahmaputra river system, whose sediment is carried through a network of underwater canyons at the edge of the continental shelf.*

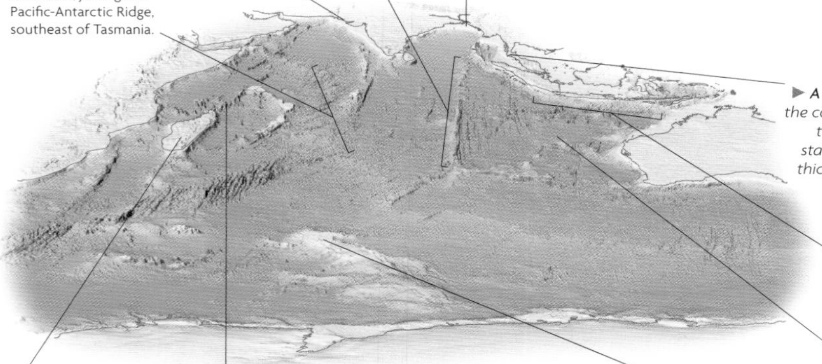

Indus River

The mid-oceanic ridge runs from the Arabian Sea. It diverges east of Madagascar. One arm runs southwest to join the Mid-Atlantic Ridge, the other branches southeast, joining the Pacific-Antarctic Ridge, southeast of Tasmania.

The Ninetyeast Ridge takes its name from the line of longitude it follows. It is the world's longest and straightest under-sea ridge.

Two of the world's largest rivers flow into the Indian Ocean; the Indus and the Ganges/ Brahmaputra. Both have deposited enormous fans of sediment.

The relief of Madagascar rises from a low-lying coastal strip in the east, to the central plateau. The plateau is also a major watershed separating Madagascar's three main river basins.

The Kerguelen Islands in the Southern Ocean were created by a hot spot in the Earth's crust. The islands were formed in succession as the Antarctic Plate moved slowly over the hot spot.

The Java Trench is the world's longest, it runs 1600 miles (2570 km) from the southwest of Java, but is only 50 miles (80 km) wide.

The circulation in the northern Indian Ocean is controlled by the monsoon winds. Biannually these winds reverse their pattern, causing a reversal in the surface currents and alternative high and low pressure conditions over Asia and Australia.

► *A large proportion of the coast of Thailand, on the Isthmus of Kra, is stabilized by mangrove thickets. They act as an important breeding ground for wildlife.*

► *The central group of the Seychelles are mountainous, granite islands. They have a narrow coastal belt and lush, tropical vegetation cloaks the highlands.*

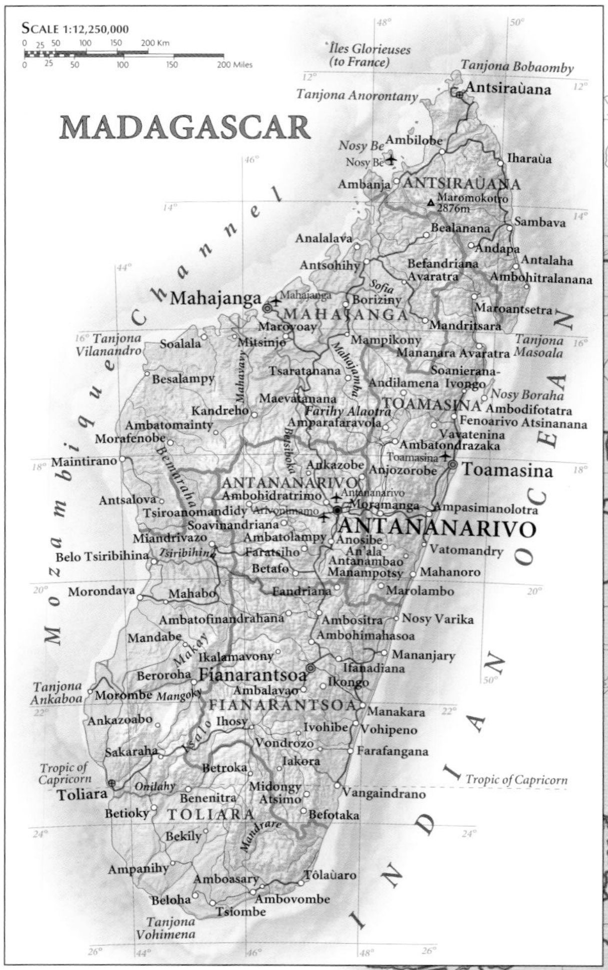

Scale 1:12,250,000
MADAGASCAR
Mozambique Channel
INDIAN OCEAN
Antsiranana
Mahajanga
Toamasina
ANTANANARIVO
Fianarantsoa
Toliara
Tropic of Capricorn

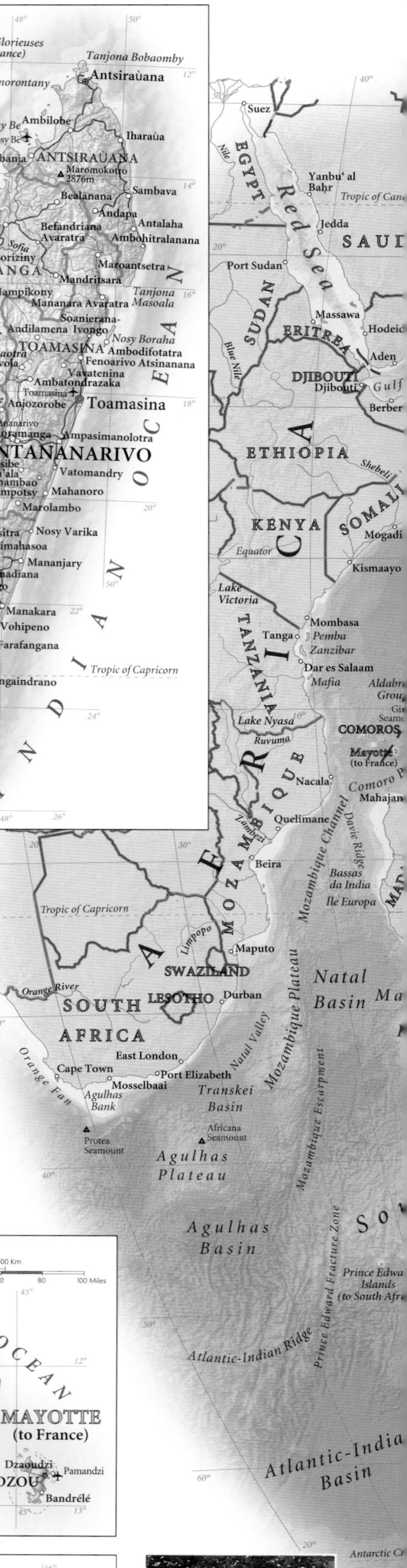

EGYPT
SUDAN
ERITREA
DJIBOUTI
ETHIOPIA
KENYA
SOMALIA
TANZANIA
MOZAMBIQUE
SWAZILAND
LESOTHO
SOUTH AFRICA
COMOROS
Red Sea
Mozambique Channel
Natal Basin
Transkei Basin
Agulhas Plateau
Agulhas Basin
Atlantic-Indian Ridge
Atlantic-Indian Basin
Tropic of Capricorn

Resources

Many of the small islands in the Indian Ocean rely exclusively on tuna-fishing and tourism to maintain their economies. Most fisheries are artisanal, although large-scale tuna-fishing does take place in the Seychelles, Mauritius and the western Indian Ocean. Other resources include oil in the Persian Gulf, pearls in the Red Sea, and tin from deposits off the shores of Myanmar, Thailand, and Indonesia.

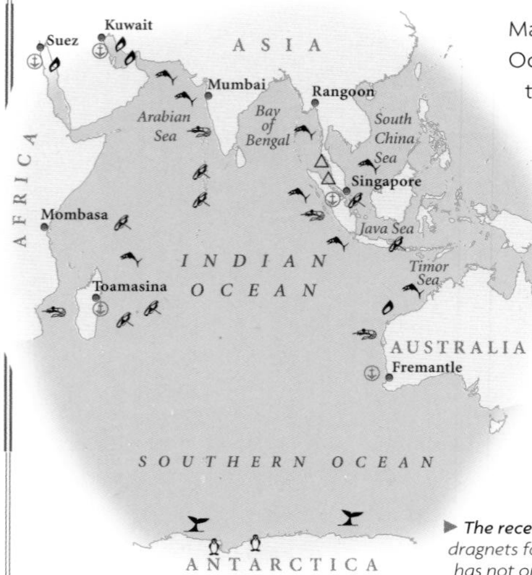

ASIA
AFRICA
INDIAN OCEAN
AUSTRALIA
SOUTHERN OCEAN
ANTARCTICA
Suez
Kuwait
Mumbai
Rangoon
Arabian Sea
Bay of Bengal
South China Sea
Singapore
Java Sea
Timor Sea
Mombasa
Toamasina
Fremantle
Resources (including wildlife)
fish
penguins
shellfish
whales
oil & gas
tin deposits
tourism
major towns
major ports

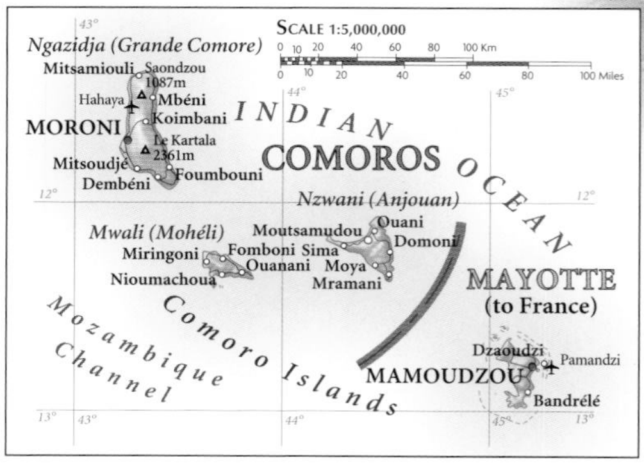

Scale 1:5,000,000
Ngazidja (Grande Comore)
MORONI
COMOROS
INDIAN OCEAN
Nzwani (Anjouan)
Mwali (Mohéli)
MAYOTTE (to France)
MAMOUDZOU
Mozambique Channel
Comoro Islands

Inner Islands
SEYCHELLES
INDIAN OCEAN
Praslin
La Digue
Silhouette
Mahé
VICTORIA
Scale 1:2,250,000

► *The recent use of large dragnets for tuna-fishing has not only threatened the livelihoods of many small-scale fisheries, but also caused widespread environmental concern about the potential impact on other marine species.*

▲ *Coral reefs support an enormous diversity of animal and plant life. Many species of tropical fish, like these squirrel fish, live and feed around the profusion of reefs and atolls in the Indian Ocean.*

◀ *The steeper eastern side of Madagascar is drained by numerous short, fast-flowing rivers. In contrast, larger, more languid rivers flow across the west. Both erode huge quantities of Madagascar's reddish soil.*

▶ *There are over 1300 small coral islands in the Maldives, but only about 200 are inhabited. They are based around an ancient submerged volcanic mountain range and all the islands are low-lying, none rising more than 6 ft (1.8 m) above sea level.*

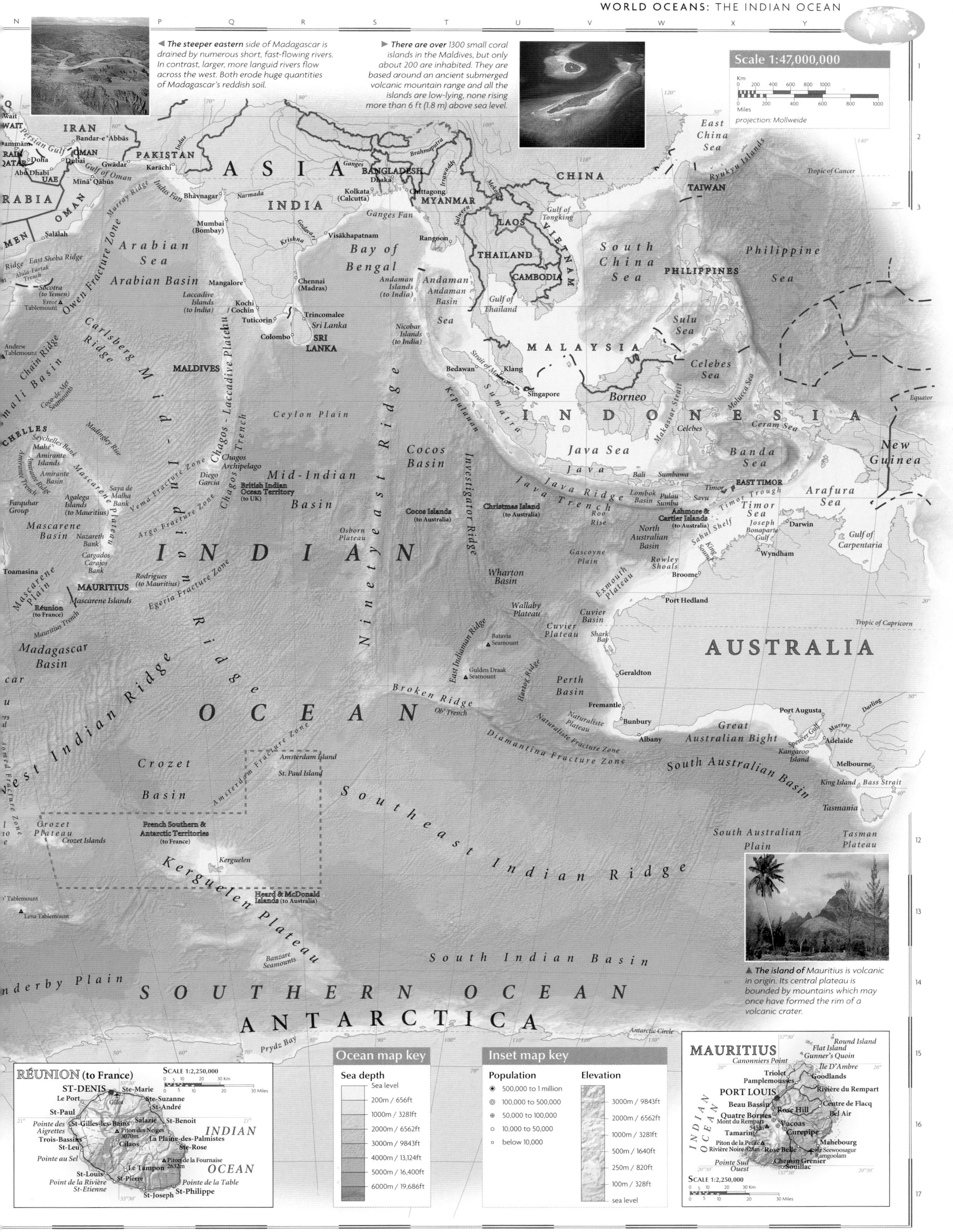
N
P
Q
R
S
T
U
V
W
X
Y
Z
ASIA
IRAN
Bandar-e 'Abbās
Persian Gulf
OMAN
Dubai
Doha
Abu Dhabi
UAE
Gwādar
Gulf of Oman
Masqaṭ
PAKISTAN
Karāchi
Indus
Mina' Qābūs
ARABIA
Murray Ridge
Indus Fan
Bhāvnagar
Narmada
INDIA
Ganges
BANGLADESH
Dhaka
Kolkata (Calcutta)
Chittagong
MYANMAR
Brahmaputra
Irrawaddy
CHINA
TAIWAN
Ryukyu Islands
East China Sea
Tropic of Cancer
Salālah
Mumbai (Bombay)
Ganges Fan
Godavari
Krishna
Visākhapatnam
Rangoon
Salween
Mekong
LAOS
VIETNAM
Gulf of Tongking
THAILAND
CAMBODIA
Gulf of Thailand
South China Sea
PHILIPPINES
Philippine Sea
Arabian Sea
Bay of Bengal
East Sheba Ridge
Alula-Fartak Trench
Owen Fracture Zone
Arabian Basin
Mangalore
Socotra (to Yemen)
Error Tablemount
Laccadive Islands (to India)
Kochi / Cochin
Chennai (Madras)
Andaman Islands (to India)
Andaman Sea
Andaman Basin
Trincomalee
Tuticorin
Colombo
Sri Lanka
SRI LANKA
Nicobar Islands (to India)
Sulu Sea
Celebes Sea
MALAYSIA
Andrew Tablemount
Chain Ridge
Carlsberg Ridge
Somali Basin
Coco-de-Mer Seamounts
MALDIVES
Laccadive Plateau
Chagos - Laccadive Plateau
Mid-Indian Ridge
Ceylon Plain
Ninetyeast Ridge
Bedawan
Strait of Malacca
Klang
Singapore
Sumatra
Kepulauan
Borneo
INDONESIA
Makassar Strait
Molucca Sea
Celebes
Ceram Sea
Equator
New Guinea
SEYCHELLES
Seychelles Bank
Mahé
Amirante Islands
Amirante Basin
Amirante Trench
Amirante Ridge
Madingley Rise
Chagos Trench
Chagos Archipelago
Diego Garcia
British Indian Ocean Territory (to UK)
Mid-Indian Basin
Cocos Basin
Investigator Ridge
Java Sea
Java
Bali
Sumbawa
Banda Sea
Timor
EAST TIMOR
Arafura Sea
Mascarene Plateau
Saya de Malha Bank
Vema Fracture Zone
Farquhar Group
Agalega Islands (to Mauritius)
Argo Fracture Zone
Cocos Islands (to Australia)
Christmas Island (to Australia)
Java Ridge
Java Trench
Lombok Basin
Pulau Sumba
Savu
Timor Trough
Timor Sea
Ashmore & Cartier Islands (to Australia)
Roo Rise
Sahul Shelf
Joseph Bonaparte Gulf
Darwin
Gulf of Carpentaria
Mascarene Basin
Nazareth Bank
Cargados Carajos Bank
Osborn Plateau
North Australian Basin
King Sound
Wyndham
Gascoyne Plain
Rowley Shoals
Broome
INDIAN
Toamasina
Mascarene Plain
MAURITIUS
Mascarene Islands
Réunion (to France)
Rodrigues (to Mauritius)
Egeria Fracture Zone
Wharton Basin
Exmouth Plateau
Port Hedland
Mauritius Trench
Madagascar Basin
Wallaby Plateau
Cuvier Basin
Cuvier Plateau
Shark Bay
Tropic of Capricorn
Batavia Seamount
East Indiaman Ridge
Gulden Draak Seamount
Hartog Ridge
AUSTRALIA
Geraldton
Perth Basin
Southwest Indian Ridge
Broken Ridge
Ob' Trench
OCEAN
Fremantle
Bunbury
Albany
Naturaliste Plateau
Naturaliste Fracture Zone
Diamantina Fracture Zone
Port Augusta
Spencer Gulf
Murray
Darling
Adelaide
Great Australian Bight
Kangaroo Island
Melbourne
South Australian Basin
King Island
Bass Strait
Tasmania
Amsterdam Fracture Zone
Amsterdam Island
St. Paul Island
Crozet Basin
Southeast Indian Ridge
Crozet Plateau
Crozet Islands
French Southern & Antarctic Territories (to France)
South Australian Plain
Tasman Plateau
Kerguelen
Kerguelen Plateau
Heard & McDonald Islands (to Australia)
Lena Tablemount
Banzare Seamounts
South Indian Basin
Enderby Plain
SOUTHERN OCEAN
ANTARCTICA
Prydz Bay
Antarctic Circle
RÉUNION (to France)
Scale 1:2,250,000
ST-DENIS
Ste-Marie
Le Port
Ste-Suzanne
St-André
St-Paul
Salazie
St-Benoit
Pointe des Aigrettes
St-Gilles-les-Bains
Piton des Neiges 3070m
Trois-Bassins
Cilaos
La Plaine-des-Palmistes
St-Leu
Ste-Rose
Pointe au Sel
Piton de la Fournaise 2632m
Le Tampon
St-Pierre
St-Louis
Point de la Rivière
St-Etienne
Pointe de la Table
St-Joseph
St-Philippe
INDIAN OCEAN
MAURITIUS
Round Island
Flat Island
Gunner's Quoin
Canonniers Point
Île D'Ambre
Triolet
Pamplemousses
Goodlands
PORT LOUIS
Rivière du Rempart
Beau Bassin
Rose Hill
Centre de Flacq
Quatre Bornes
Bel Air
Mont du Rempart 545m
Vacoas
Tamarin
Curepipe
Piton de la Petite Rivière Noire 828m
Rose Belle
Mahebourg
Ile Seewoosagur Ramgoolam
Pointe Sud Ouest
Chemin Grenier
Souillac
Scale 1:2,250,000

Scale 1:47,000,000

Km	0	200	400	600	800	1000
Miles	0	200	400	600	800	1000

projection: Mollweide

▲ *The island of Mauritius is volcanic in origin. Its central plateau is bounded by mountains which may once have formed the rim of a volcanic crater.*

Ocean map key

Sea depth

- Sea level
- 200m / 656ft
- 1000m / 3281ft
- 2000m / 6562ft
- 3000m / 9843ft
- 4000m / 13,124ft
- 5000m / 16,400ft
- 6000m / 19,686ft

Inset map key

Population

- 500,000 to 1 million
- 100,000 to 500,000
- 50,000 to 100,000
- 10,000 to 50,000
- below 10,000

Elevation

- 3000m / 9843ft
- 2000m / 6562ft
- 1000m / 3281ft
- 500m / 1640ft
- 250m / 820ft
- 100m / 328ft
- sea level

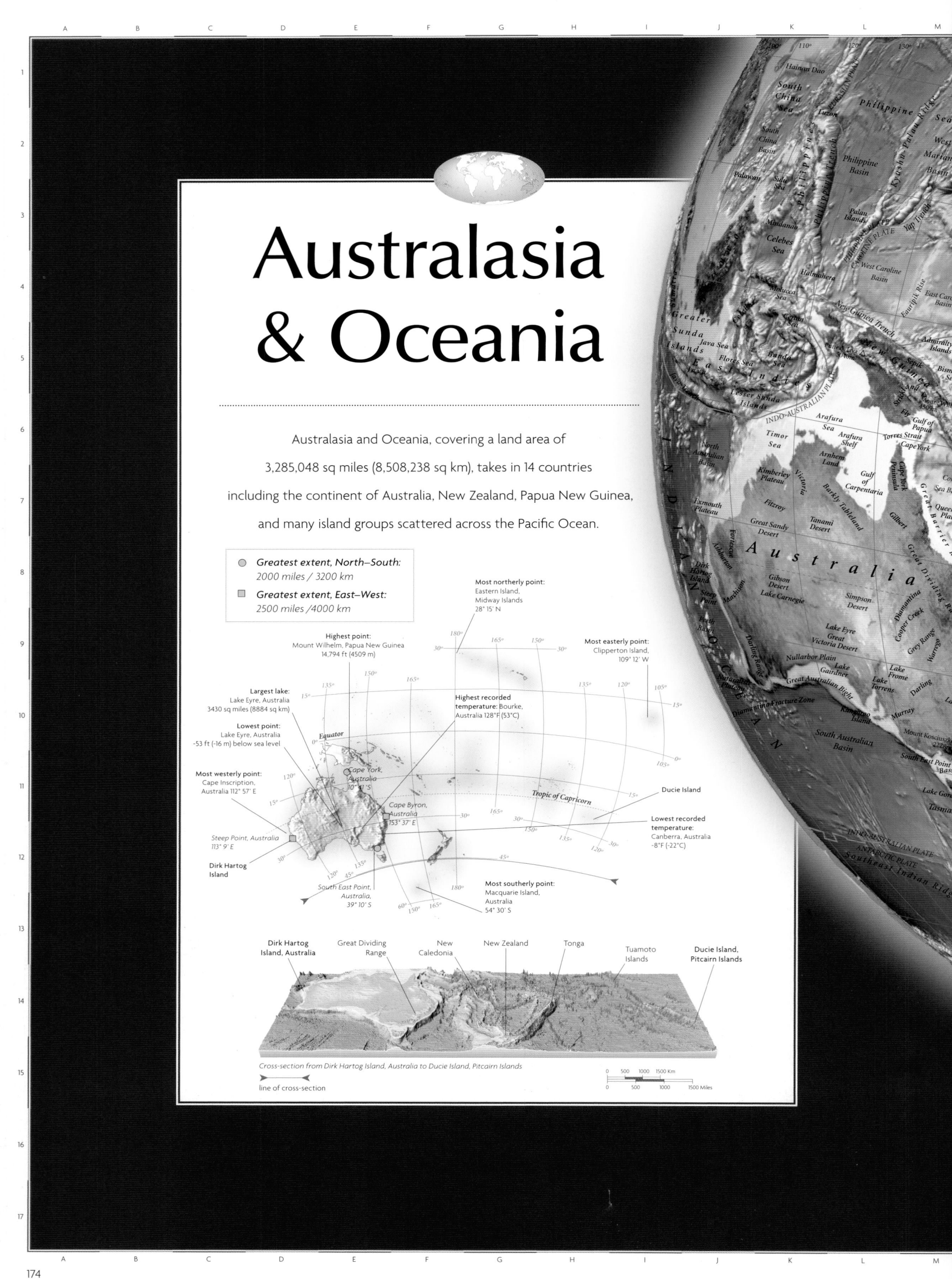

Australasia & Oceania

Australasia and Oceania, covering a land area of 3,285,048 sq miles (8,508,238 sq km), takes in 14 countries including the continent of Australia, New Zealand, Papua New Guinea, and many island groups scattered across the Pacific Ocean.

- *Greatest extent, North–South:* 2000 miles / 3200 km
- *Greatest extent, East–West:* 2500 miles /4000 km

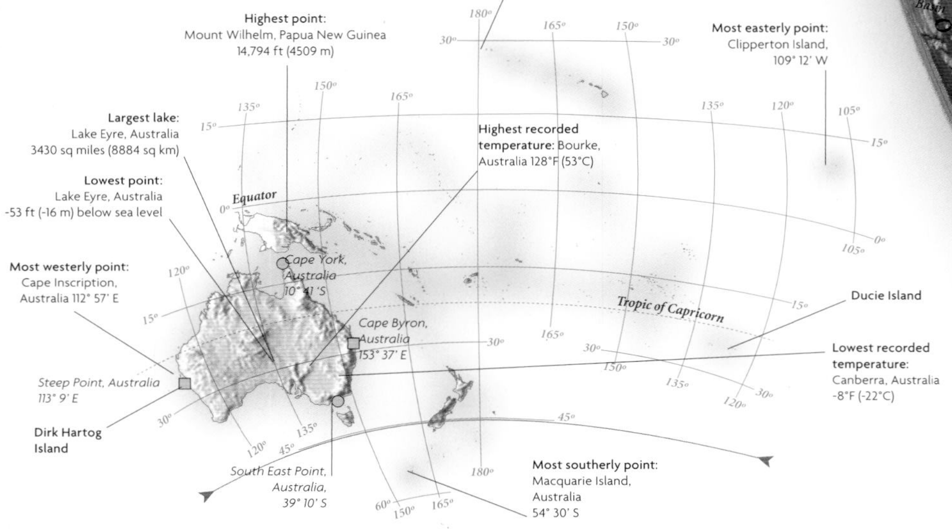

Most northerly point: Eastern Island, Midway Islands 28° 15' N
Highest point: Mount Wilhelm, Papua New Guinea 14,794 ft (4509 m)
Most easterly point: Clipperton Island, 109° 12' W
Largest lake: Lake Eyre, Australia 3430 sq miles (8884 sq km)
Highest recorded temperature: Bourke, Australia 128°F (53°C)
Lowest point: Lake Eyre, Australia -53 ft (-16 m) below sea level
Equator
Most westerly point: Cape Inscription, Australia 112° 57' E
Cape York, Australia 10° 41' S
Tropic of Capricorn
Ducie Island
Cape Byron, Australia 153° 37' E
Lowest recorded temperature: Canberra, Australia -8°F (-22°C)
Steep Point, Australia 113° 9' E
Dirk Hartog Island
South East Point, Australia, 39° 10' S
Most southerly point: Macquarie Island, Australia 54° 30' S

Dirk Hartog Island, Australia
Great Dividing Range
New Caledonia
New Zealand
Tonga
Tuamoto Islands
Ducie Island, Pitcairn Islands
0 500 1000 1500 Km
0 500 1000 1500 Miles

Cross-section from Dirk Hartog Island, Australia to Ducie Island, Pitcairn Islands

line of cross-section

Hainan Dao
South China Sea
Luzon
Philippine Sea
South China Basin
Philippine Basin
Palawan
Sulu Sea
Mindanao
Palau Islands
Celebes Sea
West Caroline Basin
Halmahera
Molucca Sea
Greater Sunda Islands
Java Sea
Flores Sea
Banda Sea
New Guinea Trench
Lesser Sunda Islands
INDO-AUSTRALIAN PLATE
Arafura Sea
Timor Sea
Torres Strait
Cape York
Arnhem Land
Gulf of Carpentaria
Kimberley Plateau
Exmouth Plateau
Great Sandy Desert
Tanami Desert
Australia
Gibson Desert
Lake Carnegie
Simpson Desert
Lake Eyre
Great Victoria Desert
Nullarbor Plain
Great Australian Bight
Kangaroo Island
South Australian Basin
Dirk Hartog Island
Steep Point
Perth Basin
Darling Range
Diamantina Fracture Zone
INDIAN OCEAN
Great Dividing Range
Murray
Darling
Lake Torrens
Lake Frome
Lake Gairdner
Mount Kosciuszko
South East Point
INDO-AUSTRALIAN PLATE
ANTARCTIC PLATE
Southeast Indian Ridge

N O P Q R S T U V W X Y Z

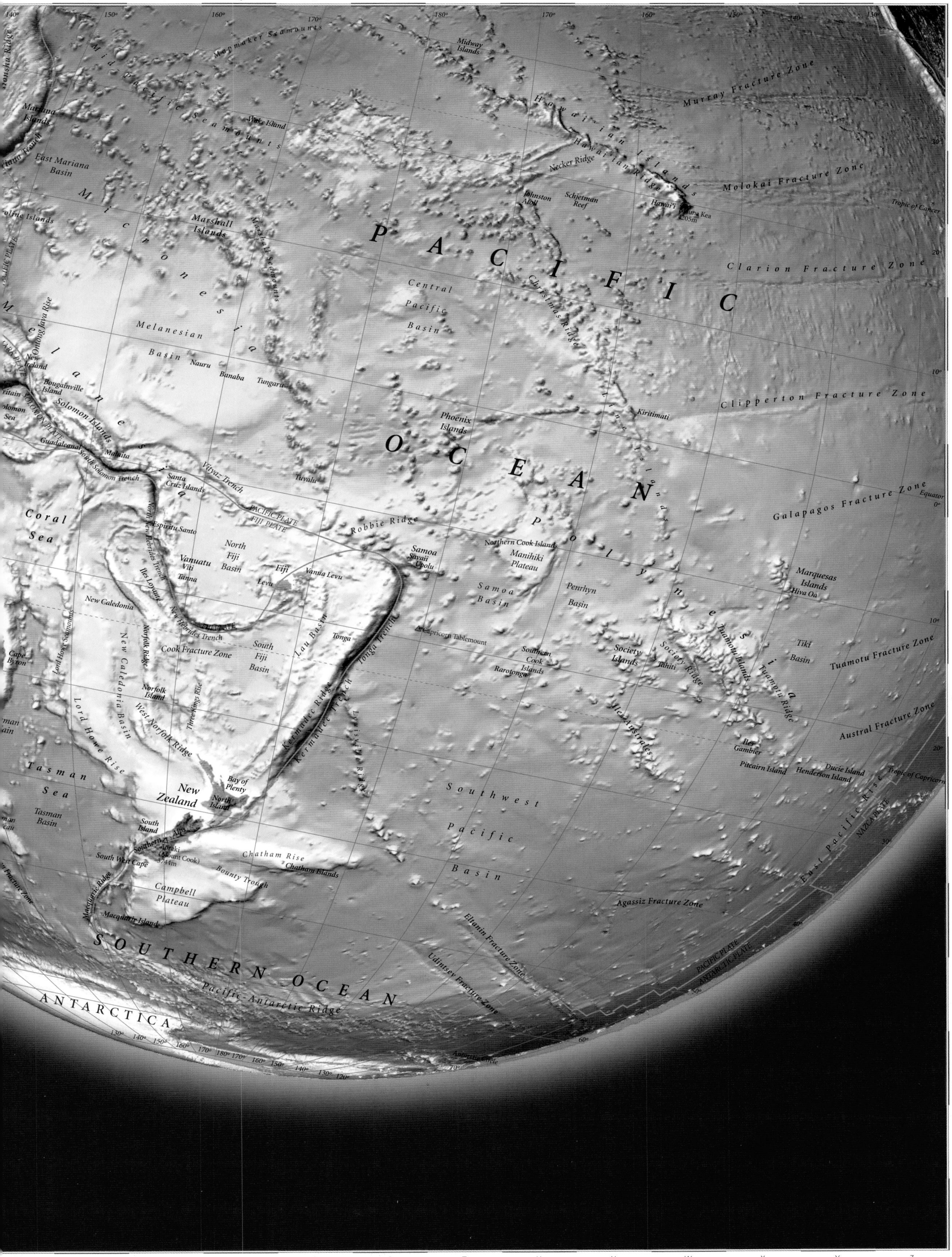

Midway Islands
Mapmaker Seamounts
Mid-Pacific Seamounts
Mariana Islands
Wake Island
East Mariana Basin
Murray Fracture Zone
Hawaiian Islands
Hawaiian Ridge
Necker Ridge
Molokai Fracture Zone
Johnston Atoll
Schjetman Reef
Hawai'i
Mauna Kea
Tropic of Cancer
Micronesia
Marshall Islands
Marshall Seamounts
PACIFIC
Clarion Fracture Zone
Central Pacific Basin
Christmas Ridge
Ontong Java Rise
Melanesian Basin
Melanesia
New Ireland
Nauru
Banaba
Tungaru
Bougainville Island
Solomon Islands
Line Islands
Clipperton Fracture Zone
Kiritimati
Phoenix Islands
OCEAN
Guadalcanal
Malaita
South Solomon Trench
Santa Cruz Islands
Vityaz Trench
Tuvalu
PACIFIC PLATE
FIJI PLATE
Galapagos Fracture Zone
Equator
Coral Sea
Espiritu Santo
North Fiji Basin
Robbie Ridge
Northern Cook Islands
Polynesia
Vanuatu
Viti Levu
Fiji
Vanua Levu
Tanna
Samoa
Savai'i
Upolu
Manihiki Plateau
Marquesas Islands
Hiva Oa
Iles Loyauté
New Caledonia
Samoa Basin
Penrhyn Basin
New Hebrides Trench
Lord Howe Seamounts
Norfolk Ridge
New Caledonia Basin
Cook Fracture Zone
South Fiji Basin
Lau Basin
Tonga
Tonga Trench
Capricorn Tablemount
Southern Cook Islands
Rarotonga
Society Islands
Tahiti
Society Ridge
Tuamotu Islands
Tuamotu Ridge
Tiki Basin
Tuamotu Fracture Zone
Cape Byron
Norfolk Island
West Norfolk Ridge
Three Kings Rise
Kermadec Ridge
Kermadec Trench
Louisville Ridge
Iles Australes
Austral Fracture Zone
Iles Gambier
Pitcairn Island
Henderson Island
Ducie Island
Tropic of Capricorn
Lord Howe Rise
Tasman Sea
Tasman Basin
New Zealand
North Island
Bay of Plenty
Southwest Pacific Basin
East Pacific Rise
NAZCA PLATE
South Island
Southern Alps
Aoraki (Mount Cook) 3,744m
South West Cape
Chatham Rise
Chatham Islands
Bounty Trough
Campbell Plateau
Macquarie Ridge
Macquarie Island
Agassiz Fracture Zone
Eltanin Fracture Zone
Udintsev Fracture Zone
SOUTHERN OCEAN
PACIFIC PLATE
ANTARCTIC PLATE
Pacific-Antarctic Ridge
ANTARCTICA
Antarctic Circle

1 2 3 4 5 6 7 8 9 10 11 12 13 14 15 16 17

N O P Q R S T U V W X Y Z

Political Australasia & Oceania

Vast expanses of ocean separate this geographically fragmented realm, characterized more by each country's isolation than by any political unity. Australia's and New Zealand's traditional ties with the United Kingdom, as members of the Commonwealth, are now being called into question as Australasian and Oceanian nations are increasingly looking to forge new relationships with neighboring Asian countries like Japan. External influences have featured strongly in the politics of the Pacific Islands; the various territories of Micronesia were largely under US control until the late 1980s, and France, New Zealand, the US, and the UK still have territories under colonial rule in Polynesia. Nuclear weapons-testing by Western superpowers was widespread during the Cold War period, but has now been discontinued.

◀ ***Western Australia's mineral*** *wealth has transformed its state capital, Perth, into one of Australia's major cities. Perth is one of the world's most isolated cities – over 2500 miles (4000 km) from the population centers of the eastern seaboard.*

Scale 1:35,500,000

Km 0 200 400 600 800
Miles 0 200 400 600 800

projection: Lambert Azimuthal Equal Area

Population

Density of settlement in the region is generally low. Australia is one of the least densely populated countries on Earth with over 80% of its population living within 25 miles (40 km) of the coast – mostly in the southeast of the country. New Zealand, and the island groups of Melanesia, Micronesia, and Polynesia, are much more densely populated, although many of the smaller islands remain uninhabited.

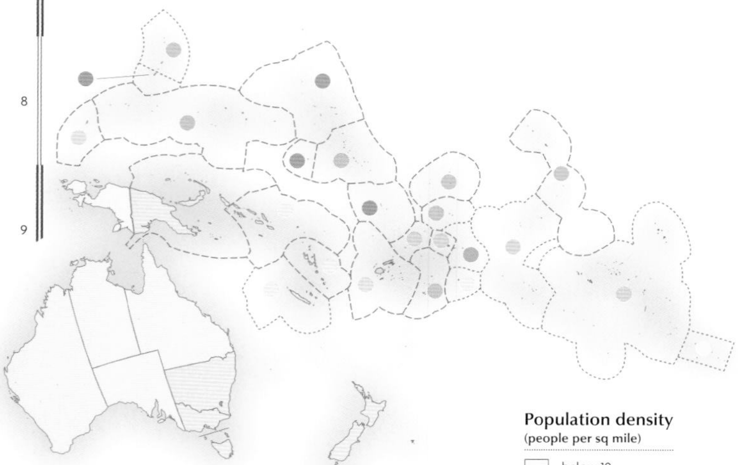

Population density
(people per sq mile)

- below 10
- 10-62
- 63-130
- 131-259
- 260-519
- 520-780
- above 780

▲ ***The myriad of*** *small coral islands that are scattered across the Pacific Ocean are often uninhabited, as they offer little shelter from the weather, often no fresh water, and only limited food supplies.*

◀ ***The planes of*** *the Australian Royal Flying Doctor Service are able to cover large expanses of barren land quickly, bringing medical treatment to the most inaccessible and far-flung places.*

Northern Mariana Islands
(to US)
Mariana Islands
Saipan
Philippine Sea
Guam
(to US)
HAGÅTÑA
Micronesia
Bikini Atoll
Ralik C
Yap
Caroline Islands
Chuuk
Pohnpei
PALIKIR
Kosrae
MELEKEOK
Babeldaob
PALAU
MICRONESIA
NAURU
YAREN
Melanesia
PAPUA NEW GUINEA
Equator
New Ireland
Bismarck Sea
Wewak
Rabaul
New Britain
Madang
New Guinea
Mount Hagen
Lae
Ubai
Arawa
Bougainville Island
Solomon Islands
Solomon Sea
Tapini
PORT MORESBY
New Georgia Islands
HONIARA
Guadalcanal
SOLOMON ISLANDS
Santa Cruz Islands
Arafura Sea
Torres Strait
Coral Sea
Cape York Peninsula
Great Barrier Reef
Wake Island
Espiritu Santo
Malekula
Efat
PORT-VIL
Errom
VANUA
Coral Sea Islands
(to Australia)
New Caledonia
(to France)
Îles Lo
NOUMÉA
Darwin
Arnhem Land
Gulf of Carpentaria
Timor Sea
Joseph Bonaparte Gulf
Katherine
Cairns
Normanton
Wyndham
Townsville
Kimberley Plateau
NORTHERN
Tennant Creek
Hughenden
Mackay
Derby
Tanami Desert
TERRITORY
Mount Isa
QUEENSLAND
Rockhampton
Broome
Barcaldine
Great Dividing Range
INDIAN OCEAN
Great Sandy Desert
Alice Springs
Simpson Desert
Charleville
Miles
Brisbane
Port Hedland
AUSTRALIA
Toowoomba
Norfolk Is
(to Austra
Cunnamulla
Grafton
Hamersley Range
Gibson Desert
Lake Eyre North
Grey Range
Bourke
Barwon
Lord Howe Island
(to Australia)
WESTERN AUSTRALIA
SOUTH AUSTRALIA
Flinders Ranges
Darling
Wilcannia
NEW SOUTH WALES
Dubbo
Newcastle
Lake Torrens
Sydney
Carnarvon
Tropic of Capricorn
Great Victoria Desert
Lake Everard
Lake Gairdner
Port Augusta
Campbelltown
Wollongong
CANBERRA
AUSTRALIAN CAPITAL TERRITORY
Ceduna
Whyalla
Murray
Wagga Wagga
Mount Magnet
Nullarbor Plain
Kalgoorlie
Great Australian Bight
Adelaide
Bendigo
Geraldton
Kangaroo Island
Horsham
VICTORIA
Ballarat
Melbourne
Geelong
Tasman Sea
Mount Gambier
Perth
Esperance
Bass Strait
Launceston
Albany
TASMANIA
Tasmania
Hobart

Languages

English is spoken throughout Australia and New Zealand. In Australia, English has been superimposed on a mosaic of Aboriginal languages. In New Zealand, the indigenous language, Maori, is the official language besides English. In Papua New Guinea, Melanesian Pidgin has become a lingua franca alongside several hundred indigenous languages. Across the region, the indigenous languages can be grouped into (1) the Aboriginal languages of Australia, (2) the Papuan languages spoken mostly inland in Papua New Guinea, and (3) the widely dispersed Austronesian, which includes coastal languages of Papua New Guinea, New Zealand Maori, and languages of Oceania.

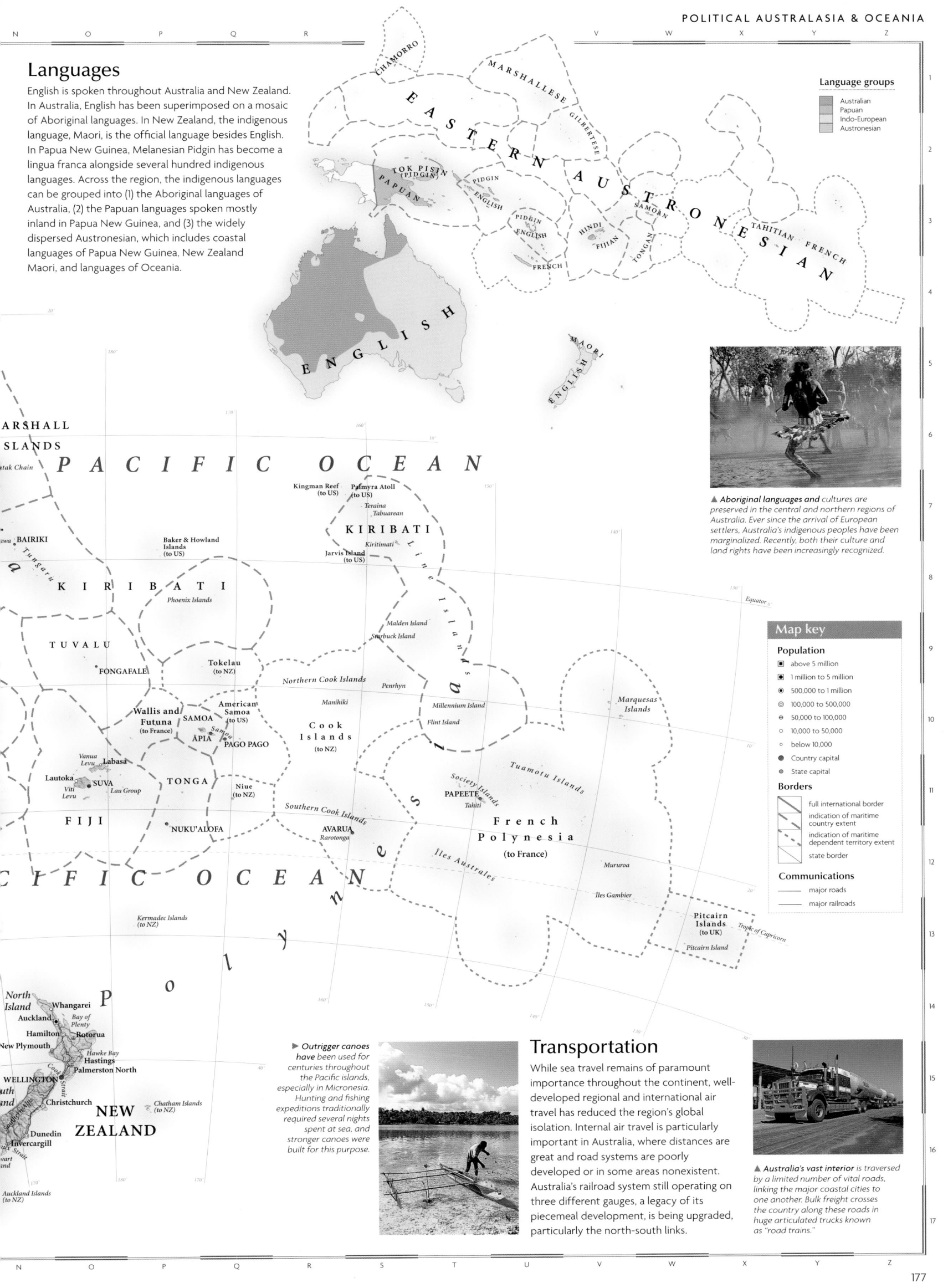

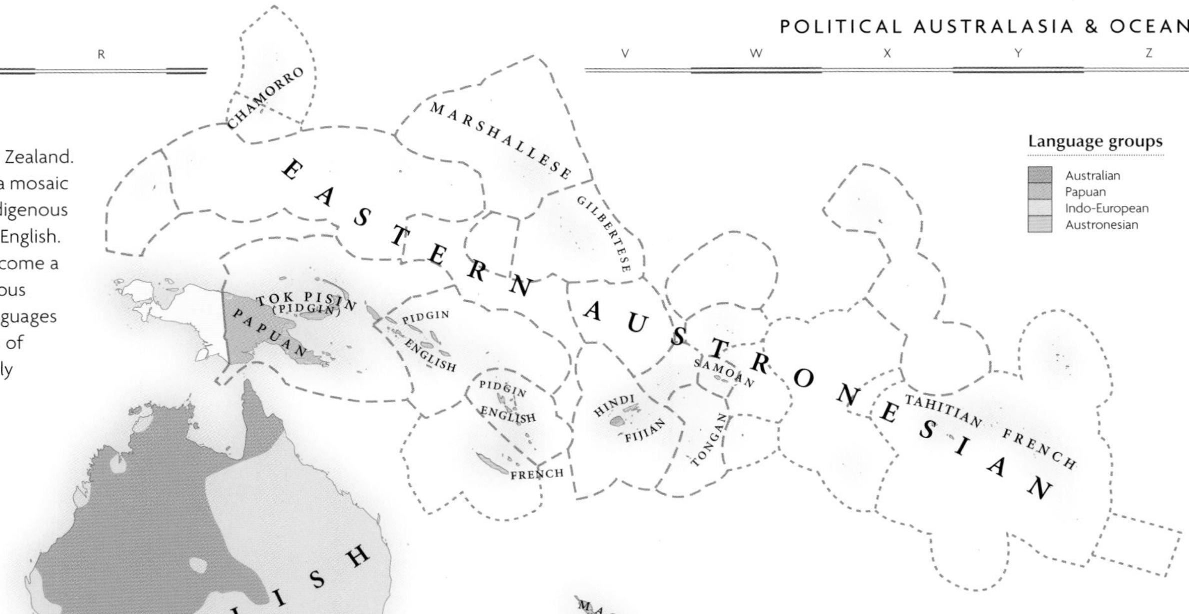

Language groups
Australian
Papuan
Indo-European
Austronesian
CHAMORRO
MARSHALLESE
GILBERTESE
EASTERN AUSTRONESIAN
TOK PISIN (PIDGIN)
PAPUAN
PIDGIN
ENGLISH
PIDGIN
ENGLISH
FRENCH
HINDI
FIJIAN
SAMOAN
TONGAN
TAHITIAN
FRENCH
ENGLISH
MAORI
ENGLISH

▲ *Aboriginal languages and cultures are preserved in the central and northern regions of Australia. Ever since the arrival of European settlers, Australia's indigenous peoples have been marginalized. Recently, both their culture and land rights have been increasingly recognized.*

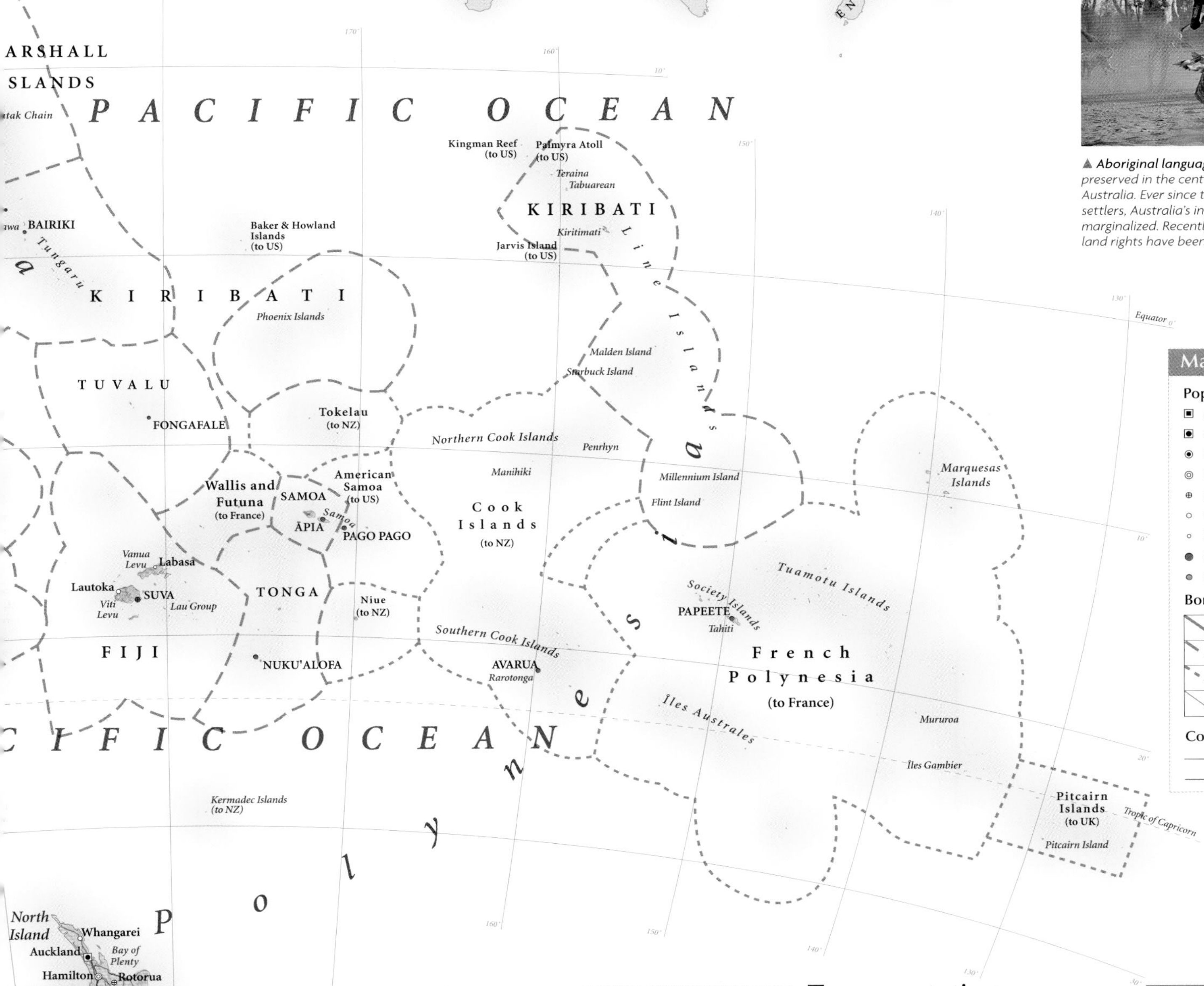

PACIFIC OCEAN
MARSHALL ISLANDS
BAIRIKI
Tungaru
KIRIBATI
Baker & Howland Islands (to US)
Phoenix Islands
Kingman Reef (to US)
Palmyra Atoll (to US)
Teraina
Tabuaeran
KIRIBATI
Kiritimati
Jarvis Island (to US)
Line Islands
Malden Island
Starbuck Island
TUVALU
FONGAFALE
Tokelau (to NZ)
Northern Cook Islands
Penrhyn
Manihiki
Millennium Island
Flint Island
Marquesas Islands
Wallis and Futuna (to France)
SAMOA
ĀPIA
Samoa
American Samoa (to US)
PAGO PAGO
Cook Islands (to NZ)
Vanua Levu
Labasa
Lautoka
SUVA
Viti Levu
Lau Group
FIJI
TONGA
Niue (to NZ)
NUKU'ALOFA
Southern Cook Islands
AVARUA
Rarotonga
Society Islands
PAPEETE
Tahiti
Tuamotu Islands
French Polynesia (to France)
Îles Australes
Mururoa
Îles Gambier
Pitcairn Islands (to UK)
Pitcairn Island
Tropic of Capricorn
Equator
PACIFIC OCEAN
Polynesia
Kermadec Islands (to NZ)
North Island
Whangarei
Auckland
Bay of Plenty
Hamilton
Rotorua
New Plymouth
Hawke Bay
Hastings
Palmerston North
Cook Strait
WELLINGTON
Christchurch
NEW ZEALAND
Chatham Islands (to NZ)
Dunedin
Invercargill
Auckland Islands (to NZ)

Map key

Population
- above 5 million
- 1 million to 5 million
- 500,000 to 1 million
- 100,000 to 500,000
- 50,000 to 100,000
- 10,000 to 50,000
- below 10,000
- Country capital
- State capital

Borders
- full international border
- indication of maritime country extent
- indication of maritime dependent territory extent
- state border

Communications
- major roads
- major railroads

▶ ***Outrigger canoes have** been used for centuries throughout the Pacific islands, especially in Micronesia. Hunting and fishing expeditions traditionally required several nights spent at sea, and stronger canoes were built for this purpose.*

Transportation

While sea travel remains of paramount importance throughout the continent, well-developed regional and international air travel has reduced the region's global isolation. Internal air travel is particularly important in Australia, where distances are great and road systems are poorly developed or in some areas nonexistent. Australia's railroad system still operating on three different gauges, a legacy of its piecemeal development, is being upgraded, particularly the north-south links.

▲ ***Australia's vast interior** is traversed by a limited number of vital roads, linking the major coastal cities to one another. Bulk freight crosses the country along these roads in huge articulated trucks known as "road trains."*

Australasian & Oceanian resources

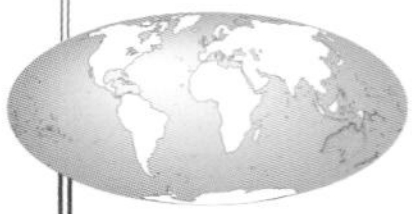

Natural resources are of major economic importance throughout Australasia and Oceania. Australia in particular is a major world exporter of raw materials such as coal, iron ore, and bauxite, while New Zealand's agricultural economy is dominated by sheep-raising. Trade with western Europe has declined significantly in the last 20 years, and the Pacific Rim countries of Southeast Asia are now the main trading partners, as well as a source of new settlers to the region. Australasia and Oceania's greatest resources are its climate and environment; tourism increasingly provides a vital source of income for the whole continent.

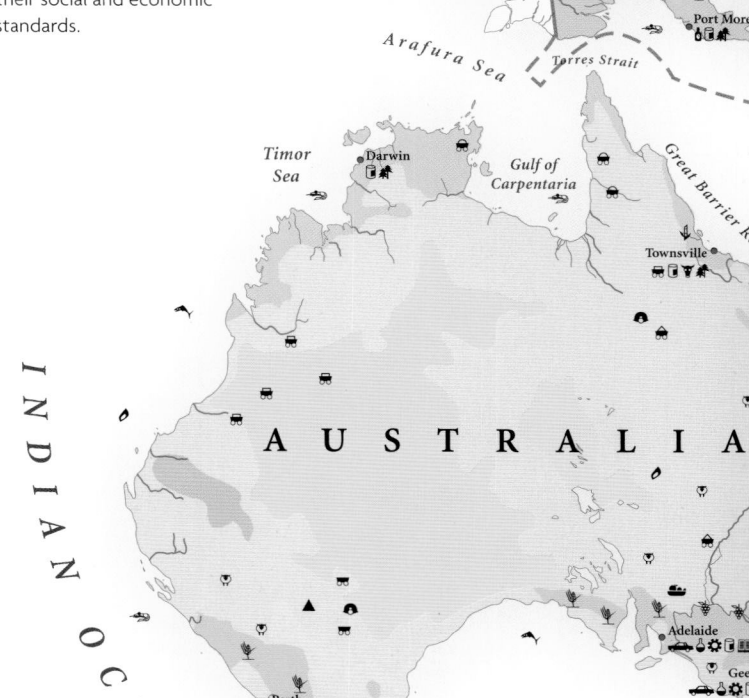

▲ ***The largely unpolluted*** *waters of the Pacific Ocean support rich and varied marine life, much of which is farmed commercially. Here, oysters are gathered for market off the coast of New Zealand's South Island.*

▶ ***Huge flocks of*** *sheep are a common sight in New Zealand, where they outnumber people by 12 to 1. New Zealand is one of the world's largest exporters of wool and frozen lamb.*

Standard of living

In marked contrast to its neighbor, Australia, with one of the world's highest life expectancies and standards of living, Papua New Guinea is one of the world's least developed countries. In addition, high population growth and urbanization rates throughout the Pacific islands contribute to overcrowding. In Australia and New Zealand, the Aboriginal and Maori people have been isolated, although recently their traditional land ownership rights have begun to be legally recognized in an effort to ease their social and economic isolation, and to improve living standards.

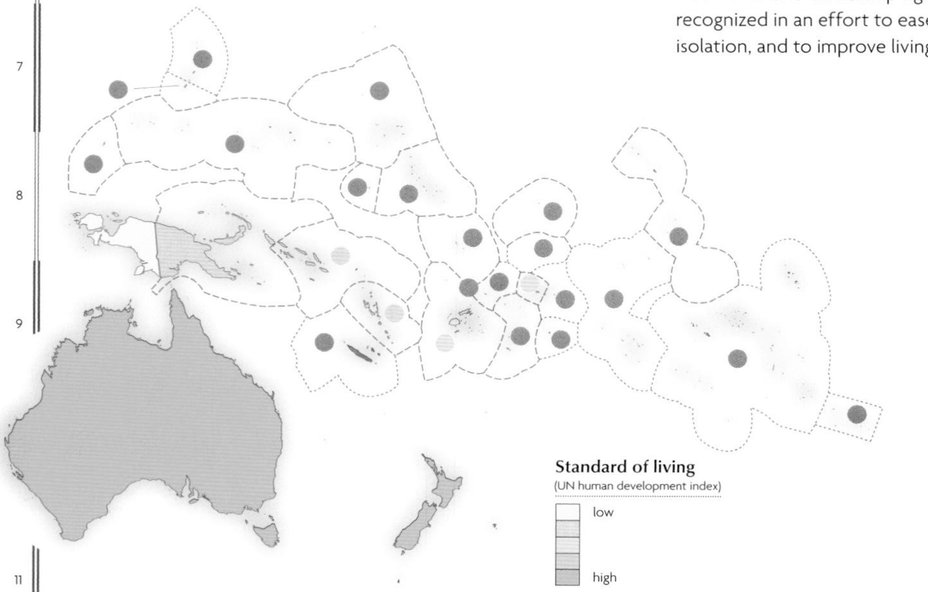

Standard of living
(UN human development index)
low
high
figures unavailable

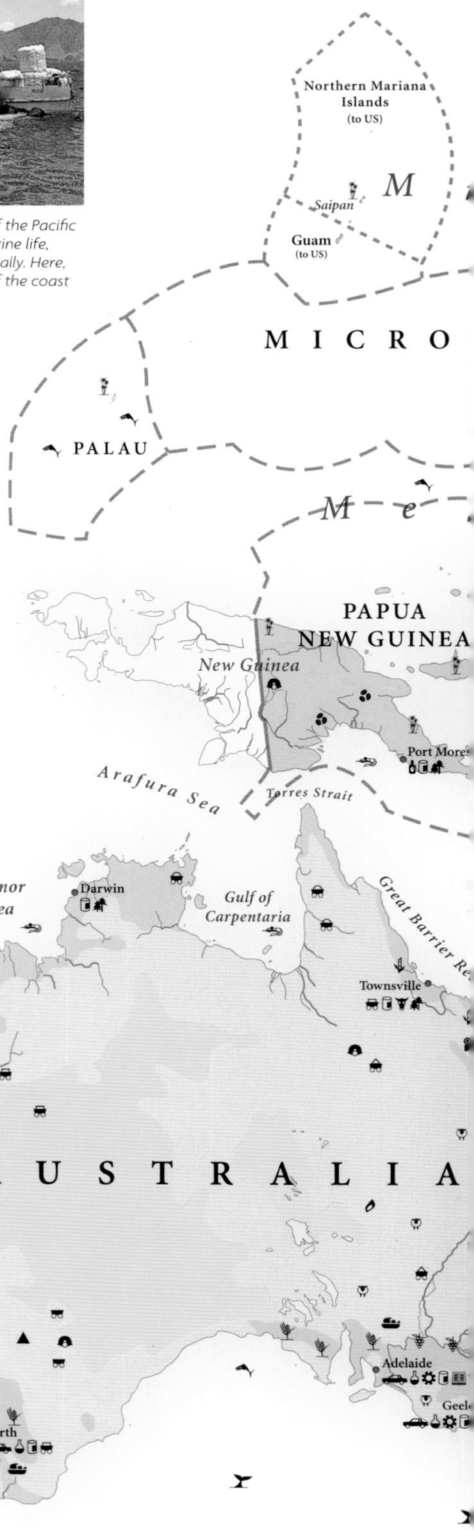

Northern Mariana Islands
(to US)
Saipan
Guam
(to US)
M
MICRO
PALAU
M e
PAPUA
NEW GUINEA
New Guinea
Port Moresby
Arafura Sea
Torres Strait
Timor
Sea
Darwin
Gulf of
Carpentaria
Great Barrier Re
Townsville
INDIAN OCEAN
AUSTRALIA
Adelaide
Geel
Perth

Environmental issues

The prospect of rising sea levels poses a threat to many low-lying islands in the Pacific. The testing of nuclear weapons, once common throughout the region, was finally discontinued in 1996. Australia's ecological balance has been irreversibly altered by the introduction of alien species. Although it has the world's largest underground water reserve, the Great Artesian Basin, the availability of fresh water in Australia remains critical. Periodic droughts combined with overgrazing lead to desertification and increase the risk of devastating bush fires, and occasional flash floods.

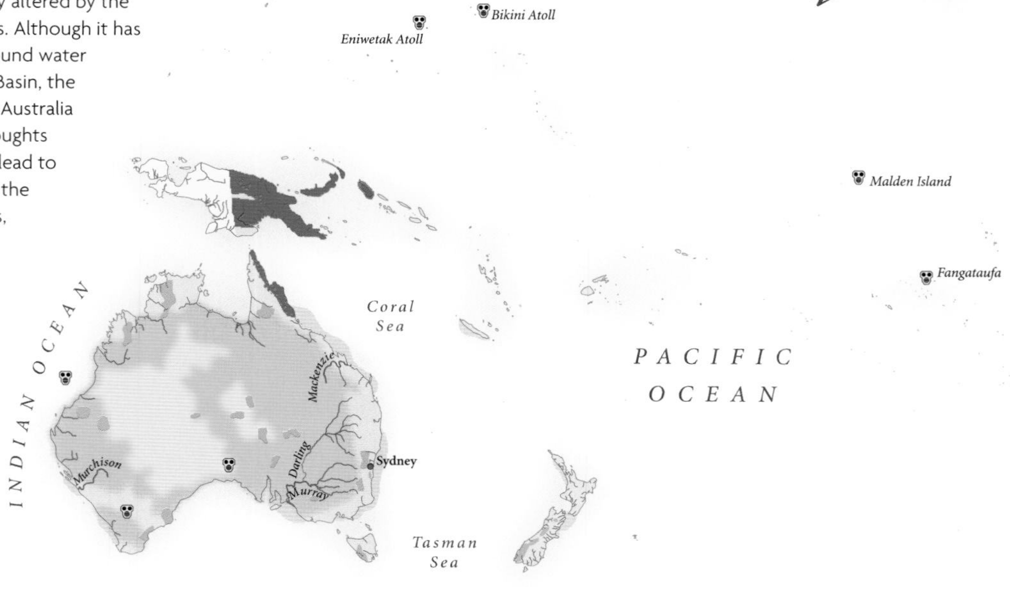

Bikini Atoll
Eniwetak Atoll
Malden Island
Fangataufa
Coral
Sea
PACIFIC
OCEAN
INDIAN OCEAN
Mackenzie
Darling
Murray
Murchison
Sydney
Tasman
Sea

Environmental issues

- national parks
- tropical forest
- forest destroyed
- desert
- desertification
- polluted rivers
- radioactive contamination
- marine pollution
- heavy marine pollution
- poor urban air quality

▲ ***In 1946 Bikini Atoll,*** *in the Marshall Islands, was chosen as the site for Operation Crossroads – investigating the effects of atomic bombs upon naval vessels. Further nuclear tests continued until the early 1990s. The long-term environmental effects are unknown.*

Agriculture, industry, and minerals

Much of the region's industry is resource-based: sheep farming for wool and meat in Australia and New Zealand; mining in Australia and Papua New Guinea and fishing throughout the Pacific islands. Manufacturing is mainly limited to the large coastal cities in Australia and New Zealand, like Sydney, Adelaide, Melbourne, Brisbane, Perth, and Auckland, although small-scale enterprises operate in the Pacific islands, concentrating on processing of fish and foods. Tourism continues to provide revenue to the area – in Fiji it accounts for 15% of GNP.

▲ ***The massive Ok Tedi*** *copper mine was opened in 1988. It is situated in the midst of remote tropical jungle in Papua New Guinea.*

▲ ***Plumes of steam*** *rise from the electricity turbines on New Zealand's North Island. New Zealand is one of the few countries in the world where geothermal energy makes a significant contribution to national energy production.*

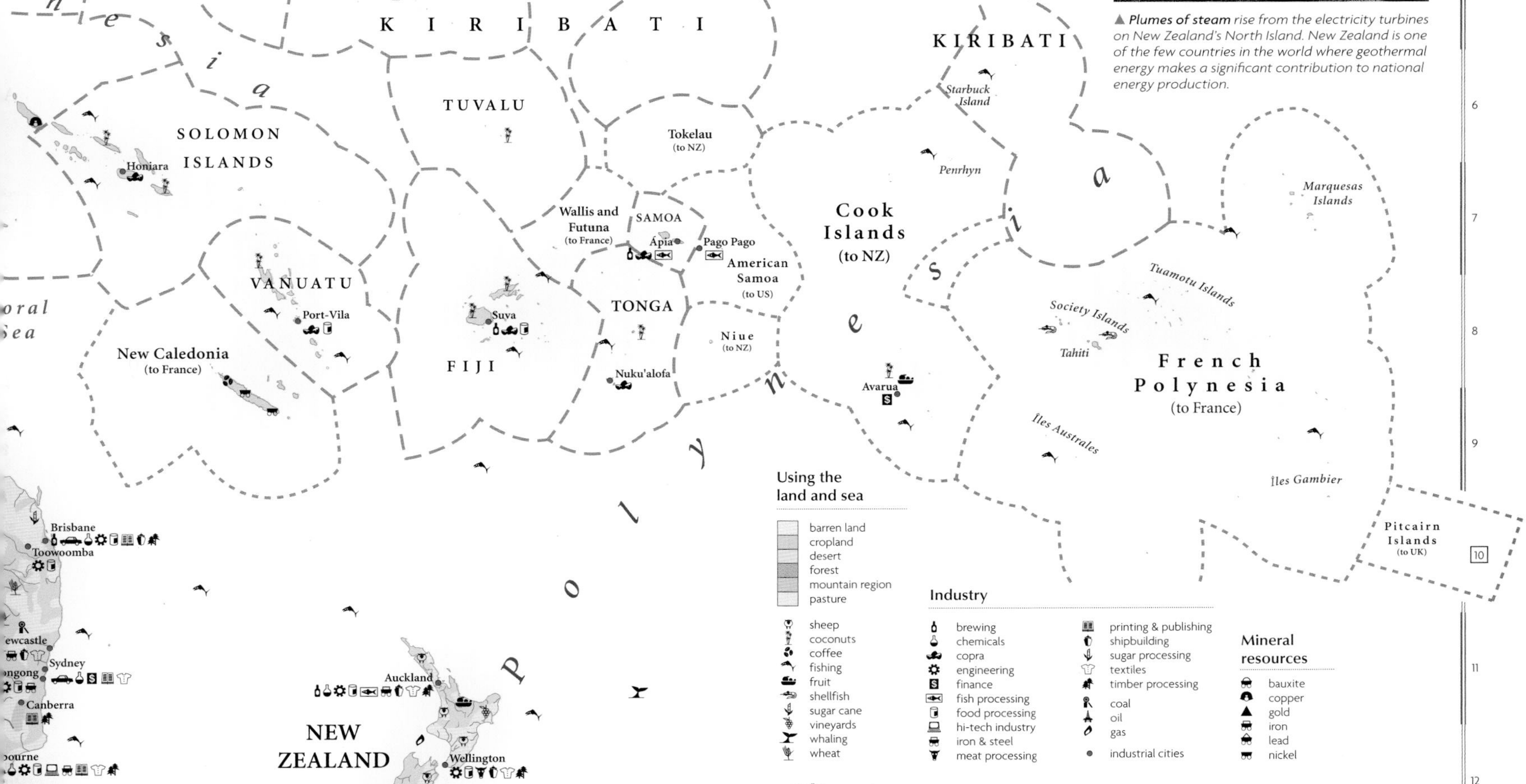

PACIFIC OCEAN
MARSHALL ISLANDS
Ralik Chain
Ratak Chain
Pohnpei
Kosrae
NAURU
KIRIBATI
Tungaru
Kiritimati
Starbuck Island
Penrhyn
TUVALU
SOLOMON ISLANDS
Honiara
Tokelau (to NZ)
Wallis and Futuna (to France)
SAMOA
Apia
Pago Pago
American Samoa (to US)
Cook Islands (to NZ)
VANUATU
Port-Vila
Suva
FIJI
TONGA
Niue (to NZ)
Nuku'alofa
Avarua
New Caledonia (to France)
Marquesas Islands
Tuamotu Islands
Society Islands
Tahiti
French Polynesia (to France)
Îles Australes
Îles Gambier
Pitcairn Islands (to UK)
Brisbane
Toowoomba
Sydney
Canberra
Launceston
Hobart
Auckland
NEW ZEALAND
Wellington
Christchurch
Dunedin
Tasman Sea
Using the land and sea
barren land
cropland
desert
forest
mountain region
pasture
sheep
coconuts
coffee
fishing
fruit
shellfish
sugar cane
vineyards
whaling
wheat
Industry
brewing
chemicals
copra
engineering
finance
fish processing
food processing
hi-tech industry
iron & steel
meat processing
printing & publishing
shipbuilding
sugar processing
textiles
timber processing
coal
oil
gas
industrial cities
Mineral resources
bauxite
copper
gold
iron
lead
nickel

Climate

Surrounded by water, the climate of most areas is profoundly affected by the moderating effects of the oceans. Australia, however, is the exception. Its dry continental interior remains isolated from the ocean; temperatures soar during the day, and droughts are common. The coastal regions, where most people live, are cooler and wetter. The numerous islands scattered across the Pacific are generally hot and humid, subject to the different air circulation patterns and ocean currents that affect the area, including the El Niño ocean current anomaly, which produces extreme aridity.

▲ ***The tourist trade*** *continues to bring valuable income to the region. Fiji, Guam, and the Cook Islands are favored destinations for Japanese, American, and Australian tourists. Surfers Paradise near Brisbane, Australia, is part of the fastest growing tourist area in the country; 40 years ago, the area was wild bushland.*

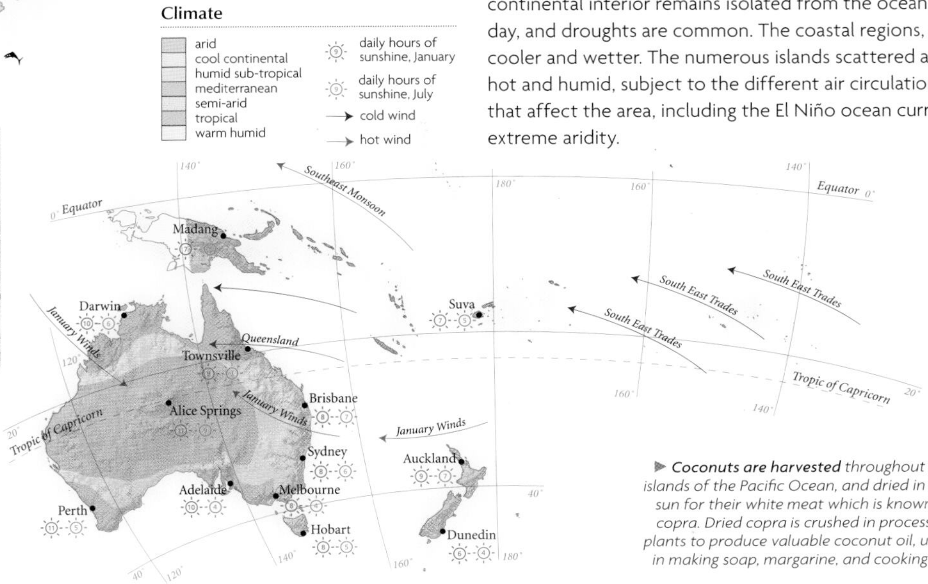

Climate
arid
cool continental
humid sub-tropical
mediterranean
semi-arid
tropical
warm humid
daily hours of sunshine, January
daily hours of sunshine, July
cold wind
hot wind
Equator
Southeast Monsoon
South East Trades
January Winds
Queensland
Tropic of Capricorn
Madang
Darwin
Townsville
Alice Springs
Brisbane
Sydney
Adelaide
Melbourne
Perth
Hobart
Suva
Auckland
Dunedin

▶ ***Coconuts are harvested*** *throughout the islands of the Pacific Ocean, and dried in the sun for their white meat which is known as copra. Dried copra is crushed in processing plants to produce valuable coconut oil, used in making soap, margarine, and cooking oil.*

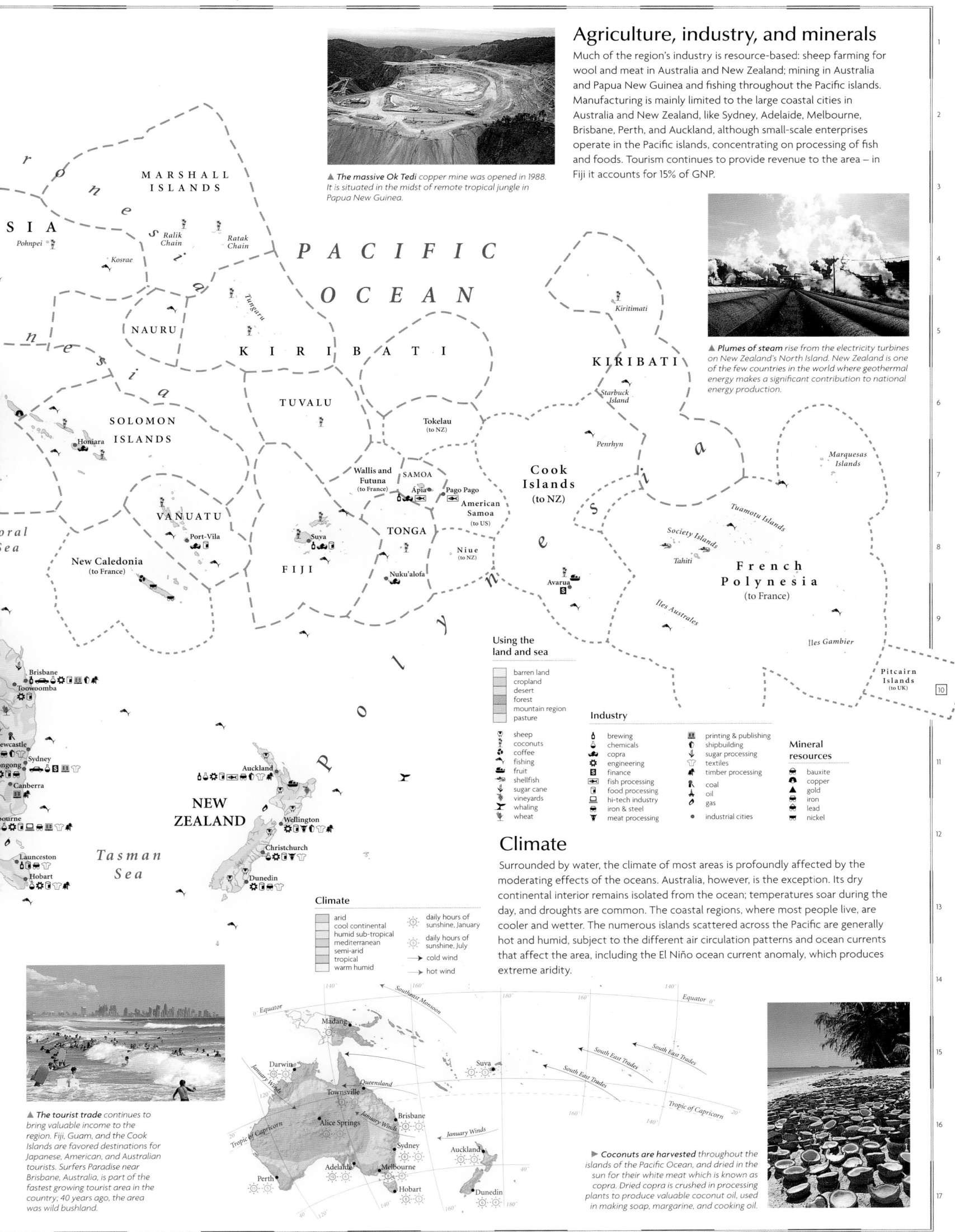

Australia

Australia is the world's smallest continent, a stable landmass lying between the Indian and Pacific oceans. Previously home to its aboriginal peoples only, since the end of the 18th century immigration has transformed the face of the country. Initially settlers came mainly from western Europe, particularly the UK, and for years Australia remained wedded to its British colonial past. More recent immigrants have come from eastern Europe, and from Asian countries such as Japan, South Korea, and Indonesia. Australia is now forging strong trading links with these "Pacific Rim" countries and its economic future seems to lie with Asia and the Americas, rather than Europe, its traditional partner.

◀ ***Uluru (Ayers Rock),*** *the world's largest free-standing rock, is a massive outcrop of red sandstone in Australia's desert center. Wind and sandstorms have ground the rock into the smooth curves seen here. Uluru is revered as a sacred site by many aboriginal peoples.*

Using the land

Over 104 million sheep are dispersed in vast herds around the country, contributing to a major export industry. Cattle-ranching is important, particularly in the west. Wheat, and grapes for Australia's wine industry, are grown mainly in the south. Much of the country is desert, unsuitable for agriculture unless irrigation is used.

The urban/rural population divide

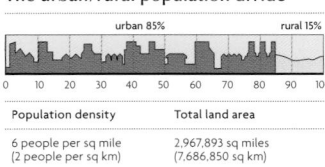

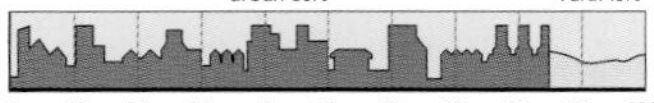

urban 85%
rural 15%
0 10 20 30 40 50 60 70 80 90 100

Population density	Total land area
6 people per sq mile (2 people per sq km)	2,967,893 sq miles (7,686,850 sq km)

Land use and agricultural distribution

- cattle
- sheep
- cereals
- sugar cane
- timber
- vineyards
- capital cities
- major towns
- pasture
- cropland
- forest
- desert
- mountain region

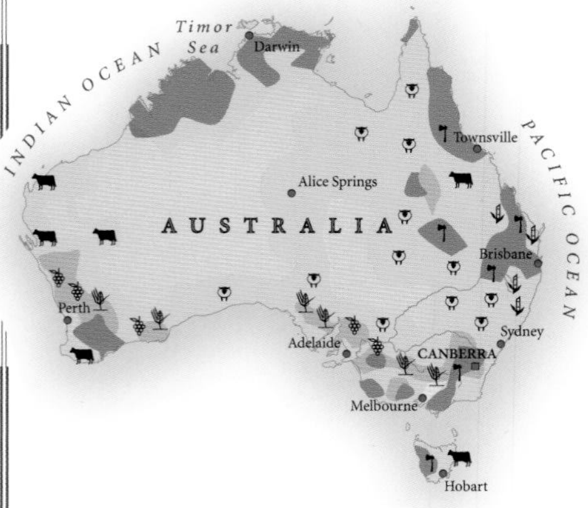

Timor Sea
INDIAN OCEAN
Darwin
Townsville
PACIFIC OCEAN
Alice Springs
AUSTRALIA
Brisbane
Perth
Sydney
Adelaide
CANBERRA
Melbourne
Hobart

▲ ***Lines of ripening*** *vines stretch for miles in Barossa Valley, a major wine-growing region near Adelaide.*

The landscape

Australia consists of many eroded plateaus, lying firmly in the middle of the Indo-Australian Plate. It is the world's flattest continent, and the driest, after Antarctica. The coasts tend to be more hilly and fertile, especially in the east. The mountains of the Great Dividing Range form a natural barrier between the eastern coastal areas and the flat, dry plains and desert regions of the Australian "outback."

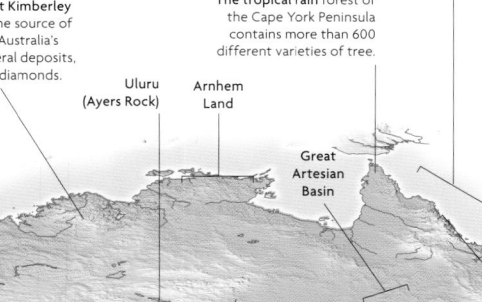

▲ ***The Great Barrier Reef*** *is the world's largest area of coral islands and reefs. It runs for about 1240 miles (2000 km) along the Queensland coast.*

▲ ***The Pinnacles are*** *a series of rugged sandstone pillars. Their strange shapes have been formed by water and wind erosion.*

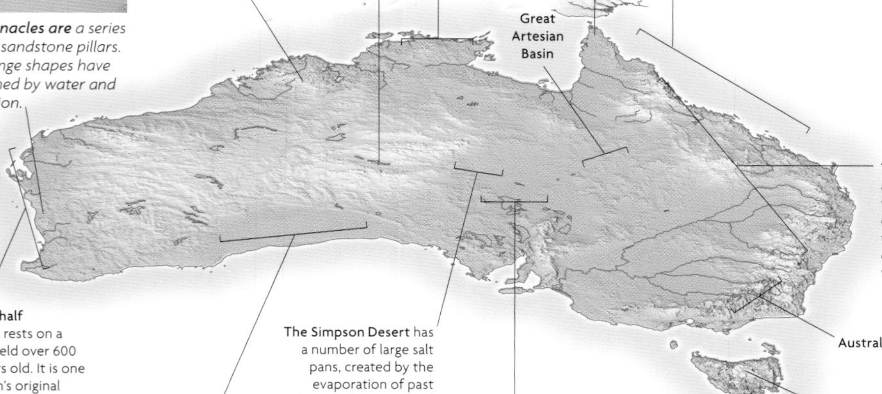

The ancient Kimberley Plateau is the source of some of Australia's richest mineral deposits, including diamonds.

Uluru (Ayers Rock)

Arnhem Land

The tropical rain forest of the Cape York Peninsula contains more than 600 different varieties of tree.

Great Artesian Basin

The Great Dividing Range forms a watershed between east- and west-flowing rivers. Erosion has created deep valleys, gorges, and waterfalls where rivers tumble over escarpments on their way to the sea.

More than half of Australia rests on a uniform shield over 600 million years old. It is one of the Earth's original geological plates.

The Nullarbor Plain is a low-lying limestone plateau which is so flat that the Trans-Australian Railway runs through it in a straight line for more than 300 miles (483 km).

The Simpson Desert has a number of large salt pans, created by the evaporation of past rivers and now sourced by seasonal rains. Some are crusted with gypsum, but most are covered by common salt crystals.

The Lake Eyre basin, lying 51 ft (16 m) below sea level, is one of the largest inland drainage systems in the world, covering an area of more than 500,000 sq miles (1,300,000 sq km).

Australian Alps

Tasmania has the same geological structure as the Australian Alps. During the last period of glaciation, 18,000 years ago, sea levels were some 300 ft (100 m) lower and it was joined to the mainland.

Scale 1:11,500,000

Km 0 25 50 100 150 200 250 300 350

0 25 50 100 150 200 250 300 350 Miles

projection: Lambert Conformal Conic

Map key

Population

- 1 million to 5 million
- 500,000 to 1 million
- 100,000 to 500,000
- 50,000 to 100,000
- 10,000 to 50,000
- below 10,000

Elevation

- 2000m / 6562ft
- 1000m / 3281ft
- 500m / 1640ft
- 250m / 820ft
- 100m / 328ft
- sea level

INDIAN OCEAN
154
Cape Londonderry
Cape Bougainville
Kalumburu
Bigge Island
Bonaparte Archipelago
Heywood Islands
Adele Island
Mount Hann 779m
Collier Bay
King Sound
Kimberley Plateau
King Leopold Range
Lombadina
Derby
Broome
Fitzroy Crossing
Fitzroy River
Eighty Mile Beach
Great Sandy Desert
Percival Lakes
De Grey River
Dampier Archipelago
Port Hedland
Wickham
Whim Creek
Dampier
Karratha
Roebourne
Marble Bar
Barrow Island
Fortescue River
Lake Dora
Lake Auld
Onslow
Wittenoom
North West Cape
Exmouth
Exmouth Gulf
Learmonth
Hamersley Range
Ashburton River
Tom Price
Mount Meharry 1251m
Paraburdoo
Newman
Lake Disappointment
Little Sandy Desert
Gibson Desert
Coral Bay
Kenneth Range
Barlee Range
WESTERN
Mount Augustus 1105m
Kumarina Roadhouse
Minilya
Tropic of Capricorn
Lake Macleod
Carnarvon Range
Waldburg Range
Gascoyne River
Gascoyne Junction
Lake Gregory
Lake Carnegie
Bernier Island
Carnarvon
Shark Bay
Robinson Range
Dorre Island
Wiluna
Lake Way
Lake Wells
Denham
Meekatharra
Dirk Hartog Island
Murchison River
Lake Annean
Lake Throssell
Lake Yeo
Lake Austin
AUSTRALIA
Kalbarri
Mount Magnet
Leonora
Lake Carey
Yalgoo
Lake Ballard
Lake Barlee
Geraldton
Mongers Lake
Menzies
Lake Rebecca
Lake Moore
Wubin
Pithara
Kalgoorlie
Coolgardie
Kitchener
Moora
The Pinnacles
Kambalda
Lake Lefroy
Southern Cross
Lake Cowan
Gingin
Merredin
Norseman
Balladonia
Wanneroo
Northam
York
Lake Johnston
Lake Dundas
Perth
Fremantle
Rockingham
Mandurah
Brookton
Kondinin
Lake Hope
Narrogin
Lake King
Tower Peak 594m
Wagin
Ravensthorpe
Esperance
Bunbury
Collie
Katanning
Busselton
Bridgetown
Manjimup
Stirling Range
Margaret River
Cape Leeuwin
Augusta
Pemberton
Mount Barker
Albany

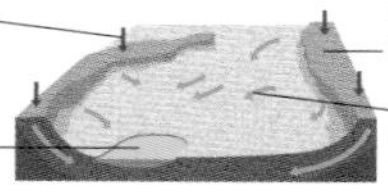

Great Artesian Basin
Rainwater replenishes aquifer
Aquifers from which artesian water is obtained
Underground water movements
Lake Eyre

▲ ***The Great Artesian Basin*** *underlies nearly 20% of the total area of Australia, providing a valuable store of underground water, essential to Australian agriculture. The ephemeral rivers which drain the northern part of the basin have highly braided courses and, in consequence, the area is known as "channel country."*

Arafura Sea
Timor Sea
Gulf of Carpentaria
Arnhem Land
Cape York Peninsula
Torres Strait
Coral Sea
Great Barrier Reef
Tasman Sea
Great Australian Bight
NORTHERN TERRITORY
QUEENSLAND
SOUTH AUSTRALIA
NEW SOUTH WALES
VICTORIA
TASMANIA
Bass Strait
AUSTRALIA
Great Dividing Range
Great Artesian Basin
Simpson Desert
Tanami Desert
Great Victoria Desert
Lake Eyre Basin
Barkly Tableland
Macdonnell Ranges
Darwin
Alice Springs
Brisbane
Sydney
CANBERRA
Melbourne
Adelaide
Hobart
Tropic of Capricorn

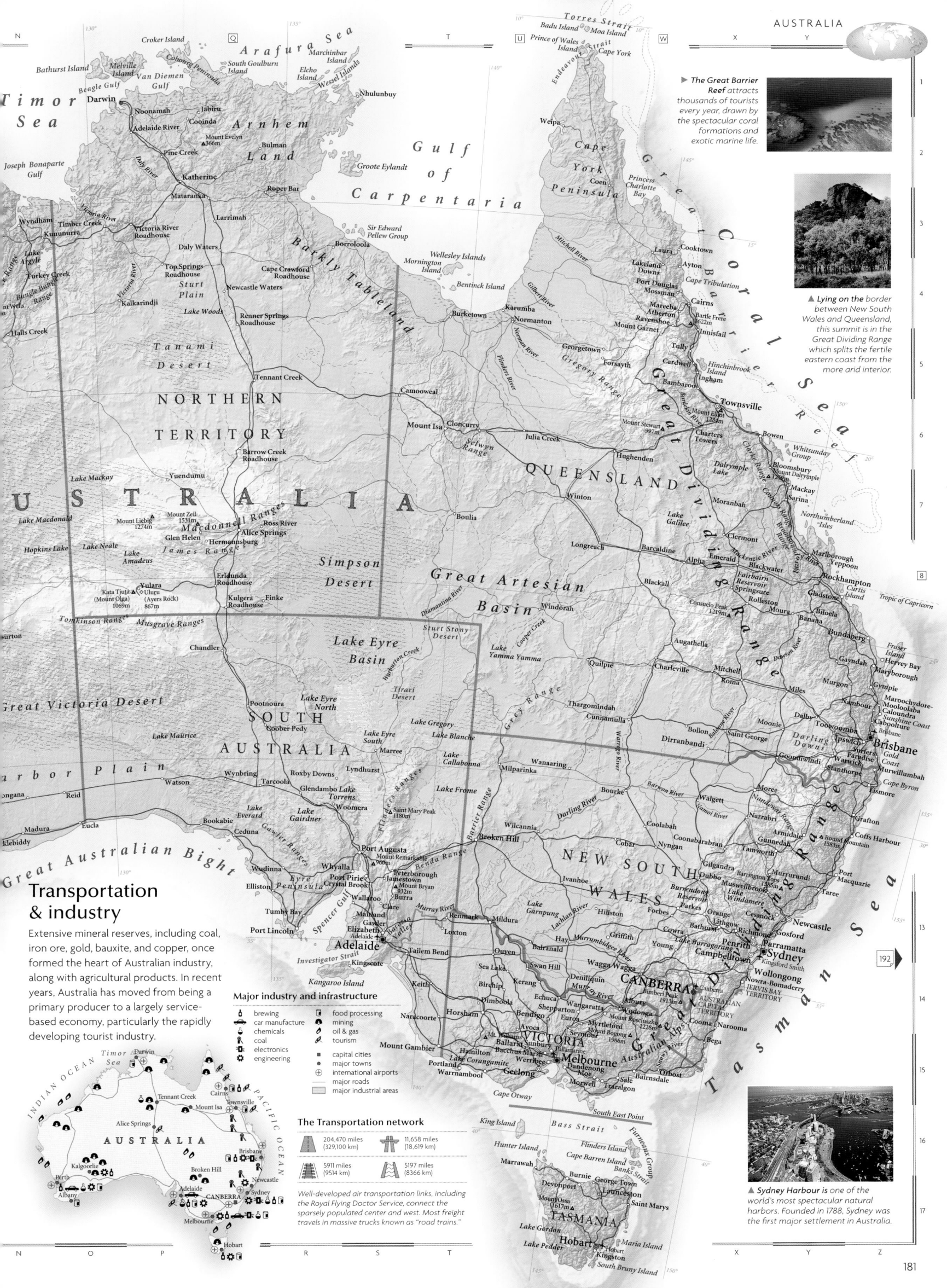

▶ **The Great Barrier Reef** attracts thousands of tourists every year, drawn by the spectacular coral formations and exotic marine life.

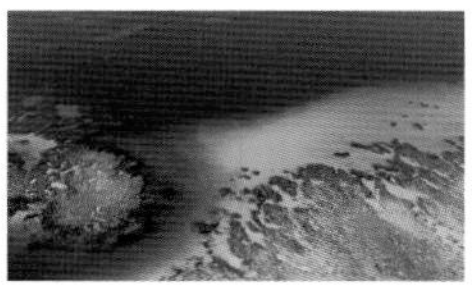

▲ **Lying on the** border between New South Wales and Queensland, this summit is in the Great Dividing Range which splits the fertile eastern coast from the more arid interior.

Transportation & industry

Extensive mineral reserves, including coal, iron ore, gold, bauxite, and copper, once formed the heart of Australian industry, along with agricultural products. In recent years, Australia has moved from being a primary producer to a largely service-based economy, particularly the rapidly developing tourist industry.

Major industry and infrastructure

- brewing
- car manufacture
- chemicals
- coal
- electronics
- engineering
- food processing
- mining
- oil & gas
- tourism
- capital cities
- major towns
- international airports
- major roads
- major industrial areas

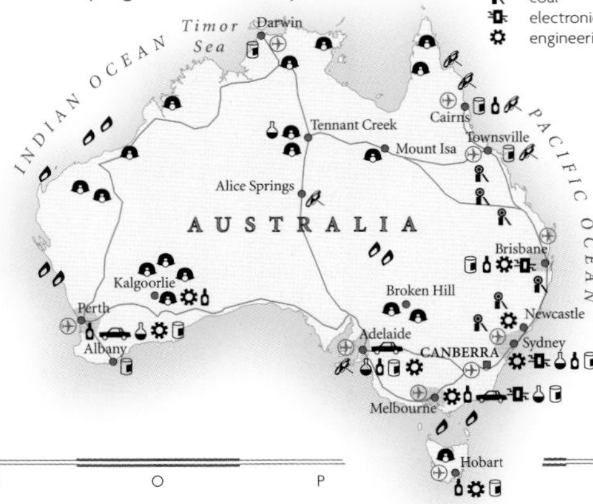
INDIAN OCEAN
PACIFIC OCEAN
Timor Sea
AUSTRALIA
Darwin
Cairns
Tennant Creek
Townsville
Mount Isa
Alice Springs
Brisbane
Kalgoorlie
Broken Hill
Newcastle
Perth
Sydney
Albany
Adelaide
CANBERRA
Melbourne
Hobart

The Transportation network

204,470 miles (329,100 km)	11,658 miles (18,619 km)
5911 miles (9514 km)	5197 miles (8366 km)

Well-developed air transportation links, including the Royal Flying Doctor Service, connect the sparsely populated center and west. Most freight travels in massive trucks known as "road trains."

▲ **Sydney Harbour is** one of the world's most spectacular natural harbors. Founded in 1788, Sydney was the first major settlement in Australia.

192

NORTHERN TERRITORY
WESTERN AUSTRALIA
SOUTH AUSTRALIA
Simpson Desert
Lake Eyre Basin
Sturt Stony Desert
Great Victoria Desert
Nullarbor Plain
Great Australian Bight
Lake Eyre North
Lake Eyre South
Lake Torrens
Lake Gairdner
Lake Frome
Flinders Ranges
Eyre Peninsula
Spencer Gulf
Gulf Saint Vincent
Kangaroo Island
Adelaide
Port Augusta
Port Pirie
Whyalla
Port Lincoln
Broken Hill
Murray River
Mount Gambier
Map key
Population
1 million to 5 million
500,000 to 1 million
100,000 to 500,000
50,000 to 100,000
10,000 to 50,000
below 10,000
Elevation
2000m / 6562ft
1000m / 3281ft
500m / 1640ft
250m / 820ft
100m / 328ft
sea level
Scale 1:6,000,000
projection: Lambert Conformal Conic

180

192

192

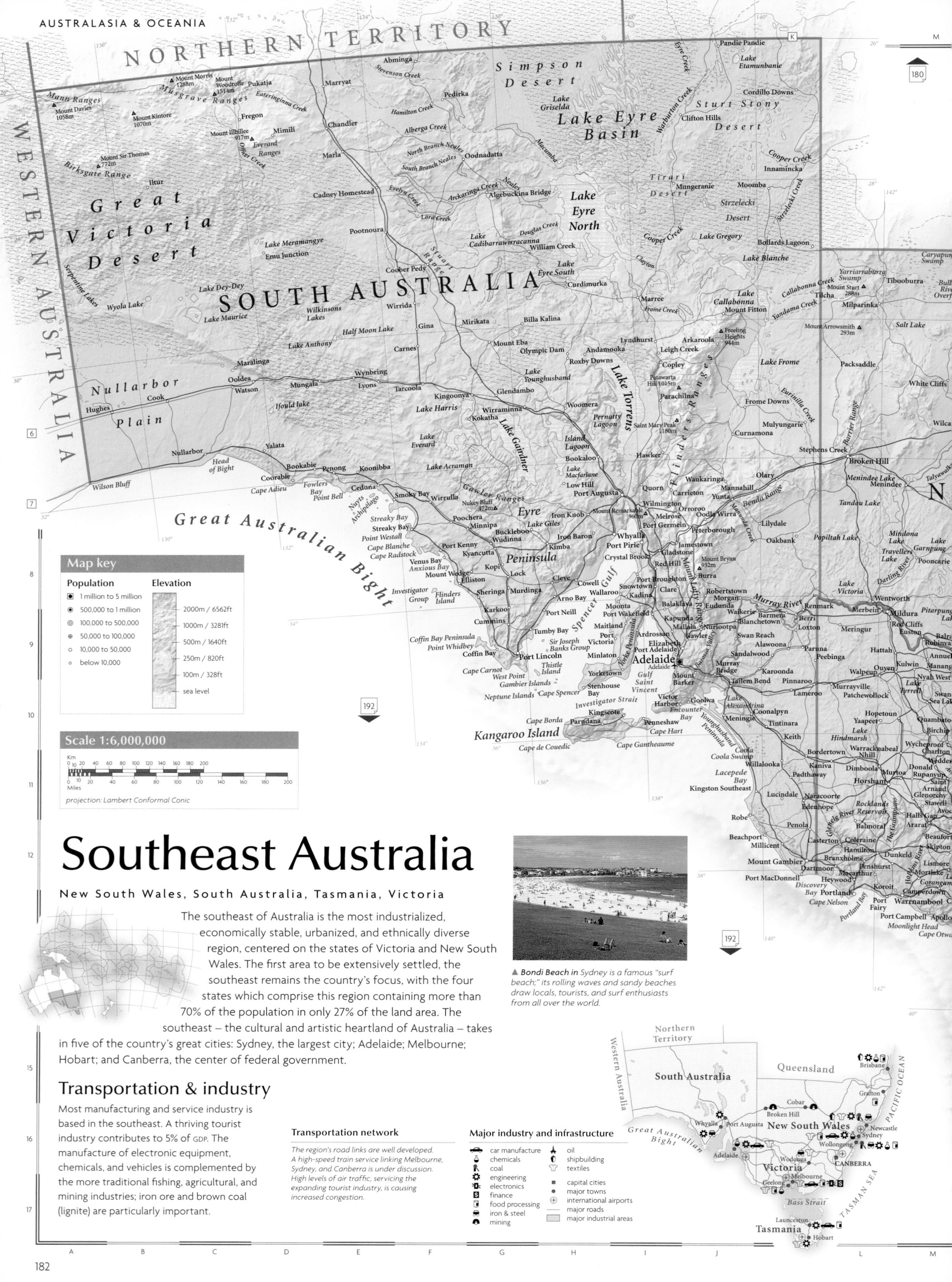

Southeast Australia

New South Wales, South Australia, Tasmania, Victoria

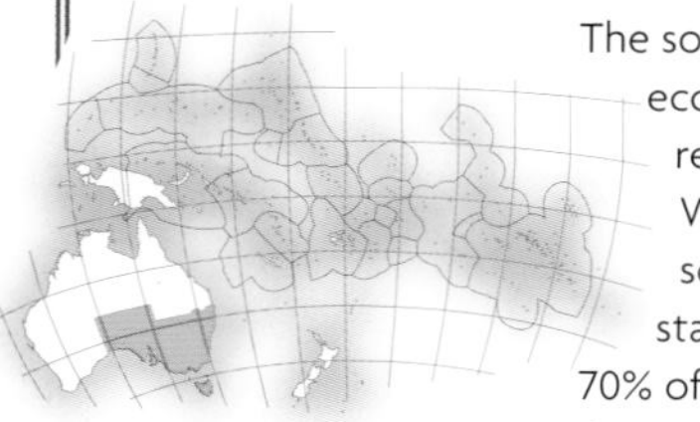

The southeast of Australia is the most industrialized, economically stable, urbanized, and ethnically diverse region, centered on the states of Victoria and New South Wales. The first area to be extensively settled, the southeast remains the country's focus, with the four states which comprise this region containing more than 70% of the population in only 27% of the land area. The southeast – the cultural and artistic heartland of Australia – takes in five of the country's great cities: Sydney, the largest city; Adelaide; Melbourne; Hobart; and Canberra, the center of federal government.

▲ **Bondi Beach in** *Sydney is a famous "surf beach;" its rolling waves and sandy beaches draw locals, tourists, and surf enthusiasts from all over the world.*

Transportation & industry

Most manufacturing and service industry is based in the southeast. A thriving tourist industry contributes to 5% of GDP. The manufacture of electronic equipment, chemicals, and vehicles is complemented by the more traditional fishing, agricultural, and mining industries; iron ore and brown coal (lignite) are particularly important.

Transportation network

The region's road links are well developed. A high-speed train service linking Melbourne, Sydney, and Canberra is under discussion. High levels of air traffic, servicing the expanding tourist industry, is causing increased congestion.

Major industry and infrastructure

- car manufacture
- chemicals
- coal
- engineering
- electronics
- finance
- food processing
- iron & steel
- mining
- oil
- shipbuilding
- textiles
- capital cities
- major towns
- international airports
- major roads
- major industrial areas

Northern Territory
Western Australia
South Australia
Queensland
New South Wales
Victoria
Tasmania
Great Australian Bight
PACIFIC OCEAN
TASMAN SEA
Bass Strait
Brisbane
Grafton
Cobar
Broken Hill
Whyalla
Port Augusta
Newcastle
Sydney
Wollongong
Adelaide
CANBERRA
Wodonga
Geelong
Melbourne
Launceston
Hobart

▲ *The fertile Darling Downs, known as the "breadbasket of Australia," support a wide range of crops including cereals, sugar cane, and fruit.*

Using the land & sea

The western flanks of the Great Dividing Range and the northern deserts of South Australia support massive herds of sheep and cattle, while more intensive stockrearing occurs near the cities. Sugar cane is the most important industrial crop, and cereal grains including wheat, corn, barley, and sorghum are also grown. Grapes, citrus, and orchard fruits are among the wide range of fruit and vegetables cultivated in this region. Tasmania's forestry and fishing contributes to over one-third of the state's exports.

QUEENSLAND
NEW SOUTH WALES
VICTORIA
TASMANIA
Tasmania
Brisbane
Sydney
CANBERRA
Melbourne
Hobart
Newcastle
Wollongong
Great Dividing Range
TASMAN SEA
Bass Strait
AUSTRALIAN CAPITAL TERRITORY
JERVIS BAY TERRITORY
Furneaux Group
New England Range
Darling Downs
Riverina
Mount Kosciuszko 2228m
Toowoomba
Tamworth
Armidale
Dubbo
Orange
Bathurst
Wagga Wagga
Albury
Bendigo
Geelong
Launceston
Devonport

▶ *The Murray River has its source in the eastern uplands of the Great Dividing Range. Fed by melting snow, it runs for 1609 miles (2589 km), and has sufficient volume to reach the ocean southeast of Adelaide despite a minimal gradient for most of its lower reaches.*

The urban/rural population divide

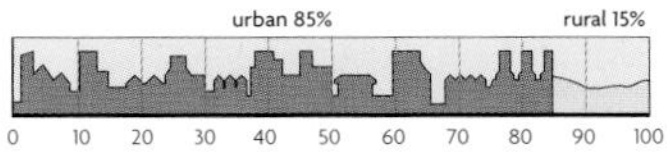
urban 85%
rural 15%
0
10
20
30
40
50
60
70
80
90
100

Population density	Total land area
18 people per sq mile (7 people per sq km)	778,022 sq miles (2,015,600 sq km)

Land use and agricultural distribution

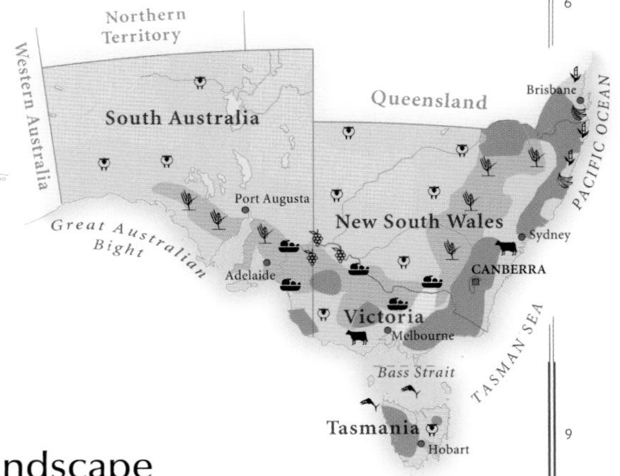
cattle
sheep
bananas
fishing
fruit
sugar cane
vineyards
wheat
capital cities
major towns
pasture
cropland
forest
desert
mountain region
Northern Territory
Western Australia
South Australia
Queensland
New South Wales
Victoria
Tasmania
Brisbane
Sydney
CANBERRA
Melbourne
Hobart
Adelaide
Port Augusta
Great Australian Bight
Bass Strait
TASMAN SEA
PACIFIC OCEAN

192

The landscape

The southern half of the Great Dividing Range runs parallel to the eastern coast of Victoria and New South Wales as far as Tasmania, which, though divided from the mainland is part of the same mountain chain. South Australia comprises the Australian shield and half of the dry, flat Nullarbor Plain. The Murray/Darling river basin is the only major river system.

◀ *The heavily folded Flinders Ranges is part of an arc of sedimentary rocks reaching northward from Kangaroo Island.*

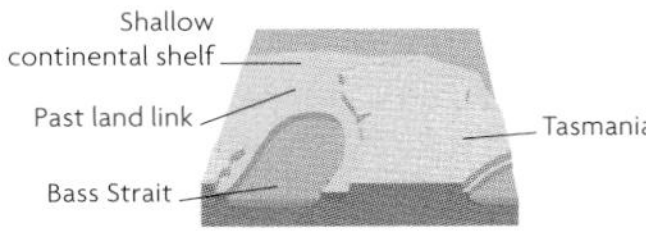
Shallow continental shelf
Past land link
Bass Strait
Tasmania

▲ *Tasmania is part of Australia's eastern highlands, separated from the mainland by 155 miles (250 km) of the Bass Strait. In the recent geological past, dry land links between Tasmania and Victoria would have been possible during periods of world-wide glaciation, when the sea level was more than 180 ft (55 m) below that of present sea levels.*

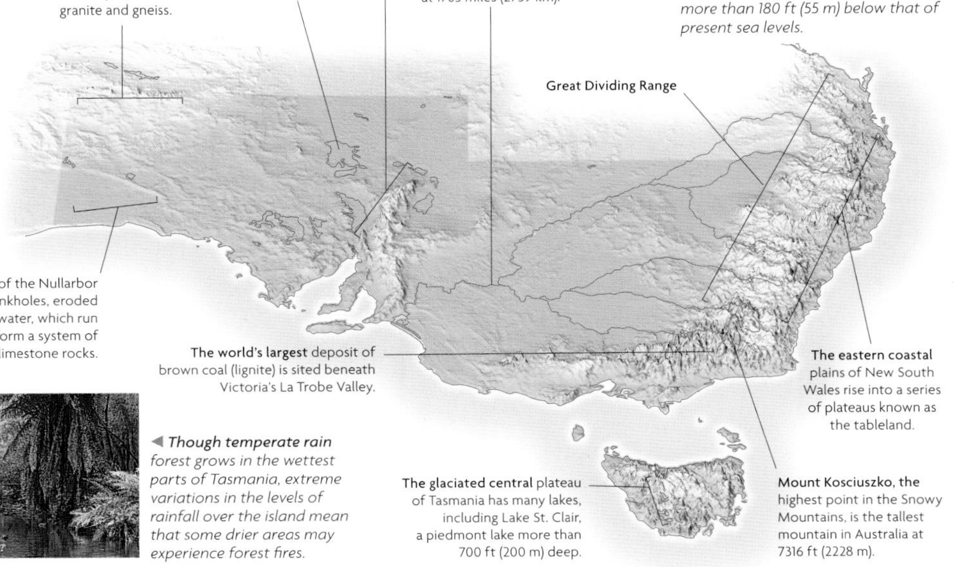

The Musgrave and Everard ranges form bare, rounded hills made up of ancient granite and gneiss.

Lake Eyre is the largest of southern Australia's dry lakes. Lying -51 ft (-16 m) below sea level, it has flooded only three times in the last century.

The Murray/Darling is Australia's longest river at 1703 miles (2739 km).

Great Dividing Range

The eastern part of the Nullarbor Plain has many sinkholes, eroded by rainwater, which run underground to form a system of long caves in the limestone rocks.

The world's largest deposit of brown coal (lignite) is sited beneath Victoria's La Trobe Valley.

The eastern coastal plains of New South Wales rise into a series of plateaus known as the tableland.

The glaciated central plateau of Tasmania has many lakes, including Lake St. Clair, a piedmont lake more than 700 ft (200 m) deep.

Mount Kosciuszko, the highest point in the Snowy Mountains, is the tallest mountain in Australia at 7316 ft (2228 m).

◀ *Though temperate rain forest grows in the wettest parts of Tasmania, extreme variations in the levels of rainfall over the island mean that some drier areas may experience forest fires.*

New Zealand

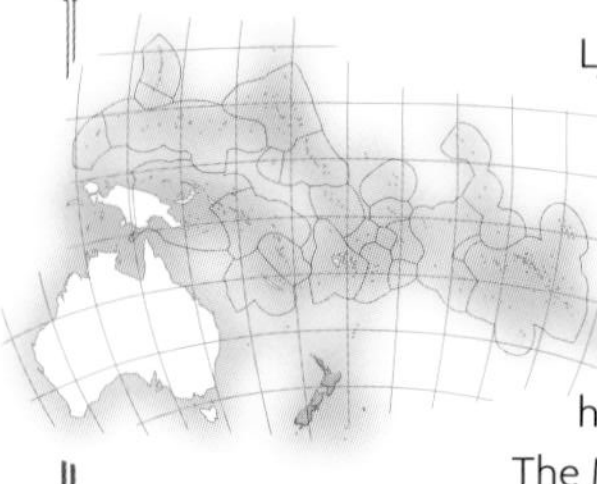

Lying 1500 miles east-southeast of Australia, New Zealand was originally settled by the Maori people of Polynesia. It was visited by Europeans for the first time only as recently as the 1770s. The islands' rugged topography means that most settlement has concentrated in coastal areas. People of European origin make up about 70% of the population of 4 million, following immigration which began in the 1920s. Many recent settlers have come from Asia, including India and China, and a number of the Pacific islands. The Maori now make up a minority of less than half a million. Their ancient claims to at least half of national territory, however, are gaining increasing legal credence.

The landscape

New Zealand comprises two large islands and many scattered smaller islands. On South Island the Alpine Fault marks the boundary between the Pacific and Indo-Australian plates. Tectonic activity has strongly influenced the formation of the Southern Alps, snowcapped mountains with several peaks over 9800 ft (3000 m). North Island has a lower and less extensive mountain region, containing forested hills, a central volcanic plateau, and downlands.

Mountain-building in the Southern Alps

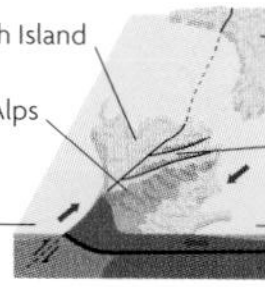
South Island
North Island
Southern Alps
Alpine Fault
Indo-Australian Plate
Pacific Plate

▲ *The Southern Alps have been formed by "slip" faulting. The Indo-Australian and Pacific plates run in opposite directions along the Alpine Fault. Although they slide past each other, they are also being thrust over one another, causing the continental crust of the Pacific Plate to be uplifted to form the Alps.*

◀ *The Northland region is characterized by many coastal inlets. These are lined by mangrove swamps, signaling the change to a subtropical climate in the far north of the island.*

◀ *The Rotorua and Taupo valleys have some of the largest and most spectacular thermal springs in New Zealand. These occur when superheated groundwater rises to the surface through joints in the rocks.*

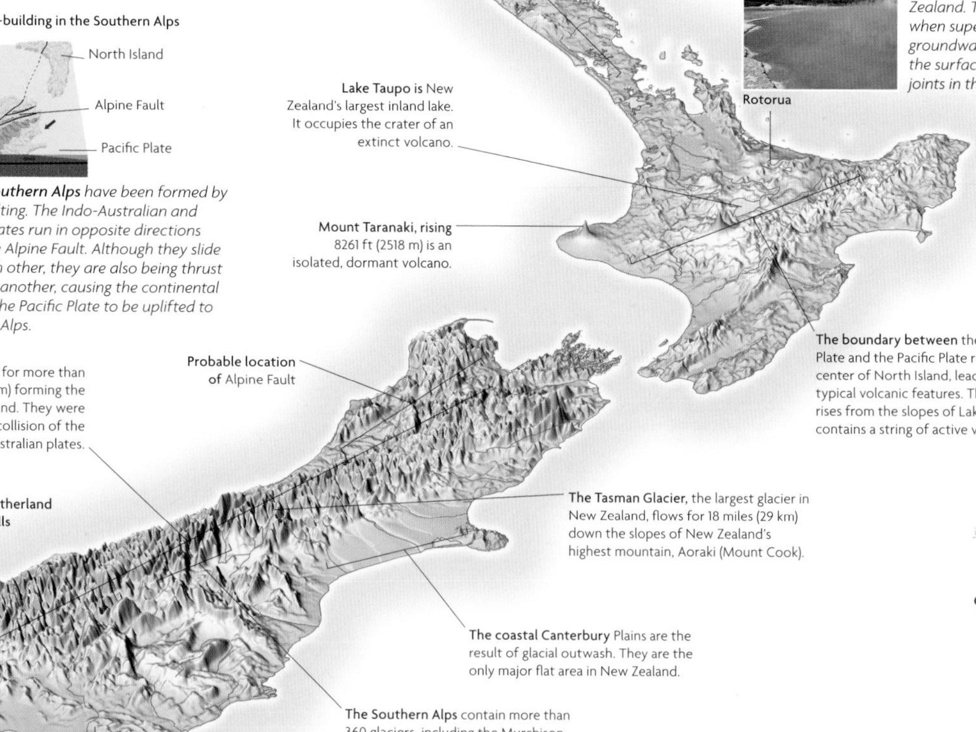
Northland
Rotorua

Lake Taupo is New Zealand's largest inland lake. It occupies the crater of an extinct volcano.

Mount Taranaki, rising 8261 ft (2518 m) is an isolated, dormant volcano.

The boundary between the Indo-Australian Plate and the Pacific Plate runs through the center of North Island, leading to many typical volcanic features. The plateau which rises from the slopes of Lake Taupo contains a string of active volcanoes.

Probable location of Alpine Fault

The Southern Alps run for more than 300 miles, (483 km) forming the backbone of South Island. They were uplifted following the collision of the Pacific and Indo-Australian plates.

Fiordland, in the far south west, contains a large number of flooded glacial valleys.

Sutherland Falls

The Tasman Glacier, the largest glacier in New Zealand, flows for 18 miles (29 km) down the slopes of New Zealand's highest mountain, Aoraki (Mount Cook).

The coastal Canterbury Plains are the result of glacial outwash. They are the only major flat area in New Zealand.

The Southern Alps contain more than 360 glaciers, including the Murchison, Mueller, and Godley glaciers on the eastern slopes and the Fox and Franz Josef glaciers to the west.

High levels of rainfall and a steep topography has made New Zealand's rivers swift-running. In the southern reaches of both islands, rivers such as the Mokoreta form broad, braided streams.

▶ *Clouds of steam rise from White Island, an active, offshore volcano lying in the Bay of Plenty, off the northern coast of North Island.*

Scale 1:3,000,000
Km
Miles
projection: Lambert Conformal Conic
192
Three Kings Islands
Cape Reinga
Cape Maria van Diemen
North Cape
Parengarenga Harbour
Te Kao
Great Exhibition Bay
Rangaunu Bay
Cape Karikari
Doubtless Bay
Mangonui
Ninety Mile Beach
Cavalli Islands
Ahipara Bay
Awanui
Kaitaia
Kaeo
Tauroa Point
Ahipara
Kerikeri
Bay of Islands
Cape Brett
Paihia
Russell
Okaihau
Whangaruru Harbour
Hokianga Harbour
Kaikohe
Kawakawa
Towai
Poor Knights Islands
Omapere
NORTHLAND
Hikurangi
Maungatapere
Whangarei
Kaihu
Portland
Bream Head
Hen and Chickens
Mokohinau Islands
Dargaville
Waiotira
Waipu
Bream Bay
Paparoa
Maungaturoto
Great Barrier Island
Little Barrier Island
Ruawai
Port Fitzroy
Kaipara Harbour
Wellsford
Cape Rodney
Leigh
Colville Channel
North Head
Warkworth
Kawau Island
Cape Colville
AUCKLAND
Hauraki Gulf
Mercury Islands
Great Mercury Island
Helensville
Orewa
Motutapu Island
Waiheke Island
Coromandel Peninsula
Coromandel
Whitianga
Muriwai Beach
Takapuna
Rangitoto Island
Ponui Island
Auckland
Papatoetoe
Manurewa
Manukau Harbour
Papakura
Firth of Thames
The Aldermen Islands
Whatipu
Thames
Pukekohe
Waiuku
Whangamata
Tuakau
Waitakaruru
Pokeno
Ngatea
Mayor Island
Kerepehi
Te Kauwhata
Paeroa
Lake Waikare
Waihi
Matakana Island
Huntly
Te Aroha
Katikati
Waitoa
Motiti Island
Pukemiro
Morrinsville
Mount Maunganui
Ngaruawahia
Tauranga
Hamilton
Bay of Plenty
Te Kaha
Raglan
Cambridge
Matamata
Te Puke
Matata
Te Awamutu
Tirau
Whakatane
Kawhia
Kawhia Harbour
Putaruru
Lake Rotoiti
Lake Rotorua
Opotiki
Otorohanga
Rotorua
Kawerau
Te Teko
Waitomo Caves
WAIKATO
Tokoroa
Lake Tarawera
BAY OF PLENTY
Te Kuiti
Kinleith
Mount Tarawera 1111m
Piopio
Mangakino
Whakamaru
Murupara
Matawai
GISBORNE
Te Karaka
Benneydale
Wairakei
Ruatahuna
Awakino
Mokau
Taupo
Okahukura
Ohura
Lake Taupo
Waitahanui
North Island
Gisborne
Whangara
Lake Waikaremoana
Poverty Bay
Young Nicks Head
North Taranaki Bight
Uruti
Taumarunui
Waitara
Urenui
Owhango
Turangi
Tarawera
Frasertown
New Plymouth
Oakura
Wairoa
Nuhaka
Inglewood
National Park
Mount Ruapehu 2797m
Table Cape
Mount Taranaki (Mount Egmont) 2518m
TARANAKI
Long Point
Mahia Peninsula
Cape Egmont
Stratford
Tutira
Hawke Bay
Portland Island
Eltham
HAWKE'S BAY
Eskdale
Opunake
Raetihi
Waiouru
Napier
MANAWATU-WANGANUI
Manaia
Hawera
Cape Kidnappers
Hastings
Havelock North
Kakaramea
Patea
Waverley
Kakatahi
Taihape
Mangaweka
Waitotara
South Taranaki Bight
Wanganui
Hunterville
Mangaweka 1733m
Ongaonga
Waipawa
Turakina
Takapau
Waipukurau
Marton
Halcombe
Bulls
Feilding
Wanstead
Dannevirke
Porangahau
Palmerston North
Woodville
Foxton
Pahiatua
Shannon
Cape Turnagain
Levin
Pongaroa
Cape Farewell
Farewell Spit
Golden
Stephens Island
Ohau
Lottin Point
Hicks Bay
Te Araroa
East Cape
Tikitiki
Ruatoria
Hikurangi 1752m
Raukumara 1413m
Arowhana 1440m
Tokomaru Bay
Mawhai Point
Tolaga Bay
Cape Runaway
White Island
TASMAN SEA
PACIFIC OCEAN
NEW ZEALAND

TASMAN SEA
PACIFIC OCEAN
Southern Alps
South Island
Fiordland
Foveaux Strait
Stewart Island
Cook Strait
WELLINGTON
NELSON
TASMAN
MARLBOROUGH
WEST COAST
CANTERBURY
Canterbury Plains
Canterbury Bight
OTAGO
SOUTHLAND
Christchurch
Dunedin
Invercargill
Timaru
Oamaru
Queenstown
Nelson
Blenheim
Greymouth
Hokitika
Westport
Kaikoura
Aoraki (Mount Cook) 3744m
Mount Aspiring 3027m
Lake Te Anau
Lake Wakatipu
Lake Wanaka
Lake Tekapo
Lake Pukaki
Milford Sound
Banks Peninsula
Otago Peninsula
192

Map key

Population

- 1 million to 5 million
- 500,000 to 1 million
- 100,000 to 500,000
- 50,000 to 100,000
- 10,000 to 50,000
- below 10,000

Elevation

- 3000m / 9843ft
- 2000m / 6562ft
- 1000m / 3281ft
- 500m / 1640ft
- 250m / 820ft
- 100m / 328ft
- sea level

▲ ***The snowcapped peak** of Aoraki (Mount Cook), on the west coast of South Island, overlooks a heath strewn with foxgloves. Though still the highest peak in New Zealand, at 12,349 ft (3744 m), a massive rock fall in 1991 reduced the height of the mountain by 66 ft (20 m).*

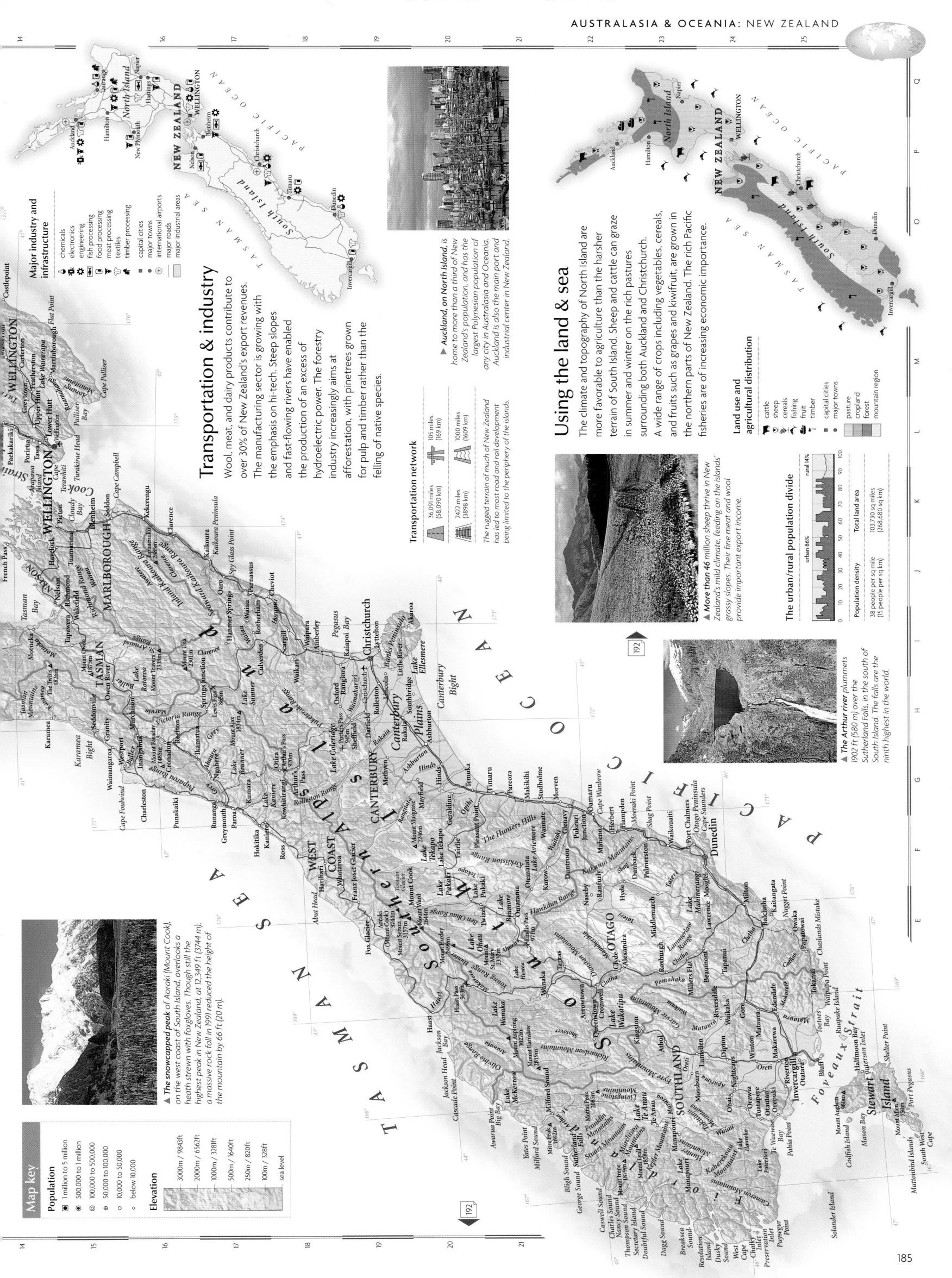

Transportation & industry

Wool, meat, and dairy products contribute to over 30% of New Zealand's export revenues. The manufacturing sector is growing with the emphasis on hi-tech. Steep slopes and fast-flowing rivers have enabled the production of an excess of hydroelectric power. The forestry industry increasingly aims at afforestation, with pinetrees grown for pulp and timber rather than the felling of native species.

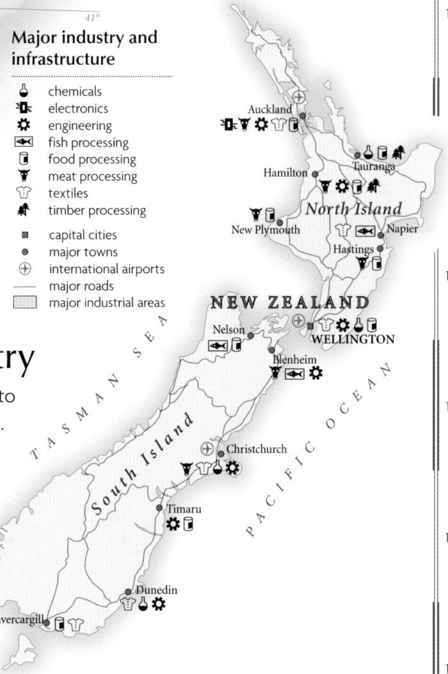
Major industry and infrastructure
chemicals
electronics
engineering
fish processing
food processing
meat processing
textiles
timber processing
capital cities
major towns
international airports
major roads
major industrial areas
NEW ZEALAND
North Island
South Island
TASMAN SEA
PACIFIC OCEAN
Auckland
Hamilton
Tauranga
New Plymouth
Napier
Hastings
WELLINGTON
Nelson
Blenheim
Christchurch
Timaru
Dunedin
Invercargill

Transportation network

36,091 miles (58,090 km)		105 miles (169 km)	
2422 miles (3898 km)		1000 miles (1609 km)	

The rugged terrain of much of New Zealand has led to most road and rail development being limited to the periphery of the islands.

▶ ***Auckland, on North Island,** is home to more than a third of New Zealand's population, and has the largest Polynesian population of any city in Australasia and Oceania. Auckland is also the main port and industrial center in New Zealand.*

192

▲ ***More than 46** million sheep thrive in New Zealand's mild climate, feeding on the islands' grassy slopes. Their fine meat and wool provide important export income.*

▲ ***The Arthur river** plummets 1902 ft (580 m) over the Sutherland Falls, in the south of South Island. The falls are the ninth highest in the world.*

Using the land & sea

The climate and topography of North Island are more favorable to agriculture than the harsher terrain of South Island. Sheep and cattle can graze in summer and winter on the rich pastures surrounding both Auckland and Christchurch. A wide range of crops including vegetables, cereals, and fruits such as grapes and kiwifruit, are grown in the northern parts of New Zealand. The rich Pacific fisheries are of increasing economic importance.

The urban/rural population divide

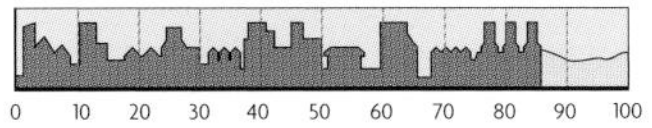
urban 86%
rural 14%
0
10
20
30
40
50
60
70
80
90
100

Population density	Total land area
38 people per sq mile (15 people per sq km)	103,730 sq miles (268,680 sq km)

Land use and agricultural distribution
cattle
sheep
cereals
fishing
fruit
timber
capital cities
major towns
pasture
cropland
forest
mountain region
NEW ZEALAND
North Island
South Island
TASMAN SEA
PACIFIC OCEAN
Auckland
Hamilton
Napier
WELLINGTON
Christchurch
Dunedin
Invercargill

Melanesia

FIJI, New Caledonia *(to France)*, PAPUA NEW GUINEA, SOLOMON ISLANDS, VANUATU

Lying in the southwest Pacific Ocean, northeast of Australia and south of the Equator, the islands of Melanesia form one of the three geographic divisions (along with Polynesia and Micronesia) of Oceania. Melanesia's name derives from the Greek melas, "black," and *nesoi*, "islands." Most of the larger islands are volcanic in origin. The smaller islands tend to be coral atolls and are mainly uninhabited. Rugged mountains, covered by dense rain forest, take up most of the land area. Melanesian's cultivate yams, taro, and sweet potatoes for local consumption and live in small, usually dispersed, homesteads.

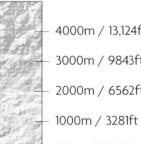

▲ *Huli tribesmen from* Southern Highlands Province in Papua New Guinea parade in ceremonial dress, their powdered wigs decorated with exotic plumage and their faces and bodies painted with colored pigments.

Map key

Population

- ◎ 100,000 to 500,000
- ⊕ 50,000 to 100,000
- ○ 10,000 to 50,000
- ○ below 10,000

Elevation

- 4000m / 13,124ft
- 3000m / 9843ft
- 2000m / 6562ft
- 1000m / 3281ft
- 500m / 1640ft
- 250m / 820ft
- 100m / 328ft
- sea level

PACIFIC OCEAN
Bismarck Archipelago
Bismarck Sea
Solomon Sea
Solomon Islands
Coral Sea
Gulf of Papua
Torres Strait
INDONESIA
AUSTRALIA
PAPUA NEW GUINEA
New Guinea
New Britain
New Ireland
Admiralty Islands
Manus Island
MANUS
Lorengau
Tulu
M'buñai
Rambutyo Island
Lou Island
Hermit Islands
Ninigo Group
Tulaghi
Aua Island
Wuvulu Island
Mussau Island
Tabalo
St.Matthias Group
Emirau Island
Ysabel Channel
New Hanover
Taskul
North Cape
Kavieng
Meteran
Dyaul Island
Tabar Islands
Lihir Group
Konos
Konogogo
Namatanai
Tanga Islands
Feni Islands
NEW IRELAND
Cape Lambert
Rabaul
Kokopo
Taron
Cape St.George
Green Islands
Nuguria Islands
Tulun Islands
Takuu Islands
Nukumanu Islands
Ontong Java Atoll
Roncador Reef
WEST NEW BRITAIN
EAST NEW BRITAIN
Witu Islands
Willaumez Peninsula
Lolobau Island
Open Bay
Kimbe Bay
Hoskins
Ulamona
Talasea
Kimbe
Gloucester
Mount Talawe 1824m
Anepmete
Arawe Islands
Kandrian
Gasmata
Sampun
Pomio
Lau
Umboi Island
Siassi
Vitiaz Strait
Sialum
Long Island
Karkar Island
Manam Island
VANIMO
Vanimo
SANDAUN
Sissano
Aitape
Torricelli Mountains
Imonda
Amanab
Green River
May River
Nuku
Dreikikir
Wewak
Maprik
Angoram
Ambunti
Kaup
Broken Water Bay
Bogia
EAST SEPIK
Yaminbot
Sepik
MADANG
Josephstaal
Madang
Aiome
Simbai
Usino
Saidor
Malalamai
Telefomin
Ok Tedi
Capella 3932m
Mount Aiyang 3325m
Star Mountains
Central Range
Wabag
Porgera
ENGA
Kandep
WESTERN HIGHLANDS
Mount Wilhelm 4509m
Ningerum
Koroba
Tari
Margarima
Mendi
Mount Hagen
Kundiawa
Goroka
Kainantu
CHIMBU
EASTERN HIGHLANDS
SOUTHERN HIGHLANDS
Nipa
Poroma
Ialibu
Kiunga
Komo
Nomad
Lake Murray
Mount Bosavi 2397m
Karimui
Wonenara
Marawaka
MOROBE
Mount Bangeta 4121m
Kabwum
Huon Peninsula
Finschhafen
Nadzab
Lae
Markham
Mumeng
Wau
Bulolo
WESTERN
Fly
Strickland
Kikori
Baimuru
Emeti
Aramia
Balimo
Weam
Morehead
Sibidiri
Daru
Oriomo
Mari
Purutu Island
Kiwai Island
GULF
Kerema
Kukipi
Kaintiba
Morobe
Hercules Bay
Tapini
CENTRAL
NORTHERN
Popondetta
Kokoda
Afore
Tufi
Mount Victoria 4072m
Owen Stanley Range
Bereina
Hisiu
NATIONAL CAPITAL DISTRICT
PORT MORESBY
Kwikila
Kupiano
Abau
Magarida
Mount Suckling 3676m
Rabaraba
Alotau
Ahioma
MILNE BAY
Eagle Point
Suau
Samarai
Bwagaoia
Louisiade Archipelago
Tagula
The Calvados Chain
Rossel Island
Tagula Island
Pocklington Reef
Lusancay Islands and Reefs
Losuia
Kiriwina Island
Trobriand Islands
D'Entrecasteaux Islands
Goodenough Island
Bolubolu
Fergusson Island
Esa'ala
Sehulea
Normanby Island
Madau Island
Woodlark Island
Guasopa
Yanaba Island
Buka Island
Lemankoa
Hutjena
NORTH SOLOMONS
Mount Balbi 2685m
Wakunai
Torokina
Arawa
Panguna
Bougainville Island
Buin
Shortland Island
Treasury Islands
Bougainville Strait
CHOISEUL
Choiseul
Taro
Nukiki
Panggoe
Luti
Vella Lavella
Kolombangara
Ranongga
Gizo
Ringgi
Mongga
Rendova
New Georgia
New Georgia Sound
New Georgia Islands
Vangunu
WESTERN
Tetepare
ISABEL
Santa Isabel
Kia
Baolo
Buala
Mount Sasari 1219m
Kaolo
CENTRAL
Yandina
Tulaghi
Cape Esperance
Tambea
HONIARA
Guadalcanal
Nduindui
Avuavu
GUADALCANAL
RENNELL AND BELLONA
Bellona
Tigoa
Lavanggu
Indispensable Reefs
168
192
180
145°
150°
155°
160°
5°
10°

◀ *Lying close to* the banks of the Sepik river in northern Papua New Guinea, this building is known as the Spirit House. It is constructed from leaves and twigs, ornately woven and trimmed into geometric patterns. The house is decorated with a mask and topped by a carved statue.

▲ *On one of* Vanuatu's many islands, beach houses stand at the water's edge, surrounded by coconut palms and other tropical vegetation. The unspoilt beaches and tranquillity of its islands are drawing ever-larger numbers of tourists to Vanuatu.

Transportation & Industry

The processing of natural resources generates significant export revenue for the countries of Melanesia. The region relies mainly on copra, tuna, and timber exports, with some production of cocoa and palm oil. The islands have substantial mineral resources including the world's largest copper reserves on Bougainville Island; gold, and potential oil and natural gas. Tourism has become the fastest growing sector in most of the countries' economies.

PACIFIC OCEAN
Bismarck Archipelago
Manus Island
Kavieng
Wewak
Bismarck Sea
Rabaul
PAPUA NEW GUINEA
Ok Tedi
Madang
Mount Hagen
Lae
New Guinea
New Britain
Solomon Sea
Bougainville Island
Panguna
Arawa
INDONESIA
PORT MORESBY
Louisiade Archipelago
Coral Sea
Auki
HONIARA
SOLOMON ISLANDS

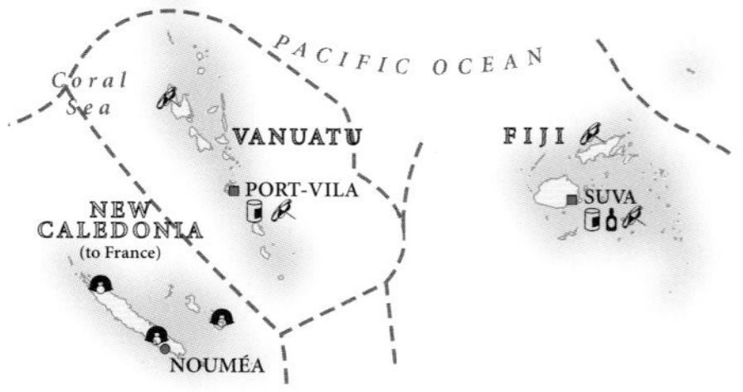

PACIFIC OCEAN
Coral Sea
VANUATU
PORT-VILA
FIJI
SUVA
NEW CALEDONIA (to France)
NOUMÉA

Transportation network

1236 miles (1990 km)	None
370 miles (595 km)	6924 miles (11,143 km)

As most of the islands of Melanesia lie off the major sea and air routes, services to and from the rest of the world are infrequent. Transportation by road on rugged terrain is difficult and expensive.

Major industry and infrastructure

- beverages
- coffee processing
- copra processing
- food processing
- mining
- textiles
- timber processing
- tourism
- capital cities
- major towns
- international airports
- major roads

◀ *On New Caledonia's* main island, relatively high interior plateaus descend to coastal plains. Nickel is the most important mineral resource, but the hills also harbor metallic deposits including chrome, cobalt, iron, gold, silver, and copper.

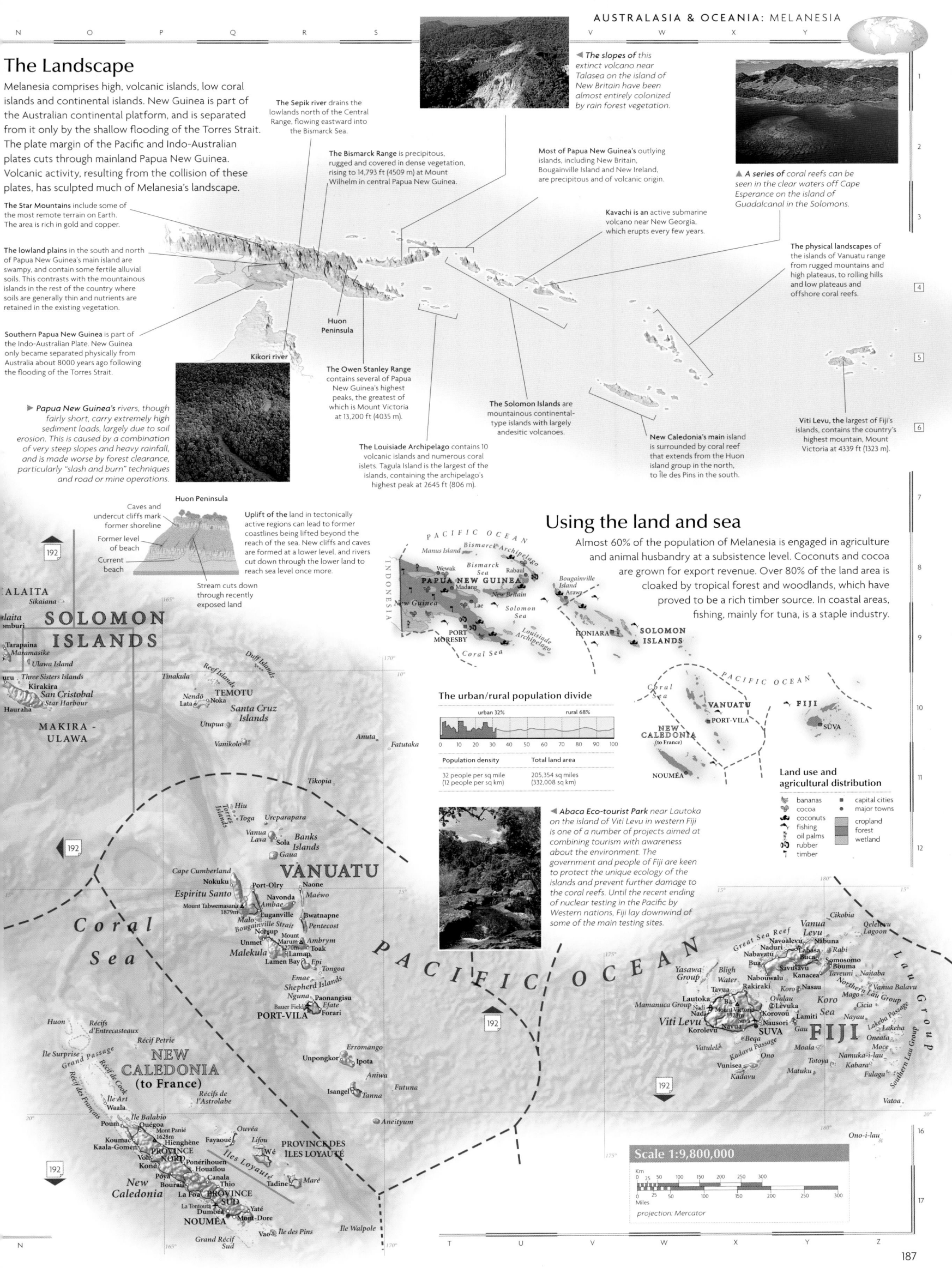

The Landscape

Melanesia comprises high, volcanic islands, low coral islands and continental islands. New Guinea is part of the Australian continental platform, and is separated from it only by the shallow flooding of the Torres Strait. The plate margin of the Pacific and Indo-Australian plates cuts through mainland Papua New Guinea. Volcanic activity, resulting from the collision of these plates, has sculpted much of Melanesia's landscape.

◀ *The slopes of this extinct volcano near Talasea on the island of New Britain have been almost entirely colonized by rain forest vegetation.*

▲ *A series of coral reefs can be seen in the clear waters off Cape Esperance on the island of Guadalcanal in the Solomons.*

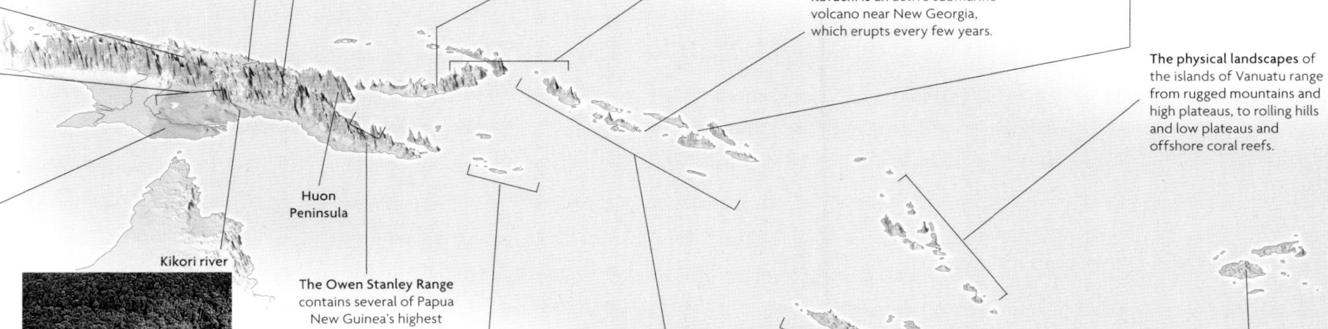

Huon Peninsula
Kikori river

The Star Mountains include some of the most remote terrain on Earth. The area is rich in gold and copper.

The lowland plains in the south and north of Papua New Guinea's main island are swampy, and contain some fertile alluvial soils. This contrasts with the mountainous islands in the rest of the country where soils are generally thin and nutrients are retained in the existing vegetation.

Southern Papua New Guinea is part of the Indo-Australian Plate. New Guinea only became separated physically from Australia about 8000 years ago following the flooding of the Torres Strait.

The Sepik river drains the lowlands north of the Central Range, flowing eastward into the Bismarck Sea.

The Bismarck Range is precipitous, rugged and covered in dense vegetation, rising to 14,793 ft (4509 m) at Mount Wilhelm in central Papua New Guinea.

Most of Papua New Guinea's outlying islands, including New Britain, Bougainville Island and New Ireland, are precipitous and of volcanic origin.

Kavachi is an active submarine volcano near New Georgia, which erupts every few years.

The physical landscapes of the islands of Vanuatu range from rugged mountains and high plateaus, to rolling hills and low plateaus and offshore coral reefs.

The Owen Stanley Range contains several of Papua New Guinea's highest peaks, the greatest of which is Mount Victoria at 13,200 ft (4035 m).

The Solomon Islands are mountainous continental-type islands with largely andesitic volcanoes.

The Louisiade Archipelago contains 10 volcanic islands and numerous coral islets. Tagula Island is the largest of the islands, containing the archipelago's highest peak at 2645 ft (806 m).

New Caledonia's main island is surrounded by coral reef that extends from the Huon island group in the north, to Île des Pins in the south.

Viti Levu, the largest of Fiji's islands, contains the country's highest mountain, Mount Victoria at 4339 ft (1323 m).

▶ *Papua New Guinea's rivers, though fairly short, carry extremely high sediment loads, largely due to soil erosion. This is caused by a combination of very steep slopes and heavy rainfall, and is made worse by forest clearance, particularly "slash and burn" techniques and road or mine operations.*

Huon Peninsula

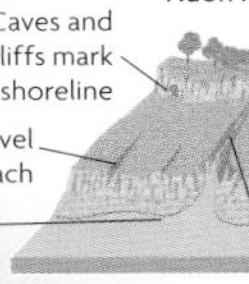

Caves and undercut cliffs mark former shoreline
Former level of beach
Current beach
Stream cuts down through recently exposed land

Uplift of the land in tectonically active regions can lead to former coastlines being lifted beyond the reach of the sea. New cliffs and caves are formed at a lower level, and rivers cut down through the lower land to reach sea level once more.

Using the land and sea

Almost 60% of the population of Melanesia is engaged in agriculture and animal husbandry at a subsistence level. Coconuts and cocoa are grown for export revenue. Over 80% of the land area is cloaked by tropical forest and woodlands, which have proved to be a rich timber source. In coastal areas, fishing, mainly for tuna, is a staple industry.

PACIFIC OCEAN
Manus Island
Bismarck Archipelago
Bismarck Sea
INDONESIA
Wewak
Rabaul
PAPUA NEW GUINEA
Madang
New Britain
New Guinea
Lae
Solomon Sea
PORT MORESBY
Louisiade Archipelago
Coral Sea
Bougainville Island
Arawa
HONIARA
SOLOMON ISLANDS

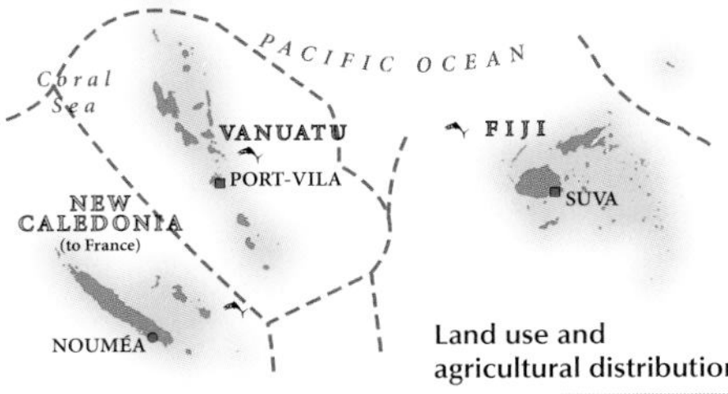

PACIFIC OCEAN
Coral Sea
VANUATU
PORT-VILA
FIJI
SUVA
NEW CALEDONIA (to France)
NOUMÉA

Land use and agricultural distribution

bananas	capital cities		
cocoa	major towns		
coconuts		cropland	
fishing		forest	
oil palms		wetland	
rubber			
timber			

The urban/rural population divide

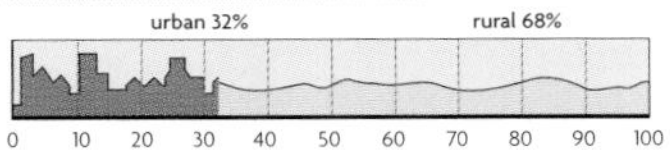

urban 32%
rural 68%
0 10 20 30 40 50 60 70 80 90 100

Population density	Total land area
32 people per sq mile (12 people per sq km)	205,354 sq miles (332,008 sq km)

◀ *Abaca Eco-tourist Park near Lautoka on the island of Viti Levu in western Fiji is one of a number of projects aimed at combining tourism with awareness about the environment. The government and people of Fiji are keen to protect the unique ecology of the islands and prevent further damage to the coral reefs. Until the recent ending of nuclear testing in the Pacific by Western nations, Fiji lay downwind of some of the main testing sites.*

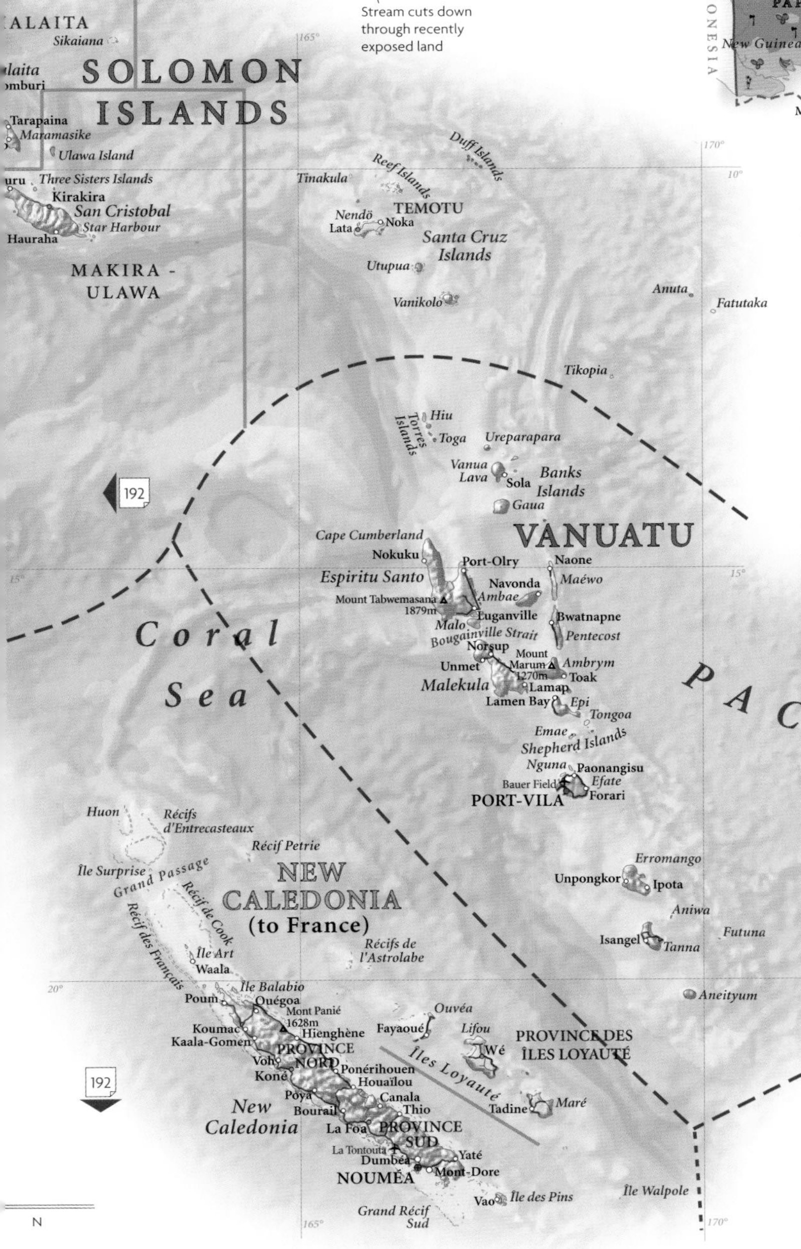

SOLOMON ISLANDS
MAKIRA - ULAWA
San Cristobal
Star Harbour
TEMOTU
Santa Cruz Islands
Duff Islands
Reef Islands
Vanikolo
Utupua
Tikopia
Anuta
Fatutaka
VANUATU
Espiritu Santo
Port-Olry
Luganville
Malekula
Ambrym
PORT-VILA
Efate
Erromango
Tanna
Aneityum
Futuna
Banks Islands
Torres Islands
Coral Sea
PACIFIC OCEAN
NEW CALEDONIA (to France)
PROVINCE NORD
PROVINCE SUD
PROVINCE DES ÎLES LOYAUTÉ
Îles Loyauté
NOUMÉA
Île des Pins
Ouvéa
Lifou
Maré
Île Walpole
FIJI
Viti Levu
Vanua Levu
SUVA
Lautoka
Nadi
Labasa
Taveuni
Kadavu
Lau Group
Koro Sea
Yasawa Group
Ono-i-lau
192

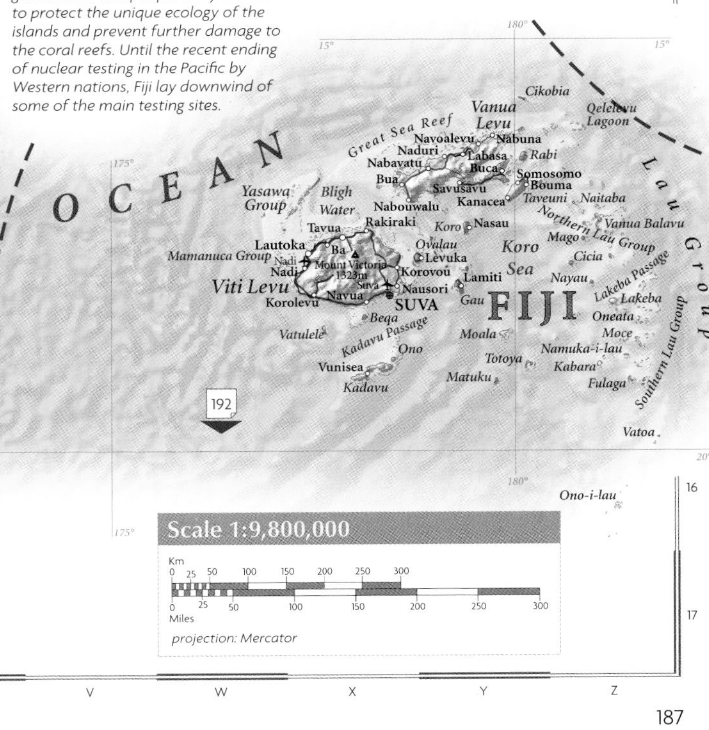

Scale 1:9,800,000

projection: Mercator

Micronesia

MARSHALL ISLANDS, MICRONESIA, NAURU, PALAU, Guam, Northern Mariana Islands, Wake Island

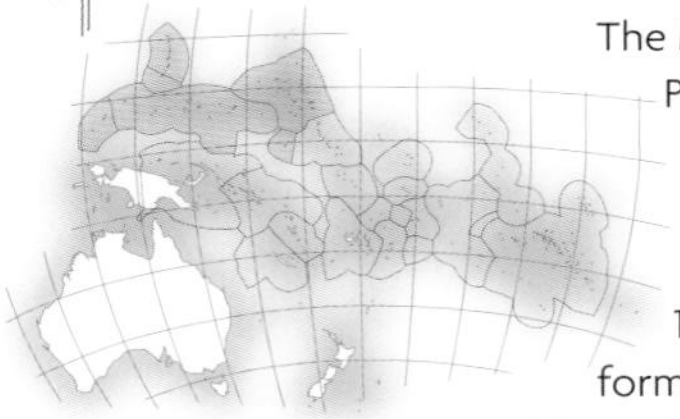

The Micronesian islands lie in the western reaches of the Pacific Ocean and are all part of the same volcanic zone. The Federated States of Micronesia is the largest group, with more than 600 atolls and forested volcanic islands in an area of more than 1120 sq miles (2900 sq km). Micronesia is a mixture of former colonies, overseas territories, and dependencies. Most of the region still relies on aid and subsidies to sustain economies limited by resources, isolation, and an emigrating population, drawn to New Zealand and Australia by the attractions of a western lifestyle.

Palau

Palau is an archipelago of over 200 islands, only eight of which are inhabited. It was the last remaining UN trust territory in the Pacific, controlled by the US until 1994, when it became independent. The economy operates on a subsistence level, with coconuts and cassava the principal crops. Fishing licenses and tourism provide foreign currency.

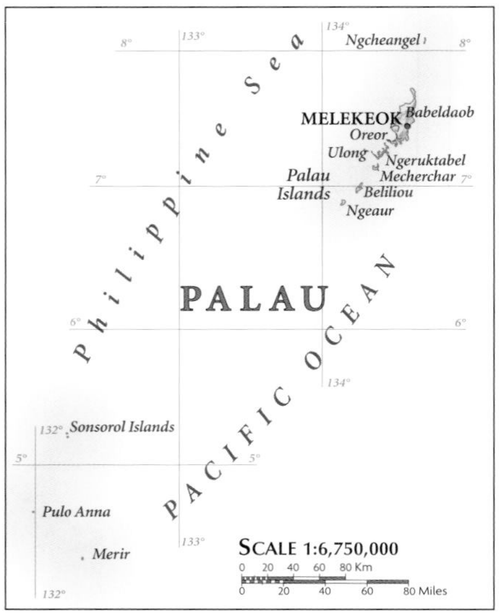
Philippine Sea
Ngcheangel
MELEKEOK
Babeldaob
Oreor
Ulong
Ngeruktabel
Mechercher
Palau Islands
Beliliou
Ngeaur
PALAU
PACIFIC OCEAN
Sonsorol Islands
Pulo Anna
Merir
SCALE 1:6,750,000
0 20 40 60 80 Km
0 20 40 60 80 Miles

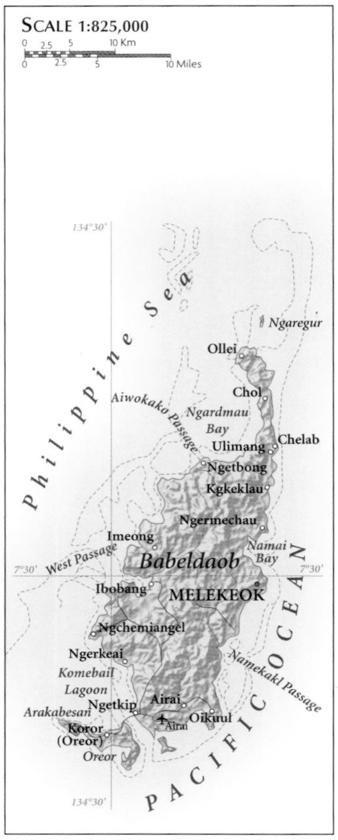
SCALE 1:825,000
0 2.5 5 10 Km
0 2.5 5 10 Miles
Philippine Sea
Ngaregur
Ollei
Aiwokako Passage
Chol
Ngardmau Bay
Ulimang
Chelab
Ngetbong
Ngkeklau
Ngerimechau
Imeong
West Passage
Namai Bay
Babeldaob
Ibobang
MELEKEOK
Ngchemiangel
Ngerkeai
Komebail Lagoon
Nameklakl Passage
Arakabesan
Ngetkip
Airai
Oikuul
Koror (Oreor)
Oreor
PACIFIC OCEAN

Northern Mariana Islands *(to US)*

A US Commonwealth territory, the Northern Marianas comprise the whole of the Mariana archipelago except for Guam. The islands retain their close links with the US and continue to receive American aid. Tourism, though bringing in much-needed revenue, has speeded the decline of the traditional subsistence economy. Most of the population lives on Saipan.

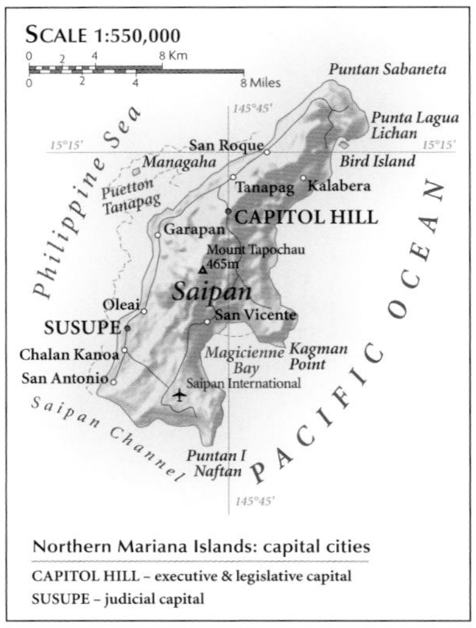
SCALE 1:550,000
0 2 4 8 Km
0 2 4 8 Miles
Puntan Sabaneta
Punta Lagua Lichan
Philippine Sea
San Roque
Managaha
Bird Island
Puetton Tanapag
Tanapag
Kalabera
CAPITOL HILL
Garapan
Mount Tapochau 465m
Saipan
Oleai
San Vicente
SUSUPE
Chalan Kanoa
Magicienne Bay
Kagman Point
San Antonio
Saipan International
Saipan Channel
Puntan I Naftan
PACIFIC OCEAN
Northern Mariana Islands: capital cities
CAPITOL HILL – executive & legislative capital
SUSUPE – judicial capital

▲ *The Palau Islands have numerous hidden lakes and lagoons. These sustain their own ecosystems which have developed in isolation. This has produced adaptations in the animals and plants that are often unique to each lake.*

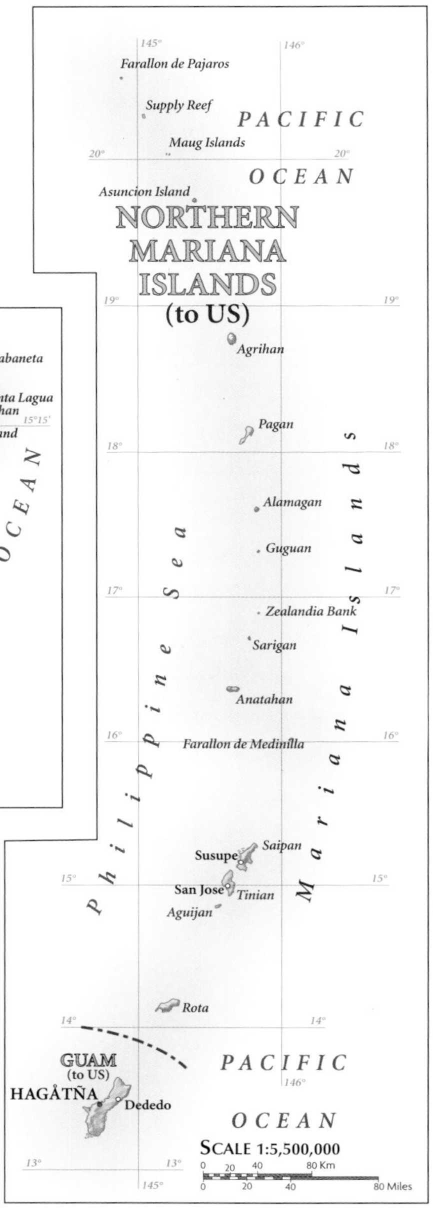
Farallon de Pajaros
Supply Reef
PACIFIC OCEAN
Maug Islands
Asuncion Island
NORTHERN MARIANA ISLANDS (to US)
Agrihan
Pagan
Alamagan
Guguan
Zealandia Bank
Sarigan
Anatahan
Farallon de Medinilla
Philippine Sea
Mariana Islands
Susupe
Saipan
San Jose
Tinian
Aguijan
Rota
GUAM (to US)
HAGÅTÑA
Dededo
PACIFIC OCEAN
SCALE 1:5,500,000
0 20 40 80 Km
0 20 40 80 Miles

Guam *(to US)*

Lying at the southern end of the Mariana Islands, Guam is an important US military base and tourist destination. Social and political life is dominated by the indigenous Chamorro, who make up just under half the population, although the increasing prevalence of western culture threatens Guam's traditional social stability.

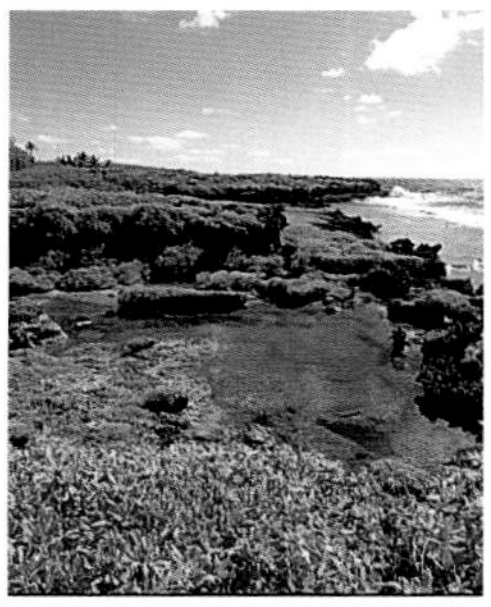

◀ *The tranquility of these coastal lagoons, at Inarajan in southern Guam, belies the fact that the island lies in a region where typhoons are common.*

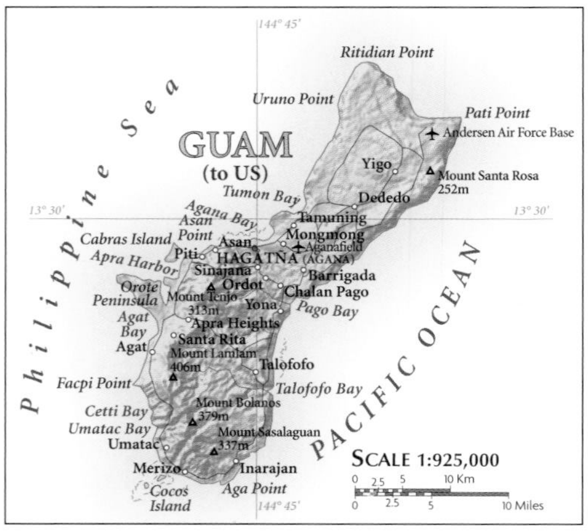
Ritidian Point
Uruno Point
Pati Point
Andersen Air Force Base
Philippine Sea
GUAM (to US)
Yigo
Tumon Bay
Dededo
Mount Santa Rosa 252m
Agana Bay
Tamuning
Asan
Asan Point
Mongmong
Cabras Island
Apra Harbor
Piti
HAGÅTÑA (AGANA)
Sinajana
Orote Peninsula
Ordot
Barrigada
Chalan Pago
Agat Bay
Yona
Pago Bay
Agat
Apra Heights
Santa Rita
Talofofo
Facpi Point
Talofofo Bay
Cetti Bay
Umatac Bay
Umatac
Merizo
Inarajan
Cocos Island
Aga Point
PACIFIC OCEAN
SCALE 1:925,000
0 2.5 5 10 Km
0 2.5 5 10 Miles

Micronesia

A mixture of high volcanic islands and low-lying coral atolls, the Federated States of Micronesia include all the Caroline Islands except Palau. Pohnpei, Kosrae, Chuuk, and Yap are the four main island cluster states, each of which has its own language, with English remaining the official language. Nearly half the population is concentrated on Pohnpei, the largest island. Independent since 1986, the islands continue to receive considerable aid from the US which supplements an economy based primarily on fishing and copra processing.

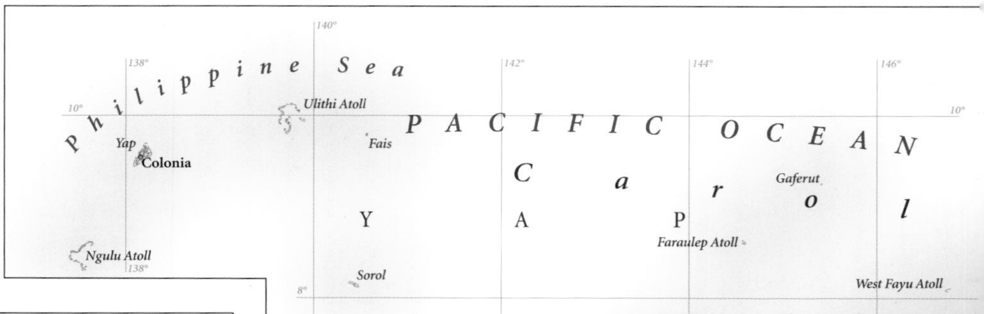
Philippine Sea
Ulithi Atoll
Yap
Colonia
Fais
PACIFIC OCEAN
YAP
Caroline
Gaferut
Ngulu Atoll
Faraulep Atoll
Sorol
West Fayu Atoll
Olimarao Atoll
Lamotrek Atoll
Woleai Atoll
Elato Atoll
Satawal
Ifalik Atoll
Eauripik Atoll

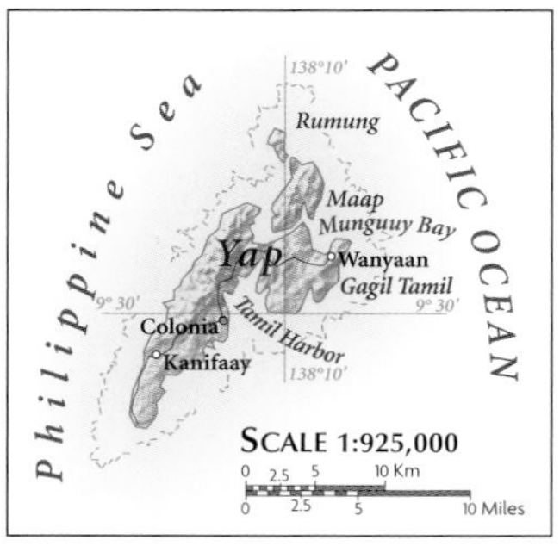
Philippine Sea
PACIFIC OCEAN
Rumung
Maap
Munguuy Bay
Yap
Wanyaan
Gagil Tamil
Tamil Harbor
Colonia
Kanifaay
SCALE 1:925,000
0 2.5 5 10 Km
0 2.5 5 10 Miles

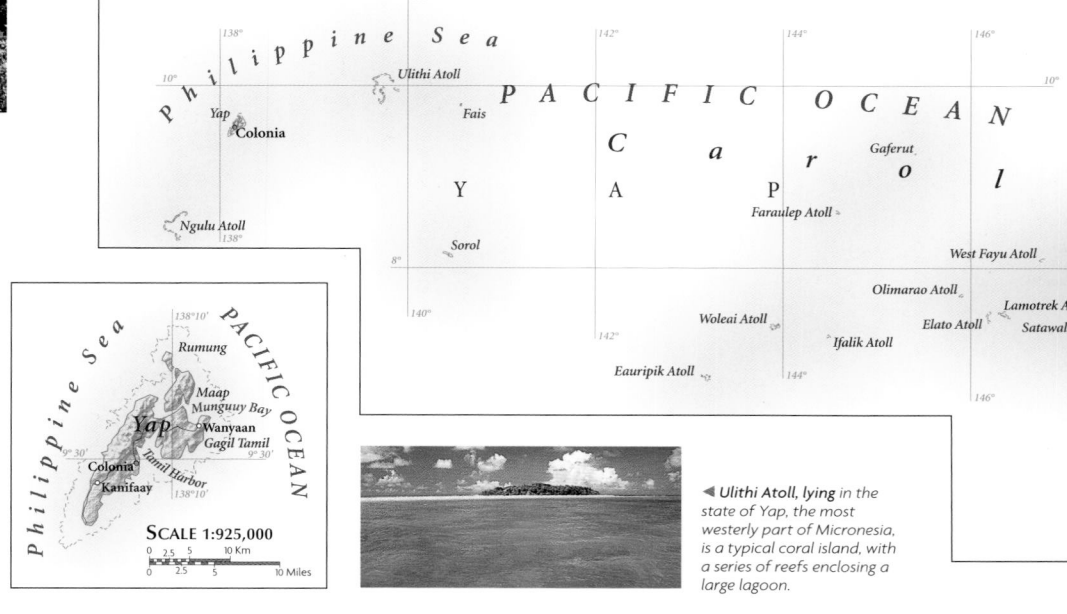

◀ ***Ulithi Atoll**, lying in the state of Yap, the most westerly part of Micronesia, is a typical coral island, with a series of reefs enclosing a large lagoon.*

Marshall Islands

A group of 34 widely-scattered atolls in the central Pacific Ocean, the Marshall Islands include some of the largest atolls in the world, formed from low coral islands with sandy beaches and enclosing vast lagoons. Formerly under US protection as part of the UN Trust Territory of the Pacific Islands, and including the former US nuclear testing sites of Bikini atoll and Enewetak Atoll, the Marshall Islands became self-governing in 1979. The economy is reliant on US aid and on the rent paid by the US for its missile base on Kwajalein atoll.

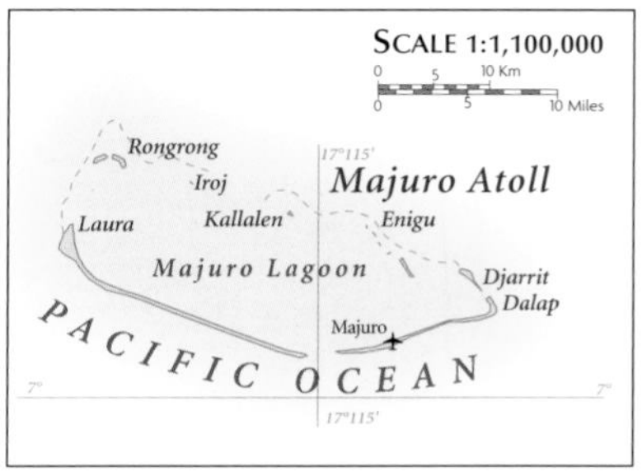
SCALE 1:1,100,000
Majuro Atoll
Rongrong
Iroj
Kallalen
Enigu
Laura
Majuro Lagoon
Djarrit
Dalap
Majuro
PACIFIC OCEAN

▲ *Majuro Atoll is the Marshall Islands' capital and commercial center. Almost half the population live on the narrow islands, often in overcrowded conditions.*

PACIFIC OCEAN
MARSHALL ISLANDS
Sibylla Island
Bokaak Atoll
Bikar Atoll
Bikini Atoll
Rongelap Atoll
Enewetak Atoll
Rongrik Atoll
Ailinginae Atoll
Utrik Atoll
Taka Atoll
Ailuk Atoll
Mejit Island
Jemo Island
Wotho Atoll
Ujelang Atoll
Likiep Atoll
Wotje Atoll
Ratak Chain
Ujae Atoll
Kwajalein Atoll
Erikub Atoll
Lae Atoll
Ralik Chain
Maloelap Atoll
Lib
Namu Atoll
Aur Atoll
Jabwot
Ailinglaplap Atoll
Majuro Atoll
Arno Atoll
Jaluit Atoll
Mili Atoll
Knox Atoll
Namorik Atoll
Kili Island
Ebon Atoll
SCALE 1:7,250,000

Nauru

A former British colony, the tiny island of Nauru, with an area of only 8.2 sq miles (21.2 sq km), has been exploited for its substantial phosphate deposits by the UK, Australia, and New Zealand. Since independence in 1968, the phosphate industry has made its citizens some of the wealthiest in the world, and scars from the vast mining operation pit the island's landscape. Phosphate reserves are now virtually exhausted and investment overseas will in future form the bulk of Nauru's income.

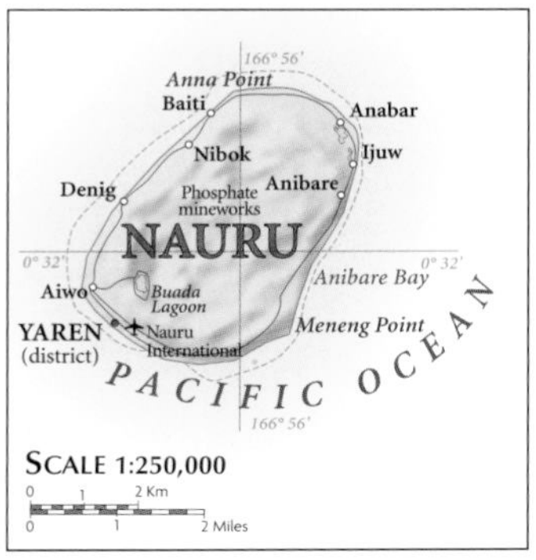
NAURU
Anna Point
Baiti
Anabar
Ijuw
Nibok
Anibare
Denig
Phosphate mineworks
Anibare Bay
Aiwo
Buada Lagoon
Meneng Point
YAREN (district)
Nauru International
PACIFIC OCEAN
SCALE 1:250,000

◀ *A series of* coral pinnacles stand exposed in the shallow water off the coast of Nauru. *Much of the island has an extraordinary "lunar" landscape, created by years of phosphate extraction.*

Wake Island *(to US)*

An unincorporated territory of the US with a tiny population, Wake Island remains strategically important to US forces, and has been used as a base in several conflicts. Formed by the rim of an extinct underwater volcano, it is now used as an emergency airstrip for trans-Pacific flights, and as a stopover for cargo planes.

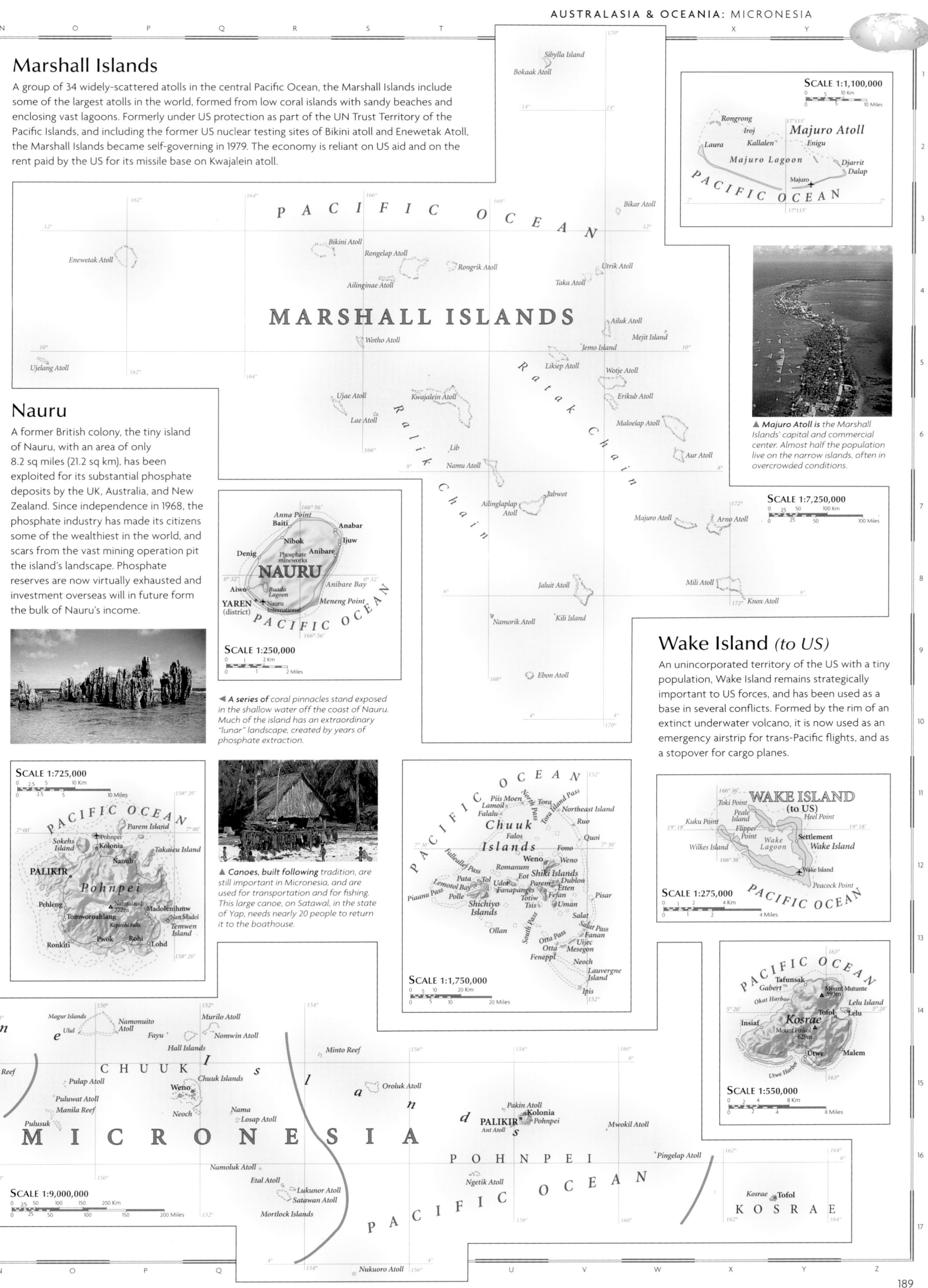

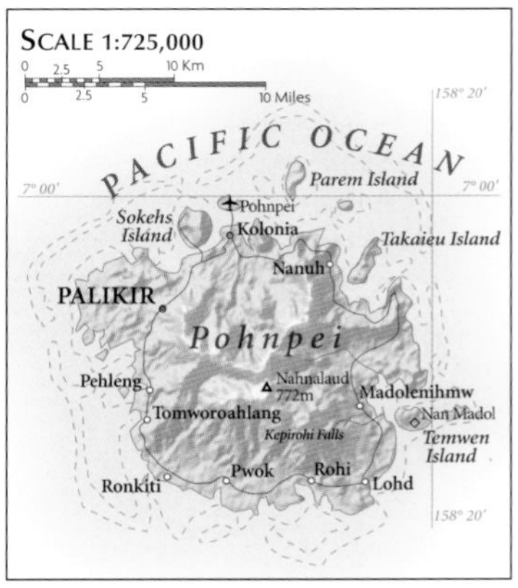
SCALE 1:725,000
PACIFIC OCEAN
Parem Island
Pohnpei
Kolonia
Sokehs Island
Takaieu Island
Nanuh
PALIKIR
Pohnpei
Pehleng
Nahnalaud 772m
Madolenihmw
Nan Madol
Tomworoahlang
Kepirohi Falls
Temwen Island
Pwok
Rohi
Lohd
Ronkiti

▲ *Canoes, built following* tradition, are still important in Micronesia, and are used for transportation and for fishing. *This large canoe, on Satawal, in the state of Yap, needs nearly 20 people to return it to the boathouse.*

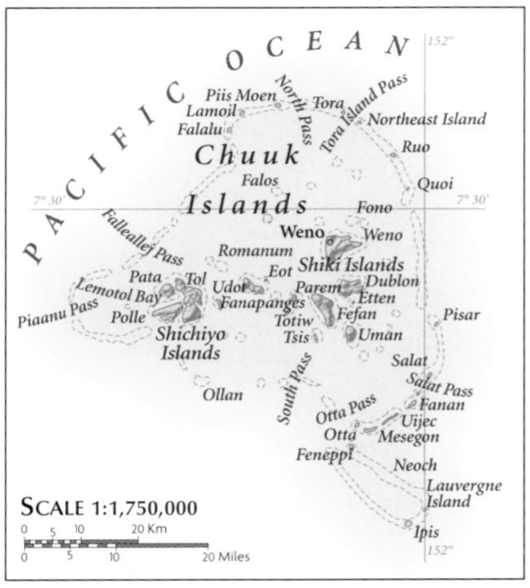
PACIFIC OCEAN
Chuuk Islands
Piis Moen
Lamoil
Falalu
North Pass
Tora
Tora Island Pass
Northeast Island
Ruo
Quoi
Falos
Fono
Weno
Romanum
Eot
Shiki Islands
Dublon
Parem
Etten
Udot
Fanapanges
Fefan
Tol
Pata
Lemotol Bay
Piaanu Pass
Polle
Totiw
Tsis
Uman
Pisar
Shichiyo Islands
Salat
Salat Pass
Fanan
Ollan
South Pass
Otta Pass
Otta
Uijec
Mesegon
Feneppi
Neoch
Lauvergne Island
Ipis
SCALE 1:1,750,000

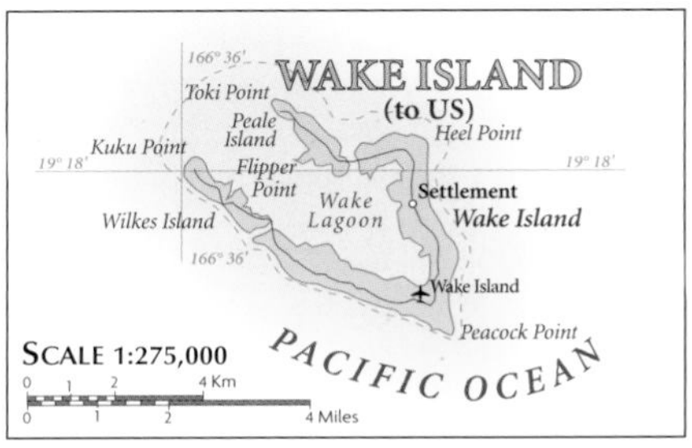
WAKE ISLAND (to US)
Toki Point
Peale Island
Kuku Point
Heel Point
Flipper Point
Wilkes Island
Wake Lagoon
Settlement
Wake Island
Wake Island
Peacock Point
PACIFIC OCEAN
SCALE 1:275,000

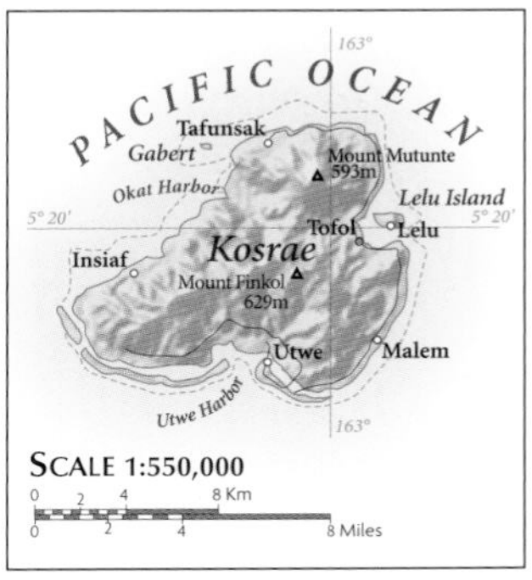
PACIFIC OCEAN
Tafunsak
Gabert
Mount Mutunte 593m
Okat Harbor
Tofol
Lelu Island
Lelu
Insiaf
Kosrae
Mount Finkol 629m
Utwe
Malem
Utwe Harbor
SCALE 1:550,000

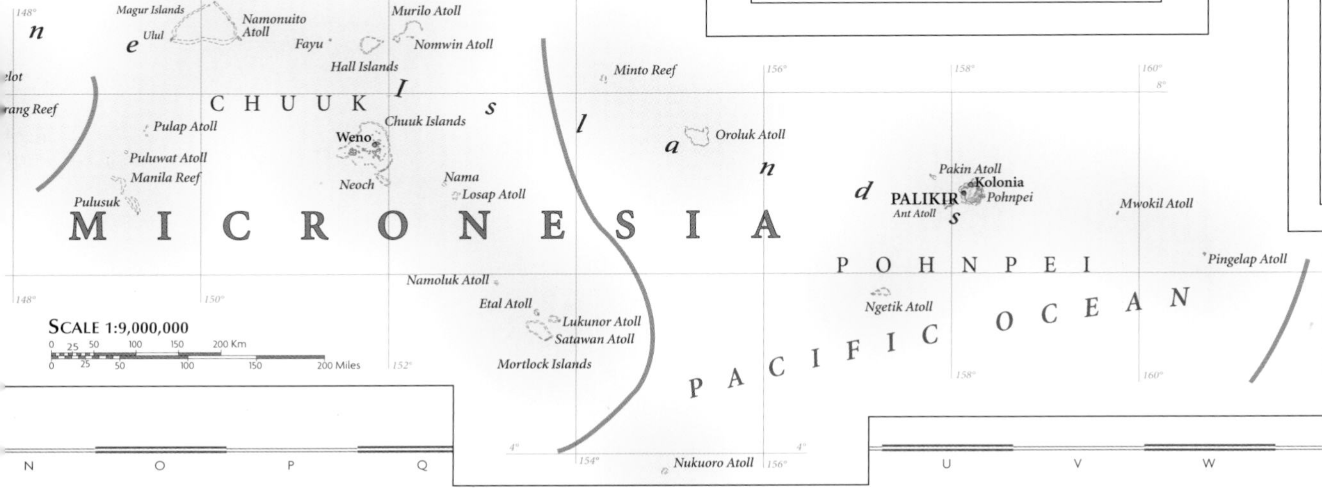
Magur Islands
Ulul
Namonuito Atoll
Fayu
Murilo Atoll
Nomwin Atoll
Hall Islands
Minto Reef
CHUUK
Islands
Chuuk Islands
Pulap Atoll
Weno
Oroluk Atoll
Puluwat Atoll
Manila Reef
Neoch
Nama
Losap Atoll
Pakin Atoll
Kolonia
Pohnpei
PALIKIR
Ant Atoll
Mwokil Atoll
Pulusuk
MICRONESIA
POHNPEI
Pingelap Atoll
Namoluk Atoll
Etal Atoll
Lukunor Atoll
Satawan Atoll
Ngetik Atoll
Mortlock Islands
PACIFIC OCEAN
Kosrae
Tofol
KOSRAE
Nukuoro Atoll
SCALE 1:9,000,000

Polynesia

KIRIBATI, TUVALU, Cook Islands, Easter Island, French Polynesia, Niue, Pitcairn Islands, Tokelau, Wallis & Futuna

The numerous island groups of Polynesia lie to the east of Australia, scattered over a vast area in the south Pacific. The islands are a mixture of low-lying coral atolls, some of which enclose lagoons, and the tips of great underwater volcanoes. The populations on the islands are small, and most people are of Polynesian origin, as are the Maori of New Zealand. Local economies remain simple, relying mainly on subsistence crops, mineral deposits, many now exhausted, fishing, and tourism.

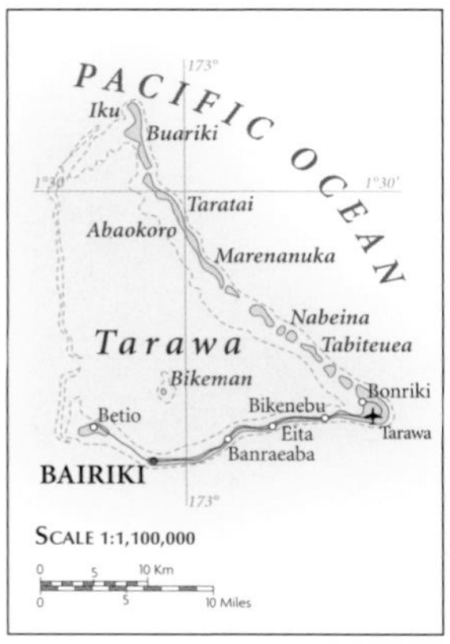
PACIFIC OCEAN
Iku
Buariki
Taratai
Abaokoro
Marenanuka
Nabeina
Tabiteuea
Tarawa
Bikeman
Bonriki
Betio
Bikenebu
Eita
Tarawa
Banraeaba
BAIRIKI
SCALE 1:1,100,000

Kiribati

A former British colony, Kiribati became independent in 1979. Banaba's phosphate deposits ran out in 1980, following decades of exploitation by the British. Economic development remains slow and most agriculture is at a subsistence level, though coconuts provide export income, and underwater agriculture is being developed.

▶ *With the exception of Banaba all the islands in Kiribati's three groups are low-lying, coral atolls. This aerial view shows the sparsely vegetated islands, intercut by many small lagoons.*

Tuvalu

A chain of nine coral atolls, 360 miles (579 km) long with a land area of just over 9 sq miles (23 sq km), Tuvalu is one of the world's smallest and most isolated states. As the Ellice Islands, Tuvalu was linked to the Gilbert Islands (now part of Kiribati) as a British colony until independence in 1978. Politically and socially conservative, Tuvaluans live by fishing and subsistence farming.

▲ ***Funafuti Atoll contains** more than 40% of Tuvalu's people, giving it an extremely high population density.*

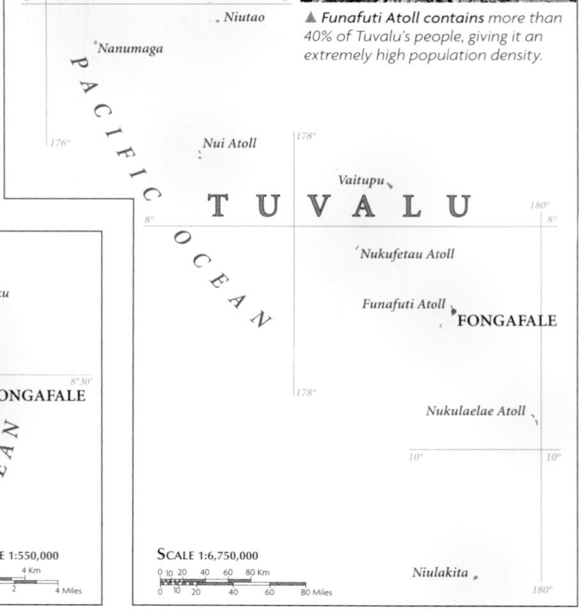
Nanumea Atoll
Niutao
Nanumaga
PACIFIC OCEAN
Nui Atoll
Vaitupu
TUVALU
Nukufetau Atoll
Funafuti Atoll
FONGAFALE
Nukulaelae Atoll
Niulakita
SCALE 1:6,750,000

Fualifeke
Te Ava I Te Lape
Amatuku
Tepuka
Fualopa
Fongafale
Funafuti
Atoll
FONGAFALE
Fuafatu
Funafuti
Te Ava Fuagea
Funangongo
Fatato
Vasafua
Te Ava Pua Pua
Fuagea
Falefatu
Tefala
Funafara
Teafuafou
Telele
PACIFIC OCEAN
SCALE 1:550,000

Tokelau *(to New Zealand)*

A low-lying coral atoll, Tokelau is a dependent territory of New Zealand with few natural resources. Although a 1990 cyclone destroyed crops and infrastructure, a tuna cannery and the sale of fishing licenses have raised revenue and a catamaran link between the islands has increased their tourism potential. Tokelau's small size and economic weakness makes independence from New Zealand unlikely.

▲ ***Fishermen cast their** nets to catch small fish in the shallow waters off Atafu Atoll, the most westerly island in Tokelau.*

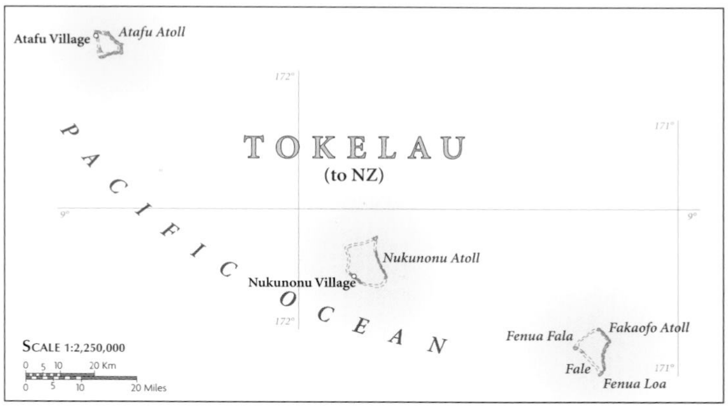
Atafu Village
Atafu Atoll
TOKELAU
(to NZ)
PACIFIC OCEAN
Nukunonu Atoll
Nukunonu Village
Fenua Fala
Fakaofo Atoll
Fale
Fenua Loa
SCALE 1:2,250,000

Wallis & Futuna *(to France)*

In contrast to other French overseas territories in the south Pacific, the inhabitants of Wallis and Futuna have shown little desire for greater autonomy. A subsistence economy produces a variety of tropical crops, while foreign currency remittances come from expatriates and from the sale of licenses to Japanese and Korean fishing fleets.

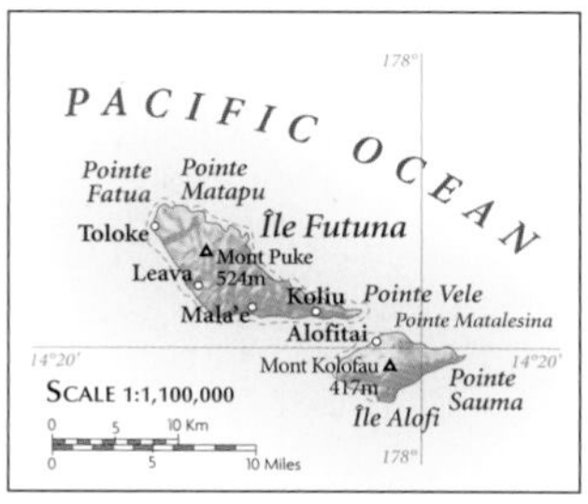
PACIFIC OCEAN
Pointe Fatua
Pointe Matapu
Toloke
Île Futuna
Mont Puke 524m
Leava
Kolia
Pointe Vele
Mala'e
Pointe Matalesina
Alofitai
Mont Kolofau 417m
Pointe Sauma
Île Alofi
SCALE 1:1,100,000

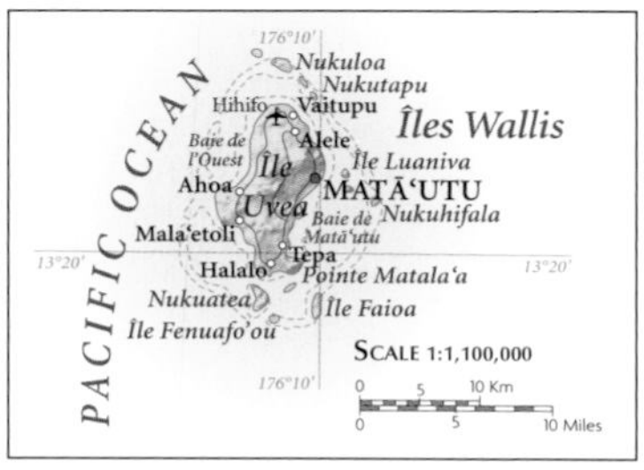
Nukuloa
Nukutapu
Hihifo
Vaitupu
Îles Wallis
Baie de l'Ouest
Alele
Île Luaniva
Ahoa
Île Uvea
MATĀ'UTU
Baie de Matā'utu
Nukuhifala
Mala'etoli
Halalo
Tepa
Pointe Matala'a
Nukuatea
Île Faioa
Île Fenuafo'ou
PACIFIC OCEAN
SCALE 1:1,100,000

Cook Islands *(to New Zealand)*

A mixture of coral atolls and volcanic peaks, the Cook Islands achieved self-government in 1965 but exist in free association with New Zealand. A diverse economy includes pearl and giant clam farming, and an ostrich farm, plus tourism and banking. A 1991 friendship treaty with France provides for French surveillance of territorial waters.

Penrhyn
Rakahanga
Manihiki
Pukapuka
Nassau
Northern Cook Islands
Suwarrow
OCEAN
COOK ISLANDS
(to NZ)
PACIFIC
Palmerston
Southern Cook Islands
Aitutaki
Manuae
Takutea
Mitiaro
Atiu
Mauke
Rarotonga
AVARUA
Mangaia
SCALE 1:22,250,000

▲ ***Palm trees fringe** the white sands of a beach on Aitutaki in the Southern Cook Islands, where tourism is of increasing economic importance.*

Niue *(to New Zealand)*

Niue, the world's largest coral island, is self-governing but exists in free association with New Zealand. Tropical fruits are grown for local consumption; tourism and the sale of postage stamps provide foreign currency. The lack of local job prospects has led more than 10,000 Niueans to emigrate to New Zealand, which has now invested heavily in Niue's economy in the hope of reversing this trend.

Hikutavake
Toi
Mutalau
Makefu
Tuapa
Makapu Point
Lakepa
Alofi Bay
ALOFI
NIUE
(to NZ)
Liku
Halagigie Point
Hanan
Tamakautoga
Avatele
Hakupu
Tepa Point
Mata Point
PACIFIC OCEAN
SCALE 1:1,100,000

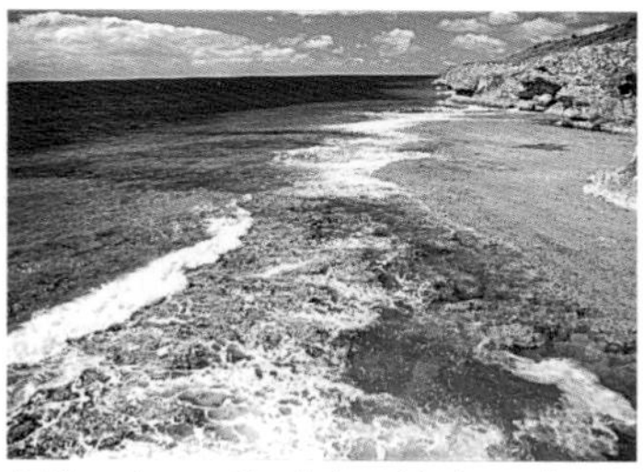

▲ ***Waves have cut** back the original coastline, exposing a sandy beach, near Mutalau in the northeast corner of Niue.*

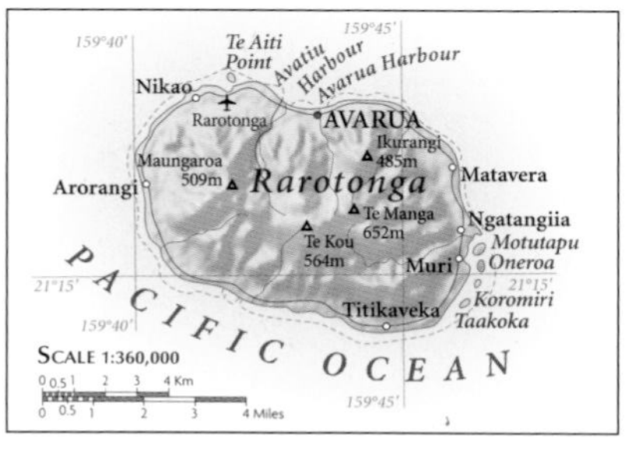
Te Aiti Point
Avatiu Harbour
Avarua Harbour
Nikao
Rarotonga
AVARUA
Ikurangi 485m
Maungaroa 509m
Rarotonga
Matavera
Arorangi
Te Manga 652m
Te Kou 564m
Ngatangiia
Motutapu
Oneroa
Muri
Koromiri
Titikaveka
Taakoka
PACIFIC OCEAN
SCALE 1:360,000

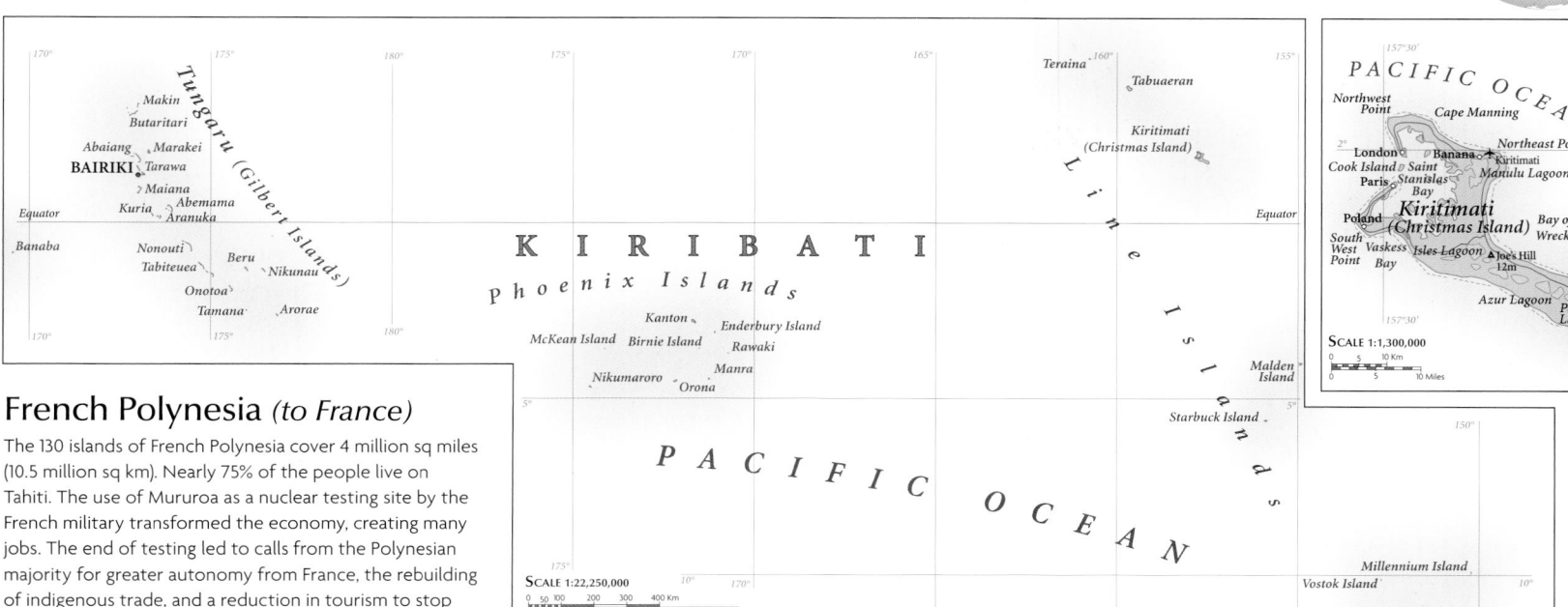

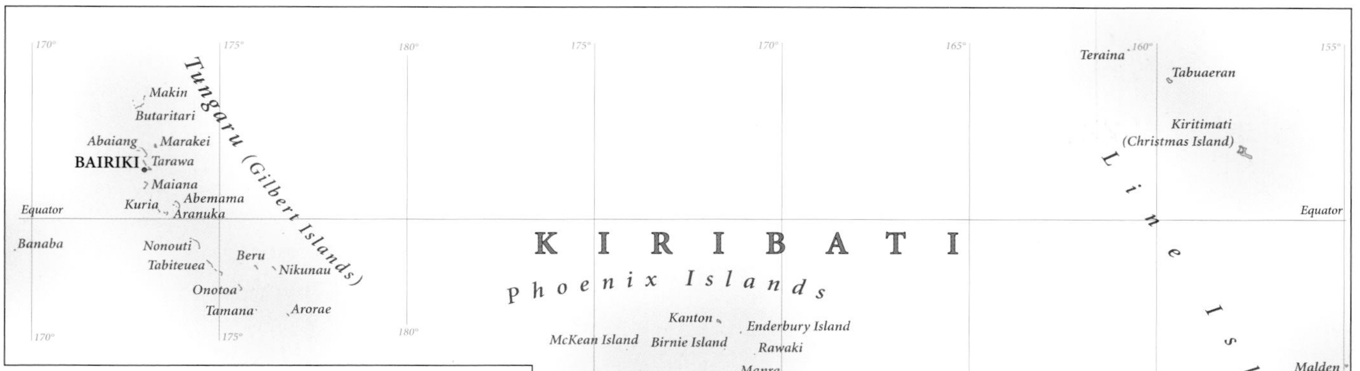
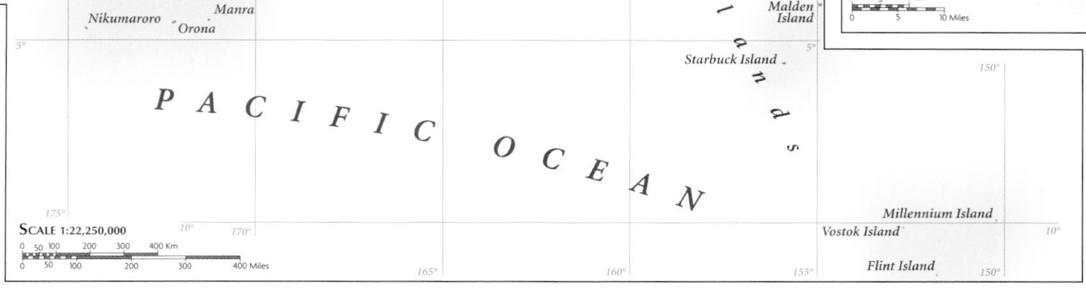
Tungaru (Gilbert Islands)
Makin
Butaritari
Abaiang
Marakei
BAIRIKI
Tarawa
Maiana
Kuria
Abemama
Aranuka
Equator
Banaba
Nonouti
Tabiteuea
Beru
Nikunau
Onotoa
Tamana
Arorae
KIRIBATI
Phoenix Islands
Kanton
Enderbury Island
McKean Island
Birnie Island
Rawaki
Manra
Nikumaroro
Orona
Teraina
Tabuaeran
Kiritimati (Christmas Island)
Line Islands
Malden Island
Starbuck Island
PACIFIC OCEAN
Millennium Island
Vostok Island
Flint Island
SCALE 1:22,250,000

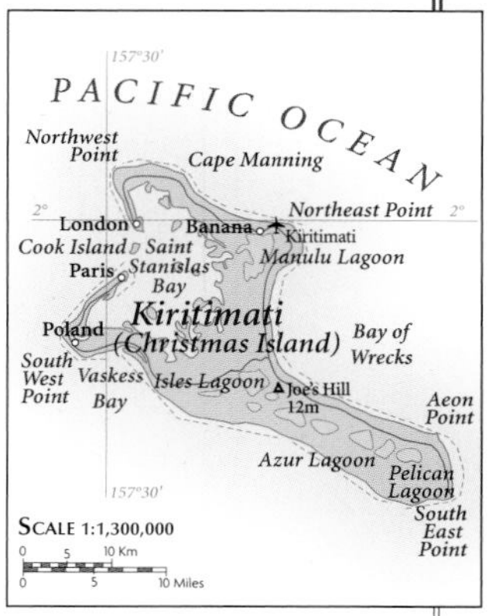
PACIFIC OCEAN
Northwest Point
Cape Manning
Northeast Point
London
Cook Island
Banana
Kiritimati
Saint Stanislas Bay
Paris
Manulu Lagoon
Poland
Kiritimati (Christmas Island)
Bay of Wrecks
South West Point
Vaskess Bay
Isles Lagoon
Joe's Hill 12m
Aeon Point
Azur Lagoon
Pelican Lagoon
South East Point
SCALE 1:1,300,000

French Polynesia *(to France)*

The 130 islands of French Polynesia cover 4 million sq miles (10.5 million sq km). Nearly 75% of the people live on Tahiti. The use of Mururoa as a nuclear testing site by the French military transformed the economy, creating many jobs. The end of testing led to calls from the Polynesian majority for greater autonomy from France, the rebuilding of indigenous trade, and a reduction in tourism to stop the erosion of the islands' traditional culture.

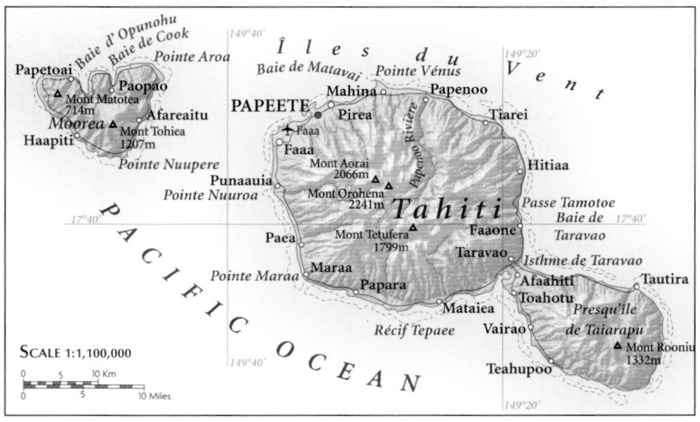
Baie d'Opunohu
Baie de Cook
Pointe Aroa
Papetoai
Paopao
Mont Matotea 714m
Moorea
Afareaitu
Mont Tohiea 1207m
Haapiti
Pointe Nuupere
Îles du Vent
Baie de Matavai
Pointe Vénus
Mahina
Papenoo
PAPEETE
Pirea
Tiarei
Faaa
Hitiaa
Punaauia
Pointe Nuuroa
Mont Aorai 2066m
Mont Orohena 2241m
Tahiti
Mont Tetufera 1799m
Passe Tamotoe
Baie de Taravao
Paea
Faaone
Taravao
Isthme de Taravao
Pointe Maraa
Maraa
Papara
Afaahiti
Toahotu
Tautira
Presqu'île de Taiarapu
Mataiea
Vairao
Récif Tepaee
Mont Rooniu 1332m
Teahupoo
PACIFIC OCEAN
SCALE 1:1,100,000

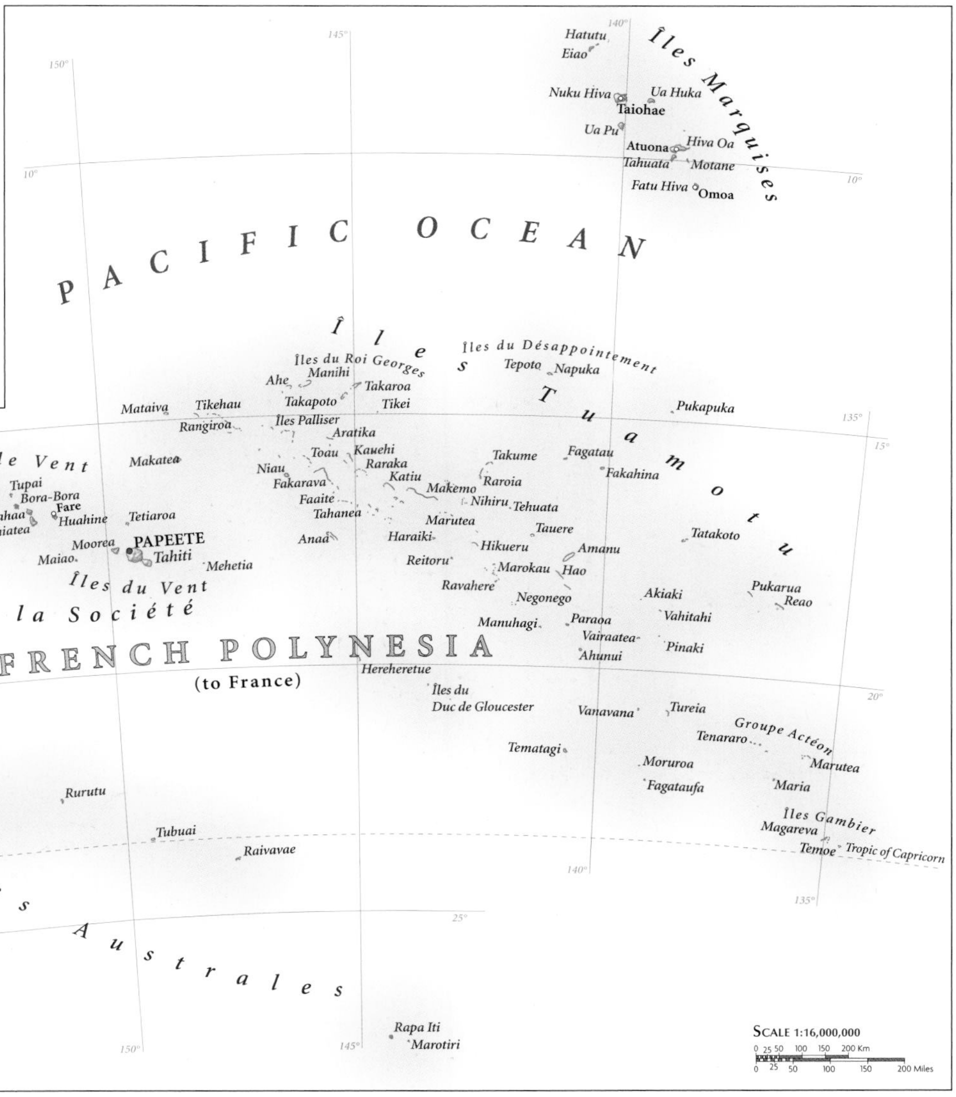
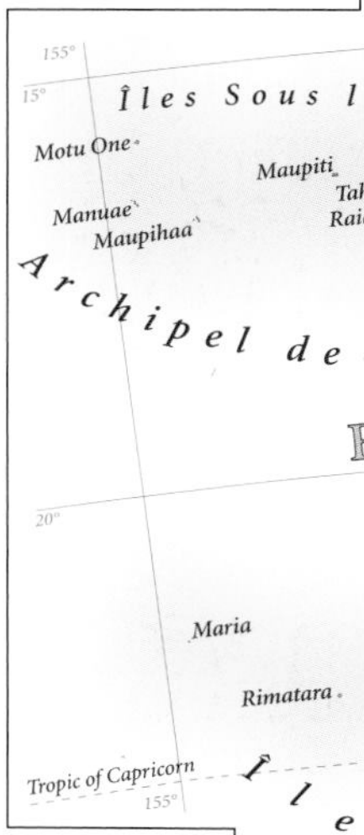
Hatutu
Eiao
Îles Marquises
Nuku Hiva
Ua Huka
Taiohae
Ua Pu
Hiva Oa
Atuona
Tahuata
Motane
Fatu Hiva
Omoa
PACIFIC OCEAN
Îles Tuamotu
Îles du Roi Georges
Manihi
Ahe
Takaroa
Takapoto
Tikei
Îles du Désappointement
Tepoto
Napuka
Pukapuka
Mataiva
Tikehau
Rangiroa
Îles Palliser
Aratika
Toau
Kauehi
Raraka
Katiu
Niau
Fakarava
Faaite
Tahanea
Anaa
Makemo
Takume
Raroia
Nihiru
Tehuata
Marutea
Fagatau
Fakahina
Îles Sous le Vent
Motu One
Tupai
Maupiti
Bora-Bora
Tahaa
Fare
Huahine
Raiatea
Manuae
Maupihaa
Makatea
Tetiaroa
Moorea
PAPEETE
Tahiti
Maiao
Mehetia
Îles du Vent
Archipel de la Société
Haraiki
Reitoru
Hikueru
Marokau
Tauere
Amanu
Hao
Tatakoto
Ravahere
Nengonego
Manuhagi
Paraoa
Vairaatea
Ahunui
Akiaki
Vahitahi
Pukarua
Reao
Pinaki
FRENCH POLYNESIA (to France)
Hereheretue
Îles du Duc de Gloucester
Vanavana
Tureia
Groupe Actéon
Tenararo
Marutea
Tematagi
Moruroa
Fagataufa
Maria
Îles Gambier
Magareva
Temoe
Maria
Rimatara
Rurutu
Tubuai
Raivavae
Tropic of Capricorn
Îles Australes
Rapa Iti
Marotiri
SCALE 1:16,000,000

◀ *The traditional Tahitian welcome for visitors, who are greeted by parties of canoes, has become a major tourist attraction.*

Pitcairn Islands *(to UK)*

Britain's most isolated dependency, Pitcairn Island was first populated by mutineers from the HMS *Bounty* in 1790. Emigration is further depleting the already limited gene pool of the island's inhabitants, with associated social and health problems. Barter, fishing, and subsistence farming form the basis of the economy although postage stamp sales provide foreign currency earnings, and offshore mineral exploitation may boost the economy in future.

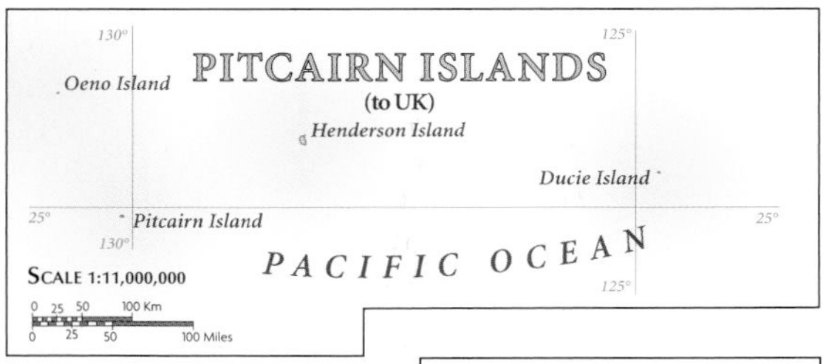
Oeno Island
PITCAIRN ISLANDS (to UK)
Henderson Island
Ducie Island
Pitcairn Island
PACIFIC OCEAN
SCALE 1:11,000,000

◀ **The Pitcairn Islanders** *rely on regular airdrops from New Zealand and periodic visits by supply vessels to provide them with basic commodities.*

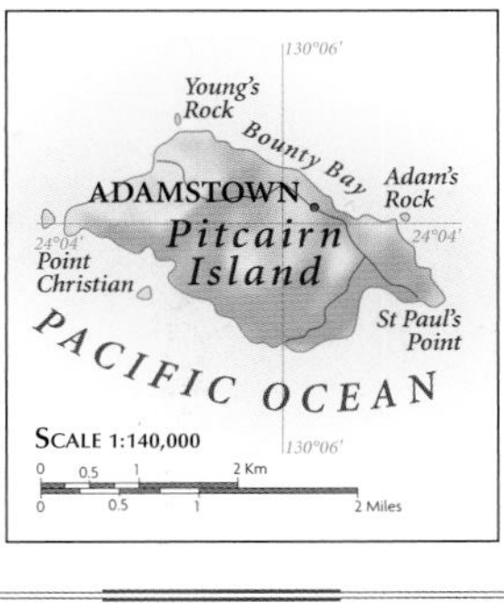
Young's Rock
Bounty Bay
Adam's Rock
ADAMSTOWN
Pitcairn Island
Point Christian
St Paul's Point
PACIFIC OCEAN
SCALE 1:140,000

Easter Island *(to Chile)*

One of the most easterly islands in Polynesia, Easter Island *(Isla de Pascua)* – also known as Rapa Nui, is part of Chile. The mainly Polynesian inhabitants support themselves by farming, which is mainly of a subsistence nature, and includes cattle rearing and crops such as sugar cane, bananas, corn, gourds, and potatoes. In recent years, tourism has become the most important source of income and the island sustains a small commercial airport.

Easter Island (Isla de Pascua) (to Chile)
Punta San Juan
Playa de Anakena
Cabo Norte
Punta Rosalia
Bahía de La Pérouse
Cabo O'Higgins
Maunga Terevaka 506m
Naunau
Maunga Pukatikei 370m
Ahu Tepeu
Motu Tautara
Ahu Akivi
Rano Raraku
Cabo Roggewein
Hanga Roa
Maunga Tangaroa 270m
Vaihu
Punta Akahanga
Punta Cuidado
Mataveri
Ahu Vinapu
Punta Baja
Rano Kau
Orongo
Cabo Sur
Motu Nui
PACIFIC OCEAN
SCALE 1:550,000

▲ **The Naunau,** *a series of huge stone statues overlook Playa de Anakena, on Easter Island. Carved from a soft volcanic rock, they were erected between 400 and 900 years ago.*

The Pacific Ocean

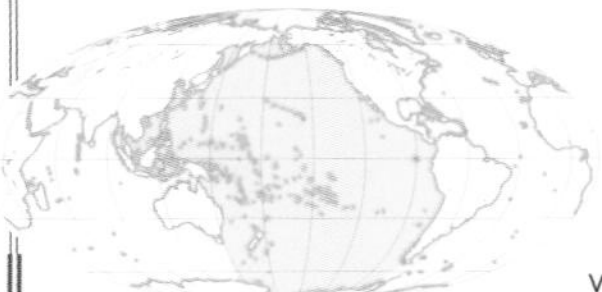

The Pacific is the world's largest and deepest ocean. It is nearly twice the area of the Atlantic and contains almost three times as much water. The ocean is dotted with islands and surrounded by some of the world's most populous states; over half the world's population lives on its shores. The Pacific is bordered by active plate margins known as the "Ring of Fire," causing earthquakes and tsunamis, and creating volcanic islands and subterranean mountain chains. The largest underwater mountains break the surface as island arcs. The fisheries of the Pacific are some of the most productive in the world and provide a vital resource for many of the Pacific islands. Since the Second World War there has been a shift in trading patterns, with a considerable growth in trade between the US and the countries of the Pacific Rim.

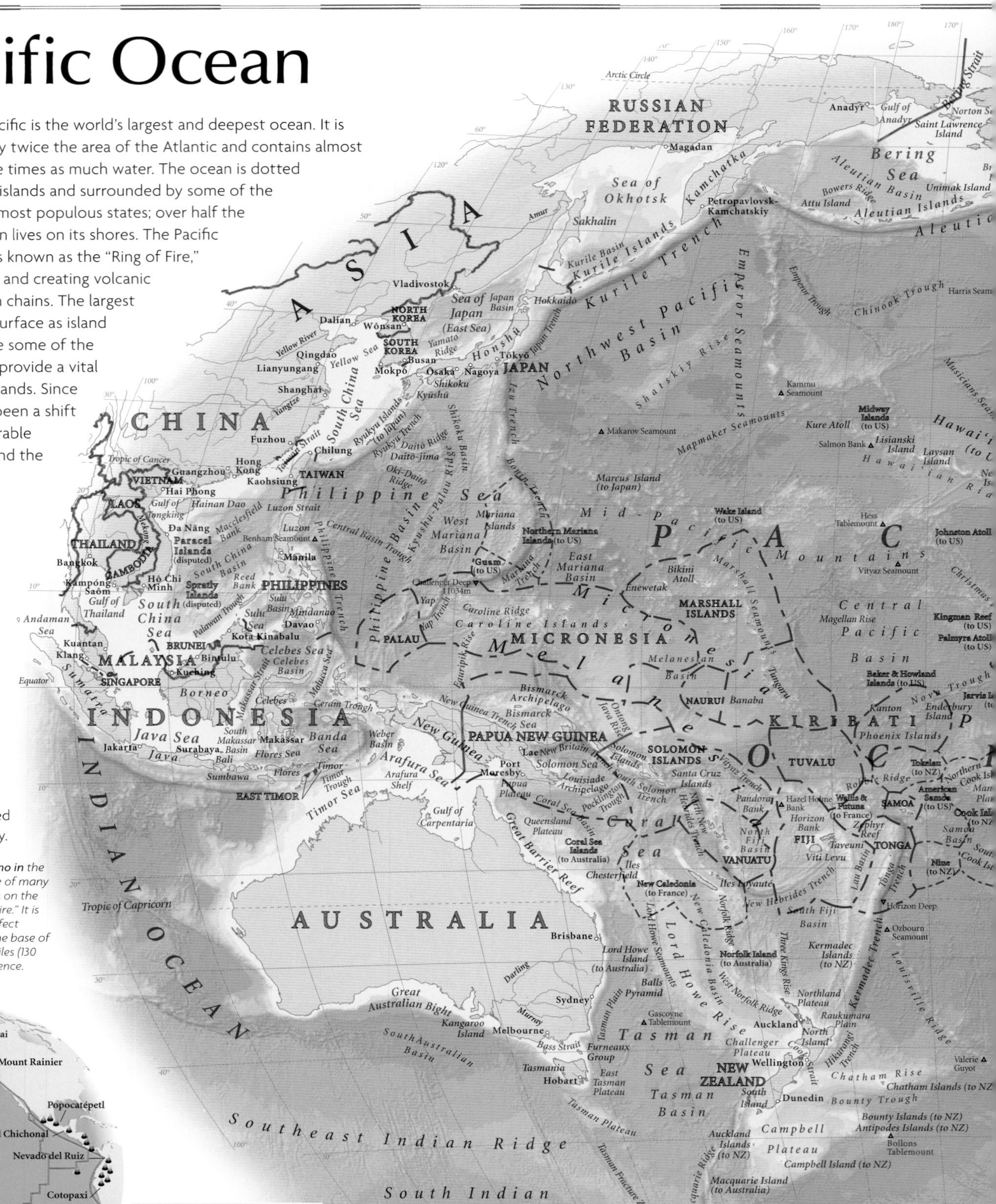

RUSSIAN FEDERATION
Arctic Circle
Magadan
Sea of Okhotsk
Kamchatka
Petropavlovsk-Kamchatskiy
Sakhalin
Amur
Anadyr
Gulf of Anadyr
Bering Strait
Saint Lawrence Island
Bering Sea
Aleutian Basin
Attu Island
Unimak Island
Aleutian Islands
ASIA
Vladivostok
Kurile Basin
Kurile Islands
Kurile Trench
Hokkaido
Sea of Japan (East Sea)
Japan Basin
Dalian
NORTH KOREA
Wŏnsan
SOUTH KOREA
Busan
Yamato Ridge
Honshu
Tokyo
JAPAN
Nagoya
Osaka
Mokpo
Shikoku
Kyushu
Qingdao
Yellow Sea
Yellow River
Lianyungang
Shanghai
Yangtze
CHINA
East China Sea
Fuzhou
Taiwan Strait
Chilung
TAIWAN
Kaohsiung
Hong Kong
Guangzhou
Tropic of Cancer
VIETNAM
Hai Phong
Hainan Dao
Gulf of Tongking
LAOS
Luzon Strait
Philippine Sea
THAILAND
Bangkok
CAMBODIA
Đa Nẵng
Paracel Islands (disputed)
Macclesfield Bank
Luzon
Manila
Benham Seamount
Hồ Chi Minh
Kampong Saôm
Gulf of Thailand
Spratly Islands (disputed)
South China Sea
Reed Bank
PHILIPPINES
Sulu Sea
Mindanao
Davao
Celebes Sea
Kota Kinabalu
BRUNEI
Kuantan
Klang
MALAYSIA
Bintulu
Kuching
SINGAPORE
Andaman Sea
Equator
Sumatra
Borneo
Celebes
Makassar Strait
INDONESIA
Java Sea
Jakarta
Java
Surabaya
Bali
Sumbawa
Flores
Flores Sea
Banda Sea
Timor
Timor Sea
Timor Trough
EAST TIMOR
Arafura Sea
Arafura Shelf
Weber Basin
New Guinea
PAPUA NEW GUINEA
Port Moresby
Gulf of Carpentaria
Coral Sea
Coral Sea Islands (to Australia)
Queensland Plateau
Great Barrier Reef
AUSTRALIA
Tropic of Capricorn
Brisbane
Sydney
Darling
Murray
Melbourne
Bass Strait
Kangaroo Island
Great Australian Bight
South Australian Basin
Tasmania
Hobart
INDIAN OCEAN
Southeast Indian Ridge
South Indian Basin
Tasman Sea
Tasman Basin
Tasman Plateau
Lord Howe Island (to Australia)
Lord Howe Rise
Norfolk Island (to Australia)
NEW ZEALAND
Auckland
Wellington
North Island
South Island
Dunedin
Chatham Rise
Chatham Islands (to NZ)
Campbell Plateau
Campbell Island (to NZ)
Auckland Islands (to NZ)
Macquarie Island (to Australia)
Bounty Islands (to NZ)
Antipodes Islands (to NZ)
Kermadec Islands (to NZ)
Kermadec Trench
New Caledonia (to France)
VANUATU
FIJI
TONGA
SAMOA
American Samoa (to US)
Wallis & Futuna (to France)
Niue (to NZ)
SOLOMON ISLANDS
Solomon Sea
NAURU
TUVALU
KIRIBATI
Phoenix Islands
Tokelau (to NZ)
Cook Islands
MARSHALL ISLANDS
MICRONESIA
PALAU
Guam (to US)
Northern Mariana Islands (to US)
Mariana Trench
Challenger Deep 11034m
Wake Island (to US)
Marcus Island (to Japan)
Micronesia
Melanesia
Melanesian Basin
Caroline Islands
Bismarck Archipelago
Northwest Pacific Basin
Emperor Seamounts
Shatsky Rise
Izu Trench
Bonin Trench
Mid-Pacific Mountains
PACIFIC
Central Pacific Basin
Midway Islands (to US)
Kure Atoll
Hawaiian Ridge
Johnston Atoll (to US)
Kingman Reef (to US)
Palmyra Atoll (to US)
Jarvis Island
Baker & Howland Islands (to US)
SOUTHERN
Pacific-Antarctic
Antarctic Circle
Balleny Islands (to NZ)
Scott Island (to NZ)
Ross Sea
ANTAR

The Ring of Fire

The active plate margins surrounding the Pacific have created numerous land and island volcanoes along its border. The actual basin of the Pacific is made up of a number of separate tectonic plates which move away from each other, colliding with other plates. When they collide, the oceanic plates, being thinner, are forced beneath the thicker continental plates, forming deep ocean trenches and high ridges. These collision zones are known as subduction zones and are characterized by intense seismic and volcanic activity.

◀ *Mayon Volcano in the Philippines is one of many active volcanoes on the Pacific "Ring of Fire." It is noted for its perfect conical shape; the base of the cone is 80 miles (130 km) in circumference.*

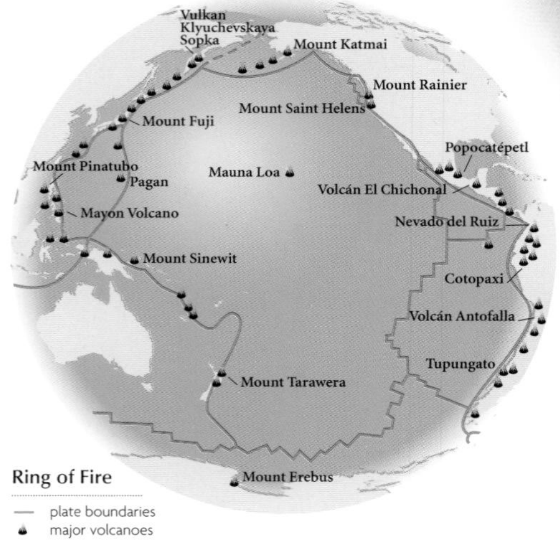

Vulkan Klyuchevskaya Sopka
Mount Katmai
Mount Rainier
Mount Saint Helens
Mount Fuji
Popocatépetl
Mount Pinatubo
Pagan
Mauna Loa
Volcán El Chichonal
Mayon Volcano
Nevado del Ruiz
Mount Sinewit
Cotopaxi
Volcán Antofalla
Tupungato
Mount Tarawera
Mount Erebus
Ring of Fire
plate boundaries
major volcanoes

◀ *The Hawai'ian volcanoes lie in the center of a plate, not on a plate margin, and are known as intraplate volcanoes. They are associated with hot spots, whereby a plume of hot molten rock rises to the surface as the plate moves over it.*

American Samoa and Samoa

American Samoa and Samoa are part of the island archipelago of Polynesia. The two most populous islands are Tutuila in American Samoa and 'Upolu in Samoa. Although the economies of both these states remain predominantly resource-based, both are expanding their light manufacturing sectors, and the US administration is the primary employer in American Samoa. Tuna fishing is particularly important: 25% of all tuna consumed in the US is processed and canned in Pago Pago.

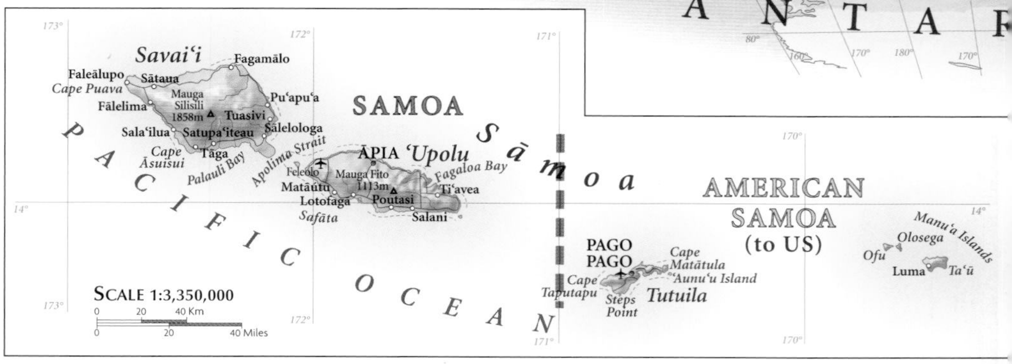

Savai'i
Fagamālo
Falealupo
Cape Puava
Sātaua
Fālelima
Mauga Silisili 1858m
Tuasivi
Pu'apu'a
SAMOA
Sala'ilua
Satupa'itea
Salelologa
Cape Āsuisui
Tāga
Palauli Bay
Apolima Strait
ĀPIA
'Upolu
Fagaloa Bay
Falelo
Mauga Fito 1113m
Matāutu
Lotofaga
Poutasi
Ti'avea
Sāfata
Salani
Sāmoa
PACIFIC OCEAN
AMERICAN SAMOA (to US)
PAGO PAGO
Cape Taputapu
Cape Matātula
Aunu'u Island
Tutuila
Steps Point
Manu'a Islands
Olosega
Ofu
Luma
Ta'ū
SCALE 1:3,350,000
20
40 Km
40 Miles

► *Many of the buildings in Samoa reflect the country's colonial past. Once a colony of New Zealand, Samoa is now an independent state; American Samoa remains an unincorporated territory of the United States.*

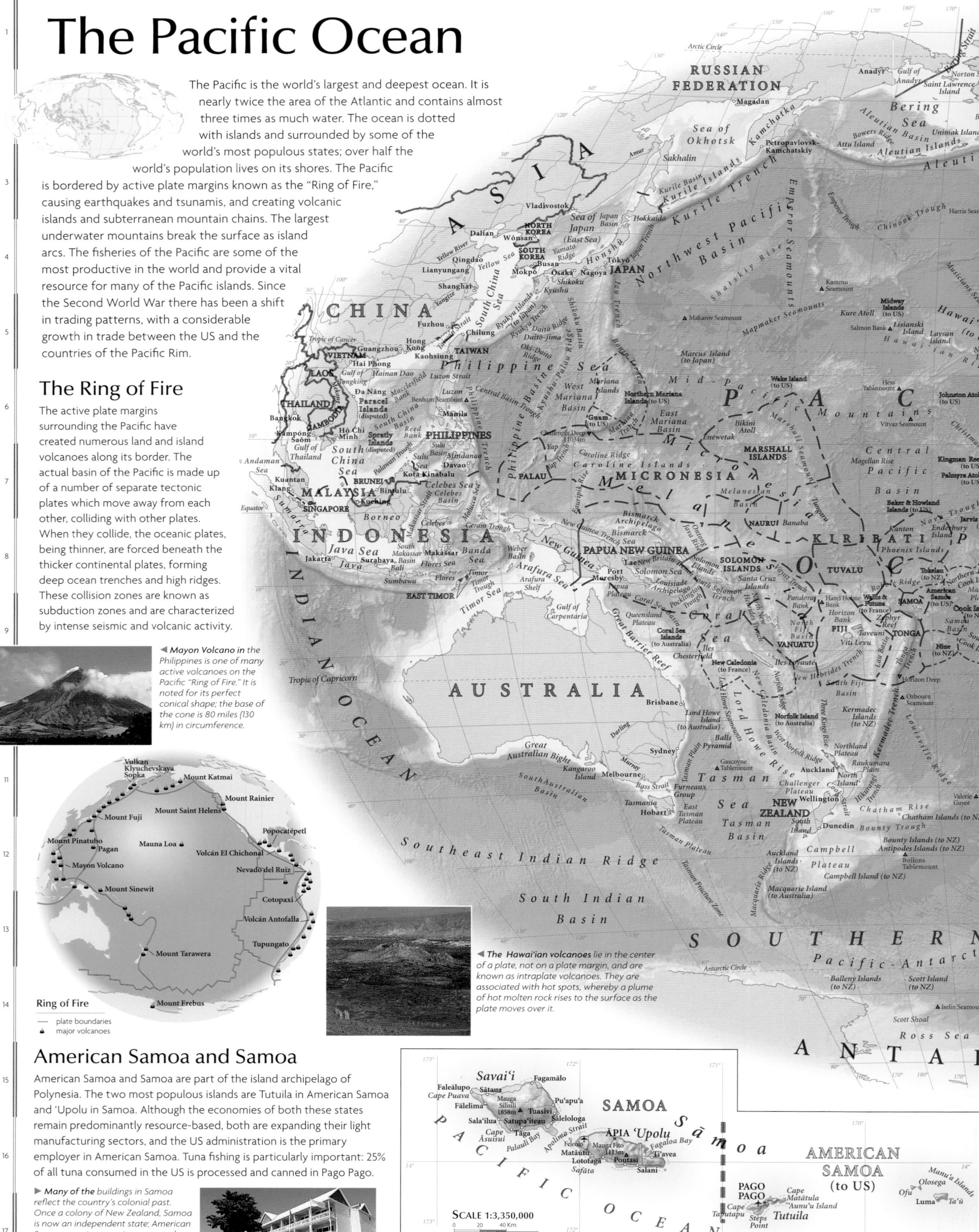

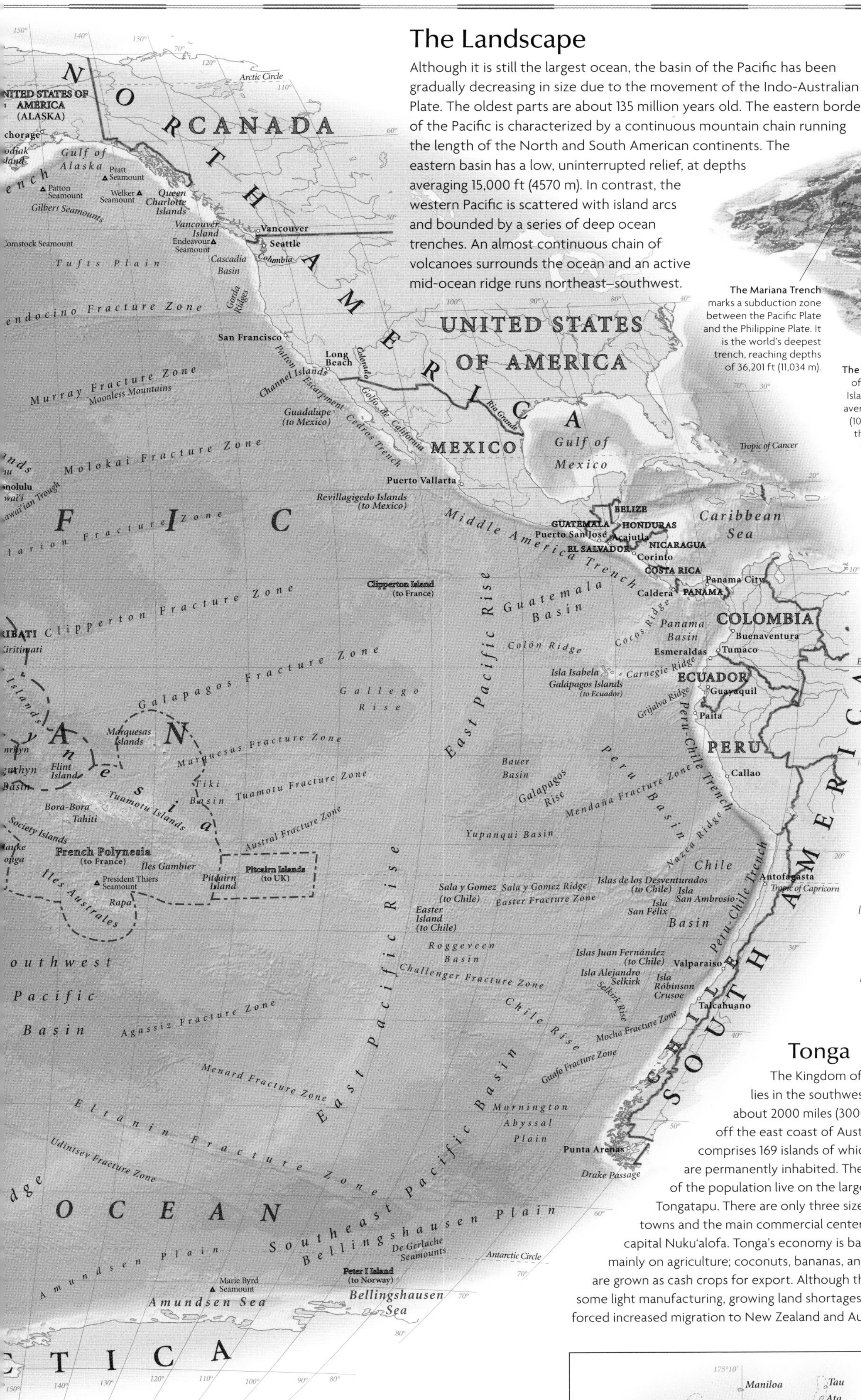
CANADA
UNITED STATES OF AMERICA (ALASKA)
Gulf of Alaska
Pratt Seamount
Patton Seamount
Welker Seamount
Queen Charlotte Islands
Gilbert Seamounts
Vancouver Island
Vancouver
Seattle
Endeavour Seamount
Comstock Seamount
Tufts Plain
Cascadia Basin
Columbia
Gorda Ridge
Mendocino Fracture Zone
San Francisco
UNITED STATES OF AMERICA
NORTH AMERICA
Long Beach
Colorado
Rio Grande
Patton Escarpment
Channel Islands
Murray Fracture Zone
Moonless Mountains
Guadalupe (to Mexico)
Cedros Trench
Golfo de California
MEXICO
Gulf of Mexico
Tropic of Cancer
Molokai Fracture Zone
Puerto Vallarta
Revillagigedo Islands (to Mexico)
Hawaiian Trough
Honolulu
PACIFIC
Clarion Fracture Zone
Middle America Trench
BELIZE
GUATEMALA
HONDURAS
Puerto San José
Acajutla
EL SALVADOR
NICARAGUA
Corinto
COSTA RICA
Caribbean Sea
Clipperton Island (to France)
Panama City
PANAMA
Caldera
Clipperton Fracture Zone
Guatemala Basin
Cocos Ridge
Panama Basin
COLOMBIA
Buenaventura
Tumaco
Esmeraldas
KIRIBATI
Kiritimati
Colón Ridge
East Pacific Rise
Galapagos Fracture Zone
Isla Isabela
Galápagos Islands (to Ecuador)
Carnegie Ridge
ECUADOR
Equator
Guayaquil
Gallego Rise
Grijalva Ridge
Paita
Peru-Chile Trench
Marquesas Islands
Marquesas Fracture Zone
PERU
Flint Island
Bauer Basin
Peru Basin
Callao
Tiki Basin
Tuamotu Fracture Zone
Galapagos Rise
Mendaña Fracture Zone
Tuamotu Islands
Bora-Bora
Tahiti
Society Islands
Austral Fracture Zone
Nazca Ridge
SOUTH AMERICA
French Polynesia (to France)
Îles Gambier
Yupanqui Basin
Chile Basin
President Thiers Seamount
Pitcairn Island
Pitcairn Islands (to UK)
Sala y Gomez (to Chile)
Sala y Gomez Ridge
Easter Fracture Zone
Islas de los Desventurados (to Chile)
Isla San Félix
Isla San Ambrosio
Antofagasta
Tropic of Capricorn
Rapa
Îles Australes
Easter Island (to Chile)
Roggeveen Basin
Islas Juan Fernández (to Chile)
Valparaíso
Isla Alejandro Selkirk
Isla Róbinson Crusoe
Southwest Pacific Basin
Challenger Fracture Zone
Selkirk Rise
Chile Rise
Talcahuano
Agassiz Fracture Zone
Mocha Fracture Zone
CHILE
Guafo Fracture Zone
Menard Fracture Zone
Eltanin Fracture Zone
Mornington Abyssal Plain
Udintsev Fracture Zone
Punta Arenas
Drake Passage
Southeast Pacific Basin
Bellingshausen Plain
OCEAN
De Gerlache Seamounts
Antarctic Circle
Amundsen Plain
Peter I Island (to Norway)
Marie Byrd Seamount
Bellingshausen Sea
Amundsen Sea
ANTARCTICA

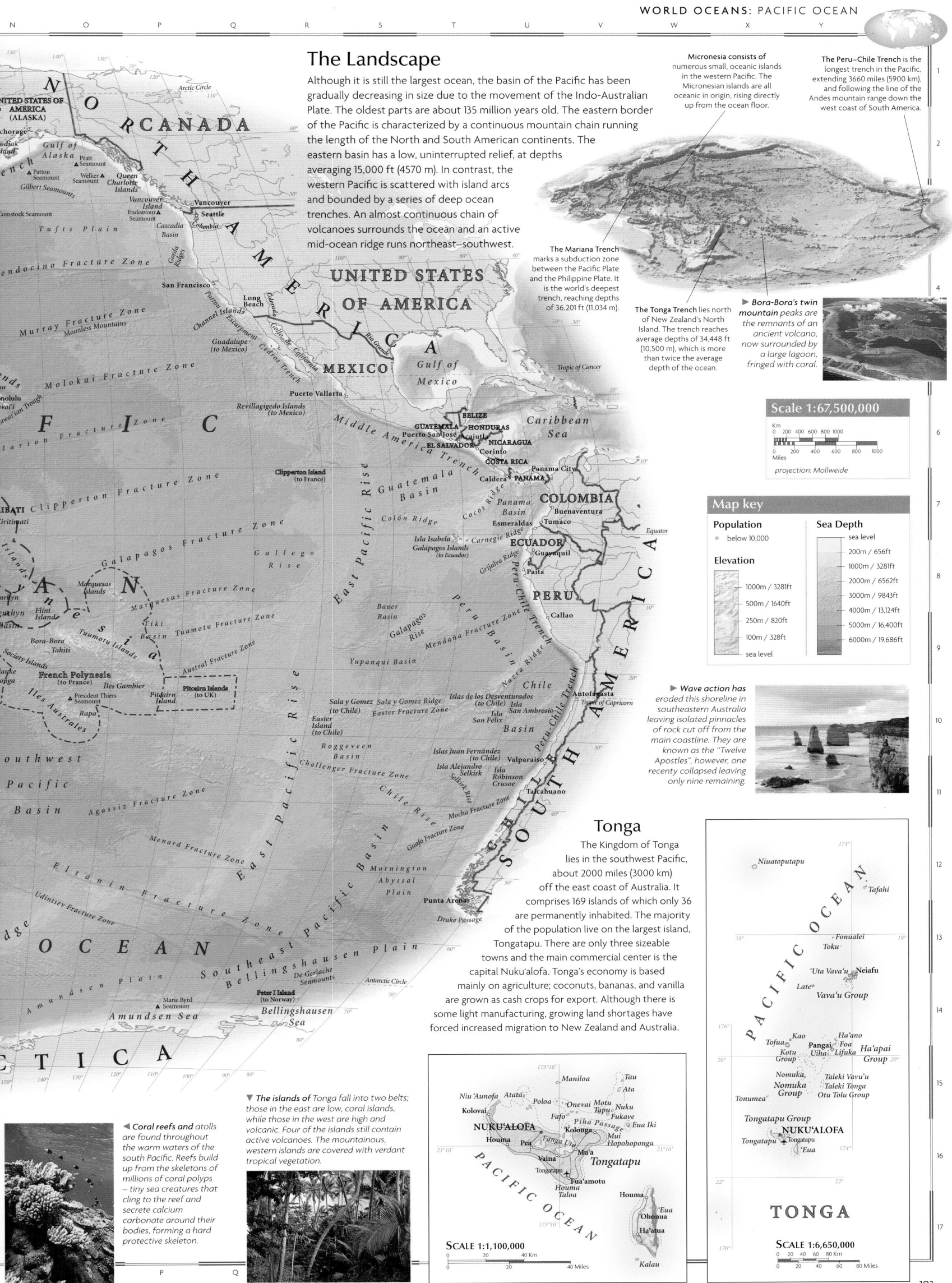

The Landscape

Although it is still the largest ocean, the basin of the Pacific has been gradually decreasing in size due to the movement of the Indo-Australian Plate. The oldest parts are about 135 million years old. The eastern border of the Pacific is characterized by a continuous mountain chain running the length of the North and South American continents. The eastern basin has a low, uninterrupted relief, at depths averaging 15,000 ft (4570 m). In contrast, the western Pacific is scattered with island arcs and bounded by a series of deep ocean trenches. An almost continuous chain of volcanoes surrounds the ocean and an active mid-ocean ridge runs northeast–southwest.

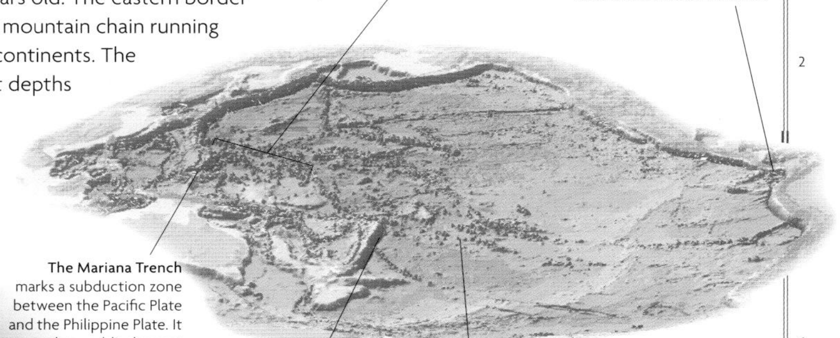

Micronesia consists of numerous small, oceanic islands in the western Pacific. The Micronesian islands are all oceanic in origin, rising directly up from the ocean floor.

The Peru–Chile Trench is the longest trench in the Pacific, extending 3660 miles (5900 km), and following the line of the Andes mountain range down the west coast of South America.

The Mariana Trench marks a subduction zone between the Pacific Plate and the Philippine Plate. It is the world's deepest trench, reaching depths of 36,201 ft (11,034 m).

The Tonga Trench lies north of New Zealand's North Island. The trench reaches average depths of 34,448 ft (10,500 m), which is more than twice the average depth of the ocean.

► ***Bora-Bora's twin mountain** peaks are the remnants of an ancient volcano, now surrounded by a large lagoon, fringed with coral.*

Scale 1:67,500,000

Km 0 200 400 600 800 1000

0 200 400 600 800 1000 Miles

projection: Mollweide

Map key

Population
- below 10,000

Elevation
- 1000m / 3281ft
- 500m / 1640ft
- 250m / 820ft
- 100m / 328ft
- sea level

Sea Depth
- sea level
- 200m / 656ft
- 1000m / 3281ft
- 2000m / 6562ft
- 3000m / 9843ft
- 4000m / 13,124ft
- 5000m / 16,400ft
- 6000m / 19,686ft

► ***Wave action has** eroded this shoreline in southeastern Australia leaving isolated pinnacles of rock cut off from the main coastline. They are known as the "Twelve Apostles", however, one recently collapsed leaving only nine remaining.*

Tonga

The Kingdom of Tonga lies in the southwest Pacific, about 2000 miles (3000 km) off the east coast of Australia. It comprises 169 islands of which only 36 are permanently inhabited. The majority of the population live on the largest island, Tongatapu. There are only three sizeable towns and the main commercial center is the capital Nuku'alofa. Tonga's economy is based mainly on agriculture; coconuts, bananas, and vanilla are grown as cash crops for export. Although there is some light manufacturing, growing land shortages have forced increased migration to New Zealand and Australia.

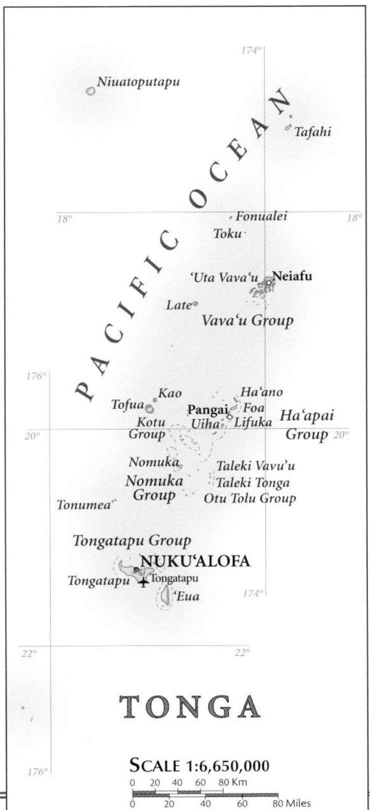
Niuatoputapu
Tafahi
PACIFIC OCEAN
Fonualei
Toku
'Uta Vava'u
Neiafu
Late
Vava'u Group
Kao
Tofua
Ha'ano
Foa
Pangai
Lifuka
Kotu Group
Uiha
Ha'apai Group
Nomuka
Nomuka Group
Taleki Vavu'u
Taleki Tonga
Otu Tolu Group
Tonumea
Tongatapu Group
NUKU'ALOFA
Tongatapu
'Eua
TONGA
SCALE 1:6,650,000
0 20 40 60 80 Km
0 20 40 60 80 Miles

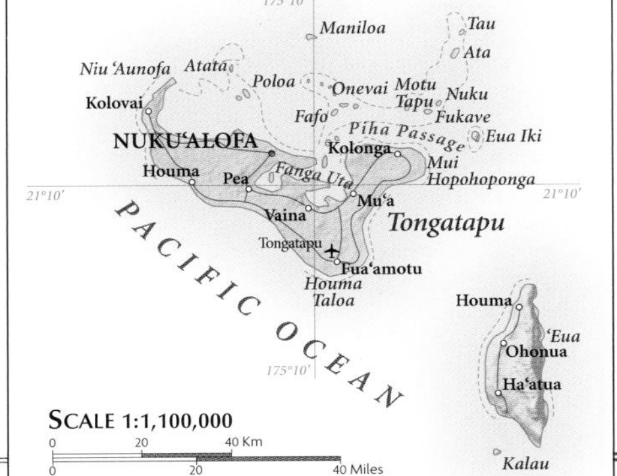
Maniloa
Tau
Ata
Niu 'Aunofa
Atata
Kolovai
Poloa
Onevai
Motu Tapu
Nuku
Fukave
Fafa
Piha Passage
Eua Iki
NUKU'ALOFA
Kolonga
Houma
Pea
Fanga Uta
Mui Hopohoponga
Vaina
Mu'a
Tongatapu
Fua'amotu
Houma Taloa
PACIFIC OCEAN
Houma
'Eua
Ohonua
Ha'atua
Kalau
SCALE 1:1,100,000
0 20 40 Km
0 20 40 Miles

◄ ***Coral reefs** and atolls are found throughout the warm waters of the south Pacific. Reefs build up from the skeletons of millions of coral polyps – tiny sea creatures that cling to the reef and secrete calcium carbonate around their bodies, forming a hard protective skeleton.*

▼ ***The islands of** Tonga fall into two belts; those in the east are low, coral islands, while those in the west are high and volcanic. Four of the islands still contain active volcanoes. The mountainous, western islands are covered with verdant tropical vegetation.*

Antarctica

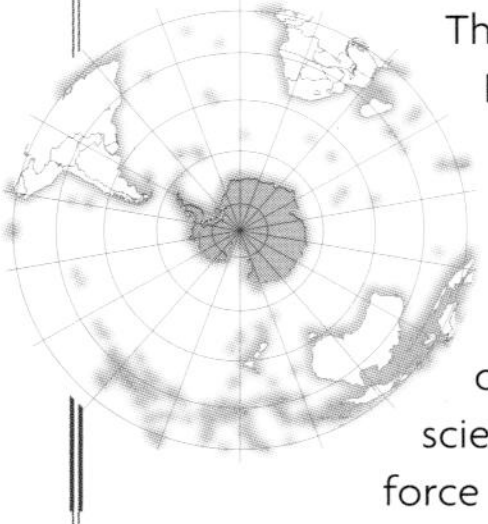

The ice-covered continent of Antarctica, which is the Earth's most southerly region, has drawn explorers and entrepreneurs seeking challenge and riches in its wintry lands for over 200 years. The extreme climate has deterred any large-scale settlement of the continent, and though commercial hunters built outposts in the past, habitation is now limited to scientific bases. The Antarctic Treaty, which came into force in 1961, provides for international governance and scientific cooperation in place of potential territorial conflict.

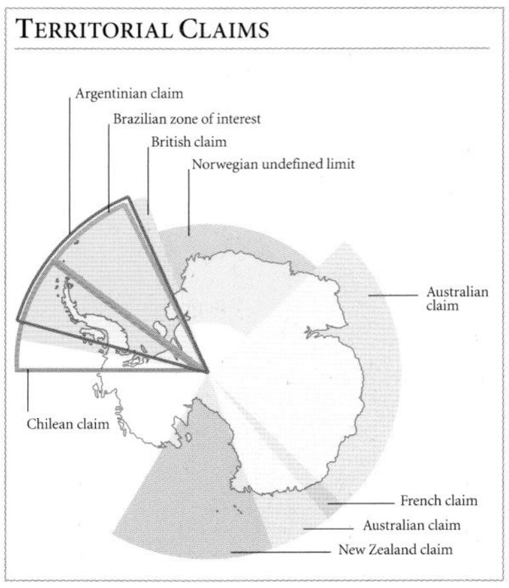
Territorial Claims
Argentinian claim
Brazilian zone of interest
British claim
Norwegian undefined limit
Australian claim
Chilean claim
French claim
Australian claim
New Zealand claim

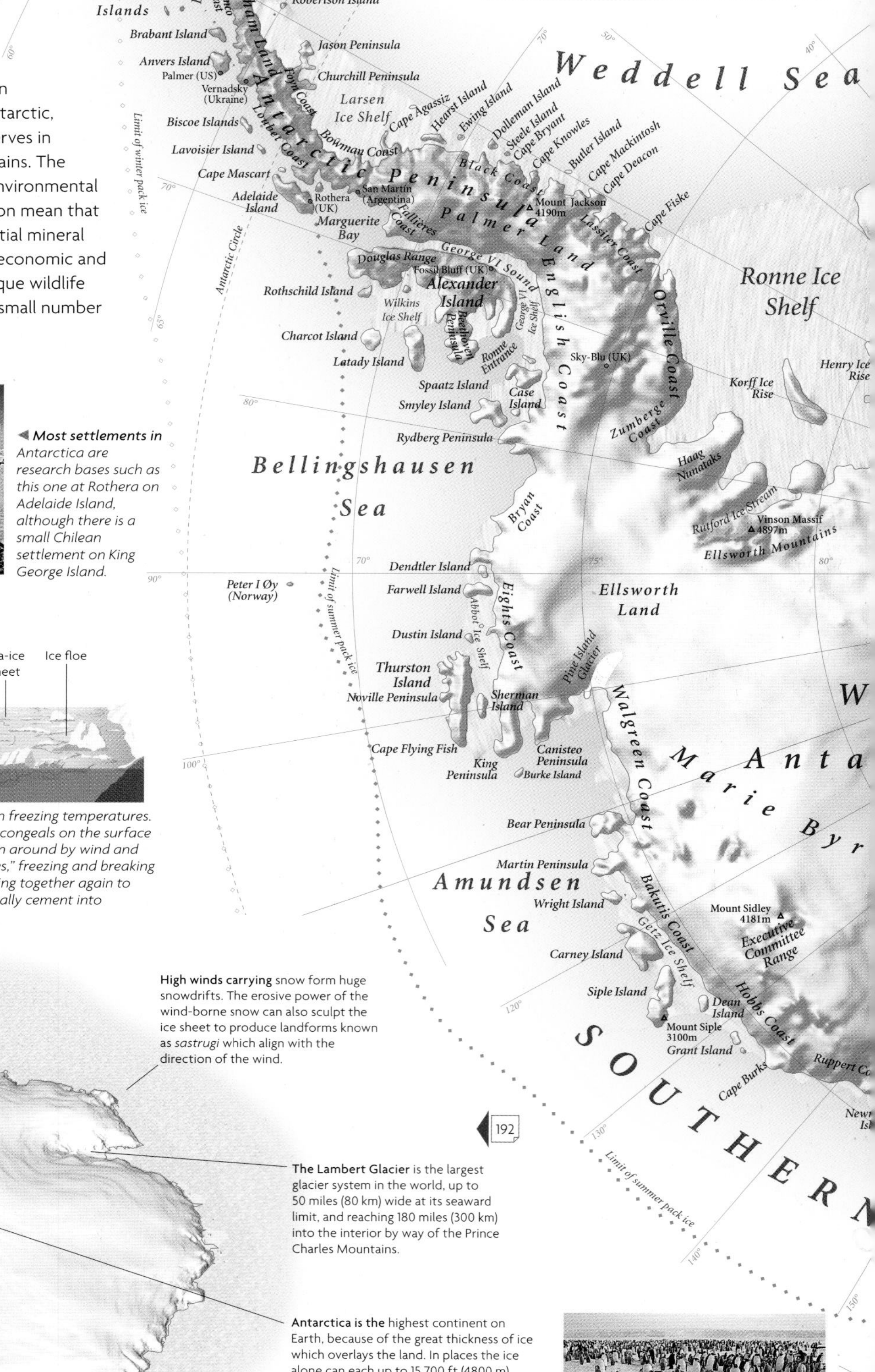
South Orkney Islands
Laurie Island
Orcadas (Argentina)
Coronation Island
Signy (UK)
Scotia Sea
Research Stations on King George Island
Arctowski (Poland)
Artigas (Uruguay)
Bellingshausen (Russian Federation)
Comandante Ferraz (Brazil)
Great Wall (China)
Jubany (Argentina)
King Sejong (South Korea)
Teniente Rodolfo Marsh (Chile)
Clarence Island
Elephant Island
Drake Passage
King George Island
Capitán Arturo Prat (Chile)
Livingston Island
South Shetland Islands
Joinville Island
Dundee Island
General Bernardo O'Higgins (Chile)
Esperanza (Argentina)
Marambio (Argentina)
Snowhill Island
James Ross Island
Robertson Island
Bransfield Strait
Davis Coast
Danco Coast
Graham Land
Brabant Island
Jason Peninsula
Anvers Island
Palmer (US)
Vernadsky (Ukraine)
Churchill Peninsula
Larsen Ice Shelf
Biscoe Islands
Lavoisier Island
Cape Mascart
Adelaide Island
Rothera (UK)
San Martin (Argentina)
Marguerite Bay
Antarctic Peninsula
Cape Agassiz
Hearst Island
Ewing Island
Dolleman Island
Steele Island
Cape Bryant
Cape Knowles
Butler Island
Cape Mackintosh
Cape Deacon
Black Coast
Mount Jackson 4190m
Palmer Land
Lassiter Coast
Cape Fiske
Weddell Sea
Fallières Coast
Douglas Range
Fossil Bluff (UK)
George VI Sound
Alexander Island
Wilkins Ice Shelf
English Coast
Ronne Ice Shelf
Orville Coast
Rothschild Island
Charcot Island
Latady Island
Sky-Blu (UK)
Henry Ice Rise
Korff Ice Rise
Spaatz Island
Smyley Island
Case Island
Rydberg Peninsula
Zumberge Coast
Haag Nunataks
Bellingshausen Sea
Bryan Coast
Rutford Ice Stream
Vinson Massif 4897m
Ellsworth Mountains
Peter I Øy (Norway)
Dendtler Island
Farwell Island
Eights Coast
Abbot Ice Shelf
Ellsworth Land
Dustin Island
Thurston Island
Noville Peninsula
Sherman Island
Pine Island Glacier
Cape Flying Fish
King Peninsula
Canisteo Peninsula
Burke Island
Walgreen Coast
Marie Byrd Land
West Antarctica
Bear Peninsula
Martin Peninsula
Amundsen Sea
Wright Island
Bakutis Coast
Getz Ice Shelf
Mount Sidley 4181m
Executive Committee Range
Carney Island
Siple Island
Dean Island
Mount Siple 3100m
Grant Island
Hobbs Coast
Ruppert Coast
Cape Burks
Southern Ocean
Antarctic Circle
Limit of winter pack ice
Limit of summer pack ice

192

Resources

Many ore minerals, including iron and gold, are found in the Antarctic, and there are also coal reserves in the Transantarctic Mountains. The severe conditions and environmental importance of the region mean that exploitation of potential mineral resources is both uneconomic and undesirable. The unique wildlife and landscape draw a small number of tourists annually.

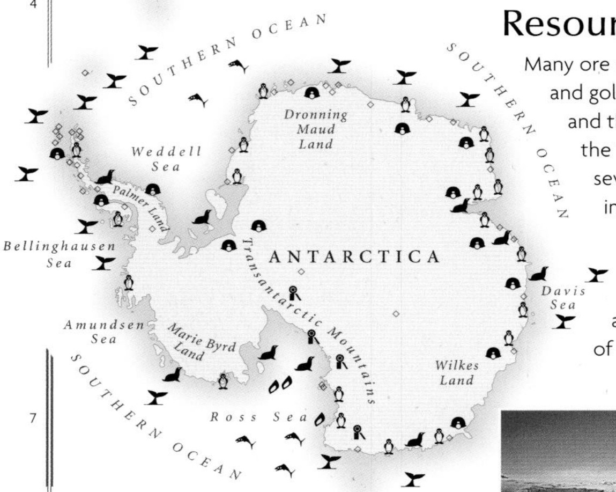
Southern Ocean
Dronning Maud Land
Weddell Sea
Palmer Land
Bellinghausen Sea
ANTARCTICA
Transantarctic Mountains
Amundsen Sea
Marie Byrd Land
Wilkes Land
Davis Sea
Ross Sea
Resources (including wildlife)
coal
fish
minerals
oil & gas
penguins
seals
whales
polar research base

Most settlements in Antarctica are research bases such as this one at Rothera on Adelaide Island, although there is a small Chilean settlement on King George Island.

The landscape

There are two distinct parts to Antarctica: West Antarctica, a series of ice-covered, mountainous islands, joined together by the ice; and the high plateau of East Antarctica. The Ross Sea and the Weddell Sea are outliers of the Southern Ocean – deep bays partially covered by thick ice shelves.

***On Elephant Island,** the coast is edged by glaciers, although the land is not permanently covered by ice.*

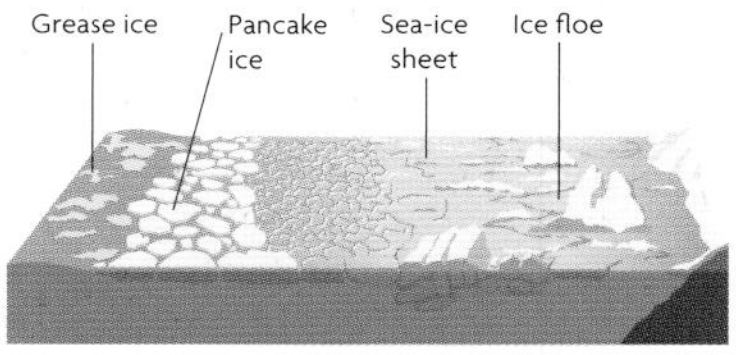
Grease ice
Pancake ice
Sea-ice sheet
Ice floe

***Pack ice forms** out at sea in freezing temperatures. At the outer limits, grease ice congeals on the surface of the ocean. This is then spun around by wind and waves into irregular "pancakes," freezing and breaking up several times before bonding together again to form sea-ice sheets, which finally cement into enormous ice floes.*

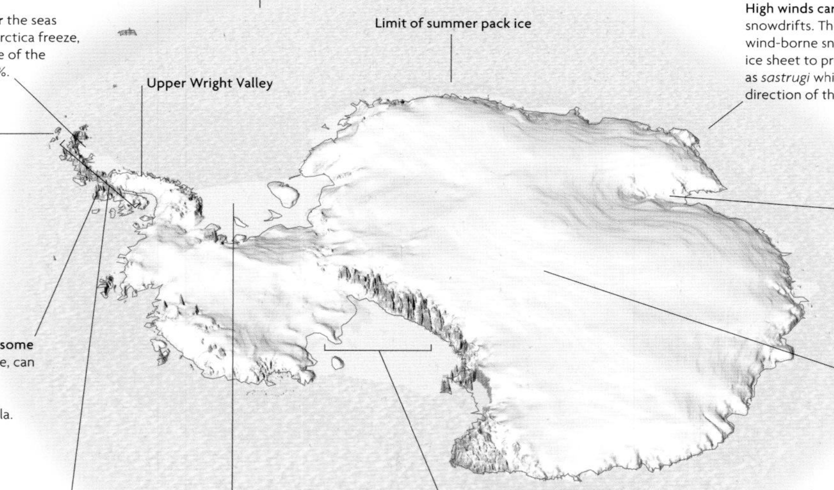
Limit of winter pack ice
Limit of summer pack ice
Upper Wright Valley
Elephant Island

During the winter the seas surrounding Antarctica freeze, increasing the size of the continent by 100%.

High winds carrying snow form huge snowdrifts. The erosive power of the wind-borne snow can also sculpt the ice sheet to produce landforms known as *sastrugi* which align with the direction of the wind.

The Lambert Glacier is the largest glacier system in the world, up to 50 miles (80 km) wide at its seaward limit, and reaching 180 miles (300 km) into the interior by way of the Prince Charles Mountains.

Many volcanoes, some of them still active, can be found in the mountains of the Antarctic Peninsula.

Antarctica is the highest continent on Earth, because of the great thickness of ice which overlays the land. In places the ice alone can each up to 15,700 ft (4800 m) thick. Much of the basement rock of west Antarctica lies below sea level, pushed down by the weight of the ice.

The mountainous Antarctic Peninsula is formed of rocks 65–225 million years old, overlain by more recent rocks and glacial deposits. It is connected to the Andes in South America by a submarine ridge.

Nearly half – 44% – of the Antarctic coastline is bounded by ice shelves, like the Ronne Ice Shelf, which float on the Ocean. These are joined to the inland ice sheet by dome-shaped ice "rises."

More than 30% of Antarctic ice is contained in the Ross Ice Shelf.

***The barren, flat-bottomed** Upper Wright Valley was once filled by a glacier, but is now dry, strewn with boulders and pebbles. In some dry valleys, there has been no rain for over 2 million years.*

***Large colonies of** seabirds live in the extremely harsh Antarctic climate. The Emperor penguins seen here, the smaller Adélie penguin, the Antarctic petrel, and the South Polar skua are the only birds that breed exclusively on the continent.*

◀ *The sun sets over the Antarctic Peninsula for more than six months during the winter. However, there are more hours of sunshine during the brief Antarctic summer than most equatorial countries experience in a whole year.*

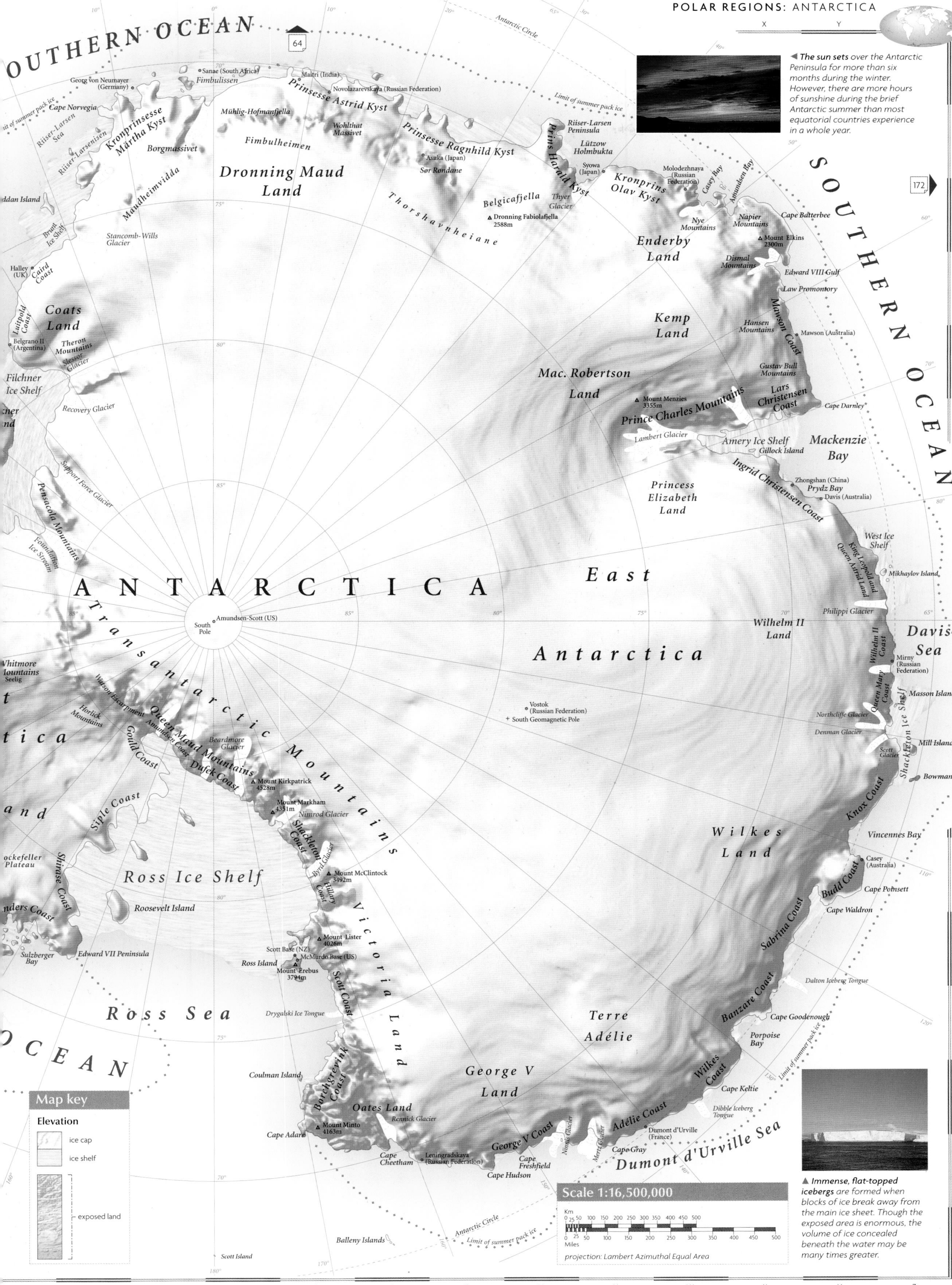
SOUTHERN OCEAN
64
172
SOUTHERN OCEAN
Antarctic Circle
Limit of summer pack ice
Georg von Neumayer (Germany)
Sanae (South Africa)
Fimbulisen
Maitri (India)
Novolazarevskaya (Russian Federation)
Prinsesse Astrid Kyst
Cape Norvegia
Riiser-Larsen Sea
Riiser-Larsenisen
Kronprinsesse Märtha Kyst
Mühlig-Hofmanfjella
Wohlthat Massivet
Fimbulheimen
Borgmassivet
Prinsesse Ragnhild Kyst
Asuka (Japan)
Sør Rondane
Riiser-Larsen Peninsula
Lützow Holmbukta
Syowa (Japan)
Prins Harald Kyst
Dronning Maud Land
Maudheimvidda
Belgicafjella
Dronning Fabiolafjella 2588m
Thorshavnheiane
Thyer Glacier
Kronprins Olav Kyst
Molodezhnaya (Russian Federation)
Casey Bay
Amundsen Bay
Nye Mountains
Napier Mountains
Cape Batterbee
Mount Elkins 2300m
Enderby Land
Dismal Mountains
Edward VIII Gulf
Law Promontory
Stancomb-Wills Glacier
Brunt Ice Shelf
Halley (UK)
Caird Coast
Coats Land
Luitpold Coast
Belgrano II (Argentina)
Theron Mountains
Slessor Glacier
Filchner Ice Shelf
Recovery Glacier
Kemp Land
Mawson Coast
Hansen Mountains
Mawson (Australia)
Mac. Robertson Land
Gustav Bull Mountains
Mount Menzies 3355m
Prince Charles Mountains
Lars Christensen Coast
Cape Darnley
Lambert Glacier
Amery Ice Shelf
Gillock Island
Mackenzie Bay
Ingrid Christensen Coast
Zhongshan (China)
Prydz Bay
Davis (Australia)
Princess Elizabeth Land
Support Force Glacier
Pensacola Mountains
Foundation Ice Stream
West Ice Shelf
King Leopold and Queen Astrid Land
Mikhaylov Island
ANTARCTICA
East Antarctica
South Pole
Amundsen-Scott (US)
Wilhelm II Land
Philippi Glacier
Davis Sea
Wilhelm II Coast
Mirny (Russian Federation)
Queen Mary Coast
Masson Island
Transantarctic Mountains
Whitmore Mountains
Watson Escarpment
Horlick Mountains
Queen Maud Mountains
Amundsen Coast
Gould Coast
Vostok (Russian Federation)
South Geomagnetic Pole
Northcliffe Glacier
Denman Glacier
Shackleton Ice Shelf
Mill Island
Scott Glacier
Bowman Island
Beardmore Glacier
Dufek Coast
Mount Kirkpatrick 4528m
Mount Markham 4351m
Nimrod Glacier
Shackleton Coast
Siple Coast
Knox Coast
Wilkes Land
Vincennes Bay
Rockefeller Plateau
Shirase Coast
Byrd Glacier
Mount McClintock 3492m
Hillary Coast
Casey (Australia)
Ross Ice Shelf
Budd Coast
Cape Poinsett
Cape Waldron
Roosevelt Island
Victoria Land
Saunders Coast
Sabrina Coast
Edward VII Peninsula
Sulzberger Bay
Mount Lister 4026m
Scott Base (NZ)
McMurdo Base (US)
Ross Island
Mount Erebus 3794m
Scott Coast
Dalton Iceberg Tongue
Ross Sea
Drygalski Ice Tongue
Banzare Coast
Cape Goodenough
Terre Adélie
Porpoise Bay
OCEAN
Coulman Island
Borchgrevink Coast
George V Land
Wilkes Coast
Cape Keltie
Oates Land
Rennick Glacier
Dibble Iceberg Tongue
Adélie Coast
Mount Minto 4163m
Cape Adare
Dumont d'Urville (France)
Ninnis Glacier
Mertz Glacier
George V Coast
Cape Gray
Dumont d'Urville Sea
Cape Cheetham
Leningradskaya (Russian Federation)
Cape Freshfield
Cape Hudson
Balleny Islands
Scott Island
Map key
Elevation
ice cap
ice shelf
exposed land
Scale 1:16,500,000
Km
Miles
projection: Lambert Azimuthal Equal Area

▲ ***Immense, flat-topped icebergs*** *are formed when blocks of ice break away from the main ice sheet. Though the exposed area is enormous, the volume of ice concealed beneath the water may be many times greater.*

The Arctic

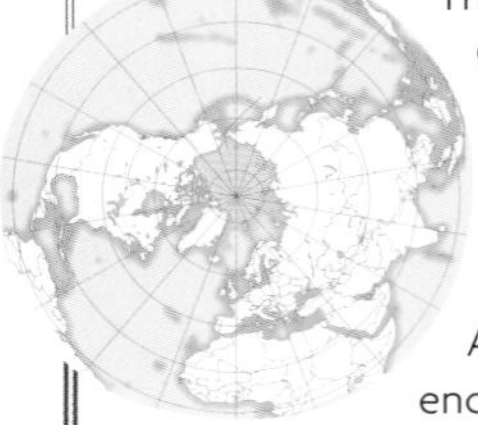

Three continents, Asia, North America, and Europe, reach into the Arctic Circle at their northernmost limits, almost entirely encircling the Arctic Ocean. Despite the region's extraordinarily harsh climate, it has been inhabited for thousands of years by peoples such as the European Lapps, the Russian Nenet, and the North American Inuit, who draw a living from fishing, herding, and hunting. More recently, particularly in the Russian Arctic, opportunities to exploit oil and other mineral reserves have encouraged immigration. Pollution of the Arctic's unique ecology and damage to the traditional lifestyles of many native peoples have been the unfortunate results of this activity, and international cooperation is needed to safeguard the future of the region.

Map key

Population

- above 5 million
- 1 million to 5 million
- 500,000 to 1 million
- 100,000 to 500,000
- 50,000 to 100,000
- 10,000 to 50,000
- below 10,000

Sea depth

- Sea level
- 200m / 656ft
- 1000m / 3281ft
- 2000m / 6562ft
- 3000m / 9843ft
- 4000m / 13,124ft
- 5000m / 16,400ft
- 6000m / 19,686ft

Scale 1:23,500,000

Km 0 100 200 300 400 500 600

Miles 0 100 200 300 400 500 600

projection: Lambert Azimuthal Equal Area

▲ *Windblown snow etches deep patterns in the ice sheet known as sastrugi. They align with the direction of the wind*

Resources

Large quantities of coal, oil, and natural gas are to be found in the basins of the Arctic Ocean, and in northern Canada, Alaska, and the Russian Federation. The cost and difficulty of extraction and, more recently, awareness of damage to the environment, have limited exploitation to coastal regions. The unfrozen waters have stocks of fish including cod, flounder, and haddock. Quotas have now been put in place to restrict the number of fish caught annually. Reindeer are herded in large numbers by many of the native Arctic peoples. Most grain and vegetables are imported from elsewhere.

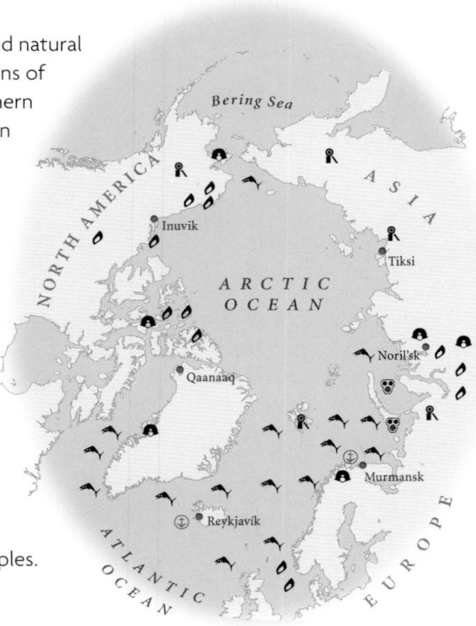
Bering Sea
NORTH AMERICA
ASIA
Inuvik
Tiksi
ARCTIC OCEAN
Noril'sk
Qaanaaq
Murmansk
Reykjavik
ATLANTIC OCEAN
EUROPE

▲ *Icebreakers are ships with specially strengthened hulls, designed to break a path through the ice. They are used to keep important routes open during the winter, when falling temperatures cause much of the Arctic Ocean to freeze over.*

Resources

- coal
- fish
- mining
- oil & gas
- radioactive contamination
- major towns
- major ports

8

The landscape

The Arctic Ocean comprises two large ocean basins divided by three submarine ridges, the greatest of which, the Lomonosov Ridge, is a huge underwater mountain range which has an average height of more than 10,000 ft (3000 m). The lands which encircle the Arctic Ocean are underlain by great shield areas of ancient rocks, which were heavily glaciated during the last Ice Age.

◀ *Icebergs are constantly broken up and reshaped by wind and the oceans. This flat-topped iceberg has been undercut, leaving a craggy ice cliff.*

The Canadian Shield underlies almost all of the Canadian Arctic. It is a very stable plateau of ancient rock, now covered by glacial lakes and sediment, which supports tundra vegetation.

The Arctic Ocean is the world's smallest ocean with a total area of 5,440,000 sq miles (15,100,000 sq km).

At a latitude of more than 75° N, the Arctic Ocean is almost permanently covered by pack ice, though high winds and the movement of the seas may cause the ice to crack and break up.

In the more southerly reaches of the Arctic, like Siberia, much of the land is covered by permafrost. In the summer, higher temperatures warm the frozen ground, causing a number of typical phenomena. These include solifluction, the fast downhill movement of top soil layers; freeze/thaw activity, which patterns the ground into regular polygonal shapes, and the formation of large domes with a frozen ice core, known as pingos.

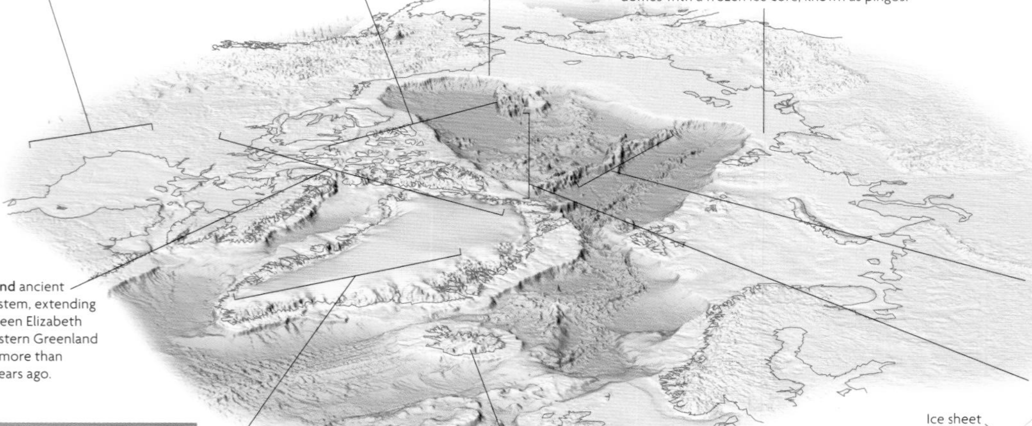

A complex and ancient mountain system, extending from the Queen Elizabeth Islands to eastern Greenland was formed more than 245 million years ago.

Lomonosov Ridge

Arctic ice shelf

◀ ***Much of Greenland** is covered by a massive ice sheet more than 650,000 sq miles (1,683,400 sq km) in extent. The weight of the ice has depressed the central land area to form a basin lying more than 1000 ft (300 m) below sea level. Only at the edges of the island is bare rock visible.*

Iceland has five major glaciers, sustained by heavy snowfall. Parts of the ice cap cover active volcanoes, such as Bárdharbunga, which periodically erupt causing the melted ice to form a great lake at the glacier margins.

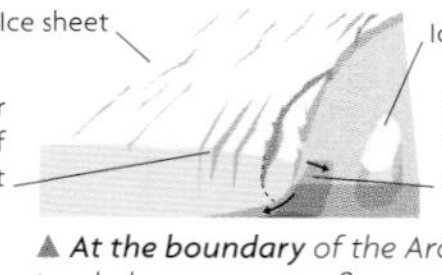
Ice sheet
Iceberg
Crevasses occur at the edge of the ice sheet
Sea water melts the edge of the ice sheet

▲ ***At the boundary** of the Arctic ice shelves, sea water flows under the ice causing melting and forming crevasses on the surface. This eventually weakens blocks of ice which break away as icebergs. This process is known as calving.*

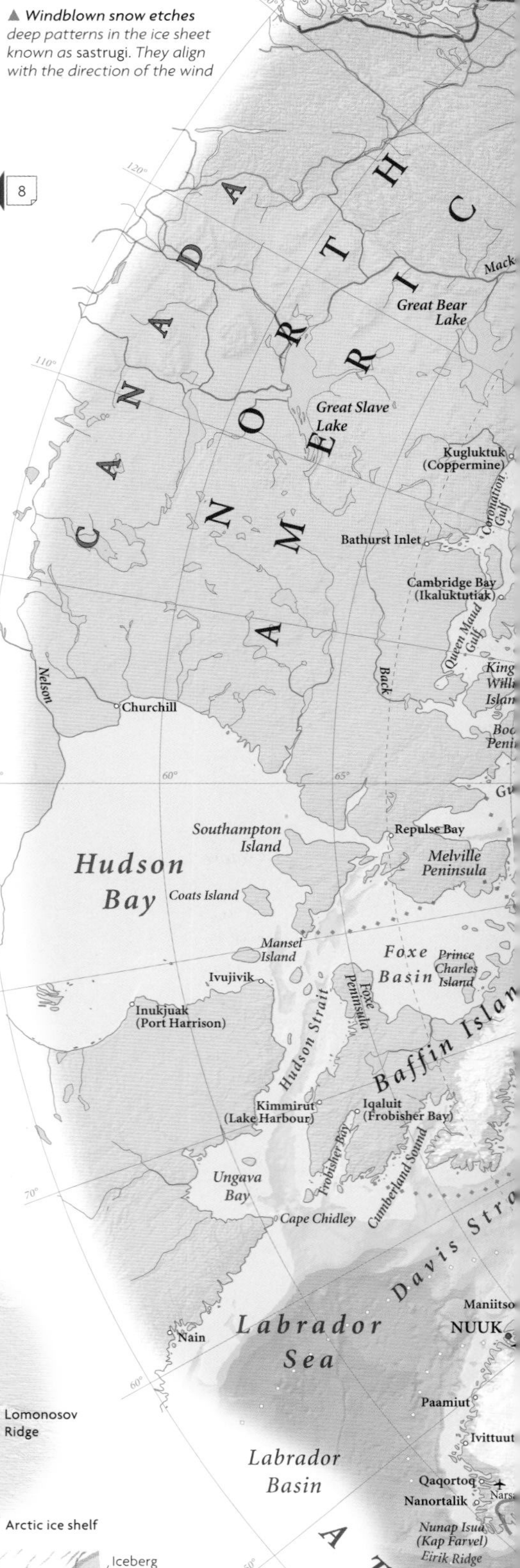
192
8
CANADA
NORTH AMERICA
Great Bear Lake
Great Slave Lake
Kugluktuk (Coppermine)
Bathurst Inlet
Cambridge Bay (Ikaluktutiak)
Queen Maud Gulf
Nelson
Back
Churchill
Southampton Island
Hudson Bay
Coats Island
Repulse Bay
Melville Peninsula
Mansel Island
Foxe Basin
Prince Charles Island
Ivujivik
Inukjuak (Port Harrison)
Hudson Strait
Foxe Peninsula
Baffin Island
Kimmirut (Lake Harbour)
Iqaluit (Frobisher Bay)
Frobisher Bay
Cumberland Sound
Ungava Bay
Cape Chidley
Davis Strait
Nain
Labrador Sea
Maniitsoq
NUUK
Paamiut
Ivittuut
Labrador Basin
Qaqortoq
Nanortalik
Nunap Isua (Kap Farvel)
Eirik Ridge
ATLANTIC
64

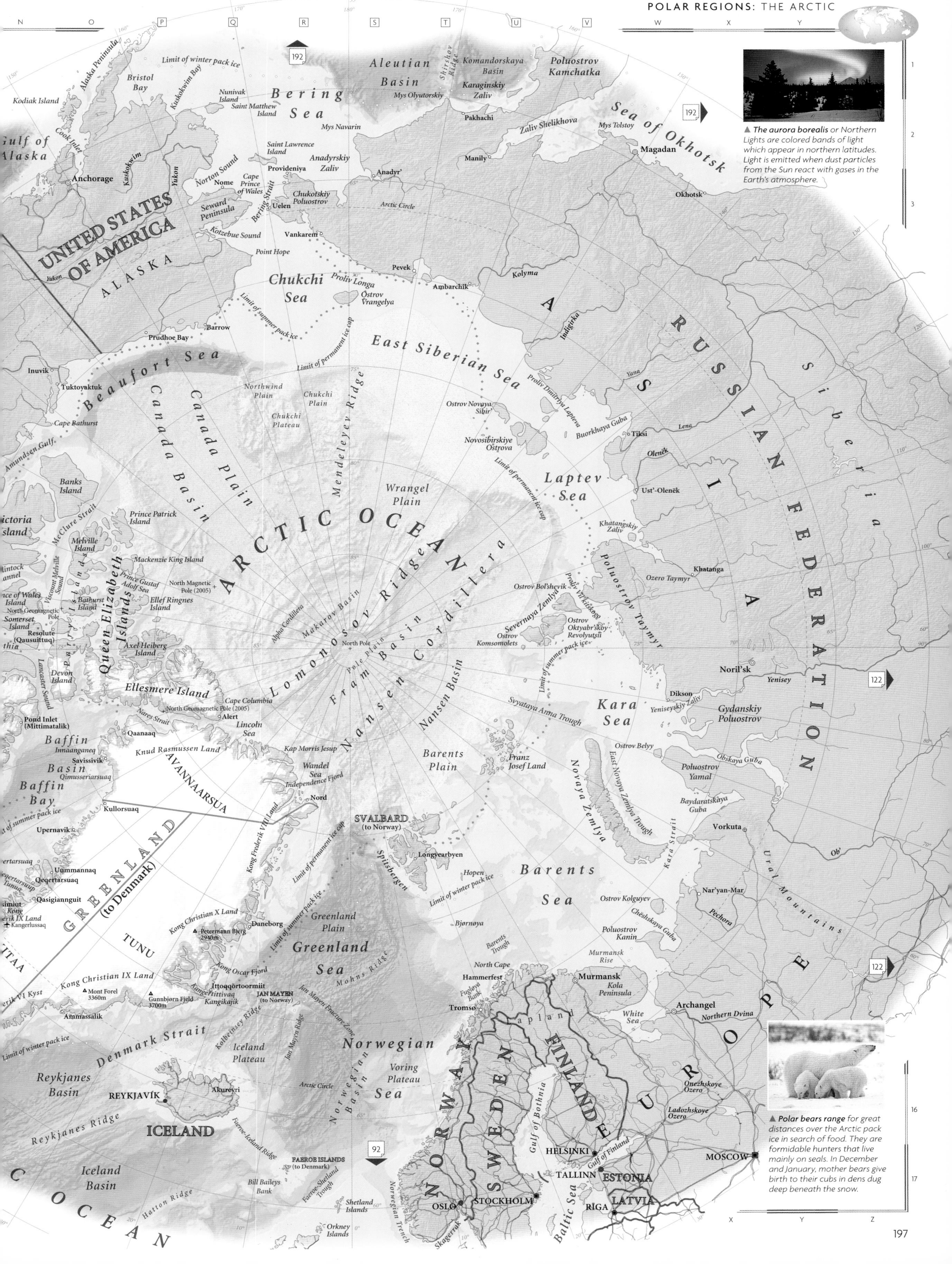

N O P Q R S T U V W X Y
Limit of winter pack ice
Alaska Peninsula
Kodiak Island
Bristol Bay
Kuskokwim Bay
Gulf of Alaska
Cook Inlet
Anchorage
Kuskokwim
Yukon
Norton Sound
Nome
Nunivak Island
Saint Matthew Island
Bering Sea
Aleutian Basin
Shirshov Ridge
Komandorskaya Basin
Karaginskiy Zaliv
Mys Olyutorskiy
Poluostrov Kamchatka
Sea of Okhotsk
Mys Tolstoy
Magadan
Okhotsk
Zaliv Shelikhova
Pakhachi
Manily
Mys Navarin
Saint Lawrence Island
Anadyrskiy Zaliv
Provideniya
Anadyr'
Cape Prince of Wales
Bering Strait
Chukotskiy Poluostrov
Uelen
Arctic Circle
Seward Peninsula
Kotzebue Sound
Vankarem
Point Hope
UNITED STATES OF AMERICA
ALASKA
Yukon
Chukchi Sea
Proliv Longa
Ostrov Vrangelya
Pevek
Ambarchik
Kolyma
Limit of summer pack ice
Limit of permanent ice cap
Barrow
Prudhoe Bay
Beaufort Sea
Inuvik
Tuktoyaktuk
Cape Bathurst
Amundsen Gulf
Banks Island
Victoria Island
McClure Strait
Prince Patrick Island
Melville Island
Viscount Melville Sound
M'Clintock Channel
Prince of Wales Island
Somerset Island
Resolute (Qausuittuq)
Parry Islands
Queen Elizabeth Islands
Mackenzie King Island
Prince Gustaf Adolf Sea
Bathurst Island
Ellef Ringnes Island
North Magnetic Pole (2005)
North Geomagnetic Pole
Axel Heiberg Island
Devon Island
Lancaster Sound
Ellesmere Island
Cape Columbia
North Geomagnetic Pole (2005)
Alert
Nares Strait
Lincoln Sea
Pond Inlet (Mittimatalik)
Baffin Inmaanganeq
Qaanaaq
Savissivik
Knud Rasmussen Land
Baffin Basin
Qimusseriarsuaq
Baffin Bay
AVANNAARSUA
Kullorsuaq
Upernavik
Uummannaq
Qeqertarsuaq
Qasigiannguit
Sisimiut
Kangerlussuaq
GREENLAND (to Denmark)
TUNU
Kong Frederik VIII Land
Kong Christian X Land
Petermann Bjerg 2940m
Daneborg
Kong Oscar Fjord
Kong Christian IX Land
Mont Forel 3360m
Gunnbjørn Fjeld 3700m
Ittoqqortoormiit
Kangertittivaq
Kangikajik
Ammassalik
Denmark Strait
Canada Basin
Canada Plain
Northwind Plain
Chukchi Plain
Chukchi Plateau
Mendeleyev Ridge
East Siberian Sea
Ostrov Novaya Sibir'
Novosibirskiye Ostrova
Proliv Dmitriya Lapteva
Indigirka
Yana
Buorkhaya Guba
Tiksi
Lena
Olenëk
Ust'-Olenëk
Laptev Sea
Wrangel Plain
ARCTIC OCEAN
Alpha Cordillera
Makarov Basin
Lomonosov Ridge
North Pole
Pole Plain
Fram Basin
Nansen Cordillera
Nansen Basin
Khatangskiy Zaliv
Khatanga
Ozero Taymyr
Poluostrov Taymyr
Ostrov Bol'shevik
Proliv Vil'kitskogo
Severnaya Zemlya
Ostrov Oktyabr'skoy Revolyutsii
Ostrov Komsomolets
Noril'sk
Yenisey
Dikson
Yeniseyskiy Zaliv
Gydanskiy Poluostrov
Kara Sea
Svyataya Anna Trough
Kap Morris Jesup
Wandel Sea
Independence Fjord
Nord
Barents Plain
Franz Josef Land
Ostrov Belyy
Obskaya Guba
Poluostrov Yamal
Baydaratskaya Guba
Novaya Zemlya
East Novaya Zemlya Trough
Kara Strait
Vorkuta
Ob'
SVALBARD (to Norway)
Longyearbyen
Spitsbergen
Hopen
Limit of winter pack ice
Barents Sea
Ostrov Kolguyev
Chëshskaya Guba
Nar'yan-Mar
Pechora
Ural Mountains
Bjørnøya
Barents Trough
Poluostrov Kanin
Murmansk Rise
Greenland Plain
Greenland Sea
Mohns Ridge
North Cape
Hammerfest
Fugløya Bank
Murmansk
Kola Peninsula
Tromsø
Lapland
White Sea
Archangel
Northern Dvina
JAN MAYEN (to Norway)
Jan Mayen Fracture Zone
Jan Mayen Ridge
Kolbeinsey Ridge
Iceland Plateau
Norwegian Sea
Norwegian Basin
Voring Plateau
Arctic Circle
Reykjanes Basin
REYKJAVÍK
Akureyri
ICELAND
Reykjanes Ridge
Faeroe-Iceland Ridge
FAEROE ISLANDS (to Denmark)
Iceland Basin
Bill Baileys Bank
Faeroe-Shetland Trough
Shetland Islands
Orkney Islands
Hatton Ridge
ATLANTIC OCEAN
Norwegian Trench
Skagerrak
NORWAY
SWEDEN
FINLAND
Gulf of Bothnia
Gulf of Finland
HELSINKI
TALLINN
ESTONIA
LATVIA
RIGA
OSLO
STOCKHOLM
Baltic Sea
Onezhskoye Ozero
Ladozhskoye Ozero
MOSCOW
EUROPE
RUSSIAN FEDERATION
ASIA
Siberia

192

192

122

122

92

▲ ***The aurora borealis*** *or Northern Lights are colored bands of light which appear in northern latitudes. Light is emitted when dust particles from the Sun react with gases in the Earth's atmosphere.*

▲ ***Polar bears range*** *for great distances over the Arctic pack ice in search of food. They are formidable hunters that live mainly on seals. In December and January, mother bears give birth to their cubs in dens dug deep beneath the snow.*

Geographical comparisons

Largest countries

Russian Federation	6,592,735 sq miles	(17,075,200 sq km)
Canada	3,855,171 sq miles	(9,984,670 sq km)
USA	3,717,792 sq miles	(9,629,091 sq km)
China	3,705,386 sq miles	(9,596,960 sq km)
Brazil	3,286,470 sq miles	(8,511,965 sq km)
Australia	2,967,893 sq miles	(7,686,850 sq km)
India	1,269,339 sq miles	(3,287,590 sq km)
Argentina	1,068,296 sq miles	(2,766,890 sq km)
Kazakhstan	1,049,150 sq miles	(2,717,300 sq km)
Algeria	919,590 sq miles	(2,381,740 sq km)

Smallest countries

Vatican City	0.17 sq miles	(0.44 sq km)
Monaco	0.75 sq miles	(1.95 sq km)
Nauru	8.2 sq miles	(21.2 sq km)
Tuvalu	10 sq miles	(26 sq km)
San Marino	24 sq miles	(61 sq km)
Liechtenstein	62 sq miles	(160 sq km)
Marshall Islands	70 sq miles	(181 sq km)
St. Kitts & Nevis	101 sq miles	(261 sq km)
Maldives	116 sq miles	(300 sq km)
Malta	124 sq miles	(320 sq km)

Largest islands

To the nearest 1000 – or 100,000 for the largest

Greenland	849,400 sq miles	(2,200,000 sq km)
New Guinea	312,000 sq miles	(808,000 sq km)
Borneo	292,222 sq miles	(757,050 sq km)
Madagascar	229,300 sq miles	(594,000 sq km)
Sumatra	202,300 sq miles	(524,000 sq km)
Baffin Island	183,800 sq miles	(476,000 sq km)
Honshu	88,800 sq miles	(230,000 sq km)
Britain	88,700 sq miles	(229,800 sq km)
Victoria Island	81,900 sq miles	(212,000 sq km)
Ellesmere Island	75,700 sq miles	(196,000 sq km)

Richest countries

GNI per capita, in US$

Monaco	188,150
Liechtenstein	137,070
Norway	88,890
Qatar	80,440
Luxembourg	78,130
Switzerland	76,380
Denmark	60,390
Sweden	53,230
Netherlands	49,730
Kuwait	48,900

Poorest countries

GNI per capita, in US$

Dem. Rep. Congo	190
Liberia	240
Burundi	250
Sierra Leone	340
Malawi	340
Niger	360
Ethiopia	400
Afghanistan	400
Madagascar	430
Eritrea	430
Guinea	440
Mozambique	470

Most populous countries

China	1,347,300,000
India	1,240,000,000
USA	314,500,000
Indonesia	237,600,000
Brazil	193,300,000
Pakistan	180,800,000
Nigeria	166,500,000
Bangladesh	152,500,000
Russian Federation	143,200,000
Japan	127,500,000

Least populous countries

Vatican City	821
Nauru	9,378
Tuvalu	10,619
Palau	21,032
Monaco	30,510
San Marino	32,140
Liechtenstein	36,713
St Kitts & Nevis	50,726
Marshall Islands	64,480
Dominica	73,126
Andorra	85,082
Antigua & Barbuda	89,018

Most densely populated countries

Monaco	40,680 people per sq mile	(15,641 per sq km)
Singapore	22,034 people per sq mile	(8525 per sq km)
Vatican City	4918 people per sq mile	(1900 per sq km)
Bahrain	4762 people per sq mile	(1841 per sq km)
Maldives	3400 people per sq mile	(1315 per sq km)
Malta	3226 people per sq mile	(1250 per sq km)
Bangladesh	2911 people per sq mile	(1124 per sq km)
Taiwan	1860 people per sq mile	(718 per sq km)
Mauritius	1811 people per sq mile	(699 per sq km)
Barbados	1807 people per sq mile	(698 per sq km)

Most sparsely populated countries

Mongolia	5 people per sq mile	(2 per sq km)
Namibia	7 people per sq mile	(3 per sq km)
Australia	8 people per sq mile	(3 per sq km)
Surinam	8 people per sq mile	(3 per sq km)
Iceland	8 people per sq mile	(3 per sq km)
Mauriania	9 people per sq mile	(4 per sq km)
Botswana	9 people per sq mile	(4 per sq km)
Libya	9 people per sq mile	(4 per sq km)
Canada	10 people per sq mile	(4 per sq km)
Guyana	11 people per sq mile	(4 per sq km)

Most widely spoken languages

1. Chinese (Mandarin)	6. Arabic
2. English	7. Bengali
3. Hindi	8. Portuguese
4. Spanish	9. Malay-Indonesian
5. Russian	10. French

Largest conurbations

Population

Tokyo	36,900,000
Delhi	21,900,000
Mexico City	20,100,000
New York - Newark	20,100,000
São Paulo	19,600,000
Shanghai	19,500,000
Mumbai	19,400,000
Beijing	15,000,000
Dhaka	14,900,000
Kolkata	14,300,000
Karachi	13,500,000
Buenos Aires	13,400,000
Los Angeles	13,200,000
Rio de Janeiro	11,800,000
Manilla	11,600,000
Moscow	11,500,000
Osaka	11,400,000
Cairo	11,400,000
Istanbul	10,900,000
Lagos	10,800,000
Paris	10,500,000
Guangzhou	10,500,000
Shenzhen	10,200,000
Seoul	9,700,000
Chongqing	9,700,000

Countries with the most land borders

14: China	(Afghanistan, Bhutan, India, Kazakhstan, Kyrgyzstan, Laos, Mongolia, Myanmar, Nepal, North Korea, Pakistan, Russian Federation, Tajikistan, Vietnam)
14: Russian Federation	(Azerbaijan, Belarus, China, Estonia, Finland, Georgia, Kazakhstan, Latvia, Lithuania, Mongolia, North Korea, Norway, Poland, Ukraine)
10: Brazil	(Argentina, Bolivia, Colombia, French Guiana, Guyana, Paraguay, Peru, Suriname, Uruguay, Venezuela)
9: Congo, Dem. Rep.	(Angola, Burundi, Central African Republic, Congo, Rwanda, South Sudan, Tanzania, Uganda, Zambia)
9: Germany	(Austria, Belgium, Czech Republic, Denmark, France, Luxembourg, Netherlands, Poland, Switzerland)
8: Austria	(Czech Republic, Germany, Hungary, Italy, Liechtenstein, Slovakia, Slovenia, Switzerland)
8: France	(Andorra, Belgium, Germany, Italy, Luxembourg, Monaco, Spain, Switzerland)
8: Tanzania	(Burundi, Dem. Rep. Congo, Kenya, Malawi, Mozambique, Rwanda, Uganda, Zambia)
8: Turkey	(Armenia, Azerbaijan, Bulgaria, Georgia, Greece, Iran, Iraq, Syria)
8: Zambia	(Angola, Botswana, Dem. Rep. Congo, Malawi, Mozambique, Namibia, Tanzania, Zimbabwe)

Longest rivers

Nile (NE Africa)	4160 miles	(6695 km)
Amazon (South America)	4049 miles	(6516 km)
Yangtze (China)	3915 miles	(6299 km)
Mississippi/Missouri (USA)	3710 miles	(5969 km)
Ob'-Irtysh (Russian Federation)	3461 miles	(5570 km)
Yellow River (China)	3395 miles	(5464 km)
Congo (Central Africa)	2900 miles	(4667 km)
Mekong (Southeast Asia)	2749 miles	(4425 km)
Lena (Russian Federation)	2734 miles	(4400 km)
Mackenzie (Canada)	2640 miles	(4250 km)
Yenisey (Russian Federation)	2541 miles	(4090km)

Highest mountains

Height above sea level

Everest	29,029 ft	(8848 m)
K2	28,253 ft	(8611 m)
Kangchenjunga I	28,210 ft	(8598 m)
Makalu I	27,767 ft	(8463 m)
Cho Oyu	26,907 ft	(8201 m)
Dhaulagiri I	26,796 ft	(8167 m)
Manaslu I	26,783 ft	(8163 m)
Nanga Parbat I	26,661 ft	(8126 m)
Annapurna I	26,547 ft	(8091 m)
Gasherbrum I	26,471 ft	(8068 m)

Largest bodies of inland water

With area and depth

Caspian Sea	143,243 sq miles (371,000 sq km)	3215 ft (980 m)
Lake Superior	31,151 sq miles (83,270 sq km)	1289 ft (393 m)
Lake Victoria	26,828 sq miles (69,484 sq km)	328 ft (100 m)
Lake Huron	23,436 sq miles (60,700 sq km)	751 ft (229 m)
Lake Michigan	22,402 sq miles (58,020 sq km)	922 ft (281 m)
Lake Tanganyika	12,703 sq miles (32,900 sq km)	4700 ft (1435 m)
Great Bear Lake	12,274 sq miles (31,790 sq km)	1047 ft (319 m)
Lake Baikal	11,776 sq miles (30,500 sq km)	5712 ft (1741 m)
Great Slave Lake	10,981 sq miles (28,440 sq km)	459 ft (140 m)
Lake Erie	9,915 sq miles (25,680 sq km)	197 ft (60 m)

Deepest ocean features

Challenger Deep, Mariana Trench (Pacific)	36,201 ft	(11,034 m)
Vityaz III Depth, Tonga Trench (Pacific)	35,704 ft	(10,882 m)
Vityaz Depth, Kurile-Kamchatka Trench (Pacific)	34,588 ft	(10,542 m)
Cape Johnson Deep, Philippine Trench (Pacific)	34,441 ft	(10,497 m)
Kermadec Trench (Pacific)	32,964 ft	(10,047 m)
Ramapo Deep, Japan Trench (Pacific)	32,758 ft	(9984 m)
Milwaukee Deep, Puerto Rico Trench (Atlantic)	30,185 ft	(9200 m)
Argo Deep, Torres Trench (Pacific)	30,070 ft	(9165 m)
Meteor Depth, South Sandwich Trench (Atlantic)	30,000 ft	(9144 m)
Planet Deep, New Britain Trench (Pacific)	29,988 ft	(9140 m)

Greatest waterfalls

Mean flow of water

Boyoma (Dem. Rep. Congo)	600,400 cu. ft/sec	(17,000 cu.m/sec)
Khône (Laos/Cambodia)	410,000 cu. ft/sec	(11,600 cu.m/sec)
Niagara (USA/Canada)	195,000 cu. ft/sec	(5500 cu.m/sec)
Grande, Salto (Uruguay)	160,000 cu. ft/sec	(4500 cu.m/sec)
Paulo Afonso (Brazil)	100,000 cu. ft/sec	(2800 cu.m/sec)
Urubupungá, Salto do (Brazil)	97,000 cu. ft/sec	(2750 cu.m/sec)
Iguaçu (Argentina/Brazil)	62,000 cu. ft/sec	(1700 cu.m/sec)
Maribondo, Cachoeira do (Brazil)	53,000 cu. ft/sec	(1500 cu.m/sec)
Victoria (Zimbabwe)	39,000 cu. ft/sec	(1100 cu.m/sec)
Murchison Falls (Uganda)	42,000 cu. ft/sec	(1200 cu.m/sec)
Churchill (Canada)	35,000 cu. ft/sec	(1000 cu.m/sec)
Kaveri Falls (India)	33,000 cu. ft/sec	(900 cu.m/sec)

Highest waterfalls

* Indicates that the total height is a single leap

Angel (Venezuela)	3212 ft	(979 m)
Tugela (South Africa)	3110 ft	(948 m)
Utigard (Norway)	2625 ft	(800 m)
Mongefossen (Norway)	2539 ft	(774 m)
Mtarazi (Zimbabwe)	2500 ft	(762 m)
Yosemite (USA)	2425 ft	(739 m)
Ostre Mardola Foss (Norway)	2156 ft	(657 m)
Tyssestrengane (Norway)	2119 ft	(646 m)
***Cuquenan** (Venezuela)	2001 ft	(610 m)
Sutherland (New Zealand)	1903 ft	(580 m)
***Kjellfossen** (Norway)	1841 ft	(561 m)

Largest deserts

NB – Most of Antarctica is a polar desert, with only 50mm of precipitation annually

Sahara	3,450,000 sq miles	(9,065,000 sq km)
Gobi	500,000 sq miles	(1,295,000 sq km)
Ar Rub al Khali	289,600 sq miles	(750,000 sq km)
Great Victorian	249,800 sq miles	(647,000 sq km)
Sonoran	120,000 sq miles	(311,000 sq km)
Kalahari	120,000 sq miles	(310,800 sq km)
Kara Kum	115,800 sq miles	(300,000 sq km)
Takla Makan	100,400 sq miles	(260,000 sq km)
Namib	52,100 sq miles	(135,000 sq km)
Thar	33,670 sq miles	(130,000 sq km)

Hottest inhabited places

Djibouti (Djibouti)	86° F	(30 °C)
Tombouctou (Mali)	84.7° F	(29.3 °C)
Tirunelveli (India)		
Tuticorin (India)		
Nellore (India)	84.5° F	(29.2 °C)
Santa Marta (Colombia)		
Aden (Yemen)	84° F	(28.9 °C)
Madurai (India)		
Niamey (Niger)		
Hodeida (Yemen)	83.8° F	(28.8 °C)
Ouagadougou (Burkina)		
Thanjavur (India)		
Tiruchchirappalli (India)		

Driest inhabited places

Aswân (Egypt)	0.02 in	(0.5 mm)
Luxor (Egypt)	0.03 in	(0.7 mm)
Arica (Chile)	0.04 in	(1.1 mm)
Ica (Peru)	0.1 in	(2.3 mm)
Antofagasta (Chile)	0.2 in	(4.9 mm)
Al Minya (Egypt)	0.2 in	(5.1 mm)
Asyut (Egypt)	0.2 in	(5.2 mm)
Callao (Peru)	0.5 in	(12.0 mm)
Trujillo (Peru)	0.55 in	(14.0 mm)
Al Fayyum (Egypt)	0.8 in	(19.0 mm)

Wettest inhabited places

Mawsynram (India)	467 in	(11,862 mm)
Mount Waialeale (Hawaii, USA)	460 in	(11,684 mm)
Cherrapunji (India)	450 in	(11,430 mm)
Cape Debundsha (Cameroon)	405 in	(10,290 mm)
Quibdo (Colombia)	354 in	(8892 mm)
Buenaventura (Colombia)	265 in	(6743 mm)
Monrovia (Liberia)	202 in	(5131 mm)
Pago Pago (American Samoa)	196 in	(4990 mm)
Mawlamyine (Myanmar)	191 in	(4852 mm)
Lae (Papua New Guinea)	183 in	(4645 mm)

The time zones

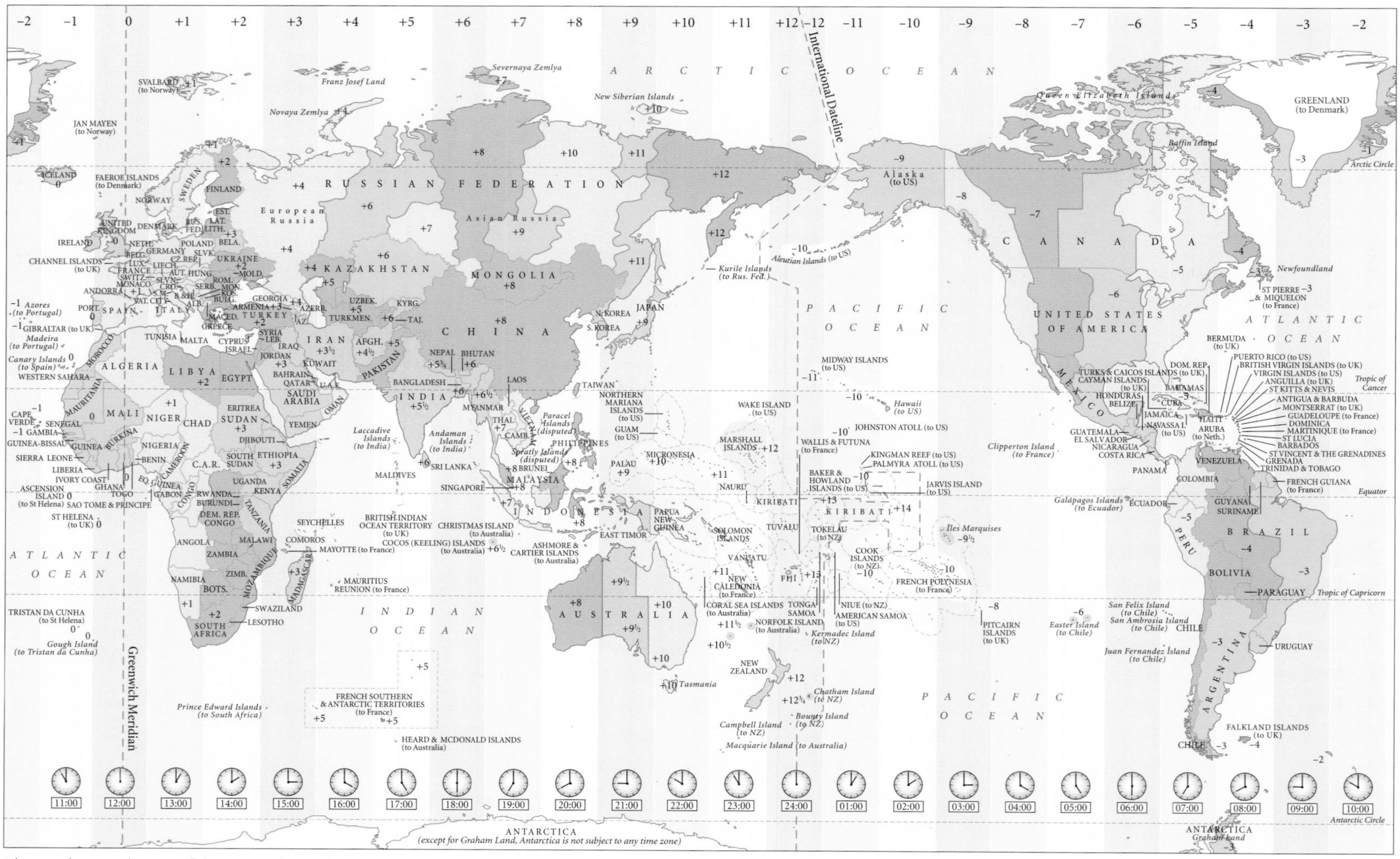

-2 -1 0 +1 +2 +3 +4 +5 +6 +7 +8 +9 +10 +11 +12 -12 -11 -10 -9 -8 -7 -6 -5 -4 -3 -2
International Dateline
Greenwich Meridian
A R C T I C O C E A N
P A C I F I C O C E A N
A T L A N T I C O C E A N
I N D I A N O C E A N
R U S S I A N F E D E R A T I O N
European Russia
Asian Russia
K A Z A K H S T A N
M O N G O L I A
C H I N A
I N D I A
I R A N
C A N A D A
U N I T E D S T A T E S O F A M E R I C A
B R A Z I L
A U S T R A L I A
NEW ZEALAND
GREENLAND (to Denmark)
ALGERIA
LIBYA
EGYPT
SOUTH AFRICA
Tropic of Cancer
Equator
Tropic of Capricorn
Arctic Circle
Antarctic Circle
11:00 12:00 13:00 14:00 15:00 16:00 17:00 18:00 19:00 20:00 21:00 22:00 23:00 24:00 01:00 02:00 03:00 04:00 05:00 06:00 07:00 08:00 09:00 10:00
ANTARCTICA
(except for Graham Land, Antarctica is not subject to any time zone)

The numbers at the top of the map indicate the number of hours each time zone is ahead or behind Coordinated Universal Time (UTC). The clocks and 24-hour times given at the bottom of the map show the time in each time zone when it is 12:00 hours noon (UTC)

Time Zones

Because Earth is a rotating sphere, the Sun shines on only half of its surface at any one time. Thus, it is simultaneously morning, evening and night time in different parts of the world *(see diagram below)*. Because of these disparities, each country or part of a country adheres to a local time.

A region of Earth's surface within which a single local time is used is called a time zone. There are 24 one hour time zones around the world, arranged roughly in longitudinal bands.

Standard Time

Standard time is the official local time in a particular country or part of a country. It is defined by the time zone or zones associated with that country or region. Although time zones are arranged roughly in longitudinal bands, in many places the borders of a zone do not fall exactly on longitudinal meridians, as can be seen on the map *(above)*, but are determined by geographical factors or by borders between countries or parts of countries. Most countries have just one time zone and one standard time, but some large countries (such as the US, Canada, and Russia) are split between several time zones, so standard time varies across those countries. For example, the coterminous United States straddles four time zones and so has four standard times, called the Eastern, Central, Mountain, and Pacific standard times. China is unusual in that just one standard time is used for the whole country, even though it extends across 60° of longitude from west to east.

Day and night around the world

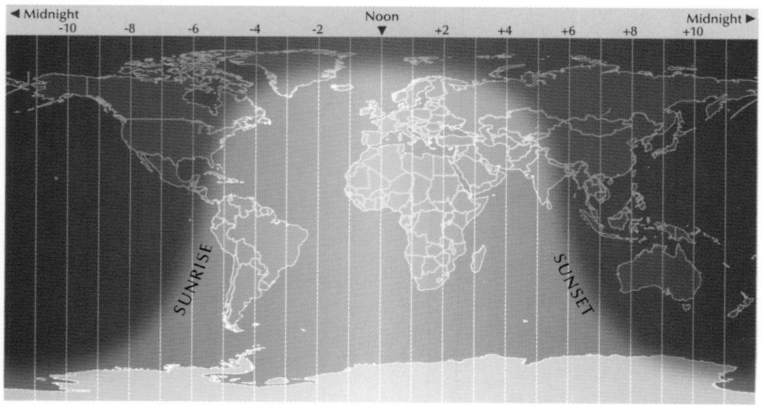

◄ Midnight -10
-8
-6
-4
-2
Noon
+2
+4
+6
+8
Midnight ► +10
SUNRISE
SUNSET

Coordinated Universal Time (UTC)

Coordinated Universal Time (UTC) is a reference by which the local time in each time zone is set. For example, Australian Western Standard Time (the local time in Western Australia) is set 8 hours ahead of UTC (it is UTC+8) whereas Eastern Standard Time in the United States is set 5 hours behind UTC (it is UTC-5). UTC is a successor to, and closely approximates, Greenwich Mean Time (GMT). However, UTC is based on an atomic clock, whereas GMT is determined by the Sun's position in the sky relative to the 0° longitudinal meridian, which runs through Greenwich, UK.

The International Dateline

The International Dateline is an imaginary line from pole to pole that roughly corresponds to the 180° longitudinal meridian. It is an arbitrary marker between calendar days. The dateline is needed because of the use of local times around the world rather than a single universal time. When moving from west to east across the dateline, travelers have to set their watches back one day. Those traveling in the opposite direction, from east to west, must add a day.

Daylight Saving Time

Daylight saving is a summertime adjustment to the local time in a country or region, designed to cause a higher proportion of its citizens' waking hours to pass during daylight. To follow the system, timepieces are advanced by an hour on a pre-decided date in spring and reverted back in the fall. About half of the world's nations use daylight saving.

Countries of the World

There are currently 196 independent countries in the world and almost 60 dependencies. Antarctica is the only land area on Earth that is not officially part of, and does not belong to, any single country.

In 1950, the world comprised 82 countries. In the decades following, many more states came into being as they achieved independence from their former colonial rulers. Most recent additions were caused by the breakup of the former Soviet Union in 1991, and the former Yugoslavia in 1992, which swelled the ranks of independent states. In July 2011, South Sudan became the latest country to be formed after declaring independence from Sudan.

Country factfile key

Formation Date of independence / date current borders were established

Population Total population / population density – based on total *land* area

Languages An asterisk (*) denotes the official language(s)

Calorie consumption Average number of calories consumed daily per person

AFGHANISTAN
Central Asia

Official name Islamic Republic of Afghanistan
Formation 1919 / 1919
Capital Kabul
Population 32.4 million / 129 people per sq mile (50 people per sq km)
Total area 250,000 sq. miles (647,500 sq. km)
Languages Pashtu*, Tajik, Dari*, Farsi, Uzbek, Turkmen
Religions Sunni Muslim 80%, Shi'a Muslim 19%, Other 1%
Ethnic mix Pashtun 38%, Tajik 25%, Hazara 19%, Uzbek and Turkmen 15%, Other 3%
Government Nonparty system
Currency Afghani = 100 puls
Literacy rate rate 28%
Calorie consumption 1539 kilocalories

ALBANIA
Southeast Europe

Official name Republic of Albania
Formation 1912 / 1921
Capital Tirana
Population 3.2 million / 302 people per sq mile (117 people per sq km)
Total area 11,100 sq. miles (28,748 sq. km)
Languages Albanian*, Greek
Religions Sunni Muslim 70%, Albanian Orthodox 20%, Roman Catholic 10%
Ethnic mix Albanian 98%, Greek 1%, Other 1%
Government Parliamentary system
Currency Lek = 100 qindarka (qintars)
Literacy rate 96%
Calorie consumption 2903 kilocalories

ALGERIA
North Africa

Official name People's Democratic Republic of Algeria
Formation 1962 / 1962
Capital Algiers
Population 36 million / 39 people per sq mile (15 people per sq km)
Total area 919,590 sq. miles (2,381,740 sq. km)
Languages Arabic*, Tamazight (Kabyle, Shawia, Tamashek), French
Religions Sunni Muslim 99%, Christian and Jewish 1%
Ethnic mix Arab 75%, Berber 24%, European and Jewish 1%
Government Presidential system
Currency Algerian dinar = 100 centimes
Literacy rate 75%
Calorie consumption 3239 kilocalories

ANDORRA
Southwest Europe

Official name Principality of Andorra
Formation 1278 / 1278
Capital Andorra la Vella
Population 85,082 / 473 people per sq mile (183 people per sq km)
Total area 181 sq. miles (468 sq. km)
Languages Spanish, Catalan*, French, Portuguese
Religions Roman Catholic 94%, Other 6%
Ethnic mix Spanish 46%, Andorran 28%, Other 18%, French 8%
Government Parliamentary system
Currency Euro = 100 cents
Literacy rate 99%
Calorie consumption Not available

ANGOLA
Southern Africa

Official name Republic of Angola
Formation 1975 / 1975
Capital Luanda
Population 19.6 million / 41 people per sq mile (16 people per sq km)
Total area 481,351 sq. miles (1,246,700 sq. km)
Languages Portuguese*, Umbundu, Kimbundu, Kikongo
Religions Roman Catholic 68%, Protestant 20%, Indigenous beliefs 12%
Ethnic mix Ovimbundu 37%, Kimbundu 25%, Other 25%, Bakongo 13%
Government Presidential system
Currency Readjusted kwanza = 100 lwei
Literacy rate 70%
Calorie consumption 2079 kilocalories

ANTIGUA & BARBUDA
West Indies

Official name Antigua and Barbuda
Formation 1981 / 1981
Capital St. John's
Population 89,018 / 524 people per sq mile (202 people per sq km)
Total area 170 sq. miles (442 sq. km)
Languages English*, English patois
Religions Anglican 45%, Other Protestant 42%, Roman Catholic 10%, Other 2%, Rastafarian 1%
Ethnic mix Black African 95%, Other 5%
Government Parliamentary system
Currency East Caribbean dollar = 100 cents
Literacy rate 99%
Calorie consumption 2373 kilocalories

ARGENTINA
South America

Official name Republic of Argentina
Formation 1816 / 1816
Capital Buenos Aires
Population 40.8 million / 39 people per sq mile (15 people per sq km)
Total area 1,068,296 sq. miles (2,766,890 sq. km)
Languages Spanish*, Italian, Amerindian languages
Religions Roman Catholic 70%, Other 18%, Protestant 9%, Muslim 2%, Jewish 1%
Ethnic mix Indo-European 97%, Mestizo 2%, Amerindian 1%
Government Presidential system
Currency Argentine peso = 100 centavos
Literacy rate 98%
Calorie consumption 2918 kilocalories

ARMENIA
Southwest Asia

Official name Republic of Armenia
Formation 1991 / 1991
Capital Yerevan
Population 3.1 million / 269 people per sq mile (104 people per sq km)
Total area 11,506 sq. miles (29,800 sq. km)
Languages Armenian*, Azeri, Russian
Religions Armenian Apostolic Church (Orthodox) 88%, Armenian Catholic Church 6%, Other 6%
Ethnic mix Armenian 98%, Other 1%, Yezidi 1%
Government Parliamentary system
Currency Dram = 100 luma
Literacy rate 99%
Calorie consumption 2806 kilocalories

AUSTRALIA
Australasia & Oceania

Official name Commonwealth of Australia
Formation 1901 / 1901
Capital Canberra
Population 22.6 million / 8 people per sq mile (3 people per sq km)
Total area 2,967,893 sq. miles (7,686,850 sq. km)
Languages English*, Italian, Cantonese, Greek, Arabic, Vietnamese, Aboriginal languages
Religions Roman Catholic 26%, Nonreligious 19%, Anglican 19%, Other 17%, Other Christian 13%, United Church 6%
Ethnic mix European 92%, Asian 7%, Aboriginal and Other 1%
Government Parliamentary system
Currency Australian dollar = 100 cents
Literacy rate 99%
Calorie consumption 3261 kilocalories

AUSTRIA
Central Europe

Official name Republic of Austria
Formation 1918 / 1919
Capital Vienna
Population 8.4 million / 263 people per sq mile (102 people per sq km)
Total area 32,378 sq. miles (83,858 sq. km)
Languages German*, Croatian, Slovenian, Hungarian (Magyar)
Religions Roman Catholic 78%, Nonreligious 9%, Other (including Jewish and Muslim) 8%, Protestant 5%
Ethnic mix Austrian 93%, Croat, Slovene, and Hungarian 6%, Other 1%
Government Parliamentary system
Currency Euro = 100 cents
Literacy rate 99%
Calorie consumption 3800 kilocalories

AZERBAIJAN
Southwest Asia

Official name Republic of Azerbaijan
Formation 1991 / 1991
Capital Baku
Population 9.3 million / 278 people per sq mile (107 people per sq km)
Total area 33,436 sq. miles (86,600 sq. km)
Languages Azeri*, Russian
Religions Shi'a Muslim 68%, Sunni Muslim 26%, Russian Orthodox 3%, Armenian Apostolic Church (Orthodox) 2%, Other 1%
Ethnic mix Azeri 91%, Other 3%, Lazs 2%, Armenian 2%, Russian 2%
Government Presidential system
Currency New manat = 100 gopik
Literacy rate 99%
Calorie consumption 3072 kilocalories

BAHAMAS
West Indies

Official name Commonwealth of the Bahamas
Formation 1973 / 1973
Capital Nassau
Population 300,000 / 78 people per sq mile (30 people per sq km)
Total area 5382 sq. miles (13,940 sq. km)
Languages English*, English Creole, French Creole
Religions Baptist 32%, Anglican 20%, Roman Catholic 19%, Other 17%, Methodist 6%, Church of God 6%
Ethnic mix Black African 85%, European 12%, Asian and Hispanic 3%
Government Parliamentary system
Currency Bahamian dollar = 100 cents
Literacy rate 96%
Calorie consumption 2750 kilocalories

BAHRAIN
Southwest Asia

Official name Kingdom of Bahrain
Formation 1971 / 1971
Capital Manama
Population 1.3 million / 4762 people per sq mile (1841 people per sq km)
Total area 239 sq. miles (620 sq. km)
Languages Arabic
Religions Muslim (mainly Shi'a) 99%, Other 1%
Ethnic mix Bahraini 63%, Asian 19%, Other Arab 10%, Iranian 8%
Government Mixed monarchical–parliamentary system
Currency Bahraini dinar = 1000 fils
Literacy rate 91%
Calorie consumption Not available

BANGLADESH
South Asia

Official name People's Republic of Bangladesh
Formation 1971 / 1971
Capital Dhaka
Population 150 million / 2911 people per sq mile (1124 people per sq km)
Total area 55,598 sq. miles (144,000 sq. km)
Languages Bengali*, Urdu, Chakma, Marma (Magh), Garo, Khasi, Santhali, Tripuri, Mro
Religions Muslim (mainly Sunni) 88%, Hindu 11%, Other 1%
Ethnic mix Bengali 98%, Other 2%
Government Parliamentary system
Currency Taka = 100 poisha
Literacy rate 56%
Calorie consumption 2481 kilocalories

BARBADOS
West Indies

Official name Barbados
Formation 1966 / 1966
Capital Bridgetown
Population 300,000 / 1807 people per sq mile (698 people per sq km)
Total area 166 sq. miles (430 sq. km)
Languages Bajan (Barbadian English), English*
Religions Anglican 40%, Other 24%, Nonreligious 17%, Pentecostal 8%, Methodist 7%, Roman Catholic 4%
Ethnic mix Black African 92%, White 3%, Other 3%, Mixed race 2%
Government Parliamentary system
Currency Barbados dollar = 100 cents
Literacy rate 99%
Calorie consumption 3021 kilocalories

BELARUS
Eastern Europe

Official name Republic of Belarus
Formation 1991 / 1991
Capital Minsk
Population 9.6 million / 120 people per sq mile (46 people per sq km)
Total area 80,154 sq. miles (207,600 sq. km)
Languages Belarussian*, Russian*
Religions Orthodox Christian 80%, Roman Catholic 14%, Other 4%, Protestant 2%
Ethnic mix Belarussian 81%, Russian 11%, Polish 4%, Ukrainian 2%, Other 2%
Government Presidential system
Currency Belarussian rouble = 100 kopeks
Literacy rate 99%
Calorie consumption 3186 kilocalories

BELGIUM
Northwest Europe

Official name Kingdom of Belgium
Formation 1830 / 1919
Capital Brussels
Population 10.8 million / 852 people per sq mile (329 people per sq km)
Total area 11,780 sq. miles (30,510 sq. km)
Languages Dutch*, French*, German*
Religions Roman Catholic 88%, Other 10%, Muslim 2%
Ethnic mix Fleming 58%, Walloon 33%, Other 6%, Italian 2%, Moroccan 1%
Government Parliamentary system
Currency Euro = 100 cents
Literacy rate 99%
Calorie consumption 3721 kilocalories

BELIZE
Central America

Official name Belize
Formation 1981 / 1981
Capital Belmopan
Population 300,000 / 34 people per sq mile (13 people per sq km)
Total area 8867 sq. miles (22,966 sq. km)
Languages English Creole, Spanish, English*, Mayan, Garifuna (Carib)
Religions Roman Catholic 62%, Other 13%, Anglican 12%, Methodist 6%, Mennonite 4%, Seventh-day Adventist 3%
Ethnic mix Mestizo 49%, Creole 25%, Maya 11%, Garifuna 6%, Other 6%, Asian Indian 3%
Government Parliamentary system
Currency Belizean dollar = 100 cents
Literacy rate 75%
Calorie consumption 2680 kilocalories

BENIN
West Africa

Official name Republic of Benin
Formation 1960 / 1960
Capital Porto-Novo
Population 9.1 million / 213 people per sq mile (82 people per sq km)
Total area 43,483 sq. miles (112,620 sq. km)
Languages Fon, Bariba, Yoruba, Adja, Houeda, Somba, French*
Religions Indigenous beliefs and Voodoo 50%, Christian 30%, Muslim 20%
Ethnic mix Fon 41%, Other 21%, Adja 16%, Yoruba 12%, Bariba 10%
Government Presidential system
Currency CFA franc = 100 centimes
Literacy rate 42%
Calorie consumption 2592 kilocalories

BHUTAN
South Asia

Official name Kingdom of Bhutan
Formation 1656 / 1865
Capital Thimphu
Population 700,000 / 39 people per sq mile (15 people per sq km)
Total area 18,147 sq. miles (47,000 sq. km)
Languages Dzongkha*, Nepali, Assamese
Religions Mahayana Buddhist 75%, Hindu 25%
Ethnic mix Bhutanese 50%, Nepalese 35%, Other 15%
Government Mixed monarchical–parliamentary system
Currency Ngultrum = 100 chetrum
Literacy rate 56%
Calorie consumption Not available

BOLIVIA
South America

Official name Plurinational State of Bolivia
Formation 1825 / 1938
Capital La Paz (administrative); Sucre (judicial)
Population 10.1 million / 24 people per sq mile (9 people per sq km)
Total area 424,162 sq. miles (1,098,580 sq. km)
Languages Aymara*, Quechua*, Spanish*
Religions Roman Catholic 93%, Other 7%
Ethnic mix Quechua 37%, Aymara 32%, Mixed race 13%, European 10%, Other 8%
Government Presidential system
Currency Boliviano = 100 centavos
Literacy rate 91%
Calorie consumption 2172 kilocalories

BOSNIA & HERZEGOVINA
Southeast Europe

Official name Bosnia and Herzegovina
Formation 1992 / 1992
Capital Sarajevo
Population 3.8 million / 192 people per sq mile (74 people per sq km)
Total area 19,741 sq. miles (51,129 sq. km)
Languages Bosnian*, Serbian*, Croatian*
Religions Muslim (mainly Sunni) 40%, Orthodox Christian 31%, Roman Catholic 15%, Other 10%, Protestant 4%
Ethnic mix Bosniak 48%, Serb 34%, Croat 16%, Other 2%
Government Parliamentary system
Currency Marka = 100 pfeninga
Literacy rate 98%
Calorie consumption 3070 kilocalories

BOTSWANA
Southern Africa

Official name Republic of Botswana
Formation 1966 / 1966
Capital Gaborone
Population 2 million / 9 people per sq mile (4 people per sq km)
Total area 231,803 sq. miles (600,370 sq. km)
Languages Setswana, English*, Shona, San, Khoikhoi, isiNdebele
Religions Christian (mainly Protestant) 70%, Nonreligious 20%, Traditional beliefs 6%, Other (including Muslim) 4%
Ethnic mix Tswana 79%, Kalanga 11%, Other 10%
Government Presidential system
Currency Pula = 100 thebe
Literacy rate 84%
Calorie consumption 2164 kilocalories

BRAZIL
South America

Official name Federative Republic of Brazil
Formation 1822 / 1828
Capital Brasília
Population 197 million / 60 people per sq mile (23 people per sq km)
Total area 3,286,470 sq. miles (8,511,965 sq. km)
Languages Portuguese*, German, Italian, Spanish, Polish, Japanese, Amerindian languages
Religions Roman Catholic 74%, Protestant 15%, Atheist 7%, Other 3%, Afro-American Spiritist 1%
Ethnic mix White 54%, Mixed race 38%, Black 6%, Other 2%
Government Presidential system
Currency Real = 100 centavos
Literacy rate 90%
Calorie consumption 3173 kilocalories

BRUNEI
Southeast Asia

Official name Sultanate of Brunei
Formation 1984 / 1984
Capital Bandar Seri Begawan
Population 400,000 / 197 people per sq mile (76 people per sq km)
Total area 2228 sq. miles (5770 sq. km)
Languages Malay*, English, Chinese
Religions Muslim (mainly Sunni) 66%, Buddhist 14%, Other 10%, Christian 10%
Ethnic mix Malay 67%, Chinese 16%, Other 11%, Indigenous 6%
Government Monarchy
Currency Brunei dollar = 100 cents
Literacy rate 95%
Calorie consumption 3088 kilocalories

BULGARIA
Southeast Europe

Official name Republic of Bulgaria
Formation 1908 / 1947
Capital Sofia
Population 7.4 million / 173 people per sq mile (67 people per sq km)
Total area 42,822 sq. miles (110,910 sq. km)
Languages Bulgarian*, Turkish, Romani
Religions Bulgarian Orthodox 83%, Muslim 12%, Other 4%, Roman Catholic 1%
Ethnic mix Bulgarian 84%, Turkish 9%, Roma 5%, Other 2%
Government Parliamentary system
Currency Lev = 100 stotinki
Literacy rate 98%
Calorie consumption 2791 kilocalories

BURKINA
West Africa

Official name Burkina Faso
Formation 1960 / 1960
Capital Ouagadougou
Population 17 million / 161 people per sq mile (62 people per sq km)
Total area 105,869 sq. miles (274,200 sq. km)
Languages Mossi, Fulani, French*, Tuare g, Dyula, Songhai
Religions Muslim 55%, Christian 25%, Traditional beliefs 20%
Ethnic mix Mossi 48%, Other 21%, Peul 10%, Lobi 7%, Bobo 7%, Mandé 7%
Government Presidential system
Currency CFA franc = 100 centimes
Literacy rate 29%
Calorie consumption 2647 kilocalories

BURUNDI
Central Africa

Official name Republic of Burundi
Formation 1962 / 1962
Capital Bujumbura
Population 8.6 million / 868 people per sq mile (335 people per sq km)
Total area 10,745 sq. miles (27,830 sq. km)
Languages Kirundi*, French*, Kiswahili
Religions Roman Catholic 62%, Traditional beliefs 23%, Muslim 10%, Protestant 5%
Ethnic mix Hutu 85%, Tutsi 14%, Twa 1%
Government Presidential system
Currency Burundian franc = 100 centimes
Literacy rate 67%
Calorie consumption 1604 kilocalories

CAMBODIA
Southeast Asia

Official name Kingdom of Cambodia
Formation 1953 / 1953
Capital Phnom Penh
Population 14.3 million / 210 people per sq mile (81 people per sq km)
Total area 69,900 sq. miles (181,040 sq. km)
Languages Khmer*, French, Chinese, Vietnamese, Cham
Religions Buddhist 93%, Muslim 6%, Christian 1%
Ethnic mix Khmer 90%, Vietnamese 5%, Other 4%, Chinese 1%
Government Parliamentary system
Currency Riel = 100 sen
Literacy rate 78%
Calorie consumption 2382 kilocalories

CAMEROON
Central Africa

Official name Republic of Cameroon
Formation 1960 / 1961
Capital Yaoundé
Population 20 million / 111 people per sq mile (43 people per sq km)
Total area 183,567 sq. miles (475,400 sq. km)
Languages Bamileke, Fang, Fulani, French*, English*
Religions Roman Catholic 35%, Traditional beliefs 25%, Muslim 22%, Protestant 18%
Ethnic mix Cameroon highlanders 31%, Other 21%, Equatorial Bantu 19%, Kirdi 11%, Fulani 10%, Northwestern Bantu 8%
Government Presidential system
Currency CFA franc = 100 centimes
Literacy rate 71%
Calorie consumption 2457 kilocalories

CANADA
North America

Official name Canada
Formation 1867 / 1949
Capital Ottawa
Population 34.3 million / 10 people per sq mile (4 people per sq km)
Total area 3,855,171 sq. miles (9,984,670 sq. km)
Languages English*, French*, Chinese, Italian, German, Ukrainian, Portuguese, Inuktitut, Cree
Religions Roman Catholic 44%, Protestant 29%, Other and nonreligious 27%
Ethnic mix European 66%, Other 32%, Amerindian 2%
Government Parliamentary system
Currency Canadian dollar = 100 cents
Literacy rate 99%
Calorie consumption 3399 kilocalories

CAPE VERDE
Atlantic Ocean

Official name Republic of Cape Verde
Formation 1975 / 1975
Capital Praia
Population 500,000 / 321 people per sq mile (124 people per sq km)
Total area 1557 sq. miles (4033 sq. km)
Languages Portuguese Creole, Portuguese*
Religions Roman Catholic 97%, Other 2%, Protestant (Church of the Nazarene) 1%
Ethnic mix Mestiço 71%, African 28%, European 1%
Government Mixed presidential–parliamentary system
Currency Escudo = 100 centavos
Literacy rate 85%
Calorie consumption 2644 kilocalories

CENTRAL AFRICAN REPUBLIC
Central Africa

Official name Central African Republic
Formation 1960 / 1960
Capital Bangui
Population 4.5 million / 19 people per sq mile (7 people per sq km)
Total area 240,534 sq. miles (622,984 sq. km)
Languages Sango, Banda, Gbaya, French*
Religions Traditional beliefs 35%, Roman Catholic 25%, Protestant 25%, Muslim 15%
Ethnic mix Baya 33%, Banda 27%, Other 17%, Mandjia 13%, Sara 10%
Government Presidential system
Currency CFA franc = 100 centimes
Literacy rate 55%
Calorie consumption 2181 kilocalories

CHAD
Central Africa

Official name Republic of Chad
Formation 1960 / 1960
Capital N'Djamena
Population 11.5 million / 24 people per sq mile (9 people per sq km)
Total area 495,752 sq. miles (1,284,000 sq. km)
Languages French*, Sara, Arabic*, Maba
Religions Muslim 51%, Christian 35%, Animist 7%, Traditional beliefs 7%
Ethnic mix Other 30%, Sara 28%, Mayo-Kebbi 12%, Arab 12%, Ouaddai 9%, Kanem-Bornou 9%
Government Presidential system
Currency CFA franc = 100 centimes
Literacy rate 34%
Calorie consumption 2074 kilocalories

CHILE
South America

Official name Republic of Chile
Formation 1818 / 1883
Capital Santiago
Population 17.3 million / 60 people per sq mile (23 people per sq km)
Total area 292,258 sq. miles (756,950 sq. km)
Languages Spanish*, Amerindian languages
Religions Roman Catholic 89%, Other and nonreligious 11%
Ethnic mix Mestizo and European 90%, Other Amerindian 9%, Mapuche 1%
Government Presidential system
Currency Chilean peso = 100 centavos
Literacy rate 99%
Calorie consumption 2908 kilocalories

CHINA
East Asia

Official name People's Republic of China
Formation 960 / 1999
Capital Beijing
Population 1.35 billion / 374 people per sq mile (144 people per sq km)
Total area 3,705,386 sq. miles (9,596,960 sq. km)
Languages Mandarin*, Wu, Cantonese, Hsiang, Min, Hakka, Kan
Religions Nonreligious 59%, Traditional beliefs 20%, Other 13%, Buddhist 6%, Muslim 2%
Ethnic mix Han 92%, Other 4%, Hui 1%, Miao 1%, Manchu 1%, Zhuang 1%
Government One-party state
Currency Renminbi (known as yuan) = 10 jiao = 100 fen
Literacy rate 94%
Calorie consumption 3036 kilocalories

COLOMBIA
South America

Official name Republic of Colombia
Formation 1819 / 1903
Capital Bogotá
Population 46.9 million / 117 people per sq mile (45 people per sq km)
Total area 439,733 sq. miles (1,138,910 sq. km)
Languages Spanish*, Wayuu, Páez, and other Amerindian languages
Religions Roman Catholic 95%, Other 5%
Ethnic mix Mestizo 58%, White 20%, European–African 14%, African 4%, African–Amerindian 3%, Amerindian 1%
Government Presidential system
Currency Colombian peso = 100 centavos
Literacy rate 93%
Calorie consumption 2717 kilocalories

COMOROS
Indian Ocean

Official name Union of the Comoros
Formation 1975 / 1975
Capital Moroni
Population 800,000 / 929 people per sq mile (359 people per sq km)
Total area 838 sq. miles (2170 sq. km)
Languages Arabic*, Comoran*, French*
Religions Muslim (mainly Sunni) 98%, Other 1%, Roman Catholic 1%
Ethnic mix Comoran 97%, Other 3%
Government Presidential system
Currency Comoros franc = 100 centimes
Literacy rate 74%
Calorie consumption 2139 kilocalories

CONGO
Central Africa

Official name Republic of the Congo
Formation 1960 / 1960
Capital Brazzaville
Population 4.1 million / 31 people per sq mile (12 people per sq km)
Total area 132,046 sq. miles (342,000 sq. km)
Languages Kongo, Teke, Lingala, French*
Religions Traditional beliefs 50%, Roman Catholic 35%, Protestant 13%, Muslim 2%
Ethnic mix Bakongo 51%, Teke 17%, Other 16%, Mbochi 11%, Mbédé 5%
Government Presidential system
Currency CFA franc = 100 centimes
Literacy rate 87%
Calorie consumption 2056 kilocalories

CONGO, DEM. REP.
Central Africa

Official name Democratic Republic of the Congo
Formation 1960 / 1960
Capital Kinshasa
Population 67.8 million / 77 people per sq mile (30 people per sq km)
Total area 905,563 sq. miles (2,345,410 sq. km)
Languages Kiswahili, Tshiluba, Kikongo, Lingala, French*
Religions Roman Catholic 50%, Protestant 20%, Traditional beliefs and other 10%, Muslim 10%, Kimbanguist 10%
Ethnic mix Other 55%, Mongo, Luba, Kongo, and Mangbetu-Azande 45%
Government Presidential system
Currency Congolese franc = 100 centimes
Literacy rate 67%
Calorie consumption 1585 kilocalories

COSTA RICA
Central America

Official name Republic of Costa Rica
Formation 1838 / 1838
Capital San José
Population 4.7 million / 238 people per sq mile (92 people per sq km)
Total area 19,730 sq. miles (51,100 sq. km)
Languages Spanish*, English Creole, Bribri, Cabecar
Religions Roman Catholic 71%, Evangelical 14%, Nonreligious 11%, Other 4%
Ethnic mix Mestizo and European 94%, Black 3%, Other 1%, Chinese 1%, Amerindian 1%
Government Presidential system
Currency Costa Rican colón = 100 céntimos
Literacy rate 96%
Calorie consumption 2886 kilocalories

CROATIA
Southeast Europe

Official name Republic of Croatia
Formation 1991 / 1991
Capital Zagreb
Population 4.4 million / 202 people per sq mile (78 people per sq km)
Total area 21,831 sq. miles (56,542 sq. km)
Languages Croatian*
Religions Roman Catholic 88%, Other 7%, Orthodox Christian 4%, Muslim 1%
Ethnic mix Croat 90%, Other 5%, Serb 5%
Government Parliamentary system
Currency Kuna = 100 lipa
Literacy rate 99%
Calorie consumption 3130 kilocalories

CUBA
West Indies

Official name Republic of Cuba
Formation 1902 / 1902
Capital Havana
Population 11.3 million / 264 people per sq mile (102 people per sq km)
Total area 42,803 sq. miles (110,860 sq. km)
Languages Spanish
Religions Nonreligious 49%, Roman Catholic 40%, Atheist 6%, Other 4%, Protestant 1%
Ethnic mix Mulatto (mixed race) 51%, White 37%, Black 11%, Chinese 1%
Government One-party state
Currency Cuban peso = 100 centavos
Literacy rate 99%
Calorie consumption 3258 kilocalories

CYPRUS
Southeast Europe

Official name Republic of Cyprus
Formation 1960 / 1960
Capital Nicosia
Population 1.1 million / 308 people per sq mile (119 people per sq km)
Total area 3571 sq. miles (9250 sq. km)
Languages Greek*, Turkish*
Religions Orthodox Christian 78%, Muslim 18%, Other 4%
Ethnic mix Greek 81%, Turkish 11%, Other 8%
Government Presidential system
Currency Euro (new Turkish lira in TRNC) = 100 cents (euro); 100 kurus (Turkish lira)
Literacy rate 98%
Calorie consumption 2678 kilocalories

CZECH REPUBLIC
Central Europe

Official name Czech Republic
Formation 1993 / 1993
Capital Prague
Population 10.5 million / 345 people per sq mile (133 people per sq km)
Total area 30,450 sq. miles (78,866 sq. km)
Languages Czech*, Slovak, Hungarian (Magyar)
Religions Roman Catholic 39%, Atheist 38%, Other 18%, Protestant 3%, Hussite 2%
Ethnic mix Czech 90%, Moravian 4%, Other 4%, Slovak 2%
Government Parliamentary system
Currency Czech koruna = 100 haleru
Literacy rate 99%
Calorie consumption 3305 kilocalories

DENMARK
Northern Europe

Official name Kingdom of Denmark
Formation 950 / 1944
Capital Copenhagen
Population 5.6 million / 342 people per sq mile (132 people per sq km)
Total area 16,639 sq. miles (43,094 sq. km)
Languages Danish
Religions Evangelical Lutheran 95%, Roman Catholic 3%, Muslim 2%
Ethnic mix Danish 96%, Other (including Scandinavian and Turkish) 3%, Faeroese and Inuit 1%
Government Parliamentary system
Currency Danish krone = 100 øre
Literacy rate 99%
Calorie consumption 3378 kilocalories

DJIBOUTI
East Africa

Official name Republic of Djibouti
Formation 1977 / 1977
Capital Djibouti
Population 900,000 / 101 people per sq mile (39 people per sq km)
Total area 8494 sq. miles (22,000 sq. km)
Languages Somali, Afar, French*, Arabic*
Religions Muslim (mainly Sunni) 94%, Christian 6%
Ethnic mix Issa 60%, Afar 35%, Other 5%
Government Presidential system
Currency Djibouti franc = 100 centimes
Literacy rate 70%
Calorie consumption 2419 kilocalories

DOMINICA
West Indies

Official name Commonwealth of Dominica
Formation 1978 / 1978
Capital Roseau
Population 73,126 / 252 people per sq mile (98 people per sq km)
Total area 291 sq. miles (754 sq. km)
Languages French Creole, English*
Religions Roman Catholic 77%, Protestant 15%, Other 8%
Ethnic mix Black 87%, Mixed race 9%, Carib 3%, Other 1%
Government Parliamentary system
Currency East Caribbean dollar = 100 cents
Literacy rate 88%
Calorie consumption 3147 kilocalories

DOMINICAN REPUBLIC
West Indies

Official name Dominican Republic
Formation 1865 / 1865
Capital Santo Domingo
Population 10.1 million / 541 people per sq mile (209 people per sq km)
Total area 18,679 sq. miles (48,380 sq. km)
Languages Spanish*, French Creole
Religions Roman Catholic 95%, Other and nonreligious 5%
Ethnic mix Mixed race 73%, European 16%, African 11%
Government Presidential system
Currency Dominican Republic peso = 100 centavos
Literacy rate 88%
Calorie consumption 2491 kilocalories

EAST TIMOR
Southeast Asia

Official name Democratic Republic of Timor-Leste
Formation 2002 / 2002
Capital Dili
Population 1.2 million / 213 people per sq mile (82 people per sq km)
Total area 5756 sq. miles (14,874 sq. km)
Languages Tetum (Portuguese/Austronesian)*, Bahasa Indonesia, Portuguese*
Religions Roman Catholic 95%, Other (including Muslim and Protestant) 5%
Ethnic mix Papuan groups approx 85%, Indonesian approx 13%, Chinese 2%
Government Parliamentary system
Currency US dollar = 100 cents
Literacy rate 51%
Calorie consumption 2076 kilocalories

ECUADOR
South America

Official name Republic of Ecuador
Formation 1830 / 1942
Capital Quito
Population 14.7 million / 138 people per sq mile (53 people per sq km)
Total area 109,483 sq. miles (283,560 sq. km)
Languages Spanish*, Quechua, other Amerindian languages
Religions Roman Catholic 95%, Protestant, Jewish, and other 5%
Ethnic mix Mestizo 77%, White 11%, Amerindian 7%, Black 5%
Government Presidential system
Currency US dollar = 100 cents
Literacy rate 84%
Calorie consumption 2267 kilocalories

EGYPT
North Africa

Official name Arab Republic of Egypt
Formation 1936 / 1982
Capital Cairo
Population 82.5 million / 215 people per sq mile (83 people per sq km)
Total area 386,660 sq. miles (1,001,450 sq. km)
Languages Arabic*, French, English, Berber
Religions Muslim (mainly Sunni) 90%, Coptic Christian and other 9%, Other Christian 1%
Ethnic mix Egyptian 99%, Nubian, Armenian, Greek, and Berber 1%
Government Transitional regime
Currency Egyptian pound = 100 piastres
Literacy rate 72%
Calorie consumption 3349 kilocalories

EL SALVADOR
Central America

Official name Republic of El Salvador
Formation 1841 / 1841
Capital San Salvador
Population 6.2 million / 775 people per sq mile (299 people per sq km)
Total area 8124 sq. miles (21,040 sq. km)
Languages Spanish
Religions Roman Catholic 80%, Evangelical 18%, Other 2%
Ethnic mix Mestizo 90%, White 9%, Amerindian 1%
Government Presidential system
Currency Salvadorean colón & US dollar = 100 centavos (colón); 100 cents (US dollar)
Literacy rate 84%
Calorie consumption 2574 kilocalories

EQUATORIAL GUINEA
Central Africa

Official name Republic of Equatorial Guinea
Formation 1968 / 1968
Capital Malabo
Population 700,000 / 65 people per sq mile (25 people per sq km)
Total area 10,830 sq. miles (28,051 sq. km)
Languages Spanish*, Fang, Bubi, French*
Religions Roman Catholic 90%, Other 10%
Ethnic mix Fang 85%, Other 11%, Bubi 4%
Government Presidential system
Currency CFA franc = 100 centimes
Literacy rate 93%
Calorie consumption Not available

ERITREA
East Africa

Official name State of Eritrea
Formation 1993 / 2002
Capital Asmara
Population 5.4 million / 119 people per sq mile (46 people per sq km)
Total area 46,842 sq. miles (121,320 sq. km)
Languages Tigrinya*, English*, Tigre, Afar, Arabic*, Saho, Bilen, Kunama, Nara, Hadareb
Religions Christian 50%, Muslim 48%, Other 2%
Ethnic mix Tigray 50%, Tigre 31%, Other 9%, Afar 5%, Saho 5%
Government Transitional regime
Currency Nakfa = 100 cents
Literacy rate 67%
Calorie consumption 1640 kilocalories

ESTONIA
Northeast Europe

Official name Republic of Estonia
Formation 1991 / 1991
Capital Tallinn
Population 1.3 million / 75 people per sq mile (29 people per sq km)
Total area 17,462 sq. miles (45,226 sq. km)
Languages Estonian*, Russian
Religions Evangelical Lutheran 56%, Orthodox Christian 25%, Other 19%
Ethnic mix Estonian 69%, Russian 25%, Other 4%, Ukrainian 2%
Government Parliamentary system
Currency Euro = 100 cents
Literacy rate 99%
Calorie consumption 3163 kilocalories

ETHIOPIA
East Africa

Official name Federal Democratic Republic of Ethiopia
Formation 1896 / 2002
Capital Addis Ababa
Population 84.7 million / 198 people per sq mile (76 people per sq km)
Total area 435,184 sq. miles (1,127,127 sq. km)
Languages Amharic*, Tigrinya, Galla, Sidamo, Somali, English, Arabic
Religions Orthodox Christian 40%, Muslim 40%, Traditional beliefs 15%, Other 5%
Ethnic mix Oromo 40%, Amhara 25%, Other 13%, Sidama 9%, Tigray 7%, Somali 6%
Government Parliamentary system
Currency Birr = 100 cents
Literacy rate 36%
Calorie consumption 2097 kilocalories

FIJI
Australasia & Oceania

Official name Republic of the Fiji Islands
Formation 1970 / 1970
Capital Suva
Population 900,000 / 128 people per sq mile (49 people per sq km)
Total area 7054 sq. miles (18,270 sq. km)
Languages Fijian, English*, Hindi, Urdu, Tamil, Telugu
Religions Hindu 38%, Methodist 37%, Roman Catholic 9%, Muslim 8%, Other 8%
Ethnic mix Melanesian 51%, Indian 44%, Other 5%
Government Transitional regime
Currency Fiji dollar = 100 cents
Literacy rate 94%
Calorie consumption 2996 kilocalories

FINLAND
Northern Europe

Official name Republic of Finland
Formation 1917 / 1947
Capital Helsinki
Population 5.4 million / 46 people per sq mile (18 people per sq km)
Total area 130,127 sq. miles (337,030 sq. km)
Languages Finnish*, Swedish*, Sámi
Religions Evangelical Lutheran 83%, Other 15%, Orthodox Christian 1%, Roman Catholic 1%
Ethnic mix Finnish 93%, Other (including Sámi) 7%
Government Parliamentary system
Currency Euro = 100 cents
Literacy rate 99%
Calorie consumption 3240 kilocalories

FRANCE
Western Europe

Official name French Republic
Formation 987 / 1919
Capital Paris
Population 63.1 million / 297 people per sq mile (115 people per sq km)
Total area 211,208 sq. miles (547,030 sq. km)
Languages French*, Provençal, German, Breton, Catalan, Basque
Religions Roman Catholic 88%, Muslim 8%, Protestant 2%, Buddhist 1%, Jewish 1%
Ethnic mix French 90%, North African (mainly Algerian) 6%, German (Alsace) 2%, Breton 1%, Other (including Corsicans) 1%
Government Mixed presidential–parliamentary system
Currency Euro = 100 cents
Literacy rate 99%
Calorie consumption 3531 kilocalories

GABON
Central Africa

Official name Gabonese Republic
Formation 1960 / 1960
Capital Libreville
Population 1.5 million / 15 people per sq mile (6 people per sq km)
Total area 103,346 sq. miles (267,667 sq. km)
Languages Fang, French*, Punu, Sira, Nzebi, Mpongwe
Religions Christian (mainly Roman Catholic) 55%, Traditional beliefs 40%, Other 4%, Muslim 1%
Ethnic mix Fang 26%, Shira-punu 24%, Other 16%, Foreign residents 15%, Nzabi-duma 11%, Mbédé-Teke 8%
Government Presidential system
Currency CFA franc = 100 centimes
Literacy rate 88%
Calorie consumption 2745 kilocalories

GAMBIA
West Africa

Official name Republic of the Gambia
Formation 1965 / 1965
Capital Banjul
Population 1.8 million / 466 people per sq mile (180 people per sq km)
Total area 4363 sq. miles (11,300 sq. km)
Languages Mandinka, Fulani, Wolof, Jola, Soninke, English*
Religions Sunni Muslim 90%, Christian 8%, Traditional beliefs 2%
Ethnic mix Mandinka 42%, Fulani 18%, Wolof 16%, Jola 10%, Serahuli 9%, Other 5%
Government Presidential system
Currency Dalasi = 100 butut
Literacy rate 46%
Calorie consumption 2643 kilocalories

GEORGIA
Southwest Asia

Official name Georgia
Formation 1991 / 1991
Capital Tbilisi
Population 4.3 million / 160 people per sq mile (62 people per sq km)
Total area 26,911 sq. miles (69,700 sq. km)
Languages Georgian*, Russian, Azeri, Armenian, Mingrelian, Ossetian, Abkhazian* (in Abkhazia)
Religions Georgian Orthodox 74%, Muslim 10%, Russian Orthodox 10%, Armenian Apostolic Church (Orthodox) 4%, Other 2%
Ethnic mix Georgian 84%, Azeri 6%, Armenian 6%, Russian 2%, Ossetian 1%, Other 1%
Government Presidential system
Currency Lari = 100 tetri
Literacy rate 99%
Calorie consumption 2743 kilocalories

GERMANY
Northern Europe

Official name Federal Republic of Germany
Formation 1871 / 1990
Capital Berlin
Population 82.2 million / 609 people per sq mile (235 people per sq km)
Total area 137,846 sq. miles (357,021 sq. km)
Languages German*, Turkish
Religions Protestant 34%, Roman Catholic 33%, Other 30%, Muslim 3%
Ethnic mix German 92%, Other European 3%, Other 3%, Turkish 2%
Government Parliamentary system
Currency Euro = 100 cents
Literacy rate 99%
Calorie consumption 3549 kilocalories

GHANA
West Africa

Official name Republic of Ghana
Formation 1957 / 1957
Capital Accra
Population 25 million / 281 people per sq mile (109 people per sq km)
Total area 92,100 sq. miles (238,540 sq. km)
Languages Twi, Fanti, Ewe, Ga, Adangbe, Gurma, Dagomba (Dagbani), English*
Religions Christian 69%, Muslim 16%, Traditional beliefs 9%, Other 6%
Ethnic mix Akan 49%, Mole-Dagbani 17%, Ewe 13%, Other 9%, Ga and Ga-Adangbe 8%, Guan 4%
Government Presidential system
Currency Cedi = 100 pesewas
Literacy rate 67%
Calorie consumption 2934 kilocalories

GREECE
Southeast Europe

Official name Hellenic Republic
Formation 1829 / 1947
Capital Athens
Population 11.4 million / 226 people per sq mile (87 people per sq km)
Total area 50,942 sq. miles (131,940 sq. km)
Languages Greek*, Turkish, Macedonian, Albanian
Religions Orthodox Christian 98%, Muslim 1%, Other 1%
Ethnic mix Greek 98%, Other 2%
Government Parliamentary system
Currency Euro = 100 cents
Literacy rate 97%
Calorie consumption 3661 kilocalories

GRENADA
West Indies

Official name Grenada
Formation 1974 / 1974
Capital St. George's
Population 109,011 / 832 people per sq mile (321 people per sq km)
Total area 131 sq. miles (340 sq. km)
Languages English*, English Creole
Religions Roman Catholic 68%, Anglican 17%, Other 15%
Ethnic mix Black African 82%, Mulatto (mixed race) 13%, East Indian 3%, Other 2%
Government Parliamentary system
Currency East Caribbean dollar = 100 cents
Literacy rate 96%
Calorie consumption 2456 kilocalories

GUATEMALA
Central America

Official name Republic of Guatemala
Formation 1838 / 1838
Capital Guatemala City
Population 14.8 million / 354 people per sq mile (136 people per sq km)
Total area 42,042 sq. miles (108,890 sq. km)
Languages Quiché, Mam, Cakchiquel, Kekchí, Spanish*
Religions Roman Catholic 65%, Protestant 33%, Other and nonreligious 2%
Ethnic mix Amerindian 60%, Mestizo 30%, Other 10%
Government Presidential system
Currency Quetzal = 100 centavos
Literacy rate 74%
Calorie consumption 2244 kilocalories

GUINEA
West Africa

Official name Republic of Guinea
Formation 1958 / 1958
Capital Conakry
Population 10.2 million / 107 people per sq mile (41 people per sq km)
Total area 94,925 sq. miles (245,857 sq. km)
Languages Pulaar, Malinké, Soussou, French*
Religions Muslim 85%, Christian 8%, Traditional beliefs 7%
Ethnic mix Peul 40%, Malinké 30%, Soussou 20%, Other 10%
Government Transitional regime
Currency Guinea franc = 100 centimes
Literacy rate 40%
Calorie consumption 2652 kilocalories

GUINEA-BISSAU
West Africa

Official name Republic of Guinea-Bissau
Formation 1974 / 1974
Capital Bissau
Population 1.5 million / 138 people per sq mile (53 people per sq km)
Total area 13,946 sq. miles (36,120 sq. km)
Languages Portuguese Creole, Balante, Fulani, Malinké, Portuguese*
Religions Traditional beliefs 50%, Muslim 40%, Christian 10%
Ethnic mix Balante 30%, Fulani 20%, Other 16%, Mandyako 14%, Mandinka 13%, Papel 7%
Government Transitional regime
Currency CFA franc = 100 centimes
Literacy rate 52%
Calorie consumption 2476 kilocalories

GUYANA
South America

Official name Cooperative Republic of Guyana
Formation 1966 / 1966
Capital Georgetown
Population 800,000 / 11 people per sq mile (4 people per sq km)
Total area 83,000 sq. miles (214,970 sq. km)
Languages English Creole, Hindi, Tamil, Amerindian languages, English*
Religions Christian 57%, Hindu 28%, Muslim 10%, Other 5%
Ethnic mix East Indian 43%, Black African 30%, Mixed race 17%, Amerindian 9%, Other 1%
Government Presidential system
Currency Guyanese dollar = 100 cents
Literacy rate 99%
Calorie consumption 2718 kilocalories

HAITI
West Indies

Official name Republic of Haiti
Formation 1804 / 1844
Capital Port-au-Prince
Population 10.1 million / 949 people per sq mile (366 people per sq km)
Total area 10,714 sq. miles (27,750 sq. km)
Languages French Creole*, French*
Religions Roman Catholic 55%, Protestant 28%, Other (including Voodoo) 16%, Nonreligious 1%
Ethnic mix Black African 95%, Mulatto (mixed race) and European 5%
Government Presidential system
Currency Gourde = 100 centimes
Literacy rate 62%
Calorie consumption 1979 kilocalories

HONDURAS
Central America

Official name Republic of Honduras
Formation 1838 / 1838
Capital Tegucigalpa
Population 7.8 million / 181 people per sq mile (70 people per sq km)
Total area 43,278 sq. miles (112,090 sq. km)
Languages Spanish*, Garífuna (Carib), English Creole
Religions Roman Catholic 97%, Protestant 3%
Ethnic mix Mestizo 90%, Black 5%, Amerindian 4%, White 1%
Government Presidential system
Currency Lempira = 100 centavos
Literacy rate 84%
Calorie consumption 2694 kilocalories

HUNGARY
Central Europe

Official name Hungary
Formation 1918 / 1947
Capital Budapest
Population 10 million / 280 people per sq mile (108 people per sq km)
Total area 35,919 sq. miles (93,030 sq. km)
Languages Hungarian (Magyar)*
Religions Roman Catholic 52%, Calvinist 16%, Other 15%, Nonreligious 14%, Lutheran 3%
Ethnic mix Magyar 90%, Roma 4%, German 3%, Serb 2%, Other 1%
Government Parliamentary system
Currency Forint = 100 fillér
Literacy rate 99%
Calorie consumption 3477 kilocalories

ICELAND
Northwest Europe

Official name Republic of Iceland
Formation 1944 / 1944
Capital Reykjavík
Population 300,000 / 8 people per sq mile (3 people per sq km)
Total area 39,768 sq. miles (103,000 sq. km)
Languages Icelandic*
Religions Evangelical Lutheran 84%, Other (mostly Christian) 10%, Roman Catholic 3%, Nonreligious 3%
Ethnic mix Icelandic 94%, Other 5%, Danish 1%
Government Parliamentary system
Currency Icelandic króna = 100 aurar
Literacy rate 99%
Calorie consumption 3376 kilocalories

INDIA
South Asia

Official name Republic of India
Formation 1947 / 1947
Capital New Delhi
Population 1.24 billion / 1081 people per sq mile (418 people per sq km)
Total area 1,269,339 sq. miles (3,287,590 sq. km)
Languages Hindi*, English*, Urdu, Bengali, Marathi, Telugu, Tamil, Bihari, Gujarati, Kanarese
Religions Hindu 81%, Muslim 13%, Christian 2%, Sikh 2%, Buddhist 1%, Other 1%
Ethnic mix Indo-Aryan 72%, Dravidian 25%, Mongoloid and other 3%
Government Parliamentary system
Currency Indian rupee = 100 paise
Literacy rate 66%
Calorie consumption 2321 kilocalories

INDONESIA
Southeast Asia

Official name Republic of Indonesia
Formation 1949 / 1999
Capital Jakarta
Population 242 million / 349 people per sq mile (135 people per sq km)
Total area 741,096 sq. miles (1,919,440 sq. km)
Languages Javanese, Sundanese, Madurese, Bahasa Indonesian*, Dutch
Religions Sunni Muslim 86%, Protestant 6%, Roman Catholic 3%, Hindu 2%, Other 2%, Buddhist 1%
Ethnic mix Javanese 41%, Other 29%, Sundanese 15%, Coastal Malays 12%, Madurese 3%
Government Presidential system
Currency Rupiah = 100 sen
Literacy rate 92%
Calorie consumption 2646 kilocalories

IRAN
Southwest Asia

Official name Islamic Republic of Iran
Formation 1502 / 1990
Capital Tehran
Population 74.8 million / 118 people per sq mile (46 people per sq km)
Total area 636,293 sq. miles (1,648,000 sq. km)
Languages Farsi*, Azeri, Luri, Gilaki, Mazanderani, Kurdish, Turkmen, Arabic, Baluchi
Religions Shi'a Muslim 89%, Sunni Muslim 9%, Other 2%
Ethnic mix Persian 51%, Azari 24%, Other 10%, Lur and Bakhtiari 8%, Kurdish 7%
Government Islamic theocracy
Currency Iranian rial = 100 dinars
Literacy rate 85%
Calorie consumption 3143 kilocalories

IRAQ
Southwest Asia

Official name Republic of Iraq
Formation 1932 / 1990
Capital Baghdad
Population 32.7 million / 194 people per sq mile (75 people per sq km)
Total area 168,753 sq. miles (437,072 sq. km)
Languages Arabic*, Kurdish*, Turkic languages, Armenian, Assyrian
Religions Shi'a Muslim 60%, Sunni Muslim 35%, Other (including Christian) 5%
Ethnic mix Arab 80%, Kurdish 15%, Turkmen 3%, Other 2%
Government Parliamentary system
Currency New Iraqi dinar = 1000 fils
Literacy rate 78%
Calorie consumption 2197 kilocalories

IRELAND
Northwest Europe

Official name Ireland
Formation 1922 / 1922
Capital Dublin
Population 4.5 million / 169 people per sq mile (65 people per sq km)
Total area 27,135 sq. miles (70,280 sq. km)
Languages English*, Irish Gaelic*
Religions Roman Catholic 87%, Other and nonreligious 10%, Anglican 3%
Ethnic mix Irish 99%, Other 1%
Government Parliamentary system
Currency Euro = 100 cents
Literacy rate 99%
Calorie consumption 3617 kilocalories

ISRAEL
Southwest Asia

Official name State of Israel
Formation 1948 / 1994
Capital Jerusalem (not internationally recognized)
Population 7.6 million / 968 people per sq mile (374 people per sq km)
Total area 8019 sq. miles (20,770 sq. km)
Languages Hebrew*, Arabic*, Yiddish, German, Russian, Polish, Romanian, Persian
Religions Jewish 76%, Muslim (mainly Sunni) 16%, Other 4%, Druze 2%, Christian 2%
Ethnic mix Jewish 76%, Arab 20%, Other 4%
Government Parliamentary system
Currency Shekel = 100 agorot
Literacy rate 99%
Calorie consumption 3569 kilocalories

ITALY
Southern Europe

Official name Italian Republic
Formation 1861 / 1947
Capital Rome
Population 60.8 million / 536 people per sq mile (207 people per sq km)
Total area 116,305 sq. miles (301,230 sq. km)
Languages Italian*, German, French, Rhaeto-Romanic, Sardinian
Religions Roman Catholic 85%, Other and nonreligious 13%, Muslim 2%
Ethnic mix Italian 94%, Other 4%, Sardinian 2%
Government Parliamentary system
Currency Euro = 100 cents
Literacy rate 99%
Calorie consumption 3627 kilocalories

IVORY COAST
West Africa

Official name Republic of Côte d'Ivoire
Formation 1960 / 1960
Capital Yamoussoukro
Population 20.2 million / 165 people per sq mile (64 people per sq km)
Total area 124,502 sq. miles (322,460 sq. km)
Languages Akan, French*, Krou, Voltaique
Religions Muslim 38%, Traditional beliefs 25%, Roman Catholic 25%, Other 6%, Protestant 6%
Ethnic mix Akan 42%, Voltaique 18%, Mandé du Nord 17%, Krou 11%, Mandé du Sud 10%, Other 2%
Government Presidential system
Currency CFA franc = 100 centimes
Literacy rate 55%
Calorie consumption 2670 kilocalories

JAMAICA
West Indies

Official name Jamaica
Formation 1962 / 1962
Capital Kingston
Population 2.8 million / 670 people per sq mile (259 people per sq km)
Total area 4243 sq. miles (10,990 sq. km)
Languages English Creole, English*
Religions Other and nonreligious 45%, Other Protestant 20%, Church of God 18%, Baptist 10%, Anglican 7%
Ethnic mix Black 91%, Mulatto (mixed race) 7%, European and Chinese 1%, East Indian 1%
Government Parliamentary system
Currency Jamaican dollar = 100 cents
Literacy rate 86%
Calorie consumption 2807 kilocalories

JAPAN
East Asia

Official name Japan
Formation 1590 / 1972
Capital Tokyo
Population 126 million / 870 people per sq mile (336 people per sq km)
Total area 145,882 sq. miles (377,835 sq. km)
Languages Japanese*, Korean, Chinese
Religions Shinto and Buddhist 76%, Buddhist 16%, Other (including Christian) 8%
Ethnic mix Japanese 99%, Other (mainly Korean) 1%
Government Parliamentary system
Currency Yen = 100 sen
Literacy rate 99%
Calorie consumption 2723 kilocalories

JORDAN
Southwest Asia

Official name Hashemite Kingdom of Jordan
Formation 1946 / 1967
Capital Amman
Population 6.3 million / 183 people per sq mile (71 people per sq km)
Total area 35,637 sq. miles (92,300 sq. km)
Languages Arabic*
Religions Sunni Muslim 92%, Christian 6%, Other 2%
Ethnic mix Arab 98%, Circassian 1%, Armenian 1%
Government Monarchy
Currency Jordanian dinar = 1000 fils
Literacy rate 92%
Calorie consumption 2977 kilocalories

KAZAKHSTAN
Central Asia

Official name Republic of Kazakhstan
Formation 1991 / 1991
Capital Astana
Population 16.2 million / 15 people per sq mile (6 people per sq km)
Total area 1,049,150 sq. miles (2,717,300 sq. km)
Languages Kazakh*, Russian, Ukrainian, German, Uzbek, Tatar, Uighur
Religions Muslim (mainly Sunni) 47%, Orthodox Christian 44%, Other 7%, Protestant 2%
Ethnic mix Kazakh 57%, Russian 27%, Other 8%, Uzbek 3%, Ukrainian 3%, German 2%
Government Presidential system
Currency Tenge = 100 tiyn
Literacy rate 99%
Calorie consumption 3284 kilocalories

KENYA
East Africa

Official name Republic of Kenya
Formation 1963 / 1963
Capital Nairobi
Population 41.6 million / 190 people per sq mile (73 people per sq km)
Total area 224,961 sq. miles (582,650 sq. km)
Languages Kiswahili*, English*, Kikuyu, Luo, Kalenjin, Kamba
Religions Christian 80%, Muslim 10%, Traditional beliefs 9%, Other 1%
Ethnic mix Other 28%, Kikuyu 22%, Luo 14%, Luhya 14%, Kalenjin 11%, Kamba 11%
Government Mixed Presidential–Parliamentary system
Currency Kenya shilling = 100 cents
Literacy rate 87%
Calorie consumption 2092 kilocalories

KIRIBATI
Australasia & Oceania

Official name Republic of Kiribati
Formation 1979 / 1979
Capital Bairiki (Tarawa Atoll)
Population 101,998 / 372 people per sq mile (144 people per sq km)
Total area 277 sq. miles (717 sq. km)
Languages English*, Kiribati
Religions Roman Catholic 55%, Kiribati Protestant Church 36%, Other 9%
Ethnic mix Micronesian 99%, Other 1%
Government Elections involving informal groupings
Currency Australian dollar = 100 cents
Literacy rate 99%
Calorie consumption 2866 kilocalories

KOSOVO (not yet recognised)
Southeast Europe

Official name Republic of Kosovo
Formation 2008 / 2008
Capital Pristina
Population 1.73 million / 412 people per sq mile (159 people per sq km)
Total area 4212 sq. miles (10,908 sq. km)
Languages Albanian*, Serbian*, Bosniak, Gorani, Roma, Turkish
Religions Muslim 92%, Roman Catholic 4%, Orthodox Christian 4%
Ethnic mix Albanian 92%, Serb 4%, Bosniak and Gorani 2%, Turkish 1%, Roma 1%
Government Parliamentary system
Currency Euro = 100 cents
Literacy rate 92%
Calorie consumption Not available

KUWAIT
Southwest Asia

Official name State of Kuwait
Formation 1961 / 1961
Capital Kuwait City
Population 2.8 million / 407 people per sq mile (157 people per sq km)
Total area 6880 sq. miles (17,820 sq. km)
Languages Arabic*, English
Religions Sunni Muslim 45%, Shi'a Muslim 40%, Christian, Hindu, and other 15%
Ethnic mix Kuwaiti 45%, Other Arab 35%, South Asian 9%, Other 7%, Iranian 4%
Government Monarchy
Currency Kuwaiti dinar = 1000 fils
Literacy rate 94%
Calorie consumption 3681 kilocalories

KYRGYZSTAN
Central Asia

Official name Kyrgyz Republic
Formation 1991 / 1991
Capital Bishkek
Population 5.4 million / 70 people per sq mile (27 people per sq km)
Total area 76,641 sq. miles (198,500 sq. km)
Languages Kyrgyz*, Russian*, Uzbek, Tatar, Ukrainian
Religions Muslim (mainly Sunni) 70%, Orthodox Christian 30%
Ethnic mix Kyrgyz 69%, Uzbek 14%, Russian 9%, Other 6%, Dungan 1%, Uighur 1%
Government Presidential system
Currency Som = 100 tyiyn
Literacy rate 99%
Calorie consumption 2791 kilocalories

LAOS
Southeast Asia

Official name Lao People's Democratic Republic
Formation 1953 / 1953
Capital Vientiane
Population 6.3 million / 71 people per sq mile (27 people per sq km)
Total area 91,428 sq. miles (236,800 sq. km)
Languages Lao*, Mon-Khmer, Yao, Vietnamese, Chinese, French
Religions Buddhist 65%, Other (including animist) 34%, Christian 1%
Ethnic mix Lao Loum 66%, Lao Theung 30%, Lao Soung 2%, Other 2%
Government One-party state
Currency New kip = 100 at
Literacy rate 73%
Calorie consumption 2377 kilocalories

LATVIA
Northeast Europe

Official name Republic of Latvia
Formation 1991 / 1991
Capital Riga
Population 2.2 million / 88 people per sq mile (34 people per sq km)
Total area 24,938 sq. miles (64,589 sq. km)
Languages Latvian*, Russian
Religions Other 43%, Lutheran 24%, Roman Catholic 18%, O rthodox Christian 15%
Ethnic mix Latvian 59%, Russian 28%, Belarussian 4%, Other 4%, Ukrainian 3%, Polish 2%
Government Parliamentary system
Currency Lats = 100 santimi
Literacy rate 99%
Calorie consumption 2923 kilocalories

LEBANON
Southwest Asia

Official name Republic of Lebanon
Formation 1941 / 1941
Capital Beirut
Population 4.3 million / 1089 people per sq mile (420 people per sq km)
Total area 4015 sq. miles (10,400 sq. km)
Languages Arabic*, French, Armenian, Assyrian
Religions Muslim 60%, Christian 39%, Other 1%
Ethnic mix Arab 95%, Armenian 4%, Other 1%
Government Parliamentary system
Currency Lebanese pound = 100 piastres
Literacy rate 90%
Calorie consumption 3153 kilocalories

LESOTHO
Southern Africa

Official name Kingdom of Lesotho
Formation 1966 / 1966
Capital Maseru
Population 2.2 million / 188 people per sq mile (72 people per sq km)
Total area 11,720 sq. miles (30,355 sq. km)
Languages English*, Sesotho*, isiZulu
Religions Christian 90%, Traditional beliefs 10%
Ethnic mix Sotho 99%, European and Asian 1%
Government Parliamentary system
Currency Loti & South African rand = 100 lisente
Literacy rate 90%
Calorie consumption 2371 kilocalories

LIBERIA
West Africa

Official name Republic of Liberia
Formation 1847 / 1847
Capital Monrovia
Population 4.1 million / 110 people per sq mile (43 people per sq km)
Total area 43,000 sq. miles (111,370 sq. km)
Languages Kpelle, Vai, Bassa, Kru, Grebo, Kissi, Gola, Loma, English*
Religions Christian 40%, Traditional beliefs 40%, Muslim 20%
Ethnic mix Indigenous tribes (12 groups) 49%, Kpellé 20%, Bassa 16%, Gio 8%, Krou 7%
Government Presidential system
Currency Liberian dollar = 100 cents
Literacy rate 59%
Calorie consumption 2261 kilocalories

LIBYA
North Africa

Official name Libya
Formation 1951 / 1951
Capital Tripoli
Population 6.4 million / 9 people per sq mile (4 people per sq km)
Total area 679,358 sq. miles (1,759,540 sq. km)
Languages Arabic*, Tuareg
Religions Muslim (mainly Sunni) 97%, Other 3%
Ethnic mix Arab and Berber 97%, Other 3%
Government Transitional regime
Currency Libyan dinar = 1000 dirhams
Literacy rate 89%
Calorie consumption 3157 kilocalories

LIECHTENSTEIN
Central Europe

Official name Principality of Liechtenstein
Formation 1719 / 1719
Capital Vaduz
Population 36,713 / 592 people per sq mile (229 people per sq km)
Total area 62 sq. miles (160 sq. km)
Languages German*, Alemannish dialect, Italian
Religions Roman Catholic 79%, Other 13%, Protestant 8%
Ethnic mix Liechtensteiner 66%, Other 12%, Swiss 10%, Austrian 6%, German 3%, Italian 3%
Government Parliamentary system
Currency Swiss franc = 100 rappen/centimes
Literacy rate 99%
Calorie consumption Not available

LITHUANIA
Northeast Europe

Official name Republic of Lithuania
Formation 1991 / 1991
Capital Vilnius
Population 3.3 million / 131 people per sq mile (51 people per sq km)
Total area 25,174 sq. miles (65,200 sq. km)
Languages Lithuanian*, Russian
Religions Roman Catholic 79%, Other 15%, Russian Orthodox 4%, Protestant 2%
Ethnic mix Lithuanian 85%, Polish 6%, Russian 5%, Other 3%, Belarussian 1%
Government Parliamentary system
Currency Litas = 100 centu
Literacy rate 99%
Calorie consumption 3486 kilocalories

LUXEMBOURG
Northwest Europe

Official name Grand Duchy of Luxembourg
Formation 1867 / 1867
Capital Luxembourg-Ville
Population 500,000 / 501 people per sq mile (193 people per sq km)
Total area 998 sq. miles (2586 sq. km)
Languages Luxembourgish*, German*, French*
Religions Roman Catholic 97%, Protestant, Orthodox Christian, and Jewish 3%
Ethnic mix Luxembourger 62%, Foreign residents 38%
Government Parliamentary system
Currency Euro = 100 cents
Literacy rate 99%
Calorie consumption 3637 kilocalories

MACEDONIA
Southeast Europe

Official name Republic of Macedonia
Formation 1991 / 1991
Capital Skopje
Population 2.1 million / 212 people per sq mile (82 people per sq km)
Total area 9781 sq. miles (25,333 sq. km)
Languages Macedonian*, Albanian*, Turkish, Romani, Serbian
Religions Orthodox Christian 65%, Muslim 29%, Roman Catholic 4%, Other 2%
Ethnic mix Macedonian 64%, Albanian 25%, Turkish 4%, Roma 3%, Serb 2%, Other 2%
Government Mixed presidential–parliamentary system
Currency Macedonian denar = 100 deni
Literacy rate 97%
Calorie consumption 2983 kilocalories

MADAGASCAR
Indian Ocean

Official name Republic of Madagascar
Formation 1960 / 1960
Capital Antananarivo
Population 21.3 million / 95 people per sq mile (37 people per sq km)
Total area 226,656 sq. miles (587,040 sq. km)
Languages Malagasy*, French*, English*
Religions Traditional beliefs 52%, Christian (mainly Roman Catholic) 41%, Muslim 7%
Ethnic mix Other Malay 46%, Merina 26%, Betsimisaraka 15%, Betsileo 12%, Other 1%
Government Transitional regime
Currency Ariary = 5 iraimbilanja
Literacy rate 64%
Calorie consumption 2117 kilocalories

MALAWI
Southern Africa

Official name Republic of Malawi
Formation 1964 / 1964
Capital Lilongwe
Population 15.4 million / 424 people per sq mile (164 people per sq km)
Total area 45,745 sq. miles (118,480 sq. km)
Languages Chewa, Lomwe, Yao, Ngoni, English*
Religions Protestant 55%, Roman Catholic 20%, Muslim 20%, Traditional beliefs 5%
Ethnic mix Bantu 99%, Other 1%
Government Presidential system
Currency Malawi kwacha = 100 tambala
Literacy rate 74%
Calorie consumption 2318 kilocalories

MALAYSIA
Southeast Asia

Official name Federation of Malaysia
Formation 1963 / 1965
Capital Kuala Lumpur; Putrajaya (administrative)
Population 28.9 million / 228 people per sq mile (88 people per sq km)
Total area 127,316 sq. miles (329,750 sq. km)
Languages Bahasa Malaysia*, Malay, Chinese, Tamil, English
Religions Muslim (mainly Sunni) 61%, Buddhist 19%, Christian 9%, Hindu 6%, Other 5%
Ethnic mix Malay 53%, Chinese 26%, Indigenous tribes 12%, Indian 8%, Other 1%
Government Parliamentary system
Currency Ringgit = 100 sen
Literacy rate 92%
Calorie consumption 2902 kilocalories

MALDIVES
Indian Ocean

Official name Republic of Maldives
Formation 1965 / 1965
Capital Male'
Population 394,491 / 3400 people per sq mile (1315 people per sq km)
Total area 116 sq. miles (300 sq. km)
Languages Dhivehi (Maldivian), Sinhala, Tamil, Arabic
Religions Sunni Muslim 100%
Ethnic mix Arab–Sinhalese–Malay 100%
Government Presidential system
Currency Rufiyaa = 100 laari
Literacy rate 97%
Calorie consumption 2720 kilocalories

MALI
West Africa

Official name Republic of Mali
Formation 1960 / 1960
Capital Bamako
Population 15.8 million / 34 people per sq mile (13 people per sq km)
Total area 478,764 sq. miles (1,240,000 sq. km)
Languages Bambara, Fulani, Senufo, Soninke, French*
Religions Muslim (mainly Sunni) 90%, Traditional beliefs 6%, Christian 4%
Ethnic mix Bambara 52%, Other 14%, Fulani 11%, Saracolé 7%, Soninka 7%, Tuareg 5%, Mianka 4%
Government Transitional regime
Currency CFA franc = 100 centimes
Literacy rate 23%
Calorie consumption 2624 kilocalories

MALTA
Southern Europe

Official name Republic of Malta
Formation 1964 / 1964
Capital Valletta
Population 400,000 / 3226 people per sq mile (1250 people per sq km)
Total area 122 sq. miles (316 sq. km)
Languages Maltese*, English*
Religions Roman Catholic 98%, Other and nonreligious 2%
Ethnic mix Maltese 96%, Other 4%
Government Parliamentary system
Currency Euro = 100 cents
Literacy rate 92%
Calorie consumption 3438 kilocalories

MARSHALL ISLANDS
Australasia & Oceania

Official name Republic of the Marshall Islands
Formation 1986 / 1986
Capital Majuro
Population 68,480 / 978 people per sq mile (378 people per sq km)
Total area 70 sq. miles (181 sq. km)
Languages Marshallese*, English*, Japanese, German
Religions Protestant 90%, Roman Catholic 8%, Other 2%
Ethnic mix Micronesian 90%, Other 10%
Government Presidential system
Currency US dollar = 100 cents
Literacy rate 91%
Calorie consumption Not available

MAURITANIA
West Africa

Official name Islamic Republic of Mauritania
Formation 1960 / 1960
Capital Nouakchott
Population 3.5 million / 9 people per sq mile (3 people per sq km)
Total area 397,953 sq. miles (1,030,700 sq. km)
Languages Hassaniyah Arabic*, Wolof, French
Religions Sunni Muslim 100%
Ethnic mix Maure 81%, Wolof 7%, Tukolor 5%, Other 4%, Soninka 3%
Government Presidential system
Currency Ouguiya = 5 khoums
Literacy rate 58%
Calorie consumption 2856 kilocalories

MAURITIUS
Indian Ocean

Official name Republic of Mauritius
Formation 1968 / 1968
Capital Port Louis
Population 1.3 million / 1811 people per sq mile (699 people per sq km)
Total area 718 sq. miles (1860 sq. km)
Languages French Creole, Hindi, Urdu, Tamil, Chinese, English*, French
Religions Hindu 48%, Roman Catholic 24%, Muslim 17%, Protestant 9%, Other 2%
Ethnic mix Indo-Mauritian 68%, Creole 27%, Sino-Mauritian 3%, Franco-Mauritian 2%
Government Parliamentary system
Currency Mauritian rupee = 100 cents
Literacy rate 88%
Calorie consumption 2993 kilocalories

MEXICO
North America

Official name United Mexican States
Formation 1836 / 1848
Capital Mexico City
Population 115 million / 156 people per sq mile (60 people per sq km)
Total area 761,602 sq. miles (1,972,550 sq. km)
Languages Spanish*, Nahuatl, Mayan, Zapotec, Mixtec, Otomi, Totonac, Tzotzil, Tzeltal
Religions Roman Catholic 77%, Other 14%, Protestant 6%, Nonreligious 3%
Ethnic mix Mestizo 60%, Amerindian 30%, European 9%, Other 1%
Government Presidential system
Currency Mexican peso = 100 centavos
Literacy rate 93%
Calorie consumption 3146 kilocalories

MICRONESIA
Australasia & Oceania

Official name Federated States of Micronesia
Formation 1986 / 1986
Capital Palikir (Pohnpei Island)
Population 106,487 / 393 people per sq mile (152 people per sq km)
Total area 271 sq. miles (702 sq. km)
Languages Trukese, Pohnpeian, Kosraean, Yapese, English*
Religions Roman Catholic 50%, Protestant 47%, Other 3%
Ethnic mix Chuukese 49%, Pohnpeian 24%, Other 14%, Kosraean 6%, Yapese 5%, Asian 2%
Government Nonparty system
Currency US dollar = 100 cents
Literacy rate 81%
Calorie consumption Not available

MOLDOVA
Southeast Europe

Official name Republic of Moldova
Formation 1991 / 1991
Capital Chisinau
Population 3.5 million / 269 people per sq mile (104 people per sq km)
Total area 13,067 sq. miles (33,843 sq. km)
Languages Moldovan*, Ukrainian, Russian
Religions Orthodox Christian 93%, Other 6%, Baptist 1%
Ethnic mix Moldovan 84%, Ukrainian 7%, Gagauz 5%, Russian 2%, Bulgarian 1%, Other 1%
Government Parliamentary system
Currency Moldovan leu = 100 bani
Literacy rate 99%
Calorie consumption 2707 kilocalories

MONACO
Southern Europe

Official name Principality of Monaco
Formation 1861 / 1861
Capital Monaco-Ville
Population 30,510 / 40680 people per sq mile (15646 people per sq km)
Total area 0.75 sq. miles (1.95 sq. km)
Languages French*, Italian, Monégasque, English
Religions Roman Catholic 89%, Protestant 6%, Other 5%
Ethnic mix French 47%, Other 21%, Italian 16%, Monégasque 16%
Government Mixed monarchical–parliamentary system
Currency Euro = 100 cents
Literacy rate 99%
Calorie consumption Not available

MONGOLIA
East Asia

Official name Mongolia
Formation 1924 / 1924
Capital Ulan Bator
Population 2.8 million / 5 people per sq mile (2 people per sq km)
Total area 604,247 sq. miles (1,565,000 sq. km)
Languages Khalkha Mongolian, Kazakh, Chinese, Russian
Religions Tibetan Buddhist 50%, Nonreligious 40%, Shamanist and Christian 6%, Muslim 4%
Ethnic mix Khalkh 95%, Kazakh 4%, Other 1%
Government Mixed presidential–parliamentary system
Currency Tugrik (tögrög) = 100 möngö
Literacy rate 98%
Calorie consumption 2434 kilocalories

MONTENEGRO
Southeast Europe

Official name Montenegro
Formation 2006 / 2006
Capital Podgorica
Population 600,000 / 113 people per sq mile (43 people per sq km)
Total area 5332 sq. miles (13,812 sq. km)
Languages Montenegrin*, Serbian, Albanian, Bosniak, Croatian
Religions Orthodox Christian 74%, Muslim 18%, Roman Catholic 4%, Other 4%
Ethnic mix Montenegrin 43%, Serb 32%, Other 12%, Bosniak 8%, Albanian 5%
Government Parliamentary system
Currency Euro = 100 cents
Literacy rate 98%
Calorie consumption 2887 kilocalories

MOROCCO
North Africa

Official name Kingdom of Morocco
Formation 1956 / 1969
Capital Rabat
Population 32.3 million / 187 people per sq mile (72 people per sq km)
Total area 172,316 sq. miles (446,300 sq. km)
Languages Arabic*, Tamazight (Berber), French, Spanish
Religions Muslim (mainly Sunni) 99%, Other (mostly Christian) 1%
Ethnic mix Arab 70%, Berber 29%, European 1%
Government Mixed monarchical–parliamentary system
Currency Moroccan dirham = 100 centimes
Literacy rate 56%
Calorie consumption 3264 kilocalories

MOZAMBIQUE
Southern Africa

Official name Republic of Mozambique
Formation 1975 / 1975
Capital Maputo
Population 23.9 million / 79 people per sq mile (30 people per sq km)
Total area 309,494 sq. miles (801,590 sq. km)
Languages Makua, Xitsonga, Sena, Lomwe, Portuguese*
Religions Traditional beliefs 56%, Christian 30%, Muslim 14%
Ethnic mix Makua Lomwe 47%, Tsonga 23%, Malawi 12%, Shona 11%, Yao 4%, Other 3%
Government Presidential system
Currency New metical = 100 centavos
Literacy rate 55%
Calorie consumption 2112 kilocalories

MYANMAR (BURMA)
Southeast Asia

Official name Union of Myanmar
Formation 1948 / 1948
Capital Nay Pyi Taw
Population 48.3 million / 190 people per sq mile (73 people per sq km)
Total area 261,969 sq. miles (678,500 sq. km)
Languages Burmese*, Shan, Karen, Rakhine, Chin, Yangbye, Kachin, Mon
Religions Buddhist 89%, Christian 4%, Muslim 4%, Other 2%, Animist 1%
Ethnic mix Burman (Bamah) 68%, Other 12%, Shan 9%, Karen 7%, Rakhine 4%
Government Presidential system
Currency Kyat = 100 pyas
Literacy rate 92%
Calorie consumption 2493 kilocalories

NAMIBIA
Southern Africa

Official name Republic of Namibia
Formation 1990 / 1994
Capital Windhoek
Population 2.3 million / 7 people per sq mile (3 people per sq km)
Total area 318,694 sq. miles (825,418 sq. km)
Languages Ovambo, Kavango, English*, Bergdama, German, Afrikaans
Religions Christian 90%, Traditional beliefs 10%
Ethnic mix Ovambo 50%, Other tribes 22%, Kavango 9%, Damara 7%, Herero 7%, Other 5%
Government Presidential system
Currency Namibian dollar & South African rand = 100 cents
Literacy rate 88%
Calorie consumption 2151 kilocalories

NAURU
Australasia & Oceania

Official name Republic of Nauru
Formation 1968 / 1968
Capital Yaren District
Population 9378 / 1158 people per sq mile (447 people per sq km)
Total area 8.1 sq. miles (21 sq. km)
Languages Nauruan*, Kiribati, Chinese, Tuvaluan, English
Religions Nauruan Congregational Church 60%, Roman Catholic 35%, Other 5%
Ethnic mix Nauruan 93%, Chinese 5%, European 1%, Other Pacific islanders 1%
Government Nonparty system
Currency Australian dollar = 100 cents
Literacy rate 95%
Calorie consumption Not available

NEPAL
South Asia

Official name Federal Democratic Republic of Nepal
Formation 1769 / 1769
Capital Kathmandu
Population 30.5 million / 577 people per sq mile (223 people per sq km)
Total area 54,363 sq. miles (140,800 sq. km)
Languages Nepali*, Maithili, Bhojpuri
Religions Hindu 81%, Buddhist 11%, Muslim 4%, Other (including Christian) 4%
Ethnic mix Other 52%, Chhetri 16%, Hill Brahman 13%, Tharu 7%, Magar 7%, Tamang 5%
Government Transitional regime
Currency Nepalese rupee = 100 paisa
Literacy rate 59%
Calorie consumption 2443 kilocalories

NETHERLANDS
Northwest Europe

Official name Kingdom of the Netherlands
Formation 1648 / 1839
Capital Amsterdam; The Hague (administrative)
Population 16.7 million / 1275 people per sq mile (492 people per sq km)
Total area 16,033 sq. miles (41,526 sq. km)
Languages Dutch*, Frisian
Religions Roman Catholic 36%, Other 34%, Protestant 27%, Muslim 3%
Ethnic mix Dutch 82%, Other 12%, Surinamese 2%, Turkish 2%, Moroccan 2%
Government Parliamentary system
Currency Euro = 100 cents
Literacy rate 99%
Calorie consumption 3261 kilocalories

NEW ZEALAND
Australasia & Oceania

Official name New Zealand
Formation 1947 / 1947
Capital Wellington
Population 4.4 million / 42 people per sq mile (16 people per sq km)
Total area 103,737 sq. miles (268,680 sq. km)
Languages English*, Maori*
Religions Anglican 24%, Other 22%, Presbyterian 18%, Nonreligious 16%, Roman Catholic 15%, Methodist 5%
Ethnic mix European 75%, Maori 15%, Other 7%, Samoan 3%
Government Parliamentary system
Currency New Zealand dollar = 100 cents
Literacy rate 99%
Calorie consumption 3172 kilocalories

NICARAGUA
Central America

Official name Republic of Nicaragua
Formation 1838 / 1838
Capital Managua
Population 5.9 million / 129 people per sq mile (50 people per sq km)
Total area 49,998 sq. miles (129,494 sq. km)
Languages Spanish*, English Creole, Miskito
Religions Roman Catholic 80%, Protestant Evangelical 17%, Other 3%
Ethnic mix Mestizo 69%, White 17%, Black 9%, Amerindian 5%
Government Presidential system
Currency Córdoba oro = 100 centavos
Literacy rate 80%
Calorie consumption 2517 kilocalories

NIGER
West Africa

Official name Republic of Niger
Formation 1960 / 1960
Capital Niamey
Population 16.1 million / 33 people per sq mile (13 people per sq km)
Total area 489,188 sq. miles (1,267,000 sq. km)
Languages Hausa, Djerma, Fulani, Tuareg, Teda, French*
Religions Muslim 99%, Other (including Christian) 1%
Ethnic mix Hausa 53%, Djerma and Songhai 21%, Tuareg 11%, Fulani 7%, Kanuri 6%, Other 2%
Government Presidential system
Currency CFA franc = 100 centimes
Literacy rate 30%
Calorie consumption 2489 kilocalories

NIGERIA
West Africa

Official name Federal Republic of Nigeria
Formation 1960 / 1961
Capital Abuja
Population 162 million / 462 people per sq mile (178 people per sq km)
Total area 356,667 sq. miles (923,768 sq. km)
Languages Hausa, English*, Yoruba, Ibo
Religions Muslim 50%, Christian 40%, Traditional beliefs 10%
Ethnic mix Other 29%, Hausa 21%, Yoruba 21%, Ibo 18%, Fulani 11%
Government Presidential system
Currency Naira = 100 kobo
Literacy rate 61%
Calorie consumption 2711 kilocalories

NORTH KOREA
East Asia

Official name Democratic People's Republic of Korea
Formation 1948 / 1953
Capital Pyongyang
Population 24.5 million / 527 people per sq mile (203 people per sq km)
Total area 46,540 sq. miles (120,540 sq. km)
Languages Korean*
Religions Atheist 100%
Ethnic mix Korean 100%
Government One-party state
Currency North Korean won = 100 chon
Literacy rate 99%
Calorie consumption 2078 kilocalories

NORWAY
Northern Europe

Official name Kingdom of Norway
Formation 1905 / 1905
Capital Oslo
Population 4.9 million / 41 people per sq mile (16 people per sq km)
Total area 125,181 sq. miles (324,220 sq. km)
Languages Norwegian* (Bokmål "book language" and Nynorsk "new Norsk"), Sámi
Religions Evangelical Lutheran 88%, Other and nonreligious 8%, Muslim 2%, Pentecostal 1%, Roman Catholic 1%
Ethnic mix Norwegian 93%, Other 6%, Sámi 1%
Government Parliamentary system
Currency Norwegian krone = 100 øre
Literacy rate 99%
Calorie consumption 3453 kilocalories

OMAN
Southwest Asia

Official name Sultanate of Oman
Formation 1951 / 1951
Capital Muscat
Population 2.8 million / 34 people per sq mile (13 people per sq km)
Total area 82,031 sq. miles (212,460 sq. km)
Languages Arabic*, Baluchi, Farsi, Hindi, Punjabi
Religions Ibadi Muslim 75%, Other Muslim and Hindu 25%
Ethnic mix Arab 88%, Baluchi 4%, Persian 3%, Indian and Pakistani 3%, African 2%
Government Monarchy
Currency Omani rial = 1000 baisa
Literacy rate 87%
Calorie consumption Not available

PAKISTAN
South Asia

Official name Islamic Republic of Pakistan
Formation 1947 / 1971
Capital Islamabad
Population 177 million / 594 people per sq mile (229 people per sq km)
Total area 310,401 sq. miles (803,940 sq. km)
Languages Punjabi, Sindhi, Pashtu, Urdu*, Baluchi, Brahui
Religions Sunni Muslim 77%, Shi'a Muslim 20%, Hindu 2%, Christian 1%
Ethnic mix Punjabi 56%, Pathan (Pashtun) 15%, Sindhi 14%, Mohajir 7%, Baluchi 4%, Other 4%
Government Presidential system
Currency Pakistani rupee = 100 paisa
Literacy rate 56%
Calorie consumption 2423 kilocalories

PALAU
Australasia & Oceania

Official name Republic of Palau
Formation 1994 / 1994
Capital Melekeok
Population 21,032 / 107 people per sq mile (41 people per sq km)
Total area 177 sq. miles (458 sq. km)
Languages Palauan, English, Japanese, Angaur, Tobi, Sonsorolese
Religions Christian 66%, Modekngei 34%
Ethnic mix Palauan 74%, Filipino 16%, Other 6%, Chinese and other Asian 4%
Government Nonparty system
Currency US dollar = 100 cents
Literacy rate 98%
Calorie consumption Not available

PANAMA
Central America

Official name Republic of Panama
Formation 1903 / 1903
Capital Panama City
Population 3.6 million / 123 people per sq mile (47 people per sq km)
Total area 30,193 sq. miles (78,200 sq. km)
Languages English Creole, Spanish*, Amerindian languages, Chibchan languages
Religions Roman Catholic 84%, Protestant 15%, Other 1%
Ethnic mix Mestizo 70%, Black 14%, White 10%, Amerindian 6%
Government Presidential system
Currency Balboa & US dollar = 100 centésimos
Literacy rate 94%
Calorie consumption 2606 kilocalories

PAPUA NEW GUINEA
Australasia & Oceania

Official name Independent State of Papua New Guinea
Formation 1975 / 1975
Capital Port Moresby
Population 7 million / 40 people per sq mile (15 people per sq km)
Total area 178,703 sq. miles (462,840 sq. km)
Languages Pidgin English, Papuan, English*, Motu, 800 (est.) native languages
Religions Protestant 60%, Roman Catholic 37%, Other 3%
Ethnic mix Melanesian and mixed race 100%
Government Parliamentary system
Currency Kina = 100 toea
Literacy rate 60%
Calorie consumption 2193 kilocalories

PARAGUAY
South America

Official name Republic of Paraguay
Formation 1811 / 1938
Capital Asunción
Population 6.6 million / 43 people per sq mile (17 people per sq km)
Total area 157,046 sq. miles (406,750 sq. km)
Languages Guarani, Spanish*, German
Religions Roman Catholic 90%, Protestant (including Mennonite) 10%
Ethnic mix Mestizo 91%, Other 7%, Amerindian 2%
Government Presidential system
Currency Guaraní = 100 céntimos
Literacy rate 95%
Calorie consumption 2518 kilocalories

PERU
South America

Official name Republic of Peru
Formation 1824 / 1941
Capital Lima
Population 29.4 million / 59 people per sq mile (23 people per sq km)
Total area 496,223 sq. miles (1,285,200 sq. km)
Languages Spanish*, Quechua*, Aymara
Religions Roman Catholic 81%, Other 19%
Ethnic mix Amerindian 45%, Mestizo 37%, White 15%, Other 3%
Government Presidential system
Currency New sol = 100 céntimos
Literacy rate 90%
Calorie consumption 2563 kilocalories

PHILIPPINES
Southeast Asia

Official name Republic of the Philippines
Formation 1946 / 1946
Capital Manila
Population 94.9 million / 824 people per sq mile (318 people per sq km)
Total area 115,830 sq. miles (300,000 sq. km)
Languages Filipino, English, Tagalog, Cebuano, Ilocano, Hiligaynon, many other local languages
Religions Roman Catholic 81%, Protestant 9%, Muslim 5%, Other (including Buddhist) 5%
Ethnic mix Other 34%, Tagalog 28%, Cebuano 13%, Ilocano 9%, Hiligaynon 8%, Bisaya 8%
Government Presidential system
Currency Philippine peso = 100 centavos
Literacy rate 95%
Calorie consumption 2580 kilocalories

POLAND
Northern Europe

Official name Republic of Poland
Formation 1918 / 1945
Capital Warsaw
Population 38.3 million / 326 people per sq mile (126 people per sq km)
Total area 120,728 sq. miles (312,685 sq. km)
Languages Polish*
Religions Roman Catholic 93%, Other and nonreligious 5%, Orthodox Christian 2%
Ethnic mix Polish 98%, Other 2%
Government Parliamentary system
Currency Zloty = 100 groszy
Literacy rate 99%
Calorie consumption 3392 kilocalories

PORTUGAL
Southwest Europe

Official name Republic of Portugal
Formation 1139 / 1640
Capital Lisbon
Population 10.7 million / 301 people per sq mile (116 people per sq km)
Total area 35,672 sq. miles (92,391 sq. km)
Languages Portuguese*
Religions Roman Catholic 92%, Protestant 4%, Nonreligious 3%, Other 1%
Ethnic mix Portuguese 98%, African and other 2%
Government Parliamentary system
Currency Euro = 100 cents
Literacy rate 95%
Calorie consumption 3617 kilocalories

QATAR
Southwest Asia

Official name State of Qatar
Formation 1971 / 1971
Capital Doha
Population 1.9 million / 447 people per sq mile (173 people per sq km)
Total area 4416 sq. miles (11,437 sq. km)
Languages Arabic*
Religions Muslim (mainly Sunni) 95%, Other 5%
Ethnic mix Qatari 20%, Indian 20%, Other Arab 20%, Nepalese 13%, Filipino 10%, Other 10%, Pakistani 7%
Government Monarchy
Currency Qatar riyal = 100 dirhams
Literacy rate 95%
Calorie consumption Not available

ROMANIA
Southeast Europe

Official name Romania
Formation 1878 / 1947
Capital Bucharest
Population 21.4 million / 241 people per sq mile (93 people per sq km)
Total area 91,699 sq. miles (237,500 sq. km)
Languages Romanian*, Hungarian (Magyar), Romani, German
Religions Romanian Orthodox 87%, Protestant 5%, Roman Catholic 5%, Greek Orthodox 1%, Greek Catholic (Uniate) 1%, Other 1%
Ethnic mix Romanian 89%, Magyar 7%, Roma 3%, Other 1%
Government Presidential system
Currency New Romanian leu = 100 bani
Literacy rate 98%
Calorie consumption 3487 kilocalories

RUSSIAN FEDERATION
Europe / Asia

Official name Russian Federation
Formation 1480 / 1991
Capital Moscow
Population 143 million / 22 people per sq mile (8 people per sq km)
Total area 6,592,735 sq. miles (17,075,200 sq. km)
Languages Russian*, Tatar, Ukrainian, Chavash, various other national languages
Religions Orthodox Christian 75%, Muslim 14%, Other 11%
Ethnic mix Russian 80%, Other 12%, Tatar 4%, Ukrainian 2%, Bashkir 1%, Chavash 1%
Government Mixed Presidential–Parliamentary system
Currency Russian rouble = 100 kopeks
Literacy rate 99%
Calorie consumption 3172 kilocalories

RWANDA
Central Africa

Official name Republic of Rwanda
Formation 1962 / 1962
Capital Kigali
Population 10.9 million / 1132 people per sq mile (437 people per sq km)
Total area 10,169 sq. miles (26,338 sq. km)
Languages Kinyarwanda*, French*, Kiswahili, English*
Religions Christian 94%, Muslim 5%, Traditional beliefs 1%
Ethnic mix Hutu 85%, Tutsi 14%, Other (including Twa) 1%
Government Presidential system
Currency Rwanda franc = 100 centimes
Literacy rate 71%
Calorie consumption 2188 kilocalories

ST KITTS & NEVIS
West Indies

Official name Federation of Saint Christopher and Nevis
Formation 1983 / 1983
Capital Basseterre
Population 50,726 / 365 people per sq mile (141 people per sq km)
Total area 101 sq. miles (261 sq. km)
Languages English*, English Creole
Religions Anglican 33%, Methodist 29%, Other 22%, Moravian 9%, Roman Catholic 7%
Ethnic mix Black 95%, Mixed race 3%, White 1%, Other and Amerindian 1%
Government Parliamentary system
Currency East Caribbean dollar = 100 cents
Literacy rate 98%
Calorie consumption 2546 kilocalories

ST LUCIA
West Indies

Official name Saint Lucia
Formation 1979 / 1979
Capital Castries
Population 162,178 / 687 people per sq mile (266 people per sq km)
Total area 239 sq. miles (620 sq. km)
Languages English*, French Creole
Religions Roman Catholic 90%, Other 10%
Ethnic mix Black 83%, Mulatto (mixed race) 13%, Asian 3%, Other 1%
Government Parliamentary system
Currency East Caribbean dollar = 100 cents
Literacy rate 95%
Calorie consumption 2710 kilocalories

ST VINCENT & THE GRENADINES
West Indies

Official name Saint Vincent and the Grenadines
Formation 1979 / 1979
Capital Kingstown
Population 103,537 / 790 people per sq mile (305 people per sq km)
Total area 150 sq. miles (389 sq. km)
Languages English*, English Creole
Religions Anglican 47%, Methodist 28%, Roman Catholic 13%, Other 12%
Ethnic mix Black 66%, Mulatto (mixed race) 19%, Other 12%, Carib 2%, Asian 1%
Government Parliamentary system
Currency East Caribbean dollar = 100 cents
Literacy rate 88%
Calorie consumption 2914 kilocalories

SAMOA
Australasia & Oceania

Official name Independent State of Samoa
Formation 1962 / 1962
Capital Apia
Population 200,000 / 183 people per sq mile (71 people per sq km)
Total area 1104 sq. miles (2860 sq. km)
Languages Samoan*, English*
Religions Christian 99%, Other 1%
Ethnic mix Polynesian 91%, Euronesian 7%, Other 2%
Government Parliamentary system
Currency Tala = 100 sene
Literacy rate 99%
Calorie consumption 2997 kilocalories

SAN MARINO
Southern Europe

Official name Republic of San Marino
Formation 1631 / 1631
Capital San Marino
Population 32,140 / 1339 people per sq mile (527 people per sq km)
Total area 23.6 sq. miles (61 sq. km)
Languages Italian*
Religions Roman Catholic 93%, Other and nonreligious 7%
Ethnic mix Sammarinese 88%, Italian 10%, Other 2%
Government Parliamentary system
Currency Euro = 100 cents
Literacy rate 99%
Calorie consumption Not available

SÃO TOMÉ & PRÍNCIPE
West Africa

Official name Democratic Republic of São Tomé and Príncipe
Formation 1975 / 1975
Capital São Tomé
Population 200,000 / 539 people per sq mile (208 people per sq km)
Total area 386 sq. miles (1001 sq. km)
Languages Portuguese Creole, Portuguese*
Religions Roman Catholic 84%, Other 16%
Ethnic mix Black 90%, Portuguese and Creole 10%
Government Presidential system
Currency Dobra = 100 céntimos
Literacy rate 89%
Calorie consumption 2734 kilocalories

SAUDI ARABIA
Southwest Asia

Official name Kingdom of Saudi Arabia
Formation 1932 / 1932
Capital Riyadh
Population 28.1 million / 34 people per sq mile (13 people per sq km)
Total area 756,981 sq. miles (1,960,582 sq. km)
Languages Arabic*
Religions Sunni Muslim 85%, Shi'a Muslim 15%
Ethnic mix Arab 72%, Foreign residents (mostly south and southeast Asian) 20%, Afro-Asian 8%
Government Monarchy
Currency Saudi riyal = 100 halalat
Literacy rate 86%
Calorie consumption 3076 kilocalories

SENEGAL
West Africa

Official name Republic of Senegal
Formation 1960 / 1960
Capital Dakar
Population 12.8 million / 172 people per sq mile (66 people per sq km)
Total area 75,749 sq. miles (196,190 sq. km)
Languages Wolof, Pulaar, Serer, Diola, Mandinka, Malinké, Soninké, French*
Religions Sunni Muslim 95%, Christian (mainly Roman Catholic) 4%, Traditional beliefs 1%
Ethnic mix Wolof 43%, Serer 15%, Peul 14%, Other 14%, Toucouleur 9%, Diola 5%
Government Presidential system
Currency CFA franc = 100 centimes
Literacy rate 50%
Calorie consumption 2479 kilocalories

SERBIA
Southeast Europe

Official name Republic of Serbia
Formation 2006 / 2008
Capital Belgrade
Population 9.9 million / 331 people per sq mile (128 people per sq km)
Total area 29,905 sq. miles (77,453 sq. km)
Languages Serbian*, Hungarian (Magyar)
Religions Orthodox Christian 85%, Roman Catholic 6%, Other 6%, Muslim 3%
Ethnic mix Serb 83%, Other 10%, Magyar 4%, Bosniak 2%, Roma 1%
Government Parliamentary system
Currency Serbian dinar = 100 para
Literacy rate 98%
Calorie consumption 2823 kilocalories

SEYCHELLES
Indian Ocean

Official name Republic of Seychelles
Formation 1976 / 1976
Capital Victoria
Population 90,024 / 866 people per sq mile (333 people per sq km)
Total area 176 sq. miles (455 sq. km)
Languages French Creole*, English*, French*
Religions Roman Catholic 82%, Anglican 6%, Other (including Muslim) 6%, Other Christian 3%, Hindu 2%, Seventh-day Adventist 1%
Ethnic mix Creole 89%, Indian 5%, Other 4%, Chinese 2%
Government Presidential system
Currency Seychelles rupee = 100 cents
Literacy rate 92%
Calorie consumption 2426 kilocalories

SIERRA LEONE
West Africa

Official name Republic of Sierra Leone
Formation 1961 / 1961
Capital Freetown
Population 6 million / 217 people per sq mile (84 people per sq km)
Total area 27,698 sq. miles (71,740 sq. km)
Languages Mende, Temne, Krio, English*
Religions Muslim 60%, Christian 30%, Traditional beliefs 10%
Ethnic mix Mende 35%, Temne 32%, Other 21%, Limba 8%, Kuranko 4%
Government Presidential system
Currency Leone = 100 cents
Literacy rate 41%
Calorie consumption 2162 kilocalories

SINGAPORE
Southeast Asia

Official name Republic of Singapore
Formation 1965 / 1965
Capital Singapore
Population 5.2 million / 22034 people per sq mile (8525 people per sq km)
Total area 250 sq. miles (648 sq. km)
Languages Mandarin*, Malay*, Tamil*, English*
Religions Buddhist 55%, Taoist 22%, Muslim 16%, Hindu, Christian, and Sikh 7%
Ethnic mix Chinese 74%, Malay 14%, Indian 9%, Other 3%
Government Parliamentary system
Currency Singapore dollar = 100 cents
Literacy rate 95%
Calorie consumption Not available

SLOVAKIA
Central Europe

Official name Slovak Republic
Formation 1993 / 1993
Capital Bratislava
Population 5.5 million / 290 people per sq mile (112 people per sq km)
Total area 18,859 sq. miles (48,845 sq. km)
Languages Slovak*, Hungarian (Magyar), Czech
Religions Roman Catholic 69%, Nonreligious 13%, Other 13%, Greek Catholic (Uniate) 4%, Orthodox Christian 1%
Ethnic mix Slovak 86%, Magyar 10%, Roma 2%, Czech 1%, Other 1%
Government Parliamentary system
Currency Euro = 100 cents
Literacy rate 99%
Calorie consumption 2881 kilocalories

SLOVENIA
Central Europe

Official name Republic of Slovenia
Formation 1991 / 1991
Capital Ljubljana
Population 2 million / 256 people per sq mile (99 people per sq km)
Total area 7820 sq. miles (20,253 sq. km)
Languages Slovenian*
Religions Roman Catholic 58%, Other 28%, Atheist 10%, Orthodox Christian 2%, Muslim 2%
Ethnic mix Slovene 83%, Other 12%, Serb 2%, Croat 2%, Bosniak 1%
Government Parliamentary system
Currency Euro = 100 cents
Literacy rate 99%
Calorie consumption 3275 kilocalories

SOLOMON ISLANDS
Australasia & Oceania

Official name Solomon Islands
Formation 1978 / 1978
Capital Honiara
Population 600,000 / 56 people per sq mile (21 people per sq km)
Total area 10,985 sq. miles (28,450 sq. km)
Languages English*, Pidgin English, Melanesian Pidgin, c.120 others
Religions Church of Melanesia (Anglican) 34%, Roman Catholic 19%, South Seas Evangelical Church 17%, Methodist 11%, Seventh-day Adventist 10%, Other 9%
Ethnic mix Melanesian 93%, Polynesian 4%, Micronesian 2%, Other 1%
Government Parliamentary system
Currency Solomon Islands dollar = 100 cents
Literacy rate 77%
Calorie consumption 2439 kilocalories

SOMALIA
East Africa

Official name Federal Republic of Somalia
Formation 1960 / 1960
Capital Mogadishu
Population 9.6 million / 40 people per sq mile (15 people per sq km)
Total area 246,199 sq. miles (637,657 sq. km)
Languages Somali*, Arabic*, English, Italian
Religions Sunni Muslim 99%, Christian 1%
Ethnic mix Somali 85%, Other 15%
Government Transitional regime
Currency Somali shilin = 100 senti
Literacy rate 24%
Calorie consumption 1762 kilocalories

SOUTH AFRICA
Southern Africa

Official name Republic of South Africa
Formation 1934 / 1994
Capital Pretoria (Tshwane); Cape Town; Bloemfontein
Population 50.5 million / 107 people per sq mile (41 people per sq km)
Total area 471,008 sq. miles (1,219,912 sq. km)
Languages English, isiZulu, isiXhosa, Afrikaans, Sepedi, Setswana, Sesotho, Xitsonga, siSwati, Tshivenda, isiNdebele
Religions Christian 68%, Traditional beliefs and animist 29%, Muslim 2%, Hindu 1%
Ethnic mix Black 89%, White 9%, Asian 2%
Government Presidential system
Currency Rand = 100 cents
Literacy rate 89%
Calorie consumption 3017 kilocalories

SOUTH KOREA
East Asia

Official name Republic of Korea
Formation 1948 / 1953
Capital Seoul
Population 48.4 million / 1270 people per sq mile (490 people per sq km)
Total area 38,023 sq. miles (98,480 sq. km)
Languages Korean*
Religions Mahayana Buddhist 47%, Protestant 38%, Roman Catholic 11%, Confucianist 3%, Other 1%
Ethnic mix Korean 100%
Government Presidential system
Currency South Korean won = 100 chon
Literacy rate 99%
Calorie consumption 3200 kilocalories

SOUTH SUDAN
East Africa

Official name Republic of South Sudan
Formation 2011 / 2011
Capital Juba
Population 8.3 million / 33 people per sq mile (13 people per sq km)
Total area 248,777 sq. miles (644,329 sq. km)
Languages Arabic, Dinka, Nuer, Zande, Bari, Shilluk, Lotuko
Religions Over half of the population follow Christian or traditional beliefs.
Ethnic mix Dinka 40%, Nuer 15%, Bari 10%, Shilluk/Anwak 10%, Azande 10%, Arab 10%, Other 5%
Government Transitional regime
Currency South Sudan pound = 100 piastres
Literacy rate 37%
Calorie consumption Not available

SPAIN
Southwest Europe

Official name Kingdom of Spain
Formation 1492 / 1713
Capital Madrid
Population 46.5 million / 241 people per sq mile (93 people per sq km)
Total area 194,896 sq. miles (504,782 sq. km)
Languages Spanish*, Catalan*, Galician*, Basque*
Religions Roman Catholic 96%, Other 4%
Ethnic mix Castilian Spanish 72%, Catalan 17%, Galician 6%, Basque 2%, Other 2%, Roma 1%
Government Parliamentary system
Currency Euro = 100 cents
Literacy rate 98%
Calorie consumption 3239 kilocalories

SRI LANKA
South Asia

Official name Democratic Socialist Republic of Sri Lanka
Formation 1948 / 1948
Capital Colombo; Sri Jayewardenapura Kotte
Population 21 million / 840 people per sq mile (324 people per sq km)
Total area 25,332 sq. miles (65,610 sq. km)
Languages Sinhala*, Tamil*, Sinhala-Tamil, English
Religions Buddhist 69%, Hindu 15%, Muslim 8%, Christian 8%
Ethnic mix Sinhalese 74%, Tamil 18%, Moor 7%, Other 1%
Government Mixed presidential–parliamentary system
Currency Sri Lanka rupee = 100 cents
Literacy rate 91%
Calorie consumption 2426 kilocalories

SUDAN
East Africa

Official name Republic of the Sudan
Formation 1956 / 2011
Capital Khartoum
Population 34 million / 47 people per sq mile (18 people per sq km)
Total area 718,722 sq. miles (1,861,481 sq. km)
Languages Arabic, Nubian, Beja, Fur
Religions Nearly the whole population is Muslim (mainly Sunni)
Ethnic mix Arab 60%, Other 18%, Nubian 10%, Beja 8%, Fur 3%, Zaghawa 1%
Government Presidential system
Currency New Sudanese pound = 100 piastres
Literacy rate 70%
Calorie consumption 2326 kilocalories

SURINAME
South America

Official name Republic of Surinam
Formation 1975 / 1975
Capital Paramaribo
Population 500,000 / 8 people per sq mile (3 people per sq km)
Total area 63,039 sq. miles (163,270 sq. km)
Languages Sranan (creole), Dutch*, Javanese, Sarnami Hindi, Saramaccan, Chinese, Carib
Religions Hindu 27%, Protestant 25%, Roman Catholic 23%, Muslim 20%, Traditional beliefs 5%
Ethnic mix East Indian 27%, Creole 18%, Black 15%, Javanese 15%, Mixed race 13%, Other 6%, Amerindian 4%, Chinese 2%
Government Parliamentary system
Currency Surinamese dollar = 100 cents
Literacy rate 95%
Calorie consumption 2548 kilocalories

SWAZILAND
Southern Africa

Official name Kingdom of Swaziland
Formation 1968 / 1968
Capital Mbabane
Population 1.2 million / 181 people per sq mile (70 people per sq km)
Total area 6704 sq. miles (17,363 sq. km)
Languages English*, siSwati*, isiZulu, Xitsonga
Religions Traditional beliefs 40%, Other 30%, Roman Catholic 20%, Muslim 10%
Ethnic mix Swazi 97%, Other 3%
Government Monarchy
Currency Lilangeni = 100 cents
Literacy rate 87%
Calorie consumption 2249 kilocalories

SWEDEN
Northern Europe

Official name Kingdom of Sweden
Formation 1523 / 1921
Capital Stockholm
Population 9.4 million / 59 people per sq mile (23 people per sq km)
Total area 173,731 sq. miles (449,964 sq. km)
Languages Swedish*, Finnish, Sámi
Religions Evangelical Lutheran 75%, Other 13%, Muslim 5%, Other Protestant 5%, Roman Catholic 2%
Ethnic mix Swedish 86%, Foreign-born or first-generation immigrant 12%, Finnish and Sámi 2%
Government Parliamentary system
Currency Swedish krona = 100 öre
Literacy rate 99%
Calorie consumption 3125 kilocalories

SWITZERLAND
Central Europe

Official name Swiss Confederation
Formation 1291 / 1857
Capital Bern
Population 7.7 million / 501 people per sq mile (194 people per sq km)
Total area 15,942 sq. miles (41,290 sq. km)
Languages German*, Swiss-German, French*, Italian*, Romansch
Religions Roman Catholic 42%, Protestant 35%, Other and nonreligious 19%, Muslim 4%
Ethnic mix German 64%, French 20%, Other 9.5%, Italian 6%, Romansch 0.5%
Government Parliamentary system
Currency Swiss franc = 100 rappen/centimes
Literacy rate 99%
Calorie consumption 3454 kilocalories

SYRIA
Southwest Asia

Official name Syrian Arab Republic
Formation 1941 / 1967
Capital Damascus
Population 20.8 million / 293 people per sq mile (113 people per sq km)
Total area 71,498 sq. miles (184,180 sq. km)
Languages Arabic*, French, Kurdish, Armenian, Circassian, Turkic languages, Assyrian, Aramaic
Religions Sunni Muslim 74%, Alawi 12%, Christian 10%, Druze 3%, Other 1%
Ethnic mix Arab 90%, Kurdish 9%, Armenian, Turkmen, and Circassian 1%
Government One-party state
Currency Syrian pound = 100 piastres
Literacy rate 84%
Calorie consumption 3212 kilocalories

TAIWAN
East Asia

Official name Republic of China (ROC)
Formation 1949 / 1949
Capital Taipei
Population 23.2 million / 1860 people per sq mile (718 people per sq km)
Total area 13,892 sq. miles (35,980 sq. km)
Languages Amoy Chinese, Mandarin Chinese*, Hakka Chinese
Religions Buddhist, Confucianist, and Taoist 93%, Christian 5%, Other 2%
Ethnic mix Han Chinese (pre-20th-century migration) 84%, Han Chinese (20th-century migration) 14%, Aboriginal 2%
Government Presidential system
Currency Taiwan dollar = 100 cents
Literacy rate 98%
Calorie consumption 2673 kilocalories

TAJIKISTAN
Central Asia

Official name Republic of Tajikistan
Formation 1991 / 1991
Capital Dushanbe
Population 7 million / 127 people per sq mile (49 people per sq km)
Total area 55,251 sq. miles (143,100 sq. km)
Languages Tajik*, Uzbek, Russian
Religions Sunni Muslim 95%, Shi'a Muslim 3%, Other 2%
Ethnic mix Tajik 80%, Uzbek 15%, Other 3%, Russian 1%, Kyrgyz 1%
Government Presidential system
Currency Somoni = 100 diram
Literacy rate 99%
Calorie consumption 2106 kilocalories

TANZANIA
East Africa

Official name United Republic of Tanzania
Formation 1964 / 1964
Capital Dodoma
Population 46.2 million / 135 people per sq mile (52 people per sq km)
Total area 364,898 sq. miles (945,087 sq. km)
Languages Kiswahili*, Sukuma, Chagga, Nyamwezi, Hehe, Makonde, Yao, Sandawe, English*
Religions Christian 63%, Muslim 35%, Other 2%
Ethnic mix Native African (over 120 tribes) 99%, European, Asian, and Arab 1%
Government Presidential system
Currency Tanzanian shilling = 100 cents
Literacy rate 73%
Calorie consumption 2137 kilocalories

THAILAND
Southeast Asia

Official name Kingdom of Thailand
Formation 1238 / 1907
Capital Bangkok
Population 69.5 million / 352 people per sq mile (136 people per sq km)
Total area 198,455 sq. miles (514,000 sq. km)
Languages Thai*, Chinese, Malay, Khmer, Mon, Karen, Miao
Religions Buddhist 95%, Muslim 4%, Other (including Christian) 1%
Ethnic mix Thai 83%, Chinese 12%, Malay 3%, Khmer and Other 2%
Government Parliamentary system
Currency Baht = 100 satang
Literacy rate 94%
Calorie consumption 2862 kilocalories

TOGO
West Africa

Official name Republic of Togo
Formation 1960 / 1960
Capital Lomé
Population 6.2 million / 295 people per sq mile (114 people per sq km)
Total area 21,924 sq. miles (56,785 sq. km)
Languages Ewe, Kabye, Gurma, French*
Religions Christian 47%, Traditional beliefs 33%, Muslim 14%, Other 6%
Ethnic mix Ewe 46%, Other African 41%, Kabye 12%, European 1%
Government Presidential system
Currency CFA franc = 100 centimes
Literacy rate 57%
Calorie consumption 2363 kilocalories

TONGA
Australasia & Oceania

Official name Kingdom of Tonga
Formation 1970 / 1970
Capital Nuku'alofa
Population 106,146 / 382 people per sq mile (147 people per sq km)
Total area 289 sq. miles (748 sq. km)
Languages English*, Tongan*
Religions Free Wesleyan 41%, Other 17%, Roman Catholic 16%, Church of Jesus Christ of Latter-day Saints 14%, Free Church of Tonga 12%
Ethnic mix Tongan 98%, Other 2%
Government Monarchy
Currency Pa'anga (Tongan dollar) = 100 seniti
Literacy rate 99%
Calorie consumption Not available

TRINIDAD & TOBAGO
West Indies

Official name Republic of Trinidad and Tobago
Formation 1962 / 1962
Capital Port-of-Spain
Population 1.3 million / 656 people per sq mile (253 people per sq km)
Total area 1980 sq. miles (5128 sq. km)
Languages English Creole, English*, Hindi, French, Spanish
Religions Roman Catholic 26%, Hindu 23%, Other and nonreligious 23%, Anglican 8%, Baptist 7%, Pentecostal 7%, Muslim 6%
Ethnic mix East Indian 40%, Black 38%, Mixed race 20%, Other 2%
Government Parliamentary system
Currency Trinidad and Tobago dollar = 100 cents
Literacy rate 99%
Calorie consumption 2751 kilocalories

TUNISIA
North Africa

Official name Republic of Tunisia
Formation 1956 / 1956
Capital Tunis
Population 10.6 million / 177 people per sq mile (68 people per sq km)
Total area 63,169 sq. miles (163,610 sq. km)
Languages Arabic*, French
Religions Muslim (mainly Sunni) 98%, Christian 1%, Jewish 1%
Ethnic mix Arab and Berber 98%, Jewish 1%, European 1%
Government Transitional regime
Currency Tunisian dinar = 1000 millimes
Literacy rate 78%
Calorie consumption 3314 kilocalories

TURKEY
Asia / Europe

Official name Republic of Turkey
Formation 1923 / 1939
Capital Ankara
Population 73.6 million / 248 people per sq mile (96 people per sq km)
Total area 301,382 sq. miles (780,580 sq. km)
Languages Turkish*, Kurdish, Arabic, Circassian, Armenian, Greek, Georgian, Ladino
Religions Muslim (mainly Sunni) 99%, Other 1%
Ethnic mix Turkish 70%, Kurdish 20%, Other 8%, Arab 2%
Government Parliamentary system
Currency Turkish lira = 100 kurus
Literacy rate 91%
Calorie consumption 3666 kilocalories

TURKMENISTAN
Central Asia

Official name Turkmenistan
Formation 1991 / 1991
Capital Ashgabat
Population 5.1 million / 27 people per sq mile (10 people per sq km)
Total area 188,455 sq. miles (488,100 sq. km)
Languages Turkmen*, Uzbek, Russian, Kazakh, Tatar
Religions Sunni Muslim 89%, Orthodox Christian 9%, Other 2%
Ethnic mix Turkmen 85%, Other 6%, Uzbek 5%, Russian 4%
Government One-party state
Currency New manat = 100 tenge
Literacy rate 99%
Calorie consumption 2878 kilocalories

TUVALU
Australasia & Oceania

Official name Tuvalu
Formation 1978 / 1978
Capital Fongafale (Funafuti Atoll)
Population 10,619 / 1062 people per sq mile (408 people per sq km)
Total area 10 sq. miles (26 sq. km)
Languages Tuvaluan, Kiribati, English*
Religions Church of Tuvalu 97%, Baha'i 1%, Seventh-day Adventist 1%, Other 1%
Ethnic mix Polynesian 96%, Micronesian 4%
Government Nonparty system
Currency Australian dollar and Tuvaluan dollar = 100 cents
Literacy rate 98%
Calorie consumption Not available

UGANDA
East Africa

Official name Republic of Uganda
Formation 1962 / 1962
Capital Kampala
Population 34.5 million / 448 people per sq mile (173 people per sq km)
Total area 91,135 sq. miles (236,040 sq. km)
Languages Luganda, Nkole, Chiga, Lango, Acholi, Teso, Lugbara, English*
Religions Christian 85%, Muslim (mainly Sunni) 12%, Other 3%
Ethnic mix Other 50%, Baganda 17%, Banyakole 10%, Basoga 9%, Iteso 7%, Bakiga 7%
Government Presidential system
Currency New Uganda shilling = 100 cents
Literacy rate 74%
Calorie consumption 2260 kilocalories

UKRAINE
Eastern Europe

Official name Ukraine
Formation 1991 / 1991
Capital Kiev
Population 45.2 million / 194 people per sq mile (75 people per sq km)
Total area 223,089 sq. miles (603,700 sq. km)
Languages Ukrainian*, Russian, Tatar
Religions Christian (mainly Orthodox) 95%, Other 5%
Ethnic mix Ukrainian 78%, Russian 17%, Other 5%
Government Presidential system
Currency Hryvna = 100 kopiykas
Literacy rate 99%
Calorie consumption 3198 kilocalories

UNITED ARAB EMIRATES
Southwest Asia

Official name United Arab Emirates
Formation 1971 / 1972
Capital Abu Dhabi
Population 7.9 million / 245 people per sq mile (94 people per sq km)
Total area 32,000 sq. miles (82,880 sq. km)
Languages Arabic*, Farsi, Indian and Pakistani languages, English
Religions Muslim (mainly Sunni) 96%, Christian, Hindu, and other 4%
Ethnic mix Asian 60%, Emirian 25%, Other Arab 12%, European 3%
Government Monarchy
Currency UAE dirham = 100 fils
Literacy rate 90%
Calorie consumption 3245 kilocalories

UNITED KINGDOM
Northwest Europe

Official name United Kingdom of Great Britain and Northern Ireland
Formation 1707 / 1922
Capital London
Population 62.4 million / 669 people per sq mile (258 people per sq km)
Total area 94,525 sq. miles (244,820 sq. km)
Languages English*, Welsh*, Scottish Gaelic, Irish Gaelic
Religions Anglican 45%, Other and nonreligious 36%, Roman Catholic 9%, Presbyterian 4%, Muslim 3%, Methodist 2%, Hindu 1%
Ethnic mix English 80%, Scottish 9%, West Indian, Asian, and other 5%, Northern Irish 3%, Welsh 3%
Government Parliamentary system
Currency Pound sterling = 100 pence
Literacy rate 99%
Calorie consumption 3432 kilocalories

UNITED STATES
North America

Official name United States of America
Formation 1776 / 1959
Capital Washington D.C.
Population 313 million / 88 people per sq mile (34 people per sq km)
Total area 3,717,792 sq. miles (9,626,091 sq. km)
Languages English, Spanish, Chinese, French, German, Tagalog, Vietnamese, Italian, Korean, Russian, Polish
Religions Protestant 52%, Roman Catholic 25%, Other and nonreligious 20%, Jewish 2%, Muslim 1%
Ethnic mix White 62%, Hispanic 13%, Black American/African 13%, Other 7%, Asian 4%, Native American 1%
Government Presidential system
Currency US dollar = 100 cents
Literacy rate 99%
Calorie consumption 3688 kilocalories

URUGUAY
South America

Official name Eastern Republic of Uruguay
Formation 1828 / 1828
Capital Montevideo
Population 3.4 million / 50 people per sq mile (19 people per sq km)
Total area 68,039 sq. miles (176,220 sq. km)
Languages Spanish*
Religions Roman Catholic 66%, Other and nonreligious 30%, Jewish 2%, Protestant 2%
Ethnic mix White 90%, Mestizo 6%, Black 4%
Government Presidential system
Currency Uruguayan peso = 100 centésimos
Literacy rate 98%
Calorie consumption 2808 kilocalories

UZBEKISTAN
Central Asia

Official name Republic of Uzbekistan
Formation 1991 / 1991
Capital Tashkent
Population 27.8 million / 161 people per sq mile (62 people per sq km)
Total area 172,741 sq. miles (447,400 sq. km)
Languages Uzbek*, Russian, Tajik, Kazakh
Religions Sunni Muslim 88%, Orthodox Christian 9%, Other 3%
Ethnic mix Uzbek 80%, Russian 6%, Other 6%, Tajik 5%, Kazakh 3%
Government Presidential system
Currency Som = 100 tiyin
Literacy rate 99%
Calorie consumption 2618 kilocalories

VANUATU
Australasia & Oceania

Official name Republic of Vanuatu
Formation 1980 / 1980
Capital Port Vila
Population 200,000 / 42 people per sq mile (16 people per sq km)
Total area 4710 sq. miles (12,200 sq. km)
Languages Bislama* (Melanesian pidgin), English*, French*, other indigenous languages
Religions Presbyterian 37%, Other 19%, Anglican 15%, Roman Catholic 15%, Traditional beliefs 8%, Seventh-day Adventist 6%
Ethnic mix ni-Vanuatu 94%, European 4%, Other 2%
Government Parliamentary system
Currency Vatu = 100 centimes
Literacy rate 82%
Calorie consumption 2841 kilocalories

VATICAN CITY
Southern Europe

Official name State of the Vatican City
Formation 1929 / 1929
Capital Vatican City
Population 836 / 4918 people per sq mile (1900 people per sq km)
Total area 0.17 sq. miles (0.44 sq. km)
Languages Italian*, Latin*
Religions Roman Catholic 100%
Ethnic mix The current pope is German, though most popes for the last 500 years have been Italian. Cardinals are from many nationalities, but Italians form the largest group. Most of the resident lay persons are Italian.
Government Papal state
Currency Euro = 100 cents
Literacy rate 99%
Calorie consumption Not available

VENEZUELA
South America

Official name Bolivarian Republic of Venezuela
Formation 1830 / 1830
Capital Caracas
Population 29.4 million / 86 people per sq mile (33 people per sq km)
Total area 352,143 sq. miles (912,050 sq. km)
Languages Spanish*, Amerindian languages
Religions Roman Catholic 96%, Protestant 2%, Other 2%
Ethnic mix Mestizo 69%, White 20%, Black 9%, Amerindian 2%
Government Presidential system
Currency Bolívar fuerte = 100 céntimos
Literacy rate 95%
Calorie consumption 3014 kilocalories

VIETNAM
Southeast Asia

Official name Socialist Republic of Vietnam
Formation 1976 / 1976
Capital Hanoi
Population 88.8 million / 707 people per sq mile (273 people per sq km)
Total area 127,243 sq. miles (329,560 sq. km)
Languages Vietnamese*, Chinese, Thai, Khmer, Muong, Nung, Miao, Yao, Jarai
Religions Other 74%, Buddhist 14%, Roman Catholic 7%, Cao Dai 3%, Protestant 2%
Ethnic mix Vietnamese 86%, Other 8%, Muong 2%, Tay 2%, Thai 2%
Government One-party state
Currency Dông = 10 hao = 100 xu
Literacy rate 93%
Calorie consumption 2690 kilocalories

YEMEN
Southwest Asia

Official name Republic of Yemen
Formation 1990 / 1990
Capital Sana
Population 24.8 million / 114 people per sq mile (44 people per sq km)
Total area 203,849 sq. miles (527,970 sq. km)
Languages Arabic*
Religions Sunni Muslim 55%, Shi'a Muslim 42%, Christian, Hindu, and Jewish 3%
Ethnic mix Arab 99%, Afro-Arab, Indian, Somali, and European 1%
Government Transitional regime
Currency Yemeni rial = 100 fils
Literacy rate 62%
Calorie consumption 2109 kilocalories

ZAMBIA
Southern Africa

Official name Republic of Zambia
Formation 1964 / 1964
Capital Lusaka
Population 13.5 million / 47 people per sq mile (18 people per sq km)
Total area 290,584 sq. miles (752,614 sq. km)
Languages Bemba, Tonga, Nyanja, Lozi, Lala-Bisa, Nsenga, English*
Religions Christian 63%, Traditional beliefs 36%, Muslim and Hindu 1%
Ethnic mix Bemba 34%, Other African 26%, Tonga 16%, Nyanja 14%, Lozi 9%, European 1%
Government Presidential system
Currency Zambian kwacha = 100 ngwee
Literacy rate 71%
Calorie consumption 1879 kilocalories

ZIMBABWE
Southern Africa

Official name Republic of Zimbabwe
Formation 1980 / 1980
Capital Harare
Population 12.8 million / 86 people per sq mile (33 people per sq km)
Total area 150,803 sq. miles (390,580 sq. km)
Languages Shona, isiNdebele, English*
Religions Syncretic (Christian/traditional beliefs) 50%, Christian 25%, Traditional beliefs 24%, Other (including Muslim) 1%
Ethnic mix Shona 71%, Ndebele 16%, Other African 11%, White 1%, Asian 1%
Government Presidential system
Currency Zimbabwe dollar suspended in 2009; US dollar, South African rand, euro, UK pound, and Botswanan pula are legal tender
Literacy rate 92%
Calorie consumption 2219 kilocalories

GLOSSARY

This glossary lists all geographical, technical, and foreign language terms which appear in the text, followed by a brief definition of the term. Any acronyms used in the text are also listed in full. Terms in italics are for cross-reference and indicate that the word is separately defined in the glossary.

A

Aboriginal The original (*indigenous*) inhabitants of a country or continent. Especially used with reference to Australia.

Abyssal plain A broad *plain* found in the depths of the ocean, more than 10,000 ft (3,000 m) below sea level.

Acid rain Rain, sleet, snow, or mist which has absorbed waste gases from fossil-fueled power stations and vehicle exhausts, becoming more acid. It causes severe environmental damage.

Adaptation The gradual evolution of plants and animals so that they become better suited to survive and reproduce in their *environment*.

Afforestation The planting of new forest in areas that were once forested but have been cleared.

Agribusiness A term applied to activities such as the growing of crops, rearing of animals, or the manufacture of farm machinery, which eventually leads to the supply of agricultural produce at market.

Air mass A huge, homogeneous mass of air, within which horizontal patterns of temperature and *humidity* are consistent. Air masses are separated by *fronts*.

Alliance An agreement between two or more states, to work together to achieve common purposes.

Alluvial fan A large fan-shaped deposit of fine sediments deposited by a river as it emerges from a narrow, mountain valley onto a broad, open *plain*.

Alluvium Material deposited by rivers. Nowadays usually only applied to finer particles of silt and clay.

Alpine Mountain *environment*, between the *treeline* and the level of permanent snow cover.

Alpine mountains Ranges of mountains formed between 30 and 65 million years ago, by *folding*, in western and central Europe.

Amerindian A term applied to people *indigenous* to North, Central, and South America.

Animal husbandry The business of rearing animals.

Antarctic circle The parallel which lies at *latitude* of 66° 32' S.

Anticline A geological *fold* that forms an arch shape, curving upward in the rock *strata*.

Anticyclone An area of relatively high atmospheric pressure.

Aquaculture Collective term for the farming of produce derived from the sea, including fish-farming, the cultivation of shellfish, and plants such as seaweed.

Aquifer A body of rock that can absorb water. Also applied to any rock strata that have sufficient porosity to yield *groundwater* through wells or springs.

Arable Land which has been plowed and is being used, or is suitable, for growing crops.

Archipelago A group or chain of islands.

Arctic Circle The parallel that lies at a *latitude* of 66° 32' N.

Arête A thin, jagged mountain ridge that divides two adjacent *cirques*, found in regions where *glaciation* has occurred.

Arid Dry. An area of low rainfall, where the rate of *evaporation* may be greater than that of *precipitation*. Often defined as those areas that receive less than one inch (25 mm) of rain a year. In these areas only drought-resistant plants can survive.

Artesian well A naturally occurring source of underground water, stored in an *aquifer*.

Artisanal Small-scale, manual operation, such as fishing, using little or no machinery.

ASEAN Association of Southeast Asian Nations. Established in 1967 to promote economic, social, and cultural cooperation. Its members include Brunei, Indonesia, Malaysia, Philippines, Singapore, and Thailand.

Aseismic A region where *earthquake* activity has ceased.

Asteroid A minor planet circling the Sun, mainly between the orbits of Mars and Jupiter.

Asthenosphere A zone of hot, partially melted rock, which underlies the *lithosphere*, within the Earth's *crust*.

Atmosphere The envelope of odorless, colorless and tasteless gases surrounding the Earth, consisting of *oxygen* (23%), *nitrogen* (75%), argon (1%), *carbon dioxide* (0.03%), as well as tiny proportions of other gases.

Atmospheric pressure The pressure created by the action of gravity on the gases surrounding the Earth.

Atoll A ring-shaped island or *coral reef* often enclosing a *lagoon* of sea water.

Avalanche The rapid movement of a mass of snow and ice down a steep slope. Similar movements of other materials are described as *rock avalanches* or *landslides* and *sand avalanches*.

B

Badlands A landscape that has been heavily eroded and dissected by rainwater, and which has little or no vegetation.

Back slope The gentler windward slope of a sand *dune* or gentler slope of a *cuesta*.

Bajos An *alluvial fan* deposited by a river at the base of mountains and hills that encircle *desert* areas.

Bar, coastal An offshore strip of sand or shingle, either above or below the water. Usually parallel to the shore but sometimes crescent-shaped or at an oblique angle.

Barchan A crescent-shaped sand *dune*, formed where wind direction is very consistent. The horns of the crescent point downwind and where there is enough sand the barchan is mobile.

Barrio A Spanish term for the shantytowns – settlements of shacks – that are clustered around many South and Central American cities (*see also Favela*).

Basalt Dark, fine-grained *igneous rock* that is formed near the Earth's surface from fast-cooling *lava*.

Base level The level below which flowing water cannot erode the land.

Basement rock A mass of ancient rock often of *PreCambrian age*, covered by a layer of more recent *sedimentary rocks*. Commonly associated with *shield* areas.

Beach Lake or sea shore where waves break and there is an accumulation of loose sand, mud, gravel, or pebbles.

Bedrock Solid, consolidated and relatively unweathered rock, found on the surface of the land or just below a layer of soil or *weathered* rock.

Biodiversity The quantity of animal or plant species in a given area.

Biomass The total mass of organic matter – plants and animals – in a given area. It is usually measured in kilogrammes per square meter. Plant biomass is proportionally greater than that of animals, except in cities.

Biosphere The zone just above and below the Earth's surface, where all plants and animals live.

Blizzard A severe windstorm with snow and sleet. Visibility is often severely restricted.

Bluff The steep bank of a *meander*, formed by the erosive action of a river.

Boreal forest Tracts of mainly coniferous forest found in northern *latitudes*.

Breccia A type of rock composed of sharp fragments, cemented by a fine-grained material such as clay.

Butte An isolated, flat-topped hill with steep or vertical sides, buttes are the eroded remnants of a former land surface

C

Caatinga Portuguese (Brazilian) term for thorny woodland growing in areas of pale granitic soils.

CACM Central American Common Market. Established in 1960 to further economic ties between its members, which are Costa Rica, El Salvador, Guatemala, Honduras, and Nicaragua.

Calcite Hexagonal crystals of calcium carbonate.

Caldera A huge volcanic vent, often containing a number of smaller vents, and sometimes a crater lake.

Carbon cycle The transfer of carbon to and from the *atmosphere*. This occurs on land through *photosynthesis*. In the sea, *carbon dioxide* is absorbed, some returning to the air and some taken up into the bodies of sea creatures.

Carbon dioxide A colorless, odorless gas (CO_2) that makes up 0.03% of the *atmosphere*.

Carbonation The process whereby rocks are broken down by carbonic acid. Carbon dioxide in the air dissolves in rainwater, forming carbonic acid. *Limestone* terrain can be rapidly eaten away.

Cash crop A single crop grown specifically for export sale, rather than for local use. Typical examples include coffee, tea, and citrus fruits.

Cassava A type of grain meal, used to produce tapioca. A staple crop in many parts of Africa.

Castle kopje Hill or rock outcrop, especially in southern Africa, where steep sides, and a summit composed of blocks, give a castle-like appearance.

Cataracts A series of stepped waterfalls created as a river flows over a band of hard, resistant rock.

Causeway A raised route through marshland or a body of water.

CEEAC Economic Community of Central African States. Established in 1983 to promote regional cooperation and if possible, establish a common market between 16 Central African nations.

Chemical weathering The chemical reactions leading to the decomposition of rocks. Types of chemical weathering include *carbonation*, *hydrolysis*, and *oxidation*.

Chernozem A fertile soil, also known as "black earth" consisting of a layer of dark topsoil, rich in decaying vegetation, overlying a lighter chalky layer.

Cirque Armchair-shaped basin, found in mountain regions, with a steep back, or rear, wall and a raised rock lip, often containing a lake (or *tarn*). The cirque floor has been eroded by a *glacier*, while the back wall is eroded both by the *glacier* and by *weathering*.

Climate The average weather conditions in a given area over a period of years, sometimes defined as 30 years or more.

Cold War A period of hostile relations between the US and the Soviet Union and their allies after the Second World War.

Composite volcano Also known as a strato-volcano, the volcanic cone is composed of alternating deposits of *lava* and *pyroclastic* material.

Compound A substance made up of *elements* chemically combined in a consistent way.

Condensation The process whereby a gas changes into a liquid. For example, water vapor in the *atmosphere* condenses around tiny airborne particles to form droplets of water.

Confluence The point at which two rivers meet.

Conglomerate Rock composed of large, water-worn or rounded pebbles, held together by a natural cement.

Coniferous forest A forest type containing trees which are generally, but not necessarily, *evergreen* and have slender, needlelike leaves. Coniferous trees reproduce by means of seeds contained in a cone.

Continental drift The theory that the continents of today are fragments of one or more prehistoric *supercontinents* which have moved across the Earth's surface, creating ocean basins. The theory has been superseded by a more sophisticated one – *plate tectonics*.

Continental shelf An area of the continental crust, below sea level, which slopes gently. It is separated from the deep ocean by a much more steeply inclined *continental slope*.

Continental slope A steep slope running from the edge of the *continental shelf* to the ocean floor.

Conurbation A vast metropolitan area created by the expansion of towns and cities into a virtually continuous urban area.

Cool continental A rainy *climate* with warm summers [warmest month below 76°F (22°C)] and often severe winters [coldest month below 32°F (0°C)].

Copra The dried, white kernel of a coconut, from which coconut oil is extracted.

Coral reef An underwater barrier created by colonies of the coral polyp. Polyps secrete a protective skeleton of calcium carbonate, and reefs develop as live polyps build on the skeletons of dead generations.

Core The center of the Earth, consisting of a dense mass of iron and nickel. It is thought that the outer core is molten or liquid, and that the hot inner core is solid due to extremely high pressures.

Coriolis effect A deflecting force caused by the rotation of the Earth. In the northern hemisphere a body, such as an *air mass* or ocean current, is deflected to the right, and in the southern hemisphere to the left. This prevents winds from blowing straight from areas of high to low pressure.

Coulées A US / Canadian term for a ravine formed by river *erosion*.

Craton A large block of the Earth's *crust* which has remained stable for a long period of *geological time*. It is made up of ancient *shield* rocks.

Cretaceous A period of *geological time* beginning about 145 million years ago and lasting until about 65 million years ago.

Crevasse A deep crack in a *glacier*.

Crust The hard, thin outer shell of the Earth. The crust floats on the *mantle*, which is softer and more dense. Under the oceans (oceanic crust) the crust is 3.7–6.8 miles (6–11 km) thick. Continental crust averages 18–24 miles (30–40 km).

Crystalline rock Rocks formed when molten *magma* crystallizes (*igneous rocks*) or when heat or pressure cause re-crystallization (*metamorphic rocks*). Crystalline rocks are distinct from *sedimentary rocks*.

Cuesta A hill which rises into a steep slope on one side but has a gentler gradient on its other slope.

Cyclone An area of low *atmospheric pressure*, occurring where the air is warm and relatively low in density, causing low level winds to spiral. *Hurricanes* and *typhoons* are tropical cyclones.

D

De facto
1 Government or other activity that takes place, or exists in actuality if not by right.
2 A border, which exists in practice, but which is not officially recognized by all the countries it adjoins.

Deciduous forest A forest of trees that shed their leaves annually at a particular time or season. In *temperate* climates the fall of leaves occurs in the autumn. Some *coniferous* trees, such as the larch, are deciduous. Deciduous vegetation contrasts with *evergreen*, which keeps its leaves for more than a year.

Defoliant Chemical spray used to remove foliage (leaves) from trees.

Deforestation The act of cutting down and clearing large areas of forest for human activities, such as agricultural land or urban development.

Delta Low-lying, fan-shaped area at a river mouth, formed by the *deposition* of successive layers of *sediment*. Slowing as it enters the sea, a river deposits sediment and may, as a result, split into numerous smaller channels, known as *distributaries*.

Denudation The combined effect of *weathering*, *erosion*, and *mass movement*, which, over long periods, exposes underlying rocks.

Deposition The laying down of material that has accumulated:
(1) after being *eroded* and then transported by physical forces such as wind, ice, or water;
(2) as organic remains, such as coal and coral;
(3) as the result of *evaporation* and chemical *precipitation*.

Depression
1 In climatic terms it is a large low pressure system.
2 A complex *fold*, producing a large valley, which incorporates both a *syncline* and an *anticline*.

Desert An *arid* region of low rainfall, with little vegetation or animal life, which is adapted to the dry conditions. The term is now applied not only to hot tropical and subtropical regions, but to arid areas of the continental interiors and to the ice deserts of the *Arctic* and *Antarctic*.

Desertification The gradual extension of *desert* conditions in *arid* or *semiarid* regions, as a result of climatic change or human activity, such as over-grazing and *deforestation*.

Despot A ruler with absolute power. Despots are often associated with oppressive regimes.

Detritus Piles of rock deposited by an erosive agent such as a river or *glacier*.

Distributary A minor branch of a river, which does not rejoin the main stream, common at *deltas*.

Diurnal Daily, something that occurs each day. Diurnal temperature refers to the variation in temperature over the course of a full day and night.

Divide A US term describing the area of high ground separating two *drainage basins*.

Donga A steep-sided *gully*, resulting from *erosion* by a river or by floods.

Dormant A term used to describe a *volcano* which is not currently erupting. They differ from extinct volcanoes as dormant volcanoes are still considered likely to erupt in the future.

Drainage basin The area drained by a single river system, its boundary is marked by a *watershed* or *divide*.

Drought A long period of continuously low rainfall.

Drumlin A long, streamlined hillock composed of material deposited by a *glacier*. They often occur in groups known as swarms.

Dune A mound or ridge of sand, shaped, and often moved, by the wind. They are found in hot *deserts* and on low-lying coasts where onshore winds blow across sandy beaches.

Dyke A wall constructed in low-lying areas to contain floodwaters or protect from high tides.

E

Earthflow The rapid movement of soil and other loose surface material down a slope, when saturated by water. Similar to a mudflow but not as fast-flowing, due to a lower percentage of water.

Earthquake Sudden movements of the Earth's *crust*, causing the ground to shake. Frequently occurring at *tectonic plate* margins. The shock, or series of shocks, spreads out from an *epicenter*.

EC The European Community (*see* EU).

Ecosystem A system of living organisms – plants and animals – interacting with their *environment*.

ECOWAS Economic Community of West African States. Established in 1975, it incorporates 16 West African states and aims to promote closer regional and economic cooperation.

Element
1 A constituent of the *climate* – *precipitation*, *humidity*, temperature, *atmospheric pressure*, or wind.
2 A substance that cannot be separated into simpler substances by chemical means.

El Niño A climatic phenomenon, the El Niño effect occurs about 14 times each century and leads to major shifts in global air circulation. It is associated with unusually warm currents off the coasts of Peru, Ecuador and Chile. The anomaly can last for up to two years.

Environment The conditions created by the surroundings (both natural and artificial) within which an organism lives. In human geography the word includes the surrounding economic, cultural, and social conditions.

Eon (aeon) Traditionally a long, but indefinite, period of *geological time*.

Ephemeral A nonpermanent feature, often used in connection with seasonal rivers or lakes in dry areas.

Epicenter The point on the Earth's surface directly above the underground origin – or focus – of an *earthquake*.

Equator The line of *latitude* which lies equidistant between the North and South Poles.

Erg An extensive area of sand *dunes*, particularly in the Sahara Desert.

Erosion The processes which wear away the surface of the land. *Glaciers*, wind, rivers, waves, and currents all carry debris which causes *erosion*. Some definitions also include *mass movement* due to gravity as an agent of erosion.

Escarpment A steep slope at the margin of a level, upland surface. In a landscape created by *folding*, escarpments (or scarps) frequently lie behind a more gentle backward slope.

Esker A narrow, winding ridge of sand and gravel deposited by streams of water flowing beneath or at the edge of a *glacier*.

Erratic A rock transported by a *glacier* and deposited some distance from its place of origin.

Eustacy A world-wide fall or rise in ocean levels.

EU The European Union. Established in 1965, it was formerly known as the EEC (European Economic Community) and then the EC (European Community). Its members are Austria, Belgium, Denmark, Finland, France, Germany, Greece, Ireland, Italy, Luxembourg, Netherlands, Portugal, Spain, Sweden, and UK. It seeks to establish an integrated European common market and eventual federation.

Evaporation The process whereby a liquid or solid is turned into a gas or vapor. Also refers to the diffusion of water vapor into the *atmosphere* from exposed water surfaces such as lakes and seas.

Evapotranspiration The loss of moisture from the Earth's surface through a combination of *evaporation*, and *transpiration* from the leaves of plants.

Evergreen Plants with long-lasting leaves, which are not shed annually or seasonally.

Exfoliation A kind of *weathering* whereby scalelike flakes of rock are peeled or broken off by the development of salt crystals in water within the rocks. *Groundwater*, which contains dissolved salts, seeps to the surface and evaporates, precipitating a film of salt crystals, which expands causing fine cracks. As these grow, flakes of rock break off.

Extrusive rock *Igneous* rock formed when molten material (*magma*) pours forth at the Earth's surface and cools rapidly. It usually has a glassy texture.

F

Factionalism The actions of one or more minority political group acting against the interests of the majority government.

Fault A fracture or crack in rock, where strains (*tectonic* movement) have caused blocks to move, vertically or laterally, relative to each other.

Fauna Collective name for the animals of a particular period of time, or region.

Favela Brazilian term for the shantytowns or temporary huts that have grown up around the edge of many South and Central American cities.

Ferrel cell A component in the global pattern of air circulation, which rises in the colder *latitudes* (60° N and S) and descends in warmer *latitudes* (30° N and S). The Ferrel cell forms part of the world's three-cell air circulation pattern, with the *Hadley* and Polar cells.

Fissure A deep crack in a rock or a *glacier*.

Fjord A deep, narrow inlet, created when the sea inundates the *U-shaped valley* created by a *glacier*.

Flash flood A sudden, short-lived rise in the water level of a river or stream, or surge of water down a dry river channel, or *wadi*, caused by heavy rainfall.

Flax A plant used to make linen.

Floodplain The broad, flat part of a river valley, adjacent to the river itself, formed by *sediment* deposited during flooding.

Flora The collective name for the plants of a particular period of time or region.

Flow The movement of a river within its banks, particularly in terms of the speed and volume of water.

Fold A bend in the rock *strata* of the Earth's *crust*, resulting from compression.

Fossil The remains, or traces,of a dead organism preserved in the Earth's *crust*.

Fossil dune A *dune* formed in a once-*arid* region which is now wetter. *Dunes* normally move with the wind, but in these cases vegetation makes them stable.

Fossil fuel Fuel – coal, natural gas or oil – composed of the fossilized remains of plants and animals.

Front The boundary between two *air masses*, which contrast sharply in temperature and *humidity*.

Frontal depression An area of low pressure caused by rising warm air. They are generally 600–1,200 miles (1,000–2,000 km) in diameter. Within *depressions* there are both warm and cold fronts.

Frost shattering A form of *weathering* where water freezes in cracks, causing expansion. As temperatures fluctuate and the ice melts and refreezes, it eventually causes the rocks to shatter and fragments of rock to break off.

G

Gaucho South American term for a stock herder or cowboy who works on the grassy *plains* of Paraguay, Uruguay, and Argentina.

Geological timescale The chronology of the Earth's history as revealed in its rocks. Geological time is divided into a number of periods: *eon*, era, period, epoch, age, and chron (the shortest). These units are not of uniform length.

Geosyncline A concave fold (*syncline*) or large depression in the Earth's *crust*, extending hundreds of miles. This basin contains a deep layer of sediment, especially at its center, from the land masses around it.

Geothermal energy Heat derived from hot rocks within the Earth's *crust* and resulting in hot springs, steam, or hot rocks at the surface. The energy is generated by rock movements, and from the breakdown of radioactive elements occurring under intense pressure.

GDP Gross Domestic Product. The total value of goods and services produced by a country excluding income from foreign countries.

Geyser A jet of steam and hot water that intermittently erupts from vents in the ground in areas that are, or were, *volcanic*. Some geysers occasionally reach heights of 196 ft (60 m).

Ghetto An area of a city or region occupied by an overwhelming majority of people from one racial or religious group, who may be subject to persecution or containment.

Glaciation The growth of *glaciers* and *ice sheets*, and their impact on the landscape.

Glacier A body of ice moving downslope under the influence of gravity and consisting of compacted and frozen snow. A glacier is distinct from an *ice sheet*, which is wider and less confined by features of the landscape.

Glacio-eustacy A world-wide change in the level of the oceans, caused when the formation of *ice sheets* takes up water or when their melting returns water to the ocean. The formation of ice sheets in the *Pleistocene* epoch, for example, caused sea level to drop by about 320 ft (100-m).

Glaciofluvial To do with glacial *meltwater*, the landforms it creates and its processes; *erosion*, transportation, and *deposition*. Glaciofluvial effects are more powerful and rapid where they occur within or beneath the *glacier*, rather than beyond its edge.

Glacis A gentle slope or *pediment*.

Global warming An increase in the average temperature of the Earth. At present the *greenhouse effect* is thought to contribute to this.

GNP Gross National Product. The total value of goods and services produced by a country.

Gondwanaland The *supercontinent* thought to have existed over 200 million years ago in the southern hemisphere. Gondwanaland is believed to have comprised today's Africa, Madagascar, Australia, parts of South America, *Antarctica*, and the Indian subcontinent.

Graben A block of rock let down between two parallel *faults*. Where the graben occurs within a valley, the structure is known as a *rift valley*.

Grease ice Slicks of ice which form in *Antarctic* seas, when ice crystals are bonded together by wind and wave action.

Greenhouse effect A change in the temperature of the *atmosphere*. Short-wave solar radiation travels through the *atmosphere* unimpeded to the Earth's surface, whereas outgoing, long-wave terrestrial radiation is absorbed by materials that reradiate it back to the Earth. Radiation trapped in this way, by water vapor, carbon dioxide, and other "greenhouse gases," keeps the Earth warm. As more *carbon dioxide* is released into the atmosphere by the burning of *fossil fuels*, the greenhouse effect may cause a global increase in temperature.

Groundwater Water that has seeped into the pores, cavities, and cracks of rocks or into soil and water held in an *aquifer*.

Gully A deep, narrow channel eroded in the landscape by *ephemeral* streams.

Guyot A small, flat-topped submarine mountain, formed as a result of subsidence which occurs during *sea-floor spreading*.

Gypsum A soft mineral *compound* (hydrated calcium sulphate), used as the basis of many forms of plaster, including plaster of Paris.

H

Hadley cell A large-scale component in the global pattern of air circulation. Warm air rises over the *Equator* and blows at high altitude toward the poles, sinking in subtropical regions (30° N and 30° S) and creating high pressure. The air then flows at the surface toward the *Equator* in the form of trade winds. There is one cell in each hemisphere. Named after G. Hadley, who published his theory in 1735.

Hamada An Arabic word for a plateau of bare rock in a *desert*.

Hanging valley A tributary valley that ends suddenly, high above the bed of the main valley. The effect is found where the main valley has been more deeply eroded by a *glacier*, than has the tributary valley. A stream in a hanging valley will descend to the floor of the main valley as a waterfall or *cataract*.

Headwards The action of a river eroding back upstream, as opposed to the normal process of downstream *erosion*. Headwards erosion is often associated with *gullying*.

Hoodos Pinnacles of rock that have been worn away by *weathering* in *semiarid* regions.

Horst A block of the Earth's *crust* which has been left upstanding by the sinking of adjoining blocks along fault lines.

Hot spot A region of the Earth's *crust* where high thermal activity occurs, often leading to volcanic eruptions. Hot spots often occur far from plate boundaries, but their movement is associated with *plate tectonics*.

Humid equatorial Rainy *climate* with no winter, where the coolest month is generally above 64°F (18°C).

Humidity The relative amount of moisture held in the Earth's *atmosphere*.

Hurricane
1 A tropical *cyclone* occurring in the Caribbean and western North Atlantic.
2 A wind of more than 65 knots (75 kmph).

Hydroelectric power Energy produced by harnessing the rapid movement of water down steep mountain slopes to drive turbines to generate electricity.

Hydrolysis The chemical breakdown of rocks in reaction with water, forming new compounds.

I

Ice Age A period in the Earth's history when surface temperatures in the temperate *latitudes* were much lower and *ice sheets* expanded considerably. There have been *ice ages* from *Pre-Cambrian* times onward. The most recent began two million years ago and ended 10,000 years ago.

Ice cap A permanent dome of ice in highland areas. The term ice cap is often seen as distinct from *ice sheet*, which denotes a much wider covering of ice; and is also used refer to the very extensive polar and Greenland ice caps.

Ice floe A large, flat mass of ice floating free on the ocean surface. It is usually formed after the break-up of winter ice by heavy storms.

Ice sheet A continuous, very thick layer of ice and snow. The term is usually used of ice masses which are continental in extent.

Ice shelf A floating mass of ice attached to the edge of a coast. The seaward edge is usually a sheer cliff up to 100 ft (30-m) high.

Ice wedge Massive blocks of ice up to 6.5-ft (2-m) wide at the top and extending 32-ft (10-m) deep. They are found in cracks in *polygonally-patterned* ground in *periglacial* regions.

Iceberg A large mass of ice in a lake or a sea, which has broken off from a floating *ice sheet* (an *ice shelf*) or from a *glacier*.

Igneous rock Rock formed when molten material, *magma*, from the hot, lower layers of the Earth's *crust*, cools, solidifies, and crystallizes, either within the Earth's *crust* (*intrusive*) or on the surface (*extrusive*).

IMF International Monetary Fund. Established in 1944 as a UN agency, it contains 182 members around the world and is concerned with world monetary stability and economic development.

Incised meander A *meander* where the river, following its original course, cuts deeply into *bedrock*. This may occur when a mature, meandering river begins to erode its bed much more vigorously after the surrounding land has been uplifted.

Indigenous People, plants, or animals native to a particular region.

Infrastructure The communications and services – roads, railroads, and telecommunications – necessary for the functioning of a country or region.

Inselberg An isolated, steep-sided hill, rising from a low *plain* in *semiarid* and *savannah* landscapes. Inselbergs are usually composed of a rock, such as granite, which resists *erosion*.

Interglacial A period of global *climate*, between two *ice ages*, when temperatures rise and *ice sheets* and *glaciers* retreat.

Intraplate volcano A *volcano* which lies in the centre of one of the Earth's *tectonic plates*, rather than, as is more common, at its edge. They are thought to have been formed by a *hot spot*.

Intrusion (intrusive igneous rock) Rock formed when molten material, *magma*, penetrates existing rocks below the Earth's surface before cooling and solidifying. These rocks cool more slowly than extrusive rock and therefore tend to have coarser grains.

Irrigation The artificial supply of agricultural water to dry areas, often involving the creation of canals and the diversion of natural watercourses.

Island arc A curved chain of islands. Typically, such an arc fringes an ocean trench, formed at the margin between two *tectonic plates*. As one plate overrides another, *earthquakes* and volcanic activity are common and the islands themselves are often volcanic cones.

Isostasy The state of equilibrium that the Earth's *crust* maintains as its lighter and heavier parts float on the denser underlying mantle.

Isthmus A narrow strip of land connecting two larger landmasses or islands.

J

Jet stream A narrow belt of westerly winds in the *troposphere*, at altitudes above 39,000 ft (12,000 m). Jet streams tend to blow more strongly in winter and include: the subtropical jet stream; the *polar* front jet stream in mid-*latitudes*; the *Arctic* jet stream; and the polar-night jet stream.

Joint A crack in a rock, formed where blocks of rock have not shifted relative to each other, as is the case with a *fault*. Joints are created by *folding*; by shrinkage in *igneous rock* as it cools or *sedimentary rock* as it dries out; and by the release of pressure in a rock mass when overlying materials are removed by *erosion*.

Jute A plant fiber used to make coarse ropes, sacks, and matting.

K

Kame A mound of stratified sand and gravel with steep sides, deposited in a *crevasse* by *meltwater* running over a *glacier*. When the ice retreats, this forms an undulating terrain of hummocks.

Karst A barren *limestone* landscape created by carbonic acid in streams and rainwater, in areas where *limestone* is close to the surface. Typical features include caverns, towerlike hills, *sinkholes*, and flat limestone pavements.

Kettle hole A round hollow formed in a glacial deposit by a detached block of glacial ice, which later melted. They can fill with water to form kettle-lakes.

L

Lagoon A shallow stretch of coastal salt-water behind a partial barrier such as a sandbank or *coral reef*. Lagoon is also used to describe the water encircled by an *atoll*.

LAIA Latin American Integration Association. Established in 1980, its members are Argentina, Bolivia, Brazil, Chile, Colombia, Ecuador, Mexico, Paraguay, Peru, Uruguay, and Venezuala. It aims to promote economic cooperation between member states.

Landslide The sudden downslope movement of a mass of rock or earth on a slope, caused either by heavy rain; the impact of waves; an *earthquake* or human activity.

Laterite A hard red deposit left by *chemical weathering* in tropical conditions, and consisting mainly of oxides of iron and aluminium.

Latitude The angular distance from the *Equator*, to a given point on the Earth's surface. Imaginary lines of *latitude* running parallel to the Equator encircle the Earth, and are measured in degrees north or south of the Equator. The Equator is 0°, the poles 90° South and North respectively. Also called parallels.

Laurasia In the theory of *continental drift*, the northern part of the great *supercontinent* of *Pangaea*. Laurasia is said to consist of N America, Greenland and all of Eurasia north of the Indian subcontinent.

Lava The molten rock, *magma*, which erupts onto the Earth's surface through a *volcano*, or through a *fault* or crack in the Earth's *crust*. Lava refers to the rock both in its molten and in its later, solidified form.

Leaching The process whereby water dissolves minerals and moves them down through layers of soil or rock.

Levée A raised bank alongside the channel of a river. Levées are either human-made or formed in times of flood when the river overflows its channel, slows and deposits much of its *sediment* load.

Lichen An organism which is the symbiotic product of an algae and a fungus. Lichens form in tight crusts on stones and trees, and are resistant to extreme cold. They are often found in tundra regions.

Lignite Low-grade coal, also known as brown coal. Found in large deposits in eastern Europe.

Limestone A porous *sedimentary* rock formed from carbonate materials.

Lingua franca The language adopted as the common language between speakers whose native languages are different. This is common in former colonial states.

Lithosphere The rigid upper layer of the Earth, comprising the *crust* and the upper part of the *mantle*.

Llanos Vast grassland *plains* of northern South America.

Loess Fine-grained, yellow deposits of unstratified silts and sands. Loess is believed to be wind-carried *sediment* created in the last *Ice Age*. Some deposits may later have been redistributed by rivers. Loess-derived soils are of high quality, fertile, and easy to work.

Longitude A division of the Earth which pinpoints how far east or west a given place is from the Prime Meridian (0°) which runs through the Royal Observatory at Greenwich, England (UK). Imaginary lines of longitude are drawn around the world from pole to pole. The world is divided into 360 degrees.

Longshore drift The movement of sand and silt along the coast, carried by waves hitting the beach at an angle.

M

Magma Underground, molten rock, which is very hot and highly charged with gas. It is generated at great pressure, at depths 10 miles (16 km) or more below the Earth's surface. It can issue as *lava* at the Earth's surface or, more often, solidify below the surface as *intrusive igneous rock*.

Mantle The layer of the Earth between the *crust* and the *core*. It is about 1,800 miles (2,900-km) thick. The uppermost layer of the mantle is the soft, 125-mile (200 km) thick *asthenosphere* on which the more rigid *lithosphere* floats.

Maquiladoras Factories on the Mexico side of the Mexico/US border, that are allowed to import raw materials and components duty-free and use low-cost labor to assemble the goods, finally exporting them for sale in the US.

Market gardening The intensive growing of fruit and vegetables close to large local markets.

Mass movement Downslope movement of weathered materials such as rock, often helped by rainfall or glacial *meltwater*. Mass movement may be a gradual process or rapid, as in a *landslide* or rockfall.

Massif A single very large mountain or an area of mountains with uniform characteristics and clearly-defined boundaries.

Meander A looplike bend in a river, which is found typically in the lower, mature reaches of a river but can form wherever the valley is wide and the slope gentle.

Mediterranean climate A temperate *climate* of hot, dry summers and warm, damp winters. This is typical of the western fringes of the world's continents in the warm temperate regions between *latitudes* of 30° and 40° (north and south).

Meltwater Water resulting from the melting of a *glacier* or *ice sheet*.

Mesa A broad, flat-topped hill, characteristic of *arid* regions.

Mesosphere A layer of the Earth's *atmosphere*, between the *stratosphere* and the *thermosphere*. Extending from about 25–50 miles (40–80 km) above the surface of the Earth.

Mestizo A person of mixed *Amerindian* and European origin.

Metallurgy The refining and working of metals.

Metamorphic rocks Rocks that have been altered from their original form, in terms of texture, composition, and structure by intense heat, pressure, or by the introduction of new chemical substances – or a combination of more than one of these.

Meteor A body of rock, metal or other material, that travels through space at great speeds. Meteors are visible as they enter the Earth's *atmosphere* as shooting stars and fireballs.

Meteorite The remains of a *meteor* that has fallen to Earth.

Meteoroid A *meteor* that is still traveling in space, outside the Earth's *atmosphere*.

Mezzogiorno A term applied to the southern portion of Italy.

Milankovitch hypothesis A theory suggesting that there are a series of cycles that slightly alter the Earth's position when rotating about the Sun. The cycles identified all affect the amount of *radiation* the Earth receives at different *latitudes*. The theory is seen as a key factor in the cause of *ice ages*.

Millet A grain-crop, forming part of the staple diet in much of Africa.

Mistral A strong, dry, cold northerly or north-westerly wind, which blows from the Massif Central of France to the Mediterranean Sea. It is common in winter and its cold blasts can cause crop damage in the Rhône Delta, in France.

Mohorovicic discontinuity (Moho) The structural divide at the margin between the Earth's *crust* and the *mantle*. On average it is 20 miles (35-km) below the continents and 6-miles (10 km) below the oceans. The different densities of the *crust* and the mantle cause *earthquake* waves to accelerate at this point.

Monarchy A form of government in which the head of state is a single hereditary monarch. The monarch may be a mere figurehead, or may retain significant authority.

Monsoon A wind that changes direction biannually. The change is caused by the reversal of pressure over landmasses and the adjacent oceans. Because the inflowing moist winds bring rain, the term monsoon is also used to refer to the rains themselves. The term is derived from and most commonly refers to the seasonal winds of south and east Asia.

Montaña Mountain areas along the west coast of South America.

Moraine Debris, transported and deposited by a *glacier* or *ice sheet* in unstratified, mixed, piles of rock, boulders, pebbles, and clay.

Mountain-building The formation of *fold* mountains by tectonic activity. Also known as orogeny, mountain-building often occurs on the margin where two *tectonic plates* collide. The periods when most mountain-building occurred are known as orogenic phases and lasted many millions of years.

Mudflow An *avalanche* of mud that occurs when a mass of soil is drenched by rain or melting snow. It is a type of *mass movement*, faster than an *earthflow* because it is lubricated by water.

N

Nappe A mass of rocks which has been overfolded by repeated thrust *faulting*.

NAFTA The North American Free Trade Association. Established in 1994 between Canada, Mexico, and the US to set up a free-trade zone.

NASA The National Aeronautical and Space Administration. It is a US government agency, established in 1958 to develop manned and unmanned space programs.

NATO The North Atlantic Treaty Organization. Established in 1949 to promote mutual defense and cooperation between its members, which are Belgium, Canada, Czech Republic, Denmark, France, Germany, Greece, Iceland, Italy, Luxembourg, the Netherlands, Norway, Portugal, Poland, Spain, Turkey, UK, and US.

Nitrogen The odorless, colorless gas that makes up 78% of the atmosphere. Within the soil, it is a vital nutrient for plants.

Nomads (nomadic) Wandering communities that move around in search of suitable pasture for their herds of animals.

Nuclear fusion A technique used to create a new nucleus by the merging of two lighter ones, resulting in the release of large quantities of energy.

O

Oasis A fertile area in the midst of a *desert*, usually watered by an underground *aquifer*.

Oceanic ridge A mid-ocean ridge formed, according to the theory of *plate tectonics*, when plates drift apart and hot *magma* pours through to form new oceanic *crust*.

Oligarchy The government of a state by a small, exclusive group of people – such as an elite class or a family group.

Onion-skin weathering The *weathering* away or *exfoliation* of a rock or outcrop by the peeling off of surface layers.

Oriente A flatter region lying to the east of the Andes in South America.

Outwash plain *Glaciofluvial* material (typically clay, sand, and gravel) carried beyond an ice sheet by *meltwater* streams, forming a broad, flat deposit.

Oxbow lake A crescent-shaped lake formed on a river *floodplain* when a river erodes the outside bend of a *meander*, making the neck of the *meander* narrower until the river cuts across the neck. The meander is cut off and is dammed off with sediment, creating an oxbow lake. Also known as a cut-off or mortlake.

Oxidation A form of *chemical weathering* where *oxygen* dissolved in water reacts with minerals in rocks – particularly iron – to form oxides. Oxidation causes brown or yellow staining on rocks, and eventually leads to the break down of the rock.

Oxygen A colorless, odorless gas which is one of the main constituents of the Earth's *atmosphere* and is essential to life on Earth.

Ozone layer A layer of enriched *oxygen* (O_3) within the stratosphere, mostly between 18–50 miles (30–80 km) above the Earth's surface. It is vital to the existence of life on Earth because it absorbs harmful shortwave ultraviolet radiation, while allowing beneficial longer wave ultraviolet radiation to penetrate to the Earth's surface.

P

Pacific Rim The name given to the economically-dynamic countries bordering the Pacific Ocean.

Pack ice Ice masses more than 10 ft (3-m) thick that form on the sea surface and are not attached to a landmass.

Pancake ice Thin discs of ice, up to 8 ft (2.4 m) wide which form when slicks of *grease ice* are tossed together by winds and stormy seas.

Pangaea In the theory of continental drift, Pangaea is the original great land mass which, about 190 million years ago, began to split into Gondwanaland in the south and Laurasia in the north, separated by the Tethys Sea.

Pastoralism Grazing of livestock– usually sheep, goats, or cattle. Pastoralists in many drier areas have traditionally been *nomadic*.

Parallel *see Latitude*.

Peat Ancient, partially-decomposed vegetation found in wet, boggy conditions where there is little *oxygen*. It is the first stage in the development of coal and is often dried for use as fuel. It is also used to improve soil quality.

Pediment A gently-sloping ramp of *bedrock* below a steeper slope, often found at mountain edges in *desert* areas, but also in other climatic zones. Pediments may include depositional elements such as *alluvial fans*.

Peninsula A thin strip of land surrounded on three of its sides by water. Large examples include Florida and Korea.

Per capita Latin term meaning "for each person."

Periglacial Regions on the edges of *ice sheets* or *glaciers* or, more commonly, cold regions experiencing intense frost action, *permafrost* or both. Periglacial climates bring long, freezing winters and short, mild summers.

Permafrost Permanently frozen ground, typical of *Arctic* regions. Although a layer of soil above the permafrost melts in summer, the melted water does not drain through the permafrost.

Permeable rocks Rocks through which water can seep, because they are either porous or cracked.

Pharmaceuticals The manufacture of medicinal drugs.

Phreatic eruption A volcanic eruption which occurs when *lava* combines with *groundwater*, superheating the water and causing a sudden emission of steam at the surface.

Physical weathering (mechanical weathering) The breakdown of rocks by physical, as opposed to chemical, processes. Examples include: changes in pressure or temperature; the effect of windblown sand; the pressure of growing salt crystals in cracks within rock; and the expansion and contraction of water within rock as it freezes and thaws.

Pingo A dome of earth with a core of ice, found in *tundra* regions. Pingos are formed either when *groundwater* freezes and expands, pushing up the land surface, or when trapped, freezing water in a lake expands and pushes up lake *sediments* to form the pingo dome.

Placer A belt of mineral-bearing rock *strata* lying at or close to the Earth's surface, from which minerals can be easily extracted.

Plain A flat, level region of land, often relatively low-lying.

Plateau A highland tract of flat land.

Plate *see Tectonic plates*.

Plate tectonics The study of *tectonic plates*, that helps to explain *continental drift*, mountain formation and volcanic activity. The movement of tectonic plates may be explained by the currents of rock rising and falling from within the Earth's *mantle*, as it heats up and then cools. The boundaries of the plates are known as plate margins and most mountains, *earthquakes*, and *volcanoes* occur at these margins. Constructive margins are moving apart; destructive margins are crunching together and conservative margins are sliding past one another.

Pleistocene A period of *geological time* spanning from about 5.2 million years ago to 1.6 million years ago.

Plutonic rock *Igneous* rocks found deep below the surface. They are coarse-grained because they cooled and solidified slowly.

Polar The zones within the *Arctic* and *Antarctic* circles.

Polje A long, broad *depression* found in *karst* (*limestone*) regions.

Polygonal patterning Typical ground patterning, found in areas where the soil is subject to severe frost action, often in *periglacial* regions.

Porosity A measure of how much water can be held within a rock or a soil. Porosity is measured as the percentage of holes or pores in a material, compared to its total volume. For example, the porosity of slate is less than 1%, whereas that of gravel is 25–35%.

Prairies Originally a French word for grassy *plains* with few or no trees.

Pre-Cambrian The earliest period of *geological time* dating from over 570-million years ago.

Precipitation The fall of moisture from the *atmosphere* onto the surface of the Earth, whether as dew, hail, rain, sleet, or snow.

Pyramidal peak A steep, isolated mountain summit, formed when the back walls of three or more *cirques* are cut back and move toward each other. The cliffs around such a horned peak, or horn, are divided by sharp *arêtes*. The Matterhorn in the Swiss Alps is an example.

Pyroclasts Fragments of rock ejected during volcanic eruptions.

Q

Quaternary The current period of *geological time*, which started about 1.6-million years ago.

R

Radiation The emission of energy in the form of particles or waves. Radiation from the sun includes heat, light, ultraviolet rays, gamma rays, and X-rays. Only some of the solar energy radiated into space reaches the Earth.

Rainforest Dense forests in tropical zones with high rainfall, temperature and *humidity*. Strictly, the term applies to the equatorial rain forest in tropical lowlands with constant rainfall and no seasonal change. The Congo and Amazon basins are examples. The term is applied more loosely to lush forest in other climates. Within rain forests organic life is dense and varied: at least 40% of all plant and animal species are found here and there may be as many as 100 tree species per hectare.

Rainshadow An area which experiences low rainfall, because of its position on the leeward side of a mountain range.

Reg A large area of stony *desert*, where tightly-packed gravel lies on top of clayey sand. A reg is formed where the wind blows away the finer sand.

Remote-sensing Method of obtaining information about the *environment* using unmanned equipment, such as a satellite, that relays the information to a point where it is collected and used.

Resistance The capacity of a rock to resist *denudation*, by processes such as *weathering* and *erosion*.

Ria A flooded *V-shaped river valley* or estuary, flooded by a rise in sea level (*eustacy*) or sinking land. It is shorter than a *fjord* and gets deeper as it meets the sea.

Rift valley A long, narrow depression in the Earth's *crust*, formed by the sinking of rocks between two *faults*.

River channel The trough which contains a river and is molded by the flow of water within it.

Roche moutonée A rock found in a glaciated valley. The side facing the flow of the *glacier* has been smoothed and rounded, while the other side has been left more rugged because the *glacier*, as it flows over it, has plucked out frozen fragments and carried them away.

Runoff Water draining from a land surface by flowing across it.

S

Sabkha The floor of an isolated *depression* that occurs in an *arid environment* – usually covered by salt deposits and devoid of vegetation.

SADC Southern African Development Community. Established in 1992 to promote economic integration between its member states, which are Angola, Botswana, Lesotho, Malawi, Mauritius, Mozambique, Namibia, South Africa, Swaziland, Tanzania, Zambia, and Zimbabwe.

Salt plug A rounded hill produced by the upward doming of rock *strata* caused by the movement of salt or other evaporite deposits under intense pressure.

Sastrugi Ice ridges formed by wind action. They lie parallel to the direction of the wind.

Savannah Open grassland found between the zone of *deserts*, and that of tropical *rain forests* in the tropics and subtropics. Scattered trees and shrubs are found in some kinds of savannah. A savannah *climate* usually has wet and dry seasons.

Scarp *see Escarpment*.

Scree Piles of rock fragments beneath a cliff or rock face, caused by mechanical *weathering*, especially *frost shattering*, where the expansion and contraction of freezing and thawing water within the rock, gradually breaks it up.

Sea-floor spreading The process whereby *tectonic plates* move apart, allowing hot *magma* to erupt and solidify. This forms a new sea floor and, ultimately, widens the ocean.

Seamount An isolated, submarine mountain or hill, probably of volcanic origin.

Season A period of time linked to regular changes in the weather, especially the intensity of solar *radiation*.

Sediment Grains of rock transported and deposited by rivers, sea, ice, or wind.

Sedimentary rocks Rocks formed from the debris of preexisting rocks or of organic material. They are found in many *environments* – on the ocean floor, on beaches, rivers, and *deserts*. Organically-formed sedimentary rocks include coal and chalk. Other sedimentary rocks, such as flint, are formed by chemical processes. Most of these rocks contain *fossils*, which can be used to date them.

Seif A sand *dune* which lies parallel to the direction of the prevailing wind. Seifs form steep-sided ridges, sometimes extending for miles.

Seismic activity Movement within the Earth, such as an *earthquake* or *tremor*.

Selva A region of wet forest found in the Amazon Basin.

Semiarid, semidesert The *climate* and landscape which lies between *savannah* and *desert* or between savannah and a *mediterranean* climate. In semiarid conditions there is a little more moisture than in a true *desert*; and more patches of drought-resistant vegetation can survive.

Shale (marine shale) A compacted *sedimentary rock*, with fine-grained particles. Marine shale is formed on the seabed. Fuel such as oil may be extracted from it.

Sheetwash Water that runs downhill in thin sheets without forming channels. It can cause *sheet erosion*.

Sheet erosion The washing away of soil by a thin film or sheet of water, known as *sheetwash*.

Shield A vast stable block of the Earth's *crust*, which has experienced little or no *mountain-building*.

Sierra The Spanish word for mountains.

Sinkhole A circular *depression* in a *limestone* region. They are formed by the collapse of an underground cave system or the *chemical weathering* of the *limestone*.

Sisal A plant-fiber used to make matting.

Slash and burn A farming technique involving the cutting down and burning of scrub forest, to create agricultural land. After a number of seasons this land is abandoned and the process is repeated. This practice is common in Africa and South America.

Slip face The steep leeward side of a sand *dune* or slope. Opposite side to a *back slope*.

Soil A thin layer of rock particles mixed with the remains of dead plants and animals. This occurs naturally on the surface of the Earth and provides a medium for plants to grow.

Soil creep The very gradual downslope movement of rock debris and soil, under the influence of gravity. This is a type of *mass movement*.

Soil erosion The wearing away of soil more quickly than it is replaced by natural processes. Soil can be carried away by wind as well as by water. Human activities, such as over-grazing and the clearing of land for farming, accelerate the process in many areas.

Solar energy Energy derived from the Sun. Solar energy is converted into other forms of energy. For example, the wind and waves, as well as the creation of plant material in photosynthesis, depend on solar energy.

Solifluction A kind of *soil creep*, where water in the surface layer has saturated the soil and rock debris which slips slowly downhill. It often happens where frozen top-layer deposits thaw, leaving frozen layers below them.

Sorghum A type of grass found in South America, similar to sugar cane. When refined it is used to make molasses.

Spit A thin linear deposit of sand or shingle extending from the sea shore. Spits are formed as angled waves shift sand along the beach, eventually extending a ridge of sand beyond a change in the angle of the coast. Spits are common where the coastline bends, especially at estuaries.

Squash A type of edible gourd.

Stack A tall, isolated pillar of rock near a coastline, created as wave action erodes away the adjacent rock.

Stalactite A tapering cylinder of mineral deposit, hanging from the roof of a cave in a *karst* area. It is formed by calcium carbonate, dissolved in water, which drips through the roof of a *limestone* cavern.

Stalagmite A cone of calcium carbonate, similar to a *stalactite*, rising from the floor of a *limestone* cavern and formed when drops of water fall from the roof of a *limestone* cave. If the water has dripped from a *stalactite* above the stalagmite, the two may join to form a continuous pillar.

Staple crop The main crop on which a country is economically and or physically reliant. For example, the major crop grown for large-scale local consumption in South Asia is rice.

Steppe Large areas of dry grassland in the northern hemisphere – particularly found in southeast Europe and central Asia.

Strata The plural of stratum, a distinct, virtually horizontal layer of deposited material, lying parallel to other layers.

Stratosphere A layer of the *atmosphere*, above the *troposphere*, extending from about 7–30 miles (11–50 km) above the Earth's surface. In the lower part of the stratosphere, the temperature is relatively stable and there is little moisture.

Strike-slip fault Occurs where plates move sideways past each other and blocks of rocks move horizontally in relation to each other, not up or down as in normal *faults*.

Subduction zone A region where two *tectonic plates* collide, forcing one beneath the other. Typically, a dense oceanic plate dips below a lighter continental plate, melting in the heat of the *asthenosphere*. This is why the zone is also called a destructive margins (*see Plate tectonics*). These zones are characterized by *earthquakes*, volcanoes, *mountain–building*, and the development of oceanic trenches and *island arcs*.

Submarine canyon A steep-sided valley, that extends along the *continental shelf* to the ocean floor. Often formed by *turbidity currents*.

Submarine fan Deposits of silt and *alluvium*, carried by large rivers forming great fan-shaped deposits on the ocean floor.

Subsistence agriculture An agricultural practice in which enough food is produced to support the farmer and his dependents, but not providing any surplus to generate an income.

Subtropical A term applied loosely to *climates* which are nearly tropical or tropical for a part of the year – areas north or south of the *tropics* but outside the *temperate zone*.

Supercontinent A large continent that breaks up to form smaller continents or that forms when smaller continents merge. In the theory of *continental drift*, the supercontinents are *Pangaea*, *Gondwanaland*, and *Laurasia*.

Sustainable development An approach to development, especially applied to economies across the world which exploit natural resources without destroying them or the *environment*.

Syncline A basin-shaped downfold in rock *strata*, created when the *strata* are compressed, for example where *tectonic plates* collide.

T

Tableland A highland area with a flat or gently undulating surface.

Taiga The belt of *coniferous* forest found in the north of Asia and North America. The conifers are adapted to survive low temperatures and long periods of snowfall.

Tarn A Scottish term for a small mountain lake, usually found at the head of a *glacier*.

Tectonic plates Plates, or tectonic plates, are the rigid slabs which form the Earth's outer shell, the *lithosphere*. Eight big plates and several smaller ones have been identified.

Temperate A moderate *climate* without extremes of temperature, typical of the mid-*latitudes* between the *tropics* and the *polar* circles.

Theocracy A state governed by religious laws – today Iran is the world's largest theocracy.

Thermokarst Subsidence created by the thawing of ground ice in *periglacial* areas, creating depressions.

Thermosphere A layer of the Earth's *atmosphere* which lies above the *mesosphere*, about 60–300 miles (100–500 km) above the Earth

Terraces Steps cut into steep slopes to create flat surfaces for cultivating crops. They also help reduce soil *erosion* on unconsolidated slopes. They are most common in heavily-populated parts of Southeast Asia.

Till Unstratified glacial deposits or drift left by a *glacier* or *ice sheet*. Till includes mixtures of clay, sand, gravel, and boulders.

Topography The typical shape and features of a given area such as land height and terrain.

Tombolo A large sand *spit* which attaches part of the mainland to an island.

Tornado A violent, spiraling windstorm, with a center of very low pressure. Wind speeds reach 200 mph (320 kmph) and there is often thunder and heavy rain.

Transform fault In *plate tectonics*, a *fault* of continental scale, occurring where two plates slide past each other, staying close together for example, the San Andreas Fault, USA. The jerky, uneven movement creates *earthquakes* but does not destroy or add to the Earth's *crust*

Transpiration The loss of water vapor through the pores (or stomata) of plants. The process helps to return moisture to the *atmosphere*.

Trap An area of fine-grained *igneous rock* that has been extruded and cooled on the Earth's surface in stages, forming a series of steps or terraces.

Treeline The line beyond which trees cannot grow, dependent on *latitude* and altitude, as well as local factors such as soil.

Tremor A slight *earthquake*.

Trench (oceanic trench) A long, deep trough in the ocean floor, formed, according to the theory of *plate tectonics*, when two plates collide and one dives under the other, creating a *subduction zone*.

Tropics The zone between the *Tropic of Cancer* and the *Tropic of Capricorn* where the *climate* is hot. Tropical climate is also applied to areas rather further north and south of the *Equator* where the climate is similar to that of the true tropics.

Tropic of Cancer A line of *latitude* or imaginary circle round the Earth, lying at 23° 28' N.

Tropic of Capricorn A line of *latitude* or imaginary circle round the Earth, lying at 23° 28' S.

Troposphere The lowest layer of the Earth's *atmosphere*. From the surface, it reaches a height of between 4–10 miles (7–16 km). It is the most turbulent zone of the atmosphere and accounts for the generation of most of the world's weather. The layer above it is called the *stratosphere*.

Tsunami A huge wave created by shock waves from an *earthquake* under the sea. Reaching speeds of up to 600 mph (960-kmph), the wave may increase to heights of 50 ft (15 m) on entering coastal waters; and it can cause great damage.

Tundra The treeless *plains* of the *Arctic Circle*, found south of the *polar* region of permanent ice and snow, and north of the belt of *coniferous* forests known as *taiga*. In this region of long, very cold winters, vegetation is usually limited to mosses, *lichens*, sedges, and rushes, although flowers and dwarf shrubs blossom in the brief summer.

Turbidity current An oceanic feature. A turbidity current is a mass of *sediment*-laden water thathas substantial erosive power. Turbidity currents are thought to contribute to the formation of *submarine canyons*.

Typhoon A kind of *hurricane* (or tropical cyclone) bringing violent winds and heavy rain, a typhoon can do great damage. They occur in the South China Sea, especially around the Philippines.

U

U-shaped valley A river valley that has been deepened and widened by a *glacier*. They are characteristically flat-bottomed and steep-sided and generally much deeper than river valleys.

UN United Nations. Established in 1945, it contains 188 nations and aims to maintain international peace and security, and promote cooperation over economic, social, cultural, and humanitarian problems.

UNICEF United Nations Children's Fund. A UN organization set up to promote family and child related programs.

Urstromtäler A German word used to describe *meltwater* channels that flowed along the front edge of the advancing *ice sheet* during the last Ice Age, 18,000–20,000 years ago.

V

V-shaped valley A typical valley eroded by a river in its upper course.

Virgin rain forest Tropical *rain-forest* in its original state, untouched by human activity such as logging, clearance for agriculture, settlement, or roadbuilding.

Viticulture The cultivation of grapes for wine.

Volcano An opening or vent in the Earth's *crust* where molten rock, *magma*, erupts. Volcanoes tend to be conical but may also be a crack in the Earth's surface or a hole blasted through a mountain. The magma is accompanied by other materials such as gas, steam, and fragments of rock, or *pyroclasts*. They tend to occur on destructive or constructive tectonic*plate* margins.

W-Z

Wadi The dry bed left by a torrent of water. Also classified as a *ephemeral* stream, found in *arid* and *semiarid* regions, which are subject to sudden and often severe flash flooding.

Warm humid climate A rainy climate with warm summers and mild winters.

Water cycle The continuous circulation of water between the Earth's surface and the *atmosphere*. The processes include *evaporation* and *transpiration* of moisture into the atmosphere, and its return as *precipitation*, some of which flows into lakes and oceans.

Water table The upper level of *groundwater* saturation in permeable rock *strata*.

Watershed The dividing line between one *drainage basin* – an area where all streams flow into a single river system – and another. In the US, watershed also means the whole drainage basin of a single river system – its catchment area.

Waterspout A rotating column of water in the form of cloud, mist, and spray which form on open water. Often has the appearance of a small *tornado*.

Weathering The decay and breakup of rocks at or near the Earth's surface, caused by water, wind, heat or ice, organic material, or the *atmosphere*. *Physical weathering* includes the effects of frost and temperature changes. Biological weathering includes the effects of plant roots, burrowing animals and the acids produced by animals, especially as they decay after death. *Carbonation* and *hydrolysis* are among many kinds of *chemical weathering*.

Geographical names

The following glossary lists all geographical terms occurring on the maps and in main-entry names in the Index-Gazetteer. These terms may precede, follow, or be run together with the proper element of the name; where they precede it the term is reversed for indexing purposes - thus Poluostrov Yamal is indexed as Yamal, Poluostrov.

Key

Geographical term
Language, Term

A

Å *Danish, Norwegian*, River
Āb *Persian*, River
Adrar *Berber*, Mountains
Agía, Ágios *Greek*, Saint
Air *Indonesian*, River
Akrotírio *Greek*, Cape, point
Alpen *German*, Alps
Alt- *German*, Old
Altiplanicie *Spanish*, Plateau
Älv, -älven *Swedish*, River
-ån *Swedish*, River
Anse *French*, Bay
'Aqabat *Arabic*, Pass
Archipiélago *Spanish*, Archipelago
Arcipelago *Italian*, Archipelago
Arquipélago *Portuguese*, Archipelago
Arrecife(s) *Spanish*, Reef(s)
Aru *Tamil*, River
Augstiene *Latvian*, Upland
Aukštuma *Lithuanian*, Upland
Aust- *Norwegian*, Eastern
Avtonomnyy Okrug *Russian*, Autonomous district
Āw *Kurdish*, River
'Ayn *Arabic*, Spring, well
'Ayoûn *Arabic*, Wells

B

Baelt *Danish*, Strait
Bahía *Spanish*, Bay
Baḩr *Arabic*, River
Baía *Portuguese*, Bay
Baie *French*, Bay
Bañado *Spanish*, Marshy land
Bandao *Chinese*, Peninsula
Banjaran *Malay*, Mountain range
Baraji *Turkish*, Dam
Barragem *Portuguese*, Reservoir
Bassin *French*, Basin
Batang *Malay*, Stream
Beinn, Ben *Gaelic*, Mountain
-berg *Afrikaans, Norwegian*, Mountain
Besar *Indonesian, Malay*, Big
Birkat, Birket *Arabic*, Lake, well, cistern
Boğazı *Turkish*, Strait, defile
Boka *Serbo-Croatian*, Bay
Bol'sh-aya, -iye, -oy, -oye *Russian*, Big
Botigh(i) *Uzbek*, Depression basin
-bre(en) *Norwegian*, Glacier
Bredning *Danish*, Bay
Bucht *German*, Bay
Bugt(en) *Danish*, Bay
Buḩayrat *Arabic*, Lake, reservoir
Buḩeirat *Arabic*, Lake
Bukit *Malay*, Mountain
-bukta *Norwegian*, Bay
bukten *Swedish*, Bay
Bulag *Mongolian*, Spring
Bulak *Uighur*, Spring
Burnu *Turkish*, Cape, point
Buuraha *Somali*, Mountains

C

Cabo *Portuguese*, Cape
Caka *Tibetan*, Salt lake
Canal *Spanish*, Channel
Cap *French*, Cape
Capo *Italian*, Cape, headland
Cascada *Portuguese*, Waterfall
Cayo(s) *Spanish*, Islet(s), rock(s)
Cerro *Spanish*, Hill
Chaîne *French*, Mountain range
Chapada *Portuguese*, Hills, upland
Chau *Cantonese*, Island
Chay *Turkish*, River
Chhâk *Cambodian*, Bay
Chhu *Tibetan*, River
-chŏsuji *Korean*, Reservoir
Chott *Arabic*, Depression, salt lake
Chŭli *Uzbek*, Grassland, steppe
Ch'ün-tao *Chinese*, Island group
Chuŏr Phnum *Cambodian*, Mountains
Ciudad *Spanish*, City, town
Co *Tibetan*, Lake
Colline(s) *French*, Hill(s)
Cordillera *Spanish*, Mountain range
Costa *Spanish*, Coast
Côte *French*, Coast
Coxilha *Portuguese*, Mountains
Cuchilla *Spanish*, Mountains

D

Daban *Mongolian, Uighur*, Pass
Daği *Azerbaijani, Turkish*, Mountain
Dağları *Azerbaijani, Turkish*, Mountains
-dake *Japanese*, Peak
-dal(en) *Norwegian*, Valley
Danau *Indonesian*, Lake
Dao *Chinese*, Island
Đao *Vietnamese*, Island
Daryā *Persian*, River
Daryācheh *Persian*, Lake
Dasht *Persian*, Desert, plain
Dawḩat *Arabic*, Bay
Denizi *Turkish*, Sea
Dere *Turkish*, Stream
Desierto *Spanish*, Desert
Dili *Azerbaijani*, Spit
-do *Korean*, Island
Dooxo *Somali*, Valley
Düzü *Azerbaijani*, Steppe
-dwīp *Bengali*, Island

E

-eilanden *Dutch*, Islands
Embalse *Spanish*, Reservoir
Ensenada *Spanish*, Bay
Erg *Arabic*, Dunes
Estany *Catalan*, Lake
Estero *Spanish*, Inlet
Estrecho *Spanish*, Strait
Étang *French*, Lagoon, lake
-ey *Icelandic*, Island
Ezero *Bulgarian, Macedonian*, Lake
Ezers *Latvian*, Lake

F

Feng *Chinese*, Peak
-fjella *Norwegian*, Mountain
Fjord *Danish*, Fjord
-fjord(en) *Danish, Norwegian, Swedish*, fjord
-fjørdhur *Icelandic*, Fjord
Fleuve *French*, River
Fliegu *Maltese*, Channel
-fljór *Icelandic*, River
-flói *Icelandic*, Bay
Forêt *French*, Forest

G

-gan *Japanese*, Rock
-gang *Korean*, River
Ganga *Hindi, Nepali, Sinhala*, River
Gaoyuan *Chinese*, Plateau
Garagumy *Turkmen*, Sands
-gawa *Japanese*, River
Gebel *Arabic*, Mountain
-gebirge *German*, Mountain range
Ghadīr *Arabic*, Well
Ghubbat *Arabic*, Bay
Gjiri *Albanian*, Bay
Gol *Mongolian*, River
Golfe *French*, Gulf
Golfo *Italian, Spanish*, Gulf
Göl(ü) *Turkish*, Lake
Golyam, -a *Bulgarian*, Big
Gora *Russian, Serbo-Croatian*, Mountain
Góra *Polish*, mountain
Gory *Russian*, Mountain
Gryada *Russian*, ridge
Guba *Russian*, Bay
-gundo *Korean*, island group
Gunung *Malay*, Mountain

H

Ḩadd *Arabic*, Spit
-haehyŏp *Korean*, Strait
Haff *German*, Lagoon
Hai *Chinese*, Bay, lake, sea
Haixia *Chinese*, Strait
Ḩammādah *Arabic*, Desert
Ḩammādat *Arabic*, Rocky plateau
Hāmūn *Persian*, Lake
-hantō *Japanese*, Peninsula
Har, Haré *Hebrew*, Mountain
Ḩarrat *Arabic*, Lava-field
Hav(et) *Danish*, Swedish, Sea
Hawr *Arabic*, Lake
Hāyk' *Amharic*, Lake
He *Chinese*, River
-hegység *Hungarian*, Mountain range
Heide *German*, Heath, moorland
Helodrano *Malagasy*, Bay
Higashi- *Japanese*, East(ern)
Ḩişā' *Arabic*, Well
Hka *Burmese*, River
-ho *Korean*, Lake
Ḩolot *Hebrew*, Dunes
Hora *Belarussian, Czech*, Mountain
Hrada *Belarussian*, Mountain, ridge
Hsi *Chinese*, River
Hu *Chinese*, Lake
Huk *Danish*, Point

I

Île(s) *French*, Island(s)
Ilha(s) *Portuguese*, Island(s)
Ilhéu(s) *Portuguese*, Islet(s)
-isen *Norwegian*, Ice shelf
Imeni *Russian*, In the name of
Inish- *Gaelic*, Island
Insel(n) *German*, Island(s)
Irmağı, Irmak *Turkish*, River
Isla(s) *Spanish*, Island(s)
Isola (Isole) *Italian*, Island(s)

J

Jabal *Arabic*, Mountain
Jāl *Arabic*, Ridge
-järv *Estonian*, Lake
-järvi *Finnish*, Lake
Jazā'ir *Arabic*, Islands
Jazīrat *Arabic*, Island
Jazīreh *Persian*, Island
Jebel *Arabic*, Mountain
Jezero *Serbo-Croatian*, Lake
Jezioro *Polish*, Lake
Jiang *Chinese*, River
-jima *Japanese*, Island
Jižní *Czech*, Southern
-jõgi *Estonian*, River
-joki *Finnish*, River
-jökull *Icelandic*, Glacier
Jūn *Arabic*, Bay
Juzur *Arabic*, Islands

K

Kaikyō *Japanese*, Strait
-kaise *Lappish*, Mountain
Kali *Nepali*, River
Kalnas *Lithuanian*, Mountain
Kalns *Latvian*, Mountain
Kang *Chinese*, Harbor
Kangri *Tibetan*, Mountain(s)
Kaôh *Cambodian*, Island
Kapp *Norwegian*, Cape
Káto *Greek*, Lower
Kavīr *Persian*, Desert
K'edi *Georgian*, Mountain range
Kediet *Arabic*, Mountain
Kepi *Albanian*, Cape, point
Kepulauan *Indonesian, Malay*, Island group
Khalīg, Khalīj *Arabic*, Gulf
Khawr *Arabic*, Inlet
Khola *Nepali*, River
Khrebet *Russian*, Mountain range
Ko *Thai*, Island
-ko *Japanese*, Inlet, lake
Kólpos *Greek*, Bay
-kopf *German*, Peak
Körfäzi *Azerbaijani*, Bay
Körfezi *Turkish*, Bay
Kõrgustik *Estonian*, Upland
Kosa *Russian, Ukrainian*, Spit
Koshi *Nepali*, River
Kou *Chinese*, River-mouth
Kowtal *Persian*, Pass
Kray *Russian*, Region, territory
Kryazh *Russian*, Ridge
Kuduk *Uighur*, Well
Kūh(hā) *Persian*, Mountain(s)
-kul' *Russian*, Lake
Kŭl(i) *Tajik, Uzbek*, Lake
-kundo *Korean*, Island group
-kysten *Norwegian*, Coast
Kyun *Burmese*, Island

L

Laaq *Somali*, Watercourse
Lac *French*, Lake
Lacul *Romanian*, Lake
Lagh *Somali*, Stream
Lago *Italian, Portuguese, Spanish*, Lake
Lagoa *Portuguese*, Lagoon
Laguna *Italian, Spanish*, Lagoon, lake
Laht *Estonian*, Bay
Laut *Indonesian*, Bay
Lembalemba *Malagasy*, Plateau
Lerr *Armenian*, Mountain
Lerrnashght'a *Armenian*, Mountain range
Les *Czech*, Forest
Lich *Armenian*, Lake
Liehtao *Chinese*, Island group
Liqeni *Albanian*, Lake
Límni *Greek*, Lake
Ling *Chinese*, Mountain range
Llano *Spanish*, Plain, prairie
Lumi *Albanian*, River
Lyman *Ukrainian*, Estuary

M

Madīnat *Arabic*, City, town
Mae Nam *Thai*, River
-mägi *Estonian*, Hill
Maja *Albanian*, Mountain
Mal *Albanian*, Mountains
Mal-aya, -oye, -yy, *Russian*, Small
-man *Korean*, Bay
Mar *Spanish*, Sea
Marios *Lithuanian*, Lake
Massif *French*, Mountains
Meer *German*, Lake
-meer *Dutch*, Lake
Melkosopochnik *Russian*, Plain
-meri *Estonian*, Sea
Mifraz *Hebrew*, Bay
Minami- *Japanese*, South(ern)
-misaki *Japanese*, Cape, point
Monkhafad *Arabic*, Depression
Montagne(s) *French*, Mountain(s)
Montañas *Spanish*, Mountains
Mont(s) *French*, Mountain(s)
Monte *Italian, Portuguese*, Mountain
More *Russian*, Sea
Mörön *Mongolian*, River
Mys *Russian*, Cape, point

N

-nada *Japanese*, Open stretch of water
Nadi *Bengali*, River
Nagor'ye *Russian*, Upland
Naḩal *Hebrew*, River
Nahr *Arabic*, River
Nam *Laotian*, River
Namakzār *Persian*, Salt desert
Né-a, -on, -os *Greek*, New
Nedre- *Norwegian*, Lower
-neem *Estonian*, Cape, point
Nehri *Turkish*, River
-nes *Norwegian*, Cape, point
Nevado *Spanish*, Mountain (snow-capped)
Nieder- *German*, Lower
Nishi- *Japanese*, West(ern)
-nísi *Greek*, Island
Nisoi *Greek*, Islands
Nizhn-eye, -iy, -iye, -yaya *Russian*, Lower
Nizmennost' *Russian*, Lowland, plain
Nord *Danish, French, German*, North
Norte *Portuguese, Spanish*, North
Nos *Bulgarian*, Point, spit
Nosy *Malagasy*, Island
Nov-a, -i, *Bulgarian, Serbo-Croatian*, New
Nov-aya, -o, -oye, -yy, -yye *Russian*, New
Now-a, -e, -y *Polish*, New
Nur *Mongolian*, Lake
Nuruu *Mongolian*, Mountains
Nuur *Mongolian*, Lake
Nyzovyna *Ukrainian*, Lowland, plain

O

-ø *Danish*, Island
Ober- *German*, Upper
Oblast' *Russian*, Province
Órmos *Greek*, Bay
Orol(i) *Uzbek*, Island
Øster- *Norwegian*, Eastern
Ostrov(a) *Russian*, Island(s)
Otok *Serbo-Croatian*, Island
Oued *Arabic*, Watercourse
-oy *Faeroese*, Island
-øy(a) *Norwegian*, Island
Oya *Sinhala*, River
Ozero *Russian, Ukrainian*, Lake

P

Passo *Italian*, Pass
Pegunungan *Indonesian, Malay*, Mountain range
Pélagos *Greek*, Sea
Pendi *Chinese*, Basin
Penisola *Italian*, Peninsula
Pertuis *French*, Strait
Peski *Russian*, Sands
Phanom *Thai*, Mountain
Phou *Laotian*, Mountain
Pi *Chinese*, Point
Pic *Catalan, French*, Peak
Pico *Portuguese, Spanish*, Peak
-piggen *Danish*, Peak
Pik *Russian*, Peak
Pivostriv *Ukrainian*, Peninsula
Planalto *Portuguese*, Plateau
Planina, Planini *Bulgarian, Macedonian, Serbo-Croatian*, Mountain range
Plato *Russian*, Plateau
Ploskogor'ye *Russian*, Upland
Poluostrov *Russian*, Peninsula
Ponta *Portuguese*, Point
Porthmós *Greek*, Strait
Pótamos *Greek*, River
Presa *Spanish*, Dam
Prokhod *Bulgarian*, Pass
Proliv *Russian*, Strait
Pulau *Indonesian, Malay*, Island
Pulu *Malay*, Island
Punta *Spanish*, Point
Pushcha *Belorussian*, Forest
Puszcza *Polish*, Forest

Q

Qā' *Arabic*, Depression
Qalamat *Arabic*, Well
Qatorkŭh(i) *Tajik*, Mountain
Qiuling *Chinese*, Hills
Qolleh *Persian*, Mountain
Qu *Tibetan*, Stream
Quan *Chinese*, Well
Qulla(i) *Tajik*, Peak
Qundao *Chinese*, Island group

R

Raas *Somali*, Cape
-rags *Latvian*, Cape
Ramlat *Arabic*, Sands
Ra's *Arabic*, Cape, headland, point
Ravnina *Bulgarian, Russian*, Plain
Récif *French*, Reef
Recife *Portuguese*, Reef
Reka *Bulgarian*, River
Represa (Rep.) *Portuguese, Spanish*, Reservoir
Reshteh *Persian*, Mountain range
Respublika *Russian*, Republic, first-order administrative division
Respublika(si) *Uzbek*, Republic, first-order administrative division
-retsugan *Japanese*, Chain of rocks
-rettō *Japanese*, Island chain
Riacho *Spanish*, Stream
Riban' *Malagasy*, Mountains
Rio *Portuguese*, River
Río *Spanish*, River
Riu *Catalan*, River
Rivier *Dutch*, River
Rivière *French*, River
Rowd *Pashtu*, River
Rt *Serbo-Croatian*, Point
Rūd *Persian*, River
Rūdkhāneh *Persian*, River
Rudohorie *Slovak*, Mountains
Ruisseau *French*, Stream

S

-saar *Estonian*, Island
-saari *Finnish*, Island
Sabkhat *Arabic*, Salt marsh
Sāgar(a) *Hindi*, Lake, reservoir
Şaḩrā' *Arabic*, Desert
Saint, Sainte *French*, Saint
Salar *Spanish*, Salt-pan
Salto *Portuguese, Spanish*, Waterfall
Samudra *Sinhala*, Reservoir
-san *Japanese, Korean*, Mountain
-sanchi *Japanese*, Mountains
-sandur *Icelandic*, Beach
Sankt *German, Swedish*, Saint
-sanmaek *Korean*, Mountain range
-sanmyaku *Japanese*, Mountain range
San, Santa, Santo *Italian, Portuguese, Spanish*, Saint
São *Portuguese*, Saint
Sarīr *Arabic*, Desert
Sebkha, Sebkhet *Arabic*, Depression, salt marsh
Sedlo *Czech*, Pass
See *German*, Lake
Selat *Indonesian*, Strait
Selatan *Indonesian*, Southern
-selkä *Finnish*, Lake, ridge
Selseleh *Persian*, Mountain range
Serra *Portuguese*, Mountain
Serranía *Spanish*, Mountain
-seto *Japanese*, Channel, strait
Sever-naya, -noye, -nyy, -o *Russian*, Northern
Sha'ib *Arabic*, Watercourse
Shākh *Kurdish*, Mountain
Shamo *Chinese*, Desert
Shan *Chinese*, Mountain(s)
Shankou *Chinese*, Pass
Shanmo *Chinese*, Mountain range
Shaţţ *Arabic*, Distributary
Shet' *Amharic*, River
Shi *Chinese*, Municipality
-shima *Japanese*, Island
Shiqqat *Arabic*, Depression
-shotō *Japanese*, Group of islands
Shuiku *Chinese*, Reservoir
Shŭrkhog(i) *Uzbek*, Salt marsh
Sierra *Spanish*, Mountains
Sint *Dutch*, Saint
-sjø(en) *Norwegian*, Lake
-sjön *Swedish*, Lake
Solonchak *Russian*, Salt lake
Solonchakovyye Vpadiny *Russian*, Salt basin, wetlands
Sơn *Vietnamese*, Mountain
Sông *Vietnamese*, River
Sør- *Norwegian*, Southern
-spitze *German*, Peak
Star-á, -é *Czech*, Old
Star-aya, -oye, -yy, -yye *Russian*, Old
Stenó *Greek*, Strait
Step' *Russian*, Steppe
Štít *Slovak*, Peak
Stœng *Cambodian*, River
Stolovaya Strana *Russian*, Plateau
Stredné *Slovak*, Middle
Střední *Czech*, Middle
Stretto *Italian*, Strait
Su Anbarı *Azerbaijani*, Reservoir
-suidō *Japanese*, Channel, strait
Sund *Swedish*, Sound, strait
Sungai *Indonesian, Malay*, River
Suu *Turkish*, River

T

Tal *Mongolian*, Plain
Tandavan' *Malagasy*, Mountain range
Tangorombohitr' *Malagasy*, Mountain massif
Tanjung *Indonesian, Malay*, Cape, point
Tao *Chinese*, Island
Ţaraq *Arabic*, Hills
Tassili *Berber*, Mountain, plateau
Tau *Russian*, Mountain(s)
Taungdan *Burmese*, Mountain range
Techníti Límni *Greek*, Reservoir
Tekojärvi *Finnish*, Reservoir
Teluk *Indonesian, Malay*, Bay
Tengah *Indonesian*, Middle
Terara *Amharic*, Mountain
Timur *Indonesian*, Eastern
-tind(an) *Norwegian*, Peak
Tizma(si) *Uzbek*, Mountain range, ridge
-tō *Japanese*, island
Tog *Somali*, Valley
-tōge *Japanese*, pass
Togh(i) *Uzbek*, mountain
Tônlé *Cambodian*, Lake
Top *Dutch*, Peak
-tunturi *Finnish*, Mountain
Ţurāq *Arabic*, hills
Tur'at *Arabic*, Channel

U

Udde(n) *Swedish*, Cape, point
'Uqlat *Arabic*, Well
Utara *Indonesian*, Northern
Uul *Mongolian*, Mountains

V

Väin *Estonian*, Strait
Vallée *French*, Valley
Varful *Romanian*, Peak
-vatn *Icelandic*, Lake
-vatnet *Norwegian*, Lake
Velayat *Turkmen*, Province
-vesi *Finnish*, Lake
Vestre- *Norwegian*, Western
-vidda *Norwegian*, Plateau
-vík *Icelandic*, Bay
-viken *Swedish*, Bay, inlet
Vinh *Vietnamese*, Bay
Víztárloló *Hungarian*, Reservoir
Vodaskhovishcha *Belarussian*, Reservoir
Vodokhranilishche (Vdkhr.) *Russian*, Reservoir
Vodoskhovyshche (Vdskh.) *Ukrainian*, Reservoir
Volcán *Spanish*, Volcano
Vostochn-o, yy *Russian*, Eastern
Vozvyshennost' *Russian*, Upland, plateau
Vozyera *Belarussian*, Lake
Vpadina *Russian*, Depression
Vrchovina *Czech*, Mountains
Vrh *Croat, Slovene*, Peak
Vychodné *Slovak*, Eastern
Vysochyna *Ukrainian*, Upland
Vysočina *Czech*, Upland

W

Waadi *Somali*, Watercourse
Wādī *Arabic* Watercourse
Wāḩat, Wâhat *Arabic*, Oasis
Wald *German*, Forest
Wan *Chinese*, Bay
Way *Indonesian*, River
Webi *Somali*, River
Wenz *Amharic*, River
Wiloyat(i) *Uzbek*, Province
Wyżyna *Polish*, Upland
Wzgórza *Polish*, Upland
Wzvyshsha *Belarussian*, Upland

X

Xé *Laotian*, River
Xi *Chinese*, Stream

Y

-yama *Japanese*, Mountain
Yanchi *Chinese*, Salt lake
Yanhu *Chinese*, Salt lake
Yarımadası *Azerbaijani, Turkish*, Peninsula
Yaylası *Turkish*, Plateau
Yazovir *Bulgarian*, Reservoir
Yoma *Burmese*, Mountains
Ytre- *Norwegian*, Outer
Yu *Chinese*, Islet
Yunhe *Chinese*, Canal
Yuzhn-o, -yy *Russian*, Southern

Z

-zaki *Japanese*, Cape, point
Zaliv *Bulgarian, Russian*, Bay
-zan *Japanese*, Mountain
Zangbo *Tibetan*, River
Zapadn-aya, -o, -yy *Russian*, Western
Západné *Slovak*, Western
Západní *Czech*, Western
Zatoka *Polish, Ukrainian*, Bay
-zee *Dutch*, Sea
Zemlya *Russian*, Earth, land
Zizhiqu *Chinese*, Autonomous region

Index

Glossary of Abbreviations

This glossary provides a comprehensive guide to the abbreviations used in this Atlas, and in the Index.

A
abbrev. abbreviated
AD Anno Domini
Afr. Afrikaans
Alb. Albanian
Amh. Amharic
anc. ancient
approx. approximately
Ar. Arabic
Arm. Armenian
ASEAN Association of South East Asian Nations
ASSR Autonomous Soviet Socialist Republic
Aust. Australian
Az. Azerbaijani
Azerb. Azerbaijan

B
Basq. Basque
BC before Christ
Bel. Belorussian
Ben. Bengali
Ber. Berber
B-H Bosnia-Herzegovina
bn billion (one thousand million)
BP British Petroleum
Bret. Breton
Brit. British
Bul. Bulgarian
Bur. Burmese

C
C central
C. Cape
°C degrees Centigrade
CACM Central America Common Market
Cam. Cambodian
Cant. Cantonese
CAR Central African Republic
Cast. Castilian
Cat. Catalan
CEEAC Central America Common Market
Chin. Chinese
CIS Commonwealth of Independent States
cm centimetre(s)
Cro. Croat
Cz. Czech
Czech Rep. Czech Republic

D
Dan. Danish
Div. Divehi
Dom. Rep. Dominican Republic
Dut. Dutch

E
E east
EC *see* EU
EEC *see* EU
ECOWAS Economic Community of West African States
ECU European Currency Unit
EMS European Monetary System
Eng. English
est estimated
Est. Estonian
EU European Union (previously European Community [EC], European Economic Community [EEC])

F
°F degrees Fahrenheit
Faer. Faeroese
Fij. Fijian
Fin. Finnish
Fr. French
Fris. Frisian
ft foot/feet
FYROM Former Yugoslav Republic of Macedonia

G
g gram(s)
Gael. Gaelic
Gal. Galician
GDP Gross Domestic Product (the total value of goods and services produced by a country excluding income from foreign countries)
Geor. Georgian
Ger. German
Gk Greek
GNP Gross National Product (the total value of goods and services produced by a country)

H
Heb. Hebrew
HEP hydro-electric power
Hind. Hindi
hist. historical
Hung. Hungarian

I
I. Island
Icel. Icelandic
in inch(es)
In. Inuit (Eskimo)
Ind. Indonesian
Intl International
Ir. Irish
Is Islands
It. Italian

J
Jap. Japanese

K
Kaz. Kazakh
kg kilogram(s)
Kir. Kirghiz
km kilometre(s)
km² square kilometre (singular)
Kor. Korean
Kurd. Kurdish

L
L. Lake
LAIA Latin American Integration Association
Lao. Laotian
Lapp. Lappish
Lat. Latin
Latv. Latvian
Liech. Liechtenstein
Lith. Lithuanian
Lus. Lusatian
Lux. Luxembourg

M
m million/metre(s)
Mac. Macedonian
Maced. Macedonia
Mal. Malay
Malg. Malagasy
Malt. Maltese
mi. mile(s)
Mong. Mongolian
Mt. Mountain
Mts Mountains

N
N north
NAFTA North American Free Trade Agreement
Nep. Nepali
Neth. Netherlands
Nic. Nicaraguan
Nor. Norwegian
NZ New Zealand

P
Pash. Pashtu
PNG Papua New Guinea
Pol. Polish
Poly. Polynesian
Port. Portuguese
prev. previously

R
Rep. Republic
Res. Reservoir
Rmsch Romansch
Rom. Romanian
Rus. Russian
Russ. Fed. Russian Federation

S
S south
SADC Southern Africa Development Community
SCr. Serbian, Croatian
Sinh. Sinhala
Slvk Slovak
Slvn. Slovene
Som. Somali
Sp. Spanish
St., St Saint
Strs Straits
Swa. Swahili
Swe. Swedish
Switz. Switzerland

T
Taj. Tajik
Th. Thai
Thai. Thailand
Tib. Tibetan
Turk. Turkish
Turkm. Turkmenistan

U
UAE United Arab Emirates
Uigh. Uighur
UK United Kingdom
Ukr. Ukrainian
UN United Nations
Urd. Urdu
US/USA United States of America
USSR Union of Soviet Socialist Republics
Uzb. Uzbek

V
var. variant
Vdkhr. Vodokhranilishche (Russian for reservoir)
Vdskh. Vodoskhovyshche (Ukrainian for reservoir)
Vtn. Vietnamese

W
W west
Wel. Welsh

This index lists all the placenames and features shown on the regional and continental maps in this Atlas. Placenames are referenced to the largest scale map on which they appear. The policy followed throughout the Atlas is to use the local spelling or local name at regional level; commonly-used English language names may occasionally be added (in parentheses) where this is an aid to identification e.g. Firenze (Florence). English names, where they exist, have been used for all international features e.g. oceans and country names; they are also used on the continental maps and in the introductory World Today section; these are then fully cross-referenced to the local names found on the regional maps. The index also contains commonly-found alternative names and variant spellings, which are also fully cross-referenced.

All main entry names are those of settlements unless otherwise indicated by the use of italicized definitions or representative symbols, which are keyed at the foot of each page.

1

10 *M16* **100 Mile House** *var.* Hundred Mile House. British Columbia, SW Canada *51°39′N 121°19′W*
25 de Mayo *see* Veinticinco de Mayo
26 Bakı Komissarı *see* Häsänabad
26 Baku Komissarlary Adyndaky *see* Uzboý

A

Aa *see* Gauja
95 *G24* **Aabenraa** *var.* Åbenrå, *Ger.* Apenrade. Syddanmark, SW Denmark *55°03′N 09°26′E*
95 *G20* **Aabybro** *var.* Åbybro. Nordjylland, N Denmark *57°09′N 09°32′E*
101 *C16* **Aachen** *Dut.* Aken, *Fr.* Aix-la-Chapelle; *anc.* Aquae Grani, Aquisgranum. Nordrhein-Westfalen, W Germany *50°47′N 06°06′E*
Aaiún *see* Laâyoune
95 *M24* **Aakirkeby** *var.* Åkirkeby. Bornholm, E Denmark *55°04′N 14°56′E*
95 *G20* **Aalborg** *var.* Ålborg, Ålborg-Nørresundby; *anc.* Alburgum. Nordjylland, N Denmark *57°03′N 09°56′E*
Aalborg Bugt *see* Ålborg Bugt
101 *J21* **Aalen** Baden-Württemberg, S Germany *48°50′N 10°06′E*
95 *G21* **Aalestrup** *var.* Ålestrup. Midtjylland, NW Denmark *56°42′N 09°31′E*
98 *I11* **Aalsmeer** Noord-Holland, C Netherlands *52°17′N 04°43′E*
99 *F18* **Aalst** Oost-Vlaanderen, C Belgium *50°57′N 04°03′E*
99 *K18* **Aalst** *Fr.* Alost. Noord-Brabant, S Netherlands *51°23′N 05°29′E*
98 *O12* **Aalten** Gelderland, E Netherlands *51°56′N 06°35′E*
99 *D17* **Aalter** Oost-Vlaanderen, NW Belgium *51°05′N 03°28′E*
Aanaar *see* Inari
Aanaarjävri *see* Inarijärvi
93 *M17* **Äänekoski** Länsi-Suomi, W Finland *62°34′N 25°45′E*
138 *H7* **Aanjar** *var.* ʻAnjar. C Lebanon *33°45′N 35°56′E*
83 *G21* **Aansluit** Northern Cape, N South Africa *26°41′S 22°24′E*
Aar *see* Aare
108 *F7* **Aarau** Aargau, N Switzerland *47°22′N 08°00′E*
108 *D8* **Aarberg** Bern, W Switzerland *47°19′N 07°54′E*
99 *D16* **Aardenburg** Zeeland, SW Netherlands *51°16′N 03°27′E*
108 *D8* **Aare** *var.* Aar. ≈ W Switzerland
108 *F7* **Aargau** *Fr.* Argovie. ◐ *canton* N Switzerland
Aarhus *see* Århus
Aarlen *see* Arlon
95 *G21* **Aars** *var.* Års. Nordjylland, N Denmark *56°49′N 09°32′E*
99 *I17* **Aarschot** Vlaams Brabant, C Belgium *50°59′N 04°50′E*
Aassi, Nahr el *see* Orontes
Aat *see* Ath
160 *G7* **Aba** *prev.* Ngawa. Sichuan, C China *32°51′N 101°46′E*
79 *P16* **Aba** Orientale, NE Dem. Rep. Congo *03°52′N 30°14′E*
77 *V17* **Aba** Abia, S Nigeria *05°06′N 07°22′E*
140 *J6* **Abā al Qazāz, Biʼr** *well* NW Saudi Arabia
Abā as Suʻūd *see* Najrān
59 *G14* **Abacaxis, Rio** ≈ NW Brazil
Abaco Island *see* Great Abaco/Little Abaco
Abaco Island *see* Great Abaco, N Bahamas
142 *K10* **Ābādān** Khūzestān, SW Iran *30°24′N 48°18′E*
146 *F13* **Abadan** *prev.* Bezmein, Büzmeýin, *Rus.* Byuzmeyin. Ahal Welaýaty, C Turkmenistan *38°08′N 57°53′E*
143 *O10* **Ābādeh** Fārs, C Iran *31°06′N 52°40′E*
74 *H8* **Abadla** W Algeria *31°04′N 02°39′W*
59 *M20* **Abaeté** Minas Gerais, SE Brazil *19°10′S 45°24′W*
62 *P7* **Abaí** Caazapá, S Paraguay *25°58′S 55°54′W*
Abai *see* Blue Nile
191 *O2* **Abaiang** *var.* Apia; *prev.* Charlotte Island. *atoll* Tungaru, W Kiribati
Abaj *see* Abay
77 *U15* **Abaji** Federal Capital District, C Nigeria *08°35′N 06°54′E*
37 *O7* **Abajo Peak** ▲ Utah, W USA *37°51′N 109°28′W*
77 *V16* **Abakaliki** Ebonyi, SE Nigeria *06°18′N 08°07′E*
122 *K13* **Abakan** Respublika Khakasiya, S Russian Federation *53°43′N 91°25′E*
77 *S11* **Abala** Tillabéri, SW Niger *14°55′N 03°27′E*
77 *U11* **Abalak** Tahoua, C Niger *15°28′N 06°18′E*
119 *N14* **Abalyanka** *Rus.* Obolyanka. ≈ N Belarus
122 *L12* **Aban** Krasnoyarskiy Kray, S Russian Federation *56°41′N 96°04′E*
143 *P9* **Āb Anbār-e Kān Sorkh** Yazd, C Iran *31°22′N 53°38′E*
57 *G16* **Abancay** Apurímac, SE Peru *13°37′S 72°52′W*
190 *H2* **Abaokoro** *atoll* Tungaru, W Kiribati
Abariringa *see* Kanton
143 *P10* **Abarkūh** Yazd, C Iran *31°07′N 53°17′E*
165 *V3* **Abashiri** *var.* Abasiri. Hokkaidō, NE Japan *44°N 144°15′E*
165 *U3* **Abashiri-ko** ◎ Hokkaidō, NE Japan
Abasiri *see* Abashiri
41 *P10* **Abasolo** Tamaulipas, C Mexico *24°02′N 98°18′W*
186 *F9* **Abau** Central, S Papua New Guinea *10°04′S 148°34′E*
145 *R10* **Abay** *var.* Abaj. Karaganda, C Kazakhstan *49°38′N 72°50′E*
81 *I15* **Ābaya Hāykʼ** *Eng.* Lake Margherita, *It.* Abbaia. ◎ SW Ethiopia
Ābay Wenz *see* Blue Nile
122 *K13* **Abaza** Respublika Khakasiya, S Russian Federation *52°40′N 89°58′E*
Abbaia *see* Ābaya Hāykʼ
143 *Q13* **Āb Bārīk** Fārs, S Iran
107 *C18* **Abbasanta** Sardegna, Italy, C Mediterranean Sea *40°08′N 08°49′E*
Abbatis Villa *see* Abbeville
30 *M3* **Abbaye, Point** *headland* Michigan, N USA *46°58′N 88°08′W*
Abbazia *see* Opatija
Abbé, Lake *see* Abhe, Lake
103 *N2* **Abbeville** *anc.* Abbatis Villa. Somme, N France *50°06′N 01°50′E*
23 *R7* **Abbeville** Alabama, S USA *31°35′N 85°16′W*
23 *U6* **Abbeville** Georgia, SE USA *31°58′N 83°18′W*
22 *I9* **Abbeville** Louisiana, S USA *29°58′N 92°08′W*
21 *P12* **Abbeville** South Carolina, SE USA *34°10′N 82°23′W*
97 *B20* **Abbeyfeale** *Ir.* Mainistir na Féile. SW Ireland *52°24′N 09°21′W*
106 *D8* **Abbiategrasso** Lombardia, NW Italy *45°24′N 08°55′E*
93 *I14* **Abborrträsk** Norrbotten, N Sweden *65°24′N 19°33′E*
194 *J9* **Abbot Ice Shelf** *ice shelf* Antarctica
10 *M17* **Abbotsford** British Columbia, SW Canada *49°02′N 122°18′W*
30 *K6* **Abbotsford** Wisconsin, N USA *44°57′N 90°19′W*
149 *U5* **Abbottābād** Khyber Pakhtunkhwa, NW Pakistan *34°12′N 73°15′E*
119 *M14* **Abchuha** *Rus.* Obchuga. Minskaya Voblastsʼ, NW Belarus *54°30′N 29°22′E*
98 *I10* **Abcoude** Utrecht, C Netherlands *52°17′N 04°59′E*
139 *N2* **ʻAbd al ʻAzīz, Jabal** ▲▲ NE Syria
141 *U17* **ʻAbd al Kūrī** *island* SE Yemen
127 *U6* **Abdulino** Orenburgskaya Oblastʼ, W Russian Federation *53°37′N 53°39′E*
78 *J10* **Abéché** *var.* Abécher, Abeshr. Ouaddaï, SE Chad *13°49′N 20°49′E*
Abécher *see* Abéché
143 *S8* **Āb-e Garm va Sard** Yazd, E Iran
77 *R8* **Abeïbara** Kidal, NE Mali *19°07′N 01°52′E*
105 *P5* **Abejar** Castilla y León, N Spain *41°48′N 02°47′W*
54 *E9* **Abejorral** Antioquia, W Colombia *05°48′N 75°28′W*
Abela *see* Ávila
Abellinum *see* Avellino
92 *Q2* **Abeløya** *island* Kong Karls Land, E Svalbard
80 *I13* **Ābeltī** Oromīya, C Ethiopia *08°09′N 37°31′E*
191 *O2* **Abemama** *var.* Apamama; *prev.* Roger Simpson Island. *atoll* Tungaru, W Kiribati
171 *Y15* **Abemaree** *var.* Abermarre. Papua, E Indonesia *07°03′S 140°10′E*
77 *O16* **Abengourou** E Ivory Coast *06°42′N 03°27′W*
Åbenrå *see* Aabenraa
101 *L22* **Abens** ≈ SE Germany
77 *S16* **Abeokuta** Ogun, SW Nigeria *07°07′N 03°21′E*
97 *I20* **Aberaeron** SW Wales, United Kingdom *52°15′N 04°15′W*
Aberbrothock *see* Arbroath
Abercorn *see* Mbala
29 *R6* **Abercrombie** North Dakota, N USA *46°25′N 96°42′W*
183 *T7* **Aberdeen** New South Wales, SE Australia *32°09′S 150°55′E*
11 *T15* **Aberdeen** Saskatchewan, S Canada *52°15′N 106°19′W*
83 *H25* **Aberdeen** Eastern Cape, S South Africa *32°30′S 24°00′E*
96 *L9* **Aberdeen** *anc.* Devana. NE Scotland, United Kingdom *57°10′N 02°04′W*
21 *X2* **Aberdeen** Maryland, NE USA *39°28′N 76°09′W*
23 *N3* **Aberdeen** Mississippi, S USA *33°49′N 88°32′W*
21 *T10* **Aberdeen** North Carolina, SE USA *35°07′N 79°25′W*
29 *P8* **Aberdeen** South Dakota, N USA *45°27′N 98°29′W*
32 *F8* **Aberdeen** Washington, NW USA *46°57′N 123°48′W*
96 *K9* **Aberdeen** *cultural region* NE Scotland, United Kingdom
8 *L8* **Aberdeen Lake** ◎ Nunavut, NE Canada
96 *J10* **Aberfeldy** C Scotland, United Kingdom *56°38′N 03°49′W*
97 *K21* **Abergavenny** *anc.* Gobannium. SE Wales, United Kingdom *51°50′N 03°W*
Abergwaun *see* Fishguard
Abermarre *see* Abemaree
25 *N5* **Abernathy** Texas, SW USA *33°49′N 101°50′W*
Abersee *see* Wolfgangsee
Abertawe *see* Swansea
Aberteifi *see* Cardigan
32 *I15* **Abert, Lake** ◎ Oregon, NW USA
97 *I20* **Aberystwyth** W Wales, United Kingdom *52°25′N 04°05′W*
Abeshr *see* Abéché
Ábeskovvu *see* Abisko
106 *F10* **Abetone** Toscana, C Italy *44°09′N 10°42′E*
125 *V5* **Abezʼ** Respublika Komi, NW Russian Federation *66°32′N 61°41′E*
142 *M5* **Āb Garm** Qazvin, N Iran
141 *N12* **Abhā** ʻAsīr, SW Saudi Arabia *18°16′N 42°32′E*
142 *M5* **Abhar** Zanjān, NW Iran *36°05′N 49°18′E*
Abhé Bad/Ābhē Bid Hāykʼ *see* Abhe, Lake
80 *K12* **Abhe, Lake** *var.* Lake Abbé, *Amh.* Ābhē Bid Hāykʼ, *Som.* Abhé Bad. ◎ Djibouti/Ethiopia
77 *V17* **Abia** ◐ *state* SE Nigeria
139 *V9* **ʻAbīd ʻAlī** Wāsiţ, E Iraq *32°20′N 45°58′E*
119 *O17* **Abidavichy** *Rus.* Obidovichi. Mahilyowskaya Voblastsʼ, E Belarus *53°20′N 30°25′E*
115 *L15* **Abide** Çanakkale, NW Turkey *40°04′N 26°13′E*
77 *N17* **Abidjan** S Ivory Coast *05°19′N 04°01′W*
Āb-i-Istāda *see* Īstādeh-ye Moqor, Āb-e-
27 *N4* **Abilene** Kansas, C USA *38°55′N 97°14′W*
25 *Q7* **Abilene** Texas, SW USA *32°27′N 99°44′W*
Abindonia *see* Abingdon
97 *M21* **Abingdon** *anc.* Abindonia. S England, United Kingdom *51°41′N 01°17′W*
30 *K12* **Abingdon** Illinois, N USA *40°48′N 90°24′W*
21 *P8* **Abingdon** Virginia, NE USA *36°42′N 81°59′W*
Abingdon *see* Pinta, Isla
18 *J15* **Abington** Pennsylvania, NE USA *40°06′N 75°05′W*
126 *K14* **Abinsk** Krasnodarskiy Kray, SW Russian Federation *44°51′N 38°12′E*
37 *R9* **Abiquiu Reservoir** ▣ New Mexico, SW USA
Āb-i-safed *see* Sefīd, Darya-ye
92 *I10* **Abisko** *Lapp.* Ábeskovvu. Norrbotten, N Sweden *68°21′N 18°50′E*
12 *G12* **Abitibi** ≈ Ontario, S Canada
12 *H12* **Abitibi, Lac** ◎ Ontario/Québec, S Canada
80 *J10* **Ābīy Ādī** Tigray, N Ethiopia *13°40′N 38°57′E*
118 *H6* **Abja-Paluoja** Viljandimaa, S Estonia *58°08′N 25°20′E*
Abkhazia *see* Apkhazeti
182 *F1* **Abminga** South Australia *26°07′S 134°49′E*
75 *W9* **Abnūb** *var.* Abnûb. C Egypt *27°18′N 31°09′E*
Abnûb *see* Abnūb
Åbo *see* Turku
152 *G9* **Abohar** Punjab, N India *30°11′N 74°14′E*
77 *O17* **Aboisso** SE Ivory Coast *05°26′N 03°13′W*
78 *H5* **Abo, Massif dʼ** ▲▲ NW Chad
77 *R16* **Abomey** S Benin *07°14′N 02°00′E*
79 *F16* **Abong Mbang** Est, SE Cameroon *03°58′N 13°10′E*
111 *L23* **Abony** Pest, C Hungary *47°10′N 20°00′E*
78 *J11* **Abou-Déïa** Salamat, SE Chad *11°30′N 19°18′E*
Aboudouhour *see* Abū aḑ Ḑuhūr
Abou Kémal *see* Abū Kamāl
Abou Simbel *see* Abū Sunbul
137 *T12* **Abovyan** C Armenia *40°16′N 44°33′E*
141 *P15* **Abrād, Wādī** *seasonal river* W Yemen
Abraham Bay *see* The Carlton
104 *G10* **Abrantes** *var.* Abrántes. Santarém, C Portugal *39°28′N 08°12′W*
62 *J4* **Abra Pampa** Jujuy, N Argentina *22°47′S 65°41′W*
Abrashlare *see* Brezovo
54 *G7* **Abrego** Norte de Santander, N Colombia *08°08′N 73°14′W*
Abrene *see* Pytalovo
40 *C7* **Abreojos, Punta** *headland* NW Mexico *26°43′N 113°36′W*
65 *J16* **Abrolhos Bank** *undersea feature* W Atlantic Ocean *18°30′S 38°45′W*
119 *H19* **Abrova** *Rus.* Obrovo. Brestskaya Voblastsʼ, SW Belarus *52°30′N 25°34′E*
116 *G11* **Abrud** *Ger.* Gross-Schlatten, *Hung.* Abrudbánya. Alba, SW Romania *46°16′N 23°05′E*
Abrudbánya *see* Abrud
118 *E6* **Abruka** *island* SW Estonia
107 *J15* **Abruzzese, Appennino** ▲▲ C Italy
107 *J14* **Abruzzo** ◐ *region* C Italy
141 *N14* **ʻAbs** *var.* Sūq ʻAbs. W Yemen *16°42′N 42°55′E*
33 *T12* **Absaroka Range** ▲▲ Montana/Wyoming, NW USA
137 *Z11* **Abşeron Yarımadası** *Rus.* Apsheronskiy Poluostrov. *peninsula* E Azerbaijan
143 *N6* **Āb Shīrīn** Eşfahān, C Iran *34°17′N 51°17′E*
139 *X10* **Abtān** Maysān, SE Iraq *31°37′N 47°06′E*
109 *R6* **Abtenau** Salzburg, NW Austria *47°33′N 13°21′E*
152 *E14* **Ābu** Rājasthān, N India *24°41′N 72°50′E*
164 *E12* **Abu** Yamaguchi, Honshū, SW Japan *34°30′N 131°26′E*
138 *I4* **Abū aḑ Ḑuhūr** *Fr.* Aboudouhour. Idlib, NW Syria *35°30′N 37°00′E*
143 *P17* **Abū al Abyaḑ** *island* C United Arab Emirates
138 *K10* **Abū al Ḩuşayn, Khabrat** ◎ N Jordan
139 *R8* **Abū al Jīr** Al Anbār, C Iraq *33°16′N 42°55′E*
139 *Y12* **Abū al Khaşīb** *var.* Abul Khasib. Al Başrah, SE Iraq *30°26′N 48°00′E*
139 *U12* **Abū at Tubrah, Thaqb** *well* S Iraq
Abu Balâs *see* Abu Ballās
75 *V11* **Abu Ballās** *var.* Abu Balâs. ▲ SW Egypt *24°28′N 27°36′E*
Abu Dhabi *see* Abū Ẓabī
139 *R8* **Abū Farūkh** Al Anbār, C Iraq *33°06′N 43°18′E*
80 *C12* **Abu Gabra** Southern Darfur, W Sudan *11°02′N 26°50′E*
139 *P10* **Abū Ghār, Shaʻīb** *dry watercourse* S Iraq
80 *G7* **Abu Hamed** River Nile, N Sudan *19°32′N 33°20′E*
139 *O5* **Abū Ḩardān** *var.* Hajîne. Dayr az Zawr, E Syria *34°45′N 40°49′E*
139 *T7* **Abū Ḩasāwīyah** Diyālá, E Iraq *33°52′N 44°47′E*
138 *K10* **Abū Ḩifnah, Wādī** *dry watercourse* N Jordan
77 *V15* **Abuja** ● (Nigeria) Federal Capital District, C Nigeria *09°04′N 07°28′E*
139 *R9* **Abū Jahaf, Wādī** *dry watercourse* C Iraq
56 *F12* **Abujao, Río** ≈ E Peru
139 *U12* **Abū Jasrah** Al Muthanná, S Iraq *30°43′N 44°50′E*
139 *O6* **Abū Kamāl** *Fr.* Abou Kémal. Dayr az Zawr, E Syria *34°29′N 40°56′E*
165 *P12* **Abukuma-sanchi** ▲▲ Honshū, C Japan
Abula *see* Ávila
Abul Khasib *see* Abū al Khaşīb
79 *K16* **Abumombazi** *var.* Abumonbazi. Equateur, N Dem. Rep. Congo *03°43′N 22°06′E*
Abumonbazi *see* Abumombazi
59 *D15* **Abunã** Rondônia, W Brazil *09°41′S 65°20′W*
56 *K13* **Abunã, Rio** *var.* Río Abuná. ≈ Bolivia/Brazil
138 *G10* **Abū Nuşayr** *var.* Abu Nuseir. ʻAmmān, W Jordan *32°03′N 35°58′E*
Abu Nuseir *see* Abū Nuşayr
139 *T12* **Abū Qabr** Al Muthanná, S Iraq *31°03′N 44°34′E*
138 *K5* **Abū Raḩbah, Jabal** ▲▲ C Syria
139 *S5* **Abū Rajāsh** Şalāḩ ad Dīn, N Iraq *34°47′N 43°36′E*
139 *W13* **Abū Raqrāq, Ghadīr** *well* S Iraq
152 *E14* **Ābu Road** Rājasthān, N India *24°29′N 72°47′E*
80 *I6* **Abu Shagara, Ras** *headland* NE Sudan *18°04′N 38°31′E*
Abu Simbel *see* Abū Sunbul
139 *U12* **Abū Sudayrah** Al Muthanná, S Iraq *30°55′N 44°58′E*
139 *T10* **Abū Şukhayr** Al Qādisīyah, S Iraq *31°54′N 44°27′E*
Abū Sunbul *see* Abū Sunbul
185 *E18* **Abut Head** *headland* South Island, New Zealand *43°06′S 170°16′E*
80 *E9* **Abu ʻUrug** Northern Kordofan, C Sudan *15°52′N 30°25′E*
80 *K12* **Ābuyē Mēda** ▲ C Ethiopia *10°28′N 39°44′E*

◆ Country
● Country Capital
◇ Dependent Territory
○ Dependent Territory Capital
◐ Administrative Regions
✕ International Airport
▲ Mountain
▲▲ Mountain Range
Volcano
≈ River
◎ Lake
▣ Reservoir

80 D11 **Abu Zabad** Southern Kordofan, C Sudan 12°21′N 29°16′E
143 P16 **Abū Ẓabī** var. Abū Ẓabī, Eng. Abu Dhabi. ● (United Arab Emirates) Abū Ẓaby, C United Arab Emirates 24°30′N 54°20′E
Abū Ẓabī see Abū Ẓabī
75 X8 **Abu Zenīma** E Egypt 29°01′N 33°08′E
95 N17 **Åby** Östergötland, S Sweden 58°40′N 16°10′E
Abyaḍ, Al Baḥr al see White Nile
Åbybro see Aabybro
80 D13 **Abyei** Southern Kordofan, S Sudan 09°35′N 28°28′E
80 D13 **Abyei Area** disputed region Southern Kordofan, S Sudan
Abyla see Ávila
Abymes see les Abymes
Abyssinia see Ethiopia
Açâba see Assaba
54 F11 **Acacias** Meta, C Colombia 03°59′N 73°46′W
58 L13 **Açailândia** Maranhão, E Brazil 04°51′S 47°26′W
Acaill see Achill Island
42 E8 **Acajutla** Sonsonate, W El Salvador 13°34′N 89°50′W
79 D17 **Acalayong** SW Equatorial Guinea 01°05′N 09°34′E
41 N13 **Acámbaro** Guanajuato, C Mexico 20°01′N 100°42′W
54 C6 **Acandí** Chocó, NW Colombia 08°32′N 77°20′W
104 H4 **A Cañiza** var. La Cañiza. Galicia, NW Spain 42°13′N 08°16′W
40 J11 **Acaponeta** Nayarit, C Mexico 22°30′N 105°21′W
40 J11 **Acaponeta, Río de** ≈ C Mexico
41 O16 **Acapulco** var. Acapulco de Juárez. Guerrero, S Mexico 16°51′N 99°53′W
Acapulco de Juárez see Acapulco
55 T13 **Acarai Mountains** Sp. Serra Acaraí. ▲▲ Brazil/Guyana
Acaraí, Serra see Acarai Mountains
58 O13 **Acaraú** Ceará, NE Brazil 04°35′S 37°37′W
54 J6 **Acarigua** Portuguesa, N Venezuela 09°35′N 69°12′W
104 H2 **A Carreira** Galicia, NW Spain 43°21′N 08°12′W
42 C6 **Acatenango, Volcán de** ⛰ S Guatemala 14°30′N 90°52′W
41 Q15 **Acatlán** var. Acatlán de Osorio. Puebla, S Mexico 18°12′N 98°02′W
Acatlán de Osorio see Acatlán
41 S15 **Acayucan** var. Acayucán. Veracruz-Llave, E Mexico 17°59′N 94°58′W
Accho see Akko
21 Y5 **Accomac** Virginia, NE USA 37°43′N 75°41′N
77 Q17 **Accra** ● (Ghana)SE Ghana 05°33′N 00°15′W
97 L17 **Accrington** NW England, United Kingdom 53°46′N 02°21′W
61 B19 **Acebal** Santa Fe, C Argentina 33°14′S 60°50′W
168 H8 **Aceh** off. Daerah Istimewa Aceh, var. Acheen, Achin, Atchin, Atjeh. ⬖ autonomous district NW Indonesia
107 M18 **Acerenza** Basilicata, S Italy 40°46′N 15°51′E
107 K17 **Acerra** anc. Acerrae. Campania, S Italy 40°56′N 14°22′E
Acerrae see Acerra
57 J17 **Achacachi** La Paz, W Bolivia 16°01′S 68°44′W
54 K7 **Achaguas** Apure, C Venezuela 07°46′N 68°14′W
154 H12 **Achalpur** prev. Elichpur, Ellichpur. Mahārāshtra, C India 21°19′N 77°30′E
61 F18 **Achar** Tacuarembó, C Uruguay 32°20′S 56°15′W
137 R10 **Ach'ara** prev. Achara, var. Ajaria. ⬖ autonomous republic SW Georgia
Achara see Ach'ara
115 H19 **Acharnés** var. Aharnes; prev. Akharnaí. Attikí, C Greece 38°09′N 23°58′E
Ach'asar Lerr see Achk'asari, Mta
Acheen see Aceh
99 K16 **Achel** Limburg, NE Belgium 51°15′N 05°31′E
115 D16 **Achelóos** var. Akhelóös, Aspropótamos; anc. Achelous. ≈ W Greece
Achelous see Achelóos
163 W8 **Acheng** Heilongjiang, NE China 45°32′N 126°56′E
109 N6 **Achenkirch** Tirol, W Austria 47°31′N 11°42′E
101 L24 **Achenpass** pass Austria/Germany
109 N7 **Achensee** ◎ W Austria
101 F22 **Achern** Baden-Württemberg, SW Germany 48°37′N 08°04′E
115 C16 **Acherón** ≈ W Greece
77 W11 **Achétinamou** ≈ S Niger
152 J12 **Achhnera** Uttar Pradesh, N India 27°10′N 77°45′E
42 C7 **Achiguate, Río** ≈ S Guatemala
97 A16 **Achill Head** Ir. Ceann Acla. headland W Ireland 53°58′N 10°14′W
97 A16 **Achill Island** Ir. Acaill. island W Ireland
100 H11 **Achim** Niedersachsen, NW Germany 53°01′N 09°01′E
149 S5 **Achīn** Nangarhār, E Afghanistan 34°04′N 70°41′E
Achin see Aceh
122 K12 **Achinsk** Krasnoyarskiy Kray, S Russian Federation 56°21′N 90°25′E
162 E5 **Achit Nuur** ◎ NW Mongolia
137 T11 **Achk'asari, Mta** Arm. Ach'asar Lerr. ▲ Armenia/Georgia 41°09′N 43°55′E
126 K13 **Achuyevo** Krasnodarskiy Kray, SW Russian Federation 46°00′N 38°01′E
81 F16 **Achwa** var. Aswa. ≈ N Uganda
136 E15 **Acıgöl** salt lake SW Turkey
107 L24 **Acireale** Sicilia, Italy, C Mediterranean Sea 37°36′N 15°10′E
Aciris see Agri
25 N7 **Ackerly** Texas, SW USA 32°31′N 101°43′W
22 M4 **Ackerman** Mississippi, S USA 33°18′N 89°10′W
29 W13 **Ackley** Iowa, C USA 42°33′N 93°03′W
44 J5 **Acklins Island** island SE Bahamas
Acla, Ceann see Achill Head
62 H11 **Aconcagua, Cerro** ▲ W Argentina 32°36′S 69°53′W
Açores/Açores, Arquipélago dos/Açores, Ilhas dos see Azores
104 H2 **A Coruña** Cast. La Coruña, Eng. Corunna; anc. Caronium. Galicia, NW Spain 43°22′N 08°24′W
104 G2 **A Coruña** Cast. La Coruña. ⬖ province Galicia, NW Spain
42 L10 **Acoyapa** Chontales, S Nicaragua 11°58′N 85°10′W
106 H13 **Acquapendente** Lazio, C Italy 42°44′N 11°52′E
106 J13 **Acquasanta Terme** Marche, C Italy 42°46′N 13°24′E
106 I13 **Acquasparta** Lazio, C Italy 42°41′N 12°31′E
106 C9 **Acqui Terme** Piemonte, NW Italy 44°41′N 08°28′E
Acrae see Palazzola Acreide
182 F7 **Acraman, Lake** salt lake South Australia
59 A15 **Acre** off. Estado do Acre. ⬖ state W Brazil
Acre see Akko
59 C16 **Acre, Rio** ≈ W Brazil
107 N20 **Acri** Calabria, SW Italy 39°30′N 16°22′E
Acte see Ágion Óros
191 Y12 **Actéon, Groupe** island group Îles Tuamotu, SE French Polynesia
15 P12 **Acton-Vale** Québec, SE Canada 45°39′N 72°31′W
41 P13 **Actopan** var. Actopán. Hidalgo, C Mexico 20°19′N 98°59′W
Açu see Assu
Acunum Acusio see Montélimar
77 Q17 **Ada** SE Ghana 05°47′N 00°42′E
112 L8 **Ada** Vojvodina, N Serbia 45°48′N 20°08′E
29 R5 **Ada** Minnesota, N USA 47°18′N 96°31′W
31 R12 **Ada** Ohio, N USA 40°46′N 83°49′W
27 O12 **Ada** Oklahoma, C USA 34°47′N 96°41′W
162 L8 **Adaatsag** var. Tavin. Dundgovĭ, C Mongolia 46°27′N 105°43′E
Ada Bazar see Adapazarı
40 D3 **Adair, Bahía de** bay NW Mexico
104 M7 **Adaja** ≈ N Spain
38 H17 **Adak Island** island Aleutian Islands, Alaska, USA
Adalia see Antalya
Adalia, Gulf of see Antalya Körfezi
141 X9 **Adam** N Oman 22°22′N 57°30′E
Adama see Nazrēt
60 I8 **Adamantina** São Paulo, S Brazil 21°41′S 51°04′W
79 E14 **Adamaoua** Eng. Adamawa. ⬖ province N Cameroon
68 F11 **Adamaoua, Massif d'** Eng. Adamawa Highlands. plateau NW Cameroon
77 Y14 **Adamawa** ⬖ state E Nigeria
Adamawa see Adamaoua
Adamawa Highlands see Adamaoua, Massif d'
106 F6 **Adamello** ▲ N Italy 46°09′N 10°33′E
81 J14 **Ādamī Tulu** Oromīya, C Ethiopia 07°52′N 38°39′E
63 M23 **Adam, Mount** var. Monte Independencia. ▲ West Falkland, Falkland Islands 51°36′S 60°00′W
29 R16 **Adams** Nebraska, C USA 40°25′N 96°30′W
18 H8 **Adams** New York, NE USA 43°48′N 75°57′W
29 Q3 **Adams** North Dakota, N USA 48°23′N 98°01′W
155 I23 **Adam's Bridge** chain of shoals NW Sri Lanka
32 H10 **Adams, Mount** ▲ Washington, NW USA 46°12′N 121°29′W
Adam's Peak see Sri Pada
191 R16 **Adam's Rock** island Pitcairn Island, Pitcairn Islands
191 P16 **Adamstown** ○ (Pitcairn Islands)Pitcairn Island, Pitcairn Islands 25°04′S 130°05′W
20 G10 **Adamsville** Tennessee, S USA 35°14′N 88°23′W
25 S9 **Adamsville** Texas, SW USA 31°15′N 98°09′W
141 O17 **'Adan** Eng. Aden. SW Yemen 12°51′N 45°05′E
136 K16 **Adana** var. Seyhan. Adana, S Turkey 37°N 35°19′E
136 K16 **Adana** var. Seyhan. ⬖ province S Turkey
Adâncata see Horlivka
169 V12 **Adang, Teluk** bay Borneo, C Indonesia
136 F11 **Adapazarı** prev. Ada Bazar. Sakarya, NW Turkey 40°49′N 30°24′E
80 H8 **Adarama** River Nile, NE Sudan 17°04′N 34°57′E
195 Q16 **Adare, Cape** cape Antarctica
Ādavāni see Ādoni
106 E6 **Adda** anc. Addua. ≈ N Italy
80 A13 **Adda** ≈ W South Sudan
143 Q17 **Aḑ Ḑab'īyah** Abū Ẓaby, C United Arab Emirates 24°17′N 54°08′E
143 O18 **Aḑ Ḑafrah** desert S United Arab Emirates
141 Q6 **Ad Dahnā'** desert E Saudi Arabia
74 A11 **Ad Dakhla** var. Dakhla. SW Western Sahara 23°46′N 15°56′W
Ad Dalanj see Dilling
Ad Damar see Ed Damer
Ad Damazīn see Ed Damazin
Ad Dāmir see Ed Damer
173 N2 **Ad Dammām** desert NE Saudi Arabia
141 R6 **Ad Dammān** var. Dammām. Ash Sharqīyah, NE Saudi Arabia 26°23′N 50°05′E
Ad Dāmūr see Damoûr
140 K5 **Ad Dār al Ḩamrā'** Tabūk, NW Saudi Arabia 27°22′N 37°46′E
140 M13 **Ad Darb** Jīzān, SW Saudi Arabia 17°45′N 42°15′E
141 O8 **Ad Dawādimī** Ar Riyāḑ, C Saudi Arabia 24°32′N 44°21′E
143 N16 **Ad Dawḩah** Eng. Doha. ● (Qatar) C Qatar 25°15′N 51°36′E
143 N16 **Ad Dawḩah** Eng. Doha. ✈ C Qatar 25°11′N 51°37′E
139 S6 **Ad Dawr** Şalāḩ ad Dīn, N Iraq 34°30′N 43°49′E
139 Y12 **Ad Dayr** var. Dayr, Shahbān. Al Başrah, E Iraq 30°45′N 47°36′E
Addi Arkay see Ādī Ārk'ay
139 X15 **Ad Dibdibah** physical region Iraq/Kuwait
Aḑ Ḑiffah see Libyan Plateau
Addis Ababa see Ādīs Ābeba
Addison see Webster Springs
139 U10 **Ad Dīwānīyah** var. Diwaniyah. C Iraq 32°00′N 44°57′E
Addoo Atoll see Addu Atoll
Addua see Adda
151 K22 **Addu Atoll** var. Addoo Atoll, Seenu Atoll. atoll S Maldives
Ad Dujail see Ad Dujayl
139 T7 **Ad Dujayl** var. Ad Dujail. Şalāḩ ad Dīn, N Iraq 33°49′N 44°16′E
Ad Duwaym/Ad Duwēm see Ed Dueim
99 D16 **Adegem** Oost-Vlaanderen, NW Belgium 51°12′N 03°31′E
23 U7 **Adel** Georgia, SE USA 31°08′N 83°25′W
29 U14 **Adel** Iowa, C USA 41°36′N 94°01′W
182 I9 **Adelaide** state capital South Australia 34°56′S 138°36′E
44 H2 **Adelaide** New Providence, N Bahamas 24°59′N 77°30′W
182 I9 **Adelaide** ✈ South Australia 34°55′S 138°31′E
194 H6 **Adelaide Island** island Antarctica
181 P2 **Adelaide River** Northern Territory, N Australia 13°12′S 131°06′E
76 M10 **'Adel Bagrou** Hodh ech Chargui, SE Mauritania 15°33′N 07°04′W
186 D6 **Adelbert Range** ▲▲ N Papua New Guinea
180 K3 **Adele Island** island Western Australia
107 O17 **Adelfia** Puglia, SE Italy 41°01′N 16°52′E
195 V16 **Adélie Coast** physical region Antarctica
195 V14 **Adélie, Terre** physical region Antarctica
Adelnau see Odolanów
Adelsberg see Postojna
Aden see Khormaksar
Aden see 'Adan
141 Q17 **Aden, Gulf of** gulf SW Arabian Sea
77 V10 **Aderbissinat** Agadez, C Niger 15°30′N 07°57′E
Adhaim see Al 'Uẓaym
143 R16 **Adh Dhayd** var. Al Dhaid. Ash Shāriqah, NE United Arab Emirates 25°19′N 55°51′E
140 M4 **'Adhfā'** spring/well NW Saudi Arabia 29°15′N 41°24′E
138 I13 **'Ādhriyāt, Jabāl al** ▲▲ S Jordan
80 I10 **Ādī Ārk'ay** var. Addi Arkay. Āmara, N Ethiopia 13°18′N 37°56′E
182 C7 **Adieu, Cape** headland South Australia 32°01′S 132°12′E
106 H8 **Adige** Ger. Etsch. ≈ N Italy
80 J10 **Ādīgrat** Tigray, N Ethiopia 14°17′N 39°27′E
154 I13 **Ādilabād** var. Ādilābād. Andhra Pradesh, C India 19°40′N 78°31′E
35 P2 **Adin** California, W USA 41°10′N 120°57′W
171 V14 **Adi, Pulau** island E Indonesia
18 K8 **Adirondack Mountains** ▲▲ New York, NE USA
80 J13 **Ādīs Ābeba** Eng. Addis Ababa. ● (Ethiopia) Ādīs Ābeba, C Ethiopia 8°59′N 38°43′E
80 J13 **Ādīs Ābeba** ✈ Ādīs Ābeba, C Ethiopia 08°58′N 38°53′E
80 I11 **Ādīs Zemen** Āmara, N Ethiopia 12°00′N 37°43′E
Adi Ugri see Mendefera
137 N15 **Adıyaman** Adıyaman, SE Turkey 37°46′N 38°15′E
137 N15 **Adıyaman** ⬖ province S Turkey
116 L11 **Adjud** Vrancea, E Romania 46°07′N 27°10′E
45 T6 **Adjuntas** C Puerto Rico 18°10′N 66°42′W
Adjuntas, Presa de las see Vicente Guerrero, Presa
Ādkup see Erikub Atoll
126 L15 **Adler** Krasnodarskiy Kray, SW Russian Federation 43°25′N 39°58′E
Adler see Orlice
108 G7 **Adliswil** Zürich, NW Switzerland 47°19′N 08°32′E
32 G7 **Admiralty Inlet** inlet Washington, NW USA
39 X13 **Admiralty Island** island Alexander Archipelago, Alaska, USA
186 E5 **Admiralty Islands** island group N Papua New Guinea
136 B14 **Adnan Menderes** ✈ (İzmir) İzmir, W Turkey 38°16′N 27°09′E
37 V6 **Adobe Creek Reservoir** ⊠ Colorado, C USA
77 T16 **Ado-Ekiti** Ekiti, SW Nigeria 07°42′N 05°13′E
Adola see Kibre Mengist
61 C23 **Adolfo González Chaues** Buenos Aires, E Argentina
155 H17 **Ādoni** var. Ādavāni. Andhra Pradesh, C India 15°38′N 77°16′E
102 K15 **Adour** anc. Aturus. ≈ SW France
Adowa see Ādwa
105 O15 **Adra** Andalucía, S Spain 36°45′N 03°01′W
107 L24 **Adrano** Sicilia, Italy, C Mediterranean Sea 37°39′N 14°49′E
74 I9 **Adrar** C Algeria 27°56′N 00°12′W
76 K7 **Adrar** ⬖ region C Mauritania
74 L11 **Adrar** ▲▲ SE Algeria
74 A12 **Adrar Souttouf** ▲▲ SW Western Sahara
Adrasman see Adrasmon
147 Q10 **Adrasmon** Rus. Adrasman. NW Tajikistan 40°38′N 69°56′E
78 K10 **Adré** Ouaddaï, E Chad 13°26′N 22°14′E
106 H9 **Adria** anc. Atria, Hadria, Hatria. Veneto, NE Italy 45°03′N 12°04′E
31 R10 **Adrian** Michigan, N USA 41°54′N 84°02′W
29 S11 **Adrian** Minnesota, N USA 43°38′N 95°55′W
27 R5 **Adrian** Missouri, C USA 38°24′N 94°21′W
24 M2 **Adrian** Texas, SW USA 35°16′N 102°39′W
21 S4 **Adrian** West Virginia, NE USA 38°53′N 80°14′W
Adrianople/Adrianopolis see Edirne
121 P7 **Adriatic Basin** undersea feature Adriatic Sea, N Mediterranean Sea 42°00′N 17°30′E
Adriatico, Mare see Adriatic Sea
106 L13 **Adriatic Sea** Alb. Deti Adriatik, It. Mare Adriatico, SCr. Jadransko More, Slvn. Jadransko Morje. sea N Mediterranean Sea
Adriatik, Deti see Adriatic Sea
Adua see Ādwa
Aduana del Sásabe see El Sásabe
79 O17 **Adusa** Orientale, NE Dem. Rep. Congo 01°25′N 28°05′E
118 J13 **Adutiškis** Vilnius, E Lithuania 55°09′N 26°34′E
27 Y7 **Advance** Missouri, C USA 37°06′N 89°54′W
65 D25 **Adventure Sound** bay East Falkland, Falkland Islands
80 J10 **Ādwa** var. Adowa, It. Adua. Tigray, N Ethiopia 14°08′N 38°51′E
123 Q8 **Adycha** ≈ NE Russian Federation
126 L14 **Adygeya, Respublika** ⬖ autonomous republic SW Russian Federation
Adzhikui see Ajyguÿy
77 N17 **Adzopé** SE Ivory Coast 06°07′N 03°49′W
125 U4 **Adz'va** ≈ NW Russian Federation
125 U5 **Adz'vavom** Respublika Komi, NW Russian Federation 66°35′N 59°13′E
Ædua see Autun
115 K19 **Aegean Islands** island group Greece/Turkey
Aegean North see Vóreion Aigaíon
115 I17 **Aegean Sea** Gk. Aigaíon Pelagos, Aigaío Pélagos, Turk. Ege Denizi. sea NE Mediterranean Sea
Aegean South see Nótion Aigaíon
118 H3 **Aegviidu** Ger. Charlottenhof. Harjumaa, NW Estonia 59°17′N 25°37′E
Aegyptus see Egypt
Aelana see Al 'Aqabah
Aelok see Ailuk Atoll
Aelōninae see Ailinginae Atoll
Aelōnlaplap see Ailinglaplap Atoll
Æmilia see Emilia-Romagna
Æmilianum see Millau
Aemona see Ljubljana
Aenaria see Ischia
Aeolian Islands see Eolie, Isole
191 Z3 **Aeon Point** headland Kiritimati, NE Kiribati 01°46′N 157°11′W
Æsernia see Isernia
104 G3 **A Estrada** Galicia, NW Spain 42°41′N 08°29′W
115 C18 **Aetós** Itháki, Iónia Nísoi, Greece, C Mediterranean Sea 38°21′N 20°40′E
191 Q8 **Afaahiti** Tahiti, W French Polynesia 17°43′S 149°18′W
139 U10 **'Afak** Al Qādisīyah, C Iraq 32°04′N 45°17′E
Afanasjevo see Afanas'yevo
125 T14 **Afanas'yevo** var. Afanasjevo. Kirovskaya Oblast', NW Russian Federation 58°55′N 53°13′E
Afándou see Afántou
115 O23 **Afántou** var. Afándou. Ródos, Dodekánisa, Greece, Aegean Sea 36°17′N 28°10′E
80 K11 **Āfar** ⬖ region NE Ethiopia
Afar Depression see Danakil Desert
191 O7 **Afareaitu** Moorea, W French Polynesia 17°33′S 149°47′W
140 L7 **'Afarīyah, Bi'r al** well NW Saudi Arabia
Afars et des Issas, Territoire Français des see Djibouti
83 D22 **Affenrücken** Karas, SW Namibia 28°05′S 15°49′E
Afghānestān, Dowlat-e Eslāmī-ye see Afghanistan
148 M6 **Afghanistan** off. Islamic Republic of Afghanistan, Per. Dowlat-e Eslāmī-ye Afghānestān; prev. Republic of Afghanistan. ◆ islamic state C Asia
Afgoi see Afgooye
81 N17 **Afgooye** It. Afgoi. Shabeellaha Hoose, S Somalia 02°09′N 45°07′E
141 N8 **'Afīf** Ar Riyāḑ, C Saudi Arabia 23°57′N 42°57′E
77 V17 **Afikpo** Ebonyi, S Nigeria 05°52′N 07°58′E
Afiun Karahissar see Afyon
109 V6 **Aflenz Kurort** Steiermark, E Austria 47°33′N 15°14′E
74 J6 **Aflou** N Algeria 34°09′N 02°06′E
81 L18 **Afmadow** Jubbada Hoose, S Somalia 0°24′N 42°04′E
39 Q14 **Afognak Island** island Alaska, USA
104 J2 **A Fonsagrada** Galicia, NW Spain 43°09′N 07°03′W
186 E9 **Afore** Northern, S Papua New Guinea 09°10′S 148°30′E
59 O15 **Afrânio** Pernambuco, E Brazil 08°32′S 40°54′W
66-67 **Africa** continent
68 L11 **Africa, Horn of** physical region Ethiopia/Somalia
172 K11 **Africana Seamount** undersea feature SW Indian Ocean 37°10′S 29°10′E
86 A14 **African Plate** tectonic plate
138 I2 **'Afrīn** Ḩalab, N Syria 36°31′N 36°51′E
136 M15 **Afşin** Kahramanmaraş, C Turkey 38°14′N 36°54′E
98 J7 **Afsluitdijk** dam N Netherlands
29 U15 **Afton** Iowa, C USA 41°01′N 94°12′W
29 W9 **Afton** Minnesota, N USA 44°54′N 92°46′W
27 R8 **Afton** Oklahoma, C USA 36°41′N 94°57′W
136 F14 **Afyon** prev. Afyonkarahisar. Afyon, W Turkey 38°46′N 30°32′E
136 F14 **Afyon** var. Afiun Karahissar, Afyonkarahisar. ⬖ province W Turkey
Afyonkarahisar see Afyon
Agadès see Agadez
77 V10 **Agadez** prev. Agadès. Agadez, C Niger 16°57′N 07°56′E
77 W8 **Agadez** ⬖ department N Niger
74 E8 **Agadir** SW Morocco 30°30′N 09°37′W
64 M9 **Agadir Canyon** undersea feature SE Atlantic Ocean 32°30′N 12°50′W
145 R12 **Agadyr'** Karaganda, C Kazakhstan 48°15′N 72°55′E
173 O7 **Agalega Islands** island group N Mauritius
42 K6 **Agalta, Sierra de** ▲▲ E Honduras
122 I10 **Agan** ≈ C Russian Federation
Agana/Agaña see Hagåtña
188 B15 **Agana Bay** bay NW Guam
171 Kk13 **Agano-gawa** ≈ Honshū, C Japan
188 B17 **Aga Point** headland S Guam
154 G9 **Agar** Madhya Pradesh, C India 23°44′N 76°01′E
81 I14 **Āgaro** Oromīya, C Ethiopia 07°52′N 36°36′E
153 V15 **Agartala** state capital Tripura, NE India 23°49′N 91°15′E
194 I5 **Agassiz, Cape** headland Antarctica 68°29′S 62°59′W
175 V13 **Agassiz Fracture Zone** tectonic feature S Pacific Ocean
9 N2 **Agassiz Ice Cap** Ice feature Nunavut, N Canada
188 B16 **Agat** W Guam 13°20′N 144°38′E
188 B16 **Agat Bay** bay W Guam
Agatha see Agde
115 M20 **Agathónisi** island Dodekánisa, Greece, Aegean Sea
171 X14 **Agats** Papua, E Indonesia 05°33′S 138°07′E
155 C21 **Agatti Island** island Lakshadweep, India, N Indian Ocean
38 D16 **Agattu Island** island Aleutian Islands, Alaska, USA
38 D16 **Agattu Strait** strait Aleutian Islands, Alaska, USA
14 B8 **Agawa** ≈ Ontario, S Canada
14 B8 **Agawa Bay** lake bay Ontario, S Canada
77 N17 **Agboville** SE Ivory Coast 05°55′N 04°15′W
137 V12 **Ağdam** Rus. Agdam. SW Azerbaijan 40°04′N 46°00′E
Agdam see Ağdam
103 P16 **Agde** anc. Agatha. Hérault, S France 43°19′N 03°29′E
103 P16 **Agde, Cap d'** headland S France 43°17′N 03°30′E
Agedabia see Ajdābiyā
102 L14 **Agen** anc. Aginnum. Lot-et-Garonne, SW France 44°12′N 00°37′E
Agendicum see Sens
165 O13 **Ageo** Saitama, Honshū, S Japan 35°58′N 139°36′E
109 R5 **Ager** ≈ N Austria
Agere Hiywet see Hāgere Hiywet
108 G8 **Ägerisee** ◎ W Switzerland
142 M10 **Āghā Jārī** Khūzestān, SW Iran 30°48′N 49°45′E
39 P15 **Aghiyuk Island** island Alaska, USA
74 B12 **Aghouinit** SE Western Sahara 22°14′N 13°10′W
Aghri Dagh see Büyükağrı Dağı
74 B10 **Aghzoumal, Sebkhet** var. Sebjet Agsumal. salt lake E Western Sahara
115 F15 **Agiá** var. Ayiá. Thessalía, C Greece 39°43′N 22°45′E
40 G7 **Agiabampo, Estero de** estuary NW Mexico
121 P3 **Agía Fýlaxis** var. Ayia Phyla. S Cyprus 34°43′N 33°02′E
Agialoúsa see Yenierenköy
115 M21 **Agía Marína** Léros, Dodekánisa, Greece, Aegean Sea 37°09′N 26°51′E
121 Q2 **Agía Nápa** var. Ayia Napa. E Cyprus 34°59′N 34°00′E
115 L16 **Agía Paraskeví** Lésvos, E Greece 39°13′N 26°19′E
115 J15 **Agías Eirínis, Akrotírio** headland Límnos, E Greece 39°47′N 25°21′E
Agiasós see Agiassós
115 L17 **Agiassós** var. Agiasós, Ayiásos, Ayiássos. Lésvos, E Greece 39°05′N 26°23′E
Aginnum see Agen
123 O14 **Aginskoye** Zabaykal'skiy Kray, S Russian Federation 51°10′N 114°32′E
115 I14 **Ágion Óros** Eng. Mount Athos. ⬖ monastic republic NE Greece
115 H14 **Ágion Óros** var. Akte, Aktí; anc. Acte. peninsula NE Greece
114 D13 **Ágios Achílleios** religious building Dytikí Makedonía, N Greece
115 J16 **Ágios Efstrátios** var. Áyios Evstrátios, Hagios Evstrátios. island E Greece 34°00′N 25°00′E
115 H20 **Ágios Geórgios** island Kykládes, Greece, Aegean Sea
Ágios Geórgios see Ro
115 E21 **Ágios Ilías** ▲ S Greece 36°57′N 22°19′E
115 K25 **Ágios Ioánnis, Akrotírio** headland Kríti, Greece, E Mediterranean Sea 35°19′N 25°46′E
115 L20 **Ágios Kírykos** var. Áyios Kírikos. Ikaría, Dodekánisa, Greece, Aegean Sea 37°34′N 26°15′E
115 K25 **Ágios Nikólaos** var. Áyios Nikólaos. Kríti, Greece, E Mediterranean Sea 35°12′N 25°43′E
115 D16 **Ágios Nikolaos** Thessalía, C Greece 39°33′N 21°21′E
115 H14 **Agíou Órous, Kólpos** gulf N Greece
107 K24 **Agira** anc. Agyrium. Sicilia, Italy, C Mediterranean Sea 37°39′N 14°32′E
115 G20 **Agkístri** island S Greece
114 G12 **Ágkistro** var. Angistro. ▲ NE Greece 41°21′N 23°29′E
103 O17 **Agly** ≈ S France
Agnetheln see Agnita
14 E10 **Agnew Lake** ◎ Ontario, S Canada
77 O16 **Agnibilékrou** E Ivory Coast 07°10′N 03°11′W
116 I11 **Agnita** Ger. Agnetheln, Hung. Szentágota. Sibiu, SW Romania 45°59′N 24°40′E
107 K15 **Agnone** Molise, C Italy 41°49′N 14°21′E
164 K14 **Ago** Mie, Honshū, SW Japan 34°18′N 136°50′E
106 C8 **Agogna** ≈ N Italy
Agoitz see Aoiz
Agoiz see Aoiz
77 P17 **Agona Swedru** var. Swedru. SE Ghana 05°31′N 00°42′W
Agordat see Ak'ordat
Agosta see Augusta
103 N15 **Agout** ≈ S France
152 J12 **Āgra** Uttar Pradesh, N India 27°09′N 78°E
Agra and Oudh, United Provinces of see Uttar Pradesh
Agram see Zagreb
105 U5 **Agramunt** Cataluña, NE Spain 41°48′N 01°07′E
105 Q5 **Agreda** Castilla y León, N Spain 41°51′N 01°55′W
137 S13 **Ağrı** var. Karaköse; prev. Karakılısse. Ağrı, NE Turkey 39°44′N 43°04′E
137 S13 **Ağrı** ⬖ province NE Turkey
107 N19 **Agri** anc. Aciris. ≈ S Italy
Agri Dagi see Büyükağrı Dağı
107 J24 **Agrigento** Gk. Akragas; prev. Girgenti. Sicilia, Italy, C Mediterranean Sea 37°19′N 13°33′E
188 K4 **Agrihan** island N Northern Mariana Islands
115 L17 **Agriliá, Akrotírio** prev. Ákra Maléas. cape Lésvos, E Greece
115 D18 **Agrínio** prev. Agrinion. Dytikí Elláda, W Greece 38°38′N 21°25′E
Agrinion see Agrínio
115 G17 **Agriovótano** Évvoia, C Greece 39°00′N 23°18′E
107 L18 **Agropoli** Campania, S Italy 40°22′N 14°59′E
127 T3 **Agryz** Udmurtskaya Respublika, NW Russian Federation 56°27′N 52°58′E
137 U11 **Ağstafa** Rus. Akstafa. NW Azerbaijan 41°06′N 45°28′E
137 X11 **Ağsu** Rus. Akhsu. C Azerbaijan
Agsumal, Sebjet see Aghzoumal, Sebkhet
40 J11 **Agua Brava, Laguna** lagoon W Mexico
54 F7 **Aguachica** Cesar, N Colombia 08°16′N 73°35′W
59 J20 **Água Clara** Mato Grosso do Sul, SW Brazil 20°21′S 52°58′W
44 D5 **Aguada de Pasajeros** Cienfuegos, C Cuba 22°23′N 80°51′W
54 J5 **Aguada Grande** Lara, N Venezuela 10°38′N 69°29′W
45 S5 **Aguadilla** W Puerto Rico 18°27′N 67°08′W
43 S16 **Aguadulce** Coclé, S Panama 08°16′N 80°31′W
104 L14 **Aguadulce** Andalucía, S Spain 37°15′N 04°59′W
41 O8 **Agualeguas** Nuevo León, NE Mexico 26°17′N 99°30′W
40 L9 **Aguanaval, Río** ≈ C Mexico
42 J5 **Aguán, Río** ≈ N Honduras
25 R16 **Agua Nueva** Texas, SW USA 26°57′N 98°34′W
60 J8 **Aguapeí, Rio** ≈ S Brazil
61 E14 **Aguapey, Río** ≈ NE Argentina
40 G3 **Agua Prieta** Sonora, NW Mexico 31°16′N 109°33′W
104 G5 **A Guarda** var. A Guardia, Laguardia, La Guardia. Galicia, NW Spain 41°54′N 08°53′W
A Guardia see A Guarda
56 E6 **Aguarico, Río** ≈ Ecuador/Peru
55 O6 **Aguasay** Monagas, NE Venezuela 09°25′N 63°44′W
40 M12 **Aguascalientes** Aguascalientes, C Mexico 21°54′N 102°17′W
40 L12 **Aguascalientes** ⬖ state C Mexico
57 I18 **Aguas Calientes, Río** ≈ S Peru
105 R7 **Aguasvivas** ≈ NE Spain
60 J7 **Água Vermelha, Represa de** ⊠ S Brazil
56 E12 **Aguaytía** Ucayali, C Peru 09°02′S 75°30′W
104 I5 **A Gudiña** var. La Gudiña. Galicia, NW Spain 42°04′N 07°08′W
104 G7 **Águeda** Aveiro, N Portugal 40°34′N 08°28′W
104 J8 **Águeda** ≈ Portugal/Spain
77 Q8 **Aguelhok** Kidal, NE Mali 19°18′N 00°50′E
77 V12 **Aguié** Maradi, S Niger 13°28′N 07°43′E
188 K8 **Aguijan** island S Northern Mariana Islands
104 M14 **Aguilar** var. Aguilar de la Frontera. Andalucía, S Spain 37°31′N 04°40′W
104 M3 **Aguilar de Campóo** Castilla y León, N Spain 42°47′N 04°15′W
Aguilar de la Frontera see Aguilar
42 F7 **Aguilares** San Salvador, C El Salvador 13°56′N 89°09′W
105 Q14 **Aguilas** Murcia, SE Spain 37°24′N 01°36′W
40 L15 **Aguililla** Michoacán, SW Mexico 18°43′N 102°45′W
Agulhas see L'Agulhas
172 J11 **Agulhas Bank** undersea feature SW Indian Ocean 35°30′S 21°00′E
172 K11 **Agulhas Basin** undersea feature SW Indian Ocean 47°00′S 27°00′E
83 F26 **Agulhas, Cape** Afr. Kaap Agulhas. headland SW South Africa 34°51′S 19°59′E
Agulhas, Kaap see Agulhas, Cape
60 O9 **Agulhas Negras, Pico das** ▲ SE Brazil 22°21′S 44°39′W
172 K11 **Agulhas Plateau** undersea feature SW Indian Ocean 40°00′S 26°00′E
165 S16 **Aguni-jima** island Nansei-shotō, SW Japan
Agurain see Salvatierra
54 G5 **Agustín Codazzi** var. Codazzi. Cesar, N Colombia 10°02′N 73°15′W
Agyrium see Agira
74 L12 **Ahaggar** high plateau region SE Algeria
146 E12 **Ahal Welaýaty** Rus. Akhalskiy Velayat. ⬖ province C Turkmenistan
142 K2 **Ahar** Āžarbāyjān-e Sharqī, NW Iran 38°25′N 47°07′E
Aharnes see Acharnés
138 J3 **Aḩaş, Jabal** ▲ NW Syria
138 J3 **Aḩaş, Jebal** ▲▲ W Syria
185 G16 **Ahaura** ≈ South Island, New Zealand
100 E13 **Ahaus** Nordrhein-Westfalen, NW Germany 52°04′N 07°01′E
191 U9 **Ahe** atoll Îles Tuamotu, C French Polynesia
184 N10 **Ahimanawa Range** ▲▲ North Island, New Zealand
119 I19 **Ahinski Kanal** Rus. Oginskiy Kanal. canal SW Belarus
186 G10 **Ahioma** SE Papua New Guinea 10°20′S 150°35′E
184 I2 **Ahipara** Northland, North Island, New Zealand 35°11′S 173°07′E
184 I2 **Ahipara Bay** bay SE Tasman Sea
Áhkájávrre see Akkajaure
Áhkká see Akka
39 N13 **Ahklun Mountains** ▲▲ Alaska, USA
137 R14 **Ahlat** Bitlis, E Turkey 38°45′N 42°28′E
101 F14 **Ahlen** Nordrhein-Westfalen, W Germany 51°46′N 07°53′E
154 D10 **Ahmadābād** var. Ahmedabad. Gujarāt, W India 23°03′N 72°40′E
143 R10 **Ahmadābād** Kermān, C Iran 35°51′N 59°36′E
Ahmadi see Al Aḩmadī
Ahmad Khel see Ḩasan Khēl
155 F14 **Ahmadnagar** var. Ahmednagar. Mahārāshtra, W India 19°08′N 74°48′E
149 T9 **Ahmadpur Siāl** Punjab, E Pakistan 30°40′N 71°52′E
77 N5 **Aḩmar, 'Erg el** desert N Mali
80 K13 **Ahmar Mountains** ▲▲ C Ethiopia
Ahmedabad see Ahmadābād
Ahmednagar see Ahmadnagar
114 N12 **Ahmetbey** Kırklareli, NW Turkey 41°26′N 27°35′E
14 H12 **Ahmic Lake** ◎ Ontario, S Canada
190 G12 **Ahoa** Île Uvea, E Wallis and Futuna 13°17′S 176°12′W
40 G8 **Ahomé** Sinaloa, C Mexico 25°55′N 109°10′W
21 X8 **Ahoskie** North Carolina, SE USA 36°17′N 76°59′W
101 D17 **Ahr** ≈ W Germany
143 N12 **Ahram** var. Ahrom. Būshehr, S Iran 28°52′N 51°18′E
100 J9 **Ahrensburg** Schleswig-Holstein, N Germany 53°41′N 10°14′E
Ahrom see Ahram
93 L17 **Ähtäri** Länsi-Suomi, W Finland 62°34′N 24°08′E
40 K12 **Ahuacatlán** Nayarit, C Mexico 21°02′N 104°30′W
42 E7 **Ahuachapán** Ahuachapán, W El Salvador 13°55′N 89°51′W
42 A9 **Ahuachapán** ⬖ department W El Salvador
191 V16 **Ahu Akivi** var. Siete Moai. ancient monument Easter Island, Chile, E Pacific Ocean
191 W11 **Ahunui** atoll Îles Tuamotu, C French Polynesia
185 E20 **Ahuriri** ≈ South Island, New Zealand
95 L22 **Åhus** Skåne, S Sweden 55°55′N 14°18′E
Ahu Tahira see Ahu Vinapu
191 V16 **Ahu Tepeu** ancient monument Easter Island, Chile, E Pacific Ocean
191 V17 **Ahu Vinapu** var. Ahu Tahira. ancient monument Easter Island, Chile, E Pacific Ocean
142 L9 **Ahvāz** var. Ahwāz; prev. Nāsiri. Khūzestān, SW Iran 31°20′N 48°38′E
Ahvenanmaa see Åland
141 Q16 **Aḩwar** SW Yemen 13°34′N 46°41′E
Ahwāz see Ahvāz
94 H7 **Åi Åfjord** var. Åi Åfjord, Årnes. Sør-Trøndelag, C Norway 63°57′N 10°12′E see also Åi Åfjord
Åi Åfjord see Åi Åfjord
149 P3 **Aibak** var. Haibak; prev. Āybak, Samangān. Samangān, NE Afghanistan 36°16′N 68°04′E
101 K22 **Aichach** Bayern, SE Germany 48°26′N 11°06′E
164 L14 **Aichi** off. Aichi-ken, var. Aiti. ⬖ prefecture Honshū, SW Japan
Aïdin see Aydın
Aidussina see Ajdovščina
Aifir, Clochán an see Giant's Causeway
Aigaíon Pelagos/Aigaío Pélagos see Aegean Sea
109 S3 **Aigen im Mülkreis** Oberösterreich, N Austria 48°39′N 13°57′E
115 G20 **Aígina** var. Aíyina, Egina. Aígina, C Greece 37°45′N 23°26′E
115 G20 **Aígina** island S Greece
115 E18 **Aígio** var. Egio; prev. Aíyion. Dytikí Elláda, S Greece 38°15′N 22°05′E
108 C10 **Aigle** Vaud, SW Switzerland 46°20′N 06°58′E
103 P14 **Aigoual, Mont** ▲ S France 44°09′N 03°34′E
173 O16 **Aigrettes, Pointe des** headland W Réunion 21°02′S 55°14′E
61 G19 **Aiguá** var. Aigua. Maldonado, S Uruguay 34°13′S 54°46′W
103 S13 **Aigues** ≈ SE France
103 N10 **Aigurande** Indre, C France 46°26′N 01°49′E
Ai-hun see Heihe
163 N10 **Aikawa** Niigata, Sado, C Japan 38°04′N 138°15′E
21 Q13 **Aiken** South Carolina, SE USA 33°34′N 81°44′W
25 N4 **Aiken** Texas, SW USA 34°06′N 101°31′W

◆ Country
● Country Capital
◇ Dependent Territory
○ Dependent Territory Capital
⬖ Administrative Regions
✈ International Airport
▲ Mountain
▲▲ Mountain Range
⛰ Volcano
≈ River
◎ Lake
⊠ Reservoir

160 F13 Ailao Shan ▲▲ SW China
189 R4 Ailinginae Atoll var. Aelōninae. atoll Ralik Chain, SW Marshall Islands
189 T7 Ailinglaplap Atoll var. Aelōnlaplap. atoll Ralik Chain, S Marshall Islands
Aillionn, Loch see Allen, Lough
96 H13 Ailsa Craig island SW Scotland, United Kingdom
189 V5 Ailuk Atoll var. Aelok. atoll Ratak Chain, NE Marshall Islands
123 R11 Aim Khabarovskiy Kray, E Russian Federation 58°45′N 134°08′E
45 Q12 Aimé Césaire ✈ (Fort-de-France) C Martinique 14°34′N 61°00′W
103 R11 Ain ◈ department E France
103 S10 Ain ~ E France
118 G7 Ainaži Est. Heinaste, Ger. Hainasch. N Latvia 57°51′N 24°24′E
74 L6 Aïn Beida NE Algeria 35°52′N 07°25′E
76 K4 ʿAïn Ben Tili Tiris Zemmour, N Mauritania 25°58′N 09°30′W
74 J5 Aïn Defla var. Aïn Eddefla. N Algeria 36°16′N 01°58′E
Aïn Eddefla see Aïn Defla
74 L5 Aïn El Bey ✈ (Constantine) NE Algeria 36°15′N 06°36′E
115 C19 Aínos ▲ Kefallonía, Iónia Nísoi, Greece, C Mediterranean Sea 38°08′N 20°39′E
105 T4 Ainsa Aragón, NE Spain 42°25′N 00°08′E
74 I7 Aïn Sefra NW Algeria 32°45′N 00°32′W
29 N13 Ainsworth Nebraska, C USA 42°33′N 99°51′W
Aintab see Gaziantep
74 H5 Aïn Témouchent N Algeria 35°18′N 01°09′W
186 C6 Aiome Madang, N Papua New Guinea 05°08′S 144°45′E
Aïoun el Atrous/Aïoun el Atroûss see ʿAyoûn el ʿAtroûs
54 E11 Aipe Huila, C Colombia 03°15′N 75°17′W
56 D9 Aipena, Río ~ N Peru
57 L19 Aiquile Cochabamba, C Bolivia 18°10′S 65°10′W
Aïr see Aïr, Massif de l'
188 E10 Airai Babeldaob, C Palau
188 E10 Airai ✈ (Oreor) Babeldaob, N Palau 07°22′N 134°34′E
168 I11 Airbangis Sumatera, NW Indonesia 0°12′N 99°22′E
11 Q16 Airdrie Alberta, SW Canada 51°20′N 114°00′W
96 I12 Airdrie S Scotland, United Kingdom 55°52′N 03°59′W
Air du Azbine see Aïr, Massif de l'
97 M17 Aire ~ N England, United Kingdom
102 K15 Aire-sur-l'Adour Landes, SW France 43°43′N 00°16′W
103 O1 Aire-sur-la-Lys Pas-de-Calais, N France 50°39′N 02°24′E
9 Q6 Air Force Island island Baffin Island, Nunavut, NE Canada
169 Q13 Airhitam, Teluk bay Borneo, C Indonesia
171 Q11 Airmadidi Sulawesi, N Indonesia 01°25′N 124°59′E
77 V8 Aïr, Massif de l' var. Aïr, Air du Azbine, Asben. ▲▲ NC Niger
108 G10 Airolo Ticino, S Switzerland 46°32′N 08°38′E
102 K9 Airvault Deux-Sèvres, W France 46°51′N 00°07′W
101 K19 Aisch ~ S Germany
63 G20 Aisén off. Región Aisén del General Carlos Ibañez del Campo, var. Aysen. ◈ region S Chile
10 H7 Aishihik Lake ◎ Yukon Territory, W Canada
103 P3 Aisne ◈ department N France
103 R4 Aisne ~ NE France
109 T4 Aist ~ N Austria
114 K13 Aisými Anatolikí Makedonía kai Thráki, NE Greece 41°00′N 25°55′E
105 S11 Aitana ▲ E Spain 38°39′N 00°15′W
186 B5 Aitape var. Eitape. Sandaun, NW Papua New Guinea 03°10′S 142°17′E
Aiti see Aichi
29 V6 Aitkin Minnesota, N USA 46°31′N 93°42′W
115 D18 Aitolikó var. Etoliko; prev. Aitolikón. Dytikí Elláda, C Greece 38°26′N 21°21′E
Aitolikón see Aitolikó
190 L15 Aitutaki island S Cook Islands
116 H11 Aiud Ger. Strassburg, Hung. Nagyenyed; prev. Engeten. Alba, SW Romania 46°19′N 23°43′E
118 I9 Aiviekste ~ C Latvia
189 Q8 Aiwo SW Nauru 0°32′S 166°54′E
188 E8 Aiwokako Passage passage Babeldaob, N Palau
Aix see Aix-en-Provence
103 S15 Aix-en-Provence var. Aix; anc. Aquae Sextiae. Bouches-du-Rhône, SE France 43°31′N 05°27′E
Aix-la-Chapelle see Aachen
103 T11 Aix-les-Bains Savoie, E France 45°40′N 05°55′E
186 A6 Aiyang, Mount ▲ NW Papua New Guinea 05°03′S 141°15′E
Aíyina see Aígina
Aíyion see Aígio
153 W15 Āīzawl state capital Mizoram, NE India 23°41′N 92°45′E
118 H9 Aizkraukle S Latvia 56°39′N 25°07′E
118 C9 Aizpute W Latvia 56°43′N 21°32′E
165 O11 Aizuwakamatsu Fukushima, Honshū, C Japan 37°30′N 139°58′E
103 X15 Ajaccio Corse, France, C Mediterranean Sea 41°54′N 08°43′E
103 X15 Ajaccio, Golfe d' gulf Corse, France, C Mediterranean Sea
41 Q15 Ajalpán Puebla, S Mexico 18°26′N 97°20′W
154 F13 Ajanta Range ▲▲ C India
Ajastan see Ach'ara
Ajastan see Armenia
93 G14 Ajaureforsen Västerbotten, N Sweden 65°31′N 15°44′E
185 H17 Ajax, Mount ▲ South Island, New Zealand 42°34′S 172°06′E
162 F9 Aj Bogd Uul ▲ SW Mongolia 44°49′N 95°01′E
75 R8 Ajdābiyā var. Agedabia, Ajdābiyah. NE Libya 30°46′N 20°14′E
Ajdābiyah see Ajdābiyā
109 S12 Ajdovščina Ger. Haidenschaft, It. Aidussina. W Slovenia 45°52′N 13°55′E
165 Q7 Ajigasawa Aomori, Honshū, C Japan 40°45′N 140°11′E
Ajjinena see El Geneina
111 H23 Ajka Veszprém, W Hungary 47°18′N 17°32′E
138 G9 ʿAjlūn Irbid, N Jordan 32°20′N 35°45′E
138 H9 ʿAjlūn, Jabal ▲▲ W Jordan
Ajluokta see Drag
143 R15 ʿAjmān var. Ajman, ʿUjmān. ʿAjmān, NE United Arab Emirates 25°36′N 55°42′E
152 G12 Ajmer var. Ajmere. Rājasthān, N India 26°29′N 74°40′E
36 J15 Ajo Arizona, SW USA 32°22′N 112°51′W
105 N2 Ajo, Cabo de headland N Spain 43°31′N 03°36′W
36 J16 Ajo Range ▲▲ Arizona, SW USA
146 C14 Ajyguýy Rus. Adzhikui. Balkan Welaýaty, W Turkmenistan 39°46′N 53°57′E
Akaba see Al ʿAqabah
165 T3 Akabira Hokkaidō, NE Japan 43°30′N 142°04′E
165 N10 Akadomari Niigata, Sado, C Japan 37°54′N 138°24′E
81 E20 Akagera ~ Rwanda/Tanzania
191 W16 Akahanga, Punta headland Easter Island, Chile, E Pacific Ocean
80 J13 Āk'ak'i Oromīya, C Ethiopia 08°50′N 38°51′E
155 G15 Akalkot Mahārāshtra, W India 17°36′N 76°10′E
Akamagaseki see Shimonoseki
165 V3 Akan Hokkaidō, NE Japan 44°06′N 144°03′E
165 U4 Akan Hokkaidō, NE Japan 43°09′N 144°08′E
165 U4 Akan-ko ◎ Hokkaidō, NE Japan
Akanthoú see Tatlısu
185 I19 Akaroa Canterbury, South Island, New Zealand 43°48′S 172°58′E
80 E6 Akasha Northern, N Sudan 21°03′N 30°46′E
164 I13 Akashi var. Akasi. Hyōgo, Honshū, SW Japan 34°39′N 135°00′E
139 N7 ʿAkāsh, Wādī var. Wādī ʿUkash. dry watercourse W Iraq
Akasi see Akashi
92 K11 Äkäsjokisuu Lappi, N Finland 67°28′N 23°44′E
137 S11 Akbaba Dağı ▲ Armenia/Turkey 41°04′N 43°28′E
Akbük Limanı see Güllük Körfezi
127 V8 Akbulak Orenburgskaya Oblast', W Russian Federation 51°01′N 55°35′E
137 O11 Akçaabat Trabzon, NE Turkey 41°00′N 39°36′E
137 N15 Akçadağ Malatya, C Turkey 38°21′N 37°59′E
136 G11 Akçakoca Düzce, NW Turkey 41°05′N 31°08′E
Akchakaya, Vpadina see Akdzhakaya, Vpadina
76 H7 Akchâr desert W Mauritania
Akchatau see Akshatau
136 L13 Akdağlar ▲▲ C Turkey
136 E17 Ak Dağları ▲▲ SW Turkey
136 K13 Akdağmadeni Yozgat, C Turkey 39°40′N 35°52′E
146 G8 Akdepe prev. Ak-Tepe, Leninsk, Turkm. Lenin. Daşoguz Welaýaty, N Turkmenistan 42°10′N 59°17′E
Ak-Dere see Byala
121 P2 Akdoğan Gk. Lýsi. C Cyprus 35°06′N 33°42′E
122 J14 Ak-Dovurak Respublika Tyva, S Russian Federation 51°09′N 90°36′E
146 F9 Akdzhakaya, Vpadina var. Vpadina Akchakaya. depression N Turkmenistan
171 S11 Akelamo Pulau Halmahera, E Indonesia 01°27′N 128°39′E
Aken see Aachen
Akermanceaster see Bath
95 P15 Åkersberga Stockholm, C Sweden 59°28′N 18°19′E
95 H15 Akershus ◈ county S Norway
79 L16 Aketi Orientale, N Dem. Rep. Congo 02°44′N 23°46′E
146 C10 Akgyr Erezi Rus. Gryada Akkyr. hill range NW Turkmenistan
Akhalskiy Velayat see Ahal Welaýaty
137 S10 Akhaltsikhe prev. Akhalts'ikhe. SW Georgia 41°39′N 43°04′E
Akhalts'ikhe see Akhaltsikhe
Akhangaran see Ohangaron
Akharnaí see Acharnés
75 R7 Akhḍar, Al Jabal al hill range NE Libya
Akhelóos see Achelóos
39 Q15 Akhiok Kodiak Island, Alaska, USA 56°57′N 154°12′W
136 C13 Akhisar Manisa, W Turkey 38°54′N 27°50′E
75 X10 Akhmīm var. Akhmîm; anc. Panopolis. C Egypt 26°35′N 31°48′E
152 H6 Akhnūr Jammu and Kashmir, NW India 32°53′N 74°46′E
Akhsu see Ağsu
114 N10 Akhtopol Burgas, E Bulgaria 42°06′N 27°57′E
127 P11 Akhtuba ~ SW Russian Federation
127 P11 Akhtubinsk Astrakhanskaya Oblast', SW Russian Federation 48°17′N 46°14′E
Akhtyrka see Okhtyrka
164 H14 Aki Kōchi, Shikoku, SW Japan 33°30′N 133°53′E
39 N12 Akiachak Alaska, USA 60°54′N 161°25′W
39 N12 Akiak Alaska, USA 60°54′N 161°12′W
191 X11 Akiaki atoll Îles Tuamotu, E French Polynesia
12 H9 Akimiski Island island Nunavut, C Canada
136 K17 Akıncı Burnu headland S Turkey 36°21′N 35°47′E
Akıncılar see Selçuk
117 U10 Akinovka Zaporiz'ka Oblast', S Ukraine
Åkirkeby see Aakirkeby
165 P8 Akita Akita, Honshū, C Japan 39°44′N 140°06′E
165 Q8 Akita off. Akita-ken. ◈ prefecture Honshū, C Japan
76 H8 Akjoujt prev. Fort-Repoux. Inchiri, W Mauritania 19°42′N 14°28′W
92 H11 Akka Lapp. Áhkká. ▲ N Sweden 67°33′N 17°27′E
92 H11 Akkajaure Lapp. Áhkájávrre. ◎ N Sweden
Akkala see Oqqal'a
155 L25 Akkaraipattu Eastern Province, E Sri Lanka 07°13′N 81°51′E
145 P13 Akkense Kaz. Aqkengse. Karaganda, C Kazakhstan 46°39′N 68°06′E
Akkerman see Bilhorod-Dnistrovs'kyy
127 W8 Akkermanovka Orenburgskaya Oblast', W Russian Federation 51°11′N 58°03′E
165 V4 Akkeshi Hokkaidō, NE Japan 43°03′N 144°49′E
165 V4 Akkeshi-ko ◎ Hokkaidō, NE Japan
165 V5 Akkeshi-wan bay NW Pacific Ocean
138 F8 ʿAkko Eng. Acre, Fr. Saint-Jean-d'Acre, Bibl. Accho, Ptolemaïs. Northern, N Israel 32°55′N 35°04′E
145 Q8 Akkol' Kaz. Aqköl; prev. Alekseyevka, Kaz. Alekseevka. Akmola, C Kazakhstan 51°58′N 70°58′E
145 T14 Akkol' Kaz. Aqköl. Almaty, SE Kazakhstan 45°01′N 75°38′E
145 Q16 Akkol' Kaz. Aqköl. Zhambyl, C Kazakhstan 43°25′N 70°47′E
144 M11 Akkol', Ozero prev. Ozero Zhaman-Akkol. ◎ C Kazakhstan
98 L6 Akkrum Fryslân, N Netherlands 53°01′N 05°52′E
145 U8 Akku Kaz. Aqqū; prev. Lebyazh'ye. Pavlodar, NE Kazakhstan 51°29′N 77°48′E
144 F12 Akkystau Kaz. Aqqystaū. Atyrau, SW Kazakhstan 47°17′N 51°03′E
8 G6 Aklavik Northwest Territories, NW Canada 68°15′N 135°02′W
118 B9 Akmenrags prev. Akmeņrags. headland W Latvia 56°49′N 21°03′E
Akmeņrags see Akmenrags
158 E9 Akmeqit Xinjiang Uygur Zizhiqu, NW China 37°10′N 76°59′E
146 J14 Akmeydan Mary Welaýaty, C Turkmenistan 37°50′N 62°08′E
145 P9 Akmola off. Akmolinskaya Oblast', Kaz. Aqmola Oblysy; prev. Tselinogradskaya Oblast. ◈ province C Kazakhstan
Akmola see Astana
Akmolinsk see Astana
Akmolinskaya Oblast' see Akmola
Aknavásár see Târgu Ocna
118 I11 Aknīste S Latvia 56°09′N 25°43′E
81 G14 Akobo Jonglei, E South Sudan 07°50′N 33°05′E
81 G14 Akobo var. Ākobowenz. ~ Ethiopia/Sudan
Ākobowenz see Akobo
154 H12 Akola Mahārāshtra, C India 20°44′N 77°00′E
80 J9 Ak'ordat var. Agordat, Akurdet. C Eritrea 15°33′N 38°01′E
77 Q16 Akosombo Dam dam SE Ghana
154 H12 Akot Mahārāshtra, C India 21°05′N 77°04′E
77 N16 Akoupé SE Ivory Coast 06°19′N 03°54′W
12 M3 Akpatok Island island Nunavut, E Canada
158 G7 Akqi Xinjiang Uygur Zizhiqu, NW China 40°51′N 78°20′E
138 I2 Akrād, Jabal al ▲▲ N Syria
Akragas see Agrigento
92 H3 Akranes Vesturland, W Iceland 64°19′N 22°01′W
139 S2 Ākrē Ar. ʿAqrah. Dahūk, N Iraq 36°46′N 43°52′E
95 C16 Åkrehamn Rogaland, S Norway 59°15′N 15°13′E
77 V9 Akrérèb Agadez, C Niger 17°45′N 09°01′E
115 D22 Akrítas, Akrotírio headland S Greece 36°43′N 21°52′E
37 V3 Akron Colorado, C USA 40°09′N 103°12′W
29 R12 Akron Iowa, C USA 42°49′N 96°33′W
31 U12 Akron Ohio, N USA 41°05′N 81°31′W
Akrotiri see Akrotírion
Akrotiri Bay see Akrotírion, Kólpos
Akrotírio Kastállou see Kástelo, Akrotírio
121 P3 Akrotírion var. Akrotiri. UK air base S Cyprus34°36′N 32°57′E
121 P3 Akrotírion, Kólpos var. Akrotiri Bay. bay S Cyprus
121 O3 Akrotiri Sovereign Base Area UK military installation S Cyprus
158 F11 Aksai Chin Chin. Aksayqin. disputed region China/India
Aksaj see Aksay
136 I15 Aksaray Aksaray, C Turkey 38°23′N 33°50′E
136 I15 Aksaray ◈ province C Turkey
144 G8 Aksay var. Aksaj, Kaz. Aqsay. Zapadnyy Kazakhstan, NW Kazakhstan 51°11′N 53°00′E
127 O11 Aksay Volgogradskaya Oblast', SW Russian Federation 47°59′N 43°54′E
147 W10 Ak-say var. Toxkan He. ~ China/Kyrgyzstan
Aksay/Aksay Kazakzu Zizhixian see Boluozhuanjing/Hongliuwan
Aksayqin see Aksai Chin
158 G11 Aksayqin Hu ◎ NW China
136 G14 Akşehir Konya, W Turkey 38°22′N 31°24′E
136 G14 Akşehir Gölü ◎ C Turkey
136 G16 Akseki Antalya, SW Turkey 37°03′N 31°46′E
123 P13 Aksenovo-Zilovskoye Zabaykal'skiy Kray, S Russian Federation 53°01′N 117°26′E
145 S12 Akshatau Kaz. Aqshataū; prev. Akchatau. Karaganda, C Kazakhstan 47°59′N 74°02′E
145 V11 Akshatau, Khrebet ▲▲ E Kazakhstan
147 Y8 Ak-Shyyrak Issyk-Kul'skaya Oblast', E Kyrgyzstan 41°46′N 78°34′E
Akstafa see Ağstafa
158 H7 Aksu Xinjiang Uygur Zizhiqu, NW China 41°17′N 80°15′E
145 R8 Aksu Kaz. Aqsū. Akmola, N Kazakhstan 52°31′N 72°00′E
145 W13 Aksu Kaz. Aqsū. Almaty, SE Kazakhstan 45°31′N 79°28′E
145 T8 Aksu var. Jermak, Kaz. Ermak; prev. Yermak. Pavlodar, NE Kazakhstan 52°03′N 76°55′E
145 V13 Aksu Kaz. Aqsū. ~ SE Kazakhstan
145 Y11 Aksuat Kaz. Aqsūat. Vostochnyy Kazakhstan, SE Kazakhstan 48°16′N 83°39′E
145 X11 Aksuat Kaz. Aqsūat. Vostochnyy Kazakhstan, E Kazakhstan 47°48′N 82°51′E
127 S4 Aksubayevo Respublika Tatarstan, W Russian Federation 54°52′N 50°50′E
158 H7 Aksu He Rus. Sary-Dzhaz. ~ China/Kyrgyzstan see also Sary-Dzhaz
80 J10 Āksum Tigray, N Ethiopia 14°06′N 38°42′E
145 O12 Aktas Kaz. Aqtas. Karaganda, C Kazakhstan 48°03′N 66°21′E
Aktash see Oqtosh
147 V9 Ak-Tash, Gora ▲ C Kyrgyzstan 40°53′N 74°39′E
145 R10 Aktau Kaz. Aqtaū. Karaganda, C Kazakhstan 50°13′N 73°06′E
144 E11 Aktau Kaz. Aqtaū; prev. Shevchenko. Mangistau, W Kazakhstan 43°37′N 51°14′E
Aktau, Khrebet see Oqtogh, Qatorkühi. SW Tajikistan
Aktau, Khrebet see Oqtov Tizmasi, C Uzbekistan
Akte see Ágion Óros
Ak-Tepe see Akdepe
147 X7 Ak-Terek Issyk-Kul'skaya Oblast', E Kyrgyzstan 42°14′N 77°46′E
Aktí see Ágion Óros
Aktjubinsk/Aktyubinsk see Aktobe
158 E8 Akto Xinjiang Uygur Zizhiqu, NW China 39°07′N 75°43′E
144 I10 Aktobe Kaz. Aqtöbe; prev. Aktjubinsk, Aktyubinsk. Aktyubinsk, NW Kazakhstan 50°18′N 57°10′E
145 V12 Aktogay Kaz. Aqtoghay. Vostochnyy Kazakhstan, E Kazakhstan 46°56′N 79°40′E
119 M18 Aktsyabrski Rus. Oktyabr'skiy; prev. Karpilovka. Homyel'skaya Voblasts', SE Belarus 52°38′N 28°53′E
144 H11 Aktyubinsk off. Aktyubinskaya Oblast', Kaz. Aqtöbe Oblysy. ◈ province W Kazakhstan
Aktyubinsk see Aktobe
147 W7 Ak-Tyuz var. Aktyuz. Chuyskaya Oblast', N Kyrgyzstan 42°50′N 76°05′E
79 J17 Akula Equateur, NW Dem. Rep. Congo 02°21′N 20°13′E
164 C15 Akune Kagoshima, Kyūshū, SW Japan 32°00′N 130°12′E
38 L16 Akun Island island Aleutian Islands, Alaska, USA
Akurdet see Ak'ordat
77 T16 Akure Ondo, SW Nigeria 07°18′N 05°13′E
92 J2 Akureyri Nordhurland Eystra, N Iceland 65°40′N 18°07′W
38 L17 Akutan Akutan Island, Alaska, USA 54°08′N 165°47′W
38 K17 Akutan Island island Aleutian Islands, Alaska, USA
77 V17 Akwa Ibom ◈ state SE Nigeria
Akyab see Sittwe
127 W7 Ak"yar Respublika Bashkortostan, W Russian Federation 51°51′N 58°13′E
144 J10 Akzhar prev. Novorossiyskiy, Novorossiyskoye. Aktyubinsk, NW Kazakhstan 50°14′N 57°57′E
145 Y11 Akzhar Kaz. Aqzhar. Vostochnyy Kazakhstan, E Kazakhstan 47°36′N 83°38′E
94 F13 Ål Buskerud, S Norway 60°37′N 08°33′E
119 N18 Ala Rus. Ola. ~ SE Belarus
23 P5 Alabama off. State of Alabama, also known as Camellia State, Heart of Dixie, The Cotton State, Yellowhammer State. ◈ state S USA
23 P6 Alabama River ~ Alabama, S USA
23 P4 Alabaster Alabama, S USA 33°14′N 86°49′W
139 U10 Al ʿAbd Allāh var. Al Abdullah. Al Qādisīyah, S Iraq 32°06′N 45°08′E
139 W14 Al Abṭīyah well S Iraq
147 S9 Ala-Buka Dzhalal-Abadskaya Oblast', W Kyrgyzstan 41°22′N 71°27′E
136 J12 Alaca Çorum, N Turkey 40°10′N 34°52′E
136 K10 Alaçam Samsun, N Turkey 41°36′N 35°35′E
Alacant see Alicante
23 V9 Alachua Florida, SE USA 29°48′N 82°29′W
137 S13 Aladağlar ▲▲ W Turkey
136 K15 Ala Dağları ▲▲ C Turkey
162 I5 Alag-Erdene var. Manhan. Hövsgöl, N Mongolia 50°05′N 100°01′E
127 O16 Alagir Respublika Severnaya Osetiya, SW Russian Federation 43°02′N 44°10′E
106 B6 Alagna Valsesia Valle d'Aosta, NW Italy 45°51′N 07°50′E
103 P12 Alagnon ~ C France
59 P16 Alagoas off. Estado de Alagoas. ◈ state E Brazil
59 P17 Alagoinhas Bahia, E Brazil 12°09′S 38°21′W
105 R5 Alagón Aragón, NE Spain 41°46′N 01°07′W
104 J9 Alagón ~ W Spain
93 K16 Alahärmä Länsi-Suomi, W Finland 63°15′N 22°50′E
al Ahdar see Al Akhḍar
Álahaeieatnu see Altaelva
142 K12 Al Aḥmadī var. Ahmadi. E Kuwait 29°02′N 48°01′E
Al Ain see Al ʿAyn
105 Z8 Alaior prev. Alayor. Menorca, Spain, W Mediterranean Sea 39°56′N 04°08′E
147 T11 Alai Range Rus. Alayskiy Khrebet. ▲▲ Kyrgyzstan/Tajikistan
Alais see Alès
141 X11 Al ʿAjā'iz E Oman 19°33′N 57°12′E
141 X11 Al ʿAjā'iz oasis SE Oman
93 L16 Alajärvi Länsi-Suomi, W Finland 63°00′N 23°50′E
118 K4 Alajõe Ida-Virumaa, NE Estonia 59°00′N 27°26′E
42 M13 Alajuela Alajuela, C Costa Rica 10°00′N 84°12′W
42 L12 Alajuela off. Provincia de Alajuela. ◈ province N Costa Rica
43 T14 Alajuela, Lago ◎ C Panama
38 M11 Alakanuk Alaska, USA 62°41′N 164°37′W
140 K5 Al Akhḍar var. al Ahdar. Tabūk, NW Saudi Arabia 28°04′N 37°13′E
Alakol' see Alakol', Ozero
145 X13 Alakol', Ozero Kaz. Alaköl. ◎ SE Kazakhstan
124 I5 Alakurtti Murmanskaya Oblast', NW Russian Federation 66°57′N 30°27′E
38 F10 Alalākeiki Channel var. Alalakeiki Channel. channel Hawaii, USA, C Pacific Ocean
75 U8 Al ʿAlamayn var. El ʿAlamein. N Egypt 30°50′N 28°57′E
139 R1 Al ʿAmādīyah Dahūk, N Iraq 37°09′N 43°27′E
188 K5 Alamagan island C Northern Mariana Islands
139 X10 Al ʿAmārah var. Amara. Maysān, E Iraq 31°51′N 47°10′E
80 J11 Alamat'ā Tigray, N Ethiopia 12°22′N 39°32′E
37 R11 Alameda New Mexico, SW USA 35°09′N 106°37′W
121 T13 ʿAlam el Rûm, Râs headland N Egypt 31°21′N 27°23′E
Alamícamba see Alamikamba
42 M8 Alamikamba var. Alamícamba. Región Autónoma Atlántico Norte, NE Nicaragua 13°26′N 84°09′W
24 K11 Alamito Creek ~ Texas, SW USA
40 M8 Alamitos, Sierra de los ▲ NE Mexico 26°15′N 102°14′W
41 Q12 Álamo Veracruz-Llave, C Mexico 20°55′N 97°41′W
35 X9 Alamo Nevada, W USA 37°21′N 115°08′W
20 F9 Alamo Tennessee, S USA 35°47′N 89°09′W
37 S14 Alamogordo New Mexico, SW USA 32°52′N 105°57′W
36 J12 Alamo Lake ⊠ Arizona, SW USA
40 H7 Álamos Sonora, NW Mexico 26°59′N 108°53′W
37 S7 Alamosa Colorado, C USA 37°25′N 105°51′W
93 J20 Åland var. Aland Islands, Fin. Ahvenanmaa. ◈ province SW Finland
88 K9 Åland var. Aland Islands, Fin. Ahvenanmaa. island group SW Finland
Aland Islands see Åland
Aland Sea see Ålands Hav
95 Q14 Ålands Hav var. Aland Sea. strait Baltic Sea/Gulf of Bothnia
43 P16 Alanje Chiriquí, SW Panama 08°26′N 82°33′W
25 O2 Alanreed Texas, SW USA 35°12′N 100°45′W
136 G17 Alanya Antalya, S Turkey 36°32′N 32°02′E
23 U7 Alapaha River ~ Florida/Georgia, SE USA
122 G10 Alapayevsk Sverdlovskaya Oblast', C Russian Federation 57°48′N 61°50′E
138 F14 Al ʿAqabah var. Akaba, Aqaba, ʿAqaba; anc. Aelana, Elath. Al ʿAqabah, SW Jordan 29°32′N 35°00′E
138 G14 Al ʿAqabah off. Muḥāfaẓat al ʿAqabah. ◈ governorate SW Jordan
Al ʿArabīyah as Suʿūdīyah see Saudi Arabia
al Araïch see Larache
105 Q10 Alarcón Castilla-La Mancha, C Spain 39°32′N 02°05′W
105 Q9 Alarcón, Embalse de ⊠ C Spain
138 J2 Al ʿArīmah Fr. Arime. Ḥalab, N Syria 36°27′N 37°41′E
75 X7 Al ʿArīsh var. El ʿArîsh. NE Egypt 33°00′N 31°00′E
141 P6 Al Arṭāwīyah Ar Riyāḍ, N Saudi Arabia 26°34′N 45°20′E
Alasca, Golfo de see Alaska, Gulf of
136 D14 Alaşehir Manisa, W Turkey 38°19′N 28°30′E
139 N5 Al ʿAshārah var. Ashara. Dayr az Zawr, E Syria 34°51′N 40°36′E
Al Ashkhara see Al Ashkharah
141 Z9 Al Ashkharah var. Al Ashkhara. NE Oman 21°47′N 59°30′E
Al ʿAṣimah see ʿAmmān
39 P8 Alaska off. State of Alaska, also known as Land of the Midnight Sun, The Last Frontier, Seward's Folly; prev. Russian America. ◈ state NW USA
39 T13 Alaska, Gulf of var. Golfo de Alasca. gulf Canada/USA
39 O15 Alaska Peninsula peninsula Alaska, USA
39 Q11 Alaska Range ▲▲ Alaska, USA
Al-Asnam see Chlef
106 B10 Alassio Liguria, NW Italy 44°01′N 08°12′E
137 Y12 Älät Rus. Alyat; prev. Alyaty-Pristan'. SE Azerbaijan 39°57′N 49°24′E
Alat see Olot
139 S13 Al ʿAthāmīn An Najaf, S Iraq 30°27′N 43°41′E
39 P7 Alatna River ~ Alaska, USA
107 J15 Alatri Lazio, C Italy 41°43′N 13°21′E
Alattio see Alta
127 P5 Alatyr' Chuvashskaya Respublika, W Russian Federation 54°50′N 46°28′E
56 C7 Alausí Chimborazo, C Ecuador 02°11′S 78°52′W
105 O3 Álava Basq. Araba. ◈ province País Vasco, N Spain
137 T11 Alaverdi N Armenia 41°06′N 44°37′E
Alavo see Alavus
93 N14 Ala-Vuokki Oulu, E Finland 64°46′N 29°29′E
93 K17 Alavus Swe. Alavo. Länsi-Suomi, W Finland 62°33′N 23°38′E
Al ʿAwābī see Awābī
139 P6 Al ʿAwānī Al Anbār, W Iraq 34°28′N 41°43′E
75 U12 Al Awaynāt SE Libya 21°46′N 24°51′E
Al Awaynāt see Al ʿUwaynāt
182 K9 Alawoona South Australia 34°45′S 140°28′E
Alaykel'/Alay-Kuu see Kek-Art
143 R17 Al ʿAyn var. Al Ain. Abū Ẓaby, E United Arab Emirates 24°13′N 55°44′E
143 R17 Al ʿAyn var. Al Ain. ✈ Abū Ẓaby, E United Arab Emirates 24°16′N 55°31′E
138 G12 Al ʿAynā Al Karak, W Jordan 30°59′N 35°43′E
Alayor see Alaior
Alayskiy Khrebet see Alai Range
123 S6 Alazeya ~ NE Russian Federation
139 U8 Al ʿAzīzīyah var. Aziziya. Wāsiṭ, E Iraq 32°54′N 45°05′E
120 M12 Al ʿAzīzīyah NW Libya 32°32′N 13°01′E
138 I10 Al Azraq al Janūbī Az Zarqā', N Jordan 31°49′N 36°48′E
106 B9 Alba anc. Alba Pompeia. Piemonte, NW Italy 44°42′N 08°02′E
25 V6 Alba Texas, SW USA 32°47′N 95°37′W
116 G11 Alba ◈ county W Romania
139 P3 Al Baʿāj Nīnawá, N Iraq 36°02′N 41°43′E
138 J2 Al Bāb Ḥalab, N Syria 36°24′N 37°32′E
116 G10 Albac Hung. Fehérvölgy; prev. Álbák. Alba, SW Romania 46°27′N 22°58′E
105 Q11 Albacete Castilla-La Mancha, C Spain 39°N 01°52′W
105 P11 Albacete ◈ province Castilla-La Mancha, C Spain
140 J4 Al Badʿ Tabūk, NW Saudi Arabia 28°28′N 35°00′E
104 L7 Alba de Tormes Castilla y León, N Spain 40°50′N 05°30′W
139 P3 Al Bādī Nīnawá, N Iraq 35°57′N 41°37′E
141 V8 Al Badīʿah ✈ (Abū Ẓaby) Abū Ẓaby, C United Arab Emirates 24°27′N 54°39′E
143 P17 Al Badīʿah var. Al Bedeiʿah. spring/well C United Arab Emirates 23°44′N 53°50′E
95 H19 Ålbæk Nordjylland, N Denmark 57°33′N 10°24′E
139 Q7 Al Baghdādī var. Khān al Baghdādī. Al Anbār, SW Iraq 33°60′N 42°50′E
Al Bāha see Al Bāḥah
140 M11 Al Bāḥah var. Al Bāha. Al Bāḥah, SW Saudi Arabia 20°01′N 41°29′E
140 M11 Al Bāḥah var. Minṭaqat al Bāḥah. ◈ province W Saudi Arabia
Al Baḥrayn see Bahrain
105 S11 Albaida Valenciana, E Spain 38°51′N 00°31′W
116 H11 Alba Iulia Ger. Weissenburg, Hung. Gyulafehérvár; prev. Bălgrad, Karlsburg, Károly-Fehérvár. Alba, W Romania 46°06′N 23°33′E
Álbák see Albac
138 G10 Al Balqā' off. Muḥāfaẓat al Balqā', var. Balqā'. ◈ governorate NW Jordan
14 F11 Alban Ontario, S Canada 46°07′N 80°37′W
103 O15 Alban Tarn, S France 43°52′N 02°30′E
12 K11 Albanel, Lac ◎ Québec, SE Canada
113 L20 Albania off. Republic of Albania, Alb. Republika e Shqipërisë, Shqipëria; prev. People's Socialist Republic of Albania. ◆ republic SE Europe
Albania see Aubagne
107 H15 Albano Laziale Lazio, C Italy 41°44′N 12°40′E
180 J14 Albany Western Australia 35°03′S 117°54′E
23 S7 Albany Georgia, SE USA 31°35′N 84°09′W
31 P13 Albany Indiana, N USA 40°18′N 85°14′W
20 L8 Albany Kentucky, S USA 36°42′N 85°08′W
29 U7 Albany Minnesota, N USA 45°39′N 94°33′W
27 R2 Albany Missouri, C USA 40°15′N 94°15′W
18 L10 Albany state capital New York, NE USA 42°39′N 73°45′W
32 G12 Albany Oregon, NW USA 44°38′N 123°06′W
25 Q6 Albany Texas, SW USA 32°44′N 99°18′W
12 F10 Albany ~ Ontario, S Canada
Alba Pompeia see Alba
Alba Regia see Székesfehérvár
138 J6 Al Bāridah var. Bāridah. Ḥimṣ, C Syria 34°15′N 37°39′E
139 Q11 Al Barīt Al Anbār, S Iraq 31°16′N 42°28′E
105 R8 Albarracín Aragón, NE Spain 40°24′N 01°25′W
139 Y12 Al Baṣrah Eng. Basra, hist. Busra, Bussora. Al Baṣrah, SE Iraq 30°30′N 47°50′E
139 V11 Al Baṭḥā' Dhī Qār, SE Iraq 31°06′N 45°54′E
141 X8 Al Bāṭinah var. Batinah. coastal region N Oman
0 H16 Albatross Plateau undersea feature E Pacific Ocean 10°00′N 103°00′W
Al Batrūn see Batroûn
121 Q12 Al Bayḍā' var. Beida. NE Libya 32°46′N 21°43′E
141 P16 Al Bayḍā' var. Al Beida. SW Yemen 13°58′N 45°38′E
Al Bedeiʿah see Al Badīʿah
Al Beida see Al Bayḍā'
21 S10 Albemarle var. Albermarle. North Carolina, SE USA 35°21′N 80°12′W
Albemarle Island see Isabela, Isla
21 N8 Albemarle Sound inlet W Atlantic Ocean
106 B10 Albenga Liguria, NW Italy 44°04′N 08°13′E
104 L8 Alberche ~ C Spain
103 O17 Albères, Chaîne des var. les Albères, Montes Albères. ▲▲ France/Spain
Albères, Montes see Albères, Chaîne des
182 F2 Alberga Creek seasonal river South Australia
104 G7 Albergaria-a-Velha Aveiro, N Portugal 40°42′N 08°28′W
105 S10 Alberic Valenciana, E Spain 39°07′N 00°31′W
Albermarle see Albemarle
107 P18 Alberobello Puglia, SE Italy 40°47′N 17°14′E
108 J7 Alberschwende Vorarlberg, W Austria 47°28′N 09°50′E
103 O3 Albert Somme, N France 50°N 02°38′E
11 O12 Alberta ◈ province SW Canada
Albert Edward Nyanza see Edward, Lake
61 C20 Alberti Buenos Aires, E Argentina 35°03′S 60°15′W
111 K23 Albertirsa Pest, C Hungary 47°15′N 19°36′E
99 I16 Albertkanaal canal N Belgium
79 P17 Albert, Lake var. Albert Nyanza, Lac Mobutu Sese Seko. ◎ Uganda/Dem. Rep. Congo
29 V11 Albert Lea Minnesota, N USA 43°39′N 93°22′W
81 F16 Albert Nile ~ NW Uganda
Albert Nyanza see Albert, Lake
103 T11 Albertville Savoie, E France 45°41′N 06°24′E
23 Q2 Albertville Alabama, S USA 34°16′N 86°12′W
Albertville see Kalemie
103 N15 Albi anc. Albiga. Tarn, S France 43°55′N 02°09′E
29 W15 Albia Iowa, C USA 41°01′N 92°48′W
Albiga see Albi
55 X9 Albina Marowijne, NE Suriname 05°29′N 54°08′W
83 A15 Albina, Ponta headland SW Angola 15°52′S 11°45′E
30 M16 Albion Illinois, N USA 38°22′N 88°03′W
31 P11 Albion Indiana, N USA 41°23′N 85°26′W
29 P14 Albion Nebraska, C USA 41°41′N 98°00′W
18 E9 Albion New York, NE USA 43°13′N 78°09′W
18 B12 Albion Pennsylvania, NE USA 41°52′N 80°18′W
Al Biqāʿ see El Beqaa
140 J4 Al Biʾr var. Biʾr Ibn Hirmās. Tabūk, NW Saudi Arabia 28°52′N 36°16′E
140 M12 Al Birk Makkah, SW Saudi Arabia 18°13′N 41°36′E
141 Q9 Al Biyāḍ desert C Saudi Arabia
98 H13 Alblasserdam Zuid-Holland, SW Netherlands 51°52′N 04°40′E
Albocácer see Albocàsser
105 T8 Albocàsser Cast. Albocácer. Valenciana, E Spain 40°21′N 00°01′E
Albona see Labin
105 O17 Alborán, Isla de island S Spain
Alborán, Mar de see Alboran Sea
105 N17 Alboran Sea Sp. Mar de Alborán. sea SW Mediterranean Sea
Ålborg see Aalborg
95 H21 Ålborg Bugt var. Aalborg Bugt. bay N Denmark
Ålborg-Nørresundby see Aalborg
143 O5 Alborz, Reshteh-ye Kūhhā-ye Eng. Elburz Mountains. ▲▲ N Iran
105 Q14 Albox Andalucía, S Spain 37°22′N 02°08′W
101 H23 Albstadt Baden-Württemberg, SW Germany 48°13′N 09°01′E
104 G14 Albufeira Beja, S Portugal 37°05′N 08°15′W
139 P5 Ālbū Gharz, Sabkhat ◎ W Iraq
105 O15 Albuñol Andalucía, S Spain 36°48′N 03°11′W
37 Q11 Albuquerque New Mexico, SW USA 35°05′N 106°38′W
141 W8 Al Buraymī var. Buraimi. N Oman 24°16′N 55°48′E
143 R17 Al Buraymī var. Buraimi. spring/well Oman/United Arab Emirates 24°27′N 55°33′E
Al Burayqah see Marsá al Burayqah
Alburgum see Aalborg
104 I10 Alburquerque Extremadura, W Spain 39°12′N 07°00′W
181 V14 Albury New South Wales, SE Australia 36°03′S 146°53′E
141 T14 Al Buzūn SE Yemen 15°40′N 50°53′E
93 G17 Alby Västernorrland, C Sweden 62°30′N 15°25′E
Albyn, Glen see Mor, Glen
104 G12 Alcácer do Sal Setúbal, W Portugal 38°22′N 08°29′W
Alcalá de Chisvert/Alcalá de Chivert see Alcalà de Xivert
104 K14 Alcalá de Guadaira Andalucía, S Spain 37°20′N 05°50′W
105 O8 Alcalá de Henares Ar. Alkal'a; anc. Complutum. Madrid, C Spain 40°28′N 03°22′W
104 K16 Alcalá de los Gazules Andalucía, S Spain 36°29′N 05°43′W
105 T8 Alcalà de Xivert var. Alcalá de Chisvert, Cast. Alcalá de Chivert. Valenciana, E Spain 40°19′N 00°13′E
105 N14 Alcalá La Real Andalucía, S Spain 37°28′N 03°55′W
107 I23 Alcamo Sicilia, Italy, C Mediterranean Sea 37°58′N 12°58′E
105 T4 Alcanadre ~ NE Spain
105 T8 Alcanar Cataluña, NE Spain 40°33′N 00°28′E
104 J5 Alcañices Castilla y León, N Spain 41°41′N 06°21′W

◆ Country ◇ Dependent Territory ◈ Administrative Regions ▲ Mountain Volcano ◎ Lake
● Country Capital ○ Dependent Territory Capital ✈ International Airport ▲▲ Mountain Range ~ River ⊠ Reservoir

105 T7 Alcañiz Aragón, NE Spain 41°03′N 00°09′W
104 I9 Alcántara Extremadura, W Spain 39°42′N 06°54′W
104 J9 Alcántara, Embalse de ▣ W Spain
105 R13 Alcantarilla Murcia, SE Spain 37°59′N 01°12′W
105 P11 Alcaraz Castilla-La Mancha, C Spain 38°40′N 02°29′W
105 P12 Alcaraz, Sierra de ▲▲ C Spain
104 I12 Alcarrache ~ SW Spain
105 T6 Alcarràs Cataluña, NE Spain 41°34′N 00°31′E
105 N14 Alcaudete Andalucía, S Spain 37°35′N 04°05′W
Alcázar see Ksar-el-Kebir
105 O10 Alcázar de San Juan anc. Alce. Castilla-La Mancha, C Spain 39°24′N 03°12′W
Alcazarquivir see Ksar-el-Kebir
Alce see Alcázar de San Juan
57 B17 Alcebo, Volcán ⛰ Galapagos Islands, Ecuador, E Pacific Ocean 0°25′S 91°06′W
139 X12 Al Chabā'ish var. Al Kaba'ish. Dhī Qār, SE Iraq 30°58′N 47°02′E
117 Y7 Alchevs'k prev. Kommunarsk, Voroshilovsk. Luhans'ka Oblast', E Ukraine 48°29′N 38°52′E
Alcira see Alzira
21 N9 Alcoa Tennessee, S USA 35°47′N 83°58′W
104 F9 Alcobaça Leiria, C Portugal 39°32′N 08°59′W
105 N8 Alcobendas Madrid, C Spain 40°32′N 03°38′W
Alcoi see Alcoy
105 P7 Alcolea del Pinar Castilla-La Mancha, C Spain 41°02′N 02°28′W
104 I11 Alconchel Extremadura, W Spain 38°31′N 07°04′W
Alcora see L'Alcora
105 N8 Alcorcón Madrid, C Spain 40°20′N 03°52′W
105 S7 Alcorisa Aragón, NE Spain 40°53′N 00°23′W
61 B19 Alcorta Santa Fe, C Argentina 33°32′S 61°07′W
104 H14 Alcoutim Faro, S Portugal 37°28′N 07°29′W
33 W15 Alcova Wyoming, C USA 42°33′N 106°40′W
105 S11 Alcoy Cat. Alcoi. Valenciana, E Spain 38°42′N 00°29′W
105 Y9 Alcúdia Mallorca, Spain, W Mediterranean Sea 39°51′N 03°06′E
105 Y9 Alcúdia, Badia d' bay Mallorca, Spain, W Mediterranean Sea
172 M7 Aldabra Group island group SW Seychelles
139 U10 Al Daghghārah Bābil, C Iraq 32°10′N 44°57′E
40 J5 Aldama Chihuahua, N Mexico 28°50′N 105°52′W
41 P11 Aldama Tamaulipas, C Mexico 22°54′N 98°05′W
123 Q11 Aldan Respublika Sakha (Yakutiya), NE Russian Federation 58°31′N 125°15′E
123 Q10 Aldan ~ NE Russian Federation
Aldar see Aldarhaan
al Dar al Baida see Rabat
162 G7 Aldarhaan var. Aldar. Dzavhan, W Mongolia 47°43′N 96°36′E
97 Q20 Aldeburgh E England, United Kingdom 52°12′N 01°36′E
105 P5 Aldehuela de Calatañazor Castilla y León, N Spain 41°42′N 02°46′W
Aldeia Nova see Aldeia Nova de São Bento
104 H13 Aldeia Nova de São Bento var. Aldeia Nova. Beja, S Portugal 37°55′N 07°24′W
29 V11 Alden Minnesota, N USA 43°40′N 93°34′W
184 N6 Aldermen Islands, The island group N New Zealand
97 L25 Alderney island Channel Islands
97 N22 Aldershot S England, United Kingdom 51°15′N 00°47′W
21 R6 Alderson West Virginia, NE USA 37°43′N 80°38′W
Al Dhaid see Adh Dhayd
98 L5 Aldtsjerk Dutch. Oudkerk. Fryslân, N Netherlands 53°16′N 05°52′E
30 J11 Aledo Illinois, N USA 41°12′N 90°45′W
76 H9 Aleg Brakna, SW Mauritania 17°03′N 13°53′W
64 Q10 Alegranza island Islas Canarias, Spain, NE Atlantic Ocean
37 P12 Alegres Mountain ▲ New Mexico, SW USA 34°09′N 108°11′W
61 F15 Alegrete Rio Grande do Sul, S Brazil 29°46′S 55°46′W
61 C16 Alejandra Santa Fe, C Argentina 29°54′S 59°50′W
193 T11 Alejandro Selkirk, Isla island Islas Juan Fernández, Chile, E Pacific Ocean
124 I12 Alëkhovshchina Leningradskaya Oblast', NW Russian Federation 60°22′N 33°57′E
39 O13 Aleknagik Alaska, USA 59°16′N 158°37′W
Aleksandriya see Oleksandriya
Aleksandropol' see Gyumri
126 L3 Aleksandrov Vladimirskaya Oblast', W Russian Federation 56°24′N 38°42′E
113 N14 Aleksandrovac Serbia, C Serbia 43°28′N 21°05′E
127 R9 Aleksandrov Gay Saratovskaya Oblast', W Russian Federation 50°08′N 48°34′E
127 U6 Aleksandrovka Orenburgskaya Oblast', W Russian Federation 52°47′N 54°14′E
Aleksandrovka see Oleksandrivka
125 V13 Aleksandrovsk Permskiy Kray, NW Russian Federation 59°12′N 57°27′E
Aleksandrovsk see Zaporizhzhya
127 N14 Aleksandrovskoye Stavropol'skiy Kray, SW Russian Federation 44°43′N 42°56′E
123 T12 Aleksandrovsk-Sakhalinskiy Ostrov Sakhalin, Sakhalinskaya Oblast', SE Russian Federation 50°55′N 142°12′E
110 J10 Aleksandrów Kujawski Kujawsko-pormorskie, C Poland 52°52′N 18°40′E
110 K12 Aleksandrów Łódzki Łódzkie, C Poland 51°49′N 19°19′E
114 J8 Aleksandŭr Stamboliyski, Yazovir ▣ N Bulgaria
Alekseevka see Akkol', Akmola, Kazakhstan
Alekseevka see Terekty
145 P7 Alekseyevka Kaz. Alekseevka. Akmola, N Kazakhstan 53°32′N 69°30′E
126 L9 Alekseyevka Belgorodskaya, W Russian Federation 50°35′N 38°41′E
127 S7 Alekseyevka Samarskaya Oblast', W Russian Federation 52°37′N 51°20′E
Alekseyevka see Akkol', Akmola, Kazakhstan
Alekseyevka see Terekty, Vostochnyy Kazakhstan, Kazakhstan
127 R4 Alekseyevskoye Respublika Tatarstan, W Russian Federation 55°18′N 50°11′E
126 K5 Aleksin Tul'skaya Oblast', W Russian Federation 54°30′N 37°08′E
113 O14 Aleksinac Serbia, SE Serbia 43°33′N 21°43′E
190 G11 Alele Île Uvea, E Wallis and Futuna 13°14′S 176°09′W
95 N20 Älem Kalmar, S Sweden 56°57′N 16°25′E
102 L6 Alençon Orne, N France 48°26′N 00°04′E
58 I12 Alenquer Pará, NE Brazil 01°58′S 54°45′W
38 G10 'Alenuihaha Channel var. Alenuihaha Channel. channel Hawai'i, USA, C Pacific Ocean
Alep/Aleppo see Ḥalab
103 Y15 Aléria Corse, France, C Mediterranean Sea 42°06′N 09°29′E
197 Q11 Alert Ellesmere Island, Nunavut, N Canada 82°28′N 62°13′W
103 Q14 Alès prev. Alais. Gard, S France 44°08′N 04°05′E
116 G9 Aleşd Hung. Élesd. Bihor, SW Romania 47°03′N 22°22′E
106 C9 Alessandria Fr. Alexandrie. Piemonte, N Italy 44°54′N 08°37′E
Ålestrup see Aalestrup
94 D9 Ålesund Møre og Romsdal, S Norway 62°28′N 06°11′E
108 E10 Aletschhorn ▲ SW Switzerland 46°33′N 08°01′E
197 S1 Aleutian Basin undersea feature Bering Sea 57°00′N 177°00′E
38 H17 Aleutian Islands island group Alaska, USA
39 P14 Aleutian Range ▲▲ Alaska, USA
0 B5 Aleutian Trench undersea feature S Bering Sea 57°00′N 177°00′W
123 T10 Alevina, Mys cape E Russian Federation
15 Q6 Alex ~ Québec, SE Canada
28 J3 Alexander North Dakota, N USA 47°48′N 103°38′W
39 W14 Alexander Archipelago island group Alaska, USA
Alexanderbaai see Alexander Bay
83 D23 Alexander Bay Afr. Alexanderbaai. Northern Cape, W South Africa 28°40′S 16°30′E
23 Q5 Alexander City Alabama, S USA 32°56′N 85°57′W
194 J6 Alexander Island island Antarctica
Alexander Range see Kirghiz Range
183 O12 Alexandra Victoria, SE Australia 37°12′S 145°43′E
185 D22 Alexandra Otago, South Island, New Zealand 45°15′S 169°25′E
115 F14 Alexándreia var. Alexándria. Kentrikí Makedonía, N Greece 40°38′N 22°27′E
Alexandretta see İskenderun
Alexandretta, Gulf of see İskenderun Körfezi
15 N13 Alexandria Ontario, SE Canada 45°19′N 74°37′W
121 U13 Alexandria Ar. Al Iskandarīyah. N Egypt 31°07′N 29°51′E
44 J12 Alexandria C Jamaica 18°18′N 77°21′W
116 J15 Alexandria Teleorman, S Romania 43°58′N 25°18′E
31 P13 Alexandria Indiana, N USA 40°15′N 85°40′W
20 M4 Alexandria Kentucky, S USA 38°59′N 84°22′W
22 H7 Alexandria Louisiana, S USA 31°19′N 92°27′W
29 T7 Alexandria Minnesota, N USA 45°54′N 95°22′W
29 Q11 Alexandria South Dakota, N USA 43°39′N 97°46′W
21 W4 Alexandria Virginia, NE USA 38°49′N 77°06′W
Alexándria see Alexándreia
18 I7 Alexandria Bay New York, NE USA 44°20′N 75°54′W
Alexandrie see Alessandria
182 J10 Alexandrina, Lake ◎ South Australia
114 K13 Alexandroúpoli var. Alexandroúpolis, Turk. Dedeagaç, Dedeagach. Anatolikí Makedonía kai Thráki, NE Greece 40°52′N 25°53′E
Alexandroúpolis see Alexandroúpoli
10 L15 Alexis Creek British Columbia, SW Canada 52°06′N 123°25′W
122 I13 Aleysk Altayskiy Kray, S Russian Federation 52°32′N 82°46′E
139 S8 Al Fallūjah var. Falluja. Al Anbār, C Iraq 33°21′N 43°46′E
105 R8 Alfambra ~ E Spain
Al Faqa see Faq'
141 R15 Al Farḍah C Yemen 14°51′N 48°33′E
105 Q4 Alfaro La Rioja, N Spain 42°13′N 01°45′W
105 U5 Alfarràs Cataluña, NE Spain 41°50′N 00°34′E
Al Fāshir see El Fasher
75 W8 Al Fashn var. El Fashn. C Egypt 28°49′N 30°54′E
114 M7 Alfatar Silistra, NE Bulgaria 43°56′N 27°17′E
139 S5 Al Fatḥah Ṣalāḥ ad Dīn, C Iraq 35°06′N 43°34′E
139 Q3 Al Fatsī Nīnawá, N Iraq 36°04′N 42°39′E
139 Z13 Al Fāw var. Fao. Al Baṣrah, SE Iraq 29°55′N 48°26′E
75 W8 Al Fayyūm var. El Faiyûm. N Egypt 29°19′N 30°50′E
115 D20 Alfeiós prev. Alfiós; anc. Alpheius, Alpheus. ~ S Greece
100 I13 Alfeld Niedersachsen, C Germany 51°58′N 09°49′E
Alfiós see Alfeiós
Alföld see Great Hungarian Plain
94 C11 Ålfotbreen glacier S Norway
19 P9 Alfred Maine, NE USA 43°29′N 70°44′W
18 F11 Alfred New York, NE USA 42°15′N 77°47′W
61 K14 Alfredo Wagner Santa Catarina, S Brazil 27°40′S 49°22′W
94 M12 Alfta Gävleborg, C Sweden 61°20′N 16°05′E
140 K12 Al Fuḥayḥīl var. Fahaheel. SE Kuwait 29°01′N 48°05′E
139 Q6 Al Fuḥaymī Al Anbār, C Iraq 34°18′N 42°09′E
143 S16 Al Fujayrah Eng. Fujairah. Al Fujayrah, NE United Arab Emirates 25°09′N 56°18′E
143 S16 Al Fujayrah Eng. Fujairah. ✈ Al Fujayrah, NE United Arab Emirates 25°04′N 56°12′E
Al-Furāt see Euphrates
144 I10 Alga Kaz. Algha. Aktyubinsk, NW Kazakhstan 49°56′N 57°19′E
144 G9 Algabas Kaz. Alghabas. Zapadnyy Kazakhstan, NW Kazakhstan 50°43′N 52°09′E
95 C17 Ålgård Rogaland, S Norway 58°45′N 05°52′E
104 G14 Algarve cultural region S Portugal
182 G3 Algebuckina Bridge South Australia 28°03′S 135°48′E
104 K16 Algeciras Andalucía, SW Spain 36°08′N 05°27′W
105 S10 Algemesí Valenciana, E Spain 39°11′N 00°27′W
Al-Genain see El Geneina
120 F9 Alger var. Algiers, El Djazaïr, Al Jazair. ● (Algeria) N Algeria 36°47′N 02°58′E
74 H9 Algeria off. Democratic and Popular Republic of Algeria. ◆ republic N Africa
Algeria, Democratic and Popular Republic of see Algeria
120 J8 Algerian Basin var. Balearic Plain. undersea feature W Mediterranean Sea
Algha see Alga
138 I4 Al Ghāb Valley NW Syria
141 X10 Al Ghābah var. Ghaba. C Oman 21°22′N 57°14′E
Alghabas see Algabas
141 U14 Al Ghayḍah E Yemen 16°15′N 52°13′E
140 M6 Al Ghazālah Ḥā'il, NW Saudi Arabia 26°55′N 41°23′E
107 B17 Alghero Sardegna, Italy, C Mediterranean Sea 40°34′N 08°19′E
95 M20 Älghult Kronoberg, S Sweden 57°00′N 15°34′E
75 X9 Al Ghurdaqah var. Ghurdaqah, Hurghada. E Egypt 27°17′N 33°47′E
Algiers see Alger
105 S10 Alginet Valenciana, E Spain 39°16′N 00°28′W
83 I26 Algoa Bay bay S South Africa
104 L15 Algodonales Andalucía, S Spain 36°54′N 05°24′W
105 N9 Algodor ~ C Spain
Al Golea see El Goléa
31 N6 Algoma Wisconsin, N USA 44°41′N 87°24′W
29 U12 Algona Iowa, C USA 43°04′N 94°13′W
20 L8 Algood Tennessee, S USA 36°12′N 85°27′W
105 O2 Algorta País Vasco, N Spain 43°20′N 03°00′W
61 E18 Algorta Río Negro, W Uruguay 32°26′S 57°18′W
Al Haba see Haba
139 Q10 Al Habbārīyah Al Anbār, S Iraq 32°16′N 42°12′E
Al Hadhar see Al Ḥaḍr
139 Q4 Al Ḥaḍr var. Al Hadhar; anc. Hatra. Nīnawýa, NW Iraq 35°34′N 42°44′E
139 T13 Al Ḥajarah desert S Iraq
141 W8 Al Ḥajar al Gharbī ▲▲ N Oman
141 Y8 Al Ḥajar ash Sharqī ▲▲ NE Oman
141 R15 Al Ḥajarayn C Yemen 15°29′N 48°24′E
138 L10 Al Ḥamād desert Jordan/Saudi Arabia
Al Hamad see Syrian Desert
75 N9 Al Ḥamādah al Ḥamrā' var. Al Ḥamrā'. desert NW Libya
105 N15 Alhama de Granada Andalucía, S Spain 37°00′N 03°59′W
105 R13 Alhama de Murcia Murcia, SE Spain 37°51′N 01°25′W
35 T15 Alhambra California, W USA 34°08′N 118°06′W
139 T12 Al Ḥammām An Najaf, S Iraq 31°09′N 44°04′E
141 X8 Al Ḥamrā' NE Oman 23°07′N 57°23′E
Al Ḥamrā' see Al Ḥamādah al Ḥamrā'
141 O6 Al Ḥamūdīyah spring/well N Saudi Arabia 27°05′N 44°24′E
140 M7 Al Ḥanākīyah Al Madīnah, W Saudi Arabia 24°55′N 40°31′E
139 W14 Al Ḥanīyah escarpment Iraq/Saudi Arabia
139 Y12 Al Ḥārithah Al Baṣrah, SE Iraq 30°43′N 47°44′E
140 L3 Al Ḥarrah desert NW Saudi Arabia
75 Q10 Al Harūj al Aswad desert C Libya
Al Hasaifin see Al Ḥusayfin
139 N2 Al Ḥasakah var. Al Hasijah, El Haseke, Fr. Hassetché. Al Ḥasakah, NE Syria 36°22′N 40°44′E
139 O2 Al Ḥasakah off. Muḥāfaẓat al Ḥasakah, var. Al Hasakah, Al Ḥasakah, Hasakah, Hassakeh. ◈ governorate NE Syria
Al Hasakah see Al Ḥasakah
Al Hasakah see 'Āmūdah
139 T9 Al Hāshimīyah Bābil, C Iraq 32°24′N 44°39′E
138 G13 Al Hāshimīyah Ma'ān, S Jordan 30°31′N 35°46′E
Al Hasijah see Al Ḥasakah
104 M15 Alhaurín el Grande Andalucía, S Spain 36°39′N 04°41′W
141 Q16 Al Ḥawrā S Yemen 13°54′N 47°36′E
139 V10 Al Ḥayy var. Kut al Hai, Kūt al Ḥayy. Wāsiṭ, E Iraq 32°11′N 46°03′E
141 U11 Al Ḥibāk desert E Saudi Arabia
138 H8 Al Hījānah var. Hejanah, Hijanah. Rīf Dimashq, W Syria 33°23′N 36°34′E
140 K7 Al Ḥijāz Eng. Hejaz. physical region NW Saudi Arabia
Al Hilbeh see 'Ulayyānīyah, Bi'r al
139 T9 Al Ḥillah var. Hilla. Bābil, C Iraq 32°28′N 44°29′E
139 T9 Al Hindīyah var. Hindiya. Bābil, C Iraq 32°32′N 44°14′E
138 G12 Al Ḥisā Aṭ Ṭafīlah, W Jordan 30°49′N 35°58′E
74 G5 Al-Hoceïma var. al Hoceima, Al-Hoceima, Alhucemas; prev. Villa Sanjurjo. N Morocco 35°14′N 03°56′W
Alhucemas see Al-Hoceïma
105 N17 Alhucemas, Peñon de island group S Spain
141 N15 Al Ḥudaydah Eng. Hodeida. W Yemen 15°N 42°50′E
141 N15 Al Ḥudaydah var. Hodeida. ✈ W Yemen 14°45′N 43°01′E
140 M4 Al Ḥudūd ash Shamālīyah var. Minṭaqat al Ḥudūd ash Shamālīyah, Eng. Northern Border Region. ◈ province N Saudi Arabia
141 S7 Al Hufūf var. Hofuf. Ash Sharqīyah, NE Saudi Arabia 25°21′N 49°34′E
al-Hurma see Al Khurmah
141 X7 Al Ḥuṣayfīn var. Al Hasaifin. N Oman 24°33′N 56°33′E
138 G9 Al Ḥuṣn var. Husn. Irbid, N Jordan 32°29′N 35°53′E
139 U9 'Alī Wāsiṭ, E Iraq 32°43′N 45°21′E
104 L10 Alia Extremadura, W Spain 39°25′N 05°12′W
143 P9 'Alīābād Yazd, C Iran 36°55′N 54°33′E
'Aliābād see Qā'emshahr
105 S7 Aliaga Aragón, NE Spain 40°40′N 00°42′W
136 B13 Aliağa İzmir, W Turkey 38°49′N 26°59′E
Aliákmon see Aliákmonas
115 F14 Aliákmonas prev. Aliákmon; anc. Haliacmon. ~ N Greece
139 W9 'Alī al Gharbī Maysān, E Iraq 32°28′N 46°42′E
139 U11 'Alī al Ḥassūnī Al Qādisīyah, S Iraq 31°25′N 44°50′E
115 G18 Alíartos Stereá Elláda, C Greece 38°23′N 23°06′E
Äli-Bayramlı see Şirvan
114 P12 Alibey Barajı ▣ NW Turkey
77 S13 Alibori ~ N Benin
112 M10 Alibunar Vojvodina, NE Serbia 45°06′N 20°59′E
105 S12 Alicante Cat. Alacant, Lat. Lucentum. Valenciana, SE Spain 38°21′N 00°29′W
105 S12 Alicante ◈ province Valenciana, SE Spain
105 S12 Alicante ✈ Murcia, E Spain 38°21′N 00°29′W
83 I25 Alice Eastern Cape, S South Africa 32°47′S 26°50′E
25 S14 Alice Texas, SW USA 27°45′N 98°06′W
83 I25 Alicedale Eastern Cape, S South Africa 33°19′S 26°05′E
65 B25 Alice, Mount hill West Falkland, Falkland Islands
107 P20 Alice, Punta headland S Italy 39°24′N 17°09′E
181 Q7 Alice Springs Northern Territory, C Australia 23°42′S 133°52′E
23 N4 Aliceville Alabama, S USA 33°07′N 88°09′W
147 U13 Alichur SE Tajikistan 37°49′N 73°45′E
147 U14 Alichuri Janubí, Qatorkŭhi Rus. Yuzhno-Alichurskiy Khrebet. ▲▲ SE Tajikistan
147 U13 Alichuri Shimolí, Qatorkŭhi Rus. Severo-Alichurskiy Khrebet. ▲▲ SE Tajikistan
107 K22 Alicudi, Isola island Isole Eolie, S Italy
Alifu Atoll see Ari Atoll
43 W14 Aligandí Kuna Yala, NE Panama 09°15′N 78°05′W
152 J11 Alīgarh Uttar Pradesh, N India 27°54′N 78°04′E
142 M7 Alīgūdarz Lorestān, W Iran 33°24′N 49°19′E
163 U5 Alihe var. Oroqen Zizhiqi. Nei Mongol Zizhiqu, N China 50°34′N 123°40′E
0 F12 Alijos, Islas islets California, SW USA
149 R6 'Alī Kbel Pash. 'Alī Khēl. Paktīkā, E Afghanistan 33°55′N 69°49′E
149 R6 'Alī Khēl var. Ali Khel, Jaji; prev. 'Alī Kheyl. Paktīyā, SE Afghanistan 33°55′N 69°46′E
'Alī Khēl see 'Alī Kbel, Paktīkā, Afghanistan
Ali Khel see 'Alī Kheyl, Paktīā, Afghanistan
'Alī Kheyl see 'Alī Khēl
141 V17 Al Ikhwān island group SE Yemen
Aliki see Alykí
79 H19 Alima ~ C Congo
Al Imārāt al 'Arabīyah al Muttaḥidah see United Arab Emirates
115 N23 Alimía island Dodekánisa, Greece, Aegean Sea
55 V12 Alimimuni Piek ▲ S Suriname 02°26′N 55°46′W
79 K15 Alindao Basse-Kotto, S Central African Republic 04°58′N 21°16′E
95 J18 Alingsås Västra Götaland, S Sweden 57°55′N 12°30′E
81 K18 Alinjugul spring/well E Kenya 0°03′S 40°31′E
149 S11 Alīpur Punjab, E Pakistan 29°22′N 70°59′E
153 T12 Alīpur Duār West Bengal, NE India 26°28′N 89°25′E
18 B14 Aliquippa Pennsylvania, NE USA 40°36′N 80°15′W
80 L12 'Ali Sabieh var. 'Alī Sabīḥ. S Djibouti 11°07′N 42°44′E
'Alī Sabīḥ see 'Ali Sabieh
140 K3 Al 'Īsāwīyah Al Jawf, NW Saudi Arabia 30°41′N 37°58′E
104 J10 Aliseda Extremadura, W Spain 39°25′N 06°42′W
139 T8 Al Iskandarīyah Bābil, C Iraq 32°53′N 44°22′E
Al Iskandarīyah see Alexandria
123 T6 Aliskerovo Chukotskiy Avtonomnyy Okrug, NE Russian Federation 67°40′N 167°37′E
75 W7 Al Ismā'īlīya var. Ismailia, Ismâ'ilîya. N Egypt 30°32′N 32°13′E
114 H13 Alistráti Kentrikí Makedonía, NE Greece 41°03′N 23°58′E
39 P15 Alitak Bay bay Kodiak Island, Alaska, USA
Al Ittiḥād see Madīnat ash Sha'b
115 H18 Alivéri var. Alivérion. Évvoia, C Greece 38°24′N 24°02′E
Alivérion see Alivéri
Aliwal-Noord see Aliwal North
83 I24 Aliwal North Afr. Aliwal-Noord. Eastern Cape, SE South Africa 30°42′S 26°43′E
121 Q13 Al Jabal al Akhḍar ▲▲ NE Libya
138 H13 Al Jafr Ma'ān, S Jordan 30°18′N 36°13′E
75 T8 Al Jaghbūb NE Libya 29°45′N 24°31′E
142 K11 Al Jahrā' var. Al Jahrah, Jahra. C Kuwait 29°18′N 47°36′E
Al Jahrah see Al Jahrā'
Al Jamāhīrīyah al 'Arabīyah al Lībīyah ash Sha'bīyah al Ishtirākīy see Libya
140 K3 Al Jarāwī spring/well NW Saudi Arabia 30°12′N 38°48′E
141 X11 Al Jawārah oasis SE Oman
140 L3 Al Jawf off. Jauf. Al Jawf, NW Saudi Arabia 29°51′N 39°49′E
140 L4 Al Jawf var. Minṭaqat al Jawf. ◈ province N Saudi Arabia
Al Jawlān see Golan Heights
Al Jazair see Alger
139 N4 Al Jazīrah physical region Iraq/Syria
104 F14 Aljezur Faro, S Portugal 37°18′N 08°49′W
139 S13 Al Jil An Najaf, S Iraq 30°28′N 43°57′E
138 G11 Al Jīzah var. Jiza. 'Ammān, N Jordan 31°42′N 35°57′E
Al Jīzah see Giza
Al Jubail see Al Jubayl
141 S6 Al Jubayl var. Al Jubail. Ash Sharqīyah, NE Saudi Arabia 27°N 49°36′E
141 T10 Āl Juḥaysh, Qalamat well SE Saudi Arabia
143 N15 Al Jumaylīyah N Qatar 25°37′N 51°05′E
Al Junaynah see El Geneina
104 G13 Aljustrel Beja, S Portugal 37°52′N 08°10′W
Al Kaba'ish see Al Chabā'ish
Al-Kadhimain see Al Kāẓimīyah
Al Kāf see El Kef
Alkal'a see Alcalá de Henares
35 W4 Alkali Flat salt flat Nevada, W USA
35 Q1 Alkali Lake ◎ Nevada, W USA
141 Z9 Al Kāmil NE Oman 22°14′N 58°15′E
138 G11 Al Karak var. El Kerak, Karak, Kerak; anc. Kir Moab, Kir of Moab. Al Karak, W Jordan 31°11′N 35°42′E
138 G12 Al Karak off. Muḥāfaẓat al Karak. ◈ governorate W Jordan
139 W8 Al Karmashīyah Wāsiṭ, E Iraq 32°57′N 46°10′E
Al-Kashaniya see Al Qash'ānīyah
Al-Kasr al-Kebir see Ksar-el-Kebir
139 T8 Al Kāẓimīyah var. Al-Kadhimain, Kadhimain. Baghdād, C Iraq 33°22′N 44°20′E
99 J18 Alken Limburg, NE Belgium 50°52′N 05°19′E
141 X8 Al Khābūrah var. Khabura. N Oman 23°57′N 57°06′E
Al Khalīl see Hebron
139 T7 Al Khāliṣ Diyālá, C Iraq 33°51′N 44°33′E
Al Khaluf see Khalūf
75 W10 Al Khārijah var. El Khârga. C Egypt 25°31′N 30°36′E
141 Q8 Al Kharj Ar Riyāḍ, C Saudi Arabia 24°12′N 47°12′E
141 W6 Al Khaṣab var. Khasab. N Oman 26°11′N 56°18′E
Al Khaur see Al Khawr
143 N15 Al Khawr var. Al Khaur, Al Khor. N Qatar 25°40′N 51°33′E
142 K12 Al Khīrān var. Al Khiran. SE Kuwait 28°34′N 48°21′E
141 W9 Al Khīrān spring/well NW Oman 22°31′N 55°42′E
Al Khiyām see El Khiyam
Al-Khobar see Al Khubar
Al Khor see Al Khawr
141 S6 Al Khubar var. Al-Khobar. Ash Sharqīyah, NE Saudi Arabia 26°00′N 50°00′E
120 M12 Al Khums var. Homs, Khoms, Khums. NW Libya 32°39′N 14°16′E
141 R15 Al Khuraybah C Yemen 15°05′N 48°17′E
140 M9 Al Khurmah var. al-Hurma. Makkah, W Saudi Arabia 21°59′N 42°00′E
141 V9 Al Kidan desert NE Saudi Arabia
127 V4 Alkino-2 Respublika Bashkortostan, W Russian Federation 54°30′N 55°40′E
98 H9 Alkmaar Noord-Holland, NW Netherlands 52°37′N 04°45′E
139 T10 Al Kūfah var. Kufa. An Najaf, S Iraq 32°02′N 44°25′E
75 T11 Al Kufrah SE Libya 24°11′N 23°19′E
141 T10 Al Kursū' desert E Saudi Arabia
139 V9 Al Kūt var. Kūt al 'Amārah, Kut al Imara. Wāsiṭ, E Iraq 32°30′N 45°51′E
Al-Kuwait see Al Kuwayt
Al Kuwayr see Guwēr
142 K11 Al Kuwayt var. Al-Kuwait, Eng. Kuwait, Kuwait City; prev. Qurein. ● (Kuwait) E Kuwait 29°23′N 48°00′E
142 K11 Al Kuwayt ✈ C Kuwait 29°13′N 47°57′E
115 G19 Alkyonídon, Kólpos gulf C Greece
141 N4 Al Labbah physical region N Saudi Arabia
138 G4 Al Lādhiqīyah Eng. Latakia, Fr. Lattaquié; anc. Laodicea, Laodicea ad Mare. Al Lādhiqīyah, W Syria 35°31′N 35°47′E
138 H4 Al Lādhiqīyah off. Muḥāfaẓat al Lādhiqīyah, var. Al Lathqiyah, Latakia, Lattakia. ◈ governorate W Syria
19 R2 Allagash River ~ Maine, NE USA
152 M13 Allahābād Uttar Pradesh, N India 25°27′N 81°50′E
143 S3 Allāh Dāgh, Reshteh-ye ▲▲ NE Iran
39 Q8 Allakaket Alaska, USA 66°34′N 152°39′W
141 X12 Al Lakbī S Oman 18°27′N 56°37′E
11 T15 Allan Saskatchewan, S Canada 51°50′N 105°59′W
Allanmyo see Aunglan
83 I22 Allanridge Free State, C South Africa 27°45′S 26°40′E
104 H4 Allariz Galicia, NW Spain 42°11′N 07°48′W
139 R11 Al Laṣaf var. Al Lussuf. An Najaf, S Iraq 31°38′N 43°16′E
Al Lathqiyah see Al Lādhiqīyah
23 S2 Allatoona Lake ▣ Georgia, SE USA
83 J19 Alldays Limpopo, NE South Africa 22°39′S 29°04′E
Alle see Łyna
31 P10 Allegan Michigan, N USA 42°31′N 85°51′W
18 E14 Allegheny Mountains ▲▲ NE USA
18 E12 Allegheny Plateau ▲▲ New York/Pennsylvania, NE USA
18 D11 Allegheny Reservoir ▣ New York/Pennsylvania, NE USA
18 E12 Allegheny River ~ New York/Pennsylvania, NE USA
22 K9 Allemands, Lac des ◎ Louisiana, S USA
25 U6 Allen Texas, SW USA 33°06′N 96°40′W
21 R14 Allendale South Carolina, SE USA 33°01′N 81°19′W
41 N6 Allende Coahuila, NE Mexico 28°22′N 100°50′W
41 O9 Allende Nuevo León, NE Mexico 25°20′N 100°01′W
97 D16 Allen, Lough Ir. Loch Aillionn. ◎ NW Ireland
185 B26 Allen, Mount ▲ Stewart Island, Southland, SW New Zealand 47°05′S 167°49′E
109 V2 Allensteig Niederösterreich, N Austria 48°40′N 15°24′E
Allenstein see Olsztyn
18 I14 Allentown Pennsylvania, NE USA 40°37′N 75°30′W
155 G23 Alleppey var. Alappuzha. Kerala, SW India 09°30′N 76°22′E see also Alappuzha
100 J12 Aller ~ NW Germany
29 V16 Allerton Iowa, C USA 40°42′N 93°22′W
99 K19 Alleur Liège, E Belgium 50°40′N 05°33′E
101 J25 Allgäuer Alpen ▲▲ Austria/Germany
28 J13 Alliance Nebraska, C USA 42°08′N 102°54′W
31 U12 Alliance Ohio, N USA 40°55′N 81°06′W
103 O10 Allier ◈ department N France
139 R13 Al Līfīyah well An Najaf, S Iraq
44 J13 Alligator Pond C Jamaica 17°52′N 77°34′W
21 Y9 Alligator River ~ North Carolina, SE USA
29 W12 Allison Iowa, C USA 42°45′N 92°48′W
14 G14 Alliston Ontario, S Canada 44°09′N 79°51′W
140 L11 Al Līth Makkah, SW Saudi Arabia 21°N 41°E
Al Liwā' see Līwā
96 J12 Alloa C Scotland, United Kingdom 56°07′N 03°49′W
103 U14 Allos Alpes-de-Haute-Provence, SE France 44°16′N 06°37′E
108 D6 Allschwil Basel Landschaft, NW Switzerland 47°34′N 07°32′E
Al Lubnān see Lebanon
141 N14 Al Luḥayyah W Yemen 15°44′N 42°45′E
14 K12 Allumettes, Île des island Québec, SE Canada
Al Lussuf see Al Laṣaf
109 S5 Alm ~ N Austria
15 Q7 Alma Québec, SE Canada 48°32′N 71°41′W
27 S10 Alma Arkansas, C USA 35°28′N 94°13′W
23 V7 Alma Georgia, SE USA 31°32′N 82°27′W
27 P4 Alma Kansas, C USA 39°01′N 96°17′W
31 Q8 Alma Michigan, N USA 43°22′N 84°39′W
29 O17 Alma Nebraska, C USA 40°06′N 99°21′W
30 I7 Alma Wisconsin, N USA 44°21′N 91°54′W
139 R12 Al Ma'ānīyah well An Najaf, S Iraq
Alma-Ata see Almaty
Alma-Atinskaya Oblast' see Almaty
105 T5 Almacelles Cataluña, NE Spain 41°44′N 00°26′E
104 F11 Almada Setúbal, W Portugal 38°40′N 09°09′W
104 L11 Almadén Castilla-La Mancha, C Spain 38°47′N 04°50′W
Al Madīnah see Medina
66 L6 Almadies, Pointe des headland W Senegal 14°44′N 17°31′W
140 L7 Al Madīnah Eng. Medina. Al Madinah, W Saudi Arabia 24°25′N 39°29′E
140 L7 Al Madīnah off. Minṭaqat al Madīnah. ◈ province W Saudi Arabia
138 H9 Al Mafraq var. Mafraq. Al Mafraq, N Jordan 32°20′N 36°12′E
138 J10 Al Mafraq off. Muḥāfaẓat al Mafraq. ◈ governorate NW Jordan
141 R15 Al Maghārim C Yemen 15°00′N 47°49′E
105 N11 Almagro Castilla-La Mancha, C Spain 38°54′N 03°43′W
Al Maḥallah al Kubrá see El Maḥalla el Kubra
139 T9 Al Maḥāwīl var. Khān al Maḥāwīl. Bābil, C Iraq 32°39′N 44°28′E
Al Mahdīyah see Mahdia
139 T8 Al Maḥmūdīyah var. Mahmudiya. Baghdād, C Iraq 33°04′N 44°22′E
141 T14 Al Mahrah ▲▲ E Yemen
141 P7 Al Majma'ah Ar Riyāḍ, C Saudi Arabia 25°55′N 45°19′E
139 Q11 Al Makmīn well S Iraq
139 Q1 Al Mālikīyah var. Malkiye. Al Ḥasakah, N Syria 37°12′N 42°13′E
Almalyk see Olmaliq
Al Mamlakah see Morocco
Al Mamlaka al Urdunīya al Hashemīyah see Jordan
143 Q18 Al Manādir var. Al Manadir. desert Oman/United Arab Emirates
142 L15 Al Manāmah Eng. Manama. ● (Bahrain) N Bahrain 26°13′N 50°33′E
139 O5 Al Manāṣif ▲▲ E Syria
35 O4 Almanor, Lake ▣ California, W USA
105 R11 Almansa Castilla-La Mancha, C Spain 38°52′N 01°06′W
75 W7 Al Manṣūrah var. Manṣūra, El Manṣûra. N Egypt 31°03′N 31°23′E
104 L3 Almanza Castilla y León, N Spain 42°40′N 05°01′W
104 L8 Almanzor ▲ W Spain 40°13′N 05°18′W
105 P14 Almanzora ~ SE Spain
139 S9 Al Mardah Karbalā', C Iraq 32°35′N 43°30′E
Al-Mariyya see Almeria
75 R7 Al Marj var. Barka, It. Barce. NE Libya 32°30′N 20°54′E
138 L2 Al Mashrafah Ar Raqqah, N Syria 36°25′N 39°07′E
141 X8 Al Maṣna'ah var. Al Muṣana'a. NE Oman 23°45′N 57°38′E
Almassora see Almazora
Almatinskaya Oblast' see Almaty
145 U15 Almaty var. Alma-Ata. Almaty, SE Kazakhstan 43°19′N 76°55′E
145 S14 Almaty off. Almatinskaya Oblast', Kaz. Almaty Oblysy; prev. Alma-Atinskaya Oblast'. ◈ province SE Kazakhstan
145 U15 Almaty ✈ Almaty, SE Kazakhstan 43°15′N 76°57′E
Almaty Oblysy see Almaty
al-Mawailih see Al Muwayliḥ
139 R3 Al Mawṣil Eng. Mosul. Nīnawá, N Iraq 36°21′N 43°08′E
139 N5 Al Mayādīn var. Mayadin, Fr. Meyadine. Dayr az Zawr, E Syria 35°00′N 40°31′E
139 X10 Al Maymūnah var. Maimuna. Maysān, SE Iraq 31°43′N 46°55′E
141 N5 Al Mayyāh Ḥā'il, N Saudi Arabia 27°57′N 42°53′E
Al Ma'zam see Al Ma'zim
105 P6 Almazán Castilla y León, N Spain 41°29′N 02°31′W
141 W8 Al Ma'zim var. Al Ma'zam. NW Oman 23°22′N 56°16′E
123 N11 Almaznyy Respublika Sakha (Yakutiya), NE Russian Federation 62°19′N 114°14′E
105 T9 Almazora Cat. Almassora. Valenciana, E Spain 39°55′N 00°02′W
Al Mazra' see Al Mazra'ah
138 G11 Al Mazra'ah var. Al Mazra', Mazra'a. Al Karak, W Jordan 31°18′N 35°32′E
101 G15 Alme ~ W Germany
104 I7 Almeida Guarda, N Portugal 40°43′N 06°53′W
104 G10 Almeirim Santarém, C Portugal 39°12′N 08°37′W
98 O10 Almelo Overijssel, E Netherlands 52°22′N 06°42′E
105 S9 Almenara Valenciana, E Spain 39°46′N 00°14′W
105 P12 Almenaras ▲ S Spain 38°31′N 02°27′W
105 P5 Almenar de Soria Castilla y León, N Spain 41°41′N 02°12′W
104 J6 Almendra, Embalse de ▣ Castilla y León, NW Spain
104 J11 Almendralejo Extremadura, W Spain 38°41′N 06°25′W
98 J10 Almere var. Almere-stad. Flevoland, C Netherlands 52°22′N 05°12′E
98 J10 Almere-Buiten Flevoland, C Netherlands 52°24′N 05°15′E
98 J10 Almere-Haven Flevoland, C Netherlands 52°20′N 05°13′E
Almere-stad see Almere
105 P15 Almería Ar. Al-Mariyya; anc. Unci, Lat. Portus Magnus. Andalucía, S Spain 36°50′N 02°26′W
105 P14 Almería ◈ province Andalucía, S Spain
105 P15 Almería, Golfo de gulf S Spain
127 S5 Al'met'yevsk Respublika Tatarstan, W Russian Federation 54°53′N 52°20′E
95 L21 Älmhult Kronoberg, S Sweden 56°32′N 14°10′E
141 U9 Al Miḥrāḍ desert NE Saudi Arabia
Al Mīnā' see El Mina
104 L17 Almina, Punta headland Ceuta, Spain, N Africa 35°54′N 05°16′W
75 W9 Al Minyā var. El Minya, Minya. C Egypt 28°06′N 30°40′E
Al Miqdādīyah see Al Muqdādiyah
43 P14 Almirante Bocas del Toro, NW Panama 09°20′N 82°22′W
Almirós see Almyrós
140 M9 Al Mislaḥ spring/well W Saudi Arabia 22°46′N 40°47′E
Almissa see Omiš
104 G13 Almodóvar var. Almodôvar. Beja, S Portugal 37°31′N 08°03′W

104 M11 **Almodóvar del Campo** Castilla-La Mancha, C Spain 38°43′N 04°10′W
105 Q9 **Almodóvar del Pinar** Castilla-La Mancha, C Spain 39°44′N 01°55′W
31 S9 **Almont** Michigan, N USA 42°53′N 83°02′W
14 L13 **Almonte** Ontario, SE Canada 45°13′N 76°12′W
104 J14 **Almonte** Andalucía, S Spain 37°16′N 06°31′W
104 K9 **Almonte** ≈ W Spain
152 K9 **Almora** Uttarakhand, N India 29°36′N 79°40′E
104 M8 **Almorox** Castilla-La Mancha, C Spain 40°13′N 04°22′W
141 S7 **Al Mubarraz** Ash Sharqīyah, E Saudi Arabia 25°28′N 49°34′E
Al Muḍaibī see Al Muḍaybī
138 G15 **Al Mudawwarah** Ma'ān, SW Jordan 29°20′N 36°E
141 Y9 **Al Muḍaybī** var. Al Muḍaibī. NE Oman 22°35′N 58°08′E
Almudébar see Almudévar
105 S5 **Almudévar** var. Almudébar. Aragón, NE Spain 42°03′N 00°34′W
141 S15 **Al Mukallā** var. Mukalla. SE Yemen 14°36′N 49°07′E
141 N16 **Al Mukhā** Eng. Mocha. SW Yemen 13°18′N 43°17′E
105 N15 **Almuñécar** Andalucía, S Spain 36°44′N 03°41′W
139 U7 **Al Muqdādīyah** var. Al Miqdādīyah. Diyālá, C Iraq 33°58′N 44°58′E
140 L3 **Al Murayr** spring/well NW Saudi Arabia 30°06′N 39°54′E
136 M12 **Almus** Tokat, N Turkey 40°22′N 36°54′E
Al Muşana'a see Al Maşna'ah
139 T9 **Al Musayyib** var. Musaiyib. Bābil, C Iraq 32°47′N 44°20′E
139 V9 **Al Muwaffaqīyah** Wāsiţ, S Iraq 32°19′N 45°22′E
138 H10 **Al Muwaqqar** var. El Muwaqqar. 'Ammān, W Jordan 31°49′N 36°06′E
140 J5 **Al Muwayliḩ** var. al-Mawailih. Tabūk, NW Saudi Arabia 27°39′N 35°33′E
115 F17 **Almyrós** var. Almiros. Thessalía, C Greece 39°11′N 22°45′E
115 I24 **Almyroú, Órmos** bay Kríti, Greece, E Mediterranean Sea
Al Nūwfalīyah see An Nawfalīyah
96 L13 **Alnwick** N England, United Kingdom 55°27′N 01°44′W
Al Obayyid see El Obeid
Al Odaid see Al 'Udayd
190 B16 **Alofi** ○ (Niue) W Niue 19°01′S 169°55′E
190 A16 **Alofi Bay** bay W Niue, C Pacific Ocean
190 E13 **Alofi, Île** island S Wallis and Futuna
190 E13 **Alofitai** Île Alofi, W Wallis and Futuna 14°21′S 178°03′W
Aloha State see Hawai'i
118 G7 **Aloja** N Latvia 57°47′N 24°53′E
153 X10 **Along** Arunāchal Pradesh, NE India 28°15′N 94°56′E
115 H16 **Alónnisos** island Vóreies Sporádes, Greece, Aegean Sea
104 M15 **Álora** Andalucía, S Spain 36°50′N 04°43′W
171 Q16 **Alor, Kepulauan** island group E Indonesia
171 Q16 **Alor, Pulau** prev. Ombai. island Kepulauan Alor, E Indonesia
171 O16 **Alor, Selat** strait Flores Sea/Savu Sea
168 I7 **Alor Setar** var. Alor Star, Alur Setar. Kedah, Peninsular Malaysia 06°06′N 100°23′E
Alor Star see Alor Setar
Alost see Aalst
154 F9 **Ālot** Madhya Pradesh, C India 23°56′N 75°40′E
186 G10 **Alotau** Milne Bay, SE Papua New Guinea 10°20′S 150°23′E
171 Y16 **Alotip** Papua, E Indonesia 08°07′S 140°06′E
Al Oued see El Oued
35 R12 **Alpaugh** California, W USA 35°52′N 119°29′W
Alpen see Alps
31 R6 **Alpena** Michigan, N USA 45°04′N 83°27′W
Alpes see Alps
103 S14 **Alpes-de-Haute-Provence** ◈ department SE France
103 U14 **Alpes-Maritimes** ◈ department SE France
181 W8 **Alpha** Queensland, E Australia 23°40′S 146°38′E
197 R9 **Alpha Cordillera** var. Alpha Ridge. undersea feature Arctic Ocean 85°30′N 125°00′W
Alpha Ridge see Alpha Cordillera
Alpheius see Alfeiós
99 I15 **Alphen** Noord-Brabant, S Netherlands 51°29′N 04°57′E
Alphen see Alphen aan den Rijn
98 H11 **Alphen aan den Rijn** var. Alphen. Zuid-Holland, C Netherlands 52°08′N 04°40′E
Alpheus see Alfeiós
Alpi see Alps
104 G10 **Alpiarça** Santarém, C Portugal 39°15′N 08°35′W
24 K10 **Alpine** Texas, SW USA 30°22′N 103°40′W
108 F8 **Alpnach** Unterwalden, W Switzerland 46°56′N 08°17′E
108 D11 **Alps** Fr. Alpes, Ger. Alpen, It. Alpi. ▲ C Europe
141 W8 **Al Qābil** var. Qabil. N Oman 23°55′N 55°50′E
Al Qaḍārif see Gedaref
75 P8 **Al Qaddāḩīyah** N Libya 31°21′N 15°16′E
Al Qāhirah see Cairo
140 K4 **Al Qalībah** Tabūk, NW Saudi Arabia 28°29′N 37°40′E
139 O1 **Al Qāmishlī** var. Kamishli, Qamishly. Al Ḩasakah, NE Syria 37°N 41°E
138 I6 **Al Qaryatayn** var. Qaryatayn, Fr. Qariateïne. Ḩimş, C Syria 34°13′N 37°13′E
142 K11 **Al Qash'ānīyah** var. Al-Kashaniya. NE Kuwait 29°59′N 47°42′E
141 N7 **Al Qaşīm** var. Minţaqat Qaşīm, Qassim. ◈ province C Saudi Arabia
75 V10 **Al Qaşr** var. Al Qaşr var. El Qasr. C Egypt 25°43′N 28°54′E
138 J5 **Al Qaşr** Ḩimş, C Syria 35°06′N 37°39′E
Al Qaşr see Al Qaşr
Al Qaşrayn see Kasserine
141 S6 **Al Qaţīf** Ash Sharqīyah, NE Saudi Arabia 26°27′N 50°01′E
138 G11 **Al Qaţrānah** var. El Qatrani, Qatrana. Al Karak, W Jordan 31°14′N 36°03′E
75 P11 **Al Qaţrūn** SW Libya 24°57′N 14°40′E
Al Qayrawān see Kairouan
Al-Qsar al-Kbir see Ksar-el-Kebir
Al Qubayyāt see Qoubaïyât
Al Quds/Al Quds ash Sharīf see Jerusalem
104 H12 **Alqueva, Barragem do** ⊞ Portugal/Spain
138 G8 **Al Qunayţirah** var. El Kuneitra, El Quneitra, Kuneitra, Qunaytra. Al Qunayţirah, SW Syria 33°08′N 35°49′E
138 G8 **Al Qunayţirah** off. Muḩāfaẓat al Qunayţirah, var. El Q'unayţirah, Qunaytirah, Fr. Kuneitra. ◈ governorate SW Syria
140 M11 **Al Qunfudhah** Makkah, SW Saudi Arabia 19°19′N 41°03′E
140 K2 **Al Qurayyāt** Al Jawf, NW Saudi Arabia 31°25′N 37°26′E
139 Y11 **Al Qurnah** var. Kurna. Al Başrah, SE Iraq 31°01′N 47°27′E
75 Y10 **Al Quşayr** var. Al Quşayr var. Qusair, Quseir. E Egypt 26°05′N 34°16′E
139 V12 **Al Quşayr** Al Muthannā, S Iraq 30°36′N 45°52′E
138 I6 **Al Quşayr** var. El Quseir, Quşayr, Fr. Kousseir. Ḩimş, W Syria 34°36′N 36°36′E
Al Quşayr see Al Quşayr
138 H7 **Al Quţayfah** var. Quţayfah, Qutayfe, Quteife, Fr. Kouteifé. Rīf Dimashq, W Syria 33°44′N 36°33′E
141 P8 **Al Quwayīyah** Ar Riyāḑ, C Saudi Arabia 24°06′N 45°18′E
Al Quwayr see Guwēr
138 F14 **Al Quwayrah** var. El Quweira. Al 'Aqabah, SW Jordan 29°47′E 35°18′E
Al Rayyan see Ar Rayyān
Al Ruweis see Ar Ruways
95 G24 **Als** Ger. Alsen. island SW Denmark
103 U5 **Alsace** Ger. Elsass; anc. Alsatia. ◈ region NE France
11 R16 **Alsask** Saskatchewan, S Canada 51°24′N 109°55′W
Alsasua see Altsasu
Alsatia see Alsace
101 C16 **Alsdorf** Nordrhein-Westfalen, W Germany 50°52′N 06°09′E
10 G8 **Alsek** ≈ Canada/USA
Alsen see Als
101 F19 **Alsenz** ≈ W Germany
101 H17 **Alsfeld** Hessen, C Germany 50°45′N 09°14′E
119 K20 **Al'shany** Rus. Ol'shany. Brestskaya Voblasts', SW Belarus 52°05′N 27°21′E
Alsókubin see Dolný Kubín
118 C9 **Alsunga** W Latvia 56°59′N 21°31′E
Alt see Olt
92 K9 **Alta** Fin. Alattio. Finnmark, N Norway 69°58′N 23°17′E
29 T12 **Alta** Iowa, C USA 42°40′N 95°17′W
108 I7 **Altach** Vorarlberg, W Austria 47°22′N 09°39′E
92 K9 **Altaelva** Lapp. Álaheaieatnu. ≈ N Norway
92 J8 **Altafjorden** fjord NE Norwegian Sea
62 K10 **Alta Gracia** Córdoba, C Argentina 31°42′S 64°25′W
42 K11 **Alta Gracia** Rivas, SW Nicaragua 11°35′N 85°38′W
54 H4 **Altagracia** Zulia, NW Venezuela 10°44′N 71°30′W
54 M5 **Altagracia de Orituco** Guárico, N Venezuela 09°54′N 66°24′W
Altai see Altai Mountains
129 T7 **Altai Mountains** var. Altai, Chin. Altay Shan, Rus. Altay. ▲ Asia/Europe
23 V6 **Altamaha River** ≈ Georgia, SE USA
58 J13 **Altamira** Pará, NE Brazil 03°13′S 52°15′W
54 D12 **Altamira** Huila, S Colombia 02°04′N 75°47′W
42 M13 **Altamira** Alajuela, N Costa Rica 10°25′N 84°21′W
41 Q11 **Altamira** Tamaulipas, C Mexico 22°25′N 97°55′W
30 L15 **Altamont** Illinois, N USA 39°03′N 88°45′W
27 Q7 **Altamont** Kansas, C USA 37°11′N 95°18′W
32 H16 **Altamont** Oregon, NW USA 42°12′N 121°44′W
20 K10 **Altamont** Tennessee, S USA 35°28′N 85°42′W
23 X11 **Altamonte Springs** Florida, SE USA 28°39′N 81°22′W
107 O17 **Altamura** anc. Lupatia. Puglia, SE Italy 40°50′N 16°33′E
40 H9 **Altamura, Isla** island C Mexico
Altan see Erdenehayrhan
Altanbulag see Bayanhayrhan
163 Q7 **Altan Emel** var. Xin Barag Youqi. Nei Mongol Zizhiqu, N China 48°37′N 116°40′E
Altan-Ovoo see Tsenher
163 N9 **Altanshiree** var. Chamdmanī. Dornigovĭ, SE Mongolia 45°36′N 110°30′E
Altanteel see Dzereg
162 D5 **Altantsögts** var. Tsagaantüngi. Bayan-Ölgiy, NW Mongolia 49°06′N 90°26′E
40 F3 **Altar** Sonora, NW Mexico 30°41′N 111°53′W
40 D2 **Altar, Desierto de** var. Sonoran Desert. desert Mexico/USA see also Sonoran Desert
Altar, Desierto de see Sonoran Desert
105 Q8 **Alta, Sierra** ▲ N Spain 40°29′N 01°36′W
40 H9 **Altata** Sinaloa, C Mexico 24°40′N 107°54′W
42 D4 **Alta Verapaz** off. Departamento de Alta Verapaz. ◈ department C Guatemala
Alta Verapaz, Departamento de see Alta Verapaz
107 L18 **Altavilla Silentia** Campania, S Italy 40°32′N 15°06′E
21 T7 **Altavista** Virginia, NE USA 37°06′N 79°17′W
158 L2 **Altay** Xinjiang Uygur Zizhiqu, NW China 47°51′N 88°06′E
162 D6 **Altay** var. Chihertey. Bayan-Ölgiy, W Mongolia 48°10′N 89°35′E
162 G8 **Altay** prev. Yösönbulag. Govĭ-Altay, W Mongolia 46°23′N 96°17′E
162 E8 **Altay** var. Bor-Üdzüür. Hovd, W Mongolia 45°46′N 92°13′E
Altay see Altai Mountains, Asia/Europe
Altay see Bayantes, Mongolia
122 J14 **Altay, Respublika** var. Gornyy Altay; prev. Gorno-Altayskaya Respublika. ◈ autonomous republic S Russian Federation
Altay Shan see Altai Mountains
123 I13 **Altayskiy Kray** ◈ territory S Russian Federation
Altbetsche see Bečej
101 L20 **Altdorf** Bayern, SE Germany 49°23′N 11°22′E
108 G8 **Altdorf** var. Altorf. Uri, C Switzerland 46°53′N 08°38′E
105 T11 **Altea** Valenciana, E Spain 38°37′N 00°03′W
100 L10 **Alte Elde** ≈ N Germany
101 M16 **Altenburg** Thüringen, E Germany 50°59′N 12°27′E
Altenburg see București, Romania
Altenburg see Baia de Criș, Romania
100 P12 **Alte Oder** ≈ NE Germany
104 H10 **Alter do Chão** Portalegre, C Portugal 39°12′N 07°40′W
92 I10 **Áltevatnet** Lapp. Álttesjávri. ◎ N Norway
27 V12 **Altheimer** Arkansas, C USA 34°19′N 91°51′W
109 T9 **Althofen** Kärnten, S Austria 46°52′N 14°27′E
114 H7 **Altimir** Vratsa, NW Bulgaria 43°33′N 23°48′E
136 K11 **Altınkaya Barajı** ⊞ N Turkey
139 S3 **Altin Köprü** var. Altun Kupri. At Ta'mīm, N Iraq 35°50′N 44°10′E
136 E13 **Altıntaş** Kütahya, W Turkey 39°05′N 30°07′E
57 K18 **Altiplano** physical region W South America
Altkanischa see Kanjiža
103 U7 **Altkirch** Haut-Rhin, NE France 47°37′N 07°14′E
Altlublau see Stará L'ubovňa
100 L12 **Altmark** cultural region N Germany
Altmoldowa see Moldova Veche
25 W8 **Alto** Texas, SW USA 31°39′N 95°04′W
104 H11 **Alto Alentejo** physical region S Portugal
59 I19 **Alto Araguaia** Mato Grosso, C Brazil 17°19′S 53°10′W
58 L12 **Alto Bonito** Pará, NE Brazil 01°48′S 46°18′W
83 O15 **Alto Molócuè** Zambézia, NE Mozambique 15°38′S 37°42′E
30 K15 **Alton** Illinois, N USA 38°53′N 90°10′W
27 W8 **Alton** Missouri, C USA 36°41′N 91°25′W
11 X17 **Altona** Manitoba, S Canada 49°06′N 97°33′W
18 E14 **Altoona** Pennsylvania, NE USA 40°32′N 78°23′W
30 J6 **Altoona** Wisconsin, N USA 44°49′N 91°22′W
62 N3 **Alto Paraguay** off. Departamento del Alto Paraguay. ◈ department N Paraguay
Alto Paraguay, Departamento del see Alto Paraguay
59 L17 **Alto Paraíso de Goiás** Goiás, S Brazil 14°04′S 47°15′W
62 P6 **Alto Paraná** off. Departamento del Alto Paraná. ◈ department E Paraguay
Alto Paraná see Paraná
Alto Paraná, Departamento del see Alto Paraná
59 L15 **Alto Parnaíba** Maranhão, E Brazil 09°08′S 45°56′W
56 H13 **Alto Purús, Río** ≈ E Peru
Altorf see Altdorf
63 H19 **Alto Río Senguer** var. Alto Río Senguerr. Chubut, S Argentina 45°01′S 70°55′W
Alto Río Senguerr see Alto Río Senguer
41 Q13 **Altotonga** Veracruz-Llave, E Mexico 19°46′N 97°14′W
101 N23 **Altötting** Bayern, SE Germany 48°12′N 12°37′E
Altpasua see Stara Pazova
Altraga see Bayandzürh
105 P3 **Altsasu** Cast. Alsasua. Navarra, N Spain 42°54′N 02°10′W
Alt-Schwanenburg see Gulbene
Altsohl see Zvolen
108 I7 **Altstätten** Sankt Gallen, NE Switzerland 47°22′N 09°33′E
Álttesjávri see Altevatnet
42 G1 **Altun Ha** ruins Belize, N Belize
Altun Kupri see Altin Köprü
158 D8 **Altun Shan** ▲ C China 39°19′N 93°37′E
158 L9 **Altun Shan** var. Altyn Tagh. ▲ NW China
35 P2 **Alturas** California, W USA 41°28′N 120°32′W
26 K12 **Altus** Oklahoma, C USA 34°39′N 99°21′W
26 K11 **Altus Lake** ⊞ Oklahoma, C USA
Altvater see Praděd
Altyn Tagh see Altun Shan
Alu see Shortland Island
al-'Ubaila see Al 'Ubaylah
139 O6 **Al 'Ubaydī** Al Anbār, W Iraq 34°22′N 41°15′E
141 T9 **Al 'Ubaylah** var. al-'Ubaila. Ash Sharqīyah, E Saudi Arabia 22°02′N 50°57′E
141 T9 **Al 'Ubaylah** spring/well E Saudi Arabia 22°02′N 50°56′E
Al Ubayyid see El Obeid
141 T7 **Al 'Udayd** var. Al Odaid. Abū Ẓaby, W United Arab Emirates 24°34′N 51°27′E
118 J8 **Alūksne** Ger. Marienburg. NE Latvia 57°26′N 27°02′E
140 K6 **Al 'Ulā** Al Madīnah, NW Saudi Arabia 26°39′N 37°55′E
173 N4 **Alula-Fartak Trench** var. Illaue Fartak Trench. undersea feature W Indian Ocean 14°04′N 51°47′E
138 I11 **Al 'Umarī** 'Ammān, E Jordan 37°30′N 31°30′E
31 S13 **Alum Creek Lake** ⊞ Ohio, N USA
63 H15 **Aluminé** Neuquén, C Argentina 39°15′S 71°00′W
95 O14 **Alunda** Uppsala, C Sweden 60°04′N 18°04′E
117 T14 **Alupka** Avtonomna Respublika Krym, S Ukraine 44°24′N 34°01′E
75 P8 **Al 'Uqaylah** N Libya 30°13′N 19°12′E
Al Uqşur see Luxor
Al Urdunn see Jordan
168 J9 **Alur Panal** bay Sumatera, W Indonesia
Alur Setar see Alor Setar
141 V10 **Al 'Urūq al Mu'tariḑah** salt lake SE Saudi Arabia
139 Q7 **Ālūs** Al Anbār, C Iraq 34°05′N 42°27′E
117 T13 **Alushta** Avtonomna Respublika Krym, S Ukraine 44°41′N 34°24′E
151 G22 **Aluva** var. Alwaye. Kerala, SW India 10°06′N 76°23′E see also Alwaye
75 N11 **Al 'Uwaynāt** var. Al Awaynāt. SW Libya 25°47′N 10°34′E
139 T6 **Al 'Uẓaym** var. Adhaim. Diyālá, E Iraq 34°12′N 44°31′E
26 L8 **Alva** Oklahoma, C USA 36°48′N 98°40′W
104 H8 **Alva** ≈ N Portugal
95 J18 **Älvängen** Västra Götaland, S Sweden 57°56′N 12°09′E
14 F14 **Alvanley** Ontario, S Canada 44°33′N 81°05′W
41 S14 **Alvarado** Veracruz-Llave, E Mexico 18°47′N 95°45′W
25 T7 **Alvarado** Texas, SW USA 32°24′N 97°12′W
58 D13 **Alvarães** Amazonas, NW Brazil 03°13′S 64°53′W
40 G6 **Álvaro Obregón, Presa** ⊞ W Mexico
94 H10 **Alvdal** Hedmark, S Norway 62°07′N 10°39′E
94 K12 **Älvdalen** Dalarna, C Sweden 61°13′N 14°04′E
61 E15 **Alvear** Corrientes, NE Argentina 29°05′S 56°35′W
104 F10 **Alverca do Ribatejo** Lisboa, C Portugal 38°56′N 09°01′W
95 L20 **Alvesta** Kronoberg, S Sweden 56°52′N 14°34′E
25 W12 **Alvin** Texas, SW USA 29°25′N 95°14′W
95 O13 **Älvkarleby** Uppsala, C Sweden 60°34′N 17°30′E
25 S5 **Alvord** Texas, SW USA 33°22′N 97°39′W
93 G18 **Älvros** Jämtland, C Sweden 62°04′N 14°30′E
92 J13 **Älvsbyn** Norrbotten, N Sweden 65°41′N 21°00′E
142 K12 **Al Wafrā'** SE Kuwait 28°38′N 47°57′E
140 J6 **Al Wajh** Tabūk, NW Saudi Arabia 26°16′N 36°30′E
143 N16 **Al Wakrah** var. Wakra. C Qatar 25°09′N 51°36′E
138 M8 **al Walaj, Sha'īb** dry watercourse W Iraq
152 I11 **Alwar** Rājasthān, N India 27°32′N 76°35′E
141 Q5 **Al Wari'ah** Ash Sharqīyah, N Saudi Arabia 27°54′N 47°23′E
155 G22 **Alwaye** var. Aluva. Kerala, SW India 10°06′N 76°23′E see also Aluva
Alxa Zuoqi see Bayan Hot
Alx Youqi see Ehen Hudag
Al Yaman see Yemen
138 G9 **Al Yarmūk** Irbid, N Jordan 32°41′N 35°55′E
Alyat/Alyaty-Pristan' see Ālāt
115 I14 **Alykí** var. Aliki. Thásos, N Greece 40°36′N 24°45′E
119 F15 **Alytus** Pol. Olita. Alytus, S Lithuania 54°24′N 24°02′E
119 F15 **Alytus** ◈ province S Lithuania
101 N23 **Alz** ≈ SE Germany
33 Y11 **Alzada** Montana, NW USA 45°00′N 104°24′W
122 L12 **Alzamay** Irkutskaya Oblast', S Russian Federation 55°33′N 98°36′E
99 M25 **Alzette** ≈ S Luxembourg
105 S10 **Alzira** var. Alcira; anc. Saetabicula, Suero. Valenciana, E Spain 39°10′N 00°27′W
Al Zubair see Az Zubayr
181 O8 **Amadeus, Lake** seasonal lake Northern Territory, C Australia
81 E15 **Amadi** Western Equatoria, SW South Sudan 05°32′N 30°20′E
9 R7 **Amadjuak Lake** ◎ Baffin Island, Nunavut, N Canada
95 J23 **Amager** island E Denmark
165 N14 **Amagi-san** ▲ Honshū, S Japan 34°51′N 138°57′E
171 S13 **Amahai** var. Masohi. Pulau Seram, E Indonesia 03°19′S 128°56′E
38 M16 **Amak Island** island Alaska, USA
164 C15 **Amakusa** prev. Hondo. Kumamoto, Shimo-jima, SW Japan 32°28′N 130°12′E
164 B14 **Amakusa-nada** gulf SW Japan
95 J16 **Åmål** Västra Götaland, S Sweden 59°04′N 12°41′E
54 E8 **Amalfi** Antioquia, N Colombia 06°54′N 75°04′W
107 L18 **Amalfi** Campania, S Italy 40°37′N 14°35′E
115 D19 **Amaliáda** var. Amaliás. Dytikí Elláda, S Greece 37°48′N 21°21′E
Amaliás see Amaliáda
154 F12 **Amalner** Mahārāshtra, C India 21°03′N 75°04′E
171 W14 **Amamapare** Papua, E Indonesia 04°51′S 136°44′E
59 H21 **Amambaí, Serra de** var. Cordillera de Amambay, Serra de Amambay. ▲ Brazil/Paraguay see also Amambay, Cordillera de
62 P4 **Amambay** off. Departamento del Amambay. ◈ department E Paraguay
62 P5 **Amambay, Cordillera de** var. Serra de Amambaí, Serra de Amambay. ▲ Brazil/Paraguay see also Amambaí, Serra de
Amambay, Departamento del see Amambay
Amambay, Serra de see Amambaí, Serra de/Amambay, Cordillera de
165 U16 **Amami-guntō** island group SW Japan
165 V15 **Amami-Ō-shima** island S Japan
186 A5 **Amanab** Sandaun, NW Papua New Guinea 03°38′S 141°16′E
106 J13 **Amandola** Marche, C Italy 42°58′N 13°22′E
107 N21 **Amantea** Calabria, SW Italy 39°06′N 16°05′E
191 W10 **Amanu** island Îles Tuamotu, C French Polynesia
58 J10 **Amapá** Amapá, NE Brazil 02°00′N 50°50′W
58 J11 **Amapá** off. Estado de Amapá; prev. Território de Amapá. ◈ state NE Brazil
Amapá, Estado de see Amapá
42 H8 **Amapala** Valle, S Honduras 13°16′N 87°39′W
Amapá, Território de see Amapá
80 J12 **Āmara** var. Amhara. ◈ N Ethiopia
Amara see Al 'Amārah
104 H6 **Amarante** Porto, N Portugal 41°16′N 08°05′W
166 M5 **Amarapura** Mandalay, C Myanmar (Burma) 21°54′N 96°01′E
Amardalay see Delgertsogt
104 I12 **Amareleja** Beja, S Portugal 38°12′N 07°13′W
35 V11 **Amargosa Range** ▲ California, W USA
25 N2 **Amarillo** Texas, SW USA 35°13′N 101°50′W
Amarinthos see Amárynthos
107 K15 **Amaro, Monte** ▲ C Italy 42°03′N 14°06′E
115 H18 **Amárynthos** var. Amarinthos. Évvoia, C Greece 38°24′N 23°53′E
Amasia see Amasya
136 K12 **Amasya** anc. Amasia. Amasya, N Turkey 40°37′N 35°50′E
136 K11 **Amasya** ◈ province N Turkey
42 F4 **Amatique, Bahía de** bay Gulf of Honduras, W Caribbean Sea
42 D6 **Amatitlán, Lago de** ◎ S Guatemala
107 J14 **Amatrice** Lazio, C Italy 42°38′N 13°19′E
190 C8 **Amatuku** atoll C Tuvalu
99 J20 **Amay** Liège, E Belgium 50°33′N 05°19′E
48 F7 **Amazon** Sp. Amazonas. ≈ Brazil/Peru
59 C14 **Amazonas** off. Estado do Amazonas. ◈ state N Brazil
54 G15 **Amazonas** off. Comisaria del Amazonas. ◈ province SE Colombia
56 C10 **Amazonas** off. Departamento de Amazonas. ◈ department N Peru
54 M12 **Amazonas** off. Territorio Amazonas. ◈ federal territory S Venezuela
Amazonas see Amazon
Amazonas, Comisaria del see Amazonas
Amazonas, Departamento de see Amazonas
Amazonas, Estado do see Amazonas
Amazonas, Territorio see Amazonas
48 F7 **Amazon Basin** basin N South America
47 V5 **Amazon Fan** undersea feature W Atlantic Ocean 05°00′N 47°30′W
58 K11 **Amazon, Mouths of the** delta NE Brazil
187 R13 **Ambae** var. Aoba, Omba. island C Vanuatu
152 I9 **Ambāla** Haryāna, NW India 30°19′N 76°49′E
155 J26 **Ambalangoda** Southern Province, SW Sri Lanka 06°14′N 80°03′E
155 K26 **Ambalantota** Southern Province, S Sri Lanka 06°07′N 81°01′E
172 I6 **Ambalavao** Fianarantsoa, C Madagascar 21°50′S 46°56′E
54 E10 **Ambalema** Tolima, C Colombia 04°49′N 74°48′W
79 E17 **Ambam** Sud, S Cameroon 02°23′N 11°17′E
172 J2 **Ambanja** Antsiranana, N Madagascar 13°40′S 48°27′E
123 T6 **Ambarchik** Respublika Sakha (Yakutiya), NE Russian Federation 69°33′N 162°08′E
62 K9 **Ambargasta, Salinas de** salt lake C Argentina
124 J6 **Ambarnyy** Respublika Kareliya, NW Russian Federation 65°53′N 33°44′E
56 C7 **Ambato** Tungurahua, C Ecuador 01°18′S 78°39′W
172 I6 **Ambato Finandrahana** Fianarantsoa, SE Madagascar 20°33′S 46°48′E
172 I5 **Ambatolampy** Antananarivo, C Madagascar 19°21′S 47°27′E
172 H4 **Ambatomainty** Mahajanga, W Madagascar 17°40′S 45°39′E
172 J4 **Ambatondrazaka** Toamasina, C Madagascar 17°49′S 48°28′E
101 L20 **Amberg** var. Amberg in der Oberpfalz. Bayern, SE Germany 49°26′N 11°52′E
Amberg in der Oberpfalz see Amberg
42 H1 **Ambergris Cay** island NE Belize
103 S11 **Ambérieu-en-Bugey** Ain, E France 45°57′N 05°21′E
185 I18 **Amberley** Canterbury, South Island, New Zealand 43°09′S 172°43′E
103 P11 **Ambert** Puy-de-Dôme, C France 45°33′N 03°45′E
Ambianum see Amiens
76 J11 **Ambidédi** Kayes, SW Mali 14°37′N 11°49′W
154 M10 **Ambikāpur** Chhattīsgarh, C India 23°09′N 83°12′E
172 J2 **Ambilobe** Antsirañana, N Madagascar 13°10′S 49°03′E
39 O7 **Ambler** Alaska, USA 67°05′N 157°51′W
Amblève see Amel
Ambo see Hägere Hiywet
172 I8 **Amboasary** Toliara, S Madagascar 25°01′S 46°23′E
172 J4 **Ambodifotatra** var. Ambodifototra. Toamasina, E Madagascar 16°59′S 49°51′E
Amboenten see Ambunten
172 I5 **Ambohidratrimo** Antananarivo, C Madagascar 18°48′S 47°26′E
172 I6 **Ambohimahasoa** Fianarantsoa, SE Madagascar 21°07′S 47°13′E
172 K3 **Ambohitralanana** Antsirañana, NE Madagascar 15°13′S 50°28′E
Amboina see Ambon
102 M8 **Amboise** Indre-et-Loire, C France 47°25′N 01°00′E
171 S13 **Ambon** prev. Amboina, Amboyna. Pulau Ambon, E Indonesia 03°41′S 128°10′E
171 S13 **Ambon, Pulau** island E Indonesia
81 I20 **Amboseli, Lake** ◎ Kenya/Tanzania
172 I6 **Ambositra** Fianarantsoa, SE Madagascar 20°31′S 47°15′E
172 I8 **Ambovombe** Toliara, S Madagascar 25°10′S 46°06′E
35 W14 **Amboy** California, W USA 34°33′N 115°44′W
30 L11 **Amboy** Illinois, N USA 41°42′N 89°19′W
Amboyna see Ambon
Ambracia see Árta
Ambre, Cap d' see Bobaomby, Tanjona
18 B14 **Ambridge** Pennsylvania, NE USA 40°33′N 80°11′W
Ambrim see Ambrym
82 A11 **Ambriz** Bengo, NW Angola 07°55′S 13°11′E
Ambrizete see N'Zeto
187 R13 **Ambrym** var. Ambrim. island C Vanuatu
169 T16 **Ambunten** prev. Amboenten. Pulau Madura, E Indonesia 06°55′S 113°45′E
186 B6 **Ambunti** East Sepik, NW Papua New Guinea 04°12′S 142°49′E
155 I20 **Āmbūr** Tamil Nādu, SE India 12°48′N 78°44′E
38 E17 **Amchitka Island** island Aleutian Islands, Alaska, USA
38 F17 **Amchitka Pass** strait Aleutian Islands, Alaska, USA
141 R15 **'Amd** C Yemen 15°10′N 47°58′E
78 J10 **Am Dam** Ouaddaï, E Chad 12°46′N 20°29′E
171 U16 **Amdassa** Pulau Yamdena, E Indonesia 07°40′S 131°24′E
125 U1 **Amderma** Nenetskiy Avtonomnyy Okrug, NW Russian Federation 69°45′N 61°36′E
159 N14 **Amdo** Xizang Zizhiqu, W China 32°15′N 91°43′E
40 K13 **Ameca** Jalisco, SW Mexico 20°34′N 104°03′W
41 P14 **Amecameca** var. Amecameca de Juárez. México, C Mexico 19°08′N 98°48′W
Amecameca de Juárez see Amecameca
61 A20 **Ameghino** Buenos Aires, E Argentina 34°51′S 62°28′W
99 M21 **Amel** Fr. Amblève. Liège, E Belgium 50°20′N 06°13′E
98 K4 **Ameland** Fris. It Amelân. island Waddeneilanden, N Netherlands
Amelân, It see Ameland
107 H14 **Amelia** Umbria, C Italy 42°33′N 12°26′E
21 V6 **Amelia Court House** Virginia, NE USA 37°20′N 77°59′W
23 W8 **Amelia Island** island Florida, SE USA
18 L12 **Amenia** New York, NE USA 41°51′N 73°31′W
America see United States of America
65 M21 **America-Antarctica Ridge** undersea feature S Atlantic Ocean
America in Miniature see Maryland
60 L9 **Americana** São Paulo, S Brazil 22°44′S 47°19′W
33 Q15 **American Falls** Idaho, NW USA 42°47′N 112°51′W
33 Q15 **American Falls Reservoir** ⊞ Idaho, NW USA
36 L3 **American Fork** Utah, W USA 40°24′N 111°47′W
192 K16 **American Samoa** ◇ US unincorporated territory W Polynesia
23 S6 **Americus** Georgia, SE USA 32°04′N 84°13′W
98 K12 **Amerongen** Utrecht, C Netherlands 52°00′N 05°30′E
98 K11 **Amersfoort** Utrecht, C Netherlands 52°09′N 05°23′E
97 N21 **Amersham** SE England, United Kingdom 51°40′N 00°37′W
30 I5 **Amery** Wisconsin, N USA 45°18′N 92°20′W
195 W6 **Amery Ice Shelf** ice shelf Antarctica
29 V13 **Ames** Iowa, C USA 42°01′N 93°37′W
19 P10 **Amesbury** Massachusetts, NE USA 42°51′N 70°55′W
Amestratus see Mistretta
115 F18 **Amfikleia** var. Amfiklia. Stereá Elláda, C Greece 38°38′N 22°35′E
Amfiklia see Amfikleia
115 D17 **Amfilochía** var. Amfilokhía. Dytikí Elláda, C Greece 38°52′N 21°09′E
Amfilokhía see Amfilochía
114 H13 **Amfípoli** anc. Amphipolis. site of ancient city Kentrikí Makedonía, NE Greece
115 F18 **Ámfissa** Stereá Elláda, C Greece 38°32′N 22°22′E
123 Q10 **Amga** Respublika Sakha (Yakutiya), NE Russian Federation 60°55′N 131°45′E
123 Q11 **Amga** ≈ NE Russian Federation
163 R7 **Amgalang** var. Xin Barag Zuoqi. Nei Mongol Zizhiqu, N China 48°12′N 118°15′E
123 V5 **Amguema** ≈ NE Russian Federation
123 S12 **Amgun'** ≈ SE Russian Federation
Amhara see Āmara
13 P15 **Amherst** Nova Scotia, SE Canada 45°50′N 64°14′W
18 M11 **Amherst** Massachusetts, NE USA 42°22′N 72°31′W
18 D10 **Amherst** New York, NE USA 42°57′N 78°47′W
24 M4 **Amherst** Texas, SW USA 33°59′N 102°24′W
21 U6 **Amherst** Virginia, NE USA 37°35′N 79°04′W
Amherst see Kyaikkami
14 C18 **Amherstburg** Ontario, S Canada 42°05′N 83°06′W
21 Q6 **Amherstdale** West Virginia, NE USA 37°46′N 81°46′W
14 K15 **Amherst Island** island Ontario, SE Canada
Amida see Diyarbakır
28 J6 **Amidon** North Dakota, N USA 46°29′N 103°19′W
103 O3 **Amiens** anc. Ambianum, Samarobriva. Somme, N France 49°54′N 02°18′E
139 P8 **'Āmij, Wādī** var. Wadi 'Amiq. dry watercourse W Iraq
136 L17 **Amik Ovasi** ◎ S Turkey
76 E9 **Amilcar Cabral** ✕ Sal, NE Cape Verde
Amilḩayt, Wādī see Umm al Ḩayt, Wādī
Amindaion/Amindeo see Amýntaio
155 C21 **Amīndīvi Islands** island group Lakshadweep, India, N Indian Ocean
139 U6 **Amīn Ḩabīb** Diyālá, E Iraq 34°17′N 45°10′E
83 E20 **Aminuis** Omaheke, E Namibia 23°43′S 19°21′E
'Amīq, Wadi see 'Āmij, Wādī
142 J7 **Amīrābād** Īlām, NW Iran 33°20′N 46°16′E
Amirante Bank see Amirante Ridge
173 N6 **Amirante Basin** undersea feature W Indian Ocean 07°00′S 54°00′E
173 N6 **Amirante Islands** var. Amirantes Group. island group C Seychelles
173 N7 **Amirante Ridge** var. Amirante Bank. undersea feature W Indian Ocean 06°00′S 53°10′E
Amirantes Group see Amirante Islands
173 N7 **Amirante Trench** undersea feature W Indian Ocean 08°00′S 52°30′E
11 U13 **Amisk Lake** ◎ Saskatchewan, C Canada
Amistad, Presa de la see Amistad Reservoir
25 O12 **Amistad Reservoir** var. Presa de la Amistad. ⊞ Mexico/USA
Amisus see Samsun
22 K8 **Amite** var. Amite City. Louisiana, S USA 30°40′N 90°30′W
Amite City see Amite
27 T12 **Amity** Arkansas, C USA 34°15′N 93°27′W
154 H11 **Amla** prev. Amulla. Madhya Pradesh, C India 21°53′N 78°10′E
38 I17 **Amlia Island** island Aleutian Islands, Alaska, USA
97 I18 **Amlwch** NW Wales, United Kingdom 53°25′N 04°23′W
Ammaia see Portalegre
138 H10 **'Ammān** var. Amman; anc. Philadelphia, Bibl. Rabbah Ammon, Rabbath Ammon. ● (Jordan) 'Ammān, NW Jordan 31°57′N 35°56′E
138 H10 **'Ammān** off. Muḩāfaẓat 'Ammān; prev. Al 'Aşimah. ◈ governorate NW Jordan
'Ammān, Muḩāfaẓat see 'Ammān
93 N14 **Ämmänsaari** Oulu, E Finland 64°51′N 28°58′E
92 H13 **Ammarnäs** Västerbotten, N Sweden 65°58′N 16°10′E
197 O15 **Ammassalik** var. Angmagssalik. Tunu, S Greenland 65°51′N 37°30′W
101 K24 **Ammer** ≈ SE Germany
101 K24 **Ammersee** ◎ SE Germany
98 J13 **Ammerzoden** Gelderland, C Netherlands 51°46′N 05°07′E
Ammóchostos see Gazimağusa
Ammóchostos, Kólpos see Gazimağusa Körfezi
Amnok-kang see Yalu
Amoea see Portalegre
Amoentai see Amuntai
Amoerang see Amurang
143 O4 **Āmol** var. Amul. Māzandarān, N Iran 36°31′N 52°24′E
115 K21 **Amorgós** Amorgós, Kykládes, Greece, Aegean Sea 36°49′N 25°54′E
115 K22 **Amorgós** island Kykládes, Greece, Aegean Sea
23 N3 **Amory** Mississippi, S USA 33°58′N 88°29′W
12 I13 **Amos** Québec, SE Canada 48°34′N 78°08′W
95 G15 **Åmot** Buskerud, S Norway 59°52′N 09°55′E
95 E15 **Åmot** Telemark, S Norway 59°34′N 07°59′E
95 J15 **Åmotfors** Värmland, C Sweden 59°46′N 12°24′E
76 L10 **Amourj** Hodh ech Chargui, SE Mauritania 16°04′N 07°12′W
Amoy see Xiamen
172 H7 **Ampanihy** Toliara, SW Madagascar 24°40′S 44°45′E
155 L25 **Ampara** var. Amparai. Eastern Province, E Sri Lanka 07°17′N 81°41′E
172 J4 **Amparafaravola** Toamasina, E Madagascar 17°33′S 48°13′E
Amparai see Ampara
60 M9 **Amparo** São Paulo, S Brazil 22°40′S 46°49′W
172 J5 **Ampasimanolotra** Toamasina, E Madagascar 18°49′S 49°04′E
57 H17 **Ampato, Nevado** ▲ S Peru 15°52′S 71°51′W
101 L23 **Amper** ≈ SE Germany
64 M9 **Ampère Seamount** undersea feature E Atlantic Ocean 35°05′N 13°00′W
Amphipolis see Amfípoli
167 X10 **Amphitrite Group** island group N Paracel Islands
171 T16 **Amplawas** var. Emplawas. Pulau Babar, E Indonesia 08°01′S 129°42′E
105 U7 **Amposta** Cataluña, NE Spain 40°43′N 00°34′E
15 V7 **Amqui** Québec, SE Canada 48°28′N 67°27′W
141 O14 **'Amrān** W Yemen 15°39′N 43°59′E
Amraoti see Amrāvati
154 H12 **Amrāvati** prev. Amraoti. Mahārāshtra, C India 20°56′N 77°45′E
154 C11 **Amreli** Gujarāt, W India 21°36′N 71°20′E

◆ Country
● Country Capital
◇ Dependent Territory
○ Dependent Territory Capital
◈ Administrative Regions
✕ International Airport
▲ Mountain
▲ Mountain Range
Volcano
≈ River
◎ Lake
⊞ Reservoir

108 H6 **Amriswil** Thurgau, NE Switzerland 47°33´N 09°18´E
138 H5 **'Amrīt** ruins Ṭarṭūs, W Syria
152 H7 **Amritsar** Punjab, N India 31°38´N 74°55´E
152 J10 **Amroha** Uttar Pradesh, N India 28°54´N 78°29´E
100 G7 **Amrum** island NW Germany
93 I15 **Åmsele** Västerbotten, N Sweden 64°31´N 19°24´E
98 I10 **Amstelveen** Noord-Holland, C Netherlands 52°18´N 04°50´E
98 I10 **Amsterdam** ● (Netherlands) Noord-Holland, C Netherlands 52°22´N 04°54´E
18 K10 **Amsterdam** New York, NE USA 42°56´N 74°11´W
173 Q11 **Amsterdam Fracture Zone** tectonic feature S Indian Ocean
173 R11 **Amsterdam Island** island NE French Southern and Antarctic Territories
109 U4 **Amstetten** Niederösterreich, N Austria 48°08´N 14°52´E
78 J11 **Am Timan** Salamat, SE Chad 11°02´N 20°17´E
146 L12 **Amu-Buxoro Kanali** var. Aral-Bukhorskiy Kanal. canal C Uzbekistan
139 O1 **'Āmūdah** var. Amude. Al Ḥasakah, N Syria 37°06´N 40°56´E
147 O15 **Amu Darya** Rus. Amudar'ya, Taj. Dar"yoi Amu, Turkm. Amyderya, Uzb. Amudaryo; anc. Oxus. ∽ C Asia
Amu-Dar'ya see Amyderýa
Amudar'ya/Amudaryo/Amu, Dar"yoi see Amu Darya
Amude see 'Āmūdah
140 L3 **'Amūd, Jabal al** ▲ NW Saudi Arabia 30°59´N 39°17´E
38 J17 **Amukta Island** island Aleutian Islands, Alaska, USA
38 I17 **Amukta Pass** strait Aleutian Islands, Alaska, USA
Amul see Āmol
Amulla see Amla
Amundsen Basin see Fram Basin
195 X3 **Amundsen Bay** bay Antarctica
195 P10 **Amundsen Coast** physical region Antarctica
193 O14 **Amundsen Plain** undersea feature S Pacific Ocean
195 Q9 **Amundsen-Scott** US research station Antarctica 89°59´S 10°00´E
194 J11 **Amundsen Sea** sea S Pacific Ocean
94 M12 **Amungen** ◎ C Sweden
169 U13 **Amuntai** prev. Amoentai. Borneo, C Indonesia 02°24´S 115°14´E
129 W6 **Amur** Chin. Heilong Jiang. ∽ China/Russian Federation
171 Q11 **Amurang** prev. Amoerang. Sulawesi, C Indonesia 01°12´N 124°37´E
105 O3 **Amurrio** País Vasco, N Spain 43°03´N 03°00´W
123 S13 **Amursk** Khabarovskiy Kray, SE Russian Federation 50°13´N 136°34´E
123 Q12 **Amurskaya Oblast'** ◈ province SE Russian Federation
80 G7 **'Amur, Wadi** ∽ NE Sudan
115 C17 **Amvrakikós Kólpos** gulf W Greece
Amvrosiyevka see Amvrosiyivka
117 X8 **Amvrosiyivka** Rus. Amvrosiyevka. Donets'ka Oblast', SE Ukraine 47°46´N 38°30´E
146 M14 **Amyderya** Rus. Amu-Dar'ya. Lebap Welaýaty, NE Turkmenistan 37°58´N 65°14´E
Amyderya see Amu Darya
114 E13 **Amýntaio** var. Amindeo; prev. Amíndaion. Dytikí Makedonía, N Greece 40°42´N 21°42´E
14 B6 **Amyot** Ontario, S Canada 48°28´N 84°58´W
191 U10 **Anaa** atoll Îles Tuamotu, C French Polynesia
Anabanoea see Anabanua
171 N14 **Anabanua** prev. Anabanoea. Sulawesi, C Indonesia 03°58´S 120°07´E
189 R8 **Anabar** NE Nauru 0°30´S 166°56´E
123 N8 **Anabar** ∽ NE Russian Federation
An Abhainn Mhór see Blackwater
55 O6 **Anaco** Anzoátegui, NE Venezuela 09°30´N 64°28´W
33 Q10 **Anaconda** Montana, NW USA 46°09´N 112°56´W
32 H7 **Anacortes** Washington, NW USA 48°30´N 122°36´W
26 M11 **Anadarko** Oklahoma, C USA 35°04´N 98°16´W
114 N12 **Ana Dere** ∽ NW Turkey
104 G8 **Anadia** Aveiro, N Portugal 40°26´N 08°27´W
Anadolu Dağları see Doğu Karadeniz Dağları
123 V6 **Anadyr'** Chukotskiy Avtonomnyy Okrug, NE Russian Federation 64°41´N 177°22´E
123 V6 **Anadyr'** ∽ NE Russian Federation
Anadyr, Gulf of see Anadyrskiy Zaliv
129 X4 **Anadyrskiy Khrebet** var. Chukot Range. ▲▲ NE Russian Federation
123 W6 **Anadyrskiy Zaliv** Eng. Gulf of Anadyr. gulf NE Russian Federation
115 K22 **Anáfi** anc. Anaphe. island Kykládes, Greece, Aegean Sea
107 J15 **Anagni** Lazio, C Italy 41°43´N 13°12´E
'Ānah see 'Annah
35 T15 **Anaheim** California, W USA 33°50´N 117°54´W
10 L15 **Anahim Lake** British Columbia, SW Canada 52°26´N 125°13´W
38 B8 **Anahola** Kaua'i, Hawai'i, USA, C Pacific Ocean 22°09´N 159°19´W
41 O7 **Anáhuac** Nuevo León, NE Mexico 27°13´N 100°09´W
25 X11 **Anahuac** Texas, SW USA 29°44´N 94°41´W
155 G22 **Anai Mudi** ▲ S India 10°16´N 77°08´E
Anaiza see 'Unayzah
155 M15 **Anakāpalle** Andhra Pradesh, E India 17°42´N 83°06´E
191 W15 **Anakena, Playa de** beach Easter Island, Chile, E Pacific Ocean
39 Q7 **Anaktuvuk Pass** Alaska, USA 68°08´N 151°44´W
39 Q6 **Anaktuvuk River** ∽ Alaska, USA
172 J3 **Analalava** Mahajanga, NW Madagascar 14°38´S 47°46´E
44 F6 **Ana Maria, Golfo de** gulf N Caribbean Sea
Anambas Islands see Anambas, Kepulauan
169 N8 **Anambas, Kepulauan** var. Anambas Islands. island group W Indonesia
77 U17 **Anambra** ◈ state SE Nigeria
29 N4 **Anamoose** North Dakota, N USA 47°50´N 100°14´W
29 Y13 **Anamosa** Iowa, C USA 42°06´N 91°17´W
136 H17 **Anamur** İçel, S Turkey 36°06´N 32°49´E
136 H17 **Anamur Burnu** headland S Turkey 36°03´N 32°49´E
154 O12 **Ānandapur** var. Anandpur. Orissa, E India 21°14´N 86°10´E
Anandpur see Ānandapur
155 H18 **Anantapur** Andhra Pradesh, S India 14°41´N 77°36´E
152 H5 **Anantnāg** var. Islamabad. Jammu and Kashmir, NW India 33°44´N 75°11´E
Ananyev see Anan'yiv
117 O9 **Anan'yiv** Rus. Ananyev. Odes'ka Oblast', SW Ukraine 47°43´N 29°51´E
126 J14 **Anapa** Krasnodarskiy Kray, SW Russian Federation 44°55´N 37°20´E
Anaphe see Anáfi
59 K18 **Anápolis** Goiás, C Brazil 16°19´S 48°58´W
143 R10 **Anār** Kermān, C Iran 30°49´N 55°18´E
Anár see Inari
143 P7 **Anārak** Eşfahān, C Iran 33°21´N 53°43´E
Anar Dara see Anār Darreh
148 J7 **Anār Darreh** var. Anar Dara. Farāh, W Afghanistan 32°45´N 61°38´E
Anárjohka see Inarijoki
23 X9 **Anastasia Island** island Florida, SE USA
188 K7 **Anatahan** island C Northern Mariana Islands
86 M6 **Anatolia** plateau C Turkey
86 F14 **Anatolian Plate** tectonic feature Asia/Europe
114 H13 **Anatolikí Makedonía kai Thráki** Eng. Macedonia East and Thrace. ◈ region NE Greece
Anatom see Aneityum
62 L8 **Añatuya** Santiago del Estero, N Argentina 28°28´S 62°52´W
An Baile Meánach see Ballymena
An Bhearú see Barrow
An Bhóinn see Boyne
An Blascaod Mór see Great Blasket Island
An Cabhán see Cavan
An Caisleán Nua see Newcastle
An Caisleán Riabhach see Castlerea, Ireland
An Caisleán Riabhach see Castlereagh
56 C13 **Ancash** off. Departamento de Ancash. ◈ department W Peru
Ancash, Departamento de see Ancash
An Cathair see Caher
102 J8 **Ancenis** Loire-Atlantique, NW France 47°23´N 01°10´W
An Chanáil Ríoga see Royal Canal
An Cheacha see Caha Mountains
39 R11 **Anchorage** Alaska, USA 61°13´N 149°52´W
39 R12 **Anchorage** ✈ Alaska, USA 61°08´N 150°00´W
39 Q13 **Anchor Point** Alaska, USA 59°46´N 151°49´W
An Chorr Chríochach see Cookstown
65 M24 **Anchorstock Point** headland W Tristan da Cunha 37°07´S 12°21´W
An Clár see Clare
An Clochán see Clifden
An Clochán Liath see Dunglow
23 U12 **Anclote Keys** island group Florida, SE USA
An Cóbh see Cobh
57 J17 **Ancohuma, Nevado de** ▲ W Bolivia 15°51´S 68°33´W
An Comar see Comber
57 D14 **Ancón** Lima, W Peru 11°45´S 77°08´W
106 J12 **Ancona** Marche, C Italy 43°38´N 13°30´E
Ancuabe see Ancuabi
82 Q13 **Ancuabi** var. Ancuabe. Cabo Delgado, NE Mozambique 13°00´S 39°50´E
63 F17 **Ancud** prev. San Carlos de Ancud. Los Lagos, S Chile 41°53´S 73°50´W
63 G17 **Ancud, Golfo de** gulf S Chile
Ancyra see Ankara
163 V8 **Anda** Heilongjiang, NE China 46°25´N 125°20´E
57 G16 **Andahuaylas** Apurímac, S Peru 13°39´S 73°24´W
An Daingean see Dingle
153 R15 **Āndāl** West Bengal, NE India 23°35´N 87°14´E
94 E9 **Åndalsnes** Møre og Romsdal, S Norway 62°33´N 07°42´E
104 K13 **Andalucía** Eng. Andalusia. ◈ autonomous community S Spain
23 P7 **Andalusia** Alabama, S USA 31°18´N 86°29´W
Andalusia see Andalucía
151 Q21 **Andaman and Nicobar Islands** var. Andamans and Nicobars. ◈ union territory India, NE Indian Ocean
173 T4 **Andaman Basin** undersea feature NE Indian Ocean 10°00´N 94°00´E
151 P19 **Andaman Islands** island group India, NE Indian Ocean
Andamans and Nicobars see Andaman and Nicobar Islands
173 T4 **Andaman Sea** sea NE Indian Ocean
57 K19 **Andamarca** Oruro, C Bolivia 18°46´S 67°31´W
182 H5 **Andamooka** South Australia 30°26´S 137°12´E
141 Y9 **'Andām, Wādī** seasonal river NE Oman
172 J3 **Andapa** Antsirañana, NE Madagascar 14°39´S 49°40´E
149 R4 **Andarāb** var. Banow. Baghlān, NE Afghanistan 35°36´N 69°18´E
Andarbag see Andarbogh
147 S13 **Andarbogh** Rus. Andarbag, Anderbak. S Tajikistan 37°51´N 71°45´E
109 Z5 **Andau** Burgenland, E Austria 47°47´N 17°02´E
108 I10 **Andeer** Graubünden, S Switzerland 46°36´N 09°24´E
92 H9 **Andenes** Nordland, C Norway 69°18´N 16°10´E
99 J20 **Andenne** Namur, SE Belgium 50°29´N 05°06´E
77 S11 **Andéramboukane** Gao, E Mali 15°24´N 03°03´E
Anderbak see Andarbogh
99 G18 **Anderlecht** Brussels, C Belgium 50°50´N 04°18´E
99 G21 **Anderlues** Hainaut, S Belgium 50°24´N 04°16´E
108 G9 **Andermatt** Uri, C Switzerland 46°39´N 08°36´E
101 E17 **Andernach** anc. Antunnacum. Rheinland-Pfalz, SW Germany 50°26´N 07°24´E
188 D15 **Andersen Air Force Base** air base NE Guam 13°34´N 144°55´E
39 R9 **Anderson** Alaska, USA 64°20´N 149°11´W
35 N4 **Anderson** California, W USA 40°26´N 122°21´W
31 P13 **Anderson** Indiana, N USA 40°06´N 85°40´W
27 R8 **Anderson** Missouri, C USA 36°39´N 94°26´W
21 P11 **Anderson** South Carolina, SE USA 34°30´N 82°39´W
25 V10 **Anderson** Texas, SW USA 30°29´N 96°00´W
95 K20 **Anderstorp** Jönköping, S Sweden 57°17´N 13°38´E
54 D9 **Andes** Antioquia, W Colombia 05°40´N 75°56´W
47 P7 **Andes** ▲▲ W South America
29 P12 **Andes, Lake** ◎ South Dakota, N USA
92 H9 **Andfjorden** fjord E Norwegian Sea
155 H16 **Andhra Pradesh** ◈ state E India
98 J8 **Andijk** Noord-Holland, NW Netherlands 52°38´N 05°00´E
147 S10 **Andijon** Rus. Andizhan. Andijon Viloyati, E Uzbekistan 40°46´N 72°19´E
147 S10 **Andijon Viloyati** Rus. Andizhanskaya Oblast'. ◈ province E Uzbekistan
Andikíthira see Antikýthira
172 J4 **Andilamena** Toamasina, C Madagascar 17°00´S 48°35´E
142 L8 **Andīmeshk** var. Andimishk; prev. Salehābād. Khūzestān, SW Iran 32°30´N 48°26´E
Andimishk see Andīmeshk
Andipáros see Antíparos
Andipaxi see Antípaxoi
Andípsara see Antípsara
136 L16 **Andırın** Kahramanmaraş, S Turkey 37°33´N 36°18´E
158 J8 **Andirlangar** Xinjiang Uygur Zizhiqu, NW China 37°38´N 83°40´E
Andírrion see Antírrio
Ándissa see Ántissa
Andizhan see Andijon
Andizhanskaya Oblast' see Andijon Viloyati
149 N2 **Andkhvoy** prev. Andkhvoy. Fāryāb, N Afghanistan 36°56´N 65°08´E
105 Q2 **Andoain** País Vasco, N Spain 43°13´N 02°02´W
163 Y15 **Andong** Jap. Antō. E South Korea 36°34´N 128°44´E
109 R4 **Andorf** Oberösterreich, N Austria 48°22´N 13°33´E
105 S7 **Andorra** Aragón, NE Spain 40°59´N 00°27´W
105 V4 **Andorra** off. Principality of Andorra, Cat. Valls d'Andorra, Fr. Vallée d'Andorre. ◆ monarchy SW Europe
Andorra see Andorra la Vella
105 V4 **Andorra la Vella** var. Andorra, Fr. Andorre la Vielle, Sp. Andorra la Vieja. ● (Andorra) C Andorra 42°30´N 01°30´E
Andorra la Vieja see Andorra la Vella
Andorra, Principality of see Andorra
Andorra, Valls d'/Andorra, Vallée d' see Andorra
Andorre la Vielle see Andorra la Vella
97 M22 **Andover** S England, United Kingdom 51°13´N 01°28´W
27 N6 **Andover** Kansas, C USA 37°42´N 97°08´W
92 G10 **Andøya** island C Norway
60 I8 **Andradina** São Paulo, S Brazil 20°54´S 51°19´W
105 X9 **Andratx** Mallorca, Spain, W Mediterranean Sea 39°35´N 02°25´E
39 N10 **Andreafsky River** ∽ Alaska, USA
38 H17 **Andreanof Islands** island group Aleutian Islands, Alaska, USA
124 H16 **Andreapol'** Tverskaya Oblast', W Russian Federation 56°38´N 32°17´E
Andreas, Cape see Zafer Burnu
Andreevka see Kabanbay
21 N10 **Andrews** North Carolina, SE USA 35°19´N 84°01´W
21 T13 **Andrews** South Carolina, SE USA 33°27´N 79°33´W
24 M7 **Andrews** Texas, SW USA 32°19´N 102°34´W
173 N5 **Andrew Tablemount** var. Gora Andryu. undersea feature W Indian Ocean 06°45´N 50°30´E
Andreyevka see Kabanbay
107 N17 **Andria** Puglia, SE Italy 41°13´N 16°17´E
113 K16 **Andrijevica** E Montenegro 42°45´N 19°45´E
115 E20 **Andrítsaina** Pelopónnisos, S Greece 37°29´N 21°52´E
An Droichead Nua see Newbridge
Andropov see Rybinsk
115 J19 **Ándros** Ándros, Kykládes, Greece, Aegean Sea 37°49´N 24°54´E
115 J20 **Ándros** island Kykládes, Greece, Aegean Sea
19 O7 **Androscoggin River** ∽ Maine/New Hampshire, NE USA
44 F3 **Andros Island** island NW Bahamas
127 R7 **Androsovka** Samarskaya Oblast', W Russian Federation 52°41´N 49°34´E
44 G3 **Andros Town** Andros Island, NW Bahamas 24°40´N 77°47´W
155 D21 **Āndrott Island** island Lakshadweep, India, N Indian Ocean
117 N5 **Andrushivka** Zhytomyrs'ka Oblast', N Ukraine 50°01´N 29°02´E
111 K17 **Andrychów** Małopolskie, S Poland 49°51´N 19°18´E
Andryu, Gora see Andrew Tablemount
92 I10 **Andselv** Troms, N Norway 69°05´N 18°30´E
79 O17 **Andudu** Orientale, NE Dem. Rep. Congo 02°26´N 28°39´E
105 N13 **Andújar** anc. Illiturgis. Andalucía, SW Spain 38°02´N 04°03´W
82 C12 **Andulo** Bié, W Angola 11°29´S 16°43´E
103 Q14 **Anduze** Gard, S France 44°03´N 03°59´E
An Earagail see Errigal Mountain
95 L19 **Aneby** Jönköping, S Sweden 57°50´N 14°45´E
Anécho see Aného
77 Q9 **Anéfis** Kidal, NE Mali 18°05´N 00°38´E
45 U8 **Anegada** island NE British Virgin Islands
61 B25 **Anegada, Bahía** bay E Argentina
45 U9 **Anegada Passage** passage Anguilla/British Virgin Islands
77 R17 **Aného** var. Anécho; prev. Petit-Popo. S Togo 06°14´N 01°36´E
197 D17 **Aneityum** var. Anatom; prev. Kéamu. island S Vanuatu
117 N10 **Anenii Noi** Rus. Novyye Aneny. C Moldova 46°52´N 29°10´E
186 F7 **Anepmete** New Britain, E Papua New Guinea 05°47´S 148°37´E
105 U4 **Aneto** ▲ NE Spain 42°36´N 00°37´E
146 F13 **Änew** Rus. Annau. Ahal Welaýaty, C Turkmenistan 37°51´N 58°22´E
Änewetak see Enewetak Atoll
77 Y8 **Aney** Agadez, NE Niger 19°22´N 13°00´E
An Fheoir see Nore
122 L12 **Angara** ∽ C Russian Federation
122 M13 **Angarsk** Irkutskaya Oblast', S Russian Federation 52°31´N 103°55´E
Angaur see Ngeaur
93 G17 **Ånge** Västernorrland, C Sweden 62°31´N 15°40´E
Angel see Úhlava
40 D4 **Ángel de la Guarda, Isla** island NW Mexico
171 O3 **Angeles** off. Angeles City. Luzon, N Philippines 15°16´N 120°37´E
Angeles City see Angeles
Angel Falls see Ángel, Salto
95 J22 **Ängelholm** Skåne, S Sweden 56°14´N 12°52´E
61 A17 **Angélica** Santa Fe, C Argentina 31°33´S 61°33´W
25 W8 **Angelina River** ∽ Texas, SW USA
55 Q9 **Ángel, Salto** Eng. Angel Falls. waterfall E Venezuela
95 M15 **Ängelsberg** Västmanland, C Sweden 59°57´N 16°01´E
35 P8 **Angels Camp** California, W USA 38°03´N 120°31´W
109 W7 **Anger** Steiermark, SE Austria 47°16´N 15°41´E
Angerapp see Ozersk
Angerburg see Węgorzewo
93 H15 **Ångermanälven** ∽ N Sweden
100 P11 **Angermünde** Brandenburg, NE Germany 53°02´N 13°59´E
102 K7 **Angers** anc. Juliomagus. Maine-et-Loire, NW France 47°30´N 00°33´W
15 W7 **Angers** ∽ Québec, SE Canada
93 J16 **Ängesön** island N Sweden
Angistro see Ágkistro
114 H13 **Angítis** ∽ NE Greece
167 R13 **Ângk Tasaôm** prev. Angtassom. Takêv, S Cambodia
185 C25 **Anglem, Mount** ▲ Stewart Island, Southland, SW New Zealand 46°44´S 167°56´E
97 I18 **Anglesey** cultural region NW Wales, United Kingdom
97 I18 **Anglesey** island NW Wales, United Kingdom
102 I15 **Anglet** Pyrénées-Atlantiques, SW France 43°29´N 01°30´W
25 W12 **Angleton** Texas, SW USA 29°10´N 95°27´W
Anglia see England
14 H9 **Angliers** Québec, SE Canada 47°33´N 79°17´W
Anglo-Egyptian Sudan see Sudan
Angmagssalik see Ammassalik
167 Q7 **Ang Nam Ngum** ◎ C Laos
79 N16 **Ango** Orientale, N Dem. Rep. Congo 04°01´N 25°52´E
83 Q15 **Angoche** Nampula, E Mozambique 16°10´S 39°58´E
63 G14 **Angol** Araucanía, C Chile 37°47´S 72°45´W
31 Q11 **Angola** Indiana, N USA 41°37´N 85°00´W
82 A9 **Angola** off. Republic of Angola; prev. People's Republic of Angola, Portuguese West Africa. ◆ republic SW Africa
65 P15 **Angola Basin** undersea feature E Atlantic Ocean 15°00´S 03°00´E
Angola, People's Republic of see Angola
Angola, Republic of see Angola
39 X13 **Angoon** Admiralty Island, Alaska, USA 57°33´N 134°30´W
147 O14 **Angor** Surkhondaryo Viloyati, S Uzbekistan 37°30´N 67°06´E
186 C6 **Angoram** East Sepik, NW Papua New Guinea 04°04´S 144°04´E
40 H8 **Angostura** Sinaloa, C Mexico 25°18´N 108°10´W
Angostura see Ciudad Bolívar
41 U17 **Angostura, Presa de la** ▣ SE Mexico
28 J11 **Angostura Reservoir** ▣ South Dakota, N USA
102 L11 **Angoulême** anc. Iculisma. Charente, W France 45°39´N 00°10´E
102 K11 **Angoumois** cultural region W France
64 O2 **Angra do Heroísmo** Terceira, Azores, Portugal, NE Atlantic Ocean 38°40´N 27°14´W
60 O10 **Angra dos Reis** Rio de Janeiro, SE Brazil 22°59´S 44°17´W
Angra Pequena see Lüderitz
147 Q10 **Angren** Toshkent Viloyati, E Uzbekistan 41°05´N 70°18´E
Angtassom see Ângk Tasaôm
167 O10 **Ang Thong** var. Angthong. Ang Thong, C Thailand 14°35´N 100°25´E
Angthong see Ang Thong
79 M16 **Angu** Orientale, N Dem. Rep. Congo 03°38´N 24°14´E
105 S5 **Angües** Aragón, NE Spain 42°07´N 00°10´W
45 U9 **Anguilla** ◇ UK dependent territory E West Indies
45 V9 **Anguilla** island E West Indies
44 F4 **Anguilla Cays** islets SW Bahamas
Angul see Anugul
161 N1 **Anguli Nur** ◎ E China
79 O18 **Angumu** Orientale, E Dem. Rep. Congo 0°10´S 27°42´E
14 G14 **Angus** Ontario, S Canada 44°19´N 79°52´W
96 J10 **Angus** cultural region E Scotland, United Kingdom
59 K19 **Anhangüera** Goiás, S Brazil 18°12´S 48°19´W
99 I21 **Anhée** Namur, S Belgium 50°18´N 04°52´E
95 I21 **Anholt** island C Denmark
160 M11 **Anhua** var. Dongping. Hunan, S China 28°25´N 111°10´E
161 P8 **Anhui** var. Anhui Sheng, Anhwei, Wan. ◈ province E China
AnhuiSheng/Anhwei Wan see Anhui
39 O11 **Aniak** Alaska, USA 61°34´N 159°31´W
39 O12 **Aniak River** ∽ Alaska, USA
An Iarmhí see Westmeath
189 R8 **Anibare** E Nauru 0°31´S 166°56´E
189 R8 **Anibare Bay** bay E Nauru, W Pacific Ocean
Anicium see le Puy
115 K22 **Ánidro** island Kykládes, Greece, Aegean Sea
77 R15 **Anié** C Togo 07°48´N 01°12´E
77 Q15 **Anié** ∽ C Togo
102 J16 **Anie, Pic d'** ▲ SW France 42°56´N 00°44´W
127 Y7 **Anikhovka** Orenburgskaya Oblast', W Russian Federation 51°27´N 60°17´E
14 G9 **Anima Nipissing Lake** ◎ Ontario, S Canada
37 O16 **Animas** New Mexico, SW USA 31°55´N 108°49´W
37 P16 **Animas Peak** ▲ New Mexico, SW USA 31°34´N 108°46´W
37 P16 **Animas Valley** valley New Mexico, SW USA
116 F13 **Anina** Ger. Steierdorf, Hung. Stájerlakanina; prev. Ştaierdorf-Anina, Steierdorf-Anina, Steyerlak-Anina. Caraş-Severin, SW Romania 45°05´N 21°51´E
29 U14 **Anita** Iowa, C USA 41°27´N 94°45´W
123 U14 **Aniva, Mys** headland Ostrov Sakhalin, SE Russian Federation 46°02´N 143°25´E
187 S15 **Aniwa** island S Vanuatu
93 M19 **Anjalankoski** Etelä-Suomi, S Finland 60°39´N 26°54´E
'Anjar see Aanjar
Anjiangying see Luanping
14 B8 **Anjigami Lake** ◎ Ontario, S Canada
149 N13 **Anjīra** Baluchistān, SW Pakistan 28°19´N 66°19´E
164 K14 **Anjō** var. Anzyô. Aichi, Honshū, SW Japan 34°56´N 137°05´E
102 J8 **Anjou** cultural region NW France
Anjouan see Nzwani
172 J4 **Anjozorobe** Antananarivo, C Madagascar 18°22´S 47°52´E
163 W13 **Anju** W North Korea 39°36´N 125°44´E
98 M5 **Anjum** Fris. Eanjum. Fryslân, N Netherlands 53°22´N 06°09´E
172 G6 **Ankaboa, Tanjona** prev./Fr. Cap Saint-Vincent. headland W Madagascar 21°57´S 43°16´E
160 L7 **Ankang** prev. Xing'an. Shaanxi, C China 32°45´N 109°00´E
136 I12 **Ankara** prev. Angora; anc. Ancyra. ● (Turkey) Ankara, C Turkey 39°55´N 32°50´E
136 H12 **Ankara** ◈ province C Turkey
95 N19 **Ankarsrum** Kalmar, S Sweden 57°40´N 16°19´E
172 H6 **Ankazoabo** Toliara, SW Madagascar 22°18´S 44°30´E
172 I4 **Ankazobe** Antananarivo, C Madagascar 18°20´S 47°07´E
29 V14 **Ankeny** Iowa, C USA 41°43´N 93°37´W
167 V11 **An Khê** Gia Lai, C Vietnam 13°57´N 108°39´E
100 O9 **Anklam** Mecklenburg-Vorpommern, NE Germany 53°51´N 13°42´E
80 K13 **Änkober** Āmara, N Ethiopia 09°36´N 39°44´E
77 O17 **Ankobra** ∽ S Ghana
79 N22 **Ankoro** Katanga, SE Dem. Rep. Congo 06°45´S 26°58´E
99 L24 **Anlier, Forêt d'** forest SE Belgium
160 I13 **Anlong** var. Xin'an. Guizhou, S China 25°05´N 105°29´E
An Longfort see Longford
167 R11 **Ânlong Vêng** Siĕmréab, NW Cambodia 14°16´N 104°08´E
An Lorgain see Lurgan
161 N8 **Anlu** Hubei, C China 31°15´N 113°41´E
An Mhí see Meath
An Mhuir Cheilteach see Celtic Sea
An Muileann gCearr see Mullingar
93 F16 **Ånn** Jämtland, C Sweden 63°19´N 12°34´E
126 M8 **Anna** Voronezhskaya Oblast', W Russian Federation 51°31´N 40°23´E
30 L17 **Anna** Illinois, N USA 37°27´N 89°15´W
25 U5 **Anna** Texas, SW USA 33°21´N 96°33´W
74 L5 **Annaba** prev. Bône. NE Algeria 36°55´N 07°47´E
An Nabatīyah at Taḥtā see Nabatîyé
101 N17 **Annaberg-Buchholz** Sachsen, E Germany 50°35´N 13°01´E
109 T9 **Annabichl** ✈ (Klagenfurt) Kärnten, S Austria 46°39´N 14°21´E
140 M5 **An Nafūd** desert NW Saudi Arabia
139 P6 **'Annah** var. 'Ānah. Al Anbār, NW Iraq 34°50´N 42°00´E
139 P6 **An Nāḥiyah** Al Anbār, W Iraq 34°24´N 41°33´E
139 T10 **An Najaf** var. Najaf. An Najaf, S Iraq 31°59´N 44°19´E
21 V5 **Anna, Lake** ▣ Virginia, NE USA
97 F16 **Annalee** ∽ N Ireland
167 S9 **Annamite Mountains** var. annamsescordillera, Fr. Chaîne Annamitique, Lao. Phou Louang. ▲▲ C Laos
Annamitique, Chaîne see Annamite Mountains
Annamses Cordillera see Annamite Mountains
97 J14 **Annan** S Scotland, United Kingdom 55°N 03°20´W
29 U8 **Annandale** Minnesota, N USA 45°15´N 94°07´W
21 W4 **Annandale** Virginia, NE USA 38°48´N 77°10´W
189 Q7 **Anna Point** headland N Nauru 0°30´S 166°56´E
21 X3 **Annapolis** state capital Maryland, NE USA 38°59´N 76°30´W
188 A10 **Anna, Pulo** island S Palau
153 O10 **Annapurṇa** ▲ C Nepal 28°30´N 83°50´E
An Nāqūrah see En Nâqoûra
31 R10 **Ann Arbor** Michigan, N USA 42°17´N 83°45´W
An Nās see Naas
139 W12 **An Nāṣirīyah** var. Nasiriya. Dhī Qār, SE Iraq 31°04´N 46°17´E
139 W11 **An Naṣr** Dhī Qār, E Iraq 31°34´N 46°08´E
Annau see Änew
121 O13 **An Nawfalīyah** var. Al Nūwfalīyah. N Libya 30°46´N 17°48´E
19 P10 **Ann, Cape** headland Massachusetts, NE USA 42°39´N 70°35´W
180 I10 **Annean, Lake** ◎ Western Australia
Anneciacum see Annecy
103 T11 **Annecy** anc. Anneciacum. Haute-Savoie, E France 45°53´N 06°09´E
103 T11 **Annecy, Lac d'** ◎ E France
103 T10 **Annemasse** Haute-Savoie, E France 46°10´N 06°13´E
39 Z14 **Annette Island** island Alexander Archipelago, Alaska, USA
An Nhon see Binh Đinh
An Nīl al Abyaḍ see White Nile
An Nīl al Azraq see Blue Nile
23 Q3 **Anniston** Alabama, S USA 33°39´N 85°49´W
79 A19 **Annobón** island W Equatorial Guinea
103 R12 **Annonay** Ardèche, E France 45°15´N 04°40´E
44 K12 **Annotto Bay** C Jamaica 18°16´N 76°47´W
141 R5 **An Nu'ayrīyah** var. Narīya. Ash Sharqīyah, NE Saudi Arabia 27°30´N 48°30´E
182 M9 **Annuello** Victoria, SE Australia 34°54´S 142°50´E
139 Q10 **An Nukhayb** Al Anbār, S Iraq 32°02´N 42°15´E
139 U9 **An Nu'mānīyah** Wāsiṭ, E Iraq 32°34´N 45°23´E
Áno Arkhánai see Archánes
115 J25 **Anógeia** var. Anogia, Anóyia. Kríti, Greece, E Mediterranean Sea 35°17´N 24°53´E
Anogia see Anógeia
29 V8 **Anoka** Minnesota, N USA 45°15´N 93°26´W
An Ómaigh see Omagh
172 I1 **Anorontany, Tanjona** Fr. Cap Saint-Sébastien. headland N Madagascar
172 J5 **Anosibe An'Ala** Toamasina, E Madagascar 19°24´S 48°11´E
Anóyia see Anógeia
An Pointe see Warrenpoint
161 P9 **Anqing** Anhui, E China 30°32´N 116°59´E
161 Q5 **Anqiu** Shandong, E China 36°25´N 119°10´E
An Ráth see Ráth Luirc
An Ribhéar see Kenmare River
An Ros see Rush
99 K19 **Ans** Liège, E Belgium 50°39´N 05°32´E
Anṣāb see Nişāb
171 W12 **Ansas** Papua, E Indonesia 01°44´S 135°52´E
101 J20 **Ansbach** Bayern, SE Germany 49°18´N 10°36´E
An Sciobairín see Skibbereen
An Scoil see Skull
An Seancheann see Old Head of Kinsale
45 Y5 **Anse-Bertrand** Grande Terre, N Guadeloupe 16°28´N 61°31´W
172 H17 **Anse Boileau** Mahé, NE Seychelles 04°43´S 55°29´E
45 S11 **Anse La Raye** NW Saint Lucia 13°57´N 61°01´W
54 D9 **Anserma** Caldas, W Colombia 05°15´N 75°47´W
109 T4 **Ansfelden** Oberösterreich, N Austria 48°12´N 14°17´E
163 U12 **Anshan** Liaoning, NE China 41°06´N 122°55´E
160 J12 **Anshun** Guizhou, S China 26°15´N 105°58´E
61 F17 **Ansina** Tacuarembó, C Uruguay 31°58´S 55°28´W
29 O15 **Ansley** Nebraska, C USA 41°16´N 99°22´W
25 P6 **Anson** Texas, SW USA 32°45´N 99°55´W
77 Q10 **Ansongo** Gao, E Mali 15°39´N 00°33´E
An Srath Bán see Strabane
21 R5 **Ansted** West Virginia, NE USA 38°08´N 81°06´W
171 Y13 **Ansudu** Papua, E Indonesia 02°09´S 139°19´E
57 G15 **Anta** Cusco, S Peru 13°30´S 72°08´W
57 G16 **Antabamba** Apurímac, C Peru 14°23´S 72°54´W
Antafalva see Kovačica
136 L17 **Antakya** anc. Antioch, Antiochia. Hatay, S Turkey 36°12´N 36°10´E
172 K3 **Antalaha** Antsirañana, NE Madagascar 14°53´S 50°16´E
136 F17 **Antalya** prev. Adalia; anc. Attaleia, Bibl. Attalia. Antalya, SW Turkey 36°53´N 30°42´E
136 F17 **Antalya** ◈ province SW Turkey
136 F16 **Antalya** ✈ Antalya, SW Turkey 36°53´N 30°45´E
121 U10 **Antalya Basin** undersea feature E Mediterranean Sea
Antalya, Gulf of see Antalya Körfezi
136 F16 **Antalya Körfezi** var. Gulf of Adalia, Eng. Gulf of Antalya. gulf SW Turkey
172 J5 **Antanambao Manampotsy** Toamasina, E Madagascar 19°30´S 48°36´E
172 I5 **Antananarivo** prev. Tananarive. ● (Madagascar) Antananarivo, C Madagascar 18°52´S 47°30´E
172 I4 **Antananarivo** ◈ province C Madagascar
172 J5 **Antananarivo** ✈ Antananarivo, C Madagascar 18°52´S 47°30´E
An tAonach see Nenagh
194-195 **Antarctica** continent
194 I5 **Antarctic Peninsula** peninsula Antarctica
61 J15 **Antas, Rio das** ∽ S Brazil
189 U16 **Ant Atoll** atoll Caroline Islands, E Micronesia
An Teampall Mór see Templemore
Antep see Gaziantep
104 M15 **Antequera** anc. Antikaria, Antiquaria. Andalucía, S Spain 37°01´N 04°34´W
Antequera see Oaxaca
37 S5 **Antero Reservoir** ▣ Colorado, C USA
26 M7 **Anthony** Kansas, C USA 37°10´N 98°02´W
37 R16 **Anthony** New Mexico, SW USA 32°00´N 106°36´W
182 D5 **Anthony, Lake** salt lake South Australia
74 E8 **Anti-Atlas** ▲▲ SW Morocco
103 U15 **Antibes** anc. Antipolis. Alpes-Maritimes, SE France 43°35´N 07°07´E
103 U15 **Antibes, Cap d'** headland SE France 43°33´N 07°08´E
Anticaria see Antequera
13 Q11 **Anticosti, Île d'** Eng. Anticosti Island. island Québec, E Canada
Anticosti Island see Anticosti, Île d'
102 K3 **Antifer, Cap d'** headland N France 49°43´N 00°10´E
30 L6 **Antigo** Wisconsin, N USA 45°10´N 89°10´W
13 Q15 **Antigonish** Nova Scotia, SE Canada 45°39´N 62°00´W
64 P11 **Antigua** Fuerteventura, Islas Canarias, NE Atlantic Ocean
45 X10 **Antigua** island S Antigua and Barbuda, Leeward Islands
Antigua see Antigua Guatemala
45 W9 **Antigua and Barbuda** ◆ commonwealth republic E West Indies
42 C6 **Antigua Guatemala** var. Antigua. Sacatepéquez, SW Guatemala 14°33´N 90°42´W
41 P11 **Antiguo Morelos** var. Antiguo-Morelos. Tamaulipas, C Mexico 22°35´N 99°08´W
115 F19 **Antíkyras, Kólpos** gulf C Greece
115 G24 **Antikýthira** var. Andikíthira. island S Greece
138 I7 **Anti-Lebanon** var. Jebel esh Sharqi, Ar. Al Jabal ash Sharqī, Fr. Anti-Liban. ▲▲ Lebanon/Syria
Anti-Liban see Anti-Lebanon
115 M22 **Antimácheia** Kos, Dodekánisa, Greece 47°19´N 07°54´E
115 I22 **Antímilos** island Kykládes, Greece, Aegean Sea
36 L6 **Antimony** Utah, W USA 38°07´N 112°00´W
An tInbhear Mór see Arklow
30 M10 **Antioch** Illinois, N USA 42°28´N 88°06´W
Antioch see Antakya
102 I10 **Antioche, Pertuis d'** inlet W France
Antiochia see Antakya
54 D8 **Antioquia** Antioquia, C Colombia 06°36´N 75°53´W
54 E8 **Antioquia** off. Departamento de Antioquia. ◈ province C Colombia
Antioquia, Departamento de see Antioquia
115 J21 **Antíparos** var. Andipáros. island Kykládes, Greece, Aegean Sea
115 B17 **Antípaxoi** var. Andipaxi. island Iónia Nísiá, Greece, C Mediterranean Sea
122 J8 **Antipayuta** Yamalo-Nenetskiy Avtonomnyy Okrug, N Russian Federation 69°08´N 76°43´E
192 L12 **Antipodes Islands** island group S New Zealand
Antipolis see Antibes
115 J18 **Antípsara** var. Andípsara. island E Greece
Antiquaria see Antequera
15 N10 **Antique, Lac** ◎ Québec, SE Canada
115 E18 **Antírrio** var. Andírrion. Dytikí Elláda, C Greece 38°20´N 21°46´E

115 K16 **Ántissa** *var.* Ándissa. Lésvos, E Greece 39°15´N 26°00´E
An tIúr *see* Newry
Antivari *see* Bar
56 C6 **Antizana** ▲ N Ecuador 0°29´S 78°08´W
27 Q13 **Antlers** Oklahoma, C USA 34°15´N 95°38´W
93 J14 **Antnäs** Norrbotten, N Sweden 65°32´N 21°53´E
Antō *see* Andong
62 G5 **Antofagasta** Antofagasta, N Chile 23°40´S 70°23´W
62 G6 **Antofagasta** *off.* Región de Antofagasta. ◆ *region* N Chile
Antofagasta, Región de *see* Antofagasta
62 I7 **Antofalla, Salar de** *salt lake* NW Argentina
99 D20 **Antoing** Hainaut, SW Belgium 50°34´N 03°26´E
43 S16 **Antón** Coclé, C Panama 08°23´N 80°15´W
24 M5 **Anton** Texas, SW USA 33°48´N 102°09´W
37 T11 **Anton Chico** New Mexico, SW USA 35°12´N 105°09´W
60 K12 **Antonina** Paraná, S Brazil 25°28´S 48°43´W
188 C16 **Antonio B. Won Pat International** ✕ (Agana) C Guam 13°28´N 144°48´E
103 O5 **Antony** Hauts-de-Seine, N France 48°45´N 02°17´E
Antratsit *see* Antratsyt
117 Y8 **Antratsyt** *Rus.* Antratsit. Luhans'ka Oblast', E Ukraine 48°07´N 39°05´E
97 G15 **Antrim** *Ir.* Aontroim. NE Northern Ireland, United Kingdom 54°43´N 06°13´W
97 G14 **Antrim** *Ir.* Aontroim. *cultural region* NE Northern Ireland, United Kingdom
97 G14 **Antrim Mountains** ▲▲ NE Northern Ireland, United Kingdom
172 H5 **Antsalova** Mahajanga, W Madagascar 18°40´S 44°37´E
Antserana *see* Antsiranana
An tSionainn *see* Shannon
172 J2 **Antsiranana** *var.* Antserana; *prev.* Antsirane, Diégo-Suarez. Antsiranana, N Madagascar 12°19´S 49°17´E
172 J2 **Antsiranana** ◆ *province* N Madagascar
Antsirane *see* Antsiranana
An tSiúir *see* Suir
118 I7 **Antsla** *Ger.* Anzen. Võrumaa, SE Estonia 57°52´N 26°33´E
An tSláine *see* Slaney
172 J3 **Antsohihy** Mahajanga, NW Madagascar 14°50´S 47°58´E
63 G14 **Antuco, Volcán** ⛰ C Chile 37°29´S 71°25´W
169 W10 **Antu, Gunung** ▲ Borneo, N Indonesia 0°57´N 118°51´E
An Tullach *see* Tullow
An-tung *see* Dandong
Antunnacum *see* Andernach
Antwerp *see* Antwerpen
99 G16 **Antwerpen** *Eng.* Antwerp, *Fr.* Anvers. Antwerpen, N Belgium 51°13´N 04°25´E
99 H16 **Antwerpen** *Eng.* Antwerp. ◆ *province* N Belgium
An Uaimh *see* Navan
154 N12 **Anugul** *var.* Angul. Orissa, E India 20°51´N 84°59´E
152 F9 **Anūpgarh** Rājasthān, NW India 29°10´N 73°14´E
154 K10 **Anūppur** Madhya Pradesh, C India 23°05´N 81°45´E
155 K24 **Anuradhapura** North Central Province, C Sri Lanka 08°20´N 80°25´E
Anvers *see* Antwerpen
194 G4 **Anvers Island** *island* Antarctica
39 N11 **Anvik** Alaska, USA 62°39´N 160°12´W
39 N10 **Anvik River** ≈ Alaska, USA
38 F17 **Anvil Peak** ▲ Semisopochnoi Island, Alaska, USA 51°59´N 179°36´E
159 P7 **Anxi** *var.* Yuanquan. Gansu, N China 40°32´N 95°50´E
182 F8 **Anxious Bay** *bay* South Australia
161 O5 **Anyang** Henan, C China 36°11´N 114°18´E
159 S11 **A'nyêmaqên Shan** ▲▲ C China
118 H12 **Anykščiai** Utena, E Lithuania 55°30´N 25°34´E
161 P13 **Anyuan** *var.* Xinshan. Jiangxi, S China 25°10´N 115°25´E
123 T7 **Anyuysk** Chukotskiy Avtonomnyy Okrug, NE Russian Federation 68°22´N 161°33´E
123 T7 **Anyuyskiy Khrebet** ▲▲ NE Russian Federation
54 D8 **Anzá** Antioquia, C Colombia 06°18´N 75°54´W
Anzen *see* Antsla
107 I16 **Anzio** Lazio, C Italy 41°28´N 12°38´E
55 O6 **Anzoátegui** *off.* Estado Anzoátegui. ◆ *state* NE Venezuela
Anzoátegui, Estado *see* Anzoátegui
147 P12 **Anzob** W Tajikistan 39°24´N 68°55´E
Anzyō *see* Anjō
Aoba *see* Ambae
165 X13 **Aoga-shima** *island* Izu-shotō, SE Japan
Aohan Qi *see* Xinhui
105 R3 **Aoiz** *Bas.* Agoitz, *var.* Agoiz. Navarra, N Spain 42°47´N 01°23´W
167 O11 **Ao Krung Thep** *var.* Krung Thep Mahanakhon, *Eng.* Bangkok. ● (Thailand) Bangkok, C Thailand 13°44´N 100°30´E
186 M9 **Aola** *var.* Tenaghau. Guadalcanal, C Solomon Islands 09°32´S 160°28´E
166 M15 **Ao Luk Nua** Krabi, SW Thailand 08°21´N 98°43´E
Aomen *see* Macao
172 N8 **Aomori** Aomori, Honshū, C Japan 40°50´N 140°43´E
172 N8 **Aomori** *off.* Aomori-ken. ◆ *prefecture* Honshū, C Japan
Aomori-ken *see* Aomori
Aontroim *see* Antrim
115 C15 **Aóos** *var.* Vijosa, Vijosë, *Alb.* Lumi i Vjosës. ≈ Albania/Greece *see also* Vjosës, Lumi i
Aóos *see* Vjosës, Lumi i
191 Q7 **Aorai, Mont** ⛰ Tahiti, W French Polynesia 17°36´S 149°29´W
185 E19 **Aoraki** *prev.* Aorangi, Mount Cook. ▲ South Island, New Zealand 43°38´S 170°05´E
167 R13 **Aôral, Phnum** *prev.* Phnom Aural. ▲ W Cambodia 12°01´N 104°10´E
Aorangi *see* Aoraki
185 L15 **Aorangi Mountains** ▲▲ North Island, New Zealand
184 H13 **Aorere** ≈ South Island, New Zealand
106 A7 **Aosta** *anc.* Augusta Praetoria. Valle d'Aosta, NW Italy 45°43´N 07°20´E
77 O11 **Aougoundou, Lac** ◎ S Mali
76 K9 **Aoukâr** *var.* Aouker. *plateau* C Mauritania
78 J13 **Aouk, Bahr** ≈ Central African Republic/Chad
Aouker *see* Aoukâr
74 B11 **Aousard** SE Western Sahara 22°42´N 14°22´W
164 H12 **Aoya** Tottori, Honshū, SW Japan 35°31´N 134°01´E
Aoyang *see* Shanggao
78 H5 **Aozou** Borkou-Ennedi-Tibesti, N Chad 22°01´N 17°11´E
26 M11 **Apache** Oklahoma, C USA 34°57´N 98°21´W
36 L14 **Apache Junction** Arizona, SW USA 33°25´N 111°33´W
24 J9 **Apache Mountains** ▲▲ Texas, SW USA
36 M16 **Apache Peak** ▲ Arizona, SW USA 31°50´N 110°25´W
116 H10 **Apahida** Cluj, NW Romania 46°49´N 23°45´E
23 T9 **Apalachee Bay** *bay* Florida, SE USA
23 T3 **Apalachee River** ≈ Georgia, SE USA
23 S10 **Apalachicola** Florida, SE USA 29°43´N 84°58´W
23 S10 **Apalachicola Bay** *bay* Florida, SE USA
23 R9 **Apalachicola River** ≈ Florida, SE USA
Apam *see* Apan
Apamama *see* Abemama
41 P14 **Apan** *var.* Apam. Hidalgo, C Mexico 19°48´N 98°25´W
42 J8 **Apanás, Lago de** ◎ NW Nicaragua
54 H14 **Apaporis, Río** ≈ Brazil/Colombia
185 C23 **Aparima** ≈ South Island, New Zealand
171 O1 **Aparri** Luzon, N Philippines 18°16´N 121°42´E
112 J9 **Apatin** Vojvodina, NW Serbia 45°40´N 19°01´E
124 J4 **Apatity** Murmanskaya Oblast', NW Russian Federation 67°34´N 33°26´E
55 X9 **Apatou** NW French Guiana 05°10´N 54°22´W
40 M14 **Apatzingán** *var.* Apatzingán de la Constitución. Michoacán, SW Mexico 19°05´N 102°20´W
Apatzingán de la Constitución *see* Apatzingán
171 X12 **Apauwar** Papua, E Indonesia 01°36´S 138°10´E
Apaxtla *see* Apaxtla de Castrejón
41 O15 **Apaxtla de Castrejón** *var.* Apaxtla. Guerrero, S Mexico 18°06´N 99°55´W
118 J7 **Ape** NE Latvia 57°32´N 26°42´E
98 L11 **Apeldoorn** Gelderland, E Netherlands 52°13´N 05°57´E
Apennines *see* Appennino
Apenrade *see* Aabenraa
57 L17 **Apere, Río** ≈ C Bolivia
55 W11 **Apetina** Sipaliwini, SE Suriname 03°30´N 55°03´W
21 U9 **Apex** North Carolina, SE USA 35°43´N 78°51´W
79 M16 **Api** Orientale, N Dem. Rep. Congo 03°40´N 25°26´E
152 M9 **Api** ▲ NW Nepal 30°07´N 80°57´E
192 H16 **Āpia** ● (Samoa) Upolu, SE Samoa 13°50´S 171°47´W
Apia *see* Abaiang
60 K11 **Apiaí** São Paulo, S Brazil 24°29´S 48°51´W
170 M16 **Api, Gunung** ▲ Pulau Sangeang, S Indonesia 08°09´S 119°03´E
187 N9 **Apio** Maramasike Island, N Solomon Islands 09°36´S 161°25´E
41 O15 **Apipilulco** Guerrero, S Mexico 18°11´N 99°40´W
41 P14 **Apizaco** Tlaxcala, S Mexico 19°26´N 98°09´W
137 Q8 **Apkhazeti** *var.* Abkhazia; *prev.* Ap'khazet'i. ◆ *autonomous republic* NW Georgia
Ap'khazet'i *see* Apkhazeti
104 I4 **A Pobla de Trives** *Cast.* Puebla de Trives. Galicia, NW Spain 42°21´N 07°16´W
55 U9 **Apoera** Sipaliwini, NW Suriname 05°12´N 57°13´W
115 O23 **Apolakkiá** Ródos, Dodekánisa, Greece, Aegean Sea 36°02´N 27°48´E
101 L16 **Apolda** Thüringen, C Germany 51°02´N 11°31´E
192 H16 **Apolima Strait** *strait* C Pacific Ocean
182 M13 **Apollo Bay** Victoria, SE Australia 38°40´S 143°44´E
Apollonia *see* Sozopol
57 J16 **Apolo** La Paz, W Bolivia 14°48´S 68°31´W
57 J16 **Apolobamba, Cordillera** ▲▲ Bolivia/Peru
171 Q8 **Apo, Mount** ⛰ Mindanao, S Philippines 06°54´N 125°16´E
23 W11 **Apopka** Florida, SE USA 28°40´N 81°30´W
23 W11 **Apopka, Lake** ◎ Florida, SE USA
59 J19 **Aporé, Rio** ≈ SW Brazil
30 K2 **Apostle Islands** *island group* Wisconsin, N USA
Apostolas Andreas, Cape *see* Zafer Burnu
61 F14 **Apóstoles** Misiones, NE Argentina 27°54´S 55°45´W
Apostólou Andréa, Akrotíri *see* Zafer Burnu
117 S9 **Apostolove** *Rus.* Apostolovo. Dnipropetrovs'ka Oblast', E Ukraine 47°40´N 33°45´E
Apostolovo *see* Apostolove
17 S10 **Appalachian Mountains** ▲▲ E USA
95 K14 **Äppelbo** Dalarna, C Sweden 60°30´N 14°00´E
98 N7 **Appelscha** *Fris.* Appelskea. Fryslân, N Netherlands 52°57´N 06°19´E
Appelskea *see* Appelscha
106 G11 **Appennino** *Eng.* Apennines. ▲▲ Italy/San Marino
107 L17 **Appennino Campano** ▲▲ C Italy
108 I7 **Appenzell** Inner-Rhoden, NW Switzerland 47°20´N 09°25´E
Appenzell *former canton see* Ausser-Rhoden, Inner-Rhoden
55 V12 **Appikalo** Sipaliwini, S Suriname 02°07´N 56°16´W
98 O5 **Appingedam** Groningen, NE Netherlands 53°18´N 06°52´E
25 X8 **Appleby** Texas, SW USA 31°43´N 94°36´W
97 L15 **Appleby-in-Westmorland** Cumbria, NW England, United Kingdom 54°35´N 02°26´W
30 K10 **Apple River** ≈ Illinois, N USA
30 I5 **Apple River** ≈ Wisconsin, N USA
25 W9 **Apple Springs** Texas, SW USA 31°13´N 94°57´W
29 S8 **Appleton** Minnesota, N USA 45°12´N 96°01´W
30 M7 **Appleton** Wisconsin, N USA 44°17´N 88°24´W
27 S5 **Appleton City** Missouri, C USA 38°11´N 94°01´W
35 U14 **Apple Valley** California, W USA 34°30´N 117°11´W
29 V9 **Apple Valley** Minnesota, N USA 44°43´N 93°13´W
21 U6 **Appomattox** Virginia, NE USA 37°21´N 78°51´W
188 B16 **Apra Harbor** *harbor* W Guam
188 B16 **Apra Heights** W Guam
106 F6 **Aprica, Passo dell'** *pass* N Italy
107 M15 **Apricena** *anc.* Hadria Picena. Puglia, SE Italy 41°47´N 15°27´E
114 I9 **Apriltsi** Lovech, N Bulgaria 42°50´N 24°54´E
126 L14 **Apsheronsk** Krasnodarskiy Kray, SW Russian Federation 44°27´N 39°45´E
Apsheronskiy Poluostrov *see* Abşeron Yarımadası
103 S15 **Apt** *anc.* Apta Julia. Vaucluse, SE France 43°54´N 05°24´E
Apta Julia *see* Apt
38 H12 **'Apua Point** *var.* Apua Point. *headland* Hawai'i, USA, C Pacific Ocean 19°15´N 155°13´W
60 I10 **Apucarana** Paraná, S Brazil 23°34´S 51°28´W
Apulia *see* Puglia
54 K8 **Apure** *off.* Estado Apure. ◆ *state* C Venezuela
Apure, Estado *see* Apure
54 J7 **Apure, Río** ≈ W Venezuela
57 F16 **Apurímac** *off.* Departamento de Apurímac. ◆ *department* C Peru
Apurímac, Departamento de *see* Apurímac
57 F15 **Apurímac, Río** ≈ S Peru
116 G10 **Apuseni, Munții** ▲▲ W Romania
Aqaba/'Aqaba *see* Al 'Aqabah
138 F15 **Aqaba, Gulf of** *var.* Gulf of Elat, *Ar.* Khalīj al 'Aqabah; *anc.* Sinus Aelaniticus. *gulf* NE Red Sea
139 R7 **'Aqabah** Al Anbār, C Iraq 33°33´N 42°55´E
'Aqabah, Khalīj al *see* Aqaba, Gulf of
149 O2 **Āqchah** *var.* Āqcheh. Jowzjān, N Afghanistan 37°N 66°07´E
Āqcheh *see* Āqchah
Aqkengse *see* Akkense
Aqköl *see* Akkol'
Aqmola *see* Astana
Aqmola Oblysy *see* Akmola
158 L10 **Aqqikkol Hu** ◎ NW China
Aqqū *see* Akku
Aqqystaū *see* Akkystau
'Aqrah *see* Ākrē
Aqsay *see* Aksay
Aqshataū *see* Akshatau
Aqsū *see* Aksu
Aqsūat *see* Aksuat
Aqtas *see* Aktas
Aqtaū *see* Aktau
Aqtöbe *see* Aktobe
Aqtöbe Oblysy *see* Aktyubinsk
Aqtoghay *see* Aktogay
Aquae Augustae *see* Dax
Aquae Calidae *see* Bath
Aquae Flaviae *see* Chaves
Aquae Grani *see* Aachen
Aquae Panoniae *see* Baden
Aquae Sextiae *see* Aix-en-Provence
Aquae Solis *see* Bath
Aquae Tarbelicae *see* Dax
36 J11 **Aquarius Mountains** ▲▲ Arizona, SW USA
62 O5 **Aquidabán, Río** ≈ E Paraguay
59 H20 **Aquidauana** Mato Grosso do Sul, S Brazil 20°27´S 55°45´W
40 L15 **Aquila** Michoacán, S Mexico 18°36´N 103°32´W
Aquila/Aquila degli Abruzzi *see* L'Aquila
25 T8 **Aquilla** Texas, SW USA 31°51´N 97°13´W
44 L9 **Aquin** S Haiti 18°16´N 73°24´W
Aquisgranum *see* Aachen
102 J13 **Aquitaine** ◆ *region* SW France
Aqzhar *see* Akzhar
153 P13 **Āra** *prev.* Arrah. Bihār, N India 25°34´N 84°40´E
105 S4 **Ara** ≈ NE Spain
23 P2 **Arab** Alabama, S USA 34°19´N 86°30´W
Araba *see* Álava
138 G12 **'Arabah, Wādī al** *Heb.* Ha'Arava. *dry watercourse* Israel/Jordan
117 U12 **Arabats'ka Strilka, Kosa** *spit* S Ukraine
117 U12 **Arabats'ka Zatoka** *gulf* S Ukraine
'Arab, Baḩr al *see* Arab, Bahr el
80 C12 **Arab, Bahr el** *var.* Baḩr al 'Arab. ≈ S Sudan
55 E7 **Arabela, Río** ≈ N Peru
173 O4 **Arabian Basin** *undersea feature* N Arabian Sea 11°30´N 65°00´E
Arabian Desert *see* Sahara el Sharqîya
141 N9 **Arabian Peninsula** *peninsula* SW Asia
85 P15 **Arabian Plate** *tectonic feature* Africa/Asia/Europe
141 W14 **Arabian Sea** *sea* NW Indian Ocean
Arabicus, Sinus *see* Red Sea
'Arabī, Khalīj al *see* Persian Gulf
Arabistan *see* Khūzestān
'Arabīyah as Su'ūdīyah, Al Mamlakah al *see* Saudi Arabia
'Arabīyah Jumhūrīyah, Mişr al *see* Egypt
138 I9 **'Arab, Jabal al** ▲▲ S Syria
Arab Republic of Egypt *see* Egypt
139 Y12 **'Arab, Shaṭṭ al** *Eng.* Shatt al Arab, *Per.* Arvand Rūd. ≈ Iran/Iraq
136 I11 **Araç** Kastamonu, N Turkey 41°14´N 33°20´E
59 P16 **Aracaju** *state capital* Sergipe, E Brazil 10°45´S 37°07´W
54 F5 **Aracataca** Magdalena, N Colombia 10°38´N 74°09´W
58 P13 **Aracati** Ceará, E Brazil 04°32´S 37°45´W
60 J8 **Araçatuba** São Paulo, S Brazil 21°12´S 50°24´W
136 I11 **Araç Çayı** ≈ N Turkey
104 J13 **Aracena** Andalucía, S Spain 37°54´N 06°33´W
115 F20 **Arachnaío** ▲▲ S Greece
115 D16 **Árachthos** *var.* Arta, *prev.* Árakhthos; *anc.* Arachthus. ≈ W Greece
Arachthus *see* Árachthos
59 N19 **Araçuaí** Minas Gerais, SE Brazil 16°52´S 42°03´W
138 F11 **Arad** Southern, S Israel 31°16´N 35°09´E
116 F11 **Arad** Arad, W Romania 46°12´N 21°20´E
116 F11 **Arad** ◆ *county* W Romania
78 J9 **Arada** Biltine, NE Chad 15°00´N 20°38´E
143 P18 **'Arādah** Abū Ẓaby, S United Arab Emirates 22°57´N 53°24´E
Aradhippou *see* Aradíppou
121 Q3 **Aradíppou** *var.* Aradhippou. SE Cyprus 34°57´N 33°37´E
174 K6 **Arafura Sea** *Ind.* Laut Arafuru. *sea* W Pacific Ocean
174 L6 **Arafura Shelf** *undersea feature* C Arafura Sea
Arafuru, Laut *see* Arafura Sea
59 J18 **Aragarças** Goiás, C Brazil 15°55´S 52°12´W
Aragats, Gora *see* Aragats Lerr
137 T12 **Aragats Lerr** *Rus.* Gora Aragats. ▲ W Armenia 40°31´N 44°06´E
32 E14 **Arago, Cape** *headland* Oregon, NW USA 43°17´N 124°25´W
105 R6 **Aragón** *autonomous community* E Spain
105 Q4 **Aragón** ≈ NE Spain
107 I24 **Aragona** Sicilia, Italy, C Mediterranean Sea 37°25´N 13°37´E
105 Q7 **Aragoncillo** ▲ C Spain 40°59´N 02°01´W
54 L5 **Aragua** *off.* Estado Aragua. ◆ *state* N Venezuela
55 N6 **Aragua de Barcelona** Anzoátegui, NE Venezuela 09°30´N 64°51´W
55 O5 **Aragua de Maturín** Monagas, NE Venezuela 09°58´N 63°30´W
Aragua, Estado *see* Aragua
59 K15 **Araguaia, Río** *var.* Araguaya. ≈ C Brazil
59 K19 **Araguari** Minas Gerais, SE Brazil 18°38´S 48°13´W
58 J11 **Araguari, Rio** ≈ SW Brazil
Araguaya *see* Araguaia, Río
104 K14 **Arahal** Andalucía, S Spain 37°15´N 05°33´W
165 N11 **Arai** Niigata, Honshū, C Japan 37°02´N 138°17´E
Árainn *see* Inishmore
Árainn Mhór *see* Aran Island
Ara Jovis *see* Aranjuez
74 J11 **Arak** C Algeria 25°17´N 03°45´E
171 Y15 **Arak** Papua, E Indonesia 07°14´S 139°40´E
142 M7 **Arāk** *prev.* Sultānābād. Markazī, W Iran 34°07´N 49°39´E
188 D10 **Arakabesan** *island* Palau Islands, N Palau
55 S7 **Arakaka** NW Guyana 07°37´N 59°58´W
Arakan State *see* Rakhine State
166 K5 **Arakan Yoma** ▲▲ W Myanmar (Burma)
165 O10 **Arakawa** Niigata, Honshū, C Japan 38°06´N 139°25´E
Árakhthos *see* Árachthos
Araks/Arak's *see* Aras
158 H7 **Aral** Xinjiang Uygur Zizhiqu, NW China 40°40´N 81°19´E
Aral *see* Aralsk, Kazakhstan
Aral *see* Vose', Tajikistan
Aral-Bukhorskiy Kanal *see* Amu-Buxoro Kanali
137 T12 **Aralık** Iğdır, E Turkey 39°54´N 44°28´E
146 H5 **Aral Sea** *Kaz.* Aral Tengizi, *Rus.* Aral'skoye More, *Uzb.* Orol Dengizi. *inland sea* Kazakhstan/Uzbekistan
144 L13 **Aral'sk** *Kaz.* Aral. Kzylorda, SW Kazakhstan 46°48´N 61°40´E
Aral'skoye More/Aral Tengizi *see* Aral Sea
41 O10 **Aramberri** Nuevo León, NE Mexico 24°05´N 99°52´W
186 B8 **Aramia** ≈ SW Papua New Guinea
105 N5 **Aranda de Duero** Castilla y León, N Spain 41°40´N 03°41´W
112 M12 **Aranđelovac** *prev.* Arandjelovac. Serbia, C Serbia 44°18´N 20°32´E
Arandjelovac *see* Aranđelovac
97 J19 **Aran Fawddwy** ▲ NW Wales, United Kingdom 52°48´N 03°42´W
97 C14 **Aran Island** *Ir.* Árainn Mhór. *island* NW Ireland
97 A18 **Aran Islands** *island group* W Ireland
105 N9 **Aranjuez** *anc.* Ara Jovis. Madrid, C Spain 40°02´N 03°37´W
83 E20 **Aranos** Hardap, SE Namibia 24°10´S 19°08´E
25 U14 **Aransas Bay** *inlet* Texas, SW USA
25 T14 **Aransas Pass** Texas, SW USA 27°54´N 97°09´W
191 O3 **Aranuka** *prev.* Nanouki. *atoll* Tungaru, W Kiribati
143 N6 **Ārān-va-Bīdgol** *var.* Golārā. Eşfahān, C Iran 34°03´N 51°30´E
167 Q11 **Aranyaprathet** Prachin Buri, S Thailand 13°42´N 102°32´E
Aranyosasztal *see* Zlatý Stôl
Aranyosgyéres *see* Câmpia Turzii
Aranyosmarót *see* Zlaté Moravce
164 C14 **Arao** Kumamoto, Kyūshū, SW Japan 32°58´N 130°26´E
77 O8 **Araouane** Tombouctou, N Mali 18°53´N 03°31´W
26 L10 **Arapaho** Oklahoma, C USA 35°34´N 98°57´W
29 N16 **Arapahoe** Nebraska, C USA 40°18´N 99°54´W
57 I16 **Arapa, Laguna** ◎ SE Peru
185 K14 **Arapawa Island** *island* C New Zealand
61 E17 **Arapey Grande, Río** ≈ N Uruguay
59 P16 **Arapiraca** Alagoas, E Brazil 09°45´S 36°40´W
140 M3 **'Ar'ar** Al Ḩudūd ash Shamālīyah, NW Saudi Arabia 31°N 41°E
54 G15 **Araracuara** Caquetá, S Colombia 0°36´S 72°24´W
61 K15 **Araranguá** Santa Catarina, S Brazil 28°56´S 49°30´W
60 L8 **Araraquara** São Paulo, S Brazil 21°46´S 48°08´W
59 O13 **Araras** Ceará, E Brazil 04°08´S 40°30´W
58 I14 **Araras** Pará, N Brazil 06°04´S 54°34´W
60 L9 **Araras** São Paulo, S Brazil 22°21´S 47°21´W
60 H11 **Araras, Serra das** ▲▲ S Brazil
137 U12 **Ararat** S Armenia 39°49´N 44°45´E
182 M12 **Ararat** Victoria, SE Australia 37°20´S 143°00´E
Ararat, Mount *see* Büyükağrı Dağı
140 M3 **'Ar'ar, Wādī** *dry watercourse* Iraq/Saudi Arabia
129 N7 **Aras** *Arm.* Arak's, *Az.* Araz Nehri, *Per.* Rūd-e Aras, *Rus.* Araks; *prev.* Araxes. ≈ SW Asia
Aras de Alpuente *see* Aras de los Olmos
105 R9 **Aras de los Olmos** *prev.* Aras de Alpuente. Valenciana, E Spain 39°55´N 01°09´W
137 S13 **Aras Güneyi Dağları** ▲▲ NE Turkey
Aras, Rūd-e *see* Aras
191 U9 **Aratika** *atoll* Îles Tuamotu, C French Polynesia
Aratürük *see* Yiwu
54 I8 **Arauca** Arauca, NE Colombia 07°03´N 70°47´W
54 I8 **Arauca** *off.* Intendencia de Arauca. ◆ *province* NE Colombia
Arauca, Intendencia de *see* Arauca
63 G15 **Araucanía** *off.* Region de la Araucanía. ◆ *region* C Chile
Araucanía, Region de la *see* Araucanía
54 L7 **Arauca, Río** ≈ Colombia/Venezuela
63 F14 **Arauco** Bío Bío, C Chile 37°15´S 73°22´W
63 F14 **Arauco, Golfo de** *gulf* S Chile
54 H8 **Arauquita** Arauca, C Colombia 06°57´N 71°19´W
Arausio *see* Orange
152 F13 **Arāvali Range** ▲▲ N India
186 I7 **Arawa** Bougainville Island, NE Papua New Guinea 06°15´S 155°35´E
185 C20 **Arawata** ≈ South Island, New Zealand
186 F7 **Arawe Islands** *island group* E Papua New Guinea
59 L20 **Araxá** Minas Gerais, SE Brazil 19°37´S 46°50´W
Araxes *see* Aras
55 O5 **Araya** Sucre, N Venezuela 10°34´N 64°15´W
Araz Nehri *see* Aras
105 R4 **Arba** ≈ N Spain
81 I15 **Ārba Minch'** Southern Nationalities, S Ethiopia 06°02´N 37°34´E
139 U4 **Arbat** As Sulaymānīyah, NE Iraq 35°26´N 45°34´E
107 D19 **Arbatax** Sardegna, Italy, C Mediterranean Sea 39°57´N 09°42´E
Arbe *see* Rab
Arbela *see* Arbīl
139 S3 **Arbīl** *var.* Erbil, Irbil, *Kurd.* Hawlēr; *anc.* Arbela. Arbīl, N Iraq 36°12´N 44°01´E
95 M16 **Arboga** Västmanland, C Sweden 59°24´N 15°50´E
95 M16 **Arbogaån** ≈ C Sweden
103 S9 **Arbois** Jura, E France 46°54´N 05°45´E
54 D6 **Arboletes** Antioquia, NW Colombia 08°52´N 76°25´W
11 X15 **Arborg** Manitoba, S Canada 50°52´N 97°20´W
94 N12 **Arbrå** Gävleborg, C Sweden 61°27´N 16°21´E
96 K10 **Arbroath** *anc.* Aberbrothock. E Scotland, United Kingdom 56°34´N 02°35´W
35 N6 **Arbuckle** California, W USA 39°00´N 122°05´W
27 N12 **Arbuckle Mountains** ▲▲ Oklahoma, C USA
162 I5 **Arbulag** *var.* Mandal. Hövsgöl, N Mongolia 49°55´N 99°21´E
Arbuzinka *see* Arbuzynka
117 Q8 **Arbuzynka** *Rus.* Arbuzinka. Mykolayivs'ka Oblast', S Ukraine 47°54´N 31°19´E
103 U12 **Arc** ≈ E France
102 J13 **Arcachon** Gironde, SW France 44°40´N 01°11´W
102 J13 **Arcachon, Bassin d'** *inlet* SW France
18 E10 **Arcade** New York, NE USA 42°32´N 78°19´W
23 W14 **Arcadia** Florida, SE USA 27°13´N 81°51´W
22 H5 **Arcadia** Louisiana, S USA 32°33´N 92°55´W
30 J7 **Arcadia** Wisconsin, N USA 44°15´N 91°30´W
Arcae Remorum *see* Châlons-en-Champagne
44 L9 **Arcahaie** C Haiti 18°46´N 72°32´W
34 K3 **Arcata** California, W USA 40°51´N 124°06´W
35 U6 **Arc Dome** ▲ Nevada, W USA 38°52´N 117°20´W
107 J16 **Arce** Lazio, C Italy 41°35´N 13°34´E
41 O15 **Arcelia** Guerrero, S Mexico 18°20´N 100°16´W
99 M15 **Arcen** Limburg, SE Netherlands 51°28´N 06°10´E
115 J25 **Archánes** *var.* Áno Arkhánai, Epáno Archánes; *prev.* Epáno Arkhánai. Kríti, Greece, E Mediterranean Sea 35°12´N 25°10´E
Archangel *see* Arkhangel'sk
Archangel Bay *see* Chëshskaya Guba
115 O23 **Archángelos** *var.* Arhangelos, Arkhángelos. Ródos, Dodekánisa, Greece, Aegean Sea 36°13´N 28°07´E
114 F7 **Archar** ≈ NW Bulgaria
31 R11 **Archbold** Ohio, N USA 41°31´N 84°18´W
105 R12 **Archena** Murcia, SE Spain 38°07´N 01°17´W
25 R5 **Archer City** Texas, SW USA 33°36´N 98°37´W
104 M14 **Archidona** Andalucía, S Spain 37°06´N 04°23´W
65 B25 **Arch Islands** *island group* SW Falkland Islands
106 G13 **Arcidosso** Toscana, C Italy 42°52´N 11°30´E
103 Q5 **Arcis-sur-Aube** Aube, N France 48°31´N 04°09´E
182 F3 **Arckaringa Creek** *seasonal river* South Australia
106 G7 **Arco** Trentino-Alto Adige, N Italy 45°53´N 10°52´E
33 Q14 **Arco** Idaho, NW USA 43°38´N 113°18´W
30 M14 **Arcola** Illinois, N USA 39°39´N 88°19´W
105 P6 **Arcos de Jalón** Castilla y León, N Spain 41°12´N 02°13´W
104 K15 **Arcos de la Frontera** Andalucía, S Spain 36°45´N 05°49´W
104 G5 **Arcos de Valdevez** Viana do Castelo, N Portugal 41°51´N 08°25´W
59 P15 **Arcoverde** Pernambuco, E Brazil 08°23´S 37°W
102 H5 **Arcovest, Pointe de l'** *headland* NW France 48°49´N 02°58´W
Arctic Mid Oceanic Ridge *see* Nansen Cordillera
197 R8 **Arctic Ocean** *ocean*
8 G7 **Arctic Red River** ≈ Northwest Territories/Yukon Territory, NW Canada
Arctic Red River *see* Tsiigehtchic
39 S6 **Arctic Village** Alaska, USA 68°07´N 145°32´W
194 H1 **Arctowski** *Polish research station* South Shetland Islands, Antarctica 61°57´S 58°23´W
114 I12 **Arda** *var.* Ardhas, *Gk.* Ardas. ≈ Bulgaria/Greece *see also* Ardas
142 L2 **Ardabīl** *var.* Ardebil. Ardabīl, NW Iran 38°15´N 48°18´E
142 L2 **Ardabīl** *off.* Ostān-e Ardabīl. ◆ *province* NW Iran
Ardabīl, Ostān-e *see* Ardabīl
137 R11 **Ardahan** Ardahan, NE Turkey 41°08´N 42°41´E
137 S11 **Ardahan** ◆ *province* Ardahan, Turkey
143 P8 **Ardakān** Yazd, C Iran 32°20´N 53°59´E
94 E12 **Årdalstangen** Sogn Og Fjordane, S Norway 61°14´N 07°45´E
137 R11 **Ardanuç** Artvin, NE Turkey 41°07´N 42°04´E
114 L12 **Ardas** *var.* Ardhas, *Bul.* Arda. ≈ Bulgaria/Greece *see also* Arda
138 I13 **Arḑ aş Şawwān** *var.* Ardh es Suwwān. *plain* S Jordan
127 P5 **Ardatov** Respublika Mordoviya, W Russian Federation 54°49´N 46°13´E
14 G12 **Ardbeg** Ontario, S Canada 45°38´N 80°05´W
Ardeal *see* Transylvania
Ardebil *see* Ardabīl
103 Q13 **Ardèche** ◆ *department* E France
103 Q13 **Ardèche** ≈ C France
97 F17 **Ardee** *Ir.* Baile Átha Fhirdhia. Louth, NE Ireland 53°52´N 06°33´W
103 Q3 **Ardennes** ◆ *department* NE France
99 J23 **Ardennes** *physical region* Belgium/France
137 Q11 **Ardeşen** Rize, NE Turkey 41°14´N 41°00´E
143 O7 **Ardestān** *var.* Ardistan. Eşfahān, C Iran 33°29´N 52°17´E
108 J9 **Ardez** Graubünden, SE Switzerland 46°47´N 10°09´E
Ardhas *see* Arda/Ardas
Ardh es Suwwān *see* Arḑ aş Şawwān
Ardila *see* Ardila, Ribeira de
104 I12 **Ardila, Ribeira de** *Sp.* Ardilla. ≈ Portugal/Spain *see also* Ardilla
Ardila, Ribeira de *see* Ardilla
11 T17 **Ardill** Saskatchewan, S Canada 49°56´N 105°49´W
104 I12 **Ardilla** *Port.* Ribeira de Ardila. ≈ Portugal/Spain *see also* Ardila, Ribeira de
40 M11 **Ardilla, Cerro la** ▲ C Mexico 22°15´N 102°33´W
114 J12 **Ardino** Kŭrdzhali, S Bulgaria 41°38´N 25°22´E
Ardistan *see* Ardestān
183 P9 **Ardlethan** New South Wales, SE Australia 34°24´S 146°52´E
Ard Mhacha *see* Armagh
23 P1 **Ardmore** Alabama, S USA 34°59´N 86°51´W
27 N13 **Ardmore** Oklahoma, C USA 34°11´N 97°08´W
20 J10 **Ardmore** Tennessee, S USA 35°00´N 86°48´W
96 G10 **Ardnamurchan, Point of** *headland* N Scotland, United Kingdom 56°42´N 06°15´W
Ardni *see* Arnøya
99 C17 **Ardooie** West-Vlaanderen, W Belgium 50°59´N 03°10´E
182 I9 **Ardrossan** South Australia 34°27´S 137°54´E
116 H9 **Ardusat** *Hung.* Erdőszáda. Maramureş, N Romania 47°36´N 23°25´E
93 F16 **Åre** Jämtland, C Sweden 63°25´N 13°04´E
79 P16 **Arebi** Orientale, NE Dem. Rep. Congo 02°47´N 29°35´E
45 T5 **Arecibo** C Puerto Rico 18°29´N 66°44´W
171 V13 **Aredo** Papua, E Indonesia 02°27´S 133°59´E
59 P14 **Areia Branca** Rio Grande do Norte, E Brazil 04°53´S 37°03´W
119 O14 **Arekhawsk** *Rus.* Orekhovsk. Vitsyebskaya Voblasts', N Belarus 54°42´N 30°30´E
Arel *see* Arlon
Arelas/Arelate *see* Arles
Arenal, Embalse de *see* Arenal Laguna
42 L12 **Arenal Laguna** *var.* Embalse de Arenal. ◎ NW Costa Rica
42 L13 **Arenal, Volcán** ⛰ NW Costa Rica 10°21´N 84°42´W
34 K6 **Arena, Point** *headland* California, W USA 38°57´N 123°44´W
59 H17 **Arenápolis** Mato Grosso, W Brazil 14°25´S 56°52´W
40 G10 **Arena, Punta** *headland* NW Mexico 23°28´N 109°24´W
104 L8 **Arenas de San Pedro** Castilla y León, N Spain 40°12´N 05°05´W
63 I24 **Arenas, Punta de** *headland* S Argentina 53°10´S 68°15´W
61 B20 **Arenaza** Buenos Aires, E Argentina 34°55´S 61°45´W
95 F17 **Arendal** Aust-Agder, S Norway 58°27´N 08°45´E
99 J16 **Arendonk** Antwerpen, N Belgium 51°18´N 05°06´E
43 T15 **Arenosa** Panamá, N Panama 09°02´N 79°57´W
Arensburg *see* Kuressaare
105 W5 **Arenys de Mar** Cataluña, NE Spain 41°35´N 02°33´E
106 C9 **Arenzano** Liguria, NW Italy 44°25´N 08°43´E
115 F22 **Areópoli** *prev.* Areópolis. Pelopónnisos, S Greece 36°40´N 22°24´E
Areópolis *see* Areópoli
57 H18 **Arequipa** Arequipa, SE Peru 16°24´S 71°33´W
57 G17 **Arequipa** *off.* Departamento de Arequipa. ◆ *department* Arequia SW Peru
Arequipa, Departamento de *see* Arequipa
61 B19 **Arequito** Santa Fe, C Argentina 33°09´S 61°28´W
104 M7 **Arévalo** Castilla y León, N Spain 41°04´N 04°44´W
106 H12 **Arezzo** *anc.* Arretium. Toscana, C Italy 43°28´N 11°50´E
105 Q4 **Arga** ≈ N Spain
Argaeus *see* Erciyes Dağı
115 G17 **Argalastí** Thessalía, C Greece 39°13´N 23°13´E
105 O10 **Argamasilla de Alba** Castilla-La Mancha, C Spain 39°08´N 03°05´W
158 L8 **Argan** Xinjiang Uygur Zizhiqu, NW China 40°09´N 88°16´E
105 O8 **Arganda** Madrid, C Spain 40°19´N 03°26´W
104 H8 **Arganil** Coimbra, N Portugal 40°13´N 08°03´W
171 P6 **Argao** Cebu, C Philippines 09°52´N 123°33´E
153 V15 **Argartala** Tripura, NE India
123 N9 **Arga-Sala** ≈ Respublika Sakha (Yakutiya), NE Russian Federation
103 P17 **Argelès-sur-Mer** Pyrénées-Orientales, S France 42°33´N 03°01´E
103 T15 **Argens** ≈ SE France
106 H9 **Argenta** Emilia-Romagna, N Italy 44°37´N 11°49´E
102 K5 **Argentan** Orne, N France 48°45´N 00°01´W
103 N12 **Argentat** Corrèze, C France 45°06´N 01°57´E
106 A9 **Argentera** Piemonte, NE Italy 44°25´N 06°57´E
103 N5 **Argenteuil** Val-d'Oise, N France 48°57´N 02°13´E
62 K13 **Argentina** *off.* Argentine Republic. ◆ *republic* S South America
Argentina Basin *see* Argentine Basin
Argentine Abyssal Plain *see* Argentine Plain
65 I19 **Argentine Basin** *var.* Argentina Basin. *undersea feature* SW Atlantic Ocean 45°00´S 45°00´W
65 I20 **Argentine Plain** *var.* Argentine Abyssal Plain. *undersea feature* SW Atlantic Ocean 47°31´S 50°00´W
Argentine Republic *see* Argentina
Argentine Rise *see* Falkland Plateau
63 H22 **Argentino, Lago** ◎ S Argentina
102 K8 **Argenton-Château** Deux-Sèvres, W France 46°59´N 00°22´W
102 M9 **Argenton-sur-Creuse** Indre, C France 46°34´N 01°32´E
Argentoratum *see* Strasbourg
116 I12 **Argeş** ◆ *county* S Romania
116 K14 **Argeş** ≈ S Romania
149 O8 **Arghandāb, Daryā-ye** ≈ SE Afghanistan
Arghastān *see* Arghistān
Arghestān *see* Arghistān
149 O8 **Arghistān** *Pash.* Arghastān; *prev.* Arghestān. ≈ SE Afghanistan
Argirocastro *see* Gjirokastër
80 E7 **Argo** Northern, N Sudan 19°31´N 30°25´E
173 P7 **Argo Fracture Zone** *tectonic feature* C Indian Ocean
115 F20 **Argolikós Kólpos** *gulf* S Greece
103 R4 **Argonne** *physical region* NE France
115 F20 **Árgos** Pelopónnisos, S Greece 37°38´N 22°43´E
139 S1 **Argōsh** Dahūk, N Iraq 37°07´N 44°13´E
115 D14 **Árgos Orestikó** Dytikí Makedonía, N Greece 40°27´N 21°15´E
115 B19 **Argostóli** *var.* Argostólion. Kefallonía, Iónia Nisiá, Greece, C Mediterranean Sea 38°13´N 20°29´E
Argostólion *see* Argostóli
Argovie *see* Aargau
35 O14 **Arguello, Point** *headland* California, W USA 34°34´N 120°39´W
127 P16 **Argun** Chechenskaya Respublika, SW Russian Federation 43°16´N 45°53´E

◆ Country
● Country Capital
◇ Dependent Territory
○ Dependent Territory Capital
◆ Administrative Regions
✕ International Airport
▲ Mountain
▲▲ Mountain Range
⛰ Volcano
≈ River
◎ Lake
⊠ Reservoir

157 *T2* **Argun** *Chin.* Ergun He, *Rus.* Argun'. ≈ China/Russian Federation
77 *T12* **Argungu** Kebbi, NW Nigeria *12°45′N 04°24′E*
Arguut *see* Guchin-Us
181 *N3* **Argyle, Lake** *salt lake* Western Australia
96 *G12* **Argyll** *cultural region* W Scotland, United Kingdom
Argyrokastron *see* Gjirokastër
162 *I7* **Arhangay** ⬖ *province* C Mongolia
Arhangelos *see* Archángelos
95 *G22* **Århus** *var.* Aarhus. Midtjylland, C Denmark *56°09′N 10°11′E*
139 *T1* **Ārī** Arbīl, E Iraq *37°07′N 44°34′E*
Aria *see* Herāt
83 *F22* **Ariamsvlei** Karas, SE Namibia *28°08′S 19°50′E*
107 *L17* **Ariano Irpino** Campania, S Italy *41°08′N 15°00′E*
54 *F11* **Ariari, Río** ≈ C Colombia
151 *K19* **Ari Atoll** *var.* Alifu Atoll. *atoll* C Maldives
77 *P11* **Aribinda** N Burkina *14°12′N 00°50′W*
62 *G2* **Arica** *hist.* San Marcos de Arica. Arica y Parinacota, N Chile *18°31′S 70°18′W*
54 *H16* **Arica** Amazonas, S Colombia *02°09′S 71°48′W*
62 *G2* **Arica** ✈ Arica y Parinacota, N Chile *18°30′S 70°20′W*
62 *H2* **Arica y Parinacota** ⬖ *region* N Chile
114 *E13* **Aridaía** *var.* Aridea, Aridhaía. Dytikí Makedonía, N Greece *40°59′N 22°04′E*
Aridea *see* Aridaía
172 *I15* **Aride, Île** *island* Inner Islands, NE Seychelles
Aridhaía *see* Aridaía
103 *N17* **Ariège** ⬖ *department* S France
102 *M16* **Ariège** *var.* la Riege. ≈ Andorra/France
116 *H11* **Arieș** ≈ W Romania
149 *U10* **Ārifwāla** Punjab, E Pakistan *30°15′N 73°08′E*
Ariguaní *see* El Difícil
138 *G11* **Arīhā** Al Karak, W Jordan *31°25′N 35°47′E*
138 *I3* **Arīḩā** *var.* Arīhā. Idlib, W Syria *35°50′N 36°36′E*
Arīhā *see* Arīḩā
Arīḩā *see* Jericho
37 *W4* **Arikaree River** ≈ Colorado/Nebraska, C USA
112 *L13* **Arilje** Serbia, W Serbia *43°45′N 20°06′E*
45 *U14* **Arima** Trinidad, Trinidad and Tobago *10°38′N 61°17′W*
Arime *see* Al 'Arīmah
Ariminum *see* Rimini
59 *H16* **Arinos, Rio** ≈ W Brazil
40 *M14* **Ario de Rosales** *var.* Ario de Rosáles. Michoacán, SW Mexico *19°12′N 101°42′W*
Ario de Rosáles *see* Ario de Rosales
118 *F12* **Ariogala** Kaunas, C Lithuania *55°16′N 23°30′E*
47 *T7* **Aripuanã** ≈ W Brazil
59 *E15* **Ariquemes** Rondônia, W Brazil *09°55′S 63°06′W*
121 *W13* **'Arīsh, Wādi el** ≈ NE Egypt
54 *K6* **Arismendi** Barinas, C Venezuela *08°29′N 68°22′W*
10 *J14* **Aristazabal Island** *island* SW Canada
60 *F13* **Aristóbulo del Valle** Misiones, NE Argentina *27°09′S 54°54′W*
172 *I5* **Arivonimamo** ✈ (Antananarivo) Antananarivo, C Madagascar *19°00′S 47°11′E*
Arixang *see* Wenquan
105 *Q6* **Ariza** Aragón, NE Spain *41°19′N 02°03′W*
62 *I6* **Arizaro, Salar de** *salt lake* NW Argentina
105 *O2* **Arizgoiti** *var.* Basauri. País Vasco, N Spain *43°13′N 02°54′W*
62 *K13* **Arizona** San Luis, C Argentina *35°44′S 65°16′W*
36 *J12* **Arizona** *off.* State of Arizona, *also known as* Copper State, Grand Canyon State. ⬖ *state* SW USA
40 *G4* **Arizpe** Sonora, NW Mexico *30°20′N 110°11′W*
95 *J16* **Årjäng** Värmland, C Sweden *59°24′N 12°09′E*
143 *P8* **Arjenān** Yazd, C Iran *32°19′N 53°48′E*
92 *I13* **Arjeplog** *Lapp.* Árjepluovve. Norrbotten, N Sweden *66°04′N 18°E*
Árjepluovve *see* Arjeplog
54 *E5* **Arjona** Bolívar, N Colombia *10°14′N 75°22′W*
105 *N13* **Arjona** Andalucía, S Spain *37°56′N 04°04′W*
123 *S10* **Arka** Khabarovskiy Kray, E Russian Federation *60°04′N 142°17′E*
22 *L2* **Arkabutla Lake** ⊠ Mississippi, S USA
127 *O7* **Arkadak** Saratovskaya Oblast', W Russian Federation *51°55′N 43°29′E*
27 *T13* **Arkadelphia** Arkansas, C USA *34°07′N 93°06′W*
115 *J25* **Arkalochóri** ; *prev.* Arkalokhórion. Kríti, Greece, E Mediterranean Sea *35°09′N 25°15′E*
Arkalohori/Arkalokhórion *see* Arkalochóri
145 *O10* **Arkalyk** *Kaz.* Arqalyq. Kostanay, N Kazakhstan *50°17′N 66°51′E*
27 *U10* **Arkansas** *off.* State of Arkansas, *also known as* The Land of Opportunity. ⬖ *state* S USA
27 *W14* **Arkansas City** Arkansas, C USA *33°36′N 91°12′W*
27 *O7* **Arkansas City** Kansas, C USA *37°03′N 97°02′W*
16 *K11* **Arkansas River** ≈ C USA
182 *J5* **Arkaroola** South Australia *30°21′S 139°20′E*
Arkhángelos *see* Archángelos
124 *L8* **Arkhangel'sk** *Eng.* Archangel. Arkhangel'skaya Oblast', NW Russian Federation *64°32′N 40°40′E*
124 *L9* **Arkhangel'skaya Oblast'** ⬖ *province* NW Russian Federation
127 *O14* **Arkhangel'skoye** Stavropol'skiy Kray, SW Russian Federation *44°37′N 44°03′E*
123 *R14* **Arkhara** Amurskaya Oblast', S Russian Federation *49°20′N 130°04′E*
97 *G19* **Arklow** *Ir.* An tInbhear Mór. SE Ireland *52°48′N 06°09′W*
115 *M20* **Arkoí** *island* Dodekánisa, Greece, Aegean Sea
27 *R11* **Arkoma** Oklahoma, C USA *35°19′N 94°27′W*
100 *O7* **Arkona, Kap** *headland* NE Germany *54°40′N 13°24′E*
95 *N17* **Arkösund** Östergötland, S Sweden *58°28′N 16°55′E*
122 *J6* **Arkticheskogo Instituta, Ostrova** *island* N Russian Federation
95 *O15* **Arlanda** ✈ (Stockholm) Stockholm, C Sweden *59°40′N 17°58′E*
146 *C11* **Arlandag** *Rus.* Gora Arlan. ▲ W Turkmenistan *39°39′N 54°28′E*
Arlan, Gora *see* Arlandag
105 *O5* **Arlanza** ≈ N Spain
105 *N5* **Arlanzón** ≈ N Spain
103 *R15* **Arles** *var.* Arles-sur-Rhône; *anc.* Arelas, Arelate. Bouches-du-Rhône, SE France *43°41′N 04°38′E*
Arles-sur-Rhône *see* Arles
103 *O17* **Arles-sur-Tech** Pyrénées-Orientales, S France *42°27′N 02°37′E*
29 *U9* **Arlington** Minnesota, N USA *44°36′N 94°04′W*
29 *R15* **Arlington** Nebraska, C USA *41°27′N 96°21′W*
32 *J11* **Arlington** Oregon, NW USA *45°43′N 120°10′W*
29 *R10* **Arlington** South Dakota, N USA *44°21′N 97°07′W*
20 *E10* **Arlington** Tennessee, S USA *35°17′N 89°40′W*
25 *T6* **Arlington** Texas, SW USA *32°44′N 97°05′W*
21 *W4* **Arlington** Virginia, NE USA *38°54′N 77°09′W*
32 *H7* **Arlington** Washington, NW USA *48°12′N 122°07′W*
30 *M10* **Arlington Heights** Illinois, N USA *42°08′N 88°03′W*
77 *U8* **Arlit** Agadez, C Niger *18°54′N 07°25′E*
99 *L24* **Arlon** *Dut.* Aarlen, *Ger.* Arel, *Lat.* Orolaunum. Luxembourg, SE Belgium *49°41′N 05°49′E*
27 *R7* **Arma** Kansas, C USA *37°32′N 94°42′W*
97 *F16* **Armagh** *Ir.* Ard Mhacha. S Northern Ireland, United Kingdom *54°15′N 06°33′W*
97 *F16* **Armagh** *cultural region* S Northern Ireland, United Kingdom
102 *K15* **Armagnac** *cultural region* S France
103 *Q7* **Armançon** ≈ C France
60 *K10* **Armando Laydner, Represa** ⊠ S Brazil
115 *M24* **Armathía** *island* SE Greece
137 *T12* **Armavir** *prev.* Hoktemberyan, *Rus.* Oktemberyan. SW Armenia *40°09′N 43°58′E*
126 *M14* **Armavir** Krasnodarskiy Kray, SW Russian Federation *44°59′N 41°07′E*
54 *E10* **Armenia** Quindío, W Colombia *04°32′N 75°40′W*
137 *T12* **Armenia** *off.* Republic of Armenia, *var.* Ajastan, *Arm.* Hayastani Hanrapetut'yun; *prev.* Armenian Soviet Socialist Republic. ◆ *republic* SW Asia
Armenian Soviet Socialist Republic *see* Armenia
Armenia, Republic of *see* Armenia
Armenierstadt *see* Gherla
103 *O1* **Armentières** Nord, N France *50°41′N 02°53′E*
40 *K14* **Armería** Colima, SW Mexico *18°55′N 103°59′W*
183 *T5* **Armidale** New South Wales, SE Australia *30°32′S 151°40′E*
29 *P11* **Armour** South Dakota, N USA *43°19′N 98°21′W*
61 *B18* **Armstrong** Santa Fe, C Argentina *32°46′S 61°39′W*
11 *N16* **Armstrong** British Columbia, SW Canada *50°27′N 119°14′W*
12 *D11* **Armstrong** Ontario, S Canada *50°20′N 89°02′W*
29 *U11* **Armstrong** Iowa, C USA *43°24′N 94°28′W*
25 *S16* **Armstrong** Texas, SW USA *26°55′N 97°47′W*
117 *S11* **Armyans'k** *Rus.* Armyansk. Avtonomna Respublika Krym, S Ukraine *46°05′N 33°43′E*
115 *H14* **Arnaía** *Cont.* Arnea. Kentrikí Makedonía, N Greece *40°30′N 23°36′E*
121 *N2* **Arnaoúti, Akrotíri** *var.* Arnaoútis, Cape Arnaouti. *headland* W Cyprus *35°06′N 32°16′E*
Arnaouti, Cape/Arnaoútis *see* Arnaoúti, Akrotíri
12 *L4* **Arnaud** ≈ Québec, E Canada
103 *Q8* **Arnay-le-Duc** Côte d'Or, C France *47°08′N 04°27′E*
Arnea *see* Arnaía
105 *Q4* **Arnedo** La Rioja, N Spain *42°14′N 02°05′W*
95 *I14* **Årnes** Akershus, S Norway *60°07′N 11°28′E*
Årnes *see* Åi Åfjord
26 *K9* **Arnett** Oklahoma, C USA *36°08′N 99°46′W*
98 *L12* **Arnhem** Gelderland, SE Netherlands *51°59′N 05°54′E*
181 *Q2* **Arnhem Land** *physical region* Northern Territory, N Australia
106 *F11* **Arno** ≈ C Italy
Arņo *see* Arno Atoll
189 *W7* **Arno Atoll** *var.* Arņo. *atoll* Ratak Chain, NE Marshall Islands
182 *H8* **Arno Bay** South Australia *33°55′S 136°31′E*
35 *Q8* **Arnold** California, W USA *38°15′N 120°19′W*
27 *X5* **Arnold** Missouri, C USA *38°25′N 90°22′W*
29 *N15* **Arnold** Nebraska, C USA *41°25′N 100°11′W*
109 *R10* **Arnoldstein** *Slvn.* Pod Klošter. Kärnten, S Austria *46°34′N 13°43′E*
103 *N9* **Arnon** ≈ C France
45 *P14* **Arnos Vale** ✈ (Kingstown) Saint Vincent, SE Saint Vincent and the Grenadines *13°08′N 61°13′W*
92 *I8* **Arnøya** *Lapp.* Árdni. *island* N Norway
14 *L12* **Arnprior** Ontario, SE Canada *45°31′N 76°11′W*
101 *G15* **Arnsberg** Nordrhein-Westfalen, W Germany *51°24′N 08°04′E*
101 *K16* **Arnstadt** Thüringen, C Germany *50°50′N 10°57′E*
Arnswalde *see* Choszczno
54 *K5* **Aroa** Yaracuy, N Venezuela *10°26′N 68°54′W*
83 *E21* **Aroab** Karas, SE Namibia *26°47′S 19°40′E*
Ároania *see* Chelmós
191 *O6* **Aroa, Pointe** *headland* Moorea, W French Polynesia *17°27′S 149°45′W*
Aroe Islands *see* Aru, Kepulauan
101 *H15* **Arolsen** Niedersachsen, C Germany *51°23′N 09°00′E*
106 *C7* **Arona** Piemonte, NE Italy *45°45′N 08°33′E*
19 *R3* **Aroostook River** ≈ Canada/USA
Arop Island *see* Long Island
38 *M12* **Aropuk Lake** ◎ Alaska, USA
191 *P4* **Arorae** *atoll* Tungaru, W Kiribati
190 *G16* **Arorangi** Rarotonga, S Cook Islands *21°13′S 159°49′W*
108 *I9* **Arosa** Graubünden, S Switzerland *46°48′N 09°42′E*
104 *F4* **Arousa, Ría de** *estuary* E Atlantic Ocean
184 *P8* **Arowhana** ▲ North Island, New Zealand *38°07′S 177°52′E*
137 *V12* **Arp'a** *Az.* Arpaçay. ≈ Armenia/Azerbaijan
137 *S11* **Arpaçay** Kars, NE Turkey *40°51′N 43°20′E*
Arpaçay *see* Arp'a
Arqalyq *see* Arkalyk
149 *N14* **Arra** ≈ SW Pakistan
Arrabona *see* Győr
Arrah *see* Āra
Ar Rahad *see* Er Rahad
139 *R9* **Ar Raḩḩālīyah** Al Anbār, C Iraq *32°53′N 43°21′E*
60 *Q10* **Arraial do Cabo** Rio de Janeiro, SE Brazil *22°57′S 42°00′W*
104 *H11* **Arraiolos** Évora, S Portugal *38°44′N 07°59′W*
139 *R8* **Ar Ramādī** *var.* Ramadi, Rumadiya. Al Anbār, SW Iraq *33°27′N 43°19′E*
138 *J6* **Ar Rāmī** Ḩimş, C Syria *34°32′N 37°54′E*
Ar Rams *see* Rams
138 *H9* **Ar Ramthā** *var.* Ramtha. Irbid, N Jordan *32°34′N 36°00′E*
96 *H13* **Arran, Isle of** *island* SW Scotland, United Kingdom
138 *L3* **Ar Raqqah** *var.* Rakka; *anc.* Nicephorium. Ar Raqqah, N Syria *35°57′N 39°03′E*
138 *L3* **Ar Raqqah** *off.* Muḩāfaẓat al Raqqah, *var.* Raqqah, *Fr.* Rakka. ⬖ *governorate* N Syria
103 *O2* **Arras** *anc.* Nemetocenna. Pas-de-Calais, N France *50°17′N 02°46′E*
105 *P3* **Arrasate** *Cast.* Mondragón. País Vasco, N Spain *43°04′N 02°30′W*
138 *G12* **Ar Rashādīyah** Aţ ţafīlah, W Jordan *30°42′N 35°38′E*
138 *I5* **Ar Rastān** *var.* Rastâne. Ḩimş, W Syria *34°57′N 36°43′E*
139 *X12* **Ar Raţāwī** Al Başrah, E Iraq *30°37′N 47°12′E*
102 *L15* **Arrats** ≈ S France
141 *N10* **Ar Rawḑah** Makkah, S Saudi Arabia *21°19′N 42°48′E*
141 *Q15* **Ar Rawḑah** S Yemen *14°26′N 47°14′E*
142 *K11* **Ar Rawḑatayn** *var.* Raudhatain. N Kuwait *29°80′N 47°50′E*
143 *N16* **Ar Rayyān** *var.* Al Rayyan. C Qatar *25°18′N 51°29′E*
102 *L17* **Arreau** Hautes-Pyrénées, S France *42°55′N 00°21′E*
64 *Q11* **Arrecife** *var.* Arrecife de Lanzarote, Puerto Arrecife. Lanzarote, Islas Canarias, NE Atlantic Ocean *28°57′N 13°33′W*
Arrecife de Lanzarote *see* Arrecife
43 *P6* **Arrecife Edinburgh** *reef* NE Nicaragua
61 *C19* **Arrecifes** Buenos Aires, E Argentina *34°06′S 60°09′W*
102 *F6* **Arrée, Monts d'** ▲▲ NW France
Ar Refā'ī *see* Ar Rifā'ī
Arretium *see* Arezzo
Arriaca *see* Guadalajara
109 *S9* **Arriach** Kärnten, S Austria *46°43′N 13°52′E*
41 *T16* **Arriaga** Chiapas, SE Mexico *16°14′N 93°54′W*
41 *N12* **Arriaga** San Luis Potosí, C Mexico *21°55′N 101°23′W*
139 *W10* **Ar Rifā'ī** *var.* Ar Refā'ī. Dhī Qār, SE Iraq *31°47′N 46°07′E*
139 *V12* **Ar Riḩāb** *salt flat* S Iraq
Arriondas *see* Les Arriondes
141 *Q7* **Ar Riyāḑ** *Eng.* Riyadh. ● (Saudi Arabia) Ar Riyāḑ, C Saudi Arabia *24°50′N 46°50′E*
141 *O8* **Ar Riyāḑ** *off.* Minţaqat ar Riyāḑ. ⬖ *province* C Saudi Arabia
141 *S15* **Ar Riyān** S Yemen *14°43′N 49°18′E*
Arrö *see* Ærø
61 *H18* **Arroio Grande** Rio Grande do Sul, S Brazil *32°15′S 53°02′W*
102 *K15* **Arros** ≈ S France
103 *Q9* **Arroux** ≈ C France
25 *R5* **Arrowhead, Lake** ⊠ Texas, SW USA
182 *L5* **Arrowsmith, Mount** *hill* New South Wales, SE Australia
185 *D21* **Arrowtown** Otago, South Island, New Zealand *44°57′S 168°51′E*
61 *D17* **Arroyo Barú** Entre Ríos, E Argentina *31°52′S 58°26′W*
104 *J10* **Arroyo de la Luz** Extremadura, W Spain *39°28′N 06°36′W*
63 *J16* **Arroyo de la Ventana** Río Negro, SE Argentina *41°41′S 66°03′W*
35 *P13* **Arroyo Grande** California, W USA *35°07′N 120°35′W*
Ar Ru'ays *see* Ar Ruways
141 *R11* **Ar Rub' al Khālī** *Eng.* Empty Quarter, Great Sandy Desert. *desert* SW Asia
139 *V13* **Ar Ruḑaymah** Al Muthanná, S Iraq *30°20′N 45°26′E*
61 *A16* **Arrufó** Santa Fe, C Argentina *30°15′S 61°45′W*
138 *I7* **Ar Ruḩaybah** *var.* Ruhaybeh, *Fr.* Rouhaïbé. Rīf Dimashq, W Syria *33°45′N 36°40′E*
139 *V15* **Ar Rukhaymīyah** *well* S Iraq
139 *U11* **Ar Rumaythah** *var.* Rumaitha. Al Muthanná, S Iraq *31°31′N 45°15′E*
141 *X8* **Ar Rustāq** *var.* Rostak, Rustaq. N Oman *23°34′N 57°25′E*
139 *N8* **Ar Ruţbah** *var.* Rutba. Al Anbār, SW Iraq *33°03′N 40°16′E*
140 *M3* **Ar Rūthīyah** *spring/well* NW Saudi Arabia *31°18′N 41°23′E*
ar-Ruwaida *see* Ar Ruwayḑah
141 *O8* **Ar Ruwayḑah** *var.* ar-Ruwaida. Jīzān, C Saudi Arabia *23°48′N 44°44′E*
143 *N15* **Ar Ruways** *var.* Al Ruweis, Ar Ru'ays, Ruwais. N Qatar *26°08′N 51°13′E*
143 *O17* **Ar Ruways** *var.* Ar Ru'ays. Abū Ẓaby, W United Arab Emirates *24°09′N 52°57′E*
Års *see* Aars
Arsanias *see* Murat Nehri
123 *S15* **Arsen'yev** Primorskiy Kray, SE Russian Federation *44°09′N 133°28′E*
155 *G19* **Arsikere** Karnātaka, W India *13°20′N 76°13′E′N*
127 *R3* **Arsk** Respublika Tatarstan, W Russian Federation *56°07′N 49°54′E*
94 *N10* **Årskogen** Gävleborg, C Sweden *62°07′N 17°19′E*
121 *O3* **Ársos** C Cyprus *34°51′N 32°46′E*
94 *N13* **Årsunda** Gävleborg, C Sweden *60°31′N 16°45′E*
115 *C17* **Árta** *anc.* Ambracia. Ípeiros, W Greece *39°08′N 20°59′E*
105 *Y9* **Artà** Mallorca, Spain, W Mediterranean Sea *39°42′N 03°20′E*
Arta *see* Árachthos
137 *T12* **Artashat** S Armenia *39°57′N 44°34′E*
40 *M15* **Arteaga** Michoacán, SW Mexico *18°22′N 102°18′W*
123 *S15* **Artem** Primorskiy Kray, SE Russian Federation *43°24′N 132°20′E*
44 *C4* **Artemisa** La Habana, W Cuba *22°49′N 82°47′W*
117 *W7* **Artemivs'k** Donets'ka Oblast', E Ukraine *48°35′N 37°58′E*
122 *K13* **Artemovsk** Krasnoyarskiy Kray, S Russian Federation *54°22′N 93°24′E*
105 *U5* **Artesa de Segre** Cataluña, NE Spain *41°54′N 01°03′E*
37 *U14* **Artesia** New Mexico, SW USA *32°50′N 104°24′W*
25 *Q14* **Artesia Wells** Texas, SW USA *28°13′N 99°18′W*
108 *G8* **Arth** Schwyz, C Switzerland *47°05′N 08°39′E*
14 *F15* **Arthur** Ontario, S Canada *43°49′N 80°31′W*
30 *M14* **Arthur** Illinois, N USA *39°42′N 88°28′W*
28 *L14* **Arthur** Nebraska, C USA *41°35′N 101°42′W*
29 *Q5* **Arthur** North Dakota, N USA *47°03′N 97°12′W*
185 *B21* **Arthur** ≈ South Island, New Zealand
18 *B13* **Arthur, Lake** ⊠ Pennsylvania, NE USA
183 *N15* **Arthur River** ≈ Tasmania, SE Australia
185 *G18* **Arthur's Pass** Canterbury, South Island, New Zealand *42°59′S 171°33′E*
185 *G17* **Arthur's Pass** *pass* South Island, New Zealand
44 *I3* **Arthur's Town** Cat Island, C Bahamas *24°34′N 75°39′W*
44 *M9* **Artibonite, Rivière de l'** ≈ C Haiti
61 *E16* **Artigas** *prev.* San Eugenio, San Eugenio del Cuareim. Artigas, N Uruguay *30°25′S 56°28′W*
61 *E16* **Artigas** ⬖ *department* N Uruguay
194 *H1* **Artigas** *Uruguayan research station* Antarctica *61°57′S 58°23′W*
137 *T11* **Art'ik** W Armenia *40°38′N 43°58′E*
187 *O16* **Art, Île** *island* Îles Belep, W New Caledonia
103 *O2* **Artois** *cultural region* N France
136 *L12* **Artova** Tokat, N Turkey *40°04′N 36°17′E*
105 *Y9* **Artrutx, Cap d'** *var.* Cabo Dartuch. *cape* Menorca, Spain, W Mediterranean Sea
Artsiz *see* Artsyz
117 *N11* **Artsyz** *Rus.* Artsiz. Odes'ka Oblast', SW Ukraine *45°59′N 29°26′E*
158 *E7* **Artux** Xinjiang Uygur Zizhiqu, NW China *39°40′N 76°10′E*
137 *R11* **Artvin** Artvin, NE Turkey *41°12′N 41°48′E*
137 *R11* **Artvın** ⬖ *province* NE Turkey
146 *G14* **Artyk** Ahal Welaýaty, C Turkmenistan *37°32′N 59°16′E*
79 *Q16* **Aru** Orientale, NE Dem. Rep. Congo *02°53′N 30°50′E*
81 *E17* **Arua** NW Uganda *03°02′N 30°56′E*
104 *I4* **A Rúa de Valdeorras** *var.* La Rúa. Galicia, NW Spain *42°22′N 07°12′W*
Aruângua *see* Luangwa
45 *O15* **Aruba** *var.* Oruba. ◇ *Dutch autonomous region* S West Indies
47 *Q4* **Aruba** *island* Aruba, Lesser Antilles
Aru Islands *see* Aru, Kepulauan
171 *W15* **Aru, Kepulauan** *Eng.* Aru Islands; *prev.* Aroe Islands. *island group* E Indonesia
153 *W10* **Arunāchal Pradesh** *prev.* North East Frontier Agency, North East Frontier Agency of Assam. ⬖ *state* NE India
Arun Qi *see* Naji
155 *H23* **Aruppukkottai** Tamil Nādu, SE India *09°31′N 78°03′E*
81 *I20* **Arusha** Arusha, N Tanzania *03°23′S 36°40′E*
81 *I21* **Arusha** ⬖ *region* E Tanzania
81 *I20* **Arusha** ✈ Arusha, N Tanzania *03°26′S 37°07′E*
54 *C9* **Arusí, Punta** *headland* NW Colombia *05°36′N 77°30′W*
155 *J23* **Aruvi Aru** ≈ NW Sri Lanka
79 *M17* **Aruwimi** *var.* Ituri (upper course). ≈ NE Dem. Rep. Congo
Árva *see* Orava
37 *T4* **Arvada** Colorado, C USA *39°48′N 105°06′W*
Arvand Rūd *see* 'Arab, Shaţţ al
162 *J8* **Arvayheer** Övörhangay, C Mongolia *46°13′N 102°47′E*
9 *O10* **Arviat** *prev.* Eskimo Point. Nunavut, C Canada *61°10′N 94°15′W*
93 *I14* **Arvidsjaur** Norrbotten, N Sweden *65°34′N 19°12′E*
95 *J15* **Arvika** Värmland, C Sweden *59°41′N 12°38′E*
92 *J8* **Årviksand** Troms, N Norway *70°10′N 20°30′E*
35 *S13* **Arvin** California, W USA *35°12′N 118°52′W*
163 *S8* **Arxan** Nei Mongol Zizhiqu, N China *47.11N 119.58′E*
145 *P7* **Arykbalyk** *Kaz.* Aryqbalyq. Severnyy Kazakhstan, N Kazakhstan *53°00′N 68°11′E*
Aryqbalyq *see* Arykbalyk
145 *P17* **'Arys'** *prev.* Arys'. Yuzhnyy Kazakhstan, S Kazakhstan *42°26′N 68°49′E*
Arys' *see* 'Arys'
Arys *see* Orzysz
Arys Köli *see* Arys, Ozero
145 *O14* **Arys, Ozero** *Kaz.* Arys Köli. ◎ C Kazakhstan
107 *D16* **Arzachena** Sardegna, Italy, C Mediterranean Sea *41°05′N 09°21′E*
127 *O4* **Arzamas** Nizhegorodskaya Oblast', W Russian Federation *55°25′N 43°51′E*
141 *V13* **Arzāt** S Oman *17°00′N 54°18′E*
104 *H3* **Arzúa** Galicia, NW Spain *42°55′N 08°10′W*
111 *A16* **Aš** *Ger.* Asch. Karlovarský Kraj, W Czech Republic *50°18′N 12°12′E*
95 *H15* **Ås** Akershus, S Norway *59°40′N 10°50′E*
Åsa *see* Asaa
95 *H20* **Asaa** *var.* Åsa. Nordjylland, N Denmark *57°07′N 10°24′E*
83 *E21* **Asab** Karas, S Namibia *25°29′S 17°59′E*
77 *U16* **Asaba** Delta, S Nigeria *06°10′N 06°44′E*
76 *J10* **Assaba** *var.* Açâba. ⬖ *region* S Mauritania
149 *S4* **Asadābād** *var.* Asaḏābād; *prev.* Chaghasarāy. Kunar, E Afghanistan *34°52′N 71°09′E*
Asaḏābād *see* Asadābād
138 *K3* **Asad, Buḩayrat al** *Eng.* Lake Assad. ◎ N Syria
63 *H20* **Asador, Pampa del** *plain* S Argentina
165 *P14* **Asahi** Chiba, Honshū, S Japan *35°43′N 140°38′E*
164 *M11* **Asahi** Toyama, Honshū, SW Japan *36°56′N 137°34′E*
165 *T13* **Asahi-dake** ▲ Hokkaidō, N Japan *43°42′N 142°50′E*
165 *T3* **Asahikawa** Hokkaidō, N Japan *43°46′N 142°23′E*
147 *S10* **Asaka** *Rus.* Assake; *prev.* Leninsk. Andijon Viloyati, E Uzbekistan *40°39′N 72°16′E*
77 *P17* **Asamankese** SE Ghana *05°47′N 00°41′W*
188 *B15* **Asan** W Guam *13°28′N 144°43′E*
188 *B15* **Asan Point** *headland* W Guam
153 *R15* **Āsānsol** West Bengal, NE India *23°40′N 86°59′E*
80 *K12* **Āsayita** Āfar, NE Ethiopia *11°35′S 41°23′E*
171 *T12* **Asbakin** Papua, E Indonesia *0°45′S 131°40′E*
Asben *see* Aïr, Massif de l'
15 *Q12* **Asbestos** Québec, SE Canada *45°46′N 71°56′W*
29 *Y13* **Asbury** Iowa, C USA *42°30′N 90°45′W*
18 *K15* **Asbury Park** New Jersey, NE USA *40°13′N 74°00′W*
41 *Z12* **Ascención, Bahiá de la** *bay* NW Caribbean Sea
40 *I3* **Ascensión** Chihuahua, N Mexico *31°07′N 107°59′W*
65 *M14* **Ascension Fracture Zone** *tectonic feature* C Atlantic Ocean
65 *G14* **Ascension Island** ◇ *dependency of St.Helena* C Atlantic Ocean
65 *N16* **Ascension Island** *island* C Atlantic Ocean
Asch *see* Aš
109 *S3* **Aschach an der Donau** Oberösterreich, N Austria *48°22′N 14°00′E*
101 *H18* **Aschaffenburg** Bayern, SW Germany *49°58′N 09°10′E*
101 *F14* **Ascheberg** Nordrhein-Westfalen, W Germany *51°46′N 07°36′E*
101 *L14* **Aschersleben** Sachsen-Anhalt, C Germany *51°46′N 11°28′E*
106 *G12* **Asciano** Toscana, C Italy *43°15′N 11°32′E*
106 *J13* **Ascoli Piceno** *anc.* Asculum Picenum. Marche, C Italy *42°51′N 13°34′E*
107 *M17* **Ascoli Satriano** *anc.* Asculub, Ausculum Apulum. Puglia, SE Italy *41°13′N 15°32′E*
108 *G11* **Ascona** Ticino, S Switzerland *46°10′N 08°45′E*
Asculub *see* Ascoli Satriano
Asculum Picenum *see* Ascoli Piceno
80 *L11* **'Aseb** *var.* Assab, *Amh.* Āseb. SE Eritrea *13°04′N 42°36′E*
95 *M20* **Åseda** Kronoberg, S Sweden *57°10′N 15°20′E*
127 *T6* **Asekeyevo** Orenburgskaya Oblast', W Russian Federation *53°36′N 52°53′E*
81 *J14* **Āsela** *var.* Asella, Aselle, Asselle. Oromīya, C Ethiopia *07°55′N 39°08′E*
93 *H15* **Åsele** Västerbotten, N Sweden *64°10′N 17°20′E*
Asella/Aselle *see* Āsela
98 *N7* **Assen** Drenthe, NE Netherlands *53°N 06°34′E*
94 *K12* **Åsen** Dalarna, C Sweden *61°18′N 13°49′E*
114 *J11* **Asenovgrad** *prev.* Stanimaka. Plovdiv, C Bulgaria *42°00′N 24°53′E*
171 *O13* **Asera** Sulawesi, C Indonesia *03°24′S 121°42′E*
95 *E17* **Åseral** Vest-Agder, S Norway *58°37′N 07°27′E*
118 *J3* **Aseri** *var.* Asserien, *Ger.* Asserin. Ida-Virumaa, NE Estonia *59°29′N 26°51′E*
104 *G3* **A Serra de Outes** Galicia, NW Spain *42°50′N 08°54′W*
40 *J10* **Aserradero** Durango, W Mexico
146 *F13* **Aşgabat** *prev.* Ashgabat, Ashkhabad, Poltoratsk. ● (Turkmenistan) Ahal Welaýaty, C Turkmenistan *37°58′N 58°22′E*
146 *F13* **Aşgabat** ✈ Ahal Welaýaty, C Turkmenistan *38°06′N 58°10′E*
95 *H16* **Åsgårdstrand** Vestfold, S Norway *59°22′N 10°27′E*
Ashara *see* Al 'Ashārah
23 *T6* **Ashburn** Georgia, SE USA *31°42′N 83°39′W*
185 *G19* **Ashburton** Canterbury, South Island, New Zealand *43°55′S 171°47′E*
185 *G19* **Ashburton** ≈ South Island, New Zealand
180 *H8* **Ashburton River** ≈ Western Australia
145 *V10* **Ashchysu** ≈ E Kazakhstan
10 *M16* **Ashcroft** British Columbia, SW Canada *50°41′N 121°17′W*
138 *E10* **Ashdod** *anc.* Azotos, *Lat.* Azotus. Central, W Israel *31°48′N 34°38′E*
27 *S14* **Ashdown** Arkansas, C USA *33°40′N 94°09′W*
21 *T9* **Asheboro** North Carolina, SE USA *35°42′N 79°50′W*
11 *X15* **Ashern** Manitoba, S Canada *51°10′N 98°22′W*
21 *P10* **Asheville** North Carolina, SE USA *35°36′N 82°33′W*
12 *E8* **Asheweig** ≈ Ontario, C Canada
27 *V9* **Ash Flat** Arkansas, C USA *36°13′N 91°36′W*
183 *T4* **Ashford** New South Wales, SE Australia *29°18′S 151°09′E*
97 *P22* **Ashford** SE England, United Kingdom *51°09′N 00°52′E*
36 *K11* **Ash Fork** Arizona, SW USA *35°12′N 112°31′W*
Ashgabat *see* Aşgabat
27 *T7* **Ash Grove** Missouri, C USA *37°19′N 93°35′W*
165 *O12* **Ashikaga** *var.* Asikaga. Tochigi, Honshū, S Japan *36°21′N 139°26′E*
165 *Q8* **Ashiro** Iwate, Honshū, C Japan *40°04′N 141°00′E*
164 *F15* **Ashizuri-misaki** Shikoku, SW Japan
138 *E10* **Ashkelon** *prev.* Ashqelon. Southern, C Israel *31°40′N 34°35′E*
Ashkhabad *see* Aşgabat
23 *Q4* **Ashland** Alabama, S USA *33°16′N 85°50′W*
26 *K7* **Ashland** Kansas, C USA *37°12′N 99°47′W*
21 *P5* **Ashland** Kentucky, S USA *38°28′N 82°40′W*
19 *S2* **Ashland** Maine, NE USA *46°36′N 68°24′W*
22 *M1* **Ashland** Mississippi, S USA *34°51′N 89°10′W*
27 *U4* **Ashland** Missouri, C USA *38°46′N 92°15′W*
29 *S15* **Ashland** Nebraska, C USA *41°01′N 96°21′W*
31 *T12* **Ashland** Ohio, N USA *40°52′N 82°19′W*
32 *G15* **Ashland** Oregon, NW USA *42°11′N 122°42′W*
21 *W6* **Ashland** Virginia, NE USA *37°45′N 77°28′W*
30 *K3* **Ashland** Wisconsin, N USA *46°34′N 90°54′W*
20 *I8* **Ashland City** Tennessee, S USA *36°16′N 87°05′W*
183 *S4* **Ashley** New South Wales, SE Australia *29°21′S 149°49′E*
29 *O7* **Ashley** North Dakota, N USA *46°00′N 99°22′W*
173 *W7* **Ashmore and Cartier Islands** ◇ *Australian external territory* E Indian Ocean
119 *I14* **Ashmyany** *Rus.* Oshmyany. Hrodzyenskaya Voblasts', W Belarus *54°24′N 25°57′E*
18 *K12* **Ashokan Reservoir** ⊠ New York, NE USA
165 *U4* **Ashoro** Hokkaidō, NE Japan *43°16′N 143°33′E*
Ashqelon *see* Ashkelon
Ashraf *see* Behshahr
139 *O3* **Ash Shadādah** *var.* Ash Shaddādah, Jisr ash Shadadi, Shaddādī, Shedadi, Tell Shedadi. Al Ḩasakah, NE Syria *36°00′N 40°42′E*
Ash Shaddādah *see* Ash Shadādah
139 *Y12* **Ash Shāfī** Al Başrah, E Iraq *30°49′N 47°30′E*
139 *R4* **Ash Shakk** *var.* Shaykh. Şalāḩ ad Dīn, C Iraq *35°15′N 43°27′E*
Ash Sham/Ash Shām *see* Rīf Dimashq
139 *T10* **Ash Shāmīyah** *var.* Shamiya. Al Qādisīyah, C Iraq *31°56′N 44°37′E*
139 *Y13* **Ash Shāmīyah** *var.* Al Bādiyah al Janūbīyah. *desert* S Iraq
139 *T11* **Ash Shanāfīyah** *var.* Ash Shināfīyah. Al Qādisīyah, S Iraq *31°35′N 44°38′E*
138 *G13* **Ash Sharāh** *var.* Esh Sharā. ▲▲ W Jordan
143 *R16* **Ash Shāriqah** *Eng.* Sharjah. Ash Shāriqah, NE United Arab Emirates *25°22′N 55°28′E*
143 *R16* **Ash Shāriqah** *var.* Sharjah. ✈ Ash Shāriqah, NE United Arab Emirates *25°19′N 55°37′E*
140 *I4* **Ash Sharmah** *var.* Šarma. Tabūk, NW Saudi Arabia *28°02′N 35°16′E*
139 *R4* **Ash Sharqāţ** Nīnawýa, NW Iraq *35°31′N 43°15′E*
141 *S10* **Ash Sharqīyah** *off.* Al Minţaqah ash Sharqīyah, *Eng.* Eastern Region. ⬖ *province* E Saudi Arabia
Ash Sharqīyah *see* Al 'Ubaylah
139 *W11* **Ash Shaţrah** *var.* Shatra. Dhī Qār, SE Iraq *31°26′N 46°10′E*
138 *G13* **Ash Shawbak** Ma'ān, W Jordan *30°32′N 35°34′E*
138 *L5* **Ash Shaykh Ibrāhīm** Ḩimş, C Syria *35°03′N 38°50′E*
141 *O17* **Ash Shaykh 'Uthmān** SW Yemen *12°53′N 45°00′E*
141 *S15* **Ash Shiḩr** SE Yemen *14°45′N 49°24′E*
Ash Shināfīyah *see* Ash Shanāfīyah
141 *V12* **Ash Shişar** *var.* Shisur. SW Oman *18°13′N 53°35′E*
139 *S13* **Ash Shubrūm** *well* S Iraq
141 *R10* **Ash Shuqqān** *desert* E Saudi Arabia
75 *O9* **Ash Shuwayrif** *var.* Ash Shwayrif. N Libya *29°54′N 14°16′E*
Ash Shwayrif *see* Ash Shuwayrif
31 *U10* **Ashtabula** Ohio, N USA *41°54′N 80°46′W*
29 *Q5* **Ashtabula, Lake** ⊠ North Dakota, N USA
137 *T12* **Ashtarak** W Armenia *40°18′N 44°22′E*
142 *M6* **Āshtīān** *var.* Āshtiyān. Markazī, W Iran *34°23′N 49°55′E*
Āshtiyān *see* Āshtīān
33 *R13* **Ashton** Idaho, NW USA *44°04′N 111°27′W*
13 *O10* **Ashuanipi Lake** ◎ Newfoundland and Labrador, E Canada
15 *P6* **Ashuapmushuan** ≈ Québec, SE Canada
23 *Q3* **Ashville** Alabama, S USA *33°50′N 86°15′W*
31 *S14* **Ashville** Ohio, N USA *39°43′N 82°57′W*
30 *K3* **Ashwabay, Mount** *hill* Wisconsin, N USA
128-129 **Asia** *continent*
171 *T11* **Asia, Kepulauan** *island group* E Indonesia
154 *N13* **Āsika** Orissa, E India *19°38′N 84°41′E*
Asikaga *see* Ashikaga
93 *M18* **Asikkala** *var.* Vääksy. Etelä-Suomi, S Finland *61°09′N 25°36′E*
74 *G5* **Asilah** N Morocco *35°32′N 06°04′W*
'Aşī, Nahr al *see* Orontes
107 *B16* **Asinara, Isola** *island* W Italy
122 *J12* **Asino** Tomskaya Oblast', C Russian Federation *56°56′N 86°02′E*
119 *O14* **Asintorf** *Rus.* Osintorf. Vitsyebskaya Voblasts', N Belarus *54°43′N 30°35′E*
119 *L17* **Asipovichy** *Rus.* Osipovichi. Mahilyowskaya Voblasts', C Belarus *53°18′N 28°40′E*
141 *N12* **'Asīr** *off.* Minţaqat 'Asīr. ⬖ *province* SW Saudi Arabia
140 *M11* **'Asīr** *Eng.* Asir. ▲▲ SW Saudi Arabia
'Asīr, Minţaqat *see* 'Asīr
139 *X10* **Askal** Maysān, E Iraq *31°45′N 47°07′E*
137 *P13* **Aşkale** Erzurum, NE Turkey *39°56′N 40°39′E*
117 *T11* **Askaniya-Nova** Khersons'ka Oblast', S Ukraine *46°27′N 33°54′E*
95 *H15* **Asker** Akershus, S Norway *59°52′N 10°26′E*
95 *L17* **Askersund** Örebro, C Sweden *58°55′N 14°55′E*
Askī Kalak *see* Eski Kaļak
95 *I15* **Askim** Østfold, S Norway *59°15′N 11°10′E*
127 *V3* **Askino** Respublika Bashkortostan, W Russian Federation *56°07′N 56°39′E*
115 *D14* **Áskio** ▲▲ N Greece
152 *L9* **Askot** Uttarakhand, N India *29°44′N 80°20′E*
94 *C12* **Askvoll** Sogn Og Fjordane, S Norway *61°21′N 05°04′E*
136 *A13* **Aslan Burnu** *headland* W Turkey *38°44′N 26°43′E*
136 *L16* **Aslantaş Barajı** ⊠ S Turkey
149 *S4* **Asmār** *var.* Bar Kunar. Kunar, E Afghanistan *34°59′N 71°29′E*
Asmara *see* Asmera
80 *I9* **Asmera** *var.* Asmara. ● (Eritrea) C Eritrea *15°15′N 38°58′E*
95 *L21* **Åsnen** ◎ S Sweden
115 *F19* **Asopós** ≈ S Greece
171 *W13* **Asori** Papua, E Indonesia *02°37′S 136°06′E*
80 *G12* **Āsosa** Bīnishangul Gumuz, W Ethiopia *10°06′N 34°27′E*
32 *M10* **Asotin** Washington, NW USA *46°18′N 117°03′W*
Aspadana *see* Eşfahān
Aspang *see* Aspang Markt
109 *X6* **Aspang Markt** *var.* Aspang. Niederösterreich, E Austria *47°34′N 16°06′E*
105 *S12* **Aspe** Valenciana, E Spain *38°21′N 00°43′W*
37 *R5* **Aspen** Colorado, C USA *39°12′N 106°49′W*
25 *P6* **Aspermont** Texas, SW USA *33°08′N 100°14′W*
Asphaltites, Lacus *see* Dead Sea
Aspinwall *see* Colón
185 *C20* **Aspiring, Mount** ▲ South Island, New Zealand *44°21′S 168°47′E*
115 *B16* **Asprókavos, Akrotírio** *headland* Kérkyra, Iónia Nísiá, Greece, C Mediterranean Sea *39°22′N 20°07′E*
Aspropótamos *see* Achelóos
Assab *see* 'Aseb
138 *L4* **As Sabkhah** *var.* Sabkha. Ar Raqqah, NE Syria *35°30′N 35°54′E*
139 *U6* **As Sa'dīyah** Diyālá, E Iraq *34°11′N 45°09′E*
Assad, Lake *see* Asad, Buḩayrat al
138 *I8* **Aş Şafā** ▲ S Syria *33°03′N 37°07′E*
138 *I10* **Aş Şafāwī** Al Mafraq, N Jordan *37°12′N 32°30′E*
75 *W8* **Aş Şaff** *var.* El Şaff. N Egypt *29°34′N 31°16′E*
139 *N2* **Aş Şafīḩ** Al Ḩasakah, N Syria *36°42′N 40°12′E*
Aş Şaḩrā' ash Sharqīyah *see* Sahara el Sharqîya
Assake *see* Asaka
As Salamīyah *see* Salamīyah
141 *Q4* **As Sālimī** *var.* Salemy. SW Kuwait *29°07′N 46°41′E*
67 *W7* **'Assal, Lac** ◎ C Djibouti
75 *T7* **As Sallūm** *var.* Salûm. NW Egypt *31°31′N 25°09′E*
139 *T13* **As Salmān** Al Muthanná, S Iraq *30°29′N 44°34′E*
138 *G10* **As Salţ** *var.* Salt. Al Balqā', NW Jordan *32°03′N 35°44′E*

◆ Country
● Country Capital
◇ Dependent Territory
○ Dependent Territory Capital
⬖ Administrative Regions
✈ International Airport
▲ Mountain
▲▲ Mountain Range
⛰ Volcano
≈ River
◎ Lake
⊠ Reservoir

142 M16 As Salwā var. Salwa, Salwah. S Qatar 24°44′N 50°52′E
153 V12 Assam ◈ state NE India
Assamaka see Assamakka
77 T8 Assamakka var. Assamaka. Agadez, NW Niger 19°24′N 05°53′E
139 U11 As Samāwah var. Samawa. Al Muthannā, S Iraq 31°17′N 45°06′E
As Saqia al Hamra see Saguia al Hamra
138 J4 Aş Şa'rān Ḩamāh, C Syria 35°15′N 37°28′E
138 G9 Aş Şarīḩ Irbid, N Jordan 32°31′N 35°54′E
21 Z5 Assateague Island island Maryland, NE USA
139 O6 As Sayyāl var. Sayyāl. Dayr az Zawr, E Syria 34°37′N 40°52′E
99 G18 Asse Vlaams Brabant, C Belgium 50°55′N 04°12′E
99 D16 Assebroek West-Vlaanderen, NW Belgium 51°12′N 03°16′E
Asselle see Āsela
107 C20 Assemini Sardegna, Italy, C Mediterranean Sea 39°16′N 08°58′E
99 E16 Assenede Oost-Vlaanderen, NW Belgium 51°15′N 03°43′E
95 G24 Assens Syddtjylland, C Denmark 55°16′N 09°54′N
Asserien/Asserin see Aseri
99 I21 Assesse Namur, SE Belgium 50°22′N 05°01′E
141 Y8 As Sīb var. Seeb. NE Oman 23°40′N 58°03′E
139 Z13 As Sībah var. Sibah. Al Başrah, SE Iraq 30°13′N 47°24′E
11 T17 Assiniboia Saskatchewan, S Canada 49°39′N 105°59′W
11 V15 Assiniboine ≈ Manitoba, S Canada
11 P16 Assiniboine, Mount ▲ Alberta/British Columbia, SW Canada 50°54′N 115°43′W
Assiout see Asyūţ
60 J9 Assis São Paulo, S Brazil 22°37′S 50°25′W
106 I13 Assisi Umbria, C Italy 43°04′N 12°36′E
Assiut see Asyūţ
Assling see Jesenice
Assouan see Aswān
59 P14 Assu var. Açu. Rio Grande do Norte, E Brazil 05°33′S 36°55′W
Assuan see Aswān
142 K12 Aş Şubayḩīyah var. Subiyah. S Kuwait 28°55′N 47°57′E
141 R16 As Sufāl S Yemen 14°06′N 48°42′E
138 L5 As Sukhnah var. Sukhne, Fr. Soukhné. Ḩimş, C Syria 34°56′N 38°52′E
139 U4 As Sulaymānīyah var. Sulaimaniya, Kurd. Slēmānī. As Sulaymānīyah, NE Iraq 35°32′N 45°27′E
141 P11 As Sulayyil Ar Riyāḑ, S Saudi Arabia 20°29′N 45°33′E
145 O13 As Sulţān N Libya 31°01′N 17°21′E
141 Q5 Aş Şummān desert N Saudi Arabia
141 Q16 Aş Şurrah SW Yemen 13°56′N 46°23′E
139 N4 Aş Şuwār var. Şuwār. Dayr az Zawr, E Syria 35°31′N 40°37′E
138 H9 As Suwaydā' var. El Suweida, Es Suweida, Suweida, Fr. Soueida. As Suwaydā', SW Syria 32°43′N 36°33′E
138 H9 As Suwaydā' off. Muḩāfaz̧at as Suwaydā', var. As Suwaydā, Suwaydā, Suweida. ◈ governorate S Syria
141 Z9 As Suwayḩ NE Oman 22°07′N 59°42′E
141 X8 As Suwayq var. Suwaik. N Oman 23°49′N 57°30′E
139 T8 Aş Şuwayrah var. Suwaira. Wāsiţ, E Iraq 32°57′N 44°47′E
As Suways see Suez
Asta Colonia see Asti
Astacus see İzmit
115 M23 Astakída island SE Greece
145 Q9 Astana prev. Akmola, Akmolinsk, Tselinograd, Aqmola. ● (Kazakhstan) Akmola, N Kazakhstan 51°13′N 71°25′E
142 M3 Āstāneh var. Āstāneh-ye Ashrafīyeh. Gīlān, NW Iran 37°17′N 49°58′E
Āstāneh-ye Ashrafīyeh see Āstāneh
Asta Pompeia see Asti
137 Y14 Astara S Azerbaijan 38°28′N 48°51′E
Astarabad see Gorgān
99 L15 Asten Noord-Brabant, SE Netherlands 51°24′N 05°45′E
Asterābād see Gorgān
106 C8 Asti anc. Asta Colonia, Asta Pompeia, Hasta Colonia, Hasta Pompeia. Piemonte, NW Italy 44°54′N 08°11′E
Astigi see Ecija
Astipálaia see Astypálaia
148 L16 Astola Island island SW Pakistan
152 H4 Astor Jammu and Kashmir, NW India 35°21′N 74°52′E
104 K4 Astorga anc. Asturica Augusta. Castilla y León, N Spain 42°27′N 06°04′W
32 F10 Astoria Oregon, NW USA 46°12′N 123°50′W
0 F8 Astoria Fan undersea feature E Pacific Ocean 45°15′N 126°15′W
95 J22 Åstorp Skåne, S Sweden 56°09′N 12°57′E
Astrabad see Gorgān
127 Q13 Astrakhan' Astrakhanskaya Oblast', SW Russian Federation 46°20′N 48°01′E
Astrakhan-Bazar see Cälilabad
127 Q11 Astrakhanskaya Oblast' ◈ province SW Russian Federation
93 J15 Åsträsk Västerbotten, N Sweden 64°38′N 20°00′E
Astrida see Butare
65 O22 Astrid Ridge undersea feature S Atlantic Ocean
187 P15 Astrolabe, Récifs de l' reef C New Caledonia
121 P2 Astromeritis N Cyprus 35°09′N 33°02′E
115 F20 Ástros Pelopónnisos, S Greece 37°24′N 22°43′E
119 G16 Astryna Rus. Ostryna. Hrodzyenskaya Voblasts', W Belarus 53°44′N 24°33′E
104 J2 Asturias ◈ autonomous community NW Spain
Asturias see Oviedo
Asturica Augusta see Astorga
115 L22 Astypálaia var. Astipálaia, It. Stampalia. island Kykládes, Greece, Aegean Sea
192 G16 Āsuisui, Cape headland Savai'i, W Samoa 13°44′S 172°29′W
195 S2 Asuka Japanese research station Antarctica 71°49′S 23°52′E
62 O6 Asunción ● (Paraguay) Central, S Paraguay 25°17′S 57°36′W
62 O6 Asunción ✈ Central, S Paraguay 25°15′S 57°40′W
188 K3 Asuncion Island island N Northern Mariana Islands
42 E6 Asunción Mita Jutiapa, SE Guatemala 14°20′N 89°42′W
Asunción Nochixtlán see Nochixtlán
40 E3 Asunción, Río ≈ NW Mexico
95 M18 Åsunden ⊚ S Sweden
118 K11 Asvyeya Rus. Osveya. Vitsyebskaya Voblasts', N Belarus 56°00′N 28°05′E
Aswa see Achwa
75 X11 Aswān var. Assouan, Assuan, Aswân; anc. Syene. SE Egypt 24°03′N 32°59′E
Aswân see Aswān
Aswan Dam see Khazzān Aswān
75 W9 Asyūţ var. Assiout, Assiut, Asyût, Siut; anc. Lycopolis. C Egypt 27°06′N 31°11′E
Asyût see Asyūţ
193 W15 Ata island Tongatapu Group, SW Tonga
62 G8 Atacama off. Región de Atacama. ◈ region C Chile
Atacama Desert see Atacama, Desierto de
62 H4 Atacama, Desierto de Eng. Atacama Desert. desert N Chile
62 I6 Atacama, Puna de ▲▲ NW Argentina
Atacama, Región de see Atacama
62 I5 Atacama, Salar de salt lake N Chile
54 E11 Ataco Tolima, C Colombia 03°36′N 75°23′W
190 H8 Atafu Atoll island NW Tokelau
190 H8 Atafu Village Atafu Atoll, NW Tokelau 08°40′S 172°40′W
74 K12 Atakor ▲▲ SE Algeria
77 R14 Atakora, Chaîne de l' var. Atakora Mountains. ▲▲ N Benin
Atakora Mountains see Atakora, Chaîne de l'
77 R16 Atakpamé C Togo 07°32′N 01°08′E
146 F11 Atakui Ahal Welaýaty, C Turkmenistan 40°04′N 58°03′E
58 B13 Atalaia do Norte Amazonas, N Brazil 04°22′S 70°10′W
146 M14 Atamyrat prev. Kerki. Lebap Welaýaty, E Turkmenistan 37°52′N 65°06′E
76 I7 Aţâr Adrar, W Mauritania 20°30′N 13°03′W
162 G10 Atas Bogd ▲ SW Mongolia 43°17′N 96°47′E
35 P12 Atascadero California, W USA 35°28′N 120°40′W
25 S13 Atascosa River ≈ Texas, SW USA
145 R11 Atasu Karaganda, C Kazakhstan 48°42′N 71°38′E
145 R12 Atasu ≈ Karaganda, C Kazakhstan
193 V15 Atata island Tongatapu Group, S Tonga
136 H10 Atatürk ✈ (İstanbul) İstanbul, NW Turkey 40°58′N 28°50′E
137 N16 Atatürk Barajı ⊡ S Turkey
115 O23 Atavýros prev. Attavyros. Ródos, Dodekánisa, Aegean Sea 36°10′N 27°50′E
115 O23 Atávyros prev. Attávyros. ▲ Ródos, Dodekánisa, Greece, Aegean Sea 36°10′N 27°50′E
Atax see Aude
80 G8 Atbara var. 'Aţbārah. River Nile, NE Sudan 17°42′N 34°E
80 H8 Atbara var. Nahr 'Aţbārah. ≈ Eritrea/Sudan
'Aţbārah/'Aţbārah, Nahr see Atbara
145 P9 Atbasar Akmola, N Kazakhstan 51°49′N 68°18′E
At-Bashi see At-Bashy
147 W9 At-Bashy var. At-Bashi. Narynskaya Oblast', C Kyrgyzstan 41°07′N 75°48′E
22 I10 Atchafalaya Bay bay Louisiana, S USA
22 I8 Atchafalaya River ≈ Louisiana, S USA
Atchin see Aceh
27 Q3 Atchison Kansas, C USA 39°31′N 95°07′W
77 P16 Atebubu C Ghana 07°47′N 01°00′W
105 Q6 Ateca Aragón, NE Spain 41°20′N 01°49′W
40 K11 Atengo, Río ≈ C Mexico
Aternum see Pescara
107 K15 Atessa Abruzzo, C Italy 42°03′N 14°25′E
Ateste see Este
99 E19 Ath var. Aat. Hainaut, SW Belgium 50°38′N 03°47′E
11 Q13 Athabasca Alberta, SW Canada 54°44′N 113°15′W
11 Q12 Athabasca var. Athabaska. ≈ Alberta, SW Canada
11 R10 Athabasca, Lake ⊚ Alberta/ Saskatchewan, SW Canada
Athabaska see Athabasca
115 C16 Athamánon ▲▲ C Greece
97 F17 Athboy Ir. Baile Átha Buí. E Ireland 53°38′N 06°55′W
Athenae see Athína
97 C18 Athenry Ir. Baile Átha an Rí. W Ireland 53°19′N 08°49′W
23 P2 Athens Alabama, S USA 34°48′N 86°58′W
23 T3 Athens Georgia, SE USA 33°57′N 83°24′W
31 T14 Athens Ohio, N USA 39°20′N 82°06′W
20 M10 Athens Tennessee, S USA 35°27′N 84°38′W
25 V7 Athens Texas, SW USA 32°12′N 95°51′W
Athens see Athína
115 B18 Athéras, Akrotírio headland Kefalloniá, Iónia Nísiá, Greece, C Mediterranean Sea 38°20′N 20°24′E
181 W4 Atherton Queensland, NE Australia 17°18′S 145°29′E
81 I19 Athi ≈ S Kenya
121 Q2 Athiénou SE Cyprus 35°01′N 33°31′E
115 H19 Athína Eng. Athens, prev. Athínai; anc. Athenae. ● (Greece) Attikí, C Greece 37°59′N 23°44′E
Athínai see Athína
139 S10 Athīyah An Najaf, C Iraq 32°01′N 44°04′E
97 D18 Athlone Ir. Baile Átha Luain. C Ireland 53°25′N 07°56′W
155 F16 Athni Karnātaka, W India 16°43′N 75°04′E
185 C23 Athol Southland, South Island, New Zealand 45°30′S 168°35′E
19 N11 Athol Massachusetts, NE USA 42°35′N 72°11′W
115 I15 Áthos ▲ NE Greece 40°10′N 24°21′E
Athos, Mount see Ágion Óros
Ath Thawrah see Madīnat ath Thawrah
141 P5 Ath Thumāmī spring/well N Saudi Arabia 27°56′N 45°06′E
99 L25 Athus Luxembourg, SE Belgium 49°34′N 05°50′E
97 E19 Athy Ir. Baile Átha Í. C Ireland 52°59′N 06°59′W
78 I10 Ati Batha, C Chad 13°11′N 18°20′E
81 F16 Atiak NW Uganda 03°14′N 32°05′E
57 G17 Atico Arequipa, SW Peru 16°13′S 73°13′W
105 O6 Atienza Castilla-La Mancha, C Spain 41°12′N 02°52′W
39 Q6 Atigun Pass pass Alaska, USA
12 B12 Atikokan Ontario, S Canada 48°45′N 91°38′W
13 O9 Atikonak Lac ⊚ Newfoundland and Labrador, E Canada
42 C6 Atitlán, Lago de ⊚ W Guatemala
190 L16 Atiu island S Cook Islands
Atjeh see Aceh
123 T9 Atka Magadanskaya Oblast', E Russian Federation 60°45′N 151°35′E
38 H17 Atka Atka Island, Alaska, USA 52°12′N 174°14′W
38 H17 Atka Island island Aleutian Islands, Alaska, USA
127 O7 Atkarsk Saratovskaya Oblast', W Russian Federation 52°15′N 43°48′E
27 U11 Atkins Arkansas, C USA 35°15′N 92°56′W
29 O13 Atkinson Nebraska, C USA 42°31′N 98°57′W
171 T12 Atkri Papua, E Indonesia 01°45′S 130°04′E
41 O13 Atlacomulco var. Atlacomulco de Fabela. México, C Mexico 19°49′N 99°54′W
Atlacomulco de Fabela see Atlacomulco
23 S3 Atlanta state capital Georgia, SE USA 33°45′N 84°23′W
31 R6 Atlanta Michigan, N USA 45°01′N 84°07′W
25 X6 Atlanta Texas, SW USA 33°06′N 94°09′W
29 T15 Atlantic Iowa, C USA 41°24′N 95°00′W
21 Y10 Atlantic North Carolina, SE USA 34°52′N 76°20′W
23 W8 Atlantic Beach Florida, SE USA 30°19′N 81°24′W
18 J17 Atlantic City New Jersey, NE USA 39°23′N 74°27′W
172 L14 Atlantic-Indian Basin undersea feature SW Indian Ocean 60°00′S 15°00′E
172 K13 Atlantic-Indian Ridge undersea feature SW Indian Ocean 53°00′S 15°00′E
54 E4 Atlántico off. Departamento del Atlántico. ◈ province NW Colombia
64-65 Atlantic Ocean ocean
Atlántico, Departamento del see Atlántico
42 K7 Atlántico Norte, Región Autónoma prev. Zelaya Norte. ◈ autonomous region NE Nicaragua
42 L10 Atlántico Sur, Región Autónoma prev. Zelaya Sur. ◈ autonomous region SE Nicaragua
42 I5 Atlántida ◈ department N Honduras
77 Y15 Atlantika Mountains ▲▲ E Nigeria
64 J10 Atlantis Fracture Zone tectonic feature NW Atlantic Ocean
74 H7 Atlas Mountains ▲▲ NW Africa
123 V11 Atlasova, Ostrov island SE Russian Federation
123 V10 Atlasovo Kamchatskiy Kray, E Russian Federation 55°42′N 159°35′E
120 G11 Atlas Saharien var. Saharan Atlas. ▲▲ Algeria/Morocco
Atlas, Tell see Atlas Tellien
120 H10 Atlas Tellien Eng. Tell Atlas. ▲▲ N Algeria
10 I9 Atlin British Columbia, W Canada 59°31′N 133°41′W
10 I9 Atlin Lake ⊚ British Columbia, W Canada
41 P14 Atlixco Puebla, S Mexico 18°55′N 98°26′W
94 B11 Atløyna island S Norway
155 I17 Ātmakūr Andhra Pradesh, C India 15°52′N 78°42′E
23 O8 Atmore Alabama, S USA 31°01′N 87°29′W
101 J20 Atmühl ≈ S Germany
94 H11 Atna ≈ S Norway
164 E13 Atō Yamaguchi, Honshū, SW Japan 34°24′N 131°42′E
57 L21 Atocha Potosí, S Bolivia 20°55′S 66°14′W
27 P12 Atoka Oklahoma, C USA 34°22′N 96°08′W
27 O12 Atoka Lake var. Atoka Reservoir. ⊡ Oklahoma, C USA
Atoka Reservoir see Atoka Lake
33 Q14 Atomic City Idaho, NW USA 43°26′N 112°48′W
40 L10 Atotonilco Zacatecas, C Mexico 24°12′N 102°46′W
Atotonilco see Atotonilco el Alto
40 M13 Atotonilco el Alto var. Atotonilco. Jalisco, SW Mexico 20°35′N 102°30′W
77 N7 Atouila, 'Erg desert N Mali
41 N16 Atoyac var. Atoyac de Alvarez. Guerrero, S Mexico 17°12′N 100°28′W
Atoyac de Alvarez see Atoyac
41 P15 Atoyac, Río ≈ S Mexico
39 O5 Atqasuk Alaska, USA 70°28′N 157°24′W
Atrak/Atrak, Rūd-e see Etrek
95 J20 Ätran ≈ S Sweden
54 C7 Atrato, Río ≈ NW Colombia
Atrek see Etrek
107 K14 Atri Abruzzo, C Italy 42°35′N 13°59′E
Atria see Adria
165 P9 Atsumi Yamagata, Honshū, C Japan 38°38′N 139°36′E
165 S3 Atsuta Hokkaidō, NE Japan 43°28′N 141°24′E
143 Q17 Aţ Ţaff desert C United Arab Emirates
138 G12 Aţ Ţafilah var. Et Tafila, Tafila. Aţ Ţafilah, W Jordan 30°52′N 35°36′E
138 G12 Aţ Ţafilah off. Muḩāfaz̧at aţ Ţafilah. ◈ governorate W Jordan
140 L10 Aţ Ţā'if Makkah, W Saudi Arabia 21°50′N 40°50′E
Attaleia/Attalia see Antalya
23 Q3 Attalla Alabama, S USA 34°01′N 86°05′W
138 L2 At Tall al Abyaḑ var. Tall al Abyaḑ, Tell Abyad, Fr. Tell Abiad. Ar Raqqah, N Syria 36°36′N 34°00′E
138 L7 Aţ Ţanf Ḩimş, S Syria 33°29′N 38°39′E
163 N9 Attanshiree Dornogovĭ, SE Mongolia 45°36′N 110°30′E
167 T10 Attapu var. Attopeu, Samakhixai. Attapu, S Laos 14°48′N 106°51′E
139 S10 At Taqtaqānah An Najaf, C Iraq 32°03′N 43°54′E
Attávyros see Atávyros
12 G9 Attawapiskat Ontario, C Canada 52°55′N 82°26′W
12 F9 Attawapiskat ≈ Ontario, S Canada
12 D9 Attawapiskat Lake ⊚ Ontario, C Canada
At Taybé see Ţayyibah
101 F16 Attendorn Nordrhein-Westfalen, W Germany 51°07′N 07°54′E
109 R5 Attersee Salzburg, NW Austria 47°55′N 13°31′E
109 R5 Attersee ⊚ N Austria
99 L24 Attert Luxembourg, SE Belgium 49°45′N 05°47′E
138 M4 At Tibnī var. Tibnī. Dayr az Zawr, NE Syria 35°30′N 39°48′E
31 N13 Attica Indiana, N USA 40°17′N 87°15′W
18 E10 Attica New York, NE USA 42°51′N 78°13′W
Attica see Attikí
13 N7 Attikamagen Lake ⊚ Newfoundland and Labrador, E Canada
115 H20 Attikí Eng. Attica. ◈ region C Greece
19 O12 Attleboro Massachusetts, NE USA 41°55′N 71°15′W
109 R5 Attnang Oberösterreich, N Austria 48°02′N 13°44′E
149 U6 Attock City Punjab, E Pakistan 33°52′N 72°20′E
Attopeu see Attapu
25 X8 Attoyac River ≈ Texas, SW USA
38 D16 Attu Attu Island, Alaska, USA 52°53′N 173°18′E
139 Y12 Aţ Ţūbah Al Başrah, E Iraq 30°29′N 47°28′E
140 K4 Aţ Ţubayq plain Jordan/ Saudi Arabia
38 C16 Attu Island island Aleutian Islands, Alaska, USA
75 X8 Aţ Ţūr var. El Ţûr. NE Egypt 28°14′N 33°36′E
155 I21 Āttūr Tamil Nādu, SE India 11°34′N 78°39′E
141 N17 At Turbah SW Yemen 12°42′N 43°31′E
62 I12 Atuel, Río ≈ C Argentina
191 X7 Atuona Hiva Oa, NE French Polynesia 09°47′S 139°03′W
Aturus see Adour
95 M18 Åtvidaberg Östergötland, S Sweden 58°12′N 16°00′E
35 P9 Atwater California, W USA 37°19′N 120°33′W
29 T8 Atwater Minnesota, N USA 45°08′N 94°48′W
26 I2 Atwood Kansas, C USA 39°48′N 101°03′W
31 U12 Atwood Lake ⊡ Ohio, N USA
127 P5 Atyashevo Respublika Mordoviya, W Russian Federation 54°36′N 46°04′E
144 F12 Atyrau prev. Gur'yev. Atyrau, W Kazakhstan 47°07′N 51°56′E
144 E11 Atyrau off. Atyrauskaya Oblast', var.Kaz. Atyraū Oblysy; prev. Gur'yevskaya Oblast'. ◈ province W Kazakhstan
Atyraū Oblysy/ Atyrauskaya Oblast' see Atyrau
Atyrauskaya Oblast' see Atyrau
108 J7 Au Vorarlberg, NW Austria 47°19′N 10°01′E
186 B4 Aua Island island NW Papua New Guinea
103 S16 Aubagne anc. Albania. Bouches-du-Rhône, SE France 43°17′N 05°35′E
99 L25 Aubange Luxembourg, SE Belgium 49°35′N 05°49′E
103 Q6 Aube ◈ department N France
103 R6 Aube ≈ N France
99 L19 Aubel Liège, E Belgium 50°45′N 05°49′E
103 Q13 Aubenas Ardèche, E France 44°37′N 04°24′E
103 O8 Aubigny-sur-Nère Cher, C France 47°30′N 02°27′E
103 O13 Aubin Aveyron, S France 44°30′N 02°18′E
103 O13 Aubrac, Monts d' ▲▲ S France
36 J10 Aubrey Cliffs cliff Arizona, SW USA
23 R5 Auburn Alabama, S USA 32°37′N 85°30′W
35 P6 Auburn California, W USA 38°53′N 121°03′W
30 K14 Auburn Illinois, N USA 39°35′N 89°45′W
31 Q11 Auburn Indiana, N USA 41°22′N 85°03′W
20 J7 Auburn Kentucky, S USA 36°52′N 86°42′W
19 P8 Auburn Maine, NE USA 44°05′N 70°15′W
19 N11 Auburn Massachusetts, NE USA 42°11′N 71°47′W
29 S16 Auburn Nebraska, C USA 40°23′N 95°50′W
18 H10 Auburn New York, NE USA 42°55′N 76°31′W
32 H8 Auburn Washington, NW USA 47°18′N 122°13′W
103 N11 Aubusson Creuse, C France 45°58′N 02°10′E
118 E10 Auce Ger. Autz. SW Latvia 56°28′N 22°54′E
102 L15 Auch Lat. Augusta Auscorum, Elimberrum. Gers, S France 43°40′N 00°37′E
77 U16 Auchi Edo, S Nigeria 07°01′N 06°17′E
23 T9 Aucilla River ≈ Florida/ Georgia, SE USA
184 L6 Auckland Auckland, North Island, New Zealand 36°53′S 174°46′E
184 K5 Auckland off. Auckland Region. ◈ region North Island, New Zealand
184 L6 Auckland ✈ Auckland, North Island, New Zealand 37°01′S 174°49′E
192 J12 Auckland Islands island group S New Zealand
Auckland Region see Auckland
103 O16 Aude ◈ department S France
103 N16 Aude anc. Atax. ≈ S France
Audenarde see Oudenaarde
Audern see Audru
102 E6 Audierne Finistère, NW France 48°01′N 04°30′W
102 E6 Audierne, Baie d' bay NW France
103 U7 Audincourt Doubs, E France 47°29′N 06°50′E
118 G5 Audru Ger. Audern. Pärnumaa, SW Estonia 58°24′N 24°22′E
29 T14 Audubon Iowa, C USA 41°44′N 94°56′W
101 N17 Aue Sachsen, E Germany 50°35′N 12°42′E
100 H12 Aue ≈ NW Germany
100 L9 Auerbach Bayern, SE Germany 49°41′N 11°41′E
101 M17 Auerbach Sachsen, E Germany 50°30′N 12°24′E
108 I10 Auererrhein ≈ SW Switzerland
101 N17 Auersberg ▲ E Germany 50°30′N 12°42′E
181 W9 Augathella Queensland, E Australia 25°54′S 146°38′E
31 Q12 Auglaize River ≈ Ohio, N USA
83 F22 Augrabies Falls waterfall W South Africa
31 R7 Au Gres River ≈ Michigan, N USA
Augsbourg see Augsburg
101 K22 Augsburg Fr. Augsbourg; anc. Augusta Vindelicorum. Bayern, S Germany 48°22′N 10°54′E
180 I14 Augusta Western Australia 34°18′S 115°10′E
107 L25 Augusta It. Agosta. Sicilia, Italy, C Mediterranean Sea 37°14′N 15°14′E
27 W11 Augusta Arkansas, C USA 35°16′N 91°21′W
23 V3 Augusta Georgia, SE USA 33°29′N 81°58′W
27 O6 Augusta Kansas, C USA 37°40′N 96°59′W
19 Q7 Augusta state capital Maine, NE USA 44°20′N 69°44′W
33 Q8 Augusta Montana, NW USA 47°28′N 112°23′W
Augusta see London
Augusta Auscorum see Auch
Augusta Emerita see Mérida
Augusta Praetoria see Aosta
Augusta Suessionum see Soissons
Augusta Trajana see Stara Zagora
Augusta Treverorum see Trier
Augusta Vangionum see Worms
Augusta Vindelicorum see Augsburg
95 G24 Augustenborg Ger. Augustenburg. Syddanmark, SW Denmark 54°57′N 09°53′E
Augustenburg see Augustenborg
39 Q13 Augustine Island island Alaska, USA
14 L9 Augustines, Lac des ⊚ Québec, SE Canada
Augustobona Tricassium see Troyes
Augustodunum see Autun
Augustodurum see Bayeux
Augustoritum Lemovicensium see Limoges
110 O8 Augustów Rus. Avgustov. Podlaskie, NE Poland 53°52′N 22°58′E
Augustow Canal see Augustowski, Kanał
110 O8 Augustowski, Kanał Eng. Augustow Canal, Rus. Avgustovskiy Kanal. canal NE Poland
180 I9 Augustus, Mount ▲ Western Australia 24°42′S 117°42′E
Aujuittuq see Grise Fiord
186 M9 Auki Malaita, N Solomon Islands 08°48′S 160°45′E
21 W8 Aulander North Carolina, SE USA 36°15′N 77°16′W
180 L7 Auld, Lake salt lake C Western Australia
Aulie Ata/Auliye-Ata see Taraz
Äūliekōl see Auliyekol'
144 M8 Auliyekol' Kaz. Äūliekōl; prev. Semiozernoye. Kostanay, N Kazakhstan 52°22′N 64°06′E
106 E10 Aulla Toscana, C Italy 44°15′N 10°00′E
102 F6 Aulne ≈ NW France
Aulong see Ulong
37 T3 Ault Colorado, C USA 40°34′N 104°43′W
95 F22 Aulum var. Avlum. Midtjylland, C Denmark 56°16′N 08°48′E
103 N3 Aumale Seine-Maritime, N France 49°45′N 01°43′E
Auminzatau, Gory see Ovminzatovo Tog'lari
77 T14 Auna Niger, W Nigeria 10°13′N 04°43′E
166 L6 Aunglan var. Allanmyo, Myaydo. Magway, C Myanmar (Burma) 19°25′N 95°13′E
95 H21 Auning Midtjylland, C Denmark 56°26′N 10°23′E
192 K17 'Aunu'u Island island W American Samoa
83 E20 Auob var. Oup. ≈ Namibia/South Africa
93 K19 Aura Länsi-Suomi, SW Finland 60°37′N 22°35′E
109 R5 Aurach ≈ N Austria
Aural, Phnom see Aôral, Phnum
153 O14 Aurangābād Bihār, N India 24°46′N 84°23′E
154 F13 Aurangābād Mahārāshtra, C India 19°52′N 75°22′E
189 V7 Aur Atoll atoll E Marshall Islands
102 G7 Auray Morbihan, NW France 47°40′N 03°00′W
94 G13 Aurdal Oppland, S Norway 60°51′N 09°25′E
94 F8 Aure Møre og Romsdal, S Norway 63°16′N 08°31′E
29 T12 Aurelia Iowa, C USA 42°42′N 95°26′W
Aurelia Aquensis see Baden-Baden
Aurelianum see Orléans
120 J10 Aurès, Massif de l' ▲▲ NE Algeria
100 F10 Aurich Niedersachsen, NW Germany 53°28′N 07°28′E
103 O13 Aurillac Cantal, C France 44°56′N 02°26′E
Aurine, Alpi see Zillertaler Alpen
Aurium see Ourense
14 H15 Aurora Ontario, S Canada 44°00′N 79°26′W
55 S8 Aurora NW Guyana 06°46′N 59°45′W
37 T4 Aurora Colorado, C USA 39°42′N 104°51′W
30 M11 Aurora Illinois, N USA 41°46′N 88°19′W
31 Q15 Aurora Indiana, N USA 39°01′N 84°55′W
29 W4 Aurora Minnesota, N USA 47°31′N 92°14′W
27 S8 Aurora Missouri, C USA 36°58′N 93°43′W
29 P16 Aurora Nebraska, C USA 40°52′N 98°00′W
36 J5 Aurora Utah, W USA 38°55′N 111°55′W
Aurora see San Francisco, Philippines
Aurora see Maéwo, Vanuatu
94 F10 Aursjøen ⊚ S Norway
94 I9 Aursunden ⊚ S Norway
83 D21 Aus Karas, SW Namibia 26°38′S 16°19′E
Ausa see Vic
14 E16 Ausable ≈ Ontario, S Canada
31 O3 Au Sable Point headland Michigan, N USA 46°40′N 86°08′W
31 S7 Au Sable Point headland Michigan, N USA 44°19′N 83°20′W
31 R6 Au Sable River ≈ Michigan, N USA
57 H16 Ausangate, Nevado ▲ C Peru 13°47′S 71°13′W
Auschwitz see Oświęcim
Ausculum Apulum see Ascoli Satriano
105 Q4 Ausejo La Rioja, N Spain 42°21′N 02°10′W
108 H7 Ausser Rhoden ◈ canton NE Switzerland
Ausser Rhoden/Inner Rhoden see Ausser Rhoden
Aussig see Ústí nad Labem
95 F17 Aust-Agder ◈ county S Norway
92 P2 Austfonna glacier NE Svalbard
31 P15 Austin Indiana, N USA 38°45′N 85°48′W
29 W11 Austin Minnesota, N USA 43°40′N 92°58′W
35 U5 Austin Nevada, W USA 39°30′N 117°05′W
25 S10 Austin state capital Texas, SW USA 30°16′N 97°45′W
180 J10 Austin, Lake salt lake Western Australia
31 V11 Austintown Ohio, N USA 41°06′N 80°45′W
25 V9 Austonio Texas, SW USA 31°09′N 95°39′W
Australes, Archipel des see Australes, Îles
Australes et Antarctiques Françaises, Terres see French Southern and Antarctic Territories
191 T14 Australes, Îles var. Archipel des Australes, Îles Tubuai, Tubuai Islands, Eng. Austral Islands. island group SW French Polynesia
175 Y11 Austral Fracture Zone tectonic feature S Pacific Ocean
174 M8 Australia continent
181 O7 Australia off. Commonwealth of Australia. ◆ commonwealth republic
Australia, Commonwealth of see Australia
183 Q12 Australian Alps ▲▲ SE Australia
183 R11 Australian Capital Territory prev. Federal Capital Territory. ◈ territory SE Australia
Australie, Bassin Nord de l' see North Australian Basin
Austral Islands see Australes, Îles
Austrava see Ostrov
109 T6 Austria off. Republic of Austria, Ger. Österreich. ◆ republic C Europe
Austria, Republic of see Austria
92 K3 Austurland ◈ region SE Iceland
92 G10 Austvågøya island C Norway
Ausuitoq see Grise Fiord
58 G13 Autazes Amazonas, N Brazil 03°37′S 59°08′W
102 M16 Auterive Haute-Garonne, S France 43°22′N 01°28′E
Autesiodorum see Auxerre
103 N2 Authie ≈ N France
Autissiodorum see Auxerre
40 K14 Autlán var. Autlán de Navarro. Jalisco, SW Mexico 19°48′N 104°20′W
Autlán de Navarro see Autlán
Autricum see Chartres
103 Q9 Autun anc. Ædua, Augustodunum. Saône-et-Loire, C France 46°58′N 04°18′E
Autz see Auce
99 H20 Auvelais Namur, S Belgium 50°27′N 04°38′E
103 P11 Auvergne ◈ region C France
102 M12 Auvézère ≈ W France
103 P7 Auxerre anc. Autesiodorum, Autissiodorum. Yonne, C France 47°48′N 03°35′E
103 N2 Auxi-le-Château Pas-de-Calais, N France 50°14′N 02°06′E
103 S8 Auxonne Côte d'Or, C France 47°12′N 05°22′E
55 P9 Auyan Tebuy ▲ SE Venezuela 05°48′N 62°27′W
103 O10 Auzances Creuse, C France 46°01′N 02°29′E
27 U8 Ava Missouri, C USA 36°57′N 92°39′W
142 M5 Āvaj Qazvīn, N Iran
95 C15 Avaldsnes Rogaland, S Norway 59°21′N 05°16′E
103 Q8 Avallon Yonne, C France 47°30′N 03°54′E
102 K6 Avaloirs, Mont des ▲ NW France 48°27′N 00°11′W
35 S16 Avalon Santa Catalina Island, California, W USA 33°20′N 118°19′W
18 J17 Avalon New Jersey, NE USA 39°04′N 74°42′W
13 V13 Avalon Peninsula peninsula Newfoundland and Labrador, E Canada
Avanersuaq see Avannaarsua
197 Q11 Avannaarsua var Avanersuaq, Dan. Nordgrønland. ◈ province N Greenland
60 K10 Avaré São Paulo, S Brazil 23°06′S 48°57′W
Avaricum see Bourges
190 H16 Avarua ○ (Cook Islands) Rarotonga, S Cook Islands 21°12′S 159°46′E
190 H16 Avarua Harbour harbor Rarotonga, S Cook Islands
Avasfelsőfalu see Negreşti-Oaş
38 L17 Avatanak Island island Aleutian Islands, Alaska, USA
190 B16 Avatele S Niue 19°06′S 169°55′E
190 H15 Avatiu Harbour harbor Rarotonga, S Cook Islands
Avdeyevka see Avdiyivka
114 J13 Ávdira Anatolikí Makedonía kai Thráki, NE Greece 40°58′N 24°58′E
117 X8 Avdiyivka Rus. Avdeyevka. Donets'ka Oblast', SE Ukraine 48°06′N 37°46′E
Avdzaga see Gurvanbulag
104 G6 Ave ≈ N Portugal
104 G7 Aveiro anc. Talabriga. Aveiro, W Portugal 40°38′N 08°40′W
104 G7 Aveiro ◈ district N Portugal
Avela see Ávila
99 D18 Avelgem West-Vlaanderen, W Belgium 50°46′N 03°25′E
61 D20 Avellaneda Buenos Aires, E Argentina 34°43′S 58°23′W
107 L17 Avellino anc. Abellinum. Campania, S Italy 40°54′N 14°46′E
35 Q12 Avenal California, W USA 36°00′N 120°07′W
Avenio see Avignon
94 E8 Averøya island S Norway
107 K17 Aversa Campania, S Italy 40°58′N 14°13′E
33 N9 Avery Idaho, NW USA 47°14′N 115°48′W
25 W5 Avery Texas, SW USA 33°33′N 94°46′W
Aves, Islas de see Las Aves, Islas
Avesnes see Avesnes-sur-Helpe
103 Q2 Avesnes-sur-Helpe var. Avesnes. Nord, N France 50°08′N 03°57′E
64 G12 Aves Ridge undersea feature SE Caribbean Sea 14°00′N 63°30′W
95 M14 Avesta Dalarna, C Sweden 60°09′N 16°10′E
103 O14 Aveyron ◈ department S France
103 N14 Aveyron ≈ S France
107 J15 Avezzano Abruzzo, C Italy 42°02′N 13°26′E
115 D16 Avgó ▲ C Greece 39°31′N 21°24′E
Avgustov see Augustów
Avgustovskiy Kanal see Augustowski, Kanał
96 J9 Aviemore N Scotland, United Kingdom 57°06′N 04°01′W
185 F21 Aviemore, Lake ⊚ South Island, New Zealand
103 R15 Avignon anc. Avenio. Vaucluse, SE France 43°57′N 04°49′E
104 M7 Ávila var. Avila; anc. Abela, Abula, Abyla, Avela. Castilla y León, C Spain 40°39′N 04°42′W
104 L8 Ávila ◈ province Castilla y León, C Spain
104 K2 Avilés Asturias, NW Spain 43°33′N 05°55′W
118 J4 Avinurme Ger. Awwinorm. Ida-Virumaa, NE Estonia 58°58′N 26°53′E
104 H10 Avis Portalegre, C Portugal 39°03′N 07°53′W
Avlum see Aulum
182 M11 Avoca Victoria, SE Australia 37°09′S 143°34′E
29 T14 Avoca Iowa, C USA 41°29′N 95°16′W
182 M11 Avoca River ≈ Victoria, SE Australia
107 L25 Avola Sicilia, Italy, C Mediterranean Sea 36°54′N 15°08′E
18 F10 Avon New York, NE USA 42°53′N 77°41′W
29 P12 Avon South Dakota, N USA 43°00′N 98°03′W
97 M23 Avon ≈ S England, United Kingdom
97 L20 Avon ≈ C England, United Kingdom
36 K13 Avondale Arizona, SW USA 33°25′N 112°20′W
23 X13 Avon Park Florida, SE USA 27°36′N 81°30′W
102 J5 Avranches Manche, N France 48°42′N 01°21′W
Avveel see Ivalo, Ivalojoki, Finland
186 M6 Avuavu var. Kolotambu. Guadalcanal, C Solomon Islands 09°52′S 160°25′E
103 O3 Avure ≈ N France

◆ Country ● Country Capital ◇ Dependent Territory ○ Dependent Territory Capital ◈ Administrative Regions ✈ International Airport ▲ Mountain ▲▲ Mountain Range Volcano ≈ River ⊚ Lake ⊡ Reservoir

Avveel see Ivalo, Finland
Avvil see Ivalo
77 O17 Awaaso var. Awaso. SW Ghana 06°10′N 02°18′W
141 X8 Awābī var. Al 'Awābī. NE Oman 23°20′N 57°35′E
184 L9 Awakino Waikato, North Island, New Zealand 38°40′S 174°37′E
142 M15 'Awālī C Bahrain 26°07′N 50°33′E
99 K19 Awans Liège, E Belgium 50°39′N 05°30′E
184 I2 Awanui Northland, North Island, New Zealand 35°01′S 173°16′E
148 M14 Awārān Baluchistān, SW Pakistan 26°31′N 65°10′E
81 K16 Awara Plain plain NE Kenya
80 M13 Āwarē Sumalē, E Ethiopia 08°12′N 44°09′E
138 M6 'Awāriḍ, Wādī dry watercourse E Syria
185 B20 Awarua Point headland South Island, New Zealand 44°15′S 168°03′E
81 J14 Āwasa Southern Nationalities, S Ethiopia 06°54′N 38°26′E
80 K13 Āwash Āfar, NE Ethiopia 08°59′N 40°16′E
80 K12 Āwash var. Hawash. ≈ C Ethiopia
Awaso see Awaaso
158 H7 Awat Xinjiang Uygur Zizhiqu, NW China 40°36′N 80°22′E
185 J15 Awatere ≈ South Island, New Zealand
75 O10 Awbārī SW Libya 26°35′N 12°46′E
75 N9 Awbārī, Idhān var. Edeyen d'Oubari. desert Algeria/Libya
80 M12 Awdal off. Gobolka Awdal. ◈ N Somalia
80 C13 Aweil Northern Bahr el Ghazal, NW South Sudan 08°42′N 27°20′E
96 H11 Awe, Loch ◎ W Scotland, United Kingdom
77 U16 Awka Anambra, SW Nigeria 06°12′N 07°04′E
39 O6 Awuna River ≈ Alaska, USA
Awwinorm see Avinurme
Ax see Dax
Axarfjördhur see Öxarfjördhur
103 N17 Axat Aude, S France 42°47′N 02°14′E
99 F16 Axel Zeeland, SW Netherlands 51°16′N 03°55′E
197 P9 Axel Heiberg Island var. Axel Heiburg. island Nunavut, N Canada
Axel Heiburg see Axel Heiberg Island
77 O17 Axim S Ghana 04°53′N 02°14′W
114 F13 Axiós var. Vardar. ≈ Greece/FYR Macedonia see also Vardar
Axiós see Vardar
103 N17 Ax-les-Thermes Ariège, S France 42°43′N 01°49′E
120 D11 Ayachi, Jbel ▲ C Morocco 32°30′N 05°00′W
61 D22 Ayacucho Buenos Aires, E Argentina 37°09′S 58°30′W
57 F15 Ayacucho Ayacucho, S Peru 13°10′S 74°15′W
57 E16 Ayacucho off. Departamento de Ayacucho. ◈ department SW Peru
Ayacucho, Departamento de see Ayacucho
145 W11 Ayagoz var. Ayaguz, Kaz. Ayaköz; prev. Sergiopol. Vostochnyy Kazakhstan, E Kazakhstan 47°54′N 80°25′E
145 V12 Ayagoz var. Ayaguz, Kaz. Ayakoz. ≈ E Kazakhstan
Ayaguz see Ayagoz
Ayakagytma see Oyoqogʻitma
Ayakkuduk see Oyoqquduq
158 L10 Ayakkum Hu ◎ NW China
Ayaköz see Ayagoz
104 H14 Ayamonte Andalucía, S Spain 37°13′N 07°24′W
123 S11 Ayan Khabarovskiy Kray, E Russian Federation 56°27′N 138°09′E
136 J10 Ayancık Sinop, N Turkey 41°56′N 34°35′E
55 S9 Ayanganna Mountain ▲ C Guyana 05°21′N 59°54′W
77 U16 Ayangba Kogi, C Nigeria 07°36′N 07°10′E
123 U7 Ayanka Krasnoyarskiy Kray, E Russian Federation 63°42′N 167°31′E
54 E7 Ayapel Córdoba, NW Colombia 08°16′N 75°10′W
136 H12 Ayaş Ankara, N Turkey 40°02′N 32°21′E
57 I16 Ayaviri Puno, S Peru 14°53′S 70°35′W
Āybak see Aibak
147 N10 Aydarkoʻl Koʻli Rus. Ozero Aydarkul'. ◎ C Uzbekistan
Aydarkul', Ozero see Aydarkoʻl Koʻli
21 W10 Ayden North Carolina, SE USA 35°28′N 77°25′W
136 C15 Aydın var. Aidin; anc. Tralles Aydın. Aydın, SW Turkey 37°51′N 27°51′E
136 C15 Aydın var. Aidin. ◈ province SW Turkey
136 I17 Aydıncık İçel, S Turkey 36°08′N 33°17′E
136 C15 Aydın Dağları ▲▲ W Turkey
158 L6 Aydingkol Hu ◎ NW China
127 X7 Aydyrlinskiy Orenburgskaya Oblast', W Russian Federation 52°03′N 59°54′E
105 S4 Ayerbe Aragón, NE Spain 42°16′N 00°41′W
Ayers Rock see Uluru
166 K8 Ayeyarwady var. Irrawaddy. ◈ division SW Myanmar (Burma)
Ayeyarwady see Irrawaddy
Ayiá see Agiá
Ayia Napa see Agía Nápa
Ayia Phyla see Agía Fýlaxis
Ayiásos/Ayiássos see Agiassós
Áyios Evstrátios see Ágios Efstrátios
Áyios Kírikos see Ágios Kírykos
Áyios Nikólaos see Ágios Nikólaos
80 I11 Āykel Āmara, N Ethiopia 12°33′N 37°01′E
123 N9 Aykhal Respublika Sakha (Yakutiya), NE Russian Federation 66°07′N 110°25′E
14 J12 Aylen Lake ◎ Ontario, SE Canada
97 N21 Aylesbury SE England, United Kingdom 51°50′N 00°50′W
105 O6 Ayllón Castilla y León, N Spain 41°25′N 03°23′W
14 F17 Aylmer Ontario, S Canada 42°46′N 80°57′W
14 L12 Aylmer Québec, SE Canada 45°23′N 75°51′W
15 R12 Aylmer, Lac ◎ Québec, SE Canada
8 L9 Aylmer Lake ◎ Northwest Territories, NW Canada
145 V14 Aynabulak Kaz. Aynabulaq. Almaty, SE Kazakhstan 44°37′N 77°59′E
Aynabulaq see Aynabulak
138 K2 'Ayn al 'Arab Ḥalab, N Syria 36°55′N 38°21′E
Aynayn see 'Aynīn
139 V12 'Ayn Ḥamūd Dhī Qār, S Iraq 30°51′N 45°37′E
147 P12 Ayni prev. Varzimanor Ayni. W Tajikistan 39°24′N 68°30′E
140 M10 'Aynīn var. Aynayn. spring/well SW Saudi Arabia 20°52′N 41°41′E
21 U12 Aynor South Carolina, SE USA 33°59′N 79°11′W
139 Q7 'Ayn Zāzūh Al Anbār, C Iraq 33°29′N 42°34′E
153 N12 Ayodhya Uttar Pradesh, N India 26°47′N 82°12′E
123 S6 Ayon, Ostrov island NE Russian Federation
105 R11 Ayora Valenciana, E Spain 39°04′N 01°04′W
77 Q11 Ayorou Tillabéri, W Niger 14°45′N 00°54′E
79 E16 Ayos Centre, S Cameroon 03°53′N 12°31′E
76 L5 'Ayoûn 'Abd el Mâlek well N Mauritania
76 K10 'Ayoûn el 'Atroûs var. Aïoun el Atrous, Aïoun el Atroûss. Hodh el Gharbi, SE Mauritania 16°38′N 09°36′W
96 I13 Ayr W Scotland, United Kingdom 55°28′N 04°38′W
96 I13 Ayr ≈ W Scotland, United Kingdom
96 I13 Ayrshire cultural region SW Scotland, United Kingdom
Aysen see Aisén
80 L12 Āysha Sumalē, E Ethiopia 10°36′N 42°31′E
144 L14 Ayteke Bi Kaz. Zhangaqazaly; prev. Novokazalinsk. Kzylorda, SW Kazakhstan 45°53′N 62°10′E
146 K8 Aytim Navoiy Viloyati, N Uzbekistan 42°15′N 63°25′E
181 W4 Ayton Queensland, NE Australia 15°54′S 145°19′E
114 M9 Aytos Burgas, E Bulgaria 42°43′N 27°14′E
171 T11 Ayu, Kepulauan island group E Indonesia
167 U12 A Yun Pa prev. Cheo Reo. Gia Lai, S Vietnam 13°19′N 108°27′E
169 V11 Ayu, Tanjung headland Borneo, N Indonesia 0°25′N 117°34′E
41 P16 Ayutlá var. Ayutla de los Libres. Guerrero, S Mexico 16°51′N 99°16′W
40 K13 Ayutla Jalisco, C Mexico 20°07′N 104°18′W
Ayutla de los Libres see Ayutlá
167 O11 Ayutthaya var. Phra Nakhon Si Ayutthaya. Phra Nakhon Si Ayutthaya, C Thailand 14°20′N 100°35′E
136 B13 Ayvalık Balıkesir, W Turkey 39°18′N 26°42′E
99 L20 Aywaille Liège, E Belgium 50°28′N 05°40′E
141 R13 'Aywat aş Şay'ar, Wādī seasonal river N Yemen
Azaffal see Azeffâl
105 T9 Azahar, Costa del coastal region E Spain
105 S6 Azaila Aragón, NE Spain 41°17′N 00°20′W
104 F10 Azambuja Lisboa, C Portugal 39°04′N 08°52′W
153 N13 Āzamgarh Uttar Pradesh, N India 26°03′N 83°10′E
77 O9 Azaouâd desert C Mali
77 S10 Azaouagh, Vallée de l' var. Azaouak. ≈ W Niger
Azaouak see Azaouagh, Vallée de l'
61 F14 Azara Misiones, NE Argentina 28°03′S 55°42′W
Azaran see Hashtrūd
Azärbaycan/Azärbaycan Respublikasī see Azerbaijan
Āzarbāyjān-e Bākhtarī see Āzarbāyjān-e Gharbī
142 I4 Āzarbāyjān-e Gharbī off. Ostān-e Āzarbāyjān-e Gharbī, Eng. West Azerbaijan; prev. Āzarbāyjān-e Bākhtarī. ◈ province NW Iran
Āzarbāyjān-e Gharbī, Ostān-e see Āzarbāyjān-e Gharbī
Āzarbāyjān-e Khāvarī see Āzarbāyjān-e Sharqī
142 J3 Āzarbāyjān-e Sharqī off. Ostān-e Āzarbāyjān-e Sharqī, Eng. East Azerbaijan; prev. Āzarbāyjān-e Khāvarī. ◈ province NW Iran
Āzarbāyjān-e Sharqī, Ostān-e see Āzarbāyjān-e Sharqī
77 W13 Azare Bauchi, N Nigeria 11°41′N 10°09′E
119 M19 Azarychy Rus. Ozarichi. Homyel'skaya Voblasts', SE Belarus 52°31′N 29°19′E
145 P13 Azat, Gory hill C Kazakhstan
102 L8 Azay-le-Rideau Indre-et-Loire, C France 47°16′N 00°25′E
138 I2 A'zāz Ḥalab, NW Syria 36°35′N 37°03′E
76 H7 Azeffâl var. Azaffal. desert Mauritania/Western Sahara
137 V12 Azerbaijan off. Azerbaijani Republic, Az. Azärbaycan, Azärbaycan Respublikasī; prev. Azerbaijan SSR. ◆ republic SE Asia
Azerbaijani Republic see Azerbaijan
Azerbaijan SSR see Azerbaijan
74 F7 Azilal C Morocco 31°58′N 06°53′W
Azimabad see Patna
19 O6 Aziscohos Lake ⊠ Maine, NE USA
Azizbekov see Vayk'
Azizie see Telish
Aziziya see Al 'Azīzīyah
127 T4 Aznakayevo Respublika Tatarstan, W Russian Federation 54°55′N 53°15′E
56 C8 Azogues Cañar, S Ecuador 02°44′S 78°48′W
64 N2 Azores var. Açores, Ilhas dos Açores, Port. Arquipélago dos Açores. island group Portugal, NE Atlantic Ocean
64 L8 Azores-Biscay Rise undersea feature E Atlantic Ocean 19°00′W 42°40′N
Azotos/Azotus see Ashdod
78 K11 Azoum, Bahr seasonal river SE Chad
126 L12 Azov Rostovskaya Oblast', SW Russian Federation 47°07′N 39°26′E
126 J13 Azov, Sea of Rus. Azovskoye More, Ukr. Azovs'ke More. sea NE Black Sea
Azovs'ke More/Azovskoye More see Azov, Sea of
138 I10 Azraq, Wāḥat al oasis N Jordan
Āzro see Āzrow
74 G6 Azrou C Morocco 33°30′N 05°12′W
149 R5 Āzrow var. Āzro. Lōgar, E Afghanistan 34°11′N 69°39′E
37 P8 Aztec New Mexico, SW USA 36°49′N 107°59′W
36 M13 Aztec Peak ▲ Arizona, SW USA 33°48′N 110°54′W
45 N9 Azua var. Azua de Compostela. S Dominican Republic 18°29′N 70°44′W
Azua de Compostela see Azua
104 K12 Azuaga Extremadura, W Spain 38°16′N 05°40′W
56 B8 Azuay ◈ province W Ecuador
164 C13 Azuchi-Ō-shima island SW Japan
43 O11 Azuer ≈ C Spain
43 S17 Azuero, Península de peninsula S Panama
62 I6 Azufre, Volcán var. Volcán Lastarria. ⛰ N Chile 25°16′S 68°35′W
116 J12 Azuga Prahova, SE Romania 45°27′N 25°34′E
61 C22 Azul Buenos Aires, E Argentina 36°46′S 59°50′W
62 I8 Azul, Cerro ▲ NW Argentina 28°28′S 68°43′W
56 E12 Azul, Cordillera ▲▲ C Peru
165 P11 Azuma-san ▲ Honshū, C Japan 37°44′N 140°05′E
103 V15 Azur, Côte d' coastal region SE France
191 Z3 Azur Lagoon ◎ Kiritimati, E Kiribati
'Azza see Gaza
Az Zāb al Kabīr see Great Zab
138 H7 Az Zabdānī var. Zabadani. Rīf Dimashq, W Syria 33°45′N 36°07′E
141 W8 Az Ẓāhirah desert NW Oman
141 S6 Az Ẓahrān Eng. Dhahran. Ash Sharqīyah, NE Saudi Arabia 26°18′N 50°02′E
141 R6 Az Ẓahrān al Khubar var. Dhahran Al Khobar. ✕ Ash Sharqīyah, NE Saudi Arabia 26°28′N 49°42′E
75 W7 Az Zaqāzīq var. Zagazig. N Egypt 30°36′N 31°32′E
138 H10 Az Zarqā' var. Zarqa. Az Zarqā', NW Jordan 32°04′N 36°06′E
138 I11 Az Zarqā' off. Muḥāfaẓat az Zarqā', var. Zarqa. ◈ governorate N Jordan
75 O7 Az Zāwiyah var. Zawia. NW Libya 32°45′N 12°44′E
141 N15 Az Zaydīyah W Yemen 15°20′N 43°03′E
74 I11 Azzel Matti, Sebkha var. Sebkha Azz el Matti. salt flat C Algeria
141 P6 Az Zilfī Ar Riyāḍ, N Saudi Arabia 26°17′N 44°48′E
139 Y13 Az Zubayr var. Al Zubair. Al Baṣrah, SE Iraq 30°24′N 47°45′E
Az Zuqur see Jabal Zuqar, Jazīrat

B

187 X15 Ba prev. Mba. Viti Levu, W Fiji 17°35′S 177°40′E
Ba see Đa Răng, Sông
171 P17 Baa Pulau Rote, C Indonesia 10°44′S 123°06′E
138 H7 Baalbek var. Ba'labakk; anc. Heliopolis. E Lebanon 34°00′N 36°15′E
108 G8 Baar Zug, N Switzerland 47°12′N 08°32′E
81 L17 Baardheere var. Bardere, It. Bardera. Gedo, SW Somalia 02°13′N 42°19′E
Baargaal see Bargaal
99 I15 Baarle-Hertog Antwerpen, N Belgium 51°26′N 04°56′E
99 I15 Baarle-Nassau Noord-Brabant, S Netherlands 51°27′N 04°56′E
98 J11 Baarn Utrecht, C Netherlands 52°13′N 05°16′E
162 H9 Baatsagaan var. Bayansayr. Bayanhongor, C Mongolia 45°36′N 99°27′E
114 D13 Baba var. Buševa, Gk. Varnoús. ▲▲ FYR Macedonia/Greece
76 H10 Bababé Brakna, W Mauritania 16°22′N 13°57′W
136 G10 Baba Burnu headland NW Turkey 41°18′N 31°24′E
117 N13 Babadag Tulcea, SE Romania 44°53′N 28°47′E
137 X10 Babadağ Dağı ▲ NE Azerbaijan 41°02′N 48°04′E
146 H14 Babadaýhan Rus. Babadaykhan; prev. Kirovsk. Ahal Welaýaty, C Turkmenistan 37°39′N 60°17′E
Babadaykhan see Babadaýhan
146 G14 Babadurmaz Ahal Welaýaty, C Turkmenistan 37°39′N 59°03′E
114 M12 Babaeski Kırklareli, NW Turkey 41°26′N 27°06′E
139 T4 Bāba Gurgur At Ta'mím, N Iraq 35°34′N 44°18′E
56 B7 Babahoyo prev. Bodegas. Los Ríos, C Ecuador 01°53′S 79°31′W
149 P5 Bābā, Kūh-e ▲▲ C Afghanistan
171 N12 Babana Sulawesi, C Indonesia 02°03′S 119°13′E
Babao see Qilian
171 Q12 Babar, Kepulauan island group E Indonesia
171 T12 Babar, Pulau island Kepulauan Babar, E Indonesia
Bābāsar Pass see Babusar Pass
Babashy, Gory see Babaşy
146 C9 Babaşy Rus. Gory Babashy. ▲▲ W Turkmenistan
168 M13 Babat Sumatera, W Indonesia 02°45′S 104°01′E
Babatag, Khrebet see Bototog', Tizmasi
81 H21 Babati Manyara, NE Tanzania 04°12′S 35°45′E
124 J13 Babayevo Vologodskaya Oblast', NW Russian Federation 59°23′N 35°52′E
127 Q15 Babayurt Respublika Dagestan, SW Russian Federation 43°38′N 46°49′E
33 P6 Babb Montana, NW USA 48°51′N 113°26′W
29 X4 Babbitt Minnesota, N USA 47°42′N 91°56′W
188 E9 Babeldaob var. Babeldaop, Babelthuap. island N Palau
Babeldaop see Babeldaob
141 N17 Bab el Mandeb strait Gulf of Aden/Red Sea
Babelthuap see Babeldaob
111 K17 Babia Góra var. Babia Hora. ▲ Poland/Slovakia 49°33′N 19°32′E
Babia Hora see Babia Góra
Babian Jiang see Black River
Babichi see Babichy
119 N19 Babichy Rus. Babichi. Homyel'skaya Voblasts', SE Belarus 52°17′N 30°00′E
112 I10 Babina Greda Vukovar-Srijem, E Croatia 45°09′N 18°33′E
10 K13 Babine Lake ◎ British Columbia, SW Canada
143 O4 Bābol var. Babul, Balfrush, Barfrush; prev. Barfurush. Māzandarān, N Iran 36°34′N 52°39′E
143 O4 Bābolsar var. Babulsar; prev. Meshed-i-Sar. Māzandarān, N Iran 36°41′N 52°39′E
36 L16 Baboquivari Peak ▲ Arizona, SW USA 31°46′N 111°36′W
79 G15 Baboua Nana-Mambéré, W Central African Republic 05°46′N 14°47′E
119 M17 Babruysk Rus. Bobruysk. Mahilyowskaya Voblasts', E Belarus 53°07′N 29°13′E
Babu see Hezhou
Babul see Bābol
Babulsar see Bābolsar
113 O19 Babuna ▲▲ C FYR Macedonia
113 O19 Babuna ≈ C FYR Macedonia
152 G4 Babusar Pass prev. Bābāsar Pass. pass India/Pakistan
148 K7 Bābūs, Dasht-e Pash. Bebas, Dasht-i. ▲▲ W Afghanistan
171 O1 Babuyan Channel channel N Philippines
171 O1 Babuyan Islands island N Philippines
139 T9 Babylon site of ancient city C Iraq
112 J9 Bač Ger. Batsch. Vojvodina, NW Serbia 45°24′N 19°17′E
58 M13 Bacabal Maranhão, E Brazil 04°15′S 44°45′W
41 Y14 Bacalar Quintana Roo, SE Mexico 18°38′N 88°17′W
41 Y14 Bacalar Chico, Boca strait SE Mexico
171 Q12 Bacan, Kepulauan island group E Indonesia
171 S12 Bacan, Pulau prev. Batjan. island Maluku, E Indonesia
116 L10 Bacău Hung. Bákó. Bacău, NE Romania 46°36′N 26°56′E
116 K11 Bacău ◈ county E Romania
Bắc Bộ, Vịnh see Tongking, Gulf of
167 T5 Bắc Can var. Bach Thong. Bắc Thai, N Vietnam 22°07′N 105°50′E
103 T5 Baccarat Meurthe-et-Moselle, NE France 48°27′N 06°46′E
183 N12 Bacchus Marsh Victoria, SE Australia 37°41′S 144°30′E
40 H4 Bacerac Sonora, NW Mexico 30°27′N 108°55′W
116 L10 Băcești Vaslui, E Romania 46°50′N 27°14′E
167 T6 Bắc Giang Ha Bắc, N Vietnam 21°17′N 106°12′E
54 J5 Bachaquero Zulia, NW Venezuela 09°57′N 71°09′W
Bacher see Pohorje
118 M13 Bacheykava Rus. Bocheykovo. Vitsyebskaya Voblasts', N Belarus 55°01′N 29°09′E
40 I5 Bachíniva Chihuahua, N Mexico 28°41′N 107°13′W
Bach Thong see Bắc Can
158 G8 Bachu Xinjiang Uygur Zizhiqu, NW China 39°46′N 78°30′E
9 N8 Back ≈ Nunavut, N Canada
112 K10 Bačka Palanka prev. Palanka. Serbia, NW Serbia 44°22′N 20°57′E
112 K8 Bačka Topola Hung. Topolya; prev. Hung. Bácstopolya. Vojvodina, N Serbia 45°48′N 19°39′E
95 J17 Bäckefors Västra Götaland, S Sweden 58°49′N 12°07′E
Bäckermühle Schulzenmühle see Żywiec
95 L16 Bäckhammar Värmland, C Sweden 59°09′N 14°13′E
112 K9 Bački Petrovac Hung. Petrőcz; prev. Petrovac, Petrovácz. Vojvodina, NW Serbia 45°22′N 19°34′E
101 I21 Backnang Baden-Württemberg, SW Germany 48°57′N 09°26′E
167 S15 Bac Liêu var. Vinh Loi. Minh Hai, S Vietnam 09°17′N 105°44′E
167 T6 Bắc Ninh Ha Bắc, N Vietnam 21°10′N 106°04′E
40 G4 Bacoachi Sonora, NW Mexico 30°36′N 110°00′W
171 P6 Bacolod off. Bacolod City. Negros, C Philippines 10°43′N 122°58′E
Bacolod City see Bacolod
171 O4 Baco, Mount ▲ Mindoro, N Philippines 12°50′N 121°08′E
111 K25 Bácsalmás Bács-Kiskun, S Hungary 46°07′N 19°20′E
Bácsjózseffalva see Žednik
111 J24 Bács-Kiskun off. Bács-Kiskun Megye. ◈ county S Hungary
Bács-Kiskun Megye see Bács-Kiskun
Bácsszenttamás see Srbobran
Bácstopolya see Bačka Topola
Bactra see Balkh
Bada see Xilin
155 F21 Badagara var. Vadakara. Kerala, SW India 11°36′N 75°34′E see also Vadakara
101 M24 Bad Aibling Bayern, SE Germany 47°52′N 12°00′E
162 I13 Badain Jaran Shamo desert N China
104 I11 Badajoz anc. Pax Augusta. Extremadura, W Spain 38°53′N 06°58′W
104 J11 Badajoz ◈ province Extremadura, W Spain
149 S2 Badakhshān ◈ province NE Afghanistan
105 W6 Badalona anc. Baetulo. Cataluña, E Spain 41°27′N 02°15′E
154 O11 Bādāmpāhārh var. Bādāmapāhārh. Orissa, E India 22°04′N 86°06′E
169 O10 Badas, Kepulauan island group W Indonesia
109 S6 Bad Aussee Salzburg, E Austria 47°35′N 13°44′E
31 S8 Bad Axe Michigan, N USA 43°48′N 83°00′W
101 G16 Bad Berleburg Nordrhein-Westfalen, W Germany 51°03′N 08°24′E
101 L17 Bad Blankenburg Thüringen, C Germany 50°43′N 11°19′E
Bad Borseck see Borsec
101 G18 Bad Camberg Hessen, W Germany 50°18′N 08°15′E
100 L8 Bad Doberan Mecklenburg-Vorpommern, N Germany 54°06′N 11°55′E
101 N14 Bad Düben Sachsen, E Germany 51°35′N 12°34′E
109 X4 Baden var. Baden bei Wien; anc. Aquae Panoniae, Thermae Pannonicae. Niederösterreich, NE Austria 48°01′N 16°14′E
108 F9 Baden Aargau, N Switzerland 47°28′N 08°19′E
101 G21 Baden-Baden anc. Aurelia Aquensis. Baden-Württemberg, SW Germany 48°46′N 08°14′E
Baden bei Wien see Baden
101 G22 Baden-Württemberg Fr. Bade-Wurtemberg. ◈ state SW Germany
112 A10 Baderna Istra, NW Croatia 45°12′N 13°45′E
Bade-Wurtemberg see Baden-Württemberg
101 H20 Bad Fredrichshall Baden-Württemberg, S Germany 49°13′N 09°15′E
100 P11 Bad Freienwalde Brandenburg, NE Germany 52°47′N 14°04′E
109 Q8 Badgastein var. Gastein. Salzburg, NW Austria 47°07′N 13°09′E
Badger State see Wisconsin
148 L4 Bādghīs ◈ province NW Afghanistan
109 T5 Bad Hall Oberösterreich, N Austria 48°03′N 14°13′E
101 J14 Bad Harzburg Niedersachsen, C Germany 51°52′N 10°34′E
101 I16 Bad Hersfeld Hessen, C Germany 50°52′N 09°42′E
98 I10 Badhoevedorp Noord-Holland, C Netherlands 52°21′N 04°46′E
109 Q8 Bad Hofgastein Salzburg, NW Austria 47°11′N 13°07′E
Bad Homburg see Bad Homburg vor der Höhe
101 G18 Bad Homburg vor der Höhe var. Bad Homburg. Hessen, W Germany 50°14′N 08°37′E
101 E17 Bad Honnef Nordrhein-Westfalen, W Germany 50°39′N 07°13′E
149 Q17 Badin Sind, SE Pakistan 24°38′N 68°53′E
21 S10 Badin Lake ⊠ North Carolina, SE USA
40 I8 Badiraguato Sinaloa, C Mexico 25°21′N 107°31′W
109 R6 Bad Ischl Oberösterreich, N Austria 47°43′N 13°36′E
Badjawa see Bajawa
Badje-Sohppar see Övre Soppero
101 J18 Bad Kissingen Bayern, SE Germany 50°12′N 10°04′E
Bad Königswart see Lázně Kynžvart
101 F19 Bad Kreuznach Rheinland-Pfalz, SW Germany 49°51′N 07°52′E
101 F24 Bad Krozingen Baden-Württemberg, SW Germany 47°55′N 07°43′E
101 G16 Bad Laasphe Nordrhein-Westfalen, W Germany 50°57′N 08°24′E
28 J6 Badlands physical region North Dakota/South Dakota, N USA
101 K16 Bad Langensalza Thüringen, C Germany 51°05′N 10°40′E
109 T3 Bad Leonfelden Oberösterreich, N Austria 48°31′N 14°17′E
101 I20 Bad Mergentheim Baden-Württemberg, SW Germany 49°30′N 09°46′E
101 H17 Bad Nauheim Hessen, W Germany 50°22′N 08°45′E
101 E17 Bad Neuenahr-Ahrweiler Rheinland-Pfalz, W Germany 50°33′N 07°07′E
Bad Neustadt see Bad Neustadt an der Saale
101 J18 Bad Neustadt an der Saale var. Bad Neustadt. Berlin, C Germany 50°21′N 10°13′E
Badnur see Betūl
100 H13 Bad Oeynhausen Nordrhein-Westfalen, NW Germany 52°12′N 08°48′E
100 J9 Bad Oldesloe Schleswig-Holstein, N Germany 53°49′N 10°22′E
77 Q16 Badou C Togo 07°37′N 00°37′E
Bad Polzin see Połczyn-Zdrój
100 H13 Bad Pyrmont Niedersachsen, C Germany 51°58′N 09°16′E
109 X9 Bad Radkersburg Steiermark, SE Austria 46°40′N 16°02′E
139 V8 Badrah Wāsiţ, E Iraq 33°06′N 45°58′E
Badrah see Tarialan
101 N24 Bad Reichenhall Bayern, SE Germany 47°43′N 12°52′E
140 K8 Badr Ḥunayn Al Madīnah, W Saudi Arabia 23°46′N 38°45′E
152 K8 Badrīnāth ▲ N India 30°44′N 79°29′E
28 M10 Bad River ≈ South Dakota, N USA
30 K4 Bad River ≈ Wisconsin, N USA
100 H13 Bad Salzuflen Nordrhein-Westfalen, NW Germany 52°06′N 08°45′E
101 J16 Bad Salzungen Thüringen, C Germany 50°48′N 10°15′E
109 V8 Bad Sankt Leonhard im Lavanttal Kärnten, S Austria 46°55′N 14°51′E
100 K9 Bad Schwartau Schleswig-Holstein, N Germany 53°55′N 10°42′E
101 L24 Bad Tölz Bayern, SE Germany 47°44′N 11°34′E
181 U1 Badu Island island Queensland, NE Australia
155 K25 Badulla Uva Province, C Sri Lanka 06°59′N 81°03′E
109 X5 Bad Vöslau Niederösterreich, NE Austria 47°58′N 16°13′E
101 I24 Bad Waldsee Baden-Württemberg, S Germany 47°54′N 09°44′E
35 U11 Badwater Basin depression California, W USA
101 J20 Bad Windsheim Bayern, C Germany 49°30′N 10°25′E
101 J23 Bad Wörishofen Bayern, S Germany 48°00′N 10°36′E
100 G10 Bad Zwischenahn Niedersachsen, NW Germany 53°10′N 08°01′E
104 M13 Baena Andalucía, S Spain 36°37′N 04°20′W
163 V15 Baengnyong-do prev. Paengnyŏng. island NW South Korea
Baeterrae/Baeterrae Septimanorum see Béziers
Baetic Cordillera/Baetic Mountains see Béticos, Sistemas
Baetulo see Badalona
57 K18 Baeza Napo, NE Ecuador 0°30′S 77°52′W
105 N13 Baeza Andalucía, S Spain 38°00′N 03°28′W
79 D15 Bafang Ouest, W Cameroon 05°10′N 10°11′E
76 H12 Bafatá C Guinea-Bissau 12°09′N 14°38′W
149 U5 Baffa Khyber Pakhtunkhwa, NW Pakistan 34°30′N 73°18′E
197 O11 Baffin Basin undersea feature N Labrador Sea
197 N12 Baffin Bay bay Canada/Greenland
25 T15 Baffin Bay inlet Texas, SW USA
196 M12 Baffin Island island Nunavut, NE Canada
79 E15 Bafia Centre, C Cameroon 04°49′N 11°14′E
77 R14 Bafilo NE Togo 09°23′N 01°20′E
76 J12 Bafing ≈ W Africa
76 J12 Bafoulabé Kayes, W Mali 13°43′N 10°49′W
79 D15 Bafoussam Ouest, W Cameroon 05°31′N 10°25′E
143 R9 Bāfq Yazd, C Iran 31°35′N 55°21′E
136 L10 Bafra Samsun, N Turkey 41°34′N 35°56′E
136 L10 Bafra Burnu headland N Turkey 41°42′N 36°02′E
143 S12 Bāft Kermān, S Iran 29°12′N 56°36′E
79 N18 Bafwabalinga Orientale, NE Dem. Rep. Congo 0°52′N 26°55′E
79 N18 Bafwaboli Orientale, NE Dem. Rep. Congo 0°36′N 26°08′E
79 N17 Bafwasende Orientale, NE Dem. Rep. Congo 01°00′N 27°09′E
42 K13 Bagaces Guanacaste, NW Costa Rica 10°31′N 85°18′W
153 O12 Bagaha Bihār, N India 27°08′N 84°04′E
155 F16 Bāgalkot Karnātaka, W India 16°11′N 75°42′E
81 J22 Bagamoyo Pwani, E Tanzania 06°26′S 38°55′E
Bagan Datok see Bagan Datuk
168 J8 Bagan Datuk var. Bagan Datok. Perak, Peninsular Malaysia 03°58′N 100°47′E
171 R7 Baganga Mindanao, S Philippines 07°31′N 126°34′E
168 J9 Bagansiapiapi var. Pasirpangarayan. Sumatera, W Indonesia 02°06′N 100°52′E
162 M8 Baganuur var. Nüürst. Töv, C Mongolia 47°44′N 108°22′E
Bagaria see Bagheria
77 T11 Bagaroua Tahoua, W Niger 14°34′N 04°24′E
79 I20 Bagata Bandundu, W Dem. Rep. Congo 03°47′S 17°57′E
Bagdad see Baghdad
123 O13 Bagdarin Respublika Buryatiya, S Russian Federation 54°27′N 113°34′E
61 G17 Bagé Rio Grande do Sul, S Brazil 31°22′S 54°06′W
Bagenalstown see Muine Bheag
153 T16 Bagerhat var. Bagherhat. Khulna, S Bangladesh 22°40′N 89°48′E
103 P16 Bages et de Sigean, Étang de ◎ S France
33 W17 Baggs Wyoming, C USA 41°02′N 107°39′W
154 F11 Bāgh Madhya Pradesh, C India 22°22′N 74°49′E
139 T8 Baghdad var. Bagdad, Eng. Baghdad. ● Baghdād, C Iraq 33°20′N 44°26′E
139 T8 Baghdād ✕ (Baghdād) Baghdād, C Iraq 33°20′N 44°26′E
Baghdad see Baghdad
Bagherhat see Bagerhat
107 J23 Bagheria var. Bagaria. Sicilia, Italy, C Mediterranean Sea 38°05′N 13°31′E
143 S10 Bāghīn Kermān, C Iran 30°50′N 57°00′E
149 Q3 Baghlān Baghlān, NE Afghanistan 36°11′N 68°44′E
149 Q3 Baghlān var. Bāghlān. ◈ province NE Afghanistan
Bāghlān see Baghlān
148 M7 Bāghrān Helmand, S Afghanistan 32°55′N 64°57′E
29 T4 Bagley Minnesota, N USA 47°31′N 95°24′W
106 H10 Bagnacavallo Emilia-Romagna, C Italy 44°00′N 12°59′E
102 K16 Bagnères-de-Bigorre Hautes-Pyrénées, S France 43°04′N 00°09′E
102 L17 Bagnères-de-Luchon Hautes-Pyrénées, S France 42°46′N 00°34′E
106 F11 Bagni di Lucca Toscana, C Italy 44°01′N 10°38′E
106 H11 Bagno di Romagna Emilia-Romagna, C Italy 43°51′N 11°57′E
103 R14 Bagnols-sur-Cèze Gard, S France 44°10′N 04°37′E
162 M14 Bag Nur ◎ N China
166 L8 Bago var. Pegu. Bago, SW Myanmar (Burma) 17°18′N 96°31′E
171 P6 Bago off. Bago City. Negros, C Philippines 10°30′N 122°49′E
166 L7 Bago var. Pegu. ◈ division S Myanmar (Burma)
Bago City see Bago
76 M13 Bagoé ≈ Ivory Coast/Mali
Bagrāmē see Bagrāmī
149 R5 Bagrāmī var. Bagrāmē. Kābōl, E Afghanistan 34°29′N 69°16′E
119 B14 Bagrationovsk Ger. Preussisch Eylau. Kaliningradskaya Oblast', W Russian Federation 54°24′N 20°39′E
Bagrax see Bohu
Bagrax Hu see Bosten Hu
56 C10 Bagua Amazonas, NE Peru 05°37′S 78°36′W
171 O2 Baguio off. Baguio City. Luzon, N Philippines 16°25′N 120°36′E
Baguio City see Baguio
77 V9 Bagzane, Monts ▲ N Niger 17°48′N 08°43′E
Bāḥah, Minṭaqat al see Al Bāḥah
Bahama Islands see Bahamas
44 H3 Bahamas off. Commonwealth of the Bahamas. ◆ commonwealth republic N West Indies
0 L13 Bahamas var. Bahama Islands. island group N West Indies
Bahamas, Commonwealth of the see Bahamas
153 S15 Baharampur prev. Berhampore. West Bengal, NE India 24°06′N 88°19′E
146 E12 Baharly var. Bäherden, Rus. Bakharden; prev. Bakherden. Ahal Welaýaty, C Turkmenistan 38°30′N 57°18′E
149 U10 Bahāwalnagar Punjab, E Pakistan 30°00′N 73°03′E
149 T11 Bahāwalpur Punjab, E Pakistan 29°25′N 71°40′E
136 L16 Bahçe Osmaniye, S Turkey 37°14′N 36°34′E
160 J8 Ba He ≈ C China
Bäherden see Baharly
59 N16 Bahia off. Estado da Bahia. ◈ state E Brazil
61 B24 Bahía Blanca Buenos Aires, E Argentina 38°43′S 62°19′W
40 L15 Bahía Bufadero Michoacán, SW Mexico
63 J19 Bahía Bustamante Chubut, SE Argentina 45°06′S 66°30′W
40 D5 Bahía de los Ángeles Baja California Norte, NW Mexico 28°55′N 113°34′W
40 C6 Bahía de Tortugas Baja California Sur, NW Mexico 27°42′N 114°54′W
Bahia, Estado da see Bahia
42 J4 Bahía, Islas de la Eng. Bay Islands. island group N Honduras
40 E5 Bahía Kino Sonora, NW Mexico 28°48′N 111°55′W
40 E9 Bahía Magdalena var. Puerto Magdalena. Baja California Sur, NW Mexico 24°34′N 112°07′W
54 C8 Bahía Solano var. Ciudad Mutis, Solano. Chocó, W Colombia 06°13′N 77°27′W
80 I11 Bahir Dar var. Bahr Dar, Bahrdar Giyorgis. Āmara, N Ethiopia 11°34′N 37°23′E
141 X8 Bahlā' var. Bahlah, Bahlat. NW Oman 22°58′N 57°16′E
Bāhla see Bālān
Bahlah/Bahlat see Bahlā'
152 M11 Bahraich Uttar Pradesh, N India 27°35′N 81°36′E
143 M14 Bahrain off. State of Bahrain, Dawlat al Bahrayn, Ar. Al Baḥrayn, prev. Bahrein; anc. Tylos, Tyros. ◆ monarchy SW Asia
142 M14 Bahrain ✕ C Bahrain 26°15′N 50°39′E
142 M15 Bahrain, Gulf of gulf Persian Gulf, NW Arabian Sea
Bahrain, State of see Bahrain
138 I7 Baḥrat Mallāḥah ◎ W Syria
Bahrayn, Dawlat al see Bahrain
Bahr Dar/Bahrdar Giyorgis see Bahir Dar
Bahrein see Bahrain
Bahr el, Azraq see Blue Nile
Bahr el Gebel see Central Equatoria
Bahr el Jebel see Central Equatoria
80 E13 Bahr ez Zaref ≈ Jonglei, E South Sudan
67 R8 Bahr Kameur ≈ N Central African Republic
Bahr Tabariya, Sea of see Tiberias, Lake
143 W15 Bāhū Kalāt Sīstān va Balūchestān, SE Iran 25°42′N 61°28′E

118 N13 Bahushewsk Rus. Bogushevsk. Vitsyebskaya Voblasts', NE Belarus 54°51'N 30°13'E
Bai see Tagow Bāy
116 G13 Baia de Aramă Mehedinţi, SW Romania 45°00'N 22°43'E
116 G11 Baia de Criş Ger. Altenburg, Hung. Körösbánya. Hunedoara, SW Romania 46°10'N 22°41'E
83 A16 Baia dos Tigres Namibe, SW Angola 16°36'S 11°44'E
82 A13 Baia Farta Benguela, W Angola 12°38'S 13°12'E
116 H9 Baia Mare Ger. Frauenbach, Hung. Nagybánya; prev. Neustadt. Maramureş, NW Romania 47°40'N 23°35'E
116 H8 Baia Sprie Ger. Mittelstadt, Hung. Felsőbánya. Maramureş, NW Romania 47°40'N 23°42'E
78 G13 Baïbokoum Logone-Oriental, SW Chad 07°46'N 15°43'E
160 F12 Baicao Ling ▲ SW China
163 U9 Baicheng var. Pai-ch'eng; prev. T'aon-an. Jilin, NE China 45°32'N 122°51'E
158 I6 Baicheng var. Bay. Xinjiang Uygur Zizhiqu, NW China 41°49'N 81°45'E
116 J13 Băicoi Prahova, SE Romania 45°02'N 25°51'E
Baidoa see Baydhabo
15 U6 Baie-Comeau Québec, SE Canada 49°12'N 68°10'W
15 U6 Baie-des-Sables Québec, SE Canada 48°41'N 67°55'W
15 T7 Baie-des-Bacon Québec, SE Canada 48°31'N 69°17'W
15 S8 Baie-des-Rochers Québec, SE Canada 47°57'N 69°50'W
Baie-du-Poste see Mistissini
172 H17 Baie Lazare Mahé, NE Seychelles 04°45'S 55°29'E
45 Y5 Baie-Mahault Basse Terre, C Guadeloupe 16°16'N 61°35'W
15 R9 Baie-St-Paul Québec, SE Canada 47°27'N 70°30'W
15 V5 Baie-Trinité Québec, SE Canada 49°25'N 67°20'W
13 T11 Baie Verte Newfoundland and Labrador, SE Canada 49°55'N 56°12'W
Baiguan see Shangyu
Baihe see Erdaobaihe
139 U11 Bā'ij al Mahdī Al Muthannā, S Iraq 31°21'N 44°57'E
Baiji see Bayjī
Baikal, Lake see Baykal, Ozero
Bailādila see Kirandul
Baile an Chaistil see Ballycastle
Baile an Róba see Ballinrobe
Baile an tSratha see Ballintra
Baile Átha an Rí see Athenry
Baile Átha Buí see Athboy
Baile Átha Cliath see Dublin
Baile Átha Fhirdhia see Ardee
Baile Átha Í see Athy
Baile Átha Luain see Athlone
Baile Átha Troim see Trim
Baile Brigín see Balbriggan
Baile Easa Dara see Ballysadare
116 I13 Băile Govora Vâlcea, SW Romania 45°00'N 24°08'E
116 F13 Băile Herculane Ger. Herkulesbad, Hung. Herkulesfürdő. Caraş-Severin, SW Romania 44°51'N 22°24'E
Baile Locha Riach see Loughrea
Baile Mhistéala see Mitchelstown
Baile Monaidh see Ballymoney
105 N12 Bailén Andalucía, S Spain 38°06'N 03°46'W
Baile na hInse see Ballynahinch
Baile na Lorgan see Castleblayney
Baile na Mainistreach see Newtownabbey
Baile Nua na hArda see Newtownards
116 I12 Băile Olăneşti Vâlcea, SW Romania 45°14'N 24°18'E
116 H14 Băileşti Dolj, SW Romania 44°01'N 23°20'E
163 N12 Bailingmiao var. Darhan Muminggan Lianheqi. Nei Mongol Zizhiqu, N China 41°41'N 110°25'E
58 K11 Bailique, Ilha island NE Brazil
103 O1 Bailleul Nord, N France 50°43'N 02°43'E
78 H12 Ba Illi Chari-Baguirmi, SW Chad 10°31'N 16°29'E
159 V12 Bailong Jiang ≈ C China
82 C13 Bailundo Port. Vila Teixeira da Silva. Huambo, C Angola 12°12'S 15°52'E
159 T13 Baima var. Sêraitang. Qinghai, C China 32°55'N 100°44'E
Baima see Baxoi
186 C8 Baimuru Gulf, S Papua New Guinea 07°34'S 144°49'E
158 M16 Bainang Xizang Zizhiqu, W China 28°57'N 89°31'E
23 S8 Bainbridge Georgia, SE USA 30°54'N 84°33'W
171 O17 Baing Pulau Sumba, SE Indonesia 10°09'S 120°34'E
158 M14 Baingoin var. Pubao. Xizang Zizhiqu, W China 31°22'N 90°00'E
104 G2 Baio Galicia, NW Spain 43°08'N 08°58'W
104 G4 Baiona Galicia, NW Spain 42°06'N 08°49'W
163 V7 Baiquan Heilongjiang, NE China 47°37'N 126°04'E
Bā'ir see Bāyir
158 I11 Bairab Co ◎ W China
25 Q7 Baird Texas, SW USA 32°23'N 99°24'W
39 N7 Baird Mountains ▲ Alaska, USA
Baireuth see Bayreuth
190 H3 Bairiki ● (Kiribati) Tarawa, NW Kiribati 01°20'N 173°01'E
Bairin Youqi see Daban
Bairin Zuoqi see Lindong
Bairkum see Bayyrkum
183 P12 Bairnsdale Victoria, SE Australia 37°51'S 147°38'E
171 P6 Bais Negros, S Philippines 09°36'N 123°07'E
102 L15 Baïse var. Baise. ≈ S France
Baise see Baïse
163 W11 Baishan prev. Hunjiang. Jilin, NE China 41°57'N 126°31'E
Baishan see Mashan
118 F12 Baisogala Šiauliai, C Lithuania 55°38'N 23°44'E
189 Q7 Baiti N Nauru 0°30'S 166°55'E
Baitou Shan see Paektu-san
104 G13 Baixo Alentejo physical region S Portugal
64 P5 Baixo, Ilhéu de island Madeira, Portugal, NE Atlantic Ocean
83 E15 Baixo Longa Cuando Cubango, SE Angola 15°39'S 18°39'E
159 V10 Baiyin Gansu, C China 36°33'N 104°11'E
160 E8 Baiyü var. Jianshe. Sichuan, C China 30°37'N 97°15'E
161 N14 Baiyun ✈ (Guangzhou) Guangdong, S China 23°12'N 113°19'E
160 K4 Baiyu Shan ▲ C China
111 J25 Baja Bács-Kiskun, S Hungary 46°13'N 18°56'E
40 C4 Baja California Eng. Lower California. peninsula NW Mexico
40 C4 Baja California Norte ◆ state NW Mexico
40 E9 Baja California Sur ◆ state NW Mexico
Bājah see Béja
Bajan see Bayan
191 V16 Baja, Punta headland Easter Island, Chile, E Pacific Ocean 27°10'S 109°21'W
40 B4 Baja, Punta headland NW Mexico 29°57'N 115°48'W
55 R5 Baja, Punta headland NE Venezuela
42 D5 Baja Verapaz off. Departamento de Baja Verapaz. ◆ department C Guatemala
Baja Verapaz, Departamento de see Baja Verapaz
171 N16 Bajawa prev. Badjawa. Flores, S Indonesia 08°46'S 120°59'E
153 S16 Baj Baj prev. Budge-Budge. West Bengal, E India 22°29'N 88°11'E
141 N15 Bājil W Yemen 15°05'N 43°16'E
183 U4 Bajimba, Mount ▲ New South Wales, SE Australia 29°19'S 152°04'E
112 K13 Bajina Bašta Serbia, W Serbia 43°58'N 19°33'E
153 U14 Bajitpur Dhaka, E Bangladesh 24°12'N 90°57'E
112 K8 Bajmok Vojvodina, NW Serbia 45°59'N 19°25'E
Bajo Boquete see Boquete
113 L17 Bajram Curri Kukës, N Albania 42°23'N 20°06'E
79 J14 Bakala Ouaka, C Central African Republic 06°03'N 20°31'E
127 T4 Bakaly Respublika Bashkortostan, W Russian Federation 55°10'N 53°46'E
Bakan see Shimonoseki
145 U14 Bakanas Kaz. Baqanas. Almaty, SE Kazakhstan 44°50'N 76°13'E
145 V12 Bakanas Kaz. Baqanas. ≈ E Kazakhstan
149 R4 Bākārak Panjshīr, NE Afghanistan 35°16'N 69°28'E
145 U14 Bakbakty Kaz. Baqbaqty. Almaty, SE Kazakhstan 44°36'N 76°41'E
122 J12 Bakchar Tomskaya Oblast', C Russian Federation 56°58'N 81°59'E
76 I11 Bakel E Senegal 14°54'N 12°26'W
35 W13 Baker California, W USA 35°15'N 116°04'W
22 J8 Baker Louisiana, S USA 30°35'N 91°10'W
33 Y9 Baker Montana, NW USA 46°22'N 104°16'W
32 L12 Baker Oregon, NW USA 44°46'N 117°50'W
192 L7 Baker and Howland Islands ◇ US unincorporated territory W Polynesia
36 L12 Baker Butte ▲ Arizona, SW USA 34°24'N 111°22'W
39 X15 Baker Island island Alexander Archipelago, Alaska, USA
9 N9 Baker Lake var. Qamanittuaq. Nunavut, N Canada 64°20'N 96°10'W
9 N9 Baker Lake ◎ Nunavut, N Canada
32 H6 Baker, Mount ▲ Washington, NW USA 48°46'N 121°48'W
35 R13 Bakersfield California, W USA 35°22'N 119°01'W
24 M9 Bakersfield Texas, SW USA 30°54'N 102°21'W
21 P9 Bakersville North Carolina, SE USA 36°01'N 82°09'W
Bākhābī see Bū Khābī
Bakharden see Baharly
Bakhardok see Bokurdak
143 U5 Bākharz, Kuhhā-ye ▲ NE Iran
152 D13 Bākhāsar Rājasthān, NW India 24°42'N 71°11'E
Bakhchisaray see Bakhchysaray
117 T13 Bakhchysaray Rus. Bakhchisaray. Avtonomna Respublika Krym, S Ukraine 44°44'N 33°53'E
Bakherden see Baharly
117 R3 Bakhmach Chernihivs'ka Oblast', N Ukraine 51°10'N 32°48'E
Bākhtarān see Kermānshāh
143 Q11 Bakhtegān, Daryācheh-ye ◎ C Iran
Bakhty see Bakty
137 Z11 Bakı Eng. Baku. ● (Azerbaijan) E Azerbaijan 40°24'N 49°51'E
80 M12 Baki Awdal, N Somalia 10°10'N 43°45'E
137 Z11 Bakı ✈ E Azerbaijan 40°26'N 49°55'E
136 C13 Bakır Çayı ≈ W Turkey
92 L1 Bakkafjörður Austurland, NE Iceland 66°01'N 14°49'W
92 L1 Bakkaflói sea area W Norwegian Sea
81 I15 Bako Southern Nationalities, S Ethiopia 05°45'N 36°39'E
76 L15 Bako NW Ivory Coast 09°08'N 07°40'W
Bákó see Bacău
111 H23 Bakony Eng. Bakony Mountains, Ger. Bakonywald. ▲ W Hungary
Bakony Mountains/ Bakonywald see Bakony
81 M16 Bakool off. Gobolka Bakool. ◆ region W Somalia
Bakool, Gobolka see Bakool
79 L15 Bakouma Mbomou, SE Central African Republic 05°42'N 22°43'E
127 N15 Baksan Kabardino-Balkarskaya Respublika, SW Russian Federation 43°43'N 43°31'E
119 I16 Bakshty Hrodzyenskaya Voblasts', W Belarus 53°56'N 26°11'E
145 X12 Bakty prev. Bakhty. Vostochnyy Kazakhstan, E Kazakhstan 46°41'N 82°45'E
Baku see Bakı
194 K12 Bakutis Coast physical region Antarctica
Bakwanga see Mbuji-Mayi
145 O15 Bakyrly Yuzhnyy Kazakhstan, S Kazakhstan 44°30'N 67°41'E
14 H13 Bala Ontario, S Canada 45°01'N 79°37'W
136 I13 Balâ Ankara, C Turkey 39°34'N 33°07'E
97 J19 Bala NW Wales, United Kingdom 52°54'N 03°31'W
170 L7 Balabac Island island W Philippines
Balabac, Selat see Balabac Strait
169 V5 Balabac Strait var. Selat Balabac. strait Malaysia/ Philippines
Ba'labakk see Baalbek
187 P16 Balabio, Île island Province Nord, W New Caledonia
116 I14 Balaci Teleorman, S Romania 44°21'N 24°55'E
139 S7 Balad Şalāḩ ad Dīn, N Iraq 34°00'N 44°07'E
139 U7 Balad Rūz Diyālá, E Iraq 33°42'N 45°04'E
154 J11 Bālāghāt Madhya Pradesh, C India 21°48'N 80°11'E
155 F14 Bālāghāt Range ▲ W India
103 X14 Balagne physical region Corse, France, C Mediterranean Sea
105 U5 Balaguer Cataluña, NE Spain 41°48'N 00°48'E
105 S3 Balaïtous var. Pic de Balaitous. ▲ France/Spain 42°51'N 00°17'W
Balaitous, Pic de see Balaïtous
Balák see Ballangen
127 O3 Balakhna Nizhegorodskaya Oblast', W Russian Federation 56°26'N 43°43'E
122 L12 Balakhta Krasnoyarskiy Kray, S Russian Federation 55°22'N 91°24'E
182 I9 Balaklava South Australia 34°10'S 138°22'E
Balakleya see Balakliya
117 V6 Balakliya Rus. Balakleya. Kharkivs'ka Oblast', E Ukraine 49°27'N 36°53'E
127 Q7 Balakovo Saratovskaya Oblast', W Russian Federation 52°03'N 47°47'E
83 P14 Balama Cabo Delgado, N Mozambique 13°18'S 38°39'E
169 U6 Balambangan, Pulau island East Malaysia
Bālā Morghāb see Bālā Murghāb
148 L3 Bālā Murghāb prev. Bālā Morghāb. Laghmān, NW Afghanistan 35°38'N 63°21'E
152 E11 Bālān prev. Bāhla. Rājasthān, NW India 27°45'N 71°32'E
116 J10 Bălan Hung. Balánbánya. Harghita, C Romania 46°39'N 25°47'E
Balánbánya see Bălan
171 O3 Balanga Luzon, N Philippines 14°40'N 120°32'E
154 M12 Balāngīr prev. Bolangir. Orissa, E India 20°41'N 83°30'E
127 N8 Balashov Saratovskaya Oblast', W Russian Federation 51°32'N 43°14'E
Balasore see Bāleshwar
111 K21 Balassagyarmat Nógrád, N Hungary 48°06'N 19°17'E
29 S10 Balaton Minnesota, N USA 44°13'N 95°52'W
111 H24 Balaton var. Lake Balaton, Ger. Plattensee. ◎ W Hungary
111 I23 Balatonfüred var. Füred. Veszprém, W Hungary 46°59'N 17°53'E
Balaton, Lake see Balaton
116 I11 Bălăuşeri Ger. Bladenmarkt, Hung. Balavásár. Mureş, C Romania 46°24'N 24°41'E
Balavásár see Bălăuşeri
105 Q11 Balazote Castilla-La Mancha, C Spain 38°54'N 02°09'W
Balázsfalva see Blaj
119 F14 Balbieriškis Kaunas, S Lithuania 54°29'N 23°52'E
186 J7 Balbi, Mount ▲ Bougainville Island, NE Papua New Guinea 05°51'S 154°58'E
58 F11 Balbina, Represa ▣ NW Brazil
43 T15 Balboa Panamá, C Panama 08°55'N 79°36'W
97 G17 Balbriggan Ir. Baile Brigín. E Ireland 53°37'N 06°11'W
Balbunar see Kubrat
81 N17 Balcad Shabeellaha Dhexe, C Somalia 02°19'N 45°19'E
61 D23 Balcarce Buenos Aires, E Argentina 37°51'S 58°16'W
11 U16 Balcarres Saskatchewan, S Canada 50°49'N 103°31'W
114 O8 Balchik Dobrich, NE Bulgaria 43°25'N 28°11'E
185 E24 Balclutha Otago, South Island, New Zealand 46°15'S 169°45'E
25 Q12 Balcones Escarpment escarpment Texas, SW USA
18 F14 Bald Eagle Creek ≈ Pennsylvania, NE USA
Baldenburg see Biały Bór
21 V12 Bald Head Island island North Carolina, SE USA
27 W10 Bald Knob Arkansas, C USA 35°18'N 91°34'W
30 K17 Bald Knob hill Illinois, N USA
Baldohn see Baldone
118 G9 Baldone Ger. Baldohn. W Latvia 56°46'N 24°18'E
22 I9 Baldwin Louisiana, S USA 29°50'N 91°32'W
31 P7 Baldwin Michigan, N USA 43°54'N 85°50'W
27 Q4 Baldwin City Kansas, C USA 38°43'N 95°12'W
39 N8 Baldwin Peninsula headland Alaska, USA 66°45'N 162°19'W
18 H9 Baldwinsville New York, NE USA 43°09'N 76°19'W
23 N2 Baldwyn Mississippi, S USA 34°30'N 88°38'W
11 W15 Baldy Mountain ▲ Manitoba, S Canada 51°29'N 100°46'W
33 T7 Baldy Mountain ▲ Montana, NW USA 48°09'N 109°39'W
37 O13 Baldy Peak ▲ Arizona, SW USA 33°56'N 109°37'W
Bâle see Basel
Balearic Plain see Algerian Basin
Baleares see Illes Baleares
105 X11 Baleares, Islas Eng. Balearic Islands. island group Spain, W Mediterranean Sea
Baleares Major see Mallorca
Balearic Islands see Baleares, Islas
Balearis Minor see Menorca
169 S9 Baleh, Batang ≈ East Malaysia
12 J8 Baleine, Grande Rivière de la ≈ Québec, E Canada
12 K7 Baleine, Petite Rivière de la ≈ Québec, SE Canada
12 K7 Baleine, Petite Rivière de la ≈ Québec, NE Canada
13 N6 Baleine, Rivière à la ≈ Québec, E Canada
99 J16 Balen Antwerpen, N Belgium 51°12'N 05°12'E
171 O3 Baler Luzon, N Philippines 15°47'N 121°30'E
154 P11 Bāleshwar prev. Balasore. Orissa, E India 21°31'N 86°59'E
77 S12 Baléyara Tillabéri, W Niger 13°48'N 02°57'E
127 T1 Balezino Udmurtskaya Respublika, NW Russian Federation 57°57'N 53°03'E
42 J4 Balfate Colón, N Honduras 15°47'N 86°24'W
11 O17 Balfour British Columbia, SW Canada 49°39'N 116°57'W
29 N3 Balfour North Dakota, N USA 47°55'N 100°34'W
Balfrush see Bābol
122 L14 Balgazyn Respublika Tyva, S Russian Federation 50°53'N 95°12'E
11 U16 Balgonie Saskatchewan, S Canada 50°30'N 104°12'W
Bălgrad see Alba Iulia
81 J19 Balguda spring/well S Kenya 01°28'S 39°50'E
158 K6 Balguntay Xinjiang Uygur Zizhiqu, NW China 42°45'N 86°18'E
141 R16 Baḩḩāf S Yemen 14°02'N 48°16'E
152 F13 Bāli Rājasthān, N India 25°10'N 73°20'E
169 U17 Bali ◆ province S Indonesia
169 T17 Bali island C Indonesia
111 K16 Balice ✈ (Kraków) Małopolskie, S Poland 49°57'N 19°49'E
171 Y14 Baliem, Sungai ≈ Papua, E Indonesia
136 C12 Balıkesir Balıkesir, W Turkey 39°38'N 27°52'E
136 C12 Balıkesir ◆ province NW Turkey
138 L3 Balīkh, Nahr ≈ N Syria
169 V12 Balikpapan Borneo, C Indonesia 01°15'S 116°50'E
169 T16 Bali, Laut Eng. Bali Sea. sea C Indonesia
171 N9 Balimbing Tawitawi, SW Philippines 05°10'N 120°00'E
186 B8 Balimo Western, SW Papua New Guinea 08°00'S 143°00'E
Bálinc see Balinţ
101 H23 Balingen Baden-Württemberg, SW Germany 48°16'N 08°51'E
116 F11 Balinţ Hung. Bálinc. Timiş, W Romania 45°48'N 21°54'E
171 O1 Balintang Channel channel N Philippines
138 K3 Bālis Ḩalab, N Syria 36°01'N 38°03'E
Bali Sea see Bali, Laut
98 K7 Balk Fryslân, N Netherlands 52°54'N 05°34'E
146 B11 Balkanabat Rus. Nebitdag. Balkan Welaýaty, W Turkmenistan 39°33'N 54°19'E
121 R6 Balkan Mountains Bul./SCr. Stara Planina. ▲ Bulgaria/Serbia
Balkanskiy Welayat see Balkan Welaýaty
146 B9 Balkan Welaýaty Rus. Balkanskiy Velayat. ◆ province W Turkmenistan
145 T13 Balkash Kaz. Balqash; prev. Balkhash. Karaganda, SE Kazakhstan 46°52'N 74°55'E
145 P8 Balkashino Akmola, N Kazakhstan 52°36'N 68°46'E
Balkash, Ozero Eng. Lake Balkhash, Kaz. Balqash; prev. Ozero Balkhash. ◎ SE Kazakhstan
149 O2 Balkh anc. Bactra. Balkh, N Afghanistan 36°46'N 66°54'E
149 P2 Balkh ◆ province N Afghanistan
Balkhash see Balkash
Balkhash, Lake see Balkash, Ozero
Balkhash, Ozero see Balkash, Ozero
Balla Balla see Mbalabala
96 H10 Ballachulish N Scotland, United Kingdom 56°40'N 05°10'W
180 M12 Balladonia Western Australia 32°21'S 123°32'E
97 C16 Ballaghaderreen Ir. Bealach an Doirín. C Ireland 53°51'N 08°29'W
92 H10 Ballangen Lapp. Bálák. Nordland, NW Norway 68°18'N 16°48'E
97 H14 Ballantrae W Scotland, United Kingdom 55°05'N 05°W
183 N12 Ballarat Victoria, SE Australia 37°36'S 143°51'E
180 K11 Ballard, Lake salt lake Western Australia
Ballari see Bellary
76 L11 Ballé Koulikoro, W Mali 15°18'N 08°31'W
40 D7 Ballenas, Bahía de bay NW Mexico
40 D5 Ballenas, Canal de channel NW Mexico
195 R17 Balleny Islands island group Antarctica
40 J7 Balleza var. San Pablo Balleza. Chihuahua, N Mexico 26°55'N 106°21'W
114 M13 Ballı Tekirdağ, NW Turkey 40°48'N 27°03'E
153 O13 Ballia Uttar Pradesh, N India 25°45'N 84°09'E
183 V4 Ballina New South Wales, SE Australia 28°50'S 153°37'E
97 C16 Ballina Ir. Béal an Átha. W Ireland 54°07'N 09°09'W
97 D16 Ballinamore Ir. Béal an Átha Móir. NW Ireland 54°03'N 07°47'W
97 D18 Ballinasloe Ir. Béal Átha na Sluaighe. W Ireland 53°20'N 08°13'W
25 P8 Ballinger Texas, SW USA 31°44'N 99°57'W
97 C17 Ballinrobe Ir. Baile an Róba. W Ireland 53°37'N 09°14'W
97 A21 Ballinskelligs Bay Ir. Bá na Scealg. inlet SW Ireland
97 D15 Ballintra Ir. Baile an tSratha. NW Ireland 54°35'N 08°07'W
103 T7 Ballon d'Alsace ▲ NE France 47°50'N 06°54'E
Ballon de Guebwiller see Grand Ballon
113 K21 Ballsh var. Ballshi. Fier, SW Albania 40°35'N 19°45'E
Ballshi see Ballsh
98 K4 Ballum Fryslân, N Netherlands 53°27'N 05°40'E
97 F16 Ballybay Ir. Béal Átha Beithe. N Ireland 54°08'N 06°54'W
97 E14 Ballybofey Ir. Bealach Féich. NW Ireland 54°49'N 07°47'W
97 G14 Ballycastle Ir. Baile an Chaistil. N Northern Ireland, United Kingdom 55°12'N 06°14'W
97 G15 Ballyclare Ir. Bealach Cláir. E Northern Ireland, United Kingdom 54°45'N 06°W
97 E16 Ballyconnell Ir. Béal Átha Conaill. N Ireland 54°07'N 07°35'W
97 C17 Ballyhaunis Ir. Beál Átha hAmhnais. W Ireland 53°45'N 08°45'W
97 G14 Ballymena Ir. An Baile Meánach. NE Northern Ireland, United Kingdom 54°52'N 06°17'W
97 F14 Ballymoney Ir. Baile Monaidh. NE Northern Ireland, United Kingdom 55°10'N 06°30'W
97 G15 Ballynahinch Ir. Baile na hInse. SE Northern Ireland, United Kingdom 54°24'N 05°54'W
97 D16 Ballysadare Ir. Baile Easa Dara. NW Ireland 54°13'N 08°30'W
97 D15 Ballyshannon Ir. Béal Átha Seanaidh. NW Ireland 54°30'N 08°11'W
63 H19 Balmaceda Aisén, S Chile 45°52'S 72°43'W
63 G23 Balmaceda, Cerro ▲ S Chile 51°27'S 73°26'W
111 N22 Balmazújváros Hajdú-Bihar, E Hungary 47°36'N 21°18'E
108 E10 Balmhorn ▲ SW Switzerland 46°27'N 07°41'E
182 L12 Balmoral Victoria, SE Australia 37°16'S 141°38'E
24 K9 Balmorhea Texas, SW USA 30°58'N 103°44'W
Balneario Claromecó see Claromecó
148 M12 Balochistān prev. Baluchistan, Beluchistan. ◆ province SW Pakistan
82 B13 Balombo Port. Norton de Matos, Vila Norton de Matos. Benguela, W Angola 12°21'S 14°46'E
82 B13 Balombo ≈ W Angola
181 X10 Balonne River ≈ Queensland, E Australia
152 E13 Bālotra Rājasthān, N India 25°50'N 72°21'E
145 V14 Balpyk Bi prev. Kirovskiy, Kaz. Kīrov. Almaty, SE Kazakhstan 44°54'N 78°13'E
Balqā'/Balqā', Muḩāfaẓat al see Al Balqā'
Balqash see Balkash/ Balkhash, Ozero
152 M12 Balrāmpur Uttar Pradesh, N India 27°25'N 82°10'E
182 M9 Balranald New South Wales, SE Australia 34°39'S 143°33'E
116 H14 Balş Olt, S Romania 44°20'N 24°06'E
14 H11 Balsam Creek Ontario, S Canada 46°26'N 79°10'W
30 I5 Balsam Lake Wisconsin, N USA 45°27'N 92°28'W
14 I14 Balsam Lake ◎ Ontario, SE Canada
59 M14 Balsas Maranhão, E Brazil 07°30'S 46°W
40 M15 Balsas, Río var. Río Mexcala. ≈ S Mexico
43 W16 Balsas, Río ≈ SE Panama
119 O18 Bal'shavik Rus. Bol'shevik. Homyel'skaya Voblasts', SE Belarus 52°34'N 30°53'E
95 O15 Bålsta Uppsala, C Sweden 59°31'N 17°32'E
108 E7 Balsthal Solothurn, NW Switzerland 47°18'N 07°42'E
117 O8 Balta Odes'ka Oblast', SW Ukraine 47°58'N 29°39'E
105 N5 Baltanás Castilla y León, N Spain 41°56'N 04°12'W
61 E16 Baltasar Brum Artigas, N Uruguay 30°44'S 57°19'W
116 M9 Bălţi Rus. Bel'tsy. N Moldova 47°45'N 27°57'E
Baltic Port see Paldiski
118 B10 Baltic Sea Ger. Ostee, Rus. Baltiskoye More. sea N Europe
21 X3 Baltimore Maryland, NE USA 39°17'N 76°37'W
31 T13 Baltimore Ohio, N USA 39°48'N 82°33'W
21 X3 Baltimore-Washington ✈ Maryland, E USA 39°10'N 76°40'W
Baltischport/Baltiski see Paldiski
Baltiskoye More see Baltic Sea
119 A14 Baltiysk Ger. Pillau. Kaliningradskaya Oblast', W Russian Federation 54°39'N 19°54'E
Baltkrievija see Belarus
119 H14 Baltoji Voke Vilnius, SE Lithuania 54°35'N 25°13'E
Balūchestān va Sīstān see Sīstān va Balūchestān
Baluchistan see Balochistān
171 P5 Balud Masbate, N Philippines 12°03'N 123°12'E
169 T9 Balui, Batang ≈ East Malaysia
153 S13 Bālurghat West Bengal, NE India 25°12'N 88°50'E
118 J8 Balvi NE Latvia 57°07'N 27°14'E
147 W7 Balykchy Kir. Ysyk-Köl; prev. Issyk-Kul', Rybach'ye. Issyk-Kul'skaya Oblast', NE Kyrgyzstan 42°29'N 76°08'E
56 B7 Balzar Guayas, W Ecuador 01°25'S 79°54'W
108 I8 Balzers S Liechtenstein 47°04'N 09°32'E
143 T12 Bam Kermān, SE Iran 29°08'N 58°27'E
77 Y13 Bama Borno, NE Nigeria 11°28'N 13°46'E
76 L12 Bamako ● (Mali) Capital District, SW Mali 12°39'N 08°02'W
77 P10 Bamba Gao, C Mali 17°03'N 01°19'W
42 M8 Bambana, Río ≈ NE Nicaragua
79 J15 Bambari Ouaka, C Central African Republic 05°45'N 20°37'E
181 W5 Bambaroo Queensland, NE Australia 19°00'S 146°16'E
101 K19 Bamberg Bayern, SE Germany 49°54'N 10°53'E
21 R14 Bamberg South Carolina, SE USA 33°16'N 81°02'W
79 M16 Bambesa Orientale, N Dem. Rep. Congo 03°25'N 25°43'E
76 G11 Bambey W Senegal 14°43'N 16°26'W
79 H16 Bambio Sangha-Mbaéré, SW Central African Republic 03°57'N 16°54'E
83 I24 Bamboesberge ▲ S South Africa 31°24'S 26°10'E
79 D14 Bamenda Nord-Ouest, W Cameroon 05°55'N 10°09'E
10 K17 Bamfield Vancouver Island, British Columbia, SW Canada 48°48'N 125°05'W
Bami see Bamy
79 J14 Bamingui Bamingui-Bangoran, C Central African Republic 07°38'N 20°06'E
78 J13 Bamingui ≈ N Central African Republic
78 J13 Bamingui-Bangoran ◆ prefecture N Central African Republic
143 V13 Bampūr Sīstān va Balūchestān, SE Iran 27°13'N 60°28'E
186 C8 Bamu ≈ SW Papua New Guinea
146 E12 Bamy Rus. Bami. Ahal Welaýaty, C Turkmenistan 38°42'N 56°47'E
149 P4 Bāmyān prev. Bāmiān. Bāmyān, NE Afghanistan 34°50'N 67°50'E
149 O4 Bāmyān prev. Bāmiān. ◆ province C Afghanistan
Bán see Bánovce nad Bebravou
81 N17 Banaadir off. Gobolka Banaadir. ◆ region S Somalia
Banaadir, Gobolka see Banaadir
191 N3 Banaba var. Ocean Island. island Tungaru, W Kiribati
59 O14 Banabuiú, Açude ▣ NE Brazil
57 O19 Bañados del Izozog salt lake SE Bolivia
97 D18 Banagher Ir. Beannchar. C Ireland 53°12'N 07°56'W
79 M17 Banalia Orientale, N Dem. Rep. Congo 01°33'N 25°23'E
76 L12 Banamba Koulikoro, W Mali 13°29'N 07°22'W
40 G4 Banámichi Sonora, NW Mexico 30°00'N 110°14'W
181 Y9 Banana Queensland, E Australia 24°33'S 150°07'E
191 Z2 Banana prev. Main Camp. Kiritimati, E Kiribati 02°00'N 157°25'W
59 K16 Bananal, Ilha do island C Brazil
23 Y12 Banana River lagoon Florida, SE USA
151 Q22 Bananga Andaman and Nicobar Islands, India, NE Indian Ocean 06°57'N 93°54'E
Banaras see Vārānasi
114 N13 Banarlı Tekirdağ, NW Turkey 41°04'N 27°21'E
152 H12 Banās ≈ N India
75 Z11 Banās, Rās headland E Egypt 23°55'N 35°47'E
112 N10 Banatski Karlovac Vojvodina, NE Serbia 45°03'N 21°02'E
141 P16 Banā, Wādī dry watercourse SW Yemen
136 E14 Banaz Uşak, W Turkey 38°47'N 29°46'E
136 E14 Banaz Çayı ≈ W Turkey
159 P14 Banbar var. Coka. Xizang Zizhiqu, W China 31°01'N 94°43'E
97 G15 Banbridge Ir. Droichead na Banna. SE Northern Ireland, United Kingdom 54°21'N 06°16'W
Ban Bua Yai see Bua Yai
97 M21 Banbury S England, United Kingdom 52°04'N 01°20'W
167 O7 Ban Chiang Dao Chiang Mai, NW Thailand 19°22'N 98°59'E
96 K9 Banchory NE Scotland, United Kingdom 58°05'N 00°35'W
14 J13 Bancroft Ontario, SE Canada 45°03'N 77°52'W
33 R15 Bancroft Idaho, NW USA 42°43'N 111°54'W
29 U11 Bancroft Iowa, C USA 43°17'N 94°13'W
154 I9 Bānda Madhya Pradesh, C India 24°01'N 78°59'E
152 L13 Bānda Uttar Pradesh, N India 25°28'N 80°20'E
168 F7 Banda Aceh var. Banda Atjeh; prev. Koetaradja, Kutaradja, Kutaraja. Sumatera, W Indonesia 05°30'N 95°20'E
Banda Atjeh see Banda Aceh
171 S14 Banda, Kepulauan island group E Indonesia
Banda, Laut see Banda Sea
77 N17 Bandama var. Bandama Fleuve. ≈ S Ivory Coast
77 N15 Bandama Blanc ≈ C Ivory Coast
Bandama Fleuve see Bandama
Bandar 'Abbās see Bandar-e 'Abbās
153 W16 Bandarban Chittagong, SE Bangladesh 22°13'N 92°13'E
80 Q13 Bandarbeyla var. Bender Beila, Bender Beyla. Bari, NE Somalia 09°28'N 50°48'E
143 R14 Bandar-e 'Abbās var. Bandar 'Abbās; prev. Gombroon. Hormozgān, S Iran 27°11'N 56°11'E
142 M3 Bandar-e Anzalī Gīlān, NW Iran 37°26'N 49°29'E
143 N12 Bandar-e Būshehr var. Būshehr, Eng. Bushire. Būshehr, S Iran 28°59'N 50°50'E
143 O13 Bandar-e Dayyer var. Deyyer. Būshehr, SE Iran 27°50'N 51°55'E
142 M11 Bandar-e Gonāveh var. Deyyer; prev. Gonāveh. Būshehr, SW Iran 29°33'N 50°39'E
143 T15 Bandar-e Jāsk var. Jāsk. Hormozgān, SE Iran 25°35'N 58°06'E
143 O13 Bandar-e Kangān var. Kangān. Būshehr, S Iran 25°50'N 57°30'E
143 R14 Bandar-e Khamīr Hormozgān, S Iran 27°00'N 55°50'E
Bandar-e Langeh see Bandar-e Lengeh
143 Q14 Bandar-e Lengeh var. Bandar-e Langeh, Lingeh. Hormozgān, S Iran 26°34'N 54°52'E
142 L10 Bandar-e Māhshahr var. Māh-Shahr; prev. Bandar-e Ma'shūr. Khūzestān, SW Iran 30°34'N 49°10'E
Bandar-e Ma'shūr see Bandar-e Māhshahr
143 O14 Bandar-e Nakhīlū Hormozgān, S Iran
Bandar-e Shāh see Bandar-e Torkaman
143 P4 Bandar-e Torkaman var. Bandar-e Torkeman, Bandar-e Torkman; prev. Bandar-e Shāh. Golestān, N Iran 36°55'N 54°05'E
Bandar-e Torkeman/ Bandar-e Torkman see Bandar-e Torkaman
Bandar Kassim see Boosaaso
168 M15 Bandar Lampung var. Bandarlampung, Tanjungkarang-Telukbetung; prev. Tandjoengkarang, Tanjungkarang, Teloekbetoeng, Telukbetung. Sumatera, W Indonesia 05°28'S 105°16'E
Bandarlampung see Bandar Lampung
Bandar Maharani see Muar
Bandar Masulipatnam see Machilīpatnam
Bandar Penggaram see Batu Pahat
169 T7 Bandar Seri Begawan prev. Brunei Town. ● (Brunei) N Brunei 04°56'N 114°58'E
169 T7 Bandar Seri Begawan ✈ N Brunei 04°56'N 114°58'E
171 R15 Banda Sea var. Laut Banda. sea E Indonesia
104 H5 Bande Galicia, NW Spain 42°01'N 07°58'W
59 G15 Bandeirantes Mato Grosso, W Brazil 09°04'S 57°53'W
59 N20 Bandeira, Pico da ▲ SE Brazil 20°25'S 41°45'W
83 K19 Bandelierkop Limpopo, NE South Africa 23°21'S 29°46'E
62 L8 Bandera Santiago del Estero, N Argentina 28°53'S 62°15'W
25 Q11 Bandera Texas, SW USA 29°44'N 99°06'W
40 J13 Banderas, Bahía de bay W Mexico
77 O11 Bandiagara Mopti, C Mali 14°20'N 03°37'W
152 I12 Bāndīkūi Rājasthān, N India 27°01'N 76°33'E
136 C11 Bandırma var. Penderma. Balıkesir, NW Turkey 40°21'N 27°58'E
Bandjarmasin see Banjarmasin
Bandoeng see Bandung
97 C21 Bandon Ir. Droicheadna Bandan. SW Ireland 51°44'N 08°44'W
32 E14 Bandon Oregon, NW USA 43°07'N 124°24'W
167 R8 Ban Dong Bang Nong Khai, E Thailand 18°00'N 104°08'E
167 Q6 Ban Donkon Oudômxai, N Laos 20°20'N 101°37'E
172 J14 Bandrélé SE Mayotte
79 H20 Bandundu prev. Banningville. Bandundu, W Dem. Rep. Congo 03°19'S 17°24'E
79 I21 Bandundu off. Région de Bandundu. ◆ region W Dem. Rep. Congo
Bandundu, Région de see Bandundu
169 O16 Bandung prev. Bandoeng. Jawa, C Indonesia 06°47'S 107°28'E
116 L15 Băneasa Constanţa, SW Romania 45°56'N 27°55'E
142 J4 Bāneh Kordestān, N Iran 35°58'N 45°54'E
44 I7 Banes Holguín, E Cuba 20°58'N 75°43'W
11 P16 Banff Alberta, SW Canada 51°10'N 115°34'W
96 K8 Banff NE Scotland, United Kingdom 57°39'N 02°33'W
96 K8 Banff cultural region NE Scotland, United Kingdom
Bánffyhunyad see Huedin
77 N14 Banfora SW Burkina 10°36'N 04°45'W
155 H19 Bangalore var. Bengalooru. state capital Karnātaka, S India 12°58'N 77°35'E
153 S16 Bangaon West Bengal, NE India 23°01'N 88°50'E
79 L15 Bangassou Mbomou, SE Central African Republic 04°51'N 22°55'E
186 D7 Bangeta, Mount ▲ C Papua New Guinea 06°11'S 147°02'E
171 P12 Banggai, Kepulauan island group C Indonesia
171 Q12 Banggai, Pulau island Kepulauan Banggai, N Indonesia
171 X13 Banggelapa Papua, E Indonesia 03°47'S 136°53'E

◆ Country
● Country Capital
◇ Dependent Territory
○ Dependent Territory Capital
◆ Administrative Regions
✈ International Airport
▲ Mountain
▲ Mountain Range
Volcano
≈ River
◎ Lake
▣ Reservoir

Banggi *see* Banggi, Pulau
169 *V6* **Banggi, Pulau** *var.* Banggi. *island* East Malaysia
152 *K5* **Banggong Co** *var.* Pangong Tso. ◎ China/India *see also* Pangong Tso
121 *P13* **Banghāzī** *Eng.* Bengazi, Benghazi, *It.* Bengasi. NE Libya *32°07′N 20°04′E*
Bang Hieng *see* Xé Banghiang
169 *O13* **Bangka-Belitung** *off.* Propinsi Bangka-Belitung. ⬖ *province* W Indonesia
169 *P11* **Bangkai, Tanjung** *var.* Bankai. *headland* Borneo, N Indonesia *0°21′N 108°53′E*
169 *S16* **Bangkalan** Pulau Madura, C Indonesia *07°05′S 112°44′E*
169 *N12* **Bangka, Pulau** *island* W Indonesia
169 *N13* **Bangka, Selat** *strait* Sumatera, W Indonesia
169 *N13* **Bangka, Selat** *var.* Selat Likupang. *strait* Sulawesi, N Indonesia
168 *J11* **Bangkinang** Sumatera, W Indonesia *0°21′N 100°52′E*
168 *K12* **Bangko** Sumatera, W Indonesia *02°05′S 102°20′E*
Bangkok *see* Ao Krung Thep
Bangkok, Bight of *see* Krung Thep, Ao
153 *T14* **Bangladesh** *off.* People's Republic of Bangladesh; *prev.* East Pakistan. ◆ *republic* S Asia
Bangladesh, People's Republic of *see* Bangladesh
167 *V13* **Ba Ngoi** Khanh Hoa, S Vietnam *11°56′N 109°07′E*
Ba Ngoi *see* Cam Ranh
Bangong Co *see* Pangong Tso
97 *I18* **Bangor** NW Wales, United Kingdom *53°13′N 04°08′W*
97 *G15* **Bangor** *Ir.* Beannchar. E Northern Ireland, United Kingdom *54°40′N 05°40′W*
19 *R6* **Bangor** Maine, NE USA *44°48′N 68°47′W*
18 *I14* **Bangor** Pennsylvania, NE USA *40°52′N 75°12′W*
67 *R8* **Bangoran** ≋ S Central African Republic
Bang Phra *see* Trat
Bang Pla Soi *see* Chon Buri
25 *Q8* **Bangs** Texas, SW USA *31°43′N 99°07′W*
167 *N13* **Bang Saphan** *var.* Bang Saphan Yai. Prachuap Khiri Khan, SW Thailand *11°10′N 99°33′E*
Bang Saphan Yai *see* Bang Saphan
36 *I8* **Bangs, Mount** ▲ Arizona, SW USA *36°47′N 113°51′W*
93 *E15* **Bangsund** Nord-Trøndelag, C Norway *64°22′N 11°22′E*
171 *O2* **Bangued** Luzon, N Philippines *17°36′N 120°40′E*
79 *I15* **Bangui** ● (Central African Republic) Ombella-Mpoko, SW Central African Republic *04°21′N 18°32′E*
79 *I15* **Bangui** ✈ Ombella-Mpoko, SW Central African Republic *04°19′N 18°34′E*
83 *N16* **Bangula** Southern, S Malawi *16°38′S 35°04′E*
Bangwaketse *see* Southern
82 *K12* **Bangweulu, Lake** *var.* Lake Bengweulu. ◎ N Zambia
121 *V13* **Banhā** *var.* Benha. N Egypt *30°28′N 31°11′E*
Ban Hat Yai *see* Hat Yai
167 *Q7* **Ban Hin Heup** Viangchan, C Laos *18°37′N 102°19′E*
Ban Houayxay/Ban Houei Sai *see* Houayxay
167 *O12* **Ban Hua Hin** *var.* Hua Hin. Prachuap Khiri Khan, SW Thailand *12°34′N 99°58′E*
79 *L14* **Bani** Haute-Kotto, E Central African Republic *07°06′N 22°51′E*
45 *O9* **Baní** S Dominican Republic *18°19′N 70°21′W*
77 *N12* **Bani** ≋ S Mali
Bāmīān *see* Bāmyān
Banias *see* Bāniyās
77 *S11* **Bani Bangou** Tillabéri, SW Niger *15°04′N 02°40′E*
76 *M12* **Banifing** *var.* Ngorolaka. ≋ Burkina/Mali
Banijska Palanka *see* Glina
77 *R13* **Banikoara** N Benin *11°18′N 02°26′E*
75 *W9* **Banī Mazār** *var.* Beni Mazâr. C Egypt *28°29′N 30°48′E*
114 *K8* **Baniski Lom** ≋ N Bulgaria
21 *U7* **Banister River** ≋ Virginia, NE USA
121 *V14* **Banī Suwayf** *var.* Beni Suef. N Egypt *29°09′N 31°04′E*
75 *O8* **Banī Walīd** NW Libya *31°46′N 13°59′E*
138 *H5* **Bāniyās** *var.* Banias, Baniyas, Paneas. Ṭarṭūs, W Syria *35°12′N 35°57′E*
113 *K14* **Banja** Serbia, W Serbia *43°33′N 19°35′E*
Banjak, Kepulauan *see* Banyak, Kepulauan
112 *J12* **Banja Koviljača** Serbia, W Serbia *44°31′N 19°11′E*
112 *G11* **Banja Luka** ⬖ Republika Srpska, NW Bosnia and Herzegovina
169 *T13* **Banjarmasin** *prev.* Bandjarmasin. Borneo, C Indonesia *03°22′S 114°33′E*
76 *F11* **Banjul** *prev.* Bathurst. ● (Gambia) W Gambia *13°26′N 16°43′W*
76 *F11* **Banjul** ✈ W Gambia *13°18′N 16°39′W*
Bank *see* Bankä
137 *Y13* **Bankä** *Rus.* Bank. SE Azerbaijan *39°25′N 49°13′E*
167 *S11* **Ban Kadian** *var.* Ban Kadiene. Champasak, S Laos *14°25′N 105°42′E*
Ban Kadiene *see* Ban Kadian
Bankai *see* Bangkai, Tanjung
166 *M14* **Ban Kam Phuam** Phangnga, SW Thailand *09°16′N 98°24′E*
Ban Kantang *see* Kantang
77 *O11* **Bankass** Mopti, S Mali *14°05′N 03°30′W*
95 *L19* **Bankeryd** Jönköping, S Sweden *57°51′N 14°07′E*
83 *K16* **Banket** Mashonaland West, N Zimbabwe *17°23′S 30°24′E*
167 *T11* **Ban Khamphô** Attapu, S Laos *14°35′N 106°18′E*
23 *O4* **Bankhead Lake** ⊠ Alabama, S USA
77 *Q11* **Bankilaré** Tillabéri, SW Niger *14°34′N 00°41′E*
Banks, Îles *see* Banks Islands
10 *I14* **Banks Island** *island* British Columbia, SW Canada
187 *R12* **Banks Islands** *Fr.* Îles Banks. *island group* N Vanuatu
23 *U8* **Banks Lake** ◎ Georgia, SE USA
32 *K8* **Banks Lake** ⊠ Washington, NW USA
185 *I19* **Banks Peninsula** *peninsula* South Island, New Zealand
183 *Q15* **Banks Strait** *strait* SW Tasman Sea
Ban Kui Nua *see* Kui Buri
153 *R16* **Bānkura** West Bengal, NE India *23°14′N 87°05′E*
167 *S8* **Ban Lakxao** *var.* Lak Sao. Bolikhamxai, C Laos *18°10′N 104°58′E*
167 *O16* **Ban Lam Phai** Songkhla, SW Thailand *06°43′N 100°57′E*
Ban Mae Sot *see* Mae Sot
Ban Mae Suai *see* Mae Suai
Ban Mak Khaeng *see* Udon Thani
166 *M3* **Banmauk** Sagaing, Myanmar (Burma) *24°26′N 95°54′E*
Banmo *see* Bhamo
167 *T10* **Ban Mun-Houamuang** S Laos *15°11′N 106°44′E*
97 *F14* **Bann** *var.* Lower Bann, Upper Bann. ≋ N Northern Ireland, United Kingdom
167 *S10* **Ban Nadou** Salavan, S Laos *15°51′N 105°38′E*
167 *S9* **Ban Nakala** Savannakhét, S Laos *16°14′N 105°09′E*
167 *Q8* **Ban Nakha** Viangchan, C Laos *18°13′N 102°29′E*
167 *S9* **Ban Nakham** Khammouan, S Laos *17°10′N 105°25′E*
167 *P7* **Ban Namoun** Xaignabouli, N Laos *18°40′N 101°34′E*
167 *O17* **Ban Nang Sata** Yala, SW Thailand *06°15′N 101°13′E*
167 *N15* **Ban Na San** Surat Thani, SW Thailand *08°53′N 99°17′E*
167 *R7* **Ban Nasi** Xiangkhoang, N Laos *19°37′N 103°33′E*
44 *I3* **Bannerman Town** Eleuthera Island, C Bahamas *24°38′N 76°09′W*
35 *V15* **Banning** California, W USA *33°55′N 116°52′W*
Banningville *see* Bandundu
167 *S11* **Ban Nongsim** Champasak, S Laos *14°45′N 106°00′E*
149 *S7* **Bannu** *prev.* Edwardesabad. Khyber Pakhtunkhwa, NW Pakistan *33°00′N 70°36′E*
Bañolas *see* Banyoles
56 *C7* **Baños** Tungurahua, C Ecuador *01°26′S 78°24′W*
Bánovce *see* Bánovce nad Bebravou
111 *I19* **Bánovce nad Bebravou** *var.* Bánovce, *Hung.* Bán. Trenčiansky Kraj, W Slovakia *48°43′N 18°15′E*
112 *I12* **Banovići** ⬖ Federacija Bosna I Hercegovina, E Bosnia and Herzegovina
Banow *see* Andarāb
Ban Pak Phanang *see* Pak Phanang
167 *O7* **Ban Pan Nua** Lampang, NW Thailand *18°51′N 99°57′E*
167 *Q9* **Ban Phai** Khon Kaen, E Thailand *16°00′N 102°42′E*
167 *Q8* **Ban Phônhông** *var.* Phônhông. C Laos *18°29′N 102°26′E*
167 *T9* **Ban Phou A Douk** Khammouan, C Laos *17°12′N 106°07′E*
167 *Q8* **Ban Phu** Uthai Thani, W Thailand
167 *O11* **Ban Pong** Ratchaburi, W Thailand *13°49′N 99°53′E*
190 *I3* **Banraeaba** Tarawa, W Kiribati *01°20′N 173°02′E*
167 *N10* **Ban Sai Yok** Kanchanaburi, W Thailand *14°24′N 98°54′E*
Ban Sattahip/Ban Sattahipp *see* Sattahip
Ban Sichon *see* Sichon
Ban Si Racha *see* Si Racha
111 *J19* **Banská Bystrica** *Ger.* Neusohl, *Hung.* Besztercebánya. Banskobystricky Kraj, C Slovakia *48°46′N 19°08′E*
111 *K20* **Banskobystrický Kraj** ⬖ *region* C Slovakia
167 *R8* **Ban Sôppheung** Bolikhamxai, C Laos *18°33′N 104°18′E*
Ban Sop Prap *see* Sop Prap
152 *G15* **Bānswāra** Rājasthān, N India *23°32′N 74°28′E*
167 *N15* **Ban Ta Khun** Surat Thani, SW Thailand *08°53′N 98°52′E*
Ban Takua Pa *see* Takua Pa
167 *S8* **Ban Talak** Khammouan, C Laos *17°33′N 105°40′E*
77 *R15* **Bantè** W Benin *08°25′N 01°58′E*
167 *Q11* **Bânteay Méan Choăy** *var.* Sisŏphŏn. Bătdâmbâng, NW Cambodia *13°37′N 102°58′E*
167 *N16* **Banten** *off.* Propinsi Banten. ⬖ *province* W Indonesia
Propinsi Banten *see* Banten
167 *Q8* **Ban Thabôk** Bolikhamxai, C Laos *18°21′N 103°12′E*
167 *T9* **Ban Tôp** Savannakhét, S Laos *16°07′N 106°07′E*
97 *B21* **Bantry** *Ir.* Beanntraí. Cork, SW Ireland *51°41′N 09°27′W*
97 *A21* **Bantry Bay** *Ir.* Bá Bheanntraí. *bay* SW Ireland
155 *F19* **Bantvāl** *var.* Bantwāl. Karnātaka, E India *12°57′N 75°04′E*
Bantwāl *see* Bantvāl
114 *N9* **Banya** Burgas, E Bulgaria *42°46′N 27°49′E*
168 *G10* **Banyak, Kepulauan** *prev.* Kepulauan Banjak. *island group* NW Indonesia
105 *U8* **Banya, La** *headland* E Spain *40°34′N 00°37′E*
79 *E14* **Banyo** Adamaoua, NW Cameroon *06°47′N 11°50′E*
105 *X4* **Banyoles** *var.* Bañolas. Cataluña, NE Spain *42°07′N 02°46′E*
167 *N16* **Ban Yong Sata** Trang, SW Thailand *07°09′N 99°42′E*
195 *X14* **Banzare Coast** *physical region* Antarctica
173 *Q14* **Banzare Seamounts** *undersea feature* S Indian Ocean
Banzart *see* Bizerte
163 *Q12* **Baochang** *var.* Taibus Qi. Nei Mongol Zizhiqu, N China *41°55′N 115°22′E*
161 *O3* **Baoding** *var.* Pao-ting; *prev.* Tsingyuan. Hebei, E China *38°47′N 115°30′E*
Baoebaoe *see* Baubau
Baoi, Oileán *see* Dursey Island
160 *J6* **Baoji** *var.* Pao-chi, Paoki. Shaanxi, C China *34°23′N 107°16′E*
163 *U9* **Baokang** *var.* Hoqin Zuoyi Zhongji. Nei Mongol Zizhiqu, N China *44°08′N 123°18′E*
186 *L8* **Baolo** Santa Isabel, N Solomon Islands *07°41′S 158°47′E*
167 *U13* **Bao Lôc** Lâm Đông, S Vietnam *11°33′N 107°48′E*
163 *Z7* **Baoqing** Heilongjiang, NE China *46°15′N 132°12′E*
Baoqing *see* Shaoyang
79 *H15* **Baoro** Nana-Mambéré, W Central African Republic *05°40′N 16°00′E*
160 *E12* **Baoshan** *var.* Pao-shan. Yunnan, SW China *25°05′N 99°07′E*
163 *N13* **Baotou** *var.* Pao-t'ou, Paotow. Nei Mongol Zizhiqu, N China *40°38′N 109°59′E*
76 *L14* **Baoulé** ≋ S Mali
76 *K12* **Baoulé** ≋ W Mali
Bao Yèn *see* Phô Rang
103 *O2* **Bapaume** Pas-de-Calais, N France *50°06′N 02°50′E*
14 *J13* **Baptiste Lake** ◎ Ontario, SE Canada
Bapu *see* Meigu
Baqanas *see* Bakanas
Baqbaqty *see* Bakbakty
159 *P14* **Baqên** *var.* Dartang. Xizang Zizhiqu, W China *31°50′N 94°08′E*
138 *F14* **Bāqir, Jabal** ▲▲ S Jordan
139 *T7* **Ba'qūbah** *var.* Qubba. Diyālá, C Iraq *33°45′N 44°40′E*
62 *H5* **Baquedano** Antofagasta, N Chile *23°20′S 69°50′W*
Baquerizo Moreno *see* Puerto Baquerizo Moreno
113 *J18* **Bar** *It.* Antivari. S Montenegro *42°02′N 19°09′E*
116 *M6* **Bar** Vinnyts'ka Oblast', C Ukraine *49°05′N 27°40′E*
80 *E10* **Bara** Northern Kordofan, C Sudan *13°42′N 30°21′E*
81 *M18* **Baraawe** *It.* Brava. Shabeellaha Hoose, S Somalia *01°10′N 43°59′E*
152 *M12* **Bāra Banki** Uttar Pradesh, N India *26°56′N 81°11′E*
30 *L8* **Baraboo** Wisconsin, N USA *43°27′N 89°45′W*
30 *K8* **Baraboo Range** *hill range* Wisconsin, N USA
Baracaldo *see* San Vicente de Barakaldo
15 *Y6* **Barachois** Québec, SE Canada *48°37′N 64°14′W*
44 *J7* **Baracoa** Guantánamo, E Cuba *20°23′N 74°31′W*
61 *C19* **Baradero** Buenos Aires, E Argentina *33°50′S 59°30′W*
183 *R6* **Baradine** New South Wales, SE Australia *30°55′S 149°03′E*
Baraf Daja Islands *see* Damar, Kepulauan
Baragarh *see* Bargarh
81 *I17* **Baragoi** Rift Valley, W Kenya *01°39′N 36°46′E*
45 *N9* **Barahona** SW Dominican Republic *18°13′N 71°07′W*
153 *W13* **Barail Range** ▲▲ NE India
Baraka *see* Barka
80 *G10* **Barakat** Gezira, C Sudan *14°18′N 33°32′E*
Barakī *see* Barakī Barak
149 *Q6* **Barakī Barak** *var.* Barakī, Baraki Rajan. Lōgar, E Afghanistan *33°58′N 68°58′E*
Baraki Rajan *see* Barakī Barak
154 *N11* **Bārākot** Orissa, E India *21°35′N 85°00′E*
55 *S7* **Barama River** ≋ N Guyana
155 *E14* **Bārāmati** Mahārāshtra, W India *18°12′N 74°39′E*
152 *H5* **Bāramūla** Jammu and Kashmir, NW India *34°15′N 74°24′E*
119 *N14* **Baran'** Vitsyebskaya Voblasts', NE Belarus *54°29′N 30°18′E*
152 *I14* **Bārān** Rājasthān, N India *25°08′N 76°32′E*
139 *U4* **Barānān, Shākh-i** ▲▲ E Iraq
119 *I17* **Baranavichy** *Pol.* Baranowicze, *Rus.* Baranovichi. Brestskaya Voblasts', SW Belarus *53°08′N 26°02′E*
123 *T6* **Baranikha** Chukotskiy Avtonomnyy Okrug, NE Russian Federation *68°29′N 168°13′E*
75 *Y11* **Baranīs** *var.* Berenice, Mînâ Baranîs. SE Egypt *23°58′N 35°29′E*
116 *M4* **Baranivka** Zhytomyrs'ka Oblast', N Ukraine *50°16′N 27°40′E*
39 *W14* **Baranof Island** *island* Alexander Archipelago, Alaska, USA
Baranovichi/Baranowicze *see* Baranavichy
111 *N15* **Baranów Sandomierski** Podkarpackie, SE Poland *50°28′N 21°31′E*
111 *I26* **Baranya** *off.* Baranya Megye. ⬖ *county* S Hungary
Baranya Megye *see* Baranya
153 *R13* **Barāri** Bihār, NE India *25°31′N 87°23′E*
22 *L10* **Barataria Bay** *bay* Louisiana, S USA
Barat Daya, Kepulauan *see* Damar, Kepulauan
118 *L12* **Baravukha** *Rus.* Borovukha. Vitsyebskaya Voblasts', N Belarus *55°34′N 28°36′E*
54 *E11* **Baraya** Huila, C Colombia *03°11′N 75°04′W*
59 *M21* **Barbacena** Minas Gerais, SE Brazil *21°13′S 43°47′W*
54 *B13* **Barbacoas** Nariño, SW Colombia *01°38′N 78°08′W*
54 *L6* **Barbacoas** Aragua, N Venezuela *09°29′N 66°58′W*
45 *Z13* **Barbados** ◆ *commonwealth republic* SE West Indies
47 *S3* **Barbados** *island* Barbados
105 *U11* **Barbaria, Cap de** *var.* Cabo de Berberia. *headland* Formentera, E Spain *38°39′N 01°24′E*
114 *N13* **Barbaros** Tekirdağ, NW Turkey *40°55′N 27°28′E*
74 *A11* **Barbas, Cap** *headland* S Western Sahara *22°14′N 16°45′W*
105 *T5* **Barbastro** Aragón, NE Spain *42°02′N 00°07′E*
104 *K16* **Barbate** ≋ SW Spain
104 *K16* **Barbate de Franco** Andalucía, S Spain *36°11′N 05°55′W*
83 *K21* **Barberton** Mpumalanga, NE South Africa *25°48′S 31°03′E*
31 *U12* **Barberton** Ohio, N USA *41°02′N 81°37′W*
102 *K12* **Barbezieux-St-Hilaire** Charente, W France *45°28′N 00°09′W*
54 *G9* **Barbosa** Boyaca, C Colombia *05°57′N 73°37′W*
21 *N7* **Barbourville** Kentucky, S USA *36°52′N 83°54′W*
45 *W9* **Barbuda** *island* N Antigua and Barbuda
181 *W8* **Barcaldine** Queensland, E Australia *23°33′S 145°21′E*
Barcarozsnyó *see* Râşnov
104 *I11* **Barcarrota** Extremadura, W Spain *38°31′N 06°51′W*
Barcău *see* Berettyó
Barce *see* Al Marj
107 *L23* **Barcellona** *var.* Barcellona Pozzo di Gotto. Sicilia, Italy, C Mediterranean Sea *38°10′N 15°15′E*
Barcellona Pozzo di Gotto *see* Barcellona
105 *W6* **Barcelona** *anc.* Barcino, Barcinona. Cataluña, E Spain *41°25′N 02°10′E*
55 *N5* **Barcelona** Anzoátegui, NE Venezuela *10°08′N 64°43′W*
105 *S5* **Barcelona** ⬖ *province* Cataluña, NE Spain
105 *W6* **Barcelona** ✈ Cataluña, E Spain *41°25′N 02°10′E*
103 *U14* **Barcelonnette** Alpes-de-Haute-Provence, SE France *44°24′N 06°37′E*
58 *E12* **Barcelos** Amazonas, N Brazil *0°59′S 62°58′W*
104 *G5* **Barcelos** Braga, N Portugal *41°32′N 08°37′W*
110 *I10* **Barcin** *Ger.* Bartschin. Kujawski-pomorskie, C Poland *52°51′N 17°55′E*
Barcino/Barcinona *see* Barcelona
Barcoo *see* Cooper Creek
111 *H26* **Barcs** Somogy, SW Hungary *45°58′N 17°26′E*
137 *W11* **Bärdä** *Rus.* Barda. C Azerbaijan *40°25′N 47°07′E*
Barda *see* Bärdä
78 *H5* **Bardaï** Borkou-Ennedi-Tibesti, N Chad *21°21′N 16°56′E*
139 *R2* **Bardaṛash** Dahūk, N Iraq *36°32′N 43°36′E*
139 *Q7* **Bardasah** Al Anbār, SW Iraq *34°02′N 42°28′E*
153 *S16* **Barddhamān** West Bengal, NE India *23°10′N 88°03′E*
111 *N18* **Bardejov** *Ger.* Bartfeld, *Hung.* Bártfa. Presovský Kraj, E Slovakia *49°17′N 21°18′E*
105 *R4* **Bárdenas Reales** *physical region* N Spain
Bardera/Bardere *see* Baardheere
Bardesīr *see* Bardsīr
92 *K3* **Bárdharbunga** ▲ C Iceland *64°39′N 17°30′W*
92 *K2* **Bárdhárdalur** ≋ C Iceland
106 *E9* **Bardi** Emilia-Romagna, C Italy *44°39′N 09°44′E*
106 *A8* **Bardonecchia** Piemonte, W Italy *45°04′N 06°40′E*
97 *H19* **Bardsey Island** *island* NW Wales, United Kingdom
143 *S11* **Bardsīr** *var.* Bardesīr, Mashīz. Kermān, C Iran *29°58′N 56°29′E*
20 *L6* **Bardstown** Kentucky, S USA *37°49′N 85°29′W*
Barduli *see* Barletta
20 *G7* **Bardwell** Kentucky, S USA *36°52′N 89°01′W*
152 *K11* **Bareilly** *var.* Bareli. Uttar Pradesh, N India *28°20′N 79°24′E*
Bareli *see* Bareilly
Baren *see* Jiashi
98 *H13* **Barendrecht** Zuid-Holland, SW Netherlands *51°52′N 04°31′E*
102 *M3* **Barentin** Seine-Maritime, N France *49°33′N 00°57′E*
92 *N3* **Barentsburg** Spitsbergen, W Svalbard *78°01′N 14°19′E*
Barentsevo More/Barents Havet *see* Barents Sea
92 *O3* **Barentsøya** *island* E Svalbard
197 *T11* **Barents Plain** *undersea feature* N Barents Sea
125 *P3* **Barents Sea** *Nor.* Barents Havet, *Rus.* Barentsevo More. *sea* Arctic Ocean
197 *U14* **Barents Trough** *undersea feature* SW Barents Sea *75°00′N 29°00′E*
80 *I9* **Barentu** W Eritrea *15°08′N 37°35′E*
102 *J3* **Barfleur** Manche, N France *49°41′N 01°18′W*
102 *J3* **Barfleur, Pointe de** *headland* N France *49°46′N 01°09′W*
Barfrush/Barfurush *see* Bābol
158 *H14* **Barga** Xizang Zizhiqu, W China *30°51′N 81°20′E*
80 *Q12* **Bargaal** *prev.* Baargaal. Bari, NE Somalia *11°12′N 51°04′E*
154 *M12* **Bargarh** *var.* Baragarh. Orissa, E India *21°25′N 83°35′E*
105 *N9* **Bargas** Castilla-La Mancha, C Spain *39°56′N 04°00′W*
81 *I15* **Bargē** Southern Nationalities, S Ethiopia *06°11′N 37°04′E*
106 *A9* **Barge** Piemonte, NE Italy *44°49′N 07°21′E*
153 *U16* **Barguna** Barisal, S Bangladesh *22°09′N 90°07′E*
Bārguşad *see* Vorotan
123 *N13* **Barguzin** Respublika Buryatiya, S Russian Federation *53°37′N 109°47′E*
153 *O13* **Barhaj** Uttar Pradesh, N India *26°16′N 83°44′E*
183 *N10* **Barham** New South Wales, SE Australia *35°39′S 144°09′E*
152 *J12* **Barhan** Uttar Pradesh, N India *27°21′N 78°11′E*
19 *S7* **Bar Harbor** Mount Desert Island, Maine, NE USA *44°23′N 68°14′W*
153 *R14* **Barharwa** Jhārkhand, NE India *24°52′N 87°47′E*
153 *P15* **Barhi** Jhārkhand, N India *24°19′N 85°25′E*
107 *O17* **Bari** *var.* Bari delle Puglie; *anc.* Barium. Puglia, SE Italy *41°06′N 16°52′E*
80 *P12* **Bari** *Off.* Gobolka Bari. ⬖ *region* NE Somalia
167 *T14* **Ba Ria** *var.* Châu Thanh. Ba Ria-Vung Tau, S Vietnam *10°30′N 107°10′E*
Bāridah *see* Al Bāridah
Bari delle Puglie *see* Bari
Bari, Gobolka *see* Bari
Barikot *see* Barīkowṯ
149 *T4* **Barīkowṯ** *var.* Barikot. Kunar, NE Afghanistan *35°18′N 71°36′E*
42 *C4* **Barillas** *var.* Santa Cruz Barillas. Huehuetenango, NW Guatemala *15°50′N 91°20′W*
54 *J6* **Barinas** Barinas, W Venezuela *08°36′N 70°15′W*
54 *I7* **Barinas** *off.* Estado Barinas; *prev.* Zamora. ⬖ *state* C Venezuela
Barinas, Estado *see* Barinas
54 *I6* **Barinitas** Barinas, NW Venezuela *08°45′N 70°26′W*
154 *P11* **Bāripada** Orissa, E India *21°56′N 86°43′E*
60 *K9* **Bariri** São Paulo, S Brazil *22°04′S 48°46′W*
75 *W11* **Bārīs** *var.* Bârîs. S Egypt *24°28′N 30°39′E*
152 *G14* **Bari Sādri** Rājasthān, N India *24°25′N 74°28′E*
153 *U16* **Barisal** Barisal, S Bangladesh *22°41′N 90°20′E*
153 *U16* **Barisal** ⬖ *division* S Bangladesh
168 *I10* **Barisan, Pegunungan** ▲▲ Sumatera, W Indonesia
169 *T12* **Barito, Sungai** ≋ Borneo, C Indonesia
Barium *see* Bari
Bårjås *see* Porjus
80 *I9* **Barka** *var.* Baraka, *Ar.* Khawr Barakah. *seasonal river* Eritrea/Sudan
Barka *see* Al Marj
160 *H8* **Barkam** Sichuan, C China *31°56′N 102°22′E*
118 *J9* **Barkava** C Latvia *56°43′N 26°34′E*
10 *M15* **Barkerville** British Columbia, SW Canada *53°06′N 121°35′W*
14 *J12* **Bark Lake** ◎ Ontario, SE Canada
20 *H7* **Barkley, Lake** ⊠ Kentucky/Tennessee, S USA
10 *K17* **Barkley Sound** *inlet* British Columbia, W Canada
83 *J24* **Barkly East** *Afr.* Barkly-Oos. Eastern Cape, SE South Africa *30°58′S 27°35′E*
Barkly-Oos *see* Barkly East
181 *S4* **Barkly Tableland** *plateau* Northern Territory/Queensland, N Australia
Barkly-Wes *see* Barkly West
83 *H22* **Barkly West** *Afr.* Barkly-Wes. Northern Cape, N South Africa *28°32′S 24°32′E*
159 *O5* **Barkol** *var.* Barkol Kazak Zizhixian. Xinjiang Uygur Zizhiqu, NW China *43°37′N 93°01′E*
159 *O5* **Barkol Hu** ◎ NW China
Barkol Kazak Zizhixian *see* Barkol
30 *J3* **Bark Point** *headland* Wisconsin, N USA *46°53′N 91°11′W*
25 *P11* **Barksdale** Texas, SW USA *29°43′N 100°03′W*
Bar Kunar *see* Asmār
116 *L11* **Bârlad** *prev.* Bîrlad. Vaslui, E Romania *46°12′N 27°39′E*
116 *M11* **Bârlad** *prev.* Bîrlad. ≋ E Romania
76 *D9* **Barlavento, Ilhas de** *var.* Windward Islands. *island group* N Cape Verde
103 *R5* **Bar-le-Duc** *var.* Bar-sur-Ornain. Meuse, NE France *48°46′N 05°10′E*
180 *K11* **Barlee, Lake** ◎ Western Australia
180 *H8* **Barlee Range** ▲▲ Western Australia
107 *N16* **Barletta** *anc.* Barduli. Puglia, SE Italy *41°20′N 16°17′E*
110 *E10* **Barlinek** *Ger.* Berlinchen. Zachodnio-pomorskie, NW Poland *53°N 15°11′E*
27 *S11* **Barling** Arkansas, C USA *35°19′N 94°18′W*
171 *U12* **Barma** Papua, E Indonesia *01°55′S 132°57′E*
183 *Q9* **Barmedman** New South Wales, SE Australia *34°09′S 147°21′E*
Barmen-Elberfeld *see* Wuppertal
152 *D12* **Bārmer** Rājasthān, NW India *25°43′N 71°25′E*
182 *K9* **Barmera** South Australia *34°14′S 140°26′E*
97 *I19* **Barmouth** NW Wales, United Kingdom *52°44′N 04°04′W*
154 *F10* **Barnagar** Madhya Pradesh, C India *23°01′N 75°28′E*
152 *H9* **Barnāla** Punjab, NW India *30°26′N 75°33′E*
97 *L15* **Barnard Castle** N England, United Kingdom *54°35′N 01°55′W*
183 *O6* **Barnato** New South Wales, SE Australia *31°39′S 145°01′E*
112 *I13* **Barnaul** Altayskiy Kray, C Russian Federation *53°21′N 83°45′E*
109 *V8* **Bärnbach** Steiermark, SE Austria *47°05′N 15°07′E*
18 *K16* **Barnegat** New Jersey, NE USA *39°43′N 74°12′W*
23 *S4* **Barnesville** Georgia, SE USA *33°03′N 84°09′W*
29 *R6* **Barnesville** Minnesota, N USA *46°39′N 96°25′W*
31 *U13* **Barnesville** Ohio, N USA *39°59′N 81°10′W*
98 *K11* **Barneveld** *var.* Barnveld. Gelderland, C Netherlands *52°08′N 05°34′E*
25 *O9* **Barnhart** Texas, SW USA *31°07′N 101°09′W*
27 *P8* **Barnsdall** Oklahoma, C USA *36°33′N 96°09′W*
97 *M17* **Barnsley** N England, United Kingdom *53°34′N 01°28′W*
19 *Q12* **Barnstable** Massachusetts, NE USA *41°42′N 70°17′W*
97 *I23* **Barnstaple** SW England, United Kingdom *51°05′N 04°04′W*
Barnveld *see* Barneveld
21 *Q14* **Barnwell** South Carolina, SE USA *33°14′N 81°21′W*
77 *U15* **Baro** Niger, C Nigeria *08°35′N 06°28′E*
67 *U8* **Baro** *var.* Baro Wenz. ≋ Ethiopia/Sudan
Baro *see* Baro Wenz
Baroda *see* Vadodara
149 *U2* **Baroghil Pass** *var.* Kowtal-e Barowghīl. *pass* Afghanistan/Pakistan
119 *Q17* **Baron'ki** *Rus.* Boron'ki. Mahilyowskaya Voblasts', E Belarus *53°09′N 32°08′E*
182 *J9* **Barossa Valley** *valley* South Australia
Baroui *see* Salisbury
81 *H14* **Baro Wenz** *var.* Baro, Nahr Barū. ≋ Ethiopia/Sudan
Baro Wenz *see* Baro
Barowghīl, Kowtal-e *see* Baroghil Pass
153 *U12* **Barpeta** Assam, NE India *26°19′N 91°05′E*
31 *S7* **Barques, Pointe Aux** *headland* Michigan, N USA *44°04′N 82°57′W*
54 *I5* **Barquisimeto** Lara, NW Venezuela *10°03′N 69°18′W*
59 *N16* **Barra** Bahia, E Brazil *11°06′S 43°15′W*
96 *E9* **Barra** *island* NW Scotland, United Kingdom
183 *T5* **Barraba** New South Wales, SE Australia *30°24′S 150°37′E*
60 *L9* **Barra Bonita** São Paulo, S Brazil *22°30′S 48°35′W*
64 *J12* **Barracuda Fracture Zone** *var.* Fifteen Twenty Fracture Zone. *tectonic feature* SW Atlantic Ocean
64 *G11* **Barracuda Ridge** *undersea feature* N Atlantic Ocean
43 *N12* **Barra del Colorado** Limón, NE Costa Rica *10°44′N 83°35′W*
43 *N9* **Barra de Río Grande** Región Autónoma Atlántico Sur, E Nicaragua *12°56′N 83°30′W*
82 *A11* **Barra do Cuanza** Luanda, NW Angola *09°12′S 13°08′E*
60 *O9* **Barra do Piraí** Rio de Janeiro, SE Brazil *22°30′S 43°47′W*
61 *D16* **Barra do Quaraí** Rio Grande do Sul, SE Brazil *31°03′S 58°10′W*
59 *G14* **Barra do São Manuel** Pará, N Brazil *07°12′S 58°03′W*
83 *N19* **Barra Falsa, Ponta da** *headland* S Mozambique *22°57′S 35°36′E*
96 *E10* **Barra Head** *headland* NW Scotland, United Kingdom *56°46′N 07°37′W*
60 *O9* **Barra Mansa** Rio de Janeiro, SE Brazil *22°25′S 44°03′W*
57 *D14* **Barranca** Lima, W Peru *10°46′S 77°46′W*
54 *F8* **Barrancabermeja** Santander, N Colombia *07°01′N 73°51′W*
54 *H4* **Barrancas** La Guajira, N Colombia *10°59′N 72°46′W*
54 *J6* **Barrancas** Barinas, NW Venezuela *08°47′N 70°07′W*
55 *Q6* **Barrancas** Monagas, NE Venezuela *08°45′N 62°12′W*
54 *F6* **Barranco de Loba** Bolívar, N Colombia *08°56′N 74°07′W*
104 *I12* **Barrancos** Beja, S Portugal *38°08′N 06°59′W*
62 *N7* **Barranqueras** Chaco, N Argentina *27°29′S 58°54′W*
54 *E4* **Barranquilla** Atlántico, N Colombia *10°59′N 74°48′W*
83 *N20* **Barra, Ponta da** *headland* S Mozambique *23°46′S 35°33′E*
105 *P11* **Barrax** Castilla-La Mancha, C Spain *39°04′N 02°12′W*
19 *N11* **Barre** Massachusetts, NE USA *42°24′N 72°06′W*
18 *M7* **Barre** Vermont, NE USA *44°09′N 72°25′W*
59 *M17* **Barreiras** Bahia, E Brazil *12°09′S 44°58′W*
104 *F11* **Barreiro** Setúbal, W Portugal *38°40′N 09°05′W*
65 *C26* **Barren Island** *island* S Falkland Islands
20 *K7* **Barren River Lake** ⊠ Kentucky, S USA
60 *L7* **Barretos** São Paulo, S Brazil *20°33′S 48°33′W*
11 *P14* **Barrhead** Alberta, SW Canada *54°10′N 114°22′W*
14 *G14* **Barrie** Ontario, S Canada *44°22′N 79°42′W*
11 *N16* **Barrière** British Columbia, SW Canada *51°10′N 120°06′W*
14 *H8* **Barrière, Lac** ◎ Québec, SE Canada
182 *L6* **Barrier Range** *hill range* New South Wales, SE Australia
42 *G3* **Barrier Reef** *reef* E Belize
188 *C16* **Barrigada** C Guam *13°27′N 144°48′E*
Barrington Island *see* Santa Fe, Isla
183 *T7* **Barrington Tops** ▲ New South Wales, SE Australia *32°06′S 151°18′E*
183 *O4* **Barringun** New South Wales, SE Australia *29°02′S 145°45′E*
59 *K18* **Barro Alto** Goiás, S Brazil *15°07′S 48°56′W*
59 *N14* **Barro Duro** Piauí, NE Brazil *05°49′S 42°30′W*
30 *I5* **Barron** Wisconsin, N USA *45°24′N 91°50′W*
14 *J12* **Barron** ≋ Ontario, SE Canada
61 *H15* **Barros Cassal** Rio Grande do Sul, S Brazil *29°12′S 52°33′W*
45 *P14* **Barrouallie** Saint Vincent , W Saint Vincent and the Grenadines *13°14′N 61°17′W*
39 *O4* **Barrow** Alaska, USA *71°17′N 156°47′W*
97 *E20* **Barrow** *Ir.* An Bhearú. ≋ SE Ireland
181 *Q6* **Barrow Creek Roadhouse** Northern Territory, N Australia *21°30′S 133°52′E*
97 *J16* **Barrow-in-Furness** NW England, United Kingdom *54°07′N 03°14′W*
180 *G7* **Barrow Island** *island* Western Australia
39 *O4* **Barrow, Point** *headland* Alaska, USA *71°23′N 156°28′W*
11 *V14* **Barrows** Manitoba, S Canada *52°49′N 101°36′W*
97 *J22* **Barry** S Wales, United Kingdom *51°24′N 03°18′W*
14 *J12* **Barry's Bay** Ontario, SE Canada *45°30′N 77°41′W*
144 *K14* **Barsakel'mes, Ostrov** *island* SW Kazakhstan
Baršć Łužyca *see* Forst
147 *S14* **Barsem** S Tajikistan *37°36′N 71°43′E*
145 *V11* **Barshatas** Vostochnyy Kazakhstan, E Kazakhstan *48°13′N 78°33′E*
155 *F14* **Bārsi** Mahārāshtra, W India *18°14′N 75°42′E*
100 *I13* **Barsinghausen** Niedersachsen, C Germany *53°19′N 09°30′E*
147 *X8* **Barskoon** Issyk-Kul'skaya Oblast', E Kyrgyzstan *42°07′N 77°34′E*
100 *F10* **Barssel** Niedersachsen, NW Germany *53°10′N 07°46′E*
35 *U14* **Barstow** California, W USA *34°52′N 117°00′W*
24 *L8* **Barstow** Texas, SW USA *31°27′N 103°23′W*
103 *R6* **Bar-sur-Aube** Aube, NE France *48°13′N 04°43′E*
Bar-sur-Ornain *see* Bar-le-Duc
103 *Q6* **Bar-sur-Seine** Aube, N France *48°06′N 04°22′E*
147 *S13* **Bartang** S Tajikistan *38°06′N 71°48′E*
147 *T13* **Bartang** ≋ SE Tajikistan
Bartenstein *see* Bartoszyce
Bártfa/Bartfeld *see* Bardejov
100 *N7* **Barth** Mecklenburg-Vorpommern, NE Germany *54°21′N 12°43′E*
27 *W13* **Bartholomew, Bayou** ≋ Arkansas/Louisiana, S USA
55 *T8* **Bartica** N Guyana *06°24′N 58°36′W*
136 *H10* **Bartın** Bartın, NW Turkey *41°37′N 32°20′E*
136 *H10* **Bartın** ⬖ *province* NW Turkey
181 *W4* **Bartle Frere** ▲ Queensland, E Australia *17°15′S 145°43′E*
27 *P8* **Bartlesville** Oklahoma, C USA *36°44′N 95°59′W*
29 *P14* **Bartlett** Nebraska, C USA *41°51′N 98°32′W*
20 *E10* **Bartlett** Tennessee, S USA *35°12′N 89°52′W*
25 *T9* **Bartlett** Texas, SW USA *30°47′N 97°25′W*
36 *L13* **Bartlett Reservoir** ⊠ Arizona, SW USA
19 *N6* **Barton** Vermont, NE USA *44°44′N 72°09′W*
110 *L7* **Bartoszyce** *Ger.* Bartenstein. Warmińsko-mazurskie, NE Poland *54°16′N 20°49′E*
23 *W12* **Bartow** Florida, SE USA *27°54′N 81°50′W*
Bartschin *see* Barcin
168 *J10* **Barumun, Sungai** ≋ Sumatera, W Indonesia
Barū, Nahr *see* Baro Wenz
169 *S17* **Barung, Nusa** *island* S Indonesia
168 *H9* **Barus** Sumatera, NW Indonesia *02°02′N 98°20′E*
162 *I9* **Baruunbayan-Ulaan** *var.* Höövör. Övörhangay, C Mongolia *45°10′N 101°19′E*
Baruunsuu *see* Tsogttsetsiy
163 *P8* **Baruun-Urt** Sühbaatar, E Mongolia *46°40′N 113°17′E*
43 *P15* **Barú, Volcán** *var.* Volcán de Chiriquí. Ѫ W Panama *08°49′N 82°32′W*
99 *K21* **Barvaux** Luxembourg, SE Belgium *50°21′N 05°30′E*
42 *M13* **Barva, Volcán** Ѫ NW Costa Rica *10°07′N 84°08′W*
117 *W6* **Barvinkove** Kharkivs'ka Oblast', E Ukraine *48°54′N 37°03′E*
154 *G11* **Barwāh** Madhya Pradesh, C India *22°17′N 76°01′E*
Bärwalde Neumark *see* Mieszkowice
154 *F11* **Barwāni** Madhya Pradesh, C India *22°02′N 74°56′E*
183 *P5* **Barwon River** ≋ New South Wales, SE Australia
119 *L15* **Barysaw** *Rus.* Borisov. Minskaya Voblasts', NE Belarus *54°14′N 28°30′E*
127 *Q6* **Barysh** Ul'yanovskaya Oblast', W Russian Federation *53°32′N 47°06′E*
117 *Q4* **Baryshivka** Kyyivs'ka Oblast', N Ukraine *50°21′N 31°21′E*
79 *J17* **Basankusu** Equateur, NW Dem. Rep. Congo *01°12′N 19°50′E*
117 *N11* **Basarabeasca** *Rus.* Bessarabka. SE Moldova *46°22′N 28°56′E*
116 *M14* **Basarabi** Constanța, SW Romania *44°10′N 28°26′E*
40 *H6* **Basaseachic** Chihuahua, NW Mexico *28°18′N 108°13′W*
Basauri *see* Arizgoiti
61 *D18* **Basavilbaso** Entre Ríos, E Argentina *32°23′S 58°55′W*
79 *F21* **Bas-Congo** *off.* Région du Bas-Congo; *prev.* Bas-Zaïre. ⬖ *region* SW Dem. Rep. Congo
108 *E6* **Basel** *Eng.* Basle, *Fr.* Bâle. Basel Stadt, NW Switzerland *47°33′N 07°36′E*
Baselland *see* Basel Landschaft
108 *E7* **Basel Landschaft** *prev.* Baselland ⬖ *canton* NW Switzerland
108 *E6* **Basel Stadt** ⬖ *canton* NW Switzerland
143 *T14* **Bashākerd, Kūhhā-ye** ▲▲ SE Iran
11 *Q15* **Bashaw** Alberta, SW Canada *52°40′N 112°53′W*
146 *K16* **Bashbedeng** Mary Welaýaty, S Turkmenistan *35°44′N 63°07′E*
161 *T15* **Bashi Channel** *Chin.* Pa-shih Hai-hsia. *channel* Philippines/Taiwan
Bashkiria *see* Bashkortostan, Respublika
122 *F11* **Bashkortostan, Respublika** *prev.* Bashkiria. ⬖ *autonomous republic* W Russian Federation
127 *N6* **Bashmakovo** Penzenskaya Oblast', W Russian Federation *53°13′N 43°00′E*
146 *J10* **Bashsakarba** Lebap Welaýaty, NE Turkmenistan *40°25′N 62°16′E*
117 *R9* **Bashtanka** Mykolayivs'ka Oblast', S Ukraine *47°24′N 32°27′E*
22 *H8* **Basile** Louisiana, S USA *30°29′N 92°36′W*
107 *M18* **Basilicata** ⬖ *region* S Italy
33 *V13* **Basin** Wyoming, C USA *44°22′N 108°02′W*
97 *N22* **Basingstoke** S England, United Kingdom *51°16′N 01°08′W*
143 *U8* **Başīrān** Khorāsān-e Janūbī, E Iran *31°57′N 59°07′E*

◆ Country
● Country Capital
◇ Dependent Territory
○ Dependent Territory Capital
⬖ Administrative Regions
✈ International Airport
▲ Mountain
▲▲ Mountain Range
Ѫ Volcano
≋ River
◎ Lake
⊠ Reservoir

112 B10 **Baška** *It.* Bescanuova. Primorje-Gorski Kotar, NW Croatia 44°58′N 14°46′E
137 T15 **Başkale** Van, SE Turkey 38°03′N 43°59′E
14 L10 **Baskatong, Réservoir** ⊞ Québec, SE Canada
137 O14 **Baskil** Elazığ, E Turkey 38°38′N 38°47′E
Basle *see* Basel
154 H9 **Bāsoda** Madhya Pradesh, C India 23°54′N 77°58′E
79 L17 **Basoko** Orientale, N Dem. Rep. Congo 01°14′N 23°26′E
Basque Country, The *see* País Vasco
Basra *see* Al Başrah
103 U5 **Bas-Rhin** ◈ *department* NE France
Bassam *see* Grand-Bassam
11 Q16 **Bassano** Alberta, SW Canada 50°48′N 112°28′W
106 H7 **Bassano del Grappa** Veneto, NE Italy 45°45′N 11°45′E
77 Q15 **Bassar** *var.* Bassari. NW Togo 09°15′N 00°47′E
Bassari *see* Bassar
172 L9 **Bassas da India** *island group* W Madagascar
108 D7 **Bassecourt** Jura, W Switzerland 47°20′N 07°16′E
Bassein *see* Pathein
79 J15 **Basse-Kotto** ◈ *prefecture* S Central African Republic
102 J5 **Basse-Normandie** *Eng.* Lower Normandy. ◈ *region* N France
45 Q11 **Basse-Pointe** N Martinique 14°52′N 61°07′W
76 H12 **Basse Santa Su** E Gambia 13°18′N 14°10′W
Basse-Saxe *see* Niedersachsen
45 X6 **Basse-Terre** ○ (Guadeloupe) Basse Terre, SW Guadeloupe 16°08′N 61°40′W
45 V10 **Basseterre** ● (Saint Kitts and Nevis) Saint Kitts, Saint Kitts and Nevis 17°16′N 62°45′W
45 X6 **Basse Terre** *island* W Guadeloupe
29 O13 **Bassett** Nebraska, C USA 42°34′N 99°32′W
21 S7 **Bassett** Virginia, NE USA 36°45′N 79°59′W
37 N15 **Bassett Peak** ▲ Arizona, SW USA 32°30′N 110°16′W
76 M10 **Bassikounou** Hodh ech Chargui, SE Mauritania 15°55′N 05°59′W
77 R15 **Bassila** W Benin 08°25′N 01°58′E
Bass, Îlots de *see* Marotiri
31 O11 **Bass Lake** Indiana, N USA 41°12′N 86°35′W
183 O14 **Bass Strait** *strait* SE Australia
100 H11 **Bassum** Niedersachsen, NW Germany 52°52′N 08°44′E
29 X3 **Basswood Lake** ◎ Canada/USA
95 J21 **Båstad** Skåne, S Sweden 56°25′N 12°50′E
139 U2 **Basţah** As Sulaymānīyah, E Iraq 36°20′N 45°14′E
153 N12 **Basti** Uttar Pradesh, N India 26°48′N 82°44′E
103 X14 **Bastia** Corse, France, C Mediterranean Sea 42°42′N 09°27′E
99 L23 **Bastogne** Luxembourg, SE Belgium 50°N 05°43′E
22 I5 **Bastrop** Louisiana, S USA 32°46′N 91°54′W
25 T11 **Bastrop** Texas, SW USA 30°07′N 97°21′W
93 J15 **Bastuträsk** Västerbotten, N Sweden 64°47′N 20°05′E
119 J19 **Bastyn’** *Rus.* Bostyn’. Brestskaya Voblasts’, SW Belarus 52°23′N 26°45′E
Basuo *see* Dongfang
Basutoland *see* Lesotho
119 O15 **Basya** ≈ E Belarus
Bas-Zaïre *see* Bas-Congo
79 D17 **Bata** NW Equatorial Guinea 01°51′N 09°48′E
79 D17 **Bata** ✈ S Equatorial Guinea 01°55′N 09°48′E
Batae Coritanorum *see* Leicester
123 Q8 **Batagay** Respublika Sakha (Yakutiya), NE Russian Federation 67°36′N 134°44′E
123 P8 **Batagay-Alyta** Respublika Sakha (Yakutiya), NE Russian Federation 67°48′N 130°15′E
112 L10 **Batajnica** Vojvodina, N Serbia 44°55′N 20°17′E
136 H15 **Bataklık Gölü** ◎ S Turkey
114 H11 **Batak, Yazovir** ⊞ SW Bulgaria
152 H7 **Batāla** Punjab, N India 31°48′N 75°12′E
104 F9 **Batalha** Leiria, C Portugal 39°40′N 08°50′W
79 N17 **Batama** Orientale, NE Dem. Rep. Congo 0°54′N 26°25′E
123 Q10 **Batamay** Respublika Sakha (Yakutiya), NE Russian Federation 63°28′N 129°33′E
160 F9 **Batang** *var.* Bazhong. Sichuan, C China 30°04′N 99°10′E
79 I14 **Batangafo** Ouham, NW Central African Republic 07°19′N 18°22′E
171 P8 **Batangas** *off.* Batangas City. Luzon, N Philippines 13°47′N 121°03′E
Batangas City *see* Batangas
Bătania *see* Battonya
171 Q10 **Batan Islands** *island group* N Philippines
60 L8 **Batatais** São Paulo, S Brazil 20°54′S 47°37′W
18 E10 **Batavia** New York, NE USA 43°00′N 78°11′W
Batavia *see* Jakarta
173 T9 **Batavia Seamount** *undersea feature* E Indian Ocean 27°42′S 100°36′E
126 L12 **Bataysk** Rostovskaya Oblast’, SW Russian Federation 47°10′N 39°46′E
14 B9 **Batchawana** ≈ Ontario, S Canada
14 B9 **Batchawana Bay** Ontario, S Canada 46°55′N 84°36′W
167 Q12 **Bătdâmbâng** *prev.* Battambang. Bătdâmbâng, NW Cambodia 13°06′N 103°13′E
79 G20 **Batéké, Plateaux** *plateau* S Congo
183 S11 **Batemans Bay** New South Wales, SE Australia 35°45′S 150°09′E
21 Q13 **Batesburg** South Carolina, SE USA 33°54′N 81°33′W
28 K12 **Batesland** South Dakota, N USA 43°05′N 102°07′W
27 V10 **Batesville** Arkansas, C USA 35°45′N 91°39′W
31 Q14 **Batesville** Indiana, N USA 39°18′N 85°13′W
22 L2 **Batesville** Mississippi, S USA 34°18′N 89°56′W
25 Q13 **Batesville** Texas, SW USA 28°56′N 99°38′W
44 L13 **Bath** E Jamaica 17°57′N 76°22′W
97 L22 **Bath** *hist.* Akermanceaster; *anc.* Aquae Calidae, Aquae Solis. SW England, United Kingdom 51°23′N 02°22′W
19 Q8 **Bath** Maine, NE USA 43°54′N 69°49′W
18 F11 **Bath** New York, NE USA 42°20′N 77°16′W
Bath *see* Berkeley Springs
78 I10 **Batha** *off.* Préfecture du Batha. ◈ *prefecture* C Chad
78 I10 **Batha** *seasonal river* C Chad
Batha, Préfecture du *see* Batha
141 Y8 **Baţhā’, Wādī al** *dry watercourse* NE Oman
152 H9 **Bathinda** Punjab, NW India 30°14′N 74°54′E
98 M11 **Bathmen** Overijssel, E Netherlands 52°15′N 06°16′E
45 Z14 **Bathsheba** E Barbados 13°13′N 59°31′W
183 R8 **Bathurst** New South Wales, SE Australia 33°32′S 149°35′E
13 O13 **Bathurst** New Brunswick, SE Canada 47°37′N 65°40′W
Bathurst *see* Banjul
8 H6 **Bathurst, Cape** *headland* Northwest Territories, NW Canada 70°33′N 128°00′W
196 L8 **Bathurst Inlet** Nunavut, N Canada 66°23′N 107°00′W
196 L8 **Bathurst Inlet** *inlet* Nunavut, N Canada
181 N1 **Bathurst Island** *island* Northern Territory, N Australia
197 O9 **Bathurst Island** *island* Parry Islands, Nunavut, N Canada
77 O14 **Batié** SW Burkina 09°53′N 02°53′W
Batinah *see* Al Bāţinah
141 Y9 **Bāţin, Wādī al** *dry watercourse* SW Asia
15 P9 **Batiscan** ≈ Québec, SE Canada
136 F16 **BatıToroslar** ▲▲ SW Turkey
Batjan *see* Bacan, Pulau
147 R11 **Batken** Batenskaya Oblast’, SW Kyrgyzstan 40°03′N 70°50′E
Batken Oblasty *see* Batkenskaya Oblast’
147 Q11 **Batkenskaya Oblast’** *Kir.* Batken Oblasty. ◈ *province* SW Kyrgyzstan
Batlle y Ordóñez *see* José Batlle y Ordóñez
183 Q10 **Batlow** New South Wales, SE Australia 35°32′S 148°09′E
137 Q15 **Batman** *var.* İluh. Batman, SE Turkey 37°52′N 41°06′E
137 Q15 **Batman** ◈ *province* SE Turkey
74 L6 **Batna** NE Algeria 35°34′N 06°10′E
163 O7 **Batnorov** *var.* Dundbürd. Hentiy, E Mongolia 47°55′N 111°37′E
Batoe *see* Batu, Kepulauan
162 K7 **Bat-Öldziy** *var.* Övt. Övörhangay, C Mongolia 46°50′N 102°15′E
Bat-Öldziyt *see* Dzaamar
22 J8 **Baton Rouge** *state capital* Louisiana, S USA 30°28′N 91°09′W
79 G15 **Batouri** Est, E Cameroon 04°26′N 14°27′E
138 G14 **Batrā’, Jibāl al** ▲▲ S Jordan
138 G6 **Batroûn** *var.* Al Batrūn. N Lebanon 34°15′N 35°42′E
Batsch *see* Bač
Batsevichi *see* Batsevichy
119 M17 **Batsevichy** *Rus.* Batsevichi. Mahilyowskaya Voblasts’, E Belarus 53°24′N 29°14′E
92 M7 **Båtsfjord** Finnmark, N Norway 70°37′N 29°42′E
Batshireet *see* Hentiy
162 L7 **Batsümber** *var.* Mandal. Töv, C Mongolia 48°24′N 106°47′E
Battambang *see* Bătdâmbâng
195 X3 **Batterbee, Cape** *headland* Antarctica
155 L24 **Batticaloa** Eastern Province, E Sri Lanka 07°44′N 81°43′E
99 L19 **Battice** Liège, E Belgium 50°39′N 05°50′E
107 L18 **Battipaglia** Campania, S Italy 40°36′N 14°59′E
11 R15 **Battle** ≈ Alberta/Saskatchewan, SW Canada
Battle Born State *see* Nevada
31 Q10 **Battle Creek** Michigan, N USA 42°20′N 85°10′W
27 T7 **Battlefield** Missouri, C USA 37°07′N 93°22′W
11 S15 **Battleford** Saskatchewan, S Canada 52°45′N 108°20′W
29 S6 **Battle Lake** Minnesota, N USA 46°16′N 95°42′W
35 U3 **Battle Mountain** Nevada, W USA 40°37′N 116°55′W
111 M25 **Battonya** *Rom.* Bătania. Békés, SE Hungary 46°16′N 21°00′E
162 J7 **Battsengel** *var.* Jargalant. Arhangay, C Mongolia 47°46′N 101°56′E
168 D11 **Batu, Kepulauan** *prev.* Batoe. *island group* W Indonesia
137 Q10 **Batumi** W Georgia 41°39′N 41°38′E
168 K10 **Batu Pahat** *prev.* Bandar Penggaram. Johor, Peninsular Malaysia 01°51′N 102°56′E
171 O12 **Baturebe** Sulawesi, N Indonesia 01°43′S 121°43′E
122 J12 **Baturino** Tomskaya Oblast’, C Russian Federation 57°46′N 85°08′E
117 R3 **Baturyn** Chernihivs’ka Oblast’, N Ukraine 51°20′N 32°54′E
138 F10 **Bat Yam** Tel Aviv, C Israel 32°01′N 34°45′E
127 Q4 **Batyrevo** Chuvashskaya Respublika, W Russian Federation 55°04′N 47°34′E
Batys Qazaqstan Oblysy *see* Zapadnyy Kazakhstan
102 F5 **Batz, Île de** *island* NW France
169 Q10 **Bau** Sarawak, East Malaysia 01°25′N 110°10′E
171 N2 **Bauang** Luzon, N Philippines 16°33′N 120°19′E
171 P14 **Baubau** *var.* Baoebaoe. Pulau Buton, C Indonesia 05°30′S 122°37′E
77 W14 **Bauchi** Bauchi, NE Nigeria 10°18′N 09°46′E
77 W14 **Bauchi** ◈ *state* C Nigeria
102 H7 **Baud** Morbihan, NW France 47°52′N 02°59′W
29 T2 **Baudette** Minnesota, N USA 48°42′N 94°36′W
193 S9 **Bauer Basin** *undersea feature* E Pacific Ocean 10°00′S 101°45′W
187 R14 **Bauer Field** *var.* Port Vila. ✈ (Port-Vila) Éfaté, C Vanuatu 17°42′S 168°21′E
13 T9 **Bauld, Cape** *headland* Newfoundland and Labrador, E Canada 51°35′N 55°22′W
103 T8 **Baume-les-Dames** Doubs, E France 47°22′N 06°20′E
101 I15 **Baunatal** Hessen, C Germany 51°15′N 09°25′E
107 D18 **Baunei** Sardegna, Italy, C Mediterranean Sea 40°04′N 09°36′E
57 M15 **Baures, Río** ≈ N Bolivia
60 K9 **Bauru** São Paulo, S Brazil 22°19′S 49°07′W
Baushar *see* Bawshar
118 G10 **Bauska** *Ger.* Bauske. S Latvia 56°25′N 24°11′E
Bauske *see* Bauska
101 Q15 **Bautzen** *Lus.* Budyšin. Sachsen, E Germany 51°11′N 14°29′E
145 Q16 **Bauyrzhan Momyshuly** *Kaz.* Baūyrzhan Momyshuly; *prev.* Burnoye. Zhambyl, S Kazakhstan 42°36′N 70°46′E
Bauzanum *see* Bolzano
Bavaria *see* Bayern
109 N7 **Bavarian Alps** *Ger.* Bayrische Alpen. ▲▲ Austria/Germany
Bavière *see* Bayern
40 H4 **Bavispe, Río** ≈ NW Mexico
127 T5 **Bavly** Respublika Tatarstan, W Russian Federation 54°20′N 53°21′E
169 P13 **Bawal, Pulau** *island* N Indonesia
169 T12 **Bawan** Borneo, C Indonesia 01°36′S 113°55′E
183 O12 **Baw Baw, Mount** ▲ Victoria, SE Australia 37°49′S 146°16′E
169 S15 **Bawean, Pulau** *island* S Indonesia
75 V9 **Bawīţī** *var.* Bawîti. N Egypt 28°19′N 28°53′E
Bawîti *see* Bawīţī
77 Q13 **Bawku** N Ghana 11°00′N 00°12′W
Bawlake *see* Bawlakhe
167 N7 **Bawlakhe** *var.* Bawlake. Kayah State, C Myanmar (Burma) 19°10′N 97°19′E
169 H11 **Bawo Ofuloa** Pulau Tanahmasa, W Indonesia 0°10′S 98°24′E
141 Y8 **Bawshar** *var.* Baushar. NE Oman 23°32′N 58°24′E
Ba Xian *see* Bazhou
Baxian *see* Bazhou
158 M8 **Baxkorgan** Xinjiang Uygur Zizhiqu, W China 39°05′N 90°00′E
23 V6 **Baxley** Georgia, SE USA 31°46′N 82°21′W
159 R15 **Baxoi** *var.* Baima. Xizang Zizhiqu, W China 30°01′N 96°53′E
29 W14 **Baxter** Iowa, C USA 41°49′N 93°09′W
29 U6 **Baxter** Minnesota, N USA 46°21′N 94°18′W
27 R8 **Baxter Springs** Kansas, C USA 37°01′N 94°45′W
81 M17 **Bay** *off.* Gobolka Bay. ◈ *region* SW Somalia
Bay *see* Baicheng
44 H7 **Bayamo** Granma, E Cuba 20°21′N 76°38′W
45 U5 **Bayamón** E Puerto Rico 18°24′N 66°09′W
163 W8 **Bayan** Heilongjiang, NE China 46°05′N 127°24′E
170 L16 **Bayan** *prev.* Bajan. Pulau Lombok, C Indonesia 08°16′S 116°28′E
162 M8 **Bayan** *var.* Maanīt. Töv, C Mongolia 47°14′N 107°34′E
Bayan *see* Hölönbuyr, Dornod, Mongolia
Bayan *see* Ihhet, Dornogovĭ, Mongolia
Bayan *see* Bayan-Uul, Govĭ-Altay, Mongolia
Bayan *see* Bayanhutag, Hentiy, Mongolia
Bayan *see* Bürentogtoh, Hövsgol, Mongolia
152 I12 **Bayāna** Rājasthān, N India 26°55′N 77°18′E
149 N5 **Bāyān, Band-e** ▲▲ C Afghanistan
162 H8 **Bayanbulag** Bayanhongor, C Mongolia 46°46′N 98°07′E
Bayanbulag *see* Ömnödelger
158 J5 **Bayanbulak** Xinjiang Uygur Zizhiqu, W China 43°05′N 84°05′E
162 L7 **Bayanchandmanĭ** *var.* Ihsüüj. Töv, C Mongolia 48°12′N 106°23′E
162 J11 **Bayandalay** *var.* Dalay. Ömnögovĭ, S Mongolia 43°27′N 103°30′E
163 O9 **Bayandelger** *var.* Shireet. Sühbaatar, SE Mongolia 45°33′N 112°19′E
162 I5 **Bayandzürh** *var.* Altraga. Hövsgöl, N Mongolia 50°08′N 98°54′E
Bayan Gol *see* Dengkou, China
Bayangol *see* Bugat, Mongolia
162 I9 **Bayangovĭ** *var.* Örgön. Bayanhongor, C Mongolia 44°43′N 100°23′E
159 R12 **Bayan Har Shan** *var.* Bayan Khar. ▲▲ C China
162 G6 **Bayanhayrhan** *var.* Altanbulag. Dzavhan, N Mongolia 49°16′N 96°22′E
162 I8 **Bayanhongor** Bayanhongor, C Mongolia 46°08′N 100°42′E
162 H9 **Bayanhongor** ◈ *province* C Mongolia
162 K14 **Bayan Hot** *var.* Alxa Zuoqi. Nei Mongol Zizhiqu, N China 38°49′N 105°40′E
163 O8 **Bayanhutag** *var.* Bayan. Hentiy, C Mongolia 47°13′N 110°57′E
163 T9 **Bayan Huxu** *var.* Horqin Zuoyi Zhongqi. Nei Mongol Zizhiqu, N China 45°02′N 121°28′E
Bayan Khar *see* Bayan Har Shan
163 N12 **Bayan Kuang** *prev.* Bayan Obo. Nei Mongol Zizhiqu, N China 41°45′N 109°58′E
168 J7 **Bayan Lepas** ✈ (George Town) Pinang, Peninsular Malaysia 05°18′N 100°15′E
162 I10 **Bayanlig** *var.* Hatansuudal. Bayanhongor, C Mongolia 44°34′N 100°41′E
162 K13 **Bayan Mod** Nei Mongol Zizhiqu, N China 40°45′N 104°29′E
163 N8 **Bayanmönh** *var.* Ulaan-Ereg. Hentiy, E Mongolia 46°50′N 109°39′E
162 L12 **Bayannur** *var.* Linhe. Nei Mongol Zizhiqu, N China 40°46′N 107°27′E
Bayan Nuru *see* Xar Burd
162 E5 **Bayannuur** *var.* Tsul-Ulaan. Bayan-Ölgiy, W Mongolia 48°51′N 91°13′E
Bayan Obo *see* Bayan Kuang
43 V15 **Bayano, Lago** ◎ E Panama
162 C5 **Bayan-Ölgiy** ◈ *province* NW Mongolia
162 H9 **Bayan-Öndör** *var.* Bulgan. Bayanhongor, C Mongolia 44°48′N 98°39′E
162 K8 **Bayan-Öndör** *var.* Bumbat. Övörhangay, C Mongolia 46°30′N 104°08′E
162 L8 **Bayan-Önjüül** *var.* Ihhayrhan. Töv, C Mongolia 46°57′N 105°51′E
163 O7 **Bayan-Ovoo** *var.* Javhlant. Hentiy, E Mongolia 47°46′N 112°06′E
162 L11 **Bayan-Ovoo** *var.* Erdenetsogt. Ömnögovĭ, S Mongolia 42°54′N 106°16′E
Bayansayr *see* Baatsagaan
159 Q9 **Bayan Shan** ▲ C China 37°36′N 96°23′E
162 J9 **Bayanteeg** Övörhangay, C Mongolia 45°39′N 101°30′E
162 G5 **Bayantes** *var.* Altay. Dzavhan, N Mongolia 49°40′N 96°21′E
Bayantöhöm *see* Büren
162 M8 **Bayantsagaan** *var.* Dzogsool. Töv, C Mongolia 46°46′N 107°18′E
163 P7 **Bayantümen** *var.* Tsagaanders. Dornod, NE Mongolia 48°03′N 114°16′E
Bayan-Uhaa *see* Ih-Uul
163 R10 **Bayan Ul** *var.* Xi Ujimqin Qi. Nei Mongol Zizhiqu, N China 44°31′N 117°36′E
Bayan-Ulaan *see* Dzüünbayan-Ulaan
163 O7 **Bayan-Uul** *var.* Javarthushuu. Dornod, NE Mongolia 49°05′N 112°40′E
162 F7 **Bayan-Uul** *var.* Bayan. Govĭ-Altay, W Mongolia 47°05′N 95°13′E
162 M8 **Bayanuur** *var.* Tsul-Ulaan. Töv, C Mongolia 47°44′N 108°22′E
28 J14 **Bayard** Nebraska, C USA 41°45′N 103°19′W
37 P15 **Bayard** New Mexico, SW USA 32°45′N 108°07′W
103 T13 **Bayard, Col** *pass* SE France
Bayasgalant *see* Mönhhaan
136 J12 **Bayat** Çorum, N Turkey 40°34′N 34°07′E
171 P6 **Bayawan** Negros, C Philippines 09°22′N 122°50′E
143 R10 **Bayāz** Kermān, C Iran 30°41′N 55°29′E
171 Q6 **Baybay** Leyte, C Philippines 10°41′N 124°49′E
21 X10 **Bayboro** North Carolina, SE USA 35°08′N 76°49′W
137 P12 **Bayburt** Bayburt, NE Turkey 40°15′N 40°16′E
137 P12 **Bayburt** ◈ *province* NE Turkey
31 R8 **Bay City** Michigan, N USA 43°35′N 83°52′W
25 V12 **Bay City** Texas, SW USA 28°59′N 96°00′W
Baydarata Bay *see* Baydaratskaya Guba
122 J7 **Baydaratskaya Guba** *var.* Baydarata Bay. *bay* N Russian Federation
81 M16 **Baydhabo** *var.* Baydhowa, Isha Baydhabo, *It.* Baidoa. Bay, SW Somalia 03°08′N 43°39′E
Baydhowa *see* Baydhabo
101 N21 **Bayerischer Wald** ▲▲ SE Germany
101 K21 **Bayern** *Eng.* Bavaria, *Fr.* Bavière. ◈ *state* SE Germany
147 V9 **Bayetovo** Narynskaya Oblast’, C Kyrgyzstan 41°14′N 74°55′E
102 K4 **Bayeux** *anc.* Augustodurum. Calvados, N France 49°16′N 00°42′W
14 E15 **Bayfield** ≈ Ontario, S Canada
145 O15 **Baygekum** *Kaz.* Bäygequm. Kzylorda, S Kazakhstan 44°15′N 66°34′E
Bäygequm *see* Baygekum
136 C14 **Bayındır** Izmır, SW Turkey 38°12′N 27°40′E
138 H12 **Bāyir** *var.* Bā’ir. Ma‘ān, S Jordan 30°46′N 36°40′E
Bay Islands *see* Bahía, Islas de la
Bayizhen *see* Nyingchi
139 R5 **Bayjī** *var.* Baiji. Şalāḩ ad Dīn, N Iraq 34°56′N 43°29′E
Baykadam *see* Saudakent
123 N13 **Baykal, Ozero** *Eng.* Lake Baikal. ◎ S Russian Federation
123 M14 **Baykal’sk** Irkutskaya Oblast’, S Russian Federation 51°30′N 104°03′E
137 R15 **Baykan** Siirt, SE Turkey 38°08′N 41°43′E
123 L11 **Baykit** Krasnoyarskiy Kray, C Russian Federation 61°37′N 96°23′E
145 N12 **Baykonur** *var.* Baykonyr. Karaganda, C Kazakhstan 47°50′N 75°33′E
Baykonur *see* Baykonyr
144 M14 **Baykonyr** *var.* Baykonur, *Kaz.* Bayqongyr; *prev.* Leninsk. Kzylorda, S Kazakhstan 45°38′N 63°20′E
Baykonyr *see* Baykonur
158 E7 **Baykurt** Xinjiang Uygur Zizhiqu, W China 39°56′N 75°33′E
14 I9 **Bay, Lac** ◎ Québec, SE Canada
127 W6 **Baymak** Respublika Bashkortostan, W Russian Federation 52°34′N 58°20′E
23 O8 **Bay Minette** Alabama, S USA 30°52′N 87°46′W
143 O17 **Baynūnah** *desert* W United Arab Emirates
184 O8 **Bay of Plenty** *off.* Bay of Plenty Region. ◈ *region* North Island, New Zealand
Bay of Plenty Region *see* Bay of Plenty
191 Z3 **Bay of Wrecks** *bay* Kiritimati, E Kiribati
Bayonnaise Rocks *see* Beyonēsu-retsugan
102 I15 **Bayonne** *anc.* Lapurdum. Pyrénées-Atlantiques, SW France 43°30′N 01°28′W
22 H4 **Bayou D’Arbonne Lake** ⊞ Louisiana, S USA
23 N9 **Bayou La Batre** Alabama, S USA 30°24′N 88°15′W
Bayou State *see* Mississippi
Bayqadam *see* Saudakent
Bayqongyr *see* Baykonyr
Bayram-Ali *see* Baýramaly
146 J14 **Baýramaly** *var.* Bayramaly; *prev.* Bayram-Ali. Mary Welaýaty, S Turkmenistan 37°33′N 62°08′E
101 L19 **Bayreuth** *var.* Baireuth. Bayern, SE Germany 49°57′N 11°34′E
Bayrische Alpen *see* Bavarian Alps
Bayrūt *see* Beyrouth
22 L9 **Bay Saint Louis** Mississippi, S USA 30°18′N 89°19′W
Baysān *see* Beit She’an
Bayshint *see* Öndörshireet
14 H13 **Bays, Lake of** ◎ Ontario, S Canada
22 M6 **Bay Springs** Mississippi, S USA 31°58′N 89°17′W
Bay State *see* Massachusetts
Baysun *see* Boysun
14 H13 **Baysville** Ontario, S Canada 45°10′N 79°03′W
141 N15 **Bayt al Faqīh** W Yemen 14°30′N 43°20′E
158 M4 **Baytik Shan** ▲▲ China/Mongolia
Bayt Laḩm *see* Bethlehem
25 W11 **Baytown** Texas, SW USA 29°43′N 94°59′W
169 V11 **Bayur, Tanjung** *headland* Borneo, N Indonesia 0°43′S 117°32′E
121 N14 **Bayy al Kabīr, Wādī** *dry watercourse* NW Libya
145 P17 **Bayyrkum** *Kaz.* Bayyrqum; *prev.* Bairkum. Yuzhnyy Kazakhstan, S Kazakhstan 41°57′N 68°05′E
Bayyrqum *see* Bayyrkum
105 P14 **Baza** Andalucía, S Spain 37°30′N 02°45′W
137 X10 **Bazardüzü Dağı** *Rus.* Gora Bazardyuzyu. ▲ N Azerbaijan 41°13′N 47°50′E
Bazardyuzyu, Gora *see* Bazardüzü Dağı
Bazargic *see* Dobrich
83 N18 **Bazaruto, Ilha do** *island* SE Mozambique
102 K14 **Bazas** Gironde, SW France 44°27′N 00°11′W
105 O14 **Baza, Sierra de** ▲▲ S Spain
160 J8 **Bazhong** *var.* Bazhou. Sichuan, C China 31°55′N 106°44′E
Bazhong *see* Batang
161 P3 **Bazhou** *prev.* Baxian, Ba Xian. Hebei, E China 39°05′N 116°24′E
Bazhou *see* Bazhong
14 M9 **Bazin** ≈ Québec, SE Canada
Bazin *see* Pezinok
139 Q7 **Bāzīyah** Al Anbār, C Iraq 33°50′N 42°41′E
138 H6 **Bcharré** *var.* Bcharreh, Bsharrī, Bsherri. NE Lebanon 34°16′N 36°01′E
Bcharreh *see* Bcharré
28 J5 **Beach** North Dakota, N USA 46°55′N 104°00′W
182 K12 **Beachport** South Australia 37°29′S 140°03′E
97 O23 **Beachy Head** *headland* SE England, United Kingdom 50°44′N 00°16′E
18 K13 **Beacon** New York, NE USA 41°30′N 73°54′W
63 J25 **Beagle Channel** *channel* Argentina/Chile
181 O1 **Beagle Gulf** *gulf* Northern Territory, N Australia
Bealach an Doirín *see* Ballaghaderreen
Bealach Cláir *see* Ballyclare
Bealach Féich *see* Ballybofey
172 J3 **Bealanana** Mahajanga, NE Madagascar 14°33′S 48°44′E
Béal an Átha *see* Ballina
Béal an Átha Móir *see* Ballinamore
Béal an Mhuirhead *see* Belmullet
Béal Átha Beithe *see* Ballybay
Béal Átha Conaill *see* Ballyconnell
Beál Átha hAmhnais *see* Ballyhaunis
Béal Átha na Sluaighe *see* Ballinasloe
Béal Átha Seanaidh *see* Ballyshannon
Bealdovuopmi *see* Peltovuoma
Béal Feirste *see* Belfast
Béal Tairbirt *see* Belturbet
Beanna Boirche *see* Mourne Mountains
Beannchar *see* Banagher, Ireland
Beannchar *see* Bangor, Northern Ireland, UK
Beanntraí *see* Bantry
Bearalváhki *see* Berlevåg
23 N2 **Bear Creek** ≈ Alabama/Mississippi, S USA
30 J13 **Bear Creek** ≈ Illinois, N USA
27 U13 **Bearden** Arkansas, C USA 33°43′N 92°37′W
195 Q10 **Beardmore Glacier** *glacier* Antarctica
30 K13 **Beardstown** Illinois, N USA 40°01′N 90°25′W
28 L14 **Bear Hill** ▲ Nebraska, C USA 41°24′N 101°49′W
Bear Island *see* Bjørnøya
14 H12 **Bear Lake** Ontario, S Canada 45°28′N 79°31′W
36 M1 **Bear Lake** ◎ Idaho/Utah, NW USA
39 U11 **Bear, Mount** ▲ Alaska, USA 61°16′N 141°09′W
102 J16 **Béarn** *cultural region* SW France
194 J11 **Bear Peninsula** *peninsula* Antarctica
152 I7 **Beās** ≈ India/Pakistan
105 P3 **Beasain** País Vasco, N Spain 43°03′N 02°11′W
105 O12 **Beas de Segura** Andalucía, S Spain 38°16′N 02°54′W
45 N10 **Beata, Cabo** *headland* SW Dominican Republic 17°34′N 71°25′W
45 N10 **Beata, Isla** *island* SW Dominican Republic
64 F11 **Beata Ridge** *undersea feature* N Caribbean Sea 16°00′N 72°30′W
29 R17 **Beatrice** Nebraska, C USA 40°14′N 96°43′W
83 L16 **Beatrice** Mashonaland East, NE Zimbabwe 18°15′S 30°55′E
11 N11 **Beatton** ≈ British Columbia, W Canada
11 N11 **Beatton River** British Columbia, W Canada 57°35′N 121°45′W
35 V10 **Beatty** Nevada, W USA 36°53′N 116°44′W
21 N6 **Beattyville** Kentucky, S USA 37°33′N 83°44′W
173 X16 **Beau Bassin** W Mauritius 20°13′S 57°27′E
103 R15 **Beaucaire** Gard, S France 43°49′N 04°37′E
14 I8 **Beauchastel, Lac** ◎ Québec, SE Canada
14 I10 **Beauchêne, Lac** ◎ Québec, SE Canada
183 V3 **Beaudesert** Queensland, E Australia 28°00′S 152°27′E
182 M12 **Beaufort** Victoria, SE Australia 37°27′S 143°24′E
21 X11 **Beaufort** North Carolina, SE USA 34°44′N 76°41′W
21 R15 **Beaufort** South Carolina, SE USA 32°23′N 80°40′W
38 M11 **Beaufort Sea** *sea* Arctic Ocean
Beaufort-Wes *see* Beaufort West
83 G25 **Beaufort West** *Afr.* Beaufort-Wes. Western Cape, SW South Africa 32°21′S 22°35′E
103 N7 **Beaugency** Loiret, C France 47°46′N 01°38′E
19 R1 **Beau Lake** ⊞ Maine, NE USA
96 I8 **Beauly** N Scotland, United Kingdom 57°29′N 04°29′W
99 G21 **Beaumont** Hainaut, S Belgium 50°12′N 04°13′E
185 E23 **Beaumont** Otago, South Island, New Zealand 45°48′S 169°32′E
22 M7 **Beaumont** Mississippi, S USA 31°10′N 88°55′W
25 X10 **Beaumont** Texas, SW USA 30°05′N 94°06′W
102 M15 **Beaumont-de-Lomagne** Tarn-et-Garonne, S France 43°54′N 01°00′E
102 L6 **Beaumont-sur-Sarthe** Sarthe, NW France 48°15′N 00°07′E
103 R8 **Beaune** Côte d’Or, C France 47°02′N 04°50′E
15 R9 **Beaupré** Québec, SE Canada 47°03′N 70°52′W
102 J8 **Beaupréau** Maine-et-Loire, NW France 47°13′N 00°57′W
99 I22 **Beauraing** Namur, SE Belgium 50°07′N 04°57′E
103 R12 **Beaurepaire** Isère, E France 45°20′N 05°03′E
11 Y16 **Beausejour** Manitoba, S Canada 50°04′N 96°30′W
103 N4 **Beauvais** *anc.* Bellovacum, Caesaromagus. Oise, N France 49°27′N 02°04′E
11 S13 **Beauval** Saskatchewan, C Canada 55°10′N 107°37′W
102 I9 **Beauvoir-sur-Mer** Vendée, NW France 46°54′N 02°03′W
39 R8 **Beaver** Alaska, USA 66°22′N 147°31′W
26 J8 **Beaver** Oklahoma, C USA 36°48′N 100°32′W
18 B14 **Beaver** Pennsylvania, NE USA 40°39′N 80°19′W
36 K6 **Beaver** Utah, W USA 38°16′N 112°38′W
10 L9 **Beaver** ≈ British Columbia/Yukon Territory, W Canada
11 S13 **Beaver** ≈ Saskatchewan, C Canada
29 N17 **Beaver City** Nebraska, C USA 40°08′N 99°49′W
10 G6 **Beaver Creek** Yukon Territory, W Canada 62°20′N 140°45′W
31 R14 **Beavercreek** Ohio, N USA 39°42′N 83°58′W
39 S8 **Beaver Creek** ≈ Alaska, USA
26 H3 **Beaver Creek** ≈ Kansas/Nebraska, C USA
28 J5 **Beaver Creek** ≈ Montana/North Dakota, N USA
29 Q14 **Beaver Creek** ≈ Nebraska, C USA
25 Q4 **Beaver Creek** ≈ Texas, SW USA
30 M8 **Beaver Dam** Wisconsin, N USA 43°28′N 88°49′W
30 M8 **Beaver Dam Lake** ◎ Wisconsin, N USA
18 B14 **Beaver Falls** Pennsylvania, NE USA 40°45′N 80°20′W
33 P12 **Beaverhead Mountains** ▲▲ Idaho/Montana, NW USA
33 Q12 **Beaverhead River** ≈ Montana, NW USA
65 A25 **Beaver Island** *island* W Falkland Islands
31 P5 **Beaver Island** *island* Michigan, N USA
27 S9 **Beaver Lake** ⊞ Arkansas, C USA
11 N13 **Beaverlodge** Alberta, W Canada 55°11′N 119°29′W
18 I8 **Beaver River** ≈ New York, NE USA
26 J8 **Beaver River** ≈ Oklahoma, C USA
18 B13 **Beaver River** ≈ Pennsylvania, NE USA
65 A25 **Beaver Settlement** Beaver Island, W Falkland Islands 51°30′S 61°15′W
Beaver State *see* Oregon
14 H14 **Beaverton** Ontario, S Canada 44°24′N 79°07′W
32 G11 **Beaverton** Oregon, NW USA 45°29′N 122°49′W
152 G12 **Beāwar** Rājasthān, N India 26°08′N 74°22′E
Bebas, Dasht-i *see* Bābūs, Dasht-e
60 L8 **Bebedouro** São Paulo, S Brazil 20°58′S 48°28′W
101 I16 **Bebra** Hessen, C Germany 50°59′N 09°46′E
41 W12 **Becal** Campeche, SE Mexico 19°49′N 90°28′W
15 Q11 **Bécancour** ≈ Québec, SE Canada
97 Q19 **Beccles** E England, United Kingdom 52°27′N 01°32′E
112 L9 **Bečej** *Ger.* Altbetsche, *Hung.* Óbecse, Rácz-Becse; *prev.* Magyar-Becse, Stari Bečej. Vojvodina, N Serbia 45°36′N 20°02′E
104 I3 **Becerréa** Galicia, NW Spain 42°51′N 07°10′W
74 H7 **Béchar** *prev.* Colomb-Béchar. W Algeria 31°38′N 02°11′W
39 O14 **Becharof Lake** ◎ Alaska, USA
116 H15 **Bechet** *var.* Bechetu. Dolj, SW Romania 43°45′N 23°57′E
Bechetu *see* Bechet
21 R6 **Beckley** West Virginia, NE USA 37°46′N 81°12′W
101 G14 **Beckum** Nordrhein-Westfalen, W Germany 51°45′N 08°03′E
25 X7 **Beckville** Texas, SW USA 32°14′N 94°27′W
35 X4 **Becky Peak** ▲ Nevada, W USA 39°59′N 114°33′W
116 I9 **Beclean** *Hung.* Bethlen; *prev.* Betlen. Bistriţa-Năsăud, N Romania 47°10′N 24°11′E
Bécs *see* Wien
111 H18 **Bečva** *Ger.* Betschau, *Pol.* Beczwa. ≈ E Czech Republic
Beczwa *see* Bečva
103 P15 **Bédarieux** Hérault, S France 43°37′N 03°10′E
120 B10 **Beddouza, Cap** *headland* W Morocco 32°35′N 09°16′W
80 I13 **Bedelē** Oromīya, C Ethiopia 08°25′N 36°21′E
147 Y8 **Bedel Pass** *Rus.* Pereval Bedel. *pass* China/Kyrgyzstan
Bedel, Pereval *see* Bedel Pass
95 H22 **Beder** Midtjylland, C Denmark 56°03′N 10°13′E
97 N20 **Bedford** E England, United Kingdom 52°08′N 00°29′W
31 O15 **Bedford** Indiana, N USA 38°51′N 86°29′W
29 U16 **Bedford** Iowa, C USA 40°40′N 94°43′W
20 L4 **Bedford** Kentucky, S USA 38°36′N 85°18′W
18 D15 **Bedford** Pennsylvania, NE USA 40°00′N 78°29′W
21 T6 **Bedford** Virginia, NE USA 37°20′N 79°31′W
97 N20 **Bedfordshire** *cultural region* E England, United Kingdom
127 N5 **Bednodem’yanovsk** Penzenskaya Oblast’, W Russian Federation 53°55′N 43°14′E
98 N5 **Bedum** Groningen, NE Netherlands 53°18′N 06°36′E
27 V11 **Beebe** Arkansas, C USA 35°04′N 91°52′W
Beechy Group *see* Chichijima-rettō
45 T9 **Beef Island** ✈ (Road Town) Tortola, E British Virgin Islands 18°25′N 64°31′W
Beehive State *see* Utah
99 L18 **Beek** Limburg, SE Netherlands 50°56′N 05°47′E
99 L18 **Beek** ✈ (Maastricht) Limburg, SE Netherlands 50°55′N 05°47′E
99 K14 **Beek-en-Donk** Noord-Brabant, S Netherlands 51°31′N 05°37′E
138 F13 **Be’er Menuha** *prev.* Be’ér Menuḩa. Southern, S Israel 30°22′N 35°09′E
Be’ér Menuḩa *see* Be’er Menuha
99 D16 **Beernem** West-Vlaanderen, NW Belgium 51°09′N 03°18′E
99 I16 **Beerse** Antwerpen, N Belgium 51°20′N 04°52′E
Beersheba *see* Be’er Sheva
138 E11 **Be’er Sheva** *var.* Beersheba, *Ar.* Bir es Saba; *prev.* Be’ér Sheva‘. Southern, S Israel 31°15′N 34°47′E
Be’ér Sheva‘ *see* Be’er Sheva
98 J13 **Beesd** Gelderland, C Netherlands 51°52′N 05°12′E
99 M16 **Beesel** Limburg, SE Netherlands 51°16′N 06°02′E
83 J21 **Beestekraal** North-West, N South Africa 25°21′S 27°40′E
194 J7 **Beethoven Peninsula** *peninsula* Alexander Island, Antarctica
Beetstersweach *see* Beetsterzwaag
98 M6 **Beetsterzwaag** *Fris.* Beetstersweach. Fryslân, N Netherlands 53°03′N 06°04′E
25 S13 **Beeville** Texas, SW USA 28°25′N 97°47′W
79 J18 **Befale** Equateur, NW Dem. Rep. Congo 0°25′N 20°48′E
Befandriana *see* Befandriana Avaratra
172 J3 **Befandriana Avaratra** *var.* Befandriana, Befandriana Nord. Mahajanga, NW Madagascar 15°14′S 48°33′E
Befandriana Nord *see* Befandriana Avaratra
79 K18 **Befori** Equateur, N Dem. Rep. Congo 0°09′N 22°18′E
172 I7 **Befotaka** Fianarantsoa, S Madagascar 23°49′S 47°00′E
183 R11 **Bega** New South Wales, SE Australia 36°43′S 149°50′E
102 G5 **Bégard** Côtes d’Armor, NW France 48°37′N 03°18′W
112 M9 **Begejski Kanal** *canal* Vojvodina, NE Serbia
94 G13 **Begna** ≈ S Norway
Begoml’ *see* Byahoml’
Begovat *see* Bekobod
153 Q13 **Begusarai** Bihār, NE India 25°25′N 86°08′E
143 R9 **Behābād** Yazd, C Iran 32°23′N 59°50′E
Behagle *see* Laï
55 Z10 **Béhague, Pointe** *headland* E French Guiana 04°38′N 51°52′W
Behar *see* Bihār
142 M10 **Behbahān** *var.* Behbehān. Khūzestān, SW Iran 30°38′N 50°07′E
Behbehān *see* Behbahān
44 G3 **Behring Point** Andros Island, W Bahamas 24°28′N 77°44′W

◆ Country
● Country Capital
◇ Dependent Territory
○ Dependent Territory Capital
◈ Administrative Regions
✈ International Airport
▲ Mountain
▲▲ Mountain Range
⛰ Volcano
≈ River
◎ Lake
⊞ Reservoir

143 P4 **Behshahr** *prev.* Ashraf. Māzandarān, N Iran 36°42′N 53°36′E
163 V6 **Bei'an** Heilongjiang, NE China 48°16′N 126°29′E
Beibunar *see* Sredishte
Beibu Wan *see* Tongking, Gulf of
Beida *see* Al Bayḍā'
80 H13 **Beigi** Oromīya, C Ethiopia 09°13′N 34°48′E
160 L16 **Beihai** Guangxi Zhuangzu Zizhiqu, S China 21°29′N 109°10′E
159 Q10 **Bei Hulsan Hu** ◎ C China
161 N13 **Bei Jiang** ~ S China
161 O2 **Beijing** *var.* Pei-ching, *Eng.* Peking; *prev.* Pei-p'ing. ● (China) Beijing Shi, E China 39°58′N 116°23′E
161 P2 **Beijing** ✈ Beijing Shi, N China 39°54′N 116°22′E
Beijing *see* Beijing Shi, China
161 O2 **Beijing Shi** *var.* Beijing, Jing, Pei-ching, *Eng.* Peking; *prev.* Pei-p'ing. ◈ *municipality* E China
76 G8 **Beïla** Trarza, W Mauritania 18°07′N 15°56′W
98 N7 **Beilen** Drenthe, NE Netherlands 52°52′N 06°27′E
160 L15 **Beiliu** *var.* Lingcheng. Guangxi Zhuangzu Zizhiqu, S China 22°50′N 110°22′E
159 O12 **Beilu He** ~ W China
Beilul *see* Beylul
163 U12 **Beining** *prev.* Beizhen. Liaoning, NE China 41°34′N 121°51′E
96 H8 **Beinn Dearg** ▲ N Scotland, United Kingdom 57°47′N 04°52′W
Beinn MacDuibh *see* Ben Macdui
160 I12 **Beipan Jiang** ~ S China
163 T12 **Beipiao** Liaoning, NE China 41°49′N 120°45′E
83 N17 **Beira** Sofala, C Mozambique 19°45′S 34°56′E
83 N17 **Beira** ✈ Sofala, C Mozambique 19°39′S 35°05′E
104 I7 **Beira Alta** *former province* N Portugal
104 H9 **Beira Baixa** *former province* C Portugal
104 G8 **Beira Litoral** *former province* N Portugal
Beirut *see* Beyrouth
Beisān *see* Beit She'an
11 Q16 **Beiseker** Alberta, SW Canada 51°20′N 113°34′W
Beitai Ding *see* Wutai Shan
83 K19 **Beitbridge** Matabeleland South, S Zimbabwe 22°10′S 30°02′E
Beit Lekhem *see* Bethlehem
138 G9 **Beit She'an** *Ar.* Baysān, Beisān; *anc.* Scythopolis, *prev.* Bet She'an. Northern, N Israel 32°30′N 35°30′E
116 G10 **Beiuş** *Hung.* Belényes. Bihor, NW Romania 46°40′N 22°21′E
Beizhen *see* Beining
104 H12 **Beja** *anc.* Pax Julia. Beja, SE Portugal 38°01′N 07°52′W
74 M5 **Béja** *var.* Bājah. N Tunisia 36°45′N 09°04′E
104 G13 **Beja** ◈ *district* S Portugal
120 I9 **Béjaïa** *var.* Bejaïa, *Fr.* Bougie; *anc.* Saldae. NE Algeria 36°49′N 05°03′E
Bejaïa *see* Béjaïa
104 K8 **Béjar** Castilla y León, N Spain 40°24′N 05°45′W
Bejraburi *see* Phetchaburi
Bekaa Valley *see* El Beqaa
Bekabad *see* Bekobod
Békás *see* Bicaz
169 O15 **Bekasi** Jawa, C Indonesia 06°14′S 106°595′E
Bek-Budi *see* Qarshi
Bekdaş/Bekdash *see* Garabogaz
147 T10 **Bek-Dzhar** Oshskaya Oblast', SW Kyrgyzstan 40°22′N 73°08′E
111 N24 **Békés** *Rom.* Bichiş. Békés, SE Hungary 46°45′N 21°09′E
111 M24 **Békés** *off.* Békés Megye. ◈ *county* SE Hungary
111 M24 **Békéscsaba** *Rom.* Bichiş-Ciaba. Békés, SE Hungary 46°40′N 21°05′E
Békés Megye *see* Békés
172 H7 **Bekily** Toliara, S Madagascar 24°12′S 45°20′E
165 W4 **Bekkai** *var.* Betsukai. Hokkaidō, NE Japan 43°23′N 145°07′E
139 S2 **Bēkma** Arbīl, E Iraq 36°40′N 44°15′E
147 Q11 **Bekobod** *Rus.* Bekabad; *prev.* Begovat. Toshkent Viloyati, E Uzbekistan 40°17′N 69°11′E
127 O7 **Bekovo** Penzenskaya Oblast', W Russian Federation 52°27′N 43°41′E
Bel *see* Beliu
152 M13 **Bela** Uttar Pradesh, N India 25°55′N 82°00′E
149 N15 **Bela** Baluchistān, SW Pakistan 26°12′N 66°20′E
79 F15 **Bélabo** Est, C Cameroon 04°54′N 13°10′E
112 N10 **Bela Crkva** *Ger.* Weisskirchen, *Hung.* Fehértemplom. Vojvodina, W Serbia 44°55′N 21°28′E
173 Y16 **Bel Air** *var.* Rivière Sèche. E Mauritius
104 L12 **Belalcázar** Andalucía, S Spain 38°33′N 05°07′W
113 P15 **Bela Palanka** Serbia, SE Serbia 43°13′N 22°19′E
119 H16 **Belarus** *off.* Republic of Belarus, *var.* Belorussia, *Latv.* Baltkrievija; *prev.* Belorussian SSR, *Rus.* Belorusskaya SSR. ◆ *republic* E Europe
Belarus, Republic of *see* Belarus
Belau *see* Palau
59 H21 **Bela Vista** Mato Grosso do Sul, SW Brazil 22°04′S 56°25′W
83 L21 **Bela Vista** Maputo, S Mozambique 26°20′S 32°40′E
168 I8 **Belawan** Sumatera, W Indonesia 03°46′N 98°44′E
Běla Woda *see* Weisswasser
127 U4 **Belaya** ~ W Russian Federation
123 R7 **Belaya Gora** Respublika Sakha (Yakutiya), NE Russian Federation 68°25′N 146°12′E
126 M11 **Belaya Kalitiva** Rostovskaya Oblast', SW Russian Federation 48°09′N 40°43′E
125 R14 **Belaya Kholunitsa** Kirovskaya Oblast', NW Russian Federation 58°54′N 50°52′E
Belaya Tserkov' *see* Bila Tserkva
77 V11 **Belbédji** Zinder, S Niger 14°35′N 08°00′E
111 K14 **Bełchatów** *var.* Belchatow. Łódzski, C Poland 51°23′N 19°20′E
Belchatow *see* Bełchatów
Belcher, Îles *see* Belcher Islands
12 H7 **Belcher Islands** *Fr.* Îles Belcher. *island group* Nunavut, SE Canada
105 S6 **Belchite** Aragón, NE Spain 41°18′N 00°45′W
29 O2 **Belcourt** North Dakota, N USA 48°50′N 99°44′W
31 P9 **Belding** Michigan, N USA 43°06′N 85°13′W
127 U5 **Belebey** Respublika Bashkortostan, W Russian Federation 54°04′N 54°13′E
81 N16 **Beledweyne** *var.* Belet Huen, *It.* Belet Uen. Hiiraan, C Somalia 04°39′N 45°12′E
146 B10 **Belek** Balkan Welaýaty, W Turkmenistan 39°57′N 53°51′E
58 L12 **Belém** *var.* Pará. *state capital* Pará, N Brazil 01°27′S 48°29′W
65 I14 **Belém Ridge** *undersea feature* C Atlantic Ocean
62 I7 **Belén** Catamarca, NW Argentina 27°36′N 67°00′W
54 G9 **Belén** Boyacá, C Colombia 06°01′N 72°55′W
42 J11 **Belén** Rivas, SW Nicaragua 11°30′N 85°55′W
62 O5 **Belén** Concepción, C Paraguay 23°25′S 57°14′W
61 D16 **Belén** Salto, N Uruguay 30°47′S 57°47′W
37 R12 **Belen** New Mexico, SW USA 34°37′N 106°46′W
61 D20 **Belén de Escobar** Buenos Aires, E Argentina 34°21′S 58°47′W
114 J7 **Belene** Pleven, N Bulgaria 43°39′N 25°09′E
114 J7 **Belene, Ostrov** *island* N Bulgaria
43 R15 **Belén, Río** ~ C Panama
Belényes *see* Beiuş
Embalse de Belesar *see* Belesar, Encoro de
104 H3 **Belesar, Encoro de** *Sp.* Embalse de Belesar. ▣ NW Spain
Belet Huen/Belet Uen *see* Beledweyne
126 J5 **Belëv** Tul'skaya Oblast', W Russian Federation 53°48′N 36°07′E
19 R7 **Belfast** Maine, NE USA 44°25′N 69°02′W
97 G15 **Belfast** *Ir.* Béal Feirste. ● E Northern Ireland, United Kingdom 54°35′N 05°55′W
97 G15 **Belfast Aldergrove** ✈ E Northern Ireland, United Kingdom 54°37′N 06°11′W
97 G15 **Belfast Lough** *Ir.* Loch Lao. *inlet* E Northern Ireland, United Kingdom
28 K5 **Belfield** North Dakota, N USA 46°53′N 103°12′W
103 U7 **Belfort** Territoire-de-Belfort, E France 47°38′N 06°52′E
Belgard *see* Białogard
155 E17 **Belgaum** Karnātaka, W India 15°52′N 74°30′E
Belgian Congo *see* Congo (Democratic Republic of)
België/Belgique *see* Belgium
99 F20 **Belgium** *off.* Kingdom of Belgium, *Dut.* België, *Fr.* Belgique. ◆ *monarchy* NW Europe
Belgium, Kingdom of *see* Belgium
126 J8 **Belgorod** Belgorodskaya Oblast', W Russian Federation 50°38′N 36°37′E
Belgorod-Dnestrovskiy *see* Bilhorod-Dnistrovs'kyy
126 J8 **Belgorodskaya Oblast'** ◈ *province* W Russian Federation
Belgrad *see* Beograd
29 T8 **Belgrade** Minnesota, N USA 45°27′N 94°59′W
33 S11 **Belgrade** Montana, NW USA 45°46′N 111°10′W
Belgrade *see* Beograd
Belgrano, Cabo *see* Meredith, Cape
195 N5 **Belgrano II** *Argentinian research station* Antarctica 77°50′S 35°25′W
21 X9 **Belhaven** North Carolina, SE USA 35°36′N 76°50′W
107 I23 **Belice** *anc.* Hypsas. ~ Sicilia, Italy, C Mediterranean Sea
Belice *see* Belize/Belize City
Beli Drim *see* Drini i Bardhë
Beligrad *see* Berat
188 C8 **Beliliou** *prev.* Peleliu. *island* S Palau
114 L8 **Beli Lom, Yazovir** ▣ NE Bulgaria
112 I8 **Beli Manastir** *Hung.* Pélmonostor; *prev.* Monostor. Osijek-Baranja, NE Croatia 45°46′N 16°38′E
102 J13 **Bélin-Béliet** Gironde, SW France 44°30′N 00°48′W
79 F17 **Bélinga** Ogooué-Ivindo, NE Gabon 01°05′N 13°12′E
21 S4 **Belington** West Virginia, NE USA 39°01′N 79°57′W
127 O6 **Belinskiy** Penzenskaya Oblast', W Russian Federation 52°58′N 43°25′E
169 N12 **Belinyu** Pulau Bangka, W Indonesia 01°37′S 105°45′E
169 O13 **Belitung, Pulau** *island* W Indonesia
116 F10 **Beliu** *Hung.* Bel. Arad, W Romania 46°31′N 21°57′E
114 J9 **Beli Vit** ~ NW Bulgaria
42 G2 **Belize** *Sp.* Belice; *prev.* British Honduras, Colony of Belize. ◆ *commonwealth republic* Central America
42 F2 **Belize** *Sp.* Belice. ◈ *district* NE Belize
42 G2 **Belize** ~ Belize/Guatemala
Belize *see* Belize City
42 G2 **Belize City** *var.* Belize, *Sp.* Belice. Belize, NE Belize 17°29′N 88°10′W
42 G2 **Belize City** ✈ Belize, NE Belize 17°31′N 88°15′W
Belize, Colony of *see* Belize
Beljak *see* Villach
39 N16 **Belkofski** Alaska, USA 55°07′N 162°04′W
123 O6 **Bel'kovskiy, Ostrov** *island* Novosibirskiye Ostrova, NE Russian Federation
14 J8 **Bell** ~ Québec, SE Canada
10 J15 **Bella Bella** British Columbia, SW Canada 52°04′N 128°07′W
102 M10 **Bellac** Haute-Vienne, C France 46°07′N 01°04′E
10 K15 **Bella Coola** British Columbia, SW Canada 52°23′N 126°46′W
106 D6 **Bellagio** Lombardia, N Italy 45°58′N 09°15′E
31 P6 **Bellaire** Michigan, N USA 44°59′N 85°12′W
106 D6 **Bellano** Lombardia, N Italy 46°06′N 09°21′E
155 G17 **Bellary** *var.* Ballari. Karnātaka, S India 15°11′N 76°54′E
183 S5 **Bellata** New South Wales, SE Australia 29°58′S 149°49′E
61 D16 **Bella Unión** Artigas, N Uruguay 30°18′S 57°35′W
61 C14 **Bella Vista** Corrientes, NE Argentina 28°30′S 59°03′W
62 J7 **Bella Vista** Tucumán, N Argentina 27°05′S 65°19′W
62 P4 **Bella Vista** Amambay, C Paraguay 22°08′S 56°20′W
56 B10 **Bellavista** Cajamarca, N Peru 05°43′S 78°48′W
56 D11 **Bellavista** San Martín, N Peru 07°04′S 76°35′W
183 U6 **Bellbrook** New South Wales, SE Australia 30°48′S 152°32′E
27 V5 **Belle** Missouri, C USA 38°17′N 91°43′W
21 Q5 **Belle** West Virginia, NE USA 38°13′N 81°32′W
31 R13 **Bellefontaine** Ohio, N USA 40°22′N 83°45′W
18 F14 **Bellefonte** Pennsylvania, NE USA 40°54′N 77°43′W
28 J9 **Belle Fourche** South Dakota, N USA 44°40′N 103°50′W
28 J9 **Belle Fourche Reservoir** ▣ South Dakota, N USA
28 K9 **Belle Fourche River** ~ South Dakota/Wyoming, N USA
103 S10 **Bellegarde-sur-Valserine** Ain, E France 46°06′N 05°49′E
23 Y14 **Belle Glade** Florida, SE USA 26°40′N 80°40′W
102 G8 **Belle Île** *island* NW France
13 T9 **Belle Isle** *island* Belle Isle, Newfoundland and Labrador, E Canada
13 S10 **Belle Isle, Strait of** *strait* Newfoundland and Labrador, E Canada
Bellenz *see* Bellinzona
29 W14 **Belle Plaine** Iowa, C USA 41°54′N 92°16′W
29 V9 **Belle Plaine** Minnesota, N USA 44°39′N 93°47′W
14 I9 **Belleterre** Québec, SE Canada 47°24′N 78°40′W
14 J15 **Belleville** Ontario, SE Canada 44°10′N 77°22′W
103 R10 **Belleville** Rhône, E France 46°09′N 04°42′E
30 K15 **Belleville** Illinois, N USA 38°31′N 89°58′W
27 N3 **Belleville** Kansas, C USA 39°51′N 97°38′W
29 Z13 **Bellevue** Iowa, C USA 42°15′N 90°25′W
29 S15 **Bellevue** Nebraska, C USA 41°08′N 95°53′W
31 S11 **Bellevue** Ohio, N USA 41°16′N 82°50′W
25 S5 **Bellevue** Texas, SW USA 33°38′N 98°00′W
32 H8 **Bellevue** Washington, NW USA 47°36′N 122°12′W
55 Y11 **Bellevue de l'Inini, Montagnes** ▲▲ S French Guiana
103 S11 **Belley** Ain, E France 45°46′N 05°41′E
Bellin *see* Kangirsuk
183 V6 **Bellingen** New South Wales, SE Australia 30°27′S 152°53′E
97 L14 **Bellingham** N England, United Kingdom 55°09′N 02°16′W
32 H6 **Bellingham** Washington, NW USA 48°46′N 122°29′W
Belling Hausen Mulde *see* Southeast Pacific Basin
194 H2 **Bellingshausen** *Russian research station* South Shetland Islands, Antarctica 61°57′S 58°23′W
Bellingshausen *see* Motu One
Bellingshausen Abyssal Plain *see* Bellingshausen Plain
196 R14 **Bellingshausen Plain** *var.* Bellingshausen Abyssal Plain. *undersea feature* SE Pacific Ocean 64°00′S 90°00′W
194 I8 **Bellingshausen Sea** *sea* Antarctica
98 P6 **Bellingwolde** Groningen, NE Netherlands 53°07′N 07°10′E
108 H11 **Bellinzona** *Ger.* Bellenz. Ticino, S Switzerland 46°12′N 09°02′E
25 T8 **Bellmead** Texas, SW USA 31°36′N 97°02′W
54 E8 **Bello** Antioquia, W Colombia 06°19′N 75°34′W
61 B21 **Bellocq** Buenos Aires, E Argentina 35°55′S 61°32′W
Bello Horizonte *see* Belo Horizonte
186 L10 **Bellona** *var.* Mungiki. *island* S Solomon Islands
Bellovacum *see* Beauvais
182 D7 **Bell, Point** *headland* South Australia 32°13′S 133°08′E
20 F9 **Bells** Tennessee, S USA 35°42′N 89°05′W
25 U5 **Bells** Texas, SW USA 33°36′N 96°24′W
92 N3 **Bellsund** *inlet* SW Svalbard
106 H6 **Belluno** Veneto, NE Italy 46°08′N 12°13′E
62 L11 **Bell Ville** Córdoba, C Argentina 32°35′S 62°41′W
83 E26 **Bellville** Western Cape, SW South Africa 33°50′S 18°43′E
25 U11 **Bellville** Texas, SW USA 29°57′N 96°15′W
104 L12 **Belmez** Andalucía, S Spain 38°16′N 05°12′W
29 V12 **Belmond** Iowa, C USA 42°51′N 93°36′W
18 E11 **Belmont** New York, NE USA 42°14′N 78°02′W
21 R10 **Belmont** North Carolina, SE USA 35°13′N 81°01′W
59 O18 **Belmonte** Bahia, E Brazil 15°53′S 38°54′W
104 I8 **Belmonte** Castelo Branco, C Portugal 40°21′N 07°20′W
105 P10 **Belmonte** Castilla-La Mancha, C Spain 39°34′N 02°43′W
42 G2 **Belmopan** ● (Belize) Cayo, C Belize 17°13′N 88°48′W
97 B16 **Belmullet** *Ir.* Béal an Mhuirhead. Mayo, W Ireland 54°14′N 09°59′W
99 E20 **Belœil** Hainaut, SW Belgium 50°33′N 03°45′E
123 R13 **Belogorsk** Amurskaya Oblast', SE Russian Federation 50°53′N 128°24′E
Belogorsk *see* Bilohirs'k
114 F7 **Belogradchik** Vidin, NW Bulgaria 43°37′N 22°42′E
172 H8 **Beloha** Toliara, S Madagascar 25°09′S 45°04′E
59 M20 **Belo Horizonte** *prev.* Bello Horizonte. *state capital* Minas Gerais, SE Brazil 19°54′S 43°54′W
26 M3 **Beloit** Kansas, C USA 39°27′N 98°06′W
30 L9 **Beloit** Wisconsin, N USA 42°31′N 89°01′W
Belokorovichi *see* Novi Bilokorovychi
124 J8 **Belomorsk** Respublika Kareliya, NW Russian Federation 64°30′N 34°43′E
124 J8 **Belomorsko-Baltiyskiy Kanal** *Eng.* White Sea-Baltic Canal, White Sea Canal. *canal* NW Russian Federation
153 V15 **Belonia** Tripura, NE India 23°15′N 91°25′E
Beloozersk *see* Byelaazyorsk
Belopol'ye *see* Bilopillya
105 O4 **Belorado** Castilla y León, N Spain 42°25′N 03°11′W
126 L14 **Belorechensk** Krasnodarskiy Kray, SW Russian Federation 44°46′N 39°53′E
127 W5 **Beloretsk** Respublika Bashkortostan, W Russian Federation 53°56′N 58°26′E
Belorussia/Belorussian SSR *see* Belarus
Belorusskaya Gryada *see* Byelaruskaya Hrada
Belorusskaya SSR *see* Belarus
Beloshchel'ye *see* Nar'yan-Mar
114 N8 **Beloslav** Varna, E Bulgaria 43°13′N 27°42′E
Belostok *see* Białystok
Belo-sur-Tsiribihina *see* Belo Tsiribihina
172 H5 **Belo Tsiribihina** *var.* Belo-sur-Tsiribihina. Toliara, W Madagascar 19°40′S 44°30′E
Belovár *see* Bjelovar
Belovezhskaya, Pushcha *see* Białowieska, Puszcza/Byelavyezhskaya, Pushcha
114 H10 **Belovo** Pazardzhik, C Bulgaria 42°10′N 24°01′E
Belovodsk *see* Bilovods'k
122 H9 **Beloyarskiy** Khanty-Mansiyskiy Avtonomnyy Okrug-Yugra, N Russian Federation 63°40′N 66°31′E
124 K7 **Beloye More** *Eng.* White Sea. *sea* NW Russian Federation
124 K13 **Beloye, Ozero** ◎ NW Russian Federation
114 J10 **Belozem** Plovdiv, C Bulgaria 42°11′N 25°00′E
124 K13 **Belozërsk** Vologodskaya Oblast', NW Russian Federation 59°59′N 37°49′E
108 D8 **Belp** Bern, W Switzerland 46°54′N 07°31′E
108 D8 **Belp** ✈ (Bern) Bern, C Switzerland 46°55′N 07°29′E
107 L24 **Belpasso** Sicilia, Italy, C Mediterranean Sea 37°35′N 14°59′E
31 U14 **Belpre** Ohio, N USA 39°14′N 81°34′W
98 M8 **Belterwijde** ◎ N Netherlands
27 R4 **Belton** Missouri, C USA 38°48′N 94°31′W
21 P11 **Belton** South Carolina, SE USA 34°31′N 82°29′W
25 T9 **Belton** Texas, SW USA 31°04′N 97°30′W
25 S9 **Belton Lake** ▣ Texas, SW USA
Bel'tsy *see* Bălţi
97 E16 **Belturbet** *Ir.* Béal Tairbirt. Cavan, N Ireland 54°06′N 07°26′W
Beluchistan *see* Balochistān
145 Z9 **Belukha, Gora** ▲ Kazakhstan/Russian Federation 49°50′N 86°44′E
107 M20 **Belvedere Marittimo** Calabria, SW Italy 39°37′N 15°52′E
30 L10 **Belvidere** Illinois, N USA 42°15′N 88°50′W
18 J14 **Belvidere** New Jersey, NE USA 40°50′N 75°05′W
Bely *see* Belyy
127 V8 **Belyayevka** Orenburgskaya Oblast', W Russian Federation 51°25′N 56°26′E
Belynichi *see* Byalynichy
124 H17 **Belyy** *var.* Bely, Beyj. Tverskaya Oblast', W Russian Federation 55°51′N 32°57′E
126 J6 **Belyye Berega** Bryanskaya Oblast', W Russian Federation 53°11′N 34°42′E
122 J6 **Belyy, Ostrov** *island* N Russian Federation
122 J11 **Belyy Yar** Tomskaya Oblast', C Russian Federation 58°26′N 84°57′E
100 N13 **Belzig** Brandenburg, NE Germany 52°09′N 12°37′E
22 K4 **Belzoni** Mississippi, S USA 33°10′N 90°29′W
172 H4 **Bemaraha** *var.* Plateau du Bemaraha. ▲▲ W Madagascar
Bemaraha, Plateau du *see* Bemaraha
82 B10 **Bembe** Uíge, NW Angola 07°03′S 14°25′E
77 S14 **Bembèrèkè** *var.* Bimbéréké. N Benin 10°10′N 02°41′E
104 K12 **Bembézar** ~ SW Spain
104 J3 **Bembibre** Castilla y León, N Spain 42°37′N 06°25′W
29 T4 **Bemidji** Minnesota, N USA 47°27′N 94°53′W
98 L12 **Bemmel** Gelderland, SE Netherlands 51°53′N 05°54′E
171 T13 **Bemu** Pulau Seram, E Indonesia 03°21′S 129°58′E
Benāb *see* Bonāb
105 T5 **Benabarre** *var.* Benavarn. Aragón, NE Spain 42°06′N 00°28′E
Benaco *see* Garda, Lago di
79 L20 **Bena-Dibele** Kasai-Oriental, C Dem. Rep. Congo 04°01′S 22°50′E
105 R9 **Benagéber, Embalse de** ▣ E Spain
183 O11 **Benalla** Victoria, SE Australia 36°33′S 146°00′E
104 M14 **Benamejí** Andalucía, S Spain 37°16′N 04°33′W
Benares *see* Vārānasi
Benavarn *see* Benabarre
104 F10 **Benavente** Santarém, C Portugal 38°59′N 08°49′W
104 K5 **Benavente** Castilla y León, N Spain 42°00′N 05°40′W
25 S15 **Benavides** Texas, SW USA 27°36′N 98°24′W
96 F8 **Benbecula** *island* NW Scotland, United Kingdom
Bencovazzo *see* Benkovac
32 H13 **Bend** Oregon, NW USA 44°04′N 121°19′W
182 K7 **Benda Range** ▲▲ South Australia
183 T6 **Bendemeer** New South Wales, SE Australia 30°54′S 151°12′E
Bender *see* Tighina
Bender Beila/Bender Beyla *see* Bandarbeyla
Bender Cassim/Bender Qaasim *see* Boosaaso
Bendery *see* Tighina
183 N11 **Bendigo** Victoria, SE Australia 36°46′S 144°19′E
118 E10 **Bēne** SW Latvia 56°30′N 23°04′E
98 K13 **Beneden-Leeuwen** Gelderland, C Netherlands 51°52′N 05°32′E
101 L24 **Benediktenwand** ▲ S Germany 47°39′N 11°28′E
Benemérita de San Cristóbal *see* San Cristóbal
77 N12 **Bénéna** Ségou, S Mali 13°04′N 04°20′W
172 I7 **Benenitra** Toliara, S Madagascar 23°25′S 45°06′E
Beneschau *see* Benešov
Beneški Zaliv *see* Venice, Gulf of
111 D17 **Benešov** *Ger.* Beneschau. Středočeský Kraj, W Czech Republic 49°48′N 14°41′E
107 L17 **Benevento** *anc.* Beneventum, Malventum. Campania, S Italy 41°07′N 14°45′E
Beneventum *see* Benevento
173 S3 **Bengal, Bay of** *bay* N Indian Ocean
Bengalooru *see* Bangalore
79 M17 **Bengamisa** Orientale, N Dem. Rep. Congo 0°58′N 25°11′E
Bengasi *see* Banghāzī
Bengazi *see* Banghāzī
161 P7 **Bengbu** *var.* Peng-pu. Anhui, E China 32°57′N 117°17′E
32 L9 **Benge** Washington, NW USA 46°55′N 118°01′W
Benghazi *see* Banghāzī
168 K10 **Bengkalis** Pulau Bengkalis, W Indonesia 01°27′N 102°10′E
168 K10 **Bengkalis, Pulau** *island* W Indonesia
169 Q10 **Bengkayang** Borneo, C Indonesia 0°45′N 109°28′E
168 K14 **Bengkulu** *prev.* Bengkoeloe, Benkoelen, Benkulen. Sumatera, W Indonesia 03°46′S 102°16′E
168 K13 **Bengkulu** *off.* Propinsi Bengkulu; *prev.* Bengkoeloe, Benkoelen, Benkulen. ◈ *province* W Indonesia
Bengkulu, Propinsi *see* Bengkulu
82 A11 **Bengo** ◈ *province* W Angola
95 J16 **Bengtsfors** Västra Götaland, S Sweden 59°03′N 12°14′E
82 B13 **Benguela** *var.* Benguella. Benguela, W Angola 12°35′S 13°30′E
83 A14 **Benguela** ◈ *province* W Angola
Benguella *see* Benguela
138 F10 **Ben Gurion** ✈ Tel Aviv, C Israel 32°04′N 34°45′E
Bengweulu, Lake *see* Bangweulu, Lake
Benha *see* Banhā
192 F6 **Benham Seamount** *undersea feature* W Philippine Sea 15°48′N 124°15′E
96 H6 **Ben Hope** ▲ N Scotland, United Kingdom 58°25′N 04°36′W
79 P18 **Beni** Nord-Kivu, NE Dem. Rep. Congo 0°31′N 29°30′E
74 H8 **Beni Abbès** W Algeria 30°07′N 02°09′W
105 T8 **Benicarló** Valenciana, E Spain 40°25′N 00°25′E
105 T9 **Benicássim** *Cat.* Benicàssim. Valenciana, E Spain 40°03′N 00°03′E
Benicàssim *see* Benicassim
105 T12 **Benidorm** Valenciana, SE Spain 38°33′N 00°09′W
Beni Mazâr *see* Banī Mazār
121 C11 **Beni-Mellal** C Morocco 32°20′N 06°21′W
77 R14 **Benin** *off.* Republic of Benin; *prev.* Dahomey. ◆ *republic* W Africa
77 S17 **Benin, Bight of** *gulf* W Africa
77 U16 **Benin City** Edo, SW Nigeria 06°23′N 05°40′E
Benin, Republic of *see* Benin
57 K16 **Beni, Río** ~ N Bolivia
120 F10 **Beni Saf** *var.* Beni-Saf. NW Algeria 35°19′N 01°23′W
Beni-Saf *see* Beni Saf
Benishangul *see* Binshangul Gumuz
105 T11 **Benissa** Valenciana, E Spain 38°43′N 00°03′E
Beni Suef *see* Banī Suwayf
11 V15 **Benito** Manitoba, S Canada 51°57′N 101°24′W
Benito *see* Uolo, Río
61 C23 **Benito Juárez** Buenos Aires, E Argentina 37°43′S 59°48′W
41 P14 **Benito Juárez Internacional** ✈ (México) México, S Mexico 19°24′N 99°02′W
25 P5 **Benjamin** Texas, SW USA 33°35′N 99°49′W
58 B13 **Benjamin Constant** Amazonas, N Brazil 04°22′S 70°02′W
40 F4 **Benjamín Hill** Sonora, NW Mexico 30°13′N 111°08′W
63 F19 **Benjamín, Isla** *island* Archipiélago de los Chonos, S Chile
164 Q4 **Benkei-misaki** *headland* Hokkaidō, NE Japan 42°49′N 140°10′E
28 L17 **Benkelman** Nebraska, C USA 40°04′N 101°30′W
96 I7 **Ben Klibreck** ▲ N Scotland, United Kingdom 58°15′N 04°23′W
Benkoelen/Bengkoeloe *see* Bengkulu
112 D13 **Benkovac** *It.* Bencovazzo. Zadar, SW Croatia 44°02′N 15°36′E
Benkulen *see* Bengkulu
96 I11 **Ben Lawers** ▲ C Scotland, United Kingdom 56°33′N 04°13′W
96 J9 **Ben Macdui** *var.* Beinn MacDuibh. ▲ C Scotland, United Kingdom 57°02′N 03°42′W
96 G11 **Ben More** ▲ W Scotland, United Kingdom 56°26′N 06°00′W
96 I11 **Ben More** ▲ C Scotland, United Kingdom 56°22′N 04°31′W
96 H7 **Ben More Assynt** ▲ N Scotland, United Kingdom 58°09′N 04°51′W
185 E20 **Benmore, Lake** ◎ South Island, New Zealand
98 L12 **Bennekom** Gelderland, SE Netherlands 52°00′N 05°40′E
123 Q5 **Bennetta, Ostrov** *island* Novosibirskiye Ostrova, NE Russian Federation
21 T11 **Bennettsville** South Carolina, SE USA 34°36′N 79°40′W
96 H10 **Ben Nevis** ▲ N Scotland, United Kingdom 56°80′N 05°00′W
184 M9 **Benneydale** Waikato, North Island, New Zealand 38°31′S 175°22′E
Bennichab *see* Bennichchâb
76 H8 **Bennichchâb** *var.* Bennichab. Inchiri, W Mauritania 19°26′N 15°21′W
18 L10 **Bennington** Vermont, NE USA 42°51′N 73°09′W
185 E20 **Ben Ohau Range** ▲▲ South Island, New Zealand
83 J21 **Benoni** Gauteng, NE South Africa 26°04′S 28°18′E
172 J2 **Be, Nosy** *var.* Nossi-Bé. *island* NW Madagascar
Bénoué *see* Benue
42 F2 **Benque Viejo del Carmen** Cayo, W Belize 17°04′N 89°08′W
101 G19 **Bensheim** Hessen, W Germany 49°41′N 08°38′E
37 N16 **Benson** Arizona, SW USA 31°55′N 110°16′W
29 S8 **Benson** Minnesota, N USA 45°19′N 95°36′W
21 U10 **Benson** North Carolina, SE USA 35°22′N 78°33′W
171 N15 **Benteng** Pulau Selayar, C Indonesia 06°07′S 120°28′E
83 A14 **Bentiaba** Namibe, SW Angola 14°18′S 12°27′E
181 T4 **Bentinck Island** *island* Wellesley Islands, Queensland, N Australia
80 E13 **Bentiu** Wahda, N South Sudan 09°14′N 29°49′E
138 G8 **Bent Jbaïl** *var.* Bint Jubayl. S Lebanon 33°07′N 35°26′E
11 Q15 **Bentley** Alberta, SW Canada 52°27′N 114°02′W
61 I15 **Bento Gonçalves** Rio Grande do Sul, S Brazil 29°12′S 51°34′W
27 U12 **Benton** Arkansas, C USA 34°34′N 92°35′W
30 L16 **Benton** Illinois, N USA 38°00′N 88°55′W
20 H7 **Benton** Kentucky, S USA 36°51′N 88°21′W
22 G5 **Benton** Louisiana, S USA 32°41′N 93°44′W
27 Y7 **Benton** Missouri, C USA 37°05′N 89°34′W
20 M10 **Benton** Tennessee, S USA 35°10′N 84°39′W
31 O10 **Benton Harbor** Michigan, N USA 42°07′N 86°27′W
27 S9 **Bentonville** Arkansas, C USA 36°23′N 94°13′W
77 V16 **Benue** ◈ *state* SE Nigeria
78 F13 **Benue** *Fr.* Bénoué. ~ Cameroon/Nigeria
163 V12 **Benxi** *prev.* Pen-ch'i, Penhsihu, Penki. Liaoning, NE China 41°20′N 123°45′E
Benyakoni *see* Byenyakoni
112 K10 **Beočin** Vojvodina, N Serbia 45°13′N 19°43′E
Beodericsworth *see* Bury St Edmunds
112 M11 **Beograd** *Eng.* Belgrade, *Ger.* Belgrad; *anc.* Singidunum. ● (Serbia) Serbia, N Serbia 44°48′N 20°27′E
112 L11 **Beograd** *Eng.* Belgrade. ✈ Serbia, N Serbia 44°45′N 20°21′E
76 M16 **Béoumi** C Ivory Coast 07°40′N 05°34′W
35 V3 **Beowawe** Nevada, W USA 40°33′N 116°31′W
164 E14 **Beppu** Ōita, Kyūshū, SW Japan 33°18′N 131°30′E
187 X15 **Beqa** *prev.* Mbengga. *island* W Fiji
45 Y14 **Bequia** *island* C Saint Vincent and the Grenadines
113 L16 **Berane** *prev.* Ivangrad. E Montenegro 42°51′N 19°51′E
113 L21 **Berat** *var.* Berati, *SCr.* Beligrad. Berat, C Albania 40°43′N 19°58′E
113 L21 **Berat** ◈ *district* C Albania
Berătău *see* Berettyó
Berati *see* Berat
Beraun *see* Berounka, Czech Republic
Beraun *see* Beroun, Czech Republic
171 U13 **Berau, Teluk** *var.* MacCluer Gulf. *bay* Papua, E Indonesia
80 G8 **Berber** River Nile, NE Sudan 18°01′N 34°00′E
80 N12 **Berbera** Woqooyi Galbeed, NW Somalia 10°24′N 45°02′E
79 H16 **Berbérati** Mambéré-Kadéï, SW Central African Republic 04°14′N 15°50′E
Berberia, Cabo de *see* Barbaria, Cap de
55 T9 **Berbice River** ~ NE Guyana
Berchid *see* Berrechid
103 N2 **Berck-Plage** Pas-de-Calais, N France 50°24′N 01°35′E
25 T13 **Berclair** Texas, SW USA 28°33′N 97°32′W
117 W10 **Berda** ~ SE Ukraine
Berdichev *see* Berdychiv
123 P10 **Berdigestyakh** Respublika Sakha (Yakutiya), NE Russian Federation 62°02′N 127°03′E
122 J12 **Berdsk** Novosibirskaya Oblast', C Russian Federation 54°42′N 82°56′E
117 W10 **Berdyans'k** *Rus.* Berdyansk; *prev.* Osipenko. Zaporiz'ka Oblast', SE Ukraine 46°46′N 36°49′E
117 W10 **Berdyans'ka Kosa** *spit* SE Ukraine
117 V10 **Berdyans'ka Zatoka** *gulf* S Ukraine
117 N5 **Berdychiv** *Rus.* Berdichev. Zhytomyrs'ka Oblast', N Ukraine 49°54′N 28°39′E
20 M6 **Berea** Kentucky, S USA 37°34′N 84°18′W
Beregovo/Beregszász *see* Berehove
116 G8 **Berehove** *Cz.* Berehovo, *Hung.* Beregszász, *Rus.* Beregovo. Zakarpats'ka Oblast', W Ukraine 48°13′N 22°39′E
Berehovo *see* Berehove
186 D9 **Bereina** Central, S Papua New Guinea 08°29′S 146°30′E
146 C11 **Bereket** *prev. Rus.* Gazandzhyk, Kazandzhik, *Turkm.* Gazanjyk. Balkan Welaýaty, W Turkmenistan 39°17′N 55°27′E
45 O12 **Berekua** S Dominica 15°14′N 61°19′W
77 O16 **Berekum** W Ghana 07°27′N 02°35′W
Berenice *see* Baranīs
11 O14 **Berens** ~ Manitoba/Ontario, C Canada
11 X14 **Berens River** Manitoba, C Canada 52°22′N 97°00′W
29 R12 **Beresford** South Dakota, N USA 43°02′N 96°45′W
116 J4 **Berestechko** Volyns'ka Oblast', NW Ukraine 50°21′N 25°06′E
116 M11 **Bereşti** Galaţi, E Romania 46°04′N 27°54′E
117 U6 **Berestova** ~ E Ukraine
Beretău *see* Berettyó
111 N23 **Berettyó** *Rom.* Barcău; *prev.* Berătău, Beretău. ~ Hungary/Romania
111 N23 **Berettyóújfalu** Hajdú-Bihar, E Hungary 47°15′N 21°33′E
Bereza/Bereza Kartuska *see* Byaroza
117 Q4 **Berezan'** Kyyivs'ka Oblast', N Ukraine 50°18′N 31°30′E
117 Q10 **Berezanka** Mykolayivs'ka Oblast', S Ukraine 46°51′N 31°24′E
116 J6 **Berezhany** *Pol.* Brzeżany. Ternopil's'ka Oblast', W Ukraine 49°29′N 25°00′E
Berezina *see* Byarezina
Berezino *see* Byerazino
117 P10 **Berezivka** *Rus.* Berezovka. Odes'ka Oblast', SW Ukraine 47°12′N 30°56′E
117 Q2 **Berezna** Chernihivs'ka Oblast', NE Ukraine 51°35′N 31°50′E
116 L3 **Berezne** Rivnens'ka Oblast', NW Ukraine 51°00′N 26°46′E
117 R9 **Bereznehuvate** Mykolayivs'ka Oblast', S Ukraine 47°18′N 32°52′E
125 N10 **Bereznik** Arkhangel'skaya Oblast', NW Russian Federation 62°50′N 42°40′E
125 U13 **Berezniki** Permskiy Kray, NW Russian Federation 59°26′N 56°49′E
Berëzovka *see* Byarozavka, Belarus
Berezovka *see* Berezivka, Ukraine
122 H9 **Berezovo** Khanty-Mansiyskiy Avtonomnyy Okrug-Yugra, N Russian Federation 63°48′N 64°38′E
127 O9 **Berezovskaya** Volgogradskaya Oblast', SW Russian Federation 50°17′N 43°58′E
123 S13 **Berezovyy** Khabarovskiy Kray, E Russian Federation 51°42′N 135°39′E
83 E25 **Berg** ~ W South Africa
Berg *see* Berg bei Rohrbach
105 V4 **Berga** Cataluña, NE Spain 42°06′N 01°41′E
95 N20 **Berga** Kalmar, S Sweden 57°13′N 16°03′E
136 B13 **Bergama** İzmir, W Turkey 39°08′N 27°10′E
106 E7 **Bergamo** *anc.* Bergomum. Lombardia, N Italy 45°42′N 09°40′E
105 P3 **Bergara** País Vasco, N Spain 43°05′N 02°25′W
109 S3 **Berg bei Rohrbach** *var.* Berg. Oberösterreich, N Austria 48°34′N 14°02′E
100 O6 **Bergen** Mecklenburg-Vorpommern, NE Germany 54°25′N 13°25′E
101 I11 **Bergen** Niedersachsen, NW Germany 52°49′N 09°57′E
98 H8 **Bergen** Noord-Holland, NW Netherlands 52°40′N 04°42′E
94 C13 **Bergen** Hordaland, S Norway 60°24′N 05°19′E
Bergen *see* Mons
55 W9 **Berg en Dal** Brokopondo, C Suriname 05°15′N 55°20′W
99 G15 **Bergen op Zoom** Noord-Brabant, S Netherlands 51°30′N 04°17′E
102 L13 **Bergerac** Dordogne, SW France 44°51′N 00°30′E
99 J16 **Bergeyk** Noord-Brabant, S Netherlands 51°19′N 05°21′E
101 D16 **Bergheim** Nordrhein-Westfalen, W Germany 50°57′N 06°39′E
55 X10 **Bergi** Sipaliwini, E Suriname 04°36′N 54°24′W
101 E16 **Bergisch Gladbach** Nordrhein-Westfalen, W Germany 50°59′N 07°09′E
101 F14 **Bergkamen** Nordrhein-Westfalen, W Germany 51°32′N 07°41′E
95 N21 **Bergkvara** Kalmar, S Sweden 56°22′N 16°04′E
Bergomum *see* Bergamo
98 K13 **Bergse Maas** ~ S Netherlands

◆ Country ● Country Capital ◇ Dependent Territory ○ Dependent Territory Capital ◈ Administrative Regions ✈ International Airport ▲ Mountain ▲▲ Mountain Range Volcano ~ River ◎ Lake ▣ Reservoir

95 P15 **Bergshamra** Stockholm, C Sweden *59°37′N 18°40′E*
94 N10 **Bergsjö** Gävleborg, C Sweden *62°00′N 17°10′E*
93 J14 **Bergsviken** Norrbotten, N Sweden *65°16′N 21°24′E*
Bergum *see* Burgum
98 M6 **Bergumer Meer** ◎ N Netherlands
94 N12 **Bergviken** ◎ C Sweden
168 M11 **Berhala, Selat** *strait* Sumatera, W Indonesia
Berhampore *see* Baharampur
99 J17 **Beringen** Limburg, NE Belgium *51°04′N 05°14′E*
39 T12 **Bering Glacier** *glacier* Alaska, USA
Beringov Proliv *see* Bering Strait
192 L2 **Bering Sea** *sea* N Pacific Ocean
38 L9 **Bering Strait** *Rus.* Beringov Proliv. *strait* Bering Sea/ Chukchi Sea
Berislav *see* Beryslav
105 O15 **Berja** Andalucía, S Spain *36°51′N 02°56′W*
94 H9 **Berkåk** Sør-Trøndelag, S Norway *62°50′N 10°01′E*
98 N11 **Berkel** ≈ Germany/ Netherlands
35 N8 **Berkeley** California, W USA *37°52′N 122°16′W*
65 E24 **Berkeley Sound** *sound* NE Falkland Islands
21 V2 **Berkeley Springs** *var.* Bath. West Virginia, NE USA *39°38′N 78°14′W*
195 N6 **Berkner Island** *island* Antarctica
114 G8 **Berkovitsa** Montana, NW Bulgaria *43°15′N 23°05′E*
97 M22 **Berkshire** *former county* S England, United Kingdom
99 H17 **Berlaar** Antwerpen, N Belgium *51°08′N 04°39′E*
Berlanga *see* Berlanga de Duero
105 P6 **Berlanga de Duero** *var.* Berlanga. Castilla y León, N Spain *41°28′N 02°51′W*
0 I16 **Berlanga Rise** *undersea feature* E Pacific Ocean *08°30′N 93°30′W*
99 F17 **Berlare** Oost-Vlaanderen, NW Belgium *51°02′N 04°01′E*
104 E9 **Berlenga, Ilha da** *island* C Portugal
92 M7 **Berlevåg** *Lapp.* Bearalváhki. Finnmark, N Norway *70°51′N 29°04′E*
100 O12 **Berlin** ● (Germany) Berlin, NE Germany *52°31′N 13°26′E*
21 Z4 **Berlin** Maryland, NE USA *38°19′N 75°13′W*
19 O7 **Berlin** New Hampshire, NE USA *44°27′N 71°13′W*
18 D16 **Berlin** Pennsylvania, NE USA *39°54′N 78°57′W*
30 L7 **Berlin** Wisconsin, N USA *43°57′N 88°59′W*
100 O12 **Berlin** ◈ *state* NE Germany
Berlinchen *see* Barlinek
31 U12 **Berlin Lake** ◎ Ohio, N USA
183 R11 **Bermagui** New South Wales, SE Australia *36°26′S 150°01′E*
40 L8 **Bermejillo** Durango, C Mexico *25°55′N 103°39′W*
62 L5 **Bermejo, Río** ≈ N Argentina
62 I10 **Bermejo, Río** ≈ W Argentina
62 M6 **Bermejo viejo, Río** ≈ N Argentina
105 P2 **Bermeo** País Vasco, N Spain *43°25′N 02°44′W*
104 K6 **Bermillo de Sayago** Castilla y León, N Spain *41°22′N 06°08′W*
106 E6 **Bermina, Pizzo** *Rmsch.* Piz Bernina. ▲ Italy/Switzerland *46°22′N 09°52′E* ***see also*** Bermina, Piz
64 A12 **Bermuda** *var.* Bermuda Islands, Bermudas; ***prev.*** Somers Islands. ◇ *UK crown colony* NW Atlantic Ocean
1 N11 **Bermuda** *var.* Great Bermuda, Long Island, Main Island. *island* Bermuda
Bermuda Islands *see* Bermuda
Bermuda-New England Seamount Arc *see* New England Seamounts
1 N11 **Bermuda Rise** *undersea feature* C Sargasso Sea *32°30′N 65°00′W*
Bermudas *see* Bermuda
108 D8 **Bern** *Fr.* Berne. ● (Switzerland) Bern, W Switzerland *46°57′N 07°26′E*
108 D9 **Bern** *Fr.* Berne. ◈ *canton* W Switzerland
37 R11 **Bernalillo** New Mexico, SW USA *35°18′N 106°33′W*
14 H12 **Bernard Lake** ◎ Ontario, S Canada
61 B18 **Bernardo de Irigoyen** Santa Fe, NE Argentina *32°09′S 61°06′W*
18 J14 **Bernardsville** New Jersey, NE USA *40°43′N 74°34′W*
63 K14 **Bernasconi** La Pampa, C Argentina *37°55′S 63°44′W*
100 O12 **Bernau** Brandenburg, NE Germany *52°41′N 13°36′E*
102 L4 **Bernay** Eure, N France *49°05′N 00°36′E*
101 L14 **Bernburg** Sachsen-Anhalt, C Germany *51°47′N 11°45′E*
109 X5 **Berndorf** Niederösterreich, NE Austria *47°58′N 16°08′E*
31 Q12 **Berne** Indiana, N USA *40°39′N 84°57′W*
Berne *see* Bern
108 D10 **Berner Alpen** *var.* Berner Oberland, *Eng.* Bernese Oberland. ▲▲ SW Switzerland
Berner Oberland/Bernese Oberland *see* Berner Alpen
109 Y2 **Bernhardsthal** Niederösterreich, N Austria *48°40′N 16°51′E*
22 H4 **Bernice** Louisiana, S USA *32°49′N 92°39′W*
27 Y8 **Bernie** Missouri, C USA *36°40′N 89°58′W*
180 G9 **Bernier Island** *island* Western Australia
Bernina Pass *see* Bernina, Passo del
108 J10 **Bernina, Passo del** *Eng.* Bernina Pass. *pass* SE Switzerland
108 J10 **Bernina, Piz** *It.* Pizzo Bernina. ▲ Italy/Switzerland *46°22′N 09°55′E* ***see also*** Bermina, Pizzo
Bernina, Piz *see* Bermina, Pizzo
99 E20 **Bernissart** Hainaut, SW Belgium *50°29′N 03°37′E*
101 E18 **Bernkastel-Kues** Rheinland-Pfalz, W Germany *49°55′N 07°04′E*
Beroea *see* Ḥalab
172 H6 **Beroroha** Toliara, SW Madagascar *21°40′S 45°10′E*
Béroubouay *see* Gbéroubouè
111 C17 **Beroun** *Ger.* Beraun. Středočeský Kraj, W Czech Republic *49°58′N 14°05′E*
111 C16 **Berounka** *Ger.* Beraun. ≈ W Czech Republic
113 Q18 **Berovo** E FYR Macedonia *41°45′N 22°50′E*
74 F6 **Berrechid** *var.* Berchid. W Morocco *33°16′N 07°32′W*
103 R15 **Berre, Étang de** ◎ SE France
103 S15 **Berre-l'Étang** Bouches-du-Rhône, SE France *43°28′N 05°10′E*
182 K9 **Berri** South Australia *34°16′S 140°35′E*
31 O10 **Berrien Springs** Michigan, N USA *41°57′N 86°20′W*
183 O10 **Berrigan** New South Wales, SE Australia *35°41′S 145°50′E*
103 N9 **Berry** *cultural region* C France
35 N7 **Berryessa, Lake** ◎ California, W USA
44 G2 **Berry Islands** *island group* N Bahamas
27 T9 **Berryville** Arkansas, C USA *36°22′N 93°35′W*
21 V3 **Berryville** Virginia, NE USA *39°08′N 77°59′W*
83 D21 **Berseba** Karas, S Namibia *26°00′S 17°46′E*
117 O8 **Bershad'** Vinnyts'ka Oblast', C Ukraine *48°20′N 29°30′E*
28 L3 **Berthold** North Dakota, N USA *48°16′N 101°48′W*
37 T3 **Berthoud** Colorado, C USA *40°18′N 105°04′W*
37 S4 **Berthoud Pass** *pass* Colorado, C USA
79 F15 **Bertoua** Est, E Cameroon *04°34′N 13°42′E*
25 S10 **Bertram** Texas, SW USA *30°44′N 98°03′W*
63 G22 **Bertrand, Cerro** ▲ S Argentina *50°00′S 73°27′W*
99 J23 **Bertrix** Luxembourg, SE Belgium *49°52′N 05°15′E*
191 P3 **Beru** *var.* Peru. *atoll* Tungaru, W Kiribati
Beruni *see* Beruniy
146 I9 **Beruniy** *var.* Biruni, *Rus.* Beruni. Qoraqalpog'iston Respublikasi, W Uzbekistan *41°48′N 60°39′E*
58 F13 **Beruri** Amazonas, NW Brazil *03°44′S 61°13′W*
18 H14 **Berwick** Pennsylvania, NE USA *41°03′N 76°13′W*
96 K12 **Berwick** *cultural region* SE Scotland, United Kingdom
96 L12 **Berwick-upon-Tweed** N England, United Kingdom *55°46′N 02°W*
117 S10 **Beryslav** *Rus.* Berislav. Khersons'ka Oblast', S Ukraine *46°51′N 33°26′E*
Berytus *see* Beyrouth
172 H4 **Besalampy** Mahajanga, W Madagascar *16°43′S 44°29′E*
103 T8 **Besançon** *anc.* Besontium, Vesontio. Doubs, E France *47°14′N 06°01′E*
103 P10 **Besbre** ≈ C France
Bescanuova *see* Baška
Besdan *see* Bezdan
Besed' *see* Byesyedz'
147 R10 **Beshariq** *Rus.* Besharyk; *prev.* Kirovo. Farg'ona Viloyati, E Uzbekistan *40°26′N 70°33′E*
Besharyk *see* Beshariq
146 L9 **Beshbuloq** *Rus.* Beshulak. Navoiy Viloyati, N Uzbekistan *41°55′N 64°13′E*
Beshenkovichi *see* Byeshankovichy
146 M13 **Beshkent** Qashqadaryo Viloyati, S Uzbekistan *38°47′N 65°42′E*
Beshulak *see* Beshbuloq
112 L10 **Beška** Vojvodina, N Serbia *45°09′N 20°04′E*
Beskra *see* Biskra
127 O16 **Beslan** Respublika Severnaya Osetiya, SW Russian Federation *43°12′N 44°33′E*
113 P16 **Besna Kobila** ▲ SE Serbia *42°30′N 22°16′E*
137 N16 **Besni** Adıyaman, S Turkey *37°42′N 37°53′E*
Besontium *see* Besançon
121 Q2 **Beşparmak Dağları** *Eng.* Kyrenia Mountains. ▲▲ N Cyprus
Bessarabka *see* Basarabeasca
92 O2 **Bessels, Kapp** *headland* C Svalbard *78°36′N 21°43′E*
23 P4 **Bessemer** Alabama, S USA *33°24′N 86°57′W*
30 K3 **Bessemer** Michigan, N USA *46°28′N 90°03′W*
21 Q10 **Bessemer City** North Carolina, SE USA *35°16′N 81°16′W*
102 M10 **Bessines-sur-Gartempe** Haute-Vienne, C France *46°06′N 01°22′E*
99 K15 **Best** Noord-Brabant, S Netherlands *51°31′N 05°24′E*
25 N9 **Best** Texas, SW USA *31°13′N 101°34′W*
125 O11 **Bestuzhevo** Arkhangel'skaya Oblast', NW Russian Federation *61°36′N 43°54′E*
123 M11 **Bestyakh** Respublika Sakha (Yakutiya), NE Russian Federation *61°25′N 129°05′E*
Besztercze *see* Bistriţa
Beszterczebánya *see* Banská Bystrica
172 I5 **Betafo** Antananarivo, C Madagascar *19°50′S 46°50′E*
104 H2 **Betanzos** Galicia, NW Spain *43°17′N 08°17′W*
104 G2 **Betanzos, Ría de** *estuary* NW Spain
79 G15 **Bétaré Oya** Est, E Cameroon *05°34′N 14°09′E*
105 S9 **Bétera** Valenciana, E Spain *39°35′N 00°28′W*
77 R15 **Bétérou** C Benin *09°13′N 02°18′E*
83 K21 **Bethal** Mpumalanga, NE South Africa *26°27′S 29°28′E*
30 K15 **Bethalto** Illinois, N USA *38°54′N 90°02′W*
83 D21 **Bethanie** *var.* Bethanien, Bethany. Karas, S Namibia *26°32′S 17°11′E*
Bethanien *see* Bethanie
27 S2 **Bethany** Missouri, C USA *40°15′N 94°03′W*
27 N10 **Bethany** Oklahoma, C USA *35°31′N 97°37′W*
Bethany *see* Bethanie
39 N12 **Bethel** Alaska, USA *60°47′N 161°45′W*
19 P7 **Bethel** Maine, NE USA *44°24′N 70°47′W*
21 W9 **Bethel** North Carolina, SE USA *35°46′N 77°21′W*
18 B15 **Bethel Park** Pennsylvania, NE USA *40°21′N 80°03′W*
21 W3 **Bethesda** Maryland, NE USA *39°00′N 77°05′W*
83 J22 **Bethlehem** Free State, C South Africa *28°12′S 28°16′E*
18 I14 **Bethlehem** Pennsylvania, NE USA *40°36′N 75°22′W*
138 F10 **Bethlehem** *var.* Beit Lekhem, *Ar.* Bayt Laḥm, ***Heb.*** Bet Leḥem. C West Bank *31°43′N 35°12′E*
Bethlen *see* Beclean
83 I24 **Bethulie** Free State, C South Africa *30°30′S 25°59′E*
103 O1 **Béthune** Pas-de-Calais, N France *50°32′N 02°38′E*
102 M3 **Béthune** ≈ N France
104 M14 **Béticos, Sistemas** *var.* Sistema Penibético, ***Eng.*** Baetic Cordillera, Baetic Mountains. ▲▲ S Spain
54 I6 **Betijoque** Trujillo, NW Venezuela *09°25′N 70°45′W*
59 M20 **Betim** Minas Gerais, SE Brazil *19°56′S 44°10′W*
190 H3 **Betio** Tarawa, W Kiribati *01°21′N 172°56′E*
172 H7 **Betioky** Toliara, S Madagascar *23°42′S 44°22′E*
Bet Leḥem *see* Bethlehem
Betlen *see* Beclean
167 O17 **Betong** Yala, SW Thailand *05°45′N 101°05′E*
79 I16 **Bétou** Likouala, N Congo *03°08′N 18°31′E*
145 P14 **Betpakdala** *prev.* Betpak-Dala ***Kaz.*** Betpaqdala. *plateau* S Kazakhstan
Betpak-Dala *see* Betpakdala
Betpaqdala *see* Betpakdala
172 H7 **Betroka** Toliara, S Madagascar *23°15′S 46°07′E*
Betschau *see* Bečva
Bet She'an *see* Beit She'an
15 T6 **Betsiamites** Québec, SE Canada *48°56′N 68°40′W*
15 T6 **Betsiamites** ≈ Québec, SE Canada
172 I4 **Betsiboka** ≈ N Madagascar
Betsukai *see* Bekkai
99 M25 **Bettembourg** Luxembourg, S Luxembourg *49°31′N 06°06′E*
99 M23 **Bettendorf** Diekirch, NE Luxembourg *49°53′N 06°13′E*
29 Z14 **Bettendorf** Iowa, C USA *41°31′N 90°31′W*
Bette, Pic *see* Bette, Picco
75 R13 **Bette, Picco** *var.* Bikkū Bīttī, Pic Bette. ▲ S Libya *22°02′N 19°07′E*
153 P12 **Bettiah** Bihār, N India *26°49′N 84°30′E*
39 Q7 **Bettles** Alaska, USA *66°54′N 151°40′W*
95 N17 **Bettna** Södermanland, C Sweden *58°52′N 16°40′E*
154 H11 **Betūl** *prev.* Badnur. Madhya Pradesh, C India *21°55′N 77°54′E*
154 H9 **Betwa** ≈ C India
101 F16 **Betzdorf** Rheinland-Pfalz, W Germany *50°47′N 07°50′E*
82 C9 **Béu** Uíge, NW Angola *06°15′S 15°32′E*
31 P6 **Beulah** Michigan, N USA *43°35′N 86°52′W*
28 L5 **Beulah** North Dakota, N USA *47°16′N 101°48′W*
98 M8 **Beulakerwijde** ◎ N Netherlands
98 L13 **Beuningen** Gelderland, SE Netherlands *51°52′N 05°47′E*
Beuthen *see* Bytom
103 N8 **Beuvron** ≈ C France
99 F16 **Beveren** Oost-Vlaanderen, N Belgium *51°13′N 04°15′E*
21 T9 **B. Everett Jordan Reservoir** *var.* Jordan Lake. ⊠ North Carolina, SE USA
97 N17 **Beverley** E England, United Kingdom *53°51′N 00°26′W*
Beverley *see* Beverly
99 J17 **Beverlo** Limburg, NE Belgium *51°06′N 05°14′E*
19 P11 **Beverly** Massachusetts, NE USA *42°33′N 70°49′W*
32 J9 **Beverly** *var.* Beverley. Washington, NW USA *46°50′N 119°57′W*
35 S15 **Beverly Hills** California, W USA *34°02′N 118°25′W*
101 I14 **Beverungen** Nordrhein-Westfalen, C Germany *51°39′N 09°22′E*
98 H9 **Beverwijk** Noord-Holland, W Netherlands *52°29′N 04°40′E*
108 C10 **Bex** Vaud, W Switzerland *46°15′N 07°00′E*
97 P23 **Bexhill** *var.* Bexhill-on-Sea. SE England, United Kingdom *50°50′N 00°28′E*
Bexhill-on-Sea *see* Bexhill
136 E17 **Bey Dağları** ▲▲ SW Turkey
Beyj *see* Belyy
136 E10 **Beykoz** İstanbul, NW Turkey *41°09′N 29°06′E*
76 K15 **Beyla** SE Guinea *08°43′N 08°41′W*
137 X12 **Beyläqan** *prev.* Zhdanov. SW Azerbaijan *39°43′N 47°38′E*
80 L10 **Beylul** *var.* Beilul. SE Eritrea *13°10′N 42°27′E*
144 H14 **Beyneu** *Kaz.* Beyneū. Mangistau, SW Kazakhstan *45°20′N 55°11′E*
Beyneū *see* Beyneu
165 X14 **Beyonēsu-retsugan** ***Eng.*** Bayonnaise Rocks. *island group* SE Japan
136 G12 **Beypazarı** Ankara, NW Turkey *40°10′N 31°56′E*
155 F21 **Beypore** Kerala, SW India *11°10′N 75°49′E*
138 G7 **Beyrouth** *var.* Bayrūt, ***Eng.*** Beirut; ***anc.*** Berytus. ● (Lebanon) W Lebanon *33°55′N 35°31′E*
138 G7 **Beyrouth** ✈ W Lebanon *33°52′N 35°30′E*
136 G15 **Beyşehir** Konya, SW Turkey *37°40′N 31°43′E*
136 G15 **Beyşehir Gölü** ◎ C Turkey
108 J7 **Bezau** Vorarlberg, NW Austria *47°24′N 09°55′E*
112 J8 **Bezdan** *Ger.* Besdan, ***Hung.*** Bezdán. Vojvodina, NW Serbia *45°51′N 19°00′E*
Bezdezh *see* Byezdzyezh
124 G15 **Bezhanitsy** Pskovskaya Oblast', W Russian Federation *56°57′N 29°53′E*
124 K15 **Bezhetsk** Tverskaya Oblast', W Russian Federation *57°47′N 36°42′E*
103 P16 **Béziers** *anc.* Baeterrae, Baeterrae Septimanorum, Julia Beterrae. Hérault, S France *43°21′N 03°13′E*
Bezmein *see* Abadan
Bezwada *see* Vijayawāda
154 P12 **Bhadrak** *var.* Bhadrakh. Orissa, E India *21°04′N 86°30′N*
Bhadrakh *see* Bhadrak
155 F19 **Bhadra Reservoir** ⊠ SW India
155 F18 **Bhadrāvati** Karnātaka, SW India *13°52′N 75°43′E*
153 R14 **Bhāgalpur** Bihār, NE India *25°14′N 86°59′E*
Bhairab *see* Bhairab Bazar
153 U14 **Bhairab Bazar** *var.* Bhairab. Dhaka, C Bangladesh *24°04′N 91°00′E*
153 O11 **Bhairahawā** Western, S Nepal *27°31′N 83°27′E*
149 S8 **Bhakkar** Punjab, E Pakistan *31°40′N 71°08′E*
153 P11 **Bhaktapur** Central, C Nepal *27°47′N 85°21′E*
167 N3 **Bhamo** *var.* Banmo. Kachin State, N Myanmar (Burma) *24°15′N 97°15′E*
Bhāmragad *see* Bhāmragarh
154 K13 **Bhāmragarh** *var.* Bhāmragad. Mahārāshtra, C India *19°28′N 80°39′E*
154 J12 **Bhandāra** Mahārāshtra, C India *21°10′N 79°41′E*
Bhārat *see* India
152 J12 **Bharatpur** *prev.* Bhurtpore. Rājasthān, N India *27°14′N 77°29′E*
154 D11 **Bharūch** Gujarāt, W India *21°48′N 72°55′E*
155 E18 **Bhatkal** Karnātaka, W India *13°59′N 74°34′E*
153 O13 **Bhatni** *var.* Bhatni Junction. Uttar Pradesh, N India *26°23′N 83°56′E*
Bhatni Junction *see* Bhatni
153 S16 **Bhātpāra** West Bengal, NE India *22°55′N 88°30′E*
149 U7 **Bhaun** Punjab, E Pakistan *32°53′N 72°48′E*
Bhaunagar *see* Bhāvnagar
Bhavānipātna *see* Bhawānipatna
155 H21 **Bhavānīsāgar** ⊠ S India
154 D11 **Bhāvnagar** *prev.* Bhaunagar. Gujarāt, W India *21°46′N 72°14′E*
154 M13 **Bhawānipātna** *var.* Bhavānipātna. Orissa, E India *19°56′N 83°09′E*
Bheanntraí, Bá *see* Bantry Bay
Bheara, Béal an *see* Gweebarra Bay
154 K12 **Bhilai** Chhattīsgarh, C India *21°12′N 81°26′E*
152 G13 **Bhīlwāra** Rājasthān, N India *25°23′N 74°39′E*
155 E14 **Bhīma** ≈ S India
155 K16 **Bhīmavaram** Andhra Pradesh, E India *16°34′N 81°35′E*
154 I7 **Bhind** Madhya Pradesh, C India *26°33′N 78°47′E*
152 E13 **Bhīnmāl** Rājasthān, N India *25°01′N 72°22′E*
Bhir *see* Bīd
154 D13 **Bhiwandi** Mahārāshtra, W India *19°21′N 73°08′E*
152 H10 **Bhiwāni** Haryāna, N India *28°50′N 76°10′E*
152 L13 **Bhognīpur** Uttar Pradesh, N India *26°12′N 79°48′E*
153 U16 **Bhola** Barisal, S Bangladesh *22°40′N 91°36′E*
154 H10 **Bhopāl** *state capital* Madhya Pradesh, C India *23°17′N 77°25′E*
155 J14 **Bhopālpatnam** Chhattīsgarh, C India *18°51′N 80°22′E*
155 E14 **Bhor** Mahārāshtra, W India *18°10′N 73°55′E*
154 O12 **Bhubaneshwar** *prev.* Bhubaneswar, Bhuvaneshwar. *state capital* Orissa, E India *20°16′N 85°51′E*
Bhubaneswar *see* Bhubaneshwar
154 B9 **Bhuj** Gujarāt, W India *23°16′N 69°40′E*
Bhuket *see* Phuket
Bhurtpore *see* Bharatpur
Bhusaval *see* Bhusāwal
154 G12 **Bhusāwal** *prev.* Bhusaval. Mahārāshtra, C India *21°01′N 75°50′E*
153 T12 **Bhutan** *off.* Kingdom of Bhutan, *var.* Druk-yul. ◆ *monarchy* S Asia
Bhutan, Kingdom of *see* Bhutan
Bhuvaneshwar *see* Bhubaneshwar
143 T15 **Bībān, Kūh-e** ▲▲ S Iran
77 V18 **Biafra, Bight of** *var.* Bight of Bonny. *bay* W Africa
171 W12 **Biak** Papua, E Indonesia *01°10′S 136°05′E*
171 W12 **Biak, Pulau** *island* E Indonesia
110 P12 **Biała Podlaska** Lubelskie, E Poland *52°03′N 23°08′E*
110 F7 **Białogard** *Ger.* Belgard. Zachodnio-pomorskie, NW Poland *54°01′N 15°59′E*
110 P10 **Białowieska, Puszcza** ***Bel.*** Byelavyezhskaya Pushcha, *Rus.* Belovezhskaya Pushcha. *physical region* Belarus/Poland ***see also*** Byelavyezhskaya, Pushcha
Białowieska, Puszcza *see* Byelavyezhskaya Pushcha
110 G8 **Biały Bór** *Ger.* Baldenburg. Zachodnio-pomorskie, NW Poland *53°53′N 16°49′E*
110 P9 **Białystok** *Rus.* Belostok, Bielostok. Podlaskie, NE Poland *53°08′N 23°09′E*
107 L24 **Biancavilla** *prev.* Inessa. Sicilia, Italy, C Mediterranean Sea *37°38′N 14°52′E*
Bianco, Monte *see* Blanc, Mont
Bianjiang *see* Xunke
76 L15 **Biankouma** W Ivory Coast *07°44′N 07°37′W*
167 R7 **Bia, Phou** *var.* Pou Bia. ▲ C Laos *18°59′N 103°09′E*
Bia, Pou *see* Bia, Phou
143 R5 **Bīārjmand** Semnān, N Iran *36°05′N 55°50′E*
105 P4 **Biarra** ≈ NE Spain
102 I15 **Biarritz** Pyrénées-Atlantiques, SW France *43°25′N 01°40′W*
108 H10 **Biasca** Ticino, S Switzerland *46°22′N 08°59′E*
61 E17 **Biassini** Salto, N Uruguay *31°18′S 57°05′W*
Biasteri *see* Laguardia
165 S3 **Bibai** Hokkaidō, NE Japan *43°21′N 141°53′E*
83 B15 **Bibala** *Port.* Vila Arriaga. Namibe, SW Angola *14°46′S 13°21′E*
104 I4 **Bibéi** ≈ NW Spain
Biberach *see* Biberach an der Riss
101 I23 **Biberach an der Riss** *var.* Biberach, *Ger.* Biberach an der Riß. Baden-Württemberg, S Germany *48°06′N 09°48′E*
108 E7 **Biberist** Solothurn, NW Switzerland *47°11′N 07°34′E*
77 O16 **Bibiani** SW Ghana *06°28′N 02°20′W*
112 C13 **Bibinje** Zadar, SW Croatia *44°04′N 15°17′E*
Biblical Gebal *see* Jbaïl
116 I5 **Bibrka** *Pol.* Bóbrka, *Rus.* Bobrka. L'vivs'ka Oblast', NW Ukraine *49°39′N 24°16′E*
117 N10 **Bic** ≈ S Moldova
113 M18 **Bicaj** Kukës, NE Albania *42°00′N 20°24′E*
116 K10 **Bicaz** *Hung.* Békás. Neamţ, NE Romania *46°53′N 26°05′E*
183 Q16 **Bicheno** Tasmania, SE Australia *41°56′S 148°15′E*
Bichiş *see* Békés
Bichiş-Ciaba *see* Békéscsaba
Bichitra *see* Phichit
137 P8 **Bich'vinta** *Prev.* Bichvint'a, ***Rus.*** Pitsunda. NW Georgia *43°12′N 40°21′E*
Bichvint'a *see* Bich'vinta
15 T7 **Bic, Île du** *island* Québec, SE Canada
32 J10 **Bickleton** Washington, NW USA *46°00′N 120°16′W*
36 L6 **Bicknell** Utah, W USA *38°20′N 111°32′W*
171 S11 **Bicoli** Pulau Halmahera, E Indonesia *0°34′N 128°33′E*
111 J22 **Bicske** Fejér, C Hungary *47°30′N 18°36′E*
155 F14 **Bīd** *prev.* Bhir. Mahārāshtra, W India *19°17′N 75°22′E*
77 U15 **Bida** Niger, C Nigeria *09°06′N 06°02′E*
155 H15 **Bīdar** Karnātaka, C India *17°56′N 77°35′E*
141 Y8 **Bidbid** NE Oman *23°25′N 58°08′E*
19 P9 **Biddeford** Maine, NE USA *43°29′N 70°27′W*
98 L9 **Biddinghuizen** Flevoland, C Netherlands *52°28′N 05°41′E*
33 X11 **Biddle** Montana, NW USA *45°04′N 105°21′W*
97 J23 **Bideford** SW England, United Kingdom *51°01′N 04°12′W*
82 D13 **Bié** ◈ *province* C Angola
35 O2 **Bieber** California, W USA *41°07′N 121°09′W*
110 O9 **Biebrza** ≈ NE Poland
165 T3 **Biei** Hokkaidō, NE Japan *43°33′N 142°28′E*
108 D8 **Biel** *Fr.* Bienne. Bern, W Switzerland *47°09′N 07°16′E*
100 G13 **Bielefeld** Nordrhein-Westfalen, NW Germany *52°01′N 08°32′E*
108 D8 **Bieler See** *Fr.* Lac de Bienne. ◎ W Switzerland
Bielitz/Bielitz-Biala *see* Bielsko-Biała
106 C7 **Biella** Piemonte, N Italy *45°34′N 08°04′E*
Bielostok *see* Białystok
111 J17 **Bielsko-Biała** *Ger.* Bielitz, Bielitz-Biala. Śląskie, S Poland *49°49′N 19°01′E*
110 P10 **Bielsk Podlaski** Białystok, E Poland *52°45′N 23°11′E*
Bien Bien *see* Điện Biên Phu
Biên Đông *see* South China Sea
11 V17 **Bienfait** Saskatchewan, S Canada *49°06′N 102°47′W*
167 T14 **Biên Hoa** Đông Nai, S Vietnam *10°58′N 106°50′E*
Bienne *see* Biel
Bienne, Lac de *see* Bieler See
12 K8 **Bienville, Lac** ◎ Québec, C Canada
82 D13 **Bié, Planalto do** *var.* Bié Plateau. *plateau* C Angola
Bié Plateau *see* Bié, Planalto do
108 B9 **Bière** Vaud, W Switzerland *46°32′N 06°19′E*
98 O4 **Bierum** Groningen, NE Netherlands *53°25′N 06°51′E*
98 I13 **Biesbos** *var.* Biesbosch. *wetland* S Netherlands
Biesbosch *see* Biesbos
99 H21 **Biesme** Namur, S Belgium *50°19′N 04°43′E*
101 H21 **Bietigheim-Bissingen** Baden-Württemberg, SW Germany *48°57′N 09°07′E*
99 I23 **Bièvre** Namur, SE Belgium *49°56′N 05°01′E*
79 D18 **Bifoun** Moyen-Ogooué, NW Gabon *0°15′S 10°24′E*
165 T2 **Bifuka** Hokkaidō, NE Japan *44°28′N 142°20′E*
136 C11 **Biga** Çanakkale, NW Turkey *40°13′N 27°14′E*
136 C13 **Bigadiç** Balıkesir, W Turkey *39°24′N 28°08′E*
26 J7 **Big Basin** *basin* Kansas, C USA
185 B20 **Big Bay** *bay* South Island, New Zealand
31 O5 **Big Bay de Noc** ◎ Michigan, N USA
31 N3 **Big Bay Point** *headland* Michigan, N USA *46°51′N 87°40′W*
33 R10 **Big Belt Mountains** ▲▲ Montana, NW USA
29 N10 **Big Bend Dam** *dam* South Dakota, N USA
24 K12 **Big Bend National Park** *national park* Texas, S USA
22 K5 **Big Black River** ≈ Mississippi, S USA
27 O3 **Big Blue River** ≈ Kansas/ Nebraska, C USA
24 M10 **Big Canyon** ≈ Texas, SW USA
33 N12 **Big Creek** Idaho, NW USA *45°05′N 115°20′W*
23 N8 **Big Creek Lake** ⊠ Alabama, S USA
23 X15 **Big Cypress Swamp** *wetland* Florida, SE USA
39 S9 **Big Delta** Alaska, USA *64°09′N 145°50′W*
30 K6 **Big Eau Pleine Reservoir** ⊠ Wisconsin, N USA
19 P5 **Bigelow Mountain** ▲ Maine, NE USA *45°09′N 70°17′W*
162 G9 **Biger** *var.* Jargalant. Govĭ-Altay, W Mongolia *45°39′N 97°10′E*
29 U3 **Big Falls** Minnesota, N USA *48°13′N 93°48′W*
33 P8 **Bigfork** Montana, NW USA *48°03′N 114°04′W*
29 U3 **Big Fork River** ≈ Minnesota, N USA
11 S15 **Biggar** Saskatchewan, S Canada *52°03′N 107°59′W*
180 L3 **Bigge Island** *island* Western Australia
35 O5 **Biggs** California, W USA *39°24′N 121°44′W*
32 I11 **Biggs** Oregon, NW USA *45°39′N 120°49′W*
14 K13 **Big Gull Lake** ◎ Ontario, SE Canada
37 P16 **Big Hachet Peak** ▲ New Mexico, SW USA *31°38′N 108°24′W*
33 P11 **Big Hole River** ≈ Montana, NW USA
33 V13 **Bighorn Basin** *basin* Wyoming, C USA
33 U11 **Bighorn Lake** ◎ Montana/ Wyoming, N USA
33 W13 **Bighorn Mountains** ▲▲ Wyoming, C USA
36 J13 **Big Horn Peak** ▲ Arizona, SW USA *33°40′N 113°01′W*
33 V11 **Bighorn River** ≈ Montana/ Wyoming, NW USA
9 S7 **Big Island** *island* Nunavut, NE Canada
39 O16 **Big Koniuji Island** *island* Shumagin Islands, Alaska, USA
25 N9 **Big Lake** Texas, SW USA *31°12′N 101°29′W*
19 T5 **Big Lake** ◎ Maine, NE USA
30 I3 **Big Manitou Falls** *waterfall* Wisconsin, N USA
35 R2 **Big Mountain** ▲ Nevada, W USA *41°18′N 119°03′W*
108 G10 **Bignasco** Ticino, S Switzerland *46°21′N 08°37′E*
29 R16 **Big Nemaha River** ≈ Nebraska, C USA
76 G12 **Bignona** SW Senegal *12°49′N 16°16′W*
Bigorra *see* Tarbes
Bigosovo *see* Bihosava
35 S10 **Big Pine** California, W USA *37°09′N 118°18′W*
35 Q14 **Big Pine Mountain** ▲ California, W USA *34°41′N 119°37′W*
27 V6 **Big Piney Creek** ≈ Missouri, C USA
65 M24 **Big Point** *headland* N Tristan da Cunha *37°10′S 12°18′W*
31 P8 **Big Rapids** Michigan, N USA *43°42′N 85°28′W*
30 K6 **Big Rib River** ≈ Wisconsin, N USA
14 L14 **Big Rideau Lake** ◎ Ontario, SE Canada
11 T14 **Big River** Saskatchewan, C Canada *53°48′N 106°55′W*
27 X5 **Big River** ≈ Missouri, C USA
31 N7 **Big Sable Point** *headland* Michigan, N USA *44°03′N 86°30′W*
33 S7 **Big Sandy** Montana, NW USA *48°08′N 110°09′W*
25 W6 **Big Sandy** Texas, SW USA *32°34′N 95°06′W*
37 V5 **Big Sandy Creek** ≈ Colorado, C USA
29 Q16 **Big Sandy Creek** ≈ Nebraska, C USA
29 V5 **Big Sandy Lake** ◎ Minnesota, N USA
36 J11 **Big Sandy River** ≈ Arizona, SW USA
21 P5 **Big Sandy River** ≈ S USA
23 V6 **Big Satilla Creek** ≈ Georgia, SE USA
29 R12 **Big Sioux River** ≈ Iowa/ South Dakota, N USA
35 U7 **Big Smoky Valley** *valley* Nevada, W USA
25 N7 **Big Spring** Texas, SW USA *32°15′N 101°30′W*
19 Q5 **Big Squaw Mountain** ▲ Maine, NE USA *45°28′N 69°42′W*
21 O7 **Big Stone Gap** Virginia, NE USA *36°52′N 82°45′W*
29 Q8 **Big Stone Lake** ◎ Minnesota/South Dakota, N USA
22 K4 **Big Sunflower River** ≈ Mississippi, S USA
33 T11 **Big Timber** Montana, NW USA *45°50′N 109°57′W*
12 D8 **Big Trout Lake** Ontario, C Canada *53°40′N 90°00′W*
14 I12 **Big Trout Lake** ◎ Ontario, SE Canada
35 O2 **Big Valley Mountains** ▲▲ California, W USA
25 Q13 **Big Wells** Texas, SW USA *28°34′N 99°34′W*
14 F11 **Bigwood** Ontario, S Canada *46°03′N 80°37′W*
112 D11 **Bihać** ◈ Federacija Bosna I Hercegovina, NW Bosnia and Herzegovina
153 P14 **Bihār** *prev.* Behar. ◈ *state* N India
Bihār *see* Bihār Sharīf
81 F20 **Biharamulo** Kagera, NW Tanzania *02°37′S 31°20′E*
153 R13 **Bihāriganj** Bihār, NE India *25°44′N 86°59′E*
153 P14 **Bihār Sharīf** *var.* Bihār. Bihār, N India *25°13′N 85°31′E*
116 F10 **Bihor** ◈ *county* NW Romania
165 V3 **Bihoro** Hokkaidō, NE Japan *43°50′N 144°05′E*
119 K11 **Bihosava** *Rus.* Bigosovo. Vitsyebskaya Voblasts', NW Belarus *55°50′N 27°46′E*
Bijagos Archipelago *see* Bijagós, Arquipélago dos
76 G13 **Bijagós, Arquipélago dos** *var.* Bijagos Archipelago. *island group* W Guinea-Bissau
155 F16 **Bijāpur** Karnātaka, C India *16°50′N 75°42′E*
142 K5 **Bījār** Kordestān, W Iran *35°52′N 47°39′E*
112 J11 **Bijeljina** Republika Srpska, NE Bosnia and Herzegovina *44°46′N 19°13′E*
113 K15 **Bijelo Polje** E Montenegro *43°03′N 19°44′E*
160 I11 **Bijie** Guizhou, S China *27°15′N 105°16′E*
152 J10 **Bijnor** Uttar Pradesh, N India *29°22′N 78°09′E*
152 F11 **Bīkāner** Rājasthān, NW India *28°01′N 73°22′E*
189 V3 **Bikar Atoll** *var.* Pikaar. *atoll* Ratak Chain, N Marshall Islands
190 H3 **Bikeman** *atoll* Tungaru, W Kiribati
190 I3 **Bikenebu** Tarawa, W Kiribati
123 S14 **Bikin** Khabarovskiy Kray, SE Russian Federation *46°45′N 134°06′E*
123 S14 **Bikin** ≈ SE Russian Federation
189 R3 **Bikini Atoll** *var.* Pikinni. *atoll* Ralik Chain, NW Marshall Islands
83 L17 **Bikita** Masvingo, E Zimbabwe *20°06′S 31°41′E*
Bikkū Bīttī *see* Bette, Picco
79 I19 **Bikoro** Equateur, W Dem. Rep. Congo *0°45′S 18°09′E*
141 Z9 **Bilād Banī Bū 'Alī** NE Oman *22°02′N 59°18′E*
141 Z9 **Bilād Banī Bū Ḥasan** NE Oman *22°09′N 59°14′E*
141 X9 **Bilād Manaḥ** *var.* Manaḥ. NE Oman *22°44′N 57°36′E*
77 Q12 **Bilanga** C Burkina *12°35′N 00°08′W*
152 F12 **Bilāra** Rājasthān, N India *26°10′N 73°48′E*
152 K10 **Bilāri** Uttar Pradesh, N India *28°37′N 78°48′E*
138 J5 **Bil'ās, Jabal al** ▲▲ C Syria
154 L11 **Bilāspur** Chhattīsgarh, C India *22°06′N 82°08′E*
152 I8 **Bilāspur** Himāchal Pradesh, N India *31°18′N 76°48′E*
168 J9 **Bila, Sungai** ≈ Sumatera, W Indonesia
137 Y13 **Biläsuvar** *Rus.* Bilyasuvar; ***prev.*** Pushkino. SE Azerbaijan *39°26′N 48°34′E*
117 O5 **Bila Tserkva** *Rus.* Belaya Tserkov'. Kyyivs'ka Oblast', N Ukraine *49°49′N 30°08′E*
167 N11 **Bilauktaung Range** *var.* Thanintari Taungdan. ▲▲ Myanmar (Burma)/ Thailand
105 O2 **Bilbao** *Basq.* Bilbo. País Vasco, N Spain *43°15′N 02°56′W*
Bilbo *see* Bilbao
92 H2 **Bíldudalur** Vestfirdhir, NW Iceland *65°40′N 23°35′W*
113 I16 **Bileća** ◈ Republika Srpska, S Bosnia and Herzegovina
136 E12 **Bilecik** Bilecik, NW Turkey *39°59′N 29°54′E*
136 F12 **Bilecik** ◈ *province* NW Turkey
116 E11 **Biled** *Ger.* Billed, ***Hung.*** Billéd. Timiş, W Romania *45°55′N 20°55′E*
111 O15 **Biłgoraj** Lubelskie, E Poland *50°31′N 22°41′E*
117 P11 **Bilhorod-Dnistrovs'kyy** ***Rus.*** Belgorod-Dnestrovskiy, ***Rom.*** Cetatea Albă, *prev.* Akkerman; *anc.* Tyras. Odes'ka Oblast', SW Ukraine *46°10′N 30°19′E*
79 M16 **Bili** Orientale, N Dem. Rep. Congo *04°07′N 25°09′E*
123 T6 **Bilibino** Chukotskiy Avtonomnyy Okrug, NE Russian Federation *67°56′N 166°45′E*
166 M8 **Bilin** Mon State, Myanmar (Burma) *17°14′N 97°12′E*
113 N21 **Bilisht** *var.* Bilishti. Korçë, SE Albania *40°36′N 21°00′E*
Bilishti *see* Bilisht
183 N10 **Billabong Creek** *var.* Moulamein Creek. *seasonal river* New South Wales, SE Australia
182 G4 **Billa Kalina** South Australia *29°57′S 136°13′E*
197 Q17 **Bill Baileys Bank** *undersea feature* N Atlantic Ocean *60°35′N 10°15′W*
Billed/Billéd *see* Biled
153 N14 **Billi** Uttar Pradesh, N India *24°30′N 82°59′E*
97 M15 **Billingham** N England, United Kingdom *54°36′N 01°17′W*
33 U11 **Billings** Montana, NW USA *45°47′N 108°32′W*
95 J16 **Billingsfors** Västra Götaland, S Sweden *58°57′N 12°14′E*
Bill of Cape Clear, The *see* Clear, Cape
28 L9 **Billsburg** South Dakota, N USA *44°22′N 101°40′W*
95 F23 **Billund** Syddtjylland, W Denmark *55°44′N 09°07′E*
36 L11 **Bill Williams Mountain** ▲ Arizona, SW USA *35°12′N 112°12′W*
36 I12 **Bill Williams River** ≈ Arizona, SW USA
77 Y8 **Bilma** Agadez, NE Niger *18°22′N 13°01′E*
77 Y8 **Bilma, Grand Erg de** *desert* NE Niger
181 Y9 **Biloela** Queensland, E Australia *24°27′S 150°31′E*
112 G8 **Bilo Gora** ▲▲ N Croatia
117 U13 **Bilohirs'k** *Rus.* Belogorsk; ***prev.*** Karasubazar. Avtonomna Respublika Krym, S Ukraine *45°04′N 34°35′E*
Bilokorovychi *see* Novi Bilokorovychi
Bilokurakine *see* Bilokurakyne
117 X5 **Bilokurakyne** *var.* Bilokurakine. Luhans'ka Oblast', E Ukraine *49°32′N 38°44′E*
117 T3 **Bilopillya** *Rus.* Belopol'ye. Sums'ka Oblast', NE Ukraine *51°09′N 34°17′E*
117 Y6 **Bilovods'k** *Rus.* Belovodsk. Luhans'ka Oblast', E Ukraine *49°11′N 39°34′E*
22 M9 **Biloxi** Mississippi, S USA *30°24′N 88°53′W*
117 R10 **Bilozerka** Khersons'ka Oblast', S Ukraine *46°36′N 32°23′E*
117 W7 **Bilozers'ke** Donets'ka Oblast', E Ukraine *48°29′N 37°03′E*
98 J11 **Bilthoven** Utrecht, C Netherlands *52°07′N 05°12′E*
78 K9 **Biltine** Biltine, E Chad *14°30′N 20°53′E*
78 J9 **Biltine** *off.* Préfecture de Biltine. ◈ *prefecture* E Chad
Biltine, Préfecture de *see* Biltine

◆ Country ● Country Capital ◇ Dependent Territory ○ Dependent Territory Capital ◈ Administrative Regions ✈ International Airport ▲ Mountain ▲▲ Mountain Range Volcano ≈ River ◎ Lake ⊠ Reservoir

Bilüü see Ulaanhus
Bilwi see Puerto Cabezas
Bilyasuvar see Biläsuvar
117 O11 **Bilyayivka** Odes'ka Oblast', SW Ukraine 46°28′N 30°11′E
99 K18 **Bilzen** Limburg, NE Belgium 50°52′N 05°31′E
Bimbéréké see Bembèrèkè
183 R10 **Bimberi Peak** ▲ New South Wales, SE Australia 35°42′S 148°46′E
77 Q15 **Bimbila** E Ghana 08°54′N 00°05′E
79 I15 **Bimbo** Ombella-Mpoko, SW Central African Republic 04°19′N 18°27′E
44 F2 **Bimini Islands** island group W Bahamas
154 I9 **Bīna** Madhya Pradesh, C India 24°09′N 78°10′E
143 T4 **Bīnālūd, Kūh-e** ▲▲ NE Iran
99 F20 **Binche** Hainaut, S Belgium 50°25′N 04°10′E
Bindloe Island see Marchena, Isla
83 L16 **Bindura** Mashonaland Central, NE Zimbabwe 17°20′S 31°21′E
105 T5 **Binefar** Aragón, NE Spain 41°51′N 00°17′E
83 J16 **Binga** Matabeleland North, W Zimbabwe 17°40′S 27°22′E
183 T5 **Bingara** New South Wales, SE Australia 29°54′S 150°36′E
101 F18 **Bingen am Rhein** Rheinland-Pfalz, SW Germany 49°58′N 07°54′E
26 M11 **Binger** Oklahoma, C USA 35°19′N 98°19′W
Bingerau see Węgrów
Bin Ghalfān, Jazā'ir see Ḩalāniyāt, Juzur al
19 Q6 **Bingham** Maine, NE USA 45°01′N 69°51′W
18 H11 **Binghamton** New York, NE USA 42°06′N 75°55′W
Bin Ghanīmah, Jabal see Bin Ghunaymah, Jabal
75 P11 **Bin Ghunaymah, Jabal** var. Jabal Bin Ghanīmah. ▲▲ C Libya
139 U3 **Bingird** As Sulaymānīyah, NE Iraq 36°03′N 45°03′E
Bingmei see Congjiang
137 P14 **Bingöl** Bingöl, E Turkey 38°54′N 40°29′E
137 P14 **Bingöl** ◈ province E Turkey
161 R6 **Binhai** var. Dongkan. Jiangsu, E China 34°00′N 119°51′E
167 V11 **Binh Đinh** var. An Nhon. Binh Đinh, C Vietnam 13°53′N 109°07′E
Binh Sơn see Châu Ô
Binimani see Bintimani
168 I8 **Binjai** Sumatera, W Indonesia 03°37′N 98°30′E
183 R6 **Binnaway** New South Wales, SE Australia 31°34′S 149°24′E
108 E6 **Binningen** Basel Landschaft, NW Switzerland 47°32′N 07°35′E
80 H12 **Bīnshangul Gumuz** var. Benishangul. ◈ W Ethiopia
168 J8 **Bintang, Banjaran** ▲▲ Peninsular Malaysia
168 M10 **Bintan, Pulau** island Kepulauan Riau, W Indonesia
76 J14 **Bintimani** var. Binimani. ▲ NE Sierra Leone 09°21′N 11°09′W
Bint Jubayl see Bent Jbaïl
169 S9 **Bintulu** Sarawak, East Malaysia 03°12′N 113°01′E
169 S9 **Bintuni** prev. Steenkool. Papua, E Indonesia 02°03′S 133°45′E
163 W8 **Binxian** prev. Binzhou. Heilongjiang, NE China 45°44′N 127°27′E
160 K14 **Binyang** var. Binzhou. Guangxi Zhuangzu Zizhiqu, S China 23°15′N 108°40′E
161 Q4 **Binzhou** Shandong, E China 37°23′N 118°03′E
Binzhou see Binyang
Binzhou see Binxian
63 G14 **Bío Bío** var. Región del Bío Bío. ◈ region C Chile
Bío Bío, Región del see Bío Bío
63 G14 **Bío Bío, Río** ≈ C Chile
79 C16 **Bioco, Isla de** var. Bioko, Eng. Fernando Po, Sp. Fernando Póo; prev. Macías Nguema Biyogo. island NW Equatorial Guinea
112 D13 **Biograd na Moru** It. Zaravecchia. Zadar, SW Croatia 43°57′N 15°27′E
Bioko see Bioco, Isla de
113 F14 **Biokovo** ▲▲ S Croatia
Biorra see Birr
Bipontium see Zweibrücken
143 W13 **Bīrag, Kūh-e** ▲▲ SE Iran
75 O10 **Birāk** var. Brak. C Libya 27°32′N 14°17′E
139 S10 **Bi'r al Islām** Karbalā', C Iraq 32°15′N 43°40′E
154 N11 **Biramitrapur** var. Birmitrapur. Orissa, E India 22°24′N 84°42′E
139 T11 **Bi'r an Niṣf** An Najaf, S Iraq 31°22′N 44°07′E
78 L12 **Birao** Vakaga, NE Central African Republic 10°14′N 22°49′E
146 J10 **Birata** Rus. Darganata, Dargan-Ata. Lebap Welaýaty, NE Turkmenistan 40°30′N 62°09′E
158 M6 **Biratar Bulak** well NW China
153 R12 **Birātnagar** Eastern, SE Nepal 26°28′N 87°16′E
165 R5 **Biratori** Hokkaidō, NE Japan 42°35′N 142°07′E
39 S8 **Birch Creek** Alaska, USA 66°17′N 145°54′W
38 M11 **Birch Creek** ≈ Alaska, USA
11 T14 **Birch Hills** Saskatchewan, S Canada 52°58′N 105°22′W
182 M10 **Birchip** Victoria, SE Australia 36°01′S 142°55′E
29 X4 **Birch Lake** ◎ Minnesota, N USA
11 Q11 **Birch Mountains** ▲▲ Alberta, W Canada
11 V15 **Birch River** Manitoba, S Canada 52°22′N 101°03′W
44 H12 **Birchs Hill** hill W Jamaica
39 R11 **Birchwood** Alaska, USA 61°24′N 149°28′W
188 I5 **Bird Island** island S Northern Mariana Islands
137 N16 **Birecik** Şanlıurfa, S Turkey 37°03′N 37°59′E
152 M10 **Birendranagar** var. Surkhet. Mid Western, W Nepal 28°35′N 81°36′E
Bir es Saba see Be'er Sheva
74 A12 **Bir-Gandouz** SW Western Sahara 21°35′N 16°27′W
153 P12 **Birganj** Central, C Nepal 27°03′N 84°53′E
81 B14 **Biri** ≈ W South Sudan
Bi'r Ibn Hirmās see Al Bi'r
143 U8 **Bīrjand** Khorāsān-e Janūbī, E Iran 32°54′N 59°14′E
139 T11 **Birkat Ḩāmid** well S Iraq
95 F18 **Birkeland** Aust-Agder, S Norway 58°18′N 08°13′E
101 E19 **Birkenfeld** Rheinland-Pfalz, SW Germany 49°39′N 07°10′E
97 K18 **Birkenhead** NW England, United Kingdom 53°24′N 03°02′W
109 W7 **Birkfeld** Steiermark, SE Austria 47°21′N 15°40′E
182 A2 **Birksgate Range** ▲▲ South Australia
Bîrlad see Bârlad
145 S15 **Birlik** var. Novotroickoje, Novotroitskoye; prev. Brlik. Zhambyl, SE Kazakhstan 43°39′N 73°45′E
97 K20 **Birmingham** C England, United Kingdom 52°30′N 01°50′W
23 P4 **Birmingham** Alabama, S USA 33°30′N 86°47′W
97 M20 **Birmingham** ✕ C England, United Kingdom 52°27′N 01°46′W
Birmitrapur see Biramitrapur
Bir Moghrein see Bîr Mogreïn
76 J4 **Bîr Mogreïn** var. Bir Moghrein; prev. Fort-Trinquet. Tiris Zemmour, N Mauritania 25°10′N 11°35′W
191 S4 **Birnie Island** atoll Phoenix Islands, C Kiribati
77 S12 **Birnin Gaouré** var. Birni-Ngaouré. Dosso, SW Niger 12°59′N 03°02′E
Birni-Ngaouré see Birnin Gaouré
77 S12 **Birnin Kebbi** Kebbi, NW Nigeria 12°28′N 04°08′E
77 T12 **Birnin Konni** var. Birni-Nkonni. Tahoua, SW Niger 13°51′N 05°15′E
Birni-Nkonni see Birnin Konni
77 W13 **Birnin Kudu** Jigawa, N Nigeria 11°28′N 09°29′E
123 S16 **Birobidzhan** Yevreyskaya Avtonomnaya Oblast', SE Russian Federation 48°42′N 132°55′E
97 D18 **Birr** var. Parsonstown, Ir. Biorra. C Ireland 53°06′N 07°55′W
183 P4 **Birrie River** ≈ New South Wales/Queensland, SE Australia
108 D7 **Birse** ≈ NW Switzerland
Birsen see Biržai
108 E6 **Birsfelden** Basel Landschaft, NW Switzerland 47°33′N 07°37′E
127 U4 **Birsk** Respublika Bashkortostan, W Russian Federation 55°24′N 55°33′E
119 F14 **Birštonas** Kaunas, C Lithuania 54°37′N 24°00′E
159 P14 **Biru** Xinjiang Uygur Zizhiqu, W China 31°30′N 93°56′E
Biruni see Beruniy
122 L12 **Biryusa** ≈ C Russian Federation
122 L12 **Biryusinsk** Irkutskaya Oblast', C Russian Federation 55°52′N 97°48′E
118 G10 **Biržai** Ger. Birsen. Panevėžys, NE Lithuania 56°12′N 24°47′E
121 P16 **Birżebbuġa** SE Malta 35°50′N 14°32′E
Bisanthe see Tekirdağ
171 R12 **Bisa, Pulau** island Maluku, E Indonesia
37 N17 **Bisbee** Arizona, SW USA 31°27′N 109°55′W
29 O2 **Bisbee** North Dakota, N USA 48°36′N 99°21′W
Biscaia, Baía de see Biscay, Bay of
102 I13 **Biscarrosse et de Parentis, Étang de** ◎ SW France
104 M1 **Biscay, Bay of** Sp. Golfo de Vizcaya, Port. Baía de Biscaia. bay France/Spain
23 Z16 **Biscayne Bay** bay Florida, SE USA
64 M7 **Biscay Plain** undersea feature SE Bay of Biscay 07°15′W 45°00′N
107 N17 **Bisceglie** Puglia, SE Italy 41°14′N 16°31′E
Bischoflack see Škofja Loka
Bischofsburg see Biskupiec
109 Q7 **Bischofshofen** Salzburg, NW Austria 47°25′N 13°13′E
101 P15 **Bischofswerda** Sachsen, E Germany 51°07′N 14°13′E
103 V5 **Bischwiller** Bas-Rhin, NE France 48°46′N 07°52′E
21 T10 **Biscoe** North Carolina, SE USA 35°20′N 79°46′W
194 G5 **Biscoe Islands** island group Antarctica
14 E9 **Biscotasi Lake** ◎ Ontario, S Canada
14 E9 **Biscotasing** Ontario, S Canada 47°16′N 82°04′W
54 J6 **Biscucuy** Portuguesa, NW Venezuela 09°22′N 69°59′W
99 M24 **Bissen** Luxembourg, C Luxembourg 49°47′N 06°04′E
114 K11 **Biser** Khaskovo, S Bulgaria 41°52′N 25°59′E
113 D15 **Biševo** It. Busi. island SW Croatia
141 N12 **Bīshah, Wādī** dry watercourse C Saudi Arabia
147 U7 **Bishkek** var. Pishpek; prev. Frunze. ● (Kyrgyzstan) Chuyskaya Oblast', N Kyrgyzstan 42°54′N 74°27′E
147 U7 **Bishkek** ✕ Chuyskaya Oblast', N Kyrgyzstan 42°55′N 74°37′E
153 R16 **Bishnupur** West Bengal, NE India 23°05′N 87°20′E
83 J25 **Bisho** Eastern Cape, S South Africa 32°46′S 27°21′E
35 S9 **Bishop** California, W USA 37°22′N 118°24′W
25 S15 **Bishop** Texas, SW USA 27°36′N 97°49′W
97 L15 **Bishop Auckland** N England, United Kingdom 54°41′N 01°41′W
Bishop's Lynn see King's Lynn
97 O21 **Bishop's Stortford** E England, United Kingdom 51°45′N 00°11′E
21 S12 **Bishopville** South Carolina, SE USA 34°18′N 80°15′W
138 M5 **Bishrī, Jabal** ▲▲ E Syria
163 U4 **Bishui** Heilongjiang, NE China 52°06′N 123°42′E
81 G17 **Bisina, Lake** prev. Lake Salisbury. ◎ E Uganda
Biskara see Biskra
74 L6 **Biskra** var. Beskra, Biskara. NE Algeria 34°51′N 05°44′E
110 M8 **Biskupiec** Ger. Bischofsburg. Warmińsko-Mazurskie, NE Poland 53°52′N 20°57′E
171 R7 **Bislig** Mindanao, S Philippines 08°10′N 126°19′E
27 X6 **Bismarck** Missouri, C USA 37°46′N 90°37′W
28 M5 **Bismarck** state capital North Dakota, N USA 46°49′N 100°47′W
186 D5 **Bismarck Archipelago** island group NE Papua New Guinea
129 Z16 **Bismarck Plate** tectonic feature W Pacific Ocean
186 D7 **Bismarck Range** ▲▲ N Papua New Guinea
186 E6 **Bismarck Sea** sea W Pacific Ocean
137 P15 **Bismil** Dıyarbakır, SE Turkey 37°53′N 40°38′E
43 N6 **Bismuna, Laguna** lagoon NE Nicaragua
Bisnulok see Phitsanulok
171 R10 **Bisoa, Tanjung** headland Pulau Halmahera, N Indonesia 02°15′N 127°57′E
28 K7 **Bison** South Dakota, N USA 45°31′N 102°27′W
93 H17 **Bispgården** Jämtland, C Sweden 63°00′N 16°40′E
76 G13 **Bissau** ● (Guinea-Bissau) W Guinea-Bissau 11°52′N 15°39′W
76 G13 **Bissau** ✕ W Guinea-Bissau 11°53′N 15°41′W
Bissojohka see Børselv
76 G12 **Bissorã** W Guinea-Bissau 12°16′N 15°35′W
11 O10 **Bistcho Lake** ◎ Alberta, W Canada
22 G5 **Bistineau, Lake** ▣ Louisiana, S USA
Bistrica see Ilirska Bistrica
116 I9 **Bistriţa** Ger. Bistritz, Hung. Beszterce; prev. Nösen. Bistriţa-Năsăud, N Romania 47°10′N 24°31′E
116 K10 **Bistriţa** Ger. Bistritz. ≈ NE Romania
116 I9 **Bistriţa-Năsăud** ◈ county N Romania
Bistritz see Bistriţa
Bistritz ober Pernstein see Bystřice nad Pernštejnem
152 L11 **Biswān** Uttar Pradesh, N India 27°30′N 81°00′E
110 M7 **Bisztynek** Warmińsko-Mazurskie, NE Poland 54°05′N 20°53′E
79 E17 **Bitam** Woleu-Ntem, N Gabon 02°05′N 11°30′E
101 D18 **Bitburg** Rheinland-Pfalz, SW Germany 49°58′N 06°31′E
103 U4 **Bitche** Moselle, NE France 49°01′N 07°27′E
78 I11 **Bitkine** Guéra, C Chad 11°59′N 18°13′E
137 R15 **Bitlis** Bitlis, SE Turkey 38°23′N 42°04′E
137 R14 **Bitlis** ◈ province E Turkey
Bitoeng see Bitung
113 N20 **Bitola** Turk. Monastir; prev. Bitolj. S FYR Macedonia 41°01′N 21°22′E
Bitolj see Bitola
107 O17 **Bitonto** anc. Butuntum. Puglia, SE Italy 41°07′N 16°41′E
77 Q13 **Bitou** var. Bittou. SE Burkina 11°19′N 00°17′W
155 C20 **Bitra Island** island Lakshadweep, India, N Indian Ocean
101 M14 **Bitterfeld** Sachsen-Anhalt, E Germany 51°37′N 12°18′E
32 O9 **Bitterroot Range** ▲▲ Idaho/Montana, NW USA
33 P10 **Bitterroot River** ≈ Montana, NW USA
107 D18 **Bitti** Sardegna, Italy, C Mediterranean Sea 40°30′N 09°31′E
Bittou see Bitou
171 Q11 **Bitung** prev. Bitoeng. Sulawesi, C Indonesia 01°28′N 125°13′E
60 I12 **Bituruna** Paraná, S Brazil 26°11′S 51°34′W
77 Y13 **Biu** Borno, E Nigeria 10°35′N 12°13′E
Biumba see Byumba
164 J13 **Biwa-ko** ◎ Honshū, SW Japan
171 X14 **Biwarlaut** Papua, E Indonesia 05°44′S 138°14′E
27 P10 **Bixby** Oklahoma, C USA 35°56′N 95°52′W
122 J13 **Biya** ≈ S Russian Federation
122 J13 **Biysk** Altayskiy Kray, S Russian Federation 52°34′N 85°09′E
164 H13 **Bizen** Okayama, Honshū, SW Japan 34°45′N 134°10′E
Bizerta see Bizerte
120 K10 **Bizerte** Ar. Banzart, Eng. Bizerta. N Tunisia 37°18′N 09°48′E
Bizkaia see Vizcaya
92 G2 **Bjargtangar** headland W Iceland 63°30′N 24°29′W
Bjärnå see Perniö
95 K22 **Bjärnum** Skåne, S Sweden 56°15′N 13°45′E
93 I16 **Bjästa** Västernorrland, C Sweden 63°12′N 18°30′E
113 I14 **Bjelašnica** ▲ SE Bosnia and Herzegovina 43°13′N 18°18′E
112 C10 **Bjelolasica** ▲ NW Croatia 45°13′N 14°56′E
112 F8 **Bjelovar** Hung. Belovár. Bjelovar-Bilogora, N Croatia 45°54′N 16°49′E
112 F8 **Bjelovar-Bilogora** off. Bjelovarsko-Bilogorska Županija. ◈ province NE Croatia
Bjelovarsko-Bilogorska Županija see Bjelovar-Bilogora
92 H10 **Bjerkvik** Nordland, C Norway 68°31′N 16°08′E
95 G21 **Bjerringbro** Midtjylland, NW Denmark 56°23′N 09°40′E
Bjeshkët e Namuna see North Albanian Alps
95 L14 **Björbo** Dalarna, C Sweden 60°28′N 14°44′E
95 I15 **Bjørkelangen** Akershus, S Norway 59°54′N 11°33′E
95 O14 **Björklinge** Uppsala, C Sweden 60°03′N 17°33′E
95 P14 **Bjørkø-Arholma** Stockholm, C Sweden 59°51′N 19°01′E
93 I14 **Björksele** Västerbotten, N Sweden 64°58′N 18°30′E
93 I16 **Björna** Västernorrland, C Sweden 63°34′N 18°38′E
95 C14 **Bjørnafjorden** fjord S Norway
95 L16 **Björneborg** Värmland, C Sweden 59°13′N 14°15′E
Björneborg see Pori
95 E14 **Bjornesfjorden** ◎ S Norway
92 M9 **Bjørnevatn** Finnmark, N Norway 69°40′N 29°57′E
197 T13 **Bjørnøya** Eng. Bear Island. island N Norway
93 I15 **Bjurholm** Västerbotten, N Sweden 63°57′N 19°16′E
95 J22 **Bjuv** Skåne, S Sweden 56°05′N 12°57′E
76 M12 **Bla** Ségou, W Mali 12°58′N 05°45′W
181 W8 **Blackall** Queensland, E Australia 24°26′S 145°32′E
29 V2 **Black Bay** lake bay Minnesota, N USA
27 N9 **Black Bear Creek** ≈ Oklahoma, C USA
97 K17 **Blackburn** NW England, United Kingdom 53°45′N 02°29′W
39 T11 **Blackburn, Mount** ▲ Alaska, USA 61°43′N 143°25′W
35 N5 **Black Butte Lake** ▣ California, W USA
194 J5 **Black Coast** physical region Antarctica
11 Q16 **Black Diamond** Alberta, SW Canada 50°42′N 114°09′W
18 K11 **Black Dome** ▲ New York, NE USA 42°16′N 74°07′W
113 L18 **Black Drin** Alb. Lumi i Drinit të Zi, SCr. Crni Drim. ≈ Albania/FYR Macedonia
29 U4 **Blackduck** Minnesota, N USA 47°45′N 94°33′W
12 D6 **Black Duck** ≈ Ontario, C Canada
33 R14 **Blackfoot** Idaho, NW USA 43°11′N 112°20′W
33 P9 **Blackfoot River** ≈ Montana, NW USA
Black Forest see Schwarzwald
28 J10 **Blackhawk** South Dakota, N USA 44°09′N 103°18′W
28 I10 **Black Hills** ▲▲ South Dakota/Wyoming, N USA
11 T10 **Black Lake** ◎ Saskatchewan, C Canada
22 G6 **Black Lake** ▣ Louisiana, S USA
31 Q5 **Black Lake** ◎ Michigan, N USA
18 I7 **Black Lake** ◎ New York, NE USA
26 F7 **Black Mesa** ▲ Oklahoma, C USA 37°00′N 103°07′W
21 P10 **Black Mountain** North Carolina, SE USA 35°37′N 82°19′W
35 P13 **Black Mountain** ▲ California, W USA 35°22′N 120°21′W
37 Q2 **Black Mountain** ▲ Colorado, C USA 40°47′N 107°23′W
96 K1 **Black Mountains** ▲▲ SE Wales, United Kingdom
36 H10 **Black Mountains** ▲▲ Arizona, SW USA
21 O7 **Black Mountains** ▲ Kentucky, E USA 36°54′N 82°53′W
33 Q16 **Black Pine Peak** ▲ Idaho, NW USA 42°07′N 113°07′W
97 K17 **Blackpool** NW England, United Kingdom 53°50′N 03°03′W
37 Q14 **Black Range** ▲▲ New Mexico, SW USA
44 I12 **Black River** W Jamaica 18°02′N 77°52′W
14 J14 **Black River** ≈ Ontario, SE Canada
129 U12 **Black River** Chin. Babian Jiang, Lixian Jiang, Fr. Rivière Noire, Vtn. Sông Đa. ≈ China/Vietnam
44 I12 **Black River** ≈ W Jamaica
39 T7 **Black River** ≈ Alaska, USA
37 N13 **Black River** ≈ Arizona, SW USA
27 X7 **Black River** ≈ Arkansas/Missouri, C USA
22 I7 **Black River** ≈ Louisiana, S USA
31 S8 **Black River** ≈ Michigan, N USA
31 Q5 **Black River** ≈ Michigan, N USA
18 I8 **Black River** ≈ New York, NE USA
21 T13 **Black River** ≈ South Carolina, SE USA
30 J7 **Black River** ≈ Wisconsin, N USA
30 J7 **Black River Falls** Wisconsin, N USA 44°18′N 90°51′W
35 R3 **Black Rock Desert** desert Nevada, W USA
Black Sand Desert see Garagum
21 S7 **Blacksburg** Virginia, NE USA 37°15′N 80°25′W
136 H10 **Black Sea** var. Euxine Sea, Bul. Cherno More, Rom. Marea Neagră, Rus. Chernoye More, Turk. Karadeniz, Ukr. Chorne More. sea Asia/Europe
117 Q10 **Black Sea Lowland** Ukr. Prychornomor'ska Nyzovyna. depression SE Europe
33 S17 **Blacks Fork** ≈ Wyoming, C USA
23 V7 **Blackshear** Georgia, SE USA 31°18′N 82°14′W
23 S6 **Blackshear, Lake** ▣ Georgia, SE USA
97 A16 **Blacksod Bay** Ir. Cuan an Fhóid Duibh. inlet W Ireland
21 V7 **Blackstone** Virginia, NE USA 37°04′N 78°00′W
77 O14 **Black Volta** var. Borongo, Mouhoun, Moun Hou, Fr. Volta Noire. ≈ W Africa
23 O5 **Black Warrior River** ≈ Alabama, S USA
181 X8 **Blackwater** Queensland, E Australia 23°34′S 148°51′E
97 D20 **Blackwater** Ir. An Abhainn Mhór. ≈ S Ireland
27 T4 **Blackwater River** ≈ Missouri, C USA
21 W7 **Blackwater River** ≈ Virginia, NE USA
Blackwater State see Nebraska
27 N8 **Blackwell** Oklahoma, C USA 36°48′N 97°16′W
25 P7 **Blackwell** Texas, SW USA 32°05′N 100°19′W
99 J15 **Bladel** Noord-Brabant, S Netherlands 51°22′N 05°13′E
Bladenmarkt see Bălăuşeri
114 G11 **Blagoevgrad** prev. Gorna Dzhumaya. Blagoevgrad, W Bulgaria 42°01′N 23°05′E
114 G11 **Blagoevgrad** ◈ province SW Bulgaria
123 Q14 **Blagoveshchensk** Amurskaya Oblast', SE Russian Federation 50°19′N 127°30′E
127 V4 **Blagoveshchensk** Respublika Bashkortostan, W Russian Federation 55°03′N 56°01′E
102 I7 **Blain** Loire-Atlantique, NW France 47°26′N 01°47′W
29 V8 **Blaine** Minnesota, N USA 45°09′N 93°13′W
32 H6 **Blaine** Washington, NW USA 48°59′N 122°45′W
11 T15 **Blaine Lake** Saskatchewan, S Canada 52°49′N 106°48′W
29 S14 **Blair** Nebraska, C USA 41°32′N 96°07′W
96 J10 **Blairgowrie** C Scotland, United Kingdom 56°19′N 03°25′W
18 C15 **Blairsville** Pennsylvania, NE USA 40°25′N 79°12′W
116 H11 **Blaj** Ger. Blasendorf, Hung. Balázsfalva. Alba, SW Romania 46°10′N 23°57′E
64 F9 **Blake-Bahama Ridge** undersea feature W Atlantic Ocean 29°00′N 73°30′W
23 S7 **Blakely** Georgia, SE USA 31°22′N 84°55′W
64 E10 **Blake Plateau** var. Blake Terrace. undersea feature W Atlantic Ocean 31°00′N 79°00′W
30 M1 **Blake Point** headland Michigan, N USA 48°11′N 88°25′W
Blake Terrace see Blake Plateau
61 B24 **Blanca, Bahía** bay E Argentina
56 C12 **Blanca, Cordillera** ▲▲ W Peru
105 T12 **Blanca, Costa** physical region SE Spain
37 S7 **Blanca Peak** ▲ Colorado, C USA 37°34′N 105°29′W
24 I9 **Blanca, Sierra** ▲ Texas, SW USA 31°15′N 105°26′W
120 K9 **Blanc, Cap** headland N Tunisia 37°20′N 09°41′E
Blanc, Cap see Nouâdhibou, Râs
31 R12 **Blanchard River** ≈ Ohio, N USA
182 E8 **Blanche, Cape** headland South Australia 33°03′S 134°10′E
182 J4 **Blanche, Lake** ◎ South Australia
31 R14 **Blanchester** Ohio, N USA 39°17′N 83°59′W
182 J9 **Blanchetown** South Australia 34°21′S 139°36′E
45 U13 **Blanchisseuse** Trinidad, Trinidad and Tobago 10°47′N 61°18′W
103 T11 **Blanc, Mont** It. Monte Bianco. ▲ France/Italy 45°45′N 06°51′E
25 R11 **Blanco** Texas, SW USA 30°06′N 98°25′W
42 K14 **Blanco, Cabo** headland NW Costa Rica 09°34′N 85°06′W
32 D14 **Blanco, Cape** headland Oregon, NW USA 42°49′N 124°33′W
62 H10 **Blanco, Río** ≈ W Argentina
56 F10 **Blanco, Río** ≈ NE Peru
15 O9 **Blanc, Réservoir** ▣ Québec, SE Canada
21 R7 **Bland** Virginia, NE USA 37°06′N 81°08′W
92 I2 **Blanda** ≈ N Iceland
37 O7 **Blanding** Utah, W USA 37°37′N 109°28′W
105 X5 **Blanes** Cataluña, NE Spain 41°41′N 02°48′E
103 N3 **Blangy-sur-Bresle** Seine-Maritime, N France 49°55′N 01°37′E
111 C18 **Blanice** Ger. Blanitz. ≈ SE Czech Republic
Blanitz see Blanice
99 C16 **Blankenberge** West-Vlaanderen, NW Belgium 51°19′N 03°08′E
101 D17 **Blankenheim** Nordrhein-Westfalen, W Germany 50°26′N 06°41′E
25 R8 **Blanket** Texas, SW USA 31°49′N 98°47′W
55 O3 **Blanquilla, Isla** var. La Blanquilla. island N Venezuela
Blanquilla, La see Blanquilla, Isla
61 F18 **Blanquillo** Durazno, C Uruguay 32°53′S 55°37′W
111 G18 **Blansko** Ger. Blanz. Jihomoravský Kraj, SE Czech Republic 49°22′N 16°39′E
83 N15 **Blantyre** var. Blantyre-Limbe. Southern, S Malawi 15°45′S 35°04′E
83 N15 **Blantyre** ✕ Southern, S Malawi 15°34′S 35°03′E
Blantyre-Limbe see Blantyre
Blanz see Blansko
98 J10 **Blaricum** Noord-Holland, C Netherlands 52°16′N 05°15′E
Blasendorf see Blaj
Blatnitsa see Durankulak
113 F15 **Blato** It. Blatta. Dubrovnik-Neretva, S Croatia 42°57′N 16°47′E
Blatta see Blato
108 E10 **Blatten** Valais, SW Switzerland 46°22′N 08°00′E
101 J20 **Blaufelden** Baden-Württemberg, SW Germany 49°21′N 10°01′E
95 E23 **Blåvands Huk** headland W Denmark 55°33′N 08°04′E
102 G6 **Blavet** ≈ NW France
102 J12 **Blaye** Gironde, SW France
183 R8 **Blayney** New South Wales, SE Australia 33°33′S 149°13′E
65 D25 **Bleaker Island** island SE Falkland Islands
109 T10 **Bled** Ger. Veldes. NW Slovenia 46°23′N 14°06′E
99 D20 **Bléharies** Hainaut, SW Belgium 50°31′N 03°25′E
109 U9 **Bleiburg** Slvn. Pliberk. Kärnten, S Austria 46°36′N 14°49′E
101 L17 **Bleiloch-stausee** ▣ C Germany
98 H12 **Bleiswijk** Zuid-Holland, W Netherlands 52°01′N 04°32′E
95 L22 **Blekinge** ◈ county S Sweden
14 D17 **Blenheim** Ontario, S Canada 42°20′N 81°59′W
185 K15 **Blenheim** Marlborough, South Island, New Zealand 41°32′S 174°E
99 M15 **Blerick** Limburg, SE Netherlands 51°22′N 06°10′E
Blesae see Blois
25 V13 **Blessing** Texas, SW USA 28°52′N 96°12′W
14 I10 **Bleu, Lac** ◎ Québec, SE Canada
Blibba see Blitta
120 H10 **Blida** var. El Boulaida, El Boulaïda. N Algeria 36°30′N 02°50′E
95 P15 **Blidö** Stockholm, C Sweden 59°37′N 18°55′E
95 K18 **Blidsberg** Västra Götaland, S Sweden 57°55′N 13°30′E
185 A21 **Bligh Sound** sound South Island, New Zealand
187 X14 **Bligh Water** strait NW Fiji
14 D11 **Blind River** Ontario, S Canada 46°12′N 82°59′W
31 R11 **Blissfield** Michigan, N USA 41°49′N 83°51′W
77 R15 **Blitta** prev. Blibba. C Togo 08°19′N 00°59′E
19 O13 **Block Island** island Rhode Island, NE USA
19 O13 **Block Island Sound** sound Rhode Island, NE USA
98 H10 **Bloemendaal** Noord-Holland, W Netherlands 52°23′N 04°39′E
83 H23 **Bloemfontein** var. Mangaung. ● (South Africa-judicial capital) Free State, C South Africa 29°07′S 26°14′E
83 I22 **Bloemhof** North-West, NW South Africa 27°39′S 25°37′E
102 M7 **Blois** anc. Blesae. Loir-et-Cher, C France 47°36′N 01°20′E
98 L8 **Blokzijl** Overijssel, N Netherlands 52°46′N 05°58′E
95 N20 **Blomstermåla** Kalmar, S Sweden 56°58′N 16°19′E
92 I2 **Blönduós** Nordhurland Vestra, N Iceland 65°39′N 20°15′W
110 L11 **Błonie** Mazowieckie, C Poland 52°13′N 20°36′E
97 C14 **Bloody Foreland** Ir. Cnoc Fola. headland NW Ireland 55°09′N 08°18′W
31 N15 **Bloomfield** Indiana, N USA 39°01′N 86°58′W
29 X16 **Bloomfield** Iowa, C USA 40°45′N 92°24′W
27 Y8 **Bloomfield** Missouri, C USA 36°54′N 89°58′W
37 P9 **Bloomfield** New Mexico, SW USA 36°42′N 108°00′W
25 U7 **Blooming Grove** Texas, SW USA 32°05′N 96°43′W
29 W10 **Blooming Prairie** Minnesota, N USA 43°52′N 93°03′W
30 L13 **Bloomington** Illinois, N USA 40°28′N 88°59′W
31 O15 **Bloomington** Indiana, N USA 39°10′N 86°31′W
29 V9 **Bloomington** Minnesota, N USA 44°50′N 93°18′W
25 U13 **Bloomington** Texas, SW USA 28°39′N 96°53′W
18 H14 **Bloomsburg** Pennsylvania, NE USA 40°59′N 76°27′W
181 X7 **Bloomsbury** Queensland, NE Australia 20°47′S 148°35′E
169 R16 **Blora** Jawa, C Indonesia 06°55′S 111°29′E
18 G12 **Blossburg** Pennsylvania, NE USA 41°38′N 77°00′W
25 V5 **Blossom** Texas, SW USA 33°39′N 95°23′W
123 T5 **Blossom, Mys** headland Ostrov Vrangelya, NE Russian Federation 70°49′N 178°49′E
23 R8 **Blountstown** Florida, SE USA 30°26′N 85°03′W
21 P8 **Blountville** Tennessee, S USA 36°31′N 82°19′W
21 Q9 **Blowing Rock** North Carolina, SE USA 36°15′N 81°53′W
108 J8 **Bludenz** Vorarlberg, W Austria 47°10′N 09°50′E
36 L6 **Blue Bell Knoll** ▲ Utah, W USA 38°11′N 111°31′W
23 Y12 **Blue Cypress Lake** ◎ Florida, SE USA
29 U11 **Blue Earth** Minnesota, N USA 43°38′N 94°06′W
21 Q7 **Bluefield** Virginia, NE USA 37°15′N 81°16′W
21 R7 **Bluefield** West Virginia, NE USA 37°16′N 81°13′W
43 N10 **Bluefields** Región Autónoma Atlántico Sur, SE Nicaragua 12°01′N 83°47′W
43 N10 **Bluefields, Bahía de** bay W Caribbean Sea
29 Z14 **Blue Grass** Iowa, C USA 41°30′N 90°46′W
Bluegrass State see Kentucky
Blue Hen State see Delaware
19 S7 **Blue Hill** Maine, NE USA 44°25′N 68°36′W
29 P16 **Blue Hill** Nebraska, C USA 40°19′N 98°27′W
30 J5 **Blue Hills** hill range Wisconsin, N USA
34 L3 **Blue Lake** California, W USA 40°52′N 124°00′W
Blue Law State see Connecticut
37 Q6 **Blue Mesa Reservoir** ▣ Colorado, C USA
27 S12 **Blue Mountain** ▲ Arkansas, C USA 34°42′N 94°04′W
19 O6 **Blue Mountain** ▲ New Hampshire, NE USA 44°48′N 71°26′W
18 K8 **Blue Mountain** ▲ New York, NE USA 43°52′N 74°24′W
18 H15 **Blue Mountain** ridge Pennsylvania, NE USA
44 H10 **Blue Mountain Peak** ▲ E Jamaica 18°02′N 76°34′W
183 S8 **Blue Mountains** ▲▲ New South Wales, SE Australia
32 L11 **Blue Mountains** ▲▲ Oregon/Washington, NW USA
80 G12 **Blue Nile** ◈ state E Sudan
80 H12 **Blue Nile** var. Abai, Bahr el, Azraq, Amh. Ābay Wenz, Ar. An Nīl al Azraq. ≈ Ethiopia/Sudan
8 J7 **Bluenose Lake** ◎ Nunavut, NW Canada
27 O3 **Blue Rapids** Kansas, C USA 39°39′N 96°38′W
23 S1 **Blue Ridge** Georgia, SE USA 34°51′N 84°19′W
17 S11 **Blue Ridge** var. Blue Ridge Mountains. ▲▲ North Carolina/Virginia, USA
23 S1 **Blue Ridge Lake** ▣ Georgia, SE USA
Blue Ridge Mountains see Blue Ridge
11 N15 **Blue River** British Columbia, SW Canada 52°03′N 119°21′W
27 O12 **Blue River** ≈ Oklahoma, C USA
27 R4 **Blue Springs** Missouri, C USA 39°01′N 94°16′W
21 R6 **Bluestone Lake** ▣ West Virginia, NE USA
185 C25 **Bluff** Southland, South Island, New Zealand 46°36′S 168°22′E
37 O8 **Bluff** Utah, W USA 37°15′N 109°36′W
21 P8 **Bluff City** Tennessee, S USA 36°28′N 82°15′W
65 E24 **Bluff Cove** East Falkland, Falkland Islands 51°45′S 58°11′W
25 S7 **Bluff Dale** Texas, SW USA 32°18′N 98°01′W
183 N15 **Bluff Hill Point** headland Tasmania, SE Australia 41°03′S 144°35′E
31 Q12 **Bluffton** Indiana, N USA 40°44′N 85°10′W
31 R12 **Bluffton** Ohio, N USA 40°54′N 83°53′W
25 T7 **Blum** Texas, SW USA 32°08′N 97°24′W
101 G24 **Blumberg** Baden-Württemberg, SW Germany 47°48′N 08°31′E
60 K13 **Blumenau** Santa Catarina, S Brazil 26°55′S 49°07′W
29 N9 **Blunt** South Dakota, N USA 44°30′N 99°58′E
32 H15 **Bly** Oregon, NW USA 42°22′N 121°04′W
39 R13 **Blying Sound** sound Alaska, USA
97 M14 **Blyth** N England, United Kingdom 55°07′N 01°30′W
35 Y16 **Blythe** California, W USA 33°35′N 114°36′W
27 Y9 **Blytheville** Arkansas, C USA 35°56′N 89°55′W
117 V7 **Blyznyuky** Kharkivs'ka Oblast', E Ukraine 48°51′N 36°32′E
95 G16 **Bø** Telemark, S Norway 59°24′N 09°04′E
76 I15 **Bo** S Sierra Leone 07°58′N 11°45′W
171 O4 **Boac** Marinduque, N Philippines 13°26′N 121°50′E
42 K10 **Boaco** Boaco, S Nicaragua 12°28′N 85°45′W
42 J10 **Boaco** ◈ department C Nicaragua
79 I15 **Boali** Ombella-Mpoko, SW Central African Republic 04°52′N 18°00′E
Boalsert see Bolsward
31 V12 **Boardman** Ohio, N USA 41°01′N 80°39′W
32 J11 **Boardman** Oregon, NW USA 45°50′N 119°42′W
14 F13 **Boat Lake** ◎ Ontario, S Canada
58 F10 **Boa Vista** state capital Roraima, NW Brazil 02°51′N 60°43′W
76 D9 **Boa Vista** island Ilhas de Barlavento, E Cape Verde
23 Q2 **Boaz** Alabama, S USA 34°12′N 86°10′W
160 L15 **Bobai** Guangxi Zhuangzu Zizhiqu, S China 22°09′N 109°57′E
172 J1 **Bobaomby, Tanjona** Fr. Cap d'Ambre. headland N Madagascar 11°58′S 49°13′E
155 M14 **Bobbili** Andhra Pradesh, E India 18°32′N 83°29′E
106 D9 **Bobbio** Emilia-Romagna, C Italy 44°48′N 09°27′E
14 I14 **Bobcaygeon** Ontario, SE Canada 44°32′N 78°33′W
Bober see Bóbr
103 O5 **Bobigny** Seine-St-Denis, N France 48°55′N 02°27′E
77 N13 **Bobo-Dioulasso** SW Burkina 11°12′N 04°21′W
110 G8 **Bobolice** Ger. Bublitz. Zachodnio-pomorskie, NW Poland 53°56′N 16°37′E
83 J19 **Bobonong** Central, E Botswana 21°58′S 28°26′E
171 R11 **Bobopayo** Pulau Halmahera, E Indonesia 01°07′N 127°26′E
113 J15 **Bobotov Kuk** ▲ N Montenegro 43°06′N 19°00′E
114 G10 **Bobovdol** Kyustendil, W Bulgaria 42°21′N 22°59′E
119 M15 **Bobr** Minskaya Voblasts', NW Belarus 54°20′N 29°16′E
119 M15 **Bobr** ≈ C Belarus
111 E14 **Bóbr** Eng. Bobrawa, Ger. Bober. ≈ SW Poland
Bobrawa see Bóbr
Bobrik see Bobryk
Bobrinets see Bobrynets'
Bobrka/Bóbrka see Bibrka
126 L8 **Bobrov** Voronezhskaya Oblast', W Russian Federation 51°10′N 40°03′E
117 Q4 **Bobrovytsya** Chernihivs'ka Oblast', N Ukraine 50°43′N 31°24′E
Bobruysk see Babruysk
119 J19 **Bobryk** Rus. Bobrik. ≈ SW Belarus
117 Q8 **Bobrynets'** Rus. Bobrinets. Kirovohrads'ka Oblast', C Ukraine 48°02′N 32°10′E
14 K14 **Bobs Lake** ◎ Ontario, SE Canada
54 I6 **Bobures** Zulia, NW Venezuela 09°15′N 71°10′W
42 H1 **Boca Bacalar Chico** headland N Belize 15°05′N 82°12′W
112 G11 **Bočac** ◈ Republika Srpska, NW Bosnia and Herzegovina
41 R14 **Boca del Río** Veracruz-Llave, S Mexico 19°08′N 96°08′W
55 O4 **Boca de Pozo** Nueva Esparta, NE Venezuela 11°00′N 64°23′W
59 C15 **Boca do Acre** Amazonas, N Brazil 08°45′S 67°23′W
55 N12 **Boca Mavaca** Amazonas, S Venezuela 02°30′N 65°11′W
79 G14 **Bocaranga** Ouham-Pendé, W Central African Republic 07°07′N 15°40′E

◆ Country
● Country Capital
◇ Dependent Territory
○ Dependent Territory Capital
◈ Administrative Regions
✕ International Airport
▲ Mountain
▲▲ Mountain Range
⊼ Volcano
≈ River
◎ Lake
▣ Reservoir

23 Z15 **Boca Raton** Florida, SE USA 26°22′N 80°05′W
43 P14 **Bocas del Toro** Bocas del Toro, NW Panama 09°20′N 82°15′W
43 P15 **Bocas del Toro** *off.* Provincia de Bocas del Toro. ◈ *province* NW Panama
43 P15 **Bocas del Toro, Archipiélago de** *island group* NW Panama
Bocas del Toro, Provincia de *see* Bocas del Toro
42 L7 **Bocay** Jinotega, N Nicaragua 14°19′N 85°08′W
105 N6 **Boceguillas** Castilla y León, N Spain 41°20′N 03°39′W
Bocheykovo *see* Bacheykava
111 L17 **Bochnia** Małopolskie, SE Poland 49°58′N 20°27′E
99 K16 **Bocholt** Limburg, NE Belgium 51°10′N 05°37′E
101 D14 **Bocholt** Nordrhein-Westfalen, W Germany 51°50′N 06°37′E
101 E15 **Bochum** Nordrhein-Westfalen, W Germany 51°29′N 07°13′E
103 Y15 **Bocognano** Corse, France, C Mediterranean Sea 42°04′N 09°03′E
54 I6 **Boconó** Trujillo, NW Venezuela 09°17′N 70°17′W
116 F12 **Bocşa** *Ger.* Bokschen, *Hung.* Boksánbánya. Caraş-Severin, SW Romania 45°23′N 21°47′E
79 H15 **Boda** Lobaye, SW Central African Republic 04°17′N 17°25′E
94 L12 **Boda** Dalarna, C Sweden 61°00′N 15°15′E
95 O20 **Böda** Kalmar, S Sweden 57°16′N 17°04′E
95 L19 **Bodafors** Jönköping, S Sweden 57°30′N 14°40′E
123 O12 **Bodaybo** Irkutskaya Oblast', E Russian Federation 57°52′N 114°05′E
22 G5 **Bodcau, Bayou** *var.* Bodcau Creek. ≈ Louisiana, S USA
Bodcau Creek *see* Bodcau, Bayou
44 D8 **Bodden Town** *var.* Boddentown. Grand Cayman, SW Cayman Islands 19°20′N 81°14′W
Boddentown *see* Bodden Town
101 K14 **Bode** ≈ C Germany
34 L7 **Bodega Head** *headland* California, W USA 38°16′N 123°04′W
Bodegas *see* Babahoyo
98 H11 **Bodegraven** Zuid-Holland, C Netherlands 52°05′N 04°45′E
78 H8 **Bodélé** *depression* W Chad
92 J13 **Boden** Norrbotten, N Sweden 65°50′N 21°44′E
Bodensee *see* Constance, Lake, C Europe
65 M15 **Bode Verde Fracture Zone** *tectonic feature* E Atlantic Ocean
155 H14 **Bodhan** Andhra Pradesh, C India 18°40′N 77°51′E
Bodī *see* Jinst
155 H22 **Bodināyakkanūr** Tamil Nādu, SE India 10°02′N 77°18′E
108 H10 **Bodio** Ticino, S Switzerland 46°23′N 08°55′E
Bodjonegoro *see* Bojonegoro
97 I24 **Bodmin** SW England, United Kingdom 50°29′N 04°43′W
97 I24 **Bodmin Moor** *moorland* SW England, United Kingdom
92 G12 **Bodø** Nordland, C Norway 67°17′N 14°22′E
59 H20 **Bodoquena, Serra da** ▲▲ SW Brazil
136 B16 **Bodrum** Muğla, SW Turkey 37°01′N 27°28′E
Bodzafordulő *see* Întorsura Buzăului
99 L14 **Boekel** Noord-Brabant, SE Netherlands 51°35′N 05°42′E
Boeloekoemba *see* Bulukumba
103 Q11 **Boën** Loire, E France 45°45′N 04°01′E
79 K18 **Boende** Equateur, C Dem. Rep. Congo 0°12′S 20°54′E
25 R11 **Boerne** Texas, SW USA 29°47′N 98°44′W
Boeroe *see* Buru, Pulau
Boetoeng *see* Buton, Pulau
22 I5 **Boeuf River** ≈ Arkansas/Louisiana, S USA
76 H14 **Boffa** W Guinea 10°12′N 14°02′W
Bó Finne, Inis *see* Inishbofin
Boga *see* Bogë
166 L9 **Bogale** Ayeyarwady, SW Myanmar (Burma) 16°16′N 95°21′E
22 L8 **Bogalusa** Louisiana, S USA 30°47′N 89°51′W
77 Q12 **Bogandé** C Burkina 13°02′N 00°08′W
79 I15 **Bogangolo** Ombella-Mpoko, C Central African Republic 05°36′N 18°17′E
183 Q7 **Bogan River** ≈ New South Wales, SE Australia
25 W5 **Bogata** Texas, SW USA 33°28′N 95°12′W
111 D14 **Bogatynia** *Ger.* Reichenau. Dolnośląskie, SW Poland 50°53′N 14°55′E
136 K13 **Boğazlıyan** Yozgat, C Turkey 39°13′N 35°17′E
79 J17 **Bogbonga** Equateur, NW Dem. Rep. Congo 01°36′N 19°24′E
158 J14 **Bogcang Zangbo** ≈ W China
162 I9 **Bogd** *var.* Horiult. Bayanhongor, C Mongolia 45°09′N 100°50′E
162 J10 **Bogd** *var.* Hovd. Övörhangay, C Mongolia 44°43′N 102°08′E
158 L5 **Bogda Feng** ▲ NW China 43°51′N 88°14′E
114 I9 **Bogdan** ▲ C Bulgaria 42°37′N 24°28′E
113 Q20 **Bogdanci** SE FYR Macedonia 41°12′N 22°34′E
158 M5 **Bogda Shan** *var.* Po-ko-to Shan. ▲▲ NW China
113 K17 **Bogë** *var.* Boga. Shkodër, N Albania 42°25′N 19°38′E
Bogeda'er *see* Wenquan
Bogendorf *see* Łuków
95 G23 **Bogense** Syddtjylland, C Denmark 55°34′N 10°06′E
183 T3 **Boggabilla** New South Wales, SE Australia 28°37′S 150°21′E
183 S6 **Boggabri** New South Wales, SE Australia 30°44′S 150°00′E
186 D6 **Bogia** Madang, N Papua New Guinea 04°16′S 144°56′E
97 N23 **Bognor Regis** SE England, United Kingdom 50°47′N 00°41′W
Bogodukhov *see* Bohodukhiv
181 V15 **Bogong, Mount** ▲ Victoria, SE Australia 36°43′S 147°19′E
169 O16 **Bogor** *Dut.* Buitenzorg. Jawa, C Indonesia 06°34′S 106°45′E
126 L5 **Bogoroditsk** Tul'skaya Oblast', W Russian Federation 53°46′N 38°09′E
127 O3 **Bogorodsk** Nizhegorodskaya Oblast', W Russian Federation 56°06′N 43°29′E
Bogorodskoje *see* Bogorodskoye
123 S12 **Bogorodskoye** Khabarovskiy Kray, SE Russian Federation 52°22′N 140°33′E
125 R15 **Bogorodskoye** *var.* Bogorodskoje. Kirovskaya Oblast', NW Russian Federation 57°50′N 50°41′E
54 F10 **Bogotá** *prev.* Santa Fe, Santa Fe de Bogotá. ● (Colombia) Cundinamarca, C Colombia 04°38′N 74°05′W
153 T14 **Bogra** Rajshahi, N Bangladesh 24°52′N 89°28′E
Bogschan *see* Boldu
122 L12 **Boguchany** Krasnoyarskiy Kray, C Russian Federation 58°20′N 97°20′E
126 M9 **Boguchar** Voronezhskaya Oblast', W Russian Federation 49°57′N 40°34′E
76 H10 **Bogué** Brakna, SW Mauritania 16°36′N 14°15′W
22 K8 **Bogue Chitto** ≈ Louisiana/Mississippi, S USA
Bogushëvsk *see* Bahushewsk
Boguslav *see* Bohuslav
44 K12 **Bog Walk** C Jamaica 18°06′N 77°01′W
161 Q3 **Bo Hai** *var.* Gulf of Chihli. *gulf* NE China
161 R3 **Bohai Haixia** *strait* NE China
161 Q3 **Bohai Wan** *bay* NE China
111 C17 **Bohemia** *Cz.* Čechy, *Ger.* Böhmen. W Czech Republic
111 B18 **Bohemian Forest** *Cz.* Ceský Les, Šumava, *Ger.* Böhmerwald. ▲▲ C Europe
Bohemian-Moravian Highlands *see* Českomoravská Vrchovina
77 R16 **Bohicon** S Benin 07°14′N 02°04′E
109 S11 **Bohinjska Bistrica** *Ger.* Wocheiner Feistritz. NW Slovenia 46°16′N 13°55′E
Bohkká *see* Pokka
Böhmen *see* Bohemia
Böhmerwald *see* Bohemian Forest
Böhmisch-Krumau *see* Český Krumlov
Böhmisch-Leipa *see* Česká Lípa
Böhmisch-Mährische Höhe *see* Českomoravská Vrchovina
Böhmisch-Trübau *see* Česká Třebová
117 U5 **Bohodukhiv** *Rus.* Bogodukhov. Kharkivs'ka Oblast', E Ukraine 50°10′N 35°32′E
171 Q6 **Bohol** *island* C Philippines
171 Q7 **Bohol Sea** *var.* Mindanao Sea. *sea* S Philippines
116 I7 **Bohorodchany** Ivano-Frankivs'ka Oblast', W Ukraine 48°46′N 24°31′E
Böhöt *see* Öndörshil
158 K6 **Bohu** *var.* Bagrax. Xinjiang Uygur Zizhiqu, NW China 42°00′N 86°28′E
111 I17 **Bohumín** *Ger.* Oderberg; *prev.* Neuoderberg, Nový Bohumín. Moravskoslezský Kraj, E Czech Republic 49°55′N 18°20′E
117 P6 **Bohuslav** *Rus.* Boguslav. Kyyivs'ka Oblast', N Ukraine 49°33′N 30°53′E
58 F11 **Boiaçu** Roraima, N Brazil 0°27′S 61°46′W
107 K16 **Boiano** Molise, C Italy 41°28′N 14°28′E
15 R8 **Boilleau** Québec, SE Canada 48°06′N 70°49′W
59 O17 **Boipeba, Ilha de** *island* SE Brazil
104 G3 **Boiro** Galicia, NW Spain 42°39′N 08°53′W
31 Q5 **Bois Blanc Island** *island* Michigan, N USA
29 R7 **Bois de Sioux River** ≈ Minnesota, N USA
33 N14 **Boise** *var.* Boise City. *state capital* Idaho, NW USA 43°39′N 116°14′W
26 G8 **Boise City** Oklahoma, C USA 36°44′N 102°31′W
Boise City *see* Boise
33 N14 **Boise River, Middle Fork** ≈ Idaho, NW USA
Bois, Lac des *see* Woods, Lake of the
Bois-le-Duc *see* 's-Hertogenbosch
11 W17 **Boissevain** Manitoba, S Canada 49°14′N 100°02′W
15 T7 **Boisvert, Pointe au** *headland* Québec, SE Canada 48°34′N 69°07′W
100 K10 **Boizenburg** Mecklenburg-Vorpommern, N Germany 53°23′N 10°43′E
Bojador *see* Boujdour
113 K18 **Bojana** *Alb.* Bunë. ≈ Albania/Montenegro *see also* Bunë
Bojana *see* Bunë, Lumi i
143 S3 **Bojnūrd** *var.* Bujnurd. Khorāsān-e Shemālī, N Iran 37°31′N 57°24′E
169 R16 **Bojonegoro** *prev.* Bodjonegoro. Jawa, C Indonesia 07°06′S 111°50′E
189 T1 **Bokaak Atoll** *var.* Bokak, Taongi. *atoll* Ratak Chain, NE Marshall Islands
Bokak *see* Bokaak Atoll
146 K8 **Bo'kantov Tog'lari** *Rus.* Gory Bukantau. ▲▲ N Uzbekistan
153 Q15 **Bokāro** Jhārkhand, N India 23°46′N 85°55′E
79 I18 **Bokatola** Equateur, NW Dem. Rep. Congo 0°37′S 18°45′E
76 H13 **Boké** W Guinea 10°56′N 14°18′W
Bokhara *see* Buxoro
183 Q4 **Bokharra River** ≈ New South Wales/Queensland, SE Australia
147 X8 **Bokonbayevo** *Kir.* Kajisay; *prev.* Kadzhi-Say. Issyk-Kul'skaya Oblast', NE Kyrgyzstan 42°07′N 76°59′E
78 H11 **Bokoro** Chari-Baguirmi, W Chad 12°23′N 17°03′E
79 K19 **Bokota** Equateur, NW Dem. Rep. Congo 0°56′S 22°24′E
167 N13 **Bokpyin** Tanintharyi, S Myanmar (Burma) 11°16′N 98°47′E
Boksánbánya/Bokschen *see* Bocşa
83 F21 **Bokspits** Kgalagadi, SW Botswana 26°50′S 20°41′E
79 K18 **Bokungu** Equateur, C Dem. Rep. Congo 0°41′S 22°19′E
146 F12 **Bokurdak** *Rus.* Bakhardok. Ahal Welaýaty, C Turkmenistan 38°51′N 58°34′E
78 G10 **Bol** Lac, W Chad 13°27′N 14°40′E
76 G13 **Bolama** SW Guinea-Bissau 11°35′N 15°30′W
Bolangir *see* Balāngīr
Bolanos *see* Bolaños, Mount, Guam
Bolaños *see* Bolaños de Calatrava, Spain
105 N11 **Bolaños de Calatrava** *var.* Bolaños. Castilla-La Mancha, C Spain 38°55′N 03°39′W
188 B17 **Bolanos, Mount** *var.* Bolanos. ▲ S Guam 13°18′N 144°41′E
40 L12 **Bolaños, Río** ≈ C Mexico
115 M14 **Bolayır** Çanakkale, NW Turkey 40°31′N 26°46′E
102 L3 **Bolbec** Seine-Maritime, N France 49°34′N 00°31′E
116 L13 **Boldu** *var.* Bogschan. Buzău, SE Romania 45°18′N 27°15′E
146 H8 **Boldumsaz** *prev.* Kalinin, Kalininsk, Porsy. Daşoguz Welaýaty, N Turkmenistan 42°12′N 59°33′E
158 I4 **Bole** *var.* Bortala. Xinjiang Uygur Zizhiqu, NW China 44°52′N 82°06′E
77 O15 **Bole** NW Ghana 09°02′N 02°29′W
79 J19 **Boleko** Equateur, W Dem. Rep. Congo 01°27′S 19°52′E
111 E14 **Bolesławiec** *Ger.* Bunzlau. Dolnośląskie, SW Poland 51°16′N 15°34′E
127 R4 **Bolgar** *prev.* Kuybyshev. Respublika Tatarstan, W Russian Federation 54°58′N 49°03′E
77 P14 **Bolgatanga** N Ghana 10°45′N 00°52′W
Bolgrad *see* Bolhrad
117 N12 **Bolhrad** *Rus.* Bolgrad. Odes'ka Oblast', SW Ukraine 45°42′N 28°35′E
163 Y8 **Boli** Heilongjiang, NE China 45°45′N 130°32′E
79 I19 **Bolia** Bandundu, W Dem. Rep. Congo 01°34′S 18°24′E
93 J14 **Boliden** Västerbotten, N Sweden 64°52′N 20°20′E
171 T13 **Bolifar** Pulau Seram, E Indonesia 03°08′S 130°34′E
171 N2 **Bolinao** Luzon, N Philippines 16°22′N 119°52′E
54 C12 **Bolívar** Cauca, SW Colombia 01°52′N 76°56′W
27 T6 **Bolivar** Missouri, C USA 37°37′N 93°25′W
20 F10 **Bolivar** Tennessee, S USA 35°17′N 88°59′W
54 F7 **Bolívar** *off.* Departmento de Bolívar. ◈ *province* N Colombia
56 A13 **Bolívar** ◈ *province* C Ecuador
55 N9 **Bolívar** *off.* Estado Bolívar. ◈ *state* SE Venezuela
Bolívar, Departmento de *see* Bolívar
Bolívar, Estado *see* Bolívar
25 X12 **Bolivar Peninsula** *headland* Texas, SW USA 29°26′N 94°41′W
54 I6 **Bolívar, Pico** ▲ W Venezuela 08°33′N 71°05′W
57 K17 **Bolivia** *off.* Republic of Bolivia. ◆ *republic* W South America
Bolivia, Republic of *see* Bolivia
112 O13 **Boljevac** Serbia, E Serbia 43°50′N 21°57′E
Bolkenhain *see* Bolków
126 J5 **Bolkhov** Orlovskaya Oblast', W Russian Federation 53°28′N 36°00′E
111 F14 **Bolków** *Ger.* Bolkenhain. Dolnośląskie, SW Poland 50°55′N 15°49′E
182 K3 **Bollards Lagoon** South Australia 28°58′S 140°52′E
103 R14 **Bollène** Vaucluse, SE France 44°16′N 04°45′E
94 N12 **Bollnäs** Gävleborg, C Sweden 61°18′N 16°27′E
181 W10 **Bollon** Queensland, C Australia 28°07′S 147°28′E
192 L12 **Bollons Tablemount** *undersea feature* S Pacific Ocean 49°40′S 176°10′W
93 H17 **Bollstabruk** Västernorrland, C Sweden 63°00′N 17°41′E
Bolluilos de Par del Condado *see* Bollulos Par del Condado
104 J14 **Bollulos Par del Condado** *var.* Bolluilos de Par del Condado. Andalucía, S Spain 37°20′N 06°32′W
95 K21 **Bolmen** ◎ S Sweden
137 T10 **Bolnisi** S Georgia 41°28′N 44°34′E
79 H19 **Bolobo** Bandundu, W Dem. Rep. Congo 02°10′S 16°17′E
106 G10 **Bologna** Emilia-Romagna, N Italy 44°30′N 11°20′E
124 I15 **Bologoye** Tverskaya Oblast', W Russian Federation 57°54′N 34°04′E
79 J18 **Bolomba** Equateur, NW Dem. Rep. Congo 0°27′N 19°13′E
41 X13 **Bolónchén de Rejón** *var.* Bolonchén de Rejón. Campeche, SE Mexico 20°00′N 89°34′W
114 J13 **Boloústra, Akrotírio** *headland* NE Greece 40°56′N 24°58′E
167 L8 **Bolovén, Phouphiang** *Fr.* Plateau des Bolovens. *plateau* S Laos
Bolovens, Plateau des *see* Bolovén, Phouphiang
106 H13 **Bolsena** Lazio, C Italy 42°39′N 11°59′E
107 G14 **Bolsena, Lago di** ◎ C Italy
126 B3 **Bol'shakovo** *Ger.* Kreuzingen; *prev.* Gross-Skaisgirren. Kaliningradskaya Oblast', W Russian Federation 54°53′N 21°38′E
Bol'shaya Berëstovitsa *see* Vyalikaya Byerastavitsa
127 S7 **Bol'shaya Chernigovka** Samarskaya Oblast', W Russian Federation 52°07′N 50°49′E
127 S7 **Bol'shaya Glushitsa** Samarskaya Oblast', W Russian Federation 52°22′N 50°29′E
124 J4 **Bol'shaya Imandra, Ozero** ◎ NW Russian Federation
Bol'shaya Khobda *see* Kobda
126 M12 **Bol'shaya Martynovka** Rostovskaya Oblast', SW Russian Federation 47°19′N 41°40′E
122 K12 **Bol'shaya Murta** Krasnoyarskiy Kray, C Russian Federation 56°51′N 93°10′E
125 V4 **Bol'shaya Rogovaya** ≈ NW Russian Federation
125 U7 **Bol'shaya Synya** ≈ NW Russian Federation
145 V9 **Bol'shaya Vladimirovka** Vostochnyy Kazakhstan, E Kazakhstan 50°53′N 79°29′E
123 V11 **Bol'sheretsk** Kamchatskiy Kray, E Russian Federation 52°20′N 156°24′E
127 W3 **Bol'sheust'ikinskoye** Respublika Bashkortostan, W Russian Federation 56°00′N 58°13′E
Bol'shevik *see* Bal'shavik
122 L5 **Bol'shevik, Ostrov** *island* Severnaya Zemlya, N Russian Federation
125 U4 **Bol'shezemel'skaya Tundra** *physical region* NW Russian Federation
144 J13 **Bol'shiye Barsuki, Peski** *desert* SW Kazakhstan
123 T7 **Bol'shoy Anyuy** ≈ NE Russian Federation
123 N7 **Bol'shoy Begichev, Ostrov** *island* NE Russian Federation
123 S15 **Bol'shoye Kamen'** Primorskiy Kray, SE Russian Federation 43°06′N 132°21′E
127 O4 **Bol'shoye Murashkino** Nizhegorodskaya Oblast', W Russian Federation 55°46′N 44°48′E
127 W4 **Bol'shoy Iremel'** ▲ W Russian Federation 54°31′N 58°47′E
127 R7 **Bol'shoy Irgiz** ≈ W Russian Federation
123 Q6 **Bol'shoy Lyakhovskiy, Ostrov** *island* NE Russian Federation
123 Q11 **Bol'shoy Nimnyr** Respublika Sakha (Yakutiya), NE Russian Federation 57°55′N 125°34′E
Bol'shoy Rozhan *see* Vyaliki Rozhan
Bol'shoy Uzen' *see* Karaozen
40 K6 **Bolsón de Mapimí** ▲▲ NW Mexico
98 K6 **Bolsward** *Fris.* Boalsert. Fryslân, N Netherlands 53°04′N 05°31′E
105 T4 **Boltaña** Aragón, NE Spain 42°28′N 00°02′E
14 G15 **Bolton** Ontario, S Canada 43°52′N 79°45′W
97 K17 **Bolton** *prev.* Bolton-le-Moors. NW England, United Kingdom 53°35′N 02°26′W
21 V12 **Bolton** North Carolina, SE USA 34°22′N 78°26′W
Bolton-le-Moors *see* Bolton
136 G11 **Bolu** Bolu, NW Turkey 40°45′N 31°38′E
136 G11 **Bolu** ◈ *province* NW Turkey
186 G9 **Bolubolu** Goodenough Island, S Papua New Guinea 09°22′S 150°22′E
92 H1 **Bolungarvík** Vestfirdhir, NW Iceland 66°09′N 23°17′W
159 O10 **Boluntay** Qinghai, W China 36°30′N 92°11′E
159 P8 **Boluozhuanjing**, Aksay Kazakzu Zizhixian. Gansu, N China 39°25′N 94°09′E
136 F14 **Bolvadin** Afyon, W Turkey 38°43′N 31°02′E
114 M10 **Bolyarovo** *prev.* Pashkeni. Yambol, E Bulgaria 42°09′N 26°49′E
106 G6 **Bolzano** *Ger.* Bozen; *anc.* Bauzanum. Trentino-Alto Adige, N Italy 46°30′N 11°22′E
79 F22 **Boma** Bas-Congo, W Dem. Rep. Congo 05°42′S 13°05′E
183 R12 **Bombala** New South Wales, SE Australia 36°54′S 149°15′E
104 F10 **Bombarral** Leiria, C Portugal 39°15′N 09°09′W
Bombay *see* Mumbai
171 U13 **Bomberai, Semenanjung** *cape* Papua, E Indonesia
81 F18 **Bombo** S Uganda 0°36′N 32°33′E
162 I8 **Bömbögör** *var.* Dzadgay. Bayanhongor, C Mongolia 46°12′N 99°29′E
79 I17 **Bomboma** Equateur, NW Dem. Rep. Congo 02°23′N 19°03′E
59 I14 **Bom Futuro** Pará, N Brazil 06°27′S 54°44′W
159 Q15 **Bomi** *var.* Bowo, Zhamo. Xizang Zizhiqu, W China 29°43′N 96°12′E
79 N17 **Bomili** Orientale, NE Dem. Rep. Congo 01°45′N 27°01′E
59 N17 **Bom Jesus da Lapa** Bahia, E Brazil 13°16′S 43°23′W
60 Q8 **Bom Jesus do Itabapoana** Rio de Janeiro, SE Brazil 21°07′S 41°43′W
95 C15 **Bømlafjorden** *fjord* S Norway
95 B15 **Bømlo** *island* S Norway
12 Q12 **Bomnak** Amurskaya Oblast', SE Russian Federation 54°43′N 128°50′E
79 I17 **Bomongo** Equateur, NW Dem. Rep. Congo 01°22′N 18°21′E
61 K14 **Bom Retiro** Santa Catarina, S Brazil 27°45′S 49°31′W
79 L15 **Bomu** *var.* Mbomou, Mbomu, M'Bomu. ≈ Central African Republic/Dem. Rep. Congo
142 J3 **Bonāb** *var.* Benāb, Bunab. Āžarbāyjān-e Sharqī, N Iran 37°30′N 46°03′E
45 S9 **Bonaire** ◈ *Dutch autonomous region* S Caribbean Sea
45 Q16 **Bonaire** *island* Lesser Antilles
39 U11 **Bona, Mount** ▲ Alaska, USA 61°22′N 141°45′W
183 Q12 **Bonang** Victoria, SE Australia 37°13′S 148°43′E
42 L7 **Bonanza** Región Autónoma Atlántico Norte, NE Nicaragua 13°59′N 84°30′W
37 O4 **Bonanza** Utah, W USA 40°01′N 109°12′W
45 O9 **Bonao** C Dominican Republic 18°55′N 70°25′W
180 L3 **Bonaparte Archipelago** *island group* Western Australia
32 K6 **Bonaparte, Mount** ▲ Washington, NW USA 48°47′N 119°07′W
39 N11 **Bonasila Dome** ▲ Alaska, USA 62°24′N 160°28′W
45 T15 **Bonasse** Trinidad, Trinidad and Tobago 10°02′N 61°48′W
15 X7 **Bonaventure** Québec, SE Canada 48°03′N 65°30′W
15 X7 **Bonaventure** ≈ Québec, SE Canada
13 V11 **Bonavista** Newfoundland, Newfoundland and Labrador, SE Canada 48°38′N 53°08′W
13 U11 **Bonavista Bay** *inlet* NW Atlantic Ocean
79 E19 **Bonda** Ogooué-Lolo, C Gabon 0°50′S 12°28′E
127 N6 **Bondari** Tambovskaya Oblast', W Russian Federation 52°58′N 42°02′E
106 G9 **Bondeno** Emilia-Romagna, C Italy 44°53′N 11°24′E
30 L4 **Bond Falls Flowage** ◎ Michigan, N USA
79 L16 **Bondo** Orientale, N Dem. Rep. Congo 03°52′N 23°41′E
171 N17 **Bondokodi** Pulau Sumba, S Indonesia 09°36′S 119°01′E
77 O15 **Bondoukou** E Ivory Coast 08°03′N 02°45′W
Bondoukui/Bondoukuy *see* Boundoukui
169 T17 **Bondowoso** Jawa, C Indonesia 07°54′S 113°50′E
33 S14 **Bondurant** Wyoming, C USA 43°14′N 110°26′W
Bône *see* Annaba, Algeria
Bone *see* Watampone, Indonesia
30 I5 **Bone Lake** ◎ Wisconsin, N USA
171 P14 **Bonelipu** Pulau Buton, C Indonesia 04°42′S 123°09′E
171 O15 **Bonerate, Kepulauan** *var.* Macan. *island group* C Indonesia
29 O12 **Bonesteel** South Dakota, N USA 43°01′N 98°55′W
62 I8 **Bonete, Cerro** ▲ N Argentina 27°58′S 68°22′W
171 O14 **Bone, Teluk** *bay* Sulawesi, C Indonesia
108 D6 **Bonfol** Jura, NW Switzerland 47°28′N 07°08′E
153 U12 **Bongaigaon** Assam, NE India 26°30′N 90°31′E
79 K17 **Bongandanga** Equateur, NW Dem. Rep. Congo 01°28′N 21°03′E
78 L13 **Bongo, Massif des** *var.* Chaîne des Mongos. ▲▲ NE Central African Republic
78 G12 **Bongor** Mayo-Kébbi, SW Chad 10°18′N 15°20′E
77 N16 **Bongouanou** E Ivory Coast 06°39′N 04°12′W
167 V11 **Bông Sơn** *var.* Hoai Nhơn. Bình Định, C Vietnam 14°28′N 109°00′E
25 U5 **Bonham** Texas, SW USA 33°36′N 96°12′W
Bonhard *see* Bonyhád
103 U6 **Bonhomme, Col du** *pass* NE France
103 Y16 **Bonifacio** Corse, France, C Mediterranean Sea 41°24′N 09°09′E
Bonifacio, Bocche de/Bonifacio, Bouches de *see* Bonifacio, Strait of
103 Y16 **Bonifacio, Strait of** *Fr.* Bouches de Bonifacio, *It.* Bocche di Bonifacio. *strait* C Mediterranean Sea
23 Q8 **Bonifay** Florida, SE USA 30°49′N 85°42′W
Bonin Islands *see* Ogasawara-shotō
192 H5 **Bonin Trench** *undersea feature* NW Pacific Ocean
23 W15 **Bonita Springs** Florida, SE USA 26°19′N 81°48′W
42 I5 **Bonito, Pico** ▲ N Honduras 15°33′N 86°55′W
101 E17 **Bonn** Nordrhein-Westfalen, W Germany 50°44′N 07°06′E
92 H11 **Bonnåsjøen** Nordland, C Norway 67°35′N 15°39′E
14 J12 **Bonnechere** Ontario, SE Canada 45°39′N 77°36′W
14 J12 **Bonnechere** ≈ Ontario, SE Canada
33 N7 **Bonners Ferry** Idaho, NW USA 48°41′N 116°19′W
27 R4 **Bonner Springs** Kansas, C USA 39°03′N 94°52′W
102 L6 **Bonnétable** Sarthe, NW France 48°09′N 00°24′E
27 X6 **Bonne Terre** Missouri, C USA 37°55′N 90°33′W
10 J5 **Bonnet Plume** ≈ Yukon Territory, NW Canada
102 M6 **Bonneval** Eure-et-Loir, C France 48°12′N 01°23′E
103 T10 **Bonneville** Haute-Savoie, E France 46°05′N 06°25′E
36 J3 **Bonneville Salt Flats** *salt flat* Utah, W USA
77 U18 **Bonny** Rivers, S Nigeria 04°25′N 07°13′E
Bonny, Bight of *see* Biafra, Bight of
37 W4 **Bonny Reservoir** ▣ Colorado, C USA
11 R14 **Bonnyville** Alberta, SW Canada 54°16′N 110°46′W
107 C18 **Bono** Sardegna, Italy, C Mediterranean Sea 40°24′N 09°01′E
Bononia *see* Vidin, Bulgaria
Bononia *see* Boulogne-sur-Mer, France
107 B18 **Bonorva** Sardegna, Italy, C Mediterranean Sea 40°27′N 08°46′E
30 M15 **Bonpas Creek** ≈ Illinois, N USA
190 I3 **Bonriki** Tarawa, W Kiribati 01°23′N 173°09′E
183 T4 **Bonshaw** New South Wales, SE Australia 29°06′S 151°15′E
76 I16 **Bonthe** SW Sierra Leone 07°32′N 12°30′W
171 N2 **Bontoc** Luzon, N Philippines 17°04′N 120°58′E
25 Y9 **Bon Wier** Texas, SW USA 30°43′N 93°40′W
111 J25 **Bonyhád** *Ger.* Bonhard. Tolna, S Hungary 46°20′N 18°31′E
Bonzabaai *see* Bonza Bay
83 J25 **Bonza Bay** *Afr.* Bonzabaai. Eastern Cape, S South Africa 32°58′S 27°58′E
182 D7 **Bookabie** South Australia 31°49′S 132°41′E
182 H6 **Bookaloo** South Australia 31°56′S 137°21′E
37 P5 **Book Cliffs** *cliff* Colorado/Utah, W USA
25 P1 **Booker** Texas, SW USA 36°27′N 100°32′W
76 K15 **Boola** SE Guinea 08°22′N 08°41′W
183 O8 **Booligal** New South Wales, SE Australia 33°56′S 144°54′E
99 G17 **Boom** Antwerpen, N Belgium 51°05′N 04°24′E
43 N6 **Boom** *var.* Boon. Región Autónoma Atlántico Norte, NE Nicaragua 14°52′N 83°36′W
183 S3 **Boomi** New South Wales, SE Australia 28°43′S 149°35′E
Boon *see* Boom
162 H9 **Böön Tsagaan Nuur** ◎ S Mongolia
29 V13 **Boone** Iowa, C USA 42°04′N 93°52′W
21 Q8 **Boone** North Carolina, SE USA 36°13′N 81°41′W
27 S11 **Booneville** Arkansas, C USA 35°09′N 93°57′W
21 N6 **Booneville** Kentucky, S USA 37°26′N 83°45′W
23 N2 **Booneville** Mississippi, S USA 34°39′N 88°34′W
21 V3 **Boonsboro** Maryland, NE USA 39°30′N 77°39′W
34 L6 **Boonville** California, W USA 38°58′N 123°21′W
31 N16 **Boonville** Indiana, N USA 38°03′N 87°16′W
27 U4 **Boonville** Missouri, C USA 38°58′N 92°43′W
18 I9 **Boonville** New York, NE USA 43°28′N 75°17′W
80 M12 **Boorama** Awdal, NW Somalia 09°58′N 43°15′E
183 O6 **Booroondarra, Mount** *hill* New South Wales, SE Australia
183 N9 **Booroorban** New South Wales, SE Australia 34°55′S 144°45′E
183 R9 **Boorowa** New South Wales, SE Australia 34°26′S 148°42′E
99 H17 **Boortmeerbeek** Vlaams Brabant, C Belgium 50°58′N 04°27′E
80 P11 **Boosaaso** *var.* Bandar Kassim, Bender Qaasim, Bosaso, *It.* Bender Cassim. Bari, N Somalia 11°26′N 49°37′E
19 Q8 **Boothbay Harbor** Maine, NE USA 43°52′N 69°35′W
Boothia Felix *see* Boothia Peninsula
9 N6 **Boothia, Gulf of** *gulf* Nunavut, NE Canada
9 N6 **Boothia Peninsula** *prev.* Boothia Felix. *peninsula* Nunavut, NE Canada
79 E18 **Booué** Ogooué-Ivindo, NE Gabon 0°03′S 11°58′E
101 J21 **Bopfingen** Baden-Württemberg, S Germany 48°51′N 10°21′E
101 F18 **Boppard** Rheinland-Pfalz, W Germany 50°13′N 07°36′E
62 M4 **Boquerón** *off.* Departamento de Boquerón. ◈ *department* W Paraguay
Boquerón, Departamento de *see* Boquerón
43 P15 **Boquete** *var.* Bajo Boquete. Chiriquí, W Panama 08°45′N 82°26′W
40 J6 **Boquilla, Presa de la** ▣ N Mexico
40 L5 **Boquillas** *var.* Boquillas del Carmen. Coahuila, NE Mexico 29°10′N 102°55′W
Boquillas del Carmen *see* Boquillas
112 P12 **Bor** Serbia, E Serbia 44°05′N 22°07′E
81 F15 **Bor** Jonglei, E South Sudan 06°12′N 31°33′E
95 L20 **Bor** Jönköping, S Sweden 57°04′N 14°10′E
136 J15 **Bor** Niğde, S Turkey 37°49′N 35°00′E
191 S10 **Bora-Bora** *island* Îles Sous le Vent, W French Polynesia
167 Q9 **Borabu** Maha Sarakham, E Thailand 16°01′N 103°06′E
172 K4 **Boraha, Nosy** *island* E Madagascar
33 P13 **Borah Peak** ▲ Idaho, NW USA 44°21′N 113°53′W
145 U16 **Boralday** *prev.* Burunday. Almaty, SE Kazakhstan 43°21′N 76°48′E
145 Y11 **Boran** *prev.* Buran. Vostochnyy Kazakhstan, E Kazakhstan 48°00′N 85°09′E
144 G13 **Borankul** *prev.* Opornyy. Mangistau, SW Kazakhstan 46°09′N 54°32′E
95 J19 **Borås** Västra Götaland, S Sweden 57°44′N 12°55′E
143 N11 **Borāzjān** *var.* Borazjān. Būshehr, S Iran 29°19′N 51°12′E
Borazjān *see* Borāzjān
58 G13 **Borba** Amazonas, N Brazil 04°39′S 59°35′W
104 H11 **Borba** Évora, S Portugal 38°48′N 07°28′W
Borbetomagus *see* Worms
55 O7 **Borbón** Bolívar, E Venezuela 07°55′N 64°03′W
59 Q15 **Borborema, Planalto da** *plateau* NE Brazil
116 M14 **Borcea, Braţul** ≈ S Romania
Borchalo *see* Marneuli
195 R15 **Borchgrevink Coast** *physical region* Antarctica
137 Q11 **Borçka** Artvin, NE Turkey 41°24′N 41°38′E
98 N11 **Borculo** Gelderland, E Netherlands 52°07′N 06°31′E
182 G10 **Borda, Cape** *headland* South Australia 35°45′S 136°34′E
102 K13 **Bordeaux** *anc.* Burdigala. Gironde, SW France 44°49′N 00°33′W
11 T15 **Borden** Saskatchewan, S Canada 52°23′N 107°10′W
14 D8 **Borden Lake** ◎ Ontario, S Canada
9 N4 **Borden Peninsula** *peninsula* Baffin Island, Nunavut, NE Canada
182 K11 **Bordertown** South Australia 36°21′S 140°48′E
92 H2 **Bordheyri** Vestfirdhir, NW Iceland 65°12′N 21°09′W
95 B18 **Bordhoy** *Dan.* Bordø. *island* NE Faeroe Islands
106 B11 **Bordighera** Liguria, NW Italy 43°48′N 07°40′E
74 K5 **Bordj-Bou-Arreridj** *var.* Bordj Bou Arreridj, Bordj Bou Arréridj. N Algeria 36°02′N 04°49′E
74 L10 **Bordj Omar Driss** E Algeria 28°09′N 06°52′E
143 N13 **Bord Khūn** Hormozgān, S Iran
Bordø *see* Bordhoy
147 V7 **Bordunskiy** Chuyskaya Oblast', N Kyrgyzstan 42°37′N 75°31′E
95 M17 **Borensberg** Östergötland, S Sweden 58°33′N 15°15′E
Borgå *see* Porvoo
92 L2 **Borgarfjördhur** Austurland, NE Iceland 65°32′N 13°46′W
92 H3 **Borgarnes** Vesturland, W Iceland 64°33′N 21°55′W
93 G14 **Børgefjell** ▲▲ C Norway
98 O7 **Borger** Drenthe, NE Netherlands 52°54′N 06°48′E
25 N2 **Borger** Texas, SW USA 35°40′N 101°24′W
95 N20 **Borgholm** Kalmar, S Sweden 56°50′N 16°41′E
107 N22 **Borgia** Calabria, SW Italy 38°48′N 16°28′E
99 J18 **Borgloon** Limburg, NE Belgium 50°48′N 05°21′E
Borg Massif *see* Borgmassivet
195 P2 **Borgmassivet** *Eng.* Borg Massif. ▲▲ Antarctica
22 L9 **Borgne, Lake** ◎ Louisiana, S USA
106 C7 **Borgomanero** Piemonte, NE Italy 45°42′N 08°33′E
106 G10 **Borgo Panigale** ✈ (Bologna) Emilia-Romagna, N Italy 44°33′N 11°16′E
107 J15 **Borgorose** Lazio, C Italy 42°10′N 13°15′E
106 A9 **Borgo San Dalmazzo** Piemonte, N Italy 44°19′N 07°29′E
106 G11 **Borgo San Lorenzo** Toscana, C Italy 43°58′N 11°22′E
106 C7 **Borgosesia** Piemonte, NE Italy 45°41′N 08°21′E
106 E9 **Borgo Val di Taro** Emilia-Romagna, C Italy 44°29′N 09°48′E
106 G6 **Borgo Valsugana** Trentino-Alto Adige, N Italy 46°04′N 11°31′E
Borhoyn Tal *see* Dzamïn-Üüd
167 R8 **Borikhan** *var.* Borikhane. Bolikhamxai, C Laos 18°36′N 103°43′E
Borikhane *see* Borikhan
144 G8 **Borili** *prev.* Burlin. Zapadnyy Kazakhstan, NW Kazakhstan 51°25′N 52°42′E
Borislav *see* Boryslav
127 N8 **Borisoglebsk** Voronezhskaya Oblast', W Russian Federation 51°23′N 42°00′E
Borisov *see* Barysaw
Borisovgrad *see* Pŭrvomay
Borispol' *see* Boryspil'
172 I3 **Boriziny** *prev./Fr.* Port-Bergé. Mahajanga, NW Madagascar 15°31′S 47°40′E
105 Q5 **Borja** Aragón, NE Spain 41°50′N 01°32′W
Borjas Blancas *see* Les Borges Blanques
137 S10 **Borjomi** *Rus.* Borzhomi. C Georgia 41°50′N 43°24′E
118 L12 **Borkavichy** *Rus.* Borkovichi. Vitsyebskaya Voblasts', N Belarus 55°40′N 28°20′E
101 H16 **Borken** Hessen, C Germany 51°01′N 09°16′E
101 E14 **Borken** Nordrhein-Westfalen, W Germany 51°51′N 06°51′E
92 H10 **Borkenes** Troms, N Norway 68°46′N 16°10′E
78 H7 **Borkou-Ennedi-Tibesti** *off.* Préfecture du Borkou-Ennedi-Tibesti. ◈ *prefecture* N Chad
Borkou-Ennedi-Tibesti, Préfecture du *see* Borkou-Ennedi-Tibesti
Borkovichi *see* Borkavichy
100 E9 **Borkum** *island* NW Germany
81 K17 **Bor, Lagh** *var.* Lak Bor. *dry watercourse* NE Kenya
Bor, Lak *see* Bor, Lagh
95 M14 **Borlänge** Dalarna, C Sweden 60°29′N 15°25′E
106 C9 **Bormida** ≈ NW Italy
106 F6 **Bormio** Lombardia, N Italy 46°27′N 10°24′E
101 M16 **Borna** Sachsen, E Germany 51°07′N 12°30′E
98 O10 **Borne** Overijssel, E Netherlands 52°18′N 06°45′E
99 F17 **Bornem** Antwerpen, N Belgium 51°06′N 04°14′E
169 S10 **Borneo** *island* Brunei/Indonesia/Malaysia
101 E16 **Bornheim** Nordrhein-Westfalen, W Germany 50°46′N 06°58′E
95 L24 **Bornholm** ◈ *county* E Denmark
95 L24 **Bornholm** *island* E Denmark
77 Y13 **Borno** ◈ *state* NE Nigeria
104 K15 **Bornos** Andalucía, S Spain 36°50′N 05°42′W
162 L7 **Bornuur** Töv, C Mongolia 48°28′N 106°15′E
117 O4 **Borodyanka** Kyyivs'ka Oblast', N Ukraine 50°40′N 29°54′E
158 I5 **Borohoro Shan** ▲▲ NW China
77 O13 **Boromo** SW Burkina 11°47′N 02°54′W
35 T13 **Boron** California, W USA 35°00′N 117°42′W
Borongo *see* Black Volta
Boron'ki *see* Baron'ki
Borosjenő *see* Ineu
Borossebes *see* Sebiş

76 L15 **Borotou** NW Ivory Coast 08°46′N 07°30′W

117 W6 **Borova** Kharkivs'ka Oblast', E Ukraine 49°22′N 37°39′E

114 H8 **Borovan** Vratsa, NW Bulgaria 43°25′N 23°45′E

124 I14 **Borovichi** Novgorodskaya Oblast', W Russian Federation 58°24′N 33°56′E

Borovlje *see* Ferlach

114 K8 **Borovo** Ruse, N Bulgaria 43°28′N 25°46′E

112 J9 **Borovo** Vukovar-Srijem, NE Croatia 45°22′N 18°57′E

Borovoye *see* Burabay

126 K4 **Borovsk** Kaluzhskaya Oblast', W Russian Federation 55°12′N 36°22′E

145 N7 **Borovskoye** Kostanay, N Kazakhstan 53°48′N 64°17′E

Borovukha *see* Baravukha

95 L23 **Borrby** Skåne, S Sweden 55°27′N 14°10′E

105 T9 **Borriana** *var.* Burriana. Valenciana, E Spain 39°54′N 00°05′W

181 R3 **Borroloola** Northern Territory, N Australia 16°09′S 136°18′E

116 F9 **Borş** Bihor, NW Romania 47°07′N 21°49′E

116 I9 **Borşa** *Hung.* Borsa. Maramureş, N Romania 47°40′N 24°37′E

116 J10 **Borsec** *Ger.* Bad Borseck, *Hung.* Borszék. Harghita, C Romania 46°58′N 25°32′E

92 K8 **Børselv** *Lapp.* Bissojohka. Finnmark, N Norway 70°18′N 25°35′E

113 L23 **Borsh** *var.* Borshi. Vlorë, S Albania 40°04′N 19°51′E

Borshchev *see* Borshchiv

116 K7 **Borshchiv** *Pol.* Borszczów, *Rus.* Borshchev. Ternopil's'ka Oblast', W Ukraine 48°48′N 26°00′E

Borshi *see* Borsh

111 L20 **Borsod-Abaúj-Zemplén** *off.* Borsod-Abaúj-Zemplén Megye. ◈ *county* NE Hungary

Borsod-Abaúj-Zemplén Megye *see* Borsod-Abaúj-Zemplén

99 E15 **Borssele** Zeeland, SW Netherlands 51°26′N 03°45′E

Borszczów *see* Borshchiv

Borszék *see* Borsec

Bortala *see* Bole

103 O12 **Bort-les-Orgues** Corrèze, C France 45°28′N 02°31′E

Bor u České Lípy *see* Nový Bor

Bor-Üdzüür *see* Altay

143 N9 **Borūjen** Chahār Maḩall va Bakhtīārī, C Iran 32°N 51°09′E

142 L7 **Borūjerd** *var.* Burujird. Lorestān, W Iran 33°55′N 48°46′E

116 H6 **Boryslav** *Pol.* Borysław, *Rus.* Borislav. L'vivs'ka Oblast', NW Ukraine 49°18′N 23°28′E

Borysław *see* Boryslav

117 P4 **Boryspil'** *Rus.* Borispol'. Kyyivs'ka Oblast', N Ukraine 50°21′N 30°59′E

117 P4 **Boryspil'** *Rus.* Borispol'. ✈ (Kyyiv) Kyyivs'ka Oblast', N Ukraine 50°21′N 30°46′E

Borzhomi *see* Borjomi

117 R3 **Borzna** Chernihivs'ka Oblast', NE Ukraine 51°15′N 32°25′E

123 O14 **Borzya** Zabaykal'skiy Kray, S Russian Federation 50°18′N 116°24′E

107 B18 **Bosa** Sardegna, Italy, C Mediterranean Sea 40°18′N 08°28′E

112 F10 **Bosanska Dubica** *var.* Kozarska Dubica. ◈ Republika Srpska, NW Bosnia and Herzegovina

112 G10 **Bosanska Gradiška** *var.* Gradiška. ◈ Republika Srpska, N Bosnia and Herzegovina

112 F10 **Bosanska Kostajnica** *var.* Srpska Kostajnica. ◈ Republika Srpska, NW Bosnia and Herzegovina

112 E11 **Bosanska Krupa** *var.* Krupa, Krupa na Uni. ◈ Federacija Bosna I Hercegovina, NW Bosnia and Herzegovina

112 H10 **Bosanski Brod** *var.* Srpski Brod. ◈ Republika Srpska, N Bosnia and Herzegovina

112 E10 **Bosanski Novi** *var.* Novi Grad. Republika Srpska, NW Bosnia and Herzegovina 45°03′N 16°23′E

112 E11 **Bosanski Petrovac** *var.* Petrovac. Federacija Bosna I Hercegovina, NW Bosnia and Herzegovina 44°34′N 16°21′E

112 I10 **Bosanski Šamac** *var.* Šamac. Republika Srpska, N Bosnia and Herzegovina 45°03′N 18°27′E

112 E12 **Bosansko Grahovo** *var.* Grahovo, Hrvatsko Grahovi. Federacija Bosna I Hercegovina, W Bosnia and Herzegovina 44°10′N 16°22′E

Bosaso *see* Boosaaso

186 B7 **Bosavi, Mount** ※ W Papua New Guinea 06°33′S 142°50′E

160 J14 **Bose** Guangxi Zhuangzu Zizhiqu, S China 23°55′N 106°32′E

161 Q5 **Boshan** Shandong, E China 36°32′N 117°47′E

113 P16 **Bosilegrad** *prev.* Bosiljgrad. Serbia, SE Serbia 42°30′N 22°30′E

Bosiljgrad *see* Bosilegrad

Bösing *see* Pezinok

98 H12 **Boskoop** Zuid-Holland, C Netherlands 52°04′N 04°40′E

111 G18 **Boskovice** *Ger.* Boskowitz. Jihomoravský Kraj, SE Czech Republic 49°30′N 16°39′E

Boskowitz *see* Boskovice

112 I10 **Bosna** ≈ N Bosnia and Herzegovina

113 G14 **Bosna I Hercegovina, Federacija** ◈ *republic* Bosnia and Herzegovina

112 H12 **Bosnia and Herzegovina** *off.* Republic of Bosnia and Herzegovina. ◆ *republic* SE Europe

Bosnia and Herzegovina, Republic of *see* Bosnia and Herzegovina

79 J16 **Bosobolo** Equateur, NW Dem. Rep. Congo 04°11′N 19°55′E

165 O14 **Bōsō-hantō** *peninsula* Honshū, S Japan

Bosora *see* Buşrá ash Shām

Bosphorus/Bosporus *see* İstanbul Boğazı

Bosporus Cimmerius *see* Kerch Strait

Bosporus Thracius *see* İstanbul Boğazı

Bosra *see* Buşrá ash Shām

79 H14 **Bossangoa** Ouham, C Central African Republic 06°32′N 17°25′E

Bossé Bangou *see* Bossey Bangou

79 I15 **Bossembélé** Ombella-Mpoko, C Central African Republic 05°13′N 17°39′E

79 H15 **Bossentélé** Ouham-Pendé, W Central African Republic 05°36′N 16°37′E

77 R12 **Bossey Bangou** *var.* Bossé Bangou. Tillabéri, SW Niger 13°22′N 01°18′E

22 G5 **Bossier City** Louisiana, S USA 32°31′N 93°43′W

83 D20 **Bossiesvlei** Hardap, S Namibia 25°02′S 16°48′E

77 Y11 **Bosso** Diffa, SE Niger 13°42′N 13°18′E

61 F15 **Bossoroca** Rio Grande do Sul, S Brazil 28°45′S 54°54′W

158 J10 **Bostan** Xinjiang Uygur Zizhiqu, W China 41°20′N 83°15′E

142 K3 **Bostānābād** Āžarbāyjān-e Sharqī, N Iran 37°52′N 46°51′E

158 K6 **Bosten Hu** *var.* Bagrax Hu. ◎ NW China

97 O18 **Boston** *prev.* St.Botolph's Town. E England, United Kingdom 52°59′N 00°01′W

19 O11 **Boston** *state capital* Massachusetts, NE USA 42°22′N 71°04′W

146 I9 **Bo'ston** *Rus.* Bustan. Qoraqalpog'iston Respublikasi, W Uzbekistan 41°49′N 60°51′E

10 M17 **Boston Bar** British Columbia, SW Canada 49°54′N 121°22′W

27 T10 **Boston Mountains** ▲▲ Arkansas, C USA

15 P8 **Bostonnais** ≈ Québec, SE Canada

Bostyn' *see* Bastyn'

112 J10 **Bosut** ≈ E Croatia

154 C11 **Botād** Gujarāt, W India 22°12′N 71°44′E

145 S10 **Botakara** *Kas.* Botaqara; *prev.* Ul'yanovskiy. Karaganda, C Kazakhstan 50°05′N 73°45′E

183 T9 **Botany Bay** *inlet* New South Wales, SE Australia

Botaqara *see* Botakara

83 G18 **Boteti** *var.* Botletle. ≈ N Botswana

114 J9 **Botev** ▲ C Bulgaria 42°45′N 24°57′E

114 H9 **Botevgrad** *prev.* Orkhaniye. Sofiya, W Bulgaria 42°55′N 23°47′E

93 J16 **Bothnia, Gulf of** *Fin.* Pohjanlahti, *Swe.* Bottniska Viken. *gulf* N Baltic Sea

183 P17 **Bothwell** Tasmania, SE Australia 42°24′S 147°01′E

104 H5 **Boticas** Vila Real, N Portugal 41°41′N 07°40′W

55 W10 **Boti-Pasi** Sipaliwini, C Suriname 04°15′N 55°27′W

Botletle *see* Boteti

127 P16 **Botlikh** Chechenskaya Respublika, SW Russian Federation 42°39′N 46°12′E

117 N10 **Botna** ≈ E Moldova

116 I9 **Botoşani** *Hung.* Botosány. Botoşani, NE Romania 47°44′N 26°41′E

116 K8 **Botoşani** ◈ *county* NE Romania

Botosány *see* Botoşani

147 P12 **Bototog', Tizmasi** *Rus.* Khrebet Babatag. ▲▲ Tajikistan/Uzbekistan

161 P4 **Botou** *prev.* Bozhen. Hebei, E China 38°09′N 116°37′E

99 M20 **Botrange** ▲ E Belgium 50°30′N 06°03′E

107 O21 **Botricello** Calabria, SW Italy 38°56′N 16°51′E

83 I23 **Botshabelo** Free State, C South Africa 29°15′S 26°51′E

93 J15 **Botsmark** Västerbotten, N Sweden 64°15′N 20°15′E

83 G19 **Botswana** *off.* Republic of Botswana. ◆ *republic* S Africa

Botswana, Republic of *see* Botswana

29 N2 **Bottineau** North Dakota, N USA 48°50′N 100°28′W

Bottniska Viken *see* Bothnia, Gulf of

60 L9 **Botucatu** São Paulo, S Brazil 22°52′S 48°30′W

76 M16 **Bouaflé** C Ivory Coast 06°59′N 05°45′W

77 N16 **Bouaké** *var.* Bwake. C Ivory Coast 07°42′N 05°00′W

79 G14 **Bouar** Nana-Mambéré, W Central African Republic 05°58′N 15°38′E

74 H7 **Bouarfa** NE Morocco 32°33′N 01°54′W

111 B19 **Boubín** ▲ SW Czech Republic 49°00′N 13°51′E

79 I14 **Bouca** Ouham, W Central African Republic 06°57′N 18°18′E

15 T5 **Boucher** ≈ Québec, SE Canada

103 R15 **Bouches-du-Rhône** ◈ *department* SE France

74 C9 **Bou Craa** *var.* Bu Craa. NW Western Sahara 26°32′N 12°52′W

77 O9 **Boû Djébéha** *oasis* C Mali

108 C8 **Boudry** Neuchâtel, W Switzerland 46°57′N 06°46′E

79 F21 **Bouenza** ◈ *province* S Congo

180 L2 **Bougainville, Cape** *cape* Western Australia

65 E24 **Bougainville, Cape** *headland* East Falkland, Falkland Islands 51°18′S 58°28′W

Bougainville, Détroit de *see* Bougainville Strait

186 J7 **Bougainville Island** *island* NE Papua New Guinea

186 I8 **Bougainville Strait** *strait* N Solomon Islands

187 Q13 **Bougainville Strait** *Fr.* Détroit de Bougainville. *strait* C Vanuatu

120 I9 **Bougaroun, Cap** *headland* NE Algeria 37°07′N 06°18′E

77 R8 **Boughessa** Kidal, NE Mali 20°05′N 02°13′E

Bougie *see* Béjaïa

76 L13 **Bougouni** Sikasso, SW Mali 11°25′N 07°28′W

99 J24 **Bouillon** Luxembourg, SE Belgium 49°47′N 05°04′E

74 K5 **Bouira** *var.* Bouïra. N Algeria 36°22′N 03°55′E

74 D8 **Bou-Izakarn** SW Morocco 29°12′N 09°43′W

74 B9 **Boujdour** *var.* Bojador. W Western Sahara 26°06′N 14°29′W

74 G5 **Boukhalef** ✈ (Tanger) N Morocco 35°45′N 05°53′W

Boukombé *see* Boukoumbé

77 R14 **Boukoumbé** *var.* Boukombé. C Benin 10°13′N 01°09′E

76 G6 **Boû Lanouâr** Dakhlet Nouâdhibou, W Mauritania 21°17′N 16°29′W

37 T4 **Boulder** Colorado, C USA 40°02′N 105°18′W

33 R10 **Boulder** Montana, NW USA 46°14′N 112°07′W

35 X12 **Boulder City** Nevada, W USA 35°58′N 114°49′W

181 T7 **Boulia** Queensland, C Australia 23°02′S 139°58′E

15 N10 **Boullé** ≈ Québec, SE Canada

102 J9 **Boulogne** ≈ NW France

Boulogne *see* Boulogne-sur-Mer

102 L16 **Boulogne-sur-Gesse** Haute-Garonne, S France 43°18′N 00°38′E

103 N1 **Boulogne-sur-Mer** *var.* Boulogne; *anc.* Bononia, Gesoriacum, Gessoriacum. Pas-de-Calais, N France 50°43′N 01°36′E

77 Q12 **Boulsa** C Burkina 12°41′N 00°29′W

77 W11 **Boultoum** Zinder, C Niger 14°43′N 10°22′E

187 Y14 **Bouma** Taveuni, N Fiji 16°49′S 179°50′W

79 G16 **Boumba** ≈ SE Cameroon

76 J9 **Boûmdeïd** *var.* Boumdeït. Assaba, S Mauritania 17°26′N 11°21′W

Boumdeït *see* Boûmdeïd

115 C17 **Boumistós** ▲ W Greece 38°48′N 20°59′E

77 O15 **Bouna** NE Ivory Coast 09°16′N 03°00′W

19 P4 **Boundary Bald Mountain** ▲ Maine, NE USA 45°45′N 70°10′W

35 S8 **Boundary Peak** ▲ Nevada, W USA 37°50′N 118°21′W

76 M14 **Boundiali** N Ivory Coast 09°30′N 06°31′W

79 G19 **Boundji** Cuvette, C Congo 01°05′S 15°18′E

77 O13 **Boundoukui** *var.* Bondoukui, Bondoukuy. W Burkina 11°51′N 03°47′W

36 L2 **Bountiful** Utah, W USA 40°53′N 111°52′W

Bounty Basin *see* Bounty Trough

191 Q16 **Bounty Bay** *bay* Pitcairn Island, C Pacific Ocean

192 L12 **Bounty Islands** *island group* S New Zealand

175 Q13 **Bounty Trough** *var.* Bounty Basin. *undersea feature* S Pacific Ocean

187 P17 **Bourail** Province Sud, C New Caledonia 21°35′S 165°29′E

27 V5 **Bourbeuse River** ≈ Missouri, C USA

103 Q9 **Bourbon-Lancy** Saône-et-Loire, C France 46°39′N 03°48′E

31 N11 **Bourbonnais** Illinois, N USA 41°08′N 87°52′W

103 O10 **Bourbonnais** *cultural region* C France

103 S7 **Bourbonne-les-Bains** Haute-Marne, N France 48°00′N 05°43′E

Bourbon Vendée *see* la Roche-sur-Yon

74 M8 **Bourdj Messaouda** E Algeria 30°18′N 09°19′E

77 Q10 **Bourem** Gao, C Mali 16°56′N 00°21′W

Bourg *see* Bourg-en-Bresse

103 N11 **Bourganeuf** Creuse, C France 45°57′N 01°47′E

Bourgas *see* Burgas

Bourge-en-Bresse *see* Bourg-en-Bresse

103 S10 **Bourg-en-Bresse** *var.* Bourg, Bourge-en-Bresse. Ain, E France 46°12′N 05°13′E

103 O8 **Bourges** *anc.* Avaricum. Cher, C France 47°06′N 02°24′E

103 T11 **Bourget, Lac du** ◎ E France

103 P8 **Bourgogne** *Eng.* Burgundy. ◈ *region* E France

103 S11 **Bourgoin-Jallieu** Isère, E France 45°34′N 05°16′E

103 R14 **Bourg-St-Andéol** Ardèche, E France 44°24′N 04°36′E

103 U11 **Bourg-St-Maurice** Savoie, E France 45°37′N 06°49′E

108 C11 **Bourg St. Pierre** Valais, SW Switzerland 45°54′N 07°10′E

76 H8 **Boû Rjeimât** *well* W Mauritania

183 P5 **Bourke** New South Wales, SE Australia 30°08′S 145°57′E

97 M24 **Bournemouth** S England, United Kingdom 50°43′N 01°54′W

99 M23 **Bourscheid** Diekirch, NE Luxembourg 49°55′N 06°04′E

74 K6 **Bou Saâda** *var.* Bou Saada. N Algeria 35°10′N 04°09′E

36 I13 **Bouse Wash** ≈ Arizona, SW USA

103 N10 **Boussac** Creuse, C France 46°20′N 02°12′E

102 M16 **Boussens** Haute-Garonne, S France 43°11′N 00°58′E

78 H12 **Bousso** *prev.* Fort-Bretonnet. Chari-Baguirmi, S Chad 10°32′N 16°45′E

76 H9 **Boutilimit** Trarza, SW Mauritania 17°33′N 14°42′W

65 D21 **Bouvet Island** ◇ *Norwegian dependency* S Atlantic Ocean

77 U11 **Bouza** Tahoua, SW Niger 14°25′N 06°09′E

109 R10 **Bovec** *Ger.* Flitsch, *It.* Plezzo. NW Slovenia 46°21′N 13°33′E

98 J8 **Bovenkarspel** Noord-Holland, NW Netherlands 52°33′N 05°03′E

29 V5 **Bovey** Minnesota, N USA 47°18′N 93°25′W

32 M9 **Bovill** Idaho, NW USA 46°50′N 116°24′W

24 L4 **Bovina** Texas, SW USA 34°30′N 102°52′W

107 M17 **Bovino** Puglia, SE Italy 41°14′N 15°19′E

61 C17 **Bovril** Entre Ríos, E Argentina 31°24′S 59°25′W

28 L2 **Bowbells** North Dakota, N USA 48°48′N 102°15′W

11 Q16 **Bow City** Alberta, SW Canada 50°27′N 112°16′W

29 O8 **Bowdle** South Dakota, N USA 45°27′N 99°39′W

181 X6 **Bowen** Queensland, NE Australia 20°S 148°10′E

192 L2 **Bowers Ridge** *undersea feature* S Bering Sea 50°00′N 180°00′W

25 S5 **Bowie** Texas, SW USA 33°33′N 97°51′W

11 R17 **Bow Island** Alberta, SW Canada 49°53′N 111°24′W

Bowkān *see* Būkān

20 J7 **Bowling Green** Kentucky, S USA 37°00′N 86°29′W

27 V3 **Bowling Green** Missouri, C USA 39°21′N 91°11′W

31 R11 **Bowling Green** Ohio, N USA 41°22′N 83°40′W

21 W5 **Bowling Green** Virginia, NE USA 38°02′N 77°22′W

28 J6 **Bowman** North Dakota, N USA 46°11′N 103°26′W

9 Q7 **Bowman Bay** *bay* NW Atlantic Ocean

194 I5 **Bowman Coast** *physical region* Antarctica

28 J7 **Bowman-Haley Lake** ⊞ North Dakota, N USA

195 Z11 **Bowman Island** *island* Antarctica

Bowo *see* Bomi

183 S9 **Bowral** New South Wales, SE Australia 34°28′S 150°52′E

186 E8 **Bowutu Mountains** ▲▲ C Papua New Guinea

83 I16 **Bowwood** Southern, S Zambia 17°09′S 26°16′E

28 I12 **Box Butte Reservoir** ⊞ Nebraska, C USA

28 J10 **Box Elder** South Dakota, N USA 44°06′N 103°04′W

95 M18 **Boxholm** Östergötland, S Sweden 58°12′N 15°05′E

Bo Xian/Boxian *see* Bozhou

161 Q4 **Boxing** Shandong, E China 37°06′N 118°05′E

99 L14 **Boxmeer** Noord-Brabant, SE Netherlands 51°39′N 05°57′E

99 J14 **Boxtel** Noord-Brabant, S Netherlands 51°36′N 05°20′E

136 J10 **Boyabat** Sinop, N Turkey 41°27′N 34°45′E

54 F9 **Boyacá** *off.* Departamento de Boyacá. ◈ *province* C Colombia

Boyacá, Departamento de *see* Boyacá

117 O4 **Boyarka** Kyyivs'ka Oblast', N Ukraine 50°19′N 30°20′E

22 H7 **Boyce** Louisiana, S USA 31°23′N 92°40′W

114 H8 **Boychinovtsi** Montana, NW Bulgaria 43°28′N 23°20′E

33 U11 **Boyd** Montana, NW USA 45°27′N 109°03′W

25 S6 **Boyd** Texas, SW USA 33°01′N 97°33′W

21 V8 **Boydton** Virginia, NE USA 36°40′N 78°26′W

Boyer Ahmadī va Kohkīlūyeh *see* Kohgīlūyeh va Bowyer Aḩmad

29 T13 **Boyer River** ≈ Iowa, C USA

21 W8 **Boykins** Virginia, NE USA 36°35′N 77°11′W

11 Q13 **Boyle** Alberta, SW Canada 54°38′N 112°45′W

97 D16 **Boyle** *Ir.* Mainistirna Búille. C Ireland 53°58′N 08°18′W

97 F17 **Boyne** *Ir.* An Bhóinn. ≈ E Ireland

31 Q5 **Boyne City** Michigan, N USA 45°13′N 85°00′W

23 Z14 **Boynton Beach** Florida, SE USA 26°31′N 80°04′W

147 O13 **Boysun** *Rus.* Baysun. Surkhondaryo Viloyati, S Uzbekistan 38°14′N 67°08′E

Bozau *see* Întorsura Buzăului

136 B12 **Bozcaada** *Island* Çanakkale, NW Turkey

136 C14 **Boz Dağları** ▲▲ W Turkey

33 S11 **Bozeman** Montana, NW USA 45°40′N 111°02′W

Bozen *see* Bolzano

79 J16 **Bozene** Equateur, NW Dem. Rep. Congo 02°56′N 19°15′E

Bozhen *see* Botou

161 P7 **Bozhou** *var.* Boxian, Bo Xian. Anhui, E China 33°46′N 115°44′E

136 H16 **Bozkır** Konya, S Turkey 37°10′N 32°15′E

136 K13 **Bozok Yaylasī** *plateau* C Turkey

79 H14 **Bozoum** Ouham-Pendé, W Central African Republic 06°17′N 16°26′E

137 N16 **Bozova** Sanlıurfa, S Turkey 37°23′N 38°33′E

Bozrah *see* Buşrá ash Shām

136 E12 **Bozüyük** Bilecik, NW Turkey 39°55′N 30°02′E

106 B9 **Bra** Piemonte, NW Italy 44°42′N 07°51′E

194 G4 **Brabant Island** *island* Antarctica

99 I20 **Brabant Walloon** ◈ *province* C Belgium

113 F15 **Brač** *var.* Brach, *It.* Brazza; *anc.* Brattia. *island* S Croatia

Bracara Augusta *see* Braga

107 H15 **Bracciano** Lazio, C Italy 42°04′N 12°12′E

107 H14 **Bracciano, Lago di** ◎ C Italy

14 H13 **Bracebridge** Ontario, S Canada 45°02′N 79°19′W

Brach *see* Brač

93 G17 **Bräcke** Jämtland, C Sweden 62°43′N 15°30′E

25 P12 **Brackettville** Texas, SW USA 29°19′N 100°27′W

97 N22 **Bracknell** S England, United Kingdom 51°26′N 00°46′W

61 K14 **Braço do Norte** Santa Catarina, S Brazil 28°16′S 49°11′W

116 G11 **Brad** *Hung.* Brád. Hunedoara, SW Romania 45°52′N 23°00′E

107 N18 **Bradano** ≈ S Italy

23 V13 **Bradenton** Florida, SE USA 27°30′N 82°34′W

45 V10 **Brades** ○ (Montserrat: *de facto* capital, *de jure* capital, Plymouth, destroyed by volcano in 1995) N Montserrat 16°45′N 62°12′W

14 H14 **Bradford** Ontario, S Canada 44°09′N 79°34′W

97 L17 **Bradford** N England, United Kingdom 53°48′N 01°45′W

27 W10 **Bradford** Arkansas, C USA 35°25′N 91°27′W

18 D12 **Bradford** Pennsylvania, NE USA 41°57′N 78°38′W

27 T15 **Bradley** Arkansas, C USA 33°06′N 93°39′W

25 P7 **Bradshaw** Texas, SW USA 32°06′N 99°52′W

25 Q9 **Brady** Texas, SW USA 31°08′N 99°22′W

25 Q9 **Brady Creek** ≈ Texas, SW USA

95 G22 **Brædstrup** Syddanmark, C Denmark 55°58′N 09°38′E

96 J10 **Braemar** NE Scotland, United Kingdom 57°12′N 02°52′W

116 K8 **Brăeşti** Botoşani, NW Romania 47°50′N 26°26′E

104 G5 **Braga** *anc.* Bracara Augusta. Braga, NW Portugal 41°32′N 08°26′W

104 G5 **Braga** ◈ *district* N Portugal

116 J15 **Bragadiru** Teleorman, S Romania 43°43′N 25°32′E

61 C20 **Bragado** Buenos Aires, E Argentina 35°10′S 60°29′W

104 J5 **Bragança** *Eng.* Braganza; *anc.* Julio Briga. Bragança, NE Portugal 41°47′N 06°46′W

104 I5 **Bragança** ◈ *district* N Portugal

60 N9 **Bragança Paulista** São Paulo, S Brazil 22°55′S 46°30′W

Braganza *see* Bragança

Bragin *see* Brahin

29 V7 **Braham** Minnesota, N USA 45°43′N 93°10′W

Brahe *see* Brda

Brahestad *see* Raahe

119 O20 **Brahin** *Rus.* Bragin. Homyel'skaya Voblasts', SE Belarus 51°47′N 30°16′E

153 U15 **Brahmanbaria** Chittagong, E Bangladesh 23°58′N 91°04′E

154 O12 **Brāhmani** ≈ E India

154 N13 **Brahmapur** Orissa, E India 19°21′N 84°51′E

129 S10 **Brahmaputra** *var.* Padma, Tsangpo, *Ben.* Jamuna, *Chin.* Yarlung Zangbo Jiang, *Ind.* Bramaputra, Dihang, Siang. ≈ S Asia

97 H19 **Braich y Pwll** *headland* NW Wales, United Kingdom 52°47′N 04°46′W

183 R10 **Braidwood** New South Wales, SE Australia 35°26′S 149°48′E

30 M11 **Braidwood** Illinois, N USA 41°16′N 88°12′W

116 M13 **Brăila** Brăila, E Romania 45°17′N 27°57′E

116 L13 **Brăila** ◈ *county* SE Romania

99 G19 **Braine-l'Alleud** Brabant Walloon, C Belgium 50°41′N 04°22′E

99 F19 **Braine-le-Comte** Hainaut, SW Belgium 50°37′N 04°08′E

29 U6 **Brainerd** Minnesota, N USA 46°22′N 94°10′W

99 J19 **Braives** Liège, E Belgium 50°37′N 05°09′E

83 H23 **Brak** ≈ C South Africa

Brak *see* Birāk

99 E18 **Brakel** Oost-Vlaanderen, SW Belgium 50°50′N 03°48′E

98 J13 **Brakel** Gelderland, C Netherlands 51°49′N 05°05′E

76 H9 **Brakna** ◈ *region* S Mauritania

95 J17 **Brålanda** Västra Götaland, S Sweden 58°32′N 12°18′E

Bramaputra *see* Brahmaputra

95 F23 **Bramming** Syddtjylland, W Denmark 55°28′N 08°42′E

14 G15 **Brampton** Ontario, S Canada 43°42′N 79°46′W

100 F12 **Bramsche** Niedersachsen, NW Germany 52°25′N 07°58′E

116 J12 **Bran** *Ger.* Törzburg, *Hung.* Törcsvár. Braşov, S Romania 45°31′N 25°23′E

29 W8 **Branch** Minnesota, N USA 45°29′N 92°57′W

21 R14 **Branchville** South Carolina, SE USA 33°15′N 80°49′W

47 Y6 **Branco, Cabo** *headland* E Brazil 07°08′S 34°45′W

58 F11 **Branco, Rio** ≈ N Brazil

108 J8 **Brand** Vorarlberg, W Austria 47°07′N 09°45′E

83 B18 **Brandberg** ▲ NW Namibia 21°20′S 14°22′E

95 H14 **Brandbu** Oppland, S Norway 60°24′N 10°30′E

95 F22 **Brande** Midtjylland, W Denmark 55°57′N 09°08′E

Brandebourg *see* Brandenburg

100 M12 **Brandenburg** *var.* Brandenburg an der Havel. Brandenburg, NE Germany 52°25′N 12°34′E

20 K5 **Brandenburg** Kentucky, S USA 38°00′N 86°11′W

100 N12 **Brandenburg** *off.* Freie und Hansestadt Hamburg, *Fr.* Brandebourg. ◈ *state* NE Germany

Brandenburg an der Havel *see* Brandenburg

83 I23 **Brandfort** Free State, C South Africa 28°42′S 26°28′E

11 W16 **Brandon** Manitoba, S Canada 49°50′N 99°57′W

23 V12 **Brandon** Florida, SE USA 27°56′N 82°17′W

22 L6 **Brandon** Mississippi, S USA 32°16′N 90°01′W

97 A20 **Brandon Mountain** *Ir.* Cnoc Bréanainn. ▲ SW Ireland 52°13′N 10°16′W

Brandsen *see* Coronel Brandsen

95 I14 **Brandval** Hedmark, S Norway 60°18′N 12°01′E

83 F24 **Brandvlei** Northern Cape, W South Africa 30°27′S 20°29′E

23 U9 **Branford** Florida, SE USA 29°57′N 82°54′W

110 K7 **Braniewo** *Ger.* Braunsberg. Warmińsko-mazurskie, N Poland 54°24′N 19°50′E

194 H3 **Bransfield Strait** *strait* Antarctica

37 U8 **Branson** Colorado, C USA 37°01′N 103°52′W

27 T8 **Branson** Missouri, C USA 36°38′N 93°13′W

14 G16 **Brantford** Ontario, S Canada 43°09′N 80°17′W

102 L12 **Brantôme** Dordogne, SW France 45°21′N 00°37′E

182 L12 **Branxholme** Victoria, SE Australia 37°51′S 141°48′E

Brasil *see* Brazil

59 C16 **Brasiléia** Acre, W Brazil 10°59′S 48°45′W

59 K18 **Brasília** ● (Brazil) Distrito Federal, C Brazil 15°45′S 47°57′W

Brasil, Repùblica Federativa do *see* Brazil

Braslav *see* Braslaw

118 J12 **Braslaw** *Pol.* Brasław, *Rus.* Braslav. Vitsyebskaya Voblasts', N Belarus 55°38′N 27°02′E

116 J12 **Braşov** *Ger.* Kronstadt, *Hung.* Brassó; *prev.* Oraşul Stalin. Braşov, C Romania 45°40′N 25°35′E

116 I12 **Braşov** ◈ *county* C Romania

77 U18 **Brass** Bayelsa, S Nigeria 04°19′N 06°21′E

99 H16 **Brasschaat** *var.* Brasschaet. Antwerpen, N Belgium 51°17′N 04°30′E

Brasschaet *see* Brasschaat

169 V8 **Brassey, Banjaran** *var.* Brassey Range. ▲▲ East Malaysia

Brassey Range *see* Brassey, Banjaran

Brassó *see* Braşov

23 T1 **Brasstown Bald** ▲ Georgia, SE USA 34°52′N 83°48′W

113 K22 **Brataj** Vlorë, SW Albania 40°18′N 19°37′E

114 J10 **Bratan** *var.* Morozov. ▲ C Bulgaria 42°31′N 25°08′E

111 F21 **Bratislava** *Ger.* Pressburg, *Hung.* Pozsony. ● (Slovakia) Bratislavský Kraj, W Slovakia 48°10′N 17°10′E

111 H21 **Bratislavský Kraj** ◈ *region* W Slovakia

114 H10 **Bratiya** ▲ C Bulgaria 42°36′N 24°08′E

122 M12 **Bratsk** Irkutskaya Oblast', C Russian Federation 56°20′N 101°50′E

117 Q8 **Brats'ke** Mykolayivs'ka Oblast', S Ukraine 47°52′N 31°34′E

122 M13 **Bratskoye Vodokhranilishche** *Eng.* Bratsk Reservoir. ⊞ S Russian Federation

Bratsk Reservoir *see* Bratskoye Vodokhranilishche

Brattia *see* Brač

94 D9 **Brattvåg** Møre og Romsdal, S Norway 62°36′N 06°21′E

112 K12 **Bratunac** ◈ Republika Srpska, E Bosnia and Herzegovina

114 J10 **Bratya Daskalovi** *prev.* Grozdovo. Stara Zagora, C Bulgaria 42°13′N 25°21′E

109 U2 **Braunau** ≈ N Austria

Braunau *see* Braunau am Inn

109 Q4 **Braunau am Inn** *var.* Braunau. Oberösterreich, N Austria 48°16′N 13°03′E

Braunsberg *see* Braniewo

100 J13 **Braunschweig** *Eng./Fr.* Brunswick. Niedersachsen, N Germany 52°16′N 10°32′E

Brava *see* Baraawe

105 Y6 **Brava, Costa** *coastal region* NE Spain

43 V16 **Brava, Punta** *headland* E Panama 08°21′N 78°22′W

95 N17 **Bråviken** *inlet* S Sweden

56 B10 **Bravo, Cerro** ▲ N Peru 05°33′S 79°10′W

Bravo del Norte, Río/Bravo, Río *see* Grande, Rio

35 X17 **Brawley** California, W USA 32°58′N 115°31′W

97 G18 **Bray** *Ir.* Bré. E Ireland 53°12′N 06°06′W

59 G16 **Brazil** *off.* Federative Republic of Brazil, *Port.* Repùblica Federativa do Brasil, *Sp.* Brasil; *prev.* United States of Brazil. ◆ *federal republic* South America

65 K15 **Brazil Basin** *var.* Brazilian Basin, Brazil'skaya Kotlovina. *undersea feature* W Atlantic Ocean 15°00′S 25°00′W

Brazil, Federative Republic of *see* Brazil

Brazilian Basin *see* Brazil Basin

Brazilian Highlands *see* Central, Planalto

Brazil'skaya Kotlovina *see* Brazil Basin

Brazil, United States of *see* Brazil

25 U10 **Brazos River** ≈ Texas, SW USA

Brazza *see* Brač

79 G21 **Brazzaville** ● (Congo) Capital District, S Congo 04°14′S 15°14′E

79 G21 **Brazzaville** ✈ Pool, S Congo 04°15′S 15°15′E

112 J11 **Brčko** ◈ Republika Srpska, NE Bosnia and Herzegovina

110 H8 **Brda** *Ger.* Brahe. ≈ N Poland

Bré *see* Bray

185 A23 **Breaksea Sound** *sound* South Island, New Zealand

184 L4 **Bream Bay** *bay* North Island, New Zealand

184 L4 **Bream Head** *headland* North Island, New Zealand 35°51′S 174°35′E

Bréanainn, Cnoc *see* Brandon Mountain

45 S6 **Brea, Punta** *headland* W Puerto Rico 17°56′N 66°55′W

22 I9 **Breaux Bridge** Louisiana, S USA 30°16′N 91°54′W

116 J13 **Breaza** Prahova, SE Romania 45°13′N 25°38′E

169 P16 **Brebes** Jawa, C Indonesia 06°54′S 109°00′E

96 K10 **Brechin** E Scotland, United Kingdom 56°45′N 02°38′W

99 H15 **Brecht** Antwerpen, N Belgium 51°21′N 04°33′E

37 S4 **Breckenridge** Colorado, C USA 39°28′N 106°02′W

29 R6 **Breckenridge** Minnesota, N USA 46°15′N 96°35′W

25 R6 **Breckenridge** Texas, SW USA 32°45′N 98°56′W

97 J21 **Brecknock** *cultural region* SE Wales, United Kingdom

63 G25 **Brecknock, Península** *headland* S Chile 54°39′S 71°48′W

111 G19 **Břeclav** *Ger.* Lundenburg. Jihomoravský Kraj, SE Czech Republic 49°05′N 16°51′E

97 J21 **Brecon** E Wales, United Kingdom 51°58′N 03°26′W

97 J21 **Brecon Beacons** ▲▲ S Wales, United Kingdom

99 I14 **Breda** Noord-Brabant, S Netherlands 51°35′N 04°46′E

95 K20 **Bredaryd** Jönköping, S Sweden 57°10′N 13°45′E

83 F26 **Bredasdorp** Western Cape, SW South Africa 34°32′S 20°02′E

93 H16 **Bredbyn** Västernorrland, N Sweden 63°28′N 18°04′E

122 F11 **Bredy** Chelyabinskaya Oblast', C Russian Federation 52°23′N 60°24′E

99 K17 **Bree** Limburg, NE Belgium 51°08′N 05°36′E

67 T15 **Breede** ≈ S South Africa

98 I7 **Breezand** Noord-Holland, NW Netherlands 52°52′N 04°47′E

113 P18 **Bregalnica** ≈ E FYR Macedonia

108 I6 **Bregenz** *anc.* Brigantium. Vorarlberg, W Austria 47°31′N 09°46′E

108 J7 **Bregenzer Wald** ▲▲ W Austria

114 F6 **Bregovo** Vidin, NW Bulgaria 44°07′N 22°40′E

102 H5 **Bréhat, Île de** *island* NW France

92 H2 **Breidhafjördhur** *bay* W Iceland

92 L3 **Breidhdalsvík** Austurland, E Iceland 64°48′N 14°02′W

108 H9 **Breil** *Ger.* Brigels. Graubünden, S Switzerland 46°46′N 09°04′E

92 J8 **Breivikbotn** Finnmark, N Norway 70°36′N 22°19′E

94 I9 **Brekken** Sør-Trøndelag, S Norway 62°39′N 11°49′E

94 G7 **Brekstad** Sør-Trøndelag, S Norway 63°42′N 09°40′E

94 B10 **Bremangerlandet** *island* S Norway

Brême *see* Bremen

100 H11 **Bremen** *Fr.* Brême. Bremen, NW Germany 53°06′N 08°48′E

23 R3 **Bremen** Georgia, SE USA 33°43′N 85°09′W

31 O11 **Bremen** Indiana, N USA 41°24′N 86°07′W

100 H10 **Bremen** *off.* Freie Hansestadt Bremen, *Fr.* Brême. ◈ *state* N Germany

100 G9 **Bremerhaven** Bremen, NW Germany 53°33′N 08°35′E

Bremersdorp *see* Manzini

32 G8 **Bremerton** Washington, NW USA 47°34′N 122°37′W

100 H10 **Bremervörde** Niedersachsen, NW Germany 53°29′N 09°06′E

25 U9 **Bremond** Texas, SW USA 31°10′N 96°40′W

25 U10 **Brenham** Texas, SW USA 30°09′N 96°24′W

108 M8 **Brenner** Tirol, W Austria 47°10′N 11°51′E

Brenner, Col du/Brennero, Passo del *see* Brenner Pass

108 M8 **Brenner Pass** *var.* Brenner Sattel, *Fr.* Col du Brenner, *Ger.* Brennerpass, *It.* Passo del Brennero. *pass* Austria/Italy

Brennerpass *see* Brenner Pass

Brenner Sattel *see* Brenner Pass

108 G10 **Brenno** ≈ SW Switzerland

106 F7 **Breno** Lombardia, N Italy 45°58′N 10°18′E

23 O5 **Brent** Alabama, S USA 32°54′N 87°10′W

106 H7 **Brenta** ≈ NE Italy

97 P21 **Brentwood** E England, United Kingdom 51°38′N 00°21′E

18 L14 **Brentwood** Long Island, New York, NE USA 40°46′N 73°12′W

106 F7 **Brescia** *anc.* Brixia. Lombardia, N Italy 45°33′N 10°13′E

99 D15 **Breskens** Zeeland, SW Netherlands 51°24′N 03°33′E

Breslau *see* Wrocław

106 H5 **Bressanone** *Ger.* Brixen. Trentino-Alto Adige, N Italy 46°44′N 11°41′E

96 M2 **Bressay** *island* NE Scotland, United Kingdom

102 K9 **Bressuire** Deux-Sèvres, W France 46°50′N 00°29′W

119 F20 **Brest** *Pol.* Brześć nad Bugiem, *Rus.* Brest-Litovsk; *prev.* Brześć Litewski. Brestskaya Voblasts', SW Belarus 52°06′N 23°42′E

102 F5 **Brest** Finistère, NW France 48°24′N 04°31′W

Brest-Litovsk *see* Brest

112 A10 **Brestova** Istra, NW Croatia 45°09′N 14°13′E

Brestskaya Oblast' *see* Brestskaya Voblasts'

119 G19 **Brestskaya Voblasts'** *prev.* *Rus.* Brestskaya Oblast'. ◈ *province* SW Belarus

102 G6 **Bretagne** *Eng.* Brittany, *Lat.* Britannia Minor. ◈ *region* NW France

116 G12 **Bretea-Română** *Hung.* Oláhbrettye; *prev.* Bretea-Romînă. Hunedoara, W Romania 45°39′N 23°00′E

Bretea-Romînă *see* Bretea-Română

103 O3 **Breteuil** Oise, N France 49°37′N 02°18′E

102 I10 **Breton, Pertuis** *inlet* W France

22 L10 **Breton Sound** *sound* Louisiana, S USA

184 K2 **Brett, Cape** *headland* North Island, New Zealand 35°11′S 174°21′E

101 G21 **Bretten** Baden-Württemberg, SW Germany 49°01′N 08°42′E

99 K15 **Breugel** Noord-Brabant, S Netherlands 51°30′N 05°30′E

106 B6 **Breuil-Cervinia** *It.* Cervinia. Valle d'Aosta, NW Italy 45°57′N 07°37′E

98 I11 **Breukelen** Utrecht, C Netherlands 52°11′N 05°01′E

21 P10 **Brevard** North Carolina, SE USA 35°13′N 82°46′W

38 L9 **Brevig Mission** Alaska, USA 65°19′N 166°29′W

95 G16 **Brevik** Telemark, S Norway 59°05′N 09°42′E

◆ Country ● Country Capital ◇ Dependent Territory ○ Dependent Territory Capital ◈ Administrative Regions ✈ International Airport ▲ Mountain ▲▲ Mountain Range ※ Volcano ≈ River ◎ Lake ⊞ Reservoir

183 P5 **Brewarrina** New South Wales, SE Australia *30°01′S 146°50′E*
19 R6 **Brewer** Maine, NE USA *44°46′N 68°44′W*
29 T11 **Brewster** Minnesota, N USA *43°43′N 95°28′W*
29 N14 **Brewster** Nebraska, C USA *41°57′N 99°52′W*
31 U12 **Brewster** Ohio, N USA *40°42′N 81°36′W*
Brewster, Kap *see* Kangikajik
183 O8 **Brewster, Lake** ◎ New South Wales, SE Australia
23 P7 **Brewton** Alabama, S USA *31°06′N 87°04′W*
Brezhnev *see* Naberezhnyye Chelny
109 W12 **Brežice** *Ger.* Rann. E Slovenia *45°54′N 15°35′E*
114 G9 **Breznik** Pernik, W Bulgaria *42°45′N 22°54′E*
111 K19 **Brezno** *Ger.* Bries, Briesen, *Hung.* Breznóbánya; *prev.* Brezno nad Hronom. Banskobystrický Kraj, C Slovakia *48°49′N 19°40′E*
Breznóbánya/Brezno nad Hronom *see* Brezno
116 I12 **Brezoi** Vâlcea, SW Romania *45°18′N 24°15′E*
114 J10 **Brezovo** *prev.* Abrashlare. Plovdiv, C Bulgaria *42°19′N 25°05′E*
79 K14 **Bria** Haute-Kotto, C Central African Republic *06°30′N 22°00′E*
103 U13 **Briançon** *anc.* Brigantio. Hautes-Alpes, SE France *44°55′N 06°37′E*
36 K7 **Brian Head** ▲ Utah, W USA *37°40′N 112°49′W*
103 O7 **Briare** Loiret, C France *47°35′N 02°46′E*
183 V2 **Bribie Island** *island* Queensland, E Australia
43 O14 **Bribrí** Limón, E Costa Rica *09°37′N 82°51′W*
116 L8 **Briceni** *var.* Brinceni, *Rus.* Brichany. N Moldova *48°21′N 27°02′E*
Bricgstow *see* Bristol
Brichany *see* Briceni
99 M24 **Bridel** Luxembourg, C Luxembourg *49°40′N 06°03′E*
97 J22 **Bridgend** S Wales, United Kingdom *51°30′N 03°37′W*
14 I14 **Bridgenorth** Ontario, SE Canada *44°21′N 78°22′W*
23 Q1 **Bridgeport** Alabama, S USA *34°57′N 85°42′W*
35 R8 **Bridgeport** California, W USA *38°14′N 119°15′W*
18 L13 **Bridgeport** Connecticut, NE USA *41°10′N 73°12′W*
31 N15 **Bridgeport** Illinois, N USA *38°42′N 87°45′W*
28 J14 **Bridgeport** Nebraska, C USA *41°37′N 103°07′W*
25 S6 **Bridgeport** Texas, SW USA *33°12′N 97°45′W*
21 S3 **Bridgeport** West Virginia, NE USA *39°17′N 80°15′W*
25 S5 **Bridgeport, Lake** ⊠ Texas, SW USA
33 U11 **Bridger** Montana, NW USA *45°16′N 108°55′W*
18 I17 **Bridgeton** New Jersey, NE USA *39°24′N 75°10′W*
180 J14 **Bridgetown** Western Australia *34°01′S 116°07′E*
45 Y14 **Bridgetown** ● (Barbados) SW Barbados *13°05′N 59°36′W*
183 P17 **Bridgewater** Tasmania, SE Australia *42°47′S 147°15′E*
13 P16 **Bridgewater** Nova Scotia, SE Canada *44°19′N 64°30′W*
19 P12 **Bridgewater** Massachusetts, NE USA *41°59′N 70°58′W*
29 Q11 **Bridgewater** South Dakota, N USA *43°33′N 97°30′W*
21 U5 **Bridgewater** Virginia, NE USA *38°22′N 78°58′W*
19 P8 **Bridgton** Maine, NE USA *44°04′N 70°43′W*
97 K23 **Bridgwater** SW England, United Kingdom *51°08′N 03°W*
97 K22 **Bridgwater Bay** *bay* SW England, United Kingdom
97 O16 **Bridlington** E England, United Kingdom *54°05′N 00°12′W*
97 O16 **Bridlington Bay** *bay* E England, United Kingdom
183 P15 **Bridport** Tasmania, SE Australia *41°03′S 147°26′E*
97 K24 **Bridport** S England, United Kingdom *50°44′N 02°43′W*
103 O5 **Brie** *cultural region* N France
Brieg *see* Brzeg
Briel *see* Brielle
98 G12 **Brielle** *var.* Briel, Bril, *Eng.* The Brill. Zuid-Holland, SW Netherlands *51°54′N 04°10′E*
108 E9 **Brienz** Bern, C Switzerland *46°45′N 08°00′E*
108 E9 **Brienzer See** ◎ SW Switzerland
Bries/Briesen *see* Brezno
Brietzig *see* Brzesko
103 S4 **Briey** Meurthe-et-Moselle, NE France *49°15′N 05°57′E*
108 E10 **Brig** *Fr.* Brigue, *It.* Briga. Valais, SW Switzerland *46°19′N 08°E*
Briga *see* Brig
101 G24 **Brigach** ≈ S Germany
18 K17 **Brigantine** New Jersey, NE USA *39°23′N 74°21′W*
Brigantio *see* Briançon
Brigantium *see* Bregenz
Brigels *see* Breil
25 S9 **Briggs** Texas, SW USA *30°52′N 97°55′W*
36 L1 **Brigham City** Utah, W USA *41°30′N 112°00′W*
14 J15 **Brighton** Ontario, SE Canada *44°01′N 77°44′W*
97 O23 **Brighton** SE England, United Kingdom *50°50′N 00°10′W*
37 T4 **Brighton** Colorado, C USA *39°58′N 104°46′W*
30 K15 **Brighton** Illinois, N USA *39°01′N 90°09′W*
103 T16 **Brignoles** Var, SE France *43°25′N 06°03′E*
Brigue *see* Brig
105 O7 **Brihuega** Castilla-La Mancha, C Spain *40°45′N 02°52′W*
112 A10 **Brijuni** *It.* Brioni. *island group* NW Croatia
76 G12 **Brikama** W Gambia *13°13′N 16°37′W*
Bril *see* Brielle
Brill, The *see* Brielle
101 G15 **Brilon** Nordrhein-Westfalen, W Germany *51°24′N 08°34′E*
Brinceni *see* Briceni
107 Q18 **Brindisi** *anc.* Brundisium, Brundusium. Puglia, SE Italy *40°39′N 17°55′E*
27 W11 **Brinkley** Arkansas, C USA *34°53′N 91°11′W*
Brioni *see* Brijuni
103 P12 **Brioude** *anc.* Brivas. Haute-Loire, C France *45°18′N 03°23′E*
Briovera *see* St-Lô
183 U2 **Brisbane** *state capital* Queensland, E Australia *27°30′S 153°00′E*
183 V2 **Brisbane** ✈ Queensland, E Australia *27°30′S 153°00′E*
25 P2 **Briscoe** Texas, SW USA *35°34′N 100°17′W*
106 H10 **Brisighella** Emilia-Romagna, C Italy *44°12′N 11°45′E*
108 G11 **Brissago** Ticino, S Switzerland *46°07′N 08°40′E*
97 K22 **Bristol** *anc.* Bricgstow. SW England, United Kingdom *51°27′N 02°35′W*
18 M12 **Bristol** Connecticut, NE USA *41°40′N 72°56′W*
23 R9 **Bristol** Florida, SE USA *30°25′N 84°58′W*
19 N9 **Bristol** New Hampshire, NE USA *43°34′N 71°42′W*
29 Q8 **Bristol** South Dakota, N USA *45°18′N 97°45′W*
21 P8 **Bristol** Tennessee, S USA *36°36′N 82°11′W*
18 M8 **Bristol** Vermont, NE USA *44°07′N 73°00′W*
39 N14 **Bristol Bay** *bay* Alaska, USA
97 I22 **Bristol Channel** *inlet* England/Wales, United Kingdom
35 W14 **Bristol Lake** ◎ California, W USA
27 P10 **Bristow** Oklahoma, C USA *35°49′N 96°23′W*
86 C10 **Britain** *var.* Great Britain. *island* United Kingdom
Britannia Minor *see* Bretagne
10 L12 **British Columbia** *Fr.* Colombie-Britannique. ◈ *province* SW Canada
British Guiana *see* Guyana
British Honduras *see* Belize
173 Q7 **British Indian Ocean Territory** ◇ *UK dependent territory* C Indian Ocean
86 B9 **British Isles** *island group* NW Europe
10 I1 **British Mountains** ▲▲ Yukon Territory, NW Canada
British North Borneo *see* Sabah
British Solomon Islands Protectorate *see* Solomon Islands
45 S8 **British Virgin Islands** *var.* Virgin Islands. ◇ *UK dependent territory* E West Indies
83 J21 **Brits** North-West, N South Africa *25°39′S 27°47′E*
83 H24 **Britstown** Northern Cape, W South Africa *30°36′S 23°30′E*
14 F12 **Britt** Ontario, S Canada *45°46′N 80°34′W*
29 V12 **Britt** Iowa, C USA *43°06′N 93°48′W*
Brittany *see* Bretagne
29 Q7 **Britton** South Dakota, N USA *45°47′N 97°45′W*
Briva Curretia *see* Brive-la-Gaillarde
Briva Isarae *see* Pontoise
Brivas *see* Brioude
Brive *see* Brive-la-Gaillarde
102 M12 **Brive-la-Gaillarde** *prev.* Brive; *anc.* Briva Curretia. Corrèze, C France *45°09′N 01°31′E*
105 O4 **Briviesca** Castilla y León, N Spain *42°33′N 03°19′W*
Brixen *see* Bressanone
Brixia *see* Brescia
Brlik *see* Birlik
Brněnský Kraj *see* Jihomoravský Kraj
111 G18 **Brno** *Ger.* Brünn. Jihomoravský Kraj, SE Czech Republic *49°11′N 16°35′E*
96 G7 **Broad Bay** *bay* NW Scotland, United Kingdom
25 X8 **Broaddus** Texas, SW USA *31°18′N 94°16′W*
183 O12 **Broadford** Victoria, SE Australia *37°07′S 145°04′E*
96 G9 **Broadford** N Scotland, United Kingdom *57°14′N 05°54′W*
96 J13 **Broad Law** ▲ S Scotland, United Kingdom *55°30′N 03°22′W*
23 U3 **Broad River** ≈ Georgia, SE USA
21 N8 **Broad River** ≈ North Carolina/South Carolina, SE USA
181 Y8 **Broadsound Range** ▲▲ Queensland, E Australia
33 X11 **Broadus** Montana, NW USA *45°28′N 105°22′W*
21 U4 **Broadway** Virginia, NE USA *38°36′N 78°48′W*
118 E9 **Brocēni** SW Latvia *56°41′N 22°31′E*
11 U11 **Brochet** Manitoba, C Canada *57°55′N 101°40′W*
11 U10 **Brochet, Lac** ◎ Manitoba, C Canada
15 S5 **Brochet, Lac au** ◎ Québec, SE Canada
101 K14 **Brocken** ▲ C Germany *51°48′N 10°38′E*
19 O12 **Brockton** Massachusetts, NE USA *42°04′N 71°01′W*
14 L14 **Brockville** Ontario, SE Canada *44°35′N 75°44′W*
18 D13 **Brockway** Pennsylvania, NE USA *41°14′N 78°45′W*
Brod/Bród *see* Slavonski Brod
9 N5 **Brodeur Peninsula** *peninsula* Baffin Island, Nunavut, NE Canada
96 H13 **Brodick** W Scotland, United Kingdom *55°34′N 05°10′W*
Brod na Savi *see* Slavonski Brod
110 K9 **Brodnica** *Ger.* Buddenbrock. Kujawski-pomorskie, C Poland *53°15′N 19°23′E*
Brod-Posavina *see* Slavonski Brod-Posavina
Brodsko-Posavska Županija *see* Slavonski Brod-Posavina
116 J5 **Brody** L'vivs'ka Oblast', NW Ukraine *50°05′N 25°08′E*
98 I10 **Broek-in-Waterland** Noord-Holland, C Netherlands *52°27′N 04°59′E*
32 L13 **Brogan** Oregon, NW USA *44°15′N 117°34′W*
110 N10 **Brok** Mazowieckie, C Poland *52°42′N 21°53′E*
27 P9 **Broken Arrow** Oklahoma, C USA *36°03′N 95°47′W*
183 T9 **Broken Bay** *bay* New South Wales, SE Australia
29 N15 **Broken Bow** Nebraska, C USA *41°24′N 99°38′W*
27 R13 **Broken Bow** Oklahoma, C USA *34°01′N 94°44′W*
27 R12 **Broken Bow Lake** ⊠ Oklahoma, C USA
182 L6 **Broken Hill** New South Wales, SE Australia *31°58′S 141°27′E*
173 S10 **Broken Ridge** *undersea feature* S Indian Ocean *31°30′S 95°00′E*
186 C6 **Broken Water Bay** *bay* W Bismarck Sea
55 W10 **Brokopondo** Brokopondo, NE Suriname *05°04′N 55°00′W*
55 W10 **Brokopondo** ◈ *district* C Suriname
Bromberg *see* Bydgoszcz
95 L22 **Bromölla** Skåne, S Sweden *56°04′N 14°28′E*
97 L20 **Bromsgrove** W England, United Kingdom *52°20′N 02°03′W*
95 G20 **Brønderslev** Nordjylland, N Denmark *57°16′N 09°58′E*
106 D8 **Broni** Lombardia, N Italy *45°04′N 09°18′E*
10 K11 **Bronlund Peak** ▲ British Columbia, W Canada *57°27′N 126°43′W*
93 F14 **Brønnøysund** Nordland, C Norway *65°38′N 12°15′E*
23 V10 **Bronson** Florida, SE USA *29°25′N 82°38′W*
31 Q11 **Bronson** Michigan, N USA *41°52′N 85°11′W*
25 X8 **Bronson** Texas, SW USA *31°20′N 94°00′W*
107 L24 **Bronte** Sicilia, Italy, C Mediterranean Sea *37°47′N 14°50′E*
25 P8 **Bronte** Texas, SW USA *31°53′N 100°17′W*
25 Y9 **Brookeland** Texas, SW USA *31°05′N 93°57′W*
170 M7 **Brooke's Point** Palawan, W Philippines *08°54′N 117°54′E*
27 T3 **Brookfield** Missouri, C USA *39°46′N 93°04′W*
22 K7 **Brookhaven** Mississippi, S USA *31°34′N 90°26′W*
32 E16 **Brookings** Oregon, NW USA *42°03′N 124°16′W*
29 R10 **Brookings** South Dakota, N USA *44°19′N 96°46′W*
29 W14 **Brooklyn** Iowa, C USA *41°43′N 92°27′W*
29 U8 **Brooklyn Park** Minnesota, N USA *45°06′N 93°18′W*
21 U7 **Brookneal** Virginia, NE USA *37°03′N 78°56′W*
11 R16 **Brooks** Alberta, SW Canada *50°35′N 111°54′W*
25 V11 **Brookshire** Texas, SW USA *29°47′N 95°57′W*
38 L8 **Brooks Mountain** ▲ Alaska, USA *65°31′N 167°24′W*
38 M11 **Brooks Range** ▲▲ Alaska, USA
31 O12 **Brookston** Indiana, N USA *40°34′N 86°53′W*
23 V11 **Brooksville** Florida, SE USA *28°33′N 82°23′W*
23 N4 **Brooksville** Mississippi, S USA *33°13′N 88°34′W*
180 J13 **Brookton** Western Australia *32°24′S 117°04′E*
31 Q14 **Brookville** Indiana, N USA *39°25′N 85°00′W*
18 D13 **Brookville** Pennsylvania, NE USA *41°07′N 79°05′W*
31 Q14 **Brookville Lake** ⊠ Indiana, N USA
180 K5 **Broome** Western Australia *17°58′S 122°15′E*
37 S4 **Broomfield** Colorado, C USA *39°55′N 105°05′W*
Broos *see* Orăştie
96 J7 **Brora** N Scotland, United Kingdom *57°59′N 04°00′W*
96 I7 **Brora** ≈ N Scotland, United Kingdom
95 F23 **Brørup** Syddtjylland, W Denmark *55°29′N 09°01′E*
95 L23 **Brösarp** Skåne, S Sweden *55°43′N 14°10′E*
116 J9 **Broşteni** Suceava, NE Romania *47°14′N 25°43′E*
102 M6 **Brou** Eure-et-Loir, C France *48°12′N 01°10′E*
Broucsella *see* Brussel/Bruxelles
Broughton Bay *see* Tongjosŏn-man
Broughton Island *see* Qikiqtarjuaq
138 G7 **Broummâna** C Lebanon *33°53′N 35°39′E*
22 I9 **Broussard** Louisiana, S USA *30°09′N 91°57′W*
98 E13 **Brouwersdam** *dam* SW Netherlands
98 E13 **Brouwershaven** Zeeland, SW Netherlands *51°44′N 03°50′E*
117 P4 **Brovary** Kyyivs'ka Oblast', N Ukraine *50°30′N 30°45′E*
95 G20 **Brovst** Nordjylland, N Denmark *57°06′N 09°32′E*
31 S8 **Brown City** Michigan, N USA *43°12′N 82°50′W*
24 M6 **Brownfield** Texas, SW USA *33°11′N 102°16′W*
33 Q7 **Browning** Montana, NW USA *48°33′N 113°00′W*
33 R6 **Brown, Mount** ▲ Montana, NW USA *48°52′N 111°08′W*
0 M9 **Browns Bank** *undersea feature* NW Atlantic Ocean *42°40′N 66°05′W*
31 O14 **Brownsburg** Indiana, N USA *39°50′N 86°24′W*
18 J16 **Browns Mills** New Jersey, NE USA *39°58′N 74°33′W*
44 J12 **Browns Town** C Jamaica *18°28′N 77°22′W*
31 P15 **Brownstown** Indiana, N USA *38°52′N 86°02′W*
29 R8 **Browns Valley** Minnesota, N USA *45°36′N 96°49′W*
20 K7 **Brownsville** Kentucky, S USA *37°10′N 86°18′W*
20 F9 **Brownsville** Tennessee, S USA *35°35′N 89°15′W*
25 T17 **Brownsville** Texas, SW USA *25°56′N 97°28′W*
55 W10 **Brownsweg** Brokopondo, C Suriname
29 U9 **Brownton** Minnesota, N USA *44°43′N 94°21′W*
19 R5 **Brownville Junction** Maine, NE USA *45°20′N 69°04′W*
25 R8 **Brownwood** Texas, SW USA *31°42′N 98°59′W*
25 R8 **Brownwood Lake** ⊠ Texas, SW USA
104 I9 **Brozas** Extremadura, W Spain *39°37′N 06°48′W*
119 M18 **Brozha** Mahilyowskaya Voblasts', E Belarus *52°57′N 29°07′E*
103 O2 **Bruay-en-Artois** Pas-de-Calais, N France *50°31′N 02°30′E*
103 P2 **Bruay-sur-l'Escaut** Nord, N France *50°24′N 03°33′E*
14 F13 **Bruce Peninsula** *peninsula* Ontario, S Canada
20 H9 **Bruceton** Tennessee, S USA *36°02′N 88°14′W*
25 T9 **Bruceville** Texas, SW USA *31°17′N 97°15′W*
101 G21 **Bruchsal** Baden-Württemberg, SW Germany *49°07′N 08°35′E*
109 Q7 **Bruck** Salzburg, NW Austria *47°18′N 12°51′E*
Bruck *see* Bruck an der Mur
109 Y4 **Bruck an der Leitha** Niederösterreich, NE Austria *48°02′N 16°47′E*
109 V7 **Bruck an der Mur** *var.* Bruck. Steiermark, C Austria *47°25′N 15°17′E*
101 M24 **Bruckmühl** Bayern, SE Germany *47°52′N 11°54′E*
168 E7 **Brueuh, Pulau** *island* NW Indonesia
Bruges *see* Brugge
108 F6 **Brugg** Aargau, NW Switzerland *47°29′N 08°13′E*
99 C16 **Brugge** *Fr.* Bruges. West-Vlaanderen, NW Belgium *51°13′N 03°14′E*
109 R9 **Bruggen** Kärnten, S Austria *46°46′N 13°13′E*
101 E16 **Brühl** Nordrhein-Westfalen, W Germany *50°50′N 06°55′E*
99 F14 **Bruinisse** Zeeland, SW Netherlands *51°40′N 04°04′E*
169 R9 **Bruit, Pulau** *island* East Malaysia
14 K10 **Brûlé, Lac** ◎ Québec, SE Canada
30 M4 **Brule River** ≈ Michigan/Wisconsin, N USA
99 H23 **Brûly** Namur, S Belgium *49°55′N 04°31′E*
59 N17 **Brumado** Bahia, E Brazil *14°14′S 41°38′W*
98 M11 **Brummen** Gelderland, E Netherlands *52°05′N 06°10′E*
94 H13 **Brumunddal** Hedmark, S Norway *60°54′N 11°00′E*
23 Q6 **Brundidge** Alabama, S USA *31°43′N 85°49′W*
Brundisium/Brundusium *see* Brindisi
33 N15 **Bruneau River** ≈ Idaho, NW USA
Bruneck *see* Brunico
169 T8 **Brunei** *off.* Brunei Darussalam, *Mal.* Negara Brunei Darussalam. ◆ *monarchy* SE Asia
169 T7 **Brunei Bay** *var.* Teluk Brunei. *bay* N Brunei
Brunei Darussalam *see* Brunei
Brunei, Teluk *see* Brunei Bay
Brunei Town *see* Bandar Seri Begawan
106 H5 **Brunico** *Ger.* Bruneck. Trentino-Alto Adige, N Italy *46°49′N 11°57′E*
Brünn *see* Brno
185 G17 **Brunner, Lake** ◎ South Island, New Zealand
99 M18 **Brunssum** Limburg, SE Netherlands *50°57′N 05°59′E*
23 W7 **Brunswick** Georgia, SE USA *31°09′N 81°30′W*
19 Q8 **Brunswick** Maine, NE USA *43°54′N 69°58′W*
21 V3 **Brunswick** Maryland, NE USA *39°18′N 77°37′W*
27 T3 **Brunswick** Missouri, C USA *39°25′N 93°07′W*
31 T11 **Brunswick** Ohio, N USA *41°14′N 81°50′W*
Brunswick *see* Braunschweig
63 H24 **Brunswick, Península** *headland* S Chile *53°30′S 71°27′W*
111 H17 **Bruntál** *Ger.* Freudenthal. Moravskoslezský Kraj, E Czech Republic *50°00′N 17°27′E*
195 N3 **Brunt Ice Shelf** *ice shelf* Antarctica
Brusa *see* Bursa
114 G7 **Brusartsi** Montana, NW Bulgaria *43°39′N 23°04′E*
37 U3 **Brush** Colorado, C USA *40°15′N 103°37′W*
42 M5 **Brus Laguna** Gracias a Dios, E Honduras *15°46′N 84°32′W*
60 K13 **Brusque** Santa Catarina, S Brazil *27°07′S 48°54′W*
Brussa *see* Bursa
99 E18 **Brussel** *var.* Brussels, *Fr.* Bruxelles, *Ger.* Brüssel; *anc.* Broucsella. ● (Belgium) Brussels, C Belgium *50°52′N 04°21′E* *see also* Bruxelles
Brussel *see* Bruxelles
Brüssel/Brussels *see* Brussel/Bruxelles
117 O5 **Brusyliv** Zhytomyrs'ka Oblast', N Ukraine *50°16′N 29°31′E*
183 Q12 **Bruthen** Victoria, SE Australia *37°43′S 147°49′E*
Bruttium *see* Calabria
Brüx *see* Most
99 E18 **Bruxelles** *var.* Brussels, *Dut.* Brussel, *Ger.* Brüssel; *anc.* Broucsella. ● Brussels, C Belgium *50°52′N 04°21′E* *see also* Brussel
Bruxelles *see* Brussel
54 J7 **Bruzual** Apure, W Venezuela *07°59′N 69°18′W*
31 R11 **Bryan** Ohio, N USA *41°30′N 84°34′W*
25 U10 **Bryan** Texas, SW USA *30°40′N 96°23′W*
194 J4 **Bryan Coast** *physical region* Antarctica
122 L11 **Bryanka** Krasnoyarskiy Kray, C Russian Federation *59°01′N 93°13′E*
117 Y7 **Bryanka** Luhans'ka Oblast', E Ukraine *48°30′N 38°45′E*
182 J8 **Bryan, Mount** ▲ South Australia *33°25′S 138°59′E*
126 I6 **Bryansk** Bryanskaya Oblast', W Russian Federation *53°16′N 34°07′E*
126 H6 **Bryanskaya Oblast'** ◈ *province* W Russian Federation
194 J5 **Bryant, Cape** *headland* Antarctica
27 U8 **Bryant Creek** ≈ Missouri, C USA
36 K8 **Bryce Canyon** *canyon* Utah, W USA
119 O15 **Bryli** Mahilyowskaya Voblasts', E Belarus *53°54′N 30°33′E*
95 C17 **Bryne** Rogaland, S Norway *58°43′N 05°40′E*
25 R6 **Bryson** Texas, SW USA *33°09′N 98°23′W*
21 N10 **Bryson City** North Carolina, SE USA *35°26′N 83°27′W*
14 K11 **Bryson, Lac** ◎ Québec, SE Canada
126 K13 **Bryukhovetskaya** Krasnodarskiy Kray, SW Russian Federation *45°49′N 38°01′E*
111 H15 **Brzeg** *Ger.* Brieg; *anc.* Civitas Altae Ripae. Opolskie, S Poland *50°52′N 17°27′E*
111 G14 **Brzeg Dolny** *Ger.* Dyhernfurth. Dolnośląskie, SW Poland *51°15′N 16°40′E*
Brześć Litewski/Brześć nad Bugiem *see* Brest
111 L17 **Brzesko** *Ger.* Brietzig. Małopolskie, SE Poland *49°59′N 20°34′E*
Brzeżany *see* Berezhany
110 K12 **Brzeziny** Łódzkie, C Poland *51°49′N 19°41′E*
Brzostowica Wielka *see* Vyalikaya Byerastavitsa
111 O17 **Brzozów** Podkarpackie, SE Poland *49°38′N 22°00′E*
Bsharrī/Bsherri *see* Bcharré
187 X14 **Bua** Vanua Levu, N Fiji *16°48′S 178°36′E*
95 J20 **Bua** Halland, S Sweden *57°14′N 12°07′E*
82 M13 **Bua** ≈ C Malawi
Bua *see* Čiovo
81 L18 **Bu'aale** *It.* Buale. Jubbada Dhexe, SW Somalia *0°52′N 42°37′E*
Buache, Mount *see* Mutunte, Mount
189 Q8 **Buada Lagoon** *lagoon* Nauru, C Pacific Ocean
186 M8 **Buala** Santa Isabel, E Solomon Islands *08°06′S 159°31′E*
Buale *see* Bu'aale
190 H1 **Buariki** *atoll* Tungaru, W Kiribati
167 Q10 **Bua Yai** *var.* Ban Bua Yai. Nakhon Ratchasima, E Thailand *15°35′N 102°25′E*
75 P8 **Bu'ayrāt al Ḩasūn** *var.* Buwayrāt al Hasūn. C Libya *31°22′N 15°41′E*
76 H13 **Buba** S Guinea-Bissau *11°36′N 14°55′W*
171 P11 **Bubaa** Sulawesi, N Indonesia *0°32′N 122°27′E*
81 D20 **Bubanza** NW Burundi *03°04′S 29°22′E*
83 K18 **Bubi** *prev.* Bubye. ≈ S Zimbabwe
142 L11 **Būbīyan, Jazīrat** *island* E Kuwait
Bublitz *see* Bobolice
Bubye *see* Bubi
187 Y13 **Buca** *prev.* Mbutha. Vanua Levu, N Fiji *16°39′S 179°51′E*
136 F16 **Bucak** Burdur, SW Turkey *37°28′N 30°37′E*
54 G8 **Bucaramanga** Santander, N Colombia *07°08′N 73°10′W*
107 M18 **Buccino** Campania, S Italy *40°37′N 15°25′E*
116 K8 **Bucecea** Botoşani, NE Romania *47°45′N 26°30′E*
116 J6 **Buchach** *Pol.* Buczacz. Ternopil's'ka Oblast', W Ukraine *49°04′N 25°23′E*
183 Q12 **Buchan** Victoria, SE Australia *37°26′S 148°11′E*
76 J17 **Buchanan** *prev.* Grand Bassa. SW Liberia *05°53′N 10°03′W*
23 R3 **Buchanan** Georgia, SE USA *33°48′N 85°11′W*
31 O11 **Buchanan** Michigan, N USA *41°49′N 86°21′W*
21 T6 **Buchanan** Virginia, NE USA *37°31′N 79°40′W*
25 R10 **Buchanan Dam** Texas, SW USA *30°42′N 98°24′W*
25 R10 **Buchanan, Lake** ⊠ Texas, SW USA
96 L8 **Buchan Ness** *headland* NE Scotland, United Kingdom *57°28′N 01°46′W*
13 T12 **Buchans** Newfoundland and Labrador, SE Canada *48°49′N 56°53′W*
Bucharest *see* Bucureşti
101 H20 **Buchen** Baden-Württemberg, SW Germany *49°31′N 09°18′E*
100 I10 **Buchholz in der Nordheide** Niedersachsen, NW Germany *53°19′N 09°52′E*
108 F7 **Buchs** Aargau, N Switzerland *47°24′N 08°04′E*
108 I8 **Buchs** Sankt Gallen, NE Switzerland *47°10′N 09°28′E*
100 H13 **Bückeburg** Niedersachsen, NW Germany *52°16′N 09°03′E*
36 K14 **Buckeye** Arizona, SW USA *33°22′N 112°34′W*
Buckeye State *see* Ohio
21 S4 **Buckhannon** West Virginia, NE USA *39°00′N 80°14′W*
25 T9 **Buckholts** Texas, SW USA *30°52′N 97°07′W*
96 K8 **Buckie** NE Scotland, United Kingdom *57°39′N 02°56′W*
14 M12 **Buckingham** Québec, SE Canada *45°35′N 75°25′W*
21 U6 **Buckingham** Virginia, NE USA *37°33′N 78°34′W*
97 N21 **Buckinghamshire** *cultural region* SE England, United Kingdom
39 N8 **Buckland** Alaska, USA *65°58′N 161°07′W*
182 G7 **Buckleboo** South Australia *32°55′S 136°11′E*
26 K7 **Bucklin** Kansas, C USA *37°33′N 99°37′W*
27 T3 **Bucklin** Missouri, C USA *39°46′N 92°53′W*
36 I12 **Buckskin Mountains** ▲▲ Arizona, SW USA
19 R7 **Bucksport** Maine, NE USA *44°34′N 68°46′W*
82 A9 **Buco Zau** Cabinda, NW Angola *04°45′S 12°34′E*
Bu Craa *see* Bou Craa
116 K14 **Bucureşti** *Eng.* Bucharest, *Ger.* Bukarest, *prev.* Altenburg; *anc.* Cetatea Damboviţei. ● (Romania) Bucureşti, S Romania *44°27′N 26°06′E*
31 S12 **Bucyrus** Ohio, N USA *40°47′N 82°57′W*
Buczacz *see* Buchach
94 E9 **Bud** Møre og Romsdal, S Norway *62°55′N 06°55′E*
25 S11 **Buda** Texas, SW USA *30°05′N 97°50′W*
119 O18 **Buda-Kashalyova** *Rus.* Buda-Koshelëvo. Homyel'skaya Voblasts', SE Belarus *52°43′N 30°34′E*
Buda-Koshelëvo *see* Buda-Kashalyova
166 L4 **Budalin** Sagaing, C Myanmar (Burma) *22°24′N 95°08′E*
111 J22 **Budapest** *off.* Budapest Főváros, *SCr.* Budimpešta. ● (Hungary) Pest, N Hungary *47°30′N 19°03′E*
Budapest Főváros *see* Budapest
152 K11 **Budaun** Uttar Pradesh, N India *28°02′N 79°07′E*
141 O9 **Budayyi'ah** *oasis* C Saudi Arabia
195 Y12 **Budd Coast** *physical region* Antarctica
Buddenbrock *see* Brodnica
107 C17 **Budduso** Sardegna, Italy, C Mediterranean Sea *40°37′N 09°19′E*
97 I23 **Bude** SW England, United Kingdom *50°50′N 04°33′W*
22 J7 **Bude** Mississippi, S USA *31°27′N 90°51′W*
Budějovický Kraj *see* Jihočeský Kraj
99 K16 **Budel** Noord-Brabant, SE Netherlands *51°17′N 05°35′E*
100 I8 **Büdelsdorf** Schleswig-Holstein, N Germany *54°20′N 09°40′E*
127 O14 **Budënnovsk** Stavropol'skiy Kray, SW Russian Federation *44°46′N 44°07′E*
116 K14 **Budeşti** Călăraşi, SE Romania *44°13′N 26°30′E*
Budge-Budge *see* Baj Baj
Budgewoi *see* Budgewoi Lake
183 T8 **Budgewoi Lake** *var.* Budgewoi. New South Wales, SE Australia *33°14′S 151°34′E*
92 I2 **Búdhardalur** Vesturland, W Iceland *65°07′N 21°45′W*
Budimpešta *see* Budapest
79 J16 **Budjala** Equateur, NW Dem. Rep. Congo *02°39′N 19°42′E*
106 G10 **Budrio** Emilia-Romagna, C Italy *44°33′N 11°34′E*
Budslav *see* Budslaw
119 K14 **Budslaw** *Rus.* Budslav. Minskaya Voblasts', N Belarus *54°47′N 27°27′E*
Budua *see* Budva
169 R9 **Budu, Tanjung** *headland* East Malaysia *02°51′N 111°42′E*
113 J17 **Budva** *It.* Budua. W Montenegro *42°17′N 18°49′E*
Budweis *see* České Budějovice
Budyšin *see* Bautzen
79 D16 **Buea** Sud-Ouest, SW Cameroon *04°09′N 09°13′E*
103 S13 **Buëch** ≈ SE France
18 J17 **Buena** New Jersey, NE USA *39°30′N 74°55′W*
62 K12 **Buena Esperanza** San Luis, C Argentina *34°45′S 65°15′W*
54 C11 **Buenaventura** Valle del Cauca, W Colombia *03°54′N 77°02′W*
40 I4 **Buenaventura** Chihuahua, N Mexico *29°50′N 107°30′W*
57 M18 **Buena Vista** Santa Cruz, C Bolivia *17°28′S 63°37′W*
40 G10 **Buenavista** Baja California Sur, NW Mexico *23°39′N 109°41′W*
37 S5 **Buena Vista** Colorado, C USA *38°50′N 106°07′W*
23 S5 **Buena Vista** Georgia, SE USA *32°19′N 84°31′W*
21 T6 **Buena Vista** Virginia, NE USA *37°44′N 79°22′W*
44 F5 **Buena Vista, Bahia de** *bay* N Cuba
35 R13 **Buena Vista Lake Bed** ◎ California, W USA
105 P8 **Buendía, Embalse de** ⊠ C Spain
63 F16 **Bueno, Río** ≈ S Chile
62 N12 **Buenos Aires** *hist.* Santa Maria del Buen Aire. ● (Argentina) Buenos Aires, E Argentina *34°40′S 58°30′W*
43 O15 **Buenos Aires** Puntarenas, SE Costa Rica *09°10′N 83°23′W*
61 C20 **Buenos Aires** *off.* Provincia de Buenos Aires. ◈ *province* E Argentina
63 H19 **Buenos Aires, Lago** *var.* Lago General Carrera. ◎ Argentina/Chile
Buenos Aires, Provincia de *see* Buenos Aires
54 C13 **Buesaco** Nariño, SW Colombia *01°22′N 77°07′W*
29 U8 **Buffalo** Minnesota, N USA *45°11′N 93°50′W*
26 T6 **Buffalo** Missouri, C USA *37°38′N 93°05′W*
18 D10 **Buffalo** New York, NE USA *42°53′N 78°53′W*
27 K8 **Buffalo** Oklahoma, C USA *36°51′N 99°38′W*
28 J7 **Buffalo** South Dakota, N USA *45°25′N 103°35′W*
25 V8 **Buffalo** Texas, SW USA *31°25′N 96°04′W*
33 W12 **Buffalo** Wyoming, C USA *44°21′N 106°40′W*
29 U11 **Buffalo Center** Iowa, C USA *43°23′N 93°57′W*
24 M3 **Buffalo Lake** ⊠ Texas, SW USA
30 K7 **Buffalo Lake** ⊠ Wisconsin, N USA
11 S12 **Buffalo Narrows** Saskatchewan, C Canada *55°52′N 108°28′W*
27 U9 **Buffalo River** ≈ Arkansas, C USA
29 R5 **Buffalo River** ≈ Minnesota, N USA
20 I10 **Buffalo River** ≈ Tennessee, S USA
30 J6 **Buffalo River** ≈ Wisconsin, N USA
44 L12 **Buff Bay** E Jamaica *18°18′N 76°40′W*
23 T3 **Buford** Georgia, SE USA *34°07′N 84°00′W*
28 J3 **Buford** North Dakota, N USA *48°00′N 103°58′W*
33 Y17 **Buford** Wyoming, C USA *41°05′N 105°17′W*
116 J14 **Buftea** Ilfov, S Romania *44°34′N 25°58′E*
84 I9 **Bug** *Bel.* Zakhodni Buh, *Eng.* Western Bug, *Rus.* Zapadnyy Bug, *Ukr.* Zakhidnyy Buh. ≈ E Europe
54 D11 **Buga** Valle del Cauca, W Colombia *03°53′N 76°17′W*
Buga *see* Dörvöljin
103 O17 **Bugarach, Pic du** ▲ S France *42°52′N 02°23′E*
162 F8 **Bugat** *var.* Bayangol. Govĭ-Altay, SW Mongolia *45°33′N 94°22′E*
146 B12 **Bugdaýly** *Rus.* Bugdayly. Balkan Welaýaty, W Turkmenistan *38°42′N 54°14′E*
Bugdayly *see* Bugdaýly
Buggs Island Lake *see* John H. Kerr Reservoir
Bughotu *see* Santa Isabel
171 O14 **Bugingkalo** Sulawesi, C Indonesia *04°49′S 121°42′E*
64 P6 **Bugio** *island* Madeira, Portugal, NE Atlantic Ocean
92 M8 **Bugøynes** Finnmark, N Norway *69°57′N 29°34′E*
125 Q3 **Bugrino** Nenetskiy Avtonomnyy Okrug, NW Russian Federation *68°48′N 49°12′E*
127 T5 **Bugul'ma** Respublika Tatarstan, W Russian Federation *54°31′N 52°45′E*
Bügür *see* Luntai
127 T6 **Buguruslan** Orenburgskaya Oblast', W Russian Federation *53°38′N 52°30′E*
159 R9 **Buh He** ≈ C China
101 F22 **Bühl** Baden-Württemberg, SW Germany *48°42′N 08°07′E*
33 O15 **Buhl** Idaho, NW USA *42°36′N 114°45′W*
116 K10 **Buhuşi** Bacău, E Romania *46°41′N 26°45′E*
Buie d'Istria *see* Buje
97 J20 **Builth Wells** E Wales, United Kingdom *52°07′N 03°28′W*
186 J8 **Buin** Bougainville Island, NE Papua New Guinea *06°52′S 155°42′E*
108 J9 **Buin, Piz** ▲ Austria/Switzerland *46°51′N 10°07′E*
127 Q4 **Buinsk** Chuvashskaya Respublika, W Russian Federation *55°09′N 47°00′E*
127 Q4 **Buinsk** Respublika Tatarstan, W Russian Federation *54°58′N 48°16′E*
163 R8 **Buir Nur** *Mong.* Buyr Nuur. ◎ China/Mongolia *see also* Buyr Nuur
Buir Nur *see* Buyr Nuur
98 M5 **Buitenpost** *Fris.* Bûtenpost. Fryslân, N Netherlands *53°15′N 06°09′E*
Buitenzorg *see* Bogor
83 F19 **Buitepos** Omaheke, E Namibia *22°17′S 19°59′E*
105 N7 **Buitrago del Lozoya** Madrid, C Spain *41°00′N 03°38′W*
Buj *see* Buy
104 M13 **Bujalance** Andalucía, S Spain *37°54′N 04°23′W*
113 O17 **Bujanovac** SE Serbia *42°29′N 21°44′E*
105 S6 **Bujaraloz** Aragón, NE Spain *41°29′N 00°10′W*
112 A9 **Buje** *It.* Buie d'Istria. Istra, NW Croatia *45°23′N 13°40′E*
Bujnurd *see* Bojnūrd
81 D21 **Bujumbura** *prev.* Usumbura. ● (Burundi) W Burundi *03°25′S 29°24′E*
81 D20 **Bujumbura** ✈ W Burundi *03°21′S 29°19′E*
159 N11 **Buka Daban** *var.* Bukadaban Feng. ▲ C China *36°09′N 90°52′E*
Bukadaban Feng *see* Buka Daban
186 J6 **Buka Island** *island* NE Papua New Guinea
81 F18 **Bukakata** S Uganda *0°18′S 31°57′E*
79 N24 **Bukama** Katanga, SE Dem. Rep. Congo *09°13′S 25°52′E*
142 J4 **Būkān** *var.* Bowkān. Āzarbāyjān-e Gharbī, NW Iran *36°31′N 46°10′E*
Bukantau, Gory *see* Bo'kantov Tog'lari
Bukarest *see* Bucureşti
79 O19 **Bukavu** *prev.* Costermansville. Sud-Kivu, E Dem. Rep. Congo *02°19′S 28°49′E*
81 F21 **Bukene** Tabora, NW Tanzania *04°15′S 32°51′E*
141 W8 **Bū Khābī** *var.* Bakhābī. NW Oman *23°29′N 56°06′E*
Bukhara *see* Buxoro
Bukharskaya Oblast' *see* Buxoro Viloyati
168 M14 **Bukitkemuning** Sumatera, W Indonesia *04°43′S 104°27′E*
168 I11 **Bukittinggi** *prev.* Fort de Kock. Sumatera, W Indonesia *0°18′S 100°20′E*
111 L21 **Bükk** ▲▲ NE Hungary
81 F19 **Bukoba** Kagera, NW Tanzania *01°19′S 31°49′E*
113 N20 **Bukovo** S FYR Macedonia *40°59′N 21°20′E*
108 G6 **Bülach** Zürich, NW Switzerland *47°31′N 08°30′E*
Bulaevo *see* Bulayevo
Bulag *see* Tünel, Hövsgöl, Mongolia
Bulag *see* Möngönmorĭt, Töv, Mongolia
Bulagiyn Denj *see* Bulgan
183 U7 **Bulahdelah** New South Wales, SE Australia *32°24′S 152°13′E*
171 P4 **Bulan** Luzon, N Philippines *12°40′N 123°55′E*
137 N11 **Bulancak** Giresun, N Turkey *40°57′N 38°14′E*
152 J10 **Bulandshahr** Uttar Pradesh, N India *28°30′N 77°49′E*
137 R14 **Bulanık** Muş, E Turkey *39°04′N 42°16′E*
127 V7 **Bulanovo** Orenburgskaya Oblast', W Russian Federation *52°27′N 55°08′E*
83 J17 **Bulawayo** *var.* Buluwayo. Bulawayo, SW Zimbabwe *20°08′S 28°37′E*
83 J17 **Bulawayo** ✈ Matabeleland North, SW Zimbabwe *20°00′S 28°36′E*

◆ Country
● Country Capital
◇ Dependent Territory
○ Dependent Territory Capital
◈ Administrative Regions
✈ International Airport
▲ Mountain
▲▲ Mountain Range
Volcano
≈ River
◎ Lake
⊠ Reservoir

145 Q6 **Bulayevo** *Kaz.* Bŭlaevo. Severnyy Kazakhstan, N Kazakhstan 54°55′N 70°29′E
136 D15 **Buldan** Denizli, SW Turkey 38°03′N 28°50′E
154 G12 **Buldāna** Mahārāshtra, C India 20°31′N 76°18′E
38 E16 **Buldir Island** *island* Aleutian Islands, Alaska, USA
Buldur *see* Burdur
162 I8 **Bulgan** *var.* Bulagiyn Denj. Arhangay, C Mongolia 47°14′N 100°56′E
162 D7 **Bulgan** *var.* Jargalant. Bayan-Ölgiy, W Mongolia 46°56′N 91°07′E
162 K6 **Bulgan** Bulgan, N Mongolia 50°31′N 101°30′E
162 F7 **Bulgan** *var.* Bürenhayrhan. Hovd, W Mongolia 46°04′N 91°34′E
162 J10 **Bulgan** Ömnögovĭ, S Mongolia 44°07′N 103°28′E
162 J7 **Bulgan** ◈ *province* N Mongolia
Bulgan *see* Bayan-Öndör, Bayanhongor, C Mongolia
Bulgan *see* Darvi, Hovd, Mongolia
Bulgan *see* Tsagaan-Üür, Hövsgöl, Mongolia
114 H10 **Bulgaria** *off.* Republic of Bulgaria, *Bul.* Bŭlgariya; *prev.* People's Republic of Bulgaria. ◆ *republic* SE Europe
Bulgaria, People's Republic of *see* Bulgaria
Bulgaria, Republic of *see* Bulgaria
Bŭlgariya *see* Bulgaria
114 L9 **Bŭlgarka** ▲ E Bulgaria 42°43′N 26°19′E
171 S11 **Buli** Pulau Halmahera, E Indonesia 0°56′N 128°17′E
171 S11 **Buli, Teluk** *bay* Pulau Halmahera, E Indonesia
160 J13 **Buliu He** ~ S China
Bullange *see* Büllingen
Bulla, Ostrov *see* Xärä Zirä Adasi
104 M11 **Bullaque** ~ C Spain
105 Q13 **Bullas** Murcia, SE Spain 38°02′N 01°40′W
80 M12 **Bullaxaar** Woqooyi Galbeed, NW Somalia 10°28′N 44°15′E
108 C9 **Bulle** Fribourg, SW Switzerland 46°37′N 07°04′E
185 G15 **Buller** ~ South Island, New Zealand
183 P12 **Buller, Mount** ▲ Victoria, SE Australia 37°10′S 146°31′E
36 H11 **Bullhead City** Arizona, SW USA 35°07′N 114°32′W
99 N21 **Büllingen** *Fr.* Bullange. Liège, E Belgium 50°23′N 06°15′E
Bullion State *see* Missouri
21 T14 **Bull Island** *island* South Carolina, SE USA
182 M4 **Bulloo River Overflow** *wetland* New South Wales, SE Australia
184 M12 **Bulls** Manawatu-Wanganui, North Island, New Zealand 40°10′S 175°22′E
21 T14 **Bulls Bay** *bay* South Carolina, SE USA
27 U9 **Bull Shoals Lake** ⊞ Arkansas/Missouri, C USA
181 Q2 **Bulman** Northern Territory, N Australia 13°39′S 134°21′E
162 I6 **Bulnayn Nuruu** ▲▲ N Mongolia
171 O11 **Bulowa, Gunung** ▲ Sulawesi, N Indonesia 0°33′N 123°39′E
Bulqiza *see* Bulqizë
113 L19 **Bulqizë** *var.* Bulqiza. Dibër, C Albania 41°30′N 20°16′E
Bulsar *see* Valsād
171 N14 **Bulukumba** *prev.* Boeloekoemba. Sulawesi, C Indonesia 05°35′S 120°13′E
147 O11 **Bulungh'ur** *Rus.* Bulungur; *prev.* Krasnogvardeysk. Samarqand Viloyati, C Uzbekistan 39°46′N 67°18′E
79 I21 **Bulungu** Bandundu, SW Dem. Rep. Congo 04°36′S 18°34′E
Bulungur *see* Bulungh'ur
Buluwayo *see* Bulawayo
79 K17 **Bumba** Equateur, N Dem. Rep. Congo 02°14′N 22°25′E
121 R12 **Bumbah, Khalīj al** *gulf* N Libya
Bumbat *see* Bayan-Öndör
81 F19 **Bumbire Island** *island* N Tanzania
169 V8 **Bum Bun, Pulau** *island* East Malaysia
81 J17 **Buna** North Eastern, NE Kenya 02°40′N 39°34′E
25 Y10 **Buna** Texas, SW USA 30°25′N 94°00′W
Bunab *see* Bonāb
Bunai *see* M'bunai
147 S13 **Bunay** S Tajikistan 38°29′N 71°41′E
180 I13 **Bunbury** Western Australia 33°24′S 115°44′E
97 E14 **Buncrana** *Ir.* Bun Cranncha. NW Ireland 55°08′N 07°27′W
Bun Cranncha *see* Buncrana
181 Z9 **Bundaberg** Queensland, E Australia 24°50′S 152°16′E
183 T5 **Bundarra** New South Wales, SE Australia 30°12′S 151°06′E
100 G13 **Bünde** Nordrhein-Westfalen, NW Germany 52°12′N 08°34′E
152 H13 **Būndi** Rājasthān, N India 25°28′N 75°42′E
Bun Dobhráin *see* Bundoran
97 D15 **Bundoran** *Ir.* Bun Dobhráin. NW Ireland 54°30′N 08°11′W
Bunë *see* Bojana
113 K18 **Bunë, Lumi i** *SCr.* Bojana. ~ Albania/Montenegro *see also* Bojana
171 Q8 **Bunga** ~ Mindanao, S Philippines
168 I12 **Bungalaut, Selat** *strait* W Indonesia
167 R8 **Bung Kan** Nong Khai, E Thailand 18°19′N 103°39′E
181 N4 **Bungle Bungle Range** ▲▲ Western Australia
82 C10 **Bungo** Uíge, NW Angola 07°30′S 15°24′E
81 G18 **Bungoma** Western, W Kenya 0°34′N 34°34′E
164 F15 **Bungo-suidō** *strait* SW Japan
164 E14 **Bungo-Takada** Ōita, Kyūshū, SW Japan 33°34′N 131°28′E
100 K8 **Bungsberg** *hill* N Germany
Bungur *see* Bunyu
79 P17 **Bunia** Orientale, NE Dem. Rep. Congo 01°33′N 30°16′E
35 U6 **Bunker Hill** ▲ Nevada, W USA 39°16′N 117°06′W
22 I7 **Bunkie** Louisiana, S USA 30°58′N 92°12′W
23 X10 **Bunnell** Florida, SE USA 29°28′N 81°15′W
105 S10 **Buñol** Valenciana, E Spain 39°25′N 00°47′W
98 K11 **Bunschoten** Utrecht, C Netherlands 52°15′N 05°23′E
136 K14 **Bünyan** Kayseri, C Turkey 38°51′N 35°50′E
169 W8 **Bunyu** *var.* Bungur. Borneo, N Indonesia 03°33′N 117°50′E
169 W8 **Bunyu, Pulau** *island* N Indonesia
Bunzlau *see* Bolesławiec
Buoddobohki *see* Patoniva
123 P7 **Buor-Khaya, Guba** *bay* N Russian Federation
123 P7 **Buor-Khaya, Guba** *bay* N Russian Federation
171 Z15 **Bupul** Papua, E Indonesia 07°24′S 140°57′E
81 K19 **Bura** Coast, SE Kenya 01°06′S 40°01′E
80 P12 **Buraan** Bari, N Somalia 10°03′N 49°08′E
145 Q7 **Burabay** *prev.* Borovoye. Akmola, N Kazakhstan 53°07′N 70°20′E
Buraida *see* Buraydah
Buraimi *see* Al Buraymī
Buran *see* Boran
158 G15 **Burang** Xizang Zizhiqu, W China 30°28′N 81°13′E
Burao *see* Burco
138 H8 **Burāq** Dar'ā, S Syria 33°11′N 36°28′E
141 O6 **Buraydah** *var.* Buraida. Al Qaşīm, N Saudi Arabia 26°50′N 44°E
35 S15 **Burbank** California, W USA 34°10′N 118°25′W
31 N11 **Burbank** Illinois, N USA 41°45′N 87°48′W
183 Q8 **Burcher** New South Wales, SE Australia 33°29′S 147°16′E
80 N13 **Burco** *var.* Burao, Bur'o. Togdheer, NW Somalia 09°29′N 45°31′E
162 K8 **Bürd** *var.* Ongon. Övörhangay, C Mongolia 46°58′N 103°45′E
146 L13 **Burdalyk** Lebap Welaýaty, E Turkmenistan 38°31′N 64°21′E
181 W6 **Burdekin River** ~ Queensland, NE Australia
27 O7 **Burden** Kansas, C USA 37°18′N 96°45′W
Burdigala *see* Bordeaux
136 E15 **Burdur** *var.* Buldur. Burdur, SW Turkey 37°44′N 30°17′E
136 E15 **Burdur** *var.* Buldur. ◈ *province* SW Turkey
136 E15 **Burdur Gölü** *salt lake* SW Turkey
65 H21 **Burdwood Bank** *undersea feature* SW Atlantic Ocean
80 I12 **Burē** Āmara, N Ethiopia 10°43′N 37°09′E
80 H13 **Burē** Oromīya, C Ethiopia 08°13′N 35°09′E
93 J15 **Bureå** Västerbotten, N Sweden 64°36′N 21°15′E
162 K7 **Büreghangay** *var.* Darhan. Bulgan, C Mongolia 48°07′N 103°54′E
101 G14 **Büren** Nordrhein-Westfalen, W Germany 51°34′N 08°34′E
162 L8 **Büren** *var.* Bayantöhöm. Töv, C Mongolia 46°57′N 105°09′E
162 K6 **Bürengiyn Nuruu** ▲▲ N Mongolia
Bürenhayrhan *see* Bulgan
162 I6 **Bürentogtoh** *var.* Bayan. Hövsgol, C Mongolia 49°36′N 99°36′E
149 U10 **Būrewāla** *var.* Mandi Būrewāla. Punjab, E Pakistan 30°05′N 72°47′E
92 J9 **Burfjord** Troms, N Norway 69°55′N 21°54′E
100 L13 **Burg** *var.* Burg an der Ihle, Burg bei Magdeburg. Sachsen-Anhalt, C Germany 52°17′N 11°51′E
Burg an der Ihle *see* Burg
114 N10 **Burgas** *var.* Bourgas. Burgas, E Bulgaria 42°31′N 27°30′E
114 M10 **Burgas** ◈ *province* E Bulgaria
114 N9 **Burgas** ✈ Burgas, E Bulgaria 42°35′N 27°33′E
114 N10 **Burgaski Zaliv** *gulf* E Bulgaria
114 M10 **Burgasko Ezero** *lagoon* E Bulgaria
21 V11 **Burgaw** North Carolina, SE USA 34°33′N 77°56′W
Burg bei Magdeburg *see* Burg
108 E8 **Burgdorf** Bern, NW Switzerland 47°03′N 07°38′E
109 Y7 **Burgenland** *off.* Land Burgenland. ◈ *state* SE Austria
13 S13 **Burgeo** Newfoundland, Newfoundland and Labrador, SE Canada 47°37′N 57°38′W
83 I24 **Burgersdorp** Eastern Cape, SE South Africa 31°00′S 26°20′E
83 K20 **Burgersfort** Mpumalanga, NE South Africa 24°39′S 30°18′E
101 N23 **Burghausen** Bayern, SE Germany 48°10′N 12°48′E
139 O5 **Burghūth, Sabkhat al** ◎ E Syria
101 M20 **Burglengenfeld** Bayern, SE Germany 49°11′N 12°01′E
41 P9 **Burgos** Tamaulipas, C Mexico 24°55′N 98°46′W
105 N4 **Burgos** Castilla y León, N Spain 42°21′N 03°41′W
105 N4 **Burgos** ◈ *province* Castilla y León, N Spain
Burgstadlberg *see* Hradiště
95 P20 **Burgsvik** Gotland, SE Sweden 57°01′N 18°18′E
98 L6 **Burgum** *Dutch.* Bergum. Fryslân, N Netherlands 53°12′N 05°59′E
Burgundy *see* Bourgogne
159 Q11 **Burhan Budai Shan** ▲▲ C China
136 B12 **Burhaniye** Balıkesir, W Turkey 39°29′N 26°59′E
154 G12 **Burhānpur** Madhya Pradesh, C India 21°18′N 76°14′E
127 W7 **Buribay** Respublika Bashkortostan, W Russian Federation 51°57′N 58°11′E
43 O17 **Burica, Punta** *headland* Costa Rica/Panama 08°02′N 82°53′W
167 Q10 **Buriram** *var.* Buri Ram, Puriramya. Buri Ram, E Thailand 15°01′N 103°06′E
Buri Ram *see* Buriram
105 S10 **Burjassot** Valenciana, E Spain 39°33′N 00°26′W
81 N16 **Burka Giibi** Hiiraan, C Somalia 03°52′N 45°07′E
147 X8 **Burkan** ~ E Kyrgyzstan
25 R4 **Burkburnett** Texas, SW USA 34°06′N 98°34′W
29 O12 **Burke** South Dakota, N USA 43°09′N 99°18′W
10 K15 **Burke Channel** *channel* British Columbia, W Canada
194 J10 **Burke Island** *island* Antarctica
20 L7 **Burkesville** Kentucky, S USA 36°48′N 85°21′W
181 T4 **Burketown** Queensland, NE Australia 17°49′S 139°28′E
25 Q8 **Burkett** Texas, SW USA 32°01′N 99°17′W
25 Y9 **Burkeville** Texas, SW USA 30°58′N 93°41′W
21 V7 **Burkeville** Virginia, NE USA 37°11′N 78°12′W
77 O12 **Burkina** *off.* Burkina Faso; *prev.* Upper Volta. ◆ *republic* W Africa
Burkina *see* Burkina Faso
Burkina Faso *see* Burkina
194 L13 **Burks, Cape** *headland* Antarctica
14 H12 **Burk's Falls** Ontario, S Canada 45°38′N 79°25′W
101 H23 **Burladingen** Baden-Württemberg, S Germany 48°18′N 09°05′E
25 T7 **Burleson** Texas, SW USA 32°32′N 97°19′W
33 P15 **Burley** Idaho, NW USA 42°32′N 113°47′W
Burlin *see* Borili
14 G16 **Burlington** Ontario, S Canada 43°19′N 79°48′W
37 W4 **Burlington** Colorado, C USA 39°17′N 102°17′W
29 Y15 **Burlington** Iowa, C USA 40°48′N 91°05′W
27 P5 **Burlington** Kansas, C USA 38°11′N 95°46′W
21 T9 **Burlington** North Carolina, SE USA 36°05′N 79°27′W
28 M3 **Burlington** North Dakota, N USA 48°16′N 101°25′W
18 L7 **Burlington** Vermont, NE USA 44°28′N 73°14′W
30 M9 **Burlington** Wisconsin, N USA 42°38′N 88°12′W
27 Q1 **Burlington Junction** Missouri, C USA 40°27′N 95°04′W
Burma *see* Myanmar
10 L17 **Burnaby** British Columbia, SW Canada 49°16′N 122°58′W
117 O12 **Burnas, Ozero** ◎ SW Ukraine
25 S10 **Burnet** Texas, SW USA 30°46′N 98°14′W
35 O3 **Burney** California, W USA 40°52′N 121°42′W
183 O16 **Burnie** Tasmania, SE Australia 41°07′S 145°52′E
97 L17 **Burnley** NW England, United Kingdom 53°48′N 02°14′W
Burnoye *see* Bauyrzhan Momyshuly
153 R15 **Burnpur** West Bengal, NE India 23°39′N 86°55′E
32 K14 **Burns** Oregon, NW USA 43°35′N 119°03′W
26 K11 **Burns Flat** Oklahoma, C USA 35°21′N 99°10′W
20 M7 **Burnside** Kentucky, S USA 36°55′N 84°34′W
8 K8 **Burnside** ~ Nunavut, NW Canada
32 L15 **Burns Junction** Oregon, NW USA 42°46′N 117°51′W
10 L13 **Burns Lake** British Columbia, SW Canada 54°14′N 125°45′W
29 V9 **Burnsville** Minnesota, N USA 44°49′N 93°14′W
21 P9 **Burnsville** North Carolina, SE USA 35°56′N 82°18′W
21 R4 **Burnsville** West Virginia, NE USA 38°50′N 80°39′W
14 I13 **Burnt River** ~ Ontario, SE Canada
14 J11 **Burntroot Lake** ◎ Ontario, SE Canada
11 W12 **Burntwood** ~ Manitoba, C Canada
Bur'o *see* Burco
158 L2 **Burqin** Xinjiang Uygur Zizhiqu, NW China 47°42′N 86°50′E
182 J8 **Burra** South Australia 33°41′S 138°54′E
183 S9 **Burragorang, Lake** ⊞ New South Wales, SE Australia
96 K5 **Burray** *island* NE Scotland, United Kingdom
113 L19 **Burrel** *var.* Burreli. Dibër, C Albania 41°36′N 20°00′E
Burreli *see* Burrel
183 R8 **Burrendong Reservoir** ⊞ New South Wales, SE Australia
183 R5 **Burren Junction** New South Wales, SE Australia 30°06′S 149°01′E
Burriana *see* Borriana
183 R10 **Burrinjuck Reservoir** ⊞ New South Wales, SE Australia
36 J12 **Burro Creek** ~ Arizona, SW USA
40 M5 **Burro, Serranías del** ▲▲ NW Mexico
62 K7 **Burruyacú** Tucumán, N Argentina 26°30′S 64°45′W
136 E12 **Bursa** *var.* Brussa, *prev.* Brusa; *anc.* Prusa. Bursa, NW Turkey 40°12′N 29°04′E
136 D12 **Bursa** *var.* Brusa, Brussa. ◈ *province* NW Turkey
75 Y9 **Būr Safājah** *var.* Būr Safājah. E Egypt 26°43′N 33°55′E
Būr Safājah *see* Būr Safājah
75 W7 **Būr Sa'īd** *var.* Port Said. N Egypt 31°17′N 32°18′E
81 O14 **Bur Tinle** Nugaal, C Somalia 07°50′N 48°01′E
31 Q5 **Burt Lake** ◎ Michigan, N USA
118 H7 **Burtnieks** *var.* Burtnieks Ezers. ◎ N Latvia
Burtnieks Ezers *see* Burtnieks
31 Q9 **Burton** Michigan, N USA 43°00′N 84°16′W
Burton on Trent *see* Burton upon Trent
97 M19 **Burton upon Trent** *var.* Burton on Trent, Burton-upon-Trent. C England, United Kingdom 52°48′N 01°36′W
93 J15 **Burträsk** Västerbotten, N Sweden 64°31′N 20°40′E
Burubaytal *see* Burybaytal
Burujird *see* Borūjerd
Burultokay *see* Fuhai
141 R15 **Burūm** SE Yemen 14°22′N 48°53′E
Burunday *see* Boralday
81 D21 **Burundi** *off.* Republic of Burundi; *prev.* Kingdom of Burundi, Urundi. ◆ *republic* C Africa
Burundi, Kingdom of *see* Burundi
Burundi, Republic of *see* Burundi
171 R13 **Buru, Pulau** *prev.* Boeroe. *island* E Indonesia
77 T17 **Burutu** Delta, S Nigeria 05°18′N 05°32′E
10 G7 **Burwash Landing** Yukon Territory, W Canada 61°26′N 139°12′W
29 O14 **Burwell** Nebraska, C USA 41°46′N 99°04′W
97 L17 **Bury** NW England, United Kingdom 53°36′N 02°17′W
123 N13 **Buryatiya, Respublika** *prev.* Buryatskaya ASSR. ◈ *autonomous republic* S Russian Federation
Buryatskaya ASSR *see* Buryatiya, Respublika
145 S14 **Burybaytal** *prev.* Burubaytal. Zhambyl, SE Kazakhstan 44°56′N 73°59′E
117 S3 **Buryn'** Sums'ka Oblast', NE Ukraine 51°13′N 33°50′E
97 P20 **Bury St Edmunds** *hist.* Beodericsworth. E England, United Kingdom 52°15′N 00°43′E
114 G8 **Bŭrziya** ~ NW Bulgaria
106 D9 **Busalla** Liguria, NW Italy 44°35′N 08°55′E
163 Z16 **Busan** *off.* Pusan-gwangyŏksi, *var.* Pusan; *prev.* Pusan, *Jap.* Fusan. SE South Korea 35°11′N 129°04′E
139 N5 **Buşayrah** Dayr az Zawr, E Syria 35°10′N 40°25′E
Buševa *see* Baba
143 N12 **Būshehr** *off.* Ostān-e Būshehr. ◈ *province* SW Iran
Būshehr/Bushire *see* Bandar-e Būshehr
Būshehr, Ostān-e *see* Būshehr
25 N2 **Bushland** Texas, SW USA 35°11′N 102°04′W
30 J12 **Bushnell** Illinois, N USA 40°33′N 90°30′W
Busi *see* Biševo
81 G18 **Busia** SE Uganda 01°20′N 34°48′E
Busiasch *see* Buziaş
79 K16 **Businga** Equateur, NW Dem. Rep. Congo 03°20′N 20°53′E
79 J18 **Busira** ~ NW Dem. Rep. Congo
116 I5 **Bus'k** *Rus.* Busk. L'vivs'ka Oblast', W Ukraine 49°59′N 24°34′E
95 E14 **Buskerud** ◈ *county* S Norway
113 F14 **Buško Jezero** ⊞ SW Bosnia and Herzegovina
111 M15 **Busko-Zdrój** Świętokrzyskie, C Poland 50°28′N 20°44′E
Busra *see* Al Başrah, Iraq
Buşrá *see* Buşrá ash Shām, Syria
138 H9 **Buşrá ash Shām** *var.* Bosora, Bosra, Bozrah, Buşrá. Dar'ā, S Syria 32°31′N 36°29′E
180 I13 **Busselton** Western Australia 33°43′S 115°15′E
81 C14 **Busseri** ~ W South Sudan
106 E9 **Busseto** Emilia-Romagna, C Italy 45°00′N 10°06′E
106 A8 **Bussoleno** Piemonte, NE Italy 45°11′N 07°07′E
Bussora *see* Al Başrah
41 N7 **Bustamante** Nuevo León, NE Mexico 26°29′N 100°30′W
63 I23 **Bustamante, Punta** *headland* S Argentina 51°35′S 68°58′W
Bustan *see* Bo'ston
116 J12 **Buşteni** Prahova, SE Romania 45°23′N 25°32′E
106 D7 **Busto Arsizio** Lombardia, N Italy 45°37′N 08°51′E
147 Q10 **Bŭston** *Rus.* Buston. NW Tajikistan 40°31′N 69°21′E
100 H8 **Büsum** Schleswig-Holstein, N Germany 54°08′N 08°52′E
98 J10 **Bussum** Noord-Holland, C Netherlands 52°17′N 05°10′E
79 M16 **Buta** Orientale, N Dem. Rep. Congo 02°50′N 24°41′E
81 E20 **Butare** *prev.* Astrida. S Rwanda 02°39′S 29°44′E
191 O2 **Butaritari** *atoll* Tungaru, W Kiribati
Butawal *see* Butwal
96 H13 **Bute** *cultural region* SW Scotland, United Kingdom
162 K6 **Büteeliyn Nuruu** ▲▲ N Mongolia
10 L16 **Bute Inlet** *fjord* British Columbia, W Canada
96 H12 **Bute, Island of** *island* SW Scotland, United Kingdom
79 P18 **Butembo** Nord-Kivu, NE Dem. Rep. Congo 0°09′N 29°17′E
Bütenpost *see* Buitenpost
107 K25 **Butera** Sicilia, Italy, C Mediterranean Sea 37°12′N 14°12′E
99 M20 **Bütgenbach** Liège, E Belgium 50°25′N 06°12′E
Butha Qi *see* Zalantun
166 J5 **Buthidaung** Rakhine State, W Myanmar (Burma) 20°50′N 92°25′E
61 I16 **Butiá** Rio Grande do Sul, S Brazil 30°09′S 51°55′W
81 F17 **Butiaba** NW Uganda 01°48′N 31°21′E
23 N6 **Butler** Alabama, S USA 32°05′N 88°13′W
23 S5 **Butler** Georgia, SE USA 32°33′N 84°14′W
31 Q11 **Butler** Indiana, N USA 41°25′N 84°52′W
27 R5 **Butler** Missouri, C USA 38°17′N 94°21′W
18 B14 **Butler** Pennsylvania, NE USA 40°51′N 79°52′W
194 K5 **Butler Island** *island* Antarctica
21 U8 **Butner** North Carolina, SE USA 36°07′N 78°45′W
171 P14 **Buton, Pulau** *var.* Pulau Butung; *prev.* Boetoeng. *island* C Indonesia
Bütow *see* Bytów
113 L23 **Butrintit, Liqeni i** ◎ S Albania
23 N3 **Buttahatchee River** ~ Alabama/Mississippi, S USA
33 Q10 **Butte** Montana, NW USA 46°01′N 112°33′W
29 O12 **Butte** Nebraska, C USA 42°54′N 98°51′W
168 J7 **Butterworth** Pinang, Peninsular Malaysia 05°24′N 100°22′E
83 J25 **Butterworth** *var.* Gcuwa. Eastern Cape, SE South Africa 32°20′S 28°09′E
13 O3 **Button Islands** *island group* Nunavut, NE Canada
35 R13 **Buttonwillow** California, W USA 35°24′N 119°26′W
171 Q7 **Butuan** *off.* Butuan City. Mindanao, S Philippines 08°57′N 125°33′E
Butuan City *see* Butuan
Butung, Pulau *see* Buton, Pulau
Butuntum *see* Bitonto
126 M8 **Buturlinovka** Voronezhskaya Oblast', W Russian Federation 50°48′N 40°33′E
153 O11 **Butwal** *var.* Butawal. Western, C Nepal 27°41′N 83°28′E
101 G17 **Butzbach** Hessen, W Germany 50°26′N 08°40′E
100 L9 **Bützow** Mecklenburg-Vorpommern, N Germany 53°49′N 11°58′E
80 N13 **Buuhoodle** Togdheer, N Somalia 08°18′N 46°15′E
81 N16 **Buulobarde** *var.* Buulo Berde. Hiiraan, C Somalia 03°52′N 45°37′E
Buulo Berde *see* Buulobarde
80 P12 **Buuraha Cal Miskaat** ▲ NE Somalia
81 L19 **Buur Gaabo** Jubbada Hoose, S Somalia 01°14′S 41°48′E
99 M22 **Buurgplaatz** ▲ N Luxembourg 50°09′N 06°02′E
162 H8 **Buutsagaan** *var.* Buyant. Bayanhongor, C Mongolia 46°07′N 98°45′E
Buwayrāt al Hasūn *see* Bu'ayrāt al Ḩasūn
146 L11 **Buxoro** *var.* Bokhara, *Rus.* Bukhara. Buxoro Viloyati, C Uzbekistan 39°51′N 64°23′E
146 J11 **Buxoro Viloyati** *Rus.* Bukharskaya Oblast'. ◈ *province* C Uzbekistan
100 I10 **Buxtehude** Niedersachsen, NW Germany 53°29′N 09°42′E
97 L18 **Buxton** C England, United Kingdom 53°18′N 01°52′W
124 M14 **Buy** *var.* Buj. Kostromskaya Oblast', NW Russian Federation 58°27′N 41°31′E
Buyanbat *see* Jargalant
162 D6 **Buyant** Bayan-Ölgiy, W Mongolia 48°31′N 89°36′E
Buyant *see* Buutsagaan, Bayanhongor, Mongolia
Buyant *see* Otgon, Dzavhan, Mongolia
Buyant *see* Galshar, Hentiy, Mongolia
163 N10 **Buyant-Uhaa** Dornogovĭ, SE Mongolia 44°52′N 110°12′E
162 M7 **Buyant Ukha** ✈ (Ulaanbaatar) Töv, N Mongolia
127 Q16 **Buynaksk** Respublika Dagestan, SW Russian Federation 42°53′N 47°03′E
119 L20 **Buynavichy** *Rus.* Buynovichi. Homyel'skaya Voblasts', SE Belarus 51°52′N 28°33′E
Buynovichi *see* Buynavichy
76 L16 **Buyo** SW Ivory Coast 06°16′N 07°03′W
76 L16 **Buyo, Lac de** ⊞ W Ivory Coast
163 R7 **Buyr Nuur** *var.* Buir Nur. ◎ China/Mongolia *see also* Buir Nur
Buyr Nuur *see* Buir Nur
137 T13 **Büyükağrı Dağı** *var.* Aghri Dagh, Agri Dagi, Koh I Noh, Masis, *Eng.* Great Ararat, Mount Ararat. ▲ E Turkey 39°43′N 44°19′E
137 R15 **Büyük Çayı** ~ NE Turkey
114 O13 **Büyük Çekmece** İstanbul, NW Turkey 41°02′N 28°35′E
114 N12 **Büyükkarıştıran** Kırklareli, NW Turkey 41°17′N 27°33′E
115 L14 **Büyükkemikli Burnu** *cape* NW Turkey
136 E15 **Büyükmenderes Nehri** ~ SW Turkey
Büyükzap Suyu *see* Great Zab
102 M9 **Buzançais** Indre, C France 46°53′N 01°25′E
116 K13 **Buzău** Buzău, SE Romania 45°08′N 26°51′E
116 K13 **Buzău** ◈ *county* SE Romania
116 L12 **Buzău** ~ E Romania
75 S11 **Buzaymah** *var.* Bzīmah. SE Libya 24°53′N 22°01′E
164 E13 **Buzen** Fukuoka, Kyūshū, SW Japan 33°37′N 131°06′E
116 F12 **Buziaş** *Ger.* Busiasch, *Hung.* Buziásfürdő; *prev.* Buziás. Timiş, W Romania 45°38′N 21°36′E
Buziás *see* Buziaş
Buziásfürdő *see* Buziaş
83 M18 **Búzi, Rio** ~ C Mozambique
117 Q10 **Buz'kyy Lyman** *bay* S Ukraine
Büzmeýin *see* Abadan
127 T6 **Buzuluk** Orenburgskaya Oblast', W Russian Federation 52°47′N 52°16′E
127 N8 **Buzuluk** ~ SW Russian Federation
Buzuluk *see* Buzylyk
145 O8 **Buzylyk** *prev.* Buzuluk. Akmola, C Kazakhstan 51°53′N 66°09′E
19 P12 **Buzzards Bay** Massachusetts, NE USA 41°45′N 70°37′W
19 P13 **Buzzards Bay** *bay* Massachusetts, NE USA
83 G16 **Bwabata** Caprivi, NE Namibia 17°52′S 22°39′E
186 H10 **Bwagaoia** Misima Island, SE Papua New Guinea 10°39′S 152°48′E
Bwake *see* Bouaké
187 R13 **Bwatnapne** Pentecost, C Vanuatu 15°42′S 168°07′E
119 K14 **Byahoml'** *Rus.* Begoml'. Vitsyebskaya Voblasts', N Belarus 54°44′N 28°04′E
114 K8 **Byala** Ruse, N Bulgaria 43°27′N 25°44′E
114 N9 **Byala** *prev.* Ak-Dere. Varna, E Bulgaria 42°52′N 27°53′E
Byala Reka *see* Erythropótamos
114 H8 **Byala Slatina** Vratsa, NW Bulgaria 43°28′N 23°56′E
119 N15 **Byalynichy** *Rus.* Belynichi. Mahilyowskaya Voblasts', E Belarus 54°00′N 29°42′E
Byan Tumen *see* Choybalsan
119 L14 **Byarezina** *prev.* Byerezino, *Rus.* Berezina. ~ C Belarus
119 G19 **Byaroza** *Pol.* Bereza Kartuska, *Rus.* Bereza. Brestskaya Voblasts', SW Belarus 52°32′N 24°59′E
119 H16 **Byarozawka** *Rus.* Berëzovka. Hrodzyenskaya Voblasts', W Belarus 53°45′N 25°30′E
Bybles *see* Jbail
111 O14 **Bychawa** Lubelskie, SE Poland 51°06′N 22°34′E
Bychikha *see* Bychykha
118 N11 **Bychykha** *Rus.* Bychikha. Vitsyebskaya Voblasts', NE Belarus 55°41′N 29°59′E
111 I14 **Byczyna** *Ger.* Pitschen. Opolskie, S Poland 51°06′N 18°13′E
110 I10 **Bydgoszcz** *Ger.* Bromberg. Kujawski-pomorskie, C Poland 53°06′N 18°00′E
119 H19 **Byelaazyorsk** *Rus.* Beloozersk. Brestskaya Voblasts', SW Belarus 52°28′N 25°10′E
119 I17 **Byelaruskaya Hrada** *Rus.* Belorusskaya Gryada. *ridge* N Belarus
119 G18 **Byelavyezhskaya Pushcha** *Pol.* Puszcza Białowieska, *Rus.* Belovezhskaya Pushcha. *forest* Belarus/Poland *see also* Białowieska, Puszcza
Byelavyezhskaya, Pushcha *see* Białowieska, Puszcza
119 H15 **Byenyakoni** *Rus.* Benyakoni. Hrodzyenskaya Voblasts', W Belarus 54°15′N 25°22′E
119 M16 **Byerazino** *Rus.* Berezino. Minskaya Voblasts', C Belarus 53°50′N 29°00′E
118 L13 **Byerazino** *Rus.* Berezino. Vitsyebskaya Voblasts', N Belarus 54°54′N 28°12′E
Byerezino *see* Byarezina
118 M13 **Byeshankovichy** *Rus.* Beshenkovichi. Vitsyebskaya Voblasts', N Belarus 55°03′N 29°27′E
31 U13 **Byesville** Ohio, N USA 39°58′N 81°32′W
119 P18 **Byesyedz'** *Rus.* Besed'. ~ SE Belarus
119 H19 **Byezdzyezh** *Rus.* Bezdezh. Brestskaya Voblasts', SW Belarus 52°19′N 25°18′E
93 J15 **Bygdeå** Västerbotten, N Sweden 64°03′N 20°49′E
94 F12 **Bygdin** ◎ S Norway
93 J15 **Bygdsiljum** Västerbotten, N Sweden 64°20′N 20°31′E
95 E17 **Bygland** Aust-Agder, S Norway 58°46′N 07°50′E
95 E17 **Byglandsfjord** Aust-Agder, S Norway 58°42′N 07°51′E
119 N16 **Bykhaw** *Rus.* Bykhov. Mahilyowskaya Voblasts', E Belarus 53°31′N 30°15′E
Bykhov *see* Bykhaw
127 P9 **Bykovo** Volgogradskaya Oblast', SW Russian Federation 49°52′N 45°24′E
123 P7 **Bykovskiy** Respublika Sakha (Yakutiya), NE Russian Federation 71°57′N 129°07′E
195 R12 **Byrd Glacier** *glacier* Antarctica
14 K10 **Byrd, Lac** ◎ Québec, SE Canada
183 P5 **Byrock** New South Wales, SE Australia 30°40′S 146°24′E
30 L10 **Byron** Illinois, N USA 42°06′N 89°15′W
183 V4 **Byron Bay** New South Wales, SE Australia 28°39′S 153°34′E
183 V4 **Byron, Cape** *headland* New South Wales, E Australia 28°37′S 153°40′E
63 F21 **Byron, Isla** *island* S Chile
Byron Island *see* Nikunau
65 B24 **Byron Sound** *sound* NW Falkland Islands
122 M6 **Byrranga, Gory** ▲▲ N Russian Federation
93 J14 **Byske** Västerbotten, N Sweden 64°58′N 21°10′E
111 K18 **Bystrá** ▲ N Slovakia 49°10′N 19°49′E
111 F18 **Bystřice nad Pernštejnem** *Ger.* Bistritz ober Pernstein. Vysočina, C Czech Republic 49°32′N 16°16′E
Bystrovka *see* Kemin
111 G16 **Bystrzyca Kłodzka** *Ger.* Habelschwerdt. Wałbrzych, SW Poland 50°19′N 16°39′E
111 I18 **Bytča** Žilinský Kraj, N Slovakia 49°15′N 18°32′E
119 L15 **Bytcha** Minskaya Voblasts', NE Belarus 54°19′N 28°24′E
Byteń/Byten' *see* Bytsyen'
111 J16 **Bytom** *Ger.* Beuthen. Śląskie, S Poland 50°21′N 18°51′E
110 H7 **Bytów** *Ger.* Bütow. Pomorskie, N Poland 54°10′N 17°30′E
119 H18 **Bytsyen'** *Pol.* Byteń, *Rus.* Byten'. Brestskaya Voblasts', SW Belarus 52°53′N 25°30′E
81 E19 **Byumba** *var.* Biumba. N Rwanda 01°37′S 30°05′E
Byuzmeyin *see* Abadan
119 O20 **Byval'ki** Homyel'skaya Voblasts', SE Belarus 51°51′N 30°38′E
95 O20 **Byxelkrok** Kalmar, S Sweden 57°18′N 17°01′E
Byzantium *see* İstanbul
Bzīmah *see* Buzaymah

C

62 O6 **Caacupé** Cordillera, S Paraguay 25°23′S 57°05′W
62 P6 **Caaguazú** *off.* Departamento de Caaguazú. ◈ *department* C Paraguay
Caaguazú, Departamento de *see* Caaguazú
82 C13 **Caála** *var.* Kaala, Robert Williams, *Port.* Vila Robert Williams. Huambo, C Angola 12°51′S 15°33′E
62 P7 **Caazapá** Caazapá, S Paraguay 26°09′S 56°21′W
62 P7 **Caazapá** *off.* Departamento de Caazapá. ◈ *department* SE Paraguay
Caazapá, Departamento de *see* Caazapá
81 P15 **Cabaad, Raas** *headland* C Somalia 06°13′N 49°01′E
55 N10 **Cabadisocaña** Amazonas, S Venezuela 04°28′N 64°45′W
44 F5 **Cabaiguán** Sancti Spíritus, C Cuba 22°04′N 79°32′W
Caballeria, Cabo *see* Cavalleria, Cap de
37 Q14 **Caballo Reservoir** ⊞ New Mexico, SW USA
40 L6 **Caballos Mesteños, Llano de los** *plain* N Mexico
104 L2 **Cabanaquinta** Asturias, N Spain 43°10′N 05°37′W
42 B9 **Cabañas** ◈ *department* E El Salvador
171 O3 **Cabanatuan** *off.* Cabanatuan City. Luzon, N Philippines 15°27′N 120°57′E
Cabanatuan City *see* Cabanatuan
15 T8 **Cabano** Québec, SE Canada 47°40′N 68°56′W
104 L11 **Cabeza del Buey** Extremadura, W Spain 38°44′N 05°13′W
45 V5 **Cabezas de San Juan** *headland* E Puerto Rico 18°23′N 65°37′W
105 N2 **Cabezón de la Sal** Cantabria, N Spain 43°19′N 04°14′W
Cabhán *see* Cavan
61 B23 **Cabildo** Buenos Aires, E Argentina 38°28′S 61°50′W
Cabillonum *see* Chalon-sur-Saône
54 H5 **Cabimas** Zulia, NW Venezuela 10°26′N 71°27′W
82 A9 **Cabinda** *var.* Kabinda. Cabinda, NW Angola 05°34′S 12°12′E
82 A9 **Cabinda** *var.* Kabinda. ◈ *province* NW Angola
33 N7 **Cabinet Mountains** ▲▲ Idaho/Montana, NW USA
82 B11 **Cabiri** Bengo, NW Angola 08°50′S 13°42′E
63 J20 **Cabo Blanco** Santa Cruz, SE Argentina 47°13′S 65°43′W
82 P13 **Cabo Delgado** *off.* Província de Cabo Delgado. ◈ *province* NE Mozambique
14 L9 **Cabonga, Réservoir** ⊞ Québec, SE Canada
27 V7 **Cabool** Missouri, C USA 37°07′N 92°06′W
183 V2 **Caboolture** Queensland, E Australia 27°05′S 152°50′E
Cabora Bassa, Lake *see* Cahora Bassa, Albufeira de
40 F3 **Caborca** Sonora, NW Mexico 30°44′N 112°06′W
Cabo San Lucas *see* San Lucas
27 V11 **Cabot** Arkansas, C USA 34°58′N 92°01′W
14 F12 **Cabot Head** *headland* Ontario, S Canada 45°13′N 81°17′W
13 R13 **Cabot Strait** *strait* E Canada
Cabo Verde, Ilhas do *see* Cape Verde
104 M14 **Cabra** Andalucía, S Spain 37°28′N 04°28′W
107 B19 **Cabras** Sardegna, Italy, C Mediterranean Sea 39°55′N 08°30′E
188 A15 **Cabras Island** *island* W Guam
45 O8 **Cabrera** N Dominican Republic 19°40′N 69°54′W
104 J4 **Cabrera** ~ NW Spain
105 X10 **Cabrera, Illa de** *anc.* Capraria. *island* Islas Baleares, Spain, W Mediterranean Sea
105 Q15 **Cabrera, Sierra** ▲▲ S Spain
11 S16 **Cabri** Saskatchewan, S Canada 50°38′N 108°28′W
105 R10 **Cabriel** ~ E Spain
54 M7 **Cabruta** Guárico, C Venezuela 07°39′N 66°19′W
171 N2 **Cabugao** Luzon, N Philippines 17°55′N 120°29′E
54 G10 **Cabuyaro** Meta, C Colombia 04°21′N 72°47′W
60 I13 **Caçador** Santa Catarina, S Brazil 26°47′S 51°00′W
42 G8 **Cacaguatique, Cordillera** *var.* Cordillera. ▲▲ NE El Salvador
112 L13 **Čačak** Serbia, C Serbia 43°52′N 20°23′E
55 Y10 **Cacao** NE French Guiana 04°37′N 52°29′W
61 H16 **Caçapava do Sul** Rio Grande do Sul, S Brazil 30°28′S 53°29′W
21 U3 **Cacapon River** ~ West Virginia, NE USA
107 J23 **Caccamo** Sicilia, Italy, C Mediterranean Sea 37°56′N 13°40′E
107 A17 **Caccia, Capo** *headland* Sardegna, Italy, C Mediterranean Sea 40°34′N 08°09′E
146 F15 **Çäçe** *var.* Chäche, *Rus.* Chaacha. Ahal Welaýaty, S Turkmenistan 36°49′N 60°33′E
59 G18 **Cáceres** Mato Grosso, W Brazil 16°05′S 57°40′W
104 J10 **Cáceres** *Ar.* Qazris. Extremadura, W Spain 39°29′N 06°23′W
104 J9 **Cáceres** ◈ *province* Extremadura, W Spain
Cachacrou *see* Scotts Head Village
61 C21 **Cacharí** Buenos Aires, E Argentina 36°24′S 59°32′W
26 L12 **Cache** Oklahoma, C USA 34°37′N 98°37′W
10 M16 **Cache Creek** British Columbia, SW Canada 50°49′N 121°20′W
35 N6 **Cache Creek** ~ California, W USA
37 S3 **Cache La Poudre River** ~ Colorado, C USA
Cacheo *see* Cacheu
27 W11 **Cache River** ~ Arkansas, C USA
30 L17 **Cache River** ~ Illinois, N USA
76 G12 **Cacheu** *var.* Cacheo. Cacheu, W Guinea-Bissau 12°12′N 16°10′W

◆ Country
● Country Capital
◇ Dependent Territory
○ Dependent Territory Capital
◈ Administrative Regions
✈ International Airport
▲ Mountain
▲▲ Mountain Range
Volcano
~ River
◎ Lake
⊞ Reservoir

59 I15 **Cachimbo** Pará, NE Brazil 09°21′S 54°58′W
59 H15 **Cachimbo, Serra do** ▲▲ C Brazil
82 D13 **Cachingues** Bié, C Angola 13°05′S 16°48′E
54 G7 **Cáchira** Norte de Santander, N Colombia 07°44′N 73°07′W
61 H16 **Cachoeira do Sul** Rio Grande do Sul, S Brazil 29°58′S 52°54′W
59 O20 **Cachoeiro de Itapemirim** Espírito Santo, SE Brazil 20°51′S 41°07′W
82 E12 **Cacolo** Lunda Sul, NE Angola 10°09′S 19°21′E
83 C14 **Caconda** Huíla, C Angola 13°43′S 15°03′E
82 A9 **Cacongo** Cabinda, NW Angola 05°13′S 12°08′E
35 U9 **Cactus Peak** ▲ Nevada, W USA 37°42′N 116°51′W
82 A11 **Cacuaco** Luanda, NW Angola 08°47′S 13°21′E
83 B14 **Cacula** Huíla, SW Angola 14°33′S 14°04′E
67 R12 **Caculuvar** ≈ SW Angola
59 O19 **Caçumba, Ilha** *island* SE Brazil
55 N10 **Cacuri** Amazonas, S Venezuela
81 N17 **Cadale** Shabeellaha Dhexe, E Somalia 02°48′N 46°19′E
105 X4 **Cadaqués** Cataluña, NE Spain 42°17′N 03°16′E
111 J18 **Čadca** *Hung.* Csaca. Zílinský Kraj, N Slovakia 49°27′N 18°46′E
27 P13 **Caddo** Oklahoma, C USA 34°07′N 96°15′W
25 R6 **Caddo** Texas, SW USA 32°42′N 98°40′W
25 X6 **Caddo Lake** ⊠ Louisiana/Texas, SW USA
27 S12 **Caddo Mountains** ▲▲ Arkansas, C USA
41 O8 **Cadereyta** Nuevo León, NE Mexico 25°35′N 99°54′W
97 J19 **Cader Idris** ▲ NW Wales, United Kingdom 52°43′N 03°57′W
182 F3 **Cadibarrawirracanna, Lake** *salt lake* South Australia
14 I7 **Cadillac** Québec, SE Canada 48°12′N 78°23′W
11 T17 **Cadillac** Saskatchewan, S Canada 49°43′N 107°41′W
102 K13 **Cadillac** Gironde, SW France 44°37′N 00°16′W
31 P7 **Cadillac** Michigan, N USA 44°15′N 85°23′W
105 V4 **Cadí, Toretta de** *prev.* Torre de Cadí. ▲ NE Spain 42°16′N 01°38′E
Torre de Cadí *see* Cadí, Toretta de
171 P5 **Cadiz** *off.* Cadiz City. Negros, C Philippines 10°58′N 123°18′E
104 J15 **Cádiz** *anc.* Gades, Gadier, Gadir, Gadire. Andalucía, SW Spain 36°32′N 06°18′W
20 H7 **Cadiz** Kentucky, S USA 36°52′N 87°50′W
31 U13 **Cadiz** Ohio, N USA 40°16′N 81°00′W
104 K15 **Cádiz** ◈ *province* Andalucía, SW Spain
104 I15 **Cadiz, Bahía de** *bay* SW Spain
Cadiz City *see* Cadiz
104 H15 **Cádiz, Golfo de** *Eng.* Gulf of Cadiz. *gulf* Portugal/Spain
Cadiz, Gulf of *see* Cádiz, Golfo de
35 X14 **Cadiz Lake** ◎ California, W USA
182 E2 **Cadney Homestead** South Australia 27°52′S 134°03′E
Cadurcum *see* Cahors
Caecae *see* Xaixai
102 K4 **Caen** Calvados, N France 49°10′N 00°20′W
Caene/Caenepolis *see* Qinā
Caerdydd *see* Cardiff
Caer Glou *see* Gloucester
Caer Gybi *see* Holyhead
Caerleon *see* Chester
Caer Luel *see* Carlisle
97 I18 **Caernarfon** *var.* Caernarvon, Carnarvon. NW Wales, United Kingdom 53°08′N 04°16′W
97 H18 **Caernarfon Bay** *bay* NW Wales, United Kingdom
97 I19 **Caernarvon** *cultural region* NW Wales, United Kingdom
Caernarvon *see* Caernarfon
Caesaraugusta *see* Zaragoza
Caesarea Mazaca *see* Kayseri
Caesarobriga *see* Talavera de la Reina
Caesarodunum *see* Tours
Caesaromagus *see* Beauvais
Caesena *see* Cesena
59 N17 **Caetité** Bahia, E Brazil 14°04′S 42°29′W
62 J6 **Cafayate** Salta, N Argentina 26°02′S 66°00′W
171 O2 **Cagayan** ≈ Luzon, N Philippines
171 Q7 **Cagayan de Oro** *off.* Cagayan de Oro City. Mindanao, S Philippines 08°29′N 124°38′E
Cagayan de Oro City *see* Cagayan de Oro
170 M8 **Cagayan de Tawi Tawi** *island* S Philippines
171 N6 **Cagayan Islands** *island group* C Philippines
31 O14 **Cagles Mill Lake** ⊠ Indiana, N USA
106 I12 **Cagli** Marche, C Italy 43°33′N 12°39′E
107 C20 **Cagliari** *anc.* Caralis. Sardegna, Italy, C Mediterranean Sea 39°15′N 09°06′E
107 C20 **Cagliari, Golfo di** *gulf* Sardegna, Italy, C Mediterranean Sea
103 U15 **Cagnes-sur-Mer** Alpes-Maritimes, SE France 43°40′N 07°09′E
54 L5 **Cagua** Aragua, N Venezuela 10°09′N 67°27′W
171 O1 **Cagua, Mount** ▲ Luzon, N Philippines 18°10′N 122°03′E
54 F13 **Caguán, Río** ≈ SW Colombia
45 U6 **Caguas** E Puerto Rico 18°14′N 66°02′W
146 C9 **Çagyl** *Rus.* Chagyl. Balkan Welaýaty, NW Turkmenistan 40°48′N 55°21′E
23 P5 **Cahaba River** ≈ Alabama, S USA
42 E5 **Cahabón, Río** ≈ C Guatemala
83 B15 **Cahama** Cunene, SW Angola 16°16′S 14°23′E
97 B21 **Caha Mountains** *Ir.* An Cheacha. ▲▲ SW Ireland
97 D20 **Caher** *Ir.* An Cathair. S Ireland 52°21′N 07°58′W
97 A21 **Caherciveen** *Ir.* Cathair Saidhbhín. SW Ireland 51°56′N 10°12′W
30 K15 **Cahokia** Illinois, N USA 38°34′N 90°11′W
83 L15 **Cahora Bassa, Albufeira de** *var.* Lake Cabora Bassa. ⊠ NW Mozambique
97 G20 **Cahore Point** *Ir.* Rinn Chathóir. *headland* SE Ireland 52°33′N 06°11′W
102 M14 **Cahors** *anc.* Cadurcum. Lot, S France 44°26′N 01°27′E
56 D9 **Cahuapanas, Río** ≈ N Peru
116 M12 **Cahul** *Rus.* Kagul. S Moldova 45°53′N 28°13′E
Cahul, Lacul *see* Kahul, Ozero
83 N16 **Caia** Sofala, C Mozambique 17°50′S 35°21′E
59 J19 **Caiapó, Serra do** ▲▲ C Brazil
44 F5 **Caibarién** Villa Clara, C Cuba 22°31′N 79°29′W
55 O5 **Caicara** Monagas, NE Venezuela 09°52′N 63°38′W
54 L5 **Caicara del Orinoco** Bolívar, C Venezuela 07°38′N 66°10′W
59 P14 **Caicó** Rio Grande do Norte, E Brazil 06°25′S 37°04′W
44 M6 **Caicos Islands** *island group* W Turks and Caicos Islands
44 L5 **Caicos Passage** *strait* Bahamas/Turks and Caicos Islands
161 O9 **Caidian** *prev.* Hanyang. Hubei, C China 30°37′N 114°02′E
Caiffa *see* Hefa
180 M12 **Caiguna** Western Australia 32°14′S 125°33′E
Caillí, Ceann *see* Hag's Head
40 J11 **Caimanero, Laguna del** *var.* Laguna del Camaronero. *lagoon* E Pacific Ocean
117 N10 **Căinari** *Rus.* Kaynary. C Moldova 46°43′N 29°00′E
57 L19 **Caine, Río** ≈ C Bolivia
Caiphas *see* Hefa
195 N4 **Caird Coast** *physical region* Antarctica
96 J9 **Cairn Gorm** ▲ C Scotland, United Kingdom 57°07′N 03°38′W
96 J9 **Cairngorm Mountains** ▲▲ C Scotland, United Kingdom
39 P12 **Cairn Mountain** ▲ Alaska, USA 61°07′N 155°23′W
181 W4 **Cairns** Queensland, NE Australia 16°51′S 145°43′E
121 V13 **Cairo** *var.* El Qâhira, *Ar.* Al Qāhirah. ● (Egypt) N Egypt 30°01′N 31°18′E
23 T8 **Cairo** Georgia, SE USA 30°52′N 84°12′W
30 L17 **Cairo** Illinois, N USA 37°00′N 89°10′W
75 V8 **Cairo** ✈ C Egypt 30°06′N 31°36′E
Caiseal *see* Cashel
Caisleán an Bharraigh *see* Castlebar
Caisleán na Finne *see* Castlefinn
96 J6 **Caithness** *cultural region* N Scotland, United Kingdom
83 D15 **Caiundo** Cuando Cubango, S Angola 15°41′S 17°28′E
56 C11 **Cajamarca** *prev.* Caxamarca. Cajamarca, NW Peru 07°09′S 78°32′W
56 B11 **Cajamarca** *off.* Departamento de Cajamarca. ◈ *department* N Peru
Cajamarca, Departamento de *see* Cajamarca
103 N14 **Cajarc** Lot, S France 44°28′N 01°51′E
42 G6 **Cajón, Represa El** ⊠ NW Honduras
58 N12 **Caju, Ilha do** *island* NE Brazil
159 R10 **Caka Yanhu** ◎ C China
112 E7 **Čakovec** *Ger.* Csakathurn, *Hung.* Csáktornya; *prev. Ger.* Tschakathurn. Medimurje, N Croatia 46°24′N 16°29′E
77 V17 **Calabar** Cross River, S Nigeria 04°56′N 08°25′E
14 K13 **Calabogie** Ontario, SE Canada 45°18′N 76°46′W
54 L6 **Calabozo** Guárico, C Venezuela 08°58′N 67°28′W
107 N20 **Calabria** *anc.* Bruttium. ◈ *region* SW Italy
104 M16 **Calaburra, Punta de** *headland* S Spain 36°30′N 04°38′W
116 G14 **Calafat** Dolj, SW Romania 43°59′N 22°57′E
Calafate *see* El Calafate
105 Q4 **Calahorra** La Rioja, N Spain 42°19′N 01°58′W
103 N1 **Calais** Pas-de-Calais, N France 51°N 01°54′E
19 T5 **Calais** Maine, NE USA 45°09′N 67°15′W
Calais, Pas de *see* Dover, Strait of
Calalen *see* Kallalen
62 H4 **Calama** Antofagasta, N Chile 22°26′S 68°54′W
Calamianes *see* Calamian Group
170 M5 **Calamian Group** *var.* Calamianes. *island group* W Philippines
105 R7 **Calamocha** Aragón, NE Spain 40°54′N 01°18′W
29 N14 **Calamus River** ≈ Nebraska, C USA
116 G12 **Călan** *Ger.* Kalan, *Hung.* Pusztakalán. Hunedoara, SW Romania 45°45′N 22°59′E
105 S7 **Calanda** Aragón, NE Spain 40°56′N 00°15′W
168 F9 **Calang** Sumatera, W Indonesia 04°37′N 95°37′E
171 N4 **Calapan** Mindoro, N Philippines 13°24′N 121°08′E
Călăras *see* Călărași
116 M9 **Călărași** *var.* Călăras, *Rus.* Kalarash. C Moldova 47°19′N 28°13′E
116 L14 **Călărași** Călărași, SE Romania 44°18′N 26°52′E
116 K14 **Călărași** ◈ *county* SE Romania
54 E10 **Calarca** Quindío, W Colombia 04°31′N 75°38′W
105 Q12 **Calasparra** Murcia, SE Spain 38°14′N 01°41′W
107 I23 **Calatafimi** Sicilia, Italy, C Mediterranean Sea 37°54′N 12°52′E
105 Q6 **Calatayud** Aragón, NE Spain 41°21′N 01°39′W
171 O4 **Calauag** Luzon, N Philippines 13°57′N 122°18′E
35 P8 **Calaveras River** ≈ California, W USA
171 N4 **Calavite, Cape** *headland* Mindoro, N Philippines 13°25′N 120°16′E
171 Q8 **Calbayog** *off.* Calbayog City. Samar, C Philippines 12°08′N 124°36′E
Calbayog City *see* Calbayog
22 G9 **Calcasieu Lake** ◎ Louisiana, S USA
22 H8 **Calcasieu River** ≈ Louisiana, S USA
56 B6 **Calceta** Manabí, W Ecuador 0°51′S 80°07′W
61 B16 **Calchaquí** Santa Fe, C Argentina 29°56′S 60°14′W
62 J6 **Calchaquí, Río** ≈ NW Argentina
58 J10 **Calçoene** Amapá, NE Brazil 02°29′N 51°01′W
153 S16 **Calcutta** ✈ West Bengal, N India 22°30′N 88°20′E
Calcutta *see* Kolkata
54 E9 **Caldas** *off.* Departamento de Caldas. ◈ *province* W Colombia
104 F10 **Caldas da Rainha** Leiria, W Portugal 39°24′N 09°08′W
Caldas, Departamento de *see* Caldas
104 G3 **Caldas de Reis** *var.* Caldas de Reyes. Galicia, NW Spain 42°36′N 08°39′W
Caldas de Reyes *see* Caldas de Reis
58 F13 **Caldeirão** Amazonas, NW Brazil 03°18′S 60°22′W
62 G7 **Caldera** Atacama, N Chile 27°05′S 70°48′W
42 L14 **Caldera** Puntarenas, W Costa Rica 09°55′N 84°51′W
105 N10 **Calderina** ▲ C Spain 39°18′N 03°49′W
137 T13 **Çaldıran** Van, E Turkey 39°10′N 43°52′E
32 M14 **Caldwell** Idaho, NW USA 43°39′N 116°41′W
27 N8 **Caldwell** Kansas, C USA 37°01′N 97°36′W
14 G15 **Caledon** Ontario, S Canada 43°51′N 79°58′W
83 I23 **Caledon** *var.* Mohokare. ≈ Lesotho/South Africa
42 G1 **Caledonia** Corozal, N Belize 18°14′N 88°29′W
14 G16 **Caledonia** Ontario, S Canada 43°04′N 79°57′W
29 X11 **Caledonia** Minnesota, N USA 43°37′N 91°30′W
105 X5 **Calella** *var.* Calella de la Costa. Cataluña, NE Spain 41°37′N 02°40′E
Calella de la Costa *see* Calella
23 P4 **Calera** Alabama, S USA 33°06′N 86°45′W
63 I19 **Caleta Olivia** Santa Cruz, SE Argentina 46°21′S 67°37′W
35 X17 **Calexico** California, W USA 32°39′N 115°28′W
97 H16 **Calf of Man** *island* SW Isle of Man
11 Q16 **Calgary** Alberta, SW Canada 51°05′N 114°05′W
11 Q16 **Calgary** ✈ Alberta, SW Canada 51°15′N 114°03′W
37 U5 **Calhan** Colorado, C USA 39°00′N 104°18′W
64 O5 **Calheta** Madeira, Portugal, NE Atlantic Ocean 32°42′N 17°12′W
23 R2 **Calhoun** Georgia, SE USA 34°30′N 84°57′W
20 I6 **Calhoun** Kentucky, S USA 37°32′N 87°15′W
22 M3 **Calhoun City** Mississippi, S USA 33°51′N 89°18′W
21 P12 **Calhoun Falls** South Carolina, SE USA 34°05′N 82°36′W
54 D11 **Cali** Valle del Cauca, W Colombia 03°24′N 76°30′W
27 V9 **Calico Rock** Arkansas, C USA 36°07′N 92°08′W
155 F21 **Calicut** *var.* Kozhikode. Kerala, SW India 11°17′N 75°49′E *see also* Kozhikode
35 Y9 **Caliente** Nevada, W USA 37°37′N 114°30′W
27 U5 **California** Missouri, C USA 38°39′N 92°35′W
18 B15 **California** Pennsylvania, NE USA 40°02′N 79°52′W
35 Q12 **California** *off.* State of California, *also known as* El Dorado, The Golden State. ◈ *state* W USA
35 P11 **California Aqueduct** *aqueduct* California, W USA
35 T13 **California City** California, W USA 35°06′N 117°55′W
40 F6 **California, Golfo de** *Eng.* Gulf of California; *prev.* Sea of Cortez. *gulf* W Mexico
California, Gulf of *see* California, Golfo de
137 Y13 **Călilabad** *Rus.* Dzhalilabad; *prev.* Astrakhan-Bazar. S Azerbaijan 39°15′N 48°30′E
116 I12 **Călimănești** Vâlcea, SW Romania 45°14′N 24°20′E
116 J9 **Călimani, Munții** ▲▲ N Romania
Calinisc *see* Cupcina
35 X17 **Calipatria** California, W USA 33°07′N 115°30′W
Calisia *see* Kalisz
34 M7 **Calistoga** California, W USA 38°34′N 122°37′W
83 G25 **Calitzdorp** Western Cape, SW South Africa 33°32′S 21°41′E
41 W12 **Calkiní** Campeche, E Mexico 20°21′N 90°03′W
182 K4 **Callabonna Creek** *var.* Tilcha Creek. *seasonal river* New South Wales/South Australia
182 J4 **Callabonna, Lake** ◎ South Australia
102 G5 **Callac** Côtes d'Armor, NW France 48°28′N 03°22′W
35 U5 **Callaghan, Mount** ▲ Nevada, W USA 39°38′N 116°57′W
Callain *see* Callan
97 E19 **Callan** *Ir.* Callain. S Ireland 52°33′N 07°23′W
14 H11 **Callander** Ontario, S Canada 46°14′N 79°21′W
96 I11 **Callander** C Scotland, United Kingdom 56°15′N 04°16′W
98 H7 **Callantsoog** Noord-Holland, NW Netherlands 52°51′N 04°41′E
57 D14 **Callao** Callao, W Peru 12°03′S 77°10′W
57 D15 **Callao** *off.* Departamento del Callao. ◈ *constitutional province* W Peru
Callao, Departamento del *see* Callao
56 F11 **Callaria, Río** ≈ E Peru
Callatis *see* Mangalia
11 Q13 **Calling Lake** Alberta, W Canada 55°12′N 113°07′W
Callosa de Ensarriá *see* Callosa d'En Sarrià
105 T11 **Callosa d'En Sarrià** *var.* Callosa de Ensarriá. Valenciana, E Spain 38°40′N 00°08′W
105 S12 **Callosa de Segura** Valenciana, E Spain 38°07′N 00°53′W
29 X11 **Calmar** Iowa, C USA 43°10′N 91°51′W
Calmar *see* Kalmar
43 R16 **Calobre** Veraguas, C Panama 08°18′N 80°49′W
23 X14 **Caloosahatchee River** ≈ Florida, SE USA
183 V2 **Caloundra** Queensland, E Australia 26°48′S 153°08′E
Calp *see* Calpe
105 T11 **Calpe** *Cat.* Calp. Valenciana, E Spain 38°39′N 00°03′E
41 P14 **Calpulalpan** Tlaxcala, S Mexico 19°36′N 98°26′W
107 K25 **Caltagirone** Sicilia, Italy, C Mediterranean Sea 37°14′N 14°31′E
107 J24 **Caltanissetta** Sicilia, Italy, C Mediterranean Sea 37°30′N 14°01′E
82 E11 **Caluango** Lunda Norte, NE Angola 08°16′S 19°36′E
82 C12 **Calucinga** Bié, W Angola 11°18′S 16°12′E
82 B12 **Calulo** Cuanza Sul, NW Angola 09°58′S 14°56′E
83 B14 **Caluquembe** Huíla, W Angola 13°47′S 14°40′E
80 Q11 **Caluula** Bari, NE Somalia 11°55′N 50°51′E
102 K4 **Calvados** ◈ *department* N France
186 I10 **Calvados Chain, The** *island group* SE Papua New Guinea
25 U9 **Calvert** Texas, SW USA 30°58′N 96°40′W
20 H7 **Calvert City** Kentucky, S USA 37°01′N 88°21′W
103 X14 **Calvi** Corse, France, C Mediterranean Sea 42°34′N 08°44′E
40 L12 **Calvillo** Aguascalientes, C Mexico 21°51′N 102°18′W
83 F24 **Calvinia** Northern Cape, W South Africa 31°25′S 19°47′E
104 K8 **Calvitero** ▲ W Spain 40°16′N 05°48′W
101 G22 **Calw** Baden-Württemberg, SW Germany 48°43′N 08°43′E
Calydon *see* Kalydón
105 N11 **Calzada de Calatrava** Castilla-La Mancha, C Spain 38°42′N 03°46′W
Cama *see* Kama
82 C11 **Camabatela** Cuanza Norte, NW Angola 08°13′S 15°23′E
64 Q5 **Camacha** Porto Santo, Madeira, Portugal, NE Atlantic Ocean 32°41′N 16°52′W
14 L8 **Camachigama, Lac** ◎ Québec, SE Canada
40 M9 **Camacho** Zacatecas, C Mexico 24°23′N 102°20′W
82 D13 **Camacupa** *var.* General Machado, *Port.* Vila General Machado. Bié, C Angola 12°S 17°31′E
54 L7 **Camaguán** Guárico, C Venezuela 08°09′N 67°37′W
44 G6 **Camagüey** *prev.* Puerto Príncipe. Camagüey, C Cuba 21°24′N 77°55′W
44 G5 **Camagüey, Archipiélago de** *island group* C Cuba
40 D5 **Camalli, Sierra de** ▲ NW Mexico 28°21′N 113°26′W
57 G18 **Camana** *var.* Camaná. Arequipa, SW Peru 16°37′S 72°42′W
29 Z14 **Camanche** Iowa, C USA 41°47′N 90°15′W
35 P8 **Camanche Reservoir** ⊠ California, W USA
61 I16 **Camaquã** Rio Grande do Sul, S Brazil 30°50′S 51°47′W
61 H16 **Camaquã, Rio** ≈ S Brazil
64 P6 **Câmara de Lobos** Madeira, Portugal, NE Atlantic Ocean 32°38′N 16°59′W
103 U16 **Camarat, Cap** *headland* SE France 43°12′N 06°42′E
41 O8 **Camargo** Tamaulipas, C Mexico 26°16′N 98°49′W
103 R15 **Camargue** *physical region* SE France
104 F2 **Camariñas** Galicia, NW Spain 43°07′N 09°10′W
Camaronero, Laguna del *see* Caimanero, Laguna del
63 J18 **Camarones** Chubut, S Argentina 44°48′S 65°42′W
63 J18 **Camarones, Bahía** *bay* S Argentina
104 J14 **Camas** Andalucía, S Spain 37°24′N 06°01′W
167 S15 **Ca Mau** *var.* Quan Long. Minh Hai, S Vietnam 09°11′N 105°09′E
82 E11 **Camaxilo** Lunda Norte, NE Angola 08°19′S 18°53′E
104 G3 **Cambados** Galicia, NW Spain 42°31′N 08°49′W
Cambay, Gulf of *see* Khambhāt, Gulf of
Camberia *see* Chambéry
97 N22 **Camberley** SE England, United Kingdom 51°21′N 00°45′W
167 R12 **Cambodia** *off.* Kingdom of Cambodia, *var.* Democratic Kampuchea, Roat Kampuchea, *Cam.* Kampuchea; *prev.* People's Democratic Republic of Kampuchea. ◆ *republic* SE Asia
Cambodia, Kingdom of *see* Cambodia
102 I16 **Cambo-les-Bains** Pyrénées-Atlantiques, SW France 43°22′N 01°24′W
103 P2 **Cambrai** *Flem.* Kambryk, *prev.* Cambray; *anc.* Cameracum. Nord, N France 50°10′N 03°14′E
Cambray *see* Cambrai
104 H2 **Cambre** Galicia, NW Spain 43°18′N 08°21′W
35 O12 **Cambria** California, W USA 35°33′N 121°04′W
97 J20 **Cambrian Mountains** ▲▲ C Wales, United Kingdom
14 G16 **Cambridge** Ontario, S Canada 43°22′N 80°20′W
44 I12 **Cambridge** W Jamaica 18°18′N 77°54′W
184 M8 **Cambridge** Waikato, North Island, New Zealand 37°53′S 175°28′E
97 O20 **Cambridge** *Lat.* Cantabrigia. E England, United Kingdom 52°12′N 00°07′E
32 M12 **Cambridge** Idaho, NW USA 44°34′N 116°42′W
30 K11 **Cambridge** Illinois, N USA 41°18′N 90°11′W
21 Y4 **Cambridge** Maryland, NE USA 38°34′N 76°04′W
19 O11 **Cambridge** Massachusetts, NE USA 42°21′N 71°05′W
29 V7 **Cambridge** Minnesota, N USA 45°34′N 93°13′W
29 N16 **Cambridge** Nebraska, C USA 40°18′N 100°10′W
31 U13 **Cambridge** Ohio, NE USA 40°00′N 81°34′W
8 L7 **Cambridge Bay** *var.* Ikaluktutiak. Victoria Island, Nunavut, NW Canada 68°56′N 105°09′W
97 O20 **Cambridgeshire** *cultural region* E England, United Kingdom
105 U6 **Cambrils** *prev.* Cambrils de Mar. Cataluña, NE Spain 41°06′N 01°02′E
Cambrils de Mar *see* Cambrils
Cambundi-Catembo *see* Nova Gaia
137 N11 **Çam Burnu** *headland* N Turkey 41°07′N 37°48′E
183 S9 **Camden** New South Wales, SE Australia 34°04′S 150°40′E
23 O6 **Camden** Alabama, S USA 31°59′N 87°17′W
27 U14 **Camden** Arkansas, C USA 33°32′N 92°49′W
21 Y3 **Camden** Delaware, NE USA 39°06′N 75°30′W
19 R7 **Camden** Maine, NE USA 44°12′N 69°04′W
18 I16 **Camden** New Jersey, NE USA 39°55′N 75°07′W
18 I9 **Camden** New York, NE USA 43°21′N 75°45′W
21 R12 **Camden** South Carolina, SE USA 34°16′N 80°36′W
20 H8 **Camden** Tennessee, S USA 36°03′N 88°07′W
25 X9 **Camden** Texas, SW USA 30°55′N 94°43′W
39 S5 **Camden Bay** *bay* S Beaufort Sea
27 U6 **Camdenton** Missouri, C USA 38°01′N 92°44′W
Camellia State *see* Alabama
18 M7 **Camels Hump** ▲ Vermont, NE USA 44°18′N 72°50′W
117 N8 **Camenca** *Rus.* Kamenka. N Moldova 48°01′N 28°43′E
Cameracum *see* Cambrai
22 G9 **Cameron** Louisiana, S USA 29°48′N 93°19′W
25 T9 **Cameron** Texas, SW USA 30°51′N 96°58′W
30 J5 **Cameron** Wisconsin, N USA 45°25′N 91°42′W
10 M12 **Cameron** ≈ British Columbia, W Canada
185 A24 **Cameron Mountains** ▲▲ South Island, New Zealand
79 D15 **Cameroon** *off.* Republic of Cameroon, *Fr.* Cameroun. ◆ *republic* W Africa
79 D15 **Cameroon Mountain** ▲ SW Cameroon 04°12′N 09°00′E
Cameroon, Republic of *see* Cameroon
Cameroon Ridge *see* Camerounaise, Dorsale
Cameroun *see* Cameroon
79 E14 **Camerounaise, Dorsale** *Eng.* Cameroon Ridge. *ridge* NW Cameroon
136 B15 **Çamiçi Gölü** ◎ SW Turkey
171 N3 **Camiling** Luzon, N Philippines 15°41′N 120°22′E
23 T7 **Camilla** Georgia, SE USA 31°13′N 84°12′W
104 G5 **Caminha** Viana do Castelo, N Portugal 41°52′N 08°50′W
35 P7 **Camino** California, W USA 38°43′N 120°39′W
107 J24 **Cammarata** Sicilia, Italy, C Mediterranean Sea 37°36′N 13°39′E
42 K10 **Camoapa** Boaco, S Nicaragua 12°25′N 85°30′W
58 O13 **Camocim** Ceará, E Brazil 02°55′S 40°50′W
106 D10 **Camogli** Liguria, NW Italy 44°21′N 09°10′E
181 S5 **Camooweal** Queensland, C Australia 19°57′S 138°14′E
55 Y11 **Camopi** E French Guiana 03°12′N 52°19′W
151 Q22 **Camorta** *island* Nicobar Islands, India, NE Indian Ocean
42 I6 **Campamento** Olancho, C Honduras 14°36′N 86°38′W
61 D19 **Campana** Buenos Aires, E Argentina 34°10′S 58°57′W
63 F21 **Campana, Isla** *island* S Chile
104 K11 **Campanario** Extremadura, W Spain 38°52′N 05°36′W
107 L17 **Campania** *Eng.* Champagne. ◈ *region* S Italy
27 Y8 **Campbell** Missouri, C USA 36°29′N 90°04′W
185 K15 **Campbell, Cape** *headland* South Island, New Zealand 41°44′S 174°16′E
14 J14 **Campbellford** Ontario, SE Canada 44°18′N 77°48′W
31 R13 **Campbell Hill** *hill* Ohio, N USA
192 K13 **Campbell Island** *island* S New Zealand
175 P13 **Campbell Plateau** *undersea feature* SW Pacific Ocean 51°00′S 170°00′E
10 K17 **Campbell River** Vancouver Island, British Columbia, SW Canada 49°59′N 125°18′W
20 L6 **Campbellsville** Kentucky, S USA 37°20′N 85°21′W
13 O13 **Campbellton** New Brunswick, SE Canada 48°00′N 66°41′W
183 S9 **Campbelltown** New South Wales, SE Australia 34°04′S 150°46′E
183 P16 **Campbell Town** Tasmania, SE Australia 41°57′S 147°30′E
96 G13 **Campbeltown** W Scotland, United Kingdom 55°26′N 05°38′W
41 W13 **Campeche** Campeche, SE Mexico 19°47′N 90°29′W
41 W14 **Campeche** ◈ *state* SE Mexico
41 T14 **Campeche, Bahía de** *Eng.* Bay of Campeche. *bay* E Mexico
Campeche, Banco de *see* Campeche Bank
64 C11 **Campeche Bank** *Sp.* Banco de Campeche, Sonda de Campeche. *undersea feature* S Gulf of Mexico 22°00′N 90°00′W
Campeche, Bay of *see* Campeche, Bahía de
Campeche, Sonda de *see* Campeche Bank
44 H7 **Campechuela** Granma, E Cuba 20°15′N 77°17′W
182 M13 **Camperdown** Victoria, SE Australia 38°16′S 143°10′E
167 U6 **Câm Pha** Quang Ninh, N Vietnam 21°04′N 107°20′E
116 H10 **Câmpia Turzii** *Ger.* Jerischmarkt, *Hung.* Aranyosgyéres; *prev.* Cîmpia Turzii, Ghiriş, Gyéres. Cluj, NW Romania 46°33′N 23°53′E
104 K12 **Campillo de Llerena** Extremadura, W Spain 38°30′N 05°48′W
104 L15 **Campillos** Andalucía, S Spain 37°04′N 04°51′W
116 J13 **Câmpina** *prev.* Cîmpina. Prahova, SE Romania 45°08′N 25°44′E
59 Q15 **Campina Grande** Paraíba, E Brazil 07°15′S 35°50′W
60 L9 **Campinas** São Paulo, S Brazil 22°54′S 47°06′W
38 L10 **Camp Kulowiye** Saint Lawrence Island, Alaska, USA 63°15′N 168°45′W
79 D17 **Campo** *var.* Kampo. Sud, SW Cameroon 02°22′N 09°50′E
Campo *see* Ntem
59 N15 **Campo Alegre de Lourdes** Bahia, E Brazil 09°28′S 43°01′W
107 L16 **Campobasso** Molise, C Italy 41°34′N 14°40′E
107 H24 **Campobello di Mazara** Sicilia, Italy, C Mediterranean Sea 37°38′N 12°45′E
Campo Criptana *see* Campo de Criptana
105 O10 **Campo de Criptana** *var.* Campo Criptana. Castilla-La Mancha, C Spain 39°25′N 03°07′W
59 I16 **Campo de Diauarum** *var.* Pôsto Diuarum. Mato Grosso, W Brazil 11°08′S 53°16′W
54 E5 **Campo de la Cruz** Atlántico, N Colombia 10°23′N 74°52′W
105 P11 **Campo de Montiel** *physical region* C Spain
60 H12 **Campo Erê** Santa Catarina, S Brazil 26°24′S 53°04′W
62 L7 **Campo Gallo** Santiago del Estero, N Argentina 26°32′S 62°51′W
59 I20 **Campo Grande** *state capital* Mato Grosso do Sul, SW Brazil 20°24′S 54°35′W
60 K12 **Campo Largo** Paraná, S Brazil 25°27′S 49°29′W
58 N13 **Campo Maior** Piauí, E Brazil 04°50′S 42°12′W
104 I10 **Campo Maior** Portalegre, C Portugal 39°01′N 07°04′W
60 H10 **Campo Mourão** Paraná, S Brazil 24°01′S 52°24′W
59 L17 **Campos Belos** Goiás, S Brazil 13°11′S 46°47′W
60 N9 **Campos do Jordão** São Paulo, S Brazil 22°45′S 45°36′W
60 Q9 **Campos dos Goytacazes** Rio de Janeiro, SE Brazil 21°46′S 41°21′W
60 I13 **Campos Novos** Santa Catarina, S Brazil 27°22′S 51°11′W
59 O14 **Campos Sales** Ceará, E Brazil 07°01′S 40°21′W
25 Q9 **Camp San Saba** Texas, SW USA 30°57′N 99°16′W
21 N6 **Campton** Kentucky, S USA 37°44′N 83°35′W
116 I13 **Câmpulung** *prev.* Câmpulung-Muşcel, Cîmpulung. Argeş, S Romania 45°16′N 25°03′E
116 J9 **Câmpulung Moldovenesc** *var.* Cîmpulung Moldovenesc, *Ger.* Kimpolung, *Hung.* Hosszúmezjő. Suceava, NE Romania 47°32′N 25°34′E
Câmpulung-Muşcel *see* Câmpulung
Campus Stellae *see* Santiago de Compostela
36 L12 **Camp Verde** Arizona, SW USA 34°33′N 111°52′W
25 P11 **Camp Wood** Texas, SW USA 29°40′N 100°00′W
167 V13 **Cam Ranh** *prev.* Ba Ngoi. Khanh Hoa, S Vietnam 11°54′N 109°14′E
11 Q15 **Camrose** Alberta, SW Canada 53°01′N 112°48′W
Camulodunum *see* Colchester
136 B12 **Çan** Çanakkale, NW Turkey 40°03′N 27°03′E
18 L12 **Canaan** Connecticut, NE USA 42°00′N 73°17′W
11 O13 **Canada** ◆ *commonwealth republic* N North America
197 P6 **Canada Basin** *undersea feature* Arctic Ocean 80°00′N 145°00′W
61 B18 **Cañada de Gómez** Santa Fe, C Argentina 32°50′S 61°23′W
197 P6 **Canada Plain** *undersea feature* Arctic Ocean
61 A18 **Cañada Rosquín** Santa Fe, C Argentina 32°04′S 61°35′W
25 P1 **Canadian** Texas, SW USA 35°54′N 100°23′W
16 K12 **Canadian River** ≈ SW USA
8 L12 **Canadian Shield** *physical region* Canada
63 I18 **Cañadón Grande, Sierra** ▲▲ S Argentina
55 P9 **Canaima** Bolívar, SE Venezuela 09°41′N 72°33′W
136 B11 **Çanakkale** *var.* Dardanelli; *prev.* Chanak, Kale Sultanie. Çanakkale, W Turkey 40°09′N 26°25′E
136 B12 **Çanakkale** ◈ *province* NW Turkey
136 B11 **Çanakkale Boğazı** *Eng.* Dardanelles. *strait* NW Turkey
187 Q17 **Canala** Province Nord, C New Caledonia 21°31′S 165°57′E
59 A15 **Canamari** Amazonas, W Brazil 07°37′S 72°33′W
18 G10 **Canandaigua** New York, NE USA 42°52′N 77°14′W
18 F10 **Canandaigua Lake** ◎ New York, NE USA
40 G3 **Cananea** Sonora, NW Mexico 30°59′N 110°20′W
56 B8 **Cañar** ◈ *province* C Ecuador
64 N10 **Canarias, Islas** *Eng.* Canary Islands. ◈ *autonomous community* Spain, NE Atlantic Ocean
Canaries Basin *see* Canary Basin
44 C6 **Canarreos, Archipiélago de los** *island group* W Cuba
Canary Islands *see* Canarias, Islas
66 K3 **Canary Basin** *var.* Canaries Basin, Monaco Basin. *undersea feature* E Atlantic Ocean 30°00′N 25°00′W
42 L13 **Cañas** Guanacaste, NW Costa Rica 10°25′N 85°07′W
18 I10 **Canastota** New York, NE USA 43°04′N 75°45′W
40 K9 **Canatlán** Durango, C Mexico 24°33′N 104°45′W
104 J9 **Cañaveral** Extremadura, W Spain 39°47′N 06°24′W
23 Y11 **Canaveral, Cape** *headland* Florida, SE USA 28°27′N 80°31′W
59 O18 **Canavieiras** Bahia, E Brazil 15°44′S 38°58′W
43 R16 **Cañazas** Veraguas, W Panama 08°25′N 81°10′W
106 H6 **Canazei** Trentino-Alto Adige, N Italy 46°29′N 11°50′E
183 P6 **Canbelego** New South Wales, SE Australia 31°36′S 146°20′E
183 R10 **Canberra** ● (Australia) Australian Capital Territory, SE Australia 35°21′S 149°08′E
183 R10 **Canberra** ✈ Australian Capital Territory, SE Australia 35°19′S 149°12′E
35 P2 **Canby** California, W USA 41°27′N 120°51′W
29 S9 **Canby** Minnesota, N USA 44°42′N 96°17′W
103 N2 **Canche** ≈ N France
102 L13 **Cancon** Lot-et-Garonne, SW France 44°33′N 00°37′E
41 Z11 **Cancún** Quintana Roo, SE Mexico 21°05′N 86°48′W
104 K2 **Candás** Asturias, N Spain 43°35′N 05°45′W
102 J7 **Cande** Maine-et-Loire, NW France 47°33′N 01°03′W
41 W14 **Candelaria** Campeche, SE Mexico 18°10′N 91°00′W
24 J11 **Candelaria** Texas, SW USA 30°05′N 104°40′W
41 W15 **Candelaria, Río** ≈ Guatemala/Mexico
104 L8 **Candeleda** Castilla y León, N Spain 40°10′N 05°14′W
Candia *see* Irákleio
41 P8 **Cándido Aguilar** Tamaulipas, C Mexico 25°30′N 97°57′W
39 N8 **Candle** Alaska, USA 65°54′N 161°55′W
11 T14 **Candle Lake** Saskatchewan, C Canada 53°43′N 105°09′W
18 L13 **Candlewood, Lake** ⊠ Connecticut, NE USA
29 O3 **Cando** North Dakota, N USA 48°29′N 99°12′W
Canea *see* Chaniá
45 O12 **Canefield** ✈ (Roseau) SW Dominica 15°20′N 61°24′W
61 F20 **Canelones** *prev.* Guadalupe. Canelones, S Uruguay 34°32′S 56°17′W
61 E20 **Canelones** ◈ *department* S Uruguay
Canendiyú *see* Canindeyú
63 F14 **Cañete** Bío Bío, C Chile 37°48′S 73°25′W
105 Q9 **Cañete** Castilla-La Mancha, C Spain 40°03′N 01°39′W
Cañete *see* San Vicente de Cañete
27 P8 **Caney** Kansas, C USA 37°00′N 95°56′W
27 P8 **Caney River** ≈ Kansas/Oklahoma, C USA
105 S3 **Canfranc-Estación** Aragón, NE Spain 42°42′N 00°31′W
83 E14 **Cangamba** *Port.* Vila de Aljustrel. Moxico, E Angola 13°40′S 19°47′E
82 C12 **Cangandala** Malanje, NW Angola 09°47′S 16°27′E
104 G4 **Cangas** Galicia, NW Spain 42°16′N 08°46′W
104 J2 **Cangas del Narcea** Asturias, N Spain 43°10′N 06°32′W
Cangas de Onís *see* Cangues d'Onís
161 S11 **Cangnan** *var.* Lingxi. Zhejiang, SE China 27°29′N 120°23′E
82 C10 **Cangola** Uíge, NW Angola 07°54′S 15°57′E
83 E14 **Cangombe** Moxico, E Angola 14°27′S 20°05′E
63 H21 **Cangrejo, Cerro** ▲ S Argentina 49°19′S 72°18′W
61 H17 **Canguçu** Rio Grande do Sul, S Brazil 31°25′S 52°37′W
104 L2 **Cangues d'Onís** *var.* Cangas de Onís. Asturias, N Spain 43°21′N 05°08′W
161 P3 **Cangzhou** Hebei, E China 38°19′N 116°54′E
12 M7 **Caniapiscau** ≈ Québec, E Canada
12 M8 **Caniapiscau, Réservoir de** ⊠ Québec, C Canada
107 J24 **Canicattì** Sicilia, Italy, C Mediterranean Sea 37°22′N 13°51′E
136 L11 **Canik Dağları** ▲▲ N Turkey
105 P14 **Caniles** Andalucía, S Spain 37°24′N 02°41′W
59 B16 **Canindé** Acre, W Brazil 10°55′S 69°45′W
62 P6 **Canindeyú** *var.* Canendiyú, Canindiyú. ◈ *department* E Paraguay
Canindiyú *see* Canindeyú
194 J10 **Canisteo Peninsula** *peninsula* Antarctica
18 F11 **Canisteo River** ≈ New York, NE USA
40 M10 **Cañitas** *var.* Cañitas de Felipe Pescador. Zacatecas, C Mexico 23°35′N 102°39′W
Cañitas de Felipe Pescador *see* Cañitas
105 P15 **Canjáyar** Andalucía, S Spain 37°00′N 02°45′W

◆ Country
● Country Capital
◇ Dependent Territory
○ Dependent Territory Capital
◈ Administrative Regions
✈ International Airport
▲ Mountain
▲▲ Mountain Range
Volcano
≈ River
◎ Lake
⊠ Reservoir

136 I12 **Çankırı** *var.* Chankiri; *anc.* Gangra, Germanicopolis. Çankın, N Turkey 40°36′N 33°35′E
136 I11 **Çankırı** *var.* Chankiri. ⬖ *province* N Turkey
171 P6 **Canlaon Volcano** ⛰ Negros, C Philippines 10°24′N 123°05′E
11 P16 **Canmore** Alberta, SW Canada 51°07′N 115°18′W
96 F9 **Canna** *island* NW Scotland, United Kingdom
155 F20 **Cannanore** *var.* Kannur, Jagatsinghapur. Kerala, SW India 11°53′N 75°23′E *see also* Kannur
31 O17 **Cannelton** Indiana, N USA 37°54′N 86°44′W
103 U15 **Cannes** Alpes-Maritimes, SE France 43°33′N 06°59′E
39 R5 **Canning River** ≈ Alaska, USA
106 C6 **Cannobio** Piemonte, NE Italy 46°04′N 08°39′E
97 L19 **Cannock** C England, United Kingdom 52°41′N 02°03′W
28 M6 **Cannonball River** ≈ North Dakota, N USA
29 W9 **Cannon Falls** Minnesota, N USA 44°30′N 92°54′W
18 I11 **Cannonsville Reservoir** ▣ New York, NE USA
183 R12 **Cann River** Victoria, SE Australia 37°34′S 149°11′E
61 I16 **Canoas** Rio Grande do Sul, S Brazil 29°42′S 51°07′W
61 I14 **Canoas, Rio** ≈ S Brazil
14 I12 **Canoe Lake** ◎ Ontario, SE Canada
60 J12 **Canoinhas** Santa Catarina, S Brazil 26°12′S 50°24′W
37 T6 **Canon City** Colorado, C USA 38°25′N 105°14′W
55 P8 **Caño Negro** Bolívar, SE Venezuela
173 X15 **Canonniers Point** *headland* N Mauritius
23 W6 **Canoochee River** ≈ Georgia, SE USA
11 V15 **Canora** Saskatchewan, S Canada 51°38′N 102°28′W
45 Y14 **Canouan** *island* S Saint Vincent and the Grenadines
13 R15 **Canso** Nova Scotia, SE Canada 45°20′N 61°00′W
104 M3 **Cantabria** ⬖ *autonomous community* N Spain
104 K3 **Cantábrica, Cordillera** ▲▲ N Spain
Cantabrigia *see* Cambridge
103 O12 **Cantal** ⬖ *department* C France
105 N6 **Cantalejo** Castilla y León, N Spain 41°15′N 03°57′W
103 O12 **Cantal, Monts du** ▲▲ C France
104 G8 **Cantanhede** Coimbra, C Portugal 40°21′N 08°37′W
Cantaño *see* Cataño
55 O6 **Cantaura** Anzoátegui, NE Venezuela 09°22′N 64°24′W
116 M11 **Cantemir** *Rus.* Kantemir. S Moldova 46°17′N 28°12′E
97 Q22 **Canterbury** *hist.* Cantwaraburh; *anc.* Durovernum, *Lat.* Cantuaria. SE England, United Kingdom 51°17′N 01°05′E
185 F19 **Canterbury** *off.* Canterbury Region. ⬖ *region* South Island, New Zealand
185 H20 **Canterbury Bight** *bight* South Island, New Zealand
185 H19 **Canterbury Plains** *plain* South Island, New Zealand
Canterbury Region *see* Canterbury
167 S14 **Cân Thơ** Cân Thơ, S Vietnam 10°03′N 105°46′E
104 K13 **Cantillana** Andalucía, S Spain 37°34′N 05°48′W
59 N15 **Canto do Buriti** Piauí, NE Brazil 08°07′S 43°00′W
23 S2 **Canton** Georgia, SE USA 34°14′N 84°29′W
30 K12 **Canton** Illinois, N USA 40°33′N 90°02′W
22 L5 **Canton** Mississippi, S USA 32°36′N 90°02′W
27 V2 **Canton** Missouri, C USA 40°07′N 91°31′W
18 J7 **Canton** New York, NE USA 44°36′N 75°10′W
21 O10 **Canton** North Carolina, SE USA 35°31′N 82°50′W
31 U12 **Canton** Ohio, N USA 40°48′N 81°23′W
26 L9 **Canton** Oklahoma, C USA 36°03′N 98°35′W
18 G12 **Canton** Pennsylvania, NE USA 41°38′N 76°49′W
29 R11 **Canton** South Dakota, N USA 43°19′N 96°33′W
25 V7 **Canton** Texas, SW USA 32°33′N 95°51′W
Canton *see* Guangzhou
Canton Island *see* Kanton
26 L9 **Canton Lake** ▣ Oklahoma, C USA
106 D7 **Cantù** Lombardia, N Italy 45°44′N 09°98′E
Cantuaria/Cantwaraburh *see* Canterbury
39 R10 **Cantwell** Alaska, USA 63°23′N 148°57′W
59 O16 **Canudos** Bahia, E Brazil 09°51′S 39°08′W
47 T7 **Canumã, Rio** ≈ N Brazil
Canusium *see* Puglia, Canosa di
24 G7 **Canutillo** Texas, SW USA 31°53′N 106°34′W
25 N3 **Canyon** Texas, SW USA 34°58′N 101°56′W
33 S12 **Canyon** Wyoming, C USA 44°44′N 110°30′W
32 K13 **Canyon City** Oregon, NW USA 44°24′N 118°58′W
33 R10 **Canyon Ferry Lake** ◎ Montana, NW USA
25 S11 **Canyon Lake** ▣ Texas, SW USA
167 T5 **Cao Băng** *var.* Caobang. Cao Băng, N Vietnam 22°40′N 106°16′E
Caobang *see* Cao Băng
160 J12 **Caodu He** ≈ S China
Caohai *see* Weining
167 S14 **Cao Lanh** Đông Thap, S Vietnam 10°35′N 105°25′E
82 C11 **Caombo** Malanje, NW Angola 08°42′S 16°33′E
Caorach, Cuan na g *see* Sheep Haven
Caozhou *see* Heze
171 Q12 **Capalulu** Pulau Mangole, E Indonesia 01°51′S 125°53′E
54 K8 **Capanaparo, Río** ≈ Colomiba/Venezuela
58 L12 **Capanema** Pará, NE Brazil 01°08′S 47°07′W
60 L10 **Capão Bonito do Sul** São Paulo, S Brazil 24°01′S 48°23′W
60 I13 **Capão Doce, Morro do** ▲ S Brazil 26°37′S 51°28′W
54 I4 **Capatárida** Falcón, N Venezuela 11°11′N 70°37′W
102 I15 **Capbreton** Landes, SW France 43°40′N 01°25′W
Cap-Breton, Île du *see* Cape Breton Island
15 W6 **Cap-Chat** Québec, SE Canada 49°04′N 66°43′W
15 P11 **Cap-de-la-Madeleine** Québec, SE Canada 46°22′N 72°31′W
103 N13 **Capdenac** Aveyron, S France 44°35′N 02°06′E
Cap des Palmès *see* Palmas, Cape
183 Q15 **Cape Barren Island** *island* Furneaux Group, Tasmania, SE Australia
65 O18 **Cape Basin** *undersea feature* S Atlantic Ocean 37°00′S 07°00′E
13 R14 **Cape Breton Island** *Fr.* Île du Cap-Breton. *island* Nova Scotia, SE Canada
23 Y11 **Cape Canaveral** Florida, SE USA 28°24′N 80°36′W
21 Y6 **Cape Charles** Virginia, NE USA 37°16′N 76°01′W
77 P17 **Cape Coast** *prev.* Cape Coast Castle. S Ghana 05°10′N 01°13′W
Cape Coast Castle *see* Cape Coast
19 Q12 **Cape Cod Bay** *bay* Massachusetts, NE USA
23 W15 **Cape Coral** Florida, SE USA 26°33′N 81°57′W
181 R4 **Cape Crawford Roadhouse** Northern Territory, N Australia 16°39′S 135°44′E
9 Q7 **Cape Dorset** *var.* Kingait. Baffin Island, Nunavut, NE Canada 76°14′N 76°32′W
21 N8 **Cape Fear River** ≈ North Carolina, SE USA
27 Y7 **Cape Girardeau** Missouri, C USA 37°19′N 89°31′W
21 T14 **Cape Island** *island* South Carolina, SE USA
186 A6 **Capella** ▲ NW Papua New Guinea 05°00′S 141°09′E
98 H12 **Capelle aan den IJssel** Zuid-Holland, SW Netherlands 51°56′N 04°36′E
83 C15 **Capelongo** Huíla, C Angola 14°45′S 15°02′E
18 J17 **Cape May** New Jersey, NE USA 38°54′N 74°54′W
18 J17 **Cape May Court House** New Jersey, NE USA 39°03′N 74°46′W
Cape Palmas *see* Harper
8 I16 **Cape Parry** Northwest Territories, N Canada 70°10′N 124°33′W
65 P19 **Cape Rise** *undersea feature* SW Indian Ocean 42°00′S 15°00′E
Cape Saint Jacques *see* Vung Tau
Capesterre *see* Capesterre-Belle-Eau
45 Y6 **Capesterre-Belle-Eau** *var.* Capesterre. Basse Terre, S Guadeloupe 16°03′N 61°34′W
83 D26 **Cape Town** *var.* Ekapa, *Afr.* Kaapstad, Kapstad. ● (South Africa-legislative capital) Western Cape, SW South Africa 33°56′S 18°28′E
83 E26 **Cape Town** ✈ Western Cape, SW South Africa 31°51′S 21°06′E
76 D9 **Cape Verde** *off.* Republic of Cape Verde, *Port.* Cabo Verde, Ilhas do Cabo Verde. ◆ *republic* E Atlantic Ocean
64 L11 **Cape Verde Basin** *undersea feature* E Atlantic Ocean 15°00′N 30°00′W
66 K5 **Cape Verde Islands** *island group* E Atlantic Ocean
64 L10 **Cape Verde Plain** *undersea feature* E Atlantic Ocean 23°00′N 26°00′W
Cape Verde Plateau/Cape Verde Rise *see* Cape Verde Terrace
Cape Verde, Republic of *see* Cape Verde
64 L11 **Cape Verde Terrace** *var.* Cape Verde Plateau, Cape Verde Rise. *undersea feature* E Atlantic Ocean 18°00′N 20°00′W
181 V2 **Cape York Peninsula** *peninsula* Queensland, N Australia
44 M8 **Cap-Haïtien** *var.* Le Cap. N Haiti 19°44′N 72°12′W
43 T15 **Capira** Panamá, C Panama 08°48′N 79°51′W
14 K8 **Capitachouane** ≈ Québec, SE Canada
14 L8 **Capitachouane, Lac** ◎ Québec, SE Canada
37 T13 **Capitan** New Mexico, SW USA 33°33′N 105°34′W
194 G3 **Capitán Arturo Prat** *Chilean research station* South Shetland Islands, Antarctica 62°24′S 59°42′W
37 S13 **Capitan Mountains** ▲▲ New Mexico, SW USA
62 M3 **Capitán Pablo Lagerenza** *var.* Mayor Pablo Lagerenza. Chaco, N Paraguay 19°55′S 60°46′W
37 T13 **Capitan Peak** ▲ New Mexico, SW USA 33°35′N 105°15′W
188 H5 **Capitol Hill** ● (Northern Mariana Islands-legislative capital) Saipan, S Northern Mariana Islands
60 I9 **Capivara, Represa** ▣ S Brazil
61 J16 **Capivari** Rio Grande do Sul, S Brazil 30°08′S 50°32′W
113 H15 **Čapljina** Federicija Bosna I Hercegovina, S Bosnia and Herzegovina 43°07′N 17°42′E
83 M15 **Capoche** *var.* Kapoche. ≈ Mozambique/Zambia
Capo Delgado, Província de *see* Cabo Delgado
107 K17 **Capodichino** ✈ (Napoli) Campania, S Italy 40°53′N 14°15′E
Capodistria *see* Koper
106 E12 **Capraia, Isola di** *island* Arcipelago Toscano, C Italy
107 B16 **Caprara, Punta** *var.* Punta dello Scorno. *headland* Isola Asinara, W Italy 41°07′N 08°19′E
Capraria *see* Cabrera, Illa de
14 F10 **Capreol** Ontario, S Canada 46°43′N 80°56′W
107 K18 **Capri** Campania, S Italy 40°33′N 14°14′E
175 S9 **Capricorn Tablemount** *undersea feature* W Pacific Ocean 18°34′S 172°12′W
107 J18 **Capri, Isola di** *island* S Italy
83 G16 **Caprivi** ⬖ *district* NE Namibia
Caprivi Concession *see* Caprivi Strip
83 F16 **Caprivi Strip** *Ger.* Caprivizipfel; *prev.* Caprivi Concession. *cultural region* NE Namibia
Caprivizipfel *see* Caprivi Strip
25 O5 **Cap Rock Escarpment** *cliffs* Texas, SW USA
15 R10 **Cap-Rouge** Québec, SE Canada 46°45′N 71°18′W
Cap Saint-Jacques *see* Vung Tau
38 F12 **Captain Cook** Hawaii, USA, C Pacific Ocean 19°30′N 155°55′W
183 R10 **Captains Flat** New South Wales, SE Australia 35°37′S 149°28′E
102 K14 **Captieux** Gironde, SW France 44°16′N 00°15′W
107 K17 **Capua** Campania, S Italy 41°06′N 14°13′E
54 F14 **Caquetá** *off.* Departamanto del Caquetá. ⬖ *province* S Colombia
Caquetá, Departamanto del *see* Caquetá
54 E13 **Caquetá, Río** *var.* Rio Japurá, Yapurá. ≈ Brazil/Colombia *see also* Japurá, Rio
Caquetá, Río *see* Japurá, Rio
CAR *see* Central African Republic
Cara *see* Kara
57 I16 **Carabaya, Cordillera** ▲▲ E Peru
54 K5 **Carabobo** *off.* Estado Carabobo. ⬖ *state* N Venezuela
Carabobo, Estado *see* Carabobo
116 I14 **Caracal** Olt, S Romania 44°07′N 24°18′E
58 F10 **Caracaraí** Rondônia, W Brazil 01°47′N 61°11′W
54 L5 **Caracas** ● (Venezuela) Distrito Federal, N Venezuela 10°29′N 66°54′W
54 I5 **Carache** Trujillo, N Venezuela 09°40′N 70°15′W
60 N10 **Caraguatatuba** São Paulo, S Brazil 23°37′S 45°24′W
48 I7 **Carajás, Serra dos** ▲▲ N Brazil
Caralis *see* Cagliari
54 E9 **Caramanta** Antioquia, W Colombia 05°36′N 75°38′W
171 P4 **Caramoan** Catanduanes Island, N Philippines 13°47′N 123°49′E
Caramurat *see* Mihail Kogălniceanu
116 F12 **Caransebeş** *Ger.* Karansebesch, *Hung.* Karánsebes. Caraş-Severin, SW Romania 45°23′N 22°13′E
Carapella *see* Carapelle
107 M16 **Carapelle** *var.* Carapella. ≈ SE Italy
55 O9 **Carapo** Bolívar, SE Venezuela
13 P13 **Caraquet** New Brunswick, SE Canada 47°48′N 64°59′W
Caras *see* Caraz
116 F12 **Caraşova** *Hung.* Krassóvár. Caraş-Severin, SW Romania 45°11′N 21°51′E
116 F12 **Caraş-Severin** ⬖ *county* SW Romania
42 M5 **Caratasca, Laguna de** *lagoon* NE Honduras
58 C13 **Carauari** Amazonas, NW Brazil 04°55′S 66°57′W
Caravaca *see* Caravaca de la Cruz
105 Q12 **Caravaca de la Cruz** *var.* Caravaca. Murcia, SE Spain 38°06′N 01°51′W
106 E7 **Caravaggio** Lombardia, N Italy 45°31′N 09°39′E
107 C18 **Caravai, Passo di** *pass* Sardegna, Italy, C Mediterranean Sea
59 O19 **Caravelas** Bahia, E Brazil 17°45′S 39°15′W
56 C12 **Caraz** *var.* Caras. Ancash, W Peru 09°03′S 77°47′W
61 H14 **Carazinho** Rio Grande do Sul, S Brazil 28°16′S 52°46′W
42 J11 **Carazo** ⬖ *department* SW Nicaragua
Carballiño *see* O Carballiño
104 G2 **Carballo** Galicia, NW Spain 43°13′N 08°41′W
11 W16 **Carberry** Manitoba, S Canada 49°52′N 99°20′W
40 F4 **Carbó** Sonora, NW Mexico 29°41′N 111°00′W
107 C20 **Carbonara, Capo** *headland* Sardegna, Italy, C Mediterranean Sea 39°06′N 09°31′E
37 Q5 **Carbondale** Colorado, C USA 39°24′N 107°12′W
30 L17 **Carbondale** Illinois, N USA 37°43′N 89°13′W
27 Q4 **Carbondale** Kansas, C USA 38°49′N 95°41′W
18 I13 **Carbondale** Pennsylvania, NE USA 41°34′N 75°30′W
13 V12 **Carbonear** Newfoundland, Newfoundland and Labrador, SE Canada 47°45′N 53°16′W
105 Q9 **Carboneras de Guadazaón** *var.* Carboneras de Guadazón. Castilla-La Mancha, C Spain 39°54′N 01°50′W
Carboneras de Guadazón *see* Carboneras de Guadazaón
23 O3 **Carbon Hill** Alabama, S USA 33°53′N 87°31′W
107 B20 **Carbonia** *var.* Carbonia Centro. Sardegna, Italy, C Mediterranean Sea 39°11′N 08°31′E
Carbonia Centro *see* Carbonia
63 I22 **Carbon, Laguna del** *depression* S Argentina 49°34′S 68°21′W
105 S10 **Carcaixent** Valenciana, E Spain 39°08′N 00°28′W
Carcaso *see* Carcassonne
65 B24 **Carcass Island** *island* NW Falkland Islands
103 O16 **Carcassonne** *anc.* Carcaso. Aude, S France 43°13′N 02°21′E
105 R12 **Carche** ▲ S Spain 38°24′N 01°11′W
56 A13 **Carchi** ⬖ *province* N Ecuador
10 I8 **Carcross** Yukon Territory, W Canada 60°11′N 134°41′W
Cardamomes, Chaîne des *see* Krâvanh, Chuŏr Phnum
155 G22 **Cardamom Hills** ▲▲ SW India
Cardamom Mountains *see* Krâvanh, Chuŏr Phnum
104 M12 **Cardeña** Andalucía, S Spain 38°16′N 04°20′W
44 D4 **Cárdenas** Matanzas, W Cuba 23°02′N 81°12′W
41 O11 **Cárdenas** San Luis Potosí, C Mexico 22°03′N 99°30′W
41 U15 **Cárdenas** Tabasco, SE Mexico 18°00′N 93°21′W
63 H21 **Cardiel, Lago** ◎ S Argentina
97 K22 **Cardiff** *Wel.* Caerdydd. ◐ S Wales, United Kingdom 51°30′N 03°13′W
97 J22 **Cardiff-Wales** ✈ S Wales, United Kingdom 51°24′N 03°22′W
97 I21 **Cardigan** *Wel.* Aberteifi. SW Wales, United Kingdom 52°06′N 04°40′W
97 I20 **Cardigan** *cultural region* W Wales, United Kingdom
97 I20 **Cardigan Bay** *bay* W Wales, United Kingdom
19 N8 **Cardigan, Mount** ▲ New Hampshire, NE USA 43°39′N 71°52′W
14 M13 **Cardinal** Ontario, SE Canada 44°48′N 75°22′W
105 V5 **Cardona** Cataluña, NE Spain 41°55′N 01°41′E
61 E19 **Cardona** Soriano, SW Uruguay 33°53′S 57°18′W
105 V4 **Cardoner** ≈ NE Spain
11 Q17 **Cardston** Alberta, SW Canada 49°14′N 113°19′W
181 W5 **Cardwell** Queensland, NE Australia 18°24′S 146°06′E
116 G8 **Carei** *Ger.* Gross-Karol, Karol, *Hung.* Nagykároly; *prev.* Careii-Mari. Satu Mare, NW Romania 47°40′N 22°28′E
Careii-Mari *see* Carei
58 F13 **Careiro** Amazonas, NW Brazil 03°40′S 60°23′W
102 J4 **Carentan** Manche, N France 49°18′N 01°15′W
104 M2 **Cares** ≈ N Spain
33 P14 **Carey** Idaho, NW USA 43°17′N 113°58′W
31 S12 **Carey** Ohio, N USA 40°57′N 83°22′W
25 P4 **Carey** Texas, SW USA 34°28′N 100°18′W
180 L11 **Carey, Lake** ◎ Western Australia
173 O8 **Cargados Carajos Bank** *undersea feature* C Indian Ocean
102 G6 **Carhaix-Plouguer** Finistère, NW France 48°16′N 03°35′W
61 A22 **Carhué** Buenos Aires, E Argentina 37°10′S 62°45′W
55 O5 **Cariaco** Sucre, NE Venezuela 10°33′N 63°37′W
107 O20 **Cariati** Calabria, SW Italy 39°30′N 16°57′E
2 H17 **Caribbean Plate** *tectonic feature*
44 I11 **Caribbean Sea** *sea* W Atlantic Ocean
11 N15 **Cariboo Mountains** ▲▲ British Columbia, SW Canada
11 W9 **Caribou** Manitoba, C Canada 59°27′N 97°43′W
19 S2 **Caribou** Maine, NE USA 46°51′N 68°00′W
11 P10 **Caribou Mountains** ▲▲ Alberta, SW Canada
Caribrod *see* Dimitrovgrad
40 I6 **Carichic** Chihuahua, N Mexico 27°57′N 107°01′W
103 R3 **Carignan** Ardennes, N France 49°38′N 05°08′E
183 Q5 **Carinda** New South Wales, SE Australia 30°26′S 147°45′E
105 R6 **Cariñena** Aragón, NE Spain 41°20′N 01°13′W
107 I23 **Carini** Sicilia, Italy, C Mediterranean Sea 38°06′N 13°09′E
107 K17 **Carinola** Campania, S Italy 41°14′N 14°03′E
Carinthi *see* Kärnten
55 O5 **Caripe** Monagas, NE Venezuela 10°13′N 63°30′W
55 P5 **Caripito** Monagas, NE Venezuela 10°03′N 63°05′W
15 W7 **Carleton** Québec, SE Canada 48°07′N 66°07′W
31 S10 **Carleton** Michigan, N USA 42°03′N 83°23′W
13 O14 **Carleton, Mount** ▲ New Brunswick, SE Canada 47°10′N 66°54′W
14 L13 **Carleton Place** Ontario, SE Canada 45°08′N 76°09′W
35 V3 **Carlin** Nevada, W USA 40°40′N 116°09′W
30 K14 **Carlinville** Illinois, N USA 39°16′N 89°52′W
97 K14 **Carlisle** *anc.* Caer Luel, Luguvallium, Luguvallum. NW England, United Kingdom 54°54′N 02°55′W
27 V11 **Carlisle** Arkansas, C USA 34°46′N 91°45′W
31 N15 **Carlisle** Indiana, N USA 38°57′N 87°23′W
29 V14 **Carlisle** Iowa, C USA 41°30′N 93°29′W
21 N5 **Carlisle** Kentucky, S USA 38°19′N 84°02′W
18 F15 **Carlisle** Pennsylvania, NE USA 40°10′N 77°10′W
21 Q11 **Carlisle** South Carolina, SE USA 34°35′N 81°27′W
38 J17 **Carlisle Island** *island* Aleutian Islands, Alaska, USA
27 R7 **Carl Junction** Missouri, C USA 37°10′N 94°34′W
107 A20 **Carloforte** Sardegna, Italy, C Mediterranean Sea 39°10′N 08°17′E
Carlopago *see* Karlobag
61 B21 **Carlos Casares** Buenos Aires, E Argentina 35°39′S 61°28′W
61 E18 **Carlos Reyles** Durazno, C Uruguay 33°00′S 56°30′W
61 A21 **Carlos Tejedor** Buenos Aires, E Argentina 35°25′S 62°25′W
97 F19 **Carlow** *Ir.* Ceatharlach. SE Ireland 52°50′N 06°55′W
97 F19 **Carlow** *Ir.* Cheatharlach. *cultural region* SE Ireland
96 F7 **Carloway** NW Scotland, United Kingdom 58°17′N 06°48′W
35 U17 **Carlsbad** California, W USA 33°09′N 117°21′W
37 U15 **Carlsbad** New Mexico, SW USA 32°24′N 104°15′W
Carlsbad *see* Karlovy Vary
129 N13 **Carlsberg Ridge** *undersea feature* S Arabian Sea 06°00′N 61°00′E
Carlsruhe *see* Karlsruhe
29 W6 **Carlton** Minnesota, N USA 46°39′N 92°25′W
11 V17 **Carlyle** Saskatchewan, S Canada 49°39′N 102°18′W
30 L15 **Carlyle** Illinois, N USA 38°36′N 89°22′W
30 L15 **Carlyle Lake** ▣ Illinois, N USA
10 H7 **Carmacks** Yukon Territory, W Canada 62°04′N 136°21′W
106 B9 **Carmagnola** Piemonte, NW Italy 44°50′N 07°43′E
11 X16 **Carman** Manitoba, S Canada 49°32′N 97°59′W
Carmana/Carmania *see* Kermān
97 I21 **Carmarthen** SW Wales, United Kingdom 51°52′N 04°19′W
97 I21 **Carmarthen** *cultural region* SW Wales, United Kingdom
97 I22 **Carmarthen Bay** *inlet* SW Wales, United Kingdom
103 N14 **Carmaux** Tarn, S France 44°03′N 02°09′E
35 N11 **Carmel** California, W USA 36°32′N 121°54′W
31 O13 **Carmel** Indiana, N USA 39°58′N 86°07′W
18 L13 **Carmel** New York, NE USA 41°25′N 73°40′W
97 H18 **Carmel Head** *headland* NW Wales, United Kingdom 53°24′N 04°35′W
42 E2 **Carmelita** Petén, N Guatemala 17°33′N 90°11′W
61 D19 **Carmelo** Colonia, SW Uruguay 34°00′S 58°20′W
41 V14 **Carmen** *var.* Ciudad del Carmen. Campeche, SE Mexico 18°38′N 91°50′W
61 A25 **Carmen de Patagones** Buenos Aires, E Argentina 40°45′S 63°00′W
40 F8 **Carmen, Isla** *island* NW Mexico
40 M5 **Carmen, Sierra del** ▲▲ NW Mexico
30 M16 **Carmi** Illinois, N USA 38°05′N 88°09′W
35 O7 **Carmichael** California, W USA 38°36′N 121°21′W
Carmiel *see* Karmi'el
25 U11 **Carmine** Texas, SW USA 30°07′N 96°40′W
104 K14 **Carmona** Andalucía, S Spain 37°28′N 05°38′W
Carmona *see* Uíge
Carnaro *see* Kvarner
180 G9 **Carnarvon** Western Australia 24°57′S 113°38′E
14 I13 **Carnarvon** Ontario, SE Canada 45°03′N 78°41′W
83 G24 **Carnarvon** Northern Cape, W South Africa 30°59′S 22°08′E
Carnarvon *see* Caernarfon
180 K9 **Carnarvon Range** ▲▲ Western Australia
Carn Domhnach *see* Carndonagh
96 E13 **Carndonagh** *Ir.* Carn Domhnach. NW Ireland 55°15′N 07°15′W
11 V17 **Carnduff** Saskatchewan, S Canada 49°11′N 101°50′W
26 L11 **Carnegie** Oklahoma, C USA 35°06′N 98°36′W
180 L9 **Carnegie, Lake** *salt lake* Western Australia
193 U8 **Carnegie Ridge** *undersea feature* E Pacific Ocean 01°00′S 85°00′W
96 H9 **Carn Eige** ▲ N Scotland, United Kingdom 57°18′N 05°04′W
182 F5 **Carnes** South Australia 30°12′S 134°31′E
194 J12 **Carney Island** *island* Antarctica
18 H16 **Carneys Point** New Jersey, NE USA 39°38′N 75°29′W
Carniche, Alpi *see* Karnische Alpen
151 Q21 **Car Nicobar** *island* Nicobar Islands, India, NE Indian Ocean
79 H15 **Carnot** Mambéré-Kadéï, W Central African Republic 04°58′N 15°55′E
182 F10 **Carnot, Cape** *headland* South Australia 34°57′S 135°39′E
96 K11 **Carnoustie** E Scotland, United Kingdom 56°30′N 02°42′W
97 F20 **Carnsore Point** *Ir.* Ceann an Chairn. *headland* SE Ireland 52°10′N 06°22′W
8 H7 **Carnwath** ≈ Northwest Territories, NW Canada
31 R8 **Caro** Michigan, N USA 43°29′N 83°24′W
23 Z15 **Carol City** Florida, SE USA 25°56′N 80°15′W
59 L14 **Carolina** Maranhão, E Brazil 07°20′S 47°25′W
45 U5 **Carolina** E Puerto Rico 18°22′N 65°57′W
21 V12 **Carolina Beach** North Carolina, SE USA 34°02′N 77°53′W
Caroline Island *see* Millennium Island
189 N15 **Caroline Islands** *island group* C Micronesia
129 Z14 **Caroline Plate** *tectonic feature*
192 H7 **Caroline Ridge** *undersea feature* E Philippine Sea 08°00′N 150°00′E
Carolopois *see* Châlons-en-Champagne
45 V14 **Caroni Arena Dam** ▣ Trinidad, Trinidad and Tobago
Caronie, Monti *see* Nebrodi, Monti
55 P7 **Caroní, Río** ≈ E Venezuela
45 U14 **Caroni River** ≈ Trinidad, Trinidad and Tobago
Caronium *see* A Coruña
54 J5 **Carora** Lara, N Venezuela 10°12′N 70°07′W
86 F12 **Carpathian Mountains** *var.* Carpathians, *Cz./Pol.* Karpaty, *Ger.* Karpaten. ▲▲ E Europe
Carpathians *see* Carpathian Mountains
Carpathos/Carpathus *see* Kárpathos
116 H12 **Carpaţii Meridionalii** *var.* Alpi Transilvaniei, Carpaţii Sudici, *Eng.* South Carpathians, Transylvanian Alps, *Ger.* Südkarpaten, Transsylvanische Alpen, *Hung.* Déli-Kárpátok, Erdélyi-Havasok. ▲▲ C Romania
Carpaţii Sudici *see* Carpaţii Meridionalii
174 L7 **Carpentaria, Gulf of** *gulf* N Australia
Carpentoracte *see* Carpentras
103 R14 **Carpentras** *anc.* Carpentoracte. Vaucluse, SE France 44°03′N 05°03′E
106 F9 **Carpi** Emilia-Romagna, N Italy 44°47′N 10°53′E
116 E11 **Cărpiniş** *Hung.* Gyertyámos. Timiş, W Romania 45°46′N 20°53′E
35 R14 **Carpinteria** California, W USA 34°24′N 119°30′W
23 S9 **Carrabelle** Florida, SE USA 29°51′N 84°39′W
Carraig Aonair *see* Fastnet Rock
Carraig Fhearghais *see* Carrickfergus
Carraig Mhachaire Rois *see* Carrickmacross
Carraig na Siúire *see* Carrick-on-Suir
Carrantual *see* Carrauntoohil
106 E10 **Carrara** Toscana, C Italy 44°05′N 10°07′E
61 F20 **Carrasco** ✈ (Montevideo) Canelones, S Uruguay 34°51′S 56°00′W
105 P9 **Carrascosa del Campo** Castilla-La Mancha, C Spain 40°02′N 02°35′W
54 H4 **Carrasquero** Zulia, NW Venezuela 11°00′N 72°01′W
183 O9 **Carrathool** New South Wales, SE Australia 34°25′S 145°30′E
Carrauntohil *see* Carrauntoohil
97 B21 **Carrauntoohil** *Ir.* Carrantual, Carrauntohil, Corrán Tuathail. ▲ SW Ireland 51°98′N 09°53′W
45 Y15 **Carriacou** *island* N Grenada
97 G15 **Carrickfergus** *Ir.* Carraig Fhearghais. NE Northern Ireland, United Kingdom 54°43′N 05°49′W
97 F16 **Carrickmacross** *Ir.* Carraig Mhachaire Rois. N Ireland 53°58′N 06°43′W
97 D16 **Carrick-on-Shannon** *Ir.* Cora Droma Rúisc. NW Ireland 53°37′N 08°05′W
97 E20 **Carrick-on-Suir** *Ir.* Carraig na Siúire. S Ireland 52°21′N 07°25′W
182 I7 **Carrieton** South Australia 32°27′S 138°33′E
40 L7 **Carrillo** Chihuahua, N Mexico 25°53′N 103°54′W
29 O4 **Carrington** North Dakota, N USA 47°27′N 99°07′W
104 M4 **Carrión** ≈ N Spain
104 M4 **Carrión de los Condes** Castilla y León, N Spain 42°20′N 04°37′W
25 P13 **Carrizo Springs** Texas, SW USA 28°33′N 99°54′W
37 S13 **Carrizozo** New Mexico, SW USA 33°38′N 105°52′W
29 T13 **Carroll** Iowa, C USA 42°04′N 94°52′W
23 N4 **Carrollton** Alabama, S USA 33°13′N 88°05′W
23 R3 **Carrollton** Georgia, SE USA 33°33′N 85°04′W
30 K14 **Carrollton** Illinois, N USA 39°18′N 90°24′W
20 L4 **Carrollton** Kentucky, S USA 38°41′N 85°09′W
31 R8 **Carrollton** Michigan, N USA 43°27′N 83°55′W
27 T3 **Carrollton** Missouri, C USA 39°20′N 93°30′W
31 U12 **Carrollton** Ohio, N USA 40°34′N 81°05′W
25 T6 **Carrollton** Texas, SW USA 32°57′N 96°53′W
11 U14 **Carrot** ≈ Saskatchewan, S Canada
11 U14 **Carrot River** Saskatchewan, C Canada 53°18′N 103°32′W
18 J7 **Carry Falls Reservoir** ▣ New York, NE USA
136 L11 **Çarşamba** Samsun, N Turkey 41°13′N 36°43′E
28 L6 **Carson** North Dakota, N USA 46°26′N 101°34′W
35 Q6 **Carson City** *state capital* Nevada, W USA 39°10′N 119°46′W
35 R6 **Carson River** ≈ Nevada, W USA
35 S5 **Carson Sink** *salt flat* Nevada, W USA
11 Q16 **Carstairs** Alberta, SW Canada 51°35′N 114°02′W
Carstensz, Puntjak *see* Jaya, Puncak
54 E5 **Cartagena** *var.* Cartagena de los Indes. Bolívar, NW Colombia 10°24′N 75°33′W
105 R13 **Cartagena** *anc.* Carthago Nova. Murcia, SE Spain 37°36′N 00°59′W
54 E13 **Cartagena de Chaira** Caquetá, S Colombia 01°19′N 74°52′W
Cartagena de los Indes *see* Cartagena
54 D10 **Cartago** Valle del Cauca, W Colombia 04°45′N 75°55′W
43 N14 **Cartago** Cartago, C Costa Rica 09°50′N 83°54′W
42 M14 **Cartago** *off.* Provincia de Cartago. ⬖ *province* C Costa Rica
Cartago, Provincia de *see* Cartago
25 O11 **Carta Valley** Texas, SW USA 29°46′N 100°37′W
104 F10 **Cartaxo** Santarém, C Portugal 39°10′N 08°47′W
104 I14 **Cartaya** Andalucía, S Spain 37°16′N 07°09′W
Carteret Islands *see* Tulun Islands
29 S15 **Carter Lake** Iowa, C USA 41°17′N 95°55′W
23 S3 **Cartersville** Georgia, SE USA 34°10′N 84°48′W
185 M14 **Carterton** Wellington, North Island, New Zealand 41°01′S 175°30′E
30 J13 **Carthage** Illinois, N USA 40°25′N 91°09′W
22 L5 **Carthage** Mississippi, S USA 32°43′N 89°31′W
27 R7 **Carthage** Missouri, C USA 37°10′N 94°20′W
18 I8 **Carthage** New York, NE USA 43°58′N 75°36′W
21 T10 **Carthage** North Carolina, SE USA 35°21′N 79°27′W
20 K8 **Carthage** Tennessee, S USA 36°14′N 85°59′W
25 X7 **Carthage** Texas, SW USA 32°10′N 94°21′W
74 M5 **Carthage** ✈ (Tunis) N Tunisia 36°51′N 10°12′E
Carthago Nova *see* Cartagena
14 E10 **Cartier** Ontario, S Canada 46°40′N 81°31′W
13 S8 **Cartwright** Newfoundland and Labrador, E Canada 53°40′N 57°W
55 P9 **Caruana de Montaña** Bolívar, SE Venezuela 05°16′N 63°12′W
59 Q15 **Caruaru** Pernambuco, E Brazil 08°15′S 35°55′W
55 P5 **Carúpano** Sucre, NE Venezuela 10°39′N 63°14′W
Carusbur *see* Cherbourg
58 M12 **Carutapera** Maranhão, E Brazil 01°12′S 45°57′W
27 Y9 **Caruthersville** Missouri, C USA 36°11′N 89°40′W
103 O1 **Carvin** Pas-de-Calais, N France 50°31′N 03°00′E
58 E12 **Carvoeiro** Amazonas, NW Brazil 01°24′S 61°59′W
104 E10 **Carvoeiro, Cabo** *headland* C Portugal 39°19′N 09°27′W
21 U9 **Cary** North Carolina, SE USA 35°47′N 78°46′W
182 M3 **Caryapundy Swamp** *wetland* New South Wales/Queensland, SE Australia
65 E24 **Carysfort, Cape** *headland* East Falkland, Falkland Islands 51°26′S 57°50′W
74 F6 **Casablanca** *Ar.* Dar-el-Beida. NW Morocco 33°39′N 07°31′W
60 M8 **Casa Branca** São Paulo, S Brazil 21°47′S 47°05′W
36 L14 **Casa Grande** Arizona, SW USA 32°52′N 111°45′W
106 C8 **Casale Monferrato** Piemonte, NW Italy 45°08′N 08°27′E
106 E8 **Casalpusterlengo** Lombardia, N Italy 45°10′N 09°37′E
54 H10 **Casanare** *off.* Intendencia de Casanare. ⬖ *province* C Colombia
Casanare, Intendencia de *see* Casanare
55 P5 **Casanay** Sucre, NE Venezuela 10°30′N 63°25′W
24 K11 **Casa Piedra** Texas, SW USA 29°43′N 104°03′W
107 Q19 **Casarano** Puglia, SE Italy 40°01′N 18°10′E
42 J11 **Casares** Carazo, W Nicaragua 11°37′N 86°19′W
105 R10 **Casas Ibáñez** Castilla-La Mancha, C Spain 39°17′N 01°28′W
61 I14 **Casca** Rio Grande do Sul, S Brazil 28°39′S 51°55′W
172 I17 **Cascade** Mahé, NE Seychelles 04°39′S 55°29′E
33 N13 **Cascade** Idaho, NW USA 44°31′N 116°02′W
29 Y13 **Cascade** Iowa, C USA 42°18′N 91°00′W
33 R9 **Cascade** Montana, NW USA 47°15′N 111°46′W
185 B20 **Cascade Point** *headland* South Island, New Zealand 44°00′S 168°23′E
32 G13 **Cascade Range** ▲▲ Oregon/Washington, NW USA
33 N12 **Cascade Reservoir** ▣ Idaho, NW USA
0 E8 **Cascadia Basin** *undersea feature* NE Pacific Ocean 47°00′N 127°30′W
104 E11 **Cascais** Lisboa, C Portugal 38°41′N 09°25′W
15 W7 **Cascapédia** ≈ Québec, SE Canada
59 I22 **Cascavel** Ceará, E Brazil 04°10′S 38°15′W
60 G11 **Cascavel** Paraná, S Brazil 24°56′S 53°28′W
106 I13 **Cascia** Umbria, C Italy 42°45′N 13°01′E
106 F11 **Cascina** Toscana, C Italy 43°40′N 10°33′E
19 Q8 **Casco Bay** *bay* Maine, NE USA
194 J7 **Case Island** *island* Antarctica
106 B8 **Caselle** ✈ (Torino) Piemonte, NW Italy 45°06′N 07°41′E
107 K17 **Caserta** Campania, S Italy 41°05′N 14°20′E
15 N8 **Casey** Québec, SE Canada 47°50′N 74°09′W
30 M14 **Casey** Illinois, N USA 39°18′N 87°59′W
195 Y12 **Casey** *Australian research station* Antarctica 65°58′S 111°04′E
195 W3 **Casey Bay** *bay* Antarctica
80 Q11 **Caseyr, Raas** *headland* NE Somalia 11°51′S 51°16′E
97 D20 **Cashel** *Ir.* Caiseal. S Ireland 52°31′N 07°53′W
54 G6 **Casigua** Zulia, W Venezuela 08°46′N 72°30′W
61 B19 **Casilda** Santa Fe, C Argentina 33°05′S 61°10′W
Casim *see* General Toshevo
183 V4 **Casino** New South Wales, SE Australia 28°50′S 153°02′E
107 J16 **Cassino** *prev.* San Germano; *anc.* Casinum. Lazio, C Italy 41°29′N 13°50′E
Casinum *see* Cassino
111 E17 **Čáslav** *Ger.* Tschaslau. Střední Čechy, C Czech Republic 49°54′N 15°23′E
56 C13 **Casma** Ancash, C Peru 09°30′S 78°18′W
167 S7 **Ca, Sông** ≈ N Vietnam
107 K17 **Casoria** Campania, S Italy 40°54′N 14°28′E
105 T6 **Caspe** Aragón, NE Spain 41°14′N 00°03′W
33 X15 **Casper** Wyoming, C USA 42°48′N 106°22′W
84 M10 **Caspian Depression** *Kaz.* Kaspīy Mangy Oypaty, *Rus.* Prikaspiyskaya Nizmennost'. *depression* Kazakhstan/Russian Federation
130 D10 **Caspian Sea** *Az.* Xäzär Dänizi, *Kaz.* Kaspiy Tengizi, *Per.* Baḩr-e Khazar, Daryā-ye Khazar, *Rus.* Kaspiyskoye More. *inland sea* Asia/Europe

◆ Country
● Country Capital
◇ Dependent Territory
○ Dependent Territory Capital
⬖ Administrative Regions
✈ International Airport
▲ Mountain
▲▲ Mountain Range
⛰ Volcano
≈ River
◎ Lake
▣ Reservoir

83 L14 **Cassacatiza** Tete, NW Mozambique 14°20′S 32°24′E
Cassai see Kasai
82 F13 **Cassamba** Moxico, E Angola 13°07′S 20°22′E
107 N20 **Cassano allo Ionio** Calabria, SE Italy 39°46′N 16°16′E
31 S8 **Cass City** Michigan, N USA 43°36′N 83°10′W
Cassel see Kassel
14 M13 **Casselman** Ontario, SE Canada 45°18′N 75°05′W
29 R5 **Casselton** North Dakota, N USA 46°53′N 97°10′W
Cássia see Santa Rita de Cassia
10 J9 **Cassiar** British Columbia, W Canada 59°16′N 129°40′W
10 K10 **Cassiar Mountains** ▲▲ British Columbia, W Canada
83 C15 **Cassinga** Huíla, SW Angola 15°08′S 16°05′E
29 T4 **Cass Lake** Minnesota, N USA 47°22′N 94°36′W
29 T4 **Cass Lake** ◎ Minnesota, N USA
31 P10 **Cassopolis** Michigan, N USA 41°56′N 86°00′W
31 S8 **Cass River** ~ Michigan, N USA
27 S8 **Cassville** Missouri, C USA 36°42′N 93°52′W
Castamoni see Kastamonu
58 L12 **Castanhal** Pará, NE Brazil 01°16′S 47°55′W
104 G8 **Castanheira de Pêra** Leiria, C Portugal 40°01′N 08°12′W
41 N7 **Castaños** Coahuila, NE Mexico 26°48′N 101°26′W
108 I10 **Castasegna** Graubünden, SE Switzerland 46°21′N 09°30′E
106 D8 **Casteggio** Lombardia, N Italy 45°02′N 09°10′E
107 K23 **Castelbuono** Sicilia, Italy, C Mediterranean Sea 37°56′N 14°05′E
107 K15 **Castel di Sangro** Abruzzo, C Italy 41°46′N 14°03′E
106 H7 **Castelfranco Veneto** Veneto, NE Italy 45°40′N 11°55′E
102 K14 **Casteljaloux** Lot-et-Garonne, SW France 44°19′N 00°03′E
107 L18 **Castellabate** var. Santa Maria di Castellabate. Campania, S Italy 40°16′N 14°57′E
107 I23 **Castellammare del Golfo** Sicilia, Italy, C Mediterranean Sea 38°02′N 12°53′E
107 H22 **Castellammare, Golfo di** gulf Sicilia, Italy, C Mediterranean Sea
103 U15 **Castellane** Alpes-de-Haute-Provence, SE France 43°49′N 06°34′E
107 O18 **Castellaneta** Puglia, SE Italy 40°38′N 16°57′E
106 E9 **Castel l'Arquato** Emilia-Romagna, C Italy 44°52′N 09°51′E
61 E21 **Castelli** Buenos Aires, E Argentina 36°07′S 57°47′W
105 S8 **Castelló de la Plana** var. Castellón de la Plana. ◐ province Valenciana, E Spain
Castelló de la Plana see Castellón de la Plana
Castellón see Castellón de la Plana
105 T9 **Castellón de la Plana** var. Castellón, Cat. Castelló de la Plana. Valenciana, E Spain 39°59′N 00°03′W
Castellón de la Plana see Castelló de la Plana
105 S7 **Castellote** Aragón, NE Spain 40°46′N 00°18′W
103 N16 **Castelnaudary** Aude, S France 43°18′N 01°57′E
102 L16 **Castelnau-Magnoac** Hautes-Pyrénées, S France 43°18′N 00°30′E
106 F10 **Castelnovo ne' Monti** Emilia-Romagna, C Italy 44°26′N 10°24′E
Castelnuovo see Herceg-Novi
104 H9 **Castelo Branco** Castelo Branco, C Portugal 39°50′N 07°30′W
104 H8 **Castelo Branco** ◐ district C Portugal
104 I10 **Castelo de Vide** Portalegre, C Portugal 39°25′N 07°27′W
104 G9 **Castelo do Bode, Barragem do** ⊠ C Portugal
106 G10 **Castel San Pietro Terme** Emilia-Romagna, C Italy 44°22′N 11°34′E
107 B17 **Castelsardo** Sardegna, Italy, C Mediterranean Sea 40°54′N 08°42′E
102 M14 **Castelsarrasin** Tarn-et-Garonne, S France 44°02′N 01°06′E
107 I24 **Casteltermini** Sicilia, Italy, C Mediterranean Sea 37°33′N 13°38′E
107 H24 **Castelvetrano** Sicilia, Italy, C Mediterranean Sea 37°40′N 12°46′E
182 L12 **Casterton** Victoria, SE Australia 37°37′S 141°22′E
102 J15 **Castets** Landes, SW France 43°55′N 01°08′W
106 H12 **Castiglione del Lago** Umbria, C Italy 43°07′N 12°02′E
106 F13 **Castiglione della Pescaia** Toscana, C Italy 42°46′N 10°53′E
106 F8 **Castiglione delle Stiviere** Lombardia, N Italy 45°24′N 10°31′E
104 M9 **Castilla-La Mancha** ◐ autonomous community NE Spain
Castilla-León see Castilla y León
105 N10 **Castilla Nueva** cultural region C Spain
105 N6 **Castilla Vieja** ◐ cultural region N Spain
104 L5 **Castilla y León** var. Castillia-León. ◐ autonomous community NW Spain
Castillo de Locubim see Castillo de Locubín
105 N14 **Castillo de Locubín** var. Castillo de Locubim. Andalucía, S Spain 37°32′N 03°56′W
102 K13 **Castillon-la-Bataille** Gironde, SW France 44°51′N 00°01′W
63 I19 **Castillo, Pampa del** plain S Argentina
61 G19 **Castillos** Rocha, SE Uruguay 34°12′S 53°52′W
97 B16 **Castlebar** Ir. Caisleán an Bharraigh. W Ireland 53°52′N 09°17′W
97 F16 **Castleblayney** Ir. Baile na Lorgan. N Ireland 54°07′N 06°44′W
45 O11 **Castle Bruce** E Dominica 15°24′N 61°26′W
36 M5 **Castle Dale** Utah, W USA 39°10′N 111°02′W
36 I14 **Castle Dome Peak** ▲ Arizona, SW USA 33°04′N 114°08′W
97 J14 **Castle Douglas** S Scotland, United Kingdom 54°56′N 03°56′W
97 E14 **Castlefinn** Ir. Caisleán na Finne. NW Ireland 54°47′N 07°35′W
97 M17 **Castleford** N England, United Kingdom 53°44′N 01°21′W
11 O17 **Castlegar** British Columbia, SW Canada 49°18′N 117°48′W
64 B12 **Castle Harbour** inlet Bermuda, NW Atlantic Ocean
21 V12 **Castle Hayne** North Carolina, SE USA 34°23′N 78°07′W
97 B20 **Castleisland** Ir. Oileán Ciarral. SW Ireland 52°12′N 09°30′W
183 N12 **Castlemaine** Victoria, SE Australia 37°06′S 144°13′E
37 R5 **Castle Peak** ▲ Colorado, C USA 39°00′N 106°51′W
33 O13 **Castle Peak** ▲ Idaho, NW USA 44°02′N 114°42′W
184 N13 **Castlepoint** Wellington, North Island, New Zealand 40°54′S 176°13′E
97 D17 **Castlerea** Ir. An Caisleán Riabhach. W Ireland 53°45′N 08°32′W
97 G15 **Castlereagh** Ir. An Caisleán Riabhach. N Northern Ireland, United Kingdom 54°33′N 05°53′W
183 R6 **Castlereagh River** ~ New South Wales, SE Australia
37 T5 **Castle Rock** Colorado, C USA 39°22′N 104°51′W
30 K7 **Castle Rock Lake** ⊠ Wisconsin, N USA
65 G25 **Castle Rock Point** headland S Saint Helena 16°02′S 05°45′W
97 I16 **Castletown** SE Isle of Man 54°05′N 04°39′W
29 R9 **Castlewood** South Dakota, N USA 44°43′N 97°01′W
11 R15 **Castor** Alberta, SW Canada 52°14′N 111°54′W
14 M13 **Castor** ~ Ontario, SE Canada
27 X7 **Castor River** ~ Missouri, C USA
Castra Albiensium see Castres
Castra Regina see Regensburg
103 N15 **Castres** anc. Castra Albiensium. Tarn, S France 43°36′N 02°15′E
98 H9 **Castricum** Noord-Holland, W Netherlands 52°33′N 04°40′E
45 S11 **Castries** ● (Saint Lucia) N Saint Lucia 14°01′N 60°59′W
60 J11 **Castro** Paraná, S Brazil 24°46′S 50°03′W
63 F17 **Castro** Los Lagos, W Chile 42°27′S 73°48′W
104 H7 **Castro Daire** Viseu, N Portugal 40°54′N 07°55′W
104 M13 **Castro del Río** Andalucía, S Spain 37°41′N 04°29′W
Castrogiovanni see Enna
104 H14 **Castro Marim** Faro, S Portugal 37°13′N 07°26′W
104 J2 **Castropol** Asturias, N Spain 43°30′N 07°01′W
105 O2 **Castro-Urdiales** var. Castro Urdiales. Cantabria, N Spain 43°23′N 03°11′W
104 G13 **Castro Verde** Beja, S Portugal 37°42′N 08°05′W
107 N19 **Castrovillari** Calabria, SW Italy 39°48′N 16°12′E
35 N10 **Castroville** California, W USA 36°46′N 121°46′W
25 R12 **Castroville** Texas, SW USA 29°21′N 98°52′W
104 K11 **Castuera** Extremadura, W Spain 38°44′N 05°33′W
61 F19 **Casupá** Florida, S Uruguay 34°09′S 55°38′W
185 A22 **Caswell Sound** sound South Island, New Zealand
137 Q13 **Çat** Erzurum, NE Turkey 39°40′N 41°03′E
42 K6 **Catacamas** Olancho, C Honduras 14°55′N 85°54′W
56 A10 **Catacaos** Piura, NW Peru 05°22′S 80°40′W
22 I7 **Catahoula Lake** ◎ Louisiana, S USA
137 S15 **Çatak** Van, SE Turkey 38°02′N 43°05′E
137 S15 **Çatak Çayi** ~ SE Turkey
114 O12 **Çatalca** İstanbul, NW Turkey 41°09′N 28°28′E
114 O12 **Çatalca Yarimadasi** physical region NW Turkey
62 H6 **Catalina** Antofagasta, N Chile 25°19′S 69°37′W
Catalonia see Cataluña
105 U5 **Cataluña** Cat. Catalunya, Eng. Catalonia. ◐ autonomous community N Spain
Catalunya see Cataluña
62 I7 **Catamarca** off. Provincia de Catamarca. ◐ province NW Argentina
Catamarca see San Fernando del Valle de Catamarca
Catamarca, Provincia de see Catamarca
83 M16 **Catandica** Manica, C Mozambique 18°05′S 33°10′E
171 P4 **Catanduanes Island** island N Philippines
60 K8 **Catanduva** São Paulo, S Brazil 21°05′S 49°00′W
107 L24 **Catania** Sicilia, Italy, C Mediterranean Sea 37°31′N 15°04′E
107 M24 **Catania, Golfo di** gulf Sicilia, Italy, C Mediterranean Sea
45 U5 **Cataño** var. Cantaño. E Puerto Rico 18°26′N 66°06′W
107 O21 **Catanzaro** Calabria, SW Italy 38°53′N 16°36′E
107 O22 **Catanzaro Marina** var. Marina di Catanzaro. Calabria, S Italy 38°48′N 16°33′E
Marina di Catanzaro see Catanzaro Marina
25 Q14 **Catarina** Texas, SW USA 28°19′N 99°36′W
171 Q5 **Catarman** Samar, C Philippines 12°29′N 124°34′E
105 S10 **Catarroja** Valenciana, E Spain 39°24′N 00°24′W
21 R11 **Catawba River** ~ North Carolina/South Carolina, SE USA
171 Q5 **Catbalogan** Samar, C Philippines 11°49′N 124°55′E
14 I14 **Catchacoma** Ontario, SE Canada 44°43′N 78°19′W
41 S15 **Catemaco** Veracruz-Llave, SE Mexico 18°28′N 95°10′W
Cathair na Mart see Westport
Cathair Saidhbhín see Caherciveen
31 P5 **Cat Head Point** headland Michigan, N USA 45°11′N 85°37′W
23 Q2 **Cathedral Caverns** cave Alabama, S USA
35 V16 **Cathedral City** California, W USA 33°45′N 116°27′W
24 K10 **Cathedral Mountain** ▲ Texas, SW USA 30°10′N 103°39′W
32 G10 **Cathlamet** Washington, NW USA 46°12′N 123°24′W
76 G13 **Catió** S Guinea-Bissau 11°13′N 15°10′W
55 O10 **Catisimiña** Bolívar, SE Venezuela 04°07′N 63°40′W
44 J3 **Cat Island** island C Bahamas
12 B9 **Cat Lake** Ontario, S Canada 51°47′N 91°52′W
21 P5 **Catlettsburg** Kentucky, S USA 38°24′N 82°37′W
185 D24 **Catlins** ~ South Island, New Zealand
35 R1 **Catnip Mountain** ▲ Nevada, W USA 41°53′N 119°19′W
41 Z11 **Catoche, Cabo** headland SE Mexico 21°36′N 87°04′W
27 P9 **Catoosa** Oklahoma, C USA 36°11′N 95°45′W
41 N10 **Catorce** San Luis Potosí, C Mexico 23°42′N 100°49′W
63 I14 **Catriel** Río Negro, C Argentina 37°54′S 67°52′W
62 K13 **Catriló** La Pampa, C Argentina 36°28′S 63°20′W
58 F11 **Catrimani** Roraima, N Brazil 0°24′N 61°30′W
58 E10 **Catrimani, Rio** ~ N Brazil
18 K11 **Catskill** New York, NE USA 42°13′N 73°52′W
18 K11 **Catskill Creek** ~ New York, NE USA
18 J11 **Catskill Mountains** ▲▲ New York, NE USA
18 D11 **Cattaraugus Creek** ~ New York, NE USA
Cattaro see Kotor
Cattaro, Bocche di see Kotorska, Boka
107 I24 **Cattolica Eraclea** Sicilia, Italy, C Mediterranean Sea 37°27′N 13°24′E
83 B14 **Catumbela** ~ W Angola
83 N14 **Catur** Niassa, N Mozambique 13°50′S 35°43′E
82 C10 **Cauale** ~ NE Angola
171 O2 **Cauayan** Luzon, N Philippines 16°55′N 121°46′E
54 C12 **Cauca** off. Departamento del Cauca. ◐ province SW Colombia
47 P5 **Cauca** ~ SE Venezuela
Cauca, Departamento del see Cauca
58 P13 **Caucaia** Ceará, E Brazil 03°44′S 38°45′W
54 E7 **Cauca, Río** ~ N Colombia
54 E7 **Caucasia** Antioquia, NW Colombia 07°59′N 75°13′W
137 Q8 **Caucasus** Rus. Kavkaz. ▲▲ Georgia/Russian Federation
62 I10 **Caucete** San Juan, W Argentina 31°38′S 68°16′W
105 R11 **Caudete** Castilla-La Mancha, C Spain 38°42′N 01°00′W
103 P2 **Caudry** Nord, N France 50°07′N 03°24′E
82 D11 **Caungula** Lunda Norte, NE Angola 08°22′S 18°37′E
62 G13 **Cauquenes** Maule, C Chile 35°58′S 72°22′W
55 N8 **Caura, Río** ~ C Venezuela
15 V7 **Causapscal** Québec, SE Canada 48°22′N 67°14′W
117 N10 **Căuşeni** Rus. Kaushany. E Moldova 46°37′N 29°21′E
102 M14 **Caussade** Tarn-et-Garonne, S France 44°10′N 01°31′E
102 K17 **Cauterets** Hautes-Pyrénées, S France 42°53′N 00°08′W
10 J15 **Caution, Cape** headland British Columbia, SW Canada 51°10′N 127°43′W
44 H7 **Cauto** ~ E Cuba
Cauvery see Kāveri
102 L3 **Caux, Pays de** physical region N France
107 L18 **Cava de' Tirreni** Campania, S Italy 40°42′N 14°42′E
104 G6 **Cávado** ~ N Portugal
Cavaia see Kavajë
103 R15 **Cavaillon** Vaucluse, SE France 43°51′N 05°01′E
103 U16 **Cavalaire-sur-Mer** Var, SE France 43°10′N 06°31′E
106 G6 **Cavalese** Ger. Gablös. Trentino-Alto Adige, N Italy 46°18′N 11°29′E
29 Q2 **Cavalier** North Dakota, N USA 48°47′N 97°37′W
76 L17 **Cavalla** var. Cavally, Cavally Fleuve. ~ Ivory Coast/ Liberia
105 Y8 **Cavalleria, Cap de** var. Cabo Caballeria. headland Menorca, Spain, W Mediterranean Sea 40°04′N 04°06′E
184 K2 **Cavalli Islands** island group N New Zealand
Cavally/Cavally Fleuve see Cavalla
97 E16 **Cavan** Ir. Cabhán. N Ireland 54°N 07°21′W
97 E16 **Cavan** Ir. An Cabhán. cultural region N Ireland
106 H8 **Cavarzere** Veneto, NE Italy 45°08′N 12°05′E
27 W9 **Cave City** Arkansas, C USA 35°56′N 91°33′W
20 K7 **Cave City** Kentucky, S USA 37°08′N 85°57′W
65 M25 **Cave Point** headland S Tristan da Cunha
21 N5 **Cave Run Lake** ⊠ Kentucky, S USA
58 K11 **Caviana de Fora, Ilha** var. Ilha Caviana. island N Brazil
Caviana, Ilha see Caviana de Fora, Ilha
113 I16 **Cavtat** It. Ragusavecchia. Dubrovnik-Neretva, SE Croatia 42°36′N 18°13′E
Cawnpore see Kānpur
Caxamarca see Cajamarca
58 A13 **Caxias** Amazonas, W Brazil 04°27′S 71°27′W
58 N13 **Caxias** Maranhão, E Brazil 04°53′S 43°20′W
61 I15 **Caxias do Sul** Rio Grande do Sul, S Brazil 29°14′S 51°10′W
42 J4 **Caxinas, Punta** headland N Honduras 16°01′N 86°02′W
82 B11 **Caxito** Bengo, NW Angola 08°34′S 13°38′E
136 F14 **Çay** Afyon, W Turkey 38°35′N 31°01′E
40 L15 **Cayacal, Punta** var. Punta Mongrove. headland S Mexico 17°55′N 102°09′W
56 C6 **Cayambe** Pichincha, N Ecuador 0°02′N 78°08′W
56 C6 **Cayambe** ▲ N Ecuador 0°00′S 77°58′W
21 R12 **Cayce** South Carolina, SE USA 33°58′N 81°04′W
55 Y10 **Cayenne** ○ (French Guiana) NE French Guiana 04°55′N 52°18′W
55 Y10 **Cayenne** ✕ NE French Guiana 04°55′N 52°18′W
44 K10 **Cayes** var. Les Cayes. SW Haiti 18°10′N 73°48′W
45 U6 **Cayey** C Puerto Rico 18°06′N 66°11′W
45 U6 **Cayey, Sierra de** ▲▲ E Puerto Rico
103 N14 **Caylus** Tarn-et-Garonne, S France 44°13′N 01°42′E
44 E8 **Cayman Brac** island E Cayman Islands
44 D8 **Cayman Islands** ◇ UK dependent territory W West Indies
64 D11 **Cayman Trench** undersea feature NW Caribbean Sea 19°00′N 80°00′W
47 O3 **Cayman Trough** undersea feature NW Caribbean Sea 18°00′N 81°00′W
80 O13 **Caynabo** Togdheer, N Somalia 08°55′N 46°28′E
42 F3 **Cayo** ◐ district SW Belize
Cayo see San Ignacio
43 N9 **Cayos Guerrero** reef E Nicaragua
43 O9 **Cayos King** reef E Nicaragua
44 E4 **Cay Sal** islet SW Bahamas
14 G16 **Cayuga** Ontario, S Canada 42°57′N 79°49′W
25 V8 **Cayuga** Texas, SW USA 31°55′N 95°57′W
18 G10 **Cayuga Lake** ◎ New York, NE USA
104 K13 **Cazalla de la Sierra** Andalucía, S Spain 37°56′N 05°46′W
116 L14 **Căzăneşti** Ialomiţa, SE Romania 44°36′N 27°03′E
102 M16 **Cazères** Haute-Garonne, S France 43°15′N 01°11′E
112 E10 **Cazin** ◐ Federacija Bosna I Hercegovina, NW Bosnia and Herzegovina
82 G13 **Cazombo** Moxico, E Angola 11°54′S 22°56′E
105 O13 **Cazorla** Andalucía, S Spain 37°55′N 03°00′W
Cazza see Sušac
104 L4 **Cea** ~ NW Spain
Ceadâr-Lunga see Ciadîr-Lunga
Ceanannas see Kells
Ceann Toirc see Kanturk
58 O13 **Ceará** off. Estado do Ceará. ◐ state C Brazil
Ceará see Fortaleza
Ceara Abyssal Plain see Ceará Plain
Ceará, Estado do see Ceará
59 Q14 **Ceará Mirim** Rio Grande do Norte, E Brazil 05°30′S 35°51′W
64 J13 **Ceará Plain** var. Ceara Abyssal Plain. undersea feature W Atlantic Ocean 0°00′ 36°30′W
64 I13 **Ceará Ridge** undersea feature C Atlantic Ocean
Ceatharlach see Carlow
43 Q17 **Cébaco, Isla** island SW Panama
40 K7 **Ceballos** Durango, C Mexico 26°33′N 104°07′W
61 G19 **Cebollatí** Rocha, E Uruguay 33°15′S 53°46′W
61 G19 **Cebollatí, Río** ~ E Uruguay
105 P5 **Cebollera** ▲ N Spain 42°01′N 02°40′W
104 M8 **Cebreros** Castilla y León, N Spain 40°27′N 04°28′W
171 P6 **Cebu** off. Cebu City. Cebu, C Philippines 10°17′N 123°46′E
171 P6 **Cebu** island C Philippines
Cebu City see Cebu
107 J16 **Ceccano** Lazio, C Italy 41°34′N 13°20′E
Čechy see Bohemia
106 F12 **Cecina** Toscana, C Italy 43°19′N 10°31′E
26 K4 **Cedar Bluff Reservoir** ⊠ Kansas, C USA
30 M8 **Cedarburg** Wisconsin, N USA 43°18′N 87°58′W
36 J7 **Cedar City** Utah, W USA 37°40′N 113°03′W
25 T11 **Cedar Creek** Texas, SW USA 30°04′N 97°30′W
28 L7 **Cedar Creek** ~ North Dakota, N USA
25 U7 **Cedar Creek Reservoir** ⊠ Texas, SW USA
29 W13 **Cedar Falls** Iowa, C USA 42°31′N 92°27′W
31 N8 **Cedar Grove** Wisconsin, N USA 43°31′N 87°48′W
21 Y6 **Cedar Island** island Virginia, NE USA
23 U11 **Cedar Key** Cedar Keys, Florida, SE USA 29°08′N 83°03′W
23 U11 **Cedar Keys** island group Florida, SE USA
11 V14 **Cedar Lake** ◎ Manitoba, C Canada
14 I11 **Cedar Lake** ◎ Ontario, SE Canada
24 M6 **Cedar Lake** ◎ Texas, SW USA
29 X13 **Cedar Rapids** Iowa, C USA 41°58′N 91°40′W
29 X14 **Cedar River** ~ Iowa/ Minnesota, C USA
29 O14 **Cedar River** ~ Nebraska, C USA
31 P8 **Cedar Springs** Michigan, N USA 43°13′N 85°33′W
23 R3 **Cedartown** Georgia, SE USA 34°00′N 85°16′W
27 O7 **Cedar Vale** Kansas, C USA 37°06′N 96°30′W
35 Q2 **Cedarville** California, W USA 41°30′N 120°10′W
104 H1 **Cedeira** Galicia, NW Spain 43°40′N 08°03′W
42 H8 **Cedeño** Choluteca, S Honduras 13°10′N 87°25′W
41 N10 **Cedral** San Luis Potosí, C Mexico 23°47′N 100°40′W
42 I6 **Cedros** Francisco Morazán, C Honduras 14°38′N 86°42′W
40 M9 **Cedros** Zacatecas, C Mexico 24°39′N 101°47′W
40 B5 **Cedros, Isla** island W Mexico
193 R5 **Cedros Trench** undersea feature E Pacific Ocean 27°45′N 115°45′W
182 E7 **Ceduna** South Australia 32°09′S 133°43′E
110 D10 **Cedynia** Ger. Zehden. Zachodnio-pomorskie, W Poland 52°54′N 14°15′E
80 P12 **Ceelaayo** Sanaag, N Somalia 11°18′N 49°20′E
81 O16 **Ceel Buur** It. El Bur. Galguduud, C Somalia 04°36′N 46°33′E
81 N15 **Ceel Dheere** var. Ceel Dher, It. El Dere. Galguduud, C Somalia 05°18′N 46°07′E
Ceel Dher see Ceel Dheere
80 O12 **Ceerigaabo** var. Erigabo, Erigavo. Sanaag, N Somalia 10°34′N 47°22′E
107 J23 **Cefalù** anc. Cephaloedium. Sicilia, Italy, C Mediterranean Sea 38°02′N 14°02′E
105 N6 **Cega** ~ Castilla y León, N Spain
111 K23 **Cegléd** prev. Czegléd. Pest, C Hungary 47°10′N 19°47′E
113 N18 **Čegrane** W FYR Macedonia 41°50′N 20°59′E
105 Q13 **Cehegín** Murcia, SE Spain 38°04′N 01°48′W
136 K12 **Çekerek** Yozgat, N Turkey 40°04′N 35°30′E
146 B13 **Çekiçler** Rus. Chekishlyar, Turkm. Chekichler. Balkan Welaýaty, W Turkmenistan 37°35′N 53°52′E
107 J15 **Celano** Abruzzo, C Italy 42°06′N 13°33′E
104 H4 **Celanova** Galicia, NW Spain 42°09′N 07°58′W
42 F6 **Celaque, Cordillera de** ▲▲ W Honduras
41 N13 **Celaya** Guanajuato, C Mexico 20°32′N 100°48′W
Celebes see Sulawesi
192 F7 **Celebes Basin** undersea feature SE South China Sea 04°00′N 122°00′E
192 F7 **Celebes Sea** Ind. Laut Sulawesi. sea Indonesia/ Philippines
41 W12 **Celestún** Yucatán, E Mexico 20°50′N 90°22′W
31 Q12 **Celina** Ohio, N USA 40°34′N 84°35′W
20 L8 **Celina** Tennessee, S USA 36°32′N 85°30′W
25 U5 **Celina** Texas, SW USA 33°19′N 96°46′W
112 G11 **Čelinac Donji** Republika Srpska, N Bosnia and Herzegovina 44°43′N 17°19′E
109 V10 **Celje** Ger. Cilli. C Slovenia 46°16′N 15°14′E
111 G23 **Celldömölk** Vas, W Hungary 47°16′N 17°10′E
100 J12 **Celle** var. Zelle. Niedersachsen, N Germany 52°38′N 10°05′E
99 D19 **Celles** Hainaut, SW Belgium 50°42′N 03°25′E
104 I7 **Celorico da Beira** Guarda, N Portugal 40°38′N 07°24′W
Celovec see Klagenfurt
64 M7 **Celtic Sea** Ir. An Mhuir Cheilteach. sea SW British Isles
64 N7 **Celtic Shelf** undersea feature E Atlantic Ocean 07°00′W 49°15′N
114 L13 **Çeltik Gölu** ◎ NW Turkey
146 J17 **Çemenibit** prev. Rus. Chemenibit. Mary Welaýaty, S Turkmenistan 35°27′N 62°19′E
113 M14 **Čemerno** ▲ C Serbia
105 Q12 **Cenajo, Embalse del** ⊠ S Spain
171 V13 **Cenderawasih, Teluk** var. Teluk Irian, Teluk Sarera. bay W Pacific Ocean
105 P4 **Cenicero** La Rioja, N Spain 42°29′N 02°38′W
106 E9 **Ceno** ~ NW Italy
102 K13 **Cenon** Gironde, SW France 44°51′N 00°33′W
14 K13 **Centennial Lake** ◎ Ontario, SE Canada
Centennial State see Colorado
37 S7 **Center** Colorado, C USA 37°45′N 106°06′W
29 Q13 **Center** Nebraska, C USA 42°33′N 97°51′W
28 M5 **Center** North Dakota, N USA 47°07′N 101°18′W
25 X8 **Center** Texas, SW USA 31°49′N 94°10′W
29 W8 **Center City** Minnesota, N USA 45°25′N 92°48′W
36 L5 **Centerfield** Utah, W USA 39°07′N 111°49′W
20 K9 **Center Hill Lake** ⊠ Tennessee, S USA
29 X13 **Center Point** Iowa, C USA 42°11′N 91°47′W
25 R11 **Center Point** Texas, SW USA 29°56′N 99°01′W
29 W16 **Centerville** Iowa, C USA 40°47′N 92°51′W
27 W7 **Centerville** Missouri, C USA 37°27′N 91°01′W
29 R12 **Centerville** South Dakota, N USA 43°07′N 96°57′W
20 I9 **Centerville** Tennessee, S USA 35°45′N 87°29′W
25 V9 **Centerville** Texas, SW USA 31°17′N 95°59′W
40 M5 **Centinela, Picacho del** ▲ NE Mexico 29°07′N 102°40′W
106 G9 **Cento** Emilia-Romagna, N Italy 44°43′N 11°16′E
Centrafricaine, République see Central African Republic
39 S8 **Central** Alaska, USA 65°34′N 144°48′W
37 P15 **Central** New Mexico, SW USA 32°46′N 108°09′W
83 H18 **Central** ◐ district E Botswana
138 E10 **Central** ◐ district C Israel
81 I19 **Central** ◐ province C Kenya
82 M13 **Central** ◐ region C Malawi
153 P12 **Central** ◐ zone C Nepal
186 E9 **Central** prev. Central. ◐ province S Papua New Guinea
63 I21 **Central** ◐ department C Paraguay
155 K25 **Central** ◐ province C Sri Lanka
83 J14 **Central** ◐ province C Zambia
117 P11 **Central** ✕ (Odesa) Odes'ka Oblast', SW Ukraine 46°26′N 30°41′E
Central see Centre
Central see Central
Central see Rennell and Bellona
79 H14 **Central African Republic** var. République Centrafricaine, abbrev. CAR; prev. Ubangi-Shari, Oubangui-Chari, Territoire de l'Oubangui-Chari. ◆ republic C Africa
192 C6 **Central Basin Trough** undersea feature W Pacific Ocean 16°45′N 130°00′E
Central Borneo see Kalimantan Tengah
149 P12 **Central Brāhui Range** ▲▲ W Pakistan
Central Celebes see Sulawesi Tengah
29 Y13 **Central City** Iowa, C USA 42°12′N 91°31′W
20 I6 **Central City** Kentucky, S USA 37°17′N 87°07′W
29 P15 **Central City** Nebraska, C USA 41°04′N 97°59′W
48 D6 **Central, Cordillera** ▲▲ W Bolivia
54 D11 **Central, Cordillera** ▲▲ W Colombia
42 M13 **Central, Cordillera** ▲▲ C Costa Rica
45 N9 **Central, Cordillera** ▲▲ C Dominican Republic
43 R16 **Central, Cordillera** ▲▲ C Panama
45 S6 **Central, Cordillera** ▲▲ Puerto Rico
42 H7 **Central District** var. Tegucigalpa. ◐ district C Honduras
81 E16 **Central Equatoria** var. Bahr el Gebel, Bahr el Jebel. ◐ state S South Sudan
Central Group see Inner Islands
30 L15 **Centralia** Illinois, N USA 38°31′N 89°07′W
27 U4 **Centralia** Missouri, C USA 39°12′N 92°08′W
32 G9 **Centralia** Washington, NW USA 46°43′N 122°57′W
Central Indian Ridge see Mid-Indian Ridge
Central Java see Jawa Tengah
Central Kalimantan see Kalimantan Tengah
148 L14 **Central Makrān Range** ▲▲ W Pakistan
192 K7 **Central Pacific Basin** undersea feature C Pacific Ocean 05°00′N 175°00′W
59 M19 **Central, Planalto** var. Brazilian Highlands. ▲▲ E Brazil
32 F15 **Central Point** Oregon, NW USA 42°22′N 122°55′W
Central Provinces and Berar see Madhya Pradesh
186 B6 **Central Range** ▲▲ NW Papua New Guinea
Central Russian Upland see Srednerusskaya Vozvyshennost'
Central Siberian Plateau/ Central Siberian Uplands see Srednesibirskoye Ploskogor'ye
104 K8 **Central, Sistema** ▲▲ C Spain
Central Sulawesi see Sulawesi Tengah
35 N3 **Central Valley** California, W USA 40°39′N 122°21′W
35 P8 **Central Valley** valley California, W USA
23 Q3 **Centre** Alabama, S USA 34°09′N 85°40′W
79 E15 **Centre** Eng. Central. ◐ province C Cameroon
102 M8 **Centre** ◐ region N France
173 Y16 **Centre de Flacq** E Mauritius 20°12′S 57°43′E
55 Y9 **Centre Spatial Guyanais** space station N French Guiana
23 O5 **Centreville** Alabama, S USA 32°58′N 87°08′W
21 X3 **Centreville** Maryland, NE USA 39°03′N 76°04′W
22 J7 **Centreville** Mississippi, S USA 31°05′N 91°04′W
Centum Cellae see Civitavecchia
160 M14 **Cenxi** Guangxi Zhuangzu Zizhiqu, S China 22°58′N 111°00′E
Ceos see Tziá
Cephaloedium see Cefalù
112 I9 **Čepin** Hung. Csepén. Osijek-Baranja, E Croatia 45°32′N 18°33′E
Ceram see Seram, Pulau
Ceram Sea see Seram, Laut
192 G8 **Ceram Trough** undersea feature W Pacific Ocean
Cerasus see Giresun
36 I10 **Cerbat Mountains** ▲▲ Arizona, SW USA
103 P17 **Cerbère, Cap** headland S France 42°28′N 03°15′E
104 F13 **Cercal do Alentejo** Setúbal, S Portugal 37°48′N 08°40′W
111 A18 **Čerchov** Ger. Czerkow. ▲ W Czech Republic 49°24′N 12°47′E
103 O13 **Cère** ~ C France
61 A16 **Ceres** Santa Fe, C Argentina 29°55′S 61°55′W
59 K18 **Ceres** Goiás, C Brazil 15°21′S 49°34′W
Ceresio see Lugano, Lago di
103 O17 **Céret** Pyrénées-Orientales, S France 42°30′N 02°44′E
54 E6 **Cereté** Córdoba, NW Colombia 08°54′N 75°51′W
172 I17 **Cerf, Île au** island Inner Islands, NE Seychelles
99 G22 **Cerfontaine** Namur, S Belgium 50°08′N 04°25′E
Cergy-Pontoise see Pontoise
107 N16 **Cerignola** Puglia, SE Italy 41°17′N 15°53′E
Cerigo see Kýthira
103 O9 **Cérilly** Allier, C France 46°38′N 02°51′E
136 I11 **Çerkeş** Çankırı, N Turkey 40°51′N 32°52′E
136 D10 **Çerkezköy** Tekirdağ, NW Turkey 41°17′N 28°00′E
109 T12 **Cerknica** Ger. Zirknitz. SW Slovenia 45°48′N 14°21′E
109 S11 **Cerkno** W Slovenia 46°07′N 13°58′E
116 F10 **Cermei** Hung. Csermő. Arad, W Romania 46°33′N 21°51′E
137 O15 **Çermik** Diyarbakır, SE Turkey 38°09′N 39°27′E
112 I10 **Cerna** Vukovar-Srijem, E Croatia 45°10′N 18°36′E
Cernăuţi see Chernivtsi
116 M14 **Cernavodă** Constanţa, SW Romania 44°20′N 28°03′E
103 U7 **Cernay** Haut-Rhin, NE France 47°49′N 07°11′E
Černice see Schwarzach
41 O8 **Cerralvo** Nuevo León, NE Mexico 26°10′N 99°40′W
40 G9 **Cerralvo, Isla** island NW Mexico
107 L16 **Cerreto Sannita** Campania, S Italy 41°17′N 14°39′E
113 L20 **Cërrik** var. Cerriku. Elbasan, C Albania 41°01′N 19°55′E
Cerriku see Cërrik
41 O11 **Cerritos** San Luis Potosí, C Mexico 22°25′N 100°16′W
60 K11 **Cerro Azul** Paraná, S Brazil 24°48′S 49°14′W
61 F18 **Cerro Chato** Treinta y Tres, E Uruguay 33°04′S 55°08′W
61 F19 **Cerro Colorado** Florida, S Uruguay 33°52′S 55°33′W
56 E13 **Cerro de Pasco** Pasco, C Peru 10°43′S 76°15′W
61 G14 **Cêrro Largo** Rio Grande do Sul, S Brazil 28°10′S 54°43′W
61 G18 **Cerro Largo** ◐ department NE Uruguay
42 E7 **Cerrón Grande, Embalse** ⊠ N El Salvador
63 I14 **Cerros Colorados, Embalse** ◎ W Argentina
105 V5 **Cervera** Cataluña, NE Spain 41°40′N 01°16′E
104 M3 **Cervera del Pisuerga** Castilla y León, N Spain 42°51′N 04°30′W
105 Q5 **Cervera del Río Alhama** La Rioja, N Spain 42°01′N 01°58′W
107 H15 **Cerveteri** Lazio, C Italy 42°00′N 12°06′E
106 H10 **Cervia** Emilia-Romagna, N Italy 44°14′N 12°22′E
106 J7 **Cervignano del Friuli** Friuli-Venezia Giulia, NE Italy 45°49′N 13°18′E
107 L17 **Cervinara** Campania, S Italy 41°02′N 14°36′E
Cervinia see Breuil-Cervinia
106 B6 **Cervino, Monte** var. Matterhorn. ▲ Italy/ Switzerland 46°00′N 07°39′E see also Matterhorn
Cervino, Monte see Matterhorn
103 Y14 **Cervione** Corse, France, C Mediterranean Sea 42°22′N 09°28′E
104 I1 **Cervo** Galicia, NW Spain 43°39′N 07°25′W
54 F5 **Cesar** off. Departamento del Cesar. ◐ province N Colombia
Cesar, Departamento del see Cesar
106 H10 **Cesena** anc. Caesena. Emilia-Romagna, N Italy 44°09′N 12°14′E
106 I10 **Cesenatico** Emilia-Romagna, N Italy 44°12′N 12°24′E
118 H8 **Cēsis** Ger. Wenden. C Latvia 57°19′N 25°17′E
111 D15 **Česká Lípa** Ger. Böhmisch-Leipa. Liberecký Kraj, N Czech Republic 50°43′N 14°35′E
Česká Republika see Czech Republic
111 F17 **Česká Třebová** Ger. Böhmisch-Trübau. Pardubický Kraj, C Czech Republic 49°54′N 16°27′E
111 D19 **České Budějovice** Ger. Budweis. Jihočeský Kraj, S Czech Republic 48°58′N 14°29′E
111 D19 **České Velenice** Jihočeský Kraj, S Czech Republic 48°49′N 14°57′E
111 E18 **Českomoravská Vrchovina** var. Českomoravská Vysočina, Eng. Bohemian-Moravian Highlands, Ger. Böhmisch-Mährische Höhe. ▲▲ S Czech Republic
Českomoravská Vysočina see Českomoravská Vrchovina
111 C19 **Český Krumlov** var. Böhmisch-Krumau, Ger. Krummau. Jihočeský Kraj, S Czech Republic 48°48′N 14°18′E
Český Les see Bohemian Forest
112 F8 **Česma** ~ N Croatia
136 A14 **Çeşme** İzmir, W Turkey 38°19′N 26°20′E
Cess see Cestos
183 T8 **Cessnock** New South Wales, SE Australia 32°51′S 151°21′E
76 K17 **Cestos** var. Cess. ~ S Liberia
118 I9 **Cesvaine** E Latvia 56°58′N 26°15′E
116 G14 **Cetate** Dolj, SW Romania 44°06′N 23°01′E
Cetatea Albă see Bilhorod-Dnistrovs'kyy
Cetatea Damboviţei see Bucureşti
113 J17 **Cetinje** It. Cettigne. S Montenegro 42°23′N 18°55′E
107 N20 **Cetraro** Calabria, S Italy 39°30′N 15°59′E
Cette see Sète
188 A17 **Cetti Bay** bay SW Guam
Cettigne see Cetinje
104 L17 **Ceuta** var. Sebta. Ceuta, Spain, N Africa 35°53′N 05°19′W
88 C16 **Ceuta** enclave Spain, N Africa
106 B9 **Ceva** Piemonte, NE Italy 44°24′N 08°01′E
103 P14 **Cévennes** ▲▲ S France
108 G10 **Cevio** Ticino, S Switzerland 46°18′N 08°36′E
136 K16 **Ceyhan** Adana, S Turkey 37°02′N 35°48′E
136 K17 **Ceyhan Nehri** ~ S Turkey
137 P17 **Ceylanpınar** Şanlıurfa, SE Turkey 36°53′N 40°02′E
Ceylon see Sri Lanka
173 R6 **Ceylon Plain** undersea feature N Indian Ocean 04°00′S 82°00′E
Ceyre to the Caribs see Marie-Galante
103 Q14 **Cèze** ~ S France
Chaacha see Çäçe

◆ Country
● Country Capital
◇ Dependent Territory
○ Dependent Territory Capital
◐ Administrative Regions
✕ International Airport
▲ Mountain
▲▲ Mountain Range
Volcano
~ River
◎ Lake
⊠ Reservoir

127 P6 Chaadayevka Penzenskaya Oblast', W Russian Federation 53°07′N 45°55′E
167 O12 Cha-Am Phetchaburi, SW Thailand 12°48′N 99°58′E
143 W15 Chābahār var. Chāh Bahār, Chahbar. Sīstān va Balūchestān, SE Iran 25°21′N 60°38′E
Chabaricha see Khabarikha
61 B19 Chabas Santa Fe, C Argentina 33°16′S 61°23′W
103 T10 Chablais physical region E France
61 B20 Chacabuco Buenos Aires, E Argentina 34°40′S 60°27′W
42 K8 Chachagón, Cerro ▲ N Nicaragua 13°18′N 85°39′W
56 C10 Chachapoyas Amazonas, NW Peru 06°13′S 77°54′W
Chäche see Çäçe
119 O18 Chachersk Rus. Chechersk. Homyel'skaya Voblasts', SE Belarus 52°54′N 30°54′E
119 N16 Chachevichy Rus. Chechevichi. Mahilyowskaya Voblasts', E Belarus 53°31′N 29°51′E
61 B14 Chaco off. Provincia de Chaco. ◈ province NE Argentina
Chaco see Gran Chaco
62 M6 Chaco Austral physical region N Argentina
62 M3 Chaco Boreal physical region N Paraguay
62 M6 Chaco Central physical region N Argentina
39 Y15 Chacon, Cape headland Prince of Wales Island, Alaska, USA 54°41′N 132°00′W
Chaco, Provincia de see Chaco
78 H9 Chad off. Republic of Chad, Fr. Tchad. ◆ republic C Africa
122 K14 Chadan Respublika Tyva, S Russian Federation 51°16′N 91°25′E
21 U12 Chadbourn North Carolina, SE USA 34°19′N 78°49′W
83 L14 Chadiza Eastern, E Zambia 14°04′S 32°27′E
67 Q7 Chad, Lake Fr. Lac Tchad. ◎ C Africa
Chad, Republic of see Chad
28 J12 Chadron Nebraska, C USA 42°48′N 102°57′W
Chadyr-Lunga see Ciadîr-Lunga
163 W14 Chaeryŏng SW North Korea 38°22′N 125°35′E
105 P17 Chafarinas, Islas island group S Spain
27 Y7 Chaffee Missouri, C USA 37°10′N 89°39′W
148 L12 Chāgai Hills var. Chāh Gay. ▲▲ Afghanistan/Pakistan
123 Q11 Chagda Respublika Sakha (Yakutiya), NE Russian Federation 58°43′N 130°38′E
Chaghasarāy see Asadābād
149 N5 Chaghcharān var. Chakhcharan, Cheghcheran, Qala Āhangarān. Gōwr, C Afghanistan 34°28′N 65°18′E
103 R9 Chagny Saône-et-Loire, C France 46°54′N 04°45′E
173 Q7 Chagos Archipelago var. Oil Islands. island group British Indian Ocean Territory
129 O15 Chagos Bank undersea feature C Indian Ocean 06°15′S 72°00′E
129 O14 Chagos-Laccadive Plateau undersea feature N Indian Ocean 03°00′S 73°00′E
173 Q7 Chagos Trench undersea feature N Indian Ocean 07°00′S 73°30′E
43 T14 Chagres, Río ≈ C Panama
45 U14 Chaguanas Trinidad, Trinidad and Tobago 10°31′N 61°25′W
54 M6 Chaguaramas Guárico, N Venezuela 09°23′N 66°18′W
Chagyl see Çagyl
Chahār Maḩāll and Bakhtiyāri see Chahār Maḩāl va Bakhtīārī
Chahār Maḩall va Bakhtīārī, Ostān-e see Chahār Maḩāl va Bakhtīārī
142 M9 Chahār Maḩāl va Bakhtīārī off. Ostān-e Chahār Maḩall va Bakhtīārī, var. Chahār Maḩāll and Bakhtiyāri. ◈ province SW Iran
Chāh Bahār/Chahbar see Chābahār
143 V13 Chāh Derāz Sīstān va Balūchestān, SE Iran 27°07′N 60°01′E
Chāh Gay see Chāgai Hills
167 P10 Chai Badan Lop Buri, C Thailand 15°08′N 101°03′E
153 Q16 Chāībāsa Jhārkhand, N India 22°31′N 85°50′E
79 E19 Chaillu, Massif du ▲ C Gabon
167 O10 Chai Nat var. Chainat, Jainat, Jayanath. Chai Nat, C Thailand 15°10′N 100°10′E
Chainat see Chai Nat
65 M14 Chain Fracture Zone tectonic feature E Atlantic Ocean
173 N5 Chain Ridge undersea feature W Indian Ocean 06°00′N 54°00′E
Chairn, Ceann an see Carnsore Point
158 L5 Chaiwopu Xinjiang Uygur Zizhiqu, W China 43°32′N 87°55′E
167 Q10 Chaiyaphum var. Jayabum. Chaiyaphum, C Thailand 15°46′N 101°55′E
62 N10 Chajarí Entre Ríos, E Argentina 30°45′S 57°57′W
42 C5 Chajul Quiché, W Guatemala 15°28′N 91°02′W
83 K16 Chakari Mashonaland West, N Zimbabwe 18°05′S 29°51′E
148 J9 Chakhānsūr Nīmrōz, SW Afghanistan 31°11′N 62°06′E
Chakhānsūr see Nīmrōz
Chakhcharan see Chaghcharān
149 V8 Chak Jhumra var. Jhumra. Punjab, E Pakistan 31°33′N 73°14′E
146 I16 Chaknakdysonga Ahal Welaýaty, S Turkmenistan 35°39′N 61°24′E
153 P16 Chakradharpur Jhārkhand, N India 22°42′N 85°38′E
152 J8 Chakrāta Uttarakhand, N India 30°42′N 77°52′E
149 U7 Chakwāl Punjab, NE Pakistan 32°56′N 72°53′E
57 F17 Chala Arequipa, SW Peru 15°52′S 74°13′W
102 K12 Chalais Charente, W France 45°16′N 00°02′E
108 D10 Chalais Valais, SW Switzerland 46°18′N 07°37′E
115 J20 Chalándri var. Halandri; prev. Khalándrion. prehistoric site Sýros, Kykládes, Greece, Aegean Sea
188 H6 Chalan Kanoa Saipan, S Northern Mariana Islands 15°08′S 145°43′E
188 C16 Chalan Pago C Guam
Chalap Dalam/Chalap Dalan see Chehel Abdālān, Kūh-e
42 F7 Chalatenango Chalatenango, N El Salvador 14°04′N 88°53′W
42 A9 Chalatenango ◈ department NW El Salvador
83 P15 Chalaua Nampula, NE Mozambique 16°04′S 39°08′E
81 I16 Chalbi Desert desert N Kenya
42 D7 Chalchuapa Santa Ana, W El Salvador 13°59′N 89°41′W
Chalcidice see Chalkidikí
Chalcis see Chalkída
Chāldarān see Sīāh Chashmeh
103 N6 Châlette-sur-Loing Loiret, C France 48°01′N 02°45′E
15 X8 Chaleur Bay Fr. Baie des Chaleurs. bay New Brunswick/Québec, E Canada
Chaleurs, Baie des see Chaleur Bay
57 G16 Chalhuanca Apurímac, S Peru 14°17′S 73°15′W
154 F12 Chālisgaon Mahārāshtra, C India 20°29′N 75°10′E
115 N23 Chálki island Dodekánisa, Greece, Aegean Sea
115 F16 Chalkiádes Thessalía, C Greece 39°24′N 22°25′E
115 H18 Chalkída var. Halkida, prev. Khalkís; anc. Chalcis. Evvoia, E Greece 38°27′N 23°38′E
115 G14 Chalkidikí var. Khalkidhikí; anc. Chalcidice. peninsula NE Greece
185 A24 Chalky Inlet inlet South Island, New Zealand
39 S7 Chalkyitsik Alaska, USA 66°39′N 143°43′W
102 I9 Challans Vendée, NW France 46°51′N 01°52′W
57 K19 Challapata Oruro, SW Bolivia 18°50′S 66°45′W
192 H6 Challenger Deep undersea feature W Pacific Ocean 11°20′N 142°12′E
Challenger Deep see Mariana Trench
193 S11 Challenger Fracture Zone tectonic feature SE Pacific Ocean
192 K11 Challenger Plateau undersea feature E Tasman Sea
33 P13 Challis Idaho, NW USA 44°31′N 114°14′W
22 L9 Chalmette Louisiana, S USA 29°56′N 89°57′W
124 J11 Chalna Respublika Kareliya, NW Russian Federation 61°53′N 33°59′E
103 Q5 Châlons-en-Champagne prev. Châlons-sur-Marne, hist. Arcae Remorum; anc. Carolopois. Marne, NE France 48°58′N 04°22′E
Châlons-sur-Marne see Châlons-en-Champagne
103 R9 Chalon-sur-Saône anc. Cabillonum. Saône-et-Loire, C France 46°47′N 04°51′E
Chaltel, Cerro see Fitzroy, Monte
102 M11 Châlus Haute-Vienne, C France 45°38′N 01°00′E
143 N4 Chālūs Māzandarān, N Iran 36°40′N 51°25′E
101 N20 Cham Bayern, SE Germany 49°13′N 12°40′E
108 F7 Cham Zug, N Switzerland 47°11′N 08°28′E
37 R8 Chama New Mexico, SW USA 36°54′N 106°34′W
Cha Mai see Thung Song
83 E22 Chamaites Karas, S Namibia 27°15′S 17°52′E
149 O9 Chaman Baluchistān, SW Pakistan 30°55′N 66°27′E
37 R9 Chama, Rio ≈ New Mexico, SW USA
152 I6 Chamba Himāchal Pradesh, N India 32°33′N 76°10′E
81 I25 Chamba Ruvuma, S Tanzania 11°33′S 37°01′E
150 H12 Chambal ≈ C India
11 U16 Chamberlain Saskatchewan, S Canada 50°49′N 105°29′W
29 O11 Chamberlain South Dakota, N USA 43°48′N 99°19′W
19 R3 Chamberlain Lake ◎ Maine, NE USA
39 S5 Chamberlin, Mount ▲ Alaska, USA 69°16′N 144°54′W
37 O11 Chambers Arizona, SW USA 35°11′N 109°25′W
18 F16 Chambersburg Pennsylvania, NE USA 39°54′N 77°39′W
31 N5 Chambers Island island Wisconsin, N USA
103 T11 Chambéry anc. Camberia. Savoie, E France 45°34′N 05°56′E
82 L12 Chambeshi Northern, NE Zambia 10°55′S 31°07′E
82 L12 Chambeshi ≈ NE Zambia
74 M6 Chambi, Jebel var. Jabal ash Sha'nabī. ▲ W Tunisia 35°16′N 08°39′E
15 Q7 Chambord Québec, SE Canada 48°25′N 72°02′W
139 U11 Chamcham Al Muthanná, S Iraq 31°17′N 45°05′E
139 T4 Chamchamāl At Ta'mím, N Iraq 35°32′N 44°50′E
Chamdmanī see Altanshiree
40 J14 Chamela Jalisco, SW Mexico 19°31′N 105°02′W
42 G5 Chamelecón, Río ≈ NW Honduras
62 J9 Chamical La Rioja, C Argentina 30°21′S 66°19′W
115 L23 Chamilí island Kykládes, Greece, Aegean Sea
167 Q13 Châmnar Kaôh Kông, SW Cambodia 11°45′N 103°32′E
152 K9 Chamoli Uttarakhand, N India 30°22′N 79°19′E
103 U11 Chamonix-Mont-Blanc Haute-Savoie, E France 45°55′N 06°52′E
154 L11 Chāmpa Chhattīsgarh, C India 22°02′N 82°42′E
10 H8 Champagne Yukon Territory, W Canada 60°48′N 136°22′W
103 Q5 Champagne cultural region N France
Champagne see Campania
103 Q5 Champagne-Ardenne ◈ region N France
103 S9 Champagnole Jura, E France 46°44′N 05°55′E
30 M13 Champaign Illinois, N USA 40°07′N 88°15′W
167 S10 Champasak Champasak, S Laos 14°50′N 105°51′E
103 U6 Champ de Feu ▲ NE France 48°24′N 07°15′E
13 O7 Champdoré, Lac ◎ Québec, NE Canada
42 B6 Champerico Retalhuleu, SW Guatemala 14°18′N 91°54′W
108 C11 Champéry Valais, SW Switzerland 46°12′N 06°52′E
18 L6 Champlain New York, NE USA 44°58′N 73°25′W
18 L9 Champlain Canal canal New York, NE USA
15 P13 Champlain, Lac ◎ Québec, Canada/USA see also Champlain, Lake
18 L7 Champlain, Lake ◎ Canada/USA see also Champlain, Lac
103 S7 Champlitte Haute-Saône, E France 47°36′N 05°31′E
41 W13 Champotón Campeche, SE Mexico 19°18′N 90°43′W
104 G10 Chamusca Santarém, C Portugal 39°21′N 08°29′W
119 O20 Chamyarysy Rus. Chemerisy. Homyel'skaya Voblasts', SE Belarus 51°42′N 30°27′E
127 P5 Chamzinka Respublika Mordoviya, W Russian Federation 54°22′N 45°22′E
Chanáil Mhór, An see Grand Canal
Chanak see Çanakkale
62 G7 Chañaral Atacama, N Chile 26°19′S 70°34′W
104 H13 Chança, Rio var. Chanza. ≈ Portugal/Spain
57 D14 Chancay Lima, W Peru 11°36′S 77°14′W
Chan-chiang/Chanchiang see Zhanjiang
62 G13 Chanco Maule, C Chile 35°43′S 72°35′W
39 R7 Chandalar Alaska, USA 67°30′N 148°29′W
39 R6 Chandalar River ≈ Alaska, USA
152 L10 Chandan Chauki Uttar Pradesh, N India 28°32′N 80°43′E
153 S16 Chandannagar prev. Chandernagore. West Bengal, E India 22°52′N 88°21′E
152 K10 Chandausi Uttar Pradesh, N India 28°27′N 78°43′E
22 M10 Chandeleur Islands island group Louisiana, S USA
22 M9 Chandeleur Sound sound N Gulf of Mexico
Chandernagore see Chandannagar
152 I8 Chandīgarh state capital Punjab, N India 30°41′N 76°51′E
153 Q16 Chāndil Jhārkhand, NE India 22°58′N 86°04′E
182 D2 Chandler South Australia 26°59′S 133°22′E
15 Y7 Chandler Québec, SE Canada 48°21′N 64°41′W
36 L14 Chandler Arizona, SW USA 33°18′N 111°50′W
27 O10 Chandler Oklahoma, C USA 35°43′N 96°54′W
25 V7 Chandler Texas, SW USA 32°18′N 95°28′W
39 Q6 Chandler River ≈ Alaska, USA
56 H13 Chandles, Río ≈ E Peru
162 H9 Chandmanĭ var. Talshand. Govĭ-Altayĭ, C Mongolia 45°21′N 98°00′E
162 E7 Chandmanĭ var. Urdgol. Hovd, W Mongolia 47°39′N 92°46′E
14 J13 Chandos Lake ◎ Ontario, SE Canada
153 U15 Chandpur Chittagong, C Bangladesh 23°13′N 90°43′E
154 I13 Chandrapur Mahārāshtra, C India 19°58′N 79°21′E
83 J15 Changa Southern, S Zambia 16°24′S 28°27′E
Chang'an see Rong'an, Guangxi Zhuangzu Zizhiqu, S China
Chang'an see Xi'an, Shaanxi, C China
155 G23 Changanācheri var. Changannassery. Kerala, SW India 09°26′N 76°31′E see also Changannassery
83 M19 Changane ≈ S Mozambique
83 M16 Changara Tete, NW Mozambique 16°54′S 33°15′E
163 X11 Changbai var. Changbai Chaoxianzu Zizhixian. Jilin, NE China 41°25′N 128°08′E
Changbai Chaoxianzu Zizhixian see Changbai
163 X11 Changbai Shan ▲▲ NE China
163 V10 Changchun var. Ch'angch'un, Ch'ang-ch'un; prev. Hsinking. province capital Jilin, NE China 43°53′N 125°18′E
Ch'angch'un/Ch'ang-ch'un see Changchun
160 M10 Changde Hunan, S China 29°04′N 111°42′E
Changhua see Zhanghua
168 L10 Changi ✈ (Singapore) E Singapore 01°22′N 103°58′E
158 L5 Changji Xinjiang Uygur Zizhiqu, NW China 44°02′N 87°12′E
160 L17 Changjiang var. Changjiang Lizu Zizhixian, Shiliu. Hainan, S China 19°16′N 109°09′E
157 R11 Chang Jiang var. Yangtze Kiang, Eng. Yangtze. ≈ C China
157 N12 Chang Jiang Eng. Yangtze. ≈ SW China
161 S8 Changjiang Kou delta E China
Changjiang Lizu Zizhixian see Changjiang
Changkiakow see Zhangjiakou
167 F12 Chang, Ko island S Thailand
161 Q2 Changli Hebei, E China 39°44′N 119°13′E
163 V10 Changling Jilin, NE China 44°15′N 124°03′E
Changning see Xunwu
161 N11 Changsha var. Ch'angsha, Ch'ang-sha. province capital Hunan, S China 28°10′N 113°E
Ch'angsha/Ch'ang-sha see Changsha
161 Q10 Changshan Zhejiang, SE China 28°54′N 118°30′E
163 V14 Changshan Qundao island group NE China
161 S8 Changshu var. Ch'ang-shu. Jiangsu, E China 31°39′N 120°45′E
Ch'ang-shu see Changshu
163 V11 Changtu Liaoning, NE China 42°50′N 123°59′E
43 P14 Changuinola Bocas del Toro, NW Panama 09°28′N 82°31′W
159 N9 Changweiliang Qinghai, W China 38°24′N 92°08′E
160 K6 Changwu var. Zhaoren. Shaanxi, C China 35°12′N 107°46′E
163 U13 Changxing Dao island N China
160 M9 Changyang var. Longzhouping. Hubei, C China 30°45′N 111°13′E
163 W14 Changyŏn SW North Korea 38°19′N 125°15′E
161 N5 Changzhi Shanxi, C China 36°10′N 113°02′E
161 R8 Changzhou Jiangsu, E China 31°45′N 119°58′E
115 H24 Chaniá var. Hania, Khaniá, Eng. Canea; anc. Cydonia. Kríti, Greece, E Mediterranean Sea 35°31′N 24°00′E
62 J5 Chañi, Nevado de ▲ NW Argentina 24°09′S 65°44′W
115 H24 Chanión, Kólpos gulf Kríti, Greece, E Mediterranean Sea
Chankiri see Çankırı
30 M11 Channahon Illinois, N USA 41°25′N 88°13′W
155 H20 Channapatna Karnātaka, E India 12°43′N 77°14′E
97 K26 Channel Islands Fr. Iles Normandes. island group S English Channel
35 R16 Channel Islands island group California, W USA
13 S13 Channel-Port aux Basques Newfoundland and Labrador, SE Canada 47°35′N 59°02′W
Channel, The see English Channel
97 Q23 Channel Tunnel tunnel France/United Kingdom
24 M2 Channing Texas, SW USA 35°41′N 102°21′W
Chantabun/Chantaburi see Chanthaburi
104 H3 Chantada Galicia, NW Spain 42°36′N 07°46′W
167 P12 Chanthaburi var. Chantabun, Chantaburi. Chantaburi, S Thailand 12°35′N 102°08′E
103 O4 Chantilly Oise, N France 49°12′N 02°28′E
139 V12 Chanūn as Sa'ūdī Dhī Qār, S Iraq 31°04′N 46°00′E
27 Q6 Chanute Kansas, C USA 37°40′N 95°27′W
Chanza see Chança, Rio
Ch'ao-an/Chaochow see Chaozhou
161 P8 Chao Hu ◎ E China
167 P11 Chao Phraya, Mae Nam ≈ C Thailand
163 T8 Chaor He prev. Qulin Gol. ≈ NE China
Chaouèn see Chefchaouen
161 P14 Chaoyang Guangdong, S China 23°17′N 116°33′E
163 T12 Chaoyang Liaoning, NE China 41°34′N 120°29′E
Chaoyang see Jiayin, Heilongjiang, China
Chaoyang see Huinan, Jilin China
161 Q14 Chaozhou var. Chaoan, Chao'an, Ch'ao-an; prev. Chaochow. Guangdong, SE China 23°42′N 116°36′E
58 N13 Chapadinha Maranhão, E Brazil 03°45′S 43°23′W
12 K12 Chapais Québec, SE Canada 49°47′N 74°54′W
40 L13 Chapala Jalisco, SW Mexico 20°20′N 103°10′W
40 L13 Chapala, Lago de ◎ C Mexico
146 F13 Chapan, Gora ▲ C Turkmenistan 37°48′N 58°03′E
57 M18 Chapare, Río ≈ C Bolivia
54 E11 Chaparral Tolima, C Colombia 03°45′N 75°30′W
144 F9 Chapayev Zapadnyy Kazakhstan, NW Kazakhstan 50°12′N 51°09′E
123 O11 Chapayevo Respublika Sakha (Yakutiya), NE Russian Federation 60°03′N 117°19′E
127 R6 Chapayevsk Samarskaya Oblast', W Russian Federation 52°57′N 49°42′E
60 H13 Chapecó Santa Catarina, S Brazil 27°14′S 52°41′W
60 I13 Chapecó, Rio ≈ S Brazil
20 J9 Chapel Hill Tennessee, S USA 35°38′N 86°40′W
44 J12 Chapelton C Jamaica 18°05′N 77°16′W
14 C8 Chapleau Ontario, SE Canada 47°50′N 83°24′W
14 D7 Chapleau ≈ Ontario, S Canada
11 T16 Chaplin Saskatchewan, S Canada 50°27′N 106°37′W
126 M6 Chaplygin Lipetskaya Oblast', W Russian Federation 53°13′N 39°58′E
117 S11 Chaplynka Khersons'ka Oblast', S Ukraine 46°20′N 33°34′E
9 O6 Chapman, Cape headland Nunavut, NE Canada 69°15′N 89°09′W
25 T15 Chapman Ranch Texas, SW USA 27°32′N 97°25′W
Chapman's see Okwa
21 P5 Chapmanville West Virginia, NE USA 37°58′N 82°01′W
28 K15 Chappell Nebraska, C USA 41°05′N 102°28′W
Chapra see Chhapra
56 D9 Chapuli, Río ≈ N Peru
76 I6 Châr well N Mauritania
123 P12 Chara Zabaykal'skiy Kray, S Russian Federation 56°57′N 118°05′E
123 O11 Chara ≈ C Russian Federation
54 G8 Charala Santander, C Colombia 06°17′N 73°09′W
41 N10 Charcas San Luis Potosí, C Mexico 23°09′N 101°10′W
25 T13 Charco Texas, SW USA 28°42′N 97°35′W
194 H7 Charcot Island island Antarctica
64 M8 Charcot Seamounts undersea feature E Atlantic Ocean 11°30′W 45°00′N
Chardara see Shardara
Chardarinskoye Vodokhranilishche see Shardarinskoye Vodokhranilishche
31 U11 Chardon Ohio, N USA 41°34′N 81°12′W
44 K9 Chardonnières SW Haiti 18°16′N 74°10′W
Chardzhev see Türkmenabat
Chardzhevskaya Oblast see Lebap Welaýaty
Chardzhou/Chardzhui see Türkmenabat
102 L11 Charente ◈ department W France
102 J11 Charente ≈ W France
102 J10 Charente-Maritime ◈ department W France
137 U12 Ch'arents'avan C Armenia 40°23′N 44°41′E
78 I12 Chari var. Shari. ≈ Central African Republic/Chad
78 G11 Chari-Baguirmi off. Préfecture du Chari-Baguirmi. ◈ prefecture SW Chad
Chari-Baguirmi, Préfecture du see Chari-Baguirmi
149 Q4 Chārīkār Parwān, NE Afghanistan 35°01′N 69°11′E
29 V15 Chariton Iowa, C USA 41°00′N 93°18′W
27 U3 Chariton River ≈ Missouri, C USA
55 T7 Charity NW Guyana 07°22′N 58°34′W
31 R7 Charity Island island Michigan, N USA
Chärjew see Türkmenabat
Chärjew Oblasty see Lebap Welaýaty
Charkhlik/Charkhliq see Ruoqiang
99 G20 Charleroi Hainaut, S Belgium 50°25′N 04°27′E
11 V12 Charles Manitoba, C Canada 55°27′N 100°58′W
15 R10 Charlesbourg Québec, SE Canada 46°50′N 71°15′W
21 Y7 Charles, Cape headland Virginia, NE USA 37°09′N 75°57′W
29 W12 Charles City Iowa, C USA 43°04′N 92°40′W
21 W6 Charles City Virginia, NE USA 37°21′N 77°05′W
103 O5 Charles de Gaulle ✈ (Paris) Seine-et-Marne, N France 49°04′N 02°36′E
12 K1 Charles Island island Nunavut, NE Canada
Charles Island see Santa María, Isla
30 K9 Charles Mound hill Illinois, N USA
185 A22 Charles Sound sound South Island, New Zealand
185 G15 Charleston West Coast, South Island, New Zealand 41°54′S 171°25′E
27 S11 Charleston Arkansas, C USA 35°19′N 94°02′W
30 M14 Charleston Illinois, N USA 39°30′N 88°10′W
22 L3 Charleston Mississippi, S USA 34°00′N 90°03′W
27 Z7 Charleston Missouri, C USA 36°54′N 89°22′W
21 T15 Charleston South Carolina, SE USA 32°48′N 79°57′W
21 Q5 Charleston state capital West Virginia, NE USA 38°21′N 81°38′W
14 L14 Charleston Lake ◎ Ontario, SE Canada
35 W11 Charleston Peak ▲ Nevada, W USA 36°16′N 115°40′W
45 W10 Charlestown Nevis, Saint Kitts and Nevis 17°08′N 62°37′W
31 P16 Charlestown Indiana, N USA 38°27′N 85°40′W
18 M9 Charlestown New Hampshire, NE USA 43°14′N 72°23′W
21 V3 Charles Town West Virginia, NE USA 39°18′N 77°54′W
181 W9 Charleville Queensland, E Australia 26°25′S 146°18′E
103 R3 Charleville-Mézières Ardennes, N France 49°45′N 04°43′E
31 P5 Charlevoix Michigan, N USA 45°19′N 85°15′W
31 Q6 Charlevoix, Lake ◎ Michigan, N USA
39 T9 Charley River ≈ Alaska, USA
64 J6 Charlie-Gibbs Fracture Zone tectonic feature N Atlantic Ocean
103 Q10 Charlieu Loire, E France 46°11′N 04°10′E
31 Q9 Charlotte Michigan, N USA 42°33′N 84°50′W
21 R10 Charlotte North Carolina, SE USA 35°14′N 80°51′W
20 I8 Charlotte Tennessee, S USA 36°11′N 87°18′W
25 R13 Charlotte Texas, SW USA 28°51′N 98°42′W
21 R10 Charlotte ✈ North Carolina, SE USA 35°12′N 80°54′W
45 T9 Charlotte Amalie prev. Saint Thomas. ○ (Virgin Islands (US)) Saint Thomas, N Virgin Islands (US) 18°22′N 64°56′W
21 U7 Charlotte Court House Virginia, NE USA 37°04′N 78°37′W
23 W14 Charlotte Harbor inlet Florida, SE USA
Charlotte Island see Abaiang
95 J15 Charlottenberg Värmland, C Sweden 59°53′N 12°17′E
Charlottenhof see Aegviidu
21 U5 Charlottesville Virginia, NE USA 38°02′N 78°29′W
13 Q14 Charlottetown province capital Prince Edward Island, Prince Edward Island, SE Canada 46°14′N 63°09′W
Charlotte Town see Roseau, Dominica
Charlotte Town see Gouyave, Grenada
45 Z16 Charlotteville Tobago, Trinidad and Tobago 11°16′N 60°33′W
182 M11 Charlton Victoria, SE Australia 36°18′S 143°19′E
12 H10 Charlton Island island Northwest Territories, C Canada
103 T6 Charmes Vosges, NE France 48°19′N 06°19′E
119 F19 Charnawchytsy Rus. Chernavchitsy. Brestskaya Voblasts', SW Belarus 52°13′N 23°44′E
15 R10 Charny Québec, SE Canada 46°43′N 71°15′W
149 T5 Chārsadda Khyber Pakhtunkhwa, NW Pakistan 34°12′N 71°46′E
Charshanga/Charshangngy/Charshangy see Köýtendag
Charsk see Shar
181 W6 Charters Towers Queensland, NE Australia 20°02′S 146°20′E
15 R12 Chartierville Québec, SE Canada 45°19′N 71°13′W
102 M6 Chartres anc. Autricum, Civitas Carnutum. Eure-et-Loir, C France 48°27′N 01°27′E
Charyn see Sharyn
Charyn see Sharyn
61 D21 Chascomús Buenos Aires, E Argentina 35°34′S 58°01′W
11 N16 Chase British Columbia, SW Canada 50°49′N 119°41′W
21 U7 Chase City Virginia, NE USA 36°48′N 78°27′W
19 S4 Chase, Mount ▲ Maine, NE USA 46°06′N 68°30′W
118 M13 Chashniki Vitsyebskaya Voblasts', N Belarus 54°52′N 29°10′E
115 D15 Chásia ▲▲ C Greece
29 V9 Chaska Minnesota, N USA 44°47′N 93°36′W
185 D25 Chaslands Mistake headland South Island, New Zealand 46°37′S 169°21′E
125 R11 Chasovo Respublika Komi, NW Russian Federation 61°58′N 50°34′E
Chasovo see Vazhgort
124 H14 Chastova Novgorodskaya Oblast', NW Russian Federation 58°37′N 32°05′E
143 R3 Chāt Golestān, N Iran 37°52′N 55°27′E
Chatak see Chhatak
Chatang see Zhanang
39 R9 Chatanika Alaska, USA 65°06′N 147°28′W
39 R9 Chatanika River ≈ Alaska, USA
147 T8 Chat-Bazar Talasskaya Oblast', NW Kyrgyzstan 42°29′N 72°37′E
45 Y14 Chateaubelair Saint Vincent, W Saint Vincent and the Grenadines 13°15′N 61°05′W
102 J7 Châteaubriant Loire-Atlantique, NW France 47°43′N 01°22′W
103 Q8 Château-Chinon Nièvre, C France 47°04′N 03°50′E
108 C10 Château d'Oex Vaud, W Switzerland 46°28′N 07°09′E
102 L7 Château-du-Loir Sarthe, NW France 47°40′N 00°25′E
102 M6 Châteaudun Eure-et-Loir, C France 48°04′N 01°20′E
102 K7 Château-Gontier Mayenne, NW France 47°49′N 00°42′W
15 O13 Châteauguay Québec, SE Canada 45°22′N 73°44′W
102 F6 Châteaulin Finistère, NW France 48°12′N 04°07′W
103 O9 Châteaumeillant Cher, C France 46°33′N 02°10′E
102 K11 Châteauneuf-sur-Charente Charente, W France 45°34′N 00°33′W
102 M7 Château-Renault Indre-et-Loire, C France 47°34′N 00°52′E
103 N9 Châteauroux prev. Indreville. Indre, C France 46°50′N 01°43′E
103 T5 Château-Salins Moselle, NE France 48°50′N 06°29′E
103 P4 Château-Thierry Aisne, N France 49°03′N 03°24′E
99 H21 Châtelet Hainaut, S Belgium 50°24′N 04°32′E
Châtelherault see Châtellerault
102 L9 Châtellerault var. Châtelherault. Vienne, W France 46°49′N 00°33′E
29 X10 Chatfield Minnesota, N USA 43°51′N 92°11′W
13 O14 Chatham New Brunswick, SE Canada 47°02′N 65°30′W
14 D17 Chatham Ontario, S Canada 42°24′N 82°11′W
97 P22 Chatham SE England, United Kingdom 51°23′N 00°31′E
30 K14 Chatham Illinois, N USA 39°40′N 89°42′W
21 T7 Chatham Virginia, NE USA 36°49′N 79°26′W
63 F22 Chatham, Isla island S Chile
175 R12 Chatham Island island Chatham Islands, New Zealand
Chatham Island see San Cristóbal, Isla
Chatham Island Rise see Chatham Rise
175 R12 Chatham Islands island group New Zealand, SW Pacific Ocean
175 Q12 Chatham Rise var. Chatham Island Rise. undersea feature S Pacific Ocean
39 X13 Chatham Strait strait Alaska, USA
Chathóir, Rinn see Cahore Point
102 M9 Châtillon-sur-Indre Indre, C France 46°58′N 01°10′E
103 Q7 Châtillon-sur-Seine Côte d'Or, C France 47°51′N 04°30′E
147 S8 Chatkal Uzb. Chotqol. ≈ Kyrgyzstan/Uzbekistan
147 R9 Chatkal Range Rus. Chatkal'skiy Khrebet. ▲▲ Kyrgyzstan/Uzbekistan
Chatkal'skiy Khrebet see Chatkal Range
23 N7 Chatom Alabama, S USA 31°28′N 88°15′W
Chatrapur see Chhatrapur
143 S10 Chatrūd Kermān, C Iran 30°39′N 56°57′E
23 S2 Chatsworth Georgia, SE USA 34°46′N 84°46′W
Chāttagām see Chittagong
23 S8 Chattahoochee Florida, SE USA 30°40′N 84°51′W
23 R8 Chattahoochee River ≈ SE USA
20 L10 Chattanooga Tennessee, S USA 35°05′N 85°16′W
147 V10 Chatyr-Kël', Ozero ◎ C Kyrgyzstan
147 W9 Chatyr-Tash Narynskaya Oblast', C Kyrgyzstan 40°54′N 76°22′E
15 R12 Chaudière ≈ Québec, SE Canada
167 S14 Châu Đôc var. Chauphu, Chau Phu. An Giang, S Vietnam 10°53′N 105°07′E
152 D13 Chauhtan prev. Chohtan. Rājasthān, NW India 25°27′N 71°08′E
166 L5 Chauk Magway, Myanmar (Burma) 20°52′N 94°50′E
103 R6 Chaumont prev. Chaumont-en-Bassigny. Haute-Marne, N France 48°07′N 05°08′E
Chaumont-en-Bassigny see Chaumont
123 T5 Chaunskaya Guba bay NE Russian Federation
103 P3 Chauny Aisne, N France 49°37′N 03°13′E
167 U10 Châu Ô var. Binh Sơn. Quang Ngai, C Vietnam 15°18′N 108°45′E
Chau Phu see Châu Đôc
102 I5 Chausey, Îles island group N France
Chausy see Chavusy
18 C11 Chautauqua Lake ◎ New York, NE USA
ChâuThanh see Ba Ria
102 L9 Chauvigny Vienne, W France 46°35′N 00°37′E
124 L6 Chavan'ga Murmanskaya Oblast', NW Russian Federation 66°07′N 37°44′E
14 K10 Chavannes, Lac ◎ Québec, SE Canada
Chavantes, Represa de see Xavantes, Represa de
61 D15 Chavarría Corrientes, NE Argentina 28°57′S 58°35′W
Chavash Respubliki see Chuvashskaya Respublika
104 I5 Chaves anc. Aquae Flaviae. Vila Real, N Portugal 41°44′N 07°28′W
Chávez, Isla see Santa Cruz, Isla
82 G13 Chavuma North Western, NW Zambia 13°04′S 22°43′E
119 O16 Chavusy Rus. Chausy. Mahilyowskaya Voblasts', E Belarus 53°48′N 30°58′E
Chayan see Shayan
147 U8 Chayek Narynskaya Oblast', C Kyrgyzstan 41°54′N 74°28′E
139 T6 Chāy Khānah Diyālá, E Iraq 34°19′N 44°33′E
125 T16 Chaykovskiy Permskiy Kray, NW Russian Federation 56°45′N 54°09′E
167 T12 Chbar Môndól Kiri, E Cambodia 12°46′N 107°10′E
23 Q4 Cheaha Mountain ▲ Alabama, S USA 33°29′N 85°48′W
Cheatharlach see Carlow
21 S2 Cheat River ≈ NE USA
111 A16 Cheb Ger. Eger. Karlovarský Kraj, W Czech Republic 50°05′N 12°23′E
127 Q3 Cheboksary Chuvashskaya Respublika, W Russian Federation 56°06′N 47°15′E
31 Q5 Cheboygan Michigan, N USA 45°40′N 84°28′W
Chechaouèn see Chefchaouen
Chechenia see Chechenskaya Respublika
127 O15 Chechenskaya Respublika Eng. Chechenia, Chechnia, Rus. Chechnya. ◈ autonomous republic SW Russian Federation
67 N4 Chech, Erg desert Algeria/Mali
Chechevichi see Chachevichy
Che-chiang see Zhejiang
Chechnia/Chechnya see Chechenskaya Respublika
Chech'ŏn see Jecheon
111 L15 Chęciny Świętokrzyskie, S Poland 50°51′N 20°31′E
27 Q10 Checotah Oklahoma, C USA 35°28′N 95°31′W
13 R15 Chedabucto Bay inlet Nova Scotia, E Canada
166 J7 Cheduba Island island W Myanmar (Burma)
37 T5 Cheesman Lake ⊠ Colorado, C USA
195 S16 Cheetham, Cape headland Antarctica 70°26′S 162°40′E
74 G5 Chefchaouen var. Chaouèn, Chechaouèn, Sp. Xauen. N Morocco 35°10′N 05°16′W
Chefoo see Yantai
38 M12 Chefornak Alaska, USA 60°09′N 164°09′W
123 R13 Chegdomyn Khabarovskiy Kray, SE Russian Federation 51°09′N 132°58′E
76 M4 Chegga Tiris Zemmour, NE Mauritania 25°27′N 05°49′W
Cheghcheran see Chaghcharān
32 G9 Chehalis Washington, NW USA 46°39′N 122°57′W
32 G9 Chehalis River ≈ Washington, NW USA
148 M6 Chehel Abdālān, Kūh-e var. Chalap Dalam, Pash. Chalap Dalan. ▲▲ C Afghanistan
115 D14 Cheimadítis, Límni var. Límni Cheimadítis. ◎ N Greece
Cheimadítis, Límni see Cheimadítis, Límni
103 U15 Cheiron, Mont ▲ SE France 43°49′N 07°00′E
163 Y17 Cheju ✈ S South Korea 33°31′N 126°29′E
Cheju see Jeju
Cheju-do see Jeju-do
Cheju-haehyeop see Jeju-haehyeop
Cheju Strait see Jeju-haehyeop
Chekiang see Zhejiang
Chekichler/Chekishlyar see Çekiçler
188 F8 Chelab Babeldaob, N Palau

◆ Country
● Country Capital
◇ Dependent Territory
○ Dependent Territory Capital
◈ Administrative Regions
✈ International Airport
▲ Mountain
▲▲ Mountain Range
⩕ Volcano
≈ River
◎ Lake
⊠ Reservoir

147 N11 Chelak Rus. Chelek. Samarqand Viloyati, C Uzbekistan 39°55′N 66°45′E
32 J7 Chelan, Lake ⊠ Washington, NW USA
Chelek see Chelak
Cheleken see Hazar
Chélif/Chéliff see Chelif, Oued
74 J5 Chelif, Oued var. Chélif, Chéliff, Chellif, Shellif. ≈ N Algeria
Chelkar see Shalkar
Chelkar Ozero see Shalkar, Ozero
Chellif see Chelif, Oued
111 P14 Chełm Rus. Kholm. Lubelskie, SE Poland 51°08′N 23°29′E
110 I9 Chełmno Ger. Culm, Kulm. Kujawski-pomorskie, C Poland 53°21′N 18°27′E
115 E19 Chelmós var. Ároania. ▲ S Greece
14 F10 Chelmsford Ontario, S Canada 46°33′N 81°16′W
97 P21 Chelmsford E England, United Kingdom 51°44′N 00°28′E
110 J9 Chełmża Ger. Culmsee, Kulmsee. Kujawski-pomorskie, C Poland 53°11′N 18°34′E
27 Q8 Chelsea Oklahoma, C USA 36°32′N 95°25′W
18 M8 Chelsea Vermont, NE USA 43°58′N 72°29′W
97 L21 Cheltenham C England, United Kingdom 51°54′N 02°04′W
105 R9 Chelva Valenciana, E Spain 39°45′N 01°00′W
122 G11 Chelyabinsk Chelyabinskaya Oblast', C Russian Federation 55°12′N 61°25′E
122 F11 Chelyabinskaya Oblast' ◈ province C Russian Federation
123 N5 Chelyuskin, Mys headland N Russian Federation 77°42′N 104°13′E
41 Y12 Chemax Yucatán, SE Mexico 20°41′N 87°54′W
83 N16 Chemba Sofala, C Mozambique 17°11′S 34°53′E
82 J13 Chembe Luapula, NE Zambia 11°58′S 28°45′E
Chemenibit see Çemenibit
Chemerisy see Chamyarysy
116 K7 Chemerivtsi Khmel'nyts'ka Oblast', W Ukraine 49°00′N 26°21′E
102 J8 Chemillé Maine-et-Loire, NW France 47°15′N 00°42′W
173 X17 Chemin Grenier S Mauritius 20°29′S 57°28′E
101 N16 Chemnitz prev. Karl-Marx-Stadt. Sachsen, E Germany 50°50′N 12°55′E
Chemulpo see Incheon
32 H14 Chemult Oregon, NW USA 43°14′N 121°48′W
18 G12 Chemung River ≈ New York/Pennsylvania, NE USA
149 U8 Chenāb ≈ India/Pakistan
39 S9 Chena Hot Springs Alaska, USA 65°06′N 146°02′W
18 I11 Chenango River ≈ New York, NE USA
168 J7 Chenderoh, Tasik ◎ Peninsular Malaysia
15 Q11 Chêne, Rivière du ≈ Québec, SE Canada
32 L8 Cheney Washington, NW USA 47°29′N 117°34′W
26 M6 Cheney Reservoir ⊠ Kansas, C USA
Chengchiatun see Liaoyuan
Ch'eng-chou/Chengchow see Zhengzhou
161 P1 Chengde var. Jehol. Hebei, E China 41°N 117°57′E
160 I9 Chengdu var. Chengtu, Ch'eng-tu. province capital Sichuan, C China 30°41′N 104°03′E
161 Q14 Chenghai Guangdong, S China 23°30′N 116°42′E
Chenghsien see Zhengzhou
160 H13 Chengjiang Yunnan, SW China 24°40′N 102°55′E
Chengjiang see Taihe
160 L17 Chengmai var. Jinjiang. Hainan, S China 19°45′N 109°56′E
Chengtu/Ch'eng-tu see Chengdu
Chengwen see Chindu
159 W12 Chengxian var. Cheng Xiang. Gansu, C China 33°42′N 105°45′E
Cheng Xiang see Chengxian
Chengyang see Juxian
Chengzhong see Ningming
Chenkiang see Zhenjiang
155 J19 Chennai prev. Madras. state capital Tamil Nādu, S India 13°05′N 80°18′E
155 J19 Chennai ✈ Tamil Nādu, S India 13°07′N 80°13′E
103 R8 Chenôve Côte d'Or, C France 47°16′N 05°00′E
Chenstokhov see Częstochowa
160 L11 Chenxi var. Chenyang. Hunan, S China 28°02′N 110°15′E
Chen Xian/Chenxian/Chen Xiang see Chenzhou
Chenyang see Chenxi
161 N12 Chenzhou var. Chenxian, Chen Xian, Chen Xiang. Hunan, S China 25°51′N 113°01′E
163 X15 Cheonan Jap. Tenan; prev. Ch'ŏnan. W South Korea 36°51′N 127°11′E
163 W13 Cheongju prev. Chŏngju. W North Korea 39°44′N 125°13′E
Cheo Reo see A Yun Pa
114 I11 Chepelare Smolyan, S Bulgaria 41°44′N 24°41′E
114 I11 Chepelarska Reka ≈ S Bulgaria
56 B11 Chepén La Libertad, C Peru 07°15′S 79°23′W
62 J10 Chepes La Rioja, C Argentina 31°19′S 66°40′W
161 O15 Chep Lap Kok ✈ S China 22°23′N 114°11′E
43 U14 Chepo Panamá, C Panama 09°09′N 79°03′W
Chepping Wycombe see High Wycombe
125 R14 Cheptsa ≈ NW Russian Federation
30 K3 Chequamegon Point headland Wisconsin, N USA 46°42′N 90°45′W
103 O8 Cher ◈ department C France
102 M8 Cher ≈ C France
Cherangani Hills see Cherangany Hills
81 H17 Cherangany Hills var. Cherangani Hills. ▲▲ W Kenya
21 S11 Cheraw South Carolina, SE USA 34°42′N 79°52′W
102 J3 Cherbourg anc. Carusbur. Manche, N France 49°40′N 01°36′W
127 R5 Cherdakly Ul'yanovskaya Oblast', W Russian Federation 54°21′N 48°54′E
125 U12 Cherdyn' Permskiy Kray, NW Russian Federation 60°21′N 56°39′E
124 J14 Cherekha ≈ W Russian Federation
122 M13 Cheremkhovo Irkutskaya Oblast', S Russian Federation 53°16′N 102°44′E
Cheren see Keren
124 K14 Cherepovets Vologodskaya Oblast', NW Russian Federation 59°09′N 37°50′E
125 O11 Cherevkovo Arkhangel'skaya Oblast', NW Russian Federation 61°45′N 45°16′E
74 I6 Chergui, Chott ech salt lake NW Algeria
Cherikov see Cherykaw
117 P6 Cherkas'ka Oblast' var. Cherkasy, Rus. Cherkasskaya Oblast'. ◈ province C Ukraine
Cherkasskaya Oblast' see Cherkas'ka Oblast'
Cherkassy see Cherkasy
117 Q6 Cherkasy Rus. Cherkassy. Cherkas'ka Oblast', C Ukraine 49°26′N 32°05′E
Cherkasy see Cherkas'ka Oblast'
126 M15 Cherkessk Karachayevo-Cherkesskaya Respublika, SW Russian Federation 44°12′N 42°06′E
122 H12 Cherlak Omskaya Oblast', C Russian Federation 54°06′N 74°59′E
122 H12 Cherlakskoye Omskaya Oblast', C Russian Federation 53°42′N 74°23′E
125 U13 Chermoz Permskiy Kray, NW Russian Federation 58°49′N 56°07′E
Chernavchitsy see Charnawchytsy
125 T3 Chernaya Nenetskiy Avtonomnyy Okrug, NW Russian Federation 68°36′N 56°34′E
125 T4 Chernaya ≈ NW Russian Federation
Chernigov see Chernihiv
Chernigovskaya Oblast' see Chernihivs'ka Oblast'
117 Q2 Chernihiv Rus. Chernigov. Chernihivs'ka Oblast', NE Ukraine 51°28′N 31°19′E
Chernihiv see Chernihivs'ka Oblast'
117 V9 Chernihivka Zaporiz'ka Oblast', SE Ukraine 47°11′N 36°10′E
117 P2 Chernihivs'ka Oblast' var. Chernihiv, Rus. Chernigovskaya Oblast'. ◈ province NE Ukraine
114 I9 Cherni Osŭm ≈ N Bulgaria
116 J8 Chernivets'ka Oblast' var. Chernivtsi, Rus. Chernovitskaya Oblast'. ◈ province W Ukraine
114 I9 Cherni Vit ≈ NW Bulgaria
114 G10 Cherni Vrŭkh ▲ W Bulgaria 42°33′N 23°18′E
116 K8 Chernivtsi Ger. Czernowitz, Rom. Cernăuţi, Rus. Chernovtsy. Chernivets'ka Oblast', W Ukraine 48°18′N 25°55′E
116 M7 Chernivtsi Vinnyts'ka Oblast', C Ukraine 48°33′N 28°06′E
Chernivtsi see Chernivets'ka Oblast'
Chernobyl' see Chornobyl'
Cherno More see Black Sea
Chernomorskoye see Chornomors'ke
145 T7 Chernoretsk prev. Chernoretskoye. Pavlodar, NE Kazakhstan 52°51′N 76°37′E
Chernoretskoye see Chernoretsk
Chernovitskaya Oblast' see Chernivets'ka Oblast'
Chernovtsy see Chernivtsi
145 U8 Chernoye Pavlodar, NE Kazakhstan 51°40′N 77°33′E
Chernoye More see Black Sea
125 U16 Chernushka Permskiy Kray, NW Russian Federation 56°30′N 56°07′E
117 N4 Chernyakhiv Rus. Chernyakhov. Zhytomyrs'ka Oblast', N Ukraine 50°30′N 28°38′E
Chernyakhov see Chernyakhiv
119 C14 Chernyakhovsk Ger. Insterburg. Kaliningradskaya Oblast', W Russian Federation 54°36′N 21°49′E
126 K8 Chernyanka Belgorodskaya Oblast', W Russian Federation 50°59′N 37°54′E
125 V5 Chernyshëva, Gryada ▲▲ NW Russian Federation
144 J14 Chernyshëva, Zaliv gulf SW Kazakhstan
123 O10 Chernyshevskiy Respublika Sakha (Yakutiya), NE Russian Federation 62°57′N 112°29′E
127 P13 Chernyye Zemli plain SW Russian Federation
Chërnyy Irtysh see Ertix He, China/Kazakhstan
Chërnyy Irtysh see Kara Irtysh, Kazakhstan
127 V7 Chernyy Otrog Orenburgskaya Oblast', W Russian Federation 52°03′N 56°09′E
29 T12 Cherokee Iowa, C USA 42°45′N 95°33′W
26 M8 Cherokee Oklahoma, C USA 36°45′N 98°22′W
25 R9 Cherokee Texas, SW USA 30°56′N 98°42′W
21 O8 Cherokee Lake ⊠ Tennessee, S USA
Cherokees, Lake O' The see Grand Lake O' The Cherokees
44 H1 Cherokee Sound Great Abaco, N Bahamas 26°16′N 77°03′W
153 V13 Cherrapunji Meghālaya, NE India 25°16′N 91°42′E
28 L9 Cherry Creek ≈ South Dakota, N USA
18 J16 Cherry Hill New Jersey, NE USA 39°55′N 75°01′W
27 Q7 Cherryvale Kansas, C USA 37°16′N 95°33′W
21 Q10 Cherryville North Carolina, SE USA 35°22′N 81°22′W
Cherski Range see Cherskogo, Khrebet
123 T6 Cherskiy Respublika Sakha (Yakutiya), NE Russian Federation 68°45′N 161°15′E
123 R8 Cherskogo, Khrebet var. Cherski Range. ▲▲ NE Russian Federation
Cherso see Cres
126 L10 Chertkovo Rostovskaya Oblast', SW Russian Federation 49°22′N 40°10′E
Cherven' see Chervyen'
114 H8 Cherven Bryag Pleven, N Bulgaria 43°16′N 24°06′E
116 M4 Chervonoarmiys'k Zhytomyrs'ka Oblast', N Ukraine 50°27′N 28°15′E
Chervonograd see Chervonohrad
116 I4 Chervonohrad Rus. Chervonograd. L'vivs'ka Oblast', NW Ukraine 50°25′N 24°10′E
117 W6 Chervonooskil's'ke Vodoskhovyshche Rus. Krasnoosol'skoye Vodokhranilishche. ⊠ NE Ukraine
Chervonoye, Ozero see Chyrvonaye, Vozyera
117 S4 Chervonozavods'ke Poltavs'ka Oblast', C Ukraine 50°24′N 33°22′E
119 L16 Chervyen' Rus. Cherven'. Minskaya Voblasts', C Belarus 53°42′N 28°26′E
119 P16 Cherykaw Rus. Cherikov. Mahilyowskaya Voblasts', E Belarus 53°34′N 31°23′E
31 R9 Chesaning Michigan, N USA 43°10′N 84°07′W
21 X5 Chesapeake Bay inlet NE USA
Chesha Bay see Chëshskaya Guba
Cheshevlya see Tsyeshawlya
97 K18 Cheshire cultural region C England, United Kingdom
125 P5 Chëshskaya Guba var. Archangel Bay, Chesha Bay, Dvina Bay. bay NW Russian Federation
14 F14 Chesley Ontario, S Canada 44°17′N 81°06′W
21 Q10 Chesnee South Carolina, SE USA 35°09′N 81°51′W
97 K18 Chester Wel. Caerleon, hist. Legaceaster, Lat. Deva, Devana Castra. C England, United Kingdom 53°12′N 02°54′W
35 O4 Chester California, W USA 40°18′N 121°14′W
30 K16 Chester Illinois, N USA 37°54′N 89°49′W
33 S7 Chester Montana, NW USA 48°30′N 110°59′W
18 I16 Chester Pennsylvania, NE USA 39°51′N 75°21′W
21 R1 Chester South Carolina, SE USA 34°43′N 81°14′W
25 X9 Chester Texas, SW USA 30°55′N 94°36′W
21 W6 Chester Virginia, NE USA 37°22′N 77°27′W
21 R11 Chester West Virginia, NE USA 40°34′N 80°33′W
97 M18 Chesterfield C England, United Kingdom 53°15′N 01°25′W
21 S11 Chesterfield South Carolina, SE USA 34°44′N 80°04′W
21 W6 Chesterfield Virginia, NE USA 37°22′N 77°31′W
192 J9 Chesterfield, Îles island group NW New Caledonia
9 O9 Chesterfield Inlet Nunavut, NW Canada 63°19′N 90°57′W
9 O9 Chesterfield Inlet inlet Nunavut, N Canada
21 Y3 Chester River ≈ Delaware/Maryland, NE USA
21 X3 Chestertown Maryland, NE USA 39°13′N 76°04′W
19 R4 Chesuncook Lake ◎ Maine, NE USA
30 J5 Chetek Wisconsin, N USA 45°19′N 91°37′W
13 R14 Chéticamp Nova Scotia, SE Canada 46°14′N 61°19′W
27 Q8 Chetopa Kansas, C USA 37°02′N 95°05′W
41 Y14 Chetumal var. Payo Obispo. Quintana Roo, SE Mexico 18°32′N 88°16′W
Chetumal, Bahia/Chetumal, Bahía de see Chetumal Bay
42 G1 Chetumal Bay var. Bahia Chetumal, Bahía de Chetumal. bay Belize/Mexico
10 M13 Chetwynd British Columbia, W Canada 55°42′N 121°36′W
38 M11 Chevak Alaska, USA 61°31′N 165°35′W
36 M12 Chevelon Creek ≈ Arizona, SW USA
185 J17 Cheviot Canterbury, South Island, New Zealand 42°48′S 173°17′E
96 L13 Cheviot Hills hill range England/Scotland, United Kingdom
96 L13 Cheviot, The ▲ NE England, United Kingdom 55°28′N 02°10′W
14 M11 Chevreuil, Lac du ◎ Québec, SE Canada
81 I16 Ch'ew Bahir var. Lake Stefanie. ◎ Ethiopia/Kenya
32 L7 Chewelah Washington, NW USA 48°16′N 117°42′W
26 K10 Cheyenne Oklahoma, C USA 35°37′N 99°43′W
33 Z17 Cheyenne state capital Wyoming, C USA 41°08′N 104°46′W
26 L5 Cheyenne Bottoms ◎ Kansas, C USA
16 J8 Cheyenne River ≈ South Dakota/Wyoming, N USA
37 W5 Cheyenne Wells Colorado, C USA 38°49′N 102°21′W
108 C9 Cheyres Vaud, W Switzerland 46°48′N 06°48′E
Chezdi-Oşorheiu see Târgu Secuiesc
153 P13 Chhapra prev. Chapra. Bihār, N India 25°50′N 84°42′E
153 V13 Chhatak var. Chatak. Sylhet, NE Bangladesh 25°02′N 91°33′E
154 J9 Chhatarpur Madhya Pradesh, C India 24°54′N 79°35′E
154 N13 Chhatrapur prev. Chatrapur. Orissa, E India 19°26′N 85°02′E
154 K2 Chhattīsgarh ◈ state E India
154 L12 Chhattīsgarh plain C India
154 I11 Chhindwāra Madhya Pradesh, C India 22°04′N 78°58′E
153 T12 Chhukha SW Bhutan 27°02′N 89°36′E
Chiai see Jiayi
Chia-i see Jiayi
Chia-mu-ssu see Jiamusi
83 B15 Chiange Port. Vila de Almoster. Huíla, SW Angola 15°44′S 13°54′E
Chiang-hsi see Jiangxi
161 S12 Chiang Kai-shek ✈ (T'aipei) N Taiwan 25°09′N 121°20′E
167 P8 Chiang Khan Loei, E Thailand 17°51′N 101°43′E
167 O7 Chiang Mai var. Chiangmai, Chiengmai, Kiangmai. Chiang Mai, NW Thailand 18°48′N 98°59′E
167 O7 Chiang Mai ✈ Chiang Mai, NW Thailand 18°44′N 98°53′E
Chiangmai see Chiang Mai
167 O6 Chiang Rai var. Chianpai, Chienrai, Muang Chiang Rai. Chiang Rai, NW Thailand 19°56′N 99°51′E
Chiang-su see Jiangsu
Chianning/Chian-ning see Nanjing
Chianpai see Chiang Rai
106 G12 Chianti cultural region C Italy
Chiapa see Chiapa de Corzo
41 U16 Chiapa de Corzo var. Chiapa. Chiapas, SE Mexico 16°42′N 92°59′W
41 V16 Chiapas ◈ state SE Mexico
106 J12 Chiaravalle Marche, C Italy 43°36′N 13°19′E
107 N22 Chiaravalle Centrale Calabria, SW Italy 38°40′N 16°25′E
106 E7 Chiari Lombardia, N Italy 45°33′N 10°00′E
108 H12 Chiasso Ticino, S Switzerland 45°51′N 09°02′E
137 S9 Chiatura prev. Chiat'ura. C Georgia 42°13′N 43°11′E
Chiat'ura see Chiatura
41 P15 Chiautla var. Chiautla de Tapia. Puebla, S Mexico 18°16′N 98°31′W
Chiautla de Tapia see Chiautla
106 D10 Chiavari Liguria, NW Italy 44°19′N 09°19′E
106 E6 Chiavenna Lombardia, N Italy 46°19′N 09°22′E
Chiayi see Jiayi
Chiazza see Piazza Armerina
165 O14 Chiba var. Tiba. Chiba, Honshū, S Japan 35°37′N 140°06′E
165 O13 Chiba off. Chiba-ken, var. Tiba. ◈ prefecture Honshū, S Japan
83 M18 Chibabava Sofala, C Mozambique 20°17′S 33°39′E
Chiba-ken see Chiba
161 O10 Chibi prev. Puqi. Hubei, C China 29°45′N 113°55′E
83 B15 Chibia Port. João de Almeida, Vila João de Almeida. Huíla, SW Angola 15°11′S 13°41′E
83 M18 Chiboma Sofala, C Mozambique 20°06′S 33°54′E
82 J12 Chibondo Luapula, N Zambia 10°42′S 28°42′E
82 K11 Chibote Luapula, NE Zambia 09°52′S 29°33′E
12 K12 Chibougamau Québec, SE Canada 49°56′N 74°24′W
164 H11 Chiburi-jima island Oki-shotō, SW Japan
83 M20 Chibuto Gaza, S Mozambique 24°40′S 33°33′E
31 N11 Chicago Illinois, N USA 41°51′N 87°39′W
31 N11 Chicago Heights Illinois, N USA 41°30′N 87°38′W
15 W6 Chic-Chocs, Monts Eng. Shickshock Mountains. ▲▲ Québec, SE Canada
39 W13 Chichagof Island island Alexander Archipelago, Alaska, USA
57 K20 Chichas, Cordillera de ▲▲ SW Bolivia
41 X12 Chichén-Itzá, Ruinas ruins Yucatán, SE Mexico
97 N23 Chichester SE England, United Kingdom 50°50′N 00°48′W
42 C5 Chichicastenango Quiché, W Guatemala 14°55′N 91°06′W
42 I9 Chichigalpa Chinandega, NW Nicaragua 12°35′N 87°04′W
Ch'i-ch'i-ha-erh see Qiqihar
165 X16 Chichijima-rettō Eng. Beechy Group. island group SE Japan
54 K4 Chichiriviche Falcón, N Venezuela 10°58′N 68°17′W
39 R11 Chickaloon Alaska, USA 61°48′N 148°27′W
20 L10 Chickamauga Lake ⊠ Tennessee, S USA
23 N7 Chickasawhay River ≈ Mississippi, S USA
26 M11 Chickasha Oklahoma, C USA 35°03′N 97°57′W
39 T9 Chicken Alaska, USA 64°04′N 141°56′W
104 J16 Chiclana de la Frontera Andalucía, S Spain 36°26′N 06°09′W
56 B11 Chiclayo Lambayeque, NW Peru 06°47′S 79°47′W
35 N5 Chico California, W USA 39°42′N 121°51′W
83 L15 Chicoa Tete, NW Mozambique 15°45′S 32°25′E
83 M20 Chicomo Gaza, S Mozambique 24°29′S 34°15′E
18 M11 Chicopee Massachusetts, NE USA 42°08′N 72°34′W
63 I19 Chico, Río ≈ SE Argentina
63 I21 Chico, Río ≈ S Argentina
27 W14 Chicot, Lake ◎ Arkansas, C USA
15 R7 Chicoutimi Québec, SE Canada 48°24′N 71°04′W
15 Q8 Chicoutimi ≈ Québec, SE Canada
83 L19 Chicualacuala Gaza, SW Mozambique 22°06′S 31°42′E
83 B14 Chicuma Benguela, C Angola 13°33′S 14°41′E
155 J21 Chidambaram Tamil Nādu, SE India 11°25′N 79°42′E
196 K13 Chidley, Cape headland Newfoundland and Labrador, E Canada 60°25′N 64°39′W
101 N24 Chiemsee ◎ SE Germany
Chiengmai see Chiang Mai
Chienrai see Chiang Rai
106 B8 Chieri Piemonte, NW Italy 45°01′N 07°49′E
106 F8 Chiese ≈ N Italy
107 K14 Chieti var. Teate. Abruzzo, C Italy 42°22′N 14°10′E
99 E19 Chièvres Hainaut, SW Belgium 50°34′N 03°49′E
163 S12 Chifeng var. Ulanhad. Nei Mongol Zizhiqu, N China 42°17′N 118°56′E
82 F13 Chifumage ≈ E Angola
82 M13 Chifunda Eastern, NE Zambia 11°57′S 32°36′E
Chiganak see Shyganak
39 P15 Chiginagak, Mount ▲ Alaska, USA 57°10′N 157°00′W
Chigirin see Chyhyryn
41 P13 Chignahuapan Puebla, S Mexico 19°52′N 98°03′W
39 O15 Chignik Alaska, USA 56°18′N 158°24′W
83 M19 Chigombe ≈ S Mozambique
54 D7 Chigorodó Antioquia, NW Colombia 07°42′N 76°45′W
83 M19 Chigubo Gaza, S Mozambique 22°50′S 33°30′E
Chihertey see Altay
Chih-fu see Yantai
Chihli see Hebei
Chihli, Gulf of see Bo Hai
40 J6 Chihuahua Chihuahua, NW Mexico 28°40′N 106°06′W
40 I6 Chihuahua ◈ state N Mexico
Chiili see Shiyeli
26 M7 Chikaskia River ≈ Kansas/Oklahoma, C USA
155 H19 Chik Ballāpur Karnātaka, W India 13°28′N 77°42′E
124 G15 Chikhachevo Pskovskaya Oblast', W Russian Federation 57°17′N 29°51′E
155 F19 Chikmagalūr Karnātaka, W India 13°20′N 75°46′E
129 V7 Chikoy ≈ C Russian Federation
83 J15 Chikumbi Lusaka, C Zambia 15°11′S 28°20′E
82 M13 Chikwa Eastern, NE Zambia 11°39′S 32°45′E
Chikwana see Chikwawa
83 N15 Chikwawa var. Chikwana. Southern, S Malawi 16°03′S 34°48′E
155 J16 Chilakalūrupet Andhra Pradesh, E India 16°09′N 80°13′E
146 L14 Chilan Lebap Welaýaty, E Turkmenistan 37°57′N 64°58′E
Chilapa see Chilapa de Alvarez
41 P16 Chilapa de Alvarez var. Chilapa. Guerrero, S Mexico 17°38′N 99°11′W
155 J25 Chilaw North Western Province, W Sri Lanka 07°34′N 79°48′E
57 D15 Chilca Lima, W Peru 12°35′S 76°41′W
23 Q4 Childersburg Alabama, S USA 33°16′N 86°21′W
25 P4 Childress Texas, SW USA 34°25′N 100°14′W
63 G14 Chile off. Republic of Chile. ◆ republic SW South America
47 R10 Chile Basin undersea feature E Pacific Ocean 33°00′S 80°00′W
63 H20 Chile Chico Aisén, W Chile 46°34′S 71°44′W
62 I9 Chilecito La Rioja, NW Argentina 29°10′S 67°30′W
62 H12 Chilecito Mendoza, W Argentina 33°53′S 69°03′W
83 L14 Chilembwe Eastern, E Zambia 13°54′S 31°38′E
Chile, Republic of see Chile
193 S11 Chile Rise undersea feature SE Pacific Ocean 40°00′S 90°00′W
117 N13 Chilia, Braţul ≈ SE Romania
Chilia-Nouă see Kiliya
Chilik see Shelek
Chilik see Shelek
154 O13 Chilika Lake var. Chilka Lake. ◎ E India
82 J13 Chililabombwe Copperbelt, C Zambia 12°20′S 27°52′E
Chi-lin see Jilin
Chilka Lake see Chilika Lake
10 H9 Chilkoot Pass pass British Columbia, W Canada
Chill Ala, Cuan see Killala Bay
62 G13 Chillán Bío Bío, C Chile 36°37′S 72°10′W
61 C22 Chillar Buenos Aires, E Argentina 37°16′S 59°58′W
Chill Chiaráin, Cuan see Kilkieran Bay
30 K12 Chillicothe Illinois, N USA 40°55′N 89°29′W
27 S3 Chillicothe Missouri, C USA 39°47′N 93°33′W
31 S14 Chillicothe Ohio, N USA 39°20′N 83°00′W
25 Q4 Chillicothe Texas, SW USA 34°15′N 99°31′W
10 M17 Chilliwack British Columbia, SW Canada 49°09′N 121°54′W
Chill Mhantáin, Ceann see Wicklow Head
Chill Mhantáin, Sléibhte see Wicklow Mountains
108 C10 Chillon Vaud, W Switzerland 46°24′N 06°56′E
Chil'mamedkum, Peski/Chilmämetgum see Çilmämmetgum
63 F17 Chiloé, Isla de var. Isla Grande de Chiloé. island W Chile
32 H15 Chiloquin Oregon, NW USA 42°33′N 121°33′W
41 O16 Chilpancingo var. Chilpancingo de los Bravos. Guerrero, S Mexico 17°33′N 99°30′W
Chilpancingo de los Bravos see Chilpancingo
97 N21 Chiltern Hills hill range S England, United Kingdom
30 M7 Chilton Wisconsin, N USA 44°04′N 88°10′W
82 F11 Chiluage Lunda Sul, NE Angola 09°32′S 21°48′E
82 N12 Chilumba prev. Deep Bay. Northern, N Malawi 10°27′S 34°12′E
Chilung see Jilong
83 N15 Chilwa, Lake var. Lago Chirua, Lake Shirwa. ◎ SE Malawi
167 R10 Chi, Mae Nam ≈ E Thailand
42 C6 Chimaltenango Chimaltenango, C Guatemala 14°40′N 90°48′W
42 A2 Chimaltenango off. Departamento de Chimaltenango. ◈ department S Guatemala
Chimaltenango, Departamento de see Chimaltenango
43 V15 Chimán Panamá, E Panama 08°42′N 78°35′W
83 M17 Chimanimani prev. Mandidzudzure, Melsetter. Manicaland, E Zimbabwe 19°48′S 32°52′E
99 G22 Chimay Hainaut, S Belgium 50°03′N 04°20′E
37 S10 Chimayo New Mexico, SW USA 36°00′N 105°55′W
Chimbay see Chimboy
56 A13 Chimborazo ◈ province C Ecuador
56 C7 Chimborazo △ C Ecuador 01°29′S 78°50′W
56 C12 Chimbote Ancash, W Peru 09°04′S 78°34′W
146 H7 Chimboy Rus. Chimbay. Qoraqalpog'iston Respublikasi, NW Uzbekistan 43°03′N 59°52′E
186 D7 Chimbu ◈ province C Papua New Guinea
54 F6 Chimichagua Cesar, N Colombia 09°19′N 73°51′W
Chimishliya see Cimişlia
Chimkent see Shymkent
Chimkentskaya Oblast' see Yuzhnyy Kazakhstan
28 I14 Chimney Rock rock Nebraska, C USA
83 M17 Chimoio Manica, C Mozambique 19°08′S 33°29′E
82 K11 Chimpembe Northern, NE Zambia 09°31′S 29°33′E
41 O8 China Nuevo León, NE Mexico 25°42′N 99°15′W
156 M9 China off. People's Republic of China, Chin. Chung-hua Jen-min Kung-ho-kuo, Zhonghua Renmin Gongheguo; prev. Chinese Empire. ◆ republic E Asia
19 Q7 China Lake ◎ Maine, NE USA
42 F8 Chinameca San Miguel, E El Salvador 13°30′N 88°20′W
Chi-nan/Chinan see Jinan
42 H9 Chinandega Chinandega, NW Nicaragua 12°37′N 87°08′W
42 H9 Chinandega ◈ department NW Nicaragua
China, People's Republic of see China
China, Republic of see Taiwan
24 J11 Chinati Mountains ▲▲ Texas, SW USA
Chinaz see Chinoz
57 E15 Chincha Alta Ica, SW Peru 13°25′S 76°07′W
11 N11 Chinchaga ≈ Alberta, SW Canada
Chin-chiang see Quanzhou
Chinchilla see Chinchilla de Monte Aragón
105 Q11 Chinchilla de Monte Aragón var. Chinchilla. Castilla-La Mancha, C Spain 38°56′N 01°44′W
54 D10 Chinchiná Caldas, W Colombia 04°59′N 75°37′W
105 O8 Chinchón Madrid, C Spain 40°08′N 03°26′W
41 Z14 Chinchorro, Banco island SE Mexico
Chin-chou/Chinchow see Jinzhou
21 Z5 Chincoteague Assateague Island, Virginia, NE USA 37°55′N 75°22′W
83 O17 Chinde Zambézia, NE Mozambique 18°35′S 36°28′E
Chin-do see Jin-do
159 R13 Chindu var. Chengwen; prev. Chuqung. Qinghai, C China 33°19′N 97°08′E
Chindwin see Chindwinn
166 M2 Chindwinn var. Chindwin. ≈ N Myanmar (Burma)
Chinese Empire see China
Ch'ing Hai see Qinghai Hu, China
Chinghai see Qinghai
Chingildi see Shengeldi
Chingirlau see Shyngghyrlau
82 J13 Chingola Copperbelt, C Zambia 12°31′S 27°53′E
Ching-Tao/Ch'ing-tao see Qingdao
82 C13 Chinguar Huambo, C Angola 12°33′S 16°25′E
76 I7 Chinguețti var. Chinguetti. Adrar, C Mauritania 20°25′N 12°24′W
Chinhae see Jinhae
166 K4 Chin Hills ▲▲ W Myanmar (Burma)
83 K16 Chinhoyi prev. Sinoia. Mashonaland West, N Zimbabwe 17°22′S 30°12′E
Chinhsien see Jinzhou
39 Q14 Chiniak, Cape headland Kodiak Island, Alaska, USA 57°37′N 152°10′W
14 G10 Chiniguchi Lake ◎ Ontario, S Canada
149 U8 Chiniot Punjab, NE Pakistan 31°40′N 73°00′E
Chinju see Jinju
Chinkai see Jinhae
78 M13 Chinko ≈ E Central African Republic
37 O9 Chinle Arizona, SW USA 36°09′N 109°33′W
Chinmen Tao see Jinmen Dao
Chinnchâr see Shinshār
Chinnereth see Tiberias, Lake
164 C12 Chino var. Tino. Nagano, Honshū, S Japan 36°00′N 138°10′E
102 L8 Chinon Indre-et-Loire, C France 47°10′N 00°15′E
33 T7 Chinook Montana, NW USA 48°35′N 109°13′W
Chinook State see Washington
192 L4 Chinook Trough undersea feature N Pacific Ocean
36 K11 Chino Valley Arizona, SW USA 34°45′N 112°27′W
147 P10 Chinoz Rus. Chinaz. Toshkent Viloyati, E Uzbekistan 40°58′N 68°46′E
82 L12 Chinsali Northern, NE Zambia 10°33′S 32°05′E
166 K5 Chin State ◈ state W Myanmar (Burma)
Chinsura see Chunchura
Chin-tō see Jin-do
54 E6 Chinú Córdoba, NW Colombia 09°07′N 75°25′W
99 K24 Chiny, Forêt de forest SE Belgium
83 M15 Chioco Tete, NW Mozambique 16°22′S 32°50′E
106 H8 Chioggia anc. Fossa Claudia. Veneto, NE Italy 45°14′N 12°17′E
114 H12 Chionótrypa ▲ NE Greece 41°16′N 24°06′E
115 L18 Chíos var. Hios, Khíos, It. Scio, Turk. Sakiz-Adasi. Chíos, E Greece 38°23′N 26°07′E
115 K18 Chíos var. Khíos. island E Greece
83 M14 Chipata prev. Fort Jameson. Eastern, E Zambia 13°40′S 32°42′E
82 C14 Chipindo Huíla, C Angola 13°53′S 15°47′E
23 R8 Chipley Florida, SE USA 30°46′N 85°32′W
155 D15 Chiplūn Mahārāshtra, W India 17°32′N 73°32′E
81 H22 Chipogolo Dodoma, C Tanzania 06°52′S 36°03′E
23 R8 Chipola River ≈ Florida, SE USA
97 L22 Chippenham S England, United Kingdom 51°28′N 02°07′W
30 J6 Chippewa Falls Wisconsin, N USA 44°56′N 91°25′W
30 J4 Chippewa, Lake ⊠ Wisconsin, N USA
31 Q8 Chippewa River ≈ Michigan, N USA
30 I6 Chippewa River ≈ Wisconsin, N USA
Chipping Wycombe see High Wycombe
114 G8 Chiprovtsi Montana, NW Bulgaria 43°23′N 22°53′E
19 T4 Chiputneticook Lakes lakes Canada/USA
56 D13 Chiquián Ancash, W Peru 10°09′S 78°08′W
41 Y11 Chiquilá Quintana Roo, SE Mexico 21°25′N 87°20′W
42 E6 Chiquimula Chiquimula, SE Guatemala 14°46′N 89°32′W
42 A3 Chiquimula off. Departamento de Chiquimula. ◈ department SE Guatemala
Chiquimula, Departamento de see Chiquimula
42 D7 Chiquimulilla Santa Rosa, S Guatemala 14°06′N 90°23′W
54 F9 Chiquinquirá Boyacá, C Colombia 05°37′N 73°51′W
155 J17 Chīrāla Andhra Pradesh, E India 15°49′N 80°21′E
149 N4 Chīras Gōwr, N Afghanistan 35°15′N 65°39′E
152 H11 Chirāwa Rājasthān, N India 28°12′N 75°42′E
Chirchik see Chirchiq
147 Q9 Chirchiq Rus. Chirchik. Toshkent Viloyati, E Uzbekistan 41°30′N 69°32′E
147 P10 Chirchiq ≈ E Uzbekistan
Chire see Shire
83 L18 Chiredzi Masvingo, SE Zimbabwe 21°00′S 31°38′E
25 X8 Chireno Texas, SW USA 31°30′N 94°21′W
77 X7 Chirfa Agadez, NE Niger 21°01′N 12°41′E
37 O16 Chiricahua Mountains ▲▲ Arizona, SW USA
37 O16 Chiricahua Peak ▲ Arizona, SW USA 31°51′N 109°17′W
54 F6 Chiriguaná Cesar, N Colombia 09°24′N 73°38′W
39 P15 Chirikof Island island Alaska, USA
43 P16 Chiriquí off. Provincia de Chiriquí. ◈ province SW Panama
43 P17 Chiriquí, Golfo de Eng. Chiriqui Gulf. gulf SW Panama
43 P15 Chiriquí Grande Bocas del Toro, W Panama 08°58′N 82°08′W
Chiriqui Gulf see Chiriquí, Golfo de
43 P15 Chiriquí, Laguna de lagoon NW Panama
Chiriquí, Provincia de see Chiriquí
43 O16 Chiriquí Viejo, Río ≈ W Panama
Chiriquí, Volcán de see Barú, Volcán
83 N15 Chiromo Southern, S Malawi 16°32′S 35°07′E
114 J10 Chirpan Stara Zagora, C Bulgaria 42°12′N 25°20′E
43 N14 Chirripó Atlántico, Río ≈ E Costa Rica
Chirripó, Cerro see Chirripó Grande, Cerro
Chirripó del Pacífico, Río see Chirripó, Río
43 N14 Chirripó Grande, Cerro var. Cerro Chirripó. ▲ SE Costa Rica 09°31′N 83°28′W
43 N13 Chirripó, Río var. Río Chirripó del Pacífico. ≈ NE Costa Rica
Chirua, Lago see Chilwa, Lake
83 J15 Chirundu Southern, S Zambia 16°03′S 28°50′E
29 W8 Chisago City Minnesota, N USA 45°22′N 92°53′W
83 J14 Chisamba Central, C Zambia 15°00′S 28°22′E
39 T10 Chisana Alaska, USA 62°09′N 142°07′W
82 I13 Chisasa North Western, NW Zambia 12°09′S 25°30′E
12 I9 Chisasibi prev. Fort George. Québec, C Canada 53°50′N 79°01′W
42 D4 Chisec Alta Verapaz, C Guatemala 15°50′N 90°18′W
127 U5 Chishmy Respublika Bashkortostan, W Russian Federation 54°33′N 55°21′E

◆ Country
● Country Capital
◇ Dependent Territory
○ Dependent Territory Capital
◈ Administrative Regions
✈ International Airport
▲ Mountain
▲▲ Mountain Range
△ Volcano
≈ River
◎ Lake
⊠ Reservoir

29 V4 **Chisholm** Minnesota, N USA *47°29′N 92°52′W*
149 U10 **Chishtiān** *var.* Chishtiān Mandi. Punjab, E Pakistan *29°44′N 72°54′E*
Chishtiān Mandi *see* Chishtiān
160 I11 **Chishui He** ≈ C China
Chisimaio/Chisimayu *see* Kismaayo
117 N10 **Chişinău** *Rus.* Kishinev. ● (Moldova) C Moldova *47°N 28°51′E*
117 N10 **Chişinău** ✈ S Moldova *46°54′N 28°56′E*
Chişinău-Criş *see* Chişineu-Criş
116 F10 **Chişineu-Criş** *Hung.* Kisjenő; *prev.* Chişinău-Criş. Arad, W Romania *46°33′N 21°30′E*
83 K14 **Chisomo** Central, C Zambia *13°30′S 30°37′E*
106 A8 **Chisone** ≈ NW Italy
24 K12 **Chisos Mountains** ▲ Texas, SW USA
39 T10 **Chistochina** Alaska, USA *62°34′N 144°39′W*
127 R4 **Chistopol'** Respublika Tatarstan, W Russian Federation *55°20′N 50°39′E*
145 O8 **Chistopol'ye** Severnyy Kazakhstan, N Kazakhstan *52°37′N 67°14′E*
123 O13 **Chita** Zabaykal'skiy Kray, S Russian Federation *52°03′N 113°35′E*
83 B16 **Chitado** Cunene, SW Angola *17°16′S 13°54′E*
Chitaldroog/Chitaldrug *see* Chitradurga
83 C15 **Chitanda** ≈ S Angola
Chitangwiza *see* Chitungwiza
82 F10 **Chitato** Lunda Norte, NE Angola *07°23′S 20°46′E*
83 C14 **Chitembo** Bié, C Angola *13°33′S 16°47′E*
39 T11 **Chitina** Alaska, USA *61°31′N 144°26′W*
39 T11 **Chitina River** ≈ Alaska, USA
82 M11 **Chitipa** Northern, NW Malawi *09°41′S 33°19′E*
165 S4 **Chitose** *var.* Titose. Hokkaidō, NE Japan *42°51′N 141°40′E*
155 G18 **Chitradurga** *prev.* Chitaldroog, Chitaldrug. Karnātaka, W India *14°16′N 76°23′E*
149 T3 **Chitrāl** Khyber Pakhtunkhwa, NW Pakistan *35°51′N 71°47′E*
43 S16 **Chitré** Herrera, S Panama *07°57′N 80°26′W*
153 V16 **Chittagong** *Ben.* Chāttagām. Chittagong, SE Bangladesh *22°20′N 91°48′E*
153 U16 **Chittagong** ❖ *division* E Bangladesh
153 Q15 **Chittaranjan** West Bengal, NE India *23°52′N 86°40′E*
152 G14 **Chittaurgarh** *var.* Chittorgarh. Rājasthān, N India *24°54′N 74°42′E*
155 I19 **Chittoor** Andhra Pradesh, E India *13°13′N 79°06′E*
Chittorgarh *see* Chittaurgarh
155 G21 **Chittūr** Kerala, SW India *10°42′N 76°46′E*
83 K16 **Chitungwiza** *prev.* Chitangwiza. Mashonaland East, NE Zimbabwe *18°S 31°06′E*
62 H4 **Chiuchiu** Antofagasta, N Chile *22°13′S 68°34′W*
82 F12 **Chiumbe** *var.* Tshiumbe. ≈ Angola/Dem. Rep. Congo
83 F15 **Chiume** Moxico, E Angola *15°08′S 21°09′E*
82 K13 **Chiundaponde** Northern, NE Zambia *12°14′S 30°40′E*
106 H13 **Chiusi** Toscana, C Italy *43°00′N 11°56′E*
54 J5 **Chivacoa** Yaracuy, N Venezuela *10°10′N 68°54′W*
106 B8 **Chivasso** Piemonte, NW Italy *45°13′N 07°54′E*
83 L17 **Chivhu** *prev.* Enkeldoorn. Midlands, C Zimbabwe *19°01′S 30°54′E*
61 C20 **Chivilcoy** Buenos Aires, E Argentina *34°55′S 60°00′W*
82 N12 **Chiweta** Northern, N Malawi *10°36′S 34°09′E*
42 D4 **Chixoy, Río** *var.* Río Negro, Río Salinas. ≈ Guatemala/Mexico
82 H13 **Chizela** North Western, NW Zambia *13°11′S 24°59′E*
125 O5 **Chizha** Nenetskiy Avtonomnyy Okrug, NW Russian Federation *67°04′N 44°19′E*
161 Q9 **Chizhou** *var.* Guichi. Anhui, E China *30°39′N 117°29′E*
164 I12 **Chizu** Tottori, Honshū, SW Japan *35°15′N 134°14′E*
Chkalov *see* Orenburg
74 J5 **Chlef** *var.* Ech Cheliff, Ech Chleff; *prev.* Al-Asnam, El Asnam, Orléansville. NW Algeria *36°11′N 01°21′E*
115 G18 **Chlómo** ▲ C Greece *38°36′N 22°57′E*
111 M15 **Chmielnik** Świętokrzyskie, C Poland *50°37′N 20°43′E*
167 S11 **Chŏâm Khsant** Preăh Vihéar, N Cambodia *14°13′N 104°56′E*
62 G10 **Choapa, Río** *var.* Choapo. ≈ C Chile
Choapas *see* Las Choapas
Choapo *see* Choapa, Río
Choarta *see* Chwārtā
67 T13 **Chobe** ≈ N Botswana
14 K8 **Chochocouane** ≈ Québec, SE Canada
110 E13 **Chocianów** *Ger.* Kotzenan. Dolnośląskie, SW Poland *51°23′N 15°55′E*
54 C9 **Chocó** *off.* Departamento del Chocó. ❖ *province* W Colombia
Chocó, Departamento del *see* Chocó
35 X16 **Chocolate Mountains** ▲ California, W USA
21 W9 **Chocowinity** North Carolina, SE USA *35°33′N 77°03′W*
27 N10 **Choctaw** Oklahoma, C USA *35°30′N 97°16′W*
23 Q8 **Choctawhatchee Bay** *bay* Florida, SE USA
23 Q8 **Choctawhatchee River** ≈ Florida, SE USA
Chodau *see* Chodov
163 V14 **Ch'o-do** *island* SW North Korea
Chodorów *see* Khodoriv
111 A16 **Chodov** *Ger.* Chodau. Karlovarský Kraj, W Czech Republic *50°15′N 12°45′E*
110 G10 **Chodzież** Wielkopolskie, C Poland *53°N 16°55′E*
63 J15 **Choele Choel** Río Negro, C Argentina *39°19′S 65°42′W*
83 L14 **Chofombo** Tete, NW Mozambique *14°43′S 31°48′E*
Chohtan *see* Chauhtan
11 U14 **Choiceland** Saskatchewan, C Canada *53°28′N 104°26′W*
186 K8 **Choiseul** ❖ *province* NW Solomon Islands
186 K8 **Choiseul** *var.* Lauru. *island* NW Solomon Islands
63 M23 **Choiseul Sound** *sound* East Falkland, Falkland Islands
40 H7 **Choix** Sinaloa, C Mexico *26°43′N 108°20′W*
110 D10 **Chojna** Zachodnio-pomorskie, W Poland *52°56′N 14°25′E*
110 H8 **Chojnice** *Ger.* Konitz. Pomorskie, N Poland *53°41′N 17°34′E*
111 F14 **Chojnów** *Ger.* Hainau, Haynau. Dolnośląskie, SW Poland *51°16′N 15°55′E*
167 Q10 **Chok Chai** Nakhon Ratchasima, C Thailand *14°45′N 102°10′E*
80 I12 **Ch'ok'ē** *var.* Choke Mountains. ▲ NW Ethiopia
25 R13 **Choke Canyon Lake** ⊠ Texas, SW USA
Choke Mountains *see* Ch'ok'ē
Chokpar *see* Shokpar
147 W7 **Chok-Tal** *var.* Choktal. Issyk-Kul'skaya Oblast', E Kyrgyzstan *42°37′N 76°45′E*
Choktal *see* Chok-Tal
Chókué *see* Chokwè
123 R7 **Chokurdakh** Respublika Sakha (Yakutiya), NE Russian Federation *70°38′N 148°18′E*
83 L20 **Chokwè** *var.* Chókué. Gaza, S Mozambique *24°27′S 32°55′E*
188 F8 **Chol** Babeldaob, N Palau
160 E8 **Chola Shan** ▲ C China
102 J8 **Cholet** Maine-et-Loire, NW France *47°03′N 00°52′W*
63 H17 **Cholila** Chubut, W Argentina *42°33′S 71°28′W*
Cholo *see* Thyolo
147 V8 **Cholpon** Narynskaya Oblast', C Kyrgyzstan *42°07′N 75°25′E*
147 X7 **Cholpon-Ata** Issyk-Kul'skaya Oblast', E Kyrgyzstan *42°39′N 77°05′E*
41 P14 **Cholula** Puebla, S Mexico *19°03′N 98°19′W*
42 I8 **Choluteca** Choluteca, S Honduras *13°15′N 87°10′W*
42 H8 **Choluteca** ❖ *department* S Honduras
42 H8 **Choluteca, Río** ≈ SW Honduras
83 I15 **Choma** Southern, S Zambia *16°48′S 26°58′E*
153 T11 **Chomo Lhari** ▲ NW Bhutan *27°59′N 89°24′E*
167 N7 **Chom Thong** Chiang Mai, NW Thailand *18°25′N 98°44′E*
111 B15 **Chomutov** *Ger.* Komotau. Ústecký Kraj, NW Czech Republic *50°28′N 13°24′E*
123 N11 **Chona** ≈ C Russian Federation
Ch'ŏnan *see* Cheonan
167 P11 **Chon Buri** *prev.* Bang Pla Soi. Chon Buri, S Thailand *13°24′N 100°59′E*
56 B6 **Chone** Manabí, W Ecuador *0°44′S 80°04′W*
Chong'an *see* Wuyishan
163 W13 **Ch'ŏngch'ŏn-gang** ≈ W North Korea
163 Y11 **Ch'ŏngjin** NE North Korea *41°48′N 129°44′E*
Chŏngju *see* Cheongju
161 S8 **Chongming Dao** *island* E China
160 J10 **Chongqing** *var.* Ch'ung-ching, Ch'ung-ch'ing, Chungking, Pahsien, Tchongking, Yuzhou. Chongqing Shi, C China *29°34′N 106°27′E*
Chŏngup *see* Chŏnju
161 O10 **Chongyang** *var.* Tiancheng. Hubei, C China *29°35′N 114°03′E*
160 J15 **Chongzuo** *prev.* Taiping. Guangxi Zhuangzu Zizhiqu, S China *22°18′N 107°23′E*
163 Y16 **Chŏnju** *prev.* Chŏnju, Chŏngup, *Jap.* Seiyu. SW South Korea *35°51′N 127°08′E*
Chŏnju *see* Chŏnju
Chŏnju *see* Jeonju
Chonnacht *see* Connaught
Chonogol *see* Erdenetsagaan
63 F19 **Chonos, Archipiélago de los** *island group* S Chile
42 K10 **Chontales** ❖ *department* S Nicaragua
167 T13 **Chơn Thanh** Sông Be, S Vietnam *11°25′N 106°38′E*
158 K17 **Cho Oyu** *var.* Qowowuyag. ▲ China/Nepal *28°07′N 86°37′E*
116 G7 **Chop** *Cz.* Čop, *Hung.* Csap. Zakarpats'ka Oblast', W Ukraine *48°26′N 22°13′E*
21 Y3 **Choptank River** ≈ Maryland, NE USA
115 J22 **Chóra** *prev.* Íos. Íos, Kykládes, Greece, Aegean Sea *36°42′N 25°16′E*
115 H25 **Chóra Sfakíon** *var.* Sfákia. Kríti, Greece, E Mediterranean Sea *35°12′N 24°05′E*
Chorcaí, Cuan *see* Cork Harbour
43 P15 **Chorcha, Cerro** ▲ W Panama *08°39′N 82°07′W*
Chorku *see* Chorkŭh
147 R11 **Chorkŭh** *Rus.* Chorku. N Tajikistan *40°04′N 70°30′E*
97 K17 **Chorley** NW England, United Kingdom *53°40′N 02°38′W*
Chorne More *see* Black Sea
117 R5 **Chornobay** Cherkas'ka Oblast', C Ukraine *49°40′N 32°20′E*
117 O3 **Chornobyl'** *Rus.* Chernobyl'. Kyyivs'ka Oblast', N Ukraine *51°17′N 30°15′E*
117 R12 **Chornomors'ke** *Rus.* Chernomorskoye. Avtonomna Respublika Krym, S Ukraine *45°29′N 32°45′E*
117 R4 **Chornukhy** Poltavs'ka Oblast', C Ukraine *50°15′N 32°57′E*
Chorokh/Chorokhi *see* Çoruh Nehri
110 O9 **Choroszcz** Podlaskie, NE Poland *53°10′N 23°E*
116 K6 **Chortkiv** *Rus.* Chortkov. Ternopil's'ka Oblast', W Ukraine *49°01′N 25°46′E*
Chortkov *see* Chortkiv
Chorum *see* Çorum
110 M9 **Chorzele** Mazowieckie, C Poland *53°16′N 20°53′E*
111 J16 **Chorzów** *Ger.* Königshütte; *prev.* Królewska Huta. Śląskie, S Poland *50°17′N 18°58′E*
163 W12 **Ch'osan** N North Korea *40°45′N 125°52′E*
Chosebuz *see* Cottbus
Chōsen-kaikyō *see* Korea Strait
164 P14 **Chōshi** *var.* Tyôsi. Chiba, Honshū, S Japan *35°44′N 140°48′E*
63 H14 **Chos Malal** Neuquén, W Argentina *37°23′S 70°16′W*
Chosŏn-minjujuŭi-inmin-kanghwaguk *see* North Korea
110 E9 **Choszczno** *Ger.* Arnswalde. Zachodnio-pomorskie, NW Poland *53°10′N 15°24′E*
153 O15 **Chota Nāgpur** *plateau* N India
33 R8 **Choteau** Montana, NW USA *47°48′N 112°40′W*
Chotqol *see* Chatkal
14 M8 **Chouart** ≈ Québec, SE Canada
76 I7 **Choûm** Adrar, C Mauritania *21°19′N 12°59′W*
27 Q9 **Chouteau** Oklahoma, C USA *36°11′N 95°20′W*
21 X8 **Chowan River** ≈ North Carolina, SE USA
35 Q10 **Chowchilla** California, W USA *37°06′N 120°15′W*
163 P7 **Choybalsan** *prev.* Byan Tumen. Dornod, E Mongolia *48°03′N 114°32′E*
163 Q7 **Choybalsan** *var.* Hulstay. Dornod, NE Mongolia *48°25′N 114°56′E*
162 M9 **Choyr** Govĭ Sumber, C Mongolia *46°20′N 108°21′E*
185 I19 **Christchurch** Canterbury, South Island, New Zealand *43°31′S 172°39′E*
97 M24 **Christchurch** S England, United Kingdom *50°44′N 01°45′W*
185 I18 **Christchurch** ✈ Canterbury, South Island, New Zealand *43°28′S 172°33′E*
44 J12 **Christiana** C Jamaica *18°13′N 77°29′W*
83 H22 **Christiana** Free State, C South Africa *27°55′S 25°10′E*
115 J23 **Christiána** *var.* Christiani. *island* Kykládes, Greece, Aegean Sea
Christiani *see* Christiána
Christiania *see* Oslo
14 G13 **Christian Island** *island* Ontario, S Canada
191 P16 **Christian, Point** *headland* Pitcairn Island, Pitcairn Islands *25°04′S 130°08′E*
38 M11 **Christian River** ≈ Alaska, USA
Christiansand *see* Kristiansand
21 S7 **Christiansburg** Virginia, NE USA *37°07′N 80°26′W*
95 G23 **Christiansfeld** Syddanmark, SW Denmark *55°21′N 09°30′E*
Christianshåb *see* Qasigiannguit
39 X14 **Christian Sound** *inlet* Alaska, USA
45 T9 **Christiansted** Saint Croix, S Virgin Islands (US) *17°43′N 64°42′W*
Christiansund *see* Kristiansund
25 R13 **Christine** Texas, SW USA *28°47′N 98°30′W*
173 U7 **Christmas Island** ◇ *Australian external territory* E Indian Ocean
129 T17 **Christmas Island** *island* E Indian Ocean
Christmas Island *see* Kiritimati
192 M7 **Christmas Ridge** *undersea feature* C Pacific Ocean
30 L16 **Christopher** Illinois, N USA *37°58′N 89°03′W*
25 P9 **Christoval** Texas, SW USA *31°09′N 100°30′W*
111 F17 **Chrudim** Pardubický Kraj, C Czech Republic *49°58′N 15°49′E*
115 K25 **Chrýsi** *island* SE Greece
121 N2 **Chrysochoú, Kólpos** *var.* Khrysokhou Bay. *bay* E Mediterranean Sea
114 I13 **Chrysoúpoli** *var.* Hrisoupoli; *prev.* Khrisoúpolis. Anatolikí Makedonía kai Thráki, NE Greece *40°59′N 24°42′E*
111 K16 **Chrzanów** *var.* Chrzanow, *Ger.* Zaumgarten. Śląskie, S Poland *50°10′N 19°21′E*
Chu *see* Shu
42 C5 **Chuacús, Sierra de** ▲ W Guatemala
153 S15 **Chuadanga** Khulna, W Bangladesh *23°38′N 88°52′E*
Chuan *see* Sichuan
Ch'uan-chou *see* Quanzhou
Chuankou *see* Minhe
39 O11 **Chuathbaluk** Alaska, USA *61°36′N 159°14′W*
Chubek *see* Moskva
63 I17 **Chubut** *off.* Provincia de Chubut. ❖ *province* S Argentina
Chubut, Provincia de *see* Chubut
63 I17 **Chubut, Río** ≈ SE Argentina
43 V15 **Chucanti, Cerro** ▲ E Panama *08°48′N 78°27′W*
Ch'u-chiang *see* Shaoguan
43 W15 **Chucunaque, Río** ≈ E Panama
Chudin *see* Chudzin
116 M5 **Chudniv** Zhytomyrs'ka Oblast', N Ukraine *50°02′N 28°06′E*
124 H13 **Chudovo** Novgorodskaya Oblast', W Russian Federation *59°07′N 31°42′E*
Chudskoye Ozero *see* Peipus, Lake
119 J18 **Chudzin** *Rus.* Chudin. Brestskaya Voblasts', SW Belarus *52°44′N 26°59′E*
39 Q13 **Chugach Islands** *island group* Alaska, USA
39 S11 **Chugach Mountains** ▲ Alaska, USA
164 G12 **Chūgoku-sanchi** ▲ Honshū, SW Japan
Chugqênsumdo *see* Jigzhi
Chuguyev *see* Chuhuyiv
117 V5 **Chuhuyiv** *var.* Chuguyev. Kharkivs'ka Oblast', E Ukraine *49°51′N 36°44′E*
61 H19 **Chuí** Rio Grande do Sul, S Brazil *33°45′S 53°23′W*
Chui *see* Chuy
Chu-Iliyskiye Gory *see* Gory Shu-Ile
Chukai *see* Cukai
Chukchi Avtonomnyy Okrug *see* Chukotskiy Avtonomnyy Okrug
Chukchi Peninsula *see* Chukotskiy Poluostrov
197 R6 **Chukchi Plain** *undersea feature* Arctic Ocean
197 R6 **Chukchi Plateau** *undersea feature* Arctic Ocean
197 R4 **Chukchi Sea** *Rus.* Chukotskoye More. *sea* Arctic Ocean
125 N14 **Chukhloma** Kostromskaya Oblast', NW Russian Federation *58°42′N 42°39′E*
Chukotka *see* Chukotskiy Avtonomnyy Okrug
Chukot Range *see* Anadyrskiy Khrebet
123 V6 **Chukotskiy Avtonomnyy Okrug** *var.* Chukchi Avtonomnyy Okrug, Chukotka. ❖ *autonomous district* NE Russian Federation
123 W5 **Chukotskiy, Mys** *headland* NE Russian Federation *64°15′N 173°03′W*
123 V5 **Chukotskiy Poluostrov** *Eng.* Chukchi Peninsula. *peninsula* NE Russian Federation
Chukotskoye More *see* Chukchi Sea
Chukurkak *see* Chuqurqoq
Chulakkurgan *see* Sholakkorgan
35 U17 **Chula Vista** California, W USA *32°38′N 117°04′W*
123 Q12 **Chul'man** Respublika Sakha (Yakutiya), NE Russian Federation *56°50′N 124°47′E*
56 B9 **Chulucanas** Piura, NW Peru *05°08′S 80°10′W*
122 J12 **Chulym** ≈ C Russian Federation
152 K6 **Chumar** Jammu and Kashmir, N India *32°38′N 78°36′E*
114 K9 **Chumerna** ▲ C Bulgaria *42°45′N 25°58′E*
123 R12 **Chumikan** Khabarovskiy Kray, E Russian Federation *54°41′N 135°12′E*
167 Q9 **Chum Phae** Khon Kaen, C Thailand *16°31′N 102°09′E*
167 N13 **Chumphon** *var.* Jumporn. Chumphon, SW Thailand *10°30′N 99°11′E*
167 O9 **Chumsaeng** *var.* Chum Saeng. Nakhon Sawan, C Thailand *15°52′N 100°18′E*
Chum Saeng *see* Chumsaeng
122 L12 **Chuna** ≈ C Russian Federation
161 R9 **Chun'an** *var.* Qiandaohu; *prev.* Pailing. Zhejiang, SE China *29°37′N 118°59′E*
Chunan *see* Zhunan
Chuncheng *see* Yangchun
163 Y14 **Chuncheon** *Jap.* Shunsen; *prev.* Ch'unch'ŏn. N South Korea *37°52′N 127°48′E*
Ch'unch'ŏn *see* Chuncheon
153 S16 **Chunchura** *prev.* Chinsura. West Bengal, NE India *22°54′N 88°20′E*
Chundzha *see* Shonzhy
Ch'ung-ch'ing/Ch'ung-ching *see* Chongqing
Chung-hua Jen-min Kung-ho-kuo *see* China
163 Y15 **Chungju** *Jap.* Chūshū; *prev.* Ch'ungju. C South Korea *36°57′N 127°50′E*
Ch'ungju *see* Chungju
Chungking *see* Chongqing
161 T14 **Chungyang Shanmo** *Chin.* Taiwan Shan. ▲ C Taiwan
149 V9 **Chūniān** Punjab, E Pakistan *30°57′N 74°01′E*
122 L12 **Chunskiy** Irkutskaya Oblast', S Russian Federation *56°10′N 99°15′E*
122 M11 **Chunya** ≈ C Russian Federation
124 J6 **Chupa** Respublika Kareliya, NW Russian Federation *66°15′N 33°02′E*
125 P8 **Chuprovo** Respublika Komi, NW Russian Federation *64°16′N 46°27′E*
57 G17 **Chuquibamba** Arequipa, SW Peru *15°47′S 72°44′W*
62 H4 **Chuquicamata** Antofagasta, N Chile *22°20′S 68°56′W*
57 L21 **Chuquisaca** ❖ *department* S Bolivia
Chuquisaca *see* Sucre
Chuqung *see* Chindu
146 I8 **Chuqurqoq** *Rus.* Chukurkak. Qoraqalpogʻiston Respublikasi, NW Uzbekistan *42°44′N 61°33′E*
127 T2 **Chur** Udmurtskaya Respublika, NW Russian Federation *57°06′N 52°57′E*
108 I9 **Chur** *Fr.* Coire, *It.* Coira, *Rmsch.* Cuera, Quera; *anc.* Curia Rhaetorum. Graubünden, E Switzerland *46°52′N 09°32′E*
123 Q10 **Churapcha** Respublika Sakha (Yakutiya), NE Russian Federation *61°59′N 132°06′E*
11 V16 **Churchbridge** Saskatchewan, S Canada *50°55′N 101°53′W*
21 O8 **Church Hill** Tennessee, S USA *36°31′N 82°42′W*
11 X9 **Churchill** Manitoba, C Canada *58°46′N 94°10′W*
11 X10 **Churchill** ≈ Manitoba/Saskatchewan, C Canada
13 P9 **Churchill** ≈ Newfoundland and Labrador, E Canada
11 Y9 **Churchill, Cape** *headland* Manitoba, C Canada *58°42′N 93°12′W*
13 P9 **Churchill Falls** Newfoundland and Labrador, E Canada *53°38′N 64°00′W*
11 S12 **Churchill Lake** ⊚ Saskatchewan, C Canada
19 Q3 **Churchill Lake** ⊠ Maine, NE USA
194 I5 **Churchill Peninsula** *peninsula* Antarctica
22 H8 **Church Point** Louisiana, S USA *30°24′N 92°13′W*
29 O3 **Churchs Ferry** North Dakota, N USA *48°15′N 99°12′W*
146 G12 **Churchuri** Ahal Welaýaty, C Turkmenistan *38°55′N 59°13′E*
21 T5 **Churchville** Virginia, NE USA *38°13′N 79°10′W*
152 G10 **Chūru** Rājasthān, NW India *28°18′N 75°00′E*
54 J4 **Churuguara** Falcón, N Venezuela *10°52′N 69°35′W*
167 U11 **Chư Sê** Gia Lai, C Vietnam *13°38′N 108°06′E*
144 J12 **Chushkakul, Gory** ▲ SW Kazakhstan
Chūshū *see* Chungju
37 O9 **Chuska Mountains** ▲ Arizona/New Mexico, SW USA
Chu, Sông *see* Sam, Nam
125 V14 **Chusovoy** Permskiy Kray, NW Russian Federation *58°17′N 57°54′E*
147 R10 **Chust** Namangan Viloyati, E Uzbekistan *40°58′N 71°12′E*
Chust *see* Khust
15 U6 **Chute-aux-Outardes** Québec, SE Canada *49°07′N 68°25′W*
117 U5 **Chutove** Poltavs'ka Oblast', C Ukraine *49°45′N 35°11′E*
167 U11 **Chư Ty** *var.* Đưc Cơ. Gia Lai, C Vietnam *13°48′N 107°41′E*
189 O15 **Chuuk** *var.* Truk. ❖ *state* C Micronesia
189 P15 **Chuuk Islands** *var.* Hogoley Islands; *prev.* Truk Islands. *island group* Caroline Islands, C Micronesia
Chuvashia *see* Chuvashskaya Respublika
Chuvashiya *see* Chuvashskaya Respublika
127 P4 **Chuvashskaya Respublika** *var.* Chuvashiya, *Eng.* Chuvashia. ❖ *autonomous republic* W Russian Federation
Chuwārtah *see* Chwārtā
Chu Xian/Chuxian *see* Chuzhou
160 G13 **Chuxiong** Yunnan, SW China *25°02′N 101°32′E*
147 V7 **Chuy** Chuyskaya Oblast', N Kyrgyzstan *42°45′N 75°11′E*
61 H19 **Chuy** *var.* Chuí. Rocha, E Uruguay *33°42′S 53°27′W*
123 O11 **Chuya** Respublika Sakha (Yakutiya), NE Russian Federation *59°30′N 112°26′E*
Chüy Oblasty *see* Chuyskaya Oblast'
147 U8 **Chuyskaya Oblast'** *Kir.* Chüy Oblasty. ❖ *province* N Kyrgyzstan
161 Q7 **Chuzhou** *var.* Chuxian, Chu Xian. Anhui, E China *32°20′N 118°18′E*
139 U3 **Chwārtā** *var.* Choarta, Chuwārtah. As Sulaymānīyah, NE Iraq *35°11′N 45°59′E*
119 N16 **Chyhirynskaye Vodaskhovishcha** ⊠ E Belarus
117 R6 **Chyhyryn** *Rus.* Chigirin. Cherkas'ka Oblast', N Ukraine *49°03′N 32°40′E*
119 J18 **Chyrvonaya Slabada** *Rus.* Krasnaya Slabada, Krasnaya Sloboda. Minskaya Voblasts', S Belarus *52°51′N 27°10′E*
119 L19 **Chyrvonaye, Vozyera** *Rus.* Ozero Chervonoye. ⊚ SE Belarus
117 N11 **Ciadîr-Lunga** *var.* Ceadâr-Lunga, *Rus.* Chadyr-Lunga. S Moldova *46°03′N 28°50′E*
169 P16 **Ciamis** *prev.* Tjiamis. Jawa, C Indonesia *07°20′S 108°21′E*
107 I16 **Ciampino** ✈ Lazio, C Italy *41°48′N 12°36′E*
169 N16 **Cianjur** *prev.* Tjiandjoer. Jawa, C Indonesia *06°50′S 107°09′E*
60 H10 **Cianorte** Paraná, S Brazil *23°42′S 52°31′W*
Ciarraí *see* Kerry
112 N13 **Ćićevac** Serbia, E Serbia *43°44′N 21°25′E*
187 Z14 **Cicia** *prev.* Thithia. *island* Lau Group, E Fiji
105 P4 **Cidacos** ≈ N Spain
136 I10 **Cide** Kastamonu, N Turkey *41°53′N 33°01′E*
110 L10 **Ciechanów** *prev.* Zichenau. Mazowieckie, C Poland *52°53′N 20°37′E*
110 O10 **Ciechanowiec** *Ger.* Rudelstadt. Podlaskie, E Poland *52°43′N 22°30′E*
110 J10 **Ciechocinek** Kujawsko-pomorskie, C Poland *52°53′N 18°49′E*
44 F6 **Ciego de Ávila** Ciego de Ávila, C Cuba *21°50′N 78°44′W*
54 F4 **Ciénaga** Magdalena, N Colombia *11°01′N 74°15′W*
54 E6 **Ciénaga de Oro** Córdoba, NW Colombia *08°54′N 75°39′W*
44 E5 **Cienfuegos** Cienfuegos, C Cuba *22°10′N 80°27′W*
104 F4 **Cíes, Illas** *island group* NW Spain
111 P16 **Cieszanów** Podkarpackie, SE Poland *50°15′N 23°09′E*
111 J17 **Cieszyn** *Cz.* Těšín, *Ger.* Teschen. Śląskie, S Poland *49°45′N 18°35′E*
105 R12 **Cieza** Murcia, SE Spain *38°14′N 01°25′W*
136 F13 **Çifteler** Eskişehir, W Turkey *39°25′N 31°00′E*
105 P7 **Cifuentes** Castilla-La Mancha, C Spain *40°47′N 02°37′W*
Çiganak *see* Shyganak
105 P9 **Cigüela** ≈ C Spain
136 H14 **Cihanbeyli** Konya, C Turkey *38°40′N 32°55′E*
136 H14 **Cihanbeyli Yaylası** *plateau* C Turkey
104 L10 **Cijara, Embalse de** ⊠ C Spain
169 P16 **Cikalong** Jawa, S Indonesia *07°46′S 108°13′E*
169 N16 **Cikawung** Jawa, S Indonesia *06°49′S 105°29′E*
187 Y13 **Cikobia** *prev.* Thikombia. *island* N Fiji
169 P17 **Cilacap** *prev.* Tjilatjap. Jawa, C Indonesia *07°44′S 109°E*
173 O16 **Cilaos** C Réunion *21°08′S 55°28′E*
137 S11 **Çıldır** Ardahan, NE Turkey *41°08′N 43°08′E*
137 S11 **Çıldır Gölü** ⊚ NE Turkey
160 M10 **Cili** Hunan, S China *29°24′N 110°59′E*
Cilician Gates *see* Gülek Boğazı
121 V10 **Cilicia Trough** *undersea feature* E Mediterranean Sea
Cill Airne *see* Killarney
Cill Chainnigh *see* Kilkenny
Cill Chaoi *see* Kilkee
Cill Choca *see* Kilcock
Cill Dara *see* Kildare
105 N3 **Cilleruelo de Bezana** Castilla y León, N Spain *42°58′N 03°50′W*
Cilli *see* Celje
Cill Mhantáin *see* Wicklow
Cill Rois *see* Kilrush
146 C11 **Çilmämmetgum** *Rus.* Peski Chil'mamedkum, *Turkm.* Chilmämetgum. *desert* Balkan Welaýaty, W Turkmenistan
137 Z11 **Çilov Adası** *Rus.* Ostrov Zhiloy. *island* E Azerbaijan
26 J6 **Cimarron** Kansas, C USA *37°49′N 100°20′W*
37 T9 **Cimarron** New Mexico, SW USA *36°30′N 104°55′W*
26 M9 **Cimarron River** ≈ Kansas/Oklahoma, C USA
117 N11 **Cimişlia** *Rus.* Chimishliya. S Moldova *46°31′N 28°45′E*
Cîmpia Turzii *see* Câmpia Turzii
Cîmpina *see* Câmpina
Cîmpulung *see* Câmpulung
Cîmpulung Moldovenesc *see* Câmpulung Moldovenesc
137 P15 **Çınar** Diyarbakır, SE Turkey *37°45′N 40°22′E*
54 J8 **Cinaruco, Río** ≈ Colombia/Venezuela
Cina Selatan, Laut *see* South China Sea
105 T5 **Cinca** ≈ NE Spain
112 G13 **Cincar** ▲ SW Bosnia and Herzegovina *43°55′N 17°05′E*
31 Q15 **Cincinnati** Ohio, N USA *39°04′N 84°34′W*
21 M4 **Cincinnati** ✈ Kentucky, S USA *39°03′N 84°39′W*
Cinco de Outubro *see* Xá-Muteba
136 C15 **Çine** Aydın, SW Turkey *37°37′N 28°03′E*
99 J21 **Ciney** Namur, SE Belgium *50°17′N 05°06′E*
104 H6 **Cinfães** Viseu, N Portugal *41°04′N 08°06′W*
106 J12 **Cingoli** Marche, C Italy *43°25′N 13°09′E*
41 U16 **Cintalapa** *var.* Cintalapa de Figueroa. Chiapas, SE Mexico *16°42′N 93°40′W*
Cintalapa de Figueroa *see* Cintalapa
103 X14 **Cinto, Monte** ▲ Corse, France, C Mediterranean Sea *42°22′N 08°57′E*
Cintra *see* Sintra
105 Q5 **Cintruénigo** Navarra, N Spain *42°05′N 01°50′W*
Cionn tSáile *see* Kinsale
116 K13 **Ciorani** Prahova, SE Romania *44°49′N 26°25′E*
113 E14 **Čiovo** *It.* Bua. *island* S Croatia
Cipiúr *see* Kippure
63 I15 **Cipolletti** Río Negro, C Argentina *38°55′S 68°W*
120 L7 **Circeo, Capo** *headland* C Italy *41°15′N 13°03′E*
39 S8 **Circle** *var.* Circle City. Alaska, USA *65°51′N 144°04′W*
33 X8 **Circle** Montana, NW USA *47°25′N 105°32′W*
Circle City *see* Circle
31 S14 **Circleville** Ohio, N USA *39°36′N 82°57′W*
36 K6 **Circleville** Utah, W USA *38°10′N 112°16′W*
169 P16 **Cirebon** *prev.* Tjirebon. Jawa, S Indonesia *06°46′S 108°33′E*
97 L21 **Cirencester** *anc.* Corinium, Corinium Dobunorum. C England, United Kingdom *51°44′N 01°59′W*
Cirkvenica *see* Crikvenica
107 O20 **Cirò** Calabria, SW Italy *39°22′N 17°02′E*
107 O20 **Cirò Marina** Calabria, S Italy *39°21′N 17°07′E*
102 K14 **Ciron** ≈ SW France
Cirquenizza *see* Crikvenica
25 R7 **Cisco** Texas, SW USA *32°23′N 98°58′W*
116 I12 **Cisnădie** *Ger.* Heltau, *Hung.* Nagydisznód. Sibiu, SW Romania *45°42′N 24°09′E*
63 G18 **Cisnes, Río** ≈ S Chile
25 T11 **Cistern** Texas, SW USA *29°46′N 97°12′W*
104 L3 **Cistierna** Castilla y León, N Spain *42°47′N 05°08′W*
Citharista *see* la Ciotat
Citlaltépetl *see* Orizaba, Volcán Pico de
55 X10 **Citron** NW French Guiana *04°49′N 53°55′W*
23 N7 **Citronelle** Alabama, S USA *31°05′N 88°13′W*
35 O7 **Citrus Heights** California, W USA *38°42′N 121°18′W*
106 H7 **Cittadella** Veneto, NE Italy *45°37′N 11°46′E*
106 H13 **Città della Pieve** Umbria, C Italy *42°57′N 12°01′E*
106 H12 **Città di Castello** Umbria, C Italy *43°27′N 12°13′E*
107 I14 **Cittaducale** Lazio, C Italy *42°24′N 12°55′E*
107 N22 **Cittanova** Calabria, SW Italy *38°21′N 16°05′E*
Cittavecchia *see* Stari Grad
116 G10 **Ciucea** *Hung.* Csucsa. Cluj, NW Romania *46°58′N 22°50′E*
116 M13 **Ciucurova** Tulcea, SE Romania *44°57′N 28°24′E*
Ciudad Acuña *see* Villa Acuña
41 N15 **Ciudad Altamirano** Guerrero, S Mexico *18°20′N 100°40′W*
42 G7 **Ciudad Barrios** San Miguel, NE El Salvador *13°46′N 88°13′W*
54 I7 **Ciudad Bolívar** Barinas, NW Venezuela *08°22′N 70°37′W*
55 N7 **Ciudad Bolívar** *prev.* Angostura. Bolívar, E Venezuela *08°08′N 63°31′W*
40 K6 **Ciudad Camargo** Chihuahua, N Mexico *27°42′N 105°10′W*
40 E8 **Ciudad Constitución** Baja California Sur, NW Mexico *25°09′N 111°43′W*
Ciudad Cortés *see* Cortés
41 V17 **Ciudad Cuauhtémoc** Chiapas, SE Mexico *15°38′N 91°59′W*
42 J9 **Ciudad Darío** *var.* Dario. Matagalpa, W Nicaragua *12°42′N 86°10′W*
Ciudad de Dolores Hidalgo *see* Dolores Hidalgo
42 C6 **Ciudad de Guatemala** *Eng.* Guatemala City; *prev.* Santiago de los Caballeros. ● (Guatemala) Guatemala, C Guatemala *14°38′N 90°29′W*
Ciudad del Carmen *see* Carmen
62 Q6 **Ciudad del Este** *prev.* Ciudad Presidente Stroessner, Presidente Stroessner, Puerto Presidente Stroessner. Alto Paraná, SE Paraguay *25°34′S 54°40′W*
62 K5 **Ciudad de Libertador General San Martín** *var.* Libertador General San Martín. Jujuy, C Argentina *23°50′S 64°45′W*
Ciudad Delicias *see* Delicias
41 O11 **Ciudad del Maíz** San Luis Potosí, C Mexico *22°26′N 99°36′W*
Ciudad de México *see* México
54 J7 **Ciudad de Nutrias** Barinas, NW Venezuela *08°03′N 69°17′W*
Ciudad de Panama *see* Panamá
55 P7 **Ciudad Guayana** *prev.* San Tomé de Guayana, Santo Tomé de Guayana. Bolívar, NE Venezuela *08°22′N 62°37′W*
40 K14 **Ciudad Guzmán** Jalisco, SW Mexico *19°40′N 103°30′W*
41 V17 **Ciudad Hidalgo** Chiapas, SE Mexico *14°40′N 92°11′W*
41 N14 **Ciudad Hidalgo** Michoacán, SW Mexico *19°40′N 100°34′W*
40 J3 **Ciudad Juárez** Chihuahua, N Mexico *31°39′N 106°26′W*
40 L8 **Ciudad Lerdo** Durango, C Mexico *25°34′N 103°30′W*
41 Q11 **Ciudad Madero** *var.* Villa Cecilia. Tamaulipas, C Mexico *22°18′N 97°56′W*
41 P11 **Ciudad Mante** Tamaulipas, C Mexico *22°43′N 99°02′W*
42 F2 **Ciudad Melchor de Mencos** *var.* Melchor de Mencos. Petén, NE Guatemala *17°03′N 89°12′W*
41 P8 **Ciudad Miguel Alemán** Tamaulipas, C Mexico *26°20′N 98°56′W*
Ciudad Mutis *see* Bahía Solano
40 G6 **Ciudad Obregón** Sonora, NW Mexico *27°32′N 109°53′W*
54 I5 **Ciudad Ojeda** Zulia, NW Venezuela *10°12′N 71°17′W*
55 P7 **Ciudad Piar** Bolívar, E Venezuela *07°25′N 63°19′W*
Ciudad Porfirio Díaz *see* Piedras Negras
Ciudad Presidente Stroessner *see* Ciudad del Este
Ciudad Quesada *see* Quesada
105 N11 **Ciudad Real** Castilla-La Mancha, C Spain *38°59′N 03°55′W*
105 N11 **Ciudad Real** ❖ *province* Castilla-La Mancha, C Spain
104 J7 **Ciudad-Rodrigo** Castilla y León, N Spain *40°36′N 06°33′W*
42 A6 **Ciudad Tecún Umán** San Marcos, SW Guatemala *14°40′N 92°06′W*
Ciudad Trujillo *see* Santo Domingo
41 P12 **Ciudad Valles** San Luis Potosí, C Mexico *21°59′N 99°01′W*
41 O10 **Ciudad Victoria** Tamaulipas, C Mexico *23°44′N 99°07′W*
42 C6 **Ciudad Vieja** Suchitepéquez, S Guatemala *14°30′N 90°46′W*
116 L8 **Ciuhuru** *var.* Reuţel. ≈ N Moldova
105 Z8 **Ciutadella** *var.* Ciutadella de Menorca. Menorca, Spain, W Mediterranean Sea *40°N 03°50′E*
Ciutadella Ciutadella de Menorca *see* Ciutadella
136 L11 **Civa Burnu** *headland* N Turkey *41°22′N 36°39′E*
106 J7 **Cividale del Friuli** Friuli-Venezia Giulia, NE Italy *46°06′N 13°25′E*
107 H14 **Civita Castellana** Lazio, C Italy *42°16′N 12°24′E*
106 J12 **Civitanova Marche** Marche, C Italy *43°18′N 13°41′E*
Civitas Altae Ripae *see* Brzeg
Civitas Carnutum *see* Chartres
Civitas Eburovicum *see* Évreux
Civitas Nemetum *see* Speyer
107 G15 **Civitavecchia** *anc.* Centum Cellae, Trajani Portus. Lazio, C Italy *42°05′N 11°47′E*
102 L10 **Civray** Vienne, W France *46°10′N 00°18′E*
136 E14 **Çivril** Denizli, W Turkey *38°18′N 29°43′E*
161 O5 **Cixian** Hebei, E China *36°19′N 114°22′E*
137 R16 **Cizre** Şırnak, SE Turkey *37°21′N 42°11′E*
Clacton *see* Clacton-on-Sea
97 Q21 **Clacton-on-Sea** *var.* Clacton. E England, United Kingdom *51°48′N 01°09′E*
22 H5 **Claiborne, Lake** ⊠ Louisiana, S USA
102 L10 **Clain** ≈ W France
11 Q11 **Claire, Lake** ⊚ Alberta, C Canada
25 O6 **Clairemont** Texas, SW USA *33°09′N 100°45′W*
34 M3 **Clair Engle Lake** ⊠ California, W USA
18 B15 **Clairton** Pennsylvania, NE USA *40°17′N 79°52′W*
32 F7 **Clallam Bay** Washington, NW USA *48°13′N 124°16′W*
103 P8 **Clamecy** Nièvre, C France *47°28′N 03°30′E*
23 P5 **Clanton** Alabama, S USA *32°50′N 86°37′W*
61 D17 **Clara** Entre Ríos, E Argentina *31°50′S 58°48′W*
97 E18 **Clara** *Ir.* Clóirtheach. C Ireland *53°20′N 07°36′W*
29 T9 **Clara City** Minnesota, N USA *44°57′N 95°22′W*

◆ Country ● Country Capital ◇ Dependent Territory ○ Dependent Territory Capital ❖ Administrative Regions ✈ International Airport ▲ Mountain ▲ Mountain Range Volcano ≈ River ⊚ Lake ⊠ Reservoir

61 D23 Claraz Buenos Aires, E Argentina 37°56′S 59°18′W
Clár Chlainne Mhuiris see Claremorris
182 I8 Clare South Australia 33°49′S 138°35′E
97 C19 Clare Ir. An Clár. cultural region W Ireland
97 C18 Clare ≈ W Ireland
97 A16 Clare Island Ir. Cliara. island W Ireland
44 J12 Claremont C Jamaica 18°23′N 77°11′W
29 W10 Claremont Minnesota, N USA 44°01′N 93°00′W
19 N9 Claremont New Hampshire, NE USA 43°21′N 72°18′W
27 Q9 Claremore Oklahoma, C USA 36°20′N 95°37′W
97 C17 Claremorris Ir. Clár Chlainne Mhuiris. W Ireland 53°47′N 09°W
185 J16 Clarence Canterbury, South Island, New Zealand 42°08′S 173°54′E
185 J16 Clarence ≈ South Island, New Zealand
65 F15 Clarence Bay bay Ascension Island, C Atlantic Ocean
63 H25 Clarence, Isla island S Chile
194 H2 Clarence Island island South Shetland Islands, Antarctica
183 V5 Clarence River ≈ New South Wales, SE Australia
44 J5 Clarence Town Long Island, C Bahamas 23°03′N 74°57′W
27 W12 Clarendon Arkansas, C USA 34°41′N 91°19′W
25 O3 Clarendon Texas, SW USA 34°57′N 100°54′W
13 U12 Clarenville Newfoundland, Newfoundland and Labrador, SE Canada 48°10′N 54°00′W
11 Q17 Claresholm Alberta, SW Canada 50°02′N 113°33′W
29 T16 Clarinda Iowa, C USA 40°44′N 95°02′W
55 N5 Clarines Anzoátegui, NE Venezuela 09°56′N 65°11′W
29 V12 Clarion Iowa, C USA 42°43′N 93°43′W
18 C13 Clarion Pennsylvania, NE USA 41°11′N 79°21′W
193 O6 Clarion Fracture Zone tectonic feature NE Pacific Ocean
18 D13 Clarion River ≈ Pennsylvania, NE USA
29 Q9 Clark South Dakota, N USA 44°50′N 97°44′W
36 K11 Clarkdale Arizona, SW USA 34°46′N 112°03′W
15 W4 Clarke City Québec, SE Canada 50°09′N 66°36′W
183 Q15 Clarke Island island Furneaux Group, Tasmania, SE Australia
181 X6 Clarke Range ⛰ Queensland, E Australia
23 T2 Clarkesville Georgia, SE USA 34°36′N 83°31′W
29 S9 Clarkfield Minnesota, N USA 44°48′N 95°49′W
33 N7 Clark Fork Idaho, NW USA 48°06′N 116°10′W
33 N8 Clark Fork ≈ Idaho/Montana, NW USA
21 P13 Clark Hill Lake var. J.Storm Thurmond Reservoir. ▣ Georgia/South Carolina, SE USA
39 Q12 Clark, Lake ◎ Alaska, USA
35 W12 Clark Mountain ▲ California, W USA 35°30′N 115°34′W
37 S3 Clark Peak ▲ Colorado, C USA 40°36′N 105°57′W
14 D14 Clark, Point headland Ontario, S Canada 44°04′N 81°45′W
21 S3 Clarksburg West Virginia, NE USA 39°16′N 80°22′W
22 K2 Clarksdale Mississippi, S USA 34°12′N 90°34′W
33 U12 Clarks Fork Yellowstone River ≈ Montana/Wyoming, NW USA
29 R14 Clarkson Nebraska, C USA 41°42′N 97°07′W
39 O13 Clarks Point Alaska, USA 58°50′N 158°33′W
18 I13 Clarks Summit Pennsylvania, NE USA 41°29′N 75°42′W
32 M10 Clarkston Washington, NW USA 46°25′N 117°02′W
44 J12 Clark's Town C Jamaica 18°25′N 77°32′W
27 T10 Clarksville Arkansas, C USA 35°29′N 93°29′W
31 P13 Clarksville Indiana, N USA 40°01′N 85°54′W
20 I8 Clarksville Tennessee, S USA 36°32′N 87°22′W
25 W5 Clarksville Texas, SW USA 33°37′N 95°04′W
21 U8 Clarksville Virginia, NE USA 36°36′N 78°36′W
21 U11 Clarkton North Carolina, SE USA 34°28′N 78°39′W
61 C24 Claromecó var. Balneario Claromecó. Buenos Aires, E Argentina 38°51′S 60°01′W
25 N3 Claude Texas, SW USA 35°06′N 101°22′W
Clausentum see Southampton
171 O1 Claveria Luzon, N Philippines 18°36′N 121°04′E
99 J20 Clavier Liège, E Belgium 50°27′N 05°21′E
23 W6 Claxton Georgia, SE USA 32°09′N 81°54′W
21 R4 Clay West Virginia, NE USA 38°28′N 81°17′W
27 N3 Clay Center Kansas, C USA 39°22′N 97°08′W
29 P16 Clay Center Nebraska, C USA 40°31′N 98°03′W
21 Y2 Claymont Delaware, NE USA 39°48′N 75°27′W
36 M14 Claypool Arizona, SW USA 33°24′N 110°50′W
23 R6 Clayton Alabama, S USA 31°52′N 85°27′W
23 T1 Clayton Georgia, SE USA 34°52′N 83°24′W
22 J5 Clayton Louisiana, S USA 31°43′N 91°32′W
27 X5 Clayton Missouri, C USA 38°39′N 90°21′W
37 V9 Clayton New Mexico, SW USA 36°27′N 103°12′W
21 V9 Clayton North Carolina, SE USA 35°39′N 78°27′W
27 Q12 Clayton Oklahoma, C USA 34°35′N 95°21′W
45 V9 Clayton J. Lloyd ✈ (The Valley) C Anguilla 18°12′N 63°02′W
182 I4 Clayton River seasonal river South Australia
21 R7 Claytor Lake ▣ Virginia, NE USA
27 P13 Clear Boggy Creek ≈ Oklahoma, C USA
97 B22 Clear, Cape var. The Bill of Cape Clear, Ir. Ceann Cléire. headland SW Ireland 51°25′N 09°31′W
36 M12 Clear Creek ≈ Arizona, SW USA
39 S12 Cleare, Cape headland Montague Island, Alaska, USA 59°46′N 147°54′W
18 E13 Clearfield Pennsylvania, NE USA 41°02′N 78°27′W
36 L2 Clearfield Utah, W USA 41°06′N 112°03′W
25 Q6 Clear Fork Brazos River ≈ Texas, SW USA
31 T12 Clear Fork Reservoir ▣ Ohio, N USA
11 N12 Clear Hills ⛰ Alberta, SW Canada
34 M6 Clearlake California, W USA 38°57′N 122°38′W
29 V12 Clear Lake Iowa, C USA 43°07′N 93°22′W
29 R9 Clear Lake South Dakota, N USA 44°45′N 96°40′W
34 M6 Clear Lake ◎ California, W USA
22 G6 Clear Lake ▣ Louisiana, S USA
35 P1 Clear Lake Reservoir ▣ California, W USA
11 N16 Clearwater British Columbia, SW Canada 51°38′N 120°02′W
23 U12 Clearwater Florida, SE USA 27°58′N 82°46′W
11 R12 Clearwater ≈ Alberta/Saskatchewan, C Canada
27 W7 Clearwater Lake ▣ Missouri, C USA
33 N10 Clearwater Mountains ⛰ Idaho, NW USA
33 N10 Clearwater River ≈ Idaho, NW USA
29 S4 Clearwater River ≈ Minnesota, N USA
25 T7 Cleburne Texas, SW USA 32°21′N 97°24′W
32 I9 Cle Elum Washington, NW USA 47°12′N 120°56′W
97 O17 Cleethorpes E England, United Kingdom 53°34′N 00°02′W
Cléire, Ceann see Clear, Cape
21 O11 Clemson South Carolina, SE USA 34°40′N 82°50′W
21 Q4 Clendenin West Virginia, NE USA 38°29′N 81°21′W
26 M9 Cleo Springs Oklahoma, C USA 36°25′N 98°25′W
Clerk Island see Onotoa
181 X8 Clermont Queensland, E Australia 22°47′S 147°41′E
15 S8 Clermont Québec, SE Canada 47°41′N 70°15′W
103 O4 Clermont Oise, N France 49°23′N 02°26′E
29 X12 Clermont Iowa, C USA 43°00′N 91°39′W
103 P11 Clermont-Ferrand Puy-de-Dôme, C France 45°47′N 03°05′E
103 Q15 Clermont-l'Hérault Hérault, S France 43°37′N 03°25′E
99 M22 Clervaux Diekirch, N Luxembourg 50°03′N 06°02′E
106 G6 Cles Trentino-Alto Adige, N Italy 46°22′N 11°04′E
182 H8 Cleve South Australia 33°43′S 136°30′E
Cleve see Kleve
23 T2 Cleveland Georgia, SE USA 34°36′N 83°45′W
22 K3 Cleveland Mississippi, S USA 33°45′N 90°43′W
31 T11 Cleveland Ohio, N USA 41°30′N 81°42′W
27 O9 Cleveland Oklahoma, C USA 36°18′N 96°27′W
20 L10 Cleveland Tennessee, S USA 35°10′N 84°51′W
25 W10 Cleveland Texas, SW USA 30°19′N 95°06′W
31 N7 Cleveland Wisconsin, N USA 43°58′N 87°45′W
31 O4 Cleveland Cliffs Basin ◎ Michigan, N USA
31 U11 Cleveland Heights Ohio, N USA 41°30′N 81°34′W
33 P6 Cleveland, Mount ▲ Montana, NW USA 48°55′N 113°51′W
Cleves see Kleve
97 B16 Clew Bay Ir. Cuan Mó. inlet W Ireland
23 Y14 Clewiston Florida, SE USA 26°45′N 80°55′W
Cliara see Clare Island
97 A17 Clifden Ir. An Clochán. Galway, W Ireland 53°29′N 10°14′W
37 O14 Clifton Arizona, SW USA 33°03′N 109°18′W
18 K14 Clifton New Jersey, NE USA 40°50′N 74°28′W
25 S8 Clifton Texas, SW USA 31°43′N 97°36′W
21 S6 Clifton Forge Virginia, NE USA 37°49′N 79°50′W
182 I1 Clifton Hills South Australia 27°03′S 138°49′E
11 S17 Climax Saskatchewan, S Canada 49°12′N 108°22′W
21 O8 Clinch River ≈ Tennessee/Virginia, S USA
25 P12 Cline Texas, SW USA 29°14′N 100°07′W
21 N10 Clingmans Dome ▲ North Carolina/Tennessee, SE USA 35°33′N 83°30′W
24 H8 Clint Texas, SW USA 31°35′N 106°13′W
10 M16 Clinton British Columbia, SW Canada 51°06′N 121°31′W
14 E15 Clinton Ontario, S Canada 43°36′N 81°33′W
27 U10 Clinton Arkansas, C USA 35°34′N 92°28′W
30 L10 Clinton Illinois, N USA 40°09′N 88°57′W
29 Z14 Clinton Iowa, C USA 41°50′N 90°11′W
20 G7 Clinton Kentucky, S USA 36°39′N 89°00′W
22 J8 Clinton Louisiana, S USA 30°52′N 91°01′W
19 N11 Clinton Massachusetts, NE USA 42°25′N 71°40′W
31 R10 Clinton Michigan, N USA 42°04′N 83°58′W
22 K5 Clinton Mississippi, S USA 32°22′N 90°22′W
27 S5 Clinton Missouri, C USA 38°22′N 93°51′W
21 V10 Clinton North Carolina, SE USA 35°00′N 78°19′W
26 L10 Clinton Oklahoma, C USA 35°31′N 98°58′W
21 Q12 Clinton South Carolina, SE USA 34°28′N 81°52′W
21 M9 Clinton Tennessee, S USA 36°07′N 84°08′W
8 L9 Clinton-Colden Lake ◎ Northwest Territories, NW Canada
10 H5 Clinton Creek Yukon Territory, NW Canada 64°24′N 140°35′W
30 L13 Clinton Lake ▣ Illinois, N USA
27 Q4 Clinton Lake ▣ Kansas, N USA
21 T11 Clio South Carolina, SE USA 34°34′N 79°33′W
193 O7 Clipperton Fracture Zone tectonic feature E Pacific Ocean
193 Q7 Clipperton Island ◇ French dependency of French Polynesia E Pacific Ocean
46 K6 Clipperton Island island E Pacific Ocean
0 F16 Clipperton Seamounts undersea feature E Pacific Ocean 08°00′N 111°00′W
102 J8 Clisson Loire-Atlantique, NW France 47°06′N 01°19′W
62 K7 Clodomira Santiago del Estero, N Argentina 27°35′S 64°14′W
Cloich na Coillte see Clonakilty
Clóirtheach see Clara
97 C21 Clonakilty Ir. Cloich na Coillte. SW Ireland 51°37′N 08°54′W
181 T6 Cloncurry Queensland, C Australia 20°45′S 140°30′E
97 F18 Clondalkin Ir. Cluain Dolcáin. E Ireland 53°19′N 06°24′W
97 E16 Clones Ir. Cluain Eois. N Ireland 54°11′N 07°14′W
97 D20 Clonmel Ir. Cluain Meala. S Ireland 52°21′N 07°42′W
100 G11 Cloppenburg Niedersachsen, NW Germany 52°51′N 08°03′E
29 W6 Cloquet Minnesota, N USA 46°43′N 92°27′W
37 S14 Cloudcroft New Mexico, SW USA 32°57′N 105°44′W
33 W12 Cloud Peak ▲ Wyoming, C USA 44°22′N 107°10′W
185 K14 Cloudy Bay inlet South Island, New Zealand
21 R10 Clover South Carolina, SE USA 35°06′N 81°13′W
34 M6 Cloverdale California, W USA 38°49′N 123°03′W
20 J5 Cloverport Kentucky, S USA 37°50′N 86°37′W
35 Q10 Clovis California, W USA 36°48′N 119°43′W
37 W12 Clovis New Mexico, SW USA 34°22′N 103°12′W
14 K13 Cloyne Ontario, SE Canada 44°48′N 77°09′W
Cluain Dolcáin see Clondalkin
Cluain Eois see Clones
Cluainín see Manorhamilton
Cluain Meala see Clonmel
116 H10 Cluj ◈ county NW Romania
Cluj see Cluj-Napoca
116 H10 Cluj-Napoca Ger. Klausenburg, Hung. Kolozsvár; prev. Cluj. Cluj, NW Romania 46°47′N 23°36′E
Clunia see Feldkirch
103 R10 Cluny Saône-et-Loire, C France 46°25′N 04°38′E
103 T10 Cluses Haute-Savoie, E France 46°04′N 06°34′E
106 E7 Clusone Lombardia, N Italy 45°56′N 10°00′E
25 W12 Clute Texas, SW USA 29°01′N 95°24′W
185 D23 Clutha ≈ South Island, New Zealand
97 J18 Clwyd cultural region NE Wales, United Kingdom
185 D22 Clyde Otago, South Island, New Zealand 45°12′S 169°21′E
27 N3 Clyde Kansas, C USA 39°35′N 97°24′W
29 P2 Clyde North Dakota, N USA 48°44′N 98°51′W
31 S11 Clyde Ohio, N USA 41°18′N 82°58′W
25 Q7 Clyde Texas, SW USA 32°24′N 99°29′W
14 K13 Clyde ≈ Ontario, SE Canada
96 J13 Clyde ≈ W Scotland, United Kingdom
96 H12 Clydebank S Scotland, United Kingdom 55°54′N 04°24′W
96 H13 Clyde, Firth of inlet S Scotland, United Kingdom
33 S11 Clyde Park Montana, NW USA 45°56′N 110°39′W
35 W16 Coachella California, W USA 33°38′N 116°10′W
35 W16 Coachella Canal canal California, W USA
40 I9 Coacoyole Durango, C Mexico 24°30′N 106°33′W
25 N7 Coahoma Texas, SW USA 32°18′N 101°18′W
10 K8 Coal ≈ Yukon Territory, NW Canada
40 L14 Coalcomán var. Coalcomán de Matamoros. Michoacán, S Mexico 18°49′N 103°13′W
Coalcomán de Matamoros see Coalcomán
39 T8 Coal Creek Alaska, USA 65°21′N 143°08′W
11 Q17 Coaldale Alberta, SW Canada 49°42′N 112°36′W
27 P12 Coalgate Oklahoma, C USA 34°33′N 96°15′W
35 P11 Coalinga California, W USA 36°08′N 120°21′W
10 L9 Coal River British Columbia, W Canada 59°38′N 126°45′W
21 Q6 Coal River ≈ West Virginia, NE USA
36 M2 Coalville Utah, W USA 40°56′N 111°22′W
58 E13 Coari Amazonas, N Brazil 04°08′S 63°07′W
104 I7 Côa, Rio ≈ N Portugal
59 D14 Coari, Rio ≈ NW Brazil
81 J20 Coast ◈ province SE Kenya
Coast see Pwani
10 G12 Coast Mountains Fr. Chaîne Côtière. ⛰ Canada/USA
16 C7 Coast Ranges ⛰ W USA
96 I12 Coatbridge S Scotland, United Kingdom 55°52′N 04°01′W
42 B6 Coatepeque Quezaltenango, SW Guatemala 14°42′N 91°50′W
18 H16 Coatesville Pennsylvania, NE USA 39°58′N 75°47′W
15 Q13 Coaticook Québec, SE Canada 45°07′N 71°46′W
9 P9 Coats Island island Nunavut, NE Canada
195 O4 Coats Land physical region Antarctica
41 T14 Coatzacoalcos var. Quetzalcoalco; prev. Puerto México. Veracruz-Llave, E Mexico 18°06′N 94°26′W
41 S14 Coatzacoalcos, Río ≈ SE Mexico
116 M15 Cobadin Constanța, SW Romania 44°05′N 28°13′E
14 H9 Cobalt Ontario, S Canada 47°24′N 79°41′W
42 D5 Cobán Alta Verapaz, C Guatemala 15°28′N 90°20′W
183 O6 Cobar New South Wales, SE Australia 31°31′S 145°51′E
18 F12 Cobb Hill ▲ Pennsylvania, NE USA 41°52′N 77°52′W
0 D8 Cobb Seamount undersea feature E Pacific Ocean 47°00′N 131°00′W
14 K12 Cobden Ontario, SE Canada 45°36′N 76°54′W
97 D21 Cobh Ir. An Cóbh; prev. Cove of Cork, Queenstown. SW Ireland 51°51′N 08°17′W
57 J14 Cobija Pando, NW Bolivia 11°04′S 68°49′W
Coblence/Coblenz see Koblenz
18 J10 Cobleskill New York, NE USA 42°40′N 74°29′W
14 I15 Cobourg Ontario, SE Canada 43°57′N 78°06′W
181 P1 Cobourg Peninsula headland Northern Territory, N Australia 11°27′S 132°33′E
183 O10 Cobram Victoria, SE Australia 35°56′S 145°36′E
82 N13 Cóbuè Niassa, N Mozambique 12°08′S 34°46′E
101 K18 Coburg Bayern, SE Germany 50°16′N 10°58′E
19 Q5 Coburn Mountain ▲ Maine, NE USA 45°28′N 70°07′W
57 H18 Cocachacra Arequipa, SW Peru 17°05′S 71°45′W
59 J17 Cocalinho Mato Grosso, W Brazil 14°22′S 51°00′W
Cocanada see Kākināda
105 S11 Cocentaina Valenciana, E Spain 38°44′N 00°27′W
57 L18 Cochabamba hist. Oropeza. Cochabamba, C Bolivia 17°23′S 66°10′W
57 K18 Cochabamba ◈ department C Bolivia
57 L18 Cochabamba, Cordillera de ⛰ C Bolivia
101 E18 Cochem Rheinland-Pfalz, W Germany 50°09′N 07°09′E
37 R6 Cochetopa Hills ⛰ Colorado, C USA
155 G22 Cochin var. Kochchi, Kochi. Kerala, SW India 09°56′N 76°15′E see also Kochi
44 D5 Cochinos, Bahía de Eng. Bay of Pigs. bay SE Cuba
37 O16 Cochise Head ▲ Arizona, SW USA 32°03′N 109°19′W
23 U5 Cochran Georgia, SE USA 32°23′N 83°21′W
11 P16 Cochrane Alberta, SW Canada 51°15′N 114°25′W
12 G12 Cochrane Ontario, S Canada 49°04′N 81°02′W
63 G20 Cochrane Aisén, S Chile 47°16′S 72°33′W
11 U10 Cochrane ≈ Manitoba/Saskatchewan, C Canada
Cochrane, Lago see Pueyrredón, Lago
Cocibolca see Nicaragua, Lago de
Cockade State see Maryland
44 M6 Cockburn Harbour South Caicos, S Turks and Caicos Islands 21°28′N 71°30′W
14 C11 Cockburn Island island Ontario, S Canada
44 J3 Cockburn Town San Salvador, E Bahamas 24°01′N 74°31′W
21 X2 Cockeysville Maryland, NE USA 39°29′N 76°34′W
181 N12 Cocklebiddy Western Australia 32°02′S 125°54′E
44 I12 Cockpit Country, The physical region W Jamaica
43 S16 Coclé off. Provincia de Coclé. ◈ province C Panama
43 S15 Coclé del Norte Colón, C Panama 09°04′N 80°32′W
Coclé, Provincia de see Coclé
23 Y12 Cocoa Florida, SE USA 28°23′N 80°44′W
23 Y12 Cocoa Beach Florida, SE USA 28°19′N 80°36′W
79 D17 Cocobeach Estuaire, NW Gabon 0°59′N 09°34′E
44 G5 Coco, Cayo island C Cuba
151 Q19 Coco Channel strait Andaman Sea/Bay of Bengal
173 N6 Coco-de-Mer Seamounts undersea feature W Indian Ocean 0°30′N 56°00′E
36 K10 Coconino Plateau plain Arizona, SW USA
43 N6 Coco, Río var. Río Wanki, Segoviao Wangkí. ≈ Honduras/Nicaragua
173 T7 Cocos Basin undersea feature E Indian Ocean 05°00′S 94°00′E
188 B17 Cocos Island island S Guam
Cocos Island Ridge see Cocos Ridge
129 S17 Cocos Islands island group E Indian Ocean
173 T8 Cocos (Keeling) Islands ◇ Australian external territory E Indian Ocean
0 G15 Cocos Plate tectonic feature
193 T7 Cocos Ridge var. Cocos Island Ridge. undersea feature E Pacific Ocean 05°30′N 86°00′W
40 K13 Cocula Jalisco, SW Mexico 20°22′N 103°50′W
107 D17 Coda Cavallo, Capo headland Sardegna, Italy, C Mediterranean Sea 40°49′N 09°43′E
58 E13 Codajás Amazonas, N Brazil 03°50′S 62°12′W
Codazzi see Agustín Codazzi
19 Q12 Cod, Cape headland Massachusetts, NE USA 41°50′N 69°56′W
185 B25 Codfish Island island SW New Zealand
106 H9 Codigoro Emilia-Romagna, N Italy 44°50′N 12°07′E
13 P5 Cod Island island Newfoundland and Labrador, E Canada
116 J12 Codlea Ger. Zeiden, Hung. Feketehalom. Brașov, C Romania 45°43′N 25°27′E
58 M13 Codó Maranhão, E Brazil 04°28′S 43°51′W
106 E8 Codogno Lombardia, N Italy 45°10′N 09°42′E
116 M10 Codrii hill range C Moldova
45 W9 Codrington Barbuda, Antigua and Barbuda 17°43′N 61°49′W
106 J7 Codroipo Friuli-Venezia Giulia, NE Italy 45°58′N 13°00′E
28 M12 Cody Nebraska, C USA 42°54′N 101°13′W
33 U12 Cody Wyoming, C USA 43°31′N 109°04′W
21 P7 Coeburn Virginia, NE USA 36°56′N 82°27′W
54 E10 Coello Tolima, W Colombia 04°15′N 74°52′W
Coemba see Cuemba
181 V2 Coen Queensland, NE Australia 14°03′S 143°16′E
101 E14 Coesfeld Nordrhein-Westfalen, W Germany 51°55′N 07°10′E
32 M8 Coeur d'Alene Idaho, NW USA 47°40′N 116°46′W
32 M8 Coeur d'Alene Lake ▣ Idaho, NW USA
98 O8 Coevorden Drenthe, NE Netherlands 52°39′N 06°45′E
10 H6 Coffee Creek Yukon Territory, W Canada 62°52′N 139°05′W
30 L15 Coffeen Lake ▣ Illinois, N USA
22 L3 Coffeeville Mississippi, S USA 33°58′N 89°40′W
27 Q8 Coffeyville Kansas, C USA 37°02′N 95°37′W
182 G9 Coffin Bay South Australia 34°39′S 135°30′E
182 F9 Coffin Bay Peninsula peninsula South Australia
183 V5 Coffs Harbour New South Wales, SE Australia 30°18′S 153°08′E
105 R10 Cofrentes Valenciana, E Spain 39°14′N 01°04′W
117 N10 Cogîlnic Ukr. Kohyl'nyk. ≈ Moldova/Ukraine
102 K11 Cognac anc. Compniacum. Charente, W France 45°42′N 00°19′W
106 B7 Cogne Valle d'Aosta, NW Italy 45°37′N 07°27′E
103 U16 Cogolin Var, SE France 43°15′N 06°30′E
105 O7 Cogolludo Castilla-La Mancha, C Spain 40°58′N 03°05′W
Cohalm see Rupea
92 K8 Čohkarášša var. Cuokkaraš ša. ▲ N Norway 69°57′N 24°38′E
Čohkkiras see Jukkasjärvi
18 F11 Cohocton River ≈ New York, NE USA
18 L10 Cohoes New York, NE USA 42°46′N 73°42′W
183 N10 Cohuna Victoria, SE Australia 35°51′S 144°15′E
43 P17 Coiba, Isla de island SW Panama
63 H23 Coig, Río ≈ S Argentina
63 G19 Coihaique var. Coyhaique. Aisén, S Chile 45°32′S 72°00′W
155 G21 Coimbatore Tamil Nādu, S India 11°N 76°57′E
104 G8 Coimbra anc. Conimbria, Conimbriga. Coimbra, W Portugal 40°12′N 08°25′W
104 G8 Coimbra ◈ district N Portugal
104 L15 Coín Andalucía, S Spain 36°40′N 04°45′W
Coin de Mire see Gunner's Quoin
57 J20 Coipasa, Laguna ◎ W Bolivia
57 J20 Coipasa, Salar de salt lake W Bolivia
Coira/Coire see Chur
Coirib, Loch see Corrib, Lough
54 K6 Cojedes off. Estado Cojedes. ◈ state N Venezuela
Cojedes, Estado see Cojedes
42 F7 Cojutepeque Cuscatlán, C El Salvador 13°43′N 88°56′W
Coka see Banbar
33 S16 Cokeville Wyoming, C USA 42°03′N 110°55′W
182 M13 Colac Victoria, SE Australia 38°22′S 143°38′E
59 O20 Colatina Espírito Santo, SE Brazil 19°35′S 40°37′W
27 O13 Colbert Oklahoma, C USA 33°51′N 96°30′W
100 L12 Colbitz-Letzinger Heide heathland N Germany
26 I3 Colby Kansas, C USA 39°24′N 101°04′W
57 H17 Colca, Río ≈ SW Peru
97 P21 Colchester hist. Colneceaste; anc. Camulodunum. E England, United Kingdom 51°54′N 00°54′E
19 N13 Colchester Connecticut, NE USA 41°34′N 72°17′W
38 M16 Cold Bay Alaska, USA 55°11′N 162°43′W
11 R14 Cold Lake Alberta, SW Canada 54°26′N 110°16′W
11 R13 Cold Lake ◎ Alberta/Saskatchewan, S Canada
29 U8 Cold Spring Minnesota, N USA 45°27′N 94°25′W
25 W10 Coldspring Texas, SW USA 30°34′N 95°10′W
11 N17 Coldstream British Columbia, SW Canada 50°13′N 119°09′W
96 L13 Coldstream SE Scotland, United Kingdom 55°39′N 02°19′W
14 H13 Coldwater Ontario, S Canada 44°43′N 79°36′W
26 K7 Coldwater Kansas, C USA 37°16′N 99°20′W
31 Q10 Coldwater Michigan, N USA 41°56′N 85°00′W
25 N1 Coldwater Creek ≈ Oklahoma/Texas, SW USA
22 K2 Coldwater River ≈ Mississippi, S USA
183 O9 Coleambally New South Wales, SE Australia 34°48′S 145°54′E
19 O6 Colebrook New Hampshire, NE USA 44°52′N 71°27′W
27 T5 Cole Camp Missouri, C USA 38°27′N 93°12′W
39 T6 Coleen River ≈ Alaska, USA
11 P17 Coleman Alberta, SW Canada 49°36′N 114°26′W
25 Q8 Coleman Texas, SW USA 31°50′N 99°27′W
Çölemerik see Hakkâri
83 K22 Colenso KwaZulu/Natal, E South Africa 28°44′S 29°50′E
182 L12 Coleraine Victoria, SE Australia 37°39′S 141°42′E
97 F14 Coleraine Ir. Cúil Raithin. N Northern Ireland, United Kingdom 55°08′N 06°40′W
185 G18 Coleridge, Lake ◎ South Island, New Zealand
83 H24 Colesberg Northern Cape, C South Africa 30°41′S 25°08′E
22 H7 Colfax Louisiana, S USA 31°31′N 92°42′W
32 L9 Colfax Washington, NW USA 46°52′N 117°21′W
30 J6 Colfax Wisconsin, N USA 45°00′N 91°44′W
63 I19 Colhué Huapí, Lago ◎ S Argentina
45 Z6 Colibris, Pointe des headland Grande Terre, E Guadeloupe 16°15′N 61°10′W
106 D6 Colico Lombardia, N Italy 46°08′N 09°24′E
99 E14 Colijnsplaat Zeeland, SW Netherlands 51°36′N 03°47′E
40 L14 Colima Colima, S Mexico 19°13′N 103°46′W
40 K14 Colima ◈ state SW Mexico
40 L14 Colima, Nevado de Ж C Mexico 19°36′N 103°36′W
59 M14 Colinas Maranhão, E Brazil 06°02′S 44°15′W
96 F10 Coll island W Scotland, United Kingdom
105 N7 Collado Villalba var. Villalba. Madrid, C Spain 40°38′N 04°00′W
183 R4 Collarenebri New South Wales, SE Australia 29°31′S 148°33′E
37 P5 Collbran Colorado, C USA 39°14′N 107°57′W
106 G12 Colle di Val d'Elsa Toscana, C Italy 43°26′N 11°06′E
39 R9 College Alaska, USA 64°49′N 148°06′W
32 K10 College Place Washington, NW USA 46°03′N 118°23′W
25 U10 College Station Texas, SW USA 30°38′N 96°21′W
183 P4 Collerina New South Wales, SE Australia 29°41′S 146°36′E
180 I13 Collie Western Australia 33°20′S 116°06′E
180 L4 Collier Bay bay Western Australia
21 F10 Collierville Tennessee, S USA 35°02′N 89°39′W
106 F11 Collina, Passo della pass C Italy
14 G14 Collingwood Ontario, S Canada 44°30′N 80°14′W
184 I13 Collingwood Tasman, South Island, New Zealand 40°40′S 172°40′E
22 L7 Collins Mississippi, S USA 31°39′N 89°33′W
30 K15 Collinsville Illinois, N USA 38°40′N 89°58′W
27 P9 Collinsville Oklahoma, C USA 36°21′N 95°50′W
20 H10 Collinwood Tennessee, S USA 35°10′N 87°44′W
Collipo see Leiria
63 G14 Collipulli Araucanía, C Chile 37°55′S 72°30′W
97 D16 Collooney Ir. Cúil Mhuine. NW Ireland 54°11′N 08°29′W
29 R10 Colman South Dakota, N USA 43°58′N 96°48′W
103 U6 Colmar Ger. Kolmar. Haut-Rhin, NE France 48°05′N 07°21′E
104 M15 Colmenar Andalucía, S Spain 36°54′N 04°20′W
Colmenar see Colmenar de Oreja
105 O9 Colmenar de Oreja var. Colmenar. Madrid, C Spain 40°06′N 03°25′W
105 N7 Colmenar Viejo Madrid, C Spain 40°39′N 03°46′W
25 X9 Colmesneil Texas, SW USA 30°54′N 94°25′W
Cöln see Köln
Colneceaste see Colchester
59 I16 Colniza Mato Grosso, W Brazil 09°16′S 59°25′W
Cologne see Köln
42 B6 Colomba Quezaltenango, SW Guatemala 14°45′N 91°39′W
Colomb-Béchar see Béchar
54 E11 Colombia Huila, C Colombia 03°24′N 74°49′W
54 G10 Colombia off. Republic of Colombia. ◆ republic N South America
64 E12 Colombian Basin undersea feature SW Caribbean Sea 13°00′N 76°00′W
Colombia, Republic of see Colombia
Colombie-Britannique see British Columbia
15 T6 Colombier Québec, SE Canada 48°51′N 68°52′W
155 J25 Colombo ● (Sri Lanka) Western Province, W Sri Lanka 06°55′N 79°52′E
155 J25 Colombo ✈ Western Province, SW Sri Lanka 06°50′N 79°59′E
29 N11 Colome South Dakota, N USA 43°13′N 99°42′W
61 B19 Colón Buenos Aires, E Argentina 33°53′S 61°06′W
61 D18 Colón Entre Ríos, E Argentina 32°10′S 58°16′W
44 D5 Colón Matanzas, C Cuba 22°43′N 80°54′W
43 T14 Colón prev. Aspinwall. Colón, C Panama 09°04′N 80°33′W
42 K5 Colón ◈ department NE Honduras
43 S15 Colón off. Provincia de Colón. ◈ province N Panama
57 A16 Colón, Archipiélago de var. Islas de los Galápagos, Eng. Galapagos Islands, Tortoise Islands. island group Ecuador, E Pacific Ocean
44 K5 Colonel Hill Crooked Island, SE Bahamas 22°43′N 74°12′W
40 C3 Colonet Baja California Norte, NW Mexico 31°00′N 116°1′W
40 B3 Colonet, Cabo headland NW Mexico 30°57′N 116°19′W
188 G14 Colonia Yap, W Micronesia 09°29′N 138°06′E
61 D19 Colonia ◈ department SW Uruguay
Colonia see Kolonia, Micronesia
Colonia see Colonia del Sacramento, Uruguay
Colonia Agrippina see Köln
61 D20 Colonia del Sacramento var. Colonia. Colonia, SW Uruguay 34°29′S 57°48′W
62 L8 Colonia Dora Santiago del Estero, N Argentina 28°34′S 62°59′W
Colonia Julia Fanestris see Fano
21 W5 Colonial Beach Virginia, NE USA 38°15′N 76°57′W
21 V6 Colonial Heights Virginia, NE USA 37°15′N 77°24′W
Colón, Provincia de see Colón
193 S7 Colón Ridge undersea feature E Pacific Ocean 02°00′N 96°00′W
96 F12 Colonsay island W Scotland, United Kingdom
57 K22 Colorada, Laguna ◎ SW Bolivia
37 R6 Colorado off. State of Colorado, also known as Centennial State, Silver State. ◈ state C USA
63 H22 Colorado, Cerro ▲ S Argentina 49°58′S 71°38′W
25 O7 Colorado City Texas, SW USA 32°24′N 100°51′W
36 M7 Colorado Plateau plateau W USA
61 A24 Colorado, Río ≈ E Argentina
43 N12 Colorado, Río ≈ NE Costa Rica
Colorado, Río see Colorado River
16 F12 Colorado River var. Río Colorado. ≈ Mexico/USA
16 K14 Colorado River ≈ Texas, SW USA
35 W15 Colorado River Aqueduct aqueduct California, W USA
44 A4 Colorados, Archipiélago de los island group NW Cuba
62 J9 Colorados, Desagües de los ◎ W Argentina
37 T5 Colorado Springs Colorado, C USA 38°50′N 104°47′W
40 L11 Colotlán Jalisco, SW Mexico 22°08′N 103°15′W
57 L19 Colquechaca Potosí, C Bolivia 18°40′S 66°00′W
23 S7 Colquitt Georgia, SE USA 31°10′N 84°43′W
29 R11 Colton South Dakota, N USA 43°47′N 96°55′W
32 M10 Colton Washington, NW USA 46°34′N 117°10′W
35 P8 Columbia California, W USA 38°01′N 120°22′W
30 K16 Columbia Illinois, N USA 38°26′N 90°12′W
20 L7 Columbia Kentucky, S USA 37°05′N 85°19′W
22 I6 Columbia Louisiana, S USA 32°05′N 92°03′W
21 W3 Columbia Maryland, NE USA 39°13′N 76°51′W
22 L7 Columbia Mississippi, S USA 31°15′N 89°50′W
27 U4 Columbia Missouri, C USA 38°56′N 92°19′W
21 Y9 Columbia North Carolina, SE USA 35°55′N 76°15′W
18 G16 Columbia Pennsylvania, NE USA 40°01′N 76°30′W
21 Q12 Columbia state capital South Carolina, SE USA 34°00′N 81°02′W
20 I9 Columbia Tennessee, S USA 35°37′N 87°02′W
0 F9 Columbia ≈ Canada/USA
32 K9 Columbia Basin basin Washington, NW USA
197 Q10 Columbia, Cape headland Ellesmere Island, Nunavut, NE Canada
31 Q12 Columbia City Indiana, N USA 41°09′N 85°29′W
21 W3 Columbia, District of ◈ federal district NE USA
33 P7 Columbia Falls Montana, NW USA 48°22′N 114°10′W
11 O15 Columbia Icefield ice field Alberta/British Columbia, S Canada
11 O15 Columbia, Mount ▲ Alberta/British Columbia, SW Canada 52°07′N 117°30′W
11 N15 Columbia Mountains ⛰ British Columbia, SW Canada
23 P4 Columbiana Alabama, S USA 33°10′N 86°36′W
31 V12 Columbiana Ohio, N USA 40°53′N 80°41′W
32 M14 Columbia Plateau plateau Idaho/Oregon, NW USA
29 P7 Columbia Road Reservoir ▣ South Dakota, N USA
65 K16 Columbia Seamount undersea feature C Atlantic Ocean 20°30′S 32°00′W
83 D25 Columbine, Cape headland SW South Africa 32°50′S 17°39′E
105 U9 Columbretes, Illes prev. Islas Columbretes. island group E Spain
Columbretes, Islas see Columbretes, Illes
23 R5 Columbus Georgia, SE USA 32°29′N 84°58′W
31 P14 Columbus Indiana, N USA 39°12′N 85°55′W
27 R7 Columbus Kansas, C USA 37°09′N 94°52′W
23 N4 Columbus Mississippi, S USA 33°30′N 88°25′W
33 U11 Columbus Montana, NW USA 45°38′N 109°15′W
29 Q15 Columbus Nebraska, C USA 41°25′N 97°22′W
37 Q16 Columbus New Mexico, SW USA 31°49′N 107°38′W
21 P10 Columbus North Carolina, SE USA 35°15′N 82°09′W
28 K2 Columbus North Dakota, N USA 48°52′N 102°47′W
31 S13 Columbus state capital Ohio, N USA 39°58′N 83°W
25 U11 Columbus Texas, SW USA 29°42′N 96°35′W
30 L8 Columbus Wisconsin, N USA 43°21′N 89°01′W
31 R12 Columbus Grove Ohio, N USA 40°55′N 84°03′W
29 Y15 Columbus Junction Iowa, C USA 41°16′N 91°21′W
44 J3 Columbus Point headland Cat Island, C Bahamas 24°07′N 75°19′W
35 T8 Columbus Salt Marsh salt marsh Nevada, W USA
35 N6 Colusa California, W USA 39°10′N 122°03′W

◆ Country
● Country Capital
◇ Dependent Territory
○ Dependent Territory Capital
◈ Administrative Regions
✈ International Airport
▲ Mountain
⛰ Mountain Range
Ж Volcano
≈ River
◎ Lake
▣ Reservoir

32 L7 Colville Washington, NW USA 48°33′N 117°54′W
184 M5 Colville, Cape headland North Island, New Zealand 36°28′S 175°20′E
184 M5 Colville Channel channel North Island, New Zealand
39 P6 Colville River ≈ Alaska, USA
97 J18 Colwyn Bay N Wales, United Kingdom 53°18′N 03°43′W
106 H9 Comacchio var. Commachio; anc. Comactium. Emilia-Romagna, N Italy 44°41′N 12°10′E
106 H9 Comacchio, Valli di lagoon Adriatic Sea, N Mediterranean Sea
Comactium see Comacchio
41 V17 Comalapa Chiapas, SE Mexico 15°42′N 92°06′W
41 U15 Comalcalco Tabasco, SE Mexico 18°16′N 93°05′W
63 H16 Comallo Río Negro, SW Argentina 40°58′S 70°13′W
26 M12 Comanche Oklahoma, C USA 34°22′N 97°57′W
25 R8 Comanche Texas, SW USA 31°55′N 98°36′W
194 H2 Comandante Ferraz Brazilian research station Antarctica 61°57′S 58°23′W
62 N6 Comandante Fontana Formosa, N Argentina 25°19′S 59°42′W
63 I22 Comandante Luis Peidra Buena Santa Cruz, S Argentina 50°04′S 68°55′W
59 O18 Comandatuba Bahia, SE Brazil 15°13′S 39°00′W
116 K11 Comănești Hung. Kománfalva. Bacău, SW Romania 46°25′N 26°29′E
57 M19 Comarapa Santa Cruz, C Bolivia 17°53′S 64°30′W
116 J13 Comarnic Prahova, SE Romania 45°18′N 25°37′E
42 H6 Comayagua Comayagua, W Honduras 14°30′N 87°39′W
42 H6 Comayagua ◈ department W Honduras
42 I6 Comayagua, Montañas de ▲▲ C Honduras
21 R15 Combahee River ≈ South Carolina, SE USA
62 G10 Combarbalá Coquimbo, C Chile 31°15′S 71°03′W
103 S7 Combeaufontaine Haute-Saône, E France 47°43′N 05°52′E
97 G15 Comber Ir. An Comar. E Northern Ireland, United Kingdom 54°33′N 05°45′W
99 K20 Comblain-au-Pont Liège, E Belgium 50°29′N 05°36′E
102 I6 Combourg Ille-et-Vilaine, NW France 48°21′N 01°44′W
44 M9 Comendador prev. Elías Piña. W Dominican Republic 18°53′N 71°42′W
Comer See see Como, Lago di
25 R11 Comfort Texas, SW USA 29°58′N 98°54′W
153 V15 Comilla Ben. Kumillā. Chittagong, E Bangladesh 23°28′N 91°10′E
99 B18 Comines Hainaut, W Belgium 50°46′N 02°58′E
Comino see Kemmuna
107 D18 Comino, Capo headland Sardegna, Italy, C Mediterranean Sea 40°32′N 09°49′E
107 K25 Comiso Sicilia, Italy, C Mediterranean Sea 36°57′N 14°37′E
41 V16 Comitán var. Comitán de Domínguez. Chiapas, SE Mexico 16°15′N 92°06′W
Comitán de Domínguez see Comitán
Commachio see Comacchio
Commander Islands see Komandorskiye Ostrova
103 O10 Commentry Allier, C France 46°18′N 02°46′E
23 T2 Commerce Georgia, SE USA 34°12′N 83°27′W
27 R8 Commerce Oklahoma, C USA 36°55′N 94°52′W
25 V5 Commerce Texas, SW USA 33°16′N 95°52′W
37 T4 Commerce City Colorado, C USA 39°45′N 104°54′W
103 S5 Commercy Meuse, NE France 48°46′N 05°36′E
55 W9 Commewijne var. Commewyne. ◈ district NE Suriname
Commewyne see Commewijne
15 P8 Commissaires, Lac des ◎ Québec, SE Canada
64 A12 Commissioner's Point headland W Bermuda
9 O7 Committee Bay bay Nunavut, N Canada
106 D7 Como anc. Comum. Lombardia, N Italy 45°48′N 09°05′E
63 J19 Comodoro Rivadavia Chubut, SE Argentina 45°50′S 67°30′W
106 D6 Como, Lago di var. Lario, Eng. Lake Como, Ger. Comer See. ◎ N Italy
Como, Lake see Como, Lago di
40 E7 Comondú Baja California Sur, NW Mexico 26°01′N 111°50′W
116 F12 Comorâște Hung. Komornok. Caraș-Severin, SW Romania 45°13′N 21°34′E
Comores, République Fédérale Islamique des see Comoros
155 G24 Comorin, Cape headland SE India 08°00′N 77°10′E
172 M8 Comoro Basin undersea feature SW Indian Ocean 14°00′S 44°00′E
172 K14 Comoro Islands island group W Indian Ocean
172 H13 Comoros off. Federal Islamic Republic of the Comoros, Fr. République Fédérale Islamique des Comores. ◆ republic W Indian Ocean
Comoros, Federal Islamic Republic of the see Comoros
10 L17 Comox Vancouver Island, British Columbia, SW Canada 49°40′N 124°55′W
103 O4 Compiègne Oise, N France 49°25′N 02°50′E
Complutum see Alcalá de Henares
Compniacum see Cognac
40 K12 Compostela Nayarit, C Mexico 21°12′N 104°52′W
Compostella see Santiago de Compostela
60 L11 Comprida, Ilha island S Brazil
117 N11 Comrat Rus. Komrat. S Moldova 46°18′N 28°40′E
25 O11 Comstock Texas, SW USA 29°39′N 101°10′W
31 P9 Comstock Park Michigan, N USA 43°00′N 85°40′W
193 N3 Comstock Seamount undersea feature N Pacific Ocean 48°15′N 156°55′W
Comum see Como
159 N17 Cona Xizang Zizhiqu, W China 27°59′N 91°54′E
76 H14 Conakry ● (Guinea) SW Guinea 09°31′N 13°43′W
76 H14 Conakry ✈ SW Guinea 09°37′N 13°32′W
Conamara see Connemara
Conca see Cuenca
25 Q12 Concan Texas, SW USA 29°27′N 99°43′W
102 F6 Concarneau Finistère, NW France 47°53′N 03°55′W
83 O17 Conceição Sofala, C Mozambique 18°47′S 36°18′E
59 K15 Conceição do Araguaia Pará, NE Brazil 08°15′S 49°15′W
58 F10 Conceição do Maú Roraima, W Brazil 03°35′N 59°52′W
61 D14 Concepción var. Concepcion. Corrientes, NE Argentina 28°25′S 57°54′W
62 J8 Concepción Tucumán, N Argentina 27°20′S 65°35′W
57 O17 Concepción Santa Cruz, E Bolivia 16°15′S 62°08′W
62 G13 Concepción Bío Bío, C Chile 36°47′S 73°01′W
54 E14 Concepción Putumayo, S Colombia 0°03′N 75°35′W
62 O5 Concepción var. Villa Concepción. Concepción, C Paraguay 23°26′S 57°24′W
62 O5 Concepción off. Departamento de Concepción. ◈ department E Paraguay
Concepción see La Concepción
Concepción de la Vega see La Vega
41 N9 Concepción del Oro Zacatecas, C Mexico 24°38′N 101°25′W
61 D18 Concepción del Uruguay Entre Ríos, E Argentina 32°30′S 58°15′W
Concepción, Departamento de see Concepción
42 K11 Concepción, Volcán ✵ SW Nicaragua 11°31′N 85°37′W
44 J4 Conception Island island C Bahamas
35 P14 Conception, Point headland California, W USA 34°27′N 120°28′W
54 H6 Concha Zulia, W Venezuela 09°02′N 71°45′W
60 L9 Conchas São Paulo, S Brazil 23°00′S 47°58′W
37 U11 Conchas Dam New Mexico, SW USA 35°21′N 104°11′W
37 U10 Conchas Lake ⊠ New Mexico, SW USA
102 M5 Conches-en-Ouche Eure, N France 49°00′N 01°00′E
37 N12 Concho Arizona, SW USA 34°28′N 109°33′W
40 J5 Conchos, Río ≈ NW Mexico
41 O8 Conchos, Río ≈ C Mexico
108 C8 Concise Vaud, W Switzerland 46°52′N 06°40′E
35 N8 Concord California, W USA 37°58′N 122°01′W
19 O9 Concord state capital New Hampshire, NE USA 43°10′N 71°32′W
21 R10 Concord North Carolina, SE USA 35°25′N 80°34′W
61 D17 Concordia Entre Ríos, E Argentina 31°25′S 58°W
60 I13 Concórdia Santa Catarina, S Brazil 27°14′S 52°01′W
54 D9 Concordia Antioquia, W Colombia 06°03′N 75°57′W
40 J10 Concordia Sinaloa, C Mexico 23°18′N 106°02′W
57 I19 Concordia Tacna, SW Peru 18°12′S 70°19′W
27 N3 Concordia Kansas, C USA 39°35′N 97°39′W
27 S4 Concordia Missouri, C USA 38°58′N 93°34′W
167 S7 Con Cuông Nghê An, N Vietnam 19°02′N 104°54′E
167 T15 Côn Đao Sơn var. Con Son. island S Vietnam
Condate see Rennes, Ille-et-Vilaine, France
Condate see St-Claude, Jura, France
Condate see Montereau-Faut-Yonne, Seine-St-Denis, France
29 P8 Conde South Dakota, N USA 45°08′N 98°07′W
42 J8 Condega Estelí, NW Nicaragua 13°19′N 86°26′W
103 P2 Condé-sur-l'Escaut Nord, N France 50°27′N 03°36′E
102 K5 Condé-sur-Noireau Calvados, N France 48°52′N 00°31′W
Condivincum see Nantes
183 P8 Condobolin New South Wales, SE Australia 33°04′S 147°08′E
102 L15 Condom Gers, S France 43°56′N 00°23′E
32 J11 Condon Oregon, NW USA 45°15′N 120°10′W
54 D9 Condoto Chocó, W Colombia 05°06′N 76°37′W
23 P7 Conecuh River ≈ Alabama/Florida, SE USA
106 H7 Conegliano Veneto, NE Italy 45°53′N 12°18′E
61 C19 Conesa Buenos Aires, E Argentina 33°36′S 60°21′W
14 F15 Conestogo ≈ Ontario, S Canada
Confluentes see Koblenz
102 L10 Confolens Charente, W France 46°00′N 00°40′E
36 J4 Confusion Range ▲▲ Utah, W USA
62 N6 Confuso, Río ≈ C Paraguay
21 R12 Congaree River ≈ South Carolina, SE USA
Công Hoa Xa Hôi Chu Nghia Viêt Nam see Vietnam
160 K12 Congjiang var. Bingmei. Guizhou, S China 25°48′N 108°55′E
79 G18 Congo off. Republic of the Congo, Fr. Moyen-Congo; prev. Middle Congo. ◆ republic C Africa
79 K19 Congo off. Democratic Republic of Congo; prev. Zaire, Belgian Congo, Congo (Kinshasa). ◆ republic C Africa
67 T11 Congo var. Kongo, Fr. Zaire. ≈ C Africa
Congo see Zaire (province) Angola
68 G12 Congo Basin drainage basin W Dem. Rep. Congo
67 Q11 Congo Canyon var. Congo Seavalley, Congo Submarine Canyon. undersea feature E Atlantic Ocean 06°00′S 11°50′E
Congo Cone see Congo Fan
Congo/Congo (Kinshasa) see Congo (Democratic Republic of)
65 P15 Congo Fan var. Congo Cone. undersea feature E Atlantic Ocean 06°00′S 09°00′E
Congo Seavalley see Congo Canyon
Congo Submarine Canyon see Congo Canyon
Coni see Cuneo
63 H18 Cónico, Cerro ▲ SW Argentina 43°12′S 71°42′W
Conimbria/Conimbriga see Coimbra
Conjeeveram see Kānchīpuram
11 R13 Conklin Alberta, C Canada 55°36′N 111°06′W
24 M1 Conlen Texas, SW USA 36°16′N 102°10′W
Con, Loch see Conn, Lough
Connacht see Connaught
97 B17 Connaught var. Connacht, Ir. Chonnacht, Cúige. cultural region W Ireland
31 V10 Conneaut Ohio, N USA 41°56′N 80°32′W
18 L13 Connecticut off. State of Connecticut, also known as Blue Law State, Constitution State, Land of Steady Habits, Nutmeg State. ◈ state NE USA
19 N8 Connecticut ≈ Canada/USA
19 O6 Connecticut Lakes lakes New Hampshire, NE USA
32 K9 Connell Washington, NW USA 46°39′N 118°51′W
97 B17 Connemara Ir. Conamara. physical region W Ireland
31 Q14 Connersville Indiana, N USA 39°38′N 85°15′W
97 B16 Conn, Lough Ir. Loch Con. ◎ W Ireland
35 X6 Connors Pass pass Nevada, W USA
181 X7 Connors Range ▲▲ Queensland, E Australia
56 E7 Cononaco, Río ≈ E Ecuador
29 W13 Conrad Iowa, C USA 42°13′N 92°52′W
33 R7 Conrad Montana, NW USA 48°10′N 111°58′W
25 W10 Conroe Texas, SW USA 30°19′N 95°28′W
25 V10 Conroe, Lake ⊠ Texas, SW USA
61 C17 Conscripto Bernardi Entre Ríos, E Argentina 31°03′S 59°05′W
59 M20 Conselheiro Lafaiete Minas Gerais, SE Brazil 20°40′S 43°48′W
Consentia see Cosenza
97 L14 Consett N England, United Kingdom 54°50′N 01°53′W
44 B5 Consolación del Sur Pinar del Río, W Cuba 22°32′N 83°32′W
Con Son see Côn Đao Sơn
11 R15 Consort Alberta, SW Canada 51°58′N 110°44′W
Constance see Konstanz
108 I6 Constance, Lake Ger. Bodensee. ◎ C Europe
104 G9 Constância Santarém, C Portugal 39°29′N 08°22′W
117 N14 Constanța var. Küstendje, Eng. Constanza, Ger. Konstanza, Turk. Küstence. Constanța, SE Romania 44°09′N 28°37′E
116 L14 Constanța ◈ county SE Romania
Constantia see Coutances
Constantia see Konstanz
104 K13 Constantina Andalucía, S Spain 37°54′N 05°36′W
74 L5 Constantine var. Qacentina, Ar. Qoussantîna. NE Algeria 36°23′N 06°44′E
39 O14 Constantine, Cape headland Alaska, USA 58°23′N 158°53′W
Constantinople see İstanbul
Constantiola see Oltenița
Constanz see Konstanz
Constanza see Constanța
62 G13 Constitución Maule, C Chile 35°20′S 72°28′W
61 D17 Constitución Salto, N Uruguay 31°05′S 57°51′W
Constitution State see Connecticut
105 N10 Consuegra Castilla-La Mancha, C Spain 39°28′N 03°36′W
181 X9 Consuelo Peak ▲ Queensland, E Australia 24°45′S 148°01′E
56 E11 Contamana Loreto, N Peru 07°19′S 75°04′W
Contrasto, Colle del see Contrasto, Portella del
107 K23 Contrasto, Portella del var. Colle del Contrasto. pass Sicilia, Italy, C Mediterranean Sea
54 G8 Contratación Santander, C Colombia 06°18′N 73°27′W
102 M8 Contres Loir-et-Cher, C France 47°24′N 01°30′E
107 O17 Conversano Puglia, SE Italy 40°58′N 17°07′E
27 U11 Conway Arkansas, C USA 35°05′N 92°27′W
19 O8 Conway New Hampshire, NE USA 43°58′N 71°05′W
21 U13 Conway South Carolina, SE USA 33°51′N 79°04′W
25 N2 Conway Texas, SW USA 35°10′N 101°23′W
27 U11 Conway, Lake ⊠ Arkansas, C USA
27 N7 Conway Springs Kansas, C USA 37°23′N 97°38′W
97 J18 Conwy N Wales, United Kingdom 53°17′N 03°51′W
23 T3 Conyers Georgia, SE USA 33°40′N 84°01′W
Coo see Kos
182 F4 Coober Pedy South Australia 29°01′S 134°47′E
181 P2 Cooinda Northern Territory, N Australia 12°54′S 132°31′E
182 B6 Cook South Australia 30°37′S 130°26′E
29 W4 Cook Minnesota, N USA 47°51′N 92°41′W
191 N6 Cook, Baie de bay Moorea, W French Polynesia
10 J16 Cook, Cape headland Vancouver Island, British Columbia, SW Canada 50°04′N 127°52′W
37 Q15 Cookes Peak ▲ New Mexico, SW USA 32°32′N 107°43′W
20 L8 Cookeville Tennessee, S USA 36°10′N 85°30′W
175 P9 Cook Fracture Zone tectonic feature S Pacific Ocean
Cook, Grand Récif de see Cook, Récif de
39 Q12 Cook Inlet inlet Alaska, USA
191 X2 Cook Island island Line Islands, E Kiribati
190 J14 Cook Islands ◇ territory in free association with New Zealand S Pacific Ocean
Cook, Mount see Aoraki
187 O15 Cook, Récif de var. Grand Récif de Cook. reef S New Caledonia
14 G14 Cookstown Ontario, S Canada 44°12′N 79°39′W
97 F15 Cookstown Ir. An Chorr Chríochach. C Northern Ireland, United Kingdom 54°39′N 06°45′W
185 K14 Cook Strait var. Raukawa. strait New Zealand
181 W3 Cooktown Queensland, NE Australia 15°28′S 145°15′E
183 P6 Coolabah New South Wales, SE Australia 31°03′S 146°42′E
182 J11 Coola Coola Swamp wetland South Australia
183 S7 Coolah New South Wales, SE Australia 31°49′S 149°43′E
183 P9 Coolamon New South Wales, SE Australia 34°49′S 147°13′E
183 T4 Coolatai New South Wales, SE Australia 29°16′S 150°45′E
180 K12 Coolgardie Western Australia 31°01′S 121°12′E
36 L14 Coolidge Arizona, SW USA 32°58′N 111°29′W
25 U8 Coolidge Texas, SW USA 31°45′N 96°39′W
183 Q11 Cooma New South Wales, SE Australia 36°16′S 149°09′E
Coomassie see Kumasi
183 R6 Coonabarabran New South Wales, SE Australia 31°19′S 149°18′E
182 J10 Coonalpyn South Australia 35°43′S 139°50′E
183 R6 Coonamble New South Wales, SE Australia 30°56′S 148°22′E
Coondapoor see Kundāpura
155 G21 Coonoor Tamil Nādu, SE India 11°21′N 76°46′E
29 U14 Coon Rapids Iowa, C USA 41°52′N 94°40′W
29 V8 Coon Rapids Minnesota, N USA 45°12′N 93°18′W
25 V5 Cooper Texas, SW USA 33°23′N 95°42′W
181 U9 Cooper Creek var. Barcoo, Cooper's Creek. seasonal river Queensland/South Australia
39 R12 Cooper Landing Alaska, USA 60°27′N 149°59′W
21 T14 Cooper River ≈ South Carolina, SE USA
Cooper's Creek see Cooper Creek
44 H1 Coopers Town Great Abaco, N Bahamas 26°46′N 77°27′W
18 J10 Cooperstown New York, NE USA 42°43′N 74°56′W
29 P4 Cooperstown North Dakota, N USA 47°26′N 98°07′W
31 P9 Coopersville Michigan, N USA 43°03′N 85°55′W
182 D7 Coorabie South Australia 31°57′S 132°18′E
23 Q3 Coosa River ≈ Alabama/Georgia, S USA
32 E14 Coos Bay Oregon, NW USA 43°22′N 124°13′W
183 Q9 Cootamundra New South Wales, SE Australia 34°41′S 148°03′E
97 E16 Cootehill Ir. Muinchille. N Ireland 54°04′N 07°05′W
Čop see Chop
57 J17 Copacabana La Paz, W Bolivia 16°11′S 69°02′W
63 H14 Copahué, Volcán ✵ C Chile 37°56′S 71°04′W
41 U16 Copainalá Chiapas, SE Mexico 17°04′N 93°13′W
32 F8 Copalis Beach Washington, NW USA 47°05′N 124°11′W
42 F6 Copán ◈ department W Honduras
Copán see Copán Ruinas
25 T14 Copano Bay bay NW Gulf of Mexico
42 F6 Copán Ruinas var. Copán. Copán, W Honduras 14°52′N 89°10′W
Copenhagen see København
107 Q19 Copertino Puglia, SE Italy 40°16′N 18°03′E
62 H7 Copiapó Atacama, N Chile 27°17′S 70°25′W
62 G8 Copiapó, Bahía bay N Chile
62 G7 Copiapó, Río ≈ N Chile
114 M12 Çöpköy Edirne, NW Turkey 41°14′N 26°51′E
182 I5 Copley South Australia 30°36′S 138°26′E
106 H9 Copparo Emilia-Romagna, C Italy 44°53′N 11°53′E
55 V10 Coppename Rivier var. Koppename. ≈ C Suriname
25 S9 Copperas Cove Texas, SW USA 31°07′N 97°54′W
82 J13 Copperbelt ◈ province C Zambia
39 S11 Copper Center Alaska, USA 61°57′N 145°21′W
8 K8 Coppermine ≈ Northwest Territories/Nunavut, N Canada
Coppermine see Kugluktuk
39 T11 Copper River ≈ Alaska, USA
Copper State see Arizona
116 I11 Copșa Mică Ger. Kleinkopisch, Hung. Kiskapus. Sibiu, C Romania 46°06′N 24°15′E
158 J14 Coqên Xizang Zizhiqu, W China 31°13′N 85°12′E
Coquilhatville see Mbandaka
32 E14 Coquille Oregon, NW USA 43°11′N 124°12′W
62 G9 Coquimbo Coquimbo, N Chile 30°S 71°18′W
62 G9 Coquimbo off. Región de Coquimbo. ◈ region C Chile
Coquimbo, Región de see Coquimbo
116 I15 Corabia Olt, S Romania 43°46′N 24°31′E
57 F17 Coracora Ayacucho, SW Peru 15°03′S 73°45′W
Cora Droma Rúisc see Carrick-on-Shannon
44 K9 Corail SW Haiti 18°34′N 73°53′W
183 V4 Coraki New South Wales, SE Australia 29°01′S 153°15′E
180 G8 Coral Bay Western Australia 23°02′S 113°51′E
23 Y16 Coral Gables Florida, SE USA 25°43′N 80°16′W
9 P8 Coral Harbour var. Salliq. Southampton Island, Nunavut, NE Canada 64°10′N 83°15′W
192 I9 Coral Sea sea SW Pacific Ocean
174 M7 Coral Sea Basin undersea feature N Coral Sea
192 H9 Coral Sea Islands ◇ Australian external territory SW Pacific Ocean
182 M12 Corangamite, Lake ◎ Victoria, SE Australia
Corantijn Rivier see Courantyne River
18 B14 Coraopolis Pennsylvania, NE USA 40°28′N 80°08′W
107 N17 Corato Puglia, SE Italy 41°09′N 16°25′E
103 O17 Corbières ▲▲ S France
103 P8 Corbigny Nièvre, C France 47°15′N 03°42′E
21 N7 Corbin Kentucky, S USA 36°57′N 84°06′W
104 L14 Corbones ≈ SW Spain
Corcaigh see Cork
35 R11 Corcoran California, W USA 36°06′N 119°33′W
47 T14 Corcovado, Golfo gulf S Chile
63 G18 Corcovado, Volcán ✵ S Chile 43°13′S 72°45′W
104 F3 Corcubión Galicia, NW Spain 42°56′N 09°12′W
Corcyra Nigra see Korčula
60 Q9 Cordeiro Rio de Janeiro, SE Brazil 22°01′S 42°20′W
23 T6 Cordele Georgia, SE USA 31°59′N 83°49′W
26 L11 Cordell Oklahoma, C USA 35°17′N 98°59′W
103 N14 Cordes Tarn, S France 44°03′N 01°57′E
62 O6 Cordillera off. Departamento de la Cordillera. ◈ department C Paraguay
Cordillera see Cacaguatique, Cordillera
Cordillera, Departamento de la see Cordillera
182 K1 Cordillo Downs South Australia 26°44′S 140°37′E
62 K10 Córdoba Córdoba, C Argentina 31°25′S 64°11′W
41 R14 Córdoba Veracruz-Llave, E Mexico 18°55′N 96°55′W
104 M13 Córdoba var. Cordoba, Eng. Cordova; anc. Corduba. Andalucía, SW Spain 37°53′N 04°46′W
62 K11 Córdoba off. Provincia de Córdoba. ◈ province C Argentina
54 D7 Córdoba off. Departamento de Córdoba. ◈ province NW Colombia
104 L13 Córdoba ◈ province Andalucía, S Spain
Córdoba, Departamento de see Córdoba
Córdoba, Provincia de see Córdoba
62 K10 Córdoba, Sierras de ▲▲ C Argentina
23 O3 Cordova Alabama, S USA 33°45′N 87°10′W
39 S12 Cordova Alaska, USA 60°32′N 145°45′W
Cordova/Cordoba see Córdoba
Corduba see Córdoba
Corentyne River see Courantyne River
Corfu see Kérkyra
104 J9 Coria Extremadura, W Spain 39°59′N 06°32′W
104 J14 Coria del Río Andalucía, S Spain 37°18′N 06°04′W
183 S8 Coricudgy, Mount ▲ New South Wales, SE Australia 32°49′S 150°28′E
107 N20 Corigliano Calabro Calabria, SW Italy 39°36′N 16°32′E
Corinium/Corinium Dobunorum see Cirencester
23 N1 Corinth Mississippi, S USA 34°56′N 88°29′W
Corinth see Kórinthos
Corinth Canal see Dióryga Korinthou
Corinth, Gulf of/Corinthiacus Sinus see Korinthiakós Kólpos
Corinthus see Kórinthos
42 I9 Corinto Chinandega, NW Nicaragua 12°29′N 87°14′W
97 C21 Cork Ir. Corcaigh. S Ireland 51°54′N 07°06′W
97 C21 Cork Ir. Corcaigh. cultural region SW Ireland
97 C21 Cork ✈ Cork, SW Ireland 51°52′N 08°25′W
97 D21 Cork Harbour Ir. Cuan Chorcaí. inlet SW Ireland
107 I23 Corleone Sicilia, Italy, C Mediterranean Sea 37°49′N 13°18′E
114 N13 Çorlu Tekirdağ, NW Turkey 41°11′N 27°48′E
114 N12 Çorlu Çayı ≈ NW Turkey
Cormaiore see Courmayeur
11 V13 Cormorant Manitoba, C Canada 54°12′N 100°33′W
23 T2 Cornelia Georgia, SE USA 34°30′N 83°31′W
60 J10 Cornélio Procópio Paraná, S Brazil 23°07′S 50°40′W
55 V9 Corneliskondre Sipaliwini, N Suriname 05°21′N 56°10′W
30 J5 Cornell Wisconsin, N USA 45°09′N 91°10′W
13 S12 Corner Brook Newfoundland, Newfoundland and Labrador, E Canada 48°58′N 57°58′W
Corner Rise Seamounts see Corner Seamounts
64 I9 Corner Seamounts var. Corner Rise Seamounts. undersea feature NW Atlantic Ocean 35°30′N 51°30′W
116 M9 Cornești Rus. Korneshty. C Moldova 47°23′N 28°00′E
Corneto see Tarquinia
Cornhusker State see Nebraska
27 X8 Corning Arkansas, C USA 36°26′N 90°35′W
35 N5 Corning California, W USA 39°54′N 122°12′W
29 U15 Corning Iowa, C USA 40°58′N 94°46′W
18 G11 Corning New York, NE USA 42°08′N 77°03′W
Corn Islands see Maíz, Islas del
107 J14 Corno Grande ▲ C Italy 42°26′N 13°29′E
15 N13 Cornwall Ontario, SE Canada 45°02′N 74°45′W
97 H25 Cornwall cultural region SW England, United Kingdom
97 G25 Cornwall, Cape headland SW England, United Kingdom 50°11′N 05°39′W
54 J4 Coro prev. Santa Ana de Coro. Falcón, NW Venezuela 11°27′N 69°41′W
57 J18 Corocoro La Paz, W Bolivia 17°10′S 68°28′W
57 K17 Coroico La Paz, W Bolivia 16°09′S 67°45′W
184 M5 Coromandel Waikato, North Island, New Zealand 36°47′S 175°30′E
155 K20 Coromandel Coast coast E India
184 M5 Coromandel Peninsula peninsula North Island, New Zealand
184 M6 Coromandel Range ▲▲ North Island, New Zealand
171 N5 Coron Busuanga Island, W Philippines 12°02′N 120°10′E
35 T15 Corona California, W USA 33°52′N 117°34′W
37 T12 Corona New Mexico, SW USA 34°15′N 105°36′W
11 U17 Coronach Saskatchewan, S Canada 49°07′N 105°33′W
35 U17 Coronado California, W USA 32°41′N 117°10′W
43 N15 Coronado, Bahía de bay S Costa Rica
11 R15 Coronation Alberta, SW Canada 52°06′N 111°25′W
8 K7 Coronation Gulf gulf Nunavut, N Canada
194 I1 Coronation Island island Antarctica
39 X14 Coronation Island island Alexander Archipelago, Alaska, USA
61 B18 Coronda Santa Fe, C Argentina 31°58′S 60°56′W
63 F14 Coronel Bío Bío, C Chile 37°01′S 73°08′W
61 D20 Coronel Brandsen var. Brandsen. Buenos Aires, E Argentina 35°08′S 58°15′W
62 K4 Coronel Cornejo Salta, N Argentina 22°46′S 63°49′W
61 B24 Coronel Dorrego Buenos Aires, E Argentina 38°38′S 61°15′W
62 P6 Coronel Oviedo Caaguazú, SE Paraguay 25°24′S 56°30′W
61 B23 Coronel Pringles Buenos Aires, E Argentina 37°56′S 61°25′W
61 B23 Coronel Suárez Buenos Aires, E Argentina 37°30′S 61°52′W
61 E22 Coronel Vidal Buenos Aires, E Argentina 37°28′S 57°45′W
55 V9 Coronie ◈ district NW Suriname
57 G17 Coropuna, Nevado ▲ S Peru 15°31′S 72°31′W
Çorovoda see Çorovodë
113 L22 Çorovodë var. Çorovoda. Berat, S Albania 40°29′N 20°15′E
183 P11 Corowa New South Wales, SE Australia 36°01′S 146°22′E
42 G1 Corozal Corozal, N Belize 18°23′N 88°23′W
54 E6 Corozal Sucre, NW Colombia 09°18′N 75°19′W
42 G1 Corozal ◈ district N Belize
25 T14 Corpus Christi Texas, SW USA 27°48′N 97°24′W
25 T14 Corpus Christi Bay inlet Texas, SW USA
25 R14 Corpus Christi, Lake ⊠ Texas, SW USA
63 F16 Corral Los Ríos, C Chile 39°55′S 73°30′W
105 O9 Corral de Almaguer Castilla-La Mancha, C Spain 39°45′N 03°10′W
104 K6 Corrales Castilla y León, N Spain 41°22′N 05°44′W
37 R11 Corrales New Mexico, SW USA 35°11′N 106°37′W
Corrán Tuathail see Carrauntoohil
106 F9 Correggio Emilia-Romagna, C Italy 44°47′N 10°46′E
59 M16 Corrente Piauí, E Brazil 10°29′S 45°11′W
59 I19 Correntes, Rio ≈ SW Brazil
103 N12 Corrèze ◈ department C France
97 C17 Corrib, Lough Ir. Loch Coirib. ◎ W Ireland
61 C14 Corrientes Corrientes, NE Argentina 27°29′S 58°42′W
61 D15 Corrientes off. Provincia de Corrientes. ◈ province NE Argentina
44 A5 Corrientes, Cabo headland W Cuba 21°48′N 84°30′W
40 I13 Corrientes, Cabo headland SW Mexico 20°25′N 105°42′W
Corrientes, Provincia de see Corrientes
61 C16 Corrientes, Río ≈ NE Argentina
56 E8 Corrientes, Río ≈ Ecuador/Peru
25 W9 Corrigan Texas, SW USA 31°00′N 94°49′W
55 U9 Corriverton E Guyana 05°55′N 57°09′W
Corriza see Korçë
183 Q11 Corryong Victoria, SE Australia 36°14′S 147°54′E
103 F2 Corse Eng. Corsica. ◈ region France, C Mediterranean Sea
101 X13 Corse Eng. Corsica. island France, C Mediterranean Sea
103 Y12 Corse, Cap headland Corse, France, C Mediterranean Sea 43°01′N 09°25′E
103 X15 Corse-du-Sud ◈ department Corse, France, C Mediterranean Sea
29 P11 Corsica South Dakota, N USA 43°25′N 98°24′W
Corsica see Corse
25 U7 Corsicana Texas, SW USA 32°05′N 96°27′W
103 Y15 Corte Corse, France, C Mediterranean Sea 42°18′N 09°08′E
63 G16 Corte Alto Los Lagos, S Chile 40°58′S 73°04′W
104 I13 Cortegana Andalucía, S Spain 37°55′N 06°49′W
43 N15 Cortés var. Ciudad Cortés. Puntarenas, SE Costa Rica 08°59′N 83°32′W
42 G5 Cortés ◈ department NW Honduras
37 P8 Cortez Colorado, C USA 37°22′N 108°36′W
Cortez, Sea of see California, Golfo de
106 H6 Cortina d'Ampezzo Veneto, NE Italy 46°33′N 12°09′E
18 H11 Cortland New York, NE USA 42°34′N 76°09′W
31 V11 Cortland Ohio, N USA 41°19′N 80°43′W
106 H12 Cortona Toscana, C Italy 43°15′N 12°01′E
76 H13 Corubal, Rio ≈ E Guinea-Bissau
104 G10 Coruche Santarém, C Portugal 38°58′N 08°31′W
Çoruh see Rize
137 R11 Çoruh Nehri Geor. Chorokh, Rus. Chorokhi. ≈ Georgia/Turkey
136 K12 Çorum var. Chorum. Çorum, N Turkey 40°31′N 34°57′E
136 J12 Çorum var. Chorum. ◈ province N Turkey
59 H19 Corumbá Mato Grosso do Sul, S Brazil 19°S 57°35′W
14 D16 Corunna Ontario, S Canada 42°49′N 82°25′W
Corunna see A Coruña
32 F12 Corvallis Oregon, NW USA 44°35′N 123°16′W
64 M1 Corvo var. Ilha do Corvo. island Azores, Portugal, NE Atlantic Ocean
Corvo, Ilha do see Corvo
31 O16 Corydon Indiana, N USA 38°12′N 86°07′W
29 V16 Corydon Iowa, C USA 40°45′N 93°19′W
Cos see Kos
40 I9 Cosalá Sinaloa, C Mexico 24°25′N 106°39′W
41 R15 Cosamaloapan var. Cosamaloapan de Carpio. Veracruz-Llave, E Mexico 18°23′N 95°50′W
Cosamaloapan de Carpio see Cosamaloapan
107 N21 Cosenza anc. Consentia. Calabria, SW Italy 39°17′N 16°15′E
31 T13 Coshocton Ohio, N USA 40°16′N 81°53′W
42 H9 Cosigüina, Punta headland NW Nicaragua 12°53′N 87°42′W
29 T9 Cosmos Minnesota, N USA 44°56′N 94°42′W
103 O8 Cosne-Cours-sur-Loire Nièvre, C France 47°25′N 02°56′E
108 B9 Cossonay Vaud, W Switzerland 46°37′N 06°28′E
Cossyra see Pantelleria
47 R4 Costa, Cordillera de la var. Cordillera de Venezuela. ▲▲ N Venezuela
42 K13 Costa Rica off. Republic of Costa Rica. ◆ republic Central America
Costa Rica, Republic of see Costa Rica
43 N15 Costeña, Fila ▲▲ S Costa Rica
Costermansville see Bukavu
116 I14 Costești Argeș, SW Romania 44°40′N 24°53′E
37 S8 Costilla New Mexico, SW USA 36°58′N 105°31′W
35 O7 Cosumnes River ≈ California, W USA
101 O16 Coswig Sachsen, E Germany 51°07′N 13°36′E
101 M14 Coswig Sachsen-Anhalt, E Germany 51°53′N 12°26′E
Cosyra see Pantelleria
171 Q7 Cotabato Mindanao, S Philippines 07°13′N 124°12′E
56 C5 Cotacachi ▲ N Ecuador 0°29′N 78°17′W
57 L21 Cotagaita Potosí, S Bolivia 20°47′S 65°40′W
103 V15 Côte d'Azur prev. Nice. ✈ (Nice) Alpes-Maritimes, SE France 43°40′N 07°12′E
Côte d'Ivoire see Ivory Coast
Côte d'Ivoire, République de la see Ivory Coast
103 R7 Côte d'Or ◈ department E France
103 R8 Côte d'Or cultural region C France
Côte Française des Somalis see Djibouti
102 J4 Cotentin peninsula N France
102 G6 Côtes d'Armor prev. Côtes-du-Nord. ◈ department NW France
Côtes-du-Nord see Côtes d'Armor
Cöthen see Köthen
Côtière, Chaine see Coast Mountains
40 M13 Cotija var. Cotija de la Paz. Michoacán, SW Mexico 19°49′N 102°39′W
Cotija de la Paz see Cotija
77 R16 Cotonou var. Kotonu. S Benin 06°24′N 02°26′E
77 R16 Cotonou ✈ S Benin 06°31′N 02°18′E
56 B6 Cotopaxi prev. León. ◈ province C Ecuador
56 C6 Cotopaxi ✵ N Ecuador 0°42′S 78°24′W
Cotrone see Crotone
97 L21 Cotswold Hills var. Cotswolds. hill range S England, United Kingdom
Cotswolds see Cotswold Hills
32 F13 Cottage Grove Oregon, NW USA 43°48′N 123°03′W
21 S14 Cottageville South Carolina, SE USA 32°55′N 80°28′W

◆ Country ● Country Capital ◇ Dependent Territory ○ Dependent Territory Capital ◈ Administrative Regions ✈ International Airport ▲ Mountain ▲▲ Mountain Range ✵ Volcano ≈ River ◎ Lake ⊠ Reservoir

101 P14 **Cottbus** *Lus.* Chośebuz; *prev.* Kottbus. Brandenburg, E Germany 51°42′N 14°22′E
27 U9 **Cotter** Arkansas, C USA 36°16′N 92°30′W
106 A9 **Cottian Alps** *Fr.* Alpes Cottiennes, *It.* Alpi Cozie. ▲▲ France/Italy
Cottiennes, Alpes *see* Cottian Alps
Cotton State, The *see* Alabama
22 G4 **Cotton Valley** Louisiana, S USA 32°49′N 93°25′W
36 L12 **Cottonwood** Arizona, SW USA 34°43′N 112°00′W
32 M10 **Cottonwood** Idaho, NW USA 46°01′N 116°20′W
29 S9 **Cottonwood** Minnesota, N USA 44°37′N 95°41′W
25 Q7 **Cottonwood** Texas, SW USA 32°12′N 99°14′W
27 O5 **Cottonwood Falls** Kansas, C USA 38°21′N 96°33′W
36 L3 **Cottonwood Heights** Utah, W USA 40°37′N 111°48′W
29 S10 **Cottonwood River** ≈ Minnesota, N USA
45 O9 **Cotuí** C Dominican Republic 19°04′N 70°10′W
25 Q13 **Cotulla** Texas, SW USA 28°27′N 99°15′W
Cotyora *see* Ordu
102 I11 **Coubre, Pointe de la** *headland* W France 45°39′N 01°23′W
18 E12 **Coudersport** Pennsylvania, NE USA 41°45′N 78°00′W
15 S9 **Coudres, Île aux** *island* Québec, SE Canada
182 G11 **Couedic, Cape de** *headland* South Australia 36°04′S 136°43′E
Couentrey *see* Coventry
102 I6 **Couesnon** ≈ NW France
32 H10 **Cougar** Washington, NW USA 46°03′N 122°18′W
102 L10 **Couhé** Vienne, W France 46°18′N 00°10′E
32 K8 **Coulee City** Washington, NW USA 47°36′N 119°18′W
195 Q15 **Coulman Island** *island* Antarctica
103 P5 **Coulommiers** Seine-et-Marne, N France 48°49′N 03°04′E
14 K11 **Coulonge** ≈ Québec, SE Canada
14 K11 **Coulonge Est** ≈ Québec, SE Canada
35 Q9 **Coulterville** California, W USA 37°41′N 120°10′W
38 M9 **Council** Alaska, USA 64°54′N 163°40′W
32 M12 **Council** Idaho, NW USA 44°45′N 116°26′W
29 S15 **Council Bluffs** Iowa, C USA 41°16′N 95°52′W
27 O5 **Council Grove** Kansas, C USA 38°41′N 96°29′W
27 O5 **Council Grove Lake** ⊠ Kansas, C USA
32 G7 **Coupeville** Washington, NW USA 48°13′N 122°41′W
55 U12 **Courantyne River** *var.* Corantijn Rivier, Corentyne River. ≈ Guyana/Suriname
99 G21 **Courcelles** Hainaut, S Belgium 50°28′N 04°23′E
108 C7 **Courgenay** Jura, NW Switzerland 47°24′N 07°09′E
126 B2 **Courland Lagoon** *Ger.* Kurisches Haff, *Rus.* Kurskiy Zaliv. *lagoon* Lithuania/Russian Federation
118 B12 **Courland Spit** *Lith.* Kuršių Nerija, *Rus.* Kurshskaya Kosa. *spit* Lithuania/Russian Federation
106 A6 **Courmayeur** *prev.* Cormaiore. Valle d'Aosta, NW Italy 45°48′N 07°00′E
108 D7 **Courroux** Jura, NW Switzerland 47°22′N 07°23′E
10 K17 **Courtenay** Vancouver Island, British Columbia, SW Canada 49°40′N 124°58′W
21 W7 **Courtland** Virginia, NE USA 36°44′N 77°06′W
25 V10 **Courtney** Texas, SW USA 30°16′N 96°04′W
30 J4 **Court Oreilles, Lac** ◎ Wisconsin, N USA
Courtrai *see* Kortrijk
99 H19 **Court-Saint-Étienne** Walloon Brabant, C Belgium 50°38′N 04°34′E
22 G6 **Coushatta** Louisiana, S USA 32°00′N 93°20′W
172 I16 **Cousin** *island* Inner Islands, NE Seychelles
172 I16 **Cousine** *island* Inner Islands, NE Seychelles
102 J4 **Coutances** *anc.* Constantia. Manche, N France 49°04′N 01°27′W
102 K12 **Coutras** Gironde, SW France 45°01′N 00°07′W
45 U14 **Couva** Trinidad, Trinidad and Tobago 10°25′N 61°27′W
108 B8 **Couvet** Neuchâtel, W Switzerland 46°57′N 06°41′E
99 H22 **Couvin** Namur, S Belgium 50°03′N 04°30′E
116 K12 **Covasna** *Ger.* Kowasna, *Hung.* Kovászna. Covasna, E Romania 45°51′N 26°11′E
116 J11 **Covasna** ◈ *county* E Romania
14 E12 **Cove Island** *island* Ontario, S Canada
34 M5 **Covelo** California, W USA 39°46′N 123°16′W
97 M20 **Coventry** *anc.* Couentrey. C England, United Kingdom 52°25′N 01°30′W
Cove of Cork *see* Cobh
21 U5 **Covesville** Virginia, NE USA 37°52′N 78°41′W
104 I8 **Covilhã** Castelo Branco, E Portugal 40°17′N 07°30′W
23 T3 **Covington** Georgia, SE USA 33°34′N 83°52′W
31 N13 **Covington** Indiana, N USA 40°08′N 87°23′W
20 M3 **Covington** Kentucky, S USA 39°04′N 84°30′W
22 K8 **Covington** Louisiana, S USA 30°28′N 90°06′W
31 Q13 **Covington** Ohio, N USA 40°07′N 84°21′W
20 F9 **Covington** Tennessee, S USA 35°32′N 89°40′W
21 S6 **Covington** Virginia, NE USA 37°48′N 80°01′W
183 Q8 **Cowal, Lake** *seasonal lake* New South Wales, SE Australia
11 W15 **Cowan** Manitoba, S Canada 51°59′N 100°36′W
18 F12 **Cowanesque River** ≈ New York/Pennsylvania, NE USA
180 L12 **Cowan, Lake** ◎ Western Australia
15 P13 **Cowansville** Québec, SE Canada 45°13′N 72°44′W
182 H8 **Cowell** South Australia 33°43′S 136°53′E
97 M23 **Cowes** S England, United Kingdom 50°45′N 01°19′W
27 Q10 **Coweta** Oklahoma, C USA 35°57′N 95°39′W
0 D6 **Cowie Seamount** *undersea feature* NE Pacific Ocean 54°15′N 149°30′W
32 G10 **Cowlitz River** ≈ Washington, NW USA
21 Q11 **Cowpens** South Carolina, SE USA 35°01′N 81°48′W
183 R8 **Cowra** New South Wales, SE Australia 33°50′S 148°45′E
Coxen Hole *see* Roatán
59 I19 **Coxim** Mato Grosso do Sul, S Brazil 18°28′S 54°45′W
59 I19 **Coxim, Rio** ≈ SW Brazil
Coxin Hole *see* Roatán
153 V17 **Cox's Bazar** Chittagong, S Bangladesh 21°25′N 91°59′E
76 H14 **Coyah** Conakry, W Guinea 09°45′N 13°26′W
40 K5 **Coyame** Chihuahua, N Mexico 29°29′N 105°07′W
24 L9 **Coyanosa Draw** ≈ Texas, SW USA
Coyhaique *see* Coihaique
42 C7 **Coyolate, Río** ≈ S Guatemala
Coyote State, The *see* South Dakota
40 I10 **Coyotitán** Sinaloa, C Mexico 23°48′N 106°37′W
41 O16 **Coyuca** *var.* Coyuca de Benítez. Guerrero, S Mexico 17°01′N 100°08′W
41 N15 **Coyuca** *var.* Coyuca de Catalán. Guerrero, S Mexico 18°21′N 100°39′W
Coyuca de Benítez/Coyuca de Catalán *see* Coyuca
29 N15 **Cozad** Nebraska, C USA 40°52′N 99°58′W
158 L14 **Cozhê** Xizang Zizhiqu, W China 31°53′N 87°51′E
Cozie, Alpi *see* Cottian Alps
Cozmeni *see* Kitsman'
40 E3 **Cozón, Cerro** ▲ NW Mexico 31°16′N 112°29′W
41 Z12 **Cozumel** Quintana Roo, E Mexico 20°29′N 86°54′W
41 Z12 **Cozumel, Isla** *island* SE Mexico
32 K8 **Crab Creek** ≈ Washington, NW USA
44 H12 **Crab Pond Point** *headland* W Jamaica 18°07′N 78°01′W
Cracovia/Cracow *see* Kraków
83 I25 **Cradock** Eastern Cape, S South Africa 32°07′S 25°38′E
39 Y14 **Craig** Prince of Wales Island, Alaska, USA 55°29′N 133°04′W
37 Q3 **Craig** Colorado, C USA 40°31′N 107°33′W
97 F15 **Craigavon** C Northern Ireland, United Kingdom 54°28′N 06°25′W
21 T5 **Craigsville** Virginia, NE USA 38°07′N 79°21′W
101 J21 **Crailsheim** Baden-Württemberg, S Germany 49°07′N 10°04′E
116 H14 **Craiova** Dolj, SW Romania 44°19′N 23°49′E
10 K12 **Cranberry Junction** British Columbia, SW Canada 55°35′N 128°21′W
18 J8 **Cranberry Lake** ◎ New York, NE USA
11 V13 **Cranberry Portage** Manitoba, C Canada 54°34′N 101°22′W
11 P17 **Cranbrook** British Columbia, SW Canada 49°29′N 115°48′W
30 M5 **Crandon** Wisconsin, N USA 45°34′N 88°54′W
32 K14 **Crane** Oregon, NW USA 43°24′N 118°35′W
24 M9 **Crane** Texas, SW USA 31°23′N 102°22′W
Crane *see* The Crane
25 S8 **Cranfills Gap** Texas, SW USA 31°46′N 97°49′W
19 O12 **Cranston** Rhode Island, NE USA 41°46′N 71°26′W
Cranz *see* Zelenogradsk
59 L15 **Craolândia** Tocantins, E Brazil 07°17′S 47°23′W
102 J7 **Craon** Mayenne, NW France 47°52′N 00°57′W
195 V16 **Crary, Cape** *headland* Antarctica
Crasna *see* Kraszna
32 G14 **Crater Lake** ◎ Oregon, NW USA
33 P14 **Craters of the Moon National Monument** *national park* Idaho, NW USA
59 O14 **Crateús** Ceará, E Brazil 05°10′S 40°39′W
Crathis *see* Crati
107 N20 **Crati** *anc.* Crathis. ≈ S Italy
11 U16 **Craven** Saskatchewan, S Canada 50°44′N 104°50′W
54 I8 **Cravo Norte** Arauca, E Colombia 06°17′N 70°15′W
28 J12 **Crawford** Nebraska, C USA 42°40′N 103°24′W
25 T8 **Crawford** Texas, SW USA 31°31′N 97°26′W
11 O17 **Crawford Bay** British Columbia, SW Canada 49°39′N 116°44′W
65 M19 **Crawford Seamount** *undersea feature* S Atlantic Ocean 40°30′S 10°00′W
31 O13 **Crawfordsville** Indiana, N USA 40°02′N 86°52′W
23 S9 **Crawfordville** Florida, SE USA 30°10′N 84°22′W
97 O23 **Crawley** SE England, United Kingdom 51°07′N 00°12′W
33 S10 **Crazy Mountains** ▲▲ Montana, NW USA
11 T11 **Cree** ≈ Saskatchewan, C Canada
37 R7 **Creede** Colorado, C USA 37°51′N 106°55′W
40 I6 **Creel** Chihuahua, N Mexico 27°45′N 107°36′W
11 S11 **Cree Lake** ◎ Saskatchewan, C Canada
11 V13 **Creighton** Saskatchewan, C Canada 54°46′N 101°54′W
29 Q13 **Creighton** Nebraska, C USA 42°28′N 97°54′W
103 O4 **Creil** Oise, N France 49°16′N 02°29′E
106 E8 **Crema** Lombardia, N Italy 45°22′N 09°40′E
106 E8 **Cremona** Lombardia, N Italy 45°08′N 10°02′E
Creole State *see* Louisiana
112 M10 **Crepaja** *Hung.* Cserépalja. Vojvodina, N Serbia 45°02′N 20°36′E
103 O4 **Crépy-en-Valois** Oise, N France 49°13′N 02°54′E
112 B10 **Cres** *It.* Cherso. Primorje-Gorski Kotar, NW Croatia 44°57′N 14°24′E
112 A11 **Cres** *It.* Cherso; *anc.* Crexa. *island* W Croatia
32 H14 **Crescent** Oregon, NW USA 43°27′N 121°40′W
34 K1 **Crescent City** California, W USA 41°45′N 124°14′W
23 W10 **Crescent City** Florida, SE USA 29°25′N 81°30′W
167 X10 **Crescent Group** *island group* C Paracel Islands
23 W10 **Crescent Lake** ◎ Florida, SE USA
29 X11 **Cresco** Iowa, C USA 43°22′N 92°06′W
61 B18 **Crespo** Entre Ríos, E Argentina 32°05′S 60°20′W
103 R13 **Crest** Drôme, E France 44°45′N 05°00′E
37 R5 **Crested Butte** Colorado, C USA 38°52′N 106°59′W
31 S12 **Crestline** Ohio, N USA 40°47′N 82°44′W
11 O17 **Creston** British Columbia, SW Canada 49°05′N 116°32′W
29 U15 **Creston** Iowa, C USA 41°03′N 94°21′W
33 V16 **Creston** Wyoming, C USA 41°40′N 107°43′W
37 S7 **Crestone Peak** ▲ Colorado, C USA 37°58′N 105°34′W
23 P8 **Crestview** Florida, SE USA 30°44′N 86°34′W
121 R10 **Cretan Trough** *undersea feature* Aegean Sea, C Mediterranean Sea
29 R16 **Crete** Nebraska, C USA 40°36′N 96°58′W
Crete *see* Kríti
103 O5 **Créteil** Val-de-Marne, N France 48°47′N 02°28′E
Crete, Sea of/Creticum, Mare *see* Kritikó Pélagos
105 X4 **Creus, Cap de** *headland* NE Spain 42°18′N 03°18′E
103 N10 **Creuse** ◈ *department* C France
102 L9 **Creuse** ≈ C France
103 T4 **Creutzwald** Moselle, NE France 49°13′N 06°41′E
105 S12 **Crevillent** *prev.* Crevillente. Valenciana, E Spain 38°15′N 00°48′W
Crevillente *see* Crevillent
97 L18 **Crewe** C England, United Kingdom 53°05′N 02°27′W
21 V7 **Crewe** Virginia, NE USA 37°10′N 78°07′W
Crexa *see* Cres
43 Q15 **Cricamola, Río** ≈ NW Panama
61 K14 **Criciúma** Santa Catarina, S Brazil 28°39′S 49°23′W
96 J11 **Crieff** C Scotland, United Kingdom 56°22′N 03°49′W
112 B10 **Crikvenica** *It.* Cirquenizza; *prev.* Cirkvenica, Crjkvenica. Primorje-Gorski Kotar, NW Croatia 45°12′N 14°40′E
Crimea/Crimean Oblast *see* Krym, Avtonomna Respublika
101 M16 **Crimmitschau** *var.* Krimmitschau. Sachsen, E Germany 50°48′N 12°23′E
116 G11 **Crişcior** *Hung.* Kristyor. Hunedoara, W Romania 46°09′N 22°54′E
21 Y5 **Crisfield** Maryland, NE USA 37°58′N 75°51′W
31 P3 **Crisp Point** *headland* Michigan, N USA 46°45′N 85°15′W
59 L19 **Cristalina** Goiás, C Brazil 16°43′S 47°37′W
44 J7 **Cristal, Sierra del** ▲▲ E Cuba
43 T14 **Cristóbal** Colón, C Panama 09°18′N 79°52′W
54 F4 **Cristóbal Colón, Pico** ▲ N Colombia 10°52′N 73°46′W
Cristur/Cristuru Săcuiesc *see* Cristuru Secuiesc
116 I11 **Cristuru Secuiesc** *prev.* Cristur, Cristuru Săcuiesc, *Ger.* Kreutz, Sitaş Cristuru, *Hung.* Székelykeresztúr, Szitás-Keresztúr. Harghita, C Romania 46°17′N 25°02′E
116 F10 **Crişul Alb** *var.* Weisse Kreisch, *Ger.* Weisse Körös, *Hung.* Fehér-Körös. ≈ Hungary/Romania
116 F10 **Crişul Negru** *Ger.* Schwarze Körös, *Hung.* Fekete-Körös. ≈ Hungary/Romania
116 G10 **Crişul Repede** *var.* Schnelle Kreisch, *Ger.* Schnelle Körös, *Hung.* Sebes-Körös. ≈ Hungary/Romania
117 N10 **Criuleni** *Rus.* Kriulyany. C Moldova 47°12′N 29°09′E
Crivadia Vulcanului *see* Vulcan
Crjkvenica *see* Crikvenica
113 J17 **Crkvice** SW Montenegro 42°34′N 18°38′E
113 O17 **Crna Gora** *Alb.* Mali i Zi. ▲▲ FYR Macedonia/Serbia
Crna Gora *see* Montenegro
113 O20 **Crna Reka** ≈ S FYR Macedonia
Crni Drim *see* Black Drin
109 V10 **Črni vrh** ▲ NE Slovenia 46°28′N 15°14′E
109 V13 **Črnomelj** *Ger.* Tschernembl. SE Slovenia 45°32′N 15°12′E
97 A17 **Croagh Patrick** *Ir.* Cruach Phádraig. ▲ W Ireland 53°45′N 09°39′W
112 D9 **Croatia** *off.* Republic of Croatia, *Ger.* Kroatien, *SCr.* Hrvatska. ◆ *republic* SE Europe
Croatia, Republic of *see* Croatia
Croce, Picco di *see* Wilde Kreuzspitze
15 P8 **Croche** ≈ Québec, SE Canada
169 V7 **Crocker, Banjaran** *var.* Crocker Range. ▲▲ East Malaysia
Crocker Range *see* Crocker, Banjaran
25 V9 **Crockett** Texas, SW USA 31°21′N 95°30′W
67 V14 **Crocodile** *var.* Krokodil. ≈ N South Africa
Crocodile *see* Limpopo
20 I7 **Crofton** Kentucky, S USA 37°01′N 87°25′W
29 Q12 **Crofton** Nebraska, C USA 42°43′N 97°30′W
Croia *see* Krujë
103 R16 **Croisette, Cap** *headland* SE France 43°12′N 05°21′E
102 G8 **Croisic, Pointe du** *headland* NW France 47°16′N 02°42′W
103 S13 **Croix Haute, Col de la** *pass* E France
15 U5 **Croix, Pointe à la** *headland* Québec, SE Canada 49°16′N 67°46′W
14 F13 **Croker, Cape** *headland* Ontario, S Canada 44°56′N 80°57′W
181 P1 **Croker Island** *island* Northern Territory, N Australia
96 I8 **Cromarty** N Scotland, United Kingdom 57°40′N 04°02′W
99 M21 **Crombach** Liège, E Belgium 50°14′N 06°07′E
97 Q18 **Cromer** E England, United Kingdom 52°56′N 01°06′E
185 D22 **Cromwell** Otago, South Island, New Zealand 45°03′S 169°14′E
185 H16 **Cronadun** West Coast, South Island, New Zealand 42°03′S 171°52′E
39 O11 **Crooked Creek** Alaska, USA 61°52′N 158°06′W
44 K5 **Crooked Island** *island* SE Bahamas
44 J5 **Crooked Island Passage** *channel* SE Bahamas
32 I13 **Crooked River** ≈ Oregon, NW USA
29 R4 **Crookston** Minnesota, N USA 47°47′N 96°36′W
28 I10 **Crooks Tower** ▲ South Dakota, N USA 44°09′N 103°55′W
31 T14 **Crooksville** Ohio, N USA 39°46′N 82°05′W
183 R9 **Crookwell** New South Wales, SE Australia 34°28′S 149°27′E
14 L14 **Crosby** Ontario, SE Canada 44°39′N 76°13′W
97 K17 **Crosby** *var.* Great Crosby. NW England, United Kingdom 53°30′N 03°02′W
29 U6 **Crosby** Minnesota, N USA 46°30′N 93°58′W
28 K2 **Crosby** North Dakota, N USA 48°54′N 103°17′W
25 O5 **Crosbyton** Texas, SW USA 33°40′N 101°16′W
77 V16 **Cross** ≈ Cameroon/Nigeria
23 U10 **Cross City** Florida, SE USA 29°37′N 83°08′W
Crossen *see* Krosno Odrzańskie
27 V14 **Crossett** Arkansas, C USA 33°08′N 91°58′W
97 K15 **Cross Fell** ▲ N England, United Kingdom 54°42′N 02°30′W
11 P16 **Crossfield** Alberta, SW Canada 51°24′N 114°03′W
21 Q12 **Cross Hill** South Carolina, SE USA 34°18′N 81°58′W
19 U6 **Cross Island** *island* Maine, NE USA
11 X13 **Cross Lake** Manitoba, C Canada 54°38′N 97°35′W
22 F5 **Cross Lake** ⊠ Louisiana, S USA
36 I12 **Crossman Peak** ▲ Arizona, SW USA 34°33′N 114°09′W
25 Q7 **Cross Plains** Texas, SW USA 32°07′N 99°10′W
77 V17 **Cross River** ◈ *state* SE Nigeria
20 L9 **Crossville** Tennessee, S USA 35°57′N 85°02′W
31 S8 **Croswell** Michigan, N USA 43°16′N 82°37′W
14 K13 **Crotch Lake** ◎ Ontario, SE Canada
Croton/Crotona *see* Crotone
107 O21 **Crotone** *var.* Cotrone; *anc.* Croton, Crotona. Calabria, SW Italy 39°05′N 17°07′E
33 V11 **Crow Agency** Montana, NW USA 45°35′N 107°28′W
183 U7 **Crowdy Head** *headland* New South Wales, SE Australia 31°52′S 152°45′E
25 Q4 **Crowell** Texas, SW USA 33°59′N 99°45′W
183 O6 **Crowl Creek** *seasonal river* New South Wales, SE Australia
22 H9 **Crowley** Louisiana, S USA 30°11′N 92°21′W
35 S9 **Crowley, Lake** ⊠ California, W USA
27 X10 **Crowleys Ridge** *hill range* Arkansas, C USA
31 N11 **Crown Point** Indiana, N USA 41°25′N 87°22′W
37 P10 **Crownpoint** New Mexico, SW USA 35°40′N 108°09′W
33 R10 **Crow Peak** ▲ Montana, NW USA 46°17′N 111°54′W
11 P17 **Crowsnest Pass** *pass* Alberta/British Columbia, SW Canada
29 T6 **Crow Wing River** ≈ Minnesota, N USA
97 O22 **Croydon** SE England, United Kingdom 51°21′N 00°06′W
Crozer, Mount *see* Finkol, Mount
173 P11 **Crozet Basin** *undersea feature* S Indian Ocean 39°00′S 60°00′E
173 O12 **Crozet Islands** *island group* French Southern and Antarctic Territories
173 N12 **Crozet Plateau** *var.* Crozet Plateaus. *undersea feature* SW Indian Ocean 46°00′S 51°00′E
Crozet Plateaus *see* Crozet Plateau
102 E6 **Crozon** Finistère, NW France 48°14′N 04°31′W
Cruacha Dubha, Na *see* Macgillycuddy's Reeks
Cruach Phádraig *see* Croagh Patrick
116 M14 **Crucea** Constanţa, SE Romania 44°30′N 28°18′E
44 E5 **Cruces** Cienfuegos, C Cuba 22°20′N 80°17′W
107 O20 **Crucoli Torretta** Calabria, SW Italy 39°26′N 17°03′E
41 P9 **Cruillas** Tamaulipas, C Mexico 24°43′N 98°26′W
64 K9 **Cruiser Tablemount** *undersea feature* E Atlantic Ocean 32°00′N 28°00′W
61 G14 **Cruz Alta** Rio Grande do Sul, S Brazil 28°38′S 53°38′W
44 G8 **Cruz, Cabo** *headland* S Cuba 19°50′N 77°43′W
60 N9 **Cruzeiro** São Paulo, S Brazil 22°33′S 44°59′W
60 H10 **Cruzeiro do Oeste** Paraná, S Brazil 23°45′S 53°03′W
59 A15 **Cruzeiro do Sul** Acre, W Brazil 07°40′S 72°39′W
23 U11 **Crystal Bay** *bay* Florida, SE USA NE Gulf of Mexico Atlantic Ocean
182 I8 **Crystal Brook** South Australia 33°24′S 138°10′E
11 X17 **Crystal City** Manitoba, S Canada 49°07′N 98°54′W
27 X5 **Crystal City** Missouri, C USA 38°13′N 90°22′W
25 P13 **Crystal City** Texas, SW USA 28°43′N 99°51′W
30 M4 **Crystal Falls** Michigan, N USA 46°06′N 88°20′W
23 Q8 **Crystal Lake** Florida, SE USA 30°26′N 85°41′W
31 O6 **Crystal Lake** ◎ Michigan, N USA
23 V11 **Crystal River** Florida, SE USA 28°54′N 82°35′W
37 Q5 **Crystal River** ≈ Colorado, C USA
22 K6 **Crystal Springs** Mississippi, S USA 31°59′N 90°21′W
Csaca *see* Čadca
Csakathurn/Csáktornya *see* Čakovec
Csap *see* Chop
Csepén *see* Čepin
Cserépalja *see* Crepaja
Csermő *see* Cermei
Csíkszereda *see* Miercurea-Ciuc
111 L24 **Csongrád** Csongrád, SE Hungary 46°42′N 20°09′E
111 L24 **Csongrád** *off.* Csongrád Megye. ◈ *county* SE Hungary
Csongrád Megye *see* Csongrád
111 H22 **Csorna** Győr-Moson-Sopron, NW Hungary 47°37′N 17°14′E
Csucsa *see* Ciucea
111 G25 **Csurgó** Somogy, SW Hungary 46°16′N 17°09′E
Csurog *see* Čurug
54 L5 **Cúa** Miranda, N Venezuela 10°14′N 66°58′W
82 C11 **Cuale** Malanje, NW Angola 08°22′S 16°10′E
67 T12 **Cuando** *var.* Kwando. ≈ S Africa
83 E15 **Cuando Cubango** *var.* Kuando-Kubango. ◈ *province* SE Angola
83 E16 **Cuangar** Cuando Cubango, S Angola 17°34′S 18°39′E
82 D11 **Cuango** Lunda Norte, NE Angola 09°10′S 17°59′E
82 C10 **Cuango** Uíge, NW Angola 06°20′S 16°42′E
82 C10 **Cuango** *var.* Kwango. ≈ Angola/Dem. Rep. Congo *see also* Kwango
Cuango *see* Kwango
Cuan, Loch *see* Strangford Lough
82 C12 **Cuanza** *var.* Kwanza. ≈ C Angola
82 B11 **Cuanza Norte** *var.* Kuanza Norte. ◈ *province* NE Angola
82 B12 **Cuanza Sul** *var.* Kuanza Sul. ◈ *province* NE Angola
61 E16 **Cuareim, Río** *var.* Rio Quaraí. ≈ Brazil/Uruguay *see also* Quaraí, Rio
Cuareim, Río *see* Quaraí, Rio
83 D15 **Cuatir** ≈ S Angola
40 M7 **Cuatro Ciénegas** *var.* Cuatro Ciénegas de Carranza. Coahuila, NE Mexico 27°00′N 102°03′W
Cuatro Ciénegas de Carranza *see* Cuatro Ciénegas
40 I6 **Cuauhtémoc** Chihuahua, N Mexico 28°22′N 106°52′W
41 P14 **Cuautla** Morelos, S Mexico 18°48′N 98°56′W
104 H12 **Cuba** Beja, S Portugal 38°10′N 07°54′W
27 W6 **Cuba** Missouri, C USA 38°03′N 91°24′W
37 R10 **Cuba** New Mexico, SW USA 36°01′N 106°57′W
44 E6 **Cuba** *off.* Republic of Cuba. ◆ *republic* W West Indies
47 O2 **Cuba** *island* W West Indies
82 B13 **Cubal** Benguela, W Angola 12°58′S 14°16′E
83 C15 **Cubango** *var.* Kuvango, *Port.* Vila Artur de Paiva, Vila da Ponte. Huíla, SW Angola 14°27′S 16°18′E
83 D16 **Cubango** *var.* Kavango, Kavengo, Kubango, Okavango, Okavanggo. ≈ S Africa *see also* Okavango
Cubango *see* Okavango
54 H8 **Cubará** Boyacá, N Colombia 07°01′N 72°07′W
Cuba, Republic of *see* Cuba
136 I12 **Çubuk** Ankara, N Turkey 40°13′N 33°02′E
83 D14 **Cuchi** Cuando Cubango, C Angola 14°40′S 16°58′E
42 C5 **Cuchumatanes, Sierra de los** ▲▲ W Guatemala
Cuculaya, Rio *see* Kukalaya, Rio
82 E12 **Cucumbi** *prev.* Trás-os-Montes. Lunda Sul, NE Angola 10°13′S 19°04′E
54 G7 **Cúcuta** *var.* San José de Cúcuta. Norte de Santander, N Colombia 07°55′N 72°31′W
31 N9 **Cudahy** Wisconsin, N USA 42°54′N 87°51′W
155 J21 **Cuddalore** Tamil Nādu, SE India 11°43′N 79°46′E
155 I18 **Cuddapah** Andhra Pradesh, S India 14°30′N 78°50′E
104 M6 **Cuéllar** Castilla y León, N Spain 41°24′N 04°19′W
82 D13 **Cuemba** *var.* Coemba. Bié, C Angola 12°09′S 18°07′E
56 B8 **Cuenca** Azuay, S Ecuador 02°54′S 79°W
105 Q9 **Cuenca** *anc.* Conca. Castilla-La Mancha, C Spain 40°04′N 02°07′W
105 P9 **Cuenca** ◈ *province* Castilla-La Mancha, C Spain
40 L9 **Cuencamé** *var.* Cuencamé de Ceniceros. Durango, C Mexico 24°53′N 103°41′W
Cuencamé de Ceniceros *see* Cuencamé
105 Q8 **Cuenca, Serrania de** ▲▲ C Spain
Cuera *see* Chur
105 P5 **Cuerda del Pozo, Embalse de la** ⊠ N Spain
41 O14 **Cuernavaca** Morelos, S Mexico 18°57′N 99°15′W
25 T12 **Cuero** Texas, SW USA 29°06′N 97°19′W
44 I7 **Cueto** Holguín, E Cuba 20°43′N 75°54′W
41 Q13 **Cuetzalán** *var.* Cuetzalán del Progreso. Puebla, S Mexico 20°00′N 97°27′W
Cuetzalán del Progreso *see* Cuetzalán
105 Q14 **Cuevas de Almanzora** Andalucía, S Spain 37°19′N 01°52′W
Cuevas de Vinromá *see* Les Coves de Vinromà
116 H12 **Cugir** *Hung.* Kudzsir. Alba, SW Romania 45°48′N 23°25′E
59 H18 **Cuiabá** *prev.* Cuyabá. *state capital* Mato Grosso, SW Brazil 15°32′S 56°05′W
59 H19 **Cuiabá, Rio** ≈ SW Brazil
41 R15 **Cuicatlán** *var.* San Juan Bautista Cuicatlán. Oaxaca, SE Mexico 17°49′N 96°59′W
191 W16 **Cuidado, Punta** *headland* Easter Island, Chile, E Pacific Ocean 27°08′S 109°18′W
Cúige *see* Connaught
Cúige Laighean *see* Leinster
Cúige Mumhan *see* Munster
Cuihua *see* Daguan
98 L13 **Cuijck** Noord-Brabant, SE Netherlands 51°41′N 05°56′E
Cúil an tSúdaire *see* Portarlington
42 D7 **Cuilapa** Santa Rosa, S Guatemala 14°16′N 90°18′W
42 B5 **Cuilco, Río** ≈ W Guatemala
Cúil Mhuine *see* Collooney
Cúil Raithin *see* Coleraine
83 C14 **Cuima** Huambo, C Angola 13°16′S 15°39′E
83 E16 **Cuito** *var.* Kwito. ≈ SE Angola
83 E15 **Cuito Cuanavale** Cuando Cubango, E Angola 15°01′S 19°07′E
41 N14 **Cuitzeo, Lago de** ◎ C Mexico
27 W4 **Cuivre River** ≈ Missouri, C USA
Çuka *see* Çukë
168 L8 **Cukai** *var.* Chukai, Kemaman. Terengganu, Peninsular Malaysia 04°15′N 103°25′E
113 L23 **Çukë** *var.* Çuka. Vlorë, S Albania 39°50′N 20°01′E
Cularo *see* Grenoble
33 Y7 **Culbertson** Montana, NW USA 48°09′N 104°30′W
28 M16 **Culbertson** Nebraska, C USA 40°13′N 100°50′W
183 P10 **Culcairn** New South Wales, SE Australia 35°41′S 147°01′E
45 W5 **Culebra** *var.* Dewey. E Puerto Rico 18°19′N 65°17′W
45 W6 **Culebra, Isla de** *island* E Puerto Rico
37 T8 **Culebra Peak** ▲ Colorado, C USA 37°07′N 105°11′W
104 J5 **Culebra, Sierra de la** ▲▲ NW Spain
98 J12 **Culemborg** Gelderland, C Netherlands 51°57′N 05°17′E
137 V14 **Culfa** *Rus.* Dzhul'fa. SW Azerbaijan 38°58′N 45°37′E
183 P4 **Culgoa River** ≈ New South Wales/Queensland, SE Australia
40 I9 **Culiacán** *var.* Culiacán Rosales, Culiacán-Rosales. Sinaloa, C Mexico 24°48′N 107°25′W
Culiacán-Rosales/Culiacán Rosales *see* Culiacán
105 P14 **Cúllar-Baza** Andalucía, S Spain 37°35′N 02°34′W
105 S10 **Cullera** Valenciana, E Spain 39°10′N 00°15′W
23 P3 **Cullman** Alabama, S USA 34°10′N 86°50′W
108 B10 **Cully** Vaud, W Switzerland 46°58′N 06°46′E
Culm *see* Chełmno
Culmsee *see* Chełmża
21 V4 **Culpeper** Virginia, NE USA 38°28′N 78°00′W
185 I17 **Culverden** Canterbury, South Island, New Zealand 42°46′S 172°51′E
83 H18 **Cum** *var.* Xhumo. Central, C Botswana 21°13′S 24°38′E
55 N5 **Cumaná** Sucre, NE Venezuela 10°29′N 64°12′W
55 O5 **Cumanacoa** Sucre, NE Venezuela 10°17′N 63°58′W
54 C13 **Cumbal, Nevado de** *elevation* S Colombia
21 O7 **Cumberland** Kentucky, S USA 36°55′N 83°00′W
21 U2 **Cumberland** Maryland, NE USA 39°40′N 78°47′W
21 V6 **Cumberland** Virginia, NE USA 37°31′N 78°16′W
187 P12 **Cumberland, Cape** *var.* Cape Nahoi. *headland* Espiritu Santo, N Vanuatu 14°39′S 166°35′E
11 V14 **Cumberland House** Saskatchewan, C Canada 53°57′N 102°21′W
23 W8 **Cumberland Island** *island* Georgia, SE USA
20 L7 **Cumberland, Lake** ⊠ Kentucky, S USA
9 R5 **Cumberland Peninsula** *peninsula* Baffin Island, Nunavut, NE Canada
2 N9 **Cumberland Plateau** *plateau* E USA
30 L1 **Cumberland Point** *headland* Michigan, N USA 47°51′N 89°14′W
21 O7 **Cumberland River** ≈ Kentucky/Tennessee, S USA
9 S6 **Cumberland Sound** *inlet* Baffin Island, Nunavut, NE Canada
96 I12 **Cumbernauld** S Scotland, United Kingdom 55°57′N 04°W
97 K15 **Cumbria** *cultural region* NW England, United Kingdom
97 K15 **Cumbrian Mountains** ▲▲ NW England, United Kingdom
23 S2 **Cumming** Georgia, SE USA 34°12′N 84°08′W
Cummin in Pommern *see* Kamień Pomorski
182 G9 **Cummins** South Australia 34°17′S 135°43′E
96 I13 **Cumnock** W Scotland, United Kingdom 55°32′N 04°28′W
40 G4 **Cumpas** Sonora, NW Mexico 30°N 109°48′W
136 H16 **Çumra** Konya, C Turkey 37°34′N 32°38′E
63 G15 **Cunco** Araucanía, C Chile 38°55′S 72°02′W
54 E9 **Cundinamarca** *off.* Departamento de Cundinamarca. ◈ *province* C Colombia
Cundinamarca, Departamento de *see* Cundinamarca
41 U15 **Cunduacán** Tabasco, SE Mexico 18°00′N 93°07′W
83 C16 **Cunene** ◈ *province* S Angola
83 A16 **Cunene** *var.* Kunene. ≈ Angola/Namibia *see also* Kunene
Cunene *see* Kunene
106 A9 **Cuneo** *Fr.* Coni. Piemonte, NW Italy 44°23′N 07°32′E
83 E15 **Cunjamba** Cuando Cubango, E Angola 15°22′S 20°07′E
181 V10 **Cunnamulla** Queensland, E Australia 28°09′S 145°44′E
Čunusavvon *see* Junosuando
Cuokkarašša *see* Čohkarášša
106 B7 **Cuorgnè** Piemonte, NE Italy 45°23′N 07°34′E
96 K11 **Cupar** E Scotland, United Kingdom 56°19′N 03°01′W
116 L8 **Cupcina** *Rus.* Kupchino; *prev.* Calinisc, Kalinisk. N Moldova 48°07′N 27°22′E
54 C8 **Cupica** Chocó, W Colombia 06°43′N 77°31′W
54 C8 **Cupica, Golfo de** *gulf* W Colombia
112 N13 **Ćuprija** Serbia, E Serbia 43°57′N 21°21′E
Cura *see* Villa de Cura
45 S9 **Curaçao** *prev.* Dutch West Indies. ◇ *Dutch autonomous region* S Caribbean Sea
45 P16 **Curaçao** *island* Lesser Antilles
56 H13 **Curanja, Río** ≈ E Peru
56 F7 **Curaray, Río** ≈ Ecuador/Peru
116 K14 **Curcani** Călăraşi, SE Romania 44°11′N 26°39′E
182 H4 **Curdimurka** South Australia 29°27′S 136°56′E
103 P7 **Cure** ≈ C France
173 Y16 **Curepipe** C Mauritius 20°19′S 57°31′E
55 R6 **Curiapo** Delta Amacuro, NE Venezuela 10°03′N 63°05′W
Curia Rhaetorum *see* Chur
62 G12 **Curicó** Maule, C Chile 35°00′S 71°15′W
Curieta *see* Krk
172 I15 **Curieuse** *island* Inner Islands, NE Seychelles
59 C16 **Curitiba** Acre, W Brazil 10°08′S 69°00′W
60 K12 **Curitiba** *prev.* Curytiba. *state capital* Paraná, S Brazil 25°25′S 49°25′W
60 J13 **Curitibanos** Santa Catarina, S Brazil 27°18′S 50°35′W
183 S6 **Curlewis** New South Wales, SE Australia 31°09′S 150°18′E
182 J6 **Curnamona** South Australia 31°39′S 139°35′E
83 A15 **Curoca** ≈ SW Angola
183 T6 **Currabubula** New South Wales, SE Australia 31°17′S 150°43′E
59 Q14 **Currais Novos** Rio Grande do Norte, E Brazil 06°12′S 36°30′W
35 W7 **Currant** Nevada, W USA 38°43′N 115°27′W
35 W6 **Currant Mountain** ▲ Nevada, W USA 38°56′N 115°19′W
44 H2 **Current** Eleuthera Island, C Bahamas 25°24′N 76°44′W
27 W8 **Current River** ≈ Arkansas/Missouri, C USA
182 M14 **Currie** Tasmania, SE Australia 39°59′S 143°51′E
21 Y8 **Currituck** North Carolina, SE USA 36°29′N 76°02′W
21 Y8 **Currituck Sound** *sound* North Carolina, SE USA
39 R11 **Curry** Alaska, USA 62°36′N 150°00′W
Curtbunar *see* Tervel
116 I13 **Curtea de Argeş** *var.* Curtea-de-Arges. Argeş, S Romania 45°06′N 24°40′E
Curtea-de-Arges *see* Curtea de Argeş
116 E10 **Curtici** *Ger.* Kurtitsch, *Hung.* Kürtös. Arad, W Romania 46°21′N 21°17′E
104 H2 **Curtis** Galicia, NW Spain 43°09′N 08°10′W
28 M16 **Curtis** Nebraska, C USA 40°36′N 100°27′W
183 O14 **Curtis Group** *island group* Tasmania, SE Australia
181 Y8 **Curtis Island** *island* Queensland, SE Australia
58 K11 **Curuá, Ilha do** *island* NE Brazil
47 U7 **Curuá, Rio** ≈ N Brazil
59 A14 **Curuçá, Rio** ≈ NW Brazil
112 L9 **Čurug** *Hung.* Csurog. Vojvodina, N Serbia 45°30′N 20°02′E
61 D16 **Curuzú Cuatiá** Corrientes, NE Argentina 29°50′S 58°05′W
59 M19 **Curvelo** Minas Gerais, SE Brazil 18°45′S 44°27′W
18 E14 **Curwensville** Pennsylvania, NE USA 40°57′N 78°29′W
30 M3 **Curwood, Mount** ▲ Michigan, N USA 46°42′N 88°14′W
Curytiba *see* Curitiba
Curzola *see* Korčula
42 A10 **Cuscatlán** ◈ *department* C El Salvador
57 H15 **Cusco** *var.* Cuzco. Cusco, C Peru 13°35′S 72°02′W
57 H15 **Cusco** *off.* Departamento de Cusco, *var.* Cuzco. ◈ *department* C Peru
Cusco, Departamento de *see* Cusco
27 O9 **Cushing** Oklahoma, C USA 36°01′N 96°46′W
25 W8 **Cushing** Texas, SW USA 31°48′N 94°50′W
40 I6 **Cusihuiriachic** Chihuahua, N Mexico 28°16′N 106°46′W
103 P10 **Cusset** Allier, C France 46°08′N 03°27′E
23 S6 **Cusseta** Georgia, SE USA 32°18′N 84°46′W
28 J10 **Custer** South Dakota, N USA 43°46′N 103°36′W
Cüstrin *see* Kostrzyn
33 Q7 **Cut Bank** Montana, NW USA 48°38′N 112°20′W
Cutch, Gulf of *see* Kachchh, Gulf of
23 S6 **Cuthbert** Georgia, SE USA 31°46′N 84°47′W
11 S15 **Cut Knife** Saskatchewan, S Canada 52°40′N 108°54′W
23 Y16 **Cutler Ridge** Florida, SE USA 25°34′N 80°21′W

◆ Country
● Country Capital
◇ Dependent Territory
○ Dependent Territory Capital
◈ Administrative Regions
✈ International Airport
▲ Mountain
▲▲ Mountain Range
Volcano
≈ River
◎ Lake
⊠ Reservoir

22 K10 **Cut Off** Louisiana, S USA 29°32′N 90°20′W
63 I15 **Cutral-Có** Neuquén, C Argentina 38°56′S 69°13′W
107 O21 **Cutro** Calabria, SW Italy 39°01′N 16°59′E
183 O4 **Cuttaburra Channels** *seasonal river* New South Wales, SE Australia
154 O12 **Cuttack** Orissa, E India 20°28′N 85°53′E
83 C15 **Cuvelai** Cunene, SW Angola 15°40′S 15°48′E
79 G18 **Cuvette** *var.* Région de la Cuvette. ◈ *province* C Congo
Cuvette, Région de la *see* Cuvette
173 V9 **Cuvier Basin** *undersea feature* E Indian Ocean
173 U9 **Cuvier Plateau** *undersea feature* E Indian Ocean
82 B12 **Cuvo** ≈ W Angola
100 H9 **Cuxhaven** Niedersachsen, NW Germany 53°51′N 08°43′E
Cuyabá *see* Cuiabá
Cuyuni, Río *see* Cuyuni River
55 S8 **Cuyuni River** *var.* Río Cuyuni. ≈ Guyana/Venezuela
Cuzco *see* Cusco
97 K22 **Cwmbran** *Wel.* Cwmbrân. SW Wales, United Kingdom 51°39′N 03°W
Cwmbrân *see* Cwmbran
28 K15 **C. W. McConaughy, Lake** ⊠ Nebraska, C USA
81 D20 **Cyangugu** SW Rwanda 02°27′S 29°00′E
110 D11 **Cybinka** *Ger.* Ziebingen. Lubuskie, W Poland 52°11′N 14°46′E
Cyclades *see* Kykládes
Cydonia *see* Chaniá
Cymru *see* Wales
20 M5 **Cynthiana** Kentucky, S USA 38°22′N 84°18′W
11 S17 **Cypress Hills** ▲▲ Alberta/Saskatchewan, SW Canada
Cypro-Syrian Basin *see* Cyprus Basin
121 U11 **Cyprus** *off.* Republic of Cyprus, *Gk.* Kypros, *Turk.* Kıbrıs, Kıbrıs Cumhuriyeti. ◆ *republic* E Mediterranean Sea
84 L14 **Cyprus** *Gk.* Kypros, *Turk.* Kıbrıs. *island* E Mediterranean Sea
121 W11 **Cyprus Basin** *var.* Cypro-Syrian Basin. *undersea feature* E Mediterranean Sea 34°00′N 34°00′E
Cyprus, Republic of *see* Cyprus
Cythera *see* Kýthira
Cythnos *see* Kýthnos
110 F9 **Czaplinek** *Ger.* Tempelburg. Zachodnio-pomorskie, NW Poland 53°33′N 16°14′E
Czarna Woda *see* Wda
110 G8 **Czarne** Pomorskie, N Poland 53°40′N 17°00′E
110 G10 **Czarnków** Wielkopolskie, C Poland 52°53′N 16°32′E
111 E17 **Czech Republic** *Cz.* Česká Republika. ◆ *republic* C Europe
Czegléd *see* Cegléd
110 G12 **Czempiń** Wielkopolskie, C Poland 52°10′N 16°46′E
Czenstochau *see* Częstochowa
Czerkow *see* Čerchov
Czernowitz *see* Chernivtsi
110 I8 **Czersk** Pomorskie, N Poland 53°48′N 17°58′E
111 J15 **Częstochowa** *Ger.* Czenstochau, Tschenstochau, *Rus.* Chenstokhov. Śląskie, S Poland 50°49′N 19°07′E
110 F10 **Człopa** *Ger.* Schloppe. Zachodnio-pomorskie, NW Poland 53°05′N 16°05′E
110 H8 **Człuchów** *Ger.* Schlochau. Pomorskie, NW Poland 53°41′N 17°20′E

D

163 V9 **Da'an** *var.* Dalai. Jilin, NE China 45°28′N 124°18′E
15 S10 **Daaquam** Québec, SE Canada 46°36′N 70°03′W
Daawo, Webi *see* Dawa Wenz
54 I4 **Dabajuro** Falcón, NW Venezuela 11°00′N 70°41′W
77 N15 **Dabakala** NE Ivory Coast 08°19′N 04°24′W
163 S11 **Daban** *var.* Bairin Youqi. Nei Mongol Zizhiqu, N China 43°33′N 118°40′E
111 K23 **Dabas** Pest, C Hungary 47°36′N 19°22′E
160 L8 **Daba Shan** ▲▲ C China
Dabba *see* Daocheng
140 J5 **Dabbāgh, Jabal** ▲ NW Saudi Arabia 27°52′N 35°48′E
54 D8 **Dabeiba** Antioquia, NW Colombia 07°01′N 76°18′W
154 E11 **Dabhoi** Gujarāt, W India 22°08′N 73°28′E
161 P8 **Dabie Shan** ▲▲ C China
76 J13 **Dabola** C Guinea 10°48′N 11°02′W
77 N17 **Dabou** S Ivory Coast 05°20′N 04°23′W
162 M15 **Dabqig** *prev.* Uxin Qi. Nei Mongol Zizhiqu, N China 38°29′N 108°48′E
110 P8 **Dąbrowa Białostocka** Podlaskie, NE Poland 53°38′N 23°18′E
111 M16 **Dąbrowa Tarnowska** Małopolskie, S Poland 50°10′N 21°E
119 M20 **Dabryn'** *Rus.* Dobryn'. Homyel'skaya Voblasts', SE Belarus 51°46′N 29°12′E
159 P10 **Dabsan Hu** ◎ C China
161 Q13 **Dabu** *var.* Huliao. Guangdong, S China 24°19′N 116°07′E
116 H15 **Dăbuleni** Dolj, SW Romania 43°48′N 24°05′E
152 G9 **Dabwāli** Haryāna, NW India 29°56′N 74°40′E
Dacca *see* Dhaka
101 L23 **Dachau** Bayern, SE Germany 48°15′N 11°26′E
Dachuan *see* Dazhou
Dacia Bank *see* Dacia Seamount
64 M10 **Dacia Seamount** *var.* Dacia Bank. *undersea feature* E Atlantic Ocean 31°10′N 13°42′W
37 T3 **Dacono** Colorado, C USA 40°04′N 104°56′W
Đắc Tô *see* Đăk Tô
Dacura *see* Dákura
23 W12 **Dade City** Florida, SE USA 28°21′N 82°12′W
152 L10 **Ḍaḍeldhurā** *var.* Dandeldhura. Far Western, W Nepal 29°12′N 80°31′E
23 Q5 **Dadeville** Alabama, S USA 32°49′N 85°45′W
Dadong *see* Donggang
103 N15 **Dadou** ≈ S France
152 D12 **Dādra and Nagar Haveli** ◈ *union territory* W India
149 P14 **Dādu** Sind, SE Pakistan 26°42′N 67°48′E
167 U11 **Da Du Boloc** Kon Tum, C Vietnam 14°06′N 107°40′E
160 G9 **Dadu He** ≈ C China
163 V15 **Daecheong-do** *prev.* Taechŏng-do. *island* NW South Korea
163 Y16 **Daegu** *Jap.* Taikyū; *prev.* Taegu. SE South Korea 35°55′N 128°33′E
163 Y15 **Daejeon** *Jap.* Taiden; *prev.* Taejŏn. C South Korea 36°20′N 127°28′E
Daerah Istimewa Aceh *see* Aceh
171 P4 **Daet** Luzon, N Philippines 14°06′N 122°57′E
160 I11 **Dafang** Guizhou, S China 27°07′N 105°40′E
Dafeng *see* Shanglin
153 W11 **Dafla Hills** ▲▲ NE India
11 U15 **Dafoe** Saskatchewan, S Canada 51°46′N 104°11′W
76 G10 **Dagana** N Senegal 16°28′N 15°35′W
Dagana *see* Massakory, Chad
Dagana *see* Dahana, Tajikistan
Dagcagoin *see* Zoigê
118 K11 **Dagda** SE Latvia 56°06′N 27°36′E
Dagden *see* Hiiumaa
Dagden-Sund *see* Soela Väin
127 P16 **Dagestan, Respublika** *prev.* Dagestanskaya ASSR, *Eng.* Daghestan. ◈ *autonomous republic* SW Russian Federation
Dagestanskaya ASSR *see* Dagestan, Respublika
127 R17 **Dagestanskiye Ogni** Respublika Dagestan, SW Russian Federation 42°09′N 48°08′E
Dagezhen *see* Fengning
185 A23 **Dagg Sound** *sound* South Island, New Zealand
Daghestan *see* Dagestan, Respublika
141 Y8 **Daghmar** NE Oman 23°09′N 59°01′E
Dağliq Quarabağ *see* Nagorno-Karabakh
Dagö *see* Hiiumaa
54 D11 **Dagua** Valle del Cauca, W Colombia 03°39′N 76°40′W
160 H11 **Daguan** *var.* Cuihua. Yunnan, SW China 27°42′N 103°51′E
171 N3 **Dagupan** *off.* Dagupan City. Luzon, N Philippines 16°05′N 120°21′E
Dagupan City *see* Dagupan
159 N16 **Dagzê** *var.* Dêqên. Xizang Zizhiqu, W China 29°38′N 91°15′E
147 Q13 **Dahana** *Rus.* Dagana, Dakhana. SW Tajikistan 38°03′N 69°51′E
163 V10 **Dahei Shan** ▲▲ N China
163 T7 **Da Hinggan Ling** *Eng.* Great Khingan Range. ▲▲ NE China
Dahlac Archipelago *see* Dahlak Archipelago
80 K9 **Dahlak Archipelago** *var.* Dahlac Archipelago. *island group* E Eritrea
23 T2 **Dahlonega** Georgia, SE USA 34°31′N 83°59′W
101 O14 **Dahme** Brandenburg, E Germany 52°10′N 13°47′E
100 O13 **Dahme** ≈ E Germany
141 O14 **Dahm, Ramlat** *desert* NW Yemen
154 E10 **Dāhod** *prev.* Dohad. Gujarāt, W India 22°48′N 74°18′E
Dahomey *see* Benin
158 G10 **Dahongliutan** Xinjiang Uygur Zizhiqu, NW China 35°59′N 79°12′E
Dahra *see* Dara
Dahraishu *see* Hongtong
139 R2 **Dahūk** *var.* Dohuk, *Kurd.* Dihōk. N Iraq 36°52′N 43°01′E
116 J15 **Daia** Giurgiu, S Romania 44°00′N 25°59′E
165 P12 **Daigo** Ibaraki, Honshū, S Japan 36°43′N 140°22′E
163 O13 **Dai Hai** ◎ N China
Daihoku *see* T'aipei
186 M8 **Dai Island** *island* N Solomon Islands
166 M8 **Daik-u** Bago, SW Myanmar (Burma) 17°46′N 96°40′E
138 H9 **Dā'īl** Dar'ā, S Syria 32°45′N 36°08′E
167 U12 **Đại Lanh** Khanh Hoa, S Vietnam 12°49′N 109°20′E
161 Q13 **Daimao Shan** ▲▲ SE China
105 N11 **Daimiel** Castilla-La Mancha, C Spain 39°04′N 03°37′W
115 F22 **Daimoniá** Pelopónnisos, S Greece 36°38′N 22°54′E
Dainan *see* Tainan
25 W6 **Daingerfield** Texas, SW USA 33°03′N 94°42′W
Daingin, Bá an *see* Dingle Bay
159 R13 **Dainkognubma** Xizang Zizhiqu, W China 32°26′N 97°58′E
164 K14 **Daiō-zaki** *headland* Honshū, SW Japan 34°15′N 136°50′E
Dairbhre *see* Valencia Island
61 B22 **Daireaux** Buenos Aires, E Argentina 36°34′S 61°40′W
Dairen *see* Dalian
Dairûţ *see* Dayrūţ
25 X10 **Daisetta** Texas, SW USA 30°06′N 94°38′W
192 G5 **Daitō-jima** *island group* SW Japan
192 G5 **Daitō Ridge** *undersea feature* N Philippine Sea 25°30′N 133°00′E
161 N3 **Daixian** *var.* Dai Xian, Shangguan. Shanxi, C China 39°10′N 112°57′E
Dai Xian *see* Daixian
Daiyue *see* Shanyin
161 Q12 **Daiyun Shan** ▲▲ SE China
44 M8 **Dajabón** NW Dominican Republic 19°35′N 71°41′W
160 G8 **Dajin Chuan** ≈ C China
148 J6 **Dāk** ◎ W Afghanistan
76 F11 **Dakar** ● (Senegal) W Senegal 14°44′N 17°27′W
76 F11 **Dakar** ✈ W Senegal 14°42′N 17°27′W
Đăk Glây *see* Đak Glei
167 U10 **Đak Glei** *prev.* Đak Glây. Kon Tum, C Vietnam 15°05′N 107°42′E
Dakhana *see* Dahana
153 U16 **Dakhin Shahbazpur Island** *island* S Bangladesh
Dakhla *see* Ad Dakhla
76 F7 **Dakhlet Nouâdhibou** ◈ *region* NW Mauritania
Đak Lap *see* Kiên Đưc
Đak Nông *see* Gia Nghia
77 U11 **Dakoro** Maradi, S Niger 14°29′N 06°45′E
29 U12 **Dakota City** Iowa, C USA 42°42′N 94°13′W
29 R13 **Dakota City** Nebraska, C USA 42°25′N 96°25′W
Đakovica *see* Gjakovë
112 I10 **Đakovo** *var.* Djakovo, *Hung.* Diakovár. Osijek-Baranja, E Croatia 45°18′N 18°24′E
Dakshin *see* Deccan
167 U11 **Đăk Tô** *var.* Đăc Tô. Kon Tum, C Vietnam 14°35′N 107°55′E
43 N7 **Dákura** *var.* Dacura. Región Autónoma Atlántico Norte, NE Nicaragua 14°22′N 83°13′W
95 I14 **Dal** Akershus, S Norway 60°19′N 11°16′E
82 E12 **Dala** Lunda Sul, E Angola 11°04′S 20°15′E
108 J8 **Dalaas** Vorarlberg, W Austria 47°08′N 10°03′E
76 I13 **Dalaba** W Guinea 10°47′N 12°12′W
Dalai *see* Da'an
162 I12 **Dalain Hob** *var.* Ejin Qi. Nei Mongol Zizhiqu, N China 41°59′N 101°04′E
Dalai Nor *see* Hulun Nur
163 Q11 **Dalai Nur** *salt lake* N China
Dala-Jarna *see* Järna
95 M14 **Dalälven** ≈ C Sweden
136 C16 **Dalaman** Muğla, SW Turkey 36°47′N 28°47′E
136 C16 **Dalaman** ✈ Muğla, SW Turkey 36°37′N 28°51′E
136 D16 **Dalaman Çayı** ≈ SW Turkey
162 K11 **Dalandzadgad** Ömnögovĭ, S Mongolia 43°35′N 104°23′E
95 D17 **Dalane** *physical region* S Norway
189 Z2 **Dalap-Uliga-Djarrit** *var.* Delap-Uliga-Darrit, D-U-D. *island group* Ratak Chain, SE Marshall Islands
94 J12 **Dalarna** *prev.* Kopparberg. ◈ *county* C Sweden
94 L13 **Dalarna** *prev. Eng.* Dalecarlia. *cultural region* C Sweden
95 P16 **Dalarö** Stockholm, C Sweden 59°07′N 18°25′E
167 U13 **Đa Lat** Lâm Đồng, S Vietnam 11°56′N 108°25′E
Dalay *see* Bayandalay
148 L12 **Dālbandin** *var.* Dāl Bandin. Baluchistān, SW Pakistan 28°48′N 64°08′E
95 J17 **Dalbosjön** *lake bay* S Sweden
181 Y10 **Dalby** Queensland, E Australia 27°11′S 151°12′E
94 D13 **Dale** Hordaland, S Norway 60°35′N 05°48′E
94 C12 **Dale** Sogn Og Fjordane, S Norway 61°22′N 05°24′E
32 K12 **Dale** Oregon, NW USA 44°58′N 118°56′W
25 T11 **Dale** Texas, SW USA 29°56′N 97°34′W
Dalecarlia *see* Dalarna
21 W4 **Dale City** Virginia, NE USA 38°38′N 77°18′W
20 L8 **Dale Hollow Lake** ⊠ Kentucky/Tennessee, S USA
98 O8 **Dalen** Drenthe, NE Netherlands 52°42′N 06°45′E
95 E15 **Dalen** Telemark, S Norway 59°25′N 07°58′E
166 K14 **Daletme** Chin State, W Myanmar (Burma) 21°44′N 92°48′E
23 Q7 **Daleville** Alabama, S USA 31°18′N 85°42′W
98 M9 **Dalfsen** Overijssel, E Netherlands 52°31′N 06°16′E
24 M1 **Dalhart** Texas, SW USA 36°05′N 102°31′W
13 O13 **Dalhousie** New Brunswick, SE Canada 48°03′N 66°22′W
152 I6 **Dalhousie** Himāchal Pradesh, N India 32°32′N 76°01′E
160 F12 **Dali** *var.* Xiaguan. Yunnan, SW China 25°34′N 100°11′E
Dali *see* Idálion
163 U14 **Dalian** *var.* Dairen, Dalien, Jay Dairen, Lüda, Ta-lien, *Rus.* Dalny. Liaoning, NE China 38°53′N 121°37′E
105 O15 **Dalías** Andalucía, S Spain 36°49′N 02°50′W
Dalien *see* Dalian
Dalijan *see* Delijān
112 J9 **Dalj** *Hung.* Dalja. Osijek-Baranja, E Croatia 45°29′N 19°00′E
Dalja *see* Dalj
32 F12 **Dallas** Oregon, NW USA 44°56′N 123°20′W
25 U6 **Dallas** Texas, SW USA 32°47′N 96°48′W
25 T7 **Dallas-Fort Worth** ✈ Texas, SW USA 32°37′N 97°16′W
154 K12 **Dalli Rājhara** *var.* Dhalli Rajhara. Chhattīsgarh, C India 20°32′N 81°10′E
39 X15 **Dall Island** *island* Alexander Archipelago, Alaska, USA
38 M12 **Dall Lake** ◎ Alaska, USA
Dállogilli *see* Korpilombolo
77 S12 **Dallol Bosso** *seasonal river* W Niger
141 U7 **Dalmā** *island* W United Arab Emirates
113 E14 **Dalmacija** *Eng.* Dalmatia, *Ger.* Dalmatien, *It.* Dalmazia. *cultural region* S Croatia
Dalmatia/Dalmatien/Dalmazia *see* Dalmacija
123 S15 **Dal'negorsk** Primorskiy Kray, SE Russian Federation 44°27′N 135°30′E
Dalny *see* Dalian
76 M16 **Daloa** C Ivory Coast 06°56′N 06°28′W
160 J11 **Dalou Shan** ▲▲ S China
181 X7 **Dalrymple Lake** ◎ Queensland, E Australia
14 H14 **Dalrymple Lake** ◎ Ontario, S Canada
181 X7 **Dalrymple, Mount** ▲ Queensland, E Australia 21°01′S 148°34′E
93 K20 **Dalsbruk** *Fin.* Taalintehdas. Länsi-Suomi, W Finland 60°02′N 22°31′E
95 K19 **Dalsjöfors** Västra Götaland, S Sweden 57°43′N 13°05′E
95 J17 **Dals Långed** *var.* Långed. Västra Götaland, S Sweden 58°54′N 12°20′E
153 O15 **Dāltenganj** *prev.* Daltonganj. Jhārkhand, N India 24°02′N 84°07′E
23 R2 **Dalton** Georgia, SE USA 34°46′N 84°58′W
Daltonganj *see* Dāltenganj
195 X14 **Dalton Iceberg Tongue** *ice feature* Antarctica
92 J1 **Dalvík** Nordhurland Eystra, N Iceland 65°58′N 18°31′W
Dálvvadis *see* Jokkmokk
35 N8 **Daly City** California, W USA 37°44′N 122°27′W
181 P2 **Daly River** ≈ Northern Territory, N Australia
181 Q3 **Daly Waters** Northern Territory, N Australia 16°21′S 133°22′E
119 F20 **Damachava** *var.* Damachova, *Pol.* Domaczewo, *Rus.* Domachëvo. Brestskaya Voblasts', SW Belarus 51°45′N 23°36′E
Damachova *see* Damachava
77 W11 **Damagaram Takaya** Zinder, S Niger 14°02′N 09°28′E
154 D12 **Damān** Damān and Diu, W India 20°25′N 72°58′E
154 B12 **Damān and Diu** ◈ *union territory* W India
75 V7 **Damanhûr** *anc.* Hermopolis Parva. N Egypt 31°03′N 30°28′E
161 O1 **Damaqun Shan** ▲▲ E China
79 I15 **Damara** Ombella-Mpoko, S Central African Republic 05°00′N 18°45′E
83 D18 **Damaraland** *physical region* C Namibia
171 S15 **Damar, Kepulauan** *var.* Baraf Daja Islands, Kepulauan Barat Daya. *island group* C Indonesia
168 J8 **Damar Laut** Perak, Peninsular Malaysia 04°13′N 100°36′E
171 S15 **Damar, Pulau** *island* Maluku, E Indonesia
Damas *see* Dimashq
77 Y12 **Damasak** Borno, NE Nigeria 13°10′N 12°40′E
Damasco *see* Dimashq
21 Q8 **Damascus** Virginia, NE USA 36°37′N 81°46′W
Damascus *see* Dimashq
77 X13 **Damaturu** Yobe, NE Nigeria 11°44′N 11°58′E
171 R9 **Damau** Pulau Kaburuang, N Indonesia 03°46′N 126°49′E
143 O5 **Damāvand, Qolleh-ye** ▲ N Iran 35°56′N 52°08′E
82 B10 **Damba** Uíge, NW Angola 06°44′S 15°20′E
114 M12 **Dambaslar** Tekirdağ, NW Turkey 41°13′N 27°13′E
116 J13 **Dâmbovița** *prev.* Dîmbovița. ◈ *county* SE Romania
116 J13 **Dâmbovița** *prev.* Dîmbovița. ≈ S Romania
173 Y15 **D'Ambre, Île** *island* NE Mauritius
155 K24 **Dambulla** Central Province, C Sri Lanka 07°51′N 80°40′E
44 K9 **Dame-Marie** SW Haiti 18°36′N 74°26′W
44 J9 **Dame Marie, Cap** *headland* SW Haiti 18°37′N 74°24′W
143 Q4 **Dāmghān** Semnān, N Iran 36°13′N 54°22′E
Damietta *see* Dumyât
138 G10 **Dāmiyā** Al Balqā', NW Jordan 32°07′N 35°33′E
146 G11 **Damla** Daşoguz Welaýaty, N Turkmenistan 40°05′N 59°15′E
Dammām *see* Ad Dammān
100 G12 **Damme** Niedersachsen, NW Germany 52°31′N 08°12′E
153 R15 **Dāmodar** ≈ NE India
154 J9 **Damoh** Madhya Pradesh, C India 23°50′N 79°30′E
77 P15 **Damongo** NW Ghana 09°05′N 01°49′W
138 G7 **Damoûr** *var.* Ad Dāmūr. W Lebanon 33°36′N 35°30′E
171 N11 **Dampal, Teluk** *bay* Sulawesi, C Indonesia
180 H7 **Dampier** Western Australia 20°40′S 116°40′E
180 H6 **Dampier Archipelago** *island group* Western Australia
141 U14 **Damqawt** *var.* Damqut. E Yemen 16°35′N 52°39′E
159 O13 **Dam Qu** ≈ C China
Damqut *see* Damqawt
167 R13 **Dâmrei, Chuŏr Phmun** *Fr.* Chaîne de l'Éléphant. ▲▲ SW Cambodia
108 C7 **Damvant** Jura, NW Switzerland 47°22′N 06°55′E
Damwâld *see* Damwoude
98 L5 **Damwoude** *Fris.* Damwâld. Fryslân, N Netherlands 53°18′N 05°59′E
159 N15 **Damxung** *var.* Gongtang. Xizang Zizhiqu, W China 30°29′N 91°02′E
80 K11 **Danakil Desert** *var.* Afar Depression, Danakil Plain. *desert* E Africa
Danakil Plain *see* Danakil Desert
35 R8 **Dana, Mount** ▲ California, W USA 37°54′N 119°13′W
76 L16 **Danané** W Ivory Coast 07°16′N 08°09′W
167 U10 **Đa Nẵng** *prev.* Tourane. Quang Nam-Đa Nẵng, C Vietnam 16°04′N 108°14′E
160 G9 **Danba** *var.* Zhanggu, *Tib.* Rongzhag. Sichuan, C China 30°54′N 101°49′E
Danborg *see* Daneborg
18 L13 **Danbury** Connecticut, NE USA 41°21′N 73°27′W
25 W12 **Danbury** Texas, SW USA 29°13′N 95°20′W
35 X15 **Danby Lake** ◎ California, W USA
194 H4 **Danco Coast** *physical region* Antarctica
82 B11 **Dande** ≈ NW Angola
Dandeldhura *see* Ḍaḍeldhurā
155 E17 **Dandeli** Karnātaka, W India 15°18′N 74°42′E
183 O12 **Dandenong** Victoria, SE Australia 38°01′S 145°13′E
163 V13 **Dandong** *var.* Tan-tung; *prev.* An-tung. Liaoning, NE China 40°10′N 124°23′E
197 Q14 **Daneborg** *var.* Danborg. ◈ Tunu, N Greenland
25 V12 **Danevang** Texas, SW USA 29°03′N 96°11′W
Dänew *see* Galkynyş
Danfeng *see* Shizong
14 L12 **Danford Lake** Québec, SE Canada 45°55′N 76°12′W
19 T4 **Danforth** Maine, USA 45°39′N 67°54′W
37 P3 **Danforth Hills** ▲ Colorado, C USA
Dangara *see* Danghara
159 V12 **Dangchang** Gansu, C China 34°01′N 104°19′E
159 P8 **Dangchengwan** *var.* Subei, Subei Mongolzu Zizhixian. Gansu, N China 39°33′N 94°50′E
82 B10 **Dange** Uíge, NW Angola 07°55′S 15°01′E
Dangerous Archipelago *see* Tuamotu, Îles
83 E26 **Danger Point** *headland* SW South Africa 34°37′S 19°20′E
147 Q13 **Danghara** *Rus.* Dangara. SW Tajikistan 38°05′N 69°14′E
159 P8 **Danghe Nanshan** ▲▲ W China
80 I12 **Dangila** *var.* Dānglā. Āmara, NW Ethiopia 11°08′N 36°51′E
159 P8 **Dangjin Shankou** *pass* N China
Dangla *see* Tanggula Shan, China
Dang La *see* Tanggula Shankou, China
Dānglā *see* Dangila, Ethiopia
Dangme Chu *see* Manās
153 Y11 **Dāngori** Assam, NE India 27°40′N 95°35′E
Dang Raek, Phanom/Dangrek, Chaîne des *see* Dângrêk, Chuŏr Phnum
167 S11 **Dângrêk, Chuŏr Phnum** *var.* Phanom Dang Raek, Phanom Dong Rak, *Fr.* Chaîne des Dangrek. ▲▲ Cambodia/Thailand
42 G3 **Dangriga** *prev.* Stann Creek. Stann Creek, E Belize 16°59′N 88°13′W
161 P6 **Dangshan** Anhui, E China 34°22′N 116°21′E
33 T15 **Daniel** Wyoming, C USA 42°49′N 110°04′W
83 H22 **Daniëlskuil** Northern Cape, N South Africa 28°11′S 23°33′E
19 N12 **Danielson** Connecticut, NE USA 41°48′N 71°53′W
124 M15 **Danilov** Yaroslavskaya Oblast', W Russian Federation 58°11′N 40°11′E
127 O9 **Danilovka** Volgogradskaya Oblast', SW Russian Federation 50°21′N 44°03′E
Danish West Indies *see* Virgin Islands (US)
160 L7 **Dan Jiang** ≈ C China
160 M7 **Danjiangkou Shuiku** ⊠ C China
141 W8 **Dank** *var.* Dhank. NW Oman 23°34′N 56°16′E
152 J7 **Dankhar** Himāchal Pradesh, N India 32°08′N 78°12′E
126 L6 **Dankov** Lipetskaya Oblast', W Russian Federation 53°17′N 39°07′E
42 J7 **Danlí** El Paraíso, S Honduras 14°02′N 86°34′W
Danmark *see* Denmark
Danmarksstraedet *see* Denmark Strait
95 O14 **Dannemora** Uppsala, C Sweden 60°13′N 17°49′E
18 L6 **Dannemora** New York, NE USA 44°42′N 73°42′W
100 K11 **Dannenberg** Niedersachsen, N Germany 53°05′N 11°06′E
184 N12 **Dannevirke** Manawatu-Wanganui, North Island, New Zealand 40°14′S 176°05′E
21 U8 **Dan River** ≈ Virginia, NE USA
167 P8 **Dan Sai** Loei, C Thailand 17°15′N 101°04′E
18 F10 **Dansville** New York, NE USA 42°34′N 77°40′W
Dantzig *see* Gdańsk
86 E12 **Danube** *Bul.* Dunav, *Cz.* Dunaj, *Ger.* Donau, *Hung.* Duna, *Rom.* Dunărea. ≈ C Europe
Danubian Plain *see* Dunavska Ravnina
166 L8 **Danubyu** Ayeyarwady, SW Myanmar (Burma) 17°15′N 95°35′E
Danum *see* Doncaster
19 P11 **Danvers** Massachusetts, NE USA 42°34′N 70°54′W
27 T11 **Danville** Arkansas, C USA 35°03′N 93°22′W
31 N13 **Danville** Illinois, N USA 40°10′N 87°37′W
31 O14 **Danville** Indiana, N USA 39°45′N 86°31′W
29 Y15 **Danville** Iowa, C USA 40°52′N 91°18′W
20 M6 **Danville** Kentucky, S USA 37°40′N 84°49′W
18 G14 **Danville** Pennsylvania, NE USA 40°57′N 76°36′W
21 T6 **Danville** Virginia, NE USA 36°34′N 79°25′W
Danxian/Dan Xian *see* Danzhou
160 L17 **Danzhou** *prev.* Danxian, Dan Xian, Nada. Hainan, S China 19°31′N 109°31′E
Danzhou *see* Yichuan
Danzig *see* Gdańsk
Danziger Bucht *see* Danzig, Gulf of
110 J6 **Danzig, Gulf of** *var.* Gulf of Gdańsk, *Ger.* Danziger Bucht, *Pol.* Zakota Gdańska, *Rus.* Gdan'skaya Bukhta. *gulf* N Poland
160 F10 **Daocheng** *var.* Jinzhu, *Tib.* Dabba. Sichuan, C China 29°05′N 100°14′E
Daojiang *see* Daoxian
Daokou *see* Huaxian
104 H7 **Dão, Rio** ≈ N Portugal
Daosa *see* Dausa
77 Y7 **Dao Timmi** Agadez, NE Niger 20°31′N 13°34′E
160 M13 **Daoxian** *var.* Daojiang. Hunan, S China 25°30′N 111°37′E
77 Q14 **Dapaong** N Togo 10°52′N 00°12′E
23 N8 **Daphne** Alabama, S USA 30°36′N 87°54′W
171 P7 **Dapitan** Mindanao, S Philippines 08°39′N 123°26′E
159 P9 **Da Qaidam** Qinghai, C China 37°50′N 95°18′E
163 V8 **Daqing** *var.* Sartu. Heilongjiang, NE China 46°35′N 125°00′E
163 O13 **Daqing Shan** ▲▲ N China
163 T11 **Daqin Tal** *var.* Naiman Qi. Nei Mongol Zizhiqu, N China 42°51′N 120°41′E
Daqm *see* Duqm
160 G8 **Da Qu** *var.* Do Qu. ≈ C China
139 T5 **Dāqūq** *var.* Tāwūq. At Ta'mím, N Iraq 35°08′N 44°27′E
76 G10 **Dara** *var.* Dahra. NW Senegal 15°20′N 15°28′W
138 H9 **Dar'ā** *var.* Der'a, *Fr.* Déraa. Dar'ā, SW Syria 32°37′N 36°06′E
138 H8 **Dar'ā** *off.* Muḥāfaẓat Dar'ā, *var.* Darā, Der'a, Derrá. ◈ *governorate* S Syria
143 Q12 **Dārāb** Fārs, S Iran 28°52′N 54°25′E
116 K8 **Darabani** Botoşani, NW Romania 48°10′N 26°39′E
Daraj *see* Dirj
Dar'ā, Muḥāfaẓat *see* Dar'ā
142 M8 **Dārān** Eşfahān, W Iran 33°00′N 50°27′E
167 U12 **Da Răng, Sông** *var.* Ba. ≈ S Vietnam
Daraut-Kurgan *see* Daroot-Korgon
77 W13 **Darazo** Bauchi, E Nigeria 11°01′N 10°27′E
139 S3 **Darband** Arbil, N Iraq 36°15′N 44°17′E
139 V4 **Darband-i Khān, Sadd** *dam* NE Iraq
139 N1 **Darbāsīyah** *var.* Derbisīye. Al Ḥasakah, N Syria 37°06′N 40°42′E
118 C11 **Darbėnai** Klaipėda, NW Lithuania 56°02′N 21°16′E
153 Q13 **Darbhanga** Bihār, N India 26°10′N 85°54′E
38 M9 **Darby, Cape** *headland* Alaska, USA 64°19′N 162°46′W
112 I9 **Darda** *Hung.* Dárda. Osijek-Baranja, E Croatia 45°37′N 18°41′E
Dárda *see* Darda
Dardanë *see* Kamenicë
27 T11 **Dardanelle** Arkansas, C USA 35°11′N 93°09′W
27 S11 **Dardanelle, Lake** ⊠ Arkansas, C USA
Dardanelles *see* Çanakkale Boğazı
Dardanelli *see* Çanakkale
Dardo *see* Kangding
Dar-el-Beida *see* Casablanca
136 M14 **Darende** Malatya, C Turkey 38°34′N 37°29′E
81 J22 **Dar es Salaam** Dar es Salaam, E Tanzania 06°51′S 39°18′E
81 J22 **Dar es Salaam** ✈ Pwani, E Tanzania 06°57′S 39°17′E
185 H18 **Darfield** Canterbury, South Island, New Zealand 43°29′S 172°07′E
106 F7 **Darfo** Lombardia, N Italy 45°54′N 10°12′E
80 B10 **Darfur** *var.* Darfur Massif. *cultural region* W Sudan
Darfur Massif *see* Darfur
Darganata/Dargan-Ata *see* Birata
143 T3 **Dargaz** *var.* Darreh Gaz; *prev.* Moḥammadābād. Khorāsān-Razavī, NE Iran 37°28′N 59°08′E
139 U4 **Dargazayn** As Sulaymānīyah, NE Iraq 35°39′N 45°00′E
183 P12 **Dargo** Victoria, SE Australia 37°29′S 147°15′E
162 L6 **Darhan** Darhan Uul, N Mongolia 49°24′N 105°57′E
163 N8 **Darhan** Hentiy, C Mongolia 46°38′N 109°25′E
Darhan *see* Büreghangay
Darhan Muminggan Lianheqi *see* Bailingmiao
162 L6 **Darhan Uul** ◈ *province* N Mongolia
23 W7 **Darien** Georgia, SE USA 31°22′N 81°25′W
43 W16 **Darién** *off.* Provincia del Darién. ◈ *province* SE Panama
Darién, Golfo del *see* Darien, Gulf of
43 X14 **Darien, Gulf of** *Sp.* Golfo del Darién. *gulf* S Caribbean Sea
Darien, Isthmus of *see* Panama, Istmo de
Darién, Provincia del *see* Darién
42 K9 **Dariense, Cordillera** ▲▲ C Nicaragua
43 W15 **Darién, Serranía del** ▲▲ Colombia/Panama
163 P10 **Dariganga** *var.* Ovoot. Sühbaatar, SE Mongolia 45°08′N 113°51′E
Dario *see* Ciudad Darío
Dariorigum *see* Vannes
Dariv *see* Darvi
Darj *see* Dirj
Darjeeling *see* Dārjiling
153 S12 **Dārjiling** *prev.* Darjeeling. West Bengal, NE India 27°00′N 88°13′E
Darkehnen *see* Ozersk
159 S12 **Darlag** *var.* Gümai. Qinghai, C China 33°43′N 99°42′E
183 T3 **Darling Downs** *hill range* Queensland, E Australia
28 M2 **Darling, Lake** ◎ North Dakota, N USA
180 I12 **Darling Range** ▲▲ Western Australia
182 K8 **Darling River** ≈ New South Wales, SE Australia
97 M15 **Darlington** N England, United Kingdom 54°31′N 01°34′W
21 T12 **Darlington** South Carolina, SE USA 34°19′N 79°53′W
30 K9 **Darlington** Wisconsin, N USA 42°41′N 90°08′W
110 G7 **Darłowo** Zachodnio-pomorskie, NW Poland 54°24′N 16°21′E
101 G19 **Darmstadt** Hessen, SW Germany 49°52′N 08°39′E
75 S7 **Darnah** *var.* Dérna. NE Libya 32°46′N 22°39′E
103 S6 **Darney** Vosges, NE France 48°06′N 05°58′E
182 M7 **Darnick** New South Wales, SE Australia 32°52′S 143°38′E
195 Y6 **Darnley, Cape** *cape* Antarctica
105 R7 **Daroca** Aragón, NE Spain 41°07′N 01°25′W
147 S11 **Daroot-Korgon** *var.* Daraut-Kurgan. Oshskaya Oblast', SW Kyrgyzstan 39°35′N 72°13′E
61 A23 **Darragueira** *var.* Darregueira. Buenos Aires, E Argentina 37°40′S 63°12′W
Darregueira *see* Darragueira
Darreh Gaz *see* Dargaz
142 K7 **Darreh Shahr** *var.* Darreh-ye Shahr. Īlām, W Iran 33°10′N 47°18′E
Darreh-ye Shahr *see* Darreh Shahr
32 I7 **Darrington** Washington, NW USA 48°15′N 121°36′W
25 P1 **Darrouzett** Texas, SW USA 36°27′N 100°19′W
153 S15 **Darsana** *var.* Darshana. Khulna, N Bangladesh 23°32′N 88°49′E
Darshana *see* Darsana
100 M7 **Darss** *peninsula* NE Germany
100 M7 **Darsser Ort** *headland* NE Germany 54°28′N 12°31′E
97 J24 **Dart** ≈ SW England, United Kingdom
Dartang *see* Baqên
97 P22 **Dartford** SE England, United Kingdom 51°27′N 00°13′E
182 L12 **Dartmoor** Victoria, SE Australia 37°56′S 141°18′E
97 I24 **Dartmoor** *moorland* SW England, United Kingdom
13 Q15 **Dartmouth** Nova Scotia, SE Canada 44°40′N 63°35′W
97 J24 **Dartmouth** SW England, United Kingdom 50°21′N 03°34′W
15 Y6 **Dartmouth** ≈ Québec, SE Canada
183 Q11 **Dartmouth Reservoir** ◎ Victoria, SE Australia
Dartuch, Cabo *see* Artrutx, Cap d'
186 C9 **Daru** Western, SW Papua New Guinea 09°05′S 143°10′E
112 G9 **Daruvar** *Hung.* Daruvár. Bjelovar-Bilogora, NE Croatia 45°34′N 17°12′E
Daruvár *see* Daruvar
Darvaza *see* Derweze, Turkmenistan
Darvaza *see* Darvoza, Uzbekistan
Darvazskiy Khrebet *see* Darvoz, Qatorkŭhi
Darvel Bay *see* Lahad Datu, Teluk
Darvel, Teluk *see* Lahad Datu, Teluk
162 F8 **Darvi** *var.* Dariv. Govĭ-Altay, W Mongolia 46°20′N 94°11′E
162 F7 **Darvi** *var.* Bulgan. Hovd, W Mongolia 46°57′N 93°40′E
Darvīshān *see* Darwēshān
147 O10 **Darvoza** *Rus.* Darvaza. Jizzax Viloyati, C Uzbekistan 40°59′N 67°19′E
147 R13 **Darvoz, Qatorkŭhi** *Rus.* Darvazskiy Khrebet. ▲▲ C Tajikistan
148 L9 **Darwēshān** , *var.* Garmser; *prev.* Darvīshān. Helmand, S Afghanistan 31°02′N 64°12′E
63 J15 **Darwin** Río Negro, S Argentina 39°13′S 65°41′W
181 O1 **Darwin** *prev.* Palmerston, Port Darwin. *territory capital* Northern Territory, N Australia 12°28′S 130°52′E
65 D24 **Darwin** *var.* Darwin Settlement. East Falkland, Falkland Islands 51°51′S 58°55′W
62 H8 **Darwin, Cordillera** ▲▲ N Chile
Darwin Settlement *see* Darwin
57 B17 **Darwin, Volcán** ✱ Galapagos Islands, Ecuador, E Pacific Ocean 0°12′S 91°17′W
149 S8 **Darya Khān** Punjab, E Pakistan 31°47′N 71°10′E
145 O15 **Dar'yalyktakyr, Ravnina** *plain* S Kazakhstan
143 T11 **Dārzīn** Kermān, S Iran 29°11′N 58°09′E
Dashhowuz *see* Daşoguz
Dashhowuz Welayaty *see* Daşoguz Welaýaty
162 K7 **Dashinchilen** *var.* Süüj. Bulgan, C Mongolia 47°49′N 104°06′E
119 O16 **Dashkawka** *Rus.* Dashkovka. Mahilyowskaya Voblasts', E Belarus 53°44′N 30°16′E
Dashkhovuz *see* Daşoguz Welaýaty
Dashkhovuzskiy Velayat *see* Daşoguz Welaýaty
Dashköpri *see* Daşköpri
Dashkovka *see* Dashkawka
148 J15 **Dasht** ≈ SW Pakistan
Dasht-i *see* Bābūs, Dasht-e
Dashtidzhum *see* Dashtijum
147 R13 **Dashtijum** *Rus.* Dashtidzhum. SW Tajikistan 38°06′N 70°11′E
149 W7 **Daska** Punjab, NE Pakistan 32°15′N 74°23′E
146 J16 **Daşköpri** *var.* Dashköpri, *Rus.* Tashkepri. Mary Welaýaty, S Turkmenistan 36°15′N 62°37′E
146 H8 **Daşoguz** *Rus.* Dashkhovuz, *Turkm.* Dashhowuz; *prev.* Tashauz. Daşoguz Welaýaty, N Turkmenistan 41°51′N 59°53′E
146 E9 **Daşoguz Welaýaty** *var.* Dashhowuz Welayaty, *Rus.* Dashkhovuz, Dashkhovuzskiy Velayat. ◈ *province* N Turkmenistan
Đa, Sông *see* Black River
77 R15 **Dassa** *var.* Dassa-Zoumé. S Benin 07°46′N 02°15′E
Dassa-Zoumé *see* Dassa
29 U8 **Dassel** Minnesota, N USA 45°06′N 94°18′W
152 H3 **Dastegil Sar** ▲ N India
136 C16 **Datça** Muğla, SW Turkey 36°46′N 27°40′E
165 R4 **Date** Hokkaidō, NE Japan 42°28′N 141°00′E
154 I8 **Datia** *prev.* Duttia. Madhya Pradesh, C India 25°41′N 78°28′E
Dåtnejaevrie *see* Tunnsjøen
159 T10 **Datong** *var.* Datong Huizu Tuzu Zizhixian, Qiaotou. Qinghai, C China 37°01′N 101°33′E

◆ Country
● Country Capital
◇ Dependent Territory
○ Dependent Territory Capital
◈ Administrative Regions
✈ International Airport
▲ Mountain
▲▲ Mountain Range
✱ Volcano
≈ River
◎ Lake
⊠ Reservoir

161 N2 Datong var. Tatung, Ta-t'ung. Shanxi, C China 40°09'N 113°17'E
Datung see Tong'an
159 S8 Datong He ≈ C China
Datong Huizu Tuzu Zizhixian see Datong
159 S9 Datong Shan ⛰ C China
169 O10 Datu, Tanjung headland Indonesia/Malaysia 02°01'N 109°37'E
Datu, Teluk see Lahad Datu, Teluk
Daua see Dawa Wenz
172 H16 Dauban, Mount ▲ Silhouette, NE Seychelles
149 T7 Dāūd Khel Punjab, E Pakistan 32°52'N 71°35'E
119 G15 Daugai Alytus, S Lithuania 54°22'N 24°20'E
Daugava see Western Dvina
118 J11 Daugavpils Ger. Dünaburg; prev. Rus. Dvinsk. SE Latvia 55°53'N 26°34'E
Dauka see Dawkah
Daulatabad see Malāyer
101 D18 Daun Rheinland-Pfalz, W Germany 50°13'N 06°50'E
155 E14 Daund prev. Dhond. Mahārāshtra, W India 18°28'N 74°38'E
166 M12 Daung Kyun island S Myanmar (Burma)
11 W15 Dauphin Manitoba, S Canada 51°09'N 100°05'W
103 S13 Dauphiné cultural region E France
23 N9 Dauphin Island island Alabama, S USA
11 X15 Dauphin River Manitoba, S Canada 51°55'N 98°03'W
77 V12 Daura Katsina, N Nigeria 13°03'N 08°18'E
152 H12 Dausa prev. Daosa. Rājasthān, N India 26°51'N 76°21'E
Dauwa see Dawwah
Dāvāçi see Şabran
155 F18 Dāvangere Karnātaka, W India 14°30'N 75°52'E
171 Q8 Davao off. Davao City. Mindanao, S Philippines 07°06'N 125°36'E
Davao City see Davao
171 Q8 Davao Gulf gulf Mindanao, S Philippines
15 Q11 Daveluyville Québec, SE Canada 46°12'N 72°07'W
29 Z14 Davenport Iowa, C USA 41°31'N 90°35'W
32 L8 Davenport Washington, NW USA 47°39'N 118°09'W
43 P16 David Chiriquí, W Panama 08°26'N 82°26'W
15 O11 David ≈ Québec, SE Canada
29 R15 David City Nebraska, C USA 41°15'N 97°07'W
David-Gorodok see Davyd-Haradok
11 T16 Davidson Saskatchewan, S Canada 51°15'N 105°59'W
21 R10 Davidson North Carolina, SE USA 35°29'N 80°49'W
26 K12 Davidson Oklahoma, C USA 34°15'N 99°06'W
39 S6 Davidson Mountains ⛰ Alaska, USA
172 M8 Davie Ridge undersea feature W Indian Ocean 17°10'S 41°45'E
182 A1 Davies, Mount ▲ South Australia 26°14'S 129°14'E
35 O7 Davis California, W USA 38°31'N 121°46'W
27 N12 Davis Oklahoma, C USA 34°30'N 97°07'W
195 Y7 Davis Australian research station Antarctica 68°30'S 78°15'E
194 H3 Davis Coast physical region Antarctica
18 C16 Davis, Mount ▲ Pennsylvania, NE USA 39°47'N 79°10'W
24 K9 Davis Mountains ⛰ Texas, SW USA
195 Z9 Davis Sea sea Antarctica
65 O20 Davis Seamounts undersea feature S Atlantic Ocean
196 M13 Davis Strait strait Baffin Bay/Labrador Sea
127 U5 Davlekanovo Respublika Bashkortostan, W Russian Federation 54°13'N 55°06'E
108 J9 Davos Rmsch. Tavau. Graubünden, E Switzerland 46°48'N 09°50'E
Davvesiida see Lebesby
119 J20 Davyd-Haradok Pol. Dawidgródek, Rus. David-Gorodok. Brestskaya Voblasts', SW Belarus 52°03'N 27°13'E
163 U12 Dawa Liaoning, NE China 40°55'N 122°02'E
141 O11 Dawāsir, Wādī ad dry watercourse S Saudi Arabia
81 K15 Dawa Wenz var. Daua, Webi Daawo. ≈ E Africa
Dawaymah, Birkat ad see Umm al Baqar, Hawr
167 N10 Dawei var. Tavoy, Htawei. Tanintharyi, S Myanmar (Burma) 14°02'N 98°12'E
119 K14 Dawhinava Rus. Dolginovo. Minskaya Voblasts', N Belarus 54°39'N 27°29'E
Dawidgródek see Davyd-Haradok
141 V12 Dawkah var. Dauka. SW Oman 18°32'N 54°03'E
Dawlat Qaṭar see Qatar
24 M3 Dawn Texas, SW USA 34°54'N 102°10'W
Dawo see Maqên
140 M11 Daws Al Bāḩah, SW Saudi Arabia 20°19'N 41°12'E
10 H5 Dawson var. Dawson City. Yukon Territory, NW Canada 64°04'N 139°24'W
23 S6 Dawson Georgia, SE USA 31°46'N 84°27'W
29 S9 Dawson Minnesota, N USA 44°55'N 96°03'W
Dawson City see Dawson
11 N13 Dawson Creek British Columbia, W Canada 55°45'N 120°07'W
10 H7 Dawson Range ⛰ Yukon Territory, W Canada
181 Y9 Dawson River ≈ Queensland, E Australia
10 J15 Dawsons Landing British Columbia, SW Canada 51°33'N 127°38'W
20 I7 Dawson Springs Kentucky, S USA 37°10'N 87°41'W
23 S2 Dawsonville Georgia, SE USA 34°28'N 84°07'W
160 G8 Dawu var. Xianshui. Sichuan, C China 30°55'N 101°08'E
Dawu see Maqên
Dawukou see Huinong
141 Y10 Dawwah var. Dauwa. W Oman 20°36'N 58°52'E
102 J15 Dax var. Ax; anc. Aquae Augustae, Aquae Tarbelicae. Landes, SW France 43°43'N 01°03'W
Daxian see Dazhou
Daxiangshan see Gangu
Daxue see Wencheng
160 G9 Daxue Shan ⛰ C China
Dayan see Lijiang
160 G12 Dayao var. Jinbi. Yunnan, SW China 25°41'N 101°23'E
Dayishan see Gaoyou
Dāykondī see Dāykundī
149 O6 Dāykundī prev. Dāykondī. ◈ province C Afghanistan
183 N12 Daylesford Victoria, SE Australia 37°24'S 144°07'E
35 U10 Daylight Pass pass California, W USA
61 D17 Daymán, Río ≈ N Uruguay
Dayong see Zhangjiajie
Dayr see Ad Dayr
138 G10 Dayr 'Allā var. Deir 'Alla. Al Balqā', N Jordan 32°39'N 36°06'E
139 N4 Dayr az Zawr var. Deir ez Zor. Dayr az Zawr, E Syria 35°12'N 40°12'E
138 M5 Dayr az Zawr off. Muḩāfaẓat Dayr az Zawr, var. Dayr Az-Zor. ◈ governorate E Syria
Dayr az Zawr, Muḩāfaẓat see Dayr az Zawr
Dayr Az-Zor see Dayr az Zawr
75 W9 Dayrūṭ var. Dairûṭ. C Egypt 27°34'N 30°48'E
11 Q15 Daysland Alberta, SW Canada 52°53'N 112°19'W
31 R14 Dayton Ohio, N USA 39°46'N 84°12'W
20 L10 Dayton Tennessee, S USA 35°30'N 85°01'W
25 W11 Dayton Texas, SW USA 30°03'N 94°53'W
32 L10 Dayton Washington, NW USA 46°19'N 117°58'W
23 X10 Daytona Beach Florida, SE USA 29°12'N 81°03'W
169 U12 Dayu Borneo, C Indonesia 01°59'S 115°04'E
161 O13 Dayu Ling ⛰ S China
161 R7 Da Yunhe Eng. Grand Canal. canal E China
161 S11 Dayu Shan island SE China
Dayyer see Bandar-e Dayyer
160 K8 Dazhou prev. Dachuan, Daxian. Sichuan, C China 31°16'N 107°31'E
160 J9 Dazhu var. Zhuyang. Sichuan, C China 30°45'N 107°11'E
161 T13 Dazhuoshui prev. Tachoshui. N Taiwan 24°26'N 121°43'E
160 J9 Dazu var. Longgang. Chongqing Shi, C China 29°47'N 106°30'E
83 H24 De Aar Northern Cape, C South Africa 30°40'S 24°01'E
194 K5 Deacon, Cape headland Antarctica
39 R5 Deadhorse Alaska, USA 70°15'N 148°28'W
33 T12 Dead Indian Peak ▲ Wyoming, C USA 44°36'N 109°45'W
23 R9 Dead Lake ◎ Florida, SE USA
44 J4 Deadman's Cay Long Island, C Bahamas 23°09'N 75°06'W
138 G11 Dead Sea var. Bahret Lut, Lacus Asphaltites, Ar. Al Baḩr al Mayyit, Baḩrat Lūt, Heb. Yam HaMelaḩ. salt lake Israel/Jordan
28 J9 Deadwood South Dakota, N USA 44°22'N 103°43'W
97 Q22 Deal SE England, United Kingdom 51°14'N 01°23'E
83 I22 Dealesville Free State, C South Africa 28°40'S 25°46'E
161 P10 De'an var. Puting. Jiangxi, S China 29°24'N 115°46'E
62 K9 Deán Funes Córdoba, C Argentina 30°25'S 64°22'W
194 L12 Dean Island island Antarctica
Deanuvuotna see Tanafjorden
31 S10 Dearborn Michigan, N USA 42°16'N 83°13'W
27 R3 Dearborn Missouri, C USA 39°31'N 94°46'W
Deargget see Tārendö
32 K9 Deary Idaho, NW USA 46°46'N 118°33'W
32 M9 Deary Washington, NW USA 46°42'N 116°36'W
10 J10 Dease ≈ British Columbia, W Canada
10 J10 Dease Lake British Columbia, W Canada 58°28'N 130°04'W
35 U11 Death Valley California, W USA 36°25'N 116°50'W
35 U11 Death Valley valley California, W USA
92 M8 Deatnu Fin. Tenojoki, Nor. Tana. ≈ Finland/Norway see also Tana, Tenojoki
Deatnu see Tana
102 L4 Deauville Calvados, N France 49°21'N 00°06'E
117 X7 Debal'tseve Rus. Debal'tsevo. Donets'ka Oblast', SE Ukraine 48°21'N 38°26'E
Debal'tsevo see Debal'tseve
113 M19 Debar Ger. Dibra, Turk. Debre. W FYR Macedonia 41°32'N 20°33'E
39 O9 Debauch Mountain ▲ Alaska, USA 64°31'N 159°52'W
De Behagle see Laï
25 X7 De Berry Texas, SW USA 32°18'N 94°09'W
Debessy see Debesy
127 T2 Debesy prev. Debessy. Udmurtskaya Respublika, NW Russian Federation 57°41'N 53°56'E
111 N16 Dębica Podkarpackie, SE Poland 50°04'N 21°24'E
De Bildt see De Bilt
98 J11 De Bilt var. De Bildt. Utrecht, C Netherlands 52°06'N 05°11'E
123 T9 Debin Magadanskaya Oblast', E Russian Federation 62°18'N 150°42'E
110 N13 Dęblin Rus. Ivangorod. Lubelskie, E Poland 51°34'N 21°50'E
110 D10 Dębno Zachodnio-pomorskie, NW Poland 52°43'N 14°42'E
39 S10 Deborah, Mount ▲ Alaska, USA 63°38'N 147°13'W
33 N8 De Borgia Montana, NW USA 47°23'N 115°24'W
Debra Birhan see Debre Birhan
Debra Marcos see Debre Mark'os
Debra Tabor see Debre Tabor
Debre see Debar
80 J13 Debre Birhan var. Debra Birhan. Āmara, N Ethiopia 09°45'N 39°40'E
111 N22 Debrecen Ger. Debreczin, Rom. Debreţin; prev. Debreczen. Hajdú-Bihar, E Hungary 47°32'N 21°38'E
Debreczen/Debreczin see Debrecen
80 I12 Debre Mark'os var. Debra Marcos. Āmara, N Ethiopia 10°18'N 37°48'E
113 N19 Debrešte SW FYR Macedonia 41°29'N 21°20'E
80 J11 Debre Tabor var. Debra Tabor. Āmara, N Ethiopia 11°46'N 38°06'E
Debreţin see Debrecen
80 J13 Debre Zeyt Oromīya, C Ethiopia 08°41'N 39°00'E
113 L16 Deçan Serb. Dečane; prev. Dečani. W Kosovo 42°33'N 20°18'E
Dečane see Deçan
Dečani see Deçan
23 P2 Decatur Alabama, S USA 34°36'N 86°58'W
23 S3 Decatur Georgia, SE USA 33°46'N 84°18'W
30 L13 Decatur Illinois, N USA 39°50'N 88°57'W
31 Q12 Decatur Indiana, N USA 40°40'N 84°57'W
22 M5 Decatur Mississippi, S USA 32°26'N 89°06'W
29 S14 Decatur Nebraska, C USA 42°00'N 96°19'W
25 S6 Decatur Texas, SW USA 33°14'N 97°35'W
20 H9 Decaturville Tennessee, S USA 35°35'N 88°08'W
103 O13 Decazeville Aveyron, S France 44°34'N 02°18'E
155 H17 Deccan Hind. Dakshin. plateau C India
14 J8 Decelles, Réservoir ⊠ Québec, SE Canada
12 K2 Déception Québec, NE Canada 62°06'N 74°36'W
160 G11 Dechang var. Dezhou. Sichuan, C China 27°24'N 102°09'E
111 C15 Děčín Ger. Tetschen. Ústecký Kraj, NW Czech Republic 50°48'N 14°15'E
103 P9 Decize Nièvre, C France 46°51'N 03°25'E
98 I6 De Cocksdorp Noord-Holland, NW Netherlands 53°09'N 04°52'E
29 X11 Decorah Iowa, C USA 43°18'N 91°47'W
Dedeagaç/Dedeagach see Alexandroúpoli
188 C15 Dededo N Guam 13°30'N 144°51'E
98 N9 Dedemsvaart Overijssel, E Netherlands 52°36'N 06°28'E
19 O11 Dedham Massachusetts, NE USA 42°14'N 71°10'W
63 H19 Dedo, Cerro ▲ SW Argentina 44°46'S 71°48'W
77 O13 Dédougou W Burkina 12°29'N 03°25'W
124 G15 Dedovichi Pskovskaya Oblast', W Russian Federation 57°31'N 29°53'E
Dedu see Wudalianchi
155 J24 Deduru Oya ≈ W Sri Lanka
83 N14 Dedza Central, S Malawi 14°20'S 34°24'E
83 N14 Dedza Mountain ▲ C Malawi 14°22'S 34°16'E
96 K9 Dee ≈ NE Scotland, United Kingdom
97 J19 Dee Wel. Afon Dyfrdwy. ≈ England/Wales, United Kingdom
Deep Bay see Chilumba
21 T3 Deep Creek Lake ⊠ Maryland, NE USA
36 J4 Deep Creek Range ⛰ Utah, W USA
27 P10 Deep Fork River ≈ Oklahoma, C USA
14 J11 Deep River Ontario, SE Canada 46°04'N 77°29'W
21 T10 Deep River ≈ North Carolina, SE USA
183 U4 Deepwater New South Wales, SE Australia 29°27'S 151°52'E
31 S14 Deer Creek Lake ◎ Ohio, N USA
23 Z15 Deerfield Beach Florida, SE USA 26°19'N 80°06'W
39 N8 Deering Alaska, USA 66°04'N 162°43'W
38 M16 Deer Island island Alaska, USA
19 S7 Deer Isle island Maine, NE USA
13 S11 Deer Lake Newfoundland and Labrador, SE Canada 49°11'N 57°27'W
99 D18 Deerlijk West-Vlaanderen, W Belgium 50°52'N 03°21'E
33 Q10 Deer Lodge Montana, NW USA 46°24'N 112°43'W
32 L8 Deer Park Washington, NW USA 47°55'N 117°28'W
29 U5 Deer River Minnesota, N USA 47°19'N 93°47'W
Deés see Dej
Defeng see Liping
31 R11 Defiance Ohio, N USA 41°17'N 84°21'W
23 Q8 De Funiak Springs Florida, SE USA 30°43'N 86°07'W
95 L23 Degeberga Skåne, S Sweden 55°48'N 14°06'E
104 H12 Degebe, Ribeira ≈ S Portugal
80 M13 Degeh Bur Sumalē, E Ethiopia 08°08'N 43°35'E
15 U9 Dégelis Québec, SE Canada 47°30'N 68°38'W
77 U17 Degema Rivers, S Nigeria 04°46'N 06°47'E
95 L16 Degerfors Örebro, C Sweden 59°14'N 14°26'E
193 R14 De Gerlache Seamounts undersea feature SE Pacific Ocean
101 N21 Deggendorf Bayern, SE Germany 48°50'N 12°58'E
80 I11 Degoma Āmara, N Ethiopia 12°22'N 37°36'E
De Gordyk see Gorredijk
27 T12 De Gray Lake ⊠ Arkansas, C USA
180 J6 De Grey River ≈ Western Australia
126 M10 Degtevo Rostovskaya Oblast', SW Russian Federation 49°12'N 40°39'E
Dehbārez see Rūdān
Deh Bīd see Şafāshahr
142 M10 Deh Dasht Kohkīlūyeh va Būyer Aḩmad, SW Iran 30°49'N 50°36'E
75 N8 Dehibat SE Tunisia 31°58'N 10°43'E
Dehli see Delhi
142 K8 Dehlorān Īlām, W Iran 32°41'N 47°18'E
147 N13 Dehqonobod Rus. Dekhkanabad. Qashqadaryo Viloyati, S Uzbekistan 38°24'N 66°31'E
152 J9 Dehra Dūn Uttaranchal, N India 30°19'N 78°04'E
153 O14 Dehri Bihār, N India 24°55'N 84°11'E
Deh Shū see Dīshū
163 W9 Dehui Jilin, NE China 44°23'N 125°42'E
99 D17 Deinze Oost-Vlaanderen, NW Belgium 50°59'N 03°32'E
Deir 'Alla see Dayr 'Allā
Deir ez Zor see Dayr az Zawr
Deirgeirt, Loch see Derg, Lough
116 H9 Dej Hung. Dés; prev. Deés. Cluj, NW Romania 47°08'N 23°55'E
95 K15 Deje Värmland, C Sweden 59°35'N 13°29'E
171 Y15 De Jongs, Tanjung headland Papua, SE Indonesia 06°56'S 138°32'E
De Jouwer see Joure
30 M10 De Kalb Illinois, N USA 41°55'N 88°45'W
22 M5 De Kalb Mississippi, S USA 32°46'N 88°39'W
25 W5 De Kalb Texas, SW USA 33°30'N 94°34'W
83 G18 Dekar var. D'Kar. Ghanzi, NW Botswana 21°31'S 21°55'E
Dekéleia see Dhekéleia
79 K20 Dekese Kasai-Occidental, C Dem. Rep. Congo 03°28'S 21°24'E
Dekhkanabad see Dehqonobod
79 I14 Dékoa Kémo, C Central African Republic 06°17'N 19°07'E
98 H6 De Koog Noord-Holland, NW Netherlands 53°06'N 04°43'E
30 M9 Delafield Wisconsin, N USA 43°03'N 88°22'W
61 C23 De La Garma Buenos Aires, E Argentina 37°58'S 60°25'W
14 K10 Delahey, Lac ◎ Québec, SE Canada
80 E11 Delami Southern Kordofan, C Sudan 11°51'N 30°30'E
23 X11 De Land Florida, SE USA 29°01'N 81°18'W
35 R12 Delano California, W USA 35°46'N 119°15'W
29 V8 Delano Minnesota, N USA 45°03'N 93°46'W
36 K6 Delano Peak ▲ Utah, W USA 38°22'N 112°21'W
Delap-Uliga-Darrit see Dalap-Uliga-Djarrit
Delārām see Dilārām
38 F17 Delarof Islands island group Aleutian Islands, Alaska, USA
30 M9 Delavan Wisconsin, N USA 42°37'N 88°37'W
31 S13 Delaware Ohio, N USA 40°18'N 83°06'W
18 I17 Delaware off. State of Delaware, also known as Blue Hen State, Diamond State, First State. ◈ state NE USA
18 I17 Delaware Bay bay NE USA
24 J8 Delaware Mountains ⛰ Texas, SW USA
18 I12 Delaware River ≈ NE USA
27 Q3 Delaware River ≈ Kansas, C USA
18 J14 Delaware Water Gap valley New Jersey/Pennsylvania, NE USA
101 G14 Delbrück Nordrhein-Westfalen, W Germany 51°46'N 08°34'E
11 Q15 Delburne Alberta, SW Canada 52°09'N 113°11'W
172 M12 Del Cano Rise undersea feature SW Indian Ocean 45°15'S 44°15'E
113 Q18 Delčevo NE FYR Macedonia 41°57'N 22°45'E
Delcommune, Lac see Nzilo, Lac
98 O10 Delden Overijssel, E Netherlands 52°16'N 06°41'E
183 R12 Delegate New South Wales, SE Australia 37°04'S 148°57'E
De Lemmer see Lemmer
108 D7 Delémont Ger. Delsberg. Jura, NW Switzerland 47°22'N 07°21'E
25 R7 De Leon Texas, SW USA 32°06'N 98°33'W
115 F18 Delfoí Stereá Elláda, C Greece 38°28'N 22°31'E
98 G12 Delft Zuid-Holland, W Netherlands 52°01'N 04°22'E
155 J23 Delft island NW Sri Lanka
98 O5 Delfzijl Groningen, NE Netherlands 53°20'N 06°55'E
0 E9 Delgada Fan undersea feature NE Pacific Ocean 39°15'N 126°00'W
42 F7 Delgado San Salvador, SW El Salvador 13°44'N 89°07'W
82 Q12 Delgado, Cabo headland N Mozambique 10°41'S 40°40'E
162 G8 Delger var. Taygan. Govĭ-Altay, C Mongolia 46°20'N 97°22'E
163 O9 Delgereh var. Hongor. Dornogovĭ, SE Mongolia 45°49'N 111°20'E
162 J8 Delgerhaan var. Hujirt. Töv, C Mongolia 46°41'N 104°40'E
162 K9 Delgerhangay var. Hashaat. Dundgovĭ, C Mongolia 45°09'N 104°51'E
162 L9 Delgertsogt var. Amardalay. Dundgovĭ, C Mongolia 46°09'N 106°24'E
80 E6 Delgo Northern, N Sudan 20°08'N 30°35'E
159 R10 Delhi var. Delingha. Qinghai, C China 37°19'N 97°22'E
152 I10 Delhi var. Dehli, Hind. Dilli, hist. Shahjahanabad. union territory capital Delhi, N India 28°40'N 77°11'E
22 J5 Delhi Louisiana, S USA 32°28'N 91°29'W
18 J11 Delhi New York, NE USA 42°16'N 74°55'W
152 I10 Delhi ◈ union territory NW India
136 J17 Deli Burnu headland S Turkey 36°43'N 34°55'E
136 J12 Delice Çayı ≈ C Turkey
55 X10 Délices C French Guiana 04°45'N 53°45'W
40 J6 Delicias var. Ciudad Delicias. Chihuahua, N Mexico 28°09'N 105°22'W
143 N7 Delījān var. Dalijan, Dilijan. Markazī, W Iran 34°02'N 50°39'E
112 P12 Deli Jovan ⛰ E Serbia
Déli-Kárpátok see Carpaţii Meridionalii
8 I8 Déline prev. Fort Franklin. Northwest Territories, NW Canada 65°10'N 123°30'W
Delingha see Delhi
15 Q7 Delisle Québec, SE Canada 48°39'N 71°42'W
11 T15 Delisle Saskatchewan, S Canada 51°54'N 107°01'W
101 M15 Delitzsch Sachsen, E Germany 51°31'N 12°19'E
33 Q12 Dell Montana, NW USA 44°41'N 112°42'W
24 I7 Dell City Texas, SW USA 31°56'N 105°12'W
103 U7 Delle Territoire-de-Belfort, E France 47°30'N 07°00'E
36 J9 Dellenbaugh, Mount ▲ Arizona, SW USA 36°06'N 113°32'W
29 R11 Dell Rapids South Dakota, N USA 43°50'N 96°42'W
21 Y4 Delmar Maryland, NE USA 38°26'N 75°32'W
18 K11 Delmar New York, NE USA 42°37'N 73°49'W
100 G11 Delmenhorst Niedersachsen, NW Germany 53°03'N 08°38'E
112 C9 Delnice Primorje-Gorski Kotar, NW Croatia 45°24'N 14°49'E
37 R7 Del Norte Colorado, C USA 37°40'N 106°21'W
39 N6 De Long Mountains ⛰ Alaska, USA
183 P16 Deloraine Tasmania, SE Australia 41°34'S 146°43'E
11 W17 Deloraine Manitoba, S Canada 49°12'N 100°28'W
31 O12 Delphi Indiana, N USA 40°35'N 86°40'W
31 Q12 Delphos Ohio, N USA 40°49'N 84°20'W
23 Z15 Delray Beach Florida, SE USA 26°27'N 80°04'W
25 O12 Del Rio Texas, SW USA 29°23'N 100°56'W
Delsberg see Delémont
94 N11 Delsbo Gävleborg, C Sweden 61°49'N 16°34'E
37 P6 Delta Colorado, C USA 38°44'N 108°04'W
36 K5 Delta Utah, W USA 39°21'N 112°34'W
77 T17 Delta ◈ state S Nigeria
55 Q6 Delta Amacuro off. Territorio Delta Amacuro. ◈ federal district NE Venezuela
Delta Amacuro, Territorio see Delta Amacuro
39 S9 Delta Junction Alaska, USA 64°02'N 145°43'W
23 X11 Deltona Florida, SE USA 28°54'N 81°15'W
183 T5 Delungra New South Wales, SE Australia 29°40'S 150°49'E
162 D6 Delüün var. Rashaant. Bayan-Ölgiy, W Mongolia 47°48'N 90°45'E
154 C12 Delvāda Gujarāt, W India 20°46'N 71°02'E
61 B21 Del Valle Buenos Aires, E Argentina 35°55'S 60°42'W
Delvina see Delvinë
115 C15 Delvináki var. Dhelvinákion; prev. Pogónion. Ípeiros, W Greece 39°57'N 20°28'E
113 L23 Delvinë var. Delvina, It. Delvino. Vlorë, S Albania 39°56'N 20°07'E
Delvino see Delvinë
116 I7 Delyatyn Ivano-Frankivs'ka Oblast', W Ukraine 48°32'N 24°38'E
127 U5 Dëma ≈ W Russian Federation
105 O5 Demanda, Sierra de la ⛰ W Spain
39 T5 Demarcation Point headland Alaska, USA 69°40'N 141°19'W
79 K21 Demba Kasai-Occidental, C Dem. Rep. Congo 05°24'S 22°16'E
172 H13 Dembéni Grande Comore, NW Comoros 11°50'S 43°25'E
79 M15 Dembia Mbomou, SE Central African Republic 05°08'N 24°25'E
Dembidollo see Dembī Dolo
80 H13 Dembī Dolo var. Dembidollo. Oromīya, C Ethiopia 08°33'N 34°49'E
152 K6 Demchok var. Dêmqog. China/India 32°30'N 79°42'E see also Dêmqog
152 L6 Demchok var. Dêmqog. disputed region China/India see also Dêmqog
98 I12 De Meern Utrecht, C Netherlands 52°06'N 05°00'E
99 I17 Demer ≈ C Belgium
64 H12 Demerara Plain undersea feature W Atlantic Ocean 10°00'N 48°00'W
64 H12 Demerara Plateau undersea feature W Atlantic Ocean
55 T9 Demerara River ≈ NE Guyana
126 H3 Demidov Smolenskaya Oblast', W Russian Federation 55°15'N 31°30'E
37 Q15 Deming New Mexico, SW USA 32°17'N 107°46'W
32 H6 Deming Washington, NW USA 48°49'N 122°13'W
58 E10 Demini, Rio ≈ NW Brazil
136 D13 Demirci Manisa, W Turkey 39°03'N 28°40'E
113 P19 Demir Kapija prev. Železna Vrata. SE FYR Macedonia 41°25'N 22°15'E
114 N11 Demirköy Kırklareli, NW Turkey 41°48'N 27°49'E
100 N9 Demmin Mecklenburg-Vorpommern, NE Germany 53°53'N 13°03'E
23 O5 Demopolis Alabama, S USA 32°31'N 87°50'W
31 N11 Demotte Indiana, N USA 41°13'N 87°07'W
158 F13 Dêmqog var. Demchok. China/India 32°36'N 79°29'E see also Demchok
152 L6 Dêmqog var. Demchok. disputed region China/India see also Demchok
171 Y13 Demta Papua, E Indonesia 02°19'S 140°06'E
121 K11 Dem'yanka ≈ C Russian Federation
124 H15 Demyansk Novgorodskaya Oblast', W Russian Federation 57°39'N 32°31'E
122 H10 Dem'yanskoye Tyumenskaya Oblast', C Russian Federation 59°39'N 69°15'E
103 P2 Denain Nord, N France 50°19'N 03°24'E
39 S10 Denali Alaska, USA 63°08'N 147°33'W
Denali see McKinley, Mount
81 M14 Denan Sumalē, E Ethiopia 06°40'N 43°31'E
Denau see Denov
97 J18 Denbigh Wel. Dinbych. NE Wales, United Kingdom 53°11'N 03°25'W
97 J18 Denbigh cultural region N Wales, United Kingdom
98 I6 Den Burg Noord-Holland, NW Netherlands 53°03'N 04°47'E
99 F18 Dender Fr. Dendre. ≈ W Belgium
99 F18 Denderleeuw Oost-Vlaanderen, NW Belgium 50°53'N 04°05'E
99 F17 Dendermonde Fr. Termonde. Oost-Vlaanderen, NW Belgium 51°02'N 04°06'E
Dendre see Dender
194 I9 Dendtler Island island Antarctica
98 P10 Denekamp Overijssel, E Netherlands 52°23'N 07°E
77 W12 Dengas Zinder, S Niger 13°15'N 09°43'E
Dêngka see Têwo
Dêngkagoin see Têwo
162 L13 Dengkou var. Bayan Gol. Nei Mongol Zizhiqu, N China 40°15'N 106°59'E
159 Q14 Dêngqên var. Gyamotang. Xizang Zizhiqu, W China 31°28'N 95°28'E
Deng Xian see Dengzhou
160 M7 Dengzhou prev. Deng Xian. Henan, C China 32°48'N 111°59'E
Dengzhou see Penglai
Den Haag see 's-Gravenhage
180 H10 Denham Western Australia 25°56'S 113°35'E
98 N9 Den Ham Overijssel, E Netherlands 52°30'N 06°31'E
44 J12 Denham, Mount ▲ C Jamaica 18°13'N 77°33'W
22 J8 Denham Springs Louisiana, S USA 30°29'N 90°57'W
98 I7 Den Helder Noord-Holland, NW Netherlands 52°54'N 04°45'E
105 T11 Dénia Valenciana, E Spain 38°51'N 00°07'E
189 Q8 Denig W Nauru
183 N10 Deniliquin New South Wales, SE Australia 35°33'S 144°58'E
29 T14 Denison Iowa, C USA 42°00'N 95°22'W
25 U5 Denison Texas, SW USA 33°45'N 96°32'W
144 L8 Denisovka prev. Ordzhonikidze. Kostanay, N Kazakhstan 52°27'N 61°42'E
136 D15 Denizli Denizli, SW Turkey 37°46'N 29°05'E
136 D15 Denizli ◈ province SW Turkey
Denjong see Sikkim
183 S7 Denman New South Wales, SE Australia 32°24'S 150°43'E
195 Y10 Denman Glacier glacier Antarctica
21 R14 Denmark South Carolina, SE USA 33°19'N 81°08'W
95 G23 Denmark off. Kingdom of Denmark, Dan. Danmark; anc. Hafnia. ◆ monarchy N Europe
Denmark, Kingdom of see Denmark
92 H1 Denmark Strait var. Danmarksstraedet. strait Greenland/Iceland
45 T11 Dennery E Saint Lucia 13°55'N 60°53'W
98 I7 Den Oever Noord-Holland, NW Netherlands 52°56'N 05°01'E
147 O13 Denov Rus. Denau. Surkhondaryo Viloyati, S Uzbekistan 38°20'N 67°48'E
169 U17 Denpasar prev. Paloe. Bali, C Indonesia 08°40'S 115°14'E
116 E12 Denta Timiş, W Romania 45°20'N 21°15'E
21 Y3 Denton Maryland, NE USA 38°53'N 75°50'W
25 T6 Denton Texas, SW USA 33°11'N 97°08'W
186 G9 D'Entrecasteaux Islands island group SE Papua New Guinea
37 T4 Denver state capital Colorado, C USA 39°45'N 105°W
37 T4 Denver ✈ Colorado, C USA 39°57'N 104°38'W
24 L6 Denver City Texas, SW USA 32°57'N 102°49'W
152 J9 Deoband Uttar Pradesh, N India 29°41'N 77°40'E
Deoghar see Devghar
163 X15 Deokjeok-gundo prev. Tŏkchŏk-kundo. island group NW South Korea
154 E13 Deolāli Mahārāshtra, W India 19°55'N 73°49'E
154 I10 Deori Madhya Pradesh, C India 23°09'N 78°39'E
153 O12 Deoria Uttar Pradesh, N India 26°31'N 83°48'E
99 A17 De Panne West-Vlaanderen, W Belgium 51°06'N 02°35'E
Departamento del Quindío see Quindío
Departamento de Narino, see Nariño
54 M5 Dependencia Federal off. Territorio Dependencia Federal. ◈ federal dependency N Venezuela
Dependencia Federal, Territorio see Dependencia Federal
30 M7 De Pere Wisconsin, N USA 44°26'N 88°03'W
18 D10 Depew New York, NE USA 42°54'N 78°41'W
99 E17 De Pinte Oost-Vlaanderen, NW Belgium 51°00'N 03°37'E
25 V5 Deport Texas, SW USA 33°31'N 95°19'W
123 Q8 Deputatskiy Respublika Sakha (Yakutiya), NE Russian Federation 69°18'N 139°48'E
Dêqên see Dagzê
27 S13 De Queen Arkansas, C USA 34°02'N 94°20'W
22 G8 De Quincy Louisiana, S USA 30°27'N 93°25'W
81 J20 Dera spring/well S Kenya 02°39'S 39°52'E
Der'a/Derá/Déraa see Dar'ā
149 S10 Dera Ghāzi Khān var. Dera Ghāzikhān. Punjab, C Pakistan 30°01'N 70°37'E
Dera Ghāzikhān see Dera Ghāzi Khān
149 S8 Dera Ismāīl Khān Khyber Pakhtunkhwa, C Pakistan 31°51'N 70°56'E
Đeravica see Gjeravicë
116 L6 Derazhnya Khmel'nyts'ka Oblast', W Ukraine 49°16'N 27°24'E
127 R17 Derbent Respublika Dagestan, SW Russian Federation 42°01'N 48°16'E
147 N13 Derbent Surkhondaryo Viloyati, S Uzbekistan 38°15'N 66°59'E
Derbisîye see Darbāsīyah
79 M15 Derbissaka Mbomou, SE Central African Republic 05°43'N 24°48'E
180 L4 Derby Western Australia 17°18'S 123°37'E
97 M19 Derby C England, United Kingdom 52°55'N 01°30'W
27 N7 Derby Kansas, C USA 37°33'N 97°16'W
97 L18 Derbyshire cultural region C England, United Kingdom
112 O11 Đerdap physical region E Serbia
Dereli see Gónnoi
162 L9 Deren var. Tsant. Dundgovĭ, C Mongolia 46°16'N 106°55'E
171 W13 Derew ≈ Papua, E Indonesia
127 R8 Dergachi Saratovskaya Oblast', W Russian Federation 51°15'N 48°58'E
Dergachi see Derhachi
97 C19 Derg, Lough Ir. Loch Deirgeirt. ◎ W Ireland
117 V5 Derhachi Rus. Dergachi. Kharkivs'ka Oblast', E Ukraine 50°09'N 36°11'E
22 G8 De Ridder Louisiana, S USA 30°51'N 93°18'W
137 P16 Derik Mardin, SE Turkey 37°22'N 40°16'E
83 E20 Derm Hardap, C Namibia 23°38'S 18°12'E
Dermentobe see Diirmentobe
27 W14 Dermott Arkansas, C USA 33°31'N 91°26'W
Dérna see Darnah
Dernberg, Cape see Dolphin Head
22 J11 Dernieres, Isles island group Louisiana, S USA
102 I4 Déroute, Passage de la strait Channel Islands/France
Derrá see Dar'ā
81 O16 Derri prev. Dirri. Galguduud, C Somalia 04°15'N 46°31'E
Derry see Londonderry
Dertona see Tortona
Dertosa see Tortosa
80 H8 Derudeb Red Sea, NE Sudan 17°31'N 36°07'E
112 H10 Derventa Republika Srpska, N Bosnia and Herzegovina 44°57'N 17°55'E
183 O16 Derwent Bridge Tasmania, SE Australia 42°10'S 146°13'E
183 O17 Derwent, River ≈ Tasmania, SE Australia
146 F10 Derweze Rus. Darvaza. Ahal Welaýaty, C Turkmenistan 40°10'N 58°27'E
Deržavinsk see Derzhavinsk
145 O9 Derzhavinsk var. Deržavinsk. ◈ Akmola, C Kazakhstan
Dés see Dej
57 J18 Desaguadero Puno, S Peru 16°35'S 69°05'W
57 J18 Desaguadero, Río ≈ Bolivia/Peru
191 W9 Désappointement, Îles du island group Îles Tuamotu, C French Polynesia
27 W11 Des Arc Arkansas, C USA 34°58'N 91°30'W
14 C10 Desbarats Ontario, S Canada 46°20'N 83°52'W
62 H13 Descabezado Grande, Volcán Ѫ C Chile 35°34'S 70°40'W
102 L9 Descartes Indre-et-Loire, C France 46°58'N 00°40'E
11 T13 Deschambault Lake ◎ Saskatchewan, C Canada
Deschnaer Koppe see Velká Deštná
32 I11 Deschutes River ≈ Oregon, NW USA
80 J12 Desē var. Desse, It. Dessie. Āmara, N Ethiopia 11°02'N 39°39'E
63 I20 Deseado, Río ≈ S Argentina
106 F8 Desenzano del Garda Lombardia, N Italy 45°28'N 10°31'E
36 K3 Deseret Peak ▲ Utah, W USA 40°27'N 112°37'W
64 P6 Deserta Grande island Madeira, Portugal, NE Atlantic Ocean
64 P6 Desertas, Ilhas island group Madeira, Portugal, NE Atlantic Ocean
35 X16 Desert Center California, W USA 33°42'N 115°22'W
35 V15 Desert Hot Springs California, W USA 33°57'N 116°33'W
14 K10 Désert, Lac ◎ Québec, SE Canada
36 J2 Desert Peak ▲ Utah, W USA 41°03'N 113°22'W
31 R11 Deshler Ohio, N USA 41°12'N 83°55'W
Deshu see Dīshū
Desiderii Fanum see St-Dizier
106 D7 Desio Lombardia, N Italy 45°37'N 09°12'E

◆ Country ● Country Capital ◇ Dependent Territory ○ Dependent Territory Capital ◈ Administrative Regions ✈ International Airport ▲ Mountain ⛰ Mountain Range Ѫ Volcano ≈ River ◎ Lake ⊠ Reservoir

115 E15 **Deskáti** *var.* Dheskáti. Dytikí Makedonía, N Greece *39°55′N 21°49′E*
28 L2 **Des Lacs River** ≈ North Dakota, N USA
27 X6 **Desloge** Missouri, C USA *37°52′N 90°31′W*
11 Q12 **Desmarais** Alberta, W Canada *55°58′N 113°56′W*
29 Q10 **De Smet** South Dakota, N USA *44°23′N 97°33′W*
29 V14 **Des Moines** *state capital* Iowa, C USA *41°36′N 93°37′W*
17 N9 **Des Moines River** ≈ C USA
117 P4 **Desna** ≈ Russian Federation/Ukraine
116 G14 **Desnăţui** ≈ S Romania
63 F24 **Desolación, Isla** *island* S Chile
29 V14 **De Soto** Iowa, C USA *41°31′N 94°00′W*
23 Q4 **De Soto Falls** *waterfall* Alabama, S USA
83 I25 **Despatch** Eastern Cape, S South Africa *33°48′S 25°28′E*
105 N12 **Despeñaperros, Desfiladero de** *pass* S Spain
31 N10 **Des Plaines** Illinois, N USA *42°01′N 87°52′W*
115 J21 **Despotikó** *island* Kykládes, Greece, Aegean Sea
112 N12 **Despotovac** Serbia, E Serbia *44°06′N 21°25′E*
101 M14 **Dessau** Sachsen-Anhalt, E Germany *51°51′N 12°15′E*
Desse *see* Desē
99 J16 **Dessel** Antwerpen, N Belgium *51°15′N 05°07′E*
Dessie *see* Desē
Destêrro *see* Florianópolis
23 P9 **Destin** Florida, SE USA *30°23′N 86°30′W*
Deštná *see* Velká Deštná
193 T10 **Desventurados, Islas de los** *island group* W Chile
103 N1 **Desvres** Pas-de-Calais, N France *50°41′N 01°48′E*
116 E12 **Deta** *Ger.* Detta. Timiș, W Romania *45°24′N 21°14′E*
101 H14 **Detmold** Nordrhein-Westfalen, W Germany *51°55′N 08°52′E*
31 S10 **Detroit** Michigan, N USA *42°20′N 83°03′W*
25 W5 **Detroit** Texas, SW USA *33°39′N 95°16′W*
31 S10 **Detroit** ≈ Canada/USA
29 S6 **Detroit Lakes** Minnesota, N USA *46°49′N 95°49′W*
31 S10 **Detroit Metropolitan** ✈ Michigan, N USA *42°12′N 83°16′W*
Detta *see* Deta
167 S10 **Det Udom** Ubon Ratchathani, E Thailand *14°54′N 105°03′E*
111 K20 **Detva** *Hung.* Gyeva. Bankobýstricky Kraj, C Slovakia *48°35′N 19°25′E*
154 G13 **Deūlgaon Rāja** Mahārāshtra, C India *20°04′N 76°08′E*
99 L15 **Deurne** Noord-Brabant, SE Netherlands *51°28′N 05°47′E*
99 H16 **Deurne** ✈ (Antwerpen) Antwerpen, N Belgium *51°10′N 04°28′E*
Deutsch-Brod *see* Havlíčkův Brod
Deutschendorf *see* Poprad
Deutsch-Eylau *see* Iława
109 Y6 **Deutschkreutz** Burgenland, E Austria *47°37′N 16°37′E*
Deutsch Krone *see* Wałcz
Deutschland/Deutschland, Bundesrepublik *see* Germany
109 V9 **Deutschlandsberg** Steiermark, SE Austria *46°52′N 15°13′E*
Deutsch-Südwestafrika *see* Namibia
109 Y3 **Deutsch-Wagram** Niederösterreich, E Austria *48°19′N 16°33′E*
Deux-Ponts *see* Zweibrücken
14 I11 **Deux Rivieres** Ontario, SE Canada *46°13′N 78°16′W*
102 K9 **Deux-Sèvres** ◈ *department* W France
116 G11 **Deva** *Ger.* Diemrich, *Hung.* Déva. Hunedoara, W Romania *45°55′N 22°55′E*
Déva *see* Deva
Deva *see* Chester
Devana *see* Aberdeen
Devana Castra *see* Chester
Đevđelija *see* Gevgelija
136 L12 **Deveci Dağları** ▲▲ N Turkey
137 P15 **Devegeçidi Barajı** ⊠ SE Turkey
136 K15 **Develi** Kayseri, C Turkey *38°22′N 35°28′E*
98 M11 **Deventer** Overijssel, E Netherlands *52°15′N 06°10′E*
15 O10 **Devenyns, Lac** ⊛ Québec, SE Canada
96 K8 **Deveron** ≈ NE Scotland, United Kingdom
153 R14 **Devghar** *prev.* Deoghar. Jhārkhand, NE India
27 R10 **Devil's Den** *plateau* Arkansas, C USA
35 R7 **Devils Gate** *pass* California, W USA
30 J2 **Devils Island** *island* Apostle Islands, Wisconsin, N USA
Devil's Island *see* Diable, Île du
29 P3 **Devils Lake** North Dakota, N USA *48°08′N 98°50′W*
31 R10 **Devils Lake** ⊛ Michigan, N USA
29 O3 **Devils Lake** ⊛ North Dakota, N USA
35 W13 **Devils Playground** *desert* California, W USA
25 O11 **Devils River** ≈ Texas, SW USA
33 Y12 **Devils Tower** ▲ Wyoming, C USA *44°33′N 104°45′W*
114 I11 **Devin** *prev.* Dovlen. Smolyan, S Bulgaria *41°45′N 24°24′E*
25 R12 **Devine** Texas, SW USA *29°08′N 98°54′W*
152 H13 **Devli** Rājasthān, N India *25°47′N 75°23′E*
Devne *see* Devnya
114 N8 **Devnya** *prev.* Devne. Varna, E Bulgaria *43°15′N 27°35′E*
31 U14 **Devola** Ohio, N USA *39°28′N 81°28′W*
Devoll *see* Devollit, Lumi i
113 M21 **Devollit, Lumi i** *var.* Devoll. ≈ SE Albania
11 Q14 **Devon** Alberta, SW Canada *53°21′N 113°47′W*
97 I23 **Devon** *cultural region* SW England, United Kingdom
197 N10 **Devon Island** *prev.* North Devon Island. *island* Parry Islands, Nunavut, NE Canada
183 O16 **Devonport** Tasmania, SE Australia *41°14′S 146°21′E*
136 H11 **Devrek** Zonguldak, N Turkey *41°14′N 31°57′E*
154 G10 **Dewās** Madhya Pradesh, C India *22°59′N 76°03′E*
De Westerein *see* Zwaagwesteinde
27 P8 **Dewey** Oklahoma, C USA *36°48′N 95°56′W*
Dewey *see* Culebra
98 M8 **De Wijk** Drenthe, NE Netherlands *52°41′N 06°13′E*
27 W12 **De Witt** Arkansas, C USA *34°17′N 91°21′W*
29 Z14 **De Witt** Iowa, C USA *41°49′N 90°32′W*
29 R16 **De Witt** Nebraska, C USA *40°23′N 96°55′W*
97 M17 **Dewsbury** N England, United Kingdom *53°42′N 01°37′W*
161 Q10 **Dexing** Jiangxi, S China *28°51′N 117°36′E*
27 Y8 **Dexter** Missouri, C USA *36°48′N 89°57′W*
37 U14 **Dexter** New Mexico, SW USA *33°12′N 104°25′W*
160 I8 **Deyang** Sichuan, C China *31°08′N 104°23′E*
182 C4 **Dey-Dey, Lake** *salt lake* South Australia
143 S7 **Deyhūk** Yazd, E Iran *33°18′N 57°30′E*
Deynau *see* Galkynyş
Deyyer *see* Bandar-e Dayyer
142 L8 **Dezfūl** *var.* Dizful. Khūzestān, SW Iran *32°23′N 48°28′E*
129 X4 **Dezhneva, Mys** *headland* NE Russian Federation *66°08′N 169°40′W*
161 P4 **Dezhou** Shandong, E China *37°28′N 116°18′E*
Dezhou *see* Dechang
Dezh Shāhpūr *see* Marīvān
Dhaalu Atoll *see* South Nilandhe Atoll
Dhahran *see* Aẓ Ẓahrān
Dhahran Al Khobar *see* Aẓ Ẓahrān al Khubar
153 U14 **Dhaka** *prev.* Dacca. ● (Bangladesh) Dhaka, C Bangladesh *23°42′N 90°22′E*
153 T15 **Dhaka** ◈ *division* C Bangladesh
Dhali *see* Idálion
Dhalli Rajhara *see* Dalli Rājhara
141 O15 **Dhamār** W Yemen *14°31′N 44°25′E*
154 K12 **Dhamtari** Chhattīsgarh, C India *20°43′N 81°36′E*
153 Q15 **Dhanbād** Jhārkhand, NE India *23°48′N 86°27′E*
152 L10 **Dhangaḍhi** *var.* Dhangarhi. Far Western, W Nepal *28°45′N 80°38′E*
Dhangarhi *see* Dhangaḍhi
Dhank *see* Ḍank
153 R12 **Dhankuṭā** Eastern, E Nepal *27°06′N 87°21′E*
152 I6 **Dhaola Dhār** ▲▲ NE India
154 F10 **Dhār** Madhya Pradesh, C India *22°32′N 75°24′E*
153 R12 **Dharān** *var.* Dharan Bazar. Eastern, E Nepal *26°51′N 87°18′E*
Dharan Bazar *see* Dharān
155 H21 **Dhārāpuram** Tamil Nādu, SE India *10°45′N 77°33′E*
155 H20 **Dharmapuri** Tamil Nādu, SE India *12°11′N 78°07′E*
155 H18 **Dharmavaram** Andhra Pradesh, E India *14°27′N 77°44′E*
154 M11 **Dharmjaygarh** Chhattīsgarh, C India *22°27′N 83°16′E*
Dharmsāla *see* Dharmshāla
152 I7 **Dharmshāla** *prev.* Dharmsāla. Himāchal Pradesh, N India *32°14′N 76°24′E*
155 F17 **Dhārwād** *prev.* Dharwar. Karnātaka, SW India *15°30′N 75°04′E*
Dharwar *see* Dhārwād
Dhaulagiri *see* Dhawalāgiri
153 O10 **Dhawalāgiri** *var.* Dhaulagiri. ▲ C Nepal *28°45′N 83°27′E*
81 L18 **Dheere Laaq** *var.* Lak Dera, *It.* Lach Dera. *seasonal river* Kenya/Somalia
121 Q3 **Dhekeleia Sovereign Base Area** *UK military installation* E Cyprus*34°59′N 33°45′E*
121 Q3 **Dhekélia** *Eng.* Dhekelia, *Gk.* Dekéleia. *UK air base* SE Cyprus*35°00′N 33°45′E*
see Dhekélia
Dhelvinákion *see* Delvináki
113 M22 **Dhëmbelit, Maja e** ▲ S Albania *40°10′N 20°22′E*
154 O12 **Dhenkānāl** Orissa, E India *20°40′N 85°36′E*
Dheskáti *see* Deskáti
138 G11 **Dhībān** Ma'dabā, NW Jordan *31°30′N 35°47′E*
Dhidhimótikhon *see* Didymóteicho
Dhíkti Ori *see* Díkti
138 I12 **Dhirwah, Wādī adh** *dry watercourse* C Jordan
Dhistomon *see* Dístomo
Dhodhekánisos *see* Dodekánisa
Dhodhóni *see* Dodóni
Dhofar *see* Ẓufār
Dhomokós *see* Domokós
Dhond *see* Daund
155 H17 **Dhone** Andhra Pradesh, C India *15°25′N 77°52′E*
154 B11 **Dhorāji** Gujarāt, W India *21°44′N 70°27′E*
Dhráma *see* Dráma
154 C10 **Dhrāngadhra** Gujarāt, W India *22°59′N 71°32′E*
Dhrepanon, Akrotírio *see* Drépano, Akrotírio
153 T13 **Dhuburi** Assam, NE India *26°06′N 89°55′E*
154 F12 **Dhule** *prev.* Dhulia. Mahārāshtra, C India *20°54′N 74°47′E*
Dhulia *see* Dhule
Dhún Dealgan, Cuan *see* Dundalk Bay
Dhún Droma, Cuan *see* Dundrum Bay
Dhún na nGall, Bá *see* Donegal Bay
Dhū Shaykh *see* Qazānīyah
80 Q13 **Dhuudo** Bari, NE Somalia *09°21′N 50°19′E*
81 N15 **Dhuusa Marreeb** *var.* Dusa Marreb, *It.* Dusa Mareb. Galguduud, C Somalia *05°33′N 46°24′E*
115 J24 **Día** *island* SE Greece
55 Y9 **Diable, Île du** *var.* Devil's Island. *island* N French Guiana
15 N12 **Diable, Rivière du** ≈ Québec, SE Canada
35 N8 **Diablo, Mount** ▲ California, W USA *37°52′N 121°57′W*
35 O9 **Diablo Range** ▲▲ California, W USA
24 I8 **Diablo, Sierra** ▲▲ Texas, SW USA
45 O11 **Diablotins, Morne** ▲ N Dominica *15°30′N 61°23′W*
77 N11 **Diafarabé** Mopti, C Mali *14°09′N 05°01′W*
77 N11 **Diaka** ≈ SW Mali
Diakovár *see* Đakovo
76 I12 **Dialakoto** S Senegal *13°21′N 13°19′W*
61 B18 **Diamante** Entre Ríos, E Argentina *32°05′S 60°40′W*
62 I12 **Diamante, Río** ≈ C Argentina
59 M19 **Diamantina** Minas Gerais, SE Brazil *18°17′S 43°37′W*
59 N17 **Diamantina, Chapada** ▲ E Brazil
173 U11 **Diamantina Fracture Zone** *tectonic feature* E Indian Ocean
181 T8 **Diamantina River** ≈ Queensland/South Australia
38 D9 **Diamond Head** *headland* O'ahu, Hawai'i, USA *21°15′N 157°48′W*
37 P2 **Diamond Peak** ▲ Colorado, C USA *40°56′N 108°56′W*
35 W5 **Diamond Peak** ▲ Nevada, W USA *39°34′N 115°46′W*
Diamond State *see* Delaware
76 J11 **Diamou** Kayes, SW Mali *14°04′N 11°16′W*
95 I23 **Dianalund** Sjælland, C Denmark *55°32′N 11°30′E*
65 G25 **Diana's Peak** ▲ C Saint Helena
160 M16 **Dianbai** *var.* Shuidong. Guangdong, S China *21°30′N 111°05′E*
160 G13 **Dian Chi** ⊛ SW China
106 B10 **Diano Marina** Liguria, NW Italy *43°55′N 08°06′E*
163 V11 **Diaobingshan** *var.* Tiefa. Liaoning, NE China *42°25′N 123°39′E*
77 R13 **Diapaga** E Burkina *12°09′N 01°48′E*
Diarbekr *see* Diyarbakır
107 J15 **Diavolo, Passo del** *pass* C Italy
61 B18 **Díaz** Santa Fe, C Argentina *32°22′S 61°05′W*
141 W6 **Dibā al Ḩiṣn** *var.* Dibāh, Dibba. Ash Shāriqah, NE United Arab Emirates *25°35′N 56°16′E*
139 S3 **Dībaga** Arbīl, N Iraq *35°51′N 43°49′E*
Dibāh *see* Dibā al Ḩiṣn
79 L22 **Dibaya** Kasai-Occidental, S Dem. Rep. Congo *06°31′S 22°57′E*
Dibba *see* Dibā al Ḩiṣn
195 W15 **Dibble Iceberg Tongue** *ice feature* Antarctica
113 L19 **Dibër** ◈ *district* E Albania
83 I20 **Dibete** Central, SE Botswana *23°45′S 26°26′E*
Dibio *see* Dijon
25 W9 **Diboll** Texas, SW USA *31°11′N 94°46′W*
Dibra *see* Debar
153 X11 **Dibrugarh** Assam, NE India *27°29′N 94°49′E*
54 G4 **Dibulla** La Guajira, N Colombia *11°14′N 73°22′W*
25 O5 **Dickens** Texas, SW USA *33°38′N 100°51′W*
19 R2 **Dickey** Maine, NE USA *47°04′N 69°05′W*
30 K9 **Dickeyville** Wisconsin, N USA *42°37′N 90°36′W*
28 K5 **Dickinson** North Dakota, N USA *46°54′N 102°48′W*
0 E6 **Dickins Seamount** *undersea feature* NE Pacific Ocean *54°30′N 137°00′W*
27 O13 **Dickson** Oklahoma, C USA *34°11′N 96°58′W*
20 I9 **Dickson** Tennessee, S USA *36°04′N 87°23′W*
Dicle *see* Tigris
Dicsőszentmárton *see* Târnăveni
98 M12 **Didam** Gelderland, E Netherlands *51°56′N 06°08′E*
163 Y8 **Didao** Heilongjiang, NE China *45°22′N 130°48′E*
76 L12 **Didiéni** Koulikoro, W Mali *13°48′N 08°01′W*
Didimo *see* Dídymo
Didimotiho *see* Didymóteicho
81 K17 **Didimtu** *spring/well* NE Kenya *02°58′N 40°07′E*
67 U9 **Didinga Hills** ▲ S Sudan
11 Q16 **Didsbury** Alberta, SW Canada *51°39′N 114°09′W*
152 G11 **Dīdwāna** Rājasthān, N India *27°23′N 74°36′E*
115 G20 **Dídymo** *var.* Didimo. ▲ S Greece *37°28′N 23°12′E*
114 L12 **Didymóteicho** *var.* Dhidhimótikhon, Didimotiho. Anatolikí Makedonía kai Thráki, NE Greece *41°22′N 26°29′E*
103 S13 **Die** Drôme, E France *44°46′N 05°21′E*
77 O13 **Diébougou** SW Burkina *11°00′N 03°12′W*
Diedenhofen *see* Thionville
11 S16 **Diefenbaker, Lake** ⊠ Saskatchewan, S Canada
62 H7 **Diego de Almagro** Atacama, N Chile *26°24′S 70°10′W*
63 F23 **Diego de Almagro, Isla** *island* S Chile
61 A20 **Diego de Alvear** Santa Fe, C Argentina *34°25′S 62°10′W*
173 Q7 **Diego Garcia** *island* S British Indian Ocean Territory
Diégo-Suarez *see* Antsiranana
99 M23 **Diekirch** Diekirch, C Luxembourg *49°52′N 06°10′E*
99 L23 **Diekirch** ◈ *district* N Luxembourg
76 K11 **Diéma** Kayes, W Mali *14°30′N 09°12′W*
101 H15 **Diemel** ≈ W Germany
98 I10 **Diemen** Noord-Holland, C Netherlands *52°21′N 04°58′E*
Diemrich *see* Deva
Điện Biên *see* Điện Biên Phu
167 R6 **Điện Biên Phu** *var.* Dien Bien, Điện Biên. Lai Châu, N Vietnam *21°23′N 103°02′E*
167 S7 **Diễn Châu** Nghệ An, N Vietnam *18°54′N 105°35′E*
99 K18 **Diepenbeek** Limburg, NE Belgium *50°54′N 05°25′E*
98 N11 **Diepenheim** Overijssel, E Netherlands *52°10′N 06°37′E*
98 M10 **Diepenveen** Overijssel, E Netherlands *52°18′N 06°09′E*
100 G12 **Diepholz** Niedersachsen, NW Germany *52°36′N 08°23′E*
102 M3 **Dieppe** Seine-Maritime, N France *49°55′N 01°05′E*
98 M12 **Dieren** Gelderland, E Netherlands *52°03′N 06°06′E*
27 S13 **Dierks** Arkansas, C USA *34°07′N 94°01′W*
99 J17 **Diest** Vlaams Brabant, C Belgium *50°58′N 05°03′E*
108 F7 **Dietikon** Zürich, NW Switzerland *47°24′N 08°25′E*
103 R13 **Dieulefit** Drôme, E France *44°30′N 05°01′E*
103 T5 **Dieuze** Moselle, NE France *48°49′N 06°41′E*
119 H15 **Dieveniškės** Vilnius, SE Lithuania *54°12′N 25°38′E*
98 N7 **Diever** Drenthe, NE Netherlands *52°49′N 06°19′E*
101 F17 **Diez** Rheinland-Pfalz, W Germany *50°22′N 08°01′E*
77 Y12 **Diffa** Diffa, SE Niger *13°19′N 12°37′E*
77 Y10 **Diffa** ◈ *department* SE Niger
99 L25 **Differdange** Luxembourg, SW Luxembourg *49°32′N 05°53′E*
13 O16 **Digby** Nova Scotia, SE Canada *44°37′N 65°47′W*
26 J5 **Dighton** Kansas, C USA *38°28′N 100°28′W*
Dignano d'Istria *see* Vodnjan
103 T14 **Digne** *var.* Digne-les-Bains. Alpes-de-Haute-Provence, SE France *44°05′N 06°14′E*
Digne-les-Bains *see* Digne
Digoel *see* Digul, Sungai
103 Q10 **Digoin** Saône-et-Loire, C France *46°30′N 04°E*
171 Q8 **Digos** Mindanao, S Philippines *06°46′N 125°21′E*
149 Q16 **Digri** Sind, SE Pakistan *25°11′N 69°10′E*
171 Y14 **Digul Barat, Sungai** ≈ Papua, E Indonesia
171 Y15 **Digul, Sungai** *prev.* Digoel. ≈ Papua, E Indonesia
171 Z14 **Digul Timur, Sungai** ≈ Papua, E Indonesia
153 X10 **Dihang** ≈ NE India
Dihang *see* Brahmaputra
Dihōk *see* Dahūk
81 L17 **Diinsoor** Bay, S Somalia *02°28′N 43°00′E*
144 M14 **Diirmentobe** *Kas.* Dürmentöbe; *prev.* Dermentobe, Dyurment'yube. Kzyl-Orda, S Kazakhstan *45°46′N 63°42′E*
Diirmentöbe *see* Diirmentobe
Dijlah *see* Tigris
99 H17 **Dijle** ≈ C Belgium
103 R8 **Dijon** *anc.* Dibio. Côte d'Or, C France *47°21′N 05°04′E*
93 H14 **Dikanäs** Västerbotten, N Sweden *65°15′N 16°00′E*
80 L12 **Dikhil** SW Djibouti *11°08′N 42°19′E*
136 B13 **Dikili** İzmir, W Turkey *39°05′N 26°52′E*
99 B17 **Diksmuide** *var.* Dixmuide, *Fr.* Dixmude. West-Vlaanderen, W Belgium *51°02′N 02°52′E*
122 K7 **Dikson** Krasnoyarskiy Kray, N Russian Federation *73°30′N 80°35′E*
115 K25 **Díkti** *var.* Dhíkti Ori. ▲▲ Kríti, Greece, E Mediterranean Sea
77 Z13 **Dikwa** Borno, NE Nigeria *12°00′N 13°57′E*
81 J15 **Dila** Southern Nationalities, S Ethiopia *06°19′N 38°16′E*
148 L7 **Dilārām** *prev.* Delārām. Nīmrōz, SW Afghanistan *32°11′N 63°27′E*
99 G18 **Dilbeek** Vlaams Brabant, C Belgium *50°51′N 04°16′E*
171 Q16 **Dili** *var.* Dilli, Dilly. ● (East Timor) N East Timor *08°33′S 125°34′E*
77 Y11 **Dilia** *var.* Dillia. ≈ SE Niger
Dilijan *see* Delijān
167 U13 **Di Linh** Lâm Đồng, S Vietnam *11°38′N 108°07′E*
101 G16 **Dillenburg** Hessen, W Germany *50°45′N 08°16′E*
25 Q13 **Dilley** Texas, SW USA *28°40′N 99°10′W*
Dilli *see* Dili, East Timor
Dilli *see* Delhi, India
Dillia *see* Dilia
80 E11 **Dilling** *var.* Ad Dalanj. Southern Kordofan, C Sudan *12°02′N 29°41′E*
101 D20 **Dillingen** Saarland, SW Germany *49°20′N 06°43′E*
101 J22 **Dillingen an der Donau** *var.* Dillingen. Bayern, S Germany *48°34′N 10°29′E*
39 O13 **Dillingham** Alaska, USA *59°03′N 158°30′W*
33 Q12 **Dillon** Montana, NW USA *45°14′N 112°38′W*
21 T12 **Dillon** South Carolina, SE USA *34°25′N 79°22′W*
31 T13 **Dillon Lake** ⊛ Ohio, N USA
Dilly *see* Dili
Dilman *see* Salmās
79 K24 **Dilolo** Katanga, S Dem. Rep. Congo *10°42′S 22°21′E*
115 J20 **Dílos** *island* Kykládes, Greece, Aegean Sea
141 Y11 **Dil', Ra's ad** *headland* E Oman *19°12′N 57°53′E*
29 R5 **Dilworth** Minnesota, N USA *46°53′N 96°38′W*
138 H7 **Dimashq** *var.* Ash Shām, Esh Sham, *Eng.* Damascus, *Fr.* Damas, *It.* Damasco. ● (Syria) Rīf Dimashq, SW Syria *33°30′N 36°19′E*
138 I7 **Dimashq** ✈ Rīf Dimashq, S Syria *33°30′N 36°19′E*
Dimashq, Muḩāfaẓat *see* Rīf Dimashq
79 L21 **Dimbelenge** Kasai-Occidental, C Dem. Rep. Congo *05°36′S 23°04′E*
77 N16 **Dimbokro** E Ivory Coast *06°43′N 04°46′W*
182 L11 **Dimboola** Victoria, SE Australia *36°29′S 142°03′E*
Dîmbovița *see* Dâmbovița
Dimitrov *see* Dymytrov
114 K11 **Dimitrovgrad** Khaskovo, S Bulgaria *42°03′N 25°36′E*
127 R5 **Dimitrovgrad** Ul'yanovskaya Oblast', W Russian Federation *54°14′N 49°37′E*
113 Q15 **Dimitrovgrad** *prev.* Caribrod. Serbia, SE Serbia *43°01′N 22°46′E*
Dimitrovo *see* Pernik
Dimlang *see* Vogel Peak
24 M3 **Dimmitt** Texas, SW USA *34°32′N 102°20′W*
114 F7 **Dimovo** Vidin, NW Bulgaria *43°46′N 22°47′E*
59 A16 **Dimpolis** Acre, W Brazil *09°52′S 71°51′W*
115 O23 **Dimyliá** Ródos, Dodekánisa, Greece, Aegean Sea *36°17′N 27°59′E*
171 Q6 **Dinagat Island** *island* S Philippines
153 S13 **Dinajpur** Rajshahi, NW Bangladesh *25°38′N 88°40′E*
102 I6 **Dinan** Côtes d'Armor, NW France *48°27′N 02°02′W*
99 I21 **Dinant** Namur, S Belgium *50°16′N 04°55′E*
136 E15 **Dinar** Afyon, SW Turkey *38°05′N 30°09′E*
112 F13 **Dinara** ▲ W Croatia *43°49′N 16°42′E*
Dinara *see* Dinaric Alps
102 I5 **Dinard** Ille-et-Vilaine, NW France *48°38′N 02°04′W*
112 F13 **Dinaric Alps** *var.* Dinara. ▲▲ Bosnia and Herzegovina/Croatia
143 N10 **Dīnār, Kūh-e** ▲ C Iran *30°51′N 51°36′E*
Dinbych *see* Denbigh
155 H22 **Dindigul** Tamil Nādu, SE India *10°23′N 78°E*
83 M19 **Dindiza** Gaza, S Mozambique *23°22′S 33°28′E*
79 H21 **Dinga** Bandundu, SW Dem. Rep. Congo *05°00′S 16°29′E*
149 V7 **Dinga** Punjab, E Pakistan *32°38′N 73°45′E*
Dingchang *see* Qinxian
158 L16 **Dinggyê** *var.* Gyangkar. Xizang Zizhiqu, W China *28°18′N 88°06′E*
97 A20 **Dingle** *Ir.* An Daingean. SW Ireland *52°09′N 10°16′W*
97 A20 **Dingle Bay** *Ir.* Bá an Daingin. *bay* SW Ireland
18 I13 **Dingmans Ferry** Pennsylvania, NE USA *41°12′N 74°51′W*
101 N22 **Dingolfing** Bayern, SE Germany *48°37′N 12°28′E*
171 O1 **Dingras** Luzon, N Philippines *18°06′N 120°43′E*
76 J13 **Dinguiraye** N Guinea *11°19′N 10°49′W*
96 I8 **Dingwall** N Scotland, United Kingdom *57°36′N 04°26′W*
159 V10 **Dingxi** Gansu, C China *35°36′N 104°33′E*
Ding Xian *see* Dingzhou
161 Q7 **Dingyuan** Anhui, E China *32°30′N 117°40′E*
161 O3 **Dingzhou** *prev.* Ding Xian. Hebei, E China *38°31′N 114°52′E*
167 U6 **Đinh Lâp** Lang Sơn, N Vietnam *21°33′N 107°03′E*
167 T13 **Đinh Quan** *var.* Tân Phu. Đông Nai, S Vietnam *11°11′N 107°20′E*
100 E13 **Dinkel** ≈ Germany/Netherlands
101 J21 **Dinkelsbühl** Bayern, S Germany *49°06′N 10°18′E*
101 D14 **Dinslaken** Nordrhein-Westfalen, W Germany *51°34′N 06°43′E*
35 R11 **Dinuba** California, W USA *36°32′N 119°23′W*
21 W7 **Dinwiddie** Virginia, NE USA *37°02′N 77°40′W*
98 N13 **Dinxperlo** Gelderland, E Netherlands *51°51′N 06°30′E*
Dio *see* Díon
Diófás *see* Nucet
76 M12 **Dioïla** Koulikoro, W Mali *12°28′N 06°43′W*
115 F14 **Díon** *var.* Dio; *anc.* Dium. *site of ancient city* Kentrikí Makedonía, N Greece
115 G19 **Dióryga Korinthou** *Eng.* Corinth Canal. *canal* S Greece
76 G12 **Diouloulou** SW Senegal *13°00′N 16°34′W*
77 N11 **Dioura** Mopti, W Mali *14°48′N 05°20′W*
76 G11 **Diourbel** W Senegal *14°39′N 16°12′W*
152 L10 **Dipāyal** Far Western, W Nepal *29°09′N 80°46′E*
121 R1 **Dipkarpaz** *Gk.* Rizokarpaso, Rizokárpason. NE Cyprus *35°36′N 34°23′E*
149 R17 **Diplo** Sind, SE Pakistan *24°29′N 69°36′E*
171 P7 **Dipolog** *var.* Dipolog City. Mindanao, S Philippines *08°31′N 123°20′E*
Dipolog City *see* Dipolog
185 C23 **Dipton** Southland, South Island, New Zealand *45°55′S 168°21′E*
77 O10 **Diré** Tombouctou, C Mali *16°12′N 03°31′W*
80 L13 **Dirē Dawa** Dirē Dawa, E Ethiopia *09°35′N 41°53′E*
Dirfis *see* Dírfys
115 H18 **Dírfys** *var.* Dirfis. ▲▲ Évvioa, C Greece
75 N9 **Dirj** *var.* Daraj, Darj. W Libya *30°09′N 10°26′E*
180 G10 **Dirk Hartog Island** *island* Western Australia
77 Y8 **Dirkou** Agadez, NE Niger *18°45′N 13°00′E*
181 X11 **Dirranbandi** Queensland, E Australia *28°37′S 148°13′E*
Dirri *see* Derri
Dirschau *see* Tczew
37 N6 **Dirty Devil River** ≈ Utah, W USA
32 E10 **Disappointment, Cape** *headland* Washington, NW USA *46°16′N 124°06′W*
180 L8 **Disappointment, Lake** *salt lake* Western Australia
183 R12 **Disaster Bay** *bay* New South Wales, SE Australia
44 J11 **Discovery Bay** C Jamaica *18°27′N 77°24′W*
182 K13 **Discovery Bay** *inlet* SE Australia
67 Y15 **Discovery II Fracture Zone** *tectonic feature* SW Indian Ocean
Discovery Seamount/Discovery Seamounts *see* Discovery Tablemounts
65 O19 **Discovery Tablemounts** *var.* Discovery Seamount, Discovery Seamounts. *undersea feature* SW Atlantic Ocean *42°00′S 00°10′E*
108 G9 **Disentis** *Rmsch.* Mustér. Graubünden, S Switzerland *46°43′N 08°52′E*
39 O10 **Dishna River** ≈ Alaska, USA
148 K10 **Dishū** *var.* Deshu; *prev.* Deh Shū. Helmand, S Afghanistan *30°28′N 63°21′E*
Disko Bugt *see* Qeqertarsuup Tunua
195 X4 **Dismal Mountains** ▲▲ Antarctica
28 M14 **Dismal River** ≈ Nebraska, C USA
Disna *see* Dzisna
99 L19 **Dison** Liège, E Belgium *50°37′N 05°52′E*
153 V12 **Dispur** *state capital* Assam, NE India *26°03′N 91°52′E*
15 R11 **Disraeli** Québec, SE Canada *45°58′N 71°21′W*
115 F18 **Dístomo** *prev.* Dhístomon. Stereá Elláda, C Greece *38°25′N 22°40′E*
Dístos, Límni *see* Dýstos, Límni
59 L18 **Distrito Federal** *Eng.* Federal District. ◈ *federal district* C Brazil
41 P14 **Distrito Federal** ◈ *federal district* S Mexico
54 L4 **Distrito Federal** *off.* Territorio Distrito Federal. ◈ *federal district* N Venezuela
Distrito Federal, Territorio *see* Distrito Federal
116 J10 **Ditrău** *Hung.* Ditró. Harghita, C Romania *46°49′N 25°31′E*
Ditró *see* Ditrău
154 B12 **Diu** Damān and Diu, W India *20°42′N 70°59′E*
Dium *see* Díon
109 S13 **Divača** SW Slovenia *45°40′N 13°58′E*
102 K5 **Dives** ≈ N France
33 Q11 **Divide** Montana, NW USA *45°44′N 112°47′W*
Divin *see* Dzivin
83 N18 **Divinhe** Sofala, E Mozambique *20°41′S 34°46′E*
59 L20 **Divinópolis** Minas Gerais, SE Brazil *20°08′S 44°55′W*
127 N13 **Divnoye** Stavropol'skiy Kray, SW Russian Federation *45°54′N 43°18′E*
76 M17 **Divo** S Ivory Coast *05°50′N 05°22′W*
Divodurum Mediomatricum *see* Metz
137 N13 **Divriği** Sivas, C Turkey *39°23′N 38°06′E*
Diwaniyah *see* Ad Dīwānīyah
14 J10 **Dix Milles, Lac** ⊛ Québec, SE Canada
14 M8 **Dix Milles, Lac des** ⊛ Québec, SE Canada
Dixmude/Dixmuide *see* Diksmuide
35 N7 **Dixon** California, W USA *38°19′N 121°49′W*
30 L10 **Dixon** Illinois, N USA *41°51′N 89°26′W*
20 I6 **Dixon** Kentucky, S USA *37°30′N 87°39′W*
27 V6 **Dixon** Missouri, C USA *37°59′N 92°05′W*
37 S9 **Dixon** New Mexico, SW USA *36°10′N 105°49′W*
39 Y15 **Dixon Entrance** *strait* Canada/USA
18 D14 **Dixonville** Pennsylvania, NE USA *40°43′N 79°01′W*
137 T13 **Diyadin** Ağrı, E Turkey *39°33′N 43°41′E*
Diyālá, Nahr *see* Sīrvān, Rūdkhāneh-ye
139 V5 **Diyālá, Sīrwan Nahr** *var.* Rudkhaneh-ye Sīrvān, Sīrwān. ≈ Iran/Iraq *see also* Sīrvān, Rudkhaneh-ye
137 P15 **Diyarbakır** *var.* Diarbekr; *anc.* Amida. Diyarbakır, SE Turkey *37°55′N 40°14′E*
137 P15 **Diyarbakır** *var.* Diarbekr. ◈ *province* SE Turkey
Dizful *see* Dezfūl
79 F16 **Dja** ≈ SE Cameroon
Djadié *see* Zadié
77 X7 **Djado** Agadez, NE Niger *21°00′N 12°11′E*
77 X6 **Djado, Plateau du** ▲ NE Niger
Djailolo *see* Halmahera, Pulau
Djajapura *see* Jayapura
Djakarta *see* Jakarta
Djakovo *see* Đakovo
79 G20 **Djambala** Plateaux, C Congo *02°32′S 14°43′E*
Djambi *see* Jambi
Djambi *see* Hari, Batang
74 M9 **Djanet** E Algeria *24°43′N 08°57′E*
74 M11 **Djanet** *prev.* Fort Charlet. SE Algeria *24°34′N 09°33′E*
Djaul *see* Dyaul Island
Djawa *see* Jawa
Djéblé *see* Jablah
78 I10 **Djédaa** Batha, C Chad *13°31′N 18°34′E*
74 J6 **Djelfa** *var.* El Djelfa. N Algeria *34°43′N 03°14′E*
79 M14 **Djéma** Haut-Mbomou, E Central African Republic *06°04′N 25°20′E*
Djember *see* Jember
Djeneponto *see* Jeneponto
77 N12 **Djenné** *var.* Jenné. Mopti, C Mali *13°55′N 04°31′W*
Djérablous *see* Jarābulus
Djerba *see* Jerba, Île de
79 F15 **Djérem** ≈ C Cameroon
Djevdjelija *see* Gevgelija
77 P11 **Djibo** N Burkina *14°09′N 01°38′W*
80 L12 **Djibouti** *var.* Jibuti. ● (Djibouti) E Djibouti *11°33′N 42°55′E*
80 L12 **Djibouti** *off.* Republic of Djibouti, *var.* Jibuti; *prev.* French Somaliland, French Territory of the Afars and Issas, *Fr.* Côte Française des Somalis, Territoire Français des Afars et des Issas. ◆ *republic* E Africa
80 L12 **Djibouti** ✈ C Djibouti *11°29′N 42°54′E*
Djibouti, Republic of *see* Djibouti
Djidjel/Djidjelli *see* Jijel
Djidji *see* Ivando
55 W10 **Djoemoe** Sipaliwini, C Surinam *04°00′N 55°27′W*
Djokjakarta *see* Yogyakarta
79 K21 **Djoku-Punda** Kasai-Occidental, S Dem. Rep. Congo *05°27′S 20°58′E*
79 K18 **Djolu** Equateur, N Dem. Rep. Congo *0°35′N 22°30′E*
Djombang *see* Jombang
Djorče Petrov *see* Đorče Petrov
79 F17 **Djoua** ≈ Congo/Gabon
77 R14 **Djougou** W Benin *09°42′N 01°38′E*
79 F16 **Djoum** Sud, S Cameroon *02°38′N 12°51′E*
78 I8 **Djourab, Erg du** *desert* N Chad
79 P17 **Djugu** Orientale, NE Dem. Rep. Congo *01°55′N 30°31′E*
Djumbir *see* Ďumbier
92 L3 **Djúpivogur** Austurland, SE Iceland *64°40′N 14°18′W*
94 L13 **Djura** Dalarna, C Sweden *60°37′N 15°00′E*
Djurdjevac *see* Đurđevac
D'Kar *see* Dekar
197 U6 **Dmitriya Lapteva, Proliv** *strait* N Russian Federation
126 J7 **Dmitriyev-L'govskiy** Kurskaya Oblast', W Russian Federation *52°08′N 35°09′E*
Dmitriyevsk *see* Makiyivka
126 K3 **Dmitrov** Moskovskaya Oblast', W Russian Federation *56°23′N 37°30′E*
Dmitrovichi *see* Dzmitravichy
126 J6 **Dmitrovsk-Orlovskiy** Orlovskaya Oblast', W Russian Federation *52°28′N 35°01′E*
117 R3 **Dmytrivka** Chernihivs'ka Oblast', N Ukraine *50°56′N 32°57′E*
Dnepr *see* Dnieper
Dneprodzerzhinsk *see* Romaniv
Dneprodzerzhinskoye Vodokhranilishche *see* Dniprodzerzhyns'ke Vodoskhovyshche
Dnepropetrovsk *see* Dnipropetrovs'k
Dnepropetrovskaya Oblast' *see* Dnipropetrovs'ka Oblast'
Dneprorudnoye *see* Dniprorudne
Dneprovskiy Liman *see* Dniprovs'kyy Lyman
Dneprovsko-Bugskiy Kanal *see* Dnyaprowska-Buhski Kanal
Dnestr *see* Dniester
Dnestrovskiy Liman *see* Dnistrovs'kyy Lyman
86 H11 **Dnieper** *Bel.* Dnyapro, *Rus.* Dnepr, *Ukr.* Dnipro. ≈ E Europe
117 P3 **Dnieper Lowland** *Bel.* Prydnyaprowskaya Nizina, *Ukr.* Prydniprovs'ka Nyzovyna. *lowlands* Belarus/Ukraine
116 M8 **Dniester** *Rom.* Nistru, *Rus.* Dnestr, *Ukr.* Dnister; *anc.* Tyras. ≈ Moldova/Ukraine
Dnipro *see* Dnieper
Dniprodzerzhyns'k *see* Romaniv
117 T7 **Dniprodzerzhyns'ke Vodoskhovyshche** *Rus.* Dneprodzerzhinskoye Vodokhranilishche. ⊠ C Ukraine
117 U7 **Dnipropetrovs'k** *Rus.* Dnepropetrovsk; *prev.* Yekaterinoslav. Dnipropetrovs'ka Oblast', E Ukraine *48°28′N 35°E*
117 U8 **Dnipropetrovs'k** ✈ Dnipropetrovs'ka Oblast', S Ukraine *48°20′N 35°04′E*
Dnipropetrovs'k *see* Dnipropetrovs'ka Oblast'
117 T7 **Dnipropetrovs'ka Oblast'** *var.* Dnipropetrovs'k, *Rus.* Dnepropetrovskaya Oblast'. ◈ *province* E Ukraine
117 U9 **Dniprorudne** *Rus.* Dneprorudnoye. Zaporiz'ka Oblast', SE Ukraine *47°21′N 35°00′E*
117 Q11 **Dniprovs'kyy Lyman** *Rus.* Dneprovskiy Liman. *bay* S Ukraine
Dnister *see* Dniester
117 O11 **Dnistrovs'kyy Lyman** *Rus.* Dnestrovskiy Liman. *inlet* S Ukraine
124 G14 **Dno** Pskovskaya Oblast', W Russian Federation *57°48′N 29°58′E*
Dnyapro *see* Dnieper
119 H20 **Dnyaprowska-Buhski Kanal** *Rus.* Dneprovsko-Bugskiy Kanal. *canal* SW Belarus
13 O14 **Doaktown** New Brunswick, SE Canada *46°34′N 66°06′W*
78 H13 **Doba** Logone-Oriental, S Chad *08°40′N 16°50′E*
118 E9 **Dobele** *Ger.* Doblen. W Latvia *56°36′N 23°14′E*
101 N16 **Döbeln** Sachsen, E Germany *51°07′N 13°07′E*
171 U12 **Doberai, Jazirah** *Dut.* Vogelkop. *peninsula* Papua, E Indonesia
110 F10 **Dobiegniew** *Ger.* Lubuskie, Woldenberg Neumark. Lubuskie, W Poland *52°58′N 15°43′E*
Doblen *see* Dobele
81 K18 **Dobli** *spring/well* SW Somalia *0°24′N 41°18′E*
112 H11 **Doboj** Republiks Srpska, N Bosnia and Herzegovina *44°45′N 18°03′E*
143 R12 **Doborjī** *var.* Fūrg. Fārs, S Iran *28°16′N 55°13′E*
110 L8 **Dobre Miasto** *Ger.* Guttstadt. Warmińsko-mazurskie, NE Poland *53°59′N 20°25′E*
114 N7 **Dobrich** *Rom.* Bazargic; *prev.* Tolbukhin. Dobrich, NE Bulgaria *43°35′N 27°49′E*
114 N7 **Dobrich** ◈ *province* NE Bulgaria
126 M8 **Dobrinka** Lipetskaya Oblast', W Russian Federation *52°10′N 40°30′E*
126 M7 **Dobrinka** Volgogradskaya Oblast', SW Russian Federation *50°52′N 41°48′E*
Dobrla Vas *see* Eberndorf
111 I15 **Dobrodzień** *Ger.* Guttentag. Opolskie, S Poland *50°43′N 18°24′E*

◆ Country
● Country Capital
◇ Dependent Territory
○ Dependent Territory Capital
◈ Administrative Regions
✈ International Airport
▲ Mountain
▲▲ Mountain Range
Volcano
≈ River
⊛ Lake
⊠ Reservoir

Dobrogea *see* Dobruja
117 W7 **Dobropillya** *Rus.* Dobropol'ye. Donets'ka Oblast', SE Ukraine *48°25′N 37°02′E*
Dobropol'ye *see* Dobropillya
117 P8 **Dobrovelychkivka** Kirovohrads'ka Oblast', C Ukraine *48°22′N 31°12′E*
Dobrudja/Dobrudzha *see* Dobruja
114 O7 **Dobruja** *var.* Dobrudja, *Bul.* Dobrudzha, *Rom.* Dobrogea. *physical region* Bulgaria/Romania
119 P19 **Dobrush** Homyel'skaya Voblasts', SE Belarus *52°25′N 31°19′E*
125 U14 **Dobryanka** Permskiy Kray, NW Russian Federation *58°28′N 56°27′E*
117 P2 **Dobryanka** Chernihivs'ka Oblast', N Ukraine *52°03′N 31°09′E*
Dobryn' *see* Dabryn'
21 R8 **Dobson** North Carolina, SE USA *36°25′N 80°45′W*
59 N20 **Doce, Rio** ≈ SE Brazil
93 I16 **Docksta** Västernorrland, C Sweden *63°06′N 18°22′E*
41 N10 **Doctor Arroyo** Nuevo León, NE Mexico *23°40′N 100°09′W*
62 L4 **Doctor Pedro P. Peña** Boquerón, W Paraguay *22°22′S 62°23′W*
171 S11 **Dodaga** Pulau Halmahera, E Indonesia *01°06′N 128°10′E*
155 G21 **Dodda Betta** ▲ S India *11°28′N 76°44′E*
Dodecanese *see* Dodekánisa
115 M22 **Dodekánisa** *var.* Nóties Sporádes, *Eng.* Dodecanese; *prev.* Dhodhekánisos, Dodekanisos. *island group* SE Greece
Dodekanisos *see* Dodekánisa
26 J6 **Dodge City** Kansas, C USA *37°45′N 100°01′W*
30 K9 **Dodgeville** Wisconsin, N USA *42°57′N 90°08′W*
97 H25 **Dodman Point** *headland* SW England, United Kingdom *50°13′N 04°47′W*
81 J14 **Dodola** Oromīya, C Ethiopia *07°00′N 39°15′E*
81 H22 **Dodoma** ● (Tanzania) Dodoma, C Tanzania *06°11′S 35°45′E*
81 H22 **Dodoma** ◈ *region* C Tanzania
115 C16 **Dodóni** *var.* Dhodhóni. *site of ancient city* Ípeiros, W Greece
33 U7 **Dodson** Montana, NW USA *48°25′N 108°18′W*
25 P3 **Dodson** Texas, SW USA *34°46′N 100°01′W*
98 M12 **Doesburg** Gelderland, E Netherlands *52°01′N 06°08′E*
98 N12 **Doetinchem** Gelderland, E Netherlands *51°58′N 06°17′E*
158 L12 **Dogai Coring** *var.* Lake Montcalm. ◎ W China
137 N15 **Doğanşehir** Malatya, C Turkey *38°07′N 37°54′E*
84 E9 **Dogger Bank** *undersea feature* C North Sea *55°00′N 03°00′E*
23 S10 **Dog Island** *island* Florida, SE USA
14 C7 **Dog Lake** ◎ Ontario, S Canada
106 B9 **Dogliani** Piemonte, NE Italy *44°33′N 07°55′E*
164 H11 **Dōgo** *island* Oki-shotō, SW Japan
143 N10 **Do Gonbadān** *var.* Dow Gonbadān, Gonbadān. Kohkīlūyeh va Būyer AḤmad, SW Iran *30°12′N 50°48′E*
77 S12 **Dogondoutchi** Dosso, SW Niger *13°36′N 04°03′E*
137 T13 **Doğubayazıt** Ağrı, E Turkey *39°33′N 44°07′E*
137 P12 **Doğu Karadeniz Dağları** *var.* Anadolu Dağları. ▲▲ NE Turkey
158 K16 **Dogxung Zangbo** ≈ W China
Doha *see* Ad Dawḩah
Doha *see* Ad Dawḩah
Dohad *see* Dāhod
Dohuk *see* Dahūk
159 N16 **Doilungdêqên** *var.* Namka. Xizang Zizhiqu, W China *29°41′N 90°58′E*
114 F12 **Doïráni, Límni** *var.* Limni Doïranis, *Bul.* Ezero Doyransko. ◎ N Greece
Doire *see* Londonderry
99 H22 **Doische** Namur, S Belgium *50°09′N 04°43′E*
59 P17 **Dois de Julho** ✈ (Salvador) Bahia, NE Brazil *12°04′S 38°58′W*
60 H12 **Dois Vizinhos** Paraná, S Brazil *25°47′S 53°03′W*
80 H10 **Doka** Gedaref, E Sudan *13°30′N 35°47′E*
Doka *see* Kéita, Bahr
139 T3 **Dokan** *var.* Dūkān. As Sulaymānīyah, E Iraq *35°55′N 44°58′E*
94 H13 **Dokka** Oppland, S Norway *60°49′N 10°04′E*
98 L5 **Dokkum** Fryslân, N Netherlands *53°20′N 06°E*
98 L5 **Dokkumer Ee** ≈ N Netherlands
76 K13 **Doko** NE Guinea *11°46′N 08°58′W*
Dokshitsy *see* Dokshytsy
118 K13 **Dokshytsy** *Rus.* Dokshitsy. Vitsyebskaya Voblasts', N Belarus *54°54′N 27°46′E*
117 X8 **Dokuchayevs'k** *var.* Dokuchayevsk. Donets'ka Oblast', SE Ukraine *47°43′N 37°41′E*
Dokuchayevsk *see* Dokuchayevs'k
Dolak, Pulau *see* Yos Sudarso, Pulau
29 P9 **Doland** South Dakota, N USA *44°51′N 98°06′W*
63 J18 **Dolavón** Chaco, S Argentina *43°16′S 65°44′W*
15 P6 **Dolbeau** Québec, SE Canada *48°52′N 72°15′W*
15 P6 **Dolbeau-Mistassini** Québec, SE Canada *48°54′N 72°13′W*
102 I5 **Dol-de-Bretagne** Ille-et-Vilaine, NW France *48°33′N 01°45′W*
64 J13 **Doldrums Fracture Zone** *tectonic feature* W Atlantic Ocean
103 S8 **Dôle** Jura, E France *47°05′N 05°30′E*
97 J19 **Dolgellau** NW Wales, United Kingdom *52°45′N 03°54′W*
Dolginovo *see* Dawhinava
Dolgi, Ostrov *see* Dolgiy, Ostrov
125 U2 **Dolgiy, Ostrov** *var.* Ostrov Dolgi. *island* NW Russian Federation
162 J9 **Dölgöön** Övörhangay, C Mongolia *45°57′N 103°14′E*
107 C20 **Dolianova** Sardegna, Italy, C Mediterranean Sea *39°23′N 09°08′E*
Dolina *see* Dolyna
123 T13 **Dolinsk** Ostrov Sakhalin, Sakhalinskaya Oblast', SE Russian Federation *47°20′N 142°52′E*
Dolinskaya *see* Dolyns'ka
79 F21 **Dolisie** *prev.* Loubomo. Niari, S Congo *04°12′S 12°41′E*
116 G14 **Dolj** ◈ *county* SW Romania
98 P5 **Dollard** *bay* NW Germany
194 J5 **Dolleman Island** *island* Antarctica
114 K8 **Dolna Oryakhovitsa** Veliko Tŭrnovo, N Bulgaria *43°09′N 25°44′E*
114 N9 **Dolni Chiflik** Varna, E Bulgaria *42°59′N 27°43′E*
114 I8 **Dolni Dŭbnik** Pleven, N Bulgaria *43°24′N 24°25′E*
114 F8 **Dolni Lom** Vidin, NW Bulgaria *43°31′N 22°46′E*
Dolnja Lendava *see* Lendava
129 F14 **Dolnośląskie** ◈ *province* SW Poland
111 K18 **Dolný Kubín** *Hung.* Alsókubin. Žilinský Kraj, N Slovakia *49°12′N 19°17′E*
106 H8 **Dolo** Veneto, NE Italy *45°25′N 12°06′E*
Dolomites/Dolomiti *see* Dolomitiche, Alpi
106 H6 **Dolomitiche, Alpi** *var.* Dolomiti, *Eng.* Dolomites. ▲▲ NE Italy
Dolonnur *see* Duolun
Doloon *see* Tsogt-Ovoo
61 E21 **Dolores** Buenos Aires, E Argentina *36°21′S 57°39′W*
42 E3 **Dolores** Petén, N Guatemala *16°33′N 89°26′W*
171 Q5 **Dolores** Samar, C Philippines *12°01′N 125°27′E*
105 S12 **Dolores** Valenciana, E Spain *38°09′N 00°45′W*
61 D19 **Dolores** Soriano, SW Uruguay *33°34′S 58°15′W*
41 N12 **Dolores Hidalgo** *var.* Ciudad de Dolores Hidalgo. Guanajuato, C Mexico *21°10′N 100°55′W*
8 J7 **Dolphin and Union Strait** *strait* Northwest Territories/Nunavut, N Canada
65 D23 **Dolphin, Cape** *headland* East Falkland, Falkland Islands *51°15′S 58°57′W*
44 H12 **Dolphin Head** *hill* W Jamaica
83 B21 **Dolphin Head** *var.* Cape Dernberg. *headland* SW Namibia *25°33′S 14°36′E*
110 G12 **Dolsk** *Ger.* Dolzig. Weilkopolskie, C Poland *51°59′N 17°03′E*
167 S8 **Đô Lương** Nghê An, N Vietnam *18°51′N 105°19′E*
116 I6 **Dolyna** *Rus.* Dolina. Ivano-Frankivs'ka Oblast', W Ukraine *48°58′N 24°01′E*
117 R8 **Dolyns'ka** *Rus.* Dolinskaya. Kirovohrads'ka Oblast', S Ukraine *48°06′N 32°46′E*
Dolzig *see* Dolsk
Domachëvo/Domaczewo *see* Damachava
117 P9 **Domanivka** Mykolayivs'ka Oblast', S Ukraine *47°40′N 30°56′E*
153 S13 **Domar** Rajshahi, N Bangladesh *26°08′N 88°57′E*
108 I9 **Domat/Ems** Graubünden, SE Switzerland *46°50′N 09°28′E*
111 A18 **Domažlice** *Ger.* Taus. Plzeňský Kraj, W Czech Republic *49°26′N 12°54′E*
127 X8 **Dombarovskiy** Orenburgskaya Oblast', W Russian Federation *50°53′N 59°18′E*
94 G10 **Dombås** Oppland, S Norway *62°04′N 09°07′E*
83 M17 **Dombe** Manica, C Mozambique *19°59′S 33°24′E*
82 A13 **Dombe Grande** Benguela, C Angola *12°57′S 13°07′E*
103 R10 **Dombes** *physical region* E France
111 I25 **Dombóvár** Tolna, S Hungary *46°24′N 18°09′E*
99 D14 **Domburg** Zeeland, SW Netherlands *51°34′N 03°30′E*
58 L13 **Dom Eliseu** Pará, NE Brazil *04°02′S 47°31′W*
Domel Island *see* Letsôk-aw Kyun
103 O11 **Dôme, Puy de** ▲ C France *45°46′N 03°00′E*
36 H13 **Dome Rock Mountains** ▲▲ Arizona, SW USA
Domesnes, Cape *see* Kolkasrags
62 G8 **Domeyko** Atacama, N Chile *28°58′S 70°54′W*
62 H5 **Domeyko, Cordillera** ▲▲ N Chile
102 K5 **Domfront** Orne, N France *48°35′N 00°39′W*
171 X13 **Dom, Gunung** ▲ Papua, E Indonesia *02°41′S 137°00′E*
45 X11 **Dominica** *off.* Commonwealth of Dominica. ◆ *republic* E West Indies
47 S3 **Dominica** *island* Dominica
Dominica Channel *see* Martinique Passage
Dominica, Commonwealth of *see* Dominica
43 N15 **Dominical** Puntarenas, SE Costa Rica *09°16′N 83°52′W*
45 Q8 **Dominican Republic** ◆ *republic* C West Indies
45 X11 **Dominica Passage** *passage* E Caribbean Sea
99 K14 **Dommel** ≈ S Netherlands
81 O14 **Domo** Sumalē, E Ethiopia *07°53′N 46°55′E*
126 L4 **Domodedovo** ✈ (Moskva) Moskovskaya Oblast', W Russian Federation *55°19′N 37°55′E*
106 C6 **Domodossola** Piemonte, NE Italy *46°07′N 08°20′E*
115 F17 **Domokós** *var.* Dhomokós. Stereá Elláda, C Greece *39°07′N 22°18′E*
172 I14 **Domoni** Anjouan, SE Comoros *12°15′S 44°39′E*
61 G16 **Dom Pedrito** Rio Grande do Sul, S Brazil *31°00′S 54°40′W*
Dompoe *see* Dompu
170 M16 **Dompu** *prev.* Dompoe. Sumbawa, C Indonesia *08°30′S 118°28′E*
Domschale *see* Domžale
62 H13 **Domuyo, Volcán** ⛰ W Argentina *36°36′S 70°22′W*
109 U11 **Domžale** *Ger.* Domschale. C Slovenia *46°09′N 14°33′E*
127 O10 **Don** *var.* Duna, Tanais. ≈ SW Russian Federation
96 K9 **Don** ≈ NE Scotland, United Kingdom
182 M11 **Donald** Victoria, SE Australia *36°27′S 143°03′E*
22 J9 **Donaldsonville** Louisiana, S USA *30°06′N 90°59′W*
23 S8 **Donalsonville** Georgia, SE USA *31°02′N 84°52′W*
Donau *see* Danube
101 G23 **Donaueschingen** Baden-Württemberg, SW Germany *47°57′N 08°30′E*
101 K22 **Donaumoos** *wetland* S Germany
101 K22 **Donauwörth** Bayern, S Germany *48°43′N 10°46′E*
109 U7 **Donawitz** Steiermark, SE Austria *47°23′N 15°00′E*
117 X7 **Donbass** *industrial region* Russian Federation/Ukraine
104 K11 **Don Benito** Extremadura, W Spain *38°57′N 05°52′W*
97 M17 **Doncaster** *anc.* Danum. N England, United Kingdom *53°32′N 01°07′W*
44 K12 **Don Christophers Point** *headland* C Jamaica *18°19′N 76°48′W*
55 V9 **Donderkamp** Sipaliwini, NW Suriname *05°18′N 56°22′W*
82 B12 **Dondo** Cuanza Norte, NW Angola *09°40′S 14°24′E*
171 O12 **Dondo** Sulawesi, N Indonesia *0°54′S 121°33′E*
83 N17 **Dondo** Sofala, C Mozambique *19°41′S 34°45′E*
155 K26 **Dondra Head** *headland* S Sri Lanka *05°57′N 80°33′E*
Donduşani *see* Donduşeni
116 M8 **Donduşeni** *var.* Donduşani, *Rus.* Dondyushany. N Moldova *48°13′N 27°38′E*
Dondyushany *see* Donduşeni
97 D15 **Donegal** *Ir.* Dún na nGall. Donegal, NW Ireland *54°39′N 08°06′W*
97 D14 **Donegal** *Ir.* Dún na nGall. *cultural region* NW Ireland
97 C15 **Donegal Bay** *Ir.* Bá Dhún na nGall. *bay* NW Ireland
84 K10 **Donets** ≈ Russian Federation/Ukraine
117 X8 **Donets'k** *Rus.* Donetsk; *prev.* Stalino. Donets'ka Oblast', E Ukraine *47°58′N 37°50′E*
117 W8 **Donets'k** ✈ Donets'ka Oblast', E Ukraine *48°03′N 37°44′E*
Donets'k *see* Donets'ka Oblast'
117 W8 **Donets'ka Oblast'** *var.* Donets'k, *Rus.* Donetskaya Oblast'; *prev. Rus.* Stalinskaya Oblast'. ◈ *province* SE Ukraine
Donetskaya Oblast' *see* Donets'ka Oblast'
67 P8 **Donga** ≈ Cameroon/Nigeria
157 O13 **Dongchuan** Yunnan, SW China *26°09′N 103°10′E*
161 Q14 **Dongchuan Dao** *prev.* Dongshan Dao. *island* SE China
99 I14 **Dongen** Noord-Brabant, S Netherlands *51°38′N 04°56′E*
160 K17 **Dongfang** *var.* Basuo. Hainan, S China *19°05′N 108°40′E*
163 Z7 **Dongfanghong** Heilongjiang, NE China *46°13′N 133°13′E*
163 W11 **Dongfeng** Jilin, NE China *42°39′N 125°33′E*
171 N12 **Donggala** Sulawesi, C Indonesia *0°40′S 119°44′E*
163 V13 **Donggang** *var.* Dadong; *prev.* Donggou. Liaoning, NE China *39°52′N 124°08′E*
Donggou *see* Donggang
161 O14 **Dongguan** Guangdong, S China *23°03′N 113°43′E*
167 T9 **Đông Ha** Quang Tri, C Vietnam *16°45′N 107°10′E*
163 Y14 **Donghae** *prev.* Tonghae. NE South Korea *37°26′N 129°09′E*
Dong Hai *see* East China Sea
160 M16 **Donghai Dao** *island* S China
Dong He *see* Omon Gol
Donghe *see* Wangcang
167 T9 **Đông Hơi** Quang Binh, C Vietnam *17°32′N 106°35′E*
Donghua *see* Huating
Donghuang *see* Xishui
108 H10 **Dongio** Ticino, S Switzerland *46°27′N 08°58′E*
Dongkan *see* Binhai
160 L11 **Dongkou** Hunan, S China *27°06′N 110°35′E*
167 S8 **Đông Lê** Quang Binh, C Vietnam *17°52′N 105°49′E*
Dongliao *see* Liaoyuan
Dong-nai *see* Đông Nai, Sông
167 U13 **Đông Nai, Sông** *var.* Dong-nai, Dong Noi, Donnai. ≈ S Vietnam
161 N14 **Dongnan Qiuling** *plateau* SE China
163 Y9 **Dongning** Heilongjiang, NE China *44°01′N 131°03′E*
Dong Noi *see* Đông Nai, Sông
83 C14 **Dongo** Huíla, C Angola *14°35′S 15°51′E*
80 E7 **Dongola** *var.* Dongola, Dunqulah. Northern, N Sudan *19°10′N 30°27′E*
79 I17 **Dongou** Likouala, NE Congo *02°05′N 18°E*
Đông Phu *see* Đông Xoai
Dongping *see* Anhua
Dong Rak, Phanom *see* Dângrêk, Chuŏr Phnum
Dongshan Dao *see* Dongchuan Dao
Dongsha Qundao *see* Tungsha Tao
Dongsheng *see* Ordos
161 S13 **Dongshi** *Jap.* Tōsei; *prev.* Tungshih. N Taiwan *24°13′N 120°54′E*
161 R7 **Dongtai** Jiangsu, E China *32°50′N 120°22′E*
161 N10 **Dongting Hu** *var.* Tung-t'ing Hu. ◎ S China
161 P10 **Dongxiang** *var.* Xiaogang. Jiangxi, S China *28°16′N 116°32′E*
167 T13 **Đông Xoai** *var.* Đông Phu. Sông Be, S Vietnam *11°31′N 106°55′E*
161 Q4 **Dongying** Shandong, E China *37°27′N 118°01′E*
27 X8 **Doniphan** Missouri, C USA *36°39′N 90°51′W*
Donja Łužica *see* Niederlausitz
10 G7 **Donjek** ≈ Yukon Territory, W Canada
112 E11 **Donji Lapac** Lika-Senj, W Croatia *44°33′N 15°58′E*
112 H8 **Donji Miholjac** Osijek-Baranja, NE Croatia *45°45′N 18°10′E*
112 P12 **Donji Milanovac** Serbia, E Serbia *44°27′N 22°06′E*
112 G12 **Donji Vakuf** *var.* Srbobran. ◈ Federacija Bosna I Hercegovina, C Bosnia and Herzegovina
98 M6 **Donkerbroek** Fryslân, N Netherlands *52°58′N 05°15′E*
167 P11 **Don Muang** ✈ (Krung Thep) Nonthaburi, C Thailand *13°51′N 100°40′E*
25 S17 **Donna** Texas, SW USA *26°10′N 98°03′W*
15 Q10 **Donnacona** Québec, SE Canada *46°41′N 71°46′W*
Donnai *see* Đông Nai, Sông
29 Y16 **Donnellson** Iowa, C USA *40°38′N 91°33′W*
11 O13 **Donnelly** Alberta, W Canada *55°42′N 117°06′W*
35 P6 **Donner Pass** *Pass* California, W USA
101 F19 **Donnersberg** ▲ W Germany *49°37′N 07°54′E*
Donoso *see* Miguel de la Borda
105 P2 **Donostia-San Sebastián** País Vasco, N Spain *43°19′N 01°59′W*
115 K21 **Donoúsa** *var.* Donoússa. *island* Kykládes, Greece, Aegean Sea
Donoússa *see* Donoúsa
35 P8 **Don Pedro Reservoir** ▣ California, W USA
Donqola *see* Dongola
126 L5 **Donskoy** Tul'skaya Oblast', W Russian Federation *54°02′N 38°27′E*
81 L16 **Doolow** Sumalē, E Ethiopia *04°10′N 42°05′E*
39 Q7 **Doonerak, Mount** ▲ Alaska, USA *67°54′N 150°33′W*
98 J12 **Doorn** Utrecht, C Netherlands *52°02′N 05°21′E*
Doornik *see* Tournai
31 N6 **Door Peninsula** *peninsula* Wisconsin, N USA
80 P13 **Dooxo Nugaaleed** *var.* Nogal Valley. *valley* E Somalia
Do Qu *see* Da Qu
106 B7 **Dora Baltea** *anc.* Duria Major. ≈ NW Italy
180 K7 **Dora, Lake** *salt lake* Western Australia
106 A8 **Dora Riparia** *anc.* Duria Minor. ≈ NW Italy
Dorbiljin *see* Emin
Dorbod/Dorbod Mongolzu Zizhixian *see* Taikang
Dorbod Mongolzu Zizhixian *see* Taikang
113 N18 **Dorče Petrov** *var.* Đjorče Petrov, Gorče Petrov. N Macedonia *42°01′N 21°21′E*
14 F16 **Dorchester** Ontario, S Canada *43°00′N 81°04′W*
97 L24 **Dorchester** *anc.* Durnovaria. S England, United Kingdom *50°43′N 02°26′W*
9 P7 **Dorchester, Cape** *headland* Baffin Island, Nunavut, NE Canada *65°25′N 77°25′W*
83 D19 **Dordabis** Khomas, C Namibia *22°57′S 17°39′E*
102 L12 **Dordogne** ◈ *department* SW France
103 N12 **Dordogne** ≈ W France
98 H13 **Dordrecht** *var.* Dordt, Dort. Zuid-Holland, SW Netherlands *51°48′N 04°40′E*
Dordt *see* Dordrecht
103 P11 **Dore** ≈ C France
11 S13 **Doré Lake** Saskatchewan, C Canada *54°37′N 107°36′W*
103 O12 **Dore, Monts** ▲▲ C France
101 M23 **Dorfen** Bayern, SE Germany *48°16′N 12°06′E*
107 D18 **Dorgali** Sardegna, Italy, C Mediterranean Sea *40°18′N 09°34′E*
159 N11 **Dorgê Co** *var.* Elsen Nur. ◎ C China
162 E6 **Dörgön** *var.* Seer. Hovd, W Mongolia *48°18′N 92°37′E*
162 F7 **Dörgön Nuur** ◎ NW Mongolia
77 Q12 **Dori** N Burkina *14°03′N 00°02′W*
83 E24 **Doring** ≈ S South Africa
101 E16 **Dormagen** Nordrhein-Westfalen, W Germany *51°06′N 06°49′E*
103 P4 **Dormans** Marne, N France *49°03′N 03°44′E*
108 E6 **Dornach** Solothurn, NW Switzerland *47°29′N 07°37′E*
Dorna Watra *see* Vatra Dornei
108 J7 **Dornbirn** Vorarlberg, W Austria *47°25′N 09°46′E*
96 I7 **Dornoch** N Scotland, United Kingdom *57°52′N 04°01′W*
96 J7 **Dornoch Firth** *inlet* N Scotland, United Kingdom
163 P7 **Dornod** ◈ *province* E Mongolia
163 N10 **Dornogovĭ** ◈ *province* SE Mongolia
77 P10 **Doro** Tombouctou, S Mali *16°07′N 00°57′W*
116 L14 **Dorobanţu** Călăraşi, S Romania *44°15′N 26°55′E*
111 J22 **Dorog** Komárom-Esztergom, N Hungary *47°43′N 18°42′E*
126 I4 **Dorogobuzh** Smolenskaya Oblast', W Russian Federation *54°56′N 33°16′E*
116 K8 **Dorohoi** Botoşani, NE Romania *47°57′N 26°24′E*
93 H15 **Dorotea** Västerbotten, N Sweden *64°17′N 16°30′E*
180 G10 **Dorre Island** *island* Western Australia
183 U5 **Dorrigo** New South Wales, SE Australia *30°22′S 152°43′E*
35 N1 **Dorris** California, W USA *41°58′N 121°54′W*
14 H13 **Dorset** Ontario, SE Canada *45°12′N 78°52′W*
97 K23 **Dorset** *cultural region* S England, United Kingdom
101 E14 **Dorsten** Nordrhein-Westfalen, W Germany *51°38′N 06°58′E*
Dort *see* Dordrecht
101 F15 **Dortmund** Nordrhein-Westfalen, W Germany *51°31′N 07°28′E*
100 F12 **Dortmund-Ems-Kanal** *canal* W Germany
136 L17 **Dörtyol** Hatay, S Turkey *36°51′N 36°11′E*
Do Rūd *see* Dow Rūd
79 O15 **Doruma** Orientale, N Dem. Rep. Congo *04°35′N 27°43′E*
15 O12 **Dorval** ✈ (Montréal) Québec, SE Canada *45°27′N 73°46′W*
162 F7 **Dörvöljin** *var.* Buga. Dzavhan, W Mongolia *47°42′N 94°53′E*
45 T5 **Dos Bocas, Lago** ◎ C Puerto Rico
104 K14 **Dos Hermanas** Andalucía, S Spain *37°16′N 05°55′W*
Dospad Dagh *see* Rhodope Mountains
35 P10 **Dos Palos** California, W USA *37°00′N 120°39′W*
114 I11 **Dospat** Smolyan, S Bulgaria *41°39′N 24°10′E*
114 H11 **Dospat, Yazovir** ▣ SW Bulgaria
100 M11 **Dosse** ≈ NE Germany
77 S12 **Dosso** Dosso, SW Niger *13°03′N 03°10′E*
77 S12 **Dosso** ◈ *department* SW Niger
144 G12 **Dossor** Atyrau, SW Kazakhstan *47°31′N 53°01′E*
147 O10 **Do'stlik** Jizzax Viloyati, C Uzbekistan *40°37′N 67°59′E*
147 V9 **Dostuk** Narynskaya Oblast', C Kyrgyzstan *41°19′N 75°40′E*
145 X13 **Dostyk** *prev.* Druzhba. Almaty, SE Kazakhstan *45°15′N 82°29′E*
23 R7 **Dothan** Alabama, S USA *31°13′N 85°23′W*
39 T9 **Dot Lake** Alaska, USA *63°39′N 144°10′W*
118 F12 **Dotnuva** Kaunas, C Lithuania *55°23′N 23°53′E*
99 D19 **Dottignies** Hainaut, W Belgium *50°43′N 03°16′E*
103 P2 **Douai** *prev.* Douay; *anc.* Duacum. Nord, N France *50°22′N 03°04′E*
14 L9 **Douaire, Lac** ◎ Québec, SE Canada
79 D16 **Douala** *var.* Duala. Littoral, W Cameroon *04°04′N 09°43′E*
79 D16 **Douala** ✈ Littoral, W Cameroon *03°57′N 09°48′E*
102 F6 **Douarnenez** Finistère, NW France *48°05′N 04°20′W*
102 E6 **Douarnenez, Baie de** *bay* NW France
Douay *see* Douai
25 O6 **Double Mountain Fork Brazos River** ≈ Texas, SW USA
23 O3 **Double Springs** Alabama, S USA *34°09′N 87°24′W*
103 T8 **Doubs** ◈ *department* E France
108 C8 **Doubs** ≈ France/Switzerland
185 A22 **Doubtful Sound** *sound* South Island, New Zealand
184 J2 **Doubtless Bay** *bay* North Island, New Zealand
25 X9 **Doucette** Texas, SW USA *30°48′N 94°25′W*
102 K8 **Doué-la-Fontaine** Maine-et-Loire, NW France *47°12′N 00°16′W*
77 O11 **Douentza** Mopti, S Mali *14°59′N 02°57′W*
65 E24 **Douglas** East Falkland, Falkland Islands
97 I16 **Douglas** ○ (Isle of Man) E Isle of Man *54°09′N 04°28′W*
83 H23 **Douglas** Northern Cape, C South Africa *29°04′S 23°47′E*
39 X13 **Douglas** Alexander Archipelago, Alaska, USA *58°12′N 134°18′W*
37 O17 **Douglas** Arizona, SW USA *31°20′N 109°32′W*
23 U7 **Douglas** Georgia, SE USA *31°30′N 82°51′W*
33 Y15 **Douglas** Wyoming, C USA *42°48′N 105°23′W*
21 O7 **Douglas Cape** *headland* Alaska, N USA *64°59′N 166°41′W*
10 J14 **Douglas Channel** *channel* British Columbia, W Canada
182 G3 **Douglas Creek** *seasonal river* South Australia
31 P5 **Douglas Lake** ◎ Michigan, N USA
21 O9 **Douglas Lake** ▣ Tennessee, S USA
39 Q13 **Douglas, Mount** ▲ Alaska, USA *58°51′N 153°31′W*
194 I6 **Douglas Range** ▲▲ Alexander Island, Antarctica
161 S14 **Douliu** *prev.* Touliu. C Taiwan *23°44′N 120°27′E*
103 O2 **Doullens** Somme, N France *50°09′N 02°21′E*
Douma *see* Dūmā
79 F15 **Doumé** Est, E Cameroon *04°14′N 13°27′E*
99 E21 **Dour** Hainaut, S Belgium *50°24′N 03°47′E*
59 K18 **Dourada, Serra** ▲▲ S Brazil
59 I21 **Dourados** Mato Grosso do Sul, S Brazil *22°09′S 54°52′W*
103 N5 **Dourdan** Essonne, N France *48°33′N 01°58′E*
104 I6 **Douro** *Sp.* Duero. ≈ Portugal/Spain *see also* Duero
Douro *see* Duero
104 G6 **Douro Litoral** *former province* N Portugal
Douvres *see* Dover
102 K15 **Douze** ≈ SW France
183 P17 **Dover** Tasmania, SE Australia *43°19′S 147°01′E*
97 Q22 **Dover** *Fr.* Douvres, *Lat.* Dubris Portus. SE England, United Kingdom *51°08′N 03°E*
21 Y3 **Dover** *state capital* Delaware, NE USA *39°09′N 75°31′W*
19 P9 **Dover** New Hampshire, NE USA *43°10′N 70°50′W*
18 J14 **Dover** New Jersey, NE USA *40°51′N 74°33′W*
31 U12 **Dover** Ohio, N USA *40°31′N 81°28′W*
20 H8 **Dover** Tennessee, S USA *36°30′N 87°50′W*
97 Q23 **Dover, Strait of** *var.* Straits of Dover, *Fr.* Pas de Calais. *strait* England, United Kingdom/France
Dover, Straits of *see* Dover, Strait of
Dovlen *see* Devin
94 G11 **Dovre** Oppland, S Norway *61°59′N 09°16′E*
94 G10 **Dovrefjell** *plateau* S Norway
Dovsk *see* Dowsk
83 M14 **Dowa** Central, C Malawi *13°40′S 33°55′E*
31 O10 **Dowagiac** Michigan, N USA *41°58′N 86°06′W*
Dow Gonbadān *see* Do Gonbadān
148 M2 **Dowlatābād** Fāryāb, N Afghanistan *36°30′N 64°51′E*
97 G16 **Down** *cultural region* SE Northern Ireland, United Kingdom
33 R16 **Downey** Idaho, NW USA *42°25′N 112°06′W*
35 P5 **Downieville** California, W USA *39°34′N 120°49′W*
97 G16 **Downpatrick** *Ir.* Dún Pádraig. SE Northern Ireland, United Kingdom *54°20′N 05°43′W*
26 M3 **Downs** Kansas, C USA *39°30′N 98°33′W*
18 J12 **Downsville** New York, NE USA *42°03′N 74°59′W*
142 L7 **Dow Rūd** *var.* Do Rūd, Durud. Lorestān, W Iran *33°28′N 49°04′E*
29 V12 **Dows** Iowa, C USA *42°39′N 93°30′W*
119 O17 **Dowsk** *Rus.* Dovsk. Homyel'skaya Voblasts', SE Belarus *53°09′N 30°28′E*
35 Q4 **Doyle** California, W USA *40°00′N 120°06′W*
18 I15 **Doylestown** Pennsylvania, NE USA *40°18′N 75°08′W*
Doyransko, Ezero *see* Doïráni, Límni
114 I8 **Doyrentsi** Lovech, N Bulgaria *43°13′N 24°46′E*
164 G11 **Dōzen** *island* Oki-shotō, SW Japan
14 K9 **Dozois, Réservoir** ▣ Québec, SE Canada
74 D9 **Drâa** *seasonal river* S Morocco
Drâa, Hammada du *see* Dra, Hamada du
Drabble *see* José Enrique Rodó
117 Q5 **Drabiv** Cherkas'ka Oblast', C Ukraine *49°57′N 32°10′E*
Drable *see* José Enrique Rodó
103 S13 **Drac** ≈ E France
Drač/Drac *see* Durrës
60 I8 **Dracena** São Paulo, S Brazil *21°27′S 51°30′W*
98 M6 **Drachten** Fryslân, N Netherlands *53°07′N 06°06′E*
92 H11 **Drag** *Lapp.* Ájluokta. Nordland, C Norway *68°02′N 16°E*
116 L14 **Dragalina** Călăraşi, SE Romania *44°26′N 27°19′E*
116 I14 **Draganesti-Olt** Olt, S Romania *44°06′N 25°00′E*
116 J14 **Drăgănești-Vlașca** Teleorman, S Romania *44°05′N 25°39′E*
116 I13 **Drăgășani** Vâlcea, SW Romania *44°40′N 24°16′E*
114 G9 **Dragoman** Sofiya, W Bulgaria *42°32′N 22°56′E*
115 L25 **Dragonáda** *island* SE Greece
Dragonera, Isla *see* Sa Dragonera
45 T14 **Dragon's Mouths, The** *strait* Trinidad and Tobago/Venezuela
95 J23 **Dragør** Sjælland, E Denmark *55°36′N 12°42′E*
114 F10 **Dragovishtitsa** Kyustendil, W Bulgaria *42°22′N 22°39′E*
103 U15 **Draguignan** Var, SE France *43°31′N 06°31′E*
74 E9 **Dra, Hamada du** *var.* Hammada du Drâa, Haut Plateau du Dra. *plateau* W Algeria
Dra, Haut Plateau du *see* Dra, Hamada du
119 H19 **Drahichyn** *Pol.* Drohiczyn Poleski, *Rus.* Drogichin. Brestskaya Voblasts', SW Belarus *52°11′N 25°10′E*
29 N4 **Drake** North Dakota, N USA *47°54′N 100°23′W*
83 K23 **Drakensberg** ▲▲ Lesotho/South Africa
194 F3 **Drake Passage** *passage* Atlantic Ocean/Pacific Ocean
114 L8 **Dralfa** Tŭrgovishte, N Bulgaria *43°17′N 26°25′E*
114 I12 **Dráma** *var.* Dhráma. Anatolikí Makedonía kai Thráki, NE Greece *41°09′N 24°10′E*
Dramburg *see* Drawsko Pomorskie
95 H15 **Drammen** Buskerud, S Norway *59°44′N 10°12′E*
95 H15 **Drammensfjorden** *fjord* S Norway
92 H1 **Drangajökull** ▲ NW Iceland *66°13′N 22°18′W*
95 F16 **Drangedal** Telemark, S Norway *59°05′N 09°05′E*
92 I2 **Drangsnes** Vestfirdhir, NW Iceland *65°42′N 21°27′W*
Drann *see* Dravinja
109 T10 **Drau** *var.* Drava, *Eng.* Drave, *Hung.* Dráva. ≈ C Europe *see also* Drava
Drau *see* Drava
84 I11 **Drava** *var.* Drau, *Eng.* Drave, *Hung.* Dráva. ≈ C Europe *see also* Drau
Dráva/Drave *see* Drau/Drava
109 W10 **Dravinja** *Ger.* Drann. ≈ NE Slovenia
109 V9 **Dravograd** *Ger.* Unterdrauburg; *prev.* Spodnji Dravograd. N Slovenia *46°36′N 15°00′E*
110 F10 **Drawa** ≈ NW Poland
110 F9 **Drawno** Zachodnio-pomorskie, NW Poland *53°12′N 15°44′E*
110 F9 **Drawsko Pomorskie** *Ger.* Dramburg. Zachodnio-pomorskie, NW Poland *53°32′N 15°48′E*
29 R3 **Drayton** North Dakota, N USA *48°34′N 97°10′W*
11 P14 **Drayton Valley** Alberta, SW Canada *53°15′N 115°00′W*
186 B6 **Dreikikir** East Sepik, NW Papua New Guinea *03°42′S 142°46′E*
Dreikirchen *see* Teiuş
98 N7 **Drenthe** ◈ *province* NE Netherlands
115 H15 **Drépano, Akrotírio** *var.* Akrotírio Dhrepanon. *headland* N Greece *39°56′N 23°57′E*
Drepanum *see* Trapani
14 D17 **Dresden** Ontario, S Canada *42°34′N 82°09′W*
101 O16 **Dresden** Sachsen, E Germany *51°03′N 13°43′E*
20 G8 **Dresden** Tennessee, S USA *36°17′N 88°42′W*
118 M11 **Dretun'** Vitsyebskaya Voblasts', N Belarus *55°41′N 29°13′E*
102 M5 **Dreux** *anc.* Drocae, Durocasses. Eure-et-Loir, C France *48°44′N 01°23′E*
94 I11 **Drevsjø** Hedmark, S Norway *61°52′N 12°01′E*
22 K3 **Drew** Mississippi, S USA *33°48′N 90°31′W*
110 F10 **Drezdenko** *Ger.* Driesen. Lubuskie, W Poland *52°51′N 15°50′E*
98 J12 **Driebergen** *var.* Driebergen-Rijsenburg. Utrecht, C Netherlands *52°03′N 05°17′E*
Driebergen-Rijsenburg *see* Driebergen
Driesen *see* Drezdenko
97 N16 **Driffield** E England, United Kingdom *54°00′N 00°28′W*
65 D25 **Driftwood Point** *headland* East Falkland, Falkland Islands *52°15′S 59°00′W*
33 S14 **Driggs** Idaho, NW USA *43°44′N 111°06′W*
Drin *see* Drinit, Lumi i
112 K12 **Drina** ≈ Bosnia and Herzegovina/Serbia
Drin, Gulf of *see* Drinit, Gjiri i
113 M16 **Drini i Bardhë** *Serb.* Beli Drim. ≈ Albania/Serbia
113 K18 **Drinit, Gjiri i** *var.* Pellg i Drinit, *Eng.* Gulf of Drin. *gulf* NW Albania
113 L17 **Drinit, Lumi i** *var.* Drin. ≈ NW Albania
Drinit, Pellg i *see* Drinit, Gjiri i
Drinit të Zi, Lumi i *see* Black Drin
113 L22 **Drino** *var.* Drino, Drínos Pótamos, *Alb.* Lumi i Drinos. ≈ Albania/Greece
Drinos, Lumi i/Drínos Pótamos *see* Drino
25 S11 **Dripping Springs** Texas, SW USA *30°11′N 98°04′W*
25 S15 **Driscoll** Texas, SW USA *27°40′N 97°45′W*
22 H5 **Driskill Mountain** ▲ Louisiana, S USA *32°25′N 92°54′W*
Drissa *see* Drysa
94 G10 **Driva** ≈ S Norway
112 E13 **Drniš** *It.* Šibenik-Knin. Šibenik-Knin, S Croatia *43°51′N 16°10′E*
95 H15 **Drøbak** Akershus, S Norway *59°40′N 10°40′E*
116 G13 **Drobeta-Turnu Severin** *prev.* Turnu Severin. Mehedinţi, SW Romania *44°39′N 22°40′E*
Drocae *see* Dreux
116 M8 **Drochia** *Rus.* Drokiya. N Moldova *48°02′N 27°46′E*
97 F17 **Drogheda** *Ir.* Droichead Átha. NE Ireland *53°43′N 06°21′W*
Drogichin *see* Drahichyn
Drogobych *see* Drohobych
Drohiczyn Poleski *see* Drahichyn
116 H6 **Drohobych** *Pol.* Drohobycz, *Rus.* Drogobych. L'vivs'ka Oblast', NW Ukraine *49°22′N 23°33′E*
Drohobycz *see* Drohobych
Droichead Átha *see* Drogheda
Droicheadna Bandan *see* Bandon
Droichead na Banna *see* Banbridge
Droim Mór *see* Dromore
Drokiya *see* Drochia
103 R13 **Drôme** ◈ *department* E France
103 S13 **Drôme** ≈ E France
97 G15 **Dromore** *Ir.* Droim Mór. SE Northern Ireland, United Kingdom *54°25′N 06°09′W*
106 A9 **Dronero** Piemonte, NE Italy *44°28′N 07°25′E*
102 L12 **Dronne** ≈ SW France
195 T3 **Dronning Fabiolafjella** *var.* Mount Victor. ▲ Antarctica *72°49′S 33°01′E*
195 Q3 **Dronning Maud Land** *physical region* Antarctica
98 K6 **Dronrijp** *Fris.* Dronryp. Fryslân, N Netherlands *53°12′N 05°37′E*
Dronryp *see* Dronrijp
98 L9 **Dronten** Flevoland, C Netherlands *52°31′N 05°41′E*
Drontheim *see* Trondheim
102 L13 **Dropt** ≈ SW France
149 T4 **Drosh** Khyber Pakhtunkhwa, NW Pakistan *35°33′N 71°48′E*
Drossen *see* Ośno Lubuskie
Drug *see* Durg
Drujba *see* Pitnak
118 I12 **Drūkšiai** ◎ NE Lithuania
Druk-yul *see* Bhutan
11 Q16 **Drumheller** Alberta, SW Canada *51°28′N 112°42′W*
33 Q10 **Drummond** Montana, NW USA *46°39′N 113°12′W*
31 R4 **Drummond Island** *island* Michigan, N USA
Drummond Island *see* Tabiteuea
21 X7 **Drummond, Lake** ◎ Virginia, NE USA
15 P12 **Drummondville** Québec, SE Canada *45°52′N 72°28′W*
39 T11 **Drum, Mount** ▲ Alaska, USA *62°11′N 144°37′W*
27 O9 **Drumright** Oklahoma, C USA *35°59′N 96°36′W*
99 J14 **Drunen** Noord-Brabant, S Netherlands *51°41′N 05°08′E*
Druskienniki *see* Druskininkai
119 F15 **Druskininkai** *Pol.* Druskienniki. Alytus, S Lithuania *54°00′N 24°00′E*
98 K13 **Druten** Gelderland, SE Netherlands *51°53′N 05°37′E*
118 K11 **Druya** Vitsyebskaya Voblasts', NW Belarus *55°47′N 27°27′E*
117 S2 **Druzhba** Sums'ka Oblast', NE Ukraine *52°01′N 33°56′E*

◆ Country
● Country Capital
◇ Dependent Territory
○ Dependent Territory Capital
◈ Administrative Regions
✈ International Airport
▲ Mountain
▲▲ Mountain Range
⛰ Volcano
≈ River
◎ Lake
▣ Reservoir

Druzhba see Dostyk, Kazakhstan
Druzhba see Pitnak, Uzbekistan
123 R7 **Druzhina** Respublika Sakha (Yakutiya), NE Russian Federation 68°01′N 144°58′E
117 X7 **Druzhkivka** Donets'ka Oblast', E Ukraine 48°38′N 37°31′E
112 E12 **Drvar** Federacija Bosna I Hercegovina, W Bosnia and Herzegovina 44°21′N 16°24′E
113 G15 **Drvenik** Split-Dalmacija, SE Croatia 43°10′N 17°13′E
114 K9 **Dryanovo** Gabrovo, N Bulgaria 42°58′N 25°28′E
26 G7 **Dry Cimarron River** ~ Kansas/Oklahoma, C USA
12 B11 **Dryden** Ontario, C Canada 49°48′N 92°48′W
24 M11 **Dryden** Texas, SW USA 30°01′N 102°06′W
195 Q14 **Drygalski Ice Tongue** *ice feature* Antarctica
118 L11 **Drysa** *Rus.* Drissa. ~ N Belarus
23 V17 **Dry Tortugas** *island* Florida, SE USA
79 D15 **Dschang** Ouest, W Cameroon 05°28′N 10°02′E
54 J5 **Duaca** Lara, N Venezuela 10°22′N 69°08′W
Duacum see Douai
Duala see Douala
45 N9 **Duarte, Pico** ▲ C Dominican Republic 19°02′N 70°57′W
140 J5 **Ḍubā** Tabūk, NW Saudi Arabia 27°26′N 35°42′E
Dubai see Dubayy
117 N9 **Dubăsari** *Rus.* Dubossary. NE Moldova 47°16′N 29°07′E
117 N9 **Dubăsari Reservoir** ⊠ NE Moldova
8 M10 **Dubawnt** ~ Nunavut, NW Canada
8 L9 **Dubawnt Lake** ◎ Northwest Territories/Nunavut, N Canada
30 L6 **Du Bay, Lake** ⊠ Wisconsin, N USA
141 U7 **Dubayy** *Eng.* Dubai. Dubayy, NE United Arab Emirates 25°11′N 55°18′E
141 W7 **Dubayy** *Eng.* Dubai. ✈ Dubayy, NE United Arab Emirates 25°15′N 55°22′E
183 R7 **Dubbo** New South Wales, SE Australia 32°16′S 148°41′E
108 G7 **Dübendorf** Zürich, NW Switzerland 47°23′N 08°37′E
97 F18 **Dublin** *Ir.* Baile Átha Cliath; *anc.* Eblana. ● (Ireland) Dublin, E Ireland 53°20′N 06°15′W
23 U5 **Dublin** Georgia, SE USA 32°32′N 82°54′W
25 R7 **Dublin** Texas, SW USA 32°05′N 98°20′W
97 G18 **Dublin** *Ir.* Baile Átha Cliath; *anc.* Eblana. *cultural region* E Ireland
97 G18 **Dublin Airport** ✈ Dublin, E Ireland 53°25′N 06°18′W
189 V12 **Dublon** *var.* Tonoas. *island* Chuuk Islands, C Micronesia
126 K2 **Dubna** Moskovskaya Oblast', W Russian Federation 56°45′N 37°09′E
111 G19 **Dubňany** *Ger.* Dubnian. Jihomoravský Kraj, SE Czech Republic 48°54′N 17°00′E
Dubnian see Dubňany
111 I19 **Dubnica nad Váhom** *Hung.* Máriatölgyes; *prev.* Dubnicz. Trenčiansky Kraj, W Slovakia 48°58′N 18°10′E
Dubnicz see Dubnica nad Váhom
116 K4 **Dubno** Rivnens'ka Oblast', NW Ukraine 50°28′N 25°40′E
33 R13 **Dubois** Idaho, NW USA 44°10′N 112°13′W
18 D13 **Du Bois** Pennsylvania, NE USA 41°07′N 78°45′W
33 T14 **Dubois** Wyoming, C USA 43°31′N 109°37′W
Dubossary see Dubăsari
127 O10 **Dubovka** Volgogradskaya Oblast', SW Russian Federation 49°10′N 48°49′E
76 H14 **Dubréka** SW Guinea 09°48′N 13°31′W
14 B7 **Dubreuilville** Ontario, S Canada 48°21′N 84°31′W
Dubris Portus see Dover
119 L20 **Dubrova** Homyel'skaya Voblasts', SE Belarus 51°47′N 28°13′E
Dubrovačko-Neretvanska Županija see Dubrovnik-Neretva
126 I5 **Dubrovka** Bryanskaya Oblast', W Russian Federation 53°44′N 33°27′E
113 H16 **Dubrovnik** *It.* Ragusa. Dubrovnik-Neretva, SE Croatia 42°40′N 18°06′E
113 I16 **Dubrovnik** ✈ Dubrovnik-Neretva, SE Croatia 42°34′N 18°17′E
113 F16 **Dubrovnik-Neretva** *off.* Dubrovačko-Neretvanska Županija. ◈ *province* SE Croatia
Dubrovno see Dubrowna
116 L2 **Dubrovytsya** Rivnens'ka Oblast', NW Ukraine 51°34′N 26°37′E
119 O14 **Dubrowna** *Rus.* Dubrovno. Vitsyebskaya Voblasts', N Belarus 54°35′N 30°41′E
29 Z13 **Dubuque** Iowa, C USA 42°30′N 90°40′W
118 E12 **Dubysa** ~ C Lithuania
Đuc Cơ see Chư Ty
191 V12 **Duc de Gloucester, Îles du** *Eng.* Duke of Gloucester Islands. *island group* C French Polynesia
111 C15 **Duchcov** *Ger.* Dux. Ústecký Kraj, NW Czech Republic 50°37′N 13°45′E
37 N3 **Duchesne** Utah, W USA 40°09′N 110°24′W
191 P17 **Ducie Island** *atoll* E Pitcairn Islands
11 W15 **Duck Bay** Manitoba, S Canada 52°11′N 100°08′W
23 X17 **Duck Key** *island* Florida Keys, Florida, SE USA
11 T14 **Duck Lake** Saskatchewan, S Canada 52°52′N 106°12′W
11 V15 **Duck Mountain** ▲▲ Manitoba, S Canada
20 I9 **Duck River** ~ Tennessee, S USA
20 M10 **Ducktown** Tennessee, S USA 35°01′N 84°24′W
167 U10 **Đức Phổ** Quang Ngai, C Vietnam 14°56′N 108°55′E
Đức Tho see Lin Camh
Đức Trong see Liên Nghia
D-U-D see Dalap-Uliga-Djarrit
153 N15 **Dūddhinagar** *var.* Dūdhi. Uttar Pradesh, N India 24°09′N 83°16′E
99 M25 **Dudelange** *var.* Forge du Sud, *Ger.* Dudelingen. Luxembourg, S Luxembourg 49°28′N 06°05′E
Dudelingen see Dudelange
101 J15 **Duderstadt** Niedersachsen, C Germany 51°31′N 10°16′E
Dūdhi see Dūddhinagar
122 K8 **Dudinka** Krasnoyarskiy Kray, N Russian Federation 69°27′N 86°13′E
97 L20 **Dudley** C England, United Kingdom 52°30′N 02°05′W
154 G13 **Dudna** ~ C India
76 L16 **Duékoué** W Ivory Coast 06°50′N 05°22′W
104 M5 **Dueñas** Castilla y León, N Spain 41°52′N 04°33′W
104 K4 **Duerna** ~ NW Spain
105 O6 **Duero** *Port.* Douro. ~ Portugal/Spain *see also* Douro
Duero see Douro
Duesseldorf see Düsseldorf
21 P12 **Due West** South Carolina, SE USA 34°19′N 82°23′W
195 P11 **Dufek Coast** *physical region* Antarctica
99 H17 **Duffel** Antwerpen, C Belgium 51°06′N 04°30′E
35 S2 **Duffer Peak** ▲ Nevada, W USA 41°40′N 118°45′W
187 Q9 **Duff Islands** *island group* E Solomon Islands
Dufour, Pizzo/Dufour, Punta see Dufour Spitze
108 E12 **Dufour Spitze** *It.* Pizzo Dufour, Punta Dufour. ▲ Italy/Switzerland 45°54′N 07°50′E
112 D9 **Duga Resa** Karlovac, C Croatia 45°25′N 15°30′E
22 H5 **Dugdemona River** ~ Louisiana, S USA
154 J12 **Duggipar** Mahārāshtra, C India 21°06′N 80°10′E
112 B13 **Dugi Otok** *var.* Isola Grossa, *It.* Isola Lunga. *island* W Croatia
113 F14 **Dugopolje** Split-Dalmacija, S Croatia 43°35′N 16°35′E
160 L8 **Du He** ~ C China
54 M11 **Duida, Cerro** ▲ S Venezuela 03°21′N 65°45′W
Duinekerke see Dunkerque
101 E15 **Duisburg** *prev.* Duisburg-Hamborn. Nordrhein-Westfalen, W Germany 51°25′N 06°47′E
Duisburg-Hamborn see Duisburg
99 F14 **Duiveland** *island* SW Netherlands
98 M12 **Duiven** Gelderland, E Netherlands 51°57′N 06°02′E
139 W10 **Dujaylah, Hawr ad** ◎ S Iraq
160 H9 **Dujiangyan** *var.* Guanxian, Guan Xian. Sichuan, C China 31°01′N 103°40′E
81 L18 **Dujuuma** Shabeellaha Hoose, S Somalia 01°04′N 42°37′E
Dūkān see Dokan
39 Z14 **Duke Island** *island* Alexander Archipelago, Alaska, USA
Dukelský Priesmy/Dukelský Průsmyk see Dukla Pass
Duke of Gloucester Islands see Duc de Gloucester, Îles du
81 F14 **Duk Faiwil** Jonglei, E South Sudan 07°30′N 31°27′E
141 T7 **Dukhān** C Qatar 25°29′N 50°48′E
Dukhan Heights see Dukhān, Jabal
143 N16 **Dukhān, Jabal** *var.* Dukhan Heights. *hill range* S Qatar
127 Q7 **Dukhovnitskoye** Saratovskaya Oblast', W Russian Federation 52°31′N 48°32′E
126 H4 **Dukhovshchina** Smolenskaya Oblast', W Russian Federation 55°15′N 32°22′E
Dukielska, Przełęcz see Dukla Pass
111 N17 **Dukla** Podkarpackie, SE Poland 49°33′N 21°40′E
Duklai Hág see Dukla Pass
111 N18 **Dukla Pass** *Cz.* Dukelský Průsmyk, *Ger.* Dukla-Pass, *Hung.* Duklai Hág, *Pol.* Przełęcz Dukielska, *Slvk.* Dukelský Priesmy. *pass* Poland/Slovakia
Dukla-Pass see Dukla Pass
Dukou see Panzhihua
118 I12 **Dūkštas** Utena, E Lithuania 55°32′N 26°21′E
Dulaan see Herlenbayan-Ulaan
159 R10 **Dulan** *var.* Qagan Us. Qinghai, C China 36°11′N 97°51′E
37 R8 **Dulce** New Mexico, SW USA 36°55′N 107°00′W
43 N16 **Dulce, Golfo** *gulf* S Costa Rica
Dulce, Golfo see Izabal, Lago de
42 K6 **Dulce Nombre de Culmí** Olancho, C Honduras 15°09′N 85°37′W
62 L9 **Dulce, Río** ~ C Argentina
123 Q9 **Dulgalakh** ~ NE Russian Federation
114 M8 **Dŭlgopol** Varna, E Bulgaria 43°05′N 27°24′E
153 V14 **Dullabchara** Assam, NE India 24°25′N 92°22′E
20 D3 **Dulles** ✈ (Washington DC)Virginia, NE USA 39°00′N 77°27′W
101 E14 **Dülmen** Nordrhein-Westfalen, W Germany 51°51′N 07°17′E
114 M7 **Dulovo** Silistra, NE Bulgaria 43°51′N 27°10′E
29 W5 **Duluth** Minnesota, N USA 46°47′N 92°06′W
138 H7 **Dūmā** *Fr.* Douma. Rīf Dimashq, SW Syria 33°33′N 36°24′E
171 O8 **Dumagasa Point** *headland* Mindanao, S Philippines 07°01′N 121°54′E
171 P6 **Dumaguete** *var.* Dumaguete City. Negros, C Philippines 09°16′N 123°17′E
Dumaguete City see Dumaguete
168 J10 **Dumai** Sumatera, W Indonesia 01°39′N 101°28′E
183 T4 **Dumaresq River** ~ New South Wales/Queensland, SE Australia
27 W13 **Dumas** Arkansas, C USA 33°53′N 91°29′W
25 N1 **Dumas** Texas, SW USA 35°51′N 101°57′W
138 I7 **Ḍumayr** Rīf Dimashq, W Syria 33°36′N 36°28′E
96 I12 **Dumbarton** W Scotland, United Kingdom 55°57′N 04°35′W
96 I12 **Dumbarton** *cultural region* C Scotland, United Kingdom
187 Q17 **Dumbéa** Province Sud, S New Caledonia 22°11′S 166°27′E
111 K19 **Ďumbier** *Ger.* Djumbir, *Hung.* Gyömbér. ▲ C Slovakia 48°54′N 19°36′E
116 I11 **Dumbrăveni** *Ger.* Elisabethstedt, *Hung.* Erzsébetváros; *prev.* Ebesfalva, Eppeschdorf, Ibaşfalău. Sibiu, C Romania 46°14′N 24°34′E
116 L12 **Dumbrăveni** Vrancea, E Romania 45°31′N 27°09′E
97 J14 **Dumfries** S Scotland, United Kingdom 55°04′N 03°37′W
97 J14 **Dumfries** *cultural region* SW Scotland, United Kingdom
153 R15 **Dumka** Jhārkhand, NE India 24°17′N 87°15′E
Dümmer see Dümmersee
100 G12 **Dümmersee** *var.* Dümmer. ◎ NW Germany
14 J11 **Dumoine** ~ Québec, SE Canada
14 J10 **Dumoine, Lac** ◎ Québec, SE Canada
195 V16 **Dumont d'Urville** *French research station* Antarctica 66°24′S 139°38′E
195 W15 **Dumont d'Urville Sea** *sea* S Pacific Ocean
14 K11 **Dumont, Lac** ◎ Québec, SE Canada
75 W7 **Dumyât** *var.* Dumyât, *Eng.* Damietta. N Egypt 31°26′N 31°48′E
Düna see Danube, C Europe
Düna see Western Dvina
Duna see Don, Russian Federation
Dünaburg see Daugavpils
111 J24 **Dunaföldvár** Tolna, C Hungary 46°48′N 18°55′E
Dunaj see Wien, Austria
Dunaj see Danube, C Europe
111 L18 **Dunajec** ~ S Poland
111 H21 **Dunajská Streda** *Hung.* Dunaszerdahely. Trnavský Kraj, W Slovakia 48°N 17°28′E
Dunapentele see Dunaújváros
Dunărea see Danube
116 M13 **Dunărea Veche, Braţul** ~ SE Romania
117 N13 **Dunării, Delta** *delta* SE Romania
Dunaszerdahely see Dunajská Streda
111 J23 **Dunaújváros** *prev.* Dunapentele, Sztálinváros. Fejér, C Hungary 47°N 18°55′E
Dunav see Danube
114 J8 **Dunavska Ravnina** *Eng.* Danubian Plain. *lowlands* N Bulgaria
114 G7 **Dunavtsi** Vidin, NW Bulgaria 43°54′N 22°49′E
123 S15 **Dunay** Primorskiy Kray, SE Russian Federation 42°53′N 132°20′E
Dunayevtsy see Dunayivtsi
116 L7 **Dunayivtsi** *Rus.* Dunayevtsy. Khmel'nyts'ka Oblast', NW Ukraine 48°56′N 26°50′E
185 F22 **Dunback** Otago, South Island, New Zealand 45°22′S 170°37′E
10 L17 **Duncan** Vancouver Island, British Columbia, SW Canada 48°46′N 123°10′W
37 O15 **Duncan** Arizona, SW USA 32°43′N 109°06′W
26 M12 **Duncan** Oklahoma, C USA 34°30′N 97°57′W
Duncan Island see Pinzón, Isla
151 Q20 **Duncan Passage** *strait* Andaman Sea/Bay of Bengal
96 K6 **Duncansby Head** *headland* N Scotland, United Kingdom 58°37′N 03°01′W
14 G12 **Dunchurch** Ontario, S Canada 45°36′N 79°54′W
118 D7 **Dundaga** NW Latvia 57°29′N 22°19′E
14 G14 **Dundalk** Ontario, S Canada 44°11′N 80°22′W
97 F16 **Dundalk** *Ir.* Dún Dealgan. Louth, NE Ireland 54°01′N 06°25′W
21 X3 **Dundalk** Maryland, NE USA 39°15′N 76°31′W
97 F16 **Dundalk Bay** *Ir.* Cuan Dhún Dealgan. *bay* NE Ireland
14 G16 **Dundas** Ontario, S Canada 43°16′N 79°55′W
180 L12 **Dundas, Lake** *salt lake* Western Australia
Dundbürd see Batnorov
Dún Dealgan see Dundalk
15 N13 **Dundee** Québec, SE Canada 45°01′N 74°27′W
83 K22 **Dundee** KwaZulu/Natal, E South Africa 28°09′S 30°12′E
96 K11 **Dundee** E Scotland, United Kingdom 56°28′N 03°W
31 R10 **Dundee** Michigan, N USA 41°57′N 83°39′W
25 R5 **Dundee** Texas, SW USA 33°43′N 98°52′W
194 H3 **Dundee Island** *island* Antarctica
162 L9 **Dundgovĭ** ◈ *province* C Mongolia
97 G16 **Dundrum Bay** *Ir.* Cuan Dhún Droma. *inlet* NW Irish Sea
11 T15 **Dundurn** Saskatchewan, S Canada 51°43′N 106°27′W
Dund-Us see Hovd
Dund-Us see Hovd
185 F23 **Dunedin** Otago, South Island, New Zealand 45°52′S 170°31′E
183 R7 **Dunedoo** New South Wales, SE Australia 32°04′S 149°23′E
97 D14 **Dunfanaghy** *Ir.* Dún Fionnachaidh. NW Ireland 55°11′N 07°59′W
96 J12 **Dunfermline** C Scotland, United Kingdom 56°04′N 03°29′W
Dún Fionnachaidh see Dunfanaghy
149 V10 **Dunga Bunga** Punjab, E Pakistan 29°51′N 73°19′E
97 F15 **Dungannon** *Ir.* Dún Geanainn. C Northern Ireland, United Kingdom 54°31′N 06°46′W
Dun Garbháin see Dungarvan
152 F15 **Dūngarpur** Rājasthān, N India 23°50′N 73°43′E
97 E21 **Dungarvan** *Ir.* Dun Garbháin. Waterford, S Ireland 52°05′N 07°37′W
101 N21 **Dungau** *cultural region* SE Germany
Dún Geanainn see Dungannon
97 P23 **Dungeness** *headland* SE England, United Kingdom 50°55′N 00°58′E
63 I23 **Dungeness, Punta** *headland* S Argentina 52°25′S 68°25′W
Dungloe see Dunglow
97 D14 **Dunglow** *var.* Dungloe, *Ir.* An Clochán Liath. Donegal, NW Ireland 54°57′N 08°22′W
183 T7 **Dungog** New South Wales, SE Australia 32°24′S 151°45′E
79 O16 **Dungu** Orientale, NE Dem. Rep. Congo 03°40′N 28°32′E
168 L8 **Dungun** *var.* Kuala Dungun. Terengganu, Peninsular Malaysia 04°47′N 103°26′E
80 I6 **Dungunab** Red Sea, NE Sudan 21°10′N 37°09′E
15 P13 **Dunham** Québec, SE Canada 45°08′N 72°48′W
Dunheved see Launceston
Dunholme see Durham
163 X10 **Dunhua** Jilin, NE China 43°22′N 128°12′E
159 P8 **Dunhuang** Gansu, N China 40°10′N 94°40′E
182 L12 **Dunkeld** Victoria, SE Australia 37°41′S 142°19′E
103 O1 **Dunkerque** *Eng.* Dunkirk, *Flem.* Duinekerke; *prev.* Dunquerque. Nord, N France 51°06′N 02°34′E
97 K23 **Dunkery Beacon** ▲ SW England, United Kingdom 51°10′N 03°36′W
18 C11 **Dunkirk** New York, NE USA 42°28′N 79°19′W
Dunkirk see Dunkerque
77 P17 **Dunkwa** SW Ghana 05°59′N 01°45′W
97 G18 **Dún Laoghaire** *Eng.* Dunleary; *prev.* Kingstown. E Ireland 53°17′N 06°08′W
29 S14 **Dunlap** Iowa, C USA 41°51′N 95°36′W
20 L10 **Dunlap** Tennessee, S USA 35°22′N 85°23′W
Dunleary see Dún Laoghaire
Dún Mánmhaí see Dunmanway
97 B21 **Dunmanway** *Ir.* Dún Mánmhaí. Cork, SW Ireland 51°43′N 09°07′W
18 I13 **Dunmore** Pennsylvania, NE USA 41°25′N 75°37′W
21 U10 **Dunn** North Carolina, SE USA 35°18′N 78°36′W
Dún na nGall see Donegal
23 V11 **Dunnellon** Florida, SE USA 29°03′N 82°27′W
96 J6 **Dunnet Head** *headland* N Scotland, United Kingdom 58°40′N 03°27′W
29 N14 **Dunning** Nebraska, C USA 41°49′N 100°04′W
65 B24 **Dunnose Head Settlement** West Falkland, Falkland Islands 51°24′S 60°29′W
14 G17 **Dunnville** Ontario, S Canada 42°54′N 79°36′W
Dún Pádraig see Downpatrick
Dunquerque see Dunkerque
Dunqulah see Dongola
96 L12 **Duns** SE Scotland, United Kingdom 55°46′N 02°13′W
29 N2 **Dunseith** North Dakota, N USA 48°48′N 100°03′W
35 N2 **Dunsmuir** California, W USA 41°12′N 122°19′W
97 N21 **Dunstable** *Lat.* Durocobrivae. E England, United Kingdom 51°53′N 00°32′W
185 D21 **Dunstan Mountains** ▲▲ South Island, New Zealand
103 O9 **Dun-sur-Auron** Cher, C France 46°52′N 02°40′E
185 F21 **Duntroon** Canterbury, South Island, New Zealand 44°52′S 170°40′E
149 T10 **Dunyāpur** Punjab, E Pakistan 29°48′N 71°48′E
163 U5 **Duobukur He** ~ NE China
163 R12 **Duolun** *var.* Dolonnur. Nei Mongol Zizhiqu, N China 42°11′N 116°30′E
167 R14 **Dương Đông** Kiên Giang, S Vietnam 10°15′N 103°58′E
114 G10 **Dupnitsa** *prev.* Marek, Stanke Dimitrov. Kyustendil, W Bulgaria 42°16′N 23°07′E
28 L8 **Dupree** South Dakota, N USA 45°03′N 101°36′W
33 Q7 **Dupuyer** Montana, NW USA 48°13′N 112°34′W
141 Y11 **Duqm** *var.* Daqm. E Oman 19°42′N 57°40′E
63 F23 **Duque de York, Isla** *island* S Chile
181 N4 **Durack Range** ▲▲ Western Australia
136 K10 **Durağan** Sinop, N Turkey 41°26′N 35°03′E
103 S15 **Durance** ~ SE France
31 R9 **Durand** Michigan, N USA 42°54′N 83°58′W
30 I6 **Durand** Wisconsin, N USA 44°37′N 91°56′W
40 K10 **Durango** *var.* Victoria de Durango. Durango, W Mexico 24°03′N 104°38′W
105 P3 **Durango** País Vasco, N Spain 43°10′N 02°38′W
37 Q8 **Durango** Colorado, C USA 37°13′N 107°51′W
40 J9 **Durango** ◈ *state* C Mexico
114 O7 **Durankulak** *Rom.* Răcari; *prev.* Blatnitsa, Duranulac. Dobrich, NE Bulgaria 43°41′N 28°31′E
22 L4 **Durant** Mississippi, S USA 33°04′N 89°51′W
27 P13 **Durant** Oklahoma, C USA 33°59′N 96°24′W
Duranulac see Durankulak
105 N6 **Duratón** ~ N Spain
61 E19 **Durazno** *var.* San Pedro de Durazno. Durazno, C Uruguay 33°22′S 56°31′W
61 E19 **Durazno** ◈ *department* C Uruguay
Durazzo see Durrës
83 K23 **Durban** *var.* Port Natal. KwaZulu/Natal, E South Africa 29°51′S 31°E
83 K23 **Durban** ✈ KwaZulu/Natal, E South Africa 29°55′S 31°01′E
118 C9 **Durbe** *Ger.* Durben. W Latvia 56°34′N 21°22′E
Durben see Durbe
99 K21 **Durbuy** Luxembourg, SE Belgium 50°21′N 05°27′E
105 N15 **Dúrcal** Andalucía, S Spain 37°00′N 03°24′W
112 F8 **Đurđevac** *Ger.* Sankt Georgen, *Hung.* Szentgyörgy; *prev.* Djurdjevac, Gjurgjevac. Koprivnica-Kri»zevci, N Croatia 46°02′N 17°03′E
113 K15 **Đurđevica Tara** N Montenegro 43°09′N 19°18′E
97 L24 **Durdle Door** *natural arch* S England, United Kingdom
158 L3 **Düre** Xinjiang Uygur Zizhiqu, W China 46°30′N 88°26′E
101 D16 **Düren** *anc.* Marcodurum. Nordrhein-Westfalen, W Germany 50°48′N 06°30′E
154 K12 **Durg** *prev.* Drug. Chhattīsgarh, C India 21°12′N 81°20′E
153 U13 **Durgapur** Dhaka, N Bangladesh 25°10′N 90°41′E
153 R15 **Durgāpur** West Bengal, NE India 23°30′N 87°20′E
14 F14 **Durham** Ontario, S Canada 44°10′N 80°48′W
97 M14 **Durham** *hist.* Dunholme. N England, United Kingdom 54°47′N 01°34′W
21 U9 **Durham** North Carolina, SE USA 36°N 78°54′W
97 L15 **Durham** *cultural region* N England, United Kingdom
168 J10 **Duri** Sumatera, W Indonesia 01°13′N 101°13′E
Duria Major see Dora Baltea
Duria Minor see Dora Riparia
Durlas see Thurles
141 P8 **Ḑurmā** Ar Riyāḑ, C Saudi Arabia 24°37′N 46°06′E
113 J15 **Durmitor** ▲ N Montenegro
96 H6 **Durness** N Scotland, United Kingdom 58°34′N 04°46′W
109 Y3 **Dürnkrut** Niederösterreich, E Austria 48°28′N 16°50′E
Durnovaria see Dorchester
Durobrivae see Rochester
Durocasses see Dreux
Durocobrivae see Dunstable
Durocortorum see Reims
Durostorum see Silistra
Durovernum see Canterbury
113 K20 **Durrës** *var.* Durrësi, Dursi, *It.* Durazzo, *SCr.* Drač, *Turk.* Draç. Durrës, W Albania 41°20′N 19°26′E
113 K19 **Durrës** ◈ *district* W Albania
Durrësi see Durrës
97 A21 **Dursey Island** *Ir.* Oileán Baoi. *island* SW Ireland
Dursi see Durrës
Duru see Wuchuan
Durud see Dow Rūd
114 P12 **Durusu** İstanbul, NW Turkey 41°18′N 28°41′E
114 O12 **Durusu Gölü** ◎ NW Turkey
138 I9 **Durūz, Jabal ad** ▲ SW Syria 37°00′N 32°30′E
185 K13 **D'Urville Island** *island* C New Zealand
171 X12 **D'Urville, Tanjung** *headland* Papua, E Indonesia 01°26′S 137°52′E
146 H14 **Duşak** *Rus.* Dushak. Ahal Welaýaty, S Turkmenistan 37°15′N 59°57′E
Dusa Mareb/Dusa Marreb see Dhuusa Marreeb
118 I11 **Dusetos** Utena, NE Lithuania 55°44′N 25°49′E
Dushak see Duşak
160 K12 **Dushan** Guizhou, S China 25°50′N 107°36′E
147 P13 **Dushanbe** *var.* Dyushambe; *prev.* Stalinabad, *Taj.* Stalinobod. ● (Tajikistan) W Tajikistan 38°35′N 68°44′E
147 P13 **Dushanbe** ✈ W Tajikistan 38°31′N 68°49′E
137 T9 **Dusheti** *prev.* Dushet'i. E Georgia 42°07′N 44°44′E
Dushet'i see Dusheti
18 H13 **Dushore** Pennsylvania, NE USA 41°30′N 76°23′W
185 A23 **Dusky Sound** *sound* South Island, New Zealand
101 E15 **Düsseldorf** *var.* Duesseldorf. Nordrhein-Westfalen, W Germany 51°14′N 06°49′E
147 P14 **Dŭsti** *Rus.* Dusti. SW Tajikistan 37°22′N 68°41′E
194 I9 **Dustin Island** *island* Antarctica
Dutch East Indies see Indonesia
Dutch Guiana see Suriname
38 L17 **Dutch Harbor** Unalaska Island, Alaska, USA 53°51′N 166°33′W
36 J3 **Dutch Mount** ▲ Utah, W USA 40°16′N 113°56′W
Dutch New Guinea see Papua
Dutch West Indies see Curaçao
83 H20 **Dutlwe** Kweneng, S Botswana 23°58′S 23°56′E
67 V16 **Du Toit Fracture Zone** *tectonic feature* SW Indian Ocean
125 U8 **Dutovo** Respublika Komi, NW Russian Federation 63°45′N 56°38′E
77 V13 **Dutsan Wai** *var.* Dutsen Wai. Kaduna, C Nigeria 10°49′N 08°15′E
77 W13 **Dutse** Jigawa, N Nigeria 11°43′N 09°25′E
Dutsen Wai see Dutsan Wai
Duttia see Datia
14 E17 **Dutton** Ontario, S Canada 42°40′N 81°28′W
36 L7 **Dutton, Mount** ▲ Utah, W USA 38°00′N 112°10′W
162 E7 **Duut** Hovd, W Mongolia 47°28′N 91°52′E
14 K11 **Duval, Lac** ◎ Québec, SE Canada
127 W3 **Duvan** Respublika Bashkortostan, W Russian Federation 55°42′N 57°56′E
138 L9 **Duwaykhilat Satih ar Ruwayshid** *seasonal river* SE Jordan
Dux see Duchcov
160 J13 **Duyang Shan** ▲▲ S China
167 T14 **Duyên Hai** Tra Vinh, S Vietnam 09°39′N 106°28′E
160 K12 **Duyun** Guizhou, S China 26°16′N 107°29′E
136 G11 **Düzce** Düzce, NW Turkey 40°51′N 31°09′E
136 K14 **Düzce** ◈ *province* NW Turkey
Duzdab see Zāhedān
Duzenkyr, Khrebet see Duzkyr, Khrebet
146 I16 **Duzkyr, Khrebet** *prev.* Khrebet Duzenkyr. ▲▲ S Turkmenistan
114 K8 **Dve Mogili** Ruse, N Bulgaria 43°35′N 25°51′E
Dvina Bay see Chëshskaya Guba
Dvinsk see Daugavpils
124 L7 **Dvinskaya Guba** *bay* NW Russian Federation
112 E10 **Dvor** Sisak-Moslavina, C Croatia 45°05′N 16°22′E
117 W5 **Dvorichna** Kharkivs'ka Oblast', E Ukraine 49°52′N 37°43′E
111 F16 **Dvůr Králové nad Labem** *Ger.* Königinhof an der Elbe. Královéhradecký Kraj, N Czech Republic 50°27′N 15°50′E
154 A10 **Dwārka** Gujarāt, W India 22°14′N 68°58′E
30 M12 **Dwight** Illinois, N USA 41°05′N 88°25′W
98 N8 **Dwingeloo** Drenthe, NE Netherlands 52°49′N 06°20′E
33 N10 **Dworshak Reservoir** ⊠ Idaho, NW USA
Dyal see Dyaul Island
Dyanev see Galkynyş
Dyatlovo see Dzyatlava
186 G5 **Dyaul Island** *var.* Djaul, Dyal. *island* NE Papua New Guinea
20 G8 **Dyer** Tennessee, S USA 36°04′N 88°59′W
9 S5 **Dyer, Cape** *headland* Baffin Island, Nunavut, NE Canada 66°37′N 61°13′W
20 F8 **Dyersburg** Tennessee, S USA 36°02′N 89°21′W
29 Y13 **Dyersville** Iowa, C USA 42°29′N 91°07′W
97 I21 **Dyfed** *cultural region* SW Wales, United Kingdom
Dyfrdwy, Afon see Dee
Dyhernfurth see Brzeg Dolny
111 E19 **Dyje** *var.* Thaya. ~ Austria/Czech Republic *see also* Thaya
Dyje see Thaya
117 T5 **Dykan'ka** Poltavs'ka Oblast', C Ukraine 49°48′N 34°33′E
127 N16 **Dykhtau** ▲ SW Russian Federation 43°01′N 42°56′E
111 A16 **Dyleń** *Ger.* Tillenberg. ▲ NW Czech Republic 49°58′N 12°31′E
110 K9 **Dylewska Góra** ▲ N Poland 53°33′N 19°57′E
117 O4 **Dymer** Kyyivs'ka Oblast', N Ukraine 50°50′N 30°20′E
117 W7 **Dymytrov** *Rus.* Dimitrov. Donets'ka Oblast', SE Ukraine 48°18′N 37°19′E
111 O17 **Dynów** Podkarpackie, SE Poland 49°49′N 22°14′E
29 X13 **Dysart** Iowa, C USA 42°10′N 92°18′W
Dysna see Dzisna
115 H18 **Dýstos, Límni** *var.* Límni Dístos. ◎ Évvoia, C Greece
115 D18 **Dytikí Elláda** *Eng.* Greece West, *var.* Dytikí Ellás. ◈ *region* C Greece
Dytikí Ellás see Dytikí Elláda
115 C14 **Dytikí Makedonía** *Eng.* Macedonia West. ◈ *region* N Greece
Dyurment'yube see Diirmentobe
127 U4 **Dyurtyuli** Respublika Bashkortostan, W Russian Federation 55°31′N 54°49′E
Dyushambe see Dushanbe
162 K7 **Dzaamar** *var.* Bat-Öldziyt. Töv, C Mongolia 48°10′N 104°49′E
Dzaanhushuu see Ihtamir
Dza Chu see Mekong
Dzadgay see Bömbögör
162 H8 **Dzag** Bayanhongor, C Mongolia 46°54′N 99°11′E
Dzalaa see Shinejinst
163 O11 **Dzamïn-Üüd** *var.* Borhoyn Tal. Dornogovĭ, SE Mongolia 43°43′N 111°53′E
172 J14 **Dzaoudzi** E Mayotte 12°48′S 45°18′E
Dzaudzhikau see Vladikavkaz
162 G7 **Dzavhan** ◈ *province* NW Mongolia
162 G7 **Dzavhan Gol** ~ NW Mongolia
162 G6 **Dzavhanmandal** *var.* Nuga. Dzavhan, W Mongolia 48°17′N 95°07′E
Dzegstey see Ögiynuur
162 E7 **Dzereg** *var.* Altanteel. Hovd, W Mongolia 47°05′N 92°57′E
127 O3 **Dzerzhinsk** Nizhegorodskaya Oblast', W Russian Federation 56°20′N 43°22′E
Dzerzhinsk see Dzyarzhynsk Belarus
Dzerzhinsk see Romaniv
Dzerzhinskiy see Nar'yan-Mar
Dzerzhinskoye see Tokzhaylau
Dzerzhinskoye see Tokzhaylau
Dzerzhyns'k see Romaniv
Dzerzhyns'k see Romaniv
Dzhetygara see Zhitikara
Dzhailgan see Jayilgan
Dzhalagash see Zhalagash
147 T10 **Dzhalal-Abad** *Kir.* Jalal-Abad. Dzhalal-Abadskaya Oblast', W Kyrgyzstan 40°56′N 73°00′E
147 S9 **Dzhalal-Abadskaya Oblast'** *Kir.* Jalal-Abad Oblasty. ◈ *province* W Kyrgyzstan
Dzhalilabad see Cälilabad
Dzhambeyty see Zhympity
Dzhambul see Taraz
Dzhambulskaya Oblast' see Zhambyl
144 D9 **Dzhanibek** *prev.* Dzhanybek, *Kaz.* Zhänibek. Zapadnyy Kazakhstan, W Kazakhstan 49°27′N 46°51′E
Dzhankel'dy see Jongeldi
117 T12 **Dzhankoy** Avtonomna Respublika Krym, S Ukraine 45°40′N 34°20′E
Dzhansugurov see Zhansugirov
147 R9 **Dzhany-Bazar** *var.* Yangibazar. Dzhalal-Abadskaya Oblast', W Kyrgyzstan 41°40′N 70°49′E
Dzhanybek see Dzhanibek
123 P8 **Dzhardzhan** Respublika Sakha (Yakutiya), NE Russian Federation 68°47′N 123°51′E
Dzharkurgan see Jarqo'rg'on
117 S11 **Dzharylhats'ka Zatoka** *gulf* S Ukraine
Dzhayilgan see Jayilgan
Dzhebel see Jebel
147 T14 **Dzhelandy** SE Tajikistan 37°34′N 72°35′E
147 Y7 **Dzhergalan** *Kir.* Jyrgalan. Issyk-Kul'skaya Oblast', NE Kyrgyzstan 42°37′N 78°56′E
Dzhetysay see Zhetysay
Dzhezkazgan see Zhezkazgan
Dzhigirbent see Jigerbent
Dzhirgatal' see Jirgatol
Dzhizak see Jizzax
Dzhizakskaya Oblast' see Jizzax Viloyati
123 P8 **Dzhugdzhur, Khrebet** ▲▲ E Russian Federation
Dzhul'fa see Culfa
Dzhuma see Juma
Dzhungarskiy Alatau see Zhetysuskiy Alatau
Dzhusaly see Zhosaly
146 J12 **Dzhynlykum, Peski** *desert* E Turkmenistan
110 L9 **Działdowo** Warmińsko-Mazurskie, C Poland 53°13′N 20°12′E
111 L16 **Działoszyce** Świętokrzyskie, C Poland 50°21′N 20°19′E
41 X11 **Dzidzantún** Yucatán, E Mexico
111 G15 **Dzierżoniów** *Ger.* Reichenbach. Dolnośląskie, SW Poland 50°43′N 16°40′E
41 X11 **Dzilam de Bravo** Yucatán, E Mexico 21°24′N 88°52′W
118 L12 **Dzisna** *Rus.* Disna. Vitsyebskaya Voblasts', N Belarus 55°33′N 28°13′E
118 K12 **Dzisna** *Lith.* Dysna, *Rus.* Disna. ~ Belarus/Lithuania
119 G20 **Dzivin** *Rus.* Divin. Brestskaya Voblasts', SW Belarus 51°58′N 24°33′E
119 M15 **Dzmitravichy** *Rus.* Dmitrovichi. Minskaya Voblasts', C Belarus 53°58′N 29°14′E
Dzogsool see Bayantsagaan
162 I5 **Dzöölön** *var.* Rinchinlhümbe. Hövsgöl, N Mongolia 51°06′N 99°40′E
129 S8 **Dzungaria** *var.* Sungaria, Zungaria. *physical region* W China
Dzungarian Basin see Junggar Pendi
Dzür see Tes
162 J8 **Dzüünbayan-Ulaan** *var.* Bayan-Ulaan. Övörhangay, C Mongolia 46°38′N 102°30′E
Dzüünbulag see Matad, Dornod, Mongolia
Dzüünbulag see Uulbayan, Sühbaatar, Mongolia
162 L8 **Dzuunmod** Töv, C Mongolia 47°45′N 107°00′E
Dzuunmod see Ider
Dzüün Soyonï Nuruu see Vostochnyy Sayan
Dzüyl see Tonhil
Dzvina see Western Dvina
119 J16 **Dzyarzhynsk Belarus** *Rus.* Dzerzhinsk; *prev.* Kaydanovo. Minskaya Voblasts', C Belarus 53°41′N 27°09′E
119 H17 **Dzyatlava** *Pol.* Zdzięcioł, *Rus.* Dyatlovo. Hrodzyenskaya Voblasts', W Belarus 53°27′N 25°23′E

E

E see Hubei
Éadan Doire see Edenderry
167 U12 **Ea Drăng** *var.* Ea H'leo. Đăc Lăc, S Vietnam 13°09′N 108°14′E
37 W6 **Eads** Colorado, C USA 38°28′N 102°46′W
37 O13 **Eagar** Arizona, SW USA 34°05′N 109°17′W
39 T8 **Eagle** Alaska, USA 64°47′N 141°12′W
13 S8 **Eagle** ~ Newfoundland and Labrador, E Canada
10 I3 **Eagle** ~ Yukon Territory, NW Canada
29 T7 **Eagle Bend** Minnesota, N USA 46°10′N 95°02′W
28 M8 **Eagle Butte** South Dakota, N USA 44°58′N 101°13′W
29 V12 **Eagle Grove** Iowa, C USA 42°39′N 93°54′W
19 R2 **Eagle Lake** Maine, NE USA 47°01′N 68°35′W
25 U11 **Eagle Lake** Texas, SW USA 29°35′N 96°19′W
12 A11 **Eagle Lake** ◎ Ontario, S Canada
35 P3 **Eagle Lake** ◎ California, W USA
19 R3 **Eagle Lake** ◎ Maine, NE USA
29 Y3 **Eagle Mountain** ▲ Minnesota, N USA 47°54′N 90°33′W
25 T6 **Eagle Mountain Lake** ⊠ Texas, SW USA
37 S9 **Eagle Nest Lake** ⊠ New Mexico, SW USA
25 P13 **Eagle Pass** Texas, SW USA 28°44′N 100°31′W
65 C25 **Eagle Passage** *passage* SW Atlantic Ocean
35 Q2 **Eagle Peak** ▲ California, W USA 41°16′N 120°12′W
35 R8 **Eagle Peak** ▲ California, W USA 38°11′N 119°22′W
37 P13 **Eagle Peak** ▲ New Mexico, SW USA 33°39′N 109°36′W
10 I4 **Eagle Plain** Yukon Territory, NW Canada 66°23′N 136°42′W
32 G15 **Eagle Point** Oregon, NW USA 42°28′N 122°48′W
186 P10 **Eagle Point** *headland* SE Papua New Guinea 10°31′S 149°53′E
39 R11 **Eagle River** Alaska, USA 61°18′N 149°38′W
30 M2 **Eagle River** Michigan, N USA 47°24′N 88°18′W
30 L4 **Eagle River** Wisconsin, N USA 45°56′N 89°15′W

◆ Country
● Country Capital
◇ Dependent Territory
○ Dependent Territory Capital
◈ Administrative Regions
✈ International Airport
▲ Mountain
▲▲ Mountain Range
Ж Volcano
~ River
◎ Lake
⊠ Reservoir

21 S6 Eagle Rock Virginia, NE USA 37°40′N 79°46′W
36 J13 Eagletail Mountains ▲▲ Arizona, SW USA
Ea H'leo see Ea Drăng
167 U12 Ea Kar Đăc Lăc, S Vietnam 12°47′N 108°26′E
Eanjum see Anjum
Eanodat see Enontekiö
12 B10 Ear Falls Ontario, C Canada 50°38′N 93°13′W
27 X10 Earle Arkansas, C USA 35°16′N 90°28′W
35 R12 Earlimart California, W USA 35°52′N 119°17′W
20 I6 Earlington Kentucky, S USA 37°16′N 87°30′W
14 H8 Earlton Ontario, S Canada 47°41′N 79°46′W
29 T13 Early Iowa, C USA 42°27′N 95°09′W
96 J11 Earn River N Scotland, United Kingdom
185 C21 Earnslaw, Mount ▲ South Island, New Zealand 44°34′S 168°26′E
24 M4 Earth Texas, SW USA 34°13′N 102°24′W
21 P11 Easley South Carolina, SE USA 34°49′N 82°36′W
East see Est
East Açores Fracture Zone see East Azores Fracture Zone
97 P19 East Anglia physical region E England, United Kingdom
15 Q12 East Angus Québec, SE Canada 45°29′N 71°39′W
195 V8 East Antarctica prev. Greater Antarctica. physical region Antarctica
18 E10 East Aurora New York, NE USA 42°44′N 78°36′W
East Australian Basin see Tasman Basin
East Azerbaijan see Āžarbāyjān-e Sharqī
64 L9 East Azores Fracture Zone var. East Açores Fracture Zone. tectonic feature E Atlantic Ocean
22 M11 East Bay bay Louisiana, S USA
25 V11 East Bernard Texas, SW USA 29°32′N 96°04′W
29 V8 East Bethel Minnesota, N USA 45°24′N 93°14′W
East Borneo see Kalimantan Timur
97 P23 Eastbourne SE England, United Kingdom 50°46′N 00°16′E
15 R11 East-Broughton Québec, SE Canada 46°14′N 71°05′W
44 M6 East Caicos island E Turks and Caicos Islands
184 R7 East Cape headland North Island, New Zealand 37°40′S 178°31′E
174 M4 East Caroline Basin undersea feature SW Pacific Ocean 04°00′N 146°45′E
192 P4 East China Sea Chin. Dong Hai. sea W Pacific Ocean
97 P19 East Dereham E England, United Kingdom 52°41′N 00°55′E
30 J9 East Dubuque Illinois, N USA 42°29′N 90°38′W
11 S17 Eastend Saskatchewan, S Canada 49°29′N 108°48′W
193 S10 Easter Fracture Zone tectonic feature E Pacific Ocean
Easter Island see Pascua, Isla de
81 J18 Eastern ◈ province Kenya
153 Q12 Eastern ◈ zone E Nepal
155 K25 Eastern ◈ province E Sri Lanka
82 L13 Eastern ◈ province E Zambia
83 H24 Eastern Cape off. Eastern Cape Province, Afr. Oos-Kaap. ◈ province SE South Africa
Eastern Cape Province see Eastern Cape
Eastern Desert see Sahara el Sharqîya
81 F15 Eastern Equatoria ◈ state SE South Sudan
Eastern Euphrates see Murat Nehri
155 J17 Eastern Ghats ▲▲ SE India
186 E7 Eastern Highlands ◈ province C Papua New Guinea
Eastern Region see Ash Sharqīyah
Eastern Sayans see Vostochnyy Sayan
Eastern Scheldt see Oosterschelde
Eastern Sierra Madre see Madre Oriental, Sierra
Eastern Transvaal see Mpumalanga
11 W14 Easterville Manitoba, C Canada 53°06′N 99°53′W
Easterwâlde see Oosterwolde
63 M23 East Falkland var. Isla Soledad. island E Falkland Islands
19 P12 East Falmouth Massachusetts, NE USA 41°34′N 70°31′W
East Fayu see Fayu
East Flanders see Oost-Vlaanderen
39 S6 East Fork Chandalar River River Alaska, USA
29 U12 East Fork Des Moines River River Iowa/Minnesota, C USA
East Frisian Islands see Ostfriesische Inseln
18 K10 East Glenville New York, NE USA 42°53′N 73°55′W
29 R4 East Grand Forks Minnesota, N USA 47°54′N 97°59′W
97 O23 East Grinstead SE England, United Kingdom 51°08′N 00°00′W
18 M12 East Hartford Connecticut, NE USA 41°45′N 72°36′W
18 M13 East Haven Connecticut, NE USA 41°16′N 72°52′W
173 T9 East Indiaman Ridge undersea feature E Indian Ocean
129 V16 East Indies island group SE Asia
East Java see Jawa Timur
31 Q6 East Jordan Michigan, N USA 45°09′N 85°07′W
East Kalimantan see Kalimantan Timur
East Kazakhstan see Vostochnyy Kazakhstan
96 I12 East Kilbride S Scotland, United Kingdom 55°46′N 04°10′W
25 R7 Eastland Texas, SW USA 32°23′N 98°50′W
31 Q9 East Lansing Michigan, N USA 42°44′N 84°28′W
35 X11 East Las Vegas Nevada, W USA 36°05′N 115°02′W
97 M23 Eastleigh S England, United Kingdom 50°58′N 01°22′W
31 V12 East Liverpool Ohio, N USA 40°37′N 80°34′W
83 J25 East London Afr. Oos-Londen; prev. Emonti, Port Rex. Eastern Cape, S South Africa 33°S 27°54′E
96 K12 East Lothian cultural region SE Scotland, United Kingdom
12 I10 Eastmain Québec, E Canada 52°11′N 78°27′W
12 J10 Eastmain River Québec, C Canada
15 P13 Eastman Québec, SE Canada 45°19′N 72°18′W
23 U6 Eastman Georgia, SE USA 32°12′N 83°10′W
175 O3 East Mariana Basin undersea feature W Pacific Ocean
30 K11 East Moline Illinois, N USA 41°30′N 90°26′W
186 H7 East New Britain ◈ province E Papua New Guinea
29 T15 East Nishnabotna River River Iowa, C USA
197 V12 East Novaya Zemlya Trough var. Novaya Zemlya Trough. undersea feature W Kara Sea
East Nusa Tenggara see Nusa Tenggara Timur
21 X4 Easton Maryland, NE USA 38°46′N 76°04′W
18 I14 Easton Pennsylvania, NE USA 40°41′N 75°13′W
193 R16 East Pacific Rise undersea feature E Pacific Ocean 20°00′S 115°00′W
East Pakistan see Bangladesh
31 V12 East Palestine Ohio, N USA 40°49′N 80°32′W
30 L12 East Peoria Illinois, N USA 40°40′N 89°34′W
23 S3 East Point Georgia, SE USA 33°40′N 84°26′W
19 U6 Eastport Maine, NE USA 44°54′N 66°59′W
27 Z8 East Prairie Missouri, C USA 36°46′N 89°23′W
19 O12 East Providence Rhode Island, NE USA 41°48′N 71°20′W
20 L11 East Ridge Tennessee, S USA 35°00′N 85°15′W
97 N16 East Riding cultural region N England, United Kingdom
18 F9 East Rochester New York, NE USA 43°06′N 77°29′W
30 K15 East Saint Louis Illinois, N USA 38°35′N 90°07′W
65 K21 East Scotia Basin undersea feature SE Scotia Sea
129 Y8 East Sea var. Sea of Japan, Rus. Yapanskoye More. Sea NW Pacific Ocean see also Japan, Sea of
186 B6 East Sepik ◈ province NW Papua New Guinea
173 N4 East Sheba Ridge undersea feature W Arabian Sea 14°30′N 56°15′E
East Siberian Sea see Vostochno-Sibirskoye More
18 I14 East Stroudsburg Pennsylvania, NE USA 41°00′N 75°10′W
East Tasmanian Rise/East Tasmania Plateau/East Tasmania Rise see East Tasman Plateau
192 I12 East Tasman Plateau var. East Tasmanian Rise, East Tasmania Plateau, East Tasmania Rise. undersea feature SW Tasman Sea
64 L7 East Thulean Rise undersea feature N Atlantic Ocean
171 R16 East Timor var. Loro Sae; prev. Portuguese Timor, Timor Timur. ◆ country S Indonesia
21 Y6 Eastville Virginia, NE USA 37°22′N 75°58′W
35 R7 East Walker River River California/Nevada, W USA
182 D1 Eateringinna Creek River South Australia
37 T3 Eaton Colorado, C USA 40°31′N 104°42′W
15 Q12 Eaton River Québec, SE Canada
11 S16 Eatonia Saskatchewan, S Canada 51°13′N 109°22′W
31 Q10 Eaton Rapids Michigan, N USA 42°30′N 84°39′W
23 U4 Eatonton Georgia, SE USA 33°19′N 83°23′W
32 H9 Eatonville Washington, NW USA 46°51′N 122°19′W
30 J6 Eau Claire Wisconsin, N USA 44°50′N 91°30′W
12 J7 Eau Claire, Lac à l' Lake Québec, SE Canada
Eau Claire, Lac à L' see St. Clair, Lake
30 L6 Eau Claire River River Wisconsin, N USA
188 J16 Eauripik Atoll atoll Caroline Islands, C Micronesia
192 H7 Eauripik Rise undersea feature W Pacific Ocean 03°00′N 142°00′E
102 K15 Eauze Gers, S France 43°52′N 00°06′E
41 P11 Ébano San Luis Potosí, C Mexico 22°16′N 98°26′W
97 K21 Ebbw Vale SE Wales, United Kingdom 51°48′N 03°13′W
79 E17 Ebebiyin NE Equatorial Guinea 02°08′N 11°15′E
95 H22 Ebeltoft Midtjylland, C Denmark 56°11′N 10°42′E
109 X5 Ebenfurth Niederösterreich, E Austria 47°53′N 16°22′E
18 D14 Ebensburg Pennsylvania, NE USA 40°28′N 78°44′W
109 S5 Ebensee Oberösterreich, N Austria 47°48′N 13°46′E
101 H20 Eberbach Baden-Württemberg, SW Germany 49°28′N 08°58′E
121 U8 Eber Gölü salt lake C Turkey
109 U9 Eberndorf Slvn. Dobrla Vas. Kärnten, S Austria 46°33′N 14°35′E
109 R4 Eberschwang Oberösterreich, N Austria 48°09′N 13°37′E
100 O11 Eberswalde-Finow Brandenburg, E Germany 52°50′N 13°48′E
Ebesfalva see Dumbrăveni
165 T4 Ebetsu var. Ebetu. Hokkaidō, NE Japan 43°08′N 141°37′E
Ebetu see Ebetsu
Ebinayon see Evinayong
158 I4 Ebinur Hu Lake NW China
138 I3 Ebla Ar. Tell Mardīkh. site of ancient city Idlib, NW Syria
Eblana see Dublin
108 H7 Ebnat Sankt Gallen, NE Switzerland 47°16′N 09°07′E
107 L18 Eboli Campania, S Italy 40°37′N 15°03′E
79 E16 Ebolowa Sud, S Cameroon 02°56′N 11°11′E
79 N21 Ebombo Kasai-Oriental, C Dem. Rep. Congo 05°42′S 26°07′E
189 T9 Ebon Atoll var. Epoon. atoll Ralik Chain, S Marshall Islands
Ebora see Évora
Eboracum see York
Eborodunum see Yverdon
101 J19 Ebrach Bayern, C Germany 49°49′N 10°30′E
109 X5 Ebreichsdorf Niederösterreich, E Austria 47°58′N 16°24′E
105 S6 Ebro River NE Spain
105 N3 Ebro, Embalse del Reservoir N Spain
120 G7 Ebro Fan undersea feature W Mediterranean Sea
Eburacum see York
Ebusus see Ibiza
Ebusus see Eivissa
99 F20 Écaussinnes-d'Enghien Hainaut, SW Belgium 50°34′N 04°10′E
Ecbatana see Hamadān
21 Q6 Eccles West Virginia, NE USA 37°46′N 81°16′W
115 L14 Eceabat Çanakkale, NW Turkey 40°12′N 26°22′E
171 O2 Echague Luzon, N Philippines 16°42′N 121°37′E
Ech Cheliff/Ech Chleff see Chlef
Echeng see Ezhou
115 C18 Echinádes island group W Greece
114 J12 Echínos var. Ehinos, Ekhínos. Anatolikí Makedonía kai Thráki, NE Greece 41°16′N 25°00′E
Echizen see Takefu
164 J12 Echizen-misaki headland Honshū, SW Japan 35°59′N 135°57′E
Echmiadzin see Vagharshapat
8 J8 Echo Bay Northwest Territories, NW Canada 66°04′N 118°W
35 Y11 Echo Bay Nevada, W USA 36°19′N 114°27′W
36 L9 Echo Cliffs cliff Arizona, SW USA
14 C10 Echo Lake Lake Ontario, S Canada
35 Q7 Echo Summit ▲ California, W USA 38°47′N 120°06′W
14 L8 Échouani, Lac Lake Québec, SE Canada
99 L17 Echt Limburg, SE Netherlands 51°07′N 05°52′E
101 H22 Echterdingen ✈ (Stuttgart) Baden-Württemberg, SW Germany 48°40′N 09°13′E
99 N24 Echternach Grevenmacher, E Luxembourg 49°49′N 06°25′E
183 N11 Echuca Victoria, SE Australia 36°10′S 144°20′E
104 L14 Écija anc. Astigi. Andalucía, SW Spain 37°33′N 05°04′W
Eckengraf see Viesīte
100 I7 Eckernförde Schleswig-Holstein, N Germany 54°28′N 09°49′E
100 J7 Eckernförder Bucht inlet N Germany
102 L7 Écommoy Sarthe, NW France 47°51′N 00°15′E
14 L10 Écorce, Lac de l' Lake Québec, SE Canada
15 Q8 Écorces, Rivière aux River Québec, SE Canada
56 C7 Ecuador off. Republic of Ecuador. ◆ republic NW South America
Ecuador, Republic of see Ecuador
95 I17 Ed Västra Götaland, S Sweden 58°55′N 11°55′E
Ed see 'Īdī
98 I9 Edam Noord-Holland, C Netherlands 52°30′N 05°02′E
96 K4 Eday island NE Scotland, United Kingdom
25 S17 Edcouch Texas, SW USA 26°17′N 97°57′W
80 C11 Ed Da'ein Southern Darfur, W Sudan 11°25′N 26°08′E
80 G11 Ed Damazin var. Ad Damazīn. Blue Nile, E Sudan 11°45′N 34°20′E
80 G8 Ed Damer var. Ad Dāmir, Ad Damar. River Nile, NE Sudan 17°37′N 33°59′E
80 E8 Ed Debba Northern, N Sudan 18°02′N 30°56′E
80 F10 Ed Dueim var. Ad Duwaym, Ad Duwēm. White Nile, C Sudan 13°38′N 32°36′E
183 Q16 Eddystone Point headland Tasmania, SE Australia 41°01′S 148°18′E
97 I25 Eddystone Rocks rocks SW England, United Kingdom
29 W15 Eddyville Iowa, C USA 41°09′N 92°37′W
20 H7 Eddyville Kentucky, S USA 37°03′N 88°02′W
98 L12 Ede Gelderland, C Netherlands 52°03′N 05°40′E
77 T16 Ede Osun, SW Nigeria 07°40′N 04°21′E
79 D16 Edéa Littoral, SW Cameroon 03°47′N 10°08′E
111 M20 Edelény Borsod-Abaúj-Zemplén, NE Hungary 48°18′N 20°40′E
183 R12 Eden New South Wales, SE Australia 37°04′S 149°51′E
21 T8 Eden North Carolina, SE USA 36°29′N 79°46′W
25 P9 Eden Texas, SW USA 31°13′N 99°51′W
97 K14 Eden River NW England, United Kingdom
83 I23 Edenburg Free State, C South Africa 29°45′S 25°57′E
185 D24 Edendale Southland, South Island, New Zealand 46°18′S 168°48′E
97 E18 Edenderry Ir. Éadan Doire. Offaly, C Ireland 53°21′N 07°03′W
182 L11 Edenhope Victoria, SE Australia 37°04′S 141°15′E
21 X8 Edenton North Carolina, SE USA 36°04′N 76°39′W
101 G16 Eder River NW Germany
101 H15 Edersee Lake W Germany
114 E13 Édessa var. Édhessa. Kentrikí Makedonía, N Greece 40°48′N 22°03′E
Edessa see Şanlıurfa
Edfu see Idfu
29 P16 Edgar Nebraska, C USA 40°22′N 97°58′W
19 P13 Edgartown Martha's Vineyard, Massachusetts, NE USA 41°23′N 70°30′W
39 X13 Edgecumbe, Mount ▲ Baranof Island, Alaska, USA 57°03′N 135°45′W
21 Q13 Edgefield South Carolina, SE USA 33°50′N 81°57′W
29 P6 Edgeley North Dakota, N USA 46°19′N 98°42′W
28 I11 Edgemont South Dakota, N USA 43°18′N 103°49′W
92 O3 Edgeøya island S Svalbard
27 Q4 Edgerton Kansas, C USA 38°45′N 95°00′W
29 S10 Edgerton Minnesota, N USA 43°52′N 96°07′W
21 X3 Edgewood Maryland, NE USA 39°20′N 76°21′W
25 V6 Edgewood Texas, SW USA 32°42′N 95°53′W
Édhessa see Édessa
29 V9 Edina Minnesota, N USA 44°53′N 93°21′W
27 U2 Edina Missouri, C USA 40°10′N 92°10′W
25 S17 Edinburg Texas, SW USA 26°18′N 98°10′W
65 M24 Edinburgh var. Settlement of Edinburgh. ○ (Tristan da Cunha) NW Tristan da Cunha 37°03′S 12°18′W
96 J12 Edinburgh ● S Scotland, United Kingdom 55°57′N 03°13′W
31 P14 Edinburgh Indiana, N USA 39°19′N 86°00′W
96 J12 Edinburgh ✈ S Scotland, United Kingdom 55°57′N 03°22′W
116 L8 Edineţ var. Edineţi, Rus. Yedintsy. NW Moldova 48°10′N 27°18′E
Edineţi see Edineţ
Edingen see Enghien
136 B9 Edirne Eng. Adrianople; anc. Adrianopolis, Hadrianopolis. Edirne, NW Turkey 41°40′N 26°34′E
136 B11 Edirne ◈ province NW Turkey
18 K15 Edison New Jersey, NE USA 40°31′N 74°24′W
21 S15 Edisto Island South Carolina, SE USA 32°34′N 80°17′W
21 R14 Edisto River River South Carolina, SE USA
33 S10 Edith, Mount ▲ Montana, NW USA 46°25′N 111°10′W
27 N10 Edmond Oklahoma, C USA 35°40′N 97°30′W
32 H8 Edmonds Washington, NW USA 47°48′N 122°22′W
11 Q14 Edmonton province capital Alberta, SW Canada 53°34′N 113°25′W
20 K7 Edmonton Kentucky, S USA 36°59′N 85°39′W
11 Q14 Edmonton ✈ Alberta, SW Canada 53°22′N 113°43′W
29 P3 Edmore North Dakota, N USA 48°22′N 98°26′W
13 N13 Edmundston New Brunswick, SE Canada 47°22′N 68°20′W
25 U12 Edna Texas, SW USA 29°00′N 96°41′W
39 X14 Edna Bay Kosciusko Island, Alaska, USA 55°54′N 133°40′W
77 U16 Edo ◈ state S Nigeria
106 F6 Edolo Lombardia, N Italy 46°13′N 10°20′E
64 L6 Edoras Bank undersea feature C Atlantic Ocean
96 G7 Edrachillis Bay bay NW Scotland, United Kingdom
136 B12 Edremit Balıkesir, NW Turkey 39°34′N 27°01′E
136 B12 Edremit Körfezi gulf NW Turkey
95 P14 Edsbro Stockholm, C Sweden 59°54′N 18°30′E
95 N18 Edsbruk Kalmar, S Sweden 58°01′N 16°30′E
94 M12 Edsbyn Gävleborg, C Sweden 61°22′N 15°45′E
11 O14 Edson Alberta, SW Canada 53°36′N 116°28′W
62 K13 Eduardo Castex La Pampa, C Argentina 35°55′S 64°18′W
58 F12 Eduardo Gomes ✈ (Manaus) Amazonas, NW Brazil 05°55′S 35°15′W
Edwardesabad see Bannu
67 U9 Edward, Lake var. Albert Edward Nyanza, Edward Nyanza, Lac Idi Amin, Lake Rutanzige. Lake Uganda/Dem. Rep. Congo
Edward Nyanza see Edward, Lake
22 K5 Edwards Mississippi, S USA 32°19′N 90°36′W
25 O10 Edwards Plateau plain Texas, SW USA
30 J11 Edwards River River Illinois, N USA
30 K15 Edwardsville Illinois, N USA 38°48′N 89°57′W
195 X4 Edward VIII Gulf bay Antarctica
195 O13 Edward VII Peninsula peninsula Antarctica
10 J11 Edziza, Mount ▲ British Columbia, W Canada 57°43′N 130°39′W
23 H16 Edzo prev. Rae-Edzo. Northwest Territories, NW Canada 62°44′N 115°55′W
39 N12 Eek Alaska, USA 60°13′N 162°01′W
99 D16 Eeklo var. Eekloo. Oost-Vlaanderen, NW Belgium 51°11′N 03°34′E
Eekloo see Eeklo
39 N12 Eek River River Alaska, USA
98 N6 Eelde Drenthe, NE Netherlands 53°07′N 06°30′E
34 L5 Eel River River California, W USA
31 P12 Eel River River Indiana, N USA
Eems see Ems
98 O4 Eemshaven Groningen, NE Netherlands 53°28′N 06°50′E
98 O5 Eems Kanaal canal NE Netherlands
98 M11 Eerbeek Gelderland, E Netherlands 52°07′N 06°04′E
99 C17 Eernegem West-Vlaanderen, W Belgium 51°08′N 03°03′E
99 J15 Eersel Noord-Brabant, S Netherlands 51°22′N 05°19′E
Eesti Vabariik see Estonia
187 R14 Efate var. Éfaté, Fr. Vaté; prev. Sandwich Island. island C Vanuatu
Efate see Efate
109 S4 Eferding Oberösterreich, N Austria 48°18′N 14°00′E
30 M15 Effingham Illinois, N USA 39°07′N 88°32′W
117 N15 Eforie-Nord Constanţa, SE Romania 44°04′N 28°37′E
117 N15 Eforie-Sud Constanţa, E Romania 44°00′N 28°38′E
Efyrnwy, Afon see Vyrnwy
Eg see Hentiy
107 G23 Egadi, Isole island group S Italy
35 X6 Egan Range ▲▲ Nevada, W USA
14 K12 Eganville Ontario, SE Canada 45°33′N 77°03′W
Ege Denizi see Aegean Sea
39 O14 Egegik Alaska, USA 58°13′N 157°22′W
111 L21 Eger Ger. Erlau. Heves, NE Hungary 47°54′N 20°22′E
Eger see Cheb, Czech Republic
Eger see Ohre, Czech Republic/Germany
173 P8 Egeria Fracture Zone tectonic feature W Indian Ocean
95 C17 Egersund Rogaland, S Norway 58°27′N 06°01′E
108 J7 Egg Vorarlberg, NW Austria 47°27′N 09°55′E
101 H14 Egge-gebirge ▲▲ C Germany
109 Q4 Eggelsberg Oberösterreich, N Austria 48°04′N 13°00′E
109 W2 Eggenburg Niederösterreich, NE Austria 48°29′N 15°49′E
101 N22 Eggenfelden Bayern, SE Germany 48°24′N 12°45′E
18 J17 Egg Harbor City New Jersey, NE USA 39°31′N 74°39′W
65 G25 Egg Island island W Saint Helena
183 N14 Egg Lagoon Tasmania, SE Australia 39°42′S 143°57′E
Egoli see Johannesburg
136 I15 Eğridir Gölü Lake W Turkey
Eğri Palanka see Kriva Palanka
95 G23 Egtved Syddanmark, C Denmark 55°34′N 09°18′E
123 U5 Egvekinot Chukotskiy Avtonomnyy Okrug, NE Russian Federation 66°13′N 178°55′W
75 V9 Egypt off. Arab Republic of Egypt, Ar. Jumhūrīyah Miṣr al 'Arabīyah, prev. United Arab Republic; anc. Aegyptus. ◆ republic NE Africa
30 L17 Egypt, Lake Of Reservoir Illinois, N USA
162 I14 Ehen Hudag var. Alx Youqi. Nei Mongol Zizhiqu, N China 39°12′N 101°40′E
164 F14 Ehime off. Ehime-ken. ◈ prefecture Shikoku, SW Japan
Ehime-ken see Ehime
101 I23 Ehingen Baden-Württemberg, S Germany 48°16′N 09°43′E
Ehinos see Echínos
21 R14 Ehrhardt South Carolina, SE USA 33°06′N 81°00′W
108 L7 Ehrwald Tirol, W Austria 47°24′N 10°52′E
191 W6 Eiao island Îles Marquises, NE French Polynesia
105 P2 Eibar País Vasco, N Spain 43°11′N 02°28′W
98 O11 Eibergen Gelderland, E Netherlands 52°06′N 06°39′E
109 V9 Eibiswald Steiermark, SE Austria 46°40′N 15°15′E
109 P8 Eichham ▲ SW Austria 47°04′N 12°24′E
101 J15 Eichsfeld hill range C Germany
101 K21 Eichstätt Bayern, SE Germany 48°53′N 11°11′E
100 H8 Eider River N Germany
94 E13 Eidfjord Hordaland, S Norway 60°26′N 07°05′E
94 D13 Eidfjorden fjord S Norway
94 F9 Eidsvåg Møre og Romsdal, S Norway 62°46′N 08°00′E
95 I14 Eidsvoll Akershus, S Norway 60°19′N 11°14′E
92 N2 Eidsvollfjellet ▲ NW Svalbard 79°13′N 13°23′E
Eier-Berg see Suur Munamägi
101 D18 Eifel plateau W Germany
108 E9 Eiger ▲ C Switzerland 46°33′N 08°02′E
96 G10 Eigg island W Scotland, United Kingdom
155 D24 Eight Degree Channel channel India/Maldives
44 G1 Eight Mile Rock Grand Bahama Island, N Bahamas 26°28′N 78°43′W
194 J9 Eights Coast physical region Antarctica
180 K6 Eighty Mile Beach beach Western Australia
99 L18 Eijsden Limburg, SE Netherlands 50°47′N 05°41′E
95 G15 Eikeren Lake S Norway
Eil see Eyl
Eilat see Elat
183 O12 Eildon Victoria, SE Australia 37°17′S 145°57′E
183 O12 Eildon, Lake Lake Victoria, SE Australia
80 E8 Eilei Northern Kordofan, C Sudan 16°33′N 30°54′E
101 N15 Eilenburg Sachsen, E Germany 51°28′N 12°37′E
Eil Malk see Mecherchar
94 H13 Eina Oppland, S Norway 60°37′N 10°37′E
138 E12 Ein Avdat prev. En 'Avedat. well S Israel
101 I14 Einbeck Niedersachsen, C Germany 51°49′N 09°52′E
99 K15 Eindhoven Noord-Brabant, S Netherlands 51°26′N 05°30′E
108 G8 Einsiedeln Schwyz, NE Switzerland 47°07′N 08°45′E
Eipel see Ipel'
Éire see Ireland
Éireann, Muir see Irish Sea
Eirik Outer Ridge see Eirik Ridge
64 I6 Eirik Ridge var. Eirik Outer Ridge. undersea feature E Labrador Sea
92 I3 Eiríksjökull ▲ C Iceland 64°47′N 20°23′W
59 B14 Eirunepé Amazonas, N Brazil 06°38′S 69°53′W
99 L17 Eisden Limburg, NE Belgium 51°05′N 05°42′E
83 F18 Eiseb River Botswana/Namibia
Eisen see Yeongcheon
101 J16 Eisenach Thüringen, C Germany 50°59′N 10°19′E
Eisenburg see Vasvár
109 U6 Eisenerz Steiermark, SE Austria 47°33′N 14°53′E
100 Q13 Eisenhüttenstadt Brandenburg, E Germany 52°09′N 14°36′E
109 U10 Eisenkappel Slvn. Železna Kapela. Kärnten, S Austria 46°27′N 14°33′E
Eisenmarkt see Hunedoara
109 Y5 Eisenstadt Burgenland, E Austria 47°50′N 16°32′E
Eishū see Yeongju
119 H15 Eišiškes Vilnius, SE Lithuania 54°10′N 24°59′E
101 L15 Eisleben Sachsen-Anhalt, C Germany 51°32′N 11°33′E
190 I3 Eita Tarawa, W Kiribati 01°21′N 173°05′E
Eitape see Aitape
105 V11 Eivissa var. Iviza, Cast. Ibiza; anc. Ebusus. Ibiza, Spain, W Mediterranean Sea 38°54′N 01°26′E
Eivissa see Ibiza
105 R4 Ejea de los Caballeros Aragón, NE Spain 42°07′N 01°09′W
40 E8 Ejido Insurgentes Baja California Sur, NW Mexico 25°18′N 111°51′W
Ejin Qi see Dalain Hob
Ejmiadzin/Ejmiatsin see Vagharshapat
77 P16 Ejura C Ghana 07°23′N 01°22′W
41 R16 Ejutla var. Ejutla de Crespo. Oaxaca, SE Mexico 16°33′N 96°40′W
Ejutla de Crespo see Ejutla
33 Y10 Ekalaka Montana, NW USA 45°52′N 104°32′W
Ekapa see Cape Town
Ekaterinodar see Krasnodar
93 L20 Ekenäs Fin. Tammisaari. Etelä-Suomi, SW Finland 60°00′N 23°30′E
146 B13 Ekerem Rus. Okarem. Balkan Welaýaty, W Turkmenistan 38°06′N 53°52′E
184 M13 Eketahuna Manawatu-Wanganui, North Island, New Zealand 40°41′S 175°40′E
Ekhínos see Echínos
Ekiatapskiy Khrebet see Ekvyvatapskiy Khrebet
Ekibastuz see Yekibastuz
123 R13 Ekimchan Amurskaya Oblast', SE Russian Federation 53°04′N 132°56′E
95 O15 Ekoln Lake C Sweden
80 I7 Ekowit Red Sea, NE Sudan 18°46′N 37°07′E
95 L19 Eksjö Jönköping, S Sweden 57°40′N 15°00′E
93 I15 Ekträsk Västerbotten, N Sweden 64°28′N 19°49′E
39 O13 Ekuk Alaska, USA 58°48′N 158°25′W
123 U5 Ekvyvatapskiy Khrebet prev. Ekiatapskiy Khrebet. ▲▲ NE Russian Federation
12 F9 Ekwan River Ontario, C Canada
39 O13 Ekwok Alaska, USA 59°21′N 157°28′W
166 M6 Ela Mandalay, C Myanmar (Burma) 19°37′N 96°15′E
El Aaiun see El Ayoun
81 N15 Ēl Ābrēd Sumalē, E Ethiopia 05°33′N 45°12′E
115 F22 Elafónisos island S Greece
115 F22 Elafonísou, Porthmós strait S Greece
El-Aïoun see El Ayoun
El 'Alamein see Al 'Alamayn
41 Q12 El Alazán Veracruz-Llave, C Mexico 21°06′N 97°43′W
57 J18 El Alto var. La Paz. ✈ (La Paz) La Paz, W Bolivia 16°31′S 68°07′W
Elam see Īlām
El Amparo see El Amparo de Apure
54 I8 El Amparo de Apure var. El Amparo. Apure, C Venezuela 07°07′N 70°47′W
171 R13 Elara Pulau Ambelau, E Indonesia 03°49′S 127°10′E
El Araïch/El Araïche see Larache
40 D6 El Arco Baja California Norte, NW Mexico 28°03′N 113°25′W
El 'Arîsh see Al 'Arīsh
115 L25 Elása island SE Greece
El Asnam see Chlef
Elassón see Elassóna
115 E15 Elassóna prev. Elassón. Thessalía, C Greece 39°53′N 22°10′E
105 N2 El Astillero Cantabria, N Spain 43°23′N 03°45′W
138 F14 Elat var. Eilat, Elath. Southern, S Israel 29°33′N 34°57′E
Elat, Gulf of see Aqaba, Gulf of
Elath see Elat, Israel
Elath see Al 'Aqabah, Jordan
115 C17 Eláti ▲ Lefkáda, Iónia Nisiá, Greece, C Mediterranean Sea 38°43′N 20°38′E
188 L16 Elato Atoll atoll Caroline Islands, C Micronesia
80 C7 El'Atrun Northern Darfur, NW Sudan 18°11′N 26°40′E
74 H6 El Ayoun var. El Aaiun, El-Aïoun, La Youne. NE Morocco 34°39′N 02°29′W
137 N14 Elâzığ var. Elazig, Elâziz. Elâzığ, E Turkey 38°41′N 39°14′E
137 O14 Elâzığ var. Elazig, Elâziz. ◈ province C Turkey
Elâzig/Elâziz see Elâzığ
23 Q7 Elba Alabama, S USA 31°24′N 86°04′W
106 E13 Elba, Isola d' island Archipelago Toscano, C Italy
123 S13 El'ban Khabarovskiy Kray, E Russian Federation 50°03′N 136°34′E
54 F6 El Banco Magdalena, N Colombia 09°00′N 74°01′W
El Barco see O Barco
104 L8 El Barco de Ávila Castilla y León, N Spain 40°21′N 05°31′W
El Barco de Valdeorras see O Barco
138 H7 El Barouk, Jabal ▲ C Lebanon
113 L20 Elbasan var. Elbasani. Elbasan, C Albania 41°07′N 20°04′E
113 L20 Elbasan ◈ district C Albania
Elbasani see Elbasan
54 K6 El Baúl Cojedes, C Venezuela 08°59′N 68°16′W
86 D11 Elbe Cz. Labe. River Czech Republic/Germany
100 L13 Elbe-Havel-Kanal canal E Germany
100 K9 Elbe-Lübeck-Kanal canal N Germany
57 L15 El Beni var. El Beni. ◈ department N Bolivia
El Beni see El Beni
138 H7 El Beqaa var. Al Biqā', Bekaa Valley. valley E Lebanon
25 R6 Elbert Texas, SW USA 33°15′N 98°58′W
37 R5 Elbert, Mount ▲ Colorado, C USA 39°07′N 106°26′W
23 U3 Elberton Georgia, SE USA 34°06′N 82°52′W
100 K11 Elbe-Seiten-Kanal canal N Germany
102 M4 Elbeuf Seine-Maritime, N France 49°16′N 01°01′E
Elbing see Elbląg
136 M15 Elbistan Kahramanmaraş, S Turkey 38°14′N 37°11′E
110 K7 Elbląg var. Elbing, Ger. Elbing. Warmińsko-Mazurskie, NE Poland 54°10′N 19°25′E
43 N10 El Bluff Región Autónoma Atlántico Sur, SE Nicaragua 12°00′N 83°40′W
63 H17 El Bolsón Río Negro, W Argentina 41°59′S 71°35′W
105 P11 El Bonillo Castilla-La Mancha, C Spain 38°57′N 02°32′W
El Bordo see Patía
El Boulaida/El Boulaïda see Blida
11 T16 Elbow Saskatchewan, S Canada 51°07′N 106°30′W
29 S7 Elbow Lake Minnesota, N USA 45°59′N 95°58′W
127 N16 El'brus var. Gora El'brus. ▲ SW Russian Federation 42°29′N 43°21′E
El'brus, Gora see El'brus
126 M15 El'brusskiy Karachayevo-Cherkesskaya Respublika, SW Russian Federation 43°36′N 42°06′E
81 D14 El Buhayrat var. Lakes State. ◈ state C South Sudan
El Bur see Ceel Buur
98 L10 Elburg Gelderland, E Netherlands 52°27′N 05°46′E
105 O6 El Burgo de Osma Castilla y León, C Spain 41°36′N 03°04′W
Elburz Mountains see Alborz, Reshteh-ye Kūhhā-ye
35 V17 El Cajon California, W USA 32°46′N 116°52′W
63 H22 El Calafate var. Calafate. Santa Cruz, S Argentina 50°20′S 72°13′W
55 Q8 El Callao Bolívar, E Venezuela 07°18′N 61°48′W
25 U12 El Campo Texas, SW USA 29°12′N 96°16′W
54 I7 El Cantón Barinas, W Venezuela 07°23′N 71°10′W
35 Q8 El Capitan ▲ California, W USA 37°46′N 119°39′W
54 H5 El Carmelo Zulia, NW Venezuela 10°20′N 71°48′W
62 J5 El Carmen Jujuy, NW Argentina 24°24′S 65°16′W
54 E5 El Carmen de Bolívar Bolívar, NW Colombia 09°43′N 75°07′W
55 O8 El Casabe Bolívar, SE Venezuela 06°26′N 63°35′W
42 M12 El Castillo de La Concepción Río San Juan, SE Nicaragua 11°01′N 84°24′W
El Cayo see San Ignacio
35 X17 El Centro California, W USA 32°47′N 115°33′W
55 N6 El Chaparro Anzoátegui, NE Venezuela 09°12′N 65°03′W
105 S12 Elche Cat. Elx; anc. Ilici, Lat. Illicis. Valenciana, E Spain 38°16′N 00°41′W
105 Q12 Elche de la Sierra Castilla-La Mancha, C Spain 38°27′N 02°03′W
41 U15 El Chichonal, Volcán Volcano SE Mexico 17°20′N 93°12′W
40 C2 El Chinero Baja California Norte, NW Mexico
181 R1 Elcho Island island Wessel Islands, Northern Territory, N Australia
63 H18 El Corcovado Chubut, SW Argentina 43°31′S 71°30′W
105 R12 Elda Valenciana, E Spain 38°29′N 00°47′W
100 M10 Elde River NE Germany
98 L12 Elden Gelderland, E Netherlands 51°57′N 05°53′E
81 J16 El Der spring/well S Ethiopia 03°55′N 39°48′E
El Dere see Ceel Dheere
40 B2 El Descanso Baja California Norte, NW Mexico 32°08′N 116°51′W
40 E3 El Desemboque Sonora, NW Mexico 30°33′N 112°59′W
54 F5 El Difícil var. Ariguaní. Magdalena, N Colombia 09°51′N 74°12′W
123 R10 El'dikan Respublika Sakha (Yakutiya), NE Russian Federation 60°46′N 135°04′E
El Djazair see Alger
El Djelfa see Djelfa
29 X15 Eldon Iowa, C USA 40°55′N 92°13′W

◆ Country ● Country Capital ◇ Dependent Territory ○ Dependent Territory Capital ◈ Administrative Regions ✈ International Airport ▲ Mountain ▲▲ Mountain Range Volcano River Lake Reservoir

27 U5 Eldon Missouri, C USA 38°21′N 92°34′W
54 E13 El Doncello Caquetá, S Colombia 01°43′N 75°17′W
29 W13 Eldora Iowa, C USA 42°21′N 93°06′W
60 G12 Eldorado Misiones, NE Argentina 26°24′S 54°38′W
40 I9 El Dorado Sinaloa, C Mexico 24°19′N 107°23′W
27 U14 El Dorado Arkansas, C USA 33°12′N 92°40′W
30 M17 Eldorado Illinois, N USA 37°48′N 88°26′W
27 O6 El Dorado Kansas, C USA 37°51′N 96°52′W
26 K12 Eldorado Oklahoma, C USA 34°28′N 99°39′W
25 O9 Eldorado Texas, SW USA 30°53′N 100°37′W
55 Q8 El Dorado Bolívar, E Venezuela 06°45′N 61°37′W
54 F10 El Dorado ✈ (Bogotá) Cundinamarca, C Colombia 01°15′N 71°52′W
El Dorado see California
27 O6 El Dorado Lake ⊠ Kansas, C USA
27 S6 El Dorado Springs Missouri, C USA 37°53′N 94°01′W
81 H18 Eldoret Rift Valley, W Kenya 0°31′N 35°17′E
29 Z14 Eldridge Iowa, C USA 41°39′N 90°34′W
95 J21 Eldsberga Halland, S Sweden 56°36′N 13°00′E
25 R4 Electra Texas, SW USA 34°01′N 98°55′W
37 Q7 Electra Lake ⊠ Colorado, C USA
38 B8 'Ele'ele var. Eleele. Kaua'i, Hawaii, USA, C Pacific Ocean 21°54′N 159°35′W
Eleele see 'Ele'ele
Elefantes see Lepelle
115 H19 Elefsína prev. Elevsís. Attikí, C Greece 38°02′N 23°33′E
115 G19 Eléftheres anc. Eleutherae. site of ancient city Attikí/Stereá Elláda, C Greece
114 I13 Eleftheroúpoli prev. Elevtheroúpolis. Anatolikí Makedonía kai Thráki, NE Greece 40°55′N 24°15′E
74 F10 El Eglab ▲ SW Algeria
118 F10 Eleja C Latvia 56°24′N 23°41′E
Elek see Yelek
119 G14 Elektrėnai Vilnius, SE Lithuania 54°47′N 24°35′E
126 L3 Elektrostal' Moskovskaya Oblast', W Russian Federation 55°47′N 38°24′E
81 H15 Elemi Triangle disputed region Kenya/Sudan
114 K9 Elena Veliko Tŭrnovo, N Bulgaria 42°55′N 25°53′E
54 G16 El Encanto Amazonas, S Colombia 01°45′S 73°12′W
37 R14 Elephant Butte Reservoir ⊠ New Mexico, SW USA
Éléphant, Chaîne de l' see Dâmrei, Chuŏr Phmun
194 G2 Elephant Island island South Shetland Islands, Antarctica
Elephant River see Olifants
El Escorial see San Lorenzo de El Escorial
Élesd see Aleşd
114 F11 Eleshnitsa ∼ W Bulgaria
137 S13 Eleşkirt Ağrı, E Turkey 39°22′N 42°48′E
42 F5 El Estor Izabal, E Guatemala 15°37′N 89°22′W
Eleutherae see Eléftheres
44 I2 Eleuthera Island island N Bahamas
37 S5 Elevenmile Canyon Reservoir ⊠ Colorado, C USA
27 W8 Eleven Point River ∼ Arkansas/Missouri, C USA
Elevsís see Elefsína
Elevtheroúpolis see Eleftheroúpoli
El Faiyûm see Al Fayyūm
80 B10 El Fasher var. Al Fāshir. Northern Darfur, W Sudan 13°37′N 25°22′E
El Fashn see Al Fashn
El Ferrol/El Ferrol del Caudillo see Ferrol
39 W13 Elfin Cove Chichagof Island, Alaska, USA 58°09′N 136°16′W
105 W4 El Fluvià ∼ NE Spain
40 H7 El Fuerte Sinaloa, W Mexico 26°28′N 108°35′W
80 D11 El Fula Southern Kordofan, C Sudan 11°44′N 28°20′E
El Gedaref see Gedaref
80 A10 El Geneina var. Ajjinena, Al-Genain, Al Junaynah. Western Darfur, W Sudan 13°27′N 22°30′E
96 J8 Elgin NE Scotland, United Kingdom 57°39′N 03°20′W
30 M10 Elgin Illinois, N USA 42°02′N 88°16′W
29 P14 Elgin Nebraska, C USA 41°58′N 98°04′W
35 Y9 Elgin Nevada, W USA 37°19′N 114°30′W
28 L6 Elgin North Dakota, N USA 46°24′N 101°51′W
26 M12 Elgin Oklahoma, C USA 34°46′N 98°17′W
25 T10 Elgin Texas, SW USA 30°21′N 97°22′W
123 R9 El'ginskiy Respublika Sakha (Yakutiya), NE Russian Federation 64°27′N 141°57′E
El Giza see Giza
74 J8 El Goléa var. Al Golea. C Algeria 30°35′N 02°59′E
40 D2 El Golfo de Santa Clara Sonora, NW Mexico 31°48′N 114°40′W
81 G18 Elgon, Mount ▲ E Uganda 01°07′N 34°29′E
94 I10 Elgpiggen ▲ S Norway 62°13′N 11°18′E
105 T4 El Grado Aragón, NE Spain 42°09′N 00°13′E
40 L6 El Guaje, Laguna ⊠ NE Mexico
54 H6 El Guayabo Zulia, W Venezuela 08°37′N 72°20′W
77 O6 El Guețțâra oasis N Mali
76 J6 El Ḥammâmi desert N Mauritania
76 M5 El Ḥank cliff N Mauritania
El Haseke see Al Ḥasakah
80 H10 El Hawata Gedaref, E Sudan 13°25′N 34°42′E
El Higo see Higos
171 T16 Eliase Pulau Selaru, E Indonesia 08°16′S 130°49′E
Elías Piña see Comendador
25 R6 Eliasville Texas, SW USA 32°55′N 98°46′W
Elichpur see Achalpur
37 V13 Elida New Mexico, SW USA 33°57′N 103°39′W
115 F18 Elikónas ▲ C Greece
67 T10 Elila ∼ W Dem. Rep. Congo
39 N9 Elim Alaska, USA 64°37′N 162°15′W
Elimberrum see Auch
Eliocroca see Lorca
61 B16 Elisa Santa Fe, C Argentina 30°42′S 61°04′W
Elisabethstedt see Dumbrăveni
Élisabethville see Lubumbashi
127 O13 Elista Respublika Kalmykiya, SW Russian Federation 46°18′N 44°09′E
182 I9 Elizabeth South Australia 34°44′S 138°39′E
21 Q3 Elizabeth West Virginia, NE USA 39°04′N 81°24′W
19 Q9 Elizabeth, Cape headland Maine, NE USA 43°34′N 70°12′W
21 Y8 Elizabeth City North Carolina, SE USA 36°18′N 76°16′W
21 P8 Elizabethton Tennessee, S USA 36°22′N 82°15′W
30 M17 Elizabethtown Illinois, N USA 37°24′N 88°21′W
20 K6 Elizabethtown Kentucky, S USA 37°41′N 85°51′W
18 L7 Elizabethtown New York, NE USA 44°13′N 73°38′W
21 U11 Elizabethtown North Carolina, SE USA 34°36′N 78°36′W
18 G15 Elizabethtown Pennsylvania, NE USA 40°08′N 76°36′W
74 E6 El-Jadida prev. Mazagan. W Morocco 33°15′N 08°27′W
El Jafr see Jafr, Qā' al
80 F11 El Jebelein White Nile, E Sudan 12°38′N 32°51′E
110 N8 Ełk Ger. Lyck. Warmińsko-mazurskie, NE Poland 53°51′N 22°20′E
110 O8 Ełk ∼ NE Poland
29 Y12 Elkader Iowa, C USA 42°51′N 91°24′W
80 G9 El Kamlin Gezira, C Sudan 15°03′N 33°11′E
33 N11 Elk City Idaho, NW USA 45°50′N 115°28′W
26 K10 Elk City Oklahoma, C USA 35°24′N 99°24′W
27 P7 Elk City Lake ⊠ Kansas, C USA
34 M5 Elk Creek California, W USA 39°34′N 122°34′W
28 J10 Elk Creek ∼ South Dakota, N USA
74 M5 El Kef var. Al Kāf, Le Kef. NW Tunisia 36°13′N 08°44′E
74 F7 El Kelâa Srarhna var. Kal al Sraghna. C Morocco 32°05′N 07°20′W
El Kerak see Al Karak
11 P17 Elkford British Columbia, SW Canada 49°58′N 114°57′W
El Khalil see Hebron
80 E7 El Khandaq Northern, N Sudan 18°34′N 30°34′E
El Khârga see Al Khārijah
31 P11 Elkhart Indiana, N USA 41°40′N 85°58′W
26 H7 Elkhart Kansas, C USA 37°00′N 101°51′W
25 V8 Elkhart Texas, SW USA 31°37′N 95°34′W
30 M7 Elkhart Lake ⊚ Wisconsin, N USA
El Khartûm see Khartoum
37 Q3 Elkhead Mountains ▲ Colorado, C USA
18 I12 Elk Hill ▲ Pennsylvania, NE USA 41°42′N 75°33′W
138 G8 El Khiyam var. Al Khiyām, Khiam. S Lebanon 33°12′N 35°42′E
29 S15 Elkhorn Nebraska, C USA 41°17′N 96°13′W
30 M9 Elkhorn Wisconsin, N USA 42°40′N 88°34′W
29 R14 Elkhorn River ∼ Nebraska, C USA
127 O16 El'khotovo Respublika Severnaya Osetiya, SW Russian Federation 43°18′N 44°17′E
114 L10 Elkhovo prev. Kizilagach. Yambol, E Bulgaria 42°10′N 26°34′E
21 R8 Elkin North Carolina, SE USA 36°14′N 80°51′W
21 S4 Elkins West Virginia, NE USA 38°56′N 79°53′W
195 X3 Elkins, Mount ▲ Antarctica 66°25′S 53°54′E
14 G8 Elk Lake Ontario, S Canada 47°44′N 80°19′W
31 P6 Elk Lake ⊚ Michigan, N USA
18 F12 Elkland Pennsylvania, NE USA 41°59′N 77°16′W
35 W3 Elko Nevada, W USA 40°48′N 115°46′W
11 R14 Elk Point Alberta, SW Canada 53°52′N 110°49′W
29 R12 Elk Point South Dakota, N USA 42°42′N 96°37′W
29 V8 Elk River Minnesota, N USA 45°18′N 93°34′W
20 J10 Elk River ∼ Alabama/Tennessee, S USA
21 R4 Elk River ∼ West Virginia, NE USA
20 I7 Elkton Kentucky, S USA 36°49′N 87°11′W
21 Y2 Elkton Maryland, NE USA 39°37′N 75°50′W
29 R10 Elkton South Dakota, N USA 44°14′N 96°28′W
20 I10 Elkton Tennessee, S USA 35°01′N 86°51′W
21 U5 Elkton Virginia, NE USA 38°22′N 78°35′W
El Kuneitra see Al Qunayṭirah
81 L15 El Kure Somali, E Ethiopia 05°37′N 42°05′E
80 D12 El Lagowa Southern Kordofan, C Sudan 11°23′N 29°10′E
39 S12 Ellamar Alaska, USA 60°54′N 146°37′W
Ellás see Greece
23 S6 Ellaville Georgia, SE USA 32°14′N 84°18′W
197 P9 Ellef Ringnes Island island Nunavut, N Canada
29 V10 Ellendale Minnesota, N USA 43°53′N 93°19′W
29 P7 Ellendale North Dakota, N USA 45°57′N 98°33′W
36 M6 Ellen, Mount ▲ Utah, W USA 38°06′N 110°48′W
32 I9 Ellensburg Washington, NW USA 47°00′N 120°34′W
18 K12 Ellenville New York, NE USA 41°43′N 74°24′W
Ellep see Lib
21 T10 Ellerbe North Carolina, SE USA 35°04′N 79°45′W
197 P10 Ellesmere Island island Queen Elizabeth Islands, Nunavut, N Canada
185 H19 Ellesmere, Lake ⊚ South Island, New Zealand
97 K18 Ellesmere Port C England, United Kingdom 53°17′N 02°54′W
31 O14 Ellettsville Indiana, N USA 39°13′N 86°37′W
99 E19 Ellezelles Hainaut, SW Belgium 50°44′N 03°40′E
8 L7 Ellice ∼ Nunavut, NE Canada
Ellice Islands see Tuvalu
Ellichpur see Achalpur
21 W3 Ellicott City Maryland, NE USA 39°16′N 76°48′W
23 S2 Ellijay Georgia, SE USA 34°42′N 84°28′W
27 W7 Ellington Missouri, C USA 37°14′N 90°58′W
26 L5 Ellinwood Kansas, C USA 38°21′N 98°34′W
83 J24 Elliot Eastern Cape, SE South Africa 31°20′S 27°51′E
14 D10 Elliot Lake Ontario, S Canada 46°24′N 82°38′W
181 X6 Elliot, Mount ▲ Queensland, E Australia 19°36′S 147°02′E
21 T5 Elliott Knob ▲ Virginia, NE USA 38°10′N 79°18′W
26 K4 Ellis Kansas, C USA 38°56′N 99°33′W
182 F8 Elliston South Australia 33°40′S 134°56′E
22 M7 Ellisville Mississippi, S USA 31°36′N 89°12′W
105 V5 El Llobregat ∼ NE Spain
96 L9 Ellon NE Scotland, United Kingdom 57°22′N 02°06′W
Ellore see Elūru
21 S13 Elloree South Carolina, SE USA 33°34′N 80°37′W
26 M4 Ellsworth Kansas, C USA 38°45′N 98°15′W
19 S7 Ellsworth Maine, NE USA 44°32′N 68°25′W
30 I6 Ellsworth Wisconsin, N USA 44°44′N 92°29′W
26 M11 Ellsworth, Lake ⊠ Oklahoma, C USA
194 K9 Ellsworth Land physical region Antarctica
194 L9 Ellsworth Mountains ▲ Antarctica
101 J21 Ellwangen Baden-Württemberg, S Germany 48°58′N 10°07′E
18 B14 Ellwood City Pennsylvania, NE USA 40°49′N 80°15′W
108 H8 Elm Glarus, NE Switzerland 46°55′N 09°09′E
32 G9 Elma Washington, NW USA 47°00′N 123°24′W
121 V13 El Maḥalla el Kubra var. Al Maḥallah al Kubrá, Mahalla el Kubra. N Egypt 30°59′N 31°10′E
74 E9 El Mahbas var. Mahbés. SW Western Sahara 27°26′N 09°09′W
63 H17 El Maitén Chubut, W Argentina 42°03′S 71°10′W
136 E16 Elmalı Antalya, SW Turkey 36°43′N 29°19′E
80 G10 El Manaqil Gezira, C Sudan 14°12′N 33°01′E
54 M12 El Mango Amazonas, S Venezuela 01°55′N 66°35′W
El Manşûra see Al Manşūrah
55 P8 El Manteco Bolívar, E Venezuela 07°27′N 62°32′W
29 O16 Elm Creek Nebraska, C USA 40°43′N 99°22′W
El Mediyya see Médéa
77 V9 Elméki Agadez, C Niger 17°52′N 08°07′E
108 K7 Elmen Tirol, W Austria 47°22′N 10°34′E
18 I16 Elmer New Jersey, NE USA 39°34′N 75°09′W
138 G6 El Mina var. Al Mīnā'. N Lebanon 34°28′N 35°49′E
El Minya see Al Minyā
14 F15 Elmira Ontario, S Canada 43°35′N 80°34′W
18 G11 Elmira New York, NE USA 42°06′N 76°50′W
36 K13 El Mirage Arizona, SW USA 33°36′N 112°19′W
29 O7 Elm Lake ⊠ South Dakota, N USA
El Mojàn see San Rafael
105 N7 El Molar Madrid, C Spain 40°43′N 03°35′W
76 L7 El Mrâyer well C Mauritania
76 L5 El Mreïti well N Mauritania
76 L8 El Mreyyé desert E Mauritania
29 P8 Elm River ∼ North Dakota/South Dakota, N USA
100 I9 Elmshorn Schleswig-Holstein, N Germany 53°45′N 09°39′E
80 D12 El Muglad Southern Kordofan, C Sudan 11°02′N 27°44′E
El Muwaqqar see Al Muwaqqar
14 G14 Elmvale Ontario, S Canada 44°34′N 79°53′W
30 K12 Elmwood Illinois, N USA 40°46′N 89°58′W
26 J8 Elmwood Oklahoma, C USA 36°37′N 100°31′W
103 P17 Elne anc. Illiberis. Pyrénées-Orientales, S France 42°36′N 02°58′E
54 F11 El Nevado, Cerro elevation C Colombia
171 N5 El Nido Palawan, W Philippines 11°10′N 119°25′E
62 I12 El Nihuil Mendoza, W Argentina 34°58′S 68°40′W
75 W7 El Nouzha ✈ (Alexandria) N Egypt 31°06′N 29°58′E
80 E10 El Obeid var. Al Obayyid, Al Ubayyiḍ. Northern Kordofan, C Sudan 13°11′N 30°10′E
41 O13 El Oro México, S Mexico 19°51′N 100°07′W
56 B8 El Oro ◆ province SW Ecuador
61 B19 Elortondo Santa Fe, C Argentina 33°42′S 61°37′W
54 J8 Elorza Apure, C Venezuela 07°02′N 69°30′W
El Ouâdi see El Oued
74 L7 El Oued var. Al Oued, El Ouâdi, El Wad. NE Algeria 33°20′N 06°53′E
36 L15 Eloy Arizona, SW USA 32°47′N 111°33′W
55 Q7 El Palmar Bolívar, E Venezuela 08°01′N 61°53′W
40 K8 El Palmito Durango, W Mexico 25°40′N 104°59′W
55 P7 El Pao Bolívar, E Venezuela 08°03′N 62°40′W
54 K5 El Pao Cojedes, N Venezuela 09°40′N 68°08′W
42 J7 El Paraíso El Paraíso, S Honduras 13°51′N 86°31′W
42 I7 El Paraíso ◆ department SE Honduras
30 L12 El Paso Illinois, N USA 40°44′N 89°01′W
24 G8 El Paso Texas, SW USA 31°45′N 106°30′W
24 G8 El Paso ✈ Texas, SW USA 31°48′N 106°24′W
105 U7 El Perelló Cataluña, NE Spain 40°53′N 00°43′E
55 P5 El Pilar Sucre, NE Venezuela 10°31′N 63°12′W
42 F7 El Pital, Cerro ▲ El Salvador/Honduras 14°19′N 89°06′W
35 Q9 El Portal California, W USA 37°40′N 119°46′W
40 J3 El Porvenir Chihuahua, N Mexico 31°15′N 105°48′W
43 U14 El Porvenir Kuna Yala, N Panama 09°33′N 78°56′W
105 W6 El Prat de Llobregat Cataluña, NE Spain 41°20′N 02°05′E
42 H5 El Progreso Yoro, NW Honduras 15°25′N 87°49′W
42 A2 El Progreso off. Departamento de El Progreso. ◆ department C Guatemala
El Progreso see Guastatoya
El Progreso, Departamento de see El Progreso
104 L9 El Puente del Arzobispo Castilla-La Mancha, C Spain 39°48′N 05°10′W
104 J15 El Puerto de Santa María Andalucía, S Spain 36°36′N 06°13′W
62 I8 El Puesto Catamarca, NW Argentina 27°57′S 67°37′W
El Qâhira see Cairo
El Qaşr see Al Qaşr
El Qatrani see Al Qaţrānah
40 I10 El Quelite Sinaloa, C Mexico 23°37′N 106°26′W
62 G9 Elqui, Río ∼ N Chile
El Q'unayţirah see Al Qunayţirah
El Quneitra see Al Qunayţirah
El Quseir see Al Quşayr
El Quweira see Al Quwayrah
141 O15 El-Rahaba ✈ (Şan'ā') W Yemen 15°28′N 44°12′E
42 M10 El Rama Región Autónoma Atlántico Sur, SE Nicaragua 12°09′N 84°15′W
43 W16 El Real var. El Real de Santa María. Darién, SE Panama 08°06′N 77°42′W
El Real de Santa María see El Real
26 M10 El Reno Oklahoma, C USA 35°32′N 97°57′W
40 K9 El Rodeo Durango, C Mexico 25°12′N 104°35′W
104 J13 El Ronquillo Andalucía, S Spain 37°43′N 06°09′W
11 S16 Elrose Saskatchewan, S Canada 51°07′N 107°59′W
30 K8 Elroy Wisconsin, N USA 43°43′N 90°16′W
25 S17 Elsa Texas, SW USA 26°17′N 97°59′W
El Şaff see Aş Şaff
40 J10 El Salto Durango, C Mexico 23°47′N 105°22′W
42 D8 El Salvador off. Republica de El Salvador. ◆ republic Central America
El Salvador, Republica de see El Salvador
54 K7 El Samán de Apure Apure, C Venezuela 07°54′N 68°44′W
14 D7 Elsas Ontario, S Canada 48°31′N 82°53′W
40 F3 El Sásabe var. Aduana del Sásabe. Sonora, NW Mexico 31°27′N 111°31′W
Elsass see Alsace
40 J5 El Sáuz Chihuahua, N Mexico 29°03′N 106°15′W
27 W4 Elsberry Missouri, C USA 39°10′N 90°46′W
45 P9 El Seibo var. Santa Cruz de El Seibo, Santa Cruz del Seibo. E Dominican Republic 18°45′N 69°04′W
42 B7 El Semillero Barra Nahualate Escuintla, SW Guatemala 14°01′N 91°28′W
Elsene see Ixelles
Elsen Nur see Dorgê Co
36 L6 Elsinore Utah, W USA 38°40′N 112°09′W
Elsinore see Helsingør
99 L18 Elsloo Limburg, SE Netherlands 50°57′N 05°46′E
60 G13 El Soberbio Misiones, NE Argentina 27°15′S 54°05′W
55 N6 El Socorro Guárico, C Venezuela 09°00′N 65°42′W
54 L6 El Sombrero Guárico, N Venezuela 09°25′N 67°06′W
98 L10 Elspeet Gelderland, E Netherlands 52°19′N 05°47′E
98 L12 Elst Gelderland, E Netherlands 51°55′N 05°51′E
101 O15 Elsterwerda Brandenburg, E Germany 51°27′N 13°32′E
40 J4 El Sueco Chihuahua, N Mexico 29°53′N 106°24′W
El Suweida see As Suwaydā'
El Suweis see Suez
54 D12 El Tambo Cauca, SW Colombia 02°25′N 76°50′W
175 T13 Eltanin Fracture Zone tectonic feature SE Pacific Ocean
105 X5 El Ter ∼ NE Spain
184 K11 Eltham Taranaki, North Island, New Zealand 39°26′S 174°25′E
55 O6 El Tigre Anzoátegui, NE Venezuela 08°55′N 64°15′W
El Tigrito see San José de Guanipa
54 J5 El Tocuyo Lara, N Venezuela 09°48′N 69°51′W
127 Q10 El'ton Volgogradskaya Oblast', SW Russian Federation 49°07′N 46°50′E
32 K10 Eltopia Washington, NW USA 46°33′N 118°59′W
El Toro see Mare de Déu del Toro
61 A18 El Trébol Santa Fe, C Argentina 32°12′S 61°40′W
40 J13 El Tuito Jalisco, SW Mexico 20°19′N 105°22′W
El Ţûr see Aţ Ţūr
161 S15 Eluan Bi Eng. Cape Olwanpi; prev. Oluan Pi. headland S Taiwan 21°57′N 120°48′E
155 K16 Elūru prev. Ellore. Andhra Pradesh, E India 16°45′N 81°10′E
118 H13 Elva Ger. Elwa. Tartumaa, SE Estonia 58°13′N 26°25′E
37 R9 El Vado Reservoir ⊠ New Mexico, SW USA
43 S15 El Valle Coclé, C Panama 08°39′N 80°08′W
104 I11 Elvas Portalegre, C Portugal 38°53′N 07°10′W
54 K7 El Venado Apure, C Venezuela 07°25′N 68°46′W
105 V6 El Vendrell Cataluña, NE Spain 41°13′N 01°32′E
94 I13 Elverum Hedmark, S Norway 60°54′N 11°33′E
42 I9 El Viejo Chinandega, NW Nicaragua 12°39′N 87°11′W
54 G7 El Viejo, Cerro ▲ C Colombia 07°31′N 72°56′W
54 H6 El Vigía Mérida, NW Venezuela 08°38′N 71°39′W
105 Q4 El Villar de Arnedo La Rioja, N Spain 42°19′N 02°05′W
59 A14 Elvira Amazonas, W Brazil 07°12′S 69°56′W
Elwa see Elva
El Wad see El Oued
81 K17 El Wak North Eastern, NE Kenya 02°46′N 40°57′E
33 R7 Elwell, Lake ⊠ Montana, NW USA
31 P13 Elwood Indiana, N USA 40°16′N 85°50′W
27 R3 Elwood Kansas, C USA 39°43′N 94°52′W
29 N16 Elwood Nebraska, C USA 40°35′N 99°51′W
Elx see Elche
97 O20 Ely E England, United Kingdom 52°24′N 00°15′E
29 X4 Ely Minnesota, N USA 47°54′N 91°52′W
35 X6 Ely Nevada, W USA 39°15′N 114°53′W
El Yopal see Yopal
31 T11 Elyria Ohio, N USA 41°22′N 82°06′W
45 S9 El Yunque ▲ E Puerto Rico 18°15′N 65°46′W
101 F23 Elz ∼ SW Germany
187 R14 Emae island Shepherd Islands, C Vanuatu
118 I5 Emajõgi Ger. Embach. ∼ SE Estonia
Emāmrūd see Shāhrūd
Emam Saheb see Imām Şāḩib
Emām Şāḩeb see Imām Şāḩib
Emāmshahr see Shāhrūd
95 M20 Emån ∼ S Sweden
144 J11 Emba Kaz. Embi. Aktyubinsk, W Kazakhstan 48°50′N 58°10′E
Emba see Zhem
Embach see Emajõgi
62 K5 Embarcación Salta, N Argentina 23°15′S 64°05′W
30 M15 Embarras River ∼ Illinois, N USA
Embi see Emba
81 I19 Embu Eastern, C Kenya 0°32′N 37°28′E
100 E10 Emden Niedersachsen, NW Germany 53°22′N 07°12′E
160 H9 Emei Shan ▲ Sichuan, C China 29°32′N 103°21′E
29 Q4 Emerado North Dakota, N USA 47°55′N 97°21′W
181 X8 Emerald Queensland, E Australia 23°33′S 148°11′E
Emerald Isle see Montserrat
57 J15 Emero, Río ∼ W Bolivia
11 Y17 Emerson Manitoba, S Canada 49°01′N 97°07′W
29 T15 Emerson Iowa, C USA 41°00′N 95°22′W
29 R13 Emerson Nebraska, C USA 42°16′N 96°43′W
36 M5 Emery Utah, W USA 38°54′N 111°16′W
Emesa see Ḩimş
136 E13 Emet Kütahya, W Turkey 39°22′N 29°15′E
186 B8 Emeti Western, SW Papua New Guinea 07°54′S 143°18′E
35 V3 Emigrant Pass pass Nevada, W USA
78 I6 Emi Koussi ▲ N Chad 19°52′N 18°34′E
Emilia see Emilia-Romagna
41 V15 Emiliano Zapata Chiapas, SE Mexico 17°42′N 91°46′W
106 E9 Emilia-Romagna prev. Emilia; anc. Æmilia. ◆ region N Italy
158 J3 Emin var. Dorbiljin. Xinjiang Uygur Zizhiqu, NW China 46°30′N 83°42′E
149 W8 Eminābād Punjab, E Pakistan 32°02′N 73°51′E
21 L5 Eminence Kentucky, S USA 38°22′N 85°10′W
27 W7 Eminence Missouri, C USA 37°09′N 91°22′W
114 N9 Emine, Nos headland E Bulgaria 42°43′N 27°53′E
158 I3 Emin He ∼ NW China
186 G4 Emirau Island island N Papua New Guinea
136 F13 Emirdağ Afyon, W Turkey 39°01′N 31°09′E
83 K22 eMkhondo prev. Piet Retief. Mpumalanga, E South Africa 27°00′S 30°49′E see also Piet Retief
95 M21 Emmaboda Kalmar, S Sweden 56°36′N 15°30′E
118 E5 Emmaste Hiiumaa, W Estonia 58°43′N 22°36′E
18 I15 Emmaus Pennsylvania, NE USA 40°32′N 75°28′W
183 U4 Emmaville New South Wales, SE Australia 29°26′S 151°38′E
108 E9 Emme ∼ W Switzerland
98 L8 Emmeloord Flevoland, N Netherlands 52°43′N 05°46′E
98 O8 Emmen Drenthe, NE Netherlands 52°48′N 06°57′E
108 F8 Emmen Luzern, C Switzerland 47°03′N 08°14′E
101 F23 Emmendingen Baden-Württemberg, SW Germany 48°07′N 07°51′E
98 P8 Emmer-Compascuum Drenthe, NE Netherlands 52°47′N 07°03′E
101 D14 Emmerich Nordrhein-Westfalen, W Germany 51°49′N 06°16′E
29 U12 Emmetsburg Iowa, C USA 43°06′N 94°40′W
32 M14 Emmett Idaho, NW USA 43°52′N 116°30′W
38 M10 Emmonak Alaska, USA 62°46′N 164°31′W
Emona see Ljubljana
Emonti see East London
24 L12 Emory Peak ▲ Texas, SW USA 29°15′N 103°18′W
40 F6 Empalme Sonora, NW Mexico 27°57′N 110°49′W
83 L23 Empangeni KwaZulu/Natal, E South Africa 28°45′S 31°54′E
61 C14 Empedrado Corrientes, NE Argentina 27°59′S 58°47′W
192 K3 Emperor Seamounts undersea feature NW Pacific Ocean 42°00′N 170°00′E
192 L3 Emperor Trough undersea feature N Pacific Ocean
35 R4 Empire Nevada, W USA 40°26′N 119°21′W
Empire State of the South see Georgia
Emplawas see Amplawas
106 F11 Empoli Toscana, C Italy 43°43′N 10°57′E
27 P5 Emporia Kansas, C USA 38°24′N 96°10′W
21 W7 Emporia Virginia, NE USA 36°42′N 77°33′W
18 E13 Emporium Pennsylvania, NE USA 41°31′N 78°14′W
Empty Quarter see Ar Rub' al Khālī
100 E10 Ems Dut. Eems. ∼ NW Germany
100 F13 Emsdetten Nordrhein-Westfalen, NW Germany 52°11′N 07°32′E
Ems-Hunte Canal see Küstenkanal
100 F10 Ems-Jade-Kanal canal NW Germany
100 F11 Emsland cultural region NW Germany
182 D3 Emu Junction South Australia 28°39′S 132°13′E
163 T3 Emur He ∼ NE China
55 R8 Enachu Landing NW Guyana 06°09′N 60°02′W
93 F16 Enafors Jämtland, C Sweden 63°17′N 12°24′E
94 N11 Enånger Gävleborg, C Sweden 61°30′N 17°10′E
96 G7 Enard Bay bay NW Scotland, United Kingdom
Enareträsk see Inarijärvi
171 X14 Enarotali Papua, E Indonesia 03°55′S 136°21′E
En 'Avedat see Ein Avdat
165 T2 Enbetsu Hokkaidō, NE Japan 44°44′N 141°47′E
61 H16 Encantadas, Serra das ▲ S Brazil
40 E7 Encantado, Cerro ▲ NW Mexico 26°46′N 112°33′W
62 P7 Encarnación Itapúa, S Paraguay 27°20′S 55°50′W
40 M12 Encarnación de Díaz Jalisco, SW Mexico 21°33′N 102°13′W
77 O17 Enchi SW Ghana 05°53′N 02°48′W
25 Q14 Encinal Texas, SW USA 28°02′N 99°21′W
35 U17 Encinitas California, W USA 33°02′N 117°17′W
25 S16 Encino Texas, SW USA 26°58′N 98°06′W
54 H6 Encontrados Zulia, NW Venezuela 09°04′N 72°16′W
182 I10 Encounter Bay inlet South Australia
61 F15 Encruzilhada Rio Grande do Sul, S Brazil 28°58′S 55°31′W
61 H16 Encruzilhada do Sul Rio Grande do Sul, S Brazil 30°30′S 52°32′W
111 M20 Encs Borsod-Abaúj-Zemplén, NE Hungary 48°21′N 21°09′E
193 P3 Endeavour Seamount undersea feature N Pacific Ocean 48°15′N 129°04′W
181 V1 Endeavour Strait strait Queensland, NE Australia
171 O16 Endeh Flores, S Indonesia 08°48′S 121°37′E
95 G23 Endelave island C Denmark
191 T4 Enderbury Island atoll Phoenix Islands, C Kiribati
11 N16 Enderby British Columbia, SW Canada 50°34′N 119°09′W
195 W4 Enderby Land physical region Antarctica
173 N14 Enderby Plain undersea feature S Indian Ocean
29 Q6 Enderlin North Dakota, N USA 46°37′N 97°36′W
Endersdorf see Jędrzejów
28 K16 Enders Reservoir ⊠ Nebraska, C USA
18 H11 Endicott New York, NE USA 42°06′N 76°03′W
39 P7 Endicott Mountains ▲ Alaska, USA
118 I5 Endla Raba wetland C Estonia
117 T9 Enerhodar Zaporiz'ka Oblast', SE Ukraine 47°30′N 34°40′E
57 F14 Ene, Río ∼ C Peru
189 N4 Enewetak Atoll var. Ānewetak, Eniwetok. atoll Ralik Chain, W Marshall Islands
114 L13 Enez Edirne, NW Turkey 40°44′N 26°05′E
21 W8 Enfield North Carolina, SE USA 36°10′N 77°40′W
186 B7 Enga ◆ province W Papua New Guinea
45 Q9 Engaño, Cabo headland E Dominican Republic 18°36′N 68°19′W
164 U3 Engaru Hokkaidō, NE Japan 44°06′N 143°30′E
108 F9 Engelberg Unterwalden, C Switzerland 46°51′N 08°25′E
21 Y9 Engelhard North Carolina, SE USA 35°30′N 76°00′W
127 P8 Engel's Saratovskaya Oblast', W Russian Federation 51°27′N 46°09′E
101 G24 Engen Baden-Württemberg, SW Germany 47°52′N 08°46′E
Engeten see Aiud
168 K15 Enggano, Pulau island W Indonesia
80 J8 Enghershatu ▲ N Eritrea 16°41′N 38°21′E
99 F19 Enghien Dut. Edingen. Hainaut, SW Belgium 50°42′N 04°03′E
27 V12 England Arkansas, C USA 34°32′N 91°58′W
97 M20 England Lat. Anglia. ◆ national region England, United Kingdom
14 H8 Englehart Ontario, S Canada 47°50′N 79°52′W
37 T4 Englewood Colorado, C USA 39°39′N 104°59′W
31 O16 English Indiana, N USA 38°20′N 86°28′W
39 Q13 English Bay Alaska, USA 59°21′N 151°55′W
English Bazar see Ingrāj Bāzār
97 N25 English Channel var. The Channel, Fr. la Manche. channel NW Europe
194 J7 English Coast physical region Antarctica
105 S11 Enguera Valenciana, E Spain 38°58′N 00°42′W
118 E8 Engure W Latvia 57°09′N 23°13′E
118 E8 Engures Ezers ⊚ NW Latvia
137 R9 Enguri Rus. Inguri. ∼ NW Georgia
Engyum see Gangi
26 M9 Enid Oklahoma, C USA 36°25′N 97°53′W
22 L3 Enid Lake ⊠ Mississippi, S USA
189 Y2 Enigu island Ratak Chain, SE Marshall Islands
Enikale Strait see Kerch Strait
147 Z8 Enil'chek Issyk-Kul'skaya Oblast', E Kyrgyzstan 42°04′N 79°01′E
115 F17 Enipéfs ∼ C Greece
165 S4 Eniwa Hokkaidō, NE Japan 42°53′N 141°14′E
Eniwetok see Enewetak Atoll
Enjiang see Yongfeng
Enkeldoorn see Chivhu
123 S11 Enken, Mys prev. Mys Enkan. headland NE Russian Federation 58°29′N 141°27′E
Enken, Mys see Enken, Mys
98 J8 Enkhuizen Noord-Holland, NW Netherlands 52°34′N 05°03′E
109 Q4 Enknach ∼ N Austria
95 N15 Enköping Uppsala, C Sweden 59°38′N 17°05′E
107 K24 Enna var. Castrogiovanni, Henna. Sicilia, Italy, C Mediterranean Sea 37°34′N 14°16′E
80 D11 En Nahud Southern Kordofan, C Sudan 12°41′N 28°28′E
138 F8 En Nâqoûra var. An Nāqūrah. SW Lebanon 33°06′N 33°30′E
En Nazira see Natzrat
78 K8 Ennedi plateau E Chad
101 E15 Ennepetal Nordrhein-Westfalen, W Germany 51°18′N 07°23′E
183 P4 Enngonia New South Wales, SE Australia 29°19′S 145°52′E
97 C19 Ennis Ir. Inis. Clare, W Ireland 52°50′N 08°59′W
33 R11 Ennis Montana, NW USA 45°21′N 111°45′W
25 U7 Ennis Texas, SW USA 32°19′N 96°37′W
97 F20 Enniscorthy Ir. Inis Córthaidh. SE Ireland 52°30′N 06°34′W
97 E15 Enniskillen var. Inniskilling, Ir. Inis Ceithleann. SW Northern Ireland, United Kingdom 54°21′N 07°38′W
97 B19 Ennistimon Ir. Inis Díomáin. Clare, W Ireland 52°57′N 09°17′W
109 T4 Enns Oberösterreich, N Austria 48°13′N 14°28′E
109 T4 Enns ∼ C Austria
93 O16 Eno Itä-Suomi, SE Finland 62°45′N 30°15′E
24 M5 Enochs Texas, SW USA 33°51′N 102°46′W
93 N17 Enonkoski Itä-Suomi, E Finland 62°04′N 28°53′E
92 K10 Enontekiö Lapp. Eanodat. Lappi, N Finland 68°25′N 23°40′E
21 Q11 Enoree South Carolina, SE USA 34°39′N 81°58′W
21 P11 Enoree River ∼ South Carolina, SE USA
18 M6 Enosburg Falls Vermont, NE USA 44°54′N 72°50′W
171 N13 Enrekang Sulawesi, C Indonesia 03°33′S 119°46′E
45 N10 Enriquillo SW Dominican Republic 17°57′N 71°13′W
45 N9 Enriquillo, Lago ⊚ SW Dominican Republic
98 L9 Ens Flevoland, N Netherlands 52°39′N 05°49′E
98 P11 Enschede Overijssel, E Netherlands 52°13′N 06°55′E
40 B2 Ensenada Baja California Norte, NW Mexico 31°52′N 116°32′W
101 E20 Ensheim ✈ (Saarbrücken) Saarland, W Germany 49°13′N 07°09′E
160 L9 Enshi Hubei, C China 30°16′N 109°26′E
164 L14 Enshū-nada gulf SW Japan
23 O8 Ensley Florida, SE USA 30°31′N 87°16′W
Enso see Svetogorsk
81 F18 Entebbe S Uganda 0°07′N 32°30′E
81 F18 Entebbe ✈ C Uganda 0°04′N 32°29′E
101 M18 Entenbühl ▲ Czech Republic/Germany 50°09′N 12°10′E
98 N10 Enter Overijssel, E Netherlands 52°19′N 06°34′E
23 Q7 Enterprise Alabama, S USA 31°19′N 85°50′W
32 L11 Enterprise Oregon, NW USA 45°25′N 117°18′W
36 J7 Enterprise Utah, W USA 37°33′N 113°42′W
32 J8 Entiat Washington, NW USA 47°39′N 120°15′W
105 P15 Entinas, Punta de las headland S Spain 36°40′N 02°44′W
108 F8 Entlebuch Luzern, W Switzerland 47°02′N 08°04′E
108 F8 Entlebuch valley C Switzerland
63 I22 Entrada, Punta headland S Argentina
103 O13 Entraygues-sur-Truyère Aveyron, S France 44°39′N 02°36′E
187 O14 Entrecasteaux, Récifs d' reef N New Caledonia

◆ Country ● Country Capital ◇ Dependent Territory ○ Dependent Territory Capital ◈ Administrative Regions ✈ International Airport ▲ Mountain ▲ Mountain Range ☒ Volcano ∼ River ⊚ Lake ⊠ Reservoir

61 C17 Entre Ríos off. Provincia de Entre Ríos. ◆ province NE Argentina
42 K7 Entre Ríos, Cordillera ▲▲ Honduras/Nicaragua
Entre Ríos, Provincia de see Entre Ríos
104 G9 Entroncamento Santarém, C Portugal 39°28′N 08°28′W
77 V16 Enugu Enugu, S Nigeria 06°24′N 07°24′E
77 U16 Enugu ◆ state SE Nigeria
123 V5 Enurmino Chukotskiy Avtonomnyy Okrug, NE Russian Federation 66°46′N 171°40′W
54 E9 Envigado Antioquia, W Colombia 06°09′N 75°38′W
59 B15 Envira Amazonas, W Brazil 07°12′S 69°59′W
Enyélé see Enyellé
79 I16 Enyellé var. Enyélé. Likouala, NE Congo 02°49′N 18°02′E
101 H21 Enz ≈ SW Germany
165 N13 Enzan var. Kōshū. Yamanashi, Honshū, S Japan 35°44′N 138°43′E
104 I2 Eo ≈ NW Spain
Eochaill see Youghal
Eochaille, Cuan see Youghal Bay
107 K22 Eolie, Isole var. Isole Lipari, Eng. Aeolian Islands, Lipari Islands. island group S Italy
189 U12 Eot island Chuuk, C Micronesia
Epáno Archánes/Epáno Arkhánai see Archánes
115 G14 Epanomí Kentrikí Makedonía, N Greece 40°25′N 22°57′E
98 M10 Epe Gelderland, E Netherlands 52°21′N 05°59′E
77 S16 Epe Lagos, S Nigeria 06°37′N 04°01′E
79 I17 Epéna Likouala, NE Congo 01°28′N 17°29′E
Eperies/Eperjes see Prešov
103 Q4 Épernay anc. Sparnacum. Marne, N France 49°02′N 03°58′E
36 L5 Ephraim Utah, W USA 39°21′N 111°35′W
18 H15 Ephrata Pennsylvania, NE USA 40°09′N 76°08′W
32 J8 Ephrata Washington, NW USA 47°19′N 119°33′W
187 R14 Epi var. Épi. island C Vanuatu
Épi see Epi
105 R6 Épila Aragón, NE Spain 41°34′N 01°19′W
103 T6 Épinal Vosges, NE France 48°10′N 06°28′E
Epiphania see Ḥamāh
Epirus see Ípeiros
121 P3 Episkopí SW Cyprus 34°37′N 32°53′E
Episkopi Bay see Episkopí, Kólpos
121 P3 Episkopí, Kólpos var. Episkopi Bay. bay SE Cyprus
Epitoli see Tshwane
Epoon see Ebon Atoll
Eporedia see Ivrea
Eppeschdorf see Dumbrăveni
101 H21 Eppingen Baden-Württemberg, SW Germany 49°09′N 08°54′E
83 E18 Epukiro Omaheke, E Namibia 21°40′S 19°09′E
29 Y13 Epworth Iowa, C USA 42°27′N 90°55′W
143 O10 Eqlīd var. Iqlid. Fārs, C Iran 30°54′N 52°40′E
Equality State see Wyoming
79 J18 Equateur off. Région de l' Equateur. ◆ region N Dem. Rep. Congo
Equateur, Région de l' see Equateur
151 K22 Equatorial Channel channel S Maldives
79 B17 Equatorial Guinea off. Equatorial Guinea, Republic of. ◆ republic C Africa
Equatorial Guinea, Republic of see Equatorial Guinea
121 V11 Eratosthenes Tablemount undersea feature E Mediterranean Sea 33°48′N 32°53′E
Erautini see Johannesburg
136 L12 Erbaa Tokat, N Turkey 40°42′N 36°37′E
101 E19 Erbeskopf ▲ W Germany 49°43′N 07°04′E
Erbil see Arbīl
121 P2 Ercan ✈ (Nicosia) N Cyprus 35°07′N 33°30′E
Ercegnovi see Herceg-Novi
137 T14 Erçek Gölü ◎ E Turkey
137 S14 Erciş Van, E Turkey 39°02′N 43°21′E
136 K14 Erciyes Dağı anc. Argaeus. ▲ C Turkey 38°32′N 35°28′E
111 J22 Érd Ger. Hanselbeck. Pest, C Hungary 47°22′N 18°56′E
163 X11 Erdaobaihe prev. Baihe. Jilin, NE China 42°24′N 128°09′E
159 O12 Erdaogou Qinghai, W China 34°30′N 92°50′E
163 X11 Erdao Jiang ≈ NE China
Erdăt-Sângeorz see Sângeorgiu de Pădure
136 C11 Erdek Balıkesir, NW Turkey 40°24′N 27°47′E
Erdély see Transylvania
Erdélyi-Havasok see Carpații Meridionali
136 J17 Erdemli İçel, S Turkey 36°35′N 34°19′E
163 O10 Erdene var. Ulaan-Uul. Dornogovĭ, SE Mongolia 44°21′N 111°06′E
162 H9 Erdene var. Sangiyn Dalay. Govĭ-Altay, C Mongolia 45°12′N 97°51′E
162 E6 Erdenebüren var. Har-Us. Hovd, W Mongolia 48°30′N 91°25′E
162 K9 Erdenedalay var. Sangiyn Dalay. Dundgovĭ, C Mongolia 45°59′N 104°58′E
162 G7 Erdenehayrhan var. Altan. Dzavhan, W Mongolia 48°05′N 95°48′E
162 J7 Erdenemandal var. Öldziyt. Arhangay, C Mongolia 48°30′N 101°25′E
162 K6 Erdenet Orhon, N Mongolia 49°01′N 104°07′E
163 Q9 Erdenetsagaan var. Chonogol. Sühbaatar, E Mongolia 45°55′N 115°19′E
162 I8 Erdenetsogt Bayanhongor, C Mongolia 46°27′N 100°53′E
Erdenetsogt see Bayan-Ovoo
78 K7 Erdi plateau NE Chad
78 L7 Erdi Ma desert NE Chad
101 M23 Erding Bayern, SE Germany 48°18′N 11°54′E
Erdőszáda see Ardusat
Erdőszentgyörgy see Sângeorgiu de Pădure
102 I7 Erdre ≈ NW France
195 R13 Erebus, Mount ⛰ Ross Island, Antarctica 78°11′S 165°09′E
61 H14 Erechim Rio Grande do Sul, S Brazil 27°35′S 52°15′W
163 O7 Ereen Davaanï Nuruu ▲▲ NE Mongolia
163 Q6 Ereentsav Dornod, NE Mongolia 49°51′N 115°41′E
136 I16 Ereğli Konya, S Turkey 37°30′N 34°02′E
115 A15 Ereíkoussa island Iónia Nisiá, Greece, C Mediterranean Sea
163 O11 Erenhot var. Erlian. Nei Mongol Zizhiqu, NE China 43°35′N 112°E
104 M6 Eresma ≈ N Spain
115 K17 Eresós var. Eressós. Lésvos, E Greece 39°11′N 25°57′E
Eressós see Eresós
Ereymentaū see Yereymentau
99 K21 Érezée Luxembourg, SE Belgium 50°16′N 05°34′E
74 G7 Erfoud SE Morocco 31°29′N 04°18′W
101 D16 Erft ≈ W Germany
101 K16 Erfurt Thüringen, C Germany 50°59′N 11°02′E
137 P15 Ergani Diyarbakır, SE Turkey 38°17′N 39°44′E
Ergel see Hatanbulag
Ergene Çayı see Ergene Irmağı
136 C10 Ergene Irmağı var. Ergene Çayı. ≈ NW Turkey
118 I9 Ērgļi C Latvia 56°55′N 25°38′E
78 H11 Erguig, Bahr ≈ SW Chad
163 S5 Ergun var. Labudalin; prev. Ergun Youqi. Nei Mongol Zizhiqu, N China 50°13′N 120°09′E
Ergun see Gegan Gol
Ergun He see Argun
Ergun Youqi see Ergun
Ergun Zuoqi see Genhe
160 F12 Er Hai ◎ SW China
104 K4 Ería ≈ NW Spain
80 H8 Eriba Kassala, NE Sudan 16°37′N 36°04′E
96 I6 Eriboll, Loch inlet NW Scotland, United Kingdom
65 Q18 Erica Seamount undersea feature SW Indian Ocean 38°15′S 14°30′E
107 H23 Erice Sicilia, Italy, C Mediterranean Sea 38°02′N 12°35′E
104 E10 Ericeira Lisboa, C Portugal 38°58′N 09°25′W
96 H10 Ericht, Loch ◎ C Scotland, United Kingdom
26 J11 Erick Oklahoma, C USA 35°13′N 99°52′W
18 B11 Erie Pennsylvania, NE USA 42°07′N 80°04′W
18 E9 Erie Canal canal New York, NE USA
Érié, Lac see Erie, Lake
31 T10 Erie, Lake Fr. Lac Érié. ◎ Canada/USA
Erigabo see Ceerigaabo
77 N8 'Erîgât desert N Mali
Erigavo see Ceerigaabo
92 P2 Erik Eriksenstretet strait E Svalbard
11 X15 Eriksdale Manitoba, S Canada 50°52′N 98°07′W
189 V6 Erikub Atoll var. Ādkup. atoll Ratak Chain, C Marshall Islands
102 G4 Er, Îles d' Island group NW France
Erimanthos see Erýmanthos
165 T6 Erimo Hokkaidō, NE Japan 42°01′N 143°07′E
165 T6 Erimo-misaki headland Hokkaidō, NE Japan 41°57′N 143°12′E
20 H8 Erin Tennessee, S USA 36°19′N 87°42′W
96 E9 Eriskay island NW Scotland, United Kingdom
Erithraí see Erythrés
80 I9 Eritrea off. State of Eritrea, Ērtra. ◆ transitional government E Africa
Eritrea, State of see Eritrea
Erivan see Yerevan
101 D16 Erkelenz Nordrhein-Westfalen, W Germany 51°04′N 06°19′E
95 P15 Erken ◎ C Sweden
101 K19 Erlangen Bayern, S Germany 49°36′N 11°E
160 G9 Erlang Shan ▲ C China 29°56′N 102°24′E
Erlau see Eger
109 V5 Erlauf ≈ NE Austria
181 Q8 Erldunda Roadhouse Northern Territory, N Australia 25°13′S 133°13′E
Erlian see Erenhot
27 T15 Erling, Lake ⊠ Arkansas, USA
109 O8 Erlsbach Tirol, W Austria 46°54′N 12°15′E
Ermak see Aksu
98 K10 Ermelo Gelderland, C Netherlands 52°18′N 05°38′E
83 K21 Ermelo Mpumalanga, NE South Africa 26°32′S 29°59′E
136 H17 Ermenek Karaman, S Turkey 36°38′N 32°55′E
Érmihályfalva see Valea lui Mihai
115 G20 Ermióni Pelopónnisos, S Greece 37°24′N 23°15′E
115 J20 Ermoúpoli var. Hermoupolis; prev. Ermoúpolis. Sýros, Kykládes, Greece, Aegean Sea 37°26′N 24°55′E
Ermoúpolis see Ermoúpoli
Ernabella see Pukatja
155 G22 Ernākulam Kerala, SW India 10°04′N 76°18′E
102 J6 Ernée Mayenne, NW France 48°18′N 00°54′W
61 H14 Ernestina, Barragem ⊠ S Brazil
54 E4 Ernesto Cortissoz ✈ (Barranquilla) Atlántico, N Colombia
155 H21 Erode Tamil Nādu, SE India 11°21′N 77°43′E
Eroj see Iroj
83 C19 Erongo ◆ district W Namibia
99 F21 Erquelinnes Hainaut, S Belgium 50°18′N 04°08′E
74 G7 Er-Rachidia var. Ksar al Soule. E Morocco 31°58′N 04°22′W
80 E11 Er Rahad var. Ar Rahad. Northern Kordofan, C Sudan 12°43′N 30°39′E
Er Ramle see Ramla
83 O15 Errego Zambézia, NE Mozambique 16°02′S 37°11′E
105 Q2 Errenteria Cast. Rentería. País Vasco, N Spain 43°17′N 01°54′W
Er Rif/Er Riff see Rif
97 D14 Errigal Mountain Ir. An Earagail. ▲ N Ireland 55°03′N 08°09′W
97 A15 Erris Head Ir. Ceann Iorrais. headland W Ireland 54°18′N 10°01′W
187 S15 Erromango island S Vanuatu
Error Guyot see Error Tablemount
173 O4 Error Tablemount var. Error Guyot. undersea feature W Indian Ocean 10°20′N 56°05′E
80 G11 Er Roseires Blue Nile, E Sudan 11°52′N 34°23′E
Erseka see Ersekë
113 M22 Ersekë var. Erseka, Kolonjë. Korçë, SE Albania 40°19′N 20°39′E
Érsekújvár see Nové Zámky
29 S4 Erskine Minnesota, N USA 47°42′N 96°00′W
103 V6 Erstein Bas-Rhin, NE France 48°24′N 07°39′E
108 G9 Erstfeld Uri, C Switzerland 46°49′N 08°41′E
158 M3 Ertai Xinjiang Uygur Zizhiqu, NW China 46°04′N 90°06′E
126 M7 Ertil' Voronezhskaya Oblast', W Russian Federation 51°51′N 40°46′E
Ertis see Irtysh, C Asia
Ertis see Irtyshsk, Kazakhstan
158 K2 Ertix He Rus. Chërnyy Irtysh. ≈ China/Kazakhstan
Ērtra see Eritrea
21 P9 Erwin North Carolina, SE USA 35°19′N 78°40′W
Erydropótamos see Erythropótamos
115 E19 Erýmanthos var. Erimanthos. ▲ S Greece 37°57′N 21°51′E
115 G19 Erythrés prev. Erithraí. Stereá Elláda, C Greece 38°18′N 23°20′E
114 L12 Erythropótamos Bul. Byala Reka, var. Erydropótamos. ≈ Bulgaria/Greece
160 F12 Eryuan var. Yuhu. Yunnan, SW China 26°09′N 100°01′E
109 U6 Erzbach ≈ W Austria
Erzerum see Erzurum
101 N17 Erzgebirge Cz. Krušné Hory, Eng. Ore Mountains. ▲▲ Czech Republic/Germany see also Krušné Hory
Erzgebirge see Krušné Hory
122 L14 Erzin Respublika Tyva, S Russian Federation 50°17′N 95°03′E
137 O13 Erzincan var. Erzinjan. Erzincan, E Turkey 39°44′N 39°30′E
137 N13 Erzincan ◆ province NE Turkey
Erzinjan see Erzincan
Erzsébetváros see Dumbrăveni
137 Q13 Erzurum prev. Erzerum. Erzurum, NE Turkey 39°57′N 41°17′E
137 Q12 Erzurum prev. Erzerum. ◆ province NE Turkey
186 G9 Esa'ala Normanby Island, SE Papua New Guinea 09°45′S 150°47′E
165 T2 Esashi Hokkaidō, NE Japan 44°57′N 142°32′E
165 Q9 Esashi var. Esasi. Iwate, Honshū, C Japan 39°13′N 141°11′E
165 Q5 Esasho Hokkaidō, N Japan
Esasi see Esashi
95 F23 Esbjerg Syddtjylland, W Denmark 55°28′N 08°28′E
Esbo see Espoo
36 L7 Escalante Utah, W USA 37°46′N 111°36′W
36 M7 Escalante River ≈ Utah, W USA
14 L12 Escalier, Réservoir l' ⊠ Québec, SE Canada
40 K7 Escalón Chihuahua, N Mexico 26°43′N 104°20′W
104 M8 Escalona Castilla-La Mancha, C Spain 40°10′N 04°24′W
23 O8 Escambia River ≈ Florida, SE USA
31 N5 Escanaba Michigan, N USA 45°45′N 87°03′W
31 N4 Escanaba River ≈ Michigan, N USA
105 R8 Escandón, Puerto de pass E Spain
41 W14 Escárcega Campeche, SE Mexico 18°33′N 90°41′W
171 O1 Escarpada Point headland Luzon, N Philippines 18°28′N 122°10′E
23 N8 Escatawpa River ≈ Alabama/Mississippi, S USA
103 P2 Escaut ≈ N France
Escaut see Scheldt
99 M25 Esch-sur-Alzette Luxembourg, S Luxembourg 49°30′N 05°59′E
101 J15 Eschwege Hessen, C Germany 51°10′N 10°03′E
101 D16 Eschweiler Nordrhein-Westfalen, W Germany 50°49′N 06°16′E
Esclaves, Grand Lac des see Great Slave Lake
45 O8 Escocesa, Bahía bay N Dominican Republic
43 W15 Escocés, Punta headland NE Panama 08°50′N 77°37′W
35 U17 Escondido California, W USA 33°07′N 117°05′W
42 M10 Escondido, Río ≈ SE Nicaragua
15 S7 Escoumins, Rivière des ≈ Québec, SE Canada
37 O13 Escudilla Mountain ▲ Arizona, SW USA 33°57′N 109°07′W
40 J11 Escuinapa var. Escuinapa de Hidalgo. Sinaloa, C Mexico 22°50′N 105°46′W
Escuinapa de Hidalgo see Escuinapa
42 C6 Escuintla Escuintla, S Guatemala 14°17′N 90°46′W
41 V17 Escuintla Chiapas, SE Mexico 15°20′N 92°40′W
42 A2 Escuintla off. Departamento de Escuintla. ◆ department S Guatemala
Escuintla, Departamento de see Escuintla
15 W7 Escuminac ≈ Québec, SE Canada
79 D16 Eséka Centre, SW Cameroon 03°40′N 10°48′E
136 I12 Esenboğa ✈ (Ankara) Ankara, C Turkey 40°05′N 33°01′E
136 D17 Eşen Çayı ≈ SW Turkey
146 B13 Esenguly Rus. Gasan-Kuli. Balkan Welaýaty, W Turkmenistan 37°29′N 53°57′E
105 T4 Ésera ≈ NE Spain
143 N8 Eşfahān Eng. Isfahan; anc. Aspadana. Eşfahān, C Iran 32°41′N 51°41′E
143 O7 Eşfahān off. Ostān-e Eşfahān. ◆ province C Iran
Eşfahān, Ostān-e see Eşfahān
105 N5 Esgueva ≈ N Spain
Eshkamesh see Ishkamish
Eshkāshem see Ishkāshim
83 L23 Eshowe KwaZulu/Natal, E South Africa 28°53′S 31°28′E
143 T5 'Eshqābād Khorāsān, NE Iran 36°00′N 59°01′E
Esh Sham see Rif Dimashq
Esh Sharā see Ash Sharāh
Esik see Yesik
Esil see Yesil'
Esil see Ishim, Kazakhstan/Russian Federation
183 V2 Esk Queensland, E Australia 27°15′S 152°23′E
184 O11 Eskdale Hawke's Bay, North Island, New Zealand 39°24′S 176°51′E
Eski Dzhumaya see Türgovishte
92 L2 Eskifjördhur Austurland, E Iceland 65°04′N 14°01′W
139 S3 Eski Kalak var. Askī Kalak, Kalak. Arbīl, N Iraq 36°16′N 43°40′E
95 N16 Eskilstuna Södermanland, C Sweden 59°22′N 16°31′E
8 H6 Eskimo Lakes ◎ Northwest Territories, NW Canada
9 O10 Eskimo Point headland Nunavut, E Canada 61°19′N 93°49′W
Eskimo Point see Arviat
139 Q2 Eski Mosul Nīnawá, N Iraq 36°31′N 42°45′E
Eski-Nookat see Nookat
136 F12 Eskişehir var. Eskishehr. Eskişehir, W Turkey 39°46′N 30°30′E
136 F13 Eskişehir var. Eski shehr. ◆ province NW Turkey
Eskishehr see Eskişehir
Eslāmābād see Eslāmābād-e Gharb
142 J6 Eslāmābād-e Gharb var. Eslāmābād; prev. Harunabad, Shāhābād. Kermānshāhān, W Iran 34°08′N 46°35′E
148 J4 Eslām Qal'eh Pash. Islam Qala. Herāt, W Afghanistan 34°41′N 61°03′E
95 K23 Eslöv Skåne, S Sweden 55°50′N 13°20′E
143 S12 Esmā'īlābād Kermān, S Iran 28°48′N 56°39′E
143 U8 Esmā'īlābād Khorāsān, E Iran 35°20′N 60°30′E
136 D14 Eşme Uşak, W Turkey 38°26′N 28°59′E
44 G6 Esmeralda Camagüey, E Cuba 21°51′N 78°10′W
63 F21 Esmeralda, Isla island S Chile
56 B5 Esmeraldas Esmeraldas, N Ecuador 0°55′N 79°40′W
56 B5 Esmeraldas ◆ province NW Ecuador
Esna see Isnā
14 B6 Esnagi Lake ◎ Ontario, S Canada
143 V14 Espakeh Sīstān va Balūchestān, SE Iran 26°54′N 60°09′E
103 O13 Espalion Aveyron, S France 44°31′N 02°45′E
España see Spain
14 E11 Espanola Ontario, S Canada 46°15′N 81°46′W
37 S10 Espanola New Mexico, SW USA 35°59′N 106°04′W
57 C18 Española, Isla var. Hood Island. island Galapagos Islands, Ecuador, E Pacific Ocean
104 M13 Espejo Andalucía, S Spain 37°40′N 04°34′W
94 C13 Espeland Hordaland, S Norway 60°22′N 05°27′E
100 G12 Espelkamp Nordrhein-Westfalen, NW Germany 52°22′N 08°37′E
38 M8 Espenberg, Cape headland Alaska, USA 66°33′N 163°36′W
180 L13 Esperance Western Australia 33°49′S 121°52′E
186 L9 Esperance, Cape headland Guadacanal, C Solomon Islands 09°09′S 159°38′E
57 P18 Esperancita Santa Cruz, E Bolivia
61 B17 Esperanza Santa Fe, C Argentina 31°29′S 61°00′W
40 G6 Esperanza Sonora, NW Mexico 27°37′N 109°51′W
24 H9 Esperanza Texas, SW USA 31°09′N 105°40′W
194 H3 Esperanza Argentinian research station Antarctica 63°29′S 56°53′W
104 E12 Espichel, Cabo headland S Portugal 38°25′N 09°15′W
54 E10 Espinal Tolima, C Colombia 04°08′N 74°53′W
48 K10 Espinhaço, Serra do ▲▲ SE Brazil
104 G6 Espinho Aveiro, N Portugal 41°01′N 08°38′W
59 N18 Espinosa Minas Gerais, SE Brazil 14°58′S 42°49′W
103 Q15 Espinouse ▲▲ S France
60 Q8 Espírito Santo off. Estado do Espírito Santo. ◆ state E Brazil
Espírito Santo, Estado do see Espírito Santo
187 P13 Espiritu Santo var. Santo. island W Vanuatu
41 Z13 Espíritu Santo, Bahía del bay SE Mexico
40 F9 Espíritu Santo, Isla del island NW Mexico
41 Y12 Espita Yucatán, SE Mexico 21°00′N 88°17′W
15 Y7 Espoir, Cap d' headland Québec, SE Canada 48°24′N 64°21′W
Esponsede/Esponsende see Esposende
93 L20 Espoo Swe. Esbo. Etelä-Suomi, S Finland 60°10′N 24°42′E
104 G5 Esposende var. Esponsede, Esponsende. Braga, N Portugal 41°32′N 08°47′W
83 M18 Espungabera Manica, SW Mozambique 20°29′S 32°48′E
63 H17 Esquel Chubut, SW Argentina 42°55′S 71°20′W
10 L17 Esquimalt Vancouver Island, British Columbia, SW Canada 48°26′N 123°27′W
61 C16 Esquina Corrientes, NE Argentina 30°00′S 59°30′W
42 E6 Esquipulas Chiquimula, SE Guatemala 14°36′N 89°22′W
42 K9 Esquipulas Matagalpa, C Nicaragua 12°30′N 85°55′W
94 I8 Essandsjøen ◎ S Norway
74 E7 Essaouira prev. Mogador. W Morocco 31°33′N 09°40′W
Esseg see Osijek
Es Semara see Smara
99 G15 Essen Antwerpen, N Belgium 51°28′N 04°28′E
101 E15 Essen var. Essen an der Ruhr. Nordrhein-Westfalen, W Germany 51°28′N 07°01′E
Essen an der Ruhr see Essen
74 I5 Es Senia ✈ (Oran) NW Algeria 35°34′N 00°42′W
55 T8 Essequibo Islands island group N Guyana
55 T11 Essequibo River ≈ C Guyana
14 C18 Essex Ontario, S Canada 42°10′N 82°50′W
29 T16 Essex Iowa, C USA 40°49′N 95°18′W
97 P21 Essex cultural region E England, United Kingdom
31 R8 Essexville Michigan, N USA 43°37′N 83°50′W
101 H22 Esslingen var. Esslingen am Neckar. Baden-Württemberg, SW Germany 48°45′N 09°19′E
Esslingen am Neckar see Esslingen
103 N6 Essonne ◆ department N France
Es Suweida see As Suwaydā'
79 F16 Est Eng. East. ◆ province SE Cameroon
104 I1 Estaca de Bares, Punta de point NW Spain
24 M5 Estacado, Llano plain New Mexico/Texas, SW USA
41 P12 Estación Tamuín San Luis Potosí, C Mexico 22°00′N 98°44′W
63 K25 Estados, Isla de los prev. Eng. Staten Island. island S Argentina
Estado Vargas see Vargas
143 P12 Eşţahbān Fārs, S Iran
14 F11 Estaire Ontario, S Canada 46°19′N 80°47′W
59 P16 Estância Sergipe, E Brazil 11°15′S 37°28′W
37 S12 Estancia New Mexico, SW USA 34°45′N 106°03′W
104 G7 Estarreja Aveiro, N Portugal 40°45′N 08°35′W
102 M17 Estats, Pica d' Sp. Pico d'Estats. ▲ France/Spain 42°39′N 01°24′E
Estats, Pico d' see Estats, Pica d'
83 K23 Estcourt KwaZulu/Natal, E South Africa 29°00′S 29°53′E
106 H8 Este anc. Ateste. Veneto, NE Italy 45°14′N 11°40′E
42 J9 Estelí Estelí, NW Nicaragua 13°05′N 86°21′W
42 J9 Estelí ◆ department NW Nicaragua
105 Q4 Estella Bas. Lizarra. Navarra, N Spain 42°41′N 02°02′W
29 R9 Estelline South Dakota, N USA 44°34′N 96°54′W
25 P4 Estelline Texas, SW USA 34°33′N 100°26′W
104 L14 Estepa Andalucía, S Spain 37°17′N 04°52′W
104 L16 Estepona Andalucía, S Spain 36°26′N 05°09′W
39 R9 Ester Alaska, USA 64°49′N 148°03′W
11 V16 Esterhazy Saskatchewan, S Canada 50°40′N 102°02′W
37 S3 Estes Park Colorado, C USA 40°22′N 105°31′W
11 V17 Estevan Saskatchewan, S Canada 49°07′N 103°05′W
29 T11 Estherville Iowa, C USA 43°24′N 94°49′W
21 R15 Estill South Carolina, SE USA 32°45′N 81°14′W
103 Q6 Estissac Aube, N France 48°17′N 03°51′E
15 T9 Est, Lac de l' ◎ Québec, SE Canada
Estland see Estonia
11 S16 Eston Saskatchewan, S Canada 51°09′N 108°42′W
118 G5 Estonia off. Republic of Estonia, Est. Eesti Vabariik, Ger. Estland, Latv. Igaunija; prev. Estonian SSR, Rus. Estonskaya SSR. ◆ republic NE Europe
Estonian SSR see Estonia
Estonia, Republic of see Estonia
Estonskaya SSR see Estonia
104 E11 Estoril Lisboa, W Portugal 38°42′N 09°23′W
59 L14 Estreito Maranhão, E Brazil 06°34′S 47°22′W
104 I8 Estrela, Serra da ▲▲ C Portugal
40 D3 Estrella, Punta headland NW Mexico 30°53′N 114°45′W
104 F10 Estremadura cultural and historical region W Portugal
Estremadura see Extremadura
104 H11 Estremoz Évora, S Portugal 38°50′N 07°35′W
79 D18 Estuaire off. Province de l'Estuaire, var. L'Estuaire. ◆ province NW Gabon
Estuaire, Province de l' see Estuaire
Eszék see Osijek
111 I22 Esztergom Ger. Gran; anc. Strigonium. Komárom-Esztergom, N Hungary 47°47′N 18°44′E
152 K11 Etah Uttar Pradesh, N India 27°33′N 78°39′E
189 R17 Etal Atoll atoll Mortlock Islands, C Micronesia
99 K24 Étalle Luxembourg, SE Belgium 49°41′N 05°36′E
103 N6 Étampes Essonne, N France 48°26′N 02°10′E
182 J1 Etamunbanie, Lake salt lake South Australia
103 N1 Étaples Pas-de-Calais, N France 50°31′N 01°39′E
152 K12 Etāwah Uttar Pradesh, N India 26°46′N 79°01′E
15 R10 Etchemin ≈ Québec, SE Canada
Etchmiadzin see Vagharshapat
40 G7 Etchojoa Sonora, NW Mexico 26°54′N 109°37′W
93 L19 Etelä-Suomi ◆ province S Finland
83 B16 Etengua Kunene, NW Namibia 17°24′S 13°05′E
99 K25 Ethe Luxembourg, SE Belgium 49°34′N 05°32′E
11 W15 Ethelbert Manitoba, S Canada 51°30′N 100°22′W
80 H12 Ethiopia off. Federal Democratic Republic of Ethiopia; prev. Abyssinia, People's Democratic Republic of Ethiopia. ◆ republic E Africa
Ethiopia, Federal Democratic Republic of see Ethiopia
80 I13 Ethiopian Highlands var. Ethiopian Plateau. plateau N Ethiopia
Ethiopian Plateau see Ethiopian Highlands
Ethiopia, People's Democratic Republic of see Ethiopia
34 M2 Etna California, W USA 41°25′N 122°53′W
18 B14 Etna Pennsylvania, NE USA 40°29′N 79°55′W
94 G12 Etna ≈ S Norway
107 L24 Etna, Monte Eng. Mount Etna. ⛰ Sicilia, Italy, C Mediterranean Sea 37°46′N 15°00′E
Etna, Mount see Etna, Monte
95 C15 Etne Hordaland, S Norway 59°40′N 05°55′E
Etoliko see Aitolikó
39 Y14 Etolin Island island Alexander Archipelago, Alaska, USA
38 L12 Etolin Strait strait Alaska, USA
83 C17 Etosha Pan salt lake N Namibia
79 G18 Etoumbi Cuvette Ouest, NW Congo 0°01′N 14°57′E
20 M10 Etowah Tennessee, S USA 35°19′N 84°31′W
23 S2 Etowah River ≈ Georgia, SE USA
146 B13 Etrek var. Gyzyletrek, Rus. Kizyl-Atrek. Balkan Welaýaty, W Turkmenistan 37°40′N 54°44′E
146 C13 Etrek Per. Rūd-e Atrak, Rus. Atrak, Atrek. ≈ Iran/Turkmenistan
102 L3 Étretat Seine-Maritime, N France 49°46′N 00°23′E
114 H9 Etropole Sofiya, W Bulgaria 42°50′N 24°00′E
Etsch see Adige
Et Tafila see Aṭ Ṭafīlah
99 M23 Ettelbrück Diekirch, C Luxembourg 49°51′N 06°06′E
189 V12 Etten atoll Chuuk Islands, C Micronesia
99 H14 Etten-Leur Noord-Brabant, S Netherlands 51°34′N 04°37′E
76 G7 Et Tîdra var. Ile Tîdra. island Dakhlet Nouâdhibou, NW Mauritania
101 G21 Ettlingen Baden-Württemberg, SW Germany 48°57′N 08°25′E
102 M2 Eu Seine-Maritime, N France 50°01′N 01°24′E
193 W16 'Eua prev. Middleburg Island. island Tongatapu Group, SE Tonga
193 W15 Eua Iki island Tongatapu Group, S Tonga
Euboea see Évvoia
181 O12 Eucla Western Australia 31°41′S 128°51′E
31 U11 Euclid Ohio, N USA 41°34′N 81°33′W
27 W14 Eudora Arkansas, C USA 33°06′N 91°15′W
27 Q4 Eudora Kansas, C USA 38°56′N 95°06′W
182 J9 Eudunda South Australia 34°11′S 139°03′E
23 R6 Eufaula Alabama, S USA 31°53′N 85°09′W
27 Q11 Eufaula Oklahoma, C USA 35°16′N 95°36′W
27 Q11 Eufaula Lake var. Eufaula Reservoir. ⊠ Oklahoma, C USA
Eufaula Reservoir see Eufaula Lake
32 F13 Eugene Oregon, NW USA 44°03′N 123°05′W
40 B6 Eugenia, Punta headland NW Mexico 27°48′N 115°03′W
183 Q8 Eugowra New South Wales, SE Australia 33°28′S 148°21′E
104 I2 Eume ≈ NW Spain
104 H2 Eume, Encoro do ⊠ NW Spain
Eumolpias see Plovdiv
59 O18 Eunápolis Bahia, SE Brazil 16°20′S 39°36′W
22 H8 Eunice Louisiana, S USA 30°29′N 92°25′W
37 W15 Eunice New Mexico, SW USA 32°26′N 103°09′W
99 M19 Eupen Liège, E Belgium 50°38′N 06°02′E
130 B10 Euphrates Ar. Al-Furāt, Turk. Fırat Nehri. ≈ SW Asia
138 L3 Euphrates Dam dam N Syria
22 M4 Eupora Mississippi, S USA 33°32′N 89°16′W
93 K19 Eura Länsi-Suomi, SW Finland 61°07′N 22°12′E
93 K19 Eurajoki Länsi-Suomi, SW Finland 61°13′N 21°45′E
0-1 Eurasian Plate tectonic feature
102 L4 Eure ◆ department N France
102 M4 Eure ≈ N France
102 M6 Eure-et-Loir ◆ department C France
34 K3 Eureka California, W USA 40°47′N 124°12′W
27 P6 Eureka Kansas, C USA 37°51′N 96°17′W
33 O6 Eureka Montana, NW USA 48°52′N 115°03′W
35 V5 Eureka Nevada, W USA 39°31′N 115°58′W
29 O7 Eureka South Dakota, N USA 45°46′N 99°37′W
36 L4 Eureka Utah, W USA 39°57′N 112°07′W
32 K10 Eureka Washington, NW USA 46°21′N 118°41′W
27 S9 Eureka Springs Arkansas, C USA 36°25′N 93°45′W
182 K6 Eurinilla Creek seasonal river South Australia
183 O11 Euroa Victoria, SE Australia 36°46′S 145°35′E
172 M9 Europa, Ile island W Madagascar
104 L3 Europa, Picos de ▲▲ N Spain
104 L16 Europa Point headland S Gibraltar 36°07′N 05°20′W
84-85 Europe continent
98 F12 Europoort Zuid-Holland, W Netherlands 51°59′N 04°08′E
Euskadi see País Vasco
101 D17 Euskirchen Nordrhein-Westfalen, W Germany 50°40′N 06°47′E
23 W11 Eustis Florida, SE USA 28°51′N 81°41′W
182 M9 Euston New South Wales, SE Australia 34°34′S 142°45′E
23 N5 Eutaw Alabama, S USA 32°50′N 87°53′W
100 K8 Eutin Schleswig-Holstein, N Germany 54°08′N 10°38′E
10 K14 Eutsuk Lake ⊠ British Columbia, SW Canada
Euxine Sea see Black Sea
83 C16 Evale Cunene, SW Angola 16°36′S 15°46′E
37 T3 Evans Colorado, C USA 40°22′N 104°41′W
11 P14 Evansburg Alberta, SW Canada 53°34′N 114°57′W
29 X13 Evansdale Iowa, C USA 42°28′N 92°16′W
183 V4 Evans Head New South Wales, SE Australia 29°07′S 153°27′E
12 J11 Evans, Lac ◎ Québec, SE Canada
37 S5 Evans, Mount ▲ Colorado, C USA 39°15′N 106°10′W
9 Q6 Evans Strait strait Nunavut, N Canada
31 N10 Evanston Illinois, N USA 42°02′N 87°41′W
33 S17 Evanston Wyoming, C USA 41°16′N 110°57′W
14 D11 Evansville Manitoulin Island, Ontario, S Canada 45°48′N 82°34′W
31 N16 Evansville Indiana, N USA 37°58′N 87°33′W
30 L9 Evansville Wisconsin, N USA 42°46′N 89°16′W
25 S8 Evant Texas, SW USA 31°28′N 98°09′W
143 P13 Evaz Fārs, S Iran 27°48′N 53°58′E
29 W4 Eveleth Minnesota, N USA 47°27′N 92°32′W
182 E3 Evelyn Creek seasonal river South Australia
181 Q2 Evelyn, Mount ▲ Northern Territory, N Australia 13°28′S 132°50′E
122 K10 Evenkiyskiy Avtonomnyy Okrug ◆ autonomous district Krasnoyarskiy Kray, N Russian Federation
183 R13 Everard, Cape headland Victoria, SE Australia 37°48′S 149°21′E
182 F6 Everard, Lake salt lake South Australia
182 C2 Everard Ranges ▲▲ South Australia
153 R11 Everest, Mount Chin. Qomolangma Feng, Nep. Sagarmāthā. ▲ China/Nepal 27°59′N 86°57′E
18 E15 Everett Pennsylvania, NE USA 40°00′N 78°22′W
32 H7 Everett Washington, NW USA 47°59′N 122°12′W
99 E17 Evergem Oost-Vlaanderen, NW Belgium 51°07′N 03°43′E
23 X16 Everglades City Florida, SE USA 25°51′N 81°22′W
23 Y16 Everglades, The wetland Florida, SE USA
23 P7 Evergreen Alabama, S USA 31°25′N 86°55′W
37 T4 Evergreen Colorado, C USA 39°37′N 105°19′W
Evergreen State see Washington
97 L21 Evesham C England, United Kingdom 52°06′N 01°57′W
103 T10 Évian-les-Bains Haute-Savoie, E France 46°22′N 06°34′E
93 K16 Evijärvi Länsi-Suomi, W Finland 63°22′N 23°30′E
79 D17 Evinayong var. Ebinayon, Evinayoung. C Equatorial Guinea 01°28′N 10°17′E
Evinayoung see Evinayong
115 E18 Évinos ≈ C Greece
95 E17 Evje Aust-Agder, S Norway 58°35′N 07°49′E
Evmolpia see Plovdiv
104 H11 Évora anc. Ebora, Lat. Liberalitas Julia. Évora, C Portugal 38°34′N 07°54′W
104 G11 Évora ◆ district S Portugal
102 M4 Évreux anc. Civitas Eburovicum. Eure, N France 49°02′N 01°10′E
102 K6 Évron Mayenne, NW France 48°10′N 00°24′W
114 L13 Évros Bul. Maritsa, Turk. Meriç; anc. Hebrus. ≈ SE Europe see also Maritsa/Meriç
Évros see Meriç
Évros see Maritsa
115 F21 Evrótas ≈ S Greece
103 O5 Évry Essonne, N France 48°38′N 02°34′E
25 O8 E. V. Spence Reservoir ⊠ Texas, SW USA
115 I18 Évvoia Lat. Euboea. island C Greece
38 D9 'Ewa Beach var. Ewa Beach. O'ahu, Hawaii, USA, C Pacific Ocean 21°19′N 158°00′W
Ewa Beach see 'Ewa Beach
32 L9 Ewan Washington, NW USA 47°06′N 117°46′W
44 K12 Ewarton C Jamaica 18°11′N 77°06′W
81 J18 Ewaso Ng'iro var. Nyiro. ≈ C Kenya
29 P13 Ewing Nebraska, C USA 42°13′N 98°20′W
194 J5 Ewing Island island Antarctica
65 P17 Ewing Seamount undersea feature E Atlantic Ocean 23°20′S 08°45′E

◆ Country ● Country Capital ◇ Dependent Territory ○ Dependent Territory Capital ◆ Administrative Regions ✈ International Airport ▲ Mountain ▲▲ Mountain Range ⛰ Volcano ≈ River ◎ Lake ⊠ Reservoir

158 L6 **Ewirgol** Xinjiang Uygur Zizhiqu, W China 42°56′N 87°39′E
79 G19 **Ewo** Cuvette, W Congo 0°55′S 14°49′E
27 S3 **Excelsior Springs** Missouri, C USA 39°20′N 94°13′W
97 J23 **Exe** ~ SW England, United Kingdom
194 L12 **Executive Committee Range** ▲ Antarctica
14 E16 **Exeter** Ontario, S Canada 43°19′N 81°26′W
97 J24 **Exeter** *anc.* Isca Damnoniorum. SW England, United Kingdom 50°43′N 03°31′W
35 R11 **Exeter** California, W USA 36°17′N 119°08′W
19 P10 **Exeter** New Hampshire, NE USA 42°57′N 70°55′W
Exin *see* Kcynia
29 T14 **Exira** Iowa, C USA 41°36′N 94°55′W
97 J23 **Exmoor** *moorland* SW England, United Kingdom
21 Y6 **Exmore** Virginia, NE USA 37°31′N 75°48′W
180 G8 **Exmouth** Western Australia 22°01′S 114°06′E
97 J24 **Exmouth** SW England, United Kingdom 50°36′N 03°25′W
180 G8 **Exmouth Gulf** *gulf* Western Australia
173 V8 **Exmouth Plateau** *undersea feature* E Indian Ocean
115 J20 **Exompourgo** *ancient monument* Tínos, Kykládes, Greece, Aegean Sea
104 I10 **Extremadura** *var.* Estremadura. ◆ *autonomous community* W Spain
78 F12 **Extrême-Nord** *Eng.* Extreme North. ◆ *province* N Cameroon
Extreme North *see* Extrême-Nord
44 I3 **Exuma Cays** *islets* C Bahamas
44 I3 **Exuma Sound** *sound* C Bahamas
81 H20 **Eyasi, Lake** ◎ N Tanzania
95 F17 **Eydehavn** Aust-Agder, S Norway 58°31′N 08°53′E
96 L12 **Eyemouth** SE Scotland, United Kingdom 55°52′N 02°07′W
96 G7 **Eye Peninsula** *peninsula* NW Scotland, United Kingdom
80 Q13 **Eyl** *It.* Eil. Nugaal, E Somalia 08°03′N 49°49′E
103 N11 **Eymoutiers** Haute-Vienne, C France 45°45′N 01°43′E
Eyo (lower course) *see* Uolo, Río
29 X10 **Eyota** Minnesota, N USA 44°00′N 92°13′W
182 H2 **Eyre Basin, Lake** *salt lake* South Australia
182 I1 **Eyre Creek** *seasonal river* Northern Territory/South Australia
174 L9 **Eyre, Lake** *salt lake* South Australia
185 C22 **Eyre Mountains** ▲ South Island, New Zealand
182 H3 **Eyre North, Lake** *salt lake* South Australia
182 G7 **Eyre Peninsula** *peninsula* South Australia
182 H4 **Eyre South, Lake** *salt lake* South Australia
95 B18 **Eysturoy** *Dan.* Østerø. *island* N Faeroe Islands
61 D20 **Ezeiza** ✈ (Buenos Aires) Buenos Aires, E Argentina 34°49′S 58°30′W
Ezeres *see* Ezeriş
116 F12 **Ezeriş** *Hung.* Ezeres. Caraş-Severin, W Romania 45°21′N 21°55′E
161 O9 **Ezhou** *prev.* Echeng. Hubei, C China 30°23′N 114°52′E
125 R11 **Ezhva** Respublika Komi, NW Russian Federation 61°45′N 50°43′E
136 B12 **Ezine** Çanakkale, NW Turkey 39°46′N 26°20′E
Ezo *see* Hokkaidō
Ezra/Ezraa *see* Izra'

F

191 P7 **Faaa** Tahiti, W French Polynesia 17°32′S 149°36′W
191 P7 **Faaa** ✈ (Papeete) Tahiti, W French Polynesia 17°31′S 149°36′W
95 H24 **Faaborg** *var.* Fåborg. Syddtjylland, C Denmark 55°06′N 10°10′E
151 K19 **Faadhippolhu Atoll** *var.* Fadiffolu, Lhaviyani Atoll. *atoll* N Maldives
191 U10 **Faaite** *atoll* Îles Tuamotu, C French Polynesia
191 Q8 **Faaone** Tahiti, W French Polynesia 17°39′S 149°18′W
24 H8 **Fabens** Texas, SW USA 31°30′N 106°09′W
94 H12 **Fåberg** Oppland, S Norway 61°15′N 10°21′E
Fåborg *see* Faaborg
106 I12 **Fabriano** Marche, C Italy 43°20′N 12°54′E
145 U16 **Fabrichnoye** *prev.* Fabrichnyy. Almaty, SE Kazakhstan 43°12′N 76°19′E
Fabrichnyy *see* Fabrichnoye
54 F10 **Facatativá** Cundinamarca, C Colombia 04°49′N 74°22′W
77 X9 **Fachi** Agadez, C Niger 18°01′N 11°36′E
188 B16 **Facpi Point** *headland* W Guam
18 I13 **Factoryville** Pennsylvania, NE USA 41°34′N 75°45′W
78 K8 **Fada** Borkou-Ennedi-Tibesti, E Chad 17°14′N 21°32′E
77 Q13 **Fada-Ngourma** E Burkina 12°05′N 00°26′E
123 N6 **Faddeya, Zaliv** *bay* N Russian Federation
123 Q5 **Faddeyevskiy, Poluostrov** *island* Novosibirskiye Ostrova, NE Russian Federation
141 W12 **Fadhī** S Oman 17°54′N 55°30′E
Fadiffolu *see* Faadhippolhu Atoll
106 H10 **Faenza** *anc.* Faventia. Emilia-Romagna, N Italy 44°17′N 11°53′E
64 M5 **Faeroe-Iceland Ridge** *undersea feature* NW Norwegian Sea 64°00′N 10°00′W
64 M5 **Faeroe Islands** *Dan.* Færøerne, *Faer.* Føroyar. ◇ *Danish external territory* N Atlantic Ocean
86 C8 **Faeroe Islands** *island group* N Atlantic Ocean
Færøerne *see* Faeroe Islands
64 N6 **Faeroe-Shetland Trough** *undersea feature* NE Atlantic Ocean
104 H6 **Fafe** Braga, N Portugal 41°27′N 08°11′W
80 K13 **Fafen Shet'** ~ E Ethiopia
193 V15 **Fafo** *island* Tongatapu Group, S Tonga
192 I16 **Fagaloa Bay** *bay* Upolu, E Samoa
192 H15 **Fagamālo** Savai'i, N Samoa 13°27′S 172°22′W
116 I12 **Făgăraş** *Ger.* Fogarasch, *Hung.* Fogaras. Braşov, C Romania 45°50′N 24°59′E
191 W10 **Fagatau** *prev.* Fangatau. *atoll* Îles Tuamotu, C French Polynesia
191 X12 **Fagataufa** *prev.* Fangataufa. *island* Îles Tuamotu, SE French Polynesia
95 M20 **Fagerhult** Kalmar, S Sweden 57°07′N 15°40′E
94 G13 **Fagernes** Oppland, S Norway 60°59′N 09°14′E
92 I9 **Fagernes** Troms, N Norway 69°31′N 19°16′E
95 M14 **Fagersta** Västmanland, C Sweden 59°59′N 15°49′E
77 W13 **Faggo** *var.* Foggo. Bauchi, N Nigeria 11°22′N 09°55′E
Faghman *see* Fughmah
Fagibina, Lake *see* Faguibine, Lac
63 J25 **Fagnano, Lago** ◎ S Argentina
99 G22 **Fagne** *hill range* S Belgium
77 N10 **Faguibine, Lac** *var.* Lake Fagibina. ◎ NW Mali
Fahaheel *see* Al Fuḩayḩīl
Fahlun *see* Falun
143 U12 **Fahraj** Kermān, SE Iran 29°00′N 59°00′E
64 P5 **Faial** Madeira, Portugal, NE Atlantic Ocean 32°47′N 16°53′W
64 N2 **Faial** *var.* Ilha do Faial. *island* Azores, Portugal, NE Atlantic Ocean
Faial, Ilha do *see* Faial
108 G10 **Faido** Ticino, S Switzerland 46°30′N 08°48′E
Faifo *see* Hôi An
Failaka Island *see* Faylakah
190 G12 **Faioa, Île** *island* N Wallis and Futuna
181 W8 **Fairbairn Reservoir** ⊠ Queensland, E Australia
39 R9 **Fairbanks** Alaska, USA 64°48′N 147°47′W
21 U12 **Fair Bluff** North Carolina, SE USA 34°18′N 79°02′W
31 R14 **Fairborn** Ohio, N USA 39°48′N 84°03′W
23 S3 **Fairburn** Georgia, SE USA 33°34′N 84°34′W
30 M12 **Fairbury** Illinois, N USA 40°45′N 88°30′W
29 Q17 **Fairbury** Nebraska, C USA 40°08′N 97°10′W
29 T9 **Fairfax** Minnesota, N USA 44°31′N 94°43′W
27 O8 **Fairfax** Oklahoma, C USA 36°34′N 96°42′W
21 R14 **Fairfax** South Carolina, SE USA 32°57′N 81°14′W
35 N8 **Fairfield** California, W USA 38°14′N 122°03′W
33 O14 **Fairfield** Idaho, NW USA 43°20′N 114°45′W
30 M16 **Fairfield** Illinois, N USA 38°22′N 88°23′W
29 X15 **Fairfield** Iowa, C USA 41°00′N 91°57′W
33 R8 **Fairfield** Montana, NW USA 47°36′N 111°59′W
31 Q14 **Fairfield** Ohio, N USA 39°21′N 84°34′W
25 U8 **Fairfield** Texas, SW USA 31°43′N 96°10′W
27 T7 **Fair Grove** Missouri, C USA 37°22′N 93°09′W
19 P12 **Fairhaven** Massachusetts, NE USA 41°38′N 70°51′W
23 N8 **Fairhope** Alabama, S USA 30°31′N 87°54′W
96 L4 **Fair Isle** *island* NE Scotland, United Kingdom
185 F20 **Fairlie** Canterbury, South Island, New Zealand 44°06′S 170°50′E
29 U11 **Fairmont** Minnesota, N USA 43°40′N 94°27′W
29 Q16 **Fairmont** Nebraska, C USA 40°37′N 97°36′W
21 S3 **Fairmont** West Virginia, NE USA 39°28′N 80°08′W
31 P13 **Fairmount** Indiana, N USA 40°25′N 85°39′W
18 H10 **Fairmount** New York, NE USA 43°03′N 76°14′W
29 R7 **Fairmount** North Dakota, N USA 46°02′N 96°36′W
37 S5 **Fairplay** Colorado, C USA 39°13′N 106°00′W
18 F9 **Fairport** New York, NE USA 43°06′N 77°26′W
11 O12 **Fairview** Alberta, W Canada 56°03′N 118°28′W
26 L9 **Fairview** Oklahoma, C USA 36°16′N 98°29′W
36 L4 **Fairview** Utah, W USA 39°37′N 111°26′W
35 T6 **Fairview Peak** ▲ Nevada, W USA 39°13′N 118°09′W
188 H14 **Fais** *atoll* Caroline Islands, W Micronesia
149 U8 **Faisalābād** *prev.* Lyallpur. Punjab, NE Pakistan 31°26′N 73°06′E
Faisaliya *see* Fayşalīyah
28 L8 **Faith** South Dakota, N USA 45°01′N 102°02′W
153 N12 **Faizābād** Uttar Pradesh, N India 26°46′N 82°08′E
Faizabad/Faizābād *see* Feizābād
45 S9 **Fajardo** E Puerto Rico 18°20′N 65°39′W
139 R9 **Fajj, Wādī al** *dry watercourse* S Iraq
140 K4 **Fajr, Bi'r** *well* NW Saudi Arabia
191 W10 **Fakahina** *atoll* Îles Tuamotu, C French Polynesia
190 L10 **Fakaofo Atoll** *island* SE Tokelau
191 U10 **Fakarava** *atoll* Îles Tuamotu, C French Polynesia
127 T2 **Fakel** Udmurtskaya Respublika, NW Russian Federation 57°35′N 53°00′E
97 P19 **Fakenham** E England, United Kingdom 52°50′N 00°51′E
171 U13 **Fakfak** Papua, E Indonesia 02°55′S 132°17′E
153 T12 **Fakīragrām** Assam, NE India 26°22′N 90°15′E
114 M10 **Fakiyska Reka** ~ SE Bulgaria
95 J24 **Fakse** Sjælland, SE Denmark 55°16′N 12°08′E
95 J24 **Fakse Bugt** *bay* SE Denmark
95 J24 **Fakse Ladeplads** Sjælland, SE Denmark 55°14′N 12°11′E
163 V11 **Faku** Liaoning, NE China 42°30′N 123°27′E
76 J14 **Falaba** N Sierra Leone 09°54′N 11°22′W
102 K5 **Falaise** Calvados, N France 48°52′N 00°12′W
114 H12 **Falakró** ▲ NE Greece
189 T12 **Falalu** *island* Chuuk, C Micronesia
166 L4 **Falam** Chin State, Myanmar (Burma) 22°58′N 93°45′E
143 N8 **Falāvarjān** Eşfahān, C Iran 32°33′N 51°28′E
116 M11 **Fălciu** Vaslui, E Romania 46°19′N 28°10′E
54 I4 **Falcón** *off.* Estado Falcón. ◆ *state* NW Venezuela
106 J12 **Falconara Marittima** Marche, C Italy 43°37′N 13°23′E
Falcone, Capo del *see* Falcone, Punta del
107 A16 **Falcone, Punta del** *var.* Capo del Falcone. *headland* Sardegna, Italy, C Mediterranean Sea 40°57′N 08°12′E
Falcón, Estado *see* Falcón
11 Y16 **Falcon Lake** Manitoba, S Canada 49°44′N 95°18′W
Falcon Lake *see* Falcón, Presa/Falcon Reservoir
41 O7 **Falcón, Presa** *var.* Falcon Lake, Falcon Reservoir. ⊠ Mexico/USA *see also* Falcon Reservoir
Falcón, Presa *see* Falcon Reservoir
25 Q16 **Falcon Reservoir** *var.* Falcon Lake, Presa Falcón. ⊠ Mexico/USA *see also* Falcón, Presa
Falcon Reservoir *see* Falcón, Presa
190 L10 **Fale** *island* Fakaofo Atoll, SE Tokelau
192 F15 **Faleālupo** Savai'i, NW Samoa 13°30′S 172°46′W
190 B10 **Falefatu** *island* Funafuti Atoll, C Tuvalu
192 G15 **Fālelima** Savai'i, NW Samoa 13°30′S 172°41′W
95 N18 **Falerum** Östergötland, S Sweden 58°07′N 16°15′E
Faleshty *see* Făleşti
116 M9 **Făleşti** *Rus.* Faleshty. NW Moldova 47°33′N 27°43′E
25 S15 **Falfurrias** Texas, SW USA 27°17′N 98°10′W
11 O13 **Falher** Alberta, W Canada 55°45′N 117°18′W
Falkenau an der Eger *see* Sokolov
95 J21 **Falkenberg** Halland, S Sweden 56°55′N 12°30′E
Falkenberg *see* Niemodlin
Falkenburg in Pommern *see* Złocieniec
100 N12 **Falkensee** Brandenburg, NE Germany 52°34′N 13°04′E
96 J12 **Falkirk** C Scotland, United Kingdom 56°N 03°48′W
65 I20 **Falkland Escarpment** *undersea feature* SW Atlantic Ocean 50°00′S 45°00′W
63 K24 **Falkland Islands** *var.* Falklands, Islas Malvinas. ◇ *UK dependent territory* SW Atlantic Ocean
47 W14 **Falkland Islands** *island group* SW Atlantic Ocean
65 I20 **Falkland Plateau** *var.* Argentine Rise. *undersea feature* SW Atlantic Ocean 51°00′S 50°00′W
Falklands *see* Falkland Islands
63 M23 **Falkland Sound** *var.* Estrecho de San Carlos. *strait* C Falkland Islands
Falknov nad Ohří *see* Sokolov
115 H21 **Falkonéra** *island* S Greece
95 K18 **Falköping** Västra Götaland, S Sweden 58°10′N 13°31′E
139 U8 **Fallāḩ** Wāsiţ, E Iraq 32°58′N 45°09′E
35 U16 **Fallbrook** California, W USA 33°22′N 117°15′W
189 U12 **Falleallej Pass** *passage* Chuuk Islands, C Micronesia
93 J14 **Fällfors** Västerbotten, N Sweden 65°07′N 20°46′E
194 I6 **Fallières Coast** *physical region* Antarctica
100 I11 **Fallingbostel** Niedersachsen, NW Germany 52°52′N 09°42′E
33 X9 **Fallon** Montana, NW USA 46°49′N 105°07′W
35 S5 **Fallon** Nevada, W USA 39°29′N 118°47′W
19 O12 **Fall River** Massachusetts, NE USA 41°42′N 71°09′W
27 P6 **Fall River Lake** ⊠ Kansas, C USA
35 O3 **Fall River Mills** California, W USA 41°00′N 121°28′W
21 W4 **Falls Church** Virginia, NE USA 38°53′N 77°11′W
29 S17 **Falls City** Nebraska, C USA 40°03′N 95°36′W
25 S12 **Falls City** Texas, SW USA 28°58′N 98°01′W
Falluja *see* Al Fallūjah
77 S12 **Falmey** Dosso, SW Niger 12°29′N 02°58′E
45 W10 **Falmouth** Antigua, Antigua and Barbuda 17°02′N 61°47′W
44 J11 **Falmouth** W Jamaica 18°28′N 77°39′W
97 H25 **Falmouth** SW England, United Kingdom 50°08′N 05°04′W
20 M4 **Falmouth** Kentucky, S USA 38°40′N 84°20′W
19 P13 **Falmouth** Massachusetts, NE USA 41°31′N 70°36′W
21 W5 **Falmouth** Virginia, NE USA 38°19′N 77°28′W
189 U12 **Falos** *island* Chuuk, C Micronesia
83 E26 **False Bay** *Afr.* Valsbaai. *bay* SW South Africa
155 K17 **False Divi Point** *headland* E India 15°46′N 80°43′E
38 M16 **False Pass** Unimak Island, Alaska, USA 54°52′N 163°15′W
154 P12 **False Point** *headland* E India 20°23′N 86°52′E
105 U6 **Falset** Cataluña, NE Spain 41°08′N 00°49′E
95 I25 **Falster** *island* SE Denmark
116 K9 **Fălticeni** *Hung.* Falticsén. Suceava, NE Romania 47°27′N 26°20′E
Falticsén *see* Fălticeni
94 M13 **Falun** *var.* Fahlun. Kopparberg, C Sweden 60°36′N 15°36′E
Famagusta *see* Gazimağusa
Famagusta Bay *see* Gazimağusa Körfezi
62 I8 **Famatina** La Rioja, NW Argentina 28°58′S 67°46′W
99 J21 **Famenne** *physical region* SE Belgium
77 X15 **Fan** ~ E Nigeria
76 M12 **Fana** Koulikoro, SW Mali 12°45′N 06°55′W
115 K19 **Fána** *ancient harbor* Chíos, SE Greece
189 V13 **Fanan** *island* Chuuk, C Micronesia
189 U12 **Fanapanges** *island* Chuuk, C Micronesia
115 L20 **Fanári, Akrotírio** *headland* Ikaría, Dodekánisa, Greece, Aegean Sea 37°40′N 26°21′E
45 Q13 **Fancy** Saint Vincent, Saint Vincent and the Grenadines 13°22′N 61°10′W
172 I5 **Fandriana** Fianarantsoa, SE Madagascar 20°14′S 47°21′E
167 O6 **Fang** Chiang Mai, NW Thailand 19°56′N 99°14′E
80 E13 **Fangak** Jonglei, E South Sudan 09°05′N 30°52′E
Fangatau *see* Fagatau
Fangataufa *see* Fagataufa
193 V15 **Fanga Uta** *bay* S Tonga
161 N7 **Fangcheng** Henan, C China 33°18′N 113°03′E
Fangcheng *see* Fangchenggang
160 K15 **Fangchenggang** *var.* Fangcheng Gezu Zizhixian; *prev.* Fangcheng. Guangxi Zhuangzu Zizhiqu, S China 21°49′N 108°21′E
Fangcheng Gezu Zizhixian *see* Fangchenggang
161 S15 **Fangshan** S Taiwan 22°19′N 120°41′E
163 X8 **Fangzheng** Heilongjiang, NE China 45°50′N 128°50′E
Fani *see* Fanit, Lumi i
119 K16 **Fanipal'** *Rus.* Fanipol'. Minskaya Voblasts', C Belarus 53°45′N 27°20′E
Fanipol' *see* Fanipal'
113 D22 **Fanit, Lumi i** *var.* Fani. ~ N Albania
25 T13 **Fannin** Texas, SW USA 28°41′N 97°13′W
Fanning Island *see* Tabuaeran
94 G8 **Fannrem** Sør-Trøndelag, S Norway 63°16′N 09°48′E
106 I11 **Fano** *anc.* Colonia Julia Fanestris, Fanum Fortunae. Marche, C Italy 43°50′N 13°E
95 E23 **Fanø** *island* W Denmark
167 R5 **Fan Si Pan** ▲ N Vietnam 22°18′N 103°36′E
Fanum Fortunae *see* Fano
Fao *see* Al Fāw
141 W7 **Faq'** *var.* Al Faqa. Dubayy, E United Arab Emirates 24°42′N 55°37′E
Farab *see* Farap
185 G16 **Faraday, Mount** ▲ South Island, New Zealand 42°01′S 171°37′E
79 P16 **Faradje** Orientale, NE Dem. Rep. Congo 03°45′N 29°43′E
Faradofay *see* Tôlañaro
172 I7 **Farafangana** Fianarantsoa, SE Madagascar 22°50′S 47°50′E
148 J7 **Farāh** *var.* Farah, Fararud. Farāh, W Afghanistan 32°22′N 62°07′E
148 K7 **Farāh** ◆ *province* W Afghanistan
148 J7 **Farāh Rūd** ~ W Afghanistan
188 K7 **Farallon de Medinilla** *island* C Northern Mariana Islands
188 J2 **Farallon de Pajaros** *var.* Uracas. *island* N Northern Mariana Islands
76 J14 **Faranah** Haute-Guinée, S Guinea 10°02′N 10°44′W
146 K12 **Farap** *Rus.* Farab. Lebap Welaýaty, NE Turkmenistan 39°15′N 63°32′E
Fararud *see* Farāh
140 M13 **Farasān, Jazā'ir** *island group* SW Saudi Arabia
172 I5 **Faratsiho** Antananarivo, C Madagascar 19°24′S 46°57′E
188 K15 **Faraulep Atoll** *atoll* Caroline Islands, C Micronesia
99 H20 **Farciennes** Hainaut, S Belgium 50°26′N 04°33′E
105 O14 **Fardes** ~ S Spain
191 S10 **Fare** Huahine, W French Polynesia 16°42′S 151°01′W
97 M23 **Fareham** S England, United Kingdom 50°51′N 01°10′W
39 P11 **Farewell** Alaska, USA 62°35′N 153°59′W
184 H13 **Farewell, Cape** *headland* South Island, New Zealand 40°30′S 172°39′E
Farewell, Cape *see* Nunap Isua
184 I13 **Farewell Spit** *spit* South Island, New Zealand
95 I17 **Färgelanda** Västra Götaland, S Sweden 58°34′N 11°59′E
Farghona, Wodii/ Farghona Valley *see* Fergana Valley
Farghona Wodiysi *see* Fergana Valley
23 V8 **Fargo** Georgia, SE USA 30°42′N 82°33′W
29 R5 **Fargo** North Dakota, N USA 46°53′N 96°47′W
147 S10 **Farg'ona** *Rus.* Fergana; *prev.* Novyy Margilan. Farg'ona Viloyati, E Uzbekistan 40°28′N 71°44′E
147 R10 **Farg'ona Viloyati** *Rus.* Ferganskaya Oblast'. ◆ *province* E Uzbekistan
29 V10 **Faribault** Minnesota, N USA 44°18′N 93°16′W
152 J11 **Farīdābād** Haryāna, N India 28°26′N 77°19′E
152 H8 **Farīdkot** Punjab, NW India 30°42′N 74°47′E
153 T15 **Faridpur** Dhaka, C Bangladesh 23°29′N 89°50′E
121 P14 **Fārigh, Wādī al** ~ N Libya
172 I4 **Farihy Alaotra** ◎ C Madagascar
94 M11 **Färila** Gävleborg, C Sweden 61°48′N 15°55′E
104 E9 **Farilhões** *island* C Portugal
76 G12 **Farim** NW Guinea-Bissau 12°30′N 15°09′W
Farish *see* Forish
141 T11 **Fāris, Qalamat** *well* SE Saudi Arabia
95 N21 **Färjestaden** Kalmar, S Sweden 56°38′N 16°30′E
149 R2 **Farkhār** Takhār, NE Afghanistan 36°39′N 69°43′E
147 Q14 **Farkhor** *Rus.* Parkhar. SW Tajikistan 37°32′N 69°22′E
116 F12 **Fârliug** *prev.* Fîrliug, *Hung.* Furluk. Caraş-Severin, SW Romania 45°21′N 21°55′E
115 M21 **Farmakonísi** *island* Dodekánisa, Greece, Aegean Sea
30 M13 **Farmer City** Illinois, N USA 40°14′N 88°38′W
31 N14 **Farmersburg** Indiana, N USA 39°14′N 87°21′W
25 U6 **Farmersville** Texas, SW USA 33°09′N 96°21′W
22 H5 **Farmerville** Louisiana, S USA 32°46′N 92°24′W
29 X16 **Farmington** Iowa, C USA 40°37′N 91°43′W
19 Q6 **Farmington** Maine, NE USA 44°40′N 70°09′W
29 V9 **Farmington** Minnesota, N USA 44°39′N 93°09′W
27 X6 **Farmington** Missouri, C USA 37°46′N 90°26′W
19 O9 **Farmington** New Hampshire, NE USA 43°23′N 71°04′W
37 P9 **Farmington** New Mexico, SW USA 36°44′N 108°13′W
36 L2 **Farmington** Utah, W USA 40°58′N 111°53′W
21 W9 **Farmville** North Carolina, SE USA 35°37′N 77°36′W
21 U6 **Farmville** Virginia, NE USA 37°17′N 78°25′W
97 N22 **Farnborough** S England, United Kingdom 51°17′N 00°46′W
97 N22 **Farnham** S England, United Kingdom 51°13′N 00°49′W
10 J7 **Faro** Yukon Territory, W Canada 62°15′N 133°30′W
104 G14 **Faro** Faro, S Portugal 37°01′N 07°56′W
95 Q18 **Fårö** Gotland, SE Sweden 57°55′N 19°10′E
104 G14 **Faro** ◆ *district* S Portugal
78 F13 **Faro** ~ Cameroon/Nigeria
104 G14 **Faro** ✈ Faro, S Portugal 37°02′N 08°01′W
Faro, Punta del *see* Peloro, Capo
95 Q18 **Fårösund** Gotland, SE Sweden 57°51′N 19°02′E
173 N7 **Farquhar Group** *island group* S Seychelles
18 B13 **Farrell** Pennsylvania, NE USA 41°12′N 80°28′W
152 K11 **Farrukhābād** Uttar Pradesh, N India 27°24′N 79°34′E
143 P11 **Fārs** *off.* Ostān-e Fārs; *anc.* Persis. ◆ *province* S Iran
115 F16 **Fársala** Thessalía, C Greece 39°17′N 22°23′E
143 R4 **Fārsīān** Golestán, N Iran
Fars, Khalīj-e *see* Persian Gulf
95 G21 **Farsø** Nordjylland, N Denmark 56°47′N 09°21′E
Fārs, Ostān-e *see* Fārs
95 D18 **Farsund** Vest-Agder, S Norway 58°05′N 06°49′E
141 U14 **Fartak, Ra's** *headland* E Yemen 15°34′N 52°19′E
60 H13 **Fartura, Serra da** ▲ S Brazil
Farvel, Kap *see* Nunap Isua
24 L4 **Farwell** Texas, SW USA 34°23′N 103°03′W
194 I9 **Farwell Island** *island* Antarctica
152 L9 **Far Western** ◆ *zone* W Nepal
148 M3 **Fāryāb** ◆ *province* N Afghanistan
143 P12 **Fasā** Fārs, S Iran 28°55′N 53°39′E
141 U12 **Fasad, Ramlat** *desert* SW Oman
107 P17 **Fasano** Puglia, SE Italy 40°50′N 17°21′E
92 L3 **Fáskrúdhsfjördhur** Austurland, E Iceland 64°55′N 14°01′W
117 O5 **Fastiv** *Rus.* Fastov. Kyyivs'ka Oblast', NW Ukraine 50°08′N 29°59′E
97 B22 **Fastnet Rock** *Ir.* Carraig Aonair. *island* SW Ireland
Fastov *see* Fastiv
190 C9 **Fatato** *island* Funafuti Atoll, C Tuvalu
152 K12 **Fatehgarh** Uttar Pradesh, N India 27°22′N 79°38′E
149 U6 **Fatehjang** Punjab, E Pakistan 33°33′N 72°43′E
152 G11 **Fatehpur** Rājasthān, N India 27°59′N 74°58′E
152 L13 **Fatehpur** Uttar Pradesh, N India 25°56′N 80°55′E
126 J7 **Fatezh** Kurskaya Oblast', W Russian Federation 52°01′N 35°51′E
76 G11 **Fatick** W Senegal 14°19′N 16°27′W
104 G9 **Fátima** Santarém, W Portugal 39°37′N 08°39′W
136 M11 **Fatsa** Ordu, N Turkey 41°02′N 37°31′E
Fatshan *see* Foshan
190 D12 **Fatua, Pointe** *var.* Pointe Nord. *headland* Île Futuna, S Wallis and Futuna
191 X7 **Fatu Hiva** *island* Îles Marquises, NE French Polynesia
Fatunda *see* Fatundu
79 H21 **Fatundu** *var.* Fatunda. Bandundu, W Dem. Rep. Congo 04°08′S 17°13′E
29 O8 **Faulkton** South Dakota, N USA 45°02′N 99°07′W
116 L13 **Făurei** *prev.* Filimon Sîrbu. Brăila, SE Romania 45°05′N 27°15′E
92 G12 **Fauske** Nordland, C Norway 67°15′N 15°27′E
11 P13 **Faust** Alberta, W Canada 55°19′N 115°33′W
99 L23 **Fauvillers** Luxembourg, SE Belgium 49°52′N 05°40′E
107 J24 **Favara** Sicilia, Italy, C Mediterranean Sea 37°19′N 13°40′E
Faventia *see* Faenza
107 G23 **Favignana, Isola** *island* Isole Egadi, S Italy
12 D8 **Fawn** ~ Ontario, SE Canada
Faxa Bay *see* Faxaflói
92 H3 **Faxaflói** *Eng.* Faxa Bay. *bay* W Iceland
78 I7 **Faya** *prev.* Faya-Largeau, Largeau. Borkou-Ennedi-Tibesti, N Chad 17°58′N 19°06′E
Faya-Largeau *see* Faya
187 Q16 **Fayaoué** Province des Îles Loyauté, C New Caledonia 20°41′S 166°31′E
138 M5 **Fayḍāt** *hill range* E Syria
23 O3 **Fayette** Alabama, S USA 33°40′N 87°49′W
29 X12 **Fayette** Iowa, C USA 42°50′N 91°48′W
22 J6 **Fayette** Mississippi, S USA 31°42′N 91°03′W
27 U4 **Fayette** Missouri, C USA 39°09′N 92°40′W
27 S9 **Fayetteville** Arkansas, C USA 36°04′N 94°10′W
21 U10 **Fayetteville** North Carolina, SE USA 35°03′N 78°53′W
20 J10 **Fayetteville** Tennessee, S USA 35°08′N 86°33′W
25 U11 **Fayetteville** Texas, SW USA 29°52′N 96°40′W
21 R5 **Fayetteville** West Virginia, NE USA 38°03′N 81°09′W
141 R4 **Faylakah** *var.* Failaka Island. *island* E Kuwait
139 T10 **Fayşalīyah** *var.* Faisaliya. Al Qādisīyah, S Iraq 31°48′N 44°36′E
189 P15 **Fayu** *var.* East Fayu. *island* Hall Islands, C Micronesia
152 G8 **Fāzilka** Punjab, NW India 30°26′N 74°04′E
Fdérick *see* Fdérik
76 I6 **Fdérik** *var.* Fdérick, *Fr.* Fort Gouraud. Tiris Zemmour, NW Mauritania 22°40′N 12°41′W
Feabhail, Loch *see* Foyle, Lough
97 B20 **Feale** ~ SW Ireland
21 V12 **Fear, Cape** *headland* Bald Head Island, North Carolina, SE USA 33°50′N 77°57′W
35 O6 **Feather River** ~ California, W USA
185 M14 **Featherston** Wellington, North Island, New Zealand 41°07′S 175°28′E
102 L3 **Fécamp** Seine-Maritime, N France 49°45′N 00°22′E
Fédala *see* Mohammedia
61 D17 **Federación** Entre Ríos, E Argentina 31°00′S 57°55′W
61 D17 **Federal** Entre Ríos, E Argentina 30°55′S 58°45′W
77 T15 **Federal Capital District** ◆ *capital territory* C Nigeria
Federal Capital Territory *see* Australian Capital Territory
Federal District *see* Distrito Federal
21 Y4 **Federalsburg** Maryland, NE USA 38°41′N 75°46′W
74 M6 **Fedjaj, Chott el** *var.* Chott el Fejaj, Shaṭṭ al Fijāj. *salt lake* C Tunisia
94 B13 **Fedje** *island* S Norway
144 M7 **Fedorovka** Kostanay, N Kazakhstan 51°12′N 52°00′E
127 U6 **Fedorovka** Respublika Bashkortostan, W Russian Federation 53°09′N 55°07′E
Fëdory *see* Fyadory
117 U11 **Fedotova Kosa** *spit* SE Ukraine
189 V13 **Fefan** *atoll* Chuuk Islands, C Micronesia
111 O21 **Fehérgyarmat** Szabolcs-Szatmár-Bereg, E Hungary 47°59′N 22°29′E
Fehér-Körös *see* Crişul Alb
Fehértemplom *see* Bela Crkva
Fehérvölgy *see* Albac
100 L7 **Fehmarn** *island* N Germany
95 H25 **Fehmarn Belt** *Dan.* Femern Bælt, *Ger.* Fehmarnbelt. *strait* Denmark /Germany *see also* Femern Bælt
Fehmarnbelt *see* Fehmarn Belt/Femer Bælt
109 X8 **Fehring** Steiermark, SE Austria 46°56′N 16°00′E
59 B15 **Feijó** Acre, W Brazil 08°07′S 70°27′W
184 M12 **Feilding** Manawatu-Wanganui, North Island, New Zealand 40°15′S 175°34′E
Feira *see* Feira de Santana
59 O17 **Feira de Santana** *var.* Feira. Bahia, E Brazil 12°17′S 38°53′W
109 X7 **Feistritz** ~ SE Austria
Feistritz *see* Ilirska Bistrica
161 P8 **Feixi** *var.* Shangpai; *prev.* Shangpaihe. Anhui, E China 31°40′N 117°08′E
149 S2 **Feizābād** *var.* Faizabad, Faizābād, Feyzabad, Fyzabad; *prev.* Feyzābād. Badakhshān, NE Afghanistan 37°06′N 70°34′E
Fejaj, Chott el *see* Fedjaj, Chott el
111 I23 **Fejér** *off.* Fejér Megye. ◆ *county* W Hungary
Fejér Megye *see* Fejér
95 I24 **Fejø** *island* SE Denmark
136 K15 **Feke** Adana, S Turkey 37°49′N 35°55′E
Feketehalom *see* Codlea
Fekete-Körös *see* Crişul Negru
105 Y9 **Felanitx** Mallorca, Spain, W Mediterranean Sea 39°28′N 03°08′E
109 T3 **Feldaist** ~ N Austria
109 W8 **Feldbach** Steiermark, SE Austria 46°58′N 15°53′E
101 F24 **Feldberg** ▲ SW Germany 47°52′N 08°01′E
116 J12 **Feldioara** *Ger.* Marienburg, *Hung.* Földvár. Braşov, C Romania 45°49′N 25°36′E
108 I7 **Feldkirch** *anc.* Clunia. Vorarlberg, W Austria 47°15′N 09°38′E
109 S9 **Feldkirchen in Kärnten** *Slvn.* Trg. Kärnten, S Austria 46°42′N 14°01′E
Félegyháza *see* Kiskunfélegyháza
192 H16 **Feleolo** ✈ (Āpia) Upolu, C Samoa 13°49′S 171°59′W
104 H6 **Felgueiras** Porto, N Portugal 41°22′N 08°12′W
Felicitas Julia *see* Lisboa
172 J16 **Félicité** *island* Inner Islands, NE Seychelles
151 K20 **Felidhu Atoll** *atoll* C Maldives
41 Y13 **Felipe Carrillo Puerto** Quintana Roo, SE Mexico 19°34′N 88°02′W
97 Q21 **Felixstowe** E England, United Kingdom 51°58′N 01°20′E
103 N11 **Felletin** Creuse, C France 45°53′N 02°12′E
Fellin *see* Viljandi
Felsőbánya *see* Baia Sprie
Felsőmuzslya *see* Mužlja
Felsővisó *see* Vişeu de Sus
35 N10 **Felton** California, W USA 37°03′N 122°04′W
106 H7 **Feltre** Veneto, NE Italy 46°01′N 11°55′E
95 H25 **Femer Bælt** *Dan.* Fehmarn Belt, *Ger.* Fehmarn. *strait* Denmark/Germany *see also* Fehmarn Belt
95 I24 **Femø** *island* SE Denmark
94 I10 **Femunden** ◎ S Norway
104 H2 **Fene** Galicia, NW Spain 43°28′N 08°10′W
14 I14 **Fenelon Falls** Ontario, SE Canada 44°34′N 78°43′W
189 U13 **Feneppi** *atoll* Chuuk Islands, C Micronesia
137 O11 **Fener Burnu** *headland* N Turkey 41°07′N 39°26′E
Fénérive *see* Fenoarivo Atsinanana
115 J14 **Fengári** ▲ Samothráki, E Greece 40°27′N 25°37′E
163 V13 **Fengcheng** *var.* Feng-cheng, Fenghwangcheng. Liaoning, NE China 40°28′N 124°01′E
Fengcheng *see* Lianjiang
Feng-cheng *see* Fengcheng
160 K11 **Fenggang** *var.* Longquan. Guizhou, S China 27°57′N 107°42′E
161 O7 **Feng He** ~ C China
161 S9 **Fenghua** Zhejiang, SE China 29°40′N 121°25′E
Fenghwangcheng *see* Fengcheng
Fengjiaba *see* Wangcang
160 L9 **Fengjie** *var.* Yong'an. Sichuan, C China 31°03′N 109°31′E
160 M14 **Fengkai** *var.* Jiangkou. Guangdong, S China 23°26′N 111°28′E
161 T13 **Fenglin** *Jap.* Hōrin. C Taiwan 23°52′N 121°30′E
161 P1 **Fengning** *prev.* Dagezhen. Hebei, E China 41°12′N 116°37′E
160 E13 **Fengqing** *var.* Fengshan. Yunnan, SW China 24°38′N 99°54′E
161 O6 **Fengqiu** Henan, C China 35°02′N 114°24′E
161 Q2 **Fengrun** Hebei, E China 39°50′N 118°10′E
Fengshan *see* Luoyuan, Fujian, China
Fengshan *see* Fengqing, Yunnan, China
163 T4 **Fengshui Shan** ▲ NE China 52°20′N 123°22′E
161 P14 **Fengshun** Guangdong, S China 23°51′N 116°11′E
Fengtien *see* Shenyang, China
Fengtien *see* Liaoning, China
160 J7 **Fengxian** *var.* Feng Xian; *prev.* Shuangshipu. Shaanxi, C China 33°50′N 106°33′E
Feng Xian *see* Fengxian
Fengxiang *see* Luobei
Fengyizhen *see* Maoxian
163 P13 **Fengzhen** Nei Mongol Zizhiqu, N China 40°25′N 113°09′E
160 M6 **Fen He** ~ C China
153 V15 **Feni** Chittagong, E Bangladesh 23°00′N 91°24′E
186 I6 **Feni Islands** *island group* NE Papua New Guinea
38 H17 **Fenimore Pass** *strait* Aleutian Islands, Alaska, USA
84 B9 **Feni Ridge** *undersea feature* N Atlantic Ocean 53°45′N 18°00′W
Fennern *see* Vändra
30 J9 **Fennimore** Wisconsin, N USA 42°58′N 90°39′W
172 J4 **Fenoarivo Atsinanana** *prev./Fr.* Fénérive. Toamasina, E Madagascar 20°52′S 46°52′E
95 I24 **Fensmark** Sjælland, SE Denmark 55°17′N 11°48′E
97 O19 **Fens, The** *wetland* E England, United Kingdom
31 R9 **Fenton** Michigan, N USA 42°48′N 83°42′W
190 K10 **Fenua Fala** *island* SE Tokelau
190 F12 **Fenua'fo'ou, Île** *island* E Wallis and Futuna
190 L10 **Fenua Loa** *island* Fakaofo Atoll, E Tokelau
160 M4 **Fenyang** Shanxi, C China 37°14′N 111°40′E
117 U13 **Feodosiya** *var.* Kefe, *It.* Kaffa; *anc.* Theodosia. Avtonomna Respublika Krym, S Ukraine 45°03′N 35°24′E
94 I10 **Feragen** ◎ S Norway
74 L5 **Fer, Cap de** *headland* NE Algeria 37°05′N 07°10′E
31 O16 **Ferdinand** Indiana, N USA 38°13′N 86°51′W
Ferdinand *see* Montana, Bulgaria
Ferdinand *see* Mihail Kogălniceanu, Romania
Ferdinandsberg *see* Oţelu Roşu
143 T7 **Ferdows** *var.* Firdaus; *prev.* Tūn. Khorāsān-Razavī, E Iran 34°00′N 58°09′E
103 Q5 **Fère-Champenoise** Marne, N France 48°45′N 03°59′E
Ferencz-Jósef Csúcs *see* Gerlachovský štít
107 J16 **Ferentino** Lazio, C Italy 41°40′N 13°16′E
114 L13 **Féres** Anatolikí Makedonía kai Thráki, NE Greece 40°54′N 26°12′E
Fergana *see* Farg'ona
147 S10 **Fergana Valley** *var.* Farghona Valley, *Rus.* Ferganskaya Dolina, *Taj.* Wodii Farghona, *Uzb.* Farghona Wodiysi. *basin* Tajikistan/Uzbekistan
Ferganskaya Dolina *see* Fergana Valley
Ferganskaya Oblast' *see* Farg'ona Viloyati
147 U9 **Ferganskiy Khrebet** ▲ C Kyrgyzstan
14 F15 **Fergus** Ontario, S Canada 43°42′N 80°22′W
29 S6 **Fergus Falls** Minnesota, N USA 46°15′N 96°02′W
186 G9 **Fergusson Island** *var.* Kaluwawa. *island* SE Papua New Guinea
111 K22 **Ferihegy** ✈ (Budapest) Budapest, C Hungary 47°25′N 19°13′E

◆ Country
● Country Capital
◇ Dependent Territory
○ Dependent Territory Capital
◆ Administrative Regions
✈ International Airport
▲ Mountain
▲ Mountain Range
Volcano
~ River
◎ Lake
⊠ Reservoir

113 N17 **Ferizaj** *Serb.* Uroševac. C Kosovo 42°23′N 21°09′E
77 N14 **Ferkessédougou** N Ivory Coast 09°36′N 05°12′W
109 T10 **Ferlach** *Slvn.* Borovlje. Kärnten, S Austria 46°31′N 14°18′E
97 E16 **Fermanagh** *cultural region* SW Northern Ireland, United Kingdom
106 J13 **Fermo** *anc.* Firmum Picenum. Marche, C Italy 43°09′N 13°44′E
104 J6 **Fermoselle** Castilla y León, N Spain 41°19′N 06°24′W
97 D20 **Fermoy** *Ir.* Mainistir Fhear Maí. SW Ireland 52°08′N 08°16′W
23 W8 **Fernandina Beach** Amelia Island, Florida, SE USA 30°40′N 81°27′W
57 A17 **Fernandina, Isla** *var.* Narborough Island. *island* Galapagos Islands, Ecuador, E Pacific Ocean
47 Y5 **Fernando de Noronha** *island* E Brazil
Fernando Po/Fernando Póo *see* Bioco, Isla de
60 J7 **Fernandópolis** São Paulo, S Brazil 20°18′S 50°13′W
104 M13 **Fernán Núñez** Andalucía, S Spain 37°40′N 04°44′W
83 Q14 **Fernão Veloso, Baía de** *bay* NE Mozambique
34 K3 **Ferndale** California, W USA 40°34′N 124°16′W
32 H6 **Ferndale** Washington, NW USA 48°51′N 122°35′W
11 P17 **Fernie** British Columbia, SW Canada 49°30′N 115°00′W
35 R5 **Fernley** Nevada, W USA 39°35′N 119°15′W
Ferozepore *see* Fīrozpur
107 N18 **Ferrandina** Basilicata, S Italy 40°30′N 16°25′E
106 G9 **Ferrara** *anc.* Forum Alieni. Emilia-Romagna, N Italy 44°50′N 11°36′E
120 F9 **Ferrat, Cap** *headland* NW Algeria 35°52′N 00°24′W
107 D20 **Ferrato, Capo** *headland* Sardegna, Italy, C Mediterranean Sea 39°18′N 09°37′E
104 G12 **Ferreira do Alentejo** Beja, S Portugal 38°04′N 08°06′W
56 B11 **Ferreñafe** Lambayeque, W Peru 06°42′S 79°45′W
108 C12 **Ferret** Valais, SW Switzerland 45°57′N 07°04′E
102 I13 **Ferret, Cap** *headland* W France 44°37′N 01°15′W
22 I6 **Ferriday** Louisiana, S USA 31°37′N 91°33′W
Ferro *see* Hierro
107 D16 **Ferro, Capo** *headland* Sardegna, Italy, C Mediterranean Sea 41°09′N 09°31′E
104 H2 **Ferrol** *var.* El Ferrol; *prev.* El Ferrol del Caudillo. Galicia, NW Spain 43°29′N 08°14′W
56 B12 **Ferrol, Península de** *peninsula* W Peru
36 M5 **Ferron** Utah, W USA 39°05′N 111°07′W
21 S7 **Ferrum** Virginia, NE USA 36°54′N 80°01′W
23 O8 **Ferry Pass** Florida, SE USA 30°30′N 87°12′W
Ferryville *see* Menzel Bourguiba
29 S4 **Fertile** Minnesota, N USA 47°32′N 96°16′W
Fertő *see* Neusiedler See
Ferwerd *see* Ferwert
98 L5 **Ferwert** *Dutch.* Ferwerd. Fryslân, N Netherlands 53°21′N 05°47′E
74 G6 **Fès** *Eng.* Fez. N Morocco 34°06′N 04°57′W
79 I22 **Feshi** Bandundu, SW Dem. Rep. Congo 06°08′S 18°12′E
29 O4 **Fessenden** North Dakota, N USA 47°36′N 99°37′W
Festenberg *see* Twardogóra
27 X5 **Festus** Missouri, C USA 38°13′N 90°24′W
116 M14 **Fetești** Ialomița, SE Romania 44°22′N 27°51′E
136 D17 **Fethiye** Muğla, SW Turkey 36°37′N 29°08′E
96 M1 **Fetlar** *island* NE Scotland, United Kingdom
95 I15 **Fetsund** Akershus, S Norway 59°55′N 11°03′E
12 L5 **Feuilles, Lac aux** ◎ Québec, E Canada
12 L5 **Feuilles, Rivière aux** ≈ Québec, E Canada
99 M23 **Feulen** Diekirch, C Luxembourg 49°52′N 06°03′E
103 Q11 **Feurs** Loire, E France 45°44′N 04°14′E
95 F18 **Fevik** Aust-Agder, S Norway 58°22′N 08°40′E
123 R13 **Fevral'sk** Amurskaya Oblast', SE Russian Federation 52°25′N 131°06′E
Feyzābād *see* Feizābād
Feyzābād *see* Feizābād
Fez *see* Fès
97 J19 **Ffestiniog** NW Wales, United Kingdom 52°55′N 03°54′W
Fhóid Duibh, Cuan an *see* Blacksod Bay
62 I8 **Fiambalá** Catamarca, NW Argentina 27°45′S 67°37′W
172 I6 **Fianarantsoa** Fianarantsoa, C Madagascar 21°27′S 47°05′E
172 H6 **Fianarantsoa** ◈ *province* SE Madagascar
78 G12 **Fianga** Mayo-Kébbi, SW Chad 09°57′N 15°09′E
Ficce *see* Fichē
80 J12 **Fichē** *It.* Ficce. Oromīya, C Ethiopia 09°48′N 38°43′E
101 N17 **Fichtelberg** ▲ Czech Republic/Germany 50°26′N 12°57′E
101 M18 **Fichtelgebirge** ▲▲ SE Germany
101 M19 **Fichtelnaab** ≈ SE Germany
106 E9 **Fidenza** Emilia-Romagna, N Italy 44°52′N 10°04′E
113 K21 **Fier** *var.* Fieri. Fier, SW Albania 40°44′N 19°34′E
113 K21 **Fier** ◈ *district* W Albania
Fieri *see* Fier
Fierza *see* Fierzë
113 L17 **Fierzë** *var.* Fierza. Shkodër, N Albania 42°15′N 20°02′E
113 L17 **Fierzës, Liqeni i** ◎ N Albania
108 F10 **Fiesch** Valais, SW Switzerland 46°25′N 08°09′E
106 G11 **Fiesole** Toscana, C Italy 43°50′N 11°18′E
138 G12 **Fifah** Aṭ Ṭafīlah, W Jordan 30°55′N 35°25′E
96 K11 **Fife** *var.* Kingdom of Fife. *cultural region* E Scotland, United Kingdom
Fife, Kingdom of *see* Fife
96 K11 **Fife Ness** *headland* E Scotland, United Kingdom 56°16′N 02°35′W
Fifteen Twenty Fracture Zone *see* Barracuda Fracture Zone
103 N13 **Figeac** Lot, S France 44°37′N 02°01′E
95 N19 **Figeholm** Kalmar, SE Sweden 57°12′N 16°34′E
Figig *see* Figuig
83 J18 **Figtree** Matabeleland South, SW Zimbabwe 20°24′S 28°21′E
104 F8 **Figueira da Foz** Coimbra, W Portugal 40°09′N 08°51′W
105 X4 **Figueres** Cataluña, E Spain 42°16′N 02°57′E
74 H7 **Figuig** *var.* Figig. E Morocco 32°09′N 01°13′W
Fijājj, Shaṭṭ al *see* Fedjaj, Chott el
187 Y15 **Fiji** *off.* Sovereign Democratic Republic of Fiji, *Fij.* Viti. ◆ *republic* SW Pacific Ocean
192 K9 **Fiji** *island group* SW Pacific Ocean
175 Q8 **Fiji Plate** *tectonic feature*
Fiji, Sovereign Democratic Republic of *see* Fiji
105 P14 **Filabres, Sierra de los** ▲▲ SE Spain
83 K18 **Filabusi** Matabeleland South, S Zimbabwe 20°34′S 29°20′E
42 K13 **Filadelfia** Guanacaste, W Costa Rica 10°28′N 85°33′W
111 K20 **Fil'akovo** *Hung.* Fülek. Banskobystrický Kraj, C Slovakia 48°15′N 19°53′E
195 N5 **Filchner Ice Shelf** *ice shelf* Antarctica
14 J11 **Fildegrand** ≈ Québec, SE Canada
33 O15 **Filer** Idaho, NW USA 42°34′N 114°36′W
Filevo *see* Vŭrbitsa
116 H14 **Filiași** Dolj, SW Romania 44°32′N 23°31′E
115 B16 **Filiátes** Ípeiros, W Greece 39°38′N 20°16′E
115 D21 **Filiatrá** Pelopónnisos, S Greece 37°09′N 21°35′E
107 K22 **Filicudi, Isola** *island* Isole Eolie, S Italy
141 Y10 **Filim** E Oman 20°37′N 58°11′E
Filimon Sîrbu *see* Făurei
77 S11 **Filingué** Tillabéri, W Niger 14°21′N 03°22′E
Filiouri *see* Líssos
114 I13 **Filippoi** *anc.* Philippi. *site of ancient city* Anatolikí Makedonía kai Thráki, NE Greece
95 L15 **Filipstad** Värmland, C Sweden 59°44′N 14°10′E
108 I9 **Filisur** Graubünden, S Switzerland 46°40′N 09°43′E
94 E12 **Fillefjell** ▲ S Norway
35 R14 **Fillmore** California, W USA 34°23′N 118°56′W
36 K5 **Fillmore** Utah, W USA 38°57′N 112°19′W
14 J10 **Fils, Lac du** ◎ Québec, SE Canada
Filyos Çayı *see* Yenice Çayı
Fimbul Ice Shelf *see* Fimbulisen
195 Q2 **Fimbutheimen** *physical region* Antarctica
106 G9 **Finale Emilia** Emilia-Romagna, C Italy 44°50′N 11°17′E
106 C10 **Finale Ligure** Liguria, NW Italy 44°11′N 08°22′E
105 P14 **Fiñana** Andalucía, S Spain 37°09′N 02°47′W
21 S6 **Fincastle** Virginia, NE USA 37°30′N 79°54′W
99 M25 **Findel** ✈ (Luxembourg) Luxembourg, C Luxembourg 49°39′N 06°16′E
96 J9 **Findhorn** ≈ N Scotland, United Kingdom
31 R12 **Findlay** Ohio, N USA 41°02′N 83°40′W
18 G11 **Finger Lakes** ◎ New York, NE USA
83 L14 **Fingoè** Tete, NW Mozambique 15°10′S 31°51′E
136 E17 **Finike** Antalya, SW Turkey 36°18′N 30°08′E
102 F6 **Finistère** ◈ *department* NW France
186 D7 **Finisterre Range** ▲▲ N Papua New Guinea
181 Q8 **Finke** Northern Territory, N Australia 25°37′S 134°35′E
109 S10 **Finkenstein** Kärnten, S Austria 46°34′N 13°53′E
189 Y15 **Finkol, Mount** *var.* Mount Crozer. ▲ Kosrae, E Micronesia 05°18′N 163°00′E
93 L17 **Finland** *off.* Republic of Finland, *Fin.* Suomen Tasavalta, Suomi. ◆ *republic* N Europe
124 F12 **Finland, Gulf of** *Est.* Soome Laht, *Fin.* Suomenlahti, *Ger.* Finnischer Meerbusen, *Rus.* Finskiy Zaliv, *Swe.* Finska Viken. *gulf* E Baltic Sea
Finland, Republic of *see* Finland
10 L11 **Finlay** ≈ British Columbia, W Canada
183 O10 **Finley** New South Wales, SE Australia 35°41′S 145°33′E
29 Q4 **Finley** North Dakota, N USA 47°30′N 97°50′W
Finnischer Meerbusen *see* Finland, Gulf of
92 K9 **Finnmark** ◈ *county* N Norway
92 K9 **Finnmarksvidda** *physical region* N Norway
92 I9 **Finnsnes** Troms, N Norway 69°16′N 18°00′E
186 E7 **Finschhafen** Morobe, C Papua New Guinea 06°35′S 147°51′E
94 E13 **Finse** Hordaland, S Norway 60°35′N 07°33′E
Finska Viken/Finskiy Zaliv *see* Finland, Gulf of
95 M17 **Finspång** Östergötland, S Sweden 58°42′N 15°45′E
108 F10 **Finsteraarhorn** ▲ Switzerland 46°33′N 08°07′E
101 O14 **Finsterwalde** Brandenburg, E Germany 51°38′N 13°43′E
185 A23 **Fiordland** *physical region* South Island, New Zealand
106 E9 **Fiorenzuola d'Arda** Emilia-Romagna, C Italy 44°57′N 09°53′E
Firat Nehri *see* Euphrates
Firdaus *see* Ferdows
18 M14 **Fire Island** *island* New York, NE USA
106 G11 **Firenze** *Eng.* Florence; *anc.* Florentia. Toscana, C Italy 43°47′N 11°15′E
106 G10 **Firenzuola** Toscana, C Italy 44°07′N 11°22′E
14 C6 **Fire River** Ontario, S Canada 48°46′N 83°34′W
Firliug *see* Fârliug
61 B19 **Firmat** Santa Fe, C Argentina 33°29′S 61°29′W
103 Q12 **Firminy** Loire, E France 45°22′N 04°18′E
Firmum Picenum *see* Fermo
152 J12 **Fīrozābād** Uttar Pradesh, N India 27°09′N 78°24′E
152 G8 **Fīrozpur** *var.* Ferozepore. Punjab, NW India 30°55′N 74°38′E
First State *see* Delaware
143 O12 **Fīrūzābād** Fārs, S Iran 28°51′N 52°35′E
Fischamend *see* Fischamend Markt
109 Y4 **Fischamend Markt** *var.* Fischamend. Niederösterreich, NE Austria 48°08′N 16°37′E
109 W6 **Fischbacher Alpen** ▲▲ E Austria
Fischhausen *see* Primorsk
83 D21 **Fish** *var.* Vis. ≈ S Namibia
83 F24 **Fish** *Afr.* Vis. ≈ SW South Africa
11 X15 **Fisher Branch** Manitoba, S Canada 51°09′N 97°34′W
11 X15 **Fisher River** Manitoba, S Canada 51°25′N 97°23′W
19 N13 **Fishers Island** *island* New York, NE USA
37 U8 **Fishers Peak** ▲ Colorado, C USA 37°06′N 104°27′W
9 P9 **Fisher Strait** *strait* Nunavut, N Canada
97 H21 **Fishguard** *Wel.* Abergwaun. SW Wales, United Kingdom 51°59′N 04°49′W
19 R2 **Fish River Lake** ◎ Maine, NE USA
194 K6 **Fiske, Cape** *headland* Antarctica 74°27′S 60°28′W
103 P4 **Fismes** Marne, N France 49°19′N 03°41′E
104 F3 **Fisterra, Cabo** *headland* NW Spain 42°53′N 09°16′W
19 N11 **Fitchburg** Massachusetts, NE USA 42°34′N 71°48′W
96 L3 **Fitful Head** *headland* NE Scotland, United Kingdom 59°57′N 01°24′W
95 C14 **Fitjar** Hordaland, S Norway 59°55′N 05°19′E
192 H16 **Fito, Mauga** ▲ Upolu, C Samoa 13°57′S 171°42′W
23 U6 **Fitzgerald** Georgia, SE USA 31°42′N 83°15′W
180 M5 **Fitzroy Crossing** Western Australia 18°10′S 125°40′E
63 G21 **Fitzroy, Monte** *var.* Cerro Chaltel. ▲ S Argentina 49°18′S 73°06′W
181 Y8 **Fitzroy River** ≈ Queensland, E Australia
180 L5 **Fitzroy River** ≈ Western Australia
14 E12 **Fitzwilliam Island** *island* Ontario, S Canada
107 J15 **Fiuggi** Lazio, C Italy 41°47′N 13°16′E
Fiume *see* Rijeka
107 H15 **Fiumicino** Lazio, C Italy 41°46′N 12°13′E
Fiumicino *see* Leonardo da Vinci
106 E10 **Fivizzano** Toscana, C Italy 44°13′N 10°06′E
79 O21 **Fizi** Sud-Kivu, E Dem. Rep. Congo 04°15′S 28°57′E
Fizuli *see* Füzuli
92 I11 **Fjällåsen** Norrbotten, N Sweden 67°31′N 20°08′E
95 G20 **Fjerritslev** Nordjylland, N Denmark 57°06′N 09°17′E
F.J.S. *see* Franz Josef Strauss
95 L16 **Fjugesta** Örebro, C Sweden 59°10′N 14°50′E
Fladstrand *see* Frederikshavn
37 V5 **Flagler** Colorado, C USA 39°17′N 103°04′W
23 X10 **Flagler Beach** Florida, SE USA 29°28′N 81°07′W
36 L11 **Flagstaff** Arizona, SW USA 35°12′N 111°39′W
65 H24 **Flagstaff Bay** *bay* N Saint Helena, C Atlantic Ocean
19 P5 **Flagstaff Lake** ◎ Maine, NE USA
94 E13 **Flåm** Sogn Og Fjordane, S Norway 60°51′N 07°06′E
15 O8 **Flamand** ≈ Québec, SE Canada
30 J5 **Flambeau River** ≈ Wisconsin, N USA
97 O16 **Flamborough Head** *headland* E England, United Kingdom 54°06′N 00°03′W
100 N13 **Fläming** *hill range* NE Germany
16 H8 **Flaming Gorge Reservoir** ▣ Utah/Wyoming, NW USA
Flanders *see* Vlaanderen
Flandre *see* Vlaanderen
29 R10 **Flandreau** South Dakota, N USA 44°03′N 96°36′W
96 D6 **Flannan Isles** *island group* NW Scotland, United Kingdom
28 M6 **Flasher** North Dakota, N USA 46°25′N 101°12′W
93 G15 **Flåsjön** ◎ N Sweden
39 O11 **Flat** Alaska, USA 62°27′N 158°00′W
92 H1 **Flateyri** Vestfirdhir, NW Iceland 66°03′N 23°28′W
33 P8 **Flathead Lake** ◎ Montana, NW USA
173 Y15 **Flat Island** *Fr.* Île Plate. *island* N Mauritius
25 T11 **Flatonia** Texas, SW USA 29°41′N 97°06′W
185 M14 **Flat Point** *headland* North Island, New Zealand 41°12′S 176°03′E
27 X6 **Flat River** Missouri, C USA 37°51′N 90°31′W
31 P8 **Flat River** ≈ Michigan, N USA
31 P14 **Flatrock River** ≈ Indiana, N USA
32 E6 **Flattery, Cape** *headland* Washington, NW USA 48°22′N 124°43′W
64 B12 **Flatts Village** *var.* The Flatts Village. C Bermuda 32°19′N 64°44′W
108 H7 **Flawil** Sankt Gallen, NE Switzerland 47°25′N 09°12′E
97 N22 **Fleet** S England, United Kingdom 51°16′N 00°50′W
97 K16 **Fleetwood** NW England, United Kingdom 53°55′N 03°02′W
18 H15 **Fleetwood** Pennsylvania, NE USA 40°27′N 75°49′W
95 D18 **Flekkefjord** Vest-Agder, S Norway 58°17′N 06°40′E
21 N5 **Flemingsburg** Kentucky, S USA 38°26′N 83°43′W
18 J15 **Flemington** New Jersey, NE USA 40°30′N 74°51′W
64 I7 **Flemish Cap** *undersea feature* NW Atlantic Ocean 47°00′N 45°00′W
95 N16 **Flen** Södermanland, C Sweden 59°04′N 16°39′E
100 I6 **Flensburg** Schleswig-Holstein, N Germany 54°47′N 09°26′E
100 J6 **Flensburger Förde** *inlet* Denmark/Germany
102 K5 **Flers** Orne, N France 48°45′N 00°34′W
95 C14 **Flesland** ✈ (Bergen) Hordaland, S Norway 60°18′N 05°15′E
Flessingue *see* Vlissingen
21 P10 **Fletcher** North Carolina, SE USA 35°24′N 82°29′W
31 R6 **Fletcher Pond** ◎ Michigan, N USA
102 L15 **Fleurance** Gers, S France 43°50′N 00°39′E
108 B8 **Fleurier** Neuchâtel, W Switzerland 46°55′N 06°37′E
99 H20 **Fleurus** Hainaut, S Belgium 50°28′N 04°33′E
103 N7 **Fleury-les-Aubrais** Loiret, C France 47°55′N 01°55′E
98 K10 **Flevoland** ◈ *province* C Netherlands
Flickertail State *see* North Dakota
108 H9 **Flims** Glarus, NE Switzerland 46°50′N 09°16′E
182 F8 **Flinders Island** *island* Investigator Group, South Australia
183 P14 **Flinders Island** *island* Furneaux Group, Tasmania, SE Australia
182 I6 **Flinders Ranges** ▲▲ South Australia
181 U5 **Flinders River** ≈ Queensland, NE Australia
11 V13 **Flin Flon** Manitoba, C Canada 54°47′N 101°51′W
97 K18 **Flint** NE Wales, United Kingdom 53°15′N 03°10′W
31 R9 **Flint** Michigan, N USA 43°01′N 83°41′W
97 J18 **Flint** *cultural region* NE Wales, United Kingdom
27 O7 **Flint Hills** *hill range* Kansas, C USA
191 Y6 **Flint Island** *island* Line Islands, E Kiribati
23 S4 **Flint River** ≈ Georgia, SE USA
31 R9 **Flint River** ≈ Michigan, N USA
189 X12 **Flipper Point** *headland* C Wake Island 19°18′N 166°37′E
94 I13 **Flisa** Hedmark, S Norway 60°36′N 12°02′E
94 J13 **Flisa** ≈ S Norway
122 J5 **Flissingskiy, Mys** *headland* Novaya Zemlya, NW Russian Federation 76°43′N 69°01′E
Flitsch *see* Bovec
105 U6 **Flix** Cataluña, NE Spain 41°13′N 00°32′E
95 J19 **Floda** Västra Götaland, S Sweden 57°47′N 12°20′E
101 O16 **Flöha** ≈ E Germany
25 O4 **Flomot** Texas, SW USA 34°13′N 100°58′W
29 V5 **Floodwood** Minnesota, N USA 46°55′N 92°55′W
30 M15 **Flora** Illinois, N USA 38°40′N 88°29′W
103 P14 **Florac** Lozère, S France 44°18′N 03°35′E
23 Q8 **Florala** Alabama, S USA 31°00′N 86°19′W
103 S4 **Florange** Moselle, NE France 49°21′N 06°06′E
Floreana, Isla *see* Santa María, Isla
23 O2 **Florence** Alabama, S USA 34°48′N 87°40′W
36 L14 **Florence** Arizona, SW USA 33°01′N 111°23′W
37 T6 **Florence** Colorado, C USA 38°20′N 105°06′W
27 O5 **Florence** Kansas, C USA 38°13′N 96°56′W
20 M4 **Florence** Kentucky, S USA 38°59′N 84°37′W
32 E13 **Florence** Oregon, NW USA 43°58′N 124°06′W
21 T12 **Florence** South Carolina, SE USA 34°12′N 79°44′W
25 S9 **Florence** Texas, SW USA 30°50′N 97°47′W
Florence *see* Firenze
54 E13 **Florencia** Caquetá, S Colombia 01°37′N 75°37′W
99 H21 **Florennes** Namur, S Belgium 50°15′N 04°36′E
Florentia *see* Firenze
63 J18 **Florentino Ameghino, Embalse** ◎ S Argentina
99 J24 **Florenville** Luxembourg, SE Belgium 49°42′N 05°19′E
42 E3 **Flores** Petén, N Guatemala 16°55′N 89°56′W
61 E19 **Flores** ◈ *department* S Uruguay
171 O16 **Flores** *island* Nusa Tenggara, C Indonesia
64 M1 **Flores** *island* Azores, Portugal, NE Atlantic Ocean
Floreshty *see* Florești
Flores, Lago de *see* Petén Itzá, Lago
Flores, Laut *see* Flores Sea
171 N15 **Flores Sea** *Ind.* Laut Flores. *sea* C Indonesia
116 M8 **Florești** *Rus.* Floreshty. N Moldova 47°52′N 28°19′E
25 S12 **Floresville** Texas, SW USA 29°09′N 98°10′W
59 N14 **Floriano** Piauí, E Brazil 06°45′S 43°W
61 K14 **Florianópolis** *prev.* Destêrro. *state capital* Santa Catarina, S Brazil 27°35′S 48°32′W
44 G6 **Florida** Camagüey, C Cuba 21°32′N 78°14′W
61 F19 **Florida** Florida, S Uruguay 34°04′S 56°14′W
61 F19 **Florida** ◈ *department* S Uruguay
23 U9 **Florida** *off.* State of Florida, *also known as* Peninsular State, Sunshine State. ◈ *state* SE USA
23 Y17 **Florida Bay** *bay* Florida, SE USA
54 G8 **Floridablanca** Santander, N Colombia 07°04′N 73°06′W
23 Y17 **Florida Keys** *island group* Florida, SE USA
37 Q16 **Florida Mountains** ▲▲ New Mexico, SW USA
64 D10 **Florida, Straits of** *strait* Atlantic Ocean/Gulf of Mexico
114 D13 **Flórina** *var.* Phlórina. Dytikí Makedonía, N Greece 40°48′N 21°26′E
27 X4 **Florissant** Missouri, C USA 38°48′N 90°20′W
94 C11 **Florø** Sogn Og Fjordane, S Norway 61°36′N 05°04′E
115 L22 **Floúda, Akrotírio** *headland* Astypálaia, Kykládes, Greece, Aegean Sea 36°38′N 26°23′E
21 S7 **Floyd** Virginia, NE USA 36°55′N 80°22′W
25 N4 **Floydada** Texas, SW USA 33°58′N 101°20′W
Flüela Wisshorn *see* Weisshorn
98 K7 **Fluessen** ◎ N Netherlands
105 S5 **Flumen** ≈ NE Spain
107 C20 **Flumendosa** ≈ Sardegna, Italy, C Mediterranean Sea
31 R9 **Flushing** Michigan, N USA 43°03′N 83°51′W
Flushing *see* Vlissingen
25 O6 **Fluvanna** Texas, SW USA 32°54′N 101°06′W
186 B8 **Fly** ≈ Indonesia/Papua New Guinea
194 I10 **Flying Fish, Cape** *headland* Thurston Island, Antarctica 72°06′S 102°25′W
Flylân *see* Vlieland
193 Y15 **Foa** *island* Ha'apai Group, C Tonga
11 U15 **Foam Lake** Saskatchewan, S Canada 51°38′N 103°31′W
113 J14 **Foča** *var.* Srbinje. SE Bosnia and Herzegovina 43°32′N 18°46′E
116 L12 **Focșani** Vrancea, E Romania 45°45′N 27°13′E
Fogaras/Fogarasch *see* Făgăraș
107 M16 **Foggia** Puglia, SE Italy 41°28′N 15°31′E
Foggo *see* Faggo
76 D10 **Fogo** *island* Ilhas de Sotavento, SW Cape Verde
13 U11 **Fogo Island** *island* Newfoundland and Labrador, E Canada
109 U7 **Fohnsdorf** Steiermark, SE Austria 47°13′N 14°40′E
100 G7 **Föhr** *island* NW Germany
104 F14 **Fóia** ▲ S Portugal 37°19′N 08°39′W
14 I10 **Foins, Lac aux** ◎ Québec, SE Canada
103 N17 **Foix** Ariège, S France 42°58′N 01°39′E
126 I5 **Fokino** Bryanskaya Oblast', W Russian Federation 53°22′N 34°22′E
123 S15 **Fokino** Primorskiy Kray, W Russian Federation 42°58′N 132°25′E
Fola, Cnoc *see* Bloody Foreland
94 E13 **Folarskardnuten** ▲ S Norway 60°34′N 07°18′E
92 G11 **Folda** *prev.* Foldafjorden. *fjord* C Norway
Foldafjorden *see* Folda
93 F14 **Foldereid** Nord-Trøndelag, C Norway 64°58′N 12°09′E
Földvár *see* Feldioara
115 J22 **Folégandros** *island* Kykládes, Greece, Aegean Sea
23 O9 **Foley** Alabama, S USA 30°24′N 87°40′W
29 U7 **Foley** Minnesota, N USA 45°39′N 93°54′W
14 E7 **Foleyet** Ontario, S Canada 48°15′N 82°26′W
95 D14 **Folgefonna** *glacier* S Norway
106 I13 **Foligno** Umbria, C Italy 42°58′N 12°40′E
97 Q23 **Folkestone** SE England, United Kingdom 51°05′N 01°11′E
23 W8 **Folkston** Georgia, SE USA 30°49′N 82°00′W
94 H10 **Folldal** Hedmark, S Norway 62°08′N 10°00′E
25 P1 **Follett** Texas, SW USA 36°25′N 100°08′W
106 F13 **Follonica** Toscana, C Italy 42°55′N 10°45′E
21 T15 **Folly Beach** South Carolina, SE USA 32°39′N 79°56′W
35 O7 **Folsom** California, W USA 38°40′N 121°11′W
116 M12 **Foltești** Galați, E Romania 45°45′N 28°00′E
172 H14 **Fomboni** Mohéli, S Comoros 12°18′S 43°46′E
18 K10 **Fonda** New York, NE USA 42°57′N 74°24′W
11 S10 **Fond-du-Lac** Saskatchewan, C Canada 59°20′N 107°09′W
30 M8 **Fond du Lac** Wisconsin, N USA 43°48′N 88°27′W
11 T10 **Fond-du-Lac** ≈ Saskatchewan, C Canada
190 C9 **Fongafale** *var.* Funafuti. ● (Tuvalu) Funafuti Atoll, SE Tuvalu 08°31′S 179°11′E
190 G8 **Fongafale** *atoll* C Tuvalu
107 C18 **Fonni** Sardegna, Italy, C Mediterranean Sea 40°07′N 09°17′E
189 V12 **Fono** *island* Chuuk, C Micronesia
54 G4 **Fonseca** La Guajira, N Colombia 10°53′N 72°51′W
Fonseca, Golfo de *see* Fonseca, Gulf of
42 H8 **Fonseca, Gulf of** *Sp.* Golfo de Fonseca. *gulf* C Central America
103 O6 **Fontainebleau** Seine-et-Marne, N France 48°24′N 02°42′E
63 G19 **Fontana, Lago** ◎ W Argentina
21 N10 **Fontana Lake** ▣ North Carolina, SE USA
107 L24 **Fontanarossa** ✈ (Catania) Sicilia, Italy, C Mediterranean Sea 37°28′N 15°04′E
11 N11 **Fontas** ≈ British Columbia, W Canada
58 D12 **Fonte Boa** Amazonas, N Brazil 02°32′S 66°01′W
102 J10 **Fontenay-le-Comte** Vendée, NW France 46°28′N 00°48′W
33 T16 **Fontenelle Reservoir** ▣ Wyoming, C USA
193 Y14 **Fonualei** *island* Vava'u Group, N Tonga
111 H24 **Fonyód** Somogy, W Hungary 46°43′N 17°32′E
Foochow *see* Fuzhou
39 Q10 **Foraker, Mount** ▲ Alaska, USA 62°57′N 151°24′W
187 R14 **Forari** Éfaté, C Vanuatu 17°42′S 168°33′E
103 U4 **Forbach** Moselle, NE France 49°11′N 06°54′E
183 Q8 **Forbes** New South Wales, SE Australia 33°24′S 148°00′E
77 T17 **Forcados** Delta, S Nigeria 05°16′N 05°25′E
103 S14 **Forcalquier** Alpes-de-Haute-Provence, SE France 43°57′N 05°46′E
101 K19 **Forchheim** Bayern, SE Germany 49°43′N 11°07′E
35 R13 **Ford City** California, W USA 35°09′N 119°27′W
94 D11 **Førde** Sogn Og Fjordane, S Norway 61°27′N 05°51′E
31 N4 **Ford River** ≈ Michigan, N USA
183 O4 **Fords Bridge** New South Wales, SE Australia 29°44′S 145°25′E
20 J6 **Fordsville** Kentucky, S USA 37°36′N 86°39′W
27 U13 **Fordyce** Arkansas, C USA 33°49′N 92°23′W
76 I14 **Forécariah** SW Guinea 09°28′N 13°06′W
197 O14 **Forel, Mont** ▲ SE Greenland 66°55′N 36°45′W
11 R17 **Foremost** Alberta, SW Canada 49°30′N 111°34′W
14 D16 **Forest** Ontario, S Canada 43°05′N 82°00′W
22 L5 **Forest** Mississippi, S USA 32°22′N 89°30′W
31 S12 **Forest** Ohio, N USA 40°47′N 83°26′W
29 V11 **Forest City** Iowa, C USA 43°15′N 93°38′W
21 Q10 **Forest City** North Carolina, SE USA 35°19′N 81°52′W
32 G11 **Forest Grove** Oregon, NW USA 45°31′N 123°06′W
183 P17 **Forestier Peninsula** *peninsula* Tasmania, SE Australia
29 V8 **Forest Lake** Minnesota, N USA 45°16′N 92°59′W
23 S3 **Forest Park** Georgia, SE USA 33°37′N 84°22′W
29 Q3 **Forest River** ≈ North Dakota, N USA
15 T6 **Forestville** Québec, SE Canada 48°45′N 69°04′W
103 Q11 **Forez, Monts du** ▲ C France
96 K10 **Forfar** E Scotland, United Kingdom 56°38′N 02°54′W
26 J8 **Forgan** Oklahoma, C USA 36°54′N 100°32′W
Forge du Sud *see* Dudelange
101 J24 **Forggensee** ◎ S Germany
147 N10 **Forish** *Rus.* Farish. Jizzax Viloyati, C Uzbekistan 40°33′N 66°52′E
20 F9 **Forked Deer River** ≈ Tennessee, S USA
32 F7 **Forks** Washington, NW USA 47°57′N 124°22′W
92 N2 **Forlandsundet** *sound* W Svalbard
106 H10 **Forlì** *anc.* Forum Livii. Emilia-Romagna, N Italy 44°14′N 12°02′E
29 Q7 **Forman** North Dakota, N USA 46°07′N 97°39′W
97 K17 **Formby** NW England, United Kingdom 53°34′N 03°05′W
105 V11 **Formentera** *anc.* Ophiusa, *Lat.* Frumentum. *island* Islas Baleares, Spain, W Mediterranean Sea
Formentor, Cabo de *see* Formentor, Cap de
105 Y9 **Formentor, Cap de** *var.* Cabo de Formentor, Cape Formentor. *headland* Mallorca, Spain, W Mediterranean Sea 39°57′N 03°12′E
Formentor, Cape *see* Formentor, Cap de
107 J16 **Formia** Lazio, C Italy 41°16′N 13°37′E
62 O7 **Formosa** Formosa, NE Argentina 26°07′S 58°14′W
62 M6 **Formosa** *off.* Provincia de Formosa. ◈ *province* NE Argentina
Formosa/Formo'sa *see* Taiwan
Formosa, Provincia de *see* Formosa
59 I17 **Formosa, Serra** ▲▲ C Brazil
Formosa Strait *see* Taiwan Strait
95 H21 **Fornæs** *headland* C Denmark 56°26′N 10°57′E
25 U6 **Forney** Texas, SW USA 32°45′N 96°28′W
106 E9 **Fornovo di Taro** Emilia-Romagna, C Italy 44°42′N 10°07′E
117 T14 **Foros** Avtonomna Respublika Krym, S Ukraine 44°24′N 33°47′E
Føroyar *see* Faeroe Islands
96 J8 **Forres** NE Scotland, United Kingdom 57°32′N 03°38′W
27 X11 **Forrest City** Arkansas, C USA 35°01′N 90°48′W
39 Y15 **Forrester Island** *island* Alexander Archipelago, Alaska, USA
25 N7 **Forsan** Texas, SW USA 32°06′N 101°22′W
181 V5 **Forsayth** Queensland, NE Australia 18°31′S 143°37′E
95 L19 **Forserum** Jönköping, S Sweden 57°42′N 14°28′E
95 K15 **Forshaga** Värmland, C Sweden 59°33′N 13°29′E
93 L19 **Forssa** Etelä-Suomi, S Finland 60°49′N 23°40′E
101 Q14 **Forst** *Lus.* Baršć Łužyca. Brandenburg, E Germany 51°43′N 14°38′E
183 U7 **Forster-Tuncurry** New South Wales, SE Australia 32°11′S 152°30′E
23 T4 **Forsyth** Georgia, SE USA 33°00′N 83°57′W
27 T8 **Forsyth** Missouri, C USA 36°41′N 93°07′W
33 W10 **Forsyth** Montana, NW USA 46°16′N 106°40′W
149 U11 **Fort Abbās** Punjab, E Pakistan 29°12′N 73°00′E
12 G10 **Fort Albany** Ontario, C Canada 52°15′N 81°35′W
56 L13 **Fortaleza** Pando, N Bolivia 09°48′S 65°29′W
58 P13 **Fortaleza** *prev.* Ceará. *state capital* Ceará, NE Brazil 03°45′S 38°35′W
59 D16 **Fortaleza** Rondônia, W Brazil 08°45′S 64°06′W
56 C13 **Fortaleza, Río** ≈ W Peru
Fort-Archambault *see* Sarh
21 U3 **Fort Ashby** West Virginia, NE USA 39°30′N 78°46′W
96 I9 **Fort Augustus** N Scotland, United Kingdom 57°14′N 04°38′W
Fort-Bayard *see* Zhanjiang
33 S8 **Fort Benton** Montana, NW USA 47°49′N 110°40′W
35 Q1 **Fort Bidwell** California, W USA 41°50′N 120°07′W
34 L5 **Fort Bragg** California, W USA 39°25′N 123°48′W
31 N16 **Fort Branch** Indiana, N USA 38°15′N 87°34′W
Fort-Bretonnet *see* Bousso
33 T17 **Fort Bridger** Wyoming, C USA 41°18′N 110°19′W
Fort-Cappolani *see* Tidjikja
Fort-Carnot *see* Ikongo
Fort Charlet *see* Djanet
Fort-Chimo *see* Kuujjuaq
11 R10 **Fort Chipewyan** Alberta, C Canada 58°42′N 111°08′W
Fort Cobb Lake *see* Fort Cobb Reservoir
26 L11 **Fort Cobb Reservoir** *var.* Fort Cobb Lake. ▣ Oklahoma, C USA
37 T3 **Fort Collins** Colorado, C USA 40°35′N 105°05′W
14 K12 **Fort-Coulonge** Québec, SE Canada 45°50′N 76°45′W
Fort-Crampel *see* Kaga Bandoro
Fort-Dauphin *see* Tôlañaro
24 K10 **Fort Davis** Texas, SW USA 30°35′N 103°54′W
37 O10 **Fort Defiance** Arizona, SW USA 35°44′N 109°04′W
45 Q12 **Fort-de-France** *prev.* Fort-Royal. ○ (Martinique) W Martinique 14°36′N 61°05′W
45 P12 **Fort-de-France, Baie de** *bay* W Martinique
Fort de Kock *see* Bukittinggi
23 P6 **Fort Deposit** Alabama, S USA 31°58′N 86°34′W
29 U13 **Fort Dodge** Iowa, C USA 42°30′N 94°10′W
13 S10 **Forteau** Québec, E Canada 51°30′N 56°55′W
106 E11 **Forte dei Marmi** Toscana, C Italy 43°59′N 10°10′E
14 H17 **Fort Erie** Ontario, S Canada 42°55′N 78°56′W
180 H7 **Fortescue River** ≈ Western Australia
19 S2 **Fort Fairfield** Maine, NE USA 46°45′N 67°51′W
Fort-Foureau *see* Kousséri
12 A11 **Fort Frances** Ontario, S Canada 48°37′N 93°23′W
Fort Franklin *see* Déljne
23 R7 **Fort Gaines** Georgia, SE USA 31°36′N 85°03′W
37 T8 **Fort Garland** Colorado, C USA 37°22′N 105°24′W
21 P5 **Fort Gay** West Virginia, NE USA 38°06′N 82°35′W
Fort George *see* La Grande Rivière
Fort George *see* Chisasibi
27 Q10 **Fort Gibson** Oklahoma, C USA 35°48′N 95°15′W
27 Q9 **Fort Gibson Lake** ▣ Oklahoma, C USA
8 H7 **Fort Good Hope** *var.* Rádeyilikóé. Northwest Territories, NW Canada 66°16′N 128°37′W
23 V4 **Fort Gordon** Georgia, SE USA 33°25′N 82°09′W
Fort Gouraud *see* Fdérik
96 I11 **Forth** ≈ C Scotland, United Kingdom
Fort Hall *see* Murang'a
24 H8 **Fort Hancock** Texas, SW USA 31°18′N 105°49′W
Fort Hertz *see* Putao
96 K12 **Forth, Firth of** *estuary* E Scotland, United Kingdom
14 L14 **Forthton** Ontario, SE Canada 44°43′N 75°31′W
14 M8 **Fortier** ≈ Québec, SE Canada
Fortín General Eugenio Garay *see* General Eugenio A. Garay
Fort Jameson *see* Chipata
Fort Johnston *see* Mangochi
19 R1 **Fort Kent** Maine, NE USA 47°15′N 68°33′W
Fort-Lamy *see* Ndjamena
23 Z15 **Fort Lauderdale** Florida, SE USA 26°07′N 80°09′W
21 R11 **Fort Lawn** South Carolina, SE USA 34°43′N 80°46′W
8 H10 **Fort Liard** *var.* Liard. Northwest Territories, W Canada 60°14′N 123°28′W
44 M8 **Fort-Liberté** NE Haiti 19°42′N 71°51′W
21 N9 **Fort Loudoun Lake** ▣ Tennessee, S USA
37 T3 **Fort Lupton** Colorado, C USA 40°04′N 104°48′W
11 R12 **Fort MacKay** Alberta, C Canada 57°12′N 111°41′W
11 Q17 **Fort Macleod** *var.* MacLeod. Alberta, SW Canada 49°44′N 113°24′W
29 Y16 **Fort Madison** Iowa, C USA 40°37′N 91°15′W
Fort Manning *see* Mchinji
25 P9 **Fort McKavett** Texas, SW USA 30°50′N 100°07′W
11 R12 **Fort McMurray** Alberta, C Canada 56°44′N 111°23′W
8 G7 **Fort McPherson** *var.* McPherson. Northwest Territories, NW Canada 67°29′N 134°50′W
21 R11 **Fort Mill** South Carolina, SE USA 35°00′N 80°57′W
Fort-Millot *see* Ngouri
37 U3 **Fort Morgan** Colorado, C USA 40°14′N 103°48′W
23 W14 **Fort Myers** Florida, SE USA 26°39′N 81°52′W
23 W15 **Fort Myers Beach** Florida, SE USA 26°27′N 81°57′W
10 M10 **Fort Nelson** British Columbia, W Canada 58°48′N 122°44′W
10 M10 **Fort Nelson** ≈ British Columbia, W Canada
Fort Norman *see* Tulita
23 Q2 **Fort Payne** Alabama, S USA 34°23′N 85°43′W
33 W7 **Fort Peck** Montana, NW USA 48°00′N 106°28′W
33 V8 **Fort Peck Lake** ▣ Montana, NW USA
23 Y13 **Fort Pierce** Florida, SE USA 27°28′N 80°20′W
29 N10 **Fort Pierre** South Dakota, N USA 44°21′N 100°22′W

◆ Country
● Country Capital
◇ Dependent Territory
○ Dependent Territory Capital
◈ Administrative Regions
✈ International Airport
▲ Mountain
▲▲ Mountain Range
Volcano
≈ River
◎ Lake
▣ Reservoir

81 E18 **Fort Portal** SW Uganda 0°39′N 30°17′E
8 J10 **Fort Providence** *var.* Providence. Northwest Territories, W Canada 61°21′N 117°39′W
11 U16 **Fort Qu'Appelle** Saskatchewan, S Canada 50°50′N 103°52′W
Fort-Repoux *see* Akjoujt
8 K10 **Fort Resolution** *var.* Resolution. Northwest Territories, W Canada 61°10′N 113°39′W
33 T13 **Fortress Mountain** ▲ Wyoming, C USA 44°20′N 109°51′W
Fort Rosebery *see* Mansa
Fort Rousset *see* Owando
Fort-Royal *see* Fort-de-France
Fort Rupert *see* Waskaganish
8 H13 **Fort St. James** British Columbia, SW Canada 54°26′N 124°15′W
11 N12 **Fort St. John** British Columbia, W Canada 56°16′N 120°52′W
Fort Sandeman *see* Zhob
11 Q14 **Fort Saskatchewan** Alberta, SW Canada 53°42′N 113°12′W
27 R6 **Fort Scott** Kansas, C USA 37°52′N 94°43′W
12 E6 **Fort Severn** Ontario, C Canada 56°N 87°40′W
31 R12 **Fort Shawnee** Ohio, N USA 40°41′N 84°08′W
144 E14 **Fort-Shevchenko** Mangistau, W Kazakhstan 44°29′N 50°16′E
Fort-Sibut *see* Sibut
8 I10 **Fort Simpson** *var.* Simpson. Northwest Territories, W Canada 61°52′N 121°23′W
8 I10 **Fort Smith** Northwest Territories, W Canada 60°01′N 111°55′W
27 R10 **Fort Smith** Arkansas, C USA 35°23′N 94°24′W
37 T13 **Fort Stanton** New Mexico, SW USA 33°28′N 105°31′W
24 L9 **Fort Stockton** Texas, SW USA 30°54′N 102°54′W
37 U12 **Fort Sumner** New Mexico, SW USA 34°28′N 104°15′W
26 K8 **Fort Supply** Oklahoma, C USA 36°34′N 99°34′W
26 K8 **Fort Supply Lake** ⊠ Oklahoma, C USA
29 O10 **Fort Thompson** South Dakota, N USA 44°01′N 99°22′W
Fort-Trinquet *see* Bir Mogreïn
105 R12 **Fortuna** Murcia, SE Spain 38°11′N 01°07′W
34 K3 **Fortuna** California, W USA 40°35′N 124°07′W
28 J2 **Fortuna** North Dakota, N USA 48°53′N 103°46′W
23 T5 **Fort Valley** Georgia, SE USA 32°33′N 83°53′W
11 P11 **Fort Vermilion** Alberta, W Canada 58°22′N 115°59′W
Fort Victoria *see* Masvingo
31 P13 **Fortville** Indiana, N USA 39°55′N 85°51′W
23 P9 **Fort Walton Beach** Florida, SE USA 30°24′N 86°37′W
31 P12 **Fort Wayne** Indiana, N USA 41°08′N 85°08′W
96 H10 **Fort William** N Scotland, United Kingdom 56°49′N 05°07′W
25 T6 **Fort Worth** Texas, SW USA 32°44′N 97°19′W
28 M7 **Fort Yates** North Dakota, N USA 46°05′N 100°37′W
39 S7 **Fort Yukon** Alaska, USA 66°35′N 145°05′W
Forum Alieni *see* Ferrara
Forum Julii *see* Fréjus
Forum Livii *see* Forlì
143 Q15 **Forūr-e Bozorg, Jazīreh-ye** *island* S Iran
94 H7 **Fosen** *physical region* S Norway
161 N14 **Foshan** *var.* Fatshan, Fo-shan, Namhoi. Guangdong, S China 23°03′N 113°08′E
Fo-shan *see* Foshan
194 J6 **Fossil Bluff** *UK research station* Antarctica 71°30′S 68°30′W
Fossa Claudia *see* Chioggia
106 B9 **Fossano** Piemonte, NW Italy 44°33′N 07°43′E
99 H21 **Fosses-la-Ville** Namur, S Belgium 50°24′N 04°42′E
32 J12 **Fossil** Oregon, NW USA 45°01′N 120°14′W
Foss Lake *see* Foss Reservoir
106 I11 **Fossombrone** Marche, C Italy 43°42′N 12°48′E
26 K10 **Foss Reservoir** *var.* Foss Lake. ⊠ Oklahoma, C USA
29 S4 **Fosston** Minnesota, N USA 47°34′N 95°45′W
183 O13 **Foster** Victoria, SE Australia 38°40′S 146°15′E
11 T12 **Foster Lakes** ◎ Saskatchewan, C Canada
31 S12 **Fostoria** Ohio, N USA 41°09′N 83°25′W
79 D19 **Fougamou** Ngounié, C Gabon 01°16′S 10°30′E
102 J6 **Fougères** Ille-et-Vilaine, NW France 48°21′N 01°12′W
Fou-hsin *see* Fuxin
27 S14 **Fouke** Arkansas, C USA 33°15′N 93°53′W
96 K2 **Foula** *island* NE Scotland, United Kingdom
65 D24 **Foul Bay** *bay* East Falkland, Falkland Islands
97 P21 **Foulness Island** *island* SE England, United Kingdom
185 F15 **Foulwind, Cape** *headland* South Island, New Zealand 41°45′S 171°28′E
79 E15 **Foumban** Ouest, NW Cameroon 05°43′N 10°50′E
172 H13 **Foumbouni** Grande Comore, NW Comoros 11°49′S 43°30′E
195 N8 **Foundation Ice Stream** *glacier* Antarctica
37 T6 **Fountain** Colorado, C USA 38°40′N 104°42′W
36 L4 **Fountain Green** Utah, W USA 39°37′N 111°37′W
21 P11 **Fountain Inn** South Carolina, SE USA 34°41′N 82°12′W
27 S11 **Fourche LaFave River** ≈ Arkansas, C USA
33 Z13 **Four Corners** Wyoming, C USA 44°04′N 104°08′W
103 Q2 **Fourmies** Nord, N France 50°01′N 04°03′E
38 J17 **Four Mountains, Islands of** *island group* Aleutian Islands, Alaska, USA
173 P17 **Fournaise, Piton de la** Ѫ SE Réunion 21°14′S 55°43′E
14 J8 **Fournière, Lac** ◎ Québec, SE Canada
115 L20 **Foúrnoi** *island* Dodekánisa, Greece, Aegean Sea
64 K13 **Four North Fracture Zone** *tectonic feature* W Atlantic Ocean
Fouron-Saint-Martin *see* Sint-Martens-Voeren
30 L3 **Fourteen Mile Point** *headland* Michigan, N USA 46°59′N 89°07′W
Fou-shan *see* Fushun
76 I13 **Fouta Djallon** *var.* Futa Jallon. ▲▲ W Guinea
185 C25 **Foveaux Strait** *strait* S New Zealand
35 Q11 **Fowler** California, W USA 36°35′N 119°40′W
37 U6 **Fowler** Colorado, C USA 38°07′N 104°01′W
31 N12 **Fowler** Indiana, N USA 40°36′N 87°20′W
182 D7 **Fowlers Bay** *bay* South Australia
25 R13 **Fowlerton** Texas, SW USA 28°27′N 98°48′W
142 M3 **Fowman** *var.* Fuman, Fumen. Gīlān, NW Iran 37°15′N 49°19′E
65 C25 **Fox Bay East** West Falkland, Falkland Islands
65 C25 **Fox Bay West** West Falkland, Falkland Islands
14 J14 **Foxboro** Ontario, SE Canada 44°16′N 77°23′W
11 O14 **Fox Creek** Alberta, W Canada 54°25′N 116°57′W
64 G5 **Foxe Basin** *sea* Nunavut, N Canada
64 G5 **Foxe Channel** *channel* Nunavut, N Canada
95 I16 **Foxen** ◎ C Sweden
9 Q7 **Foxe Peninsula** *peninsula* Baffin Island, Nunavut, NE Canada
185 E19 **Fox Glacier** West Coast, South Island, New Zealand 43°28′S 170°00′E
38 L17 **Fox Islands** *island* Aleutian Islands, Alaska, USA
30 M10 **Fox Lake** Illinois, N USA 42°24′N 88°10′W
9 V12 **Fox Mine** Manitoba, C Canada 56°36′N 101°48′W
35 R3 **Fox Mountain** ▲ Nevada, W USA 41°01′N 119°30′W
65 E25 **Fox Point** *headland* East Falkland, Falkland Islands 51°55′S 58°24′W
30 M11 **Fox River** ≈ Illinois/Wisconsin, N USA
30 L7 **Fox River** ≈ Wisconsin, N USA
184 L13 **Foxton** Manawatu-Wanganui, North Island, New Zealand 40°27′S 175°18′E
11 S16 **Fox Valley** Saskatchewan, S Canada 50°29′N 109°29′W
11 W16 **Foxwarren** Manitoba, S Canada 50°30′N 101°09′W
97 E14 **Foyle, Lough** *Ir.* Loch Feabhail. *inlet* N Ireland
194 H5 **Foyn Coast** *physical region* Antarctica
104 I2 **Foz** Galicia, NW Spain 43°33′N 07°16′W
60 I12 **Foz do Areia, Represa de** ⊠ S Brazil
59 A16 **Foz do Breu** Acre, W Brazil 09°21′S 72°41′W
83 A16 **Foz do Cunene** Namibe, SW Angola 17°11′S 11°52′E
60 G12 **Foz do Iguaçu** Paraná, S Brazil 25°33′S 54°31′W
58 C12 **Foz do Mamoriá** Amazonas, NW Brazil 02°28′S 66°06′W
105 T6 **Fraga** Aragón, NE Spain 41°32′N 00°21′E
44 F5 **Fragoso, Cayo** *island* C Cuba
61 G18 **Fraile Muerto** Cerro Largo, NE Uruguay 32°30′S 54°30′W
99 H21 **Fraire** Namur, S Belgium 50°16′N 04°30′E
99 L21 **Fraiture, Baraque de** *hill* SE Belgium
Frakštát *see* Hlohovec
197 S10 **Fram Basin** *var.* Amundsen Basin. *undersea feature* Arctic Ocean 88°00′N 90°00′E
99 F20 **Frameries** Hainaut, S Belgium 50°25′N 03°41′E
19 O11 **Framingham** Massachusetts, NE USA 42°15′N 71°24′W
60 L7 **Franca** São Paulo, S Brazil 20°33′S 47°27′W
187 O15 **Français, Récif des** *reef* W New Caledonia
107 K14 **Francavilla al Mare** Abruzzo, C Italy 42°25′N 14°16′E
107 P18 **Francavilla Fontana** Puglia, SE Italy 40°32′N 17°35′E
102 M8 **France** *off.* French Republic, *It./Sp.* Francia; *prev.* Gaul, Gaule, *Lat.* Gallia. ◆ *republic* W Europe
45 O8 **Francés Viejo, Cabo** *headland* NE Dominican Republic 19°39′N 69°57′W
79 F19 **Franceville** *var.* Massoukou, Masuku. Haut-Ogooué, E Gabon 01°40′S 13°31′E
79 F19 **Franceville** ✈ Haut-Ogooué, E Gabon 01°38′S 13°24′E
Francfort *see* Frankfurt am Main
103 T8 **Franche-Comté** ◈ *region* E France
Francia *see* France
29 O11 **Francis Case, Lake** ⊠ South Dakota, N USA
60 H12 **Francisco Beltrão** Paraná, S Brazil 26°05′S 53°04′W
Francisco I. Madero *see* Villa Madero
61 A21 **Francisco Madero** Buenos Aires, E Argentina 35°52′S 62°03′W
42 H6 **Francisco Morazán** *prev.* Tegucigalpa. ◈ *department* C Honduras
83 J18 **Francistown** North East, NE Botswana 21°08′S 27°31′E
Franconian Forest *see* Frankenwald
Franconian Jura *see* Fränkische Alb
98 K6 **Franeker** *Fris.* Frentsjer. Fryslân, N Netherlands 53°11′N 05°33′E
Frankenalb *see* Fränkische Alb
101 H16 **Frankenberg** Hessen, C Germany 51°04′N 08°49′E
101 J20 **Frankenhöhe** *hill range* C Germany
31 R8 **Frankenmuth** Michigan, N USA 43°19′N 83°44′W
101 F20 **Frankenstein** *hill* W Germany
Frankenstein/Frankenstein in Schlesien *see* Ząbkowice Śląskie
101 G20 **Frankenthal** Rheinland-Pfalz, W Germany 49°32′N 08°22′E
101 L18 **Frankenwald** *Eng.* Franconian Forest. ▲▲ C Germany
44 J12 **Frankfield** C Jamaica 18°08′N 77°22′W
14 J14 **Frankford** Ontario, SE Canada 44°12′N 77°36′W
31 O13 **Frankfort** Indiana, N USA 40°16′N 86°30′W
27 O3 **Frankfort** Kansas, C USA 39°42′N 96°25′W
20 L5 **Frankfort** *state capital* Kentucky, S USA 38°12′N 84°52′W
Frankfort on the Main *see* Frankfurt am Main
Frankfurt *see* Frankfurt am Main, Germany
Frankfurt *see* Słubice, Poland
101 G18 **Frankfurt am Main** *var.* Frankfurt, *Fr.* Francfort; *prev. Eng.* Frankfort on the Main. Hessen, SW Germany 50°07′N 08°41′E
100 Q12 **Frankfurt an der Oder** Brandenburg, E Germany 52°20′N 14°32′E
101 L21 **Fränkische Alb** *var.* Frankenalb, *Eng.* Franconian Jura. ▲▲ S Germany
101 I18 **Fränkische Saale** ≈ C Germany
101 L19 **Fränkische Schweiz** *hill range* C Germany
23 R4 **Franklin** Georgia, SE USA 33°15′N 85°06′W
31 P14 **Franklin** Indiana, N USA 39°29′N 86°02′W
20 J7 **Franklin** Kentucky, S USA 36°42′N 86°35′W
22 I9 **Franklin** Louisiana, S USA 29°48′N 91°30′W
29 O17 **Franklin** Nebraska, C USA 40°06′N 98°57′W
21 N10 **Franklin** North Carolina, SE USA 35°12′N 83°23′W
18 C13 **Franklin** Pennsylvania, NE USA 41°24′N 79°49′W
20 J9 **Franklin** Tennessee, S USA 35°55′N 86°52′W
25 U9 **Franklin** Texas, SW USA 31°02′N 96°30′W
21 X7 **Franklin** Virginia, NE USA 36°41′N 76°58′W
21 T4 **Franklin** West Virginia, NE USA 38°39′N 79°21′W
30 M9 **Franklin** Wisconsin, N USA 42°53′N 88°00′W
8 I6 **Franklin Bay** *inlet* Northwest Territories, N Canada
32 K7 **Franklin D. Roosevelt Lake** ⊠ Washington, NW USA
35 W4 **Franklin Lake** ◎ Nevada, W USA
185 B22 **Franklin Mountains** ▲▲ South Island, New Zealand
39 R5 **Franklin Mountains** ▲▲ Alaska, USA
39 N4 **Franklin, Point** *headland* Alaska, USA 70°54′N 158°48′W
183 O17 **Franklin River** ≈ Tasmania, SE Australia
22 K8 **Franklinton** Louisiana, S USA 30°51′N 90°09′W
21 U9 **Franklinton** North Carolina, SE USA 36°06′N 78°27′W
Frankstadt *see* Frenštát pod Radhoštěm
25 V7 **Frankston** Texas, SW USA 32°03′N 95°30′W
33 U12 **Frannie** Wyoming, C USA 44°57′N 108°37′W
15 U5 **Franquelin** Québec, SE Canada 49°17′N 67°52′W
15 U5 **Franquelin** ≈ Québec, SE Canada
83 C18 **Fransfontein** Kunene, NW Namibia 20°12′S 15°01′E
93 H17 **Fränsta** Västernorrland, C Sweden 62°30′N 16°06′E
122 J3 **Frantsa-Iosifa, Zemlya** *Eng.* Franz Josef Land. *island group* N Russian Federation
185 E18 **Franz Josef Glacier** West Coast, South Island, New Zealand 43°22′S 170°11′E
Franz Josef Land *see* Frantsa-Iosifa, Zemlya
Franz-Josef Spitze *see* Gerlachovský štít
101 L23 **Franz Josef Strauss** *abbrev.* F.J.S.. ✈ (München) Bayern, SE Germany 48°07′N 11°43′E
107 A19 **Frasca, Capo della** *headland* Sardegna, Italy, C Mediterranean Sea 39°46′N 08°27′E
107 I15 **Frascati** Lazio, C Italy 41°48′N 12°41′E
11 N14 **Fraser** ≈ British Columbia, SW Canada
83 G24 **Fraserburg** Western Cape, SW South Africa 31°55′S 21°31′E
96 L8 **Fraserburgh** NE Scotland, United Kingdom 57°42′N 02°20′W
181 Z9 **Fraser Island** *var.* Great Sandy Island. *island* Queensland, E Australia
10 L14 **Fraser Lake** British Columbia, SW Canada 54°00′N 124°45′W
10 L15 **Fraser Plateau** *plateau* British Columbia, SW Canada
184 P10 **Frasertown** Hawke's Bay, North Island, New Zealand 38°58′S 177°25′E
99 E19 **Frasnes-lez-Buissenal** Hainaut, SW Belgium 50°40′N 03°37′E
108 I7 **Frastanz** Vorarlberg, NW Austria 47°13′N 09°38′E
14 B8 **Frater** Ontario, S Canada 47°19′N 84°28′W
Frauenbach *see* Baia Mare
Frauenburg *see* Saldus, Latvia
Frauenburg *see* Frombork, Poland
108 H6 **Frauenfeld** Thurgau, NE Switzerland 47°34′N 08°54′E
109 Z5 **Frauenkirchen** Burgenland, E Austria 47°50′N 16°57′E
61 D19 **Fray Bentos** Río Negro, W Uruguay 33°09′S 58°14′W
61 F19 **Fray Marcos** Florida, S Uruguay 34°13′S 55°43′W
29 S6 **Frazee** Minnesota, N USA 46°42′N 95°40′W
104 M5 **Frechilla** Castilla y León, N Spain 42°08′N 04°50′W
30 I4 **Frederic** Wisconsin, N USA 45°42′N 92°30′W
95 G23 **Fredericia** Syddanmark, C Denmark 55°34′N 09°47′E
21 W3 **Frederick** Maryland, NE USA 39°25′N 77°25′W
26 L12 **Frederick** Oklahoma, C USA 34°24′N 99°03′W
29 P7 **Frederick** South Dakota, N USA 45°49′N 98°31′W
29 X12 **Fredericksburg** Iowa, C USA 42°58′N 92°12′W
25 R10 **Fredericksburg** Texas, SW USA 30°17′N 98°52′W
21 W5 **Fredericksburg** Virginia, NE USA 38°16′N 77°27′W
39 X13 **Frederick Sound** *sound* Alaska, USA
27 X6 **Fredericktown** Missouri, C USA 37°33′N 90°19′W
60 H13 **Frederico Westphalen** Rio Grande do Sul, S Brazil 27°22′S 53°20′W
13 O15 **Fredericton** *province capital* New Brunswick, SE Canada 45°57′N 66°40′W
Frederiksborgs Amt *see* Hovedstaden
Frederikshåb *see* Paamiut
95 H19 **Frederikshavn** *prev.* Fladstrand. Nordjylland, N Denmark 57°28′N 10°33′E
95 J22 **Frederikssund** Hovedstaden, E Denmark 55°51′N 12°05′E
45 T9 **Frederiksted** Saint Croix, S Virgin Islands (US) 17°41′N 64°51′W
95 I22 **Frederiksværk** *var.* Frederiksværk og Hanehoved. Hovedstaden, E Denmark 55°58′N 12°02′E
Frederiksværk og Hanehoved *see* Frederiksværk
54 E9 **Fredonia** Antioquia, W Colombia 05°57′N 75°42′W
36 K8 **Fredonia** Arizona, SW USA 36°57′N 112°31′W
27 P7 **Fredonia** Kansas, C USA 37°32′N 95°50′W
18 C11 **Fredonia** New York, NE USA 42°26′N 79°19′W
35 P4 **Fredonyer Pass** *pass* California, W USA
93 I15 **Fredrika** Västerbotten, N Sweden 64°03′N 18°25′E
95 L14 **Fredriksberg** Dalarna, C Sweden 60°07′N 14°23′E
Fredrikshald *see* Halden
Fredrikshamn *see* Hamina
95 H16 **Fredrikstad** Østfold, S Norway 59°12′N 10°57′E
30 K16 **Freeburg** Illinois, N USA 38°25′N 89°54′W
18 K15 **Freehold** New Jersey, NE USA 40°14′N 74°14′W
18 H14 **Freeland** Pennsylvania, NE USA 41°01′N 75°54′W
182 J5 **Freeling Heights** ▲ South Australia 30°09′S 139°24′E
35 Q7 **Freel Peak** ▲ California, W USA 38°52′N 119°52′W
11 Z9 **Freels, Cape** *headland* Newfoundland and Labrador, E Canada 49°16′N 53°30′W
29 Q11 **Freeman** South Dakota, N USA 43°21′N 97°26′W
44 G1 **Freeport** Grand Bahama Island, N Bahamas 26°28′N 78°43′W
30 L10 **Freeport** Illinois, N USA 42°18′N 89°37′W
25 W12 **Freeport** Texas, SW USA 28°57′N 95°21′W
44 G1 **Freeport** ✈ Grand Bahama Island, N Bahamas 26°31′N 78°48′W
25 R14 **Freer** Texas, SW USA 27°52′N 98°37′W
83 I22 **Free State** *off.* Free State Province; *prev.* Orange Free State, *Afr.* Oranje Vrystaat. ◈ *province* C South Africa
Free State *see* Maryland
Free State Province *see* Free State
76 G15 **Freetown** ● (Sierra Leone) W Sierra Leone 08°27′N 13°16′W
172 J16 **Frégate** *island* Inner Islands, NE Seychelles
104 J12 **Fregenal de la Sierra** Extremadura, W Spain 38°10′N 06°39′W
182 C2 **Fregon** South Australia 26°44′S 132°03′E
102 H5 **Fréhel, Cap** *headland* NW France 48°41′N 02°21′W
94 F8 **Frei** Møre og Romsdal, S Norway 63°02′N 07°47′E
101 O16 **Freiberg** Sachsen, E Germany 50°55′N 13°21′E
101 O16 **Freiberger Mulde** ≈ E Germany
Freiburg *see* Freiburg im Breisgau, Germany
Freiburg *see* Fribourg, Switzerland
101 F23 **Freiburg im Breisgau** *var.* Freiburg, *Fr.* Fribourg-en-Brisgau. Baden-Württemberg, SW Germany 48°N 07°52′E
Freiburg in Schlesien *see* Świebodzice
Freie Hansestadt Bremen *see* Bremen
Freie und Hansestadt Hamburg *see* Brandenburg
101 L22 **Freising** Bayern, SE Germany 48°24′N 11°45′E
109 T3 **Freistadt** Oberösterreich, N Austria 48°31′N 14°31′E
Freistadtl *see* Hlohovec
101 O16 **Freital** Sachsen, E Germany 51°00′N 13°40′E
Freiwaldau *see* Jeseník
104 I6 **Freixo de Espada à Cinta** Bragança, N Portugal 41°05′N 06°49′W
103 U15 **Fréjus** *anc.* Forum Julii. Var, SE France 43°26′N 06°44′E
180 I13 **Fremantle** Western Australia 32°07′S 115°44′E
35 N9 **Fremont** California, W USA 37°34′N 122°01′W
31 Q11 **Fremont** Indiana, N USA 41°43′N 84°54′W
29 W15 **Fremont** Iowa, C USA 41°12′N 92°26′W
31 P8 **Fremont** Michigan, N USA 43°28′N 85°56′W
29 R15 **Fremont** Nebraska, C USA 41°25′N 96°30′W
31 S11 **Fremont** Ohio, N USA 41°21′N 83°08′W
33 T14 **Fremont Peak** ▲ Wyoming, C USA 43°07′N 109°37′W
36 M6 **Fremont River** ≈ Utah, W USA
21 O9 **French Broad River** ≈ Tennessee, S USA
21 N5 **Frenchburg** Kentucky, S USA 37°58′N 83°37′W
18 C12 **French Creek** ≈ Pennsylvania, NE USA
32 K15 **Frenchglen** Oregon, NW USA 42°49′N 118°55′W
55 Y10 **French Guiana** *var.* Guiana, Guyane. ◇ *French overseas department* N South America
French Guinea *see* Guinea
31 O15 **French Lick** Indiana, N USA 38°33′N 86°37′W
185 J14 **French Pass** Marlborough, South Island, New Zealand 40°57′S 173°49′E
191 T11 **French Polynesia** ◇ *French overseas territory* S Pacific Ocean
French Republic *see* France
14 F11 **French River** ≈ Ontario, S Canada
French Somaliland *see* Djibouti
173 P12 **French Southern and Antarctic Territories** *Fr.* Terres Australes et Antarctiques Françaises. ◇ *French overseas territory* S Indian Ocean
French Sudan *see* Mali
French Territory of the Afars and Issas *see* Djibouti
French Togoland *see* Togo
74 J6 **Frenda** NW Algeria 35°04′N 01°03′E
111 I18 **Frenštát pod Radhoštěm** *Ger.* Frankstadt. Moravskoslezský Kraj, E Czech Republic 49°33′N 18°10′E
Frentsjer *see* Franeker
76 M17 **Fresco** S Ivory Coast 05°03′N 05°31′W
195 U16 **Freshfield, Cape** *headland* Antarctica
40 L10 **Fresnillo** *var.* Fresnillo de González Echeverría. Zacatecas, C Mexico 23°11′N 102°53′W
Fresnillo de González Echeverría *see* Fresnillo
35 Q10 **Fresno** California, W USA 36°45′N 119°48′W
Freu, Cabo del *see* Freu, Cap des
105 Y9 **Freu, Cap des** *var.* Cabo del Freu. *cape* Mallorca, Spain, W Mediterranean Sea
101 G22 **Freudenstadt** Baden-Württemberg, SW Germany 48°28′N 08°25′E
Freudenthal *see* Bruntál
183 Q17 **Freycinet Peninsula** *peninsula* Tasmania, SE Australia
76 H14 **Fria** W Guinea 10°27′N 13°38′W
83 A17 **Fria, Cape** *headland* NW Namibia 18°32′S 12°00′E
35 Q10 **Friant** California, W USA 36°56′N 119°44′W
62 K8 **Frías** Catamarca, N Argentina 28°41′S 65°00′W
108 D9 **Fribourg** *Ger.* Freiburg. Fribourg, W Switzerland 46°50′N 07°10′E
108 C9 **Fribourg** *Ger.* Freiburg. ◈ *canton* W Switzerland
Fribourg-en-Brisgau *see* Freiburg im Breisgau
32 G7 **Friday Harbor** San Juan Islands, Washington, NW USA 48°31′N 123°01′W
Friedau *see* Ormož
101 K23 **Friedberg** Bayern, S Germany 48°21′N 10°58′E
101 H18 **Friedberg** Hessen, W Germany 50°19′N 08°46′E
Friedeberg Neumark *see* Strzelce Krajeńskie
Friedek-Mistek *see* Frýdek-Místek
Friedland *see* Pravdinsk
101 I24 **Friedrichshafen** Baden-Württemberg, S Germany 47°39′N 09°29′E
Friedrichstadt *see* Jaunjelgava
29 Q16 **Friend** Nebraska, C USA 40°37′N 97°16′W
Friendly Islands *see* Tonga
55 V9 **Friendship** Coronie, N Suriname 05°50′N 56°16′W
30 L7 **Friendship** Wisconsin, N USA 43°58′N 89°48′W
109 T8 **Friesach** Kärnten, S Austria 46°58′N 14°24′E
Friesche Eilanden *see* Frisian Islands
101 F22 **Friesenheim** Baden-Württemberg, SW Germany 48°27′N 07°56′E
Friesische Inseln *see* Frisian Islands
Friesland *see* Fryslân
60 Q10 **Frio, Cabo** *headland* SE Brazil 23°01′S 41°59′W
24 M3 **Friona** Texas, SW USA 34°38′N 102°43′W
42 L12 **Frío, Río** ≈ N Costa Rica
25 R13 **Frio River** ≈ Texas, SW USA
99 M25 **Frisange** Luxembourg, S Luxembourg 49°31′N 06°12′E
Frisches Haff *see* Vistula Lagoon
36 J6 **Frisco Peak** ▲ Utah, W USA 38°31′N 113°17′W
84 F9 **Frisian Islands** *Dut.* Friesche Eilanden, *Ger.* Friesische Inseln. *island group* N Europe
18 L12 **Frissell, Mount** ▲ Connecticut, NE USA 42°01′N 73°25′W
95 J19 **Fristad** Västra Götaland, S Sweden 57°50′N 13°01′E
25 N2 **Fritch** Texas, SW USA 35°38′N 101°36′W
95 J19 **Fritsla** Västra Götaland, S Sweden 57°33′N 12°47′E
101 H16 **Fritzlar** Hessen, C Germany 51°09′N 09°16′E
106 H6 **Friuli-Venezia Giulia** ◈ *region* NE Italy
196 L13 **Frobisher Bay** *inlet* Baffin Island, Nunavut, NE Canada
Frobisher Bay *see* Iqaluit
11 S12 **Frobisher Lake** ◎ Saskatchewan, C Canada
94 G7 **Frohavet** *sound* C Norway
Frohenbruck *see* Veselí nad Lužnicí
109 V7 **Frohnleiten** Steiermark, SE Austria 47°17′N 15°20′E
99 G22 **Froidchapelle** Hainaut, S Belgium 50°10′N 04°18′E
127 O9 **Frolovo** Volgogradskaya Oblast', SW Russian Federation 49°46′N 43°38′E
110 K7 **Frombork** *Ger.* Frauenburg. Warmińsko-Mazurskie, NE Poland 54°21′N 19°40′E
97 L22 **Frome** SW England, United Kingdom 51°15′N 02°22′W
182 I4 **Frome Creek** *seasonal river* South Australia
182 J6 **Frome Downs** South Australia 31°17′S 139°48′E
182 J5 **Frome, Lake** *salt lake* South Australia
Fronicken *see* Wronki
104 H10 **Fronteira** Portalegre, C Portugal 39°03′N 07°39′W
40 M7 **Frontera** Coahuila, NE Mexico 26°55′N 101°27′W
41 U14 **Frontera** Tabasco, SE Mexico 18°32′N 92°39′W
40 G3 **Fronteras** Sonora, NW Mexico 30°51′N 109°33′W
103 Q16 **Frontignan** Hérault, S France 43°27′N 03°45′E
54 D8 **Frontino** Antioquia, NW Colombia 06°46′N 76°10′W
21 V4 **Front Royal** Virginia, NE USA 38°56′N 78°13′W
107 J16 **Frosinone** *anc.* Frusino. Lazio, C Italy 41°38′N 13°22′E
107 K16 **Frosolone** Molise, C Italy 41°34′N 14°25′E
25 U7 **Frost** Texas, SW USA 32°04′N 96°48′W
21 U2 **Frostburg** Maryland, NE USA 39°39′N 78°55′W
23 X13 **Frostproof** Florida, SE USA 27°45′N 81°31′W
Frostviken *see* Kvarnbergsvattnet
95 M15 **Frövi** Örebro, C Sweden 59°28′N 15°24′E
94 F7 **Frøya** *island* W Norway
37 P5 **Fruita** Colorado, C USA 39°10′N 108°42′W
28 J9 **Fruitdale** South Dakota, N USA 44°39′N 103°38′W
23 W11 **Fruitland Park** Florida, SE USA 28°51′N 81°54′W
Frumentum *see* Formentera
147 S11 **Frunze** Batkenskaya Oblast', SW Kyrgyzstan 40°07′N 71°40′E
Frunze *see* Bishkek
117 O9 **Frunzivka** Odes'ka Oblast', SW Ukraine 47°19′N 29°46′E
Frusino *see* Frosinone
108 E9 **Frutigen** Bern, W Switzerland 46°35′N 07°38′E
111 I17 **Frýdek-Místek** *Ger.* Friedek-Mistek. Moravskoslezský Kraj, E Czech Republic 49°40′N 18°22′E
98 K6 **Fryslân** *prev.* Friesland. ◈ *province* N Netherlands
193 V16 **Fua'amotu** Tongatapu, S Tonga 21°15′S 175°08′W
190 A9 **Fuafatu** *island* Funafuti Atoll, C Tuvalu
190 A9 **Fuagea** *island* Funafuti Atoll, C Tuvalu
190 B8 **Fualifeke** *atoll* C Tuvalu
190 A8 **Fualopa** *island* Funafuti Atoll, C Tuvalu
151 K22 **Fuammulah** *var.* Fuammulah, Gnaviyani. *atoll* S Maldives
Fuammulah *see* Fuammulah
161 R11 **Fu'an** Fujian, SE China 27°11′N 119°42′E
Fu-chien *see* Fujian
Fu-chou *see* Fuzhou
164 G13 **Fuchū** *var.* Hutyû. Hiroshima, Honshū, SW Japan 34°35′N 133°12′E
160 M13 **Fuchuan** *var.* Fuyang. Guangxi Zhuangzu Zizhiqu, S China 24°56′N 111°15′E
161 R9 **Fuchun Jiang** *var.* Tsien Tang. ≈ SE China
165 R8 **Fudai** Iwate, Honshū, C Japan 39°59′N 141°50′E
161 S11 **Fuding** *var.* Tongshan. Fujian, SE China 27°21′N 120°10′E
81 J20 **Fudua** *spring/well* S Kenya 02°13′S 39°43′E
104 M16 **Fuengirola** Andalucía, S Spain 36°32′N 04°38′W
104 J12 **Fuente de Cantos** Extremadura, W Spain 38°15′N 06°18′W
104 J11 **Fuente del Maestre** Extremadura, W Spain 38°31′N 06°26′W
104 L12 **Fuente Obejuna** Andalucía, S Spain 38°15′N 05°25′W
104 L6 **Fuentesaúco** Castilla y León, N Spain 41°14′N 05°30′W
62 O3 **Fuerte Olimpo** *var.* Olimpo. Alto Paraguay, NE Paraguay 21°02′S 57°51′W
40 H8 **Fuerte, Río** ≈ C Mexico
64 Q11 **Fuerteventura** *island* Islas Canarias, Spain, NE Atlantic Ocean
141 S14 **Fughmah** *var.* Faghman, Fugma. C Yemen 16°08′N 49°23′E
92 M2 **Fuglehuken** *headland* W Svalbard 78°54′N 10°30′E
Fuglø *see* Fugloy
95 B18 **Fugloy** *Dan.* Fuglø. *island* NE Faeroe Islands
197 T15 **Fugløya Bank** *undersea feature* E Norwegian Sea 71°00′N 19°20′E
Fugma *see* Fughmah
160 E11 **Fugong** Yunnan, SW China 27°00′N 98°48′E
81 K16 **Fugugo** *spring/well* NE Kenya 03°19′N 39°39′E
158 L2 **Fuhai** *var.* Burultokay. Xinjiang Uygur Zizhiqu, NW China 47°15′N 87°39′E
161 P10 **Fu He** ≈ S China
Fuhkien *see* Fujian
100 J9 **Fuhlsbüttel** ✈ (Hamburg) Hamburg, N Germany 53°37′N 09°57′E
101 L14 **Fuhne** ≈ C Germany
Fu-hsin *see* Fuxin
Fujairah *see* Al Fujayrah
164 M14 **Fuji** *var.* Huzi. Shizuoka, Honshū, S Japan 35°08′N 138°39′E
161 Q12 **Fujian** *var.* Fu-chien, Fuhkien, Fukien, Min, Fujian Sheng. ◈ *province* SE China
160 I9 **Fu Jiang** ≈ C China
Fujian Sheng *see* Fujian
164 M14 **Fujieda** *var.* Huzieda. Shizuoka, Honshū, S Japan 34°54′N 138°15′E
Fuji, Mount/Fujiyama *see* Fuji-san
163 Y7 **Fujin** Heilongjiang, NE China 47°12′N 132°01′E
164 M13 **Fujinomiya** *var.* Huzinomiya. Shizuoka, Honshū, S Japan 35°16′N 138°33′E
164 N13 **Fuji-san** *var.* Fujiyama, *Eng.* Mount Fuji. ▲ Honshū, SE Japan 35°23′N 138°44′E
165 N14 **Fujisawa** *var.* Huzisawa. Kanagawa, Honshū, S Japan 35°22′N 139°29′E
165 T3 **Fukagawa** *var.* Hukagawa. Hokkaidō, NE Japan 43°44′N 142°03′E
158 L5 **Fukang** Xinjiang Uygur Zizhiqu, W China 44°07′N 87°55′E
165 P7 **Fukaura** Aomori, Honshū, C Japan 40°38′N 139°55′E
193 W15 **Fukave** *island* Tongatapu Group, S Tonga
Fukien *see* Fujian
164 J13 **Fukuchiyama** *var.* Hukutiyama. Kyōto, Honshū, SW Japan 35°19′N 135°08′E
Fukue *see* Gotō
164 A13 **Fukue-jima** *island* Gotō-rettō, SW Japan
164 K12 **Fukui** *var.* Hukui. Fukui, Honshū, SW Japan 36°03′N 136°12′E
164 K12 **Fukui** *off.* Fukui-ken, *var.* Hukui. ◈ *prefecture* Honshū, SW Japan
Fukui-ken *see* Fukui
164 D13 **Fukuoka** *var.* Hukuoka, *hist.* Najima. Fukuoka, Kyūshū, SW Japan 33°36′N 130°24′E
164 D13 **Fukuoka** *off.* Fukuoka-ken, *var.* Hukuoka. ◈ *prefecture* Kyūshū, SW Japan
Fukuoka-ken *see* Fukuoka
165 Q6 **Fukushima** Hokkaidō, NE Japan 41°27′N 140°14′E
165 Q12 **Fukushima** *off.* Fukushima-ken, *var.* Hukusima. ◈ *prefecture* Honshū, C Japan
Fukushima-ken *see* Fukushima
164 G13 **Fukuyama** *var.* Hukuyama. Hiroshima, Honshū, SW Japan 34°29′N 133°21′E
76 G13 **Fulacunda** C Guinea-Bissau 11°44′N 15°03′W
129 P8 **Fūlādī, Kūh-e** ▲ E Afghanistan 34°38′N 67°32′E
187 Z15 **Fulaga** *island* Lau Group, E Fiji
101 I17 **Fulda** Hessen, C Germany 50°33′N 09°41′E
29 S10 **Fulda** Minnesota, N USA 43°52′N 95°36′W
101 I16 **Fulda** ≈ C Germany
Fülek *see* Fil'akovo
Fuli *see* Jixian
Fulin *see* Hanyuan
160 K10 **Fuling** Chongqing Shi, C China 29°45′N 107°23′E
35 T15 **Fullerton** California, SE USA 33°53′N 117°55′W
29 P15 **Fullerton** Nebraska, C USA 41°21′N 97°58′W
108 M8 **Fulpmes** Tirol, W Austria 47°11′N 11°22′E
20 G8 **Fulton** Kentucky, S USA 36°31′N 88°52′W
23 N2 **Fulton** Mississippi, S USA 34°16′N 88°24′W
27 V4 **Fulton** Missouri, C USA 38°50′N 91°57′W
18 H9 **Fulton** New York, NE USA 43°18′N 76°22′W
Fuman/Fumen *see* Fowman
103 R3 **Fumay** Ardennes, N France 49°58′N 04°42′E
102 M13 **Fumel** Lot-et-Garonne, SW France 44°31′N 00°58′E
190 B10 **Funafara** *atoll* C Tuvalu
190 C9 **Funafuti** ✈ Funafuti Atoll, C Tuvalu 08°30′S 179°12′E
Funafuti *see* Fongafale
190 F8 **Funafuti Atoll** *atoll* C Tuvalu
Funan *see* Fusui
190 B9 **Funangongo** *atoll* C Tuvalu
93 F17 **Funäsdalen** Jämtland, C Sweden 62°33′N 12°33′E
64 O6 **Funchal** Madeira, Portugal, NE Atlantic Ocean 32°40′N 16°55′W
64 P5 **Funchal** ✈ Madeira, Portugal, NE Atlantic Ocean 32°38′N 16°53′W
54 F5 **Fundación** Magdalena, N Colombia 10°31′N 74°09′W
104 I8 **Fundão** *var.* Fundáo. Castelo Branco, C Portugal 40°08′N 07°30′W
Fundáo *see* Fundão
13 O16 **Fundy, Bay of** *bay* Canada/USA
Fünen *see* Fyn
54 C13 **Fúnes** Nariño, SW Colombia 0°59′N 77°27′W
Fünfkirchen *see* Pécs
83 M19 **Funhalouro** Inhambane, S Mozambique 23°04′S 34°24′E
161 R6 **Funing** Jiangsu, E China 33°43′N 119°47′E
160 I14 **Funing** *var.* Xinhua. Yunnan, SW China 23°39′N 105°41′E
160 M7 **Funiu Shan** ▲▲ C China
77 U13 **Funtua** Katsina, N Nigeria 11°31′N 07°19′E
161 R12 **Fuqing** Fujian, SE China 25°40′N 119°23′E
83 M14 **Furancungo** Tete, NW Mozambique 14°51′S 33°39′E
116 J15 **Furculeşti** Teleorman, S Romania 43°51′N 25°07′E
Füred *see* Balatonfüred
165 W4 **Füren-ko** ◎ Hokkaidō, NE Japan
Fürg *see* Doborjī
Furluk *see* Fârliug
Fürmanov/Furmanovka *see* Moyynkum
Furmanovo *see* Zhalpaktal
59 L20 **Furnas, Represa de** ⊠ SE Brazil
183 Q14 **Furneaux Group** *island group* Tasmania, SE Australia
Furnes *see* Veurne
160 J10 **Furong Jiang** ≈ S China
138 I5 **Furqlus** Ḥimṣ, W Syria 34°40′N 37°02′E
100 F12 **Fürstenau** Niedersachsen, NW Germany 52°30′N 07°40′E
109 X8 **Fürstenfeld** Steiermark, SE Austria 47°03′N 16°05′E
101 L23 **Fürstenfeldbruck** Bayern, S Germany 48°10′N 11°16′E

◆ Country
● Country Capital
◇ Dependent Territory
○ Dependent Territory Capital
◈ Administrative Regions
✈ International Airport
▲ Mountain
▲▲ Mountain Range
Ѫ Volcano
≈ River
◎ Lake
⊠ Reservoir

100 P12 **Fürstenwalde** Brandenburg, NE Germany 52°22′N 14°04′E
101 K20 **Fürth** Bayern, S Germany 49°29′N 10°59′E
109 W3 **Furth bei Göttweig** Niederösterreich, NW Austria 48°22′N 15°33′E
165 R3 **Furubira** Hokkaidō, NE Japan 43°14′N 140°38′E
94 L12 **Furudal** Dalarna, C Sweden 61°10′N 15°07′E
164 L12 **Furukawa** *var.* Hida. Gifu, Honshū, SW Japan 36°13′N 137°11′E
165 Q10 **Furukawa** *var.* Hurukawa, Ōsaki. Miyagi, Honshū, C Japan 38°36′N 140°57′E
54 F10 **Fusagasugá** Cundinamarca, C Colombia 04°22′N 74°21′W
Fusan *see* Busan
Fushë-Arëzi/Fushë-Arrësi *see* Fushë-Arrëz
113 L18 **Fushë-Arrëz** *var.* Fushë-Arëzi, Fushë-Arrësi. Shkodër, N Albania 42°05′N 20°01′E
113 N16 **Fushë Kosovë** *Serb.* Kosovo Polje. C Kosovo 42°40′N 21°07′E
Fushë-Kruja *see* Fushë-Krujë
113 K19 **Fushë-Krujë** *var.* Fushë-Kruja. Durrës, C Albania 41°30′N 19°43′E
163 V12 **Fushun** *var.* Fou-shan, Fu-shun. Liaoning, NE China 41°50′N 123°54′E
Fu-shun *see* Fushun
Fusin *see* Fuxin
108 G10 **Fusio** Ticino, S Switzerland 46°27′N 08°39′E
163 X11 **Fusong** Jilin, NE China 42°20′N 127°17′E
101 K24 **Füssen** Bayern, S Germany 47°34′N 10°43′E
160 K15 **Fusui** *var.* Xinning; *prev.* Funan. Guangxi Zhuangzu Zizhiqu, S China 22°39′N 107°49′E
Futa Jallon *see* Fouta Djallon
63 G18 **Futaleufú** Los Lagos, S Chile 43°14′S 71°50′W
112 K10 **Futog** Vojvodina, NW Serbia 45°15′N 19°43′E
165 O14 **Futtsu** *var.* Huttu. Chiba, Honshū, S Japan 35°11′N 139°52′E
187 S15 **Futuna** *island* S Vanuatu
190 D12 **Futuna, Île** *island* S Wallis and Futuna
161 Q11 **Futun Xi** ≈ SE China
160 L5 **Fuxian** *var.* Fu Xian. Shaanxi, C China 36°03′N 109°19′E
Fuxian *see* Wafangdian
Fu Xian *see* Fuxian
160 G13 **Fuxian Hu** ⊠ SW China
163 U12 **Fuxin** *var.* Fou-hsin, Fu-hsin, Fusin. Liaoning, NE China 41°59′N 121°40′E
Fuxing *see* Wangmo
161 P7 **Fuyang** Anhui, E China 32°52′N 115°51′E
Fuyang *see* Fuchuan
161 O4 **Fuyang He** ≈ E China
163 U7 **Fuyu** Heilongjiang, NE China 47°48′N 124°26′E
163 Z6 **Fuyuan** Heilongjiang, NE China 48°20′N 134°22′E
Fuyu/Fu-yü *see* Songyuan
158 M3 **Fuyun** *var.* Koktokay. Xinjiang Uygur Zizhiqu, NW China 46°58′N 89°30′E
111 L22 **Füzesabony** Heves, E Hungary 47°46′N 20°25′E
161 R12 **Fuzhou** *var.* Foochow, Fu-chou. *province capital* Fujian, SE China 26°09′N 119°17′E
161 P11 **Fuzhou** *prev.* Linchuan. Jiangxi, S China 27°58′N 116°20′E
137 W13 **Füzuli** *Rus.* Fizuli. SW Azerbaijan 39°33′N 47°09′E
119 I20 **Fyadory** *Rus.* Fëdory. Brestskaya Voblasts', SW Belarus 51°57′N 26°24′E
95 G23 **Fyn** *Ger.* Fünen. *island* C Denmark
96 H12 **Fyne, Loch** *inlet* W Scotland, United Kingdom
95 E16 **Fyresvatnet** ◎ S Norway
FYR Macedonia/FYROM *see* Macedonia, FYR
Fyzabad *see* Feizābād

G

Gaafu Alifu Atoll *see* North Huvadhu Atoll
81 O14 **Gaalkacyo** *var.* Galka'yo, *It.* Galcaio. Mudug, C Somalia 06°42′N 47°24′E
146 J11 **Gabakly** *Rus.* Kabakly. Lebap Welaýaty, NE Turkmenistan 39°45′N 62°30′E
114 H8 **Gabare** Vratsa, NW Bulgaria 43°20′N 23°57′E
102 K15 **Gabas** ≈ SW France
Gabasumdo *see* Tongde
35 T7 **Gabbs** Nevada, W USA 38°51′N 117°55′W
82 B12 **Gabela** Cuanza Sul, W Angola 10°50′S 14°21′E
Gaberones *see* Gaborone
189 X14 **Gabert** *island* Caroline Islands, E Micronesia
74 M7 **Gabès** *var.* Qābis. E Tunisia 33°53′N 10°03′E
74 M6 **Gabès, Golfe de** *Ar.* Khalīj Qābis. *gulf* E Tunisia
Gablonz an der Neisse *see* Jablonec nad Nisou
Gablös *see* Cavalese
79 E18 **Gabon** *off.* Gabonese Republic. ◆ *republic* C Africa
Gabonese Republic *see* Gabon
83 I20 **Gaborone** *prev.* Gaberones. ● (Botswana) South East, SE Botswana 24°42′S 25°50′E
83 I20 **Gaborone** ✈ South East, SE Botswana 24°45′S 25°49′E
104 K8 **Gabriel y Galán, Embalse de** ⊠ W Spain
143 U15 **Gābrīk, Rūd-e** ≈ SE Iran
114 J9 **Gabrovo** Gabrovo, N Bulgaria 42°54′N 25°19′E
114 J9 **Gabrovo** ◈ *province* N Bulgaria
76 H12 **Gabú** *prev.* Nova Lamego. E Guinea-Bissau 12°16′N 14°09′W
29 O6 **Gackle** North Dakota, N USA 46°34′N 99°07′W
113 I15 **Gacko** Repulika Srpska, S Bosnia and Herzegovina 43°08′N 18°29′E
155 F17 **Gadag** Karnātaka, W India 15°25′N 75°37′E
93 G15 **Gäddede** Jämtland, C Sweden 64°30′N 14°15′E
159 S12 **Gadê** *var.* Kequ; *prev.* Pagqên. Qinghai, C China 33°56′N 99°49′E
Gades/Gadier/Gadir/Gadire *see* Cádiz
105 P15 **Gádor, Sierra de** ▲▲ S Spain
149 S15 **Gadra** Sind, SE Pakistan 25°39′N 70°28′E
23 Q3 **Gadsden** Alabama, S USA 34°00′N 86°00′W
36 H15 **Gadsden** Arizona, SW USA 32°33′N 114°45′W
Gadyach *see* Hadyach
124 J3 **Gadzhiyevo** Murmanskaya Oblast', NW Russian Federation 69°16′N 33°20′E
79 H15 **Gadzi** Mambéré-Kadéï, SW Central African Republic 04°46′N 16°42′E
116 J13 **Găeşti** Dâmboviţa, S Romania 44°42′N 25°19′E
107 J17 **Gaeta** Lazio, C Italy 41°12′N 13°35′E
107 J17 **Gaeta, Golfo di** *var.* Gulf of Gaeta. *gulf* C Italy
Gaeta, Gulf of *see* Gaeta, Golfo di
188 L14 **Gaferut** *atoll* Caroline Islands, W Micronesia
21 Q10 **Gaffney** South Carolina, SE USA 35°03′N 81°40′W
Gäfle *see* Gävle
Gäfleborg *see* Gävleborg
74 M6 **Gafsa** *var.* Qafşah. W Tunisia 34°25′N 08°52′E
Gafurov *see* Ghafurov
126 J3 **Gagarin** *prev.* Gzhatsk. Smolenskaya Oblast', W Russian Federation 53°33′N 35°00′E
147 O10 **Gagarin** Jizzax Viloyati, C Uzbekistan 40°40′N 68°04′E
116 M12 **Găgăuzia** ◈ *cultural region* S Moldavia
101 G21 **Gaggenau** Baden-Württemberg, SW Germany 48°48′N 08°19′E
188 F16 **Gagil Tamil** *var.* Gagil-Tomil. *island* Caroline Islands, W Micronesia
Gagil-Tomil *see* Gagil Tamil
127 O4 **Gagino** Nizhegorodskaya Oblast', W Russian Federation 55°18′N 45°01′E
107 Q19 **Gagliano del Capo** Puglia, SE Italy 39°49′N 18°22′E
94 L13 **Gagnef** Dalarna, C Sweden 60°34′N 15°04′E
76 M17 **Gagnoa** C Ivory Coast 06°11′N 05°56′W
13 N10 **Gagnon** Québec, E Canada 51°56′N 68°16′W
Gago Coutinho *see* Lumbala N'Guimbo
137 P8 **Gagra** NW Georgia 43°17′N 40°18′E
31 S13 **Gahanna** Ohio, N USA 40°01′N 82°52′W
143 R13 **Gahkom** Hormozgān, S Iran 28°14′N 55°48′E
Gahnpa *see* Ganta
57 Q19 **Gaíba, Laguna** ◎ E Bolivia
153 T13 **Gaibandha** *var.* Gaibanda. Rajshahi, NW Bangladesh 25°21′N 89°36′E
Gaibhlte, Cnoc Mór na n *see* Galtymore Mountain
109 R9 **Gail** ≈ S Austria
101 I21 **Gaildorf** Baden-Württemberg, S Germany 48°41′N 10°08′E
103 N15 **Gaillac** *var.* Gaillac-sur-Tarn. Tarn, S France 43°54′N 01°54′E
Gaillac-sur-Tarn *see* Gaillac
Gaillimh *see* Galway
Gaillimhe, Cuan na *see* Galway Bay
109 Q9 **Gailtaler Alpen** ▲▲ S Austria
63 J17 **Gaimán** Chaco, S Argentina 43°15′S 65°30′W
20 K8 **Gainesboro** Tennessee, S USA 36°20′N 85°41′W
23 V10 **Gainesville** Florida, SE USA 29°39′N 82°19′W
23 T2 **Gainesville** Georgia, SE USA 34°18′N 83°49′W
27 U8 **Gainesville** Missouri, C USA 36°37′N 92°28′W
25 T5 **Gainesville** Texas, SW USA 33°39′N 97°08′W
109 X5 **Gainfarn** Niederösterreich, NE Austria 47°59′N 16°11′E
97 N18 **Gainsborough** E England, United Kingdom 53°24′N 00°48′W
182 G6 **Gairdner, Lake** *salt lake* South Australia
Gaissane *see* Gáissát
92 L8 **Gáissát** *var.* Gaissane. ▲▲ N Norway
43 T15 **Gaital, Cerro** ▲ C Panama 08°37′N 80°04′W
21 W3 **Gaithersburg** Maryland, NE USA 39°08′N 77°13′W
163 U13 **Gaizhou** Liaoning, NE China 40°24′N 122°17′E
Gaizina Kalns *see* Gaiziņkalns
118 H7 **Gaiziņkalns** *var.* Gaizina Kalns. ▲ E Latvia 56°51′N 25°58′E
Gajac *see* Villeneuve-sur-Lot
39 S10 **Gakona** Alaska, USA 62°21′N 145°16′W
158 M16 **Gala** Xizang Zizhiqu, China 28°17′N 89°21′E
Galaassiya *see* Galaosiyo
Ğalāğıl *see* Jalājil
Galam, Pulau *see* Gelam, Pulau
62 J6 **Galán, Cerro** ▲ NW Argentina 25°54′S 66°45′W
111 H21 **Galanta** *Hung.* Galánta. Trnavský Kraj, W Slovakia 48°12′N 17°45′E
146 L11 **Galaosiyo** *Rus.* Galaassiya. Buxoro Viloyati, C Uzbekistan 39°53′N 64°25′E
57 B17 **Galápagos** *off.* Provincia de Galápagos. ◈ *province* W Ecuador, E Pacific Ocean
193 P8 **Galapagos Fracture Zone** *tectonic feature* E Pacific Ocean
Galapagos Islands *see* Colón, Archipiélago de
Galápagos, Islas de los *see* Colón, Archipiélago de
Galápagos, Provincia de *see* Galápagos
193 S9 **Galapagos Rise** *undersea feature* E Pacific Ocean 15°00′S 97°00′W
96 K13 **Galashiels** SE Scotland, United Kingdom 55°37′N 02°49′W
116 M12 **Galaţi** *Ger.* Galatz. Galaţi, E Romania 45°27′N 28°00′E
116 L12 **Galaţi** ◈ *county* E Romania
107 Q19 **Galatina** Puglia, SE Italy 40°10′N 18°10′E
107 Q19 **Galatone** Puglia, SE Italy 40°09′N 18°05′E
Galatz *see* Galaţi
21 R8 **Galax** Virginia, NE USA 36°40′N 88°56′W
146 J16 **Galaýmor** *Rus.* Kala-i-Mor. Mary Welaýaty, S Turkmenistan 35°40′N 62°28′E
Galcaio *see* Gaalkacyo
64 P11 **Gáldar** Gran Canaria, Islas Canarias, NE Atlantic Ocean 28°09′N 15°40′W
94 F11 **Galdhøpiggen** ▲ S Norway 61°30′N 08°08′E
40 I4 **Galeana** Chihuahua, N Mexico 30°08′N 107°38′W
41 O9 **Galeana** Nuevo León, NE Mexico 24°45′N 99°59′W
60 P9 **Galeão** ✈ (Rio de Janeiro) Rio de Janeiro, SE Brazil 22°48′S 43°16′W
171 R10 **Galela** Pulau Halmahera, E Indonesia 01°52′N 127°48′E
39 O9 **Galena** Alaska, USA 64°43′N 156°55′W
30 K10 **Galena** Illinois, N USA 42°25′N 90°25′W
27 R7 **Galena** Kansas, C USA 37°04′N 94°38′W
27 T8 **Galena** Missouri, C USA 36°45′N 93°30′W
45 V15 **Galeota Point** *headland* Trinidad, Trinidad and Tobago 10°07′N 60°59′W
105 P13 **Galera** Andalucía, S Spain 37°45′N 02°33′W
45 Y16 **Galera Point** *headland* Trinidad, Trinidad and Tobago 10°49′N 60°54′W
56 A5 **Galera, Punta** *headland* NW Ecuador 0°49′N 80°03′W
30 K12 **Galesburg** Illinois, N USA 40°57′N 90°22′W
30 J7 **Galesville** Wisconsin, N USA 44°04′N 91°21′W
18 F12 **Galeton** Pennsylvania, NE USA 41°43′N 77°38′W
116 H9 **Gâlgău** *Hung.* Galgó; *prev.* Gîlgău. Sălaj, NW Romania 47°17′N 23°43′E
Galgó *see* Gâlgău
Galgóc *see* Hlohovec
81 N15 **Galguduud** *off.* Gobolka Galguduud. ◈ *region* E Somalia
Galguduud, Gobolka *see* Galguduud
137 Q9 **Gali** W Georgia 42°40′N 41°39′E
125 N14 **Galich** Kostromskaya Oblast', NW Russian Federation 58°21′N 42°21′E
114 H7 **Galiche** Vratsa, NW Bulgaria 43°36′N 23°53′E
104 H3 **Galicia** *anc.* Gallaecia. ◈ *autonomous community* NW Spain
64 M8 **Galicia Bank** *undersea feature* E Atlantic Ocean 11°45′W 42°40′N
Galilee *see* HaGalil
181 W7 **Galilee, Lake** ◎ Queensland, NE Australia
Galilee, Sea of *see* Tiberias, Lake
106 E11 **Galileo Galilei** ✈ (Pisa) Toscana, C Italy 43°40′N 10°22′E
31 S12 **Galion** Ohio, N USA 40°43′N 82°47′W
Galka'yo *see* Gaalkacyo
146 K12 **Galkynyş** *prev. Rus.* Deynau, Dyanev, *Turkm.* Dänew. Lebap Welaýaty, NE Turkmenistan 39°16′N 63°10′E
80 H11 **Gallabat** Gedaref, E Sudan 12°57′N 36°10′E
Gallaecia *see* Galicia
147 O11 **G'allaorol** Jizzax Viloyati, C Uzbekistan 40°01′N 67°30′E
106 C7 **Gallarate** Lombardia, NW Italy 45°39′N 08°47′E
27 S2 **Gallatin** Missouri, C USA 39°54′N 93°57′W
20 J8 **Gallatin** Tennessee, S USA 36°22′N 86°28′W
33 R11 **Gallatin Peak** ▲ Montana, NW USA 45°22′N 111°21′W
33 R12 **Gallatin River** ≈ Montana/Wyoming, NW USA
155 J26 **Galle** *prev.* Point de Galle. Southern Province, SW Sri Lanka 06°04′N 80°12′E
105 S5 **Gállego** ≈ NE Spain
193 Q8 **Gallego Rise** *undersea feature* E Pacific Ocean 02°00′S 115°00′W
Gallegos *see* Río Gallegos
63 H23 **Gallegos, Río** ≈ Argentina/Chile
Gallia *see* France
22 K10 **Galliano** Louisiana, S USA 29°26′N 90°18′W
114 G13 **Gallikós** ≈ N Greece
37 S12 **Gallinas Peak** ▲ New Mexico, SW USA 34°14′N 105°47′W
54 H3 **Gallinas, Punta** *headland* NE Colombia 12°27′N 71°44′W
37 T11 **Gallinas River** ≈ New Mexico, SW USA
107 Q19 **Gallipoli** Puglia, SE Italy 40°08′N 18°E
Gallipoli *see* Gelibolu
Gallipoli Peninsula *see* Gelibolu Yarımadası
31 T15 **Gallipolis** Ohio, N USA 38°49′N 82°14′W
92 J12 **Gällivare** *Lapp.* Váhtjer. Norrbotten, N Sweden 67°08′N 20°39′E
109 T4 **Gallneukirchen** Oberösterreich, N Austria 48°22′N 14°25′E
93 G17 **Gällö** Jämtland, C Sweden 62°57′N 15°15′E
105 Q7 **Gallo** ≈ C Spain
107 I23 **Gallo, Capo** *headland* Sicilia, Italy, C Mediterranean Sea 38°13′N 13°18′E
37 P13 **Gallo Mountains** ▲▲ New Mexico, SW USA
18 G8 **Galloo Island** *island* New York, NE USA
97 H15 **Galloway, Mull of** *headland* S Scotland, United Kingdom 54°37′N 04°54′W
37 P10 **Gallup** New Mexico, SW USA 35°32′N 108°45′W
105 R5 **Gallur** Aragón, NE Spain 41°51′N 01°21′W
Gâlma *see* Guelma
163 N9 **Galshar** *var.* Buyant. Hentiy, C Mongolia 46°15′N 110°50′E
162 I6 **Galt** *var.* Ider. Hövsgöl, C Mongolia 48°45′N 99°52′E
35 O8 **Galt** California, W USA 38°13′N 121°19′W
74 C10 **Galtat-Zemmour** C Western Sahara 25°07′N 12°21′W
95 G22 **Galten** Midtjylland, C Denmark 56°09′N 09°54′E
Gålto *see* Kultsjön
97 D20 **Galtymore Mountain** *Ir.* Cnoc Mór na nGaibhlte. ▲ S Ireland 52°21′N 08°09′W
97 D20 **Galty Mountains** *Ir.* Na Gaibhlte. ▲▲ S Ireland
30 K11 **Galva** Illinois, N USA 41°10′N 90°02′W
25 X12 **Galveston** Texas, SW USA 29°17′N 94°48′W
25 W11 **Galveston Bay** *inlet* Texas, SW USA
25 W12 **Galveston Island** *island* Texas, SW USA
61 B18 **Gálvez** Santa Fe, C Argentina 32°03′S 61°14′W
97 C18 **Galway** *Ir.* Gaillimh. W Ireland 53°16′N 09°03′W
97 B18 **Galway** *Ir.* Gaillimh. *cultural region* W Ireland
97 B18 **Galway Bay** *Ir.* Cuan na Gaillimhe. *bay* W Ireland
83 F18 **Gam** Otjozondjupa, NE Namibia 20°10′S 20°51′E
164 L14 **Gamagōri** Aichi, Honshū, SW Japan 34°49′N 137°15′E
54 F7 **Gamarra** Cesar, N Colombia 08°21′N 73°46′W
Gámas *see* Kaamanen
158 L17 **Gamba** Xizang Zizhiqu, W China 28°13′N 88°32′E
Gamba *see* Zamtang
77 P14 **Gambaga** NE Ghana 10°32′N 00°28′W
80 G13 **Gambēla** Gambēla Hizboch, W Ethiopia 08°09′N 34°15′E
81 H14 **Gambēla Hizboch** ◈ *federal region* W Ethiopia
38 K10 **Gambell** Saint Lawrence Island, Alaska, USA 63°44′N 171°41′W
76 E12 **Gambia** *off.* Republic of The Gambia, The Gambia. ◆ *republic* W Africa
76 I12 **Gambia** *Fr.* Gambie. ≈ W Africa
64 K12 **Gambia Plain** *undersea feature* E Atlantic Ocean
Gambia, Republic of The *see* Gambia
Gambia, The *see* Gambia
Gambie *see* Gambia
31 T13 **Gambier** Ohio, N USA 40°22′N 82°24′W
191 Y13 **Gambier, Îles** *island group* E French Polynesia
182 G10 **Gambier Islands** *island group* South Australia
79 H19 **Gamboma** Plateaux, E Congo 01°53′S 15°51′E
79 G16 **Gamboula** Mambéré-Kadéï, SW Central African Republic 04°09′N 15°12′E
37 P10 **Gamerco** New Mexico, SW USA 35°34′N 108°45′W
137 V12 **Gamış Dağı** ▲ W Azerbaijan 40°18′N 46°15′E
Gamlakarleby *see* Kokkola
95 N18 **Gamleby** Kalmar, S Sweden 57°54′N 16°25′E
Gammelstad *see* Gammelstaden
93 J14 **Gammelstaden** *var.* Gammelstad. Norrbotten, N Sweden 65°38′N 22°05′E
Gammouda *see* Sidi Bouzid
155 J25 **Gampaha** Western Province, W Sri Lanka 07°05′N 80°00′E
155 K25 **Gampola** Central Province, C Sri Lanka 07°10′N 80°34′E
167 S5 **Gâm, Sông** ≈ N Vietnam
92 L7 **Gamvik** Finnmark, N Norway 71°04′N 28°08′E
150 H13 **Gan** Addu Atoll, C Maldives
Gan *see* Gansu, China
Gan *see* Jiangxi, China
Ganaane *see* Juba
37 O10 **Ganado** Arizona, SW USA 35°42′N 109°31′W
25 U12 **Ganado** Texas, SW USA 29°02′N 96°30′W
14 L14 **Gananoque** Ontario, SE Canada 44°21′N 76°11′W
Ganāveh *see* Bandar-e Gonāveh
137 V11 **Gäncä** *Rus.* Gyandzha; *prev.* Kirovabad, Yelisavetpol. W Azerbaijan 40°42′N 46°23′E
Ganchi *see* Ghonchí
Gand *see* Gent
82 B13 **Ganda** *var.* Mariano Machado, *Port.* Vila Mariano Machado. Benguela, W Angola 13°02′S 14°40′E
79 L22 **Gandajika** Kasai-Oriental, S Dem. Rep. Congo 06°42′S 24°01′E
153 O12 **Gandak** *Nep.* Nārāyāni. ≈ India/Nepal
13 U11 **Gander** Newfoundland and Labrador, SE Canada 48°56′N 54°33′W
13 U11 **Gander** ✈ Newfoundland and Labrador, E Canada 49°03′N 54°49′W
100 G11 **Ganderkesee** Niedersachsen, NW Germany 53°01′N 08°33′E
105 T7 **Gandesa** Cataluña, NE Spain 41°03′N 00°26′E
154 B10 **Gāndhīdhām** Gujarāt, W India 23°08′N 70°05′E
154 D10 **Gāndhīnagar** *state capital* Gujarāt, W India 23°12′N 72°37′E
154 F9 **Gāndhi Sāgar** ◎ C India
105 T11 **Gandia** *prev.* Gandía. Valenciana, E Spain 38°59′N 00°11′W
Gandía *see* Gandia
159 O10 **Gang** Qinghai, W China
152 G9 **Gangānagar** Rājasthān, NW India 29°54′N 73°56′E
152 I12 **Gangāpur** Rājasthān, N India 26°30′N 76°49′E
153 S17 **Ganga Sāgar** West Bengal, NE India 21°39′N 88°05′E
Gangavathi *see* Gangāwati
155 G17 **Gangāwati** *var.* Gangavathi. Karnātaka, C India 15°26′N 76°35′E
159 S9 **Gangca** *var.* Shaliuhe. Qinghai, C China 37°21′N 100°09′E
158 H14 **Gangdisê Shan** *Eng.* Kailas Range. ▲▲ W China
103 Q15 **Ganges** Hérault, S France 43°57′N 03°42′E
153 P13 **Ganges** *Ben.* Padma. ≈ Bangladesh/India *see also* Padma
Ganges *see* Padma
Ganges Cone *see* Ganges Fan
173 S3 **Ganges Fan** *var.* Ganges Cone. *undersea feature* N Bay of Bengal 12°00′N 87°00′E
153 U17 **Ganges, Mouths of the** *delta* Bangladesh/India
107 K23 **Gangi** *anc.* Engyum. Sicilia, Italy, C Mediterranean Sea 37°48′N 14°13′E
163 Y14 **Gangneung** *Jap.* Kōryō; *prev.* Kangnŭng. NE South Korea 37°47′N 128°51′E
152 K8 **Gangotri** Uttarakhand, N India 30°56′N 79°02′E
Gangra *see* Çankırı
153 S11 **Gangtok** *state capital* Sikkim, N India 27°20′N 88°39′E
159 W11 **Gangu** *var.* Daxiangshan. Gansu, C China 34°38′N 105°18′E
163 U5 **Gan He** ≈ NE China
171 S12 **Gani** Pulau Halmahera, E Indonesia 0°45′S 128°13′E
161 O12 **Gan Jiang** ≈ S China
163 U11 **Ganjig** *var.* Horqin Zuoyi Houqi. Nei Mongol Zizhiqu, N China 42°53′N 122°22′E
146 H15 **Gannaly** Ahal Welaýaty, S Turkmenistan 37°02′N 60°43′E
163 U7 **Gannan** Heilongjiang, NE China 47°58′N 123°36′E
103 P10 **Gannat** Allier, C France 46°06′N 03°12′E
33 T14 **Gannett Peak** ▲ Wyoming, C USA 43°10′N 109°39′W
29 O10 **Gannvalley** South Dakota, N USA 44°01′N 98°59′W
Ganqu *see* Lhünzhub
109 Y3 **Gänserndorf** Niederösterreich, NE Austria 48°21′N 16°43′E
Gansos, Lago dos *see* Goose Lake
159 T9 **Gansu** *var.* Gan, Gansu Sheng, Kansu. ◈ *province* N China
Gansu Sheng *see* Gansu
76 K16 **Ganta** *var.* Gahnpa. NE Liberia 07°15′N 08°59′W
182 H11 **Gantheaume, Cape** *headland* South Australia 36°04′S 137°28′E
Gantsevichi *see* Hantsavichy
161 Q6 **Ganyu** *var.* Qingkou. Jiangsu, E China 34°52′N 119°11′E
144 D12 **Ganyushkino** Atyrau, SW Kazakhstan 46°38′N 49°12′E
161 O12 **Ganzhou** Jiangxi, S China 25°51′N 114°59′E
Ganzhou *see* Zhangye
77 Q10 **Gao** Gao, E Mali 16°16′N 00°03′E
77 R10 **Gao** ◈ *region* SE Mali
161 O10 **Gao'an** Jiangxi, S China 28°24′N 115°27′E
Gaocheng *see* Litang
Gaoleshan *see* Xianfeng
161 R5 **Gaomi** Shandong, C China 36°23′N 119°45′E
161 N5 **Gaoping** Shanxi, C China 35°51′N 112°55′E
159 S8 **Gaotai** Gansu, N China 39°22′N 99°44′E
Gaoth Dobhair *see* Gweedore
77 O14 **Gaoua** SW Burkina 10°18′N 03°12′W
76 I13 **Gaoual** N Guinea 11°44′N 13°14′W
161 S14 **Gaoxiong** *var.* Kaohsiung, *Jap.* Takao, Takow. S Taiwan 22°36′N 120°17′E
161 S14 **Gaoxiong** ✈ S Taiwan 22°26′N 120°32′E
161 R7 **Gaoyou** *var.* Dayishan. Jiangsu, E China 32°48′N 119°26′E
161 R7 **Gaoyou Hu** ◎ E China
160 M15 **Gaozhou** Guangdong, S China 21°56′N 110°49′E
103 T13 **Gap** *anc.* Vapincum. Hautes-Alpes, SE France 44°33′N 06°05′E
146 E9 **Gaplaňgyr Platosy** *Rus.* Plato Kaplangky. *ridge* Turkmenistan/Uzbekistan
156 G13 **Gar** *var.* Shiquanhe. Xizang Zizhiqu, W China 32°31′N 80°04′E
Gar *see* Gar Xincun
Garabekevyul *see* Garabekewül
146 L13 **Garabekewül** *Rus.* Garabekevyul, Karabekaul. Lebap Welaýaty, E Turkmenistan 38°31′N 64°04′E
146 K15 **Garabil Belentligi** *Rus.* Vozvyshennost' Karabil'. ▲▲ S Turkmenistan
146 A8 **Garabogaz** *Rus.* Bekdash. Balkan Welaýaty, NW Turkmenistan 41°33′N 52°33′E
146 B9 **Garabogaz Aylagy** *Rus.* Zaliv Kara-Bogaz-Gol. *bay* NW Turkmenistan
146 A9 **Garabogazköl** *Rus.* Kara-Bogaz-Gol. Balkan Welaýaty, NW Turkmenistan 41°03′N 52°52′E
43 V16 **Garachiné** Darién, SE Panama 08°03′N 78°22′W
43 V16 **Garachiné, Punta** *headland* SE Panama 08°05′N 78°23′W
146 K12 **Garagan** *Rus.* Karagan. Ahal Welaýaty, C Turkmenistan 38°16′N 57°34′E
54 G10 **Garagoa** Boyacá, C Colombia 05°05′N 73°20′W
146 A11 **Garagöl'** *Rus.* Karagel'. Balkan Welaýaty, W Turkmenistan 39°24′N 53°13′E
146 F12 **Garagum** *var.* Garagumy, Qara Qum, *Eng.* Black Sand Desert, Kara Kum; *prev.* Peski Karakumy. *desert* C Turkmenistan
146 E12 **Garagum Kanaly** *var.* Kara Kum Canal, *Rus.* Karagumskiy Kanal, Karakumskiy Kanal. *canal* C Turkmenistan
Garagumy *see* Garagum
183 S4 **Garah** New South Wales, SE Australia 29°07′S 149°37′E
64 O11 **Garajonay** ▲ Gomera, Islas Canarias, NE Atlantic Ocean 28°07′N 17°14′W
114 M8 **Gara Khitrino** Shumen, NE Bulgaria 43°26′N 26°55′E
76 L13 **Garalo** Sikasso, SW Mali 10°58′N 07°26′W
Garam *see* Hron, Slovakia
146 L14 **Garamätnyýaz** *Rus.* Karamet-Niyaz. Lebap Welaýaty, E Turkmenistan 37°45′N 64°28′E
Garamszentkereszt *see* Žiar nad Hronom
77 Q13 **Garango** S Burkina 11°45′N 00°30′W
59 Q15 **Garanhuns** Pernambuco, E Brazil 08°53′S 36°28′W
188 H5 **Garapan** Saipan, S Northern Mariana Islands 15°12′S 145°43′E
Gárasavvon *see* Karesuando
Gárassavon *see* Kaaresuvanto
78 J13 **Garba** Bamingui-Bangoran, N Central African Republic 09°09′N 20°24′E
Garba *see* Jiulong
81 L16 **Garbahaarrey** *It.* Garba Harre. Gedo, SW Somalia 03°14′N 42°18′E
Garba Harre *see* Garbahaarrey
81 J18 **Garba Tula** Eastern, C Kenya 0°31′N 38°35′E
27 N9 **Garber** Oklahoma, C USA 36°26′N 97°35′W
34 L4 **Garberville** California, W USA 40°07′N 123°48′W
Garbo *see* Lhozhag
100 I12 **Garbsen** Niedersachsen, N Germany 52°25′N 09°36′E
60 K9 **Garça** São Paulo, S Brazil 22°14′S 49°36′W
104 L10 **García de Solá, Embalse de** ⊠ C Spain
103 Q14 **Gard** ◈ *department* S France
103 Q14 **Gard** ≈ S France
106 F7 **Garda, Lago di** *var.* Benaco, *Eng.* Lake Garda, *Ger.* Gardasee. ◎ NE Italy
Garda, Lake *see* Garda, Lago di
Gardan Divāl *see* Gardan Dīwāl
149 Q5 **Gardan Dīwāl** *var.* Gardan Divāl. Wardak, C Afghanistan 34°30′N 68°15′E
103 S15 **Gardanne** Bouches-du-Rhône, SE France 43°27′N 05°28′E
Gardasee *see* Garda, Lago di
100 L12 **Gardelegen** Sachsen-Anhalt, C Germany 52°31′N 11°25′E
14 B10 **Garden** ≈ Ontario, S Canada
23 X6 **Garden City** Georgia, SE USA 32°06′N 81°09′W
26 I6 **Garden City** Kansas, C USA 37°57′N 100°54′W
27 S5 **Garden City** Missouri, C USA 38°34′N 94°12′W
25 N8 **Garden City** Texas, SW USA 31°51′N 101°30′W
23 P3 **Gardendale** Alabama, S USA 33°39′N 86°48′W
31 P5 **Garden Island** *island* Michigan, N USA
22 M11 **Garden Island Bay** *bay* Louisiana, S USA
31 O5 **Garden Peninsula** *peninsula* Michigan, N USA
Garden State, The *see* New Jersey
95 I14 **Gardermoen** Akershus, S Norway 60°10′N 11°04′E
95 I14 **Gardermoen** ✈ (Oslo) Akershus, S Norway 60°12′N 11°05′E
Gardeyz/Gardez *see* Gardēz
149 Q6 **Gardēz** *var.* Gardeyz, Gordiaz; *prev.* Gardīz. Paktiyā, E Afghanistan 33°35′N 69°14′E
93 G14 **Gardiken** ◎ N Sweden
19 Q7 **Gardiner** Maine, NE USA 44°13′N 69°46′W
33 S12 **Gardiner** Montana, NW USA 45°02′N 110°42′W
19 N13 **Gardiners Island** *island* New York, NE USA
Gardner Island *see* Nikumaroro
19 T6 **Gardner Lake** ◎ Maine, NE USA
35 Q6 **Gardnerville** Nevada, W USA 38°55′N 119°44′W
Gardo *see* Qardho
106 F7 **Gardone Val Trompia** Lombardia, N Italy 45°40′N 10°11′E
Garegegasnjárga *see* Karigasniemi
38 F17 **Gareloi Island** *island* Aleutian Islands, Alaska, USA
Gares *see* Puente la Reina
106 B10 **Garessio** Piemonte, NE Italy 44°14′N 08°01′E
32 M9 **Garfield** Washington, NW USA 47°00′N 117°07′W
31 U11 **Garfield Heights** Ohio, N USA 41°25′N 81°36′W
Gargaliani *see* Gargaliánoi
115 D21 **Gargaliánoi** *var.* Gargaliani. Pelopónnisos, S Greece 37°04′N 21°38′E
107 N15 **Gargàno, Promontorio del** *headland* SE Italy 41°51′N 16°11′E
108 J8 **Gargellen** Graubünden, W Switzerland 46°57′N 09°55′E
93 I14 **Gargnäs** Västerbotten, N Sweden 65°19′N 18°00′E
118 C11 **Gargždai** Klaipėda, W Lithuania 55°42′N 21°24′E
154 J13 **Garhchiroli** Mahārāshtra, C India 20°14′N 79°58′E
153 O15 **Garhwa** Jhārkhand, N India 24°07′N 83°52′E
171 V13 **Gariau** Papua, E Indonesia 03°43′S 134°54′E
83 E24 **Garies** Northern Cape, W South Africa 30°30′S 18°00′E
107 K17 **Garigliano** ≈ C Italy
81 K19 **Garissa** Coast, E Kenya 0°27′S 39°39′E
21 V11 **Garland** North Carolina, SE USA 34°45′N 78°25′W
25 T6 **Garland** Texas, SW USA 32°50′N 96°37′W
36 L1 **Garland** Utah, W USA 41°43′N 112°07′W
106 D8 **Garlasco** Lombardia, N Italy 45°12′N 08°59′E
119 F14 **Garliava** Kaunas, S Lithuania 54°49′N 23°52′E
Garm *see* Gharm
142 M9 **Garm, Āb-e** *var.* Rūd-e Khersān. ≈ SW Iran
101 K25 **Garmisch-Partenkirchen** Bayern, S Germany 47°30′N 11°05′E
143 O5 **Garmsār** *prev.* Qishlaq. Semnān, N Iran 35°18′N 52°22′E
Garmser *see* Darwēshān
29 V12 **Garner** Iowa, C USA 43°06′N 93°36′W
21 U9 **Garner** North Carolina, SE USA 35°42′N 78°36′W
27 Q5 **Garnett** Kansas, C USA 38°16′N 95°15′W
99 M25 **Garnich** Luxembourg, SW Luxembourg 49°37′N 05°57′E
182 M8 **Garnpung, Lake** *salt lake* New South Wales, SE Australia
Garoe *see* Garoowe
Garoet *see* Garut
153 U13 **Gāro Hills** *hill range* NE India
102 K13 **Garonne** *anc.* Garumna. ≈ S France
80 P13 **Garoowe** *var.* Garoe. Nugaal, N Somalia 08°24′N 48°29′E
78 F12 **Garoua** *var.* Garua. Nord, N Cameroon 09°17′N 13°22′E
79 G14 **Garoua Boulaï** Est, E Cameroon 05°54′N 14°33′E
77 O10 **Garou, Lac** ◎ C Mali
95 L16 **Garphyttan** Örebro, C Sweden 59°18′N 14°54′E
29 R11 **Garretson** South Dakota, N USA 43°43′N 96°30′W
31 Q11 **Garrett** Indiana, N USA 41°21′N 85°08′W
33 Q10 **Garrison** Montana, NW USA 46°32′N 112°46′W
28 M4 **Garrison** North Dakota, N USA 47°36′N 101°25′W
25 X8 **Garrison** Texas, SW USA 31°49′N 94°29′W
28 L4 **Garrison Dam** *dam* North Dakota, N USA
104 J9 **Garrovillas** Extremadura, W Spain 39°43′N 06°33′W
Garrygala *see* Magtymguly
8 L8 **Garry Lake** ◎ Nunavut, N Canada
Gars *see* Gars am Kamp
109 W3 **Gars am Kamp** *var.* Gars. Niederösterreich, NE Austria 48°35′N 15°40′E
81 K20 **Garsen** Coast, S Kenya 02°16′S 40°07′E
Garshy *see* Garşy
14 F10 **Garson** Ontario, S Canada 46°33′N 80°51′W
109 T5 **Garsten** Oberösterreich, N Austria 48°00′N 14°24′E
146 A9 **Garşy** *var.* Garshy, *Rus.* Karshi. Balkan Welaýaty, NW Turkmenistan 40°45′N 52°50′E
Gartar *see* Qianning
102 M10 **Gartempe** ≈ C France
Gartog *see* Markam
Garua *see* Garoua
83 D21 **Garub** Karas, SW Namibia 26°33′S 16°00′E
Garumna *see* Garonne
169 P16 **Garut** *prev.* Garoet. Jawa, C Indonesia 07°15′S 107°55′E
185 C20 **Garvie Mountains** ▲▲ South Island, New Zealand
110 N12 **Garwolin** Mazowieckie, E Poland 51°54′N 21°36′E
25 U12 **Garwood** Texas, SW USA 29°25′N 96°26′W
158 G13 **Gar Xincun** *prev.* Gar. Xizang Zizhiqu, W China 32°04′N 80°01′E
31 N11 **Gary** Indiana, N USA 41°36′N 87°21′W
25 X7 **Gary** Texas, SW USA 32°00′N 94°21′W
158 G13 **Garyarsa** Xizang Zizhiqu, SW China 31°44′N 80°20′E
158 G13 **Gar Zangbo** ≈ W China
160 F8 **Garzê** Sichuan, C China 31°40′N 99°58′E
54 E12 **Garzón** Huila, S Colombia 02°14′N 75°37′W
Gasan-Kuli *see* Esenguly
31 P13 **Gas City** Indiana, N USA 40°29′N 85°36′W
102 K15 **Gascogne** *Eng.* Gascony. *cultural region* S France
26 V5 **Gasconade River** ≈ Missouri, C USA
Gascony *see* Gascogne
180 H9 **Gascoyne Junction** Western Australia 25°06′S 115°10′E
173 V8 **Gascoyne Plain** *undersea feature* E Indian Ocean
180 H9 **Gascoyne River** ≈ Western Australia
192 J11 **Gascoyne Tablemount** *undersea feature* N Tasman Sea 36°30′S 156°30′E
67 U6 **Gash** *var.* Nahr al Qāsh. ≈ W Sudan
149 X3 **Gasherbrum** ▲ NE Pakistan 35°39′N 76°34′E
Gas Hu *see* Gas Hure Hu
77 X12 **Gashua** Yobe, NE Nigeria 12°55′N 11°10′E
159 N9 **Gas Hure Hu** *var.* Gas Hu. ◎ C China
Gásluokta *see* Kjøpsvik
186 G7 **Gasmata** New Britain, E Papua New Guinea 06°12′S 150°25′E
23 V14 **Gasparilla Island** *island* Florida, SE USA
169 O13 **Gaspar, Selat** *strait* W Indonesia
15 Y6 **Gaspé** Québec, SE Canada 48°50′N 64°33′W
15 Z6 **Gaspé, Cap de** *headland* Québec, SE Canada 48°45′N 64°10′W
15 X6 **Gaspé, Péninsule de** *var.* Péninsule de la Gaspésie. *peninsula* Québec, SE Canada
Gaspésie, Péninsule de la *see* Gaspé, Péninsule de
77 W15 **Gassol** Taraba, E Nigeria 08°28′N 10°24′E
Gastein *see* Badgastein
21 R10 **Gastonia** North Carolina, SE USA 35°14′N 81°12′W
21 V8 **Gaston, Lake** ⊠ North Carolina/Virginia, SE USA
115 D19 **Gastoúni** Dytikí Elláda, S Greece 37°51′N 21°15′E
63 I17 **Gastre** Chubut, S Argentina 42°20′S 69°10′W
Gat *see* Ghāt
105 P15 **Gata, Cabo de** *cape* S Spain
Gata, Cape *see* Gátas, Akrotíri
105 T11 **Gata de Gorgos** Valenciana, E Spain 38°45′N 00°06′E
116 E12 **Gătaia** *Ger.* Gataja, *Hung.* Gátalja; *prev.* Gáttája. Timiş, W Romania 45°24′N 21°26′E
Gataja/Gátalja *see* Gătaia
121 P3 **Gátas, Akrotíri** *var.* Cape Gata. *headland* S Cyprus 34°34′N 33°03′E
104 J8 **Gata, Sierra de** ▲▲ W Spain
124 G13 **Gatchina** Leningradskaya Oblast', NW Russian Federation 59°34′N 30°06′E
21 P8 **Gate City** Virginia, NE USA 36°38′N 82°37′W
97 M14 **Gateshead** NE England, United Kingdom 54°57′N 01°37′W
21 X8 **Gatesville** North Carolina, SE USA 36°24′N 76°46′W
25 S8 **Gatesville** Texas, SW USA 31°26′N 97°46′W

◆ Country
● Country Capital
◇ Dependent Territory
○ Dependent Territory Capital
◈ Administrative Regions
✈ International Airport
▲ Mountain
▲▲ Mountain Range
Volcano
≈ River
◎ Lake
⊠ Reservoir

14 L12 **Gatineau** Québec, SE Canada 45°29′N 75°40′W
14 L11 **Gatineau** ≈ Ontario/Québec, SE Canada
21 N9 **Gatlinburg** Tennessee, S USA 35°42′N 83°30′W
Gatooma *see* Kadoma
Gáttája *see* Gătaia
43 T14 **Gatún, Lago** ▦ C Panama
59 N14 **Gaturiano** Piauí, NE Brazil 06°53′S 41°45′W
97 O22 **Gatwick** ✈ (London) SE England, United Kingdom 51°10′N 00°12′W
187 Y14 **Gau** *prev.* Ngau. *island* C Fiji
187 R12 **Gaua** *var.* Santa Maria. *Island* Banks Island, N Vanuatu
104 L16 **Gaucín** Andalucía, S Spain 36°31′N 05°19′W
Gauhāti *see* Guwāhāti
118 I8 **Gauja** *Ger.* Aa. ≈ Estonia/Latvia
118 I7 **Gaujiena** NE Latvia 57°31′N 26°24′E
94 H9 **Gauldalen** *valley* S Norway
21 R5 **Gauley River** ≈ West Virginia, NE USA
Gaul/Gaule *see* France
99 D19 **Gaurain-Ramecroix** Hainaut, SW Belgium 50°35′N 03°31′E
95 F15 **Gaustatoppen** ▲ S Norway 59°50′N 08°39′E
83 J21 **Gauteng** *off.* Gauteng Province; *prev.* Pretoria-Witwatersrand-Vereeniging. ⬖ *province* NE South Africa
Gauteng *see* Johannesburg, South Africa
Gauteng *see* Germiston, South Africa
Gauteng Province *see* Gauteng
137 U11 **Gavarr** *prev.* Kamo. C Armenia 40°21′N 45°07′E
143 P14 **Gāvbandī** Hormozgān, S Iran 27°07′N 53°21′E
115 H25 **Gavdopoúla** *island* SE Greece
115 H26 **Gávdos** *island* SE Greece
102 K16 **Gave de Pau** *var.* Gave-de-Pay. ≈ SW France
Gave-de-Pay *see* Gave de Pau
102 J16 **Gave d'Oloron** ≈ SW France
99 E18 **Gavere** Oost-Vlaanderen, NW Belgium 50°56′N 03°41′E
94 N13 **Gävle** *var.* Gäfle; *prev.* Gefle. Gävleborg, C Sweden 60°41′N 17°09′E
94 M11 **Gävleborg** *var.* Gäfleborg, Gefleborg. ⬖ *county* C Sweden
94 O13 **Gävlebukten** *bay* C Sweden
124 L16 **Gavrilov-Yam** Yaroslavskaya Oblast', W Russian Federation 57°19′N 39°52′E
182 I9 **Gawler** South Australia 34°38′S 138°44′E
182 G7 **Gawler Ranges** *hill range* South Australia
Gawso *see* Goaso
162 H11 **Gaxun Nur** ◎ N China
153 P14 **Gaya** Bihār, N India 24°48′N 85°E
77 S13 **Gaya** Dosso, SW Niger 11°52′N 03°28′E
Gaya *see* Kyjov
31 Q6 **Gaylord** Michigan, N USA 45°01′N 84°40′W
29 U9 **Gaylord** Minnesota, N USA 44°33′N 94°13′W
181 Y9 **Gayndah** Queensland, E Australia 25°37′S 151°31′E
125 T12 **Gayny** Komi-Permyatskiy Okrug, NW Russian Federation 60°19′N 54°15′E
Gaysin *see* Haysyn
Gayvorno *see* Hayvoron
138 E11 **Gaza** *Ar.* Ghazzah, *Heb.* 'Azza. NE Gaza Strip 31°30′N 34°E
83 L20 **Gaza** *off.* Província de Gaza. ⬖ *province* SW Mozambique
Gaz-Achak *see* Gazojak
147 Q9 **G'azalkent** *Rus.* Gazalkent. Toshkent Viloyati, E Uzbekistan 41°30′N 69°46′E
Gazalkent *see* G'azalkent
Gazandzhyk/Gazanjyk *see* Bereket
77 V12 **Gazaoua** Maradi, S Niger 13°28′N 07°54′E
Gaza, Província de *see* Gaza
138 E11 **Gaza Strip** *Ar.* Qita Ghazzah. *disputed region* SW Asia
136 M16 **Gaziantep** *var.* Gazi Antep; *prev.* Aintab, Antep. Gaziantep, S Turkey 37°04′N 37°21′E
136 M17 **Gaziantep** *var.* Gazi Antep. ⬖ *province* S Turkey
Gazi Antep *see* Gaziantep
114 M13 **Gaziköy** Tekirdağ, NW Turkey 40°45′N 27°18′E
121 Q2 **Gazimağusa** *var.* Famagusta, *Gk.* Ammóchostos. E Cyprus 35°07′N 33°57′E
121 Q2 **Gazimağusa Körfezi** *var.* Famagusta Bay, *Gk.* Kólpos Ammóchostos. *bay* E Cyprus
146 K11 **Gazli** Buxoro Viloyati, C Uzbekistan 40°09′N 63°28′E
146 I9 **Gazojak** *Rus.* Gaz-Achak. Lebap Welaýaty, NE Turkmenistan 41°12′N 61°24′E
79 K15 **Gbadolite** Equateur, NW Dem. Rep. Congo 04°14′N 20°59′E
76 K16 **Gbanga** *var.* Gbarnga. N Liberia 07°02′N 09°30′W
Gbarnga *see* Gbanga
77 S14 **Gbéroubouè** *var.* Béroubouay. N Benin 10°35′N 02°47′E
77 W16 **Gboko** Benue, S Nigeria 07°21′N 08°57′E
Gcuwa *see* Butterworth
110 J7 **Gdańsk** *Fr.* Dantzig, *Ger.* Danzig. Pomorskie, N Poland 54°22′N 18°35′E
Gdan'skaya Bukhta/Gdańsk, Gulf of *see* Danzig, Gulf of
Gdańska, Zakota *see* Danzig, Gulf of
Gdingen *see* Gdynia
124 F13 **Gdov** Pskovskaya Oblast', W Russian Federation 58°43′N 27°51′E
110 I6 **Gdynia** *Ger.* Gdingen. Pomorskie, N Poland 54°31′N 18°30′E
26 M10 **Geary** Oklahoma, C USA 35°37′N 98°19′W
Geavvú *see* Kevo
76 H12 **Gêba, Rio** ≈ C Guinea-Bissau
136 E11 **Gebze** Kocaeli, NW Turkey 40°48′N 29°26′E
80 H10 **Gedaref** *var.* Al Qaḍārif, El Gedaref. Gedaref, E Sudan 14°03′N 35°24′E
80 H10 **Gedaref** ⬖ *state* E Sudan
80 B11 **Gedid Ras el Fil** Southern Darfur, W Sudan 12°45′N 25°45′E
99 I23 **Gedinne** Namur, SE Belgium 49°57′N 04°55′E
136 E13 **Gediz** Kütahya, W Turkey 39°04′N 29°25′E
136 C14 **Gediz Nehri** ≈ W Turkey
81 N14 **Gedlegubē** Sumalē, E Ethiopia 06°53′N 45°08′E
81 L17 **Gedo** *off.* Gobolka Gedo. ⬖ *region* SW Somalia
Gedo, Gobolka *see* Gedo
95 I25 **Gedser** Sjælland, SE Denmark 54°34′N 11°57′E
99 I16 **Geel** *var.* Gheel. Antwerpen, N Belgium 51°10′N 04°59′E
183 N13 **Geelong** Victoria, SE Australia 38°10′S 144°21′E
Ge'e'mu *see* Golmud
99 I14 **Geertruidenberg** Noord-Brabant, S Netherlands 51°43′N 04°52′E
100 H10 **Geeste** ≈ NW Germany
100 J10 **Geesthacht** Schleswig-Holstein, N Germany 53°25′N 10°22′E
183 P17 **Geeveston** Tasmania, SE Australia 43°12′S 146°54′E
Gefle *see* Gävle
Gefleborg *see* Gävleborg
163 S5 **Gegan Gol** *prev.* Ergun, Gen He, Zuoqi. NE China
163 T5 **Gegen Gol** *prev.* Ergun Zuoqi, Genhe. Nei Mongol Zizhiqu, N China 50°48′N 121°30′E
158 G13 **Gê'gyai** Xizang Zizhiqu, W China 32°29′N 81°04′E
77 X12 **Geidam** Yobe, NE Nigeria 12°52′N 11°55′E
11 T11 **Geikie** ≈ Saskatchewan, C Canada
94 F13 **Geilo** Buskerud, S Norway 60°32′N 08°13′E
94 E10 **Geiranger** Møre og Romsdal, S Norway 62°07′N 07°12′E
101 I22 **Geislingen** *var.* Geislingen an der Steige. Baden-Württemberg, SW Germany 48°37′N 09°50′E
Geislingen an der Steige *see* Geislingen
81 F20 **Geita** Mwanza, NW Tanzania 02°52′S 32°12′E
95 G15 **Geithus** Buskerud, S Norway 59°56′N 09°58′E
160 H14 **Gejiu** *var.* Kochiu. Yunnan, S China 23°22′N 103°07′E
Gëkdepe *see* Gökdepe
146 E9 **Geklengkui, Solonchak** *var.* Solonchak Goklenkuy. *salt marsh* NW Turkmenistan
81 D14 **Gel** ≈ C South Sudan
107 K25 **Gela** *prev.* Terranova di Sicilia. Sicilia, Italy, C Mediterranean Sea 37°05′N 14°15′E
81 N14 **Geladī** SE Ethiopia 06°58′N 46°24′E
169 P13 **Gelam, Pulau** *var.* Pulau Galam. *island* N Indonesia
Gelaozu Miaozu Zhizhixian *see* Wuchuan
98 L11 **Gelderland** *prev. Eng.* Guelders. ⬖ *province* E Netherlands
98 J13 **Geldermalsen** Gelderland, C Netherlands 51°53′N 05°17′E
101 D14 **Geldern** Nordrhein-Westfalen, W Germany 51°31′N 06°19′E
99 K15 **Geldrop** Noord-Brabant, SE Netherlands 51°25′N 05°34′E
99 L17 **Geleen** Limburg, SE Netherlands 50°57′N 05°49′E
126 K14 **Gelendzhik** Krasnodarskiy Kray, SW Russian Federation 44°34′N 38°06′E
Gelib *see* Jilib
136 B11 **Gelibolu** *Eng.* Gallipoli. Çanakkale, NW Turkey 40°25′N 26°41′E
115 L14 **Gelibolu Yarımadası** *Eng.* Gallipoli Peninsula. *peninsula* NW Turkey
81 O14 **Gellinsor** Galguduud, C Somalia 06°25′N 46°44′E
101 H18 **Gelnhausen** Hessen, C Germany 50°12′N 09°12′E
101 E14 **Gelsenkirchen** Nordrhein-Westfalen, W Germany 51°30′N 07°05′E
83 C20 **Geluk** Hardap, SW Namibia 24°35′S 15°48′E
99 H20 **Gembloux** Namur, Belgium 50°34′N 04°42′E
79 J16 **Gemena** Equateur, NW Dem. Rep. Congo 03°13′N 19°49′E
99 L14 **Gemert** Noord-Brabant, SE Netherlands 51°33′N 05°41′E
136 E11 **Gemlik** Bursa, NW Turkey 40°26′N 29°10′E
Gem of the Mountains *see* Idaho
106 J6 **Gemona del Friuli** Friuli-Venezia Giulia, NE Italy 46°18′N 13°12′E
Gem State *see* Idaho
Genalē Wenz *see* Juba
169 R10 **Genali, Danau** ◎ Borneo, N Indonesia
99 G19 **Genappe** Walloon Brabant, C Belgium 50°39′N 04°27′E
137 P14 **Genç** Bingöl, E Turkey 38°44′N 40°35′E
Genck *see* Genk
98 M9 **Genemuiden** Overijssel, E Netherlands 52°38′N 06°03′E
63 K14 **General Acha** La Pampa, C Argentina 37°25′S 64°38′W
61 C21 **General Alvear** Buenos Aires, E Argentina 36°03′S 60°01′W
62 I12 **General Alvear** Mendoza, W Argentina 34°59′S 67°40′W
61 B20 **General Arenales** Buenos Aires, E Argentina 34°21′S 61°20′W
61 D21 **General Belgrano** Buenos Aires, E Argentina 35°47′S 58°30′W
194 H3 **General Bernardo O'Higgins** *Chilean research station* Antarctica 63°09′S 57°13′W
41 O8 **General Bravo** Nuevo León, NE Mexico 25°47′N 99°04′W
62 M7 **General Capdevila** Chaco, N Argentina 27°25′S 61°30′W
General Carrera, Lago *see* Buenos Aires, Lago
41 N9 **General Cepeda** Coahuila, NE Mexico 25°18′N 101°24′W
63 K15 **General Conesa** Río Negro, E Argentina 40°06′S 64°26′W
61 G18 **General Enrique Martínez** Treinta y Tres, E Uruguay 33°13′S 53°47′W
62 L3 **General Eugenio A. Garay** *var.* Fortín General Eugenio Garay; *prev.* Yrendagüé. Nueva Asunción, NW Paraguay 20°30′S 61°56′W
61 C18 **General Galarza** Entre Ríos, E Argentina 32°43′S 59°24′W
61 E22 **General Guido** Buenos Aires, E Argentina 36°36′S 57°45′W
General José F.Uriburu *see* Zárate
61 E22 **General Juan Madariaga** Buenos Aires, E Argentina 37°00′S 57°09′W
41 O16 **General Juan N Alvarez** ✈ (Acapulco) Guerrero, S Mexico 16°47′N 99°47′W
61 B22 **General La Madrid** Buenos Aires, E Argentina 37°17′S 61°20′W
61 E21 **General Lavalle** Buenos Aires, E Argentina 36°25′S 56°56′W
General Machado *see* Camacupa
62 I8 **General Manuel Belgrano, Cerro** ▲ W Argentina 29°05′S 67°05′W
41 O8 **General Mariano Escobero** ✈ (Monterrey) Nuevo León, NE Mexico 25°47′N 100°00′W
61 B20 **General O'Brien** Buenos Aires, E Argentina 34°54′S 60°45′W
62 K13 **General Pico** La Pampa, C Argentina 35°43′S 63°45′W
62 M7 **General Pinedo** Chaco, N Argentina 27°17′S 61°20′W
61 B20 **General Pinto** Buenos Aires, E Argentina 34°45′S 61°50′W
61 E22 **General Pirán** Buenos Aires, E Argentina 37°16′S 57°46′W
43 N15 **General, Río** ≈ S Costa Rica
63 I15 **General Roca** Río Negro, C Argentina 39°00′S 67°35′W
171 Q8 **General Santos** *off.* General Santos City. Mindanao, S Philippines 06°10′N 125°10′E
General Santos City *see* General Santos
41 O9 **General Terán** Nuevo León, NE Mexico 25°18′N 99°40′W
114 N7 **General Toshevo** *Rom.* I.G.Duca; *prev.* Casim, Kasimköj. Dobrich, NE Bulgaria 43°43′N 28°04′E
61 B20 **General Viamonte** Buenos Aires, E Argentina 35°01′S 61°00′W
61 A20 **General Villegas** Buenos Aires, E Argentina 35°02′S 63°01′W
Gênes *see* Genova
18 E11 **Genesee River** ≈ New York/Pennsylvania, NE USA
30 K11 **Geneseo** Illinois, N USA 41°27′N 90°08′W
18 F10 **Geneseo** New York, NE USA 42°48′N 77°46′W
57 L14 **Geneshuaya, Río** ≈ N Bolivia
23 Q8 **Geneva** Alabama, S USA 31°01′N 85°51′W
30 M10 **Geneva** Illinois, N USA 41°53′N 88°18′W
29 Q16 **Geneva** Nebraska, C USA 40°31′N 97°36′W
18 G10 **Geneva** New York, NE USA 42°52′N 76°58′W
31 U10 **Geneva** Ohio, NE USA 41°48′N 80°53′W
Geneva *see* Genève
108 B10 **Geneva, Lake** *Fr.* Lac de Genève, Lac Léman, le Léman, *Ger.* Genfer See. ◎ France/Switzerland
108 A10 **Genève** *Eng.* Geneva, *Ger.* Genf, *It.* Ginevra. Genève, SW Switzerland 46°13′N 06°09′E
108 A11 **Genève** *Eng.* Geneva, *Ger.* Genf, *It.* Ginevra. ⬖ *canton* SW Switzerland
108 A10 **Genève** *var.* Geneva. ✈ Vaud, SW Switzerland 46°13′N 06°06′E
Genève, Lac de *see* Geneva, Lake
Genf *see* Genève
Genfer See *see* Geneva, Lake
Genhe *see* Gegen Gol
Gen He *see* Gegan Gol
Genichesk *see* Heniches'k
104 L14 **Genil** ≈ S Spain
99 K18 **Genk** *var.* Genck. Limburg, NE Belgium 50°58′N 05°30′E
164 C13 **Genkai-nada** *gulf* Kyūshū, SW Japan
107 C19 **Gennargentu, Monti del** ▲▲ Sardegna, Italy, C Mediterranean Sea
99 M14 **Gennep** Limburg, SE Netherlands 51°43′N 05°58′E
30 M10 **Genoa** Illinois, N USA 42°06′N 88°41′W
29 Q15 **Genoa** Nebraska, C USA 41°27′N 97°43′W
Genoa *see* Genova
Genoa, Gulf of *see* Genova, Golfo di
106 D10 **Genova** *Eng.* Genoa; *anc.* Genua, *Fr.* Gênes. Liguria, NW Italy 44°28′N 09°E
106 D10 **Genova, Golfo di** *Eng.* Gulf of Genoa. *gulf* NW Italy
57 C17 **Genovesa, Isla** *var.* Tower Island. *island* Galapagos Islands, Ecuador, E Pacific Ocean
Genshū *see* Wonju
99 E17 **Gent** *Eng.* Ghent, *Fr.* Gand. Oost-Vlaanderen, NW Belgium 51°02′N 03°42′E
169 N16 **Genteng** Jawa, C Indonesia 07°21′S 106°20′E
100 M12 **Genthin** Sachsen-Anhalt, E Germany 52°24′N 12°10′E
27 R9 **Gentry** Arkansas, C USA 36°16′N 94°28′W
Genua *see* Genova
107 I15 **Genzano di Roma** Lazio, C Italy 41°42′N 12°42′E
163 Y17 **Geogeum-do** *prev.* Kŏgŭm-do. *island* S South Korea
163 Z16 **Geogeum-do** *Jap.* Kyōsai-tō; *prev.* Kŏje-do. *island* S South Korea
Geokchay *see* Göyçay
Geok-Tepe *see* Gökdepe
122 I3 **Georga, Zemlya** *Eng.* George Land. *island* Zemlya Frantsa-Iosifa, N Russian Federation
83 G26 **George** Western Cape, S South Africa 33°57′S 22°28′E
29 S11 **George** Iowa, C USA 43°20′N 96°00′W
13 O5 **George** ≈ Newfoundland and Labrador/Québec, E Canada
George F L Charles *see* Vigie
65 C25 **George Island** *island* S Falkland Islands
183 R10 **George, Lake** ◎ New South Wales, SE Australia
81 E18 **George, Lake** ◎ SW Uganda
23 W10 **George, Lake** ◎ Florida, SE USA
18 L8 **George, Lake** ▦ New York, NE USA
George Land *see* Georga, Zemlya
Georgenburg *see* Jurbarkas
George River *see* Kangiqsualujjuaq
64 G8 **Georges Bank** *undersea feature* W Atlantic Ocean 41°15′N 67°30′W
185 A21 **George Sound** *sound* South Island, New Zealand
65 F15 **Georgetown** ○ (Ascension Island) NW Ascension Island 17°56′S 14°25′W
181 V5 **Georgetown** Queensland, NE Australia 18°17′S 143°37′E
183 P15 **George Town** Tasmania, SE Australia 41°04′S 146°48′E
44 I4 **George Town** Great Exuma Island, C Bahamas 23°28′N 75°47′W
44 D8 **George Town** *var.* Georgetown. ○ (Cayman Islands) Grand Cayman, SW Cayman Islands 19°16′N 81°23′W
76 H12 **Georgetown** E Gambia 13°33′N 14°49′W
55 T8 **Georgetown** ● (Guyana) N Guyana 06°46′N 58°10′W
168 I7 **George Town** *var.* Penang, Pinang. Pinang, Peninsular Malaysia 05°28′N 100°20′E
45 Y14 **Georgetown** Saint Vincent, Saint Vincent and the Grenadines 13°19′N 61°09′W
21 Y4 **Georgetown** Delaware, NE USA 38°39′N 75°22′W
23 R6 **Georgetown** Georgia, SE USA 31°52′N 85°04′W
20 M5 **Georgetown** Kentucky, S USA 38°13′N 84°30′W
21 T13 **Georgetown** South Carolina, SE USA 33°23′N 79°18′W
25 S10 **Georgetown** Texas, SW USA 30°39′N 97°42′W
55 T8 **Georgetown** ✈ N Guyana 06°46′N 58°10′W
Georgetown *see* George Town
195 U16 **George V Coast** *physical region* Antarctica
194 J7 **George VI Ice Shelf** *ice shelf* Antarctica
194 J6 **George VI Sound** *sound* Antarctica
195 T15 **George V Land** *physical region* Antarctica
25 S14 **George West** Texas, SW USA 28°21′N 98°08′W
137 R9 **Georgia** *off.* Republic of Georgia, *Geor.* Sak'art'velo, *Rus.* Gruzinskaya SSR, Gruziya. ◆ *republic* SW Asia
23 S5 **Georgia** *off.* State of Georgia, *also known as* Empire State of the South, Peach State. ⬖ *state* SE USA
14 F12 **Georgian Bay** *lake bay* Ontario, S Canada
Georgia, Republic of *see* Georgia
10 L17 **Georgia, Strait of** *strait* British Columbia, W Canada
Georgi Dimitrov *see* Kostenets
Georgi Dimitrov, Yazovir *see* Koprinka, Yazovir
Georgiu-Dezh *see* Liski
145 W10 **Georgiyevka** Vostochnyy Kazakhstan, E Kazakhstan 49°19′N 81°35′E
Georgiyevka *see* Korday
127 N15 **Georgiyevsk** Stavropol'skiy Kray, SW Russian Federation 44°07′N 43°22′E
100 G13 **Georgsmarienhütte** Niedersachsen, NW Germany 52°13′N 08°02′E
195 O1 **Georg von Neumayer** *German research station* Antarctica 70°41′S 08°18′W
101 M16 **Gera** Thüringen, E Germany 50°51′N 12°13′E
101 K16 **Gera** ≈ C Germany
99 E19 **Geraardsbergen** Oost-Vlaanderen, SW Belgium 50°47′N 03°53′E
115 F21 **Geráki** Pelopónnisos, S Greece 36°56′N 22°46′E
27 W5 **Gerald** Missouri, C USA 38°24′N 91°20′W
47 V8 **Geral de Goiás, Serra** ▲▲ E Brazil
185 G20 **Geraldine** Canterbury, South Island, New Zealand 44°06′S 171°14′E
180 H11 **Geraldton** Western Australia 28°48′S 114°40′E
12 E11 **Geraldton** Ontario, S Canada 49°44′N 86°59′W
60 J12 **Geral, Serra** ▲▲ S Brazil
103 U6 **Gérardmer** Vosges, NE France 48°05′N 06°54′E
Gerasa *see* Jarash
Gerdauen *see* Zheleznodorozhnyy
39 Q11 **Gerdine, Mount** ▲ Alaska, USA 61°40′N 152°21′W
136 H11 **Gerede** Bolu, N Turkey 40°48′N 32°13′E
136 H11 **Gerede Çayı** ≈ N Turkey
148 M8 **Gereshk** Helmand, SW Afghanistan 31°50′N 64°32′E
101 L24 **Geretsried** Bayern, S Germany 47°51′N 11°28′E
105 P14 **Gérgal** Andalucía, S Spain 37°07′N 02°34′W
28 I14 **Gering** Nebraska, C USA 41°49′N 103°39′W
35 R3 **Gerlach** Nevada, W USA 40°38′N 119°21′W
Gerlachfalvi Csúcs/Gerlachovka *see* Gerlachovský štít
111 L18 **Gerlachovský štít** *var.* Gerlachovka, *Ger.* Gerlsdorfer Spitze, *Hung.* Gerlachfalvi Csúcs; *prev.* Stalinov Štít, *Ger.* Franz-Josef Spitze, *Hung.* Ferencz-Jósef Csúcs. ▲ N Slovakia 49°12′N 20°09′E
108 E8 **Gerlafingen** Solothurn, NW Switzerland 47°10′N 07°35′E
Gerlsdorfer Spitze *see* Gerlachovský štít
139 V3 **Germak** As Sulaymānīyah, E Iraq 35°49′N 46°09′E
German East Africa *see* Tanzania
Germanicopolis *see* Çankırı
Germanicum, Mare/German Ocean *see* North Sea
Germanovichi *see* Hyermanavichy
German Southwest Africa *see* Namibia
20 E10 **Germantown** Tennessee, S USA 35°06′N 89°51′W
101 I15 **Germany** *off.* Federal Republic of Germany, Bundesrepublik Deutschland, *Ger.* Deutschland. ◆ *federal republic* N Europe
Germany, Federal Republic of *see* Germany
101 L23 **Germering** Bayern, SE Germany 48°07′N 11°22′E
83 J21 **Germiston** *var.* Gauteng. Gauteng, NE South Africa 26°15′S 28°10′E
Gernika *see* Gernika-Lumo
105 P2 **Gernika-Lumo** *var.* Gernika, Guernica, Guernica y Lumo. País Vasco, N Spain 43°19′N 02°40′W
164 L12 **Gero** Gifu, Honshū, SW Japan 35°48′N 137°15′E
115 F22 **Geroliménas** Pelopónnisos, S Greece 36°28′N 22°25′E
Gerona *see* Girona
99 H21 **Gerpinnes** Hainaut, S Belgium 50°20′N 04°38′E
102 L15 **Gers** ⬖ *department* S France
102 L14 **Gers** ≈ S France
Gerunda *see* Girona
158 I13 **Gêrzê** *var.* Luring. Xizang Zizhiqu, W China 32°19′N 84°05′E
136 K10 **Gerze** Sinop, N Turkey 41°48′N 35°13′E
Gesoriacum *see* Boulogne-sur-Mer
Gessoriacum *see* Boulogne-sur-Mer
99 J21 **Gesves** Namur, SE Belgium 50°24′N 05°04′E
93 J20 **Geta** Åland, SW Finland 60°22′N 19°49′E
105 N8 **Getafe** Madrid, C Spain 40°18′N 03°44′W
95 J21 **Getinge** Halland, S Sweden 56°46′N 12°42′E
18 F16 **Gettysburg** Pennsylvania, NE USA 39°49′N 77°13′W
29 N8 **Gettysburg** South Dakota, N USA 45°00′N 99°57′W
194 K12 **Getz Ice Shelf** *ice shelf* Antarctica
137 S15 **Gevaş** Van, SE Turkey 38°16′N 43°05′E
Gevgeli *see* Gevgelija
113 Q20 **Gevgelija** *var.* Đevđelija, Djevdjelija, *Turk.* Gevgeli. SE Macedonia 41°09′N 22°30′E
103 T10 **Gex** Ain, E France 46°21′N 06°02′E
92 I3 **Geysir** *physical region* SW Iceland
136 F11 **Geyve** Sakarya, NW Turkey 40°32′N 30°18′E
80 G10 **Gezira** ⬖ *state* E Sudan
109 V3 **Gföhl** Niederösterreich, N Austria 48°30′N 15°27′E
83 H22 **Ghaap Plateau** *Afr.* Ghaapplato. *plateau* C South Africa
Ghaapplato *see* Ghaap Plateau
Ghaba *see* Al Ghābah
138 J8 **Ghāb, Tall** ▲ SE Syria 33°09′N 37°48′E
139 Q9 **Ghadaf, Wādī al** *dry watercourse* C Iraq
Ghadamès *see* Ghadāmis
74 M9 **Ghadāmis** *var.* Ghadamès, Rhadames. W Libya 30°08′N 09°30′E
141 Y10 **Ghadan** E Oman 20°20′N 57°58′E
75 O10 **Ghaddūwah** C Libya 26°36′N 14°26′E
147 Q11 **Ghafurov** *Rus.* Gafurov; *prev.* Sovetabad. NW Tajikistan 40°13′N 69°42′E
153 N12 **Ghāghara** ≈ S Asia
149 P13 **Ghaibi Dero** Sind, SE Pakistan 27°35′N 67°42′E
141 Y10 **Ghalat** E Oman 21°06′N 58°51′E
139 W11 **Ghamūkah, Hawr** ◎ S Iraq
77 P15 **Ghana** *off.* Republic of Ghana. ◆ *republic* W Africa
141 X12 **Ghānah** *spring/well* S Oman 18°35′N 56°34′E
Ghanongga *see* Ranongga
Ghansi/Ghansiland *see* Ghanzi
83 F18 **Ghanzi** *var.* Khanzi. Ghanzi, W Botswana 21°39′S 21°38′E
83 G19 **Ghanzi** *var.* Ghansi, Ghansiland, Khanzi. ⬖ *district* C Botswana
67 T14 **Ghanzi** *var.* Knanzi. ≈ Botswana/South Africa
Ghap'an *see* Kapan
138 F13 **Gharandal** Al'Aqabah, SW Jordan 30°12′N 35°18′E
139 U14 **Gharbīyah, Sha'īb al** ≈ S Iraq
Gharbt, Jabal al *see* Liban, Jebel
74 K7 **Ghardaïa** N Algeria 32°30′N 03°44′E
147 R12 **Gharm** *Rus.* Garm. C Tajikistan 39°03′N 70°25′E
149 P17 **Gharo** Sind, SE Pakistan 24°44′N 67°35′E
139 W10 **Gharrāf, Shaṭṭ al** ≈ S Iraq
Gharvān *see* Gharyān
75 O7 **Gharyān** *var.* Gharvān. NW Libya 32°10′N 13°01′E
74 M11 **Ghāt** *var.* Gat. SW Libya 24°58′N 10°11′E
Ghawdex *see* Gozo
141 U8 **Ghayathi** Abū Ẓaby, W United Arab Emirates 23°51′N 53°01′E
Ghazāl, Baḥr al *see* Ghazal, Bahr el
78 H9 **Ghazal, Bahr el** *var.* Soro. *seasonal river* C Chad
80 E13 **Ghazal, Bahr el** *var.* Baḥr al Ghazāl. ≈ N South Sudan
74 H6 **Ghazaouet** NW Algeria 35°08′N 01°50′W
152 J10 **Ghāziābād** Uttar Pradesh, N India 28°42′N 77°28′E
153 O13 **Ghāzīpur** Uttar Pradesh, N India 25°36′N 83°36′E
149 Q6 **Ghaznī** *var.* Ghazni. Ghaznī, E Afghanistan 33°31′N 68°24′E
149 P7 **Ghaznī** ⬖ *province* SE Afghanistan
Ghazzah *see* Gaza
Gheel *see* Geel
Ghelîzâne *see* Relizane
Ghent *see* Gent
Gheorghe Braṭul *see* Sfântu Gheorghe, Braṭul
Gheorghe Gheorghiu-Dej *see* Oneşti
116 J10 **Gheorgheni** *prev.* Gheorghieni, Sîn-Miclăuş, *Ger.* Niklasmarkt, *Hung.* Gyergyószentmiklós. Harghita, C Romania 46°43′N 25°36′E
Gheorghieni *see* Gheorgheni
116 H10 **Gherla** *Ger.* Neuschliss, *Hung.* Szamosújvár; *prev.* Armenierstadt. Cluj, NW Romania 47°02′N 23°55′E
Gheweifat *see* Ghuwayfāt
Ghilan *see* Gīlān
107 C18 **Ghilarza** Sardegna, Italy, C Mediterranean Sea 40°09′N 08°50′E
Ghilizane *see* Relizane
Ghimbi *see* Gīmbī
Ghiriş *see* Câmpia Turzii
103 Y15 **Ghisonaccia** Corse, France, C Mediterranean Sea 42°00′N 09°25′E
147 Q11 **Ghonchí** *Rus.* Ganchi. NW Tajikistan 39°57′N 69°10′E
153 T13 **Ghoraghat** Rajshahi, NW Bangladesh 25°18′N 89°20′E
148 J5 **Ghōrīān** *prev.* Ghūrīān. Herāt, W Afghanistan 34°20′N 61°26′E
149 R13 **Ghotki** Sind, SE Pakistan 28°00′N 69°21′E
Ghowr *see* Gōwr
147 T13 **Ghŭdara** *var.* Gudara, *Rus.* Kudara. SE Tajikistan 38°28′N 72°39′E
153 R13 **Ghugri** ≈ N India
147 S14 **Ghund** *Rus.* Gunt. ≈ SE Tajikistan
Ghurābīyah, Sha'īb al *see* Gharbīyah, Sha'īb al
Ghurdaqah *see* Al Ghurdaqah
Ghūrīān *see* Ghōrīān
141 T8 **Ghuwayfāt** *var.* Gheweifat. Abū Ẓaby, W United Arab Emirates 24°06′N 51°40′E
121 O14 **Ghuzayyil, Sabkhat** *salt lake* N Libya
126 J3 **Ghzatsk** Smolenskaya Oblast', W Russian Federation 55°33′N 35°00′E
115 G17 **Giáltra** Évvoia, C Greece 38°21′N 22°58′E
Giamame *see* Jamaame
167 U13 **Gia Nghia** *var.* Đak Nông. Đăc Lăc, S Vietnam 11°58′N 107°42′E
114 F13 **Giannitsá** *var.* Yiannitsá. Kentrikí Makedonía, N Greece 40°49′N 22°24′E
107 F14 **Giannutri, Isola di** *island* Archipelago Toscano, C Italy
96 F13 **Giant's Causeway** *Ir.* Clochán an Aifir. *lava flow* N Northern Ireland, United Kingdom
167 S15 **Gia Rai** Minh Hai, S Vietnam 09°14′N 105°28′E
107 L24 **Giarre** Sicilia, Italy, C Mediterranean Sea 37°44′N 15°12′E
44 I7 **Gibara** Holguín, E Cuba 21°09′N 76°11′W
29 O16 **Gibbon** Nebraska, C USA 40°45′N 98°50′W
32 K11 **Gibbon** Oregon, NW USA 45°40′N 118°22′W
33 P11 **Gibbonsville** Idaho, NW USA 45°33′N 113°55′W
64 A13 **Gibbs Hill** *hill* S Bermuda
92 I9 **Gibostad** Troms, N Norway 69°21′N 18°01′E
104 I14 **Gibraleón** Andalucía, S Spain 37°23′N 06°58′W
104 L16 **Gibraltar** ○ (Gibraltar) S Gibraltar 36°08′N 05°21′W
104 L16 **Gibraltar** ◇ *UK dependent territory* SW Europe
Gibraltar, Détroit de/Gibraltar, Estrecho de *see* Gibraltar, Strait of
104 J17 **Gibraltar, Strait of** *Fr.* Détroit de Gibraltar, *Sp.* Estrecho de Gibraltar. *strait* Atlantic Ocean/Mediterranean Sea
31 S11 **Gibsonburg** Ohio, N USA 41°22′N 83°19′W
30 M13 **Gibson City** Illinois, N USA 40°27′N 88°24′W
180 L8 **Gibson Desert** *desert* Western Australia
10 L17 **Gibsons** British Columbia, SW Canada 49°24′N 123°32′W
149 N12 **Gīdār** Baluchistān, SW Pakistan 28°16′N 66°00′E
155 I17 **Giddalūr** Andhra Pradesh, E India 15°24′N 78°54′E
25 U10 **Giddings** Texas, SW USA 30°12′N 96°59′W
27 Y8 **Gideon** Missouri, C USA 36°27′N 89°55′W
81 I15 **Gīdolē** Southern Nationalities, S Ethiopia 05°31′N 37°26′E
Giebnegáisi *see* Kebnekaise
118 H13 **Giedraičiai** Utena, E Lithuania 55°05′N 25°16′E
103 O7 **Gien** Loiret, C France 47°40′N 02°37′E
101 G17 **Giessen** Hessen, W Germany 50°35′N 08°41′E
98 O6 **Gieten** Drenthe, NE Netherlands 53°00′N 06°43′E
23 Y13 **Gifford** Florida, SE USA 27°40′N 80°24′W
9 O5 **Gifford** ≈ Baffin Island, Nunavut, NE Canada
100 J12 **Gifhorn** Niedersachsen, N Germany 52°28′N 10°33′E
11 P13 **Gift Lake** Alberta, W Canada 55°49′N 115°57′W
164 L13 **Gifu** *var.* Gihu. Gifu, Honshū, SW Japan 35°24′N 136°46′E
164 K13 **Gifu** *off.* Gifu-ken, *var.* Gihu. ⬖ *prefecture* Honshū, SW Japan
Gifu-ken *see* Gifu
126 M13 **Gigant** Rostovskaya Oblast', SW Russian Federation 46°29′N 41°18′E
40 E8 **Giganta, Sierra de la** ▲▲ NW Mexico
54 E12 **Gigante** Huila, S Colombia 02°24′N 75°34′W
114 I7 **Gigen** Pleven, N Bulgaria 43°40′N 24°31′E
Giggiga *see* Jijiga
96 G12 **Gigha Island** *island* SW Scotland, United Kingdom
107 E14 **Giglio, Isola del** *island* Archipelago Toscano, C Italy
Gihu *see* Gifu
146 L11 **G'ijduvon** *Rus.* Gizhduvon. Buxoro Viloyati, C Uzbekistan 40°06′N 64°38′E
104 L2 **Gijón** *var.* Xixón. Asturias, NW Spain 43°32′N 05°40′W
81 D20 **Gikongoro** SW Rwanda 02°30′S 29°32′E
36 K14 **Gila Bend** Arizona, SW USA 32°57′N 112°43′W
36 J14 **Gila Bend Mountains** ▲▲ Arizona, SW USA
36 I15 **Gila Mountains** ▲▲ Arizona, SW USA
37 N14 **Gila Mountains** ▲▲ Arizona, SW USA
142 M4 **Gīlān** *off.* Ostān-e Gīlān, *var.* Ghilan, Guilan. ⬖ *province* NW Iran
Gīlān, Ostān-e *see* Gīlān
36 L14 **Gila River** ≈ Arizona, SW USA
29 W4 **Gilbert** Minnesota, N USA 47°29′N 92°27′W
Gilbert Islands *see* Tungaru
10 L16 **Gilbert, Mount** ▲ British Columbia, SW Canada 50°49′N 124°03′W
181 U4 **Gilbert River** ≈ Queensland, NE Australia
0 C6 **Gilbert Seamounts** *undersea feature* NE Pacific Ocean 52°50′N 150°10′W
33 S7 **Gildford** Montana, NW USA 48°34′N 110°21′W
83 P15 **Gilé** Zambézia, NE Mozambique 16°10′S 28°17′E
30 K4 **Gile Flowage** ◎ Wisconsin, N USA
182 G7 **Giles, Lake** *salt lake* South Australia
Gilf Kebir Plateau *see* Haḍabat al Jilf al Kabīr
183 R6 **Gilgandra** New South Wales, SE Australia 31°43′S 148°39′E
Gilgău *see* Gâlgău
81 I19 **Gilgil** Rift Valley, SW Kenya 0°29′S 36°19′E
183 S4 **Gil Gil Creek** ≈ New South Wales, SE Australia
149 V3 **Gilgit** Jammu and Kashmir, NE Pakistan 35°54′N 74°20′E
149 V3 **Gilgit** ≈ N Pakistan
11 X11 **Gillam** Manitoba, C Canada 56°25′N 94°45′W
95 J22 **Gilleleje** Hovedstaden, E Denmark 56°05′N 12°17′E
30 K14 **Gillespie** Illinois, N USA 39°07′N 89°49′W
27 W13 **Gillett** Arkansas, C USA 34°07′N 91°22′W
33 X12 **Gillette** Wyoming, C USA 44°17′N 105°30′W
97 P22 **Gillingham** SE England, United Kingdom 51°24′N 00°33′E
195 X6 **Gillock Island** *island* Antarctica
173 O16 **Gillot** ✈ (St-Denis) N Réunion 20°53′S 55°31′E
65 H25 **Gill Point** *headland* E Saint Helena 15°59′S 05°38′W
30 M12 **Gilman** Illinois, N USA 40°44′N 87°58′W
25 W6 **Gilmer** Texas, SW USA 32°44′N 94°58′W
Gilolo *see* Halmahera, Pulau
81 G14 **Gīlo Wenz** ≈ SW Ethiopia
35 O10 **Gilroy** California, W USA 37°00′N 121°34′W
123 Q12 **Gilyuy** ≈ SE Russian Federation
99 I14 **Gilze** Noord-Brabant, S Netherlands 51°33′N 04°56′E
165 R16 **Gima** Okinawa, Kume-jima, SW Japan
80 H13 **Gīmbī** *It.* Ghimbi. Oromīya, C Ethiopia 09°13′N 35°39′E
163 Y15 **Gimcheon** *prev.* Kimch'ŏn. C South Korea 36°08′N 128°06′E
163 Z16 **Gimhae** *prev.* Kim Hae. ✈ (Busan) SE South Korea 35°10′N 128°57′E
45 T12 **Gimie, Mount** ▲ C Saint Lucia 13°51′N 61°00′W
11 X16 **Gimli** Manitoba, S Canada 50°39′N 97°00′W
Gimma *see* Jīma
95 O14 **Gimo** Uppsala, C Sweden 60°11′N 18°12′E
102 L15 **Gimone** ≈ S France
Gimpoe *see* Gimpu
171 N12 **Gimpu** *prev.* Gimpoe. Sulawesi, C Indonesia 01°38′S 120°00′E
182 F5 **Gina** South Australia 29°56′S 134°33′E
Ginevra *see* Genève
99 J19 **Gingelom** Limburg, NE Belgium 50°46′N 05°09′E
180 I12 **Gingin** Western Australia 31°22′S 115°51′E
171 Q7 **Gingoog** Mindanao, S Philippines 08°47′N 125°05′E
81 K14 **Gīnīr** Oromīya, C Ethiopia 07°12′N 40°43′E
Giohar *see* Jawhar
107 O17 **Gióia del Colle** Puglia, SE Italy 40°47′N 16°56′E
107 M22 **Gioia, Golfo di** *gulf* S Italy
Giona *see* Gkióna
115 I16 **Gioúra** *island* Vóreies Sporádes, Greece, Aegean Sea
107 O17 **Giovinazzo** Puglia, SE Italy 41°11′N 16°40′E
Gipeswic *see* Ipswich
Gipuzkoa *see* Guipúzcoa
Giran *see* Ilan
30 K14 **Girard** Illinois, N USA 39°27′N 89°46′W
27 R7 **Girard** Kansas, C USA 37°30′N 94°50′W
25 O6 **Girard** Texas, SW USA 33°18′N 100°38′W
54 E10 **Girardot** Cundinamarca, C Colombia 04°19′N 74°47′W
172 M7 **Giraud Seamount** *undersea feature* SW Indian Ocean 09°57′S 46°55′E
83 A15 **Giraul** ≈ SW Angola
96 L9 **Girdle Ness** *headland* NE Scotland, United Kingdom 57°09′N 02°04′W

◆ Country
● Country Capital
◇ Dependent Territory
○ Dependent Territory Capital
⬖ Administrative Regions
✈ International Airport
▲ Mountain
▲▲ Mountain Range
Volcano
≈ River
◎ Lake
▦ Reservoir

137 N11 **Giresun** *var.* Kerasunt; *anc.* Cerasus, Pharnacia. Giresun, NE Turkey 40°55′N 38°35′E
137 N12 **Giresun** *var.* Kerasunt. ◆ *province* NE Turkey
137 N12 **Giresun Dağları** ▲ N Turkey
Girga *see* Jirjā
Girgeh *see* Jirjā
Girgenti *see* Agrigento
153 Q15 **Girīdīh** Jhārkhand, NE India 24°10′N 86°20′E
183 P6 **Girilambone** New South Wales, SE Australia 31°19′S 146°57′E
Girin *see* Jilin
121 W10 **Girne** *Gk.* Kerýneia, Kyrenia. N Cyprus 35°20′N 33°20′E
Giron *see* Kiruna
105 X5 **Girona** *var.* Gerona; *anc.* Gerunda. Cataluña, NE Spain 41°59′N 02°49′E
105 W5 **Girona** *var.* Gerona. ◆ *province* Cataluña, NE Spain
102 J12 **Gironde** ◆ *department* SW France
102 J11 **Gironde** *estuary* SW France
105 V5 **Gironella** Cataluña, NE Spain 42°02′N 01°53′E
103 N15 **Girou** ⚡ S France
97 H14 **Girvan** W Scotland, United Kingdom 55°14′N 04°53′W
24 M9 **Girvin** Texas, SW USA 31°05′N 102°24′W
184 Q9 **Gisborne** Gisborne, North Island, New Zealand 38°41′S 178°01′E
184 P9 **Gisborne** *off.* Gisborne District. ◆ *unitary authority* North Island, New Zealand
Gisborne District *see* Gisborne
Giseifu *see* Uijeongbu
Gisenye *see* Gisenyi
81 D19 **Gisenyi** *var.* Gisenye. NW Rwanda 01°42′S 29°18′E
95 K20 **Gislaved** Jönköping, S Sweden 57°19′N 13°30′E
103 N4 **Gisors** Eure, N France 49°18′N 01°46′E
Gissar *see* Hisor
147 P12 **Gissar Range** *Rus.* Gissarskiy Khrebet. ▲ Tajikistan/Uzbekistan
Gissarskiy Khrebet *see* Gissar Range
99 B16 **Gistel** West-Vlaanderen, W Belgium 51°09′N 02°58′E
108 F9 **Giswil** Obwalden, C Switzerland 46°49′N 08°11′E
115 B16 **Gitánes** *ancient monument* Ípeiros, W Greece
81 E20 **Gitarama** C Rwanda 02°05′S 29°45′E
81 E20 **Gitega** C Burundi 03°20′S 29°56′E
Githio *see* Gýtheio
108 H11 **Giubiasco** Ticino, S Switzerland 46°11′N 09°01′E
106 K13 **Giulianova** Abruzzi, C Italy 42°45′N 13°58′E
Giulie, Alpi *see* Julian Alps
Giumri *see* Gyumri
116 M13 **Giurgeni** Ialomiţa, SE Romania 44°45′N 27°48′E
116 J15 **Giurgiu** Giurgiu, S Romania 43°54′N 25°58′E
116 J14 **Giurgiu** ◆ *county* SE Romania
95 F22 **Give** Syddanmark, C Denmark 55°51′N 09°15′E
103 R2 **Givet** Ardennes, N France 50°08′N 04°50′E
103 R11 **Givors** Rhône, E France 45°35′N 04°47′E
83 K19 **Giyani** Limpopo, NE South Africa 23°20′S 30°37′E
80 I13 **Giyon** Oromīya, C Ethiopia 08°31′N 37°56′E
75 W8 **Giza** *var.* Al Jīzah, El Giza, Gizeh. N Egypt 30°01′N 31°13′E
75 V8 **Giza, Pyramids of** *ancient monument* N Egypt
Gizhduvon *see* G'ijduvon
123 U8 **Gizhiga** Magadanskaya Oblast', E Russian Federation 61°58′N 160°16′E
123 T9 **Gizhiginskaya Guba** *bay* E Russian Federation
186 K8 **Gizo** Gizo, NW Solomon Islands 08°03′S 156°49′E
110 N7 **Giżycko** *Ger.* Lötzen. Warmińsko-Mazurskie, NE Poland 54°03′N 21°48′E
Gízymałów *see* Hrymayliv
113 M17 **Gjakovë** *Serb.* Đakovica. W Kosovo 42°22′N 20°30′E
94 F12 **Gjende** ◎ S Norway
113 L16 **Gjeravicë** *Serb.* Đeravica. ▲ Serbia 42°33′N 20°08′E
95 F17 **Gjerstad** Aust-Agder, S Norway 58°54′N 09°03′E
113 O17 **Gjilan** *Serb.* Gnjilane. E Kosovo 42°27′N 21°28′E
Gjinokastër *see* Gjirokastër
113 L23 **Gjirokastër** *var.* Gjirokastra; *prev.* Gjinokastër, *Gk.* Argyrokastron, *It.* Argirocastro. Gjirokastër, S Albania 40°04′N 20°09′E
113 L22 **Gjirokastër** ◆ *district* S Albania
Gjirokastra *see* Gjirokastër
9 N7 **Gjoa Haven** *var.* Uqsuqtuuq. King William Island, Nunavut, NW Canada 68°38′N 95°57′W
94 H13 **Gjøvik** Oppland, S Norway 60°47′N 10°40′E
113 J22 **Gjuhëzës, Kepi i** *headland* SW Albania 40°25′N 19°19′E
Gjurgjevac *see* Đurđevac
115 E18 **Gkióna** *var.* Giona. ▲ C Greece
121 R3 **Gkréko, Akrotíri** *var.* Cape Greco, Pidálion. *cape* E Cyprus
99 I18 **Glabbeek-Zuurbemde** Vlaams Brabant, C Belgium 50°54′N 04°58′E
13 R14 **Glace Bay** Cape Breton Island, Nova Scotia, SE Canada 46°12′N 59°57′W
11 O16 **Glacier** British Columbia, SW Canada 51°12′N 117°33′W
39 W12 **Glacier Bay** *inlet* Alaska, USA
32 I7 **Glacier Peak** ▲ Washington, NW USA 48°06′N 121°06′W
159 N13 **Gladaindong Feng** ▲ C China 33°24′N 91°00′E
21 Q7 **Glade Spring** Virginia, NE USA 36°47′N 81°46′W
43 W7 **Gladewater** Texas, SW USA 32°32′N 94°57′W
181 Y8 **Gladstone** Queensland, E Australia 23°52′S 151°16′E
182 I8 **Gladstone** South Australia 33°16′S 138°21′E
11 X16 **Gladstone** Manitoba, S Canada 50°12′N 98°56′W
31 O5 **Gladstone** Michigan, N USA 45°51′N 87°01′W
27 R4 **Gladstone** Missouri, C USA 39°12′N 94°33′W
31 Q7 **Gladwin** Michigan, N USA 43°58′N 84°29′W
95 J15 **Glafsfjorden** ◎ C Sweden
92 H2 **Gláma** *physical region* NW Iceland
94 I12 **Gláma** *var.* Glommen. ⚡ S Norway
112 F13 **Glamoč** Federacija Bosna I Hercegovina, NW Bosnia and Herzegovina 44°01′N 16°51′E
97 J22 **Glamorgan** *cultural region* S Wales, United Kingdom
95 G24 **Glamsbjerg** Syddtjylland, C Denmark 55°17′N 10°07′E
171 Q8 **Glan** Mindanao, S Philippines 05°49′N 125°11′E
109 T9 **Glan** ⚡ SE Austria
101 F19 **Glan** ⚡ W Germany
95 M17 **Glan** ◎ S Sweden
Glaris *see* Glarus
108 H9 **Glarner Alpen** *Eng.* Glarus Alps. ▲ E Switzerland
108 H8 **Glarus** Glarus, E Switzerland 47°03′N 09°04′E
108 H9 **Glarus** *Fr.* Glaris. ◆ *canton* C Switzerland
Glarus Alps *see* Glarner Alpen
27 N3 **Glasco** Kansas, C USA 39°21′N 97°50′W
96 I12 **Glasgow** S Scotland, United Kingdom 55°53′N 04°15′W
20 K7 **Glasgow** Kentucky, S USA 37°00′N 85°54′W
27 T4 **Glasgow** Missouri, C USA 39°13′N 92°51′W
33 W7 **Glasgow** Montana, NW USA 48°12′N 106°37′W
21 T6 **Glasgow** Virginia, NE USA 37°37′N 79°27′W
96 I12 **Glasgow** ✈ W Scotland, United Kingdom 55°52′N 04°27′W
11 S14 **Glaslyn** Saskatchewan, S Canada 53°20′N 108°18′W
18 I16 **Glassboro** New Jersey, NE USA 39°40′N 75°05′W
24 L10 **Glass Mountains** ▲ Texas, SW USA
97 K23 **Glastonbury** SW England, United Kingdom 51°09′N 02°43′W
Glatz *see* Kłodzko
101 N16 **Glauchau** Sachsen, E Germany 50°48′N 12°32′E
Glavn'a Morava *see* Velika Morava
Glavnik *see* Gllamnik
127 T1 **Glazov** Udmurtskaya Respublika, NW Russian Federation 58°06′N 52°38′E
Glda *see* Gwda
109 U8 **Gleinalpe** ▲ SE Austria
109 W8 **Gleisdorf** Steiermark, SE Austria 47°07′N 15°43′E
Gleiwitz *see* Gliwice
39 S11 **Glenallen** Alaska, USA 62°06′N 145°33′W
102 F7 **Glénan, Îles** *island group* NW France
185 G21 **Glenavy** Canterbury, South Island, New Zealand 44°53′S 171°04′E
10 H5 **Glenboyle** Yukon Territory, NW Canada 63°55′N 138°43′W
21 X3 **Glen Burnie** Maryland, NE USA 39°09′N 76°37′W
36 L8 **Glen Canyon** *canyon* Utah, W USA
36 L8 **Glen Canyon Dam** *dam* Arizona, SW USA
30 K15 **Glen Carbon** Illinois, N USA 38°45′N 89°58′W
14 E17 **Glencoe** Ontario, S Canada 42°44′N 81°42′W
83 K22 **Glencoe** KwaZulu/Natal, E South Africa 28°10′S 30°15′E
29 U9 **Glencoe** Minnesota, N USA 44°46′N 94°09′W
96 H10 **Glen Coe** *valley* N Scotland, United Kingdom
36 K13 **Glendale** Arizona, SW USA 33°32′N 112°11′W
35 S15 **Glendale** California, W USA 34°09′N 118′20′W
182 G5 **Glendambo** South Australia 30°59′S 135°45′E
33 Y8 **Glendive** Montana, NW USA 47°08′N 104°42′W
33 Y15 **Glendo** Wyoming, C USA 42°27′N 105°01′W
55 S10 **Glendor Mountains** C Guyana
182 K12 **Glenelg River** ⚡ South Australia/Victoria, SE Australia
29 P4 **Glenfield** North Dakota, N USA 47°25′N 98°33′W
25 V12 **Glen Flora** Texas, SW USA 29°22′N 96°12′W
181 P7 **Glen Helen** Northern Territory, N Australia 23°45′S 132°46′E
183 U5 **Glen Innes** New South Wales, SE Australia 29°42′S 151°45′E
31 P6 **Glen Lake** ◎ Michigan, N USA
10 I7 **Glenlyon Peak** ▲ Yukon Territory, W Canada 62°32′N 134°51′W
37 N16 **Glenn, Mount** ▲ Arizona, SW USA 31°55′N 110°00′W
33 N15 **Glenns Ferry** Idaho, NW USA 42°57′N 115°18′W
23 W6 **Glennville** Georgia, SE USA 31°56′N 81°55′W
10 J10 **Glenora** British Columbia, W Canada 57°52′N 131°16′W
182 M11 **Glenorchy** Victoria, SE Australia 36°56′S 142°39′E
183 V5 **Glenreagh** New South Wales, SE Australia 30°04′S 153°00′E
33 X15 **Glenrock** Wyoming, C USA 42°51′N 105°52′W
96 K11 **Glenrothes** E Scotland, United Kingdom 56°11′N 03°09′W
18 L9 **Glens Falls** New York, NE USA 43°18′N 73°38′W
97 D14 **Glenties** *Ir.* Na Gleannta. Donegal, NW Ireland 54°47′N 08°17′W
28 L5 **Glen Ullin** North Dakota, N USA 46°49′N 101°49′W
21 R4 **Glenville** West Virginia, NE USA 38°57′N 80°51′W
27 T12 **Glenwood** Arkansas, C USA 34°19′N 93°33′W
29 S15 **Glenwood** Iowa, C USA 41°03′N 95°44′W
29 T7 **Glenwood** Minnesota, N USA 45°39′N 95°23′W
36 L5 **Glenwood** Utah, W USA 38°45′N 111°59′W
30 I5 **Glenwood City** Wisconsin, N USA 45°04′N 92°11′W
37 Q4 **Glenwood Springs** Colorado, C USA 39°33′N 107°21′W
108 F10 **Gletsch** Valais, S Switzerland 46°34′N 08°21′E
Glevum *see* Gloucester
29 U14 **Glidden** Iowa, C USA 42°03′N 94°43′W
112 E9 **Glina** *var.* Banijska Palanka. Sisak-Moslavina, NE Croatia 45°19′N 16°07′E
94 F11 **Glittertind** ▲ S Norway 61°24′N 08°19′E
111 J16 **Gliwice** *Ger.* Gleiwitz. Śląskie, S Poland 50°19′N 18°49′E
113 N16 **Gllamnik** *Serb.* Glavnik. N Kosovo 42°53′N 21°10′E
36 M14 **Globe** Arizona, SW USA 33°24′N 110°47′W
Globino *see* Hlobyne
108 L9 **Glockturm** ▲ SW Austria 46°54′N 10°42′E
116 L9 **Glodeni** *Rus.* Glodyany. N Moldova 47°47′N 27°33′E
109 S9 **Glödnitz** Kärnten, S Austria 46°57′N 14°03′E
Glodyany *see* Glodeni
Glogau *see* Głogów
109 W6 **Gloggnitz** Niederösterreich, E Austria 47°41′N 15°57′E
110 F13 **Głogów** *Ger.* Glogau, Glogow. Dolnośląskie, SW Poland 51°40′N 16°04′E
Glogow *see* Głogów
111 I16 **Głogówek** *Ger.* Oberglogau. Opolskie, S Poland 50°21′N 17°51′E
92 G12 **Glomfjord** Nordland, C Norway 66°49′N 14°00′E
Glomma *see* Gláma
Glommen *see* Gláma
93 I14 **Glommersträsk** Norrbotten, N Sweden 65°17′N 19°40′E
172 I1 **Glorieuses, Îles** *Eng.* Glorioso Islands. *island* (to France) N Madagascar
Glorioso Islands *see* Glorieuses, Îles
65 C25 **Glorious Hill** *hill* East Falkland, Falkland Islands
38 J12 **Glory of Russia Cape** *headland* Saint Matthew Island, Alaska, USA 60°36′N 172°57′W
22 J7 **Gloster** Mississippi, S USA 31°12′N 91°01′W
183 U7 **Gloucester** New South Wales, SE Australia 32°01′S 152°00′E
186 F7 **Gloucester** New Britain, E Papua New Guinea 05°30′S 148°30′E
97 L21 **Gloucester** *hist.* Caer Glou, *Lat.* Glevum. C England, United Kingdom 51°53′N 02°14′W
19 P10 **Gloucester** Massachusetts, NE USA 42°36′N 70°36′W
21 X6 **Gloucester** Virginia, NE USA 37°26′N 76°33′W
97 K21 **Gloucestershire** *cultural region* C England, United Kingdom
31 T14 **Glouster** Ohio, N USA 39°30′N 82°04′W
42 H3 **Glovers Reef** *reef* E Belize
18 K10 **Gloversville** New York, NE USA 43°03′N 74°20′W
110 K12 **Głowno** Łódź, C Poland 51°58′N 19°43′E
111 H16 **Głubczyce** *Ger.* Leobschütz. Opolskie, S Poland 50°13′N 17°50′E
126 L11 **Glubokiy** Rostovskaya Oblast', SW Russian Federation 48°34′N 40°16′E
145 W9 **Glubokoye** Vostochnyy Kazakhstan, E Kazakhstan 50°08′N 82°16′E
Glubokoye *see* Hlybokaye
111 H16 **Głuchołazy** *Ger.* Ziegenhais. Opolskie, S Poland 50°20′N 17°23′E
100 I9 **Glückstadt** Schleswig-Holstein, N Germany 53°47′N 09°26′E
Glukhov *see* Hlukhiv
Glushkevichi *see* Hlushkavichy
Glusk/Glussk *see* Hlusk
Glybokaya *see* Hlyboka
95 F21 **Glyngøre** Midtjylland, NW Denmark 56°45′N 08°55′E
127 Q9 **Gmelinka** Volgogradskaya Oblast', SW Russian Federation 50°50′N 46°51′E
109 R8 **Gmünd** Kärnten, S Austria 46°56′N 13°32′E
109 U2 **Gmünd** Niederösterreich, N Austria 48°47′N 14°59′E
Gmünd *see* Schwäbisch Gmünd
109 S5 **Gmunden** Oberösterreich, N Austria 47°56′N 13°48′E
Gmundner See *see* Traunsee
94 N10 **Gnarp** Gävleborg, C Sweden 62°03′N 17°19′E
109 W8 **Gnas** Steiermark, SE Austria 46°53′N 15°48′E
Gnaviyani *see* Fuammulah
Gnesen *see* Gniezno
95 O16 **Gnesta** Södermanland, C Sweden 59°05′N 17°20′E
110 H11 **Gniezno** *Ger.* Gnesen. Weilkopolskie, C Poland 52°33′N 17°35′E
Gnjilane *see* Gjilan
95 K20 **Gnosjö** Jönköping, S Sweden 57°22′N 13°44′E
155 E17 **Goa** *prev.* Old Goa, Vela Goa, Velha Goa. Goa, W India 15°31′N 73°56′E
155 E17 **Goa** *var.* Old Goa. ◆ *state* W India
Goabddális *see* Kåbdalis
42 H7 **Goascorán, Río** ⚡ El Salvador/Honduras
77 O16 **Goaso** *var.* Gawso. W Ghana 06°49′N 02°27′W
81 K14 **Goba** Oromīya, C Ethiopia 07°02′N 39°58′E
83 C20 **Gobabed** Erongo, W Namibia 23°36′S 15°03′E
83 E19 **Gobabis** Omaheke, E Namibia 22°25′S 18°58′E
Gobannium *see* Abergavenny
64 M7 **Goban Spur** *undersea feature* NW Atlantic Ocean
63 H21 **Gobernador Gregores** Santa Cruz, S Argentina 48°43′S 70°21′W
61 F14 **Gobernador Ingeniero Virasoro** Corrientes, NE Argentina 28°06′S 56°00′W
162 L12 **Gobi** *desert* China/Mongolia
164 I14 **Gobō** Wakayama, Honshū, SW Japan 33°52′N 135°09′E
Gobolka Awdal *see* Awdal
Gobolka Sahil *see* Sahil
Gobolka Sool *see* Sool
101 D14 **Goch** Nordrhein-Westfalen, W Germany 51°41′N 06°10′E
83 E20 **Gochas** Hardap, S Namibia 24°54′S 18°43′E
155 I14 **Godāvari** *var.* Godavari. ⚡ C India
Godavari *see* Godāvari
155 L16 **Godāvari, Mouths of the** *delta* E India
15 V5 **Godbout** Québec, SE Canada 49°19′N 67°37′W
15 U5 **Godbout** ⚡ Québec, SE Canada
15 U5 **Godbout Est** ⚡ Québec, SE Canada
27 N6 **Goddard** Kansas, C USA 37°39′N 97°34′W
14 E15 **Goderich** Ontario, S Canada 43°43′N 81°43′W
Godhavn *see* Qeqertarsuaq
154 E10 **Godhra** Gujarāt, W India 22°49′N 73°40′E
Göding *see* Hodonín
111 K22 **Gödöllő** Pest, N Hungary 47°36′N 19°20′E
62 H11 **Godoy Cruz** Mendoza, W Argentina 32°59′S 68°49′W
11 Y11 **Gods** ⚡ Manitoba, C Canada
11 X13 **Gods Lake** ◎ Manitoba, C Canada
11 Y13 **Gods Lake Narrows** Manitoba, C Canada 54°29′N 94°21′W
Godthaab/Godthåb *see* Nuuk
Godwin Austen, Mount *see* K2
Goede Hoop, Kaap de *see* Good Hope, Cape of
Goedgegun *see* Nhlangano
Goeie Hoop, Kaap die *see* Good Hope, Cape of
13 O7 **Goëlands, Lac aux** ◎ Québec, SE Canada
98 E13 **Goeree** *island* SW Netherlands
99 F15 **Goes** Zeeland, SW Netherlands 51°30′N 03°55′E
Goettingen *see* Göttingen
19 O10 **Goffstown** New Hampshire, NE USA 43°01′N 71°34′W
14 E8 **Gogama** Ontario, S Canada 47°42′N 81°44′W
30 L3 **Gogebic, Lake** ◎ Michigan, N USA
30 K3 **Gogebic Range** *hill range* Michigan/Wisconsin, N USA
Gogi Lerr *see* Gogi, Mount
137 V13 **Gogi, Mount** *Arm.* Gogi Lerr, *Az.* Küküdağ. ▲ Armenia/Azerbaijan 39°33′N 45°35′E
124 F12 **Gogland, Ostrov** *island* NW Russian Federation
111 I15 **Gogolin** Opolskie, S Poland 50°28′N 18°04′E
Gogonou *see* Gogounou
77 S14 **Gogounou** *var.* Gogonou. N Benin 10°50′N 02°50′E
152 I10 **Gohāna** Haryāna, N India 29°06′N 76°43′E
59 K18 **Goianésia** Goiás, C Brazil 15°21′S 49°02′W
59 K18 **Goiânia** *prev.* Goyania. *state capital* Goiás, C Brazil 16°43′S 49°18′W
59 K18 **Goiás** Goiás, C Brazil 15°57′S 50°07′W
59 J18 **Goiás** *off.* Estado de Goiás; *prev.* Goiaz, Goyaz. ◆ *state* C Brazil
Goiás, Estado de *see* Goiás
Goiaz *see* Goiás
Goidhoo Atoll *see* Horsburgh Atoll
159 R14 **Goinsargoin** Xizang Zizhiqu, W China 31°56′N 98°04′E
60 H10 **Goio-Erê** Paraná, SW Brazil 24°08′S 53°07′W
99 I15 **Goirle** Noord-Brabant, S Netherlands 51°31′N 05°04′E
104 H8 **Góis** Coimbra, N Portugal 40°10′N 08°06′W
165 Q8 **Gojōme** Akita, Honshū, NW Japan 39°55′N 140°07′E
149 U9 **Gojra** Punjab, E Pakistan 31°10′N 72°43′E
136 A11 **Gökçeada** *var.* Imroz Adasī, *Gk.* Imbros. *island* NW Turkey
Gökçeada *see* Imroz
146 F13 **Gökdepe** *Rus.* Gëkdepe, Geok-Tepe. Ahal Welaýaty, C Turkmenistan 38°05′N 58°08′E
136 I10 **Gökırmak** ⚡ N Turkey
Goklenkuy, Solonchak *see* Geklengkui, Solonchak
136 C16 **Gökova Körfezi** *gulf* SW Turkey
136 K15 **Göksu** ⚡ S Turkey
136 L15 **Göksun** Kahramanmaraş, C Turkey 38°03′N 36°30′E
136 I17 **Göksu Nehri** ⚡ S Turkey
83 J16 **Gokwe** Midlands, NW Zimbabwe 18°13′S 28°55′E
94 F13 **Gol** Buskerud, S Norway 60°42′N 08°57′E
153 X12 **Golāghāt** Assam, NE India 26°31′N 93°54′E
110 H10 **Gołańcz** Wielkopolskie, C Poland 52°57′N 17°17′E
138 G8 **Golan Heights** *Ar.* Al Jawlān, *Heb.* HaGolan. ▲ SW Syria
Golārā *see* Ārān-va-Bidgol
Golaya Pristan *see* Hola Prystan'
143 T11 **Golbāf** Kermān, C Iran 29°51′N 57°44′E
136 M15 **Gölbaşı** Adıyaman, S Turkey 37°46′N 37°40′E
109 P9 **Gölbner** ▲ SW Austria 46°51′N 12°31′E
30 M17 **Golconda** Illinois, N USA 37°20′N 88°29′W
35 T3 **Golconda** Nevada, W USA 40°56′N 117°29′W
136 E11 **Gölcük** Kocaeli, NW Turkey 40°44′N 29°50′E
108 I7 **Goldach** Sankt Gallen, NE Switzerland 47°28′N 09°28′E
110 N7 **Gołdap** *Ger.* Goldap. Warmińsko-Mazurskie, NE Poland 54°19′N 22°23′E
32 E15 **Gold Beach** Oregon, NW USA 42°25′N 124°27′W
Goldberg *see* Złotoryja
183 V3 **Gold Coast** *cultural region* Queensland, E Australia
68 D12 **Gold Coast** *coastal region* S Ghana
39 R10 **Gold Creek** Alaska, USA 62°48′N 149°40′W
11 O16 **Golden** British Columbia, SW Canada 51°19′N 116°58′W
37 T4 **Golden** Colorado, C USA 39°40′N 105°12′W
184 I13 **Golden Bay** *bay* South Island, New Zealand
27 R7 **Golden City** Missouri, C USA 37°23′N 94°05′W
32 I11 **Goldendale** Washington, NW USA 45°49′N 120°49′W
Goldener Tisch *see* Zlatý Stôl
44 L13 **Golden Grove** E Jamaica 17°56′N 76°17′W
14 J12 **Golden Lake** ◎ Ontario, SE Canada
22 K10 **Golden Meadow** Louisiana, S USA 29°22′N 90°15′W
Golden State, The *see* California
83 K16 **Golden Valley** Mashonaland West, N Zimbabwe 18°11′S 29°50′E
35 U9 **Goldfield** Nevada, W USA 37°42′N 117°15′W
Goldingen *see* Kuldīga
Goldmarkt *see* Zlatna
10 K17 **Gold River** Vancouver Island, British Columbia, SW Canada 49°41′N 126°05′W
21 V10 **Goldsboro** North Carolina, SE USA 35°23′N 78°00′W
24 M8 **Goldsmith** Texas, SW USA 31°58′N 102°36′W
25 R8 **Goldthwaite** Texas, SW USA 31°28′N 98°35′W
137 R11 **Göle** Ardahan, NE Turkey 40°47′N 42°36′E
Golema Ada *see* Ostrovo
114 H9 **Golema Planina** ▲ W Bulgaria
114 F9 **Golemi Vrŭkh** ▲ W Bulgaria 42°41′N 22°38′E
110 D8 **Goleniów** *Ger.* Gollnow. Zachodnio-pomorskie, NW Poland 53°34′N 14°48′E
143 R3 **Golestān** ◆ *province* N Iran
35 Q14 **Goleta** California, W USA 34°26′N 119°50′W
43 O16 **Golfito** Puntarenas, SE Costa Rica 08°42′N 83°10′W
25 T13 **Goliad** Texas, SW USA 28°40′N 97°26′W
113 L14 **Golija** ▲ SW Serbia
Golinka *see* Gongbo'gyamda
113 O16 **Goljak** ▲ SE Serbia
136 M12 **Gölköy** Ordu, N Turkey 40°42′N 37°37′E
Gollel *see* Lavumisa
109 X3 **Göllersbach** ⚡ NE Austria
Gollnow *see* Goleniów
Golmo *see* Golmud
159 P10 **Golmud** *var.* Ge'e'mu, Golmo, *Chin.* Ko-erh-mu. Qinghai, C China 36°23′N 94°56′E
103 Y14 **Golo** ⚡ Corse, France, C Mediterranean Sea
Golovanevsk *see* Holovanivs'k
Golovchin *see* Halowchyn
39 N9 **Golovin** Alaska, USA 64°33′N 162°54′W
142 M7 **Golpāyegān** *var.* Gulpaigan. Eşfahān, W Iran 33°23′N 50°18′E
Golshan *see* Ṭabas
Gol'shany *see* Hal'shany
96 J7 **Golspie** N Scotland, United Kingdom 57°59′N 03°56′W
112 O11 **Golubac** Serbia, NE Serbia 44°38′N 21°36′E
110 J9 **Golub-Dobrzyń** Kujawski-pomorskie, C Poland 53°07′N 19°03′E
145 S7 **Golubovka** Pavlodar, N Kazakhstan 53°07′N 74°11′E
82 B11 **Golungo Alto** Cuanza Norte, NW Angola 09°10′S 14°45′E
114 M8 **Golyama Kamchiya** ⚡ E Bulgaria
114 L8 **Golyama Reka** ⚡ N Bulgaria
114 H11 **Golyama Syutkya** ▲ SW Bulgaria 41°55′N 24°03′E
114 I12 **Golyam Perelik** ▲ S Bulgaria 41°37′N 24°34′E
114 I11 **Golyam Persenk** ▲ S Bulgaria 41°50′N 24°33′E
79 P19 **Goma** Nord-Kivu, NE Dem. Rep. Congo 01°36′S 29°08′E
153 N13 **Gomati** *var.* Gumti. ⚡ N India
77 X14 **Gombe** Gombe, E Nigeria 10°19′N 11°02′E
67 U10 **Gombe** *var.* Igombe. ⚡ E Tanzania
77 Y14 **Gombi** Adamawa, E Nigeria 10°07′N 12°45′E
Gombroon *see* Bandar-e 'Abbās
Gomel' *see* Homyel'
Gomel'skaya Oblast' *see* Homyel'skaya Voblasts'
64 N11 **Gomera** *island* Islas Canarias, Spain, NE Atlantic Ocean
40 I5 **Gómez Farías** Chihuahua, N Mexico 29°25′N 107°46′W
40 L8 **Gómez Palacio** Durango, C Mexico 25°39′N 103°30′W
158 J13 **Gomo** Xizang Zizhiqu, W China 33°37′N 86°40′E
143 T6 **Gonābād** *var.* Gunabad. Khorāsān-Razavī, NE Iran 36°30′N 59°18′E
44 L8 **Gonaïves** *var.* Les Gonaïves. N Haiti 19°26′N 72°41′W
123 Q12 **Gonam** ⚡ NE Russian Federation
44 L9 **Gonâve, Canal de la** *var.* Canal de Sud. *channel* N Caribbean Sea
44 K9 **Gonâve, Golfe de la** *gulf* N Caribbean Sea
Gonāveh *see* Bandar-e Gonāveh
44 K9 **Gonâve, Île de la** *island* C Haiti
Gonbadān *see* Do Gonbadān
143 Q3 **Gonbad-e Kāvūs** *var.* Gunbad-i-Qawus. Golestān, N Iran 37°15′N 55°11′E
152 M12 **Gonda** Uttar Pradesh, N India 27°08′N 81°58′E
Gondar *see* Gonder
80 I11 **Gonder** *var.* Gondar. Āmara, NW Ethiopia 12°36′N 37°27′E
78 J13 **Gondey** Moyen-Chari, S Chad 09°07′N 19°10′E
154 J12 **Gondia** Mahārāshtra, C India 21°27′N 80°12′E
104 G6 **Gondomar** Porto, NW Portugal 41°10′N 08°35′W
136 C12 **Gönen** Balıkesir, W Turkey 40°06′N 27°39′E
136 C12 **Gönen Çayı** ⚡ NW Turkey
159 O15 **Gongbo'gyamda** *var.* Golinka. Xizang Zizhiqu, W China 30°03′N 93°10′E
Gongchang *see* Longxi
159 N16 **Gonggar** *var.* Gyixong. Xizang Zizhiqu, W China 29°18′N 90°56′E
160 G9 **Gongga Shan** ▲ C China 29°50′N 101°55′E
159 T10 **Gonghe** *var.* Qabqa. Qinghai, C China 36°20′N 100°46′E
Gongjiang *see* Yudu
158 I5 **Gongliu** *var.* Tokkuztara. Xinjiang Uygur Zizhiqu, NW China 43°29′N 82°16′E
77 W14 **Gongola** ⚡ E Nigeria
Gongoleh State *see* Jonglei
183 P5 **Gongolgon** New South Wales, SE Australia 30°19′S 146°57′E
159 Q6 **Gongpoquan** Gansu, N China 41°45′N 100°27′E
Gongquan *see* Gongxian
Gongtang *see* Damxung
160 I10 **Gongxian** *var.* Gongquan, Gong Xian. Sichuan, C China 28°25′N 104°51′E
Gong Xian *see* Gongxian
157 V10 **Gongzhuling** *prev.* Huaide. Jilin, NE China 43°30′N 124°48′E
159 S14 **Gonjo** Xizang Zizhiqu, W China 30°51′N 98°16′E
107 B20 **Gonnesa** Sardegna, Italy, C Mediterranean Sea 39°15′N 08°27′E
Gonni/Gónnos *see* Gónnoi
115 F15 **Gónnoi** *var.* Gonni, Gónnos; *prev.* Dereli. Thessalía, C Greece 39°52′N 22°27′E
Gōnoura *see* Iki
35 O11 **Gonzales** California, W USA 36°30′N 121°26′W
22 J9 **Gonzales** Louisiana, S USA 30°14′N 90°55′W
25 T12 **Gonzales** Texas, SW USA 29°31′N 97°29′W
41 P11 **González** Tamaulipas, C Mexico 22°50′N 98°25′W
21 V6 **Goochland** Virginia, NE USA 37°42′N 77°54′W
195 X14 **Goodenough, Cape** *headland* Antarctica 66°15′S 126°35′E
186 F9 **Goodenough Island** *var.* Morata. *island* SE Papua New Guinea
39 N8 **Goodhope Bay** *bay* Alaska, USA
83 D26 **Good Hope, Cape of** *Afr.* Kaap de Goede Hoop, Kaap die Goeie Hoop. *headland* SW South Africa 34°19′S 18°25′E
10 K10 **Good Hope Lake** British Columbia, W Canada 59°15′N 129°18′W
83 E23 **Goodhouse** Northern Cape, W South Africa 28°54′S 18°13′E
33 O15 **Gooding** Idaho, NW USA 42°56′N 114°42′W
26 H3 **Goodland** Kansas, C USA 39°20′N 101°43′W
173 Y15 **Goodlands** NW Mauritius 20°02′S 57°39′E
20 J8 **Goodlettsville** Tennessee, S USA 36°19′N 86°42′W
39 N13 **Goodnews** Alaska, USA 59°07′N 161°35′W
25 O3 **Goodnight** Texas, SW USA 35°00′N 101°07′W
183 Q4 **Goodooga** New South Wales, SE Australia 29°09′S 147°30′E
29 N4 **Goodrich** North Dakota, N USA 47°24′N 100°07′W
25 W10 **Goodrich** Texas, SW USA 30°36′N 94°57′W
29 X10 **Goodview** Minnesota, N USA 44°04′N 91°42′W
26 H8 **Goodwell** Oklahoma, C USA 36°36′N 101°38′W
97 N17 **Goole** E England, United Kingdom 53°43′N 00°46′W
183 O8 **Goolgowi** New South Wales, SE Australia 34°00′S 145°43′E
182 I10 **Goolwa** South Australia 35°31′S 138°43′E
181 Y11 **Goondiwindi** Queensland, E Australia 28°33′S 150°22′E
98 O11 **Goor** Overijssel, E Netherlands 52°13′N 06°33′E
Goose Bay *see* Happy Valley-Goose Bay
33 V13 **Gooseberry Creek** ⚡ Wyoming, C USA
21 S14 **Goose Creek** South Carolina, SE USA 32°58′N 80°01′W
63 M23 **Goose Green** *var.* Prado del Ganso. East Falkland, Falkland Islands 51°52′S 59°W
16 D8 **Goose Lake** *var.* Lago dos Gansos. ◎ California/Oregon, W USA
29 Q4 **Goose River** ⚡ North Dakota, N USA
153 T16 **Gopalganj** Dhaka, S Bangladesh 23°00′N 89°48′E
153 O12 **Gopālganj** Bihār, N India 26°28′N 84°26′E
Gopher State *see* Minnesota
101 I22 **Göppingen** Baden-Württemberg, SW Germany 48°42′N 09°39′E
110 G13 **Góra** *Ger.* Guhrau. Dolnośląskie, SW Poland 51°40′N 16°03′E
110 M12 **Góra Kalwaria** Mazowieckie, C Poland 52°00′N 21°14′E
153 O12 **Gorakhpur** Uttar Pradesh, N India 26°45′N 83°23′E
Gora Kyuren *see* Kürendag
Gorany *see* Harany
113 J14 **Goražde** Federacija Bosna I Hercegovina, SE Bosnia and Herzegovina 43°39′N 18°58′E
Gorbovichi *see* Harbavichy
Gorče Petrov *see* Đorče Petrov
0 E9 **Gorda Ridges** *undersea feature* NE Pacific Ocean 41°30′N 128°00′W
Gordiaz *see* Gardēz
78 K12 **Gordil** Vakaga, N Central African Republic 09°37′N 21°42′E
23 U5 **Gordon** Georgia, SE USA 32°52′N 83°19′W
28 K12 **Gordon** Nebraska, C USA 42°48′N 102°12′W
25 R7 **Gordon** Texas, SW USA 32°32′N 98°21′W
28 L13 **Gordon Creek** ⚡ Nebraska, C USA
63 I25 **Gordon, Isla** *island* S Chile
183 O17 **Gordon, Lake** ◎ Tasmania, SE Australia
183 O17 **Gordon River** ⚡ Tasmania, SE Australia
21 V5 **Gordonsville** Virginia, NE USA 38°08′N 78°11′W
78 H13 **Goré** Logone-Oriental, S Chad 07°55′N 16°38′E
80 H13 **Gorē** Oromīya, C Ethiopia 08°08′N 35°33′E
185 D24 **Gore** Southland, South Island, New Zealand 46°06′S 168°58′E
14 D11 **Gore Bay** Manitoulin Island, Ontario, S Canada 45°54′N 82°28′W
25 Q5 **Goree** Texas, SW USA 33°28′N 99°31′W
137 O11 **Görele** Giresun, NE Turkey 41°00′N 39°00′E
19 N6 **Gore Mountain** ▲ Vermont, NE USA 44°55′N 71°47′W
39 R13 **Gore Point** *headland* Alaska, USA 59°12′N 150°57′W
37 R4 **Gore Range** ▲ Colorado, C USA
97 F19 **Gorey** *Ir.* Guaire. Wexford, SE Ireland 52°40′N 06°18′W
143 R12 **Gorgāb** Kermān, S Iran
143 Q4 **Gorgān** *var.* Astarabad, Astrabad, Gurgan, *prev.* Asterābād; *anc.* Hyrcania. Golestān, N Iran 36°53′N 54°28′E
143 Q4 **Gorgān, Rūd-e** ⚡ N Iran
76 I10 **Gorgol** ◆ *region* S Mauritania
106 D12 **Gorgona, Isola di** *island* Archipelago Toscano, C Italy
19 P8 **Gorham** Maine, NE USA 43°41′N 70°27′W
137 T10 **Gori** C Georgia 42°00′N 44°07′E
98 I13 **Gorinchem** *var.* Gorkum. Zuid-Holland, C Netherlands 51°50′N 04°59′E
137 V13 **Goris** SE Armenia 39°31′N 46°20′E
124 K16 **Goritsy** Tverskaya Oblast', W Russian Federation 57°09′N 36°44′E
106 J7 **Gorizia** *Ger.* Görz. Friuli-Venezia Giulia, NE Italy 45°57′N 13°37′E
116 G13 **Gorj** ◆ *county* SW Romania
109 W12 **Gorjanci** *var.* Uskočke Planine, Žumberak, Žumberačko Gorje, *Ger.* Uskokengebirge; *prev.* Sichelburger Gerbirge. ▲ Croatia/Slovenia Europe *see also* Žumberačko Gorje
Görkau *see* Jirkov
Gorki *see* Horki
Gor'kiy *see* Nizhniy Novgorod
Gorkum *see* Gorinchem
95 I23 **Gørlev** Sjælland, E Denmark 55°33′N 11°14′E
111 M17 **Gorlice** Małopolskie, S Poland 49°40′N 21°09′E
101 Q15 **Görlitz** Sachsen, E Germany 51°09′N 14°58′E
Görlitz *see* Zgorzelec
Gorlovka *see* Horlivka
25 R7 **Gorman** Texas, SW USA 32°12′N 98°40′W
21 T3 **Gormania** West Virginia, NE USA 39°16′N 79°18′W
Gorna Dzhumaya *see* Blagoevgrad
114 K8 **Gorna Oryakhovitsa** Veliko Tŭrnovo, N Bulgaria 43°07′N 25°40′E
114 J8 **Gorna Studena** Veliko Tŭrnovo, N Bulgaria 43°26′N 25°21′E
Gornja Mužlja *see* Mužlja
109 X9 **Gornja Radgona** *Ger.* Oberradkersburg. NE Slovenia 46°39′N 16°00′E
112 M13 **Gornji Milanovac** Serbia, C Serbia 44°01′N 20°26′E
112 G13 **Gornji Vakuf** *var.* Uskoplje. Federacija Bosna I Hercegovina, SW Bosnia and Herzegovina 43°55′N 17°34′E
122 J13 **Gorno-Altaysk** Respublika Altay, S Russian Federation 51°59′N 85°56′E
Gorno-Altayskaya Respublika *see* Altay, Respublika
123 N12 **Gorno-Chuyskiy** Irkutskaya Oblast', C Russian Federation 57°33′N 111°38′E
125 V14 **Gornozavodsk** Permskiy Kray, NW Russian Federation 58°21′N 58°24′E
125 V14 **Gornozavodsk** Ostrov Sakhalin, Sakhalinskaya Oblast', SE Russian Federation 46°34′N 141°52′E
122 I13 **Gornyak** Altayskiy Kray, S Russian Federation 50°58′N 81°24′E
123 O14 **Gornyy** Chitunskaya Oblast', Russian Federation 51°42′N 114°16′E
127 R8 **Gornyy** Saratovskaya Oblast', W Russian Federation 51°42′N 48°26′E
Gornyy Altay *see* Altay, Respublika
127 O10 **Gornyy Balykley** Volgogradskaya Oblast', SW Russian Federation 49°37′N 45°03′E
80 I13 **Goroch'an** ▲ W Ethiopia 09°09′N 37°16′E
116 J7 **Gorodenka** *var.* Horodenka. Ivano-Frankivs'ka Oblast', W Ukraine 48°41′N 25°28′E
127 O3 **Gorodets** Nizhegorodskaya Oblast', W Russian Federation 56°36′N 43°27′E
Gorodets *see* Haradzyets
Gorodeya *see* Haradzyeya
127 P6 **Gorodishche** Penzenskaya Oblast', W Russian Federation 53°17′N 45°39′E
Gorodishche *see* Horodyshche
Gorodnya *see* Horodnya
Gorodok *see* Haradok
Gorodok/Gorodok Yagellonski *see* Horodok
126 M13 **Gorodovikovsk** Respublika Kalmykiya, SW Russian Federation 46°07′N 41°56′E
186 D7 **Goroka** Eastern Highlands, C Papua New Guinea 06°02′S 145°22′E
Gorokhov *see* Horokhiv
127 N3 **Gorokhovets** Vladimirskaya Oblast', W Russian Federation 56°12′N 42°40′E
77 Q11 **Gorom-Gorom** NE Burkina 14°27′N 00°14′W
171 U13 **Gorong, Kepulauan** *island group* E Indonesia
83 M17 **Gorongosa** Sofala, C Mozambique 18°40′S 34°03′E
171 P11 **Gorontalo** Sulawesi, C Indonesia 0°33′N 123°05′E
171 O11 **Gorontalo** *off.* Propinsi Gorontalo. ◆ *province* N Indonesia
Propinsi Gorontalo *see* Gorontalo
Gorontalo, Teluk *see* Tomini, Teluk

◆ Country
● Country Capital
◇ Dependent Territory
○ Dependent Territory Capital
◆ Administrative Regions
✈ International Airport
▲ Mountain
▲ Mountain Range
⚠ Volcano
⚡ River
◎ Lake
◎ Reservoir

110 L7 **Górowo Iławeckie** *Ger.* Landsberg. Warmińsko-Mazurskie, NE Poland 54°18′N 20°30′E
98 M7 **Gorredijk** *Fris.* De Gordyk. Fryslân, N Netherlands 53°00′N 06°04′E
84 C14 **Gorringe Ridge** *undersea feature* E Atlantic Ocean 36°40′N 11°35′W
98 M11 **Gorssel** Gelderland, E Netherlands 52°12′N 06°13′E
109 T8 **Görtschitz** ≈ S Austria
Goryn *see* Horyn'
145 S15 **Gory Shu-Ile** *Kaz.* Shū-Ile Taūlary; *prev.* Chu-Iliyskiye Gory. ▲▲ S Kazakhstan
Görz *see* Gorizia
110 E10 **Gorzów Wielkopolski** *Ger.* Landsberg, Landsberg an der Warthe. Lubuskie, W Poland 52°44′N 15°12′E
146 B10 **Goşabo** *var.* Goshoba, *Rus.* Koshoba. Balkan Welaýaty, NW Turkmenistan 40°28′N 54°11′E
108 G9 **Göschenen** Uri, C Switzerland 46°40′N 08°36′E
165 O11 **Gosen** Niigata, Honshū, C Japan 37°45′N 139°11′E
163 Y13 **Goseong** *prev.* Kosŏng. SE North Korea 38°41′N 128°14′E
183 T8 **Gosford** New South Wales, SE Australia 33°25′S 151°18′E
31 P11 **Goshen** Indiana, N USA 41°34′N 85°49′W
18 K13 **Goshen** New York, NE USA 41°24′N 74°17′W
Goshoba *see* Goşabo
Goshoba *see* Goşoba
165 Q7 **Goshogawara** *var.* Gosyogawara. Aomori, Honshū, C Japan 40°47′N 140°24′E
Goshquduq Qum *see* Tosquduq Qumlari
101 J14 **Goslar** Niedersachsen, C Germany 51°55′N 10°25′E
27 Y9 **Gosnell** Arkansas, C USA 35°57′N 89°58′W
146 B10 **Goşoba** *var.* Goshoba, *Rus.* Koshoba. Balkanskiy Velayat, NW Turkmenistan 40°28′N 54°11′E
112 C11 **Gospić** Lika-Senj, C Croatia 44°32′N 15°21′E
97 N23 **Gosport** S England, United Kingdom 50°48′N 01°08′W
94 D9 **Gossa** *island* S Norway
108 H7 **Gossau** Sankt Gallen, NE Switzerland 47°25′N 09°16′E
99 G20 **Gosselies** *var.* Goss'lies. Hainaut, S Belgium 50°28′N 04°26′E
77 P10 **Gossi** Tombouctou, C Mali 15°44′N 01°19′W
Goss'lies *see* Gosselies
113 N18 **Gostivar** W FYR Macedonia 41°48′N 20°55′E
Gostomel' *see* Hostomel'
110 G12 **Gostyń** *var.* Gostyn. Wielkopolskie, C Poland 51°52′N 17°00′E
Gostyn *see* Gostyń
110 K11 **Gostynin** Mazowieckie, C Poland 52°25′N 19°27′E
Gosyogawara *see* Goshogawara
95 J18 **Göta Älv** ≈ S Sweden
95 N17 **Göta kanal** *canal* S Sweden
95 K18 **Götaland** *cultural region* S Sweden
95 H17 **Göteborg** *Eng.* Gothenburg. Västra Götaland, S Sweden 57°43′N 11°58′E
77 X16 **Gotel Mountains** ▲▲ E Nigeria
95 K17 **Götene** Västra Götaland, S Sweden 58°32′N 13°29′E
Gotera *see* San Francisco
101 K16 **Gotha** Thüringen, C Germany 50°57′N 10°43′E
29 N15 **Gothenburg** Nebraska, C USA 40°57′N 100°09′W
Gothenburg *see* Göteborg
77 R12 **Gothèye** Tillabéri, SW Niger 13°52′N 01°27′E
Gothland *see* Gotland
95 P19 **Gotland** *var.* Gothland, Gottland. ◈ *county* SE Sweden
95 O18 **Gotland** *island* SE Sweden
164 A14 **Gotō** *var.* Hukue; *prev.* Fukue. Nagasaki, Fukue-jima, SW Japan 32°41′N 128°52′E
164 B13 **Gotō-rettō** *island group* SW Japan
114 H12 **Gotse Delchev** *prev.* Nevrokop. Blagoevgrad, SW Bulgaria 41°33′N 23°42′E
95 P17 **Gotska Sandön** *island* SE Sweden
101 I15 **Göttingen** *var.* Goettingen. Niedersachsen, C Germany 51°33′N 09°55′E
Gottland *see* Gotland
93 I16 **Gottne** Västernorrland, C Sweden 63°27′N 18°25′E
Gottschee *see* Kočevje
Gottwaldov *see* Zlín
146 B11 **Goturdepe** *Rus.* Koturdepe. Balkan Welaýaty, W Turkmenistan 39°32′N 53°39′E
108 I7 **Götzis** Vorarlberg, NW Austria 47°21′N 09°40′E
98 H12 **Gouda** Zuid-Holland, C Netherlands 52°01′N 04°42′E
76 I11 **Goudiri** *var.* Goudiry. E Senegal 14°12′N 12°41′W
Goudiry *see* Goudiri
77 X12 **Goudoumaria** Diffa, S Niger 13°28′N 11°15′E
15 R9 **Gouffre, Rivière du** ≈ Québec, SE Canada
65 M19 **Gough Fracture Zone** *tectonic feature* S Atlantic Ocean
65 M19 **Gough Island** *island* Tristan da Cunha, S Atlantic Ocean
15 N8 **Gouin, Réservoir** ⊠ Québec, SE Canada
14 B10 **Goulais River** Ontario, S Canada 46°41′N 84°22′W
183 R9 **Goulburn** New South Wales, SE Australia 34°45′S 149°44′E
183 O11 **Goulburn River** ≈ Victoria, SE Australia
195 O10 **Gould Coast** *physical region* Antarctica
Goulimime *see* Guelmime
114 F13 **Gouménissa** Kentrikí Makedonía, N Greece 40°56′N 22°27′E
77 O10 **Goundam** Tombouctou, NW Mali 16°27′N 03°39′W
78 H12 **Goundi** Moyen-Chari, S Chad 09°22′N 17°21′E
78 G12 **Gounou-Gaya** Mayo-Kébbi, SW Chad 09°37′N 15°30′E
Gourci *see* Goursi
Gourcy *see* Goursi
102 M13 **Gourdon** Lot, S France 44°45′N 01°22′E
77 W11 **Gouré** Zinder, SE Niger 13°59′N 10°16′E
102 G6 **Gourin** Morbihan, NW France 48°07′N 03°37′W
77 P10 **Gourma-Rharous** Tombouctou, C Mali 16°54′N 01°55′W
103 N4 **Gournay-en-Bray** Seine-Maritime, N France 49°29′N 01°42′E
78 J6 **Gouro** Borkou-Ennedi-Tibesti, N Chad 19°26′N 19°36′E
77 O12 **Goursi** *var.* Gourci, Gourcy. NW Burkina 13°13′N 02°20′W
104 H8 **Gouveia** Guarda, N Portugal 40°29′N 07°35′W
18 I7 **Gouverneur** New York, NE USA 44°20′N 75°27′W
99 L21 **Gouvy** Luxembourg, E Belgium 50°10′N 05°55′E
45 R14 **Gouyave** *var.* Charlotte Town. NW Grenada 12°10′N 61°44′W
Goverla, Gora *see* Hoverla, Hora
59 N20 **Governador Valadares** Minas Gerais, SE Brazil 18°51′S 41°57′W
171 R8 **Governor Generoso** Mindanao, S Philippines 06°36′N 126°06′E
44 I2 **Governor's Harbour** Eleuthera Island, C Bahamas 25°11′N 76°15′W
162 F9 **Govĭ-Altay** ◈ *province* SW Mongolia
162 I10 **Govĭ Altayn Nuruu** ▲▲ S Mongolia
154 L9 **Govind Ballabh Pant Sāgar** ⊠ C India
152 I7 **Govind Sāgar** ⊠ NE India
162 M8 **Govĭ-Sumber** ◈ *province* C Mongolia
Govurdak *see* Magdanly
18 D11 **Gowanda** New York, NE USA 42°25′N 78°55′W
148 J10 **Gowd-e Zereh, Dasht-e** *var.* Guad-i-Zirreh. *marsh* SW Afghanistan
14 F8 **Gowganda** Ontario, S Canada 47°41′N 80°46′W
14 G8 **Gowganda Lake** ◎ Ontario, S Canada
148 M5 **Gōwr** *prev.* Ghowr. ◈ *province* C Afghanistan
29 U13 **Gowrie** Iowa, C USA 42°16′N 94°17′W
Gowurdak *see* Magdanly
61 C15 **Goya** Corrientes, NE Argentina 29°10′S 59°15′W
Goyania *see* Goiânia
Goyaz *see* Goiás
137 X11 **Göyçay** *Rus.* Geokchay. C Azerbaijan 40°38′N 47°44′E
137 V11 **Göygöl** *prev.* Xanlar, *Rus.* Khanlar. NW Azerbaijan 40°37′N 46°18′E
146 D10 **Goymat** *Rus.* Koymat. Balkan Welaýaty, NW Turkmenistan 40°23′N 55°45′E
146 D10 **Goymatdag, Gory** *Rus.* Gory Koymatdag. *hill range* Balkan Welaýaty, NW Turkmenistan
136 F12 **Göynük** Bolu, NW Turkey 40°24′N 30°45′E
165 R9 **Goyō-san** ▲ Honshū, C Japan 39°12′N 141°40′E
78 K11 **Goz Beïda** Ouaddaï, SE Chad 12°06′N 21°22′E
146 M10 **G'ozg'on** *Rus.* Gazgan. Navoiy Viloyati, C Uzbekistan 40°36′N 65°29′E
158 H11 **Gozha Co** ◎ W China
121 O15 **Gozo** *var.* Ghawdex. *island* N Malta
80 H9 **Gōz Regeb** Kassala, NE Sudan 16°03′N 35°33′E
83 H25 **Graaff-Reinet** Eastern Cape, S South Africa 32°15′S 24°32′E
Graasten *see* Gråsten
76 L17 **Grabo** SW Ivory Coast 04°57′N 07°30′W
112 P11 **Grabovica** Serbia, E Serbia 44°30′N 22°29′E
110 I13 **Grabów nad Prosną** Wielkopolskie, C Poland 51°30′N 18°06′E
108 I8 **Grabs** Sankt Gallen, NE Switzerland 47°10′N 09°27′E
112 D12 **Gračac** Zadar, SW Croatia 44°18′N 15°52′E
112 I11 **Gračanica** Federacija Bosna I Hercegovina, NE Bosnia and Herzegovina 44°41′N 18°20′E
14 L11 **Gracefield** Québec, SE Canada 46°06′N 76°03′W
99 K19 **Grâce-Hollogne** Liège, E Belgium 50°38′N 05°30′E
23 R8 **Graceville** Florida, SE USA 30°57′N 85°31′W
29 R8 **Graceville** Minnesota, N USA 45°34′N 96°25′W
42 G6 **Gracias** Lempira, W Honduras 14°35′N 88°35′W
Gracias *see* Lempira
42 L5 **Gracias a Dios** ◈ *department* E Honduras
43 O6 **Gracias a Dios, Cabo de** *headland* Honduras/Nicaragua 15°00′N 83°10′W
64 O2 **Graciosa** *var.* Ilha Graciosa. *island* Azores, Portugal, NE Atlantic Ocean
64 Q11 **Graciosa** *island* Islas Canarias, Spain, NE Atlantic Ocean
Graciosa, Ilha *see* Graciosa
112 I11 **Gradačac** Federacija Bosna I Hercegovina, N Bosnia and Herzegovina 44°51′N 18°24′E
59 J15 **Gradaús, Serra dos** ▲▲ C Brazil
104 L3 **Gradefes** Castilla y León, N Spain 42°37′N 05°14′W
Gradiška *see* Bosanska Gradiška
Gradizhsk *see* Hradyz'k
106 J7 **Grado** Friuli-Venezia Giulia, NE Italy 45°41′N 13°24′E
Grado *see* Grau
113 P19 **Gradsko** C FYR Macedonia 41°34′N 21°56′E
37 V11 **Grady** New Mexico, SW USA 34°49′N 103°19′W
Grad Zagreb *see* Zagreb
29 T12 **Graettinger** Iowa, C USA 43°14′N 94°45′W
101 M23 **Grafing** Bayern, SE Germany 48°01′N 11°57′E
25 S6 **Graford** Texas, SW USA 32°56′N 98°15′W
183 V5 **Grafton** New South Wales, SE Australia 29°41′S 152°55′E
29 Q3 **Grafton** North Dakota, N USA 48°24′N 97°24′W
21 S3 **Grafton** West Virginia, NE USA 39°21′N 80°03′W
21 T9 **Graham** North Carolina, SE USA 36°05′N 79°25′W
25 R6 **Graham** Texas, SW USA 33°07′N 98°36′W
Graham Bell Island *see* Greem-Bell, Ostrov
10 I13 **Graham Island** *island* Queen Charlotte Islands, British Columbia, SW Canada
19 S6 **Graham Lake** ◎ Maine, NE USA
194 H4 **Graham Land** *physical region* Antarctica
37 N15 **Graham, Mount** ▲ Arizona, SW USA 32°42′N 109°52′W
Grahamstad *see* Grahamstown
83 I25 **Grahamstown** *Afr.* Grahamstad. Eastern Cape, S South Africa 33°18′S 26°32′E
Grahovo *see* Bosansko Grahovo
68 C12 **Grain Coast** *coastal region* S Liberia
169 S17 **Grajagan, Teluk** *bay* Jawa, S Indonesia
59 L14 **Grajaú** Maranhão, E Brazil 05°50′S 45°12′W
58 M13 **Grajaú, Rio** ≈ NE Brazil
110 O8 **Grajewo** Podlaskie, NE Poland 53°38′N 22°26′E
95 F24 **Gram** Syddanmark, SW Denmark 55°18′N 09°03′E
103 N13 **Gramat** Lot, S France 44°45′N 01°45′E
22 H5 **Grambling** Louisiana, S USA 32°31′N 92°43′W
115 C14 **Grámmos** ▲▲ Albania/Greece
96 I9 **Grampian Mountains** ▲▲ C Scotland, United Kingdom
182 L12 **Grampians, The** ▲▲ Victoria, SE Australia
98 O9 **Gramsbergen** Overijssel, E Netherlands 52°37′N 06°39′E
113 L21 **Gramsh** *var.* Gramshi. Elbasan, C Albania 40°52′N 20°12′E
Gramshi *see* Gramsh
Gran *see* Esztergom, Hungary
Gran *see* Hron
54 F11 **Granada** Meta, C Colombia 03°33′N 73°44′W
42 J10 **Granada** Granada, SW Nicaragua 11°55′N 85°58′W
105 N14 **Granada** Andalucía, S Spain 37°13′N 03°41′W
37 W6 **Granada** Colorado, C USA 38°00′N 102°18′W
42 J11 **Granada** ◈ *department* SW Nicaragua
105 N14 **Granada** ◈ *province* Andalucía, S Spain
63 I21 **Gran Antiplanicie Central** *plain* S Argentina
97 E17 **Granard** *Ir.* Gránard. C Ireland 53°47′N 07°30′W
Gránard *see* Granard
63 J20 **Gran Bajo** *basin* S Argentina
63 J15 **Gran Bajo del Gualicho** *basin* E Argentina
63 I21 **Gran Bajo de San Julián** *basin* SE Argentina
25 S7 **Granbury** Texas, SW USA 32°27′N 97°47′W
15 P12 **Granby** Québec, SE Canada 45°23′N 72°44′W
27 S8 **Granby** Missouri, C USA 36°55′N 94°14′W
37 S3 **Granby, Lake** ⊠ Colorado, C USA
64 O12 **Gran Canaria** *var.* Grand Canary. *island* Islas Canarias, Spain, NE Atlantic Ocean
47 T11 **Gran Chaco** *var.* Chaco. *lowland plain* South America
45 R14 **Grand Anse** SW Grenada 12°01′N 61°45′W
Grand-Anse *see* Portsmouth
44 G1 **Grand Bahama Island** *island* N Bahamas
Grand Balé *see* Tui
103 U7 **Grand Ballon** *Ger.* Ballon de Guebwiller. ▲ NE France 47°53′N 07°06′E
13 T13 **Grand Bank** Newfoundland, Newfoundland and Labrador, SE Canada 47°06′N 55°48′W
64 I7 **Grand Banks of Newfoundland** *undersea feature* NW Atlantic Ocean 45°00′N 40°00′W
Grand Bassa *see* Buchanan
77 N17 **Grand-Bassam** *var.* Bassam. SE Ivory Coast 05°14′N 03°45′W
14 E16 **Grand Bend** Ontario, S Canada 43°17′N 81°46′W
76 L17 **Grand-Bérébi** *var.* Grand-Béréby. SW Ivory Coast 04°38′N 06°55′W
Grand-Béréby *see* Grand-Bérébi
45 X11 **Grand-Bourg** Marie-Galante, SE Guadeloupe 15°53′N 61°19′W
44 M6 **Grand Caicos** *var.* Middle Caicos. *island* C Turks and Caicos Islands
14 K12 **Grand Calumet, Île du** *island* Québec, SE Canada
97 E18 **Grand Canal** *Ir.* An Chanáil Mhór. *canal* C Ireland
Grand Canal *see* Da Yunhe
Grand Canary *see* Gran Canaria
36 K10 **Grand Canyon** Arizona, SW USA 36°01′N 112°10′W
36 J9 **Grand Canyon** *canyon* Arizona, SW USA
Grand Canyon State *see* Arizona
44 D8 **Grand Cayman** *island* SW Cayman Islands
11 R14 **Grand Centre** Alberta, SW Canada 54°25′N 110°13′W
76 L17 **Grand Cess** SE Liberia 04°36′N 08°12′W
108 D12 **Grand Combin** ▲ S Switzerland 45°58′N 07°27′E
32 K8 **Grand Coulee** Washington, NW USA 47°56′N 119°00′W
32 J8 **Grand Coulee** *valley* Washington, NW USA
45 X5 **Grand Cul-de-Sac Marin** *bay* N Guadeloupe
Grand Duchy of Luxembourg *see* Luxembourg
63 I22 **Grande, Bahía** *bay* S Argentina
11 N14 **Grande Cache** Alberta, W Canada 53°53′N 119°07′W
103 U12 **Grande Casse** ▲ E France 45°22′N 06°50′E
Grande Comore *see* Ngazidja
61 G18 **Grande, Cuchilla** *hill range* E Uruguay
45 S5 **Grande de Añasco, Río** ≈ W Puerto Rico
Grande de Chiloé, Isla *see* Chiloé, Isla de
58 J12 **Grande de Gurupá, Ilha** *river island* NE Brazil
57 K21 **Grande de Lipez, Río** ≈ SW Bolivia
45 U6 **Grande de Loíza, Río** ≈ E Puerto Rico
45 T5 **Grande de Manatí, Río** ≈ C Puerto Rico
42 L9 **Grande de Matagalpa, Río** ≈ C Nicaragua
40 K12 **Grande de Santiago, Río** *var.* Santiago. ≈ C Mexico
43 O15 **Grande de Térraba, Río** *var.* Río Térraba. ≈ SE Costa Rica
12 J9 **Grande Deux, Réservoir la** ⊠ Québec, E Canada
60 O10 **Grande, Ilha** *island* SE Brazil
11 O13 **Grande Prairie** Alberta, W Canada 55°10′N 118°52′W
74 I8 **Grand Erg Occidental** *desert* W Algeria
74 L9 **Grand Erg Oriental** *desert* Algeria/Tunisia
57 M18 **Grande, Río** ≈ C Bolivia
59 J20 **Grande, Rio** ≈ S Brazil
2 F15 **Grande, Rio** *var.* Río Bravo, *Sp.* Río Bravo del Norte, Bravo del Norte. ≈ Mexico/USA
15 Y7 **Grande-Rivière** Québec, SE Canada 48°27′N 64°37′W
15 Y6 **Grande Rivière** ≈ Québec, SE Canada
44 M8 **Grande-Rivière-du-Nord** N Haiti 19°36′N 72°10′W
62 K9 **Grande, Salina** *var.* Gran Salitral. *salt lake* C Argentina
15 S7 **Grandes-Bergeronnes** Québec, SE Canada 48°16′N 69°32′W
47 W6 **Grande, Serra** ▲▲ W Brazil
40 K4 **Grande, Sierra** ▲▲ N Mexico
103 S12 **Grandes Rousses** ▲▲ E France
63 K17 **Grandes, Salinas** *salt lake* E Argentina
45 Y5 **Grande Terre** *island* E West Indies
15 X5 **Grande-Vallée** Québec, SE Canada 49°14′N 65°08′W
45 Y5 **Grande Vigie, Pointe de la** *headland* Grande Terre, N Guadeloupe 16°31′N 61°27′W
13 N14 **Grand Falls** New Brunswick, SE Canada 47°02′N 67°46′W
13 T11 **Grand Falls** Newfoundland, Newfoundland and Labrador, SE Canada 48°57′N 55°48′W
24 L9 **Grandfalls** Texas, SW USA 31°20′N 102°51′W
21 P9 **Grandfather Mountain** ▲ North Carolina, SE USA 36°06′N 81°48′W
26 L13 **Grandfield** Oklahoma, C USA 34°15′N 98°40′W
11 N17 **Grand Forks** British Columbia, SW Canada 49°02′N 118°30′W
29 R4 **Grand Forks** North Dakota, N USA 47°54′N 97°03′W
31 O9 **Grand Haven** Michigan, N USA 43°03′N 86°13′W
Grandichi *see* Hrandzichy
29 P15 **Grand Island** Nebraska, C USA 40°55′N 98°20′W
31 O3 **Grand Island** *island* Michigan, N USA
22 K10 **Grand Isle** Louisiana, S USA 29°12′N 90°00′W
65 A23 **Grand Jason** *island* Jason Islands, NW Falkland Islands
37 P5 **Grand Junction** Colorado, C USA 39°03′N 108°33′W
20 F10 **Grand Junction** Tennessee, S USA 35°03′N 89°11′W
14 J9 **Grand-Lac-Victoria** Québec, SE Canada 47°33′N 77°28′W
14 J9 **Grand lac Victoria** ◎ Québec, SE Canada
77 N17 **Grand-Lahou** *var.* Grand Lahu. S Ivory Coast 05°09′N 05°01′W
Grand Lahu *see* Grand-Lahou
37 S3 **Grand Lake** Colorado, C USA 40°15′N 105°49′W
13 S11 **Grand Lake** ◎ Newfoundland and Labrador, E Canada
22 G9 **Grand Lake** ◎ Louisiana, S USA
31 R5 **Grand Lake** ◎ Michigan, N USA
31 Q13 **Grand Lake** ◎ Ohio, N USA
27 R9 **Grand Lake O' The Cherokees** *var.* Lake O' The Cherokees. ⊠ Oklahoma, C USA
31 Q9 **Grand Ledge** Michigan, N USA 42°45′N 84°45′W
102 I8 **Grand-Lieu, Lac de** ◎ NW France
19 U6 **Grand Manan Channel** *channel* Canada/USA
13 O15 **Grand Manan Island** *island* New Brunswick, SE Canada
29 Y4 **Grand Marais** Minnesota, N USA 47°45′N 90°19′W
15 P10 **Grand-Mère** Québec, SE Canada 46°36′N 72°41′W
37 P5 **Grand Mesa** ▲ Colorado, C USA
108 C10 **Grand Muveran** ▲ W Switzerland 46°16′N 07°12′E
104 G12 **Grândola** Setúbal, S Portugal 38°10′N 08°34′W
Grand Paradis *see* Gran Paradiso
187 O15 **Grand Passage** *passage* N New Caledonia
77 R16 **Grand-Popo** S Benin 06°19′N 01°50′E
29 Z3 **Grand Portage** Minnesota, N USA 48°00′N 89°36′W
25 T6 **Grand Prairie** Texas, SW USA 32°45′N 97°00′W
11 W14 **Grand Rapids** Manitoba, C Canada 53°12′N 99°19′W
31 P9 **Grand Rapids** Michigan, N USA 42°57′N 86°40′W
29 V5 **Grand Rapids** Minnesota, N USA 47°14′N 93°31′W
14 L10 **Grand-Remous** Québec, SE Canada 46°36′N 75°53′W
14 F15 **Grand River** ≈ Ontario, S Canada
31 P9 **Grand River** ≈ Michigan, N USA
27 T3 **Grand River** ≈ Missouri, C USA
28 M7 **Grand River** ≈ South Dakota, N USA
45 Q11 **Grand' Rivière** N Martinique 14°52′N 61°11′W
32 F11 **Grand Ronde** Oregon, NW USA 45°03′N 123°43′W
32 L11 **Grand Ronde River** ≈ Oregon/Washington, NW USA
Grand-Saint-Bernard, Col du *see* Great Saint Bernard Pass
25 V6 **Grand Saline** Texas, SW USA 32°40′N 95°42′W
55 X10 **Grand-Santi** W French Guiana 04°19′N 54°24′W
Grandsee *see* Grandson
172 J16 **Grand Sœur** *island* Les Sœurs, NE Seychelles
108 B9 **Grandson** *prev.* Grandsee. Vaud, W Switzerland 46°49′N 06°39′E
33 S14 **Grand Teton** ▲ Wyoming, C USA 43°44′N 110°48′W
31 P5 **Grand Traverse Bay** *lake bay* Michigan, N USA
45 N6 **Grand Turk** ○ (Turks and Caicos Islands) Grand Turk Island, S Turks and Caicos Islands 21°24′N 71°08′W
45 N6 **Grand Turk Island** *island* SE Turks and Caicos Islands
103 S13 **Grand Veymont** ▲ E France 44°51′N 05°32′E
11 W15 **Grandview** Manitoba, S Canada 51°11′N 100°41′W
27 R4 **Grandview** Missouri, C USA 38°53′N 94°31′W
36 I10 **Grand Wash Cliffs** *cliff* Arizona, SW USA
14 J8 **Granet, Lac** ◎ Québec, SE Canada
95 L14 **Grangärde** Dalarna, C Sweden 60°15′N 15°00′E
44 H12 **Grange Hill** W Jamaica 18°19′N 78°11′W
96 J12 **Grangemouth** C Scotland, United Kingdom 56°01′N 03°44′W
25 T10 **Granger** Texas, SW USA 30°43′N 97°26′W
32 J10 **Granger** Washington, NW USA 46°20′N 120°11′W
33 T17 **Granger** Wyoming, C USA 41°37′N 109°58′W
Granges *see* Grenchen
95 L14 **Grängesberg** Dalarna, C Sweden 60°06′N 15°00′E
33 N11 **Grangeville** Idaho, NW USA 45°55′N 116°07′W
10 K13 **Granisle** British Columbia, SW Canada 54°55′N 126°14′W
30 K15 **Granite City** Illinois, N USA 38°42′N 90°09′W
29 S9 **Granite Falls** Minnesota, N USA 44°48′N 95°33′W
21 Q9 **Granite Falls** North Carolina, SE USA 35°48′N 81°25′W
36 K12 **Granite Mountain** ▲ Arizona, SW USA 34°38′N 112°34′W
33 T12 **Granite Peak** ▲ Montana, NW USA 45°09′N 109°48′W
35 T2 **Granite Peak** ▲ Nevada, W USA 41°40′N 117°35′W
36 J3 **Granite Peak** ▲ Utah, W USA 40°09′N 113°18′W
Granite State *see* New Hampshire
107 H24 **Granitola, Capo** *headland* Sicilia, Italy, C Mediterranean Sea 37°33′N 12°39′E
185 H15 **Granity** West Coast, South Island, New Zealand 41°37′S 171°53′E
Gran Lago *see* Nicaragua, Lago de
63 J18 **Gran Laguna Salada** ◎ S Argentina
Gran Malvina *see* West Falkland
95 L18 **Gränna** Jönköping, S Sweden 58°02′N 14°30′E
105 W5 **Granollers** *var.* Granollérs. Cataluña, NE Spain 41°37′N 02°18′E
Granollérs *see* Granollers
106 A7 **Gran Paradiso** *Fr.* Grand Paradis. ▲ NW Italy 45°31′N 07°13′E
Gran Pilastro *see* Hochfeiler
Gran Salitral *see* Grande, Salina
Gran San Bernardo, Passo di *see* Great Saint Bernard Pass
Gran Santiago *see* Santiago
107 J14 **Gran Sasso d'Italia** ▲▲ C Italy
100 N11 **Gransee** Brandenburg, NE Germany 53°00′N 13°10′E
28 L15 **Grant** Nebraska, C USA 40°50′N 101°43′W
27 R1 **Grant City** Missouri, C USA 40°29′N 94°25′W
97 N19 **Grantham** E England, United Kingdom 52°55′N 00°39′W
65 D24 **Grantham Sound** *sound* East Falkland, Falkland Islands
194 K13 **Grant Island** *island* Antarctica
45 Z14 **Grantley Adams** ✈ (Bridgetown) SE Barbados 13°04′N 59°29′W
35 S7 **Grant, Mount** ▲ Nevada, W USA 38°34′N 118°47′W
96 J9 **Grantown-on-Spey** N Scotland, United Kingdom 57°11′N 03°53′W
35 W8 **Grant Range** ▲▲ Nevada, W USA
37 Q11 **Grants** New Mexico, SW USA 35°09′N 107°50′W
30 I4 **Grantsburg** Wisconsin, N USA 45°47′N 92°40′W
32 F15 **Grants Pass** Oregon, NW USA 42°26′N 123°20′W
36 K3 **Grantsville** Utah, W USA 40°36′N 112°27′W
21 R4 **Grantsville** West Virginia, NE USA 38°55′N 81°07′W
102 I5 **Granville** Manche, N France 48°50′N 01°35′W
11 V12 **Granville Lake** ◎ Manitoba, C Canada
25 V8 **Grapeland** Texas, SW USA 31°29′N 95°28′W
25 T6 **Grapevine** Texas, SW USA 32°55′N 97°04′W
83 K20 **Graskop** Mpumalanga, NE South Africa 24°58′S 30°49′E
95 P14 **Gräsö** Uppsala, C Sweden 60°22′N 18°30′E
93 I19 **Gräsö** *island* C Sweden
103 U15 **Grasse** Alpes-Maritimes, SE France 43°42′N 06°52′E
18 E14 **Grassflat** Pennsylvania, NE USA 41°00′N 78°04′W
33 U9 **Grassrange** Montana, NW USA 47°02′N 108°48′W
18 J6 **Grass River** ≈ New York, NE USA
35 P6 **Grass Valley** California, W USA 39°12′N 121°04′W
183 N14 **Grassy** Tasmania, SE Australia 40°03′S 144°04′E
28 K4 **Grassy Butte** North Dakota, N USA 47°20′N 103°13′W
21 R5 **Grassy Knob** ▲ West Virginia, NE USA 38°04′N 80°31′W
95 G24 **Gråsten** *var.* Graasten. Syddanmark, SW Denmark 54°55′N 09°37′E
95 J18 **Grästorp** Västra Götaland, S Sweden 58°20′N 12°40′E
Gratianopolis *see* Grenoble
109 V8 **Gratwein** Steiermark, SE Austria 47°08′N 15°20′E
Gratz *see* Graz
104 K2 **Grau** *var.* Grado. Asturias, N Spain 43°23′N 06°04′W
108 I9 **Graubünden** *Fr.* Grisons, *It.* Grigioni. ◈ *canton* SE Switzerland
Graudenz *see* Grudziądz
103 N15 **Graulhet** Tarn, S France 43°45′N 01°58′E
105 T4 **Graus** Aragón, NE Spain 42°11′N 00°21′E
61 I16 **Gravataí** Rio Grande do Sul, S Brazil 29°55′S 51°00′W
98 L13 **Grave** Noord-Brabant, SE Netherlands 51°45′N 05°45′E
11 T17 **Gravelbourg** Saskatchewan, S Canada 49°53′N 106°33′W
103 N1 **Gravelines** Nord, N France 51°00′N 02°07′E
Graven *see* Grez-Doiceau
14 H13 **Gravenhurst** Ontario, S Canada 44°55′N 79°22′W
33 O10 **Grave Peak** ▲ Idaho, NW USA 46°24′N 114°43′W
102 I11 **Grave, Pointe de** *headland* W France 45°33′N 01°24′W
183 S4 **Gravesend** New South Wales, SE Australia 29°37′S 150°15′E
97 P22 **Gravesend** SE England, United Kingdom 51°27′N 00°24′E
107 N17 **Gravina in Puglia** Puglia, SE Italy 40°48′N 16°25′E
103 S8 **Gray** Haute-Saône, E France 47°28′N 05°34′E
23 T4 **Gray** Georgia, SE USA 33°00′N 83°31′W
195 V16 **Gray, Cape** *headland* Antarctica 67°30′N 143°30′E
32 F9 **Grayland** Washington, NW USA 46°46′N 124°07′W
39 N10 **Grayling** Alaska, USA 62°55′N 160°07′W
31 Q6 **Grayling** Michigan, N USA 44°40′N 84°43′W
32 F8 **Grays Harbor** *inlet* Washington, NW USA
21 O5 **Grayson** Kentucky, S USA 38°21′N 82°59′W
37 S4 **Grays Peak** ▲ Colorado, C USA 39°37′N 105°49′W
30 M16 **Grayville** Illinois, N USA 38°15′N 87°59′W
109 V8 **Graz** *prev.* Gratz. Steiermark, SE Austria 47°05′N 15°23′E
105 P13 **Grazalema** Andalucía, S Spain 36°46′N 05°23′W
113 P15 **Grdelica** Serbia, SE Serbia 42°54′N 22°05′E
44 H1 **Great Abaco** *var.* Abaco Island. *island* N Bahamas
Great Admiralty Island *see* Manus Island
Great Alfold *see* Great Hungarian Plain
Great Ararat *see* Büyükağrı Dağı
181 U8 **Great Artesian Basin** *lowlands* Queensland, C Australia
181 O12 **Great Australian Bight** *bight* S Australia
64 E11 **Great Bahama Bank** *undersea feature* E Gulf of Mexico 23°15′N 78°00′W
184 M4 **Great Barrier Island** *island* N New Zealand
181 X4 **Great Barrier Reef** *reef* Queensland, NE Australia
18 L11 **Great Barrington** Massachusetts, NE USA 42°11′N 73°20′W
0 F10 **Great Basin** *basin* W USA
8 I8 **Great Bear Lake** *Fr.* Grand Lac de l'Ours. ◎ Northwest Territories, NW Canada
Great Belt *see* Storebælt
26 L5 **Great Bend** Kansas, C USA 38°22′N 98°47′W
Great Bermuda *see* Bermuda
97 A20 **Great Blasket Island** *Ir.* An Blascaod Mór. *island* SW Ireland
Great Britain *see* Britain
151 Q23 **Great Channel** *channel* Andaman Sea/Indian Ocean
166 J10 **Great Coco Island** *island* SW Myanmar (Burma)
Great Crosby *see* Crosby
21 X7 **Great Dismal Swamp** *wetland* North Carolina/Virginia, SE USA
33 V16 **Great Divide Basin** *basin* Wyoming, C USA
181 W7 **Great Dividing Range** ▲▲ NE Australia
14 D12 **Great Duck Island** *island* Ontario, S Canada
Great Elder Reservoir *see* Waconda Lake
44 G8 **Greater Antilles** *island group* West Indies
129 V16 **Greater Sunda Islands** *var.* Sunda Islands. *island group* Indonesia
184 I1 **Great Exhibition Bay** *inlet* North Island, New Zealand
44 H4 **Great Exuma Island** *island* C Bahamas
33 R8 **Great Falls** Montana, NW USA 47°30′N 111°18′W
21 R11 **Great Falls** South Carolina, SE USA 34°34′N 80°54′W
84 F9 **Great Fisher Bank** *undersea feature* C North Sea 57°00′N 04°00′E
Great Glen *see* Mor, Glen
Great Grimsby *see* Grimsby
44 I4 **Great Guana Cay** *island* C Bahamas
64 I5 **Great Hellefiske Bank** *undersea feature* N Atlantic Ocean
111 L24 **Great Hungarian Plain** *var.* Great Alfold, Plain of Hungary, *Hung.* Alföld. *plain* SE Europe
44 L7 **Great Inagua** *var.* Inagua Islands. *island* S Bahamas
Great Indian Desert *see* Thar Desert
83 G25 **Great Karoo** *var.* Great Karroo, High Veld, *Afr.* Groot Karoo, Hoë Karoo. *plateau region* S South Africa
Great Karroo *see* Great Karoo
Great Kei *see* Nciba
Great Khingan Range *see* Da Hinggan Ling
14 E11 **Great La Cloche Island** *island* Ontario, S Canada
183 P16 **Great Lake** ◎ Tasmania, SE Australia
Great Lake *see* Tônlé Sap
11 R15 **Great Lakes** *lakes* Ontario, Canada/USA
Great Lakes State *see* Michigan
97 L20 **Great Malvern** W England, United Kingdom 52°07′N 02°19′W
184 M5 **Great Mercury Island** *island* N New Zealand
Great Meteor Seamount *see* Great Meteor Tablemount
64 K10 **Great Meteor Tablemount** *var.* Great Meteor Seamount. *undersea feature* E Atlantic Ocean 30°00′N 28°30′W
31 Q14 **Great Miami River** ≈ Ohio, N USA
151 Q24 **Great Nicobar** *island* Nicobar Islands, India, NE Indian Ocean
97 O19 **Great Ouse** *var.* Ouse. ≈ E England, United Kingdom
183 Q17 **Great Oyster Bay** *bay* Tasmania, SE Australia
44 I13 **Great Pedro Bluff** *headland* W Jamaica 17°51′N 77°44′W
21 T12 **Great Pee Dee River** ≈ North Carolina/South Carolina, SE USA
129 W9 **Great Plain of China** *plain* E China
0 F12 **Great Plains** *var.* High Plains. *plains* Canada/USA
37 W6 **Great Plains Reservoirs** ⊠ Colorado, C USA
19 Q13 **Great Point** *headland* Nantucket Island, Massachusetts, NE USA 41°23′N 70°03′W
68 I13 **Great Rift Valley** *var.* Rift Valley. *depression* Asia/Africa
81 I23 **Great Ruaha** ≈ S Tanzania
18 K10 **Great Sacandaga Lake** ⊠ New York, NE USA
108 C12 **Great Saint Bernard Pass** *Fr.* Col du Grand-Saint-Bernard, *It.* Passo del Gran San Bernardo. *pass* Italy/Switzerland
44 F1 **Great Sale Cay** *island* N Bahamas
Great Salt Desert *see* Kavīr, Dasht-e
36 K1 **Great Salt Lake** *salt lake* Utah, W USA
36 J3 **Great Salt Lake Desert** *plain* Utah, W USA
26 M8 **Great Salt Plains Lake** ⊠ Oklahoma, C USA
75 T9 **Great Sand Sea** *desert* Egypt/Libya
180 L6 **Great Sandy Desert** *desert* Western Australia
Great Sandy Desert *see* Ar Rub' al Khālī
Great Sandy Island *see* Fraser Island
187 Y13 **Great Sea Reef** *reef* Vanua Levu, N Fiji
38 H17 **Great Sitkin Island** *island* Aleutian Islands, Alaska, USA
8 J10 **Great Slave Lake** *Fr.* Grand Lac des Esclaves. ◎ Northwest Territories, NW Canada
21 O10 **Great Smoky Mountains** ▲▲ North Carolina/Tennessee, SE USA
10 L11 **Great Snow Mountain** ▲ British Columbia, W Canada 57°22′N 124°08′W
Great Socialist People's Libyan Arab Jamahiriya *see* Libya
64 A12 **Great Sound** *sound* Bermuda, NW Atlantic Ocean
180 M10 **Great Victoria Desert** *desert* South Australia/Western Australia
194 H2 **Great Wall** *Chinese research station* South Shetland Islands, Antarctica 61°57′S 58°23′W
19 T7 **Great Wass Island** *island* Maine, NE USA
97 Q19 **Great Yarmouth** *var.* Yarmouth. E England, United Kingdom 52°37′N 01°44′E
139 S1 **Great Zab** *Ar.* Az Zāb al Kabīr, *Kurd.* Zē-i Bādīnān, *Turk.* Büyükzap Suyu. ≈ Iraq/Turkey
95 I17 **Grebbestad** Västra Götaland, S Sweden 58°42′N 11°15′E
Grebenka *see* Hrebinka
42 M13 **Grecia** Alajuela, C Costa Rica 10°04′N 84°19′W
61 E18 **Greco** Río Negro, W Uruguay 32°49′S 57°03′W
Greco, Cape *see* Gkréko, Akrotíri
104 L8 **Gredos, Sierra de** ▲▲ W Spain
18 F9 **Greece** New York, NE USA 43°12′N 77°41′W
115 E17 **Greece** *off.* Hellenic Republic, *Gk.* Ellás; *anc.* Hellas. ◆ *republic* SE Europe
Greece Central *see* Stereá Elláda
Greece West *see* Dytikí Elláda
37 T3 **Greeley** Colorado, C USA 40°21′N 104°41′W
29 P14 **Greeley** Nebraska, C USA 41°33′N 98°31′W
122 K3 **Greem-Bell, Ostrov** *Eng.* Graham Bell Island. *island* Zemlya Frantsa-Iosifa, N Russian Federation
30 M6 **Green Bay** Wisconsin, N USA 44°32′N 88°W
31 N6 **Green Bay** *lake bay* Michigan/Wisconsin, N USA

21 S5 **Greenbrier River** ≈ West Virginia, NE USA
29 S2 **Greenbush** Minnesota, N USA *48°42′N 96°10′W*
183 R12 **Green Cape** *headland* New South Wales, SE Australia *37°15′S 150°03′E*
31 O14 **Greencastle** Indiana, N USA *39°38′N 86°51′W*
18 F16 **Greencastle** Pennsylvania, NE USA *39°47′N 77°43′W*
27 T2 **Green City** Missouri, C USA *40°16′N 92°57′W*
21 O9 **Greeneville** Tennessee, S USA *36°10′N 82°50′W*
35 O11 **Greenfield** California, W USA *36°19′N 121°15′W*
31 P14 **Greenfield** Indiana, N USA *39°47′N 85°46′W*
29 U15 **Greenfield** Iowa, C USA *41°18′N 94°27′W*
18 M11 **Greenfield** Massachusetts, NE USA *42°33′N 72°34′W*
27 S7 **Greenfield** Missouri, C USA *37°25′N 93°50′W*
31 S14 **Greenfield** Ohio, N USA *39°21′N 83°22′W*
20 G8 **Greenfield** Tennessee, S USA *36°09′N 88°48′W*
30 M9 **Greenfield** Wisconsin, N USA *42°55′N 87°59′W*
27 T9 **Green Forest** Arkansas, C USA *36°19′N 93°24′W*
37 T7 **Greenhorn Mountain** ▲ Colorado, C USA *37°50′N 104°59′W*
Green Island *see* Lü Dao
186 I6 **Green Islands** *var.* Nissan Islands. *island group* NE Papua New Guinea
11 S14 **Green Lake** Saskatchewan, C Canada *54°15′N 107°51′W*
30 L8 **Green Lake** ◎ Wisconsin, N USA
197 O14 **Greenland** *Dan.* Grønland, *Inuit* Kalaallit Nunaat. ◇ *Danish external territory* NE North America
84 D4 **Greenland** *island* NE North America
197 R13 **Greenland Plain** *undersea feature* N Greenland Sea
197 R14 **Greenland Sea** *sea* Arctic Ocean
37 R4 **Green Mountain Reservoir** ▣ Colorado, C USA
18 M8 **Green Mountains** ▲ Vermont, NE USA
Green Mountain State *see* Vermont
96 H12 **Greenock** W Scotland, United Kingdom *55°57′N 04°45′W*
39 T5 **Greenough, Mount** ▲ Alaska, USA *69°15′N 141°37′W*
186 A6 **Green River** Sandaun, NW Papua New Guinea *03°54′S 141°08′E*
37 N5 **Green River** Utah, W USA *39°00′N 110°07′W*
33 U17 **Green River** Wyoming, C USA *41°33′N 109°27′W*
16 H9 **Green River** ≈ W USA
30 K11 **Green River** ≈ Illinois, N USA
20 J7 **Green River** ≈ Kentucky, C USA
28 K5 **Green River** ≈ North Dakota, N USA
37 N6 **Green River** ≈ Utah, W USA
33 T16 **Green River** ≈ Wyoming, C USA
20 L7 **Green River Lake** ▣ Kentucky, S USA
23 O5 **Greensboro** Alabama, S USA *32°42′N 87°36′W*
23 U3 **Greensboro** Georgia, SE USA *33°34′N 83°10′W*
21 T9 **Greensboro** North Carolina, SE USA *36°04′N 79°48′W*
31 P14 **Greensburg** Indiana, N USA *39°20′N 85°28′W*
26 K6 **Greensburg** Kansas, C USA *37°36′N 99°17′W*
20 L7 **Greensburg** Kentucky, S USA *37°14′N 85°30′W*
18 C15 **Greensburg** Pennsylvania, NE USA *40°18′N 79°32′W*
37 O13 **Greens Peak** ▲ Arizona, SW USA *34°06′N 109°34′W*
21 V12 **Green Swamp** *wetland* North Carolina, SE USA
21 O4 **Greenup** Kentucky, S USA *38°34′N 82°49′W*
36 M16 **Green Valley** Arizona, SW USA *31°49′N 111°00′W*
76 K17 **Greenville** *var.* Sino, Sinoe. SE Liberia *05°01′N 09°03′W*
23 P6 **Greenville** Alabama, S USA *31°49′N 86°37′W*
23 T8 **Greenville** Florida, SE USA *30°28′N 83°37′W*
23 S4 **Greenville** Georgia, SE USA *33°03′N 84°42′W*
30 L15 **Greenville** Illinois, N USA *38°53′N 89°24′W*
20 I7 **Greenville** Kentucky, S USA *37°11′N 87°11′W*
19 Q5 **Greenville** Maine, NE USA *45°26′N 69°36′W*
31 P9 **Greenville** Michigan, N USA *43°10′N 85°15′W*
22 J4 **Greenville** Mississippi, S USA *33°24′N 91°03′W*
21 W9 **Greenville** North Carolina, SE USA *35°36′N 77°23′W*
31 Q13 **Greenville** Ohio, N USA *40°06′N 84°37′W*
19 O12 **Greenville** Rhode Island, NE USA *41°52′N 71°33′W*
21 P11 **Greenville** South Carolina, SE USA *34°51′N 82°24′W*
25 U6 **Greenville** Texas, SW USA *33°09′N 96°07′W*
31 T12 **Greenwich** Ohio, N USA *41°01′N 82°31′W*
27 S11 **Greenwood** Arkansas, C USA *35°13′N 94°15′W*
31 O14 **Greenwood** Indiana, N USA *39°38′N 86°06′W*
22 K4 **Greenwood** Mississippi, S USA *33°30′N 90°11′W*
21 P12 **Greenwood** South Carolina, SE USA *34°11′N 82°10′W*
21 Q12 **Greenwood, Lake** ▣ South Carolina, SE USA
21 P11 **Greer** South Carolina, SE USA *34°56′N 82°13′W*
27 V10 **Greers Ferry Lake** ▣ Arkansas, C USA
27 S13 **Greeson, Lake** ▣ Arkansas, C USA
45 N8 **Gregorio Luperón** ✈ N Dominican Republic *19°43′N 70°43′W*
29 O12 **Gregory** South Dakota, N USA *43°11′N 99°26′W*
182 J3 **Gregory, Lake** *salt lake* South Australia
180 J9 **Gregory Lake** ◎ Western Australia
181 V5 **Gregory Range** ▲ Queensland, E Australia
Greifenberg/Greifenberg in Pommern *see* Gryfice
Greifenhagen *see* Gryfino
100 O8 **Greifswald** Mecklenburg-Vorpommern, NE Germany *54°04′N 13°24′E*
100 O8 **Greifswalder Bodden** *bay* NE Germany
109 U4 **Grein** Oberösterreich, N Austria *48°14′N 14°50′E*
101 M17 **Greiz** Thüringen, C Germany *50°40′N 12°11′E*
125 V14 **Gremyachinsk** Permskiy Kray, NW Russian Federation *58°33′N 57°52′E*
Grenå *see* Grenaa
95 H21 **Grenaa** *var.* Grenå. Midtjylland, C Denmark *56°25′N 10°53′E*
22 L3 **Grenada** Mississippi, S USA *33°46′N 89°48′W*
45 W15 **Grenada** ◆ *commonwealth republic* SE West Indies
47 S4 **Grenada** *island* Grenada
47 R4 **Grenada Basin** *undersea feature* W Atlantic Ocean *13°30′N 62°00′W*
22 L3 **Grenada Lake** ▣ Mississippi, S USA
45 Y14 **Grenadines, The** *island group* Grenada/St Vincent and the Grenadines
108 D7 **Grenchen** *Fr.* Granges. Solothurn, NW Switzerland *47°13′N 07°24′E*
183 Q9 **Grenfell** New South Wales, SE Australia *33°54′S 148°09′E*
11 V16 **Grenfell** Saskatchewan, S Canada *50°24′N 102°56′W*
92 J1 **Grenivík** Nordhurland Eystra, N Iceland *65°57′N 18°10′W*
103 S12 **Grenoble** *anc.* Cularo, Gratianopolis. Isère, E France *45°11′N 05°42′E*
28 J2 **Grenora** North Dakota, N USA *48°36′N 103°57′W*
92 N8 **Grense-Jakobselv** Finnmark, N Norway *69°46′N 30°39′E*
45 S14 **Grenville** E Grenada *12°07′N 61°37′W*
32 G11 **Gresham** Oregon, NW USA *45°30′N 122°25′W*
Gresk *see* Hresk
106 B7 **Gressoney-St-Jean** Valle d'Aosta, NW Italy *45°48′N 07°49′E*
22 K9 **Gretna** Louisiana, S USA *29°54′N 90°03′W*
21 T7 **Gretna** Virginia, NE USA *36°57′N 79°21′W*
98 F13 **Grevelingen** *inlet* S North Sea
100 F13 **Greven** Nordrhein-Westfalen, NW Germany *52°07′N 07°38′E*
115 D15 **Grevená** Dytikí Makedonía, N Greece *40°05′N 21°26′E*
101 D16 **Grevenbroich** Nordrhein-Westfalen, W Germany *51°06′N 06°34′E*
99 N24 **Grevenmacher** Grevenmacher, E Luxembourg *49°41′N 06°27′E*
99 M24 **Grevenmacher** ◈ *district* E Luxembourg
100 K9 **Grevesmühlen** Mecklenburg-Vorpommern, N Germany *53°52′N 11°12′E*
185 H16 **Grey** ≈ South Island, New Zealand
33 V12 **Greybull** Wyoming, C USA *44°29′N 108°03′W*
33 U13 **Greybull River** ≈ Wyoming, C USA
65 A24 **Grey Channel** *sound* Falkland Islands
Greyerzer See *see* Gruyère, Lac de la
13 T10 **Grey Islands** *island group* Newfoundland and Labrador, E Canada
18 L10 **Greylock, Mount** ▲ Massachusetts, NE USA *42°38′N 73°09′W*
185 G17 **Greymouth** West Coast, South Island, New Zealand *42°29′S 171°14′E*
181 U10 **Grey Range** ▲ New South Wales/Queensland, E Australia
97 G18 **Greystones** *Ir.* Na Clocha Liatha. E Ireland *53°08′N 06°05′W*
185 M14 **Greytown** Wellington, North Island, New Zealand *41°04′S 175°29′E*
83 K23 **Greytown** KwaZulu/Natal, E South Africa *29°04′S 30°35′E*
Greytown *see* San Juan del Norte
99 H19 **Grez-Doiceau** *Dut.* Graven. Walloon Brabant, C Belgium *50°43′N 04°41′E*
115 J19 **Griá, Akrotírio** *headland* Ándros, Kykládes, Greece, Aegean Sea *37°54′N 24°57′E*
127 N8 **Gribanovskiy** Voronezhskaya Oblast', W Russian Federation *51°27′N 41°53′E*
78 I13 **Gribingui** ≈ N Central African Republic
35 O6 **Gridley** California, W USA *39°21′N 121°41′W*
83 G23 **Griekwastad** *var.* Griquatown. Northern Cape, C South Africa *28°50′S 23°16′E*
23 S4 **Griffin** Georgia, SE USA *33°15′N 84°17′W*
183 O9 **Griffith** New South Wales, SE Australia *34°18′S 146°04′E*
14 F13 **Griffith Island** *island* Ontario, S Canada
21 W10 **Grifton** North Carolina, SE USA *35°22′N 77°26′W*
Grigioni *see* Graubünden
119 H14 **Grigiškes** Vilnius, SE Lithuania *54°42′N 25°00′E*
117 N10 **Grigoriopol** C Moldova *47°09′N 29°18′E*
147 X7 **Grigor'yevka** Issyk-Kul'skaya Oblast', E Kyrgyzstan *42°43′N 77°27′E*
193 U8 **Grijalva Ridge** *undersea feature* E Pacific Ocean
41 U15 **Grijalva, Río** *var.* Tabasco. ≈ Guatemala/Mexico
98 N5 **Grijpskerk** Groningen, NE Netherlands *53°15′N 06°18′E*
83 C22 **Grillenthal** Karas, SW Namibia *26°55′S 15°24′E*
79 J15 **Grimari** Ouaka, C Central African Republic *05°44′N 20°02′E*
Grimaylov *see* Hrymayliv
99 G18 **Grimbergen** Vlaams Brabant, C Belgium *50°56′N 04°22′E*
183 N15 **Grim, Cape** *headland* Tasmania, SE Australia *40°42′S 144°42′E*
100 N8 **Grimmen** Mecklenburg-Vorpommern, NE Germany *54°06′N 13°03′E*
14 G16 **Grimsby** Ontario, S Canada *43°12′N 79°35′W*
97 O17 **Grimsby** *prev.* Great Grimsby. E England, United Kingdom *53°35′N 00°05′W*
92 J1 **Grímsey** *var.* Grimsey. *island* N Iceland
Grimsey *see* Grímsey
11 O12 **Grimshaw** Alberta, W Canada *56°11′N 117°37′W*
95 F18 **Grimstad** Aust-Agder, S Norway *58°20′N 08°35′E*
92 H4 **Grindavík** Sudurnes, W Iceland *65°57′N 18°10′W*
108 F9 **Grindelwald** Bern, S Switzerland *46°37′N 08°04′E*
95 F23 **Grindsted** Syddtjylland, W Denmark *55°46′N 08°56′E*
29 W14 **Grinnell** Iowa, C USA *41°44′N 92°43′W*
109 U10 **Grintovec** ▲ N Slovenia *46°21′N 14°31′E*
Griquatown *see* Griekwastad
9 N4 **Grise Fiord** *var* Aujuittuq. Northwest Territories, Ellesmere Island, N Canada *76°10′N 83°15′W*
182 H1 **Griselda, Lake** *salt lake* South Australia
Grisons *see* Graubünden
95 P14 **Grisslehamn** Stockholm, C Sweden *60°04′N 18°50′E*
29 T15 **Griswold** Iowa, C USA *41°14′N 95°08′W*
102 M1 **Griz Nez, Cap** *headland* N France *50°51′N 01°34′E*
112 P13 **Grljan** Serbia, E Serbia *43°52′N 22°18′E*
112 E11 **Grmeč** ▲ NW Bosnia and Herzegovina
99 H16 **Grobbendonk** Antwerpen, N Belgium *51°12′N 04°41′E*
Grobin *see* Grobiņa
118 C10 **Grobiņa** *Ger.* Grobin. W Latvia *56°32′N 21°12′E*
83 K20 **Groblersdal** Mpumalanga, NE South Africa *25°15′S 29°25′E*
83 G23 **Groblershoop** Northern Cape, W South Africa *28°51′S 22°01′E*
Gródek Jagielloński *see* Horodok
109 Q6 **Grödig** Salzburg, W Austria *47°42′N 13°06′E*
111 H15 **Grodków** Opolskie, S Poland *50°42′N 17°23′E*
Grodnenskaya Oblast' *see* Hrodzyenskaya Voblasts'
Grodno *see* Hrodna
110 L12 **Grodzisk Mazowiecki** Mazowieckie, C Poland *52°09′N 20°38′E*
110 F12 **Grodzisk Wielkopolski** Wielkopolskie, C Poland *52°13′N 16°21′E*
Grodzyanka *see* Hradzyanka
98 O12 **Groenlo** Gelderland, E Netherlands *52°02′N 06°36′E*
83 E22 **Groenrivier** Karas, SE Namibia *27°27′S 18°52′E*
25 U8 **Groesbeck** Texas, SW USA *31°31′N 96°35′W*
98 L13 **Groesbeek** Gelderland, SE Netherlands *51°47′N 05°56′E*
102 G7 **Groix, Îles de** *island group* NW France
110 M12 **Grójec** Mazowieckie, C Poland *51°51′N 20°52′E*
65 K15 **Gröll Seamount** *undersea feature* C Atlantic Ocean *12°54′S 33°24′W*
100 E13 **Gronau** *var.* Gronau in Westfalen. Nordrhein-Westfalen, NW Germany *52°13′N 07°02′E*
Gronau in Westfalen *see* Gronau
93 F15 **Grong** Nord-Trøndelag, C Norway *64°29′N 12°19′E*
95 N22 **Grönhögen** Kalmar, S Sweden *56°16′N 16°09′E*
98 N5 **Groningen** Groningen, NE Netherlands *53°13′N 06°35′E*
55 W9 **Groningen** Saramacca, N Suriname *05°45′N 55°31′W*
98 N5 **Groningen** ◈ *province* NE Netherlands
Grønland *see* Greenland
108 H11 **Grono** Graubünden, S Switzerland *46°15′N 09°07′E*
95 M20 **Grönskåra** Kalmar, S Sweden *57°04′N 15°45′E*
25 O2 **Groom** Texas, SW USA *35°12′N 101°06′W*
35 W9 **Groom Lake** ◎ Nevada, W USA
83 H25 **Groot** ≈ S South Africa
181 S2 **Groote Eylandt** *island* Northern Territory, N Australia
98 M6 **Grootegast** Groningen, NE Netherlands *53°11′N 06°12′E*
83 D17 **Grootfontein** Otjozondjupa, N Namibia *19°32′S 18°05′E*
83 E22 **Groot Karasberge** ▲ S Namibia
Groot Karoo *see* Great Karoo
Groot-Kei *see* Nciba
15 V6 **Grosses-Roches** Québec, SE Canada *48°55′N 67°06′W*
109 V2 **Gross-Siegharts** Niederösterreich, N Austria *48°48′N 15°25′E*
45 T10 **Gros Islet** N Saint Lucia *14°04′N 60°57′W*
44 L8 **Gros-Morne** NW Haiti *19°45′N 72°46′W*
13 S11 **Gros Morne** ▲ Newfoundland, Newfoundland and Labrador, E Canada *49°38′N 57°45′W*
103 R9 **Grosne** ≈ C France
45 S12 **Gros Piton** ▲ SW Saint Lucia *13°48′N 61°04′W*
Grossa, Isola *see* Dugi Otok
Grossbetschkerek *see* Zrenjanin
Grosse Isper *see* Grosse Ysper
Grosse Kokel *see* Târnava Mare
101 M21 **Grosse Laaber** *var.* Grosse Laber. ≈ SE Germany
Grosse Laber *see* Grosse Laaber
Grosse Morava *see* Velika Morava
101 O15 **Grossenhain** Sachsen, E Germany *51°18′N 13°31′E*
109 Y4 **Grossenzersdorf** Niederösterreich, NE Austria *48°12′N 16°33′E*
101 O21 **Grosser Arber** ▲ SE Germany *49°07′N 13°10′E*
101 K17 **Grosser Beerberg** ▲ C Germany *50°39′N 10°45′E*
101 G18 **Grosser Feldberg** ▲ W Germany *50°13′N 08°28′E*
109 O8 **Grosser Löffler** *It.* Monte Lovello. ▲ Austria/Italy *47°02′N 11°56′E*
109 N8 **Grosser Möseler** *var.* Mesule. ▲ Austria/Italy *47°01′N 11°52′E*
100 J8 **Grosser Plöner See** ◎ N Germany
101 O21 **Grosser Rachel** ▲ SE Germany *48°59′N 13°23′E*
Grosser Sund *see* Suur Väin
109 P8 **Grosses Wiesbachhorn** *var.* Wiesbachhorn. ▲ W Austria *47°09′N 12°44′E*
106 F13 **Grosseto** Toscana, C Italy *42°45′N 11°07′E*
101 M22 **Grosse Vils** ≈ SE Germany
109 U4 **Grosse Ysper** *var.* Grosse Isper. ≈ N Austria
101 G19 **Gross-Gerau** Hessen, W Germany *49°55′N 08°28′E*
109 U3 **Gross Gerungs** Niederösterreich, N Austria *48°33′N 14°58′E*
109 P8 **Grossglockner** ▲ W Austria *47°05′N 12°39′E*
Grosskanizsa *see* Nagykanizsa
Gross-Karol *see* Carei
Grosskikinda *see* Kikinda
109 W9 **Grossklein** Steiermark, SE Austria *46°43′N 15°24′E*
Grosskoppe *see* Velká Deštná
Grossmeseritsch *see* Velké Meziříčí
Grossmichel *see* Michalovce
101 H19 **Grossostheim** Bayern, C Germany *49°54′N 09°03′E*
109 X7 **Grosspetersdorf** Burgenland, SE Austria *47°15′N 16°19′E*
109 T5 **Grossraming** Oberösterreich, C Austria *47°54′N 14°34′E*
101 P14 **Grossräschen** Brandenburg, E Germany *51°34′N 14°00′E*
Grossrauschenbach *see* Revúca
Gross-Sankt-Johannis *see* Suure-Jaani
Gross-Schlatten *see* Abrud
Gross-Skaisgirren *see* Bol'shakovo
Gross-Steffelsdorf *see* Rimavská Sobota
Gross Strehlitz *see* Strzelce Opolskie
109 O8 **Grossvenediger** ▲ W Austria *47°07′N 12°19′E*
Grosswardein *see* Oradea
Gross Wartenberg *see* Syców
109 U11 **Grosuplje** C Slovenia *46°00′N 14°36′E*
99 H17 **Grote Nete** ≈ N Belgium
94 E10 **Grotli** Oppland, S Norway *62°02′N 07°36′E*
19 N13 **Groton** Connecticut, NE USA *41°20′N 72°03′W*
29 P8 **Groton** South Dakota, N USA *45°27′N 98°06′W*
107 P18 **Grottaglie** Puglia, SE Italy *40°32′N 17°26′E*
107 L17 **Grottaminarda** Campania, S Italy *41°04′N 15°02′E*
106 K13 **Grottammare** Marche, C Italy *43°00′N 13°52′E*
21 U5 **Grottoes** Virginia, NE USA *38°16′N 78°49′W*
98 L6 **Grou** *Dutch.* Grouw. Fryslân, N Netherlands *53°07′N 05°51′E*
13 N10 **Groulx, Monts** ▲ Québec, E Canada
14 E7 **Groundhog** ≈ Ontario, S Canada
36 J1 **Grouse Creek** Utah, W USA *41°41′N 113°52′W*
36 J1 **Grouse Creek Mountains** ▲ Utah, W USA
Grouw *see* Grou
27 R8 **Grove** Oklahoma, C USA *36°35′N 94°46′W*
31 S13 **Grove City** Ohio, N USA *39°52′N 83°05′W*
18 B13 **Grove City** Pennsylvania, NE USA *41°09′N 80°02′W*
23 O6 **Grove Hill** Alabama, S USA *31°42′N 87°46′W*
33 S15 **Grover** Wyoming, C USA *42°48′N 110°57′W*
35 P13 **Grover City** California, W USA *35°08′N 120°37′W*
25 Y11 **Groves** Texas, SW USA *29°57′N 93°55′W*
19 O7 **Groveton** New Hampshire, NE USA *44°35′N 71°28′W*
25 W9 **Groveton** Texas, SW USA *31°04′N 95°08′W*
36 J15 **Growler Mountains** ▲ Arizona, SW USA
Grozdovo *see* Bratya Daskalovi
127 P16 **Groznyy** Chechenskaya Respublika, SW Russian Federation *43°20′N 45°43′E*
Grubeshov *see* Hrubieszów
112 G9 **Grubišno Polje** Bjelovar-Bilogora, NE Croatia *45°42′N 17°09′E*
Grudovo *see* Sredets
110 J9 **Grudziądz** *Ger.* Graudenz. Kujawsko-pomorskie, C Poland *53°29′N 18°45′E*
25 R17 **Grulla** *var.* La Grulla. Texas, SW USA *26°15′N 98°37′W*
40 K14 **Grullo** Jalisco, SW Mexico *19°45′N 104°15′W*
67 V10 **Grumeti** ≈ N Tanzania
95 K16 **Grums** Värmland, C Sweden *59°22′N 13°11′E*
109 S5 **Grünau im Almtal** Oberösterreich, N Austria *47°51′N 13°56′E*
101 H17 **Grünberg** Hessen, W Germany *50°36′N 08°57′E*
Grünberg/Grünberg in Schlesien *see* Zielona Góra
92 H3 **Grundarfjördhur** Vestfirdhir, W Iceland *64°55′N 23°15′W*
21 P7 **Grundy** Virginia, NE USA *37°17′N 82°06′W*
29 W13 **Grundy Center** Iowa, C USA *42°21′N 92°46′W*
Grüneberg *see* Zielona Góra
25 N1 **Gruver** Texas, SW USA *36°16′N 101°24′W*
108 C9 **Gruyère, Lac de la** *Ger.* Greyerzer See. ◎ SW Switzerland
108 C9 **Gruyères** Fribourg, W Switzerland *46°34′N 07°04′E*
118 E11 **Gruzdžiai** Šiauliai, N Lithuania *56°06′N 23°15′E*
Gruzinskaya SSR/Gruziya *see* Georgia
Gryada Akkyr *see* Akgyr Erezi
126 L7 **Gryazi** Lipetskaya Oblast', W Russian Federation *52°27′N 39°56′E*
124 M14 **Gryazovets** Vologodskaya Oblast', NW Russian Federation *58°52′N 40°12′E*
111 M17 **Grybów** Małopolskie, SE Poland *49°35′N 20°54′E*
94 M13 **Grycksbo** Dalarna, C Sweden *60°40′N 15°30′E*
110 E8 **Gryfice** *Ger.* Greifenberg, Greifenberg in Pommern. Zachodnio-pomorskie, NW Poland *53°55′N 15°11′E*
110 D9 **Gryfino** *Ger.* Greifenhagen. Zachodnio-pomorskie, NW Poland *53°15′N 14°30′E*
92 H9 **Gryllefjord** Troms, N Norway *69°21′N 17°07′E*
95 L15 **Grythyttan** Örebro, C Sweden *59°52′N 14°31′E*
108 D10 **Gstaad** Bern, W Switzerland *46°30′N 07°16′E*
43 P14 **Guabito** Bocas del Toro, NW Panama *09°30′N 82°35′W*
44 G7 **Guacanayabo, Golfo de** *gulf* S Cuba
40 I7 **Guachochi** Chihuahua, N Mexico
104 J11 **Guadajira** ≈ SW Spain
104 M13 **Guadajoz** ≈ S Spain
40 L13 **Guadalajara** Jalisco, C Mexico *20°43′N 103°24′W*
105 O8 **Guadalajara** *Ar.* Wad Al-Hajarah; *anc.* Arriaca. Castilla-La Mancha, C Spain *40°37′N 03°10′W*
105 O7 **Guadalajara** ◈ *province* Castilla-La Mancha, C Spain
104 K12 **Guadalcanal** Andalucía, S Spain *38°06′N 05°49′W*
186 L10 **Guadalcanal** *off.* Guadalcanal Province. ◈ *province* C Solomon Islands
186 M9 **Guadalcanal** *island* C Solomon Islands
Guadalcanal Province *see* Guadalcanal
105 O12 **Guadalén** ≈ S Spain
105 R13 **Guadalentín** ≈ SE Spain
104 K15 **Guadalete** ≈ SW Spain
105 O13 **Guadalimar** ≈ S Spain
105 P12 **Guadalmena** ≈ S Spain
104 L11 **Guadalmez** ≈ W Spain
105 S7 **Guadalope** ≈ E Spain
104 K13 **Guadalquivir** ≈ W Spain
104 J14 **Guadalquivir, Marismas del** *var.* Las Marismas. *wetland* SW Spain
40 M11 **Guadalupe** Zacatecas, C Mexico *22°47′N 102°30′W*
57 E16 **Guadalupe** Ica, W Peru *13°59′S 75°49′W*
104 L10 **Guadalupe** Extremadura, W Spain *39°26′N 05°18′W*
36 L14 **Guadalupe** Arizona, SW USA *33°20′N 111°57′W*
35 P13 **Guadalupe** California, W USA *34°55′N 120°34′W*
Guadalupe *see* Canelones
40 J3 **Guadalupe Bravos** Chihuahua, N Mexico *31°22′N 106°04′W*
40 A4 **Guadalupe, Isla** *island* NW Mexico
37 U15 **Guadalupe Mountains** ▲ New Mexico/Texas, SW USA
24 J8 **Guadalupe Peak** ▲ Texas, SW USA *31°53′N 104°51′W*
25 R11 **Guadalupe River** ≈ SW USA
104 K10 **Guadalupe, Sierra de** ▲ W Spain
40 K9 **Guadalupe Victoria** Durango, C Mexico *24°30′N 104°08′W*
40 I8 **Guadalupe y Calvo** Chihuahua, N Mexico *26°04′N 106°58′W*
105 N7 **Guadarrama** Madrid, C Spain *40°40′N 04°06′W*
105 N7 **Guadarrama** ≈ C Spain
104 M7 **Guadarrama, Puerto de** *pass* C Spain
105 N9 **Guadarrama, Sierra de** ▲ C Spain
105 Q9 **Guadazaón** ≈ C Spain
45 X10 **Guadeloupe** ◇ *French overseas department* E West Indies
47 S3 **Guadeloupe** *island group* E West Indies
45 W10 **Guadeloupe Passage** *passage* E Caribbean Sea
104 H13 **Guadiana** ≈ Portugal/Spain
105 O13 **Guadiana Menor** ≈ S Spain
105 Q8 **Guadiela** ≈ C Spain
105 O14 **Guadix** Andalucía, S Spain *37°19′N 03°08′W*
Guad-i-Zirreh *see* Gowd-e Zereh, Dasht-e
193 T12 **Guafo Fracture Zone** *tectonic feature* SE Pacific Ocean
63 F18 **Guafo, Isla** *island* S Chile
42 I6 **Guaimaca** Francisco Morazán, C Honduras *14°34′N 86°49′W*
54 J12 **Guainía** *off.* Comisaría del Guainía. ◈ *province* E Colombia
Guainía, Comisaría del *see* Guainía
54 K12 **Guainía, Río** ≈ Colombia/Venezuela
55 O9 **Guaiquinima, Cerro** *elevation* SE Venezuela
60 G10 **Guaíra** Paraná, S Brazil *24°05′S 54°15′W*
60 L7 **Guaíra** São Paulo, S Brazil *20°17′S 48°21′W*
62 O7 **Guairá** *off.* Departamento del Guairá. ◈ *department* S Paraguay
Guairá, Departamento del *see* Guairá
Guaire *see* Gorey
63 F19 **Guaiteca, Isla** *island* S Chile
44 G6 **Guajaba, Cayo** *headland* C Cuba *21°50′N 77°33′W*
59 D16 **Guajará-Mirim** Rondônia, W Brazil *10°50′S 65°21′W*
Guajira *see* La Guajira
Guajira, Departamento de La *see* La Guajira
54 H3 **Guajira, Península de la** *peninsula* N Colombia
42 J6 **Gualaco** Olancho, C Honduras *15°00′N 86°03′W*
34 L7 **Gualala** California, W USA *38°45′N 123°33′W*
42 E5 **Gualán** Zacapa, C Guatemala *15°06′N 89°22′W*
61 C19 **Gualeguay** Entre Ríos, E Argentina *33°09′S 59°20′W*
61 D18 **Gualeguaychú** Entre Ríos, E Argentina *33°03′S 58°31′W*
61 C18 **Gualeguay, Río** ≈ E Argentina
63 K16 **Gualicho, Salina del** *salt lake* E Argentina
188 B15 **Guam** ◇ *US unincorporated territory* W Pacific Ocean
63 F19 **Guamblin, Isla** *island* Archipiélago de los Chonos, S Chile
61 A22 **Guaminí** Buenos Aires, E Argentina *37°01′S 62°28′W*
40 H8 **Guamúchil** Sinaloa, C Mexico *25°23′N 108°01′W*
54 H4 **Guana** *var.* Misión de Guana. Zulia, NW Venezuela *11°07′N 72°17′W*
44 C4 **Guanabacoa** La Habana, W Cuba *23°02′N 82°12′W*
42 K13 **Guanacaste** *off.* Provincia de Guanacaste. ◈ *province* NW Costa Rica
42 K12 **Guanacaste, Cordillera de** ▲ NW Costa Rica
Guanacaste, Provincia de *see* Guanacaste
40 J8 **Guanaceví** Durango, C Mexico *25°55′N 105°51′W*
44 A5 **Guanahacabibes, Golfo de** *gulf* W Cuba
42 K4 **Guanaja, Isla de** *island* Islas de la Bahía, N Honduras
44 C4 **Guanajay** La Habana, W Cuba *22°56′N 82°42′W*
41 N12 **Guanajuato** Guanajuato, C Mexico *21°N 101°19′W*
40 M12 **Guanajuato** ◈ *state* C Mexico
54 J6 **Guanare** Portuguesa, N Venezuela *09°04′N 69°45′W*
54 K7 **Guanare, Río** ≈ W Venezuela
54 J6 **Guanarito** Portuguesa, NW Venezuela *08°43′N 69°12′W*
160 M3 **Guancen Shan** ▲ C China
62 I9 **Guandacol** La Rioja, W Argentina *29°32′S 68°37′W*
44 A5 **Guane** Pinar del Río, W Cuba *22°12′N 84°05′W*
161 N14 **Guangdong** *var.* Guangdong Sheng, Kuang-tung, Kwangtung, Yue. ◈ *province* S China
Guangdong Sheng *see* Guangdong
Guanghua *see* Laohekou
Guangju *see* Gwangju
161 Q9 **Guangming Ding** ▲ Anhui, China *30°06′N 118°04′E*
160 I13 **Guangnan** *var.* Liancheng. Yunnan, SW China *24°07′N 104°54′E*
161 N8 **Guangshui** *prev.* Yinshan. Hubei, C China *31°41′N 113°53′E*
Guangxi *see* Guangxi Zhuangzu Zizhiqu
160 K14 **Guangxi Zhuangzu Zizhiqu** *var.* Guangxi, Gui, Kuang-hsi, Kwangsi, *Eng.* Kwangsi Chuang Autonomous Region. ◈ *autonomous region* S China
160 J8 **Guangyuan** *var.* Kuang-yuan, Kwangyuan. Sichuan, C China *32°27′N 105°49′E*
161 N14 **Guangzhou** *var.* Kuang-chou, Kwangchow, *Eng.* Canton. *province capital* Guangdong, S China *23°11′N 113°19′E*
59 N19 **Guanhães** Minas Gerais, SE Brazil *18°46′S 42°58′W*
160 I12 **Guanling** *var.* Guanling Bouyeizu Miaozu Zizhixian. Guizhou, S China *26°00′N 105°40′E*
Guanling Bouyeizu Miaozu Zizhixian *see* Guanling
55 N5 **Guanta** Anzoátegui, NE Venezuela *10°15′N 64°38′W*
44 J8 **Guantánamo** Guantánamo, SE Cuba *20°06′N 75°16′W*
44 J8 **Guantánamo, Bahía de** *Eng.* Guantanamo Bay. *US military base* SE Cuba*20°06′N 75°16′W*
Guantanamo Bay *see* Guantánamo, Bahía de
Guanxian/Guan Xian *see* Dujiangyan
161 Q6 **Guanyun** *var.* Yishan. Jiangsu, E China *34°18′N 119°14′E*
54 C12 **Guapí** Cauca, SW Colombia *02°36′N 77°54′W*
43 N13 **Guápiles** Limón, NE Costa Rica *10°15′N 83°46′W*
61 I15 **Guaporé** Rio Grande do Sul, S Brazil *28°55′S 51°53′W*
47 S8 **Guaporé, Rio** *var.* Río Iténez. ≈ Bolivia/Brazil *see also* Río Iténez
Guaporé, Rio *see* Iténez, Río
56 B7 **Guaranda** Bolívar, C Ecuador *01°35′S 78°59′W*
60 H11 **Guaraniaçu** Paraná, S Brazil *25°05′S 52°52′W*
59 O20 **Guarapari** Espírito Santo, SE Brazil *20°39′S 40°31′W*
60 I12 **Guarapuava** Paraná, S Brazil *25°22′S 51°28′W*
60 J8 **Guararapes** São Paulo, S Brazil *21°16′S 50°37′W*
105 N6 **Guara, Sierra de** ▲ NE Spain
60 N10 **Guaratinguetá** São Paulo, S Brazil *22°44′S 45°16′W*
104 I7 **Guarda** Guarda, N Portugal *40°32′N 07°17′W*
104 I7 **Guarda** ◈ *district* N Portugal
Guardak *see* Magdanly
104 M3 **Guardo** Castilla y León, N Spain *42°48′N 04°50′W*
104 K11 **Guareña** Extremadura, W Spain *38°51′N 06°06′W*
60 J11 **Guaricana, Pico** ▲ S Brazil *25°13′S 48°50′W*
54 L6 **Guárico** *off.* Estado Guárico. ◈ *state* N Venezuela
Guárico, Estado *see* Guárico
44 J7 **Guarico, Punta** *headland* E Cuba *20°36′N 74°43′W*
54 L7 **Guárico, Río** ≈ C Venezuela
60 M10 **Guarujá** São Paulo, SE Brazil *23°59′S 46°16′W*
61 L22 **Guarulhos** ✈ (São Paulo) São Paulo, S Brazil *23°23′S 46°32′W*
43 R17 **Guarumal** Veraguas, S Panama *07°48′N 81°15′W*
Guasapa *see* Guasopa
40 H8 **Guasave** Sinaloa, C Mexico *25°33′N 108°29′W*
54 I8 **Guasdualito** Apure, C Venezuela *07°15′N 70°40′W*
55 Q7 **Guasipati** Bolívar, E Venezuela *07°28′N 61°58′W*
186 I9 **Guasopa** *var.* Guasapa. Woodlark Island, SE Papua New Guinea *09°12′S 152°58′E*
106 F9 **Guastalla** Emilia-Romagna, C Italy *44°54′N 10°38′E*
42 D6 **Guastatoya** *var.* El Progreso. El Progreso, C Guatemala *14°51′N 90°01′W*
42 D5 **Guatemala** *off.* Republic of Guatemala. ◆ *republic* Central America
42 A2 **Guatemala** *off.* Departamento de Guatemala. ◈ *department* S Guatemala
193 S7 **Guatemala Basin** *undersea feature* E Pacific Ocean *11°00′N 95°00′W*
Guatemala City *see* Ciudad de Guatemala
Guatemala, Departamento de *see* Guatemala
Guatemala, Republic of *see* Guatemala
45 V14 **Guataro Point** *headland* Trinidad, Trinidad and Tobago *10°19′N 60°58′W*
186 B8 **Guavi** ≈ SW Papua New Guinea
54 G13 **Guaviare** *off.* Comisaría Guaviare. ◈ *province* S Colombia
Guaviare, Comisaría *see* Guaviare
54 J11 **Guaviare, Río** ≈ E Colombia
61 E15 **Guaviravi** Corrientes, NE Argentina *29°20′S 56°50′W*
54 G12 **Guayabero, Río** ≈ SW Colombia
45 U6 **Guayama** E Puerto Rico *17°59′N 66°07′W*
42 J7 **Guayambre, Río** ≈ S Honduras
Guayanas, Macizo de las *see* Guiana Highlands
45 V6 **Guayanés, Punta** *headland* E Puerto Rico *18°03′N 65°48′W*
42 J6 **Guayape, Río** ≈ C Honduras
56 B7 **Guayaquil** *var.* Santiago de Guayaquil. Guayas, SW Ecuador *02°13′S 79°54′W*
Guayaquil *see* Simon Bolivar
56 A8 **Guayaquil, Golfo de** *var.* Gulf of Guayaquil. *gulf* SW Ecuador
Guayaquil, Gulf of *see* Guayaquil, Golfo de
56 A7 **Guayas** ◈ *province* W Ecuador
62 N7 **Guaycurú, Río** ≈ NE Argentina
40 F6 **Guaymas** Sonora, NW Mexico *27°56′N 110°54′W*
45 U5 **Guaynabo** E Puerto Rico *18°19′N 66°05′W*
80 H12 **Guba** Binishangul Gumuz, W Ethiopia *11°11′N 35°21′E*
146 H8 **Gubadag** *Turkm.* Tel'man; *prev.* Tel'mansk. Daşoguz Welaýaty, N Turkmenistan *42°07′N 59°55′E*
125 V13 **Gubakha** Permskiy Kray, NW Russian Federation *58°52′N 57°35′E*
106 I12 **Gubbio** Umbria, C Italy *43°27′N 12°34′E*
100 Q13 **Guben** *var.* Wilhelm-Pieck-Stadt. Brandenburg, E Germany *51°59′N 14°42′E*
Guben *see* Gubin
110 D12 **Gubin** *Ger.* Guben. Lubuskie, W Poland *51°59′N 14°43′E*
126 K8 **Gubkin** Belgorodskaya Oblast', W Russian Federation *51°16′N 37°32′E*
162 J9 **Guchin-Us** *var.* Arguut. Övörhangay, C Mongolia *45°27′N 102°25′E*
Gudara *see* Ghŭdara
105 S8 **Gúdar, Sierra de** ▲ E Spain
137 P8 **Gudauta** *prev.* Gudaut'a. NW Georgia *43°07′N 40°35′E*
Gudaut'a *see* Gudauta
94 G12 **Gudbrandsdalen** *valley* S Norway
95 G21 **Gudenå** *var.* Gudenaa. ≈ C Denmark
Gudenaa *see* Gudenå
127 P16 **Gudermes** Chechenskaya Respublika, SW Russian Federation *43°23′N 46°06′E*
155 J18 **Gūdūr** Andhra Pradesh, E India *14°10′N 79°51′E*
146 B13 **Gudurolum** Balkan Welaýaty, W Turkmenistan *37°28′N 54°30′E*
94 D13 **Gudvangen** Sogn Og Fjordane, S Norway *60°54′N 06°49′E*
103 U7 **Guebwiller** Haut-Rhin, NE France *47°55′N 07°13′E*
Guéckédou *see* Guékédou
14 K8 **Guéguen, Lac** ◎ Québec, SE Canada
76 J15 **Guékédou** *var.* Guéckédou. Guinée-Forestière, S Guinea *08°33′N 10°08′W*
41 R16 **Guelatao** Oaxaca, SE Mexico
Guelders *see* Gelderland
78 G11 **Guélengdeng** Mayo-Kébbi, W Chad *10°55′N 15°31′E*
74 L5 **Guelma** *var.* Gâlma. NE Algeria *36°29′N 07°25′E*
74 D8 **Guelmime** *var.* Goulimime. SW Morocco *28°59′N 10°10′W*
14 G15 **Guelph** Ontario, S Canada *43°34′N 80°16′W*
102 I7 **Guéméné-Penfao** Loire-Atlantique, NW France *47°37′N 01°49′W*
102 I7 **Guer** Morbihan, NW France *47°54′N 02°07′W*
78 I11 **Guéra** *off.* Préfecture du Guéra. ◈ *prefecture* S Chad
102 H8 **Guérande** Loire-Atlantique, NW France *47°20′N 02°25′W*
Guéra, Préfecture du *see* Guéra
78 K9 **Guéréda** Biltine, E Chad *14°30′N 22°05′E*
103 N10 **Guéret** Creuse, C France *46°10′N 01°52′E*
Guernica/Guernica y Lumo *see* Gernika-Lumo
33 Z15 **Guernsey** Wyoming, C USA *42°16′N 104°44′W*
97 K25 **Guernsey** *island* Channel Islands, NW Europe
76 J10 **Guérou** Assaba, S Mauritania *16°48′N 11°40′W*
25 R16 **Guerra** Texas, SW USA *26°54′N 98°53′W*
41 O15 **Guerrero** ◈ *state* S Mexico

40 D6 **Guerrero Negro** Baja California Sur, NW Mexico *27°56′N 114°04′W*
103 P9 **Gueugnon** Saône-et-Loire, C France *46°36′N 04°03′E*
76 M17 **Guéyo** S Ivory Coast *05°25′N 06°04′W*
107 L15 **Guglionesi** Molise, C Italy *41°54′N 14°54′E*
188 K5 **Guguan** *island* C Northern Mariana Islands
Guhrau *see* Góra
Gui *see* Guangxi Zhuangzu Zizhiqu
Guiana *see* French Guiana
47 V4 **Guiana Basin** *undersea feature* W Atlantic Ocean *11°00′N 52°00′W*
48 G6 **Guiana Highlands** *var.* Macizo de las Guayanas. ▲▲ N South America
Guiba *see* Juba
102 I7 **Guichen** Ille-et-Vilaine, NW France *47°57′N 01°47′W*
Guichi *see* Chizhou
61 E18 **Guichón** Paysandú, W Uruguay *32°30′S 57°13′W*
77 U12 **Guidan-Roumji** Maradi, S Niger *13°40′N 06°41′E*
Guidder *see* Guider
159 T10 **Guide** *var.* Heyin. Qinghai, C China *36°06′N 101°25′E*
78 F12 **Guider** *var.* Guidder. Nord, N Cameroon *09°55′N 13°59′E*
76 I11 **Guidimaka** ❖ *region* S Mauritania
77 W12 **Guidimouni** Zinder, S Niger *13°40′N 09°31′E*
76 G10 **Guier, Lac de** *var.* Lac de Guiers. ◎ N Senegal
Guiers, Lac de *see* Guier, Lac de
160 L14 **Guigang** *var.* Guixian, Gui Xian. Guangxi Zhuangzu Zizhiqu, S China *23°06′N 109°36′E*
76 L16 **Guiglo** W Ivory Coast *06°33′N 07°29′W*
54 L5 **Güigüe** Carabobo, N Venezuela *10°05′N 67°48′W*
83 M20 **Guijá** Gaza, S Mozambique *24°31′S 33°02′E*
42 E7 **Güija, Lago de** ◎ El Salvador/Guatemala
160 L14 **Gui Jiang** *var.* Gui Shui. ≈ S China
104 K8 **Guijuelo** Castilla y León, N Spain *40°34′N 05°40′W*
Guilan *see* Gīlān
97 N22 **Guildford** SE England, United Kingdom *51°14′N 00°35′W*
19 R5 **Guildford** Maine, NE USA *45°10′N 69°22′W*
19 O7 **Guildhall** Vermont, NE USA *44°34′N 71°36′W*
103 R13 **Guilherand** Ardèche, E France *44°57′N 04°49′E*
160 L13 **Guilin** *var.* Kuei-lin, Kweilin. Guangxi Zhuangzu Zizhiqu, S China *25°15′N 110°16′E*
12 J6 **Guillaume-Delisle, Lac** ◎ Québec, NE Canada
103 U13 **Guillestre** Hautes-Alpes, SE France *44°41′N 06°39′E*
104 H6 **Guimarães** *var.* Guimaráes. Braga, N Portugal *41°26′N 08°19′W*
Guimaráes *see* Guimarães
58 D11 **Guimarães Rosas, Pico** ▲ NW Brazil
23 N3 **Guin** Alabama, S USA *33°58′N 87°54′W*
Güina *see* Wina
76 I14 **Guinea** *off.* Republic of Guinea, *var.* Guinée; *prev.* French Guinea, People's Revolutionary Republic of Guinea. ◆ *republic* W Africa
64 N13 **Guinea Basin** *undersea feature* E Atlantic Ocean *0°00′N 05°00′W*
76 E12 **Guinea-Bissau** *off.* Republic of Guinea-Bissau, *Fr.* Guinée-Bissau, *Port.* Guiné-Bissau; *prev.* Portuguese Guinea. ◆ *republic* W Africa
Guinea-Bissau, Republic of *see* Guinea-Bissau
66 K7 **Guinea Fracture Zone** *tectonic feature* E Atlantic Ocean
64 O13 **Guinea, Gulf of** *Fr.* Golfe de Guinée. *gulf* E Atlantic Ocean
Guinea, People's Revolutionary Republic of *see* Guinea
Guinea, Republic of *see* Guinea
Guiné-Bissau *see* Guinea-Bissau
Guinée *see* Guinea
Guinée-Bissau *see* Guinea-Bissau
Guinée, Golfe de *see* Guinea, Gulf of
44 C4 **Güines** La Habana, W Cuba *22°50′N 82°02′W*
102 G5 **Guingamp** Côtes d'Armor, NW France *48°34′N 03°09′W*
105 P3 **Guipúzcoa** *Basq.* Gipuzkoa. ❖ *province* País Vasco, N Spain
44 C5 **Güira de Melena** La Habana, W Cuba *22°47′N 82°33′W*
74 G8 **Guir, Hamada du** *desert* Algeria/Morocco
55 P5 **Güiria** Sucre, NE Venezuela *10°37′N 62°21′W*
Gui Shui *see* Gui Jiang
104 H2 **Guitiriz** Galicia, NW Spain *43°10′N 07°52′W*
77 N17 **Guitri** S Ivory Coast *05°31′N 05°14′W*
171 Q5 **Guiuan** Samar, C Philippines *11°02′N 125°45′E*
Gui Xian/Guixian *see* Guigang
160 J12 **Guiyang** *var.* Kuei-Yang, Kuei-yang, Kueyang, Kweiyang; *prev.* Kweichu. *province capital* Guizhou, S China *26°33′N 106°45′E*
160 J12 **Guizhou** *var.* Guizhou Sheng, Kuei-chou, Kweichow, Qian. ❖ *province* S China
Guizhou Sheng *see* Guizhou
102 J13 **Gujan-Mestras** Gironde, SW France *44°39′N 01°04′W*
154 B10 **Gujarāt** *var.* Gujerat. ❖ *state* W India
149 V6 **Gūjar Khān** Punjab, E Pakistan *33°19′N 73°23′E*
Gujerat *see* Gujarāt
149 V7 **Gujrānwāla** Punjab, NE Pakistan *32°11′N 74°09′E*
149 V7 **Gujrāt** Punjab, E Pakistan *32°34′N 74°04′E*
146 B8 **Gulandag** *Rus.* Gory Kulandag. ▲▲ Balkan Welaýaty, W Turkmenistan
159 U9 **Gulang** Gansu, C China *37°31′N 102°55′E*
183 R6 **Gulargambone** New South Wales, SE Australia *31°19′S 148°31′E*
155 G15 **Gulbarga** Karnātaka, C India *17°22′N 76°47′E*
118 J8 **Gulbene** *Ger.* Alt-Schwanenburg. NE Latvia *57°10′N 26°44′E*
147 U10 **Gul'cha** *Kir.* Gülchö. Oshskaya Oblast', SW Kyrgyzstan *40°16′N 73°27′E*
Gülchö *see* Gul'cha
173 T10 **Gulden Draak Seamount** *undersea feature* E Indian Ocean *33°45′S 101°00′E*
136 J16 **Gülek Boğazı** *var.* Cilician Gates. *pass* S Turkey
186 D8 **Gulf** ❖ *province* S Papua New Guinea
23 O9 **Gulf Breeze** Florida, SE USA *30°21′N 87°09′W*
Gulf of Liaotung *see* Liaodong Wan
23 V13 **Gulfport** Florida, SE USA *27°45′N 82°42′W*
22 M9 **Gulfport** Mississippi, S USA *30°22′N 89°06′W*
23 O9 **Gulf Shores** Alabama, S USA *30°15′N 87°40′W*
183 R7 **Gulgong** New South Wales, SE Australia *32°22′S 149°31′E*
160 I11 **Gulin** Sichuan, C China *28°06′N 105°47′E*
171 U14 **Gulir** Pulau Kasiui, E Indonesia *04°27′S 131°41′E*
Gulistan *see* Guliston
147 P10 **Guliston** *Rus.* Gulistan. Sirdaryo Viloyati, E Uzbekistan *40°29′N 68°46′E*
163 T6 **Guliya Shan** ▲ NE China *49°42′N 122°22′E*
Gulja *see* Yining
39 S11 **Gulkana** Alaska, USA *62°17′N 145°25′W*
11 S17 **Gull Lake** Saskatchewan, S Canada *50°05′N 108°30′W*
31 P10 **Gull Lake** ◎ Michigan, N USA
29 T6 **Gull Lake** ◎ Minnesota, N USA
95 L16 **Gullspång** Västra Götaland, S Sweden *58°58′N 14°04′E*
136 B15 **Güllük Körfezi** *prev.* Akbük Limanı. *bay* W Turkey
152 H5 **Gulmarg** Jammu and Kashmir, NW India *34°04′N 74°25′E*
Gulpaigan *see* Golpāyegān
99 L18 **Gulpen** Limburg, SE Netherlands *50°48′N 05°53′E*
Gul'shad *see* Gul'shat
145 S13 **Gul'shat** *var.* Gul'shad. Karaganda, E Kazakhstan *46°37′N 74°22′E*
81 F17 **Gulu** N Uganda *02°46′N 32°21′E*
114 K10 **Gŭlŭbovo** Stara Zagora, C Bulgaria *42°08′N 25°51′E*
114 I7 **Gulyantsi** Pleven, N Bulgaria *43°37′N 24°40′E*
Gulyaypole *see* Hulyaypole
Guma *see* Pishan
Gümai *see* Darlag
79 K16 **Gumba** Equateur, NW Dem. Rep. Congo *02°58′N 21°23′E*
Gumbinnen *see* Gusev
81 H24 **Gumbiro** Ruvuma, S Tanzania *10°19′S 35°40′E*
146 B11 **Gumdag** *prev.* Kum-Dag. Balkan Welaýaty, W Turkmenistan *39°13′N 54°35′E*
77 W12 **Gumel** Jigawa, N Nigeria *12°37′N 09°23′E*
105 N5 **Gumiel de Hizán** Castilla y León, N Spain *41°46′N 03°42′W*
153 P16 **Gumla** Jhārkhand, N India *23°03′N 84°36′E*
Gumma *see* Gunma
101 F16 **Gummersbach** Nordrhein-Westfalen, W Germany *51°01′N 07°34′E*
77 T13 **Gummi** Zamfara, NW Nigeria *12°07′N 05°07′E*
Gumpolds *see* Humpolec
Gumti *see* Gomati
Gümülcine/Gümüljina *see* Komotiní
Gümüşane *see* Gümüşhane
137 O12 **Gümüşhane** *var.* Gümüşane, Gumushkhane. Gümüşhane, NE Turkey *40°31′N 39°27′E*
137 O12 **Gümüşhane** *var.* Gümüşane, Gumushkhane. ❖ *province* NE Turkey
Gumushkhane *see* Gümüşhane
171 V14 **Gumzai** Pulau Kola, E Indonesia *05°27′S 134°38′E*
154 H9 **Guna** Madhya Pradesh, C India *24°39′N 77°18′E*
Gunabad *see* Gonābād
Gunan *see* Qijiang
Gunbad-i-Qawus *see* Gonbad-e Kāvūs
183 O9 **Gunbar** New South Wales, SE Australia *34°03′S 145°32′E*
183 O9 **Gun Creek** *seasonal river* New South Wales, SE Australia
183 Q10 **Gundagai** New South Wales, SE Australia *35°06′S 148°03′E*
79 K17 **Gundji** Equateur, N Dem. Rep. Congo *02°03′N 21°31′E*
155 G20 **Gundlupet** Karnātaka, W India *11°48′N 76°42′E*
136 G16 **Gündoğmuş** Antalya, S Turkey *36°50′N 32°07′E*
137 O14 **Güney Doğu Toroslar** ▲▲ SE Turkey
79 J21 **Gungu** Bandundu, SW Dem. Rep. Congo *05°43′S 19°20′E*
127 P17 **Gunib** Respublika Dagestan, SW Russian Federation *42°24′N 46°55′E*
112 J11 **Gunja** Vukovar-Srijem, E Croatia *44°53′N 18°51′E*
31 P9 **Gun Lake** ◎ Michigan, N USA
165 N12 **Gunma** *off.* Gunma-ken, *var.* Gumma. ❖ *prefecture* Honshū, S Japan
Gunma-ken *see* Gunma
197 P15 **Gunnbjørn Fjeld** *var.* Gunnbjörns Bjerge. ▲ C Greenland *69°03′N 29°36′W*
Gunnbjörns Bjerge *see* Gunnbjørn Fjeld
183 S6 **Gunnedah** New South Wales, SE Australia *30°59′S 150°15′E*
173 Y15 **Gunner's Quoin** *var.* Coin de Mire. *island* N Mauritius
37 R6 **Gunnison** Colorado, C USA *38°33′N 106°55′W*
36 L5 **Gunnison** Utah, W USA *39°09′N 111°49′W*
37 P5 **Gunnison River** ≈ Colorado, C USA
21 X2 **Gunpowder River** ≈ Maryland, NE USA
Güns *see* Kőszeg
163 X16 **Gunsan** *var.* Gunsan, *Jap.* Gunzan; *prev.* Kunsan. W South Korea *35°58′N 126°42′E*
Gunsan *see* Gunsan
109 S4 **Gunskirchen** Oberösterreich, N Austria *48°07′N 13°54′E*
Gunt *see* Ghund
155 H17 **Guntakal** Andhra Pradesh, C India *15°11′N 77°24′E*
23 Q2 **Guntersville** Alabama, S USA *34°21′N 86°17′W*
23 Q2 **Guntersville Lake** ▣ Alabama, S USA
109 X4 **Guntramsdorf** Niederösterreich, E Austria *48°03′N 16°19′E*
155 J16 **Guntūr** *var.* Guntur. Andhra Pradesh, SE India *16°20′N 80°27′E*
168 H10 **Gunungsitoli** Pulau Nias, W Indonesia *01°11′N 97°35′E*
155 M14 **Gunupur** Orissa, E India *19°04′N 83°52′E*
101 J23 **Günz** ≈ S Germany
Gunzan *see* Gunsan
101 J22 **Günzburg** Bayern, S Germany *48°26′N 10°18′E*
101 K21 **Gunzenhausen** Bayern, S Germany *49°07′N 10°45′E*
Guolüezhen *see* Lingbao
Guovdageaidnu *see* Kautokeino
161 P7 **Guoyang** Anhui, E China *33°30′N 116°12′E*
116 G11 **Gurahonț** *Hung.* Honctő. Arad, W Romania *46°16′N 22°21′E*
Gurahumora *see* Gura Humorului
116 K9 **Gura Humorului** *Ger.* Gurahumora. Suceava, NE Romania *47°31′N 26°00′E*
146 H8 **Gurbansoltan Eje** *prev.* Ýylanly, *Rus.* Il'yaly. Daşoguz Welaýaty, N Turkmenistan *41°57′N 59°42′E*
158 K4 **Gurbantünggüt Shamo** *desert* W China
152 H7 **Gurdāspur** Punjab, N India *32°04′N 75°28′E*
27 T13 **Gurdon** Arkansas, C USA *33°55′N 93°09′W*
Gurdzhaani *see* Gurjaani
Gurgan *see* Gorgān
152 I10 **Gurgaon** Haryāna, N India *28°27′N 77°01′E*
59 M15 **Gurguéia, Rio** ≈ NE Brazil
55 Q7 **Guri, Embalse de** ▣ E Venezuela
137 V10 **Gurjaani** *Rus.* Gurdzhaani. E Georgia *41°42′N 45°47′E*
109 T8 **Gurk** Kärnten, S Austria *46°52′N 14°17′E*
109 T9 **Gurk** *Slvn.* Krka. ≈ S Austria
Gurkfeld *see* Krško
114 K9 **Gurkovo** *prev.* Kolupchii. Stara Zagora, C Bulgaria *42°42′N 25°46′E*
109 S9 **Gurktaler Alpen** ▲▲ S Austria
146 H8 **Gurlan** *Rus.* Gurlen. Xorazm Viloyati, W Uzbekistan *41°54′N 60°18′E*
Gurlen *see* Gurlan
83 M16 **Guro** Manica, C Mozambique *17°28′S 33°18′E*
136 M14 **Gürün** Sivas, C Turkey *38°44′N 37°15′E*
59 K16 **Gurupi** Tocantins, C Brazil *11°44′S 49°01′W*
58 L12 **Gurupi, Rio** ≈ NE Brazil
152 E14 **Guru Sikhar** ▲ NW India *24°45′N 72°51′E*
162 H8 **Gurvanbulag** *var.* Höviyn Am. Bayanhongor, C Mongolia *47°08′N 98°41′E*
162 K7 **Gurvanbulag** *var.* Avdzaga. Bulgan, C Mongolia *47°43′N 103°30′E*
162 I11 **Gurvantes** *var.* Urt. Ömnögovĭ, S Mongolia *43°16′N 101°00′E*
Gur'yev/Gur'yevskaya Oblast' *see* Atyrau
77 U13 **Gusau** Zamfara, NW Nigeria *12°18′N 06°27′E*
126 C3 **Gusev** *Ger.* Gumbinnen. Kaliningradskaya Oblast', W Russian Federation *54°36′N 22°14′E*
146 J17 **Gushgy** *Rus.* Kushka. ≈ Mary Welaýaty, S Turkmenistan
Gushiago *see* Gushiegu
77 Q14 **Gushiegu** *var.* Gushiago. NE Ghana *09°54′N 00°12′W*
165 S17 **Gushikawa** Okinawa, Okinawa, SW Japan *26°21′N 127°50′E*
113 L16 **Gusinje** E Montenegro *42°34′N 19°51′E*
126 M4 **Gus'-Khrustal'nyy** Vladimirskaya Oblast', W Russian Federation *55°39′N 40°42′E*
107 B19 **Guspini** Sardegna, Italy, C Mediterranean Sea *39°33′N 08°39′E*
109 X8 **Güssing** Burgenland, SE Austria *47°03′N 16°19′E*
109 V6 **Gusswerk** Steiermark, E Austria *47°43′N 15°18′E*
92 O2 **Gustav Adolf Land** *physical region* NE Svalbard
195 X5 **Gustav Bull Mountains** ▲▲ Antarctica
39 W13 **Gustavus** Alaska, USA *58°24′N 135°44′W*
92 O1 **Gustav V Land** *physical region* NE Svalbard
35 P9 **Gustine** California, W USA *37°14′N 121°00′W*
25 R8 **Gustine** Texas, SW USA *31°51′N 98°24′W*
100 M9 **Güstrow** Mecklenburg-Vorpommern, NE Germany *53°48′N 12°12′E*
95 N18 **Gusum** Östergötland, S Sweden *58°15′N 16°30′E*
Guta/Gúta *see* Kolárovo
Gutenstein *see* Ravne na Koroškem
101 G14 **Gütersloh** Nordrhein-Westfalen, W Germany *51°54′N 08°23′E*
27 N10 **Guthrie** Oklahoma, C USA *35°53′N 97°26′W*
25 P5 **Guthrie** Texas, SW USA *33°38′N 100°21′W*
29 U14 **Guthrie Center** Iowa, C USA *41°40′N 94°30′W*
41 Q13 **Gutiérrez Zamora** Veracruz-Llave, E Mexico *20°29′N 97°07′W*
Gutta *see* Kolárovo
29 Y12 **Guttenberg** Iowa, C USA *42°47′N 91°06′W*
Guttentag *see* Dobrodzień
Guttstadt *see* Dobre Miasto
162 G8 **Guulin** Govĭ-Altay, C Mongolia *46°33′N 97°21′E*
153 V12 **Guwāhāti** *prev.* Gauhāti. Assam, NE India *26°09′N 91°42′E*
139 R3 **Guwēr** *var.* Al Kuwayr, Al Quwayr, Quwair. Arbīl, N Iraq *36°03′N 43°30′E*
146 A10 **Guwlumaýak** *Rus.* Kuuli-Mayak. Balkan Welaýaty, NW Turkmenistan *40°14′N 52°43′E*
55 R9 **Guyana** *off.* Co-operative Republic of Guyana; *prev.* British Guiana. ◆ *republic* N South America
Guyana, Co-operative Republic of *see* Guyana
21 P5 **Guyandotte River** ≈ West Virginia, NE USA
Guyane *see* French Guiana
Guyi *see* Sanjiang
26 H8 **Guymon** Oklahoma, C USA *36°42′N 101°30′W*
146 K12 **Guynuk** Lebap Welaýaty, NE Turkmenistan *39°18′N 63°00′E*
Guyong *see* Jiangle
21 O9 **Guyot, Mount** ▲ North Carolina/Tennessee, SE USA *35°42′N 83°15′W*
183 U5 **Guyra** New South Wales, SE Australia *30°13′S 151°42′E*
159 W10 **Guyuan** Ningxia, N China *35°57′N 106°13′E*
Guzar *see* G'uzor
121 P2 **Güzelyurt** *Gk.* Kólpos Mórfu, Morphou. W Cyprus *35°12′N 33°E*
121 N2 **Güzelyurt Körfezi** *var.* Morfou Bay, Morphou Bay, *Gk.* Kólpos Mórfou. *bay* W Cyprus
Guzhou *see* Rongjiang
40 I3 **Guzmán** Chihuahua, N Mexico *31°13′N 107°27′W*
147 N13 **G'uzor** *Rus.* Guzar. Qashqadaryo Viloyati, S Uzbekistan *38°41′N 66°12′E*
119 B14 **Gvardeysk** *Ger.* Tapaiu. Kaliningradskaya Oblast', W Russian Federation *54°39′N 21°02′E*
Gvardeyskoye *see* Hvardiys'ke
183 R5 **Gwabegar** New South Wales, SE Australia *30°34′S 148°58′E*
148 J16 **Gwādar** *var.* Gwadur. Baluchistān, SW Pakistan *25°09′N 62°21′E*
148 J16 **Gwādar East Bay** *bay* SW Pakistan
148 J16 **Gwādar West Bay** *bay* SW Pakistan
Gwadur *see* Gwādar
83 J17 **Gwai** Matabeleland North, W Zimbabwe *19°17′S 27°37′E*
154 I7 **Gwalior** Madhya Pradesh, C India *26°16′N 78°12′E*
83 J18 **Gwanda** Matabeleland South, SW Zimbabwe *20°56′S 29°E*
79 N15 **Gwane** Orientale, N Dem. Rep. Congo *04°40′N 25°51′E*
163 X16 **Gwangju** *off.* Kwangju-gwangyŏksi, *var.* Guangju, Kwangchu; *prev.* Kwangju, *Jap.* Kōshū. SW South Korea *35°09′N 126°53′E*
83 I17 **Gwayi** ≈ W Zimbabwe
110 G8 **Gwda** *var.* Głda, *Ger.* Küddow. ≈ NW Poland
97 C14 **Gweebarra Bay** *Ir.* Béal an Bheara. *inlet* W Ireland
97 D14 **Gweedore** *Ir.* Gaoth Dobhair. Donegal, NW Ireland *55°03′N 08°14′W*
Gwelo *see* Gweru
97 K21 **Gwent** *cultural region* S Wales, United Kingdom
83 K17 **Gweru** *prev.* Gwelo. Midlands, C Zimbabwe *19°27′S 29°49′E*
29 Q7 **Gwinner** North Dakota, N USA *46°10′N 97°42′W*
77 Y13 **Gwoza** Borno, NE Nigeria *11°07′N 13°40′E*
Gwy *see* Wye
183 R4 **Gwydir River** ≈ New South Wales, SE Australia
97 I19 **Gwynedd** *var.* Gwyneth. *cultural region* NW Wales, United Kingdom
Gwyneth *see* Gwynedd
159 O16 **Gyaca** *var.* Ngarrab. Xizang Zizhiqu, W China *29°06′N 92°37′E*
Gya'gya *see* Saga
Gyaijêpozhanggê *see* Zhidoi
Gyaisi *see* Jiulong
115 M22 **Gyalí** *var.* Yialí. *island* Dodekánisa, Greece, Aegean Sea
Gyamotang *see* Dêngqên
Gyandzha *see* Gäncä
Gyangkar *see* Dinggyê
158 M16 **Gyangzê** Xizang Zizhiqu, W China *28°50′N 89°38′E*
158 L14 **Gyaring Co** ◎ W China
159 Q12 **Gyaring Hu** ◎ C China
115 I20 **Gyáros** *var.* Yioúra. *island* Kykládes, Greece, Aegean Sea
122 J7 **Gyda** Yamalo-Nenetskiy Avtonomnyy Okrug, N Russian Federation *70°55′N 78°34′E*
122 J7 **Gydanskiy Poluostrov** *Eng.* Gyda Peninsula. *peninsula* N Russian Federation
Gyda Peninsula *see* Gydanskiy Poluostrov
Gyêgu *see* Yushu
163 W15 **Gyeonggi-man** *prev.* Kyŏnggi-man. *bay* NW South Korea
163 Z16 **Gyeongju** *Jap.* Keishū; *prev.* Kyŏngju. SE South Korea *35°49′N 129°09′E*
Gyéres *see* Câmpia Turzii
Gyergyószentmiklós *see* Gheorgheni
Gyergyótölgyes *see* Tulgheş
Gyertyámos *see* Cărpiniş
Gyeva *see* Detva
Gyigang *see* Zayü
Gyixong *see* Gonggar
95 I23 **Gyldenløveshøy** *hill range* C Denmark
181 Z10 **Gympie** Queensland, E Australia *26°05′S 152°40′E*
166 L7 **Gyobingauk** Bago, SW Myanmar (Burma) *18°14′N 95°39′E*
111 M23 **Gyomaendrőd** Békés, SE Hungary *46°56′N 20°50′E*
Gyömbér *see* Ďumbier
111 L22 **Gyöngyös** Heves, NE Hungary *47°44′N 19°49′E*
111 H22 **Győr** *Ger.* Raab, *Lat.* Arrabona. Győr-Moson-Sopron, NW Hungary *47°41′N 17°40′E*
111 G22 **Győr-Moson-Sopron** *off.* Győr-Moson-Sopron Megye. ❖ *county* NW Hungary
Győr-Moson-Sopron Megye *see* Győr-Moson-Sopron
11 X15 **Gypsumville** Manitoba, S Canada *51°47′N 98°38′W*
12 M4 **Gyrfalcon Islands** *island group* Northwest Territories, NE Canada
95 N14 **Gysinge** Gävleborg, C Sweden *60°16′N 16°55′E*
115 F22 **Gýtheio** *var.* Githio; *prev.* Yíthion. Pelopónnisos, S Greece *36°46′N 22°34′E*
146 L13 **Gyuichbirleshik** Lebap Welaýaty, E Turkmenistan *38°10′N 64°33′E*
111 N24 **Gyula** *Rom.* Jula. Békés, SE Hungary *46°39′N 21°17′E*
Gyulafehérvár *see* Alba Iulia
Gyulovo *see* Roza
137 T11 **Gyumri** *var.* Giumri, *Rus.* Kumayri; *prev.* Aleksandropol', Leninakan. W Armenia *40°48′N 43°51′E*
146 D13 **Gyunuzyndag, Gora** ▲ Balkan Welaýaty, W Turkmenistan *38°15′N 56°25′E*
146 J15 **Gyzylbaydak** *Rus.* Krasnoye Znamya. Mary Welaýaty, S Turkmenistan *36°51′N 62°24′E*
Gyzyletrek *see* Etrek
146 D10 **Gyzylgaýa** *Rus.* Kizyl-Kaya. Balkan Welaýaty, NW Turkmenistan *40°37′N 55°15′E*
146 A10 **Gyzylsuw** *Rus.* Kizyl-Su. Balkan Welaýaty, W Turkmenistan *39°49′N 53°00′E*
Gyzyrlabat *see* Serdar
Gzhatsk *see* Gagarin

H

153 T12 **Ha** W Bhutan *27°17′N 89°22′E*
Haabai *see* Ha'apai Group
99 H17 **Haacht** Vlaams Brabant, C Belgium *50°58′N 04°38′E*
109 T4 **Haag** Niederösterreich, NE Austria *48°07′N 14°32′E*
194 L8 **Haag Nunataks** ▲▲ Antarctica
92 N2 **Haakon VII Land** *physical region* NW Svalbard
98 O11 **Haaksbergen** Overijssel, E Netherlands *52°09′N 06°45′E*
99 E14 **Haamstede** Zeeland, SW Netherlands *51°43′N 03°45′E*
193 Y15 **Ha'ano** *island* Ha'apai Group, C Tonga
193 Y15 **Ha'apai Group** *var.* Haabai. *island group* C Tonga
93 L15 **Haapajärvi** Oulu, C Finland *63°45′N 25°20′E*
93 L17 **Haapamäki** Länsi-Suomi, C Finland *62°11′N 24°32′E*
93 L15 **Haapavesi** Oulu, C Finland *64°09′N 25°25′E*
191 N7 **Haapiti** Moorea, W French Polynesia *17°33′S 149°52′W*
118 F4 **Haapsalu** *Ger.* Hapsal. Läänemaa, W Estonia *58°58′N 23°32′E*
Ha'Arava *see* 'Arabah, Wādī al
95 G24 **Haarby** *var.* Hårby. Syddtjylland, C Denmark *55°13′N 10°07′E*
98 H10 **Haarlem** *prev.* Harlem. Noord-Holland, W Netherlands *52°23′N 04°39′E*
185 D19 **Haast** West Coast, South Island, New Zealand *43°53′S 169°02′E*
185 C20 **Haast** ≈ South Island, New Zealand
185 D20 **Haast Pass** *pass* South Island, New Zealand
193 W16 **Ha'atua** 'Eau, E Tonga *21°23′S 174°57′W*
149 P15 **Hab** ≈ SW Pakistan
141 W7 **Haba** *var.* Al Haba. Dubayy, NE United Arab Emirates *25°01′N 55°37′E*
158 K2 **Habahe** *var.* Kaba. Xinjiang Uygur Zizhiqu, NW China *48°04′N 86°20′E*
141 U13 **Ḩabarūt** *var.* Habrut. SW Oman *17°19′N 52°45′E*
81 J18 **Habaswein** North Eastern, NE Kenya *01°01′N 39°27′E*
99 L24 **Habay-la-Neuve** Luxembourg, SE Belgium *49°43′N 05°38′E*
139 S8 **Ḩabbānīyah, Buḩayrat** ◎ C Iraq
Habelschwerdt *see* Bystrzyca Kłodzka
153 V14 **Habiganj** Sylhet, NE Bangladesh *24°23′N 91°25′E*
163 Q12 **Habirag** Nei Mongol Zizhiqu, N China *42°18′N 115°40′E*
95 L19 **Habo** Västra Götaland, S Sweden *57°55′N 14°05′E*
123 V14 **Habomai Islands** *island group* Kuril'skiye Ostrova, SE Russian Federation
165 S2 **Haboro** Hokkaidō, NE Japan *44°19′N 141°42′E*
153 S16 **Habra** West Bengal, NE India *22°39′N 88°17′E*
Habrut *see* Ḩabarūt
143 P17 **Ḩabshān** Abū Z̧aby, C United Arab Emirates *23°51′N 53°34′E*
54 E14 **Hacha** Putumayo, S Colombia *0°02′S 75°30′W*
165 X13 **Hachijō-jima** *island* Izu-shotō, SE Japan
164 L12 **Hachiman** Gifu, Honshū, SW Japan *35°46′N 136°57′E*
165 P7 **Hachimori** Akita, Honshū, C Japan *40°22′N 139°59′E*
165 R7 **Hachinohe** Aomori, Honshū, C Japan *40°30′N 141°29′E*
165 X13 **Hachiōji** Tōkyō, Hachijō-jima, SE Japan *35°40′N 139°20′E*
137 Y12 **Hacıqabal** *prev.* Qazimämmäd. SE Azerbaijan *40°03′N 48°56′E*
93 G17 **Hackås** Jämtland, C Sweden *62°55′N 14°31′E*
18 K14 **Hackensack** New Jersey, NE USA *40°51′N 73°57′W*
75 U12 **Haḑabat al Jilf al Kabīr** *var.* Gilf Kebir Plateau. *plateau* SW Egypt
Hadama *see* Nazrēt
141 W13 **Ḩadbaram** S Oman *17°27′N 55°13′E*
139 U13 **Ḩaddānīyah** *well* S Iraq
96 K12 **Haddington** SE Scotland, United Kingdom *55°59′N 02°46′W*
141 Z8 **Ḩadd, Ra's al** *headland* NE Oman *22°28′N 59°58′E*
Haded *see* Xadeed
77 W12 **Hadejia** Jigawa, N Nigeria *12°22′N 10°02′E*
77 W12 **Hadejia** ≈ N Nigeria
138 F9 **Hadera** *var.* Khadera; *prev.* Ḩadera. Haifa, N Israel *32°26′N 34°55′E*
Ḩadera *see* Hadera
Hadersleben *see* Haderslev
95 G24 **Haderslev** *Ger.* Hadersleben. Syddanmark, SW Denmark *55°15′N 09°30′E*
151 J21 **Hadhdhunmathi Atoll** *atoll* S Maldives
141 W17 **Hadīboh** Suquţrā, SE Yemen *12°38′N 54°05′E*
158 K9 **Hadilik** Xinjiang Uygur Zizhiqu, W China *37°51′N 86°10′E*
136 H16 **Hadım** Konya, S Turkey *36°58′N 32°27′E*
140 K7 **Hadīyah** Al Madīnah, W Saudi Arabia *25°36′N 38°31′E*
8 L5 **Hadley Bay** *bay* Victoria Island, Nunavut, N Canada
167 S6 **Ha Đông** *var.* Hadong. Ha Tây, N Vietnam *20°58′N 105°46′E*
Hadong *see* Ha Đông
Hadramaut *see* Ḩaḑramawt
141 R15 **Ḩaḑramawt** *Eng.* Hadramaut. ▲▲ S Yemen
Hadria *see* Adria
Hadrianopolis *see* Edirne
Hadria Picena *see* Apricena
95 G22 **Hadsten** Midtjylland, C Denmark *56°19′N 10°03′E*
95 G21 **Hadsund** Nordjylland, N Denmark *56°43′N 10°08′E*
117 S4 **Hadyach** *Rus.* Gadyach. Poltavs'ka Oblast', NE Ukraine *50°21′N 34°00′E*
112 I13 **Hadžići** Federacija Bosna I Hercegovina, SE Bosnia and Herzegovina *43°49′N 18°12′E*
163 W14 **Haeju** S North Korea *38°04′N 125°40′E*
Haerbin/Haerhpin/Ha-erh-pin *see* Harbin
141 P5 **Ḩafar al Bāţin** Ash Sharqīyah, N Saudi Arabia *28°25′N 45°59′E*
11 T15 **Hafford** Saskatchewan, S Canada *52°43′N 107°19′W*
136 M13 **Hafik** Sivas, N Turkey *39°53′N 37°24′E*
149 V8 **Hāfizābād** Punjab, E Pakistan *32°03′N 73°42′E*
92 H4 **Hafnarfjördhur** Höfudborgarsvœdid, W Iceland *64°03′N 21°57′W*
Hafnia *see* Denmark
Hafnia *see* København
Hafren *see* Severn
Hafun *see* Xaafuun
Hafun, Ras *see* Xaafuun, Raas
80 G10 **Hag 'Abdullah** Sinnar, E Sudan *13°59′N 33°35′E*
81 K18 **Hagadera** North Eastern, E Kenya *0°06′N 40°23′E*
138 G8 **HaGalil** *Eng.* Galilee. ▲▲ N Israel
14 G10 **Hagar** Ontario, S Canada *46°27′N 80°22′W*
155 G18 **Hagari** *var.* Vedāvati. ≈ W India
188 B16 **Hagåtña**, *var.* Agaña. ○ (Guam) NW Guam *13°27′N 144°45′E*
100 M13 **Hagelberg** *hill* NE Germany
39 N14 **Hagemeister Island** *island* Alaska, USA
101 F15 **Hagen** Nordrhein-Westfalen, W Germany *51°22′N 07°27′E*
100 K10 **Hagenow** Mecklenburg-Vorpommern, N Germany *53°27′N 11°10′E*
10 K15 **Hagensborg** British Columbia, SW Canada *52°24′N 126°24′W*
80 I13 **Hāgere Hiywet** *var.* Agere Hiywet, Ambo. Oromīya, C Ethiopia *09°00′N 37°55′E*
33 O15 **Hagerman** Idaho, NW USA *42°48′N 114°53′W*
37 U14 **Hagerman** New Mexico, SW USA *33°07′N 104°19′W*
21 V2 **Hagerstown** Maryland, NE USA *39°39′N 77°44′W*
14 G16 **Hagersville** Ontario, S Canada *42°58′N 80°03′W*
102 J15 **Hagetmau** Landes, SW France *43°40′N 00°36′W*
95 K14 **Hagfors** Värmland, C Sweden *60°03′N 13°45′E*
93 G16 **Häggenås** Jämtland, C Sweden *63°24′N 14°53′E*
164 E12 **Hagi** Yamaguchi, Honshū, SW Japan *34°25′N 131°22′E*
167 S5 **Ha Giang** Ha Giang, N Vietnam *22°50′N 104°58′E*
Hagios Evstrátios *see* Ágios Efstrátios
HaGolan *see* Golan Heights
103 T4 **Hagondange** Moselle, NE France *49°16′N 06°06′E*
97 B18 **Hag's Head** *Ir.* Ceann Caillí. *headland* W Ireland *52°56′N 09°29′W*
102 I3 **Hague, Cap de la** *headland* N France *49°43′N 01°56′W*
103 V5 **Haguenau** Bas-Rhin, NE France *48°49′N 07°47′E*
165 X16 **Hahajima-rettō** *island group* SE Japan
15 R8 **Há Há, Lac** ◎ Québec, SE Canada
172 H13 **Hahaya** ✈ (Moroni) Grande Comore, NW Comoros
22 K9 **Hahnville** Louisiana, S USA *29°58′N 90°24′W*
83 E22 **Haib** Karas, S Namibia *28°12′S 18°19′E*
Haibak *see* Aibak
149 N15 **Haibo** ≈ SW Pakistan
Haibowan *see* Wuhai
163 U12 **Haicheng** Liaoning, NE China *40°53′N 122°45′E*
Haicheng *see* Haifeng
Haicheng *see* Haiyuan
Haida *see* Nový Bor
Haidarabad *see* Hyderābād
Haidenschaft *see* Ajdovščina
167 T6 **Hai Dương** Hai Hưng, N Vietnam *20°56′N 106°21′E*
138 F9 **Haifa** ❖ *district* NW Israel
Haifa *see* Hefa
Haifa, Bay of *see* Mifrats Hefa
161 P14 **Haifeng** *var.* Haicheng. Guangdong, S China *22°56′N 115°19′E*
Haifong *see* Hai Phong
161 P3 **Hai He** ≈ E China
Haikang *see* Leizhou
160 L17 **Haikou** *var.* Hai-k'ou, Hoihow, *Fr.* Hoï-Hao. *province capital* Hainan, S China *20°N 110°17′E*
Hai-k'ou *see* Haikou
140 M6 **Ḩā'il** Ḩā'il, NW Saudi Arabia *27°N 42°50′E*
141 N5 **Ḩā'il** *off.* Minţaqah Ḩā'il. ❖ *province* N Saudi Arabia
163 S6 **Hailar He** ≈ NE China
33 P14 **Hailey** Idaho, NW USA *43°31′N 114°18′W*
14 H9 **Haileybury** Ontario, S Canada *47°27′N 79°39′W*
163 X9 **Hailin** Heilongjiang, NE China *44°37′N 129°24′E*
Ḩā'il, Minţaqah *see* Ḩā'il
Hailong *see* Meihekou
93 K14 **Hailuoto** *Swe.* Karlö. *island* W Finland
Haima *see* Haymā'
Haimen *see* Taizhou
160 M17 **Hainan** *var.* Hainan Sheng, Qiong. ❖ *province* S China
160 K17 **Hainan Dao** *island* S China
Hainan Sheng *see* Hainan
Hainan Strait *see* Qiongzhou Haixia
Hainasch *see* Ainaži
Hainau *see* Chojnów
99 E20 **Hainaut** ❖ *province* SW Belgium
Hainburg *see* Hainburg an der Donau
109 Z4 **Hainburg an der Donau** *var.* Hainburg. Niederösterreich, NE Austria *48°09′N 16°57′E*
39 W12 **Haines** Alaska, USA *59°13′N 135°27′W*
32 L12 **Haines** Oregon, NW USA *44°53′N 117°56′W*
23 W12 **Haines City** Florida, SE USA *28°06′N 81°37′W*
10 H8 **Haines Junction** Yukon Territory, W Canada *60°45′N 137°30′W*
109 W4 **Hainfeld** Niederösterreich, NE Austria *48°03′N 15°47′E*
101 N16 **Hainichen** Sachsen, E Germany *50°58′N 13°08′E*
Hai Ninh *see* Mong Cai
167 T6 **Hai Phong** *var.* Haifong, Haiphong. N Vietnam *20°50′N 106°41′E*
Haiphong *see* Hai Phong
161 S12 **Haitan Dao** *island* SE China
44 K8 **Haiti** *off.* Republic of Haiti. ◆ *republic* C West Indies
Haiti, Republic of *see* Haiti
35 T11 **Haiwee Reservoir** ▣ California, W USA
80 I7 **Haiya** Red Sea, NE Sudan *18°17′N 36°21′E*
159 T10 **Haiyan** *var.* Sanjiaocheng. Qinghai, W China *36°55′N 100°54′E*
160 M13 **Haiyang Shan** ▲▲ S China
159 V10 **Haiyuan** Ningxia, N China *36°32′N 105°31′E*
Hajda *see* Nový Bor
111 M22 **Hajdú-Bihar** *off.* Hajdú-Bihar Megye. ❖ *county* E Hungary
Hajdú-Bihar Megye *see* Hajdú-Bihar
111 N22 **Hajdúböszörmény** Hajdú-Bihar, E Hungary *47°39′N 21°32′E*
111 N22 **Hajdúhadház** Hajdú-Bihar, E Hungary *47°40′N 21°40′E*
111 N21 **Hajdúnánás** Hajdú-Bihar, E Hungary *47°50′N 21°26′E*
111 N22 **Hajdúszoboszló** Hajdú-Bihar, E Hungary *47°27′N 21°24′E*
142 I3 **Ḩājī Ebrāhīm, Kūh-e** ▲ Iran/Iraq *36°53′N 44°56′E*
165 O9 **Hajiki-zaki** *headland* Sado, C Japan *38°19′N 138°28′E*
Hajîne *see* Abū Ḩardān
153 P13 **Hājīpur** Bihār, N India *25°41′N 85°13′E*
141 N14 **Ḩajjah** W Yemen *15°43′N 43°33′E*
139 U11 **Hajjama** Al Muthanná, S Iraq *31°24′N 45°20′E*
143 R12 **Ḩājjīābād** Hormozgān, C Iran
139 U14 **Ḩājj, Thaqb al** *well* S Iraq
113 L16 **Hajla** ▲▲ E Montenegro
110 P10 **Hajnówka** *Ger.* Hermhausen. Podlaskie, NE Poland *52°45′N 23°32′E*
Haka *see* Hakha
Hakapehi *see* Punaauia
Hakâri *see* Hakkâri
138 F12 **HaKatan, HaMakhtesh** *prev.* HaMakhtesh HaQatan. ▲▲ S Israel
166 K4 **Hakha** *var.* Haka. Chin State, W Myanmar (Burma) *22°42′N 93°41′E*
137 T16 **Hakkâri** *var.* Çölemerik, Hakâri. Hakkâri, SE Turkey *37°36′N 43°45′E*
137 T16 **Hakkâri** *var.* Hakkari. ❖ *province* SE Turkey
Hakkari *see* Hakkâri
92 J12 **Hakkas** Norrbotten, N Sweden *66°53′N 21°36′E*
164 J14 **Hakken-zan** ▲ Honshū, SW Japan *34°11′N 135°57′E*
165 R7 **Hakkōda-san** ▲ Honshū, C Japan *40°40′N 140°49′E*
165 T2 **Hako-dake** ▲ Hokkaidō, NE Japan *44°40′N 142°22′E*
165 R5 **Hakodate** Hokkaidō, NE Japan *41°46′N 140°43′E*
164 L11 **Hakui** Ishikawa, Honshū, SW Japan *36°55′N 136°46′E*
190 B16 **Hakupu** SE Niue *19°06′S 169°50′E*
164 L12 **Haku-san** ▲ Honshū, SW Japan *36°07′N 136°45′E*
Hakusan *see* Mattō
Hal *see* Halle
149 Q15 **Hāla** Sind, SE Pakistan *25°47′N 68°28′E*
138 J3 **Ḩalab** *Eng.* Aleppo, *Fr.* Alep; *anc.* Beroea. Ḩalab, NW Syria *36°14′N 37°10′E*
138 J3 **Ḩalab** *off.* Muḩāfaz̧at Ḩalab, *var.* Aleppo, Halab. ❖ *governorate* NW Syria
138 J3 **Ḩalab** ✈ Ḩalab, NW Syria *36°12′N 37°10′E*
Halab *see* Ḩalab

141 O8 Ḥalabān var. Halibān. Ar Riyāḍ, C Saudi Arabia 23°29´N 44°20´E
139 V4 Ḥalabja As Sulaymānīyah, NE Iraq 35°11´N 45°59´E
Ḥalab, Muḥāfaẓat see Ḥalab
146 L13 Halaç Rus. Khalach. Lebap Welaýaty, E Turkmenistan 38°05´N 64°46´E
190 A16 Halagigie Point headland W Niue
75 Z11 Halaib SE Egypt 22°10´N 36°33´E
75 Z11 Halaʻib Triangle disputed region S Egypt / N Sudan
190 G12 Halalo Île Uvea, N Wallis and Futuna 13°21´S 176°11´W
167 U10 Ha Lam Quang Nam-Đa Nāng, C Vietnam 15°42´N 108°24´E
Halandri see Chalándri
141 X13 Ḥalāniyāt, Juzur al var. Jazāʻir Bin Ghalfān, Eng. Kuria Muria Islands. island group S Oman
141 W13 Ḥalāniyāt, Khalīj al Eng. Kuria Muria Bay. bay S Oman
Halas see Kiskunhalas
38 G11 Hālawa var. Halawa. Hawaii, USA, C Pacific Ocean 20°13´N 155°46´W
Halawa see Hālawa
38 F9 Hālawa, Cape var. Cape Halawa. headland Molokaʻi, Hawaiʻi, USA 21°09´N 156°43´W
Cape Halawa see Hālawa, Cape
Halban see Tsetserleg
101 K14 Halberstadt Sachsen-Anhalt, C Germany 51°54´N 11°04´E
184 M12 Halcombe Manawatu-Wanganui, North Island, New Zealand 40°09´S 175°30´E
95 I16 Halden prev. Fredrikshald. Østfold, S Norway 59°08´N 11°20´E
100 L13 Haldensleben Sachsen-Anhalt, C Germany 52°18´N 11°25´E
Háldi see Halti
153 S17 Haldia West Bengal, NE India 22°04´N 88°02´E
152 K10 Haldwāni Uttarakhand, N India 29°13´N 79°31´E
163 P9 Haldzan Sühbaatar, E Mongolia 46°10´N 112°57´E
163 P9 Haldzan var. Hatavch. Sühbaatar, E Mongolia 46°10´N 112°57´E
38 F10 Haleakalā var. Haleakala. crater Maui, Hawaiʻi, USA
Haleakala see Haleakalā
25 N4 Hale Center Texas, SW USA 34°03´N 101°50´W
99 J18 Halen Limburg, NE Belgium 50°35´N 05°08´E
23 O2 Haleyville Alabama, S USA 34°13´N 87°37´W
77 O17 Half Assini SW Ghana 05°03´N 02°57´W
35 R8 Half Dome ▲ California, W USA 37°46´N 119°27´W
185 C25 Halfmoon Bay var. Oban. Stewart Island, Southland, New Zealand 46°53´S 168°08´E
182 E5 Half Moon Lake salt lake South Australia
163 S8 Halhgol var. Tsagaannuur. Dornod, E Mongolia 47°30´N 118°45´E
163 R7 Halhgol Dornod, E Mongolia 47°57´N 118°07´E
Haliacmon see Aliákmonas
Halibān see Ḥalabān
14 I13 Haliburton Ontario, SE Canada 45°03´N 78°20´W
14 I12 Haliburton Highlands var. Madawaska Highlands. hill range Ontario, SE Canada
13 Q15 Halifax province capital Nova Scotia, SE Canada 44°38´N 63°35´W
97 L17 Halifax N England, United Kingdom 53°44´N 01°52´W
21 W8 Halifax North Carolina, SE USA 36°19´N 77°37´W
21 U7 Halifax Virginia, NE USA 36°46´N 78°55´W
13 Q15 Halifax ✕ Nova Scotia, SE Canada 44°33´N 63°48´W
143 T13 Halīl Rūd seasonal river SE Iran
138 I6 Ḥalīmah ▲ Lebanon/Syria 34°12´N 36°37´E
162 G8 Haliun Govĭ-Altay, W Mongolia 45°55´N 96°06´E
118 I3 Haljala Ger. Halljal. Lääne-Virumaa, N Estonia 59°25´N 26°18´E
39 Q4 Halkett, Cape headland Alaska, USA 70°48´N 152°11´W
Halkida see Chalkída
96 J6 Halkirk N Scotland, United Kingdom 58°30´N 03°29´W
15 X7 Hall ≈ Québec, SE Canada
Hall see Schwäbisch Hall
93 H15 Hällabottlen Västernorrland, N Sweden 63°56´N 17°20´E
96 J6 Halladale ≈ N Scotland, United Kingdom
95 J21 Halland ◈ county S Sweden
23 Z15 Hallandale Florida, SE USA 25°58´N 80°09´W
95 K22 Hallandsås physical region S Sweden
9 P6 Hall Beach var Sanirajak. Nunavut, N Canada 68°10´N 81°56´W
99 G19 Halle Fr. Hal. Vlaams Brabant, C Belgium 50°44´N 04°14´E
101 M15 Halle var. Halle an der Saale. Sachsen-Anhalt, C Germany 51°28´N 11°58´E
Halle an der Saale see Halle
35 W3 Halleck Nevada, W USA 40°57´N 115°27´W
95 L15 Hällefors Örebro, C Sweden 59°46´N 14°30´E
95 N16 Hälleforsnäs Södermanland, C Sweden 59°10´N 16°30´E
109 Q6 Hallein Salzburg, N Austria 47°41´N 13°06´E
101 L15 Halle-Neustadt Sachsen-Anhalt, C Germany 51°29´N 11°54´E
25 U12 Hallettsville Texas, SW USA 29°27´N 96°57´W
195 N4 Halley UK research station Antarctica 75°42´S 26°30´W
28 L4 Halliday North Dakota, N USA 47°19´N 102°19´W
37 S2 Halligan Reservoir ⊠ Colorado, C USA
100 G7 Halligen island group N Germany
94 G13 Hallingdal valley S Norway
38 J12 Hall Island island Alaska, USA
Hall Island see Maiana
189 P15 Hall Islands island group C Micronesia
118 H6 Halliste ≈ S Estonia
Halljal see Haljala
93 I15 Hällnäs Västerbotten, N Sweden 64°20´N 19°41´E
29 R2 Hallock Minnesota, N USA 48°47´N 96°56´W
9 S6 Hall Peninsula peninsula Baffin Island, Nunavut, NE Canada
20 F9 Halls Tennessee, S USA 35°52´N 89°24´W
95 M16 Hallsberg Örebro, C Sweden 59°05´N 15°07´E
181 N5 Halls Creek Western Australia 18°17´S 127°39´E
182 L12 Halls Gap Victoria, SE Australia 37°09´S 142°30´E
95 N15 Hallstahammar Västmanland, C Sweden 59°37´N 16°13´E
109 R6 Hallstatt Salzburg, W Austria 47°32´N 13°39´E
109 R6 Hallstätter See ◎ C Austria
95 P14 Hallstavik Stockholm, C Sweden 60°12´N 18°45´E
25 X7 Hallsville Texas, SW USA 32°31´N 94°30´W
103 P1 Halluin Nord, N France 50°46´N 03°07´E
171 S12 Halmahera, Laut Eng. Halmahera Sea. sea E Indonesia
171 R11 Halmahera, Pulau prev. Djailolo, Gilolo, Jailolo. island E Indonesia
Halmahera Sea see Halmahera, Laut
95 J21 Halmstad Halland, S Sweden 56°41´N 12°49´E
167 T6 Ha Long prev. Hông Gai, var. Hon Gai, Hongay. Quang Ninh, N Vietnam 20°57´N 107°06´E
119 N15 Halowchyn Rus. Golovchin. Mahilyowskaya Voblasts', E Belarus 54°04´N 29°55´E
95 H20 Hals Nordjylland, N Denmark 57°00´N 10°19´E
94 F8 Halsa Møre og Romsdal, S Norway 63°04´N 08°13´E
119 I15 Hal'shany Rus. Gol'shany. Hrodzyenskaya Voblasts', W Belarus 54°15´N 26°01´E
Hälsingborg see Helsingborg
29 R5 Halstad Minnesota, N USA 47°21´N 96°49´W
27 N6 Halstead Kansas, C USA 38°00´N 97°30´W
99 G15 Halsteren Noord-Brabant, S Netherlands 51°32´N 04°16´E
93 L16 Halsua Länsi-Suomi, W Finland 63°28´N 24°10´E
101 E14 Haltern Nordrhein-Westfalen, W Germany 51°45´N 07°10´E
92 J9 Halti var. Haltiatunturi, Lapp. Háldi. ▲ Finland/Norway 69°18´N 21°19´E
Haltiatunturi see Halti
116 J6 Halych Ivano-Frankivs'ka Oblast', W Ukraine 49°08´N 24°44´E
Halycus see Platani
103 P3 Ham Somme, N France 49°46´N 03°03´E
Hama see Ḥamāh
164 F12 Hamada Shimane, Honshū, SW Japan 34°54´N 132°07´E
142 L6 Hamadān anc. Ecbatana. Hamadān, W Iran 34°51´N 48°31´E
142 L6 Hamadān off. Ostān-e Hamadān. ◈ province W Iran
Hamadān, Ostān-e see Hamadān
138 I5 Ḥamāh var. Hama; anc. Epiphania, Bibl. Hamath. Ḥamāh, W Syria 35°09´N 36°44´E
138 I5 Ḥamāh off. Muḥāfaẓat Ḥamāh, var. Hama. ◈ governorate C Syria
Ḥamāh, Muḥāfaẓat see Ḥamāh
1665 S3 Hamamasu Hokkaidō, NE Japan 43°37´N 141°24´E
164 L14 Hamamatsu var. Hamamatu. Shizuoka, Honshū, S Japan 34°43´N 137°46´E
Hamamatu see Hamamatsu
165 W14 Hamanaka Hokkaidō, NE Japan 43°05´N 145°05´E
164 L14 Hamana-ko ◎ Honshū, S Japan
94 I13 Hamar prev. Storhammer. Hedmark, S Norway 60°57´N 10°55´E
141 U10 Ḥamārīr al Kidan, Qalamat well E Saudi Arabia
164 I12 Hamasaka Hyōgo, Honshū, SW Japan 35°37´N 134°27´E
Hamath see Ḥamāh
165 T1 Hamatonbetsu Hokkaidō, NE Japan 45°07´N 142°21´E
155 K26 Hambantota Southern Province, SE Sri Lanka 06°07´N 81°07´E
Hambourg see Hamburg
100 J9 Hamburg Hamburg, N Germany 53°33´N 10°03´E
27 V14 Hamburg Arkansas, C USA 33°13´N 91°50´W
29 S16 Hamburg Iowa, C USA 40°36´N 95°39´W
18 D10 Hamburg New York, NE USA 42°40´N 78°49´W
100 I10 Hamburg Fr. Hambourg. ◈ state N Germany
148 K5 Hamdam Āb, Dasht-e Pash. Dasht-i Hamdamab. ▲▲ W Afghanistan
Hamdamab, Dasht-i see Hamdam Āb, Dasht-e
18 M13 Hamden Connecticut, NE USA 41°23´N 72°55´W
140 K6 Ḥamḍ, Wādī al dry watercourse W Saudi Arabia
93 K18 Hämeenkyrö Länsi-Suomi, W Finland 61°39´N 23°10´E
93 L19 Hämeenlinna Swe. Tavastehus. Etelä-Suomi, S Finland 61°N 24°25´E
HaMelaḥ, Yam see Dead Sea
Hamelin see Hameln
100 I13 Hameln Eng. Hamelin. Niedersachsen, N Germany 52°07´N 09°22´E
180 I8 Hamersley Range ▲▲ Western Australia
163 Y12 Hamgyŏng-sanmaek ▲▲ North Korea
163 X13 Hamhŭng C North Korea 39°53´N 127°31´E
159 O6 Hami var. Ha-mi, Uigh. Kumul, Qomul. Xinjiang Uygur Zizhiqu, NW China 42°48´N 93°27´E
Ha-mi see Hami
139 X10 Ḥāmid Amīn Maysān, E Iraq 32°06´N 46°53´E
141 W11 Hamīdān, Khawr oasis SE Saudi Arabia
114 L12 Hamidiye Edirne, NW Turkey 41°09´N 26°40´E
182 L12 Hamilton Victoria, SE Australia 37°45´S 142°04´E
64 B12 Hamilton ○ (Bermuda) C Bermuda 32°18´N 64°48´W
14 G16 Hamilton Ontario, S Canada 43°15´N 79°50´W
184 M7 Hamilton Waikato, North Island, New Zealand 37°49´S 175°16´E
96 I12 Hamilton S Scotland, United Kingdom 55°47´N 04°03´W
23 N3 Hamilton Alabama, S USA 34°08´N 87°59´W
38 M10 Hamilton Alaska, USA 62°54´N 163°53´W
30 J13 Hamilton Illinois, N USA 40°24´N 91°20´W
27 S3 Hamilton Missouri, C USA 39°44´N 94°00´W
33 P10 Hamilton Montana, NW USA 46°15´N 114°09´W
25 S8 Hamilton Texas, SW USA 31°42´N 98°08´W
14 G16 Hamilton ✕ Ontario, SE Canada 43°12´N 79°54´W
64 I6 Hamilton Bank undersea feature SE Labrador Sea
182 E1 Hamilton Creek seasonal river South Australia
13 R8 Hamilton Inlet inlet Newfoundland and Labrador, E Canada
27 T12 Hamilton, Lake ⊠ Arkansas, C USA
35 W6 Hamilton, Mount ▲ Nevada, W USA 39°15´N 115°30´W
75 S8 Ḥamīm, Wādī al ≈ NE Libya
93 N19 Hamina Swe. Fredrikshamn. Kymi, S Finland 60°33´N 27°15´E
11 W16 Hamiota Manitoba, S Canada 50°13´N 100°37´W
152 L13 Hamīrpur Uttar Pradesh, N India 25°57´N 80°08´E
Hamīs Musait see Khamis Mushayṭ
21 T11 Hamlet North Carolina, SE USA 34°52´N 79°41´W
25 P6 Hamlin Texas, SW USA 32°52´N 100°07´W
21 P5 Hamlin West Virginia, NE USA 38°16´N 82°07´W
31 O7 Hamlin Lake ◎ Michigan, N USA
101 F14 Hamm var. Hamm in Westfalen. Nordrhein-Westfalen, W Germany 51°39´N 07°49´E
Ḥammāmāt, Khalīj al see Hammamet, Golfe de
75 N5 Hammamet, Golfe de Ar. Khalīj al Ḥammāmāt. gulf NE Tunisia
139 R3 Ḥammām al 'Alīl Nīnawé, N Iraq 36°07´N 43°15´E
139 X12 Ḥammār, Hawr al ◎ SE Iraq
93 J20 Hammarland Åland, SW Finland 60°13´N 19°45´E
93 H16 Hammarstrand Jämtland, C Sweden 63°07´N 16°27´E
93 O17 Hammaslahti Itä-Suomi, SE Finland 62°26´N 29°58´E
99 F17 Hamme Oost-Vlaanderen, NW Belgium 51°06´N 04°08´E
100 H10 Hamme ≈ NW Germany
95 G22 Hammel Midtjylland, C Denmark 56°15´N 09°53´E
101 I18 Hammelburg Bayern, C Germany 50°06´N 09°50´E
99 H18 Hamme-Mille Walloon Brabant, C Belgium 50°48´N 04°42´E
100 H10 Hamme-Oste-Kanal canal NW Germany
93 G16 Hammerdal Jämtland, C Sweden 63°34´N 15°19´E
92 K8 Hammerfest Finnmark, N Norway 70°40´N 23°44´E
101 D14 Hamminkeln Nordrhein-Westfalen, W Germany 51°43´N 06°36´E
Hamm in Westfalen see Hamm
26 K10 Hammon Oklahoma, C USA 35°37´N 99°22´W
31 N11 Hammond Indiana, N USA 41°35´N 87°30´W
22 K8 Hammond Louisiana, S USA 30°30´N 90°27´W
99 K20 Hamoir Liège, E Belgium 50°28´N 05°35´E
99 J21 Hamois Namur, SE Belgium 50°21´N 05°09´E
99 K16 Hamont Limburg, NE Belgium 51°15´N 05°33´E
185 F22 Hampden Otago, South Island, New Zealand 45°18´S 170°49´E
19 R6 Hampden Maine, NE USA 44°44´N 68°51´W
97 M23 Hampshire cultural region S England, United Kingdom
13 O15 Hampton New Brunswick, SE Canada 45°30´N 65°50´W
27 U14 Hampton Arkansas, C USA 33°33´N 92°28´W
29 V12 Hampton Iowa, C USA 42°44´N 93°12´W
19 P10 Hampton New Hampshire, NE USA 42°55´N 70°48´W
21 R14 Hampton South Carolina, SE USA 32°52´N 81°06´W
21 P8 Hampton Tennessee, S USA 36°16´N 82°10´W
21 X7 Hampton Virginia, NE USA 37°02´N 76°23´W
94 L11 Hamra Gävleborg, C Sweden 61°40´N 15°00´E
80 D10 Hamrat esh Sheikh Northern Kordofan, C Sudan 14°38´N 27°56´E
139 S5 Ḥamrīn, Jabal ▲▲ N Iraq
121 P16 Hamrun C Malta 35°53´N 14°28´E
Ham Thuân Nam see Thuân Nam
Hāmūn, Daryācheh-ye see Şāberī, Hāmūn-e/Sīstān, Daryācheh-ye
Hamwih see Southampton
38 G10 Hāna var. Hana. Maui, Hawaii, USA, C Pacific Ocean 20°45´N 155°59´W
Hana see Hāna
21 S14 Hanahan South Carolina, SE USA 32°55´N 80°01´W
38 B8 Hanalei Kauaʻi, Hawaii, USA, C Pacific Ocean 22°12´N 159°30´W
165 Q9 Hanamaki Iwate, Honshū, C Japan 39°25´N 141°04´E
38 F10 Hanamanioa, Cape headland Maui, Hawaiʻi, USA 20°34´N 156°22´W
190 B16 Hanan ✕ (Alofi) SW Niue
101 H18 Hanau Hessen, W Germany 50°06´N 08°56´E
162 M11 Hanbogd var. Ih Bulag. Ömnögovĭ, S Mongolia 43°04´N 107°43´E
8 L9 Hanbury ≈ Northwest Territories, NW Canada
Hâncești see Hîncești
10 M15 Hanceville British Columbia, SW Canada 51°54´N 122°56´W
23 P3 Hanceville Alabama, S USA 34°03´N 86°46´W
Hancewicze see Hantsavichy
160 L6 Hancheng Shaanxi, C China 35°22´N 110°27´E
21 V2 Hancock Maryland, NE USA 39°42´N 78°10´W
30 M3 Hancock Michigan, N USA 47°07´N 88°34´W
29 S8 Hancock Minnesota, N USA 45°30´N 95°47´W
18 I12 Hancock New York, NE USA 41°57´N 75°15´W
80 Q12 Handa Bari, NE Somalia 10°35´N 51°09´E
161 O5 Handan var. Han-tan. Hebei, E China 36°35´N 114°28´E
95 P16 Handen Stockholm, C Sweden 59°12´N 18°09´E
81 J22 Handeni Tanga, E Tanzania 05°25´S 38°04´E
37 Q7 Handies Peak ▲ Colorado, C USA 37°54´N 107°30´W
111 J19 Handlová Ger. Krickerhäu, Hung. Nyitrabánya; prev. Kriegerhaj. Trenčiansky Kraj, C Slovakia 48°45´N 18°45´E
165 O13 Haneda ✕ (Tōkyō) Tōkyō, Honshū, S Japan 35°33´N 139°45´E
138 F13 HaNegev Eng. Negev. desert S Israel
Hanfeng see Kaixian
35 Q11 Hanford California, W USA 36°19´N 119°39´W
191 V16 Hanga Roa Easter Island, Chile, E Pacific Ocean 27°09´S 109°26´W
162 I7 Hangay var. Hunt. Arhangay, C Mongolia 47°49´N 99°24´E
162 H7 Hangayn Nuruu ▲▲ C Mongolia
Hang-chou/Hangchow see Hangzhou
95 K20 Hånger Jönköping, S Sweden 57°06´N 13°58´E
Hangö see Hanko
161 R9 Hangzhou var. Hang-chou, Hangchow. province capital Zhejiang, SE China 30°18´N 120°07´E
162 J4 Hanh var. Turt. Hövsgöl, N Mongolia 51°30´N 100°40´E
162 F5 Hanhöhiy Uul ▲▲ NW Mongolia
162 K10 Hanhongor var. Ögöömör. Ömnögovĭ, S Mongolia 43°47´N 104°31´E
146 I14 Hanhowuz Rus. Khauz-Khan. Ahal Welaýaty, S Turkmenistan 37°15´N 61°12´E
146 I14 Hanhowuz Suw Howdany Rus. Khauzkhanskoye Vodoranilishche. ⊠ S Turkmenistan
137 P15 Hani Diyarbakır, SE Turkey 38°26´N 40°23´E
Hania see Chaniá
141 R11 Ḥanīsh al Kabīr, Jazīrat al island SW Yemen
Hanka, Lake see Khanka, Lake
93 M17 Hankasalmi Länsi-Suomi, W Finland 62°25´N 26°27´E
29 R7 Hankinson North Dakota, N USA 46°04´N 96°54´W
93 K20 Hanko Swe. Hangö. Etelä-Suomi, SW Finland 59°50´N 23°E
Han-kou/Han-k'ou/Hankow see Wuhan
36 M6 Hanksville Utah, W USA 38°21´N 110°43´W
152 K6 Hanle Jammu and Kashmir, NW India 32°46´N 79°01´E
185 I17 Hanmer Springs Canterbury, South Island, New Zealand 42°31´S 172°49´E
11 R16 Hanna Alberta, SW Canada 51°38´N 111°56´W
27 V3 Hannibal Missouri, C USA 39°42´N 91°23´W
180 M3 Hann, Mount ▲ Western Australia 15°53´S 125°46´E
100 I12 Hannover Eng. Hanover. Niedersachsen, NW Germany 52°23´N 09°43´E
99 J19 Hannut Liège, C Belgium 50°40´N 05°05´E
95 L22 Hanöbukten bay S Sweden
167 T6 Ha Nôi Eng. Hanoi, Fr. Hanoï. ● (Vietnam) N Vietnam 21°01´N 105°52´E
14 F14 Hanover Ontario, S Canada 44°10´N 81°03´W
31 P15 Hanover Indiana, N USA 38°42´N 85°28´W
18 G16 Hanover Pennsylvania, NE USA 39°46´N 76°57´W
21 W6 Hanover Virginia, NE USA 37°44´N 77°21´W
Hanover see Hannover
63 G23 Hanover, Isla island S Chile
Hanselbeck see Érd
195 X5 Hansen Mountains ▲▲ Antarctica
160 M8 Han Shui ≈ C China
152 H10 Hānsi Haryāna, NW India 29°06´N 76°01´E
95 F20 Hanstholm Midtjylland, NW Denmark 57°05´N 08°39´E
Han-tan see Handan
158 H6 Hantengri Feng var. Pik Khan-Tengri. ▲ China/Kazakhstan 42°17´N 80°11´E see also Khan-Tengri, Pik
119 I18 Hantsavichy Pol. Hancewicze, Rus. Gantsevichi. Brestskaya Voblasts', SW Belarus 52°45´N 26°27´E
9 Q6 Hantzsch ≈ Baffin Island, Nunavut, NE Canada
152 G9 Hanumāngarh Rājasthān, NW India 29°33´N 74°21´E
183 O9 Hanwood New South Wales, SE Australia 34°19´S 146°03´E
Hanyang see Caidian
Hanyang see Wuhan
160 H10 Hanyuan var. Fulin. Sichuan, C China 29°29´N 102°45´E
Hanyuan see Xihe
160 J7 Hanzhong Shaanxi, C China 33°12´N 107°E
191 W11 Hao atoll Îles Tuamotu, C French Polynesia
153 S16 Hāora prev. Howrah. West Bengal, NE India 22°35´N 88°20´E
78 K8 Haouach, Ouadi dry watercourse E Chad
92 K13 Haparanda Norrbotten, N Sweden 65°49´N 24°05´E
25 N3 Happy Texas, SW USA 34°44´N 101°51´W
34 M1 Happy Camp California, W USA 41°48´N 123°24´W
13 Q9 Happy Valley-Goose Bay prev. Goose Bay. Newfoundland and Labrador, E Canada 53°19´N 60°24´W
Hapsal see Haapsalu
152 J10 Hāpur Uttar Pradesh, N India 28°43´N 77°47´E
HaQatan, HaMakhtesh see HaKatan, HaMakhtesh
140 I4 Ḥaql Tabūk, NW Saudi Arabia 29°18´N 34°58´E
171 U14 Har Pulau Kai Besar, E Indonesia 05°21´S 133°09´E
Haraat see Tsagaandelger
141 R8 Ḥaraḍ var. Haradh. Ash Sharqīyah, E Saudi Arabia 24°08´N 49°02´E
Haradh see Ḥaraḍ
118 N12 Haradok Rus. Gorodok. Vitsyebskaya Voblasts', N Belarus 55°28´N 30°00´E
92 J13 Harads Norrbotten, N Sweden 66°04´N 21°04´E
119 G19 Haradzyets Rus. Gorodets. Brestskaya Voblasts', SW Belarus 52°12´N 24°40´E
119 J17 Haradzyeya Rus. Gorodeya. Minskaya Voblasts', C Belarus 53°19´N 26°32´E
191 V10 Haraiki atoll Îles Tuamotu, C French Polynesia
165 Q11 Haramachi Fukushima, Honshū, E Japan 37°40´N 140°55´E
118 M12 Harany Rus. Gorany. Vitsyebskaya Voblasts', N Belarus 55°25´N 29°03´E
83 L16 Harare prev. Salisbury. ● (Zimbabwe) Mashonaland East, NE Zimbabwe 17°47´S 31°04´E
83 L16 Harare ✕ Mashonaland East, NE Zimbabwe 17°51´S 31°06´E
78 J10 Haraz-Djombo Batha, C Chad 14°10´N 19°35´E
119 O16 Harbavichy Rus. Gorbovichi. Mahilyowskaya Voblasts', E Belarus 53°48´N 30°42´E
76 J16 Harbel W Liberia 06°19´N 10°20´W
163 W8 Harbin var. Haerbin, Ha-erh-pin, Kharbin; prev. Haerhpin, Pingkiang, Pinkiang. province capital Heilongjiang, NE China 45°45´N 126°41´E
31 S7 Harbor Beach Michigan, N USA 43°50´N 82°39´W
13 T13 Harbour Breton Newfoundland, Newfoundland and Labrador, E Canada 47°29´N 55°50´W
65 D25 Harbours, Bay of bay East Falkland, Falkland Islands
Hårby see Haarby
36 I13 Harcuvar Mountains ▲▲ Arizona, SW USA
108 I7 Hard Vorarlberg, NW Austria 47°29´N 09°42´E
154 H11 Harda Khas Madhya Pradesh, C India 22°22´N 77°06´E
95 D14 Hardangerfjorden fjord S Norway
94 E13 Hardangerjøkulen glacier S Norway
95 E14 Hardangervidda plateau S Norway
83 D20 Hardap ◈ district S Namibia
21 R15 Hardeeville South Carolina, SE USA 32°18´N 81°04´W
Hardegarijp see Hurdegaryp
98 O9 Hardenberg Overijssel, E Netherlands 52°34´N 06°38´E
183 Q9 Harden-Murrumburrah New South Wales, SE Australia 34°33´S 148°22´E
98 K10 Harderwijk Gelderland, C Netherlands 52°21´N 05°37´E
30 J14 Hardin Illinois, N USA 39°10´N 90°38´W
33 V11 Hardin Montana, NW USA 45°44´N 107°35´W
23 R5 Harding, Lake ⊠ Alabama/Georgia, SE USA
20 J6 Hardinsburg Kentucky, S USA 37°46´N 86°29´W
98 I13 Hardinxveld-Giessendam Zuid-Holland, C Netherlands 51°52´N 04°49´E
11 R15 Hardisty Alberta, SW Canada 52°42´N 111°22´W
152 L12 Hardoi Uttar Pradesh, N India 27°23´N 80°06´E
Hardwar see Haridwār
23 U4 Hardwick Georgia, SE USA 33°03´N 83°13´W
27 W9 Hardy Arkansas, C USA 36°19´N 91°29´W
94 D10 Hareid Møre og Romsdal, S Norway 62°22´N 06°02´E
8 H7 Hare Indian ≈ Northwest Territories, NW Canada
99 D18 Harelbeke var. Harlebeke. West-Vlaanderen, W Belgium 50°51´N 03°19´E
Harem see Ḥārim
100 E11 Haren Niedersachsen, NW Germany 52°47´N 07°16´E
98 N6 Haren Groningen, NE Netherlands 53°10´N 06°37´E
80 L13 Hārer E Ethiopia 09°17´N 42°19´E
95 P14 Harg Uppsala, C Sweden 60°13´N 18°25´E
Hargeisa see Hargeysa
80 M13 Hargeysa var. Hargeisa. Woqooyi Galbeed, NW Somalia 09°32´N 44°07´E
116 J10 Harghita ◈ county NE Romania
25 S17 Hargill Texas, SW USA 26°26´N 98°00´W
162 J8 Harhorin Övörhangay, C Mongolia 47°13´N 102°48´E
159 Q9 Har Hu ◎ C China
Hariana see Haryāna
141 P15 Ḥarīb W Yemen 15°08´N 45°35´E
168 M12 Hari, Batang prev. Djambi. ≈ Sumatera, W Indonesia
152 J9 Haridwār prev. Hardwar. Uttarakhand, N India 29°58´N 78°09´E
155 F18 Harihar Karnātaka, W India 14°33´N 75°44´E
185 F18 Harihari West Coast, South Island, New Zealand 43°09´S 170°35´E
138 I3 Ḥārim var. Harem. Idlib, W Syria 36°30´N 36°30´E
98 F13 Haringvliet channel SW Netherlands
98 F13 Haringvlietdam dam SW Netherlands
149 U5 Haripur Khyber Pakhtunkhwa, NW Pakistan 34°00´N 73°01´E
148 J4 Harīrūd var. Tedzhen, Turkm. Tejen. ≈ Afghanistan/Iran see also Tejen
Harīrūd see Tejen
94 J11 Härjåhågnen Swe. Härjahågnen, var. Härjehågna. ▲ Norway/Sweden 61°43´N 12°07´E
Härjåhågnen see Østrehogna
Härjahågnen see Härjåhågnen
93 K18 Harjavalta Länsi-Suomi, W Finland 61°19´N 22°10´E
Härjehågna see Østrehogna
Härjehågna see Härjåhågnen
118 G4 Harjumaa var. Harju Maakond. ◈ province NW Estonia
Harju Maakond see Harjumaa
21 X11 Harkers Island North Carolina, SE USA 34°42´N 76°33´W
139 S1 Harki Dahūk, N Iraq 37°03´N 43°39´E
29 T14 Harlan Iowa, C USA 41°40´N 95°19´W
21 O7 Harlan Kentucky, S USA 36°50´N 83°19´W
29 N17 Harlan County Lake ⊠ Nebraska, C USA
116 L9 Hârlău var. Hîrlău. Iași, NE Romania 47°26´N 26°54´E
Harlebeke see Harelbeke
33 U7 Harlem Montana, NW USA 48°31´N 108°46´W
Harlem see Haarlem
95 G22 Harlev Midtjylland, C Denmark 56°08´N 10°00´E
98 K6 Harlingen Fris. Harns. Fryslân, N Netherlands 53°10´N 05°25´E
25 T17 Harlingen Texas, SW USA 26°12´N 97°43´W
97 O21 Harlow E England, United Kingdom 51°47´N 00°07´E
33 T10 Harlowton Montana, NW USA 46°26´N 109°49´W
94 N11 Harmånger Gävleborg, C Sweden 61°55´N 17°19´E
98 I11 Harmelen Utrecht, C Netherlands 52°06´N 04°58´E
29 X11 Harmony Minnesota, N USA 43°33´N 92°00´W
32 J14 Harney Basin basin Oregon, NW USA
32 J14 Harney Lake ◎ Oregon, NW USA
28 J10 Harney Peak ▲ South Dakota, N USA 43°52´N 103°31´W
93 H17 Härnösand var. Hernösand. Västernorrland, C Sweden 62°37´N 17°55´E
Harns see Harlingen
105 P4 Haro La Rioja, N Spain 42°34´N 02°52´W
40 F6 Haro, Cabo headland NW Mexico 27°50´N 110°55´W
94 D9 Harøy island S Norway
97 N21 Harpenden E England, United Kingdom 51°49´N 00°22´W
76 L18 Harper var. Cape Palmas. NE Liberia 04°25´N 07°43´W
26 M7 Harper Kansas, C USA 37°17´N 98°01´W
32 L13 Harper Oregon, NW USA 43°51´N 117°37´W
25 Q10 Harper Texas, SW USA 30°18´N 99°18´W
35 U13 Harper Lake salt flat California, W USA
39 T9 Harper, Mount ▲ Alaska, USA 64°18´N 143°54´W
95 J21 Harplinge Halland, S Sweden 56°45´N 12°45´E
36 J13 Harquahala Mountains ▲▲ Arizona, SW USA
141 T15 Ḥarrah SE Yemen 15°02´N 50°23´E
12 H11 Harricana ≈ Québec, SE Canada
20 M9 Harriman Tennessee, S USA 35°57´N 84°33´W
13 R11 Harrington Harbour Québec, E Canada 50°34´N 59°29´W
64 B12 Harrington Sound bay Bermuda, NW Atlantic Ocean
96 F8 Harris physical region NW Scotland, United Kingdom
27 X10 Harrisburg Arkansas, C USA 35°33´N 90°43´W
30 M17 Harrisburg Illinois, N USA 37°44´N 88°32´W
28 I14 Harrisburg Nebraska, C USA 41°33´N 103°46´W
32 F12 Harrisburg Oregon, NW USA 44°16´N 123°10´W
18 G15 Harrisburg state capital Pennsylvania, NE USA 40°16´N 76°53´W
182 F6 Harris, Lake ◎ South Australia
23 W11 Harris, Lake ◎ Florida, SE USA
83 J22 Harrismith Free State, E South Africa 28°16´S 29°08´E
27 T9 Harrison Arkansas, C USA 36°13´N 93°07´W
31 Q7 Harrison Michigan, N USA 44°02´N 84°46´W
28 I12 Harrison Nebraska, C USA 42°42´N 103°53´W
39 Q5 Harrison Bay inlet Alaska, USA
22 I6 Harrisonburg Louisiana, S USA 31°44´N 91°51´W
21 U4 Harrisonburg Virginia, NE USA 38°27´N 78°54´W
13 R7 Harrison, Cape headland Newfoundland and Labrador, E Canada 54°55´N 57°48´W
27 R5 Harrisonville Missouri, C USA 38°40´N 94°21´W
Harris Ridge see Lomonosov Ridge
192 M3 Harris Seamount undersea feature N Pacific Ocean 46°09´N 161°25´W
96 F8 Harris, Sound of strait NW Scotland, United Kingdom
31 R6 Harrisville Michigan, N USA 44°41´N 83°19´W
21 R3 Harrisville West Virginia, NE USA 39°13´N 81°04´W
20 M6 Harrodsburg Kentucky, S USA 37°45´N 84°51´W
97 M16 Harrogate N England, United Kingdom 54°N 01°33´W
25 Q4 Harrold Texas, SW USA 34°05´N 99°02´W
27 S5 Harry S. Truman Reservoir ⊠ Missouri, C USA
100 G13 Harsewinkel Nordrhein-Westfalen, W Germany 51°58´N 08°13´E
116 M14 Hârșova prev. Hîrșova. Constanța, SE Romania 44°41´N 27°56´E
92 H10 Harstad Troms, N Norway 68°48´N 16°31´E
31 O8 Hart Michigan, N USA 43°43´N 86°22´W
24 M4 Hart Texas, SW USA 34°23´N 102°07´W
10 I5 Hart ≈ Yukon Territory, NW Canada
83 F23 Hartbees ≈ C South Africa
109 X7 Hartberg Steiermark, SE Austria 47°18´N 15°58´E
182 I10 Hart, Cape headland South Australia 35°54´S 138°01´E
95 E14 Hårteigen ▲ S Norway 60°11´N 07°01´E
23 Q7 Hartford Alabama, S USA 31°06´N 85°42´W
27 R11 Hartford Arkansas, C USA 35°01´N 94°22´W
18 M12 Hartford state capital Connecticut, NE USA 41°46´N 72°41´W
20 J6 Hartford Kentucky, S USA 37°26´N 86°57´W
31 P10 Hartford Michigan, N USA 42°12´N 85°54´W
29 R11 Hartford South Dakota, N USA 43°37´N 96°56´W
30 M8 Hartford Wisconsin, N USA 43°19´N 88°25´W
31 P13 Hartford City Indiana, N USA 40°27´N 85°22´W
29 Q13 Hartington Nebraska, C USA 42°37´N 97°15´W
13 N14 Hartland New Brunswick, SE Canada 46°18´N 67°31´W
97 H23 Hartland Point headland SW England, United Kingdom 51°01´N 04°33´W
97 M15 Hartlepool N England, United Kingdom 54°41´N 01°13´W
29 T12 Hartley Iowa, C USA 43°10´N 95°28´W
24 M1 Hartley Texas, SW USA 35°52´N 102°24´W
32 J15 Hart Mountain ▲ Oregon, NW USA 42°24´N 119°46´W
173 U10 Hartog Ridge undersea feature W Indian Ocean
93 M18 Hartola Etelä-Suomi, S Finland 61°34´N 26°04´E
67 U14 Harts var. Hartz. ≈ N South Africa
23 P2 Hartselle Alabama, S USA 34°26´N 86°56´W
23 S3 Hartsfield Atlanta ✕ Georgia, SE USA 33°38´N 84°24´W
27 Q11 Hartshorne Oklahoma, C USA 34°51´N 95°33´W
21 S12 Hartsville South Carolina, SE USA 34°22´N 80°04´W
20 K8 Hartsville Tennessee, S USA 36°23´N 86°11´W
27 U7 Hartville Missouri, C USA 37°15´N 92°30´W
23 U2 Hartwell Georgia, SE USA 34°21´N 82°55´W
21 O11 Hartwell Lake ⊠ Georgia/South Carolina, SE USA
Hartz see Harts
Harunabad see Eslāmābād-e Gharb
Har-Us see Erdenebüren
162 F6 Har Us Gol ◎ Hovd, W Mongolia
162 E6 Har Us Nuur ◎ NW Mongolia
30 M10 Harvard Illinois, N USA 42°25´N 88°36´W
29 P16 Harvard Nebraska, C USA 40°37´N 98°06´W
37 R5 Harvard, Mount ▲ Colorado, C USA 38°55´N 106°19´W
31 N11 Harvey Illinois, N USA 41°36´N 87°39´W
29 N4 Harvey North Dakota, N USA 47°43´N 99°55´W
97 Q21 Harwich E England, United Kingdom 51°56´N 01°16´E
152 H10 Haryāna var. Hariana. ◈ state N India
141 Y9 Ḥaryān, Ṭawī al spring/well NE Oman 21°56´N 58°33´E
101 J14 Harz ▲▲ C Germany
Ḥasakah, Muḥāfaẓat al see Al Ḥasakah
165 Q9 Hasama Miyagi, Honshū, C Japan 38°42´N 141°09´E
137 Y13 Häsänabad prev. 26 Bakı Komissarı. SE Azerbaijan 39°18´N 49°13´E
136 J15 Hasan Dağı ▲ C Turkey 38°09´N 34°15´E
139 T9 Ḥasan Ibn Ḥassūn An Najaf, C Iraq 32°24´N 44°13´E
149 R6 Ḥasan Khēl var. Ahmad Khel. Paktīā, SE Afghanistan 33°46´N 69°37´E
100 F12 Hase ≈ NW Germany
Haselberg see Krasnoznamensk
100 F12 Haselünne Niedersachsen, NW Germany 52°40´N 07°28´E
Hashaat see Delgerhangay
Hashemite Kingdom of Jordan see Jordan
139 V8 Hāshimah Wāsiț, E Iraq 33°22´N 45°56´E
142 K3 Hashtrūd var. Azaran. Āzarbāyjān-e Khāvarī, N Iran 37°34´N 47°10´E
141 W13 Ḥāsik S Oman 17°22´N 55°18´E
149 U10 Hāsilpur Punjab, E Pakistan 29°42´N 72°40´E
27 Q10 Haskell Oklahoma, C USA 35°49´N 95°40´W
25 Q6 Haskell Texas, SW USA 33°10´N 99°45´W
114 M11 Hasköy Edirne, NW Turkey 41°37´N 26°51´E
95 L24 Hasle Bornholm, E Denmark 55°12´N 14°43´E
97 N23 Haslemere SE England, United Kingdom 51°06´N 00°45´W
102 I16 Hasparren Pyrénées-Atlantiques, SW France 43°23´N 01°18´W
Hassakeh see Al Ḥasakah

◆ Country
● Country Capital
◇ Dependent Territory
○ Dependent Territory Capital
◈ Administrative Regions
✕ International Airport
▲ Mountain
▲▲ Mountain Range
Volcano
≈ River
◎ Lake
⊠ Reservoir

155 G19 **Hassan** Karnātaka, W India 13°01′N 76°03′E
36 J13 **Hassayampa River** Arizona, SW USA
101 J18 **Hassberge** *hill range* C Germany
94 N10 **Hassela** Gävleborg, C Sweden 62°06′N 16°45′E
99 J18 **Hasselt** Limburg, NE Belgium 50°56′N 05°20′E
98 M9 **Hasselt** Overijssel, E Netherlands 52°36′N 06°06′E
Hassetché *see* Al Ḩasakah
101 J18 **Hassfurt** Bayern, C Germany 50°02′N 10°32′E
74 L9 **Hassi Bel Guebbour** E Algeria 28°41′N 06°29′E
74 L8 **Hassi Messaoud** E Algeria 31°41′N 06°10′E
95 K22 **Hässleholm** Skåne, S Sweden 56°09′N 13°45′E
Hasta Colonia/Hasta Pompeia *see* Asti
183 O13 **Hastings** Victoria, SE Australia 38°18′S 145°12′E
184 O11 **Hastings** Hawke's Bay, North Island, New Zealand 39°39′S 176°51′E
97 P23 **Hastings** SE England, United Kingdom 50°51′N 00°36′E
31 P9 **Hastings** Michigan, N USA 42°38′N 85°17′W
29 W9 **Hastings** Minnesota, N USA 44°44′N 92°51′W
29 P16 **Hastings** Nebraska, C USA 40°35′N 98°23′W
95 K22 **Hästveda** Skåne, S Sweden 56°16′N 13°55′E
92 J8 **Hasvik** Finnmark, N Norway 70°29′N 22°08′E
37 V6 **Haswell** Colorado, C USA 38°27′N 103°09′W
163 N11 **Hatanbulag** *var.* Ergel. Dornogovĭ, SE Mongolia 43°10′N 109°13′E
Hatansuudal *see* Bayanlig
Hatavch *see* Haldzan
136 K17 **Hatay** ◆ *province* S Turkey
37 R15 **Hatch** New Mexico, SW USA 32°40′N 107°10′W
36 K7 **Hatch** Utah, W USA 37°39′N 112°25′W
20 F9 **Hatchie River** Tennessee, S USA
116 G12 **Haţeg** *Ger.* Wallenthal, *Hung.* Hátszeg; *prev.* Hatzeg, Hötzing. Hunedoara, SW Romania 45°35′N 22°57′E
165 O17 **Hateruma-jima** *island* Yaeyama-shotō, SW Japan
183 N8 **Hatfield** New South Wales, SE Australia 33°54′S 143°43′E
162 I5 **Hatgal** Hövsgöl, N Mongolia 50°24′N 100°12′E
153 V16 **Hathazari** Chittagong, SE Bangladesh 22°30′N 91°46′E
141 T13 **Hathūt, Hişā'** *oasis* NE Yemen
167 R14 **Ha Tiên** Kiên Giang, S Vietnam 10°24′N 104°30′E
167 T8 **Ha Tinh** Ha Tinh, N Vietnam 18°21′N 105°55′E
Hatira, Haré *see* Hatira, Harei
138 F12 **Hatira, Harei** *prev.* Haré Hatira. *hill range* S Israel
167 R6 **Hat Lot** *var.* Mai Son. Son La, N Vietnam 21°07′N 104°10′E
45 P16 **Hato Airport** ✈ (Willemstad) Curaçao 12°10′N 68°56′W
54 H9 **Hato Corozal** Casanare, C Colombia 06°08′N 71°45′W
Hato del Volcán *see* Volcán
45 P9 **Hato Mayor** E Dominican Republic 18°49′N 69°16′W
Hatra *see* Al Ḩaḑr
Hatria *see* Adria
Hátszeg *see* Haţeg
143 R16 **Ḩattá** Dubayy, NE United Arab Emirates 24°50′N 56°06′E
182 L9 **Hattah** Victoria, SE Australia 34°49′S 142°18′E
98 M9 **Hattem** Gelderland, E Netherlands 52°29′N 06°04′E
21 Z10 **Hatteras** Hatteras Island, North Carolina, SE USA 35°13′N 75°39′W
21 Rr10 **Hatteras, Cape** *headland* North Carolina, SE USA 35°29′N 75°33′W
21 Z9 **Hatteras Island** *island* North Carolina, SE USA
64 F10 **Hatteras Plain** *undersea feature* W Atlantic Ocean 31°00′N 71°00′W
93 G14 **Hattfjelldal** Troms, N Norway 65°37′N 13°58′E
22 M7 **Hattiesburg** Mississippi, S USA 31°20′N 89°17′W
29 Q4 **Hatton** North Dakota, N USA 47°38′N 97°27′W
Hatton Bank *see* Hatton Ridge
64 L6 **Hatton Ridge** *var.* Hatton Bank. *undersea feature* N Atlantic Ocean 59°00′N 17°30′W
191 W6 **Hatutu** *island* Îles Marquises, NE French Polynesia
111 K22 **Hatvan** Heves, NE Hungary 47°40′N 19°39′E
167 O16 **Hat Yai** *var.* Ban Hat Yai. Songkhla, SW Thailand 07°01′N 100°27′E
Hatzeg *see* Haţeg
Hatzfeld *see* Jimbolia
80 N13 **Haud** *plateau* Ethiopia/Somalia
95 D18 **Hauge** Rogaland, S Norway 58°20′N 06°17′E
95 C15 **Haugesund** Rogaland, S Norway 59°24′N 05°17′E
109 X2 **Haugsdorf** Niederösterreich, NE Austria 48°41′N 16°04′E
184 M9 **Hauhungaroa Range** ▲ North Island, New Zealand
95 E15 **Haukeligrend** Telemark, S Norway 59°45′N 07°33′E
93 L14 **Haukipudas** Oulu, C Finland 65°11′N 25°21′E
93 M17 **Haukivesi** ⊗ SE Finland
93 M17 **Haukivuori** Itä-Suomi, E Finland 62°02′N 27°11′E
Hauptkanal *see* Havelländ Grosse
187 N10 **Hauraha** Makira-Ulawa, SE Solomon Islands 10°47′S 162°00′E
184 L5 **Hauraki Gulf** *gulf* North Island, N New Zealand
185 B24 **Hauroko, Lake** ⊗ South Island, New Zealand
167 S14 **Hâu, Sông** S Vietnam
92 N12 **Hautajärvi** Lappi, NE Finland 66°30′N 29°01′E
74 F7 **Haut Atlas** *Eng.* High Atlas. ▲ C Morocco
79 M17 **Haut-Congo** *off.* Région du Haut-Congo; *prev.* Haut-Zaïre. ◆ *region* NE Dem. Rep. Congo
103 Y14 **Haute-Corse** ◆ *department* Corse, France, C Mediterranean Sea
102 L16 **Haute-Garonne** ◆ *department* S France
79 K14 **Haute-Kotto** ◆ *prefecture* E Central African Republic
103 P12 **Haute-Loire** ◆ *department* C France
103 R6 **Haute-Marne** ◆ *department* N France
102 M3 **Haute-Normandie** ◆ *region* N France
15 U6 **Hauterive** Québec, SE Canada 49°11′N 68°16′W
103 T13 **Hautes-Alpes** ◆ *department* SE France
103 S7 **Haute-Saône** ◆ *department* E France
103 T10 **Haute-Savoie** ◆ *department* E France
99 M20 **Hautes Fagnes** *Ger.* Hohes Venn. ▲ E Belgium
102 K16 **Hautes-Pyrénées** ◆ *department* S France
99 L23 **Haute Sûre, Lac de la** ⊠ NW Luxembourg
102 M11 **Haute-Vienne** ◆ *department* C France
19 S8 **Haut, Isle au** *island* Maine, NE USA
79 M14 **Haut-Mbomou** ◆ *prefecture* SE Central African Republic
103 Q2 **Hautmont** Nord, N France 50°15′N 03°55′E
79 F19 **Haut-Ogooué** *off.* Province du Haut-Ogooué, *var.* Le Haut-Ogooué. ◆ *province* SE Gabon
Haut-Ogooué, Le *see* Haut-Ogooué
Haut-Ogooué, Province du *see* Haut-Ogooué
103 U7 **Haut-Rhin** ◆ *department* NE France
74 I6 **Hauts Plateaux** *plateau* Algeria/Morocco
Haut-Zaïre *see* Haut-Congo
38 D9 **Hau'ula** *var.* Hauula. O'ahu, Hawaii, USA, C Pacific Ocean 21°36′N 157°54′W
Hauula *see* Hau'ula
101 O22 **Hauzenberg** Bayern, SE Germany 48°39′N 13°37′E
30 K13 **Havana** Illinois, N USA 40°18′N 90°03′W
Havana *see* La Habana
97 N23 **Havant** S England, United Kingdom 50°51′N 00°59′W
35 Y14 **Havasu, Lake** ⊠ Arizona/California, W USA
95 J23 **Havdrup** Sjælland, E Denmark 55°33′N 12°08′E
100 N10 **Havel** NE Germany
99 J21 **Havelange** Namur, SE Belgium 50°23′N 05°14′E
100 M11 **Havelberg** Sachsen-Anhalt, NE Germany 52°49′N 12°05′E
149 U5 **Haveliān** Khyber Pakhtunkhwa, NW Pakistan 34°05′N 73°14′E
100 N12 **Havelländ Grosse** *var.* Hauptkanal. *canal* NE Germany
14 J14 **Havelock** Ontario, SE Canada 44°22′N 77°57′W
185 J14 **Havelock** Marlborough, South Island, New Zealand 41°17′S 173°46′E
21 X11 **Havelock** North Carolina, SE USA 34°52′N 76°54′W
184 O11 **Havelock North** Hawke's Bay, North Island, New Zealand 39°40′S 176°53′E
98 M8 **Havelte** Drenthe, NE Netherlands 52°46′N 06°14′E
27 N6 **Haven** Kansas, C USA 37°54′N 97°46′W
97 H21 **Haverfordwest** SW Wales, United Kingdom 51°50′N 04°57′W
97 P20 **Haverhill** E England, United Kingdom 52°05′N 00°26′E
19 O10 **Haverhill** Massachusetts, NE USA 42°46′N 71°02′W
93 G17 **Haverö** Västernorrland, C Sweden 62°25′N 15°04′E
111 I17 **Havířov** Moravskoslezský Kraj, E Czech Republic 49°47′N 18°30′E
111 E17 **Havlíčkův Brod** *Ger.* Deutsch-Brod; *prev.* Německý Brod. Vysočina, C Czech Republic 49°38′N 15°46′E
92 K7 **Havøysund** Finnmark, N Norway 70°59′N 24°39′E
99 F20 **Havré** Hainaut, S Belgium 50°29′N 04°03′E
33 T7 **Havre** Montana, NW USA 48°33′N 109°41′W
Havre *see* le Havre
13 P11 **Havre-St-Pierre** Québec, E Canada 50°16′N 63°36′W
136 B10 **Havsa** Edirne, NW Turkey 41°32′N 26°49′E
38 D8 **Hawai'i** *off.* State of Hawai'i, *also known as* Aloha State, Paradise of the Pacific, *var.* Hawaii. ◆ *state* USA, C Pacific Ocean
38 G12 **Hawai'i** *var.* Hawaii. *island* Hawaiian Islands, USA, C Pacific Ocean
192 M5 **Hawai'ian Islands** *prev.* Sandwich Islands. *island group* Hawaii, USA
192 L5 **Hawaiian Ridge** *undersea feature* N Pacific Ocean 24°00′N 165°00′W
193 N6 **Hawaiian Trough** *undersea feature* N Pacific Ocean
29 R12 **Hawarden** Iowa, C USA 43°00′N 96°29′W
Hawash *see* Āwash
139 P6 **Hawbayn al Gharbīyah** Al Anbār, C Iraq 34°24′N 42°06′E
185 D21 **Hawea, Lake** ⊗ South Island, New Zealand
184 K11 **Hawera** Taranaki, North Island, New Zealand 39°36′S 174°16′E
20 J5 **Hawesville** Kentucky, S USA 37°53′N 86°47′W
38 G11 **Hawi** Hawaii, USA, C Pacific Ocean 20°14′N 155°50′W
38 G11 **Hāwī** *var.* Hawi. Hawaii, USA, C Pacific Ocean 20°13′N 155°49′W
Hawi *see* Hāwī
96 K13 **Hawick** SE Scotland, United Kingdom 55°24′N 02°49′W
139 S4 **Ḩawījah** At Ta'mím, C Iraq 35°15′N 43°54′E
139 Y10 **Ḩawīzah, Hawr al** ⊗ S Iraq
185 E21 **Hawkdun Range** ▲ South Island, New Zealand
184 P10 **Hawke Bay** *bay* North Island, New Zealand
182 I6 **Hawker** South Australia 31°54′S 138°25′E
184 N11 **Hawke's Bay** *off.* Hawkes Bay Region. ◆ *region* North Island, New Zealand
149 O16 **Hawkes Bay** *bay* SE Pakistan
Hawkes Bay Region *see* Hawke's Bay
15 N12 **Hawkesbury** Ontario, SE Canada 45°36′N 74°38′W
Hawkeye State *see* Iowa
23 T5 **Hawkinsville** Georgia, SE USA 32°16′N 83°28′W
14 B7 **Hawk Junction** Ontario, S Canada 48°05′N 84°34′W
21 N10 **Haw Knob** ▲ North Carolina/Tennessee, SE USA 35°18′N 84°01′W
21 Q9 **Hawksbill Mountain** ▲ North Carolina, SE USA 35°54′N 81°53′W
33 Z16 **Hawk Springs** Wyoming, C USA 41°48′N 104°17′W
Hawlēr *see* Arbīl
29 S5 **Hawley** Minnesota, N USA 46°53′N 96°18′W
25 P7 **Hawley** Texas, SW USA 32°36′N 99°47′W
141 R14 **Ḩawrā'** C Yemen 15°39′N 48°21′E
139 P7 **Ḩawrān, Wadi** *dry watercourse* W Iraq
21 T9 **Haw River** North Carolina, SE USA
139 U5 **Hawshqūrah** Diyālá, E Iraq 34°34′N 45°33′E
35 S7 **Hawthorne** Nevada, W USA 38°30′N 118°38′W
37 W3 **Haxtun** Colorado, C USA 40°36′N 102°38′W
183 N9 **Hay** New South Wales, SE Australia 34°31′S 144°51′E
11 O10 **Hay** W Canada
171 S13 **Haya** Pulau Seram, E Indonesia 03°22′S 129°31′E
165 R9 **Hayachine-san** ▲ Honshū, C Japan 39°31′N 141°28′E
103 S4 **Hayange** Moselle, NE France 49°19′N 06°04′E
HaYarden *see* Jordan
Hayastani Hanrapetut'yun *see* Armenia
Hayasui-seto *see* Hōyo-kaikyō
39 N9 **Haycock** Alaska, USA 65°12′N 161°10′W
36 M14 **Hayden** Arizona, SW USA 33°00′N 110°46′W
37 Q3 **Hayden** Colorado, C USA 40°29′N 107°15′W
28 M10 **Hayes** South Dakota, N USA 44°20′N 101°01′W
9 X13 **Hayes** Manitoba, C Canada
11 P12 **Hayes** Nunavut, NE Canada
28 M16 **Hayes Center** Nebraska, C USA 40°30′N 101°02′W
39 S10 **Hayes, Mount** ▲ Alaska, USA 63°37′N 146°43′W
21 N11 **Hayesville** North Carolina, SE USA 35°03′N 83°49′W
35 X10 **Hayford Peak** ▲ Nevada, W USA 36°40′N 115°10′W
34 M3 **Hayfork** California, W USA 40°33′N 123°10′W
Hayir, Qasr al *see* Ḩayr al Gharbī, Qaşr al
Haylaastay *see* Sühbaatar
14 I12 **Hay Lake** ⊗ Ontario, SE Canada
141 X11 **Haymā'** *var.* Haima. C Oman 19°59′N 56°20′E
136 H13 **Haymana** Ankara, C Turkey 39°26′N 32°30′E
138 J7 **Ḩaymūr, Jabal** ▲ W Syria
Haynau *see* Chojnów
22 G4 **Haynesville** Louisiana, S USA 32°57′N 93°08′W
23 P6 **Hayneville** Alabama, S USA 32°13′N 86°34′W
114 M12 **Hayrabolu** Tekirdağ, NW Turkey 41°14′N 27°04′E
136 C10 **Hayrabolu Deresi** NW Turkey
138 J6 **Ḩayr al Gharbī, Qaşr al** *var.* Qasr al Hayir, Qasr al Hir al Gharbi. *ruins* Ḩimş, C Syria
138 L5 **Ḩayr ash Sharqī, Qaşr al** *var.* Qasr al Hir Ash Sharqī. *ruins* Ḩimş, C Syria
162 J7 **Hayrhan** *var.* Uubulan. Arhangay, C Mongolia 48°37′N 101°58′E
162 J9 **Hayrhandulaan** *var.* Mardzad. Övörhangay, C Mongolia 45°58′N 102°06′E
8 J10 **Hay River** Northwest Territories, W Canada 60°51′N 115°42′W
26 K4 **Hays** Kansas, C USA 38°53′N 99°20′W
28 K12 **Hay Springs** Nebraska, C USA 42°40′N 102°41′W
65 H25 **Haystack, The** ▲ NE Saint Helena 15°55′S 05°40′W
27 N7 **Haysville** Kansas, C USA 37°34′N 97°21′W
117 O7 **Haysyn** *Rus.* Gaysin. Vinnyts'ka Oblast', C Ukraine 48°50′N 29°29′E
27 Y9 **Hayti** Missouri, C USA 36°13′N 89°45′W
29 Q9 **Hayti** South Dakota, N USA 44°40′N 97°22′W
117 O8 **Hayvoron** *Rus.* Gayvorno. Kirovohrads'ka Oblast', C Ukraine 48°20′S 29°52′E
35 N9 **Hayward** California, W USA 37°40′N 122°07′W
30 J4 **Hayward** Wisconsin, N USA 46°02′N 91°26′W
97 O23 **Haywards Heath** SE England, United Kingdom 51°N 00°06′W
146 A11 **Hazar** *prev. Rus.* Cheleken. Balkan Welaýaty, W Turkmenistan 39°26′N 53°07′E
143 S11 **Hazārān, Kūh-e** *var.* Kūh-e ā Hazr. ▲ SE Iran 29°26′N 57°15′E
Hazarat Imam *see* Imām Şāḩib
21 O7 **Hazard** Kentucky, S USA 37°14′N 83°11′W
137 O15 **Hazar Gölü** ⊗ C Turkey
153 P15 **Hazārībāg** *var.* Hazāribāgh. Jhārkhand, N India 24°00′N 85°23′E
Hazārībāgh *see* Hazārībāg
103 O1 **Hazebrouck** Nord, N France 50°43′N 02°33′E
30 K9 **Hazel Green** Wisconsin, N USA 42°33′N 90°26′W
192 K9 **Hazel Holme Bank** *undersea feature* S Pacific Ocean 12°49′S 174°30′E
10 K13 **Hazelton** British Columbia, SW Canada 55°15′N 127°38′W
29 N6 **Hazelton** North Dakota, N USA 46°27′N 100°17′W
35 R5 **Hazen** Nevada, W USA 39°33′N 119°02′W
28 L5 **Hazen** North Dakota, N USA 47°18′N 101°37′W
38 L12 **Hazen Bay** *bay* E Bering Sea
9 N1 **Hazen, Lake** ⊗ Nunavut, N Canada
139 S5 **Hazīm, Bi'r** *well* C Iraq
23 V6 **Hazlehurst** Georgia, SE USA 31°51′N 82°35′W
22 K6 **Hazlehurst** Mississippi, S USA 31°51′N 90°24′W
18 K15 **Hazlet** New Jersey, NE USA 40°24′N 74°10′W
146 I9 **Hazorasp** *Rus.* Khazarasp. Xorazm Viloyati, W Uzbekistan 41°21′N 61°01′E
147 R13 **Hazratishoh, Qatorkŭhi** *var.* Khrebet Khazretishi, *Rus.* Khrebet Khozretishi. ▲ S Tajikistan
Hazr, Kūh-e ā *see* Hazārān, Kūh-e
149 U6 **Hazro** Punjab, E Pakistan 33°55′N 72°33′E
23 R7 **Headland** Alabama, S USA 31°21′N 85°20′W
182 C6 **Head of Bight** *headland* South Australia 31°33′S 131°05′E
33 N10 **Headquarters** Idaho, NW USA 46°38′N 115°52′W
34 M7 **Healdsburg** California, W USA 38°36′N 122°52′W
27 N13 **Healdton** Oklahoma, C USA 34°13′N 97°29′W
183 O12 **Healesville** Victoria, SE Australia 37°41′S 145°31′E
39 R10 **Healy** Alaska, USA 63°51′N 148°58′W
173 R13 **Heard and McDonald Islands** ◇ *Australian external territory* S Indian Ocean
173 R13 **Heard Island** *island* Heard and McDonald Islands, S Indian Ocean
25 U9 **Hearne** Texas, SW USA 30°52′N 96°35′W
12 F12 **Hearst** Ontario, S Canada 49°42′N 83°40′W
194 J5 **Hearst Island** *island* Antarctica
Heart of Dixie *see* Alabama
28 L5 **Heart River** North Dakota, N USA
31 T13 **Heath** Ohio, N USA 40°01′N 82°26′W
183 N11 **Heathcote** Victoria, SE Australia 36°57′S 144°43′E
97 N22 **Heathrow** ✈ (London) SE England, United Kingdom 51°28′N 00°27′W
21 X5 **Heathsville** Virginia, NE USA 37°55′N 76°29′W
27 R11 **Heavener** Oklahoma, C USA 34°53′N 94°36′W
25 R15 **Hebbronville** Texas, SW USA 27°19′N 98°41′W
163 Q13 **Hebei** *var.* Hebei Sheng, Hopeh, Hopei, Ji; *prev.* Chihli. ◆ *province* E China
Hebei Sheng *see* Hebei
36 M3 **Heber City** Utah, W USA 40°31′N 111°25′W
27 V10 **Heber Springs** Arkansas, C USA 35°30′N 92°01′W
161 N5 **Hebi** Henan, C China 35°57′N 114°08′E
32 F11 **Hebo** Oregon, NW USA 45°10′N 123°55′W
96 F9 **Hebrides, Sea of the** *sea* NW Scotland, United Kingdom
13 P5 **Hebron** Newfoundland and Labrador, E Canada 58°15′N 62°45′W
31 N11 **Hebron** Indiana, N USA 41°19′N 87°12′W
29 Q17 **Hebron** Nebraska, C USA 40°10′N 97°35′W
28 L5 **Hebron** North Dakota, N USA 46°54′N 102°03′W
138 F11 **Hebron** *var.* Al Khalīl, El Khalil, *Heb.* Hevron; *anc.* Kiriath-Arba. S West Bank 31°30′N 35°E
Hebrus *see* Évros/Maritsa/Meriç
95 N14 **Heby** Västmanland, C Sweden 59°56′N 16°53′E
10 I14 **Hecate Strait** *strait* British Columbia, W Canada
41 W12 **Hecelchakán** Campeche, SE Mexico 20°09′N 90°04′W
160 K13 **Hechi** *var.* Jinchengjiang. Guangxi Zhuangzu Zizhiqu, S China 24°39′N 108°02′E
101 H23 **Hechingen** Baden-Württemberg, S Germany 48°20′N 08°58′E
99 K17 **Hechtel** Limburg, NE Belgium 51°07′N 05°24′E
160 J9 **Hechuan** *var.* Heyang. Chongqing Shi, C China 30°02′N 106°15′E
29 P7 **Hecla** South Dakota, N USA 45°52′N 98°09′W
9 N1 **Hecla, Cape** *headland* Nunavut, N Canada 82°00′N 64°00′W
29 T9 **Hector** Minnesota, N USA 44°44′N 94°43′W
93 F17 **Hede** Jämtland, C Sweden 62°25′N 13°33′E
Hede *see* Sheyang
95 M14 **Hedemora** Dalarna, C Sweden 60°18′N 15°58′E
92 K13 **Hedenäset** *Finn.* Hietaniemi. Norrbotten, N Sweden 66°12′N 23°40′E
95 G23 **Hedensted** Syddanmark, C Denmark 55°47′N 09°43′E
95 N14 **Hedesunda** Gävleborg, C Sweden 60°25′N 17°00′E
95 N14 **Hedesundafjärden** ⊗ C Sweden
25 O3 **Hedley** Texas, SW USA 34°52′N 100°39′W
94 I12 **Hedmark** ◆ *county* S Norway
165 T16 **Hedo-misaki** *headland* Okinawa, SW Japan 26°55′N 128°15′E
29 X15 **Hedrick** Iowa, C USA 41°10′N 92°18′W
99 L16 **Heel** Limburg, SE Netherlands 51°12′N 06°01′E
189 Y12 **Heel Point** *point* Wake Island
98 H9 **Heemskerk** Noord-Holland, W Netherlands 52°31′N 04°40′E
98 M10 **Heerde** Gelderland, E Netherlands 52°24′N 06°02′E
98 L7 **Heerenveen** *Fris.* It Hearrenfean. Fryslân, N Netherlands 52°57′N 05°55′E
98 I8 **Heerhugowaard** Noord-Holland, NW Netherlands 52°40′N 04°50′E
92 O3 **Heer Land** *physical region* C Svalbard
99 M18 **Heerlen** Limburg, SE Netherlands 50°55′N 06°E
99 J19 **Heers** Limburg, NE Belgium 50°46′N 05°17′E
Heerwegen *see* Polkowice
98 K13 **Heesch** Noord-Brabant, S Netherlands 51°44′N 05°32′E
99 K15 **Heeze** Noord-Brabant, SE Netherlands 51°23′N 05°35′E
138 F8 **Hefa** *var.* Haifa, *hist.* Caiffa, Caiphas; *anc.* Sycaminum. Haifa, N Israel 32°49′N 34°59′E
Hefa, Mifraz *see* Mifrats Hefa
161 Q8 **Hefei** *var.* Hofei, *hist.* Luchow. *province capital* Anhui, E China 31°51′N 117°20′E
23 R3 **Heflin** Alabama, S USA 33°39′N 85°35′W
163 X7 **Hegang** Heilongjiang, NE China 47°18′N 130°16′E
164 L10 **Hegura-jima** *island* SW Japan
Heguri-jima *see* Heigun-tō
Hei *see* Heilongjiang
100 H8 **Heide** Schleswig-Holstein, N Germany 54°12′N 09°06′E
101 G20 **Heidelberg** Baden-Württemberg, SW Germany 49°24′N 08°41′E
83 J21 **Heidelberg** Gauteng, NE South Africa 26°31′S 28°21′E
22 M6 **Heidelberg** Mississippi, S USA 31°53′N 88°58′W
Heidenheim *see* Heidenheim an der Brenz
101 J22 **Heidenheim an der Brenz** *var.* Heidenheim. Baden-Württemberg, S Germany 48°41′N 10°09′E
109 U2 **Heidenreichstein** Niederösterreich, N Austria 48°53′N 15°07′E
164 F14 **Heigun-tō** *var.* Heguri-jima. *island* SW Japan
163 W5 **Heihe** *prev.* Ai-hun. Heilongjiang, NE China 50°13′N 127°29′E
162 S8 **Hei He** C China
Hei-ho *see* Nagqu
83 J22 **Heilbron** Free State, N South Africa 27°17′S 27°58′E
101 H21 **Heilbronn** Baden-Württemberg, SW Germany 49°09′N 09°13′E
Heiligenbeil *see* Mamonovo
109 Q8 **Heiligenblut** Tirol, W Austria 47°04′N 12°50′E
100 K7 **Heiligenhafen** Schleswig-Holstein, N Germany 54°22′N 10°57′E
Heiligenkreuz *see* Žiar nad Hronom
101 J15 **Heiligenstadt** Thüringen, C Germany 51°22′N 10°09′E
163 W8 **Heilongjiang** *var.* Hei, Heilongjiang Sheng, Hei-lung-chiang, Heilungkiang. ◆ *province* NE China
Heilong Jiang *see* Amur
Heilongjiang Sheng *see* Heilongjiang
98 H9 **Heiloo** Noord-Holland, NW Netherlands 52°36′N 04°43′E
Heilsberg *see* Lidzbark Warmiński
Hei-lung-chiang/Heilungkiang *see* Heilongjiang
Heimaæy *see* Heimaey
92 I4 **Heimaey** *var.* Heimaæy. *island* S Iceland
94 H8 **Heimdal** Sør-Trøndelag, S Norway 63°21′N 10°23′E
Heinaste *see* Ainaži
93 N17 **Heinävesi** Itä-Suomi, E Finland 62°22′N 28°42′E
99 M22 **Heinerscheid** Diekirch, N Luxembourg 50°06′N 06°05′E
98 M10 **Heino** Overijssel, E Netherlands 52°26′N 06°13′E
93 M18 **Heinola** Etelä-Suomi, S Finland 61°13′N 26°05′E
101 C16 **Heinsberg** Nordrhein-Westfalen, W Germany 51°02′N 06°01′E
163 U12 **Heishan** Liaoning, NE China 41°43′N 122°12′E
160 H8 **Heishui** *var.* Luhua. Sichuan, C China 32°08′N 102°54′E
99 H17 **Heist-op-den-Berg** Antwerpen, C Belgium 51°04′N 04°43′E
Heitō *see* Pingdong
171 X15 **Heitske** Papua, E Indonesia 07°02′S 138°45′E
Hejanah *see* Al Hījānah
Hejaz *see* Al Ḩijāz
160 M14 **He Jiang** S China
Hejiayan *see* Lüeyang
158 K6 **Hejing** Xinjiang Uygur Zizhiqu, NW China 42°21′N 86°19′E
Héjjasfalva *see* Vânători
Heka *see* Hoika
137 N14 **Hekimhan** Malatya, C Turkey 38°50′N 37°56′E
92 J4 **Hekla** ▲ S Iceland 63°56′N 19°42′W
Hekou *see* Yanshan, Jiangxi, China
Hekou *see* Yajiang, Sichuan, China
110 J6 **Hel** *Ger.* Hela. Pomorskie, N Poland 54°35′N 18°48′E
Hela *see* Hel
93 F17 **Helagsfjället** ▲ C Sweden 62°57′N 12°31′E
159 W8 **Helan** *var.* Xigang. Ningxia, N China 38°33′N 106°21′E
162 K14 **Helan Shan** ▲ N China
99 M16 **Helden** Limburg, SE Netherlands 51°20′N 06°00′E
27 X12 **Helena** Arkansas, C USA 34°32′N 90°34′W
33 R10 **Helena** *state capital* Montana, NW USA 46°36′N 112°02′W
96 H12 **Helensburgh** W Scotland, United Kingdom 56°00′N 04°45′W
184 K5 **Helensville** Auckland, North Island, New Zealand 36°42′S 174°26′E
95 L20 **Helgasjön** ⊗ S Sweden
100 G8 **Helgoland** *Eng.* Heligoland. *island* NW Germany
Helgoland Bay *see* Helgoländer Bucht
100 G8 **Helgoländer Bucht** *var.* Helgoland Bay, Heligoland Bight. *bay* NW Germany
Heligoland *see* Helgoland
Heligoland Bight *see* Helgoländer Bucht
Heliopolis *see* Baalbek
92 I4 **Hella** Sudhurland, SW Iceland 63°51′N 20°24′W
Hellas *see* Greece
143 N11 **Ḩelleh, Rūd-e** S Iran
98 N10 **Hellendoorn** Overijssel, E Netherlands 52°22′N 06°27′E
Hellenic Republic *see* Greece
121 Q10 **Hellenic Trough** *undersea feature* Aegean Sea, C Mediterranean Sea 22°00′E 35°30′N
94 E10 **Hellesylt** Møre og Romsdal, S Norway 62°06′N 06°51′E
98 F13 **Hellevoetsluis** Zuid-Holland, SW Netherlands 51°49′N 04°08′E
105 Q12 **Hellín** Castilla-La Mancha, C Spain 38°31′N 01°43′W
115 H19 **Hellinikon** ✈ (Athína) Attikí, C Greece 37°53′N 23°43′E
32 M12 **Hells Canyon** *valley* Idaho/Oregon, NW USA
148 L9 **Helmand** ◆ *province* S Afghanistan
148 K10 **Helmand, Daryā-ye** *var.* Rūd-e Hīrmand. Afghanistan/Iran *see also* Hirmand, Rūd-e
Helmand, Daryā-ye *see* Hirmand, Rūd-e
Helmantica *see* Salamanca
101 K15 **Helme** C Germany
99 L15 **Helmond** Noord-Brabant, S Netherlands 51°29′N 05°41′E
96 J7 **Helmsdale** N Scotland, United Kingdom 58°06′N 03°36′W
100 K13 **Helmstedt** Niedersachsen, N Germany 52°14′N 11°01′E
163 Y10 **Helong** Jilin, NE China 42°38′N 129°01′E
36 M4 **Helper** Utah, W USA 39°40′N 110°52′W
100 O10 **Helpter Berge** *hill* NE Germany
95 J22 **Helsingborg** *prev.* Hälsingborg. Skåne, S Sweden 56°N 12°48′E
Helsingfors *see* Helsinki
95 J22 **Helsingør** *Eng.* Elsinore. Hovedstaden, E Denmark 56°03′N 12°38′E
93 M20 **Helsinki** *Swe.* Helsingfors. ● (Finland) Etelä-Suomi, S Finland 60°18′N 24°58′E
97 H25 **Helston** SW England, United Kingdom 50°04′N 05°17′W
Heltau *see* Cisnădie
61 C17 **Helvecia** Santa Fe, C Argentina 31°09′S 60°09′W
97 K15 **Helvellyn** ▲ NW England, United Kingdom 54°31′N 03°00′W
Helvetia *see* Switzerland
Helwân *see* Hilwān
97 N21 **Hemel Hempstead** E England, United Kingdom 51°46′N 00°28′W
35 U16 **Hemet** California, W USA 33°45′N 116°58′W
28 J13 **Hemingford** Nebraska, C USA 42°18′N 103°02′W
21 T13 **Hemingway** South Carolina, SE USA 33°45′N 79°25′W
92 G13 **Hemnesberget** Nordland, C Norway 66°14′N 13°40′E
25 Y8 **Hemphill** Texas, SW USA 31°21′N 93°50′W
25 V11 **Hempstead** Texas, SW USA 30°06′N 96°06′W
95 P20 **Hemse** Gotland, SE Sweden 57°12′N 18°22′E
94 F13 **Hemsedal** *valley* S Norway
161 N6 **Henan** *var.* Henan Sheng, Honan, Yu. ◆ *province* C China
184 L4 **Hen and Chickens** *island group* N New Zealand
Henan Mongolzu Zizhixian/Henan Sheng *see* Yêgainnyin
105 O7 **Henares** C Spain
165 P7 **Henashi-zaki** *headland* Honshū, C Japan 40°37′N 139°51′E
102 I16 **Hendaye** Pyrénées-Atlantiques, SW France 43°22′N 01°46′W
136 F11 **Hendek** Sakarya, NW Turkey 40°47′N 30°45′E
61 B21 **Henderson** Buenos Aires, E Argentina 36°18′S 61°43′W
20 I5 **Henderson** Kentucky, S USA 37°50′N 87°35′W
35 X11 **Henderson** Nevada, W USA 36°02′N 114°58′W
21 V8 **Henderson** North Carolina, SE USA 36°20′N 78°26′W
20 G10 **Henderson** Tennessee, S USA 35°27′N 88°40′W
25 W7 **Henderson** Texas, SW USA 32°11′N 94°48′W
30 J12 **Henderson Creek** Illinois, N USA
186 M9 **Henderson Field** ✈ (Honiara) Guadalcanal, C Solomon Islands 09°28′S 160°02′E
191 O17 **Henderson Island** *atoll* N Pitcairn Islands
21 O10 **Hendersonville** North Carolina, SE USA 35°19′N 82°28′W
20 J8 **Hendersonville** Tennessee, S USA 36°18′N 86°37′W
143 O14 **Hendorābī, Jazīreh-ye** *island* S Iran
55 V10 **Hendrik Top** *var.* Hendriktop. *elevation* C Suriname
Hendriktop *see* Hendrik Top
Hendū Kosh *see* Hindu Kush
14 L12 **Heney, Lac** ⊗ Québec, SE Canada
Hengchow *see* Hengyang
161 S15 **Hengch'un** S Taiwan 22°09′N 120°43′E
159 R16 **Hengduan Shan** ▲ SW China
98 N12 **Hengelo** Gelderland, E Netherlands 52°03′N 06°19′E
98 O10 **Hengelo** Overijssel, E Netherlands 52°16′N 06°46′E
Hengnan *see* Hengyang
161 N11 **Hengshan** Hunan, S China 27°17′N 112°51′E
160 L4 **Hengshan** Shaanxi, C China 37°57′N 109°17′E
161 O4 **Hengshui** Hebei, E China 37°42′N 115°39′E
161 N12 **Hengyang** *var.* Hengnan, Heng-yang; *prev.* Hengchow. Hunan, S China 26°55′N 112°34′E
Heng-yang *see* Hengyang
117 U11 **Heniches'k** *Rus.* Genichesk. Khersons'ka Oblast', S Ukraine 46°10′N 34°49′E
21 Z4 **Henlopen, Cape** *headland* Delaware, NE USA 38°48′N 75°06′W
Henna *see* Enna
94 M10 **Hennan** Gävleborg, C Sweden 62°01′N 15°55′E
102 G7 **Hennebont** Morbihan, NW France 47°48′N 03°17′W
30 L11 **Hennepin** Illinois, N USA 41°14′N 89°21′W
26 M9 **Hennessey** Oklahoma, C USA 36°06′N 97°54′W
100 N12 **Hennigsdorf** *var.* Hennigsdorf bei Berlin. Brandenburg, NE Germany 52°37′N 13°13′E
Hennigsdorf bei Berlin *see* Hennigsdorf
19 N9 **Henniker** New Hampshire, NE USA 43°10′N 71°47′W
25 S5 **Henrietta** Texas, SW USA 33°49′N 98°13′W
Henrique de Carvalho *see* Saurimo
30 L12 **Henry** Illinois, N USA 41°06′N 89°21′W
21 Y7 **Henry, Cape** *headland* Virginia, NE USA 36°55′N 76°01′W
27 P10 **Henryetta** Oklahoma, C USA 35°26′N 95°58′W
194 M7 **Henry Ice Rise** *ice cap* Antarctica
9 R5 **Henry Kater, Cape** *headland* Baffin Island, Nunavut, NE Canada 69°09′N 66°45′W
33 R13 **Henrys Fork** Idaho, NW USA
14 E15 **Hensall** Ontario, S Canada 43°25′N 81°28′W
100 J9 **Henstedt-Ulzburg** Schleswig-Holstein, N Germany 53°45′N 09°59′E
163 N7 **Hentiy** *var.* Batshireet, Eg. ◆ *province* N Mongolia
162 M7 **Hentiyn Nuruu** ▲ N Mongolia
183 P10 **Henty** New South Wales, SE Australia 35°33′S 147°03′E
Henzada *see* Hinthada
Heping *see* Huishui
101 G19 **Heppenheim** Hessen, W Germany 49°39′N 08°38′E
32 J11 **Heppner** Oregon, NW USA 45°21′N 119°32′W
160 L15 **Hepu** *var.* Lianzhou. Guangxi Zhuangzu Zizhiqu, S China 21°40′N 109°12′E
Heracleum *see* Irákleio
92 J2 **Heradhsvötn** C Iceland
Herakleion *see* Irákleio
148 K5 **Herāt** *var.* Herat; *anc.* Aria. Herāt, W Afghanistan 34°23′N 62°11′E
148 J5 **Herāt** ◆ *province* W Afghanistan
103 P14 **Hérault** ◆ *department* S France
103 P15 **Hérault** S France
11 T16 **Herbert** Saskatchewan, S Canada 50°27′N 107°09′W
185 F22 **Herbert** Otago, South Island, New Zealand 45°14′S 170°48′E
38 J17 **Herbert Island** *island* Aleutian Islands, Alaska, USA
Herbertshöhe *see* Kokopo
15 Q7 **Herbertville** Québec, SE Canada 48°23′N 71°42′W
101 G17 **Herborn** Hessen, W Germany 50°40′N 08°18′E
113 I17 **Herceg-Novi** *It.* Castelnuovo; *prev.* Ercegnovi. SW Montenegro 42°28′N 18°35′E
11 X10 **Herchmer** Manitoba, C Canada 57°25′N 94°12′W
186 E8 **Hercules Bay** *bay* E Papua New Guinea
92 K2 **Herdhubreidh** ▲ C Iceland 65°12′N 16°26′W
42 M13 **Heredia** Heredia, C Costa Rica 10°N 84°06′W
42 M12 **Heredia** *off.* Provincia de Heredia. ◆ *province* N Costa Rica
Heredia, Provincia de *see* Heredia
97 K21 **Hereford** W England, United Kingdom 52°04′N 02°43′W
24 M3 **Hereford** Texas, SW USA 34°49′N 102°25′W
15 Q13 **Hereford, Mont** ▲ Québec, SE Canada 45°04′N 71°38′W
97 K21 **Herefordshire** *cultural region* W England, United Kingdom
191 U11 **Hereheretue** *atoll* Îles Tuamotu, C French Polynesia
105 N10 **Herencia** Castilla-La Mancha, C Spain 39°22′N 03°12′W
99 H18 **Herent** Vlaams Brabant, C Belgium 50°54′N 04°40′E
99 I16 **Herentals** *var.* Herenthals. Antwerpen, N Belgium 51°11′N 04°50′E
Herenthals *see* Herentals
99 H17 **Herenthout** Antwerpen, N Belgium 51°09′N 04°45′E
95 J23 **Herfølge** Sjælland, E Denmark 55°25′N 12°09′E
100 G13 **Herford** Nordrhein-Westfalen, NW Germany 52°07′N 08°41′E
27 O5 **Herington** Kansas, C USA 38°37′N 96°55′W
108 H7 **Herisau** *Fr.* Hérisau. Ausser Rhoden, NE Switzerland 47°23′N 09°17′E
Hérisau *see* Herisau
Hérisal *see* Herstal
99 J18 **Herk-de-Stad** Limburg, NE Belgium 50°57′N 05°12′E
Herkulesbad/Herkulesfürdő *see* Băile Herculane
162 M8 **Herlenbayan-Ulaan** *var.* Dulaan. Hentiy, C Mongolia 47°09′N 108°48′E
Herlen Gol/Herlen He *see* Kerulen
35 Q4 **Herlong** California, W USA 40°07′N 120°06′W
97 L26 **Herm** *island* Channel Islands
109 R9 **Hermagor** *Slvn.* Šmohor. Kärnten, S Austria 46°37′N 13°24′E
29 S7 **Herman** Minnesota, N USA 45°49′N 96°08′W

◆ Country ● Country Capital ◇ Dependent Territory ○ Dependent Territory Capital ◆ Administrative Regions ✈ International Airport ▲ Mountain ▲ Mountain Range Volcano River ⊗ Lake ⊠ Reservoir

96 L1 **Herma Ness** *headland* NE Scotland, United Kingdom 60°51′N 00°55′W
27 V4 **Hermann** Missouri, C USA 38°43′N 91°26′W
181 Q8 **Hermannsburg** Northern Territory, N Australia 23°59′S 132°55′E
Hermannstadt *see* Sibiu
94 E12 **Hermansverk** Sogn Og Fjordane, S Norway 61°11′N 06°52′E
138 H6 **Hermel** *var.* Hirmil. NE Lebanon 34°23′N 36°19′E
Hermhausen *see* Hajnówka
183 P6 **Hermidale** New South Wales, SE Australia 31°36′S 146°42′E
55 X9 **Herminadorp** Sipaliwini, NE Suriname 05°05′N 54°22′W
32 K11 **Hermiston** Oregon, NW USA 45°50′N 119°17′W
27 T6 **Hermitage** Missouri, C USA 37°57′N 93°21′W
186 D4 **Hermit Islands** *island group* N Papua New Guinea
25 O7 **Hermleigh** Texas, SW USA 32°37′N 100°44′W
138 G7 **Hermon, Mount** *Ar.* Jabal ash Shaykh. ▲ S Syria 35°30′N 33°30′E
Hermopolis Parva *see* Damanhûr
28 J10 **Hermosa** South Dakota, N USA 43°49′N 103°12′W
40 F5 **Hermosillo** Sonora, NW Mexico 28°59′N 110°53′W
Hermoupolis *see* Ermoúpoli
111 N20 **Hernád** *var.* Hornád, *Ger.* Kundert. ↝ Hungary/Slovakia
61 C18 **Hernández** Entre Ríos, E Argentina 32°21′S 60°02′W
23 V11 **Hernando** Florida, SE USA 28°54′N 82°22′W
22 L1 **Hernando** Mississippi, S USA 34°49′N 89°59′W
105 Q2 **Hernani** País Vasco, N Spain 43°16′N 01°59′W
99 F19 **Herne** Vlaams Brabant, C Belgium 50°45′N 04°03′E
101 E14 **Herne** Nordrhein-Westfalen, W Germany 51°32′N 07°12′E
95 F22 **Herning** Midtjylland, W Denmark 56°08′N 08°59′E
Hernösand *see* Härnösand
121 U11 **Herodotus Basin** *undersea feature* E Mediterranean Sea
121 Q12 **Herodotus Trough** *undersea feature* C Mediterranean Sea
29 T11 **Heron Lake** Minnesota, N USA 43°48′N 95°18′W
Herowābād *see* Khalkhāl
95 G16 **Herre** Telemark, S Norway 59°06′N 09°34′E
29 N7 **Herreid** South Dakota, N USA 45°49′N 100°04′W
101 H22 **Herrenberg** Baden-Württemberg, S Germany 48°36′N 08°52′E
104 L14 **Herrera** Andalucía, S Spain 37°22′N 04°50′W
43 R17 **Herrera** *off.* Provincia de Herrera. ◆ *province* S Panama
104 L10 **Herrera del Duque** Extremadura, W Spain 39°10′N 05°03′W
104 M4 **Herrera de Pisuerga** Castilla y León, N Spain 42°35′N 04°20′W
Herrera, Provincia de *see* Herrera
41 Z13 **Herrero, Punta** *headland* SE Mexico 19°15′N 87°28′W
183 P16 **Herrick** Tasmania, SE Australia 41°07′S 147°53′E
30 L17 **Herrin** Illinois, N USA 37°48′N 89°01′W
20 M6 **Herrington Lake** ⊠ Kentucky, S USA
95 K18 **Herrljunga** Västra Götaland, S Sweden 58°05′N 13°02′E
103 N16 **Hers** ↝ S France
10 I1 **Herschel Island** *island* Yukon Territory, NW Canada
99 I17 **Herselt** Antwerpen, C Belgium 51°04′N 04°53′E
18 G15 **Hershey** Pennsylvania, NE USA 40°17′N 76°39′W
99 K19 **Herstal** *Fr.* Héristal. Liège, E Belgium 50°40′N 05°38′E
97 O21 **Hertford** E England, United Kingdom 51°48′N 00°05′W
21 X8 **Hertford** North Carolina, SE USA 36°11′N 76°30′W
97 O21 **Hertfordshire** *cultural region* E England, United Kingdom
181 Z9 **Hervey Bay** Queensland, E Australia 25°17′S 152°48′E
101 O14 **Herzberg** Brandenburg, E Germany 51°42′N 13°15′E
99 E18 **Herzele** Oost-Vlaanderen, NW Belgium 50°52′N 03°52′E
101 K20 **Herzogenaurach** Bayern, SE Germany 49°34′N 10°52′E
109 W4 **Herzogenburg** Niederösterreich, NE Austria 48°18′N 15°43′E
Herzogenbusch *see* 's-Hertogenbosch
103 N2 **Hesdin** Pas-de-Calais, N France 50°21′N 02°00′E
160 K14 **Heshan** Guangxi Zhuangzu Zizhiqu, S China 23°45′N 108°58′E
159 X10 **Heshui** *var.* Xihuachi. Gansu, C China 35°42′N 108°06′E
99 M25 **Hespérange** Luxembourg, SE Luxembourg 49°34′N 06°10′E
35 U14 **Hesperia** California, W USA 34°25′N 117°17′W
37 P7 **Hesperus Mountain** ▲ Colorado, C USA 37°27′N 108°05′W
10 J6 **Hess** ↝ Yukon Territory, NW Canada
Hesse *see* Hessen
101 J21 **Hesselberg** ▲ S Germany 49°04′N 10°32′E
95 I22 **Hesselø** *island* E Denmark
101 H17 **Hessen** *Eng./Fr.* Hesse. ◆ *state* C Germany
192 L6 **Hess Tablemount** *undersea feature* C Pacific Ocean 17°49′N 174°15′W
27 N6 **Hesston** Kansas, C USA 38°08′N 97°25′W
93 G15 **Hestkjøltoppen** ▲ C Norway 64°21′N 13°57′E
97 K18 **Heswall** NW England, United Kingdom 53°20′N 03°06′W
153 P12 **Hetauda** Central, C Nepal
Hétfalu *see* Săcele
28 K7 **Hettinger** North Dakota, N USA 46°00′N 102°38′W
101 L14 **Hettstedt** Sachsen-Anhalt, C Germany 51°39′N 11°31′E
92 P3 **Heuglin, Kapp** *headland* SE Svalbard 78°15′N 22°49′E
163 W17 **Heuksan-jedo** *var.* Hŭksan-gundo. *island group* SW South Korea
187 N10 **Heuru** Makira-Ulawa, SE Solomon Islands 10°13′S 161°25′E
99 J17 **Heusden** Limburg, NE Belgium 51°02′N 05°17′E
98 J13 **Heusden** Noord-Brabant, S Netherlands 51°43′N 05°05′E
102 K3 **Hève, Cap de la** *headland* N France 49°28′N 00°13′W
99 H18 **Heverlee** Vlaams Brabant, C Belgium 50°52′N 04°41′E
111 L22 **Heves** Heves, NE Hungary 47°36′N 20°17′E
111 L22 **Heves** *off.* Heves Megye. ◆ *county* NE Hungary
Heves Megye *see* Heves
Hevron *see* Hebron
45 Y13 **Hewanorra** ✕ (Saint Lucia) S Saint Lucia 13°44′N 60°57′W
Hexian *see* Hezhou
160 L6 **Heyang** Shaanxi, C China 35°14′N 110°02′E
Heyang *see* Hechuan
Heydebrech *see* Kędzierzyn-Kozle
Heydekrug *see* Šilutė
Heyin *see* Guide
97 K16 **Heysham** NW England, United Kingdom 54°02′N 02°54′W
161 O14 **Heyuan** *var.* Yuancheng. Guangdong, S China 23°41′N 114°45′E
182 L12 **Heywood** Victoria, SE Australia 38°09′S 141°38′E
180 K3 **Heywood Islands** *island group* Western Australia
161 O6 **Heze** *var.* Caozhou. Shandong, E China 35°16′N 115°27′E
159 U11 **Hezheng** Gansu, C China 35°29′N 103°36′E
160 M13 **Hezhou** *var.* Babu; *prev.* Hexian. Guangxi Zhuangzu Zizhiqu, S China 24°33′N 11°30′E
159 U11 **Hezuo** Gansu, C China 34°55′N 102°49′E
23 Z16 **Hialeah** Florida, SE USA 25°51′N 80°16′W
27 Q3 **Hiawatha** Kansas, C USA 39°51′N 95°34′W
36 M4 **Hiawatha** Utah, W USA 39°28′N 111°00′W
29 V4 **Hibbing** Minnesota, N USA 47°25′N 92°55′W
183 N17 **Hibbs, Point** *headland* Tasmania, SE Australia 42°37′S 145°15′E
Hibernia *see* Ireland
20 F8 **Hickman** Kentucky, S USA 36°33′N 89°11′W
21 Q9 **Hickory** North Carolina, SE USA 35°44′N 81°20′W
21 Q9 **Hickory, Lake** ⊠ North Carolina, SE USA
184 Q7 **Hicks Bay** Gisborne, North Island, New Zealand 37°36′S 178°18′E
25 S8 **Hico** Texas, SW USA 31°58′N 98°01′W
Hida *see* Furukawa
165 T4 **Hidaka** Hokkaidō, NE Japan 42°53′N 142°24′E
164 I12 **Hidaka** Hyōgo, Honshū, SW Japan 35°27′N 134°43′E
165 T5 **Hidaka-sanmyaku** ▲▲ Hokkaidō, NE Japan
41 O6 **Hidalgo** *var.* Villa Hidalgo. Coahuila, NE Mexico 27°46′N 99°54′W
41 N8 **Hidalgo** Nuevo León, NE Mexico 29°59′N 100°27′W
41 O10 **Hidalgo** Tamaulipas, C Mexico 24°16′N 99°28′W
41 O13 **Hidalgo** ◆ *state* C Mexico
40 J7 **Hidalgo del Parral** *var.* Parral. Chihuahua, N Mexico 26°58′N 105°40′W
100 N7 **Hiddensee** *island* NE Germany
80 G6 **Hidiglib, Wadi** ↝ NE Sudan
109 U6 **Hieflau** Salzburg, E Austria 47°36′N 14°34′E
187 P16 **Hienghène** Province Nord, C New Caledonia 20°43′S 164°54′E
Hierosolyma *see* Jerusalem
64 N12 **Hierro** *var.* Ferro. *island* Islas Canarias, Spain, NE Atlantic Ocean
Hietaniemi *see* Hedenäset
164 G13 **Higashi-Hiroshima** *var.* Higasihirosima. Hiroshima, Honshū, SW Japan 34°27′N 132°43′E
164 C12 **Higashi-suidō** *strait* SW Japan
Higasihirosima *see* Higashi-Hiroshima
25 P1 **Higgins** Texas, SW USA 36°06′N 100°01′W
31 P7 **Higgins Lake** ⊚ Michigan, N USA
27 S4 **Higginsville** Missouri, C USA 39°04′N 93°43′W
High Atlas *see* Haut Atlas
30 M5 **High Falls Reservoir** ⊠ Wisconsin, N USA
44 K12 **Highgate** C Jamaica 18°16′N 76°53′W
25 X11 **High Island** Texas, SW USA 29°35′N 94°24′W
31 O5 **High Island** *island* Michigan, N USA
30 K15 **Highland** Illinois, N USA 38°44′N 89°40′W
31 N10 **Highland Park** Illinois, N USA 42°10′N 87°48′W
21 O10 **Highlands** North Carolina, SE USA 35°04′N 83°10′W
11 O11 **High Level** Alberta, W Canada 58°31′N 117°08′W
29 O9 **Highmore** South Dakota, N USA 44°29′N 99°26′W
171 N3 **High Peak** ▲ Luzon, N Philippines 15°28′N 120°07′E
High Plains *see* Great Plains
21 S9 **High Point** North Carolina, SE USA 35°58′N 80°00′W
18 J13 **High Point** *hill* New Jersey, NE USA
11 P13 **High Prairie** Alberta, W Canada 55°27′N 116°28′W
11 Q16 **High River** Alberta, SW Canada 50°35′N 113°50′W
21 S9 **High Rock Lake** ⊠ North Carolina, SE USA
23 V9 **High Springs** Florida, SE USA 29°49′N 82°36′W
High Veld *see* Great Karoo
97 J24 **High Willhays** ▲ SW England, United Kingdom 50°39′N 03°58′W
97 N22 **High Wycombe** *prev.* Chepping Wycombe, Chipping Wycombe. SE England, United Kingdom 51°38′N 00°46′W
41 P12 **Higos** *var.* El Higo. Veracruz-Llave, E Mexico 21°48′N 98°25′W
102 I16 **Higuer, Cap** *headland* NE Spain 43°23′N 01°46′W
45 R5 **Higüero, Punta** *headland* W Puerto Rico 18°21′N 67°15′W
45 P9 **Higüey** *var.* Salvaleón de Higüey. E Dominican Republic 18°40′N 68°43′W
190 G11 **Hihifo** ✕ (Matā'utu) Île Uvea, N Wallis and Futuna
81 N16 **Hiiraan** *off.* Gobolka Hiiraan. ◆ *region* C Somalia
Hiiraan, Gobolka *see* Hiiraan
118 E4 **Hiiumaa** *var.* Hiiumaa Maakond. ◆ *province* W Estonia
118 D4 **Hiiumaa** *Ger.* Dagden, *Swe.* Dagö. *island* W Estonia
Hiiumaa Maakond *see* Hiiumaa
Hijanah *see* Al Hījānah
105 S6 **Híjar** Aragón, NE Spain 41°10′N 00°27′W
191 V10 **Hikueru** *atoll* Îles Tuamotu, C French Polynesia
184 K3 **Hikurangi** Northland, North Island, New Zealand 35°37′S 174°16′E
184 Q8 **Hikurangi** ▲ North Island, New Zealand 37°55′S 177°59′E
192 L11 **Hikurangi Trench** *var.* Hikurangi Trough. *undersea feature* SW Pacific Ocean
Hikurangi Trough *see* Hikurangi Trench
190 B15 **Hikutavake** NW Niue
121 Q12 **Hilāl, Ra's al** *headland* N Libya 32°55′N 22°09′E
61 A24 **Hilario Ascasubi** Buenos Aires, E Argentina 39°22′S 62°39′W
101 K17 **Hildburghausen** Thüringen, C Germany 50°26′N 10°44′E
101 E15 **Hilden** Nordrhein-Westfalen, W Germany 51°12′N 06°56′E
100 I13 **Hildesheim** Niedersachsen, N Germany 52°09′N 09°57′E
33 T9 **Hilger** Montana, NW USA 47°15′N 109°18′W
153 S13 **Hili** *var.* Hilli. Rajshahi, NW Bangladesh 25°16′N 89°04′E
Hilla *see* Al Ḥillah
45 O14 **Hillaby, Mount** ▲ N Barbados 13°12′N 59°34′W
95 K19 **Hillared** Västra Götaland, S Sweden 57°37′N 13°10′E
195 R12 **Hillary Coast** *physical region* Antarctica
42 G2 **Hill Bank** Orange Walk, N Belize 17°36′N 88°43′W
33 O14 **Hill City** Idaho, NW USA 43°18′N 115°03′W
26 K3 **Hill City** Kansas, C USA 39°23′N 99°51′W
29 V5 **Hill City** Minnesota, N USA 46°59′N 93°36′W
28 J10 **Hill City** South Dakota, N USA 43°54′N 103°33′W
65 C24 **Hill Cove Settlement** West Falkland, Falkland Islands
98 H10 **Hillegom** Zuid-Holland, W Netherlands 52°18′N 04°35′E
95 J22 **Hillerød** Hovedstaden, E Denmark 55°56′N 12°19′E
36 M7 **Hillers, Mount** ▲ Utah, W USA 37°53′N 110°42′W
Hilli *see* Hili
29 R11 **Hills** Minnesota, N USA 43°31′N 96°21′W
30 L14 **Hillsboro** Illinois, N USA 39°09′N 89°29′W
27 N5 **Hillsboro** Kansas, C USA 38°21′N 97°12′W
27 X5 **Hillsboro** Missouri, C USA 38°13′N 90°33′W
19 N10 **Hillsboro** New Hampshire, NE USA 43°06′N 71°52′W
37 Q14 **Hillsboro** New Mexico, SW USA 32°55′N 107°33′W
29 R4 **Hillsboro** North Dakota, N USA 47°25′N 97°03′W
31 R14 **Hillsboro** Ohio, N USA 39°12′N 83°36′W
32 G11 **Hillsboro** Oregon, NW USA 45°32′N 122°59′W
25 T8 **Hillsboro** Texas, SW USA 32°01′N 97°08′W
30 K8 **Hillsboro** Wisconsin, N USA 43°40′N 90°21′W
23 Y14 **Hillsboro Canal** *canal* Florida, SE USA
45 Y15 **Hillsborough** Carriacou, N Grenada 12°28′N 61°28′W
97 G15 **Hillsborough** E Northern Ireland, United Kingdom 54°27′N 06°06′W
21 U9 **Hillsborough** North Carolina, SE USA 36°04′N 79°06′W
31 Q10 **Hillsdale** Michigan, N USA 41°55′N 84°37′W
183 O8 **Hillston** New South Wales, SE Australia 33°30′S 145°33′E
21 R7 **Hillsville** Virginia, NE USA 36°46′N 80°44′W
96 L2 **Hillswick** NE Scotland, United Kingdom 60°28′N 01°37′W
Hill Tippera *see* Tripura
38 H11 **Hilo** Hawaii, USA, C Pacific Ocean 19°42′N 155°04′W
18 F9 **Hilton** New York, NE USA 43°17′N 77°47′W
14 C10 **Hilton Beach** Ontario, S Canada 46°14′N 83°51′W
21 R16 **Hilton Head Island** South Carolina, SE USA 32°13′N 80°45′W
21 R16 **Hilton Head Island** *island* South Carolina, SE USA
99 J15 **Hilvarenbeek** Noord-Brabant, S Netherlands 51°29′N 05°08′E
98 J11 **Hilversum** Noord-Holland, C Netherlands 52°14′N 05°10′E
75 W8 **Hilwān** *var.* Helwan, Hilwân, Hulwan, Hulwân. N Egypt 29°51′N 31°20′E
Hilwân *see* Hilwān
152 J7 **Himāchal Pradesh** ◆ *state* NW India
Himalaya/Himalaya Shan *see* Himalayas
152 M9 **Himalayas** *var.* Himalaya, *Chin.* Himalaya Shan. ▲▲ S Asia
171 P6 **Himamaylan** Negros, C Philippines 10°04′N 122°52′E
93 K15 **Himanka** Länsi-Suomi, W Finland 64°04′N 23°40′E
Himara *see* Himarë
113 L23 **Himarë** *var.* Himara. Vlorë, S Albania 40°06′N 19°45′E
138 M2 **Ḥimār, Wādī al** *dry watercourse* N Syria
154 D9 **Himatnagar** Gujarāt, W India 23°38′N 73°02′E
109 Y4 **Himberg** Niederösterreich, E Austria 48°05′N 16°27′E
164 I13 **Himeji** *var.* Himezi. Hyōgo, Honshū, SW Japan 34°47′N 134°32′E
164 E14 **Hime-jima** *island* SW Japan
Himezi *see* Himeji
164 L13 **Himi** Toyama, Honshū, SW Japan 36°54′N 136°59′E
109 S9 **Himmelberg** Kärnten, S Austria 46°45′N 14°01′E
138 I5 **Ḥimṣ** *var.* Homs; *anc.* Emesa. Ḥimṣ, C Syria 34°44′N 36°43′E
138 K6 **Ḥimṣ** *off.* Muḥāfazat Hims, *var.* Homs. ◆ *governorate* C Syria
138 I5 **Ḥimṣ, Buḥayrat** *var.* Buhayrat Qattinah. ⊚ W Syria
171 R7 **Hinatuan** Mindanao, S Philippines 08°21′N 126°19′E
117 N10 **Hincești** *var.* Hânceşti; *prev.* Kotovsk. C Moldova 46°48′N 28°33′E
44 M9 **Hinche** C Haiti 19°07′N 72°00′W
181 X5 **Hinchinbrook Island** *island* Queensland, NE Australia
39 S12 **Hinchinbrook Island** *island* Alaska, USA
97 M19 **Hinckley** C England, United Kingdom 52°33′N 01°21′W
29 V7 **Hinckley** Minnesota, N USA 46°01′N 92°57′W
36 K5 **Hinckley** Utah, W USA 39°21′N 112°39′W
18 J9 **Hinckley Reservoir** ⊠ New York, NE USA
152 I12 **Hindaun** Rājasthān, N India 26°44′N 77°02′E
Hindenburg/Hindenburg in Oberschlesien *see* Zabrze
Hindiya *see* Al Hindīyah
21 O6 **Hindman** Kentucky, S USA 37°20′N 82°58′W
182 L10 **Hindmarsh, Lake** ⊚ Victoria, SE Australia
185 G19 **Hinds** Canterbury, South Island, New Zealand 44°01′S 171°33′E
185 G19 **Hinds** ↝ South Island, New Zealand
95 H23 **Hindsholm** *island* C Denmark
149 S4 **Hindu Kush** *Per.* Hendū Kosh. ▲▲ Afghanistan/Pakistan
155 H19 **Hindupur** Andhra Pradesh, E India 13°46′N 77°33′E
11 O12 **Hines Creek** Alberta, W Canada 56°14′N 118°36′W
23 W6 **Hinesville** Georgia, SE USA 31°51′N 81°36′W
154 I12 **Hinganghāt** Mahārāshtra, C India 20°32′N 78°52′E
149 N15 **Hingol** ↝ SW Pakistan
154 H13 **Hingoli** Mahārāshtra, C India 19°45′N 77°08′E
137 R13 **Hınıs** Erzurum, E Turkey 39°22′N 41°44′E
92 O2 **Hinlopenstretet** *strait* N Svalbard
92 G10 **Hinnøya** *Lapp.* Iinnasuolu. *island* C Norway
108 H10 **Hinterrhein** ↝ SW Switzerland
166 L8 **Hinthada** *var.* Henzada. Ayeyarwady, SW Myanmar (Burma) 17°36′N 95°26′E
11 O14 **Hinton** Alberta, SW Canada 53°24′N 117°35′W
26 M10 **Hinton** Oklahoma, C USA 35°28′N 98°21′W
21 R6 **Hinton** West Virginia, NE USA 37°42′N 80°54′W
Hios *see* Chíos
41 N8 **Hipólito** Coahuila, NE Mexico 25°42′N 101°22′W
Hipponium *see* Vibo Valentia
164 B13 **Hirado** Nagasaki, Hirado-shima, SW Japan 33°22′N 129°31′E
164 B13 **Hirado-shima** *island* SW Japan
165 P16 **Hirakubo-saki** *headland* Ishigaki-jima, SW Japan 24°36′N 124°19′E
154 M11 **Hīrākud Reservoir** ⊠ E India
Hir al Gharbi, Qasr al *see* Ḥayr al Gharbī, Qaşr al
165 Q16 **Hirara** Okinawa, Miyako-jima, SW Japan 24°48′N 125°17′E
Hir Ash Sharqī, Qasr al *see* Ḥayr ash Sharqī, Qaşr al
164 G12 **Hirata** Shimane, Honshū, SW Japan 35°25′N 132°45′E
136 I13 **Hirfanlı Barajı** ⊠ C Turkey
155 G18 **Hiriyūr** Karnātaka, W India 13°58′N 76°33′E
Hîrlău *see* Hârlău
148 K10 **Hīrmand, Rūd-e** *var.* Daryā-ye Helmand. ↝ Afghanistan/Iran *see also* Helmand, Daryā-ye
Hīrmand, Rūd-e *see* Helmand, Daryā-ye
Hirmil *see* Hermel
165 T5 **Hiroo** Hokkaidō, NE Japan 42°16′N 143°16′E
165 Q7 **Hirosaki** Aomori, Honshū, C Japan 40°34′N 140°28′E
164 G13 **Hiroshima** *var.* Hirosima. Hiroshima, Honshū, SW Japan 34°23′N 132°26′E
164 F13 **Hiroshima** *off.* Hiroshima-ken, *var.* Hirosima. ◆ *prefecture* Honshū, SW Japan
Hiroshima-ken *see* Hiroshima
Hirosima *see* Hiroshima
Hirschberg/Hirschberg im Riesengebirge/Hirschberg in Schlesien *see* Jelenia Góra
103 Q3 **Hirson** Aisne, N France 49°56′N 04°05′E
Hîrşova *see* Hârşova
95 G19 **Hirtshals** Nordjylland, N Denmark 57°34′N 09°58′E
152 H10 **Hisār** Haryāna, NW India 29°10′N 75°45′E
162 K7 **Hishig Öndör** *var.* Maanĭt. Bulgan, C Mongolia 48°17′N 103°29′E
186 E9 **Hisiu** Central, SW Papua New Guinea 09°20′S 146°48′E
147 P13 **Hisor** *Rus.* Gissar. W Tajikistan 38°34′N 68°29′E
Hispalis *see* Sevilla
Hispana/Hispania *see* Spain
44 M7 **Hispaniola** *island* Dominion Republic/Haiti
64 F11 **Hispaniola Basin** *var.* Hispaniola Trough. *undersea feature* SW Atlantic Ocean
Hispaniola Trough *see* Hispaniola Basin
Histonium *see* Vasto
139 R7 **Hīt** Al Anbār, SW Iraq 33°38′N 42°50′E
165 P14 **Hita** Ōita, Kyūshū, SW Japan 33°19′N 130°55′E
165 P12 **Hitachi** *var.* Hitati. Ibaraki, Honshū, S Japan 36°40′N 140°42′E
165 P12 **Hitachiōta** Ibaraki, Honshū, S Japan 36°32′N 140°31′E
Hitati *see* Hitachi
97 O21 **Hitchin** E England, United Kingdom 51°57′N 00°17′W
191 Q7 **Hitiaa** Tahiti, W French Polynesia 17°35′S 149°17′W
164 D15 **Hitoyoshi** *var.* Hitoyosi. Kumamoto, Kyūshū, SW Japan 32°12′N 130°48′E
Hitoyosi *see* Hitoyoshi
94 F7 **Hitra** *prev.* Hitteren. *island* S Norway
Hitteren *see* Hitra
187 Q11 **Hiu** *island* Torres Islands, N Vanuatu
165 O11 **Hiuchiga-take** ▲ Honshū, C Japan 36°57′N 139°18′E
191 X7 **Hiva Oa** *island* Îles Marquises, N French Polynesia
20 M10 **Hiwassee Lake** ⊠ North Carolina, SE USA
20 M10 **Hiwassee River** ↝ SE USA
95 H20 **Hjallerup** Nordjylland, N Denmark 57°10′N 10°10′E
95 M16 **Hjälmaren** *Eng.* Lake Hjalmar. ⊚ C Sweden
Hjalmar, Lake *see* Hjälmaren
95 C14 **Hjellestad** Hordaland, S Norway 60°15′N 05°13′E
95 D16 **Hjelmeland** Rogaland, S Norway 59°12′N 06°07′E
94 G10 **Hjerkinn** Oppland, S Norway 62°13′N 09°37′E
95 L18 **Hjo** Västra Götaland, S Sweden 58°18′N 14°17′E
95 G19 **Hjørring** Nordjylland, N Denmark 57°28′N 09°59′E
167 O1 **Hkakabo Razi** ▲ Myanmar (Burma)/China 28°17′N 97°28′E
166 M2 **Hkamti** *var.* Singkaling Hkamti. Sagaing, Myanmar (Burma) 26°00′N 95°43′E
167 N1 **Hkring Bum** ▲ N Myanmar (Burma) 27°05′N 97°16′E
83 L21 **Hlathikulu** *var.* Hlatikulu. S Swaziland 26°58′S 31°19′E
Hlatikulu *see* Hlathikulu
Hliboka *see* Hlyboka
111 F17 **Hlinsko** *var.* Hlinsko v Čechách. Pardubický Kraj, C Czech Republic 49°46′N 15°54′E
Hlinsko v Čechách *see* Hlinsko
117 S6 **Hlobyne** *Rus.* Globino. Poltavs'ka Oblast', NE Ukraine 49°24′N 33°16′E
111 H20 **Hlohovec** *Ger.* Freistadtl, *Hung.* Galgóc; *prev.* Frakštát. Trnavský Kraj, W Slovakia 48°26′N 17°49′E
83 J23 **Hlotse** *var.* Leribe. NW Lesotho 28°55′S 28°01′E
111 I17 **Hlučín** *Ger.* Hultschin, *Pol.* Hulczyn. Moravskoslezský Kraj, E Czech Republic 49°54′N 18°11′E
117 S2 **Hlukhiv** *Rus.* Glukhov. Sums'ka Oblast', NE Ukraine 51°40′N 33°53′E
119 K21 **Hlushkavichy** *Rus.* Glushkevichi. Homyel'skaya Voblasts', SE Belarus 51°34′N 27°47′E
119 L18 **Hlusk** *Rus.* Glusk, Glussk. Mahilyowskaya Voblasts', E Belarus 52°54′N 28°41′E
116 K8 **Hlyboka** *Ger.* Hliboka, *Rus.* Glybokaya. Chernivets'ka Oblast', W Ukraine 48°04′N 25°56′E
118 K13 **Hlybokaye** *Rus.* Glubokoye. Vitsyebskaya Voblasts', N Belarus 55°08′N 27°41′E
77 Q16 **Ho** SE Ghana 06°36′N 00°28′E
167 S6 **Hoa Binh** Hoa Binh, N Vietnam 20°49′N 105°20′E
83 E20 **Hoachanas** Hardap, C Namibia 23°55′S 18°04′E
Hoai Nhơn *see* Bồng Sơn
167 T8 **Hoa Lac** Quang Binh, C Vietnam 17°54′N 106°24′E
167 S5 **Hoang Liên Sơn** ▲▲ N Vietnam
83 B17 **Hoanib** ↝ NW Namibia
33 S15 **Hoback Peak** ▲ Wyoming, C USA 43°04′N 110°34′W
183 P17 **Hobart** *prev.* Hobarton, Hobart Town. *state capital* Tasmania, SE Australia 42°54′S 147°18′E
26 L11 **Hobart** Oklahoma, C USA 35°03′N 99°04′W
183 P17 **Hobart** ✕ Tasmania, SE Australia 42°52′S 147°28′E
Hobarton/Hobart Town *see* Hobart
37 W14 **Hobbs** New Mexico, SW USA 32°42′N 103°08′W
194 L12 **Hobbs Coast** *physical region* Antarctica
23 Z14 **Hobe Sound** Florida, SE USA 27°03′N 80°08′W
Hobicaurikány *see* Uricani
54 E12 **Hobo** Huila, S Colombia 02°34′N 75°28′W
99 G16 **Hoboken** Antwerpen, N Belgium 51°12′N 04°22′E
158 K3 **Hoboksar** *var.* Hoboksar Mongol Zizhixian. Xinjiang Uygur Zizhiqu, NW China 46°48′N 85°42′E
Hoboksar Mongol Zizhixian *see* Hoboksar
95 G21 **Hobro** Nordjylland, N Denmark 56°39′N 09°51′E
21 X10 **Hobucken** North Carolina, SE USA 35°15′N 76°31′W
95 O20 **Hoburgen** *headland* SE Sweden 56°54′N 18°07′E
81 P15 **Hobyo** *It.* Obbia. Mudug, E Somalia 05°16′N 48°24′E
109 R8 **Hochalmspitze** ▲ SW Austria 47°00′N 13°19′E
109 Q4 **Hochburg** Oberösterreich, N Austria 48°10′N 12°57′E
108 F8 **Hochdorf** Luzern, N Switzerland 47°10′N 08°16′E
109 N8 **Hochfeiler** *It.* Gran Pilastro. ▲ Austria/Italy 46°59′N 11°42′E
167 T14 **Hô Chi Minh** *var.* Ho Chi Minh City; *prev.* Saigon. S Vietnam 10°46′N 106°43′E
Ho Chi Minh City *see* Hô Chi Minh
108 I7 **Höchst** Vorarlberg, NW Austria 47°28′N 09°40′E
Höchstadt *see* Höchstadt an der Aisch
101 K19 **Höchstadt an der Aisch** *var.* Höchstadt. Bayern, C Germany 49°43′N 10°48′E
108 L9 **Hochwilde** *It.* L'Altissima. ▲ Austria/Italy 46°45′N 11°00′E
109 S7 **Hochwildstelle** ▲ C Austria 47°21′N 13°53′E
31 T14 **Hocking River** ↝ Ohio, N USA
Hoctúm *see* Hoctún
41 X12 **Hoctún** *var.* Hoctúm. Yucatán, E Mexico 20°48′N 89°14′W
Hodeida *see* Al Ḩudaydah
20 K6 **Hodgenville** Kentucky, S USA 37°34′N 85°45′W
11 T17 **Hodgeville** Saskatchewan, S Canada 50°06′N 106°55′W
76 L9 **Hodh ech Chargui** ◆ *region* E Mauritania
Hodh el Garbi *see* Hodh el Gharbi
76 J10 **Hodh el Gharbi** *var.* Hodh el Garbi. ◆ *region* S Mauritania
111 L25 **Hódmezővásárhely** Csongrád, SE Hungary 46°27′N 20°18′E
74 J6 **Hodna, Chott El** *var.* Chott el-Hodna, *Ar.* Shatt al-Hodna. *salt lake* N Algeria
Hodna, Chott el-/Hodna, Shatt al- *see* Hodna, Chott El
111 G19 **Hodonín** *Ger.* Göding. Jihomoravský Kraj, SE Czech Republic 48°52′N 17°07′E
Hödrögö *see* Nömrög
Hodság/Hodschag *see* Odžaci
39 R7 **Hodzana River** ↝ Alaska, USA
Hoei *see* Huy
99 H19 **Hoeilaart** Vlaams Brabant, C Belgium 50°46′N 04°28′E
Hoë Karoo *see* Great Karoo
98 F12 **Hoek van Holland** *Eng.* Hook of Holland. Zuid-Holland, W Netherlands 52°00′N 04°07′E
98 L11 **Hoenderloo** Gelderland, E Netherlands 52°08′N 05°46′E
99 L18 **Hoensbroek** Limburg, SE Netherlands 50°55′N 05°55′E
163 Y11 **Hoeryŏng** NE North Korea 42°23′N 129°46′E
99 K18 **Hoeselt** Limburg, NE Belgium 50°50′N 05°30′E
98 K11 **Hoevelaken** Gelderland, C Netherlands 52°10′N 05°27′E
Hoey *see* Huy
101 M18 **Hof** Bayern, SE Germany 50°19′N 11°55′E
Höfdhakaupstadhur *see* Skagaströnd
Hofei *see* Hefei
101 G18 **Hofheim am Taunus** Hessen, W Germany 50°04′N 08°27′E
Hofmarkt *see* Odorheiu Secuiesc
92 L3 **Höfn** Austurland, SE Iceland 64°14′N 15°17′W
94 N13 **Hofors** Gävleborg, C Sweden 60°33′N 16°21′E
92 J6 **Hofsjökull** *glacier* C Iceland
92 J1 **Hofsós** Nordhurland Vestra, N Iceland 65°54′N 19°25′W
164 E13 **Hōfu** Yamaguchi, Honshū, SW Japan 34°01′N 131°34′E
92 I4 **Hōfudhborgarsvædid** ◆ *region* SW Iceland
Hofuf *see* Al Hufūf
95 J22 **Höganäs** Skåne, S Sweden 56°11′N 12°39′E
183 P14 **Hogan Group** *island group* Tasmania, SE Australia
23 R4 **Hogansville** Georgia, SE USA 33°10′N 84°55′W
39 P8 **Hogatza River** ↝ Alaska, USA
28 I14 **Hogback Mountain** ▲ Nebraska, C USA 41°40′N 103°44′W
95 G14 **Høgevarde** ▲ S Norway 60°19′N 09°27′E
Högfors *see* Karkkila
31 P5 **Hog Island** *island* Michigan, N USA
21 Y6 **Hog Island** *island* Virginia, NE USA
Hogoley Islands *see* Chuuk Islands
95 N20 **Högsby** Kalmar, S Sweden 57°10′N 16°03′E
36 K1 **Hogup Mountains** ▲▲ Utah, W USA
101 E17 **Hohe Acht** ▲ W Germany 50°23′N 07°00′E
Hohenelbe *see* Vrchlabí
108 I7 **Hohenems** Vorarlberg, W Austria 47°23′N 09°43′E
Hohenmauth *see* Vysoké Mýto
Hohensalza *see* Inowrocław
Hohenstadt *see* Zábřeh
Hohenstein in Ostpreussen *see* Olsztynek
20 I9 **Hohenwald** Tennessee, S USA 35°33′N 87°31′W
101 L17 **Hohenwarte-Stausee** ⊠ C Germany
Hohes Venn *see* Hautes Fagnes
109 Q8 **Hohe Tauern** ▲▲ W Austria
163 O13 **Hohhot** *var.* Huhehot, Huhohaote, *Mong.* Kukukhoto; *prev.* Kweisui, Kwesui. Nei Mongol Zizhiqu, N China 40°49′N 111°37′E
162 F7 **Hohmorït** *var.* Sayn-Ust. Govĭ-Altay, W Mongolia 47°23′N 94°19′E
103 U6 **Hohneck** ▲ NE France 48°04′N 07°01′E
77 Q16 **Hohoe** E Ghana 07°08′N 00°32′E
164 E12 **Hōhoku** Yamaguchi, Honshū, SW Japan 34°15′N 130°56′E
159 O11 **Hoh Sai Hu** ⊚ C China
159 N11 **Hoh Xil Hu** ⊚ C China
158 L11 **Hoh Xil Shan** ▲▲ W China
167 U10 **Hôi An** *prev.* Faifo. Quang Nam-Đa Năng, C Vietnam 15°54′N 108°19′E
Hoï-Hao/Hoihow *see* Haikou
159 S11 **Hoika** *prev.* Heka. Qinghai, W China 35°49′N 99°50′E
81 F17 **Hoima** W Uganda 01°25′N 31°22′E
26 L5 **Hoisington** Kansas, C USA 38°31′N 98°46′W
146 D12 **Hojagala** *Rus.* Khodzhakala. Balkan Welaýaty, W Turkmenistan 38°46′N 56°14′E
146 M13 **Hojambaz** *Rus.* Khodzhambas. Lebap Welaýaty, E Turkmenistan 38°11′N 64°33′E
95 H23 **Højby** Syddtjylland, C Denmark 55°20′N 10°27′E
95 F24 **Højer** Syddanmark, SW Denmark 54°57′N 08°43′E
164 E14 **Hōjō** *var.* Hôzyô. Ehime, Shikoku, SW Japan 33°58′N 132°47′E
184 J3 **Hokianga Harbour** *inlet* SE Tasman Sea
185 F17 **Hokitika** West Coast, South Island, New Zealand 42°44′S 170°58′E
165 U4 **Hokkai-dō** ◆ *territory* Hokkaidō, NE Japan
165 T3 **Hokkaidō** *prev.* Ezo, Yeso, Yezo. *island* NE Japan
95 G15 **Hokksund** Buskerud, S Norway 59°45′N 09°55′E
143 S4 **Hokmābād** Khorāsān-Razavī, N Iran 36°37′N 57°34′E
Hokō *see* Pohang
Hoko-guntō/Hoko-shotō *see* Penghu Liedao
Hoktemberyan *see* Armavir
94 F13 **Hol** Buskerud, S Norway 60°36′N 08°18′E
117 R11 **Hola Prystan'** *Rus.* Golaya Pristan. Khersons'ka Oblast', S Ukraine 46°31′N 32°31′E
95 I23 **Holbæk** Sjælland, E Denmark 55°42′N 11°42′E
Holboo *see* Santmargats
183 P10 **Holbrook** New South Wales, SE Australia 35°45′S 147°18′E
37 N11 **Holbrook** Arizona, SW USA 34°54′N 110°09′W
27 S5 **Holden** Missouri, C USA 38°42′N 93°59′W
36 K5 **Holden** Utah, W USA 39°06′N 112°16′W
27 O11 **Holdenville** Oklahoma, C USA 35°05′N 96°25′W
29 O16 **Holdrege** Nebraska, C USA 40°28′N 99°28′W
35 X3 **Hole in the Mountain Peak** ▲ Nevada, W USA 40°54′N 115°06′W
155 G20 **Hole Narsipur** Karnātaka, W India 12°46′N 76°14′E
111 H18 **Holešov** *Ger.* Holleschau. Zlínský Kraj, E Czech Republic 49°20′N 17°35′E
45 N14 **Holetown** *prev.* Jamestown. W Barbados 13°11′N 59°38′W
31 Q12 **Holgate** Ohio, N USA 41°12′N 84°06′W
44 I7 **Holguín** Holguín, SE Cuba 20°51′N 76°16′W
23 V12 **Holiday** Florida, SE USA 28°11′N 82°44′W
163 S9 **Holin Gol** *prev.* Hulingol. Nei Mongol Zizhiqu, N China 45°36′N 119°54′E
39 O12 **Holitna River** ↝ Alaska, USA
94 J13 **Höljes** Värmland, C Sweden 60°54′N 12°34′E
109 X3 **Hollabrunn** Niederösterreich, NE Austria 48°33′N 16°06′E
36 L3 **Holladay** Utah, W USA 40°39′N 111°49′W
11 X16 **Holland** Manitoba, S Canada 49°36′N 98°52′W
31 O9 **Holland** Michigan, N USA 42°47′N 86°06′W
25 T9 **Holland** Texas, SW USA 30°52′N 97°24′W
Holland *see* Netherlands
22 K4 **Hollandale** Mississippi, S USA 33°10′N 90°51′W
Hollandia *see* Jayapura
Hollandsch Diep *see* Hollands Diep
99 H14 **Hollands Diep** *var.* Hollandsch Diep. *channel* SW Netherlands
Holleschau *see* Holešov
25 R5 **Holliday** Texas, SW USA 33°49′N 98°41′W
18 E15 **Hollidaysburg** Pennsylvania, NE USA 40°24′N 78°22′W
21 S6 **Hollins** Virginia, NE USA 37°20′N 79°56′W
26 J12 **Hollis** Oklahoma, C USA 34°42′N 99°56′W
35 O10 **Hollister** California, W USA 36°51′N 121°25′W
27 T8 **Hollister** Missouri, C USA 36°37′N 93°13′W
93 M19 **Hollola** Etelä-Suomi, S Finland 61°N 25°32′E
98 K4 **Hollum** Fryslân, N Netherlands 53°27′N 05°38′E
95 J23 **Höllviken** *prev.* Höllviksnäs. Skåne, S Sweden 55°25′N 12°57′E
Höllviksnäs *see* Höllviken
37 W6 **Holly** Colorado, C USA 38°03′N 102°07′W
31 R9 **Holly** Michigan, N USA 42°47′N 83°37′W
21 S14 **Holly Hill** South Carolina, SE USA 33°19′N 80°24′W
21 W11 **Holly Ridge** North Carolina, SE USA 34°31′N 77°31′W
22 L1 **Holly Springs** Mississippi, S USA 34°47′N 89°25′W
23 Z15 **Hollywood** Florida, SE USA 26°00′N 80°09′W
8 J6 **Holman** Victoria Island, Northwest Territories, N Canada 70°42′N 117°45′W
92 I2 **Hólmavík** Vestfirdhir, NW Iceland 65°42′N 21°43′W
30 J7 **Holmen** Wisconsin, N USA 43°57′N 91°14′W
23 R8 **Holmes Creek** ↝ Alabama/Florida, SE USA
95 H16 **Holmestrand** Vestfold, S Norway 59°29′N 10°20′E
93 J16 **Holmön** *island* N Sweden
95 E22 **Holmsland Klit** *beach* W Denmark
93 J16 **Holmsund** Västerbotten, N Sweden 63°42′N 20°26′E
95 Q18 **Holmudden** *headland* SE Sweden 57°59′N 19°14′E
138 F10 **Holon** *var.* Kholon; *prev.* Holon. Tel Aviv, C Israel 32°01′N 34°46′E
Holon *see* Holon
163 P7 **Hölönbuyr** *var.* Bayan. Dornod, E Mongolia 47°56′N 112°58′E
117 P8 **Holovanivs'k** *Rus.* Golovanevsk. Kirovohrads'ka Oblast', C Ukraine 48°21′N 30°26′E
95 F21 **Holstebro** Midtjylland, W Denmark 56°22′N 08°38′E
95 F23 **Holsted** Syddtjylland, W Denmark 55°30′N 08°54′E

◆ Country
● Country Capital
◇ Dependent Territory
○ Dependent Territory Capital
◆ Administrative Regions
✕ International Airport
▲ Mountain
▲▲ Mountain Range
⛰ Volcano
↝ River
⊚ Lake
⊠ Reservoir

29 T13 **Holstein** Iowa, C USA *42°29′N 95°32′W*
Holsteinborg/Holsteinsborg/Holstenborg/Holstensborg *see* Sisimiut
21 O8 **Holston River** ≈ Tennessee, S USA
31 Q9 **Holt** Michigan, N USA *42°38′N 84°31′W*
98 N10 **Holten** Overijssel, E Netherlands *52°16′N 06°25′E*
27 P3 **Holton** Kansas, C USA *39°27′N 95°44′W*
27 U5 **Holts Summit** Missouri, C USA *38°38′N 92°07′W*
35 X17 **Holtville** California, W USA *32°48′N 115°22′W*
98 L5 **Holwerd** *Fris.* Holwert. Fryslân, N Netherlands *53°22′N 05°51′E*
Holwert *see* Holwerd
39 O11 **Holy Cross** Alaska, USA *62°12′N 159°46′W*
37 R4 **Holy Cross, Mount Of The** ▲ Colorado, C USA *39°28′N 106°28′W*
97 I18 **Holyhead** *Wel.* Caer Gybi. NW Wales, United Kingdom *53°19′N 04°38′W*
97 H18 **Holy Island** *island* NW Wales, United Kingdom
96 L12 **Holy Island** *island* NE England, United Kingdom
37 W3 **Holyoke** Colorado, C USA *40°31′N 102°18′W*
18 M11 **Holyoke** Massachusetts, NE USA *42°12′N 72°37′W*
101 I14 **Holzminden** Niedersachsen, C Germany *51°49′N 09°27′E*
81 G19 **Homa Bay** Nyanza, W Kenya *0°31′S 34°30′E*
Homāyūnshahr *see* Khomeynīshahr
77 P11 **Hombori** Mopti, S Mali *15°13′N 01°39′W*
101 E20 **Homburg** Saarland, SW Germany *49°20′N 07°20′E*
9 R5 **Home Bay** *bay* Baffin Bay, Nunavut, NE Canada
Homenau *see* Humenné
39 Q13 **Homer** Alaska, USA *59°38′N 151°33′W*
22 H4 **Homer** Louisiana, S USA *32°47′N 93°03′W*
18 H10 **Homer** New York, NE USA *42°38′N 76°10′W*
23 V7 **Homerville** Georgia, SE USA *31°02′N 82°45′W*
23 Y16 **Homestead** Florida, SE USA *25°28′N 80°28′W*
27 O9 **Hominy** Oklahoma, C USA *36°24′N 96°24′W*
94 H8 **Hommelvik** Sør-Trøndelag, S Norway *63°24′N 10°48′E*
95 C16 **Hommersåk** Rogaland, S Norway *58°55′N 05°51′E*
155 H15 **Homnābād** Karnātaka, C India *17°46′N 77°08′E*
22 J7 **Homochitto River** ≈ Mississippi, S USA
83 N20 **Homoíne** Inhambane, SE Mozambique *23°51′S 35°04′E*
112 O12 **Homoljske Planine** ▲▲ E Serbia
Homonna *see* Humenné
Homs *see* Al Khums, Libya
Homs *see* Ḩimş
119 P19 **Homyel'** *Rus.* Gomel'. Homyel'skaya Voblasts', SE Belarus *52°25′N 31°E*
118 L12 **Homyel'** Vitsyebskaya Voblasts', N Belarus *55°20′N 28°52′E*
119 L19 **Homyel'skaya Voblasts'** *prev. Rus.* Gomel'skaya Oblast'. ◈ *province* SE Belarus
Honan *see* Henan, China
Honan *see* Luoyang, China
164 U4 **Honbetsu** Hokkaidō, NE Japan *43°09′N 143°46′E*
Honctő *see* Gurahonț
54 E9 **Honda** Tolima, C Colombia *05°12′N 74°45′W*
83 D24 **Hondeklip** *Afr.* Hondeklipbaai. Northern Cape, W South Africa *30°15′S 17°17′E*
Hondeklipbaai *see* Hondeklip
11 Q13 **Hondo** Alberta, W Canada *54°43′N 113°14′W*
25 Q12 **Hondo** Texas, SW USA *29°21′N 99°09′W*
42 G1 **Hondo** ≈ Central America
Hondo *see* Honshū
Hondo *see* Amakusa
42 G6 **Honduras** *off.* Republic of Honduras. ◆ *republic* Central America
Honduras, Golfo de *see* Honduras, Gulf of
42 H4 **Honduras, Gulf of** *Sp.* Golfo de Honduras. *gulf* W Caribbean Sea
Honduras, Republic of *see* Honduras
11 V12 **Hone** Manitoba, C Canada *56°13′N 101°12′W*
21 P12 **Honea Path** South Carolina, SE USA *34°27′N 82°23′W*
95 H14 **Hønefoss** Buskerud, S Norway *60°10′N 10°15′E*
31 S12 **Honey Creek** ≈ Ohio, N USA
25 V5 **Honey Grove** Texas, SW USA *33°34′N 95°54′W*
35 Q4 **Honey Lake** ◎ California, W USA
102 L4 **Honfleur** Calvados, N France *49°25′N 00°14′E*
Hon Gai *see* Ha Long
161 O8 **Hong'an** *prev.* Huang'an. Hubei, C China *31°20′N 114°43′E*
Hongay *see* Ha Long
Hông Gai *see* Ha Long
161 O15 **Honghai Wan** *bay* N South China Sea
Hông Hà, Sông *see* Red River
161 O7 **Hong He** ≈ C China
161 N9 **Hong Hu** ◎ C China
160 L11 **Hongjiang** Hunan, S China *27°09′N 109°58′E*
Hongjiang *see* Wangcang
161 O15 **Hong Kong** *Chin.* Xianggang. Hong Kong, S China *22°17′N 114°09′E*
160 L4 **Hongliu He** ≈ C China
160 L4 **Hongliu He** ≈ C China
159 P8 **Hongliuwan** *var.* Aksay, Aksay Kazakzu Zizhixian. Gansu, N China *39°25′N 94°09′E*
159 P7 **Hongliuyuan** Gansu, N China *41°02′N 95°24′E*
Hongor *see* Delgereh
161 S8 **Hongqiao** ✈ (Shanghai) Shanghai Shi, E China *31°28′N 121°08′E*
160 K14 **Hongshui He** ≈ S China
160 M5 **Hongtong** *var.* Dahuaishu. Shanxi, C China *36°30′N 111°42′E*
164 J15 **Hongū** Wakayama, Honshū, SW Japan *33°50′N 135°42′E*
Honguedo, Détroit d' *see* Honguedo Passage
15 Y5 **Honguedo Passage** *var.* Honguedo Strait, *Fr.* Détroit d'Honguedo. *strait* Québec, E Canada
Honguedo Strait *see* Honguedo Passage
Hongwan *see* Hongwansi
159 S8 **Hongwansi** *var.* Sunan, Sunan Yugurzu Zizhixian; *prev.* Hongwan. Gansu, N China *38°55′N 99°29′E*
163 X13 **Hongwŏn** E North Korea *40°03′N 127°54′E*
160 H7 **Hongyuan** *var.* Qiongxi; *prev.* Hurama. Sichuan, C China *32°49′N 102°40′E*
161 Q7 **Hongze Hu** *var.* Hung-tse Hu. ◎ E China
186 L9 **Honiara** ● (Solomon Islands) Guadalcanal, C Solomon Islands *09°27′S 159°56′E*
165 P8 **Honjō** *var.* Honzyô, Yurihonjō. Akita, Honshū, C Japan *39°23′N 140°03′E*
93 K18 **Honkajoki** Länsi-Suomi, SW Finland *62°00′N 22°15′E*
92 K7 **Honningsvåg** Finnmark, N Norway *70°58′N 25°59′E*
95 I19 **Hönö** Västra Götaland, S Sweden *57°42′N 11°39′E*
38 G11 **Honoka'a** Hawaii, USA, C Pacific Ocean *20°04′N 155°27′W*
38 G11 **Honoka'a** *var.* Honokaa. Hawaii, USA, C Pacific Ocean *20°04′N 155°27′W*
Honokaa *see* Honoka'a
38 D9 **Honolulu** *state capital* O'ahu, Hawaii, USA, C Pacific Ocean *21°18′N 157°52′W*
38 H11 **Honomú** *var.* Honomu. Hawaii, USA, C Pacific Ocean *19°51′N 155°06′W*
105 P10 **Honrubia** Castilla-La Mancha, C Spain *39°36′N 02°17′W*
164 M12 **Honshū** *var.* Hondo, Honsyû. *island* SW Japan
Honsyû *see* Honshū
Honte *see* Westerschelde
Honzyô *see* Honjō
8 K8 **Hood** ≈ Nunavut, NW Canada
Hood Island *see* Española, Isla
32 H11 **Hood, Mount** ▲ Oregon, NW USA *45°22′N 121°41′W*
32 H11 **Hood River** Oregon, NW USA *45°44′N 121°31′W*
98 H10 **Hoofddorp** Noord-Holland, W Netherlands *52°18′N 04°41′E*
99 G15 **Hoogerheide** Noord-Brabant, S Netherlands *51°25′N 04°19′E*
98 N8 **Hoogeveen** Drenthe, NE Netherlands *52°44′N 06°30′E*
98 O6 **Hoogezand-Sappemeer** Groningen, NE Netherlands *53°10′N 06°47′E*
98 J8 **Hoogkarspel** Noord-Holland, NW Netherlands *52°42′N 04°59′E*
98 N5 **Hoogkerk** Groningen, NE Netherlands *53°13′N 06°30′E*
98 G13 **Hoogvliet** Zuid-Holland, SW Netherlands *51°51′N 04°23′E*
26 I8 **Hooker** Oklahoma, C USA *36°51′N 101°12′W*
97 E21 **Hook Head** *Ir.* Rinn Duáin. *headland* SE Ireland *52°07′N 06°55′W*
Hook of Holland *see* Hoek van Holland
Hoolt *see* Tögrög
39 W13 **Hoonah** Chichagof Island, Alaska, USA *58°05′N 135°21′W*
38 L11 **Hooper Bay** Alaska, USA *61°31′N 166°06′W*
31 N13 **Hoopeston** Illinois, N USA *40°28′N 87°40′W*
95 K22 **Höör** Skåne, S Sweden *55°55′N 13°33′E*
98 I9 **Hoorn** Noord-Holland, NW Netherlands *52°38′N 05°04′E*
18 L10 **Hoosic River** ≈ New York, NE USA
Hoosier State *see* Indiana
35 Y11 **Hoover Dam** *dam* Arizona/Nevada, W USA
Höövör *see* Baruunbayan-Ulaan
137 Q11 **Hopa** Artvin, NE Turkey *41°23′N 41°28′E*
18 J14 **Hopatcong** New Jersey, NE USA *40°55′N 74°39′W*
10 M17 **Hope** British Columbia, SW Canada *49°21′N 121°28′W*
39 R12 **Hope** Alaska, USA *60°55′N 149°38′W*
27 T14 **Hope** Arkansas, C USA *33°40′N 93°36′W*
31 P14 **Hope** Indiana, N USA *39°18′N 85°46′W*
29 Q5 **Hope** North Dakota, N USA *47°18′N 97°42′W*
13 Q7 **Hopedale** Newfoundland and Labrador, NE Canada *55°26′N 60°14′W*
Hopeh/Hopei *see* Hebei
180 K13 **Hope, Lake** *salt lake* Western Australia
41 X13 **Hopelchén** Campeche, SE Mexico *19°46′N 89°50′W*
21 U11 **Hope Mills** North Carolina, SE USA *34°58′N 78°57′W*
183 O7 **Hope, Mount** New South Wales, SE Australia *32°49′S 145°55′E*
92 P4 **Hopen** *island* SE Svalbard
197 Q4 **Hope, Point** *headland* Alaska, USA
12 M3 **Hopes Advance, Cap** *cape* Québec, NE Canada
182 L10 **Hopetoun** Victoria, SE Australia *35°46′S 142°23′E*
83 H23 **Hopetown** Northern Cape, W South Africa *29°37′S 24°05′E*
21 W6 **Hopewell** Virginia, NE USA *37°16′N 77°15′W*
109 O7 **Hopfgarten im Brixental** Tirol, W Austria *47°28′N 12°14′E*
181 N8 **Hopkins Lake** *salt lake* Western Australia
182 M12 **Hopkins River** ≈ Victoria, SE Australia
20 I7 **Hopkinsville** Kentucky, S USA *36°50′N 87°30′W*
34 M6 **Hopland** California, W USA *38°58′N 123°09′W*
95 G24 **Hoptrup** Syddanmark, SW Denmark *55°09′N 09°27′E*
Hoqin Zuoyi Zhongji *see* Baokang
32 F9 **Hoquiam** Washington, NW USA *46°58′N 123°53′W*
29 R6 **Horace** North Dakota, N USA *46°44′N 96°54′W*
117 T14 **Hora Roman-Kosh** ▲ S Ukraine *44°37′N 34°13′E*
137 R12 **Horasan** Erzurum, NE Turkey *40°03′N 42°10′E*
101 G22 **Horb am Neckar** Baden-Württemberg, S Germany *48°27′N 08°42′E*
95 K23 **Hörby** Skåne, S Sweden *55°51′N 13°42′E*
43 P16 **Horconcitos** Chiriquí, W Panama *08°20′N 82°10′W*
95 C14 **Hordaland** ◈ *county* S Norway
116 H13 **Horezu** Vâlcea, SW Romania *45°06′N 24°00′E*
108 G7 **Horgen** Zürich, N Switzerland *47°16′N 08°36′E*
Horgo *see* Tariat
Hörin *see* Fenglin
163 O13 **Horinger** Nei Mongol Zizhiqu, N China *40°23′N 111°48′E*
Horiult *see* Bogd
11 U17 **Horizon** Saskatchewan, S Canada *49°33′N 105°05′W*
192 K9 **Horizon Bank** *undersea feature* S Pacific Ocean
192 L10 **Horizon Deep** *undersea feature* W Pacific Ocean
95 L14 **Hörken** Örebro, S Sweden *60°03′N 14°55′E*
119 O15 **Horki** *Rus.* Gorki. Mahilyowskaya Voblasts', E Belarus *54°18′N 31°E*
195 O10 **Horlick Mountains** ▲▲ Antarctica
117 X7 **Horlivka** *Rom.* Adâncata, *Rus.* Gorlovka. Donets'ka Oblast', E Ukraine *48°19′N 38°04′E*
143 V11 **Ḩormak** Sīstān va Balūchestān, SE Iran *30°00′N 60°50′E*
143 R13 **Hormozgān** *off.* Ostān-e Hormozgān. ◈ *province* S Iran
Hormozgān, Ostān-e *see* Hormozgān
Hormoz, Tangeh-ye *see* Hormuz, Strait of
141 W6 **Hormuz, Strait of** *var.* Strait of Ormuz, *Per.* Tangeh-ye Hormoz. *strait* Iran/Oman
109 W2 **Horn** Niederösterreich, NE Austria *48°40′N 15°40′E*
95 M18 **Horn** Östergötland, S Sweden *57°54′N 15°49′E*
8 I9 **Horn** ≈ Northwest Territories, NW Canada
Hornád *see* Hernád
8 I6 **Hornaday** ≈ Northwest Territories, NW Canada
92 H13 **Hornavan** ◎ N Sweden
65 C24 **Hornby Mountains** *hill range* West Falkland, Falkland Islands
Horn, Cape *see* Hornos, Cabo de
97 O18 **Horncastle** E England, United Kingdom *53°12′N 00°07′W*
95 N14 **Horndal** Dalarna, C Sweden *60°16′N 16°25′E*
93 I16 **Hörnefors** Västerbotten, N Sweden *63°37′N 19°54′E*
18 F11 **Hornell** New York, NE USA *42°19′N 77°38′W*
Horné Nové Mesto *see* Kysucké Nové Mesto
12 F12 **Hornepayne** Ontario, S Canada *49°14′N 84°48′W*
94 D10 **Hornindalsvatnet** ◎ S Norway
101 G22 **Hornisgrinde** ▲ SW Germany *48°37′N 08°13′E*
22 M9 **Horn Island** *island* Mississippi, S USA
Hornja Łužica *see* Oberlausitz
63 J26 **Hornos, Cabo de** *Eng.* Cape Horn. *headland* S Chile *55°52′S 67°00′W*
117 S10 **Hornostayivka** Khersons'ka Oblast', S Ukraine *47°00′N 33°42′E*
183 T9 **Hornsby** New South Wales, SE Australia *33°44′S 151°08′E*
97 O16 **Hornsea** E England, United Kingdom *53°54′N 00°10′W*
94 O11 **Hornslandet** *peninsula* C Sweden
95 H22 **Hornslet** Midtjylland, C Denmark *56°19′N 10°20′E*
92 O4 **Hornsundtind** ▲ S Svalbard *76°54′N 16°07′E*
Horochów *see* Horokhiv
Horodenka *see* Gorodenka
117 Q2 **Horodnya** *Rus.* Gorodnya. Chernihivs'ka Oblast', NE Ukraine *51°54′N 31°30′E*
116 K6 **Horodok** Khmel'nyts'ka Oblast', W Ukraine *49°10′N 26°34′E*
116 H5 **Horodok** *Pol.* Gródek Jagielloński, *Rus.* Gorodok, Gorodok Yagellonski. L'vivs'ka Oblast', NW Ukraine *49°48′N 23°39′E*
117 Q6 **Horodyshche** *Rus.* Gorodishche. Cherkas'ka Oblast', C Ukraine *49°19′N 31°27′E*
165 T3 **Horokanai** Hokkaidō, NE Japan *44°02′N 142°08′E*
116 J4 **Horokhiv** *Pol.* Horochów, *Rus.* Gorokhov. Volyns'ka Oblast', NW Ukraine *50°31′N 24°50′E*
165 T4 **Horoshiri-dake** *var.* Horosiri Dake. ▲ Hokkaidō, N Japan *42°43′N 142°41′E*
Horosiri Dake *see* Horoshiri-dake
111 C17 **Hořovice** *Ger.* Horowitz. Střední Čechy, W Czech Republic *49°49′N 13°53′E*
Horowitz *see* Hořovice
Horqin Zuoyi Houqi *see* Ganjig
Horqin Zuoyi Zhongqi *see* Bayan Huxu
62 O5 **Horqueta** Concepción, C Paraguay *23°24′S 56°53′W*
55 O12 **Horqueta Minas** Amazonas, S Venezuela *02°20′N 63°32′W*
95 J20 **Horred** Västra Götaland, S Sweden *57°22′N 12°25′E*
151 J19 **Horsburgh Atoll** *var.* Goidhoo Atoll. *atoll* N Maldives
20 K7 **Horse Cave** Kentucky, S USA *37°10′N 85°54′W*
37 V6 **Horse Creek** ≈ Colorado, C USA
27 S6 **Horse Creek** ≈ Missouri, C USA
18 G11 **Horseheads** New York, NE USA *42°10′N 76°49′W*
37 P13 **Horse Mount** ▲ New Mexico, SW USA *33°58′N 108°10′W*
95 G22 **Horsens** Syddanmark, C Denmark *55°53′N 09°53′E*
65 F25 **Horse Pasture Point** *headland* W Saint Helena *15°57′S 05°46′W*
33 N13 **Horseshoe Bend** Idaho, NW USA *43°55′N 116°11′W*
36 L13 **Horseshoe Reservoir** ⊠ Arizona, SW USA
64 M9 **Horseshoe Seamounts** *undersea feature* E Atlantic Ocean *36°30′N 15°00′W*
182 L11 **Horsham** Victoria, SE Australia *36°44′S 142°13′E*
97 O23 **Horsham** SE England, United Kingdom *51°01′N 00°21′W*
99 M15 **Horst** Limburg, SE Netherlands *51°30′N 06°05′E*
64 N2 **Horta** Faial, Azores, Portugal, NE Atlantic Ocean *38°32′N 28°39′W*
105 S12 **Horta, Cap de l'** *Cast.* Cabo Huertas. *headland* SE Spain *38°21′N 00°25′W*
95 H16 **Horten** Vestfold, S Norway *59°25′N 10°25′E*
111 M23 **Hortobágy-Berettyó** ≈ E Hungary
27 Q3 **Horton** Kansas, C USA *39°39′N 95°31′W*
8 I7 **Horton** ≈ Northwest Territories, NW Canada
95 I23 **Hørve** Sjælland, E Denmark *55°46′N 11°28′E*
95 L22 **Hörvik** Blekinge, S Sweden *56°01′N 14°45′E*
Horvot Haluza *see* Horvot Halutsa
14 E7 **Horwood Lake** ◎ Ontario, S Canada
116 K4 **Horyn'** *Rus.* Goryn. ≈ NW Ukraine
81 I14 **Hosa'ina** *var.* Hosseina, *It.* Hosanna. Southern Nationalities, S Ethiopia *07°38′N 37°58′E*
Hosanna *see* Hosa'ina
101 H18 **Hösbach** Bayern, C Germany *50°00′N 09°12′E*
Hose Mountains *see* Hose, Pegunungan
169 T9 **Hose, Pegunungan** *var.* Hose Mountains. ▲▲ East Malaysia
148 L15 **Hoshāb** Baluchistān, SW Pakistan *26°01′N 63°51′E*
154 H10 **Hoshangābād** Madhya Pradesh, C India *22°44′N 77°45′E*
116 L4 **Hoshcha** Rivnens'ka Oblast', NW Ukraine *50°37′N 26°38′E*
152 I7 **Hoshiārpur** Punjab, NW India *31°30′N 75°59′E*
Höshööt *see* Öldziyt
99 M23 **Hosingen** Diekirch, NE Luxembourg *50°01′N 06°05′E*
186 G7 **Hoskins** New Britain, E Papua New Guinea *05°28′S 150°25′E*
155 G17 **Hospet** Karnātaka, C India *15°16′N 76°20′E*
104 K4 **Hospital de Orbigo** Castilla y León, N Spain *42°27′N 05°53′W*
Hospitalet *see* L'Hospitalet de Llobregat
92 N13 **Hossa** Oulu, E Finland *65°28′N 29°36′E*
Hosseina *see* Hosa'ina
Hosszúmezjő *see* Câmpulung Moldovenesc
63 I25 **Hoste, Isla** *island* S Chile
117 O4 **Hostomel'** *Rus.* Gostomel'. Kyyivs'ka Oblast', N Ukraine *50°41′N 30°15′E*
155 H20 **Hosūr** Tamil Nādu, SE India *12°45′N 77°51′E*
167 N8 **Hot** Chiang Mai, NW Thailand *18°07′N 98°34′E*
158 G10 **Hotan** *var.* Khotan, *Chin.* Ho-t'ien. Xinjiang Uygur Zizhiqu, NW China *37°10′N 79°51′E*
158 H9 **Hotan He** ≈ NW China
83 G22 **Hotazel** Northern Cape, N South Africa *27°12′S 22°58′E*
37 Q5 **Hotchkiss** Colorado, C USA *38°47′N 107°43′W*
35 V7 **Hot Creek Range** ▲▲ Nevada, W USA
Hote *see* Hoti
171 T13 **Hoti** *var.* Hote. Pulau Seram, E Indonesia *02°58′S 130°19′E*
Ho-t'ien *see* Hotan
Hotin *see* Khotyn
93 H15 **Hoting** Jämtland, C Sweden *64°07′N 16°14′E*
162 L14 **Hotong Qagan Nur** ◎ N China
162 J8 **Hotont** Arhangay, C Mongolia *47°21′N 102°27′E*
27 T12 **Hot Springs** Arkansas, C USA *34°31′N 93°03′W*
28 J11 **Hot Springs** South Dakota, N USA *43°26′N 103°29′W*
21 S5 **Hot Springs** Virginia, NE USA *38°00′N 79°50′W*
35 Q4 **Hot Springs Peak** ▲ California, W USA *40°23′N 120°06′W*
27 T12 **Hot Springs Village** Arkansas, C USA *34°39′N 93°03′W*
Hotspur Bank *see* Hotspur Seamount
65 J16 **Hotspur Seamount** *var.* Hotspur Bank. *undersea feature* C Atlantic Ocean *18°00′S 35°00′W*
8 J8 **Hottah Lake** ◎ Northwest Territories, NW Canada
44 K9 **Hotte, Massif de la** ▲▲ SW Haiti
99 K21 **Hotton** Luxembourg, SE Belgium *50°18′N 05°25′E*
Hötzing *see* Hațeg
187 P17 **Houaïlou** Province Nord, C New Caledonia *21°17′S 165°37′E*
74 K5 **Houari Boumediène** ✈ (Alger) N Algeria *36°38′N 03°15′E*
167 P6 **Houayxay** *var.* Ban Houayxay. Bokèo, N Laos *20°17′N 100°27′E*
103 N5 **Houdan** Yvelines, N France *48°48′N 01°36′E*
99 F20 **Houdeng-Goegnies** *var.* Houdeng-Gœgnies. Hainaut, S Belgium *50°29′N 04°10′E*
102 K14 **Houeillès** Lot-et-Garonne, SW France *44°15′N 00°02′E*
99 L22 **Houffalize** Luxembourg, SE Belgium *50°08′N 05°47′E*
30 M3 **Houghton** Michigan, N USA *47°07′N 88°34′W*
31 Q7 **Houghton Lake** Michigan, N USA *44°18′N 84°45′W*
31 Q7 **Houghton Lake** ◎ Michigan, N USA
19 T3 **Houlton** Maine, NE USA *46°09′N 67°50′W*
160 M5 **Houma** Shanxi, C China *35°36′N 111°23′E*
193 U16 **Houma** Tongatapu, S Tonga *21°18′S 174°55′W*
22 J10 **Houma** Louisiana, S USA *29°35′N 90°44′W*
196 V16 **Houma Taloa** *headland* Tongatapu, S Tonga *21°16′S 175°08′W*
77 O13 **Houndé** SW Burkina *11°34′N 03°31′W*
102 J12 **Hourtin-Carcans, Lac d'** ◎ SW France
36 J5 **House Range** ▲▲ Utah, W USA
10 K13 **Houston** British Columbia, SW Canada *54°24′N 126°39′W*
39 R11 **Houston** Alaska, USA *61°37′N 149°50′W*
29 X10 **Houston** Minnesota, N USA *43°45′N 91°34′W*
22 M3 **Houston** Mississippi, S USA *33°54′N 89°00′W*
27 V7 **Houston** Missouri, C USA *37°19′N 91°59′W*
25 W11 **Houston** Texas, SW USA *29°46′N 95°22′W*
25 W11 **Houston** ✈ Texas, SW USA *30°03′N 95°18′W*
98 J12 **Houten** Utrecht, C Netherlands *52°02′N 05°10′E*
99 K17 **Houthalen** Limburg, NE Belgium *51°02′N 05°22′E*
99 I22 **Houyet** Namur, SE Belgium *50°10′N 05°00′E*
95 H22 **Hov** Midtjylland, C Denmark *55°54′N 10°13′E*
95 L17 **Hova** Västra Götaland, S Sweden *58°52′N 14°13′E*
162 J10 **Hovd** *var.* Dund-Us. Hovd, W Mongolia *48°06′N 91°22′E*
162 E6 **Hovd** *var.* Khovd, Kobdo; *prev.* Jirgalanta. Hovd, W Mongolia *47°59′N 91°41′E*
162 E6 **Hovd** *var.* Dund-Us. Hovd, W Mongolia *48°06′N 91°22′E*
162 E7 **Hovd** ◈ *province* W Mongolia
Hovd *see* Bogd
162 C5 **Hovd Gol** ≈ NW Mongolia
97 O23 **Hove** SE England, United Kingdom *50°49′N 00°11′W*
95 I22 **Hovedstaden** *off.* Frederiksborgs Amt. ◈ *county* E Denmark
29 N8 **Hoven** South Dakota, N USA *45°12′N 99°47′W*
116 I8 **Hoverla, Hora** *Rus.* Gora Goverla. ▲ W Ukraine *48°09′N 24°30′E*
Höviyn Am *see* Gurvanbulag
95 M21 **Hovmantorp** Kronoberg, S Sweden *56°47′N 15°08′E*
163 N11 **Hövsgöl** Dornogovĭ, SE Mongolia *43°35′N 109°40′E*
162 I5 **Hövsgöl** ◈ *province* N Mongolia
Hövsgöl, Lake *see* Hövsgöl Nuur
162 J5 **Hövsgöl Nuur** *var.* Lake Hovsgol. ◎ N Mongolia
78 L9 **Howa, Ouadi** *var.* Wādi Howar. ≈ Chad/Sudan *see also* Howar, Wādi
Howa, Ouadi *see* Howar, Wādi
27 P7 **Howard** Kansas, C USA *37°27′N 96°16′W*
29 Q10 **Howard** South Dakota, N USA *43°58′N 97°31′W*
25 N10 **Howard Draw** *valley* Texas, SW USA
29 U8 **Howard Lake** Minnesota, N USA *45°03′N 94°03′W*
80 B8 **Howar, Wādi** *var.* Ouadi Howa. ≈ Chad/Sudan *see also* Howa, Ouadi
Howar, Wādi *see* Howa, Ouadi
25 U5 **Howe** Texas, SW USA *33°29′N 96°38′W*
183 R12 **Howe, Cape** *headland* New South Wales/Victoria, SE Australia *37°30′S 149°58′E*
31 R9 **Howell** Michigan, N USA *42°36′N 83°55′W*
28 L9 **Howes** South Dakota, N USA *44°34′N 102°03′W*
83 K23 **Howick** KwaZulu/Natal, E South Africa *29°29′S 30°13′E*
Howrah *see* Hāora
167 T9 **Hô Xa** *prev.* Vinh Linh. Quang Tri, C Vietnam *17°02′N 107°03′E*
27 W9 **Hoxie** Arkansas, C USA *36°03′N 90°58′W*
26 J3 **Hoxie** Kansas, C USA *39°21′N 100°27′W*
101 I14 **Höxter** Nordrhein-Westfalen, W Germany *51°46′N 09°22′E*
158 K6 **Hoxud** *var.* Tewulike. Xinjiang Uygur Zizhiqu, NW China *42°18′N 86°51′E*
96 J5 **Hoy** *island* N Scotland, United Kingdom
43 S17 **Hoya, Cerro** ▲ S Panama *07°22′N 80°38′W*
94 D12 **Høyanger** Sogn Og Fjordane, S Norway *61°13′N 06°05′E*
101 P15 **Hoyerswerda** *Lus.* Wojerecy. Sachsen, E Germany *51°27′N 14°18′E*
164 R14 **Hōyo-kaikyō** *var.* Hayasui-seto. *strait* SW Japan
104 J8 **Hoyos** Extremadura, W Spain *40°10′N 06°43′W*
29 W4 **Hoyt Lakes** Minnesota, N USA *47°31′N 92°08′W*
87 V2 **Hoyvík** Streymoy, N Faeroe Islands
137 O14 **Hozat** Tunceli, E Turkey *39°09′N 39°13′E*
Hôzyô *see* Hōjō
167 N8 **Hpa-an** *var.* Pa-an. Kayin State, S Myanmar (Burma) *16°51′N 97°37′E*
167 N8 **Hpapun** *var.* Papun. Kayin State, S Myanmar (Burma) *18°05′N 97°26′E*
167 N7 **Hpasawng** *var.* Pasawng. Kayah State, C Myanmar (Burma) *18°50′N 97°16′E*
Hpyu *see* Phyu
111 F16 **Hradec Králové** *Ger.* Königgrätz. Královéhradecký Kraj, N Czech Republic *50°13′N 15°50′E*
Hradecký Kraj *see* Královéhradecký Kraj
111 B16 **Hradiště** *Ger.* Burgstadlberg. ▲ NW Czech Republic *50°12′N 13°04′E*
117 R6 **Hradyz'k** *Rus.* Gradizhsk. Poltavs'ka Oblast', NE Ukraine *49°14′N 33°07′E*
119 M16 **Hradzyanka** *Rus.* Grodzyanka. Mahilyowskaya Voblasts', E Belarus *53°33′N 28°45′E*
119 F16 **Hrandzichy** *Rus.* Grandichi. Hrodzyenskaya Voblasts', W Belarus *53°43′N 23°49′E*
111 H18 **Hranice** *Ger.* Mährisch-Weisskirchen. Olomoucký Kraj, E Czech Republic *49°34′N 17°45′E*
112 I13 **Hrasnica** Federacija Bosna I Hercegovina, SE Bosnia and Herzegovina *43°48′N 18°19′E*
109 V11 **Hrastnik** C Slovenia *46°09′N 15°08′E*
137 U12 **Hrazdan** *Rus.* Razdan. C Armenia *40°30′N 44°50′E*
137 T12 **Hrazdan** *var.* Zanga, *Rus.* Razdan. ≈ C Armenia
117 R5 **Hrebinka** *Rus.* Grebenka. Poltavs'ka Oblast', NE Ukraine *50°08′N 32°27′E*
119 K17 **Hresk** *Rus.* Gresk. Minskaya Voblasts', C Belarus *53°10′N 27°29′E*
Hrisoupoli *see* Chrysoúpoli
119 F16 **Hrodna** *Pol.* Grodno. Hrodzyenskaya Voblasts', W Belarus *53°40′N 23°50′E*
119 F16 **Hrodzyenskaya Voblasts'** *prev. Rus.* Grodnenskaya Oblast'. ◈ *province* W Belarus
111 J21 **Hron** *Ger.* Gran, *Hung.* Garam. ≈ C Slovakia
111 Q14 **Hrubieszów** *Rus.* Grubeshov. Lubelskie, E Poland *50°49′N 23°53′E*
112 F13 **Hrvace** Split-Dalmacija, SE Croatia *43°46′N 16°35′E*
Hrvatska *see* Croatia
112 F10 **Hrvatska Kostanjnica** *var.* Kostajnica. Sisak-Moslavina, C Croatia *45°14′N 16°35′E*
Hrvatsko Grahovi *see* Bosansko Grahovo
116 K6 **Hrymayliv** *Pol.* Gizymałów, *Rus.* Grimaylov. Ternopil's'ka Oblast', W Ukraine *49°18′N 26°02′E*
167 N4 **Hseni** *var.* Hsenwi. Shan State, E Myanmar (Burma) *23°20′N 97°59′E*
Hsenwi *see* Hseni
Hsia-men *see* Xiamen
Hsiang-t'an *see* Xiangtan
Hsi Chiang *see* Xi Jiang
167 N6 **Hsihseng** Shan State, C Myanmar (Burma) *20°07′N 97°17′E*
Hsinchu *see* Xinzhu
Hsing-K'ai Hu *see* Khanka, Lake
Hsi-ning/Hsining *see* Xining
Hsinking *see* Changchun
Hsin-yang *see* Xinyang
Hsinying *see* Xinying
167 N4 **Hsipaw** Shan State, Myanmar (Burma) *22°32′N 97°12′E*
Hsu-chou *see* Xuzhou
Hsüeh Shan *see* Xue Shan
Htawei *see* Dawei
Hu *see* Shanghai Shi
83 B18 **Huab** ≈ W Namibia
57 M21 **Huacaya** Chuquisaca, S Bolivia *20°45′S 63°42′W*
57 J19 **Huachacalla** Oruro, SW Bolivia *18°47′S 68°23′W*
159 X9 **Huachi** *var.* Rouyuan, Rouyuanchengzi. Gansu, C China *36°24′N 107°58′E*
57 N16 **Huachi, Laguna** ◎ N Bolivia
57 D14 **Huacho** Lima, W Peru *11°05′S 77°36′W*
163 Y7 **Huachuan** Heilongjiang, NE China *46°59′N 130°21′E*
163 P12 **Huade** Nei Mongol Zizhiqu, N China *41°52′N 113°58′E*
163 W10 **Huadian** Jilin, NE China *42°59′N 126°38′E*
56 E13 **Huagaruncho, Cordillera** ▲▲ C Peru
Hua Hin *see* Ban Hua Hin
191 S10 **Huahine** *island* Îles Sous le Vent, W French Polynesia
Huahua, Rio *see* Wawa, Río
167 R8 **Huai** ≈ E Thailand
161 Q7 **Huai'an** *var.* Qingjiang. Jiangsu, E China *33°33′N 119°03′E*
161 P6 **Huaibei** Anhui, E China *34°00′N 116°48′E*
Huaide *see* Gongzhuling
157 T10 **Huai He** ≈ C China
160 L11 **Huaihua** Hunan, S China *27°36′N 109°57′E*
161 N14 **Huaiji** Guangdong, S China *23°54′N 112°12′E*
161 O2 **Huailai** *var.* Shacheng. Hebei, E China *40°22′N 115°34′E*
161 P7 **Huainan** *var.* Huai-nan, Hwainan. Anhui, E China *32°37′N 116°57′E*
Huai-nan *see* Huainan
161 N2 **Huairen** *var.* Yunzhong. Shanxi, C China *35°28′N 110°29′E*
161 O7 **Huaiyang** Henan, C China *33°44′N 114°55′E*
161 Q7 **Huaiyin** Jiangsu, E China *33°31′N 119°03′E*
167 N16 **Huai Yot** Trang, SW Thailand *07°45′N 99°36′E*
41 Q15 **Huajuapan** *var.* Huajuapan de León. Oaxaca, SE Mexico *17°50′N 97°48′W*
Huajuapan de León *see* Huajuapan
41 O9 **Hualahuises** Nuevo León, NE Mexico *24°56′N 99°42′W*
36 I11 **Hualapai Mountains** ▲▲ Arizona, SW USA
36 I11 **Hualapai Peak** ▲ Arizona, SW USA *35°04′N 113°54′W*
62 J7 **Hualfin** Catamarca, N Argentina *27°15′S 66°53′W*
161 T13 **Hualian** *var.* Hualien, Hwalien, *Jap.* Karen. C Taiwan *23°58′N 121°35′E*
Hualien *see* Hualian
56 E10 **Huallaga, Río** ≈ N Peru
56 C11 **Huamachuco** La Libertad, C Peru *07°50′S 78°01′W*
41 Q14 **Huamantla** Tlaxcala, S Mexico *19°18′N 97°57′W*
82 C13 **Huambo** *Port.* Nova Lisboa. Huambo, C Angola *12°48′S 15°45′E*
82 B13 **Huambo** ◈ *province* C Angola
41 P15 **Huamuxtitlán** Guerrero, S Mexico *17°49′N 98°34′W*
163 Y8 **Huanan** Heilongjiang, NE China *46°21′N 130°43′E*
63 H17 **Huancache, Sierra** ▲▲ SW Argentina
57 I17 **Huancané** Puno, SE Peru *15°10′S 69°44′W*
57 F16 **Huancapi** Ayacucho, C Peru *13°40′S 74°05′W*
57 E15 **Huancavelica** Huancavelica, SW Peru *12°45′S 75°03′W*
57 E15 **Huancavelica** *off.* Departamento de Huancavelica. ◈ *department* W Peru
Huancavelica, Departamento de *see* Huancavelica
57 E14 **Huancayo** Junín, C Peru *12°03′S 75°14′W*
57 K20 **Huanchaca, Cerro** ▲ S Bolivia *20°12′S 66°35′W*
Huancheng *see* Huanxian
56 C12 **Huandoy, Nevado** ▲ W Peru *08°48′S 77°33′W*
Huangcheng *see* Hong'an
161 O8 **Huangchuan** Henan, C China *32°00′N 115°02′E*
161 O9 **Huanggang** Hubei, C China *30°27′N 114°48′E*
Huang Hai *see* Yellow Sea
157 Q8 **Huang He** *var.* Yellow River. ≈ C China
Huanghe *see* Madoi
161 Q4 **Huanghe Kou** *delta* E China
Huangheyan *see* Madoi
160 L5 **Huangling** Shaanxi, C China *35°40′N 109°14′E*
161 O9 **Huangpi** Hubei, C China *30°53′N 114°22′E*
163 P13 **Huangqi Hai** ◎ N China
161 Q9 **Huangshan** *var.* Tunxi. Anhui, E China *29°43′N 118°20′E*
161 O9 **Huangshi** *var.* Huang-shih, Hwangshih. Hubei, C China *30°14′N 115°E*
Huang-shih *see* Huangshi
160 L5 **Huangtu Gaoyuan** *plateau* C China
61 B22 **Huanguelén** Buenos Aires, E Argentina *37°02′S 61°57′W*
161 S10 **Huangyan** Zhejiang, SE China *28°39′N 121°19′E*
159 T10 **Huangyuan** Qinghai, C China *36°40′N 101°12′E*
159 T10 **Huangzhong** *var.* Lushar. Qinghai, C China *36°31′N 101°32′E*
163 W12 **Huanren** *var.* Huanren Manzu Zizhixian. Liaoning, NE China *41°16′N 125°25′E*
Huanren Manzu Zizhixian *see* Huanren
57 F15 **Huanta** Ayacucho, C Peru *12°54′S 74°13′W*
56 E13 **Huánuco** Huánuco, C Peru *09°58′S 76°16′W*
56 D13 **Huánuco** *off.* Departamento de Huánuco. ◈ *department* C Peru
Huánuco, Departamento de *see* Huánuco
57 K19 **Huanuni** Oruro, W Bolivia *18°15′S 66°48′W*
159 X9 **Huanxian** *var.* Huancheng. Gansu, C China *36°30′N 107°20′E*
161 S12 **Huaping Yu** *prev.* Huap'ing Yu. *island* N Taiwan
62 H3 **Huara** Tarapacá, N Chile *19°59′S 69°42′W*
57 D14 **Huaral** Lima, W Peru *11°31′S 77°10′W*
Huarás *see* Huaraz
56 D13 **Huaraz** *var.* Huarás. Ancash, W Peru *09°31′S 77°32′W*
57 I16 **Huari Huari, Río** ≈ S Peru
56 C13 **Huarmey** Ancash, W Peru *10°03′S 78°08′W*
40 H4 **Huásabas** Sonora, NW Mexico *29°47′N 109°18′W*
56 D8 **Huasaga, Río** ≈ Ecuador/Peru
167 O15 **Hua Sai** Nakhon Si Thammarat, SW Thailand *08°02′N 100°18′E*
56 D12 **Huascarán, Nevado** ▲ W Peru *09°01′S 77°27′W*
62 G8 **Huasco** Atacama, N Chile *28°30′S 71°15′W*
62 G8 **Huasco, Río** ≈ C Chile
159 S11 **Huashixia** Qinghai, W China
40 G7 **Huatabampo** Sonora, NW Mexico *26°49′N 109°40′W*
159 W10 **Huating** *var.* Donghua. Gansu, C China *35°13′N 106°39′E*
167 S7 **Huatt, Phou** ▲ N Vietnam *19°45′N 104°48′E*
41 Q14 **Huatusco** *var.* Huatusco de Chicuellar. Veracruz-Llave, C Mexico *19°13′N 96°57′W*
Huatusco de Chicuellar *see* Huatusco
41 P13 **Huauchinango** Puebla, S Mexico *20°11′N 98°04′W*
Huaunta *see* Wounta
41 R15 **Huautla** *var.* Huautla de Jiménez. Oaxaca, SE Mexico *18°10′N 96°51′W*
Huautla de Jiménez *see* Huautla
161 O5 **Huaxian** *var.* Daokou, Hua Xian. Henan, C China *35°33′N 114°30′E*
Hua Xian *see* Huaxian
Huazangsi *see* Tianzhu
29 V13 **Hubbard** Iowa, C USA *42°18′N 93°18′W*
25 U8 **Hubbard** Texas, SW USA *31°52′N 96°43′W*
25 Q6 **Hubbard Creek Lake** ◎ Texas, SW USA
31 R6 **Hubbard Lake** ◎ Michigan, N USA
160 M9 **Hubei** *var.* E, Hubei Sheng, Hupeh, Hupei. ◈ *province* C China
Hubei Sheng *see* Hubei
109 P8 **Huben** Tirol, W Austria *46°55′N 12°35′E*
31 R13 **Huber Heights** Ohio, N USA *39°50′N 84°07′W*
155 F17 **Hubli** Karnātaka, SW India *15°20′N 75°14′E*
163 X12 **Huch'ang** N North Korea *41°25′N 127°04′E*
97 M18 **Hucknall** C England, United Kingdom *53°02′N 01°11′W*

◆ Country
● Country Capital
◇ Dependent Territory
○ Dependent Territory Capital
◈ Administrative Regions
✈ International Airport
▲ Mountain
▲▲ Mountain Range
Ⓥ Volcano
≈ River
◎ Lake
⊠ Reservoir

97 L17 **Huddersfield** N England, United Kingdom 53°39′N 01°47′W
95 O16 **Huddinge** Stockholm, C Sweden 59°15′N 17°57′E
94 N11 **Hudiksvall** Gävleborg, C Sweden 61°45′N 17°12′E
29 W13 **Hudson** Iowa, C USA 42°24′N 92°27′W
19 O11 **Hudson** Massachusetts, NE USA 42°24′N 71°34′W
31 Q11 **Hudson** Michigan, N USA 41°51′N 84°21′W
30 H6 **Hudson** Wisconsin, N USA 44°59′N 92°43′W
11 V14 **Hudson Bay** Saskatchewan, S Canada 52°51′N 102°23′W
12 G6 **Hudson Bay** *bay* NE Canada
195 T16 **Hudson, Cape** *headland* Antarctica 68°15′S 154°00′E
Hudson, Détroit d' *see* Hudson Strait
27 Q9 **Hudson, Lake** ⊠ Oklahoma, C USA
18 K9 **Hudson River** ⚐ New Jersey/New York, NE USA
10 M12 **Hudson's Hope** British Columbia, W Canada 56°03′N 121°59′W
12 L2 **Hudson Strait** *Fr.* Détroit d'Hudson. *strait* Northwest Territories/Québec, NE Canada
Ḥudūd ash Shamālīyah, Minṭaqat al *see* Al Ḥudūd ash Shamālīyah
Hudur *see* Xuddur
167 U9 **Huê** Th,a Thiên-Huê, C Vietnam 16°28′N 107°35′E
104 J7 **Huebra** ⚐ W Spain
24 H8 **Hueco Mountains** ▲ Texas, SW USA
116 G10 **Huedin** *Hung.* Bánffyhunyad. Cluj, NW Romania 46°52′N 23°02′E
40 J10 **Huehuento, Cerro** ▲ C Mexico 24°04′N 105°42′W
42 B5 **Huehuetenango** Huehuetenango, W Guatemala 15°19′N 91°26′W
42 B4 **Huehuetenango** *off.* Departamento de Huehuetenango. ◆ *department* W Guatemala
Huehuetenango, Departamento de *see* Huehuetenango
40 L11 **Huejuquilla** Jalisco, SW Mexico 22°40′N 103°52′W
41 P12 **Huejutla** *var.* Huejutla de Reyes. Hidalgo, C Mexico 21°10′N 98°25′W
Huejutla de Reyes *see* Huejutla
102 G6 **Huelgoat** Finistère, NW France 48°22′N 03°45′W
105 O13 **Huelma** Andalucía, S Spain 37°39′N 03°28′W
104 I14 **Huelva** *anc.* Onuba. Andalucía, SW Spain 37°15′N 06°56′W
104 I13 **Huelva** ◆ *province* Andalucía, SW Spain
104 J13 **Huelva** ⚐ SW Spain
105 Q14 **Huercal-Overa** Andalucía, S Spain 37°23′N 01°56′W
37 Q9 **Huerfano Mountain** ▲ New Mexico, SW USA 36°25′N 107°50′W
37 T7 **Huerfano River** ⚐ Colorado, C USA
Huertas, Cabo *see* Horta, Cap de l'
105 R6 **Huerva** ⚐ N Spain
105 S4 **Huesca** *anc.* Osca. Aragón, NE Spain 42°08′N 00°25′W
105 T4 **Huesca** ◆ *province* Aragón, NE Spain
105 P13 **Huéscar** Andalucía, S Spain 37°39′N 02°32′W
41 N15 **Huetamo** *var.* Huetamo de Núñez. Michoacán, SW Mexico 18°36′N 100°54′W
Huetamo de Núñez *see* Huetamo
105 P8 **Huete** Castilla-La Mancha, C Spain 40°09′N 02°42′W
23 P4 **Hueytown** Alabama, S USA 33°27′N 87°00′W
28 L16 **Hugh Butler Lake** ⊠ Nebraska, C USA
181 V6 **Hughenden** Queensland, NE Australia 20°57′S 144°16′E
182 A6 **Hughes** South Australia 30°41′S 129°31′E
39 P8 **Hughes** Alaska, USA 66°03′N 154°15′W
27 X11 **Hughes** Arkansas, C USA 34°57′N 90°28′W
25 W6 **Hughes Springs** Texas, SW USA 33°00′N 94°37′W
37 V5 **Hugo** Colorado, C USA 39°08′N 103°28′W
27 Q13 **Hugo** Oklahoma, C USA 34°01′N 95°31′W
27 Q13 **Hugo Lake** ⊠ Oklahoma, C USA
26 H7 **Hugoton** Kansas, C USA 37°11′N 101°22′W
Huhehot/Huhohaote *see* Hohhot
Huhttán *see* Kvikkjokk
161 R13 **Hui'an** *var.* Luocheng. Fujian, SE China 25°06′N 118°45′E
184 O9 **Huiarau Range** ▲ North Island, New Zealand
83 D22 **Huib-Hoch Plateau** *plateau* S Namibia
41 O13 **Huichapán** Hidalgo, C Mexico 20°24′N 99°40′W
Huicheng *see* Shexian
163 W13 **Hŭich'ŏn** C North Korea 40°09′N 126°17′E
83 B15 **Huíla** ◆ *province* SW Angola
54 E12 **Huila** *off.* Departamento del Huila. ◆ *province* S Colombia
Huila, Departamento del *see* Huila
54 D11 **Huila, Nevado del** *elevation* C Colombia
83 B15 **Huíla Plateau** *plateau* S Angola
160 G12 **Huili** Sichuan, C China 26°39′N 102°13′E
161 P4 **Huimin** Shandong, E China 37°29′N 117°30′E
163 W11 **Huinan** *var.* Chaoyang. Jilin, NE China 42°40′N 126°03′E
62 K12 **Huinca Renancó** Córdoba, C Argentina 34°51′S 64°22′W
159 V10 **Huining** *var.* Huishi. Gansu, C China 35°42′N 105°01′E
159 W8 **Huinong** *var.* Dawukou. Ningxia, N China 39°04′N 106°22′E
Huishi *see* Huining
160 J12 **Huishui** *var.* Heping. Guizhou, S China 26°07′N 106°39′E
102 L6 **Huisne** ⚐ NW France
98 L12 **Huissen** Gelderland, SE Netherlands 51°57′N 05°57′E
159 N11 **Huiten Nur** ⊚ C China
93 K19 **Huittinen** Länsi-Suomi, SW Finland 61°11′N 22°40′E
41 O15 **Huitzuco** *var.* Huitzuco de los Figueroa. Guerrero, S Mexico 18°18′N 99°22′W
Huitzuco de los Figueroa *see* Huitzuco
159 W11 **Huixian** *var.* Hui Xian. Gansu, C China 33°48′N 106°02′E
Hui Xian *see* Huixian
41 V17 **Huixtla** Chiapas, SE Mexico 15°09′N 92°30′W
160 H12 **Huize** *var.* Zhongping. Yunnan, SW China 26°28′N 103°18′E
98 J10 **Huizen** Noord-Holland, C Netherlands 52°17′N 05°15′E
161 O14 **Huizhou** Guangdong, S China 23°02′N 114°28′E
162 J6 **Hujirt** Arhangay, C Mongolia 48°49′N 101°20′E
Hujirt *see* Tsetserleg, Övörhangay, Mongolia
Hujirt *see* Delgerhaan, Töv, Mongolia
Hukagawa *see* Fukagawa
Hūksan-gundo *see* Heuksan-jedo
Hukue *see* Gotō
Hukui *see* Fukui
83 G20 **Hukuntsi** Kgalagadi, SW Botswana 23°59′S 21°44′E
Hukuoka *see* Fukuoka
Hukusima *see* Fukushima
Hukutiyama *see* Fukuchiyama
Hukuyama *see* Fukuyama
163 W8 **Hulan** Heilongjiang, NE China 45°59′N 126°37′E
163 W8 **Hulan He** ⚐ NE China
31 Q4 **Hulbert Lake** ⊚ Michigan, N USA
Hulczyn *see* Hlučín
Huliao *see* Dabu
163 Z8 **Hulin** Heilongjiang, NE China 45°48′N 133°06′E
Hulingol *see* Holin Gol
14 L12 **Hull** Québec, SE Canada 45°26′N 75°45′W
29 S12 **Hull** Iowa, C USA 43°11′N 96°07′W
Hull *see* Kingston upon Hull
Hull Island *see* Orona
99 F16 **Hulst** Zeeland, SW Netherlands 51°17′N 04°03′E
Hulstay *see* Choybalsan
Hultschin *see* Hlučín
95 M19 **Hultsfred** Kalmar, S Sweden 57°30′N 15°50′E
163 T13 **Huludao** *prev.* Jinxi, Lianshan. Liaoning, NE China 40°46′N 120°47′E
Hulun *see* Hulun Buir
163 S6 **Hulun Buir** *var.* Hailar; *prev.* Hulun. Nei Mongol Zizhiqu, N China 49°15′N 119°41′E
Hu-lun Ch'ih *see* Hulun Nur
163 Q6 **Hulun Nur** *var.* Hu-lun Ch'ih; *prev.* Dalai Nor. ⊚ NE China
Hulwan/Hulwân *see* Hilwān
117 V8 **Hulyaypole** *Rus.* Gulyaypole. Zaporiz'ka Oblast', SE Ukraine 47°41′N 36°10′E
163 V4 **Huma** Heilongjiang, NE China 51°40′N 126°38′E
45 V6 **Humacao** E Puerto Rico 18°09′N 65°50′W
163 U4 **Huma He** ⚐ NE China
62 J5 **Humahuaca** Jujuy, N Argentina 23°13′S 65°20′W
59 E14 **Humaitá** Amazonas, N Brazil 07°33′S 63°01′W
62 N7 **Humaitá** Ñeembucú, S Paraguay 27°02′S 58°31′W
83 H26 **Humansdorp** Eastern Cape, S South Africa 34°01′S 24°45′E
27 S6 **Humansville** Missouri, C USA 37°47′N 93°34′W
40 I8 **Humaya, Río** ⚐ C Mexico
83 C16 **Humbe** Cunene, SW Angola 16°37′S 14°52′E
97 N17 **Humber** *estuary* E England, United Kingdom
97 N17 **Humberside** *cultural region* E England, United Kingdom
Humberto *see* Umberto
25 W11 **Humble** Texas, SW USA 29°58′N 95°15′W
11 U15 **Humboldt** Saskatchewan, S Canada 52°13′N 105°09′W
29 U12 **Humboldt** Iowa, C USA 42°42′N 94°13′W
27 Q6 **Humboldt** Kansas, C USA 37°48′N 95°26′W
29 S17 **Humboldt** Nebraska, C USA 40°09′N 95°56′W
35 S3 **Humboldt** Nevada, W USA 40°36′N 118°15′W
20 G9 **Humboldt** Tennessee, S USA 35°49′N 88°55′W
34 K3 **Humboldt Bay** *bay* California, W USA
35 S4 **Humboldt Lake** ⊚ Nevada, W USA
35 S4 **Humboldt River** ⚐ Nevada, W USA
35 T5 **Humboldt Salt Marsh** *wetland* Nevada, W USA
183 P11 **Hume, Lake** ⊚ New South Wales/Victoria, SE Australia
111 N19 **Humenné** *Ger.* Homenau, *Hung.* Homonna. Prešovský Kraj, E Slovakia 48°57′N 21°54′E
29 V15 **Humeston** Iowa, C USA 40°51′N 93°30′W
54 J5 **Humocaro Bajo** Lara, N Venezuela 09°41′N 70°00′W
29 Q14 **Humphrey** Nebraska, C USA 41°38′N 97°29′W
35 S9 **Humphreys, Mount** ▲ California, W USA 37°11′N 118°39′W
36 L11 **Humphreys Peak** ▲ Arizona, SW USA 35°18′N 111°40′W
111 E17 **Humpolec** *Ger.* Gumpolds, Humpoletz. Vysočina, C Czech Republic 49°33′N 15°23′E
Humpoletz *see* Humpolec
93 K19 **Humppila** Etelä-Suomi, S Finland 60°54′N 23°21′E
32 F8 **Humptulips** Washington, NW USA 47°13′N 123°57′W
42 H7 **Humuya, Río** ⚐ W Honduras
75 P9 **Hūn** N Libya 29°06′N 15°56′E
92 I1 **Húnaflói** *bay* NW Iceland
160 M11 **Hunan** *var.* Hunan Sheng, Xiang. ◆ *province* S China
Hunan Sheng *see* Hunan
163 Y10 **Hunchun** Jilin, NE China 42°51′N 130°21′E
95 I22 **Hundested** Hovedstaden, E Denmark 55°58′N 11°53′E
Hundred Mile House *see* 100 Mile House
116 G12 **Hunedoara** *Ger.* Eisenmarkt, *Hung.* Vajdahunyad. Hunedoara, SW Romania 45°45′N 22°54′E
116 G12 **Hunedoara** ◆ *county* W Romania
101 I17 **Hünfeld** Hessen, C Germany 50°41′N 09°46′E
Hungarian People's Republic *see* Hungary
111 H23 **Hungary** *off.* Republic of Hungary, *Ger.* Ungarn, *Hung.* Magyarország, *Rom.* Ungaria, *SCr.* Madarska, *Ukr.* Uhorshchyna; *prev.* Hungarian People's Republic. ◆ *republic* C Europe
Hungary, Plain of *see* Great Hungarian Plain
Hungary, Republic of *see* Hungary
Hungiy *see* Urgamal
163 X13 **Hŭngnam** E North Korea 39°50′N 127°36′E
33 P8 **Hungry Horse Reservoir** ⊠ Montana, NW USA
Hungt'ou *see* Lan Yu
Hung-tse Hu *see* Hongze Hu
167 T6 **Hưng Yên** Hai Hưng, N Vietnam 20°38′N 106°05′E
Hunjiang *see* Baishan
95 I18 **Hunnebostrand** Västra Götaland, S Sweden 58°26′N 11°19′E
101 E19 **Hunsrück** ▲ W Germany
97 P18 **Hunstanton** E England, United Kingdom 52°57′N 00°27′E
155 G20 **Hunsūr** Karnātaka, E India 12°18′N 76°15′E
Hunt *see* Hangay
100 G12 **Hunte** ⚐ NW Germany
29 Q5 **Hunter** North Dakota, N USA 47°10′N 97°11′W
25 S11 **Hunter** Texas, SW USA 29°47′N 98°01′W
185 D20 **Hunter** ⚐ South Island, New Zealand
183 N15 **Hunter Island** *island* Tasmania, SE Australia
18 K11 **Hunter Mountain** ▲ New York, NE USA 42°10′N 74°13′W
185 B23 **Hunter Mountains** ▲ South Island, New Zealand
183 S7 **Hunter River** ⚐ New South Wales, SE Australia
32 L7 **Hunters** Washington, NW USA 48°07′N 118°13′W
185 F20 **Hunters Hills, The** *hill range* South Island, New Zealand
184 M12 **Hunterville** Manawatu-Wanganui, North Island, New Zealand 39°55′S 175°34′E
31 N16 **Huntingburg** Indiana, N USA 38°18′N 86°57′W
97 O20 **Huntingdon** E England, United Kingdom 52°20′N 00°12′W
18 E15 **Huntingdon** Pennsylvania, NE USA 40°28′N 78°00′W
20 G9 **Huntingdon** Tennessee, S USA 36°00′N 88°25′W
97 O20 **Huntingdonshire** *cultural region* C England, United Kingdom
31 P12 **Huntington** Indiana, N USA 40°52′N 85°30′W
32 L13 **Huntington** Oregon, NW USA 44°22′N 117°18′W
25 X9 **Huntington** Texas, SW USA 31°16′N 94°34′W
36 M5 **Huntington** Utah, W USA 39°19′N 110°57′W
21 P5 **Huntington** West Virginia, NE USA 38°25′N 82°27′W
35 T16 **Huntington Beach** California, W USA 33°39′N 118°00′W
35 W4 **Huntington Creek** ⚐ Nevada, W USA
184 L7 **Huntly** Waikato, North Island, New Zealand 37°34′S 175°09′E
96 K8 **Huntly** NE Scotland, United Kingdom 57°25′N 02°48′W
10 K8 **Hunt, Mount** ▲ Yukon Territory, NW Canada 61°29′N 129°10′W
14 H12 **Huntsville** Ontario, S Canada 45°20′N 79°14′W
23 P2 **Huntsville** Alabama, S USA 34°44′N 86°35′W
27 S9 **Huntsville** Arkansas, C USA 36°04′N 93°46′W
27 U3 **Huntsville** Missouri, C USA 39°27′N 92°31′W
20 M8 **Huntsville** Tennessee, S USA 36°25′N 84°30′W
25 V10 **Huntsville** Texas, SW USA 30°43′N 95°34′W
36 L2 **Huntsville** Utah, W USA 41°16′N 111°47′W
41 W12 **Hunucmá** Yucatán, SE Mexico 20°59′N 89°55′W
149 W3 **Hunza** ⚐ NE Pakistan
Hunza *see* Karīmābād
Hunze *see* Oostermoers Vaart
158 H4 **Huocheng** *var.* Shuiding. Xinjiang Uygur Zizhiqu, NW China 44°03′N 80°49′E
161 N6 **Huojia** Henan, C China 35°14′N 113°38′E
186 N14 **Huon** *reef* N New Caledonia
186 E7 **Huon Peninsula** *headland* C Papua New Guinea 06°24′S 147°50′E
Huoshao Dao *see* Lü Dao
Huoshao Tao *see* Lan Yu
Hupeh/Hupei *see* Hubei
Hurama *see* Hongyuan
95 H14 **Hurdalsjøen** *prev.* Hurdalssjøen. ⊚ S Norway
Hurdalssjøen *see* Hurdalsjøen
14 E13 **Hurd, Cape** *headland* Ontario, S Canada 45°12′N 81°43′W
98 L5 **Hurdegaryp** *Dutch.* Hardegarijp. Fryslân, N Netherlands 53°13′N 05°57′E
29 N4 **Hurdsfield** North Dakota, N USA 47°24′N 99°55′W
Hüremt *see* Sayhan, Bulgan, Mongolia
Hüremt *see* Taragt, Övörhangay, Mongolia
Hurghada *see* Al Ghurdaqah
67 V9 **Huri Hills** ▲ NW Kenya
37 P15 **Hurley** New Mexico, SW USA 32°42′N 108°07′W
30 K4 **Hurley** Wisconsin, N USA 46°25′N 90°15′W
21 Y4 **Hurlock** Maryland, NE USA 38°37′N 75°51′W
162 K11 **Hürmen** *var.* Tsoohor. Ömnögovi, S Mongolia 43°15′N 104°04′E
29 P10 **Huron** South Dakota, N USA 44°19′N 98°13′W
31 S6 **Huron, Lake** ⊚ Canada/USA
31 N3 **Huron Mountains** *hill range* Michigan, N USA
36 J8 **Hurricane** Utah, W USA 37°10′N 113°18′W
21 P5 **Hurricane** West Virginia, NE USA 38°25′N 82°01′W
36 J8 **Hurricane Cliffs** *cliff* Arizona, SW USA
23 V6 **Hurricane Creek** ⚐ Georgia, SE USA
94 E12 **Hurrungane** ▲ S Norway 61°25′N 07°48′E
101 E16 **Hürth** Nordrhein-Westfalen, W Germany 50°52′N 06°49′E
Hurukawa *see* Furukawa
185 I17 **Hurunui** ⚐ South Island, New Zealand
95 F21 **Hurup** Midtjylland, NW Denmark 56°46′N 08°26′E
117 T14 **Hurzuf** Avtonomna Respublika Krym, S Ukraine 44°33′N 34°18′E
Hus *see* Huşi
95 B19 **Húsavík** *Dan.* Husevig. Sandoy, C Faeroe Islands 65°24′N 06°38′W
92 K1 **Húsavík** Nordhurland Eystra, NE Iceland 66°03′N 17°20′W
Husevig *see* Húsavík
116 M10 **Huşi** *var.* Huş. Vaslui, E Romania 46°40′N 28°05′E
95 L19 **Huskvarna** Jönköping, S Sweden 57°47′N 14°15′E
39 P8 **Huslia** Alaska, USA 65°42′N 156°24′W
Husn *see* Al Ḥuṣn
95 C15 **Husnes** Hordaland, S Norway 59°52′N 05°46′E
94 D8 **Hustadvika** *sea area* S Norway
Husté *see* Khust
100 H7 **Husum** Schleswig-Holstein, N Germany 54°29′N 09°04′E
93 I16 **Husum** Västernorrland, C Sweden 63°21′N 19°12′E
116 K6 **Husyatyn** Ternopil's'ka Oblast', W Ukraine 49°04′N 26°10′E
Huszt *see* Khust
Hutag *see* Hutag-Öndör
162 K6 **Hutag-Öndör** *var.* Hutag. Bulgan, N Mongolia 49°22′N 102°50′E
26 M6 **Hutchinson** Kansas, C USA 38°03′N 97°56′W
29 U9 **Hutchinson** Minnesota, N USA 44°53′N 94°22′W
23 Y13 **Hutchinson Island** *island* Florida, SE USA
36 L11 **Hutch Mountain** ▲ Arizona, SW USA 34°49′N 111°22′W
141 O14 **Ḥūth** NW Yemen 16°14′N 44°E
186 I7 **Hutjena** Buka Island, NE Papua New Guinea 05°19′S 154°40′E
109 T8 **Hüttenberg** Kärnten, S Austria 46°58′N 14°33′E
25 T10 **Hutto** Texas, SW USA 30°32′N 97°33′W
Huttu *see* Futtsu
108 E8 **Huttwil** Bern, W Switzerland 47°06′N 07°48′E
158 K5 **Hutubi** Xinjiang Uygur Zizhiqu, NW China 44°10′N 86°51′E
161 N4 **Hutuo He** ⚐ C China
Hutyû *see* Fuchū
185 E20 **Huxley, Mount** ▲ South Island, New Zealand 44°02′S 169°42′E
99 J20 **Huy** *Dut.* Hoei, Hoey. Liège, E Belgium 50°32′N 05°14′E
161 R8 **Huzhou** *var.* Wuxing. Zhejiang, SE China 30°52′N 120°06′E
Huzi *see* Fuji
Huzieda *see* Fujieda
Huzinomiya *see* Fujinomiya
Huzisawa *see* Fujisawa
92 I2 **Hvammstangi** Nordhurland Vestra, N Iceland 65°22′N 20°54′W
92 K4 **Hvannadalshnúkur** ⛰ S Iceland 64°01′N 16°39′W
113 E15 **Hvar** *It.* Lesina. Split-Dalmacija, S Croatia 43°10′N 16°27′E
113 F15 **Hvar** *It.* Lesina; *anc.* Pharus. *island* S Croatia
117 T13 **Hvardiys'ke** *Rus.* Gvardeyskoye. Avtonomna Respublika Krym, S Ukraine 45°08′N 34°01′E
92 I4 **Hveragerdhi** Sudhurland, SW Iceland 64°00′N 21°13′W
95 E22 **Hvide Sande** Midtjylland, W Denmark 56°00′N 08°08′E
92 I3 **Hvítá** ⚐ C Iceland
95 G15 **Hvittingfoss** Buskerud, S Norway 59°28′N 10°00′E
92 I4 **Hvolsvöllur** Sudhurland, SW Iceland 63°44′N 20°12′W
Hwach'ŏn-chŏsuji *see* Paro-ho
Hwainan *see* Huainan
Hwalien *see* Hualian
83 I16 **Hwange** *prev.* Wankie. Matabeleland North, W Zimbabwe 18°18′S 26°31′E
Hwang-Hae *see* Yellow Sea
Hwangshih *see* Huangshi
83 L17 **Hwedza** Mashonaland East, E Zimbabwe 18°35′S 31°35′E
63 G20 **Hyades, Cerro** ▲ S Chile 46°57′S 73°09′W
162 K6 **Hyalganat** *var.* Selenge. Bulgan, N Mongolia 49°34′N 104°18′E
19 Q12 **Hyannis** Massachusetts, NE USA 41°38′N 70°15′W
28 L13 **Hyannis** Nebraska, C USA 42°00′N 101°45′W
162 F6 **Hyargas Nuur** ⊚ NW Mongolia
Hybla/Hybla Major *see* Paternò
39 Y14 **Hydaburg** Prince of Wales Island, Alaska, USA 55°10′N 132°44′W
185 F22 **Hyde** Otago, South Island, New Zealand 45°17′S 170°17′E
21 O7 **Hyden** Kentucky, S USA 37°08′N 83°23′W
18 K12 **Hyde Park** New York, NE USA 41°46′N 73°52′W
39 Z14 **Hyder** Alaska, USA 55°55′N 130°01′W
155 I15 **Hyderābād** *var.* Haidarabad. *state capital* Andhra Pradesh, C India 17°22′N 78°26′E
149 Q16 **Hyderābād** *var.* Haidarabad. Sind, SE Pakistan 25°26′N 68°22′E
103 T16 **Hyères** Var, SE France 43°07′N 06°08′E
103 T16 **Hyères, Îles d'** *island group* S France
118 K12 **Hyermanavichy** *Rus.* Germanovichi. Vitsyebskaya Voblasts', N Belarus 55°24′N 27°48′E
163 X12 **Hyesan** NE North Korea 41°18′N 128°13′E
10 K8 **Hyland** ⚐ Yukon Territory, NW Canada
95 K20 **Hyltebruk** Halland, S Sweden 57°N 13°14′E
18 D16 **Hyndman** Pennsylvania, NE USA 39°49′N 78°42′W
33 P14 **Hyndman Peak** ▲ Idaho, NW USA 43°45′N 114°07′W
164 I13 **Hyōgo** *off.* Hyōgo-ken. ◆ *prefecture* Honshū, SW Japan
Hyōgo-ken *see* Hyōgo
Hypsas *see* Belice
Hyrcania *see* Gorgān
36 L1 **Hyrum** Utah, W USA 41°37′N 111°51′W
93 N14 **Hyrynsalmi** Oulu, C Finland 64°41′N 28°30′E
33 V10 **Hysham** Montana, NW USA 46°16′N 107°14′W
11 N13 **Hythe** Alberta, W Canada 55°18′N 119°44′W
97 Q23 **Hythe** SE England, United Kingdom 51°05′N 01°04′E
Hyvinge *see* Hyvinkää
93 L19 **Hyvinkää** *Swe.* Hyvinge. Etelä-Suomi, S Finland 60°37′N 24°50′E

I

116 J9 **Iacobeni** *Ger.* Jakobeny. Suceava, NE Romania 47°24′N 25°20′E
Iader *see* Zadar
172 I7 **Iakora** Fianarantsoa, SE Madagascar 23°04′S 46°40′E
116 K14 **Ialomiţa** *var.* Jalomitsa. ◆ *county* SE Romania
116 K14 **Ialomiţa** ⚐ SE Romania
117 N10 **Ialoveni** *Rus.* Yaloveny. C Moldova 46°57′N 28°47′E
117 N11 **Ialpug** *var.* Ialpugul Mare, *Rus.* Yalpug. ⚐ Moldova/Ukraine
Ialpugul Mare *see* Ialpug
23 T8 **Iamonia, Lake** ⊚ Florida, SE USA
116 L13 **Ianca** Brăila, SE Romania 45°06′N 27°29′E
116 M10 **Iaşi** *Ger.* Jassy. Iaşi, NE Romania 47°08′N 27°38′E
116 L9 **Iaşi** *Ger.* Jassy, Yassy. ◆ *county* NE Romania
114 J13 **Íasmos** Anatolikí Makedonía kai Thráki, NE Greece 41°07′N 25°12′E
22 H6 **Iatt, Lake** ⊠ Louisiana, S USA
58 B11 **Iauretê** Amazonas, NW Brazil 0°37′N 69°10′W
171 N3 **Iba** Luzon, N Philippines 15°25′N 119°55′E
77 S16 **Ibadan** Oyo, SW Nigeria 07°22′N 04°01′E
54 E10 **Ibagué** Tolima, C Colombia 04°27′N 75°14′W
60 J10 **Ibaiti** Paraná, S Brazil 23°49′S 50°15′W
36 J4 **Ibapah Peak** ▲ Utah, W USA 39°51′N 113°55′W
Ibar *see* Ibër
165 P13 **Ibaraki** *off.* Ibaraki-ken. ◆ *prefecture* Honshū, S Japan
Ibaraki-ken *see* Ibaraki
56 C5 **Ibarra** *var.* San Miguel de Ibarra. Imbabura, N Ecuador 0°23′S 78°08′W
Ibaşfalău *see* Dumbrăveni
141 O16 **Ibb** W Yemen 13°55′N 44°10′E
100 F13 **Ibbenbüren** Nordrhein-Westfalen, NW Germany 52°17′N 07°43′E
79 H16 **Ibenga** ⚐ N Congo
113 M15 **Ibër** *Serb.* Ibar. ⚐ C Serbia
57 I14 **Iberia** Madre de Dios, E Peru 11°21′S 69°36′W
Iberia *see* Spain
66 M1 **Iberian Basin** *undersea feature* E Atlantic Ocean 39°00′N 16°00′W
Iberian Mountains *see* Ibérico, Sistema
84 D12 **Iberian Peninsula** *physical region* Portugal/Spain
64 M8 **Iberian Plain** *undersea feature* E Atlantic Ocean 13°30′W 43°45′N
Ibérica, Cordillera *see* Ibérico, Sistema
105 P6 **Ibérico, Sistema** *var.* Cordillera Ibérica, *Eng.* Iberian Mountains. ▲ NE Spain
12 K7 **Iberville Lac d'** ⊚ Québec, NE Canada
77 T14 **Ibeto** Niger, W Nigeria 10°30′N 05°07′E
77 W15 **Ibi** Taraba, C Nigeria 08°13′N 09°46′E
105 S11 **Ibi** Valenciana, E Spain 38°38′N 00°35′W
59 L20 **Ibiá** Minas Gerais, SE Brazil 19°30′S 46°31′W
61 F15 **Ibicuí, Rio** ⚐ S Brazil
61 C19 **Ibicuy** Entre Ríos, E Argentina 33°44′S 59°10′W
61 F16 **Ibirapuitã** ⚐ S Brazil
105 V10 **Ibiza** *var.* Iviza, *Cast.* Eivissa; *anc.* Ebusus. *island* Islas Baleares, Spain, W Mediterranean Sea
Ibiza *see* Eivissa
138 J4 **Ibn Wardān, Qaṣr** *ruins* Ḥamāh, C Syria
Ibo *see* Sassandra
188 E9 **Ibobang** Babeldaob, N Palau
171 V13 **Ibonma** Papua, E Indonesia 03°27′S 133°30′E
59 N17 **Ibotirama** Bahia, E Brazil 12°13′S 43°12′W
141 Y8 **Ibrā** NE Oman 22°45′N 58°30′E
127 Q4 **Ibresi** Chuvashskaya Respublika, W Russian Federation 55°22′N 47°04′E
141 X8 **'Ibrī** NW Oman 23°12′N 56°28′E
164 C16 **Ibusuki** Kagoshima, Kyūshū, SW Japan 31°15′N 130°40′E
57 E16 **Ica** Ica, SW Peru 14°02′S 75°48′W
57 E16 **Ica** *off.* Departamento de Ica. ◆ *department* SW Peru
Ica, Departamento de *see* Ica
58 C11 **Içana** Amazonas, NW Brazil 0°22′N 67°25′W
Icaria *see* Ikaría
58 B13 **Içá, Rio** *var.* Río Putumayo. ⚐ NW South America *see also* Putumayo, Río
Içá, Rio *see* Putumayo, Río
136 I17 **İçel** *prev.* Ichili; *prev.* Mersin. ◆ *province* S Turkey
İçel *see* Mersin
92 I3 **Iceland** *off.* Republic of Iceland, *Dan.* Island, *Icel.* Ísland. ◆ *republic* N Atlantic Ocean
86 B6 **Iceland** *island* N Atlantic Ocean
64 L5 **Iceland Basin** *undersea feature* N Atlantic Ocean 61°00′N 19°00′W
Icelandic Plateau *see* Iceland Plateau
197 Q15 **Iceland Plateau** *var.* Icelandic Plateau. *undersea feature* S Greenland Sea 12°00′W 69°30′N
Iceland, Republic of *see* Iceland
155 E16 **Ichalkaranji** Mahārāshtra, W India 16°42′N 74°28′E
164 D15 **Ichifusa-yama** ▲ Kyūshū, SW Japan 32°18′N 131°05′E
Ichili *see* İçel
164 K13 **Ichinomiya** *var.* Itinomiya. Aichi, Honshū, SW Japan 35°18′N 136°48′E
165 Q9 **Ichinoseki** *var.* Itinoseki. Iwate, Honshū, C Japan 38°56′N 141°08′E
117 R3 **Ichnya** Chernihivs'ka Oblast', NE Ukraine 50°52′N 32°24′E
57 L17 **Ichoa, Río** ⚐ C Bolivia
Iconium *see* Konya
Iculisma *see* Angoulême
39 U12 **Icy Bay** *inlet* Alaska, USA
39 N5 **Icy Cape** *headland* Alaska, USA 70°19′N 161°52′W
39 W13 **Icy Strait** *strait* Alaska, USA
27 R13 **Idabel** Oklahoma, C USA 33°54′N 94°50′W
29 T13 **Ida Grove** Iowa, C USA 42°21′N 95°28′W
77 U16 **Idah** Kogi, S Nigeria 07°06′N 06°45′E
33 N13 **Idaho** *off.* State of Idaho, *also known as* Gem of the Mountains, Gem State. ◆ *state* NW USA
33 N14 **Idaho City** Idaho, NW USA 43°48′N 115°51′W
33 R14 **Idaho Falls** Idaho, NW USA 43°28′N 112°01′W
121 P2 **Idálion** *var.* Dali, Dhali. C Cyprus 35°00′N 33°25′E
25 N5 **Idalou** Texas, SW USA 33°40′N 101°40′W
104 I9 **Idanha-a-Nova** Castelo Branco, C Portugal 39°55′N 07°15′W
101 E19 **Idar-Oberstein** Rheinland-Pfalz, SW Germany 49°43′N 07°19′E
118 J3 **Ida-Virumaa** *var.* Ida-Viru Maakond. ◆ *province* NE Estonia
Ida-Viru Maakond *see* Ida-Virumaa
124 J8 **Idel'** Respublika Kareliya, NW Russian Federation 64°08′N 34°12′E
79 C15 **Idenao** Sud-Ouest, SW Cameroon 04°04′N 09°01′E
Idensalmi *see* Iisalmi
162 I6 **Ider** *var.* Dzuunmod. Hövsgöl, C Mongolia 48°09′N 97°22′E
Ider *see* Galt
75 X10 **Idfu** *var.* Edfu. SE Egypt 24°55′N 32°52′E
Ídhi Óros *see* Ídi
Ídhra *see* Ýdra
80 L10 **'Īdi** *var.* Ed. SE Eritrea 13°54′N 41°39′E
168 H7 **Idi** Sumatera, W Indonesia 05°00′N 98°00′E
115 I25 **Ídi** *var.* Ídhi Óros. ▲ Kríti, Greece, E Mediterranean Sea
Idi Amin, Lac *see* Edward, Lake
106 G10 **Idice** ⚐ N Italy
76 G9 **Idini** Trarza, W Mauritania 17°58′N 15°40′W
79 J21 **Idiofa** Bandundu, SW Dem. Rep. Congo 05°00′S 19°38′E
39 O10 **Iditarod River** ⚐ Alaska, USA
Idjavuotna *see* Ifjord
95 M14 **Idkerberget** Dalarna, C Sweden 60°22′N 15°15′E
138 I3 **Idlib** Idlib, NW Syria 35°57′N 36°38′E
138 I4 **Idlib** *off.* Muḥāfaẓat Idlib. ◆ *governorate* NW Syria
Idlib, Muḥāfaẓat *see* Idlib
Idra *see* Ýdra
94 J11 **Idre** Dalarna, C Sweden 61°52′N 12°45′E
Idria *see* Idrija
109 S11 **Idrija** *It.* Idria. W Slovenia 46°00′N 14°59′E
101 G18 **Idstein** Hessen, W Germany 50°10′N 08°16′E
83 J25 **Idutywa** Eastern Cape, SE South Africa 32°06′S 28°20′E
Idzhevan *see* Ijevan
118 G9 **Iecava** S Latvia 56°36′N 24°10′E
165 T16 **Ie-jima** *var.* Ii-shima. *island* Nansei-shotō, SW Japan
99 B18 **Ieper** *Fr.* Ypres. West-Vlaanderen, W Belgium 50°51′N 02°53′E
115 K25 **Ierápetra** Kríti, Greece, E Mediterranean Sea 35°00′N 25°45′E
115 G22 **Iérax, Akrotírio** *headland* S Greece 36°45′N 23°06′E
Ierisós *see* Ierissós
115 H14 **Ierissós** *var.* Ierisós. Kentrikí Makedonía, N Greece 40°24′N 23°53′E
116 I11 **Iernut** *Hung.* Radnót. Mureş, C Romania 46°27′N 24°15′E
106 J12 **Iesi** *var.* Jesi. Marche, C Italy 43°33′N 13°16′E
92 K9 **Iešjavri** ⊚ N Norway
Iesolo *see* Jesolo
188 K16 **Ifalik Atoll** *atoll* Caroline Islands, C Micronesia
172 I6 **Ifanadiana** Fianarantsoa, SE Madagascar 21°19′S 47°39′E
77 T16 **Ife** Osun, SW Nigeria 07°25′N 04°31′E
77 V8 **Iferouâne** Agadez, N Niger 19°05′N 08°24′E
Iferten *see* Yverdon
92 L8 **Ifjord** *Lapp.* Idjavuotna. Finnmark, N Norway 70°27′N 27°06′E
77 R8 **Ifôghas, Adrar des** *var.* Adrar des Iforas. ▲ NE Mali
Iforas, Adrar des *see* Ifôghas, Adrar des
182 D6 **Ifould lake** *salt lake* South Australia
74 G6 **Ifrane** C Morocco 33°31′N 05°09′W
171 S11 **Iga** Pulau Halmahera, E Indonesia 01°23′N 128°17′E
81 G18 **Iganga** SE Uganda 0°34′N 33°27′E
60 L7 **Igarapava** São Paulo, S Brazil 20°01′S 47°46′W
122 K9 **Igarka** Krasnoyarskiy Kray, N Russian Federation 67°31′N 86°33′E
Igaunija *see* Estonia
137 T12 **Iğdir** ◆ *province* NE Turkey
I.G.Duca *see* General Toshevo
Igel *see* Jihlava
94 N11 **Iggesund** Gävleborg, C Sweden 61°38′N 17°04′E
39 P7 **Igikpak, Mount** ▲ Alaska, USA 67°28′N 154°55′W
39 P13 **Igiugig** Alaska, USA 59°19′N 155°53′W
Iglau/Iglawa/Igława *see* Jihlava
107 B20 **Iglesias** Sardegna, Italy, C Mediterranean Sea 39°20′N 08°34′E
127 V4 **Iglino** Respublika Bashkortostan, W Russian Federation 54°51′N 56°29′E
Igló *see* Spišská Nová Ves
9 O6 **Igloolik** Nunavut, N Canada 69°24′N 81°55′W
12 B11 **Ignace** Ontario, S Canada 49°26′N 91°40′W
118 I12 **Ignalina** Utena, E Lithuania 55°20′N 26°10′E
127 Q5 **Ignatovka** Ul'yanovskaya Oblast', W Russian Federation 53°56′N 47°40′E
124 K12 **Ignatovo** Vologodskaya Oblast', NW Russian Federation 60°47′N 37°51′E
114 N11 **İğneada** Kırklareli, NW Turkey 41°54′N 27°58′E
121 S7 **İğneada Burnu** *headland* NW Turkey 41°54′N 28°03′E
Igombe *see* Gombe
115 B16 **Igoumenítsa** Ípeiros, W Greece 39°30′N 20°16′E
127 T2 **Igra** Udmurtskaya Respublika, NW Russian Federation 57°30′N 53°01′E
122 H9 **Igrim** Khanty-Mansiyskiy Avtonomnyy Okrug-Yugra, N Russian Federation 63°09′N 64°33′E
60 G12 **Iguaçu, Rio** *Sp.* Río Iguazú. ⚐ Argentina/Brazil *see also* Iguazú, Río
Iguaçu, Rio *see* Iguazú, Río
59 I22 **Iguaçu, Salto do** *Sp.* Cataratas del Iguazú; *prev.* Victoria Falls. *waterfall* Argentina/Brazil *see also* Iguazú, Cataratas del
Iguaçu, Salto do *see* Iguazú, Cataratas del
41 O15 **Iguala** *var.* Iguala de la Independencia. Guerrero, S Mexico 18°21′N 99°31′W
105 V5 **Igualada** Cataluña, NE Spain 41°35′N 01°37′E
Iguala de la Independencia *see* Iguala
60 G12 **Iguazú, Cataratas del** *Port.* Salto do Iguaçu; *prev.* Victoria Falls. *waterfall* Argentina/Brazil *see also* Iguaçu, Salto do
Iguazú, Cataratas del *see* Iguaçu, Salto do
62 Q6 **Iguazú, Río** *var.* Rio Iguaçu. ⚐ Argentina/Brazil *see also* Iguaçu, Rio
Iguazú, Río *see* Iguaçu, Rio
79 D19 **Iguéla** *prev.* Iguéla. Ogooué-Maritime, SW Gabon 02°00′S 09°23′E
Iguéla *see* Iguéla
Iguid, Erg *see* Iguidi, 'Erg
67 M5 **Iguidi, 'Erg** *var.* Erg Iguid. *desert* Algeria/Mauritania
172 K2 **Iharaña** *prev.* Vohémar. Antsiranana, NE Madagascar 13°22′S 50°00′E
151 K18 **Ihavandhippolhu Atoll** *var.* Ihavandiffulu Atoll. *atoll* N Maldives
Ihavandiffulu Atoll *see* Ihavandhippolhu Atoll
Ih Bulag *see* Hanbogd
165 T16 **Iheya-jima** *island* Nansei-shotō, SW Japan
Ihhayrhan *see* Bayan-Önjüül
163 N9 **Ihhet** *var.* Bayan. Dornogovĭ, SE Mongolia 46°15′N 110°16′E
172 I6 **Ihosy** Fianarantsoa, S Madagascar 22°23′S 46°09′E
Ihsüüj *see* Bayanchandmanĭ
162 I7 **Ihtamir** *var.* Dzaanhushuu. Arhangay, C Mongolia 47°36′N 101°06′E
162 H6 **Ih-Uul** *var.* Bayan-Uhaa. Dzavhan, C Mongolia 48°41′N 98°46′E
162 J6 **Ih-Uul** *var.* Selenge. Hövsgöl, N Mongolia 49°25′N 101°30′E
93 L14 **Ii** Oulu, C Finland 65°18′N 25°23′E
164 M13 **Iida** Nagano, Honshū, S Japan 35°32′N 137°48′E
93 M14 **Iijoki** ⚐ C Finland
Iinnasuolu *see* Hinnøya
118 J4 **Iisaku** *Ger.* Isaak. Ida-Virumaa, NE Estonia 59°06′N 27°19′E
93 M16 **Iisalmi** *var.* Idensalmi. Itä-Suomi, C Finland 63°32′N 27°10′E
Ii-shima *see* Ie-jima
165 N11 **Iiyama** Nagano, Honshū, S Japan 36°52′N 138°22′E
77 S16 **Ijebu-Ode** Ogun, SW Nigeria 06°46′N 03°57′E
137 U11 **Ijevan** *Rus.* Idzhevan. N Armenia 40°53′N 45°07′E
98 H9 **IJmuiden** Noord-Holland, W Netherlands 52°28′N 04°38′E
98 M12 **IJssel** *var.* Yssel. ⚐ Netherlands
98 J8 **IJsselmeer** *prev.* Zuider Zee. ⊚ N Netherlands
98 L9 **IJsselmuiden** Overijssel, E Netherlands 52°34′N 05°55′E
98 I12 **IJsselstein** Utrecht, C Netherlands 52°01′N 05°02′E
61 G14 **Ijuí** Rio Grande do Sul, S Brazil 28°23′S 53°55′W
61 G14 **Ijuí, Rio** ⚐ S Brazil
189 R8 **Ijuw** NE Nauru 0°30′S 166°57′E
99 E16 **IJzendijke** Zeeland, SW Netherlands 51°20′N 03°36′E
99 A18 **IJzer** ⚐ W Belgium
Ikaahuk *see* Sachs Harbour

◆ Country
● Country Capital
◇ Dependent Territory
○ Dependent Territory Capital
◆ Administrative Regions
✈ International Airport
▲ Mountain
▲ Mountain Range
⛰ Volcano
⚐ River
⊚ Lake
⊠ Reservoir

93 K18 **Ikaalinen** Länsi-Suomi, W Finland 61°46′N 23°05′E
172 I6 **Ikalamavony** Fianarantsoa, SE Madagascar 21°10′S 46°35′E
Ikaluktutiak *see* Cambridge Bay
185 G16 **Ikamatua** West Coast, South Island, New Zealand 42°16′S 171°42′E
145 P16 **Ikan** *prev.* Staroikan. Yuzhnyy Kazakhstan, S Kazakhstan 43°09′N 68°34′E
77 U16 **Ikare** Ondo, SW Nigeria 07°36′N 05°52′E
115 L20 **Ikaría** *var.* Kariot, Nicaria, Nikaria; *anc.* Icaria. *island* Dodekánisa, Greece, Aegean Sea
95 F22 **Ikast** Midtjylland, W Denmark 56°09′N 09°10′E
184 O9 **Ikawhenua Range** ▲▲ North Island, New Zealand
165 U4 **Ikeda** Hokkaidō, NE Japan 42°54′N 143°25′E
164 H14 **Ikeda** Tokushima, Shikoku, SW Japan 34°00′N 133°47′E
77 S16 **Ikeja** Lagos, SW Nigeria 06°36′N 03°16′E
79 L19 **Ikela** Equateur, C Dem. Rep. Congo 01°11′S 23°16′E
114 H10 **Ikhtiman** Sofiya, W Bulgaria 42°26′N 23°49′E
164 C13 **Iki** *prev.* Gônoura. Nagasaki, Iki, SW Japan 33°44′N 129°41′E
164 C13 **Iki** *island* SW Japan
127 O13 **Iki Burul** Respublika Kalmykiya, SW Russian Federation 45°48′N 44°44′E
137 P11 **İkizdere** Rize, NE Turkey 40°47′N 40°34′E
39 P14 **Ikolik, Cape** *headland* Kodiak Island, Alaska, USA 57°12′N 154°46′W
77 V17 **Ikom** Cross River, SE Nigeria 05°57′N 08°43′E
172 I6 **Ikongo** *prev.* Fort-Carnot. Fianarantsoa, SE Madagascar 21°52′S 47°27′E
39 P5 **Ikpikpuk River** ≈ Alaska, USA
190 H1 **Iku** *prev.* Lone Tree Islet. *atoll* Tungaru, W Kiribati
164 I12 **Ikuno** Hyōgo, Honshū, SW Japan 35°13′N 134°48′E
190 H16 **Ikurangi** ▲ Rarotonga, S Cook Islands 21°12′S 159°45′W
171 X14 **Ilaga** Papua, E Indonesia 03°54′S 137°30′E
171 O2 **Ilagan** Luzon, N Philippines 17°08′N 121°54′E
142 J7 **Īlām** *var.* Elam. Īlām, W Iran 33°37′N 46°27′E
153 R12 **Ilām** Eastern, E Nepal 26°52′N 87°58′E
142 J8 **Īlām** *off.* Ostān-e Īlām. ◆ *province* W Iran
Īlām, Ostān-e *see* Īlām
161 T13 **Ilan** *Jap.* Giran. N Taiwan 24°45′N 121°44′E
146 G9 **Ilanly Obvodnitel'nyy Kanal** *canal* N Turkmenistan
122 L12 **Ilanskiy** Krasnoyarskiy Kray, S Russian Federation 56°16′N 95°59′E
108 H9 **Ilanz** Graubünden, S Switzerland 46°46′N 09°10′E
77 S16 **Ilaro** Ogun, SW Nigeria 06°52′N 03°01′E
57 I17 **Ilave** Puno, S Peru 16°07′S 69°40′W
110 K8 **Iława** *Ger.* Deutsch-Eylau. Warmińsko-Mazurskie, NE Poland 53°36′N 19°35′E
121 P16 **Il-Bajja ta' Marsaxlokk** *var.* Marsaxlokk Bay. *bay* SE Malta
123 P10 **Ilbenge** Respublika Sakha (Yakutiya), NE Russian Federation 62°52′N 124°13′E
Ile *see* Ile/Ili He
Ile *see* Ili He
11 S13 **Île-à-la-Crosse** Saskatchewan, C Canada 55°29′N 108°00′W
79 J21 **Ilebo** *prev.* Port-Francqui. Kasai-Occidental, W Dem. Rep. Congo 04°19′S 20°32′E
103 N5 **Île-de-France** ◆ *region* N France
Ilek *see* Yelek
Ilerda *see* Lleida
77 T16 **Ilesha** Osun, SW Nigeria 07°35′N 04°49′E
187 Q16 **Îles Loyauté, Province des** ◆ *province* E New Caledonia
11 X12 **Ilford** Manitoba, C Canada 56°02′N 95°48′W
116 K14 **Ilfov** ◆ *county* S Romania
97 I23 **Ilfracombe** SW England, United Kingdom 51°12′N 04°10′W
136 I11 **Ilgaz Dağları** ▲▲ N Turkey
136 G15 **Ilgın** Konya, W Turkey 38°16′N 31°57′E
60 I7 **Ilha Solteira** São Paulo, S Brazil 20°28′S 51°19′W
104 G7 **Ílhavo** Aveiro, N Portugal 40°36′N 08°40′W
59 O18 **Ilhéus** Bahia, E Brazil 14°50′S 39°06′W
129 R7 **Ili** *var.* Ile, *Chin.* Ili He, *Rus.* Reka Ili. ≈ China/Kazakhstan *see also* Ili He
116 G11 **Ilia** *Hung.* Marosillye. Hunedoara, SW Romania 45°57′N 22°40′E
39 P13 **Iliamna** Alaska, USA 59°42′N 154°49′W
39 P13 **Iliamna Lake** ◎ Alaska, USA
137 N13 **İliç** Erzincan, C Turkey 39°27′N 38°34′E
Il'ichevsk *see* Şärur, Azerbaijan
Il'ichevsk *see* Illichivs'k, Ukraine
Ilici *see* Elche
37 V2 **Iliff** Colorado, C USA 40°46′N 103°04′W
171 Q7 **Iligan** *off.* Iligan City. Mindanao, S Philippines 08°12′N 124°16′E
171 Q7 **Iligan Bay** *bay* S Philippines
Iligan City *see* Iligan
158 I5 **Ili He** *var.* Ili, *Kaz.* Ile, *Rus.* Reka Ili. ≈ China/Kazakhstan *see also* Ile
Ili He *see* Ili
56 C6 **Iliniza** ▲ N Ecuador 0°37′S 78°41′W
Ilinski *see* Il'inskiy
125 U14 **Il'inskiy** *var.* Ilinski. Permskiy Kray, NW Russian Federation 58°33′N 55°31′E
125 U14 **Il'inskiy** Ostrov Sakhalin, Sakhalinskaya Oblast', SE Russian Federation 47°59′N 142°14′E
18 I10 **Ilion** New York, NE USA 43°01′N 75°02′W
38 E9 **'Ilio Point** *var.* Ilio Point. *headland* Moloka'i, Hawai'i, USA 21°13′N 157°15′W
Ilio Point *see* 'Ilio Point
109 T13 **Ilirska Bistrica** *prev.* Bistrica, *Ger.* Feistritz, Illyrisch-Feistritz, *It.* Villa del Nevoso. SW Slovenia 45°34′N 14°12′E
137 Q16 **Ilısu Barajı** ⊠ SE Turkey
155 G17 **Ilkal** Karnātaka, C India 15°59′N 76°08′E
97 M19 **Ilkeston** C England, United Kingdom 52°59′N 01°18′W
121 O16 **Il-Kullana** *headland* SW Malta 35°49′N 14°26′E
108 J8 **Ill** ≈ W Austria
103 U6 **Ill** ≈ NE France
62 G10 **Illapel** Coquimbo, C Chile 31°40′S 71°13′W
Illaue Fartak Trench *see* Alula-Fartak Trench
182 C2 **Illbillee, Mount** ▲ South Australia 27°01′S 132°13′E
102 I6 **Ille-et-Vilaine** ◆ *department* NW France
77 T11 **Illéla** Tahoua, SW Niger 14°25′N 05°10′E
101 J24 **Iller** ≈ S Germany
101 J23 **Illertissen** Bayern, S Germany 48°13′N 10°08′E
105 X9 **Illes Baleares** ◆ *autonomous community* E Spain
105 N8 **Illescas** Castilla-La Mancha, C Spain 40°08′N 03°51′W
Ille-sur-la-Têt *see* Ille-sur-Têt
103 O17 **Ille-sur-Têt** *var.* Ille-sur-la-Têt. Pyrénées-Orientales, S France 42°40′N 02°37′E
Illiberis *see* Elne
117 P11 **Illichivs'k** Rus. Il'ichevsk. Odes'ka Oblast', SW Ukraine 46°18′N 30°36′E
Illicis *see* Elche
102 M6 **Illiers-Combray** Eure-et-Loir, C France 48°18′N 01°15′E
30 K12 **Illinois** *off.* State of Illinois, *also known as* Prairie State, Sucker State. ◆ *state* C USA
30 J13 **Illinois River** ≈ Illinois, N USA
117 N6 **Illintsi** Vinnyts'ka Oblast', C Ukraine 49°07′N 29°13′E
Illiturgis *see* Andújar
74 M10 **Illizi** SE Algeria 26°30′N 08°28′E
27 Y7 **Illmo** Missouri, C USA 37°13′N 89°30′W
Illurco *see* Lorca
Illuro *see* Mataró
Illyrisch-Feistritz *see* Ilirska Bistrica
101 K16 **Ilm** ≈ C Germany
101 K17 **Ilmenau** Thüringen, C Germany 50°40′N 10°55′E
124 H14 **Il'men', Ozero** ◎ NW Russian Federation
57 H18 **Ilo** Moquegua, SW Peru 17°42′S 71°20′W
171 O6 **Iloilo** *off.* Iloilo City. Panay Island, C Philippines 10°42′N 122°34′E
Iloilo City *see* Iloilo
112 K10 **Ilok** *Hung.* Újlak. Vojvodina, NW Serbia 45°12′N 19°22′E
93 O16 **Ilomantsi** Itä-Suomi, SE Finland 62°40′N 30°55′E
42 F8 **Ilopango, Lago de** *volcanic lake* C El Salvador
77 T15 **Ilorin** Kwara, W Nigeria 08°32′N 04°35′E
117 X8 **Ilovays'k** *Rus.* Ilovaysk. Donets'ka Oblast', SE Ukraine 47°55′N 38°14′E
Ilovaysk *see* Ilovays'k
127 O10 **Ilovlya** Volgogradskaya Oblast', SW Russian Federation 49°45′N 44°19′E
127 O10 **Ilovlya** ≈ SW Russian Federation
121 N15 **Il-Ponta ta' San Dimitri** *var.* Ras San Dimitri, San Dimitri Point. *headland* Gozo, NW Malta 36°04′N 14°12′E
126 K14 **Il'skiy** Krasnodarskiy Kray, SW Russian Federation 44°52′N 38°26′E
182 B2 **Iltur** South Australia 27°33′S 130°31′E
171 Y13 **Ilugwa** Papua, E Indonesia 03°42′S 139°09′E
Iluh *see* Batman
118 I11 **Ilūkste** SE Latvia 55°58′N 26°21′E
171 Y13 **Ilur** Pulau Gorong, E Indonesia 04°00′S 131°25′E
32 F10 **Ilwaco** Washington, NW USA 46°19′N 124°03′W
Il'yaly *see* Gurbansoltan Eje
Ilyasbaba Burnu *see* Tekke Burnu
125 U9 **Ilych** ≈ NW Russian Federation
101 O21 **Ilz** ≈ SE Germany
111 M14 **Iłża** Radom, SE Poland 51°09′N 21°15′E
164 G13 **Imabari** *var.* Imaharu. Ehime, Shikoku, SW Japan 34°04′N 132°59′E
Imaharu *see* Imabari
165 O12 **Imaichi** *var.* Imaiti. Tochigi, Honshū, S Japan 36°43′N 139°41′E
Imaiti *see* Imaichi
164 K12 **Imajō** Fukui, Honshū, SW Japan 35°45′N 136°10′E
139 R9 **Imām Ibn Hāshim** Karbalā', C Iraq 32°46′N 43°21′E
149 Q2 **Imām Şāḩib** *var.* Emam Saheb, Hazarat Imam; *prev.* Emām Şāḩeb. Kunduz, NE Afghanistan 37°11′N 68°55′E
139 T11 **Imān 'Abd Allāh** Al Qādisīyah, S Iraq 31°36′N 44°34′E
164 F15 **Imano-yama** ▲ Shikoku, SW Japan 32°51′N 132°48′E
164 C13 **Imari** Saga, Kyūshū, SW Japan 33°18′N 129°51′E
Imarssuak Mid-Ocean Seachannel *see* Imarssuak Seachannel
64 J6 **Imarssuak Seachannel** *var.* Imarssuak Mid-Ocean Seachannel. *channel* N Atlantic Ocean
93 N18 **Imatra** Etelä-Suomi, SE Finland 61°14′N 28°50′E
164 K13 **Imazu** Shiga, Honshū, SW Japan 35°25′N 136°00′E
56 C6 **Imbabura** ◆ *province* N Ecuador
55 R9 **Imbaimadai** W Guyana 05°44′N 60°23′W
61 K14 **Imbituba** Santa Catarina, S Brazil 28°15′S 48°44′W
27 W9 **Imboden** Arkansas, C USA 36°12′N 91°10′W
Imbros *see* Gökçeada
Imeni 26 Bakinskikh Komissarov *see* Uzboý
125 N13 **Imeni Babushkina** Vologodskaya Oblast', NW Russian Federation 59°40′N 43°04′E
126 J7 **Imeni Karla Libknekhta** Kurskaya Oblast', W Russian Federation 51°36′N 35°28′E
Imeni Mollanepesa *see* Mollanepes Adyndaky
Imeni S. A. Niyazova *see* S. A.Nyýazow Adyndaky
Imeni Sverdlova Rudnik *see* Sverdlovs'k
188 E9 **Imeong** Babeldaob, N Palau
81 L14 **İmi** Sumalē, E Ethiopia 06°27′N 42°10′E
115 M21 **Ímia** *Turk.* Kardak. *island* Dodekánisa, Greece, Aegean Sea
Imishli *see* İmişli
137 X12 **İmişli** *Rus.* Imishli. C Azerbaijan 39°54′N 48°04′E
163 X14 **Imjin-gang** ≈ North Korea/South Korea
35 S3 **Imlay** Nevada, W USA 40°39′N 118°10′W
31 S9 **Imlay City** Michigan, N USA 43°01′N 83°04′W
23 X15 **Immokalee** Florida, SE USA 26°24′N 81°25′W
77 U17 **Imo** ◆ *state* SE Nigeria
106 G10 **Imola** Emilia-Romagna, N Italy 44°22′N 11°43′E
186 A5 **Imonda** Sandaun, NW Papua New Guinea 03°21′S 141°10′E
Imoschi *see* Imotski
113 G14 **Imotski** *It.* Imoschi. Split-Dalmacija, SE Croatia 43°28′N 17°13′E
59 L14 **Imperatriz** Maranhão, NE Brazil 05°32′S 47°28′W
106 B10 **Imperia** Liguria, NW Italy 43°53′N 08°03′E
57 E15 **Imperial** Lima, W Peru 13°04′S 76°21′W
35 X17 **Imperial** California, W USA 32°51′N 115°34′W
28 L16 **Imperial** Nebraska, C USA 40°30′N 101°37′W
24 M9 **Imperial** Texas, SW USA 31°15′N 102°40′W
35 Y17 **Imperial Dam** *dam* California, W USA
79 I17 **Impfondo** Likouala, NE Congo 01°37′N 18°04′E
153 X14 **Imphāl** *state capital* Manipur, NE India 24°47′N 93°55′E
103 P9 **Imphy** Nièvre, C France 46°55′N 03°16′E
106 G11 **Impruneta** Toscana, C Italy 43°42′N 11°16′E
115 K15 **İmroz** *var.* Gökçeada. Çanakkale, NW Turkey 40°06′N 25°50′E
Imroz Adası *see* Gökçeada
108 L7 **Imst** Tirol, W Austria 47°14′N 10°45′E
40 F3 **Imuris** Sonora, NW Mexico 30°48′N 110°52′W
164 M13 **Ina** Nagano, Honshū, S Japan 35°52′N 137°58′E
65 M18 **Inaccessible Island** *island* W Tristan da Cunha
115 F20 **Ínachos** ≈ S Greece
188 H6 **I Naftan, Puntan** *headland* Saipan, S Northern Mariana Islands
Inagua Islands *see* Little Inagua
Inagua Islands *see* Great Inagua
185 H15 **Inangahua** West Coast, South Island, New Zealand 41°51′S 171°58′E
57 I14 **Iñapari** Madre de Dios, E Peru 11°00′S 69°34′W
188 B17 **Inarajan** SE Guam 13°16′N 144°45′E
92 L10 **Inari** *Lapp.* Anár, Aanaar. Lappi, N Finland 68°54′N 27°06′E
92 L10 **Inarijärvi** *Lapp.* Aanaarjävri, *Swe.* Enareträsk. ◎ N Finland
92 L9 **Inarijoki** *Lapp.* Anárjohka. ≈ Finland/Norway
Inâu *see* Ineu
165 P11 **Inawashiro-ko** *var.* Inawasiro Ko. ◎ Honshū, C Japan
Inawasiro Ko *see* Inawashiro-ko
105 X9 **Inca** Mallorca, Spain, W Mediterranean Sea 39°43′N 02°54′E
62 H7 **Inca de Oro** Atacama, N Chile 26°45′S 69°54′W
115 J15 **İnce Burnu** *cape* NW Turkey
136 K9 **İnce Burnu** *headland* N Turkey 42°06′N 34°57′E
136 I17 **İncekum Burnu** *headland* S Turkey 36°13′N 33°57′E
163 X15 **Incheon** *Jap.* Jinsen; *prev.* Chemulpo, Inch'ŏn. NW South Korea 37°27′N 126°41′E
76 G7 **Inchiri** ◆ *region* NW Mauritania
161 X15 **Incheon** ✈ (Seoul) NW South Korea 37°37′N 126°42′E
Inch'ŏn *see* Incheon
83 M17 **Inchope** Manica, C Mozambique 19°09′S 33°54′E
Incoronata *see* Kornat
103 Y15 **Incudine, Monte** ▲ Corse, France, C Mediterranean Sea 41°52′N 09°13′E
60 M10 **Indaiatuba** São Paulo, S Brazil 23°03′S 47°14′W
93 H17 **Indal** Västernorrland, C Sweden 62°36′N 17°06′E
93 H17 **Indalsälven** ≈ C Sweden
40 K8 **Inde** Durango, C Mexico 25°55′N 105°10′W
Indefatigable Island *see* Santa Cruz, Isla
35 S10 **Independence** California, W USA 36°48′N 118°14′W
29 X13 **Independence** Iowa, C USA 42°28′N 91°42′W
27 P7 **Independence** Kansas, C USA 37°13′N 95°43′W
20 M4 **Independence** Kentucky, S USA 38°56′N 84°32′W
27 R4 **Independence** Missouri, C USA 39°04′N 94°27′W
21 R8 **Independence** Virginia, NE USA 36°38′N 81°11′W
30 J7 **Independence** Wisconsin, N USA 44°21′N 91°25′W
197 R12 **Independence Fjord** *fjord* N Greenland
Independence Island *see* Malden Island
35 W2 **Independence Mountains** ▲▲ Nevada, W USA
57 K18 **Independencia** Cochabamba, C Bolivia 17°08′S 66°52′W
57 E16 **Independencia, Bahía de la** *bay* W Peru
Independencia, Monte *see* Adam, Mount
116 M12 **Independenţa** Galaţi, SE Romania 45°29′N 27°45′E
Inderagiri *see* Indragiri, Sungai
144 F11 **Inderbor** *prev.* Inderborskiy. Atyrau, W Kazakhstan 48°35′N 51°45′E
Inderborskiy *see* Inderbor
151 I14 **India** *off.* Republic of India, *var.* Indian Union, Union of India, *Hind.* Bhārat. ◆ *republic* S Asia
India *see* Indija
18 D14 **Indiana** Pennsylvania, NE USA 40°37′N 79°09′W
31 N13 **Indiana** *off.* State of Indiana, *also known as* Hoosier State. ◆ *state* N USA
31 O14 **Indianapolis** *state capital* Indiana, N USA 39°46′N 86°09′W
11 O10 **Indian Cabins** Alberta, W Canada 59°51′N 117°06′W
42 G1 **Indian Church** Orange Walk, N Belize 17°47′N 88°39′W
Indian Desert *see* Thar Desert
11 U16 **Indian Head** Saskatchewan, S Canada 50°32′N 103°41′W
31 O4 **Indian Lake** ◎ Michigan, N USA
18 K9 **Indian Lake** ◎ New York, NE USA
31 R13 **Indian Lake** ⊠ Ohio, N USA
172-173 **Indian Ocean** *ocean*
29 V15 **Indianola** Iowa, C USA 41°21′N 93°33′W
22 K4 **Indianola** Mississippi, S USA 33°27′N 90°39′W
36 J6 **Indian Peak** ▲ Utah, W USA 38°18′N 113°52′W
23 Y13 **Indian River** *lagoon* Florida, SE USA
35 W10 **Indian Springs** Nevada, W USA 36°33′N 115°40′W
23 Y14 **Indiantown** Florida, SE USA 27°01′N 80°29′W
Indian Union *see* India
59 K19 **Indiara** Goiás, S Brazil 17°12′S 50°09′W
India, Republic of *see* India
India, Union of *see* India
125 Q4 **Indiga** Nenetskiy Avtonomnyy Okrug, NW Russian Federation 67°40′N 49°01′E
123 R9 **Indigirka** ≈ NE Russian Federation
112 L10 **Inđija** *Hung.* India; *prev.* Indjija. Vojvodina, N Serbia 45°03′N 20°04′E
35 V16 **Indio** California, W USA 33°42′N 116°13′W
42 M12 **Indio, Río** ≈ SE Nicaragua
152 I10 **Indira Gandhi** ✈ (Delhi) Delhi, N India
151 Q23 **Indira Point** *headland* Andaman and Nicobar Island, India, NE Indian Ocean 6°54′N 93°54′E
Indjija *see* Inđija
129 Q13 **Indo-Australian Plate** *tectonic feature*
173 N11 **Indomed Fracture Zone** *tectonic feature* SW Indian Ocean
170 L12 **Indonesia** *off.* Republic of Indonesia, *Ind.* Republik Indonesia; *prev.* Dutch East Indies, Netherlands East Indies, United States of Indonesia. ◆ *republic* SE Asia
Indonesian Borneo *see* Kalimantan
Indonesia, Republic of *see* Indonesia
Indonesia, Republik *see* Indonesia
Indonesia, United States of *see* Indonesia
154 G10 **Indore** Madhya Pradesh, C India 22°42′N 75°51′E
168 L11 **Indragiri, Sungai** *var.* Batang Kuantan, Inderagiri. ≈ Sumatera, W Indonesia
Indramajoe/Indramaju *see* Indramayu
169 P15 **Indramayu** *prev.* Indramajoe, Indramaju. Jawa, C Indonesia 06°22′S 108°20′E
155 K14 **Indrāvati** ≈ S India
103 N9 **Indre** ◆ *department* C France
102 M8 **Indre** ≈ C France
94 D13 **Indre Ålvik** Hordaland, S Norway 60°26′N 06°27′E
102 L8 **Indre-et-Loire** ◆ *department* C France
Indreville *see* Châteauroux
Indus *Chin.* Yindu He; *prev.* Yin-tu Ho. ≈ S Asia
Indus Cone *see* Indus Fan
173 P3 **Indus Fan** *var.* Indus Cone. *undersea feature* N Arabian Sea 16°00′N 66°30′E
149 P17 **Indus, Mouths of the** *delta* S Pakistan
83 I24 **Indwe** Eastern Cape, SE South Africa 31°28′S 27°20′E
136 I10 **İnebolu** Kastamonu, N Turkey 41°57′N 33°45′E
77 P8 **I-n-Échaï** *oasis* C Mali
114 M13 **İnecik** Tekirdağ, NW Turkey 40°55′N 27°16′E
136 E12 **İnegöl** Bursa, NW Turkey 40°06′N 29°31′E
Inessa *see* Biancavilla
116 F10 **Ineu** *Hung.* Borosjenő; *prev.* Inău. Arad, W Romania 46°26′N 21°51′E
Ineul/Ineu, Vîrful *see* Ineu, Vârful
116 J9 **Ineu, Vârful** *var.* Ineul; *prev.* Vîrful Ineu. ▲ N Romania 47°31′N 24°52′E
21 P6 **Inez** Kentucky, S USA 37°53′N 82°33′W
74 E8 **Inezgane** ✈ (Agadir) W Morocco 30°35′N 09°27′W
41 T17 **Inferior, Laguna** *lagoon* S Mexico
40 M15 **Infiernillo, Presa del** ⊠ S Mexico
Infiesto *see* L'Infiestu
93 L20 **Ingå** *Fin.* Inkoo. Etelä-Suomi, S Finland 60°01′N 24°05′E
77 U10 **Ingal** *var.* I-n-Gall. Agadez, C Niger 16°52′N 06°57′E
I-n-Gall *see* Ingal
99 C18 **Ingelmunster** West-Vlaanderen, W Belgium 50°12′N 03°15′E
79 I18 **Ingende** Equateur, W Dem. Rep. Congo 0°15′S 18°58′E
62 L5 **Ingeniero Guillermo Nueva Juárez** Formosa, N Argentina 23°55′S 61°50′W
63 H16 **Ingeniero Jacobacci** Río Negro, C Argentina 41°18′S 69°35′W
14 F16 **Ingersoll** Ontario, S Canada 43°03′N 80°53′W
Ingettolgoy *see* Selenge
181 W5 **Ingham** Queensland, NE Australia 18°35′S 146°12′E
146 M11 **Ingichka** Samarqand Viloyati, C Uzbekistan 39°46′N 65°56′E
97 L16 **Ingleborough** ▲ N England, United Kingdom 54°07′N 02°22′W
25 T14 **Ingleside** Texas, SW USA 27°52′N 97°12′W
184 K10 **Inglewood** Taranaki, North Island, New Zealand 39°07′S 174°13′E
35 S15 **Inglewood** California, W USA 33°57′N 118°21′W
101 L21 **Ingolstadt** Bayern, S Germany 48°46′N 11°26′E
33 V9 **Ingomar** Montana, NW USA 46°34′N 107°21′W
13 R14 **Ingonish Beach** Cape Breton Island, Nova Scotia, SE Canada 46°42′N 60°22′W
153 S14 **Ingrāj Bāzār** *prev.* English Bazar. West Bengal, NE India 25°00′N 88°10′E
25 Q11 **Ingram** Texas, SW USA 30°04′N 99°14′W
195 X7 **Ingrid Christensen Coast** *physical region* Antarctica
74 K14 **I-n-Guezzam** S Algeria 19°35′N 05°49′E
Ingulets *see* Inhulets'
Inguri *see* Enguri
Ingushetia/Ingushetiya, Respublika *see* Ingushetiya, Respublika
127 O15 **Ingushetiya, Respublika** *var.* Respublika Ingushetiya, *Eng.* Ingushetia. ◆ *autonomous republic* SW Russian Federation
83 N20 **Inhambane** Inhambane, SE Mozambique 23°52′S 35°31′E
83 M20 **Inhambane** *off.* Província de Inhambane. ◆ *province* S Mozambique
Inhambane, Província de *see* Inhambane
83 N17 **Inhaminga** Sofala, C Mozambique 18°24′S 35°00′E
83 N20 **Inharrime** Inhambane, SE Mozambique 24°29′S 35°01′E
83 M18 **Inhassoro** Inhambane, E Mozambique 21°32′S 35°13′E
117 S9 **Inhulets'** *Rus.* Ingulets. Dnipropetrovs'ka Oblast', E Ukraine 47°43′N 33°16′E
117 R10 **Inhulets'** *Rus.* Ingulets. ≈ S Ukraine
105 Q10 **Iniesta** Castilla-La Mancha, C Spain 39°27′N 01°45′W
I-ning *see* Yining
54 K11 **Inírida, Río** ≈ E Colombia
Inis *see* Ennis
Inis Ceithleann *see* Enniskillen
Inis Córthaidh *see* Enniscorthy
Inis Díomáin *see* Ennistimon
97 A17 **Inishbofin** *Ir.* Inis Bó Finne. *island* W Ireland
97 B18 **Inisheer** *var.* Inishere, *Ir.* Inis Oírr. *island* W Ireland
Inishere *see* Inisheer
97 B18 **Inishmaan** *Ir.* Inis Meáin. *island* W Ireland
97 A18 **Inishmore** *Ir.* Árainn. *island* W Ireland
96 E13 **Inishtrahull** *Ir.* Inis Trá Tholl. *island* NW Ireland
97 A17 **Inishturk** *Ir.* Inis Toirc. *island* W Ireland
Inkoo *see* Ingå
185 J16 **Inland Kaikoura Range** ▲▲ South Island, New Zealand
Inland Sea *see* Seto-naikai
21 P11 **Inman** South Carolina, SE USA 35°03′N 82°05′W
108 L7 **Inn** ≈ C Europe
197 O11 **Innaanganeq** *var.* Kap York. *headland* NW Greenland 75°54′N 66°27′W
182 K2 **Innamincka** South Australia 27°47′S 140°45′E
92 G12 **Inndyr** Nordland, C Norway 67°01′N 14°00′E
42 G3 **Inner Channel** *inlet* SE Belize
96 F11 **Inner Hebrides** *island group* W Scotland, United Kingdom
172 H15 **Inner Islands** *var.* Central Group. *island group* NE Seychelles
Inner Mongolia/Inner Mongolian Autonomous Region *see* Nei Mongol Zizhiqu
108 I7 **Inner-Rhoden** ◆ *canton* NE Switzerland
96 G8 **Inner Sound** *strait* NW Scotland, United Kingdom
100 J13 **Innerste** ≈ C Germany
181 W5 **Innisfail** Queensland, NE Australia 17°29′S 146°03′E
11 Q15 **Innisfail** Alberta, SW Canada 52°01′N 113°59′W
Inniskilling *see* Enniskillen
39 O11 **Innoko River** ≈ Alaska, USA
Innsbruch *see* Innsbruck
108 M7 **Innsbruck** *var.* Innsbruch. Tirol, W Austria 47°17′N 11°25′E
79 I19 **Inongo** Bandundu, W Dem. Rep. Congo 01°55′S 18°20′E
Inoucdjouac *see* Inukjuak
Inowrazlaw *see* Inowrocław
110 I10 **Inowrocław** *Ger.* Hohensalza; *prev.* Inowrazlaw. Kujawski-pomorskie, C Poland 52°47′N 18°15′E
57 K18 **Inquisivi** La Paz, W Bolivia 16°55′S 67°10′W
Inrin *see* Yuanlin
77 O8 **I-n-Sâkâne, 'Erg** *desert* N Mali
77 O8 **I-n-Sâkâne, 'Erg** *desert* N Mali
74 J10 **I-n-Salah** *var.* In Salah. C Algeria 27°11′N 02°31′E
127 O5 **Insar** Respublika Mordoviya, W Russian Federation 53°52′N 44°26′E
189 X15 **Insiaf** Kosrae, E Micronesia
94 L13 **Insjön** Dalarna, C Sweden 60°40′N 15°05′E
Insterburg *see* Chernyakhovsk
Insula *see* Lille
116 L13 **Însurăţei** Brăila, SE Romania 44°55′N 27°40′E
125 V6 **Inta** Respublika Komi, NW Russian Federation 66°00′N 60°10′E
77 R9 **I-n-Tebezas** Kidal, E Mali 17°58′N 01°51′E
Interamna *see* Teramo
Interamna Nahars *see* Terni
28 L11 **Interior** South Dakota, N USA 43°42′N 101°57′W
108 E9 **Interlaken** Bern, SW Switzerland 46°41′N 07°51′E
29 V2 **International Falls** Minnesota, N USA 48°38′N 93°26′W
167 O7 **Inthanon, Doi** ▲ NW Thailand 18°33′N 98°29′E
42 G7 **Intibucá** ◆ *department* SW Honduras
42 G8 **Intipucá** La Unión, SE El Salvador 13°10′N 88°03′W
61 B15 **Intiyaco** Santa Fe, C Argentina 28°43′S 60°04′W
116 K12 **Întorsura Buzăului** *Ger.* Bozau, *Hung.* Bodzafordulő. Covasna, E Romania 45°40′N 26°02′E
22 H9 **Intracoastal Waterway** *inland waterway system* Louisiana, S USA
25 V13 **Intracoastal Waterway** *inland waterway system* Texas, SW USA
108 G11 **Intragna** Ticino, S Switzerland 46°12′N 08°42′E
165 P14 **Inubō-zaki** *headland* Honshū, S Japan 35°42′N 140°51′E
164 E14 **Inukai** Ōita, Kyūshū, SW Japan 33°05′N 131°37′E
12 I5 **Inukjuak** *var.* Inoucdjouac; *prev.* Port Harrison. Québec, NE Canada 58°28′N 77°58′W
63 I24 **Inútil, Bahía** *bay* S Chile
Inuuvik *see* Inuvik
8 H7 **Inuvik** *var.* Inuuvik. Northwest Territories, NW Canada 68°25′N 133°35′W
164 L13 **Inuyama** Aichi, Honshū, SW Japan 35°23′N 136°56′E
56 G13 **Inuya, Río** ≈ E Peru
125 U13 **In'va** ≈ NW Russian Federation
96 H11 **Inveraray** W Scotland, United Kingdom 56°13′N 05°05′W
185 C24 **Invercargill** Southland, South Island, New Zealand 46°25′S 168°22′E
183 T5 **Inverell** New South Wales, SE Australia 29°46′S 151°10′E
96 I8 **Invergordon** N Scotland, United Kingdom 57°42′N 04°02′W
11 P16 **Invermere** British Columbia, SW Canada 50°30′N 116°00′W
13 R14 **Inverness** Cape Breton Island, Nova Scotia, SE Canada 46°14′N 61°19′W
96 I8 **Inverness** N Scotland, United Kingdom 57°27′N 04°15′W
23 V11 **Inverness** Florida, SE USA 28°50′N 82°19′W
96 J9 **Inverness** *cultural region* NW Scotland, United Kingdom
96 K9 **Inverurie** NE Scotland, United Kingdom 57°14′N 02°14′W
182 F8 **Investigator Group** *island group* South Australia
173 T7 **Investigator Ridge** *undersea feature* E Indian Ocean 11°30′S 98°10′E
182 H10 **Investigator Strait** *strait* South Australia
29 R11 **Inwood** Iowa, C USA 43°16′N 96°25′W
123 S10 **Inya** ≈ E Russian Federation
Inyanga *see* Nyanga
83 M16 **Inyangani** ▲ NE Zimbabwe 18°22′S 32°57′E
83 J17 **Inyathi** Matabeleland North, SW Zimbabwe 19°39′S 28°54′E
35 T12 **Inyokern** California, W USA 35°37′N 117°48′W
35 T10 **Inyo Mountains** ▲▲ California, W USA
127 P6 **Inza** Ul'yanovskaya Oblast', W Russian Federation 53°51′N 46°21′E
127 W5 **Inzer** Respublika Bashkortostan, W Russian Federation 54°11′N 57°37′E
127 N7 **Inzhavino** Tambovskaya Oblast', W Russian Federation 52°18′N 42°28′E
115 C16 **Ioánnina** *var.* Janina, Yannina. Ípeiros, W Greece 39°39′N 20°52′E
164 B17 **Iō-jima** *var.* Iwojima. *island* Nansei-shotō, SW Japan
124 L4 **Iokan'ga** ≈ NW Russian Federation
27 Q6 **Iola** Kansas, C USA 37°55′N 95°24′W
Iolcus *see* Iolkós
115 G16 **Iolkós** *anc.* Iolcus. *site of ancient city* Thessalía, C Greece
Iolotan' *see* Ýolöten
83 A16 **Iona** Namibe, SW Angola 16°54′S 12°39′E
96 F11 **Iona** *island* W Scotland, United Kingdom
116 M15 **Ion Corvin** Constanţa, SE Romania 44°07′N 27°50′E
35 P7 **Ione** California, W USA 38°21′N 120°55′W
116 I13 **Ioneşti** Vâlcea, SW Romania 44°52′N 24°12′E
31 Q9 **Ionia** Michigan, N USA 42°59′N 85°04′W
Ionian Basin *see* Ionian Basin
121 O10 **Ionian Basin** *var.* Ionia Basin. *undersea feature* Ionian Sea, C Mediterranean Sea 36°00′N 20°00′E
115 B17 **Iónia Nisiá** *var.* Iónioi Nísoi, *Eng.* Ionian Islands. *island group* W Greece
Iónian Islands *see* Iónia Nisiá
121 O10 **Ionian Sea** *Gk.* Iónio Pélagos, *It.* Mar Ionio. *sea* C Mediterranean Sea
115 B17 **Iónioi Nísoi** *Eng.* Ionian Islands. ◆ *region* W Greece
Iónioi Nísoi *see* Iónia Nisiá
Ionio, Mar/Iónio Pélagos *see* Ionian Sea
Iordan *see* Yordon
137 U10 **Iori** *var.* Qabırrı. ≈ Azerbaijan/Georgia
Iorrais, Ceann *see* Erris Head
115 J22 **Íos** *var.* Nio. *island* Kykládes, Greece, Aegean Sea
Íos *see* Chóra
165 U15 **Iō-Tori-shima** *prev.* Tori-shima. *island* Izu-shotō, SE Japan
115 I20 **Ioulís** *prev.* Kéa. Tziá, Kykládes, Greece, Aegean Sea 37°40′N 24°19′E
22 G9 **Iowa** Louisiana, S USA 30°12′N 93°00′W
29 V13 **Iowa** *off.* State of Iowa, *also known as* Hawkeye State. ◆ *state* C USA
29 Y14 **Iowa City** Iowa, C USA 41°40′N 91°32′W
29 V13 **Iowa Falls** Iowa, C USA 42°31′N 93°15′W
25 R4 **Iowa Park** Texas, SW USA 33°57′N 98°40′W
29 Y14 **Iowa River** ≈ Iowa, C USA
119 M19 **Ipa** *Rus.* Ipa. ≈ SE Belaeus
Ipa *see* Ipa
59 N20 **Ipatinga** Minas Gerais, SE Brazil 19°32′S 42°30′W
127 N13 **Ipatovo** Stavropol'skiy Kray, SW Russian Federation 45°40′N 42°51′E
115 C16 **Ípeiros** *Eng.* Epirus. ◆ *region* W Greece
111 J21 **Ipel'** *var.* Ipoly, *Ger.* Eipel. ≈ Hungary/Slovakia
54 C13 **Ipiales** Nariño, SW Colombia 0°52′N 77°38′W
189 V14 **Ipis** *atoll* Chuuk Islands, C Micronesia
59 A14 **Ipixuna** Amazonas, W Brazil 06°57′S 71°42′W
168 J8 **Ipoh** Perak, Peninsular Malaysia 04°36′N 101°02′E
Ipoly *see* Ipel'
187 S15 **Ipota** Erromango, S Vanuatu 18°54′S 169°19′E
79 K14 **Ippy** Ouaka, C Central African Republic 06°17′N 21°13′E
114 L13 **İpsala** Edirne, NW Turkey 40°56′N 26°23′E
Ipsario *see* Ypsário
183 V3 **Ipswich** Queensland, E Australia 27°38′S 152°40′E
97 Q20 **Ipswich** *hist.* Gipeswic. E England, United Kingdom 52°05′N 01°08′E
29 O8 **Ipswich** South Dakota, N USA 45°24′N 99°00′W
Iput' *see* Iputs'
119 P18 **Iputs'** *Rus.* Iput'. ≈ Belarus/Russian Federation
9 R7 **Iqaluit** *prev.* Frobisher Bay. *province capital* Baffin Island, Nunavut, NE Canada 63°44′N 68°28′W
Iqlid *see* Eqlīd
62 G3 **Iquique** Tarapacá, N Chile 20°15′S 70°08′W
56 G8 **Iquitos** Loreto, N Peru 03°51′S 73°13′W
25 N9 **Iraan** Texas, SW USA 30°52′N 101°52′W
79 K14 **Ira Banda** Haute-Kotto, E Central African Republic 05°57′N 22°05′E
165 P16 **Irabu-jima** *island* Miyako-shotō, SW Japan
55 Y9 **Iracoubo** N French Guiana 05°28′N 53°15′W
60 H13 **Iraí** Rio Grande do Sul, S Brazil 27°15′S 53°17′W
114 G12 **Irákleia** Kentrikí Makedonía, N Greece 41°09′N 23°16′E
115 J21 **Irákleia** *island* Kykládes, Greece, Aegean Sea
115 J25 **Irákleio** *var.* Herakleion, *Eng.* Candia; *prev.* Iráklion. Kríti, Greece, E Mediterranean Sea 35°20′N 25°08′E
115 F15 **Irákleio** *anc.* Heracleum. *castle* Kentrikí Makedonía, N Greece
115 J25 **Irákleio** ✈ Kríti, Greece, E Mediterranean Sea 35°20′N 25°10′E
Iráklion *see* Irákleio
143 O7 **Iran** *off.* Islamic Republic of Iran; *prev.* Persia. ◆ *republic* SW Asia
58 F13 **Iranduba** Amazonas, NW Brazil 03°19′S 60°09′W
85 P13 **Iranian Plate** *tectonic feature*
143 Q9 **Iranian Plateau** *var.* Plateau of Iran. *plateau* N Iran
Iran, Islamic Republic of *see* Iran
Iran Mountains *see* Iran, Pegunungan
169 U9 **Iran, Pegunungan** *var.* Iran Mountains. ▲▲ Indonesia/Malaysia
Iran, Plateau of *see* Iranian Plateau
143 W13 **Īrānshahr** Sīstān va Balūchestān, SE Iran 27°14′N 60°40′E
55 P5 **Irapa** Sucre, NE Venezuela 10°37′N 62°35′W
41 N13 **Irapuato** Guanajuato, C Mexico 20°40′N 101°23′W
139 R7 **Iraq** *off.* Republic of Iraq, *Ar.* 'Irāq. ◆ *republic* SW Asia
'Irāq *see* Iraq
Iraq, Republic of *see* Iraq
60 J12 **Irati** Paraná, S Brazil 25°25′S 50°38′W
105 R3 **Irati** ≈ N Spain
125 T8 **Irayël'** Respublika Komi, NW Russian Federation 64°28′N 55°20′E
43 N13 **Irazú, Volcán** ⚠ C Costa Rica 09°57′N 83°52′W
Irbenskiy Zaliv/Irbes Šaurums *see* Irbe Strait
118 D7 **Irbe Strait** *Est.* Kura Kurk, *Latv.* Irbes Šaurums, Irbenskiy Zaliv; *prev. Est.* Irbe Väin. *strait* Estonia/Latvia
Irbe Väin *see* Irbe Strait
138 G9 **Irbid** Irbid, N Jordan 32°33′N 35°51′E
138 G9 **Irbid** *off.* Muḩāfaẓat Irbid. ◆ *governorate* N Jordan
Irbid, Muḩāfaẓat *see* Irbid
Irbil *see* Arbīl
109 S6 **Irdning** Steiermark, SE Austria 47°29′N 14°04′E
79 I18 **Irebu** Equateur, W Dem. Rep. Congo 0°32′S 17°44′E
97 D17 **Ireland** *off.* Republic of Ireland, *Ir.* Éire. ◆ *republic* NW Europe
84 C9 **Ireland** *Lat.* Hibernia. *island* Ireland/United Kingdom
64 A12 **Ireland Island North** *island* W Bermuda
64 A12 **Ireland Island South** *island* W Bermuda

◆ Country
● Country Capital
◇ Dependent Territory
○ Dependent Territory Capital
◆ Administrative Regions
✈ International Airport
▲ Mountain
▲▲ Mountain Range
⚠ Volcano
≈ River
◎ Lake
⊠ Reservoir

Ireland, Republic of see Ireland
125 V15 **Iren'** ≈ NW Russian Federation
185 A22 **Irene, Mount** ▲ South Island, New Zealand 45°04′S 167°24′E
Irgalem see Yirga 'Alem
Irgiz see Yrghyz
Irian see New Guinea
Irian Barat see Papua
Irian Jaya see Papua
Irian, Teluk see Cenderawasih, Teluk
78 K9 **Iriba** Biltine, NE Chad 15°10′N 22°11′E
127 X7 **Iriklinskoye Vodokhranilishche** ▣ W Russian Federation
81 H23 **Iringa** Iringa, C Tanzania 07°49′S 35°39′E
81 H23 **Iringa** ◈ region S Tanzania
165 O16 **Iriomote-jima** island Sakishima-shotō, SW Japan
42 L4 **Iriona** Colón, NE Honduras 15°55′N 85°10′W
47 U7 **Iriri** ≈ N Brazil
58 I13 **Iriri, Rio** ≈ C Brazil
Iris see Yeşilırmak
35 W9 **Irish, Mount** ▲ Nevada, W USA 37°39′N 115°22′W
97 H17 **Irish Sea** Ir. Muir Éireann. sea C British Isles
139 U12 **Irjal ash Shaykhīyah** Al Muthannā, S Iraq 30°49′N 44°58′E
147 U11 **Irkeshtam** Oshskaya Oblast', SW Kyrgyzstan 39°39′N 73°49′E
122 M13 **Irkutsk** Irkutskaya Oblast', S Russian Federation 52°18′N 104°15′E
122 M12 **Irkutskaya Oblast'** ◈ province S Russian Federation
Irlir, Gora see Irlir Tog'i
146 K8 **Irlir Tog'i** var. Gora Irlir. ▲ N Uzbekistan 42°43′N 63°24′E
Irminger Basin see Reykjanes Basin
21 R12 **Irmo** South Carolina, SE USA 34°05′N 81°10′W
102 E6 **Iroise** sea NW France
189 X2 **Iroj** var. Eroj. island Ratak Chain, SE Marshall Islands
182 H7 **Iron Baron** South Australia 33°01′S 137°13′E
14 C10 **Iron Bridge** Ontario, S Canada 46°16′N 83°12′W
20 H10 **Iron City** Tennessee, S USA 35°01′N 87°34′W
14 I13 **Irondale** ≈ Ontario, SE Canada
182 H7 **Iron Knob** South Australia 32°46′S 137°08′E
30 M5 **Iron Mountain** Michigan, N USA 45°51′N 88°03′W
30 M4 **Iron River** Michigan, N USA 46°05′N 88°38′W
30 J3 **Iron River** Wisconsin, N USA 46°34′N 91°22′W
27 X6 **Ironton** Missouri, C USA 37°37′N 90°40′W
31 S15 **Ironton** Ohio, N USA 38°32′N 82°40′W
30 K4 **Ironwood** Michigan, N USA 46°27′N 90°10′W
12 H12 **Iroquois Falls** Ontario, S Canada 48°47′N 80°41′W
31 N12 **Iroquois River** ≈ Illinois/Indiana, N USA
164 M15 **Irō-zaki** headland Honshū, S Japan 34°36′N 138°49′E
Irpen' see Irpin'
117 O4 **Irpin'** Rus. Irpen'. Kyyivs'ka Oblast', N Ukraine 50°31′N 30°16′E
117 O4 **Irpin'** Rus. Irpen'. ≈ N Ukraine
141 Q16 **'Irqah** SW Yemen 13°42′N 47°21′E
166 L6 **Irrawaddy** var. Ayeyarwady. ≈ W Myanmar (Burma)
Irrawaddy see Ayeyarwady
166 K8 **Irrawaddy, Mouths of the** delta SW Myanmar (Burma)
117 N4 **Irsha** ≈ N Ukraine
116 H7 **Irshava** Zakarpats'ka Oblast', W Ukraine 48°19′N 23°03′E
107 N18 **Irsina** Basilicata, S Italy 40°42′N 16°18′E
Irtish see Yertis
Irtysh see Yertis
Irtyshsk see Yertis
79 P17 **Irumu** Orientale, E Dem. Rep. Congo 01°27′N 29°52′E
105 Q2 **Irun** Cast. Irún. País Vasco, N Spain 43°20′N 01°48′W
Irún see Irun
Iruña see Pamplona
105 Q3 **Irurtzun** Navarra, N Spain 42°55′N 01°50′W
96 I13 **Irvine** W Scotland, United Kingdom 55°37′N 04°40′W
21 N6 **Irvine** Kentucky, S USA 37°42′N 83°59′W
25 T6 **Irving** Texas, SW USA 32°47′N 96°57′W
20 K5 **Irvington** Kentucky, S USA 37°52′N 86°16′W
164 C15 **Isa** prev. Ōkuchi, Ōkuti. Kagoshima, Kyūshū, SW Japan 32°04′N 130°36′E
Isaak see Iisaku
28 L8 **Isabel** South Dakota, N USA 45°21′N 101°25′W
186 L8 **Isabel** off. Isabel Province. ◈ province N Solomon Islands
171 O8 **Isabela** Basilan Island, SW Philippines 06°41′N 122°00′E
45 S5 **Isabela** W Puerto Rico 18°30′N 67°02′W
45 N8 **Isabela, Cabo** headland NW Dominican Republic 19°54′N 71°03′W
57 A18 **Isabela, Isla** var. Albemarle Island. island Galapagos Islands, Ecuador, E Pacific Ocean
40 I12 **Isabela, Isla** island C Mexico
42 K9 **Isabella, Cordillera** ▲▲ NW Nicaragua
35 S12 **Isabella Lake** ▣ California, W USA
31 N2 **Isabelle, Point** headland Michigan, N USA 47°20′N 87°56′W
Isabel Province see Isabel
Isabel Segunda see Vieques
116 M13 **Isaccea** Tulcea, E Romania 45°16′N 28°28′E
92 H1 **Ísafjarðardjúp** inlet NW Iceland
92 H1 **Ísafjörður** Vestfirdhir, NW Iceland 66°04′N 23°09′W
164 C14 **Isahaya** Nagasaki, Kyūshū, SW Japan 32°51′N 130°02′E
149 S7 **Isa Khel** Punjab, E Pakistan 32°39′N 71°20′E
172 H7 **Isalo** var. Massif de L'Isalo. ▲ SW Madagascar
79 K20 **Isandja** Kasai-Occidental, C Dem. Rep. Congo 03°03′S 21°57′E
187 R15 **Isangel** Tanna, S Vanuatu 19°34′S 169°17′E
79 M18 **Isangi** Orientale, C Dem. Rep. Congo 0°46′N 24°15′E
101 L24 **Isar** ≈ Austria/Germany
101 M23 **Isar-Kanal** canal SE Germany
Isbarta see Isparta
Isca Damnoniorum see Exeter
107 K18 **Ischia** var. Isola d'Ischia; anc. Aenaria. Campania, S Italy 40°44′N 13°57′E
107 J18 **Ischia, Isola d'** island S Italy
54 B12 **Iscuandé** var. Santa Bárbara. Nariño, SW Colombia 02°32′N 78°00′W
164 K14 **Ise** Mie, Honshū, SW Japan 34°29′N 136°43′E
100 J12 **Ise** ≈ N Germany
95 I23 **Isefjord** fjord E Denmark
Iseghem see Izegem
192 M14 **Iselin Seamount** undersea feature S Pacific Ocean 72°30′S 179°00′W
Isenhof see Püssi
106 E7 **Iseo** Lombardia, N Italy 45°40′N 10°03′E
103 U12 **Iseran, Col de l'** pass E France
103 S11 **Isère** ◈ department E France
103 S12 **Isère** ≈ E France
101 F15 **Iserlohn** Nordrhein-Westfalen, W Germany 51°23′N 07°42′E
107 K16 **Isernia** var. Æsernia. Molise, C Italy 41°35′N 14°14′E
165 N12 **Isesaki** Gunma, Honshū, S Japan 36°19′N 139°11′E
129 Q5 **Iset'** ≈ C Russian Federation
77 S15 **Iseyin** Oyo, W Nigeria 07°56′N 03°33′E
Isfahan see Eşfahān
147 Q11 **Isfana** Batkenskaya Oblast', SW Kyrgyzstan 39°51′N 69°31′E
147 R11 **Isfara** N Tajikistan 40°06′N 70°34′E
149 O4 **Isfi Maidān** Gōwr, N Afghanistan 35°09′N 66°16′E
92 O3 **Isfjorden** fjord W Svalbard
Isgender see Kul'mach
Isha Baydhabo see Baydhabo
125 V11 **Isherim, Gora** ▲ NW Russian Federation 61°06′N 59°09′E
127 Q5 **Isheyevka** Ul'yanovskaya Oblast', W Russian Federation 54°27′N 48°18′E
165 P16 **Ishigaki** Okinawa, Ishigaki-jima, SW Japan 24°20′N 124°09′E
165 P16 **Ishigaki-jima** island Sakishima-shotō, SW Japan
165 R3 **Ishikari-wan** bay Hokkaidō, NE Japan
165 S16 **Ishikawa** var. Isikawa. Okinawa, Okinawa, SW Japan 26°25′N 127°47′E
164 K11 **Ishikawa** off. Ishikawa-ken, var. Isikawa. ◈ prefecture Honshū, SW Japan
Ishikawa-ken see Ishikawa
122 H11 **Ishim** Tyumenskaya Oblast', C Russian Federation 56°13′N 69°25′E
127 V6 **Ishimbay** Respublika Bashkortostan, W Russian Federation 53°21′N 56°03′E
145 O9 **Ishimskoye** Akmola, C Kazakhstan 51°23′N 67°07′E
165 Q10 **Ishinomaki** var. Isinomaki. Miyagi, Honshū, C Japan 38°26′N 141°17′E
165 P13 **Ishioka** var. Isioka. Ibaraki, Honshū, S Japan 36°11′N 140°16′E
149 Q3 **Ishkamish** prev. Eshkamesh. Takhār, NE Afghanistan 36°25′N 69°11′E
149 T2 **Ishkāshim** prev. Eshkāshem. Badakhshān, NE Afghanistan 36°43′N 71°34′E
Ishkashim see Ishkoshim
Ishkashimskiy Khrebet see Ishkoshim, Qatorkŭhi
147 S15 **Ishkoshim** Rus. Ishkashim. S Tajikistan 36°46′N 71°35′E
147 S15 **Ishkoshim, Qatorkŭhi** Rus. Ishkashimskiy Khrebet. ▲▲ SE Tajikistan
31 N4 **Ishpeming** Michigan, N USA 46°29′N 87°40′W
147 N11 **Ishtixon** Rus. Ishtykhan. Samarqand Viloyati, C Uzbekistan 39°59′N 66°28′E
Ishtykhan see Ishtixon
Ishurdi see Iswardi
61 G17 **Isidoro Noblia** Cerro Largo, NE Uruguay 31°58′S 54°09′W
102 J4 **Isigny-sur-Mer** Calvados, N France 49°20′N 01°06′W
Isikawa see Ishikawa
136 C11 **Işıklar Dağı** ▲▲ NW Turkey
107 C19 **Isili** Sardegna, Italy, C Mediterranean Sea 39°46′N 09°06′E
122 H12 **Isil'kul'** Omskaya Oblast', C Russian Federation 54°52′N 71°07′E
Isinomaki see Ishinomaki
Isioka see Ishioka
81 I18 **Isiolo** Eastern, C Kenya 0°20′N 37°36′E
79 O16 **Isiro** Orientale, NE Dem. Rep. Congo 02°51′N 27°47′E
92 P2 **Isispynten** headland NE Svalbard 79°51′N 26°44′E
123 P11 **Isit** Respublika Sakha (Yakutiya), NE Russian Federation 60°53′N 125°32′E
149 O2 **Iskabad Canal** canal N Afghanistan
147 Q9 **Iskandar** Rus. Iskander. Toshkent Viloyati, E Uzbekistan 41°32′N 69°46′E
Iskander see Iskandar
Iskăr see Iskŭr
121 Q2 **Iskele** var. Trikomo, Gk. Trikomon. E Cyprus 35°16′N 33°54′E
136 K17 **İskenderun** Eng. Alexandretta. Hatay, S Turkey 36°34′N 36°10′E
138 H2 **İskenderun Körfezi** Eng. Gulf of Alexandretta. gulf S Turkey
136 J11 **İskilip** Çorum, N Turkey 40°45′N 34°28′E
Iski-Nauket see Nookat
114 J11 **Iskra** prev. Popovo. Khaskovo, S Bulgaria 41°55′N 25°12′E
114 G10 **Iskŭr** var. Iskăr. ≈ NW Bulgaria
114 H10 **Iskŭr, Yazovir** prev. Yazovir Stalin. ▣ W Bulgaria
41 S15 **Isla** Veracruz-Llave, SE Mexico 18°01′N 95°30′W
119 J15 **Islach** Rus. Isloch'. ≈ C Belarus
104 H14 **Isla Cristina** Andalucía, S Spain 37°12′N 07°20′W
Isla de León see San Fernando
149 U6 **Islāmābād** ● (Pakistan) Federal Capital Territory Islāmābād, NE Pakistan 33°40′N 73°08′E
149 V6 **Islāmābād** ✈ Federal Capital Territory Islāmābād, NE Pakistan 33°40′N 73°08′E
Islamabad see Anantnāg
149 R17 **Islāmkot** Sind, SE Pakistan 24°37′N 70°04′E
23 Y17 **Islamorada** Florida Keys, Florida, SE USA 24°55′N 80°37′W
153 P14 **Islāmpur** Bihār, N India 25°09′N 85°13′E
Islam Qala see Eslām Qal'eh
18 K16 **Island Beach** spit New Jersey, NE USA
19 S4 **Island Falls** Maine, NE USA 45°59′N 68°16′W
Island/Ísland see Iceland
182 H6 **Island Lagoon** ◎ South Australia
11 Y13 **Island Lake** ◎ Manitoba, C Canada
29 W5 **Island Lake Reservoir** ▣ Minnesota, N USA
33 R13 **Island Park** Idaho, NW USA 44°27′N 111°21′W
19 N6 **Island Pond** Vermont, NE USA 44°48′N 71°51′W
184 K2 **Islands, Bay of** inlet North Island, New Zealand
103 R7 **Is-sur-Tille** Côte d'Or, C France 47°34′N 05°03′E
42 J3 **Islas de la Bahía** ◈ department N Honduras
65 L20 **Islas Orcadas Rise** undersea feature S Atlantic Ocean
96 F12 **Islay** island SW Scotland, United Kingdom
116 I15 **Islaz** Teleorman, S Romania 43°44′N 24°45′E
29 V7 **Isle** Minnesota, N USA 46°08′N 93°28′W
102 M12 **Isle** ≈ W France
97 I16 **Isle of Man** ◇ UK crown dependency NW Europe
21 X7 **Isle of Wight** Virginia, NE USA 36°54′N 76°41′W
97 M24 **Isle of Wight** cultural region S England, United Kingdom
191 Y3 **Isles Lagoon** ◎ Kiritimati, E Kiribati
37 R11 **Isleta Pueblo** New Mexico, SW USA 34°54′N 106°40′W
Isloch' see Islach
61 E19 **Ismael Cortinas** Flores, S Uruguay 33°57′S 57°05′W
Ismailia see Al Ismā'īlīya
Ismâ'ilîya see Al Ismā'īlīya
Ismail see Izmayil
147 S12 **Ismoili Somonī, Qullai** prev. Qullai Kommunizm. ▲ E Tajikistan
75 X10 **Isnā** var. Esna. SE Egypt 25°16′N 32°30′E
93 K18 **Isojoki** Länsi-Suomi, W Finland 62°07′N 22°00′E
82 M12 **Isoka** Northern, NE Zambia 10°08′S 32°43′E
Isola d'Ischia see Ischia
Isola d'Istria see Izola
Isonzo see Soča
15 U4 **Isoukustouc** ≈ Québec, SE Canada
136 F15 **Isparta** var. Isbarta. Isparta, SW Turkey 37°46′N 30°32′E
136 F15 **Isparta** var. Isbarta. ◈ province SW Turkey
114 M7 **Isperikh** prev. Kemanlar. Razgrad, N Bulgaria 43°43′N 26°49′E
107 L26 **Ispica** Sicilia, Italy, C Mediterranean Sea 36°47′N 14°55′E
148 J14 **Ispikān** Baluchistān, SW Pakistan 26°21′N 62°15′E
137 Q12 **İspir** Erzurum, NE Turkey 40°29′N 41°02′E
138 E12 **Israel** off. State of Israel, var. Medinat Israel, Heb. Yisrael, Yisra'el. ◆ republic SW Asia
Israel, State of see Israel
Issa see Vis
55 S9 **Issano** C Guyana 05°49′N 59°28′W
76 M16 **Issia** SW Ivory Coast 06°33′N 06°33′W
Issiq Kŭl see Issyk-Kul', Ozero
103 P11 **Issoire** Puy-de-Dôme, C France 45°33′N 03°15′E
103 N9 **Issoudun** anc. Uxellodunum. Indre, C France 46°57′N 01°59′E
81 H22 **Issuna** Singida, C Tanzania 05°24′S 34°48′E
Issyk see Yesik
Issyk-Kul' see Balykchy
147 X7 **Issyk-Kul', Ozero** var. Issiq Köl, Kir. Ysyk-Köl. ◎ E Kyrgyzstan
147 X7 **Issyk-Kul'skaya Oblast'** Kir. Ysyk-Köl Oblasty. ◈ province E Kyrgyzstan
149 Q7 **Istādeh-ye Moqor, Āb-e-** var. Āb-i-Istāda. ◎ SE Afghanistan
136 D11 **İstanbul** Bul. Tsarigrad, Eng. Istanbul, prev. Constantinople; anc. Byzantium. İstanbul, NW Turkey 41°02′N 28°57′E
114 P12 **İstanbul** ◈ province NW Turkey
114 P12 **İstanbul Boğazı** var. Bosporus Thracius, Eng. Bosphorus, Bosporus, Turk. Karadeniz Boğazi. strait NW Turkey
Istarska Županija see Istra
115 G19 **Isthmía** Pelopónnisos, S Greece 37°55′N 23°02′E
115 G17 **Istiaía** Évvoia, C Greece 38°57′N 23°09′E
54 D9 **Istmina** Chocó, W Colombia 05°09′N 76°42′W
23 W13 **Istokpoga, Lake** ◎ Florida, SE USA
112 A9 **Istra** off. Istarska Županija. ◈ province NW Croatia
112 I10 **Istra** Eng. Istria, Ger. Istrien. cultural region NW Croatia
103 R15 **Istres** Bouches-du-Rhône, SE France 43°30′N 04°59′E
Istria/Istrien see Istra
153 T15 **Iswardi** var. Ishurdi. Rajshahi, W Bangladesh 24°10′N 89°04′E
127 V7 **Isyangulovo** Respublika Bashkortostan, W Russian Federation 52°10′N 56°38′E
62 O6 **Itá** Central, S Paraguay 25°29′S 57°21′W
59 O17 **Itaberaba** Bahia, E Brazil 12°34′S 40°21′W
59 M20 **Itabira** prev. Presidente Vargas. Minas Gerais, SE Brazil 19°39′S 43°14′W
59 O18 **Itabuna** Bahia, E Brazil 14°48′S 39°18′W
59 J18 **Itacaiu** Mato Grosso, S Brazil 14°49′S 51°21′W
58 G12 **Itacoatiara** Amazonas, N Brazil 03°06′S 58°22′W
54 D9 **Itagüí** Antioquia, W Colombia 06°12′N 75°40′W
60 D13 **Itá Ibaté** Corrientes, NE Argentina 27°27′S 57°24′W
60 G11 **Itaipú, Represa de** ▣ Brazil/Paraguay
58 H13 **Itaituba** Pará, NE Brazil 04°15′S 55°56′W
60 K13 **Itajaí** Santa Catarina, S Brazil 26°50′S 48°39′W
Italia/Italiana, Republica/Italian Republic, The see Italy
Italian Somaliland see Somalia
25 T7 **Italy** Texas, SW USA 32°10′N 96°52′W
106 G12 **Italy** off. The Italian Republic, It. Italia, Repubblica Italiana. ◆ republic S Europe
59 O19 **Itamaraju** Bahia, E Brazil 16°58′S 39°32′W
59 C14 **Itamarati** Amazonas, W Brazil 06°13′S 68°17′W
59 M19 **Itambé, Pico de** ▲ SE Brazil 18°23′S 43°21′W
164 J13 **Itami** ✈ (Ōsaka) Ōsaka, Honshū, SW Japan 34°47′N 135°24′E
115 H15 **Ítamos** ▲ N Greece 40°06′N 23°51′E
153 W11 **Itānagar** state capital Arunāchal Pradesh, NE India 27°02′N 93°38′E
Itany see Litani
59 N19 **Itaobim** Minas Gerais, SE Brazil 16°34′S 41°27′W
59 P15 **Itaparica, Represa de** ▣ E Brazil
58 M13 **Itapecuru-Mirim** Maranhão, E Brazil 03°24′S 44°20′W
60 Q8 **Itaperuna** Rio de Janeiro, SE Brazil 21°14′S 41°51′W
59 O18 **Itapetinga** Bahia, E Brazil 15°17′S 40°16′W
60 L10 **Itapetininga** São Paulo, S Brazil 23°36′S 48°07′W
60 K10 **Itapeva** São Paulo, S Brazil 23°58′S 48°54′W
47 W6 **Itapicuru, Rio** ≈ NE Brazil
58 O13 **Itapipoca** Ceará, E Brazil 03°29′S 39°35′W
60 M9 **Itapira** São Paulo, S Brazil 22°25′S 46°46′W
60 K8 **Itápolis** São Paulo, S Brazil 21°36′S 48°43′W
60 K10 **Itaporanga** São Paulo, S Brazil 23°43′S 49°28′W
62 P7 **Itapúa** off. Departamento de Itapúa. ◈ department SE Paraguay
Itapúa, Departamento de see Itapúa
59 E15 **Itapuã do Oeste** Rondônia, W Brazil 09°21′S 63°07′W
61 E15 **Itaqui** Rio Grande do Sul, S Brazil 29°10′S 56°28′W
60 K10 **Itararé** São Paulo, S Brazil 24°07′S 49°16′W
60 K10 **Itararé, Rio** ≈ S Brazil
154 H11 **Itārsi** Madhya Pradesh, C India 22°39′N 77°48′E
25 T7 **Itasca** Texas, SW USA 32°09′N 97°09′W
Itassi see Vieille Case
60 D13 **Itatí** Corrientes, NE Argentina 27°16′S 58°15′W
60 K10 **Itatinga** São Paulo, S Brazil 23°08′S 48°36′W
115 F18 **Itéas, Kólpos** gulf C Greece
57 N15 **Iténez, Río** var. Rio Guaporé. ≈ Bolivia/Brazil see also Rio Guaporé
Iténez, Río see Guaporé, Rio
54 H11 **Iteviate, Río** ≈ C Colombia
100 I13 **Ith** hill range C Germany
31 Q8 **Ithaca** Michigan, N USA 43°17′N 84°36′W
18 H11 **Ithaca** New York, NE USA 42°26′N 76°30′W
115 C18 **Itháki** island Iónia Nisiá, Greece, C Mediterranean Sea
Itháki see Vathy
It Hearrenfean see Heerenveen
79 L17 **Itimbiri** ≈ N Dem. Rep. Congo
Itinomiya see Ichinomiya
Itinoseki see Ichinoseki
39 Q5 **Itkilik River** ≈ Alaska, USA
164 M11 **Itoigawa** Niigata, Honshū, C Japan 37°02′N 137°53′E
15 R6 **Itomamo, Lac** ◎ Québec, SE Canada
165 S17 **Itoman** Okinawa, SW Japan 26°05′N 127°40′E
102 M5 **Iton** ≈ N France
57 M16 **Itonamas Río** ≈ NE Bolivia
Itoupé, Mont see Sommet Tabulaire
Itseqqortoormiit see Ittoqqortoormiit
22 K4 **Itta Bena** Mississippi, S USA 33°30′N 90°19′W
107 B17 **Ittiri** Sardegna, Italy, C Mediterranean Sea 40°36′N 08°34′E
197 Q14 **Ittoqqortoormiit** var. Itseqqortoormiit, Dan. Scoresbysund, Eng. Scoresby Sound. Tunu, C Greenland 70°33′N 21°52′W
60 M10 **Itu** São Paulo, S Brazil 23°17′S 47°16′W
54 D8 **Ituango** Antioquia, NW Colombia 07°07′N 75°46′W
59 A14 **Ituí, Rio** ≈ NW Brazil
79 O20 **Itula** Sud-Kivu, E Dem. Rep. Congo 03°30′S 27°50′E
59 K19 **Itumbiara** Goiás, C Brazil 18°25′S 49°15′W
55 T9 **Ituni** E Guyana 05°24′N 58°18′W
41 X13 **Iturbide** Campeche, SE Mexico 19°41′N 89°29′W
Ituri see Aruwimi
123 V13 **Iturup, Ostrov** island Kuril'skiye Ostrova, SE Russian Federation
60 L7 **Ituverava** São Paulo, S Brazil 20°22′S 47°48′W
59 C15 **Ituxi, Rio** ≈ W Brazil
61 E14 **Ituzaingó** Corrientes, NE Argentina 27°34′S 56°44′W
101 K18 **Itz** ≈ C Germany
100 I9 **Itzehoe** Schleswig-Holstein, N Germany 53°56′N 09°31′E
23 N2 **Iuka** Mississippi, S USA 34°48′N 88°11′W
60 I11 **Ivaiporã** Paraná, S Brazil 24°16′S 51°46′W
60 I11 **Ivaí, Rio** ≈ S Brazil
92 L10 **Ivalo** Lapp. Avveel, Avvil. Lappi, N Finland 68°34′N 27°29′E
92 L10 **Ivalojoki** Lapp. Avveel. ≈ N Finland
119 H20 **Ivanava** Pol. Janów, Janów Poleski, Rus. Ivanovo. Brestskaya Voblasts', SW Belarus 52°09′N 25°32′E
79 F18 **Ivando** var. Djidji. ≈ Congo/Gabon
Ivangorod see Dęblin
Ivangrad see Berane
183 N7 **Ivanhoe** New South Wales, SE Australia 32°55′S 144°21′E
29 S9 **Ivanhoe** Minnesota, N USA 44°27′N 96°15′W
14 D8 **Ivanhoe** ≈ Ontario, S Canada
112 E8 **Ivanić-Grad** Sisak-Moslavina, N Croatia 45°43′N 16°23′E
117 T10 **Ivanivka** Khersons'ka Oblast', S Ukraine 46°43′N 34°28′E
117 P10 **Ivanivka** Odes'ka Oblast', SW Ukraine 46°57′N 30°26′E
113 L14 **Ivanjica** Serbia, C Serbia 43°36′N 20°14′E
112 G11 **Ivanjska** var. Potkozarje. Republika Srpska, NW Bosnia and Herzegovina 44°54′N 17°04′E
111 H21 **Ivanka** ✈ (Bratislava) Bratislavský Kraj, W Slovakia 48°10′N 17°13′E
117 O3 **Ivankiv** Rus. Ivankov. Kyyivs'ka Oblast', N Ukraine 50°55′N 29°53′E
Ivankov see Ivankiv
39 O15 **Ivanof Bay** Alaska, USA 55°55′N 159°28′W
116 J7 **Ivano-Frankivs'k** Ger. Stanislau, Pol. Stanisławów, Rus. Ivano-Frankovsk; prev. Stanislav. Ivano-Frankivs'ka Oblast', W Ukraine 48°55′N 24°45′E
Ivano-Frankivs'k see Ivano-Frankivs'ka Oblast'
116 I7 **Ivano-Frankivs'ka Oblast'** var. Ivano-Frankivs'k, Rus. Ivano-Frankovskaya Oblast'; prev. Stanislavskaya Oblast'. ◈ province W Ukraine
Ivano-Frankovsk see Ivano-Frankivs'k
Ivano-Frankovskaya Oblast' see Ivano-Frankivs'ka Oblast'
124 M16 **Ivanovo** Ivanovskaya Oblast', W Russian Federation 57°02′N 40°58′E
Ivanovo see Ivanava
124 M16 **Ivanovskaya Oblast'** ◈ province W Russian Federation
35 X12 **Ivanpah Lake** ◎ California, W USA
112 E7 **Ivanščica** ▲▲ NE Croatia
127 R7 **Ivanteyevka** Saratovskaya Oblast', W Russian Federation 52°13′N 49°06′E
Ivantsevichi/Ivatsevichi see Ivatsevichy
116 I4 **Ivanychi** Volyns'ka Oblast', NW Ukraine 50°37′N 24°22′E
119 H18 **Ivatsevichy** Pol. Iwacewicze, Rus. Ivantsevichi, Ivatsevichi. Brestskaya Voblasts', SW Belarus 52°43′N 25°21′E
114 L12 **Ivaylovgrad** Khaskovo, S Bulgaria 41°32′N 26°06′E
114 K11 **Ivaylovgrad, Yazovir** ▣ S Bulgaria
122 G9 **Ivdel'** Sverdlovskaya Oblast', C Russian Federation 60°42′N 60°07′E
Ivenets see Ivyanyets
116 L12 **Iveşti** Galaţi, E Romania 45°27′N 28°00′E
Ivgovuotna see Lyngen
Ivigtut see Ivittuut
59 I21 **Ivinheima** Mato Grosso do Sul, SW Brazil 22°16′S 53°52′W
196 M15 **Ivittuut** var. Ivigtut. Kitaa, S Greenland 61°12′N 48°10′W
Iviza see Eivissa/Ibiza
172 I6 **Ivohibe** Fianarantsoa, SE Madagascar 22°28′S 46°53′E
Ivoire, Côte d' see Ivory Coast
76 L15 **Ivory Coast** off. Republic of the Ivory Coast, Fr. Côte d'Ivoire, République de la Côte d'Ivoire. ◆ republic W Africa
68 C12 **Ivory Coast** Fr. Côte d'Ivoire. coastal region S Ivory Coast
Ivory Coast, Republic of the see Ivory Coast
95 L22 **Ivösjön** ◎ S Sweden
106 B7 **Ivrea** anc. Eporedia. Piemonte, NW Italy 45°28′N 07°52′E
12 J2 **Ivujivik** Québec, NE Canada 62°26′N 77°49′W
119 J16 **Ivyanyets** Rus. Ivenets. Minskaya Voblasts', C Belarus 53°53′N 26°45′E
Iv'ye see Iwye
Iwacewicze see Ivatsevichy
165 R8 **Iwaizumi** Iwate, Honshū, NE Japan 39°48′N 141°46′E
165 P12 **Iwaki** Fukushima, Honshū, N Japan 37°01′N 140°52′E
164 F13 **Iwakuni** Yamaguchi, Honshū, SW Japan 34°08′N 132°06′E
165 S4 **Iwamizawa** Hokkaidō, NE Japan 43°12′N 141°47′E
165 R4 **Iwanai** Hokkaidō, NE Japan 42°51′N 140°21′E
165 Q10 **Iwanuma** Miyagi, Honshū, C Japan 38°06′N 140°51′E
164 L14 **Iwata** Shizuoka, Honshū, S Japan 34°42′N 137°51′E
165 R8 **Iwate** Iwate, Honshū, N Japan 40°03′N 141°12′E
165 R8 **Iwate** off. Iwate-ken. ◈ prefecture Honshū, C Japan
Iwate-ken see Iwate
77 S16 **Iwo** Oyo, SW Nigeria 07°21′N 03°58′E
Iwojima see Iō-jima
119 I16 **Iwye** Pol. Iwje, Rus. Iv'ye. Hrodzyenskaya Voblasts', W Belarus 53°56′N 25°46′E
42 C4 **Ixcán, Río** ≈ Guatemala/Mexico
99 G18 **Ixelles** Dut. Elsene. Brussels, C Belgium 50°49′N 04°21′E
57 J16 **Ixiamas** La Paz, NW Bolivia 13°45′S 68°10′W
41 O13 **Ixmiquilpan** var. Ixmiquilpán. Hidalgo, C Mexico 20°30′N 99°15′W
Ixmiquilpán see Ixmiquilpan
83 K23 **Ixopo** KwaZulu/Natal, E South Africa 30°10′S 30°05′E
Ixtaccíhuatal, Volcán see Iztaccíhuatl, Volcán
40 M16 **Ixtapa** Guerrero, S Mexico 17°38′N 101°29′W
41 S16 **Ixtepec** Oaxaca, SE Mexico 16°32′N 95°03′W
40 K12 **Ixtlán** var. Ixtlán del Río. Nayarit, C Mexico 21°02′N 104°21′W
Ixtlán del Río see Ixtlán
122 H11 **Iyevlevo** Tyumenskaya Oblast', C Russian Federation 57°36′N 67°20′E
164 F14 **Iyo** Ehime, Shikoku, SW Japan 33°43′N 132°42′E
164 E14 **Iyo-nada** sea S Japan
42 E4 **Izabal** off. Departamento de Izabal. ◈ department E Guatemala
Izabal, Departamento de see Izabal
42 F5 **Izabal, Lago de** prev. Golfo Dulce. ◎ E Guatemala
143 O9 **Īzad Khvāst** Fārs, C Iran 31°31′N 52°09′E
41 X12 **Izamal** Yucatán, SE Mexico 20°58′N 89°00′W
127 Q16 **Izberbash** Respublika Dagestan, SW Russian Federation 42°32′N 47°51′E
99 C18 **Izegem** prev. Iseghem. West-Vlaanderen, W Belgium 50°55′N 03°13′E
142 M9 **Īzeh** Khūzestān, SW Iran 31°48′N 49°49′E
165 T16 **Izena-jima** island Nansei-shotō, SW Japan
114 N10 **Izgrev** Burgas, E Bulgaria 42°09′N 27°49′E
127 T2 **Izhevsk** prev. Ustinov. Udmurtskaya Respublika, NW Russian Federation 56°48′N 53°12′E
125 S7 **Izhma** Respublika Komi, NW Russian Federation 64°56′N 53°52′E
125 S7 **Izhma** ≈ NW Russian Federation
141 X8 **Izkī** NE Oman 22°45′N 57°36′E
Izmail see Izmayil
117 N13 **Izmayil** Rus. Izmail. Odes'ka Oblast', SW Ukraine 45°19′N 28°49′E
136 B14 **İzmir** prev. Smyrna. İzmir, W Turkey 38°25′N 27°10′E
136 C14 **İzmir** prev. Smyrna. ◈ province W Turkey
136 E11 **İzmit** var. Ismid; anc. Astacus. Kocaeli, NW Turkey 40°47′N 29°55′E
104 M14 **Iznájar** Andalucía, S Spain 37°17′N 04°16′W
104 M14 **Iznajar, Embalse de** ▣ S Spain
105 N14 **Iznalloz** Andalucía, S Spain 37°23′N 03°31′W
136 E11 **İznik** Bursa, NW Turkey 40°27′N 29°43′E
136 E12 **İznik Gölü** ◎ NW Turkey
126 M14 **Izobil'nyy** Stavropol'skiy Kray, SW Russian Federation 45°22′N 41°40′E
109 S13 **Izola** It. Isola d'Istria. SW Slovenia 45°31′N 13°40′E
138 H9 **Izra'** var. Ezra, Ezraa. Dar'ā, S Syria 32°52′N 36°15′E
41 P14 **Iztaccíhuatl, Volcán** var. Volcán Ixtaccíhuatal. Ѫ S Mexico 19°07′N 98°37′W
42 C7 **Iztapa** Escuintla, SE Guatemala 13°58′N 90°42′W
Izúcar de Matamoros see Matamoros
165 N14 **Izu-hantō** peninsula Honshū, S Japan
Izuhara see Tsushima
164 J14 **Izumiōtsu** Ōsaka, Honshū, SW Japan 34°29′N 135°25′E
164 I14 **Izumisano** Ōsaka, Honshū, SW Japan 34°23′N 135°18′E
164 G12 **Izumo** Shimane, Honshū, SW Japan 35°22′N 132°46′E
192 H5 **Izu Trench** undersea feature NW Pacific Ocean
122 K6 **Izvestiy TsIK, Ostrova** island N Russian Federation
114 G10 **Izvor** Pernik, W Bulgaria 42°27′N 22°53′E
116 L5 **Izyaslav** Khmel'nyts'ka Oblast', W Ukraine 50°08′N 26°53′E
117 W6 **Izyum** Kharkivs'ka Oblast', E Ukraine 49°12′N 37°19′E

J

93 M18 **Jaala** Etelä-Suomi, S Finland 61°04′N 26°30′E
140 J5 **Jabal ash Shifā** desert NW Saudi Arabia
141 U8 **Jabal az Ẓannah** var. Jebel Dhanna. Abū Ẓaby, W United Arab Emirates 24°10′N 52°36′E
138 E11 **Jabalia** var. Jabāliyah. NE Gaza Strip 31°32′N 34°29′E
Jabāliyah see Jabalia
105 N11 **Jabalón** ≈ C Spain
154 J10 **Jabalpur** prev. Jubbulpore. Madhya Pradesh, C India 23°10′N 79°59′E
141 N15 **Jabal Zuqar, Jazirat** var. Az Zuqur. island SW Yemen
Jabat see Jabwot
138 J3 **Jabbūl, Sabkhat al** sabkha NW Syria
181 P1 **Jabiru** Northern Territory, N Australia 12°44′S 132°48′E
138 H4 **Jablah** var. Jeble, Fr. Djéblé. Al Lādhiqīyah, W Syria 35°00′N 36°00′E
112 C11 **Jablanac** Lika-Senj, W Croatia 44°43′N 14°54′E
113 H14 **Jablanica** Federacija Bosna I Hercegovina, SW Bosnia and Herzegovina 43°39′N 17°43′E
113 M20 **Jablanica** Alb. Mali i Jablanicës, var. Malet e Jabllanicës. ▲▲ Albania/FYR Macedonia see also Jablanicës, Mali i
Jablanicës, Malet e see Jablanica/Jablanicës, Mali i
113 M20 **Jablanicës, Mali i**, Mac. Jablanica. ▲ Albania/FYR Macedonia see also Jablanica
111 E15 **Jablonec nad Nisou** Ger. Gablonz an der Neisse. Liberecký Kraj, N Czech Republic 50°44′N 15°10′E
Jabłonków/Jablunkau see Jablunkov
110 J9 **Jabłonowo Pomorskie** Kujawski-pomorskie, C Poland 53°24′N 19°08′E
111 J17 **Jablunkov** Ger. Jablunkau, Pol. Jabłonków. Moravskoslezský Kraj, E Czech Republic 49°35′N 18°46′E
59 Q15 **Jaboatão** Pernambuco, E Brazil 08°05′S 35°W
60 L8 **Jaboticabal** São Paulo, S Brazil 21°15′S 48°17′W
189 U7 **Jabwot** var. Jabat, Jebat, Jōwat. island Ralik Chain, S Marshall Islands
105 S4 **Jaca** Aragón, NE Spain 42°34′N 00°33′W
42 B4 **Jacaltenango** Huehuetenango, W Guatemala 15°39′N 91°46′W
59 G14 **Jacaré-a-Canga** Pará, NE Brazil 05°59′S 57°32′W
60 N10 **Jacareí** São Paulo, S Brazil 23°18′S 45°55′W
59 I18 **Jaciara** Mato Grosso, W Brazil 15°59′S 54°57′W
59 E15 **Jaciparaná** Rondônia, W Brazil 09°20′S 64°28′W
19 P5 **Jackman** Maine, NE USA 45°35′N 70°14′W
35 X1 **Jackpot** Nevada, W USA 41°57′N 114°41′W
20 M8 **Jacksboro** Tennessee, S USA 36°19′N 84°11′W
25 S6 **Jacksboro** Texas, SW USA 33°13′N 98°11′W
23 N7 **Jackson** Alabama, S USA 31°30′N 87°53′W
35 P7 **Jackson** California, W USA 38°19′N 120°46′W
23 T4 **Jackson** Georgia, SE USA 33°17′N 83°58′W
21 O6 **Jackson** Kentucky, S USA 37°32′N 83°24′W
22 J8 **Jackson** Louisiana, S USA 30°50′N 91°13′W
31 Q10 **Jackson** Michigan, N USA 42°15′N 84°24′W
29 T11 **Jackson** Minnesota, N USA 43°38′N 95°00′W
22 K5 **Jackson** state capital Mississippi, S USA 32°19′N 90°12′W
27 Y7 **Jackson** Missouri, C USA 37°23′N 89°40′W
21 W8 **Jackson** North Carolina, SE USA 36°24′N 77°25′W
31 T15 **Jackson** Ohio, NE USA 39°03′N 82°40′W
20 G9 **Jackson** Tennessee, S USA 35°37′N 88°50′W
33 S14 **Jackson** Wyoming, C USA 43°28′N 110°45′W
185 C19 **Jackson Bay** bay South Island, New Zealand
186 E9 **Jackson Field** ✈ (Port Moresby) Central/National Capital District, S Papua New Guinea 09°28′S 147°12′E
185 C20 **Jackson Head** headland South Island, New Zealand 43°57′S 168°38′E
23 S8 **Jackson, Lake** ◎ Florida, SE USA
33 S13 **Jackson Lake** ◎ Wyoming, C USA
194 J6 **Jackson, Mount** ▲ Antarctica 71°43′S 63°45′W
37 U3 **Jackson Reservoir** ◎ Colorado, C USA
23 Q3 **Jacksonville** Alabama, S USA 33°48′N 85°45′W
27 V11 **Jacksonville** Arkansas, C USA 34°52′N 92°08′W
23 W8 **Jacksonville** Florida, SE USA 30°20′N 81°39′W
30 K14 **Jacksonville** Illinois, N USA 39°43′N 90°13′W
21 W11 **Jacksonville** North Carolina, SE USA 34°45′N 77°26′W
25 W7 **Jacksonville** Texas, SW USA 31°57′N 95°16′W
23 X9 **Jacksonville Beach** Florida, SE USA 30°17′N 81°23′W
44 L9 **Jacmel** var. Jaquemel. S Haiti 18°13′N 72°33′W
Jacob see Nkayi
149 Q12 **Jacobābād** Sind, SE Pakistan 28°16′N 68°30′E
55 T11 **Jacobs Ladder Falls** waterfall S Guyana
45 O11 **Jaco, Pointe** headland N Dominica 15°38′N 61°25′W
15 Q9 **Jacques-Cartier** ≈ Québec, SE Canada
13 P11 **Jacques-Cartier, Détroit de** var. Jacques-Cartier Passage. strait Gulf of St. Lawrence/St. Lawrence River, Canada
15 W6 **Jacques-Cartier, Mont** ▲ Québec, SE Canada 48°58′N 66°00′W
Jacques-Cartier Passage see Jacques-Cartier, Détroit de
61 H16 **Jacuí, Rio** ≈ S Brazil
60 L11 **Jacupiranga** São Paulo, S Brazil 24°42′S 48°00′W
100 G10 **Jade** ≈ NW Germany
100 G10 **Jadebusen** bay NW Germany
Jadotville see Likasi
Jadransko More/Jadransko Morje see Adriatic Sea
105 O7 **Jadraque** Castilla-La Mancha, C Spain 40°55′N 02°55′W
95 I22 **Jægerspris** Hovedstaden, E Denmark 55°52′N 11°59′E
56 C10 **Jaén** Cajamarca, N Peru 05°45′S 78°51′W
105 N13 **Jaén** Andalucía, SW Spain 37°46′N 03°48′W
105 N13 **Jaén** ◈ province Andalucía, S Spain
95 C17 **Jæren** physical region S Norway
155 J23 **Jaffna** Northern Province, N Sri Lanka 09°42′N 80°03′E
155 K23 **Jaffna Lagoon** lagoon N Sri Lanka
19 N10 **Jaffrey** New Hampshire, NE USA 42°46′N 72°00′W
138 H13 **Jafr, Qā' al** var. El Jafr. salt pan S Jordan
152 J9 **Jagādhri** Haryāna, N India 30°11′N 77°18′E
118 H4 **Jägala** var. Jägala Jõgi, Ger. Jaggowal. ≈ NW Estonia
Jägala Jõgi see Jägala
Jagannath see Puri
155 L14 **Jagdalpur** Chhattīsgarh, C India 19°07′N 82°04′E

◆ Country
● Country Capital
◇ Dependent Territory
○ Dependent Territory Capital
◈ Administrative Regions
✈ International Airport
▲ Mountain
▲▲ Mountain Range
Ѫ Volcano
≈ River
◎ Lake
▣ Reservoir

163 U5 **Jagdaqi** Nei Mongol Zizhiqu, N China 50°26′N 124°03′E
Jägerndorf *see* Krnov
Jaggowal *see* Jägala
139 O2 **Jaghjaghah, Nahr** ≈ N Syria
112 N13 **Jagodina** *prev.* Svetozarevo. Serbia, C Serbia 43°59′N 21°15′E
112 K12 **Jagodnja** ▲▲ W Serbia
101 I20 **Jagst** ≈ SW Germany
155 I14 **Jagtiāl** Andhra Pradesh, C India 18°49′N 78°53′E
61 H18 **Jaguarão** Rio Grande do Sul, S Brazil 32°30′S 53°25′W
61 H18 **Jaguarão, Rio** *var.* Río Yaguarón. ≈ Brazil/Uruguay
60 K11 **Jaguariaíva** Paraná, S Brazil 24°15′S 49°44′W
44 D5 **Jagüey Grande** Matanzas, W Cuba 22°31′N 81°07′W
153 P14 **Jahānābād** Bihār, N India 25°13′N 84°59′E
Jahra *see* Al Jahrā'
143 P12 **Jahrom** *var.* Jahrum. Fārs, S Iran 28°35′N 53°32′E
Jahrum *see* Jahrom
Jailolo *see* Halmahera, Pulau
Jainat *see* Chai Nat
Jainti *see* Jayanti
152 H12 **Jaipur** *prev.* Jeypore. *state capital* Rājasthān, N India 26°54′N 75°47′E
153 T14 **Jaipurhat** *var.* Joypurhat. Rajshahi, NW Bangladesh 25°04′N 89°06′E
152 D11 **Jaisalmer** Rājasthān, NW India 26°55′N 70°56′E
154 O12 **Jājapur** *var.* Jajpur, Panikoilli. Orissa, E India 18°54′N 82°36′E
143 R4 **Jājarm** Khorāsān-e Shemālī, NE Iran 36°58′N 56°26′E
112 G12 **Jajce** Federacija Bosna I Hercegovina, W Bosnia and Herzegovina 44°20′N 17°16′E
Jajı *see* 'Alī Khēl
Jajpur *see* Jājapur
83 D17 **Jakalsberg** Otjozondjupa, N Namibia 19°23′S 17°28′E
169 O15 **Jakarta** *prev.* Djakarta, *Dut.* Batavia. ● (Indonesia) Jawa, C Indonesia 06°08′S 106°45′E
10 I8 **Jakes Corner** Yukon Territory, W Canada 60°18′N 134°00′W
152 H9 **Jākhal** Haryāna, NW India 29°46′N 75°51′E
Jakobeny *see* Iacobeni
93 K16 **Jakobstad** *Fin.* Pietarsaari. Länsi-Suomi, W Finland 63°41′N 22°40′E
Jakobstadt *see* Jēkabpils
113 O18 **Jakupica** ▲▲ C FYR Macedonia
37 W15 **Jal** New Mexico, SW USA 32°07′N 103°10′W
141 P7 **Jalājil** *var.* Ğalāğıl. Ar Riyāḍ, C Saudi Arabia 25°43′N 45°22′E
149 S5 **Jalālābād** *var.* Jalalabad, Jelalabad. Nangarhār, E Afghanistan 34°26′N 70°28′E
Jalal-Abad *see* Dzhalal-Abad, Dzhalal-Abadskaya Oblast', Kyrgyzstan
Jalal-Abad Oblasty *see* Dzhalal-Abadskaya Oblast'
149 V7 **Jalālpur** Punjab, E Pakistan 32°39′N 74°11′E
149 T11 **Jalālpur Pīrwāla** Punjab, E Pakistan 29°30′N 71°20′E
152 H8 **Jalandhar** *prev.* Jullundur. Punjab, N India 31°20′N 75°37′E
42 J7 **Jalán, Río** ≈ S Honduras
42 E6 **Jalapa** Jalapa, C Guatemala 14°39′N 89°59′W
42 J7 **Jalapa** Nueva Segovia, NW Nicaragua 13°56′N 86°11′W
42 A3 **Jalapa** *off.* Departamento de Jalapa. ◈ *department* SE Guatemala
Jalapa, Departamento de *see* Jalapa
42 E6 **Jalapa, Río** ≈ SE Guatemala
143 X13 **Jālaq** Sīstān va Balūchestān, SE Iran
93 K17 **Jalasjärvi** Länsi-Suomi, W Finland 62°30′N 22°50′E
149 O8 **Jaldak** Zābul, SE Afghanistan 32°00′N 66°45′E
60 J7 **Jales** São Paulo, S Brazil 20°15′S 50°34′W
154 P11 **Jaleshwar** *var.* Jaleswar. Orissa, NE India 21°51′N 87°15′E
Jaleswar *see* Jaleshwar
154 F12 **Jalgaon** Mahārāshtra, C India 21°01′N 75°34′E
139 W12 **Jalībah** Dhī Qār, S Iraq 30°37′N 46°31′E
139 W13 **Jalīb Shahāb** Al Muthannā, S Iraq 30°26′N 46°09′E
77 X15 **Jalingo** Taraba, E Nigeria 08°54′N 11°22′E
40 K13 **Jalisco** ◈ *state* SW Mexico
154 G13 **Jālna** Mahārāshtra, W India 19°50′N 75°53′E
Jalomitsa *see* Ialomiţa
105 R5 **Jalón** ≈ N Spain
152 E13 **Jālor** Rājasthān, N India 25°21′N 72°43′E
112 K11 **Jalovik** Serbia, W Serbia 44°37′N 19°48′E
40 L12 **Jalpa** Zacatecas, C Mexico 21°40′N 103°W
153 S12 **Jalpāiguri** West Bengal, NE India 26°43′N 88°24′E
41 O12 **Jalpán** *var.* Jalpan. Querétaro de Arteaga, C Mexico 21°13′N 99°28′W
Jalpan *see* Jalpán
67 P2 **Jalta** *island* N Tunisia
75 S9 **Jālū** *var.* Jūlā. NE Libya 29°02′N 21°33′E
189 U8 **Jaluit Atoll** *var.* Jālwōj. *atoll* Ralik Chain, S Marshall Islands
Jālwōj *see* Jaluit Atoll
81 L18 **Jamaame** *It.* Giamame; *prev.* Margherita. Jubbada Hoose, S Somalia 0°00′N 42°43′E
77 W13 **Jamaare** ≈ NE Nigeria
44 G9 **Jamaica** ◆ *commonwealth republic* W West Indies
47 P3 **Jamaica** *island* W West Indies
44 I9 **Jamaica Channel** *channel* Haiti/Jamaica
153 T14 **Jamalpur** Dhaka, N Bangladesh 24°54′N 89°57′E
153 Q14 **Jamālpur** Bihār, NE India 25°19′N 86°30′E
168 L9 **Jamaluang** *var.* Jemaluang. Johor, Peninsular Malaysia 02°15′N 103°50′E
59 I14 **Jamanxim, Rio** ≈ C Brazil
56 B8 **Jambelí, Canal de** *channel* S Ecuador
99 I20 **Jambes** Namur, SE Belgium 50°26′N 04°51′E
168 L12 **Jambi** *var.* Telanaipura; *prev.* Djambi. Sumatera, W Indonesia 01°34′S 103°37′E
168 K12 **Jambi** *off.* Propinsi Jambi, *var.* Djambi. ◈ *province* W Indonesia
Jambi, Propinsi *see* Jambi
Jamdena *see* Yamdena, Pulau
12 H8 **James Bay** *bay* Ontario/Québec, E Canada
63 F19 **James, Isla** *island* Archipiélago de los Chonos, S Chile
181 Q8 **James Ranges** ▲▲ Northern Territory, C Australia
29 P8 **James River** ≈ North Dakota/South Dakota, N USA
21 X7 **James River** ≈ Virginia, NE USA
194 H4 **James Ross Island** *island* Antarctica
182 I8 **Jamestown** South Australia 33°13′S 138°36′E
65 G25 **Jamestown** ○ (Saint Helena) NW Saint Helena 15°56′S 05°44′W
35 P8 **Jamestown** California, W USA 37°57′N 120°25′W
20 L7 **Jamestown** Kentucky, S USA 36°58′N 85°03′W
18 D11 **Jamestown** New York, NE USA 42°05′N 79°15′W
29 P5 **Jamestown** North Dakota, N USA 46°54′N 98°42′W
20 L8 **Jamestown** Tennessee, S USA 36°24′N 84°58′W
Jamestown *see* Holetown
15 N10 **Jamet** ≈ Québec, SE Canada
41 Q17 **Jamiltepec** *var.* Santiago Jamiltepec. Oaxaca, SE Mexico 16°18′N 97°51′W
95 F20 **Jammerbugten** *bay* Skagerrak, E North Sea
152 H6 **Jammu** *prev.* Jummoo. *state capital* Jammu and Kashmir, NW India 32°43′N 74°54′E
152 I5 **Jammu and Kashmir** *var.* Jammu-Kashmir, Kashmir. ◈ *state* NW India
149 V4 **Jammu and Kashmir** *disputed region* India/Pakistan
Jammu-Kashmir *see* Jammu and Kashmir
154 B10 **Jāmnagar** *prev.* Navanagar. Gujarāt, W India 22°28′N 70°06′E
149 S11 **Jāmpur** Punjab, E Pakistan 29°38′N 70°40′E
93 L18 **Jämsä** Länsi-Suomi, C Finland 61°51′N 25°10′E
93 L18 **Jämsänkoski** Länsi-Suomi, C Finland 61°54′N 25°10′E
153 Q16 **Jamshedpur** Jhārkhand, NE India 22°47′N 86°12′E
94 K9 **Jämtland** ◈ *county* C Sweden
153 Q14 **Jamūi** Bihār, NE India 24°57′N 86°14′E
Jamuna *see* Brahmaputra
153 T14 **Jamuna Nadi** ≈ N Bangladesh
Jamundá *see* Nhamundá, Rio
54 D11 **Jamundí** Valle del Cauca, SW Colombia 03°16′N 76°31′W
153 Q12 **Janakpur** Central, C Nepal 26°45′N 85°55′E
59 N18 **Janaúba** Minas Gerais, SE Brazil 15°47′S 43°16′W
58 K11 **Janaucu, Ilha** *island* NE Brazil
143 Q7 **Jandaq** Eşfahān, C Iran 34°04′N 54°26′E
64 Q11 **Jandia, Punta de** *headland* Fuerteventura, Islas Canarias, Spain, NE Atlantic Ocean 28°03′N 14°32′W
59 B14 **Jandiatuba, Rio** ≈ NW Brazil
105 N12 **Jándula** ≈ S Spain
29 V10 **Janesville** Minnesota, N USA 44°07′N 93°43′W
30 L9 **Janesville** Wisconsin, N USA 42°42′N 89°02′W
83 N20 **Jangamo** Inhambane, SE Mozambique 24°04′S 35°25′E
155 J14 **Jangaon** Andhra Pradesh, C India 18°47′N 79°25′E
153 S14 **Jangīpur** West Bengal, NE India 24°31′N 88°03′E
Janina *see* Ioánnina
Janischken *see* Joniškis
112 J11 **Janja** NE Bosnia and Herzegovina 44°40′N 19°15′E
Jankovac *see* Jánoshalma
197 Q15 **Jan Mayen** ◇ *Norwegian dependency* N Atlantic Ocean
84 D5 **Jan Mayen** *island* N Atlantic Ocean
197 R15 **Jan Mayen Fracture Zone** *tectonic feature* Greenland Sea/Norwegian Sea
197 R15 **Jan Mayen Ridge** *undersea feature* Greenland Sea/Norwegian Sea 69°00′N 08°00′W
40 H3 **Janos** Chihuahua, N Mexico 30°50′N 108°10′W
111 K25 **Jánoshalma** *SCr.* Jankovac. Bács-Kiskun, S Hungary 46°19′N 19°16′E
Janów *see* Ivanava, Belarus
110 H10 **Janowiec Wielkopolski** *Ger.* Janowitz. Kujawski-pomorskie, C Poland 52°47′N 17°30′E
Janowitz *see* Janowiec Wielkopolski
Janow/Janów *see* Jonava, Lithuania
111 O15 **Janów Lubelski** Lubelski, E Poland 50°42′N 22°24′E
Janów Poleski *see* Ivanava
83 H25 **Jansenville** Eastern Cape, S South Africa 32°56′S 24°40′E
59 M18 **Januária** Minas Gerais, SE Brazil 15°28′S 44°23′W
Janūbīyah, Al Bādiyah al *see* Ash Shāmīyah
102 I7 **Janzé** Ille-et-Vilaine, NW France 47°55′N 01°28′W
154 F10 **Jaora** Madhya Pradesh, C India 23°40′N 75°10′E
131 Y9 **Japan** *var.* Nippon, *Jap.* Nihon. ◆ *monarchy* E Asia
129 Y9 **Japan** *island group* E Asia
192 H4 **Japan Basin** *undersea feature* N Sea of Japan 40°00′N 135°00′E
129 Y8 **Japan, Sea of** *var.* East Sea, *Rus.* Yapanskoye More. *sea* NW Pacific Ocean *see also* East Sea
192 H4 **Japan Trench** *undersea feature* NW Pacific Ocean 37°00′N 143°00′E
Japen *see* Yapen, Pulau
59 A15 **Japiim** *var.* Máncio Lima. Acre, W Brazil 08°00′S 73°39′W
58 D12 **Japurá** Amazonas, N Brazil 01°43′S 66°14′W
58 C12 **Japurá, Rio** *var.* Río Caquetá, Yapurá. ≈ Brazil/Colombia *see also* Caquetá, Río
Japurá, Rio *see* Caquetá, Río
43 W17 **Jaqué** Darién, SE Panama 07°31′N 78°09′W
Jaquemel *see* Jacmel
Jarablos *see* Jarābulus
138 K2 **Jarābulus** *var.* Jarablos, Jerablus, *Fr.* Djérablous. Ḥalab, N Syria 36°51′N 38°02′E
60 K13 **Jaraguá do Sul** Santa Catarina, S Brazil 26°29′S 49°07′W
104 K9 **Jaraicejo** Extremadura, W Spain 39°40′N 05°49′W
104 K9 **Jaráiz de la Vera** Extremadura, W Spain 40°04′N 05°45′W
105 O7 **Jarama** ≈ C Spain
63 J20 **Jaramillo** Santa Cruz, SE Argentina 47°10′S 67°07′W
Jarandilla de la Vega *see* Jarandilla de la Vera
104 K8 **Jarandilla de la Vera** *var.* Jarandilla de la Vega. Extremadura, W Spain 40°08′N 05°39′W
149 V9 **Jarānwāla** Punjab, E Pakistan 31°20′N 73°26′E
138 G9 **Jarash** *var.* Jerash; *anc.* Gerasa. Irbid, NW Jordan 32°17′N 35°54′E
Jarbah, Jazīrat *see* Jerba, Île de
94 N13 **Järbo** Gävleborg, C Sweden 60°43′N 16°40′E
Jardan *see* Yordon
44 F7 **Jardines de la Reina, Archipiélago de los** *island group* C Cuba
162 I8 **Jargalant** Bayanhongor, C Mongolia 47°14′N 99°43′E
162 K6 **Jargalant** Bulgan, N Mongolia 49°09′N 104°19′E
162 G7 **Jargalant** *var.* Buyanbat. Govĭ-Altay, W Mongolia 47°00′N 95°57′E
162 I6 **Jargalant** *var.* Orgil. Hövsgöl, C Mongolia 48°31′N 99°19′E
Jargalant *see* Battsengel
Jargalant *see* Bulgan, Bayan-Ölgiy, Mongolia
Jargalant *see* Biger, Govĭ-Altay, Mongolia
Jarīd, Shaṭṭ al *see* Jerid, Chott el
58 I11 **Jari, Rio** *var.* Jary. ≈ N Brazil
141 N7 **Jarīr, Wādī al** *dry watercourse* C Saudi Arabia
Jarja *see* Yur'ya
94 L13 **Järna** *var.* Dala-Jarna. Dalarna, C Sweden 60°31′N 14°22′E
95 O16 **Järna** Stockholm, C Sweden 59°05′N 17°35′E
102 K11 **Jarnac** Charente, W France 45°41′N 00°10′W
110 H12 **Jarocin** Wielkopolskie, C Poland 51°59′N 17°30′E
111 F16 **Jaroměř** *Ger.* Jermer. Královéhradecký Kraj, N Czech Republic 50°22′N 15°55′E
Jaroslau *see* Jarosław
111 O16 **Jarosław** *Ger.* Jaroslau, *Rus.* Yaroslav. Podkarpackie, SE Poland 50°01′N 22°41′E
93 F16 **Järpen** Jämtland, C Sweden 63°21′N 13°30′E
147 O14 **Jarqo'rg'on** *Rus.* Dzharkurgan. Surkhondaryo Viloyati, S Uzbekistan 37°31′N 67°20′E
139 P2 **Jarrāh, Wadi** *dry watercourse* NE Syria
Jars, Plain of *see* Xiangkhoang, Plateau de
162 K14 **Jartai Yanchi** ◎ N China
59 E16 **Jaru** Rondônia, W Brazil 10°24′S 62°45′W
Jarud Qi *see* Lubei
118 I4 **Järva-Jaani** *Ger.* Sankt-Johannis. Järvamaa, N Estonia 59°03′N 25°54′E
118 G5 **Järvakandi** *Ger.* Jerwakant. Raplamaa, NW Estonia 58°45′N 24°49′E
118 H4 **Järvamaa** *var.* Järva Maakond. ◈ *province* N Estonia
Järva Maakond *see* Järvamaa
93 L19 **Järvenpää** Etelä-Suomi, S Finland 60°29′N 25°06′E
14 G17 **Jarvis** Ontario, S Canada 42°53′N 80°06′W
177 R8 **Jarvis Island** ◇ *US unincorporated territory* C Pacific Ocean
94 M11 **Järvsö** Gävleborg, C Sweden 61°43′N 16°25′E
Jary *see* Jari, Rio
112 M9 **Jaša Tomić** Vojvodina, NE Serbia 45°27′N 20°51′E
112 D12 **Jasenice** Zadar, SW Croatia 44°15′N 15°33′E
138 I11 **Jashshat al 'Adlah, Wādī al** *dry watercourse* C Jordan
77 Q16 **Jasikan** E Ghana 07°24′N 00°28′E
Jāsk *see* Bandar-e Jāsk
146 F6 **Jasliq** *Rus.* Zhaslyk. Qoraqalpog'iston Respublikasi, NW Uzbekistan 43°57′N 57°30′E
111 N17 **Jasło** Podkarpackie, SE Poland 49°45′N 21°28′E
11 U16 **Jasmin** Saskatchewan, S Canada 51°11′N 103°34′W
65 A23 **Jason Islands** *island group* NW Falkland Islands
194 I4 **Jason Peninsula** *peninsula* Antarctica
31 N15 **Jasonville** Indiana, N USA 39°09′N 87°12′W
11 O15 **Jasper** Alberta, SW Canada 52°55′N 118°05′W
14 L13 **Jasper** Ontario, SE Canada 44°50′N 75°57′W
23 O3 **Jasper** Alabama, S USA 33°49′N 87°16′W
27 T9 **Jasper** Arkansas, C USA 36°00′N 93°11′W
23 U8 **Jasper** Florida, SE USA 30°31′N 82°57′W
31 N16 **Jasper** Indiana, N USA 38°22′N 86°57′W
29 R11 **Jasper** Minnesota, N USA 43°51′N 96°24′W
27 S7 **Jasper** Missouri, C USA 37°20′N 94°18′W
20 K10 **Jasper** Tennessee, S USA 35°04′N 85°36′W
25 Y9 **Jasper** Texas, SW USA 30°55′N 94°00′W
11 O15 **Jasper National Park** *national park* Alberta/British Columbia, SW Canada
Jassy *see* Iaşi
113 N14 **Jastrebac** ▲▲ SE Serbia
112 D9 **Jastrebarsko** Zagreb, N Croatia 45°40′N 15°40′E
Jastrow *see* Jastrowie
110 G9 **Jastrowie** *Ger.* Jastrow. Wielkopolskie, C Poland 53°25′N 16°48′E
111 J17 **Jastrzębie-Zdrój** Śląskie, S Poland 49°58′N 18°34′E
111 L22 **Jászapáti** Jász-Nagykun-Szolnok, E Hungary 47°30′N 20°10′E
111 L22 **Jászberény** Jász-Nagykun-Szolnok, E Hungary 47°30′N 19°56′E
111 L23 **Jász-Nagykun-Szolnok** *off.* Jász-Nagykun-Szolnok Megye. ◈ *county* E Hungary
Jász-Nagykun-Szolnok Megye *see* Jász-Nagykun-Szolnok
59 J19 **Jataí** Goiás, C Brazil 17°58′S 51°45′W
58 G12 **Jatapu, Serra do** ▲ N Brazil
41 W16 **Jatate, Río** ≈ SE Mexico
149 P17 **Jāti** Sind, SE Pakistan 24°20′N 68°18′E
44 F6 **Jatibonico** Sancti Spíritus, C Cuba 21°56′N 79°11′W
169 O16 **Jatiluhur, Danau** ◎ Jawa, S Indonesia
Jativa *see* Xàtiva
149 S11 **Jatoi** *prev.* Jattoi. Punjab, E Pakistan 29°29′N 70°58′E
Jattoi *see* Jatoi
60 L9 **Jaú** São Paulo, S Brazil 22°11′S 48°35′W
58 F11 **Jauaperi, Rio** ≈ N Brazil
99 I19 **Jauche** Walloon Brabant, C Belgium 50°42′N 04°55′E
Jauer *see* Jawor
Jauf *see* Al Jawf
149 U7 **Jauharābād** Punjab, E Pakistan 32°16′N 72°17′E
57 E14 **Jauja** Junín, C Peru 11°48′S 75°30′W
41 O10 **Jaumave** Tamaulipas, C Mexico 23°28′N 99°22′W
118 H10 **Jaunjelgava** *Ger.* Friedrichstadt. S Latvia 56°38′N 25°03′E
Jaunlatgale *see* Pytalovo
118 I8 **Jaunpiebalga** NE Latvia 57°10′N 26°02′E
118 E9 **Jaunpils** C Latvia 56°45′N 23°03′E
153 N13 **Jaunpur** Uttar Pradesh, N India 25°44′N 82°41′E
29 N8 **Java** South Dakota, N USA 45°29′N 99°54′W
Java *see* Jawa
105 R9 **Javalambre** ▲ E Spain 40°02′N 01°06′W
173 V7 **Java Ridge** *undersea feature* E Indian Ocean
59 A14 **Javari, Rio** *var.* Yavarí. ≈ Brazil/Peru
Javarthushuu *see* Bayan-Uul
169 Q15 **Java Sea** *Ind.* Laut Jawa. *sea* W Indonesia
173 U7 **Java Trench** *var.* Sunda Trench. *undersea feature* E Indian Ocean
143 Q10 **Javazm** *var.* Jowzam. Kermān, C Iran 30°31′N 55°01′E
105 T11 **Jávea** *Cat.* Xàbia. Valenciana, E Spain 38°48′N 00°10′E
Javhlant *see* Bayan-Ovoo
63 G20 **Javier, Isla** *island* S Chile
113 L14 **Javor** ▲▲ Bosnia and Herzegovina/Serbia
111 K20 **Javorie** *Hung.* Jávoros. ▲ S Slovakia 48°26′N 19°16′E
Jávoros *see* Javorie
93 J14 **Jävre** Norrbotten, N Sweden 65°07′N 21°31′E
192 E8 **Jawa** *Eng.* Java; *prev.* Djawa. *island* C Indonesia
169 O16 **Jawa Barat** *off.* Propinsi Jawa Barat, *Eng.* West Java. ◈ *province* S Indonesia
Jawa Barat, Propinsi *see* Jawa Barat
Jawa, Laut *see* Java Sea
139 R3 **Jawān** Nīnawýa, NW Iraq 35°57′N 43°03′E
169 P16 **Jawa Tengah** *off.* Propinsi Jawa Tengah, *Eng.* Central Java. ◈ *province* S Indonesia
Jawa Tengah, Propinsi *see* Jawa Tengah
169 R16 **Jawa Timur** *off.* Propinsi Jawa Timur, *Eng.* East Java. ◈ *province* S Indonesia
Jawa Timur, Propinsi *see* Jawa Timur
81 N17 **Jawhar** *var.* Jowhar, *It.* Giohar. Shabeellaha Dhexe, S Somalia 02°37′N 45°30′E
111 F14 **Jawor** *Ger.* Jauer. Dolnośląskie, SW Poland 51°01′N 16°11′E
Jaworów *see* Yavoriv
111 J16 **Jaworzno** Śląskie, S Poland 50°13′N 19°11′E
Jaxartes *see* Syr Darya
27 R9 **Jay** Oklahoma, C USA 36°25′N 94°49′W
Jayabum *see* Chaiyaphum
Jayanath *see* Chai Nat
153 T12 **Jayanti** *prev.* Jainti. West Bengal, NE India 26°45′N 89°40′E
171 X14 **Jaya, Puncak** *prev.* Puntjak Carstensz, Puntjak Sukarno. ▲ Papua, E Indonesia 04°00′S 137°10′E
171 Z13 **Jayapura** *var.* Djajapura, *Dut.* Hollandia; *prev.* Kotabaru, Sukarnapura. Papua, E Indonesia 02°37′S 140°39′E
Jay Dairen *see* Dalian
Jayhawker State *see* Kansas
147 S12 **Jayilgan** *Rus.* Dzhailgan, Dzhayilgan. C Tajikistan 39°17′N 71°32′E
155 L14 **Jaypur** *var.* Jeypore, Jeypur. Orissa, E India 18°54′N 82°36′E
25 O6 **Jayton** Texas, SW USA 33°16′N 100°35′W
143 U13 **Jaz Mūrīān, Hāmūn-e** ◎ SE Iran
138 M4 **Jazrah** Ar Raqqah, C Syria 35°56′N 39°02′E
138 G6 **Jbaïl** *var.* Jebeil, Jubayl, Jubeil; *anc.* Biblical Gebal, Bybles. W Lebanon 34°00′N 35°45′E
25 O7 **J. B. Thomas, Lake** ⊠ Texas, SW USA
Jdaïdé *see* Judaydah
35 X12 **Jean** Nevada, W USA 35°45′N 115°20′W
22 I9 **Jeanerette** Louisiana, S USA 29°54′N 91°39′W
44 L8 **Jean-Rabel** NW Haiti 19°48′N 73°05′W
143 T12 **Jebāl Bārez, Kūh-e** ▲▲ SE Iran
Jebat *see* Jabwot
77 T15 **Jebba** Kwara, W Nigeria 09°04′N 04°50′E
Jebeil *see* Jbaïl
116 E12 **Jebel** *Hung.* Széphely; *prev. Hung.* Zsebely. Timiş, W Romania 45°33′N 21°14′E
146 B11 **Jebel** *Rus.* Dzhebel. Balkan Welaýaty, W Turkmenistan 39°42′N 54°10′E
Jebel, Bahr el *see* White Nile
Jebel Dhanna *see* Jabal az Zannah
Jeble *see* Jablah
163 Y15 **Jecheon** *Jap.* Teisen; *prev.* Chech'ŏn. N South Korea 37°06′N 128°15′E
96 K13 **Jedburgh** SE Scotland, United Kingdom 55°29′N 02°34′W
Jedda *see* Jiddah
111 L15 **Jędrzejów** *Ger.* Endersdorf. Świętokrzyskie, C Poland 50°39′N 20°18′E
100 K12 **Jeetze** *var.* Jeetzel. ≈ C Germany
Jeetzel *see* Jeetze
29 U14 **Jefferson** Iowa, C USA 42°01′N 94°22′W
21 Q8 **Jefferson** North Carolina, SE USA 36°24′N 81°33′W
25 X6 **Jefferson** Texas, SW USA 32°45′N 94°21′W
30 M9 **Jefferson** Wisconsin, N USA 43°01′N 88°48′W
27 U5 **Jefferson City** *state capital* Missouri, C USA 38°33′N 92°13′W
33 R10 **Jefferson City** Montana, NW USA 46°24′N 112°01′W
21 N9 **Jefferson City** Tennessee, S USA 36°07′N 83°29′W
35 U7 **Jefferson, Mount** ▲ Nevada, W USA 38°49′N 116°54′W
32 H12 **Jefferson, Mount** ▲ Oregon, NW USA 44°40′N 121°48′W
20 L5 **Jeffersontown** Kentucky, S USA 38°11′N 85°33′W
31 P16 **Jeffersonville** Indiana, N USA 38°16′N 85°45′W
33 V15 **Jeffrey City** Wyoming, C USA 42°29′N 107°49′W
77 T13 **Jega** Kebbi, NW Nigeria 12°15′N 04°21′E
Jehol *see* Chengde
163 X17 **Jeju** *Jap.* Saishū; *prev.* Cheju. S South Korea 33°31′N 126°34′E
163 Y17 **Jeju-do** *Jap.* Saishū; *prev.* Cheju-do, Quelpart. *island* S South Korea
163 Y17 **Jeju-haehyeop** *Eng.* Cheju Strait; *prev.* Cheju-haehyeop. *strait* S South Korea
62 P5 **Jejui-Guazú, Río** ≈ E Paraguay
118 I10 **Jēkabpils** *Ger.* Jakobstadt. S Latvia 56°30′N 25°56′E
23 W7 **Jekyll Island** *island* Georgia, SE USA
169 R13 **Jelai, Sungai** ≈ Borneo, N Indonesia
Jelalabad *see* Jalālābād
111 H14 **Jelcz-Laskowice** Dolnośląskie, SW Poland 51°01′N 17°24′E
111 E14 **Jelenia Góra** *Ger.* Hirschberg, Hirschberg im Riesengebirge, Hirschberg im Riesengebirge, Hirschberg in Schlesien. Dolnośląskie, SW Poland 50°54′N 15°48′E
153 S11 **Jelep La** *pass* N India
118 F9 **Jelgava** *Ger.* Mitau. C Latvia 56°38′N 23°47′E
112 L13 **Jelica** ▲▲ C Serbia
20 M8 **Jellico** Tennessee, S USA 36°33′N 84°06′W
95 G23 **Jelling** Syddanmark, C Denmark 55°45′N 09°24′E
169 N9 **Jemaja, Pulau** *island* W Indonesia
Jemaluang *see* Jamaluang
99 E20 **Jemappes** Hainaut, S Belgium 50°27′N 03°53′E
169 S17 **Jember** *prev.* Djember. Jawa, C Indonesia 08°07′S 113°45′E
99 I20 **Jemeppe-sur-Sambre** Namur, S Belgium 50°27′N 04°41′E
37 R10 **Jemez Pueblo** New Mexico, SW USA 35°36′N 106°43′W
158 K2 **Jeminay** *var.* Tuotiereke. Xinjiang Uygur Zizhiqu, NW China 47°28′N 85°49′E
189 U5 **Jemo Island** *atoll* Ratak Chain, C Marshall Islands
169 U11 **Jempang, Danau** ◎ Borneo, N Indonesia
101 L16 **Jena** Thüringen, C Germany 50°56′N 11°35′E
22 I6 **Jena** Louisiana, S USA 31°40′N 92°07′W
108 I8 **Jenaz** Graubünden, SE Switzerland 46°56′N 09°43′E
109 N7 **Jenbach** Tirol, W Austria 47°24′N 11°47′E
171 N15 **Jeneponto** *prev.* Djeneponto. Sulawesi, C Indonesia 05°41′S 119°42′E
138 F9 **Jenin** N West Bank 32°28′N 35°17′E
21 P7 **Jenkins** Kentucky, S USA 37°10′N 82°37′W
27 P9 **Jenks** Oklahoma, C USA 36°01′N 95°58′W
Jenné *see* Djenné
109 X8 **Jennersdorf** Burgenland, SE Austria 46°57′N 16°08′E
22 H9 **Jennings** Louisiana, S USA 30°13′N 92°39′W
11 N7 **Jenny Lind Island** *island* Nunavut, N Canada
23 Y13 **Jensen Beach** Florida, SE USA 27°15′N 80°13′W
9 P6 **Jens Munk Island** *island* Nunavut, NE Canada
163 Y15 **Jeonju** *Jap.* Zenshū; *prev.* Chŏnju. SW South Korea 35°51′N 127°08′E
59 O17 **Jequié** Bahia, E Brazil 13°52′S 40°06′W
59 O18 **Jequitinhonha, Rio** ≈ E Brazil
Jerablus *see* Jarābulus
74 H6 **Jerada** NE Morocco 34°16′N 02°07′W
Jerash *see* Jarash
75 N7 **Jerba, Île de** *var.* Djerba, Jazīrat Jarbah. *island* E Tunisia
44 K9 **Jérémie** SW Haiti 18°39′N 74°11′W
Jeréz *see* Jerez de García Salinas, Mexico
Jerez *see* Jeréz de la Frontera, Spain
40 L11 **Jerez de García Salinas** *var.* Jeréz. Zacatecas, C Mexico 22°40′N 103°00′W
104 J15 **Jerez de la Frontera** *var.* Jerez; *prev.* Xeres. Andalucía, SW Spain 36°41′N 06°08′W
104 I12 **Jerez de los Caballeros** Extremadura, W Spain 38°20′N 06°45′W
Jergucati *see* Jorgucat
138 G10 **Jericho** *Ar.* Arīḥā, *Heb.* Yeriḥo. E West Bank 31°51′N 35°27′E
74 M7 **Jerid, Chott el** *var.* Shaṭṭ al Jarīd. *salt lake* SW Tunisia
183 O10 **Jerilderie** New South Wales, SE Australia 35°24′S 145°43′E
Jerischmarkt *see* Câmpia Turzii
92 K11 **Jerisjärvi** ◎ NW Finland
Jermak *see* Aksu
Jermentau *see* Yereymentau
Jermer *see* Jaroměř
36 K11 **Jerome** Arizona, SW USA 34°45′N 112°06′W
33 O15 **Jerome** Idaho, NW USA 42°43′N 114°31′W
97 L26 **Jersey** *island* NW Europe
18 K14 **Jersey City** New Jersey, NE USA 40°42′N 74°01′W
18 F13 **Jersey Shore** Pennsylvania, NE USA 41°12′N 77°13′W
30 K14 **Jerseyville** Illinois, N USA 39°07′N 90°19′W
104 K8 **Jerte** ≈ W Spain
138 F10 **Jerusalem** *Ar.* Al Quds, Al Quds ash Sharīf, *Heb.* Yerushalayim; *anc.* Hierosolyma. ● (Israel) Jerusalem, NE Israel 31°47′N 35°13′E
138 G10 **Jerusalem** ◈ *district* E Israel
183 S10 **Jervis Bay** New South Wales, SE Australia 35°09′S 150°42′E
183 S10 **Jervis Bay Territory** ◈ *territory* SE Australia
Jerwakant *see* Järvakandi
109 S10 **Jesenice** *Ger.* Assling. NW Slovenia 46°26′N 14°01′E
111 H16 **Jeseník** *Ger.* Freiwaldau. Olomoucký Kraj, E Czech Republic 50°14′N 17°12′E
Jesi *see* Iesi
106 I8 **Jesolo** *var.* Iesolo. Veneto, NE Italy 45°32′N 12°37′E
Jesselton *see* Kota Kinabalu
95 I14 **Jessheim** Akershus, S Norway 60°07′N 11°10′E
153 T15 **Jessore** Khulna, W Bangladesh 23°10′N 89°12′E
23 W6 **Jesup** Georgia, SE USA 31°36′N 81°54′W
41 S15 **Jesús Carranza** Veracruz-Llave, SE Mexico 17°30′N 95°01′W
62 K10 **Jesús María** Córdoba, C Argentina 30°59′S 64°05′W
26 K6 **Jetmore** Kansas, C USA 38°05′N 99°55′W
103 Q2 **Jeumont** Nord, N France 50°18′N 04°06′E
95 H14 **Jevnaker** Oppland, S Norway 60°15′N 10°25′E
Jewe *see* Jõhvi
25 V9 **Jewett** Texas, SW USA 31°21′N 96°08′W
19 N12 **Jewett City** Connecticut, NE USA 41°36′N 71°58′W
Jeypore *see* Jaipur, Rājasthān, India
Jeypore/Jeypur *see* Jaypur, Orissa, India
113 L17 **Jezercës, Maja e** ▲ N Albania 42°27′N 19°49′E
111 B18 **Jezerní Hora** ▲ SW Czech Republic 49°10′N 13°11′E
154 F10 **Jhābua** Madhya Pradesh, C India 22°44′N 74°37′E
152 H14 **Jhālāwār** Rājasthān, N India 24°37′N 76°12′E
Jhang/Jhang Sadar *see* Jhang Sadr
149 U9 **Jhang Sadr** *var.* Jhang, Jhang Sadar. Punjab, NE Pakistan 31°16′N 72°19′E
152 J13 **Jhānsi** Uttar Pradesh, N India 25°27′N 78°34′E
153 O16 **Jhārkhand** ◈ *state* NE India
154 M11 **Jhārsuguda** Orissa, E India 21°56′N 84°04′E
149 V7 **Jhelum** Punjab, NE Pakistan 32°55′N 73°42′E
129 P9 **Jhelum** ≈ E Pakistan
Jhenaida *see* Jhenaidaha
153 T15 **Jhenaidaha** *var.* Jhenaida, Jhenida. Khulna, Bangladesh 23°32′N 89°09′E
Jhenaidaha *see* Jhenida
153 T15 **Jhenida** *var.* Jhenaidaha. Dhaka, W Bangladesh 23°34′N 89°39′E
Jhenida *see* Jhenaidaha
149 P16 **Jhimpir** Sind, SE Pakistan 25°00′N 68°01′E
Jhind *see* Jīnd
149 R16 **Jhudo** Sind, SE Pakistan 24°58′N 69°18′E
Jhumra *see* Chak Jhumra
152 H11 **Jhunjhunūn** Rājasthān, N India 28°05′N 75°30′E
Ji *see* Hebei, China
Ji *see* Jilin, China
Jiading *see* Xinfeng
153 S14 **Jiāganj** West Bengal, NE India 24°18′N 88°07′E
Jiaji *see* Qionghai
160 J7 **Jialing Jiang** ≈ C China
163 Y7 **Jiamusi** *var.* Chia-mu-ssu, Kiamusze. Heilongjiang, NE China 46°46′N 130°19′E
161 O11 **Ji'an** Jiangxi, S China 27°08′N 115°00′E
163 W12 **Ji'an** Jilin, NE China 41°04′N 126°07′E
163 T13 **Jianchang** Liaoning, NE China 40°48′N 119°51′E
Jianchang *see* Nancheng
Jiancheng *see* Jianyang
160 F11 **Jianchuan** *var.* Jinhuan. Yunnan, SW China 26°28′N 99°49′E
158 M4 **Jiangjunmiao** Xinjiang Uygur Zizhiqu, W China 44°42′N 90°06′E
160 K11 **Jiangkou** *var.* Shuangjiang. Guizhou, S China 27°46′N 108°53′E
Jiangkou *see* Fengkai
161 Q12 **Jiangle** *var.* Guyong. Fujian, SE China 26°44′N 117°26′E
161 N15 **Jiangmen** Guangdong, S China 22°35′N 113°02′E
Jiangna *see* Yanshan
161 Q10 **Jiangshan** Zhejiang, SE China 28°41′N 118°33′E
161 Q7 **Jiangsu** *var.* Chiang-su, Jiangsu Sheng, Kiangsu, Su. ◈ *province* E China
Jiangsu *see* Nanjing
Jiangsu Sheng *see* Jiangsu
161 O11 **Jiangxi** *var.* Chiang-hsi, Gan, Jiangxi Sheng, Kiangsi. ◈ *province* S China
Jiangxi Sheng *see* Jiangxi
160 I8 **Jiangyou** *prev.* Zhongba. Sichuan, C China 31°52′N 104°52′E
161 N9 **Jianli** *var.* Rongcheng. Hubei, C China 29°51′N 112°50′E
161 Q11 **Jian'ou** Fujian, SE China 27°04′N 118°20′E
163 S12 **Jianping** *var.* Yebaishou. Liaoning, NE China 41°13′N 119°37′E
Jianshe *see* Baiyü
160 L9 **Jianshi** *var.* Yezhou. Hubei, C China 30°37′N 109°42′E
Jiantang *see* Xamgyi'nyilha
129 V11 **Jian Xi** ≈ SE China
161 Q11 **Jianyang** Fujian, SE China 27°20′N 118°01′E
160 I9 **Jianyang** *var.* Jiancheng. Sichuan, C China 30°22′N 104°31′E
163 X10 **Jiaohe** Jilin, NE China 43°41′N 127°20′E
Jiaojiang *see* Taizhou
Jiaoxian *see* Jiaozhou
161 R5 **Jiaozhou** *prev.* Jiaoxian. Shandong, E China 36°17′N 120°00′E
161 N6 **Jiaozuo** Henan, C China 35°14′N 113°13′E
Jiashan *see* Mingguang
158 F8 **Jiashi** *var.* Baren, Payzawat. Xinjiang Uygur Zizhiqu, NW China 39°27′N 76°45′E
154 L9 **Jiāwān** Madhya Pradesh, C India 24°20′N 82°17′E
161 S9 **Jiaxing** Zhejiang, SE China 30°44′N 120°46′E
161 S14 **Jiayi** *var.* Chia-i, Chiai, Chiayi, Kiayi, *Jap.* Kagi. C Taiwan 23°29′N 120°27′E
163 X6 **Jiayin** *var.* Chaoyang. Heilongjiang, NE China 48°51′N 130°24′E
159 R8 **Jiayuguan** Gansu, N China 39°47′N 98°14′E
Jibhalanta *see* Uliastay
138 M4 **Jiblī** Ar Raqqah, C Syria 35°49′N 39°23′E
116 H9 **Jibou** *Hung.* Zsibó. Sălaj, NW Romania 47°15′N 23°17′E
141 Z9 **Jibsh, Ra's al** *headland* E Oman 21°20′N 59°23′E
Jibuti *see* Djibouti
111 E15 **Jičín** *Ger.* Jitschin. Královéhradecký Kraj, N Czech Republic 50°27′N 15°20′E
140 K10 **Jiddah** *Eng.* Jedda. (Saudi Arabia) Makkah, W Saudi Arabia 21°34′N 39°13′E
141 W11 **Jiddat al Ḥarāsīs** *desert* C Oman
Jiesjavrre *see* Iešjavri
160 M4 **Jiexiu** Shanxi, C China 37°00′N 111°50′E
161 P14 **Jieyang** Guangdong, S China 23°32′N 116°20′E
119 F14 **Jieznas** Kaunas, S Lithuania 54°37′N 24°10′E
Jīfa', Bi'r *see* Jif'īyah, Bi'r
141 P15 **Jif'īyah, Bi'r** *var.* Bi'r Jīfa'. *well* C Yemen
77 W13 **Jigawa** ◈ *state* N Nigeria
146 J10 **Jigerbent** *Rus.* Dzhigirbent. Lebap Welaýaty, NE Turkmenistan 40°44′N 61°56′E
44 I7 **Jiguaní** Granma, E Cuba 20°24′N 76°26′W
159 T12 **Jigzhi** *var.* Chugqênsumdo. Qinghai, C China 33°23′N 101°25′E
Jih-k'a-tse *see* Xigazê
111 E18 **Jihlava** *Ger.* Iglau, *Pol.* Iglawa. Vysočina, S Czech Republic 49°22′N 15°36′E
111 E18 **Jihlava** *var.* Igel, *Ger.* Iglawa. ≈ Vysočina, C Czech Republic
Jihlavský Kraj *see* Vysočina
111 C18 **Jihočeský Kraj** *prev.* Budějovický Kraj. ◈ *region* Czech Republic
111 G19 **Jihomoravský Kraj** *prev.* Brněnský Kraj. ◈ *region* SE Czech Republic
74 L5 **Jijel** *var.* Djidjel; *prev.* Djidjelli. NE Algeria 36°50′N 05°43′E
116 L9 **Jijia** ≈ N Romania
80 L13 **Jijiga** *It.* Giggiga. Sumalē, E Ethiopia 09°21′N 42°53′E
105 S12 **Jijona** *var.* Xixona. Valenciana, E Spain 38°34′N 00°29′W
81 L18 **Jilib** *It.* Gelib. Jubbada Dhexe, S Somalia 0°18′N 42°48′E
163 W10 **Jilin** *var.* Chi-lin, Girin, Kirin; *prev.* Yungki, Yunki. Jilin, NE China 43°46′N 126°32′E
163 W10 **Jilin** *var.* Chi-lin, Girin, Ji, Jilin Sheng, Kirin. ◈ *province* NE China
163 W11 **Jilin Hada Ling** ▲▲ NE China
Jilin Sheng *see* Jilin
163 S4 **Jiliu He** ≈ NE China
105 Q6 **Jiloca** ≈ N Spain
161 T12 **Jilong** *var.* Keelung, *Jap.* Kirun, Kirun'; *prev.* Chilung, *prev. Sp.* Santissima Trinidad. N Taiwan 25°10′N 121°43′E
81 I14 **Jīma** *var.* Jimma, *It.* Gimma. Oromīya, C Ethiopia 07°42′N 36°51′E
44 M9 **Jimaní** W Dominican Republic 18°29′N 71°49′W
116 E11 **Jimbolia** *Ger.* Hatzfeld, *Hung.* Zsombolya. Timiş, W Romania 45°47′N 20°43′E
104 K16 **Jimena de la Frontera** Andalucía, S Spain 36°27′N 05°28′W
40 K7 **Jiménez** Chihuahua, N Mexico 27°09′N 104°54′W
41 N5 **Jiménez** Coahuila, NE Mexico 29°05′N 100°40′W
41 P9 **Jiménez** *var.* Santander Jiménez. Tamaulipas, C Mexico 24°11′N 98°29′W
40 L10 **Jiménez del Teul** Zacatecas, C Mexico 23°13′N 103°46′W
77 Y14 **Jimeta** Adamawa, E Nigeria 09°16′N 12°25′E
Jimma *see* Jīma
158 M5 **Jimsar** Xinjiang Uygur Zizhiqu, NW China 44°05′N 88°48′E
18 I14 **Jim Thorpe** Pennsylvania, NE USA 40°51′N 75°43′W
Jin *see* Shanxi
Jin *see* Tianjin Shi

◆ Country
● Country Capital
◇ Dependent Territory
○ Dependent Territory Capital
◈ Administrative Regions
✈ International Airport
▲ Mountain
▲▲ Mountain Range
Volcano
≈ River
◎ Lake
⊠ Reservoir

161 P5 **Jinan** *var.* Chinan, Chi-nan, Tsinan. *province capital* Shandong, E China 36°43′N 116°58′E
Jin'an *see* Songpan
Jinbi *see* Dayao
159 T8 **Jinchang** Gansu, N China 38°31′N 102°07′E
161 N5 **Jincheng** Shanxi, C China 35°30′N 112°52′E
Jincheng *see* Wuding
Jinchengjiang *see* Hechi
152 I9 **Jīnd** *prev.* Jhind. Haryāna, NW India 29°29′N 76°22′E
183 Q11 **Jindabyne** New South Wales, SE Australia 36°28′S 148°36′E
163 X17 **Jin-do** *Jap.* Chin-tō; *prev.* Chin-do. *island* SW South Korea
111 O18 **Jindřichův Hradec** *Ger.* Neuhaus. Jihočeský Kraj, S Czech Republic 49°09′N 15°01′E
Jing *see* Beijing Shi
Jing *see* Jinghe, China
159 X10 **Jingchuan** Gansu, C China 35°20′N 107°45′E
161 Q10 **Jingdezhen** Jiangxi, S China 29°18′N 117°18′E
161 O12 **Jinggangshan** Jiangxi, S China 26°36′N 114°11′E
161 P3 **Jinghai** Tianjin Shi, E China 38°53′N 116°45′E
158 I4 **Jinghe** *var.* Jing. Xinjiang Uygur Zizhiqu, NW China 44°35′N 82°55′E
160 K6 **Jing He** ≈ C China
160 F15 **Jinghong** *var.* Yunjinghong. Yunnan, SW China 22°03′N 100°56′E
160 M9 **Jingmen** Hubei, C China 30°58′N 112°09′E
163 X10 **Jingpo Hu** ◉ NE China
160 M8 **Jing Shan** ▲▲ C China
159 V9 **Jingtai** *var.* Yitiaoshan. Gansu, C China 37°12′N 104°06′E
160 J14 **Jingxi** *var.* Xinjing. Guangxi Zhuangzu Zizhiqu, S China 23°10′N 106°22′E
Jing Xian *see* Jingzhou, Hunan, China
163 W11 **Jingyu** Jilin, NE China 42°23′N 126°48′E
159 V10 **Jingyuan** *var.* Wulan. Gansu, C China 36°35′N 104°40′E
160 M9 **Jingzhou** *prev.* Shashi, Shashih, Shasi. Hubei, C China 30°21′N 112°09′E
160 L12 **Jingzhou** *var.* Jing Xian, Jingzhou Miaouzu Dongzu Zizhixian, Quyang. Hunan, S China 26°35′N 109°40′E
Jingzhou Miaouzu Dongzu Zizhixian *see* Jingzhou
163 Z16 **Jinhae** *Jap.* Chinkai; *prev.* Chinhae. S South Korea 35°06′N 128°48′E
Jinhe *see* Jinping
161 R10 **Jinhua** Zhejiang, SE China 29°15′N 119°36′E
Jinhuan *see* Jianchuan
161 P5 **Jining** Shandong, E China 35°25′N 116°35′E
Jining *see* Ulan Qab
81 G18 **Jinja** S Uganda 0°27′N 33°14′E
161 R13 **Jinjiang** *var.* Qingyang. Fujian, SE China 24°53′N 118°36′E
161 O11 **Jin Jiang** ≈ S China
Jinjiang *see* Chengmai
163 Y16 **Jinju** *prev.* Chinju, *Jap.* Shinshū. S South Korea 35°12′N 128°06′E
171 V15 **Jin, Kepulauan** *island group* E Indonesia
161 R13 **Jinmen Dao** *var.* Chinmen Tao, Quemoy. *island* W Taiwan
42 J9 **Jinotega** Jinotega, NW Nicaragua 13°03′N 85°59′W
42 K7 **Jinotega** ◈ *department* N Nicaragua
42 J11 **Jinotepe** Carazo, SW Nicaragua 11°50′N 86°10′W
160 L13 **Jinping** *var.* Sanjiang. Guizhou, S China 26°42′N 109°13′E
160 H14 **Jinping** *var.* Jinhe. Yunnan, SW China 22°47′N 103°12′E
Jinsen *see* Incheon
160 J11 **Jinsha** Guizhou, S China 27°24′N 106°16′E
160 M10 **Jinshi** Hunan, S China 29°42′N 111°46′E
Jinshi *see* Xinning
162 I9 **Jinst** *var.* Bodī. Bayanhongor, C Mongolia 45°25′N 100°33′E
159 R7 **Jinta** Gansu, N China 40°01′N 98°57′E
161 Q12 **Jin Xi** ≈ SE China
Jinxi *see* Huludao
Jinxian *see* Jinzhou
161 P6 **Jinxiang** Shandong, E China 35°08′N 116°19′E
161 P8 **Jinzhai** *var.* Meishan. Anhui, E China 31°42′N 115°47′E
161 N4 **Jinzhong** *var.* Yuci. Shanxi, C China 37°34′N 112°45′E
163 T12 **Jinzhou** *var.* Chin-chou, Chinchow; *prev.* Chinhsien. Liaoning, NE China 41°07′N 121°06′E
163 U14 **Jinzhou** *prev.* Jinxian. Liaoning, NE China 39°04′N 121°45′E
Jinzhu *see* Daocheng
138 H12 **Jinz, Qā' al** ◉ C Jordan
47 S8 **Jiparaná, Rio** ≈ W Brazil
56 A7 **Jipijapa** Manabí, W Ecuador 01°23′S 80°35′W
42 F8 **Jiquilisco** Usulután, S El Salvador 13°19′N 88°35′W
Jirgalanta *see* Hovd
147 S12 **Jirgatol** *Rus.* Dzhirgatal'. C Tajikistan 39°13′N 71°09′E
75 X10 **Jirjā** *var.* Girga, Girgeh, Jirjā. C Egypt 26°17′N 31°58′E
Jirjā *see* Jirjā
111 B15 **Jirkov** *Ger.* Görkau. Ústecký Kraj, NW Czech Republic 50°30′N 13°27′E
143 T12 **Jīroft** *var.* Sabzawaran, Sabzvārān. Kermān, SE Iran 28°40′N 57°40′E
81 P14 **Jirriiban** Mudug, E Somalia 07°15′N 48°55′E
160 L11 **Jishou** Hunan, S China 28°20′N 109°43′E
Jisr ash Shadadi *see* Ash Shadādah
116 I14 **Jitaru** Olt, S Romania 44°27′N 24°32′E
Jitschin *see* Jičín
116 H14 **Jiu** *Ger.* Schil, Schyl, *Hung.* Zsil, Zsily. ≈ S Romania
161 R11 **Jiufeng Shan** ▲▲ SE China
161 P9 **Jiujiang** Jiangxi, S China 29°45′N 115°59′E
161 O10 **Jiuling Shan** ▲▲ S China
160 G10 **Jiulong** *var.* Garba, *Tib.* Gyaisi. Sichuan, C China 29°00′N 101°30′E
161 Q13 **Jiulong Jiang** ≈ SE China
161 Q12 **Jiulong Xi** ≈ SE China
159 R8 **Jiuquan** *var.* Suzhou. Gansu, N China 39°47′N 98°30′E
160 K17 **Jiusuo** Hainan, S China 18°25′N 109°55′E
163 W10 **Jiutai** Jilin, NE China 44°01′N 125°51′E
160 K13 **Jiuwan Dashan** ▲▲ S China
160 I7 **Jiuzhaigou** *var.* Nongle; *prev.* Nanping. Sichuan, C China 33°25′N 104°05′E
148 I16 **Jiwani** Baluchistān, SW Pakistan 25°05′N 61°46′E
163 Y8 **Jixi** Heilongjiang, NE China 45°17′N 131°01′E
163 Y7 **Jixian** *var.* Fuli. Heilongjiang, NE China 46°38′N 131°04′E
160 M5 **Jixian** *var.* Ji Xian. Shanxi, C China 36°15′N 110°41′E
Ji Xian *see* Jixian
Jiza *see* Al Jīzah
141 N13 **Jīzān** *var.* Qīzān. Jīzān, SW Saudi Arabia 17°50′N 42°50′E
141 N13 **Jīzān** *var.* Minṭaqat Jīzān. ◈ *province* SW Saudi Arabia
Jīzān, Minṭaqat *see* Jīzān
140 K6 **Jizl, Wādī al** *dry watercourse* W Saudi Arabia
164 H12 **Jizō-zaki** *headland* Honshū, SW Japan 35°34′N 133°16′E
141 U14 **Jiz', Wādī al** *dry watercourse* E Yemen
147 O11 **Jizzax** *Rus.* Dzhizak. Jizzax Viloyati, C Uzbekistan 40°08′N 67°47′E
147 N10 **Jizzax Viloyati** *Rus.* Dzhizakskaya Oblast'. ◈ *province* C Uzbekistan
60 I13 **Joaçaba** Santa Catarina, S Brazil 27°08′S 51°30′W
Joal *see* Joal-Fadiout
76 F11 **Joal-Fadiout** *prev.* Joal. W Senegal 14°09′N 16°50′W
76 E10 **João Barrosa** Boa Vista, E Cape Verde 16°01′N 22°44′W
João Belo *see* Xai-Xai
João de Almeida *see* Chibia
59 Q15 **João Pessoa** *prev.* Paraíba. *state capital* Paraíba, E Brazil 07°06′S 34°53′W
25 X7 **Joaquin** Texas, SW USA 31°58′N 94°03′W
62 K6 **Joaquín V. González** Salta, N Argentina 25°06′S 64°07′W
Joazeiro *see* Juazeiro
Job'urg *see* Johannesburg
109 O7 **Jochberger Ache** ≈ W Austria
Jo-ch'iang *see* Ruoqiang
92 K12 **Jock** Norrbotten, N Sweden 66°40′N 22°45′E
42 I5 **Jocón** Yoro, N Honduras 15°17′N 86°55′W
105 O13 **Jódar** Andalucía, S Spain 37°51′N 03°18′W
152 F12 **Jodhpur** Rājasthān, NW India 26°17′N 73°02′E
99 I19 **Jodoigne** Walloon Brabant, C Belgium 50°43′N 04°52′E
93 O16 **Joensuu** Itä-Suomi, SE Finland 62°36′N 29°45′E
37 W4 **Joes** Colorado, C USA 39°36′N 102°40′W
191 Z3 **Joe's Hill** *hill* Kiritimati, NE Kiribati
165 N11 **Jōetsu** *var.* Zyôetu. Niigata, Honshū, C Japan 37°09′N 138°13′E
83 M18 **Jofane** Inhambane, S Mozambique 21°16′S 34°21′E
153 R12 **Jogbani** Bihār, NE India 26°23′N 87°16′E
118 I5 **Jõgeva** *Ger.* Laisholm. Jõgevamaa, E Estonia 58°45′N 26°23′E
118 I4 **Jõgevamaa** *off.* Jõgeva Maakond. ◈ *province* E Estonia
Jõgeva Maakond *see* Jõgevamaa
155 E18 **Jog Falls** *Waterfall* Karnātaka, W India
143 S4 **Joghatāy** Khorāsān, NE Iran 36°34′N 57°00′E
153 U12 **Jogīghopa** Assam, NE India 26°14′N 90°35′E
152 I7 **Jogindarnagar** Himāchal Pradesh, N India 31°51′N 76°47′E
Jogjakarta *see* Yogyakarta
164 L11 **Jōhana** Toyama, Honshū, SW Japan 36°30′N 136°53′E
83 J21 **Johannesburg** *var.* Egoli, Erautini, Gauteng, *abbrev.* Job'urg. Gauteng, NE South Africa 26°10′S 28°02′E
35 T13 **Johannesburg** California, W USA 35°20′N 117°37′W
Johannisburg *see* Pisz
149 P14 **Johi** Sind, SE Pakistan 26°46′N 67°28′E
55 T13 **Johi Village** S Guyana 01°48′N 58°33′W
45 W10 **John A. Osborne** ✈ (Plymouth) E Montserrat 16°45′N 62°09′W
32 K13 **John Day** Oregon, NW USA 44°25′N 118°57′W
32 I11 **John Day River** ≈ Oregon, NW USA
18 L14 **John F Kennedy** ✈ (New York) Long Island, New York, NE USA 40°39′N 73°45′W
21 V8 **John H. Kerr Reservoir** *var.* Buggs Island Lake, Kerr Lake. ▣ North Carolina/Virginia, SE USA
37 V6 **John Martin Reservoir** ▣ Colorado, C USA
96 K6 **John o'Groats** N Scotland, United Kingdom 58°38′N 03°03′W
27 P5 **John Redmond Reservoir** ▣ Kansas, C USA
39 Q7 **John River** ≈ Alaska, USA
26 H6 **Johnson** Kansas, C USA 37°33′N 101°46′W
18 M7 **Johnson** Vermont, NE USA 44°39′N 72°40′W
18 D13 **Johnsonburg** Pennsylvania, NE USA 41°28′N 78°37′W
18 H11 **Johnson City** New York, NE USA 42°06′N 75°54′W
21 P8 **Johnson City** Tennessee, S USA 36°18′N 82°21′W
25 R10 **Johnson City** Texas, SW USA 30°17′N 98°27′W
35 S12 **Johnsondale** California, W USA 35°58′N 118°32′W
10 I8 **Johnsons Crossing** Yukon Territory, W Canada 60°30′N 133°15′W
21 T13 **Johnsonville** South Carolina, SE USA 33°50′N 79°26′W
21 Q13 **Johnston** South Carolina, SE USA 33°49′N 81°48′W
192 M6 **Johnston Atoll** ◇ US *unincorporated territory* C Pacific Ocean
175 Q3 **Johnston Atoll** *atoll* C Pacific Ocean
30 L17 **Johnston City** Illinois, N USA 37°49′N 88°55′W
180 K12 **Johnston, Lake** *salt lake* Western Australia
31 S13 **Johnstown** Ohio, N USA 40°08′N 82°39′W
18 D15 **Johnstown** Pennsylvania, NE USA 40°20′N 78°56′W
168 L10 **Johor** *var.* Johore. ◈ *state* Peninsular Malaysia
Johor Baharu *see* Johor Bahru
168 K10 **Johor Bahru** *var.* Johor Baharu, Johore Bahru. Johor, Peninsular Malaysia 01°29′N 103°44′E
Johore *see* Johor
Johore Bahru *see* Johor Bahru
118 K3 **Jõhvi** *Ger.* Jewe. Ida-Virumaa, NE Estonia 59°21′N 27°25′E
103 P7 **Joigny** Yonne, C France 47°58′N 03°24′E
Joinvile *see* Joinville
60 K12 **Joinville** *var.* Joinvile. Santa Catarina, S Brazil 26°20′S 48°55′W
103 R6 **Joinville** Haute-Marne, N France 48°26′N 05°07′E
194 H3 **Joinville Island** *island* Antarctica
41 O15 **Jojutla** *var.* Jojutla de Juárez. Morelos, S Mexico 18°38′N 99°10′W
Jojutla de Juárez *see* Jojutla
92 I12 **Jokkmokk** *Lapp.* Dálvvadis. Norrbotten, N Sweden 66°35′N 19°57′E
92 L2 **Jökuldalur** ≈ E Iceland
92 K2 **Jökulsá á Fjöllum** ≈ NE Iceland
Jokyakarta *see* Yogyakarta
30 M11 **Joliet** Illinois, N USA 41°33′N 88°05′W
15 O11 **Joliette** Québec, SE Canada 46°02′N 73°27′W
171 O8 **Jolo** Jolo Island, SW Philippines 06°02′N 121°00′E
94 D11 **Jølstervatnet** ◉ S Norway
169 S16 **Jombang** *prev.* Djombang. Jawa, S Indonesia 07°33′S 112°14′E
159 R14 **Jomda** Xizang Zizhiqu, W China 31°26′N 98°09′E
118 G13 **Jonava** *Ger.* Janow, *Pol.* Janów. Kaunas, C Lithuania 55°05′N 24°19′E
146 L11 **Jondor** *Rus.* Zhondor. Buxoro Viloyati, C Uzbekistan 39°46′N 64°11′E
159 V11 **Jonê** *var.* Liulin. Gansu, C China 34°36′N 103°39′E
27 X9 **Jonesboro** Arkansas, C USA 35°50′N 90°42′W
23 S4 **Jonesboro** Georgia, SE USA 33°31′N 84°21′W
30 L17 **Jonesboro** Illinois, N USA 37°25′N 89°19′W
22 H5 **Jonesboro** Louisiana, S USA 32°14′N 92°43′W
21 P8 **Jonesboro** Tennessee, S USA 36°17′N 82°28′W
19 T6 **Jonesport** Maine, NE USA 44°33′N 67°35′W
0 J4 **Jones Sound** *channel* Nunavut, N Canada
22 I6 **Jonesville** Louisiana, S USA 31°37′N 91°49′W
31 Q10 **Jonesville** Michigan, N USA 41°58′N 84°39′W
21 Q11 **Jonesville** South Carolina, SE USA 34°49′N 81°38′W
146 K10 **Jongeldi** *Rus.* Dzhankel'dy. Buxoro Viloyati, C Uzbekistan 40°50′N 63°16′E
81 F14 **Jonglei** Jonglei, E South Sudan 06°54′N 31°19′E
81 F14 **Jonglei** *var.* Gongoleh State. ◈ *state* E South Sudan
81 F14 **Jonglei Canal** *canal* E South Sudan
118 F11 **Joniškėlis** Panevėžys, N Lithuania 56°02′N 24°10′E
118 F10 **Joniškis** *Ger.* Janischken. Šiaulai, N Lithuania 56°15′N 23°36′E
95 L19 **Jönköping** Jönköping, S Sweden 57°45′N 14°10′E
95 K20 **Jönköping** ◈ *county* S Sweden
15 Q7 **Jonquière** Québec, SE Canada 48°25′N 71°16′W
41 V15 **Jonuta** Tabasco, SE Mexico 18°04′N 92°03′W
102 K12 **Jonzac** Charente-Maritime, W France 45°26′N 00°25′W
27 R7 **Joplin** Missouri, C USA 37°04′N 94°31′W
33 W8 **Jordan** Montana, NW USA 47°18′N 106°54′W
138 H12 **Jordan** *off.* Hashemite Kingdom of Jordan, *Ar.* Al Mamlaka al Urduniya al Hashemīyah, Al Urdunn; *prev.* Transjordan. ◆ *monarchy* SW Asia
138 G9 **Jordan** *Ar.* Urdunn, *Heb.* HaYarden. ≈ SW Asia
Jordan Lake *see* B. Everett Jordan Reservoir
111 K17 **Jordanów** Małopolskie, S Poland 49°39′N 19°51′E
32 M15 **Jordan Valley** Oregon, NW USA 42°59′N 117°03′W
138 G9 **Jordan Valley** *valley* N Israel
57 D15 **Jorge Chávez International** *var.* Lima. ✈ (Lima) Lima, W Peru 12°07′S 77°01′W
113 L23 **Jorgucat** *var.* Jergucati, Jorgucati. Gjirokastër, S Albania 39°57′N 20°14′E
Jorgucati *see* Jorgucat
153 X12 **Jorhāt** Assam, NE India 26°45′N 94°09′E
93 J14 **Jörn** Västerbotten, N Sweden 65°03′N 20°04′E
37 R14 **Jornada Del Muerto** *valley* New Mexico, SW USA
93 N17 **Joroinen** Itä-Suomi, E Finland 62°11′N 27°50′E
95 C16 **Jørpeland** Rogaland, S Norway 59°01′N 06°04′E
77 W14 **Jos** Plateau, C Nigeria 09°59′N 08°57′E
171 Q8 **Jose Abad Santos** *var.* Trinidad. Mindanao, S Philippines 05°51′N 125°35′E
61 F19 **José Batlle y Ordóñez** *var.* Batlle y Ordóñez. Florida, C Uruguay 33°28′S 55°08′W
63 H18 **José de San Martín** Chubut, S Argentina 44°04′S 70°29′W
61 E19 **José Enrique Rodó** *var.* Rodó, José E.Rodo; *prev.* Drabble, Drable. Soriano, SW Uruguay 33°43′S 57°33′W
José E.Rodo *see* José Enrique Rodó
Josefsdorf *see* Žabalj
44 C4 **José Martí** ✈ (La Habana) Cuidad de La Habana, N Cuba 23°03′N 82°22′W
61 F19 **José Pedro Varela** *var.* José P.Varela. Lavalleja, S Uruguay 33°30′S 54°28′W
181 N2 **Joseph Bonaparte Gulf** *gulf* N Australia
37 N11 **Joseph City** Arizona, SW USA 34°56′N 110°18′W
13 O9 **Joseph, Lake** ◉ Newfoundland and Labrador, E Canada
14 G13 **Joseph, Lake** ◉ Ontario, S Canada
186 C6 **Josephstaal** Madang, N Papua New Guinea 04°42′S 144°55′E
José P.Varela *see* José Pedro Varela
59 J14 **José Rodrigues** Pará, N Brazil 05°45′S 51°20′W
152 K9 **Joshīmath** Uttarakhand, N India 30°33′N 79°35′E
25 T7 **Joshua** Texas, SW USA 32°27′N 97°23′W
35 V15 **Joshua Tree** California, W USA 34°07′N 116°18′W
77 V14 **Jos Plateau** *plateau* C Nigeria
102 H6 **Josselin** Morbihan, NW France 47°57′N 02°35′W
Jos Sudarso *see* Yos Sudarso, Pulau
94 E11 **Jostedalsbreen** *glacier* S Norway
94 F12 **Jotunheimen** ▲▲ S Norway
138 G7 **Joûnié** *var.* Junīyah. W Lebanon 33°54′N 35°36′E
25 R13 **Jourdanton** Texas, SW USA 28°55′N 98°34′W
98 L7 **Joure** *Fris.* De Jouwer. Fryslân, N Netherlands 52°58′N 05°48′E
93 M18 **Joutsa** Länsi-Suomi, C Finland 61°46′N 26°09′E
93 N18 **Joutseno** Etelä-Suomi, SE Finland 61°06′N 28°30′E
92 M12 **Joutsijärvi** Lappi, NE Finland 66°40′N 28°00′E
108 A9 **Joux, Lac de** ◉ W Switzerland
Jovakān *see* Jowkān
44 D5 **Jovellanos** Matanzas, W Cuba 22°49′N 81°11′W
153 V13 **Jowai** Meghālaya, NE India 25°25′N 92°21′E
Jowat *see* Jabwot
Jowhar *see* Jawhar
143 O12 **Jowkān** *var.* Jovakān. Fārs, S Iran
Jowzam *see* Javazm
149 N2 **Jowzjān** ◈ *province* N Afghanistan
Joypurhat *see* Jaipurhat
Józseffalva *see* Žabalj
J.Storm Thurmond Reservoir *see* Clark Hill Lake
45 T6 **Juana Díaz** C Puerto Rico 18°03′N 66°30′W
40 L9 **Juan Aldama** Zacatecas, C Mexico 24°20′N 103°23′W
0 E9 **Juan de Fuca Plate** *tectonic feature*
32 F7 **Juan de Fuca, Strait of** *strait* Canada/USA
Juan Fernandez Islands *see* Juan Fernández, Islas
193 S11 **Juan Fernández, Islas** *Eng.* Juan Fernandez Islands. *island group* W Chile
55 O4 **Juangriego** Nueva Esparta, NE Venezuela 11°06′N 63°59′W
56 D11 **Juanjuí** *var.* Juanjuy. San Martín, N Peru 07°10′S 76°44′W
Juanjuy *see* Juanjuí
93 N16 **Juankoski** Itä-Suomi, C Finland 63°01′N 28°24′E
Juan Lacaze *see* Juan L. Lacaze
61 E20 **Juan L. Lacaze** *var.* Juan Lacaze, Puerto Sauce; *prev.* Sauce. Colonia, SW Uruguay 34°26′S 57°25′W
62 L5 **Juan Solá** Salta, N Argentina 23°30′S 62°42′W
63 F21 **Juan Stuven, Isla** *island* S Chile
59 H16 **Juará** Mato Grosso, W Brazil 11°10′S 57°28′W
41 N7 **Juárez** *var.* Villa Juárez. Coahuila, NE Mexico 27°39′N 100°43′W
40 C2 **Juárez, Sierra de** ▲▲ NW Mexico
59 O15 **Juazeiro** *prev.* Joazeiro. Bahia, E Brazil 09°25′S 40°30′W
59 P14 **Juazeiro do Norte** Ceará, E Brazil 07°10′S 39°18′W
81 F15 **Juba** *var.* Jūbā. ● (South Sudan) Central Equatoria, S South Sudan 04°50′N 31°35′E
81 L17 **Juba** *Amh.* Genalē Wenz, *It.* Guiba, *Som.* Ganaane, Webi Jubba. ≈ Ethiopia/Somalia
194 H2 **Jubany** *Argentinian research station* Antarctica 61°57′S 58°23′W
Jubayl *see* Jbail
81 L18 **Jubbada Dhexe** *off.* Gobolka Jubbada Dhexe. ◈ *region* SW Somalia
Jubbada Dhexe, Gobolka *see* Jubbada Dhexe
81 K18 **Jubbada Hoose** ◈ *region* SW Somalia
Jubba, Webi *see* Juba
Jubbulpore *see* Jabalpur
Jubeil *see* Jbail
74 B9 **Juby, Cap** *headland* SW Morocco 27°58′N 12°56′W
105 R10 **Júcar** *var.* Jucar. ≈ C Spain
40 L12 **Juchipila** Zacatecas, C Mexico 21°25′N 103°06′W
41 S16 **Juchitán** *var.* Juchitán de Zaragosa. Oaxaca, SE Mexico 16°27′N 95°W
Juchitán de Zaragosa *see* Juchitán
138 G11 **Judaea** *cultural region* Israel/West Bank
138 F11 **Judaean Hills** *Heb.* Haré Yehuda. *hill range* E Israel
138 H8 **Judaydah** *Fr.* Jdaïdé. Rīf Dimashq, W Syria 33°17′N 36°15′E
139 P11 **Judayyidat Hāmir** Al Anbār, S Iraq 31°50′N 41°50′E
109 U8 **Judenburg** Steiermark, C Austria 47°09′N 14°43′E
33 T8 **Judith River** ≈ Montana, NW USA
27 V11 **Judsonia** Arkansas, C USA 35°16′N 91°38′W
141 P14 **Jufrah, Wādī al** *dry watercourse* NW Yemen
Jugar *see* Sêrxü
Jugoslavija *see* Serbia
42 K10 **Juigalpa** Chontales, S Nicaragua 12°04′N 85°21′W
100 E9 **Juist** *island* NW Germany
Juisui *see* Ruisui
59 M21 **Juiz de Fora** Minas Gerais, SE Brazil 21°47′S 43°23′W
62 J5 **Jujuy** *off.* Provincia de Jujuy. ◈ *province* N Argentina
Jujuy *see* San Salvador de Jujuy
Jujuy, Provincia de *see* Jujuy
92 J11 **Jukkasjärvi** *Lapp.* Čohkkiras. Norrbotten, N Sweden 67°52′N 20°39′E
Jula *see* Gyula, Hungary
Jūlā *see* Jālū, Libya
37 W2 **Julesburg** Colorado, C USA 40°59′N 102°15′W
Julia Beterrae *see* Béziers
57 I17 **Juliaca** Puno, SE Peru 15°32′S 70°10′W
181 U6 **Julia Creek** Queensland, C Australia 20°40′S 141°49′E
35 V17 **Julian** California, W USA 33°04′N 116°36′W
98 H7 **Julianadorp** Noord-Holland, NW Netherlands 52°53′N 04°43′E
109 S11 **Julian Alps** *Ger.* Julische Alpen, *It.* Alpi Giulie, *Slvn.* Julijske Alpe. ▲▲ Italy/Slovenia
55 V11 **Juliana Top** ▲ C Suriname 03°39′N 56°36′W
Julianehåb *see* Qaqortoq
Julijske Alpe *see* Julian Alps
40 J6 **Julimes** Chihuahua, N Mexico 28°29′N 105°21′W
Julio Briga *see* Bragança
Juliobriga *see* Logroño
61 G15 **Júlio de Castilhos** Rio Grande do Sul, S Brazil 29°14′S 53°42′W
Juliomagus *see* Angers
Julische Alpen *see* Julian Alps
Jullundur *see* Jalandhar
147 N11 **Juma** *Rus.* Dzhuma. Samarqand Viloyati, C Uzbekistan 39°43′N 66°37′E
161 O3 **Juma He** ≈ E China
81 L18 **Jumba** *prev.* Jumboo. Jubbada Hoose, S Somalia 0°12′S 42°34′E
Jumboo *see* Jumba
35 Y11 **Jumbo Peak** ▲ Nevada, W USA 36°12′N 114°09′W
105 R12 **Jumilla** Murcia, SE Spain 38°28′N 01°19′W
153 N10 **Jumla** Mid Western, NW Nepal 29°22′N 82°13′E
Jummoo *see* Jammu
Jumna *see* Yamuna
Jumporn *see* Chumphon
30 K5 **Jump River** ≈ Wisconsin, N USA
154 B11 **Jūnāgadh** *var.* Junagarh. Gujarāt, W India 21°32′N 70°32′E
Junagarh *see* Jūnāgadh
161 Q6 **Junan** *var.* Shizilu. Shandong, E China 35°11′N 118°47′E
62 G11 **Juncal, Cerro** ▲ C Chile 33°03′S 70°02′W
25 Q10 **Junction** Texas, SW USA 30°31′N 99°48′W
36 K6 **Junction** Utah, W USA 38°14′N 112°13′W
27 O4 **Junction City** Kansas, C USA 39°02′N 96°51′W
32 F13 **Junction City** Oregon, NW USA 44°13′N 123°12′W
60 M10 **Jundiaí** São Paulo, S Brazil 23°10′S 46°54′W
39 X12 **Juneau** *state capital* Alaska, USA 58°13′N 134°11′W
30 M8 **Juneau** Wisconsin, N USA 43°23′N 88°42′W
105 U6 **Juneda** Cataluña, NE Spain 41°33′N 00°49′E
183 Q9 **Junee** New South Wales, SE Australia 34°51′S 147°33′E
35 R8 **June Lake** California, W USA 37°46′N 119°04′W
Jungbunzlau *see* Mladá Boleslav
158 L4 **Junggar Pendi** *Eng.* Dzungarian Basin. *basin* NW China
99 N24 **Junglinster** Grevenmacher, C Luxembourg 49°43′N 06°15′E
18 F14 **Juniata River** ≈ Pennsylvania, NE USA
61 B20 **Junín** Buenos Aires, E Argentina 34°36′S 61°02′W
57 E14 **Junín** Junín, C Peru 11°11′S 76°00′W
57 F14 **Junín** *off.* Departamento de Junín. ◈ *department* C Peru
63 H15 **Junín de los Andes** Neuquén, W Argentina 39°57′S 71°05′W
Junín, Departamento de *see* Junín
57 D14 **Junín, Lago de** ◉ C Peru
Junīyah *see* Joûnié
Junkseylon *see* Phuket
160 I11 **Junlian** Sichuan, C China 28°11′N 104°31′E
25 O11 **Juno** Texas, SW USA 30°09′N 101°07′W
92 J11 **Junosuando** *Lapp.* Čunusavvon. Norrbotten, N Sweden 67°25′N 22°28′E
93 H16 **Junsele** Västernorrland, C Sweden 63°42′N 16°54′E
Junten *see* Sunch'ŏn
32 L14 **Juntura** Oregon, NW USA 43°43′N 118°05′W
93 N14 **Juntusranta** Oulu, E Finland 65°12′N 29°30′E
118 H11 **Juodupė** Panevėžys, NE Lithuania 56°07′N 25°37′E
119 H14 **Juozapinės Kalnas** ▲ SE Lithuania 54°29′N 25°27′E
99 K19 **Juprelle** Liège, E Belgium 50°39′N 05°31′E
80 D13 **Jur** ≈ W South Sudan
103 S9 **Jura** ◈ *department* E France
108 C7 **Jura** ◈ *canton* NW Switzerland
108 B8 **Jura** *var.* Jura Mountains. ▲▲ France/Switzerland
96 G12 **Jura** *island* SW Scotland, United Kingdom
Juraciszki *see* Yuratsishki
54 C8 **Juradó** Chocó, NW Colombia 07°07′N 77°45′W
Jura Mountains *see* Jura
96 G12 **Jura, Sound of** *strait* W Scotland, United Kingdom
139 V15 **Juraybīyāt, Bi'r** *well* S Iraq
118 E13 **Jurbarkas** *Ger.* Georgenburg, Jurburg. Tauragė, W Lithuania 55°04′N 22°45′E
99 F20 **Jurbise** Hainaut, SW Belgium 50°33′N 03°54′E
Jurburg *see* Jurbarkas
118 F9 **Jūrmala** C Latvia 56°57′N 23°42′E
58 D13 **Juruá** Amazonas, NW Brazil 03°08′S 65°59′W
48 F7 **Juruá, Rio** *var.* Río Yuruá. ≈ Brazil/Peru
59 G16 **Juruena** Mato Grosso, W Brazil 10°32′S 58°38′W
59 G16 **Juruena, Rio** ≈ W Brazil
165 Q6 **Jūsan-ko** ◉ Honshū, C Japan
25 O6 **Justiceburg** Texas, SW USA 32°57′N 101°07′W
Justinianopolis *see* Kirşehir
62 K11 **Justo Daract** San Luis, C Argentina 33°52′S 65°12′W
59 C14 **Jutaí** Amazonas, W Brazil 05°10′S 68°45′W
58 C13 **Jutaí, Rio** ≈ NW Brazil
100 N13 **Jüterbog** Brandenburg, E Germany 51°58′N 13°06′E
42 E6 **Jutiapa** Jutiapa, S Guatemala 14°18′N 89°52′W
42 A3 **Jutiapa** *off.* Departamento de Jutiapa. ◈ *department* SE Guatemala
Jutiapa, Departamento de *see* Jutiapa
42 J6 **Juticalpa** Olancho, C Honduras 14°39′N 86°12′W
82 I13 **Jutila** North Western, NW Zambia 12°33′S 26°09′E
Jutland *see* Jylland
84 F8 **Jutland Bank** *undersea feature* SE North Sea 56°50′N 07°20′E
93 N16 **Juuka** Itä-Suomi, E Finland 63°12′N 29°17′E
93 N17 **Juva** Itä-Suomi, E Finland 61°55′N 27°54′E
Juvavum *see* Salzburg
44 A6 **Juventud, Isla de la** *var.* Isla de Pinos, *Eng.* Isle of Youth; *prev.* The Isle of the Pines. *island* W Cuba
161 Q5 **Juxian** *var.* Chengyang, Ju Xian. Shandong, E China 35°33′N 118°45′E
Ju Xian *see* Juxian
161 P6 **Juye** Shandong, E China 35°26′N 116°04′E
113 O15 **Južna Morava** *Ger.* Südliche Morava. ≈ SE Serbia
83 H20 **Jwaneng** Southern, S Botswana 24°35′N 24°45′E
95 I23 **Jyderup** Sjælland, E Denmark 55°40′N 11°25′E
95 F22 **Jylland** *Eng.* Jutland. *peninsula* W Denmark
Jyrgalan *see* Dzhergalan
93 M17 **Jyväskylä** Länsi-Suomi, C Finland 62°08′N 25°47′E

K

38 D9 **Ka'a'awa** *var.* Kaaawa. O'ahu, Hawaii, USA, C Pacific Ocean 21°33′N 157°47′W
Kaaawa *see* Ka'a'awa
81 G16 **Kaabong** NE Uganda 03°30′N 34°08′E
Kaaden *see* Kadaň
Kaafu Atoll *see* Male' Atoll
55 V9 **Kaaimanston** Sipaliwini, N Suriname 05°06′N 56°04′W
Kaakhhka *see* Kaka
Kaala *see* Caála
187 O16 **Kaala-Gomen** Province Nord, W New Caledonia 20°40′S 164°24′E
92 L9 **Kaamanen** *Lapp.* Gámas. Lappi, N Finland 69°05′N 27°16′E
Kaapstad *see* Cape Town
Kaarasjoki *see* Karasjok
Kaaresuanto *see* Karesuando
92 J10 **Kaaresuvanto** *Lapp.* Gárassavon. Lappi, N Finland 68°28′N 22°29′E
93 K19 **Kaarina** Länsi-Suomi, SW Finland 60°24′N 22°25′E
99 I14 **Kaatsheuvel** Noord-Brabant, S Netherlands 51°39′N 05°02′E
93 N16 **Kaavi** Itä-Suomi, C Finland 62°58′N 28°30′E
Kaba *see* Habahe
171 O14 **Kabaena, Pulau** *island* C Indonesia
Kabakly *see* Gabakly
76 J14 **Kabala** N Sierra Leone 09°40′N 11°36′W
81 E19 **Kabale** SW Uganda 01°15′S 29°58′E
55 U10 **Kabalebo Rivier** ≈ W Suriname
79 N22 **Kabalo** Katanga, SE Dem. Rep. Congo 06°02′S 26°55′E
79 O21 **Kabambare** Maniema, E Dem. Rep. Congo 04°40′S 27°41′E
145 W13 **Kabanbay** *Kaz.* Qabanbay; *prev.* Andreyevka, *Kaz.* Andreevka. Almaty, SE Kazakhstan 45°50′N 80°34′E
145 Q9 **Kabanbay Batyr** *prev.* Rozhdestvenka. Akmola, C Kazakhstan 50°51′N 71°25′E
187 Y15 **Kabara** *prev.* Kambara. *island* Lau Group, E Fiji
Kabardino-Balkaria *see* Kabardino-Balkarskaya Respublika
126 M15 **Kabardino-Balkarskaya Respublika** *Eng.* Kabardino-Balkaria. ◈ *autonomous republic* SW Russian Federation
79 O19 **Kabare** Sud-Kivu, E Dem. Rep. Congo 02°13′S 28°40′E
171 T11 **Kabarei** Papua, E Indonesia 0°01′S 130°58′E
171 P7 **Kabasalan** Mindanao, S Philippines 07°46′N 122°49′E
77 U15 **Kabba** Kogi, S Nigeria 07°48′N 06°07′E
92 I13 **Kåbdalis** *Lapp.* Goabddális. Norrbotten, N Sweden 66°08′N 20°03′E
138 M6 **Kabd aş Şārim** *hill range* E Syria
14 B7 **Kabenung Lake** ◉ Ontario, S Canada
29 W3 **Kabetogama Lake** ◉ Minnesota, N USA
Kabia, Pulau *see* Kabin, Pulau
79 M22 **Kabinda** Kasai-Oriental, SE Dem. Rep. Congo 06°09′S 24°29′E
Kabinda *see* Cabinda
171 O15 **Kabin, Pulau** *var.* Pulau Kabia. *island* W Indonesia
171 P16 **Kabir** Pulau Pantar, S Indonesia 08°15′S 124°12′E
149 T10 **Kabīrwāla** Punjab, E Pakistan 30°24′N 71°51′E
114 M9 **Kableshkovo** Burgas, E Bulgaria 42°65′N 27°34′E
78 I13 **Kabo** Ouham, NW Central African Republic 07°43′N 18°38′E
Kābol *see* Kābul
83 H14 **Kabompo** North Western, W Zambia 13°36′S 24°10′E
83 H14 **Kabompo** ≈ W Zambia
79 M22 **Kabongo** Katanga, SE Dem. Rep. Congo 07°20′S 25°34′E
120 K11 **Kaboudia, Rass** *headland* E Tunisia 35°13′N 11°09′E
124 J14 **Kabozha** Novgorodskaya Oblast', W Russian Federation 58°48′N 35°00′E
Kabūd Gonbad *see* Kalāt
142 L5 **Kabūd Rāhang** Hamadān, W Iran 35°12′N 48°44′E
82 L12 **Kabuko** Northern, NE Zambia 11°31′S 31°16′E
149 Q5 **Kābul** *prev.* Kābol. ● (Afghanistan) Kābul, E Afghanistan 34°34′N 69°08′E
149 Q5 **Kābul** *prev.* Kābol. ◈ *province* E Afghanistan
149 Q5 **Kābul** ✈ Kābul, E Afghanistan 34°31′N 69°11′E
149 R5 **Kabul** *var.* Daryā-ye Kābul. ≈ Afghanistan/Pakistan *see also* Kābul, Daryā-ye
Kabul *see* Kābul, Daryā-ye
149 S5 **Kābul, Daryā-ye** *var.* Kabul. ≈ Afghanistan/Pakistan *see also* Kabul
Kābul, Daryā-ye *see* Kabul
79 O25 **Kabunda** Katanga, SE Dem. Rep. Congo 12°21′S 29°14′E
171 R9 **Kaburuang, Pulau** *island* Kepulauan Talaud, N Indonesia
80 G8 **Kabushiya** River Nile, NE Sudan 16°54′N 33°41′E
83 J14 **Kabwe** Central, C Zambia 14°29′S 28°25′E
186 E7 **Kabwum** Morobe, C Papua New Guinea 06°04′S 147°09′E
113 N17 **Kačanik** *Serb.* Kačanik. S Kosovo 42°13′N 21°16′E
Kačanik *see* Kaçanik
118 F13 **Kačerginė** Kaunas, C Lithuania 54°55′N 23°40′E
117 S13 **Kacha** Avtonomna Respublika Krym, S Ukraine 44°46′N 33°33′E
154 A10 **Kachchh, Gulf of** *var.* Gulf of Cutch, Gulf of Kutch. *gulf* W India
154 I11 **Kachchhīdhāna** Madhya Pradesh, C India 21°33′N 78°54′E
149 Q11 **Kachchh, Rann of** *var.* Rann of Kachh, Rann of Kutch. *salt marsh* India/Pakistan
39 Q13 **Kachemak Bay** *bay* Alaska, USA
Kachh, Rann of *see* Kachchh, Rann of
77 V14 **Kachia** Kaduna, C Nigeria 09°52′N 08°00′E
167 N2 **Kachin State** ◈ *state* N Myanmar (Burma)
Kachiry *see* Kashyr
137 Q11 **Kaçkar Dağları** ▲▲ NE Turkey
155 C21 **Kadamatt Island** *island* Lakshadweep, India, N Indian Ocean
111 B15 **Kadaň** *Ger.* Kaaden. Ústecký Kraj, NW Czech Republic 50°24′N 13°16′E
1667 N11 **Kadan Kyun** *prev.* King Island. *island* Mergui Archipelago, S Myanmar (Burma)
187 X15 **Kadavu** *prev.* Kandavu. *island* S Fiji
187 X15 **Kadavu Passage** *channel* S Fiji
79 G16 **Kadéï** ≈ Cameroon/Central African Republic
Kadhimain *see* Al Kāẓimīyah
Kadijica *see* Kadiytsa
114 M13 **Kadīköy Barajı** ▣ NW Turkey
182 I8 **Kadina** South Australia 33°59′S 137°43′E
136 H15 **Kadınhanı** Konya, C Turkey 38°15′N 32°14′E
76 M14 **Kadiolo** Sikasso, S Mali 10°30′N 05°43′W
136 L16 **Kadirli** Osmaniye, S Turkey 37°22′N 36°05′E
114 G11 **Kadiytsa** *Mac.* Kadijica. ▲ Bulgaria/FYR Macedonia 41°48′N 22°58′E
28 L10 **Kadoka** South Dakota, N USA 43°49′N 101°30′W
127 N5 **Kadom** Ryazanskaya Oblast', W Russian Federation 54°35′N 42°27′E
83 K16 **Kadoma** *prev.* Gatooma. Mashonaland West, C Zimbabwe 18°22′S 29°55′E
80 E12 **Kadugli** Southern Kordofan, S Sudan 11°N 29°44′E
77 V14 **Kaduna** Kaduna, C Nigeria 10°32′N 07°26′E
77 V14 **Kaduna** ◈ *state* C Nigeria
77 V15 **Kaduna** ≈ N Nigeria
124 K14 **Kaduy** Vologodskaya Oblast', NW Russian Federation 59°10′N 37°11′E
154 E13 **Kadwa** ≈ W India
123 S9 **Kadykchan** Magadanskaya Oblast', E Russian Federation 62°54′N 146°53′E
Kadzharan *see* K'ajaran
125 T7 **Kadzherom** Respublika Komi, NW Russian Federation 64°42′N 55°51′E
Kadzhi-Say *see* Bokonbayevo
76 I10 **Kaédi** Gorgol, S Mauritania 16°12′N 13°32′W
78 G12 **Kaélé** Extrême-Nord, N Cameroon 10°05′N 14°28′E
38 C9 **Ka'ena Point** *var.* Kaena Point. *headland* O'ahu, Hawai'i, USA 21°34′N 158°16′W
184 J2 **Kaeo** Northland, North Island, New Zealand 35°03′S 173°40′E
163 X14 **Kaesŏng** *var.* Kaesŏng-si. S North Korea 37°58′N 126°31′E
Kaesŏng-si *see* Kaesŏng
Kaewieng *see* Kavieng
79 L24 **Kafakumba** Shaba, S Dem. Rep. Congo 09°39′S 23°43′E
Kafan *see* Kapan
77 V14 **Kafanchan** Kaduna, C Nigeria 09°32′N 08°18′E
Kaffa *see* Feodosiya
76 G11 **Kaffrine** C Senegal 14°07′N 15°27′W

◆ Country
● Country Capital
◇ Dependent Territory
○ Dependent Territory Capital
◈ Administrative Regions
✈ International Airport
▲ Mountain
▲▲ Mountain Range
Volcano
≈ River
◉ Lake
▣ Reservoir

Kafiréas, Akrotírio *see* Ntóro, Kávo
115 I19 **Kafiréos, Stenó** *strait* Évvoia/Kykládes, Greece, Aegean Sea
Kafirnigan *see* Kofarnihon
Kafo *see* Kafu
75 W7 **Kafr ash Shaykh** *var.* Kafrel Sheik, Kafr el Sheikh. N Egypt 31°07′N 30°56′E
Kafr el Sheikh *see* Kafr ash Shaykh
81 F17 **Kafu** *var.* Kafo. ≈ W Uganda
83 J15 **Kafue** Lusaka, SE Zambia 15°44′S 28°10′E
83 I14 **Kafue** ≈ C Zambia
67 T13 **Kafue Flats** *plain* C Zambia
164 K12 **Kaga** Ishikawa, Honshū, SW Japan 36°18′N 136°19′E
79 J14 **Kaga Bandoro** *prev.* Fort-Crampel. Nana-Grébizi, C Central African Republic 06°54′N 19°10′E
81 E18 **Kagadi** W Uganda 0°57′N 30°52′E
38 H17 **Kagalaska Island** *island* Aleutian Islands, Alaska, USA
Kagan *see* Kogon
Kaganovichabad *see* Kolkhozobod
Kagarlyk *see* Kaharlyk
164 H14 **Kagawa** *off.* Kagawa-ken. ◈ *prefecture* Shikoku, SW Japan
Kagawa-ken *see* Kagawa
154 J13 **Kagaznagar** Andhra Pradesh, C India 19°25′N 79°30′E
93 J14 **Kåge** Västerbotten, N Sweden 64°49′N 21°00′E
81 E19 **Kagera** *var.* Ziwa Magharibi, *Eng.* West Lake. ◈ *region* NW Tanzania
81 E19 **Kagera** *var.* Akagera. ≈ Rwanda/Tanzania *see also* Akagera
76 L5 **Kâgheṭ** *var.* Karet. *physical region* N Mauritania
Kagi *see* Jiayi
137 S12 **Kağızman** Kars, NE Turkey 40°08′N 43°07′E
188 I6 **Kagman Point** *headland* Saipan, S Northern Mariana Islands
164 C16 **Kagoshima** *var.* Kagosima. Kagoshima, Kyūshū, SW Japan 31°37′N 130°33′E
164 C16 **Kagoshima** *off.* Kagoshima-ken, *var.* Kagosima. ◈ *prefecture* Kyūshū, SW Japan
Kagoshima-ken *see* Kagoshima
Kagosima *see* Kagoshima
Kagul *see* Cahul
Kagul, Ozero *see* Kahul, Ozero
38 B8 **Kahala Point** *headland* Kaua'i, Hawai'i, USA 22°08′N 159°17′W
81 F21 **Kahama** Shinyanga, NW Tanzania 03°48′S 32°36′E
117 P5 **Kaharlyk** *Rus.* Kagarlyk. Kyyivs'ka Oblast', N Ukraine 49°50′N 30°50′E
169 T13 **Kahayan, Sungai** ≈ Borneo, C Indonesia
79 I22 **Kahemba** Bandundu, SW Dem. Rep. Congo 07°20′S 19°00′E
185 A23 **Kaherekoau Mountains** ▲▲ South Island, New Zealand
143 W14 **Kahīrī** *var.* Kūhīrī. Sīstān va Balūchestān, SE Iran 26°55′N 61°04′E
101 L16 **Kahla** Thüringen, C Germany 50°49′N 11°33′E
101 G15 **Kahler Asten** ▲ W Germany 51°11′N 08°32′E
149 Q4 **Kahmard, Daryā-ye** *prev.* Darya-i-surkhab. ≈ NE Afghanistan
143 T13 **Kahnūj** Kermān, SE Iran 28°N 57°41′E
27 V1 **Kahoka** Missouri, C USA 40°24′N 91°44′W
38 E10 **Kaho'olawe** *var.* Kahoolawe. *island* Hawai'i, USA, C Pacific Ocean
Kahoolawe *see* Kaho'olawe
136 M16 **Kahramanmaraş** *var.* Kahraman Maraş, Maraş, Marash. Kahramanmaraş, S Turkey 37°34′N 36°54′E
136 L15 **Kahramanmaraş** *var.* Kahraman Maraş, Maraş, Marash. ◈ *province* C Turkey
Kahraman Maraş *see* Kahramanmaraş
Kahror/Kahror Pakka *see* Kahror Pakka
149 T11 **Kahror Pakka** *var.* Kahror, Koror Pacca. Punjab, E Pakistan 29°38′N 71°59′E
137 N15 **Kâhta** Adıyaman, S Turkey 37°48′N 38°35′E
38 D8 **Kahuku** O'ahu, Hawaii, USA, C Pacific Ocean 21°40′N 157°57′W
38 D8 **Kahuku Point** *headland* O'ahu, Hawai'i, USA 21°42′N 157°59′W
116 M12 **Kahul, Ozero** *var.* Lacul Cahul, *Rus.* Ozero Kagul. ◎ Moldova/Ukraine
143 V11 **Kahūrak** Sīstān va Balūchestān, SE Iran 29°25′N 59°38′E
184 G13 **Kahurangi Point** *headland* South Island, New Zealand 40°41′S 171°57′E
149 V6 **Kahūta** Punjab, E Pakistan 33°38′N 73°27′E
77 S14 **Kaiama** Kwara, W Nigeria 09°37′N 03°58′E
186 D7 **Kaiapit** Morobe, C Papua New Guinea 06°12′S 146°09′E
185 I18 **Kaiapoi** Canterbury, South Island, New Zealand 43°23′S 172°40′E
36 K9 **Kaibab Plateau** *plain* Arizona, SW USA
171 U14 **Kai Besar, Pulau** *island* Kepulauan Kai, E Indonesia
36 L9 **Kaibito Plateau** *plain* Arizona, SW USA
158 K6 **Kaidu He** *var.* Karaxahar. ≈ NW China
55 S10 **Kaieteur Falls** *waterfall* C Guyana
161 O6 **Kaifeng** Henan, C China 34°47′N 114°20′E
184 J3 **Kaihu** Northland, North Island, New Zealand 35°47′S 173°39′E
Kaihua *see* Wenshan
171 U14 **Kai Kecil, Pulau** *island* Kepulauan Kai, E Indonesia
169 U16 **Kai, Kepulauan** *prev.* Kei Islands. *island group* Maluku, SE Indonesia
184 J3 **Kaikohe** Northland, North Island, New Zealand 35°25′S 173°48′E
185 J16 **Kaikoura** Canterbury, South Island, New Zealand 42°22′S 173°40′E
185 J16 **Kaikoura Peninsula** *peninsula* South Island, New Zealand
Kailas Range *see* Gangdisê Shan
160 K12 **Kaili** Guizhou, S China 26°34′N 107°58′E
38 F10 **Kailua** Maui, Hawaii, USA, C Pacific Ocean 20°53′N 156°13′W
Kailua *see* Kalaoa
38 G11 **Kailua-Kona** *var.* Kona. Hawaii, USA, C Pacific Ocean 19°43′N 155°58′W
186 B7 **Kaim** ≈ W Papua New Guinea
171 X14 **Kaima** Papua, E Indonesia 05°36′S 138°39′E
184 M7 **Kaimai Range** ▲▲ North Island, New Zealand
114 E13 **Kaïmaktsalán** *var.* Kajmakčalan. ▲ Greece/FYR Macedonia 40°57′N 21°48′E *see also* Kajmakčalan
Kaïmaktsalán *see* Kajmakčalan
185 C20 **Kaimanawa Mountains** ▲▲ North Island, New Zealand
118 E4 **Käina** *Ger.* Keinis; *prev.* Keina. Hiiumaa, W Estonia 58°50′N 22°49′E
109 V7 **Kainach** ≈ SE Austria
164 I14 **Kainan** Tokushima, Shikoku, SW Japan 33°36′N 134°20′E
164 H15 **Kainan** Wakayama, Honshū, SW Japan 34°09′N 135°12′E
147 U7 **Kaindy** *Kir.* Kayyngdy. Chuyskaya Oblast', N Kyrgyzstan 42°48′N 73°39′E
77 T14 **Kainji Dam** *dam* W Nigeria
Kainji Lake *see* Kainji Reservoir
77 T14 **Kainji Reservoir** *var.* Kainji Lake. ⊠ W Nigeria
186 D8 **Kaintiba** *var.* Kamina. Gulf, S Papua New Guinea 07°29′S 146°04′E
92 K12 **Kainulasjärvi** Norrbotten, N Sweden 67°00′N 22°31′E
184 K5 **Kaipara Harbour** *harbor* North Island, New Zealand
152 I10 **Kairāna** Uttar Pradesh, N India 29°24′N 77°10′E
74 M6 **Kairouan** *var.* Al Qayrawān. E Tunisia 35°46′N 10°11′E
Kaisaria *see* Kayseri
101 F20 **Kaiserslautern** Rheinland-Pfalz, SW Germany 49°27′N 07°46′E
118 G13 **Kaišiadorys** Kaunas, S Lithuania 54°51′N 24°27′E
184 I2 **Kaitaia** Northland, North Island, New Zealand 35°07′S 173°13′E
185 E24 **Kaitangata** Otago, South Island, New Zealand 46°18′S 169°52′E
152 I9 **Kaithal** Haryāna, NW India 29°47′N 76°26′E
Kaitong *see* Tongyu
169 N13 **Kait, Tanjung** *headland* Sumatera, W Indonesia 03°13′S 106°03′E
38 E9 **Kaiwi Channel** *channel* Hawai'i, USA, C Pacific Ocean
160 K9 **Kaixian** *var.* Hanfeng. Sichuan, C China 31°13′N 108°25′E
163 V11 **Kaiyuan** *var.* K'ai-yüan. Liaoning, NE China 42°33′N 124°04′E
160 H14 **Kaiyuan** Yunnan, SW China 23°42′N 103°14′E
K'ai-yüan *see* Kaiyuan
39 O9 **Kaiyuh Mountains** ▲▲ Alaska, USA
93 M15 **Kajaani** *Swe.* Kajana. Oulu, C Finland 64°17′N 27°46′E
149 N7 **Kajakī, Band-e** ◎ C Afghanistan
Kajan *see* Kayan, Sungai
Kajana *see* Kajaani
137 V13 **K'ajaran** *Rus.* Kadzharan. SE Armenia 39°10′N 46°09′E
Kajisay *see* Bokonbayevo
113 O20 **Kajmakčalan** *var.* Kaïmaktsalán. ▲ S FYR Macedonia 40°57′N 21°48′E *see also* Kaïmaktsalán
Kajmakčalan *see* Kaïmaktsalán
Kajnar *see* Kaynar
149 N6 **Kajrān** Dāykundī, C Afghanistan 33°12′N 65°28′E
149 N5 **Kaj Rūd** ≈ C Afghanistan
146 G14 **Kaka** *Rus.* Kaakhka. Ahal Welaýaty, S Turkmenistan 37°20′N 59°37′E
12 C12 **Kakabeka Falls** Ontario, S Canada 48°24′N 89°40′W
83 F23 **Kakamas** Northern Cape, W South Africa 28°45′S 20°33′E
81 H18 **Kakamega** Western, W Kenya 0°17′N 34°47′E
112 H13 **Kakanj** Federacija Bosna I Hercegovina, C Bosnia and Herzegovina 44°06′N 18°07′E
185 F22 **Kakanui Mountains** ▲▲ South Island, New Zealand
184 K11 **Kakaramea** Taranaki, North Island, New Zealand 39°42′S 174°27′E
76 J16 **Kakata** C Liberia 06°35′N 10°19′W
184 M11 **Kakatahi** Manawatu-Wanganui, North Island, New Zealand 39°40′S 175°20′E
113 M23 **Kakavi** Gjirokastër, S Albania 39°55′N 20°19′E
147 O14 **Kakaydi** Surkhondaryo Viloyati, S Uzbekistan 37°37′N 67°30′E
164 F13 **Kake** Hiroshima, Honshū, SW Japan 34°37′N 132°17′E
39 X13 **Kake** Kupreanof Island, Alaska, USA 56°58′N 133°57′W
171 P14 **Kakea** Pulau Wowoni, C Indonesia 04°09′S 123°06′E
164 M14 **Kakegawa** Shizuoka, Honshū, S Japan 34°47′N 138°02′E
165 V16 **Kakeroma-jima** Kagoshima, SW Japan
143 T6 **Kākhak** Khorāsān, E Iran
118 L11 **Kakhanavichy** *Rus.* Kokhanovichi. Vitsyebskaya Voblasts', N Belarus 55°52′N 28°08′E
39 P13 **Kakhonak** Alaska, USA 59°26′N 154°48′W
117 S10 **Kakhovka** Khersons'ka Oblast', S Ukraine 46°40′N 33°30′E
117 U9 **Kakhovs'ke Vodoskhovyshche** *Rus.* Kakhovskoye Vodokhranilishche. ⊠ SE Ukraine
Kakhovskoye Vodokhranilishche *see* Kakhovs'ke Vodoskhovyshche
117 T11 **Kakhovs'kyy Kanal** *canal* S Ukraine
Kakia *see* Khakhea
155 L16 **Kākināda** *prev.* Cocanada. Andhra Pradesh, E India 16°56′N 82°13′E
Käkisalmi *see* Priozersk
164 I13 **Kakogawa** Hyōgo, Honshū, SW Japan 34°49′N 134°52′E
81 F18 **Kakoge** C Uganda 01°03′N 32°30′E
145 O7 **Kak, Ozero** ◎ N Kazakhstan
Ka-Krem *see* Malyy Yenisey
Kakshaal-Too, Khrebet *see* Kokshaal-Tau
39 S5 **Kaktovik** Alaska, USA 70°08′N 143°37′W
165 Q11 **Kakuda** Miyagi, Honshū, C Japan 37°59′N 140°48′E
165 Q8 **Kakunodate** Akita, Honshū, C Japan 39°37′N 140°35′E
Kalaallit Nunaat *see* Greenland
149 T7 **Kālābāgh** Punjab, E Pakistan 33°00′N 71°35′E
171 Q16 **Kalabahi** Pulau Alor, S Indonesia 08°14′S 124°32′E
188 I5 **Kalabera** Saipan, S Northern Mariana Islands
83 G14 **Kalabo** Western, W Zambia 15°00′S 22°37′E
126 M9 **Kalach** Voronezhskaya Oblast', W Russian Federation 50°24′N 41°00′E
127 N10 **Kalach-na-Donu** Volgogradskaya Oblast', SW Russian Federation 48°45′N 43°29′E
166 K5 **Kaladan** ≈ W Myanmar (Burma)
14 K14 **Kaladar** Ontario, SE Canada 44°38′N 77°06′W
38 G13 **Ka Lae** *var.* South Cape, South Point. *headland* Hawai'i, USA, C Pacific Ocean 18°54′N 155°40′W
83 G19 **Kalahari Desert** *desert* Southern Africa
38 B8 **Kalāheo** *var.* Kalaheo. Kaua'i, Hawaii, USA, C Pacific Ocean 21°55′N 159°31′W
Kalaheo *see* Kalāheo
Kalaikhum *see* Qal'aikhum
Kala-i-Mor *see* Galaýmor
93 K15 **Kalajoki** Oulu, W Finland 64°15′N 24°E
Kalak *see* Eski Kaļak
Kal al Sraghna *see* El Kelâa Srarhna
32 G10 **Kalama** Washington, NW USA 46°00′N 122°50′W
Kalámai *see* Kalámata
115 G14 **Kalamariá** Kentrikí Makedonía, N Greece 40°37′N 22°58′E
115 C15 **Kalamás** *var.* Thiamis; *prev.* Thýamis. ≈ W Greece
115 E21 **Kalámata** *prev.* Kalámai. Pelopónnisos, S Greece 37°02′N 22°07′E
148 L16 **Kalamat, Khor** *Eng.* Kalmat Lagoon. *lagoon* SW Pakistan
148 L16 **Kalamat, Khor** *Eng.* Kalmat Lagoon. *lagoon* SW Pakistan
31 P10 **Kalamazoo** Michigan, N USA 42°17′N 85°35′W
31 P9 **Kalamazoo River** ≈ Michigan, N USA
Kalambaka *see* Kalampáka
117 S13 **Kalamits'ka Zatoka** *Rus.* Kalamitskiy Zaliv. *gulf* S Ukraine
Kalamitskiy Zaliv *see* Kalamits'ka Zatoka
115 H18 **Kálamos** Attikí, C Greece 38°16′N 23°51′E
115 C18 **Kálamos** *island* Iónioi Nísia, Greece, C Mediterranean Sea
115 D15 **Kalampáka** *var.* Kalambaka. Thessalía, C Greece 39°43′N 21°36′E
Kalan *see* Călan, Romania
Kalan *see* Tunceli, Turkey
117 S11 **Kalanchak** Khersons'ka Oblast', S Ukraine 46°14′N 33°19′E
38 G11 **Kalaoa** *var.* Kailua. Hawaii, USA, C Pacific Ocean 19°43′N 155°59′W
171 O15 **Kalaotoa, Pulau** *island* W Indonesia
155 J24 **Kala Oya** ≈ NW Sri Lanka
Kalarash *see* Călăraşi
93 H17 **Kälarne** Jämtland, C Sweden 63°00′N 16°10′E
143 V15 **Kalar Rūd** ≈ SE Iran
169 R9 **Kalasin** *var.* Muang Kalasin. Kalasin, E Thailand 16°29′N 103°31′E
143 U4 **Kalāt** *var.* Kabūd Gonbad. Khorāsān, NE Iran 37°02′N 59°46′E
149 O11 **Kālat** *var.* Kelat, Khelat. Baluchistān, SW Pakistan 29°01′N 66°38′E
Kalāt *see* Qalāt
115 J14 **Kalathriá, Ákrotirio** *headland* Samothráki, NE Greece 40°24′N 25°34′E
193 W147 **Kalau** *island* Tongatapu Group, SE Tonga
38 E9 **Kalaupapa** Moloka'i, Hawaii, USA, C Pacific Ocean 21°11′N 156°59′W
127 N13 **Kalaus** ≈ SW Russian Federation
Kalávrita *see* Kalávryta
115 E19 **Kalávryta** *var.* Kalávrita. Dytikí Elláda, S Greece 38°02′N 22°06′E
141 Y10 **Kalbān** W Oman 20°19′N 58°40′E
180 H11 **Kalbarri** Western Australia 27°43′S 114°08′E
Kalbinskiy Khrebet *see* Khrebet Kalba
144 G10 **Kaldygayty** ≈ W Kazakhstan
136 I12 **Kalecik** Ankara, N Turkey 40°08′N 33°27′E
79 O19 **Kalehe** Sud-Kivu, E Dem. Rep. Congo 02°05′S 28°52′E
79 P22 **Kalemie** *prev.* Albertville. Katanga, SE Dem. Rep. Congo 05°55′S 29°09′E
166 L4 **Kalemyo** Sagaing, Myanmar (Burma) 23°11′N 94°03′E
82 H12 **Kalene Hill** North Western, NW Zambia 11°10′S 24°12′E
167 T11 **Kalêng** *prev.* Phumĭ Kalêng. Stœng Trêng, NE Cambodia 13°57′N 106°17′E
Kale Sultanie *see* Çanakkale
124 I7 **Kalevala** Respublika Kareliya, NW Russian Federation 65°12′N 31°16′E
166 L4 **Kalewa** Sagaing, C Myanmar (Burma) 23°15′N 94°19′E
Kalgan *see* Zhangjiakou
39 Q12 **Kalgin Island** *island* Alaska, USA
180 L12 **Kalgoorlie** Western Australia 30°51′S 121°27′E
Kali *see* Sārda
115 E17 **Kaliakoúda** ▲ C Greece 38°47′N 21°42′E
114 O8 **Kaliakra, Nos** *headland* NE Bulgaria 43°22′N 28°28′E
115 F19 **Kaliánoi** Pelopónnisos, S Greece 37°55′N 22°28′E
115 N24 **Kalí Límni** ▲ Kárpathos, SE Greece 35°34′N 27°08′E
79 N20 **Kalima** Maniema, E Dem. Rep. Congo 02°34′S 26°27′E
169 S11 **Kalimantan** *Eng.* Indonesian Borneo. ◈ *geopolitical region* Borneo, C Indonesia
169 Q11 **Kalimantan Barat** *off.* Propinsi Kalimantan Berat, *Eng.* West Borneo, West Kalimantan. ◈ *province* N Indonesia
Kalimantan Barat, Propinsi *see* Kalimantan Barat
169 T13 **Kalimantan Selatan** *off.* Propinsi Kalimantan Selatan, *Eng.* South Borneo, South Kalimantan. ◈ *province* N Indonesia
Kalimantan Selatan, Propinsi *see* Kalimantan Selatan
169 R12 **Kalimantan Tengah** *off.* Propinsi Kalimantan Tengah, *Eng.* Central Borneo, Central Kalimantan. ◈ *province* N Indonesia
Kalimantan Tengah, Propinsi *see* Kalimantan Tengah
169 U10 **Kalimantan Timur** *off.* Propinsi Kalimantan Timur, *Eng.* East Borneo, East Kalimantan. ◈ *province* N Indonesia
Kalimantan Timur, Propinsi *see* Kalimantan Timur
Kálimnos *see* Kálymnos
153 S12 **Kālimpang** West Bengal, NE India 27°02′N 88°34′E
Kalinin *see* Tver'
Kalinin *see* Boldumsaz
Kalininabad *see* Kalininobod
126 B3 **Kaliningrad** Kaliningradskaya Oblast', W Russian Federation 54°48′N 21°33′E
Kaliningrad *see* Kaliningradskaya Oblast'
126 A3 **Kaliningradskaya Oblast'** *var.* Kaliningrad. ◈ *province and enclave* W Russian Federation
Kalinino *see* Tashir
147 P14 **Kalininobod** *Rus.* Kalininabad. SW Tajikistan 37°49′N 68°55′E
127 O8 **Kalininsk** Saratovskaya Oblast', W Russian Federation 51°31′N 44°25′E
Kalininsk *see* Boldumsaz
Kalinisk *see* Cupcina
119 M19 **Kalinkavichy** *Rus.* Kalinkovichi. Homyel'skaya Voblasts', SE Belarus 52°08′N 29°19′E
Kalinkovichi *see* Kalinkavichy
81 G18 **Kaliro** SE Uganda 0°54′N 33°30′E
Kalisch/Kalish *see* Kalisz
33 O7 **Kalispell** Montana, NW USA 48°12′N 114°18′W
110 I13 **Kalisz** *Ger.* Kalisch, *Rus.* Kalish; *anc.* Calisia. Wielkopolskie, C Poland 51°46′N 18°04′E
110 F9 **Kalisz Pomorski** *Ger.* Kallies. Zachodnio-pomorskie, NW Poland 53°55′N 15°55′E
126 M10 **Kalitva** ≈ SW Russian Federation
81 F21 **Kaliua** Tabora, C Tanzania 05°03′S 31°48′E
92 K13 **Kalix** Norrbotten, N Sweden 65°51′N 23°14′E
92 K12 **Kalixälven** ≈ N Sweden
92 J11 **Kalixfors** Norrbotten, N Sweden 67°45′N 20°20′E
145 T8 **Kalkaman** *Kaz.* Qalqaman. Pavlodar, NE Kazakhstan 51°57′N 75°58′E
Kalkandelen *see* Tetovo
181 O4 **Kalkarindji** Northern Territory, N Australia 17°32′S 130°40′E
31 P6 **Kalkaska** Michigan, N USA 44°44′N 85°11′W
93 F16 **Kall** Jämtland, C Sweden 63°31′N 13°16′E
189 X2 **Kallalen** *var.* Calalen. *island* Ratak Chain, SE Marshall Islands
118 J5 **Kallaste** *Ger.* Krasnogor. Tartumaa, SE Estonia 58°40′N 27°12′E
93 N16 **Kallavesi** ◎ SE Finland
115 F17 **Kallídromo** ▲▲ C Greece
Kallies *see* Kalisz Pomorski
95 M22 **Kallinge** Blekinge, S Sweden 56°14′N 15°17′E
115 L16 **Kalloní** Lésvos, E Greece 39°14′N 26°16′E
93 F16 **Kallsjön** ◎ C Sweden
95 N21 **Kalmar** *var.* Calmar. Kalmar, S Sweden 56°40′N 16°22′E
95 M19 **Kalmar** *var.* Calmar. ◈ *county* S Sweden
95 N20 **Kalmarsund** *strait* S Sweden
Kalmat Lagoon *see* Kalamat, Khor
117 X9 **Kal'mius** ≈ E Ukraine
99 H15 **Kalmthout** Antwerpen, N Belgium 51°24′N 04°27′E
Kalmykia/Kalmykiya-Khal'mg Tangch, Respublika *see* Kalmykiya, Respublika
127 O12 **Kalmykiya, Respublika** *var.* Respublika Kalmykiya-Khal'mg Tangch, *Eng.* Kalmykia; *prev.* Kalmytskaya ASSR. ◈ *autonomous republic* SW Russian Federation
Kalmytskaya ASSR *see* Kalmykiya, Respublika
118 F9 **Kalnciems** C Latvia 56°46′N 23°37′E
114 L10 **Kalnitsa** ≈ SE Bulgaria
111 J24 **Kalocsa** Bács-Kiskun, S Hungary 46°31′N 19°00′E
114 J9 **Kalofer** Plovdiv, C Bulgaria 42°36′N 25°00′E
38 E10 **Kalohi Channel** *channel* C Pacific Ocean
83 I16 **Kalomo** Southern, S Zambia 17°02′S 26°29′E
29 X14 **Kalona** Iowa, C USA 41°28′N 91°42′W
115 K22 **Kalotási, Akrotírio** *cape* Amorgós, Kykládes, Greece, Aegean Sea
152 J8 **Kalpa** Himāchal Pradesh, N India 31°33′N 78°16′E
115 C15 **Kalpáki** Ípeiros, W Greece 39°53′N 20°38′E
155 C22 **Kalpeni Island** *island* Lakshadweep, India, N Indian Ocean
152 K13 **Kālpi** Uttar Pradesh, N India 26°07′N 79°44′E
158 G7 **Kalpin** Xinjiang Uygur Zizhiqu, NW China 40°35′N 78°52′E
149 P16 **Kalri Lake** ◎ SE Pakistan
143 R5 **Kāl Shūr** ≈ N Iran
39 N11 **Kalskag** Alaska, USA 61°32′N 160°15′W
Kalsø *see* Kalsoy
95 B18 **Kalsoy** *Dan.* Kalsø. *island* N Faeroe Islands
39 O9 **Kaltag** Alaska, USA 64°19′N 158°43′W
108 H7 **Kaltbrunn** Sankt Gallen, NE Switzerland 47°11′N 09°00′E
Kaltdorf *see* Pruszków
77 X14 **Kaltungo** Gombe, E Nigeria 09°49′N 11°22′E
126 K4 **Kaluga** Kaluzhskaya Oblast', W Russian Federation 54°31′N 36°16′E
155 J26 **Kalu Ganga** ≈ S Sri Lanka
82 J13 **Kalulushi** Copperbelt, C Zambia 12°50′S 28°03′E
180 M2 **Kalumburu** Western Australia 14°11′S 126°40′E
95 H23 **Kalundborg** Sjælland, E Denmark 55°42′N 11°06′E
82 K11 **Kalungwishi** ≈ N Zambia
149 T8 **Kalūr Kot** Punjab, E Pakistan 32°08′N 71°20′E
116 I6 **Kalush** *Pol.* Kałusz. Ivano-Frankivs'ka Oblast', W Ukraine 49°02′N 24°20′E
Kałusz *see* Kalush
110 N11 **Kałuszyn** Mazowieckie, C Poland 52°12′N 21°43′E
155 J26 **Kalutara** Western Province, SW Sri Lanka 06°35′N 79°59′E
Kaluwawa *see* Fergusson Island
126 I5 **Kaluzhskaya Oblast'** ◈ *province* W Russian Federation
119 E14 **Kalvarija** *Pol.* Kalwaria. Marijampolė, S Lithuania 54°25′N 23°13′E
93 K15 **Kälviä** Länsi-Suomi, W Finland 63°53′N 23°30′E
109 U6 **Kalwang** Steiermark, E Austria 47°25′N 14°48′E
Kalwaria *see* Kalvarija
154 D13 **Kalyān** Mahārāshtra, W India 19°17′N 73°11′E
124 K16 **Kalyazin** Tverskaya Oblast', W Russian Federation 57°15′N 37°53′E
115 D18 **Kalydón** *anc.* Calydon. *site of ancient city* Dytikí Elláda, C Greece
115 M21 **Kálymnos** *var.* Kálimnos. Kálymnos, Dodekánisa, Greece, Aegean Sea 36°57′N 26°59′E
115 M21 **Kálymnos** *var.* Kálimnos. *island* Dodekánisa, Greece, Aegean Sea
117 O5 **Kalynivka** Kyyivs'ka Oblast', N Ukraine 50°14′N 30°16′E
117 N6 **Kalynivka** Vinnyts'ka Oblast', C Ukraine 49°27′N 28°32′E
145 W15 **Kalzhat** *prev.* Kol'zhat. Almaty, SE Kazakhstan 43°29′N 80°37′E
42 M10 **Kama** *var.* Cama. Región Autónoma Atlántico Sur, SE Nicaragua 12°06′N 83°55′W
165 R9 **Kamaishi** *var.* Kamaisi. Iwate, Honshū, C Japan 39°18′N 141°52′E
Kamaisi *see* Kamaishi
118 H13 **Kamajai** Utena, E Lithuania 55°49′N 25°30′E
Kamajai *see* Toliejai
149 U9 **Kamālia** Punjab, NE Pakistan 30°44′N 72°39′E
83 I14 **Kamalondo** North Western, NW Zambia 13°42′S 25°38′E
136 I13 **Kaman** Kirşehir, C Turkey 39°22′N 33°43′E
79 O20 **Kamanyola** Sud-Kivu, E Dem. Rep. Congo 02°54′S 29°04′E
141 N14 **Kamarān** *island* W Yemen
55 R9 **Kamarang** W Guyana 05°49′N 60°38′W
Kāmāreddi/Kamareddy *see* Rāmāreddi
Kama Reservoir *see* Kamskoye Vodokhranilishche
148 K13 **Kamarod** Baluchistān, SW Pakistan 27°34′N 63°36′E
171 P14 **Kamaru** Pulau Buton, C Indonesia 05°10′S 123°03′E
77 S13 **Kamba** Kebbi, NW Nigeria 11°50′N 03°44′E
Kambaeng Petch *see* Kamphaeng Phet
180 L12 **Kambalda** Western Australia 31°15′S 121°33′E
149 P13 **Kambar** *var.* Qambar. Sind, SE Pakistan 27°35′N 68°03′E
Kambara *see* Kabara
76 I14 **Kambia** W Sierra Leone 09°09′N 12°53′W
Kambos *see* Kámpos
79 N25 **Kambove** Katanga, SE Dem. Rep. Congo 10°50′S 26°39′E
Kambryk *see* Cambrai
123 V10 **Kamchatka** ≈ E Russian Federation
Kamchatka *see* Kamchatka, Poluostrov
Kamchatka Basin *see* Komandorskaya Basin
123 U10 **Kamchatka, Poluostrov** *Eng.* Kamchatka. *peninsula* E Russian Federation
123 V10 **Kamchatskiy Kray** ◈ *province* E Russian Federation
123 V10 **Kamchatskiy Zaliv** *gulf* E Russian Federation
114 N9 **Kamchiya** ≈ E Bulgaria
114 L9 **Kamchiya, Yazovir** ◎ E Bulgaria
149 T4 **Kāmdēsh** *var.* Kamdesh; *prev.* Kāmdeysh. Nūrestān, E Afghanistan 35°25′N 71°26′E
Kamdesh *see* Kāmdēsh
Kāmdeysh *see* Kāmdēsh
Kamenets *see* Kamyanyets
Kamenets-Podol'skaya Oblast' *see* Khmel'nyts'ka Oblast'
Kamenets-Podol'skiy *see* Kam"yanets'-Podil's'kyy
113 Q18 **Kamenica** NE Macedonia 42°03′N 22°34′E
113 O16 **Kamenicë** *var.* Dardanë, *Serb.* Kosovska Kamenica. E Kosovo 42°37′N 21°33′E
112 A11 **Kamenjak, Rt** *headland* NW Croatia
125 O6 **Kamenka** Arkhangel'skaya Oblast', NW Russian Federation 65°55′N 44°01′E
126 6 **Kamenka** Penzenskaya Oblast', W Russian Federation 53°12′N 44°00′E
127 L8 **Kamenka** Voronezhskaya Oblast', W Russian Federation 50°44′N 39°31′E
Kamenka *see* Taskala
Kamenka *see* Camenca
Kamenka *see* Kam"yanka
Kamenka-Bugskaya *see* Kam"yanka-Buz'ka
Kamenka Dneprovskaya *see* Kam"yanka-Dniprovs'ka
Kamen Kashirskiy *see* Kamin'-Kashyrs'kyy
Kamenka-Strumilov *see* Kam"yanka-Buz'ka
126 L15 **Kamennomostskiy** Respublika Adygeya, SW Russian Federation 44°13′N 40°12′E
126 L11 **Kamenolomni** Rostovskaya Oblast', SW Russian Federation 47°36′N 40°18′E
127 P8 **Kamenskiy** Saratovskaya Oblast', W Russian Federation 50°56′N 45°32′E
Kamenskoye *see* Romaniv
126 L11 **Kamensk-Shakhtinskiy** Rostovskaya Oblast', SW Russian Federation 48°18′N 40°16′E
101 P15 **Kamenz** Sachsen, E Germany 51°15′N 14°06′E
164 J13 **Kameoka** Kyōto, Honshū, SW Japan 35°02′N 135°35′E
126 M3 **Kameshkovo** Vladimirskaya Oblast', W Russian Federation 56°21′N 41°01′E
164 C11 **Kami-Agata** Nagasaki, Tsushima, SW Japan 34°40′N 129°27′E
33 N10 **Kamiah** Idaho, NW USA 46°13′N 116°01′W
Kamień Koszyrski *see* Kamin'-Kashyrs'kyy
110 H9 **Kamień Krajeński** *Ger.* Kamin in Westpreussen. Kujawski-pomorskie, C Poland 53°31′N 17°31′E
111 F15 **Kamienna Góra** *Ger.* Landeshut, Landeshut in Schlesien. Dolnośląskie, SW Poland 50°48′N 16°00′E
110 D8 **Kamień Pomorski** *Ger.* Cummin in Pommern. Zachodnio-pomorskie, NW Poland 53°57′N 14°44′E
165 R5 **Kamiiso** Hokkaidō, NE Japan 41°50′N 140°38′E
79 L22 **Kamiji** Kasai-Oriental, S Dem. Rep. Congo 06°39′S 23°27′E
165 T3 **Kamikawa** Hokkaidō, NE Japan 43°51′N 142°47′E
164 B15 **Kami-Koshiki-jima** *island* SW Japan
79 M23 **Kamina** Katanga, S Dem. Rep. Congo 08°42′S 25°01′E
Kamina *see* Kaintiba
42 C6 **Kaminaljuyú** *ruins* Guatemala, C Guatemala
Kamin in Westpreussen *see* Kamień Krajeński
116 J2 **Kamin'-Kashyrs'kyy** *Pol.* Kamień Koszyrski, *Rus.* Kamen Kashirskiy. Volyns'ka Oblast', NW Ukraine 51°39′N 24°59′E
Kaminka Strumiłowa *see* Kam"yanka-Buz'ka
165 Q5 **Kaminokuni** Hokkaidō, NE Japan 41°48′N 140°05′E
165 P10 **Kaminoyama** Yamagata, Honshū, C Japan 38°10′N 140°16′E
39 Q13 **Kamishak Bay** *bay* Alaska, USA
165 U4 **Kamishihoro** Hokkaidō, NE Japan 43°14′N 143°18′E
Kamishli *see* Al Qāmishlī
Kamissar *see* Kamsar
164 C11 **Kami-Tsushima** Nagasaki, Tsushima, SW Japan 34°40′N 129°27′E
79 O20 **Kamituga** Sud-Kivu, E Dem. Rep. Congo 03°07′S 28°10′E
164 B17 **Kamiyaku** Kagoshima, Yaku-shima, SW Japan 30°24′N 130°32′E
11 N16 **Kamloops** British Columbia, SW Canada 50°39′N 120°24′W
107 G25 **Kamma** Sicilia, Italy, C Mediterranean Sea 36°46′N 12°03′E
192 K4 **Kammu Seamount** *undersea feature* N Pacific Ocean 32°09′N 173°00′E
109 U11 **Kamnik** *Ger.* Stein. C Slovenia 46°13′N 14°34′E
Kamniške Alpe *see* Kamniško-Savinjske Alpe
109 T10 **Kamniško-Savinjske Alpe** *var.* Kamniške Alpe, Sanntaler Alpen, *Ger.* Steiner Alpen. ▲▲ N Slovenia
Kamo *see* Gavarr
165 R3 **Kamoenai** *var.* Kamuenai. Hokkaidō, NE Japan 43°07′N 140°25′E
165 O14 **Kamogawa** Chiba, Honshū, S Japan 35°05′N 140°04′E
149 W8 **Kāmoke** Punjab, E Pakistan 31°58′N 74°15′E
82 L13 **Kamoto** Eastern, E Zambia 13°16′S 32°04′E
109 V3 **Kamp** ≈ N Austria
81 F18 **Kampala** ● (Uganda) S Uganda 0°20′N 32°28′E
168 K11 **Kampar, Sungai** ≈ Sumatera, W Indonesia
98 L9 **Kampen** Overijssel, E Netherlands 52°33′N 05°55′E
79 N20 **Kampene** Maniema, E Dem. Rep. Congo 03°35′S 26°40′E
29 Q9 **Kampeska, Lake** ◎ South Dakota, N USA
167 O9 **Kamphaeng Phet** *var.* Kambaeng Petch. Kamphaeng Phet, W Thailand 16°28′N 99°31′E
Kampo *see* Campo, Cameroon
Kampo *see* Ntem, Cameroon/Equatorial Guinea
167 S12 **Kâmpóng Cham** *prev.* Kompong Cham. Kâmpóng Cham, C Cambodia 12°N 105°27′E
167 R12 **Kâmpóng Chhnăng** *prev.* Kompong. Kâmpóng Chhnăng, C Cambodia 12°15′N 104°40′E
167 R12 **Kâmpóng Khleăng** *prev.* Kompong Kleang. Siĕmréab, NW Cambodia 13°04′N 104°07′E
Kâmpōng Saôm *see* Sihanoukville
167 R13 **Kâmpóng Spoe** *prev.* Kompong Speu. Kâmpóng Spœ, S Cambodia 11°28′N 104°29′E
167 S12 **Kâmpóng Thum** *var.* Trâpeăng Vêng. Kâmpóng Thum, C Cambodia 12°37′N 104°58′E
167 S12 **Kâmpóng Trâbêk** *prev.* Phumĭ Kâmpóng Trâbêk, Phum Kompong Trabek. Kâmpóng Thum, C Cambodia 13°06′N 105°16′E
121 O2 **Kámpos** *var.* Kambos. NW Cyprus 35°03′N 32°44′E
167 R14 **Kâmpôt** Kâmpôt, SW Cambodia 10°37′N 104°11′E
Kamptee *see* Kāmthi
77 O14 **Kampti** SW Burkina 10°07′N 03°22′W
Kampuchea *see* Cambodia
Kampuchea, Democratic *see* Cambodia
Kampuchea, People's Democratic Republic of *see* Cambodia
169 Q9 **Kampung Sirik** Sarawak, East Malaysia 02°42′N 111°28′E
11 V15 **Kamsack** Saskatchewan, S Canada 51°34′N 101°51′W
76 H13 **Kamsar** *var.* Kamissar. Guinée-Maritime, W Guinea 10°33′N 14°34′W
127 R4 **Kamskoye Ust'ye** Respublika Tatarstan, W Russian Federation 55°13′N 49°11′E
125 U14 **Kamskoye Vodokhranilishche** *var.* Kama Reservoir. ⊠ NW Russian Federation
154 I12 **Kāmthi** *prev.* Kamptee. Mahārāshtra, C India 21°19′N 79°11′E
Kamuela *see* Waimea
Kamuenai *see* Kamoenai
165 T5 **Kamui-dake** Ѫ Hokkaidō, NE Japan 42°24′N 142°57′E
165 R3 **Kamui-misaki** *headland* Hokkaidō, NE Japan 43°20′N 140°20′E
43 O15 **Kámuk, Cerro** ▲ SE Costa Rica 09°15′N 83°01′W
116 K7 **Kam"yanets'-Podil's'kyy** *Rus.* Kamenets-Podol'skiy. Khmel'nyts'ka Oblast', W Ukraine 48°43′N 26°36′E
117 Q6 **Kam"yanka** *Rus.* Kamenka. Cherkas'ka Oblast', C Ukraine 49°03′N 32°06′E
116 I5 **Kam"yanka-Buz'ka** *prev.* Kamenka-Strumilov, *Pol.* Kaminka Strumiłowa, *Rus.* Kamenka-Bugskaya. L'vivs'ka Oblast', NW Ukraine 50°04′N 24°21′E
117 T9 **Kam"yanka-Dniprovs'ka** *Rus.* Kamenka Dneprovskaya. Zaporiz'ka Oblast', SE Ukraine 47°28′N 34°24′E
119 F19 **Kamyanyets** *Rus.* Kamenets. Brestskaya Voblasts', SW Belarus 52°24′N 23°49′E
118 M13 **Kamyen'** Vitsyebskaya Voblasts', N Belarus 55°01′N 28°53′E
127 P9 **Kamyshin** Volgogradskaya Oblast', SW Russian Federation 50°07′N 45°20′E
127 Q13 **Kamyzyak** Astrakhanskaya Oblast', SW Russian Federation 46°07′N 48°03′E
12 K8 **Kanaaupscow** ≈ Québec, C Canada
36 K8 **Kanab** Utah, W USA 37°03′N 112°31′W
36 K9 **Kanab Creek** ≈ Arizona/Utah, SW USA
187 Y14 **Kanacea** *prev.* Kanathea. Taveuni, N Fiji 16°59′S 179°54′E
38 G17 **Kanaga Island** *island* Aleutian Islands, Alaska, USA
38 G17 **Kanaga Volcano** ▲ Kanaga Island, Alaska, USA 51°55′N 177°09′W
164 N14 **Kanagawa** *off.* Kanagawa-ken. ◈ *prefecture* Honshū, S Japan
Kanagawa-ken *see* Kanagawa
13 Q8 **Kanairiktok** ≈ Newfoundland and Labrador, E Canada
Kanaky *see* New Caledonia
79 K22 **Kananga** *prev.* Luluabourg. Kasai-Occidental, S Dem. Rep. Congo 05°51′S 22°22′E
Kanara *see* Karnātaka
36 J7 **Kanarraville** Utah, W USA 37°32′N 113°10′W
127 Q4 **Kanash** Chuvashskaya Respublika, W Russian Federation 55°30′N 47°27′E
Kanathea *see* Kanacea
21 Q4 **Kanawha River** ≈ West Virginia, NE USA
164 L13 **Kanayama** Gifu, Honshū, SW Japan 35°46′N 137°15′E
164 L11 **Kanazawa** Ishikawa, Honshū, SW Japan 36°35′N 136°40′E
166 M4 **Kanbalu** Sagaing, Myanmar (Burma) 23°10′N 95°31′E
166 L8 **Kanbe** Yangon, Myanmar (Burma) 16°40′N 96°01′E
167 O11 **Kanchanaburi** Kanchanaburi, W Thailand 14°02′N 99°32′E
Kanchanjańghā/Kānchenjunga *see* Kangchenjunga
155 J19 **Kānchīpuram** *prev.* Conjeeveram. Tamil Nādu, SE India 12°50′N 79°44′E
149 N8 **Kandahār** *Per.* Qandahār. Kandahār, S Afghanistan 31°36′N 65°48′E

◆ Country
● Country Capital
◇ Dependent Territory
○ Dependent Territory Capital
◈ Administrative Regions
✕ International Airport
▲ Mountain
▲▲ Mountain Range
Ѫ Volcano
≈ River
◎ Lake
⊠ Reservoir

149 N9 **Kandahār** *Per.* Qandahār. ◈ *province* SE Afghanistan
167 S13 **Kândal** *var.* Ta Khmau. Kândal, S Cambodia 11°30′N 104°59′E
Kandalakša *see* Kandalaksha
124 I5 **Kandalaksha** *var.* Kandalakša, *Fin.* Kantalahti. Murmanskaya Oblast', NW Russian Federation 67°09′N 32°14′E
Kandalaksha Gulf/Kandalakshskaya Guba *see* Kandalakshskiy Zaliv
124 K6 **Kandalakshskiy Zaliv** *var.* Kandalakshskaya Guba, *Eng.* Kandalaksha Gulf. *bay* NW Russian Federation
83 G17 **Kandalengoti** *var.* Kandalengoti. Ngamiland, NW Botswana 19°25′S 22°12′E
Kandalengoti *see* Kandalengoti
169 U13 **Kandangan** Borneo, C Indonesia 02°50′S 115°15′E
Kandau *see* Kandava
118 E8 **Kandava** *Ger.* Kandau. W Latvia 57°02′N 22°48′E
Kandavu *see* Kadavu
77 R14 **Kandé** *var.* Kanté. NE Togo 09°55′N 01°01′E
101 F23 **Kandel** ▲ SW Germany 48°03′N 08°00′E
186 C7 **Kandep** Enga, W Papua New Guinea 05°54′S 143°34′E
149 R12 **Kandh Kot** Sind, SE Pakistan 28°15′N 69°18′E
77 S13 **Kandi** N Benin 11°05′N 02°59′E
149 P14 **Kandiāro** Sind, SE Pakistan 27°02′N 68°16′E
136 F11 **Kandıra** Kocaeli, NW Turkey 41°05′N 30°08′E
183 S8 **Kandos** New South Wales, SE Australia 32°52′S 149°58′E
148 M16 **Kandrāch** *var.* Kanrach. Baluchistān, SW Pakistan 25°26′N 65°28′E
172 I4 **Kandreho** Mahajanga, C Madagascar 17°27′S 46°06′E
186 F7 **Kandrian** New Britain, E Papua New Guinea 06°14′S 149°32′E
Kandukur *see* Kondukūr
155 K25 **Kandy** Central Province, C Sri Lanka 07°17′N 80°40′E
144 I10 **Kandyagash** *Kaz.* Qandyaghash; *prev.* Oktyab'rsk. Aktyubinsk, W Kazakhstan 49°25′N 57°24′E
18 D12 **Kane** Pennsylvania, NE USA 41°39′N 78°47′W
64 I11 **Kane Fracture Zone** *tectonic feature* NW Atlantic Ocean
Kanëka *see* Kanëvka
78 G9 **Kanem** *off.* Préfecture du Kanem. ◈ *prefecture* W Chad
Kanem, Préfecture du *see* Kanem
38 D9 **Kāne'ohe** *var.* Kaneohe. O'ahu, Hawaii, USA, C Pacific Ocean 21°25′N 157°48′W
Kanestron, Akrotírio *see* Palioúri, Akrotírio
Kanëv *see* Kaniv
124 M5 **Kanëvka** *var.* Kanëka. Murmanskaya Oblast', NW Russian Federation 67°07′N 39°43′E
126 K13 **Kanevskaya** Krasnodarskiy Kray, SW Russian Federation 46°07′N 38°57′E
Kanevskoye Vodokhranilishche *see* Kanivs'ke Vodoskhovyshche
165 P9 **Kaneyama** Yamagata, Honshū, C Japan 38°54′N 140°20′E
83 G20 **Kang** Kgalagadi, C Botswana 23°41′S 22°50′E
76 L13 **Kangaba** Koulikoro, SW Mali 11°57′N 08°24′W
136 M13 **Kangal** Sivas, C Turkey 39°15′N 37°23′E
Kangān *see* Bandar-e Kangān
168 J6 **Kangar** Perlis, Peninsular Malaysia 06°28′N 100°10′E
76 L13 **Kangaré** Sikasso, S Mali 11°39′N 08°10′W
182 F10 **Kangaroo Island** *island* South Australia
93 M17 **Kangasniemi** Itä-Suomi, E Finland 61°58′N 26°37′E
142 K6 **Kangāvar** *var.* Kangāwar. Kermānshāhān, W Iran 34°29′N 47°55′E
Kangāwar *see* Kangāvar
153 S11 **Kangchenjunga** *var.* Kānchenjunga, *Nep.* Kanchanjańghā. ▲ NE India 27°36′N 88°06′E
160 G9 **Kangding** *var.* Lucheng, *Tib.* Dardo. Sichuan, C China 30°03′N 101°56′E
169 U16 **Kangean, Kepulauan** *island group* S Indonesia
169 T16 **Kangean, Pulau** *island* Kepulauan Kangean, S Indonesia
67 U8 **Kangen** *var.* Kengen. ≈ E South Sudan
197 N14 **Kangerlussuaq** *Dan.* Søndre Strømfjord. ✈ Kitaa, W Greenland 66°59′N 50°28′E
197 Q15 **Kangertittivaq** *Dan.* Scoresby Sund. *fjord* E Greenland
167 O2 **Kangfang** Kachin State, N Myanmar (Burma) 26°09′N 98°36′E
163 X12 **Kanggye** N North Korea 40°58′N 126°37′E
197 P15 **Kangikajik** *var.* Kap Brewster. *headland* E Greenland 70°10′N 22°00′W
13 N5 **Kangiqsualujjuaq** *prev.* George River, Port-Nouveau-Québec. Québec, E Canada 58°35′N 65°59′W
12 L2 **Kangiqsujuaq** *prev.* Maricourt, Wakeham Bay. Québec, NE Canada 61°35′N 72°00′W
12 M4 **Kangirsuk** *prev.* Bellin, Payne. Québec, E Canada 60°00′N 70°01′W
Kangle *see* Wanzai
158 M16 **Kangmar** Xizang Zizhiqu, W China 28°34′N 89°40′E
Kangnŭng *see* Gangneung
79 D18 **Kango** Estuaire, NW Gabon 0°17′N 10°00′E
152 I7 **Kāngra** Himāchal Pradesh, NW India 32°04′N 76°16′E
153 Q16 **Kangsabati Reservoir** ⊠ N India
159 O17 **Kangto** ▲ China/India 27°54′N 92°33′E
159 W12 **Kangxian** *var.* Kang Xian, Zuitai, Zuitaizi. Gansu, C China 33°21′N 105°40′E
Kang Xian *see* Kangxian
76 M15 **Kani** NW Ivory Coast 08°29′N 06°36′W
166 L4 **Kani** Sagaing, C Myanmar (Burma) 22°24′N 94°55′E
79 M23 **Kaniama** Katanga, S Dem. Rep. Congo 07°32′S 24°11′E
Kanibadam *see* Konibodom
169 V6 **Kanibongan** Sabah, East Malaysia 06°40′N 117°12′E
185 F17 **Kaniere** West Coast, South Island, New Zealand 42°45′S 171°00′E
185 G17 **Kaniere, Lake** ◎ South Island, New Zealand
188 F17 **Kanifaay** Yap, W Micronesia
125 O4 **Kanin Kamen'** ▲▲ NW Russian Federation
125 N3 **Kanin Nos** Nenetskiy Avtonomnyy Okrug, NW Russian Federation 68°38′N 43°19′E
125 N3 **Kanin Nos, Mys** *cape* NW Russian Federation
125 O5 **Kanin, Poluostrov** *peninsula* NW Russian Federation
139 V8 **Kānī Sakht** Wāsiţ, E Iraq 33°19′N 46°04′E
139 T3 **Kānī Sulaymān** Arbīl, N Iraq 35°54′N 44°35′E
165 Q6 **Kanita** Aomori, Honshū, C Japan 41°04′N 140°36′E
117 Q5 **Kaniv** *Rus.* Kanëv. Cherkas'ka Oblast', C Ukraine 49°46′N 31°28′E
182 K11 **Kaniva** Victoria, SE Australia 36°25′S 141°13′E
117 Q5 **Kanivs'ke Vodoskhovyshche** *Rus.* Kanevskoye Vodokhranilishche. ⊠ C Ukraine
112 L8 **Kanjiža** *Ger.* Altkanischa, *Hung.* Magyarkanizsa, Ókanizsa; *prev.* Stara Kanjiža. Vojvodina, N Serbia 46°03′N 20°03′E
93 K18 **Kankaanpää** Länsi-Suomi, SW Finland 61°47′N 22°25′E
30 M12 **Kankakee** Illinois, N USA 41°07′N 87°51′W
31 O11 **Kankakee River** ≈ Illinois/Indiana, N USA
76 K14 **Kankan** E Guinea 10°25′N 09°19′W
154 K13 **Kānker** Chhattīsgarh, C India 20°19′N 81°29′E
76 J10 **Kankossa** Assaba, S Mauritania 15°54′N 11°31′W
169 N12 **Kanmaw Kyun** *var.* Kisseraing, Kithareng. *island* Mergui Archipelago, S Myanmar (Burma)
164 F12 **Kanmuri-yama** ▲ Kyūshū, SW Japan 34°28′N 132°03′E
21 R10 **Kannapolis** North Carolina, SE USA 35°30′N 80°36′W
93 L16 **Kannonkoski** Länsi-Suomi, C Finland 62°59′N 25°20′E
93 K15 **Kannus** Länsi-Suomi, W Finland 63°55′N 23°55′E
77 V13 **Kano** Kano, N Nigeria 11°56′N 08°31′E
77 V13 **Kano** ◈ *state* N Nigeria
77 V13 **Kano** ✈ Kano, N Nigeria 11°56′N 08°26′E
164 G14 **Kan'onji** *var.* Kanonzi. Kagawa, Shikoku, SW Japan 34°08′N 133°38′E
Kanonzi *see* Kan'onji
26 M5 **Kanopolis Lake** ⊠ Kansas, C USA
36 K5 **Kanosh** Utah, W USA 38°48′N 112°26′W
169 R9 **Kanowit** Sarawak, East Malaysia 02°03′N 112°15′E
164 C16 **Kanoya** Kagoshima, Kyūshū, SW Japan 31°22′N 130°50′E
152 L13 **Kānpur** *Eng.* Cawnpore. Uttar Pradesh, N India 26°28′N 80°21′E
Kanrach *see* Kandrāch
164 I14 **Kansai** ✈ (Ōsaka) Ōsaka, Honshū, SW Japan 34°25′N 135°13′E
27 R9 **Kansas** Oklahoma, C USA 36°14′N 94°46′W
26 L5 **Kansas** *off.* State of Kansas, *also known as* Jayhawker State, Sunflower State. ◈ *state* C USA
27 R4 **Kansas City** Kansas, C USA 39°07′N 94°38′W
27 R4 **Kansas City** Missouri, C USA 39°06′N 94°35′W
27 R3 **Kansas City** ✈ Missouri, C USA 39°18′N 94°45′W
27 P4 **Kansas River** ≈ Kansas, C USA
122 L14 **Kansk** Krasnoyarskiy Kray, S Russian Federation 56°11′N 95°32′E
Kansu *see* Gansu
147 V7 **Kant** Chuyskaya Oblast', N Kyrgyzstan 42°54′N 74°47′E
Kantalahti *see* Kandalaksha
167 N16 **Kantang** *var.* Ban Kantang. Trang, SW Thailand 07°25′N 99°30′E
115 H25 **Kántanos** Kríti, Greece, E Mediterranean Sea 35°20′N 23°42′E
77 R12 **Kantchari** E Burkina 12°47′N 01°37′E
Kanté *see* Kandé
Kantemir *see* Cantemir
126 L9 **Kantemirovka** Voronezhskaya Oblast', W Russian Federation 49°44′N 39°53′E
167 R11 **Kantharalak** Si Sa Ket, E Thailand 14°32′N 104°37′E
Kantipur *see* Kathmandu
39 Q9 **Kantishna River** ≈ Alaska, USA
191 S3 **Kanton** *var.* Abariringa, Canton Island; *prev.* Mary Island. *atoll* Phoenix Islands, C Kiribati
97 C20 **Kanturk** *Ir.* Ceann Toirc. Cork, SW Ireland 52°12′N 08°54′W
55 T11 **Kanuku Mountains** ▲▲ S Guyana
165 O12 **Kanuma** Tochigi, Honshū, S Japan 36°34′N 139°44′E
83 H20 **Kanye** Southern, SE Botswana 24°55′S 25°14′E
83 H17 **Kanyu** North-West, C Botswana 20°04′S 24°36′E
166 M7 **Kanyutkwin** Bago, Myanmar (Burma) 18°19′N 96°30′E
79 M24 **Kanzenze** Katanga, SE Dem. Rep. Congo 10°33′S 25°28′E
193 Y15 **Kao** *island* Kotu Group, W Tonga
167 Q13 **Kaôh Kŏng** *var.* Krŏng Kaôh Kŏng. Kaôh Kong, SW Cambodia 11°37′N 102°59′E
Kaohsiung *see* Gaoxiong
Kaokaona *see* Kirakira
83 B17 **Kaoko Veld** ▲▲ N Namibia
76 G11 **Kaolack** *var.* Kaolak. W Senegal 14°09′N 16°08′W
Kaolak *see* Kaolack
Kaolan *see* Lanzhou
186 M8 **Kaolo** San Jorge, N Solomon Islands 08°24′S 159°35′E
83 H14 **Kaoma** Western, W Zambia 14°50′S 24°48′E
38 B8 **Kapa'a** *var.* Kapaa. Kaua'i, Hawaii, USA, C Pacific Ocean 22°04′N 159°19′W
Kapaa *see* Kapa'a
113 J16 **Kapa Moračka** ▲ C Montenegro 42°53′N 19°01′E
137 V13 **Kapan** *Rus.* Kafan; *prev.* Ghap'an. SE Armenia 39°13′N 46°25′E
82 L13 **Kapandashila** Northern, NE Zambia 12°43′S 31°00′E
79 L23 **Kapanga** Katanga, S Dem. Rep. Congo 08°22′S 22°37′E
Kapchagay *see* Kapshagay
Kapchagayskoye Vodokhranilishche *see* Vodokhranilishche Kapshagay
99 F15 **Kapelle** Zeeland, SW Netherlands 51°29′N 03°58′E
99 G16 **Kapellen** Antwerpen, N Belgium 51°19′N 04°25′E
95 P15 **Kapellskär** Stockholm, C Sweden 59°43′N 19°03′E
81 H18 **Kapenguria** Rift Valley, W Kenya 01°14′N 35°08′E
109 V6 **Kapfenberg** Steiermark, C Austria 47°27′N 15°18′E
83 J14 **Kapiri Mposhi** Central, C Zambia 13°59′S 28°40′E
149 R4 **Kāpīsā** ◈ *province* E Afghanistan
12 G10 **Kapiskau** ≈ Ontario, C Canada
184 K13 **Kapiti Island** *island* C New Zealand
78 K9 **Kapka, Massif du** ▲▲ E Chad
Kaplamada *see* Kaubalatmada, Gunung
22 H9 **Kaplan** Louisiana, S USA 30°00′N 92°16′W
Kaplangky, Plato *see* Gaplaňgyr Platosy
111 D19 **Kaplice** *Ger.* Kaplitz. Jihočeský Kraj, S Czech Republic 48°42′N 14°27′E
Kaplitz *see* Kaplice
Kapoche *see* Capoche
171 T12 **Kapocol** Papua, E Indonesia 01°59′S 130°11′E
167 N14 **Kapoe** Ranong, SW Thailand 09°33′N 98°37′E
Kapoeas *see* Kapuas, Sungai
81 G15 **Kapoeta** Eastern Equatoria, SE South Sudan 04°50′N 33°35′E
111 I25 **Kapos** ≈ S Hungary
111 H25 **Kaposvár** Somogy, SW Hungary 46°23′N 17°54′E
94 H13 **Kapp** Oppland, S Norway 60°42′N 10°49′E
100 I7 **Kappeln** Schleswig-Holstein, N Germany 54°41′N 09°56′E
Kapronca *see* Koprivnica
109 P7 **Kaprun** Salzburg, C Austria 47°15′N 12°48′E
145 U15 **Kapshagay** *prev.* Kapchagay. Almaty, SE Kazakhstan 43°52′N 77°05′E
Kapstad *see* Cape Town
Kapsukas *see* Marijampolė
171 Y13 **Kaptiau** Papua, E Indonesia 02°23′S 139°51′E
119 L19 **Kaptsevichy** *Rus.* Koptsevichi. Homyel'skaya Voblasts', SE Belarus 52°14′N 28°19′E
Kapuas Hulu, Banjaran/Kapuas Hulu, Pegunungan *see* Kapuas Mountains
169 S10 **Kapuas Mountains** *Ind.* Banjaran Kapuas Hulu, Pegunungan Kapuas Hulu. ▲▲ Indonesia/Malaysia
169 P11 **Kapuas, Sungai** ≈ Borneo, N Indonesia
169 T13 **Kapuas, Sungai** *prev.* Kapoeas. ≈ Borneo, C Indonesia
182 J9 **Kapunda** South Australia 34°23′S 138°51′E
152 H8 **Kapūrthala** Punjab, N India 31°20′N 75°26′E
12 G12 **Kapuskasing** Ontario, S Canada 49°25′N 82°26′W
14 D6 **Kapuskasing** ≈ Ontario, S Canada
127 P11 **Kapustin Yar** Astrakhanskaya Oblast', SW Russian Federation 48°36′N 45°49′E
82 K11 **Kaputa** Northern, NE Zambia 08°28′S 29°41′E
111 G22 **Kapuvár** Győr-Moson-Sopron, NW Hungary 47°35′N 17°01′E
Kapydzhik, Gora *see* Qazangödağ
119 J17 **Kapyl'** *Rus.* Kopyl'. Minskaya Voblasts', C Belarus 53°09′N 27°05′E
43 N9 **Kara** *var.* Cara. Región Autónoma Atlántico Sur, E Nicaragua 12°50′N 83°35′W
77 R14 **Kara** *var.* Lama-Kara. NE Togo 09°33′N 01°12′E
77 Q14 **Kara** ≈ N Togo
147 U7 **Kara-Balta** Chuyskaya Oblast', N Kyrgyzstan 42°51′N 73°51′E
144 L7 **Karabalyk** *var.* Komsomolets, *Kaz.* Komsomol. Kostanay, N Kazakhstan 53°47′N 61°58′E
144 G11 **Karabau** *Kaz.* Qarabaū. Atyrau, W Kazakhstan 48°29′N 53°05′E
146 E7 **Karabaur', Uval** *Kaz.* Korabavur Pastligi, *Uzb.* Qorabovur Kirlari. *physical region* Kazakhstan/Uzbekistan
Karabekaul *see* Garabekewül
Karabil', Vozvyshennost' *see* Garabil Belentligi
Kara-Bogaz-Gol *see* Garabogazköl
Kara-Bogaz-Gol, Zaliv *see* Garabogaz Aylagy
145 R15 **Karaboget** *Kaz.* Qaraböget. Zhambyl, S Kazakhstan 44°36′N 72°03′E
136 H11 **Karabük** Karabük, NW Turkey 41°12′N 32°36′E
136 H11 **Karabük** ◈ *province* NW Turkey
122 L12 **Karabula** Krasnoyarskiy Kray, C Russian Federation 58°01′N 97°17′E
145 V14 **Karabulak** *Kaz.* Qarabulaq. Taldykorgan, SE Kazakhstan 44°53′N 78°29′E
145 Y11 **Karabulak** *Kaz.* Qarabulaq. Vostochnyy Kazakhstan, E Kazakhstan 47°34′N 84°40′E
145 Q17 **Karabulak** *Kaz.* Qarabulaq. Yuzhnyy Kazakhstan, S Kazakhstan 42°31′N 69°47′E
Karaburn *see* Yumin
136 C17 **Kara Burnu** *headland* SW Turkey 36°34′N 28°00′E
144 K10 **Karabutak** *Kaz.* Qarabutaq. Aktyubinsk, W Kazakhstan 49°55′N 60°05′E
136 D12 **Karacabey** Bursa, NW Turkey 40°14′N 28°22′E
114 O12 **Karacaköy** İstanbul, NW Turkey 41°24′N 28°21′E
114 M12 **Karacaoğlan** Kırklareli, NW Turkey 41°30′N 27°06′E
Karachay-Cherkessia *see* Karachayevo-Cherkesskaya Respublika
126 L15 **Karachayevo-Cherkesskaya Respublika** *Eng.* Karachay-Cherkessia. ◈ *autonomous republic* SW Russian Federation
126 M15 **Karachayevsk** Karachayevo-Cherkesskaya Respublika, SW Russian Federation 43°43′N 41°53′E
126 J6 **Karachev** Bryanskaya Oblast', W Russian Federation 53°07′N 35°56′E
149 O16 **Karāchi** Sind, SE Pakistan 24°51′N 67°02′E
149 O16 **Karāchi** ✈ Sind, S Pakistan 24°51′N 67°02′E
Karácsonkő *see* Piatra-Neamţ
155 E15 **Karād** Mahārāshtra, W India 17°19′N 74°15′E
136 H16 **Karadağ** ▲ S Turkey 37°00′N 33°00′E
147 T10 **Karadar'ya** *Uzb.* Qoradaryo. ≈ Kyrgyzstan/Uzbekistan
Karadeniz *see* Black Sea
Karadeniz Boğazi *see* İstanbul Boğazı
146 B13 **Karadepe** Balkan Welaýaty, W Turkmenistan 38°04′N 54°01′E
Karadzhar *see* Qorajar
Karaferiye *see* Véroia
Karagan *see* Garagan
Karaganda *see* Karagandy
Karagandinskaya Oblast' *see* Karagandy
145 R10 **Karagandy** *Kaz.* Qaraghandy; *prev.* Karaganda. Karaganda, C Kazakhstan 49°53′N 73°07′E
145 R10 **Karagandy** *off.* Karagandinskaya Oblast', *Kaz.* Qaraghandy Oblysy; *prev.* Karaganda. ◈ *province* C Kazakhstan
145 T10 **Karagayly** *Kaz.* Qaraghayly. Karaganda, C Kazakhstan 49°25′N 75°31′E
Karagel' *see* Garagöl'
123 U9 **Karaginskiy, Ostrov** *island* E Russian Federation
197 T1 **Karaginskiy Zaliv** *bay* E Russian Federation
137 P13 **Karagöl Dağları** ▲▲ NE Turkey
Karagumskiy Kanal *see* Garagum Kanaly
114 L13 **Karahisar** Edirne, NW Turkey 40°47′N 26°34′E
127 V3 **Karaidel'** Respublika Bashkortostan, W Russian Federation 55°50′N 56°55′E
114 L13 **Karaidemir Barajı** ⊠ NW Turkey
155 J21 **Kāraikāl** Pondicherry, SE India 10°58′N 79°50′E
155 I22 **Kāraikkudi** Tamil Nādu, SE India 10°04′N 78°46′E
Kara Irtysh *see* Kara Yertis
143 N5 **Karaj** Alborz, N Iran 35°44′N 51°26′E
168 K8 **Karak** Pahang, Peninsular Malaysia 03°24′N 101°59′E
Karak *see* Al Karak
147 T11 **Kara-Kabak** Oshskaya Oblast', SW Kyrgyzstan 39°40′N 72°45′E
Kara-Kala *see* Magtymguly
Karakala *see* Oqqal'a
Karakalpakstan, Respublika *see* Qoraqalpog'iston Respublikasi
Karakalpakya *see* Qoraqalpog'iston
Karakax *see* Moyu
158 G10 **Karakax He** ≈ NW China
121 X8 **Karakaya Barajı** ⊠ C Turkey
171 Q9 **Karakelong, Pulau** *island* N Indonesia
Karakılısse *see* Ağrı
Karak, Muḥāfaẓat al *see* Al Karak
147 X8 **Karakol** *var.* Karakolka. Issyk-Kul'skaya Oblast', NE Kyrgyzstan 41°30′N 77°18′E
147 Y7 **Karakol** *prev.* Przheval'sk. Issyk-Kul'skaya Oblast', NE Kyrgyzstan 42°32′N 78°21′E
Kara-Köl *see* Kara-Kul'
Karakolka *see* Karakol
149 W2 **Karakoram Highway** *road* China/Pakistan
149 Z3 **Karakoram Pass** *Chin.* Karakoram Shankou. *pass* C Asia
152 I3 **Karakoram Range** ▲▲ C Asia
Karakoram Shankou *see* Karakoram Pass
Karaköse *see* Ağrı
145 P14 **Karakoyyn, Ozero** *Kaz.* Qaraqoyyn. ◎ C Kazakhstan
83 F19 **Karakubis** Ghanzi, W Botswana 22°03′S 20°36′E
147 T9 **Kara-Kul'** *Kir.* Kara-Köl. Dzhalal-Abadskaya Oblast', W Kyrgyzstan 40°35′N 73°36′E
Karakul' *see* Qarokŭl, Tajikistan
Karakul' *see* Qorako'l, Uzbekistan
147 U10 **Kara-Kul'dzha** Oshskaya Oblast', SW Kyrgyzstan 40°32′N 73°50′E
127 T3 **Karakulino** Udmurtskaya Respublika, NW Russian Federation 56°02′N 53°45′E
Karakul', Ozero *see* Qarokŭl
Kara Kum *see* Garagum
Kara Kum Canal/Karakumskiy Kanal *see* Garagum Kanaly
Karakumy, Peski *see* Garagum
83 E17 **Karakuwisa** Okavango, NE Namibia 18°56′S 19°40′E
122 M13 **Karam** Irkutskaya Oblast', S Russian Federation 55°07′N 107°21′E
Karamai *see* Karamay
169 T14 **Karamain, Pulau** *island* N Indonesia
136 I16 **Karaman** Karaman, S Turkey 37°11′N 33°13′E
136 H16 **Karaman** ◈ *province* S Turkey
114 M8 **Karamandere** ≈ NE Bulgaria
158 J4 **Karamay** *var.* Karamai, Kelamayi; *prev. Chin.* K'o-la-ma-i. Xinjiang Uygur Zizhiqu, NW China 45°33′N 84°45′E
169 U14 **Karambu** Borneo, N Indonesia 03°48′S 116°06′E
185 H14 **Karamea** West Coast, South Island, New Zealand 41°15′S 172°07′E
185 H14 **Karamea** ≈ South Island, New Zealand
185 G15 **Karamea Bight** *gulf* South Island, New Zealand
Karamet-Niyaz *see* Garamätnyýaz
158 K10 **Karamiran He** ≈ NW China
147 S11 **Karamyk** Oshskaya Oblast', SW Kyrgyzstan 39°28′N 71°45′E
169 U17 **Karangasem** Bali, S Indonesia 08°24′S 115°40′E
154 H12 **Kāranja** Mahārāshtra, C India 20°30′N 77°26′E
Karanpur *see* Karanpura
152 F9 **Karanpura** *var.* Karanpur. Rājasthān, NW India 29°46′N 73°30′E
Karánsebes/Karansebesch *see* Caransebeş
145 T14 **Karaoy** *Kaz.* Qaraoy. Almaty, SE Kazakhstan 45°52′N 74°44′E
144 E10 **Karaozen** *Kaz.* Ülkenözen; *prev.* Bol'shoy Uzen'. ≈ Kazakhstan/Russian Federation
114 N7 **Karapelit** *Rom.* Stejarul. Dobrich, NE Bulgaria 43°40′N 27°33′E
136 I15 **Karapınar** Konya, C Turkey 37°43′N 33°34′E
83 D22 **Karas** ◈ *district* S Namibia
147 Y8 **Kara-Say** Issyk-Kul'skaya Oblast', NE Kyrgyzstan 41°34′N 77°56′E
83 E22 **Karasburg** Karas, S Namibia 27°59′S 18°46′E
Kara Sea *see* Karskoye More
92 K9 **Kárášjohka** *var.* Karašjokka. ≈ N Norway
Kárášjohka *see* Karasjok
92 L9 **Karasjok** *Fin.* Kaarasjoki, *Lapp.* Kárášjohka. Finnmark, N Norway 69°27′N 25°28′E
Karašjokka *see* Kárášjohka
Kara Strait *see* Karskiye Vorota, Proliv
145 N8 **Karasu** *Kaz.* Qarasū. Kostanay, N Kazakhstan 52°44′N 65°29′E
136 F11 **Karasu** Sakarya, NW Turkey 41°07′N 30°37′E
Kara Su *see* Mesta/Néstos
Karasubazar *see* Bilohirs'k
122 I12 **Karasuk** Novosibirskaya Oblast', C Russian Federation 53°41′N 78°04′E
145 U13 **Karatal** *Kaz.* Qaratal. ≈ SE Kazakhstan
136 K17 **Karataş** Adana, S Turkey 36°32′N 35°22′E
145 Q16 **Karatau** *Kaz.* Qarataū. Zhambyl, S Kazakhstan 43°09′N 70°28′E
Karatau *see* Karatau, Khrebet
145 P16 **Karatau, Khrebet** *var.* Karatau, *Kaz.* Qarataū. ▲▲ S Kazakhstan
144 G13 **Karaton** *Kaz.* Qaraton. Atyrau, W Kazakhstan 46°33′N 53°31′E
164 C13 **Karatsu** *var.* Karatu. Saga, Kyūshū, SW Japan 33°28′N 129°48′E
Karatu *see* Karatsu
122 K8 **Karaul** Krasnoyarskiy Kray, N Russian Federation 70°07′N 83°12′E
Karaulbazar *see* Qorowulbozor
Karauzyak *see* Qorao'zak
115 D16 **Karáva** ▲ C Greece 39°19′N 21°33′E
Karavanke *see* Karawanken
115 F22 **Karavás** Kýthira, S Greece 36°21′N 22°57′E
113 J20 **Karavastasë, Laguna e** *var.* Kënet' e Karavastas, Kravasta Lagoon. *lagoon* W Albania
Karavastas, Kënet' e *see* Karavastasë, Laguna e
118 I5 **Karavere** Tartumaa, E Estonia 58°25′N 26°29′E
115 L23 **Karavonísia** *island* Kykládes, Greece, Aegean Sea
169 O15 **Karawang** *prev.* Krawang. Jawa, C Indonesia 06°13′S 107°16′E
109 T10 **Karawanken** *Slvn.* Karavanke. ▲▲ Austria/Serbia
Karaxahar *see* Kaidu He
137 R13 **Karayazı** Erzurum, NE Turkey 39°40′N 42°09′E
145 Y11 **Kara Yertis** *Rus.* Chërnyy Irtysh *prev.* Kara Irtysh. ≈ NE Kazakhstan
145 Q12 **Karazhal** *Kaz.* Qarazhal. Karaganda, C Kazakhstan 48°002′N 70°52′E
139 S9 **Karbalā'** *var.* Kerbala, Kerbela. Karbalā', S Iraq 32°37′N 44°03′E
94 L11 **Kårböle** Gävleborg, C Sweden 61°59′N 15°16′E
111 M23 **Karcag** Jász-Nagykun-Szolnok, E Hungary 47°22′N 20°51′E
Kardak *see* Imia
114 N7 **Kardam** Dobrich, NE Bulgaria 43°45′N 28°06′E
Kardamila *see* Kardámyla
115 L18 **Kardámyla** *var.* Kardamila, Kardhámila. Chíos, E Greece 38°33′N 26°04′E
Kardeljevo *see* Ploče
Kardh *see* Qardho
Kardhámila *see* Kardámyla
Kardhítsa *see* Kardítsa
115 E16 **Kardítsa** *var.* Kardhítsa. Thessalía, C Greece 39°22′N 21°56′E
118 E4 **Kärdla** *Ger.* Kertel. Hiiumaa, W Estonia 59°00′N 22°42′E
Karelia *see* Kareliya, Respublika
119 I16 **Karelichy** *Pol.* Korelicze, *Rus.* Korelichi. Hrodzyenskaya Voblasts', W Belarus 53°34′N 26°08′E
124 I10 **Kareliya, Respublika** *prev.* Karel'skaya ASSR, *Eng.* Karelia. ◈ *autonomous republic* NW Russian Federation
Karel'skaya ASSR *see* Kareliya, Respublika
81 E22 **Karema** Rukwa, W Tanzania 06°50′S 30°25′E
Karen *see* Hualian
83 I14 **Karenda** Central, C Zambia 14°42′S 26°52′E
Karen State *see* Kayin State
92 J10 **Karesuando** *Fin.* Kaaresuanto, *Lapp.* Gárasavvon. Norrbotten, N Sweden 68°25′N 22°28′E
Karet *see* Kâghet
Kareyz-e-Elyās/Kārez Iliās *see* Kārīz-e Elyās
122 J11 **Kargasok** Tomskaya Oblast', C Russian Federation 59°01′N 80°34′E
122 I12 **Kargat** Novosibirskaya Oblast', C Russian Federation 55°07′N 80°19′E
136 J11 **Kargı** Çorum, N Turkey 41°09′N 34°32′E
152 I5 **Kargil** Jammu and Kashmir, NW India 34°34′N 76°06′E
Kargilik *see* Yecheng
124 L11 **Kargopol'** Arkhangel'skaya Oblast', NW Russian Federation 61°30′N 38°53′E
110 F12 **Kargowa** *Ger.* Unruhstadt. Lubuskie, W Poland 52°05′N 15°50′E
77 X13 **Kari** Bauchi, E Nigeria 11°13′N 10°34′E
83 J15 **Kariba** Mashonaland West, N Zimbabwe 16°29′S 28°48′E
83 J16 **Kariba, Lake** ⊠ Zambia/Zimbabwe
165 Q4 **Kariba-yama** ▲ Hokkaidō, NE Japan 42°36′N 139°55′E
83 C19 **Karibib** Erongo, C Namibia 21°56′S 15°51′E
Karies *see* Karyés
92 L9 **Karigasniemi** *Lapp.* Garegegasnjárga. Lappi, N Finland 69°24′N 25°52′E
184 J2 **Karikari, Cape** *headland* North Island, New Zealand 34°47′S 173°24′E
149 W3 **Karīmābād** *prev.* Hunza. Jammu and Kashmir, NE Pakistan 36°23′N 74°43′E
169 P12 **Karimata, Kepulauan** *island group* N Indonesia
169 P12 **Karimata, Pulau** *island* Kepulauan Karimata, N Indonesia
169 O11 **Karimata, Selat** *strait* W Indonesia
155 I14 **Karīmnagar** Andhra Pradesh, C India 18°28′N 79°09′E
186 C7 **Karimui** Chimbu, C Papua New Guinea 06°19′S 144°48′E
169 Q15 **Karimunjawa, Pulau** *island* S Indonesia
80 N12 **Karin** Woqooyi Galbeed, N Somalia 10°48′N 45°46′E
Kariot *see* Ikaría
93 L20 **Karis** *Fin.* Karjaa. Etelä-Suomi, SW Finland 60°05′N 23°39′E
Káristos *see* Kárystos
148 J4 **Kārīz-e Elyās** *var.* Kareyz-e-Elyās, Kārez Iliās. Herāt, NW Afghanistan 35°26′N 61°24′E
Karjaa *see* Karis
Karkaralinsk *see* Karkaraly
145 T10 **Karkaraly** *prev.* Karkaralinsk. Karaganda, E Kazakhstan 49°31′N 75°53′E
186 D6 **Karkar Island** *island* N Papua New Guinea
143 N7 **Karkas, Kūh-e** ▲ C Iran
142 K8 **Karkheh, Rūd-e** ≈ SW Iran
115 L20 **Karkinágri** *var.* Karkinagrio. Ikaría, Dodekánisa, Greece, Aegean Sea 37°31′N 26°01′E
Karkinagrio *see* Karkinágri
117 R12 **Karkinits'ka Zatoka** *Rus.* Karkinitskiy Zaliv. *gulf* S Ukraine
Karkinitskiy Zaliv *see* Karkinits'ka Zatoka
93 L19 **Karkkila** *Swe.* Högfors. Uusimaa, S Finland 60°32′N 24°10′E
93 M19 **Kärkölä** Etelä-Suomi, S Finland 60°52′N 25°17′E
182 G9 **Karkoo** South Australia 34°03′S 135°45′E
Karkūk *see* Kirkūk
118 D5 **Kärla** *Ger.* Kergel. Saaremaa, W Estonia 58°20′N 22°15′E
Karleby *see* Kokkola
110 F7 **Karlino** *Ger.* Körlin an der Persante. Zachodinio-pomorskie, NW Poland 54°02′N 15°52′E
137 Q13 **Karlıova** Bingöl, E Turkey 39°16′N 41°01′E
117 U6 **Karlivka** Poltavs'ka Oblast', C Ukraine 49°27′N 35°08′E
Karl-Marx-Stadt *see* Chemnitz
Karlö *see* Hailuoto
112 C11 **Karlobag** *It.* Carlopago. Lika-Senj, W Croatia 44°31′N 15°06′E
112 D9 **Karlovac** *Ger.* Karlstadt, *Hung.* Károlyváros. Karlovac, C Croatia 45°29′N 15°31′E
112 C10 **Karlovac** *off.* Karlovačka Županija. ◈ *province* C Croatia
Karlovačka Županija *see* Karlovac
111 A16 **Karlovarský Kraj** ◈ W Czech Republic
115 M19 **Karlovási** *var.* Néon Karlovási, Néon Karlovasi. Sámos, Dodekánisa, Greece, Aegean Sea 37°47′N 26°40′E
114 J9 **Karlovo** *prev.* Levskigrad. Plovdiv, C Bulgaria 42°38′N 24°49′E
111 A16 **Karlovy Vary** *Ger.* Karlsbad; *prev. Eng.* Carlsbad. Karlovarský Kraj, W Czech Republic 50°13′N 12°51′E
Karlsbad *see* Karlovy Vary
95 L17 **Karlsborg** Västra Götaland, S Sweden 58°32′N 14°32′E
Karlsburg *see* Alba Iulia
95 L22 **Karlshamn** Blekinge, S Sweden 56°10′N 14°50′E
95 L16 **Karlskoga** Örebro, C Sweden 59°19′N 14°33′E
95 M22 **Karlskrona** Blekinge, S Sweden 56°11′N 15°39′E
101 G21 **Karlsruhe** *var.* Carlsruhe. Baden-Württemberg, SW Germany 49°01′N 08°24′E
95 K16 **Karlstad** Värmland, C Sweden 59°22′N 13°36′E
29 R3 **Karlstad** Minnesota, N USA 48°34′N 96°31′W
101 I18 **Karlstadt** Bayern, C Germany 49°58′N 09°46′E
Karlstadt *see* Karlovac
39 Q14 **Karluk** Kodiak Island, Alaska, USA 57°34′N 154°27′W
Karluk *see* Qarluq
119 O17 **Karma** *Rus.* Korma. Homyel'skaya Voblasts', SE Belarus 53°07′N 30°48′E
155 F14 **Karmāla** Mahārāshtra, W India 18°26′N 75°08′E
146 M11 **Karmana** Navoiy Viloyati, C Uzbekistan 40°09′N 65°18′E
138 G8 **Karmi'el** *var.* Carmiel. Northern, N Israel 32°55′N 35°18′E
95 B16 **Karmøy** *island* S Norway
152 I9 **Karnāl** Haryāna, N India 29°41′N 76°58′E
153 W15 **Karnaphuli Reservoir** ⊠ NE India
155 F17 **Karnātaka** *var.* Kanara; *prev.* Maisur, Mysore. ◈ *state* W India
25 S13 **Karnes City** Texas, SW USA 28°54′N 97°55′W
109 P9 **Karnische Alpen** *It.* Alpi Carniche. ▲▲ Austria/Italy
114 M9 **Karnobat** Burgas, E Bulgaria 42°39′N 26°59′E
109 Q9 **Kärnten** *off.* Land Kärten, *Eng.* Carinthi, *Slvn.* Koroška. ◈ *state* S Austria
Karnul *see* Kurnool
83 K16 **Karoi** Mashonaland West, N Zimbabwe 16°50′S 29°40′E
Karol *see* Carei
Károly-Fehérvár *see* Alba Iulia
Károlyváros *see* Karlovac
82 M12 **Karonga** Northern, N Malawi 09°54′S 33°55′E
147 W10 **Karool-Dëbë** *Kas.* Karool-Döbö; *prev.* Karool-Tëbë. Narynskaya Oblast', C Kyrgyzstan 40°33′N 75°52′E
Karool-Döbö *see* Karool-Dëbë
Karool-Tëbë *see* Karool-Dëbë
182 J9 **Karoonda** South Australia 35°04′S 139°58′E
149 S9 **Karor** *var.* Koror Lāl Esan. Punjab, E Pakistan 31°15′N 70°58′E
Karosa *see* Karossa
171 N12 **Karossa** *var.* Karosa. Sulawesi, C Indonesia 01°38′S 119°21′E
Karpaten *see* Carpathian Mountains
115 L22 **Karpáthio Pélagos** *sea* Dodekánisa, Greece, Aegean Sea
115 N24 **Kárpathos** Kárpathos, SE Greece 35°30′N 27°13′E
115 N24 **Kárpathos** *It.* Scarpanto; *anc.* Carpathos, Carpathus. *island* SE Greece
Karpathos Strait *see* Karpathou, Stenó
115 N24 **Karpathou, Stenó** *var.* Karpathos Strait, Scarpanto Strait. *strait* Dodekánisa, Greece, Aegean Sea
Karpaty *see* Carpathian Mountains
115 E17 **Karpenísi** *prev.* Karpenísion. Stereá Elláda, C Greece 38°55′N 21°46′E
Karpenísion *see* Karpenísi
Karpilovka *see* Aktsyabrski
125 O8 **Karpogory** Arkhangel'skaya Oblast', NW Russian Federation 64°01′N 44°22′E
180 I7 **Karratha** Western Australia 20°44′S 116°52′E
137 S12 **Kars** *var.* Qars. Kars, NE Turkey 40°35′N 43°05′E
137 S12 **Kars** *var.* Qars. ◈ *province* NE Turkey
145 O12 **Karsakpay** *Kaz.* Qarsaqbay. Karaganda, C Kazakhstan 47°51′N 66°42′E
93 L15 **Kärsämäki** Oulu, C Finland 63°58′N 25°49′E
Karsau *see* Kārsava
118 K9 **Kārsava** *Ger.* Karsau; *prev. Rus.* Korsovka. E Latvia 56°46′N 27°39′E
Karshi *see* Garşy, Turkmenistan
Karshi *see* Qarshi, Uzbekistan
Karshinskaya Step *see* Qarshi Cho'li
Karshinskiy Kanal *see* Qarshi Kanali
84 I5 **Karskiye Vorota, Proliv** *Eng.* Kara Strait. *strait* N Russian Federation
122 J6 **Karskoye More** *Eng.* Kara Sea. *sea* Arctic Ocean
93 L17 **Karstula** Länsi-Suomi, C Finland 62°52′N 24°48′E
127 Q5 **Karsun** Ul'yanovskaya Oblast', W Russian Federation 54°12′N 47°00′E
122 F11 **Kartaly** Chelyabinskaya Oblast', C Russian Federation 53°02′N 60°42′E
18 E13 **Karthaus** Pennsylvania, NE USA 41°06′N 78°03′W
110 I7 **Kartuzy** Pomorskie, NW Poland 54°21′N 18°11′E
165 R8 **Karumai** Iwate, Honshū, C Japan 40°19′N 141°27′E
181 U4 **Karumba** Queensland, NE Australia 17°31′S 140°51′E
142 L10 **Kārūn** *var.* Rūd-e Kārūn. ≈ SW Iran
92 K13 **Karungi** Norrbotten, N Sweden 66°03′N 23°55′E
92 K13 **Karunki** Lappi, N Finland 66°01′N 24°06′E
Kārūn, Rūd-e *see* Kārūn
155 H21 **Karūr** Tamil Nādu, SE India 10°58′N 78°03′E
93 K17 **Karvia** Länsi-Suomi, SW Finland 62°07′N 22°34′E
111 J17 **Karviná** *Ger.* Karwin, *Pol.* Karwina; *prev.* Nowa Karvinná. Moravskoslezský Kraj, E Czech Republic 49°50′N 18°30′E
155 E17 **Kārwār** Karnātaka, W India 14°50′N 74°09′E
108 M7 **Karwendelgebirge** ▲▲ Austria/Germany
Karwin/Karwina *see* Karviná
115 I14 **Karyés** *var.* Karies. Ágion Óros, N Greece 40°15′N 24°15′E

◆ Country
● Country Capital
◇ Dependent Territory
○ Dependent Territory Capital
◈ Administrative Regions
✈ International Airport
▲ Mountain
▲▲ Mountain Range
Volcano
≈ River
◎ Lake
⊠ Reservoir

115 I19 **Kárystos** var. Káristos. Évvoia, C Greece 38°01′N 24°25′E
136 E17 **Kaş** Antalya, SW Turkey 36°12′N 29°38′E
39 Y14 **Kasaan** Prince of Wales Island, Alaska, USA 55°32′N 132°24′W
164 I13 **Kasai** Hyōgo, Honshū, SW Japan 34°56′N 134°49′E
79 K21 **Kasai** var. Cassai, Kassai. ~ Angola/Dem. Rep. Congo
79 K22 **Kasai-Occidental** off. Région Kasai Occidental. ◈ region S Dem. Rep. Congo
Kasai Occidental, Région see Kasai-Occidental
79 L21 **Kasai-Oriental** off. Région Kasai Oriental. ◈ region C Dem. Rep. Congo
Kasai Oriental, Région see Kasai-Oriental
79 L24 **Kasaji** Katanga, S Dem. Rep. Congo 10°22′S 23°29′E
82 L12 **Kasama** Northern, N Zambia 10°14′S 31°12′E
Kasan see Koson
83 H16 **Kasane** North-West, NE Botswana 17°48′S 20°06′E
81 E23 **Kasanga** Rukwa, W Tanzania 08°27′S 31°10′E
79 G21 **Kasangulu** Bas-Congo, W Dem. Rep. Congo 04°33′S 15°12′E
Kasansay see Kosonsoy
155 E20 **Kāsaragod** Kerala, SW India 12°30′N 74°59′E
Kasargen see Kasari
118 P13 **Kasari** var. Kasari Jõgi, Ger. Kasargen. ~ W Estonia
Kasari Jõgi see Kasari
8 L11 **Kasba Lake** ◎ Northwest Territories, Nunavut N Canada
Kaschau see Košice
Kaseda see Minamisatsuma
83 I14 **Kasempa** North Western, NW Zambia 13°27′S 25°49′E
79 O24 **Kasenga** Katanga, SE Dem. Rep. Congo 10°22′S 28°37′E
79 P17 **Kasenye** var. Kasenyi. Orientale, NE Dem. Rep. Congo 01°23′N 30°25′E
Kasenyi see Kasenye
79 O19 **Kasese** Maniema, E Dem. Rep. Congo 01°36′S 27°31′E
81 E18 **Kasese** SW Uganda 0°10′N 30°06′E
152 J11 **Kāsganj** Uttar Pradesh, N India 27°48′N 78°38′E
143 U4 **Kashaf Rūd** ~ NE Iran
143 N7 **Kāshān** Eşfahān, C Iran 33°57′N 51°31′E
126 M10 **Kashary** Rostovskaya Oblast', SW Russian Federation 49°02′N 40°58′E
39 O12 **Kashegelok** Alaska, USA 60°57′N 157°46′W
Kashgar see Kashi
158 E7 **Kashi** Chin. Kaxgar, K'o-shih, Uigh. Kashgar. Xinjiang Uygur Zizhiqu, NW China 39°32′N 75°58′E
164 J14 **Kashihara** var. Kasihara. Nara, Honshū, SW Japan 34°28′N 135°46′E
165 P13 **Kashima-nada** gulf S Japan
124 K15 **Kashin** Tverskaya Oblast', W Russian Federation 57°20′N 37°34′E
152 K10 **Kāshīpur** Uttarakhand, N India 29°13′N 78°58′E
126 L4 **Kashira** Moskovskaya Oblast', W Russian Federation 54°53′N 38°13′E
165 N11 **Kashiwazaki** var. Kasiwazaki. Niigata, Honshū, C Japan 37°22′N 138°33′E
Kashkadar'inskaya Oblast' see Qashqadaryo Viloyati
143 T5 **Kāshmar** var. Turshiz; prev. Solṭānābād, Torshiz. Khorāsān, NE Iran 35°13′N 58°25′E
Kashmir see Jammu and Kashmir
149 R12 **Kashmor** Sind, SE Pakistan 28°24′N 69°42′E
149 S5 **Kashmūnd Ghar** Eng. Kashmund Range. ▲▲ E Afghanistan
Kashmund Range see Kashmūnd Ghar
145 T7 **Kashyr** prev. Kachiry. Pavlodar, NE Kazakhstan 53°07′N 76°08′E
Kasi see Vārānasi
153 O12 **Kasia** Uttar Pradesh, N India 26°45′N 83°55′E
39 N12 **Kasigluk** Alaska, USA 60°54′N 162°31′W
Kasihara see Kashihara
39 R12 **Kasilof** Alaska, USA 60°20′N 151°16′W
Kasimköj see General Toshevo
126 M4 **Kasimov** Ryazanskaya Oblast', W Russian Federation 54°59′N 41°22′E
79 P18 **Kasindi** Nord-Kivu, E Dem. Rep. Congo 0°03′N 29°43′E
82 M12 **Kasitu** ~ N Malawi
Kasiwazaki see Kashiwazaki
30 L14 **Kaskaskia River** ~ Illinois, N USA
93 J17 **Kaskinen** Swe. Kaskö. Länsi-Suomi, W Finland 62°23′N 21°10′E
Kaskö see Kaskinen
Kas Kong see Kŏng, Kaôh
11 O17 **Kaslo** British Columbia, SW Canada 49°54′N 116°57′W
Käsmark see Kežmarok
169 T12 **Kasongan** Borneo, C Indonesia 02°01′S 113°21′E
79 N21 **Kasongo** Maniema, E Dem. Rep. Congo 04°22′S 26°42′E
79 H22 **Kasongo-Lunda** Bandundu, SW Dem. Rep. Congo 06°30′S 16°51′E
115 M24 **Kásos** island S Greece
Kasos Strait see Kásou, Stenó
115 M25 **Kásou, Stenó** var. Kasos Strait. strait Dodekánisos/Kríti, Greece, Aegean Sea
137 T10 **K'asp'i** prev. Kaspi. C Georgia 41°54′N 44°25′E
Kaspi see K'asp'i
114 M8 **Kaspichan** Shumen, NE Bulgaria 43°18′N 27°09′E
Kaspiy Mangy Oypaty see Caspian Depression
127 Q16 **Kaspiysk** Respublika Dagestan, SW Russian Federation 42°52′N 47°40′E
Kaspiyskiy see Lagan'
Kaspiyskoye More/Kaspiy Tengizi see Caspian Sea
Kassa see Košice
Kassai see Kasai
80 I9 **Kassala** Kassala, E Sudan 15°24′N 36°25′E
80 H9 **Kassala** ◈ state NE Sudan
115 G15 **Kassándra** prev. Pallíni; anc. Pallene. peninsula NE Greece
115 G15 **Kassándra** headland N Greece 39°58′N 23°22′E
115 H15 **Kassándras, Kólpos** var. Kólpos Toronaíos. gulf N Greece
139 Y11 **Kassārah** Maysān, E Iraq 31°21′N 47°25′E
101 I15 **Kassel** prev. Cassel. Hessen, C Germany 51°19′N 09°30′E
74 M6 **Kasserine** var. Al Qaşrayn. W Tunisia 35°15′N 08°52′E
14 J14 **Kasshabog Lake** ◎ Ontario, SE Canada
139 O5 **Kassīr, Sabkhat al** ◎ E Syria
29 W10 **Kasson** Minnesota, N USA 44°00′N 92°42′W
115 C17 **Kassópeia** Var. Kassópi. site of ancient city Ípeiros, W Greece
Kassópi see Kassópeia
136 I11 **Kastamonu** var. Castamoni, Kastamuni. Kastamonu, N Turkey 41°22′N 33°47′E
136 I10 **Kastamonu** var. Kastamuni. ◈ province N Turkey
Kastamuni see Kastamonu
Kastaneá see Kastaniá
115 E14 **Kastaniá** prev. Kastaneá. Kentrikí Makedonía, N Greece 40°25′N 22°09′E
Kastélli see Kíssamos
Kastellórizon see Megísti
115 N24 **Kástelo, Akrotírio** prev. Akrotírio Kastállou. headland Kárpathos, SE Greece 35°24′N 27°08′E
95 N21 **Kastlösa** Kalmar, S Sweden 56°25′N 16°25′E
115 D14 **Kastoría** Dytikí Makedonía, N Greece 40°33′N 21°15′E
126 K7 **Kastornoye** Kurskaya Oblast', W Russian Federation 51°49′N 38°07′E
115 J21 **Kástro** Sífnos, Kykládes, Greece, Aegean Sea 36°58′N 24°45′E
95 J23 **Kastrup** ✈ (København) København, E Denmark 55°36′N 12°39′E
119 Q17 **Kastsyukovichy** Rus. Kostyukovichi. Mahilyowskaya Voblasts', E Belarus 53°20′N 32°03′E
119 O18 **Kastsyukowka** Rus. Kostyukovka. Homyel'skaya Voblasts', SE Belarus 52°32′N 30°54′E
164 D13 **Kasuga** Fukuoka, Kyūshū, SW Japan 33°31′N 130°27′E
164 L13 **Kasugai** Aichi, Honshū, SW Japan 35°15′N 136°57′E
81 E21 **Kasulu** Kigoma, W Tanzania 04°33′S 30°06′E
164 I12 **Kasumi** Hyōgo, Honshū, SW Japan 35°36′N 134°37′E
127 R17 **Kasumkent** Respublika Dagestan, SW Russian Federation 41°39′N 48°09′E
82 M13 **Kasungu** Central, C Malawi 13°04′S 33°29′E
149 W9 **Kasūr** Punjab, E Pakistan 31°07′N 74°30′E
83 G15 **Kataba** Western, W Zambia 15°28′S 23°25′E
19 R4 **Katahdin, Mount** ▲ Maine, NE USA 45°55′N 68°52′W
79 M20 **Katako-Kombe** Kasai-Oriental, C Dem. Rep. Congo 03°24′S 24°25′E
39 T12 **Katalla** Alaska, USA 60°12′N 144°31′W
Katana see Qaṭanā
79 L24 **Katanga** off. Région du Katanga; prev. Shaba. ◈ region SE Dem. Rep. Congo
122 M11 **Katanga** ~ C Russian Federation
Katanga, Région du see Katanga
154 J11 **Katāngi** Madhya Pradesh, C India 21°46′N 79°50′E
180 J13 **Katanning** Western Australia 33°45′S 117°33′E
181 P8 **Kata Tjuṯa** var. Mount Olga. ▲ Northern Territory, C Australia 25°20′S 130°47′E
Katawaz see Zarghūn Shahr
151 Q22 **Katchall Island** island Nicobar Islands, India, NE Indian Ocean
115 F14 **Kateríni** Kentrikí Makedonía, N Greece 40°15′N 22°30′E
117 P7 **Katerynopil'** Cherkas'ka Oblast', C Ukraine 49°00′N 30°59′E
166 M3 **Katha** Sagaing, N Myanmar (Burma) 24°11′N 96°20′E
181 P2 **Katherine** Northern Territory, N Australia 14°29′S 132°20′E
154 B11 **Kāthiāwār Peninsula** peninsula W India
153 P11 **Kathmandu** prev. Kantipur. ● (Nepal) Central, C Nepal 27°46′N 85°17′E
152 H7 **Kathua** Jammu and Kashmir, NW India 32°23′N 75°34′E
76 L12 **Kati** Koulikoro, SW Mali 12°41′N 08°04′W
153 R13 **Katihār** Bihār, NE India 25°33′N 87°34′E
184 N7 **Katikati** Bay of Plenty, North Island, New Zealand 37°34′S 175°55′E
83 H16 **Katima Mulilo** Caprivi, NE Namibia 17°31′S 24°20′E
77 N15 **Katiola** C Ivory Coast 08°11′N 05°04′W
191 V10 **Katiu** atoll Îles Tuamotu, C French Polynesia
117 N12 **Katlabuh, Ozero** ◎ SW Ukraine
39 P14 **Katmai, Mount** ▲ Alaska, USA 58°16′N 154°57′W
154 J9 **Katni** Madhya Pradesh, C India 23°47′N 80°29′E
115 D19 **Káto Achaïa** var. Kato Ahaia, Káto Akhaía. Dytikí Elláda, S Greece 38°08′N 21°33′E
Kato Ahaia/Káto Akhaía see Káto Achaïa
121 P2 **Kato Lakatameia** var. Kato Lakatamia. C Cyprus 35°07′N 33°20′E
Kato Lakatamia see Kato Lakatameia
79 N22 **Katompi** Katanga, SE Dem. Rep. Congo 06°10′S 26°19′E
83 K14 **Katondwe** Lusaka, C Zambia 15°08′S 30°10′E
114 H12 **Káto Nevrokópi** prev. Káto Nevrokópion. Anatolikí Makedonía kai Thráki, NE Greece 41°21′N 23°51′E
Káto Nevrokópion see Káto Nevrokópi
81 E18 **Katonga** ~ S Uganda
115 F15 **Káto Olympos** ▲▲ C Greece
115 D17 **Katoúna** Dytikí Elláda, C Greece 38°47′N 21°07′E
115 E19 **Káto Vlasiá** Dytikí Makedonía, S Greece 38°02′N 21°54′E
111 J16 **Katowice** Ger. Kattowitz. Śląskie, S Poland 50°15′N 19°01′E
153 S15 **Kātoya** West Bengal, NE India 23°39′N 88°11′E
136 E16 **Katrançık Dağı** ▲▲ SW Turkey
95 N16 **Katrineholm** Södermanland, C Sweden 58°59′N 16°15′E
96 I11 **Katrine, Loch** ◎ C Scotland, United Kingdom
77 V12 **Katsina** Katsina, N Nigeria 12°59′N 07°33′E
77 U12 **Katsina** ◈ state N Nigeria
67 P8 **Katsina Ala** ~ S Nigeria
164 C13 **Katsumoto** Nagasaki, Iki, SW Japan 33°49′N 129°42′E
165 P13 **Katsuta** var. Katuta. Ibaraki, Honshū, S Japan 36°24′N 140°32′E
165 O14 **Katsuura** var. Katuura. Chiba, Honshū, S Japan 35°09′N 140°16′E
164 K12 **Katsuyama** var. Katuyama. Fukui, Honshū, SW Japan 36°00′N 136°30′E
164 H12 **Katsuyama** Okayama, Honshū, SW Japan 35°06′N 133°43′E
Kattakurgan see Kattaqo'rg'on
147 N11 **Kattaqo'rg'on** Rus. Kattakurgan. Samarqand Viloyati, C Uzbekistan 39°56′N 66°11′E
115 O23 **Kattavía** Ródos, Dodekánisa, Greece, Aegean Sea 35°56′N 27°47′E
95 I21 **Kattegat** Dan. Kattegatt. strait N Europe
Kattegatt see Kattegat
95 P19 **Katthammarsvik** Gotland, SE Sweden 57°27′N 18°54′E
Kattowitz see Katowice
122 J13 **Katun'** ~ S Russian Federation
Katuta see Katsuta
Katuura see Katsuura
Katuyama see Katsuyama
Katwijk see Katwijk aan Zee
98 G11 **Katwijk aan Zee** var. Katwijk. Zuid-Holland, W Netherlands 52°12′N 04°24′E
38 B8 **Kaua'i** var. Kauai. island Hawaiian Islands, Hawai'i, USA, C Pacific Ocean
Kauai see Kaua'i
38 C8 **Kaua'i Channel** var. Kauai Channel. channel Hawai'i, USA, C Pacific Ocean
Kauai Channel see Kaua'i Channel
171 R13 **Kaubalatmada, Gunung** var. Kapalatmada. ▲ Pulau Buru, E Indonesia 03°16′S 126°17′E
191 U10 **Kauehi** atoll Îles Tuamotu, C French Polynesia
Kauen see Kaunas
101 K24 **Kaufbeuren** Bayern, S Germany 47°53′N 10°37′E
25 U7 **Kaufman** Texas, SW USA 32°35′N 96°18′W
101 I15 **Kaufungen** Hessen, C Germany 51°16′N 09°39′E
93 K17 **Kauhajoki** Länsi-Suomi, W Finland 62°26′N 22°10′E
93 K16 **Kauhava** Länsi-Suomi, W Finland 63°06′N 23°08′E
30 M7 **Kaukauna** Wisconsin, N USA 44°18′N 88°18′W
92 L11 **Kaukonen** Lappi, N Finland 67°28′N 24°49′E
38 A8 **Kaulakahi Channel** channel Hawai'i, USA, C Pacific Ocean
38 E9 **Kaunakakai** Moloka'i, Hawaii, USA, C Pacific Ocean 21°05′N 157°01′W
38 F12 **Kaunā Point** var. Kauna Point. headland Hawai'i, USA, C Pacific Ocean 19°02′N 155°52′W
Kauna Point see Kaunā Point
118 F13 **Kaunas** Ger. Kauen, Pol. Kowno; prev. Rus. Kovno. Kaunas, C Lithuania 54°54′N 23°57′E
118 F13 **Kaunas** ◈ province C Lithuania
186 C6 **Kaup** East Sepik, NW Papua New Guinea 03°50′S 144°01′E
77 U12 **Kaura Namoda** Zamfara, NW Nigeria 12°43′N 06°17′E
Kaushany see Căuşeni
93 K16 **Kaustinen** Länsi-Suomi, W Finland 63°33′N 23°40′E
99 M23 **Kautenbach** Diekirch, NE Luxembourg 49°57′N 06°01′E
92 K10 **Kautokeino** Lapp. Guovdageaidnu. Finnmark, N Norway 69°N 23°01′E
Kavadar see Kavadarci
113 P19 **Kavadarci** Turk. Kavadar. C Macedonia 41°25′N 22°00′E
Kavaja see Kavajë
113 K20 **Kavajë** It. Cavaia, Kavaja. Tiranë, W Albania 41°11′N 19°33′E
114 M13 **Kavak Çayı** ~ NW Turkey
Kavakli see Topolovgrad
114 I13 **Kavála** prev. Kaválla. Anatolikí Makedonía kai Thráki, NE Greece 40°57′N 24°26′E
114 I13 **Kaválas, Kólpos** gulf Aegean Sea, NE Mediterranean Sea
155 J17 **Kāvali** Andhra Pradesh, E India 15°05′N 80°02′E
Kaválla see Kavála
Kavango see Cubango/Okavango
155 C21 **Kavaratti** Lakshadweep, SW India 10°33′N 72°38′E
114 O8 **Kavarna** Dobrich, NE Bulgaria 43°27′N 28°21′E
118 G12 **Kavarskas** Utena, E Lithuania 55°27′N 24°55′E
76 I13 **Kavendou** ▲ C Guinea 10°49′N 12°14′W
Kavengo see Cubango/Okavango
155 F20 **Kāveri** var. Cauvery. ~ S India
186 G5 **Kavieng** var. Kaewieng. New Ireland, NE Papua New Guinea 04°13′S 152°11′E
83 H16 **Kavimba** North-West, NE Botswana 18°02′S 24°38′E
83 I15 **Kavingu** Southern, S Zambia 15°39′S 26°03′E
143 Q6 **Kavīr, Dasht-e** var. Great Salt Desert. salt pan N Iran
Kavirondo Gulf see Winam Gulf
Kavkaz see Caucasus
95 K23 **Kävlinge** Skåne, S Sweden 55°47′N 13°05′E
82 G12 **Kavungo** Moxico, E Angola 11°31′S 22°59′E
165 Q8 **Kawabe** Akita, Honshū, C Japan 39°39′N 140°14′E
165 R9 **Kawai** Iwate, Honshū, C Japan 39°36′N 141°40′E
38 A8 **Kawaihoa Point** headland Ni'ihau, Hawai'i, USA, C Pacific Ocean 21°47′N 160°12′W
184 K3 **Kawakawa** Northland, North Island, New Zealand 35°23′S 174°06′E
82 I13 **Kawama** North Western, NW Zambia 13°04′S 25°59′E
82 K11 **Kawambwa** Luapula, N Zambia 09°45′S 29°10′E
154 K11 **Kawardha** Chhattīsgarh, C India 21°59′N 81°12′E
14 I14 **Kawartha Lakes** ◎ Ontario, SE Canada
165 O13 **Kawasaki** Kanagawa, Honshū, S Japan 35°32′N 139°41′E
171 R12 **Kawassi** Pulau Obi, E Indonesia 01°32′S 127°25′E
165 R6 **Kawauchi** Aomori, Honshū, C Japan 41°11′N 141°00′E
184 L5 **Kawau Island** island N New Zealand
184 N10 **Kaweka Range** ▲▲ North Island, New Zealand
Kawelecht see Puhja
184 O8 **Kawerau** Bay of Plenty, North Island, New Zealand 38°06′S 176°43′E
184 L8 **Kawhia** Waikato, North Island, New Zealand 38°04′S 174°49′E
184 K8 **Kawhia Harbour** inlet North Island, New Zealand
35 V8 **Kawich Peak** ▲ Nevada, W USA 38°00′N 116°27′W
35 V9 **Kawich Range** ▲▲ Nevada, W USA
14 G12 **Kawigamog Lake** ◎ Ontario, S Canada
171 P9 **Kawio, Kepulauan** island group N Indonesia
167 N9 **Kawkareik** Kayin State, S Myanmar (Burma) 16°33′N 98°18′E
27 O8 **Kaw Lake** ⊠ Oklahoma, C USA
166 M3 **Kawlin** Sagaing, N Myanmar (Burma) 23°48′N 95°41′E
Kawm Umbū see Kom Ombo
Kawthule State see Kayin State
Kaxgar see Kashi
158 D7 **Kaxgar He** ~ NW China
158 J5 **Kax He** ~ NW China
77 P12 **Kaya** C Burkina 13°04′N 01°09′W
167 N6 **Kayah State** ◈ state C Myanmar (Burma)
39 T12 **Kayak Island** island Alaska, USA
114 M11 **Kayalıköy Barajı** ⊠ NW Turkey
166 M8 **Kayan** Yangon, SW Myanmar (Burma) 16°54′N 96°35′E
Kayangel Islands see Ngcheangel
155 G23 **Kāyankulam** Kerala, SW India 09°10′N 76°31′E
169 V9 **Kayan, Sungai** prev. Kajan. ~ Borneo, C Indonesia
144 F14 **Kaydak, Sor** salt flat SW Kazakhstan
Kaydanovo see Dzyarzhynsk Belarus
37 N9 **Kayenta** Arizona, SW USA 36°43′N 110°15′W
76 J11 **Kayes** Kayes, W Mali 14°26′N 11°22′W
76 J11 **Kayes** ◈ region SW Mali
167 N8 **Kayin State** var. Kawthule State, Karen State. ◈ state S Myanmar (Burma)
145 U10 **Kaynar** Kaz. Qaynar, var. Kajnar. Vostochnyy Kazakhstan, E Kazakhstan 49°13′N 77°27′E
Kaynary see Căinari
83 H15 **Kayoya** Western, W Zambia 16°13′S 24°09′E
Kayrakkum see Qayroqqum
Kayrakkumskoye Vodokhranilishche see Qayroqqum, Obanbori
136 K14 **Kayseri** var. Kaisaria; anc. Caesarea Mazaca, Mazaca. Kayseri, C Turkey 38°42′N 35°28′E
136 K14 **Kayseri** var. Kaisaria. ◈ province C Turkey
36 L2 **Kaysville** Utah, W USA 41°10′N 111°55′W
Kayyngdy see Kaindy
14 L11 **Kazabazua** Québec, SE Canada 45°58′N 76°00′W
14 L12 **Kazabazua** ~ Québec, SE Canada
123 Q7 **Kazach'ye** Respublika Sakha (Yakutiya), NE Russian Federation 70°38′N 135°54′E
Kazakdar'ya see Qozoqdaryo
146 E9 **Kazakhlyshor, Solonchak** var. Solonchak Shorkazakhly. salt marsh NW Turkmenistan
Kazakhskaya SSR/Kazakh Soviet Socialist Republic see Kazakhstan
144 L12 **Kazakhstan** off. Republic of Kazakhstan, var. Kazakstan, Kaz. Qazaqstan, Qazaqstan Respublikasy; prev. Kazakh Soviet Socialist Republic, Rus. Kazakhskaya SSR. ◆ republic C Asia
Kazakhstan, Republic of see Kazakhstan
Kazakh Uplands see Saryarka
Kazakstan see Kazakhstan
Kazalinsk see Kazaly
144 L14 **Kazaly** prev. Kazalinsk. Kzyl-Orda, S Kazakhstan 45°45′N 62°01′E
127 R4 **Kazan'** Respublika Tatarstan, W Russian Federation 55°43′N 49°07′E
8 M10 **Kazan** ~ Nunavut, NW Canada
127 R4 **Kazan'** ✈ Respublika Tatarstan, W Russian Federation 55°46′N 49°21′E
Kazandzhik see Bereket
117 R8 **Kazanka** Mykolayivs'ka Oblast', S Ukraine 47°49′N 32°50′E
Kazanketken see Qozonketkan
Kazanlik see Kazanlŭk
114 J9 **Kazanlŭk** prev. Kazanlik. Stara Zagora, C Bulgaria 42°38′N 25°24′E
165 Y16 **Kazan-rettō** Eng. Volcano Islands. island group SE Japan
Kazantip, Mys see Kazantyp, Mys
117 V12 **Kazantyp, Mys** prev. Mys Kazantip. headland S Ukraine 45°27′N 35°50′E
147 U9 **Kazarman** Narynskaya Oblast', C Kyrgyzstan 41°21′N 74°03′E
Kazatin see Kozyatyn
Kazbegi see Kazbek
Kazbegi see Q'azbegi
137 T9 **Kazbek** var. Kazbegi, Geor. Mqinvartsveri. ▲ N Georgia 42°43′N 44°28′E
82 M13 **Kazembe** Eastern, NE Zambia 12°06′S 32°45′E
143 N11 **Kāzerūn** Fārs, S Iran 29°41′N 51°38′E
125 R12 **Kazhym** Respublika Komi, NW Russian Federation 60°19′N 51°26′E
Kazi Ahmad see Qāzi Ahmad
136 H16 **Kazımkarabekir** Karaman, S Turkey 37°13′N 32°58′E
111 M20 **Kazincbarcika** Borsod-Abaúj-Zemplén, NE Hungary 48°15′N 20°40′E
119 H17 **Kazlowshchyna** Pol. Kozłowszczyzna, Rus. Kozlovshchina. Hrodzyenskaya Voblasts', W Belarus 53°19′N 25°18′E
119 E14 **Kazlų Rūda** Marijampolė, S Lithuania 54°45′N 23°28′E
144 E9 **Kaztalovka** Zapadnyy Kazakhstan, W Kazakhstan 49°45′N 48°42′E
79 K22 **Kazumba** Kasai-Occidental, S Dem. Rep. Congo 06°25′S 22°02′E
165 Q8 **Kazuno** Akita, Honshū, C Japan 40°14′N 140°48′E
Kazvin see Qazvīn
118 J12 **Kazyany** Rus. Koz'yany. Vitsyebskaya Voblasts', NW Belarus 55°18′N 26°52′E
122 H9 **Kazym** ~ N Russian Federation
110 H10 **Kcynia** Ger. Exin. Kujawsko-pomorskie, C Poland 53°00′N 17°29′E
Kéa see Tziá
Kéa see Ioulís
38 H11 **Kea'au** var. Keaau. Hawaii, USA, C Pacific Ocean 19°36′N 155°01′W
Keaau see Kea'au
38 F11 **Keāhole Point** var. Keahole Point. headland Hawai'i, USA, C Pacific Ocean 19°43′N 156°03′W
38 G12 **Kealakekua** Hawaii, USA, C Pacific Ocean 19°31′N 155°56′W
38 H11 **Kea, Mauna** ▲ Hawai'i, USA 19°50′N 155°30′W
37 N10 **Keams** Arizona, SW USA 35°47′N 110°09′W
Kéamu see Aneityum
29 O16 **Kearney** Nebraska, C USA 40°42′N 99°06′W
36 L3 **Kearns** Utah, W USA 40°39′N 112°00′W
115 H20 **Kéas, Stenó** strait SE Greece
137 O14 **Keban Barajı** dam C Turkey
137 O14 **Keban Barajı** ⊠ C Turkey
77 S13 **Kebbi** ◈ state NW Nigeria
76 G10 **Kébémèr** NW Senegal 15°24′N 16°25′W
74 M7 **Kebili** var. Qibilī. C Tunisia 33°42′N 09°06′E
138 H4 **Kebir, Nahr el** ~ NW Syria
80 A10 **Kebkabiya** Northern Darfur, W Sudan 13°39′N 24°05′E
92 I11 **Kebnekaise** Lapp. Giebnegáisi. ▲ N Sweden 68°01′N 18°24′E
81 M14 **K'ebrī Dehar** Sumalē, E Ethiopia 06°43′N 44°15′E
148 K15 **Kech** ~ SW Pakistan
10 K10 **Kechika** ~ British Columbia, W Canada
111 K23 **Kecskemét** Bács-Kiskun, C Hungary 46°54′N 19°42′E
168 J6 **Kedah** ◈ state Peninsular Malaysia
118 F12 **Kėdainiai** Kaunas, C Lithuania 55°19′N 24°00′E
152 K8 **Kedārnāth** Uttarakhand, N India 30°44′N 79°03′E
Kedder see Kehra
13 N13 **Kedgwick** New Brunswick, SE Canada 47°38′N 67°21′W
169 R16 **Kediri** Jawa, C Indonesia 07°45′S 112°01′E
171 Y13 **Kedir Sarmi** Papua, E Indonesia 02°00′S 139°01′E
163 V7 **Kedong** Heilongjiang, NE China 48°00′N 126°15′E
76 I12 **Kédougou** SE Senegal 12°35′N 12°09′W
122 I11 **Kedrovyy** Tomskaya Oblast', C Russian Federation 57°31′N 79°45′E
111 H16 **Kędzierzyn-Koźle** Ger. Heydebrech. Opolskie, S Poland 50°20′N 18°12′E
8 H8 **Keele** ~ Northwest Territories, NW Canada
10 K6 **Keele Peak** ▲ Yukon Territory, NW Canada 63°31′N 130°21′W
Keelung see Jilong
19 N10 **Keene** New Hampshire, NE USA 42°56′N 72°14′W
99 H17 **Keerbergen** Vlaams Brabant, C Belgium 51°01′N 04°39′E
83 E21 **Keetmanshoop** Karas, S Namibia 26°36′S 18°08′E
12 A11 **Keewatin** Ontario, S Canada 49°47′N 94°30′W
29 V4 **Keewatin** Minnesota, N USA 47°24′N 93°04′W
Kefallinía see Kefallonía
115 B18 **Kefallonía** var. Kefallinía. island Iónia Nisiá, Greece, C Mediterranean Sea
115 M22 **Kéfalos** Kos, Dodekánisa, Greece, Aegean Sea 36°44′N 26°58′E
171 Q17 **Kefamenanu** Timor, C Indonesia 09°31′S 124°29′E
Kefar Sava see Kfar Saba
Kefe see Feodosiya
77 V15 **Keffi** Nassarawa, C Nigeria 08°52′N 07°54′E
92 H4 **Keflavík** Suðurnes, W Iceland 64°01′N 22°35′W
92 H4 **Keflavík** ✈ (Reykjavík) Suðurnes, W Iceland 63°58′N 22°37′W
Kegalee see Kegalla
155 J25 **Kegalla** var. Kegalee, Kegalle. Sabaragamuwa Province, C Sri Lanka 07°14′N 80°21′E
Kegalle see Kegalla
Kegayli see Kegeyli
Kegel see Keila
145 W16 **Kegen** Almaty, SE Kazakhstan 42°58′N 79°12′E
146 H7 **Kegeyli** prev. Kegayli. Qoraqalpog'iston Respublikasi, W Uzbekistan 42°46′N 59°49′E
101 F22 **Kehl** Baden-Württemberg, SW Germany 48°34′N 07°49′E
118 H3 **Kehra** Ger. Kedder. Harjumaa, NW Estonia 59°19′N 25°21′E
117 U6 **Kehychivka** Kharkivs'ka Oblast', E Ukraine 49°18′N 35°46′E
97 L17 **Keighley** N England, United Kingdom 53°51′N 01°58′W
Kei Islands see Kai, Kepulauan
Keijō see Seoul
118 G3 **Keila** Ger. Kegel. Harjumaa, NW Estonia 59°18′N 24°29′E
Keilberg see Klínovec
83 F23 **Keimoes** Northern Cape, W South Africa 28°41′S 20°59′E
Keina/Keinis see Käina
Keishū see Gyeongju
77 T11 **Keïta** Tahoua, C Niger 14°45′N 05°40′E
78 J12 **Kéita, Bahr** var. Doka. ~ S Chad
182 K10 **Keith** South Australia 36°01′S 140°22′E
96 K8 **Keith** NE Scotland, United Kingdom 57°33′N 02°57′W
26 K3 **Keith Sebelius Lake** ⊠ Kansas, C USA
32 G11 **Keizer** Oregon, NW USA 44°59′N 123°01′W
38 A8 **Kekaha** Kaua'i, Hawaii, USA, C Pacific Ocean 21°58′N 159°43′W
147 U10 **Këk-Art** prev. Alaykel', Alay-Kuu. Oshskaya Oblast', SW Kyrgyzstan 40°16′N 74°21′E
147 W10 **Këk-Aygyr** var. Keyaygyr. Narynskaya Oblast', C Kyrgyzstan 40°42′N 75°37′E
147 V9 **Këk-Dzhar** Narynskaya Oblast', C Kyrgyzstan 41°28′N 74°48′E
14 L8 **Kekek** ~ Québec, SE Canada
185 K15 **Kekerengu** Canterbury, South Island, New Zealand 41°55′S 174°05′E
111 L21 **Kékes** ▲ N Hungary 47°53′N 19°59′E
171 P17 **Kekneno, Gunung** ▲ Timor, S Indonesia
147 S9 **Këk-Tash** Kir. Kök-Tash. Dzhalal-Abadskaya Oblast', W Kyrgyzstan 41°08′N 72°25′E
81 M15 **K'elafo** Sumalē, E Ethiopia 05°36′N 44°12′E
169 U10 **Kelai, Sungai** ~ Borneo, N Indonesia
Kelamayi see Karamay
Kelang see Klang
168 K7 **Kelantan** ◈ state Peninsular Malaysia
Kelantan see Kelantan, Sungai
168 K7 **Kelantan, Sungai** var. Kelantan. ~ Peninsular Malaysia
Kelat see Kālat
Këlcyra see Këlcyrë
113 L22 **Këlcyrë** var. Këlcyra. Gjirokastër, S Albania 40°19′N 20°10′E
Kelifskiy Uzboy see Kelif Uzboýy
146 L14 **Kelif Uzboýy** Rus. Kelifskiy Uzboy. salt marsh E Turkmenistan
137 O12 **Kelkit** Gümüşhane, NE Turkey 40°07′N 39°28′E
136 M12 **Kelkit Çayı** ~ N Turkey
79 G18 **Kéllé** Cuvette-Quest, W Congo 0°04′S 14°33′E
77 W11 **Kellé** Zinder, S Niger 14°10′N 10°10′E
145 P7 **Kellerovka** Severnyy Kazakhstan, N Kazakhstan 53°51′N 69°15′E
8 I5 **Kellett, Cape** headland Banks Island, Northwest Territories, NW Canada 71°57′N 125°55′W
31 S11 **Kelleys Island** island Ohio, N USA
33 N8 **Kellogg** Idaho, NW USA 47°30′N 116°07′W
92 M12 **Kelloselkä** Lappi, N Finland 66°56′N 28°52′E
97 F17 **Kells** Ir. Ceanannas. Meath, E Ireland 53°44′N 06°53′W
118 E12 **Kelmė** Šiauliai, C Lithuania 55°39′N 22°57′E
99 M19 **Kelmis** var. La Calamine. Liège, E Belgium 50°43′N 06°01′E
78 H12 **Kélo** Tandjilé, SW Chad 09°21′N 15°50′E
83 I14 **Kelongwa** North Western, NW Zambia 13°41′S 26°19′E
11 N17 **Kelowna** British Columbia, SW Canada 49°50′N 119°29′W
11 X12 **Kelsey** Manitoba, C Canada 56°02′N 96°31′W
34 M6 **Kelseyville** California, W USA 38°58′N 122°51′W
96 K13 **Kelso** SE Scotland, United Kingdom 55°36′N 02°27′W
32 G10 **Kelso** Washington, NW USA 46°09′N 122°54′W
195 W15 **Keltie, Cape** headland Antarctica
Keltsy see Kielce
168 L9 **Keluang** var. Kluang. Johor, Peninsular Malaysia 02°01′N 103°18′E
168 M11 **Kelume** Pulau Lingga, W Indonesia 0°12′S 104°27′E
11 U15 **Kelvington** Saskatchewan, S Canada 52°10′N 103°30′W
124 J7 **Kem'** Respublika Kareliya, NW Russian Federation 64°55′N 34°18′E
124 I7 **Kem'** ~ NW Russian Federation
137 O13 **Kemah** Erzincan, E Turkey 39°35′N 39°02′E
137 N13 **Kemaliye** Erzincan, C Turkey 39°16′N 38°29′E
Kemaman see Cukai
Kemanlar see Isperikh
10 K14 **Kemano** British Columbia, SW Canada 53°39′N 127°58′W
Kemarat see Khemmarat
171 P12 **Kembani** Pulau Peleng, N Indonesia 01°32′S 122°57′E
136 F17 **Kemer** Antalya, SW Turkey 36°39′N 30°33′E
122 J12 **Kemerovo** prev. Shcheglovsk. Kemerovskaya Oblast', C Russian Federation 55°25′N 86°05′E
122 K12 **Kemerovskaya Oblast'** ◈ province S Russian Federation
92 L13 **Kemi** Lappi, NW Finland 65°46′N 24°34′E
92 M12 **Kemijärvi** Swe. Kemiträsk. Lappi, N Finland 66°41′N 27°24′E
92 M12 **Kemijärvi** ◎ N Finland
92 L13 **Kemijoki** ~ NW Finland
147 V7 **Kemin** prev. Bystrovka. Chuyskaya Oblast', N Kyrgyzstan
92 L13 **Keminmaa** Lappi, NW Finland 65°49′N 24°34′E
Kemins Island see Nikumaroro
Kemiö see Kimito
Kemiträsk see Kemijärvi
127 P5 **Kemlya** Respublika Mordoviya, W Russian Federation 54°42′N 45°16′E
99 B18 **Kemmel** West-Vlaanderen, W Belgium 50°42′N 02°51′E
33 S16 **Kemmerer** Wyoming, C USA 41°47′N 110°32′W
121 O15 **Kemmuna** var. Comino. island C Malta
79 I14 **Kémo** ◈ prefecture S Central African Republic
25 U7 **Kemp** Texas, SW USA 32°26′N 96°13′W
93 L14 **Kempele** Oulu, C Finland 64°56′N 25°26′E
101 D15 **Kempen** Nordrhein-Westfalen, W Germany 51°22′N 06°25′E
25 Q5 **Kemp, Lake** ◎ Texas, SW USA
195 W5 **Kemp Land** physical region Antarctica
25 S9 **Kempner** Texas, SW USA 31°03′N 98°01′W
44 H3 **Kemp's Bay** Andros Island, W Bahamas 24°02′N 77°32′W
183 U6 **Kempsey** New South Wales, SE Australia 31°05′S 152°50′E
101 J24 **Kempten** Bayern, S Germany 47°44′N 10°19′E
15 N9 **Kempt, Lac** ◎ Québec, SE Canada
183 P17 **Kempton** Tasmania, SE Australia 42°34′S 147°13′E
154 J9 **Ken** ~ C India
39 R12 **Kenai** Alaska, USA 60°33′N 151°15′W
0 D5 **Kenai Mountains** ▲▲ Alaska, USA
39 R12 **Kenai Peninsula** peninsula Alaska, USA
21 V11 **Kenansville** North Carolina, SE USA 34°57′N 77°54′W
146 A10 **Kenar** prev. Rus. Ufra. Balkan Welaýaty, NW Turkmenistan 40°00′N 53°05′E
121 U13 **Kenâyis, Râs el-** headland N Egypt 31°13′N 27°53′E
97 K16 **Kendal** NW England, United Kingdom 54°20′N 02°45′W
23 Y16 **Kendall** Florida, SE USA 25°39′N 80°18′W
9 O8 **Kendall, Cape** headland Nunavut, E Canada 63°31′N 87°09′W
18 J15 **Kendall Park** New Jersey, NE USA 40°25′N 74°33′W
31 Q11 **Kendallville** Indiana, N USA 41°24′N 85°10′W
171 P14 **Kendari** Sulawesi, C Indonesia 03°57′S 122°36′E
169 Q13 **Kendawangan** Borneo, C Indonesia 02°32′S 110°13′E
Kendrāpāra see Kendrāparha
154 O12 **Kendrāparha** var. Kendrāpāra. Orissa, E India 20°29′N 86°25′E
154 O11 **Kendujhargarh** prev. Keonjhargarh. Orissa, E India 21°38′N 85°40′E
25 S13 **Kenedy** Texas, SW USA 28°49′N 97°51′W
76 J15 **Kenema** SE Sierra Leone 07°55′N 11°12′W
29 P16 **Kenesaw** Nebraska, C USA 40°37′N 98°39′W
Këneurgench see Köneürgenç
79 H21 **Kenge** Bandundu, SW Dem. Rep. Congo 04°52′S 16°59′E
Kengen see Kangen
167 O5 **Kengtung** Shan State, E Myanmar (Burma) 21°18′N 99°36′E
83 F23 **Kenhardt** Northern Cape, W South Africa 29°19′S 21°08′E
76 J12 **Kéniéba** Kayes, W Mali 12°47′N 11°16′W
Kenimekh see Konimex
169 U7 **Keningau** Sabah, East Malaysia 05°21′N 116°11′E
74 F6 **Kénitra** prev. Port-Lyautey. NW Morocco 34°20′N 06°29′W
21 V9 **Kenly** North Carolina, SE USA 35°39′N 78°16′W
97 B21 **Kenmare** Ir. Neidín. S Ireland 51°53′N 09°35′W
28 L2 **Kenmare** North Dakota, N USA 48°40′N 102°04′W
97 A21 **Kenmare River** Ir. An Ribhéar. inlet NE Atlantic Ocean
18 D10 **Kenmore** New York, NE USA 42°58′N 78°52′W
25 W8 **Kennard** Texas, SW USA 31°21′N 95°10′W
29 N10 **Kennebec** South Dakota, N USA 43°53′N 99°51′W
19 Q7 **Kennebec River** ~ Maine, NE USA
19 P9 **Kennebunk** Maine, NE USA 43°22′N 70°33′W
39 R13 **Kennedy Entrance** strait Alaska, USA
166 L3 **Kennedy Peak** ▲ Myanmar (Burma) 23°18′N 93°52′E
22 K9 **Kenner** Louisiana, S USA 29°57′N 90°15′W
180 I8 **Kenneth Range** ▲▲ Western Australia
27 Y9 **Kennett** Missouri, C USA 36°15′N 90°04′W
18 I16 **Kennett Square** Pennsylvania, NE USA 39°50′N 75°40′W
32 K10 **Kennewick** Washington, NW USA 46°12′N 119°08′W
12 E11 **Kenogami** ~ Ontario, S Canada
15 Q7 **Kénogami, Lac** ◎ Québec, SE Canada
14 G8 **Kenogami Lake** Ontario, S Canada 48°04′N 80°10′W

◆ Country
● Country Capital
◇ Dependent Territory
○ Dependent Territory Capital
◈ Administrative Regions
✈ International Airport
▲ Mountain
▲▲ Mountain Range
Volcano
~ River
◎ Lake
⊠ Reservoir

14 F7 **Kenogamissi Lake** ◎ Ontario, S Canada
10 I6 **Keno Hill** Yukon Territory, NW Canada 63°54′N 135°18′W
12 A11 **Kenora** Ontario, S Canada 49°47′N 94°26′W
31 N9 **Kenosha** Wisconsin, N USA 42°34′N 87°50′W
13 P14 **Kensington** Prince Edward Island, SE Canada 46°26′N 63°39′W
26 L3 **Kensington** Kansas, C USA 39°46′N 99°01′W
32 I11 **Kent** Oregon, NW USA 45°14′N 120°43′W
24 J9 **Kent** Texas, SW USA 31°03′N 104°13′W
32 H8 **Kent** Washington, NW USA 47°22′N 122°13′W
97 P22 **Kent** *cultural region* SE England, United Kingdom
145 P16 **Kentau** Yuzhnyy Kazakhstan, S Kazakhstan 43°28′N 68°41′E
183 P14 **Kent Group** *island group* Tasmania, SE Australia
31 N12 **Kentland** Indiana, N USA 40°46′N 87°26′W
31 R12 **Kenton** Ohio, N USA 40°39′N 83°36′W
8 K7 **Kent Peninsula** *peninsula* Nunavut, N Canada
115 F14 **Kentrikí Makedonía** *Eng.* Macedonia Central. ◈ *region* N Greece
20 J6 **Kentucky** *off.* Commonwealth of Kentucky, *also known as* Bluegrass State. ◈ *state* C USA
20 H8 **Kentucky Lake** ▦ Kentucky/Tennessee, S USA
13 P15 **Kentville** Nova Scotia, SE Canada 45°04′N 64°30′W
22 K8 **Kentwood** Louisiana, S USA 30°56′N 90°30′W
31 P9 **Kentwood** Michigan, N USA 42°52′N 85°33′W
81 H17 **Kenya** *off.* Republic of Kenya. ◆ *republic* E Africa
Kenya, Mount *see* Kirinyaga
Kenya, Republic of *see* Kenya
168 L7 **Kenyir, Tasik** *var.* Tasek Kenyir. ◎ Peninsular Malaysia
29 W10 **Kenyon** Minnesota, N USA 44°16′N 92°59′W
29 Y16 **Keokuk** Iowa, C USA 40°24′N 91°22′W
Keonjihargarh *see* Kendujhargarh
Kéos *see* Tziá
29 X16 **Keosauqua** Iowa, C USA 40°43′N 91°58′W
29 X15 **Keota** Iowa, C USA 41°21′N 91°57′W
21 O11 **Keowee, Lake** ▦ South Carolina, SE USA
124 I7 **Kepa** *var.* Kepe. Respublika Kareliya, NW Russian Federation 65°09′N 32°15′E
Kepe *see* Kepa
189 O13 **Kepirohi Falls** *waterfall* Pohnpei, E Micronesia
185 B22 **Kepler Mountains** ▲▲ South Island, New Zealand
111 I14 **Kępno** Wielkopolskie, C Poland 51°17′N 17°57′E
65 C24 **Keppel Island** *island* N Falkland Islands
Keppel Island *see* Niuatoputapu
65 C23 **Keppel Sound** *sound* N Falkland Islands
136 D12 **Kepsut** Balıkesir, NW Turkey 39°41′N 28°09′E
168 M11 **Kepulauan Riau** *off.* Propinsi Kepulauan Riau. ◈ *province* NW Indonesia
Kequ *see* Gadê
171 V13 **Kerai** Papua, E Indonesia 03°53′S 134°30′E
Kerak *see* Al Karak
155 F22 **Kerala** ◈ *state* S India
165 R16 **Kerama-rettō** *island group* SW Japan
183 N10 **Kerang** Victoria, SE Australia 35°46′S 144°01′E
Kerasunt *see* Giresun
115 H19 **Keratéa** *var.* Keratea. Attikí, C Greece 37°48′N 23°58′E
Keratea *see* Keratéa
93 M19 **Kerava** *Swe.* Kervo. Etelä-Suomi, S Finland 60°25′N 25°10′E
Kerbala/Kerbela *see* Karbalā'
32 F15 **Kerby** Oregon, NW USA 42°10′N 123°39′W
117 W12 **Kerch** *Rus.* Kerch'. Avtonomna Respublika Krym, SE Ukraine 45°22′N 36°30′E
Kerch' *see* Kerch
Kerchens'ka Protska/ Kerchenskiy Proliv *see* Kerch Strait
117 V13 **Kerchens'kyy Pivostriv** *peninsula* S Ukraine
121 V4 **Kerch Strait** *var.* Bosporus Cimmerius, Enikale Strait, *Rus.* Kerchenskiy Proliv, *Ukr.* Kerchens'ka Protska. *strait* Black Sea/Sea of Azov
Kerdilio *see* Kerdýlio
114 H13 **Kerdýlio** *var.* Kerdilio. ▲ N Greece 40°46′N 23°37′E
186 D8 **Kerema** Gulf, S Papua New Guinea 07°59′S 145°46′E
Keremitlik *see* Lyulyakovo
136 I9 **Kerempe Burnu** *headland* N Turkey 42°01′N 33°20′E
80 J9 **Keren** *var.* Cheren. C Eritrea 15°45′N 38°22′E
25 U7 **Kerens** Texas, SW USA 32°07′N 96°13′W
184 M6 **Kerepehi** Waikato, North Island, New Zealand 37°18′S 175°33′E
145 P10 **Kerey, Ozero** ◎ C Kazakhstan
Kergel *see* Kärla
173 Q12 **Kerguelen** *island* C French Southern and Antarctic Territories
173 Q13 **Kerguelen Plateau** *undersea feature* S Indian Ocean
115 C20 **Kerí** Zákynthos, Iónia Nisiá, Greece, C Mediterranean Sea 37°40′N 20°48′E
81 H19 **Kericho** Rift Valley, W Kenya 0°22′S 35°19′E
184 K2 **Kerikeri** Northland, North Island, New Zealand 35°14′S 173°58′E
93 O17 **Kerimäki** Itä-Suomi, E Finland 61°56′N 29°18′E
168 K12 **Kerinci, Gunung** ▲ Sumatera, W Indonesia 02°00′S 101°40′E
Keriya *see* Yutian
158 H9 **Keriya He** ≈ NW China
98 J9 **Kerkbuurt** Noord-Holland, C Netherlands 52°29′N 05°08′E
98 J13 **Kerkdriel** Gelderland, C Netherlands 51°46′N 05°21′E
75 N6 **Kerkenah, Îles de** *var.* Kerkenna Islands, *Ar.* Juzur Qarqannah. *island group* E Tunisia
Kerkenna Islands *see* Kerkenah, Îles de
115 M20 **Kerketévs** ▲ Sámos, Dodekánisa, Greece, Aegean Sea 37°44′N 26°39′E
29 T8 **Kerkhoven** Minnesota, N USA 45°12′N 95°18′W
Kerki *see* Atamyrat
Kerkichi *see* Kerkiçi
146 M14 **Kerkiçi** *Rus.* Kerkichi. Lebap Welaýaty, E Turkmenistan 37°46′N 65°18′E
115 F16 **Kerkíneo** *prehistoric site* Thessalía, C Greece
114 G12 **Kerkíni, Límni** *var.* Límni Kerkinitis. ◎ N Greece
Kerkinitis Límni *see* Kerkíni, Límni
Kérkira *see* Kérkyra
99 M18 **Kerkrade** Limburg, SE Netherlands 50°53′N 06°04′E
Kerkuk *see* Kirkūk
115 B16 **Kérkyra** *var.* Kérkira, *Eng.* Corfu. Kérkyra, Iónia Nisiá, Greece, C Mediterranean Sea 39°37′N 19°56′E
115 B16 **Kerkyra** ✈ Kérkyra, Iónia Nisiá, Greece, C Mediterranean Sea 39°36′N 19°55′E
115 A16 **Kérkyra** *var.* Kérkira, *Eng.* Corfu. *island* Iónia Nisiá, Greece, C Mediterranean Sea
192 K10 **Kermadec Islands** *island group* New Zealand, SW Pacific Ocean
175 R10 **Kermadec Ridge** *undersea feature* SW Pacific Ocean 30°30′S 178°30′W
175 R11 **Kermadec Trench** *undersea feature* SW Pacific Ocean
143 S10 **Kermān** *var.* Kirman; *anc.* Carmana. Kermān, C Iran 30°18′N 57°05′E
143 R11 **Kermān** *off.* Ostān-e Kermān, *var.* Kirman; *anc.* Carmania. ◈ *province* SE Iran
143 U12 **Kermān, Bīābān-e** *desert* SE Iran
Kermān, Ostān-e *see* Kermān
142 K6 **Kermānshāh** *var.* Qahremānshahr; *prev.* Bākhtarān. Kermānshāhān, W Iran 34°19′N 47°04′E
143 Q9 **Kermānshāh** Yazd, C Iran 34°19′N 47°04′E
142 J6 **Kermānshāh** *off.* Ostān-e Kermānshāhān; *prev.* Bākhtarān. ◈ *province* W Iran
Kermānshāhān, Ostān-e *see* Kermānshāh
114 L10 **Kermen** Sliven, C Bulgaria 42°30′N 26°12′E
24 L8 **Kermit** Texas, SW USA 31°49′N 103°07′W
21 P6 **Kermit** West Virginia, NE USA 37°51′N 82°24′W
21 S9 **Kernersville** North Carolina, SE USA 36°12′N 80°13′W
35 S12 **Kern River** ≈ California, W USA
35 S12 **Kernville** California, W USA 35°44′N 118°25′W
115 K21 **Kéros** *island* Kykládes, Greece, Aegean Sea
76 K14 **Kérouané** SE Guinea 09°16′N 09°00′W
101 D16 **Kerpen** Nordrhein-Westfalen, W Germany 50°51′N 06°40′E
146 I11 **Kerpichli** Lebap Welaýaty, NE Turkmenistan 40°12′N 61°09′E
24 M1 **Kerrick** Texas, SW USA 36°29′N 102°14′W
Kerr Lake *see* John H. Kerr Reservoir
11 S15 **Kerrobert** Saskatchewan, S Canada 51°56′N 109°09′W
25 Q11 **Kerrville** Texas, SW USA 30°03′N 99°09′W
97 B20 **Kerry** *Ir.* Ciarraí. *cultural region* SW Ireland
21 S11 **Kershaw** South Carolina, SE USA 34°33′N 80°34′W
Kertel *see* Kärdla
95 H23 **Kerteminde** Syddtjylland, C Denmark 55°27′N 10°40′E
163 Q7 **Kerulen** *Chin.* Herlen He, *Mong.* Herlen Gol. ≈ China/ Mongolia
Kervo *see* Kerava
Kerýneia *see* Girne
12 H11 **Kesagami Lake** ◎ Ontario, SE Canada
93 O17 **Kesälahti** Itä-Suomi, SE Finland 61°54′N 29°49′E
136 B11 **Keşan** Edirne, NW Turkey 40°52′N 26°37′E
165 R9 **Kesennuma** Miyagi, Honshū, C Japan 38°55′N 141°35′E
163 V7 **Keshan** Heilongjiang, NE China 48°00′N 125°46′E
30 M6 **Keshena** Wisconsin, N USA 44°54′N 88°37′W
136 I13 **Keskin** Kırıkkale, C Turkey 39°41′N 33°36′E
Késmárk *see* Kežmarok
124 I6 **Kesten'ga** *var.* Kest Enga. Respublika Kareliya, NW Russian Federation 65°53′N 31°47′E
Kest Enga *see* Kesten'ga
98 K12 **Kesteren** Gelderland, C Netherlands 51°55′N 05°34′E
14 H14 **Keswick** Ontario, S Canada 44°15′N 79°26′W
97 K15 **Keswick** NW England, United Kingdom 54°30′N 03°04′W
111 H24 **Keszthely** Zala, SW Hungary 46°47′N 17°16′E
122 K11 **Ket'** ≈ C Russian Federation
77 R17 **Keta** SE Ghana 05°55′N 00°59′E
169 Q12 **Ketapang** Borneo, C Indonesia 01°50′S 109°59′E
127 O12 **Ketchenery** *prev.* Sovetskoye. Respublika Kalmykiya, SW Russian Federation 47°18′N 44°31′E
39 Y14 **Ketchikan** Revillagigedo Island, Alaska, USA 55°21′N 131°39′W
33 O14 **Ketchum** Idaho, NW USA 43°40′N 114°24′W
Kete/Kete Krakye *see* Kete-Krachi
77 Q15 **Kete-Krachi** *var.* Kete, Kete Krakye. E Ghana 07°50′N 00°03′W
98 L9 **Ketelmeer** *channel* E Netherlands
149 P17 **Keti Bandar** Sind, SE Pakistan 23°55′N 67°31′E
77 S16 **Kétou** SE Benin 07°25′N 02°36′E
110 M7 **Kętrzyn** *Ger.* Rastenburg. Warmińsko-Mazurskie, NE Poland 54°05′N 21°24′E
97 N20 **Kettering** C England, United Kingdom 52°24′N 00°44′W
31 R14 **Kettering** Ohio, N USA 39°41′N 84°10′W
18 F13 **Kettle Creek** ≈ Pennsylvania, NE USA
32 L7 **Kettle Falls** Washington, NW USA 48°36′N 118°03′W
14 D16 **Kettle Point** *headland* Ontario, S Canada 43°12′N 82°01′W
29 V6 **Kettle River** ≈ Minnesota, N USA
186 B7 **Ketu** ≈ W Papua New Guinea
18 G10 **Keuka Lake** ◎ New York, NE USA
Keupriya *see* Primorsko
93 L17 **Keuruu** Länsi-Suomi, C Finland 62°15′N 24°34′E
Kevevára *see* Kovin
92 L9 **Kevo** *Lapp.* Geavvú. Lappi, N Finland 69°42′N 27°08′E
44 M6 **Kew** North Caicos, N Turks and Caicos Islands 21°52′N 71°57′W
30 K11 **Kewanee** Illinois, N USA 41°15′N 89°55′W
31 N7 **Kewaunee** Wisconsin, N USA 44°27′N 87°31′W
30 M3 **Keweenaw Bay** ◎ Michigan, N USA
31 N2 **Keweenaw Peninsula** *peninsula* Michigan, N USA
31 N2 **Keweenaw Point** *peninsula* Michigan, N USA
29 N12 **Keya Paha River** ≈ Nebraska/South Dakota, N USA
Keyaygyr *see* Këk-Aygyr
23 Z16 **Key Biscayne** Florida, SE USA 25°41′N 80°09′W
26 G8 **Keyes** Oklahoma, C USA 36°48′N 102°15′W
23 Y17 **Key Largo** Key Largo, Florida, SE USA 25°06′N 80°25′W
21 U3 **Keyser** West Virginia, NE USA 39°25′N 78°59′W
27 O9 **Keystone Lake** ▦ Oklahoma, C USA
36 L16 **Keystone Peak** ▲ Arizona, SW USA 31°52′N 111°12′W
Keystone State *see* Pennsylvania
21 U7 **Keysville** Virginia, NE USA 37°02′N 78°28′W
27 T3 **Keytesville** Missouri, C USA 39°25′N 92°56′W
23 W17 **Key West** Florida Keys, Florida, SE USA 24°34′N 81°48′W
127 T1 **Kez** Udmurtskaya Respublika, NW Russian Federation 57°55′N 53°42′E
Kezdivásárhely *see* Târgu Secuiesc
122 M12 **Kezhma** Krasnoyarskiy Kray, C Russian Federation 58°57′N 101°00′E
111 L18 **Kežmarok** *Ger.* Käsmark, *Hung.* Késmárk. Prešovský Kraj, E Slovakia 49°09′N 20°25′E
Kfar Saba *see* Kfar Sava
138 F10 **Kfar Sava** *var.* Kfar Saba; *prev.* Kefar Sava. Central, C Israel 32°11′N 34°58′E
83 F20 **Kgalagadi** ◈ *district* SW Botswana
83 I20 **Kgatleng** ◈ *district* SE Botswana
188 F8 **Kgkeklau** Babeldaob, N Palau
125 R6 **Khabarikha** *var.* Chabaricha. Respublika Komi, NW Russian Federation 65°52′N 52°19′E
123 S14 **Khabarovsk** Khabarovskiy Kray, SE Russian Federation 48°32′N 135°08′E
123 R11 **Khabarovskiy Kray** ◈ *territory* E Russian Federation
141 W7 **Khabb** Abū Ẓaby, E United Arab Emirates 24°39′N 55°43′E
Khabour, Nahr al *see* Khābūr, Nahr al
Khabura *see* Al Khābūrah
139 N2 **Khābūr, Nahr al** *var.* Nahr al Khabour. ≈ Syria/Turkey
Khachmas *see* Xaçmaz
80 B12 **Khadari** ≈ W Sudan
Khadera *see* Hadera
141 X12 **Khādhil** *var.* Khudal. SE Oman 18°48′N 56°48′E
155 E14 **Khadki** *prev.* Kirkee. Mahārāshtra, W India 18°34′N 73°52′E
126 L14 **Khadyzhensk** Krasnodarskiy Kray, SW Russian Federation 44°26′N 39°31′E
114 N9 **Khadzhiyska Reka** ≈ E Bulgaria
117 P10 **Khadzhybeys'kyy Lyman** ◎ SW Ukraine
138 K3 **Khafsah** Ḥalab, N Syria 36°16′N 38°03′E
152 M13 **Khāga** Uttar Pradesh, N India 25°47′N 81°05′E
153 Q13 **Khagaria** Bihār, NE India 25°31′N 86°27′E
149 Q13 **Khairpur** Sind, SE Pakistan 27°30′N 68°50′E
122 K13 **Khakasiya, Respublika** *prev.* Khakasskaya Avtonomnaya Oblast', *Eng.* Khakassia. ◈ *autonomous republic* C Russian Federation
Khakassia/Khakasskaya Avtonomnaya Oblast' *see* Khakasiya, Respublika
167 N9 **Kha Khaeng, Khao** ▲ W Thailand 16°13′N 99°03′E
83 G20 **Khakhea** *var.* Kakia. Southern, S Botswana 24°41′S 23°29′E
Khalach *see* Halaç
Khalándrion *see* Chalándri
75 T7 **Khalīj as Sallūm** *Ar.* Gulf of Salûm. *gulf* Egypt/Libya
75 X8 **Khalīj as Suways** *var.* Suez, Gulf of. *gulf* NE Egypt
127 W7 **Khalilovo** Orenburgskaya Oblast', W Russian Federation 51°25′N 58°13′E
Khalkabad *see* Xalqobod
142 L3 **Khalkhāl** *prev.* Herowābād. Ardabīl, NW Iran 37°36′N 48°36′E
Khalkidhikí *see* Chalkidikí
Khalkís *see* Chalkída
125 W3 **Khal'mer-Yu** Respublika Komi, NW Russian Federation 68°00′N 64°45′E
119 M14 **Khalopyenichy** *Rus.* Kholopenichi. Minskaya Voblasts', NE Belarus 54°31′N 28°58′E
Khalturin *see* Orlov
141 Y10 **Khalūf** *var.* Al Khaluf. E Oman 20°27′N 57°59′E
154 K10 **Khamaria** Madhya Pradesh, C India 23°07′N 80°54′E
154 D11 **Khambhāt** Gujarāt, W India 22°19′N 72°39′E
154 C12 **Khambhāt, Gulf of** *Eng.* Gulf of Cambay. *gulf* W India
167 U10 **Khâm Đưc** *var.* Phươc Sơn. Quang Nam-Đa Năng, C Vietnam 15°28′N 107°49′E
154 G12 **Khāmgaon** Mahārāshtra, C India 20°41′N 76°34′E
141 O14 **Khamir** *var.* Khamr. W Yemen 16°N 43°56′E
141 N12 **Khamīs Mushayṭ** *var.* Hamīs Musait. 'Asīr, SW Saudi Arabia 18°19′N 42°41′E
123 P10 **Khampa** Respublika Sakha (Yakutiya), NE Russian Federation 63°43′N 123°02′E
Khamr *see* Khamir
83 C19 **Khan** ≈ W Namibia
149 Q2 **Khānābād** Kunduz, NE Afghanistan 36°42′N 69°08′E
Khân Abou Châmâte/Khan Abou Ech Cham *see* Khān Abū Shāmāt
138 I7 **Khān Abū Shāmāt** *var.* Khân Abou Châmâte, Khan Abou Ech Cham. Rīf Dimashq, W Syria 33°43′N 36°56′E
Khān al Baghdādī *see* Al Baghdādī
Khān al Maḥāwīl *see* Al Maḥāwīl
139 T7 **Khān al Mashāhidah** Baghdād, C Iraq 33°40′N 44°15′E
139 T10 **Khān al Muṣallá** An Najaf, S Iraq 32°09′N 44°20′E
139 U6 **Khānaqīn** Diyālá, E Iraq 34°22′N 45°22′E
139 T11 **Khān ar Ruḥbah** An Najaf, S Iraq 31°42′N 44°18′E
139 P2 **Khān as Sūr** Nīnawá, N Iraq 36°28′N 41°36′E
139 T8 **Khān Āzād** Baghdād, C Iraq 33°08′N 44°21′E
154 N13 **Khandaparha** *prev.* Khandpara. Orissa, E India 20°15′N 85°11′E
Khandpara *see* Khandaparha
149 T2 **Khandūd** *var.* Khandud, Wakhan. Badakhshān, NE Afghanistan 36°57′N 72°19′E
Khandud *see* Khandūd
154 G11 **Khandwa** Madhya Pradesh, C India 21°49′N 76°23′E
123 R10 **Khandyga** Respublika Sakha (Yakutiya), NE Russian Federation 62°39′N 135°30′E
149 T10 **Khānewāl** Punjab, NE Pakistan 30°18′N 71°56′E
149 S10 **Khāngarh** Punjab, E Pakistan 29°57′N 71°14′E
Khanh Hung *see* Soc Trăng
Khaniá *see* Chaniá
Khanka *see* Xonqa
163 Z8 **Khanka, Lake** *var.* Hsing-K'ai Hu, Lake Hanka, *Chin.* Xingkai Hu, *Rus.* Ozero Khanka. ◎ China/Russian Federation
Khanka, Ozero *see* Khanka, Lake
Khankendi *see* Xankändi
123 O9 **Khannya** ≈ NE Russian Federation
144 D10 **Khan Ordasy** *prev.* Urda. Zapadnyy Kazakhstan, W Kazakhstan 48°52′N 47°31′E
149 S12 **Khānpur** Punjab, E Pakistan 28°31′N 70°30′E
138 I4 **Khān Shaykhūn** *var.* Khan Sheikhun. Idlib, NW Syria 35°27′N 36°38′E
Khan Sheikhun *see* Khān Shaykhūn
Khanshyngghys *see* Khrebet Khanshyngys
145 S15 **Khantau** Zhambyl, S Kazakhstan 44°13′N 73°47′E
145 W16 **Khan Tengri, Pik** ▲ SE Kazakhstan 42°17′N 80°11′E
Khan-Tengri, Pik *see* Hantengri Feng
Khanthabouli *see* Savannakhét
127 V8 **Khanty-Mansiysk** *prev.* Ostyako-Voguls'k. Khanty-Mansiyskiy Avtonomnyy Okrug-Yugra, C Russian Federation 61°01′N 69°E
125 V8 **Khanty-Mansiyskiy Avtonomnyy Okrug-Yugra** ◈ *autonomous district* C Russian Federation
139 R4 **Khānūqah** Nīnawýé, C Iraq 35°25′N 43°15′E
138 E11 **Khān Yūnis** *var.* Khān Yūnus. S Gaza Strip 31°21′N 34°18′E
Khān Yūnus *see* Khān Yūnis
Khanzi *see* Ghanzi
139 U5 **Khān Zūr** As Sulaymānīyah, E Iraq 35°03′N 45°08′E
167 N10 **Khao Laem Reservoir** ▦ W Thailand
123 O14 **Khapcheranga** Zabaykal'skiy Kray, S Russian Federation 49°46′N 112°21′E
127 Q12 **Kharabali** Astrakhanskaya Oblast', SW Russian Federation 47°28′N 47°14′E
153 R16 **Kharagpur** West Bengal, NE India 22°30′N 87°19′E
139 V11 **Kharā'ib 'Abd al Karīm** Al Muthanná, S Iraq 31°07′N 45°33′E
143 Q8 **Kharānaq** Yazd, C Iran 31°54′N 54°21′E
Kharbin *see* Harbin
Kharchi *see* Mārwār
146 H13 **Khardzhagaz** Ahal Welaýaty, C Turkmenistan 37°54′N 60°10′E
154 F11 **Khargon** Madhya Pradesh, C India 21°49′N 75°39′E
149 V7 **Khāriān** Punjab, NE Pakistan 32°52′N 73°52′E
117 V5 **Kharkiv** *Rus.* Khar'kov. Kharkivs'ka Oblast', NE Ukraine 50°N 36°14′E
117 V5 **Kharkiv** ✈ Kharkivs'ka Oblast', E Ukraine 49°54′N 36°20′E
Kharkiv *see* Kharkivs'ka Oblast'
117 U5 **Kharkivs'ka Oblast'** *var.* Kharkiv, *Rus.* Khar'kovskaya Oblast'. ◈ *province* E Ukraine
Khar'kov *see* Kharkiv
Khar'kovskaya Oblast' *see* Kharkivs'ka Oblast'
124 L3 **Kharlovka** Murmanskaya Oblast', NW Russian Federation 68°47′N 37°09′E
114 K11 **Kharmanli** Khaskovo, S Bulgaria 41°56′N 25°54′E
114 K11 **Kharmanliyska Reka** ≈ S Bulgaria
124 M13 **Kharovsk** Vologodskaya Oblast', NW Russian Federation 59°57′N 40°05′E
80 F9 **Khartoum** *var.* El Khartûm, Khartum. ● (Sudan) Khartoum, C Sudan 15°33′N 32°32′E
80 F9 **Khartoum** ◈ *state* NE Sudan
80 F9 **Khartoum** ✈ Khartoum, C Sudan 15°36′N 32°37′E
80 F9 **Khartoum North** Khartoum, C Sudan 15°38′N 32°33′E
117 X8 **Khartsyz'k** *Rus.* Khartsyzsk. Donets'ka Oblast', SE Ukraine 48°01′N 38°10′E
117 X8 **Khartsyz'k** Donets'ka Oblast', E Ukraine 48°01′N 38°10′E
Khartsyzsk *see* Khartsyz'k
Khartum *see* Khartoum
Khasab *see* Al Khaṣab
123 S15 **Khasan** Primorskiy Kray, SE Russian Federation 42°24′N 130°45′E
127 P16 **Khasavyurt** Respublika Dagestan, SW Russian Federation 43°16′N 46°33′E
143 W12 **Khāsh** *prev.* Vāsht. Sīstān va Balūchestān, SE Iran 28°15′N 61°11′E
148 K8 **Khāsh, Dasht-e** *Eng.* Khash Desert. *desert* SW Afghanistan
Khash Desert *see* Khāsh, Dasht-e
Khashim Al Qirba/Khashm al Qirbah *see* Khashm el Girba
80 H9 **Khashm el Girba** *var.* Khashim Al Qirba, Khashm al Qirbah. Kassala, E Sudan 15°00′N 35°59′E
138 G14 **Khashsh, Jabal al** ▲▲ S Jordan
137 S10 **Khashuri** C Georgia 41°59′N 43°36′E
153 V13 **Khāsi Hills** *hill range* NE India
114 K11 **Khaskovo** Khaskovo, S Bulgaria 41°56′N 25°35′E
114 K11 **Khaskovo** ◈ *province* S Bulgaria
122 M7 **Khatanga** ≈ N Russian Federation
Khatanga, Gulf of *see* Khatangskiy Zaliv
123 N7 **Khatangskiy Zaliv** *var.* Gulf of Khatanga. *bay* N Russian Federation
141 W7 **Khatmat al Malāḥah** N Oman 24°58′N 56°22′E
143 S16 **Khaṭmat al Malāḥah** Ash Shāriqah, E United Arab Emirates
123 V7 **Khatyrka** Chukotskiy Avtonomnyy Okrug, NE Russian Federation 62°03′N 175°09′E
Khauz-Khan *see* Hanhowuz
Khauzkhanskoye Vodoranilishche *see* Hanhowuz Suw Howdany
Khavaling *see* Khovaling
Khavast *see* Xovos
139 W10 **Khawrah, Nahr al** ≈ S Iraq
Khawr Barakah *see* Barka
141 W7 **Khawr Fakkān** *var.* Khor Fakkan. Ash Shāriqah, NE United Arab Emirates 25°22′N 56°19′E
140 L6 **Khaybar** Al Madīnah, NW Saudi Arabia 25°53′N 39°16′E
Khaybar, Kowtal-e *see* Khyber Pass
147 S11 **Khaydarkan** *var.* Khaydarken. Batkenskaya Oblast', SW Kyrgyzstan 39°56′N 71°17′E
Khaydarken *see* Khaydarkan
125 U2 **Khaypudyrskaya Guba** *bay* NW Russian Federation
139 S1 **Khayrūzuk** Arbīl, E Iraq 36°58′N 44°19′E
Khazar, Baḥr-e/Khazar, Daryā-ye *see* Caspian Sea
Khazarosp *see* Hazorasp
Khazretishi, Khrebet *see* Hazratishoh, Qatorkŭhi
75 X11 **Khazzān Aswān** *var.* Aswan Dam. *dam* SE Egypt
Khelat *see* Kālat
74 F6 **Khemisset** NW Morocco 33°52′N 06°04′W
167 R10 **Khemmarat** *var.* Kemarat. Ubon Ratchathani, E Thailand 16°03′N 105°11′E
74 L6 **Khenchela** *var.* Khenchla. NE Algeria 35°22′N 07°09′E
Khenchla *see* Khenchela
74 G7 **Khénifra** C Morocco 32°59′N 05°37′W
Khersān, Rūd-e *see* Garm, Āb-e
117 R10 **Kherson** Khersons'ka Oblast', S Ukraine 46°39′N 32°38′E
Kherson *see* Khersons'ka Oblast'
117 S14 **Khersones, Mys** *Rus.* Mys Khersonesskiy. *headland* S Ukraine 44°34′N 33°24′E
Khersonesskiy, Mys *see* Khersones, Mys
117 R10 **Khersons'ka Oblast'** *var.* Kherson, *Rus.* Khersonskaya Oblast'. ◈ *province* S Ukraine
Khersonskaya Oblast' *see* Khersons'ka Oblast'
122 L8 **Kheta** ≈ N Russian Federation
149 U7 **Khewra** Punjab, E Pakistan 32°41′N 73°04′E
Khiam *see* El Khiyam
124 J4 **Khibiny** ▲▲ NW Russian Federation
126 K3 **Khimki** Moskovskaya Oblast', W Russian Federation 55°57′N 37°48′E
147 S12 **Khingov** *Rus.* Obi-Khingou. ≈ C Tajikistan
Khíos *see* Chíos
149 R15 **Khipro** Sind, SE Pakistan 25°50′N 69°24′E
139 S10 **Khirr, Wādī al** *dry watercourse* S Iraq
114 I10 **Khisarya** Plovdiv, C Bulgaria 42°33′N 24°43′E
Khiva/Khiwa *see* Xiva
167 N9 **Khlong Khlung** Kamphaeng Phet, W Thailand 16°15′N 99°41′E
167 N15 **Khlong Thom** Krabi, SW Thailand 07°55′N 99°09′E
167 P12 **Khlung** Chantaburi, S Thailand 12°25′N 102°12′E
Khmel'nik *see* Khmil'nyk
Khmel'nitskaya Oblast' *see* Khmel'nyts'ka Oblast'
Khmel'nitskiy *see* Khmel 'nyts'kyy
116 K5 **Khmel'nyts'ka Oblast'** *var.* Khmel'nyts'kyy, *Rus.* Khmel'nitskaya Oblast'; *prev.* Kamenets-Podol'skaya Oblast'. ◈ *province* NW Ukraine
116 L6 **Khmel 'nyts'kyy** *Rus.* Khmel'nitskiy; *prev.* Proskurov. Khmel'nyts'ka Oblast', W Ukraine 49°24′N 26°59′E
Khmel'nyts'kyy *see* Khmel'nyts'ka Oblast'
116 M6 **Khmil'nyk** *Rus.* Khmel'nik. Vinnyts'ka Oblast', C Ukraine 49°36′N 27°59′E
Khobda *see* Kobda
137 R9 **Khobi** W Georgia 42°20′N 41°54′E
119 P15 **Khodasy** *Rus.* Khodosy. Mahilyowskaya Voblasts', E Belarus 53°56′N 31°29′E
116 I6 **Khodoriv** *Pol.* Chodorów, *Rus.* Khodorov. L'vivs'ka Oblast', NW Ukraine 49°20′N 24°19′E
Khodorov *see* Khodoriv
Khodosy *see* Khodasy
Khodzhakala *see* Hojagala
Khodzhambas *see* Hojambaz
Khodzhent *see* Khujand
Khodzheyli *see* Xo'jayli
Khoi *see* Khvoy
Khojend *see* Khujand
Khokand *see* Qo'qon
126 L8 **Khokhol'skiy** Voronezhskaya Oblast', W Russian Federation 51°33′N 38°43′E
167 P10 **Khok Samrong** Lop Buri, C Thailand 15°03′N 100°44′E
124 H15 **Kholm** Novgorodskaya Oblast', W Russian Federation 57°10′N 31°06′E
Kholm *see* Khulm
Kholm *see* Chełm
Kholmech' *see* Kholmyech
123 T13 **Kholmsk** Ostrov Sakhalin, Sakhalinskaya Oblast', SE Russian Federation 46°57′N 142°10′E
119 O19 **Kholmyech** *Rus.* Kholmech'. Homyel'skaya Voblasts', SE Belarus 52°09′N 30°37′E
Kholon *see* Holon
Kholopenichi *see* Khalopyenichy
83 D19 **Khomas** ◈ *district* C Namibia
83 D19 **Khomas Hochland** *var.* Khomasplato. *plateau* C Namibia
Khomasplato *see* Khomas Hochland
Khomein *see* Khomeyn
142 M7 **Khomeyn** *var.* Khomein, Khumain. Markazī, W Iran 33°38′N 50°03′E
143 N8 **Khomeynīshahr** *prev.* Homāyūnshahr. Eşfahān, C Iran 32°42′N 51°28′E
Khoms *see* Al Khums
Khong Sedone *see* Muang Khôngxédôn
167 Q9 **Khon Kaen** *var.* Muang Khon Kaen. Khon Kaen, E Thailand 16°25′N 102°50′E
Khonqa *see* Xonqa
167 Q9 **Khon San** Khon Kaen, E Thailand 16°40′N 101°51′E
123 R8 **Khonuu** Respublika Sakha (Yakutiya), NE Russian Federation 66°24′N 143°15′E
127 N8 **Khopër** *var.* Khoper. ≈ SW Russian Federation
Khoper *see* Khopër
123 S14 **Khor** Khabarovskiy Kray, SE Russian Federation 47°44′N 134°48′E
143 U9 **Khorāsān-e Jonūbī** *off.* Ostan-e Khorāsān-e Janūbī. ◈ *province* E Iran
143 S3 **Khorāsān-e Shomālī** *off.* Ostan-e Khorāsān-e Shomālī. ◈ *province* NE Iran
Khorat *see* Nakhon Ratchasima
154 O13 **Khordha** *prev.* Khurda. Orissa, E India 20°10′N 85°42′E
125 U4 **Khorey-Ver** Nenetskiy Avtonomnyy Okrug, NW Russian Federation 67°25′N 58°05′E
Khorezmskaya Oblast' *see* Xorazm Viloyati
Khor Fakkan *see* Khawr Fakkān
Khorgos *see* Korgas
123 N13 **Khorinsk** Respublika Buryatiya, S Russian Federation 52°13′N 109°52′E
83 C18 **Khorixas** Kunene, NW Namibia 20°23′S 14°55′E
141 O17 **Khormaksar** *var.* Aden. ✈ ('Adan) SW Yemen 12°56′N 45°00′E
Khormal *see* Khurmāl
Khormuj *see* Khvormūj
Khorog *see* Khorugh
117 S5 **Khorol** Poltavs'ka Oblast', NE Ukraine 49°49′N 33°17′E
142 L7 **Khorramābād** *var.* Khurramabad. Lorestān, W Iran 33°29′N 48°21′E
143 R9 **Khorramdasht** Kermān, C Iran 31°41′N 56°10′E
142 K10 **Khorramshahr** *var.* Khurramshahr, Muhammerah; *prev.* Mohammerah. Khūzestān, SW Iran 30°30′N 48°09′E
147 S14 **Khorugh** *Rus.* Khorog. S Tajikistan 37°30′N 71°31′E
Khorvot Khalutsa *see* Horvot Halutsa
127 Q12 **Khosheutovo** Astrakhanskaya Oblast', SW Russian Federation 47°04′N 47°49′E
149 R6 **Khōst** *prev.* Khowst. Khōst, E Afghanistan 33°22′N 69°57′E
149 S6 **Khōst** *prev.* Khowst. ◈ *province* E Afghanistan
Khotan *see* Hotan
Khotimsk *see* Khotsimsk
Khotin *see* Khotyn
119 R16 **Khotsimsk** *Rus.* Khotimsk. Mahilyowskaya Voblasts', E Belarus 53°24′N 32°35′E
116 K7 **Khotyn** *Rom.* Hotin, *Rus.* Khotin. Chernivets'ka Oblast', W Ukraine 48°29′N 26°30′E
74 F7 **Khouribga** C Morocco 32°55′N 06°51′W
147 Q13 **Khovaling** *Rus.* Khavaling. SW Tajikistan 38°22′N 69°54′E
Khovd *see* Hovd
Khowst *see* Khōst
Khoy *see* Khvoy
119 N20 **Khoyniki** Homyel'skaya Voblasts', SE Belarus 51°54′N 29°58′E
Khozretishi, Khrebet *see* Hazratishoh, Qatorkŭhi
145 V11 **Khrebet Khanshyngys** *Kas.* Khanshyngghys; *prev.* Khrebet Kanchingiz. ▲▲ E Kazakhstan
145 X10 **Khrebet Kalba** *Kaz.* Qalba Zhotasy; *prev.* Kalbinskiy Khrebet. ▲▲ E Kazakhstan
Khrebet Kanchingiz *see* Khrebet Khanshyngys
Khrebet Ketmen *see* Khrebet Uzynkara
145 Y10 **Khrebet Naryn** *Kaz.* Naryn Zhotasy; *prev.* Narymskiy Khrebet. ▲▲ E Kazakhstan
145 W16 **Khrebet Uzynkara** *prev.* Khrebet Ketmen. ▲▲ SE Kazakhstan
Khrisoúpolis *see* Chrysoúpoli
144 J10 **Khromtau** *Kaz.* Khromtaū. Aktyubinsk, W Kazakhstan 50°14′N 58°22′E
Khromtaū *see* Khromtau
Khrysokhou Bay *see* Chrysochoú, Kólpos
117 O7 **Khrystynivka** Cherkas'ka Oblast', C Ukraine 48°49′N 29°55′E
167 R10 **Khuang Nai** Ubon Ratchathani, E Thailand 15°22′N 104°33′E
Khudal *see* Khādhil
Khudat *see* Xudat
149 W9 **Khudiān** Punjab, E Pakistan 30°59′N 74°19′E
Khudzhand *see* Khujand
83 G21 **Khuis** Kgalagadi, SW Botswana 26°37′S 21°50′E
147 Q11 **Khujand** *var.* Khodzhent, Khojend, *Rus.* Khudzhand; *prev.* Leninabad, *Taj.* Leninobod. N Tajikistan 40°17′N 69°37′E
167 R11 **Khukhan** Si Sa Ket, E Thailand 14°38′N 104°12′E
149 P2 **Khulm** *var.* Tashqurghan; *prev.* Kholm. Balkh, N Afghanistan 36°42′N 67°41′E
153 T16 **Khulna** Khulna, SW Bangladesh 22°48′N 89°32′E
153 T16 **Khulna** ◈ *division* SW Bangladesh
Khumain *see* Khomeyn
Khums *see* Al Khums
149 W2 **Khunjerāb Pass** *pass* China/ Pakistan
Khūnjerāb Pass *see* Kunjirap Daban
153 P16 **Khunti** Jhārkhand, N India 23°02′N 85°19′E
167 N7 **Khun Yuam** Mae Hong Son, NW Thailand 18°54′N 97°54′E
Khurais *see* Khurayş
141 R7 **Khurayş** *var.* Khurais. Ash Sharqīyah, C Saudi Arabia 25°06′N 48°03′E
Khurda *see* Khordha
152 J11 **Khurja** Uttar Pradesh, N India 28°15′N 77°51′E
139 V4 **Khurmāl** *var.* Khormal. As Sulaymānīyah, NE Iraq 35°19′N 46°06′E
Khurramabad *see* Khorramābād
Khurramshahr *see* Khorramshahr
149 U7 **Khushāb** Punjab, NE Pakistan 32°16′N 72°18′E
116 H8 **Khust** *var.* Husté, *Cz.* Chust, *Hung.* Huszt. Zakarpats'ka Oblast', W Ukraine 48°11′N 23°19′E
80 D11 **Khuwei** Southern Kordofan, C Sudan 13°02′N 29°13′E
149 O13 **Khuzdār** Baluchistān, SW Pakistan 27°49′N 66°39′E
142 L9 **Khūzestān** *off.* Ostān-e Khūzestān, *var.* Khuzistan, *prev.* Arabistan; *anc.* Susiana. ◈ *province* SW Iran
Khūzestān, Ostān-e *see* Khūzestān
Khuzistan *see* Khūzestān
Khvājeh Ghār *see* Khwājeh Ghār
127 Q7 **Khvalynsk** Saratovskaya Oblast', W Russian Federation 52°30′N 48°06′E
143 N12 **Khvormūj** *var.* Khormuj. Būshehr, S Iran 28°32′N 51°22′E
142 I2 **Khvoy** *var.* Khoi, Khoy. Āžarbāyjān-e Bākhtarī, NW Iran 38°36′N 45°04′E
Khwajaghar/Khwaja-i-Ghar *see* Khwājeh Ghār
149 R2 **Khwājeh Ghār** *var.* Khwajaghar, Khwaja-i-Ghar; *prev.* Khvājeh Ghār. Takhār, NE Afghanistan 37°08′N 69°24′E
149 U4 **Khyber Pakhtunkhwa** *prev.* North-West Frontier Province. ◈ *province* NW Pakistan
149 S5 **Khyber Pass** *var.* Kowtal-e Khaybar. *pass* Afghanistan/ Pakistan
186 L8 **Kia** Santa Isabel, N Solomon Islands 07°34′S 158°31′E
183 S10 **Kiama** New South Wales, SE Australia 34°41′S 150°49′E
79 O22 **Kiambi** Katanga, SE Dem. Rep. Congo 07°15′S 28°01′E
27 Q12 **Kiamichi Mountains** ▲▲ Oklahoma, C USA
27 Q12 **Kiamichi River** ≈ Oklahoma, C USA
14 M10 **Kiamika, Réservoir** ▦ Québec, SE Canada
Kiamusze *see* Jiamusi
39 N7 **Kiana** Alaska, USA 66°58′N 160°25′W
Kiangmai *see* Chiang Mai
Kiang-ning *see* Nanjing
Kiangsi *see* Jiangxi
Kiangsu *see* Jiangsu

93 M14 Kiantajärvi ◎ E Finland
115 F19 Kiáto prev. Kiáton. Pelopónnisos, S Greece 38°01′N 22°45′E
Kiáton see Kiáto
Kiayi see Jiayi
95 F22 Kibæk Midtjylland, W Denmark 56°03′N 08°52′E
67 T9 Kibali var. Uele (upper course). ≈ NE Dem. Rep. Congo
79 E20 Kibangou Niari, SW Congo 03°27′S 12°21′E
Kibarty see Kybartai
92 M8 Kiberg Finnmark, N Norway 70°17′N 30°47′E
79 N20 Kibombo Maniema, E Dem. Rep. Congo 03°52′S 25°59′E
81 E20 Kibondo Kigoma, NW Tanzania 03°34′S 30°41′E
81 J15 Kibre Mengist var. Adola. Oromīya, C Ethiopia 05°50′N 39°06′E
Kıbrıs see Cyprus
Kıbrıs/Kıbrıs Cumhuriyeti see Cyprus
81 E20 Kibungo var. Kibungu. SE Rwanda 02°09′S 30°30′E
Kibungu see Kibungo
113 N19 Kičevo SW FYR Macedonia 41°31′N 20°57′E
125 P13 Kichmengskiy Gorodok Vologodskaya Oblast', NW Russian Federation 60°00′N 45°52′E
30 J8 Kickapoo River ≈ Wisconsin, N USA
11 P16 Kicking Horse Pass pass Alberta/British Columbia, SW Canada
77 R9 Kidal Kidal, C Mali 18°22′N 01°21′E
77 Q8 Kidal ◈ region NE Mali
171 Q7 Kidapawan Mindanao, S Philippines 07°02′N 125°04′E
97 L20 Kidderminster C England, United Kingdom 52°23′N 02°14′W
76 I11 Kidira E Senegal 14°28′N 12°13′W
184 O11 Kidnappers, Cape headland North Island, New Zealand 41°13′S 175°15′E
100 J8 Kiel Schleswig-Holstein, N Germany 54°21′N 10°05′E
111 L15 Kielce Rus. Keltsy. Świętokrzyskie, C Poland 50°53′N 20°39′E
100 K7 Kieler Bucht bay N Germany
100 J7 Kieler Förde inlet N Germany
167 U13 Kiến Đưc var. Đak Lap. Đăc Lăc, S Vietnam 11°59′N 107°30′E
79 N24 Kienge Katanga, SE Dem. Rep. Congo 10°33′S 27°33′E
100 Q12 Kietz Brandenburg, NE Germany 52°33′N 14°36′E
Kiev see Kyyiv
Kiev Reservoir see Kyyivs'ke Vodoskhovyshche
76 J10 Kiffa Assaba, S Mauritania 16°38′N 11°23′W
115 H19 Kifisiá Attikí, C Greece 38°04′N 23°49′E
115 F18 Kifisós ≈ C Greece
139 U5 Kifrī At Ta'mím, N Iraq 34°44′N 44°58′E
81 D20 Kigali ● (Rwanda) C Rwanda 01°59′S 30°02′E
81 E20 Kigali ✈ C Rwanda 01°43′S 30°01′E
137 P13 Kiğı Bingöl, E Turkey 39°19′N 40°20′E
81 E21 Kigoma Kigoma, W Tanzania 04°52′S 29°36′E
81 E21 Kigoma ◈ region W Tanzania
38 F10 Kihei var. Kihei. Maui, Hawaii, USA, C Pacific Ocean 20°47′N 156°28′W
93 K17 Kihniö Länsi-Suomi, W Finland 62°11′N 23°10′E
118 F6 Kihnu var. Kihnu Saar, Ger. Kühnö. island SW Estonia
Kihnu Saar see Kihnu
38 A8 Kii Landing Ni'ihau, Hawaii, USA, C Pacific Ocean 21°58′N 160°03′W
93 L14 Kiiminki Oulu, C Finland 65°05′N 25°47′E
164 J14 Kii-Nagashima var. Nagashima. Mie, Honshū, SW Japan 34°10′N 136°18′E
164 J14 Kii-sanchi ▲▲ Honshū, SW Japan
92 L11 Kiistala Lappi, N Finland 67°52′N 25°19′E
164 I15 Kii-suidō strait S Japan
165 V16 Kikai-shima island Nansei-shotō, SW Japan
112 M8 Kikinda Ger. Grosskikinda, Hung. Nagykikinda; prev. Velika Kikinda. Vojvodina, N Serbia 45°48′N 20°29′E
Kikládhes see Kykládes
165 Q5 Kikonai Hokkaidō, NE Japan 41°40′N 140°25′E
186 C8 Kikori Gulf, S Papua New Guinea 07°25′S 144°13′E
186 C8 Kikori ≈ W Papua New Guinea
165 O14 Kikuchi var. Kikuti. Kumamoto, Kyūshū, SW Japan 33°00′N 130°49′E
Kikuti see Kikuchi
127 N8 Kikvidze Volgogradskaya Oblast', SW Russian Federation 50°47′N 42°58′E
14 I10 Kikwissi, Lac ◎ Québec, SE Canada
79 I21 Kikwit Bandundu, W Dem. Rep. Congo 05°S 18°53′E
95 K15 Kil Värmland, C Sweden 59°30′N 13°20′E
94 N12 Kilafors Gävleborg, C Sweden 61°13′N 16°34′E
38 B8 Kilauea Kaua'i, Hawaii, USA, C Pacific Ocean 22°12′N 159°24′W
38 H12 Kilauea Caldera var. Kilauea Caldera. crater Hawai'i, USA, C Pacific Ocean
Kilauea Caldera see Kilauea Caldera
109 V4 Kilb Niederösterreich, C Austria 48°06′N 15°21′E
39 O12 Kilbuck Mountains ▲▲ Alaska, USA
163 Y12 Kilchu NE North Korea 40°58′N 129°22′E
97 F18 Kilcock Ir. Cill Choca. Kildare, E Ireland 53°25′N 06°40′W
183 V2 Kilcoy Queensland, E Australia 26°58′S 152°30′E
97 F18 Kildare Ir. Cill Dara. E Ireland 53°10′N 06°55′W
97 F18 Kildare Ir. Cill Dara. cultural region E Ireland
124 K2 Kil'din, Ostrov island NW Russian Federation
25 W7 Kilgore Texas, SW USA 32°23′N 94°52′W
Kilien Mountains see Qilian Shan
114 K9 Kilifarevo Veliko Tŭrnovo, N Bulgaria 43°00′N 25°36′E
81 K20 Kilifi Coast, SE Kenya 03°37′S 39°50′E
189 U9 Kili Island var. Köle. island Ralik Chain, S Marshall Islands
149 V2 Kilik Pass pass Afghanistan/China
Kilimane see Quelimane
81 I21 Kilimanjaro ◈ region E Tanzania
81 I20 Kilimanjaro var. Uhuru Peak. 🌋 NE Tanzania 03°01′S 37°14′E
Kilimbangara see Kolombangara
Kilinailau Islands see Tulun Islands
81 K23 Kilindoni Pwani, E Tanzania 07°56′S 39°40′E
118 H6 Kilingi-Nõmme Ger. Kurkund. Pärnumaa, SW Estonia 58°07′N 24°00′E
136 M17 Kilis Kilis, S Turkey 36°43′N 37°07′E
136 M16 Kilis ◈ province S Turkey
117 N12 Kiliya Rom. Chilia-Nouă. Odes'ka Oblast', SW Ukraine 45°30′N 29°16′E
97 B19 Kilkee Ir. Cill Chaoi. Clare, W Ireland 52°41′N 09°38′W
97 E19 Kilkenny Ir. Cill Chainnigh. Kilkenny, S Ireland 52°39′N 07°15′W
97 E19 Kilkenny Ir. Cill Chainnigh. cultural region S Ireland
97 B18 Kilkieran Bay Ir. Cuan Chill Chiaráin. bay W Ireland
114 G13 Kilkís Kentrikí Makedonía, N Greece 40°59′N 22°55′E
97 C15 Killala Bay Ir. Cuan Chill Ala. inlet NW Ireland
11 R15 Killam Alberta, SW Canada 52°45′N 111°46′W
183 U3 Killarney Queensland, E Australia 28°18′S 152°15′E
11 W17 Killarney Manitoba, S Canada 49°12′N 99°40′W
14 E11 Killarney Ontario, S Canada 45°58′N 81°27′W
97 B20 Killarney Ir. Cill Airne. Kerry, SW Ireland 52°03′N 09°30′W
28 K4 Killdeer North Dakota, N USA 47°21′N 102°45′W
28 J4 Killdeer Mountains ▲▲ North Dakota, N USA
45 V15 Killdeer River ≈ Trinidad, Trinidad and Tobago
25 S9 Killeen Texas, SW USA 31°07′N 97°44′W
39 P6 Killik River ≈ Alaska, USA
11 T7 Killinek Island island Nunavut, NE Canada
Killini see Kyllíni
115 C19 Killínis, Akrotírio headland S Greece 37°55′N 21°07′E
97 D15 Killybegs Ir. Na Cealla Beaga. NW Ireland 54°38′N 08°27′W
Kilmain see Quelimane
96 I13 Kilmarnock W Scotland, United Kingdom 55°37′N 04°30′W
21 X6 Kilmarnock Virginia, NE USA 37°42′N 76°22′W
125 S16 Kil'mez' Kirovskaya Oblast', NW Russian Federation 56°55′N 51°03′E
127 S2 Kil'mez' Udmurtskaya Respublika, NW Russian Federation 57°04′N 51°22′E
125 R16 Kil'mez' ≈ NW Russian Federation
67 V11 Kilombero ≈ S Tanzania
92 J10 Kilpisjärvi Lappi, N Finland 69°03′N 20°50′E
97 B19 Kilrush Ir. Cill Rois. Clare, W Ireland 52°39′N 09°29′W
79 O24 Kilwa Katanga, SE Dem. Rep. Congo 09°22′S 28°19′E
Kilwa see Kilwa Kivinje
81 J24 Kilwa Kivinje var. Kilwa. Lindi, SE Tanzania 08°45′S 39°21′E
81 J24 Kilwa Masoko Lindi, SE Tanzania 08°55′S 39°31′E
171 T13 Kilwo Pulau Seram, E Indonesia 03°36′S 130°48′E
114 P12 Kilyos İstanbul, NW Turkey 41°15′N 29°01′E
37 V8 Kim Colorado, C USA 37°12′N 103°22′W
145 O9 Kima prev. Kiyma. Akmola, C Kazakhstan 51°37′N 67°31′E
169 U7 Kimanis, Teluk bay Sabah, East Malaysia
182 H8 Kimba South Australia 33°09′S 136°26′E
28 I15 Kimball Nebraska, C USA 41°16′N 103°40′W
29 O11 Kimball South Dakota, N USA 43°45′N 98°57′W
79 I21 Kimbao Bandundu, SW Dem. Rep. Congo 05°27′S 17°40′E
186 F7 Kimbe New Britain, E Papua New Guinea 05°36′S 150°10′E
186 G7 Kimbe Bay inlet New Britain, E Papua New Guinea
11 P17 Kimberley British Columbia, SW Canada 49°40′N 115°58′W
83 H23 Kimberley Northern Cape, C South Africa 28°45′S 24°46′E
180 M4 Kimberley Plateau plateau Western Australia
33 P15 Kimberly Idaho, NW USA 42°31′N 114°21′W
163 Y12 Kimch'aek prev. Sŏngjin. E North Korea 40°42′N 129°13′E
Kimch'ŏn see Gimcheon
Kim Hae see Gimhae
Kími see Kými
93 K20 Kimito Swe. Kemiö. Länsi-Suomi, SW Finland 60°10′N 22°45′E
9 R7 Kimmirut prev. Lake Harbour. Baffin Island, Nunavut, NE Canada 62°48′N 69°49′W
165 R4 Kimobetsu Hokkaidō, NE Japan 42°47′N 140°55′E
115 I21 Kímolos island Kykládes, Greece, Aegean Sea
115 I21 Kímolou Sífnou, Stenó strait Kykládes, Greece, Aegean Sea
126 L5 Kimovsk Tul'skaya Oblast', W Russian Federation 53°59′N 38°34′E
Kimpolung see Câmpulung Moldovenesc
124 K16 Kimry Tverskaya Oblast', W Russian Federation 56°52′N 37°21′E
79 H21 Kimvula Bas-Congo, SW Dem. Rep. Congo 05°44′S 15°58′E
169 U6 Kinabalu, Gunung ▲ East Malaysia 05°52′N 116°08′E
Kinabatangan see Kinabatangan, Sungai
169 V7 Kinabatangan, Sungai var. Kinabatangan. ≈ East Malaysia
115 L21 Kínaros island Kykládes, Greece, Aegean Sea
11 O15 Kinbasket Lake ⊠ British Columbia, SW Canada
96 I7 Kinbrace N Scotland, United Kingdom 58°16′N 02°59′W
14 E14 Kincardine Ontario, S Canada 44°11′N 81°38′W
96 K10 Kincardine cultural region E Scotland, United Kingdom
79 K21 Kinda Kasai-Occidental, SE Dem. Rep. Congo 04°48′S 21°50′E
79 M24 Kinda Katanga, SE Dem. Rep. Congo 09°20′S 25°06′E
166 L3 Kindat Sagaing, N Myanmar (Burma) 23°42′N 94°29′E
109 V6 Kindberg Steiermark, C Austria 47°31′N 15°27′E
22 H8 Kinder Louisiana, S USA 30°29′N 92°51′W
98 H13 Kinderdijk Zuid-Holland, SW Netherlands 51°52′N 04°37′E
97 M17 Kinder Scout ▲ C England, United Kingdom 53°25′N 01°52′W
11 S16 Kindersley Saskatchewan, S Canada 51°29′N 109°08′W
76 I14 Kindia Guinée-Maritime, SW Guinea 10°12′N 12°26′W
64 B11 Kindley Field air base E Bermuda
29 R6 Kindred North Dakota, N USA 46°39′N 97°01′W
79 N20 Kindu prev. Kindu-Port-Empain. Maniema, C Dem. Rep. Congo 02°57′S 25°54′E
Kindu-Port-Empain see Kindu
127 S6 Kinel' Samarskaya Oblast', W Russian Federation 53°14′N 50°40′E
125 N15 Kineshma Ivanovskaya Oblast', W Russian Federation 57°28′N 42°08′E
King see King William's Town
140 K10 King Abdul Aziz ✈ (Makkah) Makkah, W Saudi Arabia 21°44′N 39°08′E
Kingait see Cape Dorset
21 X6 King and Queen Court House Virginia, NE USA 37°40′N 76°49′W
King Charles Islands see Kong Karls Land
King Christian IX Land see Kong Christian IX Land
King Christian X Land see Kong Christian X Land
35 O11 King City California, W USA 36°12′N 121°09′W
27 R2 King City Missouri, C USA 40°03′N 94°31′W
38 M16 King Cove Alaska, USA 55°03′N 162°19′W
26 M10 Kingfisher Oklahoma, C USA 35°53′N 97°56′W
King Frederik VI Coast see Kong Frederik VI Kyst
King Frederik VIII Land see Kong Frederik VIII Land
65 B24 King George Bay bay West Falkland, Falkland Islands
194 G3 King George Island var. King George Land. island South Shetland Islands, Antarctica
12 I6 King George Islands island group Northwest Territories, C Canada
King George Land see King George Island
124 G13 Kingisepp Leningradskaya Oblast', NW Russian Federation 59°23′N 28°37′E
183 N14 King Island island Tasmania, SE Australia
10 J15 King Island island British Columbia, SW Canada
King Island see Kadan Kyun
Kingissepp see Kuressaare
141 Q7 King Khalid ✈ (Ar Riyāḍ) Ar Riyāḍ, C Saudi Arabia 25°00′N 46°40′E
35 S2 King Lear Peak ▲ Nevada, W USA 41°13′N 118°30′W
195 Y8 King Leopold and Queen Astrid Land physical region Antarctica
180 M4 King Leopold Ranges ▲▲ Western Australia
36 I11 Kingman Arizona, SW USA 35°12′N 114°02′W
26 M6 Kingman Kansas, C USA 37°39′N 98°07′W
192 L7 Kingman Reef ◇ US territory C Pacific Ocean
79 N20 Kingombe Maniema, E Dem. Rep. Congo 02°37′S 26°39′E
182 F5 Kingoonya South Australia 30°56′S 135°20′E
194 J10 King Peninsula peninsula Antarctica
39 P13 King Salmon Alaska, USA 58°41′N 156°39′W
35 Q6 Kings Beach California, W USA 39°13′N 120°02′W
35 R11 Kingsburg California, W USA 36°30′N 119°33′W
182 I10 Kingscote South Australia 35°41′S 137°36′E
King's County see Offaly
194 H2 King Sejong South Korean research station Antarctica 61°57′S 58°23′W
183 T9 Kingsford Smith ✈ (Sydney) New South Wales, SE Australia 33°58′S 151°09′E
11 P17 Kingsgate British Columbia, SW Canada 48°58′N 116°09′W
23 W8 Kingsland Georgia, SE USA 30°48′N 81°41′W
29 S13 Kingsley Iowa, C USA 42°35′N 95°58′W
97 O19 King's Lynn var. Bishop's Lynn, Kings Lynn, Lynn, Lynn Regis. E England, United Kingdom 52°45′N 00°24′E
Kings Lynn see King's Lynn
21 Q10 Kings Mountain North Carolina, SE USA 35°15′N 81°20′W
180 K4 King Sound sound Western Australia
37 N2 Kings Peak ▲ Utah, W USA 40°43′N 110°27′W
21 O8 Kingsport Tennessee, S USA 36°32′N 82°33′W
35 R11 Kings River ≈ California, W USA
183 P17 Kingston Tasmania, SE Australia 42°57′S 147°18′E
14 K14 Kingston Ontario, SE Canada 44°14′N 76°30′W
44 K13 Kingston ● (Jamaica) E Jamaica 17°58′N 76°48′W
185 C22 Kingston Otago, South Island, New Zealand 45°20′S 168°45′E
19 P12 Kingston Massachusetts, NE USA 41°59′N 70°43′W
27 S3 Kingston Missouri, C USA 39°36′N 94°02′W
18 K12 Kingston New York, NE USA 41°55′N 74°00′W
31 S14 Kingston Ohio, N USA 39°28′N 82°54′W
19 O13 Kingston Rhode Island, NE USA 41°28′N 71°31′W
20 M9 Kingston Tennessee, S USA 35°52′N 84°30′W
35 W12 Kingston Peak ▲ California, W USA 35°43′N 115°54′W
182 J11 Kingston Southeast South Australia 36°51′S 139°53′E
97 N17 Kingston upon Hull var. Hull. E England, United Kingdom 53°45′N 00°20′W
97 N22 Kingston upon Thames SE England, United Kingdom 51°26′N 00°18′W
45 P14 Kingstown ● (Saint Vincent and the Grenadines) Saint Vincent, Saint Vincent and the Grenadines 13°09′N 61°14′W
Kingstown see Dún Laoghaire
21 T13 Kingstree South Carolina, SE USA 33°40′N 79°50′W
64 L8 Kings Trough undersea feature E Atlantic Ocean 22°00′W 43°48′N
14 C18 Kingsville Ontario, S Canada 42°03′N 82°43′W
25 S15 Kingsville Texas, SW USA 27°32′N 97°53′W
21 W6 King William Virginia, NE USA 37°42′N 77°03′W
9 N7 King William Island island Nunavut, N Canada
83 I25 King William's Town var. King, Kingwilliamstown. Eastern Cape, S South Africa 32°53′S 27°24′E
Kingwilliamstown see King William's Town
21 T3 Kingwood West Virginia, NE USA 39°27′N 79°43′W
136 C13 Kınık İzmir, W Turkey 39°05′N 27°25′E
79 G21 Kinkala Pool, S Congo 04°18′S 14°49′E
165 R10 Kinka-san headland Honshū, C Japan 38°17′N 141°34′E
184 M8 Kinleith Waikato, North Island, New Zealand 38°16′S 175°53′E
95 J19 Kinna Västra Götaland, S Sweden 57°32′N 12°42′E
96 L8 Kinnaird Head var. Kinnairds Head. headland NE Scotland, United Kingdom 58°39′N 03°22′W
Kinnairds Head see Kinnaird Head
95 K20 Kinnared Halland, S Sweden 57°01′N 13°04′E
92 L7 Kinnarodden headland N Norway 71°07′N 27°40′E
Kinneret, Yam see Tiberias, Lake
155 K24 Kinniyai Eastern Province, NE Sri Lanka 08°30′N 81°11′E
93 L16 Kinnula Länsi-Suomi, C Finland 63°24′N 25°E
14 I8 Kinojévis ≈ Québec, SE Canada
164 I14 Kino-kawa ≈ Honshū, SW Japan
11 U11 Kinoosao Saskatchewan, C Canada 57°06′N 101°02′W
99 L17 Kinrooi Limburg, NE Belgium 51°09′N 05°48′E
96 J11 Kinross C Scotland, United Kingdom 56°14′N 03°27′W
96 J11 Kinross cultural region C Scotland, United Kingdom
97 C21 Kinsale Ir. Cionn tSáile. Cork, SW Ireland 51°42′N 08°32′W
95 D14 Kinsarvik Hordaland, S Norway 60°22′N 06°43′E
79 G21 Kinshasa prev. Léopoldville. ● Kinshasa, W Dem. Rep. Congo 04°21′S 15°16′E
79 G21 Kinshasa off. Ville de Kinshasa, var. Kinshasa City. ◈ region (Dem. Rep. Congo) SW Dem. Rep. Congo
79 G21 Kinshasa ✈ Kinshasa, SW Dem. Rep. Congo 04°23′S 15°30′E
Kinshasa City see Kinshasa
117 U9 Kins'ka ≈ SE Ukraine
26 K6 Kinsley Kansas, C USA 37°55′N 99°26′W
21 W10 Kinston North Carolina, SE USA 35°16′N 77°35′W
77 P15 Kintampo W Ghana 08°06′N 01°40′W
182 B1 Kintore, Mount ▲ South Australia 26°30′S 130°24′E
96 G13 Kintyre peninsula W Scotland, United Kingdom
96 G13 Kintyre, Mull of headland W Scotland, United Kingdom 55°16′N 05°46′W
166 M4 Kin-u Sagaing, C Myanmar (Burma) 22°47′N 95°36′E
12 G8 Kinushseo ≈ Ontario, C Canada
11 P13 Kinuso Alberta, W Canada 55°19′N 115°23′W
154 I13 Kinwat Mahārāshtra, C India 19°37′N 78°12′E
81 F16 Kinyeti ▲ S South Sudan 03°56′N 32°52′E
101 I17 Kinzig ≈ SW Germany
Kioga, Lake see Kyoga, Lake
26 M8 Kiowa Kansas, C USA 37°01′N 98°29′W
27 P12 Kiowa Oklahoma, C USA 34°43′N 95°54′W
Kiparissía see Kyparissía
14 H10 Kipawa, Lac ◎ Québec, SE Canada
81 G24 Kipengere Range ▲▲ SW Tanzania
81 E23 Kipili Rukwa, W Tanzania 07°30′S 30°39′E
81 K20 Kipini Coast, SE Kenya 02°30′S 40°30′E
11 V16 Kipling Saskatchewan, S Canada 50°04′N 102°45′W
38 M13 Kipnuk Alaska, USA 59°56′N 164°02′W
97 F18 Kippure Ir. Cipiúr. ▲ E Ireland 53°10′N 06°22′W
79 N25 Kipushi Katanga, SE Dem. Rep. Congo 11°45′S 27°20′E
187 N10 Kirakira var. Kaokaona. Makira-Ulawa, SE Solomon Islands 10°28′S 161°54′E
155 K14 Kirandul var. Bailādila. Chhattīsgarh, C India 18°46′N 81°18′E
155 I21 Kīranūr Tamil Nādu, SE India 11°37′N 79°10′E
119 N21 Kiraw Rus. Kirovo. Homyel'skaya Voblasts', SE Belarus 51°30′N 29°25′E
119 M17 Kirawsk Rus. Kirovsk; prev. Startsy. Mahilyowskaya Voblasts', E Belarus 53°16′N 29°29′E
118 F5 Kirbla Läänemaa, W Estonia 58°45′N 23°57′E
25 Y9 Kirbyville Texas, SW USA 30°39′N 93°53′W
114 M12 Kircasalih Edirne, NW Turkey 41°24′N 26°48′E
109 W8 Kirchbach var. Kirchbach in Steiermark. Steiermark, SE Austria 46°55′N 15°40′E
Kirchbach in Steiermark see Kirchbach
108 H7 Kirchberg Sankt Gallen, NE Switzerland 47°24′N 09°03′E
109 S5 Kirchdorf an der Krems Oberösterreich, N Austria 47°55′N 14°08′E
Kirchheim see Kirchheim unter Teck
101 I22 Kirchheim unter Teck var. Kirchheim. Baden-Württemberg, SW Germany 48°39′N 09°28′E
Kirdzhali see Kŭrdzhali
123 N13 Kirenga ≈ S Russian Federation
123 N12 Kirensk Irkutskaya Oblast', C Russian Federation 57°37′N 107°54′E
Kirghizia see Kyrgyzstan
145 S16 Kirghiz Range Rus. Kirgizskiy Khrebet; prev. Alexander Range. ▲▲ Kazakhstan/Kyrgyzstan
Kirghiz SSR see Kyrgyzstan
Kirghiz Steppe see Saryarka
Kirgizskaya SSR see Kyrgyzstan
Kirgizskiy Khrebet see Kirghiz Range
79 I19 Kiri Bandundu, W Dem. Rep. Congo 01°29′S 19°00′E
Kirihata-Arba see Hebron
191 R3 Kiribati off. Republic of Kiribati. ◆ republic C Pacific Ocean
Kiribati, Republic of see Kiribati
136 L17 Kırıkhan Hatay, S Turkey 36°30′N 36°20′E
136 I13 Kırıkkale Kırıkkale, C Turkey 39°50′N 33°31′E
136 C10 Kırıkkale ◈ province C Turkey
124 L13 Kirillov Vologodskaya Oblast', NW Russian Federation 59°52′N 38°24′E
Kirin see Jilin
81 I18 Kirinyaga prev. Mount Kenya. 🌋 C Kenya 0°02′S 37°19′E
124 H13 Kirishi var. Kirisi. Leningradskaya Oblast', NW Russian Federation 59°28′N 32°02′E
164 C16 Kirishima-yama ▲ Kyūshū, SW Japan 31°58′N 130°51′E
Kirisi see Kirishi
191 Y2 Kiritimati ✈ Kiritimati, E Kiribati 02°00′N 157°30′W
191 Y2 Kiritimati prev. Christmas Island. atoll Line Islands, E Kiribati
186 G9 Kiriwina Island Eng. Trobriand Island. island SE Papua New Guinea
186 G9 Kiriwina Islands var. Trobriand Islands. island group S Papua New Guinea
96 K12 Kirkcaldy E Scotland, United Kingdom 56°07′N 03°10′W
97 I14 Kirkcudbright S Scotland, United Kingdom 54°50′N 04°03′W
97 I14 Kirkcudbright cultural region S Scotland, United Kingdom
Kirkee see Khadki
95 I14 Kirkenær Hedmark, S Norway 60°27′N 12°04′E
92 M8 Kirkenes Fin. Kirkkoniemi. Finnmark, N Norway 69°43′N 30°02′E
92 J4 Kirkjubæjarklaustur Sudhurland, S Iceland 63°46′N 18°03′W
Kirk-Kilissa see Kırklareli
Kirkkoniemi see Kirkenes
93 L20 Kirkkonummi Swe. Kyrkslätt. Uusimaa, S Finland 60°06′N 24°20′E
14 G7 Kirkland Lake Ontario, S Canada 48°10′N 80°02′W
136 C9 Kırklareli prev. Kirk-Kilissa. Kırklareli, NW Turkey 41°45′N 27°12′E
136 I13 Kırklareli ◈ province NW Turkey
185 F20 Kirkliston Range ▲▲ South Island, New Zealand
14 D10 Kirkpatrick Lake ◎ Ontario, S Canada
195 Q11 Kirkpatrick, Mount ▲ Antarctica 84°37′S 164°36′E
27 U2 Kirksville Missouri, C USA 40°12′N 92°35′W
139 T4 Kirkūk var. Karkūk, Kerkuk. At Ta'mím, N Iraq 35°28′N 44°26′E
139 U7 Kir Kush Diyālá, E Iraq 33°42′N 45°15′E
96 K5 Kirkwall NE Scotland, United Kingdom 58°59′N 02°58′W
83 H25 Kirkwood Eastern Cape, S South Africa 33°23′S 25°19′E
27 X5 Kirkwood Missouri, C USA 38°35′N 90°24′W
Kirman see Kermān
Kir Moab/Kir of Moab see Al Karak
126 I5 Kirov Kaluzhskaya Oblast', W Russian Federation 54°02′N 34°17′E
125 R14 Kirov prev. Vyatka. Kirovskaya Oblast', NW Russian Federation 58°35′N 49°39′E
Kirov see Balpyk Bi/Ust'yevoye
Kirovabad see Gäncä
Kirovabad see Panj, Tajikistan
Kirovakan see Vanadzor
Kirov/Kirova see Kopbirlik, Kazakhstan
Kirovo see Kiraw, Belarus
Kirovo see Beshariq, Uzbekistan
125 R14 Kirovo-Chepetsk Kirovskaya Oblast', NW Russian Federation 58°33′N 50°06′E
Kirovogradskaya Oblast'/Kirovohrad see Kirovohrads'ka Oblast'
117 R7 Kirovohrad Rus. Kirovograd; prev. Kirovo, Yelizavetgrad, Zinov'yevsk. Kirovohrads'ka Oblast', C Ukraine 48°30′N 31°17′E
117 P7 Kirovohrads'ka Oblast' var. Kirovohrad, Rus. Kirovogradskaya Oblast'. ◈ province C Ukraine
Kirovo/Kirovograd see Kirovohrad
124 J4 Kirovsk Murmanskaya Oblast', NW Russian Federation 67°37′N 33°38′E
117 X7 Kirovs'k Luhans'ka Oblast', E Ukraine 48°40′N 38°39′E
Kirovsk see Kirawsk, Belarus
Kirovsk see Babadayhan, Turkmenistan
122 E9 Kirovskaya Oblast' ◈ province NW Russian Federation
117 U13 Kirovs'ke Rus. Kirovskoye. Avtonomna Respublika Krym, S Ukraine 45°13′N 35°12′E
117 X8 Kirovs'ke Donets'ka Oblast', E Ukraine 48°12′N 38°20′E
Kirovskiy see Balpyk Bi
Kirovskiy see Ust'yevoye
Kirovskoye see Kyzyl-Adyr
Kirovskoye see Kirovs'ke
146 E11 Kirpili Ahal Welaýaty, C Turkmenistan 39°31′N 57°13′E
96 K10 Kirriemuir E Scotland, United Kingdom 56°38′N 03°01′W
125 S13 Kirs Kirovskaya Oblast', NW Russian Federation 59°22′N 52°20′E
127 N7 Kirsanov Tambovskaya Oblast', W Russian Federation 52°40′N 42°48′E
136 J14 Kırşehir anc. Justinianopolis. Kırşehir, C Turkey 39°09′N 34°08′E
136 I13 Kırşehir ◈ province C Turkey
149 P4 Kīrthar Range ▲▲ S Pakistan
37 P9 Kirtland New Mexico, SW USA 36°43′N 108°21′W
92 J11 Kiruna Lapp. Giron. Norrbotten, N Sweden 67°50′N 20°16′E
79 M18 Kirundu Orientale, NE Dem. Rep. Congo 0°45′S 25°28′E
Kirun/Kirun' see Jilong
26 L3 Kirwin Reservoir ⊠ Kansas, C USA
127 Q4 Kirya Chuvashskaya Respublika, W Russian Federation 55°04′N 46°50′E
138 G8 Kiryat Shmona prev. Qiryat Shemona. Northern, N Israel 33°13′N 35°35′E
95 M18 Kisa Östergötland, S Sweden 58°N 15°39′E
165 P9 Kisakata Akita, Honshū, C Japan 39°12′N 139°55′E
Kisalföld see Little Alföld
79 L18 Kisangani prev. Stanleyville. Orientale, NE Dem. Rep. Congo 0°30′N 25°14′E
39 N12 Kisaralik River ≈ Alaska, USA
165 O14 Kisarazu Chiba, Honshū, S Japan 35°23′N 139°57′E
111 I22 Kisbér Komárom-Esztergom, NW Hungary 47°30′N 18°00′E
11 V17 Kisbey Saskatchewan, S Canada 49°41′N 102°39′W
122 J13 Kiselevsk Kemerovskaya Oblast', S Russian Federation 54°00′N 86°38′E
153 R13 Kishanganj Bihār, NE India 26°06′N 87°57′E
152 G12 Kishangarh Rājasthān, N India 26°33′N 74°52′E
Kishegyes see Mali Iđoš
77 S15 Kishi Oyo, W Nigeria 09°01′N 03°53′E
Kishinev see Chişinău
Kishiözen see Saryozen
164 I14 Kishiwada var. Kisiwada. Ōsaka, Honshū, SW Japan 34°28′N 135°22′E
143 P14 Kīsh, Jazīreh-ye var. Qey. island S Iran
145 R7 Kishkenekol' prev. Kzyltu, Kaz. Qyzyltū. Kokshetau, N Kazakhstan 53°39′N 72°22′E
138 G9 Kishon, Nahal prev. Nahal Qishon. ≈ N Israel
152 I6 Kishtwār Jammu and Kashmir, NW India 33°20′N 75°49′E
81 H19 Kisii Nyanza, SW Kenya 0°40′S 34°47′E
81 J23 Kisiju Pwani, E Tanzania 07°25′S 39°20′E
Kisiwada see Kishiwada
Kisjenő see Chişineu-Criş
38 E17 Kiska Island island Aleutian Islands, Alaska, USA
Kiskapus see Copşa Mică
111 M22 Kiskőrei-víztároló ⊠ E Hungary
Kis-Küküllo see Târnava Mică
111 L24 Kiskunfélegyháza var. Félegyháza. Bács-Kiskun, C Hungary 46°42′N 19°52′E
111 K25 Kiskunhalas var. Halas. Bács-Kiskun, S Hungary 46°26′N 19°29′E
111 K24 Kiskunmajsa Bács-Kiskun, S Hungary 46°30′N 19°46′E
127 N15 Kislovodsk Stavropol'skiy Kray, SW Russian Federation 43°55′N 42°45′E
81 L18 Kismaayo var. Chisimayu, Kismayu, It. Chisimaio. Jubbada Hoose, S Somalia 0°05′S 42°35′E
Kismayu see Kismaayo
164 M13 Kiso-sanmyaku ▲▲ Honshū, S Japan
115 H24 Kíssamos prev. Kastélli. Kríti, Greece, E Mediterranean Sea 35°30′N 23°39′E
Kisseraing see Kanmaw Kyun
76 K14 Kissidougou Guinée-Forestière, S Guinea 09°15′N 10°08′W
23 X12 Kissimmee Florida, SE USA 28°17′N 81°24′W
23 X12 Kissimmee, Lake ◎ Florida, SE USA
23 X13 Kissimmee River ≈ Florida, SE USA
11 V13 Kississing Lake ◎ Manitoba, C Canada
111 L24 Kistelek Csongrád, SE Hungary 46°27′N 19°58′E
Kistna see Krishna
111 M23 Kisújszállás Jász-Nagykun-Szolnok, E Hungary 47°14′N 20°45′E
164 G12 Kisuki var. Unnan. Shimane, Honshū, SW Japan 35°25′N 133°15′E
81 H18 Kisumu prev. Port Florence. Nyanza, W Kenya 0°02′N 34°42′E
Kisutzaneustadtl see Kysucké Nové Mesto
111 O20 Kisvárda Ger. Kleinwardein. Szabolcs-Szatmár-Bereg, E Hungary 48°13′N 22°03′E
81 J24 Kiswere Lindi, SE Tanzania 09°24′S 39°37′E
Kiszucaújhely see Kysucké Nové Mesto
76 K12 Kita Kayes, W Mali 13°00′N 09°28′W
197 N14 Kitaa ◈ province W Greenland
Kita-Akita see Takanosu
Kitab see Kitob
165 Q4 Kitahiyama Hokkaidō, NE Japan 42°25′N 139°55′E
165 P12 Kitaibaraki Ibaraki, Honshū, S Japan 36°46′N 140°45′E
165 X16 Kita-Iō-jima Eng. San Alessandro. island SE Japan
165 Q9 Kitakami Iwate, Honshū, C Japan 39°18′N 141°05′E
165 P11 Kitakata Fukushima, Honshū, C Japan 37°38′N 139°52′E
164 D13 Kitakyūshū var. Kitakyûsyû. Fukuoka, Kyūshū, SW Japan 33°51′N 130°49′E
Kitakyûsyû see Kitakyūshū
81 H18 Kitale Rift Valley, W Kenya 01°01′N 35°01′E
165 U3 Kitami Hokkaidō, NE Japan 43°52′N 143°51′E
165 T2 Kitami-sanchi ▲▲ Hokkaidō, NE Japan
37 W5 Kit Carson Colorado, C USA 38°45′N 102°47′W
180 M12 Kitchener Western Australia 31°03′S 124°00′E
14 F16 Kitchener Ontario, S Canada 43°28′N 80°27′W
93 O17 Kitee Itä-Suomi, SE Finland 62°06′N 30°09′E
81 G16 Kitgum N Uganda 03°17′N 32°54′E
Kithareng see Kanmaw Kyun
Kíthira see Kýthira
Kíthnos see Kýthnos
8 L8 Kitikmeot cultural region Nunavut, NE Canada
10 J13 Kitimat British Columbia, SW Canada 54°05′N 128°38′W
92 L11 Kitinen ≈ N Finland
147 N12 Kitob Rus. Kitab. Qashqadaryo Viloyati, S Uzbekistan 39°06′N 66°47′E
116 K7 Kitsman' Ger. Kotzman, Rom. Cozmeni, Rus. Kitsman. Chernivets'ka Oblast', W Ukraine 48°30′N 25°50′E
164 E14 Kitsuki var. Kituki. Ōita, Kyūshū, SW Japan 33°24′N 131°36′E
18 C14 Kittanning Pennsylvania, NE USA 40°48′N 79°28′W
19 P10 Kittery Maine, NE USA 43°05′N 70°44′W
92 L11 Kittilä Lappi, N Finland 67°39′N 24°53′E
109 Z4 Kittsee Burgenland, E Austria 48°06′N 17°03′E
81 J19 Kitui Eastern, S Kenya 01°25′S 38°00′E
Kituki see Kitsuki
81 G22 Kitunda Tabora, C Tanzania 06°47′S 33°13′E
10 K13 Kitwanga British Columbia, SW Canada 55°07′N 128°03′W
82 J13 Kitwe var. Kitwe-Nkana. Copperbelt, C Zambia 12°48′S 28°13′E
Kitwe-Nkana see Kitwe
109 O7 Kitzbühel Tirol, W Austria 47°27′N 12°23′E
109 O7 Kitzbüheler Alpen ▲ W Austria
101 J19 Kitzingen Bayern, SE Germany 49°45′N 10°11′E
153 Q14 Kiul Bihār, NE India 25°10′N 86°06′E
186 A7 Kiunga Western, SW Papua New Guinea 06°10′S 141°15′E
93 M16 Kiuruvesi Itä-Suomi, C Finland 63°38′N 26°40′E
38 M7 Kivalina Alaska, USA 67°44′N 164°32′W
92 L13 Kivalo ridge C Finland
9 O10 Kivalliq cultural region Nunavut, NE Canada
116 J3 Kivertsi Pol. Kiwerce, Rus. Kivertsy. Volyns'ka Oblast', NW Ukraine 50°50′N 25°31′E
Kivertsy see Kivertsi
93 L16 Kivijärvi Länsi-Suomi, C Finland 63°09′N 25°04′E
95 L23 Kivik Skåne, S Sweden 55°40′N 14°15′E
118 J3 Kiviõli Ida-Virumaa, NE Estonia 59°20′N 27°00′E
Kivu, Lac see Kivu, Lake
67 U10 Kivu, Lake Fr. Lac Kivu. ◎ Rwanda/Dem. Rep. Congo
186 C9 Kiwai Island island SW Papua New Guinea
39 N8 Kiwalik Alaska, USA 66°01′N 161°50′W
Kiwerce see Kivertsi
Kiyev see Kyyiv
145 R10 Kiyevka Karaganda, C Kazakhstan 50°15′N 71°33′E
Kiyevskaya Oblast' see Kyyivs'ka Oblast'
Kiyevskoye Vodokhranilishche see Kyyivs'ke Vodoskhovyshche
136 D10 Kıyıköy Kırklareli, NW Turkey 41°37′N 28°07′E
Kiyma see Kima
125 V13 Kizel Permskiy Kray, NW Russian Federation 58°59′N 57°37′E
125 O12 Kizema var. Kizëma. Arkhangel'skaya Oblast', NW Russian Federation 61°06′N 44°51′E
Kizëma see Kizema
Kizilagach see Elkhovo

◆ Country
● Country Capital
◇ Dependent Territory
○ Dependent Territory Capital
◈ Administrative Regions
✈ International Airport
▲ Mountain
▲▲ Mountain Range
🌋 Volcano
≈ River
◎ Lake
⊠ Reservoir

136 H12 **Kızılcahamam** Ankara, N Turkey 40°28′N 32°37′E
136 J10 **Kızıl Irmak** 🜄 C Turkey
Kizil Kum *see* Kyzyl Kum
137 P16 **Kızıltepe** Mardin, SE Turkey 37°12′N 40°36′E
Ki Zil Uzen *see* Qezel Owzan, Rūd-e
127 Q16 **Kizilyurt** Respublika Dagestan, SW Russian Federation 43°13′N 46°54′E
127 Q15 **Kizlyar** Respublika Dagestan, SW Russian Federation 43°51′N 46°39′E
127 S3 **Kizner** Udmurtskaya Respublika, NW Russian Federation 56°19′N 51°37′E
Kizyl-Arvat *see* Serdar
Kizyl-Atrek *see* Etrek
Kizyl-Kaya *see* Gyzylgaýa
Kizyl-Su *see* Gyzylsuw
95 H16 **Kjerkøy** *island* S Norway
Kjølen *see* Kölen
92 L7 **Kjøllefjord** Finnmark, N Norway 70°55′N 27°19′E
92 H11 **Kjøpsvik** *Lapp.* Gásluokta. Nordland, C Norway 68°06′N 16°21′E
169 N12 **Klabat, Teluk** *bay* Pulau Bangka, W Indonesia
112 I12 **Kladanj** ◆ Federeacija Bosna I Hercegovina, E Bosnia and Herzegovina
171 X16 **Kladar** Papua, E Indonesia 08°14′S 137°46′E
111 C16 **Kladno** Středočeský, NW Czech Republic 50°10′N 14°05′E
112 P11 **Kladovo** Serbia, E Serbia 44°37′N 22°36′E
167 P12 **Klaeng** Rayong, S Thailand 12°48′N 101°41′E
109 T9 **Klagenfurt** *Slvn.* Celovec. Kärnten, S Austria 46°38′N 14°20′E
118 B11 **Klaipėda** *Ger.* Memel. Klaipeda, NW Lithuania 55°42′N 21°09′E
118 C11 **Klaipėda** ◆ *province* W Lithuania
Klaksvig *see* Klaksvík
95 B18 **Klaksvík** *Dan.* Klaksvig. Faeroe Islands 62°13′N 06°34′W
34 L2 **Klamath** California, W USA 41°31′N 124°02′W
32 H16 **Klamath Falls** Oregon, NW USA 42°14′N 121°47′W
34 M1 **Klamath Mountains** ▲ California/Oregon, W USA
34 L2 **Klamath River** 🜄 California/Oregon, W USA
168 K9 **Klang** *var.* Kelang; *prev.* Port Swettenham. Selangor, Peninsular Malaysia 03°02′N 101°27′E
94 J13 **Klarälven** 🜄 Norway/Sweden
111 B15 **Klášterec nad Ohří** *Ger.* Klösterle an der Eger. Ústecky Kraj, NW Czech Republic 50°24′N 13°10′E
111 B18 **Klatovy** *Ger.* Klattau. Plzeňský Kraj, W Czech Republic 49°24′N 13°16′E
Klattau *see* Klatovy
Klausenburg *see* Cluj-Napoca
39 Y14 **Klawock** Prince of Wales Island, Alaska, USA 55°33′N 133°06′W
98 P8 **Klazienaveen** Drenthe, NE Netherlands 52°43′N 07°E
Kleck *see* Klyetsk
110 H11 **Kłecko** Weilkopolskie, C Poland 52°37′N 17°27′E
110 I11 **Kleczew** Wielkopolskie, C Poland 52°22′N 18°12′E
10 L15 **Kleena Kleene** British Columbia, SW Canada 51°55′N 124°54′W
83 D20 **Klein Aub** Hardap, C Namibia 23°48′S 16°39′E
Kleine Donau *see* Mosoni-Duna
101 O14 **Kleine Elster** 🜄 E Germany
Kleine Kokel *see* Târnava Mică
99 I16 **Kleine Nete** 🜄 N Belgium
Kleines Ungarisches Tiefland *see* Little Alföld
83 E22 **Klein Karas** Karas, S Namibia 27°36′S 18°05′E
Kleinkopisch *see* Copșa Mică
Klein-Marien *see* Väike-Maarja
Kleinschlatten *see* Zlatna
83 D23 **Kleinsee** Northern Cape, W South Africa 29°43′S 17°03′E
Kleinwardein *see* Kisvárda
115 C16 **Kleisoúra** Ípeiros, W Greece 39°21′N 20°52′E
95 C17 **Klepp** Rogaland, S Norway 58°46′N 05°39′E
83 I22 **Klerksdorp** North-West, N South Africa 26°52′S 26°39′E
126 I5 **Kletnya** Bryanskaya Oblast', W Russian Federation 53°25′N 32°58′E
Kletsk *see* Klyetsk
101 D14 **Kleve** *Eng.* Cleves, *Fr.* Clèves; *prev.* Cleve. Nordrhein-Westfalen, W Germany 51°47′N 06°11′E
113 J16 **Kličevo** C Montenegro 42°45′N 18°58′E
119 M16 **Klichaw** *Rus.* Klichev. Mahilyowskaya Voblasts', E Belarus 53°29′N 29°21′E
Klichev *see* Klichaw
119 Q16 **Klimavichy** *Rus.* Klimovichi. Mahilyowskaya Voblasts', E Belarus 53°37′N 31°58′E
114 M7 **Kliment** Shumen, NE Bulgaria 43°37′N 27°00′E
Klimovichi *see* Klimavichy
93 G14 **Klimpfjäll** Västerbotten, N Sweden 65°05′N 14°50′E
126 K3 **Klin** Moskovskaya Oblast', W Russian Federation 56°19′N 36°45′E
Klina *see* Klinë
113 M16 **Klinë** *Serb.* Klina. W Kosovo 42°38′N 20°35′E
111 B15 **Klínovec** *Ger.* Keilberg. ▲ NW Czech Republic 50°23′N 12°57′E
95 P19 **Klintehamn** Gotland, SE Sweden 57°22′N 18°15′E
127 R8 **Klintsovka** Saratovskaya Oblast', W Russian Federation 51°42′N 49°17′E
126 H6 **Klintsy** Bryanskaya Oblast', W Russian Federation 52°46′N 32°21′E
95 K22 **Klippan** Skåne, S Sweden 56°08′N 13°10′E
92 G13 **Klippen** Västerbotten, N Sweden 65°50′N 15°07′E
121 P2 **Klírou** W Cyprus 35°01′N 33°11′E
114 I9 **Klisura** Plovdiv, C Bulgaria 42°40′N 24°28′E
95 F20 **Klitmøller** Midtjylland, NW Denmark 57°01′N 08°29′E
112 F11 **Ključ** Federacija Bosna I Hercegovina, NW Bosnia and Herzegovina 44°32′N 16°46′E
111 J14 **Kłobuck** Śląskie, S Poland 50°56′N 18°55′E
110 J11 **Kłodawa** Wielkopolskie, C Poland 52°14′N 18°55′E
111 G16 **Kłodzko** *Ger.* Glatz. Dolnośląskie, SW Poland 50°27′N 16°37′E
95 I14 **Kløfta** Akershus, S Norway 60°04′N 11°06′E
112 P12 **Klokočevac** Serbia, E Serbia 44°19′N 22°11′E
118 G3 **Klooga** *Ger.* Lodensee. Harjumaa, NW Estonia 59°18′N 24°10′E
99 F15 **Kloosterzande** Zeeland, SW Netherlands 51°22′N 04°01′E
113 L19 **Klos** *var.* Klosi. Dibër, C Albania 41°30′N 20°07′E
Klosi *see* Klos
Klösterle an der Eger *see* Klášterec nad Ohří
109 X3 **Klosterneuburg** Niederösterreich, NE Austria 48°19′N 16°20′E
108 J9 **Klosters** Graubünden, SE Switzerland 46°54′N 09°52′E
108 G7 **Kloten** Zürich, N Switzerland 47°27′N 08°35′E
108 G7 **Kloten** ✕ (Zürich) Zürich, N Switzerland 47°25′N 08°36′E
100 K12 **Klötze** Sachsen-Anhalt, C Germany 52°37′N 11°09′E
12 K3 **Klotz, Lac** ◎ Québec, NE Canada
101 O15 **Klotzsche** ✕ (Dresden) Sachsen, E Germany 51°06′N 13°44′E
10 H7 **Kluane Lake** ◎ Yukon Territory, W Canada
Kluang *see* Keluang
111 I14 **Kluczbork** *Ger.* Kreuzburg, Kreuzburg in Oberschlesien. Opolskie, S Poland 50°59′N 18°13′E
39 W12 **Klukwan** Alaska, USA 59°24′N 135°49′W
Klyastitsy *see* Klyastsitsy
118 L11 **Klyastsitsy** *Rus.* Klyastitsy. Vitsyebskaya Voblasts', N Belarus 55°53′N 28°36′E
127 T5 **Klyavlino** Samarskaya Oblast', W Russian Federation 54°21′N 52°12′E
84 K9 **Klyaz'ma** 🜄 W Russian Federation
127 N3 **Klyaz'ma** 🜄 W Russian Federation
119 J17 **Klyetsk** *Pol.* Kleck, *Rus.* Kletsk. Minskaya Voblasts', SW Belarus 53°04′N 26°38′E
147 S8 **Klyuchevka** Talasskaya Oblast', NW Kyrgyzstan 42°34′N 71°45′E
123 V10 **Klyuchevskaya Sopka, Vulkan** ⛰ E Russian Federation 56°03′N 160°38′E
95 D17 **Knaben** Vest-Agder, S Norway 58°46′N 07°04′E
95 K21 **Knäred** Halland, S Sweden 56°30′N 13°21′E
97 M16 **Knaresborough** N England, United Kingdom 54°01′N 01°35′W
114 H8 **Knezha** Vratsa, NW Bulgaria 43°29′N 24°04′E
25 O9 **Knickerbocker** Texas, SW USA 31°18′N 100°35′W
28 K5 **Knife River** 🜄 North Dakota, N USA
10 K16 **Knight Inlet** *inlet* British Columbia, W Canada
39 S12 **Knight Island** *island* Alaska, USA
97 K20 **Knighton** E Wales, United Kingdom 52°20′N 03°01′W
35 O7 **Knights Landing** California, W USA 38°47′N 121°43′W
112 E13 **Knin** Šibenik-Knin, S Croatia 44°03′N 16°12′E
25 Q12 **Knippal** Texas, SW USA
109 U7 **Knittelfeld** Steiermark, C Austria 47°14′N 14°50′E
95 O15 **Knivsta** Uppsala, C Sweden 59°43′N 17°49′E
113 P14 **Knjaževac** Serbia, E Serbia 43°34′N 22°16′E
27 S4 **Knob Noster** Missouri, C USA 38°47′N 93°33′W
99 D15 **Knokke-Heist** West-Vlaanderen, NW Belgium 51°21′N 03°19′E
95 H20 **Knøsen** *hill* N Denmark
Knosós *see* Knossos
115 J25 **Knossos** *Gk.* Knosós. *prehistoric site* Kríti, Greece, E Mediterranean Sea
25 N7 **Knott** Texas, SW USA 32°21′N 101°35′W
194 K5 **Knowles, Cape** *headland* Antarctica 71°45′S 60°20′W
31 O11 **Knox** Indiana, N USA 41°17′N 86°37′W
29 O3 **Knox** North Dakota, N USA 48°19′N 99°43′W
18 C13 **Knox** Pennsylvania, NE USA 41°13′N 79°33′W
189 X8 **Knox Atoll** *var.* Ņadikdik, Narikrik. *atoll* Ratak Chain, SE Marshall Islands
10 H13 **Knox, Cape** *headland* Graham Island, British Columbia, SW Canada 54°05′N 133°02′W
25 P5 **Knox City** Texas, SW USA 33°25′N 99°49′W
195 Y11 **Knox Coast** *physical region* Antarctica
31 T12 **Knox Lake** ▣ Ohio, N USA
23 T5 **Knoxville** Georgia, SE USA 32°44′N 83°58′W
30 K12 **Knoxville** Illinois, N USA 40°54′N 90°16′W
29 W15 **Knoxville** Iowa, C USA 41°19′N 93°06′W
21 N9 **Knoxville** Tennessee, S USA 35°58′N 83°55′W
197 P11 **Knud Rasmussen Land** *physical region* N Greenland
Knüll *see* Knüllgebirge
101 I16 **Knüllgebirge** *var.* Knüll. ▲ C Germany
Knyazhegubskoye Vodokhranilishche ◎ NW Russian Federation
Knyazhevo *see* Sredishte
Knyazhitsy *see* Knyazhytsy
119 O15 **Knyazhytsy** *Rus.* Knyazhitsy. Mahilyowskaya Voblasts', E Belarus 54°10′N 30°28′E
83 G26 **Knysna** Western Cape, SW South Africa 34°03′S 23°03′E
Koartac *see* Quaqtaq
169 N13 **Koba** Pulau Bangka, W Indonesia 02°30′S 106°26′E
164 D16 **Kobayashi** *var.* Kobayasi. Miyazaki, Kyūshū, SW Japan 32°00′N 130°58′E
Kobayasi *see* Kobayashi
144 I10 **Kobda** *prev.* Khobda, Novoalekseyevka. Aktyubinsk, W Kazakhstan 50°09′N 55°39′E
144 H9 **Kobda** *Kaz.* Ülkenqobda; *prev.* Bol'shaya Khobda. 🜄 Kazakhstan/Russian Federation
Kobdo *see* Hovd
164 I13 **Kōbe** Hyōgo, Honshū, SW Japan 34°40′N 135°10′E
Kobelyaki *see* Kobelyaky
117 T6 **Kobelyaky** *Rus.* Kobelyaki. Poltavs'ka Oblast', NE Ukraine 49°10′N 34°13′E
95 J22 **København** *Eng.* Copenhagen; *anc.* Hafnia. ● (Denmark) Sjælland, København, E Denmark 55°43′N 12°34′E
76 K10 **Kobenni** Hodh el Gharbi, S Mauritania 15°58′N 09°24′W
171 T13 **Kobi** Pulau Seram, E Indonesia 02°56′S 129°53′E
101 F17 **Koblenz** *prev.* Coblenz, *Fr.* Coblence; *anc.* Confluentes. Rheinland-Pfalz, W Germany 50°21′N 07°36′E
108 F6 **Koblenz** Aargau, N Switzerland 47°34′N 08°16′E
Kobrin *see* Kobryn
171 V15 **Kobroor, Pulau** *island* Kepulauan Aru, E Indonesia
119 G19 **Kobryn** *Rus.* Kobrin. Brestskaya Voblasts', SW Belarus 52°13′N 24°21′E
39 O7 **Kobuk** Alaska, USA 66°54′N 156°52′W
39 O7 **Kobuk River** 🜄 Alaska, USA
137 Q10 **K'obulet'i** *prev.* K'obulet'i. W Georgia 41°47′N 41°47′E
K'obulet'i *see* Kobuleti
123 P10 **Kobyay** Respublika Sakha (Yakutiya), NE Russian Federation 63°36′N 126°33′E
136 E11 **Kocaeli** ◆ *province* NW Turkey
113 P18 **Kočani** NE FYR Macedonia 41°55′N 22°25′E
112 K12 **Koceljevo** Serbia, W Serbia 44°28′N 19°49′E
109 U12 **Kočevje** *Ger.* Gottschee. S Slovenia 45°41′N 14°48′E
153 T12 **Koch Bihār** West Bengal, NE India 26°19′N 89°26′E
Kochchi *see* Cochin/Kochi
122 M9 **Kochechum** 🜄 N Russian Federation
101 I20 **Kocher** 🜄 SW Germany
125 T13 **Kochevo** Komi-Permyatskiy Okrug, NW Russian Federation 59°37′N 54°16′E
164 G14 **Kōchi** *var.* Kôti. Kōchi, Shikoku, SW Japan 33°31′N 133°30′E
164 G14 **Kōchi** *off.* Kōchi-ken, *var.* Kôti. ◆ *prefecture* Shikoku, SW Japan
Kōchi-ken *see* Kōchi
Kochiu *see* Gejiu
Kochkor *see* Kochkorka
147 V8 **Kochkorka** *Kir.* Kochkor. Narynskaya Oblast', C Kyrgyzstan 42°09′N 75°42′E
125 V5 **Kochmes** Respublika Komi, NW Russian Federation 66°10′N 60°46′E
127 P15 **Kochubey** Respublika Dagestan, SW Russian Federation 44°25′N 46°33′E
115 J17 **Kochylas** ▲ Skýros, Vóreies Sporádes, Greece, Aegean Sea 38°50′N 24°35′E
110 O13 **Kock** Lubelskie, E Poland 51°39′N 22°26′E
81 J19 **Kodacho** *spring/well* S Kenya 01°52′S 39°22′E
155 K24 **Koddiyar Bay** *bay* NE Sri Lanka
39 Q14 **Kodiak** Kodiak Island, Alaska, USA 57°47′N 152°24′W
39 Q14 **Kodiak Island** *island* Alaska, USA
154 B12 **Kodīnār** Gujarāt, W India 20°44′N 70°46′E
124 M9 **Kodino** Arkhangel'skaya Oblast', NW Russian Federation 63°36′N 39°54′E
122 M12 **Kodinsk** Krasnoyarskiy Kray, C Russian Federation 58°37′N 99°18′E
80 F12 **Kodok** Upper Nile, NE South Sudan 09°51′N 32°07′E
117 N8 **Kodyma** Odes'ka Oblast', SW Ukraine 48°05′N 29°09′E
Koedoes *see* Kudus
99 B17 **Koekelare** West-Vlaanderen, W Belgium 51°07′N 02°58′E
Koeln *see* Köln
Koepang *see* Kupang
Ko-erh-mu *see* Golmud
99 J17 **Koersel** Limburg, NE Belgium 51°04′N 05°17′E
83 E21 **Koës** Karas, SE Namibia 25°59′S 19°08′E
Koetai *see* Mahakam, Sungai
Koetaradja *see* Banda Aceh
36 I14 **Kofa Mountains** ▲ Arizona, SW USA
171 Y15 **Kofarau** Papua, E Indonesia 07°29′S 140°28′E
147 P13 **Kofarnihon** *Rus.* Kofarnikhon; *prev.* Ordzhonikidzeabad, *Taj.* Orjonikidzeobod, Yangi-Bazar. W Tajikistan 38°32′N 68°56′E
147 P14 **Kofarnihon** *Rus.* Kafirnigan. 🜄 SW Tajikistan
Kofarnikhon *see* Kofarnihon
114 M11 **Kofçaz** Kırklareli, NW Turkey 41°58′N 27°12′E
115 J25 **Kófinas** ▲ Kríti, Greece, E Mediterranean Sea 34°58′N 25°03′E
121 P3 **Kofínou** *var.* Kophinou. S Cyprus 34°49′N 33°24′E
109 V8 **Köflach** Steiermark, SE Austria 47°04′N 15°04′E
77 Q17 **Koforidua** SE Ghana 06°01′N 00°12′W
164 H12 **Kōfu** Tottori, Honshū, SW Japan 35°16′N 133°31′E
164 M13 **Kōfu** *var.* Kôhu. Yamanashi, Honshū, S Japan 35°41′N 138°33′E
81 F22 **Koga** Tabora, C Tanzania 06°08′S 32°20′E
Kogălniceanu *see* Mihail Kogălniceanu
13 P6 **Kogaluk** 🜄 Newfoundland and Labrador, E Canada
12 J4 **Kogaluk, Rivière** 🜄 Québec, NE Canada
145 V14 **Kogaly** *Kaz.* Qoghaly; *prev.* Kugaly. Almaty, SE Kazakhstan 44°30′N 78°40′E
122 I10 **Kogalym** Khanty-Mansiyskiy Avtonomnyy Okrug-Yugra, C Russian Federation 62°13′N 74°34′E
95 J23 **Køge** Sjælland, E Denmark 55°28′N 12°12′E
95 J23 **Køge Bugt** *bay* E Denmark
77 U16 **Kogi** ◆ *state* C Nigeria
146 L11 **Kogon** *Rus.* Kagan. Buxoro Viloyati, C Uzbekistan 39°47′N 64°29′E
Kögüm-do *see* Geogeum-do
Kőhalom *see* Rupea
149 T6 **Kohāt** Khyber Pakhtunkhwa, NW Pakistan 33°37′N 71°30′E
142 L10 **Kohgīlūyeh va Bowyer Aḥmad** *off.* Ostān-e Kohkīlūyeh va Būyer Aḥmadī, *var.* Boyer Ahmadī va Kohkīlūyeh. ◆ *province* SW Iran
118 G4 **Kohila** *Ger.* Koil. Raplamaa, NW Estonia 59°09′N 24°45′E
153 X13 **Kohīma** *state capital* Nāgāland, E India 25°40′N 94°08′E
Koh I Noh *see* Büyükağrı Dağı
Kohkīlūyeh va Būyer Aḥmadī, Ostān-e *see* Kohgīlūyeh va Bowyer Aḥmad
Kohsān *see* Kūhestān
118 J3 **Kohtla-Järve** Ida-Virumaa, NE Estonia 59°22′N 27°21′E
Kōhu *see* Kōfu
Kohyl'nyk *see* Cogîlnic
165 N11 **Koide** Niigata, Honshū, C Japan 37°13′N 138°58′E
10 G7 **Koidern** Yukon Territory, W Canada 61°55′N 140°22′W
76 J15 **Koidu** E Sierra Leone 08°40′N 11°01′W
118 I4 **Koigi** Järvamaa, C Estonia 58°51′N 25°45′E
Koil *see* Kohila
172 H13 **Koimbani** Grande Comore, NW Comoros 11°37′S 43°23′E
139 T3 **Koi Sanjaq** *var.* Koysanjaq, Küysanjaq. Arbil, N Iraq 36°05′N 44°38′E
93 O16 **Koitere** ◎ E Finland
Koivisto *see* Primorsk
Kōje-do *see* Geoje-do
80 J13 **K'ok'a Hāyk'** ◎ C Ethiopia
Kokand *see* Qo'qon
182 F6 **Kokatha** South Australia 31°17′S 135°16′E
146 M10 **Ko'kcha** *Rus.* Kokcha. Buxoro Viloyati, C Uzbekistan 40°30′N 64°58′E
Kokcha *see* Ko'kcha
Kokchetav *see* Kokshetau
93 K18 **Kokemäenjoki** 🜄 SW Finland
171 W14 **Kokenau** *var.* Kokonau. Papua, E Indonesia 04°38′S 136°24′E
83 E22 **Kokerboom** Karas, SE Namibia 28°11′S 19°25′E
119 N14 **Kokhanava** *Rus.* Kokhanovo. Vitsyebskaya Voblasts', NE Belarus 54°28′N 29°59′E
Kokhanovichi *see* Kakhanavichy
Kokhanovo *see* Kokhanava
Kök-Janggak *see* Kok-Yangak
93 K16 **Kokkola** *Swe.* Karleby; *prev. Swe.* Gamlakarleby. Länsi-Suomi, W Finland 63°50′N 23°10′E
158 L3 **Kok Kuduk** *spring/well* N China 46°03′N 87°34′E
118 H9 **Kokmuiža** Cēsis, C Latvia
77 T13 **Koko** Kebbi, W Nigeria 11°25′N 04°33′E
186 E9 **Kokoda** Northern, S Papua New Guinea 08°52′S 147°44′E
76 K12 **Kokofata** Kayes, W Mali 12°48′N 09°56′W
39 N6 **Kokolik River** 🜄 Alaska, USA
31 O13 **Kokomo** Indiana, N USA 40°29′N 86°07′W
Kokonau *see* Kokenau
Koko Nor *see* Qinghai, China
Koko Nor *see* Qinghai Hu, China
186 H6 **Kokopo** *var.* Kopopo; *prev.* Herbertshöhe. New Britain, E Papua New Guinea 04°18′S 152°17′E
Kokpekti *see* Kokpekty
Kokpekti *see* Kokpekty
145 X10 **Kokpekty** *prev.* Kokpekti. Vostochnyy Kazakhstan, E Kazakhstan 48°47′N 82°28′E
145 X11 **Kokpekty** *prev.* Kokpekti. 🜄 E Kazakhstan
39 P9 **Kokrines** Alaska, USA 64°58′N 154°42′W
39 P9 **Kokrines Hills** ▲ Alaska, USA
145 P17 **Koksaray** Yuzhnyy Kazakhstan, S Kazakhstan 42°34′N 68°06′E
147 X9 **Kokshaal-Tau** *Rus.* Khrebet Kakshaal-Too. ▲ China/Kyrgyzstan
145 P7 **Kokshetau** *Kaz.* Kökshetaū; *prev.* Kokchetav. Kokshetau, N Kazakhstan 53°18′N 69°25′E
Kökshetaū *see* Kokshetau
99 A17 **Koksijde** West-Vlaanderen, W Belgium 51°07′N 02°40′E
12 M5 **Koksoak** 🜄 Québec, E Canada
83 K24 **Kokstad** KwaZulu/Natal, E South Africa 30°23′S 29°23′E
145 V14 **Koksu** *Kaz.* Rūdnīchnyy. Almaty, SE Kazakhstan 44°39′N 78°57′E
145 W15 **Koktal** *Kaz.* Köktal. Almaty, SE Kazakhstan 44°05′N 79°44′E
145 Q12 **Koktas** 🜄 C Kazakhstan
Kök-Tash *see* Këk-Tash
Koktokay *see* Fuyun
147 T9 **Kok-Yangak** *Kir.* Kök-Janggak. Dzhalal-Abadskaya Oblast', W Kyrgyzstan 41°02′N 73°11′E
158 F9 **Kokyar** Xinjiang Uygur Zizhiqu, W China 37°41′N 77°15′E
149 O13 **Kolāchi** *var.* Kulachi. 🜄 SW Pakistan
76 J15 **Kolahun** N Liberia 08°24′N 10°02′W
171 O14 **Kolaka** Sulawesi, C Indonesia 04°04′S 121°38′E
K'o-la-ma-i *see* Karamay
Kola Peninsula *see* Kol'skiy Poluostrov
155 H19 **Kolār** Karnātaka, E India 13°10′N 78°10′E
155 H19 **Kolār Gold Fields** Karnātaka, E India 12°56′N 78°16′E
92 K11 **Kolari** Lappi, NW Finland 67°20′N 23°51′E
111 I21 **Kolárovo** *Ger.* Gutta; *prev.* Guta, *Hung.* Gúta. Nitriansky Kraj, SW Slovakia 47°54′N 18°01′E
113 K16 **Kolašin** E Montenegro 42°49′N 19°32′E
Kolāyat *see* Shir Kolāyat
95 N15 **Kolbäck** Västmanland, C Sweden 59°33′N 16°15′E
Kolbcha *see* Kowbcha
197 Q15 **Kolbeinsey Ridge** *undersea feature* Denmark Strait/Norwegian Sea 69°00′N 17°30′W
Kolberg *see* Kołobrzeg
95 H15 **Kolbotn** Akershus, S Norway 62°15′N 10°24′E
111 N16 **Kolbuszowa** Podkarpackie, SE Poland 50°12′N 22°07′E
126 L3 **Kol'chugino** Vladimirskaya Oblast', W Russian Federation 56°19′N 39°24′E
76 H12 **Kolda** S Senegal 12°58′N 14°58′W
95 G23 **Kolding** Syddanmark, C Denmark 55°29′N 09°30′E
79 K20 **Kole** Kasai-Oriental, SW Dem. Rep. Congo 03°30′S 22°28′E
79 M17 **Kole** Orientale, N Dem. Rep. Congo 02°08′N 25°25′E
Kole *see* Kili Island
84 F6 **Kölen** *Nor.* Kjølen. ▲ Norway/Sweden
Kolepom, Pulau *see* Yos Sudarso, Pulau
118 H3 **Kolga Laht** *Ger.* Kolko-Wiek. *bay* N Estonia
125 Q3 **Kolguyev, Ostrov** *island* NW Russian Federation
155 E16 **Kolhāpur** Mahārāshtra, SW India 16°42′N 74°13′E
151 K21 **Kolhumadulu** *var.* Thaa Atoll. *atoll* S Maldives
93 O16 **Koli** *var.* Kolinkylä. Itä-Suomi, E Finland 63°06′N 29°46′E
39 O13 **Koliganek** Alaska, USA 59°43′N 157°16′W
111 E16 **Kolín** *Ger.* Kolin. Střední Čechy, C Czech Republic 50°02′N 15°10′E
Kolinkylä *see* Koli
190 E12 **Koliu** Île Futuna, W Wallis and Futuna
118 E7 **Kolka** NW Latvia 57°44′N 22°34′E
118 E7 **Kolkasrags** *prev. Eng.* Cape Domesnes. *headland* NW Latvia 57°45′N 22°35′E
153 S16 **Kolkata** *prev.* Calcutta. *state capital* West Bengal, NE India 22°30′N 88°20′E
Kolkhozabad *see* Kolkhozobod
147 P14 **Kolkhozobod** *Rus.* Kolkhozabad; *prev.* Kaganovichabad, Tugalan. SW Tajikistan 37°33′N 68°34′E
Kolki/Kołki *see* Kolky
Kolko-Wiek *see* Kolga Laht
116 K3 **Kolky** *Pol.* Kołki, *Rus.* Kolki. Volyns'ka Oblast', NW Ukraine 51°05′N 25°40′E
155 G20 **Kollegāl** Karnātaka, W India 12°08′N 77°06′E
98 M5 **Kollum** Fryslân, N Netherlands 53°17′N 06°09′E
Kolmar *see* Colmar
101 E16 **Köln** *var.* Koeln, *Eng./Fr.* Cologne, *prev.* Cöln; *anc.* Colonia Agrippina, Oppidum Ubiorum. Nordrhein-Westfalen, W Germany 50°57′N 06°57′E
110 N9 **Kolno** Podlaskie, NE Poland 53°24′N 21°57′E
110 J12 **Koło** Wielkopolskie, C Poland 52°11′N 18°39′E
38 B8 **Kōloa** *var.* Koloa. Kaua'i, Hawaii, USA, C Pacific Ocean 21°54′N 159°28′W
Koloa *see* Kōloa
110 E7 **Kołobrzeg** *Ger.* Kolberg. Zachodnio-pomorskie, NW Poland 54°11′N 15°34′E
126 H4 **Kolodnya** Smolenskaya Oblast', W Russian Federation 54°57′N 32°22′E
190 E13 **Kolofau, Mont** ⛰ Île Alofi, S Wallis and Futuna 14°21′S 178°02′W
125 O14 **Kologriv** Kostromskaya Oblast', NW Russian Federation 58°49′N 44°22′E
76 L12 **Kolokani** Koulikoro, W Mali 13°35′N 08°01′W
77 N13 **Koloko** W Burkina 11°06′N 05°18′W
186 K8 **Kolombangara** *var.* Kilimbangara, Nduke. *island* New Georgia Islands, NW Solomon Islands
Kolomea *see* Kolomyya
126 L4 **Kolomna** Moskovskaya Oblast', W Russian Federation 55°03′N 38°52′E
116 J7 **Kolomyya** *Ger.* Kolomea. Ivano-Frankivs'ka Oblast', W Ukraine 48°31′N 25°00′E
76 M13 **Kolondiéba** Sikasso, SW Mali 11°04′N 06°55′W
193 V15 **Kolonga** Tongatapu, S Tonga 21°07′S 175°05′W
189 U16 **Kolonia** *var.* Colonia. Pohnpei, E Micronesia 06°57′N 158°12′E
Kolonja *see* Kolonjë
113 K21 **Kolonjë** *var.* Kolonja. Fier, C Albania 40°49′N 19°37′E
Kolonjë *see* Ersekë
Kolosjoki *see* Nikel'
Kolotambu *see* Avuavu
193 U15 **Kolovai** Tongatapu, S Tonga 21°05′S 175°20′W
Kolozsvár *see* Cluj-Napoca
112 C9 **Kolpa** *Ger.* Kulpa, *SCr.* Kupa. 🜄 Croatia/Slovenia
122 J11 **Kolpashevo** Tomskaya Oblast', C Russian Federation 58°21′N 82°44′E
124 H13 **Kolpino** Leningradskaya Oblast', NW Russian Federation 59°44′N 30°39′E
100 M10 **Kölpinsee** ◎ NE Germany
Kólpos Mórfu *see* Güzelyurt Körfezi
146 K8 **Koʻlquduq** *Rus.* Kulkuduk. Navoiy Viloyati, N Uzbekistan 42°36′N 63°24′E
124 K5 **Kol'skiy Poluostrov** *Eng.* Kola Peninsula. *peninsula* NW Russian Federation
127 T6 **Koltubanovskiy** Orenburgskaya Oblast', W Russian Federation 53°00′N 52°00′E
112 L11 **Kolubara** 🜄 C Serbia
Kolupchii *see* Gurkovo
110 K13 **Koluszki** Łódźskie, C Poland 51°44′N 19°50′E
125 T6 **Kolva** 🜄 NW Russian Federation
93 E14 **Kolvereid** Nord-Trøndelag, W Norway 64°47′N 11°22′E
79 M24 **Kolwezi** Katanga, S Dem. Rep. Congo 10°43′S 25°29′E
123 S7 **Kolyma** 🜄 NE Russian Federation
Kolyma Lowland *see* Kolymskaya Nizmennost'
Kolyma Range/Kolymskiy, Khrebet *see* Kolymskoye Nagor'ye
123 S7 **Kolymskaya Nizmennost'** *Eng.* Kolyma Lowland. *lowlands* NE Russian Federation
123 S7 **Kolymskoye** Respublika Sakha (Yakutiya), NE Russian Federation 68°42′N 158°46′E
123 U8 **Kolymskoye Nagor'ye** *var.* Khrebet Kolymskiy, *Eng.* Kolyma Range. ▲ E Russian Federation
123 V5 **Kolyuchinskaya Guba** *bay* NE Russian Federation
Kol'zhat *see* Kalzhat
114 G8 **Kom** ▲ NW Bulgaria 43°10′N 23°02′E
80 I13 **Koma** Oromīya, C Ethiopia 08°19′N 36°48′E
77 X12 **Komadugu Gana** 🜄 NE Nigeria
164 M13 **Komagane** Nagano, Honshū, S Japan 35°44′N 137°54′E
79 P17 **Komanda** Orientale, NE Dem. Rep. Congo 01°25′N 29°43′E
197 U1 **Komandorskaya Basin** *var.* Kamchatka Basin. *undersea feature* SW Bering Sea 57°00′N 168°00′E
125 Pp9 **Komandorskiye Ostrova** *Eng.* Commander Islands. *island group* E Russian Federation
Komanfalva *see* Comănești
111 I22 **Komárno** *Ger.* Komorn, *Hung.* Komárom. Nitriansky Kraj, SW Slovakia 47°46′N 18°07′E
111 I22 **Komárom** Komárom-Esztergom, NW Hungary 47°43′N 18°06′E
Komárom *see* Komárno
111 I22 **Komárom-Esztergom** *off.* Komárom-Esztergom Megye. ◆ *county* N Hungary
Komárom-Esztergom Megye *see* Komárom-Esztergom
164 K11 **Komatsu** *var.* Komatu. Ishikawa, Honshū, SW Japan 36°25′N 136°27′E
Komatu *see* Komatsu
83 D17 **Kombat** Otjozondjupa, N Namibia 19°42′S 17°45′E
Kombissiguiri *see* Kombissiri
77 P13 **Kombissiri** *var.* Kombissiguiri. C Burkina 12°01′N 01°27′W
188 E10 **Komebail Lagoon** *lagoon* N Palau
81 F20 **Kome Island** *island* N Tanzania
Komeyo *see* Wandai
117 P10 **Kominternivs'ke** Odes'ka Oblast', SW Ukraine 46°52′N 30°56′E
125 R8 **Komi, Respublika** ◆ *autonomous republic* NW Russian Federation
111 I25 **Komló** Baranya, SW Hungary 46°11′N 18°15′E
Kommunarsk *see* Alchevs'k
Kommunizm, Qullai *see* Ismoili Somoní, Qullai
186 B7 **Komo** Southern Highlands, W Papua New Guinea 06°06′S 142°52′E
170 M16 **Komodo, Pulau** *island* Nusa Tenggara, S Indonesia
77 N15 **Komoé** *var.* Komoé Fleuve. 🜄 E Ivory Coast
Komoé Fleuve *see* Komoé
75 X11 **Kom Ombo** *var.* Kôm Ombo, Kawm Umbū. SE Egypt 24°26′N 32°57′E
79 F20 **Komono** Lékoumou, SW Congo 03°15′S 13°14′E
171 Y16 **Komoran** Papua, E Indonesia 08°14′S 138°51′E
171 Y16 **Komoran, Pulau** *island* E Indonesia
Komorn *see* Komárno
Komornok *see* Comorâşte
Komosolabad *see* Komsomolobod
Komotau *see* Chomutov
114 K13 **Komotiní** *var.* Gümüljina, *Turk.* Gümülcine. Anatolikí Makedonía kai Thráki, NE Greece 41°07′N 25°27′E
113 K16 **Komovi** ▲ E Montenegro
117 R8 **Kompaniyivka** Kirovohrads'ka Oblast', C Ukraine 48°16′N 32°12′E
Kompong *see* Kâmpóng Chhnăng
Kompong Cham *see* Kâmpóng Cham
Kompong Kleang *see* Kâmpóng Khleăng
Kompong Som *see* Sihanoukville
Kompong Speu *see* Kâmpóng Spoe
Komrat *see* Comrat
144 G12 **Komsomol** *prev.* Komsomol'skiy. Atyrau, W Kazakhstan 47°18′N 53°37′E
125 W4 **Komsomol** *prev.* Komsomol'skiy. Respublika Komi, NW Russian Federation 67°33′N 64°00′E
122 K14 **Komsomolets, Ostrov** *island* Severnaya Zemlya, N Russian Federation
144 F13 **Komsomolets, Zaliv** *lake gulf* SW Kazakhstan
Komsomol/Komsomolets *see* Karabalyk, Kostanay, Kazakhstan
147 Q12 **Komsomolobod** *Rus.* Komosolabad. C Tajikistan 38°51′N 69°54′E
124 M16 **Komsomol'sk** Ivanovskaya Oblast', W Russian Federation 56°58′N 40°15′E
117 S6 **Komsomol's'k** Poltavs'ka Oblast', C Ukraine 49°01′N 33°37′E
146 M11 **Komsomol'sk** Navoiy Viloyati, N Uzbekistan 40°14′N 65°10′E
Komsomol'skiy *see* Komsomol
Komsomol'skiy *see* Komsomol
123 S13 **Komsomol'sk-na-Amure** Khabarovskiy Kray, SE Russian Federation 50°32′N 136°59′E
Komsomol'sk-na-Ustyurte *see* Kubla-Ustyurt
144 K10 **Komsomol'skoye** Aktyubinsk, NW Kazakhstan
127 Q8 **Komsomol'skoye** Saratovskaya Oblast', W Russian Federation 50°45′N 47°00′E
145 P10 **Kon** 🜄 C Kazakhstan
Kona *see* Kailua-Kona
124 K16 **Konakovo** Tverskaya Oblast', W Russian Federation 56°42′N 36°44′E
Konar *see* Kunar
143 V15 **Konārak** Sīstān va Balūchestān, SE Iran 25°26′N 60°23′E
Konarhā *see* Kunar
27 O11 **Konawa** Oklahoma, C USA 34°57′N 96°45′W
122 H10 **Konda** 🜄 C Russian Federation
154 L13 **Kondagaon** Chhattīsgarh, C India 19°38′N 81°41′E
14 K10 **Kondiaronk, Lac** ◎ Québec, SE Canada
180 J13 **Kondinin** Western Australia 32°31′S 118°15′E
81 H21 **Kondoa** Dodoma, C Tanzania 04°54′S 35°46′E
127 P6 **Kondol'** Penzenskaya Oblast', W Russian Federation 52°49′N 45°03′E
114 N10 **Kondolovo** Burgas, E Bulgaria 42°07′N 27°43′E
171 Z16 **Kondomirat** Papua, E Indonesia 08°57′S 140°55′E
124 J10 **Kondopoga** Respublika Kareliya, NW Russian Federation 62°13′N 34°17′E
Kondoz *see* Kunduz
155 J17 **Kondukūr** *var.* Kandukur. Andhra Pradesh, E India 15°17′N 79°49′E
Kondūz *see* Kunduz
187 P16 **Koné** Province Nord, W New Caledonia 21°04′S 164°51′E
146 E13 **Könekesir** Balkan Welaýaty, W Turkmenistan 38°16′N 56°51′E
146 G8 **Köneürgenç** *var.* Köneürgench, *Rus.* Këneurgench; *prev.* Kunya-Urgench. Daşoguz Welaýaty, N Turkmenistan 42°21′N 59°09′E
77 N15 **Kong** N Ivory Coast 09°10′N 04°33′W
39 S5 **Kongakut River** 🜄 Alaska, USA
197 O14 **Kong Christian IX Land** *Eng.* King Christian IX Land. *physical region* SE Greenland
197 P13 **Kong Christian X Land** *Eng.* King Christian X Land. *physical region* E Greenland
197 N13 **Kong Frederik IX Land** *physical region* SW Greenland
197 Q12 **Kong Frederik VIII Land** *Eng.* King Frederik VIII Land. *physical region* NE Greenland
197 N15 **Kong Frederik VI Kyst** *Eng.* King Frederik VI Coast. *physical region* SE Greenland
167 P13 **Kŏng, Kaôh** *prev.* Kas Kong. *island* SW Cambodia
92 P2 **Kong Karls Land** *Eng.* King Charles Islands. *island group* SE Svalbard
81 G14 **Kong Kong** 🜄 E South Sudan
Kongo *see* Congo (river)
83 G16 **Kongola** Caprivi, NE Namibia 17°47′S 23°24′E
79 N21 **Kongolo** Katanga, E Dem. Rep. Congo 05°20′S 26°58′E
81 F14 **Kongor** Jonglei, E South Sudan 07°09′N 31°44′E
197 Q14 **Kong Oscar Fjord** *fjord* E Greenland
77 P12 **Kongoussi** N Burkina 13°19′N 01°31′W
95 G15 **Kongsberg** Buskerud, S Norway 59°39′N 09°38′E
92 Q2 **Kongsøya** *island* Kong Karls Land, E Svalbard
95 I14 **Kongsvinger** Hedmark, S Norway 60°10′N 12°00′E
Kongtong *see* Pingliang
167 T11 **Kông, Tônlé** *var.* Xê Kong. 🜄 Cambodia/Laos
158 E8 **Kongur Shan** ▲ NW China 38°39′N 75°21′E
81 I22 **Kongwa** Dodoma, C Tanzania 06°13′S 36°28′E
Kong, Xê *see* Kông, Tônlé
Konia *see* Konya
147 R11 **Konibodom** *Rus.* Kanibadam. N Tajikistan 40°16′N 70°20′E
111 K15 **Koniecpol nad Pilicą** Śląskie, S Poland 50°47′N 19°45′E
Konieh *see* Konya
Königgrätz *see* Hradec Králové
Königinhof an der Elbe *see* Dvůr Králové nad Labem
101 K23 **Königsbrunn** Bayern, S Germany 48°16′N 10°52′E
101 O24 **Königssee** ◎ SE Germany
Königshütte *see* Chorzów
109 S8 **Königstuhl** ▲ S Austria 46°57′N 13°47′E
109 U3 **Königswiesen** Oberösterreich, N Austria 48°25′N 14°48′E
101 E17 **Königswinter** Nordrhein-Westfalen, W Germany 50°40′N 07°12′E
146 M11 **Konimex** *Rus.* Kenimekh. Navoiy Viloyati, N Uzbekistan 40°14′N 65°10′E
110 I12 **Konin** *Ger.* Kuhnau. Weilkopolskie, C Poland 52°13′N 18°17′E
Koninkrijk der Nederlanden *see* Netherlands
113 L24 **Konispol** *var.* Konispoli. Vlorë, S Albania 39°40′N 20°10′E
Konispoli *see* Konispol
115 C15 **Kónitsa** Ípeiros, W Greece 40°04′N 20°48′E
Konitz *see* Chojnice
108 D8 **Köniz** Bern, W Switzerland 46°56′N 07°25′E

◆ Country ● Country Capital ◇ Dependent Territory ○ Dependent Territory Capital ◆ Administrative Regions ✕ International Airport ▲ Mountain ▲ Mountain Range ⛰ Volcano 🜄 River ◎ Lake ▣ Reservoir

113 *H14* **Konjic** ◈ Federacija Bosna I Hercegovina, S Bosnia and Herzegovina
92 *J10* **Könkämäälven** ≈ Finland/Sweden
155 *D14* **Konkan** *plain* W India
83 *D22* **Konkiep** ≈ S Namibia
76 *I14* **Konkouré** ≈ W Guinea
77 *O11* **Konna** Mopti, S Mali *14°58′N 03°49′W*
186 *H6* **Konogaiang, Mount** ▲ New Ireland, NE Papua New Guinea *04°05′S 152°43′E*
186 *H5* **Konogogo** New Ireland, NE Papua New Guinea *03°25′S 152°09′E*
108 *E9* **Konolfingen** Bern, W Switzerland *46°53′N 07°36′E*
77 *P16* **Konongo** C Ghana *06°39′N 01°06′W*
186 *H5* **Konos** New Ireland, NE Papua New Guinea *03°09′S 151°47′E*
124 *M12* **Konosha** Arkhangel'skaya Oblast', NW Russian Federation *60°58′N 40°09′E*
117 *R3* **Konotop** Sums'ka Oblast', NE Ukraine *51°15′N 33°14′E*
158 *L7* **Konqi He** ≈ NW China
111 *L14* **Końskie** Śiętokrzyskie, C Poland *51°12′N 20°23′E*
Konstantinovka *see* Kostyantynivka
126 *M11* **Konstantinovsk** Rostovskaya Oblast', SW Russian Federation *47°37′N 41°07′E*
101 *H24* **Konstanz** *var.* Constanz, ***Eng.*** Constance, ***hist.*** Kostnitz; ***anc.*** Constantia. Baden-Württemberg, S Germany *47°40′N 09°10′E*
Konstanza *see* Constanţa
77 *T14* **Kontagora** Niger, W Nigeria *10°25′N 05°29′E*
78 *E13* **Kontcha** Nord, N Cameroon *08°00′N 12°13′E*
99 *G17* **Kontich** Antwerpen, N Belgium *51°08′N 04°27′E*
93 *O16* **Kontiolahti** Itä-Suomi, SE Finland *62°46′N 29°51′E*
93 *M15* **Kontiomäki** Oulu, C Finland *64°20′N 28°09′E*
167 *U11* **Kon Tum** *var.* Kontum. Kon Tum, C Vietnam *14°23′N 108°00′E*
Kontum *see* Kon Tum
Konur *see* Sulakyurt
136 *H15* **Konya** *var.* Konieh, ***prev.*** Konia; ***anc.*** Iconium. Konya, C Turkey *37°51′N 32°30′E*
136 *H15* **Konya** *var.* Konia, Konieh. ◈ *province* C Turkey
151 *E15* **Konya Reservoir** ***prev.*** Shivāji Sāgar. ⊠ W India
145 *T13* **Konyrat** *var.* Kounradskiy, ***Kaz.*** Qongyrat. Karaganda, SE Kazakhstan *46°57′N 75°01′E*
145 *W15* **Konyrolen** Almaty, SE Kazakhstan *44°16′N 79°18′E*
81 *I19* **Konza** Eastern, S Kenya *01°44′S 37°07′E*
98 *I9* **Koog aan den Zaan** Noord-Holland, C Netherlands *52°28′N 04°49′E*
182 *E7* **Koonibba** South Australia *31°55′S 133°23′E*
31 *O11* **Koontz Lake** Indiana, N USA *41°25′N 86°24′W*
171 *U12* **Koor** Papua, E Indonesia *0°21′S 132°28′E*
183 *R9* **Koorawatha** New South Wales, SE Australia *34°03′S 148°33′E*
118 *J5* **Koosa** Tartumaa, E Estonia *58°31′N 27°06′E*
33 *N7* **Kootenai** *var.* Kootenay. ≈ Canada/USA ***see also*** Kootenay
Kootenai *see* Kootenay
11 *P17* **Kootenay** *var.* Kootenai. ≈ Canada/USA ***see also*** Kootenai
Kootenay *see* Kootenai
83 *F24* **Kootjieskolk** Northern Cape, W South Africa *31°16′S 20°21′E*
113 *M15* **Kopaonik** ▲▲ S Serbia
Kopar *see* Koper
92 *K1* **Kópasker** Nordhurland Eystra, N Iceland *66°15′N 16°23′W*
92 *H4* **Kópavogur** Höfudborgarsvœdid, W Iceland *64°06′N 21°47′W*
145 *U13* **Kopbirlik** ***prev.*** Kīrov, Kirova. Almaty, SE Kazakhstan *46°24′N 77°16′E*
109 *S13* **Koper** ***It.*** Capodistria; ***prev.*** Kopar. SW Slovenia *45°32′N 13°43′E*
95 *C16* **Kopervik** Rogaland, S Norway *59°17′N 05°20′E*
Köpetdag Gershi/ Kopetdag, Khrebet *see* Koppeh Dāgh
Kophinou *see* Kofínou
182 *G8* **Kopi** South Australia *33°24′S 135°40′E*
153 *W12* **Kopili** ≈ NE India
95 *M15* **Köping** Västmanland, C Sweden *59°31′N 16°00′E*
113 *K17* **Koplik** *var.* Kopliku. Shkodër, NW Albania *42°12′N 19°26′E*
Kopliku *see* Koplik
Kopopo *see* Kokopo
94 *I11* **Koppang** Hedmark, S Norway *61°34′N 11°04′E*
Kopparberg *see* Dalarna
143 *S3* **Koppeh Dāgh** ***Rus.*** Khrebet Kopetdag, ***Turkm.*** Köpetdag Gershi. ▲▲ Iran/Turkmenistan
Koppename *see* Coppename Rivier
95 *J15* **Koppom** Värmland, C Sweden *59°42′N 12°07′E*
Kopreinitz *see* Koprivnica
114 *K9* **Koprinka, Yazovir** ***prev.*** Yazovir Georgi Dimitrov. ⊠ C Bulgaria
112 *F7* **Koprivnica** ***Ger.*** Kopreinitz, ***Hung.*** Kaproncza. Koprivnica-Križevci, N Croatia *46°10′N 16°49′E*
112 *F8* **Koprivnica-Križevci** ***off.*** Koprivničko-Križevačka Županija. ◈ *province* N Croatia
111 *I17* **Kopřivnice** ***Ger.*** Nesselsdorf. Moravskoslezský Kraj, E Czech Republic *49°36′N 18°09′E*
Koprivničko-Križevačka Županija *see* Koprivnica-Križevci
Köprülü *see* Veles
Koptsevichi *see* Kaptsevichy
Kopyl' *see* Kapyl'
119 *O14* **Kopys'** Vitsyebskaya Voblasts', NE Belarus *54°19′N 30°18′E*
113 *M18* **Korab** ▲ Albania/FYR Macedonia *41°48′N 20°33′E*
Korabavur Pastligi *see* Karabaur', Uval
124 *M5* **Korabel'noye** Murmanskaya Oblast', NW Russian Federation *67°00′N 41°10′E*
81 *M14* **K'orahē** Sumalē, E Ethiopia *06°36′N 44°21′E*
115 *L16* **Kórakas, Akrotírio** *cape* Lésvos, E Greece
112 *D9* **Korana** ≈ C Croatia
155 *L14* **Korāput** Orissa, E India *18°48′N 82°41′E*
Korat *see* Nakhon Ratchasima
167 *Q9* **Korat Plateau** *plateau* E Thailand
139 *T1* **Kōrāwa, Sar-i** ▲ NE Iraq *37°08′N 44°39′E*
154 *L11* **Korba** Chhattīsgarh, C India *22°25′N 82°43′E*
101 *H15* **Korbach** Hessen, C Germany *51°16′N 08°52′E*
Korça *see* Korçë
113 *M21* **Korçë** *var.* Korça, ***Gk.*** Korytsa, ***It.*** Corriza; ***prev.*** Koritsa. Korçë, SE Albania *40°38′N 20°47′E*
113 *M21* **Korçë** ◈ *district* SE Albania
113 *G15* **Korčula** ***It.*** Curzola. Dubrovnik-Neretva, S Croatia *42°57′N 17°08′E*
113 *F15* **Korčula** ***It.*** Curzola; ***anc.*** Corcyra Nigra. *island* S Croatia
113 *F15* **Korčulanski Kanal** *channel* S Croatia
145 *T6* **Korday** ***prev.*** Georgiyevka. Zhambyl, SE Kazakhstan *43°03′N 74°43′E*
142 *J5* **Kordestān** ***off.*** Ostān-e Kordestān, ***var.*** Kurdestan. ◈ *province* W Iran
Kordestān, Ostān-e *see* Kordestān
143 *P4* **Kord Kūy** *var.* Kurd Kui. Golestán, N Iran *36°49′N 54°05′E*
163 *V13* **Korea Bay** *bay* China/North Korea
Korea, Democratic People's Republic of *see* North Korea
171 *T15* **Koreare** Pulau Yamdena, E Indonesia *07°33′S 131°13′E*
Korea, Republic of *see* South Korea
163 *Z17* **Korea Strait** ***Jap.*** Chōsen-kaikyō, ***Kor.*** Taehan-haehyŏp. *channel* Japan/South Korea
Korelichi/Korelicze *see* Karelichy
80 *J11* **Korem** Tigrai, N Ethiopia *12°32′N 39°29′E*
77 *U11* **Korén Adoua** ≈ C Niger
126 *I7* **Korenevo** Kurskaya Oblast', W Russian Federation *51°21′N 34°53′E*
126 *L13* **Korenovsk** Krasnodarskiy Kray, SW Russian Federation *45°28′N 39°25′E*
116 *L4* **Korets'** ***Pol.*** Korzec, ***Rus.*** Korets. Rivnens'ka Oblast', NW Ukraine *50°38′N 27°12′E*
Korets *see* Korets'
194 *L7* **Korff Ice Rise** *ice cap* Antarctica
145 *Q10* **Korgalzhyn** *var.* Kurgal'dzhino, Kurgal'dzhinsky, ***Kaz.*** Qorghalzhyn. Akmola, C Kazakhstan *50°33′N 69°58′E*
145 *W15* **Korgas** ; ***prev.*** Khorgos. Almaty, SE Kazakhstan *44°13′N 80°22′E*
92 *G13* **Korgen** Troms, N Norway *66°04′N 13°51′E*
147 *R9* **Korgon-Dëbë** Dzhalal-Abadskaya Oblast', W Kyrgyzstan *41°51′N 70°52′E*
76 *M14* **Korhogo** N Ivory Coast *09°29′N 05°39′W*
115 *F19* **Korinthiakós Kólpos** ***Eng.*** Gulf of Corinth; ***anc.*** Corinthiacus Sinus. *gulf* C Greece
115 *F19* **Kórinthos** ***anc.*** Corinthus ***Eng.*** Corinth. Pelopónnisos, S Greece *37°56′N 22°55′E*
113 *M18* **Koritnik** ▲ S Serbia *42°06′N 20°34′E*
Koritsa *see* Korçë
165 *P11* **Kōriyama** Fukushima, Honshū, C Japan *37°25′N 140°20′E*
136 *E16* **Korkuteli** Antalya, SW Turkey *37°07′N 30°11′E*
158 *K6* **Korla** ***Chin.*** K'u-erh-lo. Xinjiang Uygur Zizhiqu, NW China *41°48′N 86°10′E*
122 *J10* **Korliki** Khanty-Mansiyskiy Avtonomnyy Okrug-Yugra, C Russian Federation *61°28′N 82°12′E*
Körlin an der Persante *see* Karlino
Korma *see* Karma
14 *D8* **Kormak** Ontario, S Canada *47°38′N 83°00′W*
Kormakíti, Akrotíri/ Kormakiti, Cape/ Kormakítis *see* Koruçam Burnu
111 *G23* **Körmend** Vas, W Hungary *47°02′N 16°35′E*
139 *T5* **Kōrmōr** Şalāḩ ad Dīn, E Iraq *35°06′N 44°47′E*
112 *C13* **Kornat** ***It.*** Incoronata. *island* W Croatia
Korneshty *see* Corneşti
109 *X3* **Korneuburg** Niederösterreich, NE Austria *48°22′N 16°20′E*
145 *P7* **Korneyevka** Severnyy Kazakhstan, N Kazakhstan *54°01′N 68°30′E*
95 *I17* **Kornsjø** Østfold, S Norway *58°55′N 11°40′E*
77 *O11* **Koro** Mopti, S Mali *14°05′N 03°06′W*
1873 *Y14* **Koro** *island* C Fiji
186 *B7* **Koroba** Southern Highlands, W Papua New Guinea *05°46′S 142°48′E*
126 *K8* **Korocha** Belgorodskaya Oblast', W Russian Federation *50°49′N 37°08′E*
136 *H12* **Köroğlu Dağları** ▲▲ C Turkey
183 *V6* **Korogoro Point** *headland* New South Wales, SE Australia *31°03′S 153°04′E*
81 *J21* **Korogwe** Tanga, E Tanzania *05°10′S 38°30′E*
182 *L13* **Koroit** Victoria, SE Australia *38°17′S 142°22′E*
187 *X15* **Korolevu** Viti Levu, W Fiji *18°12′S 177°44′E*
190 *I17* **Koromiri** *island* S Cook Islands
171 *Q8* **Koronadal** Mindanao, S Philippines *06°23′N 124°54′E*
114 *G13* **Koróneia, Límni** *var.* Límni Korónia. ◎ N Greece
115 *E22* **Koróni** Pelopónnisos, S Greece *36°47′N 21°57′E*
Korónia, Límni *see* Koróneia, Límni
110 *I9* **Koronowo** ***Ger.*** Krone an der Brahe. Kujawski-pomorskie,C Poland *53°18′N 17°56′E*
117 *R2* **Korop** Chernihivs'ka Oblast', N Ukraine *51°35′N 32°57′E*
115 *H19* **Koropí** Attikí, C Greece *37°54′N 23°52′E*
188 *C8* **Koror** (Palau) Oreor, N Palau *07°21′N 134°28′E*
Koror *see* Oreor
Koror Lāl Esan *see* Karor
Koror Pacca *see* Kahror Pakka
111 *L23* **Körös** ≈ E Hungary
Kőrös *see* Križevci
Körösbánya *see* Baia de Criş
187 *Y14* **Koro Sea** *sea* C Fiji
Koroška *see* Kärnten
117 *N3* **Korosten'** Zhytomyrs'ka Oblast', NW Ukraine *50°56′N 28°39′E*
Korostyshev *see* Korostyshiv
117 *N4* **Korostyshiv** ***Rus.*** Korostyshev. Zhytomyrs'ka Oblast', N Ukraine *50°18′N 29°05′E*
125 *V3* **Korotaikha** ≈ NW Russian Federation
122 *J9* **Korotchayevo** Yamalo-Nenetskiy Avtonomnyy Okrug, N Russian Federation *66°00′N 78°11′E*
78 *I8* **Koro Toro** Borkou-Ennedi-Tibesti, N Chad *16°01′N 18°27′E*
39 *N16* **Korovin Island** *island* Shumagin Islands, Alaska, USA
187 *X14* **Korovou** Viti Levu, W Fiji *17°48′S 178°32′E*
93 *M17* **Korpilahti** Länsi-Suomi, C Finland *62°02′N 25°34′E*
92 *K12* **Korpilombolo** ***Lapp.*** Dállogilli. Norrbotten, N Sweden *66°51′N 23°00′E*
123 *T13* **Korsakov** Ostrov Sakhalin, Sakhalinskaya Oblast', SE Russian Federation *46°41′N 142°45′E*
93 *J16* **Korsholm** ***Fin.*** Mustasaari. Länsi-Suomi, W Finland *63°05′N 21°43′E*
95 *I23* **Korsør** Sjælland, E Denmark *55°19′N 11°09′E*
Korsovka *see* Kārsava
117 *P6* **Korsun'-Shevchenkivs'kyy** ***Rus.*** Korsun'-Shevchenkovskiy. Cherkas'ka Oblast', C Ukraine *49°26′N 31°15′E*
Korsun'-Shevchenkovskiy *see* Korsun'-Shevchenkivs'kyy
99 *C17* **Kortemark** West-Vlaanderen, W Belgium *51°03′N 03°03′E*
99 *H18* **Kortenberg** Vlaams Brabant, C Belgium *50°53′N 04°33′E*
99 *K18* **Kortessem** Limburg, NE Belgium *50°52′N 05°22′E*
99 *E14* **Kortgene** Zeeland, SW Netherlands *51°34′N 03°48′E*
80 *F8* **Korti** Northern, N Sudan *18°06′N 31°33′E*
99 *C18* **Kortrijk** ***Fr.*** Courtrai. West-Vlaanderen, W Belgium *50°50′N 03°17′E*
121 *O2* **Koruçam Burnu** *var.* Cape Kormakiti, Kormakítis, ***Gk.*** Akrotíri Kormakíti. *headland* N Cyprus *35°24′N 32°55′E*
183 *O13* **Korumburra** Victoria, SE Australia *38°27′S 145°48′E*
Koryak Range *see* Koryakskoye Nagor'ye
Koryakskiy Khrebet *see* Koryakskoye Nagor'ye
123 *V8* **Koryakskiy Okrug** ◈ *autonomous district* E Russian Federation
123 *V7* **Koryakskoye Nagor'ye** *var.* Koryakskiy Khrebet, ***Eng.*** Koryak Range. ▲▲ NE Russian Federation
125 *P11* **Koryazhma** Arkhangel'skaya Oblast', NW Russian Federation *61°16′N 47°07′E*
Kōryō *see* Gangneung
Korytsa *see* Korçë
117 *Q2* **Koryukivka** Chernihivs'ka Oblast', N Ukraine *51°45′N 32°16′E*
Korzec *see* Korets'
115 *N21* **Kos** Kos, Dodekánisa, Greece, Aegean Sea *36°53′N 27°19′E*
115 *M21* **Kos** ***It.*** Coo; ***anc.*** Cos. *island* Dodekánisa, Greece, Aegean Sea
125 *T12* **Kosa** Komi-Permyatskiy Okrug, NW Russian Federation *59°55′N 54°54′E*
125 *T13* **Kosa** ≈ NW Russian Federation
164 *B12* **Kō-saki** *headland* Nagasaki, Tsushima, SW Japan *34°06′N 129°13′E*
163 *X13* **Kosan** SE North Korea *38°50′N 127°26′E*
119 *H18* **Kosava** ***Rus.*** Kosovo. Brestskaya Voblasts', SW Belarus *52°45′N 25°16′E*
Kosch *see* Kose
Koschagyl *see* Kosshagyl
110 *G12* **Kościan** ***Ger.*** Kosten. Wielkopolskie, C Poland *52°05′N 16°38′E*
110 *I7* **Kościerzyna** Pomorskie, NW Poland *54°07′N 17°55′E*
22 *L4* **Kosciusko** Mississippi, S USA *33°03′N 89°35′W*
Kosciusko, Mount *see* Kosciuszko, Mount
183 *R11* **Kosciuszko, Mount** ***prev.*** Mount Kosciusko. ▲ New South Wales, SE Australia *36°28′S 148°15′E*
118 *H4* **Kose** ***Ger.*** Kosch. Harjumaa, NW Estonia *59°11′N 25°10′E*
25 *U9* **Kosse** Texas, SW USA *31°16′N 96°38′W*
114 *G6* **Koshava** Vidin, NW Bulgaria *44°03′N 23°00′E*
147 *U9* **Kosh-Dëbë** *var.* Koshtebë. Narynskaya Oblast', C Kyrgyzstan *41°03′N 74°08′E*
K'o-shih *see* Kashi
164 *B12* **Koshikijima-rettō** *var.* Kosikizima Rettô. *island group* SW Japan
145 *W13* **Koshkarkol', Ozero** ◎ SE Kazakhstan
30 *L9* **Koshkonong, Lake** ◎ Wisconsin, N USA
Koshoba *see* Goşabo
Koshoba *see* Goşoba
164 *M12* **Kōshoku** *var.* Kôsyoku. Nagano, Honshū, S Japan *36°33′N 138°09′E*
Koshtebë *see* Kosh-Dëbë
Kōshū *see* Enzan
Kōshū *see* Gwangju
111 *N19* **Košice** ***Ger.*** Kaschau, ***Hung.*** Kassa. Košický Kraj, E Slovakia *48°44′N 21°15′E*
111 *M20* **Košický Kraj** ◈ *region* E Slovakia
Kosikizima Rettô *see* Koshikijima-rettō
153 *R12* **Kosi Reservoir** ⊠ E Nepal
116 *J8* **Kosiv** Ivano-Frankivs'ka Oblast', W Ukraine *48°19′N 25°04′E*
145 *O11* **Koskol'** ***Kaz.*** Qosköl. Karaganda, C Kazakhstan *49°32′N 67°08′E*
125 *Q9* **Koslan** Respublika Komi, NW Russian Federation *63°27′N 48°52′E*
Köslin *see* Koszalin
146 *M12* **Koson** ***Rus.*** Kasan. Qashqadaryo Viloyati, S Uzbekistan *39°04′N 65°35′E*
Kosŏng *see* Goseong
147 *S9* **Kosonsoy** ***Rus.*** Kasansay. Namangan Viloyati, E Uzbekistan *41°15′N 71°28′E*
113 *M16* **Kosovo** ***prev.*** Autonomous Province of Kosovo and Metohija. ◆ *republic* SE Europe
Kosovo *see* Kosava
Kosovo and Metohija, Autonomous Province of *see* Kosovo
Kosovo Polje *see* Fushë Kosovë
Kosovska Kamenica *see* Kamenicë
Kosovska Mitrovica *see* Mitrovicë
189 *X17* **Kosrae** ◈ *state* E Micronesia
189 *Y14* **Kosrae** ***prev.*** Kusaie. *island* Caroline Islands, E Micronesia
109 *P6* **Kössen** Tirol, W Austria *47°40′N 12°24′E*
144 *G12* **Kosshagyl** ***prev.*** Koschagyl, ***Kaz.*** Qosshaghyl. Atyrau, W Kazakhstan *46°52′N 53°46′E*
76 *M16* **Kossou, Lac de** ◎ C Ivory Coast
Kossukavak *see* Krumovgrad
Kostajnica *see* Hrvatska Kostanjnica
Kostamus *see* Kostomuksha
144 *M7* **Kostanay** *var.* Kustanay, ***Kaz.*** Qostanay. Kostanay, N Kazakhstan *53°16′N 63°34′E*
144 *L8* **Kostanay** *var.* Kostanayskaya Oblast', ***Kaz.*** Qostanay Oblysy. ◈ *province* N Kazakhstan
Kostanayskaya Oblast' *see* Kostanay
Kosten *see* Kościan
114 *H10* **Kostenets** ***prev.*** Georgi Dimitrov. Sofiya, W Bulgaria *42°15′N 23°48′E*
80 *F10* **Kosti** White Nile, C Sudan *13°11′N 32°38′E*
Kostnitz *see* Konstanz
124 *H7* **Kostomuksha** ***Fin.*** Kostamus. Respublika Kareliya, NW Russian Federation *64°33′N 30°28′E*
116 *K3* **Kostopil'** ***Rus.*** Kostopol'. Rivnens'ka Oblast', NW Ukraine *50°20′N 26°29′E*
Kostopol' *see* Kostopil'
124 *M15* **Kostroma** Kostromskaya Oblast', NW Russian Federation *57°46′N 41°E*
125 *N14* **Kostroma** ≈ NW Russian Federation
125 *N14* **Kostromskaya Oblast'** ◈ *province* NW Russian Federation
110 *D11* **Kostrzyn** ***Ger.*** Cüstrin, Küstrin. Lubuskie, W Poland *52°35′N 14°40′E*
110 *H11* **Kostrzyn** Wielkopolskie, C Poland *52°23′N 17°13′E*
117 *X7* **Kostyantynivka** ***Rus.*** Konstantinovka. Donets'ka Oblast', SE Ukraine
Kostyukovichi *see* Kastsyukovichy
Kostyukovka *see* Kastsyukowka
Kôsyoku *see* Kōshoku
125 *U6* **Kos'yu** Respublika Komi, NW Russian Federation *65°39′N 59°01′E*
125 *U6* **Kos'yu** ≈ NW Russian Federation
110 *F7* **Koszalin** ***Ger.*** Köslin. Zachodnio-pomorskie, NW Poland *54°12′N 16°10′E*
111 *F22* **Kőszeg** ***Ger.*** Güns. Vas, W Hungary *47°23′N 16°33′E*
152 *H13* **Kota** ***prev.*** Kotah. Rājasthān, N India *25°14′N 75°52′E*
Kota Baharu *see* Kota Bharu
Kota Bahru *see* Kota Bharu
169 *U13* **Kotabaru** Pulau Laut, C Indonesia *03°15′S 116°15′E*
168 *K12* **Kota Baru** Sumatera, W Indonesia *01°07′S 101°43′E*
Kotabaru *see* Jayapura
168 *K6* **Kota Bharu** *var.* Kota Baharu, Kota Bahru. Kelantan, Peninsular Malaysia *06°07′N 102°15′E*
Kotaboemi *see* Kotabumi
168 *M14* **Kotabumi** ***prev.*** Kotaboemi. Sumatera, W Indonesia *04°50′S 104°54′E*
149 *S10* **Kot Addu** Punjab, E Pakistan *30°28′N 70°58′E*
Kotah *see* Kota
169 *U7* **Kota Kinabalu** ***prev.*** Jesselton. Sabah, East Malaysia *05°59′N 116°04′E*
169 *U7* **Kota Kinabalu** ✈ Sabah, East Malaysia *05°59′N 116°04′E*
92 *M12* **Kotala** Lappi, N Finland *67°01′N 29°00′E*
Kotamobagoe *see* Kotamobagu
171 *Q11* **Kotamobagu** ***prev.*** Kotamobagoe. Sulawesi, C Indonesia *0°46′N 124°21′E*
155 *L14* **Kotapad** *var.* Kotapārh. Orissa, E India *19°10′N 82°23′E*
Kotapārh *see* Kotapad
166 *N17* **Ko Ta Ru Tao** *island* SW Thailand
169 *R13* **Kotawaringin, Teluk** *bay* Borneo, C Indonesia
149 *Q13* **Kot Dīji** Sind, SE Pakistan *27°16′N 68°44′E*
152 *K9* **Kotdwāra** Uttarakhand, N India *29°44′N 78°33′E*
125 *Q14* **Kotel'nich** Kirovskaya Oblast', NW Russian Federation *58°19′N 48°12′E*
127 *N12* **Kotel'nikovo** Volgogradskaya Oblast', SW Russian Federation *47°37′N 43°07′E*
123 *Q6* **Kotel'nyy, Ostrov** *island* Novosibirskiye Ostrova, N Russian Federation
117 *T5* **Kotel'va** Poltavs'ka Oblast', C Ukraine *50°04′N 34°46′E*
101 *M14* **Köthen** *var.* Cöthen. Sachsen-Anhalt, C Germany *51°46′N 11°59′E*
Kôti *see* Kōchi
81 *G17* **Kotido** NE Uganda *03°03′N 34°07′E*
93 *N19* **Kotka** Etelä-Suomi, S Finland *60°28′N 26°55′E*
125 *P11* **Kotlas** Arkhangel'skaya Oblast', NW Russian Federation *61°14′N 46°43′E*
38 *M10* **Kotlik** Alaska, USA *63°01′N 163°33′W*
77 *Q17* **Kotoka** ✈ (Accra) S Ghana *05°41′N 00°10′W*
Kotonu *see* Cotonou
113 *J17* **Kotor** ***It.*** Cattaro. SW Montenegro *42°25′N 18°47′E*
Kotor *see* Kotoriba
112 *F7* **Kotoriba** ***Hung.*** Kotor. Medimurje, N Croatia *46°20′N 16°47′E*
113 *I17* **Kotorska, Boka** ***It.*** Bocche di Cattaro. *bay* SW Montenegro
112 *H11* **Kotorsko** ◈ Republika Srpska, N Bosnia and Herzegovina
112 *G11* **Kotor Varoš** ◈ Republika Srpska, N Bosnia and Herzegovina
Koto Sho/Kotosho *see* Lan Yu
126 *M7* **Kotovsk** Tambovskaya Oblast', W Russian Federation *52°39′N 41°31′E*
117 *O9* **Kotovs'k** ***Rus.*** Kotovsk. Odes'ka Oblast', SW Ukraine *47°42′N 29°30′E*
Kotovsk *see* Hînceşti
119 *G16* **Kotra** ≈ W Belarus
149 *P16* **Kotri** Sind, SE Pakistan *25°22′N 68°18′E*
109 *Q9* **Kötschach** Kärnten, S Austria *46°41′N 12°57′E*
155 *K15* **Kottagūdem** Andhra Pradesh, E India *17°36′N 80°40′E*
155 *F21* **Kottappadi** Kerala, SW India *11°38′N 76°03′E*
155 *G23* **Kottayam** Kerala, SW India *09°34′N 76°31′E*
Kottbus *see* Cottbus
79 *K15* **Kotto** ≈ Central African Republic/Dem. Rep. Congo
193 *X15* **Kotu Group** *island group* W Tonga
Koturdepe *see* Goturdepe
122 *M9* **Kotuy** ≈ N Russian Federation
83 *M16* **Kotwa** Mashonaland East, NE Zimbabwe *16°58′S 32°46′E*
39 *N7* **Kotzebue** Alaska, USA *66°54′N 162°36′W*
38 *M7* **Kotzebue Sound** *inlet* Alaska, USA
Kotzenan *see* Chocianów
Kotzman *see* Kitsman'
77 *R14* **Kouandé** NW Benin *10°20′N 01°42′E*
79 *J15* **Kouango** Ouaka, S Central African Republic *05°00′N 20°01′E*
77 *O13* **Koudougou** C Burkina *12°15′N 02°23′W*
98 *K7* **Koudum** Fryslân, N Netherlands *52°55′N 05°26′E*
115 *L25* **Koufonísi** *island* SE Greece
115 *K21* **Koufonísi** *island* Kykládes, Greece, Aegean Sea
38 *M8* **Kougarok Mountain** ▲ Alaska, USA *65°41′N 165°29′W*
79 *E21* **Kouilou** ◈ *province* SW Congo
79 *E20* **Kouilou** ≈ S Congo
167 *Q11* **Koŭk Kduŏch** ***prev.*** Phumĭ Koŭk Kduŏch. Bătdâmbâng, NW Cambodia *13°16′N 103°08′E*
121 *O3* **Koúklia** SW Cyprus *34°42′N 32°35′E*
79 *E19* **Koulamoutou** Ogooué-Lolo, C Gabon *01°07′S 12°27′E*
76 *L12* **Koulikoro** Koulikoro, SW Mali *12°55′N 07°31′W*
76 *L11* **Koulikoro** ◈ *region* SW Mali
187 *P16* **Koumac** Province Nord, W New Caledonia *20°34′S 164°18′E*
165 *N12* **Koumi** Nagano, Honshū, S Japan *36°06′N 138°27′E*
78 *I13* **Koumra** Moyen-Chari, S Chad *08°56′N 17°32′E*
Kounadougou *see* Koundougou
76 *M15* **Kounahiri** C Ivory Coast *07°47′N 05°51′W*
76 *I12* **Koundâra** Moyenne-Guinée, NW Guinea *12°28′N 13°15′W*
77 *N13* **Koundougou** *var.* Kounadougou. C Burkina *11°43′N 04°40′W*
76 *H11* **Koungheul** C Senegal *14°00′N 14°48′W*
Kounradskiy *see* Konyrat
25 *X10* **Kountze** Texas, SW USA *30°22′N 94°20′W*
77 *Q13* **Koupéla** C Burkina *12°07′N 00°21′W*
77 *N13* **Kouri** Sikasso, SW Mali *12°09′N 04°46′W*
55 *Y9* **Kourou** N French Guiana *05°08′N 52°37′W*
114 *J12* **Kouroú** ≈ NE Greece
76 *K14* **Kouroussa** C Guinea *10°40′N 09°50′W*
Kousseir *see* Al Quşayr
78 *G11* **Kousséri** ***prev.*** Fort-Foureau. Extrême-Nord, NE Cameroon *12°05′N 14°56′E*
Kouteifé *see* Al Quţayfah
76 *M13* **Koutiala** Sikasso, S Mali *12°20′N 05°23′W*
76 *M14* **Kouto** NW Ivory Coast *09°51′N 06°25′W*
93 *M19* **Kouvola** Etelä-Suomi, S Finland *60°50′N 26°48′E*
79 *G18* **Kouyou** ≈ C Congo
112 *M10* **Kovačica** ***Hung.*** Antafalva; ***prev.*** Kovacsicza. Vojvodina, N Serbia *45°08′N 20°36′E*
Kovacsicza *see* Kovačica
Kővárhosszúfalu *see* Satulung
Kovászna *see* Covasna
124 *I4* **Kovdor** Murmanskaya Oblast', NW Russian Federation *67°32′N 30°27′E*
116 *J3* **Kovel'** ***Pol.*** Kowel. Volyns'ka Oblast', NW Ukraine *51°14′N 24°43′E*
112 *M11* **Kovin** ***Hung.*** Kevevára; ***prev.*** Temes-Kubin. Vojvodina, NE Serbia *44°45′N 20°59′E*
Kovno *see* Kaunas
127 *N3* **Kovrov** Vladimirskaya Oblast', W Russian Federation *56°24′N 41°21′E*
127 *O5* **Kovylkino** Respublika Mordoviya, W Russian Federation *54°03′N 43°52′E*
110 *J11* **Kowal** Kujawsko-pomorskie, C Poland *52°31′N 19°09′E*
110 *J9* **Kowalewo Pomorskie** ***Ger.*** Schönsee. Kujawsko-pomorskie, N Poland *53°07′N 18°48′E*
Kowasna *see* Covasna
119 *M16* **Kowbcha** ***Rus.*** Kolbcha. Mahilyowskaya Voblasts', E Belarus *53°39′N 29°14′E*
Koweit *see* Kuwait
Kowel *see* Kovel'
185 *F17* **Kowhitirangi** West Coast, South Island, New Zealand *42°54′S 171°01′E*
161 *O15* **Kowloon** Hong Kong, S China
Kowno *see* Kaunas
159 *N7* **Kox Kuduk** *well* NW China
136 *D16* **Köyceğiz** Muğla, SW Turkey *36°57′N 28°40′E*
125 *N6* **Koyda** Arkhangel'skaya Oblast', NW Russian Federation *66°22′N 42°42′E*
Koymat *see* Goymat
Koymatdag, Gory *see* Goymatdag, Gory
151 *E15* **Koyna Reservoir** ⊠ W India
165 *P9* **Koyoshi-gawa** ≈ Honshū, C Japan
Koysanjaq *see* Koi Sanjaq
Koytash *see* Qo'ytosh
146 *M14* **Köýtendag** ***prev. Rus.*** Charshanga, Charshangy, ***Turkm.*** Charshangngy. Lebap Welaýaty, E Turkmenistan *37°31′N 65°58′E*
39 *N9* **Koyuk** Alaska, USA *64°55′N 161°09′W*
39 *N9* **Koyuk River** ≈ Alaska, USA
39 *O9* **Koyukuk** Alaska, USA *64°52′N 157°42′W*
39 *O9* **Koyukuk River** ≈ Alaska, USA
136 *J13* **Kozaklı** Nevşehir, C Turkey *39°12′N 34°48′E*
136 *K16* **Kozan** Adana, S Turkey *37°27′N 35°47′E*
115 *E14* **Kozáni** Dytikí Makedonía, N Greece *40°19′N 21°48′E*
112 *F10* **Kozara** ▲▲ NW Bosnia and Herzegovina
Kozarska Dubica *see* Bosanska Dubica
117 *P3* **Kozelets'** ***Rus.*** Kozelets. Chernihivs'ka Oblast', NE Ukraine *50°54′N 31°09′E*
Kozelets *see* Kozelets'
117 *S6* **Kozel'shchyna** Poltavs'ka Oblast', C Ukraine *49°13′N 33°49′E*
126 *J5* **Kozel'sk** Kaluzhskaya Oblast', W Russian Federation *54°04′N 35°51′E*
151 *F21* **Kozhikode** *var.* Calicut. Kerala, SW India *11°17′N 75°49′E* ***see also*** Calicut
Kozhimiz, Gora *see* Kozhymiz, Gora
124 *L9* **Kozhozero, Ozero** ◎ NW Russian Federation
125 *T7* **Kozhva** Respublika Komi, NW Russian Federation *65°06′N 57°00′E*
125 *T7* **Kozhva** ≈ NW Russian Federation
125 *U6* **Kozhym** Respublika Komi, NW Russian Federation *65°43′N 59°25′E*
125 *V9* **Kozhymiz, Gora** ***prev.*** Gora Kozhimiz. ▲ NW Russian Federation *63°13′N 58°54′E*
110 *N13* **Kozienice** Mazowieckie, C Poland *51°35′N 21°31′E*
109 *S13* **Kozina** SW Slovenia *45°36′N 13°56′E*
114 *H7* **Kozloduy** Vratsa, NW Bulgaria *43°48′N 23°42′E*
127 *Q3* **Kozlovka** Chuvashskaya Respublika, W Russian Federation *55°53′N 48°07′E*
Kozlovshchina/ Kozlowszczyzna *see* Kazlowshchyna
127 *P3* **Koz'modem'yansk** Respublika Mariy El, W Russian Federation *56°19′N 46°33′E*
116 *J6* **Kozova** Ternopil's'ka Oblast', W Ukraine *49°25′N 25°09′E*
113 *P20* **Kožuf** ▲▲ Greece/Macedonia
165 *N15* **Kōzu-shima** *island* E Japan
Koz'yany *see* Kazyany
117 *N5* **Kozyatyn** ***Rus.*** Kazatin. Vinnyts'ka Oblast', C Ukraine *49°41′N 28°49′E*
77 *Q16* **Kpalimé** *var.* Palimé. SW Togo *06°54′N 00°38′E*
77 *Q16* **Kpandu** E Ghana *07°00′N 00°18′E*
99 *F15* **Krabbendijke** Zeeland, SW Netherlands *51°25′N 04°07′E*
167 *N15* **Krabi** *var.* Muang Krabi. Krabi, SW Thailand *08°04′N 98°52′E*
167 *N13* **Kra Buri** Ranong, SW Thailand *10°25′N 98°48′E*
167 *S12* **Krâchéh** ***prev.*** Kratie. Krâchéh, E Cambodia *12°29′N 106°01′E*
95 *G17* **Kragerø** Telemark, S Norway *58°54′N 09°25′E*
112 *M13* **Kragujevac** Serbia, C Serbia *44°01′N 20°55′E*
Krainburg *see* Kranj
166 *N13* **Kra, Isthmus of** *isthmus* Malaysia/Thailand
112 *D12* **Krajina** *cultural region* SW Croatia
Krakatau, Pulau *see* Rakata, Pulau
Krakau *see* Kraków
111 *L16* **Kraków** ***Eng.*** Cracow, ***Ger.*** Krakau; ***anc.*** Cracovia. Małopolskie, S Poland *50°03′N 19°58′E*
100 *L9* **Krakower See** ◎ NE Germany
167 *Q11* **Krâlănh** Siĕmréab, NW Cambodia *13°35′N 103°27′E*
45 *Q16* **Kralendijk** ○ Bonaire *12°07′N 68°13′W*
112 *B10* **Kraljevica** ***It.*** Porto Re. Primorje-Gorski Kotar, NW Croatia *45°15′N 14°36′E*
112 *M13* **Kraljevo** ***prev.*** Rankovićevo. Serbia, C Serbia *43°44′N 20°40′E*
111 *E16* **Královehradecký Kraj** ***prev.*** Hradecký Kraj. ◈ *region* N Czech Republic
Kralup an der Moldau *see* Kralupy nad Vltavou
111 *C16* **Kralupy nad Vltavou** ***Ger.*** Kralup an der Moldau. Středočeský Kraj, NW Czech Republic *50°15′N 14°20′E*
117 *W7* **Kramators'k** ***Rus.*** Kramatorsk. Donets'ka Oblast', SE Ukraine *48°43′N 37°34′E*
Kramatorsk *see* Kramators'k
93 *H17* **Kramfors** Västernorrland, C Sweden *62°55′N 17°50′E*
Kranéa *see* Kraniá
108 *M7* **Kranebitten** ✈ (Innsbruck) Tirol, W Austria *47°18′N 11°21′E*
115 *D15* **Kraniá** *var.* Kranéa. Dytikí Makedonía, N Greece *39°54′N 21°21′E*
115 *G20* **Kranídi** Pelopónnisos, S Greece *37°21′N 23°09′E*
109 *T11* **Kranj** ***Ger.*** Krainburg. NW Slovenia *46°17′N 14°16′E*
115 *F16* **Krannón** *battleground* Thessalía, C Greece
Kranz *see* Zelenogradsk
112 *D7* **Krapina** Krapina-Zagorje, N Croatia *46°12′N 15°52′E*
112 *E8* **Krapina** ≈ N Croatia
112 *D8* **Krapina-Zagorje** ***off.*** Krapinsko-Zagorska Županija. ◈ *province* N Croatia
114 *L7* **Krapinets** ≈ NE Bulgaria
Krapinsko-Zagorska Županija *see* Krapina-Zagorje
111 *I15* **Krapkowice** ***Ger.*** Krappitz. Opolskie, SW Poland *50°29′N 17°56′E*
Krappitz *see* Krapkowice
125 *O12* **Krasavino** Vologodskaya Oblast', NW Russian Federation *60°56′N 46°27′E*
122 *H6* **Krasino** Novaya Zemlya, Arkhangel'skaya Oblast', N Russian Federation *70°45′N 54°16′E*
123 *S15* **Kraskino** Primorskiy Kray, SE Russian Federation *42°40′N 130°51′E*
118 *J11* **Krāslava** SE Latvia *55°56′N 27°08′E*
119 *M14* **Krasnaluki** ***Rus.*** Krasnoluki. Vitsyebskaya Voblasts', N Belarus *54°37′N 28°50′E*
119 *P17* **Krasnapollye** ***Rus.*** Krasnopol'ye. Mahilyowskaya Voblasts', E Belarus *53°20′N 31°24′E*
126 *L15* **Krasnaya Polyana** Krasnodarskiy Kray, SW Russian Federation *43°40′N 40°13′E*
Krasnaya Slabada / Krasnaya Sloboda *see* Chyrvonaya Slabada
119 *J15* **Krasnaye** ***Rus.*** Krasnoye. Minskaya Voblasts', C Belarus *54°14′N 27°05′E*
111 *O14* **Kraśnik** ***Ger.*** Kratznick. Lubelskie, E Poland *50°56′N 22°14′E*
117 *O9* **Krasni Okny** Odes'ka Oblast', SW Ukraine *47°33′N 29°28′E*
127 *P8* **Krasnoarmeysk** Saratovskaya Oblast', W Russian Federation *51°02′N 45°42′E*
Krasnoarmeysk *see* Tayynsha
Krasnoarmeysk *see* Krasnoarmiys'k/Tayynsha
123 *T6* **Krasnoarmeyskiy** Chukotskiy Avtonomnyy Okrug, NE Russian Federation *69°30′N 171°44′E*
117 *W7* **Krasnoarmiys'k** ***Rus.*** Krasnoarmeysk. Donets'ka Oblast', SE Ukraine *48°17′N 37°14′E*
125 *P11* **Krasnoborsk** Arkhangel'skaya Oblast', NW Russian Federation *61°31′N 45°57′E*
126 *K14* **Krasnodar** ***prev.*** Ekaterinodar, Yekaterinodar. Krasnodarskiy Kray, SW Russian Federation *45°06′N 39°01′E*
126 *K13* **Krasnodarskiy Kray** ◈ *territory* SW Russian Federation
117 *Z7* **Krasnodon** Luhans'ka Oblast', E Ukraine *48°17′N 39°44′E*
Krasnogor *see* Kallaste
127 *T2* **Krasnogorskoye** Udmurtskaya Respublika, NW Russian Federation *57°42′N 52°29′E*
Krasnograd *see* Krasnohrad
Krasnogvardeysk *see* Bulungh'ur
126 *M13* **Krasnogvardeyskoye** Stavropol'skiy Kray, SW Russian Federation *45°49′N 41°31′E*
Krasnogvardeyskoye *see* Krasnohvardiys'ke
117 *U6* **Krasnohrad** ***Rus.*** Krasnograd. Kharkivs'ka Oblast', E Ukraine *49°22′N 35°28′E*
117 *S12* **Krasnohvardiys'ke** ***Rus.*** Krasnogvardeyskoye. Avtonomna Respublika Krym, S Ukraine *45°30′N 34°19′E*
123 *P14* **Krasnokamensk** Zabaykal'skiy Kray, S Russian Federation *50°03′N 118°01′E*
125 *U14* **Krasnokamsk** Permskiy Kray, W Russian Federation *58°08′N 55°48′E*
127 *U8* **Krasnokholm** Orenburgskaya Oblast', W Russian Federation *51°34′N 54°11′E*
117 *U5* **Krasnokuts'k** ***Rus.*** Krasnokutsk. Kharkivs'ka Oblast', E Ukraine *50°01′N 35°03′E*

◆ Country
● Country Capital
◇ Dependent Territory
○ Dependent Territory Capital
◈ Administrative Regions
✈ International Airport
▲ Mountain
▲▲ Mountain Range
Volcano
≈ River
◎ Lake
⊠ Reservoir

Krasnokutsk *see* Krasnokuts'k
126 L7 **Krasnolesnyy** Voronezhskaya Oblast', W Russian Federation *51°53′N 39°37′E*
Krasnoluki *see* Krasnaluki
Krasnoosol'skoye Vodokhranilishche *see* Chervonooskil's'ke Vodoskhovyshche
117 S11 **Krasnoperekops'k** *Rus.* Krasnoperekopsk. Avtonomna Respublika Krym, S Ukraine *45°56′N 33°47′E*
Krasnoperekopsk *see* Krasnoperekops'k
117 U4 **Krasnopillya** Sums'ka Oblast', NE Ukraine *50°46′N 35°17′E*
Krasnopol'ye *see* Krasnapollye
124 L5 **Krasnoshchel'ye** Murmanskaya Oblast', NW Russian Federation *67°22′N 37°03′E*
127 O5 **Krasnoslobodsk** Respublika Mordoviya, W Russian Federation *54°24′N 43°51′E*
127 T2 **Krasnoslobodsk** Volgogradskaya Oblast', SW Russian Federation *48°41′N 44°34′E*
Krasnostav *see* Krasnystaw
127 V5 **Krasnousol'skiy** Respublika Bashkortostan, W Russian Federation *53°55′N 56°22′E*
125 U12 **Krasnovishersk** Permskiy Kray, NW Russian Federation *60°22′N 57°04′E*
Krasnovodsk *see* Türkmenbaşy
Krasnovodskiy Zaliv *see* Türkmenbasy Aylagy
146 B10 **Krasnovodskoye Plato** *Turkm.* Krasnowodsk Platosy. *plateau* NW Turkmenistan
Krasnowodsk Aylagy *see* Türkmenbasy Aylagy
Krasnowodsk Platosy *see* Krasnovodskoye Plato
122 K12 **Krasnoyarsk** Krasnoyarskiy Kray, S Russian Federation *56°05′N 92°46′E*
127 X7 **Krasnoyarskiy** Orenburgskaya Oblast', W Russian Federation *51°56′N 59°54′E*
122 K11 **Krasnoyarskiy Kray** ◈ *territory* C Russian Federation
Krasnoye *see* Krasnaye
Krasnoye Znamya *see* Gyzylbaýdak
125 R11 **Krasnozatonskiy** Respublika Komi, NW Russian Federation *61°39′N 51°00′E*
118 D13 **Krasnoznamensk** *prev.* Lasdehnen, *Ger.* Haselberg. Kaliningradskaya Oblast', W Russian Federation *54°57′N 22°28′E*
126 K3 **Krasnoznamensk** Moskovskaya Oblast', W Russian Federation *55°40′N 37°05′E*
117 R11 **Krasnoznam"yans'kyy Kanal** *canal* S Ukraine
111 P14 **Krasnystaw** *Rus.* Krasnostav. Lubelskie, SE Poland *51°N 23°10′E*
126 H4 **Krasnyy** Smolenskaya Oblast', W Russian Federation *54°36′N 31°27′E*
127 P2 **Krasnyye Baki** Nizhegorodskaya Oblast', W Russian Federation *57°07′N 45°12′E*
127 Q13 **Krasnyye Barrikady** Astrakhanskaya Oblast', SW Russian Federation *46°14′N 47°48′E*
124 K15 **Krasnyy Kholm** Tverskaya Oblast', W Russian Federation *58°04′N 37°05′E*
127 Q8 **Krasnyy Kut** Saratovskaya Oblast', W Russian Federation *50°54′N 46°58′E*
Krasnyy Liman *see* Krasnyy Lyman
117 Y7 **Krasnyy Luch** *prev.* Krindachevka. Luhans'ka Oblast', E Ukraine *48°09′N 38°52′E*
117 X6 **Krasnyy Lyman** *Rus.* Krasnyy Liman. Donets'ka Oblast', SE Ukraine *49°00′N 37°50′E*
127 R3 **Krasnyy Steklovar** Respublika Mariy El, W Russian Federation *56°14′N 48°49′E*
127 P8 **Krasnyy Tekstil'shchik** Saratovskaya Oblast', W Russian Federation *51°35′N 45°49′E*
127 R13 **Krasnyy Yar** Astrakhanskaya Oblast', SW Russian Federation *46°33′N 48°21′E*
Krassóvár *see* Caraşova
116 L5 **Krasyliv** Khmel'nyts'ka Oblast', W Ukraine *49°38′N 26°59′E*
111 O21 **Kraszna** *Rom.* Crasna. ≋ Hungary/Romania
Kratie *see* Krâchéh
113 P17 **Kratovo** NE FYR Macedonia *42°04′N 22°08′E*
Kratznick *see* Kraśnik
171 Y13 **Krau** Papua, E Indonesia *03°15′S 140°07′E*
167 Q13 **Krâvanh, Chuŏr Phnum** *Eng.* Cardamom Mountains, *Fr.* Chaîne des Cardamomes. ▲▲ W Cambodia
Kravasta Lagoon *see* Karavastasë, Laguna e
Krawang *see* Karawang
127 Q15 **Kraynovka** Respublika Dagestan, SW Russian Federation *43°58′N 47°24′E*
118 D12 **Kražiai** Šiaulai, C Lithuania *55°36′N 22°41′E*
27 P11 **Krebs** Oklahoma, C USA *34°55′N 95°43′W*
101 D15 **Krefeld** Nordrhein-Westfalen, W Germany *51°20′N 06°34′E*
Kreisstadt *see* Krosno Odrzańskie
115 D17 **Kremastón, Technití Límni** ⊠ C Greece
Kremenchug *see* Kremenchuk
Kremenchugskoye Vodokhranilishche/Kremenchuk Reservoir *see* Kremenchuts'ke Vodoskhovyshche
117 S6 **Kremenchuk** *Rus.* Kremenchug. Poltavs'ka Oblast', NE Ukraine *49°04′N 33°27′E*
117 R6 **Kremenchuts'ke Vodoskhovyshche** *Eng.* Kremenchuk Reservoir, *Rus.* Kremenchugskoye Vodokhranilishche. ⊠ C Ukraine
116 K5 **Kremenets'** *Pol.* Krzemieniec, *Rus.* Kremenets. Ternopil's'ka Oblast', W Ukraine *50°06′N 25°43′E*
Kremennaya *see* Kreminna
117 X6 **Kreminna** *Rus.* Kremennaya. Luhans'ka Oblast', E Ukraine *49°03′N 38°15′E*
37 R4 **Kremmling** Colorado, C USA *40°03′N 106°23′W*
109 V3 **Krems** ≋ NE Austria
Krems *see* Krems an der Donau
109 W3 **Krems an der Donau** *var.* Krems. Niederösterreich, N Austria *48°25′N 15°36′E*
Kremsier *see* Kroměříž
109 S4 **Kremsmünster** Oberösterreich, N Austria *48°04′N 14°08′E*
38 M17 **Krenitzin Islands** *island* Aleutian Islands, Alaska, USA
Kresena *see* Kresna
114 G11 **Kresna** *var.* Kresena. Blagoevgrad, SW Bulgaria *41°43′N 23°10′E*
112 O12 **Krespoljin** Serbia, E Serbia *44°22′N 21°36′E*
25 N4 **Kress** Texas, SW USA *34°21′N 101°43′W*
123 V6 **Kresta, Zaliv** *bay* E Russian Federation
115 D20 **Kréstena** *prev.* Selinoús. Dytikí Elláda, S Greece *37°36′N 21°36′E*
124 H14 **Kresttsy** Novgorodskaya Oblast', W Russian Federation *58°15′N 32°28′E*
Kretikon Delagos *see* Kritikó Pélagos
118 C11 **Kretinga** *Ger.* Krottingen. Klaipėda, NW Lithuania *55°53′N 21°13′E*
Kreutz *see* Cristuru Secuiesc
Kreuz *see* Križevci, Croatia
Kreuz *see* Risti, Estonia
Kreuzburg/Kreuzburg in Oberschlesien *see* Kluczbork
Kreuzingen *see* Bol'shakovo
108 H6 **Kreuzlingen** Thurgau, NE Switzerland *47°38′N 09°12′E*
101 K25 **Kreuzspitze** ▲ S Germany *47°30′N 10°55′E*
101 F16 **Kreuztal** Nordrhein-Westfalen, W Germany *50°58′N 08°00′E*
119 I15 **Kreva** *Rus.* Krevo. Hrodzyenskaya Voblasts', W Belarus *54°19′N 26°17′E*
Krevo *see* Kreva
Kría Vrísi *see* Krýa Vrýsi
79 D16 **Kribi** Sud, SW Cameroon *02°53′N 09°57′E*
Krichëv *see* Krychaw
Krickerhäu/Kriegerhaj *see* Handlová
109 W6 **Krieglach** Steiermark, E Austria *47°33′N 15°37′E*
108 F8 **Kriens** Luzern, W Switzerland *47°03′N 08°17′E*
Krievija *see* Russian Federation
Krimmitschau *see* Crimmitschau
98 H12 **Krimpen aan den IJssel** Zuid-Holland, SW Netherlands *51°56′N 04°39′E*
Krindachevka *see* Krasnyy Luch
115 G25 **Kríos, Akrotírio** *headland* Kríti, Greece, E Mediterranean Sea *35°17′N 23°31′E*
155 J16 **Krishna** *prev.* Kistna. ≋ C India
155 H20 **Krishnagiri** Tamil Nādu, SE India *12°33′N 78°11′E*
155 K17 **Krishna, Mouths of the** *delta* SE India
153 S15 **Krishnanagar** West Bengal, N India *23°22′N 88°32′E*
155 G20 **Krishnarājāsāgara** *var.* Paradip. ⊠ W India
95 N19 **Kristdala** Kalmar, S Sweden *57°24′N 16°12′E*
Kristiania *see* Oslo
95 E18 **Kristiansand** *var.* Christiansand. Vest-Agder, S Norway *58°08′N 07°52′E*
95 L22 **Kristianstad** Skåne, S Sweden *56°02′N 14°10′E*
94 F8 **Kristiansund** *var.* Christiansund. Møre og Romsdal, S Norway *63°07′N 07°45′E*
Kristiinankaupunki *see* Kristinestad
93 I14 **Kristineberg** Västerbotten, N Sweden *65°07′N 18°36′E*
95 L16 **Kristinehamn** Värmland, C Sweden *59°17′N 14°09′E*
93 J17 **Kristinestad** *Fin.* Kristiinankaupunki. Länsi-Suomi, W Finland *62°15′N 21°24′E*
Kristyor *see* Crişcior
115 J25 **Kríti** *Eng.* Crete. ◈ *region* Greece, Aegean Sea
115 J24 **Kríti** *Eng.* Crete. *island* Greece, Aegean Sea
115 J23 **Kritikó Pélagos** *var.* Kretikon Delagos, *Eng.* Sea of Crete; *anc.* Mare Creticum. *sea* Greece, Aegean Sea
Kriulyany *see* Criuleni
112 I12 **Krivaja** ≋ NE Bosnia and Herzegovina
Krivaja *see* Mali Idoš
113 P17 **Kriva Palanka** *Turk.* Eğri Palanka. NE Macedonia *42°13′N 22°19′E*
Krivichi *see* Kryvichy
114 H8 **Krivodol** Vratsa, NW Bulgaria *43°23′N 23°30′E*
126 M10 **Krivorozh'ye** Rostovskaya Oblast', SW Russian Federation *48°51′N 40°49′E*
Krivoshin *see* Kryvoshyn
Krivoy Rog *see* Kryvyy Rih
112 F7 **Križevci** *Ger.* Kreuz, *Hung.* Kőrös. Varaždin, NE Croatia *46°02′N 16°32′E*
112 B10 **Krk** *It.* Veglia. Primorje-Gorski Kotar, NW Croatia *45°01′N 14°36′E*
112 B10 **Krk** *It.* Veglia; *anc.* Curieta. *island* NW Croatia
109 V12 **Krka** ≋ SE Slovenia
Krka *see* Gurk
109 R11 **Krn** ▲ NW Slovenia *46°15′N 13°37′E*
111 H16 **Krnov** *Ger.* Jägerndorf. Moravskoslezský Kraj, E Czech Republic *50°05′N 17°40′E*
Kroatien *see* Croatia
95 G14 **Krøderen** Buskerud, S Norway *60°06′N 09°48′E*
95 G14 **Krøderen** ◎ S Norway
Kroi *see* Krui
95 N17 **Krokek** Östergötland, S Sweden *58°40′N 16°25′E*
Krokodil *see* Crocodile
93 G16 **Krokom** Jämtland, C Sweden *63°20′N 14°30′E*
117 S2 **Krolevets'** *Rus.* Krolevets. Sums'ka Oblast', NE Ukraine *51°34′N 33°24′E*
Krolevets *see* Krolevets'
Królewska Huta *see* Chorzów
111 H18 **Kroměříž** *Ger.* Kremsier. Zlínský Kraj, E Czech Republic *49°18′N 17°24′E*
98 I9 **Krommenie** Noord-Holland, C Netherlands *52°30′N 04°46′E*
126 J6 **Kromy** Orlovskaya Oblast', W Russian Federation *52°41′N 35°45′E*
101 L18 **Kronach** Bayern, E Germany *50°14′N 11°19′E*
Krone an der Brahe *see* Koronowo
Krŏng Kaôh Kŏng *see* Kaôh Kŏng
95 K21 **Kronoberg** ◈ *county* S Sweden
123 V10 **Kronotskiy Zaliv** *bay* E Russian Federation
195 O2 **Kronprinsesse Märtha Kyst** *physical region* Antarctica
195 V3 **Kronprins Olav Kyst** *physical region* Antarctica
124 G12 **Kronshtadt** Leningradskaya Oblast', NW Russian Federation *60°01′N 29°42′E*
Kronstadt *see* Braşov
83 I22 **Kroonstad** Free State, C South Africa *27°40′S 27°15′E*
123 O12 **Kropotkin** Irkutskaya Oblast', C Russian Federation *58°30′N 115°21′E*
126 L14 **Kropotkin** Krasnodarskiy Kray, SW Russian Federation *45°29′N 40°31′E*
110 J11 **Krośniewice** Łódzkie, C Poland *52°14′N 19°10′E*
111 N17 **Krosno** *Ger.* Krossen. Podkarpackie, SE Poland *49°40′N 21°46′E*
110 E12 **Krosno Odrzańskie** *Ger.* Crossen, Kreisstadt. Lubuskie, W Poland *52°02′N 15°06′E*
Krossen *see* Krosno
Krotoschin *see* Krotoszyn
110 H13 **Krotoszyn** *Ger.* Krotoschin. Wielkopolskie, C Poland *51°43′N 17°24′E*
Krottingen *see* Kretinga
Krousón *see* Krousónas
115 J25 **Krousónas** *prev.* Krousón, Kroussón. Kríti, Greece, E Mediterranean Sea *35°14′N 24°59′E*
Kroussón *see* Krousónas
Krraba *see* Krrabë
113 L20 **Krrabë** *var.* Krraba. Tiranë, C Albania *41°15′N 19°56′E*
113 L17 **Krrabit, Mali i** ▲▲ N Albania
109 W12 **Krško** *Ger.* Gurkfeld; *prev.* Videm-Krško. E Slovenia *45°57′N 15°31′E*
83 K19 **Kruger National Park** *national park* Northern, N South Africa
83 J21 **Krugersdorp** Gauteng, NE South Africa *26°06′S 27°46′E*
38 D16 **Krugloi Point** *headland* Agattu Island, Alaska, USA *52°30′N 173°46′E*
Krugloye *see* Kruhlaye
119 N15 **Kruhlaye** *Rus.* Krugloye. Mahilyowskaya Voblasts', E Belarus *54°15′N 29°48′E*
168 L15 **Krui** *var.* Kroi. Sumatera, SW Indonesia *05°11′S 103°55′E*
99 G16 **Kruibeke** Oost-Vlaanderen, N Belgium *51°10′N 04°18′E*
83 G25 **Kruidfontein** Western Cape, SW South Africa *32°50′S 21°59′E*
99 F15 **Kruiningen** Zeeland, SW Netherlands *51°28′N 04°01′E*
Kruja *see* Krujë
113 L19 **Krujë** *var.* Kruja, *It.* Croia. Durrës, C Albania *41°30′N 19°48′E*
Krulevshchina/Krulewshchyna *see* Krulyewshchyna
118 K13 **Krulyewshchyna** *Rus.* Krulevshchina, Krulewshchyna. Vitsyebskaya Voblasts', N Belarus *55°02′N 27°45′E*
25 T6 **Krum** Texas, SW USA *33°15′N 97°14′W*
101 J23 **Krumbach** Bayern, S Germany *48°12′N 10°21′E*
113 M17 **Krumë** Kukës, NE Albania *42°11′N 20°25′E*
Krummau *see* Český Krumlov
114 K12 **Krumovgrad** *prev.* Kossukavak. Yambol, E Bulgaria *41°27′N 25°40′E*
114 K12 **Krumovitsa** ≋ S Bulgaria
114 L10 **Krumovo** Yambol, E Bulgaria *42°16′N 26°25′E*
167 O11 **Krung Thep, Ao** *var.* Bight of Bangkok. *bay* S Thailand
Krung Thep Mahanakhon *see* Ao Krung Thep
Krupa/Krupa na Uni *see* Bosanska Krupa
119 M15 **Krupki** Minskaya Voblasts', C Belarus *54°19′N 29°08′E*
95 G24 **Kruså** *var.* Krusaa. Syddanmark, SW Denmark *54°50′N 09°25′E*
Krusaa *see* Kruså
113 N14 **Kruševac** Serbia, C Serbia *43°37′N 21°20′E*
113 N19 **Kruševo** SW FYR Macedonia *41°22′N 21°15′E*
111 A15 **Krušné Hory** *Eng.* Ore Mountains, *Ger.* Erzgebirge. ▲▲ Czech Republic/Germany *see also* Erzgebirge
Krušné Hory *see* Erzgebirge
39 W13 **Kruzof Island** *island* Alexander Archipelago, Alaska, USA
114 F13 **Krýa Vrýsi** *var.* Kría Vrísi. Kentrikí Makedonía, N Greece *40°41′N 22°18′E*
119 P16 **Krychaw** *Rus.* Krichëv. Mahilyowskaya Voblasts', E Belarus *53°42′N 31°43′E*
64 K11 **Krylov Seamount** *undersea feature* E Atlantic Ocean *17°35′N 30°07′W*
Krym *see* Krym, Avtonomna Respublika
117 S13 **Krym, Avtonomna Respublika** *var.* Krym, *Eng.* Crimea, Crimean Oblast; *prev. Rus.* Krymskaya ASSR, Krymskaya Oblast'. ◈ *province* SE Ukraine
126 K14 **Krymsk** Krasnodarskiy Kray, SW Russian Federation *44°56′N 38°02′E*
Krymskaya ASSR/Krymskaya Oblast' *see* Krym, Avtonomna Respublika
117 T13 **Kryms'ki Hory** ▲▲ S Ukraine
117 T13 **Kryms'kyy Pivostriv** *peninsula* S Ukraine
111 M18 **Krynica** *Ger.* Tannenhof. Małopolskie, S Poland *49°25′N 20°56′E*
117 P8 **Kryve Ozero** Odes'ka Oblast', SW Ukraine *47°54′N 30°19′E*
119 K14 **Kryvichy** *Rus.* Krivichi. Minskaya Voblasts', C Belarus *54°43′N 27°17′E*
119 I18 **Kryvoshyn** *Rus.* Krivoshin. Brestskaya Voblasts', SW Belarus *52°52′N 26°08′E*
117 S8 **Kryvyy Rih** *Rus.* Krivoy Rog. Dnipropetrovs'ka Oblast', SE Ukraine *47°53′N 33°24′E*
117 N8 **Kryzhopil'** Vinnyts'ka Oblast', C Ukraine *48°22′N 28°51′E*
Krzemieniec *see* Kremenets'
111 J14 **Krzepice** Śląskie, S Poland *50°58′N 18°42′E*
110 F10 **Krzyż Wielkopolskie** Wielkopolskie, W Poland *52°52′N 16°03′E*
Ksar al Kabir *see* Ksar-el-Kebir
Ksar al Soule *see* Er-Rachidia
74 J5 **Ksar El Boukhari** N Algeria *35°55′N 02°47′E*
74 G5 **Ksar-el-Kebir** *var.* Alcázar, Ksar al Kabir, Ksar-el-Kébir, *Ar.* Al-Kasr al-Kebir, Al-Qsar al-Kbir, *Sp.* Alcazarquivir. NW Morocco *35°04′N 05°56′W*
Ksar-el-Kébir *see* Ksar-el-Kebir
110 H12 **Książ Wielkopolski** *Ger.* Xions. Weilkopolskie, W Poland *52°03′N 17°10′E*
127 O3 **Kstovo** Nizhegorodskaya Oblast', W Russian Federation *56°07′N 44°12′E*
169 T8 **Kuala Belait** W Brunei *04°48′N 114°12′E*
Kuala Dungun *see* Dungun
169 S10 **Kualakeriau** Borneo, C Indonesia
169 S12 **Kualakuayan** Borneo, C Indonesia *02°01′S 112°35′E*
168 K8 **Kuala Lipis** Pahang, Peninsular Malaysia *04°11′N 102°00′E*
168 K9 **Kuala Lumpur** ● (Malaysia) Kuala Lumpur, Peninsular Malaysia *03°08′N 101°42′E*
168 K9 **Kuala Lumpur International** ✈ Selangor, Peninsular Malaysia *02°51′N 101°45′E*
Kuala Pelabohan Kelang *see* Pelabuhan Klang
169 U7 **Kuala Penyu** Sabah, East Malaysia *05°37′N 115°36′E*
38 E9 **Kualapu'u** *var.* Kualapuu. Moloka'i, Hawaii, USA, C Pacific Ocean *21°09′N 157°02′W*
Kualapuu *see* Kualapu'u
168 L7 **Kuala Terengganu** *var.* Kuala Trengganu. Terengganu, Peninsular Malaysia *05°20′N 103°07′E*
168 L11 **Kualatungkal** Sumatera, W Indonesia *0°49′S 103°22′E*
171 P11 **Kuandang** Sulawesi, N Indonesia *0°50′N 122°55′E*
163 V12 **Kuandian** *var.* Kuandian Manzu Zizhixian. Liaoning, NE China *40°41′N 124°46′E*
Kuandian Manzu Zizhixian *see* Kuandian
Kuando-Kubango *see* Cuando Cubango
Kuang-chou *see* Guangzhou
Kuang-hsi *see* Guangxi Zhuangzu Zizhiqu
Kuang-tung *see* Guangdong
Kuang-yuan *see* Guangyuan
Kuantan, Batang *see* Indragiri, Sungai
Kuanza Norte *see* Cuanza Norte
Kuanza Sul *see* Cuanza Sul
Kuanzhou *see* Qingjian
Kuba *see* Quba
Kubango *see* Cubango/Okavango
141 X8 **Kubārah** NW Oman *23°03′N 56°52′E*
93 H16 **Kubbe** Västernorrland, C Sweden *63°31′N 18°04′E*
80 A11 **Kubbum** Southern Darfur, W Sudan *11°47′N 23°47′E*
124 L13 **Kubenskoye, Ozero** ◎ NW Russian Federation
146 G6 **Kubla-Ustyurt** *Rus.* Komsomol'sk-na-Ustyurte. Qoraqalpog'iston Respublikasi, NW Uzbekistan *44°06′N 58°14′E*
164 G15 **Kubokawa** Kōchi, Shikoku, SW Japan *33°22′N 133°14′E*
114 L7 **Kubrat** *prev.* Balbunar. Razgrad, N Bulgaria *43°48′N 26°31′E*
112 O13 **Kučajske Planine** ▲▲ E Serbia
165 T1 **Kuccharo-ko** ◎ Hokkaidō, N Japan
112 O11 **Kučevo** Serbia, NE Serbia *44°29′N 21°42′E*
Kuchan *see* Qūchān
169 Q10 **Kuching** *prev.* Sarawak. Sarawak, East Malaysia *01°32′N 110°20′E*
169 Q10 **Kuching** ✈ Sarawak, East Malaysia *01°32′N 110°20′E*
164 B17 **Kuchinoerabu-jima** *island* Nansei-shotō, SW Japan
Kuchinotsu *see* Minamishimabara
109 Q6 **Kuchl** Salzburg, NW Austria *47°37′N 13°12′E*
148 L9 **Kūchnay Darwēshān** *prev.* Kūchnay Darweyshān. Helmand, S Afghanistan *31°02′N 64°10′E*
Kūchnay Darweyshān *see* Kūchnay Darwēshān
Kuchurgan *see* Kuchurhan
117 O9 **Kuchurhan** *Rus.* Kuchurgan. ≋ NE Ukraine
Kuçova *see* Kuçovë
113 L21 **Kuçovë** *var.* Kuçova; *prev.* Qyteti Stalin. Berat, C Albania *40°48′N 19°55′E*
136 D11 **Küçükçekmece** İstanbul, NW Turkey *41°01′N 28°47′E*
164 F14 **Kudamatsu** *var.* Kudamatu. Yamaguchi, Honshū, SW Japan *34°00′N 131°53′E*
Kudamatu *see* Kudamatsu
Kudara *see* Ghŭdara
169 V6 **Kudat** Sabah, East Malaysia *06°54′N 116°47′E*
Küddow *see* Gwda
155 G17 **Kūdligi** Karnātaka, W India *14°58′N 76°24′E*
Kudowa *see* Kudowa-Zdrój
111 F16 **Kudowa-Zdrój** *Ger.* Kudowa. Wałbrzych, SW Poland *50°27′N 16°20′E*
117 P9 **Kudryavtsivka** Mykolayivs'ka Oblast', S Ukraine *47°18′N 31°02′E*
169 R16 **Kudus** *prev.* Koedoes. Jawa, C Indonesia *06°46′S 110°48′E*
125 T13 **Kudymkar** Permskiy Kray, NW Russian Federation *59°01′N 54°40′E*
Kudzsir *see* Cugir
Kuei-chou *see* Guizhou
Kuei-lin *see* Guilin
Kuei-Yang/Kuei-yang *see* Guiyang
K'u-erh-lo *see* Korla
Kueyang *see* Guiyang
Kufa *see* Al Kūfah
136 E14 **Küfiçayı** ≋ C Turkey
109 O6 **Kufstein** Tirol, W Austria *47°36′N 12°10′E*
9 N7 **Kugaaruk** *prev.* Pelly Bay. Nunavut, N Canada *68°38′N 89°45′W*
Kugaly *see* Kogaly
8 K8 **Kugluktuk** *var.* Qurlurtuuq; *prev.* Coppermine. Nunavut, NW Canada *67°49′N 115°12′W*
143 Y13 **Kūhak** Sīstān va Balūchestān, SE Iran *27°10′N 63°15′E*
143 R9 **Kūhbonān** Kermān, C Iran *31°23′N 56°16′E*
148 J5 **Kūhestān** *var.* Kohsān. Herāt, W Afghanistan *34°40′N 61°11′E*
Kūhīrī *see* Kahīrī
93 N15 **Kuhmo** Oulu, E Finland *64°04′N 29°34′E*
93 L18 **Kuhmoinen** Länsi-Suomi, C Finland *61°32′N 25°09′E*
Kuhnau *see* Konin
Kühnö *see* Kihnu
143 O8 **Kūhpāyeh** Eşfahān, C Iran *32°42′N 52°25′E*
167 O12 **Kui Buri** *var.* Ban Kui Nua. Prachuap Khiri Khan, SW Thailand *12°10′N 99°49′E*
Kuibyshev *see* Kuybyshevskoye Vodokhranilishche
82 D13 **Kuito** *Port.* Silva Porto. Bié, C Angola *12°21′S 16°55′E*
39 X14 **Kuiu Island** *island* Alexander Archipelago, Alaska, USA
92 L13 **Kuivaniemi** Oulu, C Finland *65°34′N 25°13′E*
77 V14 **Kujama** Kaduna, C Nigeria *10°27′N 07°39′E*
110 I10 **Kujawsko-pomorskie** ◈ *province* C Poland
165 R8 **Kuji** *var.* Kuzi. Iwate, Honshū, C Japan *40°12′N 141°47′E*
Kujto, Ozero *see* Yushkozerskoye Vodokhranilishche
Kujū-renzan *see* Kujū-san
164 D14 **Kujū-san** *var.* Kujū-renzan. ▲ Kyūshū, SW Japan *33°07′N 131°13′E*
43 N7 **Kukalaya, Rio** *var.* Rio Cuculaya, Rio Kukulaya. ≋ NE Nicaragua
113 O16 **Kukavica** *var.* Vlajna. ▲ SE Serbia *42°46′N 21°58′E*
113 M18 **Kukës** *var.* Kukësi. Kukës, NE Albania *42°03′N 20°25′E*
113 L18 **Kukës** ◈ *district* NE Albania
Kukësi *see* Kukës
186 D8 **Kukipi** Gulf, S Papua New Guinea *08°11′S 146°09′E*
127 S3 **Kukmor** Respublika Tatarstan, W Russian Federation *56°11′N 50°56′E*
Kukong *see* Shaoguan
39 N6 **Kukpowruk River** ≋ Alaska, USA
38 M6 **Kukpuk River** ≋ Alaska, USA
Küküdağ *see* Gogi, Mount
Kukukhoto *see* Hohhot
Kukulaya, Rio *see* Kukalaya, Rio
189 W12 **Kuku Point** *headland* NW Wake Island *19°19′N 166°36′E*
146 G11 **Kukurtli** Ahal Welaýaty, C Turkmenistan *39°58′N 58°47′E*
Kül *see* Kūl, Rūd-e
114 F7 **Kula** Vidin, NW Bulgaria *43°55′N 22°32′E*
112 K9 **Kula** Vojvodina, NW Serbia *45°37′N 19°31′E*
136 D14 **Kula** Manisa, W Turkey *38°33′N 28°38′E*
149 S8 **Kulāchi** Khyber Pakhtunkhwa, NW Pakistan *31°58′N 70°30′E*
Kulachi *see* Kolāchi
Kulagino *see* Yesbol
168 L10 **Kulai** Johor, Peninsular Malaysia *01°41′N 103°33′E*
114 M7 **Kulak** ≋ NE Bulgaria
153 T11 **Kula Kangri** *var.* Kulhakangri. ▲ Bhutan/China *28°06′N 90°19′E*
144 E13 **Kulaly, Ostrov** *island* SW Kazakhstan
145 S16 **Kulan** *Kaz.* Qulan; *prev.* Lugovoy, Lugovoye. Zhambyl, S Kazakhstan *42°54′N 72°45′E*
147 V9 **Kulanak** Narynskaya Oblast', C Kyrgyzstan *41°18′N 75°38′E*
Gory Kulandag *see* Gulandag
153 V14 **Kulaura** Sylhet, NE Bangladesh *24°32′N 92°02′E*
118 D9 **Kuldīga** *Ger.* Goldingen. W Latvia *56°57′N 21°59′E*
Kuldja *see* Yining
Kul'dzhuktau, Gory *see* QuljuqtovTog'lari
127 N4 **Kulebaki** Nizhegorodskaya Oblast', W Russian Federation *55°25′N 42°31′E*
112 E11 **Kulen Vakuf** *var.* Spasovo. ◈ Federacija Bosna I Hercegovina, NW Bosnia and Herzegovina
181 Q9 **Kulgera Roadhouse** Northern Territory, N Australia *25°49′S 133°30′E*
Kulhakangri *see* Kula Kangri
127 T1 **Kuliga** Udmurtskaya Respublika, NW Russian Federation *58°14′N 53°49′E*
Kulkuduk *see* Ko'lquduq
118 G4 **Kullamaa** Läänemaa, W Estonia *58°52′N 24°05′E*
197 O12 **Kullorsuaq** *var.* Kuvdlorssuak. ◈ Kitaa, C Greenland
29 O6 **Kulm** North Dakota, N USA *46°18′N 98°57′W*
Kulm *see* Chełmno
146 D12 **Kul'mach** *prev. Turkm.* Isgender. Balkan Welaýaty, W Turkmenistan *39°04′N 55°49′E*
101 L18 **Kulmbach** Bayern, SE Germany *50°07′N 11°27′E*
Kulmsee *see* Chełmża
147 Q14 **Kŭlob** *Rus.* Kulyab. SW Tajikistan *37°55′N 68°46′E*
92 M13 **Kuloharju** Lappi, N Finland *65°51′N 28°10′E*
125 N7 **Kuloy** Arkhangel'skaya Oblast', NW Russian Federation *64°55′N 43°35′E*
125 N7 **Kuloy** ≋ NW Russian Federation
137 Q14 **Kulp** Diyarbakır, SE Turkey *38°32′N 41°01′E*
Kulpa *see* Kolpa
77 P14 **Kulpawn** ≋ N Ghana
143 R13 **Kūl, Rūd-e** *var.* Kūl. ≋ S Iran
144 G12 **Kul'sary** *Kaz.* Qulsary. Atyrau, W Kazakhstan *46°59′N 54°02′E*
153 R15 **Kulti** West Bengal, NE India *23°45′N 86°50′E*
93 G14 **Kultsjön** *Lapp.* Gålto. ◎ N Sweden
136 I14 **Kulu** Konya, W Turkey *39°06′N 33°02′E*
123 S9 **Kulu** ≋ E Russian Federation
122 I13 **Kulunda** Altayskiy Kray, S Russian Federation *52°33′N 79°04′E*
Kulunda Steppe *see* Ravnina Kulyndy
Kulundinskaya Ravnina *see* Ravnina Kulyndy
182 M9 **Kulwin** Victoria, SE Australia *35°04′S 142°37′E*
Kulyab *see* Kŭlob
117 Q3 **Kulykivka** Chernihivs'ka Oblast', N Ukraine *51°23′N 31°39′E*
Kum *see* Qom
164 F14 **Kuma** Ehime, Shikoku, SW Japan *33°36′N 132°53′E*
127 P14 **Kuma** ≋ SW Russian Federation
165 O12 **Kumagaya** Saitama, Honshū, S Japan *36°09′N 139°22′E*
165 Q5 **Kumaishi** Hokkaidō, NE Japan *42°08′N 139°57′E*
169 R13 **Kumai, Teluk** *bay* Borneo, C Indonesia
127 Y7 **Kumak** Orenburgskaya Oblast', W Russian Federation *51°16′N 60°06′E*
164 C14 **Kumamoto** Kumamoto, Kyūshū, SW Japan *32°49′N 130°41′E*
164 D15 **Kumamoto** *off.* Kumamoto-ken. ◈ *prefecture* Kyūshū, SW Japan
Kumamoto-ken *see* Kumamoto
164 J15 **Kumano** Mie, Honshū, SW Japan *33°54′N 136°08′E*
Kumanova *see* Kumanovo
113 O17 **Kumanovo** *Turk.* Kumanova. N Macedonia *42°08′N 21°43′E*
185 G17 **Kumara** West Coast, South Island, New Zealand *42°39′S 171°12′E*
180 J8 **Kumarina Roadhouse** Western Australia *24°46′S 119°39′E*
153 T15 **Kumarkhali** Khulna, W Bangladesh *23°54′N 89°16′E*
77 P16 **Kumasi** *prev.* Coomassie. C Ghana *06°41′N 01°40′W*
Kumayri *see* Gyumri
79 D15 **Kumba** Sud-Ouest, W Cameroon *04°39′N 09°26′E*
114 N13 **Kumbağ** Tekirdağ, NW Turkey *40°51′N 27°26′E*
155 J21 **Kumbakonam** Tamil Nādu, SE India *10°59′N 79°24′E*
Kum-Dag *see* Gumdag
165 R16 **Kume-jima** *island* Nansei-shotō, SW Japan
127 V6 **Kumertau** Respublika Bashkortostan, W Russian Federation *52°48′N 55°48′E*
Kumillā *see* Comilla
35 R4 **Kumiva Peak** ▲ Nevada, W USA *40°24′N 119°16′W*
159 N7 **Kum Kuduk** Xinjiang Uygur Zizhiqu, W China *40°15′N 91°55′E*
159 N8 **Kum Kuduk** *well* NW China
Kumkurgan *see* Qumqo'rg'on
95 M16 **Kumla** Örebro, C Sweden *59°08′N 15°09′E*
136 E17 **Kumluca** Antalya, SW Turkey *36°23′N 30°17′E*
100 N9 **Kummerower See** ◎ NE Germany
77 X14 **Kumo** Gombe, E Nigeria *10°03′N 11°14′E*
145 O13 **Kumola** ≋ C Kazakhstan
167 N1 **Kumon Range** ▲▲ N Myanmar (Burma)
83 F22 **Kums** Karas, SE Namibia *28°07′S 19°40′E*
155 E18 **Kumta** Karnātaka, W India *14°25′N 74°24′E*
38 H12 **Kumukahi, Cape** *headland* Hawai'i, USA, C Pacific Ocean *19°31′N 154°48′W*
127 Q17 **Kumukh** Respublika Dagestan, SW Russian Federation *42°10′N 47°07′E*
Kumul *see* Hami
158 L6 **Kümüx** Xinjiang Uygur Zizhiqu, W China
127 N9 **Kumylzhenskaya** Volgogradskaya Oblast', SW Russian Federation *49°54′N 42°35′E*
141 W6 **Kumzār** N Oman *26°19′N 56°26′E*
43 W15 **Kuna de Wargandí** ◈ *special territory* NE Panama
149 S4 **Kunar** *Per.* Konarhā; *prev.* Konar. ◈ *province* E Afghanistan
Kunashiri *see* Kunashir, Ostrov
123 U14 **Kunashir, Ostrov** *var.* Kunashiri. *island* Kuril'skiye Ostrova, SE Russian Federation
43 V14 **Kuna Yala** *prev.* San Blas. ◈ *special territory* NE Panama
118 I3 **Kunda** Lääne-Virumaa, NE Estonia *59°31′N 26°33′E*
152 M13 **Kunda** Uttar Pradesh, N India *25°43′N 81°31′E*
155 E19 **Kundāpura** *var.* Coondapoor. Karnātaka, W India *13°39′N 74°41′E*
79 O24 **Kundelungu, Monts** ▲▲ S Dem. Rep. Congo
Kundert *see* Hernád
186 D7 **Kundiawa** Chimbu, W Papua New Guinea *06°00′S 144°57′E*
Kundla *see* Sāvarkundla
Kunduk, Ozero *see* Sasyk, Ozero
Kunduk, Ozero Sasyk *see* Sasyk, Ozero
168 L10 **Kundur, Pulau** *island* W Indonesia
149 Q2 **Kunduz** *var.* Kondūz, Qondūz; *prev.* Kondoz, Kundūz. Kunduz, NE Afghanistan *36°49′N 68°50′E*
149 Q2 **Kunduz** *prev.* Kondoz. ◈ *province* NE Afghanistan
Kunduz/Kundūz *see* Kunduz
Kuneitra *see* Al Qunayţirah
83 B18 **Kunene** ◈ *district* NE Namibia
83 A16 **Kunene** *var.* Cunene. ≋ Angola/Namibia *see also* Cunene
Kunene *see* Cunene
Künes *see* Xinyuan
158 J5 **Künes He** ≋ NW China
95 I19 **Kungälv** Västra Götaland, S Sweden *57°54′N 12°00′E*
147 W7 **Kungei Ala-Tau** *Rus.* Khrebet Kyungëy Ala-Too, *Kir.* Küngöy Ala-Too. ▲▲ Kazakhstan/Kyrgyzstan
Küngöy Ala-Too *see* Kungei Ala-Tau
Kungrad *see* Qo'ng'irot
95 J19 **Kungsbacka** Halland, S Sweden *57°30′N 12°05′E*
95 I18 **Kungshamn** Västra Götaland, S Sweden *58°21′N 11°15′E*
95 M16 **Kungsör** Västmanland, C Sweden *59°25′N 16°05′E*
79 J16 **Kungu** Equateur, NW Dem. Rep. Congo *02°47′N 19°12′E*
125 V15 **Kungur** Permskiy Kray, NW Russian Federation *57°24′N 56°56′E*
166 L9 **Kungyangon** Yangon, SW Myanmar (Burma) *16°27′N 96°00′E*
111 M22 **Kunhegyes** Jász-Nagykun-Szolnok, E Hungary *47°22′N 20°36′E*
167 O5 **Kunhing** Shan State, Myanmar (Burma) *21°17′N 98°26′E*
158 D9 **Kunjirap Daban** *var.* Khūnjerāb Pass. *pass* China/Pakistan *see also* Khūnjerāb Pass
Kunjirap Daban *see* Khunjerab Pass
Kunlun Mountains *see* Kunlun Shan
158 H10 **Kunlun Shan** *Eng.* Kunlun Mountains. ▲▲ NW China
159 P11 **Kunlun Shankou** *pass* C China
160 G13 **Kunming** *var.* K'un-ming; *prev.* Yunnan. *province capital* Yunnan, SW China *25°04′N 102°41′E*
K'un-ming *see* Kunming
Kuno *see* Kunoy
95 B18 **Kunoy** *Dan.* Kunø. *island* N Faeroe Islands
Kunsan *see* Gunsan
111 L24 **Kunszentmárton** Jász-Nagykun-Szolnok, E Hungary *46°50′N 20°19′E*
111 J23 **Kunszentmiklós** Bács-Kiskun, C Hungary *47°00′N 19°07′E*
181 N3 **Kununurra** Western Australia *15°50′S 128°44′E*
Kunyang *see* Pingyang
Kunya-Urgench *see* Köneürgenç
Kunyé *see* Pins, Île des
169 T11 **Kunyi** Borneo, C Indonesia *03°23′S 119°20′E*
101 I20 **Künzelsau** Baden-Württemberg, S Germany *49°22′N 09°43′E*
161 S10 **Kuocang Shan** ▲▲ SE China
Kuolajärvi *see* Kuoloyarvi
124 H5 **Kuoloyarvi** *Finn.* Kuolajärvi, *var.* Luolajarvi. Murmanskaya Oblast', NW Russian Federation *66°58′N 29°13′E*
93 N16 **Kuopio** Itä-Suomi, C Finland *62°54′N 27°41′E*
93 K17 **Kuortane** Länsi-Suomi, W Finland *62°48′N 23°30′E*
93 M18 **Kuortti** Itä-Suomi, E Finland *61°25′N 26°25′E*
Kupa *see* Kolpa
171 P17 **Kupang** *prev.* Koepang. Timor, C Indonesia *10°13′S 123°38′E*
39 Q5 **Kuparuk River** ≋ Alaska, USA
Kupchino *see* Cupcina
186 E9 **Kupiano** Central, S Papua New Guinea *10°06′S 148°12′E*
180 M4 **Kupingarri** Western Australia *16°46′S 125°57′E*
122 I12 **Kupino** Novosibirskaya Oblast', C Russian Federation *54°22′N 77°09′E*
118 H11 **Kupiškis** Panevėžys, NE Lithuania *55°51′N 24°58′E*
114 L13 **Küplü** Edirne, NW Turkey *41°06′N 26°23′E*
39 X13 **Kupreanof Island** *island* Alexander Archipelago, Alaska, USA
39 O16 **Kupreanof Point** *headland* Alaska, USA *55°34′N 159°36′W*
112 G13 **Kupres** ◈ Federacija Bosna I Hercegovina, SW Bosnia and Herzegovina
117 W5 **Kup"yans'k** *Rus.* Kupyansk. Kharkivs'ka Oblast', E Ukraine *49°42′N 37°36′E*
Kupyansk *see* Kup"yans'k
117 W5 **Kup"yans'k-Vuzlovyy** Kharkivs'ka Oblast', E Ukraine *49°40′N 37°41′E*
158 I6 **Kuqa** Xinjiang Uygur Zizhiqu, NW China *41°43′N 82°58′E*

◆ Country
● Country Capital
◇ Dependent Territory
○ Dependent Territory Capital
◈ Administrative Regions
✈ International Airport
▲ Mountain
▲▲ Mountain Range
Volcano
≋ River
◎ Lake
⊠ Reservoir

Kür *see* Kura
137 W11 **Kura** *Az.* Kür, *Geor.* Mtkvari, *Turk.* Kura Nehri. ≈ SW Asia
55 R8 **Kuracki** NW Guyana *06°52′N 60°13′W*
Kura Kurk *see* Irbe Strait
147 Q10 **Kurama Range** *Rus.* Kuraminskiy Khrebet. ▲▲ Tajikistan/Uzbekistan
Kuraminskiy Khrebet *see* Kurama Range
Kura Nehri *see* Kura
119 J14 **Kuranyets** *Rus.* Kurenets. Minskaya Voblasts', C Belarus *54°33′N 26°57′E*
164 H13 **Kurashiki** *var.* Kurasiki. Okayama, Honshū, SW Japan *34°35′N 133°44′E*
154 L10 **Kurasia** Chhattīsgarh, C India *23°11′N 82°16′E*
Kurasiki *see* Kurashiki
164 H12 **Kurayoshi** *var.* Kurayosi. Tottori, Honshū, SW Japan *35°27′N 133°52′E*
Kurayosi *see* Kurayoshi
163 X6 **Kurbin He** ≈ NE China
Kurchum *see* Kurshim
Kurchum *see* Kurshim
137 X11 **Kürdämir** *Rus.* Kyurdamir. C Azerbaijan *40°21′N 48°08′E*
Kurdestan *see* Kordestān
139 S1 **Kurdistan** *cultural region* SW Asia
Kurd Kui *see* Kord Kūy
155 F15 **Kurduvādi** Mahārāshtra, W India *18°06′N 75°31′E*
114 J11 **Kŭrdzhali** *var.* Kirdzhali. Kŭrdzhali, S Bulgaria *41°39′N 25°23′E*
114 K11 **Kŭrdzhali** ◈ *province* S Bulgaria
114 J11 **Kŭrdzhali, Yazovir** ⊠ S Bulgaria
164 F13 **Kure** Hiroshima, Honshū, SW Japan *34°15′N 132°33′E*
192 K5 **Kure Atoll** *var.* Ocean Island. *atoll* Hawaiian Islands, Hawaii, USA
136 J10 **Küre Dağları** ▲▲ N Turkey
146 C11 **Kürendag** *Rus.* Gora Kyuren. ▲ W Turkmenistan *39°05′N 55°09′E*
Kurenets *see* Kuranyets
118 E6 **Kuressaare** *Ger.* Arensburg; *prev.* Kingissepp. Saaremaa, W Estonia *58°17′N 22°29′E*
122 K9 **Kureyka** Krasnoyarskiy Kray, N Russian Federation *66°22′N 87°21′E*
122 K9 **Kureyka** ≈ N Russian Federation
Kurgal'dzhino/Kurgal'dzhinsky *see* Korgalzhyn
122 G11 **Kurgan** Kurganskaya Oblast', C Russian Federation *55°30′N 65°20′E*
126 L14 **Kurganinsk** Krasnodarskiy Kray, SW Russian Federation *44°55′N 40°45′E*
122 G11 **Kurganskaya Oblast'** ◈ *province* C Russian Federation
Kurgan-Tyube *see* Qŭrghonteppa
191 O2 **Kuria** *prev.* Woodle Island. *island* Tungaru, W Kiribati
Kuria Muria Bay *see* Ḥalānīyāt, Khalīj al
Kuria Muria Islands *see* Ḥalāniyāt, Juzur al
153 T13 **Kurigram** Rajshahi, N Bangladesh *25°49′N 89°39′E*
93 K17 **Kurikka** Länsi-Suomi, W Finland *62°36′N 22°25′E*
192 I3 **Kurile Basin** *undersea feature* NW Pacific Ocean *47°00′N 150°00′E*
Kurile Islands *see* Kuril'skiye Ostrova
Kurile-Kamchatka Depression *see* Kurile Trench
192 J3 **Kurile Trench** *var.* Kurile-Kamchatka Depression. *undersea feature* NW Pacific Ocean *47°00′N 155°00′E*
127 Q9 **Kurilovka** Saratovskaya Oblast', W Russian Federation *50°39′N 48°02′E*
123 U13 **Kuril'sk** *Jap.* Shana. Kuril'skiye Ostrova, Sakhalinskaya Oblats', SE Russian Federation *45°10′N 147°51′E*
122 G11 **Kuril'skiye Ostrova** *Eng.* Kurile Islands. *island group* SE Russian Federation
42 M9 **Kurinwas, Río** ≈ E Nicaragua
Kurisches Haff *see* Courland Lagoon
Kurkund *see* Kilingi-Nõmme
126 M4 **Kurlovskiy** Vladimirskaya Oblast', W Russian Federation *55°25′N 40°39′E*
80 G12 **Kurmuk** Blue Nile, SE Sudan *10°36′N 34°16′E*
Kurna *see* Al Qurnah
155 H17 **Kurnool** *var.* Karnul. Andhra Pradesh, S India *15°51′N 78°01′E*
164 M11 **Kurobe** Toyama, Honshū, SW Japan *36°55′N 137°24′E*
165 Q7 **Kuroishi** *var.* Kuroisi. Aomori, Honshū, C Japan *40°37′N 140°34′E*
Kuroisi *see* Kuroishi
165 O12 **Kuroiso** Tochigi, Honshū, S Japan *36°58′N 140°02′E*
165 Q4 **Kuromatsunai** Hokkaidō, NE Japan *42°40′N 140°18′E*
164 B17 **Kuro-shima** *island* SW Japan
185 F21 **Kurow** Canterbury, South Island, New Zealand *44°44′S 170°29′E*
127 N15 **Kursavka** Stavropol'skiy Kray, SW Russian Federation *44°28′N 42°31′E*
118 E11 **Kuršėnai** Šiauliai, N Lithuania *56°00′N 22°56′E*
145 X10 **Kurshim** *prev.* Kurchum. Vostochnyy Kazakhstan, E Kazakhstan *48°35′N 83°37′E*
145 Y10 **Kurshim** *prev.* Kurchum. ≈ E Kazakhstan
Kurshskaya Kosa/Kuršių Nerija *see* Courland Spit
126 J7 **Kursk** Kurskaya Oblast', W Russian Federation *51°44′N 36°47′E*
126 I7 **Kurskaya Oblast'** ◈ *province* W Russian Federation
Kurskiy Zaliv *see* Courland Lagoon
113 N15 **Kuršumlija** Serbia, S Serbia *43°09′N 21°16′E*
137 R15 **Kurtalan** Siirt, SE Turkey *37°58′N 41°36′E*
Kurtbunar *see* Tervel
Kurt-Dere *see* Vŭlchidol
Kurtitsch/Kürtös *see* Curtici
145 U15 **Kurtty** ≈ SE Kazakhstan
93 L18 **Kuru** Länsi-Suomi, W Finland *61°51′N 23°46′E*
80 C13 **Kuru** ≈ W South Sudan
114 M13 **Kuru Dağı** ▲▲ NW Turkey
158 L7 **Kuruktag** ▲▲ NW China
83 G22 **Kuruman** Northern Cape, N South Africa *27°28′S 23°27′E*
67 T14 **Kuruman** ≈ W South Africa
164 D14 **Kurume** Fukuoka, Kyūshū, SW Japan *33°15′N 130°27′E*
123 N13 **Kurumkan** Respublika Buryatiya, S Russian Federation *54°13′N 110°21′E*
155 J25 **Kurunegala** North Western Province, C Sri Lanka *07°28′N 80°23′E*
55 T10 **Kurupukari** C Guyana *04°39′N 58°39′W*
125 U10 **Kur"ya** Respublika Komi, NW Russian Federation *61°38′N 57°12′E*
144 E15 **Kuryk** *var.* Yeraliyev, *Kaz.* Quryq. Mangistau, SW Kazakhstan *43°12′N 51°43′E*
136 B15 **Kuşadası** Aydın, SW Turkey *37°50′N 27°16′E*
115 M19 **Kuşadası Körfezi** *gulf* SW Turkey
164 A17 **Kusagaki-guntō** *island* SW Japan
Kusaie *see* Kosrae
145 T12 **Kusak** ≈ C Kazakhstan
Kusary *see* Qusar
167 P7 **Ku Sathan, Doi** ▲ NW Thailand *18°22′N 100°31′E*
164 J13 **Kusatsu** *var.* Kusatu. Shiga, Honshū, SW Japan *35°02′N 136°00′E*
Kusatu *see* Kusatsu
138 F11 **Kuseifa** Southern, C Israel *31°15′N 35°01′E*
136 C12 **Kuş Gölü** ◎ NW Turkey
126 L12 **Kushchevskaya** Krasnodarskiy Kray, SW Russian Federation *46°35′N 39°40′E*
164 D16 **Kushima** *var.* Kusima. Miyazaki, Kyūshū, SW Japan *31°28′N 131°14′E*
164 I15 **Kushimoto** Wakayama, Honshū, SW Japan *33°28′N 135°45′E*
165 V4 **Kushiro** *var.* Kusiro. Hokkaidō, NE Japan *42°58′N 144°24′E*
148 K4 **Kushk** *prev.* Kūshk. Herāt, W Afghanistan *34°55′N 62°20′E*
Kushka *see* Serhetabat
Kushka *see* Gushgy/Serhetabat
Kushmurun *see* Kusmuryn
Kushmurun, Ozero *see* Kusmuryn, Ozero
127 U4 **Kushnarenkovo** Respublika Bashkortostan, W Russian Federation *55°07′N 55°24′E*
Kushrabat *see* Qo'shrabot
Kushtia *see* Kustia
Kusima *see* Kushima
Kusiro *see* Kushiro
38 M13 **Kuskokwim Bay** *bay* Alaska, USA
39 P11 **Kuskokwim Mountains** ▲▲ Alaska, USA
39 N12 **Kuskokwim River** ≈ Alaska, USA
145 N8 **Kusmuryn** *Kaz.* Qusmuryn; *prev.* Kushmurun. Kostanay, N Kazakhstan *52°27′N 64°31′E*
145 N8 **Kusmuryn, Ozero** *Kaz.* Qusmuryn; *prev.* Ozero Kushmurun. ◎ N Kazakhstan
108 G7 **Küsnacht** Zürich, N Switzerland *47°19′N 08°34′E*
165 V4 **Kussharo-ko** *var.* Kussyaro. ◎ Hokkaidō, NE Japan
Küssnacht *see* Küssnacht am Rigi
108 F8 **Küssnacht am Rigi** *var.* Küssnacht. Schwyz, C Switzerland *47°03′N 08°25′E*
Kussyaro *see* Kussharo-ko
Kustanay *see* Kostanay
Küstence/Küstendje *see* Constanța
100 F11 **Küstenkanal** *var.* Ems-Hunte Canal. *canal* NW Germany
153 T15 **Kustia** *var.* Kushtia. Khulna, W Bangladesh *23°54′N 89°07′E*
Küstrin *see* Kostrzyn
171 R11 **Kusu** Pulau Halmahera, E Indonesia *0°51′N 127°41′E*
170 L16 **Kuta** Pulau Lombok, S Indonesia *08°53′S 116°15′E*
139 T4 **Kutabān** At Ta'mím, N Iraq *35°21′N 44°45′E*
136 E13 **Kütahya** *prev.* Kutaia. Kütahya, W Turkey *39°25′N 29°56′E*
136 E13 **Kütahya** *var.* Kutaia. ◈ *province* W Turkey
Kutai *see* Mahakam, Sungai
Kutaia *see* Kütahya
137 R9 **Kutaisi** W Georgia *42°16′N 42°42′E*
Kūt al 'Amārah *see* Al Kūt
Kut al Hai/Kūt al Ḩayy *see* Al Ḩayy
Kut al Imara *see* Al Kūt
123 Q11 **Kutana** Respublika Sakha (Yakutiya), NE Russian Federation *59°05′N 131°43′E*
Kutaradja/Kutaraja *see* Banda Aceh
165 R4 **Kutchan** Hokkaidō, NE Japan *42°54′N 140°46′E*
Kutch, Gulf of *see* Kachchh, Gulf of
Kutch, Rann of *see* Kachchh, Rann of
112 F9 **Kutina** Sisak-Moslavina, NE Croatia *45°29′N 16°45′E*
112 H9 **Kutjevo** Požega-Slavonija, NE Croatia *45°26′N 17°54′E*
111 E17 **Kutná Hora** *Ger.* Kuttenberg. Střední Čechy, C Czech Republic *49°58′N 15°18′E*
110 K12 **Kutno** Łódzkie, C Poland *52°14′N 19°23′E*
Kuttenberg *see* Kutná Hora
79 I20 **Kutu** Bandundu, W Dem. Rep. Congo *02°42′S 18°10′E*
153 V17 **Kutubdia Island** *island* SE Bangladesh
80 B10 **Kutum** Northern Darfur, W Sudan *14°10′N 24°40′E*
147 Y7 **Kuturgu** Issyk-Kul'skaya Oblast', E Kyrgyzstan *42°45′N 78°04′E*
12 M5 **Kuujjuaq** *prev.* Fort-Chimo. Québec, E Canada *58°10′N 68°15′W*
12 I7 **Kuujjuarapik** Québec, C Canada *55°07′N 78°09′W*
12 I7 **Kuujjuarapik** *prev.* Poste-de-la-Baleine. Québec, NE Canada *55°13′N 77°54′W*
Kuuli-Mayak *see* Guwlumaýak
118 I6 **Kuulsemägi** ▲ S Estonia
92 N13 **Kuusamo** Oulu, E Finland *65°57′N 29°15′E*
93 M19 **Kuusankoski** Etelä-Suomi, S Finland *60°51′N 26°40′E*
127 W7 **Kuvandyk** Orenburgskaya Oblast', W Russian Federation *51°27′N 57°18′E*
Kuvango *see* Cubango
Kuvasay *see* Quvasoy
Kuvdlorssuak *see* Kullorsuaq
124 I16 **Kuvshinovo** Tverskaya Oblast', W Russian Federation *57°03′N 34°09′E*
141 Q4 **Kuwait** *off.* State of Kuwait, *var.* Dawlat al Kuwait, Koweit, Kuweit. ◆ *monarchy* SW Asia
Kuwait *see* Al Kuwayt
Kuwait Bay *see* Kuwayt, Jūn al
Kuwait City *see* Al Kuwayt
Kuwait, Dawlat al *see* Kuwait
Kuwait, State of *see* Kuwait
Kuwajleen *see* Kwajalein Atoll
164 K13 **Kuwana** Mie, Honshū, SW Japan *35°04′N 136°40′E*
139 X9 **Kuwayt** Maysān, E Iraq *32°26′N 47°12′E*
142 K11 **Kuwayt, Jūn al** *var.* Kuwait Bay. *bay* E Kuwait
Kuweit *see* Kuwait
117 P10 **Kuyal'nyts'kyy Lyman** ◎ SW Ukraine
122 I12 **Kuybyshev** Novosibirskaya Oblast', C Russian Federation *55°28′N 77°55′E*
Kuybyshev *see* Bolgar, Respublika Tatarstan, Russian Federation
Kuybyshev *see* Samara
117 W9 **Kuybysheve** *Rus.* Kuybyshevo. Zaporiz'ka Oblast', SE Ukraine *47°20′N 36°41′E*
Kuybyshevo *see* Kuybysheve
Kuybyshev Reservoir *see* Kuybyshevskoye Vodokhranilishche
Kuybyshevskaya Oblast' *see* Samarskaya Oblast'
Kuybyshevskiy *see* Novoishimskiy
127 R4 **Kuybyshevskoye Vodokhranilishche** *var.* Kuibyshev, *Eng.* Kuybyshev Reservoir. ⊠ W Russian Federation
123 S9 **Kuydusun** Respublika Sakha (Yakutiya), NE Russian Federation *63°15′N 143°10′E*
125 U16 **Kuyeda** Permskiy Kray, NW Russian Federation *56°23′N 55°19′E*
Kūysanjaq *see* Koi Sanjaq
158 J4 **Kuytun** Xinjiang Uygur Zizhiqu, NW China *44°25′N 84°55′E*
122 M13 **Kuytun** Irkutskaya Oblast', S Russian Federation *54°18′N 101°28′E*
55 S12 **Kuyuwini Landing** S Guyana *02°06′N 59°14′W*
Kuzi *see* Kuji
38 M9 **Kuzitrin River** ≈ Alaska, USA
127 P6 **Kuznetsk** Penzenskaya Oblast', W Russian Federation *53°06′N 46°27′E*
116 K3 **Kuznetsovs'k** Rivnens'ka Oblast', NW Ukraine *51°21′N 25°51′E*
165 R8 **Kuzumaki** Iwate, Honshū, C Japan *40°04′N 141°26′E*
95 H24 **Kværndrup** Syddtjylland, C Denmark *55°10′N 10°31′E*
92 H9 **Kvaløya** *island* N Norway
92 K8 **Kvalsund** Finnmark, N Norway *70°30′N 23°56′E*
94 G11 **Kvam** Oppland, S Norway *61°42′N 09°43′E*
127 X7 **Kvarkeno** Orenburgskaya Oblast', W Russian Federation *52°09′N 59°44′E*
93 G15 **Kvarnbergsvattnet** *var.* Frostviken. ◎ N Sweden
112 A11 **Kvarner** *var.* Carnaro, *It.* Quarnero. *gulf* W Croatia
112 B11 **Kvarnerić** *channel* W Croatia
39 O14 **Kvichak Bay** *bay* Alaska, USA
92 H12 **Kvikkjokk** *Lapp.* Huhttán. Norrbotten, N Sweden *66°58′N 17°45′E*
95 D17 **Kvina** ≈ S Norway
92 Q1 **Kvitøya** *island* NE Svalbard
95 F16 **Kvitseid** Telemark, S Norway *59°23′N 08°31′E*
79 H20 **Kwa** ≈ W Dem. Rep. Congo
77 Q15 **Kwadwokurom** C Ghana *07°49′N 00°15′W*
186 M8 **Kwailibesi** Malaita, N Solomon Islands *08°25′S 160°48′E*
189 S6 **Kwajalein Atoll** *var.* Kuwajleen. *atoll* Ralik Chain, C Marshall Islands
55 W9 **Kwakoegron** Brokopondo, N Suriname *05°14′N 55°20′W*
81 J21 **Kwale** Coast, S Kenya *04°10′S 39°27′E*
77 U17 **Kwale** Delta, S Nigeria *05°51′N 06°29′E*
79 H20 **Kwamouth** Bandundu, W Dem. Rep. Congo *03°11′S 16°16′E*
Kwando *see* Cuando
Kwangchow *see* Guangzhou
Kwangchu *see* Gwangju
Kwangju *see* Gwangju
Kwangju-gwangyŏksi *see* Gwangju
79 H20 **Kwango** *Port.* Cuango. ≈ Angola/Dem. Rep. Congo *see also* Cuango
Kwango *see* Cuango
Kwangsi/Kwangsi Chuang Autonomous Region *see* Guangxi Zhuangzu Zizhiqu
Kwangtung *see* Guangdong
Kwangyuan *see* Guangyuan
81 F17 **Kwania, Lake** ◎ C Uganda
Kwanza *see* Cuanza
77 S15 **Kwara** ◈ *state* SW Nigeria
83 K22 **KwaZulu/Natal** *off.* KwaZulu/Natal Province; *prev.* Natal. ◈ *province* E South Africa
KwaZulu/Natal Province *see* KwaZulu/Natal
Kweichow *see* Guizhou
Kweichu *see* Guiyang
Kweilin *see* Guilin
Kweisui *see* Hohhot
Kweiyang *see* Guiyang
83 K17 **Kwekwe** *prev.* Que Que. Midlands, C Zimbabwe *18°56′S 29°49′E*
83 G20 **Kweneng** ◈ *district* S Botswana
Kwesui *see* Hohhot
39 N12 **Kwethluk** Alaska, USA *60°48′N 161°26′W*
39 N12 **Kwethluk River** ≈ Alaska, USA
110 J8 **Kwidzyń** *Ger.* Marienwerder. Pomorskie, N Poland *53°44′N 18°55′E*
38 M13 **Kwigillingok** Alaska, USA *59°52′N 163°08′W*
186 E9 **Kwikila** Central, S Papua New Guinea *09°51′S 147°43′E*
79 I20 **Kwilu** ≈ W Dem. Rep. Congo
Kwito *see* Cuito
171 U12 **Kwoka, Gunung** ▲ Papua, E Indonesia *0°34′S 132°25′E*
78 I12 **Kyabé** Moyen-Chari, S Chad *09°28′N 18°54′E*
183 O11 **Kyabram** Victoria, SE Australia *36°21′S 145°05′E*
166 M9 **Kyaikkami** *prev.* Amherst. Mon State, S Myanmar (Burma) *16°03′N 97°36′E*
166 L9 **Kyaiklat** Ayeyarwady, SW Myanmar (Burma) *16°25′N 95°42′E*
166 M8 **Kyaikto** Mon State, Myanmar (Burma) *17°16′N 97°01′E*
123 N14 **Kyakhta** Respublika Buryatiya, S Russian Federation *50°25′N 106°13′E*
182 G8 **Kyancutta** South Australia *33°10′S 135°33′E*
167 T8 **Ky Anh** Ha Tinh, N Vietnam *18°05′N 106°16′E*
166 L5 **Kyaukpadaung** Mandalay, C Myanmar (Burma) *20°50′N 95°08′E*
Kyaukpyu *see* Kyaunkpyu
166 M5 **Kyaukse** Mandalay, Myanmar (Burma) *21°33′N 96°06′E*
166 L8 **Kyaunggon** Ayeyarwady, SW Myanmar (Burma) *17°04′N 95°12′E*
166 J6 **Kyaunkpyu** *var.* Kyaukpyu. Rakhine State, W Myanmar (Burma) *19°27′N 93°33′E*
119 E14 **Kybartai** *Pol.* Kibarty. Marijampolė, S Lithuania *54°37′N 22°44′E*
152 I7 **Kyelang** Himāchal Pradesh, NW India *32°33′N 77°03′E*
111 G19 **Kyjov** *Ger.* Gaya. Jihomoravský Kraj, SE Czech Republic *49°00′N 17°07′E*
115 J21 **Kykládes** *var.* Kikládhes, *Eng.* Cyclades. *island group* SE Greece
25 S11 **Kyle** Texas, SW USA *29°59′N 97°52′W*
96 G9 **Kyle of Lochalsh** N Scotland, United Kingdom *57°18′N 05°39′W*
101 D18 **Kyll** ≈ W Germany
115 F19 **Kyllíni** *var.* Killini. ▲▲ S Greece
115 H18 **Kými** *prev.* Kími. Évvoia, C Greece *38°38′N 24°06′E*
93 M19 **Kymijoki** ≈ S Finland
115 H18 **Kýmis, Akrotírio** *headland* Évvoia, C Greece *38°39′N 24°08′E*
125 W14 **Kyn** Permskiy Kray, NW Russian Federation *57°48′N 58°38′E*
183 N12 **Kyneton** Victoria, SE Australia *37°14′S 144°28′E*
81 G17 **Kyoga, Lake** *var.* Lake Kioga. ◎ C Uganda
164 J12 **Kyōga-misaki** *headland* Honshū, SW Japan *35°46′N 135°13′E*
183 V4 **Kyogle** New South Wales, SE Australia *28°37′S 153°00′E*
Kyŏnggi-man *see* Gyeonggi-man
Kyŏngju *see* Gyeongju
Kyŏngsŏng *see* Seoul
Kyōsai-tō *see* Geogeum-do
81 F19 **Kyotera** S Uganda *0°38′S 31°34′E*
164 J13 **Kyōto** Kyōto, Honshū, SW Japan *35°01′N 135°46′E*
164 J13 **Kyōto** *off.* Kyōto-fu, *var.* Kyōto Hu. ◈ *urban prefecture* Honshū, SW Japan
Kyōto-fu/Kyōto Hu *see* Kyōto
115 D21 **Kyparissía** *var.* Kiparissía. Pelopónnisos, S Greece *37°15′N 21°40′E*
115 D20 **Kyparissiakós Kólpos** *gulf* S Greece
Kyperounda *see* Kyperoúnta
121 P3 **Kyperoúnta** *var.* Kyperounda. C Cyprus *34°57′N 33°02′E*
Kypros *see* Cyprus
115 H16 **Kyrá Panagía** *island* Vóreies Sporádes, Greece, Aegean Sea
Kyrenia *see* Girne
Kyrenia Mountains *see* Beşparmak Dağları
Kyrgyz Republic *see* Kyrgyzstan
147 U9 **Kyrgyzstan** *off.* Kyrgyz Republic, *var.* Kirghizia; *prev.* Kirgizskaya SSR, Kirghiz SSR, Republic of Kyrgyzstan. ◆ *republic* C Asia
Kyrgyzstan, Republic of *see* Kyrgyzstan
138 F11 **Kyriat Gat** *prev.* Qiryat Gat. Southern, C Israel *31°37′N 34°47′E*
100 M11 **Kyritz** Brandenburg, NE Germany *52°56′N 12°24′E*
94 G8 **Kyrkseterøra** Sør-Trøndelag, S Norway *63°17′N 09°06′E*
Kyrkslätt *see* Kirkkonummi
125 U8 **Kyrta** Respublika Komi, NW Russian Federation *64°03′N 57°41′E*
111 J18 **Kysucké Nové Mesto** *prev.* Horné Nové Mesto, *Ger.* Kisutzaneustadtl, Oberneustadtl, *Hung.* Kiszucaújhely. Zílinský Kraj, N Slovakia *49°18′N 18°48′E*
117 N12 **Kytay, Ozero** ◎ SW Ukraine
115 F23 **Kýthira** *var.* Kíthira, *It.* Cerigo, *Lat.* Cythera. Kńythira, S Greece *41°39′N 26°30′E*
115 F23 **Kýthira** *var.* Kíthira, *It.* Cerigo, *Lat.* Cythera. *island* S Greece
115 I20 **Kýthnos** Kńythnos, Kykládes, Greece, Aegean Sea *37°24′N 24°28′E*
115 I20 **Kýthnos** *var.* Kíthnos, Thermiá, *It.* Termia; *anc.* Cythnos. *island* Kykládes, Greece, Aegean Sea
115 I20 **Kýthnou, Stenó** *strait* Kykládes, Greece, Aegean Sea
Kyungëy Ala-Too, Khrebet *see* Kungei Ala-Tau
Kyurdamir *see* Kürdämir
164 D15 **Kyūshū** *var.* Kyûsyû. *island* SW Japan
192 H6 **Kyushu-Palau Ridge** *var.* Kyusyu-Palau Ridge. *undersea feature* W Pacific Ocean *20°00′N 136°00′E*
114 F10 **Kyustendil** *anc.* Pautalia. Kyustendil, W Bulgaria *42°17′N 22°42′E*
114 G11 **Kyustendil** ◈ *province* W Bulgaria
Kyûsyû *see* Kyūshū
Kyusyu-Palau Ridge *see* Kyushu-Palau Ridge
123 P8 **Kyusyur** Respublika Sakha (Yakutiya), NE Russian Federation *70°36′N 127°19′E*
183 P10 **Kywong** New South Wales, SE Australia *34°59′S 146°42′E*
117 P4 **Kyyiv** *Eng.* Kiev, *Rus.* Kiyev. ● (Ukraine) Kyyivs'ka Oblast', N Ukraine *50°26′N 30°32′E*
Kyyiv *see* Kyyivs'ka Oblast'
117 O4 **Kyyivs'ka Oblast'** *var.* Kyyiv, *Rus.* Kiyevskaya Oblast'. ◈ *province* N Ukraine
117 P3 **Kyyivs'ke Vodoskhovyshche** *Eng.* Kiev Reservoir, *Rus.* Kiyevskoye Vodokhranilishche. ⊠ N Ukraine
93 L16 **Kyyjärvi** Länsi-Suomi, C Finland *63°02′N 24°34′E*
122 K14 **Kyzyl** Respublika Tyva, C Russian Federation *51°45′N 94°28′E*
147 S8 **Kyzyl-Adyr** *var.* Kirovskoye. Talasskaya Oblast', NW Kyrgyzstan *42°37′N 71°34′E*
145 V14 **Kyzylagash** *Kaz.* Qyzylaghash. Almaty, SE Kazakhstan *45°20′N 78°45′E*
146 C13 **Kyzylbair** Balkan Welaýaty, W Turkmenistan *38°13′N 55°38′E*
Kyzyl-Dzhiik, Pereval *see* Uzbel Shankou
145 S7 **Kyzylkak, Ozero** ◎ NE Kazakhstan
145 X11 **Kyzylkesek** Vostochnyy Kazakhstan, E Kazakhstan *47°56′N 82°02′E*
147 S10 **Kyzyl-Kiya** *Kir.* Kyzyl-Kyya. Batkenskaya Oblast', SW Kyrgyzstan *40°15′N 72°07′E*
144 L11 **Kyzylkol', Ozero** ◎ C Kazakhstan
122 K14 **Kyzyl Kum** *var.* Kizil Kum, Qizil Qum, *Uzb.* Qizilqum. *desert* Kazakhstan/Uzbekistan
Kyzyl-Kyya *see* Kyzyl-Kiya
145 N15 **Kyzylorda** *var.* Kzyl-Orda, Qizil Orda, Qyzylorda; *prev.* Kzylorda, Perovsk. Kyzylorda, S Kazakhstan *44°54′N 65°31′E*
144 L14 **Kyzylorda** *off.* Kyzylordinskaya Oblast', *Kaz.* Qyzylorda Oblysy. ◈ *province* S Kazakhstan
Kyzylordinskaya Oblast' *see* Kyzylorda
Kyzylrabat *see* Qizilravote
Kyzylrabot *see* Qizilrabot
Kyzylsu *see* Kyzyl-Suu
147 X7 **Kyzyl-Suu** *prev.* Pokrovka. Issyk-Kul'skaya Oblast', NE Kyrgyzstan *42°20′N 77°55′E*
147 S12 **Kyzyl-Suu** *var.* Kyzylsu. ≈ Kyrgyzstan/Tajikistan
147 X8 **Kyzyl-Tuu** Issyk-Kul'skaya Oblast', E Kyrgyzstan *42°06′N 76°54′E*
145 Q12 **Kyzylzhar** *Kaz.* Qyzylzhar. Karaganda, C Kazakhstan *48°22′N 70°00′E*
Kzyl-Orda *see* Kyzylorda
Kzylorda *see* Kyzylorda
Kzyltu *see* Kishkenekol'

L

109 X2 **Laa an der Thaya** Niederösterreich, NE Austria *48°44′N 16°23′E*
63 K15 **La Adela** La Pampa, SE Argentina *38°57′S 64°02′W*
Laagen *see* Numedalslågen
109 S5 **Laakirchen** Oberösterreich, N Austria *47°59′N 13°49′E*
Laaland *see* Lolland
104 I11 **La Albuera** Extremadura, W Spain *38°43′N 06°49′W*
105 O7 **La Alcarria** *physical region* C Spain
104 K14 **La Algaba** Andalucía, S Spain *37°27′N 06°01′W*
105 P9 **La Almarcha** Castilla-La Mancha, C Spain *39°41′N 02°23′W*
105 R6 **La Almunia de Doña Godina** Aragón, NE Spain *41°28′N 01°23′W*
41 N5 **La Amistad, Presa** ⊠ NW Mexico
118 F4 **Läänemaa** *var.* Lääne Maakond. ◈ *province* NW Estonia
Lääne Maakond *see* Läänemaa
118 I3 **Lääne-Virumaa** *off.* Lääne-Viru Maakond. ◈ *province* NE Estonia
Lääne-Viru Maakond *see* Lääne-Virumaa
62 J9 **La Antigua, Salina** *salt lake* W Argentina
99 E17 **Laarne** Oost-Vlaanderen, NW Belgium *51°03′N 03°50′E*
80 O13 **Laas Caanood** Sool, N Somalia *08°33′N 47°44′E*
41 O9 **La Ascensión** Nuevo León, NE Mexico *24°15′N 99°53′W*
80 N12 **Laas Dhaareed** Togdheer, N Somalia *10°12′N 46°09′E*
55 O4 **La Asunción** Nueva Esparta, NE Venezuela *11°06′N 63°53′W*
Laatokka *see* Ladozhskoye, Ozero
100 I13 **Laatzen** Niedersachsen, NW Germany *52°19′N 09°46′E*
38 E9 **La'au Point** *var.* Laau Point. *headland* Moloka'i, Hawai'i, USA *21°06′N 157°18′W*
Laau Point *see* La'au Point
42 D6 **La Aurora** ✈ (Ciudad de Guatemala) Guatemala, C Guatemala *14°33′N 90°30′W*
74 C9 **Laâyoune** *var.* Aaiún. ● (Western Sahara) NW Western Sahara *27°10′N 13°11′W*
126 L14 **Laba** ≈ SW Russian Federation
40 M6 **La Babia** Coahuila, NE Mexico *28°39′N 102°00′W*
15 R7 **La Baie** Québec, SE Canada *48°20′N 70°54′W*
171 P16 **Labala** Pulau Lomblen, S Indonesia *08°30′S 123°27′E*
62 K8 **La Banda** Santiago del Estero, N Argentina *27°44′S 64°14′W*
La Banda Oriental *see* Uruguay
104 K4 **La Bañeza** Castilla y León, N Spain *42°18′N 05°54′W*
167 T11 **Labăng** *prev.* Phumĭ Labăng. Rôtânôkiri, NE Cambodia *13°51′N 107°01′E*
40 M13 **La Barca** Jalisco, SW Mexico *20°20′N 102°33′W*
40 K14 **La Barra de Navidad** Jalisco, C Mexico *19°12′N 104°38′W*
187 Y13 **Labasa** *prev.* Lambasa. Vanua Levu, N Fiji *16°25′S 179°24′E*
102 H8 **la Baule-Escoublac** Loire-Atlantique, NW France *47°17′N 02°24′W*
76 I13 **Labé** NW Guinea *11°19′N 12°17′W*
Labe *see* Elbe
15 N11 **Labelle** Québec, SE Canada *46°15′N 74°43′W*
23 X14 **La Belle** Florida, SE USA *26°45′N 81°26′W*
10 H7 **Laberge, Lake** ◎ Yukon Territory, W Canada
Labes *see* Łobez
Labiau *see* Polessk
112 A10 **Labin** *It.* Albona. Istra, NW Croatia *45°05′N 14°10′E*
126 L14 **Labinsk** Krasnodarskiy Kray, SW Russian Federation *44°39′N 40°43′E*
105 X5 **La Bisbal d'Empordà** Cataluña, NE Spain *41°58′N 03°02′E*
119 P16 **Labkovichy** *Rus.* Lobkovichi. Mahilyowskaya Voblasts', E Belarus *53°50′N 31°45′E*
15 S4 **La Blache, Lac de** ◎ Québec, SE Canada
171 P4 **Labo** Luzon, N Philippines *14°10′N 122°47′E*
Laboehanbadjo *see* Labuhanbajo
Laborca *see* Laborec
111 N18 **Laborec** *Hung.* Laborca. ≈ E Slovakia
108 D11 **La Borgne** ≈ S Switzerland
45 T12 **Laborie** SW Saint Lucia *13°45′N 61°00′W*
102 J14 **Labouheyre** Landes, SW France *44°12′N 00°55′W*
62 L12 **Laboulaye** Córdoba, C Argentina *34°05′S 63°20′W*
13 Q7 **Labrador** *cultural region* Newfoundland and Labrador, SW Canada
64 I6 **Labrador Basin** *var.* Labrador Sea Basin. *undersea feature* Labrador Sea *53°00′N 48°00′W*
13 N9 **Labrador City** Newfoundland and Labrador, E Canada *52°56′N 66°52′W*
13 Q5 **Labrador Sea** *sea* NW Atlantic Ocean
Labrador Sea Basin *see* Labrador Basin
Labrang *see* Xiahe
54 G9 **Labranzagrande** Boyacá, C Colombia *05°34′N 72°34′W*
59 D14 **Lábrea** Amazonas, N Brazil *07°20′S 64°46′W*
45 U15 **La Brea** Trinidad, Trinidad and Tobago *10°14′N 61°37′W*
15 S6 **Labrieville** Québec, SE Canada *49°15′N 69°31′W*
102 K14 **Labrit** Landes, SW France *44°03′N 00°29′W*
108 C9 **La Broye** ≈ SW Switzerland
103 N15 **Labruguière** Tarn, S France *43°32′N 02°15′E*
168 M11 **Labu** Pulau Singkep, W Indonesia *0°34′S 104°24′E*
169 T7 **Labuan** *var.* Victoria. Labuan, East Malaysia *05°20′N 115°14′E*
169 T7 **Labuan** ◈ *federal territory* East Malaysia
Labuan *see* Labuan, Pulau
169 T7 **Labuan, Pulau** *var.* Labuan. *island* East Malaysia
Labudalin *see* Ergun
171 N16 **Labuhanbajo** *prev.* Laboehanbadjo. Flores, S Indonesia *08°33′S 119°55′E*
168 J9 **Labuhanbilik** Sumatera, N Indonesia *02°30′N 100°10′E*
168 G8 **Labuhanhaji** Sumatera, W Indonesia *03°31′N 97°00′E*
Labuk *see* Labuk, Sungai
Labuk Bay *see* Labuk, Teluk
169 V7 **Labuk, Sungai** *var.* Labuk. ≈ East Malaysia
169 W6 **Labuk, Teluk** *var.* Labuk Bay, Telukan Labuk. *bay* S Sulu Sea
Labuk, Telukan *see* Labuk, Teluk
166 K9 **Labutta** Ayeyarwady, SW Myanmar (Burma) *16°08′N 94°45′E*
122 I8 **Labytnangi** Yamalo-Nenetskiy Avtonomnyy Okrug, N Russian Federation *66°39′N 66°26′E*
113 K19 **Laç** *var.* Laci. Lezhë, C Albania *41°37′N 19°37′E*
78 F10 **Lac** *off.* Préfecture du Lac. ◈ *prefecture* W Chad
57 K19 **Lacajahuira, Rio** ≈ W Bolivia
La Calamine *see* Kelmis
62 G11 **La Calera** Valparaíso, C Chile *32°47′S 71°16′W*
13 P11 **Lac-Allard** Québec, E Canada *50°37′N 63°26′W*
104 L13 **La Campana** Andalucía, S Spain *37°35′N 05°24′W*
102 J12 **Lacanau** Gironde, SW France *44°59′N 01°04′W*
42 C2 **Lacandón, Sierra del** ▲▲ Guatemala/Mexico
La Cañiza *see* A Cañiza
41 W16 **Lacantún, Río** ≈ SE Mexico
103 Q3 **la Capelle** Aisne, N France *49°58′N 03°55′E*
112 K10 **Laćarak** Vojvodina, NW Serbia *45°00′N 19°34′E*
62 L11 **La Carlota** Córdoba, C Argentina *33°30′S 63°15′W*
104 L13 **La Carlota** Andalucía, S Spain *37°40′N 04°56′W*
105 N12 **La Carolina** Andalucía, S Spain *38°15′N 03°37′W*
103 O15 **Lacaune** Tarn, S France *43°42′N 02°42′E*
15 P7 **Lac-Bouchette** Québec, SE Canada *48°14′N 72°11′W*
Laccadive Islands/Laccadive Minicoy and Amindivi Islands, the *see* Lakshadweep
11 Y16 **Lac du Bonnet** Manitoba, S Canada *50°13′N 96°04′W*
30 L4 **Lac du Flambeau** Wisconsin, N USA *45°58′N 89°51′W*
15 P8 **Lac-Édouard** Québec, SE Canada *47°39′N 72°16′W*
42 I4 **La Ceiba** Atlántida, N Honduras *15°45′N 86°29′W*
54 E9 **La Ceja** Antioquia, W Colombia *06°02′N 75°30′W*
182 J11 **Lacepede Bay** *bay* South Australia
32 G9 **Lacey** Washington, NW USA *47°01′N 122°49′W*
103 P12 **la Chaise-Dieu** Haute-Loire, C France *45°19′N 03°41′E*
114 G13 **Lachanás** Kentrikí Makedonía, N Greece *40°57′N 23°15′E*
124 L11 **Lacha, Ozero** ◎ NW Russian Federation
103 O8 **la Charité-sur-Loire** Nièvre, C France *47°10′N 02°59′E*
103 N9 **la Châtre** Indre, C France *46°35′N 01°59′E*
108 C8 **La Chaux-de-Fonds** Neuchâtel, W Switzerland *47°07′N 06°51′E*
Lach Dera *see* Dheere Laaq
108 G8 **Lachen** Schwyz, C Switzerland *47°12′N 08°51′E*
183 Q8 **Lachlan River** ≈ New South Wales, SE Australia
43 T15 **La Chorrera** Panamá, C Panama *08°51′N 79°46′W*
15 V7 **Lac-Humqui** Québec, SE Canada *48°21′N 67°32′W*
15 N12 **Lachute** Québec, SE Canada *45°39′N 74°21′W*
Lachyn *see* Laçın
Laci *see* Laç
137 W13 **Laçın** *Rus.* Lachyn. SW Azerbaijan *39°36′N 46°34′E*
103 S16 **la Ciotat** *anc.* Citharista. Bouches-du-Rhône, SE France *43°10′N 05°36′E*
18 D10 **Lackawanna** New York, NE USA *42°49′N 78°49′W*
11 Q13 **Lac La Biche** Alberta, SW Canada *54°46′N 111°59′W*
Lac la Martre *see* Wha Ti
15 R12 **Lac-Mégantic** *var.* Mégantic. Québec, SE Canada *45°35′N 70°53′W*
Lacobriga *see* Lagos
40 G5 **La Colorada** Sonora, NW Mexico *28°49′N 110°32′W*
11 Q15 **Lacombe** Alberta, SW Canada *52°30′N 113°42′W*
30 L12 **Lacon** Illinois, N USA *41°01′N 89°24′W*
43 P16 **La Concepción** *var.* Concepción. Chiriquí, W Panama *08°31′N 82°39′W*
54 H5 **La Concepción** Zulia, NW Venezuela *10°48′N 71°46′W*
107 C19 **Laconi** Sardegna, Italy, C Mediterranean Sea *39°52′N 09°02′E*
19 O9 **Laconia** New Hampshire, NE USA *43°32′N 71°29′W*
61 H19 **La Coronilla** Rocha, E Uruguay *33°44′S 53°31′W*
La Coruña *see* A Coruña
103 O11 **la Courtine** Creuse, C France *45°42′N 02°18′E*
Lac, Préfecture du *see* Lac
102 J16 **Lacq** Pyrénées-Atlantiques, SW France *43°25′N 00°37′W*
15 P9 **La Croche** Québec, SE Canada *47°38′N 72°42′W*
29 X3 **la Croix, Lac** ◎ Canada/USA
26 K5 **La Crosse** Kansas, C USA *38°32′N 99°19′W*
21 V7 **La Crosse** Virginia, NE USA *36°41′N 78°03′W*
32 L9 **La Crosse** Washington, NW USA *46°48′N 117°51′W*
30 J7 **La Crosse** Wisconsin, N USA *43°46′N 91°12′W*
54 C13 **La Cruz** Nariño, SW Colombia *01°33′N 76°58′W*
42 K12 **La Cruz** Guanacaste, NW Costa Rica *11°05′N 85°39′W*
40 I10 **La Cruz** Sinaloa, W Mexico *23°53′N 106°53′W*
61 F19 **La Cruz** Florida, S Uruguay *33°54′S 56°11′W*
42 M9 **La Cruz de Río Grande** Región Autónoma Atlántico Sur, E Nicaragua *13°04′N 84°12′W*
54 J4 **La Cruz de Taratara** Falcón, N Venezuela *11°03′N 69°44′W*
15 Q10 **Lac-St-Charles** Québec, SE Canada *46°56′N 71°24′W*
40 M6 **La Cuesta** Coahuila, NE Mexico *28°45′N 102°26′W*
57 A17 **La Cumbra, Volcán** ⛬ Galapagos Islands, Ecuador, E Pacific Ocean *0°21′S 91°30′W*
152 J5 **Ladākh Range** ▲▲ NE India
26 I5 **Ladder Creek** ≈ Kansas, C USA
45 X10 **la Désirade** *atoll* E Guadeloupe
Lādhiqīyah, Muḩāfaẓat al *see* Al Lādhiqīyah
Lådik *see* Lødingen
83 F25 **Ladismith** Western Cape, SW South Africa *33°30′S 12°15′E*
152 G11 **Lādnūn** Rājasthān, NW India *27°36′N 74°26′E*
Ladoga, Lake *see* Ladozhskoye, Ozero
115 E19 **Ládon** ≈ S Greece
54 E9 **La Dorada** Caldas, C Colombia *05°28′N 74°41′W*
124 H11 **Ladozhskoye, Ozero** *Eng.* Lake Ladoga, *Fin.* Laatokka. ◎ NW Russian Federation
37 R12 **Ladron Peak** ▲ New Mexico, SW USA *34°25′N 107°04′W*
124 J11 **Ladva-Vetka** Respublika Kareliya, NW Russian Federation *61°18′N 34°24′E*
183 Q15 **Lady Barron** Tasmania, SE Australia *40°12′S 148°12′E*
14 G9 **Lady Evelyn Lake** ◎ Ontario, S Canada
23 W11 **Lady Lake** Florida, SE USA *28°55′N 81°55′W*
10 L17 **Ladysmith** Vancouver Island, British Columbia, SW Canada *48°55′N 123°45′W*

◆ Country
● Country Capital
◇ Dependent Territory
○ Dependent Territory Capital
◈ Administrative Regions
✈ International Airport
▲ Mountain
▲▲ Mountain Range
⛬ Volcano
≈ River
◎ Lake
⊠ Reservoir

83 J22 **Ladysmith** KwaZulu/Natal, E South Africa 28°34′S 29°47′E
30 J5 **Ladysmith** Wisconsin, N USA 45°27′N 91°07′W
Ladyzhenka *see* Tilekey
186 E7 **Lae** Morobe, W Papua New Guinea 06°45′S 147°00′E
189 R6 **Lae Atoll** *atoll* Ralik Chain, W Marshall Islands
40 C3 **La Encantada, Cerro de** ▲ NW Mexico 31°03′N 115°25′W
55 N11 **La Esmeralda** Amazonas, S Venezuela 03°11′N 65°33′W
42 G7 **La Esperanza** Intibucá, SW Honduras 14°19′N 88°09′W
30 K8 **La Farge** Wisconsin, N USA 43°36′N 90°39′W
23 R5 **Lafayette** Alabama, S USA 32°54′N 85°24′W
37 T4 **Lafayette** Colorado, C USA 39°59′N 105°06′W
23 R2 **La Fayette** Georgia, SE USA 34°42′N 85°16′W
31 O13 **Lafayette** Indiana, N USA 40°25′N 86°52′W
22 I9 **Lafayette** Louisiana, S USA 30°13′N 92°01′W
20 K8 **Lafayette** Tennessee, S USA 36°31′N 86°01′W
19 N7 **Lafayette, Mount** ▲ New Hampshire, NE USA 44°09′N 71°37′W
La Fe *see* Santa Fé
103 P3 **la Fère** Aisne, N France 49°41′N 03°20′E
102 L6 **la Ferté-Bernard** Sarthe, NW France 48°13′N 00°40′E
102 K5 **la Ferté-Macé** Orne, N France 48°35′N 00°21′W
103 N7 **la Ferté-St-Aubin** Loiret, C France 47°42′N 01°57′E
103 P5 **la Ferté-sous-Jouarre** Seine-et-Marne, N France 48°57′N 03°08′E
77 V15 **Lafia** Nassarawa, C Nigeria 08°29′N 08°34′E
77 T15 **Lafiagi** Kwara, W Nigeria 08°52′N 05°25′E
11 T17 **Lafleche** Saskatchewan, S Canada 49°40′N 106°28′W
102 K7 **la Flèche** Sarthe, NW France 47°42′N 00°04′W
109 X7 **Lafnitz** *Hung.* Lapines. Austria/Hungary
187 P17 **La Foa** Province Sud, S New Caledonia 21°46′S 165°49′E
20 M8 **La Follette** Tennessee, S USA 36°22′N 84°07′W
15 N12 **Lafontaine** Québec, SE Canada 45°52′N 74°01′W
22 K10 **Lafourche, Bayou** Louisiana, S USA
62 K6 **La Fragua** Santiago del Estero, N Argentina 26°06′S 64°06′W
54 H7 **La Fría** Táchira, NW Venezuela 08°13′N 72°15′W
104 J7 **La Fuente de San Esteban** Castilla y León, N Spain 40°48′N 06°14′W
186 C7 **Lagaip** W Papua New Guinea
61 B15 **La Gallareta** Santa Fe, C Argentina 29°34′S 60°23′W
127 Q14 **Lagan'** *prev.* Kaspiyskiy. Respublika Kalmykiya, SW Russian Federation 45°25′N 47°19′E
95 L20 **Lagan** Kronoberg, S Sweden 56°55′N 14°01′E
95 K21 **Lågan** S Sweden
92 L2 **Lagarfljót** *var.* Lögurinn. E Iceland
37 R7 **La Garita Mountains** ▲▲ Colorado, C USA
171 O2 **Lagawe** Luzon, N Philippines 16°46′N 121°06′E
78 F13 **Lagdo** Nord, N Cameroon 09°12′N 13°43′E
78 F13 **Lagdo, Lac de** N Cameroon
100 H13 **Lage** Nordrhein-Westfalen, W Germany 52°00′N 08°48′E
94 H12 **Lågen** S Norway
61 J14 **Lages** Santa Catarina, S Brazil 27°45′S 50°16′W
Lágesvuotna *see* Laksefjorden
149 R4 **Laghmān** ◆ *province* E Afghanistan
74 J6 **Laghouat** N Algeria 33°49′N 02°59′E
105 Q10 **La Gineta** Castilla-La Mancha, C Spain 39°08′N 02°00′W
115 E21 **Lagkáda** *var.* Langada. Pelopónnisos, S Greece 36°49′N 22°19′E
114 G13 **Lagkadás** *var.* Langades, Langadhás. Kentrikí Makedonía, N Greece 40°45′N 23°04′E
115 E20 **Lagkádia** *var.* Langádhia, *cont.* Langadia. Pelopónnisos, S Greece 37°40′N 22°01′E
54 F6 **La Gloria** Cesar, N Colombia 08°37′N 73°51′W
41 O7 **La Gloria** Nuevo León, NE Mexico
92 N3 **Lågneset** *headland* W Svalbard 77°46′N 13°44′E
104 G14 **Lagoa** Faro, S Portugal 37°07′N 08°27′W
La Goagira *see* La Guajira
Lago Agrio *see* Nueva Loja
61 I14 **Lagoa Vermelha** Rio Grande do Sul, S Brazil 28°13′S 51°32′W
137 V10 **Lagodekhi** SE Georgia 41°49′N 46°15′E
42 C7 **La Gomera** Escuintla, S Guatemala 14°05′N 91°03′W
Lagone *see* Logone
107 M19 **Lagonegro** Basilicata, S Italy 40°06′N 15°42′E
63 G16 **Lago Ranco** Los Ríos, S Chile 40°21′S 72°29′W
77 S16 **Lagos** Lagos, SW Nigeria 06°24′N 03°17′E
104 F14 **Lagos** *anc.* Lacobriga. Faro, S Portugal 37°05′N 08°40′W
77 S16 **Lagos** ◆ *state* SW Nigeria
40 M12 **Lagos de Moreno** Jalisco, SW Mexico 21°21′N 101°55′W
Lagosta *see* Lastovo
74 A12 **Lagouira** SW Western Sahara 20°55′N 17°05′W
92 O1 **Lågøya** *island* N Svalbard
32 L11 **La Grande** Oregon, NW USA 45°21′N 118°05′W
103 Q14 **la Grande-Combe** Gard, S France 44°13′N 04°01′E
12 K9 **La Grande Rivière** *var.* Fort George. Québec, SE Canada
23 R4 **La Grange** Georgia, SE USA 33°02′N 85°02′W
31 P11 **Lagrange** Indiana, N USA 41°38′N 85°25′W
20 L5 **La Grange** Kentucky, S USA 38°24′N 85°23′W
27 V2 **La Grange** Missouri, C USA 40°00′N 91°31′W
21 V10 **La Grange** North Carolina, SE USA 35°18′N 77°47′W
25 U11 **La Grange** Texas, SW USA 29°55′N 96°54′W
105 N7 **La Granja** Castilla y León, N Spain 40°53′N 04°01′W
55 Q9 **La Gran Sabana** *grassland* E Venezuela
54 H7 **La Grita** Táchira, NW Venezuela 08°09′N 71°58′W
La Grulla *see* Grulla
15 R11 **La Guadeloupe** Québec, SE Canada 45°57′N 70°56′W
65 L6 **La Guaira** Distrito Federal, N Venezuela 10°35′N 66°52′W
54 G4 **La Guajira** *off.* Departamento de La Guajira, *var.* Guajira, La Goagira. ◆ *province* NE Colombia
188 I4 **Lagua Lichan, Punta** *headland* Saipan, S Northern Mariana Islands
105 P4 **Laguardia** *Basq.* Biasteri. País Vasco, N Spain 42°32′N 02°31′W
18 K14 **La Guardia** ✈ (New York) Long Island, New York, NE USA 40°44′N 73°51′W
La Guardia/Laguardia *see* A Guarda
La Gudiña *see* A Gudiña
103 O9 **la Guerche-sur-l'Aubois** Cher, C France 46°55′N 03°00′E
103 O13 **Laguiole** Aveyron, S France 44°42′N 02°51′E
83 F26 **L'Agulhas** *var.* Agulhas. Western Cape, SW South Africa 34°49′S 20°01′E
61 K14 **Laguna** Santa Catarina, S Brazil 28°29′S 48°45′W
37 Q11 **Laguna** New Mexico, SW USA 35°03′N 107°30′W
35 T16 **Laguna Beach** California, W USA 33°32′N 117°46′W
35 Y17 **Laguna Dam** *dam* Arizona/California, W USA
40 L7 **Laguna El Rey** Coahuila, N Mexico
35 V17 **Laguna Mountains** ▲▲ California, W USA
61 B17 **Laguna Paiva** Santa Fe, C Argentina 31°21′S 60°40′W
62 H3 **Lagunas** Tarapacá, N Chile 21°01′S 69°36′W
56 E9 **Lagunas** Loreto, N Peru 05°15′S 75°24′W
57 M20 **Lagunillas** Santa Cruz, SE Bolivia 19°38′S 63°39′W
54 H6 **Lagunillas** Mérida, NW Venezuela 08°31′N 71°24′W
44 C4 **La Habana** *var.* Havana. ● (Cuba) Ciudad de La Habana, W Cuba 23°07′N 82°25′W
169 W7 **Lahad Datu** Sabah, East Malaysia 05°01′N 118°20′E
169 W7 **Lahad Datu, Teluk** *var.* Telukan Lahad Datu, Teluk Darvel, Teluk Datu; *prev.* Darvel Bay. *bay* Sabah, East Malaysia, C Pacific Ocean
Lahad Datu, Telukan *see* Lahad Datu, Teluk
38 F10 **Lahaina** Maui, Hawaii, USA, C Pacific Ocean 20°52′N 156°40′W
168 L14 **Lahat** Sumatera, W Indonesia 03°46′S 103°32′E
La Haye *see* 's-Gravenhage
Lahej *see* Laḥij
62 G9 **La Higuera** Coquimbo, N Chile 29°33′S 71°15′W
141 S13 **Lahī, Ḥisā' al** *spring/well* NE Yemen 17°28′N 50°05′E
141 O16 **Laḥij** *var.* Laḥj, *Eng.* Lahej. SW Yemen 13°04′N 44°55′E
142 M3 **Lāhījān** Gīlān, NW Iran 37°12′N 50°00′E
119 I19 **Lahishyn** *Pol.* Lohiszyn, *Rus.* Logishin. Brestskaya Voblasts', SW Belarus 52°20′N 25°59′E
Laḥj *see* Laḥij
101 F18 **Lahn** W Germany
Lähn *see* Wleń
95 J21 **Laholm** Halland, S Sweden 56°30′N 13°05′E
95 J21 **Laholmsbukten** *bay* S Sweden
35 R6 **Lahontan Reservoir** Nevada, W USA
149 W8 **Lahore** Punjab, NE Pakistan 31°36′N 74°18′E
149 W8 **Lahore** ✈ Punjab, E Pakistan 31°34′N 74°22′E
55 Q6 **La Horqueta** Delta Amacuro, NE Venezuela 09°13′N 62°02′W
119 K15 **Lahoysk** *Rus.* Logoysk. Minskaya Voblasts', C Belarus 54°12′N 27°53′E
101 F22 **Lahr** Baden-Württemberg, S Germany 48°21′N 07°52′E
93 M19 **Lahti** *Swe.* Lahtis. Etelä-Suomi, S Finland 61°N 25°40′E
Lahtis *see* Lahti
40 M14 **La Huacana** Michoacán, SW Mexico 18°56′N 101°52′W
40 K14 **La Huerta** Jalisco, SW Mexico 19°29′N 104°40′W
78 H12 **Laï** *prev.* Behagle, De Behagle. Tandjilé, S Chad 09°22′N 16°14′E
Laibach *see* Ljubljana
167 Q5 **Lai Châu** Lai Châu, N Vietnam 22°04′N 103°10′E
Laichow Bay *see* Laizhou Wan
38 D9 **Lā'ie** *var.* Laie. O'ahu, Hawaii, USA, C Pacific Ocean 21°39′N 157°55′W
Laie *see* Lā'ie
102 L5 **l'Aigle** Orne, N France 48°46′N 00°37′E
103 Q7 **Laignes** Côte d'Or, C France 47°51′N 04°24′E
93 K17 **Laihia** Länsi-Suomi, W Finland 62°58′N 22°00′E
Laila *see* Laylā
83 F25 **Laingsburg** Western Cape, SW South Africa 33°12′S 20°51′E
109 U2 **Lainsitz** *Cz.* Lužnice. Austria/Czech Republic
96 I7 **Lairg** N Scotland, United Kingdom 58°02′N 04°23′W
81 I17 **Laisamis** Eastern, N Kenya 01°35′N 37°49′E
Laisberg *see* Leisi
127 R4 **Laishevo** Respublika Tatarstan, W Russian Federation 55°26′N 49°27′E
Laisholm *see* Jõgeva
92 H13 **Laisvall** Norrbotten, N Sweden 66°07′N 17°10′E
93 K19 **Laitila** Länsi-Suomi, SW Finland 60°52′N 21°40′E
161 P5 **Laiwu** Shandong, E China 36°14′N 117°40′E
161 R4 **Laixi** *var.* Shuiji. Shandong, E China 36°50′N 120°40′E
161 R4 **Laiyang** Shandong, E China 36°58′N 120°40′E
161 O3 **Laiyuan** Hebei, E China 39°19′N 114°44′E
161 R4 **Laizhou** *var.* Ye Xian. Shandong, E China 37°12′N 120°01′E
161 Q4 **Laizhou Wan** *var.* Laichow Bay. *bay* E China
37 S8 **La Jara** Colorado, C USA 37°16′N 105°57′W
61 I15 **Lajeado** Rio Grande do Sul, S Brazil 29°28′S 52°00′W
112 L12 **Lajkovac** Serbia, C Serbia 44°22′N 20°12′E
111 K23 **Lajosmizse** Bács-Kiskun, C Hungary 47°02′N 19°31′E
Lajta *see* Leitha
40 I6 **La Junta** Chihuahua, N Mexico 28°30′N 107°20′W
37 V7 **La Junta** Colorado, C USA 37°59′N 103°34′W
92 J13 **Lakaträsk** Norrbotten, N Sweden 66°16′N 21°10′E
Lak Dera *see* Dheere Laaq
Lakeamu *see* Lakekamu
29 P12 **Lake Andes** South Dakota, N USA 43°08′N 98°33′W
22 H9 **Lake Arthur** Louisiana, S USA 30°04′N 92°40′W
187 Z15 **Lakeba** *prev.* Lakemba. *island* Lau Group, E Fiji
187 Z14 **Lakeba Passage** *channel* E Fiji
29 S10 **Lake Benton** Minnesota, N USA 44°15′N 96°17′W
23 V9 **Lake Butler** Florida, SE USA 30°01′N 82°20′W
183 P8 **Lake Cargelligo** New South Wales, SE Australia 33°21′S 146°25′E
22 G9 **Lake Charles** Louisiana, S USA 30°14′N 93°13′W
27 X9 **Lake City** Arkansas, C USA 35°50′N 90°28′W
37 Q7 **Lake City** Colorado, C USA 38°01′N 107°18′W
23 V9 **Lake City** Florida, SE USA 30°12′N 82°39′W
29 U13 **Lake City** Iowa, C USA 42°16′N 94°43′W
31 P7 **Lake City** Michigan, N USA 44°22′N 85°12′W
29 W9 **Lake City** Minnesota, N USA 44°27′N 92°16′W
21 T13 **Lake City** South Carolina, SE USA 33°52′N 79°45′W
29 Q7 **Lake City** South Dakota, N USA 45°42′N 97°22′W
20 M8 **Lake City** Tennessee, S USA 36°13′N 84°09′W
10 L17 **Lake Cowichan** Vancouver Island, British Columbia, SW Canada 48°50′N 124°04′W
29 U10 **Lake Crystal** Minnesota, N USA 44°07′N 94°13′W
25 T6 **Lake Dallas** Texas, SW USA 33°06′N 97°01′W
97 K15 **Lake District** *physical region* NW England, United Kingdom
18 D10 **Lake Erie Beach** New York, NE USA 42°37′N 79°04′W
29 T11 **Lakefield** Minnesota, N USA 43°40′N 95°10′W
25 V6 **Lake Fork Reservoir** Texas, SW USA
30 M9 **Lake Geneva** Wisconsin, N USA 42°36′N 88°25′W
18 L9 **Lake George** New York, NE USA 43°25′N 73°45′W
Lake Harbour *see* Kimmirut
36 I12 **Lake Havasu City** Arizona, SW USA 34°26′N 114°20′W
25 W12 **Lake Jackson** Texas, SW USA 29°01′N 95°25′W
186 D8 **Lakekamu** *var.* Lakeamu. S Papua New Guinea
180 K13 **Lake King** Western Australia 33°09′S 119°46′E
23 V12 **Lakeland** Florida, SE USA 28°03′N 81°57′W
23 U7 **Lakeland** Georgia, SE USA 31°02′N 83°04′W
181 W4 **Lakeland Downs** Queensland, NE Australia 15°54′S 144°54′E
11 P16 **Lake Louise** Alberta, SW Canada 51°26′N 116°10′W
Lakemba *see* Lakeba
29 V11 **Lake Mills** Iowa, C USA 43°25′N 93°31′W
39 Q10 **Lake Minchumina** Alaska, USA 63°55′N 152°25′W
Lakemti *see* Nek'emtē
186 A7 **Lake Murray** Western, SW Papua New Guinea 06°35′S 141°28′E
31 R9 **Lake Orion** Michigan, N USA 42°46′N 83°14′W
190 B16 **Lakepa** NE Niue 18°59′S 169°48′E
29 T11 **Lake Park** Iowa, C USA 43°27′N 95°19′W
18 K7 **Lake Placid** New York, NE USA 44°16′N 73°57′W
18 K9 **Lake Pleasant** New York, NE USA 43°27′N 74°24′W
34 M6 **Lakeport** California, W USA 39°04′N 122°56′W
29 Q10 **Lake Preston** South Dakota, N USA 44°21′N 97°22′W
22 J5 **Lake Providence** Louisiana, S USA 32°48′N 91°10′W
185 E20 **Lake Pukaki** Canterbury, South Island, New Zealand 44°12′S 170°10′E
183 Q12 **Lakes Entrance** Victoria, SE Australia 37°52′S 147°58′E
37 N12 **Lakeside** Arizona, SW USA 34°09′N 109°58′W
35 V17 **Lakeside** California, W USA 32°50′N 116°55′W
23 S9 **Lakeside** Florida, SE USA 30°22′N 84°18′W
28 K13 **Lakeside** Nebraska, C USA 42°01′N 102°27′W
32 E13 **Lakeside** Oregon, NW USA 43°34′N 124°10′W
21 W6 **Lakeside** Virginia, NE USA 37°36′N 77°28′W
Lakes State *see* El Buhayrat
Lake State *see* Michigan
185 F20 **Lake Tekapo** Canterbury, South Island, New Zealand 44°01′S 170°29′E
21 O10 **Lake Toxaway** North Carolina, SE USA 35°06′N 82°57′W
29 T13 **Lake View** Iowa, C USA 42°18′N 95°04′W
32 I16 **Lakeview** Oregon, NW USA 42°13′N 120°21′W
25 O3 **Lakeview** Texas, SW USA 34°38′N 100°36′W
27 W14 **Lake Village** Arkansas, C USA 33°20′N 91°19′W
23 W12 **Lake Wales** Florida, SE USA 27°54′N 81°35′W
37 T4 **Lakewood** Colorado, C USA 39°38′N 105°07′W
18 K15 **Lakewood** New Jersey, NE USA 40°04′N 74°11′W
18 C11 **Lakewood** New York, NE USA 42°03′N 79°19′W
31 T11 **Lakewood** Ohio, N USA 41°28′N 81°48′W
23 Y13 **Lakewood Park** Florida, SE USA 27°32′N 80°24′W
23 Z14 **Lake Worth** Florida, SE USA 26°37′N 80°03′W
124 H11 **Lakhdenpokh'ya** Respublika Kareliya, NW Russian Federation 61°25′N 30°05′E
152 L11 **Lakhīmpur** Uttar Pradesh, N India 27°57′N 80°47′E
154 J11 **Lakhnādon** Madhya Pradesh, C India 22°34′N 79°38′E
Lakhnau *see* Lucknow
154 A9 **Lakhpat** Gujarāt, W India 23°49′N 68°54′E
119 K19 **Lakhva** Brestskaya Voblasts', SW Belarus 52°13′N 27°06′E
26 I6 **Lakin** Kansas, C USA 37°57′N 101°16′W
149 S7 **Lakki** *var.* Lakki Marwat. Khyber Pakhtunkhwa, NW Pakistan 32°35′N 70°58′E
Lakki Marwat *see* Lakki
115 F21 **Lakonía** *historical region* S Greece
115 F22 **Lakonikós Kólpos** *gulf* S Greece
76 M17 **Lakota** S Ivory Coast 05°50′N 05°40′W
29 U11 **Lakota** Iowa, C USA 43°22′N 94°04′W
29 P3 **Lakota** North Dakota, N USA 48°02′N 98°20′W
Lak Sao *see* Ban Lakxao
92 L8 **Laksefjorden** *Lapp.* Lágesvuotna. *fjord* N Norway
92 K8 **Lakselv** *Lapp.* Leavdnja. Finnmark, N Norway 70°02′N 24°57′E
155 B21 **Lakshadweep** *prev.* the Laccadive Minicoy and Amindivi Islands. ◆ *union territory* India, N Indian Ocean
155 C22 **Lakshadweep** *Eng.* Laccadive Islands. *island group* India, N Indian Ocean
153 S17 **Lakshmikāntapur** West Bengal, NE India 22°05′N 88°19′E
112 G11 **Laktaši** ◆ Republika Srpska, N Bosnia and Herzegovina
149 V7 **Lāla Mūsa** Punjab, NE Pakistan 32°41′N 74°01′E
la Laon *see* Laon
114 M11 **Lalapaşa** Edirne, NW Turkey 41°52′N 26°44′E
83 P14 **Lalaua** Nampula, N Mozambique 14°21′S 38°16′E
105 S9 **L'Alcora** *var.* Alcora. Valenciana, E Spain 40°05′N 00°14′W
105 S10 **L'Alcúdia** *var.* L'Alcudia. Valenciana, E Spain 39°10′N 00°30′W
42 E8 **La Libertad** La Libertad, SW El Salvador 13°28′N 89°20′W*
42 E3 **La Libertad** Petén, N Guatemala 16°49′N 90°08′W
42 H6 **La Libertad** Comayagua, SW Honduras 14°43′N 87°36′W
40 E4 **La Libertad** *var.* Puerto Libertad. Sonora, NW Mexico 29°52′N 112°39′W
42 K10 **La Libertad** Chontales, S Nicaragua 12°12′N 85°10′W
42 A9 **La Libertad** ◆ *department* SW El Salvador
56 B11 **La Libertad** *off.* Departamento de La Libertad. ◆ *department* W Peru
La Libertad, Departamento de *see* La Libertad
62 G11 **La Ligua** Valparaíso, C Chile 31°30′S 71°16′W
139 U5 **La'lī Khān** As Sulaymānīyah, E Iraq 34°58′N 45°36′E
104 H3 **Lalín** Galicia, NW Spain 42°40′N 08°06′W
102 L13 **Lalinde** Dordogne, SW France 44°52′N 00°42′E
104 K16 **La Línea** *var.* La Línea de la Concepción. Andalucía, S Spain 36°10′N 05°21′W
La Línea de la Concepción *see* La Línea
152 J14 **Lalitpur** Uttar Pradesh, N India 24°42′N 78°24′E
153 P11 **Lalitpur** Central, C Nepal 27°45′N 85°18′E
152 K10 **Lālkua** Uttarachal, N India 29°04′N 79°31′E
153 T12 **Lalmanirhat** Rājshāhi, N Bangladesh 25°51′N 89°34′E
11 R12 **La Loche** Saskatchewan, C Canada 56°31′N 109°27′W
102 M6 **la Loupe** Eure-et-Loir, C France 48°30′N 01°04′E
99 G20 **La Louvière** Hainaut, S Belgium 50°29′N 04°15′E
L'Altissima *see* Hochwilde
104 L14 **La Luisiana** Andalucía, S Spain 37°30′N 05°14′W
37 S14 **La Luz** New Mexico, SW USA 32°58′N 105°56′W
107 D16 **la Maddalena** Sardegna, Italy, C Mediterranean Sea 41°13′N 09°25′E
62 J7 **La Madrid** Tucumán, N Argentina 27°37′S 65°16′W
Lama-Kara *see* Kara
15 S8 **La Malbaie** Québec, SE Canada 47°39′N 70°11′W
Lamam *see* Xékong
105 P10 **La Mancha** *physical region* C Spain
la Manche *see* English Channel
187 R13 **Lamap** Malekula, C Vanuatu 16°26′S 167°47′E
37 W6 **Lamar** Colorado, C USA 38°40′N 102°37′W
27 S7 **Lamar** Missouri, C USA 37°30′N 94°18′W
21 S12 **Lamar** South Carolina, SE USA 34°10′N 80°03′W
107 C19 **La Marmora, Punta** ▲ Sardegna, Italy, C Mediterranean Sea 39°58′N 09°20′E
8 I9 **La Martre, Lac** Northwest Territories, NW Canada
56 D10 **Lamas** San Martín, N Peru 06°28′S 76°31′W
42 I5 **La Masica** Atlántida, NW Honduras 15°38′N 87°08′W
103 R12 **Lamastre** Ardèche, E France 45°00′N 04°32′E
La Matepec *see* Santa Ana, Volcán de
44 I7 **La Maya** Santiago de Cuba, E Cuba 20°11′N 75°40′W
109 S5 **Lambach** Oberösterreich, N Austria 48°06′N 13°52′E
168 I11 **Lambak** Pulau Pini, W Indonesia 0°08′N 98°36′E
102 H5 **Lamballe** Côtes d'Armor, NW France 48°28′N 02°31′W
79 D18 **Lambaréné** Moyen-Ogooué, W Gabon 0°41′S 10°13′E
Lambasa *see* Labasa
56 B11 **Lambayeque** Lambayeque, W Peru 06°42′S 79°55′W
56 A10 **Lambayeque** *off.* Departamento de Lambayeque. ◆ *department* NW Peru
Lambayeque, Departamento de *see* Lambayeque
97 G17 **Lambay Island** *Ir.* Reachrainn. *island* E Ireland
186 G6 **Lambert, Cape** *headland* New Britain, E Papua New Guinea 04°15′S 151°31′E
195 W6 **Lambert Glacier** *glacier* Antarctica
29 T10 **Lamberton** Minnesota, N USA 44°14′N 95°15′W
27 X4 **Lambert-Saint Louis** ✈ Missouri, C USA 38°43′N 90°19′W
31 R11 **Lambertville** Michigan, N USA 41°46′N 83°37′W
18 J15 **Lambertville** New Jersey, NE USA 40°20′N 74°55′W
171 N12 **Lambogo** Sulawesi, N Indonesia 0°57′S 120°23′E
106 D8 **Lambro** N Italy
33 W11 **Lame Deer** Montana, NW USA 45°37′N 106°37′W
104 H6 **Lamego** Viseu, N Portugal 41°05′N 07°49′W
187 Q14 **Lamen Bay** Épi, C Vanuatu 16°36′S 168°10′E
45 X6 **Lamentin** Basse Terre, N Guadeloupe 16°16′N 61°38′W
Lamentin *see* le Lamentin
182 K10 **Lameroo** South Australia 35°22′S 140°30′E
54 F10 **La Mesa** Cundinamarca, C Colombia 04°37′N 74°30′W
35 U17 **La Mesa** California, W USA 32°44′N 117°00′W
37 R16 **La Mesa** New Mexico, SW USA 32°03′N 106°41′W
25 N6 **Lamesa** Texas, SW USA 32°43′N 101°57′W
107 N21 **Lamezia Terme** Calabria, SE Italy 38°54′N 16°13′E
115 F17 **Lamía** Stereá Elláda, C Greece 38°54′N 22°27′E
171 O8 **Lamitan** Basilan Island, SW Philippines 06°40′N 122°07′E
187 Y14 **Lamiti** Gau, C Fiji 18°00′S 179°20′E
171 T11 **Lamlam** Papua, E Indonesia 0°03′S 130°46′E
188 B16 **Lamlam, Mount** ▲ SW Guam 13°20′N 144°40′E
109 Q6 **Lammer** E Austria
185 E23 **Lammerlaw Range** ▲▲ South Island, New Zealand
95 L20 **Lammhult** Kronoberg, S Sweden 57°09′N 14°35′E
93 L18 **Lammi** Etelä-Suomi, S Finland 61°06′N 25°00′E
189 U11 **Lamoil** *island* Chuuk, C Micronesia
35 W3 **Lamoille** Nevada, W USA 40°47′N 115°37′W
18 M7 **Lamoille River** Vermont, NE USA
30 J13 **La Moine River** Illinois, N USA
171 P4 **Lamon Bay** *bay* Luzon, N Philippines
29 V16 **Lamoni** Iowa, C USA 40°37′N 93°56′W
35 R13 **Lamont** California, W USA 35°15′N 118°54′W
27 N8 **Lamont** Oklahoma, C USA 36°41′N 97°33′W
54 E13 **La Montañita** *var.* Montañita. Caquetá, S Colombia 01°22′N 75°25′W
43 N8 **La Mosquitia** *var.* Miskito Coast, *Eng.* Mosquito Coast. *coastal region* E Nicaragua
102 I9 **la Mothe-Achard** Vendée, NW France 46°37′N 01°37′W
188 L15 **Lamotrek Atoll** *atoll* Caroline Islands, C Micronesia
29 P6 **La Moure** North Dakota, N USA 46°21′N 98°17′W
167 O8 **Lampang** *var.* Muang Lampang. Lampang, NW Thailand 18°16′N 99°30′E
167 R9 **Lam Pao Reservoir** E Thailand
25 S9 **Lampasas** Texas, SW USA 31°04′N 98°12′W
25 S9 **Lampasas River** Texas, SW USA
41 N7 **Lampazos** *var.* Lampazos de Naranjo. Nuevo León, NE Mexico 27°00′N 100°28′W
Lampazos de Naranjo *see* Lampazos
115 E19 **Lámpeia** Dytikí Elláda, S Greece 37°51′N 21°48′E
101 G19 **Lampertheim** Hessen, W Germany 49°36′N 08°28′E
97 I20 **Lampeter** SW Wales, United Kingdom 52°08′N 04°04′W
167 O7 **Lamphun** *var.* Lampun, Muang Lamphun. Lamphun, NW Thailand 18°36′N 99°02′E
11 X10 **Lamprey** Manitoba, C Canada 58°18′N 94°06′W
Lampun *see* Lamphun
168 M15 **Lampung** *off.* Propinsi Lampung. ◆ *province* SW Indonesia
Lampung, Propinsi *see* Lampung
126 K6 **Lamskoye** Lipetskaya Oblast', W Russian Federation 52°57′N 38°04′E
81 K20 **Lamu** Coast, SE Kenya 02°17′S 40°54′E
43 N14 **La Muerte, Cerro** ▲ C Costa Rica 09°33′N 83°47′W
103 S13 **la Mure** Isère, E France 44°54′N 05°48′E
37 S10 **Lamy** New Mexico, SW USA 35°27′N 105°52′W
119 J18 **Lan'** *Rus.* Lan'. C Belarus
38 E10 **Lāna'i** *var.* Lanai. *island* Hawai'i, USA, C Pacific Ocean
38 E10 **Lāna'i City** *var.* Lanai City. Lanai, Hawaii, USA, C Pacific Ocean 20°49′N 156°55′W
Lanai City *see* Lāna'i City
99 L18 **Lanaken** Limburg, NE Belgium 50°53′N 05°39′E
171 Q7 **Lanao, Lake** *var.* Lake Sultan Alonto. Mindanao, S Philippines
96 J12 **Lanark** S Scotland, United Kingdom 55°38′N 04°25′W
96 I13 **Lanark** *cultural region* C Scotland, United Kingdom
104 L9 **La Nava de Ricomalillo** Castilla-La Mancha, C Spain 39°40′N 04°59′W
166 M13 **Lanbi Kyun** *prev.* Sullivan Island. *island* Mergui Archipelago, S Myanmar (Burma)
Lancang Jiang *see* Mekong
97 K17 **Lancashire** *cultural region* N England, United Kingdom
15 N13 **Lancaster** Ontario, SE Canada 45°10′N 74°31′W
97 K16 **Lancaster** NW England, United Kingdom 54°03′N 02°48′W
35 T14 **Lancaster** California, W USA 34°42′N 118°08′W
20 M6 **Lancaster** Kentucky, S USA 37°35′N 84°34′W
27 U1 **Lancaster** Missouri, C USA 40°32′N 92°31′W
19 O7 **Lancaster** New Hampshire, NE USA 44°29′N 71°34′W
18 D10 **Lancaster** New York, NE USA 42°54′N 78°40′W
31 T14 **Lancaster** Ohio, N USA 39°42′N 82°36′W
18 H16 **Lancaster** Pennsylvania, NE USA 40°03′N 76°18′W
21 R11 **Lancaster** South Carolina, SE USA 34°43′N 80°47′W
25 U7 **Lancaster** Texas, SW USA 32°35′N 96°45′W
21 X5 **Lancaster** Virginia, NE USA 37°48′N 76°30′W
30 J9 **Lancaster** Wisconsin, N USA 42°52′N 90°43′W
197 N10 **Lancaster Sound** *sound* Nunavut, N Canada
Lan-chou/Lan-chow/Lanchow *see* Lanzhou
107 K14 **Lanciano** Abruzzo, C Italy 42°13′N 14°23′E
111 O16 **Łańcut** Podkarpackie, SE Poland 50°04′N 22°14′E
169 Q11 **Landak, Sungai** Borneo, N Indonesia
Landao *see* Lantau Island
Landau *see* Landau an der Isar
Landau *see* Landau in der Pfalz
101 N22 **Landau an der Isar** *var.* Landau. Bayern, SE Germany 48°40′N 12°41′E
101 F20 **Landau in der Pfalz** *var.* Landau. Rheinland-Pfalz, SW Germany 49°12′N 08°07′E
Land Burgenland *see* Burgenland
108 K8 **Landeck** Tirol, W Austria 47°09′N 10°35′E
99 J19 **Landen** Vlaams Brabant, C Belgium 50°45′N 05°05′E
33 U15 **Lander** Wyoming, C USA 42°49′N 108°43′W
102 F5 **Landerneau** Finistère, NW France 48°27′N 04°16′W
95 K20 **Landeryd** Halland, S Sweden 57°04′N 13°15′E
102 J15 **Landes** ◆ *department* SW France
Landeshut/Landeshut in Schlesien *see* Kamienna Góra
105 R9 **Landete** Castilla-La Mancha, C Spain 39°54′N 01°22′W
99 M18 **Landgraaf** Limburg, SE Netherlands 50°55′N 06°04′E
102 F5 **Landivisiau** Finistère, NW France 48°31′N 04°03′W
Land Kärten *see* Kärnten
Land of Enchantment *see* New Mexico
The Land of Opportunity *see* Arkansas
Land of Steady Habits *see* Connecticut
Land of the Midnight Sun *see* Alaska
108 I8 **Landquart** Graubünden, SE Switzerland 46°58′N 09°35′E
108 J9 **Landquart** Austria/Switzerland
21 P10 **Landrum** South Carolina, SE USA 35°10′N 82°11′W
Landsberg *see* Gorzów Wielkopolski, Lubuskie, Poland
Landsberg *see* Górowo Iławeckie, Warmińsko-Mazurskie, NE Poland
101 K23 **Landsberg am Lech** Bayern, S Germany 48°03′N 10°52′E
Landsberg an der Warthe *see* Gorzów Wielkopolski
97 G25 **Land's End** *headland* SW England, United Kingdom 50°02′N 05°41′W
101 M22 **Landshut** Bayern, SE Germany 48°32′N 12°09′E
Landskron *see* Lanškroun
95 J22 **Landskrona** Skåne, S Sweden 55°52′N 12°52′E
98 I10 **Landsmeer** Noord-Holland, C Netherlands 52°26′N 04°55′E
95 J19 **Landvetter** ✈ (Göteborg) Västra Götaland, S Sweden 57°39′N 12°22′E
Landwarów *see* Lentvaris
23 R5 **Lanett** Alabama, S USA 32°52′N 85°11′W
108 C8 **La Neuveville** *var.* Neuveville, *Ger.* Neuenstadt. Neuchâtel, W Switzerland 47°05′N 07°03′E
95 G21 **Langå** *var.* Langaa. Midtjylland, C Denmark 56°23′N 09°55′E
Langaa *see* Langå
158 G14 **La'nga Co** W China
Langada *see* Lagkáda
Langades/Langadhás *see* Lagkadás
Langádhia/ *see* Lagkádia
147 T14 **Langar** *Rus.* Lyangar. SE Tajikistan 37°04′N 72°39′E
146 M10 **Langar** *Rus.* Lyangar. Navoiy Viloyati, C Uzbekistan 40°27′N 65°54′E
142 M3 **Langarūd** Gīlān, NW Iran 37°10′N 50°09′E
11 V16 **Langbank** Saskatchewan, S Canada 50°01′N 102°16′W
29 P2 **Langdon** North Dakota, N USA 48°45′N 98°22′W
103 P12 **Langeac** Haute-Loire, C France 45°06′N 03°31′E
102 L8 **Langeais** Indre-et-Loire, C France 47°22′N 00°27′E
80 I8 **Langeb, Wadi** NE Sudan
Långed *see* Dals Långed
95 G25 **Langeland** *island* S Denmark
99 B18 **Langemark** West-Vlaanderen, W Belgium 50°55′N 02°55′E
101 G18 **Langen** Hessen, W Germany 49°58′N 08°40′E
101 J22 **Langenau** Baden-Württemberg, S Germany 48°30′N 10°08′E
11 V16 **Langenburg** Saskatchewan, S Canada 50°50′N 101°43′W
108 L8 **Längenfeld** Tirol, W Austria 47°04′N 10°59′E
101 E16 **Langenfeld** Nordrhein-Westfalen, W Germany 51°06′N 06°57′E
100 I12 **Langenhagen** Niedersachsen, N Germany 52°26′N 09°45′E
100 I12 **Langenhagen** ✈ (Hannover) Niedersachsen, NW Germany 52°28′N 09°40′E
109 W3 **Langenlois** Niederösterreich, NE Austria 48°29′N 15°42′E
108 E7 **Langenthal** Bern, NW Switzerland 47°13′N 07°48′E
109 W6 **Langenwang** Steiermark, E Austria 47°34′N 15°39′E
109 X3 **Langenzersdorf** Niederösterreich, E Austria 48°20′N 16°22′E
100 F9 **Langeoog** *island* NW Germany
95 H23 **Langeskov** Syddtjylland, C Denmark 55°22′N 10°36′E
95 G16 **Langesund** Telemark, S Norway 59°00′N 09°43′E
95 G17 **Langesundsfjorden** *fjord* S Norway
94 D10 **Langevågen** Møre og Romsdal, S Norway 62°26′N 06°15′E
161 P3 **Langfang** Hebei, E China 39°30′N 116°39′E
94 E9 **Langfjorden** *fjord* S Norway
29 Q8 **Langford** South Dakota, N USA 45°36′N 97°48′W
168 I10 **Langgapayung** Sumatera, W Indonesia 01°42′N 99°57′E
106 E9 **Langhirano** Emilia-Romagna, C Italy 44°37′N 10°16′E
97 K14 **Langholm** S Scotland, United Kingdom 55°14′N 03°11′W
92 I3 **Langjökull** *glacier* C Iceland
168 I6 **Langkawi, Pulau** *island* Peninsular Malaysia
166 M14 **Langkha Tuk, Khao** ▲ SW Thailand 09°19′N 98°39′E
14 L8 **Langlade** Québec, SE Canada 48°13′N 75°58′W
10 M17 **Langley** British Columbia, SW Canada 49°07′N 122°39′W
167 S7 **Lang Mô** Thanh Hoa, N Vietnam 19°36′N 105°30′E
Langnau *see* Langnau im Emmental
108 E8 **Langnau im Emmental** *var.* Langnau. Bern, W Switzerland 46°57′N 07°47′E
103 Q13 **Langogne** Lozère, S France 44°40′N 03°52′E
102 K13 **Langon** Gironde, SW France 44°33′N 00°14′W
La Ngounié *see* Ngounié
92 G10 **Langøya** *island* C Norway
158 G14 **Langqên Zangbo** China/India
Langreo *see* Llangréu
103 S7 **Langres** Haute-Marne, N France 47°53′N 05°20′E
103 R8 **Langres, Plateau de** *plateau* C France
168 H8 **Langsa** Sumatera, W Indonesia 04°30′N 97°53′E
93 H16 **Långsele** Västernorrland, C Sweden 63°11′N 17°05′E
162 L12 **Lang Shan** ▲▲ N China
95 M14 **Långshyttan** Dalarna, C Sweden 60°26′N 16°02′E
167 T5 **Lang Sơn** *var.* Langson. Lang Sơn, N Vietnam 21°50′N 106°45′E
Langson *see* Lang Sơn
167 N14 **Lang Suan** Chumphon, SW Thailand 09°55′N 99°07′E
93 J14 **Långträsk** Norrbotten, N Sweden 65°22′N 20°19′E
25 N11 **Langtry** Texas, SW USA 29°46′N 101°25′W
103 P16 **Languedoc** *cultural region* S France
103 P15 **Languedoc-Roussillon** ◆ *region* S France
27 X10 **L'Anguille River** Arkansas, C USA
93 I16 **Långviksmon** Västernorrland, N Sweden 63°39′N 18°45′E
101 K22 **Langweid** Bayern, S Germany 48°29′N 10°50′E
160 J8 **Langzhong** Sichuan, C China 31°46′N 105°55′E
Lan Hsü *see* Lan Yu
11 U15 **Lanigan** Saskatchewan, S Canada 51°50′N 105°01′W
116 K5 **Lanivtsi** Ternopil's'ka Oblast', W Ukraine 49°52′N 26°05′E
137 Y13 **Länkäran** *Rus.* Lenkoran'. S Azerbaijan 38°46′N 48°51′E
102 L16 **Lannemezan** Hautes-Pyrénées, S France 43°08′N 00°22′E
102 G5 **Lannion** Côtes d'Armor, NW France 48°44′N 03°27′W
14 M11 **L'Annonciation** Québec, SE Canada 46°22′N 74°51′W
105 V5 **L'Anoia** NE Spain
18 I15 **Lansdale** Pennsylvania, NE USA 40°14′N 75°13′W
14 L14 **Lansdowne** Ontario, SE Canada 44°25′N 76°00′W
152 K9 **Lansdowne** Uttarakhand, N India 29°50′N 78°42′E
30 M3 **L'Anse** Michigan, N USA 46°45′N 88°27′W
15 S7 **L'Anse-St-Jean** Québec, SE Canada 48°14′N 70°13′W
29 Y11 **Lansing** Iowa, C USA 43°22′N 91°11′W
27 R4 **Lansing** Kansas, C USA 39°15′N 94°54′W
31 Q9 **Lansing** *state capital* Michigan, N USA 42°44′N 84°33′W
93 K18 **Länsi-Suomi** ◆ *province* W Finland
92 J12 **Lansjärv** Norrbotten, N Sweden 66°39′N 22°10′E
111 G17 **Lanškroun** *Ger.* Landskron. Pardubický Kraj, E Czech Republic 49°55′N 16°38′E
167 N16 **Lanta, Ko** *island* S Thailand
161 O15 **Lantau Island** *Cant.* Tai Yue Shan, *Chin.* Landao. *island* Hong Kong, S China
Lantian *see* Lianyuan
Lan-ts'ang Chiang *see* Mekong

◆ Country
● Country Capital
◇ Dependent Territory
○ Dependent Territory Capital
◆ Administrative Regions
✈ International Airport
▲ Mountain
▲▲ Mountain Range
Volcano
River
Lake
Reservoir

Lantung, Gulf of *see* Liaodong Wan
171 O11 **Lanu** Sulawesi, N Indonesia 01°00′N 121°33′E
107 D19 **Lanusei** Sardegna, Italy, C Mediterranean Sea 39°55′N 09°31′E
102 H7 **Lanvaux, Landes de** *physical region* NW France
163 W8 **Lanxi** Heilongjiang, NE China 46°18′N 126°15′E
161 R10 **Lanxi** Zhejiang, SE China 29°12′N 119°27′E
La Nyanga *see* Nyanga
161 T15 **Lan Yu** *var.* Huoshao Tao, Hungt'ou, Lan Hsü, Lanyü, *Eng.* Orchid Island; *prev.* Kotosho, Koto Sho, Lan Yü. *island* SE Taiwan
Lanyü *see* Lan Yu
64 P11 **Lanzarote** *island* Islas Canarias, Spain, NE Atlantic Ocean
159 V10 **Lanzhou** *var.* Lan-chou, Lanchow, Lan-chow; *prev.* Kaolan. *province capital* Gansu, C China 36°01′N 103°52′E
106 B8 **Lanzo Torinese** Piemonte, NE Italy 45°18′N 07°26′E
171 O11 **Laoag** Luzon, N Philippines 18°11′N 120°34′E
171 Q5 **Laoang** Samar, C Philippines 12°29′N 125°01′E
167 R5 **Lao Cai** Lao Cai, N Vietnam 22°29′N 104°00′E
Laodicea/Laodicea ad Mare *see* Al Lādhiqīyah
Laoet *see* Laut, Pulau
163 T11 **Laoha He** ⚡ NE China
160 M8 **Laohekou** *var.* Guanghua. Hubei, C China 32°20′N 111°42′E
Laoi, An *see* Lee
97 E19 **Laois** *prev.* Leix, Queen's County. *cultural region* C Ireland
163 W12 **Lao Ling** ▲ N China
64 Q11 **La Oliva** *var.* Oliva. Fuerteventura, Islas Canarias, Spain, NE Atlantic Ocean 28°36′N 13°53′W
Lao, Loch *see* Belfast Lough
Laolong *see* Longchuan
Lao Mangnai *see* Mangnai
103 P3 **Laon** *var.* la Laon; *anc.* Laudunum. Aisne, N France 49°34′N 03°37′E
Lao People's Democratic Republic *see* Laos
54 M3 **La Orchila, Isla** *island* N Venezuela
64 O11 **La Orotava** Tenerife, Islas Canarias, Spain, NE Atlantic Ocean 28°23′N 16°32′W
57 E14 **La Oroya** Junín, C Peru 11°36′S 75°54′W
167 Q7 **Laos** *off.* Lao People's Democratic Republic. ◆ *republic* SE Asia
161 R5 **Laoshan Wan** *bay* E China
163 Y10 **Laoye Ling** ▲ NE China
60 J12 **Lapa** Paraná, S Brazil 25°46′S 49°44′W
103 P10 **Lapalisse** Allier, C France 46°13′N 03°39′E
54 F9 **La Palma** Cundinamarca, C Colombia 05°23′N 74°24′W
42 F7 **La Palma** Chalatenango, N El Salvador 14°19′N 89°10′W
43 W16 **La Palma** Darién, SE Panama 08°24′N 78°09′W
64 N11 **La Palma** *island* Islas Canarias, Spain, NE Atlantic Ocean
104 J14 **La Palma del Condado** Andalucía, S Spain 37°23′N 06°33′W
61 F18 **La Paloma** Durazno, C Uruguay 32°54′S 55°36′W
61 G20 **La Paloma** Rocha, E Uruguay 34°37′S 54°08′W
61 A21 **La Pampa** *off.* Provincia de La Pampa. ◆ *province* C Argentina
La Pampa, Provincia de *see* La Pampa
55 P8 **La Paragua** Bolívar, E Venezuela 06°53′N 63°16′W
119 O16 **Lapatsichy** *Rus.* Lopatichi. Mahilyowskaya Voblasts', E Belarus 53°34′N 30°53′E
61 C16 **La Paz** Entre Ríos, E Argentina 30°45′S 59°36′W
62 I11 **La Paz** Mendoza, C Argentina 33°30′S 67°36′W
57 J18 **La Paz** *var.* La Paz de Ayacucho. ● (Bolivia-legislative and administrative capital) La Paz, W Bolivia 16°30′S 68°13′W
42 H6 **La Paz** La Paz, SW Honduras 14°20′N 87°40′W
40 F9 **La Paz** Baja California Sur, NW Mexico 24°07′N 110°18′W
61 F20 **La Paz** Canelones, S Uruguay 34°46′S 56°13′W
57 J16 **La Paz** ◆ *department* W Bolivia
42 B9 **La Paz** ◆ *department* S El Salvador
42 G7 **La Paz** ◆ *department* SW Honduras
La Paz *see* El Alto, Bolivia
La Paz *see* Robles, Colombia
La Paz *see* La Paz Centro
40 F9 **La Paz, Bahía de** *bay* NW Mexico
42 I10 **La Paz Centro** *var.* La Paz. León, W Nicaragua 12°20′N 86°41′W
La Paz de Ayacucho *see* La Paz
54 J15 **La Pedrera** Amazonas, SE Colombia 01°19′S 69°31′W
31 S9 **Lapeer** Michigan, N USA 43°03′N 83°19′W
40 K6 **La Perla** Chihuahua, N Mexico 28°18′N 104°34′W
165 T1 **La Pérouse Strait** *Jap.* Sōya-kaikyō, *Rus.* Proliv Laperuza. *strait* Japan/Russian Federation
63 I14 **La Perra, Salitral de** *salt lake* C Argentina
Laperuza, Proliv *see* La Pérouse Strait
41 Q10 **La Pesca** Tamaulipas, C Mexico 23°49′N 97°45′W
40 M13 **La Piedad Cavadas** Michoacán, C Mexico 20°20′N 102°01′W
Lapines *see* Lafnitz
93 M16 **Lapinlahti** Itä-Suomi, C Finland 63°21′N 27°25′E
Lápithos *see* Lapta
22 K9 **Laplace** Louisiana, S USA 30°04′N 90°28′W
45 X12 **La Plaine** SE Dominica 15°20′N 61°15′W
173 P16 **La Plaine-des-Palmistes** C Réunion
92 K11 **Lapland** *Fin.* Lappi, *Swe.* Lappland. *cultural region* N Europe
28 M8 **La Plant** South Dakota, N USA 45°06′N 100°40′W
61 D20 **La Plata** Buenos Aires, E Argentina 34°56′S 57°55′W
54 D12 **La Plata** Huila, SW Colombia 02°33′N 75°55′W
21 W4 **La Plata** Maryland, NE USA 38°32′N 76°59′W
La Plata *see* Sucre
45 U6 **la Plata, Río de** ⚡ C Puerto Rico
105 W4 **La Pobla de Lillet** Cataluña, NE Spain 42°15′N 01°57′E
105 U4 **La Pobla de Segur** Cataluña, NE Spain 42°15′N 00°58′E
15 S9 **La Pocatière** Québec, SE Canada 47°21′N 70°04′W
104 K2 **La Pola** *prev.* Pola de Lena. Asturias, N Spain 43°10′N 05°49′W
104 L3 **La Pola de Gordón** Castilla y León, N Spain 42°50′N 05°38′W
104 L2 **La Pola Siero** *prev.* Pola de Siero. Asturias, N Spain 43°24′N 05°39′W
31 O11 **La Porte** Indiana, N USA 41°36′N 86°43′W
18 H13 **Laporte** Pennsylvania, NE USA 41°25′N 76°29′W
29 X13 **La Porte City** Iowa, C USA 42°19′N 92°11′W
62 J8 **La Posta** Catamarca, C Argentina 27°59′S 65°32′W
40 E8 **La Poza Grande** Baja California Sur, NW Mexico 25°50′N 112°00′W
93 K16 **Lappajärvi** Länsi-Suomi, W Finland 63°13′N 23°40′E
93 L16 **Lappajärvi** ◎ W Finland
93 N18 **Lappeenranta** *Swe.* Villmanstrand. Etelä-Suomi, SE Finland 61°04′N 28°15′E
93 J17 **Lappfjärd** *Fin.* Lapväärtti. Länsi-Suomi, W Finland 62°14′N 21°30′E
92 L12 **Lappi** *Swe.* Lappland. ◆ *province* N Finland
Lappi/Lappland *see* Lapland
Lappo *see* Lapua
61 C23 **Laprida** Buenos Aires, E Argentina 37°34′S 60°45′W
25 P13 **La Pryor** Texas, SW USA 28°56′N 99°51′W
136 B11 **Lâpseki** Çanakkale, NW Turkey 40°22′N 26°42′E
121 P2 **Lapta** *Gk.* Lápithos. NW Cyprus 35°20′N 33°11′E
Laptev Sea *see* Laptevykh, More
122 N6 **Laptevykh, More** *Eng.* Laptev Sea. *sea* Arctic Ocean
93 K16 **Lapua** *Swe.* Lappo. Länsi-Suomi, W Finland 62°57′N 23°E
105 P3 **La Puebla de Arganzón** País Vasco, N Spain 42°45′N 02°49′W
104 L14 **La Puebla de Cazalla** Andalucía, S Spain 37°14′N 05°18′W
104 M9 **La Puebla de Montalbán** Castilla-La Mancha, C Spain 39°52′N 04°22′W
54 I6 **La Puerta** Trujillo, NW Venezuela 09°08′N 70°46′W
Lapurdum *see* Bayonne
40 E7 **La Purísima** Baja California Sur, NW Mexico 26°10′N 112°05′W
Lapväärtti *see* Lappfjärd
110 O10 **Łapy** Podlaskie, NE Poland 53°N 22°54′E
80 D6 **Laqiya Arba'in** Northern, NW Sudan 20°01′N 28°01′E
62 J4 **La Quiaca** Jujuy, N Argentina 22°12′S 65°36′W
107 J14 **L'Aquila** *var.* Aquila, Aquila degli Abruzzi. Abruzzo, C Italy 42°21′N 13°24′E
143 Q13 **Lār** Fārs, S Iran 27°42′N 54°19′E
54 J5 **Lara** *off.* Estado Lara. ◆ *state* NW Venezuela
104 G2 **Laracha** Galicia, NW Spain 43°14′N 08°34′W
74 G5 **Larache** *var.* al Araïch, El Araïch, *prev.* El Araïche; *anc.* Lixus. NW Morocco 35°12′N 06°10′W
Lara, Estado *see* Lara
103 T14 **Laragne-Montéglin** Hautes-Alpes, SE France 44°21′N 05°46′E
104 M13 **La Rambla** Andalucía, S Spain 37°37′N 04°44′W
33 Y17 **Laramie** Wyoming, C USA 41°18′N 105°35′W
33 X15 **Laramie Mountains** ▲▲ Wyoming, C USA
33 Y16 **Laramie River** ⚡ Wyoming, C USA
60 H12 **Laranjeiras do Sul** Paraná, S Brazil 25°23′S 52°23′W
Larantoeka *see* Larantuka
171 P16 **Larantuka** *prev.* Larantoeka. Flores, C Indonesia 08°20′S 123°00′E
171 U15 **Larat** Pulau Larat, E Indonesia 07°07′S 131°46′E
171 U15 **Larat, Pulau** *island* Kepulauan Tanimbar, E Indonesia
95 P19 **Lärbro** Gotland, SE Sweden 57°46′N 18°49′E
106 A9 **Larche, Col de** *pass* France/Italy
14 H8 **Larder Lake** Ontario, S Canada 48°06′N 79°44′W
105 O2 **Laredo** Cantabria, N Spain 43°23′N 03°22′W
25 Q15 **Laredo** Texas, SW USA 27°30′N 99°30′W
40 H9 **La Reforma** Sinaloa, W Mexico 25°05′N 108°03′W
98 N11 **Laren** Gelderland, E Netherlands 52°12′N 06°22′E
98 J11 **Laren** Noord-Holland, C Netherlands 52°15′N 05°13′E
102 K13 **la Réole** Gironde, SW France 44°34′N 00°00′W
La Réunion *see* Réunion
Largeau *see* Faya
103 U13 **l'Argentière-la-Bessée** Hautes-Alpes, SE France 44°49′N 06°34′E
149 O4 **Lar Gerd** *var.* Largird. Balkh, N Afghanistan 35°36′N 66°48′E
Largird *see* Lar Gerd
23 V12 **Largo** Florida, SE USA 27°55′N 82°47′W
37 Q9 **Largo, Canon** *valley* New Mexico, SW USA
44 D6 **Largo, Cayo** *island* W Cuba
23 Z17 **Largo, Key** *island* Florida Keys, Florida, SE USA
96 H12 **Largs** W Scotland, United Kingdom 55°48′N 04°50′W
102 I16 **la Rhune** *var.* Larrún. ▲ France/Spain 43°19′N 01°36′W *see also* Larrún
la Rhune *see* Larrún
la Riege *see* Ariège
29 Q4 **Larimore** North Dakota, N USA 47°54′N 97°37′W
107 L15 **Larino** Molise, C Italy 41°46′N 14°50′E
Lario *see* Como, Lago di
62 J9 **La Rioja** La Rioja, NW Argentina 29°26′S 66°50′W
62 I9 **La Rioja** *off.* Provincia de La Rioja. ◆ *province* NW Argentina
105 O4 **La Rioja** ◆ *autonomous community* N Spain
La Rioja, Provincia de *see* La Rioja
115 F16 **Lárisa** *var.* Larissa. Thessalía, C Greece 39°38′N 22°27′E
Larissa *see* Lárisa
149 Q13 **Lārkāna** *var.* Larkhana. Sind, SE Pakistan 27°32′N 68°18′E
Larkhana *see* Lārkāna
Larnaca *see* Lárnaka
121 Q3 **Lárnaka** *var.* Larnaca, Larnax. SE Cyprus 34°55′N 33°39′E
121 Q3 **Lárnaka** ✈ SE Cyprus 34°52′N 33°38′E
Larnax *see* Lárnaka
97 G14 **Larne** *Ir.* Latharna. E Northern Ireland, United Kingdom 54°51′N 05°49′W
26 L5 **Larned** Kansas, C USA 38°12′N 99°05′W
104 L3 **La Robla** Castilla y León, N Spain 42°48′N 05°37′W
104 J10 **La Roca de la Sierra** Extremadura, W Spain 39°06′N 06°41′W
99 K22 **La Roche-en-Ardenne** Luxembourg, SE Belgium 50°11′N 05°35′E
102 L11 **la Rochefoucauld** Charente, W France 45°43′N 00°23′E
102 J10 **la Rochelle** *anc.* Rupella. Charente-Maritime, W France 46°09′N 01°07′W
102 I9 **la Roche-sur-Yon** *prev.* Bourbon Vendée, Napoléon-Vendée. Vendée, NW France 46°40′N 01°26′W
105 Q10 **La Roda** Castilla-La Mancha, C Spain 39°13′N 02°10′W
104 L14 **La Roda de Andalucía** Andalucía, S Spain 37°12′N 04°45′W
45 P9 **La Romana** E Dominican Republic 18°25′N 69°00′W
11 T13 **La Ronge** Saskatchewan, C Canada 55°07′N 105°18′W
11 U13 **La Ronge, Lac** ◎ Saskatchewan, C Canada
22 K10 **Larose** Louisiana, S USA 29°34′N 90°22′W
42 M7 **La Rosita** Región Autónoma Atlántico Norte, NE Nicaragua 13°55′N 84°23′W
181 Q3 **Larrimah** Northern Territory, N Australia 15°30′S 133°12′E
62 N11 **Larroque** Entre Ríos, E Argentina 33°05′S 59°06′W
105 Q2 **Larrún** *Fr.* la Rhune. ▲ France/Spain 43°18′N 01°35′W *see also* la Rhune
Larrún *see* la Rhune
195 X6 **Lars Christensen Coast** *physical region* Antarctica
39 Q14 **Larsen Bay** Kodiak Island, Alaska, USA 57°32′N 153°58′W
194 I5 **Larsen Ice Shelf** *ice shelf* Antarctica
8 M6 **Larsen Sound** *sound* Nunavut, N Canada
La Rúa *see* A Rúa de Valdeorras
102 K16 **Laruns** Pyrénées-Atlantiques, SW France 43°00′N 00°25′W
95 G16 **Larvik** Vestfold, S Norway 59°04′N 10°02′E
La-sa *see* Lhasa
171 S13 **Lasahata** Pulau Seram, E Indonesia 02°52′S 128°27′E
Lasahau *see* Lasihao
37 O6 **La Sal** Utah, W USA 38°19′N 109°14′W
14 C17 **La Salle** Ontario, S Canada 42°13′N 83°05′W
30 L11 **La Salle** Illinois, N USA 41°19′N 89°06′W
45 O9 **Las Americas** ✈ (Santo Domingo) S Dominican Republic 18°24′N 69°38′W
37 V6 **Las Animas** Colorado, C USA 38°04′N 103°13′W
108 D10 **La Sarine** *var.* Sarine. ⚡ SW Switzerland
108 B9 **La Sarraz** Vaud, W Switzerland 46°40′N 06°32′E
12 H12 **La Sarre** Québec, SE Canada 48°49′N 79°12′W
54 L3 **Las Aves, Islas** *var.* Islas de Aves. *island group* N Venezuela
55 N7 **Las Bonitas** Bolívar, C Venezuela 07°50′N 65°40′W
104 K15 **Las Cabezas de San Juan** Andalucía, S Spain 36°59′N 05°56′W
61 G19 **Lascano** Rocha, E Uruguay 33°40′S 54°12′W
62 I5 **Lascar, Volcán** ▲ N Chile 23°22′S 67°33′W
41 T15 **Las Choapas** *var.* Choapas. Veracruz-Llave, SE Mexico 17°51′N 94°00′W
37 R15 **Las Cruces** New Mexico, SW USA 32°19′N 106°49′W
Lasdehnen *see* Krasnoznamensk
La Selle *see* Selle, Pic de la
62 G9 **La Serena** Coquimbo, C Chile 29°54′S 71°18′W
104 K11 **La Serena** *physical region* W Spain
105 V4 **La Seu d'Urgell** *var.* La Seu d'Urgel; *prev.* Seo de Urgel. Cataluña, NE Spain 42°22′N 01°27′E
La Seu d'Urgell *see* La Seu d'Urgell
103 T16 **la Seyne-sur-Mer** Var, SE France 43°07′N 05°53′E
61 D21 **Las Flores** Buenos Aires, E Argentina 36°03′S 59°08′W
62 H9 **Las Flores** San Juan, W Argentina 30°14′S 69°10′W
11 S14 **Lashburn** Saskatchewan, S Canada 53°09′N 109°37′W
62 I11 **Las Heras** Mendoza, W Argentina 32°48′S 68°50′W
148 M8 **Lashkar Gāh** *var.* Lash-Kar-Gar'. Helmand, S Afghanistan 31°35′N 64°21′E
Lash-Kar-Gar' *see* Lashkar Gāh
171 P14 **Lasihao** *var.* Lasahau. Pulau Muna, C Indonesia 05°01′S 122°23′E
107 N21 **La Sila** ▲ SW Italy
63 H23 **La Silueta, Cerro** ▲ S Chile 52°22′S 72°09′W
42 L9 **La Sirena** Región Autónoma Atlántico Sur, E Nicaragua 12°59′N 84°35′W
110 J13 **Łask** Łódzkie, C Poland 51°36′N 19°06′E
109 V11 **Laško** *Ger.* Tüffer. C Slovenia 46°08′N 15°13′E
63 H14 **Las Lajas** Neuquén, W Argentina 38°31′S 70°22′W
63 H15 **Las Lajas, Cerro** ▲ W Argentina 38°49′S 70°42′W
62 M6 **Las Lomitas** Formosa, N Argentina 24°45′S 60°35′W
41 V16 **Las Margaritas** Chiapas, SE Mexico 16°15′N 91°58′W
Las Marismas *see* Guadalquivir, Marismas del
54 M6 **Las Mercedes** Guárico, N Venezuela 09°08′N 66°27′W
42 F6 **Las Minas, Cerro** ▲ W Honduras 14°33′N 88°41′W
105 O11 **La Solana** Castilla-La Mancha, C Spain 38°56′N 03°14′W
45 Q14 **La Soufrière** ▲ Saint Vincent, Saint Vincent and the Grenadines 13°20′N 61°11′W
102 M10 **la Souterraine** Creuse, C France 46°15′N 01°28′E
62 N7 **Las Palmas** Chaco, N Argentina 27°08′S 58°45′W
43 Q16 **Las Palmas** Veraguas, W Panama 08°09′N 81°28′W
64 P12 **Las Palmas** *var.* Las Palmas de Gran Canaria. Gran Canaria, Islas Canarias, Spain, NE Atlantic Ocean 28°08′N 15°27′W
64 P12 **Las Palmas** ◆ *province* Islas Canarias, Spain, NE Atlantic Ocean
64 Q12 **Las Palmas** ✈ Gran Canaria, Islas Canarias, Spain, NE Atlantic Ocean
Las Palmas de Gran Canaria *see* Las Palmas
40 D6 **Las Palomas** Baja California Norte, W Mexico 31°44′N 107°37′W
105 P10 **Las Pedroñeras** Castilla-La Mancha, C Spain 39°27′N 02°41′W
106 E10 **La Spezia** Liguria, NW Italy 44°08′N 09°50′E
61 F20 **Las Piedras** Canelones, S Uruguay 34°42′S 56°14′W
63 J18 **Las Plumas** Chubut, S Argentina 43°46′S 67°15′W
61 B18 **Las Rosas** Santa Fe, C Argentina 32°27′S 61°30′W
Lassa *see* Lhasa
35 O4 **Lassen Peak** ▲ California, W USA 40°27′N 121°28′W
194 K6 **Lassiter Coast** *physical region* Antarctica
109 V9 **Lassnitz** ⚡ SE Austria
15 O12 **L'Assomption** Québec, SE Canada 45°48′N 73°27′W
15 N11 **L'Assomption** ⚡ Québec, SE Canada
43 S17 **Las Tablas** Los Santos, S Panama 07°45′N 80°17′W
Lastarria, Volcán *see* Azufre, Volcán
37 V4 **Last Chance** Colorado, C USA 39°41′N 103°34′W
Last Frontier, The *see* Alaska
11 U16 **Last Mountain Lake** ◎ Saskatchewan, S Canada
62 H9 **Las Tórtolas, Cerro** ▲ W Argentina 29°57′S 69°49′W
61 C14 **Las Toscas** Santa Fe, C Argentina 28°22′S 59°20′W
79 F19 **Lastoursville** Ogooué-Lolo, E Gabon 0°50′S 12°43′E
113 F16 **Lastovo** *It.* Lagosta. *island* SW Croatia
113 F16 **Lastovski Kanal** *channel* SW Croatia
40 E6 **Las Tres Vírgenes, Volcán** ▲ NW Mexico 27°27′N 112°34′W
40 F4 **Las Trincheras** Sonora, NW Mexico 30°21′N 111°27′W
55 N8 **Las Trincheras** Bolívar, E Venezuela 06°57′N 64°49′W
44 H7 **Las Tunas** *var.* Victoria de las Tunas. Las Tunas, E Cuba 20°58′N 76°59′W
La Suisse *see* Switzerland
40 I5 **Las Varas** Chihuahua, N Mexico 29°35′N 108°01′W
40 J12 **Las Varas** Nayarit, C Mexico 21°12′N 105°10′W
62 L10 **Las Varillas** Córdoba, E Argentina 31°54′S 62°45′W
35 X11 **Las Vegas** Nevada, W USA 36°09′N 115°10′W
37 T10 **Las Vegas** New Mexico, SW USA 35°35′N 105°15′W
187 P10 **Lata** Nendö, Solomon Islands 10°45′S 165°43′E
13 R10 **La Tabatière** Québec, E Canada 50°51′N 58°59′W
56 C6 **Latacunga** Cotopaxi, C Ecuador 0°58′S 78°36′W
194 I7 **Latady Island** *island* Antarctica
54 E14 **La Tagua** Putumayo, S Colombia 0°05′S 74°39′W
Latakia *see* Al Lādhiqīyah
92 J10 **Lätäseno** ⚡ NW Finland
14 H9 **Latchford** Ontario, S Canada 47°20′N 79°45′W
14 J13 **Latchford Bridge** Ontario, SE Canada 45°16′N 77°29′W
193 Y14 **Late** *island* Vava'u Group, N Tonga
153 P15 **Lātehār** Jhārkhand, N India 23°48′N 84°28′E
15 R7 **Laterrière** Québec, SE Canada 48°17′N 71°10′W
102 J13 **la Teste** Gironde, SW France 44°38′N 01°04′W
25 V8 **Latexo** Texas, SW USA 31°24′N 95°28′W
18 L10 **Latham** New York, NE USA 42°45′N 73°45′W
Latharna *see* Larne
108 B9 **La Thielle** *var.* Thièle. ⚡ W Switzerland
27 R3 **Lathrop** Missouri, C USA 39°33′N 94°19′W
107 I16 **Latina** *prev.* Littoria. Lazio, C Italy 41°28′N 12°53′E
41 R14 **La Tinaja** Veracruz-Llave, S Mexico
106 J7 **Latisana** Friuli-Venezia Giulia, NE Italy 45°47′N 13°01′E
Latium *see* Lazio
115 K25 **Lató** *site of ancient city* Kríti, Greece, E Mediterranean Sea
187 Q17 **La Tontouta** ✈ (Noumea) Province Sud, S New Caledonia 22°06′S 166°12′E
55 N4 **La Tortuga, Isla** *var.* Isla Tortuga. *island* N Venezuela
108 C10 **La Tour-de-Peilz** *var.* La Tour de Peilz. Vaud, SW Switzerland 46°28′N 06°52′E
La Tour de Peilz *see* La Tour-de-Peilz
103 S11 **la Tour-du-Pin** Isère, E France 45°34′N 05°25′E
102 J11 **la Tremblade** Charente-Maritime, W France 45°45′N 01°07′W
102 L10 **la Trimouille** Vienne, W France 46°27′N 01°02′E
42 J9 **La Trinidad** Estelí, NW Nicaragua 12°57′N 86°15′W
41 V16 **La Trinitaria** Chiapas, SE Mexico 16°02′N 92°00′W
45 Q11 **la Trinité** E Martinique 14°44′N 60°58′W
15 U7 **La Trinité-des-Monts** Québec, SE Canada 48°07′N 68°31′W
18 C15 **Latrobe** Pennsylvania, NE USA 40°18′N 79°19′W
183 P13 **La Trobe River** ⚡ Victoria, SE Australia
Lattakia/Lattaquié *see* Al Lādhiqīyah
171 S13 **Latu** Pulau Seram, E Indonesia 03°24′S 128°37′E
15 P9 **La Tuque** Québec, SE Canada 47°26′N 72°47′W
155 G14 **Lātūr** Mahārāshtra, C India 18°24′N 76°34′E
118 G8 **Latvia** *off.* Republic of Latvia, *Ger.* Lettland, *Latv.* Latvija, Latvijas Republika; *prev.* Latvian SSR, *Rus.* Latviyskaya SSR. ◆ *republic* NE Europe
Latvian SSR/Latvija/Latvijas Republika/Latviyskaya SSR *see* Latvia
Latvia, Republic of *see* Latvia
186 H7 **Lau** New Britain, E Papua New Guinea 05°46′S 151°21′E
175 R9 **Lau Basin** *undersea feature* S Pacific Ocean
101 O15 **Lauchhammer** Brandenburg, E Germany 51°30′N 13°48′E
105 O3 **Laudio** *var.* Llodio. País Vasco, N Spain 43°08′N 02°59′W
Laudunum *see* Laon
Laudus *see* St-Lô
Lauenburg/Lauenburg in Pommern *see* Lębork
101 L20 **Lauf an der Pegnitz** Bayern, SE Germany 49°31′N 11°16′E
108 D7 **Laufen** Basel, NW Switzerland 47°26′N 07°31′E
109 P5 **Lauffen** Salzburg, NW Austria 47°54′N 12°57′E
92 I2 **Laugarbakki** Nordhurland Vestra, N Iceland 65°18′N 20°51′W
92 I4 **Laugarvatn** Sudhurland, SW Iceland 64°09′N 20°43′W
31 O3 **Laughing Fish Point** *headland* Michigan, N USA 46°31′N 87°01′W
187 Z14 **Lau Group** *island group* E Fiji
Lauis *see* Lugano
93 M17 **Laukaa** Länsi-Suomi, C Finland 62°27′N 25°58′E
118 D12 **Laukuva** Tauragė, W Lithuania 55°37′N 22°12′E
Laun *see* Louny
183 P16 **Launceston** Tasmania, SE Australia 41°25′S 147°07′E
97 I24 **Launceston** *anc.* Dunheved. SW England, United Kingdom 50°38′N 04°21′W
54 C13 **La Unión** Nariño, SW Colombia 01°35′N 77°09′W
42 H8 **La Unión** La Unión, SE El Salvador 13°20′N 87°50′W
42 I6 **La Unión** Olancho, C Honduras 15°02′N 86°40′W
40 M15 **La Unión** Guerrero, S Mexico 17°58′N 101°49′W
41 Y14 **La Unión** Quintana Roo, E Mexico 18°00′N 101°48′W
105 S13 **La Unión** Murcia, SE Spain 37°37′N 00°54′W
54 L7 **La Unión** Barinas, C Venezuela 08°15′N 67°46′W
42 B10 **La Unión** ◆ *department* E El Salvador
38 H11 **Laupāhoehoe** *var.* Laupahoehoe. Hawaii, USA, C Pacific Ocean 20°00′N 155°15′W
Laupahoehoe *see* Laupāhoehoe
101 I23 **Laupheim** Baden-Württemberg, S Germany 48°13′N 09°54′E
181 W3 **Laura** Queensland, NE Australia 15°37′S 144°34′E
189 X2 **Laura** *atoll* Majuro Atoll, SE Marshall Islands
Laurana *see* Lovran
54 L8 **La Urbana** Bolívar, C Venezuela 07°05′N 66°58′W
21 Y4 **Laurel** Delaware, NE USA 38°33′N 75°34′W
23 V14 **Laurel** Florida, SE USA 27°07′N 82°27′W
21 W3 **Laurel** Maryland, NE USA 39°06′N 76°51′W
22 M6 **Laurel** Mississippi, S USA 31°41′N 89°10′W
33 U11 **Laurel** Montana, NW USA 45°40′N 108°46′W
29 R13 **Laurel** Nebraska, C USA 42°25′N 97°04′W
18 D15 **Laureldale** Pennsylvania, NE USA 40°24′N 75°52′W
18 C16 **Laurel Hill** *ridge* Pennsylvania, NE USA
29 T12 **Laurens** Iowa, C USA 42°51′N 94°51′W
21 P11 **Laurens** South Carolina, SE USA 34°29′N 82°01′W
Laurentian Highlands *see* Laurentian Mountains
15 P10 **Laurentian Mountains** *var.* Laurentian Highlands, *Fr.* Les Laurentides. *plateau* Newfoundland and Labrador/Québec, Canada
15 O12 **Laurentides** Québec, SE Canada 45°51′N 73°49′W
Laurentides, Les *see* Laurentian Mountains
107 M19 **Lauria** Basilicata, S Italy 40°03′N 15°50′E
194 I1 **Laurie Island** *island* Antarctica
21 T11 **Laurinburg** North Carolina, SE USA 34°46′N 79°29′W
30 M2 **Laurium** Michigan, N USA 47°14′N 88°26′W
Lauru *see* Choiseul
108 B9 **Lausanne** *It.* Losanna. Vaud, SW Switzerland 46°32′N 06°39′E
101 Q16 **Lausche** *var.* Luže. ▲ Czech Republic/Germany 50°52′N 14°39′E *see also* Luže
Lausche *see* Luže
101 Q16 **Lausitzer Bergland** *var.* Lausitzer Gebirge, *Cz.* Gory Lużyckie, Lužické Hory', *Eng.* Lusatian Mountains. ▲▲ E Germany
Lausitzer Gebirge *see* Lausitzer Bergland
Lausitzer Neisse *see* Neisse
103 T12 **Lautaret, Col du** *pass* SE France
63 G15 **Lautaro** Araucanía, C Chile 38°30′S 71°30′W
101 F21 **Lauter** ⚡ W Germany
108 I7 **Lauterach** Vorarlberg, NW Austria 47°29′N 09°44′E
101 I17 **Lauterbach** Hessen, C Germany 50°37′N 09°24′E
108 E9 **Lauterbrunnen** Bern, C Switzerland 46°36′N 07°52′E
169 U14 **Laut Kecil, Kepulauan** *island group* N Indonesia
187 X14 **Lautoka** Viti Levu, W Fiji 17°36′S 177°28′E
169 O8 **Laut, Pulau** *prev.* Laoet. *island* Borneo, C Indonesia
169 V14 **Laut, Pulau** *island* Kepulauan Natuna, W Indonesia
169 U13 **Laut, Selat** *strait* Borneo, C Indonesia
168 H8 **Laut Tawar, Danau** ◎ Sumatera, NW Indonesia
189 V14 **Lauvergne Island** *island* Chuuk, C Micronesia
98 M5 **Lauwers Meer** ◎ N Netherlands
98 M4 **Lauwersoog** Groningen, NE Netherlands 53°25′N 06°14′E
102 M14 **Lauzerte** Tarn-et-Garonne, S France 44°15′N 01°08′E
25 U13 **Lavaca Bay** *bay* Texas, SW USA
25 U12 **Lavaca River** ⚡ Texas, SW USA
15 O12 **Laval** Québec, SE Canada 45°32′N 73°44′W
102 J6 **Laval** Mayenne, NW France 48°04′N 00°46′W
15 T6 **Laval** ⚡ Québec, SE Canada
105 S9 **La Vall d'Uixó** *var.* Vall D'Uxó. Valenciana, E Spain 39°49′N 00°15′W
61 F19 **Lavalleja** ◆ *department* S Uruguay
15 O12 **Lavaltrie** Québec, SE Canada 45°56′N 73°14′W
186 M10 **Lavanggu** Rennell, S Solomon Islands 11°39′S 160°13′E
143 O14 **Lāvān, Jazīreh-ye** *island* S Iran
109 U8 **Lavant** ⚡ S Austria
118 G5 **Lavassaare** *Ger.* Lawassaar. Pärnumaa, SW Estonia 58°29′N 24°22′E
104 L3 **La Vecilla de Curueño** Castilla y León, N Spain 42°51′N 05°24′W
45 N8 **La Vega** *var.* Concepción de la Vega. C Dominican Republic 19°15′N 70°33′W
La Vela *see* La Vela de Coro
54 J4 **La Vela de Coro** *var.* La Vela. Falcón, N Venezuela 11°30′N 69°33′W
103 N17 **Lavelanet** Ariège, S France 42°56′N 01°50′E
107 M17 **Lavello** Basilicata, S Italy 41°03′N 15°48′E
36 J8 **La Verkin** Utah, W USA 37°12′N 113°16′W
26 J8 **Laverne** Oklahoma, C USA 36°42′N 99°53′W
25 S12 **La Vernia** Texas, SW USA 29°19′N 98°07′W
93 K18 **Lavia** Länsi-Suomi, SW Finland 61°36′N 22°34′E
14 I12 **Lavieille, Lake** ◎ Ontario, SE Canada
94 C12 **Lavik** Sogn Og Fjordane, S Norway 61°06′N 05°25′E
La Vila Joiosa *see* Villajoyosa
33 U10 **Lavina** Montana, NW USA 46°18′N 108°55′W
194 H5 **Lavoisier Island** *island* Antarctica
23 U2 **Lavonia** Georgia, SE USA 34°26′N 83°06′W
103 R13 **la Voulte-sur-Rhône** Ardèche, E France 44°49′N 04°46′E
123 W5 **Lavrentiya** Chukotskiy Avtonomnyy Okrug, NE Russian Federation 65°33′N 171°12′W
115 H20 **Lávrio** *prev.* Lávrion. Attikí, C Greece 37°43′N 24°03′E
Lávrion *see* Lávrio
83 L22 **Lavumisa** *prev.* Gollel. SE Swaziland 27°18′S 31°55′E
149 T4 **Lawarai Pass** *pass* N Pakistan
Lawassaar *see* Lavassaare
141 P16 **Lawdar** SW Yemen 13°49′N 45°55′E
25 Q7 **Lawn** Texas, SW USA 32°07′N 99°45′W
195 Y4 **Law Promontory** *headland* Antarctica
77 O14 **Lawra** NW Ghana 10°40′N 02°49′W
185 E23 **Lawrence** Otago, South Island, New Zealand 45°53′S 169°43′E
31 P14 **Lawrence** Indiana, N USA 39°49′N 86°01′W
27 Q4 **Lawrence** Kansas, C USA 38°58′N 95°15′W
19 O10 **Lawrence** Massachusetts, NE USA 42°42′N 71°09′W
20 L5 **Lawrenceburg** Kentucky, S USA 38°02′N 84°53′W
20 I10 **Lawrenceburg** Tennessee, S USA 35°15′N 87°20′W
23 T3 **Lawrenceville** Georgia, SE USA 33°57′N 83°59′W
31 N15 **Lawrenceville** Illinois, N USA 38°43′N 87°40′W
21 V7 **Lawrenceville** Virginia, NE USA 36°45′N 77°50′W
27 S3 **Lawson** Missouri, C USA 39°26′N 94°12′W
26 L12 **Lawton** Oklahoma, C USA 34°35′N 98°20′W
140 I4 **Lawz, Jabal al** ▲ NW Saudi Arabia 28°45′N 35°20′E
95 L16 **Laxå** Örebro, C Sweden 59°00′N 14°37′E
125 T5 **Laya** ⚡ NW Russian Federation
57 I19 **La Yarada** Tacna, SW Peru 18°14′S 70°30′W
141 S15 **Layjūn** C Yemen 15°27′N 49°16′E
141 Q9 **Laylā** *var.* Laila. Ar Riyāḑ, C Saudi Arabia 22°14′N 46°40′E
23 P4 **Lay Lake** ⊠ Alabama, S USA
45 P14 **Layou** Saint Vincent, Saint Vincent and the Grenadines 13°11′N 61°16′W
La Youne *see* El Ayoun
192 L5 **Laysan Island** *island* Hawaiian Islands, Hawai'i, USA
36 L2 **Layton** Utah, W USA 41°03′N 112°00′W
34 L5 **Laytonville** California, W USA 39°39′N 123°30′W
172 H17 **Lazare, Pointe** *headland* Mahé, NE Seychelles 04°46′S 55°28′E
123 T12 **Lazarev** Khabarovskiy Kray, SE Russian Federation 52°11′N 141°18′E
112 L12 **Lazarevac** Serbia, C Serbia 44°25′N 20°17′E
65 N22 **Lazarev Sea** *sea* Antarctica
40 M15 **Lázaro Cárdenas** Michoacán, SW Mexico 17°56′N 102°13′W
119 F15 **Lazdijai** Alytus, S Lithuania 54°13′N 23°33′E
107 H15 **Lazio** *anc.* Latium. ◆ *region* C Italy
111 A16 **Lázně Kynžvart** *Ger.* Bad Königswart. Karlovarský Kraj, W Czech Republic 50°00′N 12°40′E
Lazovsk *see* Sîngerei
167 R12 **Leach** Poŭthĭsăt, W Cambodia 12°19′N 103°45′E
27 X9 **Leachville** Arkansas, C USA 35°56′N 90°15′W
28 I9 **Lead** South Dakota, N USA 44°21′N 103°45′W
11 S16 **Leader** Saskatchewan, S Canada 50°55′N 109°31′W
19 S6 **Lead Mountain** ▲ Maine, NE USA 44°53′N 68°07′W
37 R5 **Leadville** Colorado, C USA 39°15′N 106°17′W
11 V12 **Leaf Rapids** Manitoba, C Canada 56°30′N 100°02′W
22 M7 **Leaf River** ⚡ Mississippi, S USA
25 W11 **League City** Texas, SW USA 29°30′N 95°05′W
92 K8 **Leaibevuotna** *Nor.* Olderfjord. Finnmark, N Norway 70°29′N 24°58′E
23 N7 **Leakesville** Mississippi, S USA 31°09′N 88°33′W
25 Q11 **Leakey** Texas, SW USA 29°44′N 99°48′W
Leal *see* Lihula
83 G15 **Lealui** Western, W Zambia 15°12′S 22°59′E
Leamhcán *see* Lucan
14 C18 **Leamington** Ontario, S Canada 42°03′N 82°35′W
Leamington/Leamington Spa *see* Royal Leamington Spa
Leammi *see* Lemmenjoki
25 S10 **Leander** Texas, SW USA 30°34′N 97°51′W
60 F13 **Leandro N. Alem** Misiones, NE Argentina 27°34′S 55°15′W
97 A20 **Leane, Lough** *Ir.* Loch Léin. ◎ SW Ireland
180 G8 **Learmonth** Western Australia 22°17′S 114°03′E
Leau *see* Zoutleeuw
L'Eau d'Heure *see* Plate Taille, Lac de la
190 D12 **Leava** Île Futuna, S Wallis and Futuna
Leavdnja *see* Lakselv
27 R3 **Leavenworth** Kansas, C USA 39°19′N 94°55′W
32 I8 **Leavenworth** Washington, NW USA 47°36′N 120°39′W
92 K9 **Leavvajohka** *var.* Levajok. Finnmark, N Norway 69°57′N 26°18′E
27 R4 **Leawood** Kansas, C USA 38°57′N 94°37′W
110 H6 **Łeba** *Ger.* Leba. Pomorskie, N Poland 54°45′N 17°32′E
110 I6 **Łeba** *Ger.* Leba. ⚡ N Poland
Leba *see* Łeba
101 D20 **Lebach** Saarland, SW Germany 49°25′N 06°54′E
Łeba, Jezioro *see* Łebsko, Jezioro
171 P8 **Lebak** Mindanao, S Philippines 06°28′N 124°03′E
Lebanese Republic *see* Lebanon
31 O13 **Lebanon** Indiana, N USA 40°03′N 86°28′W
20 L6 **Lebanon** Kentucky, S USA 37°33′N 85°15′W
27 U6 **Lebanon** Missouri, C USA 37°40′N 92°40′W
19 N9 **Lebanon** New Hampshire, NE USA 43°40′N 72°15′W
32 G12 **Lebanon** Oregon, NW USA 44°32′N 122°54′W
18 H15 **Lebanon** Pennsylvania, NE USA 40°20′N 76°24′W
20 J8 **Lebanon** Tennessee, S USA 36°11′N 86°19′W
21 P7 **Lebanon** Virginia, NE USA 36°52′N 82°07′W
138 G6 **Lebanon** *off.* Lebanese Republic, *Ar.* Al Lubnān, *Fr.* Liban. ◆ *republic* SW Asia
20 K6 **Lebanon Junction** Kentucky, S USA 37°49′N 85°43′W
Lebanon, Mount *see* Liban, Jebel
146 J10 **Lebap** Lebapskiy Velayat, NE Turkmenistan 41°04′N 61°49′E
Lebapskiy Velayat *see* Lebap Welaýaty
146 J11 **Lebap Welaýaty** *Rus.* Lebapskiy Velayat; *prev.* *Rus.* Chardzhevskaya Oblast, *Turkm.* Chärjew Oblasty. ◆ *province* E Turkmenistan
Lebasee *see* Łebsko, Jezioro
99 F17 **Lebbeke** Oost-Vlaanderen, NW Belgium 51°00′N 04°08′E
35 S14 **Lebec** California, W USA 34°51′N 118°52′W
Lebedin *see* Lebedyn

◆ Country
● Country Capital
◇ Dependent Territory
○ Dependent Territory Capital
◆ Administrative Regions
✈ International Airport
▲ Mountain
▲▲ Mountain Range
▲ Volcano
⚡ River
◎ Lake
⊠ Reservoir

123 Q11 Lebedinyy Respublika Sakha (Yakutiya), NE Russian Federation 58°23′N 125°24′E
126 L6 Lebedyan' Lipetskaya Oblast', W Russian Federation 53°00′N 39°11′E
117 T4 Lebedyn Rus. Lebedin. Sums'ka Oblast', NE Ukraine 50°36′N 34°30′E
12 I12 Lebel-sur-Quévillon Québec, SE Canada 49°01′N 76°56′W
92 L8 Lebesby Lapp. Davvesiida. Finnmark, N Norway 70°31′N 27°00′E
102 M9 le Blanc Indre, C France 46°38′N 01°04′E
79 L15 Lebo Orientale, N Dem. Rep. Congo 04°30′N 23°58′E
27 P5 Lebo Kansas, C USA 38°22′N 95°50′W
110 H6 Lębork var. Lębórk, Ger. Lauenburg, Lauenburg in Pommern. Pomorskie, N Poland 54°32′N 17°43′E
103 O17 le Boulou Pyrénées-Orientales, S France 42°32′N 02°50′E
108 A9 Le Brassus Vaud, W Switzerland 46°35′N 06°14′E
104 J15 Lebrija Andalucía, S Spain 36°55′N 06°04′W
110 G6 Łebsko, Jezioro Ger. Lebasee; prev. Jezioro Łeba. ◎ N Poland
63 F14 Lebu Bío Bío, C Chile 37°38′S 73°43′W
Lebyazh'ye see Akku
104 F6 Leça da Palmeira Porto, N Portugal 41°12′N 08°43′W
103 U15 le Cannet Alpes-Maritimes, SE France 43°35′N 07°E
Le Cap see Cap-Haïtien
103 P2 Le Cateau-Cambrésis Nord, N France 50°05′N 03°32′E
107 Q18 Lecce Puglia, SE Italy 40°23′N 18°11′E
106 D7 Lecco Lombardia, N Italy 45°51′N 09°23′E
29 V10 Le Center Minnesota, N USA 44°23′N 93°43′W
108 J7 Lech Vorarlberg, W Austria 47°14′N 10°10′E
101 K22 Lech ≈ Austria/Germany
115 D19 Lechainá var. Lehena, Lekhainá. Dytikí Elláda, S Greece 37°57′N 21°16′E
102 J11 le Château d'Oléron Charente-Maritime, W France 45°53′N 01°12′W
103 R3 le Chesne Ardennes, N France 49°33′N 04°42′E
103 R13 le Cheylard Ardèche, E France 44°55′N 04°27′E
108 K7 Lechtaler Alpen ▲ W Austria
100 H6 Leck Schleswig-Holstein, N Germany 54°45′N 09°00′E
14 L9 Lecointre, Lac ◎ Québec, SE Canada
22 H7 Lecompte Louisiana, S USA 31°05′N 92°24′W
103 Q9 le Creusot Saône-et-Loire, C France 46°48′N 04°27′E
Lecumberri see Lekunberri
110 P13 Łęczna Lubelskie, E Poland 51°20′N 22°52′E
110 J12 Łęczyca Ger. Lentschiza, Rus. Lenchitsa. Łódzkie, C Poland 52°04′N 19°10′E
100 F10 Leda ≈ NW Germany
109 Y9 Ledava ≈ NE Slovenia
99 F17 Lede Oost-Vlaanderen, NW Belgium 50°58′N 03°59′E
104 K6 Ledesma Castilla y León, N Spain 41°05′N 06°00′W
45 Q12 le Diamant SW Martinique 14°29′N 61°02′W
172 J16 Le Digue island Inner Islands, NE Seychelles
103 Q10 le Donjon Allier, C France 46°19′N 03°50′E
102 M10 le Dorat Haute-Vienne, C France 46°14′N 01°05′E
Ledo Salinarius see Lons-le-Saunier
11 Q14 Leduc Alberta, SW Canada 53°17′N 113°30′W
123 V7 Ledyanaya, Gora ▲ E Russian Federation 61°51′N 171°03′E
97 C21 Lee Ir. An Laoi. ≈ SW Ireland
29 U5 Leech Lake ◎ Minnesota, N USA
26 K10 Leedey Oklahoma, C USA 35°54′N 99°21′W
97 M17 Leeds N England, United Kingdom 53°50′N 01°35′W
23 P4 Leeds Alabama, S USA 33°33′N 86°32′W
29 O3 Leeds North Dakota, N USA 48°19′N 99°43′W
98 N6 Leek Groningen, NE Netherlands 53°10′N 06°24′E
99 K15 Leende Noord-Brabant, SE Netherlands 51°21′N 05°34′E
100 F10 Leer Niedersachsen, NW Germany 53°14′N 07°26′E
98 J13 Leerdam Zuid-Holland, C Netherlands 51°54′N 05°06′E
98 K12 Leersum Utrecht, C Netherlands 52°01′N 05°26′E
23 W11 Leesburg Florida, SE USA 28°48′N 81°52′W
21 V3 Leesburg Virginia, NE USA 39°09′N 77°34′W
27 R4 Lees Summit Missouri, C USA 38°55′N 94°21′W
22 G7 Leesville Louisiana, S USA 31°08′N 93°15′W
25 S12 Leesville Texas, SW USA 29°22′N 97°45′W
31 U13 Leesville Lake ⊠ Ohio, N USA
Leesville Lake see Smith Mountain Lake
183 P9 Leeton New South Wales, SE Australia 34°33′S 146°24′E
98 L6 Leeuwarden Fris. Ljouwert. Fryslân, N Netherlands 53°15′N 05°48′E
180 I14 Leeuwin, Cape headland Western Australia 34°18′S 115°03′E
35 R8 Lee Vining California, W USA 37°57′N 119°07′W
45 V8 Leeward Islands island group E West Indies
Leeward Islands see Sotavento, Ilhas de
Leeward Islands see Vent, Îles Sous le
79 G20 Léfini ≈ SE Congo
115 C17 Lefkáda prev. Levkás. Lefkáda, Iónia Nisiá, Greece, C Mediterranean Sea 38°50′N 20°42′E
115 B17 Lefkáda It. Santa Maura, prev. Levkás; anc. Leucas. island Iónia Nisiá, Greece, C Mediterranean Sea
115 H25 Lefká Óri ▲ Kríti, Greece, E Mediterranean Sea
115 B16 Lefkímmi var. Levkímmi. Kérkyra, Iónia Nisiá, Greece, C Mediterranean Sea 39°26′N 20°05′E
Lefkosía/Lefkoşa see Nicosia
25 O2 Lefors Texas, SW USA 35°26′N 100°48′W
45 R12 le François E Martinique 14°36′N 60°59′W
180 L12 Lefroy, Lake salt lake Western Australia
Legaceaster see Chester
105 N8 Leganés Madrid, C Spain 40°20′N 03°46′W
Legaspi see Legazpi City
Leghorn see Livorno
110 M11 Legionowo Mazowieckie, C Poland 52°25′N 20°56′E
99 K24 Léglise Luxembourg, SE Belgium 49°48′N 05°31′E
106 G8 Legnago Lombardia, NE Italy 45°13′N 11°18′E
106 D7 Legnano Veneto, NE Italy 45°36′N 08°54′E
111 F14 Legnica Ger. Liegnitz. Dolnośląskie, SW Poland 51°12′N 16°11′E
35 Q9 Le Grand California, W USA 37°12′N 120°15′W
103 Q15 le Grau-du-Roi Gard, S France 43°32′N 04°10′E
183 U3 Legume New South Wales, SE Australia 28°24′S 152°20′E
102 L4 le Havre Eng. Havre; prev. le Havre-de-Grâce. Seine-Maritime, N France 49°30′N 00°06′E
le Havre-de-Grâce see le Havre
Lehena see Lechainá
36 L3 Lehi Utah, W USA 40°23′N 111°51′W
18 I14 Lehighton Pennsylvania, NE USA 40°49′N 75°42′W
29 O6 Lehr North Dakota, N USA 46°15′N 99°21′W
38 A8 Lehua Island island Hawaiian Islands, Hawai'i, USA
149 S9 Leiāh Punjab, NE Pakistan 30°59′N 70°58′E
109 W9 Leibnitz Steiermark, SE Austria 46°48′N 15°33′E
97 M19 Leicester Lat. Batae Coritanorum. C England, United Kingdom 52°38′N 01°05′W
97 M19 Leicestershire cultural region C England, United Kingdom
Leicheng see Leizhou
98 H11 Leiden prev. Leyden; anc. Lugdunum Batavorum. Zuid-Holland, W Netherlands 52°09′N 04°30′E
98 H11 Leiderdorp Zuid-Holland, W Netherlands 52°08′N 04°32′E
98 G11 Leidschendam Zuid-Holland, W Netherlands 52°05′N 04°24′E
99 D18 Leie Fr. Lys. ≈ Belgium/France
Leifear see Lifford
184 L4 Leigh Auckland, North Island, New Zealand 36°17′S 174°48′E
97 K17 Leigh NW England, United Kingdom 53°30′N 02°33′W
182 I5 Leigh Creek South Australia 30°27′S 138°23′E
23 O2 Leighton Alabama, S USA 34°42′N 87°31′W
97 M21 Leighton Buzzard E England, United Kingdom 51°55′N 00°41′W
Léim an Bhradáin see Leixlip
Léim An Mhadaidh see Limavady
Léime, Ceann see Loop Head, Ireland
Léime, Ceann see Slyne Head, Ireland
101 G20 Leimen Baden-Württemberg, SW Germany 49°21′N 08°40′E
100 I13 Leine ≈ NW Germany
101 J15 Leinefelde Thüringen, C Germany 51°22′N 10°19′E
Léin, Loch see Leane, Lough
97 D19 Leinster Ir. Cúige Laighean. cultural region E Ireland
97 F19 Leinster, Mount Ir. Stua Laighean. ▲ SE Ireland 52°36′N 06°45′W
119 F15 Leipalingis Alytus, S Lithuania 54°05′N 23°52′E
92 J12 Leipojärvi Norrbotten, N Sweden 67°03′N 21°15′E
31 R12 Leipsic Ohio, N USA 41°06′N 83°58′W
Leipsic see Leipzig
115 M20 Leipsoí island Dodekánisa, Greece, Aegean Sea
101 M15 Leipzig Pol. Lipsk, hist. Leipsic; anc. Lipsia. Sachsen, E Germany 51°19′N 12°24′E
101 M15 Leipzig Halle ✈ Sachsen, E Germany 51°26′N 12°14′E
104 G9 Leiria anc. Collipo. Leiria, C Portugal 39°45′N 08°49′W
104 F9 Leiria ◆ district C Portugal
95 C15 Leirvik Hordaland, S Norway 59°49′N 05°27′E
118 E5 Leisi Ger. Laisberg. Saaremaa, W Estonia 58°33′N 22°41′E
104 J3 Leitariegos, Puerto de pass NW Spain
20 J6 Leitchfield Kentucky, S USA 37°28′N 86°19′W
109 Y5 Leitha Hung. Lajta. ≈ Austria/Hungary
Leitir Ceanainn see Letterkenny
Leitmeritz see Litoměřice
Leitomischl see Litomyšl
97 D16 Leitrim Ir. Liatroim. cultural region NW Ireland
Leix see Laois
97 F18 Leixlip Eng. Salmon Leap, Ir. Léim an Bhradáin. Kildare, E Ireland 53°23′N 06°32′W
64 N8 Leixões Porto, N Portugal 41°11′N 08°41′W
161 N12 Leiyang Hunan, S China 26°23′N 112°49′E
160 L16 Leizhou var. Haikang, Leicheng. Guangdong, S China 20°54′N 110°05′E
160 L16 Leizhou Bandao var. Luichow Peninsula. peninsula S China
98 H13 Lek ≈ SW Netherlands
114 I13 Lekánis ▲ NE Greece
172 H13 Le Kartala ▲ Grande Comore, NW Comoros
Le Kef see El Kef
79 G20 Lékéti, Monts de la ▲ S Congo
Lekhainá see Lechainá
92 G11 Leknes Nordland, C Norway 68°07′N 13°36′E
79 F20 Lékoumou ◆ province SW Congo
94 L13 Leksand Dalarna, C Sweden 60°44′N 15°E
124 H8 Leksozero, Ozero ◎ NW Russian Federation
105 Q3 Lekunberri var. Lecumberri. Navarra, N Spain 43°00′N 01°54′W
171 S11 Lelai, Tanjung headland Pulau Halmahera, N Indonesia 01°32′N 128°43′E
45 Q12 le Lamentin var. Lamentin. C Martinique 14°37′N 61°01′W
31 P6 Leland Michigan, N USA 45°01′N 85°44′W
22 J4 Leland Mississippi, S USA 33°24′N 90°54′W
95 J16 Lelång var. Lelången. ◎ S Sweden
Lelången see Lelång
Lel'chitsy see Lyel'chytsy
le Léman see Geneva, Lake
Leli see Tianlin
25 O3 Lelia Lake Texas, SW USA 34°52′N 100°42′W
113 I14 Lelija ▲ SE Bosnia and Herzegovina 43°25′N 18°31′E
108 C8 Le Locle Neuchâtel, W Switzerland 47°04′N 06°45′E
189 Y14 Lelu Kosrae, E Micronesia
Lelu see Lelu Island
189 Y14 Lelu Island var. Lelu. island Kosrae, E Micronesia
55 W9 Lelydorp Wanica, N Suriname 05°36′N 55°04′W
98 K9 Lelystad Flevoland, C Netherlands 52°30′N 05°26′E
63 K25 Le Maire, Estrecho de strait S Argentina
168 L10 Lemang Pulau Rangsang, W Indonesia 01°04′N 102°44′E
186 I7 Lemankoa Buka Island, NE Papua New Guinea 05°06′S 154°23′E
Léman, Lac see Geneva, Lake
102 L6 le Mans Sarthe, NW France 48°N 00°12′E
29 S12 Le Mars Iowa, C USA 42°47′N 96°10′W
109 S3 Lembach im Mühlkreis Oberösterreich, N Austria 48°28′N 13°53′E
101 G23 Lemberg ▲ SW Germany 48°09′N 08°47′E
Lemberg see Lviv
Lemdiyya see Médéa
121 P3 Lemesós var. Limassol. SW Cyprus 34°41′N 33°02′E
100 H13 Lemgo Nordrhein-Westfalen, W Germany 52°02′N 08°54′E
33 P13 Lemhi Range ▲ Idaho, NW USA
9 S6 Lemieux Islands island group Nunavut, NE Canada
171 Q11 Lemito Sulawesi, N Indonesia 0°34′N 121°31′E
92 L10 Lemmenjoki Lapp. Leammi. ≈ NE Finland
98 L7 Lemmer Fris. De Lemmer. Fryslân, N Netherlands 52°50′N 05°43′E
28 L7 Lemmon South Dakota, N USA 45°54′N 102°08′W
36 M15 Lemmon, Mount ▲ Arizona, SW USA 32°26′N 110°47′W
Lemnos see Límnos
31 O14 Lemon, Lake ◎ Indiana, N USA
102 J5 le Mont St-Michel castle Manche, N France
35 Q11 Lemoore California, W USA 36°16′N 119°48′W
189 T13 Lemotol Bay bay Chuuk Islands, C Micronesia
45 Y5 le Moule var. Moule. Grande Terre, NE Guadeloupe 16°20′N 61°21′W
Lemovices see Limoges
Le Moyen-Ogooué see Moyen-Ogooué
12 M6 le Moyne, Lac ◎ Québec, E Canada
93 L18 Lempäälä Länsi-Suomi, W Finland 61°14′N 23°47′E
42 E7 Lempa, Río ≈ Central America
42 F7 Lempira prev. Gracias. ◆ department SW Honduras
Lemsalu see Limbaži
107 N17 Le Murge ▲ SE Italy
125 V6 Lemva ≈ NW Russian Federation
95 F21 Lemvig Midtjylland, W Denmark 56°31′N 08°19′E
166 K8 Lemyethna Ayeyarwady, SW Myanmar (Burma) 17°36′N 95°08′E
30 K10 Lena Illinois, N USA 42°22′N 89°49′W
129 V4 Lena ≈ NE Russian Federation
173 N13 Lena Tablemount undersea feature S Indian Ocean 51°06′S 56°54′E
Lenchitsa see Łęczyca
59 N17 Lençóis Bahia, E Brazil 12°36′S 41°24′W
60 K9 Lençóis Paulista São Paulo, S Brazil 22°35′S 48°51′W
109 Y9 Lendava Hung. Lendva, Ger. Unterlimbach; prev. Dolnja Lendava. NE Slovenia 46°33′N 16°27′E
83 F20 Lendepas Hardap, SE Namibia 24°41′S 19°58′E
124 H9 Lendery Finn. Lentiira. Respublika Kareliya, NW Russian Federation 63°20′N 31°18′E
Lendum see Lens
Lendva see Lendava
27 R4 Lenexa Kansas, C USA 38°57′N 94°43′W
109 Q5 Lengau Oberösterreich, N Austria 48°01′N 13°17′E
145 Q17 Lenger Yuzhnyy Kazakhstan, S Kazakhstan 42°10′N 69°54′E
Lenghu see Lenghuzhen
159 O9 Lenghuzhen var. Lenghu. Qinghai, C China 38°50′N 93°25′E
159 T9 Lenglong Ling ▲ N China 37°40′N 102°13′E
108 D7 Lengnau Bern, W Switzerland 47°12′N 07°23′E
95 M20 Lenhovda Kronoberg, S Sweden 57°00′N 15°16′E
Lenīn see Uzynkol', Kazakhstan
Lenin see Akdepe, Turkmenistan
Leninabad see Khujand
Leninakan see Gyumri
Lenina, Pik see Lenin Peak
117 V12 Lenine Rus. Lenino. Avtonomna Respublika Krym, S Ukraine 45°18′N 35°47′E
Leningor see Leninogorsk
Leningrad see Sankt-Peterburg
Leningrad see Mu'minobod
126 L13 Leningradskaya Krasnodarskiy Kray, SW Russian Federation 46°19′N 39°23′E
195 S16 Leningradskaya Russian research station Antarctica 69°30′S 159°51′E
124 H12 Leningradskaya Oblast' ◆ province NW Russian Federation
Leningradskiy see Mu'minobod
Lenino see Lyenina, Belarus
Lenino see Lenine, Ukraine
Leninobod see Khujand
145 X9 Leninogorsk Kaz. Leningor. Vostochnyy Kazakhstan, E Kazakhstan 50°20′N 83°34′E
147 T12 Lenin Peak Rus. Pik Lenina, Taj. Qullai Lenin. ▲ Kyrgyzstan/Tajikistan 39°20′N 72°50′E
147 S8 Leninpol' Talasskaya Oblast', NW Kyrgyzstan 42°29′N 71°54′E
Lenin, Qullai see Lenin Peak
127 P11 Leninsk Volgogradskaya Oblast', SW Russian Federation 48°41′N 45°18′E
Leninsk see Baykonyr, Kazakhstan
Leninsk see Akdepe, Turkmenistan
Leninsk see Asaka, Uzbekistan
122 I13 Leninsk-Kuznetskiy Kemerovskaya Oblast', S Russian Federation 54°42′N 86°16′E
125 P15 Leninskoje Kirovskaya Oblast', NW Russian Federation 58°19′N 47°03′E
Leninskoye see Uzynkol'
Lenin-Turkmenski see Türkmenabat
Leninváros see Tiszaújváros
Lenkoran' see Länkäran
101 F15 Lenne ≈ W Germany
101 G16 Lennestadt Nordrhein-Westfalen, W Germany 51°07′N 08°04′E
29 R11 Lennox South Dakota, N USA 43°21′N 96°53′W
63 J25 Lennox, Isla Eng. Lennox Island. island S Chile
Lennox Island see Lennox, Isla
21 Q9 Lenoir North Carolina, SE USA 35°56′N 81°31′W
20 M9 Lenoir City Tennessee, S USA 35°48′N 84°15′W
108 C7 Le Noirmont Jura, NW Switzerland 47°14′N 06°57′E
14 L9 Lenôtre, Lac ◎ Québec, SE Canada
29 U15 Lenox Iowa, C USA 40°52′N 94°33′W
103 O2 Lens anc. Lendum, Lentium. Pas-de-Calais, N France 50°26′N 02°50′E
123 O11 Lensk Respublika Sakha (Yakutiya), NE Russian Federation 60°43′N 115°16′E
111 F24 Lenti Zala, SW Hungary 46°38′N 16°30′E
Lentia see Linz
93 N14 Lentiira Oulu, E Finland 64°22′N 29°52′E
Lentiira see Lendery
107 L25 Lentini anc. Leontini. Sicilia, Italy, C Mediterranean Sea 37°17′N 15°00′E
Lentium see Lens
Lentschiza see Łęczyca
93 N15 Lentua ◎ E Finland
119 H14 Lentvaris Pol. Landwarów. Vilnius, SE Lithuania 54°39′N 25°04′E
108 F7 Lenzburg Aargau, N Switzerland 47°23′N 08°11′E
109 R5 Lenzing Oberösterreich, N Austria 47°58′N 13°34′E
77 P13 Léo SW Burkina 11°07′N 02°08′W
109 V7 Leoben Steiermark, C Austria 47°23′N 15°06′E
Leobschütz see Głubczyce
44 L9 Léogâne S Haiti 18°32′N 72°37′W
171 O11 Leok Sulawesi, N Indonesia 01°10′N 121°20′E
29 O7 Leola South Dakota, N USA 45°41′N 98°58′W
97 K20 Leominster W England, United Kingdom 52°09′N 02°18′W
19 N11 Leominster Massachusetts, NE USA 42°29′N 71°43′W
102 I15 Léon Landes, SW France 43°54′N 01°17′W
40 M12 León var. León de los Aldamas. Guanajuato, C Mexico 21°05′N 101°43′W
42 I10 León León, NW Nicaragua 12°24′N 86°52′W
104 L4 León Castilla y León, NW Spain 42°34′N 05°34′W
29 V16 Leon Iowa, C USA 40°44′N 93°45′W
42 I9 León ◆ department W Nicaragua
104 K4 León ◆ province Castilla y León, NW Spain
León see Cotopaxi
25 V9 Leona Texas, SW USA 31°09′N 95°58′W
25 U5 Leonard Texas, SW USA 33°22′N 96°15′W
107 H15 Leonardo da Vinci prev. Fiumicino. ✈ (Roma) Lazio, C Italy 41°48′N 12°15′E
21 X5 Leonardtown Maryland, NE USA 38°17′N 76°35′W
25 Q13 Leona River ≈ Texas, SW USA
41 Z11 Leona Vicario Quintana Roo, SE Mexico 20°57′N 87°06′W
101 H21 Leonberg Baden-Württemberg, SW Germany 48°48′N 09°01′E
62 M3 León, Cerro ▲ NW Paraguay 20°21′S 60°16′W
León de los Aldamas see León
109 T4 Leonding Oberösterreich, N Austria 48°17′N 14°15′E
107 I14 Leonessa Lazio, C Italy 42°36′N 12°56′E
107 K24 Leonforte Sicilia, Italy, C Mediterranean Sea 37°38′N 14°23′E
183 O13 Leongatha Victoria, SE Australia 38°30′S 145°56′E
Leonídi see Leonídio
115 F21 Leonídio var. Leonídi. Pelopónnisos, S Greece 37°11′N 22°50′E
104 J4 León, Montes de ▲ NW Spain
180 K11 Leonora Western Australia 28°52′S 121°16′E
25 S8 Leon River ≈ Texas, SW USA
Leontini see Lentini
Léopold II, Lac see Mai-Ndombe, Lac
99 J17 Leopoldsburg Limburg, NE Belgium 51°07′N 05°16′E
Léopoldville see Kinshasa
26 I5 Leoti Kansas, C USA 38°28′N 101°22′W
116 M11 Leova Rus. Leovo. SW Moldova 46°31′N 28°16′E
Leovo see Leova
102 G8 le Palais Morbihan, NW France 47°20′N 03°08′W
27 X10 Lepanto Arkansas, C USA 35°34′N 90°21′W
169 N13 Lepar, Pulau island W Indonesia
104 I14 Lepe Andalucía, S Spain 37°15′N 07°12′W
Lepel' see Lyepyel'
83 E25 Lepelle var. Elefantes; prev. Olifants. ≈ SW South Africa
83 I20 Lephepe var. Lephephe. Kweneng, SE Botswana 23°20′S 25°50′E
Lephephe see Lephepe
161 Q10 Leping Jiangxi, S China 28°57′N 117°07′E
Lépontiennes, Alpes/Lepontine, Alpi see Lepontine Alps
108 G10 Lepontine Alps Fr. Alpes Lépontiennes, It. Alpi Lepontine. ▲ Italy/Switzerland
79 G20 Le Pool ◆ province S Congo
173 O16 Le Port NW Réunion
103 N1 le Portel Pas-de-Calais, N France 50°42′N 01°35′E
93 N17 Leppävirta Itä-Suomi, C Finland 62°30′N 27°50′E
45 Q11 le Prêcheur NW Martinique 14°48′N 61°14′W
145 V13 Lepsi prev. Lepsy. Taldykorgan, SE Kazakhstan 46°14′N 78°56′E
145 V13 Lepsi prev. Lepsy. ≈ SE Kazakhstan
Lepsy see Lepsi
Le Puglie see Puglia
103 Q12 le Puy prev. le Puy-en-Velay, hist. Anicium, Podium Anicensis. Haute-Loire, C France 45°03′N 03°53′E
le Puy-en-Velay see le Puy
45 X11 le Raizet var. Le Raizet. ✈ (Pointe-à-Pitre) Grande Terre, C Guadeloupe 16°16′N 61°31′W
107 J24 Lercara Friddi Sicilia, Italy, C Mediterranean Sea 37°45′N 13°37′E
78 G12 Léré Mayo-Kébbi, SW Chad 09°41′N 14°17′E
Leribe see Hlotse
106 E10 Lerici Liguria, NW Italy 44°06′N 09°53′E
54 I14 Lérida Vaupés, SE Colombia 0°01′S 70°28′W
105 U5 Lérida ◆ province Cataluña, NE Spain
Lérida see Lleida
105 N5 Lerma Castilla y León, N Spain 42°02′N 03°46′W
40 M13 Lerma, Río ≈ C Mexico
Lerna see Lérni
115 F20 Lérni var. Lerna. prehistoric site Pelopónnisos, S Greece
45 R11 le Robert E Martinique 14°41′N 60°57′W
115 M21 Léros island Dodekánisa, Greece, Aegean Sea
30 L13 Le Roy Illinois, N USA 40°21′N 88°45′W
27 Q6 Le Roy Kansas, C USA 38°04′N 95°37′W
29 W11 Le Roy Minnesota, N USA 43°30′N 92°30′W
18 E10 Le Roy New York, NE USA 42°58′N 77°58′W
Lerrnayin Gharabakh see Nagorno-Karabakh
95 J19 Lerum Västra Götaland, S Sweden 57°46′N 12°12′E
96 M2 Lerwick NE Scotland, United Kingdom 60°09′N 01°09′W
45 Y6 les Abymes var. Abymes. Grande Terre, C Guadeloupe 16°16′N 61°31′W
les Albères see Albères, Chaîne des
102 M4 les Andelys Eure, N France 49°15′N 01°26′E
45 Q12 les Anses-d'Arlets SW Martinique 14°29′N 61°05′W
104 L2 Les Arriondes prev. Arriondas. Asturias, N Spain 43°23′N 05°11′W
105 U6 Les Borges Blanques var. Borjas Blancas. Cataluña, NE Spain 41°31′N 00°52′E
Lesbos see Lésvos
Les Cayes see Cayes
31 Q4 Les Cheneaux Islands island Michigan, N USA
105 T8 Les Coves de Vinromá Cast. Cuevas de Vinromá. Valenciana, E Spain 40°18′N 00°07′E
103 T12 les Écrins ▲ E France 44°54′N 06°25′E
108 C10 Le Sépey Vaud, W Switzerland 46°21′N 07°04′E
15 T7 Les Escoumins Québec, SE Canada 48°21′N 69°26′W
Les Gonaïves see Gonaïves
160 H9 Leshan Sichuan, C China 29°42′N 103°43′E
108 D11 Les Haudères Valais, SW Switzerland 46°02′N 07°27′E
102 J9 les Herbiers Vendée, NW France 46°52′N 01°01′W
Lesh/Leshi see Lezhë
125 O8 Leshukonskoye Arkhangel'skaya Oblast', NW Russian Federation 64°54′N 45°48′E
Lesina see Hvar
107 M15 Lesina, Lago di ◎ SE Italy
114 K13 Lesitse ▲ NE Greece
94 G10 Lesja Oppland, S Norway 62°07′N 08°56′E
95 L15 Lesjöfors Värmland, C Sweden 59°57′N 14°12′E
111 O18 Lesko Podkarpackie, SE Poland 49°28′N 22°19′E
113 O15 Leskovac Serbia, SE Serbia 43°00′N 21°58′E
113 M22 Leskovik var. Leskoviku. Korçë, S Albania 40°09′N 20°39′E
Leskoviku see Leskovik
33 P14 Leslie Idaho, NW USA 43°51′N 113°28′W
31 Q10 Leslie Michigan, N USA 42°27′N 84°25′W
Leśna/Lesnaya see Lyasnaya
Lesnaya see Lyasnaya
102 F5 Lesneven Finistère, NW France 48°35′N 04°19′W
112 J11 Lešnica Serbia, W Serbia 44°40′N 19°18′E
125 S13 Lesnoy Kirovskaya Oblast', NW Russian Federation 59°49′N 52°07′E
122 G10 Lesnoy Sverdlovskaya Oblast', C Russian Federation 58°40′N 59°48′E
122 K12 Lesosibirsk Krasnoyarskiy Kray, C Russian Federation 58°13′N 92°23′E
83 J23 Lesotho off. Kingdom of Lesotho; prev. Basutoland. ◆ monarchy S Africa
Lesotho, Kingdom of see Lesotho
102 J12 Lesparre-Médoc Gironde, SW France 45°18′N 00°57′W
108 C8 Les Ponts-de-Martel Neuchâtel, W Switzerland 47°00′N 06°45′E
103 P1 Lesquin ✈ Nord, N France 50°34′N 03°07′E
102 I9 les Sables-d'Olonne Vendée, NW France 46°30′N 01°47′W
109 S7 Lessach var. Lessachbach. ≈ E Austria
Lessachbach see Lessach
45 W11 les Saintes var. Îles des Saintes. island group S Guadeloupe
74 L5 Les Salines ✈ (Annaba) NE Algeria 36°45′N 07°57′E
99 J22 Lesse ≈ SE Belgium
95 M21 Lessebo Kronoberg, S Sweden 56°45′N 15°19′E
Lesser Antarctica see West Antarctica
45 P15 Lesser Antilles island group E West Indies
137 T10 Lesser Caucasus Rus. Malyy Kavkaz. ▲ SW Asia
Lesser Khingan Range see Xiao Hinggan Ling
11 P13 Lesser Slave Lake ◎ Alberta, W Canada
99 E19 Lessines Hainaut, SW Belgium 50°43′N 03°50′E
103 R16 les Stes-Maries-de-la-Mer Bouches-du-Rhône, SE France 43°27′N 04°26′E
14 G15 Lester B. Pearson var. Toronto. ✈ (Toronto) Ontario, S Canada 43°59′N 81°30′W
29 U9 Lester Prairie Minnesota, N USA 44°52′N 94°02′W
93 L16 Lestijärvi Länsi-Suomi, W Finland 63°29′N 24°41′E
L'Estuaire see Estuaire
29 U9 Le Sueur Minnesota, N USA 44°27′N 93°53′W
108 B8 Les Verrières Neuchâtel, W Switzerland 46°54′N 06°29′E
115 L17 Lésvos anc. Lesbos. island E Greece
110 G12 Leszno Ger. Lissa. Wielkopolskie, C Poland 51°51′N 16°35′E
83 L20 Letaba Northern, NE South Africa 23°44′S 31°29′E
173 P17 Le Tampon SW Réunion
97 O21 Letchworth E England, United Kingdom 51°58′N 00°14′W
111 G25 Letenye Zala, SW Hungary 46°25′N 16°44′E
11 Q17 Lethbridge Alberta, SW Canada 49°43′N 112°48′W
55 S11 Lethem S Guyana 03°24′N 59°45′W
83 H18 Letiahau ≈ W Botswana
54 J18 Leticia Amazonas, S Colombia 04°09′S 69°57′W
171 S16 Leti, Kepulauan island group E Indonesia
83 I18 Letlhakane Central, C Botswana 21°26′S 25°36′E
83 H20 Letlhakeng Kweneng, SE Botswana 24°05′S 25°03′E
114 J8 Letnitsa Lovech, N Bulgaria 43°19′N 25°02′E
103 N1 le Touquet-Paris-Plage Pas-de-Calais, N France 50°31′N 01°36′E
166 L8 Letpadan Bago, SW Myanmar (Burma) 17°46′N 94°45′E
166 K6 Letpan Rakhine State, W Myanmar (Burma) 19°22′N 94°11′E
102 M2 le Tréport Seine-Maritime, N France 50°03′N 01°21′E
166 M12 Letsôk-aw Kyun var. Letsutan Island; prev. Domel Island. island Mergui Archipelago, S Myanmar (Burma)
Letsutan Island see Letsôk-aw Kyun
97 E14 Letterkenny Ir. Leitir Ceanainn. Donegal, NW Ireland 54°57′N 07°44′W
Lettland see Latvia
116 M6 Letychiv Khmel'nyts'ka Oblast', W Ukraine 49°24′N 27°39′E
Lëtzebuerg see Luxembourg
116 H14 Leu Dolj, SW Romania 44°10′N 24°01′E
Leucas see Lefkáda
103 P17 Leucate Aude, S France 42°55′N 03°03′E
103 P17 Leucate, Étang de ◎ S France
108 E10 Leuk Valais, SW Switzerland 46°18′N 07°46′E
108 E10 Leukerbad Valais, SW Switzerland 46°22′N 07°47′E
Leusden see Leusden-Centrum
98 K11 Leusden-Centrum var. Leusden. Utrecht, C Netherlands 52°08′N 05°25′E
Leutensdorf see Litvínov
Leutschau see Levoča
99 H18 Leuven Fr. Louvain, Ger. Löwen. Vlaams Brabant, C Belgium 50°53′N 04°42′E
99 I20 Leuze Namur, C Belgium 50°33′N 04°55′E
Leuze see Leuze-en-Hainaut
99 E19 Leuze-en-Hainaut var. Leuze. Hainaut, SW Belgium 50°36′N 03°37′E
Léva see Levice
Levádia see Livádeia
Levajok see Leavvajohka
36 L4 Levan Utah, W USA 39°33′N 111°51′W
93 E16 Levanger Nord-Trøndelag, C Norway 63°45′N 11°18′E
106 D10 Levanto Liguria, W Italy 44°12′N 09°33′E
107 H23 Levanzo, Isola di island Isole Egadi, S Italy
127 Q17 Levashi Respublika Dagestan, SW Russian Federation 42°27′N 47°19′E
24 M5 Levelland Texas, SW USA 33°35′N 102°23′W
39 P13 Levelock Alaska, USA 59°07′N 156°51′W
101 E16 Leverkusen Nordrhein-Westfalen, W Germany 51°02′N 07°E
111 J21 Levice Ger. Lewentz, Hung. Léva, Lewenz. Nitriansky Kraj, SW Slovakia 48°14′N 18°38′E
106 G6 Levico Terme Trentino-Alto Adige, N Italy 46°02′N 11°19′E
115 E20 Levídi Pelopónnisos, S Greece 37°39′N 22°13′E
103 P14 le Vigan Gard, S France 43°00′N 03°36′E
184 L13 Levin Manawatu-Wanganui, North Island, New Zealand 40°38′S 175°17′E
15 R10 Lévis var. Levis. Québec, SE Canada 46°47′N 71°12′W
Levis see Lévis
21 P6 Levisa Fork ≈ Kentucky/Virginia, S USA
115 L21 Levítha island Kykládes, Greece, Aegean Sea
18 L14 Levittown Long Island, New York, NE USA 40°42′N 73°29′W
18 J15 Levittown Pennsylvania, NE USA 40°09′N 74°50′W
Levkás see Lefkáda
Levkímmi see Lefkímmi
111 L19 Levoča Ger. Leutschau, Hung. Locse. Prešovský Kraj, E Slovakia 49°01′N 20°34′E
Lévrier, Baie du see Nouâdhibou, Dakhlet
103 N9 Levroux Indre, C France 47°00′N 01°37′E
114 J8 Levski Pleven, N Bulgaria 43°21′N 25°11′E
Levskigrad see Karlovo
126 L6 Lev Tolstoy Lipetskaya Oblast', W Russian Federation 53°12′N 39°28′E
187 X14 Levuka Ovalau, C Fiji 17°42′S 178°50′E
166 L6 Lewe Mandalay, C Myanmar (Burma) 19°40′N 96°04′E
Lewentz/Lewenz see Levice
97 O23 Lewes SE England, United Kingdom 50°52′N 00°01′E
21 Z4 Lewes Delaware, NE USA 38°46′N 75°08′W
29 Q12 Lewis And Clark Lake ⊠ Nebraska/South Dakota, N USA
18 G14 Lewisburg Pennsylvania, NE USA 40°57′N 76°52′W
20 J10 Lewisburg Tennessee, S USA 35°29′N 86°49′W
21 S6 Lewisburg West Virginia, NE USA 37°49′N 80°28′W
96 F6 Lewis, Butt of headland NW Scotland, United Kingdom 58°31′N 06°18′W
96 F7 Lewis, Isle of island NW Scotland, United Kingdom
35 U4 Lewis, Mount ▲ Nevada, W USA 40°22′N 116°50′W
185 H16 Lewis Pass pass South Island, New Zealand
33 P7 Lewis Range ▲ Montana, NW USA
23 O3 Lewis Smith Lake ⊠ Alabama, S USA
32 M10 Lewiston Idaho, NW USA 46°25′N 117°01′W
19 P7 Lewiston Maine, NE USA 44°08′N 70°14′W
29 X10 Lewiston Minnesota, N USA 43°58′N 91°52′W
18 D9 Lewiston New York, NE USA 43°10′N 79°02′W
36 L1 Lewiston Utah, W USA 41°58′N 111°52′W
30 K13 Lewistown Illinois, N USA 40°23′N 90°09′W
33 T9 Lewistown Montana, NW USA 47°04′N 109°26′W
27 T14 Lewisville Arkansas, C USA 33°21′N 93°38′W
25 T6 Lewisville Texas, SW USA 33°00′N 96°57′W
25 T6 Lewisville, Lake ⊠ Texas, SW USA
Le Woleu-Ntem see Woleu-Ntem
23 U3 Lexington Georgia, SE USA 33°51′N 83°04′W
20 M5 Lexington Kentucky, S USA 38°03′N 84°30′W
22 L4 Lexington Mississippi, S USA 33°06′N 90°03′W
27 S4 Lexington Missouri, C USA 39°11′N 93°52′W
29 N16 Lexington Nebraska, C USA 40°46′N 99°44′W
20 S9 Lexington North Carolina, SE USA 35°49′N 80°15′W
27 N11 Lexington Oklahoma, C USA 35°00′N 97°20′W
21 R12 Lexington South Carolina, SE USA 33°59′N 81°15′W
20 G9 Lexington Tennessee, S USA 35°39′N 88°24′W
25 T10 Lexington Texas, SW USA 30°25′N 97°00′W
21 T6 Lexington Virginia, NE USA 37°47′N 79°27′W
21 X5 Lexington Park Maryland, NE USA 38°16′N 76°27′W
Leyden see Leiden
102 J14 Leyre ≈ SW France
171 Q5 Leyte island C Philippines
171 Q6 Leyte Gulf gulf E Philippines
111 O16 Leżajsk Podkarpackie, SE Poland 50°15′N 22°25′E
Lezha see Lezhë
113 K18 Lezhë var. Lezha; prev. Lesh, Leshi. Lezhë, NW Albania 41°46′N 19°40′E
113 K18 Lezhë ◆ district NW Albania
103 O16 Lézignan-Corbières Aude, S France 43°12′N 02°46′E
126 J7 L'gov Kurskaya Oblast', W Russian Federation 51°38′N 35°17′E
159 P15 Lhari Xizang Zizhiqu, W China 30°34′N 93°40′E
159 N16 Lhasa var. La-sa, Lassa. Xizang Zizhiqu, W China 29°41′N 91°10′E
159 O15 Lhasa He ≈ W China

◆ Country ● Country Capital ◇ Dependent Territory ○ Dependent Territory Capital ◆ Administrative Regions ✈ International Airport ▲ Mountain ▲ Mountain Range Volcano ≈ River ◎ Lake ⊠ Reservoir

Lhaviyani Atoll see Faadhippolhu Atoll
158 K16 Lhazê var. Quxar. Xizang Zizhiqu, W China 29°07′N 87°32′E
158 K14 Lhazhong Xizang Zizhiqu, W China 31°58′N 86°43′E
168 H7 Lhoksukon Sumatera, W Indonesia 05°04′N 97°19′E
159 Q15 Lhorong var. Zito. Xizang Zizhiqu, W China 30°51′N 95°41′E
105 W6 L'Hospitalet de Llobregat var. Hospitalet. Cataluña, NE Spain 41°21′N 02°06′E
153 R11 Lhotse ▲ China/Nepal 28°00′N 86°55′E
159 N17 Lhozhag var. Garbo. Xizang Zizhiqu, W China 28°21′N 90°47′E
159 O16 Lhünzê var. Xingba. Xizang Zizhiqu, W China 28°25′N 92°30′E
159 N15 Lhünzhub var. Ganqu. Xizang Zizhiqu, W China 30°14′N 91°20′E
167 N8 Li Lamphun, NW Thailand 17°46′N 98°54′E
115 L21 Liádi var. Livádi. island Kykládes, Greece, Aegean Sea
161 P12 Liancheng var. Lianfeng. Fujian, SE China 25°47′N 116°42′E
Liancheng see Lianjiang, Guangdong, China
Liancheng see Qinglong, Guizhou, China
Liancheng see Guangnan, Yunnan, China
Lianfeng see Liancheng
160 K9 Liangping var. Liangshan. Sichuan, C China 30°40′N 107°46′E
Liangshan see Liangping
Liangzhou see Wuwei
161 O9 Liangzi Hu ⊠ C China
161 R12 Lianjiang var. Fengcheng. Fujian, SE China 26°14′N 119°33′E
160 L15 Lianjiang var. Liancheng. Guangdong, S China 21°41′N 110°12′E
Lianjiang see Xingguo
161 O13 Lianping var. Yuanshan. Guangdong, S China 24°18′N 114°27′E
Lianshan see Huludao
Lian Xian see Lianzhou
160 M11 Lianyuan prev. Lantian. Hunan, S China 27°51′N 111°44′E
161 Q6 Lianyungang var. Xinpu. Jiangsu, E China 34°38′N 119°12′E
161 N13 Lianzhou var. Linxian; prev. Lian Xian. Guangdong, S China 24°48′N 112°26′E
Lianzhou see Hepu
Liao see Liaoning
161 P5 Liaocheng Shandong, E China 36°31′N 115°59′E
163 U13 Liaodong Bandao var. Liaotung Peninsula. peninsula NE China
163 T13 Liaodong Wan Eng. Gulf of Lantung, Gulf of Liaotung. gulf NE China
163 U11 Liao He ∾ NE China
163 U12 Liaoning var. Liao, Liaoning Sheng, Shengking, hist. Fengtien, Shenking. ◈ province NE China
Liaoning Sheng see Liaoning
Liaotung Peninsula see Liaodong Bandao
163 V12 Liaoyang var. Liao-yang. Liaoning, NE China 41°16′N 123°12′E
Liao-yang see Liaoyang
163 V11 Liaoyuan var. Dongliao, Shuang-liao, Jap. Chengchiatun. Jilin, NE China 42°52′N 125°09′E
163 U12 Liaozhong Liaoning, NE China 41°33′N 122°54′E
Liaqatabad see Piplān
10 M10 Liard ∾ W Canada
Liard see Fort Liard
10 L10 Liard River British Columbia, W Canada 59°23′N 126°05′W
149 O15 Liāri Baluchistān, SW Pakistan 25°43′N 66°28′E
Liatroim see Leitrim
189 S6 Lib var. Ellep. island Ralik Chain, C Marshall Islands
Liban see Lebanon
138 H6 Liban, Jebel Ar. Jabal al Gharbt, Jabal Lubnān, Eng. Mount Lebanon. ▲ C Lebanon
Libau see Liepāja
33 N7 Libby Montana, NW USA 48°25′N 115°33′W
79 I16 Libenge Equateur, NW Dem. Rep. Congo 03°39′N 18°39′E
26 I7 Liberal Kansas, C USA 37°03′N 100°56′W
27 R7 Liberal Missouri, C USA 37°33′N 94°31′W
Liberalitas Julia see Évora
111 D15 Liberec Ger. Reichenberg. Liberecký Kraj, N Czech Republic 50°45′N 15°05′E
111 D15 Liberecký Kraj ◈ region N Czech Republic
42 K12 Liberia Guanacaste, NW Costa Rica 10°36′N 85°26′W
76 K17 Liberia off. Republic of Liberia. ◆ republic W Africa
Liberia, Republic of see Liberia
61 D16 Libertad Corrientes, NE Argentina 30°01′S 57°51′W
61 E20 Libertad San José, S Uruguay 34°38′S 56°39′W
54 I7 Libertad Barinas, NW Venezuela 08°21′N 69°39′W
54 K6 Libertad Cojedes, N Venezuela 09°15′N 68°30′W
62 G12 Libertador off. Región del Libertador General Bernardo O'Higgins. ◈ region C Chile
Libertador General Bernardo O'Higgins, Región del see Libertador
Libertador General San Martín see Ciudad de Libertador General San Martín
20 L6 Liberty Kentucky, S USA 37°19′N 84°58′W
22 J7 Liberty Mississippi, S USA 31°09′N 90°49′W
27 R4 Liberty Missouri, C USA 39°15′N 94°22′W
18 J12 Liberty New York, NE USA 41°48′N 74°45′W
21 T9 Liberty North Carolina, SE USA 35°49′N 79°34′W
Libian Desert see Libyan Desert
99 J23 Libin Luxembourg, SE Belgium 50°01′N 05°13′E
Lībīyah, Aş Şahrā' al see Libyan Desert
160 K13 Libo var. Yuping. Guizhou, S China 25°28′N 107°52′E
Libohova see Libohovë
113 L23 Libohovë var. Libohova. Gjirokastër, S Albania 40°03′N 20°13′E
81 K18 Liboi North Eastern, E Kenya 0°23′N 40°55′E
102 K13 Libourne Gironde, SW France 44°55′N 00°14′W
99 K23 Libramont Luxembourg, SE Belgium 49°55′N 05°21′E
113 M20 Librazhd var. Librazhdi. Elbasan, E Albania 41°10′N 20°22′E
Librazhdi see Librazhd
79 C18 Libreville ● (Gabon) Estuaire, NW Gabon 0°25′N 09°29′E
75 P10 Libya off. Great Socialist People's Libyan Arab Jamahiriya, Ar. Al Jamāhīrīyah al 'Arabīyah al Lībīyah ash Sha'bīyah al Ishtirākīy; prev. Libyan Arab Republic. ◆ Islamic state N Africa
Libyan Arab Republic see Libya
75 T11 Libyan Desert var. Libian Desert, Ar. Aş Şahrā' al Lībīyah. desert N Africa
75 T8 Libyan Plateau var. Aḍ Diffah. plateau Egypt/Libya
62 G12 Licantén Maule, C Chile 35°00′S 72°00′W
107 J25 Licata anc. Phintias. Sicilia, Italy, C Mediterranean Sea 37°07′N 13°57′E
137 P14 Lice Diyarbakır, SE Turkey 38°29′N 40°39′E
Licheng see Lipu
97 L19 Lichfield C England, United Kingdom 52°42′N 01°48′W
83 N14 Lichinga Niassa, N Mozambique 13°19′S 35°13′E
109 V3 Lichtenau Niederösterreich, N Austria 48°29′N 15°24′E
83 I21 Lichtenburg North-West, N South Africa 26°09′S 26°11′E
101 K18 Lichtenfels Bayern, SE Germany 50°09′N 11°04′E
98 O12 Lichtenvoorde Gelderland, E Netherlands 51°59′N 06°34′E
Lichtenwald see Sevnica
99 C17 Lichtervelde West-Vlaanderen, W Belgium 51°02′N 03°09′E
160 L9 Lichuan Hubei, C China 30°20′N 108°56′E
27 V7 Licking Missouri, C USA 37°30′N 91°51′W
20 M4 Licking River ∾ Kentucky, S USA
112 C11 Lički Osik Lika-Senj, C Croatia 44°36′N 15°24′E
Ličko-Senjska Županija see Lika-Senj
107 K19 Licosa, Punta headland S Italy 40°15′N 14°54′E
119 H16 Lida Hrodzyenskaya Voblasts', W Belarus 53°53′N 25°20′E
93 H17 Liden Västernorrland, C Sweden 62°43′N 16°49′E
29 R7 Lidgerwood North Dakota, N USA 46°04′N 97°09′W
Lidhorikíon see Lidoríki
95 K21 Lidhult Kronoberg, S Sweden 56°49′N 13°25′E
95 P16 Lidingö Stockholm, C Sweden 59°22′N 18°10′E
95 K17 Lidköping Västra Götaland, S Sweden 58°30′N 13°10′E
Lido di Iesolo see Lido di Jesolo
106 I8 Lido di Jesolo var. Lido di Iesolo. Veneto, NE Italy 45°30′N 12°37′E
107 H15 Lido di Ostia Lazio, C Italy 41°42′N 12°19′E
Lidokhorikion see Lidoríki
115 E18 Lidoríki prev. Lidhorikíon, Lidokhorikion. Stereá Elláda, C Greece 38°32′N 22°12′E
110 K9 Lidzbark Warmińsko-Mazurskie, NE Poland 53°15′N 19°49′E
110 L7 Lidzbark Warmiński Ger. Heilsberg. Olsztyn, N Poland 54°08′N 20°35′E
109 U3 Liebenau Oberösterreich, N Austria 48°33′N 14°48′E
181 P7 Liebig, Mount ▲ Northern Territory, C Australia 23°19′S 131°30′E
109 V8 Lieboch Steiermark, SE Austria 47°00′N 15°21′E
108 I8 Liechtenstein off. Principality of Liechtenstein. ◆ principality C Europe
Liechtenstein, Principality of see Liechtenstein
99 F18 Liedekerke Vlaams Brabant, C Belgium 50°51′N 04°05′E
99 K19 Liège Dut. Luik, Ger. Lüttich. Liège, E Belgium 50°38′N 05°35′E
99 K20 Liège Dut. Luik. ◈ province E Belgium
Liegnitz see Legnica
93 O16 Lieksa Itä-Suomi, E Finland 63°20′N 30°E
118 F10 Lielupe ∾ Latvia/Lithuania
118 G9 Lielvārde C Latvia 56°45′N 24°48′E
167 U13 Liên Hương var. Tuy Phong. Binh Thuận, S Vietnam 11°13′N 108°40′E
167 U13 Liên Nghia var. Đưc Trong. Lâm Đông, S Vietnam 11°45′N 108°24′E
Liên Nghia see Liên Nghia
109 P9 Lienz Tirol, W Austria 46°50′N 12°45′E
118 B10 Liepāja Ger. Libau. W Latvia 56°32′N 21°02′E
99 H17 Lier Fr. Lierre. Antwerpen, N Belgium 51°08′N 04°35′E
95 H15 Lierbyen Buskerud, S Norway 59°57′N 10°14′E
99 L21 Lierneux Liège, E Belgium 50°12′N 05°51′E
Lierre see Lier
101 D18 Lieser ∾ W Germany
109 U7 Liesing ∾ E Austria
108 E6 Liestal Basel Landschaft, N Switzerland 47°29′N 07°43′E
Lietuva see Lithuania
Lievenhof see Līvāni
103 O2 Liévin Pas-de-Calais, N France 50°25′N 02°48′E
14 M9 Lièvre, Rivière du ∾ Québec, SE Canada
109 T6 Liezen Steiermark, C Austria 47°34′N 14°12′E
97 E14 Lifford Ir. Leifear. Donegal, NW Ireland 54°50′N 07°29′W
187 Q16 Lifou island Îles Loyauté, E New Caledonia
193 Y15 Lifuka island Ha'apai Group, C Tonga
171 P4 Ligao Luzon, N Philippines 13°16′N 123°30′E
Liger see Loire
42 H2 Lighthouse Reef reef E Belize
183 Q4 Lightning Ridge New South Wales, SE Australia 29°29′S 148°00′E
103 N9 Lignières Cher, C France 46°45′N 02°10′E
103 S5 Ligny-en-Barrois Meuse, NE France 48°42′N 05°22′E
83 P15 Ligonha ∾ NE Mozambique
31 P11 Ligonier Indiana, N USA 41°25′N 85°33′W
81 I25 Ligunga Ruvuma, S Tanzania 10°51′S 37°10′E
106 D9 Ligure, Appennino Eng. Ligurian Mountains. ▲▲ NW Italy
Ligure, Mar see Ligurian Sea
106 C9 Liguria ◈ region NW Italy
Ligurian Mountains see Ligure, Appennino
120 K6 Ligurian Sea Fr. Mer Ligurienne, It. Mar Ligure. sea N Mediterranean Sea
Ligurienne, Mer see Ligurian Sea
186 H5 Lihir Group island group NE Papua New Guinea
38 B8 Līhu'e var. Lihue. Kaua'i, Hawaii, USA 21°59′N 159°23′W
Lihue see Līhu'e
118 F5 Lihula Ger. Leal. Läänemaa, W Estonia 58°44′N 23°49′E
124 I2 Liinakhamari var. Linacmamari. Murmanskaya Oblast', NW Russian Federation 69°40′N 31°27′E
Liivi Laht see Riga, Gulf of
160 F11 Lijiang var. Dayan, Lijiang Naxizu Zizhixian. Yunnan, SW China 26°52′N 100°10′E
Lijiang Naxizu Zizhixian see Lijiang
112 C11 Lika-Senj off. Ličko-Senjska Županija. ◈ province W Croatia
79 N25 Likasi prev. Jadotville. Shaba, SE Dem. Rep. Congo 11°02′S 26°51′E
79 L16 Likati Orientale, N Dem. Rep. Congo 03°28′N 23°45′E
10 M15 Likely British Columbia, SW Canada 52°40′N 121°34′W
153 Y11 Likhapāni Assam, NE India 27°19′N 95°54′E
124 J16 Likhoslavl' Tverskaya Oblast', W Russian Federation 57°08′N 35°27′E
189 U5 Likiep Atoll atoll Ratak Chain, C Marshall Islands
95 D18 Liknes Vest-Agder, S Norway 58°20′N 06°58′E
79 H16 Likouala ◈ province NE Congo
79 H18 Likouala ∾ N Congo
79 H18 Likouala aux Herbes ∾ E Congo
190 B16 Liku E Niue 19°02′S 169°47′E
Likupang, Selat see Bangka, Selat
27 Y8 Lilbourn Missouri, C USA 36°35′N 89°37′W
103 X14 l'Île-Rousse Corse, France, C Mediterranean Sea 42°39′N 08°59′E
109 W5 Lilienfeld Niederösterreich, NE Austria 48°01′N 15°36′E
161 N11 Liling Hunan, S China 27°42′N 113°49′E
95 J18 Lilla Edet Västra Götaland, S Sweden 58°08′N 12°08′E
103 P1 Lille var. l'Isle, Dut. Rijssel, Flem. Ryssel, prev. Lisle; anc. Insula. Nord, N France 50°38′N 03°04′E
95 G24 Lillebælt var. Lille Bælt, Eng. Little Belt. strait S Denmark
Lille Bælt see Lillebælt
102 L3 Lillebonne Seine-Maritime, N France 49°30′N 00°34′E
94 H12 Lillehammer Oppland, S Norway 61°07′N 10°28′E
103 O1 Lillers Pas-de-Calais, N France 50°34′N 02°26′E
95 F18 Lillesand Aust-Agder, S Norway 58°15′N 08°23′E
95 I15 Lillestrøm Akershus, S Norway 59°58′N 11°05′E
93 F18 Lillhärdal Jämtland, C Sweden 61°51′N 14°04′E
21 U10 Lillington North Carolina, SE USA 35°25′N 78°50′W
105 O9 Lillo Castilla-La Mancha, C Spain 39°43′N 03°19′W
10 M16 Lillooet British Columbia, SW Canada 50°41′N 121°59′W
83 M14 Lilongwe ● (Malawi) Central, W Malawi 13°58′S 33°48′E
83 M14 Lilongwe ✈ Central, W Malawi 13°46′S 33°44′E
83 M14 Lilongwe ∾ W Malawi
171 P7 Liloy Mindanao, S Philippines 08°04′N 122°42′E
Lilybaeum see Marsala
182 J7 Lilydale South Australia 32°57′S 140°00′E
183 P16 Lilydale Tasmania, SE Australia 41°17′S 147°13′E
113 J14 Lim ∾ SE Europe
57 D15 Lima ● (Peru) Lima, W Peru 12°06′S 78°W
94 K13 Lima Dalarna, C Sweden 60°55′N 13°19′E
31 R12 Lima Ohio, NE USA 40°43′N 84°06′W
57 D14 Lima ◈ department W Peru
Lima see Jorge Chávez Internacional
137 Y13 Liman prev. Port Iliç. SE Azerbaijan 38°54′N 48°49′E
111 L17 Limanowa Małopolskie, S Poland 49°43′N 20°25′E
104 G5 Lima, Rio Sp. Limia. ∾ Portugal/Spain see also Limia
Lima, Rio see Limia
168 M11 Limas Pulau Sebangka, W Indonesia 0°09′N 104°31′E
Limassol see Lemesós
97 F14 Limavady Ir. Léim An Mhadaidh. NW Northern Ireland, United Kingdom 55°03′N 06°57′W
63 J14 Limay Mahuida La Pampa, C Argentina 37°09′S 66°40′W
63 H15 Limay, Río ∾ W Argentina
101 N16 Limbach-Oberfrohna Sachsen, E Germany 50°52′N 12°46′E
81 F22 Limba Limba ∾ C Tanzania
107 C17 Limbara, Monte ▲ Sardegna, Italy, C Mediterranean Sea 40°50′N 09°10′E
118 G7 Limbaži Est. Lemsalu. N Latvia 57°33′N 24°46′E
44 M8 Limbé N Haiti 19°44′N 72°25′W
99 L19 Limbourg Liège, E Belgium 50°37′N 05°56′E
99 K17 Limburg ◈ province NE Belgium
99 L16 Limburg ◈ province SE Netherlands
101 F17 Limburg an der Lahn Hessen, W Germany 50°22′N 08°04′E
94 K13 Limedsforsen Dalarna, C Sweden 60°52′N 13°25′E
60 L9 Limeira São Paulo, S Brazil 22°34′S 47°25′W
97 C19 Limerick Ir. Luimneach. Limerick, SW Ireland 52°40′N 08°38′W
97 C20 Limerick Ir. Luimneach. cultural region SW Ireland
19 S2 Limestone Maine, NE USA 46°52′N 67°49′W
25 U9 Limestone, Lake ◎ Texas, SW USA
39 P12 Lime Village Alaska, USA 61°21′N 155°26′W
95 F20 Limfjorden fjord N Denmark
95 J23 Limhamn Skåne, S Sweden 55°34′N 12°57′E
104 H5 Limia Port. Rio Lima. ∾ Portugal/Spain see also Lima,Rio
Limia see Lima, Rio
93 L14 Liminka Oulu, C Finland 64°48′N 25°19′E
Limín Vathéos see Sámos
115 G17 Límni Évvoia, C Greece 38°46′N 23°20′E
115 J15 Límnos anc. Lemnos. island E Greece
102 M11 Limoges anc. Augustoritum Lemovicensium, Lemovices. Haute-Vienne, C France 45°51′N 01°16′E
43 O13 Limón var. Puerto Limón. Limón, E Costa Rica 09°59′N 83°02′W
42 K4 Limón Colón, NE Honduras 15°50′N 85°31′W
37 U5 Limon Colorado, C USA 39°15′N 103°41′W
43 N13 Limón off. Provincia de Limón. ◈ province E Costa Rica
106 A10 Limone Piemonte Piemonte, NE Italy 44°12′N 07°37′E
Limones see Valdéz
Limón, Provincia de see Limón
Limonum see Poitiers
103 N11 Limousin ◈ region C France
103 N16 Limoux Aude, S France 43°03′N 02°13′E
83 J20 Limpopo off. Limpopo Province; prev. Northern, Northern Transvaal. ◈ province NE South Africa
83 L19 Limpopo var. Crocodile. ∾ S Africa
Limpopo Province see Limpopo
160 K17 Limu Ling ▲▲ S China
113 M20 Lin var. Lini. Elbasan, E Albania 41°03′N 20°37′E
Linacmamari see Liinakhamari
62 G13 Linares Maule, C Chile 35°50′S 71°37′W
54 C13 Linares Nariño, SW Colombia 01°24′N 77°30′W
41 O9 Linares Nuevo León, NE Mexico 24°54′N 99°38′W
105 N12 Linares Andalucía, S Spain 38°05′N 03°38′W
107 G15 Linaro, Capo headland C Italy 42°01′N 11°49′E
106 D8 Linate ✈ (Milano) Lombardia, N Italy 45°27′N 09°18′E
167 T8 Lin Camh prev. Đuc Tho. Ha Tinh, N Vietnam 18°30′N 105°36′E
160 F13 Lincang Yunnan, SW China 23°55′N 100°03′E
Lincheng see Lingao
Linchuan see Fuzhou
61 B20 Lincoln Buenos Aires, E Argentina 34°54′S 61°30′W
185 H19 Lincoln Canterbury, South Island, New Zealand 43°37′S 172°30′E
97 N18 Lincoln anc. Lindum, Lindum Colonia. E England, United Kingdom 53°14′N 00°33′W
35 O6 Lincoln California, W USA 38°52′N 121°18′W
30 L13 Lincoln Illinois, N USA 40°09′N 89°21′W
26 M4 Lincoln Kansas, C USA 39°03′N 98°09′W
19 S5 Lincoln Maine, NE USA 45°22′N 68°30′W
27 T5 Lincoln Missouri, C USA 38°23′N 93°19′W
29 R16 Lincoln state capital Nebraska, C USA 40°46′N 96°43′W
32 F11 Lincoln City Oregon, NW USA 44°57′N 124°01′W
167 X10 Lincoln Island island E Paracel Islands
197 Q11 Lincoln Sea sea Arctic Ocean
97 N18 Lincolnshire cultural region E England, United Kingdom
21 R10 Lincolnton North Carolina, SE USA 35°27′N 81°16′W
25 V7 Lindale Texas, SW USA 32°31′N 95°24′W
101 I25 Lindau var. Lindau am Bodensee. Bayern, S Germany 47°33′N 09°41′E
Lindau am Bodensee see Lindau
123 P9 Linde ∾ NE Russian Federation
55 T9 Linden E Guyana 05°58′N 58°12′W
23 O6 Linden Alabama, S USA 32°18′N 87°48′W
20 H9 Linden Tennessee, S USA 35°38′N 87°50′W
25 X6 Linden Texas, SW USA 33°01′N 94°22′W
44 H2 Linden Pindling ✈ New Providence, C Bahamas 25°00′N 77°26′W
18 J16 Lindenwold New Jersey, NE USA 39°47′N 74°58′W
95 M15 Lindesberg Örebro, C Sweden 59°36′N 15°15′E
95 D18 Lindesnes headland S Norway 57°58′N 07°03′E
Líndhos see Líndos
81 K24 Lindi Lindi, SE Tanzania 10°S 39°41′E
81 J24 Lindi ◈ region SE Tanzania
79 N17 Lindi ∾ NE Dem. Rep. Congo
163 V7 Lindian Heilongjiang, NE China 47°15′N 124°51′E
185 E21 Lindis Pass pass South Island, New Zealand
83 J22 Lindley Free State, C South Africa 27°52′S 27°55′E
95 J19 Lindome Västra Götaland, S Sweden 57°34′N 12°05′E
163 S10 Lindong var. Bairin Zuoqi. Nei Mongol Zizhiqu, N China 43°59′N 119°24′E
115 O23 Líndos var. Líndhos. Ródos, Dodekánisa, Greece, Aegean Sea 36°05′N 28°05′E
14 I14 Lindsay Ontario, SE Canada 44°21′N 78°44′W
35 R11 Lindsay California, W USA 36°11′N 119°06′W
33 X8 Lindsay Montana, NW USA 47°13′N 105°10′W
27 N11 Lindsay Oklahoma, C USA 34°50′N 97°37′W
27 N5 Lindsborg Kansas, C USA 38°34′N 97°39′W
95 N21 Lindsdal Kalmar, S Sweden 56°44′N 16°18′E
Lindum/Lindum Colonia see Lincoln
191 W3 Line Islands island group E Kiribati
Linëvo see Linova
160 M5 Linfen var. Lin-fen. Shanxi, C China 36°08′N 111°34′E
Lin-fen see Linfen
104 L2 L'Infiestu prev. Infiesto. Asturias, N Spain 43°21′N 05°21′W
155 F18 Linganamakki Reservoir ⊠ SW India
160 L17 Lingao var. Lincheng. Hainan, S China 19°44′N 109°23′E
171 N3 Lingayen Luzon, N Philippines 16°00′N 120°12′E
160 M6 Lingbao var. Guolüezhen. Henan, C China 34°34′N 110°50′E
94 N12 Lingbo Gävleborg, C Sweden 61°04′N 16°45′E
Lingcheng see Beiliu,Guangxi, China
Lingcheng see Lingshan, Guangxi, China
Lingeh see Bandar-e Lengeh
100 E12 Lingen var. Lingen an der Ems. Niedersachsen, NW Germany 52°31′N 07°19′E
Lingen an der Ems see Lingen
168 M11 Lingga, Kepulauan island group W Indonesia
168 L11 Lingga, Pulau island Kepulauan Lingga, W Indonesia
14 J14 Lingham Lake ◎ Ontario, SE Canada
94 M13 Linghed Dalarna, C Sweden 60°48′N 15°55′E
33 Z15 Lingle Wyoming, C USA 42°07′N 104°21′W
18 G15 Linglestown Pennsylvania, NE USA 40°20′N 76°46′W
160 M12 Lingling prev. Yongzhou, Zhishan. Hunan, S China 26°13′N 111°36′E
79 K18 Lingomo 11 Equateur, NW Dem. Rep. Congo 0°42′N 21°59′E
160 L15 Lingshan var. Lingcheng. Guangxi Zhuangzu Zizhiqu, S China 22°28′N 109°19′E
160 L17 Lingshui var. Lingshui Lizu Zizhixian. Hainan, S China 18°35′N 110°03′E
Lingshui Lizu Zizhixian see Lingshui
155 G16 Lingsugūr Karnātaka, C India 16°13′N 76°33′E
107 L23 Linguaglossa Sicilia, Italy, C Mediterranean Sea 37°51′N 15°06′E
76 H10 Linguère N Senegal 15°24′N 15°06′W
159 W8 Lingwu Ningxia, N China 38°04′N 106°21′E
Lingxi see Yongshun, Hunan, China
Lingxi see Cangnan, Zhejiang, China
Lingxian/Ling Xian see Yanling
163 S12 Lingyuan Liaoning, NE China 41°09′N 119°24′E
163 U4 Linhai Heilongjiang, NE China 51°30′N 124°18′E
161 S10 Linhai var. Taizhou. Zhejiang, SE China 28°54′N 121°08′E
59 O20 Linhares Espírito Santo, SE Brazil 19°22′S 40°04′W
Linhe see Bayannur
Lini see Lin
139 S1 Līnik, Chiyā-ê ▲ N Iraq
Linjiang see Shanghang
95 M18 Linköping Östergötland, S Sweden 58°25′N 15°37′E
163 Y8 Linkou Heilongjiang, NE China 45°18′N 130°17′E
118 F11 Linkuva Šiauliai, N Lithuania 56°06′N 23°58′E
27 V5 Linn Missouri, C USA 38°29′N 91°51′W
25 S16 Linn Texas, SW USA 26°32′N 98°06′W
27 T2 Linneus Missouri, C USA 39°53′N 93°10′W
96 H10 Linnhe, Loch inlet W Scotland, United Kingdom
119 G19 Linova Rus. Linëvo. Brestskaya Voblasts', SW Belarus 52°29′N 24°30′E
161 O5 Linqing Shandong, E China 36°51′N 115°42′E
60 K8 Lins São Paulo, S Brazil 21°40′S 49°44′W
93 F17 Linsell Jämtland, C Sweden 62°10′N 14°E
160 J9 Linshui Sichuan, C China 30°24′N 106°54′E
44 K12 Linstead C Jamaica 18°08′N 77°02′W
159 U11 Lintan Gansu, N China 34°43′N 103°27′E
159 V11 Lintao var. Taoyang. Gansu, C China 35°23′N 103°54′E
15 S12 Lintère ∾ Québec, SE Canada
108 H8 Linth ∾ NW Switzerland
108 H8 Linthal Glarus, NE Switzerland 46°59′N 08°57′E
31 N15 Linton Indiana, N USA 39°01′N 87°10′W
29 N6 Linton North Dakota, N USA 46°16′N 100°13′W
163 R11 Linxi Nei Mongol Zizhiqu, N China 43°29′N 117°59′E
159 U11 Linxia var. Linxia Huizu Zizhizhou. Gansu, C China 35°34′N 103°08′E
Linxia Huizu Zizhizhou see Linxia
Linxian see Lianzhou
161 Q6 Linyi Shandong, S China 37°06′N 118°18′E
161 P4 Linyi var. Yishi. Shandong, E China 37°12′N 116°54′E
160 M6 Linyi Shanxi, C China 35°10′N 118°18′E
109 T4 Linz anc. Lentia. Oberösterreich, N Austria 48°19′N 14°18′E
159 S8 Linze var. Shahe; prev. Shahepu. Gansu, N China 39°06′N 100°03′E
44 J13 Lionel Town C Jamaica 17°49′N 77°14′W
103 Q16 Lion, Golfe du Eng. Gulf of Lion, Gulf of Lions; anc. Sinus Gallicus. gulf S France
Lion, Gulf of/Lions, Gulf of see Lion, Golfe du
83 K16 Lions Den Mashonaland West, N Zimbabwe 17°16′S 30°00′E
14 F13 Lion's Head Ontario, S Canada 44°59′N 81°16′W
Lios Ceannúir, Bá see Liscannor Bay
Lios Mór see Lismore
Lios na gCearrbhach see Lisburn
Lios Tuathail see Listowel
79 G17 Liouesso Sangha, N Congo 01°02′N 15°43′E
Liozno see Lyozna
171 O4 Lipa off. Lipa City. Luzon, N Philippines 13°57′N 121°10′E
Lipa City see Lipa
25 S7 Lipan Texas, SW USA 32°31′N 98°03′W
Lipari Islands/Lipari, Isole see Eolie, Isole
107 L22 Lipari, Isola island Isole Eolie, S Italy
116 L8 Lipcani Rus. Lipkany. N Moldova 48°16′N 26°47′E
93 N17 Liperi Itä-Suomi, SE Finland 62°33′N 29°29′E
126 L7 Lipetsk Lipetskaya Oblast', W Russian Federation 52°37′N 39°38′E
126 K6 Lipetskaya Oblast' ◈ province W Russian Federation
57 K22 Lipez, Cordillera de ▲▲ SW Bolivia
110 E10 Lipiany Ger. Lippehne. Zachodnio-pomorskie, W Poland 53°00′N 14°58′E
112 G9 Lipik Požega-Slavonija, NE Croatia 45°24′N 17°08′E
124 L12 Lipin Bor Vologodskaya Oblast', NW Russian Federation 60°12′N 38°04′E
160 L12 Liping var. Defeng. Guizhou, S China 26°16′N 109°08′E
Lipkany see Lipcani
119 H15 Lipnishki Hrodzyenskaya Voblasts', W Belarus 54°00′N 25°37′E
110 J10 Lipno Kujawsko-pomorskie, C Poland 52°52′N 19°11′E
116 F11 Lipova Hung. Lippa. Arad, W Romania 46°05′N 21°42′E
Lipovets see Lypovets'
Lippa see Lipova
101 E14 Lippe ∾ W Germany
Lippehne see Lipiany
101 G14 Lippstadt Nordrhein-Westfalen, W Germany 51°41′N 08°20′E
25 P1 Lipscomb Texas, SW USA 36°14′N 100°16′W
Lipsia/Lipsk see Leipzig
Liptau-Sankt-Nikolaus/Liptószentmiklós see Liptovský Mikuláš
111 K19 Liptovský Mikuláš Ger. Liptau-Sankt-Nikolaus, Hung. Liptószentmiklós. Žilinský Kraj, N Slovakia 49°06′N 19°36′E
183 O13 Liptrap, Cape headland Victoria, SE Australia 38°55′S 145°58′E
160 L13 Lipu var. Licheng. Guangxi Zhuangzu Zizhiqu, S China 24°25′N 110°15′E
81 G17 Lira N Uganda 02°15′N 32°55′E
57 F15 Lircay Huancavelica, C Peru 12°59′S 74°44′W
107 K17 Liri ∾ C Italy
144 M8 Lisakovsk Kostanay, NW Kazakhstan 52°32′N 62°32′E
79 K17 Lisala Equateur, N Dem. Rep. Congo 02°10′N 21°29′E
104 F11 Lisboa Eng. Lisbon; anc. Felicitas Julia, Olisipo. ● (Portugal) Lisboa, W Portugal 38°44′N 09°08′W
104 F10 Lisboa Eng. Lisbon. ◈ district C Portugal
19 N7 Lisbon New Hampshire, NE USA 44°11′N 71°52′W
29 Q6 Lisbon North Dakota, N USA 46°27′N 97°42′W
Lisbon see Lisboa
19 Q8 Lisbon Falls Maine, NE USA 44°00′N 70°03′W
97 G15 Lisburn Ir. Lios na gCearrbhach. E Northern Ireland, United Kingdom 54°31′N 06°03′W
38 L6 Lisburne, Cape headland Alaska, USA 68°52′N 166°13′W
97 B19 Liscannor Bay Ir. Bá Lios Ceannúir. inlet W Ireland
113 Q18 Lisec ▲ E FYR Macedonia 41°46′N 22°30′E
160 F13 Lishe Jiang ∾ SW China
Lishi see Lüliang
163 V10 Lishu Jilin, NE China 43°25′N 124°19′E
161 R10 Lishui Zhejiang, SE China 28°27′N 119°25′E
192 L5 Lisianski Island island Hawaiian Islands, Hawai'i, USA
Lisichansk see Lysychans'k
102 L4 Lisieux anc. Noviomagus. Calvados, N France 49°09′N 00°13′E
126 L8 Liski prev. Georgiu-Dezh. Voronezhskaya Oblast', W Russian Federation 51°00′N 39°36′E
103 N4 l'Isle-Adam Val-d'Oise, N France 49°07′N 02°13′E
Lisle/l'Isle see Lille
103 R15 l'Isle-sur-la-Sorgue Vaucluse, SE France 43°55′N 05°03′E
15 S9 L'Islet Québec, SE Canada 47°07′N 70°18′W
183 V4 Lismore New South Wales, SE Australia 28°48′S 153°12′E
182 M12 Lismore Victoria, SE Australia 37°59′S 143°18′E
97 D20 Lismore Ir. Lios Mór. S Ireland 52°10′N 07°10′W
Lissa see Vis, Croatia
Lissa see Leszno, Poland
98 H11 Lisse Zuid-Holland, W Netherlands 52°15′N 04°33′E
114 K13 Líssos var. Filiouri. ∾ NE Greece
95 D18 Lista peninsula S Norway
95 D18 Listafjorden fjord S Norway
195 R13 Lister, Mount ▲ Antarctica 78°12′S 161°46′E
126 M8 Listopadovka Voronezhskaya Oblast', W Russian Federation 51°54′N 41°08′E
14 F15 Listowel Ontario, S Canada 43°44′N 80°57′W
97 B20 Listowel Ir. Lios Tuathail. Kerry, SW Ireland 52°27′N 09°29′W
160 L14 Litang Guangxi Zhuangzu Zizhiqu, S China 23°09′N 109°08′E
160 F9 Litang var. Gaocheng. Sichuan, C China 30°03′N 100°12′E
160 F10 Litang Qu ∾ C China
55 X12 Litani var. Itany. ∾ French Guiana/Suriname
138 G8 Lītani, Nahr el var. Nahr al Litant. ∾ C Lebanon
Litant, Nahr al see Lītani, Nahr el
Litauen see Lithuania
30 K14 Litchfield Illinois, N USA 39°17′N 89°52′W
29 U8 Litchfield Minnesota, N USA 45°09′N 94°31′W
36 K13 Litchfield Park Arizona, SW USA 33°29′N 112°21′W
183 S8 Lithgow New South Wales, SE Australia 33°30′S 150°09′E
115 I26 Líthino, Akrotírio headland Kríti, Greece, E Mediterranean Sea 34°55′N 24°43′E
118 D12 Lithuania off. Republic of Lithuania, Ger. Litauen, Lith. Lietuva, Pol. Litwa, Rus. Litva; prev. Lithuanian SSR, Rus. Litovskaya SSR. ◆ republic NE Europe
Lithuanian SSR see Lithuania
Lithuania, Republic of see Lithuania
109 U11 Litija Ger. Littai. C Slovenia 46°03′N 14°50′E
18 H15 Lititz Pennsylvania, NE USA 40°09′N 76°18′W
115 F15 Litóchoro var. Litohoro, Litókhoron. Kentrikí Makedonía, N Greece 40°06′N 22°30′E
Litohoro/Litókhoron see Litóchoro
111 C15 Litoměřice Ger. Leitmeritz. Ústecký Kraj, NW Czech Republic 50°33′N 14°10′E
111 F17 Litomyšl Ger. Leitomischl. Pardubický Kraj, C Czech Republic 49°54′N 16°18′E
111 G17 Litovel Ger. Littau. Olomoucký Kraj, E Czech Republic 49°42′N 17°05′E
123 S13 Litovko Khabarovskiy Kray, SE Russian Federation 49°22′N 135°10′E
Litovskaya SSR see Lithuania
Littai see Litija
Littau see Litovel
44 G1 Little Abaco var. Abaco Island. island N Bahamas
111 I21 Little Alföld Ger. Kleines Ungarisches Tiefland, Hung. Kisalföld, Slvk. Podunajská Rovina. plain Hungary/Slovakia
151 Q20 Little Andaman island Andaman Islands, India, NE Indian Ocean
26 M5 Little Arkansas River ∾ Kansas, C USA
184 L4 Little Barrier Island island N New Zealand
Little Belt see Lillebælt
38 M11 Little Black River ∾ Alaska, USA
27 O2 Little Blue River ∾ Kansas/Nebraska, C USA
44 D8 Little Cayman island E Cayman Islands
11 X11 Little Churchill ∾ Manitoba, C Canada
166 J10 Little Coco Island island SW Myanmar (Burma)
36 L10 Little Colorado River ∾ Arizona, SW USA
14 E11 Little Current Manitoulin Island, Ontario, S Canada 45°57′N 81°56′W
12 E11 Little Current ∾ Ontario, S Canada
38 L8 Little Diomede Island island Alaska, USA
44 I4 Little Exuma island C Bahamas
29 U7 Little Falls Minnesota, N USA 45°59′N 94°21′W
18 J10 Little Falls New York, NE USA 43°02′N 74°51′W
24 M5 Littlefield Texas, SW USA 33°56′N 102°20′W
29 V3 Littlefork Minnesota, N USA 48°24′N 93°33′W
29 V3 Little Fork River ∾ Minnesota, N USA
11 N16 Little Fort British Columbia, SW Canada 51°27′N 120°15′W
11 Y14 Little Grand Rapids Manitoba, C Canada 52°06′N 95°29′W
97 N23 Littlehampton SE England, United Kingdom 50°48′N 00°33′W
35 T2 Little Humboldt River ∾ Nevada, W USA
44 K6 Little Inagua var. Inagua Islands. island S Bahamas
21 Q4 Little Kanawha River ∾ West Virginia, NE USA
83 F25 Little Karoo plateau S South Africa
39 O16 Little Koniuji Island island Shumagin Islands, Alaska, USA
44 H12 Little London W Jamaica 18°15′N 78°13′W
13 R10 Little Mecatina Fr. Rivière du Petit Mécatina. ∾ Newfoundland and Labrador/Québec, E Canada

96 F8 **Little Minch, The** *strait* NW Scotland, United Kingdom
27 T13 **Little Missouri River** ≈ Arkansas, USA
28 J7 **Little Missouri River** ≈ NW USA
28 J3 **Little Muddy River** ≈ North Dakota, N USA
151 Q22 **Little Nicobar** *island* Nicobar Islands, India, NE Indian Ocean
27 R6 **Little Osage River** ≈ Missouri, C USA
97 P20 **Little Ouse** ≈ E England, United Kingdom
149 V2 **Little Pamir** *Pash.* Pāmīr-e Khord, *Rus.* Malyy Pamir. ▲▲ Afghanistan/Tajikistan
21 U12 **Little Pee Dee River** ≈ North Carolina/South Carolina, SE USA
27 V10 **Little Red River** ≈ Arkansas, C USA
Little Rhody *see* Rhode Island
185 I19 **Little River** Canterbury, South Island, New Zealand 43°45′S 172°49′E
21 U12 **Little River** South Carolina, SE USA 33°52′N 78°36′W
27 Y9 **Little River** ≈ Arkansas/Missouri, C USA
27 R13 **Little River** ≈ Arkansas/Oklahoma, USA
23 T7 **Little River** ≈ Georgia, SE USA
22 H6 **Little River** ≈ Louisiana, S USA
25 T10 **Little River** ≈ Texas, SW USA
27 V12 **Little Rock** *state capital* Arkansas, C USA 34°45′N 92°17′W
31 N8 **Little Sable Point** *headland* Michigan, N USA 43°38′N 86°32′W
103 U11 **Little Saint Bernard Pass** *Fr.* Col du Petit St-Bernard, *It.* Colle del Piccolo San Bernardo. *pass* France/Italy
36 K7 **Little Salt Lake** ◎ Utah, W USA
180 K8 **Little Sandy Desert** *desert* Western Australia
29 S13 **Little Sioux River** ≈ Iowa, C USA
38 E17 **Little Sitkin Island** *island* Aleutian Islands, Alaska, USA
11 O13 **Little Smoky** Alberta, W Canada 54°35′N 117°06′W
11 O14 **Little Smoky** ≈ Alberta, W Canada
37 P3 **Little Snake River** ≈ Colorado, C USA
64 A12 **Little Sound** *bay* Bermuda, NW Atlantic Ocean
37 T4 **Littleton** Colorado, C USA 39°36′N 105°01′W
19 N7 **Littleton** New Hampshire, NE USA 44°18′N 71°46′W
18 D11 **Little Valley** New York, NE USA 42°15′N 78°47′W
30 M15 **Little Wabash River** ≈ Illinois, N USA
14 D10 **Little White River** ≈ Ontario, S Canada
28 M12 **Little White River** ≈ South Dakota, N USA
25 R5 **Little Wichita River** ≈ Texas, SW USA
142 I4 **Little Zab** *Ar.* Nahraz Zāb aş Şaghīr, *Kurd.* Zē-i Kōya, *Per.* Rūdkhāneh-ye Zāb-e Kūchek. ≈ Iran/Iraq
79 D15 **Littoral** ◈ *province* W Cameroon
Littoria *see* Latina
Litva/Litwa *see* Lithuania
111 B15 **Litvínov** *Ger.* Leutensdorf. Ústecký Kraj, NW Czech Republic 50°38′N 13°30′E
116 M6 **Lityn** Vinnyts'ka Oblast', C Ukraine 49°19′N 28°06′E
Liu-chou/Liuchow *see* Liuzhou
163 W11 **Liuhe** Jilin, NE China 42°15′N 125°49′E
Liujiaxia *see* Yongjing
Liulin *see* Jonê
Liupanshui *see* Lupanshui
83 Q15 **Liúpo** Nampula, NE Mozambique 15°36′S 39°57′E
83 G14 **Liuwa Plain** *plain* W Zambia
160 L13 **Liuzhou** *var.* Liu-chou, Liuchow. Guangxi Zhuangzu Zizhiqu, S China 24°09′N 108°55′E
116 H8 **Livada** *Hung.* Sárköz. Satu Mare, NW Romania 47°52′N 23°04′E
115 J20 **Liváda, Akrotírio** *headland* Tínos, Kykládes, Greece, Aegean Sea 37°36′N 25°15′E
115 F18 **Livádeia** *prev.* Levádia. Stereá Elláda, C Greece 38°24′N 22°51′E
Livádi *see* Liádi
Livanátai *see* Livanátes
115 G18 **Livanátes** *prev.* Livanátai. Stereá Elláda, C Greece 38°43′N 23°03′E
118 I10 **Līvāni** *Ger.* Lievenhof. SE Latvia 56°22′N 26°12′E
65 E25 **Lively Island** *island* SE Falkland Islands
65 D25 **Lively Sound** *sound* SE Falkland Islands
39 R8 **Livengood** Alaska, USA 65°31′N 148°32′W
106 I7 **Livenza** ≈ NE Italy
35 O6 **Live Oak** California, W USA 39°17′N 121°41′W
23 U9 **Live Oak** Florida, SE USA 30°18′N 82°59′W
35 O9 **Livermore** California, W USA 37°40′N 121°46′W
20 I6 **Livermore** Kentucky, S USA 37°31′N 87°08′W
19 Q7 **Livermore Falls** Maine, NE USA 44°30′N 70°09′W
24 J10 **Livermore, Mount** ▲ Texas, SW USA 30°37′N 104°10′W
13 P16 **Liverpool** Nova Scotia, SE Canada 44°03′N 64°43′W
97 K17 **Liverpool** NW England, United Kingdom 53°25′N 02°55′W
183 S7 **Liverpool Range** ▲▲ New South Wales, SE Australia
42 F4 **Lívingston** Izabal, E Guatemala 15°50′N 88°44′W
96 J12 **Livingston** C Scotland, United Kingdom 55°51′N 03°31′W
23 N5 **Livingston** Alabama, S USA 32°35′N 88°12′W
35 P9 **Livingston** California, W USA 37°22′N 120°45′W
22 J8 **Livingston** Louisiana, S USA 30°30′N 90°45′W
33 S11 **Livingston** Montana, NW USA 45°40′N 110°33′W
20 L8 **Livingston** Tennessee, S USA 36°22′N 85°20′W
25 W9 **Livingston** Texas, SW USA 30°42′N 94°58′W
83 I16 **Livingstone** *var.* Maramba. Southern, S Zambia 17°51′S 25°48′E
185 B22 **Livingstone Mountains** ▲▲ South Island, New Zealand
80 K13 **Livingstone Mountains** ▲▲ S Tanzania
82 N12 **Livingstonia** Northern, N Malawi 10°29′S 34°06′E
194 G4 **Livingston Island** *island* Antarctica
25 W9 **Livingston, Lake** ⊠ Texas, SW USA
112 F13 **Livno** ◈ Federicija Bosna I Hercegovina, SW Bosnia and Herzegovina
126 K7 **Livny** Orlovskaya Oblast', W Russian Federation 52°25′N 37°42′E
93 M14 **Livojoki** ≈ C Finland
31 R10 **Livonia** Michigan, N USA 42°22′N 83°22′W
106 E11 **Livorno** *Eng.* Leghorn. Toscana, C Italy 43°32′N 10°18′E
Livramento *see* Santana do Livramento
141 U8 **Līwā** *var.* Al Liwā'. *oasis region* S United Arab Emirates
81 I24 **Liwale** Lindi, SE Tanzania 09°46′S 37°56′E
159 W9 **Liwang** Ningxia, N China 36°42′N 106°05′E
83 N15 **Liwonde** Southern, S Malawi 15°01′S 35°15′E
159 V11 **Lixian** *var.* Li Xian. Gansu, C China 34°15′N 105°07′E
160 H8 **Lixian** *var.* Li Xian, Zagunao. Sichuan, C China 31°27′N 103°06′E
Li Xian *see* Lixian
Lixian Jiang *see* Black River
115 B18 **Lixoúri** *prev.* Lixoúrion. Kefallinía, Iónia Nisiá, Greece, C Mediterranean Sea 38°14′N 20°24′E
Lixoúrion *see* Lixoúri
Lixus *see* Larache
33 U15 **Lizard Head Peak** ▲ Wyoming, C USA 42°47′N 109°12′W
97 H25 **Lizard Point** *headland* SW England, United Kingdom 49°57′N 05°12′W
Lizarra *see* Estella
112 L12 **Ljig** Serbia, C Serbia 44°14′N 20°16′E
Ljouwert *see* Leeuwarden
Ljubelj *see* Loibl Pass
109 U11 **Ljubljana** *Ger.* Laibach, *It.* Lubiana; *anc.* Aemona, Emona. ● (Slovenia) C Slovenia 46°03′N 14°29′E
109 T11 **Ljubljana** ✈ C Slovenia 46°14′N 14°26′E
113 N17 **Ljuboten** *Alb.* Luboten. ▲ S Serbia 42°12′N 21°06′E
95 P19 **Ljugarn** Gotland, SE Sweden 57°23′N 18°45′E
84 G7 **Ljungan** ≈ N Sweden
93 F17 **Ljungan** ≈ C Sweden
95 K21 **Ljungby** Kronoberg, S Sweden 56°49′N 13°55′E
95 M17 **Ljungsbro** Östergötland, S Sweden 58°31′N 15°30′E
95 I18 **Ljungskile** Västra Götaland, S Sweden 58°14′N 11°55′E
94 M11 **Ljusdal** Gävleborg, C Sweden 61°50′N 16°10′E
94 M11 **Ljusnan** ≈ C Sweden
94 N12 **Ljusne** Gävleborg, C Sweden 61°11′N 17°07′E
95 P15 **Ljusterö** Stockholm, C Sweden 59°31′N 18°40′E
109 X9 **Ljutomer** *Ger.* Luttenberg. NE Slovenia 46°31′N 16°12′E
63 G15 **Llaima, Volcán** 🌋 S Chile 39°01′S 71°38′W
105 X4 **Llançà** *var.* Llansá. Cataluña, NE Spain 42°23′N 03°08′E
97 J21 **Llandovery** C Wales, United Kingdom 52°01′N 03°47′W
97 J20 **Llandrindod Wells** E Wales, United Kingdom 52°15′N 03°23′W
97 J18 **Llandudno** N Wales, United Kingdom 53°19′N 03°49′W
97 I21 **Llanelli** *prev.* Llanelly. SW Wales, United Kingdom 51°41′N 04°12′W
Llanelly *see* Llanelli
104 M2 **Llanes** Asturias, N Spain 43°25′N 04°46′W
97 K19 **Llangollen** NE Wales, United Kingdom 52°58′N 03°10′W
104 K2 **Llangréu** *var.* Langreo, Sama de Langreo. Asturias, N Spain 43°18′N 05°40′W
25 R10 **Llano** Texas, SW USA 30°49′N 98°42′W
25 Q10 **Llano River** ≈ Texas, SW USA
54 I9 **Llanos** *physical region* Colombia/Venezuela
63 G16 **Llanquihue, Lago** ◎ S Chile
Llansá *see* Llançà
105 U5 **Lleida** *Cast.* Lérida; *anc.* Ilerda. Cataluña, NE Spain 41°38′N 00°35′E
104 K12 **Llerena** Extremadura, W Spain 38°13′N 06°00′W
105 S9 **Llíria** Valenciana, E Spain 39°38′N 00°36′W
105 W4 **Llívia** Cataluña, NE Spain 42°27′N 02°00′E
Llodio *see* Laudio
105 X5 **Lloret de Mar** Cataluña, NE Spain 41°42′N 02°51′E
Llorri *see* Toretta de l'Orrí
10 L11 **Lloyd George, Mount** ▲ British Columbia, W Canada 57°46′N 124°57′W
11 R14 **Lloydminster** Alberta/Saskatchewan, SW Canada 53°18′N 110°00′W
104 K2 **Lluanco** *var.* Luanco. Asturias, N Spain 43°36′N 05°48′W
105 X9 **Llucmajor** Mallorca, Spain, W Mediterranean Sea 39°29′N 02°53′E
36 L6 **Loa** Utah, W USA 38°24′N 111°38′W
169 S8 **Loagan Bunut** ◎ East Malaysia
38 G12 **Loa, Mauna** ▲ Hawai'i, USA 19°28′N 155°39′W
Loanda *see* Luanda
79 J22 **Loange** ≈ S Dem. Rep. Congo
79 E21 **Loango** Kouilou, S Congo 04°38′S 11°50′E
106 B10 **Loano** Liguria, NW Italy 44°07′N 08°15′E
62 H4 **Loa, Río** ≈ N Chile
83 I20 **Lobatse** *var.* Lobatsi. Kgatleng, SE Botswana 25°11′S 25°40′E
Lobatsi *see* Lobatse
101 Q15 **Löbau** Sachsen, E Germany 51°07′N 14°40′E
79 H16 **Lobaye** ◈ *prefecture* SW Central African Republic
79 I16 **Lobaye** ≈ SW Central African Republic
99 G21 **Lobbes** Hainaut, S Belgium 50°21′N 04°16′E
61 D23 **Lobería** Buenos Aires, E Argentina 38°08′S 58°48′W
110 F8 **Łobez** *Ger.* Labes. Zacodniopomorskie, NW Poland 53°38′N 15°39′E
82 A13 **Lobito** Benguela, W Angola 12°20′S 13°34′E
Lobkovichi *see* Labkovichy
Lob Nor *see* Lop Nur
171 V13 **Lobo** Papua, E Indonesia 03°41′S 134°06′E
104 J11 **Lobón** Extremadura, W Spain 38°51′N 06°38′W
61 D20 **Lobos** Buenos Aires, E Argentina 35°11′S 59°08′W
40 E4 **Lobos, Cabo** *headland* NW Mexico 29°53′N 112°43′W
40 F6 **Lobos, Isla** *island* NW Mexico
Lobositz *see* Lovosice
Lobsens *see* Łobżenica
Loburi *see* Lop Buri
110 H9 **Łobżenica** *Ger.* Lobsens. Wielkopolskie, C Poland 53°19′N 17°11′E
108 G11 **Locarno** *Ger.* Luggarus. Ticino, S Switzerland 46°11′N 08°48′E
96 E9 **Lochboisdale** NW Scotland, United Kingdom 57°08′N 07°17′W
98 N11 **Lochem** Gelderland, E Netherlands 52°10′N 06°25′E
102 M8 **Loches** Indre-et-Loire, C France 47°08′N 01°00′E
Loch Garman *see* Wexford
96 H12 **Lochgilphead** W Scotland, United Kingdom 56°02′N 05°27′W
96 H7 **Lochinver** N Scotland, United Kingdom 58°10′N 05°15′W
96 F8 **Lochmaddy** NW Scotland, United Kingdom 57°35′N 07°10′W
96 J10 **Lochnagar** ▲ C Scotland, United Kingdom 56°58′N 03°09′W
99 E17 **Lochristi** Oost-Vlaanderen, NW Belgium 51°07′N 03°49′E
96 H9 **Lochy, Loch** ◎ N Scotland, United Kingdom
182 G8 **Lock** South Australia 33°37′S 135°45′E
97 J14 **Lockerbie** S Scotland, United Kingdom 55°11′N 03°27′W
27 S13 **Lockesburg** Arkansas, C USA 33°58′N 94°10′W
183 P10 **Lockhart** New South Wales, SE Australia 35°15′S 146°43′E
25 S11 **Lockhart** Texas, SW USA 29°54′N 97°41′W
18 F13 **Lock Haven** Pennsylvania, NE USA 41°08′N 77°27′W
25 N4 **Lockney** Texas, SW USA 34°06′N 101°27′W
100 O12 **Löcknitz** ≈ NE Germany
18 E9 **Lockport** New York, NE USA 43°09′N 78°40′W
167 T13 **Lôc Ninh** Sông Be, S Vietnam 11°51′N 106°35′E
107 N23 **Locri** Calabria, SW Italy 38°16′N 16°16′E
Locse *see* Levoča
27 T2 **Locust Creek** ≈ Missouri, C USA
23 P3 **Locust Fork** ≈ Alabama, S USA
27 Q9 **Locust Grove** Oklahoma, C USA 36°12′N 95°10′W
94 E11 **Lodalskåpa** ▲ S Norway 61°47′N 07°10′E
183 N10 **Loddon River** ≈ Victoria, SE Australia
Lodensee *see* Klooga
103 P15 **Lodève** *anc.* Luteva. Hérault, S France 43°44′N 03°19′E
124 I12 **Lodeynoye Pole** Leningradskaya Oblast', NW Russian Federation 60°41′N 33°29′E
33 V11 **Lodge Grass** Montana, NW USA 45°19′N 107°20′W
28 J15 **Lodgepole Creek** ≈ Nebraska/Wyoming, C USA
149 T11 **Lodhrān** Punjab, E Pakistan 29°32′N 71°40′E
106 D8 **Lodi** Lombardia, NW Italy 45°19′N 09°30′E
35 O8 **Lodi** California, W USA 38°07′N 121°17′W
31 T12 **Lodi** Ohio, N USA 41°00′N 82°01′W
92 H10 **Lødingen** *Lapp.* Lådik. Nordland, C Norway 68°25′N 16°00′E
79 L20 **Lodja** Kasai-Oriental, C Dem. Rep. Congo 03°29′S 23°25′E
37 O3 **Lodore, Canyon of** *canyon* Colorado, C USA
105 Q4 **Lodosa** Navarra, N Spain 42°26′N 02°05′W
81 H16 **Lodwar** Rift Valley, NW Kenya 03°06′N 35°38′E
110 K13 **Łódź** *Rus.* Lodz. Łódź, C Poland 51°51′N 19°26′E
110 E12 **Łódzskie** ◈ *province* C Poland
167 P8 **Loei** *var.* Loey, Muang Loei. Loei, C Thailand 17°32′N 101°40′E
98 I11 **Loenen** Utrecht, C Netherlands 52°13′N 05°01′E
167 R9 **Loeng Nok Tha** Yasothon, E Thailand 16°12′N 104°31′E
83 F24 **Loeriesfontein** Northern Cape, W South Africa 30°59′S 19°29′E
Loewoek *see* Luwuk
Loey *see* Loei
76 J16 **Lofa** ≈ N Liberia
109 P6 **Lofer** Salzburg, C Austria 47°37′N 12°42′E
92 F11 **Lofoten** *var.* Lofoten Islands. *island group* C Norway
Lofoten Islands *see* Lofoten
95 N18 **Loftahammar** Kalmar, S Sweden 57°55′N 16°45′E
127 O10 **Log** Volgogradskaya Oblast', SW Russian Federation 49°32′N 43°52′E
77 S12 **Loga** Dosso, SW Niger 13°40′N 03°15′E
29 S14 **Logan** Iowa, C USA 41°38′N 95°47′W
26 K3 **Logan** Kansas, C USA 39°39′N 99°34′W
31 T14 **Logan** Ohio, N USA 39°32′N 82°24′W
36 L1 **Logan** Utah, W USA 41°45′N 111°50′W
21 P6 **Logan** West Virginia, NE USA 37°52′N 82°00′W
35 Y10 **Logandale** Nevada, W USA 36°36′N 114°28′W
19 O11 **Logan International** ✈ (Boston) Massachusetts, NE USA 42°22′N 71°00′W
11 N16 **Logan Lake** British Columbia, SW Canada 50°28′N 120°42′W
23 Q4 **Logan Martin Lake** ⊠ Alabama, S USA
10 G8 **Logan, Mount** ▲ Yukon Territory, W Canada 60°32′N 140°34′W
32 I7 **Logan, Mount** ▲ Washington, NW USA 48°32′N 120°57′W
33 P7 **Logan Pass** *pass* Montana, NW USA
31 O12 **Logansport** Indiana, N USA 40°44′N 86°25′W
22 F6 **Logansport** Louisiana, S USA 31°58′N 94°00′W
149 Q5 **Lōgar** *prev.* Lowgar. ◈ *province* E Afghanistan
67 R11 **Loge** ≈ NW Angola
Logishin *see* Lahishyn
Log na Coille *see* Lugnaquillia Mountain
78 G11 **Logone** *var.* Lagone. ≈ Cameroon/Chad
78 G13 **Logone-Occidental** *off.* Préfecture du Logone-Occidental. ◈ *prefecture* SW Chad
78 H13 **Logone Occidental** ≈ SW Chad
Logone-Occidental, Préfecture du *see* Logone-Occidental
78 G13 **Logone-Oriental** *off.* Préfecture du Logone-Oriental. ◈ *prefecture* SW Chad
78 H13 **Logone Oriental** ≈ SW Chad
Logone Oriental *see* Pendé
Logone-Oriental, Préfecture du *see* Logone-Oriental
L'Ogooué-Ivindo *see* Ogooué-Ivindo
L'Ogooué-Lolo *see* Ogooué-Lolo
L'Ogooué-Maritime *see* Ogooué-Maritime
Logoysk *see* Lahoysk
105 P4 **Logroño** *anc.* Vareia, *Lat.* Juliobriga. La Rioja, N Spain 42°28′N 02°26′W
104 L10 **Logrosán** Extremadura, W Spain 39°21′N 05°29′W
95 G20 **Løgstør** Nordjylland, N Denmark 56°57′N 09°19′E
95 H22 **Løgten** Midtjylland, C Denmark 56°17′N 10°20′E
95 F24 **Løgumkloster** Syddanmark, SW Denmark 55°04′N 08°58′E
Lögurinn *see* Lagarfljót
153 P15 **Lohārdaga** Jhārkhand, N India 23°27′N 84°42′E
152 H10 **Lohāru** Haryāna, N India 28°28′N 75°50′E
101 D15 **Lohausen** ✈ (Düsseldorf) Nordrhein-Westfalen, W Germany 51°18′N 06°51′E
189 O14 **Lohd** Pohnpei, E Micronesia
92 L12 **Lohiniva** Lappi, N Finland 67°09′N 25°04′E
Lohiszyn *see* Lahishyn
93 L20 **Lohja** *var.* Lojo. Etelä-Suomi, S Finland 60°14′N 24°07′E
169 V11 **Lohjanan** Borneo, C Indonesia
25 Q9 **Lohn** Texas, SW USA 31°15′N 99°22′W
100 G12 **Löhne** Niedersachsen, NW Germany 52°40′N 08°13′E
Lohr *see* Lohr am Main
101 I18 **Lohr am Main** *var.* Lohr. Bayern, C Germany 50°00′N 09°30′E
109 T10 **Loibl Pass** *Ger.* Loiblpass, *Slvn.* Ljubelj. *pass* Austria/Slovenia
Loiblpass *see* Loibl Pass
167 N6 **Loikaw** Kayah State, Myanmar (Burma) 19°40′N 97°17′E
93 K19 **Loimaa** Länsi-Suomi, SW Finland 60°51′N 23°03′E
103 O6 **Loing** ≈ C France
167 R6 **Loi, Phou** ▲ N Laos 20°18′N 103°14′E
102 L7 **Loir** ≈ C France
103 Q11 **Loire** ◈ *department* E France
102 M7 **Loire** *var.* Liger. ≈ C France
102 I7 **Loire-Atlantique** ◈ *department* NW France
103 O7 **Loiret** ◈ *department* C France
102 M8 **Loir-et-Cher** ◈ *department* C France
101 L24 **Loisach** ≈ SE Germany
56 B9 **Loja** Loja, S Ecuador 03°59′S 79°16′W
104 M14 **Loja** Andalucía, S Spain 37°10′N 04°09′W
56 B9 **Loja** ◈ *province* S Ecuador
Lojo *see* Lohja
116 J4 **Lokachi** Volyns'ka Oblast', NW Ukraine 50°44′N 24°39′E
79 M20 **Lokandu** Maniema, C Dem. Rep. Congo 02°34′S 25°44′E
92 M11 **Lokan Tekojärvi** ◎ NE Finland
137 Z11 **Lökbatan** *Rus.* Lokbatan. E Azerbaijan 40°21′N 49°43′E
Lokbatan *see* Lökbatan
99 F17 **Lokeren** Oost-Vlaanderen, NW Belgium 51°06′N 03°59′E
Lokhvitsa *see* Lokhvytsya
117 S4 **Lokhvytsya** *Rus.* Lokhvitsa. Poltavs'ka Oblast', NE Ukraine 50°22′N 33°16′E
81 H17 **Lokichar** Rift Valley, NW Kenya 02°23′N 35°40′E
81 G16 **Lokichokio** Rift Valley, NW Kenya 04°16′N 34°22′E
81 H16 **Lokitaung** Rift Valley, NW Kenya 04°15′N 35°45′E
92 M11 **Lokka** Lappi, N Finland 67°48′N 27°41′E
94 G8 **Løkken Verk** Sør-Trøndelag, S Norway 63°06′N 09°43′E
124 G16 **Loknya** Pskovskaya Oblast', W Russian Federation 56°48′N 30°08′E
77 V15 **Loko** Nassarawa, C Nigeria 08°00′N 07°48′E
77 U15 **Lokoja** Kogi, C Nigeria 07°48′N 06°45′E
81 H17 **Lokori** Rift Valley, W Kenya 01°56′N 36°03′E
77 R16 **Lokossa** S Benin 06°38′N 01°43′E
118 I3 **Loksa** *Ger.* Loxa. Harjumaa, NW Estonia 59°32′N 25°42′E
9 T7 **Loks Land** *island* Nunavut, NE Canada
80 C13 **Lol** ≈ NW South Sudan
76 K15 **Lola** SE Guinea 07°52′N 08°29′W
35 Q5 **Lola, Mount** ▲ California, W USA 39°27′N 120°20′W
81 H20 **Loliondo** Arusha, NE Tanzania 02°03′S 35°46′E
95 H25 **Lolland** *prev.* Laaland. *island* S Denmark
186 G6 **Lolobau Island** *island* E Papua New Guinea
79 E16 **Lolodorf** Sud, SW Cameroon 03°17′N 10°50′E
114 G7 **Lom** *prev.* Lom-Palanka. Montana, NW Bulgaria 43°49′N 23°16′E
114 G7 **Lom** ≈ NW Bulgaria
79 M19 **Lomami** ≈ C Dem. Rep. Congo
57 F17 **Lomas** Arequipa, SW Peru 15°29′S 74°54′W
63 I23 **Lomas, Bahía** *bay* S Chile
61 D20 **Lomas de Zamora** Buenos Aires, E Argentina 34°53′S 58°26′W
61 D20 **Loma Verde** Buenos Aires, E Argentina 35°16′S 58°24′W
180 K4 **Lombadina** Western Australia 16°39′S 122°54′E
106 E6 **Lombardia** *Eng.* Lombardy. ◈ *region* N Italy
Lombardy *see* Lombardia
102 M15 **Lombez** Gers, S France 43°29′N 00°54′E
171 Q16 **Lomblen, Pulau** *island* Nusa Tenggara, S Indonesia
173 W7 **Lombok Basin** *undersea feature* E Indian Ocean 09°50′S 116°00′E
170 L16 **Lombok, Pulau** *island* Nusa Tenggara, C Indonesia
77 Q16 **Lomé** ● (Togo) S Togo 06°08′N 01°13′E
77 Q16 **Lomé** ✈ S Togo 06°08′N 01°13′E
79 L19 **Lomela** Kasai-Oriental, C Dem. Rep. Congo 02°19′S 23°15′E
25 R9 **Lometa** Texas, SW USA 31°13′N 98°23′W
79 F16 **Lomié** Est, SE Cameroon 03°09′N 13°35′E
30 M8 **Lomira** Wisconsin, N USA 43°36′N 88°26′W
95 K23 **Lomma** Skåne, S Sweden 55°41′N 13°05′E
99 J16 **Lommel** Limburg, N Belgium 51°14′N 05°19′E
96 I11 **Lomond, Loch** ◎ C Scotland, United Kingdom
197 R9 **Lomonosov Ridge** *var.* Harris Ridge, *Rus.* Khrebet Homonsova. *undersea feature* Arctic Ocean 88°00′N 140°00′E
Lomonsova, Khrebet *see* Lomonosov Ridge
Lom-Palanka *see* Lom
Lomphat *see* Lumphăt
35 P14 **Lompoc** California, W USA 34°39′N 120°29′W
167 P9 **Lom Sak** *var.* Muang Lom Sak. Phetchabun, C Thailand 16°45′N 101°12′E
110 N9 **Łomża** *Rus.* Lomzha. Podlaskie, NE Poland 53°11′N 22°04′E
Lomzha *see* Łomża
Lonaula *see* Lonāvale
155 D14 **Lonāvale** *prev.* Lonaula. Mahārāshtra, W India 18°45′N 73°27′E
63 G15 **Loncoche** Araucanía, C Chile 39°22′S 72°34′W
63 H14 **Loncopue** Neuquén, W Argentina 38°04′S 70°43′W
99 G17 **Londerzeel** Vlaams Brabant, C Belgium 51°00′N 04°19′E
Londinium *see* London
14 E16 **London** Ontario, S Canada 42°59′N 81°13′W
191 Y2 **London** Kiritimati, E Kiribati 02°00′N 157°28′W
97 O22 **London** *anc.* Augusta, *Lat.* Londinium. ● (United Kingdom) SE England, United Kingdom 51°30′N 00°10′W
21 N7 **London** Kentucky, S USA 37°07′N 84°05′W
31 S13 **London** Ohio, NE USA 39°52′N 83°27′W
25 Q10 **London** Texas, SW USA 30°40′N 99°33′W
97 O22 **London City** ✈ SE England, United Kingdom 51°31′N 00°07′E
97 E14 **Londonderry** *var.* Derry, *Ir.* Doire. NW Northern Ireland, United Kingdom 55°N 07°19′W
97 F14 **Londonderry** *cultural region* NW Northern Ireland, United Kingdom
180 M2 **Londonderry, Cape** *cape* Western Australia
63 H25 **Londonderry, Isla** *island* S Chile
43 O7 **Londres, Cayos** *reef* NE Nicaragua
60 I10 **Londrina** Paraná, S Brazil 23°18′S 51°13′W
27 N13 **Lone Grove** Oklahoma, C USA 34°11′N 97°15′W
14 E12 **Lonely Island** *island* Ontario, S Canada
35 T8 **Lone Mountain** ▲ Nevada, W USA 38°01′N 117°28′W
25 V6 **Lone Oak** Texas, SW USA 33°02′N 95°58′W
35 T11 **Lone Pine** California, W USA 36°36′N 118°04′W
Lone Star State *see* Texas
Lone Tree Islet *see* Iku
83 D14 **Longa** Cuando Cubango, C Angola 14°44′S 18°36′E
82 B12 **Longa** ≈ W Angola
83 E15 **Longa** ≈ SE Angola
Long'an *see* Pingwu
163 W11 **Longang Shan** ▲▲ NE China
197 S4 **Longa, Proliv** *Eng.* Long Strait. *strait* NE Russian Federation
44 J13 **Long Bay** *bay* W Jamaica
21 V13 **Long Bay** *bay* North Carolina/South Carolina, E USA
35 T16 **Long Beach** California, W USA 33°46′N 118°11′W
22 M9 **Long Beach** Mississippi, S USA 30°21′N 89°09′W
18 L14 **Long Beach** Long Island, New York, NE USA 40°34′N 73°38′W
32 F9 **Long Beach** Washington, NW USA 46°21′N 124°03′W
18 K16 **Long Beach Island** *island* New Jersey, NE USA
65 M25 **Longbluff** *headland* SW Tristan da Cunha
23 U13 **Longboat Key** *island* Florida, SE USA
18 K15 **Long Branch** New Jersey, NE USA 40°18′N 73°59′W
44 J5 **Long Cay** *island* SE Bahamas
Longcheng *see* Xiaoxian
161 P14 **Longchuan** *var.* Laolong. Guangdong, S China 24°07′N 115°10′E
Longchuan *see* Nanhua
Longchuan Jiang *see* Shweli
32 K12 **Long Creek** Oregon, NW USA 44°40′N 119°07′W
159 W10 **Longde** Ningxia, N China 35°37′N 106°07′E
183 P16 **Longford** Tasmania, SE Australia 41°41′S 147°03′E
97 D17 **Longford** *Ir.* An Longfort. Longford, C Ireland 53°45′N 07°50′W
97 E17 **Longford** *Ir.* An Longfort. *cultural region* C Ireland
Longgang *see* Dazu
161 P1 **Longhua** Hebei, E China 41°18′N 117°44′E
169 U11 **Longiram** Borneo, C Indonesia 0°02′S 115°36′E
44 J4 **Long Island** *island* C Bahamas
12 H8 **Long Island** *island* Nunavut, C Canada
186 D7 **Long Island** *var.* Arop Island. *island* N Papua New Guinea
18 L14 **Long Island** *island* New York, NE USA
Long Island *see* Bermuda
18 M14 **Long Island Sound** *sound* NE USA
163 U7 **Longjiang** Heilongjiang, NE China 47°20′N 123°09′E
160 K13 **Long Jiang** ≈ S China
163 Y10 **Longjing** *var.* Yanji. Jilin, NE China 42°48′N 129°26′E
161 R4 **Longkou** Shandong, E China 37°40′N 120°21′E
12 E11 **Longlac** Ontario, S Canada 49°47′N 86°34′W
19 S1 **Long Lake** ◎ Maine, NE USA
31 O6 **Long Lake** ◎ Michigan, N USA
31 R5 **Long Lake** ◎ Michigan, N USA
29 N6 **Long Lake** ◎ North Dakota, N USA
30 J4 **Long Lake** ⊠ Wisconsin, N USA
99 K23 **Longlier** Luxembourg, SE Belgium 49°51′N 05°27′E
160 I13 **Longlin** *var.* Longlin Gezu Zizhixian, Xinzhou. Guangxi Zhuangzu Zizhiqu, S China 24°46′N 105°19′E
Longlin Gezu Zizhixian *see* Longlin
37 T3 **Longmont** Colorado, C USA 40°09′N 105°07′W
157 P10 **Longnan** *var.* Wudu. Gansu, C China 33°27′N 104°57′E
29 N13 **Long Pine** Nebraska, C USA 42°32′N 99°42′W
Longping *see* Luodian
14 K15 **Long Point** *headland* Ontario, SE Canada 43°56′N 76°53′W
14 F17 **Long Point** *headland* Ontario, S Canada 42°33′N 80°15′W
184 P10 **Long Point** *headland* North Island, New Zealand 39°07′S 177°41′E
30 L2 **Long Point** *headland* Michigan, N USA 47°50′N 89°09′W
14 G17 **Long Point Bay** *lake bay* Ontario, S Canada
29 T7 **Long Prairie** Minnesota, N USA 45°58′N 94°52′W
Longquan *see* Fenggang
Longquàn *see* Yanggao
13 S11 **Long Range Mountains** *hill range* Newfoundland and Labrador, E Canada
65 H25 **Long Range Point** *headland* SE Saint Helena 16°00′S 05°41′W
181 V8 **Longreach** Queensland, E Australia 23°31′S 144°18′E
160 H7 **Longriba** Sichuan, C China 32°32′N 102°20′E
160 L10 **Longshan** *var.* Min'an. Hunan, S China 29°25′N 109°28′E
37 S3 **Longs Peak** ▲ Colorado, C USA 40°15′N 105°37′W
Long Strait *see* Longa, Proliv
102 K8 **Longué** Maine-et-Loire, NW France 47°23′N 00°07′W
13 P11 **Longue-Pointe** Québec, E Canada 50°20′N 64°13′W
103 S4 **Longuyon** Meurthe-et-Moselle, NE France 49°25′N 05°37′E
25 W7 **Longview** Texas, SW USA 32°30′N 94°45′W
32 G10 **Longview** Washington, NW USA 46°08′N 122°56′W
65 H25 **Longwood** C Saint Helena
25 P7 **Longworth** Texas, SW USA 32°37′N 100°20′W
103 S3 **Longwy** Meurthe-et-Moselle, NE France 49°31′N 05°46′E
159 V11 **Longxi** *var.* Gongchang. Gansu, C China 35°00′N 104°34′E
Longxian *see* Wengyuan
167 S14 **Long Xuyên** *var.* Longxuyen. An Giang, S Vietnam 10°23′N 105°25′E
Longxuyen *see* Long Xuyên
161 Q13 **Longyan** Fujian, SE China 25°06′N 117°02′E
92 O3 **Longyearbyen** ○ (Svalbard) Spitsbergen, W Svalbard 78°12′N 15°39′E
160 J15 **Longzhou** Guangxi Zhuangzu Zizhiqu, S China 22°22′N 106°46′E
Longzhouping *see* Changyang
100 F12 **Löningen** Niedersachsen, NW Germany 52°43′N 07°42′E
27 V11 **Lonoke** Arkansas, C USA 34°46′N 91°56′W
95 L21 **Lönsboda** Skåne, S Sweden 56°24′N 14°19′E
103 S9 **Lons-le-Saunier** *anc.* Ledo Salinarius. Jura, E France 46°41′N 05°32′E
31 O15 **Loogootee** Indiana, N USA 38°40′N 86°54′W
31 Q9 **Looking Glass River** ≈ Michigan, N USA
21 X11 **Lookout, Cape** *headland* North Carolina, SE USA 34°36′N 76°31′W
39 O6 **Lookout Ridge** *ridge* Alaska, USA
Lookransar *see* Lūnkaransar
181 N11 **Loongana** Western Australia 30°53′S 127°15′E
99 I14 **Loon op Zand** Noord-Brabant, S Netherlands 51°38′N 05°05′E
97 A19 **Loop Head** *Ir.* Ceann Léime. *promontory* W Ireland
109 V4 **Loosdorf** Niederösterreich, NE Austria 48°13′N 15°25′E
158 G10 **Lop** Xinjiang Uygur Zizhiqu, NW China 37°06′N 80°12′E
112 J11 **Lopare** ◈ Republika Srpska, NE Bosnia and Herzegovina
Lopatichi *see* Lapatsichy
127 P7 **Lopatino** Penzenskaya Oblast', W Russian Federation 52°38′N 45°46′E
167 P10 **Lop Buri** *var.* Loburi. Lop Buri, C Thailand 14°49′N 100°37′E
25 R16 **Lopeno** Texas, SW USA 26°42′N 99°06′W
79 C18 **Lopez, Cap** *headland* W Gabon 0°39′S 08°44′E
98 I12 **Lopik** Utrecht, C Netherlands 51°58′N 04°57′E
Lop Nor *see* Lop Nur
158 M7 **Lop Nur** *var.* Lob Nor, Lop Nor, Lo-pu Po. *seasonal lake* NW China
Lopnur *see* Yuli
79 K17 **Lopori** ≈ NW Dem. Rep. Congo
98 O5 **Loppersum** Groningen, NE Netherlands 53°20′N 06°45′E
92 I8 **Lopphavet** *sound* N Norway
Lo-pu Po *see* Lop Nur
Lora *see* Lowrah
182 F3 **Lora Creek** *seasonal river* South Australia
104 K13 **Lora del Río** Andalucía, S Spain 37°39′N 05°32′W
148 M11 **Lora, Hāmūn-i** *wetland* SW Pakistan
31 T11 **Lorain** Ohio, N USA 41°27′N 82°10′W
25 O7 **Loraine** Texas, SW USA 32°24′N 100°42′W
31 R13 **Loramie, Lake** ⊠ Ohio, N USA
105 Q13 **Lorca** *Ar.* Lurka; *anc.* Eliocroca, *Lat.* Illurco. Murcia, S Spain 37°40′N 01°41′W
192 I10 **Lord Howe Island** *island* E Australia
Lord Howe Island *see* Ontong Java Atoll
175 O10 **Lord Howe Rise** *undersea feature* SW Pacific Ocean
192 J10 **Lord Howe Seamounts** *undersea feature* W Pacific Ocean
37 P15 **Lordsburg** New Mexico, SW USA 32°19′N 108°42′W
186 E5 **Lorengau** *var.* Lorungau. Manus Island, N Papua New Guinea 02°01′S 147°15′E
25 N5 **Lorenzo** Texas, SW USA 33°40′N 101°31′W
142 K7 **Lorestān** *off.* Ostān-e Lorestān, *var.* Luristan. ◈ *province* W Iran
Lorestān, Ostān-e *see* Lorestān
57 M17 **Loreto** El Beni, N Bolivia 15°13′S 64°44′W
106 J12 **Loreto** Marche, C Italy 43°25′N 13°37′E
40 F8 **Loreto** Baja California Sur, NW Mexico 25°59′N 111°22′W
40 M11 **Loreto** Zacatecas, C Mexico 22°15′N 102°00′W
56 E9 **Loreto** *off.* Departamento de Loreto. ◈ *department* NE Peru
Loreto, Departamento de *see* Loreto
81 K18 **Lorian Swamp** *swamp* E Kenya
54 E6 **Lorica** Córdoba, NW Colombia 09°14′N 75°50′W
102 G7 **Lorient** *prev.* l'Orient. Morbihan, NW France 47°45′N 03°22′W
l'Orient *see* Lorient
111 K22 **Lőrinci** Heves, NE Hungary 47°46′N 19°40′E
14 G11 **Loring** Ontario, S Canada 45°55′N 79°59′W
33 V6 **Loring** Montana, NW USA 48°49′N 107°48′W
103 R13 **Loriol-sur-Drôme** Drôme, E France 44°46′N 04°51′E
21 U12 **Loris** South Carolina, SE USA 34°03′N 78°53′W
57 I18 **Loriscota, Laguna** ◎ S Peru
183 N13 **Lorne** Victoria, SE Australia 38°33′S 143°57′E
96 G11 **Lorn, Firth of** *inlet* W Scotland, United Kingdom
Loro Sae *see* East Timor
101 F24 **Lörrach** Baden-Württemberg, S Germany 47°38′N 07°40′E
103 T5 **Lorraine** ◈ *region* NE France
Lorungau *see* Lorengau
94 L11 **Los** Gävleborg, C Sweden 61°43′N 15°15′E
35 P14 **Los Alamos** California, W USA 34°44′N 120°16′W
37 S10 **Los Alamos** New Mexico, SW USA 35°52′N 106°17′W
42 F5 **Los Amates** Izabal, E Guatemala 15°14′N 89°06′W
63 G14 **Los Ángeles** Bío Bío, C Chile 37°30′S 72°18′W
35 S15 **Los Angeles** California, W USA 34°03′N 118°15′W
35 S15 **Los Angeles** ✈ California, W USA 33°54′N 118°24′W
35 T13 **Los Angeles Aqueduct** *aqueduct* California, W USA
Losanna *see* Lausanne
63 H20 **Los Antiguos** Santa Cruz, SW Argentina 46°36′S 71°31′W
189 Q16 **Losap Atoll** *atoll* C Micronesia
35 P10 **Los Banos** California, W USA 37°00′N 120°39′W
104 K16 **Los Barrios** Andalucía, S Spain 36°11′N 05°30′W
62 L5 **Los Blancos** Salta, N Argentina 23°36′S 62°35′W
42 L12 **Los Chiles** Alajuela, NW Costa Rica 11°00′N 84°42′W
105 O2 **Los Corrales de Buelna** Cantabria, N Spain 43°15′N 04°04′W
25 T17 **Los Fresnos** Texas, SW USA 26°03′N 97°28′W
35 N9 **Los Gatos** California, W USA 37°13′N 121°58′W

◆ Country
● Country Capital
◇ Dependent Territory
○ Dependent Territory Capital
◈ Administrative Regions
✈ International Airport
▲ Mountain
▲▲ Mountain Range
🌋 Volcano
≈ River
◎ Lake
⊠ Reservoir

127 P10 **Loshchina** Volgogradskaya Oblast', SW Russian Federation 48°58′N 46°14′E
110 O11 **Łosice** Mazowieckie, C Poland 52°13′N 22°42′E
112 B11 **Lošinj** *Ger.* Lussin, *It.* Lussino. *island* W Croatia
Los Jardines *see* Ngetik Atoll
63 G15 **Los Lagos** Los Ríos, C Chile 39°50′S 72°50′W
63 F17 **Los Lagos** *off.* Región de los Lagos. ◆ *region* C Chile
los Lagos, Región de *see* Los Lagos
Loslau *see* Wodzisław Śląski
64 N11 **Los Llanos de Aridane** *var.* Los Llanos de Aridane. La Palma, Islas Canarias, Spain, NE Atlantic Ocean 28°39′N 17°54′W
Los Llanos de Aridane *see* Los Llanos de Aridane
37 R11 **Los Lunas** New Mexico, SW USA 34°48′N 106°43′W
63 I16 **Los Menucos** Río Negro, C Argentina 40°52′S 68°07′W
40 H8 **Los Mochis** Sinaloa, C Mexico 25°48′N 108°58′W
35 N4 **Los Molinos** California, W USA 40°00′N 122°05′W
104 M9 **Los Navalmorales** Castilla-La Mancha, C Spain 39°43′N 04°38′W
25 S15 **Los Olmos Creek** ≈ Texas, SW USA
Losonc/Losontz *see* Lučenec
167 S5 **Lô, Sông** *var.* Panlong Jiang. ≈ China/Vietnam
44 B5 **Los Palacios** Pinar del Río, W Cuba 22°35′N 83°16′W
104 K14 **Los Palacios y Villafranca** Andalucía, S Spain 37°10′N 05°55′W
37 R12 **Los Pinos Mountains** ▲▲ New Mexico, SW USA
37 R11 **Los Ranchos de Albuquerque** New Mexico, SW USA 35°09′N 106°37′W
40 M14 **Los Reyes** Michoacán, SW Mexico 19°36′N 102°29′W
63 G15 **Los Ríos** ◆ *region* C Chile
56 B7 **Los Ríos** ◆ *province* C Ecuador
64 O11 **Los Rodeos** ✈ (Santa Cruz de Ternerife) Tenerife, Islas Canarias, Spain, NE Atlantic Ocean 28°27′N 16°20′W
54 L4 **Los Roques, Islas** *island group* N Venezuela
43 S17 **Los Santos** Los Santos, S Panama 07°56′N 80°23′W
43 S17 **Los Santos** *off.* Provincia de Los Santos. ◆ *province* S Panama
Los Santos *see* Los Santos de Maimona
104 J12 **Los Santos de Maimona** *var.* Los Santos. Extremadura, W Spain 38°27′N 06°22′W
Los Santos, Provincia de *see* Los Santos
98 P10 **Losser** Overijssel, E Netherlands 52°16′N 06°25′E
96 J8 **Lossiemouth** NE Scotland, United Kingdom 57°43′N 03°18′W
61 B14 **Los Tábanos** Santa Fe, C Argentina 28°27′S 59°57′W
54 J4 **Los Taques** Falcón, N Venezuela 11°50′N 70°16′W
14 G11 **Lost Channel** Ontario, S Canada 45°54′N 80°20′W
54 L5 **Los Teques** Miranda, N Venezuela 10°25′N 67°01′W
35 Q12 **Lost Hills** California, W USA 35°35′N 119°40′W
36 I7 **Lost Peak** ▲ Utah, W USA 37°30′N 113°57′W
33 P11 **Lost Trail Pass** *pass* Montana, NW USA
186 G9 **Losuia** Kiriwina Island, SE Papua New Guinea 08°29′S 151°03′E
62 G10 **Los Vilos** Coquimbo, C Chile 31°56′S 71°35′W
105 N10 **Los Yébenes** Castilla-La Mancha, C Spain 39°35′N 03°52′W
103 N13 **Lot** ◆ *department* S France
103 N13 **Lot** ≈ S France
63 F14 **Lota** Bío Bío, C Chile 37°07′S 73°10′W
81 G15 **Lotagipi Swamp** *wetland* Kenya/Sudan
102 K14 **Lot-et-Garonne** ◆ *department* SW France
83 K21 **Lothair** Mpumalanga, NE South Africa 26°23′S 30°26′E
33 R7 **Lothair** Montana, NW USA 48°28′N 111°15′W
79 L20 **Loto** Kasai-Oriental, C Dem. Rep. Congo 02°48′S 22°30′E
108 E10 **Lötschbergtunnel** *tunnel* Valais, SW Switzerland
25 T9 **Lott** Texas, SW USA 31°12′N 97°02′W
124 H3 **Lotta** *var.* Lutto. ≈ Finland/Russian Federation
184 Q7 **Lottin Point** *headland* North Island, New Zealand 37°26′S 178°07′E
Lötzen *see* Giżycko
Loualaba *see* Lualaba
167 P6 **Louangnamtha** *var.* Luong Nam Tha. Louang Namtha, N Laos 20°55′N 101°24′E
167 Q7 **Louangphabang** *var.* Louangphrabang, Luang Prabang. Louangphabang, N Laos 19°51′N 102°08′E
Louangphrabang *see* Louangphabang
194 H5 **Loubet Coast** *physical region* Antarctica
Loubomo *see* Dolisie
Louch *see* Loukhi
102 H6 **Loudéac** Côtes d'Armor, NW France 48°11′N 02°45′W
160 M11 **Loudi** Hunan, S China 27°51′N 111°59′E
79 F21 **Loudima** Bouenza, S Congo 04°06′S 13°05′E
20 M9 **Loudon** Tennessee, S USA 35°43′N 84°19′W
31 T12 **Loudonville** Ohio, N USA 40°38′N 82°13′W
102 L8 **Loudun** Vienne, W France 47°01′N 00°05′E
102 K7 **Loué** Sarthe, NW France 48°00′N 00°14′W
76 G10 **Louga** NW Senegal 15°36′N 16°15′W
97 M19 **Loughborough** C England, United Kingdom 52°47′N 01°11′W
97 C18 **Loughrea** *Ir.* Baile Locha Riach. Galway, W Ireland 53°12′N 08°34′W
103 S9 **Louhans** Saône-et-Loire, C France 46°38′N 05°12′E
21 P5 **Louisa** Kentucky, S USA 38°06′N 82°37′W
21 V5 **Louisa** Virginia, NE USA 38°02′N 78°00′W
21 V9 **Louisburg** North Carolina, SE USA 36°05′N 78°18′W
25 U12 **Louise** Texas, SW USA 29°07′N 96°22′W
15 P11 **Louiseville** Québec, SE Canada 46°15′N 72°54′W
27 W3 **Louisiana** Missouri, C USA 39°25′N 91°03′W
22 G8 **Louisiana** *off.* State of Louisiana, ***also known as*** Creole State, Pelican State. ◆ *state* S USA
Louis Trichardt *see* Makhado
23 V4 **Louisville** Georgia, SE USA 33°00′N 82°24′W
30 M15 **Louisville** Illinois, N USA 38°46′N 88°32′W
20 K5 **Louisville** Kentucky, S USA 38°15′N 85°46′W
22 M4 **Louisville** Mississippi, S USA 33°07′N 89°03′W
29 S15 **Louisville** Nebraska, C USA 41°00′N 96°09′W
192 L11 **Louisville Ridge** *undersea feature* S Pacific Ocean
124 J6 **Loukhi** *var.* Louch. Respublika Kareliya, NW Russian Federation 66°05′N 33°04′E
79 H19 **Loukoléla** Cuvette, E Congo 01°04′S 17°10′E
104 G14 **Loulé** Faro, S Portugal 37°08′N 08°02′W
111 C16 **Louny** *Ger.* Laun. Ústecký Kraj, NW Czech Republic 50°22′N 13°50′E
29 O15 **Loup City** Nebraska, C USA 41°16′N 98°58′W
29 P15 **Loup River** ≈ Nebraska, C USA
15 S9 **Loup, Rivière du** ≈ Québec, SE Canada
12 K7 **Loups Marins, Lacs des** ◎ Québec, NE Canada
102 K16 **Lourdes** Hautes-Pyrénées, S France 43°06′N 00°03′W
Lourenço Marques *see* Maputo
104 F11 **Loures** Lisboa, C Portugal 38°50′N 09°10′W
104 F10 **Lourinhã** Lisboa, C Portugal 39°14′N 09°19′W
115 C16 **Loúros** ≈ W Greece
104 G8 **Lousã** Coimbra, N Portugal 40°07′N 08°15′W
Loushanguan *see* Tongzi
160 M10 **Lou Shui** ≈ C China
183 O5 **Louth** New South Wales, SE Australia 30°34′S 145°07′E
97 O18 **Louth** E England, United Kingdom 53°19′N 00°00′E
97 F17 **Louth** *Ir.* Lú. *cultural region* NE Ireland
115 H15 **Loutrá** Kentrikí Makedonía, N Greece 39°55′N 23°37′E
115 G19 **Loutráki** Pelopónnisos, S Greece 37°55′N 22°55′E
Louvain *see* Leuven
99 H19 **Louvain-la Neuve** Walloon Brabant, C Belgium 50°39′N 04°36′E
14 J8 **Louvicourt** Québec, SE Canada 48°04′N 77°22′W
102 M4 **Louviers** Eure, N France 49°13′N 01°11′E
30 K14 **Lou Yaeger, Lake** ⊠ Illinois, N USA
93 J15 **Lövånger** Västerbotten, N Sweden 64°22′N 21°19′E
124 J14 **Lovat'** ≈ NW Russian Federation
113 J17 **Lovćen** ▲ SW Montenegro 42°22′N 18°49′E
114 I8 **Lovech** Lovech, N Bulgaria 43°08′N 24°45′E
114 I9 **Lovech** ◆ *province* N Bulgaria
25 V9 **Lovelady** Texas, SW USA 31°07′N 95°27′W
37 T3 **Loveland** Colorado, C USA 40°24′N 105°04′W
33 U12 **Lovell** Wyoming, C USA 44°50′N 108°23′W
Lovello, Monte *see* Grosser Löffler
35 S4 **Lovelock** Nevada, W USA 40°11′N 118°30′W
106 E7 **Lovere** Lombardia, N Italy 45°51′N 10°06′E
30 L10 **Loves Park** Illinois, N USA 42°19′N 89°03′W
26 M2 **Lovewell Reservoir** ⊠ Kansas, C USA
93 M19 **Loviisa** *Swe.* Lovisa. Etelä-Suomi, S Finland 60°27′N 26°15′E
37 V15 **Loving** New Mexico, SW USA 32°17′N 104°06′W
21 U6 **Lovingston** Virginia, NE USA 37°46′N 78°54′W
37 V14 **Lovington** New Mexico, SW USA 32°56′N 103°21′W
Lovisa *see* Loviisa
111 C15 **Lovosice** *Ger.* Lobositz. Ústecký Kraj, NW Czech Republic 50°30′N 14°02′E
124 K4 **Lovozero** Murmanskaya Oblast', NW Russian Federation 68°00′N 35°03′E
124 K4 **Lovozero, Ozero** ◎ NW Russian Federation
112 B9 **Lovran** *It.* Laurana. Primorje-Gorski Kotar, NW Croatia 45°16′N 14°15′E
116 E11 **Lovrin** *Ger.* Lowrin. Timiș, W Romania 45°58′N 20°49′E
82 E10 **Lóvua** Lunda Norte, NE Angola 07°21′S 20°09′E
82 G12 **Lóvua** Moxico, E Angola 11°33′S 23°35′E
65 D25 **Low Bay** *bay* East Falkland, Falkland Islands
9 P9 **Low, Cape** *headland* Nunavut, E Canada 63°05′N 85°27′W
33 N10 **Lowell** Idaho, NW USA 46°07′N 115°36′W
19 O10 **Lowell** Massachusetts, NE USA 42°38′N 71°19′W
Löwen *see* Leuven
Löwenberg in Schlesien *see* Lwówek Śląski
Lower Austria *see* Niederösterreich
Lower Bann *see* Bann
Lower California *see* Baja California
Lower Danube *see* Niederösterreich
185 L14 **Lower Hutt** Wellington, North Island, New Zealand 41°13′S 174°51′E
39 N11 **Lower Kalskag** Alaska, USA 61°30′N 160°28′W
35 O1 **Lower Klamath Lake** ◎ California, W USA
35 Q2 **Lower Lake** ◎ California/Nevada, W USA
97 E15 **Lower Lough Erne** ◎ SW Northern Ireland, United Kingdom
Lower Lusatia *see* Niederlausitz
Lower Normandy *see* Basse-Normandie
10 K9 **Lower Post** British Columbia, W Canada 59°53′N 128°19′W
29 T4 **Lower Red Lake** ◎ Minnesota, N USA
Lower Rhine *see* Neder Rijn
Lower Saxony *see* Niedersachsen
97 Q19 **Lowestoft** E England, United Kingdom 52°29′N 01°45′E
Lowgar *see* Lōgar
182 H7 **Low Hill** South Australia 32°17′S 136°46′E
110 K12 **Łowicz** Łódzkie, C Poland 52°06′N 19°55′E
33 N13 **Lowman** Idaho, NW USA 44°04′N 115°37′W
149 P8 **Lowrah** *var.* Lora. ≈ SE Afghanistan
Lowrin *see* Lovrin
183 N17 **Low Rocky Point** *headland* Tasmania, SE Australia 42°59′S 145°28′E
18 I8 **Lowville** New York, NE USA 43°47′N 75°29′W
Loxa *see* Loksa
182 K9 **Loxton** South Australia 34°30′S 140°36′E
81 G21 **Loya** Tabora, C Tanzania 04°57′S 33°53′E
30 K6 **Loyal** Wisconsin, N USA 44°45′N 90°30′W
18 G13 **Loyalsock Creek** ≈ Pennsylvania, NE USA
35 Q5 **Loyalton** California, W USA 39°39′N 120°16′W
Lo-yang *see* Luoyang
187 Q16 **Loyauté, Îles** *island group* S New Caledonia
Loyev *see* Loyew
119 O20 **Loyew** *Rus.* Loyev. Homyel'skaya Voblasts', SE Belarus 51°56′N 30°48′E
125 S13 **Loyno** Kirovskaya Oblast', NW Russian Federation 59°44′N 52°42′E
103 P13 **Lozère** ◆ *department* S France
103 Q14 **Lozère, Mont** ▲ S France 44°27′N 03°44′E
112 J11 **Loznica** Serbia, W Serbia 44°32′N 19°13′E
114 L8 **Loznitsa** Razgrad, N Bulgaria 43°22′N 26°36′E
117 V7 **Lozova** *Rus.* Lozovaya. Kharkivs'ka Oblast', E Ukraine 48°54′N 36°23′E
Lozovaya *see* Lozova
105 N7 **Lozoyuela** Madrid, C Spain 40°55′N 03°36′W
Lu *see* Shandong, China
Lú *see* Louth, Ireland
82 F12 **Luacano** Moxico, E Angola 11°19′S 21°30′E
79 N21 **Lualaba** *Fr.* Loualaba. ≈ SE Dem. Rep. Congo
83 H14 **Luampa** Western, NW Zambia 15°02′S 24°27′E
83 H15 **Luampa Kuta** Western, W Zambia 15°22′S 24°40′E
161 P8 **Lu'an** Anhui, E China 31°46′N 116°31′E
Luanco *see* Lluanco
82 A11 **Luanda** *var.* Loanda, *Port.* São Paulo de Loanda. ● Luanda, NW Angola 08°48′S 13°17′E
82 A11 **Luanda** ◆ *province* (Angola) NW Angola
82 A11 **Luanda** ✈ Luanda, NW Angola 08°49′S 13°16′E
82 D12 **Luando** ≈ C Angola
Luang *see* Tapi, Mae Nam
83 G14 **Luanginga** *var.* Luanguinga. ≈ Angola/Zambia
167 N15 **Luang, Khao** ▲ SW Thailand 08°21′N 99°46′E
Luang Prabang *see* Louangphabang
167 P8 **Luang Prabang Range** *Th.* Thiukhaoluang Phrahang. ▲▲ Laos/Thailand
167 N16 **Luang, Thale** *lagoon* S Thailand
Luangua, Rio *see* Luangwa
82 E11 **Luangue** ≈ NE Angola
Luanguinga *see* Luanginga
83 K15 **Luangwa** *var.* Aruângua. Lusaka, C Zambia 15°36′S 30°27′E
83 K14 **Luangwa** *var.* Aruângua, Rio Luangua. ≈ Mozambique/Zambia
161 Q2 **Luan He** ≈ E China
190 G11 **Luaniva, Île** *island* E Wallis and Futuna
161 P2 **Luanping** *var.* Anjiangying. Hebei, E China 40°55′N 117°19′E
82 J13 **Luanshya** Copperbelt, C Zambia 13°09′S 28°24′E
62 K13 **Luan Toro** La Pampa, C Argentina 36°14′S 64°15′W
161 Q2 **Luanxian** *var.* Luan Xian. Hebei, E China 39°46′N 118°46′E
Luan Xian *see* Luanxian
82 J12 **Luapula** ◆ *province* N Zambia
79 O25 **Luapula** ≈ Dem. Rep. Congo/Zambia
104 J2 **Luarca** Asturias, N Spain 43°33′N 06°31′W
169 R10 **Luar, Danau** ◎ Borneo, N Indonesia
79 L25 **Luashi** Katanga, S Dem. Rep. Congo 10°54′S 23°55′E
82 G12 **Luau** *Port.* Vila Teixeira de Sousa. Moxico, NE Angola 10°42′S 22°12′E
79 C16 **Luba** *prev.* San Carlos. Isla de Bioco, NW Equatorial Guinea 03°26′N 08°36′E
42 F4 **Lubaantun** *ruins* Toledo, S Belize
111 P16 **Lubaczów** *var.* Lúbaczów. Podkarpackie, SE Poland 50°10′N 23°08′E
Lubale *see* Lubalo
82 E11 **Lubalo** Lunda Norte, NE Angola 09°02′S 19°11′E
82 E11 **Lubalo** *var.* Lubale. ≈ Angola/Dem. Rep. Congo
118 J9 **Lubāna** E Latvia 56°55′N 29°43′E
Lubānas Ezers *see* Lubāns
171 N4 **Lubang Island** *island* N Philippines
83 B15 **Lubango** *Port.* Sá da Bandeira. Huíla, SW Angola 14°55′S 13°33′E
118 J9 **Lubāns** *var.* Lubānas Ezers. ◎ E Latvia
79 M21 **Lubao** Kasai-Oriental, C Dem. Rep. Congo 05°21′S 25°42′E
110 O13 **Lubartów** *Ger.* Qumälisch. Lublin, E Poland 51°29′N 22°38′E
100 G13 **Lübbecke** Nordrhein-Westfalen, NW Germany 52°18′N 08°37′E
100 O13 **Lübben** Brandenburg, E Germany 51°56′N 13°52′E
101 P14 **Lübbenau** Brandenburg, E Germany 51°52′N 13°57′E
25 N5 **Lubbock** Texas, SW USA 33°35′N 101°51′W
Lubcz *see* Lyubcha
19 U6 **Lubec** Maine, NE USA 44°49′N 67°00′W
100 K9 **Lübeck** Schleswig-Holstein, N Germany 53°52′N 10°41′E
100 K8 **Lübecker Bucht** *bay* N Germany
79 M21 **Lubefu** Kasai-Oriental, C Dem. Rep. Congo 04°43′S 24°25′E
163 T10 **Lubei** *var.* Jarud Qi. Nei Mongol Zizhiqu, N China 44°25′N 121°12′E
111 O14 **Lubelska, Wyżyna** *plateau* SE Poland
110 O13 **Lubelskie** ◆ *province* E Poland
Lubembe *see* Luembe
Lüben *see* Lubin
144 H9 **Lubenka** Zapadnyy Kazakhstan, W Kazakhstan 50°27′N 54°07′E
79 P18 **Lubero** Nord-Kivu, E Dem. Rep. Congo 0°10′S 29°12′E
79 L22 **Lubi** ≈ S Dem. Rep. Congo
Lubiana *see* Ljubljana
110 J11 **Lubień Kujawski** Kujawsko-pomorskie, C Poland 52°25′N 19°10′E
67 T11 **Lubilandji** ≈ S Dem. Rep. Congo
110 F13 **Lubin** *Ger.* Lüben. Dolnośląskie, SW Poland 51°23′N 16°12′E
111 O14 **Lublin** *Rus.* Lyublin. Lubelskie, E Poland 51°15′N 22°33′E
111 J15 **Lubliniec** Śląskie, S Poland 50°41′N 18°41′E
Lubnān, Jabal *see* Liban, Jebel
117 R5 **Lubny** Poltavs'ka Oblast', NE Ukraine 50°00′N 33°00′E
Luboml *see* Lyuboml'
110 G11 **Luboń** *Ger.* Peterhof. Wielkolpolskie, C Poland 52°23′N 16°54′E
Luboten *see* Ljuboten
110 D12 **Lubsko** *Ger.* Sommerfeld. Lubuskie, W Poland 51°47′N 14°57′E
79 N24 **Lubudi** Katanga, SE Dem. Rep. Congo 09°57′S 25°59′E
168 L13 **Lubuklinggau** Sumatera, W Indonesia 03°10′S 102°52′E
79 N25 **Lubumbashi** *prev.* Élisabethville. Shaba, SE Dem. Rep. Congo 11°40′S 27°31′E
83 I14 **Lubungu** Central, C Zambia 14°28′S 26°30′E
110 E12 **Lubuskie** ◆ *province* W Poland
Lubuskie *see* Dobiegniew
79 N18 **Lubutu** Maniema, E Dem. Rep. Congo 0°48′S 26°39′E
Luca *see* Lucca
82 C11 **Lucala** ≈ W Angola
14 E16 **Lucan** Ontario, S Canada 43°10′N 81°22′W
97 F18 **Lucan** *Ir.* Leamhcán. Dublin, E Ireland 53°22′N 06°27′W
Lucanian Mountains *see* Lucano, Appennino
107 M18 **Lucano, Appennino** *Eng.* Lucanian Mountains. ▲▲ S Italy
82 F11 **Lucapa** *var.* Lukapa. Lunda Norte, NE Angola 08°24′S 20°42′E
29 V15 **Lucas** Iowa, C USA 41°01′N 93°26′W
61 C18 **Lucas González** Entre Ríos, E Argentina 32°25′S 59°33′W
65 C25 **Lucas Point** *headland* West Falkland, Falkland Islands 52°10′S 60°22′W
31 S15 **Lucasville** Ohio, N USA 38°52′N 83°00′W
106 F11 **Lucca** *anc.* Luca. Toscana, C Italy 43°50′N 10°30′E
44 H12 **Lucea** W Jamaica 18°26′N 78°11′W
97 H15 **Luce Bay** *inlet* SW Scotland, United Kingdom
22 M8 **Lucedale** Mississippi, S USA 30°55′N 88°35′W
171 O4 **Lucena** *off.* Lucena City. Luzon, N Philippines 13°57′N 121°38′E
104 M14 **Lucena** Andalucía, S Spain 37°25′N 04°29′W
Lucena City *see* Lucena
105 S8 **Lucena del Cid** Valenciana, E Spain 40°07′N 00°15′W
111 D15 **Lučenec** *Ger.* Losontz, *Hung.* Losonc. Banskobystrický Kraj, C Slovakia 48°21′N 19°37′E
Lucentum *see* Alicante
107 M16 **Lucera** Puglia, SE Italy 41°30′N 15°19′E
Lucerna/Lucerne *see* Luzern
Lucerne, Lake of *see* Vierwaldstätter See
40 J4 **Lucero** Chihuahua, N Mexico 30°50′N 106°30′W
123 S14 **Luchegorsk** Primorskiy Kray, SE Russian Federation 46°26′N 134°10′E
105 Q13 **Luchena** ≈ SE Spain
Lucheng *see* Kangding
82 N13 **Lucheringo** *var.* Luchulingo. ≈ N Mozambique
Luchesa *see* Luchosa
Luchin *see* Luchyn
118 N13 **Luchosa** *Rus.* Luchesa. ≈ N Belarus
100 K11 **Lüchow** Mecklenburg-Vorpommern, N Germany 52°57′N 11°10′E
Luchow *see* Hefei
Luchulingo *see* Lucheringo
119 N17 **Luchyn** *Rus.* Luchin. Homyel'skaya Voblasts', SE Belarus 53°01′N 30°01′E
55 U11 **Lucie Rivier** ≈ W Suriname
182 K11 **Lucindale** South Australia 36°57′S 140°20′E
83 A14 **Lucira** Namibe, SW Angola 13°51′S 12°35′E
Łuck *see* Luts'k
101 O14 **Luckau** Brandenburg, E Germany 51°50′N 13°42′E
100 N13 **Luckenwalde** Brandenburg, E Germany 52°05′N 13°11′E
14 E15 **Lucknow** Ontario, S Canada 43°58′N 81°30′W
152 L12 **Lucknow** *var.* Lakhnau. *state capital* Uttar Pradesh, N India 26°50′N 80°54′E
102 J10 **Luçon** Vendée, NW France 46°27′N 01°10′W
44 I7 **Lucrecia, Cabo** *headland* E Cuba 21°00′N 75°34′W
82 F13 **Lucusse** Moxico, E Angola 12°32′S 20°46′E
Lüda *see* Dalian
114 M9 **Luda Kamchiya** ≈ E Bulgaria
161 T14 **Lü Dao** *var.* Huoshao Dao, Lütao, *Eng.* Green Island; *prev.* Lü Tao. *island* SE Taiwan
Ludasch *see* Luduș
114 I10 **Luda Yana** ≈ C Bulgaria
112 F7 **Ludbreg** Varaždin, N Croatia 46°15′N 16°36′E
29 P7 **Ludden** North Dakota, N USA 45°58′N 98°07′W
101 F15 **Lüdenscheid** Nordrhein-Westfalen, W Germany 51°13′N 07°38′E
83 C21 **Lüderitz** *prev.* Angra Pequena. Karas, SW Namibia 26°38′S 15°10′E
152 H8 **Ludhiāna** Punjab, N India 30°56′N 75°52′E
31 O7 **Ludington** Michigan, N USA 43°58′N 86°27′W
97 K20 **Ludlow** W England, United Kingdom 52°20′N 02°28′W
35 W14 **Ludlow** California, W USA 34°43′N 116°07′W
28 J7 **Ludlow** South Dakota, N USA 45°48′N 103°21′W
18 M9 **Ludlow** Vermont, NE USA 43°24′N 72°39′W
114 L7 **Ludogorie** *physical region* NE Bulgaria
23 W6 **Ludowici** Georgia, SE USA 31°42′N 81°44′W
Ludsan *see* Ludza
116 I10 **Luduș** *Ger.* Ludasch, *Hung.* Marosludas. Mureș, C Romania 46°28′N 24°05′E
95 M14 **Ludvika** Dalarna, C Sweden 60°08′N 15°14′E
101 H21 **Ludwigsburg** Baden-Württemberg, SW Germany 48°54′N 09°12′E
100 O13 **Ludwigsfelde** Brandenburg, NE Germany 52°17′N 13°15′E
101 G20 **Ludwigshafen** *var.* Ludwigshafen am Rhein. Rheinland-Pfalz, W Germany 49°29′N 08°24′E
Ludwigshafen am Rhein *see* Ludwigshafen
101 L20 **Ludwigskanal** *canal* SE Germany
100 L10 **Ludwigslust** Mecklenburg-Vorpommern, N Germany 53°19′N 11°29′E
118 K10 **Ludza** *Ger.* Ludsan. E Latvia 56°32′N 27°41′E
79 K21 **Luebo** Kasai-Occidental, SW Dem. Rep. Congo 05°19′S 21°21′E
25 Q6 **Lueders** Texas, SW USA 32°46′N 99°38′W
79 N20 **Lueki** Maniema, C Dem. Rep. Congo 03°25′S 25°50′E
82 F10 **Luembe** *var.* Lubembe. ≈ Angola/Dem. Rep. Congo
82 E13 **Luena** *var.* Lwena, *Port.* Luso. Moxico, E Angola 11°47′S 19°52′E
79 M24 **Luena** Katanga, SE Dem. Rep. Congo 09°28′S 25°45′E
82 K12 **Luena** Northern, NE Zambia 10°40′S 30°21′E
82 F13 **Luena** ≈ E Angola
83 F16 **Luengue** ≈ SE Angola
67 V13 **Luenha** ≈ W Mozambique
83 G15 **Lueti** ≈ Angola/Zambia
160 J7 **Lüeyang** *var.* Hejiayan. Shaanxi, C China 33°12′N 106°31′E
161 P14 **Lufeng** Guangdong, S China 22°59′N 115°40′E
79 N24 **Lufira** ≈ SE Dem. Rep. Congo
79 N25 **Lufira, Lac de Retenue de la** *var.* Lac Tshangalele. ◎ SE Dem. Rep. Congo
25 W8 **Lufkin** Texas, SW USA 31°21′N 94°47′W
82 L11 **Lufubu** ≈ N Zambia
124 G14 **Luga** Leningradskaya Oblast', NW Russian Federation 58°43′N 29°46′E
124 G13 **Luga** ≈ NW Russian Federation
Luganer See *see* Lugano, Lago di
108 H11 **Lugano** *Ger.* Lauis. Ticino, S Switzerland 46°01′N 08°57′E
108 H12 **Lugano, Lago di** *var.* Ceresio, *Ger.* Luganer See. ◎ S Switzerland
Lugansk *see* Luhans'k
187 Q13 **Luganville** Espiritu Santo, C Vanuatu 15°31′S 167°12′E
Lugdunum *see* Lyon
Lugdunum Batavorum *see* Leiden
83 O15 **Lugela** Zambézia, NE Mozambique 16°27′S 36°47′E
83 O16 **Lugela** ≈ C Mozambique
82 P13 **Lugenda, Rio** ≈ N Mozambique
Luggarus *see* Locarno
Lugh Ganana *see* Luuq
97 G19 **Lugnaquillia Mountain** *Ir.* Log na Coille. ▲ E Ireland 52°58′N 06°27′W
106 H10 **Lugo** Emilia-Romagna, N Italy 44°25′N 11°53′E
104 I3 **Lugo** *anc.* Lugus Augusti. Galicia, NW Spain 43°N 07°33′W
104 I3 **Lugo** ◆ *province* Galicia, NW Spain
21 R12 **Lugoff** South Carolina, SE USA 34°13′N 80°41′W
116 F12 **Lugoj** *Ger.* Lugosch, *Hung.* Lugos. Timiș, W Romania 45°41′N 21°56′E
Lugos/Lugosch *see* Lugoj
Lugovoy/Lugovoye *see* Kulan
158 I13 **Lugu** Xizang Zizhiqu, W China 33°26′N 84°10′E
Lugus Augusti *see* Lugo
Luguvallium/Luguvallum *see* Carlisle
117 Y7 **Luhans'k** *Rus.* Lugansk; *prev.* Voroshilovgrad. Luhans'ka Oblast', E Ukraine 48°32′N 39°21′E
117 Y7 **Luhans'k** ✈ Luhans'ka Oblast', E Ukraine 48°25′N 39°24′E
Luhans'k *see* Luhans'ka Oblast'
117 X6 **Luhans'ka Oblast'** *var.* Luhans'k; *prev.* Voroshilovgrad, *Rus.* Voroshilovgradskaya Oblast'. ◆ *province* E Ukraine
161 Q7 **Luhe** Jiangsu, E China 32°20′N 118°52′E
171 S13 **Luhu** Pulau Seram, E Indonesia 03°20′S 127°58′E
Luhua *see* Heishui
160 G8 **Luhuo** *var.* Xindu, *Tib.* Zhaggo. Sichuan, C China 31°18′N 100°39′E
116 M3 **Luhyny** Zhytomyrs'ka Oblast', N Ukraine 51°06′N 28°24′E
83 G15 **Lui** ≈ W Zambia
83 G16 **Luiana** ≈ SE Angola
83 L15 **Luia, Rio** *var.* Ruya. ≈ Mozambique/Zimbabwe
Luichow Peninsula *see* Leizhou Bandao
Luik *see* Liège
82 C13 **Luimbale** Huambo, C Angola 12°15′S 15°19′E
Luimneach *see* Limerick
106 D6 **Luino** Lombardia, N Italy 46°00′N 08°45′E
82 E13 **Luio** ≈ E Angola
92 L11 **Luiro** ≈ NE Finland
79 N25 **Luishia** Katanga, SE Dem. Rep. Congo 11°18′S 27°08′E
59 M19 **Luislândia do Oeste** Minas Gerais, SE Brazil 17°59′S 45°35′W
40 K5 **Luis L. León, Presa** ⊠ N Mexico
45 U5 **Luis Muñoz Marín** *var.* Luis Muñoz Marin. ✈ NE Puerto Rico 18°27′N 66°05′W
Luis Muñoz Marin *see* Luis Muñoz Marín
195 N5 **Luitpold Coast** *physical region* Antarctica
79 K22 **Luiza** Kasai-Occidental, S Dem. Rep. Congo 07°11′S 22°27′E
61 D20 **Luján** Buenos Aires, E Argentina 34°34′S 59°07′W
79 N24 **Lukafu** Katanga, SE Dem. Rep. Congo 10°28′S 27°32′E
Lukapa *see* Lucapa
112 I11 **Lukavac** ◆ Federacija Bosna I Hercegovina, NE Bosnia and Herzegovina
79 I20 **Lukenie** ≈ C Dem. Rep. Congo
114 J11 **Lŭki** Plovdiv, C Bulgaria 40°50′N 24°49′E
79 H19 **Lukolela** Equateur, W Dem. Rep. Congo 01°10′S 17°11′E
Lukoml'skaye, Vozyera *see* Lukomskaye, Vozyera
Lukoml'skoye, Ozero *see* Lukomskaye, Vozyera
119 M14 **Lukomskaye, Vozyera** *Rus.* Ozero Lukoml'skoye; *prev.* Vozyera Lukoml'skaye. ◎ N Belarus
114 I8 **Lukovit** Lovech, N Bulgaria 43°11′N 24°10′E
110 O12 **Łuków** *Ger.* Bogendorf. Lubelskie, E Poland 51°57′N 22°22′E
127 O4 **Lukoyanov** Nizhegorodskaya Oblast', W Russian Federation 55°02′N 44°26′E
Lukransar *see* Lūnkaransar
79 N22 **Lukuga** ≈ SE Dem. Rep. Congo
79 F21 **Lukula** Bas-Congo, SW Dem. Rep. Congo 05°23′S 12°57′E
83 G14 **Lukulu** Western, NW Zambia 14°24′S 23°12′E
189 R17 **Lukunor Atoll** *atoll* Mortlock Islands, C Micronesia
82 J12 **Lukwesa** Luapula, NE Zambia 10°03′S 28°42′E
93 K14 **Luleå** Norrbotten, N Sweden 65°35′N 22°10′E
92 J13 **Luleälven** ≈ N Sweden
136 C10 **Lüleburgaz** Kırklareli, NW Turkey 41°25′N 27°22′E
160 M4 **Lüliang** *var.* Lishi. Shanxi, C China 37°27′N 111°05′E
160 M4 **Lüliang Shan** ▲▲ C China
79 O21 **Lulimba** Maniema, E Dem. Rep. Congo 04°42′S 28°38′E
22 K9 **Luling** Louisiana, S USA 29°55′N 90°22′W
25 T11 **Luling** Texas, SW USA 29°40′N 97°39′W
79 I18 **Lulonga** ≈ NW Dem. Rep. Congo
79 K22 **Lulua** ≈ S Dem. Rep. Congo
Luluabourg *see* Kananga
192 L17 **Luma** Ta'ū, E American Samoa 14°15′S 169°30′W
169 S17 **Lumajang** Jawa, C Indonesia 08°06′S 113°13′E
158 G12 **Lumajangdong Co** ◎ W China
82 G13 **Lumbala Kaquengue** Moxico, E Angola 12°40′S 22°34′E
83 F14 **Lumbala N'Guimbo** *var.* Nguimbo, Gago Coutinho, *Port.* Vila Gago Coutinho. Moxico, E Angola 14°08′S 21°25′E
21 T11 **Lumber River** ≈ North Carolina/South Carolina, SE USA
Lumber State *see* Maine
22 L8 **Lumberton** Mississippi, S USA 31°00′N 89°27′W
21 U11 **Lumberton** North Carolina, SE USA 34°37′N 79°00′W
105 R4 **Lumbier** Navarra, N Spain 42°39′N 01°19′W
83 Q15 **Lumbo** Nampula, NE Mozambique 15°S 40°40′E
124 M4 **Lumbovka** Murmanskaya Oblast', NW Russian Federation 67°41′N 40°31′E
104 J7 **Lumbrales** Castilla y León, N Spain 40°57′N 06°43′W
153 W13 **Lumding** Assam, NE India 25°46′N 93°10′E
82 F12 **Lumege** *var.* Lumeje. Moxico, E Angola 11°30′S 20°57′E
Lumeje *see* Lumege
99 J17 **Lummen** Limburg, NE Belgium 50°58′N 05°12′E
93 J20 **Lumparland** Åland, SW Finland 60°06′N 20°15′E
167 T11 **Lumphăt** *prev.* Lomphat. Rôtânôkiri, NE Cambodia 13°30′N
11 U16 **Lumsden** Saskatchewan, S Canada 50°39′N 104°52′W
185 C23 **Lumsden** Southland, South Island, New Zealand 45°43′S 168°26′E
169 N14 **Lumut, Tanjung** *headland* Sumatera, W Indonesia 03°47′S 105°55′E
157 P4 **Lün** Töv, C Mongolia 47°51′N 105°11′E
116 I13 **Lunca Corbului** Argeș, S Romania 44°41′N 24°46′E
95 K23 **Lund** Skåne, S Sweden 55°42′N 13°10′E
35 X6 **Lund** Nevada, W USA 38°50′N 115°00′W
82 D11 **Lunda Norte** ◆ *province* NE Angola
82 E12 **Lunda Sul** ◆ *province* NE Angola
82 M13 **Lundazi** Eastern, NE Zambia 12°19′S 33°11′E
95 G16 **Lunde** Telemark, S Norway 61°31′N 06°38′E
Lundenburg *see* Břeclav
95 C17 **Lundevatnet** ◎ S Norway
Lundi *see* Runde
97 I23 **Lundy** *island* SW England, United Kingdom
100 J10 **Lüneburg** Niedersachsen, N Germany 53°15′N 10°25′E
100 J11 **Lüneburger Heide** *heathland* NW Germany
103 Q15 **Lunel** Hérault, S France 43°40′N 04°08′E
101 F14 **Lünen** Nordrhein-Westfalen, W Germany 51°37′N 07°31′E
13 P16 **Lunenburg** Nova Scotia, SE Canada 44°23′N 64°21′W
21 V7 **Lunenburg** Virginia, NE USA 36°56′N 78°15′W
103 T5 **Lunéville** Meurthe-et-Moselle, NE France 48°35′N 06°30′E
83 I14 **Lunga** ≈ C Zambia
Lunga, Isola *see* Dugi Otok
158 H12 **Lungdo** Xizang Zizhiqu, W China 33°45′N 82°09′E
158 I14 **Lunggar** Xizang Zizhiqu, W China 31°10′N 84°01′E
76 I15 **Lungi** ✈ (Freetown) W Sierra Leone 08°36′N 13°10′W
Lungkiang *see* Qiqihar
Lungleh *see* Lunglei
153 W15 **Lunglei** *prev.* Lungleh. Mizoram, NE India 22°55′N 92°49′E
158 L15 **Lungsang** Xizang Zizhiqu, W China 29°50′N 88°27′E
82 E13 **Lungué-Bungo** *var.* Lungwebungu. ≈ Angola/Zambia ***see also*** Lungwebungu
Lungué-Bungo *see* Lungwebungu
83 G14 **Lungwebungu** *var.* Lungué-Bungo. ≈ Angola/Zambia ***see also*** Lungué-Bungo
Lungwebungu *see* Lungué-Bungo
152 F12 **Lūni** Rājasthān, N India 26°03′N 73°00′E
152 F12 **Lūni** ≈ N India
Luninets *see* Luninyets
35 S7 **Luning** Nevada, W USA 38°29′N 118°10′W
Łuniniec *see* Luninyets
127 P6 **Lunino** Penzenskaya Oblast', W Russian Federation 53°35′N 45°12′E
119 J19 **Luninyets** *Pol.* Łuniniec, *Rus.* Luninets. Brestskaya Voblasts', SW Belarus 52°15′N 26°48′E
152 F10 **Lūnkaransar** *var.* Lookransar, Lukransar. Rājasthān, NW India 28°32′N 73°50′E
119 G17 **Lunna** *Pol.* Łunna. Hrodzyenskaya Voblasts', W Belarus 53°27′N 24°16′E
76 I15 **Lunsar** W Sierra Leone 08°41′N 12°32′W
83 K14 **Lunsemfwa** ≈ C Zambia
158 J6 **Luntai** *var.* Bügür. Xinjiang Uygur Zizhiqu, NW China 41°48′N 84°14′E
98 K11 **Lunteren** Gelderland, C Netherlands 52°05′N 05°38′E
109 U5 **Lunz am See** Niederösterreich, C Austria 47°54′N 15°01′E
163 Y7 **Luobei** *var.* Fengxiang. Heilongjiang, NE China 47°35′N 130°50′E
Luocheng *see* Hui'an, Fujian, China
Luocheng *see* Luoding, Guangdong, China
160 J13 **Luodian** *var.* Longping. Guizhou, S China 25°25′N 106°49′E
160 M15 **Luoding** *var.* Luocheng. Guangdong, S China 22°44′N 111°28′E
161 N7 **Luohe** Henan, C China 33°37′N 114°00′E
160 M6 **Luo He** ≈ C China
160 L5 **Luo He** ≈ C China
Luolajarvi *see* Kuoloyarvi
Luong Nam Tha *see* Louangnamtha
160 L13 **Luoqing Jiang** ≈ S China
161 O8 **Luoshan** Henan, C China 32°12′N 114°30′E
161 O12 **Luoxiao Shan** ▲▲ S China
161 N6 **Luoyang** *var.* Honan, Lo-yang. Henan, C China 34°41′N 112°25′E
161 R12 **Luoyuan** *var.* Fengshan. Fujian, SE China 26°29′N 119°32′E
79 F21 **Luozi** Bas-Congo, W Dem. Rep. Congo 04°57′S 14°08′E
83 J17 **Lupane** Matabeleland North, W Zimbabwe 18°54′S 27°44′E
160 I12 **Lupanshui** *var.* Liupanshui; *prev.* Shuicheng. Guizhou, S China 26°38′N 104°49′E
169 R10 **Lupar, Batang** ≈ East Malaysia
Lupatia *see* Altamura
116 G12 **Lupeni** *Hung.* Lupény. Hunedoara, SW Romania 45°20′N 23°10′E
Lupény *see* Lupeni
82 N13 **Lupiliche** Niassa, N Mozambique 11°36′S 35°15′E
83 E14 **Lupire** Cuando Cubango, E Angola 14°39′S 19°39′E
79 L22 **Luputa** Kasai-Oriental, S Dem. Rep. Congo 07°07′S 23°43′E
121 P16 **Luqa** ✈ (Valletta) S Malta 35°53′N 14°27′E
159 U11 **Luqu** *var.* Ma'ai. Gansu, C China 34°34′N 102°27′E
45 U5 **Luquillo, Sierra de** ▲▲ E Puerto Rico
26 L4 **Luray** Kansas, C USA 39°06′N 98°41′W
21 U4 **Luray** Virginia, NE USA 38°40′N 78°28′W
103 T7 **Lure** Haute-Saône, E France 47°42′N 06°30′E

◆ Country
● Country Capital
◇ Dependent Territory
○ Dependent Territory Capital
◆ Administrative Regions
✈ International Airport
▲ Mountain
▲▲ Mountain Range
Volcano
≈ River
◎ Lake
⊠ Reservoir

82 *D11* **Luremo** Lunda Norte, NE Angola *08°32′S 17°55′E*
97 *F15* **Lurgan** *Ir.* An Lorgain. S Northern Ireland, United Kingdom *54°28′N 06°20′W*
57 *K18* **Luribay** La Paz, W Bolivia *17°05′S 67°37′W*
Luring *see* Gêrzê
83 *Q14* **Lúrio** Nampula, NE Mozambique *13°32′S 40°34′E*
83 *P14* **Lúrio, Rio** ≈ NE Mozambique
Luristan *see* Lorestān
Lurka *see* Lorca
83 *J15* **Lusaka** ● (Zambia) Lusaka, SE Zambia *15°24′S 28°17′E*
83 *J15* **Lusaka** ◈ *province* C Zambia
83 *J15* **Lusaka** ✈ Lusaka, C Zambia *15°10′S 28°22′E*
79 *L21* **Lusambo** Kasai-Oriental, C Dem. Rep. Congo *04°59′S 23°26′E*
186 *F8* **Lusancay Islands and Reefs** *island group* SE Papua New Guinea
79 *I21* **Lusanga** Bandundu, SW Dem. Rep. Congo *04°55′S 18°40′E*
79 *N21* **Lusangi** Maniema, E Dem. Rep. Congo *04°39′S 27°10′E*
Lusatian Mountains *see* Lausitzer Bergland
Lushar *see* Huangzhong
Lushnja *see* Lushnjë
113 *K21* **Lushnjë** *var.* Lushnja. Fier, C Albania *40°54′N 19°43′E*
81 *J21* **Lushoto** Tanga, E Tanzania *04°48′S 38°20′E*
102 *L10* **Lusignan** Vienne, W France *46°25′N 00°06′E*
33 *Z15* **Lusk** Wyoming, C USA *42°45′N 104°27′W*
Luso *see* Luena
102 *L10* **Lussac-les-Châteaux** Vienne, W France *46°23′N 00°44′E*
Lussin/Lussino *see* Lošinj
Lussinpiccolo *see* Mali Lošinj
108 *I7* **Lustenau** Vorarlberg, W Austria *47°26′N 09°42′E*
Lü Tao *see* Lü Dao
Lütao *see* Lü Dao
Lūt, Baḩrat/Lut, Bahret *see* Dead Sea
22 *K9* **Lutcher** Louisiana, S USA *30°02′N 90°42′W*
143 *T9* **Lūt, Dasht-e** *var.* Kavīr-e Lūt. *desert* E Iran
83 *F14* **Lutembo** Moxico, E Angola *13°30′S 21°21′E*
Lutetia/Lutetia Parisiorum *see* Paris
Luteva *see* Lodève
14 *G15* **Luther Lake** ◎ Ontario, S Canada
186 *K8* **Luti** Choiseul, NW Solomon Islands *07°13′S 157°01′E*
Lūt, Kavīr-e *see* Lūt, Dasht-e
97 *N21* **Luton** E England, United Kingdom *51°53′N 00°25′W*
97 *N21* **Luton** ✈ (London) SE England, United Kingdom *51°54′N 00°24′W*
108 *B10* **Lutry** Vaud, SW Switzerland *46°31′N 06°32′E*
8 *K10* **Lutselk'e** *prev.* Snowdrift. Northwest Territories, W Canada *62°24′N 110°42′W*
8 *K10* **Lutselk'e** *var.* Snowdrift. ≈ Northwest Territories, NW Canada
29 *Y4* **Lutsen** Minnesota, N USA *47°39′N 90°37′W*
116 *J4* **Luts'k** *Pol.* Łuck, *Rus.* Lutsk. Volyns'ka Oblast', NW Ukraine *50°45′N 25°23′E*
Lutsk *see* Luts'k
Luttenberg *see* Ljutomer
Lüttich *see* Liège
83 *G25* **Luttig** Western Cape, SW South Africa *32°33′S 22°13′E*
Lutto *see* Lotta
82 *E13* **Lutuai** Moxico, E Angola *12°38′S 20°06′E*
117 *Y7* **Lutuhyne** Luhans'ka Oblast', E Ukraine *48°24′N 39°12′E*
171 *V14* **Lutur, Pulau** *island* Kepulauan Aru, E Indonesia
23 *V12* **Lutz** Florida, SE USA *28°09′N 82°27′W*
Lutzow-Holm Bay *see* Lützow Holmbukta
195 *V2* **Lützow Holmbukta** *var.* Lutzow-Holm Bay. *bay* Antarctica
81 *L16* **Luuq** *It.* Lugh Ganana. Gedo, SW Somalia *03°42′N 42°34′E*
92 *M12* **Luusua** Lappi, NE Finland *66°28′N 27°16′E*
23 *Q6* **Luverne** Alabama, S USA *31°43′N 86°15′W*
29 *S11* **Luverne** Minnesota, N USA *43°39′N 96°12′W*
79 *O22* **Luvua** ≈ SE Dem. Rep. Congo
82 *F13* **Luvuei** Moxico, E Angola *13°08′S 21°09′E*
81 *H24* **Luwego** ≈ S Tanzania
82 *K12* **Luwingu** Northern, NE Zambia *10°13′S 29°58′E*
171 *P12* **Luwuk** *prev.* Loewoek. Sulawesi, C Indonesia *0°56′S 122°47′E*
23 *N3* **Luxapallila Creek** ≈ Alabama/Mississippi, S USA
99 *M25* **Luxembourg** ● (Luxembourg) Luxembourg, S Luxembourg *49°37′N 06°08′E*
99 *M25* **Luxembourg** *off.* Grand Duchy of Luxembourg, *var.* Lëtzebuerg, Luxemburg. ◆ *monarchy* NW Europe
99 *J23* **Luxembourg** ◈ *province* SE Belgium
99 *L24* **Luxembourg** ◈ *district* S Luxembourg
31 *N6* **Luxemburg** Wisconsin, N USA *44°32′N 87°42′W*
Luxemburg *see* Luxembourg
103 *U7* **Luxeuil-les-Bains** Haute-Saône, E France *47°49′N 06°22′E*
160 *E13* **Luxi** *prev.* Mangshi. Yunnan, SW China *24°27′N 98°31′E*
82 *E10* **Luxico** ≈ Angola/Dem. Rep. Congo
75 *X10* **Luxor** *Ar.* Al Uqṣur. E Egypt *25°39′N 32°39′E*
75 *X10* **Luxor** ✈ C Egypt *25°39′N 32°48′E*
160 *M4* **Luya Shan** ▲▲ C China
102 *J15* **Luy de Béarn** ≈ SW France
102 *J15* **Luy de France** ≈ SW France
125 *P12* **Luza** Kirovskaya Oblast', NW Russian Federation *60°38′N 47°13′E*
125 *Q12* **Luza** ≈ NW Russian Federation
104 *I16* **Luz, Costa de la** *coastal region* SW Spain
111 *K20* **Luže** *var.* Lausche. ▲ Czech Republic/Germany *50°51′N 14°40′E* *see also* Lausche
Luže *see* Lausche
108 *F8* **Luzern** *Fr.* Lucerne, *It.* Lucerna. Luzern, C Switzerland *47°03′N 08°17′E*
108 *E8* **Luzern** *Fr.* Lucerne. ◈ *canton* C Switzerland
160 *L13* **Luzhai** Guangxi Zhuangzu Zizhiqu, S China *24°31′N 109°46′E*
118 *K12* **Luzhki** Vitsyebskaya Voblasts', N Belarus *55°21′N 27°52′E*
160 *I10* **Luzhou** Sichuan, C China *28°55′N 105°25′E*
Lužická Nisa *see* Neisse
Lužické Hory' *see* Lausitzer Bergland
Lužnice *see* Lainsitz
171 *O2* **Luzon** *island* N Philippines
171 *N1* **Luzon Strait** *strait* Philippines/Taiwan
Lužyckie, Gory *see* Lausitzer Bergland
116 *I5* **L'viv** *Ger.* Lemberg, *Pol.* Lwów, *Rus.* L'vov. L'vivs'ka Oblast', W Ukraine *49°49′N 24°05′E*
L'viv *see* L'vivs'ka Oblast'
116 *I4* **L'vivs'ka Oblast'** *var.* L'viv, *Rus.* L'vovskaya Oblast'. ◈ *province* NW Ukraine
L'vov *see* L'viv
L'vovskaya Oblast' *see* L'vivs'ka Oblast'
Lwena *see* Luena
Lwów *see* L'viv
110 *F11* **Lwówek** *Ger.* Neustadt bei Pinne. Wielkopolskie, C Poland *52°27′N 16°10′E*
111 *E14* **Lwówek Śląski** *Ger.* Löwenberg in Schlesien. Jelenia Góra, SW Poland *51°06′N 15°35′E*
119 *I18* **Lyakhavichy** *Rus.* Lyakhovichi. Brestskaya Voblasts', SW Belarus *53°02′N 26°16′E*
Lyakhovichi *see* Lyakhavichy
185 *B22* **Lyall, Mount** ▲ South Island, New Zealand *45°14′S 167°31′E*
Lyallpur *see* Faisalābād
Lyangar *see* Langar
124 *H11* **Lyaskelya** Respublika Kareliya, NW Russian Federation *61°42′N 31°06′E*
119 *I18* **Lyasnaya** *Rus.* Lesnaya. Brestskaya Voblasts', SW Belarus *52°59′N 25°46′E*
119 *F19* **Lyasnaya** *Pol.* Leśna, *Rus.* Lesnaya. ≈ SW Belarus
124 *H15* **Lychkovo** Novgorodskaya Oblast', W Russian Federation *57°55′N 32°24′E*
Lyck *see* Ełk
93 *I15* **Lycksele** Västerbotten, N Sweden *64°34′N 18°40′E*
18 *G13* **Lycoming Creek** ≈ Pennsylvania, NE USA
Lycopolis *see* Asyūṭ
195 *N3* **Lyddan Island** *island* Antarctica
Lydenburg *see* Mashishing
119 *L20* **Lyel'chytsy** *Rus.* Lel'chitsy. Homyel'skaya Voblasts', SE Belarus *51°47′N 28°20′E*
119 *P14* **Lyenina** *Rus.* Lenino. Mahilyowskaya Voblasts', E Belarus *54°25′N 31°08′E*
118 *L13* **Lyepyel'** *Rus.* Lepel'. Vitsyebskaya Voblasts', N Belarus *54°54′N 28°44′E*
25 *S17* **Lyford** Texas, SW USA *26°24′N 97°47′W*
95 *E17* **Lygna** ≈ S Norway
18 *G14* **Lykens** Pennsylvania, NE USA *40°33′N 76°42′W*
115 *E21* **Lykódimo** ▲ S Greece *36°56′N 21°49′E*
97 *K24* **Lyme Bay** *bay* S England, United Kingdom
97 *K24* **Lyme Regis** S England, United Kingdom *50°44′N 02°56′W*
110 *L7* **Łyna** *Ger.* Alle. ≈ N Poland
29 *P12* **Lynch** Nebraska, C USA *42°49′N 98°27′W*
20 *J10* **Lynchburg** Tennessee, S USA *35°17′N 86°22′W*
21 *T6* **Lynchburg** Virginia, NE USA *37°24′N 79°09′W*
21 *T12* **Lynches River** ≈ South Carolina, SE USA
32 *H6* **Lynden** Washington, NW USA *48°57′N 122°27′W*
182 *I5* **Lyndhurst** South Australia *30°19′S 138°20′E*
27 *Q5* **Lyndon** Kansas, C USA *38°37′N 95°40′W*
19 *N7* **Lyndonville** Vermont, NE USA *44°31′N 71°58′W*
95 *D18* **Lyngdal** Vest-Agder, S Norway *58°10′N 07°08′E*
92 *I9* **Lyngen** *Lapp.* Ivgovuotna. *inlet* Arctic Ocean
95 *G17* **Lyngør** Aust-Agder, S Norway *58°38′N 09°05′E*
92 *I9* **Lyngseidet** Troms, N Norway *69°36′N 20°07′E*
19 *P11* **Lynn** Massachusetts, NE USA *42°28′N 70°57′W*
Lynn *see* King's Lynn
23 *R9* **Lynn Haven** Florida, SE USA *30°15′N 85°39′W*
11 *V11* **Lynn Lake** Manitoba, C Canada *56°51′N 101°01′W*
Lynn Regis *see* King's Lynn
118 *I13* **Lyntupy** Vitsyebskaya Voblasts', NW Belarus *55°03′N 26°19′E*
103 *R11* **Lyon** *Eng.* Lyons; *anc.* Lugdunum. Rhône, E France *45°46′N 04°50′E*
8 *I6* **Lyon, Cape** *headland* Northwest Territories, NW Canada *69°47′N 123°10′W*
18 *K6* **Lyon Mountain** ▲ New York, NE USA *44°42′N 73°52′W*
103 *Q11* **Lyonnais, Monts du** ▲▲ C France
65 *N25* **Lyon Point** *headland* SE Tristan da Cunha *37°06′S 12°13′W*
182 *E5* **Lyons** South Australia *30°40′S 133°50′E*
37 *T3* **Lyons** Colorado, C USA *40°13′N 105°16′W*
23 *V6* **Lyons** Georgia, SE USA *32°12′N 82°19′W*
26 *M5* **Lyons** Kansas, C USA *38°22′N 98°13′W*
29 *R14* **Lyons** Nebraska, C USA *41°56′N 96°28′W*
18 *G10* **Lyons** New York, NE USA *43°03′N 76°58′W*
Lyons *see* Lyon
118 *O13* **Lyozna** *Rus.* Liozno. Vitsyebskaya Voblasts', NE Belarus *55°02′N 30°48′E*
117 *S4* **Lypova Dolyna** Sums'ka Oblast', NE Ukraine *50°36′N 33°50′E*
117 *N6* **Lypovets'** *Rus.* Lipovets. Vinnyts'ka Oblast', C Ukraine *49°13′N 29°06′E*
Lys *see* Leie
111 *I18* **Lysá Hora** ▲ E Czech Republic *49°31′N 18°27′E*
95 *D16* **Lysefjorden** *fjord* S Norway
95 *I18* **Lysekil** Västra Götaland, S Sweden *58°16′N 11°26′E*
Lysi *see* Akdoğan
33 *V14* **Lysite** Wyoming, C USA *43°16′N 107°42′W*
127 *P3* **Lyskovo** Nizhegorodskaya Oblast', W Russian Federation *56°04′N 45°01′E*
108 *D8* **Lyss** Bern, W Switzerland *47°04′N 07°19′E*
95 *H22* **Lystrup** Midtjylland, C Denmark *56°14′N 10°14′E*
125 *V14* **Lys'va** Permskiy Kray, NW Russian Federation *58°04′N 57°48′E*
117 *P6* **Lysyanka** Cherkas'ka Oblast', C Ukraine *49°15′N 30°50′E*
117 *X6* **Lysychans'k** *Rus.* Lisichansk. Luhans'ka Oblast', E Ukraine *48°52′N 38°27′E*
97 *K17* **Lytham St Anne's** NW England, United Kingdom *53°45′N 03°01′W*
185 *I19* **Lyttelton** South Island, New Zealand *43°35′S 172°44′E*
10 *M17* **Lytton** British Columbia, SW Canada *50°12′N 121°34′W*
119 *L18* **Lyuban'** Minskaya Voblasts', S Belarus *52°48′N 28°00′E*
119 *L18* **Lyubanskaye Vodaskhovishcha** ⊠ C Belarus
116 *M5* **Lyubar** Zhytomyrs'ka Oblast', N Ukraine *49°54′N 27°48′E*
Lyubashëvka *see* Lyubashivka
117 *O8* **Lyubashivka** *Rus.* Lyubashëvka. Odes'ka Oblast', SW Ukraine *47°49′N 30°18′E*
119 *I16* **Lyubcha** *Pol.* Lubcz. Hrodzyenskaya Voblasts', W Belarus *53°45′N 26°04′E*
126 *L4* **Lyubertsy** Moskovskaya Oblast', W Russian Federation *55°37′N 38°02′E*
116 *K2* **Lyubeshiv** Volyns'ka Oblast', NW Ukraine *51°46′N 25°33′E*
124 *M14* **Lyubim** Yaroslavskaya Oblast', NW Russian Federation *58°21′N 40°46′E*
114 *K11* **Lyubimets** Khaskovo, S Bulgaria *41°51′N 26°03′E*
Lyublin *see* Lublin
116 *I3* **Lyuboml'** *Pol.* Luboml. Volyns'ka Oblast', NW Ukraine *51°12′N 24°01′E*
Lyubotin *see* Lyubotyn
117 *U5* **Lyubotyn** *Rus.* Lyubotin. Kharkivs'ka Oblast', E Ukraine *49°57′N 35°57′E*
126 *I5* **Lyudinovo** Kaluzhskaya Oblast', W Russian Federation *53°52′N 34°28′E*
127 *T2* **Lyuk** Udmurtskaya Respublika, NW Russian Federation *56°55′N 52°45′E*
114 *M9* **Lyulyakovo** *prev.* Keremitlik. Burgas, E Bulgaria *42°53′N 27°05′E*
119 *I18* **Lyusina** *Rus.* Lyusino. Brestskaya Voblasts', SW Belarus *52°38′N 26°31′E*
Lyusino *see* Lyusina

M

138 *G9* **Ma'ād** Irbid, N Jordan *32°37′N 35°36′E*
Ma'ai *see* Luqu
Maalahti *see* Malax
Maale *see* Male'
138 *G13* **Ma'ān** Ma'ān, SW Jordan *30°11′N 35°45′E*
138 *H13* **Ma'ān** *off.* Muḩāfaẓat Ma'ān, *var.* Ma'an, Ma'ān. ◈ *governorate* S Jordan
93 *M16* **Maaninka** Itä-Suomi, C Finland *63°10′N 27°19′E*
Maanit *see* Bayan, Töv, Mongolia
Maanit *see* Hishig Öndör, Bulgan, Mongolia
Ma'ān, Muḩāfaẓat *see* Ma'ān
93 *N15* **Maanselkä** Oulu, C Finland *63°54′N 28°28′E*
161 *Q8* **Ma'anshan** Anhui, E China *31°45′N 118°32′E*
188 *F16* **Maap** *island* Caroline Islands, W Micronesia
118 *H3* **Maardu** *Ger.* Maart. Harjumaa, NW Estonia *59°28′N 24°56′E*
Ma'aret-en-Nu'man *see* Ma'arrat an Nu'mān
99 *K16* **Maarheeze** Noord-Brabant, SE Netherlands *51°19′N 05°37′E*
Maarianhamina *see* Mariehamn
138 *I4* **Ma'arrat an Nu'mān** *var.* Ma'aret-en-Nu'man, *Fr.* Maarret enn Naamâne. Idlib, NW Syria *35°40′N 36°40′E*
Maarret enn Naamâne *see* Ma'arrat an Nu'mān
98 *I11* **Maarssen** Utrecht, C Netherlands *52°08′N 05°03′E*
Maart *see* Maardu
99 *L17* **Maas** *Fr.* Meuse. ≈ W Europe *see also* Meuse
Maas *see* Meuse
99 *M15* **Maasbree** Limburg, SE Netherlands *51°22′N 06°03′E*
99 *L17* **Maaseik** *prev.* Maeseyck. Limburg, NE Belgium *51°05′N 05°48′E*
171 *Q6* **Maasin** Leyte, C Philippines *10°10′N 124°55′E*
99 *L17* **Maasmechelen** Limburg, NE Belgium *50°58′N 05°42′E*
98 *G12* **Maassluis** Zuid-Holland, SW Netherlands *51°55′N 04°15′E*
99 *L18* **Maastricht** *var.* Maestricht; *anc.* Traiectum ad Mosam, Traiectum Tungorum. Limburg, SE Netherlands *50°51′N 05°42′E*
183 *N18* **Maatsuyker Group** *island group* Tasmania, SE Australia
Maba *see* Qujiang
83 *L20* **Mabalane** Gaza, S Mozambique *23°43′S 32°37′E*
25 *V7* **Mabank** Texas, SW USA *32°22′N 96°06′W*
97 *O18* **Mablethorpe** E England, United Kingdom *53°21′N 00°14′E*
171 *V12* **Maboi** Papua, E Indonesia *01°00′S 134°02′E*
83 *M19* **Mabote** Inhambane, S Mozambique *22°03′S 34°09′E*
32 *J10* **Mabton** Washington, NW USA *46°13′N 120°00′W*
83 *H20* **Mabutsane** Southern, S Botswana *24°24′S 23°34′E*
63 *G19* **Macá, Cerro** ▲ S Chile *45°07′S 73°11′W*
60 *Q9* **Macaé** Rio de Janeiro, SE Brazil *22°21′S 41°48′W*
82 *N13* **Macaloge** Niassa, N Mozambique *12°27′S 35°25′E*
Macan *see* Bonerate, Kepulauan
161 *N15* **Macao** *Chin.* Aomen, *Port.* Macau. Guangdong, SE China *22°06′N 113°30′E*
104 *H9* **Mação** Santarém, C Portugal *39°33′N 08°00′W*
58 *J11* **Macapá** *state capital* Amapá, N Brazil *0°04′N 51°04′W*
43 *S17* **Macaracas** Los Santos, S Panama *07°46′N 80°31′W*
55 *P6* **Macare, Caño** ≈ NE Venezuela
55 *Q6* **Macareo, Caño** ≈ NE Venezuela
Macarsca *see* Makarska
182 *L12* **MacArthur** Victoria, SE Australia *38°04′S 142°02′E*
MacArthur *see* Ormoc
56 *C7* **Macas** Morona Santiago, SE Ecuador *02°22′S 78°08′W*
Macassar *see* Makassar
59 *Q14* **Macau** Rio Grande do Norte, E Brazil *05°05′S 36°37′W*
Macău *see* Makó, Hungary
Macau *see* Macao
65 *E24* **Macbride Head** *headland* East Falkland, Falkland Islands *51°25′S 57°55′W*
23 *V9* **Macclenny** Florida, SE USA *30°16′N 82°07′W*
97 *L18* **Macclesfield** C England, United Kingdom *53°16′N 02°07′W*
192 *F6* **Macclesfield Bank** *undersea feature* N South China Sea *15°50′N 114°20′E*
MacCluer Gulf *see* Berau, Teluk
181 *N7* **Macdonald, Lake** *salt lake* Western Australia
181 *Q7* **Macdonnell Ranges** ▲▲ Northern Territory, C Australia
96 *K8* **Macduff** NE Scotland, United Kingdom *57°40′N 02°29′W*
104 *I6* **Macedo de Cavaleiros** Bragança, N Portugal *41°31′N 06°57′W*
Macedonia *see* Macedonia, FYR
Macedonia Central *see* Kentrikí Makedonía
Macedonia East and Thrace *see* Anatolikí Makedonía kai Thráki
113 *O19* **Macedonia, FYR** *off.* the Former Yugoslav Republic of Macedonia, *var.* Macedonia, *Mac.* Makedonija, *abbrev.* FYR Macedonia, FYROM. ◆ *republic* SE Europe
Macedonia, the Former Yugoslav Republic of *see* Macedonia, FYR
Macedonia West *see* Dytikí Makedonía
59 *Q16* **Maceió** *state capital* Alagoas, E Brazil *09°40′S 35°44′W*
76 *K15* **Macenta** SE Guinea *08°31′N 09°32′W*
106 *J12* **Macerata** Marche, C Italy *43°18′N 13°27′E*
11 *S11* **MacFarlane** ≈ Saskatchewan, C Canada
182 *H7* **Macfarlane, Lake** *var.* Lake Mcfarlane. ◎ South Australia
Macgillicuddy's Reeks Mountains *see* Macgillycuddy's Reeks
97 *B21* **Macgillycuddy's Reeks** *var.* Macgillicuddy's Reeks Mountains, *Ir.* Na Cruacha Dubha. ▲▲ SW Ireland
11 *X16* **MacGregor** Manitoba, S Canada *49°58′N 98°49′W*
149 *O10* **Mach** Baluchistān, SW Pakistan *29°52′N 67°20′E*
56 *C6* **Machachi** Pichincha, C Ecuador *0°33′S 78°34′W*
83 *M19* **Machaila** Gaza, S Mozambique *22°15′S 32°57′E*
Machaire Fíolta *see* Magherafelt
Machaire Rátha *see* Maghera
81 *I19* **Machakos** Eastern, S Kenya *01°31′S 37°16′E*
56 *B8* **Machala** El Oro, SW Ecuador *03°20′S 79°57′W*
83 *J19* **Machaneng** Central, SE Botswana *23°12′S 27°30′E*
83 *M18* **Machanga** Sofala, E Mozambique *20°56′S 35°04′E*
80 *G13* **Machar Marshes** *wetland* SE Sudan
102 *I8* **Machecoul** Loire-Atlantique, NW France *46°59′N 01°51′W*
161 *O8* **Macheng** Hubei, C China *31°10′N 115°00′E*
155 *I16* **Mācherla** Andhra Pradesh, C India *16°29′N 79°25′E*
153 *O11* **Māchhāpuchhre** ▲ C Nepal *28°30′N 83°57′E*
19 *T6* **Machias** Maine, NE USA *44°44′N 67°28′W*
19 *T6* **Machias River** ≈ Maine, NE USA
19 *R3* **Machias River** ≈ Maine, NE USA
64 *P5* **Machico** Madeira, Portugal, NE Atlantic Ocean *32°43′N 16°47′W*
155 *K16* **Machilīpatnam** *var.* Bandar Masulipatnam. Andhra Pradesh, E India *16°12′N 81°11′E*
54 *G5* **Machiques** Zulia, NW Venezuela *10°04′N 72°37′W*
57 *G15* **Machu Picchu** Cusco, C Peru *13°08′S 72°30′W*
83 *M20* **Macia** *var.* Vila de Macia. Gaza, S Mozambique *25°02′S 33°08′E*
Macías Nguema Biyogo *see* Bioco, Isla de
116 *M13* **Măcin** Tulcea, SE Romania *45°15′N 28°09′E*
183 *T4* **Macintyre River** ≈ New South Wales/Queensland, SE Australia
181 *Y7* **Mackay** Queensland, NE Australia *21°10′S 149°10′E*
181 *O7* **Mackay, Lake** *salt lake* Northern Territory/Western Australia
10 *M13* **Mackenzie** British Columbia, W Canada *55°18′N 123°09′W*
8 *I9* **Mackenzie** ≈ Northwest Territories, NW Canada
195 *Y6* **Mackenzie Bay** *bay* Antarctica
10 *J1* **Mackenzie Bay** *bay* NW Canada
2 *D9* **Mackenzie Delta** *delta* Northwest Territories, NW Canada
197 *P8* **Mackenzie King Island** *island* Queen Elizabeth Islands, Northwest Territories, N Canada
8 *H8* **Mackenzie Mountains** ▲▲ Northwest Territories, NW Canada
31 *Q5* **Mackinac, Straits of** ◎ Michigan, N USA
194 *K5* **Mackintosh, Cape** *headland* Antarctica *72°52′S 60°00′W*
11 *R15* **Macklin** Saskatchewan, S Canada *52°19′N 109°51′W*
183 *V6* **Macksville** New South Wales, SE Australia *30°39′S 152°54′E*
183 *V5* **Maclean** New South Wales, SE Australia *29°30′S 153°15′E*
83 *J24* **Maclear** Eastern Cape, SE South Africa *31°05′S 28°22′E*
183 *U6* **Macleay River** ≈ New South Wales, SE Australia
MacLeod *see* Fort Macleod
180 *G9* **Macleod, Lake** ◎ Western Australia
10 *I6* **Macmillan** ≈ Yukon Territory, NW Canada
30 *J12* **Macomb** Illinois, N USA *40°27′N 90°40′W*
107 *B18* **Macomer** Sardegna, Italy, C Mediterranean Sea *40°15′N 08°47′E*
82 *Q13* **Macomia** Cabo Delgado, NE Mozambique *12°15′S 40°06′E*
103 *R10* **Mâcon** *anc.* Matisco, Matisco Ædourum. Saône-et-Loire, C France *46°19′N 04°49′E*
23 *T5* **Macon** Georgia, SE USA *32°49′N 83°41′W*
23 *N4* **Macon** Mississippi, S USA *33°06′N 88°33′W*
27 *U3* **Macon** Missouri, C USA *39°44′N 92°27′W*
22 *J6* **Macon, Bayou** ≈ Arkansas/Louisiana, S USA
82 *G13* **Macondo** Moxico, E Angola *12°31′S 23°45′E*
83 *M16* **Macossa** Manica, C Mozambique *17°51′S 33°54′E*
11 *T12* **Macoun Lake** ◎ Saskatchewan, C Canada
30 *K14* **Macoupin Creek** ≈ Illinois, N USA
Macouria *see* Tonate
83 *N18* **Macovane** Inhambane, SE Mozambique *21°30′S 35°07′E*
183 *N17* **Macquarie Harbour** *inlet* Tasmania, SE Australia
192 *J13* **Macquarie Island** *island* New Zealand, SW Pacific Ocean
183 *T8* **Macquarie, Lake** *lagoon* New South Wales, SE Australia
183 *Q6* **Macquarie Marshes** *wetland* New South Wales, SE Australia
175 *O13* **Macquarie Ridge** *undersea feature* SW Pacific Ocean *57°00′S 159°00′E*
183 *Q6* **Macquarie River** ≈ New South Wales, SE Australia
183 *P17* **Macquarie River** ≈ Tasmania, SE Australia
195 *V5* **Mac. Robertson Land** *physical region* Antarctica
97 *C21* **Macroom** *Ir.* Maigh Chromtha. Cork, SW Ireland *51°54′N 08°57′W*
42 *G5* **Macuelizo** Santa Bárbara, NW Honduras *15°21′N 88°31′W*
182 *G2* **Macumba River** ≈ South Australia
57 *I16* **Macusani** Puno, S Peru *14°05′S 70°24′W*
56 *E8* **Macusari, Río** ≈ N Peru
41 *U15* **Macuspana** Tabasco, SE Mexico *17°43′N 92°36′W*
138 *G10* **Ma'dabā** *var.* Mādabā, Madeba; *anc.* Medeba. Ma'dabā, NW Jordan *31°44′N 35°48′E*
138 *G11* **Ma'dabā** *off.* Muḩāfaẓat Ma'dabā. ◈ *governorate* C Jordan
Mādabā *see* Ma'dabā
172 *G2* **Madagascar** *off.* Democratic Republic of Madagascar, *Malg.* Madagasikara; *prev.* Malagasy Republic. ◆ *republic* W Indian Ocean
172 *I5* **Madagascar** *island* W Indian Ocean
128 *L17* **Madagascar Basin** *undersea feature* W Indian Ocean *27°00′S 53°00′E*
Madagascar, Democratic Republic of *see* Madagascar
128 *L16* **Madagascar Plain** *undersea feature* W Indian Ocean *19°00′S 52°00′E*
67 *Y14* **Madagascar Plateau** *var.* Madagascar Ridge, Madagascar Rise, *Rus.* Madagaskarskiy Khrebet. *undersea feature* W Indian Ocean *30°00′S 45°00′E*
Madagascar Rise/Madagascar Ridge *see* Madagascar Plateau
Madagasikara *see* Madagascar
Madagaskarskiy Khrebet *see* Madagascar Plateau
64 *N2* **Madalena** Pico, Azores, Portugal, NE Atlantic Ocean *38°32′N 28°15′W*
77 *Y6* **Madama** Agadez, NE Niger *21°54′N 13°43′E*
114 *J12* **Madan** Smolyan, S Bulgaria *41°29′N 24°56′E*
155 *I19* **Madanapalle** Andhra Pradesh, E India *13°33′N 78°31′E*
186 *D7* **Madang** Madang, N Papua New Guinea *05°14′S 145°45′E*
186 *C6* **Madang** ◈ *province* N Papua New Guinea
146 *G7* **Madaniyat** *Rus.* Madeniyet. Qoraqalpog'iston Respublikasi, W Uzbekistan *42°48′N 59°00′E*
Madanīyīn *see* Médenine
77 *U11* **Madaoua** Tahoua, SW Niger *14°06′N 06°01′E*
Madaras *see* Vtáčnik
153 *U15* **Madaripur** Dhaka, C Bangladesh *23°09′N 90°11′E*
77 *U12* **Madarounfa** Maradi, S Niger *13°16′N 07°07′E*
Madarska *see* Hungary
146 *B13* **Madau** Balkan Welaýaty, W Turkmenistan *38°11′N 54°46′E*
186 *H9* **Madau Island** *island* SE Papua New Guinea
19 *S1* **Madawaska** Maine, NE USA *47°19′N 68°19′W*
14 *J13* **Madawaska** ≈ Ontario, SE Canada
Madawaska Highlands *see* Haliburton Highlands
166 *M4* **Madaya** Mandalay, Myanmar (Burma) *22°12′N 96°05′E*
107 *K17* **Maddaloni** Campania, S Italy *41°03′N 14°23′E*
29 *O3* **Maddock** North Dakota, N USA *47°57′N 99°31′W*
99 *I14* **Made** Noord-Brabant, S Netherlands *51°41′N 04°48′E*
Madeba *see* Ma'dabā
64 *L9* **Madeira** *var.* Ilha de Madeira. *island* Madeira, Portugal, NE Atlantic Ocean
Madeira, Ilha de *see* Madeira
64 *O5* **Madeira Islands** *Port.* Região Autoónoma da Madeira. ◈ *autonomous region* Madeira, Portugal, NE Atlantic Ocean
64 *L9* **Madeira Plain** *undersea feature* E Atlantic Ocean
Madeira, Região Autoónoma da *see* Madeira Islands
64 *L9* **Madeira Ridge** *undersea feature* E Atlantic Ocean *35°30′N 15°45′W*
59 *F14* **Madeira, Rio** *var.* Río Madera. ≈ Bolivia/Brazil *see also* Madera, Río
Madeira, Rio *see* Madera, Río
101 *J25* **Mädelegabel** ▲ Austria/Germany *47°18′N 10°19′E*
15 *X6* **Madeleine** ≈ Québec, SE Canada
15 *X5* **Madeleine, Cap de la** *headland* Québec, SE Canada *49°13′N 65°20′W*
13 *Q13* **Madeleine, Îles de la** *Eng.* Magdalen Islands. *island group* Québec, E Canada
29 *U10* **Madelia** Minnesota, N USA *44°03′N 94°26′W*
35 *P3* **Madeline** California, W USA *41°02′N 120°28′W*
30 *K3* **Madeline Island** *island* Apostle Islands, Wisconsin, N USA
137 *O15* **Maden** Elazığ, SE Turkey *38°24′N 39°42′E*
145 *V12* **Madeniyet** Vostochnyy Kazakhstan, E Kazakhstan *47°51′N 78°37′E*
Madeniyet *see* Madaniyat
40 *H5* **Madera** Chihuahua, N Mexico *29°10′N 108°10′W*
35 *Q10* **Madera** California, W USA *36°57′N 120°02′W*
56 *L13* **Madera, Río** *Port.* Rio Madeira. ≈ Bolivia/Brazil *see also* Madeira, Rio
Madera, Río *see* Madeira, Rio
106 *D6* **Madesimo** Lombardia, N Italy *46°20′N 09°26′E*
141 *O14* **Madhāb, Wādī** *dry watercourse* NW Yemen
153 *R13* **Madhepura** *prev.* Madhipure. Bihār, NE India *25°56′N 86°48′E*
Madhipure *see* Madhepura
153 *Q13* **Madhubani** Bihār, N India *26°21′N 86°05′E*
153 *Q15* **Madhupur** Jhārkhand, NE India *24°17′N 86°38′E*
154 *I10* **Madhya Pradesh** *prev.* Central Provinces and Berar. ◈ *state* C India
57 *K15* **Madidi, Río** ≈ W Bolivia
155 *F20* **Madikeri** *prev.* Mercara. Karnātaka, W India *12°29′N 75°40′E*
27 *O13* **Madill** Oklahoma, C USA *34°06′N 96°46′W*
79 *G21* **Madimba** Bas-Congo, SW Dem. Rep. Congo *04°58′S 15°08′E*
138 *M4* **Ma'dīn** Ar Raqqah, C Syria *35°45′N 39°36′E*
Madīnah, Minṭaqat al *see* Al Madīnah
76 *M14* **Madinani** NW Ivory Coast *09°37′N 06°57′W*
141 *O17* **Madīnat ash Sha'b** *prev.* Al Ittiḩād. SW Yemen *12°52′N 44°55′E*
138 *K3* **Madīnat ath Thawrah** *var.* Ath Thawrah. Ar Raqqah, N Syria *35°36′N 39°00′E*
173 *O6* **Madingley Rise** *undersea feature* W Indian Ocean
79 *E21* **Madingo-Kayes** Kouilou, S Congo *04°27′S 11°43′E*
79 *F21* **Madingou** Bouenza, S Congo *04°10′S 13°33′E*
Madioen *see* Madiun
23 *U8* **Madison** Florida, SE USA *30°27′N 83°24′W*
23 *T3* **Madison** Georgia, SE USA *33°37′N 83°28′W*
31 *P15* **Madison** Indiana, N USA *38°44′N 85°22′W*
27 *P6* **Madison** Kansas, C USA *45′01′N 96′11′W*
19 *Q6* **Madison** Maine, NE USA *44°48′N 69°52′W*
29 *S9* **Madison** Minnesota, N USA *45°00′N 96°12′W*
22 *K5* **Madison** Mississippi, S USA *32°27′N 90°07′W*
29 *Q14* **Madison** Nebraska, C USA *41°49′N 97°27′W*
29 *R10* **Madison** South Dakota, N USA *44°00′N 97°06′W*
21 *V5* **Madison** Virginia, NE USA *38°23′N 78°16′W*
21 *Q5* **Madison** West Virginia, NE USA *38°03′N 81°50′W*
30 *L9* **Madison** *state capital* Wisconsin, N USA *43°04′N 89°22′W*
21 *T6* **Madison Heights** Virginia, NE USA *37°25′N 79°07′W*
20 *I6* **Madisonville** Kentucky, S USA *37°20′N 87°30′W*
20 *M10* **Madisonville** Tennessee, S USA *35°31′N 84°21′W*
25 *V9* **Madisonville** Texas, SW USA *30°58′N 95°56′W*
Madisonville *see* Taiohae
169 *R16* **Madiun** *prev.* Madioen. Jawa, C Indonesia *07°37′S 111°33′E*
Madjene *see* Majene
14 *J14* **Madoc** Ontario, SE Canada *44°31′N 77°27′W*
Madoera *see* Madura, Pulau
81 *J18* **Mado Gashi** North Eastern, E Kenya *0°40′N 39°09′E*
159 *R11* **Madoi** *var.* Huanghe; *prev.* Huangheyan. Qinghai, C China *34°53′N 98°07′E*
189 *O13* **Madolenihmw** Pohnpei, E Micronesia
118 *I9* **Madona** *Ger.* Modohn. E Latvia *56°51′N 26°10′E*
107 *J23* **Madonie** ▲▲ Sicilia, Italy, C Mediterranean Sea
141 *Y11* **Madrakah, Ra's** *headland* E Oman *18°56′N 57°54′E*
32 *I12* **Madras** Oregon, NW USA *44°39′N 121°08′W*
Madras *see* Chennai
Madras *see* Tamil Nādu
57 *H14* **Madre de Dios** *off.* Departamento de Madre de Dios. ◈ *department* E Peru
Madre de Dios, Departamento de *see* Madre de Dios
63 *F22* **Madre de Dios, Isla** *island* S Chile
57 *J14* **Madre de Dios, Río** ≈ Bolivia/Peru
0 *H15* **Madre del Sur, Sierra** ▲▲ S Mexico
41 *Q9* **Madre, Laguna** *lagoon* NE Mexico
25 *T16* **Madre, Laguna** *lagoon* Texas, SW USA
37 *Q12* **Madre Mount** ▲ New Mexico, SW USA *34°18′N 107°54′W*
0 *H13* **Madre Occidental, Sierra** *var.* Western Sierra Madre. ▲▲ C Mexico
0 *H13* **Madre Oriental, Sierra** *var.* Eastern Sierra Madre. ▲▲ C Mexico
41 *U17* **Madre, Sierra** *var.* Sierra de Soconusco. ▲▲ Guatemala/Mexico
37 *R2* **Madre, Sierra** ▲▲ Colorado/Wyoming, C USA
105 *N8* **Madrid** ● (Spain) Madrid, C Spain *40°25′N 03°43′W*
29 *V14* **Madrid** Iowa, C USA *41°52′N 93°49′W*
105 *N7* **Madrid** ◈ *autonomous community* C Spain
105 *N10* **Madridejos** Castilla-La Mancha, C Spain *39°29′N 03°32′W*
104 *L7* **Madrigal de las Altas Torres** Castilla y León, N Spain *41°05′N 05°00′W*
104 *K10* **Madrigalejo** Extremadura, W Spain *39°08′N 05°36′W*
34 *L3* **Mad River** ≈ California, W USA
42 *J8* **Madriz** ◈ *department* NW Nicaragua
104 *K10* **Madroñera** Extremadura, W Spain *39°25′N 05°46′W*
181 *N12* **Madura** Western Australia *31°52′S 127°01′E*
Madura *see* Madurai
155 *H22* **Madurai** *prev.* Madura, Mathurai. Tamil Nādu, S India *09°55′N 78°07′E*
169 *S16* **Madura, Pulau** *prev.* Madoera. *island* C Indonesia
169 *S16* **Madura, Selat** *strait* C Indonesia
127 *Q17* **Madzhalis** Respublika Dagestan, SW Russian Federation *42°12′N 47°46′E*
114 *K12* **Madzharovo** Khaskovo, S Bulgaria *41°36′N 25°52′E*
83 *M14* **Madzimoyo** Eastern, E Zambia *13°42′S 32°34′E*
165 *O12* **Maebashi** *var.* Maebasi, Mayebashi. Gunma, Honshū, S Japan *36°24′N 139°02′E*
Maebasi *see* Maebashi
167 *O6* **Mae Chan** Chiang Rai, NW Thailand *20°13′N 99°52′E*
167 *N7* **Mae Hong Son** *var.* Maehongson, Muai To. Mae Hong Son, NW Thailand *19°16′N 97°56′E*
Maehongson *see* Mae Hong Son
Mae Nam Khong *see* Mekong
167 *Q7* **Mae Nam Nan** ≈ NW Thailand
167 *O10* **Mae Nam Tha Chin** ≈ W Thailand
167 *P7* **Mae Nam Yom** ≈ W Thailand
37 *O3* **Maeser** Utah, W USA *40°28′N 109°35′W*
Maeseyck *see* Maaseik
167 *N9* **Mae Sot** *var.* Ban Mae Sot. Tak, W Thailand *16°44′N 98°32′E*
44 *H8* **Maestra, Sierra** ▲▲ E Cuba
Maestricht *see* Maastricht
167 *O7* **Mae Suai** *var.* Ban Mae Suai. Chiang Rai, NW Thailand *19°43′N 99°30′E*
167 *O7* **Mae Tho, Doi** ▲ NW Thailand *18°56′N 99°20′E*
172 *I4* **Maevatanana** Mahajanga, C Madagascar *16°57′S 46°50′E*
187 *R13* **Maéwo** *prev.* Aurora. *island* C Vanuatu
171 *S11* **Mafa** Pulau Halmahera, E Indonesia *0°01′N 127°50′E*
83 *I23* **Mafeteng** W Lesotho *29°48′S 27°15′E*
99 *J21* **Maffe** Namur, SE Belgium *50°21′N 05°19′E*
183 *P12* **Maffra** Victoria, SE Australia *37°59′S 147°03′E*
81 *K23* **Mafia** *island* E Tanzania
81 *J23* **Mafia Channel** *sea waterway* E Tanzania
83 *I21* **Mafikeng** North-West, N South Africa *25°53′S 25°39′E*
60 *J12* **Mafra** Santa Catarina, S Brazil *26°08′S 49°47′W*
104 *F10* **Mafra** Lisboa, C Portugal *38°57′N 09°19′W*
143 *Q17* **Mafraq** Abū Ẓaby, C United Arab Emirates *24°21′N 54°33′E*
Mafraq/Muḩāfaẓat al Mafraq *see* Al Mafraq
123 *T10* **Magadan** Magadanskaya Oblast', E Russian Federation *59°38′N 150°50′E*
123 *T9* **Magadanskaya Oblast'** ◈ *province* E Russian Federation

◆ Country
● Country Capital
◇ Dependent Territory
○ Dependent Territory Capital
◈ Administrative Regions
✈ International Airport
▲ Mountain
▲▲ Mountain Range
Volcano
≈ River
◎ Lake
⊠ Reservoir

108 G11 **Magadino** Ticino, S Switzerland 46°09′N 08°50′E
63 G23 **Magallanes** *var.* Región de Magallanes y de la Antártica Chilena. ◈ *region* S Chile
Magallanes *see* Punta Arenas
Magallanes, Estrecho de *see* Magellan, Strait of
Magallanes y de la Antártica Chilena, Región de *see* Magallanes
14 I10 **Maganasipi, Lac** ◎ Québec, SE Canada
54 F6 **Magangué** Bolívar, N Colombia 09°14′N 74°46′W
191 Y13 **Magareva** *var.* Mangareva. *island* Îles Tuamotu, SE French Polynesia
77 V12 **Magaria** Zinder, S Niger 13°00′N 08°55′E
186 F10 **Magarida** Central, SW Papua New Guinea 10°10′S 149°21′E
171 O2 **Magat** ≈ Luzon, N Philippines
27 T11 **Magazine Mountain** ▲ Arkansas, C USA 35°10′N 93°38′W
76 I15 **Magburaka** C Sierra Leone 08°44′N 11°57′W
123 Q13 **Magdagachi** Amurskaya Oblast', SE Russian Federation 53°25′N 125°41′E
62 O12 **Magdalena** Buenos Aires, E Argentina 35°05′S 57°30′W
57 M15 **Magdalena** El Beni, N Bolivia 13°22′S 64°07′W
40 F4 **Magdalena** Sonora, NW Mexico 30°38′N 110°59′W
37 Q13 **Magdalena** New Mexico, SW USA 34°07′N 107°14′W
54 F5 **Magdalena** *off.* Departamento del Magdalena. ◈ *province* N Colombia
40 E9 **Magdalena, Bahía** *bay* W Mexico
Magdalena, Departamento del *see* Magdalena
63 G19 **Magdalena, Isla** *island* Archipiélago de los Chonos, S Chile
40 D8 **Magdalena, Isla** *island* NW Mexico
47 P6 **Magdalena, Río** ≈ C Colombia
40 F4 **Magdalena, Río** ≈ NW Mexico
Magdalen Islands *see* Madeleine, Îles de la
147 N14 **Magdanly** *Rus.* Govurdak; *prev.* gowurdak, Guardak. Lebap Welaýaty, E Turkmenistan 37°50′N 66°06′E
100 L13 **Magdeburg** Sachsen-Anhalt, C Germany 52°08′N 11°39′E
22 L6 **Magee** Mississippi, S USA 31°52′N 89°43′W
169 Q16 **Magelang** Jawa, C Indonesia 07°28′S 110°11′E
192 K7 **Magellan Rise** *undersea feature* C Pacific Ocean
63 H24 **Magellan, Strait of** *Sp.* Estrecho de Magallanes. *strait* Argentina/Chile
106 D7 **Magenta** Lombardia, NW Italy 45°28′N 08°52′E
Magerøy *see* Magerøya
92 K7 **Magerøya** *var.* Magerøy, *Lapp.* Máhkarávju. *island* N Norway
164 C17 **Mage-shima** *island* Nansei-shotō, SW Japan
108 G11 **Maggia** Ticino, S Switzerland 46°15′N 08°42′E
108 G10 **Maggia** ≈ SW Switzerland
Maggiore, Lago *see* Maggiore, Lake
106 C6 **Maggiore, Lake** *It.* Lago Maggiore. ◎ Italy/Switzerland
44 I12 **Maggotty** W Jamaica 18°09′N 77°46′W
76 I10 **Maghama** Gorgol, S Mauritania 15°31′N 12°50′W
97 F14 **Maghera** *Ir.* Machaire Rátha. C Northern Ireland, United Kingdom 54°51′N 06°40′W
97 F15 **Magherafelt** *Ir.* Machaire Fíolta. C Northern Ireland, United Kingdom 54°45′N 06°36′W
188 H6 **Magicienne Bay** *bay* Saipan, S Northern Mariana Islands
105 O13 **Magina** ▲ S Spain 37°43′N 03°24′W
81 H24 **Magingo** Ruvuma, S Tanzania 09°57′S 35°23′E
112 H11 **Maglaj** ◈ Federacija Bosna I Hercegovina, N Bosnia and Herzegovina
107 Q19 **Maglie** Puglia, SE Italy 40°07′N 18°18′E
36 L2 **Magna** Utah, W USA 40°42′N 112°06′W
Magnesia *see* Manisa
14 G12 **Magnetawan** ≈ Ontario, S Canada
27 T14 **Magnolia** Arkansas, C USA 33°17′N 93°16′W
22 K7 **Magnolia** Mississippi, S USA 31°08′N 90°27′W
25 V10 **Magnolia** Texas, SW USA 30°12′N 95°46′W
Magnolia State *see* Mississippi
95 J15 **Magnor** Hedmark, S Norway 59°57′N 12°14′E
187 Y14 **Mago** *prev.* Mango. *island* Lau Group, E Fiji
83 L15 **Màgoé** Tete, NW Mozambique 15°50′S 31°42′E
15 Q13 **Magog** Québec, SE Canada 45°16′N 72°09′W
83 J15 **Magoye** Southern, S Zambia 16°00′S 27°34′E
41 Q12 **Magozal** Veracruz-Llave, C Mexico 21°33′N 97°57′W
14 B7 **Magpie** ≈ Ontario, S Canada
11 Q17 **Magrath** Alberta, SW Canada 49°27′N 112°52′W
105 R10 **Magre** ≈ Valenciana, E Spain
76 J9 **Magta' Lahjar** *var.* Magta Lahjar, Magta' Lahjar, Magtá Lahjar. Brakna, SW Mauritania 17°27′N 13°07′W
146 D12 **Magtymguly** *prev.* Garrygala, *Rus.* Kara-Kala. Balkan Welaýaty, W Turkmenistan 38°27′N 56°15′E
83 L20 **Magude** Maputo, S Mozambique 25°02′S 32°40′E
77 Y12 **Magumeri** Borno, NE Nigeria 12°07′N 12°48′E
189 O14 **Magur Islands** *island group* Caroline Islands, C Micronesia
166 L6 **Magway** *var.* Magwe. Magway, W Myanmar (Burma) 20°08′N 94°55′E
166 L6 **Magway** *var.* Magwe. ◈ *division* C Myanmar (Burma)
Magwe *see* Magway
Magyar-Becse *see* Bečej
Magyarkanizsa *see* Kanjiža
Magyarország *see* Hungary
Magyarzsombor *see* Zimbor
142 J4 **Mahābād** *var.* Mehabad; *prev.* Sāūjbulāgh. Āžarbāyjān-e Gharbī, NW Iran 36°44′N 45°44′E
Maha Chai *see* Samut Sakhon
172 H5 **Mahabo** Toliara, W Madagascar 20°22′S 44°39′E
155 D14 **Mahād** Mahārāshtra, W India 18°04′N 73°21′E
81 N17 **Mahadday Weyne** Shabeellaha Dhexe, C Somalia 02°55′N 45°30′E
79 Q17 **Mahagi** Orientale, NE Dem. Rep. Congo 02°16′N 30°59′E
Mahāil *see* Muhāyil
172 I4 **Mahajamba** *seasonal river* NW Madagascar
152 G10 **Mahājan** Rājasthān, NW India 28°47′N 73°50′E
172 I3 **Mahajanga** *var.* Majunga. Mahajanga, NW Madagascar 15°40′S 46°20′E
172 I3 **Mahajanga** ◈ *province* W Madagascar
172 I3 **Mahajanga** ✈ Mahajanga, NW Madagascar 15°40′S 46°20′E
169 U10 **Mahakam, Sungai** *var.* Koetai, Kutai. ≈ Borneo, C Indonesia
83 I19 **Mahalapye** *var.* Mahalatswe. Central, SE Botswana 23°02′S 26°53′E
Mahalatswe *see* Mahalapye
Mahalla el Kubra *see* El Maḥalla el Kubra
171 O13 **Mahalona** Sulawesi, C Indonesia 02°37′S 121°26′E
Mahameru *see* Semeru, Gunung
143 S11 **Māhān** Kermān, E Iran 30°00′N 57°00′E
154 N12 **Mahanādi** ≈ E India
172 J5 **Mahanoro** Toamasina, E Madagascar 19°53′S 48°48′E
153 P13 **Mahārājganj** Bihār, N India 26°07′N 84°31′E
154 G13 **Mahārāshtra** ◈ *state* W India
172 I4 **Mahavavy** *seasonal river* N Madagascar
155 K24 **Mahaweli Ganga** ≈ C Sri Lanka
Mahbés *see* El Mahbas
155 J15 **Mahbūbābād** Andhra Pradesh, E India 17°35′N 80°00′E
155 H16 **Mahbūbnagar** Andhra Pradesh, C India 16°46′N 78°01′E
140 M8 **Mahd adh Dhahab** Al Madīnah, W Saudi Arabia 23°33′N 40°56′E
55 S9 **Mahdia** C Guyana 05°16′N 59°08′W
75 N6 **Mahdia** *var.* Al Mahdīyah, Mehdia. NE Tunisia 35°14′N 11°06′E
155 F20 **Mahe** *Fr.* Mahé; *prev.* Mayyali. Pondicherry, SW India 11°41′N 75°31′E
172 I16 **Mahé** ✈ Mahé, NE Seychelles 04°37′S 55°27′E
172 H16 **Mahé** *island* Inner Islands, NE Seychelles
Mahé *see* Mahe
173 Y17 **Mahebourg** SE Mauritius 20°24′S 57°42′E
152 I11 **Mahendragarh** *prev.* Mohendergarh. Haryāna, N India 28°17′N 76°14′E
152 L10 **Mahendranagar** Far Western, W Nepal 28°58′N 80°13′E
81 I23 **Mahenge** Morogoro, SE Tanzania 08°41′S 36°41′E
185 F22 **Maheno** Otago, South Island, New Zealand 45°10′S 170°51′E
154 D9 **Mahesāna** Gujarāt, W India 23°37′N 72°28′E
154 F11 **Maheshwar** Madhya Pradesh, C India 22°11′N 75°40′E
153 V17 **Maheskhali Island** *var.* Maiskhal Island. *island* SE Bangladesh
151 F14 **Mahi** ≈ N India
184 Q10 **Mahia Peninsula** *peninsula* North Island, New Zealand
119 O16 **Mahilyow** *Rus.* Mogilëv. Mahilyowskaya Voblasts', E Belarus 53°55′N 30°23′E
119 M16 **Mahilyowskaya Voblasts'** *prev. Rus.* Mogilëvskaya Oblast'. ◈ *province* E Belarus
191 P7 **Mahina** Tahiti, W French Polynesia 17°29′S 149°27′W
185 E23 **Mahinerangi, Lake** ◎ South Island, New Zealand
Máhkarávju *see* Magerøya
83 L22 **Mahlabatini** KwaZulu/Natal, E South Africa 28°15′S 31°28′E
166 L5 **Mahlaing** Mandalay, C Myanmar (Burma) 21°03′N 95°44′E
109 X8 **Mahldorf** Steiermark, SE Austria 46°54′N 15°55′E
Maḥmūd-e 'Erāqī *see* Maḥmūd-e Rāqī
149 R4 **Maḥmūd-e Rāqī** *var.* Mahmūd-e 'Erāqī. Kāpīsā, NE Afghanistan 35°01′N 69°20′E
Mahmudiya *see* Al Maḥmūdīyah
29 S5 **Mahnomen** Minnesota, N USA 47°19′N 95°58′W
152 K14 **Mahoba** Uttar Pradesh, N India 25°18′N 79°53′E
Mahón *see* Maó
18 D14 **Mahoning Creek Lake** ⊠ Pennsylvania, NE USA
105 Q10 **Mahora** Castilla-La Mancha, C Spain 39°13′N 01°44′W
Mähren *see* Moravia
Mährisch-Budwitz *see* Moravské Budějovice
Mährisch-Kromau *see* Moravský Krumlov
Mährisch-Neustadt *see* Uničov
Mährisch-Schönberg *see* Šumperk
Mährisch-Trübau *see* Moravská Třebová
Mährisch-Weisskirchen *see* Hranice
Māh-Shahr *see* Bandar-e Māhshahr
79 N19 **Mahulu** Maniema, E Dem. Rep. Congo 01°04′S 27°10′E
154 C12 **Mahuva** Gujarāt, W India 21°06′N 71°46′E
114 N11 **Mahya Dağı** ▲ NW Turkey 41°47′N 27°34′E
105 T6 **Maials** *var.* Mayals. Cataluña, NE Spain 41°22′N 00°30′E
191 O2 **Maiana** *prev.* Hall Island. *atoll* Tungaru, W Kiribati
191 S11 **Maiao** *var.* Tapuaemanu, Tubuai-Manu. *island* Îles du Vent, W French Polynesia
54 H4 **Maicao** La Guajira, N Colombia 11°23′N 72°16′W
Mai Ceu/Mai Chio *see* Maych'ew
103 U8 **Maîche** Doubs, E France 47°15′N 06°43′E
149 Q5 **Maīdān Shahr** *var.* Maydān Shahr; *prev.* Meydān Shahr. Wardak, E Afghanistan 34°27′N 68°48′E
97 N22 **Maidenhead** S England, United Kingdom 51°32′N 00°44′W
11 S15 **Maidstone** Saskatchewan, S Canada 53°06′N 109°21′W
97 P22 **Maidstone** SE England, United Kingdom 51°17′N 00°31′E
77 Y13 **Maiduguri** Borno, NE Nigeria 11°51′N 13°10′E
108 I8 **Maienfeld** Sankt Gallen, NE Switzerland 47°01′N 09°30′E
116 J12 **Măieruş** *Hung.* Szászmagyarós. Braşov, C Romania 45°55′N 25°30′E
Maigh Chromtha *see* Macroom
Maigh Eo *see* Mayo
55 N9 **Maigualida, Sierra** ▲▲ S Venezuela
154 K9 **Maihar** Madhya Pradesh, C India 24°18′N 80°46′E
154 K11 **Maikala Range** ▲▲ C India
67 T10 **Maiko** ≈ W Dem. Rep. Congo
Mailand *see* Milano
152 L11 **Mailāni** Uttar Pradesh, N India 28°17′N 80°20′E
149 U10 **Māilsi** Punjab, E Pakistan 29°46′N 72°15′E
147 R8 **Maimak** Talasskaya Oblast', NW Kyrgyzstan 42°40′N 71°12′E
Maimāna *see* Maīmanah
148 M3 **Maīmanah** *var.* Maimāna, Maymana; *prev.* Meymaneh. Fāryāb, NW Afghanistan 35°57′N 64°48′E
171 V13 **Maimawa** Papua, E Indonesia 03°21′S 133°36′E
Maimuna *see* Al Maymūnah
101 G18 **Main** ≈ C Germany
115 F22 **Maïna** *ancient monument* Pelopónnisos, S Greece
115 E20 **Maïnalo** ▲▲ S Greece
101 L22 **Mainburg** Bayern, SE Germany 48°40′N 11°48′E
Main Camp *see* Banana
14 E12 **Main Channel** *lake channel* Ontario, S Canada
79 I20 **Mai-Ndombe, Lac** *prev.* Lac Léopold II. ◎ W Dem. Rep. Congo
101 K20 **Main-Donau-Kanal** *canal* SE Germany
19 R6 **Maine** *off.* State of Maine, *also known as* Lumber State, Pine Tree State. ◈ *state* NE USA
102 K6 **Maine** *cultural region* NW France
102 J7 **Maine-et-Loire** ◈ *department* NW France
19 Q9 **Maine, Gulf of** *gulf* NE USA
77 X12 **Maïné-Soroa** Diffa, SE Niger 13°14′N 12°00′E
167 N2 **Maingkwan** *var.* Mungkawn. Kachin State, N Myanmar (Burma) 26°20′N 96°37′E
Main Island *see* Bermuda
Mainistir Fhear Maí *see* Fermoy
Mainistirna Búille *see* Boyle
Mainistir na Corann *see* Midleton
Mainistir na Féile *see* Abbeyfeale
96 J5 **Mainland** *island* N Scotland, United Kingdom
96 L2 **Mainland** *island* NE Scotland, United Kingdom
159 P16 **Mainling** *var.* Tungdor. Xizang Zizhiqu, W China 29°12′N 94°06′E
152 K12 **Mainpuri** Uttar Pradesh, N India 27°14′N 79°01′E
103 N5 **Maintenon** Eure-et-Loir, C France 48°35′N 01°34′E
172 H4 **Maintirano** Mahajanga, W Madagascar 18°01′S 44°03′E
93 M15 **Mainua** Oulu, C Finland 64°05′N 27°28′E
101 G18 **Mainz** *Fr.* Mayence. Rheinland-Pfalz, SW Germany 50°00′N 08°16′E
76 I9 **Maio** *var.* Vila do Maio. Maio, S Cape Verde 15°07′N 23°12′W
76 E10 **Maio** *var.* Mayo. *island* Ilhas de Sotavento, SE Cape Verde
62 G12 **Maipo, Río** ≈ C Chile
62 H12 **Maipo, Volcán** ▲ W Argentina 34°09′S 69°51′W
61 E22 **Maipú** Buenos Aires, E Argentina 36°52′S 57°52′W
62 I11 **Maipú** Mendoza, E Argentina 33°00′S 68°46′W
62 H11 **Maipú** Santiago, C Chile 33°30′S 70°52′W
106 A9 **Maira** ≈ NW Italy
108 I10 **Maira** *It.* Mera. ≈ Italy/Switzerland
153 V12 **Mairābari** Assam, NE India 26°28′N 92°22′E
44 K7 **Maisí** Guantánamo, E Cuba 20°13′N 74°08′W
118 H13 **Maišiagala** Vilnius, SE Lithuania 54°52′N 25°03′E
Maiskhal Island *see* Maheskhali Island
167 N13 **Mai Sombun** Chumphon, SW Thailand 10°49′N 99°13′E
Mai Son *see* Hat Lot
Maisur *see* Mysore, India
Maisur *see* Karnātaka, India
183 T8 **Maitland** New South Wales, SE Australia 32°33′S 151°33′E
182 I9 **Maitland** South Australia 34°21′S 137°42′E
14 F15 **Maitland** ≈ Ontario, S Canada
195 R1 **Maitri** *Indian research station* Antarctica 70°03′S 08°59′E
159 N15 **Maizhokunggar** Xizang Zizhiqu, W China 29°50′N 91°40′E
43 O10 **Maíz, Islas del** *var.* Corn Islands. *island group* SE Nicaragua
164 J12 **Maizuru** Kyōto, Honshū, SW Japan 35°30′N 135°20′E
54 F6 **Majagual** Sucre, N Colombia 08°36′N 74°39′W
41 Z13 **Majahual** Quintana Roo, E Mexico 18°43′N 87°43′W
Mājeej *see* Mejit Island
171 N13 **Majene** *prev.* Madjene. Sulawesi, C Indonesia 03°33′S 118°59′E
43 V15 **Majé, Serranía de** ▲▲ E Panama
112 I11 **Majevica** ▲▲ NE Bosnia and Herzegovina
81 H15 **Majī** Southern Nationalities, S Ethiopia 06°11′N 35°32′E
141 X7 **Majis** NW Oman 24°25′N 56°34′E
Majorca *see* Mallorca
105 X9 **Major, Puig** ▲ Mallorca, Spain, W Mediterranean Sea 39°50′N 2°50′E
Mājro *see* Majuro Atoll
Majunga *see* Mahajanga
189 Y3 **Majuro** ✈ Majuro Atoll, SE Marshall Islands 07°05′N 171°08′E
189 Y2 **Majuro Atoll** *var.* Mājro. *atoll* Ratak Chain, SE Marshall Islands
189 X2 **Majuro Lagoon** *lagoon* Majuro Atoll, SE Marshall Islands
76 H11 **Maka** C Senegal 13°40′N 14°12′W
79 F20 **Makabana** Niari, SW Congo 03°28′S 12°36′E
38 D9 **Mākaha** *var.* Makaha. O'ahu, Hawaii, USA, C Pacific Ocean 21°28′N 158°13′W
38 B8 **Makahū'ena Point** *var.* Makahuena Point. *headland* Kaua'i, Hawai'i, USA 21°52′N 159°28′W
38 D9 **Makakilo City** O'ahu, Hawaii, USA, C Pacific Ocean 21°21′N 158°05′W
83 H18 **Makalamabedi** Central, C Botswana 20°19′S 23°51′E
Makale *see* Mek'elē
158 K17 **Makalu** *Chin.* Makaru Shan. ▲ China/Nepal 27°53′N 87°09′E
81 G23 **Makampi** Mbeya, S Tanzania 08°00′S 33°17′E
Makanchi *see* Makanshy
145 X12 **Makanshy** *prev.* Makanchi. Vostochnyy Kazakhstan, E Kazakhstan 46°47′N 82°00′E
42 M8 **Makantaka** Región Autónoma Atlántico Norte, NE Nicaragua 13°13′N 84°04′W
190 B16 **Makapu Point** *headland* W Niue 18°59′S 169°56′E
185 C24 **Makarewa** Southland, South Island, New Zealand 46°17′S 168°16′E
117 O4 **Makariv** Kyyivs'ka Oblast', N Ukraine 50°28′N 29°49′E
185 D20 **Makarora** ≈ South Island, New Zealand
123 T13 **Makarov** Ostrov Sakhalin, Sakhalinskaya Oblast', SE Russian Federation 48°24′N 142°37′E
197 R9 **Makarov Basin** *undersea feature* Arctic Ocean
192 I5 **Makarov Seamount** *undersea feature* W Pacific Ocean 29°30′N 153°30′E
113 F15 **Makarska** *It.* Macarsca. Split-Dalmacija, SE Croatia 43°18′N 17°00′E
Makaru Shan *see* Makalu
125 O15 **Makar'yev** Kostromskaya Oblast', NW Russian Federation 57°52′N 43°46′E
82 L11 **Makasa** Northern, NE Zambia 09°42′S 31°54′E
Makasar *see* Makassar
Makasar, Selat *see* Makassar Straits
170 M14 **Makassar** *var.* Macassar, Makasar; *prev.* Ujungpandang. Sulawesi, C Indonesia 05°09′S 119°28′E
192 F7 **Makassar Straits** *Ind.* Makassar Selat. *strait* C Indonesia
144 G12 **Makat** *Kaz.* Maqat. Atyrau, SW Kazakhstan 47°40′N 53°28′E
191 T10 **Makatea** *island* Îles Tuamotu, C French Polynesia
139 U7 **Makātū** Diyālá, E Iraq 33°55′N 45°25′E
172 H6 **Makay** *var.* Massif du Makay. ▲▲ SW Madagascar
Makay, Massif du *see* Makay
114 J12 **Makaza** *pass* Bulgaria/Greece
Makedonija *see* Macedonia, FYR
190 B16 **Makefu** W Niue 18°59′S 169°55′W
191 V10 **Makemo** *atoll* Îles Tuamotu, C French Polynesia
76 I15 **Makeni** C Sierra Leone 08°57′N 12°02′W
Makenzen *see* Orlyak
Makeyevka *see* Makiyivka
127 Q16 **Makhachkala** *prev.* Petrovsk-Port. Respublika Dagestan, SW Russian Federation 42°58′N 47°30′E
83 K19 **Makhado** *prev.* Louis Trichardt. Northern, NE South Africa 23°01′S 29°43′E
144 F11 **Makhambet** Atyrau, W Kazakhstan 47°35′N 51°35′E
Makharadze *see* Ozurgeti
139 W13 **Makhfar al Buṣayyah** Al Muthannā, S Iraq 30°09′N 46°09′E
139 R4 **Makhmūr** Arbīl, N Iraq 35°47′N 43°32′E
138 I11 **Makhrūq, Wadi al** *dry watercourse* E Jordan
139 R4 **Makhūl, Jabal** ▲▲ C Iraq
141 R13 **Makhyah, Wādī** *dry watercourse* N Yemen
171 V13 **Maki** Papua, E Indonesia 03°00′S 134°10′E
185 G21 **Makikihi** Canterbury, South Island, New Zealand 44°36′S 171°09′E
191 O2 **Makin** *prev.* Pitt Island. *atoll* Tungaru, W Kiribati
81 I20 **Makindu** Eastern, S Kenya 02°15′S 37°49′E
145 Q8 **Makinsk** Akmola, N Kazakhstan 52°40′N 70°28′E
Makira *see* Makira-Ulawa
Makira *see* San Cristobal
187 N10 **Makira-Ulawa** *prev.* Makira. ◈ *province* SE Solomon Islands
117 X8 **Makiyivka** *Rus.* Makeyevka; *prev.* Dmitriyevsk. Donets'ka Oblast', E Ukraine 47°57′N 37°47′E
140 L10 **Makkah** *Eng.* Mecca. Makkah, W Saudi Arabia 21°28′N 39°50′E
140 M10 **Makkah** *var.* Minṭaqat Makkah. ◈ *province* W Saudi Arabia
Makkah, Minṭaqat *see* Makkah
13 R7 **Makkovik** Newfoundland and Labrador, NE Canada 55°06′N 59°07′W
98 K6 **Makkum** Fryslân, N Netherlands 53°03′N 05°25′E
111 M25 **Makó** *Rom.* Macău. Csongrád, SE Hungary 46°14′N 20°28′E
Mako *see* Makung
14 G9 **Makobe Lake** ◎ Ontario, S Canada
79 F18 **Makokou** Ogooué-Ivindo, NE Gabon 0°38′N 12°47′E
81 G23 **Makongolosi** Mbeya, S Tanzania 08°24′S 33°09′E
81 E19 **Makota** SW Uganda 0°37′S 30°12′E
79 G18 **Makoua** Cuvette, C Congo 0°01′S 15°40′E
110 M10 **Maków Mazowiecki** Mazowieckie, C Poland 52°51′N 21°06′E
111 K17 **Maków Podhalański** Małopolskie, S Poland 49°43′N 19°40′E
143 V14 **Makran** *cultural region* Iran/Pakistan
152 G12 **Makrāna** Rājasthān, N India 27°02′N 74°44′E
143 U15 **Makran Coast** *coastal region* SE Iran
119 F20 **Makrany** *Rus.* Mokrany. Brestskaya Voblasts', SW Belarus 51°50′N 24°15′E
Makrinoros *see* Makrynóros
115 H20 **Makrónisosi** *island* Kykládes, Greece, Aegean Sea
115 D17 **Makrynóros** *var.* Makrinoros. ▲▲ C Greece
115 G19 **Makryplági** ▲ C Greece 38°00′N 23°06′E
Maksamaa *see* Maxmo
Maksatha *see* Maksatikha
Maksaticha *see* Maksatikha
124 J15 **Maksatikha** *var.* Maksatha, Maksaticha. Tverskaya Oblast', W Russian Federation 57°49′N 35°46′E
154 G10 **Maksi** Madhya Pradesh, C India 23°20′N 76°36′E
142 I1 **Mākū** Āžarbāyjān-e Gharbī, NW Iran 39°20′N 44°50′E
153 Y11 **Mākum** Assam, NE India 27°28′N 95°28′E
Makun *see* Makung
161 R14 **Makung** *prev.* Mako, Makun. W Taiwan 23°35′N 119°35′E
164 B16 **Makurazaki** Kagoshima, Kyūshū, SW Japan 31°16′N 130°18′E
77 V15 **Makurdi** Benue, C Nigeria 07°42′N 08°36′E
38 L17 **Makushin Volcano** ▲ Unalaska Island, Alaska, USA 53°53′N 166°55′W
83 K16 **Makwiro** Mashonaland West, N Zimbabwe 17°58′S 30°25′E
57 D15 **Mala** Lima, W Peru 12°40′S 76°36′W
93 I14 **Malå** Västerbotten, N Sweden 65°12′N 18°45′E
Mala *see* Mallow, Ireland
Mala *see* Malaita, Solomon Islands
171 P8 **Malabang** Mindanao, S Philippines
155 E21 **Malabār Coast** *coast* SW India
79 C16 **Malabo** *prev.* Santa Isabel. ● (Equatorial Guinea) Isla de Bioco, NW Equatorial Guinea 03°43′N 08°52′E
79 C16 **Malabo** ✈ Isla de Bioco, N Equatorial Guinea 03°44′N 08°51′E
Malaca *see* Málaga
Malacca *see* Melaka
168 I7 **Malacca, Strait of** *Ind.* Selat Malaka. *strait* Indonesia/Malaysia
Malacka *see* Malacky
111 G20 **Malacky** *Hung.* Malacka. Bratislavský Kraj, W Slovakia 48°26′N 17°01′E
33 R16 **Malad City** Idaho, NW USA 42°10′N 112°16′W
117 Q4 **Mala Divytsya** Chernihivs'ka Oblast', N Ukraine 50°40′N 32°13′E
119 J15 **Maladzyechna** *Pol.* Molodeczno, *Rus.* Molodechno. Minskaya Voblasts', C Belarus 54°19′N 26°51′E
190 D12 **Malaee** Île Futuna, N Wallis and Futuna
190 G12 **Mala'etoli** Île Uvea, E Wallis and Futuna
54 G8 **Málaga** Santander, C Colombia 06°44′N 72°45′W
104 M15 **Málaga** *anc.* Malaca. Andalucía, S Spain 36°43′N 04°25′W
37 V15 **Malaga** New Mexico, SW USA 32°10′N 104°04′W
104 L15 **Málaga** ◈ *province* Andalucía, S Spain
104 M15 **Málaga** ✈ Andalucía, S Spain 36°38′N 04°36′W
Malagasy Republic *see* Madagascar
105 N10 **Malagón** Castilla-La Mancha, C Spain 39°10′N 03°51′W
97 G18 **Malahide** *Ir.* Mullach Íde. Dublin, E Ireland 53°27′N 06°09′W
187 N9 **Malaita** *off.* Malaita Province. ◈ *province* N Solomon Islands
187 N8 **Malaita** *var.* Mala. *island* N Solomon Islands
Malaita Province *see* Malaita
80 F13 **Malakal** Upper Nile, NE South Sudan 09°31′N 31°40′E
112 C10 **Mala Kapela** ▲▲ NW Croatia
25 V7 **Malakoff** Texas, SW USA 32°10′N 96°00′W
Malakula *see* Malekula
149 V7 **Malakwāl** *var.* Mālikwāla. Punjab, E Pakistan 32°32′N 73°18′E
186 E7 **Malalamai** Madang, W Papua New Guinea 05°49′S 146°44′E
171 O13 **Malamala** Sulawesi, C Indonesia 03°21′S 120°58′E
169 S17 **Malang** Jawa, C Indonesia 07°59′S 112°45′E
83 O14 **Malanga** Niassa, N Mozambique 13°27′S 36°05′E
Malange *see* Malanje
92 I9 **Malangen** *sound* N Norway
82 C11 **Malanje** *var.* Malange. Malanje, NW Angola 09°34′S 16°25′E
82 C11 **Malanje** *var.* Malange. ◈ *province* N Angola
148 M16 **Malān, Rās** *cape* SW Pakistan
77 S13 **Malanville** NE Benin 11°50′N 03°23′E
Malapane *see* Ozimek
155 F21 **Malappuram** Kerala, SW India 11°00′N 76°02′E
43 T17 **Mala, Punta** *headland* S Panama 07°28′N 79°58′W
148 L15 **Malar** Baluchistān, SW Pakistan 26°19′N 64°55′E
95 N16 **Mälaren** ◎ C Sweden
62 H13 **Malargüe** Mendoza, W Argentina 35°32′S 69°35′W
14 J8 **Malartic** Québec, SE Canada 48°09′N 78°09′W
119 F20 **Malaryta** *Pol.* Maloryta, *Rus.* Malorita. Brestskaya Voblasts', SW Belarus 51°47′N 24°05′E
63 J19 **Malaspina** Chubut, SE Argentina 44°56′S 66°52′W
10 G8 **Malaspina Glacier** *glacier* Yukon Territory, W Canada
39 U12 **Malaspina Glacier** *glacier* Alaska, USA
137 N15 **Malatya** *anc.* Melitene. Malatya, SE Turkey 38°22′N 38°18′E
136 M14 **Malatya** ◈ *province* C Turkey
Malavate *see* Pédima
117 Q7 **Mala Vyska** *Rus.* Malaya Viska. Kirovohrads'ka Oblast', S Ukraine 48°37′N 31°36′E
83 M14 **Malawi** *off.* Republic of Malawi; *prev.* Nyasaland, Nyasaland Protectorate. ◆ *republic* S Africa
Malawi, Lake *see* Nyasa, Lake
Malaŵi, Republic of *see* Malawi
93 J17 **Malax** *Fin.* Maalahti. Länsi-Suomi, W Finland 62°55′N 21°30′E
124 H14 **Malaya Vishera** Novgorodskaya Oblast', W Russian Federation 58°52′N 32°12′E
Malaya Viska *see* Mala Vyska
171 Q7 **Malaybalay** Mindanao, S Philippines 08°10′N 125°08′E
142 L6 **Malāyer** *prev.* Daulatabad. Hamadān, W Iran 34°20′N 48°47′E
168 J7 **Malay Peninsula** *peninsula* Malaysia/Thailand
168 L7 **Malaysia** *off.* Malaysia, *var.* Federation of Malaysia; *prev.* the separate territories of Federation of Malaya, Sarawak and Sabah (North Borneo) and Singapore. ◆ *monarchy* SE Asia
Malaysia, Federation of *see* Malaysia
137 R14 **Malazgirt** Muş, E Turkey 39°09′N 42°30′E
15 R8 **Malbaie** ≈ Québec, SE Canada
77 T12 **Malbaza** Tahoua, S Niger 13°57′N 05°32′E
110 J7 **Malbork** *Ger.* Marienburg, Marienburg in Westpreussen. Pomorskie, N Poland 54°01′N 19°03′E
100 N9 **Malchin** Mecklenburg-Vorpommern, N Germany 53°43′N 12°46′E
100 M9 **Malchiner See** ◎ NE Germany
99 D16 **Maldegem** Oost-Vlaanderen, NW Belgium 51°12′N 03°27′E
98 L13 **Malden** Gelderland, SE Netherlands 51°47′N 05°51′E
19 O11 **Malden** Massachusetts, NE USA 42°25′N 71°04′W
27 Y8 **Malden** Missouri, C USA 36°33′N 89°58′W
191 X4 **Malden Island** *prev.* Independence Island. *atoll* E Kiribati
173 Q6 **Maldives** *off.* Maldivian Divehi, Republic of Maldives. ◆ *republic* N Indian Ocean
Maldives, Republic of *see* Maldives
Maldivian Divehi *see* Maldives
97 P21 **Maldon** E England, United Kingdom 51°44′N 00°40′E
61 G20 **Maldonado** Maldonado, S Uruguay 34°57′S 54°59′W
61 G20 **Maldonado** ◈ *department* S Uruguay
41 P17 **Maldonado, Punta** *headland* S Mexico 16°18′N 98°31′W
106 G6 **Malè** Trentino-Alto Adige, N Italy 46°21′N 10°51′E
151 K19 **Male'** *Div.* Maale. ● (Maldives) Male' Atoll, C Maldives 04°10′N 73°29′E
76 K13 **Maléa** *var.* Maléya. NE Guinea 11°46′N 09°43′W
Maléas, Ákra *see* Agriliá, Akrotírio
115 G22 **Maléas, Akrotírio** *headland* S Greece 36°25′N 23°11′E
151 K19 **Male' Atoll** *var.* Kaafu Atoll. *atoll* C Maldives
Malebo, Pool *see* Stanley Pool
154 E12 **Mālegaon** Mahārāshtra, W India 20°33′N 74°32′E
81 F15 **Malek** Jonglei, E South Sudan 06°04′N 31°36′E
187 Q13 **Malekula** *var.* Malakula; *prev.* Mallicolo. *island* W Vanuatu
189 Y15 **Malem** Kosrae, E Micronesia 05°16′N 163°01′E
83 O15 **Malema** Nampula, N Mozambique 14°57′S 37°28′E
79 N23 **Malemba-Nkulu** Katanga, SE Dem. Rep. Congo 08°01′S 26°48′E
124 K9 **Malen'ga** Respublika Kareliya, NW Russian Federation 63°50′N 36°21′E
95 M20 **Målerås** Kalmar, S Sweden 56°55′N 15°34′E
103 O6 **Malesherbes** Loiret, C France 48°18′N 02°25′E
115 G18 **Malesína** Stereá Elláda, E Greece 38°37′N 23°15′E
Maléya *see* Maléa
127 O15 **Malgobek** Respublika Ingushetiya, SW Russian Federation 43°34′N 44°34′E
105 X5 **Malgrat de Mar** Cataluña, NE Spain 41°39′N 02°45′E
80 C9 **Malha** Northern Darfur, W Sudan 15°07′N 26°00′E
139 Q5 **Malḥāh** *var.* Malḥāt. Ṣalāḥ ad Dīn, C Iraq 34°44′N 42°41′E
Malḥāt *see* Malḥāh
32 K14 **Malheur Lake** ◎ Oregon, NW USA
32 L14 **Malheur River** ≈ Oregon, NW USA
76 I13 **Mali** NW Guinea 12°08′N 12°29′W
77 O9 **Mali** *off.* Republic of Mali, *Fr.* République du Mali; *prev.* French Sudan, Sudanese Republic. ◆ *republic* W Africa
171 Q16 **Maliana** W East Timor 08°57′S 125°25′E
167 O2 **Mali Hka** ≈ N Myanmar (Burma)
Mali Idjoš *see* Mali Iđoš
112 K8 **Mali Iđoš** *var.* Mali Idjoš, *Hung.* Kishegyes; *prev.* Krivaja. Vojvodina, N Serbia 45°43′N 19°40′E
113 M18 **Mali i Sharrit** *Serb.* Šar Planina. ▲▲ FYR Macedonia/Serbia
Mali i Zi *see* Crna Gora
112 K9 **Mali Kanal** *canal* N Serbia
171 P12 **Maliku** Sulawesi, N Indonesia 0°36′S 123°13′E
Malik, Wadi al *see* Milk, Wadi el
Mālikwāla *see* Malakwāl
167 N11 **Mali Kyun** *var.* Tavoy Island. *island* Mergui Archipelago, S Myanmar (Burma)
95 M19 **Målilla** Kalmar, S Sweden 57°24′N 15°49′E
112 B11 **Mali Lošinj** *It.* Lussinpiccolo. Primorje-Gorski Kotar, W Croatia 44°31′N 14°28′E
Malin *see* Malyn
171 P7 **Malindang, Mount** ▲ Mindanao, S Philippines 08°12′N 123°37′E
81 K20 **Malindi** Coast, SE Kenya 03°14′S 40°05′E
Malines *see* Mechelen
96 E13 **Malin Head** *Ir.* Cionn Mhálanna. *headland* NW Ireland 55°37′N 07°37′W
171 O11 **Malino, Gunung** ▲ Sulawesi, N Indonesia 0°44′N 120°45′E
113 M21 **Maliq** *var.* Maliqi. Korçë, SE Albania 40°45′N 20°45′E
Maliqi *see* Maliq
Mali, Republic of *see* Mali
Mali, République du *see* Mali
171 Q8 **Malita** Mindanao, S Philippines 06°13′N 125°39′E
154 G12 **Malkāpur** Mahārāshtra, C India 20°52′N 76°18′E
136 B10 **Malkara** Tekirdağ, NW Turkey 40°54′N 26°54′E
119 J19 **Mal'kavichy** *Rus.* Mal'kovichi. Brestskaya Voblasts', SW Belarus 52°31′N 26°36′E
Malkiye *see* Al Mālikīyah
114 L11 **Malko Sharkovo, Yazovir** ⊠ SE Bulgaria
114 N11 **Malko Tŭrnovo** Burgas, E Bulgaria 42°00′N 27°33′E
Mal'kovichi *see* Mal'kavichy
183 R12 **Mallacoota** Victoria, SE Australia 37°34′S 149°45′E
96 G10 **Mallaig** N Scotland, United Kingdom 57°04′N 05°48′W
182 I9 **Mallala** South Australia 34°29′S 138°30′E
75 W9 **Mallawī** *var.* Mallawi. C Egypt 27°44′N 30°50′E
Mallawi *see* Mallawī
105 R5 **Mallén** Aragón, NE Spain 41°53′N 01°25′W
106 F5 **Malles Venosta** *Ger.* Mals im Vinschgau. Trentino-Alto Adige, N Italy 46°40′N 10°37′E
Mallicolo *see* Malekula
109 Q8 **Mallnitz** Salzburg, S Austria 46°58′N 13°09′E
105 W9 **Mallorca** *Eng.* Majorca; *anc.* Baleares Major. *island* Islas Baleares, Spain, W Mediterranean Sea
97 C20 **Mallow** *Ir.* Mala. SW Ireland 52°08′N 08°39′W
93 E15 **Malm** Nord-Trøndelag, C Norway 64°04′N 11°12′E
95 L19 **Malmbäck** Jönköping, S Sweden 57°34′N 14°30′E
92 J12 **Malmberget** *Lapp.* Malmivaara. Norrbotten, N Sweden 67°09′N 20°39′E
99 M20 **Malmédy** Liège, E Belgium 50°26′N 06°02′E
83 E25 **Malmesbury** Western Cape, SW South Africa 33°28′S 18°43′E
Malmivaara *see* Malmberget
95 N16 **Malmköping** Södermanland, C Sweden 59°08′N 16°49′E
95 K23 **Malmö** Skåne, S Sweden 55°36′N 13°E
95 K23 **Malmo** ✈ Skåne, S Sweden 55°33′N 13°23′E
45 Q16 **Malmok** *headland* N Bonaire 12°16′N 68°21′W
95 M18 **Malmslätt** Östergötland, S Sweden 58°25′N 15°30′E
125 R16 **Malmyzh** Kirovskaya Oblast', NW Russian Federation 56°30′N 50°37′E
187 Q13 **Malo** *island* W Vanuatu
126 J7 **Maloarkhangel'sk** Orlovskaya Oblast', W Russian Federation 52°25′N 36°37′E
Maloelap *see* Maloelap Atoll
189 V6 **Maloelap Atoll** *var.* Maloelap. *atoll* E Marshall Islands
Maloenda *see* Malunda
108 I10 **Maloja** Graubünden, S Switzerland 46°25′N 09°42′E
82 L12 **Malole** Northern, NE Zambia 10°05′S 31°37′E
171 O3 **Malolos** Luzon, N Philippines 14°51′N 120°49′E
18 K6 **Malone** New York, NE USA 44°51′N 74°18′W
79 K25 **Malonga** Katanga, S Dem. Rep. Congo 10°26′S 23°10′E
111 L17 **Małopolskie** ◈ *province* SE Poland

◆ Country ● Country Capital ◇ Dependent Territory ○ Dependent Territory Capital ◈ Administrative Regions ✈ International Airport ▲ Mountain ▲▲ Mountain Range ▲ Volcano ≈ River ◎ Lake ⊠ Reservoir

Malorita/Maloryta *see* Malaryta
124 K9 **Maloshuyka** Arkhangel'skaya Oblast', NW Russian Federation 63°43′N 37°20′E
114 G10 **Mal'ovitsa** ▲ W Bulgaria 42°12′N 23°19′E
145 V15 **Malovodnoye** Almaty, SE Kazakhstan 43°31′N 77°42′E
94 C10 **Måløy** Sogn Og Fjordane, S Norway 61°57′N 05°06′E
126 K4 **Maloyaroslavets** Kaluzhskaya Oblast', W Russian Federation 55°03′N 36°31′E
122 G7 **Malozemel'skaya Tundra** *physical region* NW Russian Federation
104 J10 **Malpartida de Cáceres** Extremadura, W Spain 39°26′N 06°30′W
104 K9 **Malpartida de Plasencia** Extremadura, W Spain 39°59′N 06°03′W
106 C7 **Malpensa** ✈ (Milano) Lombardia, N Italy 45°41′N 08°40′E
76 J6 **Malqteïr** *desert* N Mauritania
Mals im Vinschgau *see* Malles Venosta
118 J10 **Malta** SE Latvia 56°19′N 27°11′E
33 V7 **Malta** Montana, NW USA 48°21′N 107°52′W
120 M11 **Malta** *off.* Republic of Malta. ◆ *republic* C Mediterranean Sea
109 R8 **Malta** *var.* Maltabach. S Austria
120 M11 **Malta** *island* Malta, C Mediterranean Sea
Maltabach *see* Malta
Malta, Canale di *see* Malta Channel
120 M11 **Malta Channel** *It.* Canale di Malta. *strait* Italy/Malta
83 D20 **Maltahöhe** Hardap, SW Namibia 24°50′S 17°00′E
Malta, Republic of *see* Malta
97 N16 **Malton** N England, United Kingdom 54°07′N 00°50′W
171 R13 **Maluku** *off.* Propinsi Maluku, *Dut.* Molukken, *Eng.* Moluccas. ◈ *province* E Indonesia
171 R13 **Maluku** *Dut.* Molukken, *Eng.* Moluccas; *prev.* Spice Islands. *island group* E Indonesia
Maluku, Laut *see* Molucca Sea
Maluku, Propinsi *see* Maluku
171 R11 **Maluku Utara** *off.* Propinsi Maluku Utara. ◈ *province* E Indonesia
Maluku Utara, Propinsi *see* Maluku Utara
77 V13 **Malumfashi** Katsina, N Nigeria 11°51′N 07°39′E
171 N13 **Malunda** *prev.* Maloenda. Sulawesi, C Indonesia 02°58′S 118°52′E
94 K13 **Malung** Dalarna, C Sweden 60°40′N 13°45′E
94 K13 **Malungsfors** Dalarna, C Sweden 60°43′N 13°34′E
186 M8 **Maluu** *var.* Malu'u. Malaita, N Solomon Islands 08°22′S 160°39′E
Malu'u *see* Maluu
155 D16 **Mālvan** Mahārāshtra, W India 16°05′N 73°28′E
Malventum *see* Benevento
27 U12 **Malvern** Arkansas, C USA 34°21′N 92°50′W
29 S15 **Malvern** Iowa, C USA 40°59′N 95°36′W
44 I13 **Malvern** ▲ W Jamaica 17°59′N 77°42′W
Malvina, Isla Gran *see* West Falkland
Malvinas, Islas *see* Falkland Islands
117 N4 **Malyn** *Rus.* Malin. Zhytomyrs'ka Oblast', N Ukraine 50°46′N 29°14′E
127 O11 **Malyye Derbety** Respublika Kalmykiya, SW Russian Federation 47°57′N 44°39′E
Malyy Kavkaz *see* Lesser Caucasus
123 Q6 **Malyy Lyakhovskiy, Ostrov** *island* NE Russian Federation
Malyy Pamir *see* Little Pamir
122 N5 **Malyy Taymyr, Ostrov** *island* Severnaya Zemlya, N Russian Federation
Malyy Uzen' *see* Saryozen
122 L14 **Malyy Yenisey** *var.* Ka-Krem. S Russian Federation
127 S3 **Mamadysh** Respublika Tatarstan, W Russian Federation 55°46′N 51°22′E
117 N14 **Mamaia** Constanța, E Romania 44°13′N 28°37′E
187 W14 **Mamanuca Group** *island group* Yasawa Group, W Fiji
146 L13 **Mamash** Lebap Welaýaty, E Turkmenistan 38°24′N 64°12′E
79 O17 **Mambasa** Orientale, NE Dem. Rep. Congo 01°20′N 29°05′E
171 X13 **Mamberamo, Sungai** Papua, E Indonesia
79 G15 **Mambéré** SW Central African Republic
79 G15 **Mambéré-Kadéï** ◈ *prefecture* SW Central African Republic
Mambij *see* Manbij
79 H18 **Mambili** W Congo
83 N18 **Mambone** *var.* Nova Mambone. Inhambane, E Mozambique 20°59′S 35°04′E
171 O4 **Mamburao** Mindoro, N Philippines 13°16′N 120°36′E
172 I16 **Mamelles** *island* Inner Islands, NE Seychelles
99 M25 **Mamer** Luxembourg, SW Luxembourg 49°37′N 06°01′E
102 L6 **Mamers** Sarthe, NW France 48°21′N 00°22′E
79 D15 **Mamfe** Sud-Ouest, W Cameroon 05°46′N 09°18′E
145 P6 **Mamlyutka** Severnyy Kazakhstan, N Kazakhstan 54°54′N 68°36′E
36 M15 **Mammoth** Arizona, SW USA 32°43′N 110°38′W
33 S12 **Mammoth Hot Springs** Wyoming, C USA 44°57′N 110°40′W
Mamoedjoe *see* Mamuju
119 A14 **Mamonovo** *Ger.* Heiligenbeil. Kaliningradskaya Oblast', W Russian Federation 54°28′N 19°57′E
57 L14 **Mamoré, Rio** Bolivia/Brazil
76 I14 **Mamou** W Guinea 10°24′N 12°05′W
22 H8 **Mamou** Louisiana, S USA 30°37′N 92°25′W
172 I14 **Mamoudzou** ○ (Mayotte) C Mayotte 12°48′S 45°E
172 I3 **Mampikony** Mahajanga, N Madagascar 16°03′S 47°39′E
77 P16 **Mampong** C Ghana 07°06′N 01°20′W
110 M7 **Mamry, Jezioro** *Ger.* Mauersee. ◎ NE Poland
171 N13 **Mamuju** *prev.* Mamoedjoe. Sulawesi, S Indonesia 02°41′S 118°55′E
83 F19 **Mamuno** Ghanzi, W Botswana 22°15′S 20°02′E
113 K19 **Mamuras** *var.* Mamurasi, Mamurras. Lezhë, C Albania 41°34′N 19°42′E
Mamurasi/Mamurras *see* Mamuras
76 L16 **Man** W Ivory Coast 07°24′N 07°33′W
55 X9 **Mana** NW French Guiana 05°40′N 53°49′W
56 A6 **Manabí** ◈ *province* W Ecuador
42 G4 **Manabique, Punta** *var.* Cabo Tres Puntas. *headland* E Guatemala 15°57′N 88°37′W
54 G11 **Manacacías, Río** C Colombia
58 F13 **Manacapuru** Amazonas, N Brazil 03°16′S 60°37′W
105 Y9 **Manacor** Mallorca, Spain, W Mediterranean Sea 39°35′N 03°12′E
171 Q11 **Manado** *prev.* Menado. Sulawesi, C Indonesia 01°32′N 124°55′E
188 H5 **Managaha** *island* S Northern Mariana Islands
99 G20 **Manage** Hainaut, S Belgium 50°30′N 04°14′E
42 J10 **Managua** ● (Nicaragua) Managua, W Nicaragua 12°08′N 86°15′W
42 J10 **Managua** ◈ *department* W Nicaragua
42 J10 **Managua** ✈ Managua, W Nicaragua 12°07′N 86°11′W
42 J10 **Managua, Lago de** *var.* Xolotlán. ◎ W Nicaragua
Manah *see* Bilād Manah
18 K16 **Manahawkin** New Jersey, NE USA 39°39′N 74°12′W
184 K11 **Manaia** Taranaki, North Island, New Zealand 39°33′S 174°07′E
172 J6 **Manakara** Fianarantsoa, SE Madagascar 22°09′S 48°E
152 J7 **Manāli** Himāchal Pradesh, NW India 32°12′N 77°06′E
Ma, Nam *see* Sông Ma
Manama *see* Al Manāmah
186 D6 **Manam Island** *island* N Papua New Guinea
67 Y13 **Mananara Avaratra** SE Madagascar
182 M9 **Manangatang** Victoria, SE Australia 35°04′S 142°53′E
172 J6 **Mananjary** Fianarantsoa, SE Madagascar 21°13′S 48°20′E
76 L14 **Manankoro** Sikasso, SW Mali 10°33′N 07°25′W
76 J12 **Manantali, Lac de** ⊠ W Mali
Manáos *see* Manaus
185 B23 **Manapouri** Southland, South Island, New Zealand 45°33′S 167°38′E
185 B23 **Manapouri, Lake** ◎ South Island, New Zealand
58 F13 **Manaquiri** Amazonas, NW Brazil 03°27′S 60°37′W
Manar *see* Mannar
158 K5 **Manas** Xinjiang Uygur Zizhiqu, NW China 44°16′N 86°12′E
153 U12 **Manās** *var.* Dangme Chu. Bhutan/India
153 P10 **Manāsalu** *var.* Manaslu. ▲ C Nepal 28°33′N 84°33′E
147 R8 **Manas, Gora** ▲ Kyrgyzstan/Uzbekistan 42°17′N 71°04′E
158 K3 **Manas Hu** ◎ NW China
Manaslu *see* Manāsalu
37 S8 **Manassa** Colorado, C USA 37°10′N 105°56′W
21 W4 **Manassas** Virginia, NE USA 38°45′N 77°28′W
45 T5 **Manatí** C Puerto Rico 18°26′N 66°29′W
186 E8 **Manau** Northern, S Papua New Guinea 08°02′S 148°00′E
54 H4 **Manaure** La Guajira, N Colombia 11°46′N 72°28′W
58 F12 **Manaus** *prev.* Manáos. *state capital* Amazonas, NW Brazil 03°06′S 60°W
136 G17 **Manavgat** Antalya, SW Turkey 36°47′N 31°28′E
184 M13 **Manawatu** North Island, New Zealand
184 L11 **Manawatu-Wanganui** *off.* Manawatu-Wanganui Region. ◈ *region* North Island, New Zealand
Manawatu-Wanganui Region *see* Manawatu-Wanganui
171 R7 **Manay** Mindanao, S Philippines 07°12′N 126°29′E
138 K2 **Manbij** *var.* Mambij, *Fr.* Membidj. Ḩalab, N Syria 36°32′N 37°55′E
105 N13 **Mancha Real** Andalucía, S Spain 37°47′N 03°37′W
102 I4 **Manche** ◈ *department* N France
97 L17 **Manchester** *Lat.* Mancunium. NW England, United Kingdom 53°30′N 02°15′W
23 S5 **Manchester** Georgia, SE USA 32°51′N 84°37′W
29 Y13 **Manchester** Iowa, C USA 42°28′N 91°27′W
21 N7 **Manchester** Kentucky, S USA 37°09′N 83°46′W
19 O10 **Manchester** New Hampshire, NE USA 42°59′N 71°26′W
20 K10 **Manchester** Tennessee, S USA 35°28′N 86°05′W
18 M9 **Manchester** Vermont, NE USA 43°09′N 73°03′W
97 L18 **Manchester** ✈ NW England, United Kingdom 53°21′N 02°16′W
149 P15 **Manchhar Lake** ◎ SE Pakistan
Man-chou-li *see* Manzhouli
129 X7 **Manchurian Plain** *plain* NE China
Máncio Lima *see* Japiim
Mancunium *see* Manchester
148 J15 **Mand** Baluchistān, SW Pakistan 26°06′N 61°58′E
Mand *see* Mand, Rūd-e
81 H25 **Manda** Iringa, SW Tanzania 10°30′S 34°37′E
172 H6 **Mandabe** Toliara, W Madagascar 21°02′S 44°56′E
162 M10 **Mandah** *var.* Töhöm. Dornogovĭ, SE Mongolia 44°25′N 108°18′E
95 E18 **Mandal** Vest-Agder, S Norway 58°02′N 07°30′E
Mandal *see* Arbulag, Hövsgöl, Mongolia
Mandal *see* Batsümber, Töv, Mongolia
166 L5 **Mandalay** Mandalay, C Myanmar (Burma) 21°57′N 96°04′E
166 M6 **Mandalay** ◈ *division* C Myanmar (Burma)
162 L9 **Mandalgovĭ** Dundgovĭ, C Mongolia 45°47′N 106°18′E
139 V7 **Mandalī** Diyālá, E Iraq 33°43′N 45°33′E
162 K10 **Mandal-Ovoo** *var.* Sharhulsan. Ömnögovĭ, S Mongolia 44°43′N 104°06′E
95 E18 **Mandalselva** S Norway
163 P11 **Mandalt** *var.* Sonid Zuoqi. Nei Mongol Zizhiqu, N China 43°49′N 113°36′E
28 M5 **Mandan** North Dakota, N USA 46°49′N 100°53′W
Mandargiri Hill *see* Mandār Hill
153 R14 **Mandār Hill** *prev.* Mandargiri Hill. Bihār, NE India 24°51′N 87°03′E
170 M13 **Mandar, Teluk** *bay* Sulawesi, C Indonesia
107 C19 **Mandas** Sardegna, Italy, C Mediterranean Sea 39°40′N 09°07′E
Mandasor *see* Mandsaur
81 L16 **Mandera** North Eastern, NE Kenya 03°56′N 41°53′E
33 V13 **Manderson** Wyoming, C USA 44°13′N 107°55′W
44 J12 **Mandeville** C Jamaica 18°02′N 77°31′W
22 K9 **Mandeville** Louisiana, S USA 30°21′N 90°04′W
152 I7 **Mandi** Himāchal Pradesh, NW India 31°40′N 76°59′E
76 K14 **Mandiana** E Guinea 10°37′N 08°39′W
Mandi Būrewāla *see* Būrewāla
Mandidzudzure *see* Chimanimani
83 M15 **Mandié** Manica, NW Mozambique 16°27′S 33°28′E
83 N14 **Mandimba** Niassa, N Mozambique 14°21′S 35°40′E
57 Q19 **Mandioré, Laguna** ◎ E Bolivia
154 J10 **Mandla** Madhya Pradesh, C India 22°36′N 80°23′E
83 M20 **Mandlakazi** *var.* Manjacaze. Gaza, S Mozambique 24°47′S 33°50′E
95 E24 **Mandø** *var.* Manø. *island* W Denmark
Mandoúdhion/Mandoudi *see* Mantoúdi
115 G19 **Mándra** Attikí, C Greece 38°04′N 23°30′E
172 I7 **Mandrare** S Madagascar
114 M10 **Mandra, Yazovir** *salt lake* SE Bulgaria
107 L23 **Mandrazzi, Portella** *pass* Sicilia, Italy, C Mediterranean Sea
172 J3 **Mandritsara** Mahajanga, N Madagascar 15°49′S 48°50′E
143 O13 **Mand, Rūd-e** *var.* Mand. S Iran
154 F9 **Mandsaur** *prev.* Mandasor. Madhya Pradesh, C India 24°03′N 75°10′E
154 F11 **Māndu** Madhya Pradesh, C India 22°22′N 75°24′E
169 W8 **Mandul, Pulau** *island* N Indonesia
83 G15 **Mandundu** Western, W Zambia 16°34′S 22°18′E
180 I13 **Mandurah** Western Australia 32°31′S 115°41′E
107 P18 **Manduria** Puglia, SE Italy 40°24′N 17°38′E
155 G20 **Mandya** Karnātaka, C India 12°34′N 76°55′E
77 P12 **Mané** C Burkina 12°59′N 01°21′W
106 E8 **Manerbio** Lombardia, NW Italy 45°22′N 10°09′E
Manevichi *see* Manevychi
116 K3 **Manevychi** *Pol.* Maniewicze, *Rus.* Manevichi. Volyns'ka Oblast', NW Ukraine 51°18′N 25°29′E
107 N16 **Manfredonia** Puglia, SE Italy 41°38′N 15°54′E
107 N16 **Manfredonia, Golfo di** *gulf* Adriatic Sea, N Mediterranean Sea
77 P13 **Manga** C Burkina 11°41′N 01°04′W
59 L16 **Mangabeiras, Chapada das** ▲▲ E Brazil
79 J20 **Mangai** Bandundu, W Dem. Rep. Congo 03°58′S 19°32′E
190 L17 **Mangaia** *island group* S Cook Islands
184 M9 **Mangakino** Waikato, North Island, New Zealand 38°23′S 175°47′E
116 M15 **Mangalia** *anc.* Callatis. Constanța, SE Romania 43°48′N 28°35′E
78 J11 **Mangalmé** Guéra, SE Chad 12°26′N 19°37′E
155 E19 **Mangalore** Karnātaka, W India 12°54′N 74°51′E
Mangareva *see* Magareva
83 I23 **Mangaung** Free State, C South Africa 29°10′S 26°19′E
Mangaung *see* Bloemfontein
154 K9 **Mangawān** Madhya Pradesh, C India 24°39′N 81°33′E
184 M11 **Mangaweka** Manawatu-Wanganui, North Island, New Zealand 39°49′S 175°47′E
184 N11 **Mangaweka** ▲ North Island, New Zealand 39°51′S 176°06′E
79 P17 **Mangbwalu** Orientale, NE Dem. Rep. Congo 02°06′N 30°04′E
101 L24 **Mangfall** SE Germany
169 P13 **Manggar** Pulau Belitung, W Indonesia 02°52′S 108°13′E
Mangghystaū Üstirti' *see* Mangystau, Plato
166 M2 **Mangin Range** ▲▲ N Myanmar (Burma)
139 R1 **Mangish** Dahūk, N Iraq 37°03′N 43°04′E
Mangistau *see* Mangystau
146 H8 **Mang'it** *Rus.* Mangit. Qoraqalpog'iston Respublikasi, W Uzbekistan 42°06′N 60°02′E
Mangit *see* Mang'it
54 A13 **Manglares, Cabo** *headland* SW Colombia 01°36′N 79°02′W
149 V6 **Mangla Reservoir** ⊠ NE Pakistan
159 N9 **Mangnai** *var.* Lao Mangnai. Qinghai, C China 37°52′N 91°45′E
Mango *see* Mago, Fiji
Mango *see* Sansanné-Mango, Togo
Mangoche *see* Mangochi
83 N14 **Mangochi** *var.* Mangoche; *prev.* Fort Johnston. Southern, SE Malawi 14°30′S 35°15′E
77 N14 **Mangodara** SW Burkina 09°49′N 04°22′W
172 H6 **Mangoky** W Madagascar
171 Q12 **Mangole, Pulau** *island* Kepulauan Sula, E Indonesia
184 J2 **Mangonui** Northland, North Island, New Zealand 35°00′S 173°30′E
Mangqystaū Oblysy *see* Mangystau
Mangqystaū Shyghanaghy *see* Mangystau Zaliv
Mangshi *see* Luxi
104 H7 **Mangualde** Viseu, N Portugal 40°36′N 07°46′W
61 H18 **Mangueira, Lagoa** ◎ S Brazil
77 X6 **Manguéni, Plateau du** ▲▲ NE Niger
163 T4 **Mangui** Nei Mongol Zizhiqu, N China 52°02′N 122°13′E
26 K11 **Mangum** Oklahoma, C USA 34°52′N 99°30′W
79 O18 **Manguredjipa** Nord-Kivu, E Dem. Rep. Congo 0°28′N 28°33′E
83 L16 **Mangwendi** Mashonaland East, E Zimbabwe 18°22′S 31°24′E
Mangyshlak, Plato *see* Mangystau, Plato
Mangyshlakskiy Zaliv *see* Mangystau Zaliv
Mangyshlaskaya *see* Mangystau
144 F15 **Mangystau** *Kaz.* Mangqystaū Oblysy *prev.* Mangistau; *prev.* Mangyshlaskaya. ◈ *province* SW Kazakhstan
144 F15 **Mangystau, Plato** *plateau* SW Kazakhstan
144 E14 **Mangystau Zaliv** *Kaz.* Mangqystaū Shyghanaghy; *prev.* Mangyshlakskiy Zaliv. *gulf* SW Kazakhstan
162 E7 **Manhan** *var.* Tögrög. Hovd, W Mongolia 47°24′N 92°06′E
Manhan *see* Alag-Erdene
27 O4 **Manhattan** Kansas, C USA 39°11′N 96°35′W
99 L21 **Manhay** Luxembourg, SE Belgium 50°13′N 05°43′E
83 L21 **Manhiça** *prev.* Vila de Manhiça. Maputo, S Mozambique 25°25′S 32°49′E
83 L21 **Manhoca** Maputo, S Mozambique 26°49′S 32°36′E
59 N20 **Manhuaçu** Minas Gerais, SE Brazil 20°16′S 42°01′W
117 W9 **Manhush** *prev.* Pershotravneve. Donets'ka Oblast', E Ukraine 47°03′N 37°20′E
54 H10 **Maní** Casanare, C Colombia 04°50′N 72°15′W
143 R11 **Mānī** Kermān, C Iran
83 M17 **Manica** *var.* Vila de Manica. Manica, W Mozambique 18°56′S 32°52′E
83 M17 **Manica** *off.* Província de Manica. ◈ *province* W Mozambique
83 L17 **Manicaland** ◈ *province* E Zimbabwe
Manica, Província de *see* Manica
15 U5 **Manic Deux, Réservoir** ⊠ Québec, SE Canada
Manich *see* Manych
59 F14 **Manicoré** Amazonas, N Brazil 05°48′S 61°16′W
13 N11 **Manicouagan** Québec, SE Canada 50°40′N 68°46′W
13 N11 **Manicouagan** Québec, SE Canada
15 U6 **Manicouagan, Péninsule de** *peninsula* Québec, SE Canada
13 N11 **Manicouagan, Réservoir** ◎ Québec, E Canada
15 T4 **Manic Trois, Réservoir** ⊠ Québec, SE Canada
79 M20 **Maniema** *off.* Région du Maniema. ◈ *region* E Dem. Rep. Congo
Maniema, Région du *see* Maniema
Maniewicze *see* Manevychi
160 F8 **Maniganggo** Sichuan, C China 32°01′N 99°04′E
11 Y15 **Manigotagan** Manitoba, S Canada 51°06′N 96°18′W
153 R13 **Manihāri** Bihār, N India 25°21′N 87°37′E
191 U9 **Manihi** *island* Îles Tuamotu, C French Polynesia
190 L13 **Manihiki** *atoll* N Cook Islands
175 U8 **Manihiki Plateau** *undersea feature* C Pacific Ocean
196 M14 **Maniitsoq** *var.* Manîtsoq, *Dan.* Sukkertoppen. ◈ Kitaa, S Greenland
153 T15 **Manikganj** Dhaka, C Bangladesh 23°52′N 90°00′E
152 M14 **Mānikpur** Uttar Pradesh, N India 25°04′N 81°06′E
171 N4 **Manila** *off.* City of Manila. ● (Philippines) Luzon, N Philippines 14°34′N 120°59′E
27 Y9 **Manila** Arkansas, C USA 35°52′N 90°10′W
Manila, City of *see* Manila
189 N16 **Manila Reef** *reef* W Micronesia
183 T6 **Manilla** New South Wales, SE Australia 30°44′S 150°43′E
192 P6 **Maniloa** *island* Tongatapu Group, S Tonga
123 U8 **Manily** Krasnoyarskiy Kray, E Russian Federation 62°33′N 165°03′E
171 V12 **Manim, Pulau** *island* E Indonesia
168 I11 **Maninjau, Danau** ◎ Sumatera, W Indonesia
153 W13 **Manipur** ◈ *state* NE India
153 X14 **Manipur Hills** *hill range* E India
136 C14 **Manisa** *var.* Manissa, *prev.* Saruhan; *anc.* Magnesia. Manisa, W Turkey 38°36′N 27°29′E
136 C13 **Manisa** *var.* Manissa. ◈ *province* W Turkey
Manissa *see* Manisa
31 O7 **Manistee** Michigan, N USA 44°14′N 86°19′W
31 P7 **Manistee River** Michigan, N USA
31 O4 **Manistique** Michigan, N USA 45°57′N 86°15′W
31 P4 **Manistique Lake** ◎ Michigan, N USA
11 W13 **Manitoba** ◈ *province* S Canada
11 X16 **Manitoba, Lake** ◎ Manitoba, S Canada
11 X17 **Manitou** Manitoba, S Canada 49°12′N 98°28′W
31 N2 **Manitou Island** *island* Michigan, N USA
14 H11 **Manitou Lake** ◎ Ontario, SE Canada
12 G15 **Manitoulin Island** *island* Ontario, S Canada
37 T5 **Manitou Springs** Colorado, C USA 38°51′N 104°56′W
14 G12 **Manitouwabing Lake** ◎ Ontario, S Canada
12 E12 **Manitouwadge** Ontario, S Canada 49°14′N 85°51′W
12 G15 **Manitowaning** Manitoulin Island, Ontario, S Canada 45°44′N 81°50′W
14 B7 **Manitowik Lake** ◎ Ontario, S Canada
31 N7 **Manitowoc** Wisconsin, N USA 44°04′N 87°40′W
Manîtsoq *see* Maniitsoq
139 O7 **Mānī', Wādī al** *dry watercourse* W Iraq
12 J14 **Maniwaki** Québec, SE Canada 46°22′N 75°58′W
171 W13 **Maniwori** Papua, E Indonesia 02°49′S 136°00′E
54 E10 **Manizales** Caldas, W Colombia 05°03′N 73°52′W
112 F11 **Manjača** ▲▲ NW Bosnia and Herzegovina
Manjacaze *see* Mandlakazi
180 J14 **Manjimup** Western Australia 34°18′S 116°14′E
109 V4 **Mank** Niederösterreich, C Austria 48°06′N 15°13′E
79 I17 **Mankanza** Equateur, NW Dem. Rep. Congo 01°40′N 19°08′E
153 N12 **Mankāpur** Uttar Pradesh, N India 27°03′N 82°12′E
26 M3 **Mankato** Kansas, C USA 39°48′N 98°13′W
29 U10 **Mankato** Minnesota, N USA 44°10′N 94°00′W
117 O7 **Man'kivka** Cherkas'ka Oblast', C Ukraine 48°58′N 30°10′E
76 M15 **Mankono** C Ivory Coast 08°01′N 06°09′W
11 T17 **Mankota** Saskatchewan, S Canada 49°25′N 107°05′W
155 K23 **Mankulam** Northern Province, N Sri Lanka 09°07′N 80°27′E
162 L10 **Manlay** *var.* Üydzen. Ömnögovĭ, S Mongolia 44°08′N 106°48′E
39 Q9 **Manley Hot Springs** Alaska, USA 65°00′N 150°37′W
18 H10 **Manlius** New York, NE USA 43°00′N 75°58′W
105 W5 **Manlleu** Cataluña, NE Spain 41°59′N 02°17′E
29 V11 **Manly** Iowa, C USA 43°17′N 93°12′W
154 E13 **Manmād** Mahārāshtra, W India 20°15′N 74°29′E
182 J7 **Mannahill** South Australia 32°29′S 139°58′E
155 J23 **Mannar** *var.* Manar. Northern Province, NW Sri Lanka 09°01′N 79°53′E
155 I24 **Mannar, Gulf of** *gulf* India/Sri Lanka
155 J23 **Mannar Island** *island* N Sri Lanka
Mannersdorf *see* Mannersdorf am Leithagebirge
109 Y5 **Mannersdorf am Leithagebirge** *var.* Mannersdorf. Niederösterreich, E Austria 47°59′N 16°36′E
109 Y6 **Mannersdorf an der Rabnitz** Burgenland, E Austria 47°25′N 16°32′E
101 G20 **Mannheim** Baden-Württemberg, SW Germany 49°29′N 08°29′E
11 O12 **Manning** Alberta, W Canada 56°53′N 117°39′W
29 T14 **Manning** Iowa, C USA 41°54′N 95°03′W
28 K5 **Manning** North Dakota, N USA 47°15′N 102°48′W
21 S13 **Manning** South Carolina, SE USA 33°42′N 80°12′W
191 Y2 **Manning, Cape** *headland* Kiritimati, NE Kiribati 02°02′N 157°26′W
21 S3 **Mannington** West Virginia, NE USA 39°31′N 80°20′W
182 A1 **Mann Ranges** ▲▲ South Australia
107 C19 **Mannu** Sardegna, Italy, C Mediterranean Sea
11 R14 **Mannville** Alberta, SW Canada 53°19′N 111°08′W
76 J15 **Mano** Liberia/Sierra Leone
Manø *see* Mandø
61 F15 **Manoel Viana** Rio Grande do Sul, S Brazil 29°33′S 55°28′W
39 O13 **Manokotak** Alaska, USA 59°00′N 158°58′W
171 V12 **Manokwari** Papua, E Indonesia 0°53′S 134°05′S
79 N22 **Manono** Shaba, SE Dem. Rep. Congo 07°18′S 27°25′E
25 T10 **Manor** Texas, SW USA 30°20′N 97°33′W
97 D16 **Manorhamilton** *Ir.* Cluainín. Leitrim, NW Ireland 54°18′N 08°10′W
103 S15 **Manosque** Alpes-de-Haute-Provence, SE France 43°50′N 05°47′E
12 L11 **Manouane, Lac** ◎ Québec, SE Canada
163 W12 **Manp'o** *var.* Manp'ojin. NW North Korea 41°10′N 126°24′E
Manp'ojin *see* Manp'o
191 T4 **Manra** *prev.* Sydney Island. *atoll* Phoenix Islands, C Kiribati
105 V5 **Manresa** Cataluña, NE Spain 41°43′N 01°50′E
152 H9 **Mānsa** Punjab, NW India 30°00′N 75°25′E
82 J12 **Mansa** *prev.* Fort Rosebery. Luapula, N Zambia 11°14′S 28°55′E
76 G12 **Mansa Konko** C Gambia 13°26′N 15°29′W
15 Q11 **Manseau** Québec, SE Canada 46°23′N 71°59′W
149 U5 **Mānsehra** Khyber Pakhtunkhwa, NW Pakistan 34°23′N 73°18′E
9 Q9 **Mansel Island** *island* Nunavut, NE Canada
183 O12 **Mansfield** Victoria, SE Australia 37°04′S 146°06′E
97 M18 **Mansfield** C England, United Kingdom 53°09′N 01°11′W
27 S11 **Mansfield** Arkansas, C USA 35°03′N 94°15′W
22 G6 **Mansfield** Louisiana, S USA 32°02′N 93°42′W
19 O12 **Mansfield** Massachusetts, NE USA 42°00′N 71°11′W
31 T12 **Mansfield** Ohio, N USA 40°45′N 82°31′W
18 G12 **Mansfield** Pennsylvania, NE USA 41°46′N 77°02′W
18 M7 **Mansfield, Mount** ▲ Vermont, NE USA 44°31′N 72°49′W
59 M16 **Mansidão** Bahia, E Brazil 10°46′S 44°04′W
102 L11 **Mansle** Charente, W France 45°52′N 00°11′E
76 G12 **Mansôa** C Guinea-Bissau 12°08′N 15°18′W
47 V8 **Manso, Rio** C Brazil
Manṣûra *see* Al Manṣūrah
Mansurabad *see* Mehrān, Rūd-e
56 A6 **Manta** Manabí, W Ecuador 0°59′S 80°44′W
56 A6 **Manta, Bahía de** *bay* W Ecuador
57 F14 **Mantaro, Río** C Peru
35 O8 **Manteca** California, W USA 37°48′N 121°13′W
54 J7 **Mantecal** Apure, C Venezuela 07°34′N 69°07′W
31 N11 **Manteno** Illinois, N USA 41°15′N 87°49′W
21 Y9 **Manteo** Roanoke Island, North Carolina, SE USA 35°54′N 75°42′W
Mantes-Gassicourt *see* Mantes-la-Jolie
103 N5 **Mantes-la-Jolie** *prev.* Mantes-Gassicourt, Mantes-sur-Seine; *anc.* Medunta. Yvelines, N France 48°59′N 01°43′E
Mantes-sur-Seine *see* Mantes-la-Jolie
36 L5 **Manti** Utah, W USA 39°16′N 111°38′W
Mantinea *see* Mantíneia
115 F20 **Mantíneia** *anc.* Mantinea. *site of ancient city* Pelopónnisos, S Greece
59 M21 **Mantiqueira, Serra da** ▲▲ S Brazil
29 W10 **Mantorville** Minnesota, N USA 44°04′N 92°45′W
115 G17 **Mantoúdi** *var.* Mandoudi; *prev.* Mandoúdhion. Évvoia, C Greece 38°47′N 23°29′E
Mantoue *see* Mantova
106 F8 **Mantova** *Eng.* Mantua, *Fr.* Mantoue. Lombardia, NW Italy 45°10′N 10°47′E
93 M19 **Mäntsälä** Etelä-Suomi, S Finland 60°38′N 25°21′E
93 L17 **Mänttä** Länsi-Suomi, W Finland 62°00′N 24°36′E
Mantua *see* Mantova
125 O14 **Manturovo** Kostromskaya Oblast', NW Russian Federation 58°19′N 44°42′E
93 M18 **Mäntyharju** Itä-Suomi, SE Finland 61°25′N 26°53′E
92 M13 **Mäntyjärvi** Lappi, N Finland 66°00′N 27°35′E
190 L16 **Manuae** *island* S Cook Islands
191 Q10 **Manuae** *atoll* Îles Sous le Vent, W French Polynesia
192 L16 **Manu'a Islands** *island group* E American Samoa
40 L5 **Manuel Benavides** Chihuahua, N Mexico 29°07′N 103°52′W
61 D21 **Manuel J. Cobo** Buenos Aires, E Argentina 35°49′S 57°54′W
58 M12 **Manuel Luís, Recife** *reef* E Brazil
59 I14 **Manuel Zinho** Pará, N Brazil 07°21′S 54°47′W
191 V11 **Manuhagi** *prev.* Manuhangi. *atoll* Îles Tuamotu, C French Polynesia
Manuhangi *see* Manuhagi
185 E22 **Manuherikia** South Island, New Zealand
171 P13 **Manui, Pulau** *island* N Indonesia
Manukau *see* Manurewa
184 L6 **Manukau Harbour** *harbor* North Island, New Zealand
191 Z2 **Manulu Lagoon** ◎ Kiritimati, E Kiribati
182 J7 **Manunda Creek** *seasonal river* South Australia
57 K15 **Manupari, Río** N Bolivia
184 L6 **Manurewa** *var.* Manukau. Auckland, North Island, New Zealand 37°01′S 174°55′E
57 K15 **Manurimi, Río** NW Bolivia
186 D5 **Manus** ◈ *province* N Papua New Guinea
186 D5 **Manus Island** *var.* Great Admiralty Island. *island* N Papua New Guinea
171 T16 **Manuwui** Pulau Babar, E Indonesia 07°47′S 129°39′E
29 Q3 **Manvel** North Dakota, N USA 48°07′N 97°15′W
33 Z14 **Manville** Wyoming, C USA 42°45′N 104°38′W
22 G6 **Many** Louisiana, S USA 31°34′N 93°28′W
81 H21 **Manyara, Lake** ◎ NE Tanzania
126 L12 **Manych** *var.* Manich. SW Russian Federation
83 H14 **Manyinga** North Western, NW Zambia 13°28′S 24°18′E
105 O11 **Manzanares** Castilla-La Mancha, C Spain 39°N 03°23′W
44 H7 **Manzanillo** Granma, E Cuba 20°21′N 77°07′W
40 K14 **Manzanillo** Colima, SW Mexico 19°00′N 104°19′W
40 K14 **Manzanillo, Bahía** *bay* SW Mexico
37 S11 **Manzano Mountains** ▲▲ New Mexico, SW USA
37 R12 **Manzano Peak** ▲ New Mexico, SW USA 34°35′N 106°27′W
163 R6 **Manzhouli** *var.* Man-chou-li. Nei Mongol Zizhiqu, N China 49°36′N 117°28′E
Manzil Bū Ruqaybah *see* Menzel Bourguiba
139 X9 **Manzilīyah** Maysān, E Iraq 32°26′N 47°01′E
83 L21 **Manzini** *prev.* Bremersdorp. C Swaziland 26°30′S 31°22′E
83 L21 **Manzini** ✈ (Mbabane) C Swaziland 26°36′S 31°25′E
78 G10 **Mao** Kanem, W Chad 14°06′N 15°17′E
45 N8 **Mao** NW Dominican Republic 19°37′N 71°04′W
105 Z9 **Maó** *Cast.* Mahón, *Eng.* Port Mahon; *anc.* Portus Magonis. Menorca, Spain, W Mediterranean Sea 39°54′N 04°15′E
Maoemere *see* Maumere
159 W9 **Maojing** Gansu, N China 36°26′N 106°36′E
171 Y14 **Maoke, Pegunungan** *Dut.* Sneeuw-gebergte, *Eng.* Snow Mountains. ▲▲ Papua, E Indonesia
Maol Réidh, Caoc *see* Mweelrea
160 M15 **Maoming** Guangdong, S China 21°46′N 110°51′E
160 H8 **Maoxian** *var.* Mao Xian; *prev.* Fengyizhen. Sichuan, C China 31°42′N 103°48′E
Mao Xian *see* Maoxian
83 L19 **Mapai** Gaza, SW Mozambique 22°52′S 32°00′E
158 H15 **Mapam Yumco** ◎ W China
83 I15 **Mapanza** Southern, S Zambia 16°16′S 26°54′E
54 J4 **Mapararí** Falcón, N Venezuela 10°52′N 69°27′W
41 U17 **Mapastepec** Chiapas, SE Mexico 15°28′N 93°00′W
169 V9 **Mapat, Pulau** *island* N Indonesia
171 Y15 **Mapi** Papua, E Indonesia 07°02′S 139°24′E
171 V11 **Mapia, Kepulauan** *island group* E Indonesia
40 L8 **Mapimí** Durango, C Mexico 25°50′N 103°50′W
83 N19 **Mapinhane** Inhambane, SE Mozambique 22°14′S 35°07′E
55 N7 **Mapire** Monagas, NE Venezuela 07°48′N 64°40′W
11 S17 **Maple Creek** Saskatchewan, S Canada 49°55′N 109°28′W
31 Q9 **Maple River** Michigan, N USA
29 P7 **Maple River** North Dakota/South Dakota, N USA
29 S13 **Mapleton** Iowa, C USA 42°10′N 95°47′W
29 U10 **Mapleton** Minnesota, N USA 43°55′N 93°57′W
29 R5 **Mapleton** North Dakota, N USA 46°51′N 97°04′W
32 F13 **Mapleton** Oregon, NW USA 44°01′N 123°56′W
36 L3 **Mapleton** Utah, W USA 40°07′N 111°37′W
192 K5 **Mapmaker Seamounts** *undersea feature* N Pacific Ocean 25°00′N 165°00′E
186 B6 **Maprik** East Sepik, NW Papua New Guinea 03°38′S 143°02′E
83 L21 **Maputo** *prev.* Lourenço Marques. ● (Mozambique) Maputo, S Mozambique 25°58′S 32°35′E
83 L21 **Maputo** ◈ *province* S Mozambique
67 V14 **Maputo** S Mozambique
83 L21 **Maputo** ✈ Maputo, S Mozambique 25°47′S 32°36′E
Maqat *see* Makat
113 M19 **Maqellarë** Dibër, C Albania 41°36′N 20°29′E
159 S12 **Maqên** *var.* Dawo; *prev.* Dawu. Qinghai, C China 34°32′N 100°17′E
159 S11 **Maqên Kangri** ▲ C China 34°44′N 99°25′E
141 X7 **Maqiz al Kurbá** N Oman 24°13′N 56°48′E
159 U12 **Maqu** *var.* Nyinma. Gansu, C China 34°02′N 102°00′E
104 M9 **Maqueda** Castilla-La Mancha, C Spain 40°04′N 04°22′W
82 B9 **Maquela do Zombo** Uíge, NW Angola 06°06′S 15°12′E
63 I16 **Maquinchao** Río Negro, C Argentina 41°19′S 68°47′W
29 Z13 **Maquoketa** Iowa, C USA 42°03′N 90°42′W
29 Y13 **Maquoketa River** Iowa, C USA
14 F13 **Mar** Ontario, S Canada 44°48′N 81°12′W
95 F14 **Mår** ◎ S Norway
81 G19 **Mara** ◈ *region* N Tanzania
58 D12 **Maraã** Amazonas, NW Brazil 01°48′S 65°21′W
191 P8 **Maraa** Tahiti, W French Polynesia 17°44′S 149°34′W
191 O8 **Maraa, Pointe** *headland* Tahiti, W French Polynesia 17°44′S 149°34′W
59 K14 **Marabá** Pará, NE Brazil 05°23′S 49°10′W
54 H5 **Maracaibo** Zulia, NW Venezuela 10°40′N 71°39′W
Maracaibo, Gulf of *see* Venezuela, Golfo de
54 H5 **Maracaibo, Lago de** *var.* Lake Maracaibo. *inlet* NW Venezuela
Maracaibo, Lake *see* Maracaibo, Lago de
58 K10 **Maracá, Ilha de** *island* NE Brazil
59 H20 **Maracaju, Serra de** ▲▲ S Brazil
58 I11 **Maracanaquará, Planalto** ▲▲ NE Brazil
54 L5 **Maracay** Aragua, N Venezuela 10°15′N 67°36′W
Marada *see* Marādah
75 R9 **Marādah** *var.* Marada. N Libya 29°16′N 19°29′E
77 U12 **Maradi** Maradi, S Niger 13°30′N 07°05′E
77 U11 **Maradi** ◈ *department* S Niger
81 E21 **Maragarazi** *var.* Muragarazi. Burundi/Tanzania
Maragha *see* Marāgheh
142 J3 **Marāgheh** *var.* Maragha. Āžarbāyjān-e Khāvarī, NW Iran 37°21′N 46°14′E
141 P7 **Marāh** *var.* Marrāt. Ar Riyāḑ, C Saudi Arabia 25°04′N 45°30′E

◆ Country
● Country Capital
◇ Dependent Territory
○ Dependent Territory Capital
◈ Administrative Regions
✈ International Airport
▲ Mountain
▲▲ Mountain Range
Volcano
River
◎ Lake
⊠ Reservoir

55 N11 **Marahuaca, Cerro** ▲ S Venezuela *03°37′N 65°25′W*
27 R5 **Marais des Cygnes River** ≈ Kansas/Missouri, C USA
58 L11 **Marajó, Baía de** *bay* N Brazil
59 K12 **Marajó, Ilha de** *island* N Brazil
191 O2 **Marakei** *atoll* Tungaru, W Kiribati
Marakesh *see* Marrakech
81 I18 **Maralal** Rift Valley, C Kenya *01°05′N 36°42′E*
83 G21 **Maralaleng** Kgalagadi, S Botswana *25°42′S 22°39′E*
145 U8 **Maraldy, Ozero** ◎ NE Kazakhstan
182 C5 **Maralinga** South Australia *30°16′S 131°35′E*
Máramarossziget *see* Sighetu Marmaţiei
187 N9 **Maramasike** *var.* Small Malaita. *island* N Solomon Islands
Maramba *see* Livingstone
194 H3 **Marambio** *Argentinian research station* Antarctica *64°22′S 57°18′W*
116 H9 **Maramureș** ◈ *county* NW Romania
36 L15 **Marana** Arizona, SW USA *32°24′N 111°12′W*
105 P7 **Maranchón** Castilla-La Mancha, C Spain *41°02′N 02°11′W*
142 J2 **Marand** *var.* Merend. Āzarbāyjān-e Sharqī, NW Iran *38°25′N 45°40′E*
Marandellas *see* Marondera
58 L13 **Maranhão** *off.* Estado do Maranhão. ◈ *state* E Brazil
104 H10 **Maranhão, Barragem do** ▣ C Portugal
Maranhão, Estado do *see* Maranhão
149 O11 **Mārān, Koh-i** ▲ SW Pakistan *29°24′N 66°50′E*
106 J7 **Marano, Laguna di** *lagoon* NE Italy
56 E9 **Marañón, Río** ≈ N Peru
102 J10 **Marans** Charente-Maritime, W France *46°19′N 00°58′W*
83 M20 **Marão** Inhambane, S Mozambique *24°15′S 34°09′E*
185 B23 **Mararoa** ≈ South Island, New Zealand
Maraş/Marash *see* Kahramanmaraş
107 M19 **Maratea** Basilicata, S Italy *39°57′N 15°44′E*
104 G11 **Marateca** Setúbal, S Portugal *38°34′N 08°40′W*
115 B20 **Marathiá, Akrotírio** *headland* Zákynthos, Iónia Nisiá, Greece, C Mediterranean Sea *37°39′N 20°49′E*
12 E12 **Marathon** Ontario, S Canada *48°44′N 86°23′W*
23 Y17 **Marathon** Florida Keys, Florida, SE USA *24°42′N 81°05′W*
24 L10 **Marathon** Texas, SW USA *30°10′N 103°14′W*
Marathón *see* Marathónas
115 H19 **Marathónas** *prev.* Marathón. Attikí, C Greece *38°09′N 23°57′E*
169 W9 **Maratua, Pulau** *island* N Indonesia
59 O18 **Maraú** Bahia, SE Brazil *14°07′S 39°02′W*
143 R3 **Marāveh Tappeh** Golestán, N Iran *37°53′N 55°57′E*
24 L11 **Maravillas Creek** ≈ Texas, SW USA
186 D8 **Marawaka** Eastern Highlands, C Papua New Guinea *06°56′S 145°54′E*
171 Q7 **Marawi** Mindanao, S Philippines *07°59′N 124°16′E*
Mārāzā *see* Qobustan
Marbat *see* Mirbāţ
104 L16 **Marbella** Andalucía, S Spain *36°31′N 04°50′W*
180 J7 **Marble Bar** Western Australia *21°13′S 119°48′E*
36 L9 **Marble Canyon** *canyon* Arizona, SW USA
25 S10 **Marble Falls** Texas, SW USA *30°34′N 98°16′W*
27 Y7 **Marble Hill** Missouri, C USA *37°18′N 89°58′W*
33 T15 **Marbleton** Wyoming, C USA *42°31′N 110°06′W*
Marburg *see* Marburg an der Lahn, Germany
Marburg *see* Maribor, Slovenia
101 H16 **Marburg an der Lahn** *hist.* Marburg. Hessen, W Germany *50°49′N 08°46′E*
111 H23 **Marcal** ≈ W Hungary
42 G7 **Marcala** La Paz, SW Honduras *14°11′N 88°00′W*
111 H24 **Marcali** Somogy, SW Hungary *46°33′N 17°29′E*
83 A16 **Marca, Ponta da** *headland* SW Angola *16°31′S 11°42′E*
59 I16 **Marcelândia** Mato Grosso, W Brazil *11°18′S 54°49′W*
27 T3 **Marceline** Missouri, C USA *39°42′N 92°57′W*
60 I13 **Marcelino Ramos** Rio Grande do Sul, S Brazil *27°31′S 51°57′W*
55 Y12 **Marcel, Mont** ▲ S French Guiana *02°32′N 53°00′W*
97 O19 **March** E England, United Kingdom *52°37′N 00°13′E*
109 Z3 **March** *var.* Morava. ≈ C Europe *see also* Morava
March *see* Morava
106 I12 **Marche** *Eng.* Marches. ◈ *region* C Italy
103 N11 **Marche** *cultural region* C France
99 J21 **Marche-en-Famenne** Luxembourg, SE Belgium *50°13′N 05°21′E*
104 K14 **Marchena** Andalucía, S Spain *37°20′N 05°24′W*
57 B17 **Marchena, Isla** *var.* Bindloe Island. *island* Galapagos Islands, Ecuador, E Pacific Ocean
Marches *see* Marche
99 J20 **Marchin** Liège, E Belgium *50°30′N 05°17′E*
181 S1 **Marchinbar Island** *island* Wessel Islands, Northern Territory, N Australia
62 L9 **Mar Chiquita, Laguna** ◎ C Argentina
103 Q10 **Marcigny** Saône-et-Loire, C France *46°16′N 04°04′E*
23 W16 **Marco** Florida, SE USA *25°56′N 81°43′W*
Marcodurum *see* Düren
59 O15 **Marcolândia** Pernambuco, E Brazil *07°21′S 40°40′W*
106 I8 **Marco Polo** ✈ (Venezia) Veneto, NE Italy *45°30′N 12°21′E*
Marcounda *see* Markounda
Marcq *see* Mark
116 M8 **Mărculeşti** *Rus.* Markuleshty. N Moldova *47°54′N 28°14′E*
29 S12 **Marcus** Iowa, C USA *42°49′N 95°48′W*
39 S11 **Marcus Baker, Mount** ▲ Alaska, USA *61°26′N 147°45′W*
192 I5 **Marcus Island** *var.* Minami Tori Shima. *island* E Japan
18 K8 **Marcy, Mount** ▲ New York, NE USA *44°06′N 73°55′W*
149 T5 **Mardān** Khyber Pakhtunkhwa, N Pakistan *34°14′N 71°59′E*
63 N14 **Mar del Plata** Buenos Aires, E Argentina *38°S 57°32′W*
137 Q16 **Mardin** Mardin, SE Turkey *37°19′N 40°43′E*
137 Q16 **Mardin** ◈ *province* SE Turkey
137 Q16 **Mardin Dağlari** ▲▲ SE Turkey
Mardzad *see* Hayrhandulaan
187 R17 **Maré** *island* Îles Loyauté, E New Caledonia
Marea Neagră *see* Black Sea
105 Z8 **Mare de Déu del Toro** *var.* El Toro. ▲ Menorca, Spain, W Mediterranean Sea *39°59′N 04°06′E*
181 W4 **Mareeba** Queensland, NE Australia *17°03′S 145°30′E*
96 G8 **Maree, Loch** ◎ N Scotland, United Kingdom
Mareeq *see* Mereeg
Marek *see* Dupnitsa
76 J11 **Maréna** Kayes, W Mali *14°36′N 10°57′W*
190 I2 **Marenanuka** *atoll* Tungaru, W Kiribati
29 X14 **Marengo** Iowa, C USA *41°48′N 92°04′W*
102 J11 **Marennes** Charente-Maritime, W France *45°47′N 01°04′W*
107 G23 **Marettimo, Isola** *island* Isole Egadi, S Italy
24 K10 **Marfa** Texas, SW USA *30°19′N 104°03′W*
57 P17 **Marfil, Laguna** ◎ E Bolivia
Marganets *see* Marhanets'
25 Q4 **Margaret** Texas, SW USA *34°00′N 99°38′W*
180 I14 **Margaret River** Western Australia *33°58′S 115°10′E*
186 C7 **Margarima** Southern Highlands, W Papua New Guinea *06°00′S 143°23′E*
55 N4 **Margarita, Isla de** *island* N Venezuela
115 I25 **Margarítes** Kríti, Greece, E Mediterranean Sea *35°19′N 24°40′E*
97 Q22 **Margate** *prev.* Mergate. SE England, United Kingdom *51°24′N 01°24′E*
23 Z15 **Margate** Florida, SE USA *26°14′N 80°12′W*
Margelan *see* Marg'ilon
103 P13 **Margeride, Montagnes de la** ▲ C France
Margherita *see* Jamaame
107 N16 **Margherita di Savoia** Puglia, SE Italy *41°23′N 16°09′E*
Margherita, Lake *see* Ābaya Hāyk'
81 E18 **Margherita Peak** *Fr.* Pic Marguerite. ▲ Uganda/Dem. Rep. Congo *0°28′N 29°58′E*
149 O4 **Marghī** Bāmyān, N Afghanistan *35°10′N 66°26′E*
116 G9 **Marghita** *Hung.* Margitta. Bihor, NW Romania *47°20′N 22°20′E*
Margilan *see* Marg'ilon
147 S10 **Marg'ilon** *var.* Margelan, *Rus.* Margilan. Farg'ona Viloyati, E Uzbekistan *40°29′N 71°43′E*
116 K8 **Marginea** Suceava, NE Romania *47°49′N 25°47′E*
Margitta *see* Marghita
148 K9 **Mārgow, Dasht-e** *desert* SW Afghanistan
99 L18 **Margraten** Limburg, SE Netherlands *50°49′N 05°49′E*
10 M15 **Marguerite** British Columbia, SW Canada *52°17′N 122°10′W*
15 V3 **Marguerite** ≈ Québec, SE Canada
194 I6 **Marguerite Bay** *bay* Antarctica
Marguerite, Pic *see* Margherita Peak
117 T9 **Marhanets'** *Rus.* Marganets. Dnipropetrovs'ka Oblast', E Ukraine *47°35′N 34°37′E*
186 B9 **Mari** Western, SW Papua New Guinea *09°10′S 141°39′E*
191 Y12 **Maria** *atoll* Groupe Actéon, SE French Polynesia
191 R12 **Maria** *island* Îles Australes, SW French Polynesia
40 I12 **María Cleofas, Isla** *island* C Mexico
62 H4 **María Elena** *var.* Oficina María Elena. Antofagasta, N Chile *22°18′S 69°40′W*
95 G21 **Mariager** Midtjylland, C Denmark *56°39′N 09°59′E*
61 C22 **María Ignacia** Buenos Aires, E Argentina *37°24′S 59°30′W*
183 P17 **Maria Island** *island* Tasmania, SE Australia
40 H12 **María Madre, Isla** *island* C Mexico
40 I12 **María Magdalena, Isla** *island* C Mexico
192 H6 **Mariana Islands** *island group* Guam/Northern Mariana Islands
175 N3 **Mariana Trench** *var.* Challenger Deep. *undersea feature* W Pacific Ocean *15°00′N 147°30′E*
153 X12 **Mariāni** Assam, NE India *26°39′N 94°18′E*
27 X11 **Marianna** Arkansas, C USA *34°46′N 90°49′W*
23 R8 **Marianna** Florida, SE USA *30°46′N 85°13′W*
172 J16 **Marianne** *island* Inner Islands, NE Seychelles
95 M19 **Mariannelund** Jönköping, S Sweden *57°37′N 15°33′E*
61 D15 **Mariano I. Loza** Corrientes, NE Argentina *29°22′S 58°12′W*
Mariano Machado *see* Ganda
111 A16 **Mariánské Lázně** *Ger.* Marienbad. Karlovarský Kraj, W Czech Republic *49°57′N 12°43′E*
Máriaradna *see* Radna
33 S7 **Marias River** ≈ Montana, NW USA
Maria-Theresiopel *see* Subotica
Máriatölgyes *see* Dubnica nad Váhom
184 H1 **Maria van Diemen, Cape** *headland* North Island, New Zealand *34°27′S 172°38′E*
109 V5 **Mariazell** Steiermark, E Austria *47°47′N 15°20′E*
141 P15 **Ma'rib** W Yemen *15°28′N 45°25′E*
95 I25 **Maribo** Sjælland, S Denmark *54°47′N 11°30′E*
109 W9 **Maribor** *Ger.* Marburg. NE Slovenia *46°34′N 15°40′E*
Marica *see* Maritsa
35 R13 **Maricopa** California, W USA *35°03′N 119°24′W*
Maricourt *see* Kangiqsujuaq
81 D15 **Maridi** Western Equatoria, SW South Sudan *04°55′N 29°30′E*
194 M11 **Marie Byrd Land** *physical region* Antarctica
193 P14 **Marie Byrd Seamount** *undersea feature* N Amundsen Sea *70°00′S 118°00′W*
45 X11 **Marie-Galante** *var.* Ceyre to the Caribs. *island* SE Guadeloupe
45 Y6 **Marie-Galante, Canal de** *channel* S Guadeloupe
93 J20 **Mariehamn** *Fin.* Maarianhamina. Åland, SW Finland *60°05′N 19°55′E*
44 C4 **Mariel** La Habana, W Cuba *23°02′N 82°44′W*
99 H22 **Mariembourg** Namur, S Belgium *50°07′N 04°30′E*
Marienbad *see* Mariánské Lázně
Marienburg *see* Alūksne, Latvia
Marienburg *see* Malbork, Poland
Marienburg *see* Feldioara, Romania
Marienburg in Westpreussen *see* Malbork
Marienhausen *see* Viļaka
83 D20 **Mariental** Hardap, SW Namibia *24°35′S 17°56′E*
18 D13 **Marienville** Pennsylvania, NE USA *41°27′N 79°07′W*
Marienwerder *see* Kwidzyń
58 C12 **Marié, Rio** ≈ NW Brazil
95 K17 **Mariestad** Västra Götaland, S Sweden *58°42′N 13°50′E*
23 S3 **Marietta** Georgia, SE USA *33°57′N 84°34′W*
31 U14 **Marietta** Ohio, N USA *39°25′N 81°27′W*
27 N13 **Marietta** Oklahoma, C USA *33°57′N 97°08′W*
81 H18 **Marigat** Rift Valley, W Kenya *0°29′S 35°59′E*
103 S16 **Marignane** Bouches-du-Rhône, SE France *43°25′N 05°12′E*
Marignano *see* Melegnano
45 O11 **Marigot** NE Dominica *15°32′N 61°18′W*
122 K12 **Mariinsk** Kemerovskaya Oblast', S Russian Federation *56°13′N 87°27′E*
127 Q3 **Mariinskiy Posad** Respublika Mariy El, W Russian Federation *56°07′N 47°44′E*
119 E14 **Marijampolė** *prev.* Kapsukas. Marijampolė, S Lithuania *54°33′N 23°21′E*
Marikostenovo *see* Marikostinovo
114 G12 **Marikostinovo** *prev.* Marikostenovo. Blagoevgrad, SW Bulgaria *41°25′N 23°21′E*
60 J9 **Marília** São Paulo, S Brazil *22°13′S 49°58′W*
82 D11 **Marimba** Malanje, NW Angola *08°18′S 16°58′E*
139 T1 **Marī Mīlā** Arbīl, E Iraq *36°58′N 44°42′E*
104 G4 **Marín** Galicia, NW Spain *42°23′N 08°43′W*
35 N10 **Marina** California, W USA *36°40′N 121°48′W*
Mar'ina Gorka *see* Mar"ina Horka
119 L17 **Mar"ina Horka** *Rus.* Mar'ina Gorka. Minskaya Voblasts', C Belarus *53°31′N 28°09′E*
171 O4 **Marinduque** *island* C Philippines
31 S9 **Marine City** Michigan, N USA *42°43′N 82°29′W*
31 N6 **Marinette** Wisconsin, N USA *45°06′N 87°38′W*
60 I10 **Maringá** Paraná, S Brazil *23°26′S 51°55′W*
83 N16 **Maringuè** Sofala, C Mozambique *17°57′S 34°23′E*
104 F9 **Marinha Grande** Leiria, C Portugal *39°45′N 08°55′W*
107 I15 **Marino** Lazio, C Italy *41°46′N 12°40′E*
59 A15 **Mário Lobão** Acre, W Brazil *08°21′S 72°58′W*
23 O5 **Marion** Alabama, S USA *32°37′N 87°19′W*
27 Y11 **Marion** Arkansas, C USA *35°12′N 90°12′W*
30 L17 **Marion** Illinois, N USA *37°43′N 88°55′W*
31 P13 **Marion** Indiana, N USA *40°32′N 85°40′W*
29 X13 **Marion** Iowa, C USA *42°01′N 91°36′W*
27 O5 **Marion** Kansas, C USA *38°22′N 97°02′W*
20 H6 **Marion** Kentucky, S USA *37°19′N 88°06′W*
21 P9 **Marion** North Carolina, SE USA *35°43′N 82°00′W*
31 S12 **Marion** Ohio, N USA *40°35′N 83°08′W*
21 T12 **Marion** South Carolina, SE USA *34°11′N 79°23′W*
21 Q7 **Marion** Virginia, NE USA *36°51′N 81°30′W*
27 O5 **Marion Lake** ▣ Kansas, C USA
21 S13 **Marion, Lake** ▣ South Carolina, SE USA
27 S8 **Marionville** Missouri, C USA *37°00′N 93°38′W*
55 N7 **Maripa** Bolívar, E Venezuela *07°27′N 65°10′W*
55 X11 **Maripasoula** W French Guiana *03°43′N 54°04′W*
35 Q9 **Mariposa** California, W USA *37°28′N 119°59′W*
61 G19 **Mariscala** Lavalleja, S Uruguay *34°03′S 54°47′W*
62 M4 **Mariscal Estigarribia** Boquerón, NW Paraguay *22°03′S 60°39′W*
56 C6 **Mariscal Sucre** *var.* Quito. ✈ (Quito) Pichincha, C Ecuador *0°21′S 78°37′W*
30 K16 **Marissa** Illinois, N USA *38°15′N 89°45′W*
103 U14 **Maritime Alps** *Fr.* Alpes Maritimes, *It.* Alpi Marittime. ▲▲ France/Italy
Maritimes, Alpes *see* Maritime Alps
Maritime Territory *see* Primorskiy Kray
114 K11 **Maritsa** *var.* Marica, *Gk.* Évros, *Turk.* Meriç; *anc.* Hebrus. ≈ SW Europe *see also* Évros/Meriç
Maritsa *see* Simeonovgrad, Bulgaria
Marittime, Alpi *see* Maritime Alps
Maritzburg *see* Pietermaritzburg
117 X9 **Mariupol'** *prev.* Zhdanov. Donets'ka Oblast', SE Ukraine *47°06′N 37°34′E*
55 Q6 **Mariusa, Caño** ≈ NE Venezuela
142 J5 **Marīvān** *prev.* Dezh Shāhpūr. Kordestān, W Iran *35°30′N 46°09′E*
127 R3 **Mariyets** Respublika Mariy El, W Russian Federation *56°31′N 49°48′E*
118 G4 **Märjamaa** *Ger.* Merjama. Raplamaa, NW Estonia *58°54′N 24°21′E*
99 I15 **Mark** *Fr.* Marcq. ≈ Belgium/Netherlands
81 N17 **Marka** *var.* Merca. Shabeellaha Hoose, S Somalia *01°43′N 44°45′E*
145 Z10 **Markakol', Ozero** *Kaz.* Marqakōl. ◎ E Kazakhstan
76 M12 **Markala** Ségou, W Mali *13°38′N 06°07′W*
159 S15 **Markam** *var.* Gartog. Xizang Zizhiqu, W China *29°40′N 98°33′E*
95 K21 **Markaryd** Kronoberg, S Sweden *56°26′N 13°35′E*
142 L7 **Markazī** *off.* Ostān-e Markazī. ◈ *province* W Iran
Markazī, Ostān-e *see* Markazī
14 F14 **Markdale** Ontario, S Canada *44°19′N 80°37′W*
27 X10 **Marked Tree** Arkansas, C USA *35°31′N 90°25′W*
98 N11 **Markelo** Overijssel, E Netherlands *52°15′N 06°30′E*
98 J9 **Markermeer** ◎ C Netherlands
97 N20 **Market Harborough** C England, United Kingdom *52°30′N 00°57′W*
97 N18 **Market Rasen** E England, United Kingdom *53°23′N 00°21′W*
123 O10 **Markha** ≈ NE Russian Federation
12 H16 **Markham** Ontario, S Canada *43°54′N 79°16′W*
25 V12 **Markham** Texas, SW USA *28°57′N 96°04′W*
186 E7 **Markham** ≈ C Papua New Guinea
195 Q11 **Markham, Mount** ▲ Antarctica *82°58′S 163°30′E*
110 M11 **Marki** Mazowieckie, C Poland *52°20′N 21°07′E*
158 F8 **Markit** Xinjiang Uygur Zizhiqu, NW China *38°55′N 77°40′E*
117 Y5 **Markivka** *Rus.* Markovka. Luhans'ka Oblast', E Ukraine *49°34′N 39°35′E*
35 Q7 **Markleeville** California, W USA *38°41′N 119°46′W*
98 L8 **Marknesse** Flevoland, N Netherlands *52°44′N 05°54′E*
79 H14 **Markounda** *var.* Marcounda. Ouham, NW Central African Republic *07°38′N 17°00′E*
Markovka *see* Markivka
123 U7 **Markovo** Chukotskiy Avtonomnyy Okrug, NE Russian Federation *64°43′N 170°13′E*
127 P8 **Marks** Saratovskaya Oblast', W Russian Federation *51°40′N 46°44′E*
22 K2 **Marks** Mississippi, S USA *34°15′N 90°16′W*
22 I7 **Marksville** Louisiana, S USA *31°07′N 92°04′W*
101 I19 **Marktheidenfeld** Bayern, C Germany *49°50′N 09°36′E*
101 J24 **Marktoberdorf** Bayern, S Germany *47°45′N 10°36′E*
101 M18 **Marktredwitz** Bayern, E Germany *50°00′N 12°04′E*
Markt-Übelbach *see* Übelbach
27 V3 **Mark Twain Lake** ▣ Missouri, C USA
Markuleshty *see* Mărculeşti
101 E14 **Marl** Nordrhein-Westfalen, W Germany *51°38′N 07°06′E*
182 E2 **Marla** South Australia *27°19′S 133°35′E*
181 Y8 **Marlborough** Queensland, E Australia *22°55′S 150°07′E*
97 M22 **Marlborough** S England, United Kingdom *51°25′N 01°45′W*
185 I15 **Marlborough** *off.* Marlborough District. ◈ *unitary authority* South Island, New Zealand
Marlborough District *see* Marlborough
103 P3 **Marle** Aisne, N France *49°44′N 03°47′E*
31 S8 **Marlette** Michigan, N USA *43°20′N 83°05′W*
25 T9 **Marlin** Texas, SW USA *31°20′N 96°55′W*
21 S5 **Marlinton** West Virginia, NE USA *38°14′N 80°06′W*
26 M12 **Marlow** Oklahoma, C USA *34°39′N 97°57′W*
155 E17 **Marmagao** Goa, W India *15°26′N 73°50′E*
Marmanda *see* Marmande
102 L13 **Marmande** *anc.* Marmanda. Lot-et-Garonne, SW France *44°30′N 00°10′E*
136 C11 **Marmara** Balıkesir, NW Turkey *40°36′N 27°34′E*
136 D11 **Marmara Denizi** *Eng.* Sea of Marmara. *sea* NW Turkey
114 N13 **Marmaraereğlisi** Tekirdağ, NW Turkey *40°59′N 27°57′E*
Marmara, Sea of *see* Marmara Denizi
136 C16 **Marmaris** Muğla, SW Turkey *36°52′N 28°17′E*
28 J6 **Marmarth** North Dakota, N USA *46°17′N 103°55′W*
21 Q5 **Marmet** West Virginia, NE USA *38°12′N 81°31′W*
106 H5 **Marmolada, Monte** ▲ N Italy *46°36′N 11°58′E*
104 M13 **Marmolejo** Andalucía, S Spain *38°03′N 04°10′W*
14 J14 **Marmora** Ontario, SE Canada *44°29′N 77°40′W*
39 Q14 **Marmot Bay** *bay* Alaska, USA
103 Q4 **Marne** ◈ *department* N France
103 Q4 **Marne** ≈ N France
137 U10 **Marneuli** *prev.* Borchalo, Sarvani. S Georgia *41°28′N 44°45′E*
78 I13 **Maro** Moyen-Chari, S Chad *08°25′N 18°46′E*
54 L12 **Maroa** Amazonas, S Venezuela *02°40′N 67°33′W*
172 J3 **Maroantsetra** Toamasina, NE Madagascar *15°23′S 49°44′E*
191 W11 **Marokau** *atoll* Îles Tuamotu, C French Polynesia
172 J5 **Marolambo** Toamasina, E Madagascar *20°03′S 48°08′E*
172 J2 **Maromokotro** ▲ N Madagascar
83 L16 **Marondera** *prev.* Marandellas. Mashonaland East, NE Zimbabwe *18°11′S 31°33′E*
55 X9 **Maroni** *Dut.* Marowijne. ≈ French Guiana/Suriname
183 V2 **Maroochydore-Mooloolaba** Queensland, E Australia *26°36′S 153°04′E*
171 N14 **Maros** Sulawesi, C Indonesia *04°59′S 119°35′E*
116 H11 **Maros** *var.* Mureş, Mureşul, *Ger.* Marosch, Mieresch. ≈ Hungary/Romania *see also* Mureş
Marosch *see* Maros/Mureş
Marosheviz *see* Toplița
Marosillye *see* Ilia
Marosludas *see* Luduş
Marosújvár/Marosújvárakna *see* Ocna Mureş
Marosvásárhely *see* Târgu Mureş
191 V14 **Marotiri** *var.* Îlots de Bass, Morotiri. *island group* Îles Australes, SW French Polynesia
78 G12 **Maroua** Extrême-Nord, N Cameroon *10°35′N 14°20′E*
55 X12 **Marouini Rivier** ≈ SE Suriname
172 I3 **Marovoay** Mahajanga, NW Madagascar *16°05′S 46°40′E*
55 W9 **Marowijne** ◈ *district* NE Suriname
Marowijne *see* Maroni
Marqakōl *see* Markakol', Ozero
193 P8 **Marquesas Fracture Zone** *tectonic feature* E Pacific Ocean
Marquesas Islands *see* Marquises, Îles
23 W17 **Marquesas Keys** *island group* Florida, SE USA
29 Y12 **Marquette** Iowa, C USA *43°02′N 91°10′W*
31 N3 **Marquette** Michigan, N USA *46°32′N 87°24′W*
103 N1 **Marquise** Pas-de-Calais, N France *50°49′N 01°42′E*
191 X7 **Marquises, Îles** *Eng.* Marquesas Islands. *island group* N French Polynesia
183 Q6 **Marra Creek** ≈ New South Wales, SE Australia
80 B10 **Marra Hills** *plateau* W Sudan
80 B11 **Marra, Jebel** ▲ W Sudan *12°59′N 24°16′E*
74 E7 **Marrakech** *var.* Marakesh, *Eng.* Marrakesh; *prev.* Morocco. W Morocco *31°39′N 07°58′W*
Marrakesh *see* Marrakech
Marrāt *see* Marāh
183 N15 **Marrawah** Tasmania, SE Australia *40°56′S 144°41′E*
182 I4 **Marree** South Australia *29°40′S 138°06′E*
81 L17 **Marrehan** ▲▲ SW Somalia
83 N17 **Marromeu** Sofala, C Mozambique *18°18′S 35°58′E*
104 J17 **Marroquí, Punta** *headland* SW Spain *36°01′N 05°39′W*
183 N8 **Marrowie Creek** *seasonal river* New South Wales, SE Australia
83 O14 **Marrupa** Niassa, N Mozambique *13°10′S 37°30′E*
182 D1 **Marryat** South Australia *26°22′S 133°22′E*
75 Y10 **Marsā al 'Alam** *var.* Marsa 'Alam. SE Egypt *25°03′N 33°44′E*
Marsa 'Alam *see* Marsā al 'Alam
75 R8 **Marsá al Burayqah** *var.* Al Burayqah. N Libya *30°21′N 19°37′E*
81 J17 **Marsabit** Eastern, N Kenya *02°20′N 37°59′E*
107 H23 **Marsala** *anc.* Lilybaeum. Sicilia, Italy, C Mediterranean Sea *37°48′N 12°26′E*
75 U7 **Marsā Maṭrūḥ** *var.* Maṭrūḥ; *anc.* Paraetonium. NW Egypt *31°21′N 27°15′E*
Marsaxlokk Bay *see* Il-Bajja ta' Marsaxlokk
65 G15 **Mars Bay** *bay* Ascension Island, C Atlantic Ocean
101 H15 **Marsberg** Nordrhein-Westfalen, W Germany *51°28′N 08°51′E*
11 R15 **Marsden** Saskatchewan, S Canada *52°50′N 109°45′W*
98 H7 **Marsdiep** *strait* NW Netherlands
103 R16 **Marseille** *Eng.* Marseilles; *anc.* Massilia. Bouches-du-Rhône, SE France *43°19′N 05°22′E*
Marseille-Marigrane *see* Provence
30 M11 **Marseilles** Illinois, N USA *41°19′N 88°42′W*
Marseilles *see* Marseille
76 J16 **Marshall** W Liberia *06°10′N 10°23′W*
39 N11 **Marshall** Alaska, USA *61°52′N 162°04′W*
27 U9 **Marshall** Arkansas, C USA *35°54′N 92°40′W*
31 N14 **Marshall** Illinois, N USA *39°23′N 87°41′W*
31 Q10 **Marshall** Michigan, N USA *42°16′N 84°57′W*
29 S9 **Marshall** Minnesota, N USA *44°26′N 95°48′W*
27 T4 **Marshall** Missouri, C USA *39°07′N 93°12′W*
21 O9 **Marshall** North Carolina, SE USA *35°48′N 82°43′W*
25 X6 **Marshall** Texas, SW USA *32°33′N 94°22′W*
189 S4 **Marshall Islands** *off.* Republic of the Marshall Islands. ◆ *republic* W Pacific Ocean
175 Q3 **Marshall Islands** *island group* W Pacific Ocean
Marshall Islands, Republic of the *see* Marshall Islands
192 K6 **Marshall Seamounts** *undersea feature* SW Pacific Ocean *10°00′N 165°00′E*
29 W13 **Marshalltown** Iowa, C USA *42°01′N 92°54′W*
19 P12 **Marshfield** Massachusetts, NE USA *42°04′N 70°40′W*
27 T7 **Marshfield** Missouri, C USA *37°20′N 92°55′W*
30 K6 **Marshfield** Wisconsin, N USA *44°41′N 90°12′W*
44 H1 **Marsh Harbour** Great Abaco, W Bahamas *26°31′N 77°03′W*
19 S3 **Mars Hill** Maine, NE USA *46°31′N 67°51′W*
21 P9 **Mars Hill** North Carolina, SE USA *35°49′N 82°33′W*
22 H10 **Marsh Island** *island* Louisiana, S USA
21 S11 **Marshville** North Carolina, SE USA *34°59′N 80°22′W*
15 W5 **Marsoui** Québec, SE Canada *49°12′N 65°58′W*
15 R8 **Mars, Rivière à** ≈ Québec, SE Canada
95 O15 **Märsta** Stockholm, C Sweden *59°37′N 17°52′E*
95 H24 **Marstal** Syddtjylland, C Denmark *54°52′N 10°32′E*
95 I19 **Marstrand** Västra Götaland, S Sweden *57°54′N 11°31′E*
25 U8 **Mart** Texas, SW USA *31°32′N 96°49′W*
Martaban *see* Mottama
Martaban, Gulf of *see* Mottama, Gulf of
107 Q19 **Martano** Puglia, SE Italy *40°12′N 18°19′E*
Martapoera *see* Martapura
169 T13 **Martapura** *prev.* Martapoera. Borneo, C Indonesia *03°25′S 114°51′E*
99 L23 **Martelange** Luxembourg, SE Belgium *49°50′N 05°43′E*
114 L7 **Marten** Ruse, N Bulgaria *43°57′N 26°08′E*
14 H10 **Marten River** Ontario, S Canada *46°43′N 79°45′W*
11 T15 **Martensville** Saskatchewan, S Canada *52°15′N 106°42′W*
Marteskirch *see* Târnăveni
Martes Tolosane *see* Martres-Tolosane
115 K25 **Mártha** Kríti, Greece, E Mediterranean Sea *35°03′N 25°22′E*
183 Q6 **Marthaguy Creek** ≈ New South Wales, SE Australia
19 P13 **Martha's Vineyard** *island* Massachusetts, NE USA
108 C11 **Martigny** Valais, SW Switzerland *46°06′N 07°04′E*
103 R16 **Martigues** Bouches-du-Rhône, SE France *43°24′N 05°03′E*
111 J19 **Martin** *Ger.* Sankt Martin, *Hung.* Turócszentmárton; *prev.* Turčianský Svätý Martin. Zilinský Kraj, N Slovakia *49°03′N 18°54′E*
28 L11 **Martin** South Dakota, N USA *43°10′N 101°43′W*
20 G8 **Martin** Tennessee, S USA *36°20′N 88°51′W*
105 S7 **Martín** ≈ E Spain
107 P18 **Martina Franca** Puglia, SE Italy *40°42′N 17°20′E*
185 M14 **Martinborough** Wellington, North Island, New Zealand *41°12′S 175°28′E*
25 S11 **Martindale** Texas, SW USA *29°49′N 97°49′W*
35 N8 **Martinez** California, W USA *38°00′N 122°12′W*
23 V3 **Martinez** Georgia, SE USA *33°31′N 82°04′W*
41 Q13 **Martínez de La Torre** Veracruz-Llave, E Mexico *20°05′N 97°02′W*
45 Y12 **Martinique** ◇ *French overseas department* E West Indies
1 O15 **Martinique** *island* E West Indies
Martinique Channel *see* Martinique Passage
45 X12 **Martinique Passage** *var.* Dominica Channel, Martinique Channel. *channel* Dominica/Martinique
23 Q5 **Martin Lake** ▣ Alabama, S USA
115 G18 **Martíno** *prev.* Martínon. Stereá Elláda, C Greece *38°34′N 23°13′E*
Martínon *see* Martíno
194 J11 **Martin Peninsula** *peninsula* Antarctica
39 S5 **Martin Point** *headland* Alaska, USA *70°06′N 143°04′W*
109 V3 **Martinsberg** Niederösterreich, NE Austria *48°23′N 15°09′E*
21 V3 **Martinsburg** West Virginia, NE USA *39°28′N 77°59′W*
31 V13 **Martins Ferry** Ohio, N USA *40°06′N 80°43′W*
Martinskirch *see* Târnăveni
31 O14 **Martinsville** Indiana, N USA *39°25′N 86°25′W*
21 S8 **Martinsville** Virginia, NE USA *36°43′N 79°53′W*
65 K16 **Martin Vaz, Ilhas** *island group* E Brazil
144 I9 **Martok** *prev.* Martuk. Aktyubinsk, NW Kazakhstan *50°45′N 56°30′E*
184 M12 **Marton** Manawatu-Wanganui, North Island, New Zealand *40°05′S 175°22′E*
105 N13 **Martos** Andalucía, S Spain *37°44′N 03°58′W*
102 M16 **Martres-Tolosane** *var.* Martes Tolosane. Haute-Garonne, S France *43°13′N 01°00′E*
92 M11 **Martti** Lappi, NE Finland *67°28′N 28°20′E*
Martuk *see* Martok
137 U12 **Martuni** E Armenia *40°07′N 45°20′E*
58 L11 **Marudá** Pará, E Brazil *05°25′S 49°04′W*
169 V6 **Marudu, Teluk** *bay* East Malaysia
149 O8 **Ma'rūf** Kandahār, SE Afghanistan *31°34′N 67°06′E*
164 H13 **Marugame** Kagawa, Shikoku, SW Japan *34°17′N 133°46′E*
185 H16 **Maruia** ≈ South Island, New Zealand
98 M6 **Marum** Groningen, NE Netherlands *53°07′N 06°16′E*
187 R13 **Marum, Mount** ▲ Ambrym, C Vanuatu *16°15′S 168°07′E*
79 P23 **Marungu** ▲▲ SE Dem. Rep. Congo
191 Y12 **Marutea** *atoll* Groupe Actéon, C French Polynesia
143 O11 **Marv Dasht** *var.* Mervdasht. Fārs, S Iran *29°50′N 52°40′E*
103 P13 **Marvejols** Lozère, S France *44°35′N 03°16′E*
27 X12 **Marvell** Arkansas, C USA *34°33′N 90°52′W*
36 L6 **Marvine, Mount** ▲ Utah, W USA *38°40′N 111°38′W*
139 Q7 **Marwānīyah** Al Anbār, C Iraq *33°58′N 42°31′E*
152 F13 **Mārwār** *var.* Kharchi, Marwar Junction. Rājasthān, N India *25°41′N 73°42′E*
Marwar Junction *see* Mārwār
11 R14 **Marwayne** Alberta, SW Canada *53°30′N 110°25′W*
146 I14 **Mary** *prev.* Merv. Mary Welaýaty, S Turkmenistan *37°25′N 61°48′E*
Mary *see* Mary Welaýaty
181 Z9 **Maryborough** Queensland, E Australia *25°32′S 152°36′E*
182 M11 **Maryborough** Victoria, SE Australia *37°05′S 143°47′E*
Maryborough *see* Port Laoise
83 G23 **Marydale** Northern Cape, W South Africa *29°25′S 22°06′E*
117 W8 **Mar"yinka** Donets'ka Oblast', E Ukraine *47°57′N 37°27′E*
Mary Island *see* Kanton
21 W4 **Maryland** *off.* State of Maryland, *also known as* America in Miniature, Cockade State, Free State, Old Line State. ◈ *state* NE USA
Maryland, State of *see* Maryland
25 P7 **Maryneal** Texas, SW USA *32°12′N 100°25′W*
97 J15 **Maryport** NW England, United Kingdom *54°45′N 03°28′W*
13 U13 **Marystown** Newfoundland, Newfoundland and Labrador, SE Canada *47°10′N 55°10′W*
36 K6 **Marysvale** Utah, W USA *38°26′N 112°14′W*
35 O6 **Marysville** California, W USA *39°07′N 121°35′W*
27 O3 **Marysville** Kansas, C USA *39°48′N 96°37′W*
31 S13 **Marysville** Michigan, N USA *42°54′N 82°29′W*
31 S9 **Marysville** Ohio, NE USA *40°13′N 83°22′W*
32 H7 **Marysville** Washington, NW USA *48°03′N 122°10′W*
27 R2 **Maryville** Missouri, C USA *40°20′N 94°53′W*
21 N9 **Maryville** Tennessee, S USA *35°45′N 83°59′W*
146 I15 **Mary Welaýaty** *var.* Mary, *Rus.* Maryyskiy Velayat. ◈ *province* S Turkmenistan
Maryyskiy Velayat *see* Mary Welaýaty
Marzūq *see* Murzuq
42 J11 **Masachapa** *var.* Puerto Masachapa. Managua, W Nicaragua *11°47′N 86°31′W*
81 G19 **Masai Mara National Reserve** *reserve* C Kenya
81 I21 **Masai Steppe** *grassland* NW Tanzania
81 F19 **Masaka** SW Uganda *0°20′S 31°46′E*
169 T15 **Masalembo Besar, Pulau** *island* S Indonesia
137 Y13 **Masallı** *Rus.* Masally. S Azerbaijan *39°03′N 48°39′E*
Masally *see* Masallı
171 N13 **Masamba** Sulawesi, C Indonesia *02°33′S 120°20′E*
Masampo *see* Masan
163 Y16 **Masan** *prev.* Masampo. S South Korea *35°11′N 128°36′E*
Masandam Peninsula *see* Musandam Peninsula
81 J25 **Masasi** Mtwara, SE Tanzania *10°43′S 38°48′E*
Masawa/Massawa *see* Mits'iwa
42 J10 **Masaya** Masaya, W Nicaragua *11°59′N 86°06′W*
42 J10 **Masaya** ◈ *department* W Nicaragua
171 P5 **Masbate** Masbate, N Philippines *12°21′N 123°34′E*
171 P5 **Masbate** *island* C Philippines
74 I6 **Mascara** *var.* Mouaskar. NW Algeria *35°20′N 00°09′E*
173 O7 **Mascarene Basin** *undersea feature* W Indian Ocean *15°00′S 56°00′E*
173 O9 **Mascarene Islands** *island group* W Indian Ocean
173 N9 **Mascarene Plain** *undersea feature* W Indian Ocean *19°00′S 52°00′E*
173 O7 **Mascarene Plateau** *undersea feature* W Indian Ocean *10°00′S 60°00′E*
194 H5 **Mascart, Cape** *headland* Adelaide Island, Antarctica
62 J10 **Mascasín, Salinas de** *salt lake* C Argentina
40 K13 **Mascota** Jalisco, C Mexico *20°31′N 104°46′W*
15 O12 **Mascouche** Québec, SE Canada *45°46′N 73°37′W*
124 J9 **Masel'gskaya** Respublika Kareliya, NW Russian Federation *63°09′N 34°22′E*
83 J23 **Maseru** ● (Lesotho) W Lesotho *29°21′S 27°35′E*
83 J23 **Maseru** ✈ W Lesotho *29°27′S 27°37′E*
Mashaba *see* Mashava
160 K14 **Mashan** *var.* Baishan. Guangxi Zhuangzu Zizhiqu, S China *23°40′N 108°10′E*
83 K17 **Mashava** *prev.* Mashaba. Masvingo, SE Zimbabwe *20°03′S 30°29′E*
143 U4 **Mashhad** *var.* Meshed. Khorāsān-Razavī, NE Iran *36°16′N 59°34′E*
165 S3 **Mashike** Hokkaidō, NE Japan *43°51′N 141°30′E*

◆ Country ● Country Capital ◇ Dependent Territory ○ Dependent Territory Capital ◈ Administrative Regions ✈ International Airport ▲ Mountain ▲▲ Mountain Range Volcano ≈ River ◎ Lake ▣ Reservoir

83 K20 **Mashishing** prev. Lydenburg. Mpumalanga, NE South Africa 25°10′S 30°29′E
Mashīz see Bardsīr
149 N14 **Mashkai** ≋ SW Pakistan
143 X13 **Māshkel** var. Rūd-i Māshkel, Rūd-e Māshkīd. ≋ Iran/Pakistan
148 K12 **Māshkel, Hāmūn-i** salt marsh SW Pakistan
Māshkel, Rūd-i/Māshkīd, Rūd-e see Māshkel
83 K15 **Mashonaland Central** ◈ province N Zimbabwe
83 K16 **Mashonaland East** ◈ province NE Zimbabwe
83 J16 **Mashonaland West** ◈ province NW Zimbabwe
Mashtagi see Maştağa
141 S14 **Masīlah, Wādī al** dry watercourse SE Yemen
79 I21 **Masi-Manimba** Bandundu, SW Dem. Rep. Congo 04°47′S 17°54′E
81 F17 **Masindi** W Uganda 01°41′N 31°45′E
81 I19 **Masinga Reservoir** ⊠ S Kenya
Masīra see Maşīrah, Jazīrat
Masira, Gulf of see Maşīrah, Khalīj
141 Y10 **Maşīrah, Jazīrat** var. Masīra. island E Oman
141 Y10 **Maşīrah, Khalīj** var. Gulf of Masira. bay E Oman
Masis see Büyükağrı Dağı
79 O19 **Masisi** Nord-Kivu, E Dem. Rep. Congo 01°25′S 28°50′E
Masjed-e Soleymān see Masjed Soleymān
142 L9 **Masjed Soleymān** var. Masjed-e Soleymān, Masjid-i Sulaiman. Khūzestān, SW Iran 31°59′N 49°18′E
Masjid-i Sulaiman see Masjed Soleymān
Maskat see Masqaţ
139 Q7 **Maskhān** Al Anbār, C Iraq 33°41′N 42°46′E
141 X8 **Maskin** var. Miskin. NW Oman 23°28′N 56°46′E
97 B17 **Mask, Lough** Ir. Loch Measca. ◎ W Ireland
114 N10 **Maslen Nos** headland E Bulgaria 42°19′N 27°47′E
172 K3 **Masoala, Tanjona** headland NE Madagascar 15°59′N 50°13′E
Masohi see Amahai
31 Q9 **Mason** Michigan, N USA 42°33′N 84°25′W
31 R14 **Mason** Ohio, N USA 39°21′N 84°18′W
25 Q10 **Mason** Texas, SW USA 30°45′N 99°15′W
21 P4 **Mason** West Virginia, NE USA 39°01′N 82°01′W
185 B25 **Mason Bay** bay Stewart Island, New Zealand
30 K13 **Mason City** Illinois, N USA 40°12′N 89°42′W
29 V12 **Mason City** Iowa, C USA 43°09′N 93°12′W
18 B16 **Masontown** Pennsylvania, NE USA 39°49′N 79°53′W
141 Y8 **Masqaţ** var. Maskat, Eng. Muscat. ● (Oman) NE Oman 23°35′N 58°36′E
106 E10 **Massa** Toscana, C Italy 44°02′N 10°07′E
18 M11 **Massachusetts** off. Commonwealth of Massachusetts, also known as Bay State, Old Bay State, Old Colony State. ◈ state NE USA
19 P11 **Massachusetts Bay** bay Massachusetts, NE USA
35 R2 **Massacre Lake** ◎ Nevada, W USA
107 O18 **Massafra** Puglia, SE Italy 40°35′N 17°08′E
108 G11 **Massagno** Ticino, S Switzerland 46°01′N 08°55′E
78 G11 **Massaguet** Chari-Baguirmi, W Chad 12°28′N 15°26′E
Massakori see Massakory
78 G10 **Massakory** var. Massakori; prev. Dagana. Chari-Baguirmi, W Chad 13°02′N 15°43′E
78 H11 **Massalassef** Chari-Baguirmi, SW Chad 11°37′N 17°09′E
106 F13 **Massa Marittima** Toscana, C Italy 43°03′N 10°55′E
82 B11 **Massangano** Cuanza Norte, NW Angola 09°40′S 14°13′E
83 M18 **Massangena** Gaza, S Mozambique 21°34′S 32°57′E
80 K9 **Massawa Channel** channel E Eritrea
18 J6 **Massena** New York, NE USA 44°55′N 74°53′W
78 H11 **Massenya** Chari-Baguirmi, SW Chad 11°21′N 16°09′E
10 I13 **Masset** Graham Island, British Columbia, SW Canada 54°00′N 132°09′W
102 L16 **Masseube** Gers, S France 43°26′N 00°33′E
14 E11 **Massey** Ontario, S Canada 46°13′N 82°06′W
103 P12 **Massiac** Cantal, C France 45°16′N 03°13′E
103 P12 **Massif Central** plateau C France
Massif de L'Isalo see Isalo
Massilia see Marseille
31 U12 **Massillon** Ohio, N USA 40°48′N 81°31′W
77 N12 **Massina** Ségou, W Mali 13°58′N 05°24′W
83 N19 **Massinga** Inhambane, SE Mozambique 23°20′S 35°25′E
83 L20 **Massingir** Gaza, SW Mozambique 23°51′S 31°58′E
195 Z10 **Masson Island** island Antarctica
Massoukou see Franceville
137 Z11 **Maştağa** Rus. Mashtagi, Mastaga. E Azerbaijan 40°31′N 50°01′E
Mastanli see Momchilgrad
184 M13 **Masterton** Wellington, North Island, New Zealand 40°56′S 175°40′E
18 M14 **Mastic** Long Island, New York, NE USA 40°48′N 72°50′W
149 O10 **Mastung** Baluchistān, SW Pakistan 29°44′N 66°56′E
119 J20 **Mastva** Rus. Mostva. ≋ SW Belarus
119 G17 **Masty** Rus. Mosty. Hrodzyenskaya Voblasts′, W Belarus 53°25′N 24°32′E
164 F12 **Masuda** Shimane, Honshū, SW Japan 34°40′N 131°50′E
92 J11 **Masugnsbyn** Norrbotten, N Sweden 67°28′N 22°01′E
Masuku see Franceville
83 K17 **Masvingo** prev. Fort Victoria, Nyanda, Victoria. Masvingo, SE Zimbabwe 20°05′S 30°50′E
83 K18 **Masvingo** prev. Victoria. ◈ province SE Zimbabwe
138 H5 **Maşyāf** Fr. Misiaf. Ḩamāh, C Syria 35°04′N 36°21′E
110 E9 **Maszewo** Zachodniopomorskie, NW Poland 53°29′N 15°01′E
83 I17 **Matabeleland North** ◈ province W Zimbabwe
83 J18 **Matabeleland South** ◈ province S Zimbabwe
82 O13 **Mataca** Niassa, N Mozambique 12°27′S 36°13′E
14 G8 **Matachewan** Ontario, S Canada 47°58′N 80°37′W
163 Q8 **Matad** var. Dzüünbulag. Dornod, E Mongolia 46°48′N 115°21′E
79 F22 **Matadi** Bas-Congo, W Dem. Rep. Congo 05°49′S 13°31′E
25 O4 **Matador** Texas, SW USA 34°01′N 100°50′W
42 J9 **Matagalpa** Matagalpa, C Nicaragua 12°53′N 85°56′W
42 K9 **Matagalpa** ◈ department W Nicaragua
12 I12 **Matagami** Québec, S Canada 49°47′N 77°38′W
25 U13 **Matagorda** Texas, SW USA 28°40′N 96°57′W
25 U13 **Matagorda Bay** inlet Texas, SW USA
25 U14 **Matagorda Island** island Texas, SW USA
25 V13 **Matagorda Peninsula** headland Texas, SW USA 28°34′N 96°01′W
191 Q8 **Mataiea** Tahiti, W French Polynesia 17°46′S 149°25′W
191 T9 **Mataiva** atoll Îles Tuamotu, C French Polynesia
183 O7 **Matakana** New South Wales, SE Australia 32°59′S 145°53′E
184 N7 **Matakana Island** island NE New Zealand
83 C15 **Matala** Huíla, SW Angola 14°45′S 15°02′E
190 G12 **Matala'a Pointe** headland Île Uvea, N Wallis and Futuna 13°20′S 176°08′W
155 K25 **Matale** Central Province, C Sri Lanka 07°29′N 80°38′E
190 E12 **Matalesina, Pointe** headland Île Alofi, W Wallis and Futuna
76 I10 **Matam** NE Senegal 15°40′N 13°18′W
184 M8 **Matamata** Waikato, North Island, New Zealand 37°49′S 175°45′E
77 V12 **Matamey** Zinder, S Niger 13°27′N 08°27′E
40 L8 **Matamoros** Coahuila, NE Mexico 25°34′N 103°13′W
41 P15 **Matamoros** var. Izúcar de Matamoros. Puebla, S Mexico 18°38′N 98°30′W
41 Q8 **Matamoros** Tamaulipas, C Mexico 25°50′N 97°31′W
75 S13 **Ma'ţan as Sārah** SE Libya 21°45′N 21°55′E
82 J12 **Matanda** Luapula, N Zambia 11°24′S 28°25′E
81 J24 **Matandu** ≋ S Tanzania
15 V6 **Matane** Québec, SE Canada 48°50′N 67°31′W
15 V6 **Matane** ≋ Québec, SE Canada
77 S12 **Matankari** Dosso, SW Niger 13°39′N 04°03′E
39 R11 **Matanuska River** ≋ Alaska, USA
54 G7 **Matanza** Santander, N Colombia 07°22′N 73°02′W
44 D4 **Matanzas** Matanzas, NW Cuba 23°N 81°32′W
15 V7 **Matapédia** ≋ Québec, SE Canada
15 V6 **Matapédia, Lac** ◎ Québec, SE Canada
190 B17 **Mata Point** headland SE Niue 19°07′S 169°51′E
190 D12 **Matapu, Pointe** headland Île Futuna, W Wallis and Futuna
62 G12 **Mataquito, Río** ≋ C Chile
155 K26 **Matara** Southern Province, S Sri Lanka 05°58′N 80°33′E
115 D18 **Matarágka** var. Mataránga. Dytikí Elláda, C Greece 38°32′N 21°28′E
171 K16 **Mataram** Pulau Lombok, C Indonesia 08°36′S 116°07′E
Mataránga see Matarágka
181 Q3 **Mataranka** Northern Territory, N Australia 14°55′S 133°03′E
105 W6 **Mataró** anc. Illuro. Cataluña, E Spain 41°32′N 02°27′E
184 O8 **Matata** Bay of Plenty, North Island, New Zealand 37°54′S 176°45′E
192 K16 **Matātula, Cape** headland Tutuila, W American Samoa 14°15′S 170°35′W
185 D24 **Mataura** Southland, South Island, New Zealand 46°12′S 168°53′E
185 D24 **Mataura** ≋ South Island, New Zealand
Mata Uta see Matā'utu
192 H16 **Matāutu** Upolu, C Samoa 13°57′S 171°55′W
190 G11 **Matā'utu** var. Mata Uta. ○ (Wallis and Futuna) Île Uvea, Wallis and Futuna 13°22′S 176°12′W
190 G12 **Matā'utu, Baie de** bay Île Uvea, Wallis and Futuna
191 P7 **Matavai, Baie de** bay Tahiti, W French Polynesia
190 I16 **Matavera** Rarotonga, S Cook Islands 21°13′S 159°44′W
191 V16 **Mataveri** Easter Island, Chile, E Pacific Ocean 27°10′S 109°27′W
191 V17 **Mataveri** ✈ (Easter Island) Easter Island, Chile, E Pacific Ocean 27°10′S 109°27′W
184 P9 **Matawai** Gisborne, North Island, New Zealand 38°23′S 177°31′E
15 O10 **Matawin** ≋ Québec, SE Canada
145 V13 **Matay** Almaty, SE Kazakhstan 45°53′N 78°45′E
14 K8 **Matchi-Manitou, Lac** ◎ Québec, SE Canada
41 O10 **Matehuala** San Luis Potosí, C Mexico 23°40′N 100°40′W
45 V13 **Matelot** Trinidad, Trinidad and Tobago 10°48′N 61°06′W
83 M15 **Matenge** Tete, NW Mozambique 15°22′S 33°47′E
107 O18 **Matera** Basilicata, S Italy 40°39′N 16°35′E
111 O21 **Mátészalka** Szabolcs-Szatmár-Bereg, E Hungary 47°58′N 22°17′E
93 H17 **Matfors** Västernorrland, C Sweden 62°21′N 17°02′E
102 K11 **Matha** Charente-Maritime, W France 45°50′N 00°13′W
0 F15 **Mathematicians Seamounts** undersea feature E Pacific Ocean 15°00′N 111°00′W
21 X6 **Mathews** Virginia, NE USA 37°26′N 76°20′W
25 S14 **Mathis** Texas, SW USA 28°05′N 97°49′W
152 J11 **Mathura** prev. Muttra. Uttar Pradesh, N India 27°30′N 77°42′E
Mathurai see Madurai
171 R7 **Mati** Mindanao, S Philippines 06°58′N 126°11′E
Matianus see Orūmīyeh, Daryācheh-ye
Matiara see Matiāri
149 Q15 **Matiāri** var. Matiara. Sind, SE Pakistan 25°38′N 68°29′E
41 S16 **Matías Romero** Oaxaca, SE Mexico 16°53′N 95°02′W
43 O13 **Matina** Limón, E Costa Rica 10°06′N 83°18′W
14 D10 **Matinenda Lake** ◎ Ontario, S Canada
19 R8 **Matinicus Island** island Maine, NE USA
Matisco/Matisco Ædourum see Mâcon
113 K19 **Matit, Lumi i** ≋ NW Albania
149 Q16 **Mātli** Sind, SE Pakistan 25°06′N 68°37′E
97 M18 **Matlock** C England, United Kingdom 53°08′N 01°32′W
59 F18 **Mato Grosso** prev. Vila Bela da Santissima Trindade. Mato Grosso, W Brazil 14°53′S 59°58′W
59 G17 **Mato Grosso** off. Estado de Mato Grosso; prev. Matto Grosso. ◈ state W Brazil
60 H8 **Mato Grosso do Sul** off. Estado de Mato Grosso do Sul. ◈ state S Brazil
Mato Grosso do Sul, Estado de see Mato Grosso do Sul
Mato Grosso, Estado de see Mato Grosso
59 I18 **Mato Grosso, Planalto de** plateau C Brazil
83 L21 **Matola** Maputo, S Mozambique 25°57′S 32°27′E
104 G6 **Matosinhos** prev. Matozinhos. Porto, NW Portugal 41°11′N 08°42′W
Matou see Pingguo
55 Z10 **Matoury** NE French Guiana 04°49′N 52°17′W
Matozinhos see Matosinhos
111 L21 **Mátra** ▲▲ N Hungary
141 Y8 **Maţraḩ** var. Mutrah. NE Oman 23°35′N 58°31′E
116 L12 **Mătrăşeşti** Vrancea, E Romania 45°53′N 27°14′E
108 M8 **Matrei am Brenner** Tirol, W Austria 47°09′N 11°28′E
109 P8 **Matrei in Osttirol** Tirol, W Austria 47°04′N 12°31′E
76 I15 **Matru** SW Sierra Leone 07°37′N 12°08′W
Maţrūḩ see Marsā Maţrūḩ
165 U16 **Matsubara** var. Matubara. Kagoshima, Tokuno-shima, SW Japan 32°58′N 129°56′E
161 S12 **Matsu Dao** var. Mazu Tao; prev. Matsu Tao. island NW Taiwan
164 G12 **Matsue** var. Matsuye, Matue. Shimane, Honshū, SW Japan 35°27′N 133°04′E
165 Q6 **Matsumae** Hokkaidō, NE Japan 41°27′N 140°04′E
164 M12 **Matsumoto** var. Matumoto. Nagano, Honshū, S Japan 36°18′N 137°58′E
164 K14 **Matsusaka** var. Matsuzaka, Matusaka. Mie, Honshū, SW Japan 34°33′N 136°31′E
Matsu Tao see Matsu Dao
Matsutō see Mattō
164 F14 **Matsuyama** var. Matuyama. Ehime, Shikoku, SW Japan 33°50′N 132°47′E
Matsuye see Matsue
Matsuzaka see Matsusaka
164 M14 **Matsuzaki** Shizuoka, Honshū, S Japan 34°43′N 138°45′E
14 F8 **Mattagami** ≋ Ontario, S Canada
14 F8 **Mattagami Lake** ◎ Ontario, S Canada
62 K12 **Mattaldi** Córdoba, C Argentina 34°26′S 64°14′W
21 Y9 **Mattamuskeet, Lake** ◎ North Carolina, SE USA
21 W6 **Mattaponi River** ≋ Virginia, NE USA
15 I11 **Mattawa** Ontario, SE Canada 46°19′N 78°42′W
14 I11 **Mattawa** ≋ Ontario, SE Canada
19 S5 **Mattawamkeag** Maine, NE USA 45°30′N 68°20′W
19 S4 **Mattawamkeag Lake** ◎ Maine, NE USA
108 D11 **Matterhorn** It. Monte Cervino. ▲ Italy/Switzerland 45°58′N 07°36′E see also Cervino, Monte
32 L12 **Matterhorn** var. Sacajawea Peak. ▲ Oregon, NW USA 45°12′N 117°18′W
35 W1 **Matterhorn** ▲ Nevada, W USA 41°48′N 115°22′W
Matterhorn see Cervino, Monte
35 R8 **Matterhorn Peak** ▲ California, W USA 38°06′N 119°19′W
109 Y5 **Mattersburg** Burgenland, E Austria 47°45′N 16°24′E
108 E11 **Matter Vispa** ≋ S Switzerland
55 R7 **Matthews Ridge** N Guyana 07°30′N 60°07′W
44 K7 **Matthew Town** Great Inagua, S Bahamas 20°56′N 73°41′W
109 Q4 **Mattighofen** Oberösterreich, NW Austria 48°07′N 13°09′E
107 N16 **Mattinata** Puglia, SE Italy 41°41′N 16°01′E
141 T9 **Maţţī, Sabkhat** salt flat Saudi Arabia/United Arab Emirates
18 M14 **Mattituck** Long Island, New York, NE USA 40°59′N 72°31′W
164 L11 **Mattō** var. Hakusan, Matsutō. Ishikawa, Honshū, SW Japan 36°31′N 136°34′E
Matto Grosso see Mato Grosso
30 M14 **Mattoon** Illinois, N USA 39°28′N 88°22′W
57 L16 **Mattos, Río** ≋ C Bolivia
Mattu see Metu
169 R9 **Matu** Sarawak, East Malaysia 02°39′N 111°31′E
Matubara see Matsubara
57 E14 **Matucana** Lima, W Peru 11°54′S 76°25′W
Matue see Matsue
187 Y15 **Matuku** island S Fiji
112 B9 **Matulji** Primorje-Gorski Kotar, NW Croatia 45°21′N 14°18′E
Matumoto see Matsumoto
55 P5 **Maturín** Monagas, NE Venezuela 09°45′N 63°10′W
Matusaka see Matsusaka
Matuyama see Matsuyama
126 K11 **Matveyev Kurgan** Rostovskaya Oblast', SW Russian Federation 47°31′N 38°55′E
127 O8 **Matyshevo** Volgogradskaya Oblast', SW Russian Federation 50°53′N 44°09′E
153 O13 **Mau** var. Maunāth Bhanjan. Uttar Pradesh, N India 25°57′N 83°33′E
83 O14 **Maúa** Niassa, N Mozambique 13°53′S 37°10′E
102 M17 **Maubermé, Pic de** var. Tuc de Moubermé, Sp. Pico Mauberme; prev. Tuc de Maubermé. ▲ France/Spain 42°48′N 00°54′E see also Moubermé, Tuc de
Maubermé, Pic de see Moubermé, Tuc de
Mauberme, Pico see Maubermé, Pic de/Moubermé, Tuc de
Maubermé, Tuc de see Maubermé, Pic de/Moubermé, Tuc de
103 Q2 **Maubeuge** Nord, N France 50°16′N 04°00′E
166 L8 **Maubin** Ayeyarwady, SW Myanmar (Burma) 16°44′N 95°37′E
152 L13 **Maudaha** Uttar Pradesh, N India 25°41′N 80°07′E
183 N9 **Maude** New South Wales, SE Australia 34°30′S 144°20′E
195 P3 **Maudheimvidda** physical region Antarctica
65 N22 **Maud Rise** undersea feature S Atlantic Ocean
109 Q4 **Mauerkirchen** Oberösterreich, NW Austria 48°11′N 13°08′E
Mauersee see Mamry, Jezioro
188 K2 **Maug Islands** island group N Northern Mariana Islands
103 Q15 **Mauguio** Hérault, S France 43°37′N 04°01′E
193 N5 **Maui** island Hawai'i, USA, C Pacific Ocean
190 M16 **Mauke** atoll S Cook Islands
62 G13 **Maule** var. Región del Maule. ◈ region C Chile
102 J9 **Mauléon** Deux-Sèvres, W France 46°55′N 00°45′W
102 J16 **Mauléon-Licharre** Pyrénées-Atlantiques, SW France 43°14′N 00°51′W
Maule, Región del see Maule
62 G13 **Maule, Río** ≋ C Chile
63 G17 **Maullín** Los Lagos, S Chile 41°38′S 73°35′W
31 R11 **Maumee** Ohio, N USA 41°34′N 83°40′W
31 Q12 **Maumee River** ≋ Indiana/Ohio, N USA
27 U11 **Maumelle** Arkansas, C USA 34°51′N 92°24′W
27 T11 **Maumelle, Lake** ⊠ Arkansas, C USA
171 O16 **Maumere** prev. Maoemere. Flores, S Indonesia 08°35′S 122°13′E
83 G17 **Maun** North-West, C Botswana 20°01′S 23°28′E
Maunāth Bhanjan see Mau
Maunawai see Waimea
190 H16 **Maungaroa** ▲ Rarotonga, S Cook Islands 21°13′S 159°48′W
184 K3 **Maungatapere** Northland, North Island, New Zealand 35°46′S 174°10′E
184 K4 **Maungaturoto** Northland, North Island, New Zealand 36°06′S 174°21′E
166 J5 **Maungdaw** var. Zullapara. Rakhine State, W Myanmar (Burma) 20°51′N 92°23′E
191 R10 **Maupiti** var. Maurua. island Îles Sous le Vent, W French Polynesia
152 K14 **Mau Rānīpur** Uttar Pradesh, N India 25°14′N 79°07′E
22 K9 **Maurepas, Lake** ◎ Louisiana, S USA
103 T16 **Maures** ▲▲ SE France
103 O12 **Mauriac** Cantal, C France 45°13′N 02°21′E
Maurice see Mauritius
65 J20 **Maurice Ewing Bank** undersea feature SW Atlantic Ocean 51°00′S 43°00′W
182 C4 **Maurice, Lake** salt lake South Australia
18 I17 **Maurice River** ≋ New Jersey, NE USA
25 Y10 **Mauriceville** Texas, SW USA 30°13′N 93°52′W
98 K12 **Maurik** Gelderland, C Netherlands 51°57′N 05°25′E
76 H8 **Mauritania** off. Islamic Republic of Mauritania, Ar. Mūrītānīyah. ◆ republic W Africa
Mauritania, Islamic Republic of see Mauritania
173 W15 **Mauritius** off. Republic of Mauritius, Fr. Maurice. ◆ republic W Indian Ocean
128 M17 **Mauritius** island W Indian Ocean
Mauritius, Republic of see Mauritius
173 N9 **Mauritius Trench** undersea feature W Indian Ocean
102 H6 **Mauron** Morbihan, NW France 48°06′N 02°16′W
103 N13 **Maurs** Cantal, C France 44°45′N 02°12′E
Maurua see Maupiti
Maury Mid-Ocean Channel see Maury Seachannel
64 L6 **Maury Seachannel** var. Maury Mid-Ocean Channel. undersea feature N Atlantic Ocean 56°33′N 24°00′W
30 K8 **Mauston** Wisconsin, N USA 43°46′N 90°06′W
109 R8 **Mauterndorf** Salzburg, NW Austria 47°09′N 13°39′E
109 T4 **Mauthausen** Oberösterreich, N Austria 48°13′N 14°30′E
109 Q9 **Mauthen** Kärnten, S Austria 46°39′N 12°58′E
83 F15 **Mavinga** Cuando Cubango, SE Angola 15°44′S 20°21′E
83 M17 **Mavita** Manica, W Mozambique 19°31′S 33°09′E
115 K22 **Mavrópetra, Akrotírio** headland Santoríni, Kykládes, Greece, Aegean Sea 36°28′N 25°22′E
115 F16 **Mavrovoúni** ▲ C Greece 39°37′N 22°45′E
184 Q8 **Mawhai Point** headland North Island, New Zealand 38°08′S 178°24′E
166 L3 **Mawlaik** Sagaing, Myanmar (Burma) 23°40′N 94°26′E
Mawlamyaing see Mawlamyine
166 M9 **Mawlamyine** var. Mawlamyaing, Moulmein. Mon State, S Myanmar (Burma) 16°30′N 97°39′E
166 L8 **Mawlamyinegyunn** var. Moulmeingyun. Ayeyarwady, SW Myanmar (Burma) 16°24′N 95°15′E
141 N14 **Mawr, Wādī** dry watercourse NW Yemen
195 X5 **Mawson** Australian research station Antarctica 67°24′S 63°16′E
195 X5 **Mawson Coast** physical region Antarctica
28 M4 **Max** North Dakota, N USA 47°48′N 101°18′W
41 W12 **Maxcanú** Yucatán, SE Mexico 20°35′N 90°00′W
Maxesibebi see Mount Ayliff
109 Q5 **Maxglan** ✈ (Salzburg) Salzburg, W Austria 47°46′N 13°00′E
93 K16 **Maxmo** Fin. Maksamaa. Länsi-Suomi, W Finland 63°13′N 22°04′E
21 T11 **Maxton** North Carolina, SE USA 34°47′N 79°34′W
25 R8 **May** Texas, SW USA 31°58′N 98°54′W
186 B6 **May** ≋ NW Papua New Guinea
123 R10 **Maya** ≋ E Russian Federation
151 Q19 **Māyābandar** Andaman and Nicobar Islands, India, E Indian Ocean 12°43′N 92°52′E
Mayadin see Al Mayādīn
44 L5 **Mayaguana** island SE Bahamas
44 L5 **Mayaguana Passage** passage SE Bahamas
45 S6 **Mayagüez** W Puerto Rico 18°12′N 67°08′W
45 R6 **Mayagüez, Bahía de** bay W Puerto Rico
Mayals see Maials
79 G20 **Mayama** Pool, SE Congo 03°50′S 14°52′E
37 V8 **Maya, Mesa De** ▲ Colorado, C USA 37°06′N 103°30′W
143 R4 **Mayamey** Semnān, N Iran 36°50′N 55°50′E
42 F3 **Maya Mountains** Sp. Montañas Mayas. ▲▲ Belize/Guatemala
44 I7 **Mayarí** Holguín, E Cuba 20°41′N 75°42′W
Mayas, Montañas see Maya Mountains
18 I17 **May, Cape** headland New Jersey, NE USA 38°55′N 74°57′W
80 J11 **Maych'ew** var. Mai Chio, It. Mai Ceu. Tigray, N Ethiopia 12°55′N 39°30′E
138 I2 **Maydān Ikbiz** Ḩalab, N Syria 36°51′N 36°40′E
Maydān Shahr see Maīdān Shahr
80 O12 **Maydh** Sanaag, N Somalia 10°57′N 47°07′E
Maydī see Mīdī
Mayebashi see Maebashi
Mayence see Mainz
102 K6 **Mayenne** Mayenne, NW France 48°18′N 00°37′W
102 J6 **Mayenne** ◈ department NW France
102 J7 **Mayenne** ≋ N France
36 K12 **Mayer** Arizona, SW USA 34°25′N 112°15′W
22 J4 **Mayersville** Mississippi, S USA 32°54′N 91°04′W
11 P14 **Mayerthorpe** Alberta, SW Canada 53°59′N 115°06′W
21 S12 **Mayesville** South Carolina, SE USA 34°00′N 80°10′W
185 G19 **Mayfield** Canterbury, South Island, New Zealand 43°50′S 171°24′E
33 N14 **Mayfield** Idaho, NW USA 43°24′N 115°56′W
20 G7 **Mayfield** Kentucky, S USA 36°45′N 88°40′W
36 L5 **Mayfield** Utah, W USA 39°06′N 111°42′W
Mayhan see Sant
37 T14 **Mayhill** New Mexico, SW USA 32°52′N 105°28′W
Maykain see Maykayyn
145 T9 **Maykayyn** Kaz. Mayqayyng prev. Maykain. Pavlodar, NE Kazakhstan 51°27′N 75°52′E
126 L14 **Maykop** Respublika Adygeya, SW Russian Federation 44°36′N 40°07′E
Maylibash see Maylybas
Mayli-Say see Mayluu-Suu
147 T9 **Mayluu-Suu** prev. Mayli-Say, Kir. Mayly-Say. Dzhalal-Abadskaya Oblast', W Kyrgyzstan 41°16′N 72°27′E
144 L14 **Maylybas** prev. Maylibash. Kzylorda, S Kazakhstan 45°51′N 62°37′E
Mayly-Say see Mayluu-Suu
Maymana see Meymaneh
Maymyo see Pyin-Oo-Lwin
123 V7 **Mayn** ≋ NE Russian Federation
127 Q5 **Mayna** Ul'yanovskaya Oblast', W Russian Federation 54°04′N 47°20′E
21 N8 **Maynardville** Tennessee, S USA 36°15′N 83°48′W
14 J13 **Maynooth** Ontario, SE Canada 45°14′N 77°54′W
10 I6 **Mayo** Yukon Territory, NW Canada 63°37′N 135°48′W
23 U9 **Mayo** Florida, SE USA 30°03′N 83°10′W
97 B16 **Mayo** Ir. Maigh Eo. cultural region W Ireland
Mayo see Maio
78 G12 **Mayo-Kébbi** off. Préfecture du Mayo-Kébbu, var. Mayo-Kébi. ◈ prefecture SW Chad
Mayo-Kébbu, Préfecture du see Mayo-Kébbi
Mayo-Kébi see Mayo-Kébbi
79 F19 **Mayoko** Niari, SW Congo 02°19′S 12°47′E
171 P4 **Mayon Volcano** ⚠ Luzon, N Philippines 13°15′N 123°41′E
61 A24 **Mayor Buratovich** Buenos Aires, E Argentina 39°15′S 62°35′W
104 L4 **Mayorga** Castilla y León, N Spain 42°10′N 05°16′W
184 N6 **Mayor Island** island NE New Zealand
Mayor Pablo Lagerenza see Capitán Pablo Lagerenza
173 I14 **Mayotte** ◇ French territorial collectivity E Africa
Mayoumba see Mayumba
44 J13 **May Pen** C Jamaica 17°58′N 77°15′W
Mayqayyng see Maykayyn
171 O1 **Mayraira Point** headland Luzon, N Philippines 18°36′N 120°47′E
109 N8 **Mayrhofen** Tirol, W Austria 47°09′N 11°52′E
186 A6 **May River** East Sepik, NW Papua New Guinea 04°24′S 141°52′E
123 R13 **Mayskiy** Amurskaya Oblast', SE Russian Federation 52°13′N 129°30′E
127 O15 **Mayskiy** Kabardino-Balkarskaya Respublika, SW Russian Federation 43°37′N 44°04′E
145 U9 **Mayskoye** Pavlodar, NE Kazakhstan 50°55′N 78°11′E
18 J17 **Mays Landing** New Jersey, NE USA 39°27′N 74°44′W
21 N4 **Maysville** Kentucky, S USA 38°38′N 83°46′W
27 R2 **Maysville** Missouri, C USA 39°53′N 94°21′W
79 D20 **Mayumba** var. Mayoumba. Nyanga, S Gabon 03°23′S 10°38′E
31 S8 **Mayville** Michigan, N USA 43°18′N 83°16′W
18 C11 **Mayville** New York, NE USA 42°15′N 79°32′W
29 Q4 **Mayville** North Dakota, N USA 47°27′N 97°17′W
Mayyali see Mahe
Mayyit, Al Baḩr al see Dead Sea
83 J15 **Mazabuka** Southern, S Zambia 15°52′S 27°46′E
Mazaca see Kayseri
Mazagan see El-Jadida
32 J7 **Mazama** Washington, NW USA 48°34′N 120°26′W
103 O15 **Mazamet** Tarn, S France 43°30′N 02°21′E
143 O4 **Māzandarān** off. Ostān-e Māzandarān. ◈ province N Iran
Māzandarān, Ostān-e see Māzandarān
156 F7 **Mazar** Xinjiang Uygur Zizhiqu, NW China 36°28′N 77°00′E
107 H24 **Mazara del Vallo** Sicilia, Italy, C Mediterranean Sea 37°39′N 12°36′E
149 O2 **Mazār-e Sharīf** var. Mazār-i Sharif. Balkh, N Afghanistan 36°44′N 67°06′E
Mazār-i Sharif see Mazār-e Sharīf
105 R13 **Mazarrón** Murcia, SE Spain 37°36′N 01°19′W
105 R14 **Mazarrón, Golfo de** gulf SE Spain
55 S9 **Mazaruni River** ≋ N Guyana
42 B6 **Mazatenango** Suchitepéquez, SW Guatemala 14°31′N 91°30′W
40 I10 **Mazatlán** Sinaloa, C Mexico 23°15′N 106°24′W
36 L12 **Mazatzal Mountains** ▲▲ Arizona, SW USA
118 D10 **Mažeikiai** Telšiai, NW Lithuania 56°19′N 22°22′E
118 D7 **Mazirbe** NW Latvia 57°39′N 22°16′E
40 G5 **Mazocahui** Sonora, NW Mexico 29°32′N 110°09′W
57 I18 **Mazocruz** Puno, S Peru 16°41′S 69°42′W
Mazoe, Rio see Mazowe
79 N21 **Mazomeno** Maniema, E Dem. Rep. Congo 04°54′S 27°13′E
159 Q6 **Mazong Shan** ▲ N China 41°40′N 97°10′E
83 L16 **Mazowe** var. Rio Mazoe. ≋ Mozambique/Zimbabwe
110 M11 **Mazowieckie** ◈ province C Poland
Mazra'a see Al Mazra'ah
138 G6 **Mazraat Kfar Debiâne** C Lebanon 34°00′N 35°51′E
118 H7 **Mazsalaca** Est. Väike-Salatsi, Ger. Salisburg. N Latvia 57°52′N 25°03′E
110 L9 **Mazury** physical region NE Poland
Mazu Tao see Matsu Dao
119 M20 **Mazyr** Rus. Mozyr'. Homyel'skaya Voblasts', SE Belarus 52°04′N 29°15′E
107 K25 **Mazzarino** Sicilia, Italy, C Mediterranean Sea 37°18′N 14°13′E
Mba see Ba
83 L21 **Mbabane** ● (Swaziland) NW Swaziland 26°24′S 31°13′E
Mbacké see Mbaké
77 N16 **Mbahiakro** E Ivory Coast 07°33′N 04°19′W
79 I16 **Mbaïki** var. M'Baiki. Lobaye, SW Central African Republic 03°52′N 17°58′E
M'Baiki see Mbaïki
79 F14 **Mbakaou, Lac de** ◎ C Cameroon
76 G11 **Mbaké** var. Mbacké. W Senegal 14°47′N 15°54′W
82 L11 **Mbala** prev. Abercorn. Northern, NE Zambia 08°50′S 31°23′E
83 J18 **Mbalabala** prev. Balla Balla. Matabeleland South, SW Zimbabwe 20°27′S 29°03′E
81 G18 **Mbale** E Uganda 01°04′N 34°12′E
79 E16 **Mbalmayo** var. M'Balmayo. Centre, S Cameroon 03°30′N 11°31′E
M'Balmayo see Mbalmayo
81 H25 **Mbamba Bay** Ruvuma, S Tanzania 11°15′S 34°44′E
79 I18 **Mbandaka** prev. Coquilhatville. Equateur, NW Dem. Rep. Congo 00°07′N 18°12′E
82 B9 **M'Banza Congo** var. Mbanza Congo; prev. São Salvador, São Salvador do Congo. Dem. Rep. Congo, NW Angola 06°11′S 14°16′E
79 G21 **Mbanza-Ngungu** Bas-Congo, W Dem. Rep. Congo 05°19′S 14°45′E
67 V11 **Mbarangandu** ≋ E Tanzania
81 E19 **Mbarara** SW Uganda 00°36′S 30°40′E
79 L15 **Mbari** ≋ SE Central African Republic
81 I24 **Mbarika Mountains** ▲▲ S Tanzania
78 F13 **Mbé** Nord, N Cameroon 07°51′N 13°36′E
81 J24 **Mbemkuru** var. Mbwemkuru. ≋ S Tanzania
Mbengga see Beqa
172 H13 **Mbéni** Grande Comore, NW Comoros
83 K18 **Mberengwa** Midlands, S Zimbabwe 20°29′S 29°55′E
81 G24 **Mbeya** Mbeya, SW Tanzania 08°54′S 33°29′E
81 G23 **Mbeya** ◈ region S Tanzania
83 J24 **Mbhashe** prev. Mbashe. ≋ S South Africa
79 E19 **Mbigou** Ngounié, C Gabon 01°54′S 12°00′E
Mbilua see Vella Lavella
79 F19 **Mbinda** Niari, SW Congo 02°07′S 12°52′E
79 D17 **Mbini** W Equatorial Guinea 01°34′N 09°39′E
Mbini see Uolo, Río
83 L18 **Mbizi** Masvingo, SE Zimbabwe 21°23′S 30°54′E
81 G23 **Mbogo** Mbeya, W Tanzania 07°24′S 33°26′E
79 N15 **Mboki** Haut-Mbomou, SE Central African Republic 05°18′N 25°52′E
79 G18 **Mbomo** Cuvette, NW Congo 0°25′N 14°42′E
79 L15 **Mbomou** ◈ prefecture SE Central African Republic
Mbomou/M'Bomu/Mbomu see Bomu
76 F11 **Mbour** W Senegal 14°22′N 16°54′W
76 I10 **Mbout** Gorgol, S Mauritania 16°02′N 12°38′W
79 J14 **Mbrès** var. Mbrés. Nana-Grébizi, C Central African Republic 06°40′N 19°46′E
Mbrés see Mbrès
79 L22 **Mbuji-Mayi** prev. Bakwanga. Kasai-Oriental, S Dem. Rep. Congo 06°05′S 23°30′E
81 H21 **Mbulu** Manyara, N Tanzania 03°45′S 35°33′E
186 E5 **M'bunai** var. Bunai. Manus Island, N Papua New Guinea 02°08′S 147°13′E
62 N8 **Mburucuyá** Corrientes, NE Argentina 28°03′S 58°15′W
Mbutha see Buca
Mbwemkuru see Mbemkuru
81 G21 **Mbwikwe** Singida, C Tanzania 05°19′S 34°09′E
13 O15 **McAdam** New Brunswick, SE Canada 45°34′N 67°20′W
25 O5 **McAdoo** Texas, SW USA 33°41′N 100°58′W
35 V2 **McAfee Peak** ▲ Nevada, W USA 41°31′N 115°57′W
27 P11 **McAlester** Oklahoma, C USA 34°56′N 95°46′W
25 S17 **McAllen** Texas, SW USA 26°12′N 98°14′W
21 S11 **McBee** South Carolina, SE USA 34°30′N 80°12′W
11 N14 **McBride** British Columbia, SW Canada 53°21′N 120°19′W
24 M9 **McCamey** Texas, SW USA 31°08′N 102°13′W
33 R15 **McCammon** Idaho, NW USA 42°38′N 112°10′W
35 X11 **McCarran** ✈ (Las Vegas) Nevada, W USA 36°04′N 115°07′W
39 T11 **McCarthy** Alaska, USA 61°25′N 142°55′W
30 M5 **McCaslin Mountain** hill Wisconsin, N USA
25 O2 **McClellan Creek** ≋ Texas, SW USA
21 T14 **McClellanville** South Carolina, SE USA 33°07′N 79°27′W
195 R12 **McClintock, Mount** ▲ Antarctica 80°09′S 156°42′E
35 N2 **McCloud** California, W USA 41°15′N 122°09′W
35 N3 **McCloud River** ≋ California, W USA
35 Q9 **McClure, Lake** ⊠ California, W USA
197 O8 **McClure Strait** strait Northwest Territories, N Canada
29 N4 **McClusky** North Dakota, N USA 47°27′N 100°25′W
21 T11 **McColl** South Carolina, SE USA 34°40′N 79°33′W
22 K7 **McComb** Mississippi, S USA 31°14′N 90°27′W
18 E16 **McConnellsburg** Pennsylvania, NE USA 39°56′N 78°00′W
31 T14 **McConnelsville** Ohio, N USA 39°39′N 81°51′W
28 M17 **McCook** Nebraska, C USA 40°12′N 100°38′W
21 P13 **McCormick** South Carolina, SE USA 33°55′N 82°19′W
11 W16 **McCreary** Manitoba, S Canada 50°48′N 99°34′W
27 W11 **McCrory** Arkansas, C USA 35°15′N 91°12′W
25 T10 **McDade** Texas, SW USA 30°15′N 97°15′W
23 O8 **McDavid** Florida, SE USA 30°51′N 87°18′W
35 T1 **McDermitt** Nevada, W USA 41°57′N 117°43′W
23 S4 **McDonough** Georgia, SE USA 33°27′N 84°09′W
36 L12 **McDowell Mountains** ▲▲ Arizona, SW USA
20 H8 **McEwen** Tennessee, S USA 36°06′N 87°37′W
35 R12 **McFarland** California, W USA 35°41′N 119°14′W
Mcfarlane, Lake see Macfarlane, Lake
27 P12 **McGee Creek Lake** ⊠ Oklahoma, C USA
27 W13 **McGehee** Arkansas, C USA 33°37′N 91°24′W
35 X5 **McGill** Nevada, USA 39°24′N 114°46′W

14 K11 McGillivray, Lac ◎ Québec, SE Canada
39 P10 McGrath Alaska, USA 62°57′N 155°36′W
25 T8 McGregor Texas, SW USA 31°26′N 97°24′W
33 O12 McGuire, Mount ▲ Idaho, NW USA 45°10′N 114°36′W
83 M14 Mchinji prev. Fort Manning. Central, W Malawi 13°48′S 32°55′E
28 M7 McIntosh South Dakota, N USA 45°56′N 101°21′W
9 S7 McKeand ≈ Baffin Island, Nunavut, NE Canada
191 R4 McKean Island island Phoenix Islands, C Kiribati
30 J13 McKee Creek ≈ Illinois, N USA
18 C15 Mckeesport Pennsylvania, NE USA 40°18′N 79°48′W
21 V7 McKenney Virginia, NE USA 36°57′N 77°42′W
20 G8 McKenzie Tennessee, S USA 36°07′N 88°31′W
185 B20 McKerrow, Lake ◎ South Island, New Zealand
39 Q10 McKinley, Mount var. Denali. ▲ Alaska, USA 63°04′N 151°00′W
39 R10 McKinley Park Alaska, USA 63°42′N 149°01′W
34 K3 McKinleyville California, W USA 40°56′N 124°06′W
25 U6 McKinney Texas, SW USA 33°14′N 96°37′W
26 I5 McKinney, Lake ◎ Kansas, C USA
28 M7 McLaughlin South Dakota, N USA 45°48′N 100°48′W
25 O2 McLean Texas, SW USA 35°13′N 100°36′W
30 M16 Mcleansboro Illinois, N USA 38°05′N 88°32′W
11 O13 McLennan Alberta, W Canada 55°42′N 116°50′W
14 L9 McLennan, Lac ◎ Québec, SE Canada
10 M13 McLeod Lake British Columbia, W Canada 55°03′N 123°02′W
8 L6 M'Clintock Channel channel Nunavut, N Canada
27 N10 McLoud Oklahoma, C USA 35°26′N 97°05′W
32 G15 McLoughlin, Mount ▲ Oregon, NW USA 42°27′N 122°18′W
37 U15 McMillan, Lake ▣ New Mexico, SW USA
32 G11 McMinnville Oregon, NW USA 45°14′N 123°12′W
20 K9 McMinnville Tennessee, S USA 35°40′N 85°49′W
195 R13 McMurdo US research station Antarctica 77°40′S 167°16′E
37 N13 Mcnary Arizona, SW USA 34°04′N 109°51′W
24 H9 McNary Texas, SW USA 31°15′N 105°46′W
27 N5 McPherson Kansas, C USA 38°22′N 97°41′W
McPherson see Fort McPherson
23 U6 McRae Georgia, SE USA 32°04′N 82°54′W
29 P4 McVille North Dakota, N USA 47°45′N 98°10′W
83 J25 Mdantsane Eastern Cape, SE South Africa 32°55′S 27°39′E
167 T6 Me Ninh Binh, N Vietnam 20°21′N 105°49′E
26 J7 Meade Kansas, C USA 37°17′N 100°21′W
39 O5 Meade River ≈ Alaska, USA
35 Y11 Mead, Lake ▣ Arizona/Nevada, W USA
24 M5 Meadow Texas, SW USA 33°20′N 102°12′W
11 S14 Meadow Lake Saskatchewan, C Canada 54°90′N 108°30′W
35 Y10 Meadow Valley Wash ≈ Nevada, W USA
22 J7 Meadville Mississippi, S USA 31°28′N 90°51′W
18 B12 Meadville Pennsylvania, NE USA 41°38′N 80°09′W
14 F14 Meaford Ontario, S Canada 44°35′N 80°35′W
Meáin, Inis see Inishmaan
104 G8 Mealhada Aveiro, N Portugal 40°22′N 08°27′W
13 R8 Mealy Mountains ▲ Newfoundland and Labrador, E Canada
11 O10 Meander River Alberta, W Canada 59°02′N 117°42′W
32 E11 Meares, Cape headland Oregon, NW USA 45°29′N 123°59′W
47 V6 Mearim, Rio ≈ NE Brazil
Measca, Loch see Mask, Lough
97 F17 Meath Ir. An Mhí. cultural region E Ireland
11 T14 Meath Park Saskatchewan, S Canada 53°25′N 105°18′W
103 O5 Meaux Seine-et-Marne, N France 48°47′N 02°54′E
21 T9 Mebane North Carolina, SE USA 36°06′N 79°16′W
171 U12 Mebo, Gunung ▲ Papua, E Indonesia 01°10′S 133°53′E
94 I8 Mebonden Sør-Trøndelag, S Norway 63°13′N 11°00′E
82 A10 Mebridege ≈ NW Angola
35 W16 Mecca California, W USA 33°34′N 116°04′W
Mecca see Makkah
29 Y14 Mechanicsville Iowa, C USA 41°54′N 91°15′W
18 L10 Mechanicville New York, NE USA 42°54′N 73°41′W
99 H17 Mechelen Eng. Mechlin, Fr. Malines. Antwerpen, C Belgium 51°02′N 04°29′E
188 C8 Mecherchar var. Eil Malk. island Palau Islands, Palau
101 D17 Mechernich Nordrhein-Westfalen, W Germany 50°36′N 06°39′E
126 L12 Mechetinskaya Rostovskaya Oblast', SW Russian Federation 46°46′N 40°30′E
114 J11 Mechka ≈ S Bulgaria
Mechlin see Mechelen
61 D23 Mechongué Buenos Aires, E Argentina 38°09′S 58°13′W
115 L14 Mecidiye Edirne, NW Turkey 40°39′N 26°33′E
101 I24 Meckenbeuren Baden-Württemberg, S Germany 47°42′N 09°34′E
100 L8 Mecklenburger Bucht bay N Germany
100 M10 Mecklenburgische Seenplatte wetland NE Germany
100 L9 Mecklenburg-Vorpommern ◆ state NE Germany
83 Q15 Meconta Nampula, NE Mozambique 15°01′S 39°52′E
111 I25 Mecsek ▲ SW Hungary
83 P14 Mecubúri ≈ N Mozambique
83 Q14 Mecúfi Cabo Delgado, NE Mozambique 13°20′S 40°32′E
82 O13 Mecula Niassa, N Mozambique 12°03′S 37°37′E
168 I8 Medan Sumatera, E Indonesia 03°35′N 98°39′E
61 A24 Médanos var. Medanos. Buenos Aires, E Argentina 38°52′S 62°45′W
61 C19 Médanos Entre Ríos, E Argentina 33°28′S 59°07′W
155 K24 Medawachchiya North Central Province, N Sri Lanka 08°32′N 80°30′E
106 C8 Mede Lombardia, N Italy 45°06′N 08°43′E
74 J5 Médéa var. El Mediyya, Lemdiyya. N Algeria 36°15′N 02°48′E
Medeba see Ma'dabā
54 E8 Medellín Antioquia, NW Colombia 06°15′N 75°36′W
100 H9 Medem ≈ NW Germany
98 J8 Medemblik Noord-Holland, NW Netherlands 52°47′N 05°06′E
75 N7 Médenine var. Madanīyīn. SE Tunisia 33°23′N 10°30′E
76 G9 Mederdra Trarza, SW Mauritania 16°56′N 15°40′W
Medeshamstede see Peterborough
42 F4 Medesto Mendez Izabal, NE Guatemala 15°54′N 89°13′W
19 O11 Medford Massachusetts, NE USA 42°25′N 71°08′W
27 N8 Medford Oklahoma, C USA 36°48′N 97°45′W
32 G15 Medford Oregon, NW USA 42°20′N 122°52′W
30 K6 Medford Wisconsin, N USA 45°08′N 90°22′W
39 P10 Medfra Alaska, USA 63°06′N 154°42′W
116 M14 Medgidia Constanța, SE Romania 44°15′N 28°16′E
Medgyes see Mediaș
43 O5 Media Luna, Arrecifes de la reef E Honduras
60 G11 Medianeira Paraná, S Brazil 25°15′S 54°07′W
29 Y15 Mediapolis Iowa, C USA 41°00′N 91°09′W
116 I11 Mediaș Ger. Mediasch, Hung. Medgyes. Sibiu, C Romania 46°10′N 24°20′E
41 S15 Medias Aguas Veracruz-Llave, SE Mexico 17°40′N 95°02′W
Mediasch see Mediaș
106 G10 Medicina Emilia-Romagna, C Italy 44°29′N 11°41′E
33 X16 Medicine Bow Wyoming, C USA 41°52′N 106°11′W
37 S2 Medicine Bow Mountains ▲ Colorado/Wyoming, C USA
33 X16 Medicine Bow River ≈ Wyoming, C USA
11 R17 Medicine Hat Alberta, SW Canada 50°03′N 110°41′W
26 L7 Medicine Lodge Kansas, C USA 37°18′N 98°35′W
26 L7 Medicine Lodge River ≈ Kansas/Oklahoma, C USA
112 E7 Medimurje off. Medimurska Županija. ◆ province N Croatia
Medimurska Županija see Medimurje
54 G10 Medina Cundinamarca, C Colombia 04°31′N 73°21′W
18 E9 Medina New York, NE USA 43°13′N 78°23′W
29 O5 Medina North Dakota, N USA 46°53′N 99°18′W
31 T11 Medina Ohio, N USA 41°08′N 81°51′W
25 Q11 Medina Texas, SW USA 29°46′N 99°14′W
Medina see Al Madīnah
105 P6 Medinaceli Castilla y León, N Spain 41°10′N 02°26′W
104 L6 Medina del Campo Castilla y León, N Spain 41°18′N 04°55′W
104 L5 Medina de Ríoseco Castilla y León, N Spain 41°53′N 05°03′W
Médina Gonassé see Médina Gounas
76 H12 Médina Gounas var. Médina Gonassé. S Senegal 13°06′N 13°49′W
25 S12 Medina River ≈ Texas, SW USA
104 K16 Medina Sidonia Andalucía, S Spain 36°28′N 05°55′W
Medinat Israel see Israel
119 H14 Medininkai Vilnius, SE Lithuania 54°32′N 25°40′E
153 R16 Medinīpur West Bengal, NE India 22°25′N 87°24′E
Mediolanum see Saintes, France
Mediolanum see Milano, Italy
Mediomatrica see Metz
121 Q11 Mediterranean Ridge undersea feature C Mediterranean Sea 34°00′N 23°00′E
121 O16 Mediterranean Sea Fr. Mer Méditerranée. sea Africa/Asia/Europe
Méditerranée, Mer see Mediterranean Sea
79 N17 Medje Orientale, NE Dem. Rep. Congo 02°27′N 27°14′E
Medjerda, Oued see Mejerda
114 G7 Medkovets Montana, NW Bulgaria 43°39′N 23°22′E
93 J15 Medle Västerbotten, N Sweden 64°45′N 20°45′E
127 W7 Mednogorsk Orenburgskaya Oblast', W Russian Federation 51°24′N 57°37′E
123 W9 Mednyy, Ostrov island E Russian Federation
102 J12 Médoc cultural region SW France
159 Q16 Mêdog Xizang Zizhiqu, W China 29°26′N 95°26′E
28 J5 Medora North Dakota, N USA 46°56′N 103°40′W
79 E17 Médouneu Woleu-Ntem, N Gabon 0°58′N 10°50′E
106 I7 Meduna ≈ NE Italy
Medunta see Mantes-la-Jolie
Medvedica see Medveditsa
124 J16 Medveditsa var. Medvedica. ≈ W Russian Federation
127 O9 Medveditsa ≈ SW Russian Federation
112 E8 Medvednica ▲ NE Croatia
125 R15 Medvedok Kirovskaya Oblast', NW Russian Federation 57°23′N 50°01′E
123 S6 Medvezh'i, Ostrova island group NE Russian Federation
124 J9 Medvezh'yegorsk Respublika Kareliya, NW Russian Federation 62°56′N 34°26′E
109 T11 Medvode Ger. Zwischenwässern. NW Slovenia 46°09′N 14°21′E
126 J4 Medyn' Kaluzhskaya Oblast', W Russian Federation 54°59′N 35°52′E
180 J10 Meekatharra Western Australia 26°37′S 118°35′E
37 Q4 Meeker Colorado, C USA 40°02′N 107°54′W
13 T12 Meelpaeg Lake ◎ Newfoundland, Newfoundland and Labrador, E Canada
Meemu Atoll see Mulakatholhu
Meenen see Menen
101 M16 Meerane Sachsen, E Germany 50°50′N 12°28′E
101 D15 Meerbusch Nordrhein-Westfalen, W Germany 51°19′N 06°43′E
98 I12 Meerkerk Zuid-Holland, C Netherlands 51°55′N 05°00′E
99 L18 Meerssen var. Mersen. Limburg, SE Netherlands 50°53′N 05°45′E
152 J10 Meerut Uttar Pradesh, N India 29°01′N 77°41′E
33 U13 Meeteetse Wyoming, C USA 44°10′N 108°53′W
99 K17 Meeuwen Limburg, NE Belgium 51°04′N 05°36′E
81 J16 Mēga Oromīya, C Ethiopia 04°03′N 38°15′E
81 J16 Mēga Escarpment escarpment S Ethiopia
Megála Kalívia see Megála Kalývia
115 E16 Megála Kalývia var. Megála Kalívia. Thessalía, C Greece 39°30′N 21°48′E
115 H14 Megáli Panagiá var. Megáli Panayía. Kentrikí Makedonía, N Greece 40°24′N 23°42′E
Megáli Panayía see Megáli Panagiá
Megáli Préspa, Límni see Prespa, Lake
114 K12 Megálo Livádi ▲ Bulgaria/Greece 41°18′N 25°51′E
115 E20 Megalópoli prev. Megalópolis. Pelopónnisos, S Greece 37°24′N 22°08′E
Megalópolis see Megalópoli
171 U12 Megamo Papua, E Indonesia 0°55′S 131°46′E
115 C18 Meganísi island Iónia Nisiá, Greece, C Mediterranean Sea
Meganom, Mys see Mehanom, Mys
Mégantic see Lac-Mégantic
15 R12 Mégantic, Mont ▲ Québec, SE Canada 45°27′N 71°09′W
115 G19 Mégara Attikí, C Greece 38°00′N 23°20′E
25 R5 Megargel Texas, SW USA 33°27′N 98°55′W
98 K13 Megen Noord-Brabant, S Netherlands 51°49′N 05°34′E
153 U13 Meghālaya ◆ state NE India
153 U16 Meghna Nadi ≈ S Bangladesh
137 V14 Meghri Rus. Megri. SE Armenia 38°57′N 46°15′E
115 Q23 Megísti var. Kastellórizon. island SE Greece
Megri see Meghri
Mehabad see Mahābād
116 F13 Mehadia Hung. Mehádia. Caraș-Severin, SW Romania 44°53′N 22°20′E
Mehádia see Mehadia
92 L7 Mehamn Finnmark, N Norway 71°01′N 27°46′E
117 U13 Mehanom, Mys Rus. Mys Meganom. headland S Ukraine 44°48′N 35°04′E
149 P14 Mehar Sind, SE Pakistan 27°12′N 67°51′E
180 J8 Meharry, Mount ▲ Western Australia 23°17′S 118°48′E
Mehdia see Mahdia
116 G14 Mehedinți ◆ county SW Romania
153 S15 Meherpur Khulna, W Bangladesh 23°47′N 88°40′E
21 W8 Meherrin River ≈ North Carolina/Virginia, SE USA
191 T11 Mehetia island Îles du Vent, W French Polynesia
118 K6 Mehikoorma Tartumaa, E Estonia 58°14′N 27°29′E
Me Hka see Nmai Hka
143 N5 Mehrabad ✈ (Tehrān) Tehrān, N Iran 35°46′N 51°07′E
142 J7 Mehrān Īlām, W Iran 33°07′N 46°10′E
143 Q14 Mehrān, Rūd-e prev. Mansurabad. ≈ W Iran
143 Q9 Mehrīz Yazd, C Iran 31°32′N 54°28′E
149 R5 Mehtar Lām var. Mehtarlām, Meterlam, Metharlam, Metharlam. Laghmān, E Afghanistan 34°39′N 70°10′E
Mehtarlām see Mehtar Lām
103 N8 Mehun-sur-Yèvre Cher, C France 47°09′N 02°15′E
79 G14 Meiganga Adamaoua, NE Cameroon 06°31′N 14°07′E
160 H10 Meigu var. Bapu. Sichuan, C China 28°16′N 103°20′E
163 W11 Meihekou var. Hailong. Jilin, NE China 42°31′N 125°40′E
99 L15 Meijel Limburg, SE Netherlands 51°22′N 05°52′E
Meijiang see Ningdu
166 M5 Meiktila Mandalay, Myanmar (Burma) 20°53′N 95°54′E
Meilbhe, Loch see Melvin, Lough
108 G7 Meilen Zürich, N Switzerland 47°17′N 08°39′E
Meilu see Wuchuan
101 J17 Meiningen Thüringen, C Germany 50°34′N 10°25′E
108 F9 Meiringen Bern, S Switzerland 46°42′N 08°13′E
Meishan see Jinzhai
101 O15 Meissen Ger. Meißen. Sachsen, E Germany 51°10′N 13°28′E
Meißen see Meissen
101 I15 Meissner ▲ C Germany 51°13′N 09°52′E
99 K25 Meix-devant-Virton Luxembourg, SE Belgium 49°36′N 05°27′E
Meixian see Meizhou
Meixing see Xinjin
161 P13 Meizhou var. Meixian, Mei Xian. Guangdong, S China 24°21′N 116°05′E
67 P2 Mejerda var. Oued Medjerda, Wādī Majardah. ≈ Algeria/Tunisia see also Medjerda, Oued
42 F7 Mejicanos San Salvador, C El Salvador 13°50′N 89°13′W
Méjico see Mexico
62 G5 Mejillones Antofagasta, N Chile 23°03′S 70°25′W
189 V5 Mejit Island var. Mājeej. island Ratak Chain, NE Marshall Islands
79 F17 Mékambo Ogooué-Ivindo, NE Gabon 01°03′N 13°50′E
80 J10 Mek'elē var. Makale. Tigray, N Ethiopia 13°36′N 39°29′E
74 I10 Mekerrhane, Sebkha var. Sebkha Meqerghane, Sebkra Mekerrhane. salt flat C Algeria
Mekerrhane, Sebkra see Mekerrhane, Sebkha
76 G10 Mékhé NW Senegal 15°02′N 16°40′W
146 G14 Mekhinli Ahal Welaýaty, C Turkmenistan 37°28′N 59°20′E
15 P9 Mékinac, Lac ◎ Québec, SE Canada
Meklong see Samut Songkhram
74 G6 Meknès N Morocco 33°54′N 05°27′W
129 U12 Mekong var. Lan-ts'ang Chiang, Cam. Mékôngk, Chin. Lancang Jiang, Lao. Mènam Khong, Nam Khong, Th. Mae Nam Khong, Tib. Dza Chu, Vtn. Sông Tiên Giang. ≈ SE Asia
Mékôngk see Mekong
167 T15 Mekong, Mouths of the delta S Vietnam
38 L12 Mekoryuk Nunivak Island, Alaska, USA 60°23′N 166°11′W
77 R14 Mékrou ≈ N Benin
168 K9 Melaka var. Malacca. Melaka, Peninsular Malaysia 02°14′N 102°14′E
168 L9 Melaka var. Malacca. ◆ state Peninsular Malaysia
Melaka, Selat see Malacca, Strait of
175 O6 Melanesia island group W Pacific Ocean
175 P5 Melanesian Basin undersea feature W Pacific Ocean 0°05′N 160°35′E
171 R9 Melanguane Pulau Karakelang, N Indonesia 04°02′N 126°43′E
169 R11 Melawi, Sungai ≈ Borneo, N Indonesia
183 N12 Melbourne state capital Victoria, SE Australia 37°51′S 144°56′E
27 V9 Melbourne Arkansas, C USA 36°04′N 91°54′W
23 Y12 Melbourne Florida, SE USA 28°04′N 80°36′W
29 W14 Melbourne Iowa, C USA 41°57′N 93°07′W
92 G10 Melbu Nordland, C Norway 68°31′N 14°50′E
Melchor de Mencos see Ciudad Melchor de Mencos
63 F19 Melchor, Isla island Archipiélago de los Chonos, S Chile
40 M9 Melchor Ocampo Zacatecas, C Mexico 24°45′N 101°38′W
14 C11 Meldrum Bay Manitoulin Island, Ontario, S Canada 45°55′N 83°06′W
Meleda see Mljet
106 D8 Melegnano prev. Marignano. Lombardia, N Italy 45°22′N 09°19′E
188 F9 Melekeok ● Babeldaob, N Palau 07°30′N 134°37′E
112 L9 Melenci Hung. Melencze. Vojvodina, N Serbia 45°32′N 20°18′E
Melencze see Melenci
127 N4 Melenki Vladimirskaya Oblast', W Russian Federation 55°21′N 41°37′E
127 V6 Meleuz Respublika Bashkortostan, W Russian Federation 52°55′N 55°54′E
12 L6 Mélèzes, Rivière aux ≈ Québec, C Canada
78 I11 Melfi Guéra, S Chad 11°05′N 17°57′E
107 M17 Melfi Basilicata, S Italy 41°00′N 15°33′E
11 U14 Melfort Saskatchewan, S Canada 52°52′N 104°38′W
104 H4 Melgaço Viana do Castelo, N Portugal 42°07′N 08°15′W
105 N4 Melgar de Fernamental Castilla y León, N Spain 42°24′N 04°15′W
74 L6 Melghir, Chott var. Chott Melrhir. salt lake E Algeria
94 H8 Melhus Sør-Trøndelag, S Norway 63°17′N 10°18′E
104 H3 Melide Galicia, NW Spain 42°54′N 08°01′W
Meligalá see Meligalás
115 E21 Meligalás prev. Meligalá. Pelopónnisos, S Greece 37°13′N 21°58′E
60 L12 Mel, Ilha do island S Brazil
120 E10 Melilla anc. Rusaddir, Russadir. Melilla, Spain, N Africa 35°18′N 02°56′W
71 N1 Melilla enclave Spain, N Africa
63 G18 Melimoyu, Monte ▲ S Chile 44°06′S 72°49′W
169 V11 Melintang, Danau ◎ Borneo, N Indonesia
117 U7 Melioratyvne Dnipropetrovs'ka Oblast', E Ukraine 48°35′N 35°18′E
62 G11 Melipilla Santiago, C Chile 33°42′S 71°15′W
115 I25 Mélissa, Akrotírio headland Kríti, Greece, E Mediterranean Sea 35°06′N 24°33′E
11 W17 Melita Manitoba, S Canada 49°16′N 100°59′W
Melita see Mljet
Melitene see Malatya
107 M23 Melito di Porto Salvo Calabria, SW Italy 37°55′N 15°48′E
117 U10 Melitopol' Zaporiz'ka Oblast', SE Ukraine 46°49′N 35°23′E
109 V4 Melk Niederösterreich, NE Austria 48°14′N 15°21′E
95 K15 Mellan-Fryken ◎ C Sweden
99 E17 Melle Oost-Vlaanderen, NW Belgium 51°N 03°48′E
100 G13 Melle Niedersachsen, NW Germany 52°12′N 08°19′E
95 J17 Mellerud Västra Götaland, S Sweden 58°42′N 12°27′E
102 K10 Melle-sur-Bretonne Deux-Sèvres, W France 46°13′N 00°07′W
29 P8 Mellette South Dakota, N USA 45°07′N 98°29′W
121 O15 Mellieha E Malta 35°58′N 14°21′E
80 B10 Mellit Northern Darfur, W Sudan 14°07′N 25°34′E
75 N7 Mellita ✈ SE Tunisia 33°47′N 10°51′E
63 G21 Mellizo Sur, Cerro ▲ S Chile 48°27′S 73°10′W
100 G9 Mellum island NW Germany
83 L22 Melmoth KwaZulu/Natal, E South Africa 28°35′S 31°25′E
111 D16 Mělník Ger. Melnik. Středočeský Kraj, NW Czech Republic 50°21′N 14°30′E
122 J12 Mel'nikovo Tomskaya Oblast', C Russian Federation 56°35′N 84°11′E
61 G18 Melo Cerro Largo, NE Uruguay 32°22′S 54°10′W
Melodunum see Melun
Melrhir, Chott see Melghir, Chott
183 P7 Melrose New South Wales, SE Australia 32°41′S 146°58′E
182 I7 Melrose South Australia 32°52′S 138°16′E
29 T7 Melrose Minnesota, N USA 45°40′N 94°46′W
33 Q11 Melrose Montana, NW USA 45°33′N 112°41′W
37 V12 Melrose New Mexico, SW USA 34°25′N 103°37′W
108 I8 Mels Sankt Gallen, NE Switzerland 47°03′N 09°26′E
Melsetter see Chimanimani
33 V9 Melstone Montana, NW USA 46°37′N 107°49′W
101 I16 Melsungen Hessen, C Germany 51°08′N 09°33′E
92 L12 Meltaus Lappi, NW Finland 66°54′N 25°18′E
97 N19 Melton Mowbray C England, United Kingdom 52°46′N 01°04′W
82 Q13 Meluco Cabo Delgado, NE Mozambique 12°31′S 39°39′E
103 O5 Melun anc. Melodunum. Seine-et-Marne, N France 48°32′N 02°40′E
80 F12 Melut Upper Nile, NE South Sudan 10°27′N 32°13′E
27 P5 Melvern Lake ▣ Kansas, C USA
11 V16 Melville Saskatchewan, S Canada 50°57′N 102°49′W
Melville Bay/Melville Bugt see Qimusseriarsuaq
45 O11 Melville Hall ✈ (Dominica) NE Dominica 15°33′N 61°19′W
181 O1 Melville Island island Northern Territory, N Australia
197 O8 Melville Island island Parry Islands, Northwest Territories, NW Canada
11 W9 Melville, Lake ◎ Newfoundland and Labrador, E Canada
9 O7 Melville Peninsula peninsula Nunavut, NE Canada
Melville Sound see Viscount Melville Sound
25 Q9 Melvin Texas, SW USA 31°12′N 99°34′W
97 D15 Melvin, Lough Ir. Loch Meilbhe. ◎ S Northern Ireland, United Kingdom/Ireland
169 S12 Memala Borneo, C Indonesia 01°44′S 112°36′E
113 L22 Memaliaj Gjirokastër, S Albania 40°21′N 19°56′E
83 Q14 Memba Nampula, NE Mozambique 14°07′S 40°33′E
83 Q14 Memba, Baia de inlet NE Mozambique
Membidj see Manbij
Memel see Neman, NE Europe
Memel see Klaipėda, Lithuania
101 J23 Memmingen Bayern, S Germany 47°59′N 10°11′E
27 U1 Memphis Missouri, C USA 40°28′N 92°11′W
20 E10 Memphis Tennessee, S USA 35°09′N 90°03′W
25 P3 Memphis Texas, SW USA 34°43′N 100°34′W
20 E10 Memphis ✈ Tennessee, S USA 35°02′N 89°57′W
15 Q13 Memphrémagog, Lac var. Lake Memphremagog. ◎ Canada/USA see also Lake Memphremagog
19 N6 Memphremagog, Lake var. Lac Memphrémagog. ◎ Canada/USA see also Memphrémagog, Lac
117 Q2 Mena Chernihivs'ka Oblast', NE Ukraine 51°30′N 32°15′E
27 S12 Mena Arkansas, C USA 34°40′N 94°15′W
Menaam see Menaldum
Menado see Manado
106 D6 Menaggio Lombardia, N Italy 46°03′N 09°14′E
29 T6 Menahga Minnesota, N USA 46°45′N 95°06′W
77 R10 Ménaka Goa, E Mali 15°55′N 02°25′E
98 K5 Menaldum Fris. Menaam. Fryslân, N Netherlands 53°14′N 05°38′E
Mènam Khong see Mekong
74 E7 Menara ✈ (Marrakech) C Morocco 31°36′N 08°00′W
25 Q9 Menard Texas, SW USA 30°56′N 99°48′W
193 Q12 Menard Fracture Zone tectonic feature E Pacific Ocean
30 M7 Menasha Wisconsin, N USA 44°13′N 88°25′W
Mencezi Garagum see Merkezi Garagumy
193 U9 Mendaña Fracture Zone tectonic feature E Pacific Ocean
169 S13 Mendawai, Sungai ≈ Borneo, C Indonesia
103 P13 Mende anc. Mimatum. Lozère, S France 44°32′N 03°30′E
81 J14 Mendebo ▲ C Ethiopia
80 J9 Mendefera prev. Adi Ugri. S Eritrea 14°53′N 38°51′E
197 S7 Mendeleyev Ridge undersea feature Arctic Ocean
127 T3 Mendeleyevsk Respublika Tatarstan, W Russian Federation 55°54′N 52°19′E
101 F15 Menden Nordrhein-Westfalen, W Germany 51°26′N 07°47′E
22 L6 Mendenhall Mississippi, S USA 31°57′N 89°52′W
38 L13 Mendenhall, Cape headland Nunivak Island, Alaska, USA 59°45′N 166°10′W
41 P9 Méndez var. Villa de Méndez. Tamaulipas, C Mexico 25°06′N 98°32′W
80 H13 Mendī Oromīya C Ethiopia 09°43′N 35°07′E
186 C7 Mendi Southern Highlands, W Papua New Guinea 06°13′S 143°39′E
97 K22 Mendip Hills var. Mendips. hill range S England, United Kingdom
Mendips see Mendip Hills
34 L6 Mendocino California, W USA 39°18′N 123°48′W
34 J3 Mendocino, Cape headland California, W USA 40°26′N 124°24′W
0 B8 Mendocino Fracture Zone tectonic feature NE Pacific Ocean
35 P10 Mendota California, W USA 36°44′N 120°24′W
30 L11 Mendota Illinois, N USA 41°32′N 89°04′W
30 K8 Mendota, Lake ◎ Wisconsin, N USA
62 I11 Mendoza Mendoza, W Argentina 33°00′S 68°47′W
62 I12 Mendoza off. Provincia de Mendoza. ◆ province W Argentina
Mendoza, Provincia de see Mendoza
108 H12 Mendrisio Ticino, S Switzerland 45°53′N 08°59′E
168 L10 Mendung Pulau Mendol, W Indonesia 0°33′N 103°09′E
54 I5 Mene de Mauroa Falcón, NW Venezuela 10°39′N 71°04′W
54 I5 Mene Grande Zulia, NW Venezuela 09°51′N 70°57′W
136 B14 Menemen İzmir, W Turkey 38°34′N 27°03′E
99 C18 Menen var. Meenen, Fr. Menin. West-Vlaanderen, W Belgium 50°48′N 03°07′E
163 Q8 Menengiyn Tal plain E Mongolia
189 R9 Meneng Point headland SW Nauru 0°33′S 166°57′E
92 L10 Menesjärvi Lapp. Menešjávri. Lappi, N Finland 68°39′N 26°22′E
Menešjávri see Menesjärvi
107 I24 Menfi Sicilia, Italy, C Mediterranean Sea 37°36′N 12°59′E
161 P7 Mengcheng Anhui, E China 33°15′N 116°33′E
160 F15 Menghai Yunnan, SW China 22°02′N 100°18′E
160 F15 Mengla Yunnan, SW China 21°30′N 101°33′E
65 F24 Menguera Point headland East Falkland, Falkland Islands
160 M13 Mengzhu Ling ▲ S China
160 H14 Mengzi Yunnan, SW China 23°20′N 103°32′E
114 H13 Menikio var. Menoíkio. ▲ NE Greece 40°50′N 12°40′E
Menin see Menen
182 L7 Menindee New South Wales, SE Australia 32°24′S 142°25′E
182 L7 Menindee Lake ◎ New South Wales, SE Australia
182 J10 Meningie South Australia 35°43′S 139°20′E
103 O5 Mennecy Essonne, N France 48°34′N 02°25′E
29 Q12 Menno South Dakota, N USA 43°14′N 97°34′W
114 H13 Menoíkio ▲ NE Greece
Menoíkio see Menikio
31 N5 Menominee Michigan, N USA 45°06′N 87°36′W
30 M5 Menominee River ≈ Michigan/Wisconsin, N USA
30 M8 Menomonee Falls Wisconsin, N USA 43°11′N 88°09′W
30 I6 Menomonie Wisconsin, N USA 44°52′N 91°55′W
83 D14 Menongue var. Vila Serpa Pinto, Port. Serpa Pinto. Cuando Cubango, C Angola 14°38′S 17°39′E
120 H8 Menorca Eng. Minorca; anc. Balearis Minor. island Islas Baleares, Spain, W Mediterranean Sea
105 S13 Menor, Mar lagoon SE Spain
39 S10 Mentasta Lake ◎ Alaska, USA
39 S10 Mentasta Mountains ▲ Alaska, USA
168 I13 Mentawai, Kepulauan island group W Indonesia
168 I12 Mentawai, Selat strait W Indonesia
168 M12 Mentok Pulau Bangka, W Indonesia 02°01′S 105°10′E
103 V15 Menton It. Mentone. Alpes-Maritimes, SE France 43°47′N 07°30′E
24 K8 Mentone Texas, SW USA 31°42′N 103°36′W
Mentone see Menton
31 U11 Mentor Ohio, N USA 41°40′N 81°20′W
169 U10 Menyapa, Gunung ▲ Borneo, N Indonesia 01°04′N 116°01′E
159 T9 Menyuan var. Menyuan Huizu Zizhixian. Qinghai, C China 37°27′N 101°33′E
Menyuan Huizu Zizhixian see Menyuan
74 M5 Menzel Bourguiba var. Manzil Bū Ruqaybah; prev. Ferryville. N Tunisia 37°09′N 09°51′E
136 M15 Menzelet Barajı ▣ C Turkey
127 T4 Menzelinsk Respublika Tatarstan, W Russian Federation 55°44′N 53°00′E
180 K11 Menzies Western Australia 29°42′S 121°04′E
195 V6 Menzies, Mount ▲ Antarctica 73°32′S 61°02′E
40 J6 Meoqui Chihuahua, N Mexico 28°18′N 105°30′W
83 N14 Meponda Niassa, NE Mozambique 13°20′S 34°53′E
98 M8 Meppel Drenthe, NE Netherlands 52°42′N 06°12′E
100 E12 Meppen Niedersachsen, NW Germany 52°42′N 07°18′E
Meqerghane, Sebkha see Mekerrhane, Sebkha
105 T6 Mequinenza, Embalse de ▣ NE Spain
30 M8 Mequon Wisconsin, N USA 43°13′N 87°57′W
Mera see Maira
182 D3 Meramangye, Lake salt lake South Australia
27 W5 Meramec River ≈ Missouri, C USA
Meran see Merano
168 K13 Merangin ≈ Sumatera, W Indonesia
106 G5 Merano Ger. Meran. Trentino-Alto Adige, N Italy 46°40′N 11°10′E
168 K8 Merapuh Lama Pahang, Peninsular Malaysia 04°37′N 101°58′E
106 D7 Merate Lombardia, N Italy 45°42′N 09°26′E
169 U13 Meratus, Pegunungan ▲ Borneo, N Indonesia
171 Y16 Merauke, Sungai ≈ Papua, E Indonesia
182 L9 Merbein Victoria, SE Australia 34°11′S 142°03′E
99 F21 Merbes-le-Château Hainaut, S Belgium 50°19′N 04°09′E
Merca see Marka
54 C13 Mercaderes Cauca, SW Colombia 01°46′N 77°09′W
Mercara see Madikeri
35 P9 Merced California, W USA 37°17′N 120°30′W
61 C20 Mercedes Buenos Aires, E Argentina 34°42′S 59°30′W
61 D15 Mercedes Corrientes, NE Argentina 29°09′S 58°05′W
61 D19 Mercedes Soriano, SW Uruguay 33°16′S 58°01′W
25 S17 Mercedes Texas, SW USA 26°09′N 97°54′W
Mercedes see Villa Mercedes
35 R9 Merced Peak ▲ California, W USA 37°34′N 119°30′W
35 P9 Merced River ≈ California, W USA
18 B13 Mercer Pennsylvania, NE USA 41°14′N 80°14′W
99 G18 Merchtem Vlaams Brabant, C Belgium 50°57′N 04°14′E
15 O13 Mercier Québec, SE Canada 45°15′N 73°45′W
25 Q9 Mercury Texas, SW USA 31°23′N 99°09′W
184 M5 Mercury Islands island group N New Zealand
19 O9 Meredith New Hampshire, NE USA 43°36′N 71°28′W
65 B25 Meredith, Cape var. Cabo Belgrano. headland West Falkland, Falkland Islands 52°15′S 60°40′W
37 V6 Meredith, Lake ◎ Colorado, C USA
25 N2 Meredith, Lake ▣ Texas, SW USA
81 O16 Mereeg var. Mareeq, It. Meregh. Galguduud, E Somalia 03°47′N 47°19′E
117 V5 Merefa Kharkivs'ka Oblast', E Ukraine 49°49′N 36°05′E
Meregh see Mereeg
99 E17 Merelbeke Oost-Vlaanderen, NW Belgium 51°00′N 03°45′E
Merend see Marand
167 T12 Méreuch Môndól Kiri, E Cambodia 13°01′N 107°26′E
Mergate see Margate
Mergui see Myeik
Mergui Archipelago see Myeik Archipelago
114 L12 Meriç Edirne, NW Turkey 41°12′N 26°24′E
114 L12 Meriç Bul. Maritsa, Gk. Évros; anc. Hebrus. ≈ SE Europe see also Évros/Maritsa
41 X12 Mérida Yucatán, SW Mexico 20°58′N 89°35′W
104 J11 Mérida anc. Augusta Emerita. Extremadura, W Spain 38°55′N 06°20′W
54 I6 Mérida Mérida, W Venezuela 08°36′N 71°08′W
54 H7 Mérida off. Estado Mérida. ◆ state W Venezuela
Mérida, Estado see Mérida
18 M13 Meriden Connecticut, NE USA 41°32′N 72°48′W
22 M5 Meridian Mississippi, S USA 32°24′N 88°43′W
25 S8 Meridian Texas, SW USA 31°56′N 97°40′W
102 J13 Mérignac Gironde, SW France 44°50′N 00°40′W
102 J13 Mérignac ✈ (Bordeaux) Gironde, SW France 44°51′N 00°44′W
93 J18 Merikarvia Länsi-Suomi, SW Finland 61°51′N 21°30′E
183 R12 Merimbula New South Wales, SE Australia 36°52′S 149°51′E
182 L9 Meringur Victoria, SE Australia 34°26′S 141°19′E
Merín, Laguna see Mirim Lagoon
97 I19 Merioneth cultural region W Wales, United Kingdom
188 A11 Merir island Palau Islands, N Palau
188 B17 Merizo SW Guam 13°15′N 144°40′E
Merjama see Märjamaa
Merke see Merki
25 P7 Merkel Texas, SW USA 32°28′N 100°00′W
146 E12 Merkezi Garagumy var. Mencezi Garagum, Rus. Tsentral'nye Nizmennyye Garagumy. desert C Turkmenistan
145 S16 Merki prev. Merke. Zhambyl, S Kazakhstan 42°48′N 73°10′E
119 F15 Merkinė Alytus, S Lithuania 54°09′N 24°11′E
99 G16 Merksem Antwerpen, N Belgium 51°17′N 04°26′E

◆ Country
● Country Capital
◇ Dependent Territory
○ Dependent Territory Capital
◆ Administrative Regions
✈ International Airport
▲ Mountain
▲ Mountain Range
▲ Volcano
≈ River
◎ Lake
▣ Reservoir

99 I15 **Merksplas** Antwerpen, N Belgium 51°22′N 04°54′E
Merkulovichi *see* Myerkulavichy
119 G15 **Merkys** ≈ S Lithuania
32 F15 **Merlin** Oregon, NW USA 42°34′N 123°23′W
61 C20 **Merlo** Buenos Aires, E Argentina 34°39′S 58°45′W
138 G8 **Meron, Harei** *prev.* Haré Meron. ▲ N Israel 35°06′N 33°00′E
74 K6 **Merouane, Chott** *salt lake* NE Algeria
80 F7 **Merowe** Northern, N Sudan 18°29′N 31°49′E
180 J12 **Merredin** Western Australia 31°31′S 118°18′E
97 I14 **Merrick** ▲ S Scotland, United Kingdom 55°09′N 04°28′W
32 H16 **Merrill** Oregon, NW USA 42°00′N 121°37′W
30 L5 **Merrill** Wisconsin, N USA 45°12′N 89°43′W
31 N11 **Merrillville** Indiana, N USA 41°28′N 87°19′W
19 O10 **Merrimack River** ≈ Massachusetts/New Hampshire, NE USA
28 L12 **Merriman** Nebraska, C USA 42°54′N 101°42′W
11 N17 **Merritt** British Columbia, SW Canada 50°09′N 120°49′W
23 Y12 **Merritt Island** Florida, SE USA 28°21′N 80°42′W
23 Y11 **Merritt Island** *island* Florida, SE USA
28 M12 **Merritt Reservoir** ▣ Nebraska, C USA
183 S7 **Merriwa** New South Wales, SE Australia 32°09′S 150°24′E
183 O8 **Merriwagga** New South Wales, SE Australia 33°51′S 145°38′E
22 G8 **Merryville** Louisiana, S USA 30°45′N 93°32′W
80 K9 **Mersa Fat'ma** E Eritrea 14°52′N 40°16′E
102 M7 **Mer St-Aubin** Loir-et-Cher, C France 47°42′N 01°31′E
99 M24 **Mersch** Luxembourg, C Luxembourg 49°45′N 06°06′E
101 M15 **Merseburg** Sachsen-Anhalt, C Germany 51°22′N 12°00′E
Mersen *see* Meerssen
97 K18 **Mersey** ≈ NW England, United Kingdom
136 J17 **Mersin** *var.* İçel. İçel, S Turkey 36°50′N 34°39′E
Mersin *see* İçel
168 L9 **Mersing** Johor, Peninsular Malaysia 02°25′N 103°50′E
118 E8 **Mērsrags** NW Latvia 57°21′N 23°05′E
Merta *see* Merta City
152 G12 **Merta City** *var.* Merta. Rājasthān, N India 26°40′N 74°04′E
152 F12 **Merta Road** Rājasthān, N India 26°42′N 73°54′E
97 J21 **Merthyr Tydfil** S Wales, United Kingdom 51°46′N 03°23′W
104 H13 **Mértola** Beja, S Portugal 37°38′N 07°40′W
144 G14 **Mertvyy Kultuk, Sor** *salt flat* SW Kazakhstan
195 V16 **Mertz Glacier** *glacier* Antarctica
99 M24 **Mertzig** Diekirch, C Luxembourg 49°50′N 06°00′E
25 O9 **Mertzon** Texas, SW USA 31°16′N 100°50′W
103 N4 **Méru** Oise, N France 49°15′N 02°07′E
81 I18 **Meru** Eastern, C Kenya 0°03′N 37°38′E
81 I20 **Meru, Mount** ▲ NE Tanzania 03°12′S 36°45′E
Merv *see* Mary
Mervdasht *see* Marv Dasht
136 K11 **Merzifon** Amasya, N Turkey 40°52′N 35°28′E
101 D20 **Merzig** Saarland, SW Germany 49°27′N 06°39′E
36 L14 **Mesa** Arizona, SW USA 33°25′N 111°49′W
29 V4 **Mesabi Range** ▲ Minnesota, N USA
54 H6 **Mesa Bolívar** Mérida, NW Venezuela 08°30′N 71°38′W
107 Q18 **Mesagne** Puglia, SE Italy 40°33′N 17°49′E
39 P12 **Mesa Mountain** ▲ Alaska, USA 60°26′N 155°14′W
115 J25 **Mesará** *lowland* Kríti, Greece, E Mediterranean Sea
37 S14 **Mescalero** New Mexico, SW USA 33°09′N 105°46′W
101 G15 **Meschede** Nordrhein-Westfalen, W Germany 51°21′N 08°16′E
137 Q12 **Mescit Dağları** ▲ NE Turkey
189 V13 **Mesegon** *island* Chuuk, C Micronesia
Meseritz *see* Międzyrzecz
54 F11 **Mesetas** Meta, C Colombia 03°14′N 74°09′W
Meshchera Lowland *see* Meshcherskaya Nizmennost'
Meshcherskaya Nizina *see* Meshcherskaya Nizmennost'
126 M4 **Meshcherskaya Nizmennost'** *var.* Meshcherskaya Nizina, *Eng.* Meshchera Lowland. *basin* W Russian Federation
126 J5 **Meshchovsk** Kaluzhskaya Oblast', W Russian Federation 54°21′N 35°23′E
125 R9 **Meshchura** Respublika Komi, NW Russian Federation 63°18′N 50°56′E
Meshed *see* Mashhad
Meshed-i-Sar *see* Bābolsar
80 E13 **Meshra'er Req** Warap, W South Sudan 08°30′N 29°27′E
37 R15 **Mesilla** New Mexico, SW USA 32°15′N 106°49′W
108 H10 **Mesocco** *Ger.* Misox. Ticino, S Switzerland 46°18′N 09°13′E
115 D18 **Mesolóngi** *prev.* Mesolóngion. Dytikí Elláda, W Greece 38°21′N 21°26′E
Mesolóngion *see* Mesolóngi
14 E8 **Mesomikenda Lake** ◎ Ontario, S Canada
61 D15 **Mesopotamia** *var.* Mesopotamia Argentina. *physical region* NE Argentina
Mesopotamia Argentina *see* Mesopotamia
35 Y10 **Mesquite** Nevada, W USA 36°47′N 114°04′W
82 Q13 **Messalo, Rio** *var.* Mualo. ≈ NE Mozambique
Messana/Messene *see* Messina
99 L25 **Messancy** Luxembourg, SE Belgium 49°36′N 05°49′E
107 M23 **Messina** *var.* Messana, Messene; *anc.* Zancle. Sicilia, Italy, C Mediterranean Sea 38°12′N 15°33′E
Messina *see* Musina
Messina, Strait of *see* Messina, Stretto di
107 M23 **Messina, Stretto di** *Eng.* Strait of Messina. *strait* SW Italy
115 E21 **Messíni** Pelopónnisos, S Greece 37°03′N 22°00′E
115 E21 **Messinía** *peninsula* S Greece
115 E22 **Messiniakós Kólpos** *gulf* S Greece
122 J8 **Messoyakha** ≈ N Russian Federation
114 H11 **Mesta** *Gk.* Néstos, *Turk.* Kara Su. ≈ Bulgaria/Greece *see also* Néstos
Mesta *see* Néstos
Mestghanem *see* Mostaganem
137 R8 **Mest'ia** *prev.* Mestia, *var.* Mestiya. N Georgia 43°03′N 42°50′E
Mestia *see* Mest'ia
Mestiya *see* Mest'ia
115 K18 **Mestón, Akrotírio** *cape* Chíos, E Greece
106 H8 **Mestre** Veneto, NE Italy 45°30′N 12°14′E
59 M16 **Mestre, Espigão** ▲ E Brazil
169 N14 **Mesuji** ≈ Sumatera, W Indonesia
Mesule *see* Grosser Möseler
10 J10 **Meszah Peak** ▲ British Columbia, W Canada 58°31′N 131°28′W
54 G11 **Meta** *off.* Departamento del Meta. ◆ *province* C Colombia
15 Q8 **Metabetchouane** ≈ Québec, SE Canada
Meta, Departamento del *see* Meta
9 S7 **Meta Incognita Peninsula** *peninsula* Baffin Island, Nunavut, NE Canada
22 K9 **Metairie** Louisiana, S USA 29°58′N 90°09′W
32 M6 **Metaline Falls** Washington, NW USA 48°51′N 117°21′W
62 K6 **Metán** Salta, N Argentina 25°29′S 64°57′W
82 N13 **Metangula** Niassa, N Mozambique 12°41′S 34°50′E
42 E7 **Metapán** Santa Ana, NW El Salvador 14°20′N 89°28′W
54 K9 **Meta, Río** ≈ Colombia/Venezuela
106 I11 **Metauro** ≈ C Italy
80 H11 **Metema** Āmara, N Ethiopia 12°53′N 36°10′E
115 D15 **Metéora** *religious building* Thessalía, C Greece
65 O20 **Meteor Rise** *undersea feature* SW Indian Ocean 46°00′S 05°30′E
186 G5 **Meteran** New Hanover, NE Papua New Guinea 02°40′S 150°12′E
Meterlam *see* Mehtar Lām
115 G20 **Methanon** *peninsula* S Greece
Methariam/Metharlam *see* Mehtar Lām
32 J6 **Methow River** ≈ Washington, NW USA
19 O10 **Methuen** Massachusetts, NE USA 42°43′N 71°10′W
185 G19 **Methven** Canterbury, South Island, New Zealand 43°37′S 171°38′E
Metis *see* Metz
113 G15 **Metković** Dubrovnik-Neretva, SE Croatia 43°02′N 17°37′E
39 Y14 **Metlakatla** Annette Island, Alaska, USA 55°07′N 131°34′W
109 V13 **Metlika** *Ger.* Möttling. SE Slovenia 45°38′N 15°18′E
109 T8 **Metnitz** Kärnten, S Austria 46°58′N 14°09′E
27 W12 **Meto, Bayou** ≈ Arkansas, C USA
168 M15 **Metro** Sumatera, W Indonesia 05°05′S 105°20′E
30 M17 **Metropolis** Illinois, N USA 37°09′N 88°43′W
Metropolitan *see* Santiago
35 N8 **Metropolitan Oakland** ✈ California, W USA 37°42′N 122°13′W
115 D15 **Métsovo** *prev.* Métsovon. Ípeiros, C Greece 39°47′N 21°12′E
Métsovon *see* Métsovo
23 V5 **Metter** Georgia, SE USA 32°24′N 82°03′W
99 H21 **Mettet** Namur, S Belgium 50°19′N 04°43′E
101 D20 **Mettlach** Saarland, SW Germany 49°28′N 06°37′E
Mettu *see* Metu
80 H13 **Metu** *var.* Mattu, Mettu. Oromīya, C Ethiopia 08°18′N 35°39′E
138 G8 **Metula** *prev.* Metulla. Northern, N Israel 33°16′N 35°35′E
169 T10 **Metulang** Borneo, N Indonesia 01°28′N 114°40′E
Metulla *see* Metula
103 T4 **Metz** *anc.* Divodurum Mediomatricum, Mediomatrica, Metis. Moselle, NE France 49°07′N 06°09′E
101 H22 **Metzingen** Baden-Württemberg, S Germany 48°31′N 09°16′E
168 G8 **Meulaboh** Sumatera, W Indonesia 04°10′N 96°09′E
99 D18 **Meulebeke** West-Vlaanderen, W Belgium 50°57′N 03°18′E
103 U6 **Meurthe** ≈ NE France
103 S5 **Meurthe-et-Moselle** ◆ *department* NE France
103 S4 **Meuse** ◆ *department* NE France
84 F10 **Meuse** *Dut.* Maas. ≈ W Europe *see also* Maas
Meuse *see* Maas
Mexcala, Río *see* Balsas, Río
25 U8 **Mexia** Texas, SW USA 31°40′N 96°28′W
58 K11 **Mexiana, Ilha** *island* NE Brazil
40 C1 **Mexicali** Baja California Norte, NW Mexico 32°34′N 115°26′W
Mexicanos, Estados Unidos *see* Mexico
41 O14 **México** *var.* Ciudad de México, *Eng.* Mexico City. ● (Mexico) México, C Mexico 19°26′N 99°08′W
27 V4 **Mexico** Missouri, C USA 19°10′N 99°04′W
18 H9 **Mexico** New York, NE USA 43°27′N 76°14′W
40 L7 **Mexico** *off.* United Mexican States, *var.* Méjico, México, *Sp.* Estados Unidos Mexicanos. ◆ *federal republic* N Central America
41 O13 **México** ◆ *state* S Mexico
México *see* Mexico
0 J13 **Mexico Basin** *var.* Sigsbee Deep. *undersea feature* C Gulf of Mexico 25°00′N 92°00′W
Mexico City *see* México
México, Golfo de *see* Mexico, Gulf of
44 B4 **Mexico, Gulf of** *Sp.* Golfo de México. *gulf* W Atlantic Ocean
Meyadine *see* Al Mayādīn
Meydān Shahr *see* Maīdān Shahr
39 Y14 **Meyers Chuck** Etolin Island, Alaska, USA 55°44′N 132°15′W
Meymaneh *see* Maīmanah
143 N7 **Meymeh** Eşfahān, C Iran 33°29′N 51°09′E
123 V7 **Meynypil'gyno** Chukotskiy Avtonomnyy Okrug, NE Russian Federation 62°33′N 177°00′E
108 A10 **Meyrin** Genève, SW Switzerland 46°14′N 06°05′E
166 L7 **Mezaligon** Ayeyarwady, SW Myanmar (Burma) 17°53′N 95°12′E
41 O15 **Mezcala** Guerrero, S Mexico 17°55′N 99°34′W
114 H8 **Mezdra** Vratsa, NW Bulgaria 43°08′N 23°42′E
103 P16 **Mèze** Hérault, S France 43°26′N 03°37′E
125 O6 **Mezen'** Arkhangel'skaya Oblast', NW Russian Federation 65°54′N 44°10′E
125 P8 **Mezen'** ≈ NW Russian Federation
Mezen, Bay of *see* Mezenskaya Guba
103 Q13 **Mézenc, Mont** ▲ C France 44°57′N 04°15′E
125 O8 **Mezenskaya Guba** *var.* Bay of Mezen. *bay* NW Russian Federation
Mezha *see* Myazha
122 H6 **Mezhdusharskiy, Ostrov** *island* Novaya Zemlya, N Russian Federation
Mezhëvo *see* Myezhava
Mezhgor'ye *see* Mizhhir"ya
117 V8 **Mezhova** Dnipropetrovs'ka Oblast', E Ukraine 48°15′N 36°44′E
10 J12 **Meziadin Junction** British Columbia, W Canada 56°06′N 129°15′W
111 G16 **Mezileské Sedlo** *var.* Przełęcz Międzyleska. *pass* Czech Republic/Poland
102 L14 **Mézin** Lot-et-Garonne, SW France 44°03′N 00°16′E
111 M24 **Mezőberény** Békés, SE Hungary 46°49′N 21°00′E
111 M25 **Mezőhegyes** Békés, SE Hungary 46°20′N 20°48′E
111 M25 **Mezőkovácsháza** Békés, SE Hungary 46°24′N 20°52′E
111 M21 **Mezőkövesd** Borsod-Abaúj-Zemplén, NE Hungary 47°49′N 20°32′E
Mezőtelegd *see* Tileagd
111 M23 **Mezőtúr** Jász-Nagykun-Szolnok, E Hungary 47°N 20°37′E
40 K10 **Mezquital** Durango, C Mexico 23°31′N 104°19′W
106 G6 **Mezzolombardo** Trentino-Alto Adige, N Italy 46°13′N 11°08′E
82 L13 **Mfuwe** Northern, N Zambia 13°00′S 31°45′E
121 O15 **Mġarr** Gozo, N Malta 36°01′N 14°18′E
126 H6 **Mglin** Bryanskaya Oblast', W Russian Federation 53°01′N 32°54′E
Mhálanna, Cionn *see* Malin Head
154 G10 **Mhow** Madhya Pradesh, C India 22°32′N 75°49′E
Miadzioł Nowy *see* Myadzyel
171 O6 **Miagao** Panay Island, C Philippines 10°40′N 122°15′E
41 R17 **Miahuatlán** *var.* Miahuatlán de Porfirio Díaz. Oaxaca, SE Mexico 16°21′N 96°36′W
Miahuatlán de Porfirio Díaz *see* Miahuatlán
104 K10 **Miajadas** Extremadura, W Spain 39°10′N 05°54′W
Miajlar *see* Myājlār
36 M14 **Miami** Arizona, SW USA 33°23′N 110°53′W
23 Z16 **Miami** Florida, SE USA 25°46′N 80°12′W
27 R8 **Miami** Oklahoma, C USA 36°53′N 94°54′W
25 O2 **Miami** Texas, SW USA 35°42′N 100°37′W
23 Z16 **Miami** ✈ Florida, SE USA 25°47′N 80°16′W
23 Z16 **Miami Beach** Florida, SE USA 25°47′N 80°08′W
23 Y15 **Miami Canal** *canal* Florida, SE USA
31 R14 **Miamisburg** Ohio, N USA 39°38′N 84°17′W
149 U10 **Miān Channūn** Punjab, E Pakistan 30°24′N 72°27′E
142 J4 **Miāndowāb** *var.* Miandub, Miyāndoāb. Āžarbāyjān-e Gharbī, NW Iran 36°57′N 46°06′E
172 H5 **Miandrivazo** Toliara, C Madagascar 19°31′S 45°29′E
Miandub *see* Miāndowāb
142 K3 **Miāneh** *var.* Miyāneh. Āžarbāyjān-e Sharqī, NW Iran 37°23′N 47°45′E
149 O16 **Miāni Hōr** *lagoon* S Pakistan
160 G10 **Mianning** Sichuan, C China 28°34′N 102°12′E
149 T7 **Miānwāli** Punjab, NE Pakistan 32°32′N 71°33′E
160 J7 **Mianxian** *var.* Mian Xian. Shaanxi, C China 33°12′N 106°36′E
Mian Xian *see* Mianxian
160 I8 **Mianyang** Sichuan, C China 31°29′N 104°43′E
Mianyang *see* Xiantao
161 R3 **Miaodao Qundao** *island group* E China
161 S13 **Miaoli** N Taiwan 24°33′N 120°48′E
122 F11 **Miass** Chelyabinskaya Oblast', C Russian Federation 55°00′N 59°55′E
110 G8 **Miastko** *Ger.* Rummelsburg in Pommern. Pomorskie, N Poland 54°N 16°58′E
Miava *see* Myjava
11 O15 **Mica Creek** British Columbia, SW Canada 51°58′N 118°29′W
160 J7 **Micang Shan** ▲ C China
Mi Chai *see* Nong Khai
111 O19 **Michalovce** *Ger.* Grossmichel, *Hung.* Nagymihály. Košický Kraj, E Slovakia 48°46′N 21°55′E
99 M20 **Michel, Baraque** *hill* E Belgium
39 S5 **Michelson, Mount** ▲ Alaska, USA 69°19′N 144°16′W
45 P9 **Miches** E Dominican Republic 18°59′N 69°03′W
30 M4 **Michigamme, Lake** ◎ Michigan, N USA
30 M4 **Michigamme Reservoir** ▣ Michigan, N USA
31 N4 **Michigamme River** ≈ Michigan, N USA
31 O7 **Michigan** *off.* State of Michigan, *also known as* Great Lakes State, Lake State, Wolverine State. ◆ *state* N USA
31 O11 **Michigan City** Indiana, N USA 41°43′N 86°52′W
31 O8 **Michigan, Lake** ◎ N USA
31 P2 **Michipicoten Bay** *lake bay* Ontario, N Canada
14 A8 **Michipicoten Island** *island* Ontario, S Canada
14 B7 **Michipicoten River** Ontario, S Canada 47°56′N 84°48′W
Michurin *see* Tsarevo
126 M6 **Michurinsk** Tambovskaya Oblast', W Russian Federation 52°56′N 40°31′E
Mico, Punta/Mico, Punto *see* Monkey Point
42 L10 **Mico, Río** ≈ SE Nicaragua
45 T12 **Micoud** SE Saint Lucia 13°49′N 60°54′W
189 N16 **Micronesia** *off.* Federated States of Micronesia. ◆ *federation* W Pacific Ocean
175 P4 **Micronesia** *island group* W Pacific Ocean
Micronesia, Federated States of *see* Micronesia
169 O9 **Midai, Pulau** *island* Kepulauan Natuna, W Indonesia
65 M17 **Mid-Atlantic Cordillera** *see* Mid-Atlantic Ridge
65 M17 **Mid-Atlantic Ridge** *var.* Mid-Atlantic Cordillera, Mid-Atlantic Rise, Mid-Atlantic Swell. *undersea feature* Atlantic Ocean 0°00′N 20°00′W
Mid-Atlantic Rise/ Mid-Atlantic Swell *see* Mid-Atlantic Ridge
99 E15 **Middelburg** Zeeland, SW Netherlands 51°30′N 03°36′E
83 H24 **Middelburg** Eastern Cape, S South Africa 31°28′S 25°01′E
83 K21 **Middelburg** Mpumalanga, NE South Africa 25°47′S 29°28′E
95 G23 **Middelfart** Syddtjylland, C Denmark 55°30′N 09°44′E
98 G13 **Middelharnis** Zuid-Holland, SW Netherlands 51°45′N 04°10′E
99 B16 **Middelkerke** West-Vlaanderen, W Belgium 51°12′N 02°51′E
98 I9 **Middenbeemster** Noord-Holland, C Netherlands 52°33′N 04°55′E
98 I8 **Middenmeer** Noord-Holland, NW Netherlands 52°48′N 04°58′E
35 Q2 **Middle Alkali Lake** ◎ California, W USA
193 S6 **Middle America Trench** *undersea feature* E Pacific Ocean 15°00′N 95°00′W
151 P19 **Middle Andaman** *island* Andaman Islands, India, NE Indian Ocean
Middle Atlas *see* Moyen Atlas
21 R3 **Middlebourne** West Virginia, NE USA 39°30′N 80°53′W
23 W9 **Middleburg** Florida, SE USA 30°03′N 81°55′W
Middleburg Island *see* 'Eua
Middle Caicos *see* Grand Caicos
25 N8 **Middle Concho River** ≈ Texas, SW USA
Middle Congo *see* Congo (Republic of)
39 R6 **Middle Fork Chandalar River** ≈ Alaska, USA
39 Q7 **Middle Fork Koyukuk River** ≈ Alaska, USA
33 O12 **Middle Fork Salmon River** ≈ Idaho, NW USA
11 T15 **Middle Lake** Saskatchewan, S Canada 52°31′N 105°16′W
28 L13 **Middle Loup River** ≈ Nebraska, C USA
185 E22 **Middlemarch** Otago, South Island, New Zealand 45°30′S 170°07′E
31 T15 **Middleport** Ohio, N USA 39°00′N 82°03′W
29 U14 **Middle Raccoon River** ≈ Iowa, C USA
29 R3 **Middle River** ≈ Minnesota, N USA
21 N8 **Middlesboro** Kentucky, S USA 36°37′N 83°42′W
97 M15 **Middlesbrough** N England, United Kingdom 54°35′N 01°14′W
42 G3 **Middlesex** Stann Creek, C Belize 17°00′N 88°31′W
97 N22 **Middlesex** *cultural region* SE England, United Kingdom
13 P15 **Middleton** Nova Scotia, SE Canada 44°56′N 65°04′W
20 F10 **Middleton** Tennessee, S USA 35°05′N 88°57′W
30 L9 **Middleton** Wisconsin, N USA 43°06′N 89°30′W
39 S13 **Middleton Island** *island* Alaska, USA
34 M7 **Middletown** California, W USA 38°44′N 122°39′W
21 Y2 **Middletown** Delaware, NE USA 39°25′N 75°39′W
18 K15 **Middletown** New Jersey, NE USA 40°23′N 74°08′W
18 K13 **Middletown** New York, NE USA 41°27′N 74°25′W
31 R14 **Middletown** Ohio, N USA 39°33′N 84°19′W
18 G15 **Middletown** Pennsylvania, NE USA 40°11′N 76°42′W
141 N14 **Midī** *var.* Maydī. NW Yemen 16°18′N 42°51′E
103 O16 **Midi, Canal du** *canal* S France
102 K17 **Midi de Bigorre, Pic du** ▲ S France 42°57′N 00°08′E
102 K17 **Midi d'Ossau, Pic du** ▲ SW France 42°51′N 00°27′W
173 R7 **Mid-Indian Basin** *undersea feature* N Indian Ocean 10°00′S 80°00′E
173 P7 **Mid-Indian Ridge** *var.* Central Indian Ridge. *undersea feature* C Indian Ocean 12°00′S 66°00′E
103 N14 **Midi-Pyrénées** ◆ *region* S France
25 N8 **Midkiff** Texas, SW USA 31°35′N 101°51′W
14 G13 **Midland** Ontario, S Canada 44°45′N 79°53′W
31 R8 **Midland** Michigan, N USA 43°37′N 84°15′W
28 M10 **Midland** South Dakota, N USA 44°04′N 101°07′W
24 M8 **Midland** Texas, SW USA 32°N 102°05′W
83 K17 **Midlands** ◆ *province* C Zimbabwe
97 D21 **Midleton** *Ir.* Mainistir na Corann. SW Ireland 51°55′N 08°10′W
25 T7 **Midlothian** Texas, SW USA 32°28′N 96°59′W
96 K12 **Midlothian** *cultural region* S Scotland, United Kingdom
172 I7 **Midongy Atsimo** Fianarantsoa, S Madagascar 21°58′S 47°47′E
102 K15 **Midou** ≈ SW France
192 J6 **Mid-Pacific Mountains** *var.* Mid-Pacific Seamounts. *undersea feature* NW Pacific Ocean 20°00′N 178°00′W
Mid-Pacific Seamounts *see* Mid-Pacific Mountains
171 Q7 **Midsayap** Mindanao, S Philippines 07°12′N 124°31′E
95 F21 **Midtjylland** ◆ *region* NW Denmark
36 L3 **Midway** Utah, W USA 40°30′N 111°28′W
192 L5 **Midway Islands** ◇ *US territory* C Pacific Ocean
33 X14 **Midwest** Wyoming, C USA 43°24′N 106°15′W
27 N10 **Midwest City** Oklahoma, C USA 35°28′N 98°24′W
152 M10 **Mid Western** ◆ *zone* W Nepal
98 P5 **Midwolda** Groningen, NE Netherlands 53°12′N 07°00′E
137 Q16 **Midyat** Mardin, SE Turkey 37°25′N 41°20′E
114 F8 **Midzhur** *SCr.* Midžor. ▲ Bulgaria/Serbia 43°24′N 22°41′E *see also* Midžor
Midzhur *see* Midžor
113 Q14 **Midžor** *Bul.* Midzhur. ▲ Bulgaria/Serbia 43°24′N 22°40′E *see also* Midzhur
Midžor *see* Midzhur
164 K14 **Mie** *off.* Mie-ken. ◆ *prefecture* Honshū, SW Japan
111 L16 **Miechów** Małopolskie, S Poland 50°21′N 20°01′E
110 F11 **Międzychód** *Ger.* Mitteldorf. Wielkopolskie, C Poland 52°36′N 15°53′E
Międzyleska, Przełęcz *see* Mezileské Sedlo
110 O12 **Międzyrzec Podlaski** Lubelskie, E Poland 52°N 22°47′E
110 E11 **Międzyrzecz** *Ger.* Meseritz. Lubuskie, W Poland 52°26′N 15°33′E
Mie-ken *see* Mie
102 L16 **Miélan** Gers, S France 43°26′N 00°19′E
111 N16 **Mielec** Podkarpackie, SE Poland 50°18′N 21°27′E
95 L21 **Mien** ◎ S Sweden
161 T12 **Mienhua Yü** *island* N Taiwan
41 O8 **Mier** Tamaulipas, C Mexico 26°28′N 99°10′W
116 J11 **Miercurea-Ciuc** *Ger.* Szeklerburg, *Hung.* Csíkszereda. Harghita, C Romania 46°24′N 25°48′E
Mieresch *see* Maros/Mureş
104 K2 **Mieres del Camín** *var.* Mieres del Camino. Asturias, NW Spain 43°15′N 05°46′W
Mieres del Camino *see* Mieres del Camín
99 K15 **Mierlo** Noord-Brabant, SE Netherlands 51°27′N 05°37′E
41 O10 **Mier y Noriega** Nuevo León, NE Mexico 23°24′N 100°06′W
Mies *see* Stříbro
80 K13 **Mī'ēso** *var.* Meheso, Miesso. Oromīya, C Ethiopia 09°13′N 40°47′E
Miesso *see* Mī'ēso
110 D10 **Mieszkowice** *Ger.* Bärwalde Neumark. Zachodnio-pomorskie, W Poland 52°45′N 14°24′E
18 G14 **Mifflinburg** Pennsylvania, NE USA 40°55′N 77°03′W
18 F14 **Mifflintown** Pennsylvania, NE USA 40°34′N 77°24′W
138 F8 **Mifrats Hefa** *Eng.* Bay of Haifa; *prev.* Mifraz Hefa. *bay* N Israel
41 R15 **Miguel Alemán, Presa** ▣ SE Mexico
40 L9 **Miguel Asua** *var.* Miguel Auza. Zacatecas, C Mexico 24°17′N 103°29′W
Miguel Auza *see* Miguel Asua
43 S15 **Miguel de la Borda** *var.* Donoso. Colón, C Panama 09°09′N 80°20′W
41 N13 **Miguel Hidalgo** ✈ (Guadalajara) Jalisco, SW Mexico 20°52′N 101°09′W
40 H7 **Miguel Hidalgo, Presa** ▣ W Mexico
116 J14 **Mihăileşti** Giurgiu, S Romania 44°20′N 25°54′E
116 M14 **Mihail Kogălniceanu** *var.* Kogălniceanu; *prev.* Caramurat, Ferdinand. Constanţa, SE Romania 44°22′N 28°27′E
117 N14 **Mihai Viteazu** Constanţa, SE Romania 44°37′N 28°41′E
136 G12 **Mihalıççık** Eskişehir, NW Turkey 39°52′N 31°30′E
164 G13 **Mihara** Hiroshima, Honshū, SW Japan 34°24′N 133°04′E
165 N14 **Mihara-yama** ▲ Miyako-jima, SE Japan 34°43′N 139°23′E
105 S8 **Mijares** ≈ E Spain
98 I11 **Mijdrecht** Utrecht, C Netherlands 52°12′N 04°52′E
165 S4 **Mikasa** Hokkaidō, NE Japan 43°15′N 141°57′E
Mikashevichi *see* Mikashevichy
119 K19 **Mikashevichy** *Pol.* Mikaszewicze, *Rus.* Mikashevichi. Brestskaya Voblasts', SW Belarus 52°13′N 27°28′E
Mikaszewicze *see* Mikashevichy
126 L5 **Mikhaylov** Ryazanskaya Oblast', W Russian Federation 54°12′N 39°03′E
Mikhaylovgrad *see* Montana
195 Z8 **Mikhaylov Island** *island* Antarctica
145 T6 **Mikhaylovka** Pavlodar, N Kazakhstan 53°49′N 76°31′E
127 N9 **Mikhaylovka** Volgogradskaya Oblast', SW Russian Federation 50°06′N 43°17′E
Mikhaylovka *see* Mykhaylivka
81 K24 **Mikindani** Mtwara, SE Tanzania 10°16′S 40°05′E
93 N18 **Mikkeli** *Swe.* Sankt Michel. Itä-Suomi, SE Finland 61°41′N 27°14′E
110 M8 **Mikołajki** *Ger.* Nikolaiken. Warmińsko-Mazurskie, NE Poland 53°49′N 21°31′E
Míkonos *see* Mýkonos
114 I9 **Mikre** Lovech, N Bulgaria 43°01′N 24°31′E
114 C13 **Mikrí Préspa, Límni** ◎ N Greece
125 P4 **Mikulkin, Mys** *headland* NW Russian Federation 67°50′N 46°36′E
81 I23 **Mikumi** Morogoro, SE Tanzania 07°22′S 37°00′E
125 R10 **Mikun'** Respublika Komi, NW Russian Federation 62°20′N 50°02′E
164 K13 **Mikuni** Fukui, Honshū, SW Japan 36°12′N 136°09′E
165 X13 **Mikura-jima** *island* E Japan
29 V7 **Milaca** Minnesota, N USA 45°45′N 93°40′W
62 J10 **Milagro** La Rioja, C Argentina 31°00′S 66°01′W
56 B7 **Milagro** Guayas, SW Ecuador 02°11′S 79°36′W
31 P4 **Milakokia Lake** ◎ Michigan, N USA
30 J1 **Milan** Illinois, N USA 41°27′N 90°33′W
31 R10 **Milan** Michigan, N USA 42°05′N 83°40′W
27 T2 **Milan** Missouri, C USA 40°12′N 93°08′W
37 Q11 **Milan** New Mexico, SW USA 35°10′N 107°53′W
20 G9 **Milan** Tennessee, S USA 35°55′N 88°45′W
Milan *see* Milano
95 F15 **Miland** Telemark, S Norway 59°57′N 08°48′E
83 N15 **Milange** Zambézia, NE Mozambique 16°09′S 35°44′E
106 D8 **Milano** *Eng.* Milan, *Ger.* Mailand; *anc.* Mediolanum. Lombardia, N Italy 45°28′N 09°10′E
25 U10 **Milano** Texas, SW USA 30°42′N 96°51′W
136 C15 **Milas** Muğla, SW Turkey 37°17′N 27°46′E
119 K21 **Milashavichy** *Rus.* Milashevichi. Homyel'skaya Voblasts', SE Belarus 51°39′N 27°56′E
Milashevichi *see* Milashavichy
119 I18 **Milavidy** *Rus.* Milovidy. Brestskaya Voblasts', SW Belarus 52°54′N 25°51′E
107 L23 **Milazzo** *anc.* Mylae. Sicilia, Italy, C Mediterranean Sea 38°13′N 15°15′E
29 R8 **Milbank** South Dakota, N USA 45°12′N 96°36′W
19 T7 **Milbridge** Maine, NE USA 44°31′N 67°55′W
100 L11 **Milde** ≈ C Germany
14 F14 **Mildmay** Ontario, S Canada 44°03′N 81°07′W
182 L9 **Mildura** Victoria, SE Australia 34°13′S 142°09′E
137 X12 **Mil Düzü** *Rus.* Mil'skaya Ravnina, Mil'skaya Step'. *physical region* C Azerbaijan
160 H13 **Mile** *var.* Miyang. Yunnan, SW China 24°28′N 103°26′E
Mile *see* Mili Atoll
181 Y10 **Miles** Queensland, E Australia 26°41′S 150°15′E
25 P8 **Miles** Texas, SW USA 31°36′N 100°10′W
33 X9 **Miles City** Montana, NW USA 46°24′N 105°48′W
11 U17 **Milestone** Saskatchewan, S Canada 50°00′N 104°24′W
107 N22 **Mileto** Calabria, SW Italy 38°35′N 16°03′E
107 K16 **Miletto, Monte** ▲ C Italy 41°28′N 14°21′E
18 M13 **Milford** Connecticut, NE USA 41°12′N 73°01′W
21 Y3 **Milford** *var.* Milford City. Delaware, NE USA 38°54′N 75°25′W
29 T11 **Milford** Iowa, C USA 43°19′N 95°09′W
19 S6 **Milford** Maine, NE USA 44°57′N 68°37′W
29 R16 **Milford** Nebraska, C USA 40°46′N 97°03′W
19 O10 **Milford** New Hampshire, NE USA 42°49′N 71°38′W
18 J13 **Milford** Pennsylvania, NE USA 41°20′N 74°48′W
25 T7 **Milford** Texas, SW USA 32°07′N 96°57′W
36 K6 **Milford** Utah, W USA 38°22′N 112°57′W
Milford *see* Milford Haven
Milford City *see* Milford
97 H21 **Milford Haven** *prev.* Milford. SW Wales, United Kingdom 51°44′N 05°02′W
27 O4 **Milford Lake** ▣ Kansas, C USA
185 B21 **Milford Sound** Southland, South Island, New Zealand 44°41′S 167°57′E
185 B21 **Milford Sound** *inlet* South Island, New Zealand
Milhau *see* Millau
Milḩ, Baḩr al *see* Razāzah, Buḩayrat ar
139 T10 **Milḩ, Wādī al** *dry watercourse* S Iraq
189 W8 **Mili Atoll** *var.* Mile. *atoll* Ratak Chain, SE Marshall Islands
110 H13 **Milicz** Dolnośląskie, SW Poland 51°32′N 17°15′E
107 L25 **Militello in Val di Catania** Sicilia, Italy, C Mediterranean Sea 37°17′N 14°47′E
11 R17 **Milk River** Alberta, SW Canada 49°10′N 112°06′W
44 J13 **Milk River** ≈ C Jamaica
33 W7 **Milk River** ≈ Montana, NW USA
80 D9 **Milk, Wadi el** *var.* Wadi al Malik. ≈ C Sudan
99 L14 **Mill** Noord-Brabant, SE Netherlands 51°42′N 05°46′E
103 P14 **Millau** *var.* Milhau; *anc.* Æmilianum. Aveyron, S France 44°06′N 03°05′E
14 I14 **Millbrook** Ontario, SE Canada 44°09′N 78°26′W
23 U4 **Milledgeville** Georgia, SE USA 33°04′N 83°13′W
12 C12 **Mille Lacs, Lac des** ◎ Ontario, S Canada
29 V6 **Mille Lacs Lake** ◎ Minnesota, N USA
23 V4 **Millen** Georgia, SE USA 32°50′N 81°56′W
191 Y5 **Millennium Island** *prev.* Caroline Island, Thornton Island. *atoll* Line Islands, E Kiribati
29 O9 **Miller** South Dakota, N USA 44°31′N 98°59′W
30 K5 **Miller Dam Flowage** ◎ Wisconsin, N USA
39 U12 **Miller, Mount** ▲ Alaska, USA 60°29′N 142°16′W
126 L10 **Millerovo** Rostovskaya Oblast', SW Russian Federation 48°57′N 40°26′E
37 N17 **Miller Peak** ▲ Arizona, SW USA 31°23′N 110°17′W
31 T12 **Millersburg** Ohio, N USA 40°33′N 81°55′W
18 G15 **Millersburg** Pennsylvania, NE USA 40°31′N 76°56′W
185 D23 **Millers Flat** Otago, South Island, New Zealand 45°42′S 169°25′E
25 Q8 **Millersview** Texas, SW USA 31°26′N 99°44′W
106 B10 **Millesimo** Piemonte, NE Italy 44°24′N 08°09′E
12 C12 **Milles Lacs, Lac des** ◎ Ontario, SW Canada
25 Q13 **Millett** Texas, SW USA 28°33′N 99°10′W
103 N11 **Millevaches, Plateau de** *plateau* C France
182 K12 **Millicent** South Australia 37°29′S 140°01′E
98 M13 **Millingen aan den Rijn** Gelderland, SE Netherlands 51°52′N 06°02′E
20 E10 **Millington** Tennessee, S USA 35°20′N 89°54′W
19 R4 **Millinocket** Maine, NE USA 45°38′N 68°45′W
19 R4 **Millinocket Lake** ◎ Maine, NE USA
195 Z11 **Mill Island** *island* Antarctica
183 T3 **Millmerran** Queensland, E Australia 27°53′S 151°15′E
109 R9 **Millstatt** Kärnten, S Austria 46°45′N 13°36′E
97 B19 **Milltown Malbay** *Ir.* Sráid na Cathrach. W Ireland 52°51′N 09°23′W
18 J17 **Millville** New Jersey, NE USA 39°24′N 75°01′W
27 S13 **Millwood Lake** ▣ Arkansas, C USA
Milne Bank *see* Milne Seamounts
186 G10 **Milne Bay** ◆ *province* SE Papua New Guinea
64 J8 **Milne Seamounts** *var.* Milne Bank. *undersea feature* N Atlantic Ocean
29 Q6 **Milnor** North Dakota, N USA 46°15′N 97°27′W
19 R5 **Milo** Maine, NE USA 45°15′N 69°01′W
115 I22 **Mílos** *island* Kykládes, Greece, Aegean Sea
Mílos *see* Pláka
110 H11 **Miłosław** Wielkopolskie, C Poland 52°13′N 17°28′E
113 K19 **Milot** *var.* Miloti. Lezhë, C Albania 41°42′N 19°43′E
Miloti *see* Milot
117 Z5 **Milove** Luhans'ka Oblast', E Ukraine 49°22′N 40°09′E
Milovidy *see* Milavidy
182 L4 **Milparinka** New South Wales, SE Australia 29°48′S 141°57′E
35 N9 **Milpitas** California, W USA 37°25′N 121°54′W
Mil'skaya Ravnina/ Mil'skaya Step' *see* Mil Düzü
14 G15 **Milton** Ontario, S Canada 43°31′N 79°53′W
185 E24 **Milton** Otago, South Island, New Zealand 46°08′S 169°59′E
21 Y4 **Milton** Delaware, NE USA 38°48′N 75°21′W
23 P8 **Milton** Florida, SE USA 30°37′N 87°02′W
18 G14 **Milton** Pennsylvania, NE USA 41°01′N 76°49′W
18 L7 **Milton** Vermont, NE USA 44°37′N 73°04′W
32 K11 **Milton-Freewater** Oregon, NW USA 45°54′N 118°24′W
97 N21 **Milton Keynes** SE England, United Kingdom 52°N 00°43′W
27 N3 **Miltonvale** Kansas, C USA 39°21′N 97°27′W
161 N10 **Miluo** Hunan, S China 28°52′N 113°00′E
30 M9 **Milwaukee** Wisconsin, N USA 43°03′N 87°56′W
Milyang *see* Miryang
Mimatum *see* Mende
37 Q15 **Mimbres Mountains** ▲ New Mexico, SW USA
182 D2 **Mimili** South Australia 27°01′S 132°33′E
102 J14 **Mimizan** Landes, SW France 44°12′N 01°12′W
Mimmaya *see* Minmaya
79 E19 **Mimongo** Ngounié, C Gabon 01°36′S 11°44′E
Min *see* Fujian
35 T7 **Mina** Nevada, W USA 38°23′N 118°07′W
143 S14 **Mīnāb** Hormozgān, SE Iran 27°08′N 57°02′E
Mina Baranīs *see* Baranīs
149 R9 **Mīna Bāzār** Baluchistān, SW Pakistan 30°58′N 69°11′E
Minami-Awaji *see* Nandan

◆ Country ● Country Capital ◇ Dependent Territory ○ Dependent Territory Capital ◆ Administrative Regions ✈ International Airport ▲ Mountain ▲ Mountain Range ♒ Volcano ≈ River ◎ Lake ▣ Reservoir

165 X17 **Minami-Iō-jima** *Eng.* San Augustine. *island* SE Japan
165 R5 **Minami-Kayabe** Hokkaidō, NE Japan 41°54′N 140°58′E
164 B16 **Minamisatsuma** *var.* Kaseda. Kagoshima, Kyūshū, SW Japan 31°25′N 130°17′E
164 C14 **Minamishimabara** *var.* Kuchinotsu. Nagasaki, Kyūshū, SW Japan 32°36′N 130°11′E
164 C17 **Minamitane** Kagoshima, Tanega-shima, SW Japan 30°23′N 130°54′E
Minami Tori Shima *see* Marcus Island
Min'an *see* Longshan
62 J4 **Mina Pirquitas** Jujuy, NW Argentina 22°48′S 66°24′W
173 O3 **Mīnā' Qābūs** NE Oman
61 F19 **Minas** Lavalleja, S Uruguay 34°20′S 55°15′W
13 P15 **Minas Basin** *bay* Nova Scotia, SE Canada
61 F17 **Minas de Corrales** Rivera, NE Uruguay 31°35′S 55°20′W
44 A5 **Minas de Matahambre** Pinar del Río, W Cuba 22°34′N 83°57′W
104 J13 **Minas de Ríotinto** Andalucía, S Spain 37°40′N 06°36′W
60 K7 **Minas Gerais** *off.* Estado de Minas Gerais. ◆ *state* E Brazil
Minas Gerais, Estado de *see* Minas Gerais
42 E5 **Minas, Sierra de las** ▲ E Guatemala
41 T15 **Minatitlán** Veracruz-Llave, E Mexico 17°59′N 94°32′W
166 L6 **Minbu** Magway, W Myanmar (Burma) 20°09′N 94°52′E
149 V10 **Minchinābād** Punjab, E Pakistan 30°10′N 73°40′E
63 G17 **Minchinmávida, Volcán** ⚠ S Chile 42°51′S 72°23′W
96 G7 **Minch, The** *var.* North Minch. *strait* NW Scotland, United Kingdom
106 F8 **Mincio** *anc.* Mincius. ⇝ N Italy
Mincius *see* Mincio
26 M11 **Minco** Oklahoma, C USA 35°18′N 97°56′W
171 Q7 **Mindanao** *island* S Philippines
Mindanao Sea *see* Bohol Sea
101 J23 **Mindel** ⇝ S Germany
101 J23 **Mindelheim** Bayern, S Germany 48°03′N 10°30′E
Mindello *see* Mindelo
76 C9 **Mindelo** *var.* Mindello; *prev.* Porto Grande. São Vicente, N Cape Verde 16°54′N 25°01′W
14 I13 **Minden** Ontario, SE Canada 44°54′N 78°41′W
100 H13 **Minden** *anc.* Minthun. Nordrhein-Westfalen, NW Germany 52°18′N 08°55′E
22 G5 **Minden** Louisiana, S USA 32°37′N 93°17′W
29 O16 **Minden** Nebraska, C USA 40°30′N 98°57′W
35 Q6 **Minden** Nevada, W USA 38°58′N 119°47′W
182 L8 **Mindona Lake** *seasonal lake* New South Wales, SE Australia
171 O4 **Mindoro** *island* N Philippines
171 N5 **Mindoro Strait** *strait* W Philippines
97 J23 **Minehead** SW England, United Kingdom 51°13′N 03°29′W
97 E21 **Mine Head** *Ir.* Mionn Ard. *headland* S Ireland 51°58′N 07°36′W
59 J19 **Mineiros** Goiás, C Brazil 17°34′S 52°33′W
25 V6 **Mineola** Texas, SW USA 32°39′N 95°29′W
25 S13 **Mineral** Texas, SW USA 28°32′N 97°54′W
127 N15 **Mineral'nyye Vody** Stavropol'skiy Kray, SW Russian Federation 44°13′N 43°06′E
30 K9 **Mineral Point** Wisconsin, N USA 42°54′N 90°09′W
25 S6 **Mineral Wells** Texas, SW USA 32°48′N 98°06′W
36 K6 **Minersville** Utah, W USA 38°12′N 112°56′W
31 U12 **Minerva** Ohio, N USA 40°43′N 81°06′W
107 N17 **Minervino Murge** Puglia, SE Italy 41°06′N 16°05′E
103 O16 **Minervois** *physical region* S France
158 I10 **Minfeng** *var.* Niya. Xinjiang Uygur Zizhiqu, NW China 37°07′N 82°43′E
79 O25 **Minga** Katanga, SE Dem. Rep. Congo 11°06′S 27°57′E
137 W11 **Mingäçevir** *Rus.* Mingechaur, Mingechevir. C Azerbaijan 40°46′N 47°02′E
137 W11 **Mingäçevir Su Anbarı** *Rus.* Mingechaurskoye Vodokhranilishche, Mingechevirskoye Vodokhranilishche. ⊠ NW Azerbaijan
166 L8 **Mingaladon** ✈ (Yangon) Yangon, SW Myanmar (Burma) 16°55′N 96°11′E
13 P11 **Mingan** Québec, E Canada 50°19′N 64°02′W
Mingāora *see* Saīdu
146 K8 **Mingbuloq** *Rus.* Mynbulak. Navoiy Viloyati, N Uzbekistan 42°18′N 62°53′E
146 K9 **Mingbuloq Botig'I** *Rus.* Vpadina Mynbulak. *depression* N Uzbekistan
Mingechaur/Mingechevir *see* Mingäçevir
Mingechaurskoye Vodokhranilishche/ Mingechevirskoye Vodokhranilishche *see* Mingäçevir Su Anbarı
161 Q7 **Mingguang** *prev.* Jiashan. Anhui, SE China 32°45′N 117°59′E
166 L4 **Mingin** Sagaing, C Myanmar (Burma) 22°51′N 94°30′E
105 Q10 **Minglanilla** Castilla-La Mancha, C Spain 39°32′N 01°36′W
31 V13 **Mingo Junction** Ohio, N USA 40°19′N 80°36′W
Mingora *see* Saīdu
163 V7 **Mingshui** Heilongjiang, NE China 47°10′N 125°53′E
Mingtekl Daban *see* Mintaka Pass
Mingu *see* Zhenfeng
83 Q14 **Minguri** Nampula, NE Mozambique 14°30′S 40°37′E
Mingzhou *see* Suide
159 U10 **Minhe** *var.* Chuankou; *prev.* Minhe Huizu Tuzu Zizhixian, Shangchuankou. Qinghai, C China 36°21′N 102°40′E
Minhe Huizu Tuzu Zizhixian *see* Minhe
166 L6 **Minhla** Magway, W Myanmar (Burma) 19°58′N 95°03′E
167 S14 **Minh Lương** Kiên Giang, S Vietnam 09°52′N 105°10′E
104 G5 **Minho** *former province* N Portugal
104 G5 **Minho, Rio** *Sp.* Miño. ⇝ Portugal/Spain *see also* Miño
Minho, Rio *see* Miño
155 C24 **Minicoy Island** *island* SW India
33 P15 **Minidoka** Idaho, NW USA 42°45′N 113°29′W
118 C11 **Minija** ⇝ W Lithuania
180 G9 **Minilya** Western Australia 23°45′S 114°03′E
14 E8 **Minisinakwa Lake** ⊚ Ontario, S Canada
45 T12 **Ministre Point** *headland* S Saint Lucia 13°42′N 60°57′W
11 V15 **Minitonas** Manitoba, S Canada 52°07′N 101°02′W
Minius *see* Miño
161 R12 **Min Jiang** ⇝ SE China
160 H10 **Min Jiang** ⇝ C China
182 H9 **Minlaton** South Australia 34°52′S 137°33′E
159 S9 **Minle** Gansu, N China
165 Q6 **Minmaya** *var.* Mimmaya. Aomori, Honshū, C Japan 41°10′N 140°24′E
77 U14 **Minna** Niger, C Nigeria 09°33′N 06°33′E
165 P16 **Minna-jima** *island* Sakishima-shotō, SW Japan
27 N4 **Minneapolis** Kansas, C USA 39°08′N 97°43′W
29 U9 **Minneapolis** Minnesota, N USA 44°59′N 93°16′W
29 V8 **Minneapolis-Saint Paul** ✈ Minnesota, N USA 44°53′N 93°13′W
11 W16 **Minnedosa** Manitoba, S Canada 50°14′N 99°50′W
26 J7 **Minneola** Kansas, C USA 37°26′N 100°00′W
29 S7 **Minnesota** *off.* State of Minnesota, *also known as* Gopher State, New England of the West, North Star State. ◆ *state* N USA
29 S9 **Minnesota River** ⇝ Minnesota/South Dakota, N USA
29 V9 **Minnetonka** Minnesota, N USA 44°55′N 93°28′W
29 O3 **Minnewaukan** North Dakota, N USA 48°04′N 99°14′W
182 F7 **Minnipa** South Australia 32°52′S 135°07′E
104 G5 **Miño** *var.* Mino, Minius, *Port.* Rio Minho. ⇝ Portugal/Spain *see also* Minho, Rio
Miño *see* Minho, Rio
30 L4 **Minocqua** Wisconsin, N USA 45°53′N 89°42′W
30 L12 **Minonk** Illinois, N USA 40°54′N 89°01′W
Minorca *see* Menorca
28 M3 **Minot** North Dakota, N USA 48°15′N 101°19′W
159 U8 **Minqin** Gansu, N China 38°35′N 103°07′E
119 J16 **Minsk** ● (Belarus) Minskaya Voblasts', C Belarus 53°52′N 27°34′E
119 L16 **Minsk** ✈ Minskaya Voblasts', C Belarus 53°52′N 27°58′E
Minskaya Oblast' *see* Minskaya Voblasts'
119 K16 **Minskaya Voblasts'** *prev. Rus.* Minskaya Oblast'. ◆ *province* C Belarus
119 J16 **Minskaya Wzvyshsha** ▲ C Belarus
110 N12 **Mińsk Mazowiecki** *var.* Nowo-Minsk. Mazowieckie, C Poland 52°10′N 21°31′E
31 Q13 **Minster** Ohio, N USA 40°23′N 84°22′W
79 F15 **Minta** Centre, C Cameroon 04°34′N 12°54′E
149 W2 **Mintaka Pass** *Chin.* Mingtekl Daban. *pass* China/Pakistan
115 D20 **Mínthi** ▲ S Greece
Minthun *see* Minden
13 O14 **Minto** New Brunswick, SE Canada 46°05′N 66°05′W
10 H6 **Minto** Yukon Territory, W Canada 62°33′N 136°45′W
39 R9 **Minto** Alaska, USA 65°07′N 149°22′W
29 Q3 **Minto** North Dakota, N USA 48°17′N 97°22′W
12 K6 **Minto, Lac** ⊚ Québec, C Canada
195 R16 **Minto, Mount** ▲ Antarctica 71°38′S 169°11′E
11 U17 **Minton** Saskatchewan, S Canada 49°12′N 104°33′W
189 R15 **Minto Reef** *atoll* Caroline Islands, C Micronesia
37 R4 **Minturn** Colorado, C USA 39°34′N 106°21′W
107 J16 **Minturno** Lazio, C Italy 41°15′N 13°47′E
122 K13 **Minusinsk** Krasnoyarskiy Kray, S Russian Federation 53°37′N 91°49′E
108 G11 **Minusio** Ticino, S Switzerland 46°11′N 08°47′E
79 E17 **Minvoul** Woleu-Ntem, N Gabon 02°08′N 12°12′E
141 R13 **Minwakh** N Yemen 16°55′N 48°04′E
159 V11 **Minxian** *var.* Min Xian, Minyang. Gansu, C China 34°20′N 104°09′E
Min Xian *see* Minxian
Minya *see* Al Minyā
Minyang *see* Minxian
31 R6 **Mio** Michigan, N USA 44°40′N 84°09′W
Mionn Ard *see* Mine Head
158 L5 **Miquan** Xinjiang Uygur Zizhiqu, NW China 44°04′N 87°40′E
119 I17 **Mir** Hrodzyenskaya Voblasts', W Belarus 53°25′N 26°28′E
106 H8 **Mira** Veneto, NE Italy 45°25′N 12°07′E
12 K15 **Mirabel** *var.* Montreal. ✈ (Montréal) Québec, SE Canada 45°27′N 73°47′W
60 Q8 **Miracema** Rio de Janeiro, SE Brazil 21°24′S 42°10′W
54 G9 **Miraflores** Boyacá, C Colombia 05°07′N 73°09′W
40 G10 **Miraflores** Baja California Sur, NW Mexico 23°24′N 109°45′W
44 L9 **Miragoâne** S Haiti 18°25′N 73°07′W
155 E16 **Miraj** Mahārāshtra, W India 16°51′N 74°42′E
61 E23 **Miramar** Buenos Aires, E Argentina 38°15′S 57°50′W
103 R15 **Miramas** Bouches-du-Rhône, SE France 43°33′N 05°02′E
102 K12 **Mirambeau** Charente-Maritime, W France 45°23′N 00°33′W
102 L13 **Miramont-de-Guyenne** Lot-et-Garonne, SW France 44°34′N 00°20′E
115 L25 **Mirampéllou Kólpos** *gulf* Kríti, Greece, E Mediterranean Sea
158 L8 **Miran** Xinjiang Uygur Zizhiqu, NW China 39°13′N 88°58′E
54 M5 **Miranda** *off.* Estado Miranda. ◆ *state* N Venezuela
Miranda de Corvo *see* Miranda do Corvo
105 O3 **Miranda de Ebro** La Rioja, N Spain 42°41′N 02°57′W
104 G8 **Miranda do Corvo** *var.* Miranda de Corvo. Coimbra, N Portugal 40°05′N 08°20′W
104 J6 **Miranda do Douro** Bragança, N Portugal 41°30′N 06°16′W
Miranda, Estado *see* Miranda
102 L15 **Mirande** Gers, S France 43°31′N 00°25′E
104 I6 **Mirandela** Bragança, N Portugal 41°28′N 07°10′W
25 R15 **Mirando City** Texas, SW USA 27°24′N 99°00′W
106 G9 **Mirandola** Emilia-Romagna, N Italy 44°52′N 11°04′E
60 I8 **Mirandópolis** São Paulo, S Brazil 21°10′S 51°03′W
104 G13 **Mira, Rio** ⇝ S Portugal
60 K8 **Mirassol** São Paulo, S Brazil 20°50′S 49°30′W
104 J3 **Miravalles** ▲ NW Spain 42°52′N 06°45′W
42 L12 **Miravalles, Volcán** ⚠ NW Costa Rica 10°43′N 85°07′W
141 W13 **Mirbāṭ** *var.* Marbat. S Oman 17°03′N 54°44′E
44 M9 **Mirebalais** C Haiti 18°51′N 72°08′W
103 T6 **Mirecourt** Vosges, NE France 48°19′N 06°04′E
103 N16 **Mirepoix** Ariège, S France 43°05′N 01°51′E
Mirgorod *see* Myrhorod
139 W10 **Mīr Ḥājī Khalīl** Wāsiṭ, E Iraq 32°11′N 46°19′E
169 T8 **Miri** Sarawak, East Malaysia 04°23′N 113°59′E
77 W12 **Miria** Zinder, S Niger 13°39′N 09°15′E
182 F5 **Mirikata** South Australia 29°56′S 135°13′E
54 K4 **Mirimire** Falcón, N Venezuela 11°14′N 68°39′W
61 H18 **Mirim Lagoon** *var.* Lake Mirim, *Sp.* Laguna Merín. *lagoon* Brazil/Uruguay
Mirim, Lake *see* Mirim Lagoon
Mírina *see* Mýrina
172 H14 **Miringoni** Mohéli, S Comoros 12°17′S 93°39′E
143 W11 **Mīrjāveh** Sīstān va Balūchestān, SE Iran 29°04′N 61°24′E
195 Z9 **Mirny** *Russian research station* Antarctica 66°25′S 93°09′E
124 M10 **Mirnyy** Arkhangel'skaya Oblast', NW Russian Federation 62°50′N 40°20′E
123 O10 **Mirnyy** Respublika Sakha (Yakutiya), NE Russian Federation 62°30′N 113°58′E
Mironovka *see* Myronivka
110 F9 **Mirosławiec** Zachodnio-pomorskie, NW Poland 53°21′N 16°04′E
Mirovo *see* Vrattsa
100 N10 **Mirow** Mecklenburg-Vorpommern, N Germany 53°16′N 12°48′E
152 G6 **Mīrpur** Jammu and Kashmir, NW India 33°06′N 73°49′E
Mīrpur *see* New Mīrpur
149 P17 **Mīrpur Batoro** Sind, SE Pakistan 24°40′N 68°15′E
149 Q16 **Mīrpur Khās** Sind, SE Pakistan 25°31′N 69°01′E
149 P17 **Mīrpur Sakro** Sind, SE Pakistan 24°32′N 67°38′E
143 T14 **Mīr Shahdād** Hormozgān, S Iran 26°15′N 58°29′E
Mirtoan Sea *see* Mirtóo Pélagos
115 G21 **Mirtóo Pélagos** *Eng.* Mirtoan Sea; *anc.* Myrtoum Mare. *sea* S Greece
163 Z16 **Miryang** *var.* Milyang, *Jap.* Mitsuō. SE South Korea 35°30′N 128°46′E
Mirzachirla *see* Murzechirla
164 E14 **Misaki** Ehime, Shikoku, SW Japan 33°22′N 132°04′E
41 Q13 **Misantla** Veracruz-Llave, E Mexico 19°54′N 96°51′W
165 R7 **Misawa** Aomori, Honshū, C Japan 40°42′N 141°26′E
57 G14 **Mishagua, Río** ⇝ C Peru
163 Z8 **Mishan** Heilongjiang, NE China 45°30′N 131°53′E
31 O11 **Mishawaka** Indiana, N USA 41°40′N 86°10′W
39 N6 **Misheguk Mountain** ▲ Alaska, USA 68°13′N 161°11′W
165 N14 **Mishima** *var.* Misima. Shizuoka, Honshū, S Japan 35°08′N 138°54′E
164 E12 **Mi-shima** *island* SW Japan
127 V4 **Mishkino** Respublika Bashkortostan, W Russian Federation 55°31′N 55°57′E
153 Y10 **Mishmi Hills** *hill range* NE India
161 N11 **Mi Shui** ⇝ S China
Misiaf *see* Maṣyāf
107 J23 **Misilmeri** Sicilia, Italy, C Mediterranean Sea 38°03′N 13°27′E
Misima *see* Mishima
14 C7 **Missinaibi Lake** ⊚ Ontario, S Canada
Misión de Guana *see* Guana
60 F13 **Misiones** *off.* Provincia de Misiones. ◆ *province* NE Argentina
62 P8 **Misiones** *off.* Departamento de las Misiones. ◆ *department* S Paraguay
Misiones, Departamento de las *see* Misiones
Misiones, Provincia de *see* Misiones
Misión San Fernando *see* San Fernando
Miskin *see* Maskin
Miskito Coast *see* La Mosquitia
43 O7 **Miskitos, Cayos** *island group* NE Nicaragua
111 M21 **Miskolc** Borsod-Abaúj-Zemplén, NE Hungary 48°05′N 20°46′E
171 T12 **Misool, Pulau** *island* Maluku, E Indonesia
Misox *see* Mesocco
29 Y3 **Misquah Hills** *hill range* Minnesota, N USA
75 P7 **Miṣrātah** *var.* Misurata. NW Libya 32°23′N 15°06′E
75 P7 **Miṣrātah, Râs** *headland* N Libya 32°22′N 15°16′E
14 C7 **Missanabie** Ontario, S Canada 48°18′N 84°04′W
58 E10 **Missão Catrimani** Roraima, N Brazil 01°26′N 62°05′W
14 D6 **Missinaibi** ⇝ Ontario, S Canada
11 T13 **Missinipe** Saskatchewan, C Canada 55°36′N 104°45′W
28 M11 **Mission** South Dakota, N USA 43°16′N 100°38′W
25 S17 **Mission** Texas, SW USA 26°13′N 98°19′W
12 F10 **Missisa Lake** ⊚ Ontario, C Canada
18 M6 **Missisquoi Bay** *lake bay* Canada/USA
14 C10 **Mississagi** ⇝ Ontario, S Canada
14 G15 **Mississauga** Ontario, S Canada 43°38′N 79°36′W
31 P12 **Mississinewa Lake** ⊠ Indiana, N USA
31 P12 **Mississinewa River** ⇝ Indiana/Ohio, N USA
22 K4 **Mississippi** *off.* State of Mississippi, *also known as* Bayou State, Magnolia State. ◆ *state* SE USA
14 K13 **Mississippi** ⇝ Ontario, SE Canada
47 N1 **Mississippi Fan** *undersea feature* N Gulf of Mexico 26°45′N 88°30′W
14 L13 **Mississippi Lake** ⊚ Ontario, SE Canada
22 M10 **Mississippi Delta** *delta* Louisiana, S USA
0 J11 **Mississippi River** ⇝ C USA
22 M9 **Mississippi Sound** *sound* Alabama/Mississippi, S USA
33 P9 **Missoula** Montana, NW USA 46°54′N 114°03′W
27 T5 **Missouri** *off.* State of Missouri, *also known as* Bullion State, Show Me State. ◆ *state* C USA
25 V11 **Missouri City** Texas, SW USA 29°37′N 95°32′W
0 J10 **Missouri River** ⇝ C USA
15 Q6 **Mistassibi** ⇝ Québec, SE Canada
15 P6 **Mistassini** ⇝ Québec, SE Canada
12 J11 **Mistassini, Lac** ⊚ Québec, SE Canada
109 Y3 **Mistelbach an der Zaya** Niederösterreich, NE Austria 48°34′N 16°33′E
107 L24 **Misterbianco** Sicilia, Italy, C Mediterranean Sea 37°31′N 15°01′E
95 N19 **Misterhult** Kalmar, S Sweden 57°28′N 16°34′E
12 K11 **Mistissini** *var.* Baie-du-Poste. Québec, SE Canada 50°20′N 73°50′W
57 H17 **Misti, Volcán** ⚠ S Peru 16°20′S 71°22′W
Mistras *see* Mystrás
107 K23 **Mistretta** *anc.* Amestratus. Sicilia, Italy, C Mediterranean Sea 37°56′N 14°22′E
164 F12 **Misumi** Shimane, Honshū, SW Japan 34°47′N 132°00′E
Misurata *see* Miṣrātah
83 O14 **Mitande** Niassa, N Mozambique 14°06′S 36°03′E
40 J13 **Mita, Punta de** *headland* C Mexico 20°46′N 105°31′W
55 W12 **Mitaraka, Massif du** ▲ NE South America 02°18′N 54°31′W
Mitau *see* Jelgava
181 X9 **Mitchell** Queensland, E Australia 26°29′S 148°00′E
14 E15 **Mitchell** Ontario, S Canada 43°28′N 81°11′W
28 I13 **Mitchell** Nebraska, C USA 41°56′N 103°48′W
32 J12 **Mitchell** Oregon, NW USA 44°34′N 120°09′W
29 P11 **Mitchell** South Dakota, N USA 43°42′N 98°01′W
23 P5 **Mitchell Lake** ⊠ Alabama, S USA
31 P7 **Mitchell, Lake** ⊚ Michigan, N USA
21 P9 **Mitchell, Mount** ▲ North Carolina, SE USA 35°46′N 82°16′W
181 V3 **Mitchell River** ⇝ Queensland, NE Australia
97 D20 **Mitchelstown** *Ir.* Baile Mhistéala. SW Ireland 52°20′N 08°16′W
14 M9 **Mitchinamécus, Lac** ⊚ Québec, SE Canada
Mitèmboni *see* Mitemele, Río
79 D17 **Mitemele, Río** *var.* Mitèmboni, Temboni, Utamboni. ⇝ S Equatorial Guinea
149 S12 **Mithān Kot** Punjab, E Pakistan 28°53′N 70°25′E
149 T7 **Mitha Tiwāna** Punjab, E Pakistan 32°18′N 72°08′E
149 R17 **Mithi** Sind, SE Pakistan 24°43′N 69°53′E
Míthimna *see* Míthymna
Mi Tho *see* My Tho
115 L16 **Míthymna** *var.* Míthimna. Lésvos, E Greece 39°20′N 26°12′E
190 L16 **Mitiaro** *island* S Cook Islands
Mitilíni *see* Mytilíni
15 U7 **Mitis** ⇝ Québec, SE Canada
41 R16 **Mitla** Oaxaca, SE Mexico 16°56′N 96°19′W
165 P13 **Mito** Ibaraki, Honshū, S Japan 36°21′N 140°26′E
92 N2 **Mitra, Kapp** *headland* W Svalbard 79°07′N 11°11′E
184 M13 **Mitre** ▲ North Island, New Zealand 40°46′S 175°27′E
185 B21 **Mitre Peak** ▲ South Island, New Zealand 44°37′S 167°45′E
39 O15 **Mitrofania Island** *island* Alaska, USA
Mitrovica/Mitrovicë *see* Kosovska Mitrovica, Serbia
Mitrovica/Mitrowitz *see* Sremska Mitrovica, Serbia
113 M16 **Mitrovicë** *Serb.* Mitrovica, Kosovska Mitrovica, Titova Mitrovica. N Kosovo 42°54′N 20°52′E
172 H12 **Mitsamiouli** Grande Comore, NW Comoros 11°22′S 43°19′E
172 I3 **Mitsinjo** Mahajanga, NW Madagascar 16°00′S 45°52′E
80 J9 **Mits'iwa** *var.* Masawa, Massawa. E Eritrea 15°37′N 39°27′E
172 H13 **Mitsoudjé** Grande Comore, NW Comoros
138 F12 **Mitspe Ramon** *prev.* Mizpe Ramon. Southern, S Israel 30°38′N 34°47′E
165 T5 **Mitsuishi** Hokkaidō, NE Japan 42°12′N 142°40′E
165 O11 **Mitsuke** *var.* Mituke. Niigata, Honshū, C Japan 37°30′N 138°54′E
Mitsuō *see* Miryang
164 C12 **Mitsushima** Nagasaki, Tsushima, SW Japan 34°16′N 129°18′E
100 G12 **Mittelandkanal** *canal* NW Germany
108 J7 **Mittelberg** Vorarlberg, NW Austria 47°19′N 10°09′E
Mitteldorf *see* Międzychód
Mittelstadt *see* Baia Sprie
Mitterburg *see* Pazin
109 P7 **Mittersill** Salzburg, NW Austria 47°16′N 12°27′E
Mittimatalik *see* Pond Inlet
101 N16 **Mittweida** Sachsen, E Germany 50°59′N 12°57′E
54 J13 **Mitú** Vaupés, SE Colombia 01°07′N 70°05′W
Mituke *see* Mitsuke
Mitumba, Chaîne des/ Mitumba Range *see* Mitumba, Monts
79 O22 **Mitumba, Monts** *var.* Chaîne des Mitumba, Mitumba Range. ▲ E Dem. Rep. Congo
79 N23 **Mitwaba** Katanga, SE Dem. Rep. Congo 08°37′S 27°20′E
79 E18 **Mitzic** Woleu-Ntem, N Gabon 00°48′N 11°30′E
82 K11 **Miueru Wantipa, Lake** ⊚ N Zambia
165 N14 **Miura** Kanagawa, Honshū, S Japan 35°08′N 139°37′E
165 Q10 **Miyagi** *off.* Miyagi-ken. ◆ *prefecture* Honshū, C Japan
Miyagi-ken *see* Miyagi
138 M7 **Miyāh, Wādī al** *dry watercourse* E Syria
165 X13 **Miyake** Tōkyō, Miyako-jima, SE Japan 34°35′N 135°33′E
165 Q16 **Miyake-jima** *island* Sakishima-shotō, SW Japan
165 R8 **Miyako** Iwate, Honshū, C Japan 39°39′N 141°57′E
164 D16 **Miyakonojō** *var.* Miyakonzyô. Miyazaki, Kyūshū, SW Japan 31°42′N 131°04′E
Miyakonzyô *see* Miyakonojō
165 Q16 **Miyako-shotō** *island group* SW Japan
144 G11 **Miyaly** Atyrau, W Kazakhstan 48°52′N 53°55′E
Miyāndoāb *see* Mīāndowāb
Miyāneh *see* Mīāneh
Miyang *see* Mile
164 D16 **Miyazaki** Miyazaki, Kyūshū, SW Japan 31°55′N 131°24′E
164 D16 **Miyazaki** *off.* Miyazaki-ken. ◆ *prefecture* Kyūshū, SW Japan
Miyazaki-ken *see* Miyazaki
164 J12 **Miyazu** Kyōto, Honshū, SW Japan 35°33′N 135°12′E
Miyory *see* Myory
164 G12 **Miyoshi** *var.* Miyosi. Hiroshima, Honshū, SW Japan 34°48′N 132°51′E
Miyosi *see* Miyoshi
Miza *see* Mizë
81 H14 **Mīzan Teferī** Southern Nationalities, S Ethiopia 06°57′N 35°30′E
Mizda *see* Mizdah
75 O8 **Mizdah** *var.* Mizda. NW Libya 31°26′N 12°59′E
113 K20 **Mizë** *var.* Miza. Fier, W Albania 40°58′N 19°32′E
97 A22 **Mizen Head** *Ir.* Carn Uí Néid. *headland* SW Ireland 51°26′N 09°50′W
116 H7 **Mizhhir"ya** *Rus.* Mezhgor'ye. Zakarpats'ka Oblast', W Ukraine 48°30′N 23°30′E
160 L4 **Mizhi** Shaanxi, C China 37°50′N 110°03′E
116 K13 **Mizil** Prahova, SE Romania 45°00′N 26°29′E
114 H7 **Miziya** Vratsa, NW Bulgaria 43°42′N 23°52′E
153 W15 **Mizo Hills** *hill range* E India
153 W15 **Mizoram** ◆ *state* NE India
Mizpe Ramon *see* Mitspe Ramon
57 L19 **Mizque** Cochabamba, C Bolivia 17°57′S 65°10′W
57 M19 **Mizque, Río** ⇝ C Bolivia
165 Q9 **Mizusawa** *var.* Ōshū. Iwate, Honshū, C Japan 39°10′N 141°07′E
95 M18 **Mjölby** Östergötland, S Sweden 58°19′N 15°10′E
95 G15 **Mjøndalen** Buskerud, S Norway 59°45′N 09°58′E
95 J19 **Mjörn** ⊚ S Sweden
94 I13 **Mjøsa** *var.* Mjøsen. ⊚ S Norway
Mjøsen *see* Mjøsa
81 G21 **Mkalama** Singida, C Tanzania 04°09′S 34°35′E
80 K13 **Mkata** ⇝ C Tanzania
83 K14 **Mkushi** Central, C Zambia 13°40′S 29°26′E
83 L22 **Mkuze** KwaZulu/Natal, E South Africa 27°37′S 32°03′E
81 J22 **Mkwaja** Tanga, E Tanzania 05°42′S 38°48′E
111 D16 **Mladá Boleslav** *Ger.* Jungbunzlau. Středočeský Kraj, N Czech Republic 50°26′N 14°55′E
112 M12 **Mladenovac** Serbia, C Serbia 44°27′N 20°42′E
114 L11 **Mladinovo** Khaskovo, S Bulgaria 41°57′N 26°13′E
113 O17 **Mlado Nagoričane** N FYR Macedonia 42°11′N 21°49′E
Mlanje *see* Mulanje
112 N12 **Mlava** ⇝ E Serbia
110 L9 **Mława** Mazowieckie, C Poland 53°07′N 20°23′E
113 G16 **Mljet** *It.* Meleda; *anc.* Melita. *island* S Croatia
167 S11 **Mlu Prey** *prev.* Phumĭ Mlu Prey. Preăh Vihéar, N Cambodia 13°48′N 105°16′E
116 K4 **Mlyniv** Rivnens'ka Oblast', NW Ukraine 50°31′N 25°36′E
83 I21 **Mmabatho** North-West, N South Africa 25°51′S 25°37′E
83 I19 **Mmashoro** Central, E Botswana 21°56′S 26°39′E
44 J7 **Moa** Holguín, E Cuba 20°42′N 74°57′W
76 J15 **Moa** ⇝ Guinea/Sierra Leone
37 O6 **Moab** Utah, W USA 38°35′N 109°34′W
181 V1 **Moa Island** *island* Queensland, NE Australia
187 Y15 **Moala** *island* S Fiji
83 L21 **Moamba** Maputo, SW Mozambique 25°35′S 32°13′E
79 F19 **Moanda** *var.* Mouanda. Haut-Ogooué, SE Gabon 01°31′S 13°07′E
83 M15 **Moatize** Tete, NW Mozambique 16°04′S 33°43′E
79 P22 **Moba** Katanga, E Dem. Rep. Congo 07°03′S 29°52′E
Mobay *see* Montego Bay
79 K15 **Mobaye** Basse-Kotto, S Central African Republic 04°19′N 21°17′E
79 K15 **Mobayi-Mbongo** Equateur, NW Dem. Rep. Congo 04°21′N 21°10′E
25 P2 **Mobeetie** Texas, SW USA 35°33′N 100°25′W
27 U3 **Moberly** Missouri, C USA 39°25′N 92°26′W
23 N8 **Mobile** Alabama, S USA 30°42′N 88°03′W
23 N9 **Mobile Bay** *bay* Alabama, S USA
23 N8 **Mobile River** ⇝ Alabama, S USA
29 N8 **Mobridge** South Dakota, N USA 45°32′N 100°25′W
Mobutu Sese Seko, Lac *see* Albert, Lake
45 N8 **Moca** N Dominican Republic 19°26′N 70°33′W
83 Q15 **Moçambique** Nampula, NE Mozambique 15°00′S 40°44′E
Moçâmedes *see* Namibe
167 S6 **Môc Châu** Sơn La, N Vietnam 20°49′N 104°38′E
187 Z15 **Moce** *island* Lau Group, E Fiji
Moce *see* Al Mukhā
193 T11 **Mocha Fracture Zone** *tectonic feature* SE Pacific Ocean
63 F14 **Mocha, Isla** *island* C Chile
56 C12 **Moche, Río** ⇝ W Peru
167 S14 **Mộc Hoa** Long An, S Vietnam 10°46′N 105°56′E
83 I20 **Mochudi** Kgatleng, SE Botswana 24°25′S 26°07′E
82 Q13 **Mocímboa da Praia** *var.* Vila de Mocímboa da Praia. Cabo Delgado, N Mozambique 11°17′S 40°21′E
94 L13 **Mockfjärd** Dalarna, C Sweden 60°30′N 14°57′E
21 R9 **Mocksville** North Carolina, SE USA 35°53′N 80°33′W
32 F8 **Moclips** Washington, NW USA 47°11′N 124°13′W
82 C13 **Môco** *var.* Morro de Môco. ▲ W Angola 12°36′S 15°09′E
54 D13 **Mocoa** Putumayo, SW Colombia 01°07′N 76°38′W
60 M8 **Mococa** São Paulo, S Brazil 21°30′S 47°00′W
Môco, Morro de *see* Môco
40 H8 **Mocorito** Sinaloa, C Mexico 25°24′N 107°55′W
40 J4 **Moctezuma** Chihuahua, N Mexico 30°10′N 106°28′W
41 N11 **Moctezuma** San Luis Potosí, C Mexico 22°46′N 101°06′W
40 G4 **Moctezuma** Sonora, NW Mexico 29°50′N 109°40′W
41 P12 **Moctezuma, Río** ⇝ C Mexico
Mó, Cuan *see* Clew Bay
83 O16 **Mocuba** Zambézia, NE Mozambique 16°50′S 37°02′E
103 U12 **Modane** Savoie, E France 45°14′N 06°41′E
106 F9 **Modena** *anc.* Mutina. Emilia-Romagna, N Italy 44°39′N 10°55′E
36 I7 **Modena** Utah, W USA 37°46′N 113°54′W
35 O9 **Modesto** California, W USA 37°38′N 121°02′W
107 L25 **Modica** *anc.* Motyca. Sicilia, Italy, C Mediterranean Sea 36°52′N 14°45′E
83 J20 **Modimolle** *prev.* Nylstroom. Limpopo, NE South Africa 24°39′N 28°23′E
79 K17 **Modjamboli** Equateur, N Dem. Rep. Congo 02°27′N 22°03′E
109 X4 **Mödling** Niederösterreich, NE Austria 48°06′N 16°18′E
Modohn *see* Madona
Modot *see* Tsenhermandal
171 V14 **Modowi** Papua, E Indonesia 04°05′S 134°39′E
112 I12 **Modračko Jezero** ⊠ NE Bosnia and Herzegovina
112 I10 **Modriča** Republika Srpska, N Bosnia and Herzegovina 44°57′N 18°17′E
183 O13 **Moe** Victoria, SE Australia 38°11′S 146°18′E
Moearatewe *see* Muaratewe
Moei, Mae Nam *see* Thaungyin
94 H13 **Moelv** Hedmark, S Norway 60°55′N 10°47′E
92 I10 **Moen** Troms, N Norway 69°08′N 18°35′E
Möen *see* Møn, Denmark
Moen *see* Weno, Micronesia
Moena *see* Muna, Pulau
36 M10 **Moenkopi Wash** ⇝ Arizona, SW USA
185 F22 **Moeraki Point** *headland* South Island, New Zealand 45°23′S 170°52′E
99 F16 **Moerbeke** Oost-Vlaanderen, NW Belgium 51°11′N 03°57′E
99 H14 **Moerdijk** Noord-Brabant, S Netherlands 51°42′N 04°37′E
Moero, Lac *see* Mweru, Lake
101 D15 **Moers** *var.* Mörs. Nordrhein-Westfalen, W Germany 51°27′N 06°36′E
Moesi *see* Musi, Air
Moeskroen *see* Mouscron
96 J13 **Moffat** SE Scotland, United Kingdom 55°29′N 03°36′W
185 C22 **Moffat Peak** ▲ South Island, New Zealand 44°57′S 168°10′E
79 N19 **Moga** Sud-Kivu, E Dem. Rep. Congo 02°16′S 26°54′E
152 H8 **Moga** Punjab, N India 30°49′N 75°13′E
Mogadiscio/Mogadishu *see* Muqdisho
Mogador *see* Essaouira
104 J6 **Mogadouro** Bragança, N Portugal 41°20′N 06°43′W
167 N2 **Mogaung** Kachin State, N Myanmar (Burma) 25°20′N 96°54′E
110 L13 **Mogielnica** Mazowieckie, C Poland 51°40′N 20°42′E
Mogilëv *see* Mahilyow
Mogilev-Podol'skiy *see* Mohyliv-Podil's'kyy
Mogilëvskaya Oblast' *see* Mahilyowskaya Voblasts'
110 I11 **Mogilno** Kujawsko-pomorskie, C Poland 52°39′N 17°58′E
83 Q15 **Mogincual** Nampula, NE Mozambique 15°33′S 40°28′E
114 E13 **Moglenítsas** ⇝ N Greece
106 H8 **Mogliano Veneto** Veneto, NE Italy 45°34′N 12°14′E
113 M21 **Moglicë** Korçë, SE Albania 40°43′N 20°22′E
123 O13 **Mogocha** Zabaykal'skiy Kray, S Russian Federation 53°39′N 119°47′E
122 J11 **Mogochin** Tomskaya Oblast', C Russian Federation 57°42′N 83°24′E
80 F13 **Mogogh** Jonglei, E South Sudan 08°26′N 31°19′E
171 U12 **Mogoi** Papua, E Indonesia 01°44′S 133°13′E
166 M4 **Mogok** Mandalay, Myanmar (Burma) 22°55′N 96°29′E
37 P14 **Mogollon Mountains** ▲ New Mexico, SW USA
36 M12 **Mogollon Rim** *cliff* Arizona, SW USA
61 E23 **Mogotes, Punta** *headland* E Argentina 38°03′S 57°31′W
42 J8 **Mogotón** ▲ NW Nicaragua 13°45′N 86°22′W
104 I14 **Moguer** Andalucía, S Spain 37°15′N 06°52′W
111 J26 **Mohács** Baranya, SW Hungary 46°N 18°40′E
185 C20 **Mohaka** ⇝ North Island, New Zealand
28 M2 **Mohall** North Dakota, N USA 48°45′N 101°30′W
Moḥammadābād *see* Dargaz
143 U12 **Moḥammadābād-e Rīgān** Kermān, SE Iran 28°39′N 59°01′E
74 F6 **Mohammedia** *prev.* Fédala. NW Morocco 33°46′N 07°16′W
74 F6 **Mohammed V** ✈ (Casablanca) W Morocco 33°07′N 08°28′W
Mohammerah *see* Khorramshahr
36 H10 **Mohave, Lake** ⊠ Arizona/Nevada, W USA
36 I12 **Mohave Mountains** ▲ Arizona, SW USA
36 I15 **Mohawk Mountains** ▲ Arizona, SW USA
18 I10 **Mohawk River** ⇝ New York, NE USA
163 T3 **Mohe** *var.* Xilinji. Heilongjiang, NE China 53°01′N 122°26′E
95 L20 **Moheda** Kronoberg, S Sweden 57°00′N 14°34′E
Mohéli *see* Mwali
Mohendergarh *see* Mahendragarh
38 K12 **Mohican, Cape** *headland* Nunivak Island, Alaska, USA 60°12′N 167°25′W
Mohn *see* Muhu
101 G15 **Möhne** ⇝ W Germany
101 G15 **Möhne-Stausee** ⊠ W Germany
92 P2 **Mohn, Kapp** *headland* NW Svalbard 79°26′N 25°44′E
197 S14 **Mohns Ridge** *undersea feature* Greenland Sea/Norwegian Sea 72°30′N 05°00′E
57 I17 **Moho** Puno, SE Peru 15°21′S 69°32′W
Mohokare *see* Caledon
95 L17 **Moholm** Västra Götaland, S Sweden 58°37′N 14°04′E
36 J11 **Mohon Peak** ▲ Arizona, SW USA 34°55′N 113°07′W
81 J23 **Mohoro** Pwani, E Tanzania 08°09′S 39°10′E
Mohra *see* Moravice
Mohrungen *see* Morąg
116 M7 **Mohyliv-Podil's'kyy** *Rus.* Mogilev-Podol'skiy. Vinnyts'ka Oblast', C Ukraine 48°29′N 27°49′E
95 D17 **Moi** Rogaland, S Norway 58°27′N 06°32′E
Moili *see* Mwali
116 K11 **Moinești** *Hung.* Mojnest. Bacău, E Romania 46°27′N 26°31′E
Móinteach Mílic *see* Mountmellick
14 J14 **Moira** ⇝ Ontario, SE Canada
92 G13 **Mo i Rana** Nordland, C Norway 66°19′N 14°10′E
153 X14 **Moirāng** Manipur, NE India 24°29′N 93°45′E
115 J25 **Moíres** Kríti, Greece, E Mediterranean Sea 35°03′N 24°51′E
118 H6 **Mõisaküla** *Ger.* Moiseküll. Viljandimaa, S Estonia 58°05′N 25°12′E
Moiseküll *see* Mõisaküla
15 W4 **Moisie** Québec, E Canada 50°12′N 66°06′W
15 W3 **Moisie** ⇝ Québec, SE Canada
102 M14 **Moissac** Tarn-et-Garonne, S France 44°07′N 01°05′E
78 I13 **Moïssala** Moyen-Chari, S Chad 08°21′N 17°46′E
55 O7 **Moitaco** Bolívar, E Venezuela 08°00′N 64°22′W
95 P15 **Möja** Stockholm, C Sweden 59°25′N 18°55′E
105 Q14 **Mojácar** Andalucía, S Spain 37°09′N 01°50′W
35 T13 **Mojave** California, W USA 35°03′N 118°10′W
35 V13 **Mojave Desert** *plain* California, W USA

◆ Country
● Country Capital
◇ Dependent Territory
○ Dependent Territory Capital
◆ Administrative Regions
✈ International Airport
▲ Mountain
▲ Mountain Range
⚠ Volcano
⇝ River
⊚ Lake
⊠ Reservoir

35 V13 **Mojave River** California, W USA
60 L9 **Moji-Mirim** *var.* Moji-Mirim. São Paulo, S Brazil 22°26′S 46°55′W
Moji-Mirim *see* Moji-Mirim
113 K15 **Mojkovac** E Montenegro 42°57′N 19°34′E
Mojnest *see* Moinești
Mōka *see* Mooka
153 Q13 **Mokāma** *prev.* Mokameh, Mukama. Bihār, N India 25°24′N 85°55′E
79 O25 **Mokambo** Katanga, SE Dem. Rep. Congo 12°23′S 28°21′E
Mokameh *see* Mokāma
38 D9 **Mōkapu Point** *var.* Mokapu Point. *headland* O'ahu, Hawai'i, USA 21°27′N 157°43′W
184 L9 **Mokau** Waikato, North Island, New Zealand 38°42′S 174°37′E
184 L9 **Mokau** North Island, New Zealand
35 P7 **Mokelumne River** California, W USA
83 J23 **Mokhotlong** NE Lesotho 29°19′S 29°06′E
Mokil Atoll *see* Mwokil Atoll
95 N14 **Möklinta** Västmanland, C Sweden 60°04′N 16°34′E
Mokna *see* Mokra Gora
184 L4 **Mokohinau Islands** *island group* N New Zealand
153 X12 **Mokokchūng** Nāgāland, NE India 26°20′N 94°30′E
78 F12 **Mokolo** Extrême-Nord, N Cameroon 10°49′N 13°54′E
83 J20 **Mokopane** *prev.* Potgietersrus. Limpopo, NE South Africa 24°09′S 28°58′E
185 D24 **Mokoreta** South Island, New Zealand
163 X17 **Mokp'o** *Jap.* Moppo; *prev.* Mokp'o. SW South Korea 34°50′N 126°26′E
Mokp'o *see* Mokpo
113 L16 **Mokra Gora** *Alb.* Mokna. ▲ S Serbia
Mokrany *see* Makrany
127 O5 **Moksha** W Russian Federation
143 X12 **Mok Sukhteh-ye Pāyīn** Sīstān va Balūchestān, SE Iran
Moktama *see* Mottama
77 T14 **Mokwa** Niger, W Nigeria 09°19′N 05°01′E
99 J16 **Mol** *prev.* Moll. Antwerpen, N Belgium 51°11′N 05°07′E
107 O17 **Mola di Bari** Puglia, SE Italy 41°03′N 17°05′E
Molai *see* Moláoi
41 P13 **Molango** Hidalgo, C Mexico 20°48′N 98°44′W
115 F22 **Moláoi** *var.* Molai. Pelopónnisos, S Greece 36°48′N 22°51′E
41 Z12 **Molas del Norte, Punta** *var.* Punta Molas. *headland* SE Mexico 20°34′N 86°43′W
Molas, Punta *see* Molas del Norte, Punta
105 R11 **Molatón** ▲ C Spain 38°58′N 01°19′W
97 K18 **Mold** NE Wales, United Kingdom 53°10′N 03°08′W
Moldau *see* Vltava, Czech Republic
Moldau *see* Moldova
Moldavia *see* Moldova
Moldavian SSR/ Moldavskaya SSR *see* Moldova
94 E9 **Molde** Møre og Romsdal, S Norway 62°44′N 07°08′E
Moldotau, Khrebet *see* Moldo-Too, Khrebet
147 V9 **Moldo-Too, Khrebet** *prev.* Khrebet Moldotau. ▲▲ C Kyrgyzstan
116 L9 **Moldova** *off.* Republic of Moldova, *var.* Moldavia; *prev.* Moldavian SSR, *Rus.* Moldavskaya SSR. ◆ *republic* SE Europe
116 K9 **Moldova** *Eng.* Moldavia, *Ger.* Moldau. *former province* NE Romania
116 K9 **Moldova** N Romania
116 F13 **Moldova Nouă** *Ger.* Neumoldowa, *Hung.* Újmoldova. Caraș-Severin, SW Romania 44°45′N 21°39′E
Moldova, Republic of *see* Moldova
116 F13 **Moldova Veche** *Ger.* Altmoldowa, *Hung.* Ómoldova. Caraș-Severin, SW Romania 44°45′N 21°13′E
Moldoveanul *see* Vârful Moldoveanu
83 I20 **Molepolole** Kweneng, SE Botswana 24°25′S 25°30′E
44 L8 **Môle-St-Nicolas** NW Haiti 19°46′N 73°19′W
118 H13 **Molėtai** Utena, E Lithuania 55°14′N 25°25′E
107 O17 **Molfetta** Puglia, SE Italy 41°12′N 16°35′E
171 P11 **Molibagu** Sulawesi, N Indonesia 0°25′N 123°57′E
62 G12 **Molina** Maule, C Chile 35°06′S 71°18′W
105 Q7 **Molina de Aragón** Castilla-La Mancha, C Spain 40°50′N 01°54′W
105 R13 **Molina de Segura** Murcia, SE Spain 38°03′N 01°11′W
30 J11 **Moline** Illinois, N USA 41°30′N 90°31′W
27 P7 **Moline** Kansas, C USA 37°21′N 96°18′W
79 P23 **Moliro** Katanga, SE Dem. Rep. Congo 08°11′S 30°31′E
107 K16 **Molise** ◈ *region* S Italy
95 K15 **Molkom** Värmland, C Sweden 59°36′N 13°43′E
109 Q9 **Möll** S Austria
Moll *see* Mol
146 I14 **Mollanepes Adyndaky** *Rus.* Imeni Mollanepesa. Mary Welaýaty, S Turkmenistan 37°36′N 61°54′E
95 J22 **Mölle** Skåne, S Sweden 56°15′N 12°19′E
57 H18 **Mollendo** Arequipa, SW Peru 17°02′S 72°01′W
105 U5 **Mollerussa** Cataluña, NE Spain 41°37′N 00°53′E
108 H8 **Mollis** Glarus, NE Switzerland 47°05′N 09°03′E
95 J19 **Mölndal** Västra Götaland, S Sweden 57°39′N 12°05′E
95 J19 **Mölnlycke** Västra Götaland, S Sweden 57°39′N 12°09′E
117 U9 **Molochans'k** *Rus.* Molochansk. Zaporiz'ka Oblast', SE Ukraine 47°10′N 35°38′E
117 U10 **Molochna** *Rus.* Molochnaya. S Ukraine
Molochnaya *see* Molochna
117 U10 **Molochnyy Lyman** *bay* N Black Sea
Molodechno/Molodeczno *see* Maladzyechna
195 V3 **Molodezhnaya** *Russian research station* Antarctica 67°33′S 46°12′E
124 J14 **Mologa** NW Russian Federation
38 E9 **Moloka'i** *var.* Molokai. *island* Hawaiian Islands, Hawai'i, USA
175 X3 **Molokai Fracture Zone** *tectonic feature* NE Pacific Ocean
124 K15 **Molokovo** Tverskaya Oblast', W Russian Federation 58°10′N 36°43′E
125 Q14 **Moloma** NW Russian Federation
183 R8 **Molong** New South Wales, SE Australia 33°07′S 148°52′E
83 H21 **Molopo** *seasonal river* Botswana/South Africa
115 F17 **Mólos** Stereá Elláda, C Greece 38°48′N 22°39′E
171 O11 **Molosipat** Sulawesi, N Indonesia 0°28′N 121°08′E
Molotov *see* Severodvinsk, Arkhangel'skaya Oblast', Russian Federation
Molotov *see* Perm', Permskaya Oblast', Russian Federation
79 G17 **Moloundou** Est, SE Cameroon 02°03′N 15°14′E
103 U5 **Molsheim** Bas-Rhin, NE France 48°33′N 07°30′E
11 X13 **Molson Lake** Manitoba, C Canada
Moluccas *see* Maluku
171 Q12 **Molucca Sea** *Ind.* Laut Maluku. *sea* E Indonesia
Molukken *see* Maluku
83 O15 **Molumbo** Zambézia, N Mozambique 15°33′S 36°19′E
171 T15 **Molu, Pulau** *island* Maluku, E Indonesia
83 P16 **Moma** Nampula, NE Mozambique 16°42′S 39°12′E
171 X14 **Momats** Papua, E Indonesia
42 J11 **Mombacho, Volcán** SW Nicaragua 11°49′N 85°58′W
81 K21 **Mombasa** Coast, SE Kenya 04°04′N 39°40′E
81 J21 **Mombasa** ✈ Coast, SE Kenya 04°01′S 39°31′E
Mombetsu *see* Monbetsu
114 J12 **Momchilgrad** *prev.* Mastanli. Kŭrdzhali, S Bulgaria 41°33′N 25°25′E
99 F23 **Momignies** Hainaut, S Belgium 50°02′N 04°10′E
54 E6 **Momil** Córdoba, NW Colombia 09°15′N 75°40′W
42 I10 **Momotombo, Volcán** W Nicaragua 12°25′N 86°33′W
56 B5 **Mompiche, Ensenada de** *bay* NW Ecuador
79 K18 **Mompono** Equateur, NW Dem. Rep. Congo 0°11′N 21°31′E
54 F6 **Mompós** Bolívar, NW Colombia 09°15′N 74°29′W
95 J24 **Møn** *prev.* Möen. *island* SE Denmark
36 L4 **Mona** Utah, W USA 39°49′N 111°52′W
Mona, Canal de la *see* Mona Passage
96 E8 **Monach Islands** *island group* NW Scotland, United Kingdom
103 V14 **Monaco** *var.* Monaco-Ville; *anc.* Monoecus. ● (Monaco) S Monaco 43°46′N 07°23′E
103 V14 **Monaco** *off.* Principality of Monaco. ◆ *monarchy* W Europe
Monaco *see* München
Monaco Basin *see* Canary Basin
Monaco, Principality of *see* Monaco
Monaco-Ville *see* Monaco
96 I9 **Monadhliath Mountains** ▲▲ N Scotland, United Kingdom
55 O6 **Monagas** *off.* Estado Monagas. ◈ *state* NE Venezuela
Monagas, Estado *see* Monagas
97 F16 **Monaghan** *Ir.* Muineachán. Monaghan, N Ireland 54°15′N 06°58′W
97 E16 **Monaghan** *Ir.* Muineachán. *cultural region* N Ireland
43 S16 **Monagrillo** Herrera, S Panama 08°00′N 80°28′W
24 L8 **Monahans** Texas, SW USA 31°35′N 102°54′W
45 Q9 **Mona, Isla** *island* W Puerto Rico
45 Q9 **Mona Passage** *Sp.* Canal de la Mona. *channel* Dominican Republic/Puerto Rico
43 O14 **Mona, Punta** *headland* E Costa Rica 09°44′N 82°48′W
155 K25 **Monaragala** Uva Province, SE Sri Lanka 06°52′N 81°22′E
33 S9 **Monarch** Montana, NW USA 47°04′N 110°51′W
10 H14 **Monarch Mountain** ▲ British Columbia, SW Canada 51°59′N 125°56′W
Monasterio *see* Monesterio
Monasterzyska *see* Monastyrys'ka
Monastir *see* Bitola
Monastyriska *see* Monastyrys'ka
117 O7 **Monastyryshche** Cherkas'ka Oblast', C Ukraine 48°59′N 29°47′E
116 J6 **Monastyrys'ka** *Pol.* Monasterzyska, *Rus.* Monastyriska. Ternopil's'ka Oblast', W Ukraine 49°05′N 25°10′E
79 E15 **Monatélé** Centre, SW Cameroon 04°16′N 11°12′E
165 U2 **Monbetsu** *var.* Mombetsu, Monbetu. Hokkaidō, NE Japan 44°23′N 143°22′E
Monbetu *see* Monbetsu
106 B8 **Moncalieri** Piemonte, NW Italy 45°N 07°41′E
104 G4 **Monção** Viana do Castelo, N Portugal 42°03′N 08°29′W
105 Q5 **Moncayo** ▲ N Spain 41°43′N 01°51′W
105 Q5 **Moncayo, Sierra del** ▲▲ N Spain
124 J4 **Monchegorsk** Murmanskaya Oblast', NW Russian Federation 67°56′N 32°47′E
101 D15 **Mönchengladbach** *prev.* München-Gladbach. Nordrhein-Westfalen, W Germany 51°12′N 06°35′E
104 F14 **Monchique** Faro, S Portugal 37°19′N 08°33′W
104 G14 **Monchique, Serra de** ▲▲ S Portugal
21 S14 **Moncks Corner** South Carolina, SE USA 33°12′N 80°00′W
41 N7 **Monclova** Coahuila, NE Mexico 26°55′N 101°25′W
Moncorvo *see* Torre de Moncorvo
13 P14 **Moncton** New Brunswick, SE Canada 46°04′N 64°50′W
104 F8 **Mondego, Cabo** *headland* N Portugal 40°10′N 08°58′W
104 G8 **Mondego, Rio** N Portugal
104 I2 **Mondoñedo** Galicia, NW Spain 43°25′N 07°22′W
99 N25 **Mondorf-les-Bains** Grevenmacher, SE Luxembourg 49°30′N 06°16′E
102 M7 **Mondoubleau** Loir-et-Cher, C France 48°00′N 00°49′E
106 B9 **Mondovì** Piemonte, NW Italy 44°23′N 07°56′E
30 J6 **Mondovi** Wisconsin, N USA 44°34′N 91°40′W
Mondragón *see* Arrasate
107 J17 **Mondragone** Campania, S Italy 41°07′N 13°53′E
109 R5 **Mondsee** N Austria
115 G22 **Monemvasiá** *var.* Monemvasia. Pelopónnisos, S Greece 36°22′N 23°03′E
18 B15 **Monessen** Pennsylvania, NE USA 40°07′N 79°51′W
104 J12 **Monesterio** *var.* Monasterio. Extremadura, W Spain 38°05′N 06°16′W
14 L8 **Monet** Québec, SE Canada 48°09′N 75°37′W
27 S8 **Monett** Missouri, C USA 36°55′N 93°55′W
27 X9 **Monette** Arkansas, C USA 35°53′N 90°20′W
14 G11 **Monetville** Ontario, S Canada 46°08′N 80°24′W
106 J7 **Monfalcone** Friuli-Venezia Giulia, NE Italy 45°49′N 13°32′E
104 H10 **Monforte** Portalegre, C Portugal 39°03′N 07°26′W
104 I4 **Monforte de Lemos** Galicia, NW Spain 42°32′N 07°30′W
79 L16 **Monga** Orientale, N Dem. Rep. Congo 04°12′N 22°49′E
81 I24 **Monga** Lindi, SE Tanzania 09°05′S 37°51′E
81 F15 **Mongalla** Central Equatoria, S South Sudan 05°12′N 31°42′E
153 U11 **Mongar** E Bhutan 27°16′N 91°07′E
167 U6 **Mong Cai** *var.* Hai Ninh. Quang Ninh, N Vietnam 21°33′N 107°56′E
180 I11 **Mongers Lake** *salt lake* Western Australia
186 K8 **Mongga** Kolombangara, NW Solomon Islands 07°51′S 157°00′E
167 O6 **Möng Hpayak** Shan State, E Myanmar (Burma) 20°56′N 100°00′E
Monghyr *see* Munger
106 B10 **Mongioie** ▲ NW Italy 44°13′N 07°46′E
153 T16 **Mongla** *var.* Mungla. Khulna, S Bangladesh 22°18′N 89°34′E
188 C15 **Mongmong** C Guam
167 N6 **Möng Nai** Shan State, E Myanmar (Burma) 20°28′N 97°51′E
78 I11 **Mongo** Guéra, C Chad 12°12′N 18°40′E
76 I14 **Mongo** N Sierra Leone
163 I8 **Mongolia** *Mong.* Mongol Uls. ◆ *republic* E Asia
129 V8 **Mongolia, Plateau of** *plateau* E Mongolia
Mongolküre *see* Zhaosu
Mongol Uls *see* Mongolia
79 E17 **Mongomo** E Equatorial Guinea 01°39′N 11°18′E
162 M7 **Möngönmorit** *var.* Bulag. Töv, C Mongolia 48°09′N 108°33′E
77 Y12 **Mongonu** *var.* Monguno. Borno, NE Nigeria 12°42′N 13°37′E
Mongora *see* Saïdu
78 K11 **Mongororo** Ouaddaï, SE Chad 12°03′N 22°26′E
Mongos, Chaîne des *see* Bongo, Massif des
79 I16 **Mongoumba** Lobaye, SW Central African Republic 03°39′N 18°30′E
Mongrove, Punta *see* Cayacal, Punta
83 G15 **Mongu** Western, W Zambia 15°13′S 23°09′E
76 I10 **Mônguel** Gorgol, SW Mauritania 16°25′N 13°08′W
Monguno *see* Mongonu
167 N4 **Möng Yai** Shan State, E Myanmar (Burma) 22°25′N 98°02′E
167 O5 **Möng Yang** Shan State, E Myanmar (Burma) 21°52′N 99°31′E
167 N3 **Möng Yu** Shan State, E Myanmar (Burma) 24°00′N 97°57′E
Mönhbulag *see* Yösöndzüyl
163 O8 **Mönhhaan** *var.* Bayasgalant. Sühbaatar, E Mongolia 46°55′N 112°11′E
162 E7 **Mönhhayrhan** *var.* Tsenher. Hovd, W Mongolia 47°07′N 92°04′E
Mönh Sarīdag *see* Munku-Sardyk, Gora
186 P9 **Moni** S Papau New Guinea
115 I15 **Moní Megístis Lávras** *monastery* Kentrikí Makedonía, N Greece
115 F18 **Moní Osíou Loúkas** *monastery* Stereá Elláda, C Greece
54 F9 **Moniquirá** Boyacá, C Colombia 05°54′N 73°35′W
103 Q12 **Monistrol-sur-Loire** Haute-Loire, C France 45°19′N 04°12′E
35 V7 **Monitor Range** ▲▲ Nevada, W USA
115 I14 **Moní Vatopedíou** *monastery* Kentrikí Makedonía, N Greece
Monkchester *see* Newcastle upon Tyne
83 N14 **Monkey Bay** Southern, SE Malawi 14°09′S 34°53′E
43 N11 **Monkey Point** *var.* Punta Mico, Punte Mono, Punto Mico. *headland* SE Nicaragua 11°37′N 83°39′W
Monkey River *see* Monkey River Town
42 G3 **Monkey River Town** *var.* Monkey River. Toledo, SE Belize 16°22′N 88°29′W
14 M13 **Monkland** Ontario, SE Canada 45°11′N 74°51′W
79 J19 **Monkoto** Equateur, NW Dem. Rep. Congo 01°39′S 20°41′E
97 K21 **Monmouth** *Wel.* Trefynwy. SE Wales, United Kingdom 51°50′N 02°43′W
30 J12 **Monmouth** Illinois, N USA 40°54′N 90°39′W
32 F12 **Monmouth** Oregon, NW USA 44°51′N 123°13′W
97 K21 **Monmouth** *cultural region* SE Wales, United Kingdom
98 I10 **Monnickendam** Noord-Holland, C Netherlands 52°28′N 05°02′E
77 R15 **Mono** C Togo
Monoecus *see* Monaco
35 R8 **Mono Lake** California, W USA
115 O23 **Monólithos** Ródos, Dodekánisa, Greece, Aegean Sea 36°08′N 27°45′E
19 Q12 **Monomoy Island** *island* Massachusetts, NE USA
31 O12 **Monon** Indiana, N USA 40°52′N 86°54′W
29 Y12 **Monona** Iowa, C USA 43°03′N 91°23′W
30 L9 **Monona** Wisconsin, N USA 43°03′N 89°18′W
18 B15 **Monongahela** Pennsylvania, NE USA 40°10′N 79°54′W
18 B16 **Monongahela River** NE USA
107 P17 **Monopoli** Puglia, SE Italy 40°57′N 17°18′E
Mono, Punte *see* Monkey Point
111 K23 **Monor** Pest, C Hungary 47°21′N 19°27′E
Monostor *see* Beli Manastir
78 K8 **Monou** Borkou-Ennedi-Tibesti, NE Chad 16°22′N 22°15′E
105 S12 **Monóvar** *Cat.* Monòver. Valenciana, E Spain 38°26′N 00°50′W
Monòver *see* Monóvar
105 R7 **Monreal del Campo** Aragón, NE Spain 40°47′N 01°20′W
107 I23 **Monreale** Sicilia, Italy, C Mediterranean Sea 38°05′N 13°17′E
23 T3 **Monroe** Georgia, SE USA 33°47′N 83°42′W
29 W14 **Monroe** Iowa, C USA 41°31′N 93°06′W
22 I5 **Monroe** Louisiana, S USA 32°32′N 92°06′W
31 S10 **Monroe** Michigan, N USA 41°55′N 83°24′W
18 K13 **Monroe** New York, NE USA 41°18′N 74°09′W
21 S11 **Monroe** North Carolina, SE USA 35°00′N 80°35′W
36 L6 **Monroe** Utah, W USA 38°37′N 112°07′W
32 H7 **Monroe** Washington, NW USA 47°51′N 121°58′W
30 L9 **Monroe** Wisconsin, N USA 42°35′N 89°39′W
27 V3 **Monroe City** Missouri, C USA 39°39′N 91°43′W
31 O15 **Monroe Lake** Indiana, N USA
23 O7 **Monroeville** Alabama, S USA 31°31′N 87°19′W
18 C15 **Monroeville** Pennsylvania, NE USA 40°24′N 79°44′W
76 J16 **Monrovia** ● (Liberia) W Liberia 06°18′N 10°48′W
76 J16 **Monrovia** ✈ W Liberia 06°22′N 10°50′W
105 T7 **Monroyo** Aragón, NE Spain 40°47′N 00°03′W
99 F20 **Mons** *Dut.* Bergen. Hainaut, S Belgium 50°28′N 03°58′E
104 I8 **Monsanto** Castelo Branco, C Portugal 40°02′N 07°07′W
106 H8 **Monselice** Veneto, NE Italy 45°15′N 11°47′E
166 M9 **Mon State** ◈ *state* S Myanmar (Burma)
98 G12 **Monster** Zuid-Holland, W Netherlands 52°01′N 04°10′E
95 N20 **Mönsterås** Kalmar, S Sweden 57°03′N 16°27′E
101 F17 **Montabaur** Rheinland-Pfalz, W Germany 50°25′N 07°48′E
106 G8 **Montagnana** Veneto, NE Italy 45°14′N 11°31′E
35 N1 **Montague** California, W USA 41°43′N 122°31′W
25 S5 **Montague** Texas, SW USA 33°40′N 97°44′W
183 S11 **Montague Island** *island* New South Wales, SE Australia
39 S12 **Montague Island** *island* Alaska, USA
39 S13 **Montague Strait** *strait* N Gulf of Alaska
102 J8 **Montaigu** Vendée, NW France 46°58′N 01°18′W
Montaigu *see* Scherpenheuvel
105 S7 **Montalbán** Aragón, NE Spain 40°49′N 00°48′W
106 G13 **Montalcino** Toscana, C Italy 43°01′N 11°34′E
104 H5 **Montalegre** Vila Real, N Portugal 41°49′N 07°48′W
114 G8 **Montana** *prev.* Ferdinand, Mikhaylovgrad. Montana, NW Bulgaria 43°25′N 23°14′E
108 D10 **Montana** Valais, SW Switzerland 46°23′N 07°29′E
39 R11 **Montana** Alaska, USA 62°06′N 150°03′W
114 G8 **Montana** ◈ *province* NW Bulgaria
33 T9 **Montana** *off.* State of Montana, *also known as* Mountain State, Treasure State. ◈ *state* NW USA
104 J10 **Montánchez** Extremadura, W Spain 39°15′N 06°07′W
Montañita *see* La Montañita
15 Q8 **Mont-Apica** Québec, SE Canada 47°57′N 71°24′W
104 G10 **Montargil** Portalegre, C Portugal 39°05′N 08°10′W
104 G10 **Montargil, Barragem de** ⊞ C Portugal
103 O7 **Montargis** Loiret, C France 48°N 02°44′E
103 O4 **Montataire** Oise, N France 49°16′N 02°24′E
102 M14 **Montauban** Tarn-et-Garonne, S France 44°01′N 01°20′E
19 N14 **Montauk** Long Island, New York, NE USA 41°01′N 71°58′W
19 N14 **Montauk Point** *headland* Long Island, New York, NE USA 41°04′N 71°51′W
103 Q7 **Montbard** Côte d'Or, C France 47°35′N 04°25′E
103 U7 **Montbéliard** Doubs, E France 47°31′N 06°49′E
25 W11 **Mont Belvieu** Texas, SW USA 29°51′N 94°53′W
105 U6 **Montblanc** *prev.* Montblanch. Cataluña, NE Spain 41°23′N 01°10′E
Montblanch *see* Montblanc
103 Q11 **Montbrison** Loire, E France 45°37′N 04°04′E
Montcalm, Lake *see* Dogai Coring
103 Q9 **Montceau-les-Mines** Saône-et-Loire, C France 46°40′N 04°19′E
103 U12 **Mont Cenis, Col du** *pass* E France
102 K15 **Mont-de-Marsan** Landes, SW France 43°54′N 00°30′W
103 O3 **Montdidier** Somme, N France 49°39′N 02°35′E
187 Q17 **Mont-Dore** Province Sud, S New Caledonia 22°18′S 166°34′E
20 K10 **Monteagle** Tennessee, S USA 35°15′N 85°47′W
57 M20 **Monteagudo** Chuquisaca, S Bolivia 19°48′S 63°57′W
41 R16 **Monte Albán** *ruins* Oaxaca, S Mexico
105 R11 **Montealegre del Castillo** Castilla-La Mancha, C Spain 38°48′N 01°18′W
59 N18 **Monte Azul** Minas Gerais, SE Brazil 15°13′S 42°53′W
14 M12 **Montebello** Québec, SE Canada 45°40′N 74°56′W
106 H7 **Montebelluna** Veneto, NE Italy 45°46′N 12°03′E
60 G13 **Montecarlo** Misiones, NE Argentina 26°38′S 54°45′W
61 D16 **Monte Caseros** Corrientes, NE Argentina 30°15′S 57°39′W
60 J13 **Monte Castelo** Santa Catarina, S Brazil 26°34′S 50°12′W
106 F11 **Montecatini Terme** Toscana, C Italy 43°53′N 10°46′E
42 H7 **Montecillos, Cordillera de** ▲▲ W Honduras
62 I12 **Monte Comán** Mendoza, W Argentina 34°35′S 67°53′W
44 M8 **Monte Cristi** *var.* San Fernando de Monte Cristi. NW Dominican Republic 19°52′N 71°39′W
58 C13 **Monte Cristo** Amazonas, W Brazil 03°14′S 68°00′W
107 E14 **Montecristo, Isola di** *island* Archipelago Toscano, C Italy
Monte Croce Carnico, Passo di *see* Plöcken Pass
58 J12 **Monte Dourado** Pará, NE Brazil 0°48′S 52°32′W
40 L11 **Monte Escobedo** Zacatecas, C Mexico 22°19′N 103°30′W
106 I13 **Montefalco** Umbria, C Italy 42°54′N 12°40′E
107 H14 **Montefiascone** Lazio, C Italy 42°33′N 12°01′E
105 N14 **Montefrío** Andalucía, S Spain 37°19′N 04°00′W
44 I11 **Montego Bay** *var.* Mobay. W Jamaica 18°28′N 77°55′W
Montego Bay *see* Sangster
104 J8 **Montehermoso** Extremadura, W Spain 40°05′N 06°20′W
104 F10 **Montejunto, Serra de** ▲ C Portugal 39°10′N 09°01′W
Monteleone di Calabria *see* Vibo Valentia
54 E7 **Montelíbano** Córdoba, NW Colombia 08°02′N 75°29′W
103 R13 **Montélimar** *anc.* Acunum Acusio, Montilium Adhemari. Drôme, E France 44°33′N 04°45′E
104 K15 **Montellano** Andalucía, S Spain 37°00′N 05°34′W
35 Y2 **Montello** Nevada, W USA 41°18′N 114°10′W
30 L8 **Montello** Wisconsin, N USA 43°47′N 89°20′W
63 J18 **Montemayor, Meseta de** *plain* SE Argentina
41 O9 **Montemorelos** Nuevo León, NE Mexico 25°10′N 99°52′W
104 G11 **Montemor-o-Novo** Évora, S Portugal 38°38′N 08°13′W
104 G8 **Montemor-o-Velho** *var.* Montemor-o-Vélho. Coimbra, N Portugal 40°11′N 08°41′W
Montemor-o-Vélho *see* Montemor-o-Velho
104 H7 **Montemuro, Serra de** ▲ N Portugal 40°59′N 07°59′W
102 K12 **Montendre** Charente-Maritime, W France 45°17′N 00°24′W
61 I15 **Montenegro** Rio Grande do Sul, S Brazil 29°40′S 51°32′W
113 J16 **Montenegro** *Serb.* Crna Gora. ◆ *republic* SW Europe
62 G10 **Monte Patria** Coquimbo, N Chile 30°40′S 71°00′W
45 O9 **Monte Plata** E Dominican Republic 18°50′N 69°47′W
83 P14 **Montepuez** Cabo Delgado, N Mozambique 13°09′S 39°00′E
83 P14 **Montepuez** N Mozambique
106 G13 **Montepulciano** Toscana, C Italy 43°02′N 11°51′E
62 L6 **Monte Quemado** Santiago del Estero, N Argentina 25°48′S 62°52′W
103 O6 **Montereau-Faut-Yonne** *anc.* Condate. Seine-St-Denis, N France 48°23′N 02°57′E
35 N11 **Monterey** California, W USA 36°36′N 121°53′W
20 L9 **Monterey** Tennessee, S USA 36°09′N 85°16′W
21 T5 **Monterey** Virginia, NE USA 38°24′N 79°36′W
Monterey *see* Monterrey
35 N10 **Monterey Bay** *bay* California, W USA
54 D6 **Montería** Córdoba, NW Colombia 08°45′N 75°54′W
57 N18 **Montero** Santa Cruz, C Bolivia 17°20′S 63°15′W
62 J7 **Monteros** Tucumán, C Argentina 27°12′S 65°30′W
104 I5 **Monterrei** Galicia, NW Spain 41°56′N 07°27′W
41 O8 **Monterrey** *var.* Monterey. Nuevo León, NE Mexico 25°41′N 100°16′W
32 F9 **Montesano** Washington, NW USA 46°58′N 123°37′W
107 M19 **Montesano sulla Marcellana** Campania, S Italy 40°15′N 15°41′E
107 N16 **Monte Sant' Angelo** Puglia, SE Italy 41°43′N 15°58′E
59 O16 **Monte Santo** Bahia, E Brazil 10°25′S 39°18′W
107 D18 **Monte Santu, Capo di** *headland* Sardegna, Italy, C Mediterranean Sea 40°05′N 09°43′E
59 M19 **Montes Claros** Minas Gerais, SE Brazil 16°45′S 43°52′W
107 K14 **Montesilvano Marina** Abruzzo, C Italy 42°28′N 14°07′E
23 P4 **Montevallo** Alabama, S USA 33°06′N 86°51′W
106 G12 **Montevarchi** Toscana, C Italy 43°32′N 11°34′E
61 F20 **Montevideo** ● (Uruguay) Montevideo, S Uruguay 34°55′S 56°10′W
29 S9 **Montevideo** Minnesota, N USA 44°56′N 95°43′W
37 S7 **Monte Vista** Colorado, C USA 37°33′N 106°08′W
23 T5 **Montezuma** Georgia, SE USA 32°18′N 84°01′W
29 W14 **Montezuma** Iowa, C USA 41°35′N 92°31′W
26 J6 **Montezuma** Kansas, C USA 37°33′N 100°25′W
103 U12 **Montgenèvre, Col de** *pass* France/Italy
97 K20 **Montgomery** E Wales, United Kingdom 52°38′N 03°05′W
23 Q5 **Montgomery** *state capital* Alabama, S USA 32°22′N 86°18′W
29 V9 **Montgomery** Minnesota, N USA 44°26′N 93°34′W
18 G13 **Montgomery** Pennsylvania, NE USA 41°08′N 76°52′W
21 Q5 **Montgomery** West Virginia, NE USA 38°07′N 81°19′W
97 K19 **Montgomery** *cultural region* E Wales, United Kingdom
Montgomery *see* Sāhīwāl
27 V4 **Montgomery City** Missouri, C USA 38°57′N 91°27′W
35 S8 **Montgomery Pass** *pass* Nevada, W USA
102 K12 **Montguyon** Charente-Maritime, W France 45°12′N 00°13′W
108 C10 **Monthey** Valais, SW Switzerland 46°15′N 06°56′E
27 V13 **Monticello** Arkansas, C USA 33°38′N 91°49′W
23 T4 **Monticello** Florida, SE USA 30°33′N 83°52′W
23 T8 **Monticello** Georgia, SE USA 33°18′N 83°40′W
30 M13 **Monticello** Illinois, N USA 40°01′N 88°34′W
31 O12 **Monticello** Indiana, N USA 40°45′N 86°46′W
29 Y13 **Monticello** Iowa, C USA 42°14′N 91°11′W
20 L7 **Monticello** Kentucky, S USA 36°50′N 84°50′W
29 V8 **Monticello** Minnesota, N USA 45°19′N 93°48′W
22 K7 **Monticello** Mississippi, S USA 31°33′N 90°06′W
27 V2 **Monticello** Missouri, C USA 40°07′N 91°42′W
18 J12 **Monticello** New York, NE USA 41°39′N 74°41′W
37 O7 **Monticello** Utah, W USA 37°52′N 109°20′W
106 F8 **Montichiari** Lombardia, N Italy 45°24′N 10°27′E
102 M12 **Montignac** Dordogne, SW France 45°24′N 00°54′E
99 G21 **Montignies-le-Tilleul** *var.* Montigny-le-Tilleul. Hainaut, S Belgium 50°22′N 04°23′E
14 J8 **Montigny, Lac de** Québec, SE Canada
103 S6 **Montigny-le-Roi** Haute-Marne, N France 48°02′N 05°28′E
Montigny-le-Tilleul *see* Montignies-le-Tilleul
43 R16 **Montijo** Veraguas, S Panama 07°59′N 80°58′W
104 F11 **Montijo** Setúbal, W Portugal 38°42′N 08°59′W
104 J11 **Montijo** Extremadura, W Spain 38°55′N 06°38′W
Montilium Adhemari *see* Montélimar
104 M13 **Montilla** Andalucía, S Spain 37°36′N 04°39′W
102 L3 **Montivilliers** Seine-Maritime, N France 49°31′N 00°10′E
15 U7 **Mont-Joli** Québec, SE Canada 48°36′N 68°14′W
14 M10 **Mont-Laurier** Québec, SE Canada 46°33′N 75°31′W
15 X5 **Mont-Louis** Québec, SE Canada 49°15′N 65°46′W
103 N17 **Mont-Louis** *var.* Mont Louis. Pyrénées-Orientales, S France 42°30′N 02°08′E
103 O10 **Montluçon** Allier, C France 46°21′N 02°37′E
15 R10 **Montmagny** Québec, SE Canada 46°58′N 70°31′W
103 S3 **Montmédy** Meuse, NE France 49°31′N 05°21′E
103 P5 **Montmirail** Marne, N France 48°53′N 03°31′E
15 R9 **Montmorency** Québec, SE Canada
102 M10 **Montmorillon** Vienne, W France 46°26′N 00°52′E
107 J14 **Montorio al Vomano** Abruzzo, C Italy 42°31′N 13°39′E
104 M13 **Montoro** Andalucía, S Spain 38°00′N 04°21′W
33 S16 **Montpelier** Idaho, NW USA 42°19′N 111°18′W
29 P6 **Montpelier** North Dakota, N USA 46°40′N 98°34′W
18 M7 **Montpelier** *state capital* Vermont, NE USA 44°16′N 72°32′W
103 Q15 **Montpellier** Hérault, S France 43°37′N 03°52′E
102 L12 **Montpon-Ménestérol** Dordogne, SW France 45°01′N 00°10′E
12 K15 **Montréal** *Eng.* Montreal. Québec, SE Canada 45°30′N 73°36′W
14 G8 **Montreal** Ontario, S Canada
Montreal *see* Mirabel
11 T14 **Montreal Lake** Saskatchewan, C Canada
14 B9 **Montreal River** Ontario, S Canada 47°13′N 84°36′W
103 N2 **Montreuil** Pas-de-Calais, N France 50°28′N 01°46′E
102 K8 **Montreuil-Bellay** Maine-et-Loire, NW France 47°07′N 00°10′W
108 C10 **Montreux** Vaud, SW Switzerland 46°27′N 06°55′E
108 B9 **Montricher** Vaud, W Switzerland 46°37′N 06°24′E
96 K10 **Montrose** E Scotland, United Kingdom 56°43′N 02°29′W
27 W14 **Montrose** Arkansas, C USA 33°18′N 91°29′W
37 Q6 **Montrose** Colorado, C USA 38°29′N 107°53′W
29 Y16 **Montrose** Iowa, C USA 40°31′N 91°24′W
18 H12 **Montrose** Pennsylvania, NE USA 41°49′N 75°53′W
21 X5 **Montross** Virginia, NE USA 38°04′N 76°51′W
15 O12 **Mont-St-Hilaire** Québec, SE Canada 45°34′N 73°10′W
103 S3 **Mont-St-Martin** Meurthe-et-Moselle, NE France 49°31′N 05°51′E
45 V10 **Montserrat** *var.* Emerald Isle. ◇ *UK dependent territory* E West Indies
105 V5 **Montserrat** ▲ NE Spain 41°39′N 01°44′E
104 M7 **Montuenga** Castilla y León, N Spain 41°04′N 04°38′W
99 M19 **Montzen** Liège, E Belgium 50°42′N 05°59′E
37 N8 **Monument Valley** *valley* Arizona/Utah, SW USA
166 L4 **Monywa** Sagaing, Myanmar (Burma) 22°05′N 95°12′E
106 D7 **Monza** Lombardia, N Italy 45°35′N 09°16′E
83 J15 **Monze** Southern, S Zambia 16°20′S 27°29′E
105 T5 **Monzón** Aragón, NE Spain 41°54′N 00°12′E
25 T9 **Moody** Texas, SW USA 31°18′N 97°21′W
98 L13 **Mook** Limburg, SE Netherlands 51°45′N 05°52′E
165 O12 **Mooka** *var.* Mōka. Tochigi, Honshū, S Japan 36°27′N 139°59′E
182 K3 **Moomba** South Australia 28°07′S 140°12′E
14 G13 **Moon** Ontario, S Canada
Moon *see* Muhu
181 Y10 **Moonie** Queensland, E Australia 27°46′S 150°22′E
193 O5 **Moonless Mountains** *undersea feature* E Pacific Ocean 30°40′N 140°00′W
182 L13 **Moonlight Head** *headland* Victoria, SE Australia 38°47′S 143°12′E
Moon-Sund *see* Väinameri
182 H8 **Moonta** South Australia 34°03′S 137°36′E
Moor *see* Mór
180 I12 **Moora** Western Australia 30°23′S 116°05′E
98 H12 **Moordrecht** Zuid-Holland, C Netherlands 51°59′N 04°40′E
33 T9 **Moore** Montana, NW USA 47°00′N 109°40′W
27 N11 **Moore** Oklahoma, C USA 35°21′N 97°30′W
25 R12 **Moore** Texas, SW USA 29°03′N 99°01′W
191 S10 **Moorea** *island* Îles du Vent, W French Polynesia
21 U3 **Moorefield** West Virginia, NE USA 39°04′N 78°59′W
23 X14 **Moore Haven** Florida, SE USA 26°49′N 81°05′W
180 J11 **Moore, Lake** Western Australia
19 N7 **Moore Reservoir** ⊞ New Hampshire/Vermont, NE USA
44 G1 **Moores Island** *island* N Bahamas
21 R10 **Mooresville** North Carolina, SE USA 35°34′N 80°48′W
29 R5 **Moorhead** Minnesota, N USA 46°51′N 96°44′W
22 K4 **Moorhead** Mississippi, S USA 33°27′N 90°30′W
99 F18 **Moorsel** Oost-Vlaanderen, C Belgium 50°58′N 04°06′E
99 C18 **Moorslede** West-Vlaanderen, W Belgium 50°53′N 03°03′E
18 L8 **Moosalamoo, Mount** ▲ Vermont, NE USA 43°55′N 73°03′W
101 M22 **Moosburg in der Isar** Bayern, SE Germany 48°28′N 11°55′E
33 S14 **Moose** Wyoming, C USA 43°38′N 110°42′W
12 H11 **Moose** Ontario, S Canada
12 H10 **Moose Factory** Ontario, S Canada 51°16′N 80°32′W
19 Q4 **Moosehead Lake** Maine, NE USA
11 U16 **Moose Jaw** Saskatchewan, S Canada 50°23′N 105°35′W
11 V14 **Moose Lake** Manitoba, C Canada 53°42′N 100°22′W
29 W6 **Moose Lake** Minnesota, N USA 46°28′N 92°46′W
19 P6 **Mooselookmeguntic Lake** Maine, NE USA
39 R12 **Moose Pass** Alaska, USA 60°28′N 149°21′W
19 P5 **Moose River** Maine, NE USA
18 J9 **Moose River** New York, NE USA
11 V16 **Moosomin** Saskatchewan, S Canada 50°09′N 101°41′W
12 H10 **Moosonee** Ontario, SE Canada 51°18′N 80°40′W
19 N12 **Moosup** Connecticut, NE USA 41°42′N 71°51′W
83 N16 **Mopeia** Zambézia, NE Mozambique 17°59′S 35°43′E
83 H18 **Mopipi** Central, C Botswana 21°07′S 24°55′E
Moppo *see* Mokpo
77 N11 **Mopti** Mopti, C Mali 14°30′N 04°15′W
77 O11 **Mopti** ◈ *region* S Mali
57 H18 **Moquegua** Moquegua, SE Peru 17°07′S 70°55′W

◆ Country ● Country Capital ◇ Dependent Territory ○ Dependent Territory Capital ◈ Administrative Regions ✈ International Airport ▲ Mountain ▲▲ Mountain Range Volcano River Lake ⊞ Reservoir

57 H18 **Moquegua** *off.* Departamento de Moquegua. ◆ *department* S Peru
Moquegua, Departamento de *see* Moquegua
111 I23 **Mór** *Ger.* Moor. Fejér, C Hungary 47°21′N 18°12′E
78 G11 **Mora** Extrême-Nord, N Cameroon 11°02′N 14°07′E
104 G11 **Mora** Évora, S Portugal 38°56′N 08°10′W
105 N9 **Mora** Castilla-La Mancha, C Spain 39°40′N 03°46′W
94 L12 **Mora** Dalarna, C Sweden 61°N 14°30′E
29 V7 **Mora** Minnesota, N USA 45°52′N 93°18′W
37 T10 **Mora** New Mexico, SW USA 35°56′N 105°16′W
113 J17 **Morača** ⚓ S Montenegro
152 K10 **Morādābād** Uttar Pradesh, N India 28°50′N 78°45′E
105 U6 **Móra d'Ebre** *var.* Mora de Ebro. Cataluña, NE Spain 41°05′N 00°38′E
Mora de Ebro *see* Móra d'Ebre
105 S8 **Mora de Rubielos** Aragón, NE Spain 40°15′N 00°45′W
172 H4 **Morafenobe** Mahajanga, W Madagascar 17°49′S 44°54′E
110 K8 **Morąg** *Ger.* Mohrungen. Warmińsko-Mazurskie, N Poland 53°55′N 19°56′E
111 L25 **Mórahalom** Csongrád, S Hungary 46°14′N 19°52′E
105 N11 **Moral de Calatrava** Castilla-La Mancha, C Spain 38°50′N 03°34′W
63 G19 **Moraleda, Canal** *strait* SE Pacific Ocean
54 J3 **Morales** Bolívar, N Colombia 08°17′N 73°52′W
54 D12 **Morales** Cauca, SW Colombia 02°46′N 76°44′W
42 F5 **Morales** Izabal, E Guatemala 15°28′N 88°46′W
172 J5 **Moramanga** Toamasina, E Madagascar 18°57′S 48°13′E
27 Q6 **Moran** Kansas, C USA 37°55′N 95°10′W
25 Q7 **Moran** Texas, SW USA 32°33′N 99°10′W
181 X7 **Moranbah** Queensland, NE Australia 22°01′S 148°08′E
44 L13 **Morant Bay** E Jamaica 17°53′N 76°25′W
96 G10 **Morar, Loch** ◎ N Scotland, United Kingdom
Morata *see* Goodenough Island
105 Q12 **Moratalla** Murcia, SE Spain 38°11′N 01°53′W
108 C8 **Morat, Lac de** *Ger.* Murtensee. ◎ W Switzerland
84 I11 **Morava** *var.* March. ⚓ C Europe *see also* March
Morava *see* March
Morava *see* Moravia, Czech Republic
Morava *see* Velika Morava, Serbia
29 W15 **Moravia** Iowa, C USA 40°53′N 92°49′W
111 F18 **Moravia** *Cz.* Morava, *Ger.* Mähren. *cultural region* E Czech Republic
111 H17 **Moravice** *Ger.* Mohra. ⚓ NE Czech Republic
116 E12 **Moraviţa** Timiş, SW Romania 45°15′N 21°17′E
111 G17 **Moravská Třebová** *Ger.* Mährisch-Trübau. Pardubický Kraj, C Czech Republic 49°47′N 16°40′E
111 E19 **Moravské Budějovice** *Ger.* Mährisch-Budwitz. Vysočina, C Czech Republic 49°03′N 15°48′E
111 H17 **Moravskoslezský Kraj** *prev.* Ostravský Kraj. ◆ *region* E Czech Republic
111 F19 **Moravský Krumlov** *Ger.* Mährisch-Kromau. Jihomoravský Kraj, SE Czech Republic 48°58′N 16°30′E
96 J8 **Moray** *cultural region* N Scotland, United Kingdom
96 J8 **Moray Firth** *inlet* N Scotland, United Kingdom
42 B10 **Morazán** ◆ *department* NE El Salvador
154 C10 **Morbi** Gujarāt, W India 22°51′N 70°49′E
102 G7 **Morbihan** ◆ *department* NW France
Mörbisch *see* Mörbisch am See
109 Y5 **Mörbisch am See** *var.* Mörbisch. Burgenland, E Austria 47°43′N 16°40′E
95 N21 **Mörbylånga** Kalmar, S Sweden 56°31′N 16°25′E
102 J14 **Morcenx** Landes, SW France 44°04′N 00°55′W
Morcheh Khort *see* Mūrcheh Khvort
163 T5 **Mordaga** Nei Mongol Zizhiqu, N China 51°15′N 120°47′E
11 X17 **Morden** Manitoba, S Canada 49°12′N 98°05′W
Mordovia *see* Mordoviya, Respublika
127 N5 **Mordoviya, Respublika** *prev.* Mordovskaya ASSR, *Eng.* Mordovia, Mordvinia. ◆ *autonomous republic* W Russian Federation
126 M7 **Mordovo** Tambovskaya Oblast', W Russian Federation 52°05′N 40°49′E
Mordovskaya ASSR/ Mordvinia *see* Mordoviya, Respublika
Morea *see* Pelopónnisos
28 K8 **Moreau River** ⚓ South Dakota, N USA
97 K16 **Morecambe** NW England, United Kingdom 54°04′N 02°53′W
97 K16 **Morecambe Bay** *inlet* NW England, United Kingdom
183 S4 **Moree** New South Wales, SE Australia 29°29′S 149°53′E
21 N5 **Morehead** Kentucky, S USA 38°11′N 83°27′W
21 X11 **Morehead City** North Carolina, SE USA 34°43′N 76°43′W
27 Y8 **Morehouse** Missouri, C USA 36°51′N 89°41′W
108 E10 **Mörel** Valais, SW Switzerland 46°22′N 08°03′E
54 D13 **Morelia** Caquetá, S Colombia 01°30′N 75°43′W
41 N14 **Morelia** Michoacán, S Mexico 19°40′N 101°11′W
105 T7 **Morella** Valenciana, E Spain 40°37′N 00°06′W
40 I7 **Morelos** Chihuahua, N Mexico 26°37′N 107°37′W
41 O15 **Morelos** ◆ *state* S Mexico
154 H7 **Morena** Madhya Pradesh, C India 26°30′N 78°04′E
104 L12 **Morena, Sierra** ▲ S Spain
37 O14 **Morenci** Arizona, SW USA 33°05′N 109°21′W
31 R11 **Morenci** Michigan, N USA 41°43′N 84°13′W
116 J13 **Moreni** Dâmboviţa, S Romania 44°59′N 25°39′E
94 D9 **Møre og Romsdal** ◆ *county* S Norway
10 I14 **Moresby Island** *island* Queen Charlotte Islands, British Columbia, SW Canada
183 W2 **Moreton Island** *island* Queensland, E Australia
103 O3 **Moreuil** Somme, N France 49°47′N 02°28′E
35 V7 **Morey Peak** ▲ Nevada, W USA 38°40′N 116°16′W
125 U4 **More-Yu** ⚓ NW Russian Federation
103 T9 **Morez** Jura, E France 46°33′N 06°01′E
Morfou Bay/Mórfou, Kólpos *see* Güzelyurt Körfezi
182 J8 **Morgan** South Australia 34°02′S 139°39′E
23 S7 **Morgan** Georgia, SE USA 31°31′N 84°34′W
25 S8 **Morgan** Texas, SW USA 32°01′N 97°36′W
22 J10 **Morgan City** Louisiana, S USA 29°42′N 91°12′W
20 H6 **Morganfield** Kentucky, S USA 37°41′N 87°55′W
35 O10 **Morgan Hill** California, W USA 37°05′N 121°38′W
21 Q9 **Morganton** North Carolina, SE USA 35°44′N 81°43′W
20 J7 **Morgantown** Kentucky, S USA 37°12′N 86°42′W
21 S2 **Morgantown** West Virginia, NE USA 39°38′N 79°57′W
108 B10 **Morges** Vaud, SW Switzerland 46°31′N 06°30′E
Morghāb, Daryā-ye *see* Murgap
Morghāb, Daryā-ye *see* Murghāb, Daryā-ye
96 I9 **Mor, Glen** *var.* Glen Albyn, Great Glen. *valley* N Scotland, United Kingdom
103 T5 **Morhange** Moselle, NE France 48°56′N 06°37′E
158 M5 **Mori** *var.* Mori Kazak Zizhixian. Xinjiang Uygur Zizhiqu, NW China 43°48′N 90°21′E
165 R5 **Mori** Hokkaidō, NE Japan 42°04′N 140°36′E
35 Y6 **Moriah, Mount** ▲ Nevada, W USA 39°16′N 114°10′W
37 S11 **Moriarty** New Mexico, SW USA 34°59′N 106°03′W
54 J12 **Morichal** Guaviare, E Colombia 02°09′N 70°35′W
Mori Kazak Zizhixian *see* Mori
Morin Dawa Daurzu Zizhiqi *see* Nirji
11 Q14 **Morinville** Alberta, SW Canada 53°48′N 113°38′W
165 R8 **Morioka** Iwate, Honshū, C Japan 39°42′N 141°08′E
183 T8 **Morisset** New South Wales, SE Australia 33°07′S 151°32′E
165 Q8 **Moriyoshi-zan** ▲ Honshū, C Japan 39°58′N 140°32′E
92 K13 **Morjärv** Norrbotten, N Sweden 66°03′N 22°45′E
127 R3 **Morki** Respublika Mariy El, W Russian Federation 56°27′N 49°01′E
123 N10 **Morkoka** ⚓ NE Russian Federation
102 F5 **Morlaix** Finistère, NW France 48°35′N 03°50′W
95 M20 **Mörlunda** Kalmar, S Sweden 57°19′N 15°52′E
107 N19 **Mormanno** Calabria, SW Italy 39°54′N 15°58′E
36 L11 **Mormon Lake** ◎ Arizona, SW USA
35 Y10 **Mormon Peak** ▲ Nevada, W USA 36°59′N 114°25′W
Mormon State *see* Utah
45 Y5 **Morne-à-l'Eau** Grande Terre, N Guadeloupe 16°20′N 61°31′W
29 Y15 **Morning Sun** Iowa, C USA 41°06′N 91°15′W
193 S12 **Mornington Abyssal Plain** *undersea feature* SE Pacific Ocean 50°00′S 90°00′W
63 F22 **Mornington, Isla** *island* S Chile
181 T4 **Mornington Island** *island* Wellesley Islands, Queensland, N Australia
115 E18 **Mórnos** ⚓ C Greece
149 P14 **Moro** Sind, SE Pakistan 26°36′N 67°59′E
32 I11 **Moro** Oregon, NW USA 45°30′N 120°46′W
186 E8 **Morobe** Morobe, C Papua New Guinea 07°46′S 147°35′E
186 E8 **Morobe** ◆ *province* C Papua New Guinea
31 N12 **Morocco** Indiana, N USA 40°57′N 87°27′W
74 E8 **Morocco** *off.* Kingdom of Morocco, *Ar.* Al Mamlakah. ◆ *monarchy* N Africa
Morocco *see* Marrakech
Morocco, Kingdom of *see* Morocco
81 I22 **Morogoro** Morogoro, E Tanzania 06°49′S 37°40′E
81 H24 **Morogoro** ◆ *region* SE Tanzania
171 Q7 **Moro Gulf** *gulf* S Philippines
41 N13 **Moroleón** Guanajuato, C Mexico 20°00′N 101°13′W
172 H6 **Morombe** Toliara, W Madagascar 21°47′S 43°21′E
44 G5 **Morón** Ciego de Ávila, C Cuba 22°08′N 78°39′W
163 N8 **Mörön** Hentiy, C Mongolia 47°21′N 110°21′E
162 I6 **Mörön** Hövsgöl, N Mongolia 49°39′N 100°08′E
54 K5 **Morón** Carabobo, N Venezuela 10°29′N 68°11′W
Morón *see* Morón de la Frontera
56 D8 **Morona, Río** ⚓ N Peru
56 C8 **Morona Santiago** ◆ *province* E Ecuador
172 H5 **Morondava** Toliara, W Madagascar 20°19′S 44°17′E
104 K14 **Morón de la Frontera** *var.* Morón. Andalucía, S Spain 37°07′N 05°27′W
172 G13 **Moroni** ● (Comoros) Grande Comore, NW Comoros 11°41′S 43°16′E
171 S10 **Morotai, Pulau** *island* Maluku, E Indonesia
Morotiri *see* Marotiri
81 H17 **Moroto** NE Uganda 02°32′N 34°41′E
Morozov *see* Bratan
126 M11 **Morozovsk** Rostovskaya Oblast', SW Russian Federation 48°21′N 41°54′E
97 L14 **Morpeth** N England, United Kingdom 55°10′N 01°41′W
Morphou *see* Güzelyurt
Morphou Bay *see* Güzelyurt Körfezi
28 I13 **Morrill** Nebraska, C USA 41°57′N 103°55′W
27 U11 **Morrilton** Arkansas, C USA 35°09′N 92°45′W
11 Q16 **Morrin** Alberta, SW Canada 51°40′N 112°45′W
184 M7 **Morrinsville** Waikato, North Island, New Zealand 37°41′S 175°32′E
11 X16 **Morris** Manitoba, S Canada 49°22′N 94°21′W
30 M11 **Morris** Illinois, N USA 41°21′N 88°25′W
29 S8 **Morris** Minnesota, N USA 45°32′N 95°53′W
14 M13 **Morrisburg** Ontario, SE Canada 44°55′N 75°07′W
197 R11 **Morris Jesup, Kap** *headland* N Greenland 83°33′N 32°40′W
182 B1 **Morris, Mount** ▲ South Australia 26°04′S 131°03′E
30 K10 **Morrison** Illinois, N USA 41°48′N 89°58′W
36 K13 **Morristown** Arizona, SW USA 33°48′N 112°34′W
18 J14 **Morristown** New Jersey, NE USA 40°48′N 74°29′W
21 O8 **Morristown** Tennessee, S USA 36°13′N 83°18′W
42 L11 **Morrito** Río San Juan, SW Nicaragua 11°37′N 85°05′W
35 P13 **Morro Bay** California, W USA 35°21′N 120°51′W
95 L22 **Mörrum** Blekinge, S Sweden 56°11′N 14°45′E
83 N16 **Morrumbala** Zambézia, NE Mozambique 17°17′S 35°35′E
83 N20 **Morrumbene** Inhambane, SE Mozambique 23°41′S 35°25′E
95 F21 **Mors** *island* NW Denmark
Mörs *see* Moers
25 N1 **Morse** Texas, SW USA 36°03′N 101°28′W
127 N6 **Morshansk** Tambovskaya Oblast', W Russian Federation 53°27′N 41°46′E
102 L5 **Mortagne-au-Perche** Orne, N France 48°32′N 00°31′E
102 J8 **Mortagne-sur-Sèvre** Vendée, NW France 47°00′N 00°57′W
104 G8 **Mortágua** Viseu, N Portugal 40°24′N 08°14′W
102 J5 **Mortain** Manche, N France 48°39′N 00°51′W
106 C8 **Mortara** Lombardia, N Italy 45°15′N 08°44′E
59 J17 **Mortes, Rio das** ⚓ C Brazil
182 M12 **Mortlake** Victoria, SE Australia 38°06′S 142°48′E
Mortlock Group *see* Takuu Islands
189 Q17 **Mortlock Islands** *prev.* Nomoi Islands. *island group* C Micronesia
29 T9 **Morton** Minnesota, N USA 44°33′N 94°58′W
22 L5 **Morton** Mississippi, S USA 32°21′N 89°39′W
24 M5 **Morton** Texas, SW USA 33°40′N 102°45′W
32 H9 **Morton** Washington, NW USA 46°33′N 122°16′W
0 D7 **Morton Seamount** *undersea feature* NE Pacific Ocean 50°15′N 142°45′W
45 U15 **Moruga** Trinidad, Trinidad and Tobago 10°04′N 61°16′W
183 P9 **Morundah** New South Wales, SE Australia 34°57′S 146°18′E
191 X12 **Moruroa** *var.* Mururoa. *atoll* Îles Tuamotu, SE French Polynesia
183 S11 **Moruya** New South Wales, SE Australia 35°55′S 150°04′E
103 Q8 **Morvan** *physical region* C France
185 G21 **Morven** Canterbury, South Island, New Zealand 44°51′S 171°07′E
183 O13 **Morwell** Victoria, SE Australia 38°14′S 146°25′E
125 N6 **Morzhovets, Ostrov** *island* NW Russian Federation
126 J4 **Mosal'sk** Kaluzhskaya Oblast', W Russian Federation 54°30′N 34°55′E
101 H20 **Mosbach** Baden-Württemberg, SW Germany 49°21′N 09°06′E
95 E18 **Mosby** Vest-Agder, S Norway 58°12′N 07°55′E
33 V9 **Mosby** Montana, NW USA 46°58′N 107°53′W
32 M9 **Moscow** Idaho, NW USA 46°43′N 117°00′W
20 F10 **Moscow** Tennessee, S USA 35°04′N 89°27′W
Moscow *see* Moskva
101 D19 **Mosel** *Fr.* Moselle. ⚓ W Europe *see also* Moselle
Mosel *see* Moselle
103 T4 **Moselle** ◆ *department* NE France
103 T6 **Moselle** *Ger.* Mosel. ⚓ W Europe *see also* Mosel
Moselle *see* Mosel
32 K9 **Moses Lake** ◎ Washington, NW USA
83 I18 **Mosetse** Central, E Botswana 20°40′S 26°38′E
92 H4 **Mosfellsbær** Hofudborgarsvædid, SW Iceland 65°09′N 21°43′W
183 N8 **Mossgiel** New South Wales, SE Australia 33°16′S 144°34′E
185 F23 **Mosgiel** Otago, South Island, New Zealand 45°51′S 170°22′E
124 M11 **Mosha** ⚓ NW Russian Federation
81 I20 **Moshi** Kilimanjaro, NE Tanzania 03°21′S 37°19′E
110 G12 **Mosina** Wielkolpolskie, C Poland 52°15′N 16°50′E
30 L6 **Mosinee** Wisconsin, N USA 44°45′N 89°39′W
92 F13 **Mosjøen** Nordland, C Norway 65°49′N 13°12′E
123 S12 **Moskal'vo** Ostrov Sakhalin, Sakhalinskaya Oblast', SE Russian Federation 53°36′N 142°31′E
92 I13 **Moskosel** Norrbotten, N Sweden 65°52′N 19°30′E
126 K4 **Moskovskaya Oblast'** ◆ *province* W Russian Federation
Moskovskiy *see* Moskva
126 J3 **Moskva** *Eng.* Moscow. ● (Russian Federation) Gorod Moskva, W Russian Federation 55°45′N 37°42′E
147 Q14 **Moskva** *Rus.* Moskovskiy; *prev.* Chubek. SW Tajikistan 37°41′N 69°33′E
126 L4 **Moskva** ⚓ W Russian Federation
83 I20 **Mosomane** Kgatleng, SE Botswana 24°04′S 26°15′E
Moson and Magyaróvár *see* Mosonmagyaróvár
111 H21 **Mosoni-Duna** *Ger.* Kleine Donau. ⚓ NW Hungary
111 H21 **Mosonmagyaróvár** *Ger.* Wieselburg-Ungarisch-Altenburg; *prev.* Moson and Magyaróvár, *Ger.* Wieselburg and Ungarisch-Altenburg. Győr-Moson-Sopron, NW Hungary 47°52′N 17°15′E
Mospino *see* Mospyne
117 X8 **Mospyne** *Rus.* Mospino. Donets'ka Oblast', E Ukraine 47°53′N 38°03′E
54 B12 **Mosquera** Nariño, SW Colombia 02°32′N 78°24′W
37 U10 **Mosquero** New Mexico, SW USA 35°46′N 103°57′W
Mosquito Coast *see* La Mosquitia
31 U11 **Mosquito Creek Lake** ▣ Ohio, N USA
Mosquito Gulf *see* Mosquitos, Golfo de los
23 X11 **Mosquito Lagoon** *wetland* Florida, SE USA
43 N10 **Mosquito, Punta** *headland* E Nicaragua 12°18′N 83°38′W
43 W14 **Mosquito, Punta** *headland* NE Panama 09°06′N 77°52′W
43 Q15 **Mosquitos, Golfo de los** *Eng.* Mosquito Gulf. *gulf* N Panama
95 H16 **Moss** Østfold, S Norway 59°25′N 10°40′E
Mossâmedes *see* Namibe
22 G8 **Moss Bluff** Louisiana, S USA 30°18′N 93°11′W
185 C23 **Mossburn** Southland, South Island, New Zealand 45°40′S 168°15′E
83 G26 **Mosselbaai** *var.* Mosselbai, *Eng.* Mossel Bay. Western Cape, SW South Africa 34°11′S 22°08′E
Mosselbai/Mossel Bay *see* Mosselbaai
79 F20 **Mossendjo** Niari, SW Congo 02°57′S 12°40′E
101 H22 **Mössingen** Baden-Württemberg, S Germany 48°22′N 09°01′E
181 W4 **Mossman** Queensland, NE Australia 16°34′S 145°27′E
59 P14 **Mossoró** Rio Grande do Norte, NE Brazil 05°11′S 37°20′W
23 N9 **Moss Point** Mississippi, S USA 30°24′N 88°31′W
183 S9 **Moss Vale** New South Wales, SE Australia 34°33′S 150°20′E
32 G9 **Mossyrock** Washington, NW USA 46°32′N 122°30′W
111 B15 **Most** *Ger.* Brüx. Ústecký Kraj, NW Czech Republic 50°30′N 13°37′E
162 E7 **Möst** *var.* Ulaantolgoy. Hovd, W Mongolia 46°39′N 92°50′E
121 P16 **Mosta** *var.* Musta. C Malta 35°54′N 14°25′E
74 I5 **Mostaganem** *var.* Mestghanem. NW Algeria 35°54′N 00°05′E
113 H14 **Mostar** Federacija Bosna I Hercegovina, S Bosnia and Herzegovina 43°21′N 17°47′E
61 J17 **Mostardas** Rio Grande do Sul, S Brazil 31°02′S 50°51′W
116 K14 **Mostiştea** ⚓ S Romania
Mostva *see* Mastva
Mosty *see* Masty
116 H5 **Mostys'ka** L'vivs'ka Oblast', W Ukraine 49°47′N 23°09′E
Mosul *see* Al Mawşil
95 F15 **Møsvatnet** ◎ S Norway
80 J12 **Mot'a** Āmara, N Ethiopia 11°03′N 38°03′E
79 H16 **Motaba** ⚓ N Congo
105 O10 **Mota del Cuervo** Castilla-La Mancha, C Spain 39°30′N 02°52′W
104 L5 **Mota del Marqués** Castilla y León, N Spain 41°38′N 05°11′W
42 F5 **Motagua, Río** ⚓ Guatemala/Honduras
119 H19 **Motal'** Brestskaya Voblasts', SW Belarus 52°13′N 25°34′E
95 L17 **Motala** Östergötland, S Sweden 58°34′N 15°05′E
191 X7 **Motane** *island* Îles Marquises, NE French Polynesia
152 K13 **Moth** Uttar Pradesh, N India 25°44′N 78°56′E
Mother of Presidents/ Mother of States *see* Virginia
96 I12 **Motherwell** C Scotland, United Kingdom 55°48′N 04°W
153 P12 **Motīhāri** Bihār, N India 26°40′N 84°55′E
105 Q10 **Motilla del Palancar** Castilla-La Mancha, C Spain 39°34′N 01°55′W
184 N7 **Motiti Island** *island* NE New Zealand
65 E25 **Motley Island** *island* SE Falkland Islands
83 J19 **Motloutse** ⚓ E Botswana
41 V17 **Motozintla de Mendoza** Chiapas, SE Mexico 15°21′N 92°14′W
105 N15 **Motril** Andalucía, S Spain 36°45′N 03°30′W
116 G13 **Motru** Gorj, SW Romania 44°49′N 22°56′E
165 Q4 **Motsuta-misaki** *headland* Hokkaidō, NE Japan 42°36′N 139°48′E
28 L6 **Mott** North Dakota, N USA 46°21′N 102°17′W
166 M9 **Mottama** *var.* Martaban, Moktama. Mon State, S Myanmar (Burma) 16°32′N 97°35′E
166 L9 **Mottama, Gulf of** *var.* Gulf of Martaban. *gulf* S Myanmar (Burma)
Möttling *see* Metlika
107 O18 **Mottola** Puglia, SE Italy 40°38′N 17°02′E
184 P8 **Motu** ⚓ North Island, New Zealand
185 I14 **Motueka** Tasman, South Island, New Zealand 41°08′S 173°00′E
185 I14 **Motueka** ⚓ South Island, New Zealand
Motu Iti *see* Tupai
41 X12 **Motul** *var.* Motul de Felipe Carrillo Puerto. Yucatán, SE Mexico 21°06′N 89°17′W
Motul de Felipe Carrillo Puerto *see* Motul
191 U17 **Motu Nui** *island* Easter Island, Chile, E Pacific Ocean
191 Q10 **Motu One** *var.* Bellingshausen. *atoll* Îles Sous le Vent, W French Polynesia
190 I16 **Motutapu** *island* E Cook Islands
193 V15 **Motu Tapu** *island* Tongatapu Group, S Tonga
184 L5 **Motutapu Island** *island* N New Zealand
Motyca *see* Modica
Mouanda *see* Moanda
Mouaskar *see* Mascara
105 U3 **Moubermé, Tuc de** *Fr.* Pic de Maubermé, *Sp.* Pico Mauberme; *prev.* Tuc de Maubermé. ▲ France/ Spain 42°48′N 00°57′E *see also* Maubermé, Pic de
Moubermé, Tuc de *see* Maubermé, Pic de
45 N7 **Mouchoir Passage** *passage* SE Turks and Caicos Islands
76 I9 **Moudjéria** Tagant, SW Mauritania 17°52′N 12°20′W
108 C9 **Moudon** Vaud, W Switzerland 46°41′N 06°49′E
Mouhoun *see* Black Volta
79 E19 **Mouila** Ngounié, C Gabon 01°50′S 11°02′E
79 K14 **Mouka** Haute-Kotto, C Central African Republic 07°12′N 21°52′E
Moukden *see* Shenyang
183 N10 **Moulamein** New South Wales, SE Australia 35°06′S 144°03′E
Moulamein Creek *see* Billabong Creek
74 F6 **Moulay-Bousselham** NW Morocco 35°00′N 06°22′W
Moule *see* le Moule
80 M11 **Moulhoulé** N Djibouti 12°34′N 43°06′E
103 P9 **Moulins** Allier, C France 46°34′N 03°20′E
Moulmein *see* Mawlamyine
Moulmeingyun *see* Mawlamyinegyunn
74 G6 **Moulouya** *var.* Mulucha, Muluya, Mulwiya. *seasonal river* NE Morocco
23 O2 **Moulton** Alabama, S USA 34°28′N 87°18′W
29 W16 **Moulton** Iowa, C USA 40°41′N 92°40′W
25 T11 **Moulton** Texas, SW USA 29°34′N 97°08′W
23 T7 **Moultrie** Georgia, SE USA 31°10′N 83°47′W
21 S14 **Moultrie, Lake** ▣ South Carolina, SE USA
22 K3 **Mound Bayou** Mississippi, S USA 33°52′N 90°43′W
30 L17 **Mound City** Illinois, N USA 37°06′N 89°09′W
27 R6 **Mound City** Kansas, C USA 38°07′N 94°49′W
27 Q2 **Mound City** Missouri, C USA 40°07′N 95°13′W
29 N7 **Mound City** South Dakota, N USA 45°44′N 100°03′W
78 H13 **Moundou** Logone-Occidental, SW Chad 08°35′N 16°01′E
27 P10 **Mounds** Oklahoma, C USA 35°52′N 96°03′W
21 R2 **Moundsville** West Virginia, NE USA 39°54′N 80°44′W
167 R11 **Moŭng** *prev.* Phumĭ Moŭng. Siĕmréab, NW Cambodia 13°45′N 103°35′E
167 Q12 **Moŭng Roessei** Bătdâmbâng, W Cambodia 12°47′N 103°28′E
Moun Hou *see* Black Volta
8 H8 **Mountain** ⚓ Northwest Territories, NW Canada
37 S12 **Mountainair** New Mexico, SW USA 34°31′N 106°14′W
35 V1 **Mountain City** Nevada, W USA 41°48′N 115°58′W
21 Q8 **Mountain City** Tennessee, S USA 36°28′N 81°48′W
27 U7 **Mountain Grove** Missouri, C USA 37°07′N 92°15′W
27 U9 **Mountain Home** Arkansas, C USA 36°19′N 92°24′W
33 N15 **Mountain Home** Idaho, NW USA 43°07′N 115°42′W
25 Q11 **Mountain Home** Texas, SW USA 30°11′N 99°19′W
29 W4 **Mountain Iron** Minnesota, N USA 47°31′N 92°37′W
29 T10 **Mountain Lake** Minnesota, N USA 43°57′N 94°54′W
23 S3 **Mountain Park** Georgia, SE USA 34°04′N 84°24′W
35 W12 **Mountain Pass** *pass* California, W USA
27 T12 **Mountain Pine** Arkansas, C USA 34°34′N 93°10′W
39 Y14 **Mountain Point** Annette Island, Alaska, USA 55°17′N 131°31′W
Mountain State *see* Montana
Mountain State *see* West Virginia
27 V7 **Mountain View** Arkansas, C USA 35°52′N 92°07′W
38 H12 **Mountain View** Hawaii, USA, C Pacific Ocean 19°32′N 155°03′W
27 V10 **Mountain View** Missouri, C USA 37°00′N 91°42′W
38 M11 **Mountain Village** Alaska, USA 62°06′N 163°42′W
21 R8 **Mount Airy** North Carolina, SE USA 36°30′N 80°36′W
83 K24 **Mount Ayliff** *Xh.* Maxesibebi. Eastern Cape, SE South Africa 30°48′S 29°23′E
29 U16 **Mount Ayr** Iowa, C USA 40°42′N 94°14′W
182 J9 **Mount Barker** South Australia 35°06′S 138°52′E
180 J14 **Mount Barker** Western Australia 34°42′S 117°40′E
183 P11 **Mount Beauty** Victoria, SE Australia 36°47′S 147°12′E
14 E16 **Mount Brydges** Ontario, S Canada 42°54′N 81°29′W
31 N16 **Mount Carmel** Illinois, N USA 38°23′N 87°46′W
30 K10 **Mount Carroll** Illinois, N USA 42°05′N 89°59′W
31 S9 **Mount Clemens** Michigan, N USA 42°36′N 82°52′W
185 E19 **Mount Cook** Canterbury, South Island, New Zealand 43°47′S 170°06′E
83 L16 **Mount Darwin** Mashonaland Central, NE Zimbabwe 16°45′S 31°39′E
19 S7 **Mount Desert Island** *island* Maine, NE USA
23 W11 **Mount Dora** Florida, SE USA 28°48′N 81°38′W
182 G5 **Mount Eba** South Australia 30°11′S 135°40′E
25 W8 **Mount Enterprise** Texas, SW USA 31°53′N 94°40′W
182 J4 **Mount Fitton** South Australia 29°55′S 139°26′E
83 J24 **Mount Fletcher** Eastern Cape, SE South Africa 30°41′S 28°30′E
14 F15 **Mount Forest** Ontario, S Canada 43°58′N 80°44′W
182 K12 **Mount Gambier** South Australia 37°47′S 140°49′E
181 W5 **Mount Garnet** Queensland, NE Australia 17°41′S 145°07′E
21 P6 **Mount Gay** West Virginia, NE USA 37°49′N 82°00′W
31 S12 **Mount Gilead** Ohio, N USA 40°33′N 82°49′W
186 C7 **Mount Hagen** Western Highlands, C Papua New Guinea 05°54′S 144°13′E
18 J16 **Mount Holly** New Jersey, NE USA 39°59′N 74°46′W
21 R10 **Mount Holly** North Carolina, SE USA 35°18′N 81°01′W
27 T12 **Mount Ida** Arkansas, C USA 34°32′N 93°38′W
181 T6 **Mount Isa** Queensland, C Australia 20°48′S 139°32′E
21 U4 **Mount Jackson** Virginia, NE USA 38°45′N 78°38′W
18 D12 **Mount Jewett** Pennsylvania, NE USA 41°43′N 78°37′W
18 L13 **Mount Kisco** New York, NE USA 41°12′N 73°42′W
18 B15 **Mount Lebanon** Pennsylvania, NE USA 40°21′N 80°03′W
182 J8 **Mount Lofty Ranges** ▲ South Australia
180 J10 **Mount Magnet** Western Australia 28°09′S 117°52′E
184 N7 **Mount Maunganui** Bay of Plenty, North Island, New Zealand 37°39′S 176°11′E
97 E18 **Mountmellick** *Ir.* Móinteach Mílic. Laois, C Ireland 53°07′N 07°20′W
30 L10 **Mount Morris** Illinois, N USA 42°03′N 89°25′W
31 R9 **Mount Morris** Michigan, N USA 43°07′N 83°42′W
18 F10 **Mount Morris** New York, NE USA 42°43′N 77°51′W
18 B16 **Mount Morris** Pennsylvania, NE USA 39°43′N 80°06′W
30 K15 **Mount Olive** Illinois, N USA 39°04′N 89°43′W
21 V10 **Mount Olive** North Carolina, SE USA 35°12′N 78°03′W
21 N4 **Mount Olivet** Kentucky, S USA 38°32′N 84°01′W
29 Y15 **Mount Pleasant** Iowa, C USA 40°57′N 91°33′W
31 Q8 **Mount Pleasant** Michigan, N USA 43°36′N 84°46′W
18 C15 **Mount Pleasant** Pennsylvania, NE USA 40°07′N 79°33′W
21 T14 **Mount Pleasant** South Carolina, SE USA 32°47′N 79°51′W
20 I9 **Mount Pleasant** Tennessee, S USA 35°32′N 87°11′W
25 W6 **Mount Pleasant** Texas, SW USA 33°10′N 94°49′W
36 L4 **Mount Pleasant** Utah, W USA 39°33′N 111°27′W
63 N23 **Mount Pleasant** ✈ (Stanley) East Falkland, Falkland Islands
97 G25 **Mount's Bay** *inlet* SW England, United Kingdom
35 N2 **Mount Shasta** California, W USA 41°18′N 122°19′W
30 J13 **Mount Sterling** Illinois, N USA 39°59′N 90°44′W
21 N5 **Mount Sterling** Kentucky, S USA 38°03′N 83°56′W
18 E15 **Mount Union** Pennsylvania, NE USA 40°21′N 77°51′W
23 V6 **Mount Vernon** Georgia, SE USA 32°10′N 82°35′W
30 L16 **Mount Vernon** Illinois, N USA 38°19′N 88°54′W
20 M6 **Mount Vernon** Kentucky, S USA 37°20′N 84°20′W
27 S7 **Mount Vernon** Missouri, C USA 37°05′N 93°49′W
31 T13 **Mount Vernon** Ohio, N USA 40°23′N 82°29′W
32 K13 **Mount Vernon** Oregon, NW USA 44°22′N 119°07′W
25 W6 **Mount Vernon** Texas, SW USA 33°11′N 95°13′W
32 H7 **Mount Vernon** Washington, NW USA 48°25′N 122°19′W
20 L5 **Mount Washington** Kentucky, S USA 38°03′N 85°33′W
182 F8 **Mount Wedge** South Australia 33°29′S 135°08′E
30 L14 **Mount Zion** Illinois, N USA 39°46′N 88°52′W
181 Y9 **Moura** Queensland, NE Australia 24°34′S 149°57′E
58 F12 **Moura** Amazonas, NW Brazil 01°32′S 61°43′W
104 H12 **Moura** Beja, S Portugal 38°08′N 07°27′W
104 I12 **Mourão** Évora, S Portugal 38°22′N 07°20′W
76 L11 **Mourdiah** Koulikoro, W Mali 14°28′N 07°31′W
78 K7 **Mourdi, Dépression du** *desert lowland* Chad/Sudan
102 J16 **Mourenx** Pyrénées-Atlantiques, SW France 43°24′N 00°37′W
Mourgana *see* Mourgkána
115 C15 **Mourgkána** *var.* Mourgana. ▲ Albania/Greece 39°48′N 20°24′E
97 G16 **Mourne Mountains** *Ir.* Beanna Boirche. ▲ SE Northern Ireland, United Kingdom
115 I15 **Moúrtzeflos, Akrotírio** *headland* Límnos, E Greece 40°00′N 25°02′E
99 C19 **Mouscron** *Dut.* Moeskroen. Hainaut, W Belgium 50°44′N 03°14′E
Mouse River *see* Souris River
78 H10 **Moussoro** Kanem, W Chad 13°41′N 16°31′E
103 T11 **Moûtiers** Savoie, E France 45°28′N 06°31′E
172 J14 **Moutsamoudou** *var.* Moutsamudu. Anjouan, SE Comoros 12°10′S 44°25′E
Moutsamudou *see* Moutsamoudou
74 K11 **Mouydir, Monts de** ▲ S Algeria
79 F20 **Mouyondzi** Bouenza, S Congo 03°58′S 13°57′E
115 E16 **Mouzáki** *prev.* Mouzákion. Thessalía, C Greece 39°25′N 21°40′E
Mouzákion *see* Mouzáki
29 S13 **Moville** Iowa, C USA 42°30′N 96°04′W
82 E13 **Moxico** ◆ *province* E Angola
172 I14 **Moya** Anjouan, SE Comoros 12°18′S 44°27′E
40 L12 **Moyahua** Zacatecas, C Mexico 21°18′N 103°09′W
81 J16 **Moyalē** Oromīya, C Ethiopia 03°34′N 38°58′E
76 I15 **Moyamba** W Sierra Leone 08°04′N 12°30′W
74 G7 **Moyen Atlas** *Eng.* Middle Atlas. ▲ N Morocco
78 H13 **Moyen-Chari** *off.* Préfecture du Moyen-Chari. ◆ *prefecture* S Chad
Moyen-Chari, Préfecture du *see* Moyen-Chari
Moyen-Congo *see* Congo (Republic of)
83 J24 **Moyeni** *var.* Quthing. SW Lesotho 30°25′S 27°43′E
79 D18 **Moyen-Ogooué** *off.* Province du Moyen-Ogooué, *var.* Le Moyen-Ogooué. ◆ *province* C Gabon
Moyen-Ogooué, Province du *see* Moyen-Ogooué
103 S4 **Moyeuvre-Grande** Moselle, NE France 49°15′N 06°03′E
33 N7 **Moyie Springs** Idaho, NW USA 48°43′N 116°15′W
146 G6 **Mo'ynoq** *Rus.* Muynak. Qoraqalpog'iston Respublikasi, NW Uzbekistan 43°45′N 59°03′E
81 F16 **Moyo** NW Uganda 03°38′N 31°43′E
56 D10 **Moyobamba** San Martín, NW Peru 06°04′S 76°56′W
78 H10 **Moyto** Chari-Baguirmi, W Chad 12°35′N 16°33′E
158 G9 **Moyu** *var.* Karakax. Xinjiang Uygur Zizhiqu, NW China 37°16′N 79°39′E
122 M9 **Moyyero** ⚓ N Russian Federation
145 S15 **Moyynkum** *var.* Furmanovka, *Kaz.* Fūrmanov. Zhambyl, S Kazakhstan 44°15′N 72°55′E
145 Q15 **Moyynkum, Peski** *Kaz.* Moyynqum. *desert* S Kazakhstan
Moyynqum *see* Moyynkum, Peski
145 S12 **Moyynty** Karaganda, C Kazakhstan 47°10′N 73°24′E
145 S12 **Moyynty** ⚓ Karaganda, C Kazakhstan
Mozambika, Lakandranon' i *see* Mozambique Channel
83 M18 **Mozambique** *off.* Republic of Mozambique; *prev.* People's Republic of Mozambique, Portuguese East Africa. ◆ *republic* S Africa
Mozambique Basin *see* Natal Basin
Mozambique, Canal de *see* Mozambique Channel
83 P17 **Mozambique Channel** *Fr.* Canal de Mozambique, *Mal.* Lakandranon' i Mozambika. *strait* W Indian Ocean
172 L11 **Mozambique Escarpment** *var.* Mozambique Scarp. *undersea feature* SW Indian Ocean 33°00′S 36°30′E
Mozambique, People's Republic of *see* Mozambique
172 L10 **Mozambique Plateau** *var.* Mozambique Rise. *undersea feature* SW Indian Ocean 32°00′S 35°00′E
Mozambique, Republic of *see* Mozambique
Mozambique Rise *see* Mozambique Plateau
Mozambique Scarp *see* Mozambique Escarpment
127 O15 **Mozdok** Respublika Severnaya Osetiya, SW Russian Federation 43°48′N 44°42′E
57 K17 **Mozetenes, Serranías de** ▲ C Bolivia
126 J4 **Mozhaysk** Moskovskaya Oblast', W Russian Federation 55°31′N 36°01′E
127 T3 **Mozhga** Udmurtskaya Respublika, NW Russian Federation 56°24′N 52°13′E
Mozyr' *see* Mazyr
79 P22 **Mpala** Katanga, E Dem. Rep. Congo 06°43′S 29°28′E
79 G19 **Mpama** ⚓ C Congo
81 E22 **Mpanda** Rukwa, W Tanzania 06°21′S 31°01′E
82 L11 **Mpande** Northern, NE Zambia 09°13′S 31°42′E
83 J18 **Mphoengs** Matabeleland South, SW Zimbabwe 21°04′S 27°56′E
81 F18 **Mpigi** S Uganda 0°14′N 32°19′E
82 L13 **Mpika** Northern, NE Zambia 11°50′S 31°30′E
83 J14 **Mpima** Central, C Zambia 14°25′S 28°34′E
82 J13 **Mpongwe** Copperbelt, C Zambia 13°25′S 28°13′E
82 K11 **Mporokoso** Northern, N Zambia 09°22′S 30°06′E
79 H20 **Mpouya** Plateaux, SE Congo 02°38′S 16°13′E
77 P16 **Mpraeso** C Ghana 06°36′N 00°43′W
82 L11 **Mpulungu** Northern, N Zambia 08°50′S 31°06′E
83 K21 **Mpumalanga** *prev.* Eastern Transvaal, *Afr.* Oos-Transvaal. ◆ *province* NE South Africa
83 D16 **Mpungu** Okavango, N Namibia 17°36′S 18°16′E
81 I22 **Mpwapwa** Dodoma, C Tanzania 06°21′S 36°29′E
Mqinvartsveri *see* Kazbek
110 M8 **Mrągowo** *Ger.* Sensburg. Warmińsko-Mazurskie, NE Poland 53°53′N 21°19′E
127 V6 **Mrakovo** Respublika Bashkortostan, W Russian Federation 52°43′N 56°36′E

◆ Country ● Country Capital ◇ Dependent Territory ○ Dependent Territory Capital ◆ Administrative Regions ✈ International Airport ▲ Mountain ▲ Mountain Range ⛰ Volcano ⚓ River ◎ Lake ▣ Reservoir

172 I13 **Mramani** Anjouan, E Comoros 12°18′N 44°39′E
166 K5 **Mrauk-oo** *var.* Mrauk U, Myohaung. Rakhine State, W Myanmar (Burma) 20°35′N 93°12′E
Mrauk U *see* Mrauk-oo
112 F12 **Mrkonjić Grad** ⬖ Republika Srpska, W Bosnia and Herzegovina
110 H9 **Mrocza** Kujawsko-pomorskie, C Poland 53°15′N 17°38′E
124 I14 **Msta** ≈ NW Russian Federation
Mstislavl' *see* Mstsislaw
119 P15 **Mstsislaw** *Rus.* Mstislavl'. Mahilyowskaya Voblasts', E Belarus 54°01′N 31°43′E
83 J24 **Mthatha** *prev.* Umtata. Eastern Cape, SE South Africa 31°33′S 28°47′E *see also* Umtata
Mtkvari *see* Kura
Mtoko *see* Mutoko
126 K6 **Mtsensk** Orlovskaya Oblast', W Russian Federation 53°17′N 36°34′E
81 K24 **Mtwara** Mtwara, SE Tanzania 10°17′S 40°11′E
81 J25 **Mtwara** ⬖ *region* SE Tanzania
104 G14 **Mu** ▲ S Portugal 37°24′N 08°04′W
193 V15 **Mu'a** Tongatapu, S Tonga 21°11′S 175°07′W
Muai To *see* Mae Hong Son
83 P16 **Mualama** Zambézia, NE Mozambique 16°51′S 38°21′E
Mualo *see* Messalo, Rio
79 E22 **Muanda** Bas-Congo, SW Dem. Rep. Congo 05°53′S 12°17′E
Muang Chiang Rai *see* Chiang Rai
167 R6 **Muang Ham** Houaphan, N Laos 20°19′N 104°00′E
167 S8 **Muang Hinboun** Khammouan, C Laos 17°37′N 104°37′E
Muang Kalasin *see* Kalasin
Muang Khammouan *see* Thakhèk
167 S11 **Muang Không** Champasak, S Laos 14°08′N 105°48′E
167 S10 **Muang Khôngxédôn** *var.* Khong Sedone. Salavan, S Laos 15°34′N 105°46′E
Muang Khon Kaen *see* Khon Kaen
167 Q6 **Muang Khoua** Phôngsali, N Laos 21°07′N 102°31′E
Muang Krabi *see* Krabi
Muang Lampang *see* Lampang
Muang Lamphun *see* Lamphun
Muang Loei *see* Loei
Muang Lom Sak *see* Lom Sak
Muang Nakhon Sawan *see* Nakhon Sawan
167 Q6 **Muang Namo** Oudômxai, N Laos 20°58′N 101°46′E
Muang Nan *see* Nan
167 Q6 **Muang Ngoy** Louangphabang, N Laos 20°43′N 102°42′E
167 Q5 **Muang Ou Tai** Phôngsali, N Laos 22°06′N 101°59′E
Muang Pak Lay *see* Pak Lay
Muang Pakxan *see* Pakxan
167 T10 **Muang Pakxong** Champasak, S Laos 15°10′N 106°17′E
167 S9 **Muang Phalan** *var.* Muang Phalane. Savannakhét, S Laos 16°40′N 105°33′E
Muang Phalane *see* Muang Phalan
Muang Phan *see* Phan
Muang Phayao *see* Phayao
Muang Phichit *see* Phichit
167 T9 **Muang Phin** Savannakhét, S Laos 16°31′N 106°01′E
Muang Phitsanulok *see* Phitsanulok
Muang Phrae *see* Phrae
Muang Roi Et *see* Roi Et
Muang Sakon Nakhon *see* Sakon Nakhon
Muang Samut Prakan *see* Samut Prakan
167 P6 **Muang Sing** Louang Namtha, N Laos 21°12′N 101°09′E
Muang Ubon *see* Ubon Ratchathani
Muang Uthai Thani *see* Uthai Thani
167 P7 **Muang Vangviang** Viangchan, C Laos 18°53′N 102°27′E
Muang Xaignabouri *see* Xaignabouli
Muang Xay *see* Oudômxai
167 S9 **Muang Xépôn** *var.* Sepone. Savannakhét, S Laos 16°40′N 106°15′E
168 K10 **Muar** *var.* Bandar Maharani. Johor, Peninsular Malaysia 02°01′N 102°35′E
168 J9 **Muara** Sumatera, W Indonesia 02°18′N 98°54′E
168 L13 **Muarabeliti** Sumatera, W Indonesia 03°13′S 103°00′E
168 K12 **Muarabungo** Sumatera, W Indonesia 01°28′S 102°06′E
168 L13 **Muaraenim** Sumatera, W Indonesia 03°40′S 103°48′E
169 T11 **Muarajuloi** Borneo, C Indonesia 0°12′S 114°03′E
169 U12 **Muarakaman** Borneo, C Indonesia 0°09′S 116°43′E
168 H12 **Muarasigep** Pulau Siberut, W Indonesia 01°01′S 98°48′E
168 L12 **Muaratembesi** Sumatera, W Indonesia 01°40′S 103°08′E
169 T12 **Muaratewe** *var.* Muarateweh; *prev.* Moearatewe. Borneo, C Indonesia 0°58′S 114°52′E
Muarateweh *see* Muaratewe
169 U10 **Muarawahau** Borneo, N Indonesia 01°03′N 116°48′E
138 G13 **Mubārak, Jabal** ▲ S Jordan 29°19′N 35°13′E
153 N13 **Mubārakpur** Uttar Pradesh, N India 26°05′N 83°19′E
Mubarek *see* Muborak
81 F18 **Mubende** SW Uganda 0°35′N 31°24′E
77 Y14 **Mubi** Adamawa, NE Nigeria 10°15′N 13°18′E
146 M12 **Muborak** *Rus.* Mubarek. Qashqadaryo Viloyati, S Uzbekistan 39°17′N 65°10′E
171 U12 **Mubrani** Papua, E Indonesia 0°42′S 133°25′E
67 U12 **Muchinga Escarpment** *escarpment* NE Zambia
127 N7 **Muchkapskiy** Tambovskaya Oblast', W Russian Federation 51°51′N 42°25′E
96 G10 **Muck** *island* W Scotland, United Kingdom
82 Q13 **Mucojo** Cabo Delgado, N Mozambique 12°05′S 40°30′E
82 F12 **Muconda** Lunda Sul, NE Angola 10°37′S 21°19′E
54 I10 **Muco, Río** ≈ E Colombia
83 O16 **Mucubela** Zambézia, NE Mozambique 16°51′S 37°48′E
42 J5 **Mucupina, Monte** ▲ N Honduras 15°07′N 86°36′W
136 J14 **Mucur** Kirşehir, C Turkey 39°05′N 34°25′E
143 U8 **Mūd** Khorāsān-e Janūbī, E Iran 32°41′N 59°30′E
163 Y9 **Mudanjiang** *var.* Mu-tan-chiang. Heilongjiang, NE China 44°33′N 129°40′E
163 Y9 **Mudan Jiang** ≈ NE China
136 D11 **Mudanya** Bursa, NW Turkey 40°23′N 28°53′E
28 K8 **Mud Butte** South Dakota, N USA 45°00′N 102°51′W
155 G16 **Muddebihāl** Karnātaka, C India 16°26′N 76°07′E
27 P12 **Muddy Boggy Creek** ≈ Oklahoma, C USA
36 M6 **Muddy Creek** ≈ Utah, W USA
37 V7 **Muddy Creek Reservoir** ▣ Colorado, C USA
33 W15 **Muddy Gap** Wyoming, C USA 42°21′N 107°27′W
35 Y11 **Muddy Peak** ▲ Nevada, W USA 36°17′N 114°40′W
183 R7 **Mudgee** New South Wales, SE Australia 32°37′S 149°36′E
29 S3 **Mud Lake** ◎ Minnesota, N USA
29 P7 **Mud Lake Reservoir** ▣ South Dakota, N USA
167 N9 **Mudon** Mon State, Myanmar (Burma) 16°17′N 97°40′E
81 O14 **Mudug** *off.* Gobolka Mudug. ⬖ *region* NE Somalia
81 O14 **Mudug** *var.* Mudugh. *plain* N Somalia
Mudug, Gobolka *see* Mudug
Mudugh *see* Mudug
83 Q15 **Muecate** Nampula, NE Mozambique 14°56′S 39°38′E
82 Q13 **Mueda** Cabo Delgado, NE Mozambique 11°40′S 39°31′E
42 L10 **Muelle de los Bueyes** Región Autónoma Atlántico Sur, SE Nicaragua 12°03′N 84°34′W
Muenchen *see* München
83 M14 **Muende** Tete, NW Mozambique 14°22′S 33°00′E
25 T5 **Muenster** Texas, SW USA 33°39′N 97°22′W
Muenster *see* Münster
43 O6 **Muerto, Cayo** *reef* NE Nicaragua
41 T17 **Muerto, Mar** *lagoon* SE Mexico
64 F11 **Muertos Trough** *undersea feature* N Caribbean Sea
83 H14 **Mufaya Kuta** Western, NW Zambia 14°30′S 24°18′E
82 J13 **Mufulira** Copperbelt, C Zambia 12°33′S 28°16′E
161 O10 **Mufu Shan** ▲▲ C China
Mugalla *see* Yutian
Mugalzhar Taūlary *see* Mugodzhary, Gory
137 Y12 **Muğan Düzü** *Rus.* Muganskaya Ravnina, Muganskaya Step'. *physical region* S Azerbaijan
Muganskaya Ravnina/Muganskaya Step' *see* Muğan Düzü
106 K8 **Múggia** Friuli-Venezia Giulia, NE Italy 45°36′N 13°48′E
153 N14 **Mughal Sarāi** Uttar Pradesh, N India 25°18′N 83°07′E
Mughla *see* Muğla
141 W11 **Mughshin** *var.* Muqshin. S Oman 19°26′N 54°38′E
147 S12 **Mughsu** *Rus.* Muksu. ≈ C Tajikistan
164 H14 **Mugi** Tokushima, Shikoku, SW Japan 33°39′N 134°24′E
136 C16 **Muğla** *var.* Mughla. Muğla, SW Turkey 37°13′N 28°22′E
136 C16 **Muğla** *var.* Mughla. ⬖ *province* SW Turkey
114 K10 **Mŭglizh** Stara Zagora, C Bulgaria 42°36′N 25°32′E
144 J11 **Mugodzhary, Gory** *Kaz.* Mugalzhar Taūlary. ▲▲ W Kazakhstan
83 O15 **Mugulama** Zambézia, NE Mozambique 16°01′S 37°33′E
Muḥāfazat Hims *see* Ḥimṣ
Muḥāfazat Ma'dabā *see* Ma'dabā
139 U9 **Muḥammad** Wāsiṭ, E Iraq 32°46′N 45°14′E
139 R8 **Muḥammadīyah** Al Anbār, C Iraq 33°22′N 42°48′E
80 I6 **Muhammad Qol** Red Sea, NE Sudan 20°53′N 37°09′E
75 Y9 **Muḥammad, Râs** *headland* E Egypt 27°45′N 34°18′E
Muhammerah *see* Khorramshahr
Muḥātazat Al 'Aqabah *see* Al 'Aqabah
140 M12 **Muhāyil** *var.* Mahāil. 'Asīr, SW Saudi Arabia 18°34′N 42°01′E
139 O7 **Muḥaywīr** Al Anbār, W Iraq 33°35′N 41°06′E
101 H21 **Mühlacker** Baden-Württemberg, SW Germany 48°57′N 08°51′E
Mühlbach *see* Sebeş
Mühldorf *see* Mühldorf am Inn
101 N23 **Mühldorf am Inn** *var.* Mühldorf. Bayern, SE Germany 48°14′N 12°32′E
101 J15 **Mühlhausen** *var.* Mühlhausen in Thüringen. Thüringen, C Germany 51°13′N 10°28′E
Mühlhausen in Thüringen *see* Mühlhausen
195 Q2 **Mühlig-Hofmanfjella** *Eng.* Mülig-Hofmann Mountains. ▲▲ Antarctica
93 L14 **Muhos** Oulu, C Finland 64°48′N 26°00′E
138 K6 **Mūḥ, Sabkhat al** ◎ C Syria
118 E5 **Muhu** *Ger.* Mohn, Moon. *island* W Estonia
81 F19 **Muhutwe** Kagera, NW Tanzania 01°31′S 31°41′E
Muhu Väin *see* Väinameri
98 J10 **Muiden** Noord-Holland, C Netherlands 52°19′N 05°04′E
193 W15 **Mui Hopohoponga** *headland* Tongatapu, S Tonga 21°09′S 175°02′W
Muinchille *see* Cootehill
Muineachán *see* Monaghan
97 F19 **Muine Bheag** *Eng.* Bagenalstown. Carlow, SE Ireland 52°42′N 06°57′W
56 B5 **Muisne** Esmeraldas, NW Ecuador 0°35′N 79°58′W
83 P14 **Muite** Nampula, NE Mozambique 14°02′S 39°06′E
41 Z11 **Mujeres, Isla** *island* E Mexico
116 G7 **Mukacheve** *Hung.* Munkács, *Rus.* Mukachevo. Zakarpats'ka Oblast', W Ukraine 48°27′N 22°45′E
Mukachevo *see* Mukacheve
169 R9 **Mukah** Sarawak, East Malaysia 02°56′N 112°02′E
Mukalla *see* Al Mukallā
Mukama *see* Mokāma
Mukāshafa/Mukashshafah *see* Mukayshīfah
139 S6 **Mukayshīfah** *var.* Mukāshafa, Mukashshafah. Şalāḩ ad Dīn, N Iraq 34°24′N 43°44′E
167 R9 **Mukdahan** Mukdahan, E Thailand 16°31′N 104°43′E
Mukden *see* Shenyang
165 Y15 **Mukojima-rettō** *Eng.* Parry group. *island group* SE Japan
146 M14 **Mukry** Lebap Welaýaty, E Turkmenistan 37°39′N 65°37′E
Muksu *see* Mughsu
Muktagacha *see* Muktagachha
153 U14 **Muktagachha** *var.* Muktagacha. N Bangladesh 24°46′N 90°16′E
82 K13 **Mukuku** Central, C Zambia 12°10′S 29°50′E
82 K11 **Mukupa Kaoma** Northern, NE Zambia 09°55′S 30°19′E
81 I18 **Mukutan** Rift Valley, W Kenya 01°06′N 36°16′E
83 F16 **Mukwe** Caprivi, NE Namibia 18°01′S 21°24′E
105 R13 **Mula** Murcia, SE Spain 38°02′N 01°29′W
151 K20 **Mulakatholhu** *var.* Meemu Atoll, Mulaku Atoll. *atoll* C Maldives
Mulaku Atoll *see* Mulakatholhu
83 J15 **Mulalika** Lusaka, C Zambia 15°37′S 28°48′E
163 X8 **Mulan** Heilongjiang, NE China 45°57′N 128°00′E
83 N15 **Mulanje** *var.* Mlanje. Southern, S Malawi 16°05′S 35°29′E
40 H5 **Mulatos** Sonora, NW Mexico 28°42′N 108°44′W
23 P3 **Mulberry Fork** ≈ Alabama, S USA
39 P12 **Mulchatna River** ≈ Alaska, USA
125 W4 **Mul'da** Respublika Komi, NW Russian Federation 67°29′N 63°55′E
101 M14 **Mulde** ≈ E Germany
27 R10 **Muldrow** Oklahoma, C USA 35°25′N 94°34′W
40 E7 **Mulegé** Baja California Sur, NW Mexico 26°54′N 112°00′W
108 I10 **Mulegns** Graubünden, S Switzerland 46°30′N 09°36′E
79 M21 **Mulenda** Kasai-Oriental, C Dem. Rep. Congo 04°19′S 24°55′E
24 M4 **Muleshoe** Texas, SW USA 34°13′N 102°43′W
83 O15 **Mulevala** Zambézia, NE Mozambique 16°25′S 37°35′E
183 P5 **Mulgoa Creek** *seasonal river* New South Wales, SE Australia
105 O15 **Mulhacén** *var.* Cerro de Mulhacén. ▲ S Spain 37°07′N 03°11′W
Mulhacén, Cerro de *see* Mulhacén
Mülhausen *see* Mulhouse
101 E24 **Mülheim** Baden-Württemberg, SW Germany 47°50′N 07°37′E
101 E15 **Mülheim** *var.* Mulheim an der Ruhr. Nordrhein-Westfalen, W Germany 51°25′N 06°50′E
Mulheim an der Ruhr *see* Mülheim
103 U7 **Mulhouse** *Ger.* Mülhausen. Haut-Rhin, NE France 47°45′N 07°20′E
160 G11 **Muli** *var.* Qiaowa, Muli Zangzu Zizhixian. Sichuan, C China 27°49′N 101°10′E
171 X15 **Muli** *channel* Papua, E Indonesia
Mülig-Hofmann Mountains *see* Mühlig-Hofmanfjella
163 Y9 **Muling** Heilongjiang, NE China 44°54′N 130°35′E
Muli Zangzu Zizhixian *see* Muli
Mullach Íde *see* Malahide
Mullaitivu *see* Mullaittivu
155 K23 **Mullaittivu** *var.* Mullaitivu. Northern Province, N Sri Lanka 09°15′N 80°48′E
33 N8 **Mullan** Idaho, NW USA 47°28′N 115°48′W
28 M13 **Mullen** Nebraska, C USA 42°02′N 101°01′W
183 Q6 **Mullengudgery** New South Wales, SE Australia 31°42′S 147°24′E
21 Q6 **Mullens** West Virginia, NE USA 37°34′N 81°22′W
Müller-gerbergte *see* Muller, Pegunungan
169 T10 **Muller, Pegunungan** *Dut.* Müller-gerbergte. ▲▲ Borneo, C Indonesia
31 Q5 **Mullett Lake** ◎ Michigan, N USA
18 J16 **Mullica River** ≈ New Jersey, NE USA
25 R8 **Mullin** Texas, SW USA 31°33′N 98°40′W
97 E17 **Mullingar** *Ir.* An Muileann gCearr. C Ireland 53°32′N 07°20′W
21 T12 **Mullins** South Carolina, SE USA 34°12′N 79°15′W
96 G11 **Mull, Isle of** *island* W Scotland, United Kingdom
127 R5 **Mullovka** Ul'yanovskaya Oblast', W Russian Federation 54°13′N 49°19′E
95 K19 **Mullsjö** Västra Götaland, S Sweden 57°56′N 13°55′E
183 V4 **Mullumbimby** New South Wales, SE Australia 28°34′S 153°28′E
83 H15 **Mulobezi** Western, SW Zambia 16°48′S 25°11′E
83 C15 **Mulondo** Huíla, SW Angola 15°41′S 15°09′E
83 G15 **Mulonga Plain** *plain* W Zambia
79 N23 **Mulongo** Katanga, SE Dem. Rep. Congo 07°44′S 26°57′E
149 T10 **Multān** Punjab, E Pakistan 30°12′N 71°30′E
93 L17 **Multia** Länsi-Suomi, C Finland 62°27′N 24°49′E
Mulucha *see* Moulouya
83 J14 **Mulungushi** Central, C Zambia 14°15′S 28°27′E
83 K14 **Mulungwe** Central, C Zambia 13°57′S 29°51′E
Muluya *see* Moulouya
27 N7 **Mulvane** Kansas, C USA 37°28′N 97°14′W
183 O10 **Mulwala** New South Wales, SE Australia 35°59′S 146°00′E
Mulwiya *see* Moulouya
182 K6 **Mulyungarie** South Australia 31°29′S 140°45′E
154 D13 **Mumbai** *prev.* Bombay. *state capital* Mahārāshtra, W India 18°56′N 72°51′E
154 D13 **Mumbai** ✈ Mahārāshtra, W India 19°10′N 72°51′E
83 D14 **Mumbué** Bié, C Angola 13°52′S 17°15′E
186 E8 **Mumeng** Morobe, C Papua New Guinea 06°57′S 146°34′E
171 V12 **Mumi** Papua, E Indonesia 01°33′S 134°09′E
Muminabad/Mŭ'minobod *see* Mu'minobod
147 Q13 **Mu'minobod** *Rus.* Leningradskiy, Muminabad; *prev.* Leningrad. SW Tajikistan 38°03′N 69°50′E
127 Q13 **Mumra** Astrakhanskaya Oblast', SW Russian Federation 45°46′N 47°46′E
41 X12 **Muna** Yucatán, SE Mexico 20°29′N 89°41′W
123 O9 **Muna** ≈ NE Russian Federation
152 C12 **Munābāo** Rājasthān, NW India 25°46′N 70°19′E
Munamägi *see* Suur Munamägi
171 O14 **Muna, Pulau** *prev.* Moena. *island* C Indonesia
101 L18 **Münchberg** Bayern, E Germany 50°10′N 11°50′E
101 L23 **München** *var.* Muenchen, *Eng.* Munich, *It.* Monaco. Bayern, SE Germany 48°09′N 11°34′E
München-Gladbach *see* Mönchengladbach
108 E6 **Münchenstein** Basel Landschaft, NW Switzerland 47°31′N 07°38′E
10 L10 **Muncho Lake** British Columbia, W Canada 58°52′N 125°40′W
31 P13 **Muncie** Indiana, N USA 40°11′N 85°22′W
18 G13 **Muncy** Pennsylvania, NE USA 41°10′N 76°46′W
11 Q14 **Mundare** Alberta, SW Canada 53°34′N 112°20′W
25 Q5 **Munday** Texas, SW USA 33°27′N 99°37′W
31 N10 **Mundelein** Illinois, N USA 42°15′N 88°00′W
101 I15 **Münden** Niedersachsen, C Germany 52°16′N 08°54′E
105 Q12 **Mundo** ≈ S Spain
82 B12 **Munenga** Cuanza Sul, NW Angola 10°03′S 14°40′E
105 P11 **Munera** Castilla-La Mancha, C Spain 39°03′N 02°29′W
20 E9 **Munford** Tennessee, S USA 35°27′N 89°49′W
20 K7 **Munfordville** Kentucky, S USA 37°17′N 85°55′W
182 D5 **Mungala** South Australia 30°36′S 132°57′E
83 M16 **Mungári** Manica, C Mozambique 17°09′S 33°33′E
79 O16 **Mungbere** Orientale, NE Dem. Rep. Congo 02°38′N 28°30′E
153 Q13 **Munger** *prev.* Monghyr. Bihār, NE India 25°23′N 86°28′E
182 I2 **Mungeranie** South Australia 28°02′S 138°42′E
Mu Nggava *see* Rennell
169 O10 **Mungguresak, Tanjung** *headland* Borneo, N Indonesia 01°57′N 109°19′E
Mungiki *see* Bellona
183 R4 **Mungindi** New South Wales, SE Australia 28°59′S 149°00′E
Mungkawn *see* Maingkwan
Mungla *see* Mongla
82 C13 **Mungo** Huambo, W Angola 11°49′S 16°16′E
188 F16 **Munguuy Bay** *bay* Yap, W Micronesia
82 E13 **Munhango** Bié, C Angola 12°12′S 18°34′E
Munich *see* München
105 S7 **Muniesa** Aragón, NE Spain 41°02′N 00°49′W
31 O4 **Munising** Michigan, N USA 46°24′N 86°39′W
Munkács *see* Mukacheve
95 I17 **Munkedal** Västra Götaland, S Sweden 58°28′N 11°38′E
95 K15 **Munkfors** Värmland, C Sweden 59°50′N 13°35′E
122 M14 **Munku-Sardyk, Gora** *var.* Mönh Sarĭdag. ▲ Mongolia/Russian Federation 51°45′N 100°22′E
99 E18 **Munkzwalm** Oost-Vlaanderen, NW Belgium 50°53′N 03°44′E
167 R10 **Mun, Mae Nam** ≈ E Thailand
153 U15 **Munshiganj** Dhaka, C Bangladesh 23°32′N 90°32′E
108 D8 **Münsingen** Bern, W Switzerland 46°53′N 07°34′E
103 U6 **Munster** Haut-Rhin, NE France 48°03′N 07°09′E
100 J11 **Münster** Niedersachsen, NW Germany 52°59′N 10°07′E
100 F13 **Münster** *var.* Muenster, Münster in Westfalen. Nordrhein-Westfalen, W Germany 51°58′N 07°38′E
108 F10 **Münster** Valais, S Switzerland 46°31′N 08°18′E
97 B20 **Munster** *Ir.* Cúige Mumhan. *cultural region* S Ireland
Münsterberg in Schlesien *see* Ziębice
Münster in Westfalen *see* Münster
100 E13 **Münsterland** *cultural region* NW Germany
100 F13 **Münster-Osnabruck** ✈ Nordrhein-Westfalen, NW Germany 52°08′N 07°41′E
31 R4 **Munuscong Lake** ◎ Michigan, N USA
83 K17 **Munyati** ≈ C Zimbabwe
109 R3 **Münzkirchen** Oberösterreich, N Austria 48°29′N 13°37′E
92 K11 **Muodoslompolo** Norrbotten, N Sweden 67°57′N 23°31′E
92 M13 **Muojärvi** ◎ NE Finland
167 S6 **Mương Khên** Hoa Binh, N Vietnam 20°34′N 105°18′E
Muong Sai *see* Oudômxai
167 Q7 **Muong Xiang Ngeun** *var.* Xieng Ngeun. Louangphabang, N Laos 19°43′N 102°09′E
92 K11 **Muonio** Lappi, N Finland 67°58′N 23°40′E
Muonioälv/Muoniojoki *see* Muonionjoki
92 K11 **Muonionjoki** *var.* Muoniojoki, *Swe.* Muonioälv. ≈ Finland/Sweden
Muorjek *see* Murjek
83 N17 **Mupa** ≈ C Mozambique
83 E16 **Mupini** Okavango, NE Namibia 17°55′S 19°34′E
80 F8 **Muqaddam, Wadi** ≈ N Sudan
138 K9 **Muqāṭ** Al Mafraq, E Jordan 32°28′N 38°04′E
81 N17 **Muqdisho** *Eng.* Mogadishu, *It.* Mogadiscio. ● (Somalia) Banaadir, S Somalia 02°06′N 45°27′E
81 N17 **Muqdisho** ✈ Banaadir, E Somalia 01°58′N 45°18′E
Muqshin *see* Mughshin
109 T8 **Mur** *SCr.* Mura. ≈ C Europe
109 X9 **Mura** ≈ NE Slovenia
Mura *see* Mur
137 T14 **Muradiye** Van, E Turkey 39°N 43°44′E
Muragarazi *see* Maragarazi
165 O10 **Murakami** Niigata, Honshū, C Japan 38°13′N 139°28′E
63 G22 **Murallón, Cerro** ▲ S Argentina 49°49′S 73°25′W
81 E20 **Muramvya** C Burundi 03°18′S 29°41′E
81 I19 **Murang'a** *prev.* Fort Hall. Central, SW Kenya 0°43′S 37°10′E
81 H16 **Murangering** Rift Valley, NW Kenya 03°48′N 35°29′E
Murapara *see* Murupara
140 M5 **Murār, Bi'r al** *well* NW Saudi Arabia
125 Q13 **Murashi** Kirovskaya Oblast', NW Russian Federation 59°27′N 48°02′E
103 O12 **Murat** Cantal, C France 45°07′N 02°52′E
114 N12 **Muratlı** Tekirdağ, NW Turkey 41°12′N 27°30′E
137 R14 **Murat Nehri** *var.* Eastern Euphrates; *anc.* Arsanias. ≈ NE Turkey
107 D20 **Muravera** Sardegna, Italy, C Mediterranean Sea 39°24′N 09°34′E
165 P10 **Murayama** Yamagata, Honshū, C Japan 38°29′N 140°21′E
121 R13 **Muraysah, Ra's al** *headland* N Libya 31°58′N 25°00′E
104 I6 **Murça** Vila Real, N Portugal 41°24′N 07°28′W
80 Q11 **Murcanyo** Bari, NE Somalia 11°39′N 50°27′E
143 N8 **Mūrcheh Khvort** *var.* Morcheh Khort. Eşfahān, C Iran 33°07′N 51°26′E
185 H15 **Murchison** Tasman, South Island, New Zealand 41°48′S 172°19′E
185 B22 **Murchison Mountains** ▲▲ South Island, New Zealand
180 I10 **Murchison River** ≈ Western Australia
105 R13 **Murcia** Murcia, SE Spain 37°59′N 01°08′W
105 Q13 **Murcia** ⬖ *autonomous community* SE Spain
103 O13 **Mur-de-Barrez** Aveyron, S France 44°48′N 02°39′E
182 G8 **Murdinga** South Australia 33°46′S 135°46′E
28 M10 **Murdo** South Dakota, N USA 43°53′N 100°42′W
15 X6 **Murdochville** Québec, SE Canada 48°57′N 65°30′W
109 W9 **Mureck** Steiermark, SE Austria 46°42′N 15°46′E
114 M13 **Mürefte** Tekirdağ, NW Turkey 40°40′N 27°15′E
116 I10 **Mureş** ⬖ *county* N Romania
84 J11 **Mureş** ≈ Hungary/Romania
Mureş *see* Maros
Mureşul *see* Maros/Mureş
102 M16 **Muret** Haute-Garonne, S France 43°28′N 01°19′E
27 T13 **Murfreesboro** Arkansas, C USA 34°04′N 93°42′W
21 W8 **Murfreesboro** North Carolina, SE USA 36°26′N 77°06′W
20 J9 **Murfreesboro** Tennessee, S USA 35°50′N 86°25′W
Murgab *see* Morghāb, Daryā-ye/Murgap
Murgab *see* Murghob
146 I14 **Murgap** Mary Welaýaty, S Turkmenistan 37°19′N 61°48′E
146 J16 **Murgap** *var.* Deryasy Murgap, Murghab, *Pash.* Daryā-ye Morghāb, *Rus.* Murgab. ≈ Afghanistan/Turkmenistan *see also* Morghāb, Daryā-ye
Murgap *see* Murghāb, Daryā-ye
Murgap, Deryasy *see* Morghāb, Daryā-ye/Murgap
114 H9 **Murgash** ▲ W Bulgaria 42°51′N 23°58′E
Murghab *see* Morghāb, Daryā-ye/Murgap
148 M4 **Murghāb, Daryā-ye** *Rus.* Murgab, Murghab, *Turk.* Murgap, Deryasy Murgap; *prev.* Morghāb, Daryā-ye. ≈ Afghanistan/Turkmenistan *see also* Murgap
147 U13 **Murghob** *Rus.* Murgab. SE Tajikistan 38°11′N 74°E
147 U13 **Murghob** *Rus.* Murgab. ≈ SE Tajikistan
181 Z10 **Murgon** Queensland, E Australia 26°08′S 152°04′E
190 I16 **Muri** Rarotonga, S Cook Islands 21°15′S 159°44′W
108 F7 **Muri** Aargau, W Switzerland 47°16′N 08°21′E
108 D8 **Muri** *var.* Muri bei Bern. Bern, W Switzerland 46°55′N 07°30′E
104 K3 **Murias de Paredes** Castilla y León, N Spain 42°51′N 06°11′W
Muri bei Bern *see* Muri
82 F11 **Muriege** Lunda Sul, NE Angola 09°55′S 21°12′E
189 P14 **Murilo Atoll** *atoll* Hall Islands, C Micronesia
Mūrītānīyah *see* Mauritania
100 N10 **Müritz** *var.* Müritzee. ◎ NE Germany
Müritzee *see* Müritz
100 L10 **Müritz-Elde-Wasserstrasse** *canal* N Germany
184 K6 **Muriwai Beach** Auckland, North Island, New Zealand 36°56′S 174°28′E
92 J13 **Murjek** *Lapp.* Muorjek. Norrbotten, N Sweden 66°27′N 20°54′E
124 J3 **Murmansk** Murmanskaya Oblast', NW Russian Federation 68°59′N 33°08′E
124 I4 **Murmanskaya Oblast'** ⬖ *province* NW Russian Federation
197 V14 **Murmansk Rise** *undersea feature* SW Barents Sea 71°00′N 37°00′E
124 J3 **Murmashi** Murmanskaya Oblast', NW Russian Federation 68°49′N 32°43′E
126 M5 **Murmino** Ryazanskaya Oblast', W Russian Federation 54°31′N 40°01′E
101 K24 **Murnau** Bayern, SE Germany 47°41′N 11°12′E
103 X16 **Muro, Capo di** *headland* Corse, France, C Mediterranean Sea 41°45′N 08°40′E
107 M18 **Muro Lucano** Basilicata, S Italy 40°48′N 15°33′E
127 N4 **Murom** Vladimirskaya Oblast', W Russian Federation 55°33′N 42°03′E
122 I11 **Muromtsevo** Omskaya Oblast', C Russian Federation 56°18′N 75°15′E
165 R5 **Muroran** Hokkaidō, NE Japan 42°20′N 140°58′E
104 G3 **Muros** Galicia, NW Spain 42°47′N 09°04′W
104 F3 **Muros e Noia, Ría de** *estuary* NW Spain
164 H15 **Muroto** Kōchi, Shikoku, SW Japan 33°16′N 134°10′E
164 H15 **Muroto-zaki** Shikoku, SW Japan
116 L7 **Murovani Kurylivtsi** Vinnyts'ka Oblast', C Ukraine 48°43′N 27°31′E
110 G11 **Murowana Goślina** Wielkolpolskie, W Poland 52°33′N 16°59′E
32 M14 **Murphy** Idaho, NW USA 43°14′N 116°36′W
21 N10 **Murphy** North Carolina, SE USA 35°05′N 84°02′W
35 P8 **Murphys** California, W USA 38°07′N 120°27′W
30 L17 **Murphysboro** Illinois, N USA 37°45′N 89°20′W
29 V15 **Murray** Iowa, C USA 41°03′N 93°56′W
20 H8 **Murray** Kentucky, S USA 36°35′N 88°20′W
182 J10 **Murray Bridge** South Australia 35°10′S 139°17′E
175 X2 **Murray Fracture Zone** *tectonic feature* NE Pacific Ocean
192 H11 **Murray, Lake** ◎ SW Papua New Guinea
21 P12 **Murray, Lake** ▣ South Carolina, SE USA
10 K8 **Murray, Mount** ▲ Yukon Territory, NW Canada 60°49′N 128°57′W
Murray Range *see* Murray Ridge
173 O3 **Murray Ridge** *var.* Murray Range. *undersea feature* N Arabian Sea 21°45′N 61°50′E
183 N10 **Murray River** ≈ SE Australia
182 K10 **Murrayville** Victoria, SE Australia 35°17′S 141°12′E
149 U5 **Murree** Punjab, E Pakistan 33°55′N 73°26′E
101 I21 **Murrhardt** Baden-Württemberg, S Germany 49°00′N 09°34′E
183 O9 **Murrumbidgee River** ≈ New South Wales, SE Australia
83 P15 **Murrupula** Nampula, NE Mozambique 15°26′S 38°46′E
183 T7 **Murrurundi** New South Wales, SE Australia 31°47′S 150°51′E
109 X9 **Murska Sobota** *Ger.* Olsnitz. NE Slovenia 46°41′N 16°09′E
154 G12 **Murtajāpur** *prev.* Murtazapur. Mahārāshtra, C India 20°43′N 77°28′E
77 S16 **Murtala Muhammed** ✈ (Lagos) Ogun, SW Nigeria 06°31′N 03°12′E
Murtazapur *see* Murtajāpur
108 C8 **Murten** Neuchâtel, W Switzerland 46°55′N 07°06′E
Murtensee *see* Morat, Lac de
182 L11 **Murtoa** Victoria, SE Australia 36°39′S 142°27′E
92 N13 **Murtovaara** Oulu, E Finland 65°40′N 29°25′E
Murua Island *see* Woodlark Island
155 D14 **Murud** Mahārāshtra, W India 18°27′N 72°56′E
184 O9 **Murupara** *var.* Murapara. Bay of Plenty, North Island, New Zealand 38°27′S 176°41′E
Mururoa *see* Moruroa
Murviedro *see* Sagunto
154 J9 **Murwāra** Madhya Pradesh, N India 23°50′N 80°23′E
183 V4 **Murwillumbah** New South Wales, SE Australia 28°20′S 153°24′E
146 H11 **Murzechirla** *prev.* Mirzachirla. Ahal Welaýaty, C Turkmenistan 39°33′N 60°02′E
Murzuk *see* Murzuq
75 O11 **Murzuq** *var.* Marzūq, Murzuk. SW Libya 25°55′N 13°55′E
Murzuq, Edeyin *see* Murzuq, Idhān
75 N11 **Murzuq, Ḥammādat** *plateau* W Libya
75 O11 **Murzuq, Idhān** *var.* Edeyin Murzuq. *desert* SW Libya
109 W6 **Mürzzuschlag** Steiermark, E Austria 47°35′N 15°41′E
137 Q14 **Muş** *var.* Mush. Muş, E Turkey 38°45′N 41°30′E
137 Q14 **Muş** *var.* Mush. ⬖ *province* E Turkey
118 G11 **Mūša** ≈ Latvia/Lithuania
186 F9 **Musa** ≈ S Papua New Guinea
Mûsa, Gebel *see* Mūsá, Jabal
Musaiyib *see* Al Musayyib
75 X8 **Mūsá, Jabal** *var.* Gebel Mûsa. ▲ NE Egypt 28°33′N 33°51′E
149 R9 **Musā Khel** *var.* Mūsa Khel Bāzār. Baluchistān, SW Pakistan 30°53′N 69°52′E
Mūsa Khel Bāzār *see* Musā Khel
139 Z13 **Mūsá, Khowr-e** *bay* Iraq/Kuwait
114 H10 **Musala** ▲ W Bulgaria 42°12′N 23°36′E
168 H10 **Musala, Pulau** *island* W Indonesia
83 I15 **Musale** Southern, S Zambia 15°27′S 26°50′E
141 Y9 **Muşalla** NE Oman 22°20′N 58°03′E
141 W6 **Musandam Peninsula** *Ar.* Masandam Peninsula. *peninsula* N Oman
Musay'īd *see* Umm Sa'īd
Muscat *see* Masqaţ
Muscat and Oman *see* Oman
29 Y14 **Muscatine** Iowa, C USA 41°25′N 91°03′W
Muscat Sīb Airport *see* Seeb
31 O15 **Muscatuck River** ≈ Indiana, N USA
30 K8 **Muscoda** Wisconsin, N USA 43°11′N 90°27′W
185 F19 **Musgrave, Mount** ▲ South Island, New Zealand 43°48′S 170°43′E
181 P9 **Musgrave Ranges** ▲▲ South Australia
Mush *see* Muş
138 H12 **Mushayyish, Qaşr al** *castle* Ma'ān, C Jordan
79 H20 **Mushie** Bandundu, W Dem. Rep. Congo 03°00′S 16°55′E
168 M13 **Musi, Air** *prev.* Moesi. ≈ Sumatera, W Indonesia
192 M4 **Musicians Seamounts** *undersea feature* N Pacific Ocean
83 K19 **Musina** *prev.* Messina. Limpopo, NE South Africa 22°18′S 30°02′E
54 D8 **Musinga, Alto** ▲ NW Colombia 06°49′N 76°24′W
29 T2 **Muskeg Bay** *lake bay* Minnesota, N USA
31 O8 **Muskegon** Michigan, N USA 43°13′N 86°15′W
31 O8 **Muskegon Heights** Michigan, N USA 43°12′N 86°14′W
31 P8 **Muskegon River** ≈ Michigan, N USA
31 T14 **Muskingum River** ≈ Ohio, N USA
95 P16 **Muskö** Stockholm, C Sweden 58°58′N 18°10′E
Muskogean *see* Tallahassee
27 Q10 **Muskogee** Oklahoma, C USA 35°45′N 95°21′W
14 H13 **Muskoka, Lake** ◎ Ontario, S Canada
80 H8 **Musmar** Red Sea, NE Sudan 18°13′N 35°40′E
83 K14 **Musofu** Central, C Zambia 13°31′S 29°02′E
81 G19 **Musoma** Mara, N Tanzania 01°31′S 33°49′E
82 L13 **Musoro** Central, C Zambia 13°21′S 31°04′E
186 F4 **Mussau Island** *island* NE Papua New Guinea
98 P7 **Musselkanaal** Groningen, NE Netherlands 52°55′N 07°01′E
33 V9 **Musselshell River** ≈ Montana, NW USA
82 C12 **Mussende** Cuanza Sul, NW Angola 10°33′S 16°02′E
102 L12 **Mussidan** Dordogne, SW France 45°03′N 00°22′E
99 L25 **Musson** Luxembourg, SE Belgium 49°33′N 05°42′E
152 J9 **Mussoorie** Uttarakhand, N India 30°26′N 78°04′E
Musta *see* Mosta
152 M13 **Mustafābād** Uttar Pradesh, N India 25°54′N 81°17′E
136 D12 **Mustafakemalpaşa** Bursa, NW Turkey 40°03′N 28°25′E
Mustafa-Pasha *see* Svilengrad
81 M15 **Mustahīl** Sumalē, E Ethiopia 05°18′N 44°34′E
24 M7 **Mustang Draw** *valley* Texas, SW USA
25 T14 **Mustang Island** *island* Texas, SW USA
Mustasaari *see* Korsholm
Mustér *see* Disentis
63 I19 **Musters, Lago** ◎ S Argentina
45 Y14 **Mustique** *island* C Saint Vincent and the Grenadines
118 I6 **Mustla** Viljandimaa, S Estonia 58°12′N 25°50′E
118 J4 **Mustvee** *Ger.* Tschorna. Jõgevamaa, E Estonia 58°51′N 26°59′E
42 L9 **Musún, Cerro** ▲ NE Nicaragua 13°01′N 85°02′W
183 T7 **Muswellbrook** New South Wales, SE Australia 32°17′S 150°55′E
111 M18 **Muszyna** Małopolskie, SE Poland 49°21′N 20°54′E
75 V10 **Mūţ** *var.* Mut. C Egypt 25°28′N 28°58′E
136 I17 **Mut** İçel, S Turkey 36°38′N 33°27′E
109 V9 **Muta** N Slovenia 46°37′N 15°09′E
190 B15 **Mutalau** N Niue 18°56′S 169°50′E
Mu-tan-chiang *see* Mudanjiang
82 I13 **Mutanda** North Western, NW Zambia 12°24′S 26°13′E
59 O17 **Mutá, Ponta do** *headland* E Brazil 13°54′S 38°54′W
83 L17 **Mutare** *var.* Mutari; *prev.* Umtali. Manicaland, E Zimbabwe 18°55′S 32°36′E
Mutari *see* Mutare
54 D8 **Mutatá** Antioquia, NW Colombia 07°16′N 76°32′W
Mutina *see* Modena
83 L16 **Mutoko** *prev.* Mtoko. Mashonaland East, NE Zimbabwe 17°24′S 32°13′E

◆ Country
● Country Capital
◇ Dependent Territory
○ Dependent Territory Capital
⬖ Administrative Regions
✈ International Airport
▲ Mountain
▲▲ Mountain Range
Volcano
≈ River
◎ Lake
▣ Reservoir

81 J20 **Mutomo** Eastern, S Kenya 01°50′S 38°13′E
Mutrah *see* Maṭraḥ
79 M24 **Mutshatsha** Katanga, S Dem. Rep. Congo 10°40′S 24°26′E
165 R6 **Mutsu** *var.* Mutu. Aomori, Honshū, N Japan 41°18′N 141°11′E
165 R6 **Mutsu-wan** *bay* N Japan
108 E6 **Muttenz** Basel Landschaft, NW Switzerland 47°31′N 07°39′E
185 A26 **Muttonbird Islands** *island group* SW New Zealand
Muttra *see* Mathura
Mutu *see* Mutsu
83 O15 **Mutuáli** Nampula, N Mozambique 14°51′S 37°01′E
82 D13 **Mutumbo** Bié, C Angola 13°10′S 17°22′E
189 Y14 **Mutunte, Mount** *var.* Mount Buache. ▲ Kosrae, E Micronesia 05°21′N 163°00′E
155 K24 **Mutur** Eastern Province, E Sri Lanka 08°27′N 81°15′E
92 L13 **Muurola** Lappi, NW Finland 66°22′N 25°20′E
162 M14 **Mu Us Shadi** *var.* Ordos Desert; *prev.* Mu Us Shamo. *desert* N China
Mu Us Shamo *see* Mu Us Shadi
82 B11 **Muxima** Bengo, NW Angola 09°33′S 13°58′E
124 I8 **Muyezerskiy** Respublika Kareliya, NW Russian Federation 63°54′N 32°00′E
81 E20 **Muyinga** NE Burundi 02°54′S 30°19′E
42 K9 **Muy Muy** Matagalpa, C Nicaragua 12°43′N 85°35′W
Muynak *see* Mo'ynoq
79 N22 **Muyumba** Katanga, SE Dem. Rep. Congo 07°13′S 27°02′E
149 V5 **Muzaffarābād** Jammu and Kashmir, NE Pakistan 34°23′N 73°34′E
149 S10 **Muzaffargarh** Punjab, E Pakistan 30°04′N 71°15′E
152 J9 **Muzaffarnagar** Uttar Pradesh, N India 29°28′N 77°42′E
153 P13 **Muzaffarpur** Bihār, N India 26°07′N 85°23′E
158 H6 **Muzat He** W China
83 L15 **Muze** Tete, NW Mozambique 15°05′S 31°16′E
122 H8 **Muzhi** Yamalo-Nenetskiy Avtonomnyy Okrug, N Russian Federation 65°25′N 64°28′E
102 H7 **Muzillac** Morbihan, NW France 47°34′N 02°30′W
Muzkol, Khrebet *see* Muzqūl, Qatorkūhi
112 L9 **Mužlja** *Hung.* Felsőmuzslya; *prev.* Gornja Mužlja. Vojvodina, N Serbia 45°21′N 20°25′E
54 F9 **Muzo** Boyacá, C Colombia 05°34′N 74°07′W
83 J15 **Muzoka** Southern, S Zambia 16°39′S 27°18′E
39 Y15 **Muzon, Cape** *headland* Dall Island, Alaska, USA 54°39′N 132°41′W
40 M6 **Múzquiz** Coahuila, NE Mexico 27°54′N 101°30′W
147 U13 **Muzqūl, Qatorkūhi** *Rus.* Khrebet Muzkol. ▲ SE Tajikistan
Muztag *see* Muztag Feng
158 D8 **Muztagata** ▲ NW China 38°16′N 75°03′E
158 K10 **Muztag Feng** *var.* Muztag. ▲ W China 36°26′N 87°15′E
83 K17 **Mvuma** *prev.* Umvuma. Midlands, C Zimbabwe 19°17′S 30°32′E
172 H13 **Mwali** *var.* Moili, *Fr.* Mohéli. *island* S Comoros
82 L13 **Mwanya** Eastern, E Zambia 12°40′S 32°15′E
79 N23 **Mwanza** Katanga, SE Dem. Rep. Congo 07°49′S 26°49′E
81 G20 **Mwanza** Mwanza, NW Tanzania 02°31′S 32°56′E
81 F20 **Mwanza** ◆ *region* N Tanzania
82 M13 **Mwase Lundazi** Eastern, E Zambia 12°26′S 33°20′E
97 B17 **Mweelrea** *Ir.* Caoc Maol Réidh. ▲ W Ireland 53°37′N 09°47′W
79 K21 **Mweka** Kasai-Occidental, C Dem. Rep. Congo 04°52′S 21°38′E
82 K12 **Mwenda** Luapula, N Zambia 10°30′S 30°21′E
79 L22 **Mwene-Ditu** Kasai-Oriental, S Dem. Rep. Congo 07°06′S 23°34′E
83 L18 **Mwenezi** S Zimbabwe
79 O20 **Mwenga** Sud-Kivu, E Dem. Rep. Congo 03°00′S 28°28′E
82 K11 **Mweru, Lake** *var.* Lac Moero. ◎ Dem. Rep. Congo/ Zambia
82 H13 **Mwinilunga** North Western, NW Zambia 11°44′S 24°24′E
189 V16 **Mwokil Atoll** *prev.* Mokil Atoll. *atoll* Caroline Islands, E Micronesia
Myadel' *see* Myadzyel
118 J13 **Myadzyel** *Pol.* Miadzioł Nowy, *Rus.* Myadel'. Minskaya Voblasts', N Belarus 54°51′N 26°51′E
152 C12 **Myājlār** *var.* Miajlar. Rājasthān, NW India 26°16′N 70°21′E
123 T9 **Myakit** Magadanskaya Oblast', E Russian Federation 61°23′N 151°58′E
23 W13 **Myakka River** Florida, SE USA
124 L14 **Myaksa** Vologodskaya Oblast', NW Russian Federation 58°54′N 38°15′E
183 U8 **Myall Lake** ◎ New South Wales, SE Australia
166 L7 **Myanaung** Ayeyarwady, SW Myanmar (Burma) 18°17′N 95°19′E
166 M4 **Myanmar** *off.* Union of Myanmar, *var.* Burma. ◆ *republic* SE Asia
166 K8 **Myaungmya** Ayeyarwady, SW Myanmar (Burma) 16°33′N 94°55′E
Myaydo *see* Aunglan
118 N11 **Myazha** *Rus.* Mezha. Vitsyebskaya Voblasts', NE Belarus 55°41′N 30°25′E
167 N12 **Myeik** *var.* Mergui. Tanintharyi, S Myanmar (Burma) 12°26′N 98°34′E
166 M12 **Myeik Archipelago** *var.* Mergui Archipelago. *island group* S Myanmar (Burma)
119 O18 **Myerkulavichy** *Rus.* Merkulovichi. Homyel'skaya Voblasts', SE Belarus 52°58′N 30°36′E
119 N14 **Myezhava** *Rus.* Mezhëvo. Vitsyebskaya Voblasts', NE Belarus 54°38′N 30°20′E
Myggenaes *see* Mykines
166 L5 **Myingyan** Mandalay, C Myanmar (Burma) 21°25′N 95°20′E
167 N12 **Myitkyina** Kachin State, N Myanmar (Burma) 25°24′N 97°25′E
166 M5 **Myittha** Mandalay, Myanmar (Burma) 21°21′N 96°06′E
111 H19 **Myjava** *Hung.* Miava. Trenčiansky Kraj, W Slovakia 48°45′N 17°35′E
Myjeldino *see* Myyëldino
117 U9 **Mykhaylivka** *Rus.* Mikhaylovka. Zaporiz'ka Oblast', SE Ukraine 47°16′N 35°14′E
95 A18 **Mykines** *Dan.* Myggenaes. *island* W Faeroe Islands
116 I5 **Mykolayiv** L'vivs'ka Oblast', W Ukraine 49°34′N 23°58′E
117 Q10 **Mykolayiv** *Rus.* Nikolayev. Mykolayivs'ka Oblast', S Ukraine 46°58′N 31°59′E
117 Q10 **Mykolayiv** ✕ Mykolayivs'ka Oblast', S Ukraine 47°02′N 31°54′E
Mykolayiv *see* Mykolayivs'ka Oblast'
117 S13 **Mykolayivka** Avtonomna Respublika Krym, S Ukraine 44°58′N 33°37′E
117 P9 **Mykolayivka** Odes'ka Oblast', SW Ukraine 47°34′N 30°48′E
117 P9 **Mykolayivs'ka Oblast'** *var.* Mykolayiv, *Rus.* Nikolayevskaya Oblast'. ◆ *province* S Ukraine
115 J20 **Mýkonos** Mýkonos, Kykládes, Greece, Aegean Sea 37°27′N 25°20′E
115 K20 **Mýkonos** *var.* Míkonos. *island* Kykládes, Greece, Aegean Sea
125 R7 **Myla** Respublika Komi, NW Russian Federation 65°24′N 50°51′E
Mylae *see* Milazzo
93 M19 **Myllykoski** Etelä-Suomi, S Finland 60°45′N 26°52′E
153 U14 **Mymensing** *var.* Mymensingh. Dhaka, N Bangladesh 24°45′N 90°23′E
Mymensingh *see* Mymensing
93 K19 **Mynämäki** Länsi-Suomi, SW Finland 60°41′N 22°00′E
145 S14 **Mynaral** *Kaz.* Myngaral. Zhambyl, S Kazakhstan 45°25′N 73°37′E
Mynbulak *see* Mingbuloq
Mynbulak, Vpadina *see* Mingbuloq Botig'I
Myngaral *see* Mynaral
Myohaung *see* Mrauk-oo
163 W13 **Myohyang-sanmaek** ▲ C North Korea
164 M11 **Myōkō-san** ▲ Honshū, S Japan 36°54′N 138°05′E
81 J15 **Myooye** Central, C Zambia 15°11′S 27°10′E
118 K12 **Myory** *prev.* Miyory. Vitsyebskaya Voblasts', N Belarus 55°39′N 27°39′E
92 J4 **Mýrdalsjökull** *glacier* S Iceland
92 G10 **Myre** Nordland, C Norway 68°54′N 15°04′E
117 S5 **Myrhorod** *Rus.* Mirgorod. Poltavs'ka Oblast', NE Ukraine 49°58′N 33°37′E
115 J15 **Mýrina** *var.* Mírina. Límnos, SE Greece 39°52′N 25°04′E
117 P5 **Myronivka** *Rus.* Mironovka. Kyyivs'ka Oblast', N Ukraine 49°40′N 30°59′E
21 U13 **Myrtle Beach** South Carolina, SE USA 33°41′N 78°53′W
32 F14 **Myrtle Creek** Oregon, NW USA 43°01′N 123°19′W
183 P11 **Myrtleford** Victoria, SE Australia 36°34′S 146°45′E
32 E14 **Myrtle Point** Oregon, NW USA 43°04′N 124°08′W
115 K25 **Mýrtos** Kríti, Greece, E Mediterranean Sea 35°00′N 25°34′E
Myrtoum Mare *see* Mirtóo Pélagos
93 G17 **Myrviken** Jämtland, C Sweden 62°59′N 14°19′E
95 I15 **Mysen** Østfold, S Norway 59°33′N 11°20′E
124 L15 **Myshkin** Yaroslavskaya Oblast', NW Russian Federation 57°47′N 38°28′E
111 K17 **Myślenice** Malopolskie, S Poland 49°50′N 19°55′E
110 D10 **Myślibórz** Zachodnio-pomorskie, NW Poland 52°55′N 14°51′E
155 G20 **Mysore** *var.* Maisur. Karnātaka, W India 12°18′N 76°37′E
Mysore *see* Karnātaka
115 F21 **Mystrás** *var.* Mistras. Pelopónnisos, S Greece 37°03′N 22°22′E
111 K15 **Myszków** Śląskie, S Poland 50°36′N 19°20′E
167 T14 **My Tho** *var.* Mi Tho. Tiền Giang, S Vietnam 10°21′N 106°21′E
Mytilene *see* Mytilíni
115 L17 **Mytilíni** *var.* Mitilíni; *anc.* Mytilene. Lésvos, E Greece 39°06′N 26°33′E
126 K3 **Mytishchi** Moskovskaya Oblast', W Russian Federation 56°00′N 37°51′E
37 N3 **Myton** Utah, W USA 40°11′N 110°03′W
92 K2 **Mývatn** ◎ C Iceland
125 T11 **Myyëldino** *var.* Myjeldino. Respublika Komi, NW Russian Federation 61°46′N 54°48′E
82 M13 **Mzimba** Northern, NW Malawi 11°56′S 33°36′E
82 M12 **Mzuzu** Northern, N Malawi 11°23′S 34°03′E

N

101 M19 **Naab** SE Germany
98 G12 **Naaldwijk** Zuid-Holland, W Netherlands 52°00′N 04°13′E
38 G12 **Nā'ālehu** *var.* Naalehu. Hawaii, USA, C Pacific Ocean 19°04′N 155°36′W
93 K19 **Naantali** *Swe.* Nådendal. Länsi-Suomi, SW Finland 60°28′N 22°05′E
98 J10 **Naarden** Noord-Holland, C Netherlands 52°18′N 05°10′E
109 U4 **Naarn** N Austria
97 F18 **Naas** *Ir.* An Nás, Nás na Ríogh. Kildare, C Ireland 53°13′N 06°39′W
92 M9 **Näätämöjoki** *Lapp.* Njávdám. NE Finland
83 E23 **Nababeep** *var.* Nababiep. Northern Cape, W South Africa 29°36′S 17°46′E
Nababiep *see* Nababeep
Nabadwip *see* Navadwip
164 J14 **Nabari** Mie, Honshū, SW Japan 34°37′N 136°05′E
Nabatié *see* Nabatīyé
138 G8 **Nabatīyé** *var.* An Nabatīyah at Taḥtā, Nabatié, Nabatiyet et Tahta. SW Lebanon 33°18′N 35°36′E
Nabatiyet et Tahta *see* Nabatīyé
187 X14 **Nabavatu** Vanua Levu, N Fiji 16°35′S 178°55′E
190 I2 **Nabeina** *island* Tungaru, W Kiribati
127 T4 **Naberezhnyye Chelny** *prev.* Brezhnev. Respublika Tatarstan, W Russian Federation 55°43′N 52°21′E
39 T10 **Nabesna** Alaska, USA 62°22′N 143°00′W
39 T10 **Nabesna River** Alaska, USA
75 N5 **Nabeul** *var.* Nābul. NE Tunisia 36°32′N 10°45′E
152 I9 **Nābha** Punjab, NW India 30°22′N 76°12′E
171 W13 **Nabire** Papua, E Indonesia 03°23′S 135°31′E
141 O15 **Nabī Shu'ayb, Jabal an** ▲ W Yemen 15°24′N 44°04′E
138 F10 **Nablus** *var.* Nābulus, *Heb.* Shekhem; *anc.* Neapolis, *Bibl.* Shechem. N West Bank 32°13′N 35°16′E
187 X14 **Nabouwalu** Vanua Levu, N Fiji 17°00′S 178°43′E
Nābul *see* Nabeul
Nābulus *see* Nablus
187 Y13 **Nabuna** Vanua Levu, N Fiji 16°13′S 179°46′E
83 Q14 **Nacala** Nampula, NE Mozambique 14°30′S 40°37′E
42 H8 **Nacaome** Valle, S Honduras 13°30′N 87°31′W
Na Cealla Beaga *see* Killybegs
Na-Ch'ii *see* Nagqu
164 J15 **Nachikatsuura** *var.* Nachi-Katsuura. Wakayama, Honshū, SE Japan 33°37′N 135°54′E
Nachi-Katsuura *see* Nachikatsuura
81 J24 **Nachingwea** Lindi, SE Tanzania 10°21′S 38°46′E
111 F16 **Náchod** Královéhradecký Kraj, N Czech Republic 50°26′N 16°10′E
Na Clocha Liatha *see* Greystones
40 G3 **Naco** Sonora, NW Mexico 31°16′N 109°56′W
25 X8 **Nacogdoches** Texas, SW USA 31°36′N 94°40′W
40 G4 **Nacozari de García** Sonora, NW Mexico 30°27′N 109°43′W
Nada *see* Danzhou
77 O14 **Nadawli** NW Ghana 10°30′N 02°40′W
104 I3 **Nadela** Galicia, NW Spain 42°58′N 07°33′W
Nådendal *see* Naantali
144 M7 **Nadezhdinka** *prev.* Nadezhdinskiy. Kostanay, N Kazakhstan 53°46′N 63°44′E
Nadezhdinskiy *see* Nadezhdinka
Nadgan *see* Nadqān, Qalamat
187 W14 **Nadi** *prev.* Nandi. Viti Levu, W Fiji 17°47′S 177°32′E
187 X14 **Nadi** *prev.* Nandi. ✕ Viti Levu, W Fiji 17°46′S 177°28′E
154 D10 **Nadiād** Gujarāt, W India 22°42′N 72°55′E
Nadikdik *see* Knox Atoll
116 E11 **Nădlac** *Ger.* Nadlak, *Hung.* Nagylak. Arad, W Romania 46°10′N 20°47′E
Nadlak *see* Nădlac
74 H6 **Nador** *prev.* Villa Nador. NE Morocco 35°10′N 05°22′W
141 S9 **Nadqān, Qalamat** *var.* Nadgan. *well* E Saudi Arabia
111 N22 **Nádudvar** Hajdú-Bihar, E Hungary 47°36′N 21°09′E
121 O15 **Nadur** Gozo, N Malta 36°03′N 14°18′E
187 X13 **Naduri** *prev.* Nanduri. Vanua Levu, N Fiji 16°26′S 179°08′E
116 I7 **Nadvirna** *Pol.* Nadwórna, *Rus.* Nadvornaya. Ivano-Frankivs'ka Oblast', W Ukraine 48°27′N 24°30′E
124 J8 **Nadvoitsy** Respublika Kareliya, NW Russian Federation 63°53′N 34°17′E
Nadvornaya/Nadwórna *see* Nadvirna
122 I9 **Nadym** Yamalo-Nenetskiy Avtonomnyy Okrug, N Russian Federation 65°25′N 72°40′E
122 I9 **Nadym** C Russian Federation
186 E7 **Nadzab** Morobe, C Papua New Guinea 06°36′S 146°46′E
95 C17 **Nærbø** Rogaland, S Norway 58°40′N 05°39′E
95 I24 **Næstved** Sjælland, SE Denmark 55°12′N 11°47′E
77 X13 **Nafada** Gombe, E Nigeria 11°02′N 11°18′E
108 H8 **Näfels** Glarus, NE Switzerland 47°06′N 09°04′E
115 E18 **Náfpaktos** *var.* Návpaktos. Dytikí Elláda, C Greece 38°23′N 21°50′E
115 F20 **Náfplio** *prev.* Návplion. Pelopónnisos, S Greece 37°34′N 22°50′E
139 U6 **Naft Khāneh** Diyālá, E Iraq 34°01′N 45°26′E
149 N13 **Nāg** Baluchistān, SW Pakistan 27°43′N 65°31′E
171 P4 **Naga** *off.* Naga City; *prev.* Nueva Caceres. Luzon, N Philippines 13°36′N 123°10′E
Nagaarzê *see* Nagarzê
Naga City *see* Naga
12 F11 **Nagagami** Ontario, S Canada
164 F14 **Nagahama** Ehime, Shikoku, SW Japan 33°36′N 132°29′E
153 X12 **Nāga Hills** ▲ NE India
165 P10 **Nagai** Yamagata, Honshū, C Japan 38°08′N 140°00′E
Na Gaibhlte *see* Galty Mountains
39 N16 **Nagai Island** *island* Shumagin Islands, Alaska, USA
153 X12 **Nāgāland** ◇ *state* NE India
164 M11 **Nagano** Nagano, Honshū, S Japan 36°39′N 138°11′E
164 M12 **Nagano** *off.* Nagano-ken. ◇ *prefecture* Honshū, S Japan
Nagano-ken *see* Nagano
165 N11 **Nagaoka** Niigata, Honshū, C Japan 37°26′N 138°48′E
153 W12 **Nagaon** *prev.* Nowgong. Assam, NE India 26°21′N 92°41′E
155 J21 **Nāgappattinam** *var.* Negapatam, Negapattinam. Tamil Nādu, SE India 10°45′N 79°50′E
Nagara Nayok *see* Nakhon Nayok
Nagara Panom *see* Nakhon Phanom
Nagara Pathom *see* Nakhon Pathom
Nagara Sridharmaraj *see* Nakhon Si Thammarat
Nagara Svarga *see* Nakhon Sawan
155 H16 **Nāgārjuna Sāgar** ⊠ E India
42 I10 **Nagarote** León, SW Nicaragua 12°15′N 86°35′W
158 M16 **Nagarzê** *var.* Nagaarzê. Xizang Zizhiqu, W China 28°57′N 90°26′E
164 C14 **Nagasaki** Nagasaki, Kyūshū, SW Japan 32°45′N 129°52′E
164 C14 **Nagasaki** *off.* Nagasaki-ken. ◇ *prefecture* Kyūshū, SW Japan
Nagasaki-ken *see* Nagasaki
Nagashima *see* Kii-Nagashima
164 E12 **Nagato** Yamaguchi, Honshū, SW Japan 34°22′N 131°10′E
152 F11 **Nāgaur** Rājasthān, NW India 27°12′N 73°48′E
154 F10 **Nāgda** Madhya Pradesh, C India 23°30′N 75°29′E
98 L8 **Nagele** Flevoland, N Netherlands 52°39′N 05°43′E
155 H24 **Nāgercoil** Tamil Nādu, SE India 08°11′N 77°30′E
153 X12 **Nāginimāra** Nāgāland, NE India 26°44′N 94°51′E
Na Gleannta *see* Glenties
165 T16 **Nago** Okinawa, Okinawa, SW Japan 26°36′N 127°59′E
154 K9 **Nāgod** Madhya Pradesh, C India 24°34′N 80°34′E
155 J26 **Nagoda** Southern Province, S Sri Lanka 06°13′N 80°13′E
101 G22 **Nagold** Baden-Württemberg, SW Germany 48°33′N 08°43′E
137 V12 **Nagorno-Karabakh** *var.* Nagorno- Karabakhskaya Avtonomnaya Oblast, *Arm.* Lerrnayin Gharabakh, *Az.* Dağliq Quarabağ, *Rus.* Nagornyy Karabakh. *former autonomous region* SW Azerbaijan
Nagorno- Karabakhskaya Avtonomnaya Oblast *see* Nagorno-Karabakh
123 Q12 **Nagornyy** Respublika Sakha (Yakutiya), NE Russian Federation 55°53′N 124°58′E
Nagornyy Karabakh *see* Nagorno-Karabakh
125 R13 **Nagorsk** Kirovskaya Oblast', NW Russian Federation 59°18′N 50°49′E
164 K13 **Nagoya** Aichi, Honshū, SW Japan 35°10′N 136°53′E
154 I12 **Nāgpur** Mahārāshtra, C India 21°09′N 79°06′E
156 K10 **Nagqu** *Chin.* Na-Ch'ii; *prev.* Hei-ho. Xizang Zizhiqu, W China 31°30′N 91°57′E
152 J8 **Nāg Tibba Range** ▲ N India
45 O8 **Nagua** NE Dominican Republic 19°25′N 69°49′W
111 H25 **Nagyatád** Somogy, SW Hungary 46°15′N 17°25′E
Nagybánya *see* Baia Mare
Nagybecskerek *see* Zrenjanin
Nagydisznód *see* Cisnădie
Nagyenyed *see* Aiud
111 N21 **Nagykálló** Szabolcs-Szatmár-Bereg, E Hungary 47°50′N 21°47′E
111 G25 **Nagykanizsa** *Ger.* Grosskanizsa. Zala, SW Hungary 46°27′N 17°E
Nagykároly *see* Carei
111 K22 **Nagykáta** Pest, C Hungary 47°25′N 19°45′E
Nagykikinda *see* Kikinda
111 K23 **Nagykőrös** Pest, C Hungary 47°01′N 19°46′E
Nagy-Küküllő *see* Târnava Mare
Nagylak *see* Nădlac
Nagymihály *see* Michalovce
Nagyrőce *see* Revúca
Nagysomkút *see* Şomcuta Mare
Nagysurány *see* Šurany
Nagyszalonta *see* Salonta
Nagyszeben *see* Sibiu
Nagyszentmiklós *see* Sânnicolau Mare
Nagyszöllös *see* Vynohradiv
Nagyszombat *see* Trnava
Nagytapolcsány *see* Topoľčany
Nagyvárad *see* Oradea
165 S17 **Naha** Okinawa, Okinawa, SW Japan 26°10′N 127°40′E
152 J8 **Nāhan** Himāchal Pradesh, NW India 30°33′N 77°18′E
Nahang, Rūd-e *see* Nihing
138 F8 **Nahariya** *prev.* Nahariyya. Northern, N Israel 33°01′N 35°05′E
Nahariyya *see* Nahariya
142 L6 **Nahāvand** *var.* Nehavend. Hamadān, W Iran 34°13′N 48°21′E
101 F19 **Nahe** SW Germany
Na H-Iarmhidhe *see* Westmeath
189 O13 **Nahnalaud** ▲ Pohnpei, E Micronesia
Nahoi, Cape *see* Cumberland, Cape
Nahtavárr *see* Nattavaara
63 H16 **Nahuel Huapí, Lago** ◎ W Argentina
23 W7 **Nahunta** Georgia, SE USA 31°11′N 81°58′W
40 J6 **Naica** Chihuahua, N Mexico 27°53′N 105°30′W
11 U15 **Naicam** Saskatchewan, S Canada 52°26′N 104°30′W
Naiman Qi *see* Daqin Tal
158 M4 **Naimin Bulak** *spring* NW China
13 P6 **Nain** Newfoundland and Labrador, NE Canada 56°33′N 61°46′W
143 P8 **Nā'īn** Eşfahān, C Iran 32°52′N 53°05′E
152 K10 **Naini Tāl** Uttarakhand, N India 29°22′N 79°26′E
154 J11 **Nainpur** Madhya Pradesh, C India 22°26′N 80°10′E
96 J8 **Nairn** N Scotland, United Kingdom 57°36′N 03°51′W
96 I8 **Nairn** *cultural region* NE Scotland, United Kingdom
81 I19 **Nairobi** ● (Kenya) Nairobi Area, S Kenya 01°17′S 36°50′E
81 I19 **Nairobi** ✕ Nairobi Area, S Kenya 01°21′S 37°01′E
82 P13 **Nairoto** Cabo Delgado, NE Mozambique 12°22′S 39°05′E
118 G3 **Naissaar** *island* N Estonia
Naissus *see* Niš
187 Z14 **Naitaba** *var.* Naitauba; *prev.* Naitamba. *island* Lau Group, E Fiji
Naitamba/Naitauba *see* Naitaba
81 I19 **Naivasha** Rift Valley, SW Kenya 0°44′S 36°26′E
81 H19 **Naivasha, Lake** ◎ SW Kenya
Najaf *see* An Najaf
143 N8 **Najafābād** *var.* Nejafabad. Eşfahān, C Iran 32°38′N 51°23′E
141 N7 **Najd** *var.* Nejd. *cultural region* C Saudi Arabia
105 O4 **Nájera** La Rioja, N Spain 42°25′N 02°45′W
105 P4 **Najerilla** N Spain
163 U7 **Naji** *var.* Arun Qi. Nei Mongol Zizhiqu, N China 48°05′N 123°28′E
152 J9 **Najībābād** Uttar Pradesh, N India 29°37′N 78°19′E
Najima *see* Fukuoka
163 Y11 **Najin** NE North Korea 42°13′N 130°16′E
139 T9 **Najm al Ḥassūn** Bābil, C Iraq 32°24′N 44°13′E
141 O13 **Najrān** *var.* Abā as Su'ūd. Najrān, S Saudi Arabia 17°31′N 44°09′E
141 P12 **Najrān** *var.* Minṭaqat al Najrān. ◇ *province* S Saudi Arabia
Najrān, Minṭaqat al *see* Najrān
165 T2 **Nakagawa** Hokkaidō, NE Japan 44°49′N 142°04′E
38 F9 **Nākālele Point** *var.* Nakalele Point. *headland* Maui, Hawai'i, USA 21°01′N 156°35′W
164 D13 **Nakama** Fukuoka, Kyūshū, SW Japan 33°53′N 130°48′E
Nakambé *see* White Volta
Nakamti *see* Nek'emtē
164 F15 **Nakamura** *var.* Shimanto. Kōchi, Shikoku, SW Japan 33°00′N 132°55′E
186 H7 **Nakanai Mountains** ▲ New Britain, E Papua New Guinea
164 H11 **Nakano-shima** *island* Oki-shotō, SW Japan
165 Q6 **Nakasato** Aomori, Honshū, C Japan 40°58′N 140°26′E
165 T5 **Nakasatsunai** Hokkaidō, NE Japan 42°42′N 143°09′E
165 W4 **Nakashibetsu** Hokkaidō, NE Japan 43°31′N 144°58′E
81 F18 **Nakasongola** C Uganda 01°19′N 32°28′E
165 T1 **Nakatonbetsu** Hokkaidō, NE Japan 44°58′N 142°18′E
164 L13 **Nakatsugawa** *var.* Nakatugawa. Gifu, Honshū, SW Japan 35°30′N 137°29′E
Nakatugawa *see* Nakatsugawa
Nakdong *see* Nakdong-gang
163 Y15 **Nakdong-gang** *var.* Nakdong, *Jap.* Rakutō-kō; *prev.* Naktong-gang. C South Korea
Nakel *see* Nakło nad Notecią
Nakfa *see* Nakh'fa
80 J8 **Nakh'fa** *var.* Nakfa. N Eritrea 16°38′N 38°26′E
Nakhichevan' *see* Naxçıvan
123 S15 **Nakhodka** Primorskiy Kray, SE Russian Federation 42°46′N 132°48′E
122 J8 **Nakhodka** Yamalo-Nenetskiy Avtonomnyy Okrug, N Russian Federation 67°48′N 77°48′E
Nakhon Navok *see* Nakhon Nayok
167 P11 **Nakhon Nayok** *var.* Nagara Nayok, Nakhon Navok. Nakhon Nayok, C Thailand 14°15′N 101°12′E
167 O11 **Nakhon Pathom** *var.* Nagara Pathom, Nakorn Pathom. Nakhon Pathom, W Thailand 13°49′N 100°06′E
167 R8 **Nakhon Phanom** *var.* Nagara Panom. Nakhon Phanom, E Thailand 17°22′N 104°46′E
167 Q10 **Nakhon Ratchasima** *var.* Khorat, Korat. Nakhon Ratchasima, E Thailand 15°N 102°06′E
167 O9 **Nakhon Sawan** *var.* Muang Nakhon Sawan, Nagara Svarga. Nakhon Sawan, W Thailand 15°42′N 100°06′E
167 N15 **Nakhon Si Thammarat** *var.* Nagara Sridharmaraj, Nakhon Sithamnaraj. Nakhon Si Thammarat, SW Thailand 08°24′N 99°58′E
Nakhon Sithamnaraj *see* Nakhon Si Thammarat
139 Y11 **Nakhrash** Al Başrah, SE Iraq 31°13′N 47°24′E
10 I9 **Nakina** British Columbia, W Canada 59°12′N 132°48′W
110 H9 **Nakło nad Notecią** *Ger.* Nakel. Kujawsko-pomorskie, C Poland 53°08′N 17°35′E
39 P13 **Naknek** Alaska, USA 58°45′N 157°01′W
152 H8 **Nakodar** Punjab, NW India 31°06′N 75°31′E
82 M11 **Nakonde** Northern, NE Zambia 09°22′S 42°47′E
Nakorn Pathom *see* Nakhon Pathom
95 H24 **Nakskov** Sjælland, SE Denmark 54°50′N 11°10′E
Naktong-gang *see* Nakdong-gang
81 H18 **Nakuru** Rift Valley, SW Kenya 0°16′S 36°04′E
81 H19 **Nakuru, Lake** ◎ Rift Valley, C Kenya
11 O17 **Nakusp** British Columbia, SW Canada 50°14′N 117°48′W
149 N15 **Nāl** W Pakistan
162 M7 **Nalayh** Töv, C Mongolia 47°48′N 107°17′E
153 V12 **Nalbāri** Assam, NE India 26°36′N 91°49′E
63 G19 **Nalcayec, Isla** *island* Archipiélago de los Chonos, S Chile
127 N15 **Nal'chik** Kabardino-Balkarskaya Respublika, SW Russian Federation 43°30′N 43°39′E
155 I16 **Nalgonda** Andhra Pradesh, C India 17°04′N 79°15′E
153 S14 **Nalhāti** West Bengal, NE India 24°19′N 87°53′E
153 U14 **Nalitabari** Dhaka, N Bangladesh 25°06′N 90°11′E
155 I17 **Nallamala Hills** ▲ E India
136 G12 **Nallıhan** Ankara, NW Turkey 40°12′N 31°22′E
104 K2 **Nalón** NW Spain
167 N3 **Nalong** Kachin State, N Myanmar (Burma) 24°42′N 97°27′E
75 N8 **Nālūt** NW Libya 31°52′N 10°59′E
171 T14 **Nama** Pulau Manawoka, E Indonesia 04°07′S 131°22′E
189 Q16 **Nama** *island* C Micronesia
83 O16 **Namacurra** Zambézia, NE Mozambique 17°31′S 37°03′E
188 F9 **Namai Bay** *bay* Babeldaob, N Palau
29 W2 **Namakan Lake** ◎ Canada/ USA
143 O6 **Namak, Daryācheh-ye** *marsh* N Iran
143 T6 **Namak, Kavīr-e** *salt pan* NE Iran
167 O6 **Namaklwe** Shan State, E Myanmar (Burma) 19°45′N 99°01′E
Namaksār, Kowl-e/ Namakzār, Daryācheh-ye *see* Namakzar
148 J5 **Namakzar** *Pash.* Daryācheh-ye Namakzār, Kowl-e Namaksār. *marsh* Afghanistan/Iran
171 V15 **Namalau** Pulau Jursian, E Indonesia 05°50′S 134°43′E
81 I20 **Namanga** Rift Valley, S Kenya 02°33′S 36°48′E
147 S10 **Namangan** Namangan Viloyati, E Uzbekistan 40°59′N 71°34′E
Namanganskaya Oblast' *see* Namangan Viloyati
147 R10 **Namangan Viloyati** *Rus.* Namanganskaya Oblast'. ◇ *province* E Uzbekistan
83 Q14 **Namapa** Nampula, NE Mozambique 13°43′S 39°48′E
83 C21 **Namaqualand** *physical region* S Namibia
81 G18 **Namasagali** C Uganda 01°02′N 32°58′E
186 H6 **Namatanai** New Ireland, NE Papua New Guinea 03°40′S 152°26′E
83 I14 **Nambala** Central, C Zambia 15°04′S 26°56′E
81 J23 **Nambanje** Lindi, SE Tanzania 08°37′S 38°21′E
183 V2 **Nambour** Queensland, E Australia 26°40′S 152°52′E
183 V6 **Nambucca Heads** New South Wales, SE Australia 30°37′S 153°00′E
159 N15 **Nam Co** ◎ W China
167 R5 **Nâm Cum** Lai Châu, N Vietnam 22°37′N 103°12′E
Namdik *see* Namorik Atoll
167 T6 **Nam Định** Nam Ha, N Vietnam 20°25′N 106°12′E
99 I20 **Namêche** Namur, SE Belgium 50°29′N 05°02′E
30 J4 **Namekagon Lake** ◎ Wisconsin, N USA
188 F10 **Namekakl Passage** *passage* Babeldaob, N Palau
Namen *see* Namur
83 P15 **Nametil** Nampula, NE Mozambique 15°46′S 39°21′E
163 X14 **Nam-gang** C North Korea
163 Y16 **Nam-gang** South Korea
163 Y17 **Namhae-do** *Jap.* Nankai-tō. *island* S South Korea
Namhoi *see* Foshan
83 C19 **Namib Desert** *desert* W Namibia
83 A15 **Namibe** *Port.* Moçâmedes, Mossâmedes. Namibe, SW Angola 15°10′S 12°09′E
83 A15 **Namibe** ◇ *province* SE Angola
83 C18 **Namibia** *off.* Republic of Namibia, *var.* South West Africa, *Afr.* Suidwes-Afrika, *Ger.* Deutsch-Südwestafrika; *prev.* German Southwest Africa, South-West Africa. ◆ *republic* S Africa
65 O17 **Namibia Plain** *undersea feature* S Atlantic Ocean
Namibia, Republic of *see* Namibia
165 Q11 **Namie** Fukushima, Honshū, C Japan 37°29′N 140°58′E
165 Q7 **Namioka** Aomori, Honshū, C Japan 40°43′N 140°34′E
40 I5 **Namiquipa** Chihuahua, N Mexico 29°15′N 107°25′W
159 P15 **Namjagbarwa Feng** ▲ W China 29°39′N 95°00′E
Namka *see* Doilungdêqên
Nam Khong *see* Mekong
171 R13 **Namlea** Pulau Buru, E Indonesia 03°12′S 127°06′E
158 L16 **Namling** Xizang Zizhiqu, W China 29°40′N 88°58′E
Namnetes *see* Nantes
167 R8 **Nam Ngum** C Laos
Namo *see* Namu Atoll
183 R5 **Namoi River** New South Wales, SE Australia
189 Q17 **Namoluk Atoll** *atoll* Mortlock Islands, C Micronesia
189 O15 **Namonuito Atoll** *atoll* Caroline Islands, C Micronesia
189 T9 **Namorik Atoll** *var.* Namdik. *atoll* Ralik Chain, S Marshall Islands
167 Q6 **Nam Ou** N Laos
32 M14 **Nampa** Idaho, NW USA 43°32′N 116°33′W
76 M11 **Nampala** Ségou, W Mali 15°21′N 05°32′W
163 W14 **Namp'o** SW North Korea 38°46′N 125°25′E
83 P15 **Nampula** Nampula, NE Mozambique 15°09′S 39°14′E
83 P15 **Nampula** *off.* Província de Nampula. ◇ *province* NE Mozambique
Nampula, Província de *see* Nampula
163 W13 **Namsan-ni** NW North Korea 40°25′N 125°01′E
Namslau *see* Namysłów
93 E15 **Namsos** Nord-Trøndelag, C Norway 64°28′N 11°31′E
93 F14 **Namsskogan** Nord-Trøndelag, C Norway 64°57′N 13°04′E
167 O6 **Nam Teng** E Myanmar (Burma)
167 P6 **Nam Tha** N Laos
123 Q10 **Namtsy** Respublika Sakha (Yakutiya), NE Russian Federation 62°42′N 129°30′E
167 N4 **Namtu** Shan State, Myanmar (Burma) 23°04′N 97°26′E
10 J15 **Namu** British Columbia, SW Canada 51°46′N 127°49′W
189 T7 **Namu Atoll** *var.* Namo. *atoll* Ralik Chain, C Marshall Islands
187 Y15 **Namuka-i-Lau** *island* Lau Group, E Fiji
83 O15 **Namuli, Mont** ▲ NE Mozambique 15°15′S 37°33′E
83 P14 **Namuno** Cabo Delgado, N Mozambique 13°39′S 38°50′E
99 I20 **Namur** *Dut.* Namen. Namur, SE Belgium 50°28′N 04°52′E
99 H21 **Namur** *Dut.* Namen. ◇ *province* S Belgium
83 D17 **Namutoni** Kunene, N Namibia 18°49′S 16°55′E
163 Y16 **Namwon** *Jap.* Nangen; *prev.* Namwŏn. S South Korea 35°24′N 127°20′E
Namwŏn *see* Namwon
111 H14 **Namysłów** *Ger.* Namslau. Opole, SW Poland 51°03′N 17°41′E
167 P7 **Nan** *var.* Muang Nan. Nan, NW Thailand 18°47′N 100°50′E
79 G15 **Nana** W Central African Republic
165 R4 **Nanae** Hokkaidō, NE Japan 41°55′N 140°40′E
79 I14 **Nana-Grébizi** ◇ *prefecture* N Central African Republic
10 L17 **Nanaimo** Vancouver Island, British Columbia, SW Canada 49°08′N 123°58′W
38 C9 **Nānākuli** *var.* Nanakuli. O'ahu, Hawaii, USA, C Pacific Ocean 21°23′N 158°09′W
79 G15 **Nana-Mambéré** ◇ *prefecture* W Central African Republic
161 R13 **Nan'an** Fujian, SE China 24°57′N 118°22′E
183 U2 **Nanango** Queensland, E Australia 26°42′S 151°58′E
164 L11 **Nanao** Ishikawa, Honshū, SW Japan 37°03′N 136°58′E
161 Q14 **Nan'ao Dao** *island* S China
164 L10 **Nanatsu-shima** *island* SW Japan
56 F8 **Nanay, Río** NE Peru
160 J8 **Nanbu** Sichuan, C China 31°19′N 106°02′E
163 X7 **Nancha** Heilongjiang, NE China 47°09′N 129°17′E
161 P10 **Nanchang** *var.* Nan-ch'ang, Nanch'ang-hsien. *province capital* Jiangxi, S China 28°38′N 115°58′E
Nan-ch'ang *see* Nanchang
Nanch'ang-hsien *see* Nanchang
161 P11 **Nancheng** *var.* Jianchang. Jiangxi, S China 27°37′N 116°37′E
Nan-ching *see* Nanjing
160 J9 **Nanchong** Sichuan, C China 30°47′N 106°03′E
160 J10 **Nanchuan** Chongqing Shi, C China 29°06′N 107°13′E
103 T5 **Nancy** Meurthe-et-Moselle, NE France 48°40′N 06°11′E
185 A22 **Nancy Sound** *sound* South Island, New Zealand
152 L9 **Nanda Devi** ▲ NW India 30°27′N 80°00′E
42 J11 **Nandaime** Granada, SW Nicaragua 11°45′N 86°02′W
160 K13 **Nandan** *var.* Minami-Awaji. Guangxi Zhuangzu Zizhiqu, S China 25°03′N 107°31′E
155 H14 **Nānded** Mahārāshtra, C India 19°11′N 77°21′E
183 S5 **Nandewar Range** ▲ New South Wales, SE Australia
Nandi *see* Nadi
160 E13 **Nanding He** China/ Vietnam
Nándorhgy *see* Oțelu Roșu
154 E11 **Nandurbār** Mahārāshtra, W India 21°22′N 74°18′E
Nanduri *see* Naduri
155 I17 **Nandyāl** Andhra Pradesh, E India 15°30′N 78°28′E
161 P11 **Nanfeng** *var.* Qincheng. Jiangxi, S China 27°15′N 116°16′E
Nang *see* Nangxian
79 E15 **Nanga Eboko** Centre, C Cameroon 04°38′N 12°21′E
Nangah Serawai *see* Nangaserawai
149 W4 **Nanga Parbat** ▲ India/ Pakistan 35°15′N 74°36′E
169 R11 **Nangapinoh** Borneo, C Indonesia 0°21′S 111°44′E
149 R5 **Nangarhār** ◇ *province* E Afghanistan
169 S11 **Nangaserawai** *var.* Nangah Serawai. Borneo, C Indonesia 0°20′S 112°26′E
169 Q12 **Nangatayap** Borneo, C Indonesia 01°30′S 110°33′E
Nangen *see* Namwon
103 P5 **Nangis** Seine-et-Marne, N France 48°36′N 03°02′E
163 X13 **Nangnim-sanmaek** ▲ C North Korea
161 O4 **Nangong** Hebei, E China 37°22′N 115°20′E
159 Q14 **Nangqên** *var.* Xangda. Qinghai, C China 32°05′N 96°28′E
167 Q10 **Nang Rong** Buri Ram, E Thailand 14°37′N 102°48′E
159 O16 **Nangxian** *var.* Nang. Xizang Zizhiqu, W China 29°04′N 93°03′E
Nan Hai *see* South China Sea
160 L8 **Nan He** C China
160 F12 **Nanhua** *var.* Longchuan. Yunnan, SW China 25°15′N 101°15′E
Naniwa *see* Ōsaka
155 G20 **Nanjangūd** Karnātaka, W India 12°07′N 76°40′E

◆ Country
● Country Capital
◇ Dependent Territory
○ Dependent Territory Capital
◇ Administrative Regions
✕ International Airport
▲ Mountain
▲ Mountain Range
Volcano
River
◎ Lake
⊠ Reservoir

161 Q8 **Nanjing** *var.* Nan-ching, Nanking; *prev.* Chianning, Chian-ning, Kiang-ning, Jiangsu. *province capital* Jiangsu, E China 32°03′N 118°47′E
Nankai-tō *see* Namhae-do
161 O12 **Nankang** *var.* Rongjiang. Jiangxi, S China 25°42′N 114°45′E
Nanking *see* Nanjing
161 N13 **Nan Ling** ▲▲ S China
160 L15 **Nanliu Jiang** ~ S China
189 P13 **Nan Madol** *ruins* Temwen Island, E Micronesia
160 K15 **Nanning** *var.* Nan-ning; *prev.* Yung-ning. Guangxi Zhuangzu Zizhiqu, S China 22°50′N 108°19′E
Nan-ning *see* Nanning
196 M15 **Nanortalik** Kitaa, S Greenland 60°08′M 45°14′W
Nanouki *see* Aranuka
160 H13 **Nanpan Jiang** ~ S China
152 M11 **Nānpāra** Uttar Pradesh, N India 27°51′N 81°30′E
161 Q12 **Nanping** *var.* Nan-p'ing; *prev.* Yenping. Fujian, SE China 26°40′N 118°07′E
Nan-p'ing *see* Nanping
Nanping *see* Jiuzhaigou
Nanpu *see* Pucheng
161 R12 **Nanri Dao** *island* SE China
165 S16 **Nansei-shotō** *Eng.* Ryukyu Islands. *island group* SW Japan
Nansei Syotō Trench *see* Ryukyu Trench
197 T10 **Nansen Basin** *undersea feature* Arctic Ocean
197 T10 **Nansen Cordillera** *var.* Arctic Mid Oceanic Ridge, Nansen Ridge. *undersea feature* Arctic Ocean 87°00′N 90°00′E
Nansen Ridge *see* Nansen Cordillera
129 T9 **Nan Shan** ▲▲ C China
Nansha Qundao *see* Spratly Islands
12 K3 **Nantais, Lac** ◎ Québec, NE Canada
103 N5 **Nanterre** Hauts-de-Seine, N France 48°53′N 02°13′E
102 I8 **Nantes** *Bret.* Naoned; *anc.* Condivincum, Namnetes. Loire-Atlantique, NW France 47°12′N 01°32′W
14 G17 **Nanticoke** Ontario, S Canada 42°49′N 80°04′W
18 H13 **Nanticoke** Pennsylvania, NE USA 41°12′N 76°00′W
21 Y4 **Nanticoke River** ~ Delaware/Maryland, NE USA
11 Q17 **Nanton** Alberta, SW Canada 50°21′N 113°47′W
161 S8 **Nantong** Jiangsu, E China 32°00′N 120°52′E
161 S13 **Nantou** *prev.* Nant'ou. W Taiwan 23°54′N 120°51′E
Nant'ou *see* Nantou
103 S10 **Nantua** Ain, E France 46°10′N 05°34′E
19 Q13 **Nantucket** Nantucket Island, Massachusetts, NE USA 41°15′N 70°05′W
19 Q13 **Nantucket Island** *island* Massachusetts, NE USA
19 Q13 **Nantucket Sound** *sound* Massachusetts, NE USA
82 P13 **Nantulo** Cabo Delgado, N Mozambique 12°30′S 39°03′E
189 O12 **Nanuh** Pohnpei, E Micronesia
190 D6 **Nanumaga** *var.* Nanumanga. *atoll* NW Tuvalu
Nanumanga *see* Nanumaga
190 D5 **Nanumea Atoll** *atoll* NW Tuvalu
59 O19 **Nanuque** Minas Gerais, SE Brazil 17°49′S 40°21′W
171 R10 **Nanusa, Kepulauan** *island group* N Indonesia
163 U4 **Nanweng He** ~ NE China
160 I10 **Nanxi** Sichuan, C China 28°54′N 104°59′E
161 N10 **Nanxian** *var.* Nan Xian, Nanzhou. Hunan, S China 29°23′N 112°18′E
Nan Xian *see* Nanxian
161 N7 **Nanyang** *var.* Nan-yang. Henan, C China 32°59′N 112°29′E
Nan-yang *see* Nanyang
161 P6 **Nanyang Hu** ◎ E China
165 P10 **Nan'yō** Yamagata, Honshū, C Japan 38°04′N 140°06′E
81 I18 **Nanyuki** Central, C Kenya 0°01′N 37°05′E
160 M8 **Nanzhang** Hubei, C China 31°47′N 111°48′E
Nanzhou *see* Nanxian
105 T11 **Nao, Cabo de La** *headland* E Spain 38°43′N 00°13′E
12 M9 **Naococane, Lac** ◎ Québec, E Canada
153 S14 **Naogaon** Rajshahi, NW Bangladesh 24°49′N 88°59′E
Naokot *see* Naukot
187 R13 **Naone** Maewo, C Vanuatu 15°03′S 168°06′E
Naoned *see* Nantes
115 E14 **Náousa** Kentrikí Makedonía, N Greece 40°38′N 22°04′E
35 N8 **Napa** California, W USA 38°15′N 122°17′W
39 O11 **Napaimiut** Alaska, USA 61°32′N 158°46′W
39 N12 **Napakiak** Alaska, USA 60°42′N 161°57′W
122 J7 **Napalkovo** Yamalo-Nenetskiy Avtonomnyy Okrug, N Russian Federation 70°06′N 73°43′E
12 I16 **Napanee** Ontario, SE Canada 44°13′N 76°57′W
39 N12 **Napaskiak** Alaska, USA 60°42′N 161°46′W
167 S5 **Na Phắc** Cao Bằng, N Vietnam 22°24′N 105°54′E
184 O11 **Napier** Hawke's Bay, North Island, New Zealand 39°30′S 176°55′E
195 X3 **Napier Mountains** ▲▲ Antarctica
15 O13 **Napierville** Québec, SE Canada 45°12′N 73°25′W
23 W15 **Naples** Florida, SE USA 26°08′N 81°48′W
25 W5 **Naples** Texas, SW USA 33°12′N 94°40′W
Naples *see* Napoli
160 I14 **Napo** Guangxi Zhuangzu Zizhiqu, S China 23°21′N 105°47′E
56 C6 **Napo** ◆ *province* NE Ecuador
29 O6 **Napoleon** North Dakota, N USA 46°30′N 99°46′W
31 R11 **Napoleon** Ohio, N USA 41°23′N 84°07′W
Napoléon-Vendée *see* la Roche-sur-Yon
22 J9 **Napoleonville** Louisiana, S USA 29°55′N 91°01′W
107 K17 **Napoli** *Eng.* Naples, *Ger.* Neapel; *anc.* Neapolis. Campania, S Italy 40°52′N 14°15′E
107 J18 **Napoli, Golfo di** *gulf* S Italy
57 F7 **Napo, Río** ~ Ecuador/Peru
191 W9 **Napuka** *island* Îles Tuamotu, C French Polynesia
142 J3 **Naqadeh** Āžarbāyjān-e Bākhtarī, NW Iran 36°57′N 45°24′E
139 U6 **Naqnah** Diyālá, E Iraq 34°13′N 45°33′E
Nar *see* Nera
164 J14 **Nara** Nara, Honshū, SW Japan 34°41′N 135°49′E
76 L11 **Nara** Koulikoro, W Mali 15°04′N 07°19′W
149 R14 **Nāra Canal** *irrigation canal* S Pakistan
182 K11 **Naracoorte** South Australia 37°02′S 140°45′E
183 P8 **Naradhan** New South Wales, SE Australia 33°37′S 146°19′E
Naradhivas *see* Narathiwat
56 B8 **Naranjal** Guayas, W Ecuador 02°43′S 79°38′W
57 Q19 **Naranjos** Santa Cruz, E Bolivia
41 Q12 **Naranjos** Veracruz-Llave, E Mexico 21°21′N 97°41′W
159 Q6 **Naran Sebstein Bulag** *spring* NW China
164 B14 **Narao** Nagasaki, Nakadōri-jima, SW Japan 32°40′N 129°03′E
155 J16 **Narasaraopet** Andhra Pradesh, E India 16°16′N 80°06′E
158 J5 **Narat** Xinjiang Uygur Zizhiqu, W China 43°20′N 84°02′E
167 P17 **Narathiwat** *var.* Naradhivas. Narathiwat, SW Thailand 06°25′N 101°48′E
37 V10 **Nara Visa** New Mexico, SW USA 35°35′N 103°06′W
Nārāyāni *see* Gandak
Narbada *see* Narmada
Narbo Martius *see* Narbonne
103 P16 **Narbonne** *anc.* Narbo Martius. Aude, S France 43°11′N 03°E
Narborough Island *see* Fernandina, Isla
104 J2 **Narcea** ~ NW Spain
152 J9 **Narendranagar** Uttarakhand, N India 30°10′N 78°21′E
Nares Abyssal Plain *see* Nares Plain
64 G11 **Nares Plain** *var.* Nares Abyssal Plain. *undersea feature* NW Atlantic Ocean 23°30′N 63°00′W
Nares Stræde *see* Nares Strait
197 P10 **Nares Strait** *Dan.* Nares Stræde. *strait* Canada/Greenland
110 O9 **Narew** ~ E Poland
155 F17 **Nargund** Karnātaka, W India 15°43′N 75°23′E
83 D20 **Narib** Hardap, S Namibia 24°11′S 17°46′E
Narikrik *see* Knox Atoll
Narin Gol *see* Omon Gol
54 B13 **Nariño** *off.* Departamento de Nariño. ◆ *province* SW Colombia
165 P13 **Narita** Chiba, Honshū, S Japan 35°46′N 140°20′E
165 P13 **Narita** ✈ (Tōkyō) Chiba, Honshū, S Japan 35°45′N 140°23′E
Nariya *see* An Nu'ayrīyah
162 F5 **Nariyn Gol** ~ Mongolia/Russian Federation
162 J8 **Nariynteel** *var.* Tsagaan-Ovoo. Övörhangay, C Mongolia 45°57′N 101°25′E
152 J8 **Nārkanda** Himāchal Pradesh, NW India 31°14′N 77°27′E
92 L13 **Narkaus** Lappi, NW Finland 66°13′N 26°09′E
154 E11 **Narmada** *var.* Narbada. ~ C India
152 H11 **Narnaul** *var.* Nārnaul. Haryāna, N India 28°04′N 76°10′E
107 I14 **Narni** Umbria, C Italy 42°31′N 12°31′E
107 J24 **Naro** Sicilia, Italy, C Mediterranean Sea 37°18′N 13°48′E
Narodichi *see* Narodychi
125 V7 **Narodnaya, Gora** ▲ NW Russian Federation 65°04′N 60°12′E
117 N3 **Narodychi** *Rus.* Narodichi. Zhytomyrs'ka Oblast', N Ukraine 51°11′N 29°01′E
126 J4 **Naro-Fominsk** Moskovskaya Oblast', W Russian Federation 55°25′N 36°41′E
81 H19 **Narok** Rift Valley, SW Kenya 01°04′S 35°54′E
104 H2 **Narón** Galicia, NW Spain 43°31′N 08°08′W
183 S11 **Narooma** New South Wales, SE Australia 36°16′S 150°08′E
Narova *see* Narva
Narovlya *see* Narowlya
149 W8 **Nārowāl** Punjab, E Pakistan 32°04′N 74°54′E
119 N20 **Narowlya** *Rus.* Narovlya. Homyel'skaya Voblasts', SE Belarus 51°48′N 29°30′E
93 J17 **Närpes** *Fin.* Närpiö. Länsi-Suomi, W Finland 62°28′N 21°19′E
Närpiö *see* Närpes
183 S5 **Narrabri** New South Wales, SE Australia 30°21′S 149°48′E
183 P9 **Narrandera** New South Wales, SE Australia 34°46′S 146°32′E
183 Q4 **Narran Lake** ◎ New South Wales, SE Australia
183 Q4 **Narran River** ~ New South Wales/Queensland, SE Australia
180 J13 **Narrogin** Western Australia 32°53′S 117°17′E
183 Q7 **Narromine** New South Wales, SE Australia 32°16′S 148°15′E
21 R6 **Narrows** Virginia, NE USA 37°19′N 80°48′W
196 M15 **Narsarsuaq** ✈ Kitaa, S Greenland 61°07′N 45°03′W
154 I10 **Narsimhapur** Madhya Pradesh, C India 22°58′N 79°15′E
153 U15 **Narsingdi** *var.* Narsinghdi. Dhaka, C Bangladesh 23°56′N 90°40′E
Narsinghdi *see* Narsingdi
154 H9 **Narsinghgarh** Madhya Pradesh, C India 23°42′N 77°08′E
163 Q11 **Nart** Nei Mongol Zizhiqu, N China 42°54′N 115°55′E
Nartës, Gjol i/Nartës, Laguna e *see* Nartës, Liqeni i
113 J22 **Nartës, Liqeni i** *var.* Gjol i Nartës, Laguna e Nartës. ◎ SW Albania
115 F17 **Narthákі** ▲ C Greece 39°12′N 22°24′E
127 O15 **Nartkala** Kabardino-Balkarskaya Respublika, SW Russian Federation 43°34′N 43°55′E
118 K3 **Narva** Ida-Virumaa, NE Estonia 59°23′N 28°12′E
118 K4 **Narva** *prev.* Narova. ~ Estonia/Russian Federation
118 J3 **Narva Bay** *Est.* Narva Laht, *Ger.* Narwa-Bucht, *Rus.* Narvskiy Zaliv. *bay* Estonia/Russian Federation
Narva Laht *see* Narva Bay
124 F13 **Narva Reservoir** *Est.* Narva Veehoidla, *Rus.* Narvskoye Vodokhranilishche. ⊠ Estonia/Russian Federation
Narva Veehoidla *see* Narva Reservoir
92 H10 **Narvik** Nordland, C Norway 68°26′N 17°24′E
Narvskiy Zaliv *see* Narva Bay
Narvskoye Vodokhranilishche *see* Narva Reservoir
Narwa-Bucht *see* Narva Bay
152 I9 **Narwāna** Haryāna, NW India 29°36′N 76°11′E
125 R4 **Nar'yan-Mar** *prev.* Beloshchel'ye, Dzerzhinskiy. Nenetskiy Avtonomnyy Okrug, NW Russian Federation 67°38′N 53°E
122 J12 **Narym** Tomskaya Oblast', C Russian Federation 58°59′N 81°20′E
Narymskiy Khrebet *see* Khrebet Naryn
147 W9 **Naryn** Narynskaya Oblast', C Kyrgyzstan 41°24′N 76°E
147 U8 **Naryn** ~ Kyrgyzstan/Uzbekistan
145 W16 **Narynkol** *Kaz.* Narynqol. Almaty, SE Kazakhstan 42°45′N 80°12′E
Naryn Oblasty *see* Narynskaya Oblast'
Narynqol *see* Narynkol
147 V9 **Narynskaya Oblast'** *Kir.* Naryn Oblasty. ◆ *province* C Kyrgyzstan
Naryn Zhotasy *see* Khrebet Naryn
126 J6 **Naryshkino** Orlovskaya Oblast', W Russian Federation 53°00′N 35°41′E
95 L14 **Nås** Dalarna, C Sweden 60°28′N 14°30′E
10 J11 **Nass** ~ British Columbia, SW Canada
92 G13 **Nasafjellet** *Lapp.* Násávárre. ▲ C Norway 66°29′N 15°23′E
93 H16 **Nåsåker** Västernorrland, C Sweden 63°27′N 16°55′E
44 H2 **Nassau** ● (Bahamas) New Providence, N Bahamas 25°03′N 77°21′W
187 Y14 **Nasau** Koro, C Fiji 17°20′S 179°26′E
190 J13 **Nassau** *island* N Cook Islands
116 I9 **Năsăud** *Ger.* Nussdorf, *Hung.* Naszód. Bistriţa-Năsăud, N Romania 47°16′N 24°24′E
Násávárre *see* Nasafjellet
103 P13 **Nasbinals** Lozère, S France 44°40′N 03°03′E
Na Sceirí *see* Skerries
Nase *see* Naze
185 E22 **Naseby** Otago, South Island, New Zealand 45°02′S 170°09′E
143 R10 **Nāşerīyeh** Kermān, C Iran
25 X5 **Nash** Texas, SW USA 33°26′N 94°04′W
154 E13 **Nāshik** *prev.* Nāsik. Mahārāshtra, W India 20°05′N 73°48′E
56 E7 **Nashiño, Río** ~ Ecuador/Peru
29 W12 **Nashua** Iowa, C USA 42°57′N 92°32′W
33 W7 **Nashua** Montana, NW USA 48°06′N 106°16′W
19 O10 **Nashua** New Hampshire, NE USA 42°45′N 71°26′W
27 S13 **Nashville** Arkansas, C USA 33°57′N 93°50′W
23 U7 **Nashville** Georgia, SE USA 31°12′N 83°15′W
30 L16 **Nashville** Illinois, N USA 38°20′N 89°22′W
31 O14 **Nashville** Indiana, N USA 39°13′N 86°15′W
21 V9 **Nashville** North Carolina, SE USA 35°58′N 78°00′W
20 J8 **Nashville** *state capital* Tennessee, S USA 36°11′N 86°48′W
20 J9 **Nashville** ✈ Tennessee, S USA 36°06′N 86°44′W
64 H10 **Nashville Seamount** *undersea feature* NW Atlantic Ocean 30°00′N 57°20′W
112 H9 **Našice** Osijek-Baranja, E Croatia 45°29′N 18°05′E
110 M11 **Nasielsk** Mazowieckie, C Poland 52°33′N 20°46′E
93 K18 **Näsijärvi** ◎ SW Finland
Nāsik *see* Nāshik
80 G13 **Nasir** Upper Nile, NE South Sudan 08°37′N 33°06′E
148 K15 **Nasīrābād** Baluchistān, SW Pakistan 26°15′N 62°32′E
Nasir, Buhayrat/Nâşir, Buheiret *see* Nasser, Lake
Nāsiri *see* Ahvāz
Nasiriya *see* An Nāşirīyah
Nás na Ríogh *see* Naas
107 L23 **Naso** Sicilia, Italy, C Mediterranean Sea 38°07′N 14°46′E
Nasratabad *see* Zābol
77 V15 **Nassarawa** Nassarawa, C Nigeria 08°33′N 07°42′E
23 W8 **Nassau Sound** *sound* Florida, SE USA
108 L7 **Nassereith** Tirol, W Austria 47°19′N 10°51′E
80 F5 **Nasser, Lake** *var.* Buhayrat Nasir, Buḩayrat Nāşir, Buḩeiret Nâşir. ◎ Egypt/Sudan
95 L19 **Nässjö** Jönköping, S Sweden 57°39′N 14°40′E
99 K22 **Nassogne** Luxembourg, SE Belgium 50°08′N 05°19′E
12 J6 **Nastapoka Islands** *island group* Northwest Territories, C Canada
93 M19 **Nastola** Etelä-Suomi, S Finland 60°57′N 25°56′E
171 O4 **Nasugbu** Luzon, N Philippines 14°03′N 120°39′E
94 N11 **Näsviken** Gävleborg, C Sweden 61°46′N 16°55′E
Naszód *see* Năsăud
83 I17 **Nata** Central, NE Botswana 20°11′S 26°10′E
54 E11 **Natagaima** Tolima, C Colombia 03°38′N 75°07′W
59 Q14 **Natal** *state capital* Rio Grande do Norte, E Brazil 05°46′S 35°15′W
168 I11 **Natal** Sumatera, N Indonesia 0°32′N 99°07′E
Natal *see* KwaZulu/Natal
173 L10 **Natal Basin** *var.* Mozambique Basin. *undersea feature* W Indian Ocean 30°00′S 40°00′E
25 R12 **Natalia** Texas, SW USA 29°11′N 98°51′W
67 W15 **Natal Valley** *undersea feature* SW Indian Ocean 31°00′S 33°15′E
Natanya *see* Netanya
143 O7 **Naţanz** Eşfahān, C Iran 33°31′N 51°55′E
13 Q11 **Natashquan** Québec, E Canada 50°10′N 61°50′W
13 Q10 **Natashquan** ~ Newfoundland and Labrador/Québec, E Canada
22 J7 **Natchez** Mississippi, S USA 31°34′N 91°24′W
22 G6 **Natchitoches** Louisiana, S USA 31°45′N 93°05′W
108 E10 **Naters** Valais, S Switzerland 46°22′N 08°00′E
Nathanya *see* Netanya
92 O3 **Nathorst Land** *physical region* W Svalbard
186 E9 **National Capital District** ◆ *province* S Papua New Guinea
35 U17 **National City** California, W USA 32°40′N 117°06′W
184 M10 **National Park** Manawatu-Wanganui, North Island, New Zealand 39°11′S 175°22′E
77 R14 **Natitingou** NW Benin 10°21′N 01°26′E
40 B5 **Natividad, Isla** *island* NW Mexico
165 Q10 **Natori** Miyagi, Honshū, C Japan 38°12′N 140°51′E
18 C14 **Natrona Heights** Pennsylvania, NE USA 40°37′N 79°42′W
81 H20 **Natron, Lake** ◎ Kenya/Tanzania
Natsrat *see* Natzrat
166 L7 **Nattalin** Bago, C Myanmar (Burma) 18°25′N 95°34′E
92 J12 **Nattavaara** *Lapp.* Nahtavárr. Norrbotten, N Sweden 66°45′N 20°58′E
109 S3 **Natternbach** Oberösterreich, N Austria 48°26′N 13°44′E
95 M22 **Nättraby** Blekinge, S Sweden 56°12′N 15°30′E
169 P10 **Natuna Besar, Pulau** *island* Kepulauan Natuna, W Indonesia
Natuna Islands *see* Natuna, Kepulauan
169 O9 **Natuna, Kepulauan** *var.* Natuna Islands. *island group* W Indonesia
169 N9 **Natuna, Laut** *Eng.* Natuna Sea. *sea* W Indonesia
Natuna Sea *see* Natuna, Laut
21 N6 **Natural Bridge** *tourist site* Kentucky, C USA
173 V11 **Naturaliste Fracture Zone** *tectonic feature* E Indian Ocean
174 J10 **Naturaliste Plateau** *undersea feature* E Indian Ocean
138 G9 **Natzrat** *var.* Natsrat, *Ar.* En Nazira, *Eng.* Nazareth; *prev.* Nazerat. Northern, N Israel 32°42′N 35°18′E
Nau *see* Nov
103 O14 **Naucelle** Aveyron, S France 44°10′N 02°19′E
83 D20 **Nauchas** Hardap, C Namibia 23°40′S 16°19′E
108 K9 **Nauders** Tirol, W Austria 46°52′N 10°31′E
Naugard *see* Nowogard
118 F12 **Naujamiestis** Panevėžys, C Lithuania 55°42′N 24°10′E
118 E10 **Naujoji Akmenė** Šiaulai, NW Lithuania 56°20′N 22°57′E
149 R16 **Naukot** *var.* Naokot. Sind, SE Pakistan 24°52′N 69°27′E
101 L16 **Naumburg** *var.* Naumburg an der Saale. Sachsen-Anhalt, C Germany 51°09′N 11°48′E
Naumburg am Queis *see* Nowogrodziec
Naumburg an der Saale *see* Naumburg
191 W15 **Naunau** *ancient monument* Easter Island, Chile, E Pacific Ocean
138 G10 **Nā'ūr** 'Ammān, W Jordan 31°52′N 35°50′E
189 Q8 **Nauru** *off.* Republic of Nauru; *prev.* Pleasant Island. ◆ *republic* W Pacific Ocean
175 P5 **Nauru** *island* W Pacific Ocean
189 Q9 **Nauru International** ✈ S Nauru
Nauru, Republic of *see* Nauru
Nausari *see* Navsāri
19 Q12 **Nauset Beach** *beach* Massachusetts, NE USA
Naushahra *see* Nowshera
149 P14 **Naushahro Firoz** Sind, SE Pakistan 26°51′N 68°11′E
Naushara *see* Nowshera
187 X14 **Nausori** Viti Levu, W Fiji 18°01′S 178°31′E
56 F9 **Nauta** Loreto, N Peru 04°31′S 73°36′W
153 O12 **Nautanwa** Uttar Pradesh, N India 27°26′N 83°25′E
41 R13 **Nautla** Veracruz-Llave, E Mexico 20°15′N 96°45′W
Nauzad *see* Now Zād
41 N6 **Nava** Coahuila, NE Mexico 28°28′N 100°45′W
Navabad *see* Navobod
104 L6 **Nava del Rey** Castilla y León, N Spain 41°19′N 05°04′W
153 S15 **Navadwīp** *prev.* Nabadwip. West Bengal, NE India 23°24′N 88°23′E
104 M9 **Navahermosa** Castilla-La Mancha, C Spain 39°39′N 04°25′W
119 I16 **Navahrudak** *Pol.* Nowogródek, *Rus.* Novogrudok. Hrodzyenskaya Voblasts', W Belarus 53°36′N 25°50′E
119 I16 **Navahrudskaye Wzvyshsha** ▲▲ W Belarus
36 M8 **Navajo Mount** ▲ Utah, W USA 37°00′N 110°52′W
37 Q9 **Navajo Reservoir** ⊠ New Mexico, SW USA
104 K9 **Navalmoral de la Mata** Extremadura, W Spain 39°54′N 05°33′W
104 K10 **Navalvillar de Pelea** Extremadura, W Spain 39°05′N 05°27′W
97 F17 **Navan** *Ir.* An Uaimh. E Ireland 53°39′N 06°41′W
Navanagar *see* Jāmnagar
118 L12 **Navapolatsk** *Rus.* Novopolotsk. Vitsyebskaya Voblasts', N Belarus 55°34′N 28°35′E
149 P6 **Nāvar, Dasht-e** *Pash.* Dasht-i-Nawar. *desert* C Afghanistan
123 W6 **Navarin, Mys** *headland* NE Russian Federation 62°18′N 179°06′E
63 I25 **Navarino, Isla** *island* S Chile
105 Q4 **Navarra** *Eng./Fr.* Navarre. ◆ *autonomous community* N Spain
Navarre *see* Navarra
105 P4 **Navarrete** La Rioja, N Spain 42°26′N 02°34′W
61 C20 **Navarro** Buenos Aires, E Argentina 35°00′S 59°15′W
105 O12 **Navas de San Juan** Andalucía, S Spain 38°11′N 03°19′W
25 V10 **Navasota** Texas, SW USA 30°23′N 96°05′W
25 U9 **Navasota River** ~ Texas, SW USA
44 J10 **Navassa Island** ◇ *US unincorporated territory* C West Indies
119 L19 **Navasyolki** *Rus.* Novosëlki. Homyel'skaya Voblasts', SE Belarus 52°24′N 28°33′E
119 H17 **Navayel'nya** *Pol.* Nowojelnia, *Rus.* Novoyel'nya. Hrodzyenskaya Voblasts', W Belarus 53°28′N 25°35′E
171 Y13 **Naver** Papua, E Indonesia 03°27′S 139°45′E
118 H5 **Navesti** ~ C Estonia
104 J2 **Navia** Asturias, N Spain 43°33′N 06°43′W
104 J2 **Navia** ~ NW Spain
59 I21 **Naviraí** Mato Grosso do Sul, SW Brazil 23°01′S 54°09′W
126 I6 **Navlya** Bryanskaya Oblast', W Russian Federation 52°47′N 34°28′E
187 X13 **Navoalevu** Vanua Levu, N Fiji 16°22′S 179°28′E
147 R12 **Navobod** *Rus.* Navabad, Novabad. C Tajikistan 39°00′N 70°06′E
147 P13 **Navobod** *Rus.* Navabad. W Tajikistan 38°37′N 68°42′E
Navoi *see* Navoiy
146 M11 **Navoiy** *Rus.* Navoi. Navoiy Viloyati, C Uzbekistan 40°05′N 65°23′E
Navoiyskaya Oblast' *see* Navoiy Viloyati
146 K8 **Navoiy Viloyati** *Rus.* Navoiyskaya Oblast'. ◆ *province* N Uzbekistan
40 G7 **Navojoa** Sonora, NW Mexico 27°04′N 109°28′W
Navolat *see* Navolato
40 H9 **Navolato** *var.* Navolat. Sinaloa, C Mexico 24°46′N 107°42′W
187 Q13 **Navonda** Ambae, C Vanuatu 15°21′S 167°58′E
Návpaktos *see* Náfpaktos
Návplion *see* Náfplio
77 P14 **Navrongo** N Ghana 10°51′N 01°03′W
154 D12 **Navsāri** *var.* Nausari. Gujarāt, W India 20°55′N 72°55′E
187 X15 **Navua** Viti Levu, W Fiji 18°15′S 178°10′E
138 H8 **Nawá** Dar'ā, S Syria 32°53′N 36°03′E
Nawabashah *see* Nawābshāh
153 S14 **Nawabganj** Rajshahi, NW Bangladesh 24°35′N 88°21′E
153 N12 **Nawābganj** Uttar Pradesh, N India 26°52′N 82°09′E
149 Q15 **Nawābshāh** *var.* Nawabashah. Sind, S Pakistan 26°15′N 68°26′E
153 P14 **Nawāda** Bihār, N India 24°54′N 85°33′E
152 H11 **Nawalgarh** Rājasthān, N India 27°48′N 75°21′E
Nawāl, Sabkhat an *see* Noual, Sebkhet en
Nawar, Dasht-i- *see* Nāvar, Dasht-e
167 N4 **Nawngkhio** *var.* Nawngkio. Shan State, C Myanmar (Burma) 22°17′N 96°50′E
Nawngkio *see* Nawngkhio
137 U13 **Naxçıvan** *Rus.* Nakhichevan'. SW Azerbaijan 39°14′N 45°24′E
160 I10 **Naxi** Sichuan, C China 28°50′N 105°20′E
115 K21 **Náxos** *var.* Naxos. Náxos, Kykládes, Greece, Aegean Sea 37°06′N 25°24′E
115 K21 **Náxos** *island* Kykládes, Greece, Aegean Sea
40 J11 **Nayarit** ◆ *state* C Mexico
187 Y14 **Nayau** *island* Lau Group, E Fiji
143 S8 **Nāy Band** Yazd, E Iran 32°26′N 57°30′E
165 T2 **Nayoro** Hokkaidō, NE Japan 44°22′N 142°27′E
166 M7 **Nay Pyi Taw** ● (Myanmar) C Myanmar (Burma) 19°45′N 96°06′E
104 F9 **Nazaré** *var.* Nazare. Leiria, C Portugal 39°36′N 09°04′W
24 M4 **Nazareth** Texas, SW USA 34°32′N 102°06′W
Nazareth *see* Natzrat
173 O8 **Nazareth Bank** *undersea feature* W Indian Ocean
40 K9 **Nazas** Durango, C Mexico 25°15′N 104°06′W
57 F16 **Nazca** Ica, S Peru 14°53′S 74°54′W
0 L17 **Nazca Plate** *tectonic feature*
193 U9 **Nazca Ridge** *undersea feature* E Pacific Ocean 22°00′S 82°00′W
165 V15 **Naze** *var.* Nase. Kagoshima, Amami-ōshima, SW Japan 28°21′N 129°30′E
Nazerat *see* Natzrat
137 R14 **Nazik Gölü** ◎ E Turkey
136 C15 **Nazilli** Aydın, SW Turkey 37°55′N 28°20′E
137 P14 **Nazımiye** Tunceli, E Turkey 39°12′N 39°51′E
Nazinon *see* Red Volta
10 L15 **Nazko** British Columbia, SW Canada 52°57′N 123°44′W
127 O16 **Nazran'** Respublika Ingushetiya, SW Russian Federation 43°14′N 44°47′E
80 J13 **Nazrēt** *var.* Adama, Hadama. Oromīya, C Ethiopia 08°31′N 39°20′E
Nazwāh *see* Nizwa
82 J13 **Nchanga** Copperbelt, C Zambia 12°30′S 27°53′E
82 J11 **Nchelenge** Luapula, N Zambia 09°20′S 28°50′E
Ncheu *see* Ntcheu
83 J25 **Nciba** *Eng.* Great Kei; *prev.* Groot-Kei. ~ South Africa
Ndaghamcha, Sebkra de *see* Te-n-Dghâmcha, Sebkhet
81 G21 **Ndala** Tabora, C Tanzania 04°45′S 33°15′E
82 B11 **N'Dalatando** *Port.* Salazar, Vila Salazar. Cuanza Norte, NW Angola 09°19′S 14°48′E
77 S14 **Ndali** C Benin 09°50′N 02°46′E
81 E18 **Ndeke** SW Uganda 0°11′S 30°04′E
78 J13 **Ndélé** Bamingui-Bangoran, N Central African Republic 08°24′N 20°41′E
79 E19 **Ndendé** Ngounié, S Gabon 02°21′S 11°20′E
79 E20 **Ndindi** Nyanga, S Gabon 03°47′S 11°06′E
78 G11 **Ndjamena** *var.* N'Djamena; *prev.* Fort-Lamy. ● (Chad) Chari-Baguirmi, W Chad 12°08′N 15°02′E
78 G11 **Ndjamena** ✈ Chari-Baguirmi, W Chad 12°09′N 15°00′E
N'Djamena *see* Ndjamena
79 D18 **Ndjolé** Moyen-Ogooué, W Gabon 0°07′S 10°45′E
82 J13 **Ndola** Copperbelt, C Zambia 12°59′S 28°35′E
Ndrhamcha, Sebkha de *see* Te-n-Dghâmcha, Sebkhet
79 L15 **Ndu** Orientale, N Dem. Rep. Congo 04°36′N 22°49′E
81 H21 **Nduguti** Singida, C Tanzania 04°19′S 34°40′E
186 M9 **Nduindui** Guadalcanal, C Solomon Islands 09°46′S 159°54′E
Nduke *see* Kolombangara
Ndzouani *see* Nzwani
115 F16 **Néa Anchíalos** *var.* Nea Anhialos, Néa Anhíalos. Thessalía, C Greece 39°16′N 22°49′E
Nea Anhialos/Néa Anhíalos *see* Néa Anchíalos
115 H18 **Néa Artáki** Évvoia, C Greece 38°31′N 23°39′E
97 F15 **Neagh, Lough** ◎ E Northern Ireland, United Kingdom
32 F7 **Neah Bay** Washington, NW USA 48°21′N 124°39′W
115 J22 **Nea Kaméni** *island* Kykládes, Greece, Aegean Sea
181 O8 **Neale, Lake** ◎ Northern Territory, C Australia
182 G2 **Neales River** *seasonal river* South Australia
115 G14 **Néa Moudanía** *var.* Néa Moudhaniá. Kentrikí Makedonía, N Greece 40°14′N 23°17′E
Néa Moudhaniá *see* Néa Moudanía
116 K10 **Neamţ** ◆ *county* NE Romania
Neapel *see* Napoli
115 D14 **Neápoli** *prev.* Neápolis. Dytikí Makedonía, N Greece 40°19′N 21°23′E
115 K25 **Neápoli** Kríti, Greece, E Mediterranean Sea 35°15′N 25°37′E
115 G22 **Neápoli** Pelopónnisos, S Greece 36°29′N 23°05′E
Neápolis *see* Neápoli, Greece
Neapolis *see* Napoli, Italy
Neapolis *see* Nablus, West Bank
38 D16 **Near Islands** *island group* Aleutian Islands, Alaska, USA
97 J21 **Neath** S Wales, United Kingdom 51°40′N 03°48′W
114 H13 **Néa Zíchni** *var.* Néa Zíkhni; *prev.* Néa Zíkhna. Kentrikí Makedonía, NE Greece 41°02′N 23°50′E
Néa Zíkhna/Néa Zíkhni *see* Néa Zíchni
42 C5 **Nebaj** Quiché, W Guatemala 15°25′N 91°05′W
77 P13 **Nebbou** S Burkina 11°22′N 01°49′W
Nebitdag *see* Balkanabat
54 M13 **Neblina, Pico da** ▲ NW Brazil 0°49′N 66°31′W
124 I13 **Nebolchi** Novgorodskaya Oblast', W Russian Federation 59°08′N 33°19′E
36 L4 **Nebo, Mount** ▲ Utah, W USA 39°47′N 111°46′W
28 L14 **Nebraska** *off.* State of Nebraska, *also known as* Blackwater State, Cornhusker State, Tree Planters State. ◆ *state* C USA
29 S16 **Nebraska City** Nebraska, C USA 40°38′N 95°52′W
107 K23 **Nebrodi, Monti** *var.* Monti Caronie. ▲▲ Sicilia, Italy, C Mediterranean Sea
10 L14 **Nechako** ~ British Columbia, SW Canada
29 Q2 **Neche** North Dakota, N USA 48°57′N 97°33′W
25 V8 **Neches** Texas, SW USA 31°51′N 95°28′W
25 W8 **Neches River** ~ Texas, SW USA
101 H20 **Neckar** ~ SW Germany
101 H20 **Neckarsulm** Baden-Württemberg, SW Germany 49°12′N 09°13′E
192 L5 **Necker Island** *island* C British Virgin Islands
175 U3 **Necker Ridge** *undersea feature* N Pacific Ocean
61 D23 **Necochea** Buenos Aires, E Argentina 38°34′S 58°42′W
104 H2 **Neda** Galicia, NW Spain 43°29′N 08°09′W
115 E20 **Néda** *var.* Nédas. ~ S Greece
Nédas *see* Néda
114 J12 **Nedelino** Smolyan, S Bulgaria 41°27′N 25°05′E
25 Y11 **Nederland** Texas, SW USA 29°58′N 93°59′W
Nederland *see* Netherlands
98 K12 **Neder Rijn** *Eng.* Lower Rhine. ~ C Netherlands
99 L16 **Nederweert** Limburg, SE Netherlands 51°17′N 05°45′E
95 G16 **Nedre Tokke** ◎ S Norway
Nedrigaylov *see* Nedryhayliv
117 S3 **Nedryhayliv** *Rus.* Nedrigaylov. Sums'ka Oblast', NE Ukraine 50°51′N 33°54′E
98 O11 **Neede** Gelderland, E Netherlands 52°08′N 06°36′E
33 T13 **Needle Mountain** ▲ Wyoming, C USA 44°03′N 109°33′W
35 Y14 **Needles** California, W USA 34°50′N 114°37′W
97 M24 **Needles, The** *rocks* S England, United Kingdom
62 O7 **Ñeembucú** *off.* Departamento de Ñeembucú. ◆ *department* SW Paraguay
Ñeembucú, Departamento de *see* Ñeembucú
30 M7 **Neenah** Wisconsin, N USA 44°09′N 88°26′W
11 W16 **Neepawa** Manitoba, S Canada 50°14′N 99°29′W
99 K16 **Neerpelt** Limburg, NE Belgium 51°13′N 05°26′E
74 M6 **Nefta** ✈ W Tunisia 34°03′N 08°05′E
126 L15 **Neftegorsk** Krasnodarskiy Kray, SW Russian Federation 44°21′N 39°40′E
127 U3 **Neftekamsk** Respublika Bashkortostan, W Russian Federation 56°07′N 54°13′E
127 O14 **Neftekumsk** Stavropol'skiy Kray, SW Russian Federation 44°45′N 45°00′E
Neftezavodsk *see* Seýdi
82 C10 **Negage** *var.* N'Gage. Uíge, NW Angola 07°47′S 15°27′E
Negapatam/Negapattinam *see* Nāgappattinam
169 T17 **Negara** Bali, Indonesia 08°21′S 114°35′E
169 T13 **Negara** Borneo, C Indonesia 02°40′S 115°05′E
Negara Brunei Darussalam *see* Brunei
31 N4 **Negaunee** Michigan, N USA 46°30′N 87°36′W
81 J15 **Negēlē** *var.* Negelli, *It.* Neghelli. Oromīya, C Ethiopia 05°13′N 39°43′E
Negelli *see* Negēlē
Negeri Pahang Darul Makmur *see* Pahang
Negeri Selangor Darul Ehsan *see* Selangor
168 K9 **Negeri Sembilan** *var.* Negri Sembilan. ◆ *state* Peninsular Malaysia
92 P3 **Negerpynten** *headland* S Svalbard 77°15′N 22°40′E
Negev *see* HaNegev
Neghelli *see* Negēlē
116 I12 **Negoiu** *var.* Negoiul. ▲ S Romania 45°34′N 24°34′E
Negoiul *see* Negoiu
82 P13 **Negomane** *var.* Negomano. Cabo Delgado, N Mozambique 11°22′S 38°32′E
Negomano *see* Negomane
155 J25 **Negombo** Western Province, SW Sri Lanka 07°13′N 79°51′E
191 W11 **Negonego** *prev.* Nengonengo. *atoll* Îles Tuamotu, C French Polynesia
Negoreloye *see* Nyeharelaye
112 P12 **Negotin** Serbia, E Serbia 44°14′N 22°31′E
113 P19 **Negotino** C Macedonia 41°29′N 22°04′E
56 A10 **Negra, Punta** *headland* NW Peru 06°03′S 81°08′W
104 G3 **Negreira** Galicia, NW Spain 42°54′N 08°46′W
116 L10 **Negreşti** Vaslui, E Romania 46°50′N 27°28′E
Negreşti *see* Negreşti-Oaş
116 H8 **Negreşti-Oaş** *Hung.* Avasfelsőfalu; *prev.* Negreşti. Satu Mare, NE Romania 47°56′N 23°22′E
44 H12 **Negril** W Jamaica 18°16′N 78°21′W
Negri Sembilan *see* Negeri Sembilan
63 K15 **Negro, Río** ~ E Argentina
62 N7 **Negro, Río** ~ NE Argentina
57 N17 **Negro, Río** ~ E Bolivia
48 F6 **Negro, Río** ~ N South America
61 E18 **Negro, Río** ~ Brazil/Uruguay
62 O5 **Negro, Río** ~ C Paraguay
Negro, Río *see* Chixoy, Río, Guatemala/Mexico
Negro, Río *see* Sico Tinto, Río, Honduras
171 P6 **Negros** *island* C Philippines
116 M15 **Negru Vodă** Constanţa, SE Romania 43°49′N 28°12′E
13 P13 **Neguac** New Brunswick, SE Canada 47°16′N 65°04′W
14 B7 **Negwazu, Lake** ◎ Ontario, S Canada
Négyfalu *see* Săcele
32 F10 **Nehalem** Oregon, NW USA 45°42′N 123°55′W
32 F10 **Nehalem River** ~ Oregon, NW USA
Nehavend *see* Nahāvand
143 V9 **Nehbandān** Khorāsān, E Iran 31°00′N 60°00′E
163 V6 **Nehe** Heilongjiang, NE China 48°28′N 124°52′E
193 Y14 **Neiafu** 'Uta Vava'u, N Tonga 18°36′S 173°58′W
45 N9 **Neiba** *var.* Neyba. SW Dominican Republic 18°31′N 71°25′W
Néid, Carn Uí *see* Mizen Head
92 M9 **Neiden** Finnmark, N Norway 69°41′N 29°23′E
Neidín *see* Kenmare
Néifinn *see* Nephin
103 S10 **Neige, Crêt de la** ▲ E France 46°18′N 05°58′E
173 O16 **Neiges, Piton des** ▲ C Réunion 21°05′S 55°28′E
15 R9 **Neiges, Rivière des** ~ Québec, SE Canada
160 I10 **Neijiang** Sichuan, C China 29°32′N 105°03′E
30 K6 **Neillsville** Wisconsin, N USA 44°34′N 90°36′W
Nei Monggol Zizhiqu/Nei Mongol *see* Nei Mongol Zizhiqu

◆ Country ● Country Capital ◇ Dependent Territory ○ Dependent Territory Capital ◆ Administrative Regions ✈ International Airport ▲ Mountain ▲▲ Mountain Range Volcano ~ River ◎ Lake ⊠ Reservoir

163 Q10 Nei Mongol Gaoyuan plateau NE China
163 O12 Nei Mongol Zizhiqu var. Nei Mongol, Eng. Inner Mongolia, Inner Mongolian Autonomous Region; prev. Nei Monggol Zizhiqu. ◈ autonomous region N China
161 O4 Neiqiu Hebei, E China 37°22′N 114°34′E
Neiriz see Neyrīz
101 Q16 Neisse Cz. Lužická Nisa Pol. Nisa, Ger. Lausitzer Neisse, Nysa Łużycka. ≈ C Europe
Neisse see Nysa
54 E11 Neiva Huila, S Colombia 02°58′N 75°15′W
160 M7 Neixiang Henan, C China 33°08′N 111°50′E
Nejafabad see Najafābād
11 V9 Nejanilini Lake ◎ Manitoba, C Canada
Nejd see Najd
80 I13 Nek'emtē var. Lakemti, Nakamti. Oromīya, C Ethiopia 09°06′N 36°31′E
126 M9 Nekhayevskaya Volgogradskaya Oblast', SW Russian Federation 50°25′N 41°44′E
30 K7 Nekoosa Wisconsin, N USA 44°19′N 89°54′W
Neksø Bornholm see Nexø
104 H7 Nelas Viseu, N Portugal 40°32′N 07°52′W
124 H16 Nelidovo Tverskaya Oblast', W Russian Federation 56°13′N 32°45′E
29 P13 Neligh Nebraska, C USA 42°07′N 98°01′W
123 R11 Nel'kan Khabarovskiy Kray, E Russian Federation 57°44′N 136°09′E
92 M10 Nellim var. Nellimö, Lapp. Njellim. Lappi, N Finland 68°49′N 28°18′E
Nellimö see Nellim
155 J18 Nellore Andhra Pradesh, E India 14°29′N 80°E
61 B17 Nelson Santa Fe, C Argentina 31°16′S 60°45′W
11 O17 Nelson British Columbia, SW Canada 49°29′N 117°17′W
185 I14 Nelson Nelson, South Island, New Zealand 41°17′S 173°17′E
97 L17 Nelson NW England, United Kingdom 53°51′N 02°13′W
29 P17 Nelson Nebraska, C USA 40°12′N 98°04′W
185 J14 Nelson ◈ unitary authority South Island, New Zealand
11 X12 Nelson ≈ Manitoba, C Canada
183 U8 Nelson Bay New South Wales, SE Australia 32°48′S 152°10′E
182 K13 Nelson, Cape headland Victoria, SE Australia 38°25′S 141°33′E
63 G23 Nelson, Estrecho strait SE Pacific Ocean
11 W12 Nelson House Manitoba, C Canada 55°49′N 98°51′W
30 J4 Nelson Lake ◎ Wisconsin, N USA
31 T14 Nelsonville Ohio, N USA 39°27′N 82°13′W
27 S2 Nelsoon River ≈ Iowa/Missouri, C USA
83 K21 Nelspruit Mpumalanga, NE South Africa 25°28′S 30°58′E
76 L10 Néma Hodh ech Chargui, SE Mauritania 16°32′N 07°12′W
118 D13 Neman Ger. Ragnit. Kaliningradskaya Oblast', W Russian Federation 55°01′N 22°00′E
84 I9 Neman Bel. Nyoman, Ger. Memel, Lith. Nemunas, Pol. Niemen. ≈ NE Europe
Nemausus see Nîmes
115 F19 Neméa Pelopónnisos, S Greece 37°49′N 22°40′E
Německý Brod see Havlíčkův Brod
14 D7 Nemegosenda ≈ Ontario, S Canada
14 D8 Nemegosenda Lake ◎ Ontario, S Canada
119 H14 Nemenčinė Vilnius, SE Lithuania 54°50′N 25°29′E
Nemetocenna see Arras
Nemirov see Nemyriv
103 O6 Nemours Seine-et-Marne, N France 48°16′N 02°41′E
Nemunas see Neman
165 W4 Nemuro Hokkaidō, NE Japan 43°20′N 145°35′E
165 W4 Nemuro-hantō peninsula Hokkaidō, NE Japan
165 W3 Nemuro-kaikyō strait Japan/Russian Federation
165 W4 Nemuro-wan bay N Japan
116 H5 Nemyriv Rus. Nemirov. L'vivs'ka Oblast', NW Ukraine 50°08′N 23°28′E
117 N7 Nemyriv Rus. Nemirov. Vinnyts'ka Oblast', C Ukraine 48°58′N 28°50′E
97 D19 Nenagh Ir. An tAonach. Tipperary, C Ireland 52°52′N 08°12′W
39 R9 Nenana Alaska, USA 64°33′N 149°05′W
39 R9 Nenana River ≈ Alaska, USA
187 P10 Nendö var. Swallow Island. island Santa Cruz Islands, E Solomon Islands
97 O19 Nene ≈ E England, United Kingdom
125 R4 Nenetskiy Avtonomnyy Okrug ◈ autonomous district Arkhangel'skaya Oblast', NW Russian Federation
Nengonengo see Negonego
163 V6 Nenjiang Heilongjiang, NE China 49°11′N 125°18′E
163 U6 Nen Jiang var. Nonni. ≈ NE China
189 P16 Neoch atoll Caroline Islands, C Micronesia
115 D18 Neochóri Dytikí Elláda, C Greece 38°23′N 21°14′E
27 Q7 Neodesha Kansas, C USA 37°25′N 95°40′W
29 S14 Neola Iowa, C USA 41°27′N 95°40′W
115 E16 Néo Monastíri var. Néon Monastiri. Thessalía, C Greece 39°22′N 21°55′E
Néon Karlovasi/Néon Karlovásion see Karlovási
Néon Monastiri see Néo Monastíri
27 R8 Neosho Missouri, C USA 36°53′N 94°24′W
27 Q7 Neosho River ≈ Kansas/Oklahoma, C USA
123 N12 Nepa ≈ C Russian Federation
153 N10 Nepal off. Nepal. ◆ monarchy S Asia
Nepal see Nepal
152 M11 Nepālganj Mid Western, SW Nepal 28°04′N 81°37′E
14 L13 Nepean Ontario, SE Canada 45°19′N 75°54′W
36 L4 Nephi Utah, W USA 39°43′N 111°50′W
97 B16 Nephin Ir. Néifinn. ▲ W Ireland 54°00′N 09°21′W
67 T9 Nepoko ≈ NE Dem. Rep. Congo
18 K15 Neptune New Jersey, NE USA 40°10′N 74°03′W
182 G10 Neptune Islands island group South Australia
107 I14 Nera anc. Nar. ≈ C Italy
102 L14 Nérac Lot-et-Garonne, SW France 44°08′N 00°21′E
111 D16 Neratovice Ger. Neratowitz. Středocesky Kraj, C Czech Republic 50°16′N 14°31′E
Neratowitz see Neratovice
123 O13 Nercha ≈ S Russian Federation
123 O13 Nerchinsk Zabaykal'skiy Kray, S Russian Federation 52°01′N 116°25′E
123 P14 Nerchinskiy Zavod Zabaykal'skiy Kray, S Russian Federation 51°13′N 119°25′E
124 M15 Nerekhta Kostromskaya Oblast', NW Russian Federation 57°27′N 40°33′E
118 H10 Nereta S Latvia 56°12′N 25°18′E
106 K13 Nereto Abruzzo, C Italy 42°49′N 13°50′E
113 H15 Neretva ≈ Bosnia and Herzegovina/Croatia
115 C17 Nerikós ruins Lefkáda, Iónia Nisiá, Greece, C Mediterranean Sea
83 F15 Neriquinha Cuando Cubango, SE Angola 15°44′S 21°34′E
118 I13 Neris Bel. Viliya, Pol. Wilia; prev. Pol. Wilja. ≈ Belarus/Lithuania
Neris see Viliya
105 N15 Nerja Andalucía, S Spain 36°45′N 03°35′W
124 L16 Nerl' ≈ W Russian Federation
105 P12 Nerpio Castilla-La Mancha, C Spain 38°08′N 02°18′W
104 J13 Nerva Andalucía, S Spain 37°40′N 06°31′W
98 L4 Nes Fryslân, N Netherlands 53°28′N 05°46′E
94 G13 Nesbyen Buskerud, S Norway 60°36′N 09°35′E
114 M9 Nesebŭr Burgas, E Bulgaria 42°40′N 27°43′E
92 L2 Neskaupstadhur Austurland, E Iceland 65°08′N 13°45′W
92 F13 Nesna Nordland, C Norway 66°11′N 12°54′E
26 K5 Ness City Kansas, C USA 38°27′N 99°54′W
Nesselsdorf see Kopřivnice
108 H7 Nesslau Sankt Gallen, NE Switzerland 47°13′N 09°12′E
96 I9 Ness, Loch ◎ N Scotland, United Kingdom
Nesterov see Zhovkva
114 I12 Néstos Bul. Mesta, Turk. Kara Su. ≈ Bulgaria/Greece see also Mesta
Néstos see Mesta
95 C14 Nesttun Hordaland, S Norway 60°19′N 05°16′E
Nesvizh see Nyasvizh
138 F9 Netanya var. Natanya, Nathanya. Central, C Israel 32°20′N 34°51′E
98 I9 Netherlands off. Kingdom of the Netherlands, var. Holland, Dut. Koninkrijk der Nederlanden, Nederland. ◆ monarchy NW Europe
Netherlands East Indies see Indonesia
Netherlands Guiana see Suriname
Netherlands, Kingdom of the see Netherlands
Netherlands New Guinea see Papua
116 L4 Netishyn Khmel'nyts'ka Oblast', W Ukraine 50°20′N 26°38′E
138 E11 Netivot Southern, S Israel 31°26′N 34°36′E
107 O21 Neto ≈ S Italy
9 Q6 Nettilling Lake ◎ Baffin Island, Nunavut, N Canada
29 V3 Nett Lake ◎ Minnesota, N USA
107 I16 Nettuno Lazio, C Italy 41°27′N 12°40′E
Netum see Noto
41 U16 Netzahualcóyotl, Presa ⊠ SE Mexico
Netze see Noteć
Neu Amerika see Puławy
Neubetsche see Novi Bečej
Neubidschow see Nový Bydžov
Neubistritz see Nová Bystřice
100 N9 Neubrandenburg Mecklenburg-Vorpommern, NE Germany 53°33′N 13°16′E
101 K22 Neuburg an der Donau Bayern, S Germany 48°43′N 11°10′E
108 C8 Neuchâtel Ger. Neuenburg. Neuchâtel, W Switzerland 46°59′N 06°55′E
108 C8 Neuchâtel Ger. Neuenburg. ◈ canton W Switzerland
108 C8 Neuchâtel, Lac de Ger. Neuenburger See. ◎ W Switzerland
Neudorf see Spišská Nová Ves
100 L10 Neue Elde canal N Germany
Neuenburg see Neuchâtel
Neuenburg an der Elbe see Nymburk
Neuenburger See see Neuchâtel, Lac de
108 F7 Neuenhof Aargau, N Switzerland 47°27′N 08°17′E
100 H11 Neuenland ✈ (Bremen) Bremen, NW Germany 53°03′N 08°46′E
Neuenstadt see La Neuveville
101 C18 Neuerburg Rheinland-Pfalz, W Germany 50°01′N 06°13′E
99 K24 Neufchâteau Luxembourg, SE Belgium 49°50′N 05°26′E
103 S6 Neufchâteau Vosges, NE France 48°21′N 05°42′E
102 M3 Neufchâtel-en-Bray Seine-Maritime, N France 49°44′N 01°26′E
109 S3 Neufelden Oberösterreich, N Austria 48°27′N 14°01′E
Neugradisk see Nova Gradiška
Neuhaus see Jindřichův Hradec
Neuhäusel see Nové Zámky
108 G6 Neuhausen var. Neuhausen am Rheinfall. Schaffhausen, N Switzerland 47°24′N 08°37′E
Neuhausen am Rheinfall see Neuhausen
101 I17 Neuhof Hessen, C Germany 50°26′N 09°34′E
Neuhof see Zgierz
Neukuhren see Pionerskiy
Neu-Langenburg see Tukuyu
109 W4 Neulengbach Niederösterreich, NE Austria 48°10′N 15°53′E
113 G15 Neum Federacija Bosna I Hercegovina, S Bosnia and Herzegovina 42°57′N 17°33′E
Neumark see Nowy Targ, Małopolskie, Poland
Neumark see Nowe Miasto Lubawskie, Warmińsko-Mazurskie, Poland
Neumarkt see Neumarkt im Hausruckkreis, Oberösterreich, Austria
Neumarkt see Neumarkt am Wallersee, Salzburg, Austria
Neumarkt see Sroda Śląska, Dolnośląskie, Poland
Neumarkt see Târgu Secuiesc, Covasna, Romania
Neumarkt see Târgu Mureş
109 Q5 Neumarkt am Wallersee var. Neumarkt. Salzburg, NW Austria 47°55′N 13°16′E
109 R4 Neumarkt im Hausruckkreis var. Neumarkt. Oberösterreich, N Austria 48°16′N 13°40′E
101 L20 Neumarkt in der Oberpfalz Bayern, SE Germany 49°16′N 11°28′E
Neumarktl see Tržič
Neumoldowa see Moldova Nouă
100 J8 Neumünster Schleswig-Holstein, N Germany 54°04′N 09°59′E
109 X5 Neunkirchen var. Neunkirchen am Steinfeld. Niederösterreich, E Austria 47°44′N 16°05′E
101 E20 Neunkirchen Saarland, SW Germany 49°21′N 07°11′E
Neunkirchen am Steinfeld see Neunkirchen
Neuoderberg see Bohumín
63 I15 Neuquén Neuquén, SE Argentina 39°03′S 68°36′W
63 H14 Neuquén off. Provincia de Neuquén. ◈ province W Argentina
Neuquén, Provincia de see Neuquén
63 H14 Neuquén, Río ≈ W Argentina
Neurode see Nowa Ruda
100 N11 Neuruppin Brandenburg, NE Germany 52°56′N 12°49′E
Neusalz an der Oder see Nowa Sól
Neu Sandec see Nowy Sącz
101 K22 Neusäss Bayern, S Germany 48°24′N 10°49′E
Neusatz see Novi Sad
Neuschliss see Gherla
21 N8 Neuse River ≈ North Carolina, SE USA
109 Z5 Neusiedl am See Burgenland, E Austria 47°58′N 16°51′E
111 G22 Neusiedler See Hung. Fertő. ◎ Austria/Hungary
Neusohl see Banská Bystrica
101 D15 Neuss anc. Novaesium, Novesium. Nordrhein-Westfalen, W Germany 51°12′N 06°42′E
Neuss see Nyon
Neustadt see Neustadt bei Coburg, Bayern, Germany
Neustadt see Neustadt an der Aisch, Bayern, Germany
Neustadt see Prudnik, Opole, Poland
Neustadt see Baia Mare, Maramureş, Romania
100 I12 Neustadt am Rübenberge Niedersachsen, N Germany 52°30′N 09°28′E
101 J19 Neustadt an der Aisch var. Neustadt. Bayern, C Germany 49°34′N 10°36′E
Neustadt an der Haardt see Neustadt an der Weinstrasse
101 F20 Neustadt an der Weinstrasse prev. Neustadt an der Haardt, hist. Niewenstat; anc. Nova Civitas. Rheinland-Pfalz, SW Germany 49°21′N 08°09′E
101 K18 Neustadt bei Coburg var. Neustadt. Bayern, C Germany 50°19′N 11°06′E
Neustadt bei Pinne see Lwówek
Neustadt in Oberschlesien see Prudnik
Neustadtl see Novo mesto
Neustadtl in Mähren see Nové Město na Moravě
Neustettin see Szczecinek
108 M8 Neustift im Stubaital var. Stubaital. Tirol, W Austria 47°07′N 11°26′E
100 N10 Neustrelitz Mecklenburg-Vorpommern, NE Germany 53°22′N 13°05′E
Neutitschein see Nový Jičín
Neutra see Nitra
101 J22 Neu-Ulm Bayern, S Germany 48°23′N 10°02′E
Neuveville see La Neuveville
103 N12 Neuvic Corrèze, C France 45°23′N 02°16′E
Neuwarp see Nowe Warpno
100 G9 Neuwerk island NW Germany
101 E17 Neuwied Rheinland-Pfalz, W Germany 50°26′N 07°28′E
Neuzen see Terneuzen
124 H12 Neva ≈ NW Russian Federation
29 V14 Nevada Iowa, C USA 42°01′N 93°27′W
27 R6 Nevada Missouri, C USA 37°51′N 94°22′W
35 R5 Nevada off. State of Nevada, also known as Battle Born State, Sagebrush State, Silver State. ◈ state W USA
35 P6 Nevada City California, W USA 39°15′N 121°02′W
105 O14 NevadaSierra ▲▲ S Spain
35 P6 Nevada, Sierra ▲▲ W USA
62 I13 Nevado, Sierra del ▲▲ W Argentina
124 G16 Nevel' Pskovskaya Oblast', W Russian Federation 56°01′N 29°54′E
123 T14 Nevel'sk Ostrov Sakhalin, Sakhalinskaya Oblast', SE Russian Federation 46°41′N 141°54′E
123 Q13 Never Amurskaya Oblast', SE Russian Federation 53°58′N 124°04′E
127 Q6 Neverkino Penzenskaya Oblast', W Russian Federation 52°53′N 46°46′E
103 P9 Nevers anc. Noviodunum. Nièvre, C France 47°N 03°09′E
18 J12 Neversink River ≈ New York, NE USA
183 Q6 Nevertire New South Wales, SE Australia 31°52′S 147°42′E
113 H15 Nevesinje ◈ Republika Srpska, S Bosnia and Herzegovina
118 G12 Nevėžis ≈ C Lithuania
138 F11 Neve Zohar prev. Newé Zohar. Southern, E Israel 31°07′N 35°23′E
126 M14 Nevinnomyssk Stavropol'skiy Kray, SW Russian Federation 44°39′N 41°57′E
45 W10 Nevis island Saint Kitts and Nevis
Nevoso, Monte see Veliki Snežnik
Nevrokop see Gotse Delchev
136 J14 Nevşehir var. Nevshehr. Nevşehir, C Turkey 38°38′N 34°43′E
136 J14 Nevşehir var. Nevshehr. ◈ province C Turkey
Nevshehr see Nevşehir
122 G10 Nev'yansk Sverdlovskaya Oblast', C Russian Federation 57°26′N 60°15′E
81 J25 Newala Mtwara, SE Tanzania 10°59′S 39°18′E
31 P16 New Albany Indiana, N USA 38°17′N 85°50′W
22 M2 New Albany Mississippi, S USA 34°29′N 89°00′W
29 Y11 New Albin Iowa, C USA 43°30′N 91°17′W
55 U8 New Amsterdam E Guyana 06°17′N 57°31′W
183 Q4 New Angledool New South Wales, SE Australia 29°06′S 147°54′E
21 Y2 Newark Delaware, NE USA 39°42′N 75°45′W
18 K14 Newark New Jersey, NE USA 40°42′N 74°12′W
18 G10 Newark New York, NE USA 43°01′N 77°04′W
31 T13 Newark Ohio, N USA 40°03′N 82°24′W
Newark see Newark-on-Trent
35 W5 Newark Lake ◎ Nevada, W USA
97 N18 Newark-on-Trent var. Newark. C England, United Kingdom 53°05′N 00°49′W
22 M7 New Augusta Mississippi, S USA 31°12′N 89°03′W
19 P12 New Bedford Massachusetts, NE USA 41°38′N 70°55′W
32 G11 Newberg Oregon, NW USA 45°18′N 122°58′W
21 X10 New Bern North Carolina, SE USA 35°05′N 77°04′W
20 F8 Newbern Tennessee, S USA 36°06′N 89°15′W
31 P4 Newberry Michigan, N USA 46°21′N 85°30′W
21 Q12 Newberry South Carolina, SE USA 34°17′N 81°39′W
18 F15 New Bloomfield Pennsylvania, NE USA 40°24′N 77°08′W
25 X5 New Boston Texas, SW USA 33°27′N 94°25′W
25 S11 New Braunfels Texas, SW USA 29°43′N 98°09′W
31 Q13 New Bremen Ohio, N USA 40°26′N 84°22′W
97 F18 Newbridge Ir. An Droichead Nua. Kildare, C Ireland 53°11′N 06°48′W
18 B14 New Brighton Pennsylvania, NE USA 40°42′N 80°18′W
18 M12 New Britain Connecticut, NE USA 41°37′N 72°45′W
186 G7 New Britain island E Papua New Guinea
192 I8 New Britain Trench undersea feature W Pacific Ocean
18 J15 New Brunswick New Jersey, NE USA 40°29′N 74°27′W
15 V8 New Brunswick Fr. Nouveau-Brunswick. ◈ province SE Canada
18 K13 Newburgh New York, NE USA 41°30′N 74°00′W
97 M22 Newbury S England, United Kingdom 51°25′N 01°20′W
19 P10 Newburyport Massachusetts, NE USA 42°49′N 70°53′W
77 T14 New Bussa Niger, W Nigeria 09°50′N 04°32′E
187 O17 New Caledonia var. Kanaky, Fr. Nouvelle-Calédonie. ◇ French overseas territory SW Pacific Ocean
187 O15 New Caledonia island SW Pacific Ocean
175 O10 New Caledonia Basin undersea feature W Pacific Ocean
183 T8 Newcastle New South Wales, SE Australia 32°55′S 151°46′E
13 O14 Newcastle New Brunswick, SE Canada 47°01′N 65°36′W
14 I15 Newcastle Ontario, SE Canada 43°55′N 78°35′W
83 K22 Newcastle KwaZulu/Natal, E South Africa 27°45′S 29°55′E
97 G16 Newcastle Ir. An Caisleán Nua. SE Northern Ireland, United Kingdom 54°12′N 05°54′W
31 P13 New Castle Indiana, N USA 39°56′N 85°21′W
20 L5 New Castle Kentucky, S USA 38°28′N 85°10′W
27 N11 Newcastle Oklahoma, C USA 35°15′N 97°36′W
18 B13 New Castle Pennsylvania, NE USA 41°00′N 80°22′W
25 R6 Newcastle Texas, SW USA 33°11′N 98°44′W
36 J7 Newcastle Utah, W USA 37°40′N 113°31′W
21 S6 New Castle Virginia, NE USA 37°31′N 80°09′W
33 Z13 Newcastle Wyoming, C USA 43°52′N 104°14′W
97 L14 Newcastle ✈ NE England, United Kingdom 55°03′N 01°42′W
Newcastle see Newcastle upon Tyne
97 L18 Newcastle-under-Lyme C England, United Kingdom 53°N 02°14′W
97 M14 Newcastle upon Tyne var. Newcastle, hist. Monkchester, Lat. Pons Aelii. NE England, United Kingdom 54°59′N 01°35′W
181 Q4 Newcastle Waters Northern Territory, N Australia 17°20′S 133°26′E
Newchwang see Yingkou
18 K13 New City New York, NE USA 41°08′N 73°57′W
31 U13 Newcomerstown Ohio, N USA 40°16′N 81°36′W
18 G15 New Cumberland Pennsylvania, NE USA 40°13′N 76°52′W
21 R1 New Cumberland West Virginia, NE USA 40°30′N 80°35′W
152 I10 New Delhi ● (India) Delhi, N India 28°35′N 77°15′E
11 O17 New Denver British Columbia, SW Canada 49°58′N 117°21′W
28 J9 Newell South Dakota, N USA 44°42′N 103°25′W
21 Q13 New Ellenton South Carolina, SE USA 33°25′N 81°41′W
22 J6 Newellton Louisiana, S USA 32°04′N 91°14′W
28 K6 New England North Dakota, N USA 46°32′N 102°52′W
19 P8 New England cultural region NE USA
New England of the West see Minnesota
183 U5 New England Range ▲▲ New South Wales, SE Australia
64 G9 New England Seamounts var. Bermuda-New England Seamount Arc. undersea feature W Atlantic Ocean 38°00′N 61°00′W
38 M14 Newenham, Cape headland Alaska, USA 58°39′N 162°10′W
Newé Zohar see Neve Zohar
18 D9 Newfane New York, NE USA 43°16′N 78°40′W
97 M23 New Forest physical region S England, United Kingdom
13 T12 Newfoundland Fr. Terre-Neuve. island Newfoundland and Labrador, SE Canada
13 R9 Newfoundland and Labrador Fr. Terre Neuve. ◈ province E Canada
65 J8 Newfoundland Basin undersea feature NW Atlantic Ocean 45°00′N 40°00′W
64 I8 Newfoundland Ridge undersea feature NW Atlantic Ocean
64 J8 Newfoundland Seamounts undersea feature N Sargasso Sea
18 G16 New Freedom Pennsylvania, NE USA 39°43′N 76°41′W
186 K9 New Georgia island New Georgia Islands, NW Solomon Islands
186 K8 New Georgia Islands island group NW Solomon Islands
186 L8 New Georgia Sound var. The Slot. sound E Solomon Sea
30 L9 New Glarus Wisconsin, N USA 42°50′N 89°38′W
13 Q15 New Glasgow Nova Scotia, SE Canada 45°36′N 62°38′W
New Goa see Panaji
186 A6 New Guinea Dut. Nieuw Guinea, Ind. Irian. island Indonesia/Papua New Guinea
192 H8 New Guinea Trench undersea feature SW Pacific Ocean
32 I6 Newhalem Washington, NW USA 48°40′N 121°18′W
39 P13 Newhalen Alaska, USA 59°43′N 154°54′W
29 X13 Newhall Iowa, C USA 42°00′N 91°58′W
14 F16 New Hamburg Ontario, S Canada 43°24′N 80°37′W
19 N9 New Hampshire off. State of New Hampshire, also known as Granite State. ◈ state NE USA
29 W12 New Hampton Iowa, C USA 43°03′N 92°19′W
186 G5 New Hanover island NE Papua New Guinea
97 P23 Newhaven SE England, United Kingdom 50°48′N 00°00′E
18 M13 New Haven Connecticut, NE USA 41°18′N 72°55′W
31 Q12 New Haven Indiana, N USA 41°02′N 84°59′W
27 W5 New Haven Missouri, C USA 38°34′N 91°15′W
10 K13 New Hazelton British Columbia, SW Canada 55°15′N 127°30′W
New Hebrides see Vanuatu
175 P9 New Hebrides Trench undersea feature N Coral Sea
18 H15 New Holland Pennsylvania, NE USA 40°06′N 76°05′W
22 I9 New Iberia Louisiana, S USA 30°00′N 91°51′W
186 G5 New Ireland ◈ province NE Papua New Guinea
186 G5 New Ireland island NE Papua New Guinea
65 A24 New Island island W Falkland Islands
18 J15 New Jersey off. State of New Jersey, also known as The Garden State. ◈ state NE USA
18 C14 New Kensington Pennsylvania, NE USA 40°33′N 79°45′W
21 W6 New Kent Virginia, NE USA 37°32′N 76°59′W
27 O8 Newkirk Oklahoma, C USA 36°54′N 97°03′W
21 Q9 Newland North Carolina, SE USA 36°04′N 81°50′W
28 L6 New Leipzig North Dakota, N USA 46°21′N 101°54′W
14 H9 New Liskeard Ontario, S Canada 47°31′N 79°41′W
22 G7 Newllano Louisiana, S USA 31°06′N 93°16′W
19 N13 New London Connecticut, NE USA 41°21′N 72°04′W
29 Y15 New London Iowa, C USA 40°55′N 91°24′W
29 T8 New London Minnesota, N USA 45°18′N 94°56′W
27 V3 New London Missouri, C USA 39°34′N 91°24′W
30 M7 New London Wisconsin, N USA 44°25′N 88°44′W
27 Y8 New Madrid Missouri, C USA 36°34′N 89°32′W
180 J8 Newman Western Australia 23°18′S 119°45′E
194 M13 Newman Island island Antarctica
14 H15 Newmarket Ontario, S Canada 44°03′N 79°27′W
97 P20 Newmarket E England, United Kingdom 52°18′N 00°28′E
19 P10 Newmarket New Hampshire, NE USA 43°04′N 70°53′W
21 U4 New Market Virginia, NE USA 38°39′N 78°40′W
21 R2 New Martinsville West Virginia, NE USA 39°39′N 80°52′W
31 U14 New Matamoras Ohio, N USA 39°32′N 81°04′W
32 M12 New Meadows Idaho, NW USA 44°57′N 116°16′W
26 R12 New Mexico off. State of New Mexico, also known as Land of Enchantment, Sunshine State. ◈ state SW USA
149 V6 New Mirpur var. Mirpur. Sind, SE Pakistan 33°11′N 73°46′E
151 N15 New Moore Island Island E India
23 S4 Newnan Georgia, SE USA 33°22′N 84°48′W
183 P17 New Norfolk Tasmania, SE Australia 42°46′S 147°02′E
22 K9 New Orleans Louisiana, S USA 30°00′N 90°01′W
22 K9 New Orleans ✈ Louisiana, S USA 29°59′N 90°17′W
18 K12 New Paltz New York, NE USA 41°44′N 74°04′W
31 U12 New Philadelphia Ohio, N USA 40°29′N 81°27′W
184 K10 New Plymouth Taranaki, North Island, New Zealand 39°04′S 174°06′E
97 M24 Newport S England, United Kingdom 50°42′N 01°18′W
97 K22 Newport SE Wales, United Kingdom 51°35′N 03°W
27 W10 Newport Arkansas, C USA 35°36′N 91°16′W
31 N13 Newport Indiana, N USA 39°52′N 87°24′W
20 M3 Newport Kentucky, S USA 39°05′N 84°27′W
29 W9 Newport Minnesota, N USA 44°52′N 93°00′W
32 F12 Newport Oregon, NW USA 44°39′N 124°04′W
19 O13 Newport Rhode Island, NE USA 41°29′N 71°17′W
21 O9 Newport Tennessee, S USA 35°58′N 83°13′W
19 N6 Newport Vermont, NE USA 44°56′N 72°13′W
32 M7 Newport Washington, NW USA 48°08′N 117°05′W
21 X7 Newport News Virginia, NE USA 36°59′N 76°26′W
97 N20 Newport Pagnell SE England, United Kingdom 52°05′N 00°44′W
23 U12 New Port Richey Florida, SE USA 28°14′N 82°42′W
29 V9 New Prague Minnesota, N USA 44°32′N 93°34′W
44 H3 New Providence island N Bahamas
97 I20 New Quay SW Wales, United Kingdom 52°13′N 04°22′W
97 H24 Newquay SW England, United Kingdom 50°27′N 05°03′W
29 V10 New Richland Minnesota, N USA 43°53′N 93°29′W
15 X7 New-Richmond Québec, SE Canada 48°12′N 65°52′W
31 R15 New Richmond Ohio, N USA 38°57′N 84°16′W
30 I5 New Richmond Wisconsin, N USA 45°09′N 92°31′W
42 G1 New River ≈ N Belize
55 T12 New River ≈ SE Guyana
21 R6 New River ≈ West Virginia, NE USA
42 G1 New River Lagoon ◎ N Belize
22 J8 New Roads Louisiana, S USA 30°42′N 91°26′W
18 L14 New Rochelle New York, NE USA 40°55′N 73°44′W
29 O4 New Rockford North Dakota, N USA 47°40′N 99°08′W
97 P23 New Romney SE England, United Kingdom 50°58′N 00°56′E
97 F20 New Ross Ir. Ros Mhic Thriúin. Wexford, SE Ireland 52°24′N 06°56′W
97 F16 Newry Ir. An tIúr. SE Northern Ireland, United Kingdom 54°11′N 06°20′W
28 M5 New Salem North Dakota, N USA 46°51′N 101°24′W
New Sarum see Salisbury
29 W14 New Sharon Iowa, C USA 41°28′N 92°39′W
New Siberian Islands see Novosibirskiye Ostrova
23 X11 New Smyrna Beach Florida, SE USA 29°01′N 80°55′W
183 O7 New South Wales ◈ state SE Australia
39 O13 New Stuyahok Alaska, USA 59°27′N 157°18′W
21 N8 New Tazewell Tennessee, S USA 36°26′N 83°36′W
152 K9 New Tehri prev. Tehri. Uttarakhand, N India 30°12′N 78°29′E
38 M12 Newtok Alaska, USA 60°56′N 164°37′W
23 S7 Newton Georgia, SE USA 31°18′N 84°20′W
29 W14 Newton Iowa, C USA 41°42′N 93°03′W
27 N6 Newton Kansas, C USA 38°02′N 97°22′W
19 O11 Newton Massachusetts, NE USA 42°19′N 71°10′W
22 M5 Newton Mississippi, S USA 32°19′N 89°09′W
18 J14 Newton New Jersey, NE USA 41°03′N 74°45′W
21 R9 Newton North Carolina, SE USA 35°42′N 81°14′W
25 Y9 Newton Texas, SW USA 30°51′N 93°45′W
97 J24 Newton Abbot SW England, United Kingdom 50°33′N 03°34′W
96 K13 Newton St Boswells SE Scotland, United Kingdom 55°34′N 02°40′W
97 I14 Newton Stewart S Scotland, United Kingdom 54°58′N 04°30′W
92 O2 Newtontoppen ▲ C Svalbard 78°57′N 17°34′E
97 J20 Newtown E Wales, United Kingdom 52°32′N 03°19′W
28 K3 New Town North Dakota, N USA 47°58′N 102°30′W
97 G15 Newtownabbey Ir. Baile na Mainistreach. E Northern Ireland, United Kingdom 54°40′N 05°57′W
97 G15 Newtownards Ir. Baile Nua na hArda. SE Northern Ireland, United Kingdom 54°36′N 05°41′W
29 U10 New Ulm Minnesota, N USA 44°20′N 94°28′W
28 K10 New Underwood South Dakota, N USA 44°05′N 102°46′W
25 V10 New Waverly Texas, SW USA 30°32′N 95°28′W
18 K14 New York New York, NE USA 40°45′N 73°57′W
18 G10 New York ◈ state NE USA
35 X13 New York Mountains ▲▲ California, W USA
184 K12 New Zealand ◆ commonwealth republic SW Pacific Ocean
95 M24 Nexø var. Neksø. Bornholm, E Denmark 55°04′N 15°09′E
125 O15 Neya Kostromskaya Oblast', NW Russian Federation 58°19′N 43°51′E
Neyba see Neiba
143 Q12 Neyrīz var. Neiriz, Niriz. Fārs, S Iran 29°14′N 54°18′E
143 T4 Neyshābūr var. Nishapur. Khorāsān-Razavī, NE Iran 36°15′N 58°47′E
155 J21 Neyveli Tamil Nādu, SE India 11°36′N 79°26′E
Nezhin see Nizhyn
33 N10 Nezperce Idaho, NW USA 46°14′N 116°15′W
22 H8 Nezpique, Bayou ≈ Louisiana, S USA
77 Y13 Ngadda ≈ NE Nigeria
N'Gage see Negage
185 G16 Ngahere West Coast, South Island, New Zealand 42°22′S 171°29′E
77 Z12 Ngala Borno, NE Nigeria 12°19′N 14°11′E
158 K16 Ngamring Xizang Zizhiqu, W China 29°16′N 87°10′E
81 K19 Ngangerabeli Plain plain SE Kenya
158 I14 Ngangla Ringco ◎ W China
158 H13 Nganglong Kangri ▲ W China 32°55′N 81°00′E
158 K15 Ngangzê Co ◎ W China
79 F14 Ngaoundéré var. N'Gaoundéré. Adamaoua, N Cameroon 07°20′N 13°35′E
N'Gaoundéré see Ngaoundéré
81 E20 Ngara Kagera, NW Tanzania 02°30′S 30°40′E
188 F8 Ngardmau Bay bay Babeldaob, N Palau
188 F7 Ngaregur island Palau Islands, N Palau
Ngarrab see Gyaca
184 L7 Ngaruawahia Waikato, North Island, New Zealand 37°41′S 175°10′E
184 N11 Ngaruroro ≈ North Island, New Zealand
190 I16 Ngatangiia Rarotonga, S Cook Islands 21°14′S 159°44′W
184 M6 Ngatea Waikato, North Island, New Zealand 37°16′S 175°29′E
166 L8 Ngathainggyaung Ayeyarwady, SW Myanmar (Burma) 17°22′N 95°04′E
Ngatik see Ngetik Atoll
Ngau see Gau
Ngawa see Aba
172 G12 Ngazidja Fr. Grande Comore, var. Njazidja. island NW Comoros
188 C7 Ngcheangel var. Kayangel Islands. island Palau Islands, N Palau
188 E10 Ngchemiangel Babeldaob, N Palau
188 C8 Ngeaur var. Angaur. island Palau Islands, S Palau
188 E10 Ngerkeai Babeldaob, N Palau
188 F9 Ngermechau Babeldaob, N Palau 07°35′N 134°39′E
188 C8 Ngeruktabel prev. Urukthapel. island Palau Islands, S Palau
188 F8 Ngetbong Babeldaob, N Palau 07°37′N 134°35′E
189 T17 Ngetik Atoll var. Ngatik; prev. Los Jardines. atoll Caroline Islands, E Micronesia
188 E10 Ngetkip Babeldaob, N Palau
Nghia Dan see Thai Hoa
83 C16 N'Giva var. Ondjiva, Port. Vila Pereira de Eça. Cunene, S Angola 17°02′S 15°42′E
79 G20 Ngo Plateaux, SE Congo 02°28′S 15°43′E
167 S7 Ngoc Lăc Thanh Hoa, N Vietnam 20°06′N 105°21′E
79 G17 Ngoko ≈ Cameroon/Congo
81 H19 Ngorengore Rift Valley, SW Kenya 01°01′S 35°26′E
159 Q11 Ngoring Hu ◎ C China
Ngorolaka see Banifing
81 H20 Ngorongoro Crater crater N Tanzania
79 D19 Ngounié off. Province de la Ngounié, var. La Ngounié. ◈ province S Gabon
79 D19 Ngounié ≈ Congo/Gabon
Ngounié, Province de la see Ngounié
78 H10 Ngoura var. NGoura. Chari-Baguirmi, W Chad 12°52′N 16°27′E
NGoura see Ngoura
78 G10 Ngouri var. NGouri; prev. Fort-Millot. Lac, W Chad 13°42′N 15°19′E
NGouri see Ngouri
77 Y10 Ngourti Diffa, E Niger 15°22′N 13°13′E
77 Y11 Nguigmi var. N'Guigmi. Diffa, SE Niger 14°17′N 13°07′E
N'Guigmi see Nguigmi
Nguimbo see Lumbala N'Guimbo
188 F15 Ngulu Atoll atoll Caroline Islands, W Micronesia
187 R14 Nguna island C Vanuatu
N'Gunza see Sumbe
169 U17 Ngurah Rai ✈ (Bali) Bali, S Indonesia 08°40′S 115°14′E

◆ Country
● Country Capital
◇ Dependent Territory
○ Dependent Territory Capital
◈ Administrative Regions
✈ International Airport
▲ Mountain
▲▲ Mountain Range
Ѫ Volcano
≈ River
◎ Lake
⊠ Reservoir

77 W12 **Nguru** Yobe, NE Nigeria 12°55′N 10°31′E
Ngwaketse see Southern
83 I16 **Ngweze** ∽ S Zambia
83 M17 **Nhamatanda** Sofala, C Mozambique 19°16′S 34°10′E
58 G12 **Nhamundá, Rio** var. Jamundá, Yamundá. ∽ N Brazil
60 J7 **Nhandeara** São Paulo, S Brazil 20°40′S 50°03′W
82 D12 **Nharêa** var. N'Harea, Nhareia. Bié, W Angola 11°38′S 16°58′E
N'Harea see Nharêa
Nhareia see Nharêa
167 V12 **Nha Trang** Khanh Hoa, S Vietnam 12°15′N 109°10′E
182 L11 **Nhill** Victoria, SE Australia 36°21′S 141°38′E
83 L22 **Nhlangano** prev. Goedgegun. SW Swaziland 27°06′S 31°12′E
181 S1 **Nhulunbuy** Northern Territory, N Australia 12°16′S 136°46′E
77 N10 **Niafounké** Tombouctou, W Mali 15°54′N 03°58′W
31 N5 **Niagara** Wisconsin, N USA 45°45′N 87°57′W
14 H16 **Niagara** ∽ Ontario, S Canada
14 G15 **Niagara Escarpment** *hill range* Ontario, S Canada
14 H16 **Niagara Falls** Ontario, S Canada 43°05′N 79°06′W
18 D9 **Niagara Falls** New York, NE USA 43°06′N 79°04′W
14 H16 **Niagara Falls** *waterfall* Canada/USA
76 K12 **Niagassola** var. Nyagassola. Haute-Guinée, NE Guinea 12°24′N 09°03′W
77 R12 **Niamey** ● (Niger) Niamey, SW Niger 13°28′N 02°03′E
77 R12 **Niamey** ✕ Niamey, SW Niger 13°28′N 02°14′E
77 R14 **Niamtougou** N Togo 09°50′N 01°08′E
79 O16 **Niangara** Orientale, NE Dem. Rep. Congo 03°45′N 27°54′E
77 O10 **Niangay, Lac** ◎ E Mali
77 N14 **Niangoloko** SW Burkina 10°15′N 04°53′W
27 U6 **Niangua River** ∽ Missouri, C USA
79 O17 **Nia-Nia** Orientale, NE Dem. Rep. Congo 01°26′N 27°38′E
19 N13 **Niantic** Connecticut, NE USA 41°19′N 72°11′W
163 U7 **Nianzishan** Heilongjiang, NE China 47°31′N 122°53′E
79 E20 **Niari** ⬖ *province* SW Congo
168 H10 **Nias, Pulau** *island* W Indonesia
82 O13 **Niassa** off. Província do Niassa. ⬖ *province* N Mozambique
Niassa, Província do see Niassa
191 U10 **Niau** *island* Îles Tuamotu, C French Polynesia
95 G20 **Nibe** Nordjylland, N Denmark 56°59′N 09°39′E
189 Q8 **Nibok** N Nauru 0°31′S 166°55′E
118 C10 **Nīca** W Latvia 56°21′N 21°03′E
Nicaea see Nice
42 J9 **Nicaragua** off. Republic of Nicaragua. ◆ *republic* Central America
42 K11 **Nicaragua, Lago de** var. Cocibolca, Gran Lago, Eng. Lake Nicaragua. ◎ S Nicaragua
Nicaragua, Lake see Nicaragua, Lago de
64 D11 **Nicaraguan Rise** *undersea feature* NW Caribbean Sea 16°00′N 80°00′W
Nicaragua, Republic of see Nicaragua
Nicaria see Ikaría
107 N21 **Nicastro** Calabria, SW Italy 38°59′N 16°20′E
103 V15 **Nice** It. Nizza; anc. Nicaea. Alpes-Maritimes, SE France 43°43′N 07°13′E
Nice see Côte d'Azur
Nicephorium see Ar Raqqah
12 M9 **Nichicun, Lac** ◎ Québec, E Canada
164 D16 **Nichinan** var. Nitinan. Miyazaki, Kyūshū, SW Japan 31°36′N 131°23′E
44 E4 **Nicholas Channel** *channel* N Cuba
Nicholas II Land see Severnaya Zemlya
149 U2 **Nicholas Range** Pash. Selselehye Kuhe Vākhān, Taj. Qatorkŭhi Vakhon. ▲▲ Afghanistan/Tajikistan
20 M6 **Nicholasville** Kentucky, S USA 37°52′N 84°34′W
44 G2 **Nicholls Town** Andros Island, NW Bahamas 25°07′N 78°01′W
21 U12 **Nichols** South Carolina, SE USA 34°13′N 79°09′W
55 U9 **Nickerie** ⬖ *district* NW Suriname
55 V9 **Nickerie Rivier** ∽ NW Suriname
151 P22 **Nicobar Islands** *island group* India, E Indian Ocean
116 L9 **Nicolae Bălcescu** Botoşani, NE Romania 47°33′N 26°52′E
15 P11 **Nicolet** Québec, SE Canada 46°13′N 72°37′W
15 Q12 **Nicolet** ∽ Québec, SE Canada
31 Q4 **Nicolet, Lake** ◎ Michigan, N USA
29 U10 **Nicollet** Minnesota, N USA 44°16′N 94°11′W
61 F19 **Nico Pérez** Florida, S Uruguay 33°30′S 55°10′W
Nicopolis see Nikopol, Bulgaria
Nicopolis see Nikópoli, Greece
121 P2 **Nicosia** Gk. Lefkosía, Turk. Lefkoşa. ● (Cyprus) C Cyprus 35°10′N 33°23′E
107 K24 **Nicosia** Sicilia, Italy, C Mediterranean Sea 37°45′N 14°24′E
107 N22 **Nicotera** Calabria, SW Italy 38°33′N 15°55′E
42 K13 **Nicoya** Guanacaste, W Costa Rica 10°09′N 85°26′W
42 L14 **Nicoya, Golfo de** *gulf* W Costa Rica
42 L14 **Nicoya, Península de** *peninsula* NW Costa Rica
Nictheroy see Niterói
118 B12 **Nida** Ger. Nidden. Klaipėda, SW Lithuania 55°20′N 21°00′E
111 L15 **Nida** ∽ S Poland
Nidaros see Trondheim
108 D8 **Nidau** Bern, W Switzerland 47°07′N 07°15′E
101 H17 **Nidda** ∽ W Germany
Nidden see Nida
95 F17 **Nidelva** ∽ S Norway
108 F9 **Nidwalden** ⬖ *canton* C Switzerland
Nidwalden/Unterwalden see Nidwalden
110 L9 **Nidzica** Ger. Niedenburg. Warmińsko-Mazurskie, NE Poland 53°22′N 20°27′E
100 H6 **Niebüll** Schleswig-Holstein, N Germany 54°47′N 08°51′E
Niedenburg see Nidzica
99 N25 **Niederanven** Luxembourg, C Luxembourg 49°39′N 06°15′E
103 V4 **Niederbronn-les-Bains** Bas-Rhin, NE France 48°57′N 07°37′E
Niederdonau see Niederösterreich
109 S7 **Niedere Tauern** ▲▲ C Austria
101 P14 **Niederlausitz** Eng. Lower Lusatia, Lus. Donja Łužica. *physical region* E Germany
109 U5 **Niederösterreich** off. Land Niederösterreich, Eng. Lower Austria, Ger. Niederdonau; prev. Lower Danube. ⬖ *state* NE Austria
Niederösterreich, Land see Niederösterreich
100 G12 **Niedersachsen** Eng. Lower Saxony, Fr. Basse-Saxe. ⬖ *state* NW Germany
79 D17 **Niefang** var. Sevilla de Niefang. NW Equatorial Guinea 01°52′N 10°12′E
83 G23 **Niekerkshoop** Northern Cape, W South Africa 29°21′S 22°49′E
99 G17 **Niel** Antwerpen, N Belgium 51°07′N 04°20′E
Niélé see Niellé
76 M14 **Niellé** var. Niélé. N Ivory Coast 10°12′N 05°38′W
79 O22 **Niemba** Katanga, E Dem. Rep. Congo 05°58′S 28°24′E
111 G15 **Niemcza** Ger. Nimptsch. Dolnośląskie, SW Poland 50°45′N 16°52′E
Niemen see Neman
92 J13 **Niemisel** Norrbotten, N Sweden 66°00′N 22°00′E
111 H15 **Niemodlin** Ger. Falkenberg. Opolskie, SW Poland 50°37′N 17°45′E
76 M13 **Niéna** Sikasso, SW Mali 11°24′N 06°20′W
100 H12 **Nienburg** Niedersachsen, N Germany 52°37′N 09°12′E
100 N13 **Nieplitz** ∽ NE Germany
111 L16 **Niepołomice** Małopolskie, S Poland 50°02′N 20°12′E
101 D14 **Niers** ∽ Germany/Netherlands
101 Q15 **Niesky** Lus. Niska. Sachsen, E Germany 51°16′N 14°49′E
Nieśwież see Nyasvizh
Nieuport see Nieuwpoort
98 O8 **Nieuw-Amsterdam** Drenthe, NE Netherlands 52°43′N 06°52′E
55 W9 **Nieuw Amsterdam** Commewijne, NE Suriname 05°53′N 55°05′W
99 M14 **Nieuw-Bergen** Limburg, SE Netherlands 51°36′N 06°04′E
98 O7 **Nieuw-Buinen** Drenthe, NE Netherlands 52°57′N 06°55′E
98 J12 **Nieuwegein** Utrecht, C Netherlands 52°03′N 05°06′E
98 P6 **Nieuwe Pekela** Groningen, NE Netherlands 53°04′N 06°58′E
98 P5 **Nieuweschans** Groningen, NE Netherlands 53°10′N 07°10′E
Nieuw Guinea see New Guinea
98 I11 **Nieuwkoop** Zuid-Holland, C Netherlands 52°09′N 04°46′E
98 M9 **Nieuwleusen** Overijssel, S Netherlands 52°34′N 06°16′E
98 J11 **Nieuw-Loosdrecht** Noord-Holland, C Netherlands 52°12′N 05°08′E
55 U9 **Nieuw Nickerie** Nickerie, NW Suriname 05°56′N 57°W
98 P5 **Nieuwolda** Groningen, NE Netherlands 53°15′N 06°58′E
99 B17 **Nieuwpoort** var. Nieuport. West-Vlaanderen, W Belgium 51°08′N 02°45′E
99 G14 **Nieuw-Vossemeer** Noord-Brabant, S Netherlands 51°34′N 04°13′E
98 P7 **Nieuw-Weerdinge** Drenthe, NE Netherlands 52°51′N 07°00′E
40 L10 **Nieves** Zacatecas, C Mexico 24°00′N 102°57′W
64 O11 **Nieves, Pico de las** ▲ Gran Canaria, Islas Canarias, Spain, NE Atlantic Ocean 27°58′N 15°34′W
103 P8 **Nièvre** ⬖ *department* C France
Niewenstat see Neustadt an der Weinstrasse
136 J15 **Niğde** Niğde, C Turkey 37°58′N 34°42′E
136 J15 **Niğde** ⬖ *province* C Turkey
83 J21 **Nigel** Gauteng, NE South Africa 26°25′S 28°28′E
77 V10 **Niger** off. Republic of Niger. ◆ *republic* W Africa
77 T14 **Niger** ⬖ *state* C Nigeria
67 P8 **Niger** ∽ W Africa
Niger Cone see Niger Fan
77 T18 **Niger Delta** *delta* S Nigeria
67 P9 **Niger Fan** var. Niger Cone. *undersea feature* E Atlantic Ocean 04°15′N 05°00′E
77 T13 **Nigeria** off. Federal Republic of Nigeria. ◆ *federal republic* W Africa
Nigeria, Federal Republic of see Nigeria
77 T17 **Niger, Mouths of the** *delta* S Nigeria
Niger, Republic of see Niger
185 C24 **Nightcaps** Southland, South Island, New Zealand 45°58′S 168°03′E
14 F7 **Night Hawk Lake** ◎ Ontario, S Canada
65 M19 **Nightingale Island** *island* S Tristan da Cunha, S Atlantic Ocean
38 M12 **Nightmute** Alaska, USA 60°28′N 164°43′W
114 G13 **Nigrita** Kentrikí Makedonía, NE Greece 40°54′N 23°29′E
148 J15 **Nihing** Per. Rūd-e Nahang. ∽ Iran/Pakistan
191 V10 **Nihiru** *atoll* Îles Tuamotu, C French Polynesia
Nihommatsu see Nihonmatsu
Nihon see Japan
165 P11 **Nihonmatsu** var. Nihommatsu, Nihonmatu. Fukushima, Honshū, C Japan 37°34′N 140°25′E
Nihonmatu see Nihonmatsu
62 I12 **Nihuil, Embalse del** ⊠ W Argentina
165 O10 **Niigata** Niigata, Honshū, C Japan 37°55′N 139°01′E
165 O11 **Niigata** off. Niigata-ken. ⬖ *prefecture* Honshū, C Japan
Niigata-ken see Niigata
165 G14 **Niihama** Ehime, Shikoku, SW Japan 33°57′N 133°15′E
38 A8 **Ni'ihau** var. Niihau. *island* Hawai'i, USA, C Pacific Ocean
165 X12 **Nii-jima** *island* E Japan
165 H12 **Niimi** Okayama, Honshū, SW Japan 35°00′N 133°27′E
165 O10 **Niitsu** var. Niitu. Niigata, Honshū, C Japan 37°48′N 139°09′E
Niitu see Niitsu
105 P15 **Níjar** Andalucía, S Spain 36°57′N 02°13′W
98 K11 **Nijkerk** Gelderland, C Netherlands 52°13′N 05°30′E
99 H16 **Nijlen** Antwerpen, N Belgium 51°10′N 04°40′E
98 L13 **Nijmegen** Ger. Nimwegen; anc. Noviomagus. Gelderland, SE Netherlands 51°50′N 05°52′E
98 N10 **Nijverdal** Overijssel, E Netherlands 52°22′N 06°28′E
190 G16 **Nikao** Rarotonga, S Cook Islands
Nikaria see Ikaría
124 I2 **Nikel'** Finn. Kolosjoki. Murmanskaya Oblast', NW Russian Federation 69°25′N 30°12′E
171 Q17 **Nikiniki** Timor, S Indonesia 10°S 124°30′E
129 Q15 **Nikitin Seamount** *undersea feature* E Indian Ocean 05°48′S 84°48′E
77 S14 **Nikki** E Benin 09°55′N 03°12′E
Niklasmarkt see Gheorgheni
39 P10 **Nikolai** Alaska, USA 63°00′N 154°22′W
Nikolaiken see Mikołajki
Nikolainkaupunki see Vaasa
Nikolayev see Mykolayiv
145 O6 **Nikolayevka** Severnyy Kazakhstan, N Kazakhstan
Nikolayevka see Zhetigen
127 P9 **Nikolayevsk** Volgogradskaya Oblast', SW Russian Federation 50°03′N 45°30′E
Nikolayevskaya Oblast' see Mykolayivs'ka Oblast'
123 S12 **Nikolayevsk-na-Amure** Khabarovskiy Kray, SE Russian Federation 53°04′N 140°39′E
127 P6 **Nikol'sk** Penzenskaya Oblast', W Russian Federation 53°46′N 46°03′E
125 O13 **Nikol'sk** Vologodskaya Oblast', NW Russian Federation 59°35′N 45°31′E
Nikol'sk see Ussuriysk
38 K17 **Nikolski** Umnak Island, Alaska, USA 52°56′N 168°52′W
Nikol'skiy see Satpayev
127 V7 **Nikol'skoye** Orenburgskaya Oblast', W Russian Federation 52°01′N 55°48′E
Nikol'sk-Ussuriyskiy see Ussuriysk
114 J7 **Nikopol** anc. Nicopolis. Pleven, N Bulgaria 43°43′N 24°55′E
117 S9 **Nikopol'** Dnipropetrovs'ka Oblast', SE Ukraine 47°34′N 34°23′E
115 C17 **Nikópoli** anc. Nicopolis. *site of ancient city* Ípeiros, W Greece
136 M12 **Niksar** Tokat, N Turkey 40°35′N 36°59′E
143 V14 **Nīkshahr** Sīstān va Balūchestān, SE Iran 26°15′N 60°10′E
113 J16 **Nikšić** C Montenegro 42°47′N 18°56′E
191 R4 **Nikumaroro** ; prev. Gardner Island. *atoll* Phoenix Islands, C Kiribati
191 P3 **Nikunau** var. Nukunau; prev. Byron Island. *atoll* Tungaru, W Kiribati
155 G21 **Nilambūr** Kerala, SW India 11°17′N 76°15′E
35 X16 **Niland** California, W USA 33°14′N 115°31′W
80 G8 **Nile** *former province* NW Uganda
67 T3 **Nile** Ar. Nahr an Nīl. ∽ N Africa
75 W7 **Nile Delta** *delta* N Egypt
67 T3 **Nile Fan** *undersea feature* E Mediterranean Sea 33°00′N 31°00′E
31 O11 **Niles** Michigan, N USA 41°49′N 86°15′W
31 V11 **Niles** Ohio, N USA 41°10′N 80°46′W
155 F20 **Nīleswaram** Kerala, SW India 12°18′N 75°07′E
14 K10 **Nilgaut, Lac** ◎ Québec, SE Canada
149 O6 **Nīlī** Dāykundī, C Afghanistan 33°43′N 66°07′E
158 I5 **Nilka** Xinjiang Uygur Zizhiqu, NW China 43°46′N 82°33′E
Nīl, Nahr an see Nile
93 N16 **Nilsiä** Itä-Suomi, C Finland 63°13′N 28°00′E
154 F9 **Nīmach** Madhya Pradesh, C India 24°27′N 74°56′E
152 G14 **Nimbāhera** Rājasthān, N India 24°38′N 74°45′E
76 L15 **Nimba, Monts** var. Nimba Mountains. ▲▲ W Africa
Nimba Mountains see Nimba, Monts
Nimburg see Nymburk
103 Q15 **Nîmes** anc. Nemausus, Nismes. Gard, S France 43°49′N 04°20′E
152 H11 **Nīm ka Thāna** Rājasthān, N India 27°42′N 75°50′E
183 R11 **Nimmitabel** New South Wales, SE Australia 36°34′S 149°18′E
Nimptsch see Niemcza
195 R11 **Nimrod Glacier** *glacier* Antarctica
148 K8 **Nīmrōz** var. Nimroze; prev. Chakhānsūr, Nīmrūz. ⬖ *province* SW Afghanistan
Nimroze see Nīmrōz
Nīmrūz see Nīmrōz
81 F16 **Nimule** Eastern Equatoria, S South Sudan 03°35′N 32°03′E
Nimwegen see Nijmegen
155 C23 **Nine Degree Channel** *channel* India/Maldives
18 G9 **Ninemile Point** *headland* New York, NE USA 43°31′N 76°22′W
173 S8 **Ninetyeast Ridge** *undersea feature* E Indian Ocean 04°00′S 90°00′E
183 P13 **Ninety Mile Beach** *beach* Victoria, SE Australia
184 I2 **Ninety Mile Beach** *beach* North Island, New Zealand
21 P12 **Ninety Six** South Carolina, SE USA 34°10′N 82°01′W
163 Y9 **Ning'an** Heilongjiang, NE China 44°20′N 129°28′E
161 S9 **Ningbo** var. Ning-po, Yin-hsien; prev. Ninghsien. Zhejiang, SE China 29°54′N 121°33′E
161 U12 **Ningde** Fujian, SE China 26°48′N 119°33′E
161 P12 **Ningdu** var. Meijiang. Jiangxi, S China 26°28′N 115°53′E
Ning'er see Pu'er
186 A7 **Ningerum** Western, SW Papua New Guinea 05°40′S 141°10′E
161 R9 **Ningguo** Anhui, E China 30°33′N 118°58′E
161 S9 **Ninghai** Zhejiang, SE China 29°18′N 121°26′E
Ning-hsia see Ningxia
Ninghsien see Ningbo
160 J15 **Ningming** var. Chengzhong. Guangxi Zhuangzu Zizhiqu, S China 22°07′N 107°06′E
160 H11 **Ningnan** var. Pisha. Sichuan, C China 26°59′N 102°49′E
Ning-po see Ningbo
Ningsia/Ningsia Hui/Ningsia Hui Autonomous Region see Ningxia
160 J5 **Ningxia** off. Ningxia Huizu Zizhiqu, var. Ning-hsia, Ningsia, Eng. Ningsia Hui, Ningsia Hui Autonomous Region. ⬖ *autonomous region* N China
Ningxia Huizu Zizhiqu see Ningxia
159 X10 **Ningxian** var. Xinning. Gansu, N China 35°30′N 108°05′E
167 T7 **Ninh Bình** Ninh Bình, N Vietnam 20°14′N 106°00′E
167 V12 **Ninh Hoa** Khanh Hoa, S Vietnam 12°28′N 109°07′E
186 C4 **Ninigo Group** *island group* N Papua New Guinea
39 Q12 **Ninilchik** Alaska, USA 60°03′N 151°40′W
27 N7 **Ninnescah River** ∽ Kansas, C USA
195 U16 **Ninnis Glacier** *glacier* Antarctica
165 R8 **Ninohe** Iwate, Honshū, C Japan 40°16′N 141°18′E
99 F18 **Ninove** Oost-Vlaanderen, C Belgium 50°50′N 04°02′E
171 O4 **Ninoy Aquino** ✕ (Manila) Luzon, N Philippines 14°26′N 121°00′E
Nio see Íos
29 P12 **Niobrara** Nebraska, C USA 42°43′N 97°59′W
28 M12 **Niobrara River** ∽ Nebraska/Wyoming, C USA
79 I20 **Nioki** Bandundu, W Dem. Rep. Congo 02°44′S 17°42′E
76 M11 **Niono** Ségou, C Mali 14°18′N 05°59′W
76 K11 **Nioro** var. Nioro du Sahel. Kayes, W Mali 15°13′N 09°39′W
76 G11 **Nioro du Rip** SW Senegal 13°44′N 15°48′W
Nioro du Sahel see Nioro
102 K10 **Niort** Deux-Sèvres, W France 46°21′N 00°25′W
172 H14 **Nioumachoua** Mohéli, S Comoros 12°21′S 43°43′E
186 C7 **Nipa** Southern Highlands, W Papua New Guinea 06°11′S 143°27′E
11 U14 **Nipawin** Saskatchewan, S Canada 52°23′N 104°01′W
12 D12 **Nipigon** Ontario, S Canada 49°02′N 88°15′W
12 D11 **Nipigon, Lake** ◎ Ontario, S Canada
11 S13 **Nipin** ∽ Saskatchewan, C Canada
14 G11 **Nipissing, Lake** ◎ Ontario, S Canada
35 P13 **Nipomo** California, W USA 35°02′N 120°28′W
Nippon see Japan
138 K6 **Niqniqīyah, Jabal an** ▲ C Syria
62 I9 **Niquivil** San Juan, W Argentina 30°25′S 68°42′W
171 Y13 **Nirabotong** Papua, E Indonesia 02°35′S 140°08′E
Niriz see Neyrīz
163 U7 **Nirji** var. Morin Dawa Daurzu Zizhiqi. Nei Mongol Zizhiqu, N China 48°21′N 124°32′E
155 I14 **Nirmal** Andhra Pradesh, C India 19°04′N 78°21′E
153 Q13 **Nirmāli** Bihār, NE India 26°18′N 86°35′E
113 O14 **Niš** Eng. Nish, Ger. Nisch; anc. Naissus. Serbia, SE Serbia 43°21′N 21°53′E
104 H9 **Nisa** Portalegre, C Portugal 39°31′N 07°39′W
Nisa see Neisse
141 P4 **Nişab** Al Ḩudūd ash Shamālīyah, N Saudi Arabia 29°11′N 44°43′E
141 Q15 **Nişāb** var. Anşāb. SW Yemen 14°24′N 46°47′E
113 P14 **Nišava** Bul. Nishava. ∽ Bulgaria/Serbia see also Nishava
Nišava see Nishava
107 K25 **Niscemi** Sicilia, Italy, C Mediterranean Sea 37°09′N 14°23′E
Nisch/Nish see Niš
165 R4 **Niseko** Hokkaidō, NE Japan 42°50′N 140°43′E
Nishapur see Neyshābūr
114 G9 **Nishava** var. Nišava. ∽ Bulgaria/Serbia see also Nišava
Nishava see Nišava
118 L11 **Nishcha** ∽ N Belarus
165 C17 **Nishinoomote** Kagoshima, Tanega-shima, SW Japan 30°42′N 130°59′E
165 X15 **Nishino-shima** Eng. Rosario. *island* Ogasawara-shotō, SE Japan
165 I13 **Nishiwaki** var. Nisiwaki. Hyōgo, Honshū, SW Japan 34°59′N 134°58′E
141 U14 **Nishtūn** SE Yemen 15°47′N 52°08′E
Nisibin see Nusaybin
Nisiros see Nísyros
Nisiwaki see Nishiwaki
Niska see Niesky
113 O14 **Niška Banja** Serbia, SE Serbia 43°18′N 22°01′E
12 D6 **Niskibi** ∽ Ontario, C Canada
111 O15 **Nisko** Podkrapackie, SE Poland 50°31′N 22°09′E
10 H7 **Nisling** ∽ Yukon Territory, W Canada
99 H22 **Nismes** Namur, S Belgium 50°04′N 04°31′E
Nismes see Nîmes
116 M10 **Nisporeni** Rus. Nisporeny. W Moldova 47°04′N 28°10′E
Nisporeny see Nisporeni
95 K20 **Nissan** ∽ S Sweden
Nissan Islands see Green Islands
95 F16 **Nisser** ◎ S Norway
95 E21 **Nissum Bredning** *inlet* NW Denmark
29 U6 **Nisswa** Minnesota, N USA 46°31′N 94°17′W
Nistru see Dniester
115 M22 **Nísyros** var. Nisiros. *island* Dodekánisa, Greece, Aegean Sea
118 H8 **Nītaure** C Latvia 57°05′N 25°12′E
60 P10 **Niterói** prev. Nictheroy. Rio de Janeiro, SE Brazil 22°54′S 43°06′W
14 F16 **Nith** ∽ Ontario, S Canada
96 J13 **Nith** ∽ S Scotland, United Kingdom
Nitinan see Nichinan
111 I21 **Nitra** Ger. Neutra, Hung. Nyitra. Nitriansky Kraj, SW Slovakia 48°20′N 18°05′E
111 I20 **Nitra** Ger. Neutra, Hung. Nyitra. ∽ W Slovakia
111 I21 **Nitriansky Kraj** ⬖ *region* SW Slovakia
21 Q5 **Nitro** West Virginia, NE USA 38°24′N 81°50′W
Niuatobutabu see Niuatoputapu
193 X13 **Niuatoputapu** var. Niuatobutabu; prev. Keppel Island. *island* N Tonga
193 U15 **Niu'Aunofa** *headland* Tongatapu, S Tonga 21°03′S 175°19′W
Niuchwang see Yingkou
190 B16 **Niue** ◇ *self-governing territory in free association with New Zealand* S Pacific Ocean
190 F10 **Niulakita** var. Nurakita. *atoll* S Tuvalu
190 E6 **Niutao** *atoll* NW Tuvalu
93 L15 **Nivala** Oulu, C Finland 63°56′N 25°00′E
102 I15 **Nive** ∽ SW France
99 G19 **Nivelles** Walloon Brabant, C Belgium 50°36′N 04°04′E
103 P8 **Nivernais** *cultural region* C France
15 N8 **Niverville, Lac** ◎ Québec, SE Canada
27 T7 **Nixa** Missouri, C USA 37°02′N 93°17′W
35 R5 **Nixon** Nevada, W USA 39°48′N 119°24′W
25 S12 **Nixon** Texas, SW USA 29°16′N 97°45′W
Niya see Minfeng
Niyazov see Nyýazow
155 H14 **Nizāmābād** Andhra Pradesh, C India 18°40′N 78°05′E
155 H15 **Nizām Sāgar** ◎ C India
125 N16 **Nizhegorodskaya Oblast'** ⬖ *province* W Russian Federation
Nizhnegorskiy see Nyzhn'ohirs'kyy
127 S4 **Nizhnekamsk** Respublika Tatarstan, W Russian Federation 55°36′N 51°45′E
127 U3 **Nizhnekamskoye Vodokhranilishche** ⊠ W Russian Federation
123 S14 **Nizhneleninskoye** Yevreyskaya Avtonomnaya Oblast', SE Russian Federation 47°50′N 132°30′E
122 L13 **Nizhneudinsk** Irkutskaya Oblast', S Russian Federation 54°48′N 98°51′E
122 I10 **Nizhnevartovsk** Khanty-Mansiyskiy Avtonomnyy Okrug-Yugra, C Russian Federation 60°57′N 76°40′E
123 Q7 **Nizhneyansk** Respublika Sakha (Yakutiya), NE Russian Federation 71°25′N 135°59′E
127 Q11 **Nizhniy Baskunchak** Astrakhanskaya Oblast', SW Russian Federation 48°15′N 46°49′E
127 O6 **Nizhniy Lomov** Penzenskaya Oblast', W Russian Federation 53°32′N 43°39′E
127 P3 **Nizhniy Novgorod** prev. Gor'kiy. Nizhegorodskaya Oblast', W Russian Federation 56°17′N 44°E
125 T8 **Nizhniy Odes** Respublika Komi, NW Russian Federation 63°42′N 54°59′E
Nizhniy Pyandzh see Panji Poyon
122 G10 **Nizhniy Tagil** Sverdlovskaya Oblast', C Russian Federation 57°57′N 59°51′E
125 T9 **Nizhnyaya-Omra** Respublika Komi, NW Russian Federation 62°46′N 55°54′E
125 P5 **Nizhnyaya Pësha** Nenetskiy Avtonomnyy Okrug, NW Russian Federation 66°54′N 47°37′E
117 Q3 **Nizhyn** Rus. Nezhin. Chernihivs'ka Oblast', NE Ukraine 51°03′N 31°54′E
136 M17 **Nizip** Gaziantep, S Turkey 37°02′N 37°47′E
141 X8 **Nizwa** var. Nazwāh. NE Oman 23°00′N 57°50′E
Nizza see Nice
106 C9 **Nizza Monferrato** Piemonte, NE Italy 44°47′N 08°22′E
Njávdám see Näätämöjoki
Njazidja see Ngazidja
Njellim see Nellim
81 H24 **Njombe** Iringa, S Tanzania 09°20′S 34°47′E
81 G23 **Njombe** ∽ C Tanzania
Njuk, Ozero see Nyuk, Ozero
Njuksenica see Nyuksenitsa
92 I10 **Njunis** ▲ N Norway 68°47′N 19°24′E
Njurunda see Njurundabommen
93 H17 **Njurundabommen** prev. Njurunda. Västernorrland, C Sweden 62°15′N 17°24′E
94 N11 **Njutånger** Gävleborg, C Sweden 61°37′N 17°04′E
79 D14 **Nkambe** Nord-Ouest, NW Cameroon 06°35′N 10°44′E
Nkata Bay see Nkhata Bay
79 F21 **Nkayi** prev. Jacob. Bouenza, S Congo 04°11′S 13°17′E
83 J17 **Nkayi** Matabeleland North, W Zimbabwe 19°00′S 28°54′E
82 N13 **Nkhata Bay** var. Nkata Bay. Northern, N Malawi 11°37′S 34°20′E
81 E22 **Nkonde** Kigoma, N Tanzania 06°16′S 30°17′E
79 D15 **Nkongsamba** var. N'Kongsamba. Littoral, W Cameroon 04°59′N 09°53′E
N'Kongsamba see Nkongsamba
83 E16 **Nkurenkuru** Okavango, N Namibia 17°38′S 18°39′E
77 Q15 **Nkwanta** E Ghana 08°18′N 00°27′E
167 O2 **Nmai Hka** var. Me Hka. ∽ N Myanmar (Burma)
Noardwâlde see Noordwolde
39 N7 **Noatak** Alaska, USA 67°34′N 162°58′W
39 N7 **Noatak River** ∽ Alaska, USA
164 E15 **Nobeoka** Miyazaki, Kyūshū, SW Japan 32°34′N 131°37′E
27 N11 **Noble** Oklahoma, C USA 35°08′N 97°23′W
31 P13 **Noblesville** Indiana, N USA 40°03′N 86°00′W
165 R5 **Noboribetsu** var. Noboribetu. Hokkaidō, NE Japan 42°27′N 141°08′E
Noboribetu see Noboribetsu
59 H18 **Nobres** Mato Grosso, W Brazil 14°44′S 56°15′W
107 N21 **Nocera Terinese** Calabria, S Italy 39°03′N 16°10′E
41 Q16 **Nochixtlán** var. Asunción Nochixtlán. Oaxaca, SE Mexico 17°29′N 97°17′W
25 S5 **Nocona** Texas, SW USA 33°47′N 97°43′W
63 K21 **Nodales, Bahía de los** *bay* S Argentina
27 Q2 **Nodaway River** ∽ Iowa/Missouri, C USA
27 R8 **Noel** Missouri, C USA 36°33′N 94°29′W
40 H3 **Nogales** Chihuahua, NW Mexico 18°50′N 97°12′W
40 F3 **Nogales** Sonora, NW Mexico 31°17′N 110°53′W
36 M17 **Nogales** Arizona, SW USA 31°20′N 110°55′W
Nogal Valley see Dooxo Nugaaleed
102 K15 **Nogaro** Gers, S France 43°46′N 00°01′W
110 J7 **Nogat** ∽ N Poland
164 D12 **Nōgata** Fukuoka, Kyūshū, SW Japan 33°46′N 130°42′E
127 P15 **Nogayskaya Step'** *steppe* SW Russian Federation
102 M6 **Nogent-le-Rotrou** Eure-et-Loir, C France 48°19′N 00°50′E
103 O4 **Nogent-sur-Oise** Oise, N France 49°16′N 02°28′E
103 P6 **Nogent-sur-Seine** Aube, N France 48°30′N 03°31′E
122 L10 **Noginsk** Krasnoyarskiy Kray, N Russian Federation 64°28′N 91°09′E
126 L3 **Noginsk** Moskovskaya Oblast', W Russian Federation 55°51′N 38°23′E
123 T12 **Nogliki** Ostrov Sakhalin, Sakhalinskaya Oblast', SE Russian Federation 51°44′N 143°14′E
164 K12 **Nōgōhaku-san** ▲ Honshū, SW Japan 35°46′N 136°30′E
162 D5 **Nogoonnuur** Bayan-Ölgiy, NW Mongolia 49°31′N 89°48′E
61 C18 **Nogoyá** Entre Ríos, E Argentina 32°25′S 59°50′W
111 K21 **Nógrád** off. Nógrád Megye. ⬖ *county* N Hungary
Nógrád Megye see Nógrád
105 U5 **Noguera Pallaresa** ∽ NE Spain
105 U4 **Noguera Ribagorçana** ∽ NE Spain
101 E19 **Nohfelden** Saarland, SW Germany 49°35′N 07°08′E
38 A8 **Nohili Point** *headland* Kaua'i, Hawai'i, USA 22°03′N 159°48′W
104 G3 **Noia** Galicia, NW Spain 42°48′N 08°52′W
103 N16 **Noire, Montagne** ▲ S France
14 J10 **Noire, Rivière** ∽ Québec, SE Canada
15 P12 **Noire, Rivière** ∽ Québec, SE Canada
Noire, Rivi`ere see Black River
102 G6 **Noires, Montagnes** ▲ NW France
102 H8 **Noirmoutier-en-l'Île** Vendée, NW France 47°00′N 02°15′W
102 H8 **Noirmoutier, Île de** *island* NW France
187 Q10 **Noka** Nendö, E Solomon Islands 10°42′S 165°57′E
83 G17 **Nokaneng** North West, NW Botswana 19°40′S 22°12′E
93 L18 **Nokia** Länsi-Suomi, W Finland 61°29′N 23°30′E
148 K11 **Nok Kundi** Baluchistān, SW Pakistan 28°49′N 62°39′E
30 L14 **Nokomis** Illinois, N USA 39°18′N 89°17′W
30 K5 **Nokomis, Lake** ⊠ Wisconsin, N USA
78 G9 **Nokou** Kanem, W Chad 14°36′N 14°45′E
187 Q12 **Nokuku** Espiritu Santo, W Vanuatu 14°56′S 166°34′E
95 J18 **Nol** Västra Götaland, S Sweden 57°55′N 12°03′E
79 H16 **Nola** Sangha-Mbaéré, SW Central African Republic 03°29′N 16°05′E
25 P7 **Nolan** Texas, SW USA 32°15′N 100°15′W
125 R15 **Nolinsk** Kirovskaya Oblast', NW Russian Federation 57°35′N 49°54′E
Nolsø see Nólsoy
95 B19 **Nólsoy** Dan. Nolsø. *island* E Faeroe Islands
186 B7 **Nomad** Western, SW Papua New Guinea 06°11′S 142°13′E
164 B16 **Noma-zaki** Kyūshū, SW Japan
40 K10 **Nombre de Dios** Durango, C Mexico 23°51′N 104°14′W
42 I5 **Nombre de Dios, Cordillera** ▲▲ N Honduras
38 M9 **Nome** Alaska, USA 64°30′N 165°24′W
29 Q6 **Nome** North Dakota, N USA 46°39′N 97°49′W
38 M9 **Nome, Cape** *headland* Alaska, USA 64°25′N 165°00′W
162 K11 **Nomgon** var. Sangiyn Dalay. Ömnögovĭ, S Mongolia 42°50′N 105°04′E
14 M11 **Nominingue, Lac** ◎ Québec, SE Canada
Nomoi Islands see Mortlock Islands
164 B16 **Nomo-zaki** *headland* Kyūshū, SW Japan 32°34′N 129°45′E
162 G6 **Nömrög** var. Hödrögö. Dzavhan, N Mongolia 48°51′N 96°48′E
193 X15 **Nomuka** *island* Nomuka Group, C Tonga
193 X15 **Nomuka Group** *island group* W Tonga
189 Q15 **Nomwin Atoll** *atoll* Hall Islands, C Micronesia
8 L10 **Nonacho Lake** ◎ Northwest Territories, NW Canada
Nondaburi see Nonthaburi
39 P12 **Nondalton** Alaska, USA 59°58′N 154°51′W
163 V10 **Nong'an** Jilin, NE China 44°25′N 125°10′E
169 P10 **Nong Bua Khok** Nakhon Ratchasima, C Thailand 15°23′N 101°51′E
167 Q9 **Nong Bua Lamphu** Udon Thani, E Thailand 17°11′N 102°27′E
167 R7 **Nông Hèt** Xiangkhoang, N Laos 19°27′N 104°02′E
Nongkaya see Nong Khai
167 Q8 **Nong Khai** var. Mi Chai, Nongkaya. Nong Khai, E Thailand 17°52′N 102°44′E
Nongle see Jiuzhaigou
167 N14 **Nong Met** Surat Thani, SW Thailand 09°27′N 99°09′E
83 L22 **Nongoma** KwaZulu/Natal, E South Africa 27°54′S 31°40′E
167 P9 **Nong Phai** Phetchabun, C Thailand 15°58′N 101°02′E
153 U13 **Nongstoin** Meghālaya, NE India 25°24′N 91°19′E
83 C19 **Nonidas** Erongo, N Namibia 22°36′S 14°40′E
Nonni see Nen Jiang
40 I7 **Nonoava** Chihuahua, N Mexico 27°24′N 106°18′W
191 O3 **Nonouti** prev. Sydenham Island. *atoll* Tungaru, W Kiribati
167 O11 **Nonthaburi** var. Nondaburi, Nontha Buri. Nonthaburi, C Thailand 13°48′N 100°11′E
Nontha Buri see Nonthaburi
102 L11 **Nontron** Dordogne, SW France 45°34′N 00°41′E
147 T10 **Nookat** var. Iski-Nauket; prev. Eski-Nookat. Oshskaya Oblast', SW Kyrgyzstan 40°18′N 72°29′E
181 P1 **Noonamah** Northern Territory, N Australia 12°46′S 131°08′E
28 K2 **Noonan** North Dakota, N USA 48°51′N 102°57′W
Noonu see South Miladhunmadulu Atoll
99 E14 **Noord-Beveland** var. Noordbeveland. *island* SW Netherlands
99 J14 **Noord-Brabant** Eng. North Brabant. ⬖ *province* S Netherlands
98 H7 **Noorder Haaks** *spit* NW Netherlands
98 H9 **Noord-Holland** Eng. North Holland. ⬖ *province* NW Netherlands
Noordhollandsch Kanaal see Noordhollands Kanaal
98 H8 **Noordhollands Kanaal** var. Noordhollandsch Kanaal. *canal* NW Netherlands
Noord-Kaap see Northern Cape
98 L8 **Noordoostpolder** *island* N Netherlands
45 P16 **Noordpunt** *headland* Curaçao, C Netherlands Antilles 12°21′N 69°08′W
98 I8 **Noord-Scharwoude** Noord-Holland, NW Netherlands 52°42′N 04°48′E
Noordwes see North-West
98 G11 **Noordwijk aan Zee** Zuid-Holland, W Netherlands 52°15′N 04°25′E
98 H11 **Noordwijkerhout** Zuid-Holland, W Netherlands 52°16′N 04°30′E
98 M7 **Noordwolde** Fris. Noardwâlde. Fryslân, N Netherlands 52°54′N 06°10′E
Noordzee see North Sea
98 H10 **Noordzee-Kanaal** *canal* NW Netherlands
93 K18 **Noormarkku** Swe. Norrmark. Länsi-Suomi, SW Finland 61°35′N 21°54′E
39 N8 **Noorvik** Alaska, USA 66°50′N 161°01′W
10 J17 **Nootka Sound** *inlet* British Columbia, W Canada
82 A9 **Nóqui** Dem. Rep. Congo, NW Angola 05°54′S 13°30′E
95 L15 **Nora** Örebro, C Sweden 59°31′N 15°02′E
147 Q13 **Norak** Rus. Nurek. W Tajikistan 38°23′N 69°14′E
13 I13 **Noranda** Québec, SE Canada 48°16′N 79°03′W
29 W12 **Nora Springs** Iowa, C USA 43°08′N 93°00′W
95 M14 **Norberg** Västmanland, C Sweden 60°04′N 15°56′E
14 K13 **Norcan Lake** ◎ Ontario, SE Canada
197 R12 **Nord** Avannaarsua, N Greenland 81°38′N 12°51′W
78 F13 **Nord** Eng. North. ⬖ *province* N Cameroon
103 P2 **Nord** ⬖ *department* N France
92 P1 **Nordaustlandet** *island* NE Svalbard
95 G24 **Nordborg** Ger. Nordburg. Syddanmark, SW Denmark 55°04′N 09°41′E
Nordburg see Nordborg
95 F23 **Nordby** Syddtjylland, W Denmark 55°27′N 08°25′E
11 P15 **Nordegg** Alberta, SW Canada 52°27′N 116°06′W
100 E9 **Norden** Niedersachsen, NW Germany 53°36′N 07°12′E

◆ Country
● Country Capital
◇ Dependent Territory
○ Dependent Territory Capital
⬖ Administrative Regions
✕ International Airport
▲ Mountain
▲▲ Mountain Range
Volcano
∽ River
◎ Lake
⊠ Reservoir

100 G10 **Nordenham** Niedersachsen, NW Germany 53°30′N 08°29′E
122 M6 **Nordenshel'da, Arkhipelag** *island group* N Russian Federation
92 O3 **Nordenskiold Land** *physical region* W Svalbard
100 E9 **Norderney** *island* NW Germany
100 J9 **Norderstedt** Schleswig-Holstein, N Germany 53°42′N 09°59′E
94 D11 **Nordfjord** *fjord* S Norway
94 C11 **Nordfjord** *physical region* S Norway
94 D11 **Nordfjordeid** Sogn og Fjordane, S Norway 61°54′N 06°E
92 G11 **Nordfold** Nordland, C Norway 67°48′N 15°16′E
Nordfriesische Inseln *see* North Frisian Islands
100 H7 **Nordfriesland** *cultural region* N Germany
Nordgrønland *see* Avannaarsua
101 K15 **Nordhausen** Thüringen, C Germany 51°31′N 10°48′E
25 T13 **Nordheim** Texas, SW USA 28°55′N 97°36′W
94 C13 **Nordhordland** *physical region* S Norway
100 E12 **Nordhorn** Niedersachsen, NW Germany 52°26′N 07°04′E
92 I1 **Nordhurfjördhur** Vestfirdhir, NW Iceland 66°01′N 21°33′W
92 J1 **Nordhurland Eystra** ◈ *region* N Iceland
92 I2 **Nordhurland Vestra** ◈ *region* N Iceland
172 H16 **Nord, Île du** *island* Inner Islands, NE Seychelles
95 F20 **Nordjylland** ◈ *region* N Denmark
Nordjyllands Amt *see* Nordjylland
92 K7 **Nordkapp** *Eng.* North Cape. *headland* N Norway 25°47′E 71°10′N
92 O1 **Nordkapp** *headland* N Svalbard 80°31′N 19°58′E
79 N19 **Nord-Kivu** *off.* Région du Nord Kivu. ◈ *region* E Dem. Rep. Congo
Nord Kivu, Région du *see* Nord-Kivu
92 G12 **Nordland** ◈ *county* C Norway
101 J21 **Nördlingen** Bayern, S Germany 48°49′N 10°28′E
93 I16 **Nordmaling** Västerbotten, N Sweden 63°35′N 19°30′E
95 K15 **Nordmark** Värmland, C Sweden 59°52′N 14°04′E
Nord, Mer du *see* North Sea
94 F8 **Nordmøre** *physical region* S Norway
100 I8 **Nord-Ostee-Kanal** *canal* N Germany
0 J3 **Nordøstrundingen** *cape* NE Greenland
79 D14 **Nord-Ouest** *Eng.* North-West. ◈ *province* NW Cameroon
Nord-Ouest, Territoires du *see* Northwest Territories
103 N2 **Nord-Pas-de-Calais** ◈ *region* N France
101 F19 **Nordpfälzer Bergland** ▲▲ W Germany
Nord, Pointe *see* Fatua, Pointe
187 P16 **Nord, Province** ◈ *province* C New Caledonia
101 D14 **Nordrhein-Westfalen** *Eng.* North Rhine-Westphalia, *Fr.* Rhénanie du Nord-Westphalie. ◈ *state* W Germany
Nordsee/Nordsjøen/ Nordsøen *see* North Sea
100 H7 **Nordstrand** *island* N Germany
93 E15 **Nord-Trøndelag** ◈ *county* C Norway
97 E19 **Nore** *Ir.* An Fheoir. ≈ S Ireland
29 Q14 **Norfolk** Nebraska, C USA 42°01′N 97°25′W
21 X7 **Norfolk** Virginia, NE USA 36°51′N 76°17′W
97 P19 **Norfolk** *cultural region* E England, United Kingdom
192 K10 **Norfolk Island** ◇ *Australian external territory* SW Pacific Ocean
175 P9 **Norfolk Ridge** *undersea feature* W Pacific Ocean
27 U8 **Norfork Lake** ⊠ Arkansas/ Missouri, C USA
98 N6 **Norg** Drenthe, NE Netherlands 53°04′N 06°28′E
Norge *see* Norway
95 D14 **Norheimsund** Hordaland, S Norway 60°22′N 06°09′E
25 S16 **Norias** Texas, SW USA 26°47′N 97°45′W
164 L12 **Norikura-dake** ▲ Honshū, S Japan 36°06′N 137°33′E
122 K8 **Noril'sk** Krasnoyarskiy Kray, N Russian Federation 69°21′N 88°02′E
14 I13 **Norland** Ontario, SE Canada 44°46′N 78°48′W
21 V8 **Norlina** North Carolina, SE USA 36°26′N 78°11′W
30 L13 **Normal** Illinois, N USA 40°30′N 88°59′W
27 N11 **Norman** Oklahoma, C USA 35°13′N 97°27′W
Norman *see* Tulita
186 G9 **Normanby Island** *island* SE Papua New Guinea
Normandes, Îles *see* Channel Islands
58 G9 **Normandia** Roraima, N Brazil 03°57′N 59°39′W
102 L5 **Normandie** *Eng.* Normandy. *cultural region* N France
102 J5 **Normandie, Collines de** *hill range* NW France
Normandy *see* Normandie
25 V9 **Normangee** Texas, SW USA 31°01′N 96°06′W
21 Q10 **Norman, Lake** ⊠ North Carolina, SE USA
44 K13 **Norman Manley** ✈ (Kingston) E Jamaica 17°55′N 76°46′W
181 U5 **Norman River** ≈ Queensland, NE Australia
181 U4 **Normanton** Queensland, NE Australia 17°49′S 141°08′E
8 I8 **Norman Wells** Northwest Territories, NW Canada 65°18′N 126°42′W
12 H12 **Normétal** Québec, S Canada 48°59′N 79°23′W
163 O7 **Norovlin** *var.* Uldz. Hentiy, NE Mongolia 48°47′N 112°01′E
11 V15 **Norquay** Saskatchewan, S Canada 51°51′N 102°04′W
93 G15 **Norråker** Jämtland, C Sweden 64°25′N 15°40′E
94 N12 **Norrala** Gävleborg, C Sweden 61°22′N 17°04′E
Norra Ny *see* Stöllet
92 G13 **Norra Storfjället** ▲ N Sweden 65°57′N 15°15′E
92 I13 **Norrbotten** ◈ *county* N Sweden
94 N11 **Norrdellen** ◎ C Sweden
95 G23 **Nørre Aaby** *var.* Nørre Åby. Syddtjylland, C Denmark 55°28′N 09°53′E
Nørre Åby *see* Nørre Aaby
95 I24 **Nørre Alslev** Sjælland, SE Denmark 54°54′N 11°53′E
95 E23 **Nørre Nebel** Syddtjylland, W Denmark 55°45′N 08°16′E
95 G20 **Nørresundby** Nordjylland, N Denmark 57°05′N 09°55′E
21 N8 **Norris Lake** ⊠ Tennessee, S USA
18 I15 **Norristown** Pennsylvania, NE USA 40°07′N 75°20′W
95 N17 **Norrköping** Östergötland, S Sweden 58°35′N 16°10′E
Norrmark *see* Noormarkku
94 N13 **Norrsundet** Gävleborg, C Sweden 60°55′N 17°09′E
95 P15 **Norrtälje** Stockholm, C Sweden 59°46′N 18°42′E
180 L12 **Norseman** Western Australia 32°16′S 121°46′E
93 I14 **Norsjö** Västerbotten, N Sweden 64°55′N 19°30′E
95 G16 **Norsjø** ◎ S Norway
123 R13 **Norsk** Amurskaya Oblast', SE Russian Federation 52°20′N 129°57′E
Norske Havet *see* Norwegian Sea
187 Q13 **Norsup** Malekula, C Vanuatu 16°05′S 167°24′E
191 V15 **Norte, Cabo** *headland* Easter Island, Chile, E Pacific Ocean 27°03′S 109°24′W
54 F7 **Norte de Santander** *off.* Departamento de Norte de Santander. ◈ *province* N Colombia
Norte de Santander, Departamento de *see* Norte de Santander
61 E21 **Norte, Punta** *headland* E Argentina 36°17′S 56°46′W
21 R13 **North** South Carolina, SE USA 33°37′N 81°06′W
North *see* Nord
18 L10 **North Adams** Massachusetts, NE USA 42°40′N 73°06′W
113 L17 **North Albanian Alps** *Alb.* Bjeshkët e Namuna, *SCr.* Prokletije. ▲▲ SE Europe
97 M15 **Northallerton** N England, United Kingdom 54°20′N 01°26′W
180 J12 **Northam** Western Australia 31°40′S 116°40′E
83 J20 **Northam** Northern, N South Africa 24°56′S 27°18′E
1 **North America** *continent*
1 N12 **North American Basin** *undersea feature* W Sargasso Sea 30°00′N 60°00′W
0 C5 **North American Plate** *tectonic feature*
18 M11 **North Amherst** Massachusetts, NE USA 42°24′N 72°31′W
97 N20 **Northampton** C England, United Kingdom 52°14′N 00°54′W
97 M20 **Northamptonshire** *cultural region* C England, United Kingdom
151 P18 **North Andaman** *island* Andaman Islands, India, NE Indian Ocean
65 D25 **North Arm** East Falkland, Falkland Islands 52°06′S 59°21′W
21 Q13 **North Augusta** South Carolina, SE USA 33°30′N 81°58′W
173 W8 **North Australian Basin** *Fr.* Bassin Nord de l' Australie. *undersea feature* E Indian Ocean
31 R11 **North Baltimore** Ohio, N USA 41°10′N 83°40′W
11 T15 **North Battleford** Saskatchewan, S Canada 52°47′N 108°19′W
14 H11 **North Bay** Ontario, S Canada 46°20′N 79°28′W
12 H6 **North Belcher Islands** *island group* Belcher Islands, Nunavut, C Canada
29 R15 **North Bend** Nebraska, C USA 41°27′N 96°46′W
32 E14 **North Bend** Oregon, NW USA 43°24′N 124°13′W
96 K12 **North Berwick** SE Scotland, United Kingdom 56°04′N 02°44′W
North Beveland *see* Noord-Beveland
North Borneo *see* Sabah
183 P5 **North Bourke** New South Wales, SE Australia 30°03′S 145°56′E
North Brabant *see* Noord-Brabant
182 F2 **North Branch Neales** *seasonal river* South Australia
44 M6 **North Caicos** *island* NW Turks and Caicos Islands
26 L10 **North Canadian River** ≈ Oklahoma, C USA
31 U12 **North Canton** Ohio, N USA 40°52′N 81°24′W
13 R13 **North, Cape** *headland* Cape Breton Island, Nova Scotia, SE Canada 47°06′N 60°24′W
184 I1 **North Cape** *headland* North Island, New Zealand 34°23′S 173°02′E
186 G5 **North Cape** *headland* New Ireland, NE Papua New Guinea 02°33′S 150°48′E
North Cape *see* Nordkapp
18 J17 **North Cape May** New Jersey, NE USA 38°59′N 74°55′W
12 C9 **North Caribou Lake** ◎ Ontario, C Canada
21 U10 **North Carolina** *off.* State of North Carolina, *also known as* Old North State, Tar Heel State, Turpentine State. ◈ *state* SE USA
North Celebes *see* Sulawesi Utara
155 J24 **North Central** ◈ *province* N Sri Lanka
31 S4 **North Channel** *lake channel* Canada/USA
97 G14 **North Channel** *strait* Northern Ireland/Scotland, United Kingdom
21 S14 **North Charleston** South Carolina, SE USA 32°53′N 79°59′W
31 N10 **North Chicago** Illinois, N USA 42°19′N 87°50′W
195 Y10 **Northcliffe Glacier** *glacier* Antarctica
31 Q14 **North College Hill** Ohio, N USA 39°13′N 84°33′W
25 O8 **North Concho River** ≈ Texas, SW USA
19 O8 **North Conway** New Hampshire, NE USA 44°03′N 71°06′W
27 V14 **North Crossett** Arkansas, C USA 33°10′N 91°56′W
28 L4 **North Dakota** *off.* State of North Dakota, *also known as* Flickertail State, Peace Garden State, Sioux State. ◈ *state* N USA
North Devon Island *see* Devon Island
97 O22 **North Downs** *hill range* SE England, United Kingdom
18 C11 **North East** Pennsylvania, NE USA 42°13′N 79°49′W
83 I18 **North East** ◈ *district* NE Botswana
65 G15 **North East Bay** *bay* Ascension Island, C Atlantic Ocean
38 L10 **Northeast Cape** *headland* Saint Lawrence Island, Alaska, USA 63°16′N 168°50′W
81 J17 **North Eastern** ◈ *province* Kenya
North East Frontier Agency/North East Frontier Agency of Assam *see* Arunāchal Pradesh
65 E25 **North East Island** *island* E Falkland Islands
189 V11 **Northeast Island** *island* Chuuk, C Micronesia
44 L6 **Northeast Point** *headland* Great Inagua, S Bahamas 21°18′N 73°01′W
44 K5 **Northeast Point** *headland* Acklins Island, SE Bahamas 22°43′N 73°50′W
44 L12 **North East Point** *headland* E Jamaica 18°09′N 76°19′W
191 Z2 **Northeast Point** *headland* Kiritimati, E Kiribati 10°23′S 105°45′E
44 H2 **Northeast Providence Channel** *channel* N Bahamas
101 J14 **Northeim** Niedersachsen, C Germany 51°42′N 10°E
29 X14 **North English** Iowa, C USA 41°30′N 92°04′W
138 G8 **Northern** ◈ *district* N Israel
82 M12 **Northern** ◈ *region* N Malawi
186 F8 **Northern** ◈ *province* S Papua New Guinea
155 J23 **Northern** ◈ *province* N Sri Lanka
80 D7 **Northern** ◈ *state* N Sudan
82 K12 **Northern** ◈ *province* NE Zambia
Northern *see* Limpopo
80 B13 **Northern Bahr el Ghazal** ◈ *state* NW South Sudan
Northern Border Region *see* Al Ḩudūd ash Shamālīyah
83 F24 **Northern Cape** *off.* Northern Cape Province, *Afr.* Noord-Kaap. ◈ *province* W South Africa
Northern Cape Province *see* Northern Cape
190 K14 **Northern Cook Islands** *island group* N Cook Islands
80 B8 **Northern Darfur** ◈ *state* NW Sudan
Northern Dvina *see* Severnaya Dvina
97 F14 **Northern Ireland** *var.* The Six Counties. *cultural region* Northern Ireland, United Kingdom
97 F14 **Northern Ireland** *var.* The Six Counties. ◈ *political division* Northern Ireland, United Kingdom
80 D9 **Northern Kordofan** ◈ *state* C Sudan
187 Z14 **Northern Lau Group** *island group* Lau Group, NE Fiji
188 K3 **Northern Mariana Islands** ◇ *US commonwealth territory* W Pacific Ocean
Northern Rhodesia *see* Zambia
Northern Sporades *see* Vóreies Sporádes
182 D1 **Northern Territory** ◈ *territory* N Australia
Northern Transvaal *see* Limpopo
Northern Ural Hills *see* Severnyye Uvaly
84 I9 **North European Plain** *plain* N Europe
27 V2 **North Fabius River** ≈ Missouri, C USA
65 D24 **North Falkland Sound** *sound* N Falkland Islands
29 V9 **Northfield** Minnesota, N USA 44°27′N 93°10′W
19 O9 **Northfield** New Hampshire, NE USA 43°26′N 71°34′W
175 Q8 **North Fiji Basin** *undersea feature* N Coral Sea
97 Q22 **North Foreland** *headland* SE England, United Kingdom 51°22′N 01°26′E
35 P6 **North Fork American River** ≈ California, W USA
39 R7 **North Fork Chandalar River** ≈ Alaska, USA
28 K7 **North Fork Grand River** ≈ North Dakota/South Dakota, N USA
21 O6 **North Fork Kentucky River** ≈ Kentucky, S USA
39 Q7 **North Fork Koyukuk River** ≈ Alaska, USA
39 Q10 **North Fork Kuskokwim River** ≈ Alaska, USA
26 K11 **North Fork Red River** ≈ Oklahoma/Texas, SW USA
26 K3 **North Fork Solomon River** ≈ Kansas, C USA
23 W14 **North Fort Myers** Florida, SE USA 26°40′N 81°52′W
31 P5 **North Fox Island** *island* Michigan, N USA
100 G6 **North Frisian Islands** *var.* Nordfriesische Inseln. *island group* N Germany
197 N9 **North Geomagnetic Pole** *pole* Arctic Ocean
18 M13 **North Haven** Connecticut, NE USA 41°25′N 72°51′W
184 J5 **North Head** *headland* North Island, New Zealand 36°23′S 174°01′E
18 L6 **North Hero** Vermont, NE USA 44°49′N 73°14′W
35 O7 **North Highlands** California, W USA 38°40′N 121°25′W
North Holland *see* Noord-Holland
81 I16 **North Horr** Eastern, N Kenya 03°17′N 37°08′E
151 K21 **North Huvadhu Atoll** *var.* Gaafu Alifu Atoll. *atoll* S Maldives
65 A24 **North Island** *island* W Falkland Islands
184 N9 **North Island** *island* N New Zealand
21 U14 **North Island** *island* South Carolina, SE USA
31 O11 **North Judson** Indiana, N USA 41°12′N 86°44′W
North Kazakhstan *see* Severnyy Kazakhstan
31 V10 **North Kingsville** Ohio, N USA 41°54′N 80°41′W
163 Y13 **North Korea** *off.* Democratic People's Republic of Korea, *Kor.* Chosŏn-minjujuŭi-inmin-kanghwaguk. ◆ *republic* E Asia
153 X11 **North Lakhimpur** Assam, NE India 27°10′N 94°00′E
184 J3 **Northland** *off.* Northland Region. ◈ *region* North Island, New Zealand
192 K11 **Northland Plateau** *undersea feature* S Pacific Ocean
Northland Region *see* Northland
35 X11 **North Las Vegas** Nevada, W USA 36°12′N 115°07′W
31 O11 **North Liberty** Indiana, N USA 41°36′N 86°22′W
29 X14 **North Liberty** Iowa, C USA 41°45′N 91°36′W
27 V12 **North Little Rock** Arkansas, C USA 34°46′N 92°15′W
28 M13 **North Loup River** ≈ Nebraska, C USA
151 K18 **North Maalhosmadulu Atoll** *var.* North Malosmadulu Atoll, Raa Atoll. *atoll* N Maldives
31 U10 **North Madison** Ohio, N USA 41°48′N 81°03′W
North Malosmadulu Atoll *see* North Maalhosmadulu Atoll
31 P12 **North Manchester** Indiana, N USA 41°00′N 85°45′W
31 P6 **North Manitou Island** *island* Michigan, N USA
29 U10 **North Mankato** Minnesota, N USA 44°11′N 94°03′W
23 Z15 **North Miami** Florida, SE USA 25°54′N 80°11′W
151 K18 **North Miladhunmadulu Atoll** *var.* Shaviyani Atoll. *atoll* N Maldives
North Minch *see* Minch, The
23 W15 **North Naples** Florida, SE USA 26°13′N 81°47′W
175 P8 **North New Hebrides Trench** *undersea feature* N Coral Sea
23 Y15 **North New River Canal** ≈ Florida, SE USA
151 K20 **North Nilandhe Atoll** *atoll* C Maldives
36 L2 **North Ogden** Utah, W USA 41°18′N 111°57′W
North Ossetia *see* Severnaya Osetiya-Alaniya, Respublika
35 S10 **North Palisade** ▲ California, W USA 37°06′N 118°31′W
189 U11 **North Pass** *passage* Chuuk Islands, C Micronesia
28 M15 **North Platte** Nebraska, C USA 41°07′N 100°46′W
33 X17 **North Platte River** ≈ C USA
65 G14 **North Point** *headland* Ascension Island, C Atlantic Ocean
172 I16 **North Point** *headland* Mahé, NE Seychelles 04°23′S 55°28′E
31 S6 **North Point** *headland* Michigan, N USA 45°01′N 83°16′W
31 R5 **North Point** *headland* Michigan, N USA 45°21′N 83°30′W
39 S9 **North Pole** Alaska, USA 64°42′N 147°09′W
197 R9 **North Pole** *pole* Arctic Ocean
23 O4 **Northport** Alabama, S USA 33°13′N 87°34′W
23 W14 **North Port** Florida, SE USA 27°03′N 82°15′W
32 L6 **Northport** Washington, NW USA 48°54′N 117°48′W
32 L12 **North Powder** Oregon, NW USA 45°00′N 117°56′W
29 U13 **North Raccoon River** ≈ Iowa, C USA
North Rhine-Westphalia *see* Nordrhein-Westfalen
97 M16 **North Riding** *cultural region* N England, United Kingdom
96 G5 **North Rona** *island* NW Scotland, United Kingdom
96 K4 **North Ronaldsay** *island* NE Scotland, United Kingdom
36 L2 **North Salt Lake** Utah, W USA 40°51′N 111°54′W
11 P15 **North Saskatchewan** ≈ Alberta/Saskatchewan, S Canada
35 X5 **North Schell Peak** ▲ Nevada, W USA 39°25′N 114°34′W
North Scotia Ridge *see* South Georgia Ridge
86 D10 **North Sea** *Dan.* Nordsøen, *Dut.* Noordzee, *Fr.* Mer du Nord, *Ger.* Nordsee, *Nor.* Nordsjøen; *prev.* German Ocean, *Lat.* Mare Germanicum. *sea* NW Europe
35 T6 **North Shoshone Peak** ▲ Nevada, W USA 39°08′N 117°28′W
North Siberian Lowland/ North Siberian Plain *see* Severo-Sibirskaya Nizmennost'
29 R13 **North Sioux City** South Dakota, N USA 42°31′N 96°28′W
96 K4 **North Sound, The** *sound* N Scotland, United Kingdom
183 T4 **North Star** New South Wales, SE Australia 28°55′S 150°25′E
North Star State *see* Minnesota
183 V3 **North Stradbroke Island** *island* Queensland, E Australia
North Sulawesi *see* Sulawesi Utara
North Sumatra *see* Sumatera Utara
14 D17 **North Sydenham** ≈ Ontario, S Canada
18 H9 **North Syracuse** New York, NE USA 43°07′N 76°07′W
184 K9 **North Taranaki Bight** *gulf* North Island, New Zealand
12 H9 **North Twin Island** *island* Nunavut, C Canada
96 E8 **North Uist** *island* NW Scotland, United Kingdom
97 L14 **Northumberland** *cultural region* N England, United Kingdom
181 Y7 **Northumberland Isles** *island group* Queensland, NE Australia
13 Q14 **Northumberland Strait** *strait* SE Canada
32 G14 **North Umpqua River** ≈ Oregon, NW USA
45 Q13 **North Union** Saint Vincent, Saint Vincent and the Grenadines 13°15′N 61°07′W
10 L17 **North Vancouver** British Columbia, SW Canada 49°21′N 123°05′W
18 K9 **Northville** New York, NE USA 43°13′N 74°08′W
97 Q19 **North Walsham** E England, United Kingdom 52°49′N 01°22′E
39 T10 **Northway** Alaska, USA 62°57′N 141°56′W
83 G17 **North-West** ◈ *district* NW Botswana
83 G21 **North-West** *off.* North-West Province, *Afr.* Noordwes. ◈ *province* N South Africa
North-West *see* Nord-Ouest
64 I6 **Northwest Atlantic Mid-Ocean Canyon** *undersea feature* N Atlantic Ocean
180 G8 **North West Cape** *cape* Western Australia
38 J9 **Northwest Cape** *headland* Saint Lawrence Island, Alaska, USA 63°46′N 171°45′W
155 J24 **North Western** ◈ *province* W Sri Lanka
82 H13 **North Western** ◈ *province* W Zambia
North-West Frontier Province *see* Khyber Pakhtunkhwa
96 H8 **North West Highlands** ▲▲ N Scotland, United Kingdom
192 J4 **Northwest Pacific Basin** *undersea feature* NW Pacific Ocean 40°00′N 150°00′E
191 Y2 **Northwest Point** *headland* Kiritimati, E Kiribati 10°25′S 105°35′E
44 G1 **Northwest Providence Channel** *channel* N Bahamas
North-West Province *see* North-West
13 Q8 **North West River** Newfoundland and Labrador, E Canada 53°30′N 60°10′W
8 J9 **Northwest Territories** *Fr.* Territoires du Nord-Ouest. ◈ *territory* NW Canada
97 K18 **Northwich** C England, United Kingdom 53°16′N 02°32′W
25 Q5 **North Wichita River** ≈ Texas, SW USA
18 J17 **North Wildwood** New Jersey, NE USA 39°00′N 74°45′W
21 R9 **North Wilkesboro** North Carolina, SE USA 36°09′N 81°09′W
19 P8 **North Windham** Maine, NE USA 43°51′N 70°25′W
197 Q6 **Northwind Plain** *undersea feature* Arctic Ocean
29 V11 **Northwood** Iowa, C USA 43°26′N 93°13′W
29 Q4 **Northwood** North Dakota, N USA 47°43′N 97°34′W
97 M15 **North York Moors** *moorland* N England, United Kingdom
25 V9 **North Zulch** Texas, SW USA 30°54′N 96°06′W
26 K2 **Norton** Kansas, C USA 39°51′N 99°53′W
31 S13 **Norton** Ohio, N USA 40°25′N 83°04′W
21 P7 **Norton** Virginia, NE USA 36°56′N 82°37′W
39 N9 **Norton Bay** *bay* Alaska, USA
Norton de Matos *see* Balombo
31 O9 **Norton Shores** Michigan, N USA 43°10′N 86°15′W
38 M10 **Norton Sound** *inlet* Alaska, USA
27 Q3 **Nortonville** Kansas, C USA 39°25′N 95°19′W
102 I8 **Nort-sur-Erdre** Loire-Atlantique, NW France 47°27′N 01°30′W
195 N2 **Norvegia, Cape** *headland* Antarctica 71°16′S 12°25′W
18 L13 **Norwalk** Connecticut, NE USA 41°08′N 73°28′W
29 V14 **Norwalk** Iowa, C USA 41°28′N 93°40′W
31 S11 **Norwalk** Ohio, N USA 41°14′N 82°37′W
19 P7 **Norway** Maine, NE USA 44°13′N 70°30′W
31 N5 **Norway** Michigan, N USA 45°47′N 87°54′W
93 E17 **Norway** *off.* Kingdom of Norway, *Nor.* Norge. ◆ *monarchy* N Europe
11 X13 **Norway House** Manitoba, C Canada 53°59′N 97°50′W
Norway, Kingdom of *see* Norway
197 R16 **Norwegian Basin** *undersea feature* NW Norwegian Sea 68°00′N 02°00′W
84 D6 **Norwegian Sea** *var.* Norske Havet. *sea* NE Atlantic Ocean
197 S17 **Norwegian Trench** *undersea feature* NE North Sea 59°00′N 04°30′E
14 F16 **Norwich** Ontario, S Canada 42°57′N 80°37′W
97 Q19 **Norwich** E England, United Kingdom 52°38′N 01°18′E
19 N13 **Norwich** Connecticut, NE USA 41°30′N 72°02′W
18 I11 **Norwich** New York, NE USA 42°31′N 75°31′W
29 U9 **Norwood** Minnesota, N USA 44°46′N 93°55′W
31 Q15 **Norwood** Ohio, N USA 39°07′N 84°27′W
14 H11 **Nosbonsing, Lake** ◎ Ontario, S Canada
Nösen *see* Bistriţa
165 T1 **Noshappu-misaki** *headland* Hokkaidō, NE Japan 45°26′N 141°38′E
165 P7 **Noshiro** *var.* Nosiro; *prev.* Noshirominato. Akita, Honshū, C Japan 40°11′N 140°02′E
Noshirominato/Nosiro *see* Noshiro
117 Q3 **Nosivka** *Rus.* Nosovka. Chernihivs'ka Oblast', NE Ukraine 50°55′N 31°37′E
67 T14 **Nosop** *var.* Nossob, Nossop. ≈ Botswana/Namibia
83 E20 **Nossop** ≈ E Namibia
125 S4 **Nosovaya** Nenetskiy Avtonomnyy Okrug, NW Russian Federation 68°12′N 54°33′E
Nosovka *see* Nosivka
143 V11 **Noşratābād** Sīstān va Balūchestān, E Iran 29°53′N 59°57′E
95 J18 **Nossebro** Västra Götaland, S Sweden 58°12′N 12°42′E
96 K6 **Noss Head** *headland* N Scotland, United Kingdom 58°29′N 03°03′W
Nossi-Bé *see* Be, Nosy
Nossob/Nossop *see* Nosop
172 J2 **Nosy Be** ✈ Antsiränana, N Madagascar 23°36′S 47°36′E
172 J6 **Nosy Varika** Fianarantsoa, SE Madagascar 20°36′S 48°31′E
14 L10 **Notawassi** ≈ Québec, SE Canada
14 M9 **Notawassi, Lac** ◎ Québec, SE Canada
36 J5 **Notch Peak** ▲ Utah, W USA 39°08′N 113°24′W
110 G10 **Noteć** *Ger.* Netze. ≈ NW Poland
Nótíes Sporádes *see* Dodekánisa
115 J22 **Nótion Aigaíon** *Eng.* Aegean South. ◈ *region* E Greece
115 H18 **Nótios Evvoïkós Kólpos** *gulf* E Greece
115 B16 **Nótio Stenó Kérkyras** *strait* W Greece
107 L25 **Noto** *anc.* Netum. Sicilia, Italy, C Mediterranean Sea 36°53′N 15°05′E
164 M10 **Noto** Ishikawa, Honshū, SW Japan 37°18′N 137°11′E
95 G15 **Notodden** Telemark, S Norway 59°35′N 09°18′E
107 L25 **Noto, Golfo di** *gulf* Sicilia, Italy, C Mediterranean Sea
164 L10 **Noto-hantō** *peninsula* Honshū, SW Japan
164 L11 **Noto-jima** *island* SW Japan
13 T11 **Notre Dame Bay** *bay* Newfoundland, Newfoundland and Labrador, E Canada
15 P6 **Notre-Dame-de-Lorette** Québec, SE Canada 49°05′N 72°24′W
14 L11 **Notre-Dame-de-Pontmain** Québec, SE Canada 46°18′N 75°37′W
15 T8 **Notre-Dame-du-Lac** Québec, SE Canada 47°36′N 68°48′W
15 Q6 **Notre-Dame-du-Rosaire** Québec, SE Canada 48°48′N 71°27′W
15 U8 **Notre-Dame, Monts** ▲▲ Québec, S Canada
77 R16 **Notsé** S Togo 06°59′N 01°12′E
14 G14 **Nottawasaga** ≈ Ontario, S Canada
14 G14 **Nottawasaga Bay** *lake bay* Ontario, S Canada
12 I11 **Nottaway** ≈ Québec, SE Canada
23 S1 **Nottely Lake** ⊠ Georgia, SE USA
95 H16 **Nøtterøy** *island* S Norway
97 M19 **Nottingham** C England, United Kingdom 52°58′N 01°10′W
9 E14 **Nottingham Island** *island* Nunavut, NE Canada
97 N18 **Nottinghamshire** *cultural region* C England, United Kingdom
21 V7 **Nottoway** Virginia, NE USA 37°07′N 78°03′W
21 V7 **Nottoway River** ≈ Virginia, NE USA
76 G7 **Nouâdhibou** *prev.* Port-Étienne. Dakhlet Nouâdhibou, W Mauritania 20°54′N 17°01′W
76 G7 **Nouâdhibou** ✈ Dakhlet Nouâdhibou, W Mauritania 20°59′N 17°02′W
76 F7 **Nouâdhibou, Dakhlet** *prev.* Baie du Lévrier. *bay* W Mauritania
76 F7 **Nouâdhibou, Râs** *prev.* Cap Blanc. *headland* NW Mauritania 20°48′N 17°03′W
76 G9 **Nouakchott** ● (Mauritania) Nouakchott District, SW Mauritania 18°09′N 15°58′W
76 G9 **Nouakchott** ✈ Trarza, SW Mauritania 18°18′N 15°54′W
120 J11 **Noual, Sebkhet en** *var.* Sabkhat an Nawāl. *salt flat* C Tunisia
76 G8 **Nouâmghâr** *var.* Nouamrhar. Dakhlet Nouâdhibou, W Mauritania 19°22′N 16°31′W
Nouamrhar *see* Nouâmghâr
Nouă Sulița *see* Novoselytsya
187 Q17 **Nouméa** ○ (New Caledonia) Province Sud, S New Caledonia 22°13′S 166°29′E
79 E15 **Noun** ≈ C Cameroon
77 N12 **Nouna** W Burkina 12°44′N 03°54′W
83 H24 **Noupoort** Northern Cape, C South Africa 31°11′S 24°57′E
Nouveau-Brunswick *see* New Brunswick
Nouveau-Comptoir *see* Wemindji
15 T4 **Nouvel, Lacs** ◎ Québec, SE Canada
15 W7 **Nouvelle** Québec, SE Canada 48°07′N 66°16′W
15 W7 **Nouvelle** ≈ Québec, SE Canada
Nouvelle-Calédonie *see* New Caledonia
Nouvelle Écosse *see* Nova Scotia
103 R3 **Nouzonville** Ardennes, N France 49°49′N 04°45′E
147 Q11 **Nov** *Rus.* Nau. NW Tajikistan 40°10′N 69°16′E
59 I21 **Nova Alvorada** Mato Grosso do Sul, SW Brazil 21°25′S 54°19′W
Novabad *see* Navobod
111 D19 **Nová Bystřice** *Ger.* Neubistritz. Jihočeský Kraj, S Czech Republic 49°N 15°05′E
116 H13 **Novaci** Gorj, SW Romania 45°07′N 23°37′E
Nova Civitas *see* Neustadt an der Weinstrasse
Novaesium *see* Neuss
60 H10 **Nova Esperança** Paraná, S Brazil 23°09′S 52°13′W
106 H11 **Novafeltria** Marche, C Italy 43°54′N 12°18′E
60 Q9 **Nova Friburgo** Rio de Janeiro, SE Brazil 22°16′S 42°34′W
82 D12 **Nova Gaia** *var.* Cambundi-Catembo. Malanje, NE Angola 10°09′S 17°31′E
109 S12 **Nova Gorica** W Slovenia 45°57′N 13°40′E
112 G10 **Nova Gradiška** *Ger.* Neugradisk, *Hung.* Újgradiska. Brod-Posavina, NE Croatia 45°15′N 17°23′E
60 K7 **Nova Granada** São Paulo, S Brazil 20°33′S 49°19′W
60 O10 **Nova Iguaçu** Rio de Janeiro, SE Brazil 22°31′S 44°05′W
117 S10 **Nova Kakhovka** *Rus.* Novaya Kakhovka. Khersons'ka Oblast', SE Ukraine 46°45′N 33°20′E
Nová Karvinná *see* Karviná
Nova Lamego *see* Gabú
Nova Lisboa *see* Huambo
112 C11 **Novalja** Lika-Senj, W Croatia 44°33′N 14°53′E
119 M14 **Novalukoml'** *Rus.* Novolukoml'. Vitsyebskaya Voblasts', N Belarus 54°40′N 29°09′E
Nova Mambone *see* Mambone
83 P16 **Nova Nabúri** Zambézia, NE Mozambique 16°47′S 38°55′E
117 Q9 **Nova Odesa** *var.* Novaya Odessa. Mykolayivs'ka Oblast', S Ukraine 47°19′N 31°45′E
60 H10 **Nova Olímpia** Paraná, S Brazil 23°28′S 53°12′W
61 I15 **Nova Prata** Rio Grande do Sul, S Brazil 28°45′S 51°37′W
14 H12 **Novar** Ontario, S Canada 45°26′N 79°14′W
106 C7 **Novara** *anc.* Novaria. Piemonte, NW Italy 45°27′N 08°36′E
Novaria *see* Novara
13 P15 **Nova Scotia** *Fr.* Nouvelle Écosse. ◈ *province* SE Canada
0 M9 **Nova Scotia** *physical region* SE Canada
34 M8 **Novato** California, W USA 38°06′N 122°35′W
192 M7 **Nova Trough** *undersea feature* W Pacific Ocean
116 L7 **Nova Ushytsya** Khmel'nyts'ka Oblast', W Ukraine 48°50′N 27°16′E
83 M17 **Nova Vanduzi** Manica, C Mozambique 18°54′S 33°18′E
117 U5 **Nova Vodolaha** *Rus.* Novaya Vodolaga. Kharkivs'ka Oblast', E Ukraine 49°43′N 35°49′E
123 O12 **Novaya Chara** Zabaykal'skiy Kray, S Russian Federation 56°45′N 117°58′E
122 M12 **Novaya Igirma** Irkutskaya Oblast', C Russian Federation 57°08′N 103°52′E
Novaya Kakhovka *see* Nova Kakhovka
Novaya Kazanka *see* Zhanakazan
124 I12 **Novaya Ladoga** Leningradskaya Oblast', NW Russian Federation 60°03′N 32°15′E
127 R5 **Novaya Malykla** Ul'yanovskaya Oblast', W Russian Federation 54°13′N 49°55′E
Novaya Odessa *see* Nova Odesa
123 Q5 **Novaya Sibir', Ostrov** *island* Novosibirskiye Ostrova, NE Russian Federation
Novaya Vodolaga *see* Nova Vodolaha
122 I6 **Novaya Zemlya** *island group* N Russian Federation
Novaya Zemlya Trough *see* East Novaya Zemlya Trough
114 K10 **Nova Zagora** Sliven, C Bulgaria 42°29′N 26°00′E
105 S12 **Novelda** Valenciana, E Spain 38°24′N 00°45′W
111 H19 **Nové Mesto nad Váhom** *Ger.* Waagneustadtl, *Hung.* Vágújhely. Trenčiansky Kraj, W Slovakia 48°46′N 17°50′E
111 F17 **Nové Město na Moravě** *Ger.* Neustadtl in Mähren. Vysočina, C Czech Republic 49°34′N 16°05′E
Novesium *see* Neuss
111 I21 **Nové Zámky** *Ger.* Neuhäusel, *Hung.* Érsekújvár. Nitriansky Kraj, SW Slovakia 49°00′N 18°10′E
Novgorod *see* Velikiy Novgorod
Novgorod-Severskiy *see* Novhorod-Sivers'kyy
122 C7 **Novgorodskaya Oblast'** ◈ *province* W Russian Federation
117 R8 **Novhorodka** Kirovohrads'ka Oblast', C Ukraine 48°21′N 32°38′E
117 R2 **Novhorod-Sivers'kyy** *Rus.* Novgorod-Severskiy. Chernihivs'ka Oblast', NE Ukraine 52°00′N 33°15′E
31 R10 **Novi** Michigan, N USA 42°28′N 83°28′W
Novi *see* Novi Vinodolski
112 L9 **Novi Bečej** *prev.* Új-Becse, Vološinovo, *Ger.* Neubetsche, *Hung.* Törökbecse. Vojvodina, N Serbia 45°36′N 20°09′E
116 M3 **Novi Bilokorovychi** *Rus.* Belokorovichi; *prev.* Bilokorovychi. Zhytomyrs'ka Oblast', N Ukraine 51°07′N 28°02′E
25 Q8 **Novice** Texas, SW USA 32°00′N 99°38′W

◆ Country
● Country Capital
◇ Dependent Territory
○ Dependent Territory Capital
◈ Administrative Regions
✈ International Airport
▲ Mountain
▲▲ Mountain Range
Volcano
≈ River
◎ Lake
⊠ Reservoir

112 A9 **Novigrad** Istra, NW Croatia 45°19′N 13°33′E
Novi Grad see Bosanski Novi
114 G9 **Novi Iskŭr** Sofiya-Grad, W Bulgaria 42°46′N 23°19′E
106 C9 **Novi Ligure** Piemonte, NW Italy 44°46′N 08°47′E
99 L22 **Noville** Luxembourg, SE Belgium 50°04′N 05°46′E
194 I10 **Noville Peninsula** *peninsula* Thurston Island, Antarctica
Noviodunum see Soissons, Aisne, France
Noviodunum see Nevers, Nièvre, France
Noviodunum see Nyon, Vaud, Switzerland
Noviomagus see Lisieux, Calvados, France
Noviomagus see Nijmegen, Netherlands
114 M8 **Novi Pazar** Shumen, NE Bulgaria 43°20′N 27°12′E
113 M15 **Novi Pazar** *Turk.* Yenipazar. Serbia, S Serbia 43°09′N 20°31′E
112 K10 **Novi Sad** *Ger.* Neusatz, *Hung.* Újvidék. Vojvodina, N Serbia 45°16′N 19°49′E
117 T6 **Novi Sanzhary** Poltavs'ka Oblast', C Ukraine 49°21′N 34°18′E
112 H12 **Novi Travnik** *prev.* Pučarevo. Federacija Bosna I Hercegovina, C Bosnia and Herzegovina 44°12′N 17°39′E
112 B10 **Novi Vinodolski** *var.* Novi. Primorje-Gorski Kotar, NW Croatia 45°08′N 14°46′E
58 F12 **Novo Airão** Amazonas, N Brazil 02°06′S 61°20′W
Novoalekseyevka see Kobda
127 N9 **Novoanninskiy** Volgogradskaya Oblast', SW Russian Federation 50°31′N 42°43′E
58 F13 **Novo Aripuanã** Amazonas, N Brazil 05°05′S 60°20′W
117 P7 **Novoarkhangel's'k** Kirovohrads'ka Oblast', C Ukraine 48°39′N 30°48′E
117 Y6 **Novoaydar** Luhans'ka Oblast', E Ukraine 49°00′N 39°00′E
117 X9 **Novoazovs'k** *Rus.* Novoazovsk. Donets'ka Oblast', E Ukraine 47°07′N 38°06′E
123 R14 **Novobureyskiy** Amurskaya Oblast', SE Russian Federation 49°42′N 129°46′E
127 Q3 **Novocheboksarsk** Chuvashskaya Respublika, W Russian Federation 56°07′N 47°33′E
127 R5 **Novocheremshansk** Ul'yanovskaya Oblast', W Russian Federation 54°23′N 50°08′E
126 L12 **Novocherkassk** Rostovskaya Oblast', SW Russian Federation 47°23′N 40°E
127 R6 **Novodevich'ye** Samarskaya Oblast', W Russian Federation 53°33′N 48°51′E
124 M8 **Novodvinsk** Arkhangel'skaya Oblast', NW Russian Federation 64°22′N 40°49′E
Novograd-Volynskiy see Novohrad-Volyns'kyy
Novogrudok see Navahrudak
61 I15 **Novo Hamburgo** Rio Grande do Sul, S Brazil 29°42′S 51°07′W
59 H16 **Novo Horizonte** Mato Grosso, W Brazil 11°19′S 57°11′W
60 K8 **Novo Horizonte** São Paulo, S Brazil 21°27′S 49°14′W
116 M4 **Novohrad-Volyns'kyy** *Rus.* Novograd-Volynskiy. Zhytomyrs'ka Oblast', N Ukraine 50°34′N 27°32′E
145 O7 **Novoishimskiy** *prev.* Kuybyshevskiy. Severnyy Kazakhstan, N Kazakhstan 53°15′N 66°51′E
Novokazalinsk see Ayteke Bi
126 M8 **Novokhopersk** Voronezhskaya Oblast', W Russian Federation 51°09′N 41°34′E
127 R6 **Novokuybyshevsk** Samarskaya Oblast', W Russian Federation 53°06′N 49°56′E
122 J13 **Novokuznetsk** *prev.* Stalinsk. Kemerovskaya Oblast', S Russian Federation 53°45′N 87°12′E
195 R1 **Novolazarevskaya** *Russian research station* Antarctica 70°42′S 11°31′E
Novolukoml' see Novalukoml'
109 V12 **Novo mesto** *Ger.* Rudolfswert; *prev. Ger.* Neustadtl. SE Slovenia 45°49′N 15°09′E
126 K15 **Novomikhaylovskiy** Krasnodarskiy Kray, SW Russian Federation 44°18′N 38°49′E
112 L8 **Novo Miloševo** Vojvodina, N Serbia 45°43′N 20°20′E
Novomirgorod see Novomyrhorod
126 L5 **Novomoskovsk** Tul'skaya Oblast', W Russian Federation 54°05′N 38°23′E
117 U7 **Novomoskovs'k** *Rus.* Novomoskovsk. Dnipropetrovs'ka Oblast', E Ukraine 48°38′N 35°15′E
117 V8 **Novomykolayivka** Zaporiz'ka Oblast', SE Ukraine 47°58′N 35°54′E
117 Q7 **Novomyrhorod** *Rus.* Novomirgorod. Kirovohrads'ka Oblast', S Ukraine 48°46′N 31°39′E
127 N8 **Novonikolayevskiy** Volgogradskaya Oblast', SW Russian Federation 50°55′N 42°24′E
127 P10 **Novonikol'skoye** Volgogradskaya Oblast', SW Russian Federation 49°23′N 45°06′E
127 X7 **Novoorsk** Orenburgskaya Oblast', W Russian Federation 51°21′N 59°03′E
126 M13 **Novopokrovskaya** Krasnodarskiy Kray, SW Russian Federation 45°58′N 40°43′E
Novopolotsk see Navapolatsk
117 Y5 **Novopskov** Luhans'ka Oblast', E Ukraine 49°33′N 39°07′E
Novoradomsk see Radomsko
127 R8 **Novorepnoye** Saratovskaya Oblast', W Russian Federation 51°04′N 48°34′E
126 K14 **Novorossiysk** Krasnodarskiy Kray, SW Russian Federation 44°50′N 37°38′E
Novorossiyskiy/Novorossiyskoye see Akzhar
124 F15 **Novorzhev** Pskovskaya Oblast', W Russian Federation 57°01′N 29°19′E
Novoselitsa see Novoselytsya
117 S12 **Novoselivs'ke** Avtonomna Respublika Krym, S Ukraine 45°26′N 33°37′E
Novosëlki see Navasyolki
114 G6 **Novo Selo** Vidin, NW Bulgaria 44°08′N 22°48′E
113 M14 **Novo Selo** Serbia, C Serbia 43°39′N 20°54′E
116 K8 **Novoselytsya** *Rom.* Nouă Suliţa, *Rus.* Novoselitsa. Chernivets'ka Oblast', W Ukraine 48°14′N 26°18′E
127 U7 **Novosergiyevka** Orenburgskaya Oblast', W Russian Federation 52°04′N 53°40′E
126 L11 **Novoshakhtinsk** Rostovskaya Oblast', SW Russian Federation 47°48′N 39°51′E
122 J12 **Novosibirsk** Novosibirskaya Oblast', C Russian Federation 55°04′N 83°05′E
122 J12 **Novosibirskaya Oblast'** ◆ *province* C Russian Federation
122 M4 **Novosibirskiye Ostrova** *Eng.* New Siberian Islands. *island group* N Russian Federation
126 K6 **Novosil'** Orlovskaya Oblast', W Russian Federation 53°00′N 37°59′E
124 G16 **Novosokol'niki** Pskovskaya Oblast', W Russian Federation 56°21′N 30°07′E
127 Q6 **Novospasskoye** Ul'yanovskaya Oblast', W Russian Federation 53°08′N 47°48′E
Novotroickoje see Birlik
127 X8 **Novotroitsk** Orenburgskaya Oblast', W Russian Federation 51°10′N 58°18′E
Novotroitskoye see Brlik, Kazakhstan
Novotroitskoye see Novotroyits'ke, Ukraine
117 T11 **Novotroyits'ke** *Rus.* Novotroitskoye. Khersons'ka Oblast', S Ukraine 46°21′N 34°21′E
Novoukrainka see Novoukrayinka
117 Q8 **Novoukrayinka** *Rus.* Novoukrainka. Kirovohrads'ka Oblast', C Ukraine 48°19′N 31°33′E
127 Q5 **Novoul'yanovsk** Ul'yanovskaya Oblast', W Russian Federation 54°10′N 48°19′E
127 W8 **Novoural'sk** Orenburgskaya Oblast', W Russian Federation 51°19′N 56°57′E
Novo-Urgench see Urganch
116 I4 **Novovolyns'k** *Rus.* Novovolynsk. Volyns'ka Oblast', NW Ukraine 50°46′N 24°09′E
117 S9 **Novovorontsovka** Khersons'ka Oblast', S Ukraine 47°28′N 33°55′E
147 Y7 **Novovoznesenovka** Issyk-Kul'skaya Oblast', E Kyrgyzstan 42°36′N 78°44′E
125 R14 **Novovyatsk** Kirovskaya Oblast', NW Russian Federation 58°30′N 49°42′E
Novoyel'nya see Navayel'nya
117 O6 **Novozhyvotiv** Vinnyts'ka Oblast', C Ukraine 49°16′N 29°31′E
126 H6 **Novozybkov** Bryanskaya Oblast', W Russian Federation 52°36′N 31°58′E
112 F9 **Novska** Sisak-Moslavina, NE Croatia 45°20′N 16°58′E
Nový Bohumín see Bohumín
111 D15 **Nový Bor** *Ger.* Haida; *prev.* Bor u České Lípy, Hajda. Liberecký Kraj, N Czech Republic 50°46′N 14°32′E
111 E16 **Nový Bydžov** *Ger.* Neubidschow. Královéhradecký Kraj, N Czech Republic 50°15′N 15°27′E
119 G18 **Novy Dvor** *Rus.* Novyy Dvor. Hrodzyenskaya Voblasts', W Belarus 53°48′N 24°34′E
111 I17 **Nový Jičín** *Ger.* Neutitschein. Moravskoslezský Kraj, E Czech Republic 49°36′N 18°00′E
118 K12 **Novy Pahost** *Rus.* Novyy Pogost. Vitsyebskaya Voblasts', NW Belarus 55°30′N 27°29′E
Novyy Bug see Novyy Buh
117 R9 **Novyy Buh** *Rus.* Novyy Bug. Mykolayivs'ka Oblast', S Ukraine 47°40′N 32°30′E
117 Q4 **Novyy Bykiv** Chernihivs'ka Oblast', N Ukraine 50°36′N 31°39′E
Novyy Dvor see Novy Dvor
Novyye Aneny see Anenii Noi
127 P7 **Novyye Burasy** Saratovskaya Oblast', W Russian Federation 52°10′N 46°00′E
Novyy Margilan see Farg'ona
126 K8 **Novyy Oskol** Belgorodskaya Oblast', W Russian Federation 50°43′N 37°55′E
Novyy Pogost see Novy Pahost
127 R2 **Novyy Tor''yal** Respublika Mariy El, W Russian Federation 56°59′N 48°53′E
123 N12 **Novyy Uoyan** Respublika Buryatiya, S Russian Federation 56°06′N 111°27′E
122 J9 **Novyy Urengoy** Yamalo-Nenetskiy Avtonomnyy Okrug, N Russian Federation 66°06′N 76°25′E
Novyy Uzen' see Zhanaozen
111 N16 **Nowa Dęba** Podkarpackie, SE Poland 50°31′N 21°53′E
111 G15 **Nowa Ruda** *Ger.* Neurode. Dolnośląskie, SW Poland 50°34′N 16°30′E
110 F12 **Nowa Sól** *var.* Nowasól, *Ger.* Neusalz an der Oder. Lubuskie, W Poland 51°47′N 15°43′E
Nowasól see Nowa Sól
27 Q8 **Nowata** Oklahoma, C USA 36°42′N 95°36′W
142 M6 **Nowbarān** Markazī, W Iran 35°07′N 49°51′E
110 J8 **Nowe** Kujawski-pomorskie, N Poland 53°40′N 18°44′E
110 K9 **Nowe Miasto Lubawskie** *Ger.* Neumark. Warmińsko-Mazurskie, NE Poland 53°24′N 19°36′E
110 L13 **Nowe Miasto nad Pilicą** Mazowieckie, C Poland 51°37′N 20°34′E
110 D8 **Nowe Warpno** *Ger.* Neuwarp. Zachodnio-pomorskie, NW Poland 53°52′N 14°12′E
Nowgong see Nagaon
110 E8 **Nowogard** *var.* Nowógard, *Ger.* Naugard. Zachodnio-pomorskie, NW Poland 53°41′N 15°09′E
110 N9 **Nowogród** Podlaskie, NE Poland 53°14′N 21°52′E
Nowogródek see Navahrudak
111 E14 **Nowogrodziec** *Ger.* Naumburg am Queis. Dolnośląskie, SW Poland 51°12′N 15°24′E
Nowojelnia see Navayel'nya
Nowo-Minsk see Mińsk Mazowiecki
33 V13 **Nowood River** ≈ Wyoming, C USA
Nowo-Święciany see Švenčionėliai
183 S10 **Nowra-Bomaderry** New South Wales, SE Australia 34°51′S 150°41′E
149 T5 **Nowshera** *var.* Naushahra, Naushara. Khyber Pakhtunkhwa, NE Pakistan 34°00′N 72°00′E
110 J7 **Nowy Dwór Gdański** *Ger.* Tiegenhof. Pomorskie, N Poland 54°12′N 19°03′E
110 L11 **Nowy Dwór Mazowiecki** Mazowieckie, C Poland 52°26′N 20°43′E
111 M17 **Nowy Sącz** *Ger.* Neu Sandec. Małopolskie, S Poland 49°36′N 20°42′E
111 L18 **Nowy Targ** *Ger.* Neumark. Małopolskie, S Poland 49°28′N 20°00′E
110 F11 **Nowy Tomyśl** *var.* Nowy Tomysl. Wielkopolskie, C Poland 52°18′N 16°07′E
Nowy Tomysl see Nowy Tomyśl
148 M7 **Now Zād** *var.* Nauzad. Helmand, S Afghanistan 32°22′N 64°32′E
23 N4 **Noxubee River** ≈ Alabama/Mississippi, S USA
122 I10 **Noyabr'sk** Yamalo-Nenetskiy Avtonomnyy Okrug, N Russian Federation 63°08′N 75°19′E
102 L8 **Noyant** Maine-et-Loire, NW France 47°28′N 00°08′W
39 X14 **Noyes Island** *island* Alexander Archipelago, Alaska, USA
103 O3 **Noyon** Oise, N France 49°35′N 03°E
102 I7 **Nozay** Loire-Atlantique, NW France 47°34′N 01°36′W
82 L12 **Nsando** Northern, NE Zambia 10°22′S 31°14′E
83 N16 **Nsanje** Southern, S Malawi 16°57′S 35°10′E
77 Q17 **Nsawam** SE Ghana 05°47′N 00°19′W
79 E16 **Nsimalen** ✈ Centre, C Cameroon 19°15′N 81°22′E
82 K12 **Nsombo** Northern, NE Zambia 10°35′S 29°58′E
82 H13 **Ntambu** North Western, NW Zambia 12°21′S 25°03′E
83 N14 **Ntcheu** *var.* Ncheu. Central, S Malawi 14°49′S 34°37′E
79 D17 **Ntem** *prev.* Campo, Kampo. ≈ Cameroon/Equatorial Guinea
83 I14 **Ntemwa** North Western, NW Zambia 14°03′S 26°13′E
Ntlenyana, Mount see Thabana Ntlenyana
79 I19 **Ntomba, Lac** *var.* Lac Tumba. ◎ NW Dem. Rep. Congo
115 I19 **Ntóro, Kávo** *prev.* Akrotírio Kafiréas. *cape* Évvoia, C Greece
81 E19 **Ntungamo** SW Uganda 0°54′S 30°16′E
81 E18 **Ntusi** SW Uganda 0°05′N 31°13′E
83 H18 **Ntwetwe Pan** *salt lake* NE Botswana
93 M15 **Nuasjärvi** ◎ C Finland
80 F11 **Nuba Mountains** ▲▲ C Sudan
68 J9 **Nubian Desert** *desert* NE Sudan
116 G10 **Nucet** *Hung.* Diófás. Bihor, W Romania 46°28′N 22°35′E
Nu Chiang see Salween
145 U9 **Nuclear Testing Ground** *nuclear site* Pavlodar, E Kazakhstan
56 E9 **Nucuray, Río** ≈ N Peru
25 R14 **Nueces River** ≈ Texas, SW USA
9 V9 **Nueltin Lake** ◎ Manitoba/Northwest Territories, C Canada
99 K15 **Nuenen** Noord-Brabant, S Netherlands 51°29′N 05°36′E
62 G6 **Nuestra Señora, Bahía** *bay* N Chile
61 D14 **Nuestra Señora Rosario de Caa Catí** Corrientes, NE Argentina 27°48′S 57°42′W
54 J9 **Nueva Antioquia** Vichada, E Colombia 06°04′N 69°30′W
Nueva Caceres see Naga
41 O7 **Nueva Ciudad Guerrera** Tamaulipas, C Mexico 26°32′N 99°13′W
55 N4 **Nueva Esparta** *off.* Estado Nueva Esparta. ◆ *state* NE Venezuela
Nueva Esparta, Estado see Nueva Esparta
44 C5 **Nueva Gerona** Isla de la Juventud, S Cuba 21°49′N 82°49′W
42 H8 **Nueva Guadalupe** San Miguel, E El Salvador 13°30′N 88°21′W
42 M11 **Nueva Guinea** Región Autónoma Atlántico Sur, SE Nicaragua 11°40′N 84°22′W
61 D19 **Nueva Helvecia** Colonia, SW Uruguay 34°16′S 57°53′W
63 J25 **Nueva, Isla** *island* S Chile
40 M14 **Nueva Italia** Michoacán, SW Mexico 19°01′N 102°06′W
56 D6 **Nueva Loja** *var.* Lago Agrio. Sucumbíos, NE Ecuador
42 F6 **Nueva Ocotepeque** *prev.* Ocotepeque. Ocotepeque, W Honduras 14°25′N 89°10′W
61 D19 **Nueva Palmira** Colonia, SW Uruguay 33°53′S 58°25′W
41 N6 **Nueva Rosita** Coahuila, NE Mexico 27°58′N 101°11′W
42 E7 **Nueva San Salvador** *prev.* Santa Tecla. La Libertad, SW El Salvador 13°40′N 89°18′W
42 J8 **Nueva Segovia** ◆ *department* NW Nicaragua
Nueva Tabarca see Plana, Isla
Nueva Villa de Padilla see Nuevo Padilla
61 B21 **Nueve de Julio** Buenos Aires, E Argentina 35°29′S 60°52′W
44 H6 **Nuevitas** Camagüey, E Cuba 21°34′N 77°18′W
61 D18 **Nuevo Berlín** Río Negro, W Uruguay 32°59′S 58°03′W
40 I4 **Nuevo Casas Grandes** Chihuahua, N Mexico 30°23′N 107°54′W
43 T14 **Nuevo Chagres** Colón, C Panama 09°14′N 80°05′W
41 W15 **Nuevo Coahuila** Campeche, E Mexico 17°53′N 90°46′W
63 K17 **Nuevo, Golfo** *gulf* S Argentina
41 O7 **Nuevo Laredo** Tamaulipas, NE Mexico 27°28′N 99°32′W
41 N8 **Nuevo León** ◆ *state* NE Mexico
41 P10 **Nuevo Padilla** *var.* Nueva Villa de Padilla. Tamaulipas, C Mexico 24°01′N 98°48′W
56 E6 **Nuevo Rocafuerte** Orellana, E Ecuador 0°59′S 75°27′W
Nuga see Dzavhanmandal
80 O13 **Nugaal** *off.* Gobolka Nugaal. ◆ *region* N Somalia
Nugaal, Gobolka see Nugaal
185 E24 **Nugget Point** *headland* South Island, New Zealand 46°26′S 169°49′E
186 J5 **Nuguria Islands** *island group* E Papua New Guinea
184 P10 **Nuhaka** Hawke's Bay, North Island, New Zealand 39°03′S 177°43′E
138 M10 **Nuhaydayn, Wādī an** *dry watercourse* W Iraq
190 E7 **Nui Atoll** *atoll* W Tuvalu
Nu Jiang see Salween
Nûk see Nuuk
182 G7 **Nukey Bluff** *hill* South Australia
Nukha see Şäki
123 T9 **Nukh Yablonevyy, Gora** ▲ E Russian Federation 60°26′N 151°45′E
186 K7 **Nukiki** Choiseul, NW Solomon Islands 06°45′S 156°30′E
186 B6 **Nuku** Sandaun, NW Papua New Guinea 03°48′S 142°23′E
193 W15 **Nuku** *island* Tongatapu Group, NE Tonga
193 Y16 **Nuku'alofa** ● (Tonga) Tongatapu, S Tonga 21°08′S 175°13′W
193 U15 **Nuku'alofa** Tongatapu, S Tonga 21°09′S 175°14′W
190 G12 **Nukuatea** *island* N Wallis and Futuna
190 F7 **Nukufetau Atoll** *atoll* C Tuvalu
190 G12 **Nukuhifala** *island* E Wallis and Futuna
191 W7 **Nuku Hiva** *island* Îles Marquises, NE French Polynesia
191 W7 **Nuku Hiva Island** *island* Îles Marquises, N French Polynesia
190 F9 **Nukulaelae Atoll** *var.* Nukulailai. *atoll* E Tuvalu
Nukulailai see Nukulaelae Atoll
190 G11 **Nukuloa** *island* N Wallis and Futuna
186 L6 **Nukumanu Islands** *prev.* Tasman Group. *island group* NE Papua New Guinea
Nukunau see Nikunau
190 J9 **Nukunonu Atoll** *island* C Tokelau
190 J9 **Nukunonu Village** Nukunonu Atoll, C Tokelau
189 S18 **Nukuoro Atoll** *atoll* Caroline Islands, S Micronesia
146 H8 **Nukus** Qoraqalpog'iston Respublikasi, W Uzbekistan 42°29′N 59°32′E
190 G11 **Nukutapu** *island* N Wallis and Futuna
39 O9 **Nulato** Alaska, USA 64°43′N 158°06′W
39 O10 **Nulato Hills** ▲▲ Alaska, USA
105 T9 **Nules** Valenciana, E Spain 39°52′N 00°10′W
Nuling see Sultan Kudarat
182 C6 **Nullarbor** South Australia 31°28′S 130°57′E
180 M11 **Nullarbor Plain** *plateau* South Australia/Western Australia
163 S12 **Nulu'erhu Shan** ▲▲ N China
77 X14 **Numan** Adamawa, E Nigeria 09°26′N 11°58′E
165 S3 **Numata** Hokkaidō, NE Japan 43°48′N 141°55′E
81 C15 **Numatinna** ≈ W South Sudan
95 F14 **Numedalen** *valley* S Norway
95 G14 **Numedalslågen** *var.* Laagen. ≈ S Norway
93 L19 **Nummela** Etelä-Suomi, S Finland 60°21′N 24°20′E
183 O11 **Numurkah** Victoria, SE Australia 36°04′S 145°28′E
196 L16 **Nunap Isua** *var.* Uummannarsuaq, *Dan.* Kap Farvel, *Eng.* Cape Farewell. *cape* S Greenland
9 N8 **Nunavut** ◆ *territory* N Canada
54 H9 **Nunchía** Casanare, C Colombia 05°37′N 72°13′W
97 M20 **Nuneaton** C England, United Kingdom 52°32′N 01°28′W
153 W14 **Nungba** Manipur, NE India 24°46′N 93°25′E
38 L12 **Nunivak Island** *island* Alaska, USA
152 I5 **Nun Kun** ▲ NW India 34°01′N 76°04′E
98 L10 **Nunspeet** Gelderland, E Netherlands 52°21′N 05°45′E
107 C18 **Nuoro** Sardegna, Italy, C Mediterranean Sea 40°20′N 09°20′E
75 R12 **Nuqayy, Jabal** *hill range* S Libya
54 C9 **Nuquí** Chocó, W Colombia 05°44′N 77°16′W
143 O4 **Nūr** Māzandarān, N Iran 36°32′N 52°00′E
145 Q9 **Nura** ≈ N Kazakhstan
143 N11 **Nūrābād** Fārs, C Iran 30°08′N 51°30′E
Nurakita see Niulakita
Nurata see Nurota
Nuratau, Khrebet see Nurota Tizmasi
136 L17 **Nur Dağları** ▲▲ S Turkey
Nurek see Norak
Nuremberg see Nürnberg
Nürestān see Nūristān
136 M15 **Nurhak** Kahramanmaraş, S Turkey 37°57′N 37°21′E
182 J9 **Nuriootpa** South Australia 34°28′S 139°00′E
149 S4 **Nūristān** *prev.* Nūrestān. ◆ *province* C Afghanistan
127 S5 **Nurlat** Respublika Tatarstan, W Russian Federation 54°26′N 50°48′E
93 N15 **Nurmes** Itä-Suomi, E Finland 63°31′N 29°10′E
101 K20 **Nürnberg** *Eng.* Nuremberg. Bayern, S Germany 49°27′N 11°05′E
101 K20 **Nürnberg** ✈ Bayern, SE Germany 49°29′N 11°04′E
146 M10 **Nurota** *Rus.* Nurata. Navoiy Viloyati, C Uzbekistan 40°41′N 65°43′E
147 N10 **Nurota Tizmasi** *Rus.* Khrebet Nuratau. ▲▲ C Uzbekistan
149 T8 **Nūrpur** Punjab, E Pakistan 31°54′N 71°55′E
183 P6 **Nurri, Mount** *hill* New South Wales, SE Australia
25 T13 **Nursery** Texas, SW USA 28°55′N 97°05′W
169 V17 **Nusa Tenggara Barat** *off.* Propinsi Nusa Tenggara Barat, *Eng.* West Nusa Tenggara. ◆ *province* S Indonesia
Nusa Tenggara Barat, Propinsi see Nusa Tenggara Barat
171 O16 **Nusa Tenggara Timur** *off.* Propinsi Nusa Tenggara Timur, *Eng.* East Nusa Tenggara. ◆ *province* S Indonesia
Nusa Tenggara Timur, Propinsi see Nusa Tenggara Timur
171 U14 **Nusawulan** Papua, E Indonesia 04°03′S 132°56′E
137 Q16 **Nusaybin** *var.* Nisibin. Manisa, SE Turkey 37°08′N 41°11′E
39 O14 **Nushagak Bay** *bay* Alaska, USA
39 O13 **Nushagak Peninsula** *headland* Alaska, USA 58°39′N 159°03′W
39 O13 **Nushagak River** ≈ Alaska, USA
160 E11 **Nu Shan** ▲▲ SW China
149 N11 **Nushki** Baluchistān, SW Pakistan 29°33′N 66°01′E
Nussdorf see Năsăud
112 J9 **Nuštar** Vukovar-Srijem, E Croatia 45°20′N 18°48′E
99 L18 **Nuth** Limburg, SE Netherlands 50°55′N 05°52′E
100 N13 **Nuthe** ≈ NE Germany
Nutmeg State see Connecticut
39 T10 **Nutzotin Mountains** ▲▲ Alaska, USA
64 I5 **Nuuk** *var.* Nûk, *Dan.* Godthaab, Godthåb. ○ (Greenland) Kitaa, SW Greenland 64°15′N 51°35′W
92 L13 **Nuupas** Lappi, NW Finland 66°01′N 26°19′E
191 O7 **Nuupere, Pointe** *headland* Moorea, W French Polynesia 17°35′S 149°47′W
191 O7 **Nuuroa, Pointe** *headland* Tahiti, W French Polynesia
Nüürst see Baganuur
Nuwara see Nuwara Eliya
155 K25 **Nuwara Eliya** *var.* Nuwara. Central Province, S Sri Lanka 06°58′N 80°46′E
182 E7 **Nuyts Archipelago** *island group* South Australia
83 F17 **Nxaunxau** North West, NW Botswana 18°57′S 21°18′E
39 N12 **Nyac** Alaska, USA 61°00′N 159°56′W
122 H9 **Nyagan'** Khanty-Mansiyskiy Avtonomnyy Okrug-Yugra, N Russian Federation 62°10′N 65°32′E
Nyagassola see Niagassola
Nyagquka see Yajiang
81 I18 **Nyahururu** Central, W Kenya 0°04′N 36°22′E
182 M10 **Nyah West** Victoria, SE Australia 35°14′S 143°18′E
158 M15 **Nyainqêntanglha Feng** ▲ W China 30°20′N 90°28′E
159 N15 **Nyainqêntanglha Shan** ▲▲ W China
80 B11 **Nyala** Southern Darfur, W Sudan 12°01′N 24°50′E
83 M16 **Nyamapanda** Mashonaland East, NE Zimbabwe 16°59′S 32°52′E
81 H25 **Nyamtumbo** Ruvuma, S Tanzania 10°33′S 36°08′E
Nyanda see Masvingo
124 M11 **Nyandoma** Arkhangel'skaya Oblast', NW Russian Federation 61°39′N 40°10′E
83 M16 **Nyanga** *prev.* Inyanga. Manicaland, E Zimbabwe 18°13′S 32°46′E
79 D20 **Nyanga** *off.* Province de la Nyanga, *var.* La Nyanga. ◆ *province* SW Gabon
79 E20 **Nyanga** ≈ Congo/Gabon
Nyanga, Province de la see Nyanga
81 F20 **Nyantakara** Kagera, NW Tanzania 03°05′S 31°23′E
81 G19 **Nyanza** ◆ *province* W Kenya
81 E21 **Nyanza-Lac** S Burundi 04°16′S 29°38′E
68 J14 **Nyasa, Lake** *var.* Lake Malawi; *prev.* Lago Nyassa. ◎ E Africa
Nyasaland/Nyasaland Protectorate see Malawi
Nyassa, Lago see Nyasa, Lake
119 J17 **Nyasvizh** *Pol.* Nieśwież, *Rus.* Nesvizh. Minskaya Voblasts', C Belarus 53°13′N 26°40′E
166 M8 **Nyaunglebin** Bago, SW Myanmar (Burma) 17°59′N 96°44′E
166 M5 **Nyaung-u** Magway, C Myanmar (Burma) 21°03′N 95°44′E
95 H24 **Nyborg** Syddtjylland, C Denmark 55°19′N 10°48′E
95 N21 **Nybro** Kalmar, S Sweden 56°45′N 15°54′E
119 J16 **Nyeharelaye** *Rus.* Negoreloye. Minskaya Voblasts', C Belarus 53°36′N 27°04′E
195 W3 **Nye Mountains** ▲▲ Antarctica
81 I19 **Nyeri** Central, C Kenya 0°25′S 36°56′E
118 M11 **Nyeshcharda, Vozyera** ◎ N Belarus
92 O2 **Ny-Friesland** *physical region* N Svalbard
95 L14 **Nyhammar** Dalarna, C Sweden 60°19′N 14°55′E
160 F7 **Nyikog Qu** ≈ C China
83 L14 **Nyimba** Eastern, E Zambia 14°33′S 30°49′E
159 P15 **Nyingchi** *var.* Bayizhen. Xizang Zizhiqu, W China 29°27′N 94°43′E
159 P15 **Nyingchi** *var.* Pula. Xizang Zizhiqu, W China 29°34′N 94°33′E
Nyinma see Maqu
111 O21 **Nyírbátor** Szabolcs-Szatmár-Bereg, E Hungary 47°50′N 22°09′E
111 N21 **Nyíregyháza** Szabolcs-Szatmár-Bereg, NE Hungary 47°57′N 21°43′E
Nyiro see Ewaso Ng'iro
Nyitra see Nitra
Nyitrabánya see Handlová
93 K16 **Nykarleby** *Fin.* Uusikaarlepyy. Länsi-Suomi, W Finland 63°22′N 22°30′E
95 F21 **Nykøbing** Midtjylland, NW Denmark 56°48′N 08°52′E
95 I25 **Nykøbing** Sjælland, SE Denmark 54°47′N 11°53′E
95 I22 **Nykøbing** Sjælland, C Denmark 55°56′N 11°41′E
95 N17 **Nyköping** Södermanland, S Sweden 58°45′N 17°03′E
95 L15 **Nykroppa** Värmland, C Sweden 59°37′N 14°18′E
Nylstroom see Modimolle
183 P7 **Nymagee** New South Wales, SE Australia 32°06′S 146°19′E
183 V5 **Nymboida** New South Wales, SE Australia 29°57′S 152°45′E
183 U5 **Nymboida River** ≈ New South Wales, SE Australia
111 D16 **Nymburk** *var.* Neuenburg an der Elbe, *Ger.* Nimburg. Středočeský Kraj, C Czech Republic 50°12′N 15°00′E
95 O16 **Nynäshamn** Stockholm, C Sweden 58°54′N 17°55′E
183 Q6 **Nyngan** New South Wales, SE Australia 31°36′S 147°07′E
Nyoman see Neman
108 A10 **Nyon** *Ger.* Neuss; *anc.* Noviodunum. Vaud, SW Switzerland 46°23′N 06°15′E
79 D16 **Nyong** ≈ SW Cameroon
103 S14 **Nyons** Drôme, E France 44°22′N 05°06′E
79 D14 **Nyos, Lac** *Eng.* Lake Nyos. ◎ NW Cameroon
Nyos, Lake see Nyos, Lac
125 U11 **Nyrob** *var.* Nyrov. Permskiy Kray, NW Russian Federation 60°41′N 56°42′E
Nyrov see Nyrob
111 H15 **Nysa** *Ger.* Neisse. Opolskie, S Poland 50°28′N 17°20′E
32 M13 **Nyssa** Oregon, NW USA 43°52′N 116°59′W
Nysa Łużycka see Neisse
Nyslott see Savonlinna
Nystad see Uusikaupunki
95 I25 **Nysted** Sjælland, SE Denmark 54°40′N 11°41′E
125 U14 **Nytva** Permskiy Kray, NW Russian Federation 57°56′N 55°22′E
165 P8 **Nyūdō-zaki** *headland* Honshū, C Japan 39°59′N 139°40′E
125 P9 **Nyukhcha** Arkhangel'skaya Oblast', NW Russian Federation 63°24′N 46°34′E
124 H8 **Nyuk, Ozero** *var.* Ozero Njuk. ◎ NW Russian Federation
125 O12 **Nyuksenitsa** *var.* Njuksenica. Vologodskaya Oblast', NW Russian Federation 60°25′N 44°12′E
79 O22 **Nyunzu** Katanga, SE Dem. Rep. Congo 05°55′S 28°00′E
123 O10 **Nyurba** Respublika Sakha (Yakutiya), NE Russian Federation 63°17′N 118°15′E
123 O11 **Nyuya** Respublika Sakha (Yakutiya), NE Russian Federation 60°33′N 116°10′E
146 K12 **Nyýazow** *Rus.* Niyazov. Lebap Welaýaty, NE Turkmenistan 39°13′N 63°16′E
117 T10 **Nyzhni Sirohozy** Khersons'ka Oblast', S Ukraine 46°49′N 34°21′E
117 U12 **Nyzhn'ohirs'kyy** *Rus.* Nizhnegorskiy. Avtonomna Respublika Krym, S Ukraine 45°26′N 34°42′E
NZ see New Zealand
81 G21 **Nzega** Tabora, C Tanzania 04°13′S 33°11′E
76 K15 **Nzérékoré** SE Guinea 07°45′N 08°49′W
82 A10 **N'Zeto** *prev.* Ambrizete. Zaire, NW Angola 07°14′S 12°52′E
79 M24 **Nzilo, Lac** *prev.* Lac Delcommune. ◎ SE Dem. Rep. Congo
172 I13 **Nzwani** *Fr.* Anjouan, *var.* Ndzouani. *island* SE Comoros

O

29 O11 **Oacoma** South Dakota, N USA 43°49′N 99°25′W
29 N9 **Oahe Dam** *dam* South Dakota, N USA
28 M9 **Oahe, Lake** ◎ North Dakota/South Dakota, N USA
38 C9 **Oa'hu** *var.* Oahu. *island* Hawai'ian Islands, Hawai'i, USA
165 V4 **O-Akan-dake** ▲ Hokkaidō, NE Japan 43°26′N 144°09′E
182 K8 **Oakbank** South Australia 34°58′S 140°36′E
19 P13 **Oak Bluffs** Martha's Vineyard, New York, NE USA 41°25′N 70°32′W
36 K4 **Oak City** Utah, W USA 39°22′N 112°19′W
37 R3 **Oak Creek** Colorado, C USA 40°16′N 106°57′W
35 P8 **Oakdale** California, W USA 37°46′N 120°51′W
22 H8 **Oakdale** Louisiana, S USA 30°49′N 92°39′W
29 P7 **Oakes** North Dakota, N USA 46°08′N 98°05′W
22 J4 **Oak Grove** Louisiana, S USA 32°51′N 91°25′W
97 N19 **Oakham** C England, United Kingdom 52°41′N 00°45′W
32 H7 **Oak Harbor** Washington, NW USA 48°17′N 122°38′W
21 R5 **Oak Hill** West Virginia, NE USA 37°59′N 81°09′W
35 N8 **Oakland** California, W USA 37°48′N 122°16′W
29 T15 **Oakland** Iowa, C USA 41°18′N 95°22′W
19 Q7 **Oakland** Maine, NE USA 44°32′N 69°43′W
21 W3 **Oakland** Maryland, NE USA 39°24′N 79°25′W
29 R14 **Oakland** Nebraska, C USA 41°50′N 96°28′W
31 N11 **Oak Lawn** Illinois, N USA 41°43′N 87°45′W
33 P16 **Oakley** Idaho, NW USA 42°13′N 113°54′W
26 I4 **Oakley** Kansas, C USA 39°08′N 100°53′W
31 N10 **Oak Park** Illinois, N USA 41°53′N 87°46′W
11 X16 **Oak Point** Manitoba, S Canada 50°23′N 97°00′W
32 G13 **Oakridge** Oregon, NW USA 43°45′N 122°27′W
20 M9 **Oak Ridge** Tennessee, S USA 36°02′N 84°12′W
184 K10 **Oakura** Taranaki, North Island, New Zealand 39°07′S 173°58′E
22 L7 **Oak Vale** Mississippi, S USA 31°26′N 89°57′W
14 G16 **Oakville** Ontario, S Canada 43°27′N 79°41′W
25 V8 **Oakwood** Texas, SW USA 31°34′N 95°51′W
185 F22 **Oamaru** Otago, South Island, New Zealand 45°10′S 170°51′E
96 F13 **Oa, Mull of** *headland* W Scotland, United Kingdom 55°35′N 06°20′W
171 O11 **Oan** Sulawesi, N Indonesia 01°16′N 121°25′E
185 J17 **Oaro** Canterbury, South Island, New Zealand 42°29′S 173°30′E
35 X2 **Oasis** Nevada, W USA 41°01′N 114°29′W
195 S15 **Oates Land** *physical region* Antarctica
183 P17 **Oatlands** Tasmania, SE Australia 42°21′S 147°23′E
36 I11 **Oatman** Arizona, SW USA 35°03′N 114°19′W
41 R16 **Oaxaca** *var.* Oaxaca de Juárez; *prev.* Antequera. Oaxaca, SE Mexico 17°04′N 96°41′W
41 Q16 **Oaxaca** ◆ *state* SE Mexico
Oaxaca de Juárez see Oaxaca
122 I19 **Ob'** ≈ C Russian Federation
145 X9 **Oba** *prev.* Uba. ≈ E Kazakhstan
14 G9 **Obabika Lake** ◎ Ontario, S Canada
Obagan see Ubagan
118 M12 **Obal'** *Rus.* Obol'. Vitsyebskaya Voblasts', N Belarus 55°22′N 29°17′E
79 E16 **Obala** Centre, SW Cameroon 04°09′N 11°32′E
14 C6 **Oba Lake** ◎ Ontario, S Canada
164 J12 **Obama** Fukui, Honshū, SW Japan 35°32′N 135°45′E
96 H11 **Oban** W Scotland, United Kingdom 56°25′N 05°29′W
Oban see Halfmoon Bay
Obando see Puerto Inírida
104 I4 **O Barco** *var.* El Barco, El Barco de Valdeorras, O Barco de Valdeorras. Galicia, NW Spain 42°24′N 07°00′W
O Barco de Valdeorras see O Barco
Obbia see Hobyo
93 J16 **Obbola** Västerbotten, N Sweden 63°41′N 20°16′E
Obbrovazzo see Obrovac
Obchuga see Abchuha
Obdorsk see Salekhard
Óbecse see Bečej
118 I11 **Obeliai** Panevėžys, NE Lithuania 55°57′N 25°47′E
60 F13 **Oberá** Misiones, NE Argentina 27°29′S 55°08′W
108 E8 **Oberburg** Bern, W Switzerland 47°00′N 07°37′E
109 Q9 **Oberdrauburg** Salzburg, S Austria 46°45′N 12°59′E
Oberglogau see Głogówek
109 W4 **Ober Grafendorf** Niederösterreich, NE Austria 48°09′N 15°33′E
101 E15 **Oberhausen** Nordrhein-Westfalen, W Germany 51°27′N 06°50′E
Oberhollabrunn see Tulln
Oberlaibach see Vrhnika
101 Q15 **Oberlausitz** *var.* Hornja Łužica. *physical region* E Germany
26 J2 **Oberlin** Kansas, C USA 39°49′N 100°33′W
22 H8 **Oberlin** Louisiana, S USA 30°37′N 92°45′W
31 T11 **Oberlin** Ohio, N USA 41°17′N 82°13′W
103 U5 **Obernai** Bas-Rhin, NE France 48°28′N 07°30′E
109 R4 **Obernberg am Inn** Oberösterreich, N Austria 48°19′N 13°20′E
Oberndorf see Oberndorf am Neckar
101 G23 **Oberndorf am Neckar** *var.* Oberndorf. Baden-Württemberg, SW Germany 48°18′N 08°32′E
109 Q5 **Oberndorf bei Salzburg** Salzburg, W Austria 47°57′N 12°57′E
Oberneustadtl see Kysucké Nové Mesto
183 S8 **Oberon** New South Wales, SE Australia 33°42′S 149°50′E
109 Q4 **Oberösterreich** *off.* Land Oberösterreich, *Eng.* Upper Austria. ◆ *state* NW Austria

◆ Country
● Country Capital
◇ Dependent Territory
○ Dependent Territory Capital
◆ Administrative Regions
✈ International Airport
▲ Mountain
▲▲ Mountain Range
Volcano
≈ River
◎ Lake
◎ Reservoir

Oberösterreich, Land see Oberösterreich
Oberpahlen see Põltsamaa
101 M19 Oberpfälzer Wald ▲ SE Germany
109 Y6 Oberpullendorf Burgenland, E Austria 47°32′N 16°30′E
Oberradkersburg see Gornja Radgona
101 G18 Oberursel Hessen, W Germany 50°12′N 08°34′E
109 Q8 Obervellach Salzburg, S Austria 46°56′N 13°10′E
109 X7 Oberwart Burgenland, SE Austria 47°18′N 16°12′E
Oberwischau see Vişeu de Sus
109 T7 Oberwölz var. Oberwölz-Stadt. Steiermark, SE Austria 47°12′N 14°20′E
Oberwölz-Stadt see Oberwölz
31 S13 Obetz Ohio, N USA 39°52′N 82°57′W
Ob', Gulf of see Obskaya Guba
58 H12 Óbidos Pará, NE Brazil 01°52′S 55°30′W
104 F10 Óbidos Leiria, C Portugal 39°21′N 09°09′W
Obidovichi see Abidavichy
147 Q13 Obigarm W Tajikistan 38°42′N 69°34′E
165 T2 Obihiro Hokkaidō, NE Japan 42°56′N 143°10′E
Obi-Khingou see Khingov
147 P13 Obikiik SW Tajikistan 38°07′N 68°36′E
Obilić see Obiliq
113 N16 Obiliq Serb. Obilić. N Kosovo 42°50′N 20°57′E
127 O12 Obil'noye Respublika Kalmykiya, SW Russian Federation 47°31′N 44°24′E
20 F8 Obion Tennessee, S USA 36°15′N 89°11′W
20 F8 Obion River ≈ Tennessee, S USA
171 S12 Obi, Pulau island Maluku, E Indonesia
165 S2 Obira Hokkaidō, NE Japan 44°01′N 141°39′E
127 N11 Oblivskaya Rostovskaya Oblast', SW Russian Federation 48°34′N 42°31′E
123 R14 Obluch'ye Yevreyskaya Avtonomnaya Oblast', SE Russian Federation 48°59′N 131°18′E
126 K4 Obninsk Kaluzhskaya Oblast', W Russian Federation 55°06′N 36°40′E
114 J8 Obnova Pleven, N Bulgaria 43°26′N 25°04′E
79 N15 Obo Haut-Mbomou, E Central African Republic 05°20′N 26°29′E
159 T9 Obo Qinghai, C China 37°57′N 101°03′E
80 M11 Obock E Djibouti 11°57′N 43°09′E
Obol' see Obal'
Obolyanka see Abalyanka
171 V13 Obome Papua, E Indonesia 03°42′S 133°21′E
110 G11 Oborniki Wielkolpolskie, W Poland 52°38′N 16°48′E
79 G19 Obouya Cuvette, C Congo 0°56′S 15°41′E
126 J8 Oboyan' Kurskaya Oblast', W Russian Federation 51°12′N 36°15′E
124 M9 Obozerskiy Arkhangel'skaya Oblast', NW Russian Federation 63°26′N 40°20′E
112 L11 Obrenovac Serbia, N Serbia 44°39′N 20°12′E
112 D12 Obrovac It. Obbrovazzo. Zadar, SW Croatia 44°12′N 15°40′E
Obrovo see Abrova
35 Q3 Observation Peak ▲ California, W USA 40°48′N 120°07′W
122 J8 Obskaya Guba Eng. Gulf of Ob. gulf N Russian Federation
173 N13 Ob' Tablemount undersea feature S Indian Ocean 50°16′S 51°59′E
173 T10 Ob' Trench undersea feature E Indian Ocean
77 P16 Obuasi S Ghana 06°15′N 01°36′W
117 P5 Obukhiv Rus. Obukhov. Kyyivs'ka Oblast', N Ukraine 50°05′N 30°37′E
Obukhov see Obukhiv
125 U14 Obva ≈ NW Russian Federation
108 F8 Obwalden ◆ canton C Switzerland
117 V10 Obytichna Kosa spit SE Ukraine
117 V10 Obytichna Zatoka gulf SE Ukraine
114 N9 Obzor Burgas, E Bulgaria 42°52′N 27°53′E
105 O3 Oca ≈ N Spain
23 W10 Ocala Florida, SE USA 29°11′N 82°08′W
40 M7 Ocampo Coahuila, NE Mexico 27°18′N 102°24′W
54 G7 Ocaña Norte de Santander, N Colombia 08°16′N 73°21′W
105 N9 Ocaña Castilla-La Mancha, C Spain 39°57′N 03°30′W
104 H4 O Carballiño Cast. Carballiño. Galicia, NW Spain 42°26′N 08°05′W
37 T9 Ocate New Mexico, SW USA 36°09′N 105°03′W
Ocavango see Okavango
57 D14 Occidental, Cordillera ▲ W South America
21 Q6 Oceana West Virginia, NE USA 37°41′N 81°37′W
21 Z4 Ocean City Maryland, NE USA 38°20′N 75°05′W
18 J17 Ocean City New Jersey, NE USA 39°15′N 74°33′W
10 K15 Ocean Falls British Columbia, SW Canada 52°24′N 127°42′W
Ocean Island see Banaba
Ocean Island see Kure Atoll
64 J9 Oceanographer Fracture Zone tectonic feature NW Atlantic Ocean
35 U17 Oceanside California, W USA 33°12′N 117°23′W
22 M9 Ocean Springs Mississippi, S USA 30°24′N 88°49′W
Ocean State see Rhode Island
25 O9 O C Fisher Lake ⊠ Texas, SW USA
117 Q10 Ochakiv Rus. Ochakov. Mykolayivs'ka Oblast', S Ukraine 46°36′N 31°33′E
Ochakov see Ochakiv
Ochamchira see Ochamchire
137 Q9 Ochamchire Rus. Ochamchira; prev. Och'amch'ire. W Georgia 42°45′N 41°30′E
Och'amch'ire see Ochamchire
Ochansk see Okhansk
125 T15 Ocher Permskiy Kray, NW Russian Federation 57°54′N 54°40′E
115 I19 Óchi ▲ Évvoia, C Greece 38°03′N 24°27′E
165 W4 Ochiishi-misaki headland Hokkaidō, NE Japan 43°10′N 145°29′E
23 S9 Ochlockonee River ≈ Florida/Georgia, SE USA
44 K12 Ocho Rios C Jamaica 18°24′N 77°06′W
Ochrida see Ohrid
Ochrida, Lake see Ohrid, Lake
101 J19 Ochsenfurt Bayern, C Germany 49°39′N 10°03′E
23 U7 Ocilla Georgia, SE USA 31°35′N 83°15′W
94 N13 Ockelbo Gävleborg, C Sweden 60°51′N 16°46′E
Ocker see Oker
95 I19 Öckerö Västra Götaland, S Sweden 57°43′N 11°39′E
23 U6 Ocmulgee River ≈ Georgia, SE USA
116 H11 Ocna Mureş Hung. Marosújvár; prev. Ocna Mureşului, prev. Hung. Marosújvárakna. Alba, C Romania 46°25′N 23°53′E
Ocna Mureşului see Ocna Mureş
116 H11 Ocna Sibiului Ger. Salzburg, Hung. Vizakna. Sibiu, C Romania 45°52′N 23°59′E
116 H13 Ocnele Mari prev. Vioara. Vâlcea, S Romania 45°03′N 24°18′E
116 L7 Ocniţa Rus. Oknitsa. N Moldova 48°25′N 27°30′E
23 U4 Oconee, Lake ⊠ Georgia, SE USA
23 U5 Oconee River ≈ Georgia, SE USA
30 M9 Oconomowoc Wisconsin, N USA 43°06′N 88°29′W
30 M6 Oconto Wisconsin, N USA 44°55′N 87°52′W
30 M6 Oconto Falls Wisconsin, N USA 44°52′N 88°06′W
30 M6 Oconto River ≈ Wisconsin, N USA
104 I3 O Corgo Galicia, NW Spain 42°56′N 07°25′W
41 V16 Ocosingo Chiapas, SE Mexico 17°04′N 92°15′W
42 J8 Ocotal Nueva Segovia, NW Nicaragua 13°38′N 86°28′W
42 F6 Ocotepeque ◆ department W Honduras
Ocotepeque see Nueva Ocotepeque
40 L13 Ocotlán Jalisco, SW Mexico 20°21′N 102°42′W
41 R16 Ocotlán var. Ocotlán de Morelos. Oaxaca, SE Mexico 16°49′N 96°49′W
Ocotlán de Morelos see Ocotlán
41 U16 Ocozocuautla Chiapas, SE Mexico 16°46′N 93°22′W
21 Y10 Ocracoke Island island North Carolina, SE USA
102 I3 Octeville Manche, N France 49°37′N 01°39′W
October Revolution Island see Oktyabr'skoy Revolyutsii, Ostrov
43 R17 Ocú Herrera, S Panama 07°55′N 80°43′W
83 Q14 Ocua Cabo Delgado, NE Mozambique 13°37′S 39°44′E
Ocumare see Ocumare del Tuy
54 M5 Ocumare del Tuy var. Ocumare. Miranda, N Venezuela 10°07′N 66°47′W
77 P17 Oda SE Ghana 05°55′N 00°56′W
165 G12 Ōda var. Ōda. Shimane, Honshū, SW Japan 35°10′N 132°29′E
92 K3 Ódadhahraun lava flow C Iceland
165 Q7 Ōdate Akita, Honshū, C Japan 40°18′N 140°34′E
165 N14 Odawara Kanagawa, Honshū, S Japan 35°15′N 139°08′E
95 D14 Odda Hordaland, S Norway 60°03′N 06°34′E
95 G22 Odder Midtjylland, C Denmark 55°59′N 10°10′E
Oddur see Xuddur
29 T13 Odebolt Iowa, C USA 42°18′N 95°15′W
104 H14 Odeleite Faro, S Portugal 37°02′N 07°29′W
25 Q4 Odell Texas, SW USA 34°19′N 99°24′W
25 T14 Odem Texas, SW USA 27°57′N 97°34′W
104 F13 Odemira Beja, S Portugal 37°35′N 08°38′W
136 C14 Ödemiş İzmir, SW Turkey 38°11′N 27°58′E
Ödenburg see Sopron
83 I22 Odendaalsrus Free State, C South Africa 27°52′S 26°42′E
Odenpäh see Otepää
95 H23 Odense Syddtjylland, C Denmark 55°24′N 10°23′E
101 H19 Odenwald ▲ W Germany
84 H10 Oder Cz./Pol. Odra. ≈ C Europe
Oderberg see Bohumín
100 P11 Oderbruch wetland Germany/Poland
Oderhaff see Szczeciński, Zalew
100 O11 Oder-Havel-Kanal canal NE Germany
Oderhellen see Odorheiu Secuiesc
100 P13 Oder-Spree-Kanal canal NE Germany
Odertal see Zdzieszowice
106 I7 Oderzo Veneto, NE Italy 45°48′N 12°33′E
117 P10 Odesa Rus. Odessa. Odes'ka Oblast', SW Ukraine 46°29′N 30°44′E
24 M8 Odessa Texas, SW USA 31°51′N 102°22′W
32 K8 Odessa Washington, NW USA 47°19′N 118°41′W
Odesa see Odes'ka Oblast'
95 L18 Ödeshög Östergötland, S Sweden 58°13′N 14°40′E
117 O9 Odes'ka Oblast' var. Odesa, Rus. Odesskaya Oblast'. ◆ province SW Ukraine
Odessa see Odesa
Odesskaya Oblast' see Odes'ka Oblast'
122 H12 Odesskoye Omskaya Oblast', C Russian Federation 54°15′N 72°45′E
Odessus see Varna
102 F6 Odet ≈ NW France
104 I14 Odiel ≈ SW Spain
76 L14 Odienné NW Ivory Coast 09°32′N 07°35′W
171 O4 Odiongan Tablas Island, C Philippines 12°23′N 122°01′E
Odisha see Orissa
116 L12 Odobeşti Vrancea, E Romania 45°46′N 27°06′E
110 H13 Odolanów Ger. Adelnau. Wielkopolskie, C Poland 51°35′N 17°42′E
167 R13 Ŏdôngk Kâmpóng Spoe, S Cambodia 11°48′N 104°45′E
25 N6 O'donnell Texas, SW USA 32°57′N 101°49′W
98 O7 Odoorn Drenthe, NE Netherlands 52°52′N 06°49′E
Odorhei see Odorheiu Secuiesc
116 J11 Odorheiu Secuiesc Ger. Oderhellen, Hung. Vámosudvarhely; prev. Odorhei, Ger. Hofmarkt. Harghita, C Romania 46°18′N 25°19′E
Odra see Oder
112 J9 Odžaci Ger. Hodschag, Hung. Hodság. Vojvodina, NW Serbia 45°31′N 19°15′E
59 N14 Oeiras Piauí, E Brazil 07°00′S 42°07′W
104 F11 Oeiras Lisboa, C Portugal 38°41′N 09°18′W
101 G14 Oelde Nordrhein-Westfalen, W Germany 51°49′N 08°09′E
28 J11 Oelrichs South Dakota, N USA 43°08′N 103°13′W
101 M17 Oelsnitz Sachsen, E Germany 50°22′N 12°12′E
Oels/Oels in Schlesien see Oleśnica
29 X12 Oelwein Iowa, C USA 42°40′N 91°54′W
Oeniadae see Oiniádes
191 N17 Oeno Island atoll Pitcairn Islands, C Pacific Ocean
Oesel see Saaremaa
108 L7 Oetz var. Ötz. Tirol, W Austria 47°15′N 10°56′E
137 P11 Of Trabzon, NE Turkey 40°57′N 40°17′E
30 K15 O'Fallon Illinois, N USA 38°35′N 89°54′W
27 W4 O'Fallon Missouri, C USA 38°54′N 90°31′W
107 N16 Ofanto ≈ S Italy
97 D18 Offaly Ir. Ua Uíbh Fhailí; prev. King's County. cultural region C Ireland
101 H18 Offenbach var. Offenbach am Main. Hessen, W Germany 50°06′N 08°46′E
Offenbach am Main see Offenbach
101 F22 Offenburg Baden-Württemberg, SW Germany 48°28′N 07°57′E
182 C2 Officer Creek seasonal river South Australia
Oficina María Elena see María Elena
Oficina Pedro de Valdivia see Pedro de Valdivia
115 K22 Ofidoússa island Kykládes, Greece, Aegean Sea
Ofiral see Sharm ash Shaykh
92 H10 Ofotfjorden fjord N Norway
192 L16 Ofu island Manua Islands, E American Samoa
165 R9 Ōfunato Iwate, Honshū, C Japan 39°04′N 141°43′E
165 P8 Oga Akita, Honshū, C Japan 39°56′N 139°47′E
Ogaadeen see Ogaden
165 Q9 Ogachi Akita, Honshū, C Japan 39°03′N 140°26′E
165 P9 Ogachi-tōge pass Honshū, C Japan
81 N14 Ogaden Som. Ogaadeen. plateau Ethiopia/Somalia
165 P8 Oga-hantō peninsula Honshū, C Japan
165 K13 Ōgaki Gifu, Honshū, SW Japan 35°22′N 136°35′E
28 L15 Ogallala Nebraska, C USA 41°09′N 101°44′W
168 M14 Ogan, Air ≈ Sumatera, W Indonesia
165 Y15 Ogasawara-shotō Eng. Bonin Islands. island group SE Japan
14 I9 Ogascanane, Lac ⊠ Québec, SE Canada
165 R7 Ogawara-ko ◎ Honshū, C Japan
77 T15 Ogbomosho var. Ogmoboso. Oyo, W Nigeria 08°10′N 04°16′E
29 U13 Ogden Iowa, C USA 42°03′N 94°01′W
36 L2 Ogden Utah, W USA 41°09′N 111°58′W
18 I6 Ogdensburg New York, NE USA 44°42′N 75°25′W
23 W5 Ogeechee River ≈ Georgia, SE USA
Oger see Ogre
165 N10 Ogi Niigata, Sado, C Japan 37°49′N 138°16′E
10 H5 Ogilvie Yukon Territory, NW Canada 63°34′N 139°44′W
10 H4 Ogilvie ≈ Yukon Territory, NW Canada
10 H5 Ogilvie Mountains ▲ Yukon Territory, NW Canada
Oginskiy Kanal see Ahinski Kanal
162 J7 Ögiynuur var. Dzegstey. Arhangay, C Mongolia 47°38′N 102°31′E
146 F6 Og'iyon Sho'rxogi wetland NW Uzbekistan
146 B10 Oglanly Balkan Welaýaty, W Turkmenistan 39°56′N 54°25′E
23 T5 Oglethorpe Georgia, SE USA 32°17′N 84°03′W
23 T2 Oglethorpe, Mount ▲ Georgia, SE USA 34°29′N 84°19′W
106 F7 Oglio anc. Ollius. ≈ N Italy
Ogmoboso see Ogbomosho
103 T8 Ognon ≈ E France
123 R13 Ogodzha Amurskaya Oblast', S Russian Federation 52°51′N 132°49′E
77 W16 Ogoja Cross River, S Nigeria 06°37′N 08°48′E
12 C10 Ogoki ≈ Ontario, S Canada
12 D11 Ogoki Lake ◎ Ontario, C Canada
Ögöömör see Hanhongor
79 F19 Ogooué ≈ Congo/Gabon
79 E18 Ogooué-Ivindo off. Province de l'Ogooué-Ivindo, var. L'Ogooué-Ivindo. ◈ province N Gabon
Ogooué-Ivindo, Province de l' see Ogooué-Ivindo
79 E19 Ogooué-Lolo off. Province de l'Ogooué-Lolo, var. L'Ogooué-Lolo. ◈ province C Gabon
Ogooué-Lolo, Province de l' see Ogooué-Lolo
79 C19 Ogooué-Maritime off. Province de l'Ogooué-Maritime, var. L'Ogooué-Maritime. ◈ province W Gabon
Ogooué-Maritime, Province de l' see Ogooué-Maritime
165 D14 Ogōri Fukuoka, Kyūshū, SW Japan 33°24′N 130°34′E
114 H7 Ogosta ≈ NW Bulgaria
112 Q9 Ograzhden Bul. Ograzhdén. ▲ Bulgaria/FYR Macedonia see also Ograzhden
114 G12 Ograzhden Mac. Orgražden. ▲ Bulgaria/FYR Macedonia see also Ograzhden
Ograzhden see Ograzhden
118 G9 Ogre Ger. Oger. C Latvia 56°49′N 24°36′E
118 H9 Ogre ≈ C Latvia
112 C10 Ogulin Karlovac, NW Croatia 45°15′N 15°13′E
77 S16 Ogun ◈ state SW Nigeria
Ogurdzhaly, Ostrov see Ogurjaly Adasy
146 A12 Ogurjaly Adasy Rus. Ogurdzhaly, Ostrov. island W Turkmenistan
77 U16 Ogwashi-Uku Delta, S Nigeria 06°08′N 06°38′E
Okarem see Ekerem
185 B23 Ohai Southland, South Island, New Zealand 45°56′S 167°59′E
147 Q10 Ohangaron Rus. Akhangaran. Toshkent Viloyati, E Uzbekistan 40°56′N 69°37′E
147 Q10 Ohangaron Rus. Akhangaran. ≈ E Uzbekistan
83 C16 Ohangwena ◈ district N Namibia
30 M10 O'Hare ✈ (Chicago) Illinois, N USA 41°59′N 87°56′W
165 R6 Ōhata Aomori, Honshū, C Japan 41°23′N 141°09′E
184 L13 Ohau Manawatu-Wanganui, North Island, New Zealand 40°40′S 175°15′E
185 E20 Ohau, Lake ◎ South Island, New Zealand
Ohcejohka see Utsjoki
99 J20 Ohey Namur, SE Belgium 50°26′N 05°07′E
191 X15 O'Higgins, Cabo headland Easter Island, Chile, E Pacific Ocean 27°05′S 109°15′W
O'Higgins, Lago see San Martín, Lago
31 S12 Ohio off. State of Ohio, also known as Buckeye State. ◈ state N USA
0 L10 Ohio River ≈ N USA
101 H16 Ohm ≈ C Germany
193 W16 Ohonua 'Eua, E Tonga 21°20′S 174°57′W
23 V5 Ohoopee River ≈ Georgia, SE USA
100 L12 Ohre Ger. Eger. ≈ Czech Republic/Germany
Ohri see Ohrid
113 M20 Ohrid Turk. Ochrida, Ohri. SW FYR Macedonia 41°07′N 20°48′E
113 M20 Ohrid, Lake var. Lake Ochrida, Alb. Liqeni i Ohrit, Mac. Ohridsko Ezero. ◎ Albania/FYR Macedonia
Ohridsko Ezero/Ohrit, Liqeni i see Ohrid, Lake
184 L9 Ohura Manawatu-Wanganui, North Island, New Zealand 38°51′S 174°58′E
58 J9 Oiapoque Amapá, E Brazil 03°54′N 51°46′W
58 J10 Oiapoque, Rio var. Fleuve l'Oyapok, Oyapock. ≈ Brazil/French Guiana see also Oyapok, Fleuve l'
Oiapoque, Rio see Oyapok, Fleuve l'
54 G8 Oiba Santander, C Colombia 06°16′N 73°18′W
15 O9 Oies, Île aux island Québec, SE Canada
92 L13 Oijärvi Oulu, C Finland 65°38′N 26°05′E
92 L12 Oikarainen Lappi, N Finland 66°30′N 25°46′E
188 F10 Oikuul Babeldaob, N Palau 07°24′N 134°36′E
18 C13 Oil City Pennsylvania, NE USA 41°25′N 79°42′W
18 C12 Oil Creek ≈ Pennsylvania, NE USA
35 R13 Oildale California, W USA 35°25′N 119°01′W
Oileán Ciarral see Castleisland
Oil Islands see Chagos Archipelago
115 D18 Oiniádes anc. Oeniadae. site of ancient city Dytikí Elláda, W Greece
115 L18 Oinoússes island E Greece
Oírr, Inis see Inisheer
99 J15 Oirschot Noord-Brabant, S Netherlands 51°30′N 05°18′E
103 N4 Oise ◈ department N France
103 P3 Oise ≈ N France
99 J14 Oisterwijk Noord-Brabant, S Netherlands 51°35′N 05°12′E
45 O14 Oistins S Barbados 13°04′N 59°33′W
165 E4 Ōita Ōita, Kyūshū, SW Japan 33°15′N 131°35′E
165 D14 Ōita off. Ōita-ken. ◈ prefecture Kyūshū, SW Japan
Ōita-ken see Ōita
115 E17 Oíti ▲ C Greece 38°48′N 22°12′E
165 S4 Oiwake Hokkaidō, NE Japan 42°54′N 141°49′E
35 R14 Ojai California, W USA 34°25′N 119°15′W
94 K13 Öje Dalarna, C Sweden 60°49′N 13°54′E
93 J14 Öjebyn Norrbotten, N Sweden 65°20′N 21°26′E
165 B13 Ojika-jima island SW Japan
40 K5 Ojinaga Chihuahua, N Mexico 29°31′N 104°26′W
40 M11 Ojo Caliente var. Ojocaliente. Zacatecas, C Mexico 22°35′N 102°18′W
Ojocaliente see Ojo Caliente
40 D6 Ojo de Liebre, Laguna var. Laguna Scammon, Scammon Lagoon. lagoon NW Mexico
62 I7 Ojos del Salado, Cerro ▲ W Argentina 27°04′S 68°34′W
105 R7 Ojos Negros Aragón, NE Spain 40°43′N 01°30′W
40 M12 Ojuelos de Jalisco Aguascalientes, C Mexico 21°52′N 101°40′W
127 N4 Oka ≈ W Russian Federation
83 D19 Okahandja Otjozondjupa, C Namibia 21°58′S 16°55′E
184 L9 Okahukura Manawatu-Wanganui, North Island, New Zealand 38°48′S 175°13′E
184 J3 Okaihau Northland, North Island, New Zealand 35°19′S 173°45′E
83 D18 Okakarara Otjozondjupa, N Namibia 20°33′S 17°20′E
13 P5 Okak Islands island group Newfoundland and Labrador, E Canada
10 M17 Okanagan ≈ British Columbia, SW Canada
11 N17 Okanagan Lake ◎ British Columbia, SW Canada
Ókanizsa see Kanjiža
83 C16 Okankolo Oshikoto, N Namibia 17°57′S 16°28′E
32 K6 Okanogan River ≈ Washington, NW USA
83 D18 Okaputa Otjozondjupa, N Namibia 20°09′S 16°56′E
149 V9 Okāra Punjab, E Pakistan 30°49′N 73°31′E
26 M10 Okarche Oklahoma, C USA 35°43′N 97°58′W
Okarem see Ekerem
189 X14 Okat Harbor harbor Kosrae, E Micronesia
22 M5 Okatibbee Creek ≈ Mississippi, S USA
83 C17 Okaukuejo Kunene, N Namibia 19°10′S 15°23′E
Okavanggo see Cubango/Okavango
83 E17 Okavango ◈ district NW Namibia
83 G17 Okavango var. Cubango, Kavango, Kavengo, Kubango, Okavanggo, Port. Ocavango. ≈ S Africa see also Cubango
Okavango see Cubango
83 G17 Okavango Delta wetland N Botswana
164 M12 Okaya Nagano, Honshū, S Japan 36°03′N 138°00′E
164 H13 Okayama Okayama, Honshū, SW Japan 34°40′N 133°54′E
164 H13 Okayama off. Okayama-ken. ◈ prefecture Honshū, SW Japan
Okayama-ken see Okayama
164 L14 Okazaki Aichi, Honshū, C Japan 34°58′N 137°10′E
110 M12 Okęcie ✈ (Warszawa) Mazowieckie, C Poland 52°08′N 20°57′E
23 Y13 Okeechobee Florida, SE USA 27°14′N 80°49′W
23 Y14 Okeechobee, Lake ◎ Florida, SE USA
26 M9 Okeene Oklahoma, C USA 36°07′N 98°19′W
23 V8 Okefenokee Swamp wetland Georgia, SE USA
97 J24 Okehampton SW England, United Kingdom 50°44′N 04°W
27 P10 Okemah Oklahoma, C USA 35°25′N 96°20′W
77 U16 Okene Kogi, S Nigeria 07°31′N 06°15′E
100 K13 Oker var. Ocker. ≈ NW Germany
101 J14 Oker-Stausee ◎ C Germany
123 T12 Okha Ostrov Sakhalin, Sakhalinskaya Oblast', SE Russian Federation 53°33′N 142°55′E
125 U15 Okhansk var. Ochansk. Permskiy Kray, NW Russian Federation 57°44′N 55°20′E
123 S10 Okhotsk Khabarovskiy Kray, E Russian Federation 59°21′N 143°15′E
192 J2 Okhotsk, Sea of sea NW Pacific Ocean
117 T4 Okhtyrka Rus. Akhtyrka. Sums'ka Oblast', NE Ukraine 50°19′N 34°54′E
83 E23 Okiep Northern Cape, W South Africa 29°39′S 17°53′E
Oki-guntō see Oki-shotō
164 H11 Oki-kaikyō strait SW Japan
165 P16 Okinawa Okinawa, SW Japan 26°20′N 127°47′E
165 S16 Okinawa off. Okinawa-ken. ◈ prefecture Okinawa, SW Japan
165 S16 Okinawa island SW Japan
Okinawa-ken see Okinawa
165 U16 Okinoerabu-jima island Nansei-shotō, SW Japan
164 F15 Okino-shima island SW Japan
164 H11 Oki-shotō var. Oki-guntō. island group SW Japan
77 T16 Okitipupa Ondo, SW Nigeria 06°33′N 04°43′E
166 L8 Okkan Bago, SW Myanmar (Burma) 17°30′N 95°52′E
27 N10 Oklahoma off. State of Oklahoma, also known as The Sooner State. ◈ state C USA
27 N11 Oklahoma City state capital Oklahoma, C USA 35°28′N 97°31′W
25 Q4 Oklaunion Texas, SW USA 34°07′N 99°07′W
23 W10 Oklawaha River ≈ Florida, SE USA
27 P10 Okmulgee Oklahoma, C USA 35°38′N 95°59′W
Oknitsa see Ocniţa
22 M3 Okolona Mississippi, S USA 34°00′N 88°45′W
165 U2 Okoppe Hokkaidō, NE Japan 44°27′N 143°06′E
11 Q16 Okotoks Alberta, SW Canada 50°46′N 113°57′W
80 H6 Oko, Wadi ≈ NE Sudan
79 G19 Okoyo Cuvette, W Congo 01°28′S 15°04′E
77 S15 Okpara ≈ Benin/Nigeria
92 J8 Øksfjord Finnmark, N Norway 70°13′N 22°22′E
125 R4 Oksino Nenetskiy Avtonomnyy Okrug, NW Russian Federation 67°33′N 52°15′E
92 G13 Oksskolten ▲ C Norway 66°00′N 14°18′E
Oksu see Oqsu
144 M8 Oktaybr'skiy Kostanay, N Kazakhstan
186 B7 Ok Tedi Western, W Papua New Guinea
Oktemberyan see Armavir
166 M7 Oktwin Bago, C Myanmar (Burma) 18°47′N 96°21′E
127 R6 Oktyabr'sk Samarskaya Oblast', W Russian Federation 53°13′N 48°36′E
Oktyabr'sk see Kandyagash
125 N12 Oktyabr'skiy Arkhangel'skaya Oblast', NW Russian Federation 61°03′N 43°16′E
122 E10 Oktyabr'skiy Kamchatskiy Kray, E Russian Federation 52°35′N 156°18′E
127 T5 Oktyabr'skiy Respublika Bashkortostan, W Russian Federation 54°28′N 53°29′E
127 O11 Oktyabr'skiy Volgogradskaya Oblast', SW Russian Federation 48°00′N 43°35′E
Oktyabr'skiy see Aktsyabrski
127 V7 Oktyabr'skoye Orenburgskaya Oblast', W Russian Federation 52°22′N 55°39′E
122 M5 Oktyabr'skoy Revolyutsii, Ostrov Eng. October Revolution Island. island Severnaya Zemlya, N Russian Federation
Okuchi see Isa
124 I14 Okulovka var. Okulovka. Novgorodskaya Oblast', W Russian Federation 58°24′N 33°16′E
Okulovka see Okulovka
165 Q4 Okushiri-tō var. Okusiri Tô. island NE Japan
Okusiri Tô see Okushiri-tō
77 S15 Okuta Kwara, W Nigeria 09°18′N 03°09′E
Ōkuti see Isa
83 F19 Okwa var. Chapman's. ≈ Botswana/Namibia
123 T10 Ola Magadanskaya Oblast', E Russian Federation 59°36′N 151°18′E
27 T11 Ola Arkansas, C USA 35°01′N 93°13′W
Ola see Ala
35 T11 Olacha Peak ▲ California, W USA 36°15′N 118°07′W
92 J1 Ólafsfjörður Nordhurland Eystra, N Iceland 66°04′N 18°36′W
92 H3 Ólafsvík Vesturland, W Iceland 64°52′N 23°45′W
Oláhbrettye see Bretea-Română
Oláhszentgyörgy see Sângeorz-Băi
Oláh-Toplicza see Toplița
118 F9 Olaine C Latvia 56°47′N 23°56′E
35 T11 Olancha California, W USA 36°16′N 118°00′W
42 J5 Olanchito Yoro, C Honduras 15°30′N 86°34′W
42 J6 Olancho ◈ department E Honduras
95 O20 Öland island S Sweden
95 O19 Ölands norra udde headland S Sweden 57°21′N 17°06′E
95 N22 Ölands södra udde headland S Sweden 56°12′N 16°26′E
182 K7 Olary South Australia 32°18′S 140°16′E
27 R4 Olathe Kansas, C USA 38°52′N 94°50′W
61 C22 Olavarría Buenos Aires, E Argentina 36°57′S 60°20′W
92 O2 Olav V Land physical region C Svalbard
111 H14 Oława Ger. Ohlau. Dolnośląskie, SW Poland 50°57′N 17°18′E
107 D17 Olbia prev. Terranova Pausania. Sardegna, Italy, C Mediterranean Sea 40°55′N 09°30′E
44 G5 Old Bahama Channel channel Bahamas/Cuba
Old Bay State/Old Colony State see Massachusetts
10 H2 Old Crow Yukon Territory, NW Canada 67°34′N 139°55′W
Old Dominion see Virginia
Oldeberkeap see Oldeberkoop
98 M7 Oldeberkoop Fris. Oldeberkeap. Fryslân, N Netherlands 52°55′N 06°07′E
98 L10 Oldebroek Gelderland, E Netherlands 52°27′N 05°54′E
98 L8 Oldemarkt Overijssel, N Netherlands 52°49′N 05°58′E
94 E11 Olden Sogn Og Fjordane, C Norway 61°52′N 06°44′E
100 G10 Oldenburg Niedersachsen, NW Germany 53°09′N 08°13′E
100 K8 Oldenburg var. Oldenburg in Holstein. Schleswig-Holstein, N Germany 54°17′N 10°55′E
Oldenburg in Holstein see Oldenburg
98 P10 Oldenzaal Overijssel, E Netherlands 52°19′N 06°53′E
Olderfjord see Leaibevuotna
18 J8 Old Forge New York, NE USA 43°42′N 74°59′W
Old Goa see Goa
97 L17 Oldham NW England, United Kingdom 53°36′N 02°W
39 Q14 Old Harbor Kodiak Island, Alaska, USA 57°12′N 153°18′W
44 J13 Old Harbour C Jamaica 17°56′N 77°06′W
97 C22 Old Head of Kinsale Ir. An Seancheann. headland SW Ireland 51°37′N 08°33′W
20 J8 Old Hickory Lake ⊠ Tennessee, S USA
Old Line State see Maryland
Old North State see North Carolina
81 I17 Ol Doinyo Lengeyo ▲ C Kenya
11 Q16 Olds Alberta, SW Canada 51°50′N 114°06′W
19 O7 Old Speck Mountain ▲ Maine, NE USA 44°34′N 70°55′W
19 S6 Old Town Maine, NE USA 44°55′N 68°39′W
11 T17 Old Wives Lake ◎ Saskatchewan, S Canada
162 J7 Öldziyt var. Hōshōōt. Arhangay, C Mongolia 48°06′N 102°34′E
162 I8 Öldziyt var. Ulaan-Uul. Bayanhongor, C Mongolia 46°03′N 100°52′E
162 L10 Öldziyt var. Rashaant. Dundgovĭ, C Mongolia 44°54′N 106°32′E
162 K8 Öldziyt var. Sangiyn Dalay. Övörhangay, C Mongolia 46°35′N 103°18′E
Öldziyt see Erdenemandal, Arhangay, Mongolia
Öldziyt see Sayhandulaan, Dornogovĭ, Mongolia
188 H6 Oleai var. San Jose. Saipan, S Northern Mariana Islands
18 E11 Olean New York, NE USA 42°04′N 78°24′W
110 O7 Olecko Ger. Treuburg. Warmińsko-Mazurskie, NE Poland 54°02′N 22°29′E
106 C7 Oleggio Piemonte, NE Italy 45°36′N 08°37′E
123 P11 Olëkma Amurskaya Oblast', SE Russian Federation 57°00′N 120°27′E
123 P12 Olëkma ≈ C Russian Federation
123 P11 Olëkminsk Respublika Sakha (Yakutiya), NE Russian Federation 60°25′N 120°25′E
117 W7 Oleksandrivka Donets'ka Oblast', E Ukraine 48°42′N 36°56′E
117 R7 Oleksandrivka Rus. Aleksandrovka. Kirovohrads'ka Oblast', C Ukraine 48°59′N 32°14′E
117 Q9 Oleksandrivka Mykolayivs'ka Oblast', S Ukraine 47°42′N 31°17′E
117 S7 Oleksandriya Rus. Aleksandriya. Kirovohrads'ka Oblast', C Ukraine 48°42′N 33°07′E
93 B20 Ølen Hordaland, S Norway 59°36′N 05°48′E
124 J4 Olenegorsk Murmanskaya Oblast', NW Russian Federation 68°06′N 33°15′E
123 N9 Olenëk Respublika Sakha (Yakutiya), NE Russian Federation 68°28′N 112°18′E
123 N9 Olenëk ≈ NE Russian Federation
123 O7 Olenëkskiy Zaliv bay N Russian Federation
124 K6 Olenitsa Murmanskaya Oblast', NW Russian Federation 66°27′N 35°21′E
102 I11 Oléron, Île d' island W France
111 H14 Oleśnica Ger. Oels, Oels in Schlesien. Dolnośląskie, SW Poland 51°13′N 17°20′E
111 I15 Olesno Ger. Rosenberg. Opolskie, S Poland 50°53′N 18°23′E
116 M3 Olevs'k Rus. Olevsk. Zhytomyrs'ka Oblast', N Ukraine 51°12′N 27°38′E
Olevsk see Olevs'k
123 S15 Ol'ga Primorskiy Kray, SE Russian Federation 43°41′N 135°06′E
Olga, Mount see Kata Tjuṯa
92 P2 Olgastretet strait E Svalbard
162 D5 Ölgiy Bayan-Ölgiy, W Mongolia 48°57′N 89°59′E
95 F23 Ølgod Syddtjylland, W Denmark 55°44′N 08°37′E
104 H14 Olhão Faro, S Portugal 37°01′N 07°50′W
93 L14 Olhava Oulu, C Finland 65°28′N 25°25′E
105 V5 Oliana Cataluña, NE Spain 42°04′N 01°19′E
112 B12 Olib It. Ulbo. island W Croatia
83 B16 Olifa Kunene, NW Namibia 17°25′S 14°27′E
83 E20 Olifants var. Elephant River. ≈ E Namibia
Olifants see Lepelle
83 I20 Olifants Drift var. Oliphants Drift. Kgatleng, SE Botswana 24°13′S 26°52′E
83 G22 Olifantshoek Northern Cape, N South Africa 27°56′S 22°45′E
188 L15 Olimarao Atoll atoll Caroline Islands, C Micronesia
Ólimbos see Ólympos
Olimpo see Fuerte Olimpo
59 Q15 Olinda Pernambuco, E Brazil 08°34′S 34°51′W
Olinthos see Ólynthos
Oliphants Drift see Olifants Drift
Olisipo see Lisboa
Olita see Alytus
105 Q4 Olite Navarra, N Spain 42°29′N 01°40′W
62 K10 Oliva Córdoba, C Argentina 32°03′S 63°34′W
105 T11 Oliva Valenciana, E Spain 38°55′N 00°09′W
Oliva see La Oliva
104 I12 Oliva de la Frontera Extremadura, W Spain 38°17′N 06°54′W
Olivares see Olivares de Júcar
62 H9 Olivares, Cerro de ▲ N Chile 30°25′S 69°52′W
105 P9 Olivares de Júcar var. Olivares. Castilla-La Mancha, C Spain 39°45′N 02°21′W
22 L1 Olive Branch Mississippi, S USA 34°58′N 89°49′W
21 O5 Olive Hill Kentucky, S USA 38°18′N 83°10′W
35 O6 Olivehurst California, W USA 39°05′N 121°33′W
104 G7 Oliveira de Azeméis Aveiro, N Portugal 40°49′N 08°29′W
104 I11 Olivenza Extremadura, W Spain 38°41′N 07°06′W
11 N17 Oliver British Columbia, SW Canada 49°10′N 119°37′W
103 N7 Olivet Loiret, C France 47°53′N 01°53′E
29 Q12 Olivet South Dakota, N USA 43°14′N 97°40′W
29 T9 Olivia Minnesota, N USA 44°46′N 94°59′W
185 C20 Olivine Range ▲ South Island, New Zealand
108 H10 Olivone Ticino, S Switzerland 46°32′N 08°55′E
Öl'keyek see Ol'keyyek
144 L11 Ol'keyyek Kaz. Ölkeyek; prev. Ul'kayak. ≈ C Kazakhstan

◆ Country ● Country Capital ◇ Dependent Territory ○ Dependent Territory Capital ◈ Administrative Regions ✈ International Airport ▲ Mountain ▲ Mountain Range ⛰ Volcano ≈ River ◎ Lake ⊠ Reservoir

127 O9 **Ol'khovka** Volgogradskaya Oblast', SW Russian Federation 49°54′N 44°36′E
111 K16 **Olkusz** Małopolskie, S Poland 50°18′N 19°33′E
22 I6 **Olla** Louisiana, S USA 31°54′N 92°14′W
62 I4 **Ollagüe, Volcán** *var.* Oyahue, Volcán Oyahue. ▲ N Chile 21°25′S 68°10′W
189 U13 **Ollan** *island* Chuuk, C Micronesia
188 F7 **Ollei** Babeldaob, N Palau 07°43′N 134°37′E
Ollius *see* Oglio
108 C10 **Ollon** Vaud, W Switzerland 46°19′N 07°00′E
147 Q10 **Olmaliq** *Rus.* Almalyk. Toshkent Viloyati, E Uzbekistan 40°51′N 69°39′E
104 M6 **Olmedo** Castilla y León, N Spain 41°17′N 04°41′W
56 B10 **Olmos** Lambayeque, W Peru 06°00′S 79°43′W
Olmütz *see* Olomouc
30 M15 **Olney** Illinois, N USA 38°43′N 88°05′W
25 R5 **Olney** Texas, SW USA 33°22′N 98°45′W
95 L22 **Olofström** Blekinge, S Sweden 56°16′N 14°33′E
187 N9 **Olomburi** Malaita, N Solomon Islands 09°00′S 161°09′E
111 H17 **Olomouc** *Ger.* Olmütz, *Pol.* Ołomuniec. Olomoucký Kraj, E Czech Republic 49°36′N 17°13′E
111 H18 **Olomoucký Kraj** ◆ *region* E Czech Republic
Ołomuniec *see* Olomouc
122 D7 **Olonets** Respublika Kareliya, NW Russian Federation 60°58′N 33°01′E
171 N3 **Olongapo** *off.* Olongapo City. Luzon, N Philippines 14°52′N 120°16′E
Olongapo City *see* Olongapo
102 J16 **Oloron-Ste-Marie** Pyrénées-Atlantiques, SW France 43°12′N 00°35′W
192 L16 **Olosega** *island* Manua Islands, E American Samoa
105 W4 **Olot** Cataluña, NE Spain 42°11′N 02°30′E
146 K12 **Olot** *Rus.* Alat. Buxoro Viloyati, C Uzbekistan 39°22′N 63°42′E
112 I12 **Olovo** Federacija Bosna I Hercegovina, E Bosnia and Herzegovina 44°08′N 18°35′E
123 O14 **Olovyannaya** Zabaykal'skiy Kray, S Russian Federation 50°59′N 115°24′E
123 T7 **Oloy** ⚡ NE Russian Federation
101 F16 **Olpe** Nordrhein-Westfalen, W Germany 51°02′N 07°51′E
109 N8 **Olperer** ▲ SW Austria 47°03′N 11°36′E
Olshanka *see* Vil'shanka
Ol'shany *see* Al'shany
Olsnitz *see* Murska Sobota
98 M10 **Olst** Overijssel, E Netherlands 52°19′N 06°06′E
110 L8 **Olsztyn** *Ger.* Allenstein. Warmińsko-Mazurskie, N Poland 53°46′N 20°28′E
110 L8 **Olsztynek** *Ger.* Hohenstein in Ostpreussen. Warmińsko-Mazurskie, N Poland 53°35′N 20°17′E
116 I14 **Olt** ◆ *county* SW Romania
116 I14 **Olt** *var.* Oltul, *Ger.* Alt. ⚡ S Romania
108 E7 **Olten** Solothurn, NW Switzerland 47°22′N 07°55′E
116 K14 **Oltenița** *prev. Eng.* Oltenitsa; *anc.* Constantiola. Călărași, SE Romania 44°05′N 26°40′E
Oltenitsa *see* Oltenița
116 H14 **Olteț** ⚡ S Romania
24 M4 **Olton** Texas, SW USA 34°10′N 102°07′W
137 R12 **Oltu** Erzurum, NE Turkey 40°34′N 41°59′E
Oltul *see* Olt
146 G7 **Oltynko'l** Qoraqalpog'iston Respublikasi, NW Uzbekistan 43°04′N 58°51′E
Oluan Pi *see* Eluan Bi
Ólubló *see* Stará Ľubovňa
137 R11 **Olur** Erzurum, NE Turkey 40°49′N 42°08′E
104 L15 **Olvera** Andalucía, S Spain 36°56′N 05°15′W
Ol'viopol' *see* Pervomays'k
Olwanpi, Cape *see* Eluan Bi
115 D20 **Olympia** Dytikí Elláda, S Greece 37°39′N 21°36′E
32 G9 **Olympia** *state capital* Washington, NW USA 47°02′N 122°54′W
182 H5 **Olympic Dam** South Australia 30°25′S 136°56′E
32 F7 **Olympic Mountains** ▲ Washington, NW USA
121 O3 **Olympos** *var.* Troodos, *Eng.* Mount Olympus. ▲ C Cyprus 34°55′N 32°49′E
115 F15 **Olympos** *var.* Ólimbos, *Eng.* Mount Olympus. ▲ N Greece 40°04′N 22°24′E
115 L17 **Olympos** ▲ Lésvos, E Greece 39°03′N 26°20′E
16 C5 **Olympus, Mount** ▲ Washington, NW USA 47°48′N 123°42′W
Olympus, Mount *see* Ólympos
115 G14 **Olynthos** *var.* Olinthos; *anc.* Olynthus. *site of ancient city* Kentrikí Makedonía, N Greece
Olynthus *see* Ólynthos
117 Q3 **Olyshivka** Chernihivs'ka Oblast', N Ukraine 51°13′N 31°19′E
123 W8 **Olyutorskiy, Mys** *headland* E Russian Federation 59°56′N 170°22′E
123 V8 **Olyutorskiy Zaliv** *bay* E Russian Federation
186 M10 **Om** ⚡ W Papua New Guinea
129 S6 **Om'** ⚡ N Russian Federation
158 I13 **Oma** Xizang Zizhiqu, W China 32°30′N 83°14′E
165 R6 **Ōma** Aomori, Honshū, C Japan 41°31′N 140°54′E
125 P6 **Oma** ⚡ NW Russian Federation
164 M12 **Ōmachi** *var.* Ōmati. Nagano, Honshū, S Japan 36°30′N 137°51′E
165 Q8 **Ōmagari** Akita, Honshū, C Japan 39°29′N 140°29′E
97 E15 **Omagh** *Ir.* An Ómaigh. W Northern Ireland, United Kingdom 54°36′N 07°18′W
29 S15 **Omaha** Nebraska, C USA 41°14′N 95°57′W
83 E19 **Omaheke** ◆ *district* W Namibia
141 W10 **Oman** *off.* Sultanate of Oman, *Ar.* Salṭanat 'Umān; *prev.* Muscat and Oman. ◆ *monarchy* SW Asia
129 O10 **Oman Basin** *var.* Bassin d'Oman. *undersea feature* N Indian Ocean 23°20′N 63°00′E
Oman, Bassin d' *see* Oman Basin
129 N10 **Oman, Gulf of** *Ar.* Khalīj 'Umān. *gulf* N Arabian Sea
Oman, Sultanate of *see* Oman
184 J3 **Omapere** Northland, North Island, New Zealand 35°32′S 173°24′E
185 E20 **Omarama** Canterbury, South Island, New Zealand 44°29′S 169°57′E
112 F11 **Omarska** ◆ Republika Srpska, NW Bosnia and Herzegovina
83 C18 **Omaruru** Erongo, NW Namibia 21°28′S 15°56′E
83 C19 **Omaruru** ⚡ W Namibia
83 E17 **Omatako** ⚡ NE Namibia
Ōmati *see* Ōmachi
83 E18 **Omawewozonyanda** Omaheke, E Namibia 21°30′S 19°34′E
165 R6 **Ōma-zaki** *headland* Honshū, C Japan 41°32′N 140°53′E
Omba *see* Ambae
Ombai *see* Alor, Pulau
83 C16 **Ombalantu** Omusati, N Namibia 17°33′S 14°58′E
79 H15 **Ombella-Mpoko** ◆ *prefecture* S Central African Republic
Ombetsu *see* Onbetsu
83 B17 **Ombombo** Kunene, NW Namibia 18°43′S 13°53′E
79 D19 **Omboué** Ogooué-Maritime, W Gabon 01°38′S 09°20′E
106 G13 **Ombrone** ⚡ C Italy
80 F9 **Omdurman** *var.* Umm Durmān. Khartoum, C Sudan 15°37′N 32°29′E
165 N13 **Ōme** Tōkyō, Honshū, S Japan 35°48′N 139°17′E
106 C6 **Omegna** Piemonte, NE Italy 45°54′N 08°25′E
183 P12 **Omeo** Victoria, SE Australia 37°09′S 147°36′E
138 F11 **Omer** Southern, C Israel 31°16′N 34°51′E
41 P16 **Ometepec** Guerrero, S Mexico 16°39′N 98°23′W
42 K11 **Ometepe, Isla de** *island* S Nicaragua
Om Hager *see* Om Hajer
80 I10 **Om Hajer** *var.* Om Hager. SW Eritrea 14°19′N 36°46′E
165 J13 **Ōmihachiman** Shiga, Honshū, SW Japan 35°08′N 136°04′E
10 L12 **Omineca Mountains** ▲ British Columbia, W Canada
113 F14 **Omiš** *It.* Almissa. Split-Dalmacija, S Croatia 43°27′N 16°41′E
112 B10 **Omišalj** Primorje-Gorski Kotar, NW Croatia 45°10′N 14°33′E
83 D19 **Omitara** Khomas, C Namibia 22°18′S 18°01′E
41 O16 **Omitlán, Río** ⚡ S Mexico
39 X14 **Ommaney, Cape** *headland* Baranof Island, Alaska, USA 56°10′N 134°40′W
98 N9 **Ommen** Overijssel, E Netherlands 52°31′N 06°25′E
163 N7 **Ömnödelger** *var.* Bayanbulag. Hentiy, C Mongolia 47°54′N 109°51′E
162 K11 **Ömnögovĭ** ◆ *province* S Mongolia
191 X7 **Omoa** Fatu Hira, NE French Polynesia 10°30′S 138°41′E
Omo Botego *see* Omo Wenz
Ómolddova *see* Moldova Veche
123 T7 **Omolon** Chukotskiy Avtonomnyy Okrug, NE Russian Federation 65°11′N 160°33′E
123 T7 **Omolon** ⚡ NE Russian Federation
123 Q8 **Omoloy** ⚡ NE Russian Federation
162 I12 **Omon Gol** *Chin.* Dong He, *var.* Narin Gol. ⚡ N China
165 P8 **Omono-gawa** ⚡ Honshū, C Japan
81 I14 **Omo Wenz** *var.* Omo Botego. ⚡ Ethiopia/Kenya
122 H12 **Omsk** Omskaya Oblast', C Russian Federation 55°N 73°22′E
122 H11 **Omskaya Oblast'** ◆ *province* C Russian Federation
165 U2 **Ōmu** Hokkaidō, NE Japan 44°36′N 142°55′E
110 M9 **Omulew** ⚡ NE Poland
116 J12 **Omul, Vârful** *prev.* Vîrful Omu. ▲ C Romania 45°24′N 25°26′E
83 D16 **Omundaungilo** Ohangwena, N Namibia 17°28′S 16°39′E
164 C14 **Ōmura** Nagasaki, Kyūshū, SW Japan 32°56′N 129°58′E
83 B17 **Omusati** ◆ *district* N Namibia
164 C14 **Ōmuta** Fukuoka, Kyūshū, SW Japan 33°01′N 130°27′E
125 S14 **Omutninsk** Kirovskaya Oblast', NW Russian Federation 58°37′N 52°08′E
Omu, Virful *see* Omul, Vârful
29 V7 **Onamia** Minnesota, N USA 46°04′N 93°40′W
21 Y5 **Onancock** Virginia, NE USA 37°42′N 75°45′W
14 E10 **Onaping Lake** ◎ Ontario, S Canada
30 M12 **Onarga** Illinois, N USA 40°39′N 88°00′W
15 R6 **Onatchiway, Lac** ◎ Québec, SE Canada
29 S14 **Onawa** Iowa, C USA 42°01′N 96°06′W
165 U5 **Onbetsu** *var.* Ombetsu. Hokkaidō, NE Japan 42°52′N 143°54′E
83 B16 **Oncócua** Cunene, SW Angola 16°37′S 13°23′E
105 S9 **Onda** Valenciana, E Spain 39°58′N 00°17′W
111 N18 **Ondava** ⚡ NE Slovakia
Ondjiva *see* N'Giva
77 T16 **Ondo** Ondo, SW Nigeria 07°07′N 04°50′E
77 T16 **Ondo** ◆ *state* SW Nigeria
163 N8 **Öndörhaan** *var.* Undur Khan; *prev.* Tsetsen Khan. Hentiy, E Mongolia 47°21′N 110°42′E
162 M9 **Öndörshil** *var.* Böhöt. Dundgovĭ, C Mongolia 45°13′N 108°12′E
162 L8 **Öndörshireet** *var.* Bayshint. Töv, C Mongolia 47°22′N 105°04′E
162 I7 **Öndör-Ulaan** *var.* Teel. Arhangay, C Mongolia 48°01′N 100°30′E
83 D18 **Ondundazongonda** Otjozondjupa, N Namibia 20°28′S 18°00′E
151 K21 **One and Half Degree Channel** *channel* S Maldives
187 Z15 **Oneata** *island* Lau Group, E Fiji
124 L9 **Onega** Arkhangel'skaya Oblast', NW Russian Federation 63°54′N 37°59′E
124 L9 **Onega** ⚡ NW Russian Federation
Onega Bay *see* Onezhskaya Guba
Onega, Lake *see* Onezhskoye Ozero
18 I10 **Oneida** New York, NE USA 43°05′N 75°39′W
20 M8 **Oneida** Tennessee, S USA 36°30′N 84°30′W
18 H9 **Oneida Lake** ◎ New York, NE USA
29 P13 **O'Neill** Nebraska, C USA 42°28′N 98°38′W
123 V12 **Onekotan, Ostrov** *island* Kuril'skiye Ostrova, SE Russian Federation
23 P3 **Oneonta** Alabama, S USA 33°57′N 86°28′W
18 J11 **Oneonta** New York, NE USA 42°27′N 75°03′W
190 I16 **Oneroa** *island* S Cook Islands
116 K11 **Onești** *Hung.* Onyest; *prev.* Gheorghe Gheorghiu-Dej. Bacău, E Romania 46°14′N 26°46′E
193 V15 **Onevai** *island* Tongatapu Group, S Tonga
108 A11 **Onex** Genève, SW Switzerland 46°12′N 06°04′E
124 K8 **Onezhskaya Guba** *Eng.* Onega Bay. *bay* NW Russian Federation
122 D7 **Onezhskoye Ozero** *Eng.* Lake Onega. ◎ NW Russian Federation
83 C16 **Ongandjera** Omusati, N Namibia 17°49′S 15°06′E
184 N12 **Ongaonga** Hawke's Bay, North Island, New Zealand 39°57′S 176°21′E
Ongi *see* Sayhan-Ovoo, Dundgovĭ, Mongolia
Ongi *see* Uyanga
163 W14 **Ongjin** SW North Korea 37°56′N 125°22′E
155 J17 **Ongole** Andhra Pradesh, E India 15°33′N 80°03′E
Ongon *see* Bürd
Ongtüstik Qazaqstan Oblysy *see* Yuzhnyy Kazakhstan
99 I21 **Onhaye** Namur, S Belgium 50°15′N 04°51′E
166 M8 **Onhne** Bago, SW Myanmar (Burma) 17°02′N 96°28′E
137 S9 **Oni** N Georgia 42°36′N 43°13′E
29 N9 **Onida** South Dakota, N USA 44°42′N 100°03′W
164 F15 **Onigajō-yama** ▲ Shikoku, SW Japan 33°10′N 132°37′E
172 H7 **Onilahy** ⚡ S Madagascar
77 U16 **Onitsha** Anambra, S Nigeria 06°09′N 06°48′E
164 K12 **Ōno** Fukui, Honshū, SW Japan 35°59′N 136°30′E
164 I13 **Ono** Hyōgo, Honshū, SW Japan 34°52′N 134°55′E
187 K15 **Ono** *island* SW Fiji
164 E13 **Onoda** Yamaguchi, Honshū, SW Japan 34°00′N 131°11′E
187 Z16 **Ono-i-lau** *island* SE Fiji
164 D13 **Ōnojō** *var.* Ōnozyô. Fukuoka, Kyūshū, SW Japan 33°34′N 130°29′E
163 O7 **Onon Gol** ⚡ N Mongolia
Ononte *see* Orontes
55 N6 **Onoto** Anzoátegui, NE Venezuela 09°36′N 65°12′W
191 O3 **Onotoa** *prev.* Clerk Island. *atoll* Tungaru, W Kiribati
Ōnozyô *see* Ōnojō
83 E23 **Onseepkans** Northern Cape, W South Africa 28°44′S 19°18′E
104 F4 **Ons, Illa de** *island* NW Spain
180 H7 **Onslow** Western Australia 21°42′S 115°08′E
21 W11 **Onslow Bay** *bay* North Carolina, E USA
98 P6 **Onstwedde** Groningen, NE Netherlands 53°01′N 07°04′E
164 C16 **On-take** ▲ Kyūshū, SW Japan 31°35′N 130°39′E
35 T15 **Ontario** California, W USA 34°03′N 117°39′W
32 M13 **Ontario** Oregon, NW USA 44°01′N 116°57′W
12 D10 **Ontario** ◆ *province* S Canada
11 P14 **Ontario, Lake** ◎ Canada/ USA
0 L9 **Ontario Peninsula** *peninsula* Canada/USA
Onteniente *see* Ontinyent
105 S11 **Ontinyent** *var.* Onteniente. Valenciana, E Spain 38°49′N 00°37′W
93 N15 **Ontojärvi** ◎ E Finland
30 L3 **Ontonagon** Michigan, N USA 46°52′N 89°18′W
30 L3 **Ontonagon River** ⚡ Michigan, N USA
186 M7 **Ontong Java Atoll** *prev.* Lord Howe Island. *atoll* N Solomon Islands
175 N5 **Ontong Java Rise** *undersea feature* W Pacific Ocean 01°00′N 157°00′E
Onuba *see* Huelva
55 W9 **Onverwacht** Para, N Suriname 05°36′N 55°12′W
Onyest *see* Onești
Oodeypore *see* Udaipur
182 J7 **Oodla Wirra** South Australia 32°52′S 139°05′E
182 F2 **Oodnadatta** South Australia 27°34′S 135°27′E
182 C5 **Ooldea** South Australia 30°29′S 131°50′E
27 Q8 **Oologah Lake** ▣ Oklahoma, C USA
Oos-Kaap *see* Eastern Cape
Oos-Londen *see* East London
99 E17 **Oostakker** Oost-Vlaanderen, NW Belgium 51°06′N 03°46′E
99 D15 **Oostburg** Zeeland, SW Netherlands 51°20′N 03°30′E
98 K9 **Oostelijk-Flevoland** *polder* C Netherlands
99 B16 **Oostende** *Eng.* Ostend, *Fr.* Ostende. West-Vlaanderen, NW Belgium 51°13′N 02°55′E
99 B16 **Oostende** ✈ West-Vlaanderen, NW Belgium 51°12′N 02°55′E
98 L12 **Oosterbeek** Gelderland, SE Netherlands 51°59′N 05°51′E
99 I14 **Oosterhout** Noord-Brabant, S Netherlands 51°38′N 04°51′E
98 O6 **Oostermoers Vaart** *var.* Hunze. ⚡ NE Netherlands
99 F14 **Oosterschelde** *Eng.* Eastern Scheldt. *inlet* SW Netherlands
99 E14 **Oosterscheldedam** *dam* SW Netherlands
98 M7 **Oosterwolde** *Fris.* Easterwâlde. Fryslân, N Netherlands 53°01′N 06°15′E
98 I9 **Oosthuizen** Noord-Holland, NW Netherlands 52°34′N 05°00′E
99 H16 **Oostmalle** Antwerpen, N Belgium 51°18′N 04°44′E
Oos-Transvaal *see* Mpumalanga
99 E15 **Oost-Souburg** Zeeland, SW Netherlands 51°28′N 03°36′E
99 E17 **Oost-Vlaanderen** *Eng.* East Flanders. ◆ *province* NW Belgium
98 J5 **Oost-Vlieland** Fryslân, N Netherlands 53°19′N 05°02′E
98 F12 **Oostvoorne** Zuid-Holland, SW Netherlands 51°55′N 04°06′E
Ootacamund *see* Udagamandalam
98 O10 **Ootmarsum** Overijssel, E Netherlands 52°25′N 06°55′E
10 K14 **Ootsa Lake** ▣ British Columbia, SW Canada
Ooty *see* Udagamandalam
114 L8 **Opaka** Tŭrgovishte, N Bulgaria 43°26′N 26°12′E
79 M18 **Opala** Orientale, C Dem. Rep. Congo 0°40′S 24°20′E
125 Q13 **Oparino** Kirovskaya Oblast', NW Russian Federation 59°52′N 48°14′E
14 H8 **Opasatica, Lac** ◎ Québec, SE Canada
112 B9 **Opatija** *It.* Abbazia. Primorje-Gorski Kotar, NW Croatia 45°18′N 14°15′E
111 N15 **Opatów** Świętokrzyskie, C Poland 50°45′N 21°27′E
111 I17 **Opava** *Ger.* Troppau. Moravskoslezský Kraj, E Czech Republic 49°56′N 17°53′E
111 H16 **Opava** *Ger.* Oppa. ⚡ NE Czech Republic
Opazova *see* Stara Pazova
Opécska *see* Pecica
14 E8 **Opeepeesway Lake** ◎ Ontario, S Canada
23 R5 **Opelika** Alabama, S USA 32°39′N 85°22′W
22 I8 **Opelousas** Louisiana, S USA 30°31′N 92°04′W
186 G6 **Open Bay** *bay* New Britain, E Papua New Guinea
14 I12 **Opeongo Lake** ◎ Ontario, SE Canada
99 K17 **Opglabbeek** Limburg, NE Belgium 51°04′N 05°39′E
33 W6 **Opheim** Montana, NW USA 48°50′N 106°24′W
39 P10 **Ophir** Alaska, USA 63°08′N 156°31′W
Ophiusa *see* Formentera
79 N18 **Opienge** Orientale, E Dem. Rep. Congo 0°15′N 27°25′E
185 G20 **Opihi** ⚡ South Island, New Zealand
12 J9 **Opinaca** ⚡ Québec, C Canada
12 J10 **Opinaca, Réservoir** ▣ Québec, E Canada
117 T5 **Opishnya** *Rus.* Oposhnya. Poltavs'ka Oblast', NE Ukraine 49°58′N 34°37′E
98 I8 **Opmeer** Noord-Holland, NW Netherlands 52°43′N 04°56′E
77 V17 **Opobo** Akwa Ibom, S Nigeria 04°36′N 07°37′E
124 F16 **Opochka** Pskovskaya Oblast', W Russian Federation 56°42′N 28°40′E
110 L13 **Opoczno** Łodzkie, C Poland 51°24′N 20°18′E
111 I15 **Opole** *Ger.* Oppeln. Opolskie, S Poland 50°40′N 17°56′E
111 H15 **Opolskie** ◆ *province* S Poland
Opornyy *see* Borankul
104 G4 **O Porriño** *var.* Porriño. Galicia, NW Spain 42°10′N 08°38′W
Oporto *see* Porto
Oposhnya *see* Opishnya
184 P8 **Opotiki** Bay of Plenty, North Island, New Zealand 38°02′S 177°18′E
23 Q7 **Opp** Alabama, S USA 31°16′N 86°14′W
Oppa *see* Opava
94 G9 **Oppdal** Sør-Trøndelag, S Norway 62°36′N 09°41′E
Oppeln *see* Opole
107 N23 **Oppido Mamertina** Calabria, SW Italy 38°17′N 15°58′E
Oppidum Ubiorum *see* Köln
94 F12 **Oppland** ◆ *county* S Norway
118 J12 **Opsa** Vitsyebskaya Voblasts', NW Belarus 55°32′N 26°50′E
26 I8 **Optima Lake** ▣ Oklahoma, C USA
184 J11 **Opunake** Taranaki, North Island, New Zealand 39°27′S 173°52′E
191 N6 **Opunohu, Baie d'** *bay* Moorea, W French Polynesia
83 B17 **Opuwo** Kunene, NW Namibia 18°03′S 13°54′E
146 H6 **Oqqal'a** *var.* Akkala, *Rus.* Karakala. Qoraqalpog'iston Respublikasi, NW Uzbekistan 43°43′N 59°25′E
147 V13 **Oqsu** *Rus.* Oksu. ⚡ SE Tajikistan
147 P14 **Oqtogh, Qatorkŭhi** *Rus.* Khrebet Aktau. ▲ SW Tajikistan
146 M11 **Oqtosh** *Rus.* Aktash. Samarqand Viloyati, C Uzbekistan 39°22′N 65°46′E
147 N11 **Oqtov Tizmasi** *var.* Khrebet Aktau. ▲ C Uzbekistan
30 J12 **Oquawka** Illinois, N USA 40°56′N 90°56′W
144 J10 **Or'** *Kaz.* Or. ⚡ Kazakhstan/ Russian Federation
36 M15 **Oracle** Arizona, SW USA 32°36′N 110°46′W
147 N13 **O'radaryo** *Rus.* Uradar'ya. ⚡ S Uzbekistan
116 F9 **Oradea** *prev.* Oradea Mare, *Ger.* Grosswardein, *Hung.* Nagyvárad. Bihor, NW Romania 47°03′N 21°56′E
Oradea Mare *see* Oradea
Orahovac *see* Rahovec
112 H9 **Orahovica** Virovitica-Podravina, NE Croatia 45°33′N 17°54′E
152 K13 **Orai** Uttar Pradesh, N India 26°00′N 79°26′E
92 K12 **Orajärvi** Lappi, NW Finland 66°54′N 24°04′E
138 F9 **Or'Akiva** *prev.* Or 'Aqiva. Haifa, N Israel 32°40′N 34°58′E
Oral *see* Ural'sk
74 I5 **Oran** *var.* Ouahran, Wahran. NW Algeria 35°42′N 00°37′W
183 R8 **Orange** New South Wales, SE Australia 33°16′S 149°06′E
103 R14 **Orange** *anc.* Arausio. Vaucluse, SE France 44°06′N 04°52′E
25 Y10 **Orange** Texas, SW USA 30°05′N 93°43′W
21 V5 **Orange** Virginia, NE USA 38°14′N 78°07′W
21 R13 **Orangeburg** South Carolina, SE USA 33°28′N 80°53′W
58 J9 **Orange, Cabo** *headland* NE Brazil 04°24′N 51°33′W
29 S12 **Orange City** Iowa, C USA 43°00′N 96°03′W
Orange Cone *see* Orange Fan
172 J10 **Orange Fan** *var.* Orange Cone. *undersea feature* SW Indian Ocean 32°00′S 12°00′E
Orange Free State *see* Free State
25 S14 **Orange Grove** Texas, SW USA 27°57′N 97°56′W
18 K13 **Orange Lake** New York, NE USA 41°32′N 74°06′W
23 V10 **Orange Lake** ◎ Florida, SE USA
Orange Mouth/ Orangemund *see* Oranjemund
23 W9 **Orange Park** Florida, SE USA 30°10′N 81°42′W
83 E23 **Orange River** *Afr.* Oranjerivier. ⚡ S Africa
14 G15 **Orangeville** Ontario, S Canada 43°55′N 80°06′W
36 M5 **Orangeville** Utah, W USA 39°14′N 111°03′W
42 G1 **Orange Walk** Orange Walk, N Belize 18°06′N 88°30′W
42 F1 **Orange Walk** ◆ *district* NW Belize
100 N11 **Oranienburg** Brandenburg, NE Germany 52°46′N 13°15′E
98 O7 **Oranjekanaal** *canal* NE Netherlands
83 D23 **Oranjemund** *var.* Orangemund; *prev.* Orange Mouth. Karas, SW Namibia 28°33′S 16°28′E
Oranjerivier *see* Orange River
45 N16 **Oranjestad** ○ (Aruba) W Aruba 12°31′N 70°W
Oranje Vrystaat *see* Free State
Orany *see* Varėna
83 H18 **Orapa** Central, C Botswana 21°16′S 25°22′E
Or 'Aqiva *see* Or'Akiva
112 I10 **Orašje** ◆ Federacija Bosna I Herecegovina, N Bosnia and Herzegovina
116 G11 **Orăștie** *Ger.* Broos, *Hung.* Szászváros. Hunedoara, W Romania 45°50′N 23°11′E
Orașul Stalin *see* Brașov
111 K18 **Orava** *Hung.* Árva, *Pol.* Orawa. ⚡ N Slovakia
Oravainen *see* Oravais
93 K16 **Oravais** *Fin.* Oravainen. Länsi-Suomi, W Finland 63°18′N 22°25′E
Oravicabánya *see* Oravița
116 F13 **Oravița** *Ger.* Orawitza, *Hung.* Oravicabánya. Caraș-Severin, SW Romania 45°02′N 21°43′E
Orawa *see* Orava
185 B24 **Orawia** Southland, South Island, New Zealand 46°03′S 167°49′E
Orawitza *see* Oravița
103 P16 **Orb** ⚡ S France
106 C9 **Orba** ⚡ NW Italy
158 H12 **Orba Co** ◎ W China
108 B9 **Orbe** Vaud, W Switzerland 46°42′N 06°28′E
107 G14 **Orbetello** Toscana, C Italy 42°28′N 11°15′E
104 K3 **Órbigo** ⚡ NW Spain
183 Q12 **Orbost** Victoria, SE Australia 37°44′S 148°28′E
95 O14 **Örbyhus** Uppsala, C Sweden 60°15′N 17°43′E
194 I1 **Orcadas** *Argentinian research station* South Orkney Islands, Antarctica 60°37′S 44°48′W
105 P12 **Orcera** Andalucía, S Spain 38°20′N 02°36′W
33 P9 **Orchard Homes** Montana, NW USA 46°52′N 114°01′W
37 P5 **Orchard Mesa** Colorado, C USA 39°02′N 108°33′W
18 D10 **Orchard Park** New York, NE USA 42°46′N 78°44′W
Orchid Island *see* Lan Yu
115 G18 **Orchómenos** *var.* Orhomenos, Orkhómenos, *prev.* Skripón; *anc.* Orchomenus. Stereá Elláda, C Greece 38°29′N 22°58′E
Orchomenus *see* Orchómenos
106 B7 **Orco** ⚡ NW Italy
103 R8 **Or, Côte d'** *physical region* C France
29 O14 **Ord** Nebraska, C USA 41°36′N 98°55′W
119 O15 **Ordats'** *Rus.* Ordat'. Mahilyowskaya Voblasts', E Belarus 54°10′N 30°42′E
36 K8 **Orderville** Utah, W USA 37°16′N 112°38′W
104 H2 **Ordes** Galicia, NW Spain 43°04′N 08°25′W
35 V14 **Ord Mountain** ▲ California, W USA 34°41′N 116°46′W
163 N14 **Ordos** *prev.* Dongsheng. Nei Mongol Zizhiqu, N China 39°51′N 110°00′E
Ordos Desert *see* Mu Us Shadi
188 B16 **Ordot** C Guam
137 N11 **Ordu** *anc.* Cotyora. Ordu, N Turkey 41°N 37°52′E
136 M11 **Ordu** ◆ *province* N Turkey
137 V14 **Ordubad** SW Azerbaijan 38°55′N 46°00′E
Orduña *see* Urduña
37 U6 **Ordway** Colorado, C USA 38°13′N 103°45′W
117 T9 **Ordzhonikidze** Dnipropetrovs'ka Oblast', E Ukraine 47°39′N 34°08′E
Ordzhonikidze *see* Denisovka, Kazakhstan
Ordzhonikidze *see* Vladikavkaz, Russian Federation
Ordzhonikidze *see* Yenakiyeve, Ukraine
Ordzhonikidzeabad *see* Kofarnihon
55 U9 **Orealla** E Guyana 05°13′N 57°17′W
113 G15 **Orebić** *It.* Sabbioncello. Dubrovnik-Neretva, S Croatia 42°58′N 17°12′E
95 M16 **Örebro** Örebro, C Sweden 59°18′N 15°12′E
95 L16 **Örebro** ◆ *county* C Sweden
25 W6 **Ore City** Texas, SW USA 32°48′N 94°43′W
30 L10 **Oregon** Illinois, N USA 42°00′N 89°19′W
27 Q2 **Oregon** Missouri, C USA 39°59′N 95°08′W
31 R11 **Oregon** Ohio, N USA 41°38′N 83°29′W
32 H13 **Oregon** *off.* State of Oregon, *also known as* Beaver State, Sunset State, Valentine State, Webfoot State. ◆ *state* NW USA
32 G11 **Oregon City** Oregon, NW USA 45°21′N 122°36′W
Oregon, State of *see* Oregon
95 P14 **Öregrund** Uppsala, C Sweden 60°19′N 18°30′E
Orekhov *see* Orikhiv
126 L3 **Orekhovo-Zuyevo** Moskovskaya Oblast', W Russian Federation 55°46′N 39°01′E
Orekhovsk *see* Arekhawsk
126 J6 **Orël** Orlovskaya Oblast', W Russian Federation 52°57′N 36°06′E
Orel *see* Oril'
56 E11 **Orellana** Loreto, N Peru 06°53′S 75°10′W
56 E6 **Orellana** ◆ *province* NE Ecuador
104 L11 **Orellana, Embalse de** ▣ W Spain
36 L3 **Orem** Utah, W USA 40°18′N 111°42′W
Ore Mountains *see* Erzgebirge/Krušné Hory
127 V7 **Orenburg** *prev.* Chkalov. Orenburgskaya Oblast', W Russian Federation 51°46′N 55°12′E
127 V7 **Orenburg** ✈ Orenburgskaya Oblast', W Russian Federation 51°54′N 55°15′E
127 T7 **Orenburgskaya Oblast'** ◆ *province* W Russian Federation
Orense *see* Ourense
188 C8 **Oreor** *var.* Koror. *island* N Palau
185 B24 **Orepuki** Southland, South Island, New Zealand 46°17′S 167°45′E
114 L12 **Orestiáda** *prev.* Orestiás. Anatolikí Makedonía kai Thráki, NE Greece 41°30′N 26°31′E
Orestiás *see* Orestiáda
Öresund/Øresund *see* Sound, The
185 C23 **Oreti** ⚡ South Island, New Zealand
184 L5 **Orewa** Auckland, North Island, New Zealand 36°34′S 174°43′E
65 A25 **Orford, Cape** *headland* West Falkland, Falkland Islands 52°00′S 61°04′W
44 B5 **Órganos, Sierra de los** ▲ W Cuba
37 R15 **Organ Peak** ▲ New Mexico, SW USA 32°17′N 106°35′W
105 N9 **Orgaz** Castilla-La Mancha, C Spain 39°39′N 03°52′W
Orgeyev *see* Orhei
Orgil *see* Jargalant
105 O15 **Órgiva** *var.* Orjiva. Andalucía, S Spain 36°54′N 03°25′W
163 O10 **Örgön** *var.* Senj. Dornogovĭ, SE Mongolia 44°34′N 110°58′E
Örgön *see* Bayangovĭ
Orgražden *see* Ograzhden
117 N9 **Orhei** *var.* Orheiu, *Rus.* Orgeyev. N Moldova 47°25′N 28°48′E
Orheiu *see* Orhei
105 R3 **Orhi** *var.* Orhy, Pico de Orhy, Pic d'Orhy. ▲ France/ Spain 42°55′N 01°01′W *see also* Orhy
Orhomenos *see* Orchómenos
162 K6 **Orhon** ◆ *province* N Mongolia
162 L6 **Orhon Gol** ⚡ N Mongolia
102 J16 **Orhy** *var.* Orhi, Pico de Orhy, Pic d'Orhy. ▲ France/ Spain 43°00′N 01°00′W *see also* Orhi
Orhy *see* Orhi
Orhy, Pic d'/Orhy, Pico de *see* Orhi/Orhy
34 L2 **Orick** California, W USA 41°16′N 124°03′W
32 L6 **Orient** Washington, NW USA 48°51′N 118°14′W
48 D6 **Oriental, Cordillera** ▲ Bolivia/Peru
48 D6 **Oriental, Cordillera** ▲ C Colombia
57 H16 **Oriental, Cordillera** ▲ C Peru
63 M15 **Oriente** Buenos Aires, E Argentina 38°45′S 60°37′W
105 R12 **Orihuela** Valenciana, E Spain 38°05′N 00°56′W
117 V9 **Orikhiv** *Rus.* Orekhov. Zaporiz'ka Oblast', SE Ukraine 47°32′N 35°48′E
113 K22 **Orikum** *var.* Orikumi. Vlorë, SW Albania 40°20′N 19°28′E
Orikumi *see* Orikum
117 V6 **Oril'** *Rus.* Orel. ⚡ E Ukraine
14 H14 **Orillia** Ontario, S Canada 44°36′N 79°26′W
93 M19 **Orimattila** Etelä-Suomi, S Finland 60°48′N 25°40′E
33 Y15 **Orin** Wyoming, C USA 42°39′N 105°10′W
47 R4 **Orinoco, Río** ⚡ Colombia/ Venezuela
186 C9 **Oriomo** Western, SW Papua New Guinea 08°53′S 143°13′E
30 K11 **Orion** Illinois, N USA 41°21′N 90°22′W
29 Q5 **Oriska** North Dakota, N USA 46°54′N 97°46′W
153 P17 **Orissa** *var.* Odisha. ◆ *state* NE India
Orissaar *see* Orissaare
118 E5 **Orissaare** *Ger.* Orissaar. Saaremaa, W Estonia 58°34′N 23°05′E
107 B19 **Oristano** Sardegna, Italy, C Mediterranean Sea 39°54′N 08°35′E
107 A19 **Oristano, Golfo di** *gulf* Sardegna, Italy, C Mediterranean Sea
54 D13 **Orito** Putumayo, SW Colombia 0°49′N 76°57′W
93 L18 **Orivesi** Häme, W Finland 61°39′N 24°21′E
93 N17 **Orivesi** ◎ Länsi-Suomi, SE Finland
58 H12 **Oriximiná** Pará, NE Brazil 01°45′S 55°50′W
41 Q14 **Orizaba** Veracruz-Llave, E Mexico 18°51′N 97°08′W
41 Q14 **Orizaba, Volcán Pico de** *var.* Citlaltépetl. ▲ S Mexico 19°00′N 97°15′W
95 I16 **Ørje** Østfold, S Norway 59°28′N 11°40′E
113 I16 **Orjen** ▲ Bosnia and Herzegovina/Montenegro
Orjiva *see* Órgiva
Orjonikidzeobod *see* Kofarnihon
94 G8 **Orkanger** Sør-Trøndelag, S Norway 63°17′N 09°52′E
94 G8 **Orkdalen** *valley* S Norway
95 K22 **Örkelljunga** Skåne, S Sweden 56°17′N 13°20′E
Orkhaniye *see* Botevgrad
Orkhómenos *see* Orchómenos
94 H9 **Orkla** ⚡ S Norway
Orkney *see* Orkney Islands
65 J22 **Orkney Deep** *undersea feature* Scotia Sea/Weddell Sea
96 J4 **Orkney Islands** *var.* Orkney, Orkneys. *island group* N Scotland, United Kingdom
Orkneys *see* Orkney Islands
24 K8 **Orla** Texas, SW USA 31°48′N 103°55′W
35 N5 **Orland** California, W USA 39°43′N 122°12′W
23 X11 **Orlando** Florida, SE USA 28°32′N 81°23′W
23 X12 **Orlando** ✈ Florida, SE USA 28°24′N 81°16′W
107 K23 **Orlando, Capo d'** *headland* Sicilia, Italy, C Mediterranean Sea 38°10′N 14°44′E
Orlau *see* Orlová
103 N6 **Orléanais** *cultural region* C France
103 N7 **Orléans** *anc.* Aurelianum. Loiret, C France 47°54′N 01°53′E
34 L2 **Orleans** California, W USA 41°16′N 123°36′W
19 Q12 **Orleans** Massachusetts, NE USA 41°48′N 69°57′W
15 R10 **Orléans, Île d'** *island* Québec, SE Canada
Orléansville *see* Chlef
111 F16 **Orlice** *Ger.* Adler. ⚡ NE Czech Republic
122 L13 **Orlik** Respublika Buryatiya, S Russian Federation 52°32′N 99°36′E
125 Q14 **Orlov** *prev.* Khalturin. Kirovskaya Oblast', NW Russian Federation 58°34′N 48°57′E
111 I17 **Orlová** *Ger.* Orlau, *Pol.* Orłowa. Moravskoslezský Kraj, E Czech Republic 49°50′N 18°21′E
Orlov, Mys *see* Orlovskiy, Mys
126 I6 **Orlovskaya Oblast'** ◆ *province* W Russian Federation
124 M5 **Orlovskiy, Mys** *var.* Mys Orlov. *headland* NW Russian Federation 67°14′N 41°17′E
Orłowa *see* Orlová
103 O5 **Orly** ✈ (Paris) Essonne, N France 48°43′N 02°24′E
119 G16 **Orlya** Hrodzyenskaya Voblasts', W Belarus 53°30′N 24°59′E
114 M7 **Orlyak** *prev.* Makenzen, Trubchular, *Rom.* Trupcilar. Dobrich, NE Bulgaria 43°39′N 27°21′E
148 L16 **Ormāra** Baluchistān, SW Pakistan 25°14′N 64°36′E
171 P5 **Ormoc** *off.* Ormoc City, *var.* MacArthur. Leyte, C Philippines 11°02′N 124°35′E
Ormoc City *see* Ormoc
23 X10 **Ormond Beach** Florida, SE USA 29°16′N 81°04′W
109 X10 **Ormož** *Ger.* Friedau. NE Slovenia 46°24′N 16°09′E
14 J13 **Ormsby** Ontario, SE Canada 44°52′N 77°45′W
97 K17 **Ormskirk** NW England, United Kingdom 53°35′N 02°54′W
Ormsö *see* Vormsi
15 N13 **Ormstown** Québec, SE Canada 45°08′N 73°57′W
Ormuz, Strait of *see* Hormuz, Strait of
103 T8 **Ornans** Doubs, E France 47°06′N 06°06′E
102 K5 **Orne** ◆ *department* N France
102 K5 **Orne** ⚡ N France
92 G12 **Ørnes** Nordland, C Norway 66°51′N 13°43′E
110 L7 **Orneta** Warmińsko-Mazurskie, NE Poland 54°07′N 20°10′E
95 P16 **Ornö** Stockholm, C Sweden 59°03′N 18°28′E
37 Q3 **Orno Peak** ▲ Colorado, C USA 40°06′N 107°06′W

◆ Country
● Country Capital
◇ Dependent Territory
○ Dependent Territory Capital
◆ Administrative Regions
✈ International Airport
▲ Mountain
▲ Mountain Range
⚡ Volcano
⚡ River
◎ Lake
▣ Reservoir

93 I16 **Örnsköldsvik** Västernorrland, C Sweden 63°16′N 18°45′E
163 X13 **Oro** E North Korea 39°59′N 127°27′E
45 T6 **Orocovis** C Puerto Rico 18°13′N 66°22′W
54 H10 **Orocué** Casanare, E Colombia 04°51′N 71°21′W
77 N13 **Orodara** SW Burkina 11°00′N 04°54′W
105 S4 **Oroel, Peña de** ▲ N Spain 42°30′N 00°31′W
33 N10 **Orofino** Idaho, NW USA 46°28′N 116°15′W
162 I9 **Orog Nuur** ◎ S Mongolia
35 U14 **Oro Grande** California, W USA 34°36′N 117°19′W
37 S15 **Orogrande** New Mexico, SW USA 32°24′N 106°04′W
191 Q7 **Orohena, Mont** 🌋 Tahiti, W French Polynesia 17°37′S 149°27′W
Orolaunum *see* Arlon
Orol Dengizi *see* Aral Sea
189 S15 **Oroluk Atoll** *atoll* Caroline Islands, C Micronesia
80 J13 **Oromīya** *var.* Oromo. ◈ C Ethiopia
Oromo *see* Oromīya
13 O15 **Oromocto** New Brunswick, SE Canada 45°50′N 66°28′W
191 S4 **Orona** *prev.* Hull Island. *atoll* Phoenix Islands, C Kiribati
191 V17 **Orongo** *ancient monument* Easter Island, Chile, E Pacific Ocean
138 I3 **Orontes** *var.* Ononte, Nahr el Aassi, *Ar.* Nahr al ʻAṣī. ≈ SW Asia
104 L9 **Oropesa** Castilla-La Mancha, C Spain 39°55′N 05°10′W
Oropesa *see* Oropesa del Mar
105 T8 **Oropesa del Mar** *var.* Oropesa, Orpesa, *Cat.* Orpes. Valenciana, E Spain 40°06′N 00°07′E
Oropeza *see* Cochabamba
Oroqen Zizhiqi *see* Alihe
171 P7 **Oroquieta** *var.* Oroquieta City. Mindanao, S Philippines 08°27′N 123°46′E
Oroquieta City *see* Oroquieta
40 J8 **Oro, Río del** ≈ C Mexico
59 O14 **Orós, Açude** ▩ E Brazil
107 D18 **Orosei, Golfo di** *gulf* Tyrrhenian Sea, C Mediterranean Sea
111 M24 **Orosháza** Békés, SE Hungary 46°33′N 20°40′E
Orosirá Rodhópis *see* Rhodope Mountains
111 I22 **Oroszlány** Komárom-Esztergom, W Hungary 47°28′N 18°16′E
188 B16 **Orote Peninsula** *peninsula* W Guam
123 T9 **Orotukan** Magadanskaya Oblast', E Russian Federation 62°18′N 150°46′E
35 O5 **Oroville** California, W USA 39°29′N 121°35′W
32 K6 **Oroville** Washington, NW USA 48°56′N 119°25′W
35 O5 **Oroville, Lake** ▩ California, W USA
0 G15 **Orozco Fracture Zone** *tectonic feature* E Pacific Ocean
Orpes *see* Oropesa del Mar
Orpesa *see* Oropesa del Mar
64 I7 **Orphan Knoll** *undersea feature* NW Atlantic Ocean 51°00′N 47°00′W
29 V3 **Orr** Minnesota, N USA 48°03′N 92°48′W
95 M21 **Orrefors** Kalmar, S Sweden 56°48′N 15°45′E
182 I7 **Orroroo** South Australia 32°46′S 138°38′E
31 T12 **Orrville** Ohio, N USA 40°50′N 81°45′W
94 L12 **Orsa** Dalarna, C Sweden 61°07′N 14°40′E
Orschowa *see* Orşova
Orschütz *see* Orzyc
119 O14 **Orsha** Vitsyebskaya Voblasts', NE Belarus 54°30′N 30°26′E
127 Q2 **Orshanka** Respublika Mariy El, W Russian Federation 56°54′N 47°54′E
108 C11 **Orsières** Valais, SW Switzerland 46°00′N 07°09′E
127 X8 **Orsk** Orenburgskaya Oblast', W Russian Federation 51°13′N 58°35′E
116 F13 **Orşova** *Ger.* Orschowa, *Hung.* Orsova. Mehedinţi, SW Romania 44°42′N 22°22′E
94 D10 **Ørsta** Møre og Romsdal, S Norway 62°12′N 06°09′E
95 O15 **Örsundsbro** Uppsala, C Sweden 59°45′N 17°19′E
136 D16 **Ortaca** Muğla, SW Turkey 36°49′N 28°43′E
83 I21 **O.R. Tambo** ✈ (Johannesburg) Gauteng, NE South Africa 26°08′S 28°01′E
107 M16 **Orta Nova** Puglia, SE Italy 41°20′N 15°43′E
136 I17 **Orta Toroslar** ▲▲ S Turkey
54 E11 **Ortega** Tolima, W Colombia 03°57′N 75°11′W
104 H1 **Ortegal, Cabo** *headland* NW Spain 43°46′N 07°54′W
Ortelsburg *see* Szczytno
102 J15 **Orthez** Pyrénées-Atlantiques, SW France 43°29′N 00°46′W
60 J10 **Ortigueira** Paraná, S Brazil 24°10′S 50°55′W
104 H1 **Ortigueira** Galicia, NW Spain 43°40′N 07°50′W
106 H5 **Ortisei** *Ger.* Sankt-Ulrich. Trentino-Alto Adige, N Italy 46°35′N 11°42′E
40 F6 **Ortiz** Sonora, NW Mexico 28°18′N 110°40′W
54 L5 **Ortiz** Guárico, N Venezuela 09°37′N 67°20′W
Ortler *see* Ortles
106 F5 **Ortles** *Ger.* Ortler. ▲ N Italy 46°29′N 10°33′E
107 K14 **Ortona** Abruzzo, C Italy 42°21′N 14°24′E
57 K14 **Ortón, Río** ≈ N Bolivia
29 R8 **Ortonville** Minnesota, N USA 45°18′N 96°26′W
147 W8 **Orto-Tokoy** Issyk-Kul'skaya Oblast', NE Kyrgyzstan 42°20′N 76°03′E
93 I15 **Orträsk** Västerbotten, N Sweden 64°10′N 19°00′E
100 J12 **Örtze** ≈ NW Germany
Oruba *see* Aruba
142 I3 **Orūmīyeh** *var.* Rizaiyeh, Urmia, Urmiyeh; *prev.* Reẕā'īyeh. Āžarbāyjān-e Gharbī, NW Iran 37°33′N 45°06′E
142 J3 **Orūmīyeh, Daryācheh-ye** *var.* Matianus, Sha Hi, Urumi Yeh, *Eng.* Lake Urmia; *prev.* Daryācheh-ye Reẕā'īyeh. ◎ NW Iran
57 K19 **Oruro** Oruro, W Bolivia 17°58′S 67°06′W
57 J19 **Oruro** ◈ *department* W Bolivia
95 I18 **Orust** *island* S Sweden
Orūzgān *see* Uruzgān
106 H13 **Orvieto** *anc.* Velsuna. Umbria, C Italy 42°43′N 12°06′E
194 K7 **Orville Coast** *physical region* Antarctica
114 H7 **Oryakhovo** Vratsa, NW Bulgaria 43°44′N 23°58′E
Oryokko *see* Yalu
117 R5 **Orzhytsya** Poltavs'ka Oblast', C Ukraine 49°48′N 32°40′E
110 M9 **Orzyc** *Ger.* Orschütz. ≈ NE Poland
110 N8 **Orzysz** *Ger.* Arys. Warmińsko-Mazurskie, NE Poland 53°49′N 21°54′E
98 K13 **Oss** Noord-Brabant, S Netherlands 51°46′N 05°32′E
94 I10 **Os** Hedmark, S Norway 62°29′N 11°14′E
125 U15 **Osa** Permskiy Kray, NW Russian Federation 57°16′N 55°22′E
115 F15 **Óssa** ▲▲ C Greece
104 H11 **Ossa** ▲ S Portugal 38°43′N 07°33′W
29 W11 **Osage** Iowa, C USA 43°16′N 92°48′W
27 U5 **Osage Beach** Missouri, C USA 38°09′N 92°37′W
27 P5 **Osage City** Kansas, C USA 38°37′N 95°49′W
27 U7 **Osage Fork River** ≈ Missouri, C USA
27 U5 **Osage River** ≈ Missouri, C USA
164 J13 **Ōsaka** *hist.* Naniwa. Ōsaka, Honshū, SW Japan 34°38′N 135°28′E
164 I13 **Ōsaka** *off.* Ōsaka-fu, *var.* Ōsaka Hu. ◈ *urban prefecture* Honshū, SW Japan
Ōsaka-fu/Ōsaka Hu *see* Ōsaka
145 R10 **Osakarovka** Karaganda, C Kazakhstan 50°32′N 72°39′E
Ōsaki *see* Furukawa
29 T7 **Osakis** Minnesota, N USA 45°51′N 95°08′W
43 N16 **Osa, Península de** *peninsula* S Costa Rica
60 M10 **Osasco** São Paulo, S Brazil 23°32′S 46°46′W
27 R5 **Osawatomie** Kansas, C USA 38°30′N 94°57′W
26 L3 **Osborne** Kansas, C USA 39°26′N 98°42′W
173 S8 **Osborn Plateau** *undersea feature* E Indian Ocean
95 L21 **Osby** Skåne, S Sweden 56°24′N 14°00′E
Osca *see* Huesca
92 N2 **Oscar II Land** *physical region* W Svalbard
27 Y10 **Osceola** Arkansas, C USA 35°43′N 89°58′W
29 V15 **Osceola** Iowa, C USA 41°01′N 93°45′W
27 S6 **Osceola** Missouri, C USA 38°01′N 93°41′W
29 Q15 **Osceola** Nebraska, C USA 41°09′N 97°28′W
101 N15 **Oschatz** Sachsen, E Germany 51°17′N 13°10′E
100 K13 **Oschersleben** Sachsen-Anhalt, C Germany 52°02′N 11°14′E
31 R7 **Oscoda** Michigan, N USA 44°25′N 83°19′W
Ösel *see* Saaremaa
94 H6 **Osen** Sør-Trøndelag, S Norway 64°17′N 10°29′E
94 I12 **Osensjøen** ◎ S Norway
164 A14 **Ōse-zaki** Fukue-jima, SW Japan
147 T10 **Osh** Oshskaya Oblast', SW Kyrgyzstan 40°34′N 72°46′E
83 C16 **Oshakati** Oshana, N Namibia 17°46′S 15°43′E
83 C16 **Oshana** ◈ *district* N Namibia
14 H15 **Oshawa** Ontario, SE Canada 43°54′N 78°50′W
165 R10 **Oshika-hantō** *peninsula* Honshū, C Japan
83 C16 **Oshikango** Ohangwena, N Namibia 17°29′S 15°54′E
83 C17 **Oshikoto** *var.* Otjikoto. ◈ *district* N Namibia
165 P5 **Ō-shima** *island* NE Japan
165 N14 **Ō-shima** *island* S Japan
165 Q5 **Oshima-hantō** ▲▲ Hokkaidō, NE Japan
83 D17 **Oshivelo** Oshikoto, N Namibia 18°37′S 17°10′E
28 K14 **Oshkosh** Nebraska, C USA 41°25′N 102°21′W
30 M7 **Oshkosh** Wisconsin, N USA 44°01′N 88°32′W
Oshmyany *see* Ashmyany
Osh Oblasty *see* Oshskaya Oblast'
77 T16 **Oshogbo** *var.* Osogbo. Osun, W Nigeria 07°42′N 04°31′E
147 S11 **Oshskaya Oblast'** *Kir.* Osh Oblasty. ◈ *province* SW Kyrgyzstan
Ōshū *see* Mizusawa
Oshun *see* Osun
79 J20 **Oshwe** Bandundu, C Dem. Rep. Congo 03°24′S 19°32′E
Osiek *see* Osijek
112 I9 **Osijek** *prev.* Osiek, Osjek, *Ger.* Esseg, *Hung.* Eszék. Osijek-Baranja, E Croatia 45°33′N 18°41′E
112 I9 **Osijek-Baranja** *off.* Osječko-Baranjska Županija. ◈ *province* E Croatia
106 J12 **Osimo** Marche, C Italy 43°28′N 13°29′E
122 M12 **Osinovka** Irkutskaya Oblast', C Russian Federation 56°19′N 101°55′E
Osintorf *see* Asintorf
112 N11 **Osipaonica** Serbia, NE Serbia 44°34′N 21°00′E
Osipenko *see* Berdyans'k
Osipovichi *see* Asipovichy
Osječko-Baranjska Županija *see* Osijek-Baranja
Osjek *see* Osijek
29 W15 **Oskaloosa** Iowa, C USA 41°17′N 92°38′W
27 Q4 **Oskaloosa** Kansas, C USA 39°14′N 95°21′W
95 N20 **Oskarshamn** Kalmar, S Sweden 57°16′N 16°25′E
95 J21 **Oskarström** Halland, S Sweden 56°48′N 13°00′E
14 M8 **Oskélanéo** Québec, SE Canada 48°06′N 75°12′W
Öskemen *see* Ust'-Kamenogorsk
117 W5 **Oskil** *Rus.* Oskil. ≈ Russian Federation/Ukraine
Oskil *see* Oskil
93 D20 **Oslo** *prev.* Christiania, Kristiania. ● (Norway) Oslo, S Norway 59°54′N 10°44′E
93 D20 **Oslo** ◈ *county* S Norway
93 D21 **Oslofjorden** *fjord* S Norway
155 G15 **Osmānābād** Mahārāshtra, C India 18°09′N 76°06′E
136 J11 **Osmancık** Çorum, N Turkey 40°58′N 34°50′E
136 L16 **Osmaniye** Osmaniye, S Turkey 37°04′N 36°15′E
136 L16 **Osmaniye** ◈ *province* S Turkey
95 O16 **Ösmo** Stockholm, C Sweden 58°58′N 17°55′E
118 E3 **Osmussaar** *island* W Estonia
100 G13 **Osnabrück** Niedersachsen, NW Germany 52°09′N 07°42′E
110 D11 **Ośno Lubuskie** *Ger.* Drossen. Lubuskie, W Poland 52°28′N 14°51′E
Osogbo *see* Oshogbo
113 P19 **Osogov Mountains** *var.* Osogovske Planine, Osogovski Planina, *Mac.* Osogovski Planini. ▲▲ Bulgaria/FYR Macedonia
Osogovske Planine/Osogovski Planina/Osogovski Planini *see* Osogov Mountains
165 R6 **Osore-zan** ▲ Honshū, C Japan 41°18′N 141°06′E
Oşorhei *see* Târgu Mureş
61 J16 **Osório** Rio Grande do Sul, S Brazil 29°53′S 50°17′W
63 G16 **Osorno** Los Lagos, C Chile 40°39′S 73°05′W
104 M4 **Osorno** Castilla y León, N Spain 42°24′N 04°22′W
11 N17 **Osoyoos** British Columbia, SW Canada 49°02′N 119°31′W
95 C14 **Osøyro** Hordaland, S Norway 60°11′N 05°30′E
54 J6 **Ospino** Portuguesa, N Venezuela 09°17′N 69°26′W
23 X6 **Ossabaw Island** *island* Georgia, SE USA
23 X6 **Ossabaw Sound** *sound* Georgia, SE USA
183 O16 **Ossa, Mount** ▲ Tasmania, SE Australia 41°55′S 146°03′E
104 H11 **Ossa, Serra d'** ▲▲ SE Portugal
77 U16 **Osse** ≈ S Nigeria
30 J6 **Osseo** Wisconsin, N USA 44°33′N 91°13′W
109 S9 **Ossiacher See** ◎ S Austria
18 K13 **Ossining** New York, NE USA 41°10′N 73°50′W
123 V9 **Ossora** Krasnoyarskiy Kray, E Russian Federation 59°16′N 163°02′E
124 I15 **Ostashkov** Tverskaya Oblast', W Russian Federation 57°08′N 33°10′E
100 H9 **Oste** ≈ NW Germany
Ostee *see* Baltic Sea
Ostend/Ostende *see* Oostende
117 P3 **Oster** Chernihivs'ka Oblast', N Ukraine 50°57′N 30°55′E
95 O14 **Österbybruk** Uppsala, C Sweden 60°13′N 17°55′E
95 M19 **Österbymo** Östergotland, S Sweden 57°49′N 15°15′E
94 K12 **Österdalälven** ≈ C Sweden
94 I12 **Østerdalen** *valley* S Norway
95 L18 **Östergötland** ◈ *county* S Sweden
100 H10 **Osterholz-Scharmbeck** Niedersachsen, NW Germany 53°13′N 08°46′E
Östermark *see* Teuva
Östermyra *see* Seinäjoki
Østerø *see* Eysturoy
101 J14 **Osterode am Harz** Niedersachsen, C Germany 51°43′N 10°15′E
Osterode/Osterode in Ostpreussen *see* Ostróda
Osterøy *see* Osterøyni
94 C13 **Osterøyni** *prev.* Osterøy. *island* S Norway
Österreich *see* Austria
93 G16 **Östersund** Jämtland, C Sweden 63°10′N 14°44′E
95 N14 **Östervåla** Västmanland, C Sweden 60°10′N 17°13′E
101 H22 **Ostfildern** Baden-Württemberg, SW Germany 48°43′N 09°16′E
95 H16 **Østfold** ◈ *county* S Norway
100 E9 **Ostfriesische Inseln** *Eng.* East Frisian Islands. *island group* NW Germany
100 F10 **Ostfriesland** *historical region* NW Germany
95 P14 **Östhammar** Uppsala, C Sweden 60°15′N 18°25′E
Ostia Aterni *see* Pescara
106 G8 **Ostiglia** Lombardia, N Italy 45°04′N 11°09′E
95 J14 **Östmark** Värmland, C Sweden 60°15′N 12°45′E
95 K22 **Östra Ringsjön** ◎ S Sweden
111 I17 **Ostrava** Moravskoslezský Kraj, E Czech Republic 49°50′N 18°15′E
Ostravský Kraj *see* Moravskoslezský Kraj
94 J11 **Østrehogna** *Swe.* Härjahågnen, Härjehågna. ▲ Norway/Sweden 61°43′N 12°07′E
110 K8 **Ostróda** *Ger.* Osterode, Osterode in Ostpreussen. Warmińsko-Mazurskie, NE Poland 53°42′N 19°59′E
Ostrog/Ostróg *see* Ostroh
126 L8 **Ostrogozhsk** Voronezhskaya Oblast', W Russian Federation 50°52′N 39°00′E
116 L4 **Ostroh** *Pol.* Ostróg, *Rus.* Ostrog. Rivnens'ka Oblast', NW Ukraine 50°20′N 26°29′E
110 N9 **Ostrołęka** *Ger.* Wiesenhof, *Rus.* Ostrolenka. Mazowieckie, C Poland 53°06′N 21°34′E
Ostrolenka *see* Ostrołęka
111 A16 **Ostrov** *Ger.* Schlackenwerth. Karlovarský Kraj, W Czech Republic 50°18′N 12°56′E
124 F15 **Ostrov** *Latv.* Austrava. Pskovskaya Oblast', W Russian Federation 57°21′N 28°18′E
Ostrovets *see* Ostrowiec Świętokrzyski
113 M21 **Ostrovicës, Mali i** ▲ SE Albania 40°36′N 20°25′E
165 Z2 **Ostrov Iturup** *island* NE Russian Federation
124 M4 **Ostrovnoy** Murmanskaya Oblast', NW Russian Federation 68°00′N 39°40′E
114 L7 **Ostrovo** *prev.* Golema Ada. Razgrad, N Bulgaria 43°40′N 26°37′E
125 N15 **Ostrovskoye** Kostromskaya Oblast', NW Russian Federation 57°46′N 42°18′E
Ostrów *see* Ostrów Wielkopolski
Ostrowiec *see* Ostrowiec Świętokrzyski
111 M14 **Ostrowiec Świętokrzyski** *var.* Ostrowiec, *Rus.* Ostrovets. Świętokrzyskie, C Poland 50°55′N 21°23′E
110 P13 **Ostrów Lubelski** Lubelskie, E Poland 51°29′N 22°57′E
110 N10 **Ostrów Mazowiecka** *var.* Ostrów Mazowiecki. Mazowieckie, NE Poland 52°49′N 21°53′E
Ostrów Mazowiecki *see* Ostrów Mazowiecka
Ostrowo *see* Ostrów Wielkopolski
110 H13 **Ostrów Wielkopolski** *var.* Ostrów, *Ger.* Ostrowo. Wielkopolskie, C Poland 51°40′N 17°47′E
Ostryna *see* Astryna
110 I13 **Ostrzeszów** Wielkopolskie, C Poland 51°25′N 17°55′E
107 P18 **Ostuni** Puglia, SE Italy 40°44′N 17°35′E
Ostyako-Voguls'k *see* Khanty-Mansiysk
114 I9 **Osŭm** ≈ N Bulgaria
Osum *see* Osumit, Lumi i
164 C17 **Ōsumi-hantō** ▲▲ Kyūshū, SW Japan
164 C17 **Ōsumi-kaikyō** *strait* SW Japan
113 L22 **Osumit, Lumi i** *var.* Osum. ≈ SE Albania
77 T16 **Osun** *var.* Oshun. ◈ *state* SW Nigeria
104 L14 **Osuna** Andalucía, S Spain 37°14′N 05°06′W
60 J8 **Osvaldo Cruz** São Paulo, S Brazil 21°49′S 50°52′W
Osveya *see* Asvyeya
18 J7 **Oswegatchie River** ≈ New York, NE USA
27 Q7 **Oswego** Kansas, C USA 37°11′N 95°10′W
18 H9 **Oswego** New York, NE USA 43°27′N 76°13′W
97 K19 **Oswestry** W England, United Kingdom 52°51′N 03°06′W
111 J16 **Oświęcim** *Ger.* Auschwitz. Małopolskie, S Poland 50°02′N 19°11′E
185 E22 **Otago** *off.* Otago Region. ◈ *region* South Island, New Zealand
185 F23 **Otago Peninsula** *peninsula* South Island, New Zealand
Otago Region *see* Otago
165 F13 **Ōtake** Hiroshima, Honshū, SW Japan 34°13′N 132°12′E
184 L13 **Otaki** Wellington, North Island, New Zealand 40°46′S 175°08′E
93 M15 **Otanmäki** Oulu, C Finland 64°07′N 27°04′E
145 T15 **Otar** Zhambyl, SE Kazakhstan 43°30′N 75°13′E
165 R4 **Otaru** Hokkaidō, NE Japan 43°14′N 140°59′E
185 C24 **Otatara** Southland, South Island, New Zealand 46°26′S 168°18′E
185 C24 **Otautau** Southland, South Island, New Zealand 46°10′S 168°01′E
93 M18 **Otava** Itä-Suomi, E Finland 61°37′N 27°07′E
111 B18 **Otava** *Ger.* Wottawa. ≈ SW Czech Republic
56 C6 **Otavalo** Imbabura, N Ecuador 0°13′N 78°15′W
83 D17 **Otavi** Otjozondjupa, N Namibia 19°35′S 17°25′E
165 P12 **Ōtawara** Tochigi, Honshū, S Japan 36°52′N 140°01′E
83 B16 **Otchinjau** Cunene, SW Angola 16°31′S 13°54′E
116 F12 **Oţelu Roşu** *Ger.* Ferdinandsberg, *Hung.* Nándorhgy. Caras-Severin, SW Romania 45°30′N 22°22′E
185 E21 **Otematata** Canterbury, South Island, New Zealand 44°37′S 170°12′E
118 I6 **Otepää** *Ger.* Odenpäh. Valgamaa, SE Estonia 58°01′N 26°30′E
144 G14 **Otes** *Kaz.* Say-Ötesh; *prev.* Say-Utës. Mangistau, SW Kazakhstan 44°20′N 53°32′E
162 H7 **Otgon** *var.* Buyant. Dzavhan, C Mongolia 47°14′N 97°14′E
32 K9 **Othello** Washington, NW USA 46°49′N 119°10′W
83 K23 **oThongathi** *prev.* Tongaat, *var.* uThongathi. KwaZulu/Natal, E South Africa 29°35′S 31°07′E *see also* Tongaat
115 A15 **Othonoí** *island* Iónia Nisiá, Greece, C Mediterranean Sea
Othris *see* Óthrys
115 F17 **Óthrys** *var.* Othris. ▲▲ C Greece
77 Q14 **Oti** ≈ N Togo
40 K10 **Otinapa** Durango, C Mexico 24°01′N 104°58′W
185 G17 **Otira** West Coast, South Island, New Zealand 42°52′S 171°33′E
37 V3 **Otis** Colorado, C USA 40°09′N 102°57′W
12 L10 **Otish, Monts** ▲▲ Québec, E Canada
83 C17 **Otjikondo** Kunene, N Namibia 19°50′S 15°23′E
Otjikoto *see* Oshikoto
83 E18 **Otjinene** Omaheke, NE Namibia 21°10′S 18°43′E
83 D18 **Otjiwarongo** Otjozondjupa, N Namibia 20°29′S 16°36′E
83 D18 **Otjosondu** *var.* Otjosundu. Otjozondjupa, C Namibia 21°19′S 17°51′E
Otjosundu *see* Otjosondu
83 D18 **Otjozondjupa** ◈ *district* C Namibia
112 C11 **Otočac** Lika-Senj, W Croatia 44°52′N 15°13′E
Otog Qi *see* Ulan
112 J10 **Otok** Vukovar-Srijem, E Croatia 45°10′N 18°52′E
116 K14 **Otopeni** ✈ (Bucureşti) Ilfov, S Romania 44°34′N 26°09′E
184 L8 **Otorohanga** Waikato, North Island, New Zealand 38°10′S 175°14′E
12 D9 **Otoskwin** ≈ Ontario, C Canada
165 G14 **Ōtoyo** Kōchi, Shikoku, SW Japan 33°45′N 133°42′E
95 E16 **Otra** ≈ S Norway
107 R19 **Otranto** Puglia, SE Italy 40°08′N 18°28′E
Otranto, Canale d' *see* Otranto, Strait of
107 Q18 **Otranto, Strait of** *It.* Canale d'Otranto. *strait* Albania/Italy
111 H18 **Otrokovice** *Ger.* Otrokowitz. Zlínský Kraj, E Czech Republic 49°13′N 17°33′E
Otrokowitz *see* Otrokovice
31 P10 **Otsego** Michigan, N USA 42°27′N 85°42′W
31 Q6 **Otsego Lake** ◎ Michigan, N USA
18 I11 **Otselic River** ≈ New York, NE USA
164 J14 **Ōtsu** *var.* Ôtu. Shiga, Honshū, SW Japan 35°03′N 135°49′E
94 G11 **Otta** Oppland, S Norway 61°46′N 09°33′E
189 U13 **Otta** *island* Chuuk, C Micronesia
94 F11 **Otta** ≈ S Norway
189 U13 **Otta Pass** *passage* Chuuk Islands, C Micronesia
95 J22 **Ottarp** Skåne, S Sweden 55°55′N 12°55′E
14 L12 **Ottawa** ● (Canada) Ontario, SE Canada 45°24′N 75°41′W
30 L11 **Ottawa** Illinois, N USA 41°21′N 88°50′W
27 Q5 **Ottawa** Kansas, C USA 38°35′N 95°16′W
31 R12 **Ottawa** Ohio, N USA 41°01′N 84°03′W
14 L12 **Ottawa** *var.* Uplands. ✈ Ontario, SE Canada 45°19′N 75°39′W
14 M12 **Ottawa** *Fr.* Outaouais. ≈ Ontario/Québec, SE Canada
9 R10 **Ottawa Islands** *island group* Nunavut, C Canada
18 L8 **Otter Creek** ≈ Vermont, NE USA
36 L6 **Otter Creek Reservoir** ▩ Utah, W USA
98 L11 **Otterlo** Gelderland, E Netherlands 52°06′N 05°46′E
94 D9 **Otterøya** *island* S Norway
29 S6 **Otter Tail Lake** ◎ Minnesota, N USA
29 R7 **Otter Tail River** ≈ Minnesota, C USA
95 H23 **Otterup** Syddtjylland, C Denmark 55°31′N 10°25′E
99 H19 **Ottignies** Wallon Brabant, C Belgium 50°40′N 04°34′E
101 L23 **Ottobrunn** Bayern, SE Germany 48°02′N 11°40′E
29 X15 **Ottumwa** Iowa, C USA 41°00′N 92°24′W
Ôtu *see* Ōtsu
83 B16 **Otuazuma** Kunene, NW Namibia 17°52′S 13°16′E
77 V16 **Oturkpo** Benue, S Nigeria 07°12′N 08°06′E
193 Y15 **Otu Tolu Group** *island group* SE Tonga
182 M13 **Otway, Cape** *headland* Victoria, SE Australia 38°52′S 143°31′E
63 H24 **Otway, Seno** *inlet* S Chile
Ötz *see* Oetz
108 L8 **Ötztaler Ache** ≈ W Austria
108 L9 **Ötztaler Alpen** *It.* Alpi Venoste. ▲▲ SW Austria
27 T12 **Ouachita, Lake** ▩ Arkansas, C USA
27 R11 **Ouachita Mountains** ▲▲ Arkansas/Oklahoma, C USA
27 U13 **Ouachita River** ≈ Arkansas/Louisiana, C USA
Ouadaï *see* Ouaddaï
76 J7 **Ouadâne** *var.* Ouadane. Adrar, C Mauritania 20°57′N 11°35′W
78 K13 **Ouadda** Haute-Kotto, N Central African Republic 08°02′N 22°22′E
78 J10 **Ouaddaï** *off.* Préfecture du Ouaddaï, *var.* Ouadaï, Wadai. ◈ *prefecture* SE Chad
Ouaddaï, Préfecture du *see* Ouaddaï
77 P13 **Ouagadougou** *var.* Wagadugu. ● (Burkina) C Burkina 12°20′N 01°32′W
77 P13 **Ouagadougou** ✈ C Burkina 12°21′N 01°27′W
77 O12 **Ouahigouya** NW Burkina 13°31′N 02°20′W
Ouahran *see* Oran
79 J14 **Ouaka** ◈ *prefecture* C Central African Republic
79 J15 **Ouaka** ≈ S Central African Republic
Oualam *see* Ouallam
76 M9 **Oualâta** *var.* Oualata. Hodh ech Chargui, SE Mauritania 17°18′N 07°00′W
77 R11 **Ouallam** *var.* Oualam. Tillabéri, W Niger 14°23′N 02°09′E
172 H14 **Ouanani** Mohéli, S Comoros 12°19′S 93°98′E
55 Z10 **Ouanary** E French Guiana 04°11′N 51°40′W
78 L13 **Ouanda Djallé** Vakaga, NE Central African Republic 08°53′N 22°47′E
79 N14 **Ouando** Haut-Mbomou, SE Central African Republic 05°57′N 25°57′E
79 L15 **Ouango** Mbomou, S Central African Republic 04°19′N 22°30′E
77 N14 **Ouangolodougou** *var.* Wangolodougou. N Ivory Coast 09°58′N 05°09′W
172 I13 **Ouani** Anjouan, SE Comoros
79 M15 **Ouara** ≈ E Central African Republic
76 K7 **Ouarâne** *desert* C Mauritania
15 O11 **Ouareau** ≈ Québec, SE Canada
74 K7 **Ouargla** *var.* Wargla. NE Algeria 32°N 05°16′E
74 F8 **Ouarzazate** S Morocco 30°54′N 06°55′W
77 Q11 **Ouatagouna** Gao, E Mali 15°06′N 00°41′E
74 G6 **Ouazzane** *var.* Ouezzane, *Ar.* Wazan, Wazzan. N Morocco 34°52′N 05°35′W
Oubangui *see* Ubangi
Oubangui-Chari *see* Central African Republic
Oubangui-Chari, Territoire de l' *see* Central African Republic
Oubari, Edeyen d' *see* Awbāri, Idhān
98 G13 **Oud-Beijerland** Zuid-Holland, SW Netherlands 51°50′N 04°25′E
98 F13 **Ouddorp** Zuid-Holland, SW Netherlands 51°49′N 03°55′E
77 P9 **Oudeïka** *oasis* C Mali
98 G13 **Oude Maas** ≈ SW Netherlands
99 E18 **Oudenaarde** *Fr.* Audenarde. Oost-Vlaanderen, SW Belgium 50°50′N 03°37′E
99 H14 **Oudenbosch** Noord-Brabant, S Netherlands 51°35′N 04°32′E
98 P6 **Oude Pekela** Groningen, NE Netherlands 53°06′N 07°00′E
Ouderkerk *see* Ouderkerk aan den Amstel
98 I10 **Ouderkerk aan den Amstel** *var.* Ouderkerk. Noord-Holland, C Netherlands 52°18′N 04°54′E
98 I6 **Oudeschild** Noord-Holland, NW Netherlands 53°01′N 04°51′E
99 G14 **Oude-Tonge** Zuid-Holland, SW Netherlands 51°40′N 04°13′E
98 I12 **Oudewater** Utrecht, C Netherlands 52°02′N 04°54′E
Oudjda *see* Oujda
Oudkerk *see* Aldtsjerk
167 Q6 **Oudômxai** *var.* Muang Xay, Muong Sai, Xai. Oudômxai, N Laos 20°41′N 102°00′E
102 J7 **Oudon** ≈ NW France
98 I9 **Oudorp** Noord-Holland, NW Netherlands 52°39′N 04°47′E
83 G25 **Oudtshoorn** Western Cape, SW South Africa 33°35′S 22°14′E
99 I16 **Oud-Turnhout** Antwerpen, N Belgium 51°19′N 05°01′E
74 F7 **Oued-Zem** C Morocco 32°53′N 06°30′W
187 P16 **Ouégoa** Province Nord, C New Caledonia 20°22′S 164°25′E
76 L13 **Ouéléssébougou** *var.* Ouolossébougou. Koulikoro, SW Mali 11°58′N 07°51′W
77 N16 **Ouéllé** E Ivory Coast 07°18′N 04°01′W
77 R16 **Ouémé** ≈ C Benin
77 O13 **Ouessa** S Burkina 11°02′N 02°44′W
102 D5 **Ouessant, Île d'** *Eng.* Ushant. *island* NW France
79 H17 **Ouésso** Sangha, NW Congo 01°38′N 16°03′E
79 D15 **Ouest** *Eng.* West. ◈ *province* W Cameroon
190 G11 **Ouest, Baie del'** *bay* Îles Wallis, E Wallis and Futuna
15 Y7 **Ouest, Pointe de l'** *headland* Québec, SE Canada 48°08′N 64°57′W
Ouezzane *see* Ouazzane
99 K20 **Ouffet** Liège, E Belgium 50°30′N 05°31′E
79 H14 **Ouham** ◈ *prefecture* NW Central African Republic
78 I13 **Ouham** ≈ Central African Republic/Chad
79 G14 **Ouham-Pendé** ◈ *prefecture* W Central African Republic
77 R16 **Ouidah** *Eng.* Whydah, Wida. S Benin 06°23′N 02°08′E
74 H6 **Oujda** *Ar.* Oudjda, Ujda. NE Morocco 34°45′N 01°53′W
76 I7 **Oujeft** Adrar, C Mauritania 20°05′N 13°00′W
93 L15 **Oulainen** Oulu, C Finland 64°14′N 24°50′E
Ould Yanja *see* Ould Yenjé
76 J10 **Ould Yenjé** *var.* Ould Yanja. Guidimaka, S Mauritania 15°33′N 11°43′W
93 L14 **Oulu** *Swe.* Uleåborg. Oulu, C Finland 65°01′N 25°28′E
93 M14 **Oulu** *Swe.* Uleåborg. ◈ *province* N Finland
93 L15 **Oulujärvi** *Swe.* Uleträsk. ◎ C Finland
93 M14 **Oulujoki** *Swe.* Uleälv. ≈ C Finland
93 L14 **Oulunsalo** Oulu, C Finland 64°55′N 25°19′E
106 A8 **Oulx** Piemonte, NE Italy 45°05′N 06°41′E
78 J9 **Oum-Chalouba** Borkou-Ennedi-Tibesti, NE Chad 15°48′N 20°46′E
76 M16 **Oumé** C Ivory Coast 06°25′N 05°23′W
74 F7 **Oum er Rbia** ≈ C Morocco
78 J10 **Oum-Hadjer** Batha, E Chad 13°18′N 19°41′E
92 K10 **Ounasjoki** ≈ N Finland
78 J7 **Ounianga Kébir** Borkou-Ennedi-Tibesti, N Chad 19°06′N 20°29′E
Ouolossébougou *see* Ouéléssébougou
Oup *see* Auob
99 K19 **Oupeye** Liège, E Belgium 50°42′N 05°38′E
99 N21 **Our** ≈ NW Europe
37 Q7 **Ouray** Colorado, C USA 38°01′N 107°40′W
103 R7 **Ource** ≈ C France
104 G9 **Ourém** Santarém, C Portugal 39°40′N 08°32′W
104 H4 **Ourense** *Cast.* Orense, *Lat.* Aurium. Galicia, NW Spain 42°20′N 07°52′W
104 I4 **Ourense** *Cast.* Orense. ◈ *province* Galicia, NW Spain
59 O15 **Ouricuri** Pernambuco, E Brazil 07°51′S 40°05′W
60 J9 **Ourinhos** São Paulo, S Brazil 22°59′S 49°52′W
104 G13 **Ourique** Beja, S Portugal 37°38′N 08°13′W
59 M20 **Ouro Preto** Minas Gerais, NE Brazil 20°25′S 43°30′W
Ours, Grand Lac de l' *see* Great Bear Lake
99 K20 **Ourthe** ≈ E Belgium
165 Q9 **Ōu-sanmyaku** ▲▲ Honshū, C Japan
97 M17 **Ouse** ≈ N England, United Kingdom
Ouse *see* Great Ouse
102 H7 **Oust** ≈ NW France
Outaouais *see* Ottawa
15 T4 **Outardes Quatre, Réservoir** ▩ Québec, SE Canada
15 T5 **Outardes, Rivière aux** ≈ Québec, SE Canada
96 E8 **Outer Hebrides** *var.* Western Isles. *island group* NW Scotland, United Kingdom
30 K3 **Outer Island** *island* Apostle Islands, Wisconsin, N USA
35 S16 **Outer Santa Barbara Passage** *passage* California, SW USA
83 C18 **Outjo** Kunene, N Namibia 20°08′S 16°08′E
11 T16 **Outlook** Saskatchewan, S Canada 51°30′N 107°03′W
93 N16 **Outokumpu** Itä-Suomi, E Finland 62°43′N 29°05′E
96 M2 **Out Skerries** *island group* NE Scotland, United Kingdom
187 Q16 **Ouvéa** *island* Îles Loyauté, NE New Caledonia
103 S14 **Ouvèze** ≈ SE France
182 L9 **Ouyen** Victoria, SE Australia 35°07′S 142°19′E
39 Q14 **Ouzinkie** Kodiak Island, Alaska, USA 57°54′N 152°27′W
137 O13 **Ovacık** Tunceli, E Turkey 39°23′N 39°13′E
106 C9 **Ovada** Piemonte, NE Italy 44°41′N 08°39′E
187 X14 **Ovalau** *island* C Fiji
62 G9 **Ovalle** Coquimbo, N Chile 30°33′S 71°16′W
83 C17 **Ovamboland** *physical region* N Namibia
54 L10 **Ovana, Cerro** ▲ S Venezuela 04°41′N 66°54′W
104 G7 **Ovar** Aveiro, N Portugal 40°52′N 08°38′W
114 L10 **Ovcharitsa, Yazovir** ▩ SE Bulgaria
54 E6 **Ovejas** Sucre, NW Colombia 09°32′N 75°14′W
101 E16 **Overath** Nordrhein-Westfalen, W Germany 50°55′N 07°16′E
98 F13 **Overflakkee** *island* SW Netherlands
99 H19 **Overijse** Vlaams Brabant, C Belgium 50°46′N 04°32′E
98 N10 **Overijssel** ◈ *province* E Netherlands
98 M9 **Overijssels Kanaal** *canal* E Netherlands
92 K13 **Överkalix** Norrbotten, N Sweden 66°19′N 22°49′E
27 R4 **Overland Park** Kansas, C USA 38°57′N 94°41′W
99 L14 **Overloon** Noord-Brabant, SE Netherlands 51°35′N 05°54′E
99 K16 **Overpelt** Limburg, NE Belgium 51°13′N 05°24′E
35 Y10 **Overton** Nevada, W USA 36°32′N 114°25′W
25 W7 **Overton** Texas, SW USA 32°16′N 94°58′W
92 K13 **Övertorneå** Norrbotten, N Sweden 66°22′N 23°40′E
95 N18 **Överum** Kalmar, S Sweden 57°58′N 16°20′E
92 G13 **Överuman** ◎ N Sweden
117 P11 **Ovidiopol'** Odes'ka Oblast', SW Ukraine 46°15′N 30°27′E
116 M14 **Ovidiu** Constanţa, SE Romania 44°16′N 28°34′E
45 N10 **Oviedo** SW Dominican Republic 17°47′N 71°22′W
104 K2 **Oviedo** *anc.* Asturias. Asturias, NW Spain 43°21′N 05°50′W
104 K2 **Oviedo** ✈ Asturias, N Spain 43°21′N 05°50′W
Ovilava *see* Wels
118 D7 **Ovīši** W Latvia 57°34′N 21°43′E
146 K10 **Ovminzatovo Tog'lari** *Rus.* Gory Auminzatau. ▲▲ N Uzbekistan
Övögdiy *see* Telmen
Ovoot *see* Darīganga
157 O4 **Övörhangay** ◈ *province* C Mongolia
94 E12 **Øvre Årdal** Sogn Og Fjordane, S Norway 61°18′N 07°48′E
95 J14 **Övre Fryken** ◎ C Sweden
92 J11 **Övre Soppero** *Lapp.* Badje-Sohppar. Norrbotten, N Sweden 68°07′N 21°40′E
117 N3 **Ovruch** Zhytomyrs'ka Oblast', N Ukraine 51°20′N 58°50′E
Övt *see* Bat-Öldziy
185 E24 **Owaka** Otago, South Island, New Zealand 46°27′S 169°42′E
79 H18 **Owando** *prev.* Fort Rousset. Cuvette, C Congo 0°29′S 15°55′E
164 J14 **Owase** Mie, Honshū, SW Japan 34°04′N 136°11′E
27 P9 **Owasso** Oklahoma, C USA 36°16′N 95°51′W
29 V10 **Owatonna** Minnesota, N USA 44°04′N 93°13′W
173 O4 **Owen Fracture Zone** *tectonic feature* W Arabian Sea
185 H15 **Owen, Mount** ▲ South Island, New Zealand 41°32′S 172°33′E
185 H15 **Owen River** Tasman, South Island, New Zealand 41°40′S 172°28′E
44 D8 **Owen Roberts** ✈ Grand Cayman, Cayman Islands 19°15′N 81°22′W
20 I6 **Owensboro** Kentucky, S USA 37°46′N 87°07′W
35 T11 **Owens Lake** *salt flat* California, W USA
14 F14 **Owen Sound** Ontario, S Canada 44°34′N 80°56′W
14 F13 **Owen Sound** ◎ Ontario, S Canada
35 T10 **Owens River** ≈ California, W USA
186 F9 **Owen Stanley Range** ▲▲ S Papua New Guinea
27 V5 **Owensville** Missouri, C USA 38°21′N 91°30′W
20 M4 **Owenton** Kentucky, S USA 38°33′N 84°50′W
77 U17 **Owerri** Imo, S Nigeria 05°19′N 07°07′E
184 M10 **Owhango** Manawatu-Wanganui, North Island, New Zealand 39°01′S 175°22′E
21 N5 **Owingsville** Kentucky, S USA 38°09′N 83°46′W
77 T16 **Owo** Ondo, SW Nigeria 07°10′N 05°31′E

◆ Country
● Country Capital
◇ Dependent Territory
○ Dependent Territory Capital
◈ Administrative Regions
✈ International Airport
▲ Mountain
▲▲ Mountain Range
🌋 Volcano
≈ River
◎ Lake
▩ Reservoir

31 R9 **Owosso** Michigan, N USA 43°00′N 84°10′W
35 V1 **Owyhee** Nevada, W USA 41°57′N 116°07′W
32 L14 **Owyhee, Lake** ◎ Oregon, NW USA
32 L15 **Owyhee River** ≈ Idaho/Oregon, NW USA
92 K1 **Öxarfjördhur** *var.* Axarfjördhur. *fjord* N Iceland
94 K12 **Oxberg** Dalarna, C Sweden 61°07′N 14°10′E
11 V17 **Oxbow** Saskatchewan, S Canada 49°16′N 102°12′W
95 O17 **Oxelösund** Södermanland, S Sweden 58°40′N 17°10′E
185 H18 **Oxford** Canterbury, South Island, New Zealand 43°18′S 172°10′E
97 M21 **Oxford** *Lat.* Oxonia. S England, United Kingdom 51°46′N 01°15′W
23 Q3 **Oxford** Alabama, S USA 33°36′N 85°50′W
22 L2 **Oxford** Mississippi, S USA 34°23′N 89°30′W
29 N16 **Oxford** Nebraska, C USA 40°15′N 99°37′W
18 I11 **Oxford** New York, NE USA 42°21′N 75°39′W
21 U8 **Oxford** North Carolina, SE USA 36°22′N 78°37′W
31 Q14 **Oxford** Ohio, N USA 39°30′N 84°45′W
18 H16 **Oxford** Pennsylvania, NE USA 39°46′N 75°57′W
11 X12 **Oxford House** Manitoba, C Canada 54°55′N 95°13′W
29 Y13 **Oxford Junction** Iowa, C USA 41°58′N 90°57′W
11 X12 **Oxford Lake** ◎ Manitoba, C Canada
97 M21 **Oxfordshire** *cultural region* S England, United Kingdom
Oxia *see* Oxyá
41 X12 **Oxkutzcab** Yucatán, SE Mexico 20°18′N 89°26′W
35 R15 **Oxnard** California, W USA 34°12′N 119°10′W
Oxonia *see* Oxford
14 I12 **Oxtongue** ≈ Ontario, SE Canada
Oxus *see* Amu Darya
115 E15 **Oxyá** *var.* Oxia. ▲ C Greece 39°46′N 21°56′E
164 L11 **Oyabe** Toyama, Honshū, SW Japan 36°42′N 136°52′E
Oyahue/Oyahue, Volcán *see* Ollagüe, Volcán
165 O12 **Oyama** Tochigi, Honshū, S Japan 36°19′N 139°46′E
47 U5 **Oyapock** ≈ E French Guiana
Oyapock *see* Oiapoque, Rio/Oyapok, Fleuve l'
55 Z10 **Oyapok, Baie de L'** *bay* Brazil/French Guiana South America W Atlantic Ocean
55 Z11 **Oyapok, Fleuve l'** *var.* Rio Oiapoque, Oyapock. ≈ Brazil/French Guiana *see also* Oiapoque, Rio
Oyapok, Fleuve l' *see* Oiapoque, Rio
79 E17 **Oyem** Woleu-Ntem, N Gabon 01°34′N 11°31′E
11 R16 **Oyen** Alberta, SW Canada 51°20′N 110°28′W
95 I15 **Øyeren** ◎ S Norway
Oygon *see* Tüdevtey
96 I7 **Oykel** ≈ N Scotland, United Kingdom
123 R9 **Oymyakon** Respublika Sakha (Yakutiya), NE Russian Federation 63°28′N 142°22′E
79 H19 **Oyo** Cuvette, C Congo 01°17′S 16°00′E
77 S15 **Oyo** Oyo, W Nigeria 07°51′N 03°57′E
77 S15 **Oyo** ◈ *state* SW Nigeria
56 D13 **Oyón** Lima, C Peru 10°39′S 76°44′W
103 S10 **Oyonnax** Ain, E France 46°16′N 05°39′E
146 L10 **Oyoqog'itma** *Rus.* Ayakagytma. Buxoro Viloyati, C Uzbekistan 40°37′N 64°26′E
146 M9 **Oyoqquduq** *Rus.* Ayakkuduk. Navoiy Viloyati, N Uzbekistan 41°16′N 65°12′E
32 F9 **Oysterville** Washington, NW USA 46°33′N 124°03′W
95 D14 **Øystese** Hordaland, S Norway 60°23′N 06°13′E
145 S16 **Oytal** Zhambyl, S Kazakhstan 42°54′N 73°21′E
147 U10 **Oy-Tal** Oshskaya Oblast', SW Kyrgyzstan 40°23′N 74°04′E
147 T10 **Oy-Tal** ≈ SW Kyrgyzstan
145 Q15 **Oyyk** *prev.* Uyuk. Zhambyl, S Kazakhstan 43°46′N 70°55′E
144 H10 **Oyyl** *prev.* Uil. Aktyubinsk, W Kazakhstan 49°06′N 54°41′E
144 H10 **Oyyl** *prev.* Uil. ≈ W Kazakhstan
Ozarichi *see* Azarychy
23 R7 **Ozark** Alabama, S USA 31°27′N 85°38′W
27 S10 **Ozark** Arkansas, C USA 35°30′N 93°50′W
27 T8 **Ozark** Missouri, C USA 37°01′N 93°12′W
27 T8 **Ozark Plateau** *plain* Arkansas/Missouri, C USA
27 T6 **Ozarks, Lake of the** ⊠ Missouri, C USA
192 L10 **Ozbourn Seamount** *undersea feature* W Pacific Ocean 26°00′S 174°49′W
111 L20 **Ózd** Borsod-Abaúj-Zemplén, NE Hungary 48°15′N 20°18′E
112 D11 **Ozeblin** ▲ C Croatia 44°37′N 15°52′E
123 V11 **Ozernovskiy** Kamchatskiy Kray, E Russian Federation 51°28′N 156°32′E
144 M7 **Ozërnoye** *var.* Ozërnyy. Kostanay, N Kazakhstan 53°29′N 63°14′E
124 J15 **Ozërnyy** Tverskaya Oblast', W Russian Federation 57°55′N 33°45′E
Ozërnyy *see* Ozërnoye
Ozero Azhbulat *see* Ozero Ul'ken Azhibolat
Ozero Segozero *see* Segozerskoye Vodokhranilishche
115 D18 **Ozerós, Límni** ◎ W Greece
145 T7 **Ozero Ul'ken Azhibolat** *prev.* Ozero Azhbulat. ◎ NE Kazakhstan
122 G11 **Ozërsk** Chelyabinskaya Oblast', C Russian Federation 55°44′N 60°59′E
119 D14 **Ozersk** *prev.* Darkehnen, *Ger.* Angerapp. Kaliningradskaya Oblast', W Russian Federation 54°23′N 21°59′E
126 L4 **Ozery** Moskovskaya Oblast', W Russian Federation 54°51′N 38°37′E
Özgön *see* Uzgen
107 C17 **Ozieri** Sardegna, Italy, C Mediterranean Sea 40°35′N 09°01′E
111 I15 **Ozimek** *Ger.* Malapane. Opolskie, SW Poland 50°41′N 18°16′E
127 R8 **Ozinki** Saratovskaya Oblast', W Russian Federation 51°16′N 49°45′E
25 O10 **Ozona** Texas, SW USA 30°43′N 101°13′W
Ozorkov *see* Ozorków
110 J12 **Ozorków** *Rus.* Ozorkov. Łódźyz, C Poland 52°00′N 19°17′E
164 F14 **Ōzu** Ehime, Shikoku, SW Japan 33°30′N 132°33′E
137 R10 **Ozurgeti** *prev.* Makharadze, Ozurget'i. W Georgia 41°57′N 42°01′E
Ozurget'i *see* Ozurgeti

P

99 J17 **Paal** Limburg, NE Belgium 51°03′N 05°08′E
196 M14 **Paamiut** *var.* Pâmiut, *Dan.* Frederikshåb. S Greenland 61°59′N 49°40′W
Pa-an *see* Hpa-an
101 L22 **Paar** ≈ SE Germany
83 E26 **Paarl** Western Cape, SW South Africa 33°45′S 18°58′E
93 L15 **Paavola** Oulu, C Finland 64°34′N 25°15′E
96 E8 **Pabbay** *island* NW Scotland, United Kingdom
153 T15 **Pabna** Rajshahi, W Bangladesh 24°02′N 89°15′E
109 U4 **Pabneukirchen** Oberösterreich, N Austria 48°19′N 14°49′E
118 H13 **Pabradė** *Pol.* Podbrodzie. Vilnius, SE Lithuania 54°58′N 25°43′E
56 L13 **Pacahuaras, Río** ≈ N Bolivia
Pacaraima, Sierra/Pacaraim, Serra *see* Pakaraima Mountains
56 B11 **Pacasmayo** La Libertad, W Peru 07°27′S 79°33′W
42 D6 **Pacaya, Volcán de** ⛰ S Guatemala 14°19′N 90°36′W
115 K23 **Pacheía** *var.* Pachía. *island* Kykládes, Greece, Aegean Sea
Pachía *see* Pacheía
107 L26 **Pachino** Sicilia, Italy, C Mediterranean Sea 36°43′N 15°06′E
56 F12 **Pachitea, Río** ≈ C Peru
154 I11 **Pachmarhi** Madhya Pradesh, C India 22°36′N 78°18′E
121 P3 **Páchna** *var.* Pakhna. SW Cyprus 34°47′N 32°48′E
115 H25 **Páchnes** ▲ Kríti, Greece, E Mediterranean Sea 35°19′N 24°00′E
54 F9 **Pacho** Cundinamarca, C Colombia 05°09′N 74°08′W
154 F12 **Pāchora** Mahārāshtra, C India 20°52′N 75°28′E
41 P13 **Pachuca** *var.* Pachuca de Soto. Hidalgo, C Mexico 20°05′N 98°46′W
Pachuca de Soto *see* Pachuca
27 W5 **Pacific** Missouri, C USA 38°28′N 90°44′W
192 L14 **Pacific-Antarctic Ridge** *undersea feature* S Pacific Ocean 62°00′S 157°00′W
32 F8 **Pacific Beach** Washington, NW USA 47°09′N 124°12′W
35 N10 **Pacific Grove** California, W USA 36°35′N 121°54′W
29 S15 **Pacific Junction** Iowa, C USA 41°01′N 95°48′W
192-193 **Pacific Ocean** *ocean*
129 Z10 **Pacific Plate** *tectonic feature*
113 J15 **Pačir** ▲ N Montenegro 43°19′N 19°07′E
182 L5 **Packsaddle** New South Wales, SE Australia 30°42′S 141°55′E
32 H9 **Packwood** Washington, NW USA 46°37′N 121°38′W
Padalung *see* Phatthalung
168 J12 **Padang** Sumatera, W Indonesia 01°S 100°21′E
168 L9 **Padang Endau** Pahang, Peninsular Malaysia 02°38′N 103°37′E
Padangpandjang *see* Padangpanjang
168 I11 **Padangpanjang** *prev.* Padangpandjang. Sumatera, W Indonesia 0°30′S 100°26′E
168 I10 **Padangsidempuan** *prev.* Padangsidimpoean. Sumatera, W Indonesia 01°23′N 99°15′E
Padangsidimpoean *see* Padangsidempuan
124 I9 **Padany** Respublika Kareliya, NW Russian Federation 63°18′N 33°20′E
93 M18 **Padasjoki** Etelä-Suomi, S Finland 61°20′N 25°21′E
57 M22 **Padcaya** Tarija, S Bolivia 21°52′S 64°46′W
101 H14 **Paderborn** Nordrhein-Westfalen, NW Germany 51°43′N 08°45′E
Padeşul/Padeş, Vîrful *see* Padeş, Vârful
116 F12 **Padeş, Vârful** *var.* Padeşul; *prev.* Vîrful Padeş. ▲ W Romania 45°39′N 22°19′E
112 L10 **Padinska Skela** Serbia, N Serbia 44°58′N 20°25′E
153 S14 **Padma** *var.* Ganges. ≈ Bangladesh/India *see also* Ganges
Padma *see* Brahmaputra
Padma *see* Ganges
106 H8 **Padova** *Eng.* Padua; *anc.* Patavium. Veneto, NE Italy 45°24′N 11°52′E
82 A10 **Padrão, Ponta do** *headland* NW Angola 06°06′S 12°18′E
25 T16 **Padre Island** *island* Texas, SW USA
104 G3 **Padrón** Galicia, NW Spain 42°44′N 08°40′W
118 K13 **Padsvillye** *Rus.* Podsvil'ye. Vitsyebskaya Voblasts', N Belarus 55°09′N 27°58′E
182 K11 **Padthaway** South Australia 36°39′S 140°30′E
Padua *see* Padova
20 G7 **Paducah** Kentucky, S USA 37°03′N 88°36′W
25 P4 **Paducah** Texas, SW USA 34°01′N 100°18′W
105 N15 **Padul** Andalucía, S Spain 37°02′N 03°37′W
191 P8 **Paea** Tahiti, W French Polynesia 17°41′S 149°35′W
185 L14 **Paekakariki** Wellington, North Island, New Zealand 41°00′S 174°58′E
163 X11 **Paektu-san** *var.* Baitou Shan. ▲ China/North Korea 42°00′N 128°03′W
Paengnyŏng *see* Baengnyong-do
184 M7 **Paeroa** Waikato, North Island, New Zealand 37°23′S 175°39′E
54 D12 **Páez** Cauca, SW Colombia 02°37′N 76°00′W
121 O3 **Páfos** *var.* Paphos. W Cyprus 34°46′N 32°26′E
121 O3 **Páfos** ✈ SW Cyprus 34°46′N 32°25′E
83 L19 **Pafúri** Gaza, SW Mozambique 22°27′S 31°21′E
112 C12 **Pag** *It.* Pago. Lika-Senj, SW Croatia 44°26′N 15°01′E
112 B11 **Pag** *It.* Pago. *island* Zadar, C Croatia
171 P7 **Pagadian** Mindanao, S Philippines 07°47′N 123°22′E
168 J13 **Pagai Selatan, Pulau** *island* Kepulauan Mentawai, W Indonesia
168 J13 **Pagai Utara, Pulau** *island* Kepulauan Mentawai, W Indonesia
188 K4 **Pagan** *island* C Northern Mariana Islands
115 G16 **Pagasitikós Kólpos** *gulf* E Greece
36 L8 **Page** Arizona, SW USA 36°54′N 111°28′W
29 Q5 **Page** North Dakota, N USA 47°09′N 97°33′W
118 D13 **Pagėgiai** *Ger.* Pogegen. Tauragė, SW Lithuania 55°08′N 21°54′E
21 S11 **Pageland** South Carolina, SE USA 34°46′N 80°23′W
81 G16 **Pager** ≈ NE Uganda
149 Q5 **Paghmān** Kābul, E Afghanistan 34°33′N 68°55′E
Pago *see* Pag
188 C16 **Pago Bay** *bay* E Guam, W Pacific Ocean
115 M20 **Pagóndas** *var.* Pagóndhas. Sámos, Dodekánisa, Greece, Aegean Sea 37°41′N 26°50′E
Pagóndhas *see* Pagóndas
192 J16 **Pago Pago** ○ (American Samoa) Tutuila, W American Samoa 14°16′S 170°43′W
37 R8 **Pagosa Springs** Colorado, C USA 37°13′N 107°01′W
Pagqên *see* Gadê
38 H12 **Pāhala** *var.* Pahala. Hawaii, USA, C Pacific Ocean 19°12′N 155°28′W
168 K8 **Pahang** *var.* Negeri Pahang Darul Makmur. ◈ *state* Peninsular Malaysia
Pahang *see* Pahang, Sungai
168 L8 **Pahang, Sungai** *var.* Pahang, Sungei Pahang. ≈ Peninsular Malaysia
149 S8 **Pahārpur** Khyber Pakhtunkhwa, NW Pakistan 32°06′N 71°00′E
185 B24 **Pahia Point** *headland* South Island, New Zealand 46°19′S 167°42′E
184 M13 **Pahiatua** Manawatu-Wanganui, North Island, New Zealand 40°30′S 175°49′E
38 H12 **Pāhoa** *var.* Pahoa. Hawaii, USA, C Pacific Ocean 19°29′N 154°56′W
23 Y14 **Pahokee** Florida, SE USA 26°49′N 80°40′W
35 X9 **Pahranagat Range** ▲▲ Nevada, W USA
35 W11 **Pahrump** Nevada, W USA 36°11′N 115°58′W
Pahsien *see* Chongqing
35 V9 **Pahute Mesa** ▲▲ Nevada, W USA
167 N7 **Pai** Mae Hong Son, NW Thailand 19°24′N 98°26′E
38 F10 **Pa'ia** *var.* Paia. Maui, Hawaii, USA, C Pacific Ocean 20°54′N 156°22′W
Paia *see* Pa'ia
Pai-ch'eng *see* Baicheng
118 H4 **Paide** *Ger.* Weissenstein. Järvamaa, N Estonia 58°55′N 25°36′E
97 J24 **Paignton** SW England, United Kingdom 50°26′N 03°34′W
184 K3 **Paihia** Northland, North Island, New Zealand 35°18′S 174°06′E
93 M18 **Päijänne** ◎ S Finland
114 F13 **Páïko** ▲▲ N Greece
57 M17 **Paila, Río** ≈ C Bolivia
167 Q12 **Pailĭn** Bătdâmbâng, W Cambodia 12°51′N 102°34′E
Pailing *see* Chun'an
54 F6 **Pailitas** Cesar, N Colombia 08°58′N 73°38′W
38 F9 **Pailolo Channel** *channel* Hawai'i, USA, C Pacific Ocean
93 K19 **Paimio** *Swe.* Pemar. Länsi-Suomi, SW Finland 60°27′N 22°42′E
165 O16 **Paimi-saki** *var.* Yaeme-saki. *headland* Iriomote-jima, SW Japan 24°18′N 123°40′E
102 G5 **Paimpol** Côtes d'Armor, NW France 48°47′N 03°03′W
168 J12 **Painan** Sumatera, W Indonesia 01°22′S 100°33′E
63 G23 **Paine, Cerro** ▲ S Chile 51°01′S 72°57′W
31 U11 **Painesville** Ohio, N USA 41°43′N 81°15′W
31 S14 **Paint Creek** ≈ Ohio, N USA
36 L10 **Painted Desert** *desert* Arizona, SW USA
Paint Hills *see* Wemindji
30 M4 **Paint River** ≈ Michigan, N USA
25 P8 **Paint Rock** Texas, SW USA 31°32′N 99°56′W
21 O6 **Paintsville** Kentucky, S USA 37°48′N 82°48′W
Paisance *see* Piacenza
96 I12 **Paisley** W Scotland, United Kingdom 55°50′N 04°26′W
32 I15 **Paisley** Oregon, NW USA 42°40′N 120°31′W
105 O3 **País Vasco** *Basq.* Euskadi, *Eng.* The Basque Country, *Sp.* Provincias Vascongadas. ◈ *autonomous community* N Spain
56 A9 **Paita** Piura, NW Peru 05°11′S 81°09′W
169 V6 **Paitan, Teluk** *bay* Sabah, East Malaysia
104 H7 **Paiva, Rio** ≈ N Portugal
92 K12 **Pajala** Norrbotten, N Sweden 67°12′N 23°19′E
104 K3 **Pajares, Puerto de** *pass* NW Spain
54 G9 **Pajarito** Boyacá, C Colombia 05°18′N 72°43′W
54 G4 **Pajaro** La Guajira, S Colombia 11°41′N 72°37′W
Pakanbaru *see* Pekanbaru
Pākaur *see* Pākur
55 Q10 **Pakaraima Mountains** *var.* Serra Pacaraim, Sierra Pacaraima. ▲▲ N South America
167 P10 **Pak Chong** Nakhon Ratchasima, C Thailand 14°38′N 101°22′E
123 V8 **Pakhachi** Krasnoyarskiy Kray, E Russian Federation 60°36′N 168°59′E
Pakhna *see* Páchna
189 U16 **Pakin Atoll** *atoll* Caroline Islands, E Micronesia
149 Q12 **Pakistan** *off.* Islamic Republic of Pakistan, *var.* Islami Jamhuriya e Pakistan. ◆ *republic* S Asia
Pakistan, Islamic Republic of *see* Pakistan
Pakistan, Islami Jamhuriya e *see* Pakistan
167 P8 **Pak Lay** *var.* Muang Pak Lay. Xaignabouli, C Laos 18°06′N 101°21′E
Paknam *see* Samut Prakan
166 L5 **Pakokku** Magway, Myanmar (Burma) 21°20′N 95°05′E
110 I10 **Pakość** *Ger.* Pakosch. Kujawski-pomorskie, C Poland 52°47′N 18°03′E
Pakosch *see* Pakość
149 V10 **Pākpattan** Punjab, E Pakistan 30°20′N 73°27′E
167 O15 **Pak Phanang** *var.* Ban Pak Phanang. Nakhon Si Thammarat, SW Thailand 08°20′N 100°10′E
112 G9 **Pakrac** *Hung.* Pakrácz. Požega-Slavonija, NE Croatia 45°26′N 17°09′E
Pakrácz *see* Pakrac
118 F11 **Pakruojis** Šiaulai, N Lithuania 56°N 23°51′E
111 J24 **Paks** Tolna, S Hungary 46°38′N 18°51′E
Pak Sane *see* Pakxan
Paksé *see* Pakxé
167 Q10 **Pak Thong Chai** Nakhon Ratchasima, C Thailand 14°43′N 102°01′E
Paktīā *see* Paktiyā
149 Q7 **Paktīkā** ◈ *province* SE Afghanistan
149 R6 **Paktiyā** *prev.* Paktīā. ◈ *province* SE Afghanistan
171 N12 **Pakuli** Sulawesi, C Indonesia 01°14′S 119°55′E
153 S14 **Pākur** *var.* Pākaur. Jharkhand, N India 24°48′N 87°14′E
81 F17 **Pakwach** NW Uganda 02°28′N 31°28′E
167 R8 **Pakxan** *var.* Muang Pakxan, Pak Sane. Bolikhamxai, C Laos 18°27′N 103°38′E
167 S10 **Pakxé** *var.* Paksé. Champasak, S Laos 15°09′N 105°49′E
78 G12 **Pala** Mayo-Kébbi, SW Chad 09°22′N 14°54′E
61 A17 **Palacios** Santa Fe, C Argentina 30°43′S 61°37′W
25 V13 **Palacios** Texas, SW USA 28°42′N 96°13′W
105 X5 **Palafrugell** Cataluña, NE Spain 41°55′N 03°10′E
107 L24 **Palagonia** Sicilia, Italy, C Mediterranean Sea 37°20′N 14°45′E
113 E17 **Palagruža** *It.* Pelagosa. *island* SW Croatia
115 G20 **Palaiá Epídavros** Pelopónnisos, S Greece 37°38′N 23°09′E
121 P3 **Palaichóri** *var.* Palekhori. C Cyprus 34°55′N 33°06′E
115 H25 **Palaiochóra** Kríti, Greece, E Mediterranean Sea 35°14′N 23°37′E
115 A15 **Palaiolastrítsa** *religious building* Kérkyra, Iónia Nisiá, Greece, C Mediterranean Sea
115 J19 **Palaiópoli** Ándros, Kykládes, Greece, Aegean Sea 37°49′N 24°49′E
103 N5 **Palaiseau** Essonne, N France 48°41′N 02°14′E
154 N11 **Pāla Laharha** Orissa, E India 21°25′N 85°18′E
83 G19 **Palamakoloi** Ghanzi, C Botswana 23°10′S 22°22′E
115 E16 **Palamás** Thessalía, C Greece 39°28′N 22°05′E
105 X5 **Palamós** Cataluña, NE Spain 41°51′N 03°06′E
118 J5 **Palamuse** *Ger.* Sankt-Bartholomäi. Jõgevamaa, E Estonia 58°41′N 26°35′E
183 Q14 **Palana** Tasmania, SE Australia 39°48′S 147°54′E
123 U9 **Palana** Krasnoyarskiy Kray, E Russian Federation 59°05′N 159°59′E
118 C11 **Palanga** *Ger.* Polangen. Klaipėda, NW Lithuania 05°54′N 21°05′E
143 V10 **Palangān, Kūh-e** ▲▲ E Iran
Palangkaraja *see* Palangkaraya
169 T12 **Palangkaraya** *prev.* Palangkaraja. Borneo, C Indonesia 02°16′S 113°55′E
155 H22 **Palani** Tamil Nādu, SE India 10°30′N 77°24′E
Palanka *see* Bačka Palanka
154 D9 **Pālanpur** Gujarāt, W India 24°12′N 72°29′E
Palantia *see* Palencia
83 I19 **Palapye** Central, SE Botswana 22°37′S 27°06′E
155 J19 **Pālār** ≈ SE India
104 H3 **Palas de Rei** Galicia, NW Spain 42°52′N 07°51′W
123 T9 **Palatka** Magadanskaya Oblast', E Russian Federation 60°09′N 150°33′E
23 W10 **Palatka** Florida, SE USA 29°39′N 81°38′W
188 B9 **Palau** *var.* Belau. ◆ *republic* W Pacific Ocean
Palau *see* Palau Islands
129 Y14 **Palau Islands** *var.* Palau. *island group* N Palau
192 G16 **Palauli Bay** *bay* Savai'i, C Samoa, C Pacific Ocean
167 N11 **Palaw** Tanintharyi, Myanmar (Burma) 12°57′N 98°39′E
170 M6 **Palawan** *island* W Philippines
171 N6 **Palawan Passage** *passage* W Philippines
192 E7 **Palawan Trough** *undersea feature* S South China Sea 07°00′N 115°00′E
155 H23 **Pālayankottai** Tamil Nādu, SE India 08°42′N 77°46′E
107 L25 **Palazzola Acreide** *anc.* Acrae. Sicilia, Italy, C Mediterranean Sea 37°04′N 14°54′E
118 G3 **Paldiski** *prev.* Baltiski, *Eng.* Baltic Port, *Ger.* Baltischport. Harjumaa, NW Estonia 59°22′N 24°08′E
112 I13 **Pale** Republika Srpska, SE Bosnia and Herzegovina 43°49′N 18°35′E
Palekhori *see* Palaichóri
168 L13 **Palembang** Sumatera, W Indonesia 02°59′S 104°45′E
63 G18 **Palena** Los Lagos, S Chile 43°40′S 71°50′W
63 G18 **Palena, Río** ≈ S Chile
104 M5 **Palencia** *anc.* Palantia, Pallantia. Castilla y León, NW Spain 42°23′N 04°32′W
104 M3 **Palencia** ◈ *province* Castilla y León, N Spain
35 X15 **Palen Dry Lake** ◎ California, W USA
41 V15 **Palenque** Chiapas, SE Mexico 17°32′N 91°59′W
41 V15 **Palenque** *var.* Ruinas de Palenque. *ruins* Chiapas, SE Mexico
45 O9 **Palenque, Punta** *headland* S Dominican Republic 18°13′N 70°08′W
Palenque, Ruinas de *see* Palenque
Palerme *see* Palermo
107 I23 **Palermo** *Fr.* Palerme; *anc.* Panhormus, Panormus. Sicilia, Italy, C Mediterranean Sea 38°08′N 13°23′E
25 V8 **Palestine** Texas, SW USA 31°45′N 93°39′W
25 V7 **Palestine, Lake** ⊠ Texas, SW USA
107 I15 **Palestrina** Lazio, C Italy 41°49′N 12°53′E
166 K5 **Paletwa** Chin State, W Myanmar (Burma) 21°25′N 92°49′E
155 G21 **Pālghāt** *var.* Palakkad. Kerala, SW India 10°46′N 76°42′E *see also* Palakkad
152 F13 **Pāli** Rājasthān, N India 25°48′N 73°21′E
167 N16 **Palian** Trang, SW Thailand
189 O12 **Palikir** ● (Micronesia) Pohnpei, E Micronesia 06°58′N 158°13′E
Palimé *see* Kpalimé
107 L19 **Palinuro, Capo** *headland* S Italy 40°02′N 15°16′E
115 H15 **Palioúri, Akrotírio** *var.* Akrotírio Kanestron. *headland* N Greece 39°55′N 23°45′E
33 R14 **Palisades Reservoir** ⊠ Idaho, NW USA
99 J23 **Paliseul** Luxembourg, SE Belgium 49°55′N 05°09′E
154 C11 **Pālitāna** Gujarāt, W India 21°30′N 71°50′E
118 F4 **Palivere** Läänemaa, W Estonia 58°59′N 23°58′E
41 V14 **Palizada** Campeche, SE Mexico 18°15′N 92°03′W
93 L18 **Pälkäne** Länsi-Suomi, W Finland 61°22′N 24°16′E
155 J22 **Palk Strait** *strait* India/Sri Lanka
155 J23 **Pallai** Northern Province, NW Sri Lanka 09°35′N 80°20′E
Pallantia *see* Palencia
106 C6 **Pallanza** Piemonte, NE Italy 45°57′N 08°32′E
127 Q9 **Pallasovka** Volgogradskaya Oblast', SW Russian Federation 50°06′N 46°52′E
Pallene/Pallíni *see* Kassándra
185 L15 **Palliser Bay** *bay* North Island, New Zealand
185 L15 **Palliser, Cape** *headland* North Island, New Zealand 41°37′S 175°16′E
191 U9 **Palliser, Îles** *island group* Îles Tuamotu, C French Polynesia
82 Q12 **Palma** Cabo Delgado, N Mozambique 10°46′S 40°30′E
105 X9 **Palma** *var.* Palma de Mallorca. Mallorca, Spain, W Mediterranean Sea 39°35′N 02°39′E
105 X9 **Palma** ✈ Mallorca, Spain, W Mediterranean Sea
105 X10 **Palma, Badia de** *bay* Mallorca, Spain, W Mediterranean Sea
104 L13 **Palma del Río** Andalucía, S Spain 37°42′N 05°16′W
Palma de Mallorca *see* Palma
107 J25 **Palma di Montechiaro** Sicilia, Italy, C Mediterranean Sea 37°12′N 13°46′E
106 J7 **Palmanova** Friuli-Venezia Giulia, NE Italy 45°54′N 13°20′E
54 J7 **Palmarito** Apure, C Venezuela 07°36′N 70°08′W
43 N15 **Palmar Sur** Puntarenas, SE Costa Rica 08°54′N 83°27′W
60 I12 **Palmas** Paraná, S Brazil 26°29′S 52°00′W
59 K16 **Palmas** *var.* Palmas do Tocantins. Tocantins, C Brazil 10°24′S 48°19′W
76 L18 **Palmas, Cape** *Fr.* Cap des Palmès. *headland* SW Ivory Coast 04°18′N 07°31′W
Palmas do Tocantins *see* Palmas
54 D11 **Palmaseca** ✈ (Cali) Valle del Cauca, SW Colombia 03°31′N 76°27′W
107 B21 **Palmas, Golfo di** *gulf* Sardegna, Italy, C Mediterranean Sea
44 I7 **Palma Soriano** Santiago de Cuba, E Cuba 20°10′N 76°00′W
23 Y12 **Palm Bay** Florida, SE USA 28°01′N 80°35′W
35 T14 **Palmdale** California, W USA 34°34′N 118°07′W
61 H14 **Palmeira das Missões** Rio Grande do Sul, S Brazil 27°54′S 53°20′W
82 A11 **Palmeirinhas, Ponta das** *headland* NW Angola 09°04′S 13°02′E
39 R11 **Palmer** Alaska, USA 61°36′N 149°06′W
19 N11 **Palmer** Massachusetts, NE USA 42°09′N 72°19′W
25 U7 **Palmer** Texas, SW USA 32°25′N 96°40′W
194 H4 **Palmer** *US research station* Antarctica 64°37′S 64°01′W
15 R11 **Palmer** ≈ Québec, SE Canada
37 T5 **Palmer Lake** Colorado, C USA 39°07′N 104°55′W
194 J6 **Palmer Land** *physical region* Antarctica
14 F15 **Palmerston** Ontario, SE Canada 43°51′N 80°49′W
185 F22 **Palmerston** Otago, South Island, New Zealand 45°27′S 170°42′E
190 K15 **Palmerston** *island* S Cook Islands
Palmerston *see* Darwin
184 M12 **Palmerston North** Manawatu-Wanganui, North Island, New Zealand 40°20′S 175°52′E
23 V13 **Palmetto** Florida, SE USA 27°31′N 82°34′W
The Palmetto State *see* South Carolina
107 M22 **Palmi** Calabria, SW Italy 38°21′N 15°51′E
54 D11 **Palmira** Valle del Cauca, W Colombia 03°33′N 76°17′W
56 F8 **Palmira, Río** ≈ N Peru
61 D19 **Palmitas** Soriano, SW Uruguay 33°27′S 57°48′W
Palmnicken *see* Yantarnyy
35 V15 **Palm Springs** California, W USA 33°48′N 116°33′W
27 V2 **Palmyra** Missouri, C USA 39°48′N 91°31′W
18 G10 **Palmyra** New York, NE USA 43°02′N 77°13′W
18 G15 **Palmyra** Pennsylvania, NE USA 40°18′N 76°35′W
21 V5 **Palmyra** Virginia, NE USA 37°53′N 78°17′W
Palmyra *see* Tudmur
192 L7 **Palmyra Atoll** ◇ *US privately owned unincorporated territory* C Pacific Ocean
154 P12 **Palmyras Point** *headland* E India 20°46′N 87°00′E
35 N9 **Palo Alto** California, W USA 37°26′N 122°08′W
25 O1 **Palo Duro Creek** ≈ Texas, SW USA
Paloe *see* Denpasar, Bali, C Indonesia
Paloe *see* Palu
168 L9 **Paloh** Johor, Peninsular Malaysia 02°10′N 103°11′E
80 F12 **Paloich** Upper Nile, NE South Sudan 10°29′N 32°31′E
40 I3 **Palomas** Chihuahua, N Mexico 31°45′N 107°38′W
107 I15 **Palombara Sabina** Lazio, C Italy 42°04′N 12°45′E
105 S13 **Palos, Cabo de** *headland* SE Spain 37°38′N 00°42′W
104 I14 **Palos de la Frontera** Andalucía, S Spain 37°14′N 06°53′W
60 G11 **Palotina** Paraná, S Brazil 24°16′S 53°49′W
32 M9 **Palouse** Washington, NW USA 46°54′N 117°04′W
32 L9 **Palouse River** ≈ Washington, NW USA
35 Y16 **Palo Verde** California, W USA 33°25′N 114°43′W
57 E16 **Palpa** Ica, W Peru 14°35′S 75°09′W
95 M16 **Pålsboda** Örebro, C Sweden 59°04′N 15°21′E
93 M15 **Paltamo** Oulu, C Finland 64°25′N 27°50′E
171 N12 **Palu** *prev.* Paloe. Sulawesi, C Indonesia 0°54′S 119°52′E
137 P14 **Palu** Elazığ, E Turkey 38°43′N 39°56′E
152 I11 **Palwal** Haryāna, N India 28°15′N 77°18′E
123 U6 **Palyavaam** ≈ NE Russian Federation
77 Q13 **Pama** SE Burkina 11°13′N 00°46′E
172 J14 **Pamandzi** ✈ (Mamoudzou) Petite-Terre, E Mayotte
Pamangkat *see* Pemangkat
143 R11 **Pā Mazār** Kermān, C Iran
83 N19 **Pambarra** Inhambane, SE Mozambique 21°57′S 35°06′E
171 X12 **Pamdai** Papua, E Indonesia 01°58′S 137°19′E
103 N16 **Pamiers** Ariège, S France 43°07′N 01°37′E
147 T14 **Pamir** *var.* Daryā-ye Pāmīr, *Taj.* Dar"yoi Pomir. ≈ Afghanistan/Tajikistan *see also* Pāmīr, Daryā-ye
Pamir *see* Pāmīr, Daryā-ye
149 U1 **Pāmīr, Daryā-ye** *var.* Pamir, *Taj.* Dar"yoi Pomir. ≈ Afghanistan/Tajikistan *see also* Pamir
Pāmīr, Daryā-ye *see* Pamir
Pāmīr-e Khord *see* Little Pamir
Pamir/Pāmīr, Daryā-ye *see* Pamirs
129 Q8 **Pamirs** *Pash.* Daryā-ye Pāmīr, *Rus.* Pamir. ▲▲ C Asia
Pâmiut *see* Paamiut
21 X10 **Pamlico River** ≈ North Carolina, SE USA
21 Y10 **Pamlico Sound** *sound* North Carolina, SE USA
25 O2 **Pampa** Texas, SW USA 35°32′N 100°58′W
Pampa Aullagas, Lago *see* Poopó, Lago
61 B21 **Pampa Húmeda** *grassland* E Argentina
56 A10 **Pampa las Salinas** *salt lake* NW Peru
57 F15 **Pampas** Huancavelica, C Peru 12°22′S 74°53′W
62 K13 **Pampas** *plain* C Argentina
55 O4 **Pampatar** Nueva Esparta, NE Venezuela 11°03′N 63°51′W
Pampeluna *see* Pamplona
104 H8 **Pampilhosa da Serra** *var.* Pampilhosa de Serra. Coimbra, N Portugal 40°03′N 07°58′W
173 Y15 **Pamplemousses** N Mauritius 20°06′S 57°34′E
54 G7 **Pamplona** Norte de Santander, N Colombia 07°24′N 72°38′W
105 Q3 **Pamplona** *Basq.* Iruña, *prev.* Pampeluna; *anc.* Pompaelo. Navarra, N Spain 42°49′N 01°39′W
114 I11 **Pamporovo** *prev.* Vasil Kolarov. Smolyan, S Bulgaria 41°39′N 24°45′E
136 D15 **Pamukkale** Denizli, W Turkey 37°51′N 29°13′E
21 W5 **Pamunkey River** ≈ Virginia, NE USA
152 K5 **Pamzal** Jammu and Kashmir, NW India 34°17′N 78°50′E
30 L14 **Pana** Illinois, N USA 39°23′N 89°04′W
41 Y11 **Panabá** Yucatán, SE Mexico 21°20′N 88°16′W
35 Y8 **Panaca** Nevada, W USA 37°47′N 114°24′W
115 E19 **Panachaikó** ▲▲ S Greece
14 F11 **Panache Lake** ◎ Ontario, S Canada
114 I10 **Panagyurishte** Pazardzhik, C Bulgaria 42°30′N 24°11′E
168 M16 **Panaitan, Pulau** *island* S Indonesia
115 D18 **Panaitolikó** ▲▲ C Greece
155 E17 **Panaji** *var.* Pangim, Panjim, New Goa. *state capital* Goa, W India 15°31′N 73°52′E
43 T15 **Panamá** *var.* Ciudad de Panama, *Eng.* Panama City. ● (Panama) Panamá, C Panama 08°57′N 79°33′W
43 T14 **Panama** *off.* Republic of Panama. ◆ *republic* Central America
43 U14 **Panamá** *off.* Provincia de Panamá. ◈ *province* E Panama
43 U15 **Panamá, Bahía de** *bay* N Gulf of Panama
193 T7 **Panama Basin** *undersea feature* E Pacific Ocean 05°00′N 83°30′W
43 T15 **Panama Canal** *canal* E Panama
23 R9 **Panama City** Florida, SE USA 30°09′N 85°39′W
43 T14 **Panama City** ✈ Panamá, C Panama 09°02′N 79°24′W
Panama City *see* Panamá
23 Q9 **Panama City Beach** Florida, SE USA 30°10′N 85°48′W
43 T17 **Panamá, Golfo de** *var.* Gulf of Panama. *gulf* S Panama
Panama, Gulf of *see* Panamá, Golfo de
Panama, Isthmus of *see* Panama, Istmo de
43 T15 **Panama, Istmo de** *Eng.* Isthmus of Panama; *prev.* Isthmus of Darien. *isthmus* E Panama
Panamá, Provincia de *see* Panamá
Panama, Republic of *see* Panama
35 U11 **Panamint Range** ▲▲ California, W USA
107 L22 **Panarea, Isola** *island* Isole Eolie, S Italy
106 G9 **Panaro** ≈ N Italy
171 P5 **Panay Island** *island* C Philippines
35 W7 **Pancake Range** ▲▲ Nevada, W USA
112 M11 **Pančevo** *Ger.* Pantschowa, *Hung.* Pancsova. Vojvodina, N Serbia 44°53′N 20°40′E
113 M15 **Pančićev Vrh** ▲ SW Serbia 43°16′N 20°49′E
116 L12 **Panciu** Vrancea, E Romania 45°54′N 27°08′E
116 F10 **Pâncota** *Hung.* Pankota; *prev.* Pîncota. Arad, W Romania 46°20′N 21°45′E
Pancsova *see* Pančevo
83 N20 **Panda** Inhambane, SE Mozambique 24°02′S 34°45′E
171 X12 **Pandaidori, Kepulauan** *island group* E Indonesia
25 N11 **Pandale** Texas, SW USA 30°09′N 101°34′W
169 P12 **Pandang Tikar, Pulau** *island* N Indonesia
61 F20 **Pan de Azúcar** Maldonado, S Uruguay 34°45′S 55°14′W
118 H11 **Pandėlys** Panevėžys, NE Lithuania 56°04′N 25°18′E
155 F15 **Pandharpur** Mahārāshtra, W India 17°42′N 75°24′E
182 J1 **Pandie Pandie** South Australia 26°06′S 139°26′E
171 O12 **Pandiri** Sulawesi, C Indonesia 01°32′S 120°47′E
61 F20 **Pando** Canelones, S Uruguay 34°44′S 55°58′W
57 J14 **Pando** ◈ *department* N Bolivia
192 K9 **Pandora Bank** *undersea feature* W Pacific Ocean
95 G20 **Pandrup** Nordjylland, N Denmark 57°14′N 09°42′E
79 J15 **Pandu** Equateur, NW Dem. Rep. Congo 05°03′N 19°14′E
153 V12 **Pandu** Assam, NE India 26°08′N 91°37′E
Paneas *see* Bāniyās
59 F15 **Panelas** Mato Grosso, W Brazil 09°06′S 60°41′W
118 G12 **Panevėžys** Panevėžys, C Lithuania 55°44′N 24°21′E
118 G11 **Panevėžys** ◈ *province* NW Lithuania
Panfilov *see* Zharkent
127 N9 **Panfilovo** Volgogradskaya Oblast', SW Russian Federation 50°25′N 42°55′E
79 N17 **Panga** Orientale, N Dem. Rep. Congo 01°52′N 26°18′E
193 Y15 **Pangai** Lifuka, C Tonga 19°50′S 174°23′W
114 H13 **Pangaío** ▲▲ N Greece
79 G20 **Pangala** Pool, S Congo 03°26′S 14°38′E
81 J22 **Pangani** Tanga, E Tanzania 05°27′S 39°00′E
81 I21 **Pangani** ≈ NE Tanzania
186 K8 **Panggoe** Choiseul, NW Solomon Islands 07°00′S 157°05′E
79 N20 **Pangi** Maniema, E Dem. Rep. Congo 03°12′S 26°39′E
Pangim *see* Panaji
168 H8 **Pangkalanbrandan** Sumatera, W Indonesia 04°00′N 98°15′E
Pangkalanbun *see* Pangkalanbuun
169 R13 **Pangkalanbuun** *var.* Pangkalanbun. Borneo, C Indonesia 02°43′S 111°38′E

◆ Country
● Country Capital
◇ Dependent Territory
○ Dependent Territory Capital
◈ Administrative Regions
✈ International Airport
▲ Mountain
▲▲ Mountain Range
⛰ Volcano
≈ River
◎ Lake
⊠ Reservoir

169 N12 **Pangkalpinang** Pulau Bangka, W Indonesia 02°05′S 106°09′E
11 U17 **Pangman** Saskatchewan, S Canada 49°37′N 104°33′W
Pang-Nga *see* Phang-Nga
9 S6 **Pangnirtung** Baffin Island, Nunavut, NE Canada 66°05′N 65°45′W
152 K6 **Pangong Tso** *var.* Bangong Co. ◎ China/India *see also* Bangong Co
Pangong Tso *see* Banggong Co
36 K7 **Panguitch** Utah, W USA 37°49′N 112°26′W
186 J7 **Panguna** Bougainville Island, NE Papua New Guinea 06°22′S 155°20′E
171 N8 **Pangutaran Group** *island group* Sulu Archipelago, SW Philippines
25 N2 **Panhandle** Texas, SW USA 35°21′N 101°24′W
Panhormus *see* Palermo
171 W14 **Paniai, Danau** ◎ Papua, E Indonesia
79 L21 **Pania-Mutombo** Kasai-Oriental, C Dem. Rep. Congo 05°09′S 23°49′E
187 P16 **Panié, Mont** ▲ C New Caledonia 20°33′S 164°41′E
Panikoilli *see* Jājapur
152 I10 **Pānīpat** Haryāna, N India 29°18′N 77°00′E
147 Q14 **Panj** *Rus.* Pyandzh; *prev.* Kirovabad. SW Tajikistan 37°39′N 69°55′E
147 P15 **Panj** *Rus.* Pyandzh. ≈ Afghanistan/Tajikistan
149 O5 **Panjāb** Bāmyān, C Afghanistan 34°21′N 67°00′E
147 O12 **Panjakent** *Rus.* Pendzhikent. W Tajikistan 39°28′N 67°33′E
148 L14 **Panjgūr** Baluchistān, SW Pakistan 26°58′N 64°05′E
Panjim *see* Panaji
163 U12 **Panjin** Liaoning, NE China 41°11′N 122°05′E
147 P14 **Panji Poyon** *Rus.* Nizhniy Pyandzh. SW Tajikistan 37°14′N 68°32′E
149 Q4 **Panjshayr** *prev.* Panjshīr. ≈ E Afghanistan
149 S4 **Panjshīr** ◈ *province* NE Afghanistan
Panjshīr *see* Panjshayr
Pankota *see* Pâncota
77 W14 **Pankshin** Plateau, C Nigeria 09°21′N 09°27′E
163 Y10 **Pan Ling** ▲▲ N China
Panlong Jiang *see* Lô, Sông
154 J9 **Panna** Madhya Pradesh, C India 24°43′N 80°11′E
99 M16 **Panningen** Limburg, SE Netherlands 51°20′N 05°59′E
149 R13 **Pāno Āqil** Sind, SE Pakistan 27°55′N 69°18′E
121 P3 **Páno Léfkara** S Cyprus 34°52′N 33°18′E
121 O3 **Páno Panagiá** *var.* Pano Panayia. W Cyprus 34°55′N 32°38′E
Pano Panayia *see* Páno Panagiá
Panopolis *see* Akhmīm
29 U14 **Panora** Iowa, C USA 41°41′N 94°21′W
60 I8 **Panorama** São Paulo, S Brazil 21°22′S 51°51′W
115 I24 **Pánormos** Kríti, Greece, E Mediterranean Sea 35°24′N 24°42′E
Panormus *see* Palermo
163 W11 **Panshi** Jilin, NE China 42°56′N 126°02′E
59 H19 **Pantanal** *var.* Pantanalmato-Grossense. *swamp* SW Brazil
Pantanalmato-Grossense *see* Pantanal
61 H16 **Pântano Grande** Rio Grande do Sul, S Brazil 30°12′S 52°24′W
171 Q16 **Pantar, Pulau** *island* Kepulauan Alor, S Indonesia
21 X9 **Pantego** North Carolina, SE USA 35°34′N 76°39′E
107 G25 **Pantelleria** *anc.* Cossyra, Cosyra. Sicilia, Italy, C Mediterranean Sea 36°47′N 12°00′E
107 G25 **Pantelleria, Isola di** *island* SW Italy
Pante Makasar/Pante Macassar/Pante Makassar *see* Ponte Macassar
152 K10 **Pantnagar** Uttarakhand, N India 29°00′N 79°28′E
115 A15 **Pantokrátoras** ▲ Kérkyra, Iónia Nisiá, Greece, C Mediterranean Sea 39°45′N 19°51′E
Pantschowa *see* Pančevo
41 P11 **Pánuco** Veracruz-Llave, E Mexico 22°01′N 98°13′W
41 P11 **Pánuco, Río** ≈ C Mexico
160 I12 **Panxian** Guizhou, S China 25°45′N 104°39′E
168 I10 **Panyabungan** Sumatera, N Indonesia 0°55′N 99°30′E
77 W14 **Panyam** Plateau, C Nigeria 09°28′N 09°13′E
157 N13 **Panzhihua** *prev.* Dukou, Tu-k'ou. Sichuan, C China 26°35′N 101°41′E
79 I22 **Panzi** Bandundu, SW Dem. Rep. Congo 07°10′S 17°55′E
42 E5 **Panzós** Alta Verapaz, E Guatemala 15°21′N 89°40′W
Pao-chi/Paoki *see* Baoji
Pao-king *see* Shaoyang
107 N20 **Paola** Calabria, SW Italy 39°21′N 16°03′E
121 P16 **Paola** E Malta 35°52′N 14°30′E
27 R5 **Paola** Kansas, C USA 38°34′N 94°54′W
31 O15 **Paoli** Indiana, N USA 38°35′N 86°25′W
187 R14 **Paonangisu** Éfaté, C Vanuatu 17°33′S 168°23′E
171 S13 **Paoni** *var.* Pauni. Pulau Seram, E Indonesia 02°48′S 129°03′E
37 Q5 **Paonia** Colorado, C USA 38°52′N 107°35′W
191 O7 **Paopao** Moorea, W French Polynesia 17°28′S 149°48′W
Pao-shan *see* Baoshan
Pao-ting *see* Baoding
Pao-t'ou/Paotow *see* Baotou
79 H14 **Paoua** Ouham-Pendé, W Central African Republic 07°22′N 16°25′E
Pap *see* Pop
111 H23 **Pápa** Veszprém, W Hungary 47°20′N 17°29′E
42 J12 **Papagayo, Golfo de** *gulf* NW Costa Rica
38 H11 **Pāpa'ikou** *var.* Papaikou. Hawaii, USA, C Pacific Ocean 19°45′N 155°06′W
41 R15 **Papaloapan, Río** ≈ S Mexico
184 L6 **Papakura** Auckland, North Island, New Zealand 37°03′S 174°57′E
41 Q13 **Papantla** *var.* Papantla de Olarte. Veracruz-Llave, E Mexico 20°30′N 97°21′W
Papantla de Olarte *see* Papantla
191 P8 **Papara** Tahiti, W French Polynesia 17°45′S 149°33′W
184 K4 **Paparoa** Northland, North Island, New Zealand 36°06′S 174°12′E
185 G16 **Paparoa Range** ▲▲ South Island, New Zealand
115 K20 **Pápas, Akrotírio** *headland* Ikaría, Dodekánisa, Greece, Aegean Sea 37°31′N 25°58′E
96 L2 **Papa Stour** *island* NE Scotland, United Kingdom
184 L6 **Papatoetoe** Auckland, North Island, New Zealand 36°58′S 174°52′E
185 E25 **Papatowai** Otago, South Island, New Zealand 46°33′S 169°33′E
96 K4 **Papa Westray** *island* NE Scotland, United Kingdom
191 T10 **Papeete** ○ (French Polynesia) Tahiti, W French Polynesia 17°32′S 149°34′W
100 F11 **Papenburg** Niedersachsen, NW Germany 53°04′N 07°24′E
98 H13 **Papendrecht** Zuid-Holland, SW Netherlands 51°50′N 04°42′E
191 Q7 **Papenoo** Tahiti, W French Polynesia 17°29′S 149°25′W
191 Q7 **Papenoo Rivière** ≈ Tahiti, W French Polynesia
191 N7 **Papetoai** Moorea, W French Polynesia 17°29′S 149°52′W
92 L3 **Papey** *island* E Iceland
Paphos *see* Páfos
40 H5 **Papigochic, Río** ≈ NW Mexico
118 E10 **Papilė** Šiauliai, NW Lithuania 56°08′N 22°51′E
29 S15 **Papillion** Nebraska, C USA 41°09′N 96°02′W
15 T5 **Papinachois** ≈ Québec, SE Canada
171 X13 **Papua** *var.* Irian Barat, West Irian, West New Guinea, West Papua; *prev.* Dutch New Guinea, Irian Jaya, Netherlands New Guinea. ◈ *province* E Indonesia
Papua and New Guinea, Territory of *see* Papua New Guinea
170 V10 **Papua Barat** *off.* Propinsi Irian Jaya Barat, *Eng.* West Irian Jaya. ◈ *province* E Indonesia
186 C9 **Papua, Gulf of** *gulf* S Papua New Guinea
186 C8 **Papua New Guinea** *off.* Independent State of Papua New Guinea; *prev.* Territory of Papua and New Guinea. ◆ *commonwealth republic* NW Melanesia
Papua New Guinea, Independent State of *see* Papua New Guinea
192 H8 **Papua Plateau** *undersea feature* N Coral Sea
112 G9 **Papuk** ▲▲ NE Croatia
Papun *see* Hpapun
42 L14 **Paquera** Puntarenas, W Costa Rica 09°52′N 84°56′W
58 I13 **Pará** *off.* Estado do Pará. ◈ *state* NE Brazil
55 V9 **Para** ◈ *district* N Suriname
Pará *see* Belém
180 I8 **Paraburdoo** Western Australia 23°07′S 117°40′E
57 E16 **Paracas, Península de** *peninsula* W Peru
59 L19 **Paracatu** Minas Gerais, NE Brazil 17°14′S 46°52′W
192 E6 **Paracel Islands** ◇ *disputed territory* SE Asia
182 I6 **Parachilna** South Australia 31°09′S 138°23′E
149 R6 **Pārachinār** Khyber Pakhtunkhwa, NW Pakistan 33°56′N 70°04′E
112 N13 **Paraćin** Serbia, C Serbia 43°51′N 21°25′E
Paradip *see* Krishnarājāsāgara
14 K8 **Paradis** Québec, SE Canada 48°13′N 76°36′W
39 N11 **Paradise** *var.* Paradise Hill. Alaska, USA 62°28′N 160°09′W
35 O5 **Paradise** California, W USA 39°42′N 121°39′W
35 X11 **Paradise** Nevada, W USA 36°05′N 115°10′W
Paradise Hill *see* Paradise
37 R11 **Paradise Hills** New Mexico, SW USA 35°12′N 106°42′W
Paradise of the Pacific *see* Hawai'i
36 L13 **Paradise Valley** Arizona, SW USA 33°31′N 111°56′W
35 T2 **Paradise Valley** Nevada, W USA 41°30′N 117°30′W
115 O22 **Paradisi** ✈ (Ródos) Ródos, Dodekánisa, Greece, Aegean Sea 36°24′N 28°08′E
154 P12 **Pārādwīp** Orissa, E India 20°17′N 86°42′E
Paraetonium *see* Marsā Maṭrūḥ
117 R4 **Parafiyivka** Chernihivs'ka Oblast', N Ukraine 50°53′N 32°40′E
36 K7 **Paragonah** Utah, W USA 37°53′N 112°46′W
27 X9 **Paragould** Arkansas, C USA 36°02′N 90°30′W
47 X8 **Paraguaçu** *var.* Paraguassú. ≈ E Brazil
60 J9 **Paraguaçu Paulista** São Paulo, S Brazil 22°22′S 50°35′W
54 H4 **Paraguaipoa** Zulia, NW Venezuela 11°21′N 71°58′W
62 O6 **Paraguarí** Paraguarí, S Paraguay 25°36′S 57°06′W
62 O7 **Paraguarí** *off.* Departamento de Paraguarí. ◈ *department* S Paraguay
Paraguarí, Departamento de *see* Paraguarí
57 O16 **Paraguá, Río** ≈ NE Bolivia
55 O8 **Paragua, Río** ≈ SE Venezuela
Paraguassú *see* Paraguaçu
62 N5 **Paraguay** ◆ *republic* C South America
47 U10 **Paraguay** *var.* Río Paraguay. ≈ C South America
Paraguay, Río *see* Paraguay
Parahiba/Parahyba *see* Paraíba
59 P15 **Paraíba** *off.* Estado da Paraíba; *prev.* Parahiba, Parahyba. ◈ *state* E Brazil
Paraíba *see* João Pessoa
60 P9 **Paraíba do Sul, Rio** ≈ SE Brazil
Paraíba, Estado da *see* Paraíba
Parainen *see* Pargas
43 N14 **Paraíso** Cartago, C Costa Rica 09°51′N 83°50′W
41 U14 **Paraíso** Tabasco, SE Mexico 18°26′N 93°10′W
57 O17 **Paraíso, Río** ≈ E Bolivia
Parajd *see* Praid
77 S14 **Parakou** C Benin 09°23′N 02°40′E
115 F20 **Paralía Tyrou** Pelopónnisos, S Greece 37°17′N 22°50′E
121 Q2 **Paralímni** E Cyprus 35°02′N 34°00′E
115 G18 **Paralímni, Límni** ◎ C Greece
55 W8 **Paramaribo** ● (Suriname) Paramaribo, N Suriname 05°52′N 55°14′W
55 W9 **Paramaribo** ◈ *district* N Suriname
55 W9 **Paramaribo** ✈ Paramaribo, N Suriname 05°52′N 55°14′W
Paramithiá *see* Paramythiá
56 C13 **Paramonga** Lima, W Peru 10°42′S 77°50′W
123 V12 **Paramushir, Ostrov** *island* SE Russian Federation
115 C16 **Paramythiá** *var.* Paramithiá. Ípeiros, W Greece 39°28′N 20°31′E
62 M10 **Paraná** Entre Ríos, E Argentina 31°48′S 60°29′W
60 H11 **Paraná** *off.* Estado do Paraná. ◈ *state* S Brazil
47 U11 **Paraná** *var.* Alto Paraná. ≈ C South America
Paraná, Estado do *see* Paraná
60 K12 **Paranaguá** Paraná, S Brazil 25°32′S 48°36′W
59 J20 **Paranaíba, Rio** ≈ E Brazil
61 C19 **Paraná Ibicuy, Río** ≈ E Argentina
59 H15 **Paranaíta** Mato Grosso, W Brazil 09°35′S 57°01′W
60 H9 **Paranapanema, Rio** ≈ S Brazil
60 K11 **Paranapiacaba, Serra do** ▲▲ S Brazil
60 H9 **Paranavaí** Paraná, S Brazil 23°02′S 52°36′W
143 N5 **Parandak** Markazī, W Iran 35°19′N 50°40′E
114 I12 **Paranésti** *var.* Paranestio. Anatolikí Makedonía kai Thráki, NE Greece 41°16′N 24°31′E
Paranestio *see* Paranésti
191 W11 **Paraoa** *atoll* Îles Tuamotu, C French Polynesia
184 L13 **Paraparaumu** Wellington, North Island, New Zealand 40°55′S 175°01′E
57 N20 **Parapeti, Río** ≈ SE Bolivia
54 L10 **Paraque, Cerro** ▲ W Venezuela 06°00′S 67°00′W
154 I11 **Parāsiya** Madhya Pradesh, C India 22°11′N 78°50′E
115 M23 **Paraspóri, Akrotírio** *headland* Kárpathos, SE Greece 35°54′N 27°15′E
60 O10 **Parati** Rio de Janeiro, SE Brazil 23°15′S 44°42′W
59 K14 **Parauapebas** Pará, N Brazil 06°03′S 49°48′W
103 Q10 **Paray-le-Monial** Saône-et-Loire, C France 46°27′N 04°07′E
Parbatsar *see* Parvatsar
154 H13 **Parbhani** Mahārāshtra, C India 19°16′N 76°51′E
100 L10 **Parchim** Mecklenburg-Vorpommern, N Germany 53°26′N 11°51′E
Parchwitz *see* Prochowice
110 P13 **Parczew** Lubelskie, E Poland 51°40′N 23°E
60 L8 **Pardo, Rio** ≈ S Brazil
111 E16 **Pardubice** *Ger.* Pardubitz. Pardubický Kraj, C Czech Republic 50°01′N 15°47′E
111 E17 **Pardubický Kraj** ◈ *region* N Czech Republic
Pardubitz *see* Pardubice
119 F16 **Parechcha** *Pol.* Porzecze, *Rus.* Porech'ye. Hrodzyenskaya Voblasts', W Belarus 53°53′N 24°08′E
59 F17 **Parecis, Chapada dos** *var.* Serra dos Parecis. ▲▲ W Brazil
Parecis, Serra dos *see* Parecis, Chapada dos
104 M4 **Paredes de Nava** Castilla y León, N Spain 42°09′N 04°42′W
189 U12 **Parem** *island* Chuuk, C Micronesia
189 O12 **Parem Island** *island* E Micronesia
184 I1 **Parengarenga Harbour** *inlet* North Island, New Zealand
15 N8 **Parent** Québec, SE Canada 47°55′N 74°36′W
102 J14 **Parentis-en-Born** Landes, SW France 44°22′N 01°04′W
Parenzo *see* Poreč
185 G20 **Pareora** Canterbury, South Island, New Zealand 44°28′S 171°12′E
171 N14 **Parepare** Sulawesi, C Indonesia 04°S 119°40′E
115 B16 **Párga** Ípeiros, W Greece 39°18′N 20°19′E
93 K20 **Pargas** *Swe.* Parainen. Länsi-Suomi, SW Finland 60°18′N 22°20′E
64 O5 **Pargo, Ponta do** *headland* Madeira, Portugal, NE Atlantic Ocean 32°48′N 17°17′W
Paria, Golfo de *see* Paria, Gulf of
55 N6 **Pariaguán** Anzoátegui, NE Venezuela 08°51′N 64°43′W
45 X17 **Paria, Gulf of** *var.* Golfo de Paria. *gulf* Trinidad and Tobago/Venezuela
57 I15 **Pariamanu, Río** ≈ E Peru
36 L8 **Paria River** ≈ Utah, W USA
Parichi *see* Parychy
40 M14 **Paricutín, Volcán** ⛰ C Mexico 19°25′N 102°20′W
43 P16 **Parida, Isla** *island* SW Panama
55 T8 **Parika** NE Guyana 06°51′N 58°25′W
93 O18 **Parikkala** Etelä-Suomi, SE Finland 61°33′N 29°34′E
58 E10 **Parima, Serra** *var.* Sierra Parima. ▲ Brazil/Venezuela *see also* Parima, Sierra
55 N11 **Parima, Sierra** *var.* Serra Parima. ▲ Brazil/Venezuela *see also* Parima, Serra
57 F17 **Parinacochas, Laguna** ◎ SW Peru
56 A9 **Pariñas, Punta** *headland* NW Peru 04°45′S 81°22′W
58 H12 **Parintins** Amazonas, N Brazil 02°38′S 56°45′W
103 O5 **Paris** *anc.* Lutetia, Lutetia Parisiorum, Parisii. ● (France) Paris, N France 48°52′N 02°19′E
191 Y2 **Paris** Kiritimati, E Kiribati 01°55′N 157°30′W
27 S11 **Paris** Arkansas, C USA 35°17′N 93°46′W
33 S16 **Paris** Idaho, NW USA 42°14′N 111°24′W
31 N14 **Paris** Illinois, N USA 39°36′N 87°42′W
20 M5 **Paris** Kentucky, S USA 38°13′N 84°15′W
27 V3 **Paris** Missouri, C USA 39°28′N 92°00′W
20 H8 **Paris** Tennessee, S USA 36°19′N 88°20′W
25 V5 **Paris** Texas, SW USA 33°41′N 95°33′W
Parisii *see* Paris
43 S16 **Parita** Herrera, S Panama 08°01′N 80°30′W
43 S16 **Parita, Bahía de** *bay* S Panama
93 K18 **Parkano** Länsi-Suomi, W Finland 62°03′N 23°E
Parkan/Párkány *see* Štúrovo
27 N6 **Park City** Kansas, C USA 37°48′N 97°19′W
36 L3 **Park City** Utah, W USA 40°39′N 111°30′W
36 I12 **Parker** Arizona, SW USA 34°07′N 114°16′W
23 R9 **Parker** Florida, SE USA 30°07′N 85°36′W
29 R11 **Parker** South Dakota, N USA 43°24′N 97°08′W
35 Z14 **Parker Dam** California, W USA 34°17′N 114°08′W
29 W13 **Parkersburg** Iowa, C USA 42°34′N 92°47′W
21 Q3 **Parkersburg** West Virginia, NE USA 39°17′N 81°33′W
29 T7 **Parkers Prairie** Minnesota, N USA 46°09′N 95°19′W
171 P8 **Parker Volcano** ⛰ Mindanao, S Philippines 06°09′N 124°52′E
181 W13 **Parkes** New South Wales, SE Australia 33°10′S 148°10′E
30 K4 **Park Falls** Wisconsin, N USA 45°57′N 90°25′W
Parkhar *see* Farkhor
14 E16 **Parkhill** Ontario, S Canada 43°11′N 81°39′W
29 T5 **Park Rapids** Minnesota, N USA 46°55′N 95°03′W
29 Q3 **Park River** North Dakota, N USA 48°24′N 97°44′W
29 Q11 **Parkston** South Dakota, N USA 43°24′N 97°58′W
10 L17 **Parksville** Vancouver Island, British Columbia, SW Canada 49°20′N 124°19′W
37 S3 **Parkview Mountain** ▲ Colorado, C USA 40°19′N 106°08′W
105 N8 **Parla** Madrid, C Spain 40°13′N 03°48′W
29 S8 **Parle, Lac qui** ▣ Minnesota, N USA
155 G14 **Parli Vaijnāth** Mahārāshtra, C India 18°53′N 76°36′E
106 F9 **Parma** Emilia-Romagna, N Italy 44°50′N 10°20′E
31 T11 **Parma** Ohio, N USA 41°24′N 81°43′W
Parnahyba *see* Parnaíba
58 N13 **Parnaíba** *var.* Parnahyba. Piauí, E Brazil 02°58′S 41°46′W
65 J14 **Parnaíba Ridge** *undersea feature* C Atlantic Ocean
58 N13 **Parnaíba, Rio** ≈ NE Brazil
115 F18 **Parnassós** ▲ C Greece
185 J17 **Parnassus** Canterbury, South Island, New Zealand 42°41′S 173°18′E
182 H10 **Parndana** South Australia 35°48′S 137°13′E
115 H19 **Párnitha** ▲▲ C Greece
Parnon *see* Párnonas
115 F21 **Párnonas** *var.* Parnon. ▲▲ S Greece
118 G5 **Pärnu** *Ger.* Pernau, *Latv.* Pērnava; *prev. Rus.* Pernov. Pärnumaa, SW Estonia 58°24′N 24°32′E
118 G6 **Pärnu** *var.* Parnu Jõgi, *Ger.* Pernau. ≈ SW Estonia
118 G5 **Pärnu-Jaagupi** *Ger.* Sankt-Jakobi. Pärnumaa, SW Estonia 58°36′N 24°30′E
Parnu Jõgi *see* Pärnu
118 G5 **Pärnu Laht** *Ger.* Pernauer Bucht. *bay* SW Estonia
118 F5 **Pärnumaa** *var.* Pärnu Maakond. ◈ *province* SW Estonia
Pärnu Maakond *see* Pärnumaa
153 T11 **Paro** W Bhutan 27°23′N 89°31′E
153 T11 **Paro** ✈ (Thimphu) W Bhutan 27°23′N 89°31′E
185 G17 **Paroa** West Coast, South Island, New Zealand 42°31′S 171°10′E
163 X14 **Paro-ho** *var.* Hwach'ŏn-chŏsuji; *prev.* P'aro-ho. ▣ N South Korea
P'aro-ho *see* Paro-ho
115 J21 **Pároikiá** *prev.* Páros. Páros, Kykládes, Greece, Aegean Sea 37°04′N 25°06′E
183 N6 **Paroo River** *seasonal river* New South Wales/Queensland, SE Australia
Paropamisus Range *see* Sefīd Kūh, Selseleh-ye
Paropamisus Range *see* Sefīd Kūh, Selseleh-ye
115 J21 **Páros** *island* Kykládes, Greece, Aegean Sea
Páros *see* Pároikiá
36 K7 **Parowan** Utah, W USA 37°50′N 112°49′W
103 U13 **Parpaillon** ▲▲ SE France
108 I9 **Parpan** Graubünden, S Switzerland 46°46′N 09°32′E
62 G13 **Parral** Maule, C Chile 36°08′S 71°52′W
Parral *see* Hidalgo del Parral
183 T9 **Parramatta** New South Wales, SE Australia 33°49′S 150°59′E
21 Y6 **Parramore Island** *island* Virginia, NE USA
40 M8 **Parras** *var.* Parras de la Fuente. Coahuila, NE Mexico 25°26′N 102°07′W
Parras de la Fuente *see* Parras
42 M14 **Parrita** Puntarenas, S Costa Rica 09°30′N 84°20′W
Parry group *see* Mukojima-rettō
14 G13 **Parry Island** *island* Ontario, S Canada
197 O9 **Parry Islands** *island group* Nunavut, NW Canada
14 G12 **Parry Sound** Ontario, S Canada 45°21′N 80°03′W
110 F7 **Parsęta** *Ger.* Persante. ≈ NW Poland
28 L3 **Parshall** North Dakota, N USA 47°57′N 102°07′W
27 Q7 **Parsons** Kansas, C USA 37°20′N 95°15′W
20 H9 **Parsons** Tennessee, S USA 35°39′N 88°07′W
21 T3 **Parsons** West Virginia, NE USA 39°06′N 79°43′W
Parsonstown *see* Birr
100 P11 **Parsteiner See** ◎ NE Germany
107 I24 **Partanna** Sicilia, Italy, C Mediterranean Sea 37°43′N 12°54′E
108 J8 **Partenen** Graubünden, E Switzerland 46°58′N 10°01′E
102 K9 **Parthenay** Deux-Sèvres, W France 46°39′N 00°13′W
95 J19 **Partille** Västra Götaland, S Sweden 57°43′N 12°12′E
107 I23 **Partinico** Sicilia, Italy, C Mediterranean Sea 38°03′N 13°07′E
111 I20 **Partizánske** *prev.* Šimonovany, *Hung.* Simony. Trenčiansky Kraj, W Slovakia 48°35′N 18°23′E
58 H11 **Paru de Oeste, Rio** ≈ N Brazil
182 K9 **Paruna** South Australia 34°45′S 140°43′E
58 I11 **Paru, Rio** ≈ N Brazil
Parvān *see* Parwān
155 M14 **Pārvatīpuram** Andhra Pradesh, E India 17°01′N 81°47′E
152 G12 **Parvatsar** *prev.* Parbatsar. Rājasthān, N India 26°52′N 74°49′E
149 Q5 **Parwān** *prev.* Parvān. ◈ *province* E Afghanistan
158 I15 **Paryang** Xizang Zizhiqu, W China 30°04′N 83°28′E
119 M18 **Parychy** *Rus.* Parichi. Homyel'skaya Voblasts', SE Belarus 52°48′N 29°25′E
83 J21 **Parys** Free State, C South Africa 26°55′S 27°28′E
35 T15 **Pasadena** California, W USA 34°09′N 118°09′W
25 W11 **Pasadena** Texas, SW USA 29°41′N 95°13′W
56 B8 **Pasaje** El Oro, SW Ecuador 03°23′S 79°50′W
137 T9 **P'asanauri** *prev.* P'asanauri. N Georgia 42°21′N 44°40′E
P'asanauri *see* Pasanauri
168 I13 **Pasapuat** Pulau Pagai Utara, W Indonesia 02°36′S 99°58′E
Pasawng *see* Hpasawng
114 L13 **Paşayiğit** Edirne, NW Turkey 40°58′N 26°38′E
23 N9 **Pascagoula** Mississippi, S USA 30°21′N 88°32′W
22 M8 **Pascagoula River** ≈ Mississippi, S USA
116 F12 **Paşcani** *Hung.* Páskán. Iaşi, NE Romania 47°14′N 26°46′E
109 T4 **Pasching** Oberösterreich, N Austria 48°16′N 14°10′E
32 K10 **Pasco** Washington, NW USA 46°13′N 119°06′W
56 E13 **Pasco** *off.* Departamento de Pasco. ◈ *department* C Peru
Pasco, Departamento de *see* Pasco
191 N11 **Pascua, Isla de** *var.* Rapa Nui, Easter Island. *island* E Pacific Ocean
63 G21 **Pascua, Río** ≈ S Chile
103 N1 **Pas-de-Calais** ◈ *department* N France
100 P10 **Pasewalk** Mecklenburg-Vorpommern, NE Germany 53°31′N 13°59′E
11 T10 **Pasfield Lake** ◎ Saskatchewan, C Canada
Pa-shih Hai-hsia *see* Bashi Channel
Pashkeni *see* Bolyarovo
Pashmakli *see* Smolyan
153 X10 **Pāsighāt** Arunāchel Pradesh, NE India 28°08′N 95°13′E
137 Q12 **Pasinler** Erzurum, NE Turkey 39°59′N 41°41′E
Pasi Oloy, Qatorkŭhi *see* Zaalayskiy Khrebet
42 E3 **Pasión, Río de la** ≈ N Guatemala
168 J12 **Pasirganting** Sumatera, W Indonesia 02°04′S 100°51′E
Pasirpangarayan *see* Bagansiapiapi
168 K6 **Pasir Puteh** *var.* Pasir Putih. Kelantan, Peninsular Malaysia 05°50′N 102°24′E
Pasir Putih *see* Pasir Puteh
169 R9 **Pasir, Tanjung** *headland* East Malaysia 02°24′N 111°12′E
95 N20 **Påskallavik** Kalmar, S Sweden 57°10′N 16°25′E
Páskán *see* Paşcani
Paskevicha, Zaliv *see* Tushchybas, Zaliv
110 K7 **Pasłęk** *Ger.* Preußisch Holland. Warmińsko-Mazurskie, NE Poland 54°03′N 19°40′E
110 K7 **Pasłęka** *Ger.* Passarge. ≈ N Poland
148 K16 **Pasni** Baluchistān, SW Pakistan 25°13′N 63°30′E
63 I18 **Paso de Indios** Chubut, S Argentina 43°52′S 69°06′W
54 L7 **Paso del Caballo** Guárico, N Venezuela 08°19′N 67°08′W
61 E15 **Paso de los Libres** Corrientes, NE Argentina 29°43′S 57°09′W
61 E18 **Paso de los Toros** Tacuarembó, C Uruguay 32°45′S 56°30′W
Pasoeroean *see* Pasuruan
35 P12 **Paso Robles** California, W USA 35°37′N 120°42′W
15 Y7 **Paspébiac** Québec, SE Canada 48°03′N 65°10′W
11 U14 **Pasquia Hills** ▲ Saskatchewan, S Canada
149 W7 **Pasrūr** Punjab, E Pakistan 32°12′N 74°42′E
30 M1 **Passage Island** *island* Michigan, N USA
65 B24 **Passage Islands** *island group* W Falkland Islands
8 K5 **Passage Point** *headland* Banks Island, Northwest Territories, NW Canada 73°31′N 115°12′W
Passarge *see* Pasłęka
115 C15 **Passarón** *ancient monument* Ípeiros, W Greece
Passarowitz *see* Požarevac
101 O22 **Passau** Bayern, SE Germany 48°34′N 13°28′E
22 M9 **Pass Christian** Mississippi, S USA 30°19′N 89°15′W
107 L26 **Passero, Capo** *headland* Sicilia, Italy, C Mediterranean Sea 36°40′N 15°09′E
171 P5 **Passi** Panay Island, C Philippines 11°05′N 122°37′E
61 H14 **Passo Fundo** Rio Grande do Sul, S Brazil 28°16′S 52°20′W
60 H13 **Passo Fundo, Barragem de** ▣ S Brazil
61 H15 **Passo Real, Barragem de** ▣ S Brazil
59 L20 **Passos** Minas Gerais, NE Brazil 20°45′S 46°38′W
167 X10 **Passu Keah** *island* S Paracel Islands
118 J13 **Pastavy** *Pol.* Postawy, *Rus.* Postavy. Vitsyebskaya Voblasts', NW Belarus 55°07′N 26°50′E
56 D7 **Pastaza** ◈ *province* E Ecuador
56 D9 **Pastaza, Río** ≈ Ecuador/Peru
61 A21 **Pasteur** Buenos Aires, E Argentina 35°10′S 62°14′W
15 V3 **Pasteur** ≈ Québec, SE Canada
147 Q12 **Pastigav** *Rus.* Pastigov. W Tajikistan 39°27′N 69°16′E
Pastigov *see* Pastigav
54 C13 **Pasto** Nariño, SW Colombia 01°12′N 77°17′W
38 M10 **Pastol Bay** *bay* Alaska, USA
37 O8 **Pastora Peak** ▲ Arizona, SW USA 36°48′N 109°10′W
105 O8 **Pastrana** Castilla-La Mancha, C Spain 40°24′N 02°55′W
169 S16 **Pasuruan** *prev.* Pasoeroean. Jawa, C Indonesia 07°38′S 112°44′E
118 F11 **Pasvalys** Panevėžys, N Lithuania 56°03′N 24°24′E
111 K21 **Pásztó** Nógrád, N Hungary 47°57′N 19°41′E
189 U12 **Pata** *var.* Patta. *atoll* Chuuk Islands, C Micronesia
36 M16 **Patagonia** Arizona, SW USA 31°32′N 110°45′W
63 H20 **Patagonia** *physical region* Argentina/Chile
Patalung *see* Phatthalung
154 D9 **Pātan** Gujarāt, W India 23°51′N 72°11′E
154 J10 **Pātan** Madhya Pradesh, C India 23°19′N 79°41′E
171 S11 **Patani** Pulau Halmahera, E Indonesia 0°19′N 128°46′E
Patani *see* Pattani
15 V7 **Patapédia Est** ≈ Québec, SE Canada
116 K13 **Pătâriagele** *prev.* Pătîriagele. Buzău, SE Romania 45°19′N 26°21′E
Patavium *see* Padova
182 I5 **Patawarta Hill** ▲ South Australia 30°57′S 138°42′E
182 L10 **Patchewollock** Victoria, SE Australia 35°24′S 142°11′E
184 K11 **Patea** Taranaki, North Island, New Zealand 39°48′S 174°35′E
184 K11 **Patea** ≈ North Island, New Zealand
77 U15 **Pategi** Kwara, C Nigeria 08°39′N 05°46′E
81 K20 **Pate Island** *var.* Patta Island. *island* SE Kenya
105 S10 **Paterna** Valenciana, E Spain 39°30′N 00°24′W
109 R9 **Paternion** *Slvn.* Špatrjan. Kärnten, S Austria 46°40′N 13°43′E
107 L24 **Paternò** *anc.* Hybla, Hybla Major. Sicilia, Italy, C Mediterranean Sea 37°34′N 14°55′E
32 J7 **Pateros** Washington, NW USA 48°01′N 119°55′W
18 J14 **Paterson** New Jersey, NE USA 40°55′N 74°12′W
32 J10 **Paterson** Washington, NW USA 45°56′N 119°37′W
185 C25 **Paterson Inlet** *inlet* Stewart Island, New Zealand
98 N6 **Paterswolde** Drenthe, NE Netherlands 53°07′N 06°32′E
152 H7 **Pathānkot** Himāchal Pradesh, N India 32°16′N 75°43′E
166 K8 **Pathein** *var.* Bassein. Ayeyarwady, SW Myanmar (Burma) 16°46′N 94°45′E
33 W15 **Pathfinder Reservoir** ▣ Wyoming, C USA
167 O11 **Pathum Thani** *var.* Patumdhani, Prathum Thani. Pathum Thani, C Thailand 14°03′N 100°29′E
54 C12 **Patía** *var.* El Bordo. Cauca, SW Colombia 02°07′N 76°57′W
152 I9 **Patiāla** *var.* Puttiala. Punjab, NW India 30°21′N 76°27′E
54 B12 **Patía, Río** ≈ SW Colombia
188 D15 **Pati Point** *headland* NE Guam 13°36′N 144°39′E
Pātiriagele *see* Pătâriagele
56 C13 **Pativilca** Lima, W Peru 10°44′S 77°45′W
166 M1 **Patkai Bum** *var.* Patkai Range. ▲▲ Myanmar (Burma)/India
Patkai Range *see* Patkai Bum
115 L20 **Pátmos** Pátmos, Dodekánisa, Greece, Aegean Sea 37°18′N 26°32′E
115 L20 **Pátmos** *island* Dodekánisa, Greece, Aegean Sea
153 P13 **Patna** *var.* Azimabad. *state capital* Bihār, N India 25°36′N 85°11′E
154 M12 **Patnāgarh** Orissa, E India 20°42′N 83°12′E
171 O5 **Patnongon** Panay Island, C Philippines 10°56′N 122°03′E
137 S13 **Patnos** Ağri, E Turkey 39°14′N 42°52′E
60 H12 **Pato Branco** Paraná, S Brazil 26°20′S 52°40′W
31 O16 **Patoka Lake** ◎ Indiana, N USA
92 L9 **Patoniva** *Lapp.* Buoddobohki. Lappi, N Finland 69°44′N 27°01′E
113 K21 **Patos** *var.* Patosi. Fier, SW Albania 40°40′N 19°37′E
Patos *see* Patos de Minas
59 K19 **Patos de Minas** *var.* Patos. Minas Gerais, NE Brazil 18°35′S 46°32′W
Patosi *see* Patos
61 I17 **Patos, Lagoa dos** *lagoon* S Brazil
62 J9 **Patquía** La Rioja, C Argentina 30°02′S 66°54′W
115 E19 **Pátra** *Eng.* Patras; *prev.* Pátrai. Dytikí Elláda, S Greece 38°14′N 21°45′E
115 D18 **Patraïkós Kólpos** *gulf* S Greece
Pátrai/Patras *see* Pátra
92 G2 **Patreksfjördhur** Vestfirdhir, W Iceland 65°33′N 23°54′W
24 M7 **Patricia** Texas, SW USA 32°34′N 102°00′W
63 F21 **Patricio Lynch, Isla** *island* S Chile
Patta *see* Pata
Patta Island *see* Pate Island
167 O16 **Pattani** *var.* Patani. Pattani, SW Thailand 06°50′N 101°20′E
167 P12 **Pattaya** Chon Buri, S Thailand 12°57′N 100°53′E
19 S4 **Patten** Maine, NE USA 45°58′N 68°27′W
35 O9 **Patterson** California, W USA 37°27′N 121°07′W
22 J10 **Patterson** Louisiana, S USA 29°41′N 91°18′W
35 R7 **Patterson, Mount** ▲ California, W USA 38°27′N 119°16′W
31 P4 **Patterson, Point** *headland* Michigan, N USA 45°58′N 85°39′W
107 L23 **Patti** Sicilia, Italy, C Mediterranean Sea 38°08′N 14°58′E
107 L23 **Patti, Golfo di** *gulf* Sicilia, Italy
93 L14 **Pattijoki** Oulu, W Finland 64°41′N 24°40′E
193 Q4 **Patton Escarpment** *undersea feature* E Pacific Ocean
27 S2 **Pattonsburg** Missouri, C USA 40°03′N 94°08′W
0 D6 **Patton Seamount** *undersea feature* NE Pacific Ocean 54°40′N 150°30′W
10 J12 **Pattullo, Mount** ▲ British Columbia, W Canada 56°18′N 129°43′W
153 U16 **Patuakhali** *var.* Patukhali. Barisal, S Bangladesh 22°20′N 90°20′E
42 M5 **Patuca, Río** ≈ E Honduras
Patukhali *see* Patuakhali
Patumdhani *see* Pathum Thani
40 M14 **Pátzcuaro** Michoacán, SW Mexico 19°30′N 101°38′W
42 C6 **Patzicía** Chimaltenango, S Guatemala 14°38′N 90°52′W
102 K16 **Pau** Pyrénées-Atlantiques, SW France 43°18′N 00°22′W
102 J12 **Pauillac** Gironde, SW France 45°12′N 00°44′W
166 L5 **Pauk** Magway, W Myanmar (Burma) 21°25′N 94°30′E
8 I6 **Paulatuk** Northwest Territories, NW Canada 69°23′N 124°W
42 K5 **Paulayá, Río** ≈ NE Honduras
22 M6 **Paulding** Mississippi, S USA 32°01′N 89°01′W
31 Q12 **Paulding** Ohio, N USA 41°08′N 84°34′W
29 S12 **Paullina** Iowa, C USA 42°58′N 95°41′W
59 P15 **Paulo Afonso** Bahia, E Brazil 09°21′S 38°14′W
38 M16 **Pauloff Harbor** *var.* Pavlor Harbour. Sanak Island, Alaska, USA 54°26′N 162°43′W
27 N12 **Pauls Valley** Oklahoma, C USA 34°46′N 97°14′W
166 L7 **Paungde** Bago, C Myanmar (Burma) 18°30′N 95°30′E
Pauni *see* Paoni
152 K9 **Pauri** Uttaranchal, N India 30°08′N 78°48′E
Pautalia *see* Kyustendil
142 J5 **Pāveh** Kermānshāhān, NW Iran 35°02′N 46°15′E
114 J9 **Pavel Banya** Stara Zagora, C Bulgaria 42°35′N 25°19′E
126 L5 **Pavelets** Ryazanskaya Oblast', W Russian Federation 53°47′N 39°22′E
106 D8 **Pavia** *anc.* Ticinum. Lombardia, N Italy 45°10′N 09°10′E
118 C9 **Pāvilosta** W Latvia 56°52′N 21°12′E
125 P14 **Pavino** Kostromskaya Oblast', NW Russian Federation 59°10′N 46°09′E
114 J8 **Pavlikeni** Veliko Tŭrnovo, N Bulgaria 43°14′N 25°20′E
145 T8 **Pavlodar** Pavlodar, NE Kazakhstan 52°21′N 76°59′E
145 S9 **Pavlodar** *off.* Pavlodarskaya Oblast', *Kaz.* Pavlodar Oblysy. ◈ *province* NE Kazakhstan
Pavlodar Oblysy/Pavlodarskaya Oblast' *see* Pavlodar
Pavlograd *see* Pavlohrad
117 U7 **Pavlohrad** *Rus.* Pavlograd. Dnipropetrovs'ka Oblast', E Ukraine 48°32′N 35°50′E
Pavlor Harbour *see* Pauloff Harbor
145 R9 **Pavlovka** Akmola, C Kazakhstan 51°22′N 72°35′E
127 V4 **Pavlovka** Respublika Bashkortostan, W Russian Federation 55°28′N 56°36′E
127 Q7 **Pavlovka** Ul'yanovskaya Oblast', W Russian Federation 52°40′N 47°08′E
127 N3 **Pavlovo** Nizhegorodskaya Oblast', W Russian Federation 55°59′N 43°03′E
126 L9 **Pavlovsk** Voronezhskaya Oblast', W Russian Federation 50°26′N 40°08′E
126 L13 **Pavlovskaya** Krasnodarskiy Kray, SW Russian Federation 46°06′N 39°52′E
117 S7 **Pavlysh** Kirovohrads'ka Oblast', C Ukraine 48°54′N 33°20′E

◆ Country ● Country Capital ◇ Dependent Territory ○ Dependent Territory Capital ◈ Administrative Regions ✈ International Airport ▲ Mountain ▲▲ Mountain Range ⛰ Volcano ≈ River ◎ Lake ▣ Reservoir

106 F10 **Pavullo nel Frignano** Emilia-Romagna, C Italy 44°19′N 10°52′E
27 P8 **Pawhuska** Oklahoma, C USA 36°42′N 96°21′W
21 U13 **Pawleys Island** South Carolina, SE USA 33°27′N 79°07′W
30 K14 **Pawnee** Illinois, N USA 39°35′N 89°34′W
27 O9 **Pawnee** Oklahoma, C USA 36°21′N 96°50′W
37 U2 **Pawnee Buttes** ▲ Colorado, C USA 40°49′N 103°58′W
29 S17 **Pawnee City** Nebraska, C USA 40°06′N 96°09′W
26 K5 **Pawnee River** ≈ Kansas, C USA
167 N6 **Pawn, Nam** ≈ C Myanmar (Burma)
31 O10 **Paw Paw** Michigan, N USA 42°12′N 86°09′W
31 O10 **Paw Paw Lake** Michigan, N USA 42°12′N 86°16′W
19 O12 **Pawtucket** Rhode Island, NE USA 41°52′N 71°22′W
Pax Augusta see Badajoz
115 I25 **Paximádia** island SE Greece
Pax Julia see Beja
115 B16 **Paxoí** island Iónia Nisiá, Greece, C Mediterranean Sea
39 S10 **Paxson** Alaska, USA 62°58′N 145°27′W
147 O11 **Paxtakor** Jizzax Viloyati, C Uzbekistan 40°21′N 67°54′E
30 M13 **Paxton** Illinois, N USA 40°27′N 88°06′W
124 J11 **Pay** Respublika Kareliya, NW Russian Federation 61°10′N 34°24′E
166 M8 **Payagyi** Bago, SW Myanmar (Burma) 17°28′N 96°32′E
108 C9 **Payerne** Ger. Peterlingen. Vaud, W Switzerland 46°49′N 06°57′E
32 M13 **Payette** Idaho, NW USA 44°04′N 116°55′W
32 M13 **Payette River** ≈ Idaho, NW USA
125 V2 **Pay-Khoy, Khrebet** ▲▲ NW Russian Federation
Payne see Kangirsuk
12 K4 **Payne, Lac** ◎ Québec, NE Canada
29 T8 **Paynesville** Minnesota, N USA 45°22′N 94°42′W
169 S8 **Payong, Tanjung** cape East Malaysia
Payo Obispo see Chetumal
61 D18 **Paysandú** Paysandú, W Uruguay 32°21′S 58°05′W
61 D17 **Paysandú** ◆ department W Uruguay
102 I7 **Pays de la Loire** ◆ region NW France
36 L12 **Payson** Arizona, SW USA 34°13′N 111°19′W
36 L4 **Payson** Utah, W USA 40°02′N 111°43′W
125 W4 **Payyer, Gora** ▲ NW Russian Federation 66°49′N 64°33′E
Payzawat see Jiashi
137 Q11 **Pazar** Rize, NE Turkey 41°10′N 40°53′E
136 F10 **Pazarbaşı Burnu** headland NW Turkey 41°12′N 30°18′E
136 M16 **Pazarcık** Kahramanmaraş, S Turkey 37°31′N 37°19′E
114 I10 **Pazardzhik** prev. Tatar Pazardzhik. Pazardzhik, SW Bulgaria 42°11′N 24°21′E
64 H11 **Pazardzhik** ◆ province C Bulgaria
54 H9 **Paz de Ariporo** Casanare, E Colombia 05°54′N 71°52′W
112 A10 **Pazin** Ger. Mitterburg, It. Pisino. Istra, NW Croatia 45°14′N 13°56′E
42 D7 **Paz, Río** ≈ El Salvador/Guatemala
113 O18 **Pčinja** ≈ N Macedonia
193 V15 **Pea** Tongatapu, S Tonga 21°10′S 175°14′W
27 O6 **Peabody** Kansas, C USA 38°10′N 97°06′W
11 O12 **Peace** ≈ Alberta/British Columbia, W Canada
Peace Garden State see North Dakota
11 Q10 **Peace Point** Alberta, C Canada 59°11′N 112°12′W
11 O12 **Peace River** Alberta, W Canada 56°15′N 117°18′W
23 W13 **Peace River** ≈ Florida, SE USA
11 N17 **Peachland** British Columbia, SW Canada 49°49′N 119°48′W
36 I10 **Peach Springs** Arizona, SW USA 35°33′N 113°27′W
Peach State see Georgia
23 S4 **Peachtree City** Georgia, SE USA 33°24′N 84°36′W
189 Y13 **Peacock Point** point SE Wake Island
97 M18 **Peak District** physical region C England, United Kingdom
183 Q7 **Peak Hill** New South Wales, SE Australia 32°39′S 148°12′E
65 G15 **Peak, The** ▲ C Ascension Island
105 O13 **Peal de Becerro** Andalucía, S Spain 37°55′N 03°08′W
189 X11 **Peale Island** island N Wake Island
37 O6 **Peale, Mount** ▲ Utah, W USA 38°26′N 109°13′W
39 O4 **Peard Bay** bay Alaska, USA
23 Q7 **Pea River** ≈ Alabama/Florida, S USA
25 W11 **Pearland** Texas, SW USA 29°33′N 95°17′W
38 D9 **Pearl City** O'ahu, Hawaii, USA, C Pacific Ocean 21°24′N 157°58′W
38 D9 **Pearl Harbor** inlet O'ahu, Hawai'i, USA, C Pacific Ocean
Pearl Islands see Perlas, Archipiélago de las
Pearl Lagoon see Perlas, Laguna de
22 M5 **Pearl River** ≈ Louisiana/Mississippi, S USA
25 Q13 **Pearsall** Texas, SW USA 28°54′N 99°07′W
23 U7 **Pearson** Georgia, SE USA 31°18′N 82°51′W
25 P4 **Pease River** ≈ Texas, SW USA
12 F7 **Peawanuck** Ontario, C Canada 54°55′N 85°31′W
12 E8 **Peawanuk** ≈ Ontario, S Canada
83 P16 **Pebane** Zambézia, NE Mozambique 17°14′S 38°10′E
65 C23 **Pebble Island** island N Falkland Islands
65 C23 **Pebble Island Settlement** Pebble Island, N Falkland Islands 51°20′S 59°40′W
Peć see Pejë
25 R8 **Pecan Bayou** ≈ Texas, SW USA
22 H10 **Pecan Island** Louisiana, S USA 29°39′N 92°26′W
60 L12 **Peças, Ilha das** island S Brazil
30 L10 **Pecatonica River** ≈ Illinois/Wisconsin, N USA
108 G10 **Peccia** Ticino, S Switzerland 46°24′N 08°39′E
Pechenegi see Pechenihy
Pechenezhskoye Vodokhranilishche see Pechenizʹke Vodoskhovyshche
124 I2 **Pechenga** Fin. Petsamo. Murmanskaya Oblast', NW Russian Federation 69°34′N 31°14′E
117 V5 **Pechenihy** Rus. Pechenegi. Kharkivs'ka Oblast', E Ukraine 49°49′N 36°57′E
117 V5 **Pechenizʹke Vodoskhovyshche** Rus. Pechenezhskoye Vodokhranilishche. ⊠ E Ukraine
125 U7 **Pechora** Respublika Komi, NW Russian Federation 65°09′N 57°09′E
125 R6 **Pechora** ≈ NW Russian Federation
Pechora Bay see Pechorskaya Guba
Pechora Sea see Pechorskoye More
125 S3 **Pechorskaya Guba** Eng. Pechora Bay. bay NW Russian Federation
122 H7 **Pechorskoye More** Eng. Pechora Sea. sea NW Russian Federation
116 E11 **Pecica** Ger. Petschka, Hung. Ópécska. Arad, W Romania 46°09′N 21°06′E
24 K8 **Pecos** Texas, SW USA 31°25′N 103°30′W
25 N11 **Pecos River** ≈ New Mexico/Texas, SW USA
111 I25 **Pécs** Ger. Fünfkirchen, Lat. Sopianae. Baranya, SW Hungary 46°05′N 18°11′E
43 T17 **Pedasí** Los Santos, S Panama 07°36′N 80°04′W
Pedde see Pedja
183 O17 **Pedder, Lake** ◎ Tasmania, SE Australia
44 M10 **Pedernales** SW Dominican Republic 18°02′N 71°41′W
55 Q5 **Pedernales** Delta Amacuro, NE Venezuela 09°58′N 62°15′W
25 R10 **Pedernales River** ≈ Texas, SW USA
62 H6 **Pedernales, Salar de** salt lake N Chile
Pedhoulas see Pedoulás
55 X11 **Pédima** var. Malavate. SW French Guiana 03°15′N 54°08′W
182 F1 **Pedirka** South Australia 26°41′S 135°11′E
171 S11 **Pediwang** Pulau Halmahera, E Indonesia 01°29′N 127°57′E
118 I5 **Pedja** var. Pedja Jõgi, Ger. Pedde. ≈ E Estonia
Pedja Jõgi see Pedja
121 O3 **Pedoulás** var. Pedhoulas. W Cyprus 34°58′N 32°51′E
59 N18 **Pedra Azul** Minas Gerais, NE Brazil 16°02′S 41°17′W
104 I3 **Pedrafita, Porto de** var. Puerto de Piedrafita. pass NW Spain
76 E9 **Pedra Lume** Sal, NE Cape Verde 16°47′N 22°54′W
43 P16 **Pedregal** Chiriquí, W Panama 09°04′N 79°25′W
54 J4 **Pedregal** Falcón, N Venezuela 11°04′N 70°08′W
40 L9 **Pedriceña** Durango, C Mexico 25°08′N 103°46′W
60 L11 **Pedro Barros** São Paulo, S Brazil 24°12′S 47°22′W
39 Q13 **Pedro Bay** Alaska, USA 59°47′N 154°06′W
62 H4 **Pedro de Valdivia** var. Oficina Pedro de Valdivia. Antofagasta, N Chile 22°33′S 69°38′W
62 P4 **Pedro Juan Caballero** Amambay, E Paraguay 22°34′S 55°41′W
63 L15 **Pedro Luro** Buenos Aires, E Argentina 39°30′S 62°38′W
105 O10 **Pedro Muñoz** Castilla-La Mancha, C Spain 39°25′N 02°56′W
155 J22 **Pedro, Point** headland NW Sri Lanka 09°54′N 80°08′E
182 K9 **Peebinga** South Australia 34°56′S 140°56′E
96 J13 **Peebles** SE Scotland, United Kingdom 55°40′N 03°15′W
31 S15 **Peebles** Ohio, N USA 38°57′N 83°23′W
96 J12 **Peebles** cultural region SE Scotland, United Kingdom
18 K13 **Peekskill** New York, NE USA 41°17′N 73°54′W
97 I16 **Peel** W Isle of Man 54°13′N 04°04′W
8 G7 **Peel** ≈ Northwest Territories/Yukon Territory, NW Canada
8 K5 **Peel Point** headland Victoria Island, Northwest Territories, NW Canada 73°22′N 114°33′W
8 M5 **Peel Sound** passage Nunavut, N Canada
100 N9 **Peene** ≈ NE Germany
99 K17 **Peer** Limburg, NE Belgium 51°08′N 05°29′E
14 H14 **Pefferlaw** Ontario, S Canada 44°18′N 79°11′W
185 I18 **Pegasus Bay** bay South Island, New Zealand
121 O3 **Pégeia** var. Peyia. SW Cyprus 34°52′N 32°24′E
109 V7 **Peggau** Steiermark, SE Austria 47°10′N 15°20′E
101 L19 **Pegnitz** Bayern, SE Germany 49°45′N 11°33′E
101 L19 **Pegnitz** ≈ SE Germany
105 T11 **Pego** Valenciana, E Spain 38°51′N 00°08′W
Pegu see Bago
Pegu see Bago
189 N13 **Pehleng** Pohnpei, E Micronesia
114 M12 **Pehlivanköy** Kırklareli, NW Turkey 41°21′N 26°55′E
77 R14 **Péhonko** C Benin 10°14′N 01°57′E
61 B21 **Pehuajó** Buenos Aires, E Argentina 35°48′S 61°53′W
Pei-ching see Beijing/Beijing Shi
100 J13 **Peine** Niedersachsen, C Germany 52°19′N 10°14′E
Pei-p'ing see Beijing/Beijing Shi
Peipsi Järv/Peipus-See see Peipus, Lake
118 J5 **Peipus, Lake** Est. Peipsi Järv, Ger. Peipus-See, Rus. Chudskoye Ozero. ◎ Estonia/Russian Federation
115 H19 **Peiraías** prev. Piraiévs, Eng. Piraeus. Attikí, C Greece 37°57′N 23°42′E
Peisern see Pyzdry
60 I8 **Peixe, Rio do** ≈ S Brazil
59 I16 **Peixoto de Azevedo** Mato Grosso, W Brazil 10°18′S 55°03′W
168 O11 **Pejantan, Pulau** island W Indonesia
113 L16 **Pejë** Serb. Peć. W Kosovo 42°40′N 20°19′E
112 N11 **Pek** ≈ E Serbia
Pèk see Phônsaven
169 Q16 **Pekalongan** Jawa, C Indonesia 06°54′S 109°37′E
168 K11 **Pekanbaru** var. Pakanbaru. Sumatera, W Indonesia 0°31′N 101°27′E
30 L12 **Pekin** Illinois, N USA 40°34′N 89°38′W
Peking see Beijing/Beijing Shi
Pelabohan Kelang/Pelabuhan Kelang see Pelabuhan Klang
168 J9 **Pelabuhan Klang** var. Kuala Pelabohan Kelang, Pelabohan Kelang, Pelabuhan Kelang, Port Klang, Port Swettenham. Selangor, Peninsular Malaysia 02°57′N 101°24′E
120 L11 **Pelagie, Isole** island group SW Italy
Pelagosa see Palagruža
22 L5 **Pelahatchie** Mississippi, S USA 32°19′N 89°48′W
169 T14 **Pelaihari** var. Pleihari. Borneo, C Indonesia 03°48′S 114°45′E
103 U14 **Pelat, Mont** ▲ SE France 44°16′N 06°46′E
116 F12 **Peleaga, Vârful** prev. Vîrful Peleaga. ▲ W Romania 45°23′N 22°52′E
Peleaga, Vîrful see Peleaga, Vârful
123 O11 **Peleduy** Respublika Sakha (Yakutiya), NE Russian Federation 59°39′N 112°36′E
14 C18 **Pelee Island** island Ontario, S Canada
45 Q11 **Pelée, Montagne** ▲ N Martinique 14°47′N 61°10′W
14 D18 **Pelee, Point** headland Ontario, S Canada 41°56′N 82°30′W
171 P12 **Pelei** Pulau Peleng, N Indonesia 01°26′S 123°27′E
Peleliu see Beliliou
171 P12 **Peleng, Pulau** island Kepulauan Banggai, N Indonesia
23 T7 **Pelham** Georgia, SE USA 31°07′N 84°09′W
111 E18 **Pelhřimov** Ger. Pilgram. Vysočina, C Czech Republic 49°26′N 15°14′E
39 W13 **Pelican** Chichagof Island, Alaska, USA 57°52′N 136°05′W
191 Z3 **Pelican Lagoon** ◎ Kiritimati, E Kiribati
29 U6 **Pelican Lake** ◎ Minnesota, N USA
29 V3 **Pelican Lake** ◎ Minnesota, N USA
30 L5 **Pelican Lake** ◎ Wisconsin, N USA
44 G1 **Pelican Point** Grand Bahama Island, N Bahamas 26°39′N 78°09′W
83 B19 **Pelican Point** headland W Namibia 22°55′S 14°25′E
29 S6 **Pelican Rapids** Minnesota, N USA 46°34′N 96°04′W
Pelican State see Louisiana
11 U13 **Pelikan Narrows** Saskatchewan, C Canada 55°11′N 102°51′W
115 L18 **Pelinaío** ▲ Chíos, E Greece 38°31′N 26°01′E
Pelinnaeum see Pelinnaío
115 E16 **Pelinnaío** anc. Pelinnaeum. ruins Thessalía, C Greece
113 N20 **Pelister** ▲ SW FYR Macedonia 41°00′N 21°12′E
113 G15 **Pelješac** peninsula S Croatia
92 M12 **Pelkosenniemi** Lappi, NE Finland 67°06′N 27°30′E
29 W15 **Pella** Iowa, C USA 41°24′N 92°55′W
114 F13 **Pélla** site of ancient city Kentrikí Makedonía, N Greece
23 P3 **Pell City** Alabama, S USA 33°35′N 86°17′W
61 A22 **Pellegrini** Buenos Aires, E Argentina 36°16′S 63°07′W
92 K12 **Pello** Lappi, NW Finland 66°47′N 24°E
100 G7 **Pellworm** island N Germany
10 H6 **Pelly** ≈ Yukon Territory, NW Canada
Pelly Bay see Kugaaruk
10 I8 **Pelly Mountains** ▲▲ Yukon Territory, W Canada
Pélmonostor see Beli Manastir
37 P13 **Pelona Mountain** ▲ New Mexico, SW USA 33°40′N 108°06′W
Peloponnese/Peloponnesus see Pelopónnisos
115 E20 **Pelopónnisos** Eng. Peloponnese. ◆ region S Greece
115 E20 **Pelopónnisos** var. Morea, Eng. Peloponnese; anc. Peloponnesus. peninsula S Greece
107 L23 **Peloritani, Monti** anc. Pelorus and Neptunius. ▲ Sicilia, Italy, C Mediterranean Sea
107 M22 **Peloro, Capo** var. Punta del Faro. headland S Italy 38°15′N 15°39′E
Pelorus and Neptunius see Peloritani, Monti
61 H17 **Pelotas** Rio Grande do Sul, S Brazil 31°45′S 52°20′W
61 I14 **Pelotas, Rio** ≈ S Brazil
92 K10 **Peltovuoma** Lapp. Bealdovuopmi. Lappi, N Finland 68°23′N 24°12′E
19 R4 **Pemadumcook Lake** ◎ Maine, NE USA
169 Q16 **Pemalang** Jawa, C Indonesia 06°53′S 109°07′E
169 P10 **Pemangkat** var. Pamangkat. Borneo, C Indonesia 01°11′N 109°00′E
Pemar see Paimio
168 I9 **Pematangsiantar** Sumatera, W Indonesia 02°59′N 99°01′E
83 Q14 **Pemba** prev. Port Amelia, Porto Amélia. Cabo Delgado, NE Mozambique 13°S 40°35′E
81 J22 **Pemba** ◆ region E Tanzania
81 K21 **Pemba** island E Tanzania
83 Q14 **Pemba, Baia de** inlet NE Mozambique
81 J21 **Pemba Channel** channel E Tanzania
180 J14 **Pemberton** Western Australia 34°27′S 116°09′E
10 M16 **Pemberton** British Columbia, SW Canada 50°19′N 122°49′W
29 Q2 **Pembina** North Dakota, N USA 48°58′N 97°14′W
11 P15 **Pembina** ≈ Alberta, SW Canada
29 Q2 **Pembina** ≈ Canada/USA
171 X16 **Pembre** Papua, E Indonesia 07°49′S 138°01′E
14 K12 **Pembroke** Ontario, SE Canada 45°49′N 77°08′W
97 H21 **Pembroke** SW Wales, United Kingdom 51°41′N 04°55′W
23 W6 **Pembroke** Georgia, SE USA 32°09′N 81°35′W
21 U11 **Pembroke** North Carolina, SE USA 34°40′N 79°12′W
21 R7 **Pembroke** Virginia, NE USA 37°19′N 80°38′W
97 H21 **Pembroke** cultural region SW Wales, United Kingdom
Pembuang, Sungai see Seruyan, Sungai
43 S15 **Peña Blanca, Cerro** ▲ C Panama 08°39′N 80°39′W
104 K8 **Peña de Francia, Sierra de la** ▲ W Spain
104 G6 **Penafiel** var. Peñafiel. Porto, N Portugal 41°12′N 08°17′W
105 N6 **Peñafiel** Castilla y León, N Spain 41°36′N 04°07′W
Peñafiel see Penafiel
Peñagolosa see Penyagolosa
105 N7 **Peñalara, Pico de** ▲ C Spain 40°52′N 03°55′W
171 X16 **Penambo, Banjaran** var. Banjaran Tama Abu, Penambo Range. ▲▲ Indonesia/Malaysia
Penambo Range see Penambo, Banjaran
41 O10 **Peña Nevada, Cerro** ▲ C Mexico 23°46′N 99°52′W
Penang see Pinang, Pulau, Peninsular Malaysia
Penang see Pinang
Penang see George Town
60 J8 **Penápolis** São Paulo, S Brazil 21°23′S 50°02′W
104 L7 **Peñaranda de Bracamonte** Castilla y León, N Spain 40°54′N 05°13′W
105 S8 **Peñarroya** ▲ E Spain 40°24′N 00°42′W
104 L12 **Peñarroya-Pueblonuevo** Andalucía, S Spain 38°21′N 05°18′W
97 K22 **Penarth** S Wales, United Kingdom 51°27′N 03°11′W
104 K1 **Peñas, Cabo de** headland N Spain 43°39′N 05°52′W
63 F20 **Penas, Golfo de** gulf S Chile
Pen-ch'i see Benxi
79 H14 **Pendé** var. Logone Oriental. ≈ Central African Republic/Chad
76 I14 **Pendembu** E Sierra Leone 09°06′N 12°12′W
29 R13 **Pender** Nebraska, C USA 42°06′N 96°42′W
Penderma see Bandırma
32 K11 **Pendleton** Oregon, NW USA 45°40′N 118°47′W
32 M7 **Pend Oreille, Lake** ◎ Idaho, NW USA
32 M7 **Pend Oreille River** ≈ Idaho/Washington, NW USA
Pendzhikent see Panjakent
Peneius see Pineiós
104 G8 **Penela** Coimbra, N Portugal 40°02′N 08°23′W
14 G13 **Penetanguishene** Ontario, S Canada 44°45′N 79°55′W
151 H15 **Penganga** ≈ C India
P'engchia Yu see Pengjia Yu
79 M21 **Penge** Kasai-Oriental, C Dem. Rep. Congo 05°29′S 24°38′E
Penghu Archipelago/P'enghu Ch'üntao/Penghu Islands see Penghu Liedao
161 R14 **Penghu Liedao** var. P'enghu Ch'üntao, Penghu Islands, P'enghu Liehtao, Eng. Penghu Archipelago, Pescadores, Jap. Hoko-guntō, Hoko-shotō. island group W Taiwan
P'enghu Liehtao see Penghu Liedao
161 S14 **Penghu Shuidao** var. Pescadores Channel, P'enghu Shuitao. channel W Taiwan
P'enghu Shuitao see Penghu Shuidao
161 T12 **Pengjia Yu** prev. P'engchia Yu. island N Taiwan
161 R4 **Penglai** var. Dengzhou. Shandong, E China 37°50′N 120°45′E
Peng-pu see Bengbu
Penhsihu see Benxi
Penibético, Sistema see Béticos, Sistemas
104 F10 **Peniche** Leiria, W Portugal 39°21′N 09°23′W
169 U17 **Penida, Nusa** island S Indonesia
Peninsular State see Florida
105 T8 **Peñíscola** var. Peñiscola. Valenciana, E Spain 40°22′N 00°24′E
40 M13 **Pénjamo** Guanajuato, C Mexico 20°26′N 101°44′W
Penki see Benxi
102 F7 **Penmarch, Pointe de** headland NW France 47°46′N 04°34′W
107 L15 **Penna, Punta della** headland C Italy 42°10′N 14°43′E
107 K14 **Penne** Abruzzo, C Italy 42°28′N 13°57′E
Penner see Penneru
155 J18 **Penneru** var. Penner. ≈ C India
182 I10 **Penneshaw** South Australia 35°45′S 137°57′E
18 C14 **Penn Hills** Pennsylvania, NE USA 40°28′N 79°53′W
Penninae, Alpes/Pennine, Alpi see Pennine Alps
108 D11 **Pennine Alps** Fr. Alpes Pennines, It. Alpi Pennine, Lat. Alpes Penninae. ▲▲ Italy/Switzerland
Pennine Chain see Pennines
97 L15 **Pennines** var. Pennine Chain. ▲▲ N England, United Kingdom
Pennines, Alpes see Pennine Alps
21 O8 **Pennington Gap** Virginia, NE USA 36°45′N 83°01′W
18 I16 **Penns Grove** New Jersey, NE USA 39°42′N 75°27′W
18 I16 **Pennsville** New Jersey, NE USA 39°37′N 75°29′W
18 E14 **Pennsylvania** off. Commonwealth of Pennsylvania, also known as Keystone State. ◆ state NE USA
18 G10 **Penn Yan** New York, NE USA 42°39′N 77°02′W
124 H16 **Peno** Tverskaya Oblast', W Russian Federation 56°55′N 32°44′E
19 R7 **Penobscot Bay** bay Maine, NE USA
19 S5 **Penobscot River** ≈ Maine, NE USA
182 K12 **Penola** South Australia 37°24′S 140°50′E
40 K9 **Peñón Blanco** Durango, C Mexico 25°12′N 100°50′W
182 E7 **Penong** South Australia 31°57′S 133°01′E
43 S16 **Penonomé** Coclé, C Panama 08°29′N 80°22′W
190 L13 **Penrhyn** atoll N Cook Islands
192 M9 **Penrhyn Basin** undersea feature C Pacific Ocean
183 S9 **Penrith** New South Wales, SE Australia 33°45′S 150°48′E
97 K15 **Penrith** NW England, United Kingdom 54°40′N 02°44′W
23 O9 **Pensacola** Florida, SE USA 30°25′N 87°13′W
23 O9 **Pensacola Bay** bay Florida, SE USA
195 N7 **Pensacola Mountains** ▲▲ Antarctica
182 L12 **Penshurst** Victoria, SE Australia 37°54′S 142°19′E
187 R13 **Pentecost** Fr. Pentecôte. island C Vanuatu
15 V4 **Pentecôte** ≈ Québec, SE Canada
Pentecôte see Pentecost
15 V4 **Pentecôte, Lac** ◎ Québec, SE Canada
8 H15 **Penticton** British Columbia, SW Canada 49°29′N 119°38′W
96 J6 **Pentland Firth** strait N Scotland, United Kingdom
96 J12 **Pentland Hills** hill range S Scotland, United Kingdom
171 Q12 **Penu** Pulau Taliabu, E Indonesia 01°43′S 125°09′E
155 H18 **Penukonda** Andhra Pradesh, E India 14°04′N 77°38′E
166 L7 **Penwegon** Bago, C Myanmar (Burma) 18°14′N 96°34′E
24 M8 **Penwell** Texas, SW USA 31°45′N 102°32′W
105 S8 **Penyagolosa** var. Peñagolosa. ▲ E Spain 40°10′N 00°15′W
97 J21 **Pen y Fan** ▲ SE Wales, United Kingdom 51°52′N 03°25′W
97 L16 **Pen-y-ghent** ▲ N England, United Kingdom 54°11′N 02°15′W
127 O6 **Penza** Penzenskaya Oblast', W Russian Federation 53°11′N 45°E
97 G25 **Penzance** SW England, United Kingdom 50°08′N 05°33′W
127 N6 **Penzenskaya Oblast'** ◆ province W Russian Federation
123 U7 **Penzhina** ≈ E Russian Federation
123 U9 **Penzhinskaya Guba** bay E Russian Federation
Penzig see Pieńsk
36 K13 **Peoria** Arizona, SW USA 33°34′N 112°14′W
30 L12 **Peoria** Illinois, N USA 40°42′N 89°35′W
30 L12 **Peoria Heights** Illinois, N USA 40°45′N 89°34′W
31 N11 **Peotone** Illinois, N USA 41°19′N 87°47′W
18 J11 **Pepacton Reservoir** ⊠ New York, NE USA
76 I15 **Pepel** W Sierra Leone 08°39′N 13°04′W
30 I6 **Pepin, Lake** ⊠ Minnesota/Wisconsin, N USA
99 L20 **Pepinster** Liège, E Belgium 50°34′N 05°49′E
113 L20 **Peqin** var. Peqini. Elbasan, C Albania 41°03′N 19°46′E
Peqini see Peqin
40 D7 **Pequeña, Punta** headland NW Mexico 26°13′N 112°34′W
168 J8 **Perak** ◆ state Peninsular Malaysia
105 R7 **Perales del Alfambra** Aragón, NE Spain 40°38′N 01°00′W
115 C15 **Pérama** var. Perama. Ípeiros, W Greece 39°42′N 20°51′E
Perama see Pérama
92 M13 **Perä-Posio** Lappi, NE Finland 66°10′N 27°56′E
15 Z6 **Percé** Québec, SE Canada 48°32′N 64°14′W
15 Z6 **Percé, Rocher** island Québec, S Canada
102 L5 **Perche, Collines de** ▲ N France
109 X4 **Perchtoldsdorf** Niederösterreich, NE Austria 48°06′N 16°16′E
180 L6 **Percival Lakes** lakes Western Australia
105 T3 **Perdido, Monte** ▲ NE Spain 42°41′N 00°01′E
23 O8 **Perdido River** ≈ Alabama/Florida, S USA
Perece Vela Basin see West Mariana Basin
116 G7 **Perechyn** Zakarpats'ka Oblast', W Ukraine 48°45′N 22°28′E
54 E10 **Pereira** Risaralda, W Colombia 04°47′N 75°46′W
60 I7 **Pereira Barreto** São Paulo, S Brazil 20°37′S 51°07′W
59 G15 **Pereirinha** Pará, N Brazil 08°18′S 57°30′W
127 N10 **Perelazovskiy** Volgogradskaya Oblast', SW Russian Federation 49°10′N 42°30′E
127 S7 **Perelyub** Saratovskaya Oblast', W Russian Federation 51°52′N 50°19′E
31 P7 **Pere Marquette River** ≈ Michigan, N USA
Peremyshl see Przemyśl
116 I5 **Peremyshlyany** L'vivs'ka Oblast', W Ukraine 49°42′N 24°33′E
Pereshchepino see Pereshchepyne
116 L9 **Pereshchepyne** Rus. Pereshchepino. Dnipropetrovs'ka Oblast', E Ukraine 48°59′N 35°22′E
124 L16 **Pereslavl'-Zalesskiy** Yaroslavskaya Oblast', W Russian Federation 56°42′N 38°45′E
117 Y7 **Pereval's'k** Luhans'ka Oblast', E Ukraine 48°28′N 38°54′E
127 U7 **Perevolotskiy** Orenburgskaya Oblast', W Russian Federation 51°54′N 54°05′E
Pereyaslav-Khmel'nitskiy see Pereyaslav-Khmel'nyts'kyy
117 Q5 **Pereyaslav-Khmel'nyts'kyy** Rus. Pereyaslav-Khmel'nitskiy. Kyyivs'ka Oblast', N Ukraine 50°05′N 31°28′E
109 U4 **Perg** Oberösterreich, N Austria 48°15′N 14°38′E
61 B19 **Pergamino** Buenos Aires, E Argentina 33°56′S 60°38′W
106 G6 **Pergine Valsugana** Ger. Persen. Trentino-Alto Adige, N Italy 46°04′N 11°13′E
29 S6 **Perham** Minnesota, N USA 46°35′N 95°34′W
93 L16 **Perho** Länsi-Suomi, W Finland 63°15′N 24°25′E
116 E11 **Periam** Ger. Perjamosch, Hung. Perjámos. Timiș, W Romania 46°02′N 20°54′E
15 Q6 **Péribonca** ≈ Québec, SE Canada
12 L11 **Péribonca, Lac** ◎ Québec, SE Canada
15 Q6 **Péribonca, Petite Rivière** ≈ Québec, SE Canada
15 Q7 **Péribonka** Québec, SE Canada 48°45′N 72°01′W
40 I9 **Pericos** Sinaloa, C Mexico 25°03′N 107°42′W
169 Q10 **Perigi** Borneo, C Indonesia
102 L12 **Périgueux** anc. Vesuna. Dordogne, SW France 45°12′N 00°41′E
54 G5 **Perijá, Serranía de** ▲▲ Columbia/Venezuela
115 H17 **Peristéra** island Vóreies Sporádes, Greece, Aegean Sea
63 H20 **Perito Moreno** Santa Cruz, S Argentina 46°35′S 71°W
155 G22 **Periyāl** var. Periyār. ≈ SW India
Periyār see Periyāl
155 G23 **Periyār Lake** ◎ S India
Perjámos/Perjamosch see Periam
27 O9 **Perkins** Oklahoma, C USA 35°58′N 97°01′W
116 L7 **Perkivtsi** Chernivets'ka Oblast', W Ukraine 48°28′N 26°48′E
43 U15 **Perlas, Archipiélago de las** Eng. Pearl Islands. island group SE Panama
43 O10 **Perlas, Cayos de** reef SE Nicaragua
43 N9 **Perlas, Laguna de** Eng. Pearl Lagoon. lagoon E Nicaragua
43 N10 **Perlas, Punta de** headland E Nicaragua 12°22′N 83°30′W
100 L11 **Perleberg** Brandenburg, N Germany 53°04′N 11°52′E
Perlepe see Prilep
168 I6 **Perlis** ◆ state Peninsular Malaysia
125 U14 **Perm'** prev. Molotov. Permskiy Kray, NW Russian Federation 58°01′N 56°10′E
113 M22 **Përmet** var. Përmeti, Prëmet. Gjirokastër, S Albania 40°12′N 20°24′E
Përmeti see Përmet
125 U15 **Permskiy Kray** ◆ province NW Russian Federation
59 P15 **Pernambuco** off. Estado de Pernambuco. ◆ state E Brazil
Pernambuco see Recife
Pernambuco Abyssal Plain see Pernambuco Plain
Pernambuco, Estado de see Pernambuco
47 Y6 **Pernambuco Plain** var. Pernambuco Abyssal Plain. undersea feature E Atlantic Ocean 07°30′S 27°00′W
65 K15 **Pernambuco Seamounts** undersea feature C Atlantic Ocean
182 H6 **Pernatty Lagoon** salt lake South Australia
Pernau see Pärnu
Pernauer Bucht see Pärnu Laht
Pērnava see Pärnu
114 G9 **Pernik** prev. Dimitrovo. Pernik, W Bulgaria 42°36′N 23°02′E
114 G10 **Pernik** ◆ province W Bulgaria
93 K20 **Perniö** Swe. Bjärnå. Länsi-Suomi, SW Finland 60°13′N 23°10′E
109 X5 **Pernitz** Niederösterreich, E Austria 47°54′N 15°58′E
Pernov see Pärnu
103 O3 **Péronne** Somme, N France 49°56′N 02°57′E
14 L8 **Péronne, Lac** ◎ Québec, SE Canada
106 A8 **Perosa Argentina** Piemonte, NE Italy 45°02′N 07°10′E
41 Q14 **Perote** Veracruz-Llave, E Mexico 19°32′N 97°16′W
Pérouse see Perugia
191 W15 **Pérouse, Bahía de la** bay Easter Island, Chile, E Pacific Ocean
Perovsk see Kyzylorda
103 O17 **Perpignan** Pyrénées-Orientales, S France 42°41′N 02°53′E
113 M20 **Përrenjas** var. Përrenjasi, Prenjas, Prenjasi. Elbasan, E Albania 41°04′N 20°34′E
Përrenjasi see Përrenjas
92 O2 **Perriertoppen** ▲ C Svalbard 79°10′N 17°01′E
25 S6 **Perrin** Texas, SW USA 32°59′N 98°03′W
23 Y16 **Perrine** Florida, SE USA 25°36′N 80°21′W
37 S12 **Perro, Laguna del** ◎ New Mexico, SW USA
102 G5 **Perros-Guirec** Côtes d'Armor, NW France 48°49′N 03°28′W
23 T9 **Perry** Florida, SE USA 30°07′N 83°34′W
23 T5 **Perry** Georgia, SE USA 32°27′N 83°43′W
29 U14 **Perry** Iowa, C USA 41°50′N 94°06′W
18 E10 **Perry** New York, NE USA 42°43′N 78°00′W
27 N9 **Perry** Oklahoma, C USA 36°17′N 97°18′W
27 Q3 **Perry Lake** ⊠ Kansas, C USA
31 R11 **Perrysburg** Ohio, N USA 41°33′N 83°37′W
25 O1 **Perryton** Texas, SW USA 36°23′N 100°48′W
39 O15 **Perryville** Alaska, USA 55°55′N 159°08′W
27 U11 **Perryville** Arkansas, C USA 35°00′N 92°48′W
27 Y6 **Perryville** Missouri, C USA 37°43′N 89°51′W
Persante see Parsęta
Persen see Pergine Valsugana
Pershay see Pyarshai
117 V7 **Pershotravens'k** Dnipropetrovs'ka Oblast', E Ukraine 48°19′N 36°22′E
Pershotravneve see Manhush
Persia see Iran
141 T5 **Persian Gulf** var. Gulf, The, Ar. Khalīj al 'Arabī, Per. Khalīj-e Fars. gulf SW Asia see also Persian Gulf
141 T5 **Persian Gulf** var. The Gulf, Ar. Khalīj al 'Arabī, Per. Khalīj-e Fars. Gulf SW Asia see also Gulf, The
Persis see Fārs
95 K22 **Perstorp** Skåne, S Sweden 56°08′N 13°23′E
137 O14 **Pertek** Tunceli, C Turkey 38°53′N 39°19′E
183 P16 **Perth** Tasmania, SE Australia 41°39′S 147°11′E
180 I13 **Perth** state capital Western Australia 31°58′S 115°49′E
14 L13 **Perth** Ontario, SE Canada 44°54′N 76°15′W
96 J11 **Perth** C Scotland, United Kingdom 56°24′N 03°28′W
96 J10 **Perth** cultural region C Scotland, United Kingdom
180 I12 **Perth** ✈ Western Australia 31°51′S 116°06′E
173 V10 **Perth Basin** undersea feature SE Indian Ocean 28°30′S 110°00′E
103 S15 **Pertuis** Vaucluse, SE France 43°42′N 05°30′E
103 Y16 **Pertusato, Capo** headland Corse, France, C Mediterranean Sea 41°22′N 09°10′E
30 L11 **Peru** Illinois, N USA 41°18′N 89°09′W
31 P12 **Peru** Indiana, N USA 40°45′N 86°04′W
57 E13 **Peru** off. Republic of Peru. ◆ republic W South America
Peru see Beru
193 T9 **Peru Basin** undersea feature E Pacific Ocean 15°00′S 85°00′W
193 U8 **Peru-Chile Trench** undersea feature E Pacific Ocean 20°00′S 73°00′W
112 F13 **Perućko Jezero** ◎ S Croatia
106 H13 **Perugia** Fr. Pérouse; anc. Perusia. Umbria, C Italy 43°06′N 12°24′E
Perugia, Lake of see Trasimeno, Lago
61 D15 **Perugorría** Corrientes, NE Argentina 29°21′S 58°35′W
60 M11 **Peruíbe** São Paulo, S Brazil 24°18′S 47°01′W
155 B21 **Perumalpār** reef India, N Indian Ocean
Peru, Republic of see Peru
Perusia see Perugia
99 D20 **Péruwelz** Hainaut, SW Belgium 50°30′N 03°35′E
137 R15 **Pervari** Siirt, SE Turkey 37°55′N 42°32′E
127 O4 **Pervomaysk** Nizhegorodskaya Oblast', W Russian Federation 54°52′N 43°49′E
117 X7 **Pervomays'k** Luhans'ka Oblast', E Ukraine 48°38′N 38°36′E
117 P8 **Pervomays'k** prev. Ol'viopol'. Mykolayivs'ka Oblast', S Ukraine 48°02′N 30°51′E
117 S12 **Pervomays'ke** Avtonomna Respublika Krym, S Ukraine 45°43′N 33°49′E
127 V7 **Pervomayskiy** Orenburgskaya Oblast', W Russian Federation 51°32′N 54°58′E
126 M6 **Pervomayskiy** Tambovskaya Oblast', W Russian Federation 53°15′N 40°20′E
117 V6 **Pervomays'kyy** Kharkivs'ka Oblast', E Ukraine 49°24′N 36°12′E
122 F10 **Pervoural'sk** Sverdlovskaya Oblast', C Russian Federation 56°58′N 59°50′E
123 V11 **Pervyy Kuril'skiy Proliv** strait E Russian Federation
99 I19 **Perwez** Walloon Brabant, C Belgium 50°39′N 04°49′E
106 I11 **Pesaro** anc. Pisaurum. Marche, C Italy 43°55′N 12°53′E
35 N9 **Pescadero** California, W USA 37°15′N 122°23′W
Pescadores see Penghu Liedao
Pescadores Channel see Penghu Shuidao
107 K14 **Pescara** anc. Aternum, Ostia Aterni. Abruzzo, C Italy 42°28′N 14°13′E
107 K15 **Pescara** ≈ C Italy
106 F11 **Pescia** Toscana, C Italy 43°54′N 10°41′E
108 C8 **Peseux** Neuchâtel, W Switzerland 46°59′N 06°53′E
125 P6 **Pësha** ≈ NW Russian Federation
149 T5 **Peshāwar** Khyber Pakhtunkhwa, N Pakistan 34°01′N 71°33′E
149 T6 **Peshāwar** ✈ Khyber Pakhtunkhwa, N Pakistan 34°01′N 71°40′E

113 M19 **Peshkopi** *var.* Peshkopia, Peshkopija. Dibër, NE Albania 41°40′N 20°25′E
Peshkopia/Peshkopija *see* Peshkopi
114 I11 **Peshtera** Pazardzhik, C Bulgaria 42°02′N 24°18′E
31 N6 **Peshtigo** Wisconsin, N USA 45°04′N 87°43′W
31 N6 **Peshtigo River** ≈ Wisconsin, N USA
Peski *see* Pyaski
125 S13 **Peskovka** Kirovskaya Oblast', NW Russian Federation 59°04′N 52°17′E
103 S8 **Pesmes** Haute-Saône, E France 47°17′N 05°33′E
104 H6 **Peso da Régua** *var.* Pêso da Regua. Vila Real, N Portugal 41°10′N 07°47′W
40 F5 **Pesqueira** Sonora, NW Mexico 29°22′N 110°58′W
102 J13 **Pessac** Gironde, SW France 44°46′N 00°42′W
111 J23 **Pest** *off.* Pest Megye. ⬖ *county* C Hungary
Pest Megye *see* Pest
124 J14 **Pestovo** Novgorodskaya Oblast', W Russian Federation 58°37′N 35°48′E
40 M15 **Petacalco, Bahía** *bay* W Mexico
Petach-Tikva *see* Petah Tikva
138 F10 **Petah Tikva** *var.* Petach-Tikva, Petah Tiqva, Petakh Tikva; *prev.* Petah Tiqwa. Tel Aviv, C Israel 32°05′N 34°53′E
Petah Tiqwa *see* Petah Tikva
93 L17 **Petäjävesi** Länsi-Suomi, C Finland 62°17′N 25°10′E
Petakh Tikva/Petah Tiqva *see* Petah Tikva
22 M7 **Petal** Mississippi, S USA 31°21′N 89°15′W
115 I19 **Petalioí** *island* C Greece
115 H19 **Petalión, Kólpos** *gulf* E Greece
115 J19 **Pétalo** ▲ Ándros, Kykládes, Greece, Aegean Sea 37°51′N 24°50′E
34 M8 **Petaluma** California, W USA 38°15′N 122°37′W
99 L25 **Pétange** Luxembourg, SW Luxembourg 49°33′N 05°53′E
54 M5 **Petare** Miranda, N Venezuela 10°31′N 66°50′W
41 N16 **Petatlán** Guerrero, S Mexico 17°31′N 101°16′W
83 L14 **Petauke** Eastern, E Zambia 14°12′S 31°16′E
14 J12 **Petawawa** Ontario, SE Canada 45°54′N 77°18′W
14 J11 **Petawawa** ≈ Ontario, SE Canada
Petchaburi *see* Phetchaburi
42 D2 **Petén** *off.* Departamento del Petén. ⬖ *department* N Guatemala
Petén, Departamento del *see* Petén
42 D2 **Petén Itzá, Lago** *var.* Lago de Flores. ⊛ N Guatemala
30 K7 **Petenwell Lake** ⊠ Wisconsin, N USA
14 D6 **Peterbell** Ontario, S Canada 48°34′N 83°19′W
182 I7 **Peterborough** South Australia 32°59′S 138°51′E
14 I14 **Peterborough** Ontario, SE Canada 44°19′N 78°20′W
97 N20 **Peterborough** *prev.* Medeshamstede. E England, United Kingdom 52°35′N 00°15′W
19 N10 **Peterborough** New Hampshire, NE USA 42°51′N 71°54′W
96 L8 **Peterhead** NE Scotland, United Kingdom 57°30′N 01°46′W
Peterhof *see* Luboń
Peter I øy *see* Peter I Øy
193 Q14 **Peter I Øy** ◇ *Norwegian dependency* Antarctica
194 H9 **Peter I Øy** *var.* Peter I øy. *island* Antarctica
97 M14 **Peterlee** N England, United Kingdom 54°45′N 01°18′W
Peterlingen *see* Payerne
197 P14 **Petermann Bjerg** ▲ C Greenland 73°16′N 27°59′W
11 S12 **Peter Pond Lake** ⊛ Saskatchewan, C Canada
39 X13 **Petersburg** Mytkof Island, Alaska, USA 56°43′N 132°51′W
30 K13 **Petersburg** Illinois, N USA 40°01′N 89°52′W
31 N16 **Petersburg** Indiana, N USA 38°30′N 87°16′W
29 Q3 **Petersburg** North Dakota, N USA 47°59′N 97°59′W
25 N5 **Petersburg** Texas, SW USA 33°52′N 101°36′W
21 V7 **Petersburg** Virginia, NE USA 37°14′N 77°24′W
21 T4 **Petersburg** West Virginia, NE USA 39°01′N 79°09′W
100 H12 **Petershagen** Nordrhein-Westfalen, NW Germany 52°22′N 08°58′E
55 S9 **Peters Mine** *var.* Peter's Mine. N Guyana 06°13′N 59°18′W
107 O21 **Petilia Policastro** Calabria, SW Italy 39°07′N 16°48′E
44 M9 **Pétionville** S Haiti 18°29′N 72°16′W
45 X6 **Petit-Bourg** Basse Terre, C Guadeloupe 16°12′N 61°36′W
15 Y5 **Petit-Cap** Québec, SE Canada 49°00′N 64°26′W
45 Y6 **Petit Cul-de-Sac Marin** *bay* C Guadeloupe
44 M9 **Petite-Rivière-de-l'Artibonite** C Haiti 19°10′N 72°30′W
173 X16 **Petite Rivière Noire, Piton de la** ▲ C Mauritius
15 R9 **Petite-Rivière-St-François** Québec, SE Canada 47°18′N 70°34′W
44 L9 **Petit-Goâve** S Haiti 18°27′N 72°51′W
Petitjean *see* Sidi-Kacem
13 N10 **Petit Lac Manicouagan** ⊛ Québec, E Canada
19 T7 **Petit Manan Point** *headland* Maine, NE USA 44°23′N 67°54′W
Petit Mécatina, Rivière du *see* Little Mecatina
11 N10 **Petitot** ≈ Alberta/British Columbia, W Canada
45 S12 **Petit Piton** ▲ SW Saint Lucia 13°49′N 61°03′W
Petit-Popo *see* Aného
Petit St-Bernard, Col du *see* Little Saint Bernard Pass
13 O8 **Petitsikapau Lake** ⊛ Newfoundland and Labrador, E Canada
92 L11 **Petkula** Lappi, N Finland 67°41′N 26°44′E
41 X12 **Peto** Yucatán, SE Mexico 20°09′N 88°55′W
62 G10 **Petorca** Valparaíso, C Chile 32°18′S 70°49′W
31 Q5 **Petoskey** Michigan, N USA 45°51′N 88°03′W
138 G14 **Petra** *archaeological site* Ma'ān, W Jordan
Petra *see* Wādī Mūsā
115 F14 **Pétras, Sténa** *pass* N Greece
123 S16 **Petra Velikogo, Zaliv** *bay* SE Russian Federation
Petrel *see* Petrer
14 K15 **Petre, Point** *headland* Ontario, SE Canada 43°49′N 77°07′W
105 S12 **Petrer** *var.* Petrel. Valenciana, E Spain 38°28′N 00°46′W
125 U11 **Petretsovo** Permskiy Kray, NW Russian Federation 61°22′N 57°21′E
114 G12 **Petrich** Blagoevgrad, SW Bulgaria 41°25′N 23°12′E
187 P15 **Petrie, Récif** *reef* N New Caledonia
37 N11 **Petrified Forest** *prehistoric site* Arizona, SW USA
Petrikau *see* Piotrków Trybunalski
Petrikov *see* Pyetrykaw
116 H12 **Petrila** *Hung.* Petrilla. Hunedoara, W Romania 45°27′N 23°25′E
Petrilla *see* Petrila
112 E9 **Petrinja** Sisak-Moslavina, C Croatia 45°27′N 16°14′E
Petroaleksandrovsk *see* To'rtkok'l
Petrőcz *see* Bački Petrovac
124 G12 **Petrodvorets** *Fin.* Pietarhovi. Leningradskaya Oblast', NW Russian Federation 59°53′N 29°52′E
Petrograd *see* Sankt-Peterburg
Petrokov *see* Piotrków Trybunalski
54 G6 **Petrólea** Norte de Santander, NE Colombia 08°30′N 72°35′W
14 D16 **Petrolia** Ontario, S Canada 42°54′N 82°07′W
25 S4 **Petrolia** Texas, SW USA 34°00′N 98°13′W
59 O15 **Petrolina** Pernambuco, E Brazil 09°22′S 40°30′W
45 T6 **Petrona, Punta** *headland* C Puerto Rico 17°57′N 66°23′W
Petropavl *see* Petropavlovsk
117 V7 **Petropavlivka** Dnipropetrovs'ka Oblast', E Ukraine 48°28′N 36°28′E
145 P6 **Petropavlovsk** *Kaz.* Petropavl. Severnyy Kazakhstan, N Kazakhstan 54°47′N 69°06′E
123 V11 **Petropavlovsk-Kamchatskiy** Kamchatskiy Kray, E Russian Federation 53°03′N 158°43′E
60 P9 **Petrópolis** Rio de Janeiro, SE Brazil 22°30′S 43°28′W
116 H12 **Petroşani** *var.* Petroşeni, *Ger.* Petroschen, *Hung.* Petrozsény. Hunedoara, W Romania 45°25′N 23°22′E
Petroschen/Petroşeni *see* Petroşani
Petroskoi *see* Petrozavodsk
112 N12 **Petrovac** Serbia, E Serbia 42°22′N 21°25′E
Petrovac *see* Bosanski Petrovac
113 J17 **Petrovac na Moru** S Montenegro 42°11′N 19°00′E
Petrovac/Petrovácz *see* Bački Petrovac
117 S8 **Petrove** Kirovohrads'ka Oblast', C Ukraine 48°22′N 33°12′E
113 O18 **Petrovec** C FYR Macedonia 41°57′N 21°37′E
Petrovgrad *see* Zrenjanin
127 P7 **Petrovsk** Saratovskaya Oblast', W Russian Federation 52°20′N 45°23′E
Petrovsk-Port *see* Makhachkala
127 P9 **Petrov Val** Volgogradskaya Oblast', SW Russian Federation 50°10′N 45°16′E
124 J11 **Petrozavodsk** *Fin.* Petroskoi. Respublika Kareliya, NW Russian Federation 61°46′N 34°19′E
Petrozsény *see* Petroşani
83 D20 **Petrusdal** Hardap, C Namibia 23°42′S 17°23′E
117 T7 **Petrykivka** Dnipropetrovs'ka Oblast', E Ukraine 48°44′N 34°42′E
Petsamo *see* Pechenga
Petschka *see* Pecica
Pettau *see* Ptuj
109 S5 **Pettenbach** Oberösterreich, C Austria 47°58′N 14°03′E
25 S13 **Pettus** Texas, SW USA 28°34′N 97°49′W
122 G12 **Petukhovo** Kurganskaya Oblast', C Russian Federation 55°04′N 67°49′E
Petuna *see* Songyuan
109 R4 **Peuerbach** Oberösterreich, N Austria 48°19′N 13°45′E
62 G12 **Peumo** Libertador, C Chile 34°20′S 71°12′W
123 T6 **Pevek** Chukotskiy Avtonomnyy Okrug, NE Russian Federation 69°41′N 170°19′E
27 X5 **Pevely** Missouri, C USA 38°16′N 90°24′W
Peyia *see* Pégeia
102 J15 **Peyrehorade** Landes, SW France 43°33′N 01°05′W
124 J14 **Peza** ≈ NW Russian Federation
103 P16 **Pézenas** Hérault, S France 43°28′N 03°25′E
111 H20 **Pezinok** *Ger.* Bösing, *Hung.* Bazin. Bratislavský Kraj, W Slovakia 48°17′N 17°15′E
101 L22 **Pfaffenhofen an der Ilm** Bayern, SE Germany 48°31′N 11°30′E
108 G7 **Pfäffikon** Schwyz, C Switzerland 47°11′N 08°46′E
101 F20 **Pfälzer Wald** *hill range* W Germany
101 N22 **Pfarrkirchen** Bayern, SE Germany 48°25′N 12°56′E
101 G21 **Pforzheim** Baden-Württemberg, SW Germany 48°53′N 08°42′E
101 H24 **Pfullendorf** Baden-Württemberg, S Germany 47°55′N 09°16′E
108 K8 **Pfunds** Tirol, W Austria 46°56′N 10°30′E
101 G19 **Pfungstadt** Hessen, W Germany 49°48′N 08°36′E
83 L20 **Phalaborwa** Limpopo, NE South Africa 23°59′S 31°04′E
152 E11 **Phalodi** Rājasthān, NW India 27°06′N 72°22′E
152 E12 **Phalsund** Rājasthān, NW India 26°22′N 71°56′E
155 E15 **Phaltan** Mahārāshtra, W India 18°01′N 74°31′E
167 O7 **Phan** *var.* Muang Phan. Chiang Rai, NW Thailand 19°34′N 99°44′E
167 O14 **Phangan, Ko** *island* SW Thailand
166 M15 **Phang-Nga** *var.* Pang-Nga, Phangnga. Phangnga, SW Thailand 08°29′N 98°31′E
Phangnga *see* Phang-Nga
Phan Rang/Phanrang *see* Phan Rang-Thap Cham
167 V13 **Phan Rang-Thap Cham** *var.* Phanrang, Phan Rang, Phan Rang Thap Cham. Ninh Thuân, S Vietnam 11°34′N 109°00′E
167 U13 **Phan Ri** Binh Thuân, S Vietnam 11°11′N 108°31′E
167 U13 **Phan Thiêt** Binh Thuân, S Vietnam 10°56′N 108°06′E
Pharnacia *see* Giresun
25 S17 **Pharr** Texas, SW USA 26°11′N 98°10′W
Pharus *see* Hvar
167 N16 **Phatthalung** *var.* Padalung, Patalung. Phatthalung, SW Thailand 07°38′N 100°04′E
167 O7 **Phayao** *var.* Muang Phayao. Phayao, NW Thailand 19°10′N 99°55′E
11 U10 **Phelps Lake** ⊛ Saskatchewan, C Canada
21 X9 **Phelps Lake** ⊛ North Carolina, SE USA
23 R5 **Phenix City** Alabama, S USA 32°28′N 85°00′W
Phet Buri *see* Phetchaburi
167 O11 **Phetchaburi** *var.* Bejraburi, Petchaburi, Phet Buri. Phetchaburi, SW Thailand 13°05′N 99°58′E
167 O9 **Phichit** *var.* Bichitra, Muang Phichit, Pichit. Phichit, C Thailand 16°29′N 100°21′E
22 M5 **Philadelphia** Mississippi, S USA 32°45′N 89°06′W
18 I7 **Philadelphia** New York, NE USA 44°10′N 75°40′W
18 I16 **Philadelphia** Pennsylvania, NE USA 40°N 75°10′W
18 I16 **Philadelphia** ✈ Pennsylvania, NE USA 39°51′N 75°13′W
Philadelphia *see* 'Amman
28 L10 **Philip** South Dakota, N USA 44°02′N 101°39′W
99 H22 **Philippeville** Namur, S Belgium 50°12′N 04°33′E
Philippeville *see* Skikda
21 S3 **Philippi** West Virginia, NE USA 39°08′N 80°03′W
Philippi *see* Fílippoi
195 Y9 **Philippi Glacier** *glacier* Antarctica
192 G6 **Philippine Basin** *undersea feature* W Pacific Ocean 17°00′N 132°00′E
129 X12 **Philippine Plate** *tectonic feature*
171 O5 **Philippines** *off.* Republic of the Philippines. ◆ *republic* SE Asia
129 X13 **Philippines** *island group* W Pacific Ocean
171 P3 **Philippine Sea** *sea* W Pacific Ocean
Philippines, Republic of the *see* Philippines
192 F6 **Philippine Trench** *undersea feature* W Philippine Sea
83 H23 **Philippolis** Free State, C South Africa 30°16′S 25°16′E
Philippopolis *see* Plovdiv
Philippopolis *see* Shahbā', Syria
45 V9 **Philipsburg** ○ Sint Maarten 17°58′N 63°02′W
33 P10 **Philipsburg** Montana, NW USA 46°19′N 113°17′W
39 R6 **Philip Smith Mountains** ▲▲ Alaska, USA
152 H8 **Phillaur** Punjab, N India 31°02′N 75°50′E
183 N13 **Phillip Island** *island* Victoria, SE Australia
25 N2 **Phillips** Texas, SW USA 35°39′N 101°21′W
30 K5 **Phillips** Wisconsin, N USA 45°42′N 90°23′W
26 K3 **Phillipsburg** Kansas, C USA 39°45′N 99°19′W
18 I14 **Phillipsburg** New Jersey, NE USA 40°39′N 75°09′W
21 S7 **Philpott Lake** ⊠ Virginia, NE USA
Phintias *see* Licata
167 P9 **Phitsanulok** *var.* Bisnulok, Muang Phitsanulok, Pitsanulok. Phitsanulok, C Thailand 16°49′N 100°15′E
Phlórina *see* Flórina
Phnom Penh *see* Phnum Penh
167 S13 **Phnum Penh** *var.* Phnom Penh. ● (Cambodia) Phnum Penh, S Cambodia 11°35′N 104°55′E
167 S11 **Phnum Tbêng Meanchey** Preăh Vihéar, N Cambodia 13°45′N 104°58′E
36 K13 **Phoenix** *state capital* Arizona, SW USA 33°27′N 112°04′W
Phoenix Island *see* Rawaki
191 R3 **Phoenix Islands** *island group* C Kiribati
18 I15 **Phoenixville** Pennsylvania, NE USA 40°07′N 75°31′W
83 K22 **Phofung** *var.* Mont-aux-Sources. ▲ N Lesotho 28°47′S 28°52′E
167 Q10 **Phon** Khon Kaen, E Thailand 15°47′N 102°35′E
167 Q5 **Phôngsali** *var.* Phong Saly. Phôngsali, N Laos 21°40′N 102°04′E
Phong Saly *see* Phôngsali
Phônhông *see* Ban Phônhông
167 R7 **Phônsaven** *var.* Pèk, Xieng Khouang; *prev.* Xiangkhoang. Xiangkhoang, N Laos 19°19′N 103°23′E
167 R5 **Phô Rang** *var.* Bao Yên. Lao Cai, N Vietnam 22°12′N 104°27′E
Phort Láirge, Cuan *see* Waterford Harbour
Phou Louang *see* Annamite Mountains
167 N10 **Phra Chedi Sam Ong** Kanchanaburi, W Thailand 15°18′N 98°26′E
167 O8 **Phrae** *var.* Muang Phrae, Prae. Phrae, NW Thailand 18°07′N 100°09′E
Phra Nakhon Si Ayutthaya *see* Ayutthaya
167 M14 **Phra Thong, Ko** *island* SW Thailand
Phu Cŭơng *see* Thu Dâu Môt
166 M15 **Phuket** *var.* Bhuket, Puket, *Mal.* Ujung Salang; *prev.* Junkseylon, Salang. Phuket, SW Thailand 07°52′N 98°22′E
166 M15 **Phuket** ✈ Phuket, SW Thailand 08°03′N 98°16′E
166 M15 **Phuket, Ko** *island* SW Thailand
154 N12 **Phulabāni** *prev.* Phulbani. Orissa, E India 20°30′N 84°18′E
Phulbani *see* Phulabāni
167 U9 **Phu Lôc** Th,a Thiên-Huê, C Vietnam 16°13′N 107°53′E
167 R13 **Phumĭ Chŏâm** Kâmpóng Spœ, SW Cambodia 11°42′N 103°58′E
Phumĭ Kalêng *see* Kalêng
Phumĭ Kâmpóng Trâbêk *see* Kâmpóng Trâbêk
Phumĭ Koŭk Kduŏch *see* Koŭk Kduŏch
Phumĭ Labăng *see* Labăng
Phumĭ Mlu Prey *see* Mlu Prey
Phumĭ Moŭng *see* Moŭng
Phumĭ Prâmaôy *see* Prâmaôy
Phumĭ Samĭt *see* Samĭt
Phumĭ Sâmraông *see* Sâmraông
Phumĭ Siĕmbok *see* Siĕmbok
Phumĭ Thalabârĭvăt *see* Thalabârĭvăt
Phumĭ Veal Renh *see* Veal Renh
Phumĭ Yeay Sên *see* Yeay Sên
Phum Kompong Trabek *see* Kâmpóng Trâbêk
Phum Samrong *see* Sâmraông
167 V11 **Phu My** Binh Đinh, C Vietnam 14°07′N 109°05′E
Phung Hiêp *see* Tân Hiêp
153 T12 **Phuntsholing** SW Bhutan 26°52′N 89°26′E
167 V13 **Phư ơ c Dân** Ninh Thuân, S Vietnam 11°28′N 108°53′E
167 R15 **Phươc Long** Minh Hai, S Vietnam 09°27′N 105°25′E
Phươc Sơn *see* Khâm Đưc
167 R14 **Phu Quôc, Đao** *var.* Phu Quoc Island. *island* S Vietnam
Phu Quoc Island *see* Phu Quôc, Đao
167 S6 **Phu Tho** Vinh Phu, N Vietnam 21°23′N 105°13′E
Phu Vinh *see* Tra Vinh
166 M7 **Phyu** *var.* Hpyu, Pyu. Bago, C Myanmar (Burma) 18°29′N 96°28′E
189 T13 **Piaanu Pass** *passage* Chuuk Islands, C Micronesia
106 E8 **Piacenza** *Fr.* Paisance; *anc.* Placentia. Emilia-Romagna, N Italy 45°02′N 09°42′E
107 K14 **Pianella** Abruzzo, C Italy 42°23′N 14°04′E
107 M15 **Pianosa, Isola** *island* Archipelago Toscano, C Italy
171 U13 **Piar** Papua, E Indonesia 02°49′S 132°46′E
45 U14 **Piarco** *var.* Port of Spain. ✈ (Port-of-Spain) Trinidad, Trinidad and Tobago 10°36′N 61°21′W
110 M12 **Piaseczno** Mazowieckie, C Poland 52°03′N 21°00′E
116 I15 **Piatra** Teleorman, S Romania 43°49′N 25°10′E
116 L10 **Piatra-Neamţ** *Hung.* Karácsonkő. Neamţ, NE Romania 46°54′N 26°23′E
Piauhy *see* Piauí
59 N15 **Piauí** *off.* Estado do Piauí; *prev.* Piauhy. ⬖ *state* E Brazil
Piauí, Estado do *see* Piauí
106 I7 **Piave** ≈ NE Italy
107 K24 **Piazza Armerina** *var.* Chiazza. Sicilia, Italy, C Mediterranean Sea 37°23′N 14°22′E
81 G14 **Pibor** *Amh.* Pībor Wenz. ≈ Ethiopia/South Sudan
81 G14 **Pibor Post** Jonglei, E South Sudan 06°50′N 33°06′E
Pībor Wenz *see* Pibor
Pibrans *see* Příbram
36 K11 **Picacho Butte** ▲ Arizona, SW USA 35°12′N 112°44′W
40 D4 **Picachos, Cerro** ▲ NW Mexico 29°15′N 114°04′W
103 O4 **Picardie** *Eng.* Picardy. ⬖ *region* N France
Picardy *see* Picardie
22 L8 **Picayune** Mississippi, S USA 30°31′N 89°40′W
Piccolo San Bernardo, Colle di *see* Little Saint Bernard Pass
PicdeBälaitous *see* Balaïtous
62 K5 **Pichanal** Salta, N Argentina 23°18′S 64°10′W
147 P12 **Pichandar** W Tajikistan 38°44′N 68°51′E
27 R8 **Picher** Oklahoma, C USA 36°59′N 94°49′W
62 G12 **Pichilemu** Libertador, C Chile 34°25′S 72°00′W
40 F9 **Pichilingue** Baja California Sur, NW Mexico 24°20′N 110°17′W
56 B6 **Pichincha** ⬖ *province* N Ecuador
56 C6 **Pichincha** ▲ N Ecuador 0°12′S 78°39′W
Pichit *see* Phichit
41 U15 **Pichucalco** Chiapas, SE Mexico 17°32′N 93°07′W
22 L5 **Pickens** Mississippi, S USA 32°52′N 89°58′W
21 O11 **Pickens** South Carolina, SE USA 34°53′N 82°42′W
14 G11 **Pickerel** ≈ Ontario, S Canada
14 H15 **Pickering** Ontario, S Canada 43°50′N 79°03′W
97 N16 **Pickering** N England, United Kingdom 54°14′N 00°47′W
31 S13 **Pickerington** Ohio, N USA 39°52′N 82°45′W
12 C10 **Pickle Lake** Ontario, C Canada 51°30′N 90°10′W
29 P12 **Pickstown** South Dakota, N USA 43°02′N 98°31′W
25 V6 **Pickton** Texas, SW USA 33°01′N 95°19′W
23 N1 **Pickwick Lake** ⊠ S USA
64 N2 **Pico** *var.* Ilha do Pico. *island* Azores, Portugal, NE Atlantic Ocean
63 J19 **Pico de Salamanca** Chubut, SE Argentina 45°26′S 67°26′W
1 P9 **Pico Fracture Zone** *tectonic feature* NW Atlantic Ocean
Pico, Ilha do *see* Pico
59 O14 **Picos** Piauí, E Brazil 07°05′S 41°24′W
63 I20 **Pico Truncado** Santa Cruz, SE Argentina 46°45′S 68°00′W
183 S9 **Picton** New South Wales, SE Australia 34°12′S 150°36′E
14 K15 **Picton** Ontario, SE Canada 43°59′N 77°09′W
185 K14 **Picton** Marlborough, South Island, New Zealand 41°18′S 174°00′E
63 H15 **Pićun Leufú, Arroyo** ≈ SW Argentina
Pidálion *see* Gkréko, Akrotíri
155 K25 **Pidurutalagala** ▲ S Sri Lanka 07°03′N 80°47′E
116 K6 **Pidvolochys'k** Ternopil's'ka Oblast', W Ukraine 49°31′N 26°09′E
107 K16 **Piedimonte Matese** Campania, S Italy 41°20′N 14°30′E
27 X7 **Piedmont** Missouri, C USA 37°09′N 90°42′W
21 P11 **Piedmont** South Carolina, SE USA 34°42′N 82°27′W
17 S12 **Piedmont** *escarpment* E USA
Piedmont *see* Piemonte
31 U13 **Piedmont Lake** ⊠ Ohio, N USA
104 M11 **Piedrabuena** Castilla-La Mancha, C Spain 39°02′N 04°10′W
Piedrafita, Puerto de *see* Pedrafita, Porto de
104 L8 **Piedrahita** Castilla y León, N Spain 40°27′N 05°20′W
41 N6 **Piedras Negras** *var.* Ciudad Porfirio Díaz. Coahuila, NE Mexico 28°40′N 100°32′W
61 E21 **Piedras, Punta** *headland* E Argentina 35°27′S 57°04′W
57 I14 **Piedras, Río de las** ≈ E Peru
111 J16 **Piekary Śląskie** Śląskie, S Poland 50°24′N 18°58′E
93 M17 **Pieksämäki** Itä-Suomi, E Finland 62°18′N 27°10′E
109 V5 **Pielach** ≈ NE Austria
93 M16 **Pielavesi** Itä-Suomi, C Finland 63°14′N 26°45′E
93 M16 **Pielavesi** ⊛ C Finland
93 N16 **Pielinen** *var.* Pielisjärvi. ⊛ E Finland
Pielisjärvi *see* Pielinen
106 A8 **Piemonte** *Eng.* Piedmont. ⬖ *region* NW Italy
111 L18 **Pieniny** ▲▲ S Poland
111 E14 **Pieńsk** *Ger.* Penzig. Dolnośląskie, SW Poland 51°14′N 15°03′E
29 Q13 **Pierce** Nebraska, C USA 42°12′N 97°31′W
11 R14 **Pierceland** Saskatchewan, C Canada
115 E14 **Piéria** ▲▲ N Greece
29 N10 **Pierre** *state capital* South Dakota, N USA 44°22′N 100°21′W
102 K16 **Pierrefitte-Nestalas** Hautes-Pyrénées, S France 42°57′N 00°04′W
103 R14 **Pierrelatte** Drôme, E France 44°22′N 04°40′E
15 P11 **Pierreville** Québec, SE Canada 46°05′N 72°48′W
15 O7 **Pierriche** ≈ Québec, SE Canada
111 H20 **Piešt'any** *Ger.* Pistyan, *Hung.* Pöstyén. Tranavský Kraj, W Slovakia 48°37′N 17°48′E
109 X5 **Piesting** ≈ E Austria
Pietarhovi *see* Petrodvorets
Pietari *see* Sankt-Peterburg
Pietarsaari *see* Jakobstad
83 K23 **Pietermaritzburg** *var.* Maritzburg. KwaZulu/Natal, E South Africa 29°35′S 30°23′E
Pietersburg *see* Polokwane
107 K24 **Pietraperzia** Sicilia, Italy, C Mediterranean Sea 37°25′N 14°08′E
107 N22 **Pietra Spada, Passo della** *pass* SW Italy
Piet Retief *see* eMkhondo
116 J10 **Pietrosul, Vârful** *prev.* Vîrful Pietrosu. ▲ N Romania 47°06′N 25°09′E
106 I6 **Pieve di Cadore** Veneto, NE Italy 46°27′N 12°22′E
14 C18 **Pigeon Bay** *lake bay* Ontario, S Canada
27 X8 **Piggott** Arkansas, C USA 36°22′N 90°11′W
83 L21 **Piggs Peak** NW Swaziland 25°58′S 31°17′E
Pigs, Bay of *see* Cochinos, Bahía de
61 A23 **Pigüé** Buenos Aires, E Argentina 37°38′S 62°27′W
41 O12 **Piguícas** ▲ C Mexico 21°08′N 99°37′W
193 W15 **Piha Passage** *passage* S Tonga
Pihkva Järv *see* Pskov, Lake
93 N18 **Pihlajavesi** ⊛ SE Finland
93 J18 **Pihlava** Länsi-Suomi, SW Finland 61°33′N 21°36′E
93 L16 **Pihtipudas** Länsi-Suomi, C Finland 63°20′N 25°37′E
40 L14 **Pihuamo** Jalisco, SW Mexico 19°20′N 103°21′W
189 U11 **Piis Moen** *var.* Pis. *atoll* Chuuk Islands, C Micronesia
41 U17 **Pijijiapán** Chiapas, SE Mexico 15°42′N 93°12′W
98 G12 **Pijnacker** Zuid-Holland, W Netherlands 52°01′N 04°26′E
42 H5 **Pijol, Pico** ▲ NW Honduras 15°07′N 87°39′W
Pikaar *see* Bikar Atoll
124 I13 **Pikalevo** Leningradskaya Oblast', NW Russian Federation 59°33′N 34°04′E
188 M15 **Pikelot** *island* Caroline Islands, C Micronesia
30 M5 **Pike River** ≈ Wisconsin, N USA
37 T5 **Pikes Peak** ▲ Colorado, C USA 38°51′N 105°06′W
21 P6 **Pikeville** Kentucky, S USA 37°29′N 82°33′W
20 L9 **Pikeville** Tennessee, S USA 35°35′N 85°11′W
Pikinni *see* Bikini Atoll
79 H18 **Pikounda** Sangha, C Congo 0°30′N 16°44′E
110 G9 **Piła** *Ger.* Schneidemühl. Wielkopolskie, C Poland 53°09′N 16°44′E
62 N6 **Pilagá, Riacho** ≈ NE Argentina
61 D20 **Pilar** Buenos Aires, E Argentina 34°28′S 58°55′W
62 N7 **Pilar** *var.* Villa del Pilar. Ñeembucú, S Paraguay 26°55′S 58°20′W
62 N6 **Pilcomayo, Rio** ≈ C South America
147 R12 **Pildon** *Rus.* Pil'don. C Tajikistan 39°10′N 71°00′E
Piles *see* Pylés
Pilgram *see* Pelhřimov
152 L10 **Pīlībhīt** Uttar Pradesh, N India 28°37′N 79°48′E
110 M13 **Pilica** ≈ C Poland
115 G16 **Pílio** ▲▲ C Greece
111 J22 **Pilisvörösvár** Pest, N Hungary 47°38′N 18°55′E
65 G15 **Pillar Bay** *bay* Ascension Island, C Atlantic Ocean
183 P17 **Pillar, Cape** *headland* Tasmania, SE Australia 43°13′S 147°58′E
Pillau *see* Baltiysk
183 R5 **Pilliga** New South Wales, SE Australia 30°22′S 148°53′E
44 H8 **Pilón** Granma, E Cuba 19°54′N 77°20′W
Pilos *see* Pýlos
11 W17 **Pilot Mound** Manitoba, S Canada 49°12′N 98°49′W
21 S8 **Pilot Mountain** North Carolina, SE USA 36°23′N 80°28′W
39 O14 **Pilot Point** Alaska, USA 57°33′N 157°34′W
25 T5 **Pilot Point** Texas, SW USA 33°24′N 96°57′W
32 K11 **Pilot Rock** Oregon, NW USA 45°28′N 118°49′W
38 M11 **Pilot Station** Alaska, USA 61°56′N 162°52′W
Pilsen *see* Plzeň
111 K18 **Pilsko** ▲ N Slovakia 49°31′N 19°21′E
Pilten *see* Piltene
118 D8 **Piltene** *Ger.* Pilten. W Latvia 57°14′N 21°41′E
111 M16 **Pilzno** Podkarpackie, SE Poland 49°58′N 21°18′E
Pilzno *see* Plzeň
37 N14 **Pima** Arizona, SW USA 32°49′N 109°50′W
58 H13 **Pimenta** Pará, N Brazil 04°32′S 56°17′W
59 F16 **Pimenta Bueno** Rondônia, W Brazil 11°40′S 61°14′W
56 B11 **Pimentel** Lambayeque, W Peru 06°51′S 79°53′W
105 S6 **Pina** Aragón, NE Spain 41°28′N 00°31′W
119 I20 **Pina** ≈ SW Belarus
40 E2 **Pinacate, Sierra del** ▲ NW Mexico 31°49′N 113°30′W
63 H22 **Pináculo, Cerro** ▲ S Argentina 50°46′S 72°07′W
191 X11 **Pinaki** *atoll* Îles Tuamotu, E French Polynesia
37 N15 **Pinaleno Mountains** ▲▲ Arizona, SW USA
171 P4 **Pinamalayan** Mindoro, N Philippines 13°00′N 121°30′E
169 Q10 **Pinang** Borneo, C Indonesia 0°36′N 109°11′W
168 J7 **Pinang** *var.* Penang. ⬖ *state* Peninsular Malaysia
Pinang *see* Pinang, Pulau, Peninsular Malaysia
Pinang *see* George Town
168 J7 **Pinang, Pulau** *var.* Penang, Pinang; *prev.* Prince of Wales Island. *island* Peninsular Malaysia
44 B5 **Pinar del Río** Pinar del Río, W Cuba 22°24′N 83°42′W
114 N11 **Pınarhisar** Kırklareli, NW Turkey 41°37′N 27°32′E
171 O3 **Pinatubo, Mount** ⛰ Luzon, N Philippines 15°08′N 120°21′E
11 Y16 **Pinawa** Manitoba, S Canada 50°09′N 95°52′W
11 Q17 **Pincher Creek** Alberta, SW Canada 49°31′N 113°53′W
30 L16 **Pinckneyville** Illinois, N USA 38°04′N 89°22′W
Pîncota *see* Pâncota
111 L15 **Pińczów** Świętokrzyskie, C Poland 50°30′N 20°30′E
149 U7 **Pind Dādan Khān** Punjab, E Pakistan 32°36′N 73°07′E
Píndhos/Píndhos Óros *see* Píndos
149 V8 **Pindi Bhattiān** Punjab, E Pakistan 31°54′N 73°20′E
149 U6 **Pindi Gheb** Punjab, E Pakistan 33°16′N 72°21′E
115 D15 **Píndos** *var.* Píndhos Óros, *Eng.* Pindus Mountains; *prev.* Píndhos. ▲▲ C Greece
Pindus Mountains *see* Píndos
18 J16 **Pine Barrens** *physical region* New Jersey, NE USA
27 V12 **Pine Bluff** Arkansas, C USA 34°15′N 92°00′W
23 X11 **Pine Castle** Florida, SE USA 28°28′N 81°22′W
29 V7 **Pine City** Minnesota, N USA 45°49′N 92°55′W
181 P2 **Pine Creek** Northern Territory, N Australia 13°51′S 131°51′E
35 V4 **Pine Creek** ≈ Nevada, W USA
18 F13 **Pine Creek** ≈ Pennsylvania, NE USA
27 Q13 **Pine Creek Lake** ⊠ Oklahoma, C USA
33 T15 **Pinedale** Wyoming, C USA 42°52′N 109°51′W
11 X15 **Pine Dock** Manitoba, S Canada 51°34′N 96°47′W
11 Y16 **Pine Falls** Manitoba, S Canada 50°29′N 96°12′W
35 R10 **Pine Flat Lake** ⊠ California, W USA
125 N8 **Pinega** Arkhangel'skaya Oblast', NW Russian Federation 64°40′N 43°24′E
125 N8 **Pinega** ≈ NW Russian Federation
15 N12 **Pine Hill** Québec, SE Canada 45°44′N 74°30′W
11 T12 **Pinehouse Lake** ⊛ Saskatchewan, C Canada
21 T10 **Pinehurst** North Carolina, SE USA 35°12′N 79°28′W
115 D19 **Pineiós** ≈ S Greece
115 E16 **Pineiós** *var.* Piniós; *anc.* Peneius. ≈ C Greece
29 W10 **Pine Island** Minnesota, N USA 44°12′N 92°39′W
23 V15 **Pine Island** *island* Florida, SE USA
194 K10 **Pine Island Glacier** *glacier* Antarctica
25 X9 **Pineland** Texas, SW USA 31°15′N 93°58′W
23 V13 **Pinellas Park** Florida, SE USA 27°50′N 82°42′W
10 M13 **Pine Pass** *pass* British Columbia, W Canada
8 J10 **Pine Point** Northwest Territories, W Canada 60°52′N 114°30′W
28 K12 **Pine Ridge** South Dakota, N USA 43°01′N 102°33′W
29 U6 **Pine River** Minnesota, N USA 46°43′N 94°24′W
31 Q8 **Pine River** ≈ Michigan, N USA
30 M4 **Pine River** ≈ Wisconsin, N USA
106 A8 **Pinerolo** Piemonte, NE Italy 44°56′N 07°21′E
115 I15 **Pínes, Akrotírio** *var.* Akrotírio Pínnes. *headland* N Greece 40°06′N 24°19′E
25 W6 **Pines, Lake O' the** ⊠ Texas, SW USA
Pines, The Isle of the *see* Juventud, Isla de la
Pine Tree State *see* Maine
21 N7 **Pineville** Kentucky, S USA 36°47′N 83°43′W
22 H7 **Pineville** Louisiana, S USA 31°19′N 92°25′W
27 R8 **Pineville** Missouri, C USA 36°36′N 94°23′W
21 R10 **Pineville** North Carolina, SE USA 35°04′N 80°53′W
21 Q6 **Pineville** West Virginia, NE USA 37°35′N 81°34′W
33 V8 **Piney Buttes** *physical region* Montana, NW USA
163 W9 **Ping'an** Jilin, NE China 44°36′N 127°13′E
160 H14 **Pingbian** *var.* Pingbian Miaozu Zizhixian, Yuping. Yunnan, SW China 22°51′N 103°28′E
Pingbian Miaozu Zizhixian *see* Pingbian
157 S9 **Pingdingshan** Henan, C China 33°52′N 113°20′E
161 S14 **Pingdong** *Jap.* Heitō; *prev.* P'ingtung. S Taiwan 22°40′N 120°30′E
161 R4 **Pingdu** Shandong, E China 36°50′N 119°55′E
189 W16 **Pingelap Atoll** *atoll* Caroline Islands, E Micronesia
160 K14 **Pingguo** *var.* Matou. Guangxi Zhuangzu Zizhiqu, S China 23°24′N 107°30′E
161 Q13 **Pinghe** *var.* Xiaoxi. Fujian, SE China 24°30′N 117°19′E
P'ing-hsiang *see* Pingxiang
161 N10 **Pingjiang** Hunan, S China 28°44′N 113°33′E
Pingkiang *see* Harbin
160 L8 **Pingli** Shaanxi, C China 32°27′N 109°21′E
159 W10 **Pingliang** *var.* Kongtong, P'ing-liang. Gansu, C China 35°27′N 106°38′E
P'ing-liang *see* Pingliang
159 W8 **Pingluo** Ningxia, N China 38°55′N 106°31′E
Pingma *see* Tiandong
167 O7 **Ping, Mae Nam** ≈ W Thailand
161 Q1 **Pingquan** Hebei, E China 41°02′N 118°35′E
29 P5 **Pingree** North Dakota, N USA 47°07′N 98°54′W
Pingsiang *see* Pingxiang
P'ingtung *see* Pingdong
160 I8 **Pingwu** *var.* Long'an. Sichuan, C China 32°33′N 104°32′E
160 J15 **Pingxiang** Guangxi Zhuangzu Zizhiqu, S China 22°03′N 106°44′E
161 O11 **Pingxiang** *var.* P'ing-hsiang; *prev.* Pingsiang. Jiangxi, S China 27°42′N 113°50′E
Pingxiang *see* Tongwei
161 S11 **Pingyang** *var.* Kunyang. Zhejiang, SE China 27°46′N 120°37′E
161 P5 **Pingyi** Shandong, E China 35°30′N 117°38′E
161 P5 **Pingyin** Shandong, E China 36°18′N 116°24′E
60 H13 **Pinhalzinho** Santa Catarina, S Brazil 26°53′S 52°57′W
60 I12 **Pinhão** Paraná, S Brazil 25°46′S 51°32′W
61 H17 **Pinheiro Machado** Rio Grande do Sul, S Brazil 31°34′S 53°22′W
104 I7 **Pinhel** Guarda, N Portugal 40°47′N 07°03′W
Piniós *see* Pineiós
168 I11 **Pini, Pulau** *island* Kepulauan Batu, W Indonesia
109 Y7 **Pinka** ≈ SE Austria
109 X7 **Pinkafeld** Burgenland, SE Austria 47°23′N 16°08′E
Pinkiang *see* Harbin
10 M12 **Pink Mountain** British Columbia, W Canada 57°10′N 122°36′W
166 M3 **Pinlebu** Sagaing, N Myanmar (Burma) 24°02′N 95°21′E
38 J12 **Pinnacle Island** *island* Alaska, USA
180 I12 **Pinnacles, The** *tourist site* Western Australia
182 K10 **Pinnaroo** South Australia 35°17′S 140°54′E
Pinne *see* Pniewy
100 I9 **Pinneberg** Schleswig-Holstein, N Germany 53°40′N 09°49′E
Pínnes, Akrotírio *see* Pínes, Akrotírio
Pinos, Isla de *see* Juventud, Isla de la
35 R14 **Pinos, Mount** ▲ California, W USA 34°48′N 119°09′W
105 R12 **Pinoso** Valenciana, E Spain 38°25′N 01°02′W
105 N14 **Pinos-Puente** Andalucía, S Spain 37°16′N 03°46′W
41 Q17 **Pinotepa Nacional** *var.* Santiago Pinotepa Nacional. Oaxaca, SE Mexico 16°20′N 98°02′W
114 F13 **Pínovo** ▲ N Greece 41°06′N 22°19′E
187 R17 **Pins, Île des** *var.* Kunyé. *island* E New Caledonia

◆ Country
● Country Capital
◇ Dependent Territory
○ Dependent Territory Capital
⬖ Administrative Regions
✈ International Airport
▲ Mountain
▲▲ Mountain Range
⛰ Volcano
≈ River
⊛ Lake
⊠ Reservoir

119 I20 **Pinsk** *Pol.* Pińsk. Brestskaya Voblasts', SW Belarus 52°07′N 26°07′E
14 D18 **Pins, Pointe aux** *headland* Ontario, S Canada 42°14′N 81°53′W
57 B16 **Pinta, Isla** *var.* Abingdon. *island* Galapagos Islands, Ecuador, E Pacific Ocean
125 Q12 **Pinyug** Kirovskaya Oblast', NW Russian Federation 60°12′N 47°45′E
57 B17 **Pinzón, Isla** *var.* Duncan Island. *island* Galapagos Islands, Ecuador, E Pacific Ocean
35 Y8 **Pioche** Nevada, W USA 37°57′N 114°30′W
106 F13 **Piombino** Toscana, C Italy 42°54′N 10°30′E
0 C9 **Pioneer Fracture Zone** *tectonic feature* NE Pacific Ocean
122 L5 **Pioner, Ostrov** *island* Severnaya Zemlya, N Russian Federation
118 A13 **Pionerskiy** *Ger.* Neukuhren. Kaliningradskaya Oblast', W Russian Federation 54°57′N 20°16′E
110 N13 **Pionki** Mazowieckie, C Poland 51°30′N 21°27′E
184 L9 **Piopio** Waikato, North Island, New Zealand 38°27′S 175°00′E
110 K13 **Piotrków Trybunalski** *Ger.* Petrikau, *Rus.* Petrokov. Łodzkie, C Poland 51°25′N 19°42′E
152 F12 **Pīpār Road** Rājasthān, N India 26°25′N 73°29′E
115 I16 **Pipéri** *island* Vóreies Sporádes, Greece, Aegean Sea
29 S10 **Pipestone** Minnesota, N USA 44°00′N 96°19′W
12 C9 **Pipestone** ♣ Ontario, C Canada
61 E21 **Pipinas** Buenos Aires, E Argentina 35°32′S 57°20′W
149 T7 **Piplān** *prev.* Liaqatabad. Punjab, E Pakistan 32°17′N 71°24′E
15 R5 **Pipmuacan, Réservoir** ◙ Québec, SE Canada
Piqan *see* Shanshan
31 R13 **Piqua** Ohio, N USA 40°08′N 84°14′W
105 P5 **Piqueras, Puerto de** *pass* N Spain
60 H11 **Piquiri, Rio** ♣ S Brazil
60 L9 **Piracicaba** São Paulo, S Brazil 22°45′S 47°40′W
Piraeus/Piraiévs *see* Peiraías
60 K10 **Piraju** São Paulo, S Brazil 23°12′S 49°24′W
60 K9 **Pirajuí** São Paulo, S Brazil 21°58′S 49°27′W
63 G21 **Pirámide, Cerro** ▲ S Chile 49°06′S 73°32′W
Piramiva *see* Pyramíva
109 R13 **Piran** *It.* Pirano. SW Slovenia 45°35′N 13°35′E
62 N6 **Piraná** Formosa, N Argentina 25°42′S 59°06′W
59 J18 **Piranhas** Goiás, S Brazil 16°24′S 51°51′W
Pirano *see* Piran
142 I4 **Pīrānshahr** Āzarbāyjān-e Gharbī, NW Iran 36°41′N 45°08′E
59 M19 **Pirapora** Minas Gerais, NE Brazil 17°20′S 44°54′W
60 I9 **Pirapòzinho** São Paulo, S Brazil 22°17′S 51°31′W
61 G19 **Piraraja** Lavalleja, S Uruguay 33°44′S 54°45′W
60 L9 **Pirassununga** São Paulo, S Brazil 21°58′S 47°23′W
45 V6 **Pirata, Monte** ▲ E Puerto Rico 18°06′N 65°33′W
60 I13 **Piratuba** Santa Catarina, S Brazil 27°26′S 51°47′W
114 I9 **Pirdop** *prev.* Strednogorie. Sofiya, W Bulgaria 42°44′N 24°09′E
191 P7 **Pirea** Tahiti, W French Polynesia
59 K18 **Pirenópolis** Goiás, S Brazil 15°48′S 49°00′W
153 S13 **Pirganj** Rajshahi, NW Bangladesh 25°51′N 88°25′E
Pirgi *see* Pyrgí
Pírgos *see* Pýrgos
61 F20 **Piriápolis** Maldonado, S Uruguay 34°51′S 55°15′W
114 G11 **Pirin** ▲▲ SW Bulgaria
Pirineos *see* Pyrenees
58 N13 **Piripiri** Piauí, E Brazil 04°15′S 41°46′W
118 H4 **Pirita** *var.* Pirita Jõgi. ♣ NW Estonia
Pirita Jõgi *see* Pirita
54 J6 **Píritu** Portuguesa, N Venezuela 09°21′N 69°16′W
93 L18 **Pirkkala** Länsi-Suomi, W Finland 61°27′N 23°47′E
101 F20 **Pirmasens** Rheinland-Pfalz, SW Germany 49°12′N 07°37′E
101 P16 **Pirna** Sachsen, E Germany 50°57′N 13°56′E
Piroe *see* Piru
113 Q15 **Pirot** Serbia, SE Serbia 43°12′N 22°34′E
152 H6 **Pīr Panjāl Range** ▲▲ NE India
43 W16 **Pirre, Cerro** ▲ SE Panama 07°54′N 77°42′W
137 Y11 **Pirsaat** *Rus.* Pirsagat. ♣ E Azerbaijan
Pirsagat *see* Pirsaat
143 V11 **Pīr Shūrān, Selseleh-ye** ▲▲ SE Iran
92 M12 **Pirttikoski** Lappi, N Finland 66°20′N 27°08′E
Pirttikylä *see* Pörtom
171 R13 **Piru** *prev.* Piroe. Pulau Seram, E Indonesia 03°01′S 128°10′E
Piryatin *see* Pyryatyn
Pis *see* Piis Moen
106 F11 **Pisa** *var.* Pisae. Toscana, C Italy 43°43′N 10°23′E
Pisae *see* Pisa
189 V12 **Pisar** *atoll* Chuuk Islands, C Micronesia
Pisaurum *see* Pesaro
14 M10 **Piscatosine, Lac** ◎ Québec, SE Canada
109 W7 **Pischeldorf** Steiermark, SE Austria 47°11′N 15°48′E
Pischk *see* Simeria
107 L19 **Pisciotta** Campania, S Italy 40°07′N 15°13′E
57 E16 **Pisco** Ica, SW Peru 13°46′S 76°12′W
116 G9 **Pişcolt** *Hung.* Piskolt. Satu Mare, NW Romania 47°35′N 22°18′E
57 E16 **Pisco, Río** ♣ E Peru
111 C18 **Písek** Budějovický Kraj, S Czech Republic 49°19′N 14°07′E
31 R14 **Pisgah** Ohio, N USA 39°19′N 84°22′W
Pisha *see* Ningnan
158 F9 **Pishan** *var.* Guma. Xinjiang Uygur Zizhiqu, NW China 37°36′N 78°45′E
117 N8 **Pishchanka** Vinnyts'ka Oblast', C Ukraine 48°12′N 28°52′E
113 K21 **Pishë** Fier, SW Albania 40°40′N 19°22′E
143 X14 **Pīshīn** Sīstān va Balūchestān, SE Iran 26°05′N 61°46′E
149 O9 **Pishīn** Khyber Pakhtunkhwa, NW Pakistan 30°33′N 67°01′E
149 N11 **Pishin Lora** *var.* Psein Lora, *Pash.* Pseyn Bowr. ♣ SW Pakistan
Pishma *see* Pizhma
Pishpek *see* Bishkek
171 O14 **Pising** Pulau Kabaena, C Indonesia 05°07′S 121°50′E
Pisino *see* Pazin
Piski *see* Simeria
Piskolt *see* Pişcolt
147 Q9 **Piskom** *Rus.* Pskem. ♣ E Uzbekistan
Piskom Tizmasi *see* Pskemskiy Khrebet
35 P13 **Pismo Beach** California, W USA 35°08′N 120°38′W
77 P12 **Pissila** C Burkina 13°07′N 00°51′W
62 H8 **Pissis, Monte** ▲ N Argentina 27°45′S 68°43′W
41 X12 **Piste** Yucatán, E Mexico 20°40′N 88°34′W
107 O18 **Pisticci** Basilicata, S Italy 40°23′N 16°33′E
106 F11 **Pistoia** *anc.* Pistoria, Pistoriæ. Toscana, C Italy 43°57′N 10°53′E
32 E15 **Pistol River** Oregon, NW USA 42°13′N 124°23′W
Pistoria/Pistoriæ *see* Pistoia
15 U5 **Pistuacanis** ♣ Québec, SE Canada
Pistyan *see* Piešt'any
104 M5 **Pisuerga** ♣ N Spain
110 N8 **Pisz** *Ger.* Johannisburg. Warmińsko-Mazurskie, NE Poland 53°37′N 21°49′E
76 I13 **Pita** NW Guinea 11°05′N 12°15′W
54 D12 **Pitalito** Huila, S Colombia 01°51′N 76°01′W
60 I11 **Pitanga** Paraná, S Brazil 24°45′S 51°43′W
182 M9 **Pitarpunga Lake** *salt lake* New South Wales, SE Australia
193 P10 **Pitcairn Island** *island* S Pitcairn Islands
193 P10 **Pitcairn Islands** ◇ UK *dependent territory* C Pacific Ocean
93 J14 **Piteå** Norrbotten, N Sweden 65°19′N 21°30′E
92 I13 **Piteälven** ♣ N Sweden
116 I13 **Pitești** Argeș, S Romania 44°53′N 24°49′E
Pithagorio *see* Pythagóreio
180 I12 **Pithara** Western Australia 30°31′S 116°38′E
103 N6 **Pithiviers** Loiret, C France 48°10′N 02°15′E
152 L9 **Pithorāgarh** Uttarakhand, N India 29°35′N 80°12′E
188 B16 **Piti** W Guam 13°28′N 144°42′E
106 G13 **Pitigliano** Toscana, C Italy 42°38′N 11°40′E
40 F3 **Pitiquito** Sonora, NW Mexico 30°39′N 112°00′W
Pitkäranta *see* Pitkyaranta
38 M11 **Pitkas Point** Alaska, USA 62°01′N 163°17′W
124 H11 **Pitkyaranta** *Fin.* Pitkäranta. Respublika Kareliya, NW Russian Federation 61°34′N 31°27′E
96 J10 **Pitlochry** C Scotland, United Kingdom 56°47′N 03°48′W
18 I16 **Pitman** New Jersey, NE USA 39°43′N 75°06′W
146 I9 **Pitnak** *var.* Drujba, *Rus.* Druzhba. Xorazm Viloyati, W Uzbekistan 41°14′N 61°13′E
112 G8 **Pitomača** Virovitica-Podravina, NE Croatia 45°57′N 17°14′E
35 O2 **Pit River** ♣ California, W USA
63 G15 **Pitrufquén** Araucanía, S Chile 38°59′S 72°40′W
Pitsanulok *see* Phitsanulok
Pitschen *see* Byczyna
Pitsunda *see* Bich'vinta
109 X6 **Pitten** ♣ E Austria
10 J14 **Pitt Island** *island* British Columbia, W Canada
Pitt Island *see* Makin
22 M3 **Pittsboro** Mississippi, S USA 33°55′N 89°20′W
21 T9 **Pittsboro** North Carolina, SE USA 35°46′N 79°12′W
27 R7 **Pittsburg** Kansas, C USA 37°24′N 94°42′W
25 W6 **Pittsburg** Texas, SW USA 33°00′N 94°58′W
18 B14 **Pittsburgh** Pennsylvania, NE USA 40°26′N 80°W
30 J14 **Pittsfield** Illinois, N USA 39°36′N 90°48′W
19 R6 **Pittsfield** Maine, NE USA 44°46′N 69°22′W
18 L11 **Pittsfield** Massachusetts, NE USA 42°27′N 73°15′W
183 U3 **Pittsworth** Queensland, E Australia 27°43′S 151°36′E
62 I8 **Pituil** La Rioja, NW Argentina 28°33′S 67°24′W
56 A10 **Piura** Piura, NW Peru 05°11′S 80°41′W
56 A9 **Piura** *off.* Departamento de Piura. ◆ *department* NW Peru
Piura, Departamento de *see* Piura
35 S13 **Piute Peak** ▲ California, W USA 35°27′N 118°24′W
113 J15 **Piva** ♣ NW Montenegro
117 V5 **Pivdenne** Kharkivs'ka Oblast', E Ukraine 49°52′N 36°04′E
117 P8 **Pivdennyy Buh** *Rus.* Yuzhnyy Bug. ♣ S Ukraine
54 F5 **Pivijay** Magdalena, N Colombia 10°31′N 74°36′W
109 T13 **Pivka** *prev.* Šent Peter, *Ger.* Sankt Peter, *It.* San Pietro del Carso. SW Slovenia 45°41′N 14°12′E
117 U13 **Pivnichno-Kryms'kyy Kanal** *canal* S Ukraine
113 J15 **Pivsko Jezero** ◎ NW Montenegro
111 M18 **Piwniczna** Małopolskie, S Poland 49°26′N 20°43′E
35 R12 **Pixley** California, W USA 35°58′N 119°18′W
125 Q15 **Pizhma** *var.* Pishma. ♣ NW Russian Federation
13 U13 **Placentia** Newfoundland, Newfoundland and Labrador, SE Canada 47°12′N 53°58′W
Placentia *see* Piacenza
13 U13 **Placentia Bay** *inlet* Newfoundland, Newfoundland and Labrador, SE Canada
171 P5 **Placer** Masbate, N Philippines 11°54′N 123°54′E
35 P7 **Placerville** California, W USA 38°42′N 120°48′W
44 F5 **Placetas** Villa Clara, C Cuba 22°18′N 79°40′W
113 Q18 **Plačkovica** ▲▲ E Macedonia
36 L2 **Plain City** Utah, W USA 41°18′N 112°05′W
22 G4 **Plain Dealing** Louisiana, S USA 32°54′N 93°42′W
31 O14 **Plainfield** Indiana, N USA 39°42′N 86°18′W
18 K14 **Plainfield** New Jersey, NE USA 40°37′N 74°25′W
33 O8 **Plains** Montana, NW USA 47°27′N 114°52′W
24 L6 **Plains** Texas, SW USA 33°12′N 102°50′W
29 X10 **Plainview** Minnesota, N USA 44°10′N 92°10′W
29 Q13 **Plainview** Nebraska, C USA 42°21′N 97°47′W
25 N4 **Plainview** Texas, SW USA 34°12′N 101°43′W
26 K4 **Plainville** Kansas, C USA 39°13′N 99°18′W
115 I22 **Pláka** *var.* Mílos. Mílos, Kykládes, Greece, Aegean Sea 36°44′N 24°25′E
115 J15 **Pláka, Akrotírio** *headland* Límnos, E Greece 40°02′N 25°25′E
113 N19 **Plakenska Planina** ▲▲ SW Macedonia
44 K5 **Plana Cays** *islets* SE Bahamas
105 S12 **Plana, Isla** *var.* Nueva Tabarca. *island* E Spain
59 L18 **Planaltina** Goiás, S Brazil 15°35′S 47°28′W
83 O14 **Planalto Moçambicano** *plateau* N Mozambique
112 N10 **Plandište** Vojvodina, NE Serbia 45°13′N 21°07′E
100 N13 **Plane** ♣ NE Germany
54 E6 **Planeta Rica** Córdoba, NW Colombia 08°24′N 75°39′W
29 P11 **Plankinton** South Dakota, N USA 43°43′N 98°28′W
30 M11 **Plano** Illinois, N USA 41°39′N 88°32′W
25 U6 **Plano** Texas, SW USA 33°01′N 96°42′W
23 W12 **Plant City** Florida, SE USA 28°01′N 82°06′W
22 J9 **Plaquemine** Louisiana, S USA 30°17′N 91°13′W
104 K9 **Plasencia** Extremadura, W Spain 40°02′N 06°05′W
110 P7 **Płaska** Podlaskie, NE Poland 53°55′N 23°18′E
112 C10 **Plaški** Karlovac, C Croatia 45°04′N 15°21′E
113 N19 **Plasnica** SW FYR Macedonia 41°28′N 21°07′E
13 N14 **Plaster Rock** New Brunswick, SE Canada 46°55′N 67°24′W
107 J24 **Platani** *anc.* Halycus. ♣ Sicilia, Italy, C Mediterranean Sea
115 G17 **Platania** Thessalía, C Greece 39°09′N 23°15′E
115 G24 **Plátanos** Kríti, Greece, E Mediterranean Sea 35°27′N 23°34′E
65 H18 **Plata, Río de la** *var.* River Plate. *estuary* Argentina/Uruguay
77 V15 **Plateau** ◆ *state* C Nigeria
79 G19 **Plateaux** *var.* Région des Plateaux. ◆ *province* C Congo
Plateaux, Région des *see* Plateaux
Plate, Île *see* Flat Island
92 P1 **Platen, Kapp** *headland* NE Svalbard 80°30′N 22°46′E
Plate, River *see* Plata, Río de la
99 G22 **Plate Taille, Lac de la** *var.* L'Eau d'Heure. ◎ SE Belgium
Plathe *see* Płoty
39 N13 **Platinum** Alaska, USA 59°01′N 161°49′W
54 F5 **Plato** Magdalena, N Colombia 09°47′N 74°47′W
29 O11 **Platte** South Dakota, N USA 43°20′N 98°51′W
27 R3 **Platte City** Missouri, C USA 39°22′N 94°47′W
Plattensee *see* Balaton
27 R3 **Platte River** ♣ Iowa/Missouri, USA
29 Q15 **Platte River** ♣ Nebraska, C USA
37 T3 **Platteville** Colorado, C USA 40°13′N 104°49′W
30 K9 **Platteville** Wisconsin, N USA 42°44′N 90°27′W
101 N21 **Plattling** Bayern, SE Germany 48°45′N 12°52′E
27 R3 **Plattsburg** Missouri, C USA 39°33′N 94°27′W
18 L6 **Plattsburgh** New York, NE USA 44°42′N 73°29′W
29 S15 **Plattsmouth** Nebraska, C USA 41°00′N 95°52′W
101 M17 **Plauen** *var.* Plauen im Vogtland. Sachsen, E Germany 50°31′N 12°08′E
Plauen im Vogtland *see* Plauen
100 M10 **Plauer See** ◎ NE Germany
113 L16 **Plav** E Montenegro 42°36′N 19°57′E
118 I10 **Pļaviņas** *Ger.* Stockmannshof. S Latvia 56°37′N 25°40′E
126 K5 **Plavsk** Tul'skaya Oblast', W Russian Federation 53°42′N 37°21′E
41 Z12 **Playa del Carmen** Quintana Roo, E Mexico 20°37′N 87°04′W
40 J12 **Playa Los Corchos** Nayarit, SW Mexico 21°91′N 105°28′W
37 P16 **Playas Lake** ◎ New Mexico, SW USA
55 J15 **Playa Vicenté** Veracruz-Llave, SE Mexico 17°42′N 95°01′W
Plây Cu *see* Plei Ku
28 L3 **Plaza** North Dakota, N USA 48°00′N 102°00′W
63 I15 **Plaza Huincul** Neuquén, C Argentina 38°55′S 69°14′W
36 L3 **Pleasant Grove** Utah, W USA 40°21′N 111°44′W
29 V14 **Pleasant Hill** Iowa, C USA 41°34′N 93°31′W
27 R4 **Pleasant Hill** Missouri, C USA 38°47′N 94°16′W
Pleasant Island *see* Nauru
36 K13 **Pleasant, Lake** ◙ Arizona, SW USA
19 P8 **Pleasant Mountain** ▲ Maine, NE USA 44°01′N 70°47′W
27 R5 **Pleasanton** Kansas, C USA 38°09′N 94°43′W
25 R12 **Pleasanton** Texas, SW USA 28°58′N 98°28′W
185 G20 **Pleasant Point** Canterbury, South Island, New Zealand 44°16′S 171°09′E
19 R5 **Pleasant River** ♣ Maine, NE USA
18 J17 **Pleasantville** New Jersey, NE USA 39°22′N 74°31′W
103 N12 **Pléaux** Cantal, C France 45°08′N 02°10′E
111 B19 **Plechý** *var.* Plöckenstein. ▲ Austria/Czech Republic 48°45′N 13°50′E
Pleebo *see* Plibo
Pleihari *see* Pelaihari
167 U11 **Plei Ku** *prev.* Plây Cu. Gia Lai, C Vietnam 13°57′N 108°01′E
101 M16 **Pleisse** ♣ E Germany
Plencia *see* Plentzia
184 O7 **Plenty, Bay of** *bay* North Island, New Zealand
33 Y6 **Plentywood** Montana, NW USA 48°46′N 104°33′W
105 O2 **Plentzia** *var.* Plencia. País Vasco, N Spain 43°25′N 02°56′W
102 H5 **Plérin** Côtes d'Armor, NW France 48°33′N 02°46′W
124 M10 **Plesetsk** Arkhangel'skaya Oblast', NW Russian Federation 62°41′N 40°14′E
Pleshchenitsy *see* Plyeshchanitsy
Pleskau *see* Pskov
Pleskauer See *see* Pskov, Lake
Pleskava *see* Pskov
112 E8 **Pleso International** ✈ (Zagreb) Zagreb, NW Croatia 45°45′N 16°00′E
Pless *see* Pszczyna
15 Q11 **Plessisville** Québec, SE Canada 46°14′N 71°46′W
110 H12 **Pleszew** Wielkopolskie, C Poland 51°54′N 17°47′E
12 L10 **Plétipi, Lac** ◎ Québec, SE Canada
101 F15 **Plettenberg** Nordrhein-Westfalen, W Germany 51°13′N 07°52′E
114 I8 **Pleven** *prev.* Plevna. Pleven, N Bulgaria 43°25′N 24°36′E
114 I8 **Pleven** ◆ *province* N Bulgaria
Plevlja/Plevlje *see* Pljevlja
Plevna *see* Pleven
Plezzo *see* Bovec
Pliberk *see* Bleiburg
76 L17 **Plibo** *var.* Pleebo. SE Liberia 04°38′N 07°41′W
121 R11 **Pliny Trench** *undersea feature* C Mediterranean Sea
118 K13 **Plisa** *Rus.* Plissa. Vitsyebskaya Voblasts', N Belarus 55°13′N 27°57′E
Plissa *see* Plisa
112 D11 **Plitvica Selo** Lika-Senj, W Croatia 44°53′N 15°36′E
112 D11 **Plješevica** ▲▲ C Croatia
113 K14 **Pljevlja** *prev.* Plevlja, Plevlje. N Montenegro 43°21′N 19°21′E
Ploça *see* Ploçë
Plocce *see* Ploče
113 K22 **Ploçë** *var.* Ploça. Vlorë, SW Albania 40°24′N 19°41′E
113 G15 **Ploče** *It.* Plocce; *prev.* Kardeljevo. Dubrovnik-Neretva, SE Croatia 43°02′N 17°25′E
110 K11 **Płock** *Ger.* Plozk. Mazowieckie, C Poland 52°32′N 19°40′E
109 Q10 **Plöcken Pass** *Ger.* Plöckenpass, *It.* Passo di Monte Croce Carnico. *pass* SW Austria
Plöckenpass *see* Plöcken Pass
Plöckenstein *see* Plechý
99 B19 **Ploegsteert** Hainaut, W Belgium 50°45′N 02°52′E
102 H6 **Ploërmel** Morbihan, NW France 47°57′N 02°24′W
Ploești *see* Ploiești
116 K13 **Ploiești** *prev.* Ploești. Prahova, SE Romania 44°56′N 26°03′E
115 L17 **Plomári** *prev.* Plomárion. Lésvos, E Greece 38°58′N 26°24′E
Plomárion *see* Plomári
103 O12 **Plomb du Cantal** ▲ C France 45°03′N 02°48′E
183 V6 **Plomer, Point** *headland* New South Wales, SE Australia 31°19′S 153°00′E
100 J8 **Plön** Schleswig-Holstein, N Germany 54°10′N 10°25′E
110 L11 **Płońsk** Mazowieckie, C Poland 52°38′N 20°23′E
119 J20 **Plotnitsa** Brestskaya Voblasts', SW Belarus 52°03′N 26°39′E
110 E8 **Płoty** *Ger.* Plathe. Zachodnio-pomorskie, NW Poland 53°48′N 15°16′E
102 G7 **Plouay** Morbihan, NW France 47°54′N 03°14′W
111 D15 **Ploučnice** *Ger.* Polzen. ♣ NE Czech Republic
114 I10 **Plovdiv** *prev.* Eumolpias; *anc.* Evmolpia, Philippopolis, *Lat.* Trimontium. Plovdiv, C Bulgaria 42°09′N 24°47′E
114 I11 **Plovdiv** ◆ *province* C Bulgaria
30 L6 **Plover** Wisconsin, N USA 44°30′N 89°33′W
Plozk *see* Płock
27 U11 **Plumerville** Arkansas, C USA 35°09′N 92°38′W
19 P10 **Plum Island** *island* Massachusetts, NE USA
32 M9 **Plummer** Idaho, NW USA 47°19′N 116°54′W
83 J18 **Plumtree** Matabeleland South, SW Zimbabwe 20°30′S 27°50′E
118 D11 **Plungė** Telšiai, W Lithuania 55°55′N 21°53′E
113 J15 **Plužine** NW Montenegro 43°08′N 18°49′E
119 K14 **Plyeshchanitsy** *Rus.* Pleshchenitsy. Minskaya Voblasts', N Belarus 54°25′N 27°50′E
97 I24 **Plymouth** SW England, United Kingdom 50°23′N 04°10′W
31 O11 **Plymouth** Indiana, N USA 41°20′N 86°19′W
19 P12 **Plymouth** Massachusetts, NE USA 41°57′N 70°40′W
19 N8 **Plymouth** New Hampshire, NE USA 43°43′N 71°39′W
21 X9 **Plymouth** North Carolina, SE USA 35°53′N 76°46′W
30 M8 **Plymouth** Wisconsin, N USA 43°48′N 87°58′W
Plymouth ○ (Montserrat) *see* Brades
97 J20 **Plynlimon** ▲ C Wales, United Kingdom 52°27′N 03°48′W
124 G14 **Plyussa** Pskovskaya Oblast', W Russian Federation 58°27′N 29°21′E
111 B17 **Plzeň** *Ger.* Pilsen, *Pol.* Pilzno. Plzeňský Kraj, W Czech Republic 49°45′N 13°23′E
111 B17 **Plzeňský Kraj** ◆ *region* W Czech Republic
110 F11 **Pniewy** *Ger.* Pinne. Wielkolpolskie, W Poland 52°31′N 16°14′E
77 P13 **Pô** S Burkina 11°11′N 01°10′W
106 D8 **Po** ♣ N Italy
42 M13 **Poás, Volcán** 🌋 NW Costa Rica 10°12′N 84°12′W
77 S16 **Pobè** S Benin 07°00′N 02°41′E
123 S8 **Pobeda, Gora** ▲ NE Russian Federation 65°28′N 145°44′E
Pobeda Peak *see* Pobedy, Pik/Tomur Feng
147 Z7 **Pobedy, Pik** *Chin.* Tomür Feng. ▲ China/Kyrgyzstan 42°02′N 80°02′E *see also* Tomür Feng
Pobedy, Pik *see* Tomür Feng
110 H11 **Pobiedziska** *Ger.* Pudewitz. Wielkolpolskie, C Poland 52°30′N 17°19′E
Po, Bocche del *see* Po, Foci del
27 W9 **Pocahontas** Arkansas, C USA 36°15′N 91°00′W
29 U12 **Pocahontas** Iowa, C USA 42°44′N 94°40′W
33 Q15 **Pocatello** Idaho, NW USA 42°52′N 112°27′W
167 S13 **Pochentong** ✈ (Phnum Penh) Phnum Penh, S Cambodia 11°24′N 104°52′E
126 I6 **Pochep** Bryanskaya Oblast', W Russian Federation 52°56′N 33°20′E
126 H4 **Pochinok** Smolenskaya Oblast', W Russian Federation 54°21′N 32°29′E
41 R17 **Pochutla** *var.* San Pedro Pochutla. Oaxaca, SE Mexico 15°45′N 96°30′W
62 I6 **Pocitos, Salar** *var.* Salar Quiróm. *salt lake* NW Argentina
101 O22 **Pocking** Bayern, SE Germany 48°22′N 13°17′E
186 I10 **Pocklington Reef** *reef* SE Papua New Guinea
59 P15 **Poço da Cruz, Açude** ◙ E Brazil
27 R11 **Pocola** Oklahoma, C USA 35°13′N 94°28′W
21 Y5 **Pocomoke City** Maryland, NE USA 38°04′N 75°34′W
59 L21 **Poços de Caldas** Minas Gerais, NE Brazil 21°48′S 46°33′W
124 H14 **Podberez'ye** Novgorodskaya Oblast', NW Russian Federation 58°42′N 31°22′E
Podbrodzie *see* Pabradė
125 U8 **Podcher'ye** Respublika Komi, NW Russian Federation 63°55′N 57°34′E
111 E16 **Poděbrady** *Ger.* Podiebrad. Středočeský Kraj, C Czech Republic 50°10′N 15°06′E
126 L9 **Podgorenskiy** Voronezhskaya Oblast', W Russian Federation 50°22′N 39°43′E
113 J17 **Podgorica** *prev.* Titograd. ● S Montenegro 42°25′N 19°16′E
113 K17 **Podgorica** ✈ S Montenegro 42°22′N 19°16′E
109 T13 **Podgrad** SW Slovenia 45°31′N 14°09′E
Podiebrad *see* Poděbrady
116 M5 **Podil's'ka Vysochina** *plateau* W Ukraine
Podium Anicensis *see* le Puy
122 L11 **Podkamennaya Tunguska** *Eng.* Stony Tunguska. ♣ C Russian Federation
111 N17 **Podkarpackie** ◆ *province* SE Poland
Pod Klošter *see* Arnoldstein
110 P9 **Podlaskie** ◆ *province* Mazowieckie, C Poland
127 Q8 **Podlesnoye** Saratovskaya Oblast', W Russian Federation 51°51′N 47°03′E
126 K4 **Podol'sk** Moskovskaya Oblast', W Russian Federation 55°24′N 37°30′E
76 H10 **Podor** N Senegal 16°40′N 14°57′W
125 P12 **Podosinovets** Kirovskaya Oblast', NW Russian Federation 60°15′N 47°06′E
124 I12 **Podporozh'ye** Leningradskaya Oblast', NW Russian Federation 60°52′N 34°00′E
Podravska Slatina *see* Slatina
112 J13 **Podromanlja** Republika Srpska, SE Bosnia and Herzegovina 43°55′N 18°46′E
Podsvil'ye *see* Padsvillye
116 L9 **Podu Iloaiei** *prev.* Podul Iloaiei. Iași, NE Romania 47°13′N 27°16′E
113 N15 **Podujevë** *Serb.* Podujevo. N Kosovo 42°56′N 21°13′E
Podujevo *see* Podujevë
Podul Iloaiei *see* Podu Iloaiei
Podunajská Rovina *see* Little Alföld
124 M12 **Podyuga** Arkhangel'skaya Oblast', NW Russian Federation 61°04′N 40°46′E
56 A9 **Poechos, Embalse** ◎ NW Peru
55 W10 **Poeketi** Sipaliwini, E Suriname
100 L8 **Poel** *island* N Germany
83 M20 **Poelela, Lagoa** ◎ S Mozambique
Poerwodadi *see* Purwodadi
Poerwokerto *see* Purwokerto
Poerworedjo *see* Purworejo
Poetovio *see* Ptuj
83 E23 **Pofadder** Northern Cape, W South Africa 29°09′S 19°25′E
106 I9 **Po, Foci del** *var.* Bocche del Po. ♣ NE Italy
116 E12 **Pogăniș** ♣ W Romania
Pogegen *see* Pagėgiai
106 G12 **Poggibonsi** Toscana, C Italy 43°28′N 11°09′E
107 I14 **Poggio Mirteto** Lazio, C Italy 42°17′N 12°42′E
109 V4 **Pöggstall** Niederösterreich, N Austria 48°19′N 15°10′E
116 L13 **Pogoanele** Buzău, SE Romania 44°55′N 27°00′E
Pogónion *see* Delvinákі
113 M21 **Pogradec** *var.* Pogradeci. Korçë, SE Albania 40°54′N 20°40′E
Pogradeci *see* Pogradec
123 S15 **Pogranichnyy** Primorskiy Kray, SE Russian Federation 44°18′N 131°33′E
38 M16 **Pogromni Volcano** ▲ Unimak Island, Alaska, USA 54°34′N 164°41′W
163 Z15 **Pohang** *Jap.* Hokō; *prev.* P'ohang. E South Korea 36°02′N 129°20′E
P'ohang *see* Pohang
15 T9 **Pohénégamook, Lac** ◎ Québec, SE Canada
93 L20 **Pohja** *Swe.* Pojo. Etelä-Suomi, SW Finland 60°07′N 23°30′E
Pohjanlahti *see* Bothnia, Gulf of
189 U16 **Pohnpei** ◆ *state* E Micronesia
189 O12 **Pohnpei** ✕ Pohnpei, E Micronesia
189 O12 **Pohnpei** *prev.* Ponape Ascension Island. *island* E Micronesia
111 F19 **Pohořelice** *Ger.* Pohrlitz. Jihomoravský Kraj, SE Czech Republic 48°58′N 16°30′E
109 V10 **Pohorje** *Ger.* Bacher. ▲▲ N Slovenia
117 N6 **Pohrebyshche** Vinnyts'ka Oblast', C Ukraine 49°31′N 29°16′E
Pohrlitz *see* Pohořelice
161 P9 **Po Hu** ◙ E China
116 G15 **Poiana Mare** Dolj, S Romania 43°55′N 23°02′E
Poictiers *see* Poitiers
127 N6 **Poim** Penzenskaya Oblast', W Russian Federation 53°03′N 43°11′E
159 N15 **Poindo** Xigzang Zizhiqu, W China 29°58′N 91°20′E
195 Y13 **Poinsett, Cape** *headland* Antarctica 65°35′S 113°00′E
29 R9 **Poinsett, Lake** ◎ South Dakota, N USA
22 I10 **Point Au Fer Island** *island* Louisiana, S USA
39 X14 **Point Baker** Prince of Wales Island, Alaska, USA 56°19′N 133°31′W
25 U13 **Point Comfort** Texas, SW USA 28°40′N 96°33′W
Point de Galle *see* Galle
44 K10 **Pointe à Gravois** *headland* SW Haiti 18°00′N 73°53′W
22 L10 **Pointe a la Hache** Louisiana, S USA 29°34′N 89°48′W
45 Y6 **Pointe-à-Pitre** Grande Terre, C Guadeloupe 16°14′N 61°32′W
15 U7 **Pointe-au-Père** Québec, SE Canada 48°31′N 68°27′W
15 V5 **Pointe-aux-Anglais** Québec, SE Canada 49°40′N 67°09′W
45 T10 **Pointe Du Cap** *headland* N Saint Lucia 14°06′N 60°56′W
79 E21 **Pointe-Noire** Kouilou, S Congo 04°46′S 11°53′E
45 X6 **Pointe Noire** Basse Terre, W Guadeloupe 16°14′N 61°47′W
79 E21 **Pointe-Noire** ✕ Kouilou, S Congo 04°45′S 11°55′E
45 U15 **Point Fortin** Trinidad, Trinidad and Tobago 10°12′N 61°41′W
38 M6 **Point Hope** Alaska, USA 68°21′N 166°48′W
39 N5 **Point Lay** Alaska, USA 69°42′N 162°57′W
18 B16 **Point Marion** Pennsylvania, NE USA 39°44′N 79°53′W
18 K16 **Point Pleasant** New Jersey, NE USA 40°04′N 74°00′W
21 P4 **Point Pleasant** West Virginia, NE USA 38°53′N 82°07′W
45 R14 **Point Salines** ✕ (St. George's) SW Grenada 12°00′N 61°47′W
102 L9 **Poitiers** *prev.* Poictiers; *anc.* Limonum. Vienne, W France 46°35′N 00°19′E
102 K9 **Poitou** *cultural region* W France
102 K10 **Poitou-Charentes** ◆ *region* W France
103 N3 **Poix-de-Picardie** Somme, N France 49°47′N 01°58′E
Pojo *see* Pohja
37 S10 **Pojoaque** New Mexico, SW USA 35°52′N 106°01′W
152 E11 **Pokaran** Rājasthān, NW India 26°55′N 71°55′E
183 R4 **Pokataroo** New South Wales, SE Australia 29°37′S 148°43′E
119 P18 **Pokats' Rus.** Pokot'. ♣ SE Belarus
29 V5 **Pokegama Lake** ◎ Minnesota, N USA
184 L6 **Pokeno** Waikato, North Island, New Zealand 37°15′S 175°01′E
153 O11 **Pokharā** Western, C Nepal 28°14′N 84°E
127 T6 **Pokhvistnevo** Samarskaya Oblast', W Russian Federation 53°38′N 52°07′E
55 W10 **Pokigron** Sipaliwini, C Suriname 04°31′N 55°23′W
92 L10 **Pokka** *Lapp.* Bohkká. Lappi, N Finland 68°11′N 25°45′E
79 N16 **Poko** Orientale, NE Dem. Rep. Congo 03°08′N 26°52′E
Pokot' *see* Pokats'
Po-ko-to Shan *see* Bogda Shan
147 S7 **Pokrovka** Talasskaya Oblast', NW Kyrgyzstan 42°45′N 71°33′E
Pokrovka *see* Kyzyl-Suu
117 V8 **Pokrovs'ke** *Rus.* Pokrovskoye. Dnipropetrovs'ka Oblast', E Ukraine 47°58′N 36°15′E
Pokrovskoye *see* Pokrovs'ke
Pola *see* Pula
37 N10 **Polacca** Arizona, SW USA 35°49′N 110°21′W
Pola de Laviana *see* Pola de Llaviana
Pola de Lena *see* La Pola
104 L2 **Pola de Llaviana** *var.* Pola de Laviana. Asturias, N Spain 43°15′N 05°33′W
Pola de Siero *see* La Pola Siero
191 Y3 **Poland** Kiritimati, E Kiribati 01°52′N 157°33′W
110 H12 **Poland** *off.* Republic of Poland, *var.* Polish Republic, *Pol.* Polska, Rzeczpospolita Polska; *prev. Pol.* Polska Rzeczpospolita Ludowa, The Polish People's Republic. ◆ *republic* C Europe
Poland, Republic of *see* Poland
Polangen *see* Palanga
110 G7 **Polanów** *Ger.* Pollnow. Zachodnio-pomorskie, NW Poland 54°07′N 16°38′E
136 H13 **Polatlı** Ankara, C Turkey 39°34′N 32°08′E
118 L12 **Polatsk** *Rus.* Polotsk. Vitsyebskaya Voblasts', N Belarus 55°29′N 28°47′E
110 F8 **Połczyn-Zdrój** *Ger.* Bad Polzin. Zachodnio-pomorskie, NW Poland 53°44′N 16°02′E
Pol-e-'Alam *see* Pul-e-'Alam
Polekhatum *see* Pulhatyn
Pol-e Khomrī *see* Pul-e Khumrī
197 S10 **Pole Plain** *undersea feature* Arctic Ocean
Pol-e-Safid *see* Pol-e Sefid
143 P5 **Pol-e Sefid** *var.* Pol-e-Safid, Pul-i-Sefid. Māzandarān, N Iran 36°05′N 53°01′E
118 B13 **Polessk** *Ger.* Labiau. Kaliningradskaya Oblast', W Russian Federation 54°52′N 21°06′E
Polesskoye *see* Polis'ke
171 N13 **Polewali** Sulawesi, C Indonesia 03°26′S 119°23′E
114 G11 **Polezhan** ▲ SW Bulgaria 41°42′N 23°28′E
78 F13 **Poli** Nord, N Cameroon 09°31′N 13°10′E
Poli *see* Pólis
107 M19 **Policastro, Golfo di** *gulf* S Italy
110 D8 **Police** *Ger.* Politz. Zachodnio-pomorskie, NW Poland 53°34′N 14°34′E
172 I17 **Police, Pointe** *headland* Mahé, NE Seychelles 04°48′S 55°31′E
115 L17 **Polichnítos** *var.* Polihnitos, Políkhnitos. Lésvos, E Greece 39°04′N 26°10′E
Poligiros *see* Polýgyros
107 P17 **Polignano a Mare** Puglia, SE Italy 40°59′N 17°13′E
103 S9 **Poligny** Jura, E France 46°51′N 05°42′E
Polihnitos *see* Polichnítos
Polikastro/Políkastron *see* Polýkastro
Políkhnitos *see* Polichnítos
171 O3 **Polillo Islands** *island group* N Philippines
109 Q9 **Polinik** ▲ SW Austria 46°54′N 13°10′E
115 J15 **Políochni** *var.* Polýochni. *site of ancient city* Límnos, E Greece
121 O2 **Pólis** *var.* Poli. W Cyprus 35°02′N 32°27′E
Polish People's Republic, The *see* Poland
Polish Republic *see* Poland
117 O3 **Polis'ke** *Rus.* Polesskoye. Kyyivs'ka Oblast', N Ukraine 51°16′N 29°27′E
107 N22 **Polistena** Calabria, SW Italy 38°25′N 16°05′E
Politz *see* Police
Políyiros *see* Polýgyros
29 V14 **Polk City** Iowa, C USA 41°46′N 93°42′W
110 F13 **Polkowice** *Ger.* Heerwegen. Dolnośląskie, W Poland 51°32′N 16°06′E
155 G22 **Pollāchi** Tamil Nādu, SE India 10°38′N 77°00′E
109 W7 **Pöllau** Steiermark, SE Austria 47°18′N 15°46′E
189 T13 **Pollé** *atoll* Chuuk Islands, C Micronesia
105 X9 **Pollença** Mallorca, Spain, W Mediterranean Sea 39°52′N 03°01′E
Pollnow *see* Polanów
29 N7 **Pollock** South Dakota, N USA 45°53′N 100°15′W
92 L8 **Polmak** Finnmark, N Norway 70°01′N 28°04′E
30 L10 **Polo** Illinois, N USA 41°59′N 89°34′W
193 V15 **Poloa** *island* Tongatapu Group, N Tonga
42 E5 **Polochic, Río** ♣ C Guatemala
Pologi *see* Polohy
117 V9 **Polohy** *Rus.* Pologi. Zaporiz'ka Oblast', SE Ukraine 47°30′N 36°18′E
83 K20 **Polokwane** *prev.* Pietersburg. Limpopo, NE South Africa 23°54′S 29°23′E
14 M10 **Polonais, Lac des** ◎ Québec, SE Canada
61 G20 **Polonio, Cabo** *headland* E Uruguay 34°22′S 53°46′W
155 K24 **Polonnaruwa** North Central Province, C Sri Lanka 07°56′N 81°02′E
116 L5 **Polonne** *Rus.* Polonnoye. Khmel'nyts'ka Oblast', NW Ukraine 50°10′N 27°30′E
Polonnoye *see* Polonne
Polotsk *see* Polatsk
Polovinka *see* Ugleural'skiy
109 T7 **Pöls** *var.* Pölsbach. ♣ E Austria
Pölsbach *see* Pöls
Polska/Polska, Rzeczpospolita/Polska Rzeczpospolita Ludowa *see* Poland
114 L10 **Polski Gradets** Stara Zagora, C Bulgaria 42°12′N 26°06′E
114 K8 **Polski Trŭmbesh** Ruse, N Bulgaria 43°22′N 25°38′E
33 P8 **Polson** Montana, NW USA 47°41′N 114°09′W

◆ Country
● Country Capital
◇ Dependent Territory
○ Dependent Territory Capital
◆ Administrative Regions
✈ International Airport
▲ Mountain
▲▲ Mountain Range
🌋 Volcano
♣ River
◎ Lake
◙ Reservoir

117 *T6* **Poltava** Poltavs'ka Oblast', NE Ukraine *49°33′N 34°32′E*
Poltava *see* Poltavs'ka Oblast'
117 *R5* **Poltavs'ka Oblast'** *var.* Poltava, ***Rus.*** Poltavskaya Oblast'. ◈ *province* NE Ukraine
Poltavskaya Oblast' *see* Poltavs'ka Oblast'
Poltoratsk *see* Aşgabat
118 *I5* **Põltsamaa** *Ger.* Oberpahlen. Jõgevamaa, E Estonia *58°40′N 26°00′E*
118 *I4* **Põltsamaa** *var.* Põltsamaa Jõgi. ≈ C Estonia
Põltsamaa Jõgi *see* Põltsamaa
122 *I8* **Poluy** ≈ N Russian Federation
118 *J6* **Põlva** *Ger.* Pölwe. Põlvamaa, SE Estonia *58°04′N 27°06′E*
93 *N16* **Polvijärvi** Itä-Suomi, SE Finland *62°53′N 29°20′E*
Pölwe *see* Põlva
115 *I22* **Polýaigos** *island* Kykládes, Greece, Aegean Sea
115 *I22* **Polyaígou Folégandrou, Stenó** *strait* Kykládes, Greece, Aegean Sea
124 *J3* **Polyarnyy** Murmanskaya Oblast', NW Russian Federation *69°10′N 33°21′E*
125 *W5* **Polyarnyy Ural** ▲▲ NW Russian Federation
115 *G14* **Polýgyros** *var.* Poligiros, Políyiros. Kentrikí Makedonía, N Greece *40°21′N 23°27′E*
114 *F13* **Polýkastro** *var.* Polikastro; ***prev.*** Políkastron. Kentrikí Makedonía, N Greece *41°01′N 22°33′E*
193 *O9* **Polynesia** *island group* C Pacific Ocean
Polýochni *see* Políochni
41 *Y13* **Polyuc** Quintana Roo, E Mexico
109 *V10* **Polzela** C Slovenia *46°18′N 15°04′E*
Polzen *see* Ploučnice
56 *D12* **Pomabamba** Ancash, C Peru *08°48′S 77°30′W*
185 *D23* **Pomahaka** ≈ South Island, New Zealand
106 *F12* **Pomarance** Toscana, C Italy *43°19′N 10°53′E*
104 *G9* **Pombal** Leiria, C Portugal *39°55′N 08°38′W*
76 *D9* **Pombas** Santo Antão, NW Cape Verde *17°09′N 25°02′W*
83 *N19* **Pomene** Inhambane, SE Mozambique *22°57′S 35°34′E*
110 *G8* **Pomerania** *cultural region* Germany/Poland
110 *D7* **Pomeranian Bay** *Ger.* Pommersche Bucht, ***Pol.*** Zatoka Pomorska. *bay* Germany/Poland
31 *T15* **Pomeroy** Ohio, N USA *39°01′N 82°01′W*
32 *L10* **Pomeroy** Washington, NW USA *46°28′N 117°36′W*
117 *Q8* **Pomichna** Kirovohrads'ka Oblast', C Ukraine *48°07′N 31°25′E*
186 *H7* **Pomio** New Britain, E Papua New Guinea *05°31′S 151°30′E*
Pomir, Dar''yoi *see* Pamir/Pāmīr, Daryā-ye
27 *T6* **Pomme de Terre Lake** ⊞ Missouri, C USA
29 *S8* **Pomme de Terre River** ≈ Minnesota, N USA
Pommersche Bucht *see* Pomeranian Bay
35 *T15* **Pomona** California, W USA *34°03′N 117°45′W*
114 *N9* **Pomorie** Burgas, E Bulgaria *42°32′N 27°39′E*
Pomorska, Zatoka *see* Pomeranian Bay
110 *H8* **Pomorskie** ◈ *province* N Poland
125 *Q4* **Pomorskiy Proliv** *strait* NW Russian Federation
125 *T10* **Pomozdino** Respublika Komi, NW Russian Federation *62°11′N 54°13′E*
Pompaelo *see* Pamplona
23 *Z15* **Pompano Beach** Florida, SE USA *26°14′N 80°06′W*
107 *K18* **Pompei** Campania, S Italy *40°45′N 14°27′E*
33 *V10* **Pompeys Pillar** Montana, NW USA *45°58′N 107°55′W*
Ponape Ascension Island *see* Pohnpei
29 *R13* **Ponca** Nebraska, C USA *42°35′N 96°42′W*
27 *O8* **Ponca City** Oklahoma, C USA *36°41′N 97°04′W*
45 *T6* **Ponce** C Puerto Rico *18°01′N 66°36′W*
23 *X10* **Ponce de Leon Inlet** *inlet* Florida, SE USA
22 *K8* **Ponchatoula** Louisiana, S USA *30°26′N 90°26′W*
26 *M8* **Pond Creek** Oklahoma, C USA *36°40′N 97°48′W*
155 *J20* **Pondicherry** *var.* Puduchcheri, ***Fr.*** Pondichéry. Pondicherry, SE India *11°59′N 79°50′E*
151 *I20* **Pondicherry** *var.* Puduchcheri, ***Fr.*** Pondichéry. ◈ *union territory* India
Pondichéry *see* Pondicherry
197 *N11* **Pond Inlet** *var.* Mittimatalik. Baffin Island, Nunavut, NE Canada *72°37′N 77°56′W*
187 *P16* **Ponérihouen** Province Nord, C New Caledonia *21°04′S 165°24′E*
104 *J4* **Ponferrada** Castilla y León, NW Spain *42°33′N 06°35′W*
184 *N13* **Pongaroa** Manawatu-Wanganui, North Island, New Zealand *40°36′S 176°08′E*
167 *Q12* **Pong Nam Ron** Chantaburi, S Thailand *12°55′N 102°15′E*
81 *C14* **Pongo** ≈ W South Sudan
152 *I7* **Pong Reservoir** ⊞ N India
111 *N14* **Poniatowa** Lubelskie, E Poland *51°11′N 22°05′E*
167 *R12* **Pônley** Kâmpóng Chhnăng, C Cambodia *12°26′N 104°25′E*
155 *I20* **Ponnaiyār** ≈ SE India
11 *Q15* **Ponoka** Alberta, SW Canada *52°42′N 113°33′W*
127 *U6* **Ponomarevka** Orenburgskaya Oblast', W Russian Federation *53°16′N 54°10′E*
169 *Q17* **Ponorogo** Jawa, C Indonesia *07°51′S 111°30′E*
122 *F6* **Ponoy** ≈ NW Russian Federation
102 *K11* **Pons** Charente-Maritime, W France *45°31′N 00°31′W*
Pons *see* Ponts
Pons Aelii *see* Newcastle upon Tyne
Pons Vetus *see* Pontevedra
99 *G20* **Pont-à-Celles** Hainaut, S Belgium *50°31′N 04°21′E*
102 *K16* **Pontacq** Pyrénées-Atlantiques, SW France *43°11′N 00°06′W*
64 *P3* **Ponta Delgada** São Miguel, Azores, Portugal, NE Atlantic Ocean *37°29′N 25°40′W*
64 *P3* **Ponta Delgado** ✈ São Miguel, Azores, Portugal, NE Atlantic Ocean *37°28′N 25°40′W*
64 *N2* **Ponta do Pico** ▲ Pico, Azores, Portugal, NE Atlantic Ocean *38°28′N 28°25′W*
60 *J11* **Ponta Grossa** Paraná, S Brazil *25°07′S 50°09′W*
103 *S5* **Pont-à-Mousson** Meurthe-et-Moselle, NE France *48°55′N 06°03′E*
103 *T9* **Pontarlier** Doubs, E France *46°54′N 06°20′E*
106 *G11* **Pontassieve** Toscana, C Italy *43°46′N 11°28′E*
102 *L4* **Pont-Audemer** Eure, N France *49°22′N 00°31′E*
22 *K9* **Pontchartrain, Lake** ◎ Louisiana, S USA
102 *I8* **Pontchâteau** Loire-Atlantique, NW France *47°26′N 02°04′W*
103 *R10* **Pont-de-Vaux** Ain, E France *46°25′N 04°57′E*
104 *G4* **Ponteareas** Galicia, NW Spain *42°11′N 08°29′W*
106 *J6* **Pontebba** Friuli-Venezia Giulia, NE Italy *46°32′N 13°18′E*
104 *G4* **Ponte Caldelas** Galicia, NW Spain *42°23′N 08°30′W*
107 *J16* **Pontecorvo** Lazio, C Italy *41°27′N 13°40′E*
104 *G5* **Ponte da Barca** Viana do Castelo, N Portugal *41°48′N 08°25′W*
104 *G5* **Ponte de Lima** Viana do Castelo, N Portugal *41°46′N 08°35′W*
106 *F11* **Pontedera** Toscana, C Italy *43°40′N 10°38′E*
104 *H10* **Ponte de Sor** Portalegre, C Portugal *39°15′N 08°01′W*
104 *H2* **Pontedeume** Galicia, NW Spain *43°22′N 08°09′W*
106 *F6* **Ponte di Legno** Lombardia, N Italy *46°16′N 10°31′E*
11 *T17* **Ponteix** Saskatchewan, S Canada *49°43′N 107°22′W*
171 *Q16* **Ponte Macassar** *var.* Pante Macassar, Pante Makasar, Pante Makassar. W East Timor *09°11′S 124°27′E*
59 *N20* **Ponte Nova** Minas Gerais, NE Brazil *20°25′S 42°54′W*
59 *G18* **Pontes e Lacerda** Mato Grosso, W Brazil *15°14′S 59°21′W*
104 *G4* **Pontevedra** *anc.* Pons Vetus. Galicia, NW Spain *42°25′N 08°39′W*
104 *G3* **Pontevedra** ◈ *province* Galicia, NW Spain
104 *G4* **Pontevedra, Ría de** *estuary* NW Spain
30 *M12* **Pontiac** Illinois, N USA *40°54′N 88°36′W*
31 *R9* **Pontiac** Michigan, N USA *42°38′N 83°17′W*
169 *P11* **Pontianak** Borneo, C Indonesia *0°05′S 109°16′E*
107 *I16* **Pontino, Agro** *plain* C Italy
Pontisarae *see* Pontoise
102 *H6* **Pontivy** Morbihan, NW France *48°04′N 02°58′W*
102 *F6* **Pont-l'Abbé** Finistère, NW France *47°52′N 04°14′W*
103 *N4* **Pontoise** *anc.* Briva Isarae, Cergy-Pontoise, Pontisarae. Val-d'Oise, N France *49°03′N 02°05′E*
11 *W13* **Ponton** Manitoba, C Canada *54°36′N 99°02′W*
102 *J5* **Pontorson** Manche, N France *48°33′N 01°31′W*
22 *M2* **Pontotoc** Mississippi, S USA *34°15′N 89°00′W*
25 *R9* **Pontotoc** Texas, SW USA *30°52′N 98°57′W*
106 *E10* **Pontremoli** Toscana, C Italy *44°24′N 09°55′E*
108 *J10* **Pontresina** Graubünden, S Switzerland *46°29′N 09°52′E*
105 *U5* **Ponts** *var.* Pons. Cataluña, NE Spain *41°55′N 01°12′E*
103 *R14* **Pont-St-Esprit** Gard, S France *44°15′N 04°37′E*
97 *K21* **Pontypool** *Wel.* Pontypŵl. SE Wales, United Kingdom *51°43′N 03°02′W*
97 *J22* **Pontypridd** S Wales, United Kingdom *51°37′N 03°22′W*
Pontypŵl *see* Pontypool
43 *R17* **Ponuga** Veraguas, SE Panama *07°50′N 80°58′W*
184 *L6* **Ponui Island** *island* N New Zealand
119 *K14* **Ponya** ≈ N Belarus
107 *I17* **Ponza, Isola di** *Island* Isole Ponziane, S Italy
107 *I17* **Ponziane, Isole** *island* C Italy
182 *F7* **Poochera** South Australia *32°45′S 134°51′E*
97 *L24* **Poole** S England, United Kingdom *50°43′N 01°59′W*
25 *S6* **Poolville** Texas, SW USA *33°00′N 97°55′W*
Poona *see* Pune
182 *M8* **Pooncarie** New South Wales, SE Australia *33°26′S 142°37′E*
183 *N6* **Poopelloe Lake** *seasonal lake* New South Wales, SE Australia
57 *K19* **Poopó** Oruro, C Bolivia *18°23′S 66°58′W*
57 *K19* **Poopó, Lago** *var.* Lago Pampa Aullagas. ◎ W Bolivia
184 *L3* **Poor Knights Islands** *island* N New Zealand
39 *P10* **Poorman** Alaska, USA *64°05′N 155°34′W*
182 *E3* **Pootnoura** South Australia *28°31′S 134°09′E*
147 *R10* **Pop** *Rus.* Pap. Namangan Viloyati, E Uzbekistan *40°49′N 71°06′E*
117 *X7* **Popasna** *Rus.* Popasnaya. Luhans'ka Oblast', E Ukraine *48°38′N 38°24′E*
Popasnaya *see* Popasna
54 *D12* **Popayán** Cauca, SW Colombia *02°27′N 76°32′W*
99 *B18* **Poperinge** West-Vlaanderen, W Belgium *50°52′N 02°44′E*
123 *N7* **Popigay** Krasnoyarskiy Kray, N Russian Federation *71°54′N 110°45′E*
123 *N7* **Popigay** ≈ N Russian Federation
117 *O5* **Popil'nya** Zhytomyrs'ka Oblast', N Ukraine *49°57′N 29°24′E*
182 *K8* **Popiltah Lake** *seasonal lake* New South Wales, SE Australia
33 *X7* **Poplar** Montana, NW USA *48°06′N 105°12′W*
11 *Y14* **Poplar** ≈ Manitoba, C Canada
27 *X8* **Poplar Bluff** Missouri, C USA *36°45′N 90°23′W*
33 *X6* **Poplar River** ≈ Montana, NW USA
41 *P14* **Popocatépetl** ⛰ S Mexico *18°59′N 98°37′W*
79 *H21* **Popokabaka** Bandundu, SW Dem. Rep. Congo *05°42′S 16°35′E*
107 *J15* **Popoli** Abruzzo, C Italy *42°09′N 13°51′E*
186 *F9* **Popondetta** Northern, S Papua New Guinea *08°45′S 148°15′E*
112 *F9* **Popovača** Sisak-Moslavina, NE Croatia *45°35′N 16°37′E*
114 *L8* **Popovo** Tŭrgovishte, N Bulgaria *43°20′N 26°14′E*
Popovo *see* Iskra
Popper *see* Poprad
30 *M5* **Popple River** ≈ Wisconsin, N USA
111 *L19* **Poprad** *Ger.* Deutschendorf, ***Hung.*** Poprád. Prešovský Kraj, E Slovakia *49°04′N 20°16′E*
111 *L18* **Poprad** *Ger.* Popper, ***Hung.*** Poprád. ≈ Poland/Slovakia
111 *L19* **Poprad-Tatry** ✈ (Poprad) Prešovský Kraj, E Slovakia *49°04′N 20°21′E*
21 *X7* **Poquoson** Virginia, NE USA *37°08′N 76°21′W*
149 *O15* **Porāli** ≈ SW Pakistan
184 *N12* **Porangahau** Hawke's Bay, North Island, New Zealand *40°19′S 176°36′E*
59 *K17* **Porangatu** Goiás, C Brazil *13°28′S 49°14′W*
119 *G18* **Porazava** *Pol.* Porozow, ***Rus.*** Porozovo. Hrodzyenskaya Voblasts', W Belarus *52°56′N 24°22′E*
154 *A11* **Porbandar** Gujarāt, W India *21°40′N 69°40′E*
10 *I13* **Porcher Island** *island* British Columbia, SW Canada
104 *M13* **Porcuna** Andalucía, S Spain *37°52′N 04°12′W*
14 *F7* **Porcupine** Ontario, S Canada *48°31′N 81°07′W*
64 *M6* **Porcupine Bank** *undersea feature* N Atlantic Ocean
11 *V15* **Porcupine Hills** ▲▲ Manitoba/Saskatchewan, S Canada
30 *L3* **Porcupine Mountains** *hill range* Michigan, N USA
64 *M7* **Porcupine Plain** *undersea feature* E Atlantic Ocean *16°00′W 49°00′N*
8 *G7* **Porcupine River** ≈ Canada/USA
106 *I7* **Pordenone** *anc.* Portenau. Friuli-Venezia Giulia, NE Italy *45°58′N 12°39′E*
54 *H9* **Pore** Casanare, E Colombia *05°42′N 71°59′W*
112 *A9* **Poreč** *It.* Parenzo. Istra, NW Croatia *45°16′N 13°36′E*
60 *I9* **Porecatu** Paraná, S Brazil *22°46′S 51°22′W*
Porech'ye *see* Parechcha
127 *P4* **Poretskoye** Chuvashskaya Respublika, W Russian Federation *55°12′N 46°20′E*
77 *Q13* **Porga** N Benin *11°04′N 00°58′E*
186 *B7* **Porgera** Enga, W Papua New Guinea *05°32′S 143°08′E*
93 *K18* **Pori** *Swe.* Björneborg. Länsi-Suomi, SW Finland *61°28′N 21°50′E*
185 *L14* **Porirua** Wellington, North Island, New Zealand *41°08′S 174°51′E*
92 *I12* **Porjus** *Lapp.* Bårjås. Norrbotten, N Sweden *66°55′N 19°55′E*
124 *G14* **Porkhov** Pskovskaya Oblast', W Russian Federation *57°46′N 29°27′E*
55 *O4* **Porlamar** Nueva Esparta, NE Venezuela *10°57′N 63°51′W*
102 *I8* **Pornic** Loire-Atlantique, NW France *47°07′N 02°07′W*
186 *B7* **Poroma** Southern Highlands, W Papua New Guinea *06°15′S 143°34′E*
123 *T13* **Poronaysk** Ostrov Sakhalin, Sakhalinskaya Oblast', SE Russian Federation *49°15′N 143°00′E*
115 *G20* **Póros** Póros, S Greece *37°30′N 23°27′E*
115 *C19* **Póros** Kefallinía, Iónia Nisiá, Greece, C Mediterranean Sea *38°09′N 20°46′E*
115 *G20* **Póros** *island* S Greece
81 *G24* **Poroto Mountains** ▲▲ SW Tanzania
112 *B10* **Porozina** Primorje-Gorski Kotar, NW Croatia *45°07′N 14°17′E*
Porozovo/Porozow *see* Porazava
195 *X15* **Porpoise Bay** *bay* Antarctica
65 *G15* **Porpoise Point** *headland* NE Ascension Island *07°54′S 14°22′W*
65 *C25* **Porpoise Point** *headland* East Falkland, Falkland Islands *52°20′S 59°18′W*
108 *C6* **Porrentruy** Jura, NW Switzerland *47°25′N 07°06′E*
106 *F10* **Porretta Terme** Emilia-Romagna, C Italy *44°10′N 11°01′E*
Porriño *see* O Porriño
92 *L7* **Porsangenfjorden** *Lapp.* Porsángguvuotna. *fjord* N Norway
92 *K8* **Porsangerhalvøya** *peninsula* N Norway
Porsángguvuotna *see* Porsangenfjorden
95 *G16* **Porsgrunn** Telemark, S Norway *59°08′N 09°38′E*
136 *E13* **Porsuk Çayı** ≈ C Turkey
Porsy *see* Boldumsaz
57 *N18* **Portachuelo** Santa Cruz, C Bolivia *17°21′S 63°24′W*
182 *I9* **Port Adelaide** South Australia *34°49′S 138°31′E*
97 *F15* **Portadown** *Ir.* Port An Dúnáin. S Northern Ireland, United Kingdom *54°26′N 06°27′W*
31 *P10* **Portage** Michigan, N USA *42°12′N 85°34′W*
18 *D15* **Portage** Pennsylvania, NE USA *40°23′N 78°40′W*
30 *K8* **Portage** Wisconsin, N USA *43°33′N 89°29′W*
30 *M3* **Portage Lake** ◎ Michigan, N USA
11 *X16* **Portage la Prairie** Manitoba, S Canada *49°58′N 98°20′W*
31 *R11* **Portage River** ≈ Ohio, N USA
27 *Y8* **Portageville** Missouri, C USA *36°25′N 89°42′W*
28 *L2* **Portal** North Dakota, N USA *48°57′N 102°33′W*
10 *L17* **Port Alberni** Vancouver Island, British Columbia, SW Canada *49°11′N 124°49′W*
14 *E15* **Port Albert** Ontario, S Canada *43°51′N 81°42′W*
104 *I10* **Portalegre** *anc.* Ammaia, Amoea. Portalegre, E Portugal *39°17′N 07°25′W*
104 *H10* **Portalegre** ◈ *district* C Portugal
37 *V12* **Portales** New Mexico, SW USA *34°11′N 103°19′W*
39 *X14* **Port Alexander** Baranof Island, Alaska, USA *56°15′N 134°39′W*
83 *I25* **Port Alfred** Eastern Cape, S South Africa *33°31′S 26°55′E*
10 *J16* **Port Alice** Vancouver Island, British Columbia, SW Canada *50°23′N 127°24′W*
22 *J8* **Port Allen** Louisiana, S USA *30°27′N 91°12′W*
Port Amelia *see* Pemba
Port An Dúnáin *see* Portadown
32 *G7* **Port Angeles** Washington, NW USA *48°06′N 123°26′W*
44 *L12* **Port Antonio** NE Jamaica *18°10′N 76°27′W*
115 *D16* **Pórta Panagiá** *religious building* Thessalía, C Greece
25 *T14* **Port Aransas** Texas, SW USA *27°49′N 97°03′W*
97 *E18* **Portarlington** *Ir.* Cúil an tSúdaire. Laois/Offaly, C Ireland *53°10′N 07°11′W*
183 *P17* **Port Arthur** Tasmania, SE Australia *43°09′S 147°51′E*
25 *Y11* **Port Arthur** Texas, SW USA *29°55′N 93°56′W*
96 *G12* **Port Askaig** W Scotland, United Kingdom *55°51′N 06°06′W*
182 *I7* **Port Augusta** South Australia *32°29′S 137°44′E*
44 *M9* **Port-au-Prince** ● (Haiti) C Haiti *18°33′N 72°20′W*
22 *I8* **Port Barre** Louisiana, S USA *30°33′N 91°57′W*
Port-Bergé *see* Boriziny
151 *Q19* **Port Blair** Andaman and Nicobar Islands, SE India *11°40′N 92°44′E*
25 *X12* **Port Bolivar** Texas, SW USA *29°21′N 94°45′W*
105 *X4* **Portbou** Cataluña, NE Spain *42°26′N 03°10′E*
77 *N17* **Port Bouet** ✈ (Abidjan) SE Ivory Coast *05°17′N 03°55′W*
182 *I8* **Port Broughton** South Australia *33°39′S 137°55′E*
14 *F17* **Port Burwell** Ontario, S Canada *42°39′N 80°47′W*
12 *G17* **Port Burwell** Québec, NE Canada *60°25′N 64°49′W*
182 *M13* **Port Campbell** Victoria, SE Australia *38°37′S 143°00′E*
15 *V4* **Port-Cartier** Québec, SE Canada *50°00′N 66°55′W*
185 *F23* **Port Chalmers** Otago, South Island, New Zealand *45°46′S 170°37′E*
23 *W14* **Port Charlotte** Florida, SE USA *27°00′N 82°07′W*
38 *L9* **Port Clarence** Alaska, USA *65°15′N 166°51′W*
10 *I13* **Port Clements** Graham Island, British Columbia, SW Canada *53°37′N 132°12′W*
31 *S11* **Port Clinton** Ohio, N USA *41°30′N 82°56′W*
14 *H17* **Port Colborne** Ontario, S Canada *42°51′N 79°16′W*
15 *Y7* **Port-Daniel** Québec, SE Canada *48°10′N 64°58′W*
Port Darwin *see* Darwin
183 *O17* **Port Davey** *headland* Tasmania, SE Australia *43°19′S 145°54′E*
44 *K8* **Port-de-Paix** NW Haiti *19°56′N 72°52′W*
181 *W4* **Port Douglas** Queensland, NE Australia *16°33′S 145°27′E*
10 *J13* **Port Edward** British Columbia, SW Canada *54°11′N 130°16′W*
83 *K24* **Port Edward** KwaZulu/Natal, SE South Africa *31°03′S 30°14′E*
58 *J12* **Portel** Pará, NE Brazil *01°58′S 50°45′W*
104 *H12* **Portel** Évora, S Portugal *38°18′N 07°42′W*
14 *E14* **Port Elgin** Ontario, S Canada *44°26′N 81°22′W*
45 *Y14* **Port Elizabeth** Bequia, Saint Vincent and the Grenadines *13°01′N 61°15′W*
83 *I26* **Port Elizabeth** Eastern Cape, S South Africa *33°58′S 25°36′E*
96 *G13* **Port Ellen** W Scotland, United Kingdom *55°37′N 06°12′W*
Portenau *see* Pordenone
97 *H16* **Port Erin** SW Isle of Man *54°05′N 04°47′W*
45 *Q13* **Porter Point** *headland* Saint Vincent, Saint Vincent and the Grenadines *13°22′N 61°10′W*
185 *G18* **Porters Pass** *pass* South Island, New Zealand
83 *E25* **Porterville** Western Cape, SW South Africa *33°03′S 19°00′E*
35 *R12* **Porterville** California, W USA *36°03′N 119°03′W*
Port-Étienne *see* Nouâdhibou
182 *L13* **Port Fairy** Victoria, SE Australia *38°24′S 142°13′E*
184 *M4* **Port Fitzroy** Great Barrier Island, Auckland, NE New Zealand *36°10′S 175°21′E*
Port Florence *see* Kisumu
Port-Francqui *see* Ilebo
79 *C18* **Port-Gentil** Ogooué-Maritime, W Gabon *0°40′S 08°50′E*
182 *I7* **Port Germein** South Australia *33°02′S 138°01′E*
22 *J6* **Port Gibson** Mississippi, S USA *31°57′N 90°58′W*
39 *Q13* **Port Graham** Alaska, USA *59°21′N 151°49′W*
77 *U17* **Port Harcourt** Rivers, S Nigeria *04°43′N 07°02′E*
10 *J16* **Port Hardy** Vancouver Island, British Columbia, SW Canada *50°41′N 127°30′W*
Port Harrison *see* Inukjuak
13 *R14* **Port Hawkesbury** Cape Breton Island, Nova Scotia, SE Canada *45°36′N 61°22′W*
180 *I6* **Port Hedland** Western Australia *20°23′S 118°40′E*
39 *O15* **Port Heiden** Alaska, USA *56°54′N 158°40′W*
97 *I19* **Porthmadog** *var.* Portmadoc. NW Wales, United Kingdom *52°55′N 04°08′W*
14 *I15* **Port Hope** Ontario, SE Canada *43°58′N 78°18′W*
13 *S9* **Port Hope Simpson** Newfoundland and Labrador, E Canada *52°30′N 56°18′W*
65 *C24* **Port Howard Settlement** West Falkland, Falkland Islands
31 *T9* **Port Huron** Michigan, N USA *42°58′N 82°25′W*
107 *K17* **Portici** Campania, S Italy *40°48′N 14°20′E*
Port-İliç *see* Liman
104 *G14* **Portimão** *var.* Vila Nova de Portimão. Faro, S Portugal *37°08′N 08°32′W*
25 *T17* **Port Isabel** Texas, SW USA *26°04′N 97°13′W*
18 *J13* **Port Jervis** New York, NE USA *41°22′N 74°39′W*
55 *S7* **Port Kaituma** NW Guyana *07°42′N 59°52′W*
126 *K12* **Port Katon** Rostovskaya Oblast', SW Russian Federation *46°52′N 38°46′E*
183 *S9* **Port Kembla** New South Wales, SE Australia *34°30′S 150°54′E*
182 *F8* **Port Kenny** South Australia *33°09′S 134°38′E*
Port Klang *see* Pelabuhan Klang
Port Láirge *see* Waterford
183 *S8* **Portland** New South Wales, SE Australia *33°24′S 150°00′E*
182 *L13* **Portland** Victoria, SE Australia *38°21′S 141°38′E*
184 *K4* **Portland** Northland, North Island, New Zealand *35°48′S 174°19′E*
31 *Q13* **Portland** Indiana, N USA *40°25′N 84°58′W*
19 *P8* **Portland** Maine, NE USA *43°41′N 70°16′W*
31 *Q9* **Portland** Michigan, N USA *42°51′N 84°52′W*
29 *Q4* **Portland** North Dakota, N USA *47°28′N 97°22′W*
32 *G11* **Portland** Oregon, NW USA *45°31′N 122°41′W*
20 *J8* **Portland** Tennessee, S USA *36°34′N 86°31′W*
25 *T14* **Portland** Texas, SW USA *27°52′N 97°19′W*
32 *G11* **Portland** ✈ Oregon, NW USA *45°36′N 122°34′W*
182 *L13* **Portland Bay** *bay* Victoria, SE Australia
44 *K13* **Portland Bight** *bay* S Jamaica
97 *L24* **Portland Bill** *var.* Bill of Portland. *headland* S England, United Kingdom *50°31′N 02°28′W*
Portland, Bill of *see* Portland Bill
183 *P15* **Portland, Cape** *headland* Tasmania, SE Australia *40°46′S 147°58′E*
10 *J12* **Portland Inlet** *inlet* British Columbia, W Canada
184 *P11* **Portland Island** *island* E New Zealand
65 *F15* **Portland Point** *headland* SW Ascension Island
44 *J13* **Portland Point** *headland* C Jamaica *17°42′N 77°10′W*
103 *P16* **Port-la-Nouvelle** Aude, S France *43°01′N 03°04′E*
Portlaoighise *see* Port Laoise
97 *E18* **Port Laoise** *var.* Portlaoise, ***Ir.*** Portlaoighise; ***prev.*** Maryborough. C Ireland *53°02′N 07°17′W*
Portlaoise *see* Port Laoise
25 *U13* **Port Lavaca** Texas, SW USA *28°36′N 96°39′W*
182 *G9* **Port Lincoln** South Australia *34°43′S 135°49′E*
39 *Q14* **Port Lions** Kodiak Island, Alaska, USA *57°55′N 152°48′W*
76 *I15* **Port Loko** W Sierra Leone *08°50′N 12°50′W*
65 *E24* **Port Louis** East Falkland, Falkland Islands *51°31′S 58°07′W*
45 *Y5* **Port-Louis** Grande Terre, N Guadeloupe *16°25′N 61°32′W*
173 *X16* **Port Louis** ● (Mauritius) NW Mauritius *20°10′S 57°30′E*
Port Louis *see* Scarborough
Port-Lyautey *see* Kénitra
182 *K12* **Port MacDonnell** South Australia *38°04′S 140°40′E*
183 *U7* **Port Macquarie** New South Wales, SE Australia *31°26′S 152°55′E*
Portmadoc *see* Porthmadog
Port Mahon *see* Maó
44 *K12* **Port Maria** C Jamaica *18°22′N 76°54′W*
10 *K16* **Port McNeill** Vancouver Island, British Columbia, SW Canada *50°34′N 127°06′W*
13 *P11* **Port-Menier** Île d'Anticosti, Québec, E Canada *49°49′N 64°19′W*
39 *N15* **Port Moller** Alaska, USA *56°00′N 160°31′W*
44 *L13* **Port Morant** E Jamaica *17°53′N 76°20′W*
44 *K13* **Portmore** C Jamaica *17°58′N 76°52′W*
186 *D9* **Port Moresby** ● (Papua New Guinea) Central/National Capital District, SW Papua New Guinea *09°28′S 147°12′E*
Port Natal *see* Durban
25 *Y11* **Port Neches** Texas, SW USA *29°59′N 93°57′W*
182 *G9* **Port Neill** South Australia *34°06′S 136°19′E*
15 *S6* **Portneuf** ≈ Québec, SE Canada
15 *R6* **Portneuf, Lac** ◎ Québec, SE Canada
83 *D23* **Port Nolloth** Northern Cape, W South Africa *29°17′S 16°51′E*
18 *J17* **Port Norris** New Jersey, NE USA *39°13′N 75°00′W*
Port-Nouveau-Québec *see* Kangiqsualujjuaq
104 *G6* **Porto** *Eng.* Oporto; *anc.* Portus Cale. Porto, NW Portugal *41°09′N 08°37′W*
104 *G6* **Porto** *var.* Pôrto. ◈ *district* N Portugal
104 *G6* **Porto** ✈ Porto, W Portugal *41°09′N 08°37′W*
Pôrto *see* Porto
61 *I16* **Porto Alegre** *var.* Pôrto Alegre. *state capital* Rio Grande do Sul, S Brazil *30°03′S 51°10′W*
Porto Alexandre *see* Tombua
82 *B12* **Porto Amboim** Cuanza Sul, NW Angola *10°47′S 13°43′E*
Porto Amélia *see* Pemba
Porto Bello *see* Portobelo
43 *T14* **Portobelo** *var.* Porto Bello, Puerto Bello. Colón, N Panama *09°33′N 79°37′W*
60 *G10* **Pôrto Camargo** Paraná, S Brazil *23°23′S 53°47′W*
25 *U13* **Port O'Connor** Texas, SW USA *28°26′N 96°26′W*
Pôrto de Mós *see* Porto de Moz
58 *J12* **Porto de Moz** *var.* Pôrto de Mós. Pará, NE Brazil *01°45′S 52°15′W*
64 *O5* **Porto do Moniz** Madeira, Portugal, NE Atlantic Ocean
59 *H16* **Porto dos Gaúchos** Mato Grosso, W Brazil *11°32′S 57°16′W*
Porto Edda *see* Sarandë
107 *J24* **Porto Empedocle** Sicilia, Italy, C Mediterranean Sea *37°18′N 13°32′E*
59 *H20* **Porto Esperança** Mato Grosso do Sul, SW Brazil *19°36′S 57°24′W*
106 *E13* **Portoferraio** Toscana, C Italy *42°49′N 10°18′E*
96 *G6* **Port of Ness** NW Scotland, United Kingdom *58°29′N 06°15′W*
45 *U14* **Port-of-Spain** ● (Trinidad and Tobago) Trinidad, Trinidad and Tobago *10°39′N 61°30′W*
Port of Spain *see* Piarco
103 *X15* **Porto, Golfe de** *gulf* Corse, France, C Mediterranean Sea
Porto Grande *see* Mindelo
106 *I7* **Portogruaro** Veneto, NE Italy *45°46′N 12°50′E*
35 *P5* **Portola** California, W USA *39°48′N 120°28′W*
187 *Q13* **Port-Olry** Espiritu Santo, C Vanuatu *15°03′S 167°04′E*
93 *J17* **Pörtom** *Fin.* Pirttikylä. Länsi-Suomi, W Finland *62°42′N 21°40′E*
Port Omna *see* Portumna
59 *G21* **Porto Murtinho** Mato Grosso do Sul, SW Brazil *21°42′S 57°52′W*
59 *K16* **Porto Nacional** Tocantins, C Brazil *10°41′S 48°19′W*
77 *S16* **Porto-Novo** ● (Benin) S Benin *06°29′N 02°37′E*
23 *X10* **Port Orange** Florida, SE USA *29°06′N 80°59′W*
32 *G8* **Port Orchard** Washington, NW USA *47°32′N 122°38′W*
Porto Re *see* Kraljevica
32 *E15* **Port Orford** Oregon, NW USA *42°45′N 124°30′W*
Porto Rico *see* Puerto Rico
106 *J13* **Porto San Giorgio** Marche, C Italy *43°10′N 13°47′E*
107 *F14* **Porto San Stefano** Toscana, C Italy *42°26′N 11°09′E*
64 *P5* **Porto Santo** *var.* Vila Baleira. Porto Santo, Madeira, Portugal, NE Atlantic Ocean *33°04′N 16°20′W*
64 *Q5* **Porto Santo** ✈ Porto Santo, Madeira, Portugal, NE Atlantic Ocean *33°04′N 16°20′W*
64 *P5* **Porto Santo** *var.* Ilha do Porto Santo. *island* Madeira, Portugal, NE Atlantic Ocean
Porto Santo, Ilha do *see* Porto Santo
60 *H9* **Porto São José** Paraná, S Brazil *22°43′S 53°10′W*
59 *O19* **Porto Seguro** Bahia, E Brazil *16°25′S 39°07′W*
107 *B17* **Porto Torres** Sardegna, Italy, C Mediterranean Sea *40°50′N 08°23′E*
59 *J23* **Porto União** Santa Catarina, S Brazil *26°15′S 51°04′W*
103 *Y16* **Porto-Vecchio** Corse, France, C Mediterranean Sea *41°35′N 09°17′E*
59 *E15* **Porto Velho** *var.* Velho. *state capital* Rondônia, W Brazil *08°45′S 63°54′W*
56 *A6* **Portoviejo** *var.* Puertoviejo. Manabí, W Ecuador *01°03′S 80°31′W*
185 *B26* **Port Pegasus** *bay* Stewart Island, New Zealand
14 *H15* **Port Perry** Ontario, SE Canada *44°08′N 78°57′W*
183 *N12* **Port Phillip Bay** *harbor* Victoria, SE Australia
182 *I8* **Port Pirie** South Australia *33°11′S 138°01′E*
96 *G9* **Portree** N Scotland, United Kingdom *57°26′N 06°12′W*
Port Rex *see* East London
Port Rois *see* Portrush
44 *K13* **Port Royal** E Jamaica *17°55′N 76°52′W*
21 *R15* **Port Royal** South Carolina, SE USA *32°22′N 80°41′W*
21 *R15* **Port Royal Sound** *inlet* South Carolina, SE USA
97 *F14* **Portrush** *Ir.* Port Rois. N Northern Ireland, United Kingdom *55°12′N 06°40′W*
Port Said *see* Būr Sa'īd
23 *R9* **Port Saint Joe** Florida, SE USA *29°49′N 85°18′W*
23 *Y11* **Port Saint John** Florida, SE USA *28°28′N 80°46′W*
103 *R16* **Port-St-Louis-du-Rhône** Bouches-du-Rhône, SE France *43°22′N 04°48′E*
44 *K10* **Port Salut** SW Haiti *18°04′N 73°55′W*
65 *E24* **Port Salvador** *inlet* East Falkland, Falkland Islands
65 *D24* **Port San Carlos** East Falkland, Falkland Islands *51°30′S 58°59′W*
13 *S10* **Port Saunders** Newfoundland, Newfoundland and Labrador, SE Canada *50°40′N 57°17′W*
83 *K24* **Port Shepstone** KwaZulu/Natal, E South Africa *30°44′S 30°28′E*
45 *O11* **Portsmouth** *var.* Grand-Anse. NW Dominica *15°34′N 61°27′W*
97 *N24* **Portsmouth** S England, United Kingdom *50°48′N 01°05′W*
19 *P10* **Portsmouth** New Hampshire, NE USA *43°04′N 70°47′W*
31 *S15* **Portsmouth** Ohio, N USA *38°43′N 83°00′W*
21 *X7* **Portsmouth** Virginia, NE USA *36°50′N 76°18′W*
14 *E17* **Port Stanley** Ontario, S Canada *42°39′N 81°12′W*
Port Stanley *see* Stanley
65 *B25* **Port Stephens** *inlet* West Falkland, Falkland Islands
65 *B25* **Port Stephens Settlement** West Falkland, Falkland Islands
97 *F14* **Portstewart** *Ir.* Port Stíobhaird. N Northern Ireland, United Kingdom *55°11′N 06°43′W*
Port Stíobhaird *see* Portstewart
83 *K24* **Port St. Johns** Eastern Cape, SE South Africa *31°37′S 29°32′E*
80 *I7* **Port Sudan** Red Sea, NE Sudan *19°37′N 37°14′E*
22 *L10* **Port Sulphur** Louisiana, S USA *29°28′N 89°41′W*
Port Swettenham *see* Klang/Pelabuhan Klang
97 *J22* **Port Talbot** S Wales, United Kingdom *51°36′N 03°47′W*
92 *L11* **Porttipahdan Tekojärvi** ◎ N Finland
32 *G7* **Port Townsend** Washington, NW USA *48°07′N 122°45′W*
104 *H9* **Portugal** *off.* Portuguese Republic. ◆ *republic* SW Europe
105 *O2* **Portugalete** País Vasco, N Spain *43°19′N 03°01′W*
54 *J6* **Portuguesa** *off.* Estado Portuguesa. ◈ *state* N Venezuela
Portuguesa, Estado *see* Portuguesa
Portuguese East Africa *see* Mozambique
Portuguese Guinea *see* Guinea-Bissau
Portuguese Republic *see* Portugal
Portuguese Timor *see* East Timor
Portuguese West Africa *see* Angola
97 *D18* **Portumna** *Ir.* Port Omna. Galway, W Ireland *53°06′N 08°13′W*
Portus Cale *see* Porto
Portus Magnus *see* Almería
Portus Magonis *see* Maó
103 *P17* **Port-Vendres** *var.* Port Vendres. Pyrénées-Orientales, S France *42°31′N 03°06′E*
182 *H9* **Port Victoria** South Australia *34°34′S 137°31′E*
187 *Q14* **Port-Vila** *var.* Vila. ● (Vanuatu) Éfaté, C Vanuatu *17°45′S 168°21′E*
Port Vila *see* Bauer Field
182 *I9* **Port Wakefield** South Australia *34°13′S 138°10′E*
31 *N8* **Port Washington** Wisconsin, N USA *43°23′N 87°54′W*
57 *J14* **Porvenir** Pando, NW Bolivia *11°15′S 68°43′W*
63 *I24* **Porvenir** Magallanes, S Chile *53°18′S 70°22′W*
61 *D18* **Porvenir** Paysandú, W Uruguay *32°23′S 57°59′W*
93 *M19* **Porvoo** *Swe.* Borgå. Etelä-Suomi, S Finland *60°25′N 25°40′E*
Porzecze *see* Parechcha
104 *M10* **Porzuna** Castilla-La Mancha, C Spain *39°10′N 04°10′W*
61 *E14* **Posadas** Misiones, NE Argentina *27°27′S 55°52′W*
104 *L13* **Posadas** Andalucía, S Spain *37°48′N 05°06′W*
Poschega *see* Požega
108 *J11* **Poschiavino** ≈ Italy/Switzerland
108 *J10* **Poschiavo** *Ger.* Puschlav. Graubünden, S Switzerland *46°19′N 10°02′E*
112 *D12* **Posedarje** Zadar, SW Croatia *44°12′N 15°27′E*
Posen *see* Poznań
124 *L14* **Poshekhon'ye** Yaroslavskaya Oblast', W Russian Federation *58°31′N 39°07′E*
92 *M13* **Posio** Lappi, NE Finland *66°06′N 28°16′E*
Poskam *see* Zepu
Posnania *see* Poznań
1713 *O12* **Poso** Sulawesi, C Indonesia *01°23′S 120°45′E*
171 *O12* **Poso, Danau** ◎ Sulawesi, C Indonesia
137 *R10* **Posof** Ardahan, NE Turkey *41°30′N 42°33′E*
25 *R6* **Possum Kingdom Lake** ⊞ Texas, SW USA
25 *N6* **Post** Texas, SW USA *33°14′N 101°24′W*
Postavy/Postawy *see* Pastavy
Poste-de-la-Baleine *see* Kuujjuarapik
99 *M17* **Posterholt** Limburg, SE Netherlands *51°07′N 06°02′E*
83 *G22* **Postmasburg** Northern Cape, N South Africa *28°20′S 23°05′E*
Pôsto Diuarum *see* Campo de Diauarum
59 *I16* **Pôsto Jacaré** Mato Grosso, W Brazil *12°S 53°27′W*
109 *T12* **Postojna** *Ger.* Adelsberg, ***It.*** Postumia. SW Slovenia *45°48′N 14°12′E*
Postumia *see* Postojna
29 *X12* **Postville** Iowa, C USA *43°04′N 91°34′W*
Pöstyén *see* Piešťany
113 *G14* **Posušje** Federacija Bosna I Hercegovina, SW Bosnia and Herzegovina *43°28′N 17°20′E*
171 *O16* **Pota** Flores, C Indonesia *08°21′S 120°50′E*
115 *G23* **Potamós** Antikýthira, S Greece *35°53′N 23°17′E*

◆ Country
● Country Capital
◇ Dependent Territory
○ Dependent Territory Capital
◈ Administrative Regions
✈ International Airport
▲ Mountain
▲▲ Mountain Range
⛰ Volcano
≈ River
◎ Lake
⊞ Reservoir

55 *S9* **Potaru River** ≈ C Guyana
83 *I21* **Potchefstroom** North-West, N South Africa *26°42′S 27°06′E*
27 *R11* **Poteau** Oklahoma, C USA *35°03′N 94°36′W*
25 *R12* **Poteet** Texas, SW USA *29°02′N 98°34′W*
115 *G14* **Poteídaia** *site of ancient city* Kentrikí Makedonía, N Greece
Potentia *see* Potenza
107 *M18* **Potenza** *anc.* Potentia. Basilicata, S Italy *40°40′N 15°50′E*
185 *A24* **Poteriteri, Lake** ◎ South Island, New Zealand
104 *M2* **Potes** Cantabria, N Spain *43°10′N 04°41′W*
Potgietersrus *see* Mokopane
25 *S12* **Poth** Texas, SW USA *29°04′N 98°04′W*
32 *J9* **Potholes Reservoir** ⊠ Washington, NW USA
137 *Q9* **Poti** *prev.* P'ot'i. W Georgia *42°10′N 41°42′E*
P'ot'i *see* Poti
77 *X13* **Potiskum** Yobe, NE Nigeria *11°38′N 11°07′E*
Potkozarje *see* Ivanjska
32 *M9* **Potlatch** Idaho, NW USA *46°55′N 116°51′W*
33 *N9* **Pot Mountain** ▲ Idaho, NW USA *46°44′N 115°24′W*
113 *H14* **Potoci** Federacija Bosna I Hercegovina, S Bosnia and Herzegovina *43°24′N 17°52′E*
21 *V3* **Potomac River** ≈ NE USA
57 *L20* **Potosí** Potosí, S Bolivia *19°35′S 65°51′W*
42 *H9* **Potosí** Chinandega, NW Nicaragua *12°58′N 87°30′W*
27 *W6* **Potosi** Missouri, C USA *37°57′N 90°49′W*
57 *K21* **Potosí** ◈ *department* SW Bolivia
62 *H7* **Potrerillos** Atacama, N Chile *26°30′S 69°25′W*
42 *H5* **Potrerillos** Cortés, NW Honduras *15°10′N 87°58′W*
62 *H8* **Potro, Cerro del** ▲ N Chile *28°22′S 69°34′W*
100 *N12* **Potsdam** Brandenburg, NE Germany *52°24′N 13°04′E*
18 *J7* **Potsdam** New York, NE USA *44°40′N 74°58′W*
109 *X5* **Pottendorf** Niederösterreich, E Austria *47°55′N 16°23′E*
109 *X5* **Pottenstein** Niederösterreich, E Austria *47°58′N 16°07′E*
18 *I15* **Pottstown** Pennsylvania, NE USA *40°15′N 75°39′W*
18 *H14* **Pottsville** Pennsylvania, NE USA *40°40′N 76°10′W*
155 *L25* **Pottuvil** Eastern Province, SE Sri Lanka *06°53′N 81°49′E*
149 *U6* **Potwar Plateau** *plateau* NE Pakistan
102 *J7* **Pouancé** Maine-et-Loire, W France *47°46′N 01°11′W*
15 *R6* **Poulin de Courval, Lac** ◎ Québec, SE Canada
18 *L9* **Poultney** Vermont, NE USA *43°31′N 73°12′W*
187 *O16* **Poum** Province Nord, W New Caledonia *20°15′S 164°03′E*
59 *L21* **Pouso Alegre** Minas Gerais, NE Brazil *22°13′S 45°56′W*
192 *I16* **Poutasi** Upolu, SE Samoa *14°00′S 171°43′W*
167 *R12* **Poŭthĭsăt** *prev.* Pursat. Poŭthĭsăt, W Cambodia *12°32′N 103°55′E*
167 *R12* **Poŭthĭsăt, Stœ̆ng** *prev.* Pursat. ≈ W Cambodia
102 *J9* **Pouzauges** Vendée, NW France *46°47′N 00°54′W*
Po, Valle del *see* Po Valley
106 *F8* **Po Valley** *It.* Valle del Po. *valley* N Italy
111 *I19* **Považská Bystrica** *Ger.* Waagbistritz, *Hung.* Vágbeszterce. Trenčiansky Kraj, W Slovakia *49°07′N 18°26′E*
124 *J10* **Povenets** Respublika Kareliya, NW Russian Federation *62°50′N 34°47′E*
184 *Q9* **Poverty Bay** *inlet* North Island, New Zealand
112 *K12* **Povlen** ▲▲ W Serbia
104 *G6* **Póvoa de Varzim** Porto, NW Portugal *41°22′N 08°46′W*
127 *N8* **Povorino** Voronezhskaya Oblast', W Russian Federation *51°10′N 42°16′E*
Povungnituk *see* Puvirnituq
Rivière de Povungnituk *see* Puvirnituq, Riviere de
14 *H11* **Powassan** Ontario, S Canada *46°05′N 79°21′W*
35 *U17* **Poway** California, W USA *32°57′N 117°02′W*
33 *W14* **Powder River** Wyoming, C USA *43°01′N 106°57′W*
33 *Y10* **Powder River** ≈ Montana/Wyoming, NW USA
32 *L12* **Powder River** ≈ Oregon, NW USA
33 *W13* **Powder River Pass** *pass* Wyoming, C USA
33 *U12* **Powell** Wyoming, C USA *44°45′N 108°45′W*
65 *I22* **Powell Basin** *undersea feature* NW Weddell Sea
36 *M8* **Powell, Lake** ◎ Utah, W USA
37 *R4* **Powell, Mount** ▲ Colorado, C USA *39°25′N 106°20′W*
10 *L17* **Powell River** British Columbia, SW Canada *49°54′N 124°34′W*
31 *N5* **Powers** Michigan, N USA *45°40′N 87°29′W*
28 *K2* **Powers Lake** North Dakota, N USA *48°33′N 102°37′W*
21 *V6* **Powhatan** Virginia, NE USA *37°33′N 77°56′W*
31 *V13* **Powhatan Point** Ohio, N USA *39°49′N 80°49′W*
97 *J20* **Powys** *cultural region* E Wales, United Kingdom
187 *P17* **Poya** Province Nord, C New Caledonia *21°19′S 165°07′E*
161 *P10* **Poyang Hu** ◎ S China
30 *L7* **Poygan, Lake** ◎ Wisconsin, N USA
109 *Y2* **Poysdorf** Niederösterreich, NE Austria *48°40′N 16°38′E*
112 *N11* **Požarevac** *Ger.* Passarowitz. Serbia, NE Serbia *44°37′N 21°11′E*
41 *Q13* **Poza Rica** *var.* Poza Rica de Hidalgo. Veracruz-Llave, E Mexico *20°34′N 97°26′W*
Poza Rica de Hidalgo *see* Poza Rica
112 *L13* **Požega** *prev.* Slavonska Požega, *Ger.* Poschega, *Hung.* Pozsega. Požega-Slavonija, NE Croatia *45°19′N 17°42′E*
112 *H9* **Požega-Slavonija** *off.* Požeško-Slavonska Županija. ◈ *province* NE Croatia
Požeško-Slavonska Županija *see* Požega-Slavonija
125 *U13* **Pozhva** Komi-Permyatskiy Okrug, NW Russian Federation *59°07′N 56°04′E*
110 *G11* **Poznań** *Ger.* Posen, Posnania. Wielkolpolskie, C Poland *52°24′N 16°56′E*
105 *O13* **Pozo Alcón** Andalucía, S Spain *37°43′N 02°55′W*
62 *H3* **Pozo Almonte** Tarapacá, N Chile *20°16′S 69°50′W*
104 *L12* **Pozoblanco** Andalucía, S Spain *38°23′N 04°48′W*
105 *Q11* **Pozo Cañada** Castilla-La Mancha, C Spain *38°49′N 01°45′W*
62 *N5* **Pozo Colorado** Presidente Hayes, C Paraguay *23°26′S 58°51′W*
63 *J20* **Pozos, Punta** *headland* S Argentina *47°55′S 65°46′W*
Pozsega *see* Požega
Pozsony *see* Bratislava
55 *N5* **Pozuelos** Anzoátegui, NE Venezuela *10°11′N 64°39′W*
107 *L26* **Pozzallo** Sicilia, Italy, C Mediterranean Sea *36°44′N 14°51′E*
107 *K17* **Pozzuoli** *anc.* Puteoli. Campania, S Italy *40°49′N 14°07′E*
77 *P17* **Pra** ≈ S Ghana
111 *C19* **Prachatice** *Ger.* Prachatitz. Jihočeský Kraj, S Czech Republic *49°01′N 14°02′E*
Prachatitz *see* Prachatice
167 *P11* **Prachin Buri** *var.* Prachinburi. Prachin Buri, C Thailand *14°05′N 101°23′E*
Prachinburi *see* Prachin Buri
Prachuab Girikhand *see* Prachuap Khiri Khan
167 *O12* **Prachuap Khiri Khan** *var.* Prachuab Girikhand. Prachuap Khiri Khan, SW Thailand *11°50′N 99°49′E*
111 *H16* **Praděd** *Ger.* Altvater. ▲ NE Czech Republic *50°06′N 17°14′E*
54 *D11* **Pradera** Valle del Cauca, SW Colombia *03°23′N 76°11′W*
103 *O17* **Prades** Pyrénées-Orientales, S France *42°36′N 02°22′E*
59 *O19* **Prado** Bahia, SE Brazil *17°13′S 39°15′W*
54 *E11* **Prado** Tolima, C Colombia *03°45′N 74°55′W*
Prado del Ganso *see* Goose Green
Prae *see* Phrae
95 *I24* **Præstø** Sjælland, SE Denmark *55°08′N 12°03′E*
Prag/Praga/Prague *see* Praha
27 *O10* **Prague** Oklahoma, C USA *35°29′N 96°40′W*
111 *D16* **Praha** *Eng.* Prague, *Ger.* Prag, *Pol.* Praga. ● (Czech Republic) Středočeský Kraj, NW Czech Republic *50°06′N 14°26′E*
116 *J13* **Prahova** ◈ *county* SE Romania
116 *J13* **Prahova** ≈ S Romania
76 *E10* **Praia** ● (Cape Verde) Santiago, S Cape Verde *14°55′N 23°31′W*
83 *M21* **Praia do Bilene** Gaza, S Mozambique *25°18′S 33°10′E*
83 *M20* **Praia do Xai-Xai** Gaza, S Mozambique *25°04′S 33°43′E*
116 *J10* **Praid** *Hung.* Parajd. Harghita, C Romania *46°33′N 25°06′E*
26 *J3* **Prairie Dog Creek** ≈ Kansas/Nebraska, C USA
30 *J9* **Prairie du Chien** Wisconsin, N USA *43°02′N 91°08′W*
27 *S9* **Prairie Grove** Arkansas, C USA *35°58′N 94°19′W*
31 *P10* **Prairie River** ≈ Michigan, N USA
Prairie State *see* Illinois
25 *V11* **Prairie View** Texas, SW USA *30°05′N 95°59′W*
167 *Q10* **Prakhon Chai** Buri Ram, E Thailand *14°36′N 103°04′E*
109 *R4* **Pram** ≈ N Austria
167 *Q12* **Prâmaôy** *prev.* Phumĭ Prâmaôy. Poŭthĭsăt, W Cambodia *12°13′N 103°05′E*
109 *S4* **Prambachkirchen** Oberösterreich, N Austria *48°18′N 13°50′E*
118 *H2* **Prangli** *island* N Estonia
154 *J13* **Prānhita** ≈ C India
172 *I15* **Praslin** *island* Inner Islands, NE Seychelles
115 *O23* **Prasonísi, Akrotírio** *cape* Ródos, Dodekánisa, Greece, Aegean Sea
111 *I14* **Praszka** Opolskie, S Poland *51°05′N 18°29′E*
Pratas Island *see* Tungsha Tao
119 *M18* **Pratasy** *Rus.* Protasy. Homyel'skaya Voblasts', SE Belarus *52°47′N 29°05′E*
167 *Q10* **Prathai** Nakhon Ratchasima, E Thailand *15°31′N 102°42′E*
Prathet Thai *see* Thailand
Prathum Thani *see* Pathum Thani
63 *F21* **Prat, Isla** *island* S Chile
106 *G11* **Prato** Toscana, C Italy *43°53′N 11°05′E*
103 *O17* **Prats-de-Mollo-la-Preste** Pyrénées-Orientales, S France *42°25′N 02°28′E*
26 *L6* **Pratt** Kansas, C USA *37°40′N 98°45′W*
108 *E6* **Pratteln** Basel Landschaft, NW Switzerland *47°32′N 07°42′E*
193 *O2* **Pratt Seamount** *undersea feature* N Pacific Ocean *56°09′N 142°30′W*
23 *P5* **Prattville** Alabama, S USA *32°27′N 86°27′W*
Praust *see* Pruszcz Gdański
119 *B14* **Pravdinsk** *Ger.* Friedland. Kaliningradskaya Oblast', W Russian Federation *54°26′N 21°01′E*
104 *K2* **Pravia** Asturias, N Spain *43°30′N 06°06′W*
118 *L12* **Prazaroki** *Rus.* Prozoroki. Vitsyebskaya Voblasts', N Belarus *55°18′N 28°13′E*
Prázsmár *see* Prejmer
167 *S11* **Preăh Vihéar** Preăh Vihéar, N Cambodia *13°57′N 104°48′E*
116 *J12* **Predeal** *Hung.* Predeál. Brașov, C Romania *45°30′N 25°31′E*
109 *S8* **Predlitz** Steiermark, SE Austria *47°04′N 13°54′E*
11 *V15* **Preeceville** Saskatchewan, S Canada *51°58′N 102°40′W*
Preenkuln *see* Priekule
102 *K6* **Pré-en-Pail** Mayenne, NW France *48°27′N 00°15′W*
109 *T4* **Pregarten** Oberösterreich, N Austria *48°21′N 14°31′E*
54 *H7* **Pregonero** Táchira, NW Venezuela *08°02′N 71°35′W*
118 *J10* **Preiļi** *Ger.* Preli. SE Latvia *56°17′N 26°52′E*
116 *J12* **Prejmer** *Ger.* Tartlau, *Hung.* Prázsmár. Brașov, S Romania *45°42′N 25°49′E*
113 *J16* **Prekornica** ▲▲ C Montenegro
Preli *see* Preiļi
Prëmet *see* Përmet
100 *M12* **Premnitz** Brandenburg, NE Germany *52°33′N 12°22′E*
25 *S15* **Premont** Texas, SW USA *27°21′N 98°07′W*
113 *H14* **Prenj** ▲▲ S Bosnia and Herzegovina
Prenjas/Prenjasi *see* Përrenjas
22 *L7* **Prentiss** Mississippi, S USA *31°36′N 89°52′W*
Preny *see* Prienai
100 *O10* **Prenzlau** Brandenburg, NE Germany *53°19′N 13°52′E*
123 *N11* **Preobrazhenka** Irkutskaya Oblast', C Russian Federation *60°01′N 108°00′E*
166 *J9* **Preparis Island** *island* SW Myanmar (Burma)
Prerau *see* Přerov
111 *H18* **Přerov** *Ger.* Prerau. Olomoucký Kraj, E Czech Republic *49°27′N 17°27′E*
Preschau *see* Prešov
14 *M14* **Prescott** Ontario, SE Canada *44°43′N 75°33′W*
36 *K12* **Prescott** Arizona, SW USA *34°33′N 112°26′W*
27 *T13* **Prescott** Arkansas, C USA *33°49′N 93°25′W*
32 *L10* **Prescott** Washington, NW USA *46°17′N 118°21′W*
30 *H6* **Prescott** Wisconsin, N USA *44°46′N 92°45′W*
185 *A24* **Preservation Inlet** *inlet* South Island, New Zealand
112 *O7* **Preševo** Serbia, SE Serbia *42°20′N 21°38′E*
29 *N10* **Presho** South Dakota, N USA *43°54′N 100°03′W*
58 *M13* **Presidente Dutra** Maranhão, E Brazil *05°17′S 44°30′W*
60 *I8* **Presidente Epitácio** São Paulo, S Brazil *21°45′S 52°07′W*
62 *N5* **Presidente Hayes** *off.* Departamento de Presidente Hayes. ◈ *department* C Paraguay
Presidente Hayes, Departamento de *see* Presidente Hayes
60 *I9* **Presidente Prudente** São Paulo, S Brazil *22°09′S 51°24′W*
Presidente Stroessner *see* Ciudad del Este
Presidente Vargas *see* Itabira
60 *I8* **Presidente Venceslau** São Paulo, S Brazil *21°52′S 51°51′W*
193 *O10* **President Thiers Seamount** *undersea feature* C Pacific Ocean *24°39′S 145°50′W*
24 *J11* **Presidio** Texas, SW USA *29°33′N 104°22′W*
Preslav *see* Veliki Preslav
111 *M19* **Prešov** *var.* Preschau, *Ger.* Eperies, *Hung.* Eperjes. Prešovský Kraj, E Slovakia *49°N 21°14′E*
111 *M19* **Prešovský Kraj** ◈ *region* E Slovakia
113 *N20* **Prespa, Lake** *Alb.* Liqen i Prespës, *Gk.* Límni Megáli Préspa, Limni Prespa, *Mac.* Prespansko Ezero, *Serb.* Prespansko Jezero. ◎ SE Europe
Prespa, Limni/Prespansko Ezero/Prespansko Jezero/Prespës, Liqen i *see* Prespa, Lake
19 *S2* **Presque Isle** Maine, NE USA *46°40′N 68°01′W*
18 *B11* **Presque Isle** *headland* Pennsylvania, NE USA *42°09′N 80°06′W*
Pressburg *see* Bratislava
77 *P17* **Prestea** SW Ghana *05°22′N 02°07′W*
111 *B17* **Přeštice** *Ger.* Pschestitz. Plzeňský Kraj, W Czech Republic *49°36′N 13°19′E*
97 *K17* **Preston** NW England, United Kingdom *53°46′N 02°42′W*
23 *S6* **Preston** Georgia, SE USA *32°03′N 84°32′W*
33 *R16* **Preston** Idaho, NW USA *42°06′N 111°52′W*
29 *Z13* **Preston** Iowa, C USA *42°03′N 90°24′W*
29 *X11* **Preston** Minnesota, N USA *43°41′N 92°06′W*
21 *O6* **Prestonsburg** Kentucky, S USA *37°40′N 82°46′W*
96 *I13* **Prestwick** W Scotland, United Kingdom *55°31′N 04°39′W*
83 *145* **Pretoria** *var.* Epitoli, Tshwane. ● Gauteng, NE South Africa *25°41′S 28°12′E* *see also* Tshwane
Pretoria-Witwatersrand-Vereeniging *see* Gauteng
Pretusha *see* Pretushë
113 *M21* **Pretushë** *var.* Pretusha. Korçë, SE Albania *40°50′N 20°45′E*
Preussisch Eylau *see* Bagrationovsk
Preußisch Holland *see* Pasłęk
Preussisch-Stargard *see* Starogard Gdański
115 *C17* **Préveza** Ípeiros, W Greece *38°59′N 20°44′E*
37 *V3* **Prewitt Reservoir** ⊠ Colorado, C USA
167 *S13* **Prey Vêng** Prey Vêng, S Cambodia *11°30′N 105°20′E*
Priaral'skiye Karakumy, Peski *see* Priaral'skiy Karakum
144 *M12* **Priaral'skiy Karakum** *prev.* Priaral'skiye Karakumy, Peski. *desert* SW Kazakhstan
123 *P14* **Priargunsk** Zabaykal'skiy Kray, S Russian Federation *50°25′N 119°12′E*
38 *K14* **Pribilof Islands** *island group* Alaska, USA
113 *K14* **Priboj** Serbia, W Serbia *43°34′N 19°33′E*
111 *C17* **Příbram** *Ger.* Pibrans. Středočeský Kraj, W Czech Republic *49°41′N 14°02′E*
36 *M4* **Price** Utah, W USA *39°35′N 110°49′W*
37 *N5* **Price River** ≈ Utah, W USA
23 *N8* **Prichard** Alabama, S USA *30°44′N 88°04′W*
25 *R8* **Priddy** Texas, SW USA *31°39′N 98°30′W*
105 *P8* **Priego** Castilla-La Mancha, C Spain *40°26′N 02°19′W*
104 *M14* **Priego de Córdoba** Andalucía, S Spain *37°27′N 04°12′W*
118 *C10* **Priekule** *Ger.* Preenkuln. SW Latvia *56°26′N 21°36′E*
118 *C12* **Priekulė** *Ger.* Prökuls. Klaipėda, W Lithuania *55°36′N 21°16′E*
119 *F14* **Prienai** *Pol.* Preny. Kaunas, S Lithuania *54°37′N 23°56′E*
83 *G23* **Prieska** Northern Cape, C South Africa *29°40′S 22°45′E*
32 *M7* **Priest Lake** ⊠ Idaho, NW USA
32 *M7* **Priest River** Idaho, NW USA *48°10′N 117°02′W*
104 *M3* **Prieta, Peña** ▲ N Spain *43°01′N 04°42′W*
40 *J10* **Prieto, Cerro** ▲ C Mexico *24°10′N 105°21′W*
111 *J19* **Prievidza** *var.* Priewitz, *Ger.* Priwitz, *Hung.* Privigye. Trenčiansky Kraj, W Slovakia *48°47′N 18°35′E*
Priewitz *see* Prievidza
112 *F10* **Prijedor** ◈ Republika Srpska, NW Bosnia and Herzegovina
113 *K14* **Prijepolje** Serbia, W Serbia *43°24′N 19°39′E*
Prikaspiyskaya Nizmennost' *see* Caspian Depression
113 *O19* **Prilep** *Turk.* Perlepe. S FYR Macedonia *41°21′N 21°34′E*
108 *B9* **Prilly** Vaud, SW Switzerland *46°32′N 06°38′E*
Priluki *see* Pryluky
62 *L10* **Primero, Río** ≈ C Argentina
29 *S12* **Primghar** Iowa, C USA *43°05′N 95°37′W*
112 *B9* **Primorje-Gorski Kotar** *off.* Primorsko-Goranska Županija. ◈ *province* NW Croatia
118 *A13* **Primorsk** *Ger.* Fischhausen. Kaliningradskaya Oblast', W Russian Federation *54°45′N 20°00′E*
124 *G12* **Primorsk** *Fin.* Koivisto. Leningradskaya Oblast', NW Russian Federation *60°20′N 28°39′E*
123 *S14* **Primorskiy Kray** *prev.* *Eng.* Maritime Territory. ◈ *territory* SE Russian Federation
114 *N10* **Primorsko** *prev.* Keupriya. Burgas, E Bulgaria *42°15′N 27°45′E*
126 *K13* **Primorsko-Akhtarsk** Krasnodarskiy Kray, SW Russian Federation *46°03′N 38°44′E*
Primorsko-Goranska Županija *see* Primorje-Gorski Kotar
Primorsk/Primorskoye *see* Prymors'k
113 *D14* **Primošten** Šibenik-Knin, S Croatia *43°34′N 15°57′E*
11 *R13* **Primrose Lake** ◎ Saskatchewan, C Canada
11 *T14* **Prince Albert** Saskatchewan, S Canada *53°09′N 105°43′W*
83 *G25* **Prince Albert** Western Cape, SW South Africa *33°13′S 22°03′E*
8 *J5* **Prince Albert Peninsula** *peninsula* Victoria Island, Northwest Territories, NW Canada
8 *J6* **Prince Albert Sound** *inlet* Northwest Territories, N Canada
J5 *8* **Prince Alfred, Cape** *headland* Northwest Territories, NW Canada
9 *P6* **Prince Charles Island** *island* Nunavut, NE Canada
195 *W6* **Prince Charles Mountains** ▲▲ Antarctica
Prince-Édouard, Île-du *see* Prince Edward Island
172 *M13* **Prince Edward Fracture Zone** *tectonic feature* SW Indian Ocean
13 *P14* **Prince Edward Island** *Fr.* Île-du Prince-Édouard. ◈ *province* SE Canada
13 *Q14* **Prince Edward Island** *Fr.* Île-du Prince-Édouard. *island* SE Canada
173 *M12* **Prince Edward Islands** *island group* S South Africa
21 *X4* **Prince Frederick** Maryland, NE USA *38°32′N 76°35′W*
10 *M14* **Prince George** British Columbia, SW Canada *53°55′N 122°49′W*
21 *W6* **Prince George** Virginia, NE USA *37°13′N 77°13′W*
197 *O8* **Prince Gustaf Adolf Sea** *sea* Nunavut, N Canada
197 *Q3* **Prince of Wales, Cape** *headland* Alaska, USA *65°39′N 168°12′W*
181 *V1* **Prince of Wales Island** *island* Queensland, E Australia
8 *L5* **Prince of Wales Island** *island* Queen Elizabeth Islands, Nunavut, NW Canada
39 *Y14* **Prince of Wales Island** *island* Alexander Archipelago, Alaska, USA
Prince of Wales Island *see* Pinang, Pulau
8 *J5* **Prince of Wales Strait** *strait* Northwest Territories, N Canada
197 *O8* **Prince Patrick Island** *island* Parry Islands, Northwest Territories, NW Canada
9 *N5* **Prince Regent Inlet** *channel* Nunavut, N Canada
10 *J13* **Prince Rupert** British Columbia, SW Canada *54°18′N 130°17′W*
Prince's Island *see* Príncipe
21 *Y5* **Princess Anne** Maryland, NE USA *38°12′N 75°42′W*
Princess Astrid Coast *see* Prinsesse Astrid Kyst
181 *W2* **Princess Charlotte Bay** *bay* Queensland, NE Australia
195 *W7* **Princess Elizabeth Land** *physical region* Antarctica
10 *J14* **Princess Royal Island** *island* British Columbia, SW Canada
45 *U15* **Princes Town** Trinidad, Trinidad and Tobago *10°16′N 61°23′W*
11 *N17* **Princeton** British Columbia, SW Canada *49°25′N 120°35′W*
30 *L11* **Princeton** Illinois, N USA *41°22′N 89°27′W*
31 *N16* **Princeton** Indiana, N USA *38°21′N 87°33′W*
29 *Z14* **Princeton** Iowa, C USA *41°40′N 90°21′W*
20 *H7* **Princeton** Kentucky, S USA *37°06′N 87°52′W*
29 *V8* **Princeton** Minnesota, N USA *45°34′N 93°34′W*
27 *S1* **Princeton** Missouri, C USA *40°22′N 93°37′W*
18 *J15* **Princeton** New Jersey, NE USA *40°21′N 74°39′W*
21 *R6* **Princeton** West Virginia, NE USA *37°23′N 81°06′W*
39 *S12* **Prince William Sound** *inlet* Alaska, USA
67 *P9* **Príncipe** *var.* Príncipe Island, *Eng.* Prince's Island. *island* N Sao Tome and Principe
Príncipe Island *see* Príncipe
32 *I13* **Prineville** Oregon, NW USA *44°19′N 120°50′W*
28 *J11* **Pringle** South Dakota, N USA *43°34′N 103°34′W*
25 *N1* **Pringle** Texas, SW USA *35°55′N 101°28′W*
99 *H14* **Prinsenbeek** Noord-Brabant, S Netherlands *51°36′N 04°42′E*
98 *L6* **Prinses Margriet Kanaal** *canal* N Netherlands
195 *R1* **Prinsesse Astrid Kyst** *Eng.* Princess Astrid Coast. *physical region* Antarctica
195 *T2* **Prinsesse Ragnhild Kyst** *physical region* Antarctica
195 *U2* **Prins Harald Kyst** *physical region* Antarctica
92 *N2* **Prins Karls Forland** *island* W Svalbard
43 *N8* **Prinzapolka** Región Autónoma Atlántico Norte, NE Nicaragua *13°19′N 83°35′W*
42 *L8* **Prinzapolka, Río** ≈ NE Nicaragua
122 *H9* **Priob'ye** Khanty-Mansiyskiy Avtonomnyy Okrug-Yugra, N Russian Federation *62°25′N 65°36′E*
104 *H1* **Prior, Cabo** *headland* NW Spain *43°33′N 08°21′W*
29 *V9* **Prior Lake** Minnesota, N USA *44°42′N 93°25′W*
124 *H11* **Priozersk** *Fin.* Käkisalmi. Leningradskaya Oblast', NW Russian Federation *61°02′N 30°07′E*
119 *J20* **Pripet** *Bel.* Prypyats', *Ukr.* Pryp"yat'. ≈ Belarus/Ukraine
119 *J20* **Pripet Marshes** *wetland* Belarus/Ukraine
113 *N16* **Prishtinë** *Serb.* Priština. C Kosovo *42°40′N 21°10′E*
126 *J8* **Pristen'** Kurskaya Oblast', W Russian Federation *51°15′N 36°47′E*
Priština *see* Prishtinë
100 *M10* **Pritzwalk** Brandenburg, NE Germany *53°10′N 12°11′E*
103 *R13* **Privas** Ardèche, E France *44°45′N 04°35′E*
107 *I16* **Priverno** Lazio, C Italy *41°28′N 13°11′E*
Privigye *see* Prievidza
112 *C12* **Privlaka** Zadar, SW Croatia *44°15′N 15°07′E*
124 *M15* **Privolzhsk** Ivanovskaya Oblast', NW Russian Federation *57°24′N 41°16′E*
127 *P7* **Privolzhskaya Vozvyshennost'** *var.* Volga Uplands. ▲▲ W Russian Federation
127 *P8* **Privolzhskoye** Saratovskaya Oblast', W Russian Federation *51°08′N 45°57′E*
Priwitz *see* Prievidza
127 *N13* **Priyutnoye** Respublika Kalmykiya, SW Russian Federation *46°08′N 43°33′E*
113 *M17* **Prizren** S Kosovo *42°14′N 20°46′E*
107 *I24* **Prizzi** Sicilia, Italy, C Mediterranean Sea *37°44′N 13°26′E*
113 *P18* **Probištip** NE FYR Macedonia *42°00′N 22°06′E*
169 *S16* **Probolinggo** Jawa, C Indonesia *07°45′S 113°12′E*
Probstberg *see* Wyszków
111 *F14* **Prochowice** *Ger.* Parchwitz. Dolnośląskie, SW Poland *51°15′N 16°22′E*
29 *W5* **Proctor** Minnesota, N USA *46°46′N 92°13′W*
25 *R8* **Proctor** Texas, SW USA *31°57′N 98°25′W*
25 *R8* **Proctor Lake** ⊠ Texas, SW USA
155 *I18* **Proddatūr** Andhra Pradesh, E India *14°45′N 78°34′E*
104 *H9* **Proença-a-Nova** *var.* Proença a Nova. Castelo Branco, C Portugal *39°45′N 07°56′W*
Proença a Nova *see* Proença-a-Nova
99 *I21* **Profondeville** Namur, SE Belgium *50°22′N 04°52′E*
41 *W11* **Progreso** Yucatán, SE Mexico *21°14′N 89°41′W*
123 *R14* **Progress** Amurskaya Oblast', SE Russian Federation *49°40′N 129°30′E*
127 *O15* **Prokhladnyy** Kabardino-Balkarskaya Respublika, SW Russian Federation *43°48′N 44°02′E*
Prokletije *see* North Albanian Alps
Prökuls *see* Priekulė
113 *O15* **Prokuplje** Serbia, SE Serbia *43°15′N 21°35′E*
124 *H14* **Proletariy** Novgorodskaya Oblast', W Russian Federation *58°24′N 31°40′E*
126 *M12* **Proletarsk** Rostovskaya Oblast', SW Russian Federation *46°42′N 41°48′E*
127 *N13* **Proletarskoye Vodokhranilishche** *salt lake* SW Russian Federation
Prome *see* Pyay
60 *J8* **Promissão** São Paulo, S Brazil *21°33′S 49°51′W*
60 *J8* **Promissão, Represa de** ⊠ S Brazil
125 *V4* **Promyshlennyy** Respublika Komi, NW Russian Federation *67°36′N 64°E*
119 *O16* **Pronya** ≈ E Belarus
10 *M11* **Prophet River** British Columbia, W Canada *58°07′N 122°39′W*
30 *K11* **Prophetstown** Illinois, N USA *41°40′N 89°56′W*
Propinsi Irian Jaya Barat *see* Papua Barat
Propinsi Kepulauan Riau *see* Kepulauan Riau
59 *P16* **Propriá** Sergipe, E Brazil *10°15′S 36°51′W*
103 *X16* **Propriano** Corse, France, C Mediterranean Sea *41°41′N 08°54′E*
Prościejów *see* Prostějov
Proskurov *see* Khmel 'nyts'kyy
114 *H12* **Prosotsáni** Anatolikí Makedonía kai Thráki, NE Greece *41°11′N 23°59′E*
171 *Q7* **Prosperidad** Mindanao, S Philippines *08°36′N 125°54′E*
32 *J10* **Prosser** Washington, NW USA *46°12′N 119°46′W*
Prossnitz *see* Prostějov
111 *G18* **Prostějov** *Ger.* Prossnitz, *Pol.* Prościejów. Olomoucký Kraj, E Czech Republic *49°29′N 17°08′E*
117 *V8* **Prosyana** Dnipropetrovs'ka Oblast', E Ukraine *48°07′N 36°22′E*
111 *L16* **Proszowice** Malopolskie, S Poland *50°12′N 20°15′E*
Protasy *see* Pratasy
172 *J11* **Protea Seamount** *undersea feature* SW Indian Ocean *36°50′S 18°05′E*
115 *D21* **Próti** *island* S Greece
114 *N8* **Provadiya** Varna, E Bulgaria *43°10′N 27°29′E*
103 *T14* **Provence** *cultural region* SE France
103 *S15* **Provence** *prev.* Marseille-Marigrane. ✈ (Marseille) Bouches-du-Rhône, SE France *43°25′N 05°15′E*
103 *T14* **Provence-Alpes-Côte d'Azur** ◈ *region* SE France
20 *H6* **Providence** Kentucky, S USA *37°23′N 87°47′W*
19 *N12* **Providence** *state capital* Rhode Island, NE USA *41°50′N 71°26′W*
36 *L1* **Providence** Utah, W USA *41°42′N 111°49′W*
Providence *see* Fort Providence
Providence *see* Providence Atoll
67 *X10* **Providence Atoll** *var.* Providence. *atoll* S Seychelles
14 *D12* **Providence Bay** Manitoulin Island, Ontario, S Canada *45°39′N 82°16′W*
23 *R6* **Providence Canyon** *valley* Alabama/Georgia, S USA
22 *I5* **Providence, Lake** ◎ Louisiana, S USA
35 *X13* **Providence Mountains** ▲▲ California, W USA
44 *L6* **Providenciales** *island* W Turks and Caicos Islands
19 *Q12* **Provincetown** Massachusetts, NE USA *42°01′N 70°10′W*
103 *P5* **Provins** Seine-et-Marne, N France *48°34′N 03°18′E*
36 *L3* **Provo** Utah, W USA *40°14′N 111°39′W*
11 *R15* **Provost** Alberta, SW Canada *52°24′N 110°16′W*
112 *G13* **Prozor** Federacija Bosna I Hercegovina, SW Bosnia and Herzegovina *43°46′N 17°38′E*
Prozoroki *see* Prazaroki
60 *I11* **Prudentópolis** Paraná, S Brazil *25°12′S 50°58′W*
39 *R5* **Prudhoe Bay** Alaska, USA *70°16′N 148°18′W*
39 *R4* **Prudhoe Bay** *bay* Alaska, USA
111 *H16* **Prudnik** *Ger.* Neustadt, Neustadt in Oberschlesien. Opole, SW Poland *50°20′N 17°34′E*
119 *J16* **Prudy** Minskaya Voblasts', C Belarus *53°47′N 26°32′E*
101 *D18* **Prüm** Rheinland-Pfalz, W Germany *50°15′N 06°27′E*
101 *D18* **Prüm** ≈ W Germany
Prusa *see* Bursa
110 *J7* **Pruszcz Gdański** *Ger.* Praust. Pomorskie, N Poland *54°16′N 18°36′E*
110 *M12* **Pruszków** *Ger.* Kaltdorf. Mazowieckie, C Poland *52°09′N 20°49′E*
116 *K8* **Prut** *Ger.* Pruth. ≈ E Europe
Pruth *see* Prut
108 *L8* **Prutz** Tirol, W Austria *47°07′N 10°42′E*
Prużana *see* Pruzhany
119 *G19* **Pruzhany** *Pol.* Prużana. Brestskaya Voblasts', SW Belarus *52°33′N 24°28′E*
124 *I11* **Pryazha** Respublika Kareliya, NW Russian Federation *61°42′N 33°39′E*
117 *U10* **Pryazovs'ke** Zaporiz'ka Oblast', SE Ukraine *46°43′N 35°39′E*
Prychornomor'ska Nyzovyna *see* Black Sea Lowland
Prydniprovs'ka Nyzovyna/Prydnyaprowskaya Nizina *see* Dnieper Lowland
195 *Y7* **Prydz Bay** *bay* Antarctica
117 *R4* **Pryluky** *Rus.* Priluki. Chernihivs'ka Oblast', NE Ukraine *50°35′N 32°23′E*
117 *V10* **Prymors'k** *Rus.* Primorsk; *prev.* Primorskoye. Zaporiz'ka Oblast', SE Ukraine *46°44′N 36°19′E*
117 *U13* **Prymors'kyy** Avtonomna Respublika Krym, S Ukraine *45°09′N 35°33′E*
27 *Q9* **Pryor** Oklahoma, C USA *36°19′N 95°19′W*
33 *U11* **Pryor Creek** ≈ Montana, NW USA
Pryp"yat'/Prypyats' *see* Pripet
110 *M10* **Przasnysz** Mazowieckie, C Poland *53°01′N 20°51′E*
111 *K14* **Przedbórz** Łodzkie, S Poland *51°04′N 19°51′E*
111 *P17* **Przemyśl** *Rus.* Peremyshl. Podkarpackie, C Poland *49°47′N 22°47′E*
111 *O16* **Przeworsk** Podkarpackie, SE Poland *50°04′N 22°30′E*
Przheval'sk *see* Karakol
110 *L13* **Przysucha** Mazowieckie, SE Poland *51°22′N 20°36′E*
115 *H18* **Psachná** *var.* Psahna, Psakhná. Évvoia, C Greece *38°35′N 23°39′E*
Psahna/Psakhná *see* Psachná
115 *K18* **Psará** *island* E Greece
115 *I16* **Psathoúra** *island* Vóreies Sporádes, Greece, Aegean Sea
Pschestitz *see* Přeštice
Psein Lora *see* Pishin Lora
117 *S5* **Psel** *Rus.* Psël. ≈ Russian Federation/Ukraine
Psël *see* Psel
115 *M21* **Psérimos** *island* Dodekánisa, Greece, Aegean Sea
Pseyn Bowr *see* Pishin Lora
Pskem *see* Piskom
147 *R8* **Pskemskiy Khrebet** *Uzb.* Piskom Tizmasi. ▲▲ Kyrgyzstan/Uzbekistan
124 *F14* **Pskov** *Ger.* Pleskau, *Latv.* Pleskava. Pskovskaya Oblast', W Russian Federation *58°32′N 31°15′E*
118 *K6* **Pskov, Lake** *Est.* Pihkva Järv, *Ger.* Pleskauer See, *Rus.* Pskovskoye Ozero. ◎ Estonia/Russian Federation
124 *F15* **Pskovskaya Oblast'** ◈ *province* W Russian Federation
Pskovskoye Ozero *see* Pskov, Lake
112 *G9* **Psunj** ▲▲ NE Croatia
111 *J17* **Pszczyna** *Ger.* Pless. Śląskie, S Poland *49°59′N 18°54′E*
Ptačnik/Ptacsnik *see* Vtáčnik
115 *D17* **Ptéri** ▲ C Greece *39°08′N 21°32′E*
Ptich' *see* Ptsich
115 *E14* **Ptolemaïda** *prev.* Ptolemaïs. Dytikí Makedonía, N Greece *40°34′N 21°42′E*
Ptolemaïs *see* Ptolemaïda, Greece
Ptolemaïs *see* 'Akko, Israel
119 *M19* **Ptsich** *Rus.* Ptich'. Homyel'skaya Voblasts', SE Belarus *52°11′N 28°49′E*
119 *M18* **Ptsich** *Rus.* Ptich'. ≈ SE Belarus
109 *X10* **Ptuj** *Ger.* Pettau; *anc.* Poetovio. NE Slovenia *46°26′N 15°54′E*
61 *A23* **Puán** Buenos Aires, E Argentina *37°35′S 62°45′W*
192 *H15* **Pu'apu'a** Savai'i, C Samoa *13°32′S 172°09′W*
192 *G15* **Puava, Cape** *headland* Savai'i, NW Samoa
Pubao *see* Baingoin
56 *F12* **Pucallpa** Ucayali, C Peru *08°21′S 74°33′W*
57 *J17* **Pucarani** La Paz, NW Bolivia *16°25′S 68°29′W*
Pučarevo *see* Novi Travnik
157 *U12* **Pucheng** Shaanxi, SE China *35°00′N 109°34′E*
160 *L6* **Pucheng** *var.* Nanpu. Fujian, C China *27°59′N 118°31′E*
125 *N16* **Puchezh** Ivanovskaya Oblast', W Russian Federation *56°58′N 41°08′E*
111 *I19* **Púchov** *Hung.* Puhó. Trenčiansky Kraj, W Slovakia *49°08′N 18°15′E*
116 *J13* **Pucioasa** Dâmbovița, S Romania *45°04′N 25°23′E*
110 *I6* **Puck** Pomorskie, N Poland *54°43′N 18°24′E*
30 *L8* **Puckaway Lake** ◎ Wisconsin, N USA
63 *G15* **Pucón** Araucanía, S Chile *39°18′S 71°52′W*
93 *M14* **Pudasjärvi** Oulu, C Finland *65°20′N 27°02′E*
148 *L8* **Pūdeh Tal, Shelleh-ye** ≈ SW Afghanistan
127 *S1* **Pudem** Udmurtskaya Respublika, NW Russian Federation *58°18′N 52°08′E*
Pudewitz *see* Pobiedziska
124 *K11* **Pudozh** Respublika Kareliya, NW Russian Federation *61°48′N 36°30′E*
97 *M17* **Pudsey** N England, United Kingdom *53°48′N 01°40′W*
Puduchcheri *see* Pondicherry
151 *H21* **Pudukkottai** Tamil Nādu, SE India *10°23′N 78°47′E*
171 *Z13* **Pue** Papua, E Indonesia *02°42′S 140°36′E*
41 *P14* **Puebla** *var.* Puebla de Zaragoza. Puebla, S Mexico *19°02′N 98°13′W*
41 *P15* **Puebla** ◈ *state* S Mexico
104 *L11* **Puebla de Alcocer** Extremadura, W Spain *38°59′N 05°14′W*
Puebla de Don Fabrique *see* Puebla de Don Fadrique
105 *P13* **Puebla de Don Fadrique** *var.* Puebla de Don Fabrique. Andalucía, S Spain *37°58′N 02°25′W*
104 *J11* **Puebla de la Calzada** Extremadura, W Spain *38°54′N 06°38′W*
104 *J5* **Puebla de Sanabria** Castilla y León, N Spain *42°04′N 06°38′W*
Puebla de Trives *see* A Pobla de Trives
Puebla de Zaragoza *see* Puebla
37 *T6* **Pueblo** Colorado, C USA *38°15′N 104°37′W*
37 *N10* **Pueblo Colorado Wash** *valley* Arizona, SW USA
61 *C16* **Pueblo Libertador** Corrientes, NE Argentina *30°13′S 59°23′W*
40 *J10* **Pueblo Nuevo** Durango, C Mexico *23°24′N 105°21′W*
42 *J8* **Pueblo Nuevo** Estelí, NW Nicaragua *13°21′N 86°30′W*
54 *J3* **Pueblo Nuevo** Falcón, N Venezuela *11°59′N 69°57′W*

◆ Country
● Country Capital
◇ Dependent Territory
○ Dependent Territory Capital
◈ Administrative Regions
✈ International Airport
▲ Mountain
▲▲ Mountain Range
⩚ Volcano
≈ River
◎ Lake
⊠ Reservoir

42 B6 Pueblo Nuevo Tiquisate var. Tiquisate. Escuintla, SW Guatemala 14°16′N 91°21′W
41 Q11 Pueblo Viejo, Laguna de lagoon E Mexico
63 J14 Puelches La Pampa, C Argentina 38°08′S 65°56′W
104 L14 Puente-Genil Andalucía, S Spain 37°23′N 04°45′W
105 Q3 Puente la Reina Bas. Gares. Navarra, N Spain 42°40′N 01°49′W
104 L12 Puente Nuevo, Embalse de ⊠ S Spain
57 D14 Puente Piedra Lima, W Peru 11°49′S 77°01′W
160 F14 Pu'er var. Ning'er. Yunnan, SW China 23°09′N 100°58′E
45 V6 Puerca, Punta headland E Puerto Rico 18°13′N 65°36′W
37 R12 Puerco, Rio ≈ New Mexico, SW USA
57 J17 Puerto Acosta La Paz, W Bolivia 15°33′S 69°15′W
63 G19 Puerto Aisén Aisén, S Chile 45°24′S 72°42′W
41 R17 Puerto Ángel Oaxaca, SE Mexico 15°39′N 96°29′W
Puerto Argentino see Stanley
41 T17 Puerto Arista Chiapas, SE Mexico 15°55′N 93°47′W
43 O16 Puerto Armuelles Chiriquí, SW Panama 08°19′N 82°51′W
Puerto Arrecife see Arrecife
54 D14 Puerto Asís Putumayo, SW Colombia 0°31′N 76°31′W
54 L9 Puerto Ayacucho Amazonas, SW Venezuela 05°45′N 67°37′W
57 C18 Puerto Ayora Galapagos Islands, Ecuador, E Pacific Ocean 0°45′S 90°19′W
57 C18 Puerto Baquerizo Moreno var. Baquerizo Moreno. Galapagos Islands, Ecuador, E Pacific Ocean 0°54′S 89°37′W
42 G4 Puerto Barrios Izabal, E Guatemala 15°42′N 88°34′W
Puerto Bello see Portobelo
54 F8 Puerto Berrío Antioquia, C Colombia 06°28′N 74°28′W
54 F9 Puerto Boyacá Boyacá, C Colombia 05°58′N 74°36′W
54 K4 Puerto Cabello Carabobo, N Venezuela 10°29′N 68°02′W
43 N7 Puerto Cabezas var. Bilwi. Región Autónoma Atlántico Norte, NE Nicaragua 14°05′N 83°22′W
54 L9 Puerto Carreño Vichada, E Colombia 06°08′N 67°30′W
54 E4 Puerto Colombia Atlántico, N Colombia 10°59′N 74°57′W
42 H4 Puerto Cortés Cortés, NW Honduras 15°50′N 87°55′W
54 J4 Puerto Cumarebo Falcón, N Venezuela 11°29′N 69°21′W
Puerto de Cabras see Puerto del Rosario
55 Q5 Puerto de Hierro Sucre, NE Venezuela 10°40′N 62°03′W
64 O11 Puerto de la Cruz Tenerife, Islas Canarias, Spain, NE Atlantic Ocean 28°24′N 16°33′W
64 Q11 Puerto del Rosario var. Puerto de Cabras. Fuerteventura, Islas Canarias, Spain, NE Atlantic Ocean 28°29′N 13°52′W
63 J20 Puerto Deseado Santa Cruz, SE Argentina 47°46′S 65°53′W
40 F8 Puerto Escondido Baja California Sur, NW Mexico 25°48′N 111°20′W
41 R17 Puerto Escondido Oaxaca, SE Mexico 15°48′N 96°57′W
60 G12 Puerto Esperanza Misiones, NE Argentina 26°01′S 54°39′W
54 H10 Puerto Gaitán Meta, C Colombia 04°20′N 72°10′W
Puerto Gallegos see Río Gallegos
60 G12 Puerto Iguazú Misiones, NE Argentina 25°39′S 54°35′W
56 F12 Puerto Inca Huánuco, N Peru 09°22′S 74°54′W
54 L11 Puerto Inírida var. Obando. Guainía, E Colombia 03°48′N 67°54′W
42 K13 Puerto Jesús Guanacaste, NW Costa Rica 10°08′N 85°26′W
41 Z11 Puerto Juárez Quintana Roo, SE Mexico 21°06′N 86°46′W
55 N5 Puerto La Cruz Anzoátegui, NE Venezuela 10°14′N 64°40′W
54 E14 Puerto Leguízamo Putumayo, S Colombia 0°14′S 74°45′W
43 N5 Puerto Lempira Gracias a Dios, E Honduras 15°14′N 83°48′W
Puerto Libertad see La Libertad
54 I11 Puerto Limón Meta, E Colombia 04°00′N 71°09′W
54 D13 Puerto Limón Putumayo, SW Colombia 01°02′N 76°30′W
Puerto Limón see Limón
105 N11 Puertollano Castilla-La Mancha, C Spain 38°41′N 04°07′W
63 K17 Puerto Lobos Chubut, SE Argentina 42°00′S 64°58′W
54 I3 Puerto López La Guajira, N Colombia 11°54′N 71°21′W
105 Q14 Puerto Lumbreras Murcia, SE Spain 37°35′N 01°49′W
41 V17 Puerto Madero Chiapas, SE Mexico 14°44′N 92°25′W
63 K17 Puerto Madryn Chubut, S Argentina 42°45′S 65°02′W
Puerto Magdalena see Bahía Magdalena
57 J15 Puerto Maldonado Madre de Dios, E Peru 12°37′S 69°11′W
Puerto Masachapa see Masachapa
Puerto México see Coatzacoalcos
63 G17 Puerto Montt Los Lagos, C Chile 41°28′S 72°57′W
41 Z12 Puerto Morelos Quintana Roo, SE Mexico 20°47′N 86°54′W
54 L10 Puerto Nariño Vichada, E Colombia 04°57′N 67°51′W
63 H23 Puerto Natales Magallanes, S Chile 51°42′S 72°28′W
43 X15 Puerto Obaldía Kuna Yala, NE Panama 08°38′N 77°26′W
44 H6 Puerto Padre Las Tunas, E Cuba 21°13′N 76°35′W
54 L9 Puerto Páez Apure, C Venezuela 06°10′N 67°30′W
40 E3 Puerto Peñasco Sonora, NW Mexico 31°20′N 113°35′W
55 N5 Puerto Píritu Anzoátegui, NE Venezuela 10°04′N 65°00′W
45 N8 Puerto Plata var. San Felipe de Puerto Plata. N Dominican Republic 19°46′N 70°42′W
Puerto Presidente Stroessner see Ciudad del Este
171 N6 Puerto Princesa off. Puerto Princesa City. Palawan, W Philippines 09°48′N 118°43′E
Puerto Princesa City see Puerto Princesa
Puerto Príncipe see Camagüey
Puerto Quellón see Quellón
60 F13 Puerto Rico Misiones, NE Argentina 26°48′S 54°59′W
57 K14 Puerto Rico Pando, N Bolivia 11°07′S 67°32′W
54 E12 Puerto Rico Caquetá, S Colombia 01°54′N 75°13′W
45 U5 Puerto Rico off. Commonwealth of Puerto Rico; prev. Porto Rico. ◇ US commonwealth territory C West Indies
64 F11 Puerto Rico island C West Indies
Puerto Rico, Commonwealth of see Puerto Rico
64 G11 Puerto Rico Trench undersea feature NE Caribbean Sea
54 I8 Puerto Rondón Arauca, E Colombia 06°16′N 71°05′W
Puerto San José see San José
63 J21 Puerto San Julián var. San Julián. Santa Cruz, SE Argentina 49°14′S 67°41′W
63 I22 Puerto Santa Cruz var. Santa Cruz. Santa Cruz, SE Argentina 50°05′S 68°31′W
Puerto Sauce see Juan L. Lacaze
57 Q20 Puerto Suárez Santa Cruz, E Bolivia 18°59′S 57°47′W
54 D13 Puerto Umbría Putumayo, SW Colombia 0°52′N 76°36′W
40 J13 Puerto Vallarta Jalisco, SW Mexico 20°36′N 105°15′W
63 G16 Puerto Varas Los Lagos, C Chile 41°20′S 73°00′W
42 M13 Puerto Viejo Heredia, NE Costa Rica 10°27′N 84°00′W
Puertoviejo see Portoviejo
57 B18 Puerto Villamil var. Villamil. Galapagos Islands, Ecuador, E Pacific Ocean 0°57′S 91°00′W
54 F8 Puerto Wilches Santander, N Colombia 07°22′N 73°53′W
63 H20 Pueyrredón, Lago var. Lago Cochrane. ◎ S Argentina
127 R7 Pugachëv Saratovskaya Oblast', W Russian Federation 52°06′N 48°50′E
127 T3 Pugachëvo Udmurtskaya Respublika, NW Russian Federation 56°38′N 53°03′E
32 H8 Puget Sound sound Washington, NW USA
107 O17 Puglia var. Le Puglie, Eng. Apulia. ◆ region SE Italy
107 N17 Puglia, Canosa di anc. Canusium. Puglia, SE Italy 41°13′N 16°04′E
118 I6 Puhja Ger. Kawelecht. Tartumaa, SE Estonia 58°20′N 26°19′E
Puhó see Púchov
105 V4 Puigcerdà Cataluña, NE Spain 42°25′N 01°53′E
Puigmal see Puigmal d'Err
103 N17 Puigmal d'Err var. Puigmal. ▲ S France 42°24′N 02°07′E
76 I16 Pujehun S Sierra Leone 07°23′N 11°44′W
Puka see Pukë
185 E20 Pukaki, Lake ◎ South Island, New Zealand
38 F10 Pukalani Maui, Hawaii, USA, C Pacific Ocean 20°50′N 156°20′W
190 J13 Pukapuka atoll N Cook Islands
191 X9 Pukapuka atoll Îles Tuamotu, E French Polynesia
Pukari Neem see Purekkari Neem
191 X11 Pukarua var. Pukaruha. atoll Îles Tuamotu, E French Polynesia
Pukaruha see Pukarua
14 A7 Pukaskwa ≈ Ontario, S Canada
11 V12 Pukatawagan Manitoba, C Canada 55°46′N 101°14′W
191 X16 Pukatikei, Maunga ▲ Easter Island, Chile, E Pacific Ocean
182 C1 Pukatja var. Ernabella. South Australia 26°18′S 132°13′E
163 Y12 Pukch'ŏng E North Korea 40°13′N 128°20′E
113 L18 Pukë var. Puka. Shkodër, N Albania 42°03′N 19°53′E
184 L6 Pukekohe Auckland, North Island, New Zealand 37°12′S 174°54′E
184 L7 Pukemiro Waikato, North Island, New Zealand 37°37′S 175°02′E
190 D12 Puke, Mont ▲ Île Futuna, W Wallis and Futuna
Puket see Phuket
185 C20 Puketeraki Range ▲▲ South Island, New Zealand
184 N13 Puketoi Range ▲▲ North Island, New Zealand
185 F21 Pukeuri Junction Otago, South Island, New Zealand 45°01′S 171°01′E
119 L16 Pukhavichy Rus. Pukhovichi. Minskaya Voblasts', C Belarus 53°32′N 28°15′E
Pukhovichi see Pukhavichy
124 M10 Puksoozero Arkhangel'skaya Oblast', NW Russian Federation 62°37′N 40°29′E
112 A10 Pula It. Pola; prev. Pulj. Istra, NW Croatia 44°53′N 13°51′E
Pula see Nyingchi
163 U14 Pulandian var. Xinjin. Liaoning, NE China 39°25′N 121°58′E
163 T14 Pulandian Wan bay NE China
189 O15 Pulap Atoll atoll Caroline Islands, C Micronesia
18 H9 Pulaski New York, NE USA 43°34′N 76°06′W
20 I10 Pulaski Tennessee, S USA 35°11′N 87°00′W
21 R7 Pulaski Virginia, NE USA 37°03′N 80°47′W
171 Y14 Pulau, Sungai ≈ Papua, E Indonesia
110 N13 Puławy Ger. Neu Amerika. Lubelskie, E Poland 51°25′N 21°57′E
149 R5 Pul-e-'Alam prev. Pol-e-'Alam. Lōgar, E Afghanistan 33°59′N 69°02′E
149 Q3 Pul-e Khumrī prev. Pol-e-Khomrī. Baghlān, NE Afghanistan 35°55′N 68°45′E
146 I16 Pulhatyn Rus. Polekhatum; prev. Pul'-I-Khatum. Ahal Welaýaty, S Turkmenistan 36°01′N 61°08′E
101 E16 Pulheim Nordrhein-Westfalen, W Germany 51°00′N 06°48′E
155 J19 Pulicat Lake lagoon SE India
Pul'-I-Khatum see Pulhatyn
Pul-i-Sefid see Pol-e Sefid
Pulj see Pula
109 W2 Pulkau ≈ NE Austria
93 L15 Pulkkila Oulu, C Finland 64°15′N 25°53′E
122 C7 Pulkovo ✈ (Sankt-Peterburg) Leningradskaya Oblast', NW Russian Federation 60°06′N 30°23′E
32 M9 Pullman Washington, NW USA 46°43′N 117°10′W
108 B10 Pully Vaud, SW Switzerland 46°31′N 06°40′E
40 F7 Púlpita, Punta headland NW Mexico 26°30′N 111°28′W
110 M10 Pułtusk Mazowieckie, C Poland 52°41′N 21°04′E
158 H10 Pulu Xinjiang Uygur Zizhiqu, W China 36°10′N 81°29′E
137 P13 Pülümür Tunceli, E Turkey 39°30′N 39°54′E
189 N16 Pulusuk island Caroline Islands, C Micronesia
189 N16 Puluwat Atoll atoll Caroline Islands, C Micronesia
25 N11 Pumpville Texas, SW USA 29°55′N 101°43′W
191 P7 Punaauia var. Hakapehi. Tahiti, W French Polynesia 17°38′S 149°37′W
56 B8 Puná, Isla island SW Ecuador
185 G16 Punakaiki West Coast, South Island, New Zealand 42°07′S 171°21′E
153 T11 Punakha C Bhutan 27°38′N 89°50′E
57 L18 Punata Cochabamba, C Bolivia 17°32′S 65°50′W
155 E14 Pune prev. Poona. Mahārāshtra, W India 18°32′N 73°52′E
83 M17 Pungoè, Rio var. Púnguè, Pungwe. ≈ C Mozambique
21 X10 Pungo River ≈ North Carolina, SE USA
Púnguè/Pungwe see Pungoè, Rio
79 N19 Punia Maniema, E Dem. Rep. Congo 01°28′S 26°25′E
62 H8 Punilla, Sierra de la ▲▲ W Argentina
161 P14 Puning Guangdong, S China 23°24′N 116°14′E
62 G10 Punitaqui Coquimbo, C Chile 30°50′S 71°29′W
149 T9 Punjab prev. West Punjab, Western Punjab. ◆ province E Pakistan
152 H8 Punjab state NW India
129 Q9 Punjab Plains plain N India
93 O17 Punkaharju var. Punkasalmi. Itä-Suomi, E Finland 61°45′N 29°21′E
Punkasalmi see Punkaharju
57 I17 Puno Puno, SE Peru 15°53′S 70°03′W
57 H17 Puno off. Departamento de Puno. ◆ department S Peru
Puno, Departamento de see Puno
61 B24 Punta Alta Buenos Aires, E Argentina 38°54′S 62°01′W
63 H24 Punta Arenas prev. Magallanes. Magallanes, S Chile 53°10′S 70°56′W
45 T6 Punta, Cerro de ▲ C Puerto Rico 18°10′N 66°36′W
43 T15 Punta Chame Panamá, C Panama 08°39′N 79°42′W
57 G17 Punta Colorada Arequipa, SW Peru 16°17′S 72°31′W
40 F9 Punta Coyote Baja California Sur, NW Mexico
62 G8 Punta de Díaz Atacama, N Chile 28°03′S 70°36′W
61 G20 Punta del Este Maldonado, S Uruguay 34°59′S 54°58′W
63 K17 Punta Delgada Chubut, SE Argentina 42°46′S 63°40′W
55 O5 Punta de Mata Monagas, NE Venezuela 09°48′N 63°38′W
55 O4 Punta de Piedras Nueva Esparta, NE Venezuela 10°57′N 64°06′W
42 F4 Punta Gorda Toledo, SE Belize 16°07′N 88°47′W
43 N11 Punta Gorda Región Autónoma Atlántico Sur, SE Nicaragua 11°31′N 83°46′W
23 W14 Punta Gorda Florida, SE USA 26°55′N 82°03′W
42 M11 Punta Gorda, Río ≈ SE Nicaragua
62 H6 Punta Negra, Salar de salt lake N Chile
40 D5 Punta Prieta Baja California Norte, NW Mexico 28°56′N 114°11′W
42 L13 Puntarenas Puntarenas, W Costa Rica 09°58′N 84°50′W
42 L13 Puntarenas off. Provincia de Puntarenas. ◆ province W Costa Rica
Puntarenas, Provincia de see Puntarenas
80 P13 Puntland cultural region NE Somalia
54 J4 Punto Fijo Falcón, N Venezuela 11°42′N 70°13′W
105 S4 Puntón de Guara ▲ N Spain 42°18′N 00°13′W
18 D14 Punxsutawney Pennsylvania, NE USA 40°55′N 78°57′W
93 M14 Puolanka Oulu, C Finland 64°51′N 27°42′E
57 J17 Pupuya, Nevado ▲ W Bolivia 15°04′S 69°01′W
Puqi see Chibi
57 F16 Puquio Ayacucho, S Peru 14°44′S 74°07′W
122 J9 Pur ≈ N Russian Federation
186 D7 Purari ≈ S Papua New Guinea
27 N11 Purcell Oklahoma, C USA 35°00′N 97°21′W
11 O16 Purcell Mountains ▲▲ British Columbia, SW Canada
105 P14 Purchena Andalucía, S Spain 37°21′N 02°21′W
27 S8 Purdy Missouri, C USA 36°49′N 93°55′W
118 I2 Purekkari Neem prev. Pukari Neem. headland N Estonia 59°33′N 24°49′E
37 U7 Purgatoire River ≈ Colorado, C USA
Purgstall see Purgstall an der Erlauf
109 V5 Purgstall an der Erlauf var. Purgstall. Niederösterreich, NE Austria 48°01′N 15°08′E
154 O13 Puri var. Jagannath. Orissa, E India 19°52′N 85°49′E
Puriramya see Buriram
109 X4 Purkersdorf Niederösterreich, NE Austria 48°13′N 16°12′E
98 I9 Purmerend Noord-Holland, C Netherlands 52°30′N 04°56′E
151 G16 Pūrna ≈ C India
Purnea see Pūrnia
153 R13 Pūrnia prev. Purnea. Bihār, NE India 25°47′N 87°28′E
Pursat see Poŭthĭsăt, Stœng, W Cambodia
Pursat see Poŭthĭsăt, Poŭthĭsăt, W Cambodia
Purulia see Puruliya
150 L13 Puruliya prev. Purulia. West Bengal, NE India 23°20′N 86°24′E
47 G7 Purus, Rio var. Río Purús. ≈ Brazil/Peru
186 C9 Purutu Island island SW Papua New Guinea
93 N17 Puruvesi ◎ SE Finland
22 L7 Purvis Mississippi, S USA 31°08′N 89°24′W
114 J11 Pŭrvomay prev. Borisovgrad. Plovdiv, C Bulgaria 42°06′N 25°13′E
169 R16 Purwodadi prev. Poerwodadi. Jawa, C Indonesia 07°05′S 110°53′E
169 P16 Purwokerto prev. Poerwokerto. Jawa, C Indonesia 07°25′S 109°14′E
169 P16 Purworejo prev. Poerworedjo. Jawa, C Indonesia 07°45′S 110°04′E
20 H8 Puryear Tennessee, S USA 36°25′N 88°21′W
154 H13 Pusad Mahārāshtra, C India 19°56′N 77°40′E
Pusan see Busan
Pusan-gwangyŏksi see Busan
168 H7 Pusatgajo, Pegunungan ▲▲ Sumatera, NW Indonesia
Puschlav see Poschiavo
124 G13 Pushkin prev. Tsarskoye Selo. Leningradskaya Oblast', NW Russian Federation 59°42′N 30°24′E
126 L3 Pushkino Moskovskaya Oblast', W Russian Federation 55°57′N 37°45′E
127 Q8 Pushkino Saratovskaya Oblast', W Russian Federation 51°09′N 47°00′E
Pushkino see Biläsuvar
111 M22 Püspökladány Hajdú-Bihar, E Hungary 47°20′N 21°05′E
118 J3 Püssi Ger. Isenhof. Ida-Virumaa, NE Estonia 59°22′N 27°04′E
116 I5 Pustomyty L'vivs'ka Oblast', W Ukraine 49°43′N 23°55′E
124 F16 Pustoshka Pskovskaya Oblast', W Russian Federation 56°21′N 29°16′E
Pusztakalán see Călan
167 N1 Putao prev. Fort Hertz. Kachin State, N Myanmar (Burma) 27°22′N 97°24′E
184 M8 Putaruru Waikato, North Island, New Zealand 38°03′S 175°48′E
Puteoli see Pozzuoli
161 R12 Putian Fujian, SE China 25°32′N 119°02′E
107 O17 Putignano Puglia, SE Italy 40°51′N 17°08′E
Puting see De'an
Putivl' see Putyvl'
41 Q16 Putla var. Putla de Guerrero. Oaxaca, SE Mexico 17°01′N 97°56′W
Putla de Guerrero see Putla
19 N12 Putnam Connecticut, NE USA 41°56′N 71°52′W
25 Q7 Putnam Texas, SW USA 32°22′N 99°11′W
18 M10 Putney Vermont, NE USA 42°59′N 72°30′W
111 L20 Putnok Borsod-Abaúj-Zemplén, NE Hungary 48°18′N 20°25′E
Putorana, Gory/Putorana Mountains see Putorana, Plato
122 L8 Putorana, Plato var. Gory Putorana, Eng. Putorana Mountains. ▲▲ N Russian Federation
168 K9 Putrajaya ● (Malaysia) Kuala Lumpur, Peninsular Malaysia 02°57′N 101°42′E
62 H2 Putre Arica y Parinacota, N Chile 18°11′S 69°30′W
155 J24 Puttalam North Western Province, W Sri Lanka 08°02′N 79°55′E
155 J24 Puttalam Lagoon lagoon W Sri Lanka
99 H17 Putte Antwerpen, C Belgium 51°04′N 04°39′E
94 E10 Puttegga ▲ S Norway 62°13′N 07°40′E
98 K11 Putten Gelderland, C Netherlands 52°15′N 05°36′E
100 K7 Puttgarden Schleswig-Holstein, N Germany 54°30′N 11°13′E
Puttiala see Patiāla
101 D20 Püttlingen Saarland, SW Germany 49°16′N 06°52′E
54 D14 Putumayo off. Intendencia del Putumayo. ◆ province S Colombia
Putumayo, Intendencia del see Putumayo
48 E7 Putumayo, Río var. Içá, Rio. ≈ NW South America see also Içá, Rio
Putumayo, Río see Içá, Rio
169 P11 Putus, Tanjung headland Borneo, N Indonesia 0°27′S 109°04′E
116 J8 Putyla Chernivets'ka Oblast', W Ukraine 47°59′N 25°04′E
117 S3 Putyvl' Rus. Putivl'. Sums'ka Oblast', NE Ukraine 51°21′N 33°53′E
93 M18 Puula ◎ SE Finland
93 N18 Puumala Itä-Suomi, E Finland 61°31′N 28°12′E
118 I5 Puurmani Ger. Talkhof. Jõgevamaa, E Estonia 58°36′N 26°17′E
99 G17 Puurs Antwerpen, N Belgium 51°05′N 04°17′E
38 F10 Pu'u 'Ula'ula var. Red Hill. ▲ Maui, Hawai'i, USA 20°42′N 156°16′W
38 A8 Pu'uwai var. Puuwai. Ni'ihau, Hawaii, USA, C Pacific Ocean 21°54′N 160°11′W
12 J4 Puvirnituq prev. Povungnituk. Québec, NE Canada 60°10′N 77°20′W
12 J3 Puvirnituq, Riviere de prev. Rivière de Povungnituk. ≈ Québec, NE Canada
32 H8 Puyallup Washington, NW USA 47°11′N 122°17′W
161 O5 Puyang Henan, C China 35°40′N 115°00′E
103 O11 Puy-de-Dôme ◆ department C France
103 N15 Puylaurens Tarn, S France 43°33′N 02°01′E
102 M13 Puy-l'Evêque Lot, S France 44°31′N 01°10′E
103 N17 Puymorens, Col de pass S France
56 C7 Puyo Pastaza, C Ecuador 01°30′S 77°58′W
185 A24 Puysegur Point headland South Island, New Zealand 46°09′S 166°38′E
148 J8 Pūzak, Hāmūn-e Pash. Hāmūn-i-Puzak. ◎ SW Afghanistan
Puzak, Hāmūn-i- see Pūzak, Hāmūn-e
81 J23 Pwani Eng. Coast. ◆ region E Tanzania
79 O23 Pweto Katanga, SE Dem. Rep. Congo 08°28′S 28°52′E
97 I19 Pwllheli NW Wales, United Kingdom 52°54′N 04°23′W
189 O14 Pwok Pohnpei, E Micronesia
122 I9 Pyakupur ≈ N Russian Federation
124 M6 Pyalitsa Murmanskaya Oblast', NW Russian Federation 66°17′N 39°56′E
124 K10 Pyal'ma Respublika Kareliya, NW Russian Federation 62°24′N 35°56′E
Pyandzh see Panj
166 L9 Pyapon Ayeyarwady, SW Myanmar (Burma) 16°15′N 95°40′E
119 J15 Pyarshai Rus. Pershay. Minskaya Voblasts', C Belarus 54°02′N 26°41′E
122 K8 Pyasina ≈ N Russian Federation
119 G17 Pyaski Rus. Peski; prev. Pyeski. Hrodzyenskaya Voblasts', W Belarus 53°21′N 24°38′E
114 I10 Pyasŭchnik, Yazovir ⊠ C Bulgaria
Pyatikhatki see P"yatykhatky
117 S7 P"yatykhatky Rus. Pyatikhatki. Dnipropetrovs'ka Oblast', E Ukraine 48°23′N 33°43′E
166 M6 Pyawbwe Mandalay, C Myanmar (Burma) 20°39′N 96°04′E
166 L7 Pyay var. Prome, Pye. Bago, C Myanmar (Burma) 18°50′N 95°14′E
127 T3 Pychas Udmurtskaya Respublika, NW Russian Federation 56°30′N 52°33′E
166 K6 Pyechin Chin State, W Myanmar (Burma) 20°01′N 93°36′E
Pye see Pyay
163 X15 Pyeongtaek prev. P'yŏngt'aek. NW South Korea 37°00′N 127°04′E
Pyeski see Pyaski
119 L19 Pyetrykaw Rus. Petrikov. Homyel'skaya Voblasts', SE Belarus 52°08′N 28°30′E
93 O17 Pyhäjärvi ◎ SE Finland
93 M16 Pyhäjärvi ◎ C Finland
93 L15 Pyhäjoki Oulu, W Finland 64°28′N 24°15′E
93 L15 Pyhäjoki ≈ W Finland
93 M15 Pyhäntä Oulu, C Finland 64°07′N 26°19′E
93 M16 Pyhäsalmi Oulu, C Finland 63°38′N 26°E
93 O17 Pyhäselkä ◎ SE Finland
93 M19 Pyhtää Swe. Pyttis. Etelä-Suomi, S Finland 60°29′N 26°40′E
166 M5 Pyin-Oo-Lwin var. Maymyo. Mandalay, C Myanmar (Burma) 22°03′N 96°30′E
115 N24 Pylés var. Piles. Kárpathos, SE Greece 35°31′N 27°08′E
115 D21 Pýlos var. Pilos. Pelopónnisos, S Greece 36°55′N 21°42′E
18 B12 Pymatuning Reservoir ⊠ Ohio/Pennsylvania, NE USA
P'yŏngt'aek see Pyeongtaek
163 V14 P'yŏngyang var. P'yŏngyang-si, Eng. Pyongyang. ● (North Korea) SW North Korea 39°04′N 125°46′E
P'yŏngyang-si see P'yŏngyang
35 Q4 Pyramid Lake ◎ Nevada, W USA
37 P15 Pyramid Mountains ▲▲ New Mexico, SW USA
37 R5 Pyramid Peak ▲ Colorado, C USA 39°04′N 106°57′W
115 D17 Pyramíva var. Piramiva. ▲ C Greece 39°08′N 21°18′E
Pyrenaei Montes see Pyrenees
86 B12 Pyrenees Fr. Pyrénées, Sp. Pirineos; anc. Pyrenaei Montes. ▲▲ SW Europe
102 J16 Pyrénées-Atlantiques ◆ department SW France
103 N17 Pyrénées-Orientales ◆ department S France
115 L19 Pyrgí var. Pirgi. Chíos, E Greece 38°13′N 26°01′E
115 D20 Pýrgos var. Pírgos. Dytikí Elláda, S Greece 37°40′N 21°27′E
Pyritz see Pyrzyce
115 E19 Pýrros ≈ S Greece
117 R4 Pyryatyn Rus. Piryatin. Poltavs'ka Oblast', NE Ukraine 50°14′N 32°31′E
110 D9 Pyrzyce Ger. Pyritz. Zachodnio-pomorskie, NW Poland 53°09′N 14°53′E
124 F15 Pytalovo Latv. Abrene; prev. Jaunlatgale. Pskovskaya Oblast', W Russian Federation 57°06′N 27°55′E
115 M20 Pythagóreio var. Pithagorio. Sámos, Dodekánisa, Greece, Aegean Sea 37°42′N 26°57′E
14 L11 Pythonga, Lac ◎ Québec, SE Canada
Pyttis see Pyhtää
Pyu see Phyu
166 M8 Pyuntaza Bago, Myanmar (Burma) 17°51′N 96°44′E
153 N11 Pyuthān Mid Western, W Nepal 28°09′N 82°50′E
110 H12 Pyzdry Ger. Peisern. Wielkopolskie, C Poland 52°10′N 17°42′E

Q

138 H13 Qāʿ al Jafr ◎ S Jordan
197 O11 Qaanaaq var. Qânâq, Dan. Thule. ◆ Avannaarsua, N Greenland
Qabanbay see Kabanbay
138 G7 Qabb Eliâs E Lebanon 33°46′N 35°49′E
Qabil see Al Qābil
Qabırrı see Iori
Qābis see Gabès
Qābis, Khalīj see Gabès, Golfe de
Qabqa see Gonghe
141 S14 Qabr Hūd C Yemen 16°02′N 49°36′E
Qacentina see Constantine
Qādes see Qādis
148 L4 Qādis prev. Qādes. Bādghīs, NW Afghanistan 34°48′N 63°26′E
139 T11 Qādisīyah, Al Qādisīyah, S Iraq 31°43′N 44°28′E
143 O4 Qā'emshahr prev. 'Alīābad, Shāhī. Māzandarān, N Iran 36°31′N 52°49′E
143 U7 Qā'en var. Qain, Qāyen. Khorāsān-Razavī, E Iran 33°43′N 59°07′E
141 U13 Qafa spring/well SW Oman 17°46′N 52°55′E
Qafsah see Gafsa
Qagan Nur see Qiemo
163 Q12 Qagan Nur var. Xulun Hobot Qagan, Zhengxiangbai Qi. Nei Mongol Zizhiqu, N China 42°10′N 114°57′E
163 V9 Qagan Nur ◎ NE China
163 Q11 Qagan Nur ◎ N China
Qagan Us see Dulan
158 H13 Qagcaka Xizang Zizhiqu, W China 32°32′N 81°52′E
Qagchêng see Xiangcheng
Qahremānshahr see Kermānshāh
159 Q10 Qaidam He ≈ C China
156 L8 Qaidam Pendi basin C China
Qain see Qā'en
Qala Āhangarān see Chaghcharān
139 U3 Qaļā Diza var. Qal' at Dīzah. As Sulaymānīyah, NE Iraq 36°11′N 45°07′E
Qal'ah Sālih see Qal'at Ṣāliḥ
149 N4 Qal'ah Shahr Pash. Qala Shāhar; prev. Qal'eh Shahr. Sar-e Pul, N Afghanistan 35°34′N 65°38′E
148 L4 Qal'ah-ye Now var. Qala Nau; prev. Qal'eh-ye Now. Bādghīs, NW Afghanistan 35°N 63°08′E
147 R13 Qal'aikhum Rus. Kalaikhum. S Tajikistan 38°28′N 70°49′E
Qala Nau see Qal'ah-ye Now
141 V17 Qalansīyah Suquṭrā, W Yemen 12°40′N 53°30′E
Qala Panja see Qal'eh-ye Panjeh
Qala Shāhar see Qal'ah Shahr
149 O8 Qalāt Per. Kalāt. Zābul, S Afghanistan 32°10′N 66°54′E
139 W9 Qal'at Aḥmad Maysān, E Iraq 32°24′N 46°46′E
141 N11 Qal'at Bīshah 'Asīr, SW Saudi Arabia 19°59′N 42°38′E
138 H4 Qal'at Burzay Ḥamāh, W Syria 35°37′N 36°16′E
Qal 'at Dīzah see Qaļā Diza
139 W9 Qal'at Ḥuṣayn Maysān, E Iraq 32°19′N 46°46′E
139 V10 Qal'at Majnūnah Al Qādisīyah, S Iraq 31°39′N 45°44′E
139 X11 Qal'at Ṣāliḥ var. Qal'ah Sālih. Maysān, E Iraq 31°30′N 47°24′E
139 V10 Qal'at Sukkar Dhī Qār, SE Iraq 31°52′N 46°05′E
Qalba Zhotasy see Khrebet Kalba
143 Q12 Qal'eh Biābān Fārs, S Iran
Qal'eh Shahr see Qal'ah Shahr
Qal'eh-ye Now see Qal'ah-ye Now
149 T2 Qal'eh-ye Panjeh var. Qala Panja. Badakhshān, NE Afghanistan 36°56′N 72°15′E
Qalqaman see Kalkaman
Qamanittuaq see Baker Lake
Qamar Bay see Qamar, Ghubbat al
141 U14 Qamar, Ghubbat al Eng. Qamar Bay. bay Oman/Yemen
141 V13 Qamar, Jabal al ▲▲ SW Oman
147 N12 Qamashi Qashqadaryo Viloyati, S Uzbekistan 38°52′N 66°30′E
Qambar see Kambar
159 R14 Qamdo Xizang Zizhiqu, W China 31°09′N 97°09′E
75 R7 Qamīnis NE Libya 31°48′N 20°04′E
Qamishly see Al Qāmishlī
Qânâq see Qaanaaq
Qandahār see Kandahār
80 Q11 Qandala Bari, NE Somalia 11°30′N 50°00′E
Qandyaghash see Kandyagash
138 L2 Qanṭarī Ar Raqqah, N Syria 36°24′N 39°16′E
Qapiciğ Dağı see Qazangödağ
158 H5 Qapqal var. Qapqal Xibe Zizhixian. Xinjiang Uygur Zizhiqu, NW China 43°46′N 81°09′E
Qapqal Xibe Zizhixian see Qapqal
Qapshagay Böyeni see Vodokhranilishche Kapshagay
Qapugtang see Zadoi
196 M15 Qaqortoq Dan. Julianehåb. ◆ Kitaa, S Greenland
139 T4 Qara Anjīr At Ta'mīm, N Iraq 35°30′N 44°37′E
Qarabāgh see Qarah Bāgh
Qarabaŭ see Karabau
Qaraböget see Karaboget
Qarabulaq see Karabulak
Qarabutaq see Karabutak
Qaraghandy/Qaraghandy Oblysy see Karagandy
Qaraghayly see Karagayly
139 U4 Qara Gol As Sulaymānīyah, NE Iraq 35°21′N 45°38′E
75 U8 Qārah var. Qâra. NW Egypt 29°34′N 26°28′E
Qârah see Qārah
148 J4 Qarah Bāgh var. Qarabāgh. Herāt, NW Afghanistan 35°06′N 61°33′E
138 G7 Qaraoun, Lac de var. Buḥayrat al Qir'awn. ◎ S Lebanon
Qaraoy see Karaoy
Qaraqoyyn see Karakoyyn, Ozero
Qara Qum see Garagum
Qarasū see Karasu
Qaratal see Karatal
Qarataū see Karatau, Khrebet, Kazakhstan
Qarataū see Karatau, Zhambyl, Kazakhstan
Qaraton see Karaton
Qarazhal see Karazhal
80 P13 Qardho var. Kardh, It. Gardo. Bari, N Somalia 09°34′N 49°30′E
142 M6 Qareh Chāy ≈ N Iran
142 K2 Qareh Sū ≈ NW Iran
Qariateïne see Al Qaryatayn
Qarkilik see Ruoqiang
147 O13 Qarluq Rus. Karluk. Surkhondaryo Viloyati, S Uzbekistan 38°17′N 67°39′E
147 U12 Qarokŭl Rus. Karakul'. E Tajikistan 39°07′N 73°33′E
147 T12 Qarokŭl Rus. Ozero Karakul'. ◎ E Tajikistan
Qarqan see Qiemo
158 K9 Qarqan He ≈ NW China
Qarqannah, Juzur see Kerkenah, Îles de
149 O1 Qarqīn Jowzjān, N Afghanistan 37°25′N 66°03′E
Qars see Kars
Qarsaqbay see Karsakpay
146 M12 Qarshi Rus. Karshi; prev. Bek-Budi. Qashqadaryo Viloyati, S Uzbekistan 38°54′N 65°48′E
146 L12 Qarshi Cho'li Rus. Karshinskaya Step. grassland S Uzbekistan
146 M13 Qarshi Kanali Rus. Karshinskiy Kanal. canal Turkmenistan/Uzbekistan
Qaryatayn see Al Qaryatayn
Qāsh, Nahr al see Gash
146 M12 Qashqadaryo Viloyati Rus. Kashkadar'inskaya Oblast'. ◆ province S Uzbekistan
Qasigianguit see Qasigiannguit
197 N13 Qasigiannguit var. Qasigianguit, Dan. Christianshåb. ◆ Kitaa, C Greenland
Qaşim, Minţaqat see Al Qaşim
75 V10 Qaşr al Farāfirah var. Qasr Farâfra. W Egypt 27°00′N 27°59′E
139 P8 Qaşr 'Amīj Al Anbār, C Iraq 33°30′N 41°52′E
139 R9 Qaşr Darwīshāh Karbalā', C Iraq 32°36′N 43°27′E
142 J6 Qaşr-e Shīrīn Kermānshāhān, W Iran 34°32′N 45°36′E
Qasr Farâfra see Qaşr al Farāfirah
Qassim see Al Qaşim
141 O16 Qa'ṭabah SW Yemen 13°51′N 44°42′E
138 H7 Qaṭanā var. Katana. Rīf Dimashq, S Syria 33°27′N 36°04′E
143 N15 Qatar off. State of Qatar, Ar. Dawlat Qaṭar. ◆ monarchy SW Asia
Qatar, State of see Qatar
Qatrana see Al Qaṭrānah
143 Q12 Qaṭrūyeh Fārs, S Iran 29°08′N 54°42′E
Qattara Depression/Qaṭṭārah, Munkhafaḍ al see Qaṭṭārah, Munkhafaḍ al
75 U8 Qaṭṭārah, Munkhafaḍ al var. Monkhafad el Qaṭṭâra, var. Munkhafaḍ al Qaṭṭārah, Eng. Qattara Depression. desert NW Egypt
Qaṭṭâra, Monkhafad el see Qaṭṭārah, Munkhafaḍ al
Qattinah, Buhayrat see Ḥimş, Buḥayrat
Qausuittuq see Resolute
Qaydār see Qeydār
Qāyen see Qā'en
Qaynar see Kaynar
147 Q11 Qayroqqum Rus. Kayrakkum. NW Tajikistan 40°16′N 69°46′E
147 Q10 Qayroqqum, Obanbori Rus. Kayrakkumskoye Vodokhranilishche. ⊠ NW Tajikistan
137 V13 Qazangödağ Rus. Gora Kapydzhik, Turk. Qapiciğ Dağı. ▲ SW Azerbaijan 39°18′N 46°00′E
139 U7 Qazānīyah var. Dhū Shaykh. Diyālá, E Iraq 33°39′N 45°33′E
Qazaqstan/Qazaqstan Respublikasy see Kazakhstan
137 T9 Q'azbegi Rus. Kazbegi; prev. Qazbegi. NE Georgia 42°39′N 44°36′E
Qazbegi see Q'azbegi
149 P15 Qāzi Ahmad var. Kazi Ahmad. Sind, SE Pakistan 26°19′N 68°08′E
Qazris see Cáceres
Qazimämmäd see Hacıqabal
142 M4 Qazvīn var. Kazvin. Qazvīn, N Iran 36°16′N 50°E
142 M5 Qazvīn ◆ province N Iran

◆ Country ● Country Capital ◇ Dependent Territory ○ Dependent Territory Capital ◆ Administrative Regions ✈ International Airport ▲ Mountain ▲▲ Mountain Range Volcano ≈ River ◎ Lake ⊠ Reservoir

187 *Z13* **Qelelevu Lagoon** *lagoon* NE Fiji
Qena *see* Qinā
113 *L23* **Qeparo** Vlorë, S Albania *40°04′N 19°49′E*
Qeqertarssuaq *see* Qeqertarsuaq
197 *N13* **Qeqertarsuaq** *var.* Qeqertarssuaq, *Dan.* Godhavn. ⬖ Kitaa, S Greenland
196 *M13* **Qeqertarsuaq** *island* W Greenland
197 *N13* **Qeqertarsuup Tunua** *Dan.* Disko Bugt. *inlet* W Greenland
Qerveh *see* Qorveh
143 *S14* **Qeshm** Hormozgān, S Iran *26°58′N 56°17′E*
143 *R14* **Qeshm** *var.* Jazīreh-ye Qeshm, Qeshm Island. *island* S Iran
Qeshm Island/Qeshm, Jazīreh-ye *see* Qeshm
Qey *see* Kīsh, Jazīreh-ye
142 *L4* **Qeydār** *var.* Qaydār. Zanjān, NW Iran *36°50′N 47°40′E*
142 *K5* **Qezel Owzan, Rūd-e** *var.* Ki Zil Uzen, Qi Zil Uzun. ∿ NW Iran
Qian *see* Guizhou
161 *Q2* **Qian’an** Heilongjiang, E China *45°00′N 124°00′E*
161 *R10* **Qiandao Hu** *prev.* Xin’anjiang Shuiku. ⊠ SE China
Qiandaohu *see* Chun’an
Qian Gorlo/Qian Gorlos/Qian Gorlos Mongolzu Zizhixian/Quianguozhen *see* Qianguo
163 *V9* **Qianguo** *var.* Qian Gorlo, Qian Gorlos, Qian Gorlos Mongolzu Zizhixian, Quianguozhen. Jilin, NE China *45°08′N 124°48′E*
161 *N9* **Qianjiang** Hubei, C China *30°23′N 112°58′E*
160 *K10* **Qianjiang** Sichuan, C China *29°30′N 108°45′E*
160 *L14* **Qian Jiang** ∿ S China
160 *G9* **Qianning** *var.* Gartar. Sichuan, C China *30°27′N 101°24′E*
163 *U13* **Qian Shan** ▲▲ NE China
160 *H10* **Qianwei** *var.* Yujin. Sichuan, C China *29°15′N 103°52′E*
160 *J11* **Qianxi** Guizhou, S China *27°00′N 106°01′E*
Qiaotou *see* Datong
Qiaowa *see* Muli
159 *Q7* **Qiaowan** Gansu, N China *40°37′N 96°40′E*
Qibilī *see* Kebili
158 *K9* **Qiemo** *var.* Qarqan. Xinjiang Uygur Zizhiqu, NW China *38°09′N 85°30′E*
160 *J10* **Qijiang** *var.* Gunan. Chongqing Shi, C China *29°01′N 106°40′E*
159 *N5* **Qijiaojing** Xinjiang Uygur Zizhiqu, NW China *43°29′N 91°35′E*
Qike *see* Xunke
9 *N5* **Qikiqtaaluk** *cultural region* Nunavut, N Canada
9 *R5* **Qikiqtarjuaq** *prev.* Broughton Island. Nunavut, NE Canada *67°35′N 63°55′W*
149 *P9* **Qila Saifullāh** Baluchistān, SW Pakistan *30°45′N 68°08′E*
159 *S9* **Qilian** *var.* Babao. Qinghai, C China *38°09′N 100°08′E*
159 *N8* **Qilian Shan** *var.* Kilien Mountains. ▲▲ N China
197 *O11* **Qimusseriarsuaq** *Dan.* Melville Bugt, *Eng.* Melville Bay. *bay* NW Greenland
75 *X10* **Qinā** *var.* Qena; *anc.* Caene, Caenepolis. E Egypt *26°12′N 32°49′E*
159 *W11* **Qin’an** Gansu, C China *34°49′N 105°50′E*
Qincheng *see* Nanfeng
Qing *see* Qinghai
163 *W7* **Qing’an** Heilongjiang, NE China *46°53′N 127°29′E*
159 *X10* **Qingcheng** *var.* Xifeng. Gansu, C China *35°46′N 107°35′E*
161 *R5* **Qingdao** *var.* Ching-Tao, Ch’ing-tao, Tsingtao, Tsintao, *Ger.* Tsingtau. Shandong, E China *36°31′N 120°55′E*
163 *V8* **Qinggang** Heilongjiang, NE China *46°41′N 126°05′E*
Qinggil *see* Qinghe
159 *P11* **Qinghai** *var.* Chinghai, Koko Nor, Qing, Qinghai Sheng, Tsinghai. ⬖ *province* C China
159 *S10* **Qinghai Hu** *var.* Ch’ing Hai, Tsing Hai, *Mong.* Koko Nor. ◎ C China
Qinghai Sheng *see* Qinghai
158 *M3* **Qinghe** *var.* Qinggil. Xinjiang Uygur Zizhiqu, NW China *46°42′N 90°19′E*
160 *L4* **Qingjian** *var.* Kuanzhou; *prev.* Xiuyan. Shaanxi, C China *37°10′N 110°09′E*
160 *L9* **Qing Jiang** ∿ C China
Qingjiang *see* Huai’an
Qingkou *see* Ganyu
160 *I12* **Qinglong** *var.* Liancheng. Guizhou, S China *25°49′N 105°10′E*
161 *Q2* **Qinglong** Hebei, E China *40°24′N 118°57′E*
Qingshan *see* Wudalianchi
159 *R12* **Qingshuihe** Qinghai, C China *33°47′N 97°10′E*
Qingyang *see* Jinjiang
161 *N14* **Qingyuan** Guangdong, S China *23°42′N 113°02′E*
163 *V11* **Qingyuan** *var.* Qingyuan Manzu Zizhixian. Liaoning, NE China *42°08′N 124°55′E*
Qingyuan *see* Weiyuan
Qingyuan *see* Shandan
Qingyuan Manzu Zizhixian *see* Qingyuan
158 *L13* **Qingzang Gaoyuan** *var.* Xizang Gaoyuan, *Eng.* Plateau of Tibet. *plateau* W China
161 *Q4* **Qingzhou** *prev.* Yidu. Shandong, E China *36°41′N 118°29′E*
157 *R9* **Qin He** ∿ C China
161 *Q2* **Qinhuangdao** Hebei, E China *39°57′N 119°31′E*
160 *K7* **Qin Ling** ▲▲ C China
161 *N5* **Qinxian** *var.* Dingchang, Qin Xian. Shanxi, C China *36°46′N 112°42′E*
Qin Xian *see* Qinxian
161 *N6* **Qinyang** Henan, C China *35°05′N 112°56′E*
160 *K15* **Qinzhou** Guangxi Zhuangzu Zizhiqu, S China *22°09′N 108°36′E*
Qiong *see* Hainan
160 *L17* **Qionghai** *prev.* Jiaji. Hainan, S China *19°12′N 110°26′E*
160 *H9* **Qionglai** Sichuan, C China *30°24′N 103°28′E*
160 *H8* **Qionglai Shan** ▲▲ C China
Qiongxi *see* Hongyuan
160 *L17* **Qiongzhou Haixia** *var.* Hainan Strait. *strait* S China
163 *U7* **Qiqihar** *var.* Ch’i-ch’i-ha-erh, Tsitsihar; *prev.* Lungkiang. Heilongjiang, NE China *47°23′N 124°E*
Qir *see* Qīr-va-Kārzīn
158 *H10* **Qira** Xinjiang Uygur Zizhiqu, NW China *37°05′N 80°45′E*
Qir‘awn, Buḩayrat al *see* Qaraoun, Lac de
143 *P12* **Qīr-va-Kārzīn** *var.* Qir. Fārs, S Iran *28°27′N 53°04′E*
Qiryat Gat *see* Kyriat Gat
Qiryat Shemona *see* Kiryat Shmona
Qishlaq *see* Garmsār
141 *U14* **Qishn** SE Yemen *15°29′N 51°44′E*
Qishon, Naḩal *see* Kishon, Nahal
Qita Ghazzah *see* Gaza Strip
156 *K5* **Qitai** Xinjiang Uygur Zizhiqu, NW China *44°N 89°34′E*
163 *Y8* **Qitaihe** Heilongjiang, NE China *45°45′N 130°53′E*
141 *W12* **Qitbīt, Wādī** *dry watercourse* S Oman
161 *O5* **Qixian** *var.* Qi Xian, Zhaoge. Henan, C China *35°35′N 114°10′E*
Qi Xian *see* Qixian
Qīzān *see* Jīzān
Qizil Orda *see* Kyzylorda
Qizil Qum/Qizilqum *see* Kyzyl Kum
147 *V14* **Qizilrabot** *Rus.* Kyzylrabot. SE Tajikistan *37°29′N 74°44′E*
146 *J10* **Qizilravote** *Rus.* Kyzylrabat. Buxoro Viloyati, C Uzbekistan *40°35′N 62°09′E*
Qi Zil Uzun *see* Qezel Owzan, Rūd-e
139 *S4* **Qizil Yār** At Ta’mím, N Iraq *35°26′N 44°12′E*
164 *J12* **Qkutango-hantō** *peninsula* Honshū, SW Japan
137 *Y11* **Qobustan** *Rus.* Märäzä. E Azerbaijan *40°32′N 48°56′E*
Qoghaly *see* Kogaly
Qogir Feng *see* K2
143 *N6* **Qom** *var.* Kum, Qum. Qom, N Iran *34°43′N 50°54′E*
143 *N6* **Qom** ⬖ *province* N Iran
Qomisheh *see* Shahreẕā
Qomolangma Feng *see* Everest, Mount
142 *M7* **Qom, Rūd-e** ∿ C Iran
Qomsheh *see* Shahreẕā
Qomul *see* Hami
Qondūz *see* Kunduz
146 *G7* **Qo‘ng‘irot** *Rus.* Kungrad. Qoraqalpog‘iston Respublikasi, NW Uzbekistan *43°01′N 58°49′E*
Qongyrat *see* Konyrat
Qoqek *see* Tacheng
147 *R10* **Qo‘qon** *var.* Khokand, *Rus.* Kokand. Farg’ona Viloyati, E Uzbekistan *40°34′N 70°55′E*
Qorabowur Kirlari *see* Karabaur’, Uval
Qoradaryo *see* Karadar’ya
146 *G6* **Qorajar** *Rus.* Karadzhar. Qoraqalpog‘iston Respublikasi, NW Uzbekistan *43°34′N 58°35′E*
146 *K12* **Qorako‘l** *Rus.* Karakul’. Buxoro Viloyati, C Uzbekistan *39°27′N 63°45′E*
146 *H7* **Qorao‘zak** *Rus.* Karauzyak. Qoraqalpog‘iston Respublikasi, NW Uzbekistan *43°07′N 60°03′E*
146 *E5* **Qoraqalpog‘iston** *Rus.* Karakalpakya. Qoraqalpog‘iston Respublikasi, NW Uzbekistan *44°45′N 56°06′E*
146 *G7* **Qoraqalpog‘iston Respublikasi** *Rus.* Respublika Karakalpakstan. ⬖ *autonomous republic* NW Uzbekistan
Qorghalzhyn *see* Korgalzhyn
138 *H6* **Qornet es Saouda** ▲ NE Lebanon *36°06′N 34°06′E*
146 *L12* **Qorowulbozor** *Rus.* Karaulbazar. Buxoro Viloyati, C Uzbekistan *39°28′N 64°49′E*
142 *K5* **Qorveh** *var.* Qerveh, Qurveh. Kordestān, W Iran *35°09′N 47°48′E*
147 *N11* **Qo‘shrabot** *Rus.* Kushrabat. Samarqand Viloyati, C Uzbekistan *40°15′N 66°40′E*
Qosköl *see* Koskol’
Qosshaghyl *see* Kosshagyl
Qostanay/Qostanay Oblysy *see* Kostanay
143 *P12* **Qoṭbābād** Fārs, S Iran *28°52′N 53°40′E*
143 *R13* **Qoṭbābād** Hormozgān, S Iran *27°49′N 56°00′E*
138 *H6* **Qoubaïyât** *var.* Al Qubayyāt. N Lebanon *37°00′N 34°30′E*
Qoussantîna *see* Constantine
Qowowuyag *see* Cho Oyu
147 *O11* **Qo‘ytosh** *Rus.* Koytash. Jizzax Viloyati, C Uzbekistan *40°13′N 67°19′E*
146 *G7* **Qozonketkan** *Rus.* Kazanketken. Qoraqalpog‘iston Respublikasi, W Uzbekistan *42°59′N 59°21′E*
146 *H6* **Qozoqdaryo** *Rus.* Kazakdar’ya. Qoraqalpog‘iston Respublikasi, NW Uzbekistan *43°26′N 59°47′E*
19 *N11* **Quabbin Reservoir** ⊠ Massachusetts, NE USA
100 *F12* **Quakenbrück** Niedersachsen, NW Germany *52°41′N 07°57′E*
18 *I15* **Quakertown** Pennsylvania, NE USA *40°26′N 75°17′W*
182 *M10* **Quambatook** Victoria, SE Australia *35°52′S 143°28′E*
25 *Q4* **Quanah** Texas, SW USA *34°17′N 99°46′W*
167 *V10* **Quang Ngai** *var.* Quangngai, Quang Nghia. Quang Ngai, C Vietnam *15°09′N 108°50′E*
Quangngai *see* Quang Ngai
Quang Nghia *see* Quang Ngai
167 *T9* **Quang Tri** *var.* Triệu Hai. Quang Tri, C Vietnam *16°46′N 107°11′E*
Quanjiang *see* Suichuan
Quan Long *see* Ca Mau
152 *L4* **Quanshuigou** China/India *35°40′N 79°28′E*
161 *R13* **Quanzhou** *var.* Ch’uan-chou, Tsinkiang; *prev.* Chin-chiang. Fujian, SE China *24°56′N 118°31′E*
160 *M12* **Quanzhou** Guangxi Zhuangzu Zizhiqu, S China *25°59′N 111°02′E*
11 *V16* **Qu’Appelle** ∿ Saskatchewan, S Canada
12 *M3* **Quaqtaq** *prev.* Koartac. Québec, NE Canada *60°50′N 69°30′W*
61 *E16* **Quaraí** Rio Grande do Sul, S Brazil *30°38′S 56°25′W*
59 *H24* **Quaraí, Rio** *Sp.* Río Cuareim. ∿ Brazil/Uruguay *see also* Cuareim, Río
Quaraí, Rio *see* Cuareim, Río
171 *N13* **Quarles, Pegunungan** ▲▲ Sulawesi, C Indonesia
Quarnero *see* Kvarner
107 *C20* **Quartu Sant’ Elena** Sardegna, Italy, C Mediterranean Sea *39°15′N 09°12′E*
29 *X13* **Quasqueton** Iowa, C USA *42°23′N 91°45′W*
173 *X16* **Quatre Bornes** W Mauritius *20°15′S 57°28′E*
172 *I17* **Quatre Bornes** Mahé, NE Seychelles
137 *X10* **Quba** *Rus.* Kuba. N Azerbaijan *41°22′N 48°30′E*
Qubba *see* Ba‘qūbah
143 *T3* **Qūchān** *var.* Kuchan. Khorāsān-Razavī, NE Iran *37°12′N 58°28′E*
183 *R10* **Queanbeyan** New South Wales, SE Australia *35°24′S 149°17′E*
15 *Q10* **Québec** *var.* Quebec. *province capital* Québec, SE Canada *46°50′N 71°15′W*
14 *K10* **Québec** *var.* Quebec. ⬖ *province* SE Canada
61 *D17* **Quebracho** Paysandú, W Uruguay *31°58′S 57°53′W*
101 *K14* **Quedlinburg** Sachsen-Anhalt, C Germany *51°48′N 11°09′E*
138 *H10* **Queen Alia** ✈ (‘Ammān) ‘Ammān, C Jordan
10 *L16* **Queen Bess, Mount** ▲ British Columbia, SW Canada *51°15′N 124°29′W*
10 *I14* **Queen Charlotte** British Columbia, SW Canada *53°18′N 132°04′W*
65 *B24* **Queen Charlotte Bay** *bay* West Falkland, W Falkland Islands
10 *H14* **Queen Charlotte Islands** *Fr.* Îles de la Reine-Charlotte. *island group* British Columbia, SW Canada
10 *I15* **Queen Charlotte Sound** *sea area* British Columbia, W Canada
10 *J16* **Queen Charlotte Strait** *strait* British Columbia, W Canada
27 *U1* **Queen City** Missouri, C USA *40°24′N 92°34′W*
25 *X5* **Queen City** Texas, SW USA *33°09′N 94°09′W*
197 *O9* **Queen Elizabeth Islands** *Fr.* Îles de la Reine-Élisabeth. *island group* Nunavut, N Canada
195 *Y10* **Queen Mary Coast** *physical region* Antarctica
65 *N24* **Queen Mary’s Peak** ▲ C Tristan da Cunha
196 *M8* **Queen Maud Gulf** *gulf* Arctic Ocean
195 *P11* **Queen Maud Mountains** ▲▲ Antarctica
Queen’s County *see* Laois
181 *U7* **Queensland** ⬖ *state* N Australia
192 *I9* **Queensland Plateau** *undersea feature* N Coral Sea
183 *O16* **Queenstown** Tasmania, SE Australia *42°06′S 145°33′E*
185 *C22* **Queenstown** Otago, South Island, New Zealand *45°01′S 168°44′E*
83 *I24* **Queenstown** Eastern Cape, S South Africa *31°52′S 26°50′E*
Queenstown *see* Cobh
32 *F8* **Queets** Washington, NW USA *47°31′N 124°19′W*
61 *D18* **Queguay Grande, Río** ∿ W Uruguay
59 *O16* **Queimadas** Bahia, E Brazil *10°59′S 39°38′W*
82 *D11* **Quela** Malanje, NW Angola *09°18′S 17°07′E*
83 *O16* **Quelimane** *var.* Kilimane, Kilmain, Quilimane. Zambézia, NE Mozambique *17°53′S 36°51′E*
63 *G18* **Quellón** *var.* Puerto Quellón. Los Lagos, S Chile *43°05′S 73°38′W*
Quelpart *see* Jeju-do
37 *P12* **Quemado** New Mexico, SW USA *34°18′N 108°29′W*
25 *O12* **Quemado** Texas, SW USA *28°58′N 100°36′W*
44 *K7* **Quemado, Punta de** *headland* E Cuba *20°13′N 74°07′W*
Quemoy *see* Jinmen Dao
62 *K13* **Quemú Quemú** La Pampa, E Argentina *36°03′S 63°36′W*
155 *E17* **Quepem** Goa, W India *15°13′N 74°03′E*
42 *M14* **Quepos** Puntarenas, S Costa Rica *09°28′N 84°10′W*
Que Que *see* Kwekwe
61 *D23* **Quequén** Buenos Aires, E Argentina *38°30′S 58°44′W*
61 *D23* **Quequén Grande, Río** ∿ E Argentina
61 *C23* **Quequén Salado, Río** ∿ E Argentina
Quera *see* Chur
41 *N13* **Querétaro** Querétaro de Arteaga, C Mexico *20°36′N 100°24′W*
40 *F4* **Querobabi** Sonora, NW Mexico *30°02′N 111°02′W*
42 *M13* **Quesada** *var.* Ciudad Quesada, San Carlos. Alajuela, N Costa Rica *10°19′N 84°26′W*
105 *O13* **Quesada** Andalucía, S Spain *37°52′N 03°05′W*
161 *O7* **Queshan** Henan, C China *32°48′N 114°03′E*
10 *M15* **Quesnel** British Columbia, SW Canada *52°59′N 122°30′W*
37 *S9* **Questa** New Mexico, SW USA *36°41′N 105°37′W*
102 *H7* **Questembert** Morbihan, NW France *47°39′N 02°24′W*
57 *K22* **Quetena, Río** ∿ SW Bolivia
149 *O10* **Quetta** Baluchistān, SW Pakistan *30°15′N 67°E*
Quetzalcoalco *see* Coatzacoalcos
Quetzaltenango *see* Quezaltenango
56 *B6* **Quevedo** Los Ríos, C Ecuador *01°02′S 79°27′W*
42 *B6* **Quezaltenango** *var.* Quetzaltenango. Quezaltenango, W Guatemala *14°50′N 91°30′W*
42 *A2* **Quezaltenango** *off.* Departamento de Quezaltenango, *var.* Quetzaltenango. ⬖ *department* SW Guatemala
Quezaltenango, Departamento de *see* Quezaltenango
42 *E6* **Quezaltepeque** Chiquimula, SE Guatemala *14°38′N 89°25′W*
170 *M6* **Quezon** Palawan, W Philippines *09°13′N 118°01′E*
161 *P5* **Qufu** Shandong, E China *35°37′N 117°05′E*
82 *B12* **Quibala** Cuanza Sul, NW Angola *10°44′S 14°58′E*
82 *B11* **Quibaxe** *var.* Quibaxi. Cuanza Norte, NW Angola *08°30′S 14°36′E*
Quibaxi *see* Quibaxe
54 *D9* **Quibdó** Chocó, W Colombia *05°40′N 76°38′W*
102 *G7* **Quiberon** Morbihan, NW France *47°30′N 03°07′W*
102 *G7* **Quiberon, Baie de** *bay* NW France
54 *J5* **Quíbor** Lara, N Venezuela *09°55′N 69°35′W*
42 *C4* **Quiché** *off.* Departamento del Quiché. ⬖ *department* W Guatemala
Quiché, Departamento del *see* Quiché
99 *E21* **Quiévrain** Hainaut, S Belgium *50°25′N 03°41′E*
40 *I9* **Quila** Sinaloa, C Mexico *24°24′N 107°11′W*
83 *B14* **Quilengues** Huíla, SW Angola *14°09′S 14°04′E*
Quilimane *see* Quelimane
57 *G15* **Quillabamba** Cusco, C Peru *12°49′S 72°41′W*
57 *L18* **Quillacollo** Cochabamba, C Bolivia *17°26′S 66°16′W*
62 *H4* **Quillagua** Antofagasta, N Chile *21°33′S 69°32′W*
103 *N17* **Quillan** Aude, S France *42°52′N 02°11′E*
11 *U15* **Quill Lakes** ◎ Saskatchewan, S Canada
62 *G11* **Quillota** Valparaíso, C Chile *32°54′S 71°16′W*
155 *G23* **Quilon** *var.* Kollam. Kerala, SW India *08°57′N 76°37′E* *see also* Kollam
181 *V9* **Quilpie** Queensland, C Australia *26°39′S 144°15′E*
149 *O4* **Quil-Qala** Bāmyān, N Afghanistan *35°13′N 67°02′E*
62 *L7* **Quimilí** Santiago del Estero, C Argentina *27°35′S 62°25′W*
57 *O19* **Quimome** Santa Cruz, E Bolivia *17°45′S 61°15′W*
102 *F6* **Quimper** *anc.* Quimper Corentin. Finistère, NW France *48°00′N 04°05′W*
Quimper Corentin *see* Quimper
102 *G7* **Quimperlé** Finistère, NW France *47°52′N 03°33′W*
32 *F8* **Quinault** Washington, NW USA *47°27′N 123°53′W*
32 *F8* **Quinault River** ∿ Washington, NW USA
35 *P5* **Quincy** California, W USA *39°56′N 120°56′W*
23 *S8* **Quincy** Florida, SE USA *30°35′N 84°34′W*
30 *I13* **Quincy** Illinois, N USA *39°56′N 91°24′W*
19 *O11* **Quincy** Massachusetts, NE USA *42°15′N 71°00′W*
32 *J9* **Quincy** Washington, NW USA *47°13′N 119°51′W*
54 *E10* **Quindío** *off.* Departamento del Quindío. ⬖ *province* C Colombia
54 *E10* **Quindío, Nevado del** ▲ C Colombia *04°42′N 75°25′W*
62 *J10* **Quines** San Luis, C Argentina *32°15′S 65°46′W*
39 *N13* **Quinhagak** Alaska, USA *59°45′N 161°55′W*
76 *G13* **Quinhámel** W Guinea-Bissau *11°52′N 15°52′W*
Qui Nhon/Quinhon *see* Quy Nhơn
Quinindé *see* Rosa Zárate
25 *U6* **Quinlan** Texas, SW USA *32°54′N 96°08′W*
61 *H17* **Quinta** Rio Grande do Sul, S Brazil *32°05′S 52°18′W*
105 *O10* **Quintanar de la Orden** Castilla-La Mancha, C Spain *39°36′N 03°03′W*
41 *X13* **Quintana Roo** ⬖ *state* SE Mexico
105 *S6* **Quinto** Aragón, NE Spain *41°25′N 00°31′W*
108 *G10* **Quinto** Ticino, S Switzerland *46°32′N 08°44′E*
27 *Q11* **Quinton** Oklahoma, C USA *35°07′N 95°22′W*
62 *K12* **Quinto, Río** ∿ C Argentina
82 *A10* **Quinzau** Dem. Rep. Congo, NW Angola *06°50′S 12°48′E*
14 *H8* **Quinze, Lac des** ◎ Québec, SE Canada
83 *B15* **Quipungo** Huíla, C Angola *14°49′S 14°29′E*
62 *G13* **Quirihue** Bío Bío, C Chile *36°15′S 72°35′W*
82 *D12* **Quirima** Malanje, NW Angola *10°51′S 18°06′E*
183 *T6* **Quirindi** New South Wales, SE Australia *31°29′S 150°40′E*
55 *P5* **Quiriquire** Monagas, NE Venezuela *09°59′N 63°14′W*
14 *D10* **Quirke Lake** ◎ Ontario, S Canada
61 *B21* **Quiroga** Buenos Aires, E Argentina *35°18′S 61°22′W*
104 *I4* **Quiroga** Galicia, NW Spain *42°28′N 07°15′W*
Quiróm, Salar *see* Pocitos, Salar
56 *B9* **Quiroz, Río** ∿ NW Peru
82 *Q13* **Quissanga** Cabo Delgado, NE Mozambique *12°24′S 40°33′E*
83 *M20* **Quissico** Inhambane, S Mozambique *24°42′S 34°44′E*
25 *O4* **Quitaque** Texas, SW USA *34°22′N 101°03′W*
82 *Q13* **Quiterajo** Cabo Delgado, NE Mozambique *11°37′S 40°22′E*
23 *T6* **Quitman** Georgia, SE USA *30°46′N 83°33′W*
22 *M6* **Quitman** Mississippi, S USA *32°02′N 88°43′W*
25 *V6* **Quitman** Texas, SW USA *32°37′N 95°26′W*
56 *C6* **Quito** ● (Ecuador) Pichincha, N Ecuador *0°14′S 78°30′W*
Quito *see* Mariscal Sucre
58 *P13* **Quixadá** Ceará, E Brazil *04°57′S 39°04′W*
83 *Q15* **Quixaxe** Nampula, NE Mozambique *15°15′S 40°07′E*
161 *N13* **Qujiang** *var.* Maba. Guangdong, S China *24°47′N 113°34′E*
160 *J9* **Qu Jiang** ∿ C China
161 *R10* **Qu Jiang** ∿ SE China
160 *H12* **Qujing** Yunnan, SW China *25°39′N 103°52′E*
Qulan *see* Kulan
Qulin Gol *see* Chaor He
146 *L10* **QuljuqtovTog‘lari** *Rus.* Gory Kul’dzhuktau. ▲▲ C Uzbekistan
Qulsary *see* Kul’sary
Qulyndy Zhazyghy *see* Ravnina Kulyndy
Qum *see* Qom
Qumälisch *see* Lubartów
159 *P11* **Qumar He** ∿ C China
159 *Q12* **Qumarlêb** *var.* Yuegai; *prev.* Yuegaitan. Qinghai, C China *34°06′N 95°54′E*
Qumisheh *see* Shahreẕā
147 *O14* **Qumqo‘rg‘on** *Rus.* Kumkurgan. Surkhondaryo Viloyati, S Uzbekistan *37°54′N 67°31′E*
Qunaytirah/Qunayṭirah, Muḩāfaẓat al *see* Al Qunayṭirah
189 *V12* **Quoi** *island* Chuuk, C Micronesia
9 *N8* **Quoich** ∿ Nunavut, NE Canada
83 *E26* **Quoin Point** *headland* SW South Africa *34°48′S 19°39′E*
182 *I7* **Quorn** South Australia *32°22′S 138°03′E*
Qurein *see* Al Kuwayt
147 *P14* **Qŭrghonteppa** *Rus.* Kurgan-Tyube. SW Tajikistan *37°51′N 68°42′E*
Qurlurtuuq *see* Kugluktuk
Qurveh *see* Qorveh
Quryq *see* Kuryk
Qusair *see* Al Quşayr
137 *X10* **Qusar** *Rus.* Kusary. NE Azerbaijan *41°26′N 48°27′E*
Quşayr *see* Al Quşayr
Quseir *see* Al Quşayr
142 *I2* **Qūshchī** Āẕarbāyjān-e Gharbi, N Iran *37°59′N 45°05′E*
Qusmuryn *see* Kusmuryn, Ozero
Qusmuryn *see* Kushmurun, Kostanay, Kazakhstan
Quṭayfah/Qutayfe/Quteife *see* Al Quṭayfah
Quthing *see* Moyeni
147 *S10* **Quvasoy** *Rus.* Kuvasay. Farg’ona Viloyati, E Uzbekistan *40°17′N 71°53′E*
Quwair *see* Guwēr
Quxar *see* Lhazê
Qu Xian *see* Quzhou
159 *N16* **Qüxü** *var.* Xoi. Xizang Zizhiqu, W China *29°25′N 90°48′E*
Quyang *see* Jingzhou
167 *V11* **Quy Nhơn** *var.* Quinhon, Qui Nhon. Binh Định, C Vietnam *13°47′N 109°11′E*
161 *R10* **Quzhou** *var.* Qu Xian. Zhejiang, SE China *28°55′N 118°54′E*
Qyteti Stalin *see* Kuçovë
Qyzylaghash *see* Kyzylagash
Qyzylorda *see* Kyzylorda
Qyzyltū *see* Kishkenekol’
Qyzylzhar *see* Kyzylzhar

R

Raa Atoll *see* North Maalhosmadulu Atoll
109 *R4* **Raab** Oberösterreich, N Austria *48°19′N 13°40′E*
109 *X8* **Raab** *Hung.* Rába. ∿ Austria/Hungary *see also* Rába
Raab *see* Rába
Raab *see* Győr
109 *V2* **Raabs an der Thaya** Niederösterreich, E Austria *48°51′N 15°28′E*
93 *L14* **Raahe** *Swe.* Brahestad. Oulu, W Finland *64°42′N 24°31′E*
98 *M10* **Raalte** Overijssel, E Netherlands *52°23′N 06°16′E*
99 *I14* **Raamsdonksveer** Noord-Brabant, S Netherlands *51°42′N 04°54′E*
92 *L12* **Raanujärvi** Lappi, NW Finland *66°39′N 24°40′E*
96 *G9* **Raasay** *island* NW Scotland, United Kingdom
118 *H3* **Raasiku** *Ger.* Rasik. Harjumaa, NW Estonia *59°22′N 25°11′E*
112 *B11* **Rab** *It.* Arbe. Primorje-Gorski Kotar, NW Croatia *44°46′N 14°46′E*
112 *B11* **Rab** *It.* Arbe. *island* NW Croatia
171 *N16* **Raba** Sumbawa, S Indonesia *08°27′S 118°45′E*
111 *G22* **Rába** *Ger.* Raab. ∿ Austria/Hungary *see also* Raab
Rába *see* Raab
112 *A10* **Rabac** Istra, NW Croatia *45°03′N 14°09′E*
104 *I2* **Rábade** Galicia, NW Spain *43°07′N 07°37′W*
80 *F10* **Rabak** White Nile, C Sudan *13°12′N 32°44′E*
186 *G9* **Rabaraba** Milne Bay, SE Papua New Guinea *10°00′S 149°50′E*
102 *K16* **Rabastens-de-Bigorre** Hautes-Pyrénées, S France *43°23′N 00°10′E*
121 *O16* **Rabat** W Malta *35°51′N 14°25′E*
74 *F6* **Rabat** *var.* al Dar al Baida. ● (Morocco) NW Morocco *34°02′N 06°51′W*
Rabat *see* Victoria
186 *H6* **Rabaul** New Britain, E Papua New Guinea *04°13′S 152°11′E*
Rabbah Ammon/Rabbath Ammon *see* ‘Amman
28 *K8* **Rabbit Creek** ∿ South Dakota, N USA
14 *H10* **Rabbit Lake** ◎ Ontario, S Canada
187 *Y14* **Rabi** *prev.* Rambi. *island* N Fiji
140 *K9* **Rābigh** Makkah, W Saudi Arabia *22°51′N 39°E*
42 *D5* **Rabinal** Baja Verapaz, C Guatemala *15°05′N 90°26′W*
168 *G9* **Rabi, Pulau** *island* NW Indonesia, East Indies
111 *L17* **Rabka** Małopolskie, S Poland *49°38′N 20°E*
155 *F16* **Rabkavi** Karnātaka, W India *16°40′N 75°03′E*
Râbniţa *see* Rîbniţa
109 *Y6* **Rabnitz** ∿ E Austria
124 *J7* **Rabocheostrovsk** Respublika Kareliya, NW Russian Federation *64°58′N 34°46′E*
23 *U1* **Rabun Bald** ▲ Georgia, SE USA *34°58′N 83°18′W*
75 *S11* **Rabyānah** SE Libya *24°07′N 21°58′E*
75 *S11* **Rabyānah, Ramlat** *var.* Rebiana Sand Sea, Şaḩrā’ Rabyānah. *desert* SE Libya
Rabyānah, Şaḩrā’ *see* Rabyānah, Ramlat
116 *L11* **Răcăciuni** Bacău, E Romania *46°20′N 27°00′E*
Racaka *see* Riwoqê
107 *J24* **Racalmuto** Sicilia, Italy, C Mediterranean Sea *37°25′N 13°44′E*
116 *J14* **Răcari** Dâmboviţa, SE Romania *44°37′N 25°43′E*
Răcari *see* Durankulak
116 *F13* **Răcăşdia** *Hung.* Rakasd. Caraş-Severin, SW Romania *44°58′N 21°36′E*
106 *B9* **Racconigi** Piemonte, NE Italy *44°45′N 07°41′E*
31 *T15* **Raccoon Creek** ∿ Ohio, N USA
13 *V13* **Race, Cape** *headland* Newfoundland, Newfoundland and Labrador, E Canada *46°40′N 53°05′W*
22 *K10* **Raceland** Louisiana, S USA *29°43′N 90°36′W*
19 *Q12* **Race Point** *headland* Massachusetts, NE USA *42°03′N 70°14′W*
167 *S14* **Rach Gia** Kiên Giang, S Vietnam *10°01′N 105°05′E*
167 *S14* **Rach Gia, Vinh** *bay* S Vietnam
76 *J8* **Rachid** Tagant, C Mauritania *18°48′N 11°41′W*
110 *L10* **Raciąż** Mazowieckie, C Poland *52°46′N 20°04′E*
111 *I16* **Racibórz** *Ger.* Ratibor. Śląskie, S Poland *50°05′N 18°10′E*
31 *N9* **Racine** Wisconsin, N USA *42°42′N 87°50′W*
14 *D7* **Racine Lake** ◎ Ontario, S Canada
111 *J23* **Ráckeve** Pest, C Hungary *47°10′N 18°58′E*
Rácz-Becse *see* Bečej
141 *O15* **Radā’** *var.* Ridā’. W Yemen *14°24′N 44°49′E*
113 *O15* **Radan** ▲ SE Serbia *42°59′N 21°31′E*
63 *J19* **Rada Tilly** Chubut, SE Argentina *45°54′S 67°33′W*
116 *K8* **Rădăuţi** *Ger.* Radautz, *Hung.* Rádóc. Suceava, N Romania *47°49′N 25°58′E*
116 *L8* **Rădăuţi-Prut** Botoşani, NE Romania *48°14′N 26°47′E*
Radautz *see* Rădăuţi
Radbusa *see* Radbuza
111 *A17* **Radbuza** *Ger.* Radbusa. ∿ SE Czech Republic
20 *K6* **Radcliff** Kentucky, S USA *37°50′N 85°57′W*
139 *O2* **Radd, Wādī ar** *dry watercourse* N Syria
95 *H16* **Råde** Østfold, S Norway *59°21′N 10°53′E*
109 *V11* **Radeče** *Ger.* Ratschach. C Slovenia *46°01′N 15°10′E*
Radein *see* Radenci
116 *J4* **Radekhiv** *Pol.* Radziechów, *Rus.* Radekhov. L’vivs’ka Oblast’, W Ukraine *50°17′N 24°39′E*
Radekhov *see* Radekhiv
109 *X9* **Radenci** *Ger.* Radein; *prev.* Radinci. NE Slovenia *46°36′N 16°02′E*
109 *S9* **Radenthein** Kärnten, S Austria *46°48′N 13°42′E*
Rádeyilikóé *see* Fort Good Hope
21 *R7* **Radford** Virginia, NE USA *37°07′N 80°34′W*
154 *C9* **Rādhanpur** Gujarāt, W India *23°52′N 71°49′E*
Radinci *see* Radenci
127 *Q6* **Radishchevo** Ul’yanovskaya Oblast’, W Russian Federation *52°49′N 47°54′E*
12 *I9* **Radisson** Québec, E Canada *53°47′N 77°35′W*
11 *P16* **Radium Hot Springs** British Columbia, SW Canada *50°39′N 116°09′W*
116 *F11* **Radna** *Hung.* Máriaradna. Arad, W Romania *46°05′N 21°41′E*
Rádnávrre *see* Randijaure
114 *K10* **Radnevo** Stara Zagora, C Bulgaria *42°17′N 25°58′E*
97 *J20* **Radnor** *cultural region* E Wales, United Kingdom
Radnót *see* Iernut
Rádóc *see* Rădăuţi
101 *H24* **Radolfzell am Bodensee** Baden-Württemberg, S Germany *47°43′N 08°58′E*
110 *M13* **Radom** Mazowieckie, C Poland *51°23′N 21°08′E*
116 *I14* **Radomireşti** Olt, S Romania *44°06′N 25°00′E*
111 *K14* **Radomsko** *Rus.* Novoradomsk. Łódzkie, C Poland *51°04′N 19°25′E*
117 *N4* **Radomyshl’** Zhytomyrs’ka Oblast’, N Ukraine *50°30′N 29°16′E*
113 *P19* **Radoviš** *prev.* Radovište. E Macedonia *41°39′N 22°26′E*
Radovište *see* Radoviš
Radøy *see* Radøyni
94 *B13* **Radøyni** *prev.* Radøy. *island* S Norway
109 *R7* **Radstadt** Salzburg, NW Austria *47°24′N 13°31′E*
182 *E8* **Radstock, Cape** *headland* South Australia *33°11′S 134°18′E*
109 *U10* **Raduha** ▲ N Slovenia *46°24′N 14°46′E*
119 *G15* **Radun’** Hrodzyenskaya Voblasts’, W Belarus *54°03′N 25°00′E*
126 *M3* **Raduzhnyy** Vladimirskaya Oblast’, W Russian Federation *55°59′N 40°15′E*
118 *F11* **Radviliškis** Šiaulai, N Lithuania *55°48′N 23°32′E*
11 *U17* **Radville** Saskatchewan, S Canada *49°28′N 104°19′W*
140 *K7* **Raḑwā, Jabal** ▲ W Saudi Arabia *24°31′N 38°21′E*
111 *P16* **Radymno** Podkarpackie, SE Poland *49°57′N 22°49′E*
116 *J5* **Radyvyliv** Rivnens’ka Oblast’, NW Ukraine *50°07′N 25°12′E*
Radziechów *see* Radekhiv
110 *I11* **Radziejów** Kujawskio-pomorskie, C Poland *52°36′N 18°33′E*
110 *O12* **Radzyń Podlaski** Lubelskie, E Poland *51°48′N 22°37′E*
8 *J7* **Rae** ∿ Nunavut, NW Canada
152 *M13* **Rāe Bareli** Uttar Pradesh, N India *26°14′N 81°14′E*
Rae-Edzo *see* Edzo
21 *T11* **Raeford** North Carolina, SE USA *34°59′N 79°15′W*
99 *M19* **Raeren** Liège, E Belgium *50°42′N 06°06′E*
9 *N7* **Rae Strait** *strait* Nunavut, N Canada
184 *L11* **Raetihi** Manawatu-Wanganui, North Island, New Zealand *39°29′S 175°16′E*
Raevavae *see* Raivavae
Rafa *see* Rafah
62 *M10* **Rafaela** Santa Fe, E Argentina *31°16′S 61°25′W*
54 *E5* **Rafael Núñez** ✈ (Cartagena) Bolívar, NW Colombia *10°27′N 75°31′W*
138 *E11* **Rafah** *var.* Rafa, Rafaḩ, *Heb.* Rafiaḩ, Raphiah. SW Gaza Strip *31°18′N 34°15′E*
79 *L15* **Rafaï** Mbomou, SE Central African Republic *05°01′N 23°51′E*
141 *O4* **Rafḩah** Al Ḩudūd ash Shamālīyah, N Saudi Arabia *29°41′N 43°29′E*
Rafiaḩ *see* Rafah
143 *R10* **Rafsanjān** Kermān, C Iran *30°25′N 56°E*
80 *B13* **Raga** Western Bahr el Ghazal, W South Sudan *08°28′N 25°41′E*
19 *S8* **Ragged Island** *island* Maine, NE USA
44 *I5* **Ragged Island Range** *island group* S Bahamas
184 *L7* **Raglan** Waikato, North Island, New Zealand *37°48′S 174°54′E*
22 *G8* **Ragley** Louisiana, S USA *30°31′N 93°13′W*
Ragnit *see* Neman
107 *K25* **Ragusa** Sicilia, Italy, C Mediterranean Sea *36°56′N 14°42′E*
Ragusa *see* Dubrovnik
Ragusavecchia *see* Cavtat
171 *P14* **Raha** Pulau Muna, C Indonesia *04°50′S 122°43′E*
119 *N17* **Rahachow** *Rus.* Rogachëv. Homyel’skaya Voblasts’, SE Belarus *53°03′N 30°03′E*
67 *U6* **Rahad** *var.* Nahr ar Rahad. ∿ W Sudan
Rahad, Nahr ar *see* Rahad
Rahaeng *see* Tak
138 *F11* **Rahat** Southern, C Israel *31°20′N 34°43′E*
140 *L8* **Rahaṭ, Ḩarrat** *lava flow* W Saudi Arabia
149 *S12* **Rahīmyār Khān** Punjab, SE Pakistan *28°27′N 70°21′E*
95 *I14* **Råholt** Akershus, S Norway *60°16′N 11°10′E*
113 *M17* **Rahovec** *Serb.* Orahovac. W Kosovo *42°24′N 20°40′E*
191 *S10* **Raiatea** *island* Îles Sous le Vent, W French Polynesia
155 *H16* **Rāichūr** Karnātaka, C India *16°15′N 77°20′E*
Raidestos *see* Tekirdağ
153 *S13* **Rāiganj** West Bengal, NE India *25°38′N 88°11′E*
154 *M11* **Raigarh** Chhattīsgarh, C India *21°53′N 83°28′E*
183 *O16* **Railton** Tasmania, SE Australia *41°24′S 146°28′E*
36 *L8* **Rainbow Bridge** *natural arch* Utah, W USA
23 *Q3* **Rainbow City** Alabama, S USA *33°57′N 86°02′W*
11 *N11* **Rainbow Lake** Alberta, W Canada *58°30′N 119°24′W*
21 *R5* **Rainelle** West Virginia, NE USA *37°57′N 80°46′W*
32 *G10* **Rainier** Oregon, NW USA *46°05′N 122°55′W*
32 *H9* **Rainier, Mount** ⛰ Washington, NW USA *46°51′N 121°45′W*
23 *Q2* **Rainsville** Alabama, S USA *34°29′N 85°51′W*
12 *B11* **Rainy Lake** ◎ Canada/USA
12 *A11* **Rainy River** Ontario, C Canada *48°44′N 94°33′W*
Raippaluoto *see* Replot
154 *K12* **Raipur** Chhattīsgarh, C India *21°16′N 81°42′E*
154 *H10* **Raisen** Madhya Pradesh, C India *23°21′N 77°49′E*
15 *N13* **Raisin** ∿ Ontario, SE Canada
31 *R11* **Raisin, River** ∿ Michigan, N USA
191 *U13* **Raivavae** *var.* Raevavae. Îles Australes, SW French Polynesia
149 *W9* **Rāiwind** Punjab, E Pakistan *31°14′N 74°10′E*
171 *T12* **Raja Ampat, Kepulauan** *island group* E Indonesia
155 *L16* **Rājahmundry** Andhra Pradesh, E India *17°05′N 81°42′E*
155 *I18* **Rājampet** Andhra Pradesh, E India *14°09′N 79°10′E*
Rajang *see* Rajang, Batang
169 *S9* **Rajang, Batang** *var.* Rajang. ∿ East Malaysia
149 *S11* **Rājanpur** Punjab, E Pakistan *29°05′N 70°25′E*
155 *H23* **Rājapālaiyam** Tamil Nādu, SE India *09°26′N 77°36′E*

◆ Country
● Country Capital
◇ Dependent Territory
○ Dependent Territory Capital
⬖ Administrative Regions
✈ International Airport
▲ Mountain
▲▲ Mountain Range
⛰ Volcano
∿ River
◎ Lake
⊠ Reservoir

152 E12 **Rājasthān** ◆ *state* NW India
153 T15 **Rajbari** Dhaka, C Bangladesh *23°47′N 89°39′E*
153 R12 **Rajbiraj** Eastern, E Nepal *26°34′N 86°52′E*
154 G9 **Rājgarh** Madhya Pradesh, C India *24°01′N 76°42′E*
152 H10 **Rājgarh** Rājasthān, NW India *28°38′N 75°21′E*
153 P14 **Rājgīr** Bihār, N India *25°01′N 85°26′E*
110 O8 **Rajgród** Podlaskie, NE Poland *53°43′N 22°40′E*
154 L12 **Rājim** Chhattīsgarh, C India *20°57′N 81°58′E*
112 C11 **Rajinac, Mali** ▲ W Croatia *44°47′N 15°04′E*
154 B10 **Rājkot** Gujarāt, W India *22°18′N 70°47′E*
153 R14 **Rājmahal** Jhārkhand, NE India *25°03′N 87°49′E*
153 Q14 **Rājmahāl Hills** *hill range* N India
154 K12 **Rāj Nāndgaon** Chhattīsgarh, C India *21°06′N 81°02′E*
152 I8 **Rājpura** Punjab, NW India *30°29′N 76°40′E*
153 S14 **Rajshahi** *prev.* Rampur Boalia. Rajshahi, W Bangladesh *24°24′N 88°40′E*
153 S13 **Rajshahi** ◆ *division* NW Bangladesh
190 K13 **Rakahanga** *atoll* N Cook Islands
185 H19 **Rakaia** Canterbury, South Island, New Zealand *43°45′S 172°02′E*
185 G19 **Rakaia** 🌊 South Island, New Zealand
152 H3 **Rakaposhi** ▲ N India *36°06′N 74°31′E*
Rakasd *see* Răcăşdia
169 N15 **Rakata, Pulau** *var.* Pulau Krakatau. *island* S Indonesia
141 U10 **Rakbah, Qalamat ar** *well* SE Saudi Arabia
166 K6 **Rakhine State** *var.* Arakan State. ◆ *state* W Myanmar (Burma)
116 I8 **Rakhiv** Zakarpats'ka Oblast', W Ukraine *48°05′N 24°15′E*
141 V13 **Rakhyūt** SW Oman *16°41′N 53°09′E*
192 K9 **Rakiraki** Viti Levu, W Fiji *17°22′S 178°10′E*
126 J8 **Rakitnoye** Belgorodskaya Oblast', W Russian Federation *50°50′N 35°51′E*
Rakka *see* Ar Raqqah
118 I4 **Rakke** Lääne-Virumaa, NE Estonia *58°58′N 26°14′E*
95 I16 **Rakkestad** Østfold, S Norway *59°25′N 11°17′E*
110 F12 **Rakoniewice** *Ger.* Rakwitz. Wielkopolskie, C Poland *52°09′N 16°10′E*
Rakonitz *see* Rakovník
83 H18 **Rakops** Central, C Botswana *21°01′S 24°20′E*
111 C16 **Rakovník** *Ger.* Rakonitz. Středočeský Kraj, W Czech Republic *50°07′N 13°44′E*
114 J10 **Rakovski** Plovdiv, C Bulgaria *42°16′N 24°58′E*
Rakutō-kō *see* Nakdong-gang
118 I3 **Rakvere** *Ger.* Wesenberg. Lääne-Virumaa, N Estonia *59°21′N 26°20′E*
Rakwitz *see* Rakoniewice
22 L6 **Raleigh** Mississippi, S USA *32°01′N 89°30′W*
21 U9 **Raleigh** *state capital* North Carolina, SE USA *35°46′N 78°38′W*
21 Y11 **Raleigh Bay** *bay* North Carolina, SE USA
21 U9 **Raleigh-Durham** ✈ North Carolina, SE USA *35°54′N 78°45′W*
189 S6 **Ralik Chain** *island group* Ralik Chain, W Marshall Islands
25 N5 **Ralls** Texas, SW USA *33°40′N 101°23′W*
18 G13 **Ralston** Pennsylvania, NE USA *41°29′N 76°57′W*
141 O16 **Ramādah** W Yemen *13°35′N 43°50′E*
Ramadi *see* Ar Ramādī
105 N2 **Ramales de la Victoria** Cantabria, N Spain *43°15′N 03°28′W*
138 F10 **Ramallah** C West Bank *31°55′N 35°12′E*
61 C19 **Ramallo** Buenos Aires, E Argentina *33°30′S 60°01′W*
155 H20 **Rāmanagaram** Karnātaka, E India *12°45′N 77°16′E*
155 I23 **Rāmanāthapuram** Tamil Nādu, SE India *09°23′N 78°53′E*
154 N12 **Rāmapur** Orissa, E India *21°48′N 84°00′E*
155 I14 **Rāmāreddi** *var.* Kāmāreddi, Kamareddy. Andhra Pradesh, C India *18°19′N 78°23′E*
138 F10 **Ramat Gan** Tel Aviv, W Israel *32°04′N 34°48′E*
103 T6 **Rambervillers** Vosges, NE France *48°15′N 06°50′E*
Rambi *see* Rabi
103 N5 **Rambouillet** Yvelines, N France *48°39′N 01°50′E*
186 E5 **Rambutyo Island** *island* N Papua New Guinea
153 Q12 **Ramechhāp** Central, C Nepal *27°20′N 86°05′E*
183 R12 **Rame Head** *headland* Victoria, SE Australia *37°48′S 149°30′E*
126 L4 **Ramenskoye** Moskovskaya Oblast', W Russian Federation *55°31′N 38°24′E*
124 J15 **Rameshki** Tverskaya Oblast', W Russian Federation *57°21′N 36°05′E*
153 P14 **Rāmgarh** Jhārkhand, N India *23°37′N 85°32′E*
152 D11 **Rāmgarh** Rājasthān, NW India *27°29′N 70°38′E*
142 M9 **Rāmhormoz** *var.* Ram Hormuz, Ramuz. Khūzestān, SW Iran *31°15′N 49°38′E*
Ram Hormuz *see* Rāmhormoz
Ram, Jebel *see* Ramm, Jabal
138 F10 **Ramla** *var.* Ramle, Ramleh, *Ar.* Er Ramle. Central, C Israel *31°56′N 34°52′E*
Ramle/Ramleh *see* Ramla
138 F14 **Ramm, Jabal** *var.* Jebel Ram. ▲ SW Jordan *29°34′N 35°24′E*
152 K10 **Rāmnagar** Uttarakhand, N India *29°23′N 79°07′E*
95 N15 **Ramnäs** Västmanland, C Sweden *59°46′N 16°16′E*
Râmnicul-Sărat *see* Râmnicu Sărat
116 L12 **Râmnicu Sărat** *prev.* Râmnicul-Sărat, Rîmnicu-Sărat. Buzău, E Romania *45°24′N 27°06′E*
116 I13 **Râmnicu Vâlcea** *prev.* Rîmnicu Vîlcea. Vâlcea, C Romania *45°04′N 24°32′E*
Ramokgwebana *see* Ramokgwebane
83 J18 **Ramokgwebane** *var.* Ramokgwebana. Central, NE Botswana *20°38′S 27°40′E*
126 L7 **Ramon'** Voronezhskaya Oblast', W Russian Federation *51°51′N 39°18′E*
35 V17 **Ramona** California, W USA *33°02′N 116°52′W*
56 A10 **Ramón, Laguna** ◎ NW Peru
14 G7 **Ramore** Ontario, S Canada *48°26′N 80°19′W*
40 M11 **Ramos** San Luis Potosí, C Mexico *22°48′N 101°55′W*
41 N8 **Ramos Arizpe** Coahuila, NE Mexico *25°35′N 100°59′W*
40 J9 **Ramos, Río de** 🌊 C Mexico
83 J21 **Ramotswa** South East, S Botswana *24°56′S 25°50′E*
39 R8 **Rampart** Alaska, USA *65°30′N 150°10′W*
8 H8 **Ramparts** 🌊 Northwest Territories, NW Canada
152 K10 **Rāmpur** Uttar Pradesh, N India *28°48′N 79°03′E*
154 F9 **Rāmpura** Madhya Pradesh, C India *24°30′N 75°32′E*
Rampur Boalia *see* Rajshahi
166 K6 **Ramree Island** *island* W Myanmar (Burma)
141 W6 **Rams** *var.* Ar Rams. Ra's al Khaymah, NE United Arab Emirates *25°52′N 56°01′E*
143 N4 **Rāmsar** *prev.* Sakhtsar. Māzandarān, N Iran *36°55′N 50°39′E*
93 H16 **Ramsele** Västernorrland, N Sweden *63°33′N 16°35′E*
21 T9 **Ramseur** North Carolina, SE USA *35°43′N 79°39′W*
97 I16 **Ramsey** NE Isle of Man *54°19′N 04°24′W*
97 I16 **Ramsey Bay** *bay* NE Isle of Man
14 E9 **Ramsey Lake** ◎ Ontario, S Canada
97 Q22 **Ramsgate** SE England, United Kingdom *51°20′N 01°25′E*
94 M10 **Ramsjö** Gävleborg, C Sweden *62°10′N 15°40′E*
154 I12 **Rāmtek** Mahārāshtra, C India *21°28′N 79°28′E*
Ramtha *see* Ar Ramthā
Ramuz *see* Rāmhormoz
118 G12 **Ramygala** Panevėžys, C Lithuania *55°30′N 24°18′E*
152 H14 **Rāna Pratāp Sāgar** ◎ N India
169 V7 **Ranau** Sabah, East Malaysia *05°56′N 116°43′E*
168 L14 **Ranau, Danau** ◎ Sumatera, W Indonesia
62 H12 **Rancagua** Libertador, C Chile *34°10′S 70°45′W*
99 G22 **Rance** Hainaut, S Belgium *50°09′N 04°16′E*
102 H6 **Rance** 🌊 NW France
60 J9 **Rancharia** São Paulo, S Brazil *22°13′S 50°53′W*
153 P15 **Rānchi** Jhārkhand, N India *23°22′N 85°20′E*
61 D21 **Ranchos** Buenos Aires, E Argentina *35°32′S 58°22′W*
37 S9 **Ranchos De Taos** New Mexico, SW USA *36°21′N 105°36′W*
63 G16 **Ranco, Lago** ◎ C Chile
95 C16 **Randaberg** Rogaland, S Norway *59°00′N 05°38′E*
29 U7 **Randall** Minnesota, N USA *46°05′N 94°30′W*
107 L23 **Randazzo** Sicilia, Italy, C Mediterranean Sea *37°52′N 14°57′E*
95 G21 **Randers** Midtjylland, C Denmark *56°28′N 10°03′E*
92 I12 **Randijaure** *Lapp.* Ráddnávrre. ◎ N Sweden
21 T9 **Randleman** North Carolina, SE USA *35°49′N 79°48′W*
19 O11 **Randolph** Massachusetts, NE USA *42°09′N 71°02′W*
29 Q13 **Randolph** Nebraska, C USA *42°25′N 97°05′W*
36 M1 **Randolph** Utah, W USA *41°40′N 111°10′W*
100 P9 **Randow** 🌊 NE Germany
95 H14 **Randsfjorden** ◎ S Norway
93 K13 **Råneå** Norrbotten, N Sweden *65°52′N 22°17′E*
92 G12 **Ranelva** 🌊 C Norway
93 F15 **Ranemsletta** Nord-Trøndelag, C Norway *64°36′N 11°55′E*
76 H10 **Ranérou** C Senegal *15°17′N 14°00′W*
Råneš *see* Ringvassøya
185 E22 **Ranfurly** Otago, South Island, New Zealand *45°07′S 170°06′E*
167 P17 **Rangae** Narathiwat, SW Thailand *06°15′N 101°45′E*
153 V16 **Rangamati** Chittagong, SE Bangladesh *22°40′N 92°10′E*
184 I2 **Rangaunu Bay** *bay* North Island, New Zealand
19 P6 **Rangeley** Maine, NE USA *44°58′N 70°37′W*
37 O4 **Rangely** Colorado, C USA *40°05′N 108°48′W*
25 R7 **Ranger** Texas, SW USA *32°28′N 98°40′W*
14 C9 **Ranger Lake** Ontario, S Canada *46°51′N 83°34′W*
14 C9 **Ranger Lake** ◎ Ontario, S Canada
153 V12 **Rangia** Assam, NE India *26°26′N 91°38′E*
185 I18 **Rangiora** Canterbury, South Island, New Zealand *43°19′S 172°34′E*
191 T9 **Rangiroa** *atoll* Îles Tuamotu, W French Polynesia
184 N9 **Rangitaiki** 🌊 North Island, New Zealand
185 F19 **Rangitata** 🌊 South Island, New Zealand
184 M12 **Rangitikei** 🌊 North Island, New Zealand
184 L6 **Rangitoto Island** *island* N New Zealand
Rangkasbitoeng *see* Rangkasbitung
169 N16 **Rangkasbitung** *prev.* Rangkasbitoeng. Jawa, SW Indonesia *06°21′S 106°12′E*
167 P9 **Rang, Khao** ▲ C Thailand *16°13′N 99°03′E*
147 V13 **Rangkŭl** *Rus.* Rangkul'. SE Tajikistan *38°30′N 74°24′E*
Rangkul' *see* Rangkŭl
Rangoon *see* Yangon
153 T13 **Rangpur** Rajshahi, N Bangladesh *25°46′N 89°20′E*
155 F18 **Rānībennur** Karnātaka, W India *14°36′N 75°39′E*
153 R15 **Rāniganj** West Bengal, NE India *23°34′N 87°13′E*
149 Q13 **Rānīpur** Sind, SE Pakistan *27°17′N 68°34′E*
Rāniyah *see* Rānya
25 N9 **Rankin** Texas, SW USA *31°14′N 101°56′W*
9 O9 **Rankin Inlet** Nunavut, C Canada *62°52′N 92°14′W*
183 P8 **Rankins Springs** New South Wales, SE Australia *33°51′S 146°16′E*
Rankovićevo *see* Kraljevo
108 I7 **Rankweil** Vorarlberg, W Austria *47°17′N 09°40′E*
Rann *see* Brežice
127 T8 **Ranneye** Orenburgskaya Oblast', W Russian Federation *51°28′N 52°29′E*
96 I10 **Rannoch, Loch** ◎ C Scotland, United Kingdom
191 U17 **Rano Kau** *var.* Rano Kao. *crater* Easter Island, Chile, E Pacific Ocean
167 N14 **Ranong** Ranong, SW Thailand *09°59′N 98°40′E*
186 J8 **Ranongga** *var.* Ghanongga. *island* NW Solomon Islands
191 W16 **Rano Raraku** *ancient monument* Easter Island, Chile, E Pacific Ocean
171 V12 **Ransiki** Papua, E Indonesia *01°27′S 134°12′E*
92 K12 **Rantajärvi** Norrbotten, N Sweden *66°45′N 23°39′E*
93 N17 **Rantasalmi** Itä-Suomi, SE Finland *62°02′N 28°22′E*
169 U13 **Rantau** Borneo, C Indonesia *02°56′S 115°09′E*
168 L10 **Rantau, Pulau** *var.* Pulau Tebingtinggi. *island* W Indonesia
171 N13 **Rantepao** Sulawesi, C Indonesia *02°58′S 119°58′E*
30 M13 **Rantoul** Illinois, N USA *40°19′N 88°08′W*
93 L15 **Rantsila** Oulu, C Finland *64°31′N 25°40′E*
92 L13 **Ranua** Lappi, NW Finland *65°55′N 26°34′E*
139 T3 **Rānya** *var.* Rāniyah. As Sulaymānīyah, NE Iraq *36°15′N 44°53′E*
157 X3 **Raohe** Heilongjiang, NE China *46°49′N 134°00′E*
74 H9 **Raoui, Erg er** *desert* W Algeria
193 O10 **Rapa** *island* Îles Australes, S French Polynesia
191 V14 **Rapa Iti** *island* Îles Australes, SW French Polynesia
106 D10 **Rapallo** Liguria, NW Italy *44°21′N 09°13′E*
Rapa Nui *see* Pascua, Isla de
Raphiah *see* Rafah
21 V5 **Rapidan River** 🌊 Virginia, NE USA
28 J10 **Rapid City** South Dakota, N USA *44°05′N 103°14′W*
15 P8 **Rapide-Blanc** Québec, SE Canada *47°48′N 72°57′W*
14 I8 **Rapide-Deux** Québec, SE Canada *47°56′N 78°33′W*
118 K6 **Räpina** *Ger.* Rappin. Põlvamaa, SE Estonia *58°06′N 27°27′E*
118 G4 **Rapla** *Ger.* Rappel. Raplamaa, NW Estonia *59°00′N 24°46′E*
118 G4 **Raplamaa** *var.* Rapla Maakond. ◆ *province* NW Estonia
Rapla Maakond *see* Raplamaa
21 X6 **Rappahannock River** 🌊 Virginia, NE USA
Rappel *see* Rapla
108 G7 **Rapperswil** Sankt Gallen, NE Switzerland *47°14′N 08°50′E*
Rappin *see* Räpina
153 N12 **Rāpti** 🌊 N India
57 K16 **Rápulo, Río** 🌊 E Bolivia
Raqqah/Raqqah, Muḥāfaẓat al *see* Ar Raqqah
18 J8 **Raquette Lake** ◎ New York, NE USA
18 J6 **Raquette River** 🌊 New York, NE USA
191 V10 **Raraka** *atoll* Îles Tuamotu, C French Polynesia
191 V10 **Raroia** *atoll* Îles Tuamotu, C French Polynesia
190 H15 **Rarotonga** ✈ Rarotonga, S Cook Islands, C Pacific Ocean *21°15′S 159°45′W*
190 H16 **Rarotonga** *island* S Cook Islands, C Pacific Ocean
147 P12 **Rarz** W Tajikistan *39°23′N 68°43′E*
Ras al 'Ain *see* Ra's al 'Ayn
139 N2 **Ra's al 'Ayn** *var.* Ras al'Ain. Al Ḥasakah, N Syria *36°52′N 40°05′E*
138 H3 **Ra's al Basīṭ** Al Lādhiqīyah, W Syria *35°57′N 35°55′E*
Ra's al-Hafğī *see* Ra's al Khafjī
141 R5 **Ra's al Khafjī** *var.* Ra's al-Hafğī. Ash Sharqīyah, NE Saudi Arabia *28°22′N 48°30′E*
Ras al-Khaimah/Ras al Khaimah *see* Ra's al Khaymah
143 R15 **Ra's al Khaymah** *var.* Ras al Khaimah. Ra's al Khaymah, NE United Arab Emirates *25°44′N 55°55′E*
143 R15 **Ra's al Khaymah** *var.* Ras al-Khaimah. ✈ Ra's al Khaymah, NE United Arab Emirates *25°37′N 55°51′E*
138 G13 **Ra's an Naqb** Ma'ān, S Jordan *30°00′N 35°29′E*
61 B26 **Rasa, Punta** *headland* E Argentina *40°50′S 62°15′W*
171 V12 **Rasawi** Papua, E Indonesia *02°04′S 134°02′E*
Râşcani *see* Rîşcani
80 J10 **Ras Dashen Terara** ▲ N Ethiopia *13°12′N 38°09′E*
Rasdhoo Atoll *see* Rasdu Atoll
151 K19 **Rasdu Atoll** *var.* Rasdhoo Atoll. *atoll* C Maldives
118 E12 **Raseiniai** Kaunas, C Lithuania *55°23′N 23°06′E*
75 X8 **Ra's Ghārib** *var.* Râs Ghârib. E Egypt *28°16′N 33°01′E*
Râs Ghârib *see* Ra's Ghārib
162 J6 **Rashaant** Hövsgöl, N Mongolia *49°08′N 101°27′E*
Rashaant *see* Delüün, Bayan-Ölgiy, Mongolia
Rashaant *see* Öldziyt, Dundgovĭ, Mongolia
75 V7 **Rashīd** *Eng.* Rosetta. N Egypt *31°25′N 30°25′E*
139 Y11 **Rashīd** Al Başrah, E Iraq *31°15′N 47°31′E*
142 M3 **Rasht** *var.* Resht. Gīlān, NW Iran *37°18′N 49°38′E*
139 S2 **Rashwan** Arbīl, N Iraq *36°28′N 43°54′E*
Rasik *see* Raasiku
113 M15 **Raška** Serbia, C Serbia *43°18′N 20°37′E*
119 P15 **Rasna** *Rus.* Ryasna. Mahilyowskaya Voblasts', E Belarus *54°01′N 31°12′E*
116 J12 **Râşnov** *prev.* Rîşno, Rozsnyó, *Hung.* Barcarozsnyó. Braşov, C Romania *45°35′N 25°27′E*
118 L11 **Rasony** *Rus.* Rossony. Vitsyebskaya Voblasts', N Belarus *55°53′N 28°50′E*
Ra's Shamrah *see* Ugarit
127 N7 **Rasskazovo** Tambovskaya Oblast', W Russian Federation *52°42′N 41°45′E*
119 O16 **Rasta** 🌊 E Belarus
Rastadt *see* Rastatt
Rastâne *see* Ar Rastān
141 S6 **Ra's Tannūrah** *Eng.* Ras Tanura. Ash Sharqīyah, NE Saudi Arabia *26°44′N 50°04′E*
Ras Tanura *see* Ra's Tannūrah
101 G21 **Rastatt** *var.* Rastadt. Baden-Württemberg, SW Germany *48°51′N 08°13′E*
Rastenburg *see* Kętrzyn
149 V7 **Rasūlnagar** Punjab, E Pakistan *32°20′N 73°51′E*
189 U6 **Ratak Chain** *island group* Ratak Chain, E Marshall Islands
119 K15 **Ratamka** *Rus.* Ratomka. Minskaya Voblasts', C Belarus *53°56′N 27°21′E*
93 G17 **Ratan** Jämtland, C Sweden *62°28′N 14°35′E*
152 G11 **Ratangarh** Rājasthān, NW India *28°02′N 74°39′E*
Rat Buri *see* Ratchaburi
167 O11 **Ratchaburi** *var.* Rat Buri. Ratchaburi, W Thailand *13°30′N 99°50′E*
29 W15 **Rathbun Lake** ⊠ Iowa, C USA
Ráth Caola *see* Rathkeale
166 K5 **Rathedaung** Rakhine State, W Myanmar (Burma) *20°30′N 92°48′E*
100 M12 **Rathenow** Brandenburg, NE Germany *52°37′N 12°21′E*
97 C19 **Rathkeale** *Ir.* Ráth Caola. Limerick, SW Ireland *52°32′N 08°56′W*
96 F13 **Rathlin Island** *Ir.* Reachlainn. *island* N Northern Ireland, United Kingdom
97 C20 **Ráth Luirc** *Ir.* An Ráth. Cork, SW Ireland *52°22′N 08°44′W*
Ratibor *see* Racibórz
Ratisbon/Ratisbona/Ratisbonne *see* Regensburg
Rätische Alpen *see* Rhaetian Alps
38 E17 **Rat Island** *island* Aleutian Islands, Alaska, USA
38 E17 **Rat Islands** *island group* Aleutian Islands, Alaska, USA
154 F10 **Ratlām** *prev.* Rutlam. Madhya Pradesh, C India *23°23′N 75°04′E*
155 D15 **Ratnāgiri** Mahārāshtra, W India *17°00′N 73°20′E*
155 K26 **Ratnapura** Sabaragamuwa Province, S Sri Lanka *06°41′N 80°25′E*
Ratne *see* Ratno
116 J2 **Ratno** *var.* Ratne. Volyns'ka Oblast', NW Ukraine *51°40′N 24°33′E*
Ratomka *see* Ratamka
37 U8 **Raton** New Mexico, SW USA *36°54′N 104°27′W*
139 O7 **Ratqah, Wādī ar** *dry watercourse* W Iraq
Ratschach *see* Radeče
167 O16 **Rattaphum** Songkhla, SW Thailand *07°07′N 100°16′E*
26 L6 **Rattlesnake Creek** 🌊 Kansas, C USA
94 L13 **Rättvik** Dalarna, C Sweden *60°53′N 15°12′E*
100 K9 **Ratzeburg** Mecklenburg-Vorpommern, N Germany *53°41′N 10°48′E*
100 K9 **Ratzeburger See** ◎ N Germany
10 J10 **Ratz, Mount** ▲ British Columbia, SW Canada *57°22′N 132°17′W*
61 D22 **Rauch** Buenos Aires, E Argentina *36°45′S 59°05′W*
41 U16 **Raudales** Chiapas, SE Mexico
Raudhatain *see* Ar Rawḍatayn
Raudnitz an der Elbe *see* Roudnice nad Labem
92 K1 **Raufarhöfn** Nordhurland Eystra, NE Iceland *66°27′N 15°58′W*
94 H13 **Raufoss** Oppland, S Norway *60°44′N 10°39′E*
Raukawa *see* Cook Strait
184 Q8 **Raukumara** ▲ North Island, New Zealand *37°46′S 178°07′E*
192 K11 **Raukumara Plain** *undersea feature* N Coral Sea
184 P8 **Raukumara Range** ▲▲ North Island, New Zealand
Räulakela *see* Rāurkela
95 F15 **Rauland** Telemark, S Norway *59°41′N 07°57′E*
93 J19 **Rauma** *Swe.* Raumo. Länsi-Suomi, SW Finland *61°09′N 21°30′E*
94 F10 **Rauma** 🌊 S Norway
Raumo *see* Rauma
118 H8 **Rauna** C Latvia *57°19′N 25°34′E*
169 T17 **Raung, Gunung** ▲ Jawa, S Indonesia *08°00′S 114°07′E*
154 N11 **Rāurkela** *var.* Räulakela, Rourkela. Orissa, E India *22°13′N 84°53′E*
95 J22 **Raus** Skåne, S Sweden *56°01′N 12°48′E*
165 W3 **Rausu** Hokkaidō, NE Japan *44°00′N 145°06′E*
165 W3 **Rausu-dake** ▲ Hokkaidō, NE Japan *44°06′N 145°04′E*
116 M9 **Răut** *var.* Răuţel. 🌊 C Moldova
93 M17 **Rautalampi** Itä-Suomi, C Finland *62°37′N 26°48′E*
93 N16 **Rautavaara** Itä-Suomi, C Finland *63°30′N 28°19′E*
Răuţel *see* Răut
93 O18 **Rautjärvi** Etelä-Suomi, SE Finland *61°21′N 29°20′E*
Rautu *see* Sosnovo
191 V11 **Ravahere** *atoll* Îles Tuamotu, C French Polynesia
107 J25 **Ravanusa** Sicilia, Italy, C Mediterranean Sea *37°16′N 13°59′E*
143 S9 **Rāvar** Kermān, C Iran *31°15′N 56°51′E*
147 Q11 **Ravat** Batkenskaya Oblast', SW Kyrgyzstan *39°54′N 70°06′E*
18 K11 **Ravena** New York, NE USA *42°28′N 73°49′W*
106 H10 **Ravenna** Emilia-Romagna, N Italy *44°28′N 12°15′E*
29 O15 **Ravenna** Nebraska, C USA *41°01′N 98°54′W*
31 U11 **Ravenna** Ohio, N USA *41°09′N 81°14′W*
101 I24 **Ravensburg** Baden-Württemberg, S Germany *47°47′N 09°37′E*
181 W4 **Ravenshoe** Queensland, NE Australia *17°29′S 145°28′E*
180 K13 **Ravensthorpe** Western Australia *33°37′S 120°03′E*
21 Q4 **Ravenswood** West Virginia, NE USA *38°57′N 81°45′W*
149 U9 **Rāvi** 🌊 India/Pakistan
112 C9 **Ravna Gora** Primorje-Gorski Kotar, NW Croatia *45°20′N 14°54′E*
109 U10 **Ravne na Koroškem** *Ger.* Gutenstein. N Slovenia *46°33′N 14°57′E*
145 T7 **Ravnina Kulyndy** *prev.* Kulunda Steppe, *Kaz.* Qulyndy Zhazyghy, *Rus.* Kulundinskaya Ravnina. *grassland* Kazakhstan/Russian Federation
139 P6 **Rāwah** Al Anbār, W Iraq *34°32′N 41°54′E*
191 T4 **Rawaki** *prev.* Phoenix Island. *atoll* Phoenix Islands, C Kiribati
149 U6 **Rāwalpindi** Punjab, NE Pakistan *33°38′N 73°06′E*
110 L13 **Rawa Mazowiecka** Łódzkie, C Poland *51°47′N 20°16′E*
139 T2 **Ŗawāndiz** *var.* Rawandoz, Rawāndūz. Arbīl, N Iraq *36°38′N 44°32′E*
Rawandoz/Rawāndūz *see* Ŗawāndiz
171 U12 **Rawas** Papua, E Indonesia *01°07′S 132°12′E*
139 O4 **Rawḍah** ◎ E Syria
110 G13 **Rawicz** *Ger.* Rawitsch. Wielkopolskie, C Poland *51°37′N 16°51′E*
Rawitsch *see* Rawicz
180 M11 **Rawlinna** Western Australia *31°01′S 125°36′E*
33 W16 **Rawlins** Wyoming, C USA *41°47′N 107°14′W*
63 K17 **Rawson** Chubut, SE Argentina *43°22′S 65°01′W*
159 R16 **Rawu** Xizang Zizhiqu, W China *29°30′N 96°42′E*
153 P12 **Raxaul** Bihār, N India *26°58′N 84°51′E*
28 K3 **Ray** North Dakota, N USA *48°19′N 103°11′W*
169 S11 **Raya, Bukit** ▲ Borneo, C Indonesia *0°40′S 112°40′E*
155 I18 **Rāyachoti** Andhra Pradesh, E India *14°03′N 78°43′E*
Rāyadrug *see* Rāyagarha
Rāyagada *see* Rāyagarha
155 M14 **Rāyagarha** *prev.* Rāyadrug, *var.* Rāyagada. Orissa, E India *19°10′N 83°28′E*
138 H7 **Rayak** *var.* Rayaq, Riyāq. E Lebanon *33°51′N 36°03′E*
Rayaq *see* Rayak
139 T2 **Rāyat** Arbīl, E Iraq *36°39′N 44°56′E*
169 N12 **Raya, Tanjung** *cape* Pulau Bangka, W Indonesia
13 R13 **Ray, Cape** *headland* Newfoundland, Newfoundland and Labrador, E Canada *47°38′N 59°15′W*
123 Q13 **Raychikhinsk** Amurskaya Oblast', SE Russian Federation *49°47′N 129°19′E*
127 U5 **Rayevskiy** Respublika Bashkortostan, W Russian Federation *54°04′N 54°58′E*
11 Q17 **Raymond** Alberta, SW Canada *49°30′N 112°41′W*
22 K6 **Raymond** Mississippi, S USA *32°15′N 90°25′W*
32 F9 **Raymond** Washington, NW USA *46°41′N 123°43′W*
183 T8 **Raymond Terrace** New South Wales, SE Australia *32°47′S 151°45′E*
25 T17 **Raymondville** Texas, SW USA *26°30′N 97°48′W*
11 U16 **Raymore** Saskatchewan, S Canada *51°24′N 104°34′W*
39 Q8 **Ray Mountains** ▲▲ Alaska, USA
22 H9 **Rayne** Louisiana, S USA *30°13′N 92°15′W*
41 O12 **Rayón** San Luis Potosí, C Mexico *21°54′N 99°33′W*
40 G4 **Rayón** Sonora, NW Mexico *29°45′N 110°33′W*
167 P12 **Rayong** Rayong, S Thailand *12°42′N 101°17′E*
25 T5 **Ray Roberts, Lake** ◎ Texas, SW USA
18 E15 **Raystown Lake** ⊠ Pennsylvania, NE USA
141 V13 **Raysūt** SW Oman *16°58′N 54°02′E*
27 R4 **Raytown** Missouri, C USA *39°00′N 94°27′W*
22 I5 **Rayville** Louisiana, S USA *32°29′N 91°45′W*
142 L5 **Razan** Hamadān, W Iran *35°22′N 48°58′E*
139 S9 **Razāzah, Buḩayrat ar** *var.* Baḩr al Milḩ. ◎ C Iraq
114 L9 **Razboyna** ▲ E Bulgaria *42°54′N 26°31′E*
Razdan *see* Hrazdan
Razdolnoye *see* Rozdol'ne
Razelm, Lacul *see* Razim, Lacul
139 U2 **Razga** As Sulaymānīyah, E Iraq *36°25′N 45°06′E*
114 L8 **Razgrad** Razgrad, N Bulgaria *43°33′N 26°31′E*
114 L8 **Razgrad** ◆ *province* NE Bulgaria
117 N13 **Razim, Lacul** *prev.* Lacul Razelm. *lagoon* NW Black Sea
114 G11 **Razlog** Blagoevgrad, SW Bulgaria *41°53′N 23°28′E*
118 K10 **Rāznas Ezers** ◎ SE Latvia
102 E6 **Raz, Pointe du** *headland* NW France *48°06′N 04°52′W*
Reachlainn *see* Rathlin Island
Reachrainn *see* Lambay Island
97 N22 **Reading** S England, United Kingdom *51°28′N 00°59′W*
18 H15 **Reading** Pennsylvania, NE USA *40°20′N 75°55′W*
48 C7 **Real, Cordillera** ▲▲ C Ecuador
62 K12 **Realicó** La Pampa, C Argentina *35°02′S 64°14′W*
25 R15 **Realitos** Texas, SW USA *27°26′N 98°31′W*
108 G9 **Realp** Uri, C Switzerland *46°36′N 08°32′E*
167 Q12 **Reăng Kesei** Bătdâmbâng, W Cambodia *12°57′N 103°15′E*
191 Y11 **Reao** *atoll* Îles Tuamotu, E French Polynesia
Reate *see* Rieti
Greater Antarctica *see* East Antarctica
180 L11 **Rebecca, Lake** ◎ Western Australia
Rebiana Sand Sea *see* Rabyānah, Ramlat
124 H8 **Reboly** *Finn.* Repola. Respublika Kareliya, NW Russian Federation *63°51′N 30°49′E*
165 S1 **Rebun** Rebun-tō, NE Japan *45°19′N 141°02′E*
165 S1 **Rebun-tō** *island* NE Japan
106 J12 **Recanati** Marche, C Italy *43°23′N 13°34′E*
Rechitsa *see* Rechytsa
109 Y7 **Rechnitz** Burgenland, SE Austria *47°19′N 16°26′E*
119 J20 **Rechytsa** *Rus.* Rechitsa. Brestskaya Voblasts', SW Belarus *51°51′N 26°48′E*
119 O19 **Rechytsa** *Rus.* Rechitsa. Homyel'skaya Voblasts', SE Belarus *52°22′N 30°23′E*
59 Q15 **Recife** *prev.* Pernambuco. *state capital* Pernambuco, E Brazil *08°06′S 34°53′W*
83 I26 **Recife, Cape** *Afr.* Kaap Recife. *headland* S South Africa *34°03′S 25°37′E*
Recife, Kaap *see* Recife, Cape
172 I16 **Récifs, Îles aux** *island* Inner Islands, NE Seychelles
101 E14 **Recklinghausen** Nordrhein-Westfalen, W Germany *51°37′N 07°12′E*
100 M8 **Recknitz** 🌊 NE Germany
99 K23 **Recogne** Luxembourg, SE Belgium *49°56′N 05°20′E*
61 C15 **Reconquista** Santa Fe, C Argentina *29°08′S 59°38′W*
195 O6 **Recovery Glacier** *glacier* Antarctica
59 G15 **Recreio** Mato Grosso, W Brazil *08°13′S 58°15′W*
27 X9 **Rector** Arkansas, C USA *36°15′N 90°17′W*
110 E9 **Recz** *Ger.* Reetz Neumark. Zachodnio-pomorskie, NW Poland *53°16′N 15°32′E*
99 L24 **Redange** *var.* Redange-sur-Attert. Diekirch, W Luxembourg *49°46′N 05°53′E*
Redange-sur-Attert *see* Redange
18 C13 **Redbank Creek** 🌊 Pennsylvania, NE USA
13 S9 **Red Bay** Québec, E Canada *51°40′N 56°37′W*
23 N2 **Red Bay** Alabama, S USA *34°26′N 88°08′W*
35 N4 **Red Bluff** California, W USA *40°09′N 122°14′W*
24 J8 **Red Bluff Reservoir** ◎ New Mexico/Texas, SW USA
30 K16 **Red Bud** Illinois, N USA *38°12′N 89°59′W*
30 J5 **Red Cedar River** 🌊 Wisconsin, N USA
11 R17 **Redcliff** Alberta, SW Canada *50°06′N 110°48′W*
83 K17 **Redcliff** Midlands, C Zimbabwe *19°00′S 29°49′E*
182 L9 **Red Cliffs** Victoria, SE Australia *34°21′S 142°12′E*
29 P17 **Red Cloud** Nebraska, C USA *40°05′N 98°31′W*
22 L8 **Red Creek** 🌊 Mississippi, S USA
11 P15 **Red Deer** Alberta, SW Canada *52°15′N 113°48′W*
11 Q16 **Red Deer** 🌊 Alberta, SW Canada
39 O11 **Red Devil** Alaska, USA *61°45′N 157°18′W*
35 N3 **Redding** California, W USA *40°33′N 122°26′W*
97 L20 **Redditch** W England, United Kingdom *52°19′N 01°56′W*
29 P9 **Redfield** South Dakota, N USA *44°51′N 98°31′W*
24 J12 **Redford** Texas, SW USA *29°31′N 104°19′W*
45 V13 **Redhead** Trinidad, Trinidad and Tobago *10°44′N 60°58′W*
182 I8 **Red Hill** South Australia *33°34′S 138°13′E*
Red Hill *see* Pu'u 'Ula'ula
26 K7 **Red Hills** *hill range* Kansas, C USA
13 T12 **Red Indian Lake** ◎ Newfoundland, Newfoundland and Labrador, E Canada
124 J16 **Redkino** Tverskaya Oblast', W Russian Federation *56°41′N 36°07′E*
12 A10 **Red Lake** Ontario, C Canada *51°00′N 93°55′W*
36 I10 **Red Lake** *salt flat* Arizona, SW USA
29 S4 **Red Lake Falls** Minnesota, N USA *47°52′N 96°16′W*
29 R4 **Red Lake River** 🌊 Minnesota, N USA
35 U15 **Redlands** California, W USA *34°03′N 117°10′W*
18 G16 **Red Lion** Pennsylvania, NE USA *39°53′N 76°36′W*
33 U11 **Red Lodge** Montana, NW USA *45°11′N 109°15′W*
32 H13 **Redmond** Oregon, NW USA *44°16′N 121°10′W*
36 L5 **Redmond** Utah, W USA *39°00′N 111°51′W*
32 H8 **Redmond** Washington, NW USA *47°40′N 122°07′W*
Rednitz *see* Regnitz
29 T15 **Red Oak** Iowa, C USA *41°00′N 95°10′W*
18 K12 **Red Oaks Mill** New York, NE USA *41°39′N 73°52′W*
102 I7 **Redon** Ille-et-Vilaine, NW France *47°39′N 02°05′W*
45 W10 **Redonda** *island* SW Antigua and Barbuda
104 G4 **Redondela** Galicia, NW Spain *42°17′N 08°36′W*
104 H11 **Redondo** Évora, S Portugal *38°38′N 07°32′W*
39 Q12 **Redoubt Volcano** ▲ Alaska, USA *60°29′N 152°44′W*
11 Y16 **Red River** 🌊 Canada/USA
129 U12 **Red River** *var.* Yuan, *Chin.* Yuan Jiang, *Vtn.* Sông Hông Hà. 🌊 China/Vietnam
25 W4 **Red River** 🌊 S USA
22 H7 **Red River** 🌊 Louisiana, S USA
30 M6 **Red River** 🌊 Wisconsin, N USA
Red Rock, Lake *see* Red Rock Reservoir
29 W14 **Red Rock Reservoir** *var.* Lake Red Rock. ⊠ Iowa, C USA
80 H7 **Red Sea** ◆ *state* NE Sudan
75 Y9 **Red Sea** *var.* Sinus Arabicus. *sea* Africa/Asia
21 T11 **Red Springs** North Carolina, SE USA *34°49′N 79°10′W*
8 I9 **Redstone** 🌊 Northwest Territories, NW Canada
11 V17 **Redvers** Saskatchewan, S Canada *49°31′N 101°33′W*
77 P13 **Red Volta** *var.* Nazinon, *Fr.* Volta Rouge. 🌊 Burkina/Ghana
11 Q14 **Redwater** Alberta, SW Canada *53°57′N 113°06′W*
28 M16 **Red Willow Creek** 🌊 Nebraska, C USA
29 W9 **Red Wing** Minnesota, N USA *44°33′N 92°31′W*
35 N9 **Redwood City** California, W USA *37°29′N 122°13′W*
29 T9 **Redwood Falls** Minnesota, N USA *44°33′N 95°07′W*
31 P7 **Reed City** Michigan, N USA *43°52′N 85°30′W*
28 K6 **Reeder** North Dakota, N USA *46°03′N 102°55′W*
35 R11 **Reedley** California, W USA *36°35′N 119°27′W*
33 T11 **Reedpoint** Montana, NW USA *45°41′N 109°33′W*
30 K8 **Reedsburg** Wisconsin, N USA *43°33′N 90°03′W*
32 E13 **Reedsport** Oregon, NW USA *43°42′N 124°06′W*
187 Q9 **Reef Islands** *island group* Santa Cruz Islands, E Solomon Islands
185 H16 **Reefton** West Coast, South Island, New Zealand *42°07′S 171°53′E*
20 F8 **Reelfoot Lake** ◎ Tennessee, S USA
97 D17 **Ree, Lough** *Ir.* Loch Rí. ◎ C Ireland
Reengus *see* Rīngas
35 U4 **Reese River** 🌊 Nevada, W USA
98 M8 **Reest** 🌊 E Netherlands
Reetz Neumark *see* Recz
Reevhtse *see* Røssvatnet
137 N13 **Refahiye** Erzincan, C Turkey *39°54′N 38°45′E*
23 N4 **Reform** Alabama, S USA *33°22′N 88°01′W*
95 K20 **Reftele** Jönköping, S Sweden *57°10′N 13°34′E*
25 T14 **Refugio** Texas, SW USA *28°19′N 97°18′W*
110 E8 **Rega** 🌊 NW Poland
Regar *see* Tursunzoda
101 O21 **Regen** Bayern, SE Germany *48°57′N 13°10′E*
101 M20 **Regen** 🌊 SE Germany
101 M21 **Regensburg** *Eng.* Ratisbon, *Fr.* Ratisbonne, *hist.* Ratisbona; *anc.* Castra Regina, Reginum. Bayern, SE Germany *49°01′N 12°06′E*
101 M21 **Regenstauf** Bayern, SE Germany *49°06′N 12°07′E*
148 M10 **Rēgestān** *var.* Rigestan, *prev.* Rīgestān. *desert region* S Afghanistan
74 I10 **Reggane** C Algeria *26°46′N 00°09′E*
98 N9 **Regge** 🌊 E Netherlands
Reggio *see* Reggio nell'Emilia
Reggio Calabria *see* Reggio di Calabria
107 M23 **Reggio di Calabria** *var.* Reggio Calabria, *Gk.* Rhegion; *anc.* Regium, Rhegium. Calabria, SW Italy *38°06′N 15°39′E*
Reggio Emilia *see* Reggio nell'Emilia
106 F9 **Reggio nell'Emilia** *var.* Reggio Emilia, *abbrev.* Reggio; *anc.* Regium Lepidum. Emilia-Romagna, N Italy *44°42′N 10°37′E*
116 I10 **Reghin** *Ger.* Sächsisch-Reen, *Hung.* Szászrégen; *prev.* Reghinul Săsesc, *Ger.* Sächsisch-Regen. Mureş, C Romania *46°46′N 24°41′E*
Reghinul Săsesc *see* Reghin
11 U16 **Regina** *province capital* Saskatchewan, S Canada *50°25′N 104°39′W*
55 Z10 **Régina** E French Guiana *04°20′N 52°07′W*
11 U16 **Regina** ✈ Saskatchewan, S Canada *50°21′N 104°43′W*
11 U16 **Regina Beach** Saskatchewan, S Canada *50°44′N 105°03′W*
Reginum *see* Regensburg
Région du Haut-Congo *see* Haut-Congo
Registan *see* Rēgestān
60 L11 **Registro** São Paulo, S Brazil *24°30′S 47°50′W*
Regium *see* Reggio di Calabria
Regium Lepidum *see* Reggio nell'Emilia
101 K19 **Regnitz** *var.* Rednitz. 🌊 SE Germany
40 K10 **Regocijo** Durango, W Mexico *23°35′N 105°11′W*
104 H12 **Reguengos de Monsaraz** Évora, S Portugal *38°25′N 07°32′W*
101 M18 **Rehau** Bayern, E Germany *50°15′N 12°03′E*
83 D19 **Rehoboth** Hardap, C Namibia *23°18′S 17°03′E*
21 Z4 **Rehoboth Beach** Delaware, NE USA *38°42′N 75°03′W*

◆ Country
● Country Capital
◇ Dependent Territory
○ Dependent Territory Capital
◆ Administrative Regions
✈ International Airport
▲ Mountain
▲▲ Mountain Range
Volcano
🌊 River
◎ Lake
⊠ Reservoir

138 F10 **Rehovot**; *prev.* Reḥovot. Central, C Israel 31°54′N 34°49′E
Reḥovot *see* Rehovot
81 J20 **Rei** *spring/well* S Kenya 03°24′S 39°18′E
Reichenau *see* Rychnov nad Kněžnou
Reichenau *see* Bogatynia, Poland
101 M17 **Reichenbach** *var.* Reichenbach im Vogtland. Sachsen, E Germany 50°36′N 12°18′E
Reichenbach *see* Dzierżoniów
Reichenbach im Vogtland *see* Reichenbach
Reichenberg *see* Liberec
181 O11 **Reid** Western Australia 30°49′S 128°24′E
23 V6 **Reidsville** Georgia, SE USA 32°05′N 82°07′W
21 T8 **Reidsville** North Carolina, SE USA 36°21′N 79°39′W
Reifnitz *see* Ribnica
97 O22 **Reigate** SE England, United Kingdom 51°14′N 00°13′W
Reikjavik *see* Reykjavík
102 I10 **Ré, Île de** *island* W France
37 N15 **Reiley Peak** ▲ Arizona, SW USA 32°24′N 110°09′W
103 Q4 **Reims** *Eng.* Rheims; *anc.* Durocortorum, Remi. Marne, N France 49°16′N 04°01′E
63 G23 **Reina Adelaida, Archipiélago** *island group* S Chile
45 O16 **Reina Beatrix** ✕ (Oranjestad) C Aruba 12°30′N 69°57′W
108 F7 **Reinach** Aargau, W Switzerland 47°16′N 08°12′E
108 E6 **Reinach** Basel Landschaft, NW Switzerland 47°30′N 07°36′E
64 O11 **Reina Sofía** ✕ (Tenerife) Tenerife, Islas Canarias, Spain, NE Atlantic Ocean
29 W13 **Reinbeck** Iowa, C USA 42°19′N 92°36′W
100 J10 **Reinbek** Schleswig-Holstein, N Germany 53°31′N 10°15′E
11 U12 **Reindeer** ↝ Saskatchewan, C Canada
11 U11 **Reindeer Lake** ◎ Manitoba/ Saskatchewan, C Canada
Reine-Charlotte, Îles de la *see* Queen Charlotte Islands
Reine-Élisabeth, Îles de la *see* Queen Elizabeth Islands
94 F13 **Reineskarvet** ▲ S Norway 60°38′N 07°48′E
184 H1 **Reinga, Cape** *headland* North Island, New Zealand 34°24′S 172°40′E
105 N3 **Reinosa** Cantabria, N Spain 43°01′N 04°09′W
109 R8 **Reisseck** ▲ S Austria 46°57′N 13°21′E
21 W3 **Reisterstown** Maryland, NE USA 39°27′N 76°46′W
Reisui *see* Yeosu
98 N5 **Reitdiep** ↝ NE Netherlands
191 V10 **Reitoru** *atoll* Îles Tuamotu, C French Polynesia
95 M17 **Rejmyre** Östergötland, S Sweden 58°49′N 15°55′E
Reka *see* Rijeka
Reka Ili *see* Ile/Ili He
Rekarne *see* Tumbo
Rekhovot *see* Rehovot
8 K9 **Reliance** Northwest Territories, C Canada 62°45′N 109°08′W
33 U16 **Reliance** Wyoming, C USA 41°42′N 109°13′W
74 I5 **Relizane** *var.* Ghelîzâne, Ghilizane. NW Algeria 35°45′N 00°33′E
182 I7 **Remarkable, Mount** ▲ South Australia 32°46′S 138°08′E
54 E8 **Remedios** Antioquia, N Colombia 07°02′N 74°42′W
43 Q16 **Remedios** Veraguas, W Panama 08°13′N 81°48′W
42 D8 **Remedios, Punta** *headland* SW El Salvador 13°31′N 89°48′W
Remi *see* Reims
99 N25 **Remich** Grevenmacher, SE Luxembourg 49°33′N 06°23′E
99 J19 **Remicourt** Liège, E Belgium 50°40′N 05°19′E
14 H8 **Rémigny, Lac** ◎ Québec, SE Canada
55 Z10 **Rémire** NE French Guiana 04°52′N 52°16′W
127 N13 **Remontnoye** Rostovskaya Oblast', SW Russian Federation 46°35′N 43°38′E
171 U14 **Remoon** Pulau Kur, E Indonesia 05°18′S 131°59′E
99 L20 **Remouchamps** Liège, E Belgium 50°29′N 05°43′E
103 R15 **Remoulins** Gard, S France 43°56′N 04°34′E
173 X16 **Rempart, Mont du** *hill* W Mauritius
101 E15 **Remscheid** Nordrhein-Westfalen, W Germany 51°10′N 07°11′E
29 S12 **Remsen** Iowa, C USA 42°48′N 95°58′W
94 I12 **Rena** Hedmark, S Norway 61°08′N 11°21′E
94 I11 **Renåa** ↝ S Norway
Renaix *see* Ronse
118 H7 **Rencēni** N Latvia 57°43′N 25°25′E
118 D9 **Renda** W Latvia 57°04′N 22°18′E
107 N20 **Rende** Calabria, SW Italy 39°19′N 16°10′E
99 K21 **Rendeux** Luxembourg, SE Belgium 50°15′N 05°28′E
Rendina *see* Rentína
30 L16 **Rend Lake** ▣ Illinois, N USA
186 K9 **Rendova** *island* New Georgia Islands, NW Solomon Islands
100 I8 **Rendsburg** Schleswig-Holstein, N Germany 54°18′N 09°40′E
108 B9 **Renens** Vaud, SW Switzerland 46°32′N 06°36′E
14 K12 **Renfrew** Ontario, SE Canada 45°28′N 76°44′W
96 I12 **Renfrew** *cultural region* Scotland, United Kingdom
168 L11 **Rengat** Sumatera, W Indonesia 0°26′S 102°38′E
153 W12 **Rengma Hills** ▲▲ NE India
62 H12 **Rengo** Libertador, C Chile 34°24′S 70°50′W
116 M12 **Reni** Odes'ka Oblast', SW Ukraine 45°30′N 28°18′E
80 F11 **Renk** Upper Nile, NE South Sudan 11°48′N 32°49′E
93 L19 **Renko** Etelä-Suomi, S Finland 60°52′N 24°16′E
98 L12 **Renkum** Gelderland, SE Netherlands 51°58′N 05°43′E
182 K9 **Renmark** South Australia 34°12′S 140°43′E
186 L10 **Rennell** *var.* Mu Nggava. *island* S Solomon Islands
186 M9 **Rennell and Bellona** *prev.* Central. ◈ *province* S Solomon Islands
181 Q4 **Renner Springs Roadhouse** Northern Territory, N Australia 18°12′S 133°48′E
102 I6 **Rennes** *Bret.* Roazon; *anc.* Condate. Ille-et-Vilaine, NW France 48°08′N 01°40′W
195 S16 **Rennick Glacier** *glacier* Antarctica
11 Y16 **Rennie** Manitoba, S Canada 49°51′N 95°28′W
35 Q5 **Reno** Nevada, W USA 39°32′N 119°49′W
106 H10 **Reno** ↝ N Italy
35 Q5 **Reno-Cannon** ✕ Nevada, W USA 39°26′N 119°42′W
83 F24 **Renoster** ↝ SW South Africa
15 T5 **Renouard, Lac** ◎ Québec, SE Canada
18 F13 **Renovo** Pennsylvania, NE USA 41°19′N 77°42′W
161 O3 **Renqiu** Hebei, E China 38°49′N 116°02′E
160 I9 **Renshou** Sichuan, C China 30°02′N 104°09′E
31 N12 **Rensselaer** Indiana, N USA 40°57′N 87°09′W
18 L11 **Rensselaer** New York, NE USA 42°38′N 73°44′W
Rentería *see* Errenteria
115 E17 **Rentína** *var.* Rendina. Thessalía, C Greece 39°04′N 21°58′E
29 T9 **Renville** Minnesota, N USA 44°48′N 95°13′W
77 O13 **Réo** W Burkina 12°20′N 02°28′W
15 O12 **Repentigny** Québec, SE Canada 45°42′N 73°28′W
146 K13 **Repetek** Lebap Welaýaty, E Turkmenistan 38°40′N 63°12′E
93 J16 **Replot** *Fin.* Raippaluoto. *island* W Finland
Repola *see* Reboly
Reppen *see* Rzepin
Reps *see* Rupea
27 T7 **Republic** Missouri, C USA 37°07′N 93°28′W
32 K7 **Republic** Washington, NW USA 48°39′N 118°44′W
27 N3 **Republican River** ↝ Kansas/Nebraska, C USA
9 O7 **Repulse Bay** Northwest Territories, N Canada 66°35′N 86°20′W
56 F9 **Requena** Loreto, NE Peru 05°05′S 73°52′W
105 R10 **Requena** Valenciana, E Spain 39°29′N 01°08′W
103 O14 **Réquista** Aveyron, S France 44°00′N 02°31′E
136 M12 **Reşadiye** Tokat, N Turkey 40°24′N 37°19′E
Reschenpass *see* Resia, Passo di
Reschitza *see* Reşiţa
113 N20 **Resen** *Turk.* Resne. SW FYR Macedonia 41°07′N 21°00′E
60 J11 **Reserva** Paraná, S Brazil 24°40′S 50°52′W
11 V15 **Reserve** Saskatchewan, S Canada 52°24′N 102°37′W
37 P13 **Reserve** New Mexico, SW USA 33°42′N 108°45′W
Reshetilovka *see* Reshetylivka
117 S6 **Reshetylivka** *Rus.* Reshetilovka. Poltavs'ka Oblast', NE Ukraine 49°34′N 34°05′E
Resht *see* Rasht
106 F5 **Resia, Passo di** *Ger.* Reschenpass. *pass* Austria/ Italy
Resicabánya *see* Reşiţa
62 N7 **Resistencia** Chaco, NE Argentina 27°27′S 58°56′W
116 F12 **Reşiţa** *Ger.* Reschitza, *Hung.* Resicabánya. Caraş-Severin, W Romania 45°14′N 21°58′E
Resne *see* Resen
197 N9 **Resolute** *Inuit* Qausuittuq. Cornwallis Island, Nunavut, N Canada 74°41′N 94°54′W
Resolution *see* Fort Resolution
9 T7 **Resolution Island** *island* Nunavut, NE Canada
185 A23 **Resolution Island** *island* SW New Zealand
15 W7 **Restigouche** Québec, SE Canada 48°02′N 66°42′W
11 W17 **Reston** Manitoba, S Canada 49°33′N 101°03′W
14 H11 **Restoule Lake** ◎ Ontario, S Canada
54 F10 **Restrepo** Meta, C Colombia 04°20′N 73°29′W
42 B6 **Retalhuleu** Retalhuleu, SW Guatemala 14°31′N 91°40′W
42 A1 **Retalhuleu** *off.* Departamento de Retalhuleu. ◈ *department* SW Guatemala
Retalhuleu, Departamento de *see* Retalhuleu
97 N18 **Retford** C England, United Kingdom 53°18′N 00°52′W
103 Q3 **Rethel** Ardennes, N France 49°31′N 04°22′E
Rethimno/Réthimnon *see* Réthymno
115 I25 **Réthymno** *prev.* Rethimno, Réthimnon. Kríti, Greece, E Mediterranean Sea 35°21′N 24°29′E
Retiche, Alpi *see* Rhaetian Alps
99 J16 **Retie** Antwerpen, N Belgium 51°18′N 05°05′E
111 J21 **Rétság** Nógrád, N Hungary 47°57′N 19°08′E
109 W2 **Retz** Niederösterreich, NE Austria 48°46′N 15°58′E
173 N15 **Réunion** *off.* La Réunion. ◇ *French overseas department* W Indian Ocean
128 L17 **Réunion** *island* W Indian Ocean
105 U6 **Reus** Cataluña, E Spain 41°10′N 01°06′E
108 F7 **Reuss** ↝ NW Switzerland
99 J15 **Reusel** Noord-Brabant, S Netherlands 51°21′N 05°10′E
Reutel *see* Ciuhuru
101 H22 **Reutlingen** Baden-Württemberg, S Germany 48°30′N 09°13′E
108 L7 **Reutte** Tirol, W Austria 47°30′N 10°44′E
99 M16 **Reuver** Limburg, SE Netherlands 51°17′N 06°05′E
28 K7 **Reva** South Dakota, N USA 45°30′N 103°03′W
Reval/Revel *see* Tallinn
124 J4 **Revda** Murmanskaya Oblast', NW Russian Federation 67°57′N 34°29′E
122 F6 **Revda** Sverdlovskaya Oblast', C Russian Federation 56°48′N 59°42′E
103 N16 **Revel** Haute-Garonne, S France 43°27′N 01°59′E
11 O16 **Revelstoke** British Columbia, SW Canada 51°02′N 118°12′W
43 N13 **Reventazón, Río** ↝ E Costa Rica
106 G9 **Revere** Lombardia, N Italy 45°03′N 11°07′E
39 Y14 **Revillagigedo Island** *island* Alexander Archipelago, Alaska, USA
193 R7 **Revillagigedo Islands** Mexico
103 R3 **Revin** Ardennes, N France 49°57′N 04°39′E
92 O3 **Revnosa** *headland* C Svalbard 78°03′N 18°52′E
Revolyutsii, Pik *see* Revolyutsiya, Qullai
147 T13 **Revolyutsiya, Qullai** *Rus.* Pik Revolyutsii. ▲ SE Tajikistan 38°40′N 72°26′E
111 L19 **Revúca** *Ger.* Grossrauschenbach, *Hung.* Nagyrőce. Banskobystrický Kraj, C Slovakia 48°40′N 20°10′E
154 K9 **Rewa** Madhya Pradesh, C India 24°32′N 81°18′E
152 I11 **Rewāri** Haryāna, N India 28°14′N 76°38′E
33 R14 **Rexburg** Idaho, NW USA 43°49′N 111°47′W
78 G13 **Rey Bouba** Nord, NE Cameroon 08°40′N 14°11′E
92 L3 **Reydharfjördhur** Austurland, E Iceland 65°02′N 14°12′W
57 K16 **Reyes** El Beni, NW Bolivia 14°17′S 67°18′W
34 L8 **Reyes, Point** *headland* California, W USA 37°59′N 123°01′W
54 B12 **Reyes, Punta** *headland* SW Colombia 02°44′N 78°08′W
136 L17 **Reyhanlı** Hatay, S Turkey 36°16′N 36°35′E
43 U16 **Rey, Isla del** *island* Archipiélago de las Perlas, SE Panama
92 H2 **Reykhólar** Vestfirdhir, W Iceland 65°28′N 22°12′W
92 K2 **Reykjahlídh** Nordhurland Eystra, NE Iceland 65°37′N 16°54′W
197 O16 **Reykjanes Basin** *var.* Irminger Basin. *undersea feature* N Atlantic Ocean 62°30′N 33°30′W
197 N17 **Reykjanes Ridge** *undersea feature* N Atlantic Ocean 62°00′N 27°00′W
92 H4 **Reykjavík** *var.* Reikjavik. ● (Iceland) Höfudhborgarsvaedhi, W Iceland 64°08′N 21°54′W
18 D13 **Reynoldsville** Pennsylvania, NE USA 41°04′N 78°51′W
41 P8 **Reynosa** Tamaulipas, C Mexico 26°03′N 98°19′W
Reẕā'īyeh *see* Orūmīyeh
Reẕā'īyeh, Daryācheh-ye *see* Orūmīyeh, Daryācheh-ye
102 I8 **Rezé** Loire-Atlantique, NW France 47°10′N 01°36′W
118 K10 **Rēzekne** *Ger.* Rositten; *prev. Rus.* Rezhitsa. SE Latvia 56°31′N 27°22′E
Rezhitsa *see* Rēzekne
117 N9 **Rezina** NE Moldova 47°44′N 28°58′E
114 N11 **Rezovo** *Turk.* Rezve. Burgas, E Bulgaria 42°00′N 28°00′E
114 N11 **Rezovska Reka** *Turk.* Rezve Deresi. ↝ Bulgaria/Turkey *see also* Rezve Deresi
Rezovska Reka *see* Rezve Deresi
Rezve *see* Rezovo
114 N11 **Rezve Deresi** *Bul.* Rezovska Reka. ↝ Bulgaria/Turkey *see also* Rezovska Reka
Rezve Deresi *see* Rezovska Reka
Rhadames *see* Ghadāmis
Rhaedestus *see* Tekirdağ
108 J10 **Rhaetian Alps** *Fr.* Alpes Rhétiques, *Ger.* Rätische Alpen, *It.* Alpi Retiche. ▲▲ C Europe
108 I8 **Rhätikon** ▲▲ C Europe
101 G14 **Rheda-Wiedenbrück** Nordrhein-Westfalen, W Germany 51°51′N 08°17′E
98 M12 **Rheden** Gelderland, E Netherlands 52°01′N 06°03′E
Rhegion/Rhegium *see* Reggio di Calabria
Rheims *see* Reims
Rhein *see* Rhine
101 E17 **Rheinbach** Nordrhein-Westfalen, W Germany 50°37′N 06°57′E
100 F13 **Rheine** *var.* Rheine in Westfalen. Nordrhein-Westfalen, NW Germany 52°17′N 07°27′E
Rheine in Westfalen *see* Rheine
Rheinfeld *see* Rheinfelden
101 F24 **Rheinfelden** Baden-Württemberg, S Germany 47°34′N 07°46′E
108 E6 **Rheinfelden** *var.* Rheinfeld. Aargau, N Switzerland 47°33′N 07°47′E
101 E17 **Rheinisches Schiefergebirge** *var.* Rhine State Uplands, *Eng.* Rhenish Slate Mountains. ▲▲ W Germany
101 D18 **Rheinland-Pfalz** *Eng.* Rhineland-Palatinate, *Fr.* Rhénanie-Palatinat. ◈ *state* W Germany
101 G18 **Rhein Main** ✕ (Frankfurt am Main) Hessen, W Germany 50°03′N 08°33′E
Rhénanie du Nord-Westphalie *see* Nordrhein-Westfalen
Rhénanie-Palatinat *see* Rheinland-Pfalz
98 K12 **Rhenen** Utrecht, C Netherlands 52°01′N 06°02′E
Rhenish Slate Mountains *see* Rheinisches Schiefergebirge
Rhétiques, Alpes *see* Rhaetian Alps
100 N10 **Rhin** ↝ NE Germany
Rhin *see* Rhine
84 F10 **Rhine** *Dut.* Rijn, *Fr.* Rhin, *Ger.* Rhein. ↝ W Europe
30 L5 **Rhinelander** Wisconsin, N USA 45°39′N 89°23′W
Rhineland-Palatinate *see* Rheinland-Pfalz
Rhine State Uplands *see* Rheinisches Schiefergebirge
100 N11 **Rhinkanal** *canal* NE Germany
81 F17 **Rhino Camp** NW Uganda 02°58′N 31°24′E
74 D7 **Rhir, Cap** *headland* W Morocco 30°40′N 09°54′W
106 D7 **Rho** Lombardia, N Italy 45°32′N 09°02′E
19 N12 **Rhode Island** *off.* State of Rhode Island and Providence Plantations, *also known as* Little Rhody, Ocean State. ◈ *state* NE USA
19 O13 **Rhode Island** *island* Rhode Island, NE USA
19 O13 **Rhode Island Sound** *sound* Maine/Rhode Island, NE USA
Rhodes *see* Ródos
Rhode-Saint-Genèse *see* Sint-Genesius-Rode
84 L14 **Rhodes Basin** *undersea feature* E Mediterranean Sea 35°55′N 28°30′E
Rhodesia *see* Zimbabwe
114 I12 **Rhodope Mountains** *var.* Rodhópi Óri, *Bul.* Rhodope Planina, Rodopi, *Gk.* Orosirá Rodhópis, *Turk.* Dospad Dagh. ▲▲ Bulgaria/Greece
Rhodope Planina *see* Rhodope Mountains
101 I18 **Rhön** ▲▲ C Germany
103 Q10 **Rhône** ◈ *department* E France
86 C12 **Rhône** ↝ France/ Switzerland
103 R12 **Rhône-Alpes** ◈ *region* E France
98 G13 **Rhoon** Zuid-Holland, SW Netherlands 51°52′N 04°25′E
96 G9 **Rhum** *var.* Rum. *island* W Scotland, United Kingdom
Rhuthun *see* Ruthin
97 J18 **Rhyl** NE Wales, United Kingdom 53°19′N 03°28′W
59 K18 **Rialma** Goiás, S Brazil 15°22′S 49°35′W
104 L3 **Riaño** Castilla y León, N Spain 42°59′N 05°00′W
105 O9 **Riansáres** ↝ C Spain
152 H6 **Riāsi** Jammu and Kashmir, NW India 33°03′N 74°51′E
168 K10 **Riau** *off.* Propinsi Riau. ◈ *province* W Indonesia
Riau Archipelago *see* Riau, Kepulauan
168 M11 **Riau, Kepulauan** *var.* Riau Archipelago, *Dut.* Riouw-Archipel. *island group* W Indonesia
Riau, Propinsi *see* Riau
105 O6 **Riaza** Castilla y León, N Spain 41°17′N 03°29′W
105 N6 **Riaza** ↝ N Spain
81 K17 **Riba** *spring/well* NE Kenya 01°56′N 40°38′E
104 H4 **Ribadavia** Galicia, NW Spain 42°17′N 08°08′W
104 J2 **Ribadeo** Galicia, NW Spain 43°32′N 07°04′W
104 L2 **Ribadesella** *var.* Ribeseya. Asturias, N Spain 43°27′N 05°04′W
104 G10 **Ribatejo** *former province* C Portugal
83 P15 **Ribáuè** Nampula, N Mozambique 14°56′S 38°19′E
97 K17 **Ribble** ↝ NW England, United Kingdom
95 F23 **Ribe** Syddtjylland, W Denmark 55°20′N 08°47′E
Ribeira *see* Sanata Uxía de Ribeira
64 O5 **Ribeira Brava** Madeira, Portugal, NE Atlantic Ocean 32°39′N 17°04′W
64 P3 **Ribeira Grande** São Miguel, Azores, Portugal, NE Atlantic Ocean 37°34′N 25°32′W
60 L8 **Ribeirão Preto** São Paulo, S Brazil 21°09′S 47°48′W
60 L11 **Ribeira, Rio** ↝ S Brazil
107 I24 **Ribera** Sicilia, Italy, C Mediterranean Sea 37°31′N 13°16′E
57 L14 **Riberalta** El Beni, N Bolivia 11°01′S 66°04′W
105 W4 **Ribes de Freser** Cataluña, NE Spain 42°18′N 02°11′E
Ribeseya *see* Ribadesella
30 L6 **Rib Mountain** ▲ Wisconsin, N USA 44°55′N 89°41′W
109 U12 **Ribnica** *Ger.* Reifnitz. S Slovenia 45°46′N 14°40′E
117 N9 **Ribniţa** *var.* Râbniţa, *Rus.* Rybnitsa. NE Moldova 47°46′N 29°01′E
100 M8 **Ribnitz-Damgarten** Mecklenburg-Vorpommern, NE Germany 54°14′N 12°25′E
111 D16 **Říčany** *Ger.* Ritschan. Středočeský Kraj, W Czech Republic 49°59′N 14°40′E
29 U7 **Rice** Minnesota, N USA 45°42′N 94°10′W
30 J5 **Rice Lake** Wisconsin, N USA 45°33′N 91°43′W
14 E8 **Rice Lake** ◎ Ontario, S Canada
14 I15 **Rice Lake** ◎ Ontario, SE Canada
23 V3 **Richard B. Russell Lake** ▣ Georgia, SE USA
25 U6 **Richardson** Texas, SW USA 32°55′N 96°44′W
11 R11 **Richardson** ↝ Alberta, C Canada
10 I3 **Richardson Mountains** ▲▲ Yukon Territory, NW Canada
185 C21 **Richardson Mountains** ▲▲ South Island, New Zealand
42 F3 **Richardson Peak** ▲ SE Belize 16°34′N 88°46′W
76 G10 **Richard Toll** N Senegal 16°28′N 15°44′W
28 L5 **Richardton** North Dakota, N USA 46°52′N 102°19′W
14 F13 **Rich, Cape** *headland* Ontario, S Canada 44°42′N 80°37′W
102 L8 **Richelieu** Indre-et-Loire, C France 47°01′N 00°18′E
33 P15 **Richfield** Idaho, NW USA 43°03′N 114°11′W
36 K5 **Richfield** Utah, W USA 38°45′N 112°05′W
18 J10 **Richfield Springs** New York, NE USA 42°52′N 74°57′W
18 M6 **Richford** Vermont, NE USA 44°59′N 72°37′W
27 R6 **Rich Hill** Missouri, C USA 38°06′N 94°22′W
13 P14 **Richibucto** New Brunswick, SE Canada 46°42′N 64°54′W
108 G8 **Richisau** Glarus, NE Switzerland 47°00′N 08°54′E
23 S6 **Richland** Georgia, SE USA 32°05′N 84°40′W
27 U6 **Richland** Missouri, C USA 37°51′N 92°24′W
25 U8 **Richland** Texas, SW USA 31°55′N 96°25′W
32 K10 **Richland** Washington, NW USA 46°17′N 119°16′W
30 K8 **Richland Center** Wisconsin, N USA 43°22′N 90°24′W
21 W11 **Richlands** North Carolina, SE USA 34°52′N 77°33′W
21 Q7 **Richlands** Virginia, NE USA 37°05′N 81°47′W
25 R9 **Richland Springs** Texas, SW USA 31°16′N 98°56′W
183 S8 **Richmond** New South Wales, SE Australia 33°36′S 150°44′E
10 L17 **Richmond** British Columbia, SW Canada 49°07′N 123°09′W
14 L13 **Richmond** Ontario, SE Canada 45°12′N 75°49′W
15 Q12 **Richmond** Québec, SE Canada 45°39′N 72°07′W
185 I14 **Richmond** Tasman, South Island, New Zealand 41°25′S 173°04′E
35 N8 **Richmond** California, W USA 37°57′N 122°22′W
31 Q14 **Richmond** Indiana, N USA 39°50′N 84°51′W
20 M6 **Richmond** Kentucky, S USA 37°45′N 84°19′W
27 S4 **Richmond** Missouri, C USA 39°15′N 93°59′W
25 V11 **Richmond** Texas, SW USA 29°36′N 95°48′W
36 L1 **Richmond** Utah, W USA 41°55′N 111°51′W
21 W6 **Richmond** *state capital* Virginia, NE USA 37°33′N 77°28′W
14 H15 **Richmond Hill** Ontario, S Canada 43°51′N 79°24′W
185 J15 **Richmond Range** ▲▲ South Island, New Zealand
27 S12 **Rich Mountain** ▲ Arkansas, C USA 34°37′N 94°17′W
31 S13 **Richwood** Ohio, N USA 40°25′N 83°18′W
21 R5 **Richwood** West Virginia, NE USA 38°13′N 80°31′W
104 K5 **Ricobayo, Embalse de** ▣ NW Spain
Ricomagus *see* Riom
Ridā' *see* Radā'
127 T5 **Ridder** Respublika Tatarstan, W Russian Federation 54°34′N 52°27′E
98 H13 **Ridderkerk** Zuid-Holland, SW Netherlands 51°52′N 04°35′E
33 N16 **Riddle** Idaho, NW USA 42°07′N 116°09′W
32 F14 **Riddle** Oregon, NW USA 42°57′N 123°21′W
14 L13 **Rideau** ↝ Ontario, SE Canada
35 T12 **Ridgecrest** California, W USA 35°37′N 117°40′W
18 L13 **Ridgefield** Connecticut, NE USA 41°16′N 73°30′W
22 K5 **Ridgeland** Mississippi, S USA 32°25′N 90°07′W
21 R15 **Ridgeland** South Carolina, SE USA 32°30′N 80°59′W
20 F8 **Ridgely** Tennessee, S USA 36°15′N 89°29′W
14 D17 **Ridgetown** Ontario, S Canada 42°27′N 81°52′W
21 R12 **Ridgeway** South Carolina, SE USA 34°17′N 80°56′W
Ridgeway *see* Ridgway
18 D13 **Ridgway** *var.* Ridgeway. Pennsylvania, NE USA 41°24′N 78°40′W
11 W16 **Riding Mountain** ▲▲ Manitoba, S Canada
Ried *see* Ried im Innkreis
109 R4 **Ried im Innkreis** *var.* Ried. Oberösterreich, NW Austria 48°13′N 13°29′E
109 X8 **Riegersburg** Steiermark, SE Austria 47°03′N 15°52′E
108 E6 **Riehen** Basel-Stadt, NW Switzerland 47°35′N 07°39′E
92 J9 **Riehppegáisá** *var.* Rieppe. ▲ N Norway 69°38′N 21°31′E
99 K18 **Riemst** Limburg, NE Belgium 50°49′N 05°36′E
Rieppe *see* Riehppegáisá
101 O15 **Riesa** Sachsen, E Germany 51°18′N 13°18′E
63 H24 **Riesco, Isla** *island* S Chile
107 K25 **Riesi** Sicilia, Italy, C Mediterranean Sea 37°17′N 14°05′E
83 F25 **Riet** ↝ SW South Africa
83 I23 **Riet** ↝ SW South Africa
118 D11 **Rietavas** Telšiai, W Lithuania 55°43′N 21°56′E
83 F19 **Rietfontein** Omaheke, E Namibia 21°58′S 20°58′E
107 I14 **Rieti** *anc.* Reate. Lazio, C Italy 42°24′N 12°51′E
84 D14 **Rif** *var.* Riff, Er Rif, Er Riff. ▲▲ N Morocco
138 I8 **Rif Dimashq** *off.* Muḩāfaẓat Dimashq, *var.* Damascus, *Ar.* Ash Sham, Ash Shām, Damasco, Esh Sham, *Fr.* Damas. ◈ *governorate* S Syria
Riff *see* Rif
37 Q4 **Rifle** Colorado, C USA 39°30′N 107°46′W
31 R7 **Rifle River** ↝ Michigan, N USA
81 H18 **Rift Valley** ◈ *province* Kenya
Rift Valley *see* Great Rift Valley
118 F9 **Rīga** *Eng.* Riga. ● C Latvia 56°57′N 24°08′E
Rigaer Bucht *see* Riga, Gulf of
118 F6 **Riga, Gulf of** *Est.* Liivi Laht, *Ger.* Rigaer Bucht, *Latv.* Rīgas Jūras Līcis, *Rus.* Rizhskiy Zaliv; *prev. Est.* Riia Laht. *gulf* Estonia/Latvia
Rīgas Jūras Līcis *see* Riga, Gulf of
15 N12 **Rigaud** ↝ Ontario/Québec, SE Canada
33 R14 **Rigby** Idaho, NW USA 43°40′N 111°54′W
Rīgestān *see* Rēgestān
32 M11 **Riggins** Idaho, NW USA 45°24′N 116°18′W
13 R8 **Rigolet** Newfoundland and Labrador, NE Canada 54°10′N 58°25′W
78 G9 **Rig-Rig** Kanem, W Chad 14°16′N 14°21′E
118 F4 **Riguldi** Läänemaa, W Estonia 59°07′N 23°34′E
Riia Laht *see* Riga, Gulf of
93 L19 **Riihimäki** Etelä-Suomi, S Finland 60°45′N 24°45′E
195 U2 **Riiser-Larsen Peninsula** *peninsula* Antarctica
65 P22 **Riiser-Larsen Sea** *sea* Antarctica
Riisser Larsen Ice Shelf *see* Riiser-Larsenisen
40 D2 **Riíto** Sonora, NW Mexico 32°06′N 114°57′W
112 B9 **Rijeka** *Ger.* Sankt Veit am Flaum, *It.* Fiume, *Slvn.* Reka; *anc.* Tarsatica. Primorje-Gorski Kotar, NW Croatia 45°20′N 14°26′E
99 I14 **Rijen** Noord-Brabant, S Netherlands 51°35′N 04°55′E
99 H15 **Rijkevorsel** Antwerpen, N Belgium 51°23′N 04°43′E
Rijn *see* Rhine
98 G11 **Rijnsburg** Zuid-Holland, W Netherlands 52°12′N 04°27′E
Rijssel *see* Lille
98 N10 **Rijssen** Overijssel, E Netherlands 52°19′N 06°30′E
98 G12 **Rijswijk** *Eng.* Ryswick. Zuid-Holland, W Netherlands 52°03′N 04°20′E
92 I10 **Riksgränsen** Norrbotten, N Sweden 68°24′N 18°15′E
165 U4 **Rikubetsu** Hokkaidō, NE Japan 43°30′N 143°43′E
165 R9 **Rikuzen-Takata** Iwate, Honshū, C Japan 39°03′N 141°38′E
27 O4 **Riley** Kansas, C USA 39°18′N 96°49′W
99 I17 **Rillaar** Vlaams Brabant, C Belgium 50°58′N 04°58′E
Rí, Loch *see* Ree, Lough
114 G11 **Rilska Reka** ↝ W Bulgaria
77 T12 **Rima** ↝ N Nigeria
141 N7 **Rimah, Wādī ar** *var.* Wādī ar Rummah. *dry watercourse* C Saudi Arabia
Rimaszombat *see* Rimavská Sobota
191 R12 **Rimatara** *island* Îles Australes, SW French Polynesia
111 L20 **Rimavská Sobota** *Ger.* Gross-Steffelsdorf, *Hung.* Rimaszombat. Banskobystrický Kraj, C Slovakia 48°24′N 20°01′E
11 Q15 **Rimbey** Alberta, SW Canada 52°39′N 114°10′W
95 P15 **Rimbo** Stockholm, C Sweden 59°44′N 18°21′E
95 M18 **Rimforsa** Östergötland, S Sweden 58°06′N 15°40′E
106 I11 **Rimini** *anc.* Ariminum. Emilia-Romagna, N Italy 44°03′N 12°33′E
Rîmnicu-Sărat *see* Râmnicu Sărat
Rîmnicu Vîlcea *see* Râmnicu Vâlcea
149 Y3 **Rimo Muztāgh** ▲▲ India/ Pakistan
15 U7 **Rimouski** Québec, SE Canada 48°26′N 68°32′W
158 M16 **Rinbung** Xizang Zizhiqu, W China 29°15′N 89°40′E
Rinchinlhumbe *see* Dzöölön
62 I5 **Rincón, Cerro** ▲ N Chile 24°01′S 67°19′W
104 M15 **Rincón de la Victoria** Andalucía, S Spain 36°43′N 04°18′W
Rincón del Bonete, Lago Artificial de *see* Río Negro, Embalse del
105 Q4 **Rincón de Soto** La Rioja, N Spain 42°15′N 01°50′W
94 G8 **Rindal** Møre og Romsdal, S Norway 63°02′N 09°09′E
115 J20 **Rineia** *island* Kykládes, Greece, Aegean Sea
152 H11 **Rīngas** *prev.* Reengus, Ringus. Rājasthān, N India 27°18′N 75°27′E
95 H24 **Ringe** Syddtjylland, C Denmark 55°14′N 10°30′E
94 H11 **Ringebu** Oppland, S Norway 61°31′N 10°09′E
Ringen *see* Rõngu
186 K8 **Ringgi** Kolombangara, NW Solomon Islands 08°03′S 157°08′E
23 R1 **Ringgold** Georgia, SE USA 34°55′N 85°06′W
22 G5 **Ringgold** Louisiana, S USA 32°19′N 93°16′W
25 S5 **Ringgold** Texas, SW USA 33°47′N 97°56′W
95 E22 **Ringkøbing** Midtjylland, W Denmark 56°04′N 08°22′E
95 E22 **Ringkøbing Fjord** *fjord* W Denmark
33 S10 **Ringling** Montana, NW USA 46°15′N 110°48′W
27 N13 **Ringling** Oklahoma, C USA 34°12′N 97°35′W
94 H13 **Ringsaker** Hedmark, S Norway 60°54′N 10°45′E
95 I23 **Ringsted** Sjælland, E Denmark 55°28′N 11°48′E
Ringus *see* Rīngas
92 I9 **Ringvassøya** *Lapp.* Ráneš. *island* N Norway
18 K13 **Ringwood** New Jersey, NE USA 41°06′N 74°15′W
Rinn Duáin *see* Hook Head
100 H13 **Rinteln** Niedersachsen, NW Germany 52°10′N 09°04′E
115 E18 **Río** Dytikí Elláda, S Greece 38°18′N 21°48′E
Rio *see* Rio de Janeiro
56 C7 **Riobamba** Chimborazo, C Ecuador 01°44′S 78°40′W
60 P9 **Rio Bonito** Rio de Janeiro, SE Brazil 22°42′S 42°38′W
59 C16 **Rio Branco** *state capital* Acre, W Brazil 09°59′S 67°49′W
61 H18 **Río Branco** Cerro Largo, NE Uruguay 32°32′S 53°28′W
Rio Branco, Território de *see* Roraima
41 P8 **Río Bravo** Tamaulipas, C Mexico 25°57′N 98°03′W
63 G16 **Río Bueno** Los Ríos, C Chile 40°20′S 72°55′W
55 P5 **Río Caribe** Sucre, NE Venezuela 10°43′N 63°06′W
54 M5 **Río Chico** Miranda, N Venezuela 10°18′N 66°00′W
63 H18 **Río Cisnes** Aisén, S Chile 44°29′S 71°15′W
60 L9 **Rio Claro** São Paulo, S Brazil 22°19′S 47°35′W
45 V14 **Rio Claro** Trinidad, Trinidad and Tobago 10°18′N 61°11′W
54 J5 **Río Claro** Lara, N Venezuela 09°54′N 69°23′W
63 K15 **Río Colorado** Río Negro, E Argentina 39°01′S 64°05′W
62 K11 **Río Cuarto** Córdoba, C Argentina 33°06′S 64°20′W
60 P10 **Rio de Janeiro** *var.* Rio. *state capital* Rio de Janeiro, SE Brazil 22°53′S 43°17′W
60 P9 **Rio de Janeiro** *off.* Estado do Rio de Janeiro. ◈ *state* SE Brazil
Rio de Janeiro, Estado do *see* Rio de Janeiro
43 R17 **Río de Jesús** Veraguas, S Panama 07°58′N 81°01′W
34 K3 **Rio Dell** California, W USA 40°30′N 124°07′W
60 K13 **Rio do Sul** Santa Catarina, S Brazil 27°15′S 49°37′W
63 I23 **Río Gallegos** *var.* Gallegos, Puerto Gallegos. Santa Cruz, S Argentina 51°40′S 69°21′W
63 J24 **Río Grande** Tierra del Fuego, S Argentina 53°45′S 67°46′W
61 I18 **Rio Grande** *var.* São Pedro do Rio Grande do Sul. Rio Grande do Sul, S Brazil 32°03′S 52°08′W
40 L10 **Río Grande** Zacatecas, C Mexico 23°50′N 103°20′W
42 J9 **Río Grande** León, NW Nicaragua 12°59′N 86°34′W
45 V5 **Río Grande** E Puerto Rico 18°23′N 65°51′W
24 I9 **Rio Grande** ↝ Texas, SW USA
25 R17 **Rio Grande City** Texas, SW USA 26°24′N 98°50′W
59 P14 **Rio Grande do Norte** *off.* Estado do Rio Grande do Norte. ◈ *state* E Brazil
Rio Grande do Norte, Estado do *see* Rio Grande do Norte
61 G15 **Rio Grande do Sul** *off.* Estado do Rio Grande do Sul. ◈ *state* S Brazil
Rio Grande do Sul, Estado do *see* Rio Grande do Sul
65 M17 **Rio Grande Fracture Zone** *tectonic feature* C Atlantic Ocean
65 J18 **Rio Grande Gap** *undersea feature* S Atlantic Ocean
Rio Grande Plateau *see* Rio Grande Rise
65 J18 **Rio Grande Rise** *var.* Rio Grande Plateau. *undersea feature* SW Atlantic Ocean 31°00′S 35°00′W
54 G4 **Ríohacha** La Guajira, N Colombia 11°23′N 72°47′W
43 S16 **Río Hato** Coclé, C Panama 08°21′N 80°10′W
25 T17 **Rio Hondo** Texas, SW USA 26°14′N 97°34′W
56 D10 **Rioja** San Martín, N Peru 06°02′S 77°10′W
41 Y11 **Río Lagartos** Yucatán, SE Mexico 21°35′N 88°08′W
103 P11 **Riom** *anc.* Ricomagus. Puy-de-Dôme, C France 45°54′N 03°06′E
104 F10 **Rio Maior** Santarém, C Portugal 39°20′N 08°55′W
103 O12 **Riom-ès-Montagnes** Cantal, C France 45°15′N 02°39′E
60 J12 **Rio Negro** Paraná, S Brazil 26°06′S 49°46′W
63 I15 **Río Negro** *off.* Provincia de Río Negro. ◈ *province* C Argentina
61 D18 **Río Negro** ◈ *department* W Uruguay
47 V12 **Río Negro, Embalse del** *var.* Lago Artificial de Rincón del Bonete. ▣ C Uruguay
Río Negro, Provincia de *see* Río Negro
107 M17 **Rionero in Vulture** Basilicata, S Italy 40°55′N 15°40′E
137 S9 **Rioni** ↝ W Georgia
105 P12 **Riópar** Castilla-La Mancha, C Spain 38°31′N 02°27′W
61 H16 **Rio Pardo** Rio Grande do Sul, S Brazil 29°41′S 52°25′W
37 R11 **Rio Rancho Estates** New Mexico, SW USA 35°14′N 106°40′W
42 L11 **Río San Juan** ◈ *department* S Nicaragua
54 E9 **Ríosucio** Caldas, W Colombia 05°26′N 75°44′W
54 C7 **Ríosucio** Chocó, NW Colombia 07°25′N 77°05′W
62 K10 **Río Tercero** Córdoba, C Argentina 32°15′S 64°08′W
42 K5 **Río Tinto, Sierra** ▲▲ NE Honduras
54 J5 **Río Tocuyo** Lara, N Venezuela 10°18′N 70°00′W
Riouw-Archipel *see* Riau, Kepulauan
59 J19 **Rio Verde** Goiás, C Brazil 17°50′S 50°55′W
41 O12 **Río Verde** *var.* Rioverde. San Luis Potosí, C Mexico 21°58′N 100°W
Rioverde *see* Río Verde
35 O8 **Rio Vista** California, W USA 38°09′N 121°42′W
112 M11 **Ripanj** Serbia, N Serbia 44°37′N 20°30′E
106 J13 **Ripatransone** Marche, C Italy 43°00′N 13°45′E
22 M2 **Ripley** Mississippi, S USA 34°43′N 88°57′W
31 R15 **Ripley** Ohio, N USA 38°45′N 83°51′W
20 F9 **Ripley** Tennessee, S USA 35°43′N 89°30′W
21 Q4 **Ripley** West Virginia, NE USA 38°49′N 81°44′W

◆ Country
● Country Capital
◇ Dependent Territory
○ Dependent Territory Capital
◈ Administrative Regions
✕ International Airport
▲ Mountain
▲▲ Mountain Range
Volcano
↝ River
◎ Lake
▣ Reservoir

105 W4 **Ripoll** Cataluña, NE Spain *42°12′N 02°12′E*
97 M16 **Ripon** N England, United Kingdom *54°07′N 01°31′W*
30 M7 **Ripon** Wisconsin, N USA *43°52′N 88°48′W*
107 L24 **Riposto** Sicilia, Italy, C Mediterranean Sea *37°44′N 15°13′E*
99 L14 **Rips** Noord-Brabant, SE Netherlands *51°31′N 05°49′E*
54 D9 **Risaralda** ***off.*** Departamento de Risaralda. ◈ *province* C Colombia
Risaralda, Departamento de ***see*** Risaralda
116 L8 **Rîşcani** ***var.*** Râşcani, ***Rus.*** Ryshkany. NW Moldova *47°55′N 27°31′E*
152 J9 **Rishikesh** Uttarakhand, N India *30°06′N 78°16′E*
165 S1 **Rishiri-tō** ***var.*** Risiri Tô. *island* NE Japan
165 S1 **Rishiri-yama** ⛰ Rishiri-tō, NE Japan *45°11′N 141°11′E*
25 R7 **Rising Star** Texas, SW USA *32°06′N 98°57′W*
31 Q15 **Rising Sun** Indiana, N USA *38°58′N 84°53′W*
Risiri Tô ***see*** Rishiri-tō
102 L4 **Risle** ≈ N France
Rîşno ***see*** Râşnov
27 V13 **Rison** Arkansas, C USA *33°58′N 92°11′W*
95 G17 **Risør** Aust-Agder, S Norway *58°44′N 09°15′E*
92 H10 **Risøyhamn** Nordland, C Norway *69°00′N 15°37′E*
101 I23 **Riss** ≈ S Germany
118 G4 **Risti** ***Ger.*** Kreuz. Läänemaa, W Estonia *59°01′N 24°01′E*
15 V8 **Ristigouche** ≈ Québec, SE Canada
93 N18 **Ristiina** Itä-Suomi, E Finland *61°32′N 27°15′E*
93 N14 **Ristijärvi** Oulu, C Finland *64°30′N 28°15′E*
188 C14 **Ritidian Point** *headland* N Guam *13°39′N 144°51′E*
Ritschan ***see*** Říčany
35 R9 **Ritter, Mount** ▲ California, W USA *37°40′N 119°10′W*
31 T12 **Rittman** Ohio, N USA *40°58′N 81°46′W*
32 L9 **Ritzville** Washington, NW USA *47°07′N 118°22′W*
Riva ***see*** Riva del Garda
61 A21 **Rivadavia** Buenos Aires, E Argentina *35°29′S 62°59′W*
106 F7 **Riva del Garda** ***var.*** Riva. Trentino-Alto Adige, N Italy *45°54′N 10°50′E*
106 B8 **Rivarolo Canavese** Piemonte, W Italy *45°21′N 07°42′E*
42 K11 **Rivas** Rivas, SW Nicaragua *11°26′N 85°50′W*
42 J11 **Rivas** ◈ *department* SW Nicaragua
103 R11 **Rive-de-Gier** Loire, E France *45°31′N 04°36′E*
61 A22 **Rivera** Buenos Aires, E Argentina *37°13′S 63°14′W*
61 F16 **Rivera** Rivera, NE Uruguay *30°54′S 55°31′W*
61 F17 **Rivera** ◈ *department* NE Uruguay
35 P9 **Riverbank** California, W USA *37°43′N 120°59′W*
76 K17 **River Cess** SW Liberia *05°28′N 09°32′W*
28 M4 **Riverdale** North Dakota, N USA *47°29′N 101°22′W*
30 I6 **River Falls** Wisconsin, N USA *44°52′N 92°38′W*
11 T16 **Riverhurst** Saskatchewan, S Canada *50°52′N 106°49′W*
183 O10 **Riverina** *physical region* New South Wales, SE Australia
80 G8 **River Nile** ◈ *state* NE Sudan
63 F19 **Rivero, Isla** *island* Archipiélago de los Chonos, S Chile
11 W16 **Rivers** Manitoba, S Canada *50°02′N 100°14′W*
77 U17 **Rivers** ◈ *state* S Nigeria
185 D23 **Riversdale** Southland, South Island, New Zealand *45°54′S 168°44′E*
83 F26 **Riversdale** Western Cape, SW South Africa *34°05′S 21°15′E*
35 U15 **Riverside** California, W USA *33°58′N 117°25′W*
25 W9 **Riverside** Texas, SW USA *30°51′N 95°24′W*
37 U3 **Riverside Reservoir** ⊠ Colorado, C USA
10 K15 **Rivers Inlet** British Columbia, SW Canada *51°43′N 127°19′W*
10 K15 **Rivers Inlet** *inlet* British Columbia, SW Canada
11 X15 **Riverton** Manitoba, S Canada *51°00′N 97°00′W*
185 C24 **Riverton** Southland, South Island, New Zealand *46°20′S 168°02′E*
30 L13 **Riverton** Illinois, N USA *39°50′N 89°31′W*
36 L3 **Riverton** Utah, W USA *40°32′N 111°57′W*
33 V15 **Riverton** Wyoming, C USA *43°01′N 108°22′W*
14 G10 **River Valley** Ontario, S Canada *46°36′N 80°09′W*
13 P14 **Riverview** New Brunswick, SE Canada *46°03′N 64°47′W*
103 O17 **Rivesaltes** Pyrénées-Orientales, S France *42°46′N 02°48′E*
36 H11 **Riviera** Arizona, SW USA *35°06′N 114°36′W*
25 S15 **Riviera** Texas, SW USA *27°15′N 97°48′W*
23 Z14 **Riviera Beach** Florida, SE USA *26°46′N 80°03′W*
15 Q10 **Rivière-à-Pierre** Québec, SE Canada *46°59′N 72°12′W*
15 T9 **Rivière-Bleue** Québec, SE Canada *47°26′N 69°02′W*
15 T8 **Rivière-du-Loup** Québec, SE Canada *47°49′N 69°32′W*
173 Y15 **Rivière du Rempart** NE Mauritius *20°06′S 57°41′E*
45 R12 **Rivière-Pilote** S Martinique *14°29′N 60°54′W*
173 O17 **Rivière St-Etienne, Pointe de la** *headland* SW Réunion
13 S10 **Rivière-St-Paul** Québec, E Canada *51°26′N 57°52′W*
Rivière Sèche ***see*** Bel Air
116 K4 **Rivne** ***Pol.*** Równe, ***Rus.*** Rovno. Rivnens'ka Oblast', NW Ukraine *50°37′N 26°16′E*
Rivne ***see*** Rivnens'ka Oblast'
116 K3 **Rivnens'ka Oblast'** ***var.*** Rivne, ***Rus.*** Rovenskaya Oblast'. ◈ *province* NW Ukraine
106 B8 **Rivoli** Piemonte, NW Italy *45°04′N 07°31′E*
159 Q14 **Riwoqê** ***var.*** Racaka. Xizang Zizhiqu, W China *31°10′N 96°25′E*
99 H19 **Rixensart** Walloon Brabant, C Belgium *50°43′N 04°32′E*
Riyadh/Riyāḍ, Minṭaqat ar ***see*** Ar Riyāḍ
Riyāq ***see*** Rayak
Rizaiyeh ***see*** Orūmīyeh
137 P11 **Rize** Rize, NE Turkey *41°03′N 40°33′E*
137 P11 **Rize** ***prev.*** Çoruh. ◈ *province* NE Turkey
161 R5 **Rizhao** Shandong, E China *35°23′N 119°32′E*
Rizhskiy Zaliv ***see*** Riga, Gulf of
Rizokarpaso/Rizokárpason ***see*** Dipkarpaz
107 O21 **Rizzuto, Capo** *headland* S Italy *38°54′N 17°05′E*
95 F15 **Rjukan** Telemark, S Norway *59°54′N 08°33′E*
95 D16 **Rjuven** ▲▲ S Norway
76 H9 **Rkîz** Trarza, W Mauritania *16°50′N 15°20′W*
115 Q23 **Ro** ***prev.*** Ágios Geórgios. *island* SE Greece
95 H14 **Roa** Oppland, S Norway *60°16′N 10°38′E*
105 N5 **Roa** Castilla y León, N Spain *41°42′N 03°55′W*
45 T9 **Road Town** ○ (British Virgin Islands) Tortola, C British Virgin Islands *18°28′N 64°39′W*
96 F6 **Roag, Loch** *inlet* NW Scotland, United Kingdom
37 O5 **Roan Cliffs** *cliff* Colorado/Utah, W USA
21 P9 **Roan High Knob** ***var.*** Roan Mountain. ▲ North Carolina/Tennessee, SE USA *36°09′N 82°07′W*
Roan Mountain ***see*** Roan High Knob
103 Q10 **Roanne** ***anc.*** Rodunma. Loire, E France *46°03′N 04°04′E*
23 R4 **Roanoke** Alabama, S USA *33°09′N 85°22′W*
21 S7 **Roanoke** Virginia, NE USA *37°16′N 79°57′W*
21 Z9 **Roanoke Island** *island* North Carolina, SE USA
21 W8 **Roanoke Rapids** North Carolina, SE USA *36°27′N 77°39′W*
21 X9 **Roanoke River** ≈ North Carolina/Virginia, SE USA
37 O4 **Roan Plateau** *plain* Utah, W USA
37 R5 **Roaring Fork River** ≈ Colorado, C USA
25 O5 **Roaring Springs** Texas, SW USA *33°54′N 100°51′W*
42 J4 **Roatán** ***var.*** Coxen Hole, Coxin Hole. Islas de la Bahía, N Honduras *16°19′N 86°33′W*
42 I4 **Roatán, Isla de** *island* Islas de la Bahía, N Honduras
Roat Kampuchea ***see*** Cambodia
Roazon ***see*** Rennes
143 T7 **Robāṭ-e Chāh Gonbad** Yazd, E Iran *33°24′N 57°43′E*
143 R7 **Robāṭ-e Khān** Yazd, C Iran *33°24′N 56°04′E*
143 T7 **Robāṭ-e Khvosh Āb** Yazd, E Iran
143 R8 **Robāṭ-e Posht-e Bādām** Yazd, NE Iran *33°01′N 55°34′E*
143 Q8 **Robāṭ-e Rīzāb** Yazd, C Iran
175 S8 **Robbie Ridge** *undersea feature* W Pacific Ocean
21 T10 **Robbins** North Carolina, SE USA *35°25′N 79°35′W*
183 N15 **Robbins Island** *island* Tasmania, SE Australia
21 N10 **Robbinsville** North Carolina, SE USA *35°18′N 83°49′W*
182 J12 **Robe** South Australia *37°11′S 139°48′E*
21 W9 **Robersonville** North Carolina, SE USA *35°49′N 77°15′W*
45 V10 **Robert L. Bradshaw** ✈ (Basseterre) Saint Kitts, Saint Kitts and Nevis *17°16′N 62°43′W*
25 P8 **Robert Lee** Texas, SW USA *31°50′N 100°30′W*
35 V5 **Roberts Creek Mountain** ▲ Nevada, W USA *39°52′N 116°16′W*
93 J15 **Robertsfors** Västerbotten, N Sweden *64°12′N 20°50′E*
27 R11 **Robert S. Kerr Reservoir** ⊠ Oklahoma, C USA
38 L12 **Roberts Mountain** ▲ Nunivak Island, Alaska, USA *60°01′N 166°15′W*
83 F26 **Robertson** Western Cape, SW South Africa *33°48′S 19°53′E*
194 H4 **Robertson Island** *island* Antarctica
76 J16 **Robertsport** W Liberia *06°45′N 11°15′W*
182 J8 **Robertstown** South Australia *34°00′S 139°04′E*
Robert Williams ***see*** Caála
15 P7 **Roberval** Québec, SE Canada *48°31′N 72°16′W*
31 N15 **Robinson** Illinois, N USA *39°00′N 87°44′W*
193 U11 **Róbinson Crusoe, Isla** *island* Islas Juan Fernández, Chile, E Pacific Ocean
180 J9 **Robinson Range** ▲▲ Western Australia
182 M9 **Robinvale** Victoria, SE Australia *34°37′S 142°45′E*
105 P11 **Robledo** Castilla-La Mancha, C Spain *38°45′N 02°27′W*
54 G5 **Robles** ***var.*** La Paz, Robles La Paz. Cesar, N Colombia *10°24′N 73°11′W*
Robles La Paz ***see*** Robles
11 V15 **Roblin** Manitoba, S Canada *51°15′N 101°20′W*
11 S17 **Robsart** Saskatchewan, S Canada *49°22′N 109°15′W*
11 N15 **Robson, Mount** ▲ British Columbia, SW Canada *53°09′N 119°16′W*
25 T14 **Robstown** Texas, SW USA *27°47′N 97°40′W*
25 P6 **Roby** Texas, SW USA *32°42′N 100°23′W*
104 E11 **Roca, Cabo da** *cape* C Portugal
Rocadas ***see*** Xangongo
41 S14 **Roca Partida, Punta** *headland* C Mexico *18°43′N 95°11′W*
47 X6 **Rocas, Atol das** *island* E Brazil
107 L18 **Roccadaspide** ***var.*** Rocca d'Aspide. Campania, S Italy *40°25′N 15°12′E*
Rocca d'Aspide ***see*** Roccadaspide
107 K15 **Roccaraso** Abruzzo, C Italy *41°49′N 14°01′E*
106 H10 **Rocca San Casciano** Emilia-Romagna, C Italy *44°06′N 11°51′E*
106 G13 **Roccastrada** Toscana, C Italy *43°00′N 11°09′E*
61 G20 **Rocha** Rocha, E Uruguay *34°30′S 54°22′W*
61 G19 **Rocha** ◈ *department* E Uruguay
97 L17 **Rochdale** NW England, United Kingdom *53°38′N 02°09′W*
102 L11 **Rochechouart** Haute-Vienne, C France *45°49′N 00°49′E*
99 J22 **Rochefort** Namur, SE Belgium *50°10′N 05°13′E*
102 J11 **Rochefort** ***var.*** Rochefort sur Mer. Charente-Maritime, W France *45°57′N 00°58′W*
Rochefort sur Mer ***see*** Rochefort
125 N10 **Rochegda** Arkhangel'skaya Oblast', NW Russian Federation *62°37′N 43°21′E*
30 L10 **Rochelle** Illinois, N USA *41°54′N 89°03′W*
25 Q9 **Rochelle** Texas, SW USA *31°13′N 99°10′W*
15 V3 **Rochers Ouest, Rivière aux** ≈ Québec, SE Canada
97 O22 **Rochester** ***anc.*** Durobrivae. SE England, United Kingdom *51°24′N 00°30′E*
31 O12 **Rochester** Indiana, N USA *41°03′N 86°13′W*
29 W10 **Rochester** Minnesota, N USA *44°01′N 92°28′W*
19 O9 **Rochester** New Hampshire, NE USA *43°18′N 70°58′W*
18 F9 **Rochester** New York, NE USA *43°09′N 77°37′W*
25 P5 **Rochester** Texas, SW USA *33°19′N 99°51′W*
31 S9 **Rochester Hills** Michigan, N USA *42°39′N 83°04′W*
Rocheuses, Montagnes/Rockies ***see*** Rocky Mountains
64 M6 **Rockall** *island* N Atlantic Ocean, United Kingdom
64 L6 **Rockall Bank** *undersea feature* N Atlantic Ocean
84 B8 **Rockall Rise** *undersea feature* N Atlantic Ocean *59°00′N 14°00′W*
84 C9 **Rockall Trough** *undersea feature* N Atlantic Ocean *57°00′N 12°00′W*
35 U2 **Rock Creek** ≈ Nevada, W USA
25 T10 **Rockdale** Texas, SW USA *30°39′N 96°58′W*
195 N12 **Rockefeller Plateau** *plateau* Antarctica
30 K11 **Rock Falls** Illinois, N USA *41°46′N 89°41′W*
23 Q5 **Rockford** Alabama, S USA *32°53′N 86°11′W*
30 L10 **Rockford** Illinois, N USA *42°16′N 89°06′W*
15 Q12 **Rock Forest** Québec, SE Canada *45°21′N 71°58′W*
11 T17 **Rockglen** Saskatchewan, S Canada *49°11′N 105°57′W*
181 Y8 **Rockhampton** Queensland, E Australia *23°31′S 150°31′E*
21 R11 **Rock Hill** South Carolina, SE USA *34°55′N 81°01′W*
180 I13 **Rockingham** Western Australia *32°16′S 115°21′E*
21 T11 **Rockingham** North Carolina, SE USA *34°56′N 79°47′W*
30 J11 **Rock Island** Illinois, N USA *41°30′N 90°34′W*
25 U12 **Rock Island** Texas, SW USA *29°31′N 96°33′W*
14 C10 **Rock Lake** Ontario, S Canada *46°25′N 83°49′W*
29 O2 **Rock Lake** North Dakota, N USA *48°45′N 99°12′W*
14 I12 **Rock Lake** ◎ Ontario, SE Canada
14 M12 **Rockland** Ontario, SE Canada *45°33′N 75°16′W*
19 R7 **Rockland** Maine, NE USA *44°08′N 69°06′W*
182 L11 **Rocklands Reservoir** ⊠ Victoria, SE Australia
35 O7 **Rocklin** California, W USA *38°48′N 121°13′W*
23 R3 **Rockmart** Georgia, SE USA *34°00′N 85°02′W*
31 N16 **Rockport** Indiana, N USA *37°53′N 87°04′W*
27 Q1 **Rock Port** Missouri, C USA *40°26′N 95°30′W*
25 T14 **Rockport** Texas, SW USA *28°02′N 99°04′W*
32 I7 **Rockport** Washington, NW USA *48°28′N 121°36′W*
29 S11 **Rock Rapids** Iowa, C USA *43°25′N 96°10′W*
30 K11 **Rock River** ≈ Illinois/Wisconsin, N USA
44 I3 **Rock Sound** Eleuthera Island, C Bahamas *24°52′N 76°10′W*
25 P11 **Rocksprings** Texas, SW USA *30°02′N 100°14′W*
33 U17 **Rock Springs** Wyoming, C USA *41°35′N 109°12′W*
55 T9 **Rockstone** C Guyana *05°58′N 58°33′W*
29 S12 **Rock Valley** Iowa, C USA *43°12′N 96°17′W*
31 N14 **Rockville** Indiana, N USA *39°45′N 87°15′W*
21 W3 **Rockville** Maryland, NE USA *39°05′N 77°10′W*
25 U6 **Rockwall** Texas, SW USA *32°56′N 96°27′W*
29 U13 **Rockwell City** Iowa, C USA *42°24′N 94°37′W*
31 S10 **Rockwood** Michigan, N USA *42°04′N 83°15′W*
20 M9 **Rockwood** Tennessee, S USA *35°52′N 84°41′W*
25 Q8 **Rockwood** Texas, SW USA *31°29′N 99°23′W*
37 U6 **Rocky Ford** Colorado, C USA *38°03′N 103°45′W*
14 D9 **Rocky Island Lake** ◎ Ontario, S Canada
21 V9 **Rocky Mount** North Carolina, SE USA *35°56′N 77°48′W*
21 S7 **Rocky Mount** Virginia, NE USA *37°00′N 79°53′W*
33 Q8 **Rocky Mountain** ▲ Montana, NW USA *47°45′N 112°46′W*
11 P15 **Rocky Mountain House** Alberta, SW Canada *52°24′N 114°52′W*
37 T3 **Rocky Mountain National Park** *national park* Colorado, C USA
2 E12 **Rocky Mountains** ***var.*** Rockies, ***Fr.*** Montagnes Rocheuses. ▲▲ Canada/USA
42 H1 **Rocky Point** *headland* NE Belize *18°21′N 88°04′W*
83 A17 **Rocky Point** *headland* NW Namibia *19°01′S 12°27′E*
95 F14 **Rødberg** Buskerud, S Norway *60°16′N 09°00′E*
95 I25 **Rødby** Sjælland, SE Denmark *54°42′N 11°24′E*
95 I25 **Rødbyhavn** Sjælland, SE Denmark *54°39′N 11°24′E*
13 T10 **Roddickton** Newfoundland, Newfoundland and Labrador, SE Canada *50°51′N 56°03′W*
95 F23 **Rødding** Syddanmark, SW Denmark *55°22′N 09°04′E*
95 M22 **Rödeby** Blekinge, S Sweden *56°16′N 15°35′E*
98 N6 **Roden** Drenthe, NE Netherlands *53°08′N 06°26′E*
62 H9 **Rodeo** San Juan, W Argentina *30°12′S 69°06′W*
103 O14 **Rodez** ***anc.*** Segodunum. Aveyron, S France *44°21′N 02°34′E*
Rodholívos ***see*** Rodolívos
Rodhópi Óri ***see*** Rhodope Mountains
Ródhos/Rodi ***see*** Ródos
107 N15 **Rodi Gargancio** Puglia, SE Italy *41°54′N 15°51′E*
101 N20 **Roding** Bayern, SE Germany *49°12′N 12°30′E*
113 J19 **Rodinit, Kepi i** *headland* W Albania *41°35′N 19°27′E*
116 I9 **Rodnei, Munţii** ▲▲ N Romania
184 L4 **Rodney, Cape** *headland* North Island, New Zealand *36°16′S 174°48′E*
38 L9 **Rodney, Cape** *headland* Alaska, USA *64°39′N 166°24′W*
124 M16 **Rodniki** Ivanovskaya Oblast', W Russian Federation *57°04′N 41°45′E*
119 Q16 **Rodnya** Mahilyowskaya Voblasts', E Belarus *53°31′N 32°07′E*
Rodó ***see*** José Enrique Rodó
114 H13 **Rodolívos** ***var.*** Rodholívos. Kentrikí Makedonía, NE Greece *40°55′N 24°00′E*
Rodopi ***see*** Rhodope Mountains
115 O22 **Ródos** ***var.*** Ródhos, ***Eng.*** Rhodes, ***It.*** Rodi. Ródos, Dodekánisa, Greece, Aegean Sea *36°26′N 28°14′E*
115 O22 **Ródos** ***var.*** Ródhos, ***Eng.*** Rhodes, ***It.*** Rodi; ***anc.*** Rhodos. *island* Dodekánisa, Greece, Aegean Sea
Rodosto ***see*** Tekirdağ
59 A14 **Rodrigues** Amazonas, W Brazil *06°50′S 73°45′W*
173 P8 **Rodrigues** ***var.*** Rodriquez. *island* E Mauritius
Rodriquez ***see*** Rodrigues
Rodunma ***see*** Roanne
180 I7 **Roebourne** Western Australia *20°49′S 117°04′E*
83 J20 **Roedtan** Limpopo, NE South Africa *24°37′S 29°05′E*
98 H11 **Roelofarendsveen** Zuid-Holland, W Netherlands *52°12′N 04°37′E*
Roepat ***see*** Rupat, Pulau
Roer ***see*** Rur
99 M16 **Roermond** Limburg, SE Netherlands *51°12′N 06°E*
99 C18 **Roeselare** ***Fr.*** Roulers; ***prev.*** Rousselaere. West-Vlaanderen, W Belgium *50°57′N 03°08′E*
9 P8 **Roes Welcome Sound** *strait* Nunavut, N Canada
Roeteng ***see*** Ruteng
Rofreit ***see*** Rovereto
Rogachëv ***see*** Rahachow
57 L15 **Rogagua, Laguna** ◎ NW Bolivia
95 C16 **Rogaland** ◈ *county* S Norway
25 Y9 **Roganville** Texas, SW USA *30°49′N 93°54′W*
109 W11 **Rogaška Slatina** ***Ger.*** Rohitsch-Sauerbrunn; ***prev.*** Rogatec-Slatina. E Slovenia *46°13′N 15°38′E*
Rogatec-Slatina ***see*** Rogaška Slatina
112 J13 **Rogatica** Republika Srpska, SE Bosnia and Herzegovina *43°50′N 18°55′E*
Rogatin ***see*** Rohatyn
93 F17 **Rogen** ◎ C Sweden
27 S9 **Rogers** Arkansas, C USA *36°19′N 94°07′W*
29 P5 **Rogers** North Dakota, N USA *47°03′N 98°12′W*
25 T9 **Rogers** Texas, SW USA *30°53′N 97°10′W*
31 R5 **Rogers City** Michigan, N USA *45°25′N 83°49′W*
Roger Simpson Island ***see*** Abemama
35 T14 **Rogers Lake** *salt flat* California, W USA
21 Q8 **Rogers, Mount** ▲ Virginia, NE USA *36°39′N 81°32′W*
33 O16 **Rogerson** Idaho, NW USA *42°11′N 114°36′W*
11 O16 **Rogers Pass** *pass* British Columbia, SW Canada
21 O8 **Rogersville** Tennessee, S USA *36°26′N 83°01′W*
99 L16 **Roggel** Limburg, SE Netherlands *51°16′N 05°55′E*
Roggeveen ***see*** Roggewein, Cabo
193 R10 **Roggeveen Basin** *undersea feature* E Pacific Ocean *31°30′S 95°30′W*
191 X16 **Roggewein, Cabo** ***var.*** Roggeveen. *headland* Easter Island, Chile, E Pacific Ocean *27°07′S 109°15′W*
103 Y13 **Rogliano** Corse, France, C Mediterranean Sea *42°58′N 09°25′E*
107 N21 **Rogliano** Calabria, SW Italy *39°09′N 16°18′E*
92 G12 **Rognan** Nordland, C Norway *67°04′N 15°21′E*
100 K10 **Rögnitz** ≈ N Germany
Rogozhina/Rogozhinë ***see*** Rrogozhinë
110 G10 **Rogoźno** Wielkopolskie, C Poland *52°46′N 16°58′E*
32 E15 **Rogue River** ≈ Oregon, NW USA
116 I6 **Rohatyn** ***Rus.*** Rogatin. Ivano-Frankivs'ka Oblast', W Ukraine *49°25′N 24°35′E*
189 O14 **Rohi** Pohnpei, E Micronesia
Rohitsch-Sauerbrunn ***see*** Rogaška Slatina
149 Q13 **Rohri** Sind, SE Pakistan *27°39′N 68°57′E*
152 I10 **Rohtak** Haryāna, N India *28°57′N 76°38′E*
Roi Ed ***see*** Roi Et
167 R9 **Roi Et** ***var.*** Muang Roi Et, Roi Ed. Roi Et, E Thailand *16°05′N 103°38′E*
191 U9 **Roi Georges, Îles du** *island group* Îles Tuamotu, C French Polynesia
153 Y10 **Roing** Arunāchal Pradesh, NE India *28°06′N 95°46′E*
118 E7 **Roja** NW Latvia *57°31′N 22°44′E*
61 B20 **Rojas** Buenos Aires, E Argentina *34°10′S 60°45′W*
149 R12 **Rojhān** Punjab, E Pakistan *28°39′N 70°00′E*
41 Q12 **Rojo, Cabo** *headland* C Mexico *21°33′N 97°19′W*
45 Q10 **Rojo, Cabo** *headland* W Puerto Rico *17°57′N 67°10′W*
168 K10 **Rokan Kiri, Sungai** ≈ Sumatera, W Indonesia
118 I11 **Rokiškis** Panevėžys, NE Lithuania *55°58′N 25°35′E*
165 R7 **Rokkasho** Aomori, Honshū, C Japan *40°59′N 141°22′E*
111 B17 **Rokycany** ***Ger.*** Rokytzan. Plzeňský Kraj, W Czech Republic *49°45′N 13°36′E*
117 P6 **Rokytne** Kyyivs'ka Oblast', N Ukraine *49°40′N 30°29′E*
116 L3 **Rokytne** Rivnens'ka Oblast', NW Ukraine *51°19′N 27°09′E*
Rokytzan ***see*** Rokycany
158 L11 **Rola Co** ◎ W China
29 V13 **Roland** Iowa, C USA *42°10′N 93°30′W*
95 D15 **Røldal** Hordaland, S Norway *59°52′N 06°49′E*
98 O7 **Rolde** Drenthe, NE Netherlands *52°58′N 06°39′E*
29 O2 **Rolette** North Dakota, N USA *48°39′N 99°50′W*
27 V6 **Rolla** Missouri, C USA *37°56′N 91°47′W*
29 O2 **Rolla** North Dakota, N USA *48°51′N 99°37′W*
108 A10 **Rolle** Vaud, W Switzerland *46°27′N 06°19′E*
181 X8 **Rolleston** Queensland, E Australia *24°30′S 148°36′E*
185 H19 **Rolleston** Canterbury, South Island, New Zealand *43°34′S 172°24′E*
185 G18 **Rolleston Range** ▲▲ South Island, New Zealand
14 H8 **Rollet** Québec, SE Canada *47°56′N 79°14′W*
22 J4 **Rolling Fork** Mississippi, S USA *32°54′N 90°52′W*
20 L6 **Rolling Fork** ≈ Kentucky, S USA
14 J11 **Rolphton** Ontario, SE Canada *46°09′N 77°43′W*
Röm ***see*** Rømø
181 X10 **Roma** Queensland, E Australia *26°37′S 148°54′E*
107 I15 **Roma** ***Eng.*** Rome. ● (Italy) Lazio, C Italy *41°53′N 12°30′E*
95 P19 **Roma** Gotland, SE Sweden *57°31′N 18°28′E*
21 T14 **Romain, Cape** *headland* South Carolina, SE USA *33°00′N 79°21′W*
13 P11 **Romaine** ≈ Newfoundland and Labrador/Québec, E Canada
25 R17 **Roma Los Saenz** Texas, SW USA *26°24′N 99°01′W*
114 H8 **Roman** Vratsa, NW Bulgaria *43°09′N 23°56′E*
116 L10 **Roman** ***Hung.*** Románvásár. Neamţ, NE Romania *46°46′N 26°56′E*
64 M13 **Romanche Fracture Zone** *tectonic feature* E Atlantic Ocean
61 C15 **Romang** Santa Fe, C Argentina *29°30′S 59°46′W*
171 R15 **Romang, Pulau** ***var.*** Pulau Roma. *island* Kepulauan Damar, E Indonesia
171 R15 **Romang, Selat** *strait* Nusa Tenggara, S Indonesia
116 J11 **Romania** ***Bul.*** Rumŭniya, ***Ger.*** Rumänien, ***Hung.*** Románia, ***Rom.*** România, ***SCr.*** Rumunjska, ***Ukr.*** Rumuniya, ***prev.*** Republica Socialistă România, Roumania, Rumania, Socialist Republic of Romania, ***prev.Rom.*** Romînia. ◆ *republic* SE Europe
România, Republica Socialistă ***see*** Romania
Romania, Socialist Republic of ***see*** Romania
117 T7 **Romaniv** ***Rus.*** Dneprodzerzhinsk, ***prev.*** Dniprodzerzhyns'k, ***prev.*** Kamenskoye. Dnipropetrovs'ka Oblast', E Ukraine *48°30′N 34°35′E*
117 X7 **Romaniv** ***Rus.*** Dzerzhinsk; ***prev.*** Dzerzhyns'k. Donets'ka Oblast', SE Ukraine *48°21′N 37°50′E*
116 M5 **Romaniv** ***prev.*** Dzerzhyns'k. Zhytomyrs'ka Oblast', N Ukraine *50°07′N 27°56′E*
23 W16 **Romano, Cape** *headland* Florida, SE USA *25°51′N 81°40′W*
44 G5 **Romano, Cayo** *island* C Cuba
123 O13 **Romanovka** Respublika Buryatiya, S Russian Federation *53°10′N 112°34′E*
127 N8 **Romanovka** Saratovskaya Oblast', W Russian Federation *51°45′N 42°45′E*
108 I6 **Romanshorn** Thurgau, NE Switzerland *47°34′N 09°23′E*
103 R12 **Romans-sur-Isère** Drôme, E France *45°03′N 05°03′E*
189 U12 **Romanum** *island* Chuuk, C Micronesia
Románvásár ***see*** Roman
39 S5 **Romanzof Mountains** ▲▲ Alaska, USA
Roma, Pulau ***see*** Romang, Pulau
103 S4 **Rombas** Moselle, NE France *49°15′N 06°04′E*
23 R2 **Rome** Georgia, SE USA *34°01′N 85°02′W*
18 I9 **Rome** New York, NE USA *43°13′N 75°28′W*
Rome ***see*** Roma
31 S9 **Romeo** Michigan, N USA *42°48′N 83°00′W*
Römerstadt ***see*** Rýmařov
Rometan ***see*** Romiton
103 P5 **Romilly-sur-Seine** Aube, N France *48°31′N 03°44′E*
Romînia ***see*** Romania
146 L11 **Romiton** ***Rus.*** Rometan. Buxoro Viloyati, C Uzbekistan *39°56′N 64°21′E*
21 U3 **Romney** West Virginia, NE USA *39°21′N 78°44′W*
117 S4 **Romny** Sums'ka Oblast', NE Ukraine *50°45′N 33°30′E*
95 E24 **Rømø** ***Ger.*** Röm. *island* SW Denmark
117 S5 **Romodan** Poltavs'ka Oblast', NE Ukraine *50°00′N 33°20′E*
127 P5 **Romodanovo** Respublika Mordoviya, W Russian Federation *54°25′N 45°24′E*
Romorantin ***see*** Romorantin-Lanthenay
103 N8 **Romorantin-Lanthenay** ***var.*** Romorantin. Loir-et-Cher, C France *47°22′N 01°44′E*
94 F9 **Romsdal** *physical region* S Norway
94 F10 **Romsdalen** *valley* S Norway
94 E9 **Romsdalsfjorden** *fjord* S Norway
33 P8 **Ronan** Montana, NW USA *47°31′N 114°06′W*
59 M14 **Roncador** Maranhão, E Brazil *05°48′S 45°08′W*
186 M7 **Roncador Reef** *reef* N Solomon Islands
59 J17 **Roncador, Serra do** ▲▲ C Brazil
21 S6 **Ronceverte** West Virginia, NE USA *37°45′N 80°27′W*
107 H14 **Ronciglione** Lazio, C Italy *42°16′N 12°15′E*
104 L15 **Ronda** Andalucía, S Spain *36°45′N 05°10′W*
94 G11 **Rondane** ▲▲ S Norway
104 L15 **Ronda, Serranía de** ▲▲ S Spain
95 H22 **Rønde** Midtjylland, C Denmark *56°18′N 10°28′E*
Ronde, Île ***see*** Round Island
Rōṇdik ***see*** Rongrik Atoll
59 E16 **Rondônia** ***off.*** Estado de Rondônia; ***prev.*** Território de Rondônia. ◈ *state* W Brazil
Rondônia, Estado de ***see*** Rondônia
Rondônia, Território de ***see*** Rondônia
59 I18 **Rondonópolis** Mato Grosso, W Brazil *16°29′S 54°37′W*
94 G11 **Rondslottet** ▲ S Norway *61°54′N 09°48′E*
95 P20 **Ronehamn** Gotland, SE Sweden *57°10′N 18°30′E*
160 L13 **Rong'an** ***var.*** Chang'an, Rongan. Guangxi Zhuangzu Zizhiqu, S China *25°14′N 109°20′E*
Rongan ***see*** Rong'an
Rongcheng ***see*** Rongxian, Guangxi, China
Rongcheng ***see*** Jianli, Hubei, China
189 R4 **Rongelap Atoll** ***var.*** Rōnlap. *atoll* Ralik Chain, NW Marshall Islands
Rongerik ***see*** Rongrik Atoll
160 K12 **Rongjiang** ***var.*** Guzhou. Guizhou, S China *25°59′N 108°27′E*
160 L13 **Rong Jiang** ≈ S China
Rongjiang ***see*** Nankang
Rong, Kas ***see*** Rŭng, Kaôh
167 P8 **Rong Kwang** Phrae, NW Thailand *18°19′N 100°18′E*
189 T4 **Rongrik Atoll** ***var.*** Rōṇdik, Rongerik. *atoll* Ralik Chain, N Marshall Islands
189 X2 **Rongrong** *island* SE Marshall Islands
160 L13 **Rongshui** ***var.*** Rongshui Miaozu Zizhixian. Guangxi Zhuangzu Zizhiqu, S China *25°05′N 109°09′E*
Rongshui Miaozu Zizhixian ***see*** Rongshui
118 I6 **Rõngu** ***Ger.*** Ringen. Tartumaa, SE Estonia *58°10′N 26°17′E*
Rongwo ***see*** Tongren
160 L15 **Rongxian** ***var.*** Rongzhou; ***prev.*** Rongcheng. Guangxi Zhuangzu Zizhiqu, S China *22°52′N 110°33′E*
Rongzhag ***see*** Danba
Rongzhou ***see*** Rongxian
Roniu, Mont ***see*** Rooniu, Mont
189 N13 **Ronkiti** Pohnpei, E Micronesia *06°48′N 158°10′E*
Rōnlap ***see*** Rongelap Atoll
95 L24 **Rønne** Bornholm, E Denmark *55°07′N 14°43′E*
95 M22 **Ronneby** Blekinge, S Sweden *56°12′N 15°18′E*
194 J7 **Ronne Entrance** *inlet* Antarctica
194 L6 **Ronne Ice Shelf** *ice shelf* Antarctica
99 E19 **Ronse** ***Fr.*** Renaix. Oost-Vlaanderen, SW Belgium *50°45′N 03°36′E*
30 K14 **Roodhouse** Illinois, N USA *39°28′N 90°22′W*
83 C19 **Rooibank** Erongo, W Namibia *23°04′S 14°34′E*
Rooke Island ***see*** Umboi Island
65 N24 **Rookery Point** *headland* NE Tristan da Cunha *37°03′S 12°15′W*
191 R8 **Rooniu, Mont** ***prev.*** Mont Roniu. ⛰ Tahiti, W French Polynesia *17°49′S 149°12′W*
171 V13 **Roon, Pulau** *island* E Indonesia
173 V7 **Roo Rise** *undersea feature* E Indian Ocean
152 J9 **Roorkee** Uttarakhand, N India *29°51′N 77°54′E*
99 H15 **Roosendaal** Noord-Brabant, S Netherlands *51°32′N 04°29′E*
25 P10 **Roosevelt** Texas, SW USA *30°28′N 100°06′W*
37 N3 **Roosevelt** Utah, W USA *40°18′N 109°59′W*
47 T8 **Roosevelt** ≈ W Brazil
195 O13 **Roosevelt Island** *island* Antarctica
10 L10 **Roosevelt, Mount** ▲ British Columbia, W Canada *58°28′N 125°22′W*
11 P17 **Roosville** British Columbia, SW Canada *48°59′N 115°03′W*
29 X10 **Root River** ≈ Minnesota, N USA
Ropar ***see*** Rūpnagar
111 N16 **Ropczyce** Podkarpackie, SE Poland *50°04′N 21°31′E*
181 Q3 **Roper Bar** Northern Territory, N Australia *14°45′S 134°30′E*
24 M5 **Ropesville** Texas, SW USA *33°24′N 102°09′W*
102 K14 **Roquefort** Landes, SW France *44°01′N 00°18′W*
61 C21 **Roque Pérez** Buenos Aires, E Argentina *35°25′S 59°24′W*
58 E10 **Roraima** ***off.*** Estado de Roraima; ***prev.*** Território de Rio Branco, Território de Roraima. ◈ *state* N Brazil
Roraima, Estado de ***see*** Roraima
58 F9 **Roraima, Mount** ▲ N South America *05°10′N 60°36′W*
Roraima, Território de ***see*** Roraima
94 I9 **Røros** Sør-Trøndelag, S Norway *62°37′N 11°25′E*
108 I7 **Rorschach** Sankt Gallen, NE Switzerland *47°28′N 09°30′E*
93 E14 **Rørvik** Nord-Trøndelag, C Norway *64°54′N 11°15′E*
119 G17 **Ros'** ***Rus.*** Ross'. Hrodzyenskaya Voblasts', W Belarus *53°25′N 24°24′E*
185 F17 **Ross** West Coast, South Island, New Zealand *42°54′S 170°52′E*
119 G17 **Ros'** ***Rus.*** Ross'. ≈ W Belarus
10 J7 **Ross** ≈ Yukon Territory, W Canada
117 O6 **Ros'** ≈ N Ukraine
44 K7 **Rosa, Lake** ◎ Great Inagua, S Bahamas
32 M9 **Rosalia** Washington, NW USA *47°14′N 117°22′W*
191 W15 **Rosalia, Punta** *headland* Easter Island, Chile, E Pacific Ocean *27°04′S 109°19′W*
45 P12 **Rosalie** E Dominica *15°22′N 61°15′W*
35 T14 **Rosamond** California, W USA *34°51′N 118°09′W*
35 S14 **Rosamond Lake** *salt flat* California, W USA
96 H8 **Ross and Cromarty** *cultural region* N Scotland, United Kingdom
61 B18 **Rosario** Santa Fe, C Argentina *32°56′S 60°39′W*
40 J11 **Rosario** Sinaloa, C Mexico *23°00′N 105°51′W*
40 G6 **Rosario** Sonora, NW Mexico *27°53′N 109°18′W*
62 O6 **Rosario** San Pedro, C Paraguay *24°26′S 57°06′W*
61 E20 **Rosario** Colonia, SW Uruguay *34°20′S 57°26′W*
54 H5 **Rosario** Zulia, NW Venezuela *10°18′N 72°19′W*
Rosario ***see*** Nishino-shima
Rosario ***see*** Rosarito
40 B4 **Rosario, Bahía del** *bay* NW Mexico
62 K6 **Rosario de la Frontera** Salta, N Argentina *25°50′S 65°00′W*
61 C18 **Rosario del Tala** Entre Ríos, E Argentina *32°20′S 59°10′W*
61 F16 **Rosário do Sul** Rio Grande do Sul, S Brazil *30°15′S 54°55′W*
59 H18 **Rosário Oeste** Mato Grosso, W Brazil *14°50′S 56°25′W*
40 D5 **Rosarito** Baja California Norte, NW Mexico *28°27′N 113°58′W*
40 B1 **Rosarito** ***var.*** Rosario. Baja California Norte, NW Mexico *32°25′N 117°04′W*
40 F7 **Rosarito** Baja California Sur, NW Mexico *26°28′N 111°41′W*
104 L9 **Rosarito, Embalse del** ⊠ W Spain
107 N22 **Rosarno** Calabria, SW Italy *38°29′N 15°59′E*
56 B5 **Rosa Zárate** ***var.*** Quinindé. Esmeraldas, SW Ecuador *0°14′N 79°28′W*
Roscianum ***see*** Rossano
29 O8 **Roscoe** South Dakota, N USA *45°24′N 99°19′W*
25 P7 **Roscoe** Texas, SW USA *32°27′N 100°32′W*
102 F5 **Roscoff** Finistère, NW France *48°43′N 04°00′W*
Ros Comáin ***see*** Roscommon
97 C17 **Roscommon** ***Ir.*** Ros Comáin. C Ireland *53°38′N 08°11′W*
31 Q7 **Roscommon** Michigan, N USA *44°30′N 84°35′W*
97 C17 **Roscommon** ***Ir.*** Ros Comáin. *cultural region* C Ireland
Ros. Cré ***see*** Roscrea
97 D19 **Roscrea** ***Ir.*** Ros. Cré. C Ireland *52°57′N 07°47′W*
14 H13 **Rosseau** Ontario, S Canada *45°15′N 79°38′W*
45 X12 **Roseau** ***prev.*** Charlotte Town. ● (Dominica) SW Dominica *15°17′N 61°23′W*
29 S2 **Roseau** Minnesota, N USA *48°51′N 95°45′W*
173 Y16 **Rose Belle** SE Mauritius *20°24′S 57°36′E*
183 O16 **Rosebery** Tasmania, SE Australia *41°51′S 145°33′E*
21 U11 **Roseboro** North Carolina, SE USA *34°58′N 78°31′W*
25 T9 **Rosebud** Texas, SW USA *31°04′N 96°58′W*
33 W10 **Rosebud Creek** ≈ Montana, NW USA
32 F14 **Roseburg** Oregon, NW USA *43°13′N 123°21′W*
22 J3 **Rosedale** Mississippi, S USA *33°51′N 91°01′W*
99 H21 **Rosée** Namur, S Belgium *50°15′N 04°43′E*
55 U8 **Rose Hall** E Guyana *06°14′N 57°30′W*
173 X16 **Rose Hill** W Mauritius *20°14′S 57°29′E*
80 H12 **Roseires, Reservoir** ***var.*** Lake Rusayris. ⊠ E Sudan
Rosenau ***see*** Rožnov pod Radhoštěm
Rosenau ***see*** Rožňava

◆ Country
● Country Capital
◇ Dependent Territory
○ Dependent Territory Capital
◈ Administrative Regions
✈ International Airport
▲ Mountain
▲▲ Mountain Range
⛰ Volcano
≈ River
◎ Lake
⊠ Reservoir

25 V11 **Rosenberg** Texas, SW USA 29°33′N 95°48′W
Rosenberg *see* Olesno, Poland
Rosenberg *see* Ružomberok, Slovakia
100 I10 **Rosengarten** Niedersachsen, N Germany 53°24′N 09°54′E
101 M24 **Rosenheim** Bayern, S Germany 47°51′N 12°08′E
Rosenhof *see* Zilupe
105 X4 **Roses** Cataluña, NE Spain 42°15′N 03°11′E
105 X4 **Roses, Golf de** *gulf* NE Spain
107 K14 **Roseto degli Abruzzi** Abruzzo, C Italy 42°39′N 14°01′E
11 S16 **Rosetown** Saskatchewan, S Canada 51°34′N 107°59′W
Rosetta *see* Rashīd
35 O7 **Roseville** California, W USA 38°44′N 121°16′W
30 J12 **Roseville** Illinois, N USA 40°42′N 90°40′W
29 V8 **Roseville** Minnesota, N USA 45°00′N 93°09′W
29 R7 **Rosholt** South Dakota, N USA 45°51′N 96°42′W
106 F12 **Rosignano Marittimo** Toscana, C Italy 43°24′N 10°28′E
116 I14 **Roşiori de Vede** Teleorman, S Romania 44°06′N 25°00′E
114 K8 **Rositsa** ≈ N Bulgaria
Rositten *see* Rēzekne
95 J23 **Roskilde** Sjælland, E Denmark 55°39′N 12°07′E
Ros Láir *see* Rosslare
126 H5 **Roslavl'** Smolenskaya Oblast', W Russian Federation 54°N 32°57′E
32 I8 **Roslyn** Washington, NW USA 47°13′N 120°52′W
99 K14 **Rosmalen** Noord-Brabant, S Netherlands 51°43′N 05°21′E
Ros Mhic Thriúin *see* New Ross
113 P19 **Rosoman** C FYR Macedonia 41°31′N 21°55′E
102 F6 **Rosporden** Finistère, NW France 47°58′N 03°54′W
Ross' *see* Ros'
107 O20 **Rossano** *anc.* Roscianum. Calabria, SW Italy 39°35′N 16°38′E
22 L5 **Ross Barnett Reservoir** ⊠ Mississippi, S USA
11 W16 **Rossburn** Manitoba, S Canada 50°42′N 100°49′W
14 H13 **Rosseau, Lake** ◎ Ontario, S Canada
186 I10 **Rossel Island** *prev.* Yela Island. *island* SE Papua New Guinea
195 P12 **Ross Ice Shelf** *ice shelf* Antarctica
13 P16 **Rossignol, Lake** ◎ Nova Scotia, SE Canada
83 C19 **Rössing** Erongo, W Namibia 22°31′S 14°52′E
195 Q14 **Ross Island** *island* Antarctica
Rossitten *see* Rybachiy
Rossiyskaya Federatsiya *see* Russian Federation
11 N17 **Rossland** British Columbia, SW Canada 49°03′N 117°49′W
97 F20 **Rosslare** *Ir.* Ros Láir. Wexford, SE Ireland 52°16′N 06°23′W
97 F20 **Rosslare Harbour** Wexford, SE Ireland 52°15′N 06°20′W
101 M14 **Rosslau** Sachsen-Anhalt, E Germany 51°52′N 12°15′E
76 G10 **Rosso** Trarza, SW Mauritania 16°36′N 15°50′W
103 X14 **Rosso, Cap** *headland* Corse, France, C Mediterranean Sea 42°25′N 08°22′E
93 H16 **Rossön** Jämtland, C Sweden 63°54′N 16°21′E
97 K21 **Ross-on-Wye** W England, United Kingdom 51°55′N 02°34′W
Rossony *see* Rasony
126 L9 **Rossosh'** Voronezhskaya Oblast', W Russian Federation 50°10′N 39°34′E
181 Q7 **Ross River** Northern Territory, N Australia 23°36′S 134°30′E
10 J7 **Ross River** Yukon Territory, W Canada 61°57′N 132°26′W
195 O15 **Ross Sea** *sea* Antarctica
92 G13 **Røssvatnet** *Lapp.* Reevhtse. ◎ C Norway
23 R1 **Rossville** Georgia, SE USA 34°59′N 85°22′W
Rostak *see* Ar Rustāq
143 P14 **Rostāq** Hormozgān, S Iran 26°48′N 53°50′E
117 N5 **Rostavytsya** ≈ N Ukraine
11 T15 **Rosthern** Saskatchewan, S Canada 52°40′N 106°20′W
100 M8 **Rostock** Mecklenburg-Vorpommern, NE Germany 54°05′N 12°08′E
124 L16 **Rostov** Yaroslavskaya Oblast', W Russian Federation 57°11′N 39°19′E
Rostov *see* Rostov-na-Donu
126 L12 **Rostov-na-Donu** *var.* Rostov, *Eng.* Rostov-on-Don. Rostovskaya Oblast', SW Russian Federation 47°16′N 39°45′E
Rostov-on-Don *see* Rostov-na-Donu
126 L10 **Rostovskaya Oblast'** ◈ *province* SW Russian Federation
93 J14 **Rosvik** Norrbotten, N Sweden 65°26′N 21°48′E
23 S3 **Roswell** Georgia, SE USA 34°01′N 84°21′W
37 U14 **Roswell** New Mexico, SW USA 33°23′N 104°31′W
94 K12 **Rot** Dalarna, C Sweden 61°16′N 14°04′E
101 I23 **Rot** ≈ S Germany
104 J15 **Rota** Andalucía, S Spain 36°39′N 06°20′W
188 K9 **Rota** *island* S Northern Mariana Islands
25 P6 **Rotan** Texas, SW USA 32°51′N 100°28′W
Rotcher Island *see* Tamana
100 I11 **Rotenburg** Niedersachsen, NW Germany 53°06′N 09°25′E
Rotenburg *see* Rotenburg an der Fulda
101 I16 **Rotenburg an der Fulda** *var.* Rotenburg. Thüringen, C Germany 51°00′N 09°43′E
101 L18 **Roter Main** ≈ E Germany
101 K20 **Roth** Bayern, SE Germany 49°15′N 11°06′E
101 G16 **Rothaargebirge** ▲▲ W Germany
Rothenburg *see* Rothenburg ob der Tauber
101 J20 **Rothenburg ob der Tauber** *var.* Rothenburg. Bayern, S Germany 49°23′N 10°10′E
194 H6 **Rothera** *UK research station* Antarctica 67°28′S 68°31′W
185 I17 **Rotherham** Canterbury, South Island, New Zealand 42°42′S 172°56′E
97 M17 **Rotherham** N England, United Kingdom 53°26′N 01°20′W
96 H12 **Rothesay** W Scotland, United Kingdom 55°49′N 05°03′W
108 E7 **Rothrist** Aargau, N Switzerland 47°18′N 07°54′E
194 H6 **Rothschild Island** *island* Antarctica
171 P17 **Roti, Pulau** *island* S Indonesia
95 H14 **Rotnes** Akershus, S Norway 60°08′N 10°45′E
183 O8 **Roto** New South Wales, SE Australia 33°04′S 145°27′E
184 N8 **Rotoiti, Lake** ◎ North Island, New Zealand
Rotomagus *see* Rouen
107 N19 **Rotondella** Basilicata, S Italy 40°12′N 16°30′E
103 X15 **Rotondo, Monte** ▲ Corse, France, C Mediterranean Sea 42°15′N 09°03′E
185 I15 **Rotoroa, Lake** ◎ South Island, New Zealand
184 N8 **Rotorua** Bay of Plenty, North Island, New Zealand 38°10′S 176°14′E
184 N8 **Rotorua, Lake** ◎ North Island, New Zealand
101 N22 **Rott** ≈ SE Germany
108 F10 **Rotten** ≈ S Switzerland
109 T6 **Rottenmann** Steiermark, E Austria 47°31′N 14°18′E
98 H12 **Rotterdam** Zuid-Holland, SW Netherlands 51°55′N 04°30′E
18 K10 **Rotterdam** New York, NE USA 42°46′N 73°57′W
95 M21 **Rottnen** ◎ S Sweden
98 N4 **Rottumeroog** *island* Waddeneilanden, NE Netherlands
98 N4 **Rottumerplaat** *island* Waddeneilanden, NE Netherlands
101 G23 **Rottweil** Baden-Württemberg, S Germany 48°10′N 08°38′E
191 O7 **Rotui, Mont** ⛰ Moorea, W French Polynesia 17°30′S 149°50′W
103 P1 **Roubaix** Nord, N France 50°42′N 03°10′E
111 C15 **Roudnice nad Labem** *Ger.* Raudnitz an der Elbe. Ústecký Kraj, NW Czech Republic 50°25′N 14°14′E
102 M4 **Rouen** *anc.* Rotomagus. Seine-Maritime, N France 49°26′N 01°05′E
171 X13 **Rouffaer Reserves** *reserve* Papua, E Indonesia
15 N10 **Rouge, Rivière** ≈ Québec, SE Canada
20 J6 **Rough River** ≈ Kentucky, S USA
20 J6 **Rough River Lake** ⊠ Kentucky, S USA
Rouhaïbé *see* Ar Ruḩaybah
102 K11 **Rouillac** Charente, W France 45°46′N 00°04′W
Roulers *see* Roeselare
Roumania *see* Romania
173 Y15 **Round Island** *var.* Île Ronde. *island* NE Mauritius
14 J12 **Round Lake** ◎ Ontario, SE Canada
35 U7 **Round Mountain** Nevada, W USA 38°42′N 117°04′W
25 R10 **Round Mountain** Texas, SW USA 30°25′N 98°20′W
183 U5 **Round Mountain** ▲ New South Wales, SE Australia 30°22′S 152°13′E
25 S10 **Round Rock** Texas, SW USA 30°30′N 97°40′W
33 U10 **Roundup** Montana, NW USA 46°27′N 108°32′W
55 Y10 **Roura** NE French Guiana 04°44′N 52°16′W
Rourkela *see* Rāurkela
96 J4 **Rousay** *island* N Scotland, United Kingdom
Rousselaere *see* Roeselare
103 O17 **Roussillon** *cultural region* S France
15 V7 **Routhierville** Québec, SE Canada 48°09′N 67°07′W
99 K25 **Rouvroy** Luxembourg, SE Belgium 49°33′N 05°28′E
14 I7 **Rouyn-Noranda** Québec, SE Canada 48°16′N 79°03′W
Rouyuan *see* Huachi
Rouyuanchengzi *see* Huachi
92 L12 **Rovaniemi** Lappi, N Finland 66°29′N 25°40′E
106 E7 **Rovato** Lombardia, N Italy 45°34′N 10°03′E
125 N11 **Rovdino** Arkhangel'skaya Oblast', NW Russian Federation 61°36′N 42°28′E
Roven'ki *see* Roven'ky
117 Y8 **Roven'ky** *var.* Roven'ki. Luhans'ka Oblast', E Ukraine 48°05′N 39°20′E
Rovenskaya Oblast' *see* Rivnens'ka Oblast'
Rovenskaya Sloboda *see* Rovyenskaya Slabada
106 G7 **Rovereto** *Ger.* Rofreit. Trentino-Alto Adige, N Italy 45°53′N 11°03′E
167 S12 **Rôviĕng Tbong** Preăh Vihéar, N Cambodia 13°18′N 105°06′E
Rovigno *see* Rovinj
106 H8 **Rovigo** Veneto, NE Italy 45°04′N 11°48′E
112 A10 **Rovinj** *It.* Rovigno. Istra, NW Croatia 45°06′N 13°39′E
54 E10 **Rovira** Tolima, C Colombia 04°15′N 75°15′W
Rovno *see* Rivne
127 P9 **Rovnoye** Saratovskaya Oblast', W Russian Federation 50°43′N 46°03′E
82 Q12 **Rovuma, Rio** *var.* Ruvuma. ≈ Mozambique/Tanzania *see also* Ruvuma
Rovuma, Rio *see* Ruvuma
119 O19 **Rovyenskaya Slabada** *Rus.* Rovenskaya Sloboda. Homyel'skaya Voblasts', SE Belarus 52°13′N 30°19′E
183 R5 **Rowena** New South Wales, SE Australia 29°51′S 148°55′E
21 T11 **Rowland** North Carolina, SE USA 34°32′N 79°17′W
9 P5 **Rowley** ≈ Baffin Island, Nunavut, NE Canada
9 P6 **Rowley Island** *island* Nunavut, NE Canada
173 W8 **Rowley Shoals** *reef* NW Australia
Równe *see* Rivne
171 O4 **Roxas** Mindoro, N Philippines 12°36′N 121°29′E
171 P5 **Roxas City** Panay Island, C Philippines 11°33′N 122°43′E
21 U8 **Roxboro** North Carolina, SE USA 36°24′N 79°00′W
185 D23 **Roxburgh** Otago, South Island, New Zealand 45°32′S 169°18′E
96 K13 **Roxburgh** *cultural region* SE Scotland, United Kingdom
182 H5 **Roxby Downs** South Australia 30°29′S 136°56′E
95 M17 **Roxen** ◎ S Sweden
25 V5 **Roxton** Texas, SW USA 33°33′N 95°43′W
15 P12 **Roxton-Sud** Québec, SE Canada 45°30′N 72°35′W
33 U8 **Roy** Montana, NW USA 47°19′N 108°55′W
37 U10 **Roy** New Mexico, SW USA 35°56′N 104°12′W
97 E17 **Royal Canal** *Ir.* An Chanáil Ríoga. *canal* C Ireland
30 L1 **Royale, Isle** *island* Michigan, N USA
37 S6 **Royal Gorge** *valley* Colorado, C USA
97 M20 **Royal Leamington Spa** *var.* Leamington, Leamington Spa. C England, United Kingdom 52°18′N 01°31′W
97 O23 **Royal Tunbridge Wells** *var.* Tunbridge Wells. SE England, United Kingdom 51°08′N 00°16′E
24 L9 **Royalty** Texas, SW USA 31°21′N 102°51′W
102 J11 **Royan** Charente-Maritime, W France 45°37′N 01°01′W
65 B24 **Roy Cove Settlement** West Falkland, Falkland Islands 51°32′S 60°23′W
103 O3 **Roye** Somme, N France 49°42′N 02°46′E
95 H15 **Røyken** Buskerud, S Norway 59°47′N 10°21′E
93 F14 **Røyrvik** Nord-Trøndelag, C Norway 64°53′N 13°30′E
25 U6 **Royse City** Texas, SW USA 32°58′N 96°19′W
97 O21 **Royston** E England, United Kingdom 52°05′N 00°01′W
23 U2 **Royston** Georgia, SE USA 34°17′N 83°06′W
114 L10 **Roza** *prev.* Gyulovo. Yambol, E Bulgaria 42°29′N 26°30′E
113 L16 **Rožaje** E Montenegro 42°51′N 20°11′E
110 M10 **Różan** Mazowieckie, C Poland 52°36′N 21°27′E
117 O10 **Rozdil'na** Odes'ka Oblast', SW Ukraine 46°51′N 30°03′E
117 S12 **Rozdol'ne** *Rus.* Razdolnoye. Avtonomna Respublika Krym, S Ukraine 45°45′N 33°27′E
Rozhdestvenka *see* Kabanbay Batyr
116 I6 **Rozhnyativ** Ivano-Frankivs'ka Oblast', W Ukraine 48°58′N 24°07′E
116 J3 **Rozhyshche** Volyns'ka Oblast', NW Ukraine 50°54′N 25°16′E
Roznau am Radhost *see* Rožnov pod Radhoštěm
111 L19 **Rožňava** *Ger.* Rosenau, *Hung.* Rozsnyó. Košický Kraj, E Slovakia 48°41′N 20°32′E
116 K10 **Roznov** Neamţ, NE Romania 46°47′N 26°33′E
111 I18 **Rožnov pod Radhoštěm** *Ger.* Rosenau, Roznau am Radhost. Zlínský Kraj, E Czech Republic 49°28′N 18°09′E
Rózsahegy *see* Ružomberok
Rozsnyó *see* Râşnov, Romania
Rozsnyó *see* Rožňava, Slovakia
113 K18 **Rranxë** Shkodër, NW Albania 41°58′N 19°27′E
113 L18 **Rrëshen** *var.* Rresheni, Rrshen. Lezhë, C Albania 41°46′N 19°54′E
Rresheni *see* Rrëshen
Rrogozhina *see* Rrogozhinë
113 K20 **Rrogozhinë** *var.* Rogozhina, Rogozhinë, Rrogozhina. Tiranë, W Albania 41°04′N 19°40′E
Rrshen *see* Rrëshen
112 O13 **Rtanj** ▲ E Serbia 43°45′N 21°54′E
127 O7 **Rtishchevo** Saratovskaya Oblast', W Russian Federation 52°16′N 43°46′E
184 N12 **Ruahine Range** *var.* Ruarine. ▲▲ North Island, New Zealand
185 L14 **Ruamahanga** ≈ North Island, New Zealand
Ruanda *see* Rwanda
184 M10 **Ruapehu, Mount** ⛰ North Island, New Zealand 39°15′S 175°33′E
185 C25 **Ruapuke Island** *island* SW New Zealand
Ruarine *see* Ruahine Range
184 O9 **Ruatahuna** Bay of Plenty, North Island, New Zealand 38°38′S 176°56′E
184 Q8 **Ruatoria** Gisborne, North Island, New Zealand 37°54′S 178°18′E
184 K4 **Ruawai** Northland, North Island, New Zealand 36°08′S 174°04′E
15 N8 **Ruban** ≈ Québec, SE Canada
81 I22 **Rubeho Mountains** ▲▲ C Tanzania
165 U3 **Rubeshibe** Hokkaidō, NE Japan 43°49′N 143°37′E
Rubezhnoye *see* Rubizhne
113 L18 **Rubik** Lezhë, C Albania 41°46′N 19°48′E
54 H7 **Rubio** Táchira, W Venezuela 07°42′N 72°23′W
117 X6 **Rubizhne** *Rus.* Rubezhnoye. Luhans'ka Oblast', E Ukraine 49°01′N 38°22′E
81 F20 **Rubondo Island** *island* N Tanzania
122 I13 **Rubtsovsk** Altayskiy Kray, S Russian Federation 51°34′N 81°11′E
39 P9 **Ruby** Alaska, USA 64°44′N 155°29′W
35 W3 **Ruby Dome** ▲ Nevada, W USA 40°35′N 115°25′W
35 W4 **Ruby Lake** ◎ Nevada, W USA
35 W4 **Ruby Mountains** ▲▲ Nevada, W USA
33 Q12 **Ruby Range** ▲▲ Montana, NW USA
118 C10 **Rucava** SW Latvia 56°09′N 21°10′E
143 S13 **Rūdān** *var.* Dehbārez. Hormozgān, S Iran 27°30′N 57°10′E
Rudelstadt *see* Ciechanowiec
Rudensk *see* Rudzyensk
119 G14 **Rūdiškės** Vilnius, S Lithuania 54°31′N 24°49′E
95 H24 **Rudkøbing** Syddtjylland, C Denmark 54°57′N 10°43′E
125 S13 **Rudnichnyy** Kirovskaya Oblast', NW Russian Federation 59°37′N 52°28′E
Rūdnīchnyy *see* Koksu
Rudny *see* Rudnyy
126 H4 **Rudnya** Smolenskaya Oblast', W Russian Federation 54°55′N 31°10′E
127 O8 **Rudnya** Volgogradskaya Oblast', SW Russian Federation 50°54′N 44°27′E
144 M7 **Rudnyy** *var.* Rudny. Kostanay, N Kazakhstan 53°N 63°05′E
122 K3 **Rudol'fa, Ostrov** *island* Zemlya Frantsa-Iosifa, NW Russian Federation
Rudolf, Lake *see* Turkana, Lake
Rudolfswert *see* Novo mesto
101 L17 **Rudolstadt** Thüringen, C Germany 50°44′N 11°20′E
31 Q4 **Rudyard** Michigan, N USA 46°15′N 84°36′W
33 S7 **Rudyard** Montana, NW USA 48°33′N 110°37′W
119 K16 **Rudzyensk** *Rus.* Rudensk. Minskaya Voblasts', C Belarus 53°36′N 27°52′E
104 L6 **Rueda** Castilla y León, N Spain 41°24′N 04°58′W
114 F10 **Ruen** ▲ Bulgaria/FYR Macedonia 42°10′N 22°31′E
80 G10 **Rufa'a** Gezira, C Sudan 14°49′N 33°21′E
102 L10 **Ruffec** Charente, W France 46°01′N 00°10′E
21 R14 **Ruffin** South Carolina, SE USA 33°00′N 80°48′W
81 J23 **Rufiji** ≈ E Tanzania
61 A20 **Rufino** Santa Fe, C Argentina 34°16′S 62°45′W
76 F11 **Rufisque** W Senegal 14°44′N 17°18′W
83 K14 **Rufunsa** Lusaka, C Zambia 15°02′S 29°35′E
118 J9 **Rugāji** E Latvia 57°01′N 27°07′E
161 R7 **Rugao** Jiangsu, E China 32°27′N 120°35′E
97 M20 **Rugby** C England, United Kingdom 52°22′N 01°18′W
29 N3 **Rugby** North Dakota, N USA 48°24′N 100°00′W
100 N7 **Rügen** *headland* NE Germany 54°25′N 13°21′E
Ruhaybeh *see* Ar Ruḩaybah
81 E19 **Ruhengeri** NW Rwanda 01°39′S 29°16′E
Ruhja *see* Rūjiena
100 M10 **Ruhner Berg** *hill* N Germany
118 F7 **Ruhnu** *var.* Ruhnu Saar, *Swe.* Runö. *island* SW Estonia
Ruhnu Saar *see* Ruhnu
101 G15 **Ruhr** ≈ W Germany
91 W6 **Ruhr Valley** *industrial region* W Germany
161 S11 **Rui'an** *var.* Rui an. Zhejiang, SE China 27°51′N 120°39′E
Rui an *see* Rui'an
161 P10 **Ruichang** Jiangxi, S China 29°46′N 115°37′E
24 J11 **Ruidosa** Texas, SW USA 30°00′N 104°40′W
37 S14 **Ruidoso** New Mexico, SW USA 33°19′N 105°40′W
161 P12 **Ruijin** Jiangxi, S China 25°52′N 116°01′E
160 D13 **Ruili** Yunnan, SW China 24°04′N 97°49′E
98 N8 **Ruinen** Drenthe, NE Netherlands 52°46′N 06°19′E
99 D17 **Ruiselede** West-Vlaanderen, W Belgium 51°03′N 03°21′E
161 T13 **Ruisui** *prev.* Juisui. C Taiwan 23°43′N 121°28′E
64 P5 **Ruivo de Santana, Pico** ▲ Madeira, Portugal, NE Atlantic Ocean 32°46′N 16°57′W
40 J12 **Ruiz** Nayarit, SW Mexico 22°00′N 105°09′W
54 E10 **Ruiz, Nevado del** ⛰ W Colombia 04°53′N 75°22′W
138 J9 **Rujaylah, Ḩarrat ar** *salt lake* N Jordan
Rujen *see* Rūjiena
118 H7 **Rūjiena** *Est.* Ruhja, *Ger.* Rujen. N Latvia 57°54′N 25°22′E
79 I18 **Ruki** ≈ W Dem. Rep. Congo
81 E22 **Rukwa** ◈ *region* SW Tanzania
81 F23 **Rukwa, Lake** ◎ SE Tanzania
25 P6 **Rule** Texas, SW USA 33°10′N 99°53′W
22 K3 **Ruleville** Mississippi, S USA 33°43′N 90°33′W
Rum *see* Rhum
112 K10 **Ruma** Vojvodina, N Serbia 45°02′N 19°51′E
Rumadiya *see* Ar Ramādī
141 Q7 **Rumāḩ** Ar Riyāḑ, C Saudi Arabia 25°35′N 47°09′E
Rumaitha *see* Ar Rumaythah
Rumania/Rumänien *see* Romania
Rumänisch-Sankt-Georgen *see* Sângeorz-Băi
139 Y13 **Rumaylah** Al Başrah, SE Iraq 30°16′N 47°22′E
139 P2 **Rumaylah, Wādī** *dry watercourse* NE Syria
171 U13 **Rumbati** Papua, E Indonesia 02°44′S 132°04′E
81 E14 **Rumbek** El Buhayrat, C South Sudan 06°50′N 29°42′E
Rumburg *see* Rumburk
111 D14 **Rumburk** *Ger.* Rumburg. Ústecký Kraj, NW Czech Republic 50°58′N 14°35′E
44 J4 **Rum Cay** *island* C Bahamas
99 M26 **Rumelange** Luxembourg, S Luxembourg 49°28′N 06°02′E
99 D20 **Rumes** Hainaut, SW Belgium 50°33′N 03°19′E
19 P7 **Rumford** Maine, NE USA 44°31′N 70°31′W
110 I6 **Rumia** Pomorskie, N Poland 54°36′N 18°21′E
113 J17 **Rumija** ▲▲ S Montenegro
103 T11 **Rumilly** Haute-Savoie, E France 45°52′N 05°57′E
139 O6 **Rūmiyah** Al Anbār, W Iraq 34°28′N 41°17′E
Rummah, Wādī ar *see* Rimah, Wādī ar
Rummelsburg in Pommern *see* Miastko
165 S3 **Rumoi** Hokkaidō, NE Japan 43°57′N 141°40′E
82 M12 **Rumphi** *var.* Rumpi. Northern, N Malawi 11°00′S 33°51′E
Rumpi *see* Rumphi
29 V7 **Rum River** ≈ Minnesota, N USA
188 F16 **Rumung** *island* Caroline Islands, W Micronesia
Rumuniya/Rumŭniya/Rumunjska *see* Romania
185 G16 **Runanga** West Coast, South Island, New Zealand 42°25′S 171°15′E
184 P7 **Runaway, Cape** *headland* North Island, New Zealand 37°33′S 177°59′E
97 K18 **Runcorn** C England, United Kingdom 53°20′N 02°44′W
118 K10 **Rundāni** *var.* Rundāni. E Latvia 56°19′N 27°51′E
Rundāni *see* Rundāni
83 L18 **Runde** *var.* Lundi. ≈ SE Zimbabwe
83 E16 **Rundu** *var.* Runtu. Okavango, NE Namibia 17°55′S 19°45′E
93 I16 **Rundvik** Västerbotten, N Sweden 63°31′N 19°22′E
81 G20 **Runere** Mwanza, N Tanzania 03°06′S 33°18′E
25 S13 **Runge** Texas, SW USA 28°52′N 97°42′W
167 Q13 **Rŭng, Kaôh** *prev.* Kas Rong. *island* SW Cambodia
79 O16 **Rungu** Orientale, NE Dem. Rep. Congo 03°11′N 27°52′E
81 F23 **Rungwa** Rukwa, W Tanzania 07°18′S 31°40′E
81 G22 **Rungwa** Singida, C Tanzania 06°54′S 33°33′E
94 M14 **Runn** ◎ C Sweden
24 M4 **Running Water Draw** *valley* New Mexico/Texas, SW USA
Runö *see* Ruhnu
Runtu *see* Rundu
189 V12 **Ruo** *island* Caroline Islands, C Micronesia
158 L9 **Ruoqiang** *var.* Jo-ch'iang, *Uigh.* Charkhlik, Charkhliq, Qarkilik. Xinjiang Uygur Zizhiqu, NW China 38°59′N 88°08′E
159 S7 **Ruo Shui** ≈ N China
92 L8 **Ruostekfielbmá** *var.* Rustefjelbma Finnmark. Finnmark, N Norway 70°25′N 28°10′E
93 L18 **Ruovesi** Länsi-Suomi, W Finland 61°59′N 24°05′E
112 B9 **Rupa** Primorje-Gorski Kotar, NW Croatia 45°29′N 14°15′E
182 M11 **Rupanyup** Victoria, SE Australia 36°38′S 142°37′E
168 K9 **Rupat, Pulau** *prev.* Roepat. *island* W Indonesia
168 K10 **Rupat, Selat** *strait* Sumatera, W Indonesia
116 J11 **Rupea** *Ger.* Reps, *Hung.* Kőhalom; *prev.* Cohalm. Braşov, C Romania 46°02′N 25°13′E
99 G17 **Rupel** ≈ N Belgium
Rupella *see* la Rochelle
33 P15 **Rupert** Idaho, NW USA 42°37′N 113°40′W
21 R5 **Rupert** West Virginia, NE USA 37°57′N 80°40′W
Rupert House *see* Waskaganish
12 J10 **Rupert, Rivière de** ≈ Québec, C Canada
152 I8 **Rūpnagar** *var.* Ropar. Punjab, India
194 M13 **Ruppert Coast** *physical region* Antarctica
100 N11 **Ruppiner Kanal** *canal* NE Germany
55 S11 **Rupununi River** ≈ S Guyana
101 D16 **Rur** *Dut.* Roer. ≈ Germany/Netherlands
58 H13 **Rurópolis Presidente Medici** Pará, N Brazil 04°05′S 55°26′W
191 S12 **Rurutu** *island* Îles Australes, SW French Polynesia
Rusaddir *see* Melilla
83 L17 **Rusape** Manicaland, E Zimbabwe 18°32′S 32°07′E
Rusayris, Lake *see* Roseires, Reservoir
Ruschuk/Rusçuk *see* Ruse
114 K7 **Ruse** *var.* Ruschuk, Rustchuk, *Turk.* Rusçuk. Ruse, N Bulgaria 43°50′N 25°59′E
109 W10 **Ruše** NE Slovenia 46°31′N 15°30′E
114 L7 **Ruse** ◈ *province* N Bulgaria
114 K7 **Rusenski Lom** ≈ N Bulgaria
97 G17 **Rush** *Ir.* An Ros. Dublin, E Ireland 53°32′N 06°06′W
161 S4 **Rushan** *var.* Xiacun. Shandong, E China 36°55′N 121°26′E
Rushan *see* Rŭshon
Rushanskiy Khrebet *see* Rushon, Qatorkŭhi
29 V7 **Rush City** Minnesota, N USA 45°41′N 92°56′W
37 V5 **Rush Creek** ≈ Colorado, C USA
29 X10 **Rushford** Minnesota, N USA 43°48′N 91°45′W
154 N13 **Rushikulya** ≈ E India
14 D8 **Rush Lake** ◎ Ontario, S Canada
30 M7 **Rush Lake** ◎ Wisconsin, N USA
28 J10 **Rushmore, Mount** ▲ South Dakota, N USA 43°52′N 103°27′W
147 S13 **Rŭshon** *Rus.* Rushan. S Tajikistan 37°58′N 71°31′E
147 S14 **Rushon, Qatorkŭhi** *Rus.* Rushanskiy Khrebet. ▲▲ SE Tajikistan
26 M12 **Rush Springs** Oklahoma, C USA 34°46′N 97°57′W
45 V15 **Rushville** Trinidad, Trinidad and Tobago 10°07′N 61°03′W
30 J13 **Rushville** Illinois, N USA 40°07′N 90°33′W
28 K12 **Rushville** Nebraska, C USA 42°41′N 102°28′W
183 O11 **Rushworth** Victoria, SE Australia 36°36′S 145°03′E
25 W8 **Rusk** Texas, SW USA 31°49′N 95°11′W
93 I14 **Rusksele** Västerbotten, N Sweden 64°49′N 18°55′E
118 C12 **Rusnė** Klaipėda, W Lithuania 55°18′N 21°19′E
114 M10 **Rusokastrenska Reka** ≈ E Bulgaria
Russadir *see* Melilla
109 X3 **Russbach** ≈ NE Austria
11 V16 **Russell** Manitoba, S Canada 50°47′N 101°17′W
184 K2 **Russell** Northland, North Island, New Zealand 35°17′S 174°07′E
26 L4 **Russell** Kansas, C USA 38°54′N 98°51′W
21 O4 **Russell** Kentucky, S USA 38°30′N 82°43′W
20 L7 **Russell Springs** Kentucky, S USA 37°02′N 85°03′W
23 O2 **Russellville** Alabama, S USA 34°30′N 87°43′W
27 T11 **Russellville** Arkansas, C USA 35°17′N 93°06′W
20 J7 **Russellville** Kentucky, S USA 36°50′N 86°54′W
101 G18 **Rüsselsheim** Hessen, W Germany 50°00′N 08°25′E
Russia *see* Russian Federation
Russian America *see* Alaska
122 J11 **Russian Federation** *off.* Russian Federation, *var.* Russia, *Latv.* Krievija, *Rus.* Rossiyskaya Federatsiya. ◆ *republic* Asia/Europe
Russian Federation *see* Russian Federation
39 N11 **Russian Mission** Alaska, USA 61°48′N 161°23′W
34 M7 **Russian River** ≈ California, W USA
122 J5 **Russkaya Gavan'** Novaya Zemlya, Arkhangel'skaya Oblast', N Russian Federation 76°13′N 62°48′E
122 J5 **Russkiy, Ostrov** *island* N Russian Federation
109 Y5 **Rust** Burgenland, E Austria 47°48′N 16°42′E
Rustaq *see* Ar Rustāq
137 U10 **Rustavi** *prev.* Rust'avi. SE Georgia 41°36′N 45°00′E
Rust'avi *see* Rustavi
21 T7 **Rustburg** Virginia, NE USA 37°17′N 79°07′W
Rustchuk *see* Ruse
Rustefjelbma Finnmark *see* Ruostekfielbmá
83 I21 **Rustenburg** North-West, N South Africa 25°40′S 27°15′E
22 H5 **Ruston** Louisiana, S USA 32°31′N 92°38′W
81 E21 **Rutana** SE Burundi 04°01′S 30°01′E
62 I4 **Rutana, Volcán** ⛰ N Chile 22°43′S 67°52′W
Rutanzige, Lake *see* Edward, Lake
Rutba *see* Ar Ruţbah
104 M14 **Rute** Andalucía, S Spain 37°20′N 04°23′W
171 N16 **Ruteng** *prev.* Roeteng. Flores, C Indonesia 08°35′S 120°28′E
194 L8 **Rutford Ice Stream** *ice feature* Antarctica
35 X6 **Ruth** Nevada, W USA 39°15′N 115°00′W
101 G15 **Rüthen** Nordrhein-Westfalen, W Germany 51°30′N 08°28′E
14 D17 **Rutherford** Ontario, S Canada 42°39′N 82°06′W
21 Q10 **Rutherfordton** North Carolina, SE USA 35°23′N 81°57′W
97 J18 **Ruthin** *Wel.* Rhuthun. NE Wales, United Kingdom 53°05′N 03°18′W
108 G7 **Rüti** Zürich, N Switzerland 47°16′N 08°51′E
Rutlam *see* Ratlām
18 M9 **Rutland** Vermont, NE USA 43°37′N 72°59′W
97 N19 **Rutland** *cultural region* C England, United Kingdom
21 N8 **Rutledge** Tennessee, S USA 36°16′N 83°31′W
158 G12 **Rutog** *var.* Rutög, Rutok. Xizang Zizhiqu, W China 33°27′N 79°43′E
Rutok *see* Rutog
79 P19 **Rutshuru** Nord-Kivu, E Dem. Rep. Congo 01°11′S 29°28′E
98 L8 **Rutten** Flevoland, N Netherlands 52°49′N 05°44′E
127 Q17 **Rutul** Respublika Dagestan, SW Russian Federation 41°35′N 47°30′E
93 L14 **Ruukki** Oulu, C Finland 64°40′N 25°35′E
98 N11 **Ruurlo** Gelderland, E Netherlands 52°04′N 06°27′E
143 S15 **Ru'ūs al Jibāl** *cape* Oman/United Arab Emirates
138 I7 **Ru'ūs aţ Ţiwāl, Jabal** ▲▲ W Syria
81 H23 **Ruvuma** ◈ *region* SE Tanzania
81 I25 **Ruvuma** *var.* Rio Rovuma. ≈ Mozambique/Tanzania *see also* Rovuma, Rio
Ruvuma *see* Rovuma, Rio
Ruwais *see* Ar Ruways
138 L9 **Ruwayshid, Wadi ar** *dry watercourse* NE Jordan
141 Z10 **Ruways, Ra's ar** *headland* E Oman 20°58′N 59°00′E
79 P18 **Ruwenzori** ▲▲ Dem. Rep. Congo/Uganda
141 Y8 **Ruwī** NE Oman 23°33′N 58°31′E
114 F9 **Ruy** ▲ Bulgaria/Serbia 42°52′N 22°35′E
Ruya *see* Luia, Rio
81 E20 **Ruyigi** E Burundi 03°28′S 30°19′E
127 P5 **Ruzayevka** Respublika Mordoviya, W Russian Federation 54°04′N 44°56′E
119 G18 **Ruzhany** Brestskaya Voblasts', SW Belarus 52°52′N 24°53′E
114 I10 **Rŭzhevo Konare** Plovdiv, C Bulgaria 42°16′N 24°58′E
Ruzhin *see* Ruzhyn
114 G7 **Ruzhintsi** Vidin, NW Bulgaria 43°38′N 22°50′E
161 N6 **Ruzhou** Henan, C China 34°10′N 112°51′E
117 N5 **Ruzhyn** *Rus.* Ruzhin. Zhytomyrs'ka Oblast', N Ukraine 49°42′N 29°01′E
111 K19 **Ružomberok** *Ger.* Rosenberg, *Hung.* Rózsahegy. Zilinský Kraj, N Slovakia 49°04′N 19°19′E
111 C16 **Ruzyně** ✈ (Praha) Praha, C Czech Republic
81 D19 **Rwanda** *off.* Rwandese Republic; *prev.* Ruanda. ◆ *republic* C Africa
Rwandese Republic *see* Rwanda
95 G22 **Ry** Midtjylland, C Denmark 56°06′N 09°46′E
Ryasna *see* Rasna
126 L5 **Ryazan'** Ryazanskaya Oblast', W Russian Federation 54°37′N 39°37′E
126 L5 **Ryazanskaya Oblast'** ◈ *province* W Russian Federation
126 M6 **Ryazhsk** Ryazanskaya Oblast', W Russian Federation 53°42′N 40°09′E
118 B13 **Rybachiy** *Ger.* Rossitten. Kaliningradskaya Oblast', W Russian Federation 55°09′N 20°49′E
124 J2 **Rybachiy, Poluostrov** *peninsula* NW Russian Federation
Rybach'ye *see* Balykchy
124 L15 **Rybinsk** *prev.* Andropov. Yaroslavskaya Oblast', W Russian Federation 58°03′N 38°53′E
124 K14 **Rybinskoye Vodokhranilishche** *Eng.* Rybinsk Reservoir, Rybinsk Sea. ⊠ W Russian Federation
Rybinsk Reservoir/Rybinsk Sea *see* Rybinskoye Vodokhranilishche
111 I16 **Rybnik** Śląskie, S Poland 50°05′N 18°31′E
Rybnitsa *see* Rîbniţa
111 F16 **Rychnov nad Kněžnou** *Ger.* Reichenau. Královéhradecký Kraj, N Czech Republic 50°10′N 16°17′E
110 I12 **Rychwał** Wielkopolskie, C Poland 52°04′N 18°10′E
11 O13 **Rycroft** Alberta, W Canada 55°45′N 118°42′W
95 L21 **Ryd** Kronoberg, S Sweden 56°27′N 14°44′E
95 L20 **Rydaholm** Jönköping, S Sweden 56°57′N 14°19′E
194 I8 **Rydberg Peninsula** *peninsula* Antarctica
97 P23 **Rye** SE England, United Kingdom 50°57′N 00°42′E
33 T10 **Ryegate** Montana, NW USA 46°21′N 109°12′W
35 S3 **Rye Patch Reservoir** ⊠ Nevada, W USA
95 D15 **Ryfylke** *physical region* S Norway
95 H16 **Rygge** Østfold, S Norway 59°22′N 10°45′E
110 N13 **Ryki** Lubelskie, E Poland 51°38′N 21°57′E
Rykovo *see* Yenakiyeve
126 I7 **Ryl'sk** Kurskaya Oblast', W Russian Federation 51°34′N 34°41′E
183 S8 **Rylstone** New South Wales, SE Australia 32°48′S 149°58′E
111 H17 **Rýmařov** *Ger.* Römerstadt. Moravskoslezský Kraj, E Czech Republic 49°56′N 17°15′E
144 E11 **Ryn-Peski** *desert* W Kazakhstan
165 N10 **Ryōtsu** *var.* Ryôtu. Niigata, Sado, C Japan 38°06′N 138°28′E
Ryôtu *see* Ryōtsu
110 K10 **Rypin** Kujawsko-pomorskie, C Poland 53°03′N 19°25′E
Ryshkany *see* Rîşcani
Ryssel *see* Lille
Ryswick *see* Rijswijk
95 M24 **Rytterknægten** *hill* E Denmark
Ryukyu Islands *see* Nansei-shotō
192 G5 **Ryukyu Trench** *var.* Nansei Syotō Trench. *undersea feature* S East China Sea 24°45′N 128°00′E
110 D11 **Rzepin** *Ger.* Reppen. Lubuskie, W Poland 52°20′N 14°48′E
111 N16 **Rzeszów** Podkarpackie, SE Poland 50°03′N 22°01′E
124 I16 **Rzhev** Tverskaya Oblast', W Russian Federation 56°17′N 34°22′E
Rzhishchev *see* Rzhyshchiv
117 P5 **Rzhyshchiv** *Rus.* Rzhishchev. Kyyivs'ka Oblast', N Ukraine 49°58′N 31°02′E

S

138 E11 **Sa'ad** Southern, W Israel 31°27′N 34°31′E
109 P7 **Saalach** ≈ W Austria
101 L14 **Saale** ≈ C Germany
101 L17 **Saalfeld** *var.* Saalfeld an der Saale. Thüringen, C Germany 50°39′N 11°22′E
Saalfeld *see* Zalewo
Saalfeld an der Saale *see* Saalfeld
108 C8 **Saane** ≈ W Switzerland
101 D19 **Saar** *Fr.* Sarre. ≈ France/Germany
101 E20 **Saarbrücken** *Fr.* Sarrebruck. Saarland, SW Germany 49°13′N 07°01′E
Saarburg *see* Sarrebourg
118 D6 **Sääre** *var.* Sjar. Saaremaa, W Estonia 57°57′N 21°53′E
Saare *see* Saaremaa
118 D5 **Saaremaa** *off.* Saare Maakond. ◈ *province* W Estonia
118 E6 **Saaremaa** *Ger.* Oesel, Ösel; *prev.* Saare. *island* W Estonia
Saare Maakond *see* Saaremaa
92 L12 **Saarenkylä** Lappi, N Finland 66°31′N 25°51′E
Saargemund *see* Sarreguemines
93 L17 **Saarijärvi** Länsi-Suomi, C Finland 62°42′N 25°16′E
Saar in Mähren *see* Žd'ár nad Sázavou
92 M10 **Saariselkä** *Lapp.* Suoločielgi. Lappi, N Finland 68°27′N 27°29′E
92 L10 **Saariselkä** *hill range* NE Finland
101 D20 **Saarland** *Fr.* Sarre. ◈ *state* SW Germany
Saarlautern *see* Saarlouis

◆ Country
● Country Capital
◇ Dependent Territory
○ Dependent Territory Capital
◈ Administrative Regions
✈ International Airport
▲ Mountain
▲▲ Mountain Range
⛰ Volcano
≈ River
◎ Lake
⊠ Reservoir

101 D20 **Saarlouis** *prev.* Saarlautern. Saarland, SW Germany *49°19′N 06°45′E*
108 E11 **Saaser Vispa** ≈ S Switzerland
137 X12 **Saatlı** *Rus.* Saatly. C Azerbaijan *39°57′N 48°24′E*
Saatly *see* Saatlı
Saaz *see* Žatec
45 V9 **Saba** *island* Sint Maarten
138 J7 **Sab' Ābār** *var.* Sab'a Biyar, Sa'b Bi'ār. Ḥimṣ, C Syria *33°46′N 37°41′E*
Sab'a Biyar *see* Sab' Ābār
112 K11 **Šabac** Serbia, W Serbia *44°45′N 19°42′E*
105 W5 **Sabadell** Cataluña, E Spain *41°33′N 02°07′E*
164 K12 **Sabae** Fukui, Honshū, SW Japan *36°00′N 136°12′E*
169 V7 **Sabah** *prev.* British North Borneo, North Borneo. ⬖ *state* East Malaysia
168 J8 **Sabak** *var.* Sabak Bernam. Selangor, Peninsular Malaysia *03°45′N 100°59′E*
Sabak Bernam *see* Sabak
38 D16 **Sabak, Cape** *headland* Agattu Island, Alaska, USA *52°21′N 173°43′E*
81 J20 **Sabaki** ≈ S Kenya
142 L2 **Sabalān, Kuhhā-ye** ▲ NW Iran *38°21′N 47°47′E*
154 H7 **Sabalgarh** Madhya Pradesh, C India *26°18′N 77°28′E*
44 E4 **Sabana, Archipiélago de** *island group* C Cuba
42 H7 **Sabanagrande** *var.* Sabana Grande. Francisco Morazán, S Honduras *13°48′N 87°15′W*
Sabana Grande *see* Sabanagrande
54 E5 **Sabanalarga** Atlántico, N Colombia *10°38′N 74°55′W*
41 W14 **Sabancuy** Campeche, SE Mexico *18°58′N 91°11′W*
45 N8 **Sabaneta** NW Dominican Republic *19°30′N 71°21′W*
54 J4 **Sabaneta** Falcón, N Venezuela *11°17′N 70°00′W*
188 H4 **Sabaneta, Puntan** *prev.* Ushi Point. *headland* Saipan, S Northern Mariana Islands *15°17′N 145°49′E*
171 X14 **Sabang** Papua, E Indonesia *04°33′S 138°42′E*
116 L10 **Săbăoani** Neamţ, NE Romania *47°01′N 26°51′E*
155 J26 **Sabaragamuwa** ⬖ *province* C Sri Lanka
Sabaria *see* Szombathely
154 D10 **Sābarmati** ≈ NW India
171 S10 **Sabatai** Pulau Morotai, E Indonesia *02°04′N 128°23′E*
141 Q15 **Sab'atayn, Ramlat as** *desert* C Yemen
107 I16 **Sabaudia** Lazio, C Italy *41°17′N 13°02′E*
57 J19 **Sabaya** Oruro, S Bolivia *19°09′S 68°21′W*
Sa'b Bi'ār *see* Sab' Ābār
Sabbioncello *see* Orebić
148 I8 **Šāberī, Hāmūn-e** *var.* Daryācheh-ye Hāmun, Daryācheh-ye Sīstān. ◎ Afghanistan/Iran *see also* Sīstān, Daryācheh-ye
Šāberī, Hāmūn-e *see* Sīstān, Daryācheh-ye
27 P2 **Sabetha** Kansas, C USA *39°54′N 95°48′W*
75 P10 **Sabhā** C Libya *27°02′N 14°26′E*
67 V13 **Sabi** *var.* Save. ≈ Mozambique/Zimbabwe *see also* Save
Sabi *see* Save
118 E8 **Sabile** *Ger.* Zabeln. NW Latvia *57°03′N 22°33′E*
31 R14 **Sabina** Ohio, N USA *39°29′N 83°38′W*
40 I3 **Sabinal** Chihuahua, N Mexico *30°59′N 107°29′W*
25 Q12 **Sabinal** Texas, SW USA *29°19′N 99°28′W*
25 Q11 **Sabinal River** ≈ Texas, SW USA
105 S4 **Sabiñánigo** Aragón, NE Spain *42°31′N 00°22′W*
41 N6 **Sabinas** Coahuila, NE Mexico *27°52′N 101°04′W*
41 O8 **Sabinas Hidalgo** Nuevo León, NE Mexico *26°29′N 100°09′W*
41 N6 **Sabinas, Río** ≈ NE Mexico
22 F9 **Sabine Lake** ◎ Louisiana/Texas, S USA
92 O3 **Sabine Land** *physical region* C Svalbard
25 W7 **Sabine River** ≈ Louisiana/Texas, SW USA
137 X12 **Sabirabad** C Azerbaijan *40°00′N 48°27′E*
Sabkha *see* As Sabkhah
171 O4 **Sablayan** Mindoro, N Philippines *12°48′N 120°48′E*
13 P16 **Sable, Cape** *headland* Newfoundland and Labrador, SE Canada *43°21′N 65°40′W*
23 X17 **Sable, Cape** *headland* Florida, SE USA *25°12′N 81°06′W*
13 R16 **Sable Island** *island* Nova Scotia, SE Canada
14 L11 **Sables, Lac des** ◎ Québec, SE Canada
14 E10 **Sables, Rivière aux** ≈ Ontario, S Canada
102 K7 **Sable-sur-Sarthe** Sarthe, NW France *47°49′N 00°19′W*
125 U7 **Sablya, Gora** ▲ NW Russian Federation *64°46′N 58°52′E*
77 U14 **Sabon Birnin Gwari** Kaduna, C Nigeria *10°43′N 06°39′E*
77 V11 **Sabon Kafi** Zinder, C Niger *14°37′N 08°46′E*
104 I6 **Sabor, Rio** ≈ N Portugal
14 J8 **Sabourin, Lac** ◎ Québec, SE Canada
137 Y10 **Şabran** *prev.* Däväçi. NE Azerbaijan *41°15′N 48°58′E*
102 J14 **Sabres** Landes, SW France *44°07′N 00°46′W*
195 X13 **Sabrina Coast** *physical region* Antarctica
140 M11 **Sabt al Ulāyā** 'Asīr, SW Saudi Arabia *19°33′N 41°58′E*
104 I8 **Sabugal** Guarda, N Portugal *40°20′N 07°05′W*
29 Z13 **Sabula** Iowa, C USA *42°04′N 90°10′W*
141 N13 **Şabyā** Jīzān, SW Saudi Arabia *17°50′N 42°50′E*
Sabzawar *see* Sabzevār
Sabzawaran *see* Jīroft
143 S4 **Sabzevār** *var.* Sabzawar. Khorāsān-Razavī, NE Iran *36°13′N 57°38′E*
Sabzvārān *see* Jīroft
Sacajawea Peak *see* Matterhorn
82 C9 **Sacandica** Uíge, NW Angola *06°01′S 15°57′E*
42 A2 **Sacatepéquez** *off.* Departamento de Sacatepéquez. ⬖ *department* S Guatemala
Sacatepéquez, Departamento de *see* Sacatepéquez
104 F11 **Sacavém** Lisboa, W Portugal *38°47′N 09°06′W*
29 T13 **Sac City** Iowa, C USA *42°25′N 94°59′W*
105 P8 **Sacedón** Castilla-La Mancha, C Spain *40°29′N 02°44′W*
116 J12 **Săcele** *Ger.* Vierdörfer, *Hung.* Négyfalu; *prev. Ger.* Sieben Dörfer, *Hung.* Hétfalu. Braşov, C Romania *45°36′N 25°40′E*
163 Y16 **Sacheon** *Jap.* Sansenhō; *prev.* Sach'ŏn, Samch'ŏnpŏ. S South Korea *34°55′N 128°07′E*
12 C7 **Sachigo** ≈ Ontario, C Canada
12 C8 **Sachigo Lake** Ontario, C Canada *53°52′N 92°16′W*
12 C8 **Sachigo Lake** ◎ Ontario, C Canada
Sach'ŏn *see* Sacheon
101 O15 **Sachsen** *Eng.* Saxony, *Fr.* Saxe. ⬖ *state* E Germany
101 K14 **Sachsen-Anhalt** *Eng.* Saxony-Anhalt. ⬖ *state* C Germany
109 R9 **Sachsenburg** Salzburg, S Austria *46°49′N 13°23′E*
Sachsenfeld *see* Žalec
8 I5 **Sachs Harbour** *var.* Ikaahuk. Banks Island, Northwest Territories, N Canada *72°N 125°14′W*
Sächsisch-Reen/Sächsisch-Regen *see* Reghin
18 H8 **Sackets Harbor** New York, NE USA *43°57′N 76°06′W*
13 P14 **Sackville** New Brunswick, SE Canada *45°54′N 64°23′W*
19 P9 **Saco** Maine, NE USA *43°32′N 70°25′W*
19 P8 **Saco River** ≈ Maine/New Hampshire, NE USA
35 O7 **Sacramento** *state capital* California, W USA *38°35′N 121°30′W*
37 T14 **Sacramento Mountains** ▲▲ New Mexico, SW USA
35 N6 **Sacramento River** ≈ California, W USA
35 N5 **Sacramento Valley** *valley* California, W USA
36 I10 **Sacramento Wash** *valley* Arizona, SW USA
105 N15 **Sacratif, Cabo** *headland* S Spain *36°41′N 03°30′W*
116 F9 **Săcueni** *prev.* Săcuieni, *Hung.* Székelyhid. Bihor, W Romania *47°20′N 22°05′E*
Săcuieni *see* Săcueni
105 R4 **Sádaba** Aragón, NE Spain *42°15′N 01°16′W*
Sá da Bandeira *see* Lubango
138 I6 **Şadad** Ḥimş, W Syria *34°19′N 36°52′E*
141 O13 **Şa'dah** NW Yemen *16°59′N 43°45′E*
167 O16 **Sadao** Songkhla, SW Thailand *06°39′N 100°30′E*
142 L8 **Sadd-e Dez, Daryācheh-ye** ◎ W Iran
19 S3 **Saddleback Mountain** *hill* Maine, NE USA
19 P6 **Saddleback Mountain** ▲ Maine, NE USA *44°57′N 70°27′W*
141 W13 **Sadḩ** S Oman *17°11′N 55°08′E*
76 J11 **Sadiola** Kayes, W Mali *13°48′N 11°47′W*
149 R12 **Sādiqābād** Punjab, E Pakistan *28°16′N 70°10′E*
153 Y10 **Sadiya** Assam, NE India *27°49′N 95°38′E*
139 W9 **Sa'dīyah, Hawr as** ◎ E Iraq
Sado *see* Sadoga-shima
165 N9 **Sadoga-shima** *var.* Sado. *island* C Japan
104 F12 **Sado, Rio** ≈ S Portugal
114 I8 **Sadovets** Pleven, N Bulgaria *43°19′N 24°21′E*
114 J11 **Sadovo** Plovdiv, C Bulgaria *42°07′N 24°56′E*
127 O11 **Sadovoye** Respublika Kalmykiya, SW Russian Federation *47°51′N 44°34′E*
105 W9 **Sa Dragonera** *var.* Isla Dragonera. *island* Islas Baleares, Spain, W Mediterranean Sea
105 P9 **Saelices** Castilla-La Mancha, C Spain *39°55′N 02°49′W*
Saena Julia *see* Siena
Saetabicula *see* Alzira
114 O12 **Safaalan** Tekirdağ, NW Turkey *41°26′N 28°07′E*
Safad *see* Tsefat
Şafāqis *see* Sfax
143 P10 **Şafāshahr** *var.* Deh Bīd. Fārs, C Iran *30°50′N 53°50′E*
192 I16 **Safata Bay** *bay* Upolu, Samoa, C Pacific Ocean
Safed *see* Tsefat
139 X11 **Şaffāf, Ḩawr aş** *marshy lake* S Iraq
95 J16 **Säffle** Värmland, C Sweden *59°08′N 12°55′E*
37 N15 **Safford** Arizona, SW USA *32°46′N 109°41′W*
74 E7 **Safi** W Morocco *32°19′N 09°14′W*
126 I4 **Safonovo** Smolenskaya Oblast', W Russian Federation *55°05′N 33°12′E*
136 H11 **Safranbolu** Karabük, NW Turkey *41°16′N 32°41′E*
139 Y13 **Safwān** Al Başrah, SE Iraq *30°06′N 47°44′E*
158 J16 **Saga** *var.* Gya'gya. Xizang Zizhiqu, W China *29°22′N 85°19′E*
164 C14 **Saga** Saga, Kyūshū, SW Japan *33°14′N 130°16′E*
164 C13 **Saga** *off.* Saga-ken. ⬖ *prefecture* Kyūshū, SW Japan
165 P10 **Sagae** Yamagata, Honshū, C Japan *38°22′N 140°12′E*
166 L3 **Sagaing** Sagaing, C Myanmar (Burma) *21°55′N 95°56′E*
166 L5 **Sagaing** ⬖ *division* N Myanmar (Burma)
Saga-ken *see* Saga
165 N13 **Sagamihara** Kanagawa, Honshū, S Japan *35°34′N 139°22′E*
165 N14 **Sagami-nada** *inlet* SW Japan
Sagan *see* Żagań
29 Y3 **Saganaga Lake** ◎ Minnesota, N USA
155 F18 **Sāgar** Karnātaka, W India *14°09′N 75°02′E*
154 I9 **Sāgar** *prev.* Saugor. Madhya Pradesh, C India *23°53′N 78°46′E*
15 S8 **Sagard** Québec, SE Canada *48°01′N 70°03′W*
Sagarmāthā *see* Everest, Mount
Sagebrush State *see* Nevada
143 V11 **Säghand** Yazd, C Iran *32°33′N 55°12′E*
19 N14 **Sag Harbor** Long Island, New York, NE USA *40°59′N 72°15′W*
Saghez *see* Saqqez
31 R8 **Saginaw** Michigan, N USA *43°25′N 83°57′W*
31 R8 **Saginaw Bay** *lake bay* Michigan, N USA
Sagiz *see* Sagyz
64 H6 **Saglek Bank** *undersea feature* W Labrador Sea
13 P5 **Saglek Bay** *bay* SW Labrador Sea
Saglouc/Sagluk *see* Salluit
103 X15 **Sagonne, Golfe de** *gulf* Corse, France, C Mediterranean Sea
105 P13 **Sagra** ▲ S Spain *37°59′N 02°33′W*
104 F14 **Sagres** Faro, S Portugal *37°01′N 08°56′W*
37 S7 **Saguache** Colorado, C USA *38°05′N 106°05′W*
44 J7 **Sagua de Tánamo** Holguín, E Cuba *20°38′N 75°14′W*
44 E5 **Sagua la Grande** Villa Clara, C Cuba *22°48′N 80°06′W*
15 R7 **Saguenay** ≈ Québec, SE Canada
74 C9 **Saguia al Hamra** *var.* As Saqia al Hamra. ≈ N Western Sahara
105 S9 **Sagunto** *Cat.* Sagunt, *Ar.* Murviedro; *anc.* Saguntum. Valenciana, E Spain *39°40′N 00°17′W*
Sagunt/Saguntum *see* Sagunto
144 H11 **Sagyz** *prev.* Sagiz. Atyrau, W Kazakhstan *48°12′N 54°56′E*
138 H10 **Saḩāb** 'Ammān, NW Jordan *31°52′N 36°00′E*
54 E6 **Sahagún** Córdoba, NW Colombia *08°58′N 75°30′W*
104 L4 **Sahagún** Castilla y León, N Spain *42°23′N 05°02′W*
141 X8 **Şaḩam** N Oman *24°06′N 56°52′E*
68 F9 **Sahara** *desert* Libya/Algeria
Sahara el Gharbîya *see* Şaḩrā' al Gharbīyah
75 X9 **Sahara el Sharqîya** *var.* Aş Şaḩrā' ash Sharqīyah, *Eng.* Arabian Desert, Eastern Desert. *desert* E Egypt
Saharan Atlas *see* Atlas Saharien
152 J9 **Sahāranpur** Uttar Pradesh, N India *29°58′N 77°33′E*
64 L10 **Saharan Seamounts** *var.* Saharian Seamounts. *undersea feature* E Atlantic Ocean *25°00′N 20°00′W*
Saharian Seamounts *see* Saharan Seamounts
153 Q13 **Saharsa** Bihār, NE India *25°54′N 86°36′E*
67 O7 **Sahel** *physical region* C Africa
153 R14 **Sāhibganj** Jhārkhand, NE India *25°15′N 87°40′E*
139 Q7 **Sahīliyah** Al Anbār, C Iraq *33°43′N 42°42′E*
138 H4 **Şāḩilīyah, Jibāl as** ▲▲ NW Syria
114 M13 **Şahin** Tekirdağ, NW Turkey *41°01′N 26°51′E*
149 U9 **Sāhīwāl** *prev.* Montgomery. Punjab, E Pakistan *30°40′N 73°05′E*
149 U8 **Sāhīwāl** Punjab, E Pakistan *31°57′N 72°22′E*
141 W11 **Şaḩmah, Ramlat as** *desert* C Oman
75 U9 **Şaḩrā' al Gharbīyah** *var.* Sahara el Gharbîya, *Eng.* Western Desert. *desert* C Egypt
139 T13 **Şaḩrā' al Ḩijārah** *desert* S Iraq
40 H5 **Sahuaripa** Sonora, NW Mexico *29°02′N 109°14′W*
36 M16 **Sahuarita** Arizona, SW USA *31°24′N 110°55′W*
40 L13 **Sahuayo** *var.* Sahuayo de José María Morelos; *prev.* Sahuayo de Díaz, Sahuayo de Porfirio Díaz. Michoacán, SW Mexico *20°05′N 102°42′W*
Sahuayo de Díaz/Sahuayo de José María Morelos/Sahuayo de Porfirio Díaz *see* Sahuayo
173 W8 **Sahul Shelf** *undersea feature* N Timor Sea
167 P17 **Sai Buri** Pattani, SW Thailand *06°42′N 101°37′E*
74 I6 **Saïda** NW Algeria *34°50′N 00°10′E*
138 G7 **Saïda** *var.* Şaydā, Sayida; *anc.* Sidon. W Lebanon *33°20′N 35°24′E*
Sa'īdābād *see* Sīrjān
80 B13 **Sa'id Bundas** Western Bahr el Ghazal, W South Sudan *08°24′N 24°53′E*
186 E7 **Saidor** Madang, N Papua New Guinea *05°38′S 146°28′E*
153 S13 **Saidpur** *var.* Syedpur. Rajshahi, NW Bangladesh *25°48′N 89°E*
149 U5 **Saīdu** *var.* Mingora, Mongora; *prev.* Mingāora. Khyber Pakhtunkhwa, N Pakistan *34°45′N 72°21′E*
108 C7 **Saignelégier** Jura, NW Switzerland *47°18′N 07°03′E*
164 H11 **Saigō** Shimane, Dōgo, SW Japan *36°12′N 133°18′E*
Saigon *see* Hô Chi Minh
163 P11 **SaihanTal** *var.* Sonid Youqi. Nei Mongol Zizhiqu, N China *42°45′N 112°36′E*
162 I12 **Saihan Toroi** Nei Mongol Zizhiqu, N China *41°44′N 100°29′E*
Sai Hun *see* Syr Darya
92 M11 **Saija** Lappi, NE Finland *67°07′N 28°46′E*
164 G14 **Saijō** Ehime, Shikoku, SW Japan *33°55′N 133°10′E*
164 E15 **Saiki** Ōita, Kyūshū, SW Japan *32°57′N 131°52′E*
93 N18 **Saimaa** ◎ SE Finland
93 N18 **Saimaa Canal** *Fin.* Saimaan Kanava, *Rus.* Saymenskiy Kanal. *canal* Finland/Russian Federation
Saimaan Kanava *see* Saimaa Canal
40 L10 **Saín Alto** Zacatecas, C Mexico *23°36′N 103°14′W*
96 L12 **St Abb's Head** *headland* SE Scotland, United Kingdom *55°54′N 02°07′W*
11 Y16 **St. Adolphe** Manitoba, S Canada *49°39′N 96°55′W*
103 O15 **St-Affrique** Aveyron, S France *43°57′N 02°52′E*
15 Q10 **St-Agapit** Québec, SE Canada *46°22′N 71°37′W*
97 O21 **St Albans** *anc.* Verulamium. E England, United Kingdom *51°46′N 00°21′W*
18 L6 **Saint Albans** Vermont, NE USA *44°49′N 73°07′W*
21 Q5 **Saint Albans** West Virginia, NE USA *38°21′N 81°47′W*
St. Alban's Head *see* St Aldhelm's Head
11 Q14 **St. Albert** Alberta, SW Canada *53°38′N 113°38′W*
97 M24 **St Aldhelm's Head** *var.* St. Alban's Head. *headland* S England, United Kingdom *50°34′N 02°04′W*
15 O11 **St-Alexis-des-Monts** Québec, SE Canada *46°30′N 73°08′W*
103 P2 **St-Amand-les-Eaux** Nord, N France *50°27′N 03°25′E*
103 O9 **St-Amand-Montrond** *var.* St-Amand-Mont-Rond. Cher, C France *46°43′N 02°29′E*
173 P16 **St-André** NE Réunion
14 M12 **St-André-Avellin** Québec, SE Canada *45°45′N 75°04′W*
Saint-André, Cap *see* Vilanandro, Tanjona
102 K12 **St-André-de-Cubzac** Gironde, SW France *45°01′N 00°26′W*
96 K11 **St Andrews** E Scotland, United Kingdom *56°20′N 02°49′W*
23 Q9 **Saint Andrews Bay** *bay* Florida, SE USA
23 W7 **Saint Andrew Sound** *sound* Georgia, SE USA
Saint Anna Trough *see* Svyataya Anna Trough
44 J11 **St. Ann's Bay** C Jamaica *18°26′N 77°12′W*
13 T10 **St. Anthony** Newfoundland and Labrador, SE Canada *51°22′N 55°34′W*
33 R13 **Saint Anthony** Idaho, NW USA *43°56′N 111°38′W*
182 M11 **Saint Arnaud** Victoria, SE Australia *36°39′S 143°15′E*
185 I15 **St.Arnaud Range** ▲▲ South Island, New Zealand
13 R10 **St-Augustin** Québec, E Canada *51°13′N 58°39′W*
23 X9 **Saint Augustine** Florida, SE USA *29°54′N 81°19′W*
97 H24 **St Austell** SW England, United Kingdom *50°21′N 04°47′W*
103 T4 **St-Avold** Moselle, NE France *49°06′N 06°43′E*
103 N17 **St-Barthélemy** ▲ S France
102 L17 **St-Béat** Haute-Garonne, S France *42°55′N 00°39′E*
97 I15 **St Bees Head** *headland* NW England, United Kingdom *54°30′N 03°39′W*
173 P16 **St-Benoit** E Réunion
103 T13 **St-Bonnet** Hautes-Alpes, SE France *44°41′N 06°04′E*
St.Botolph's Town *see* Boston
97 G21 **St Brides Bay** *inlet* SW Wales, United Kingdom
102 H5 **St-Brieuc** Côtes d'Armor, NW France *48°31′N 02°45′W*
102 H5 **St-Brieuc, Baie de** *bay* NW France
102 L7 **St-Calais** Sarthe, NW France *47°55′N 00°48′E*
15 Q10 **St-Casimir** Québec, SE Canada *46°40′N 72°05′W*
14 H16 **St. Catharines** Ontario, S Canada *43°10′N 79°15′W*
45 S14 **St. Catherine, Mount** ▲ N Grenada *12°10′N 61°41′W*
64 C11 **St Catherine Point** *headland* E Bermuda
23 X6 **Saint Catherines Island** *island* Georgia, SE USA
97 M24 **St Catherine's Point** *headland* S England, United Kingdom *50°34′N 01°17′W*
103 N13 **St-Céré** Lot, S France *44°52′N 01°53′E*
108 A10 **St. Cergue** Vaud, W Switzerland *46°25′N 06°10′E*
103 R11 **St-Chamond** Loire, E France *45°29′N 04°32′E*
33 S16 **Saint Charles** Idaho, NW USA *42°05′N 111°23′W*
27 X4 **Saint Charles** Missouri, C USA *38°48′N 90°29′W*
103 P13 **St-Chély-d'Apcher** Lozère, S France *44°51′N 03°16′E*
Saint Christopher and Nevis, Federation of *see* Saint Kitts and Nevis
Saint Christopher-Nevis *see* Saint Kitts and Nevis
31 S9 **Saint Clair** Michigan, N USA *42°49′N 82°29′W*
183 O17 **St. Clair, Lake** ◎ Tasmania, SE Australia
14 C17 **St. Clair, Lake** *var.* Lac à L'Eau Claire. ◎ Canada/USA
31 S10 **Saint Clair Shores** Michigan, N USA *42°30′N 82°53′W*
103 S10 **St-Claude** *anc.* Condate. Jura, E France *46°23′N 05°52′E*
45 X6 **St-Claude** Basse Terre, SW Guadeloupe *16°02′N 61°42′W*
23 X12 **Saint Cloud** Florida, SE USA *28°15′N 81°15′W*
29 U8 **Saint Cloud** Minnesota, N USA *45°34′N 94°10′W*
45 T9 **Saint Croix** *island* S Virgin Islands (US)
30 J4 **Saint Croix Flowage** ⊠ Wisconsin, N USA
19 T5 **Saint Croix River** ≈ Canada/USA
29 W7 **Saint Croix River** ≈ Minnesota/Wisconsin, N USA
45 S14 **St.David's** SE Grenada *12°01′N 61°40′W*
97 H21 **St David's** SW Wales, United Kingdom *51°53′N 05°16′W*
97 G21 **St David's Head** *headland* SW Wales, United Kingdom *51°54′N 05°19′W*
64 C12 **St David's Island** *island* E Bermuda
173 O16 **St-Denis** ○ (Réunion) NW Réunion *20°55′S 14°34′E*
103 U6 **St-Dié** Vosges, NE France *48°17′N 06°57′E*
103 R5 **St-Dizier** *anc.* Desiderii Fanum. Haute-Marne, N France *48°39′N 05°00′E*
15 N11 **St-Donat** Québec, SE Canada *46°19′N 74°15′W*
15 N11 **Ste-Adèle** Québec, SE Canada *45°58′N 74°10′W*
15 N11 **Ste-Agathe-des-Monts** Québec, SE Canada *46°03′N 74°19′W*
11 Y16 **Ste. Anne** Manitoba, S Canada *49°40′N 96°40′W*
45 R12 **Ste-Anne** Grande Terre, E Guadeloupe *16°13′N 61°23′W*
45 Y6 **Ste-Anne** SE Martinique *14°26′N 60°53′W*
15 Q10 **Ste-Anne** ≈ Québec, SE Canada
172 I16 **Sainte Anne** *island* Inner Islands, NE Seychelles
15 W6 **Ste-Anne-des-Monts** Québec, SE Canada *49°07′N 66°29′W*
14 M10 **Ste-Anne-du-Lac** Québec, SE Canada *46°51′N 75°20′W*
15 S10 **Ste-Apolline** Québec, SE Canada *46°47′N 70°15′W*
15 R10 **Ste-Claire** Québec, SE Canada *46°30′N 70°40′W*
15 Q10 **Ste-Croix** Québec, SE Canada *46°36′N 71°42′W*
108 B8 **Ste. Croix** Vaud, SW Switzerland *46°50′N 06°31′E*
103 P14 **Ste-Énimie** Lozère, S France *44°21′N 03°26′E*
27 Y6 **Sainte Genevieve** Missouri, C USA *37°57′N 90°01′W*
103 S12 **St-Egrève** Isère, E France *45°15′N 05°41′E*
39 T12 **Saint Elias, Cape** *headland* Kayak Island, Alaska, USA *59°48′N 144°36′W*
39 U11 **St Elias, Mount** ▲ Alaska, USA *60°18′N 140°57′W*
10 G8 **Saint Elias Mountains** ▲▲ Canada/USA
55 Y10 **St-Élie** N French Guiana *04°50′N 53°21′W*
103 O10 **St-Eloy-les-Mines** Puy-de-Dôme, C France *46°07′N 02°50′E*
15 R10 **Ste-Marie** Québec, SE Canada *46°28′N 71°00′W*
45 Q11 **Ste-Marie** NE Martinique *14°47′N 61°00′W*
173 P16 **Ste-Marie** NE Réunion
103 U6 **Ste-Marie-aux-Mines** Haut-Rhin, NE France *48°16′N 07°12′E*
Sainte Marie, Cap *see* Vohimena, Tanjona
102 L8 **Ste-Maure-de-Touraine** Indre-et-Loire, C France *47°06′N 00°38′E*
103 R4 **Ste-Menehould** Marne, NE France *49°06′N 04°54′E*
Ste-Perpétue *see* Ste-Perpétue-de-l'Islet
15 S9 **Ste-Perpétue-de-l'Islet** *var.* Ste-Perpétue. Québec, SE Canada *47°02′N 69°58′W*
45 X11 **Ste-Rose** Basse Terre, N Guadeloupe *16°20′N 61°42′W*
173 P16 **Ste-Rose** E Réunion
11 W15 **Ste. Rose du Lac** Manitoba, S Canada *51°04′N 99°31′W*
102 J11 **Saintes** *anc.* Mediolanum. Charente-Maritime, W France *45°45′N 00°37′W*
45 X7 **Saintes, Canal des** *channel* SW Guadeloupe
Saintes, Îles des *see* les Saintes
173 P16 **Ste-Suzanne** N Réunion
15 P10 **Ste-Thècle** Québec, SE Canada *46°48′N 72°31′W*
103 Q12 **St-Étienne** Loire, E France *45°26′N 04°23′E*
102 M4 **St-Étienne-du-Rouvray** Seine-Maritime, N France *49°22′N 01°07′E*
Saint Eustatius *see* Sint Eustatius
14 M11 **Ste-Véronique** Québec, SE Canada *46°30′N 74°58′W*
15 P7 **St-Félicien** Québec, SE Canada *48°38′N 72°29′W*
15 O11 **St-Félix-de-Valois** Québec, SE Canada *46°10′N 73°26′W*
103 Y14 **St-Florent** Corse, France, C Mediterranean Sea *42°41′N 09°19′E*
103 Y14 **St-Florent, Golfe de** *gulf* Corse, France, C Mediterranean Sea
103 P6 **St-Florentin** Yonne, C France *48°00′N 03°46′E*
103 N9 **St-Florent-sur-Cher** Cher, C France *47°00′N 02°13′E*
103 P12 **St-Flour** Cantal, C France *45°02′N 03°05′E*
26 H2 **Saint Francis** Kansas, C USA *39°45′N 101°31′W*
83 H26 **St. Francis, Cape** *headland* S South Africa *34°11′S 24°45′E*
27 X10 **Saint Francis River** ≈ Arkansas/Missouri, C USA
22 J8 **Saint Francisville** Louisiana, S USA *30°46′N 91°22′W*
45 Y6 **St-François** Grande Terre, E Guadeloupe *16°15′N 61°17′W*
15 Q12 **St-François** ≈ Québec, SE Canada
27 X7 **Saint Francois Mountains** ▲▲ Missouri, C USA
St-Gall *see* Sankt Gall/Saint Gall/St.Gallen
St-Gall/Saint Gall/St. Gallen *see* Sankt Gallen
102 L16 **St-Gaudens** Haute-Garonne, S France *43°07′N 00°43′E*
15 R12 **St-Gédéon** Québec, SE Canada *45°51′N 70°36′W*
181 X10 **Saint George** Queensland, E Australia *28°05′S 148°40′E*
64 B12 **St George** N Bermuda *32°24′N 64°42′W*
38 K15 **Saint George** Saint George Island, Alaska, USA *56°34′N 169°30′W*
21 S14 **Saint George** South Carolina, SE USA *33°12′N 80°34′W*
36 J8 **Saint George** Utah, W USA *37°06′N 113°35′W*
13 R12 **St. George, Cape** *headland* Newfoundland and Labrador, E Canada *48°26′N 59°17′W*
186 I6 **St. George, Cape** *headland* New Ireland, NE Papua New Guinea *04°49′S 152°52′E*
38 J15 **Saint George Island** *island* Pribilof Islands, Alaska, USA
23 S10 **Saint George Island** *island* Florida, SE USA
99 J19 **Saint-Georges** Liège, E Belgium *50°36′N 05°20′E*
15 R11 **St-Georges** Québec, SE Canada *46°08′N 70°40′W*
55 Z11 **St-Georges** E French Guiana *03°55′N 51°49′W*
45 R14 **St. George's** ● (Grenada) SW Grenada *12°04′N 61°45′W*
13 R12 **St. George's Bay** *inlet* Newfoundland and Labrador, E Canada
97 G21 **Saint George's Channel** *channel* Ireland/Wales, United Kingdom
186 H6 **St. George's Channel** *channel* NE Papua New Guinea
64 B11 **St George's Island** *island* E Bermuda
99 I21 **Saint-Gérard** Namur, S Belgium *50°20′N 04°47′E*
St-Germain *see* St-Germain-en-Laye
15 P12 **St-Germain-de-Grantham** Québec, SE Canada *45°49′N 72°32′W*
103 N5 **St-Germain-en-Laye** *var.* St-Germain. Yvelines, N France *48°53′N 02°04′E*
102 H8 **St-Gildas, Pointe du** *headland* NW France *47°09′N 02°25′W*
103 R15 **St-Gilles** Gard, S France *43°41′N 04°24′E*
102 I9 **St-Gilles-Croix-de-Vie** Vendée, NW France *46°41′N 01°55′W*
173 O16 **St-Gilles-les-Bains** W Réunion *21°02′S 55°14′E*
102 M16 **St-Girons** Ariège, S France *42°58′N 01°07′E*
Saint Gotthard *see* Szentgotthárd
108 G9 **St. Gotthard Tunnel** *tunnel* Ticino, S Switzerland
97 H22 **St Govan's Head** *headland* SW Wales, United Kingdom *51°35′N 04°55′W*
34 M7 **Saint Helena** California, W USA *38°29′N 122°30′W*
65 F24 **Saint Helena** ◇ UK *dependent territory* C Atlantic Ocean
67 O12 **Saint Helena** *island* C Atlantic Ocean
65 M16 **Saint Helena Fracture Zone** *tectonic feature* C Atlantic Ocean
34 M7 **Saint Helena, Mount** ▲ California, W USA *38°40′N 122°39′W*
21 S15 **Saint Helena Sound** *inlet* South Carolina, SE USA
31 Q7 **Saint Helen, Lake** ◎ Michigan, N USA
183 Q16 **Saint Helens** Tasmania, SE Australia *41°21′S 148°15′E*
97 K18 **St Helens** NW England, United Kingdom *53°28′N 02°44′W*
32 G10 **Saint Helens** Oregon, NW USA *45°54′N 122°50′W*
32 H10 **Saint Helens, Mount** ▲ Washington, NW USA *46°24′N 121°49′W*
97 L26 **St Helier** ○ (Jersey) S Jersey, Channel Islands *49°12′N 02°07′W*
15 S9 **St-Hilarion** Québec, SE Canada *47°34′N 70°24′W*
99 K22 **Saint-Hubert** Luxembourg, SE Belgium *50°02′N 05°23′E*
15 P12 **St-Hyacinthe** Québec, SE Canada *45°38′N 72°57′W*
St.Iago de la Vega *see* Spanish Town
31 Q4 **Saint Ignace** Michigan, N USA *45°53′N 84°44′W*
15 O10 **St-Ignace-du-Lac** Québec, SE Canada *46°43′N 73°49′W*
12 D12 **St. Ignace Island** *island* Ontario, S Canada
108 C7 **St. Imier** Bern, W Switzerland *47°09′N 06°55′E*
97 G25 **St Ives** SW England, United Kingdom *50°12′N 05°29′W*
29 U10 **Saint James** Minnesota, N USA *44°00′N 94°36′W*
10 I15 **St. James, Cape** *headland* Graham Island, British Columbia, SW Canada *51°57′N 131°04′W*
15 O13 **St-Jean** *var.* St-Jean-sur-Richelieu. Québec, SE Canada *45°15′N 73°16′W*
55 X9 **St-Jean** NW French Guiana *05°25′N 54°05′W*
Saint-Jean-d'Acre *see* Akko
102 K11 **St-Jean-d'Angély** Charente-Maritime, W France *45°57′N 00°31′W*
103 N7 **St-Jean-de-Braye** Loiret, C France *47°54′N 01°58′E*
102 I16 **St-Jean-de-Luz** Pyrénées-Atlantiques, SW France *43°24′N 01°40′W*
103 T12 **St-Jean-de-Maurienne** Savoie, E France *45°17′N 06°21′E*
102 I9 **St-Jean-de-Monts** Vendée, NW France *46°45′N 02°00′W*
103 Q14 **St-Jean-du-Gard** Gard, S France *44°06′N 03°49′E*
15 Q7 **St-Jean, Lac** ◎ Québec, SE Canada
102 I16 **St-Jean-Pied-de-Port** Pyrénées-Atlantiques, SW France *43°10′N 01°14′W*
15 S9 **St-Jean-Port-Joli** Québec, SE Canada *47°13′N 70°16′W*
St-Jean-sur-Richelieu *see* St-Jean
15 N12 **St-Jérôme** Québec, SE Canada *45°47′N 74°01′W*
25 T5 **Saint Jo** Texas, SW USA *33°42′N 97°33′W*
13 O15 **St. John** New Brunswick, SE Canada *45°16′N 66°03′W*
26 L6 **Saint John** Kansas, C USA *37°59′N 98°44′W*
19 Q2 **Saint John** *Fr.* Saint-John. ≈ Canada/USA
76 K16 **Saint John** ≈ C Liberia
45 T9 **Saint John** *island* C Virgin Islands (US)
Saint-John *see* Saint John
22 I6 **Saint John, Lake** ◎ Louisiana, S USA
45 W10 **St John's** ● (Antigua and Barbuda) Antigua, Antigua and Barbuda *17°06′N 61°50′W*
13 V12 **St. John's** *province capital* Newfoundland and Labrador, E Canada *47°34′N 52°41′W*
37 O12 **Saint Johns** Arizona, SW USA *34°28′N 109°22′W*
31 Q9 **Saint Johns** Michigan, N USA *43°01′N 84°31′W*
13 V12 **St. John's** ✈ Newfoundland and Labrador, E Canada *47°22′N 52°45′W*
23 X11 **Saint Johns River** ≈ Florida, SE USA
103 Q11 **St-Jost-St-Rambert** Loire, E France *45°30′N 04°13′E*
45 N12 **St. Joseph** W Dominica *15°24′N 61°26′W*
173 P17 **St-Joseph** S Réunion
22 J6 **Saint Joseph** Louisiana, S USA *31°56′N 91°14′W*
31 O10 **Saint Joseph** Michigan, N USA *42°05′N 86°30′W*
27 R3 **Saint Joseph** Missouri, C USA *39°46′N 94°49′W*
20 I10 **Saint Joseph** Tennessee, S USA *35°02′N 87°29′W*
22 R9 **Saint Joseph Bay** *bay* Florida, SE USA
15 R11 **St-Joseph-de-Beauce** Québec, SE Canada *46°20′N 70°52′W*
12 C10 **St. Joseph, Lake** ◎ Ontario, C Canada
31 Q11 **Saint Joseph River** ≈ N USA
14 C11 **Saint Joseph's Island** *island* Ontario, S Canada
15 N11 **St-Jovite** Québec, SE Canada *46°07′N 74°35′W*
St Julian's *see* San Giljan
St-Julien *see* St-Julien-en-Genevois
103 T10 **St-Julien-en-Genevois** *var.* St-Julien. Haute-Savoie, E France *46°07′N 06°06′E*
102 M11 **St-Junien** Haute-Vienne, C France *45°52′N 00°54′E*
96 D8 **St Kilda** *island* NW Scotland, United Kingdom
45 V10 **Saint Kitts** *island* Saint Kitts and Nevis
45 U10 **Saint Kitts and Nevis** *off.* Federation of Saint Christopher and Nevis, *var.* Saint Christopher-Nevis. ◆ *commonwealth republic* E West Indies
11 X16 **St. Laurent** Manitoba, S Canada *50°20′N 97°55′W*
St-Laurent *see* St-Laurent-du-Maroni
55 X9 **St-Laurent-du-Maroni** *var.* St-Laurent. NW French Guiana *05°29′N 54°03′W*
St-Laurent, Fleuve *see* St. Lawrence
102 J12 **St-Laurent-Médoc** Gironde, SW France *45°11′N 00°50′W*
13 N12 **St. Lawrence** *Fr.* Fleuve St-Laurent. ≈ Canada/USA
13 Q12 **St. Lawrence, Gulf of** *gulf* NW Atlantic Ocean
38 K10 **Saint Lawrence Island** *island* Alaska, USA
14 M14 **Saint Lawrence River** ≈ Canada/USA
99 L25 **Saint-Léger** Luxembourg, SE Belgium *49°36′N 05°39′E*
13 N14 **St. Léonard** New Brunswick, SE Canada *47°10′N 67°55′W*
15 P11 **St-Léonard** Québec, SE Canada *46°06′N 72°18′W*
173 O17 **St-Leu** W Réunion *21°09′S 55°17′E*
102 J4 **St-Lô** *anc.* Briovera, Laudus. Manche, N France *49°07′N 01°08′W*
11 T15 **St. Louis** Saskatchewan, S Canada *52°50′N 105°43′W*
103 V7 **St-Louis** Haut-Rhin, NE France *47°35′N 07°34′E*
173 O17 **St-Louis** S Réunion
76 G10 **Saint Louis** NW Senegal *15°59′N 16°30′W*
27 X4 **Saint Louis** Missouri, C USA *38°38′N 90°15′W*
29 W5 **Saint Louis River** ≈ Minnesota, N USA
103 T7 **St-Loup-sur-Semouse** Haute-Saône, E France *47°53′N 06°15′E*
15 O12 **St-Luc** Québec, SE Canada *45°19′N 73°18′W*
45 X13 **Saint Lucia** ◆ *commonwealth republic* SE West Indies
47 S3 **Saint Lucia** *island* SE West Indies
83 L22 **St. Lucia, Cape** *headland* E South Africa *28°29′S 32°26′E*
45 Y13 **Saint Lucia Channel** *channel* Martinique/Saint Lucia
23 Y14 **Saint Lucie Canal** *canal* Florida, SE USA
23 Z13 **Saint Lucie Inlet** *inlet* Florida, SE USA
96 L2 **St Magnus Bay** *bay* N Scotland, United Kingdom
102 K10 **St-Maixent-l'École** Deux-Sèvres, W France *46°24′N 00°13′W*
11 Y16 **St. Malo** Manitoba, S Canada *49°16′N 96°58′W*
102 I5 **St-Malo** Ille-et-Vilaine, NW France *48°39′N 02°00′W*
102 H4 **St-Malo, Golfe de** *gulf* NW France
44 L9 **St-Marc** C Haiti *19°08′N 72°41′W*
44 L9 **St-Marc, Canal de** *channel* W Haiti
103 S12 **St-Marcellin-le-Mollard** Isère, E France *45°12′N 05°18′E*
55 Y12 **Saint-Marcel, Mont** ▲ S French Guiana *2°32′N 53°00′E*
96 K5 **St Margaret's Hope** NE Scotland, United Kingdom *58°50′N 02°57′W*
32 M9 **Saint Maries** Idaho, NW USA *47°19′N 116°37′W*
23 T9 **Saint Marks** Florida, SE USA *30°09′N 84°12′W*
108 D11 **St. Martin** Valais, SW Switzerland *46°09′N 07°27′E*
Saint Martin *see* Sint Maarten
31 O5 **Saint Martin Island** *island* Michigan, N USA
22 I9 **Saint Martinville** Louisiana, S USA *30°09′N 91°51′W*
185 E20 **St. Mary, Mount** ▲ South Island, New Zealand *44°16′S 169°42′E*
186 E8 **St. Mary, Mount** ▲ S Papua New Guinea *08°06′S 147°00′E*
182 I6 **Saint Mary Peak** ▲ South Australia *31°35′S 138°39′E*
183 Q16 **Saint Marys** Tasmania, SE Australia *41°34′S 148°13′E*
14 E16 **St. Marys** Ontario, S Canada *43°15′N 81°08′W*

◆ Country
● Country Capital
◇ Dependent Territory
○ Dependent Territory Capital
⬖ Administrative Regions
✈ International Airport
▲ Mountain
▲▲ Mountain Range
⛰ Volcano
≈ River
◎ Lake
⊠ Reservoir

38 M11 **Saint Marys** Alaska, USA 62°03′N 163°10′W
23 W8 **Saint Marys** Georgia, SE USA 30°44′N 81°30′W
27 P4 **Saint Marys** Kansas, C USA 39°09′N 96°00′W
31 Q4 **Saint Marys** Ohio, N USA 40°31′N 84°22′W
21 R3 **Saint Marys** West Virginia, NE USA 39°24′N 81°13′W
23 W8 **Saint Marys River** ≋ Florida/Georgia, SE USA
31 Q4 **Saint Marys River** ≋ Michigan, N USA
102 D6 **St-Mathieu, Pointe** *headland* NW France 48°17′N 04°56′W
38 J12 **Saint Matthew Island** *island* Alaska, USA
21 R13 **Saint Matthews** South Carolina, SE USA 33°40′N 80°44′W
St.Matthew's Island *see* Zadetkyi Kyun
186 G4 **St.Matthias Group** *island group* NE Papua New Guinea
108 C11 **St. Maurice** Valais, SW Switzerland 46°09′N 07°28′E
15 P9 **St-Maurice** ≋ Québec, SE Canada
102 J13 **St-Médard-en-Jalles** Gironde, SW France 44°54′N 00°43′W
39 N10 **Saint Michael** Alaska, USA 63°28′N 162°02′W
15 N10 **St-Michel-des-Saints** Québec, SE Canada 46°39′N 73°54′W
103 S5 **St-Mihiel** Meuse, NE France 48°57′N 05°33′E
108 J10 **St. Moritz** *Ger.* Sankt Moritz, *Rmsch.* San Murezzan. Graubünden, SE Switzerland 46°30′N 09°51′E
102 H8 **St-Nazaire** Loire-Atlantique, NW France 47°17′N 02°12′W
Saint Nicholas *see* São Nicolau
Saint-Nicolas *see* Sint-Niklaas
103 N1 **St-Omer** Pas-de-Calais, N France 50°45′N 02°15′E
102 J11 **Saintonge** *cultural region* W France
15 S9 **St-Pacôme** Québec, SE Canada 47°22′N 69°56′W
15 S10 **St-Pamphile** Québec, SE Canada 46°57′N 69°46′W
15 S9 **St-Pascal** Québec, SE Canada 47°32B 69°48′W
15 J11 **St-Patrice, Lac** ◎ Québec, SE Canada
11 R14 **St. Paul** Alberta, SW Canada 54°00′N 111°18′W
173 O16 **St-Paul** NW Réunion
38 K14 **Saint Paul** Saint Paul Island, Alaska, USA 57°08′N 170°13′W
29 V8 **Saint Paul** *state capital* Minnesota, N USA 45°N 93°10′W
29 P15 **Saint Paul** Nebraska, C USA 41°13′N 98°26′W
21 P7 **Saint Paul** Virginia, NE USA 36°53′N 82°18′W
77 Q17 **Saint Paul, Cape** *headland* S Ghana 05°44′N 00°55′E
103 O17 **St-Paul-de-Fenouillet** Pyrénées-Orientales, S France 42°49′N 02°29′E
65 K14 **Saint Paul Fracture Zone** *tectonic feature* E Atlantic Ocean
38 J14 **Saint Paul Island** *island* Pribilof Islands, Alaska, USA
102 J15 **St-Paul-les-Dax** Landes, SW France 43°45′N 01°01′W
21 U11 **Saint Pauls** North Carolina, SE USA 34°45′N 78°56′W
Saint Paul's Bay *see* San Pawl il Bahar
191 R16 **St Paul's Point** *headland* Pitcairn Island, Pitcairn Islands
29 U10 **Saint Peter** Minnesota, N USA 44°21′N 93°58′W
97 L26 **St Peter Port** ○ (Guernsey) C Guernsey, Channel Islands 49°28′N 02°33′W
23 V13 **Saint Petersburg** Florida, SE USA 27°47′N 82°37′W
Saint Petersburg *see* Sankt-Peterburg
23 V13 **Saint Petersburg Beach** Florida, SE USA 27°43′N 82°43′W
173 P17 **St-Philippe** SE Réunion 21°21′S 55°46′E
45 Q11 **St-Pierre** NW Martinique 14°44′N 61°11′W
173 O17 **St-Pierre** SW Réunion
13 S13 **St-Pierre and Miquelon** *Fr.* Îles St-Pierre et Miquelon. ◇ *French territorial collectivity* NE North America
15 P11 **St-Pierre, Lac** ◎ Québec, SE Canada
102 F5 **St-Pol-de-Léon** Finistère, NW France 48°42′N 04°00′W
103 O2 **St-Pol-sur-Ternoise** Pas-de-Calais, N France 50°22′N 02°21′E
St. Pons *see* St-Pons-de-Thomières
103 O16 **St-Pons-de-Thomières** *var.* St. Pons. Hérault, S France 43°28′N 02°48′E
103 P10 **St-Pourçain-sur-Sioule** Allier, C France 46°19′N 03°16′E
15 S11 **St-Prosper** Québec, SE Canada 46°14′N 70°28′W
103 P3 **St-Quentin** Aisne, N France 49°51′N 03°17′E
15 R10 **St-Raphaël** Québec, SE Canada 46°47′N 70°46′W
103 U15 **St-Raphaël** Var, SE France 43°26′N 06°46′E
15 Q10 **St-Raymond** Québec, SE Canada 46°53′N 71°49′W
33 O9 **Saint Regis** Montana, NW USA 47°18′N 115°06′W
18 J7 **Saint Regis River** ≋ New York, NE USA
103 R15 **St-Rémy-de-Provence** Bouches-du-Rhône, SE France 43°48′N 04°49′E
102 M9 **St-Savin** Vienne, W France 46°34′N 00°53′E
Saint-Sébastien,Cap *see* Anorontany, Tanjona
23 X7 **Saint Simons Island** *island* Georgia, SE USA
191 Y2 **Saint Stanislas Bay** *bay* Kiritimati, E Kiribati
13 O15 **St. Stephen** New Brunswick, SE Canada 45°12′N 67°18′W
39 X12 **Saint Terese** Alaska, USA 58°28′N 134°46′W
14 E17 **St. Thomas** Ontario, S Canada 42°46′N 81°12′W
29 Q2 **Saint Thomas** North Dakota, N USA 48°37′N 97°28′W
45 T9 **Saint Thomas** *island* W Virgin Islands (US)
Saint Thomas *see* São Tomé, Sao Tome and Principe
Saint Thomas *see* Charlotte Amalie, Virgin Islands (US)
15 P10 **St-Tite** Québec, SE Canada 46°42′N 72°32′W
Saint-Trond *see* Sint-Truiden
103 U16 **St-Tropez** Var, SE France 43°16′N 06°39′E
St. Ubes *see* Setúbal
102 L3 **St-Valéry-en-Caux** Seine-Maritime, N France 49°53′N 00°42′E
103 Q9 **St-Vallier** Saône-et-Loire, C France 46°39′N 04°19′E
106 B7 **St-Vincent** Valle d'Aosta, NW Italy 45°47′N 07°42′E
45 Q14 **Saint Vincent** *island* N Saint Vincent and the Grenadines
Saint Vincent *see* São Vicente
45 W14 **Saint Vincent and the Grenadines** ◆ *commonwealth republic* SE West Indies
Saint-Vincent, Cap *see* Ankaboa, Tanjona
Saint Vincent, Cape *see* São Vicente, Cabo de
102 I15 **St-Vincent-de-Tyrosse** Landes, SW France 43°39′N 01°16′W
182 I9 **Saint Vincent, Gulf** *gulf* South Australia
23 R10 **Saint Vincent Island** *island* Florida, SE USA
45 T12 **Saint Vincent Passage** *passage* Saint Lucia/Saint Vincent and the Grenadines
183 N18 **Saint Vincent, Point** *headland* Tasmania, SE Australia 43°19′S 145°50′E
Saint-Vith *see* Sankt-Vith
11 S14 **St. Walburg** Saskatchewan, S Canada 53°38′N 109°12′W
St Wolfgangsee *see* Wolfgangsee
102 M11 **St-Yrieix-la-Perche** Haute-Vienne, C France 45°31′N 01°12′E
Saint Yves *see* Setúbal
188 H5 **Saipan** *island* ● (Northern Mariana Islands) S Northern Mariana Islands
188 H6 **Saipan Channel** *channel* S Northern Mariana Islands
188 H6 **Saipan International** ✈ Saipan, S Northern Mariana Islands
74 G6 **Saïs** ✈ (Fès) C Morocco 33°58′N 04°48′W
Saishū *see* Jeju-do
Saishū *see* Jeju
102 J16 **Saison** ≋ SW France
169 R10 **Sai, Sungai** ≋ Borneo, N Indonesia
165 N13 **Saitama** *off.* Saitama-ken. ◈ *prefecture* Honshū, S Japan
Saitama-ken *see* Saitama
Saiyid Abid *see* Sayyid 'Abīd
57 J19 **Sajama, Nevado** ▲ W Bolivia 17°57′S 68°51′W
141 V13 **Sājir, Ras** *headland* S Oman 16°42′N 53°40′E
111 M20 **Sajószentpéter** Borsod-Abaúj-Zemplén, NE Hungary 48°13′N 20°43′E
83 F24 **Sak** ≋ SW South Africa
81 J18 **Saka** Coast, E Kenya 0°11′S 39°27′E
167 P11 **Sa Kaeo** Prachin Buri, C Thailand 13°47′N 102°03′E
164 J14 **Sakai** Ōsaka, Honshū, SW Japan 34°35′N 135°28′E
164 H14 **Sakaide** Kagawa, Shikoku, SW Japan 34°19′N 133°50′E
164 H12 **Sakaiminato** Tottori, Honshū, SW Japan 35°34′N 133°12′E
140 M3 **Sakākah** Al Jawf, NW Saudi Arabia 29°56′N 40°10′E
28 L4 **Sakakawea, Lake** ⊠ North Dakota, N USA
12 J9 **Sakami, Lac** ◎ Québec, C Canada
79 O26 **Sakania** Katanga, SE Dem. Rep. Congo 12°44′S 28°34′E
146 K12 **Sakar** Lebap Welaýaty, E Turkmenistan 38°57′N 63°46′E
172 H7 **Sakaraha** Toliara, SW Madagascar 22°54′S 44°31′E
146 I14 **Sakarçäge** *var.* Sakarchäge, *Rus.* Sakar-Chaga. Mary Welaýaty, C Turkmenistan 37°40′N 61°33′E
Sakar-Chaga/Sakarchäge *see* Sakarçäge
Sak'art'velo *see* Georgia
136 F11 **Sakarya** ◈ *province* NW Turkey
136 F12 **Sakarya Nehri** ≋ NW Turkey
165 P9 **Sakata** Yamagata, Honshū, C Japan 38°54′N 139°51′E
123 P9 **Sakha (Yakutiya), Respublika** *var.* Respublika Yakutiya, *Eng.* Yakutia. ◈ *autonomous republic* NE Russian Federation
Sakhalin *see* Sakhalin, Ostrov
192 I3 **Sakhalin, Ostrov** *var.* Sakhalin. *island* SE Russian Federation
123 U12 **Sakhalinskaya Oblast'** ◈ *province* SE Russian Federation
123 T12 **Sakhalinskiy Zaliv** *gulf* E Russian Federation
Sakhnovshchina *see* Sakhnovshchyna
117 U6 **Sakhnovshchyna** *Rus.* Sakhnovshchina. Kharkivs'ka Oblast', E Ukraine 49°08′N 35°52′E
Sakhon Nakhon *see* Sakon Nakhon
Sakhtsar *see* Rāmsar
137 W10 **Şäki** *Rus.* Sheki; *prev.* Nukha. NW Azerbaijan 41°09′N 47°10′E
Saki *see* Saky
118 E13 **Šakiai** *Ger.* Schaken. Marijampolė, S Lithuania 54°57′N 23°04′E
165 O16 **Sakishima-shotō** *var.* Sakisima Syotô. *island group* SW Japan
Sakisima Syotô *see* Sakishima-shotō
Sakiz *see* Saqqez
Sakiz-Adasi *see* Chíos
155 F19 **Sakleshpur** Karnātaka, E India 12°58′N 75°45′E
167 S9 **Sakon Nakhon** *var.* Muang Sakon Nakhon, Sakhon Nakhon. Sakon Nakhon, E Thailand 17°10′N 104°08′E
149 P15 **Sakrand** Sind, SE Pakistan 26°06′N 68°20′E
83 F24 **Sak River** *Afr.* Sakrivier. Northern Cape, W South Africa 30°49′S 20°24′E
Sakrivier *see* Sak River
Saksaul'skiy *see* Saksaul'skoye
144 K13 **Saksaul'skoye** *var.* Saksaul'skiy, *Kaz.* Sekseüil. Kzylorda, S Kazakhstan 47°07′N 61°06′E
95 I25 **Sakskøbing** Sjælland, SE Denmark 54°48′N 11°39′E
165 N12 **Saku** Nagano, Honshū, S Japan 36°17′N 138°29′E
117 S13 **Saky** *Rus.* Saki. Avtonomna Respublika Krym, S Ukraine 45°09′N 33°36′E
76 E9 **Sal** *island* Ilhas de Barlavento, NE Cape Verde
127 N12 **Sal** ≋ SW Russian Federation
111 I21 **Sal'a** *Hung.* Sellye, Vágsellye. Nitriansky Kraj, SW Slovakia 48°09′N 17°51′E
95 N15 **Sala** Västmanland, C Sweden 59°55′N 16°38′E
15 N13 **Salaberry-de-Valleyfield** *var.* Valleyfield. Québec, SE Canada 45°15′N 74°07′W
118 G7 **Salacgrīva** *Est.* Salatsi. N Latvia 57°45′N 24°21′E
107 M18 **Sala Consilina** Campania, S Italy 40°23′N 15°35′E
40 C2 **Salada, Laguna** ◎ NW Mexico
61 D14 **Saladas** Corrientes, NE Argentina 28°15′S 58°40′W
61 C21 **Saladillo** Buenos Aires, E Argentina 35°40′S 59°50′W
61 B16 **Saladillo, Río** ≋ C Argentina
25 T9 **Salado** Texas, SW USA 30°57′N 97°32′W
63 J16 **Salado, Arroyo** ≋ SE Argentina
61 D21 **Salado, Río** ≋ E Argentina
62 L12 **Salado, Río** ≋ C Argentina
41 N7 **Salado, Río** ≋ NE Mexico
37 Q12 **Salado, Río** ≋ New Mexico, SW USA
143 N6 **Salafchegān** *var.* Sarafjagān. Quom, N Iran 34°28′N 50°28′E
77 Q15 **Salaga** C Ghana 08°31′N 00°37′W
192 G5 **Sala'ilua** Savai'i, W Samoa 13°39′S 172°33′W
116 G9 **Sălaj** ◈ *county* NW Romania
83 H20 **Salajwe** Kweneng, SE Botswana 23°40′S 24°46′E
78 H9 **Salal** Kanem, W Chad 14°48′N 17°12′E
80 I6 **Salala** Red Sea, NE Sudan 21°17′N 36°16′E
141 V13 **Şalālah** SW Oman 17°01′N 54°04′E
42 D5 **Salamá** Baja Verapaz, C Guatemala 15°06′N 90°18′W
42 J6 **Salamá** Olancho, C Honduras 14°48′N 86°34′W
62 G10 **Salamanca** Coquimbo, C Chile 31°47′S 70°58′W
41 N13 **Salamanca** Guanajuato, C Mexico 20°34′N 101°12′W
104 K7 **Salamanca** *anc.* Helmantica, Salmantica. Castilla y León, NW Spain 40°58′N 05°40′W
18 D11 **Salamanca** New York, NE USA 42°09′N 78°43′W
104 J7 **Salamanca** ◈ *province* Castilla y León, W Spain
63 J19 **Salamanca, Pampa de** *plain* S Argentina
78 J12 **Salamat** *off.* Préfecture du Salamat. ◈ *préfecture* SE Chad
78 I12 **Salamat, Bahr** ≋ S Chad
Salamat, Préfecture du *see* Salamat
54 F5 **Salamina** Magdalena, N Colombia 10°30′N 74°48′W
115 G19 **Salamina** *var.* Salamís. Salamína, C Greece 37°58′N 23°29′E
115 G19 **Salamína** *island* C Greece
Salamís *see* Salamína
138 I5 **Salamīyah** *var.* As Salamīyah. Ḥamāh, W Syria 35°01′N 37°02′E
31 P12 **Salamonie Lake** ⊠ Indiana, N USA
31 P12 **Salamonie River** ≋ Indiana, N USA
Salang *see* Phuket
192 I16 **Salani** Upolu, SE Samoa 14°00′S 171°35′W
118 C11 **Salantai** Klaipėda, NW Lithuania 56°05′N 21°36′E
104 K2 **Salas** Asturias, N Spain 43°25′N 06°15′W
105 O5 **Salas de los Infantes** Castilla y León, N Spain 42°02′N 03°17′W
102 M16 **Salat** ≋ S France
189 V13 **Salat** *island* Chuuk, C Micronesia
169 Q16 **Salatiga** Jawa, C Indonesia 07°15′S 110°34′E
189 V13 **Salat Pass** *passage* W Pacific Ocean
Salatsi *see* Salacgrīva
167 T10 **Salavan** *var.* Saravan, Saravane. Salavan, S Laos 15°43′N 106°26′E
127 V6 **Salavat** Respublika Bashkortostan, W Russian Federation 53°20′N 55°54′E
56 C12 **Salaverry** La Libertad, N Peru 08°14′S 78°55′W
171 T12 **Salawati, Pulau** *island* E Indonesia
193 R10 **Sala y Gomez** *island* Chile, E Pacific Ocean
Sala y Gomez Fracture Zone *see* Sala y Gomez Ridge
193 S10 **Sala y Gomez Ridge** *var.* Sala y Gomez Fracture Zone. *tectonic feature* SE Pacific Ocean
61 A22 **Salazar** Buenos Aires, E Argentina 36°20′S 62°11′W
54 G7 **Salazar** Norte de Santander, N Colombia 07°46′N 72°46′W
Salazar *see* N'Dalatando
173 P16 **Salazie** C Réunion 21°02′S 55°33′E
103 N8 **Salbris** Loir-et-Cher, C France 47°25′N 02°02′E
57 G15 **Salcantay, Nevado** ▲ C Peru 13°21′S 72°31′W
45 O8 **Salcedo** N Dominican Republic 19°26′N 70°25′W
39 S9 **Salcha River** ≋ Alaska, USA
119 H15 **Šalčininkai** Vilnius, SE Lithuania 54°20′N 25°26′E
Saldae *see* Béjaïa
54 E11 **Saldaña** Tolima, C Colombia 03°57′N 75°01′W
104 M4 **Saldaña** Castilla y León, N Spain 42°31′N 04°44′W
83 E25 **Saldanha** Western Cape, SW South Africa 33°00′S 17°56′E
Salduba *see* Zaragoza
61 B23 **Saldungaray** Buenos Aires, E Argentina 38°15′S 61°45′W
118 D9 **Saldus** *Ger.* Frauenburg. W Latvia 56°40′N 22°29′E
183 P13 **Sale** Victoria, SE Australia 38°06′S 147°06′E
74 F6 **Salé** NW Morocco 34°07′N 06°40′W
74 F6 **Salé** ✈ (Rabat) W Morocco 34°09′N 06°30′W
Salehābād *see* Andīmeshk
170 M16 **Saleh, Teluk** *bay* Nusa Tenggara, S Indonesia
122 H8 **Salekhard** *prev.* Obdorsk. Yamalo-Nenetskiy Avtonomnyy Okrug, N Russian Federation 66°33′N 66°35′E
192 H16 **Sālelologa** Savai'i, C Samoa 13°42′S 172°10′W
155 H21 **Salem** Tamil Nādu, SE India 11°38′N 78°08′E
27 V9 **Salem** Arkansas, C USA 36°21′N 91°49′W
30 L15 **Salem** Illinois, N USA 38°37′N 88°57′W
31 P15 **Salem** Indiana, N USA 38°38′N 86°06′W
19 P11 **Salem** Massachusetts, NE USA 42°30′N 70°51′W
27 V6 **Salem** Missouri, C USA 37°39′N 91°32′W
18 I16 **Salem** New Jersey, NE USA 39°33′N 75°26′W
31 U12 **Salem** Ohio, N USA 40°52′N 80°51′W
32 G12 **Salem** *state capital* Oregon, NW USA 44°57′N 123°01′W
29 Q11 **Salem** South Dakota, N USA 43°43′N 97°23′W
36 L4 **Salem** Utah, W USA 40°03′N 111°40′W
21 S7 **Salem** Virginia, NE USA 37°16′N 80°00′W
21 R3 **Salem** West Virginia, NE USA 39°15′N 80°32′W
107 H23 **Salemi** Sicilia, Italy, C Mediterranean Sea 37°48′N 12°48′E
Salemy *see* As Sālimī
94 K12 **Sälen** Dalarna, C Sweden 61°11′N 13°14′E
107 Q18 **Salentina, Campi** Puglia, SE Italy 40°23′N 18°01′E
107 Q18 **Salentina, Penisola** *peninsula* SE Italy
107 L18 **Salerno** *anc.* Salernum. Campania, S Italy 40°40′N 14°44′E
107 L18 **Salerno, Golfo di** *Eng.* Gulf of Salerno. *gulf* S Italy
Salerno, Gulf of *see* Salerno, Golfo di
Salernum *see* Salerno
97 K17 **Salford** NW England, United Kingdom 53°30′N 02°16′W
Salgir *see* Salhyr
111 K21 **Salgótarján** Nógrád, N Hungary 48°07′N 19°47′E
59 O15 **Salgueiro** Pernambuco, E Brazil 08°04′S 39°05′W
94 C13 **Salhus** Hordaland, S Norway 60°30′N 05°15′E
117 T12 **Salhyr** *Rus.* Salgir. ≋ S Ukraine
171 Q9 **Salibabu, Pulau** *island* N Indonesia
37 S6 **Salida** Colorado, C USA 38°29′N 105°57′W
102 J15 **Salies-de-Béarn** Pyrénées-Atlantiques, SW France 43°28′N 00°55′W
136 C14 **Salihli** Manisa, W Turkey 38°29′N 28°08′E
119 K18 **Salihorsk** *Rus.* Soligorsk. Minskaya Voblasts', S Belarus 52°48′N 27°32′E
119 K18 **Salihorskaye Vodaskhovishcha** ⊠ C Belarus
83 N14 **Salima** Central, C Malawi 13°44′S 34°21′E
166 L5 **Salin** Magway, W Myanmar (Burma) 20°30′N 94°40′E
27 N4 **Salina** Kansas, C USA 38°53′N 97°36′W
36 L5 **Salina** Utah, W USA 38°57′N 111°54′W
41 S17 **Salina Cruz** Oaxaca, SE Mexico 16°11′N 95°12′W
107 L22 **Salina, Isola** *island* Isole Eolie, S Italy
44 J5 **Salina Point** *headland* Acklins Island, SE Bahamas 22°10′N 74°16′W
56 A7 **Salinas** Guayas, W Ecuador 02°15′S 80°58′W
40 M11 **Salinas** *var.* Salinas de Hidalgo. San Luis Potosí, C Mexico 22°36′N 101°41′W
45 T6 **Salinas** C Puerto Rico 17°57′N 66°18′W
35 O10 **Salinas** California, W USA 36°41′N 121°40′W
Salinas, Cabo de *see* Salines, Cap de ses
Salinas de Hidalgo *see* Salinas
82 A13 **Salinas, Ponta das** *headland* W Angola 12°50′S 12°57′E
45 O10 **Salinas, Punta** *headland* S Dominican Republic 18°11′N 70°32′W
Salinas, Río *see* Chixoy, Río
35 O11 **Salinas River** ≋ California, W USA
22 H6 **Saline Lake** ◎ Louisiana, S USA
25 R17 **Salineno** Texas, SW USA 26°29′N 99°06′W
27 V14 **Saline River** ≋ Arkansas, C USA
30 M17 **Saline River** ≋ Illinois, N USA
105 X10 **Salines, Cap de ses** *var.* Cabo de Salinas. *headland* Mallorca, Spain, W Mediterranean Sea 39°15′N 03°03′E
Salisburg *see* Mazsalaca
45 O12 **Salisbury** *var.* Baroui. W Dominica 15°26′N 61°27′W
97 M23 **Salisbury** *var.* New Sarum. S England, United Kingdom 51°05′N 01°48′W
21 Y4 **Salisbury** Maryland, NE USA 38°22′N 75°37′W
27 T3 **Salisbury** Missouri, C USA 39°25′N 92°48′W
21 S9 **Salisbury** North Carolina, SE USA 35°40′N 80°28′W
Salisbury *see* Harare
9 Q7 **Salisbury Island** *island* Nunavut, NE Canada
Salisbury, Lake *see* Bisina, Lake
97 L23 **Salisbury Plain** *plain* S England, United Kingdom
21 R14 **Salkehatchie River** ≋ South Carolina, SE USA
138 I9 **Şalkhad** As Suwaydā', SW Syria 32°29′N 36°42′E
92 M12 **Salla** Lappi, NE Finland 66°50′N 28°40′E
Sállan *see* Sørøya
103 U11 **Sallanches** Haute-Savoie, E France 45°55′N 06°37′E
105 V5 **Sallent** Cataluña, NE Spain 41°48′N 01°52′E
Salliq *see* Coral Harbour
61 A22 **Salliqueló** Buenos Aires, E Argentina 36°45′S 62°55′W
27 R10 **Sallisaw** Oklahoma, C USA 35°27′N 94°49′W
80 I7 **Sallom** Red Sea, NE Sudan 19°17′N 37°02′E
12 J2 **Salluit** *prev.* Saglouc, Sagluk. Québec, NE Canada 62°10′N 75°40′W
Sallyana *see* Şalyān
13 S11 **Sally's Cove** Newfoundland and Labrador, E Canada 49°43′N 58°00′W
139 W9 **Salmān Bin 'Arāzah** Maysān, E Iraq 32°33′N 46°36′E
Salmantica *see* Salamanca
142 I2 **Salmās** *prev.* Dilman, Shāpūr. Āžarbāyjān-e Gharbī, NW Iran 38°13′N 44°50′E
124 I11 **Salmi** Respublika Kareliya, NW Russian Federation 61°21′N 31°55′E
33 P12 **Salmon** Idaho, NW USA 45°10′N 113°54′W
11 N16 **Salmon Arm** British Columbia, SW Canada 50°41′N 119°18′W
192 L5 **Salmon Bank** *undersea feature* N Pacific Ocean 26°55′N 176°28′W
Salmon Leap *see* Leixlip
34 L2 **Salmon Mountains** ▲▲ California, W USA
14 J15 **Salmon Point** *headland* Ontario, SE Canada 43°51′N 77°15′W
33 N11 **Salmon River** ≋ Idaho, NW USA
18 K6 **Salmon River** ≋ New York, NE USA
33 N12 **Salmon River Mountains** ▲▲ Idaho, NW USA
18 I9 **Salmon River Reservoir** ⊠ New York, NE USA
93 K19 **Salo** Länsi-Suomi, SW Finland 60°23′N 23°10′E
106 F7 **Salò** Lombardia, N Italy 45°37′N 10°30′E
Salona/Salonae *see* Solin
103 S15 **Salon-de-Provence** Bouches-du-Rhône, SE France 43°39′N 05°05′E
Salonica/Salonika *see* Thessaloníki
115 I14 **Salonikiós, Akrotírio** *var.* Akrotírio Salonikós. *headland* Thásos, E Greece 40°34′N 24°39′E
Salonikós, Akrotírio *see* Salonikiós, Akrotírio
116 F10 **Salonta** *Hung.* Nagyszalonta. Bihor, W Romania 46°49′N 21°40′E
104 I9 **Salor** ≋ W Spain
105 U6 **Salou** Cataluña, NE Spain 41°05′N 01°08′E
76 H11 **Saloum** ≋ C Senegal
42 H4 **Sal, Punta** *headland* NW Honduras 15°55′N 87°36′W
92 N3 **Salpynten** *headland* W Svalbard 78°12′N 12°11′E
138 I3 **Salqīn** Idlib, W Syria 36°09′N 36°27′E
93 F14 **Salsbruket** Nord-Trøndelag, C Norway 64°49′N 11°48′E
126 M13 **Sal'sk** Rostovskaya Oblast', SW Russian Federation 46°30′N 41°31′E
107 J25 **Salso** ≋ Sicilia, Italy, C Mediterranean Sea
107 K25 **Salso** ≋ Sicilia, Italy, C Mediterranean Sea
106 E9 **Salsomaggiore Terme** Emilia-Romagna, N Italy 44°49′N 09°58′E
Salt *see* As Salṭ
62 J6 **Salta** Salta, NW Argentina 24°47′S 65°23′W
62 K6 **Salta** *off.* Provincia de Salta. ◈ *province* N Argentina
Salta, Provincia de *see* Salta
97 I24 **Saltash** SW England, United Kingdom 50°26′N 04°14′W
24 J9 **Salt Basin** *basin* Texas, SW USA
11 V16 **Saltcoats** Saskatchewan, S Canada 51°06′N 102°12′W
30 L13 **Salt Creek** ≋ Illinois, N USA
24 J9 **Salt Draw** ≋ Texas, SW USA
97 F21 **Saltee Islands** *island group* SE Ireland
92 G12 **Saltfjorden** *inlet* C Norway
24 I8 **Salt Flat** Texas, SW USA 31°43′N 105°05′W
27 N8 **Salt Fork Arkansas River** ≋ Oklahoma, C USA
31 T13 **Salt Fork Lake** ⊠ Ohio, N USA
26 J11 **Salt Fork Red River** ≋ Oklahoma/Texas, C USA
95 J23 **Saltholm** *island* E Denmark
41 N8 **Saltillo** Coahuila, NE Mexico 25°30′N 101°W
182 L5 **Salt Lake** *salt lake* New South Wales, SE Australia
37 V15 **Salt Lake** ◎ New Mexico, SW USA
36 K2 **Salt Lake City** *state capital* Utah, W USA 40°45′N 111°54′W
61 C20 **Salto** Buenos Aires, E Argentina 34°18′S 60°17′W
61 D17 **Salto** Salto, N Uruguay 31°23′S 57°58′W
61 E17 **Salto** ◈ *department* N Uruguay
107 I14 **Salto** ≋ C Italy
62 Q6 **Salto del Guairá** Canindeyú, E Paraguay 24°06′S 54°22′W
61 D17 **Salto Grande, Embalse de** *var.* Lago de Salto Grande. ⊠ Argentina/Uruguay
Salto Grande, Lago de *see* Salto Grande, Embalse de
35 W16 **Salton Sea** ◎ California, W USA
60 I12 **Salto Santiago, Represa de** ⊠ S Brazil
149 U7 **Salt Range** ▲▲ E Pakistan
36 M13 **Salt River** ≋ Arizona, SW USA
20 L5 **Salt River** ≋ Kentucky, S USA
27 V3 **Salt River** ≋ Missouri, C USA
95 F17 **Saltrød** Aust-Agder, S Norway 58°28′N 08°49′E
95 P16 **Saltsjöbaden** Stockholm, C Sweden 59°15′N 18°20′E
92 G12 **Saltstraumen** Nordland, C Norway 67°16′N 14°42′E
21 Q7 **Saltville** Virginia, NE USA 36°52′N 81°48′W
Saluces/Saluciae *see* Saluzzo
21 Q12 **Saluda** South Carolina, SE USA 34°00′N 81°47′W
21 X6 **Saluda** Virginia, NE USA 37°36′N 76°36′W
21 Q12 **Saluda River** ≋ South Carolina, SE USA
Salûm *see* As Sallūm
152 F14 **Sālumbar** Rājasthān, N India 24°16′N 74°04′E
Salûm, Gulf of *see* Khalīj as Sallūm
171 O11 **Salumpaga** Sulawesi, N Indonesia 01°18′N 120°58′E
155 M14 **Sālūr** Andhra Pradesh, E India 18°31′N 83°16′E
55 Y9 **Salut, Îles du** *island group* N French Guiana
106 A9 **Saluzzo** *Fr.* Saluces; *anc.* Saluciae. Piemonte, NW Italy 44°39′N 07°29′E
63 F23 **Salvación, Bahía** *bay* S Chile
59 P17 **Salvador** *prev.* São Salvador. *state capital* Bahia, E Brazil 12°58′S 38°29′W
65 E24 **Salvador** East Falkland, Falkland Islands 51°28′S 58°22′W
22 K10 **Salvador, Lake** ◎ Louisiana, S USA
Salvaleón de Higüey *see* Higüey
104 F10 **Salvaterra de Magos** Santarém, C Portugal 39°01′N 08°47′W
41 N13 **Salvatierra** Guanajuato, C Mexico 20°14′N 100°52′W
105 P3 **Salvatierra** *Basq.* Agurain. País Vasco, N Spain 42°52′N 02°23′W
Salwa/Salwah *see* As Salwā
166 M7 **Salween** *Bur.* Thanlwin, *Chin.* Nu Chiang, Nu Jiang. ≋ SE Asia
137 Y12 **Salyan** *Rus.* Sal'yany. SE Azerbaijan 39°36′N 48°57′E
153 N11 **Şalyān** *var.* Sallyana. Mid Western, W Nepal 28°22′N 82°10′E
Sal'yany *see* Salyan
21 O6 **Salyersville** Kentucky, S USA 37°43′N 83°06′W
109 V6 **Salza** ≋ E Austria
109 Q7 **Salzach** ≋ Austria/Germany
109 Q6 **Salzburg** *anc.* Juvavum. Salzburg, N Austria 47°48′N 13°03′E
109 O8 **Salzburg** *off.* Land Salzburg. ◈ *state* C Austria
Salzburg *see* Ocna Sibiului
Salzburg Alps *see* Salzburger Kalkalpen
109 Q7 **Salzburger Kalkalpen** *Eng.* Salzburg Alps. ▲▲ C Austria
Salzburg, Land *see* Salzburg
100 J13 **Salzgitter** *prev.* Watenstedt-Salzgitter. Niedersachsen, C Germany 52°07′N 10°24′E
101 G14 **Salzkotten** Nordrhein-Westfalen, W Germany 51°40′N 08°36′E
100 K11 **Salzwedel** Sachsen-Anhalt, N Germany 52°51′N 11°10′E
152 D11 **Sām** Rājasthān, NW India 26°50′N 70°30′E
Šamac *see* Bosanski Šamac
54 G9 **Samacá** Boyacá, C Colombia 05°28′N 73°33′W
40 I7 **Samachique** Chihuahua, N Mexico 27°17′N 107°28′W
141 Y8 **Şamad** NE Oman 22°47′N 58°12′E
Sama de Langreo *see* Sama, Spain
Samaden *see* Samedan
57 M19 **Samaipata** Santa Cruz, C Bolivia 18°08′S 63°53′W
Samakhixai *see* Attapu
Samakov *see* Samokov
42 B6 **Samalá, Río** ≋ SW Guatemala
40 J3 **Samalayuca** Chihuahua, N Mexico 31°25′N 106°30′W
155 L16 **Sāmalkot** Andhra Pradesh, E India 17°03′N 82°15′E
45 P8 **Samaná** *var.* Santa Bárbara de Samaná. E Dominican Republic 19°14′N 69°20′W
45 P8 **Samaná, Bahía de** *bay* E Dominican Republic
44 K4 **Samana Cay** *island* SE Bahamas
136 K17 **Samandağı** Hatay, S Turkey 36°07′N 35°55′E
149 P3 **Samangān** ◈ *province* N Afghanistan
Samangān *see* Aibak
165 T5 **Samani** Hokkaidō, NE Japan 42°07′N 142°57′E
54 C13 **Samaniego** Nariño, SW Colombia 01°22′N 77°35′W
171 Q5 **Samar** *island* C Philippines
127 S6 **Samara** *prev.* Kuybyshev. Samarskaya Oblast', W Russian Federation 53°15′N 50°15′E
127 T7 **Samara** ≋ W Russian Federation
127 S6 **Samara** ✈ Samarskaya Oblast', W Russian Federation 53°11′N 50°27′E
117 V7 **Samara** ≋ E Ukraine
186 G10 **Samarai** Milne Bay, SE Papua New Guinea 10°36′S 150°39′E
Samarang *see* Semarang
123 T14 **Samarga** Khabarovskiy Kray, SE Russian Federation 47°43′N 139°08′E
138 G9 **Samaria Hills** *hill range* N Israel
54 L9 **Samariapo** Amazonas, C Venezuela 05°16′N 67°43′W
169 V11 **Samarinda** Borneo, C Indonesia 0°30′S 117°09′E
Samarkand *see* Samarqand
Samarkandskaya Oblast' *see* Samarqand Viloyati
Samarkandski/Samarkandskoye *see* Temirtau
Samarobriva *see* Amiens
147 N11 **Samarqand** *Rus.* Samarkand. Samarqand Viloyati, C Uzbekistan 39°40′N 66°56′E
146 M11 **Samarqand Viloyati** *Rus.* Samarkandskaya Oblast'. ◈ *province* C Uzbekistan
139 S6 **Sāmarrā'** Ṣalāḥ ad Dīn, C Iraq 34°13′N 43°52′E
127 R7 **Samarskaya Oblast'** *prev.* Kuybyshevskaya Oblast'. ◈ *province* W Russian Federation
153 Q13 **Samastīpur** Bihār, N India 25°52′N 85°47′E
76 L14 **Samatiguila** NW Ivory Coast 09°51′N 07°36′W
Samawa *see* As Samāwah
137 Y11 **Şamaxı** *Rus.* Shemakha. E Azerbaijan 40°38′N 48°34′E
79 K18 **Samba** Equateur, NW Dem. Rep. Congo 0°13′N 21°17′E
79 N21 **Samba** Maniema, E Dem. Rep. Congo 04°41′S 26°23′E
152 H6 **Samba** Jammu and Kashmir, NW India 32°32′N 75°08′E
169 W10 **Sambaliung, Pegunungan** ▲▲ Borneo, N Indonesia
154 M11 **Sambalpur** Orissa, E India 21°28′N 84°04′E
67 X12 **Sambao** ≋ W Madagascar
169 Q10 **Sambas, Sungai** ≋ Borneo, N Indonesia
172 K2 **Sambava** Antsiranana, NE Madagascar 14°16′S 50°10′E
152 J10 **Sambhal** Uttar Pradesh, N India 28°35′N 78°34′E
152 H12 **Sāmbhar Salt Lake** ◎ N India
107 N21 **Sambiase** Calabria, SW Italy 38°58′N 16°16′E
116 H5 **Sambir** *Rus.* Sambor. L'vivs'ka Oblast', NW Ukraine 49°31′N 23°10′E
82 C13 **Sambo** Huambo, C Angola 13°07′S 16°06′E
Sambor *see* Sambir
61 E21 **Samborombón, Bahía** *bay* NE Argentina
99 H20 **Sambre** ≋ Belgium/France
43 V16 **Sambú, Río** ≋ SE Panama
163 Z14 **Samcheok** *Jap.* Sanchoku; *prev.* Samch'ŏk. NE South Korea 37°21′N 129°12′E
Samch'ŏk *see* Samcheok
Samch'ŏnpŏ *see* Sacheon
81 I21 **Same** Kilimanjaro, NE Tanzania 04°04′S 37°41′E
108 J10 **Samedan** *Ger.* Samaden. Graubünden, S Switzerland 46°31′N 09°51′E
82 K12 **Samfya** Luapula, N Zambia 11°22′S 29°34′E
141 W13 **Samḥān, Jabal** ▲▲ SW Oman
115 C18 **Sámi** Kefallonía, Iónia Nisiá, Greece, C Mediterranean Sea 38°15′N 20°39′E
56 F10 **Samiria, Río** ≋ N Peru
Samirum *see* Semīrom
167 Q13 **Samīt** *prev.* Phumĭ Samĭt. Kaôh Kŏng, SW Cambodia 10°54′N 103°09′E
137 V11 **Şämkir** *Rus.* Shamkhor. NW Azerbaijan 40°51′N 46°03′E
167 S7 **Sam, Nam** *Vtn.* Sông Chu. ≋ Laos/Vietnam
Samnān *see* Semnān
Sam Neua *see* Xam Nua
75 P10 **Samnū** C Libya 27°19′N 15°01′E
192 H15 **Samoa** *off.* Independent State of Samoa, *var.* Sāmoa; *prev.* Western Samoa. ◆ *monarchy* W Polynesia
192 L9 **Sāmoa** *island group* C Pacific Ocean
Sāmoa *see* Samoa
175 T9 **Samoa Basin** *undersea feature* W Pacific Ocean
Samoa, Independent State of *see* Samoa
112 D8 **Samobor** Zagreb, N Croatia 45°48′N 15°38′E
114 H10 **Samokov** *var.* Samakov. Sofiya, W Bulgaria 42°19′N 23°34′E
111 H21 **Šamorín** *Ger.* Sommerein, *Hung.* Somorja. Trnavský Kraj, W Slovakia 48°01′N 17°18′E
115 M19 **Sámos** *prev.* Limín Vathéos. Sámos, Dodekánisa, Greece, Aegean Sea 37°45′N 26°58′E
115 M20 **Sámos** *island* Dodekánisa, Greece, Aegean Sea
Samosch *see* Szamos
168 I9 **Samosir, Pulau** *island* W Indonesia
Samothrace *see* Samothráki
115 K14 **Samothráki** Samothráki, NE Greece 40°28′N 25°31′E
115 J14 **Samothráki** *anc.* Samothrace. *island* NE Greece
115 A15 **Samothráki** *island* Iónia Nisiá, Greece, C Mediterranean Sea
Samotschin *see* Szamocin
Sampê *see* Xiangcheng
169 S13 **Sampit** Borneo, C Indonesia 02°30′S 112°30′E
169 S12 **Sampit, Sungai** ≋ Borneo, N Indonesia
Sampoku *see* Sanpoku
186 H7 **Sampun** New Britain, E Papua New Guinea 05°19′S 152°06′E
79 N24 **Sampwe** Katanga, SE Dem. Rep. Congo 09°17′S 27°22′E
167 R11 **Sâmraông** *prev.* Phumĭ Sâmraông, Phum Samrong. Siĕmréab, NW Cambodia 14°11′N 103°31′E
25 X8 **Sam Rayburn Reservoir** ⊠ Texas, SW USA
167 Q6 **Sam Sao, Phou** ▲▲ Laos/Thailand
95 H22 **Samsø** *island* E Denmark
95 H23 **Samsø Bælt** *channel* E Denmark
167 T7 **Sâm Sơn** Thanh Hoa, N Vietnam 19°44′N 105°53′E
136 L11 **Samsun** *anc.* Amisus. Samsun, N Turkey 41°17′N 36°22′E
136 K11 **Samsun** ◈ *province* N Turkey
137 R9 **Samt'redia** *prev.* Samtredia. W Georgia 42°09′N 42°20′E
Samtredia *see* Samt'redia

◆ Country
● Country Capital
◇ Dependent Territory
○ Dependent Territory Capital
◈ Administrative Regions
✈ International Airport
▲ Mountain
▲▲ Mountain Range
Ѫ Volcano
≋ River
◎ Lake
⊠ Reservoir

59 E15 **Samuel, Represa de** ⊠ W Brazil
167 O14 **Samui, Ko** *island* SW Thailand
Samundari *see* Samundri
149 U9 **Samundri** *var.* Samundari. Punjab, E Pakistan 31°04′N 72°58′E
137 X10 **Samur** ≈ Azerbaijan/Russian Federation
137 Y11 **Samur-Abşeron Kanalı** *Rus.* Sam ur-Apsheronskiy Kanal. *canal* E Azerbaijan
Sam ur-Apsheronskiy Kanal *see* Samur-Abşeron Kanalı
167 O11 **Samut Prakan** *var.* Muang Samut Prakan, Paknam. Samut Prakan, C Thailand 13°36′N 100°36′E
167 O11 **Samut Sakhon** *var.* Maha Chai, Samut Sakorn, Tha Chin. Samut Sakhon, C Thailand 13°31′N 100°15′E
Samut Sakorn *see* Samut Sakhon
167 O11 **Samut Songkhram** *prev.* Meklong. Samut Songkhram, SW Thailand 13°25′N 100°01′E
77 N12 **San** Ségou, C Mali 13°21′N 04°57′W
111 O15 **San** ≈ SE Poland
141 O15 **Şan'ā'** *Eng.* Sana. ● (Yemen) W Yemen 15°24′N 44°14′E
112 F11 **Sana** ≈ NW Bosnia and Herzegovina
80 O12 **Sanaag** *off.* Gobolka Sanaag. ◈ *region* N Somalia
Sanaag, Gobolka *see* Sanaag
114 J8 **Sanadinovo** Pleven, N Bulgaria 43°33′N 25°00′E
195 P1 **Sanae** *South African research station* Antarctica 70°19′S 01°31′W
139 Y10 **Sanāf, Hawr as** ◎ S Iraq
79 E15 **Sanaga** ≈ C Cameroon
54 D12 **San Agustín** Huila, SW Colombia 01°53′N 76°14′W
171 R8 **San Agustin, Cape** *headland* Mindanao, S Philippines 06°17′N 126°12′E
37 Q13 **San Agustin, Plains of** *plain* New Mexico, SW USA
38 M16 **Sanak Islands** *island* Aleutian Islands, Alaska, USA
San Alessandro *see* Kita-Iō-jima
193 U10 **San Ambrosio, Isla** *Eng.* San Ambrosio Island. *island* W Chile
San Ambrosio Island *see* San Ambrosio, Isla
171 Q12 **Sanana** Pulau Sanana, E Indonesia 02°04′S 125°58′E
171 Q12 **Sanana, Pulau** *island* Maluku, E Indonesia
142 K5 **Sanandaj** *prev.* Sinneh. Kordestān, W Iran 35°18′N 47°01′E
35 P8 **San Andreas** California, W USA 38°10′N 120°40′W
2 C13 **San Andreas Fault** *fault* W USA
54 G8 **San Andrés** Santander, C Colombia 06°52′N 72°53′W
61 C20 **San Andrés de Giles** Buenos Aires, E Argentina 34°27′S 59°27′W
37 R14 **San Andres Mountains** ▲▲ New Mexico, SW USA
41 S15 **San Andrés Tuxtla** *var.* Tuxtla. Veracruz-Llave, E Mexico 18°28′N 95°15′W
25 P8 **San Angelo** Texas, SW USA 31°28′N 100°26′W
107 A20 **San Antioco, Isola di** *island* W Italy
42 F4 **San Antonio** Toledo, S Belize 16°13′N 89°02′W
62 G11 **San Antonio** Valparaíso, C Chile 33°35′S 71°38′W
188 H6 **San Antonio** Saipan, S Northern Mariana Islands
37 R13 **San Antonio** New Mexico, SW USA 33°53′N 106°52′W
25 R12 **San Antonio** Texas, SW USA 29°25′N 98°30′W
54 M11 **San Antonio** Amazonas, S Venezuela 03°31′N 66°47′W
54 I7 **San Antonio** Barinas, C Venezuela 07°24′N 71°28′W
55 O5 **San Antonio** Monagas, NE Venezuela 10°03′N 63°45′W
25 S12 **San Antonio** ✈ Texas, SW USA 29°31′N 98°11′W
San Antonio *see* San Antonio del Táchira
San Antonio Abad *see* Sant Antoni de Portmany
25 U13 **San Antonio Bay** *inlet* Texas, SW USA
61 E22 **San Antonio, Cabo** *headland* E Argentina 36°45′S 56°40′W
44 A5 **San Antonio, Cabo de** *headland* W Cuba 21°51′N 84°58′W
105 T11 **San Antonio, Cabo de** *headland* E Spain 38°50′N 00°09′E
54 H7 **San Antonio de Caparo** Táchira, W Venezuela 07°34′N 71°28′W
62 J5 **San Antonio de los Cobres** Salta, NE Argentina 24°10′S 66°17′W
54 H7 **San Antonio del Táchira** *var.* San Antonio. Táchira, W Venezuela 07°48′N 72°28′W
35 T15 **San Antonio, Mount** ▲ California, W USA 34°18′N 117°37′W
63 K16 **San Antonio Oeste** Río Negro, E Argentina 40°45′S 64°58′W
25 T13 **San Antonio River** ≈ Texas, SW USA
54 J5 **Sanare** Lara, N Venezuela 09°45′N 69°39′W
103 T16 **Sanary-sur-Mer** Var, SE France 43°07′N 05°48′E
104 G3 **Sanata Uxía de Ribeira** *var.* Ribeira. Galicia, NW Spain 42°33′N 09°01′W
25 X8 **San Augustine** Texas, SW USA 31°32′N 94°09′W
San Augustine *see* Minami-Iō-jima
141 T13 **Sanāw** *var.* Sanaw. NE Yemen 18°N 51°E
41 O11 **San Bartolo** San Luis Potosí, C Mexico 22°20′N 100°05′W
107 L16 **San Bartolomeo in Galdo** Campania, S Italy 41°24′N 15°01′E
106 K13 **San Benedetto del Tronto** Marche, C Italy 42°57′N 13°53′E
42 E3 **San Benito** Petén, N Guatemala 16°56′N 89°53′W
25 T17 **San Benito** Texas, SW USA 26°07′N 97°37′W
54 E6 **San Benito Abad** Sucre, N Colombia 08°56′N 75°02′W
35 P11 **San Benito Mountain** ▲ California, W USA 36°21′N 120°37′W
35 O10 **San Benito River** ≈ California, W USA
108 H10 **San Bernardino** Graubünden, S Switzerland 46°21′N 09°13′E
35 U15 **San Bernardino** California, W USA 34°06′N 117°15′W
35 U15 **San Bernardino Mountains** ▲▲ California, W USA
62 H11 **San Bernardo** Santiago, C Chile 33°37′S 70°45′W
40 J8 **San Bernardo** Durango, C Mexico 25°58′N 105°27′W
164 G12 **Sanbe-san** ▲ Kyūshū, SW Japan 35°09′N 132°36′E
San Bizenti-Barakaldo *see* San Vicente de Barakaldo
40 J12 **San Blas** Nayarit, C Mexico 21°35′N 105°20′W
40 H8 **San Blas** Sinaloa, C Mexico 26°05′N 108°44′W
San Blas *see* Kuna Yala
43 U14 **San Blas, Archipiélago de** *island group* NE Panama
23 Q10 **San Blas, Cape** *headland* Florida, SE USA 29°39′N 85°21′W
43 V14 **San Blas, Cordillera de** ▲▲ NE Panama
62 J8 **San Blas de los Sauces** Catamarca, NW Argentina 28°18′S 67°12′W
106 G8 **San Bonifacio** Veneto, NE Italy 45°22′N 11°14′E
29 S12 **Sanborn** Iowa, C USA 43°10′N 95°39′W
40 M7 **San Buenaventura** Coahuila, NE Mexico 27°04′N 101°32′W
105 S5 **San Caprasio** ▲ N Spain 41°45′N 00°26′W
62 G13 **San Carlos** Bío Bío, C Chile 36°25′S 71°58′W
40 E9 **San Carlos** Baja California Sur, NW Mexico 24°52′N 112°15′W
41 N5 **San Carlos** Coahuila, NE Mexico 29°00′N 100°51′W
41 P9 **San Carlos** Tamaulipas, C Mexico 24°36′N 98°42′W
42 L12 **San Carlos** Río San Juan, S Nicaragua 11°06′N 84°46′W
43 T16 **San Carlos** Panamá, C Panama 08°29′N 79°58′W
171 N3 **San Carlos** *off.* San Carlos City. Luzon, N Philippines 15°57′N 120°18′E
61 G20 **San Carlos** Maldonado, S Uruguay 34°46′S 54°58′W
36 M14 **San Carlos** Arizona, SW USA 33°21′N 110°27′W
54 K5 **San Carlos** Cojedes, N Venezuela 09°39′N 68°35′W
San Carlos *see* Quesada, Costa Rica
San Carlos *see* Luba, Equatorial Guinea
61 B17 **San Carlos Centro** Santa Fe, C Argentina 31°45′S 61°05′W
171 P6 **San Carlos City** Negros, C Philippines 10°34′N 123°24′E
San Carlos City *see* San Carlos
San Carlos de Ancud *see* Ancud
63 H16 **San Carlos de Bariloche** Río Negro, SW Argentina 41°08′S 71°15′W
61 B21 **San Carlos de Bolívar** Buenos Aires, E Argentina 36°15′S 61°06′W
54 H6 **San Carlos del Zulia** Zulia, W Venezuela 09°01′N 71°58′W
54 L12 **San Carlos de Río Negro** Amazonas, S Venezuela 01°54′N 67°54′W
San Carlos, Estrecho de *see* Falkland Sound
36 M14 **San Carlos Reservoir** ⊠ Arizona, SW USA
42 M12 **San Carlos, Río** ≈ N Costa Rica
65 D24 **San Carlos Settlement** East Falkland, Falkland Islands
61 C23 **San Cayetano** Buenos Aires, E Argentina 38°20′S 59°37′W
103 O8 **Sancerre** Cher, C France 47°19′N 02°53′E
158 G7 **Sanchakou** Xinjiang Uygur Zizhiqu, NW China 39°56′N 78°28′E
Sanchoku *see* Samcheok
41 O12 **San Ciro** San Luis Potosí, C Mexico 21°40′N 99°50′W
105 P10 **San Clemente** Castilla-La Mancha, C Spain 39°24′N 02°25′W
35 T16 **San Clemente** California, W USA 33°25′N 117°36′W
61 E21 **San Clemente del Tuyú** Buenos Aires, E Argentina 36°22′S 56°43′W
35 S17 **San Clemente Island** *island* Channel Islands, California, W USA
103 O9 **Sancoins** Cher, C France 46°49′N 03°00′E
61 B16 **San Cristóbal** Santa Fe, C Argentina 30°20′S 61°14′W
44 B4 **San Cristóbal** Pinar del Río, W Cuba 22°43′N 83°03′W
45 O9 **San Cristóbal** *var.* Benemérita de San Cristóbal. S Dominican Republic 18°27′N 70°07′W
54 H7 **San Cristóbal** Táchira, W Venezuela 07°46′N 72°15′W
187 N10 **San Cristobal** *var.* Makira. *island* SE Solomon Islands
San Cristóbal *see* San Cristóbal de Las Casas
41 U16 **San Cristóbal de Las Casas** *var.* San Cristóbal. Chiapas, SE Mexico 16°44′N 92°40′W
187 N10 **San Cristóbal, Isla** *var.* Chatham Island. *island* Galapagos Islands, Ecuador, E Pacific Ocean
42 D5 **San Cristóbal Verapaz** Alta Verapaz, C Guatemala 15°21′N 90°22′W
44 F6 **Sancti Spíritus** Sancti Spíritus, C Cuba 21°54′N 79°27′W
103 O11 **Sancy, Puy de** ▲ C France 45°33′N 02°48′E
95 D15 **Sand** Rogaland, S Norway 59°28′N 06°16′E
169 W7 **Sandakan** Sabah, East Malaysia 05°52′N 118°04′E
182 K9 **Sandalwood** South Australia 34°51′S 140°13′E
Sandalwood Island *see* Sumba, Pulau
94 D11 **Sandane** Sogn Og Fjordane, S Norway 61°47′N 06°14′E
114 G12 **Sandanski** *prev.* Sveti Vrach. Blagoevgrad, SW Bulgaria 41°36′N 23°19′E
Sandaohezi *see* Shawan
76 J11 **Sandaré** Kayes, W Mali 14°36′N 10°22′W
95 J19 **Sandared** Västra Götaland, S Sweden 57°43′N 12°47′E
94 N12 **Sandarne** Gävleborg, C Sweden 61°15′N 17°10′E
186 B5 **Sandaun** *prev.* West Sepik. ◈ *province* NW Papua New Guinea
96 K4 **Sanday** *island* NE Scotland, United Kingdom
31 P15 **Sand Creek** ≈ Indiana, N USA
95 H15 **Sande** Vestfold, S Norway 59°34′N 10°13′E
95 H16 **Sandefjord** Vestfold, S Norway 59°10′N 10°15′E
77 O15 **Sandégué** E Ivory Coast 07°59′N 03°33′W
77 P14 **Sandema** N Ghana 10°42′N 01°17′W
37 O11 **Sanders** Arizona, SW USA 35°13′N 109°21′W
24 M11 **Sanderson** Texas, SW USA 30°08′N 102°25′W
23 U4 **Sandersville** Georgia, SE USA 32°58′N 82°48′W
92 H4 **Sandgerdhi** Sudurnes, SW Iceland 64°01′N 22°42′W
28 K14 **Sand Hills** ▲▲ Nebraska, C USA
25 S14 **Sandia** Texas, SW USA 27°59′N 97°52′W
35 T17 **San Diego** California, W USA 32°43′N 117°09′W
25 S14 **San Diego** Texas, SW USA 27°47′N 98°15′W
136 F14 **Sandıklı** Afyon, W Turkey 38°28′N 30°17′E
152 L12 **Sandila** Uttar Pradesh, N India 27°05′N 80°37′E
San Dimitri Point *see* Il-Ponta ta' San Dimitri
San Dimitri, Ras *see* Il-Ponta ta' San Dimitri
168 J13 **Sanding, Selat** *strait* W Indonesia
30 J3 **Sand Island** *island* Apostle Islands, Wisconsin, N USA
95 C16 **Sandnes** Rogaland, S Norway 58°51′N 05°45′E
92 F13 **Sandnessjøen** Nordland, C Norway 66°00′N 12°37′E
Sandø *see* Sandoy
79 L24 **Sandoa** Katanga, S Dem. Rep. Congo 09°41′S 22°56′E
111 N15 **Sandomierz** *Rus.* Sandomir. Świętokrzyskie, C Poland 50°42′N 21°45′E
Sandomir *see* Sandomierz
54 C13 **Sandoná** Nariño, SW Colombia 01°18′N 77°28′W
106 I7 **San Donà di Piave** Veneto, NE Italy 45°38′N 12°34′E
124 K14 **Sandovo** Tverskaya Oblast', W Russian Federation 58°26′N 36°30′E
Sandoway *see* Thandwe
97 M24 **Sandown** S England, United Kingdom 50°40′N 01°11′W
95 B19 **Sandoy** *Dan.* Sandø. *island* C Faeroe Islands
39 N16 **Sand Point** Popof Island, Alaska, USA 55°20′N 160°30′W
32 M7 **Sandpoint** Idaho, NW USA 48°16′N 116°33′W
65 N24 **Sand Point** *headland* E Tristan da Cunha
31 R7 **Sand Point** *headland* Michigan, N USA 43°54′N 83°24′W
93 H14 **Sandsele** Västerbotten, N Sweden 65°16′N 17°40′E
10 I14 **Sandspit** Moresby Island, British Columbia, SW Canada 53°14′N 131°50′W
27 P9 **Sand Springs** Oklahoma, C USA 36°08′N 96°06′W
29 W7 **Sandstone** Minnesota, N USA 46°07′N 92°51′W
36 K15 **Sand Tank Mountains** ▲▲ Arizona, SW USA
31 S8 **Sandusky** Michigan, N USA 43°26′N 82°50′W
31 S11 **Sandusky** Ohio, N USA 41°27′N 82°42′W
31 S12 **Sandusky River** ≈ Ohio, N USA
83 D22 **Sandverhaar** Karas, S Namibia 26°50′S 17°25′E
95 L24 **Sandvig** Bornholm, E Denmark 55°15′N 14°45′E
95 H15 **Sandvika** Akershus, S Norway 59°54′N 10°29′E
94 N13 **Sandviken** Gävleborg, C Sweden 60°38′N 16°50′E
30 M11 **Sandwich** Illinois, N USA 41°39′N 88°37′W
Sandwich Island *see* Efate
Sandwich Islands *see* Hawai'ian Islands
153 V16 **Sandwip** *island* SE Bangladesh
11 U12 **Sandy Bay** Saskatchewan, C Canada 55°31′N 102°14′W
183 N16 **Sandy Cape** *headland* Tasmania, SE Australia 41°27′S 144°43′E
36 L3 **Sandy City** Utah, W USA 40°36′N 111°53′W
31 U12 **Sandy Creek** ≈ Ohio, N USA
21 O5 **Sandy Hook** Kentucky, S USA 38°05′N 83°09′W
18 K15 **Sandy Hook** *headland* New Jersey, NE USA 40°27′N 73°59′W
Sandykachi/Sandykgachy *see* Sandykgaçy
146 J15 **Sandykgaçy** *var.* Sandykgachy, *Rus.* Sandykachi. Maryyskiy Velayat, S Turkmenistan 36°34′N 62°28′E
Sandykgachy *see* Sandykgaçy
146 J15 **Sandykgaçy** *var.* Sandykgachy, *Rus.* Sandykachi. Mary Welaýaty, S Turkmenistan 36°34′N 62°28′E
146 L13 **Sandykly Gumy** *Rus.* Peski Sandykly. *desert* E Turkmenistan
Sandykly, Peski *see* Sandykly Gumy
11 Q13 **Sandy Lake** Alberta, W Canada 55°50′N 113°30′W
12 B8 **Sandy Lake** Ontario, C Canada 53°00′N 93°25′W
12 B8 **Sandy Lake** ◎ Ontario, C Canada
23 S3 **Sandy Springs** Georgia, SE USA 33°57′N 84°23′W
24 H8 **San Elizario** Texas, SW USA 31°35′N 106°16′W
99 L25 **Sanem** Luxembourg, SW Luxembourg 49°33′N 05°56′E
42 K5 **San Esteban** Olancho, C Honduras 15°19′N 85°52′W
105 O6 **San Esteban de Gormaz** Castilla y León, N Spain 41°34′N 03°13′W
40 E5 **San Esteban, Isla** *island* NW Mexico
San Eugenio/San Eugenio del Cuareim *see* Artigas
62 H11 **San Felipe** *var.* San Felipe de Aconcagua. Valparaíso, C Chile 32°45′S 70°42′W
40 D3 **San Felipe** Baja California Norte, NW Mexico 31°03′N 114°52′W
40 N12 **San Felipe** Guanajuato, C Mexico 21°30′N 101°15′W
54 K5 **San Felipe** Yaracuy, NW Venezuela 10°25′N 68°40′W
44 B5 **San Felipe, Cayos de** *island group* W Cuba
San Felipe de Aconcagua *see* San Felipe
San Felipe de Puerto Plata *see* Puerto Plata
37 R11 **San Felipe Pueblo** New Mexico, SW USA 35°25′N 106°27′W
San Feliú de Guixols *see* Sant Feliu de Guíxols
193 T10 **San Félix, Isla** *Eng.* San Felix Island. *island* W Chile
San Felix Island *see* San Félix, Isla
40 C4 **San Fernando** *var.* Misión San Fernando. Baja California Norte, NW Mexico 29°58′N 115°14′W
41 P9 **San Fernando** Tamaulipas, C Mexico 24°50′N 98°10′W
171 N2 **San Fernando** Luzon, N Philippines 16°45′N 120°21′E
171 O3 **San Fernando** Luzon, N Philippines 15°01′N 120°41′E
104 J16 **San Fernando** *prev.* Isla de León. Andalucía, S Spain 36°28′N 06°12′W
45 U14 **San Fernando** Trinidad, Trinidad and Tobago 10°17′N 61°27′W
35 S15 **San Fernando** California, W USA 34°16′N 118°26′W
54 L7 **San Fernando** *var.* San Fernando de Apure. Apure, C Venezuela 07°54′N 67°28′W
San Fernando de Apure *see* San Fernando
54 L11 **San Fernando de Atabapo** Amazonas, S Venezuela 04°00′N 67°42′W
62 L8 **San Fernando del Valle de Catamarca** *var.* Catamarca. Catamarca, NW Argentina 28°28′S 65°46′W
San Fernando de Monte Cristi *see* Monte Cristi
41 P9 **San Fernando, Río** ≈ C Mexico
23 X11 **Sanford** Florida, SE USA 28°48′N 81°16′W
19 P9 **Sanford** Maine, NE USA 43°26′N 70°46′W
21 T10 **Sanford** North Carolina, SE USA 35°29′N 79°10′W
25 N2 **Sanford** Texas, SW USA 35°42′N 101°31′W
39 T10 **Sanford, Mount** ▲ Alaska, USA 62°21′N 144°12′W
42 G8 **San Francisco** *var.* Gotera, San Francisco Gotera. Morazán, E El Salvador 13°41′N 88°06′W
43 R16 **San Francisco** Veraguas, C Panama 08°19′N 80°59′W
171 N2 **San Francisco** *var.* Aurora. Luzon, N Philippines 13°22′N 122°31′E
35 L8 **San Francisco** California, W USA 37°47′N 122°25′W
54 H5 **San Francisco** Zulia, NW Venezuela 10°36′N 71°39′W
34 M8 **San Francisco** ✈ California, W USA 37°37′N 122°23′W
35 N9 **San Francisco Bay** *bay* California, W USA
61 C24 **San Francisco de Bellocq** Buenos Aires, E Argentina 38°42′S 60°01′W
40 I6 **San Francisco de Borja** Chihuahua, N Mexico 27°57′N 106°42′W
42 J6 **San Francisco de la Paz** Olancho, C Honduras 14°55′N 86°14′W
40 J7 **San Francisco del Oro** Chihuahua, N Mexico 26°52′N 105°50′W
40 M12 **San Francisco del Rincón** Jalisco, SW Mexico 21°00′N 101°51′W
45 O8 **San Francisco de Macorís** C Dominican Republic 19°19′N 70°15′W
San Francisco de Satipo *see* Satipo
San Francisco Gotera *see* San Francisco
San Francisco Telixtlahuaca *see* Telixtlahuaca
107 K23 **San Fratello** Sicilia, Italy, C Mediterranean Sea 38°00′N 14°35′E
San Fructuoso *see* Tacuarembó
82 C12 **Sanga** Cuanza Sul, NW Angola 11°10′S 15°27′E
56 C5 **San Gabriel** Carchi, N Ecuador 0°35′N 77°48′W
159 S15 **Sa'ngain** Xizang Zizhiqu, W China 30°47′N 98°45′E
154 E13 **Sangamner** Mahārāshtra, W India 19°37′N 74°18′E
152 H12 **Sangāner** Rājasthān, N India 26°48′N 75°48′E
Sangān, Koh-i- *see* Sangān, Kūh-e
149 N6 **Sangān, Kūh-e** *Pash.* Koh-i-Sangan. ▲ C Afghanistan
123 P10 **Sangar** Respublika Sakha (Yakutiya), NE Russian Federation 63°48′N 127°37′E
169 V11 **Sangasanga** Borneo, C Indonesia 0°36′S 117°12′E
103 N1 **Sangatte** Pas-de-Calais, N France 50°56′N 01°41′E
107 B19 **San Gavino Monreale** Sardegna, Italy, C Mediterranean Sea 39°33′N 08°47′E
57 D16 **Sangayan, Isla** *island* W Peru
30 L14 **Sangchris Lake** ⊠ Illinois, N USA
171 N16 **Sangeang, Pulau** *island* S Indonesia
116 I10 **Sângeorgiu de Pădure** *prev.* Erdăt-Sângeorz, Sîngeorgiu de Pădure, *Hung.* Erdőszentgyörgy. Mureş, C Romania 46°27′N 24°50′E
116 I9 **Sângeorz-Băi** *var.* Singeroz Băi, *Ger.* Rumänisch-Sankt-Georgen, *Hung.* Oláhszentgyörgy; *prev.* Sîngeorz-Băi. Bistriţa-Năsăud, N Romania 47°24′N 24°40′E
35 R10 **Sanger** California, W USA 36°42′N 119°33′W
25 T5 **Sanger** Texas, SW USA 33°21′N 97°10′W
Sângerei *see* Sîngerei
101 L15 **Sangerhausen** Sachsen-Anhalt, C Germany 51°29′N 11°18′E
45 S6 **San Germán** W Puerto Rico 18°05′N 67°02′W
San Germano *see* Cassino
161 N2 **Sanggan He** ≈ E China
169 Q11 **Sanggau** Borneo, C Indonesia 0°08′N 110°35′E
79 G17 **Sangha** ◈ *province* N Congo
79 H16 **Sangha** ≈ Central African Republic/Congo
79 G16 **Sangha-Mbaéré** ◈ *prefecture* SW Central African Republic
149 Q15 **Sānghar** Sind, SE Pakistan 26°10′N 68°59′E
115 F22 **Sangiás** ▲ S Greece 36°39′N 22°24′E
Sangihe, Kepulauan *see* Sangir, Kepulauan
171 Q9 **Sangihe, Pulau** *var.* Sangir. *island* N Indonesia
54 G8 **San Gil** Santander, C Colombia 06°35′N 73°08′W
121 P16 **San Ġiljan** *var.* St Julian's. N Malta 35°55′N 14°29′E
106 F12 **San Gimignano** Toscana, C Italy 43°30′N 11°00′E
148 M8 **Sangīn** *var.* Sangin. Helmand, S Afghanistan 32°03′N 64°50′E
Sangin *see* Sangīn
107 O21 **San Giovanni in Fiore** Calabria, SW Italy 39°15′N 16°42′E
107 M16 **San Giovanni Rotondo** Puglia, SE Italy 41°43′N 15°44′E
106 G12 **San Giovanni Valdarno** Toscana, C Italy 43°34′N 11°31′E
Sangir *see* Sangihe, Pulau
171 Q10 **Sangir, Kepulauan** *var.* Kepulauan Sangihe. *island group* N Indonesia
Sangiyn Dalay *see* Erdenedalay, Dundgovĭ, Mongolia
Sangiyn Dalay *see* Erdene, Govĭ-Altay, Mongolia
Sangiyn Dalay *see* Nomgon, Ömnögovĭ, Mongolia
Sangiyn Dalay *see* Öldziyt, Övörhangay, Mongolia
163 Y15 **Sangju** *Jap.* Shōshū. C South Korea 36°26′N 128°09′E
167 R11 **Sangkha** Surin, E Thailand 14°36′N 103°43′E
169 W10 **Sangkulirang** Borneo, N Indonesia 01°00′N 117°56′E
169 W10 **Sangkulirang, Teluk** *bay* Borneo, N Indonesia
155 E16 **Sāngli** Mahārāshtra, W India 16°55′N 74°37′E
79 E16 **Sangmélima** Sud, S Cameroon 02°57′N 11°56′E
35 V15 **San Gorgonio Mountain** ▲ California, W USA 34°06′N 116°50′W
37 T8 **Sangre de Cristo Mountains** ▲▲ Colorado/New Mexico, C USA
61 A20 **San Gregorio** Santa Fe, C Argentina 34°18′S 62°02′W
61 F18 **San Gregorio de Polanco** Tacuarembó, C Uruguay 32°37′S 55°50′W
45 V14 **Sangre Grande** Trinidad, Trinidad and Tobago 10°35′N 61°08′W
159 N16 **Sangri** Xizang Zizhiqu, W China 29°17′N 92°01′E
152 H9 **Sangrūr** Punjab, NW India 30°16′N 75°52′E
44 I11 **Sangster** *off.* Sir Donald Sangster International Airport, *var.* Montego Bay. ✈ (Montego Bay) W Jamaica 18°30′N 77°54′W
59 G17 **Sangue, Rio do** ≈ W Brazil
105 R4 **Sangüesa** *Bas.* Zangoza. Navarra, N Spain 42°34′N 01°17′W
61 C16 **San Gustavo** Entre Ríos, E Argentina 30°41′S 59°23′W
Sangyuan *see* Wuqiao
40 C6 **San Hipólito, Punta** *headland* NW Mexico 26°57′N 114°00′W
23 W15 **Sanibel** Sanibel Island, Florida, SE USA 26°27′N 82°01′W
23 V15 **Sanibel Island** *island* Florida, SE USA
60 F13 **San Ignacio** Misiones, NE Argentina 27°15′S 55°32′W
42 F2 **San Ignacio** *prev.* Cayo, El Cayo. Cayo, W Belize 17°09′N 89°02′W
57 L16 **San Ignacio** El Beni, N Bolivia 14°54′S 65°35′W
57 O18 **San Ignacio** Santa Cruz, E Bolivia 16°23′S 60°59′W
42 M14 **San Ignacio** *var.* San Ignacio de Acosta. San José, W Costa Rica 09°46′N 84°10′W
40 E6 **San Ignacio** Baja California Sur, NW Mexico 27°18′N 112°51′W
40 J10 **San Ignacio** Sinaloa, W Mexico 23°55′N 106°25′W
56 B9 **San Ignacio** Cajamarca, N Peru 05°09′S 79°00′W
San Ignacio de Acosta *see* San Ignacio
40 D7 **San Ignacio, Laguna** *lagoon* W Mexico
12 I6 **Sanikiluaq** Belcher Islands, Nunavut, C Canada 55°20′N 77°50′W
171 O3 **San Ildefonso Peninsula** *peninsula* Luzon, N Philippines
Saniquillie *see* Sanniquellie
Sanirajak *see* Hall Beach
61 D20 **San Isidro** Buenos Aires, E Argentina 34°28′S 58°31′W
43 N14 **San Isidro** *var.* San Isidro de El General. San José, SE Costa Rica 09°28′N 83°42′W
San Isidro de El General *see* San Isidro
54 E5 **San Jacinto** Bolívar, N Colombia 09°53′N 75°06′W
35 U16 **San Jacinto** California, W USA 33°47′N 116°58′W
35 V15 **San Jacinto Peak** ▲ California, W USA 33°48′N 116°40′W
61 F14 **San Javier** Misiones, NE Argentina 27°50′S 55°06′W
61 C16 **San Javier** Santa Fe, C Argentina 30°35′S 59°59′W
105 S13 **San Javier** Murcia, SE Spain 37°49′N 00°50′W
61 D18 **San Javier** Río Negro, W Uruguay 32°41′S 58°08′W
61 C16 **San Javier, Río** ≈ C Argentina
160 L12 **Sanjiang** *var.* Guyi, Sanjiang Dongzu Zizhixian. Guangxi Zhuangzu Zizhiqu, S China 25°46′N 109°26′E
Sanjiang *see* Jinping, Guizhou
Sanjiang Dongzu Zizhixian *see* Sanjiang
Sanjiaocheng *see* Haiyan
165 N11 **Sanjō** *var.* Sanzyô. Niigata, Honshū, C Japan 37°39′N 139°00′E
57 M15 **San Joaquín** El Beni, N Bolivia 13°06′S 64°46′W
55 O6 **San Joaquín** Anzoátegui, NE Venezuela 09°21′N 64°30′W
35 O9 **San Joaquin River** ≈ California, W USA
35 P10 **San Joaquin Valley** *valley* California, W USA
61 A18 **San Jorge** Santa Fe, C Argentina 31°50′S 61°50′W
40 D3 **San Jorge, Bahía de** *bay* NW Mexico
63 J19 **San Jorge, Golfo** *var.* Gulf of San Jorge. *gulf* S Argentina
San Jorge, Gulf of *see* San Jorge, Golfo
San Jorge, Isla de *see* Weddell Island
61 F14 **San José** Misiones, NE Argentina 27°46′S 55°47′W
57 P19 **San José** *var.* San José de Chiquitos. Santa Cruz, E Bolivia 14°13′S 68°05′W
42 M14 **San José** ● (Costa Rica) San José, C Costa Rica 09°55′N 84°05′W
42 C7 **San José** *var.* Puerto San José. Escuintla, S Guatemala 14°00′N 90°50′W
40 G6 **San José** Sonora, NW Mexico 27°32′N 110°09′W
188 K8 **San Jose** Tinian, S Northern Mariana Islands 15°00′S 145°38′E
105 U11 **San José** Eivissa, Spain, W Mediterranean Sea 38°55′N 01°18′E
35 N9 **San Jose** California, W USA 37°18′N 121°53′W
54 H5 **San José** Zulia, NW Venezuela 10°02′N 72°24′W
42 M14 **San José** *off.* Provincia de San José. ◈ *province* W Costa Rica
61 E19 **San José** ◈ *department* S Uruguay
42 M13 **San José** ✈ Alajuela, C Costa Rica 10°03′N 84°12′W
San José *see* San José del Guaviare, Colombia
San Jose *see* Oleai
San Jose *see* Sant Josep de sa Talaia, Ibiza, Spain
San José *see* San José de Mayo, Uruguay
171 O3 **San Jose City** Luzon, N Philippines 15°49′N 120°57′E
San José de Chiquitos *see* San José
San José de Cúcuta *see* Cúcuta
61 D16 **San José de Feliciano** Entre Ríos, E Argentina 30°26′S 58°46′W
55 O6 **San José de Guanipa** *var.* El Tigrito. Anzoátegui, NE Venezuela 08°54′N 64°10′W
62 I9 **San José de Jáchal** San Juan, W Argentina 30°15′S 68°46′W
40 G10 **San José del Cabo** Baja California Sur, NW Mexico 23°01′N 109°40′W
54 G12 **San José del Guaviare** *var.* San José. Guaviare, S Colombia 02°34′N 72°38′W
61 E20 **San José de Mayo** *var.* San José. San José, S Uruguay 34°20′S 56°42′W
54 I10 **San José de Ocuné** Vichada, E Colombia 04°10′N 70°21′W
41 O9 **San José de Raíces** Nuevo León, NE Mexico 24°32′N 100°15′W
63 K17 **San José, Golfo** *gulf* E Argentina
40 F9 **San José, Isla** *island* NW Mexico
43 U16 **San José, Isla** *island* SE Panama
25 U14 **San Jose Island** *island* Texas, SW USA
San José, Provincia de *see* San José
62 I10 **San Juan** San Juan, W Argentina 31°37′S 68°27′W
45 N9 **San Juan** *var.* San Juan de la Maguana. C Dominican Republic 18°49′N 71°12′W
57 E17 **San Juan** Ica, S Peru 15°22′S 75°07′W
45 U5 **San Juan** ○ (Puerto Rico) NE Puerto Rico 18°28′N 66°06′W
62 H10 **San Juan** *off.* Provincia de San Juan. ◈ *province* W Argentina
San Juan *see* San Juan de los Morros
62 O7 **San Juan Bautista** Misiones, S Paraguay 26°40′S 57°08′W
35 O10 **San Juan Bautista** California, W USA 36°50′N 121°34′W
San Juan Bautista *see* Villahermosa
San Juan Bautista Cuicatlán *see* Cuicatlán
San Juan Bautista Tuxtepec *see* Tuxtepec
79 C17 **San Juan, Cabo** *headland* S Equatorial Guinea 01°09′N 09°25′E
San Juan de Alicante *see* Sant Joan d'Alacant
54 H7 **San Juan de Colón** Táchira, NW Venezuela 08°02′N 72°17′W
40 L9 **San Juan de Guadalupe** Durango, C Mexico 25°12′N 100°50′W
San Juan de la Maguana *see* San Juan
54 G4 **San Juan del Cesar** La Guajira, N Colombia 10°45′N 73°00′W
40 L15 **San Juan de Lima, Punta** *headland* SW Mexico 18°34′N 103°40′W
42 I8 **San Juan de Limay** Estelí, NW Nicaragua 13°10′N 86°36′W
43 N12 **San Juan del Norte** *var.* Greytown. Río San Juan, SE Nicaragua 10°58′N 83°40′W
54 K4 **San Juan de los Cayos** Falcón, N Venezuela 11°11′N 68°27′W
40 M12 **San Juan de los Lagos** Jalisco, C Mexico 21°15′N 102°15′W
54 L5 **San Juan de los Morros** *var.* San Juan. Guárico, N Venezuela 09°53′N 67°23′W
40 K9 **San Juan del Río** Durango, C Mexico 25°12′N 100°50′W
41 O13 **San Juan del Río** Querétaro de Arteaga, C Mexico 20°24′N 100°00′W
42 J11 **San Juan del Sur** Rivas, SW Nicaragua 11°16′N 85°51′W
54 M9 **San Juan de Manapiare** Amazonas, S Venezuela 05°15′N 66°05′W
40 E7 **San Juanico** Baja California Sur, NW Mexico
40 D7 **San Juanico, Punta** *headland* NW Mexico 26°01′N 112°17′W
32 G6 **San Juan Islands** *island group* Washington, NW USA
40 I6 **San Juanito** Chihuahua, N Mexico
40 I12 **San Juanito, Isla** *island* C Mexico
37 R8 **San Juan Mountains** ▲▲ Colorado, C USA
54 E5 **San Juan Nepomuceno** Bolívar, NW Colombia 09°57′N 75°06′W
44 E5 **San Juan, Pico** ▲ C Cuba 21°58′N 80°10′W
San Juan, Provincia de *see* San Juan
191 W15 **San Juan, Punta** *headland* Easter Island, Chile, E Pacific Ocean 27°03′S 109°22′W
42 M12 **San Juan, Río** ≈ Costa Rica/Nicaragua
41 S15 **San Juan, Río** ≈ SE Mexico
37 O8 **San Juan River** ≈ Colorado/Utah, W USA
San Julián *see* Puerto San Julián
61 B17 **San Justo** Santa Fe, C Argentina 30°47′S 60°32′W
109 W5 **Sankt Aegyd am Neuwalde** Niederösterreich, E Austria 47°51′N 15°34′E
109 U9 **Sankt Andrä** *Slvn.* Šent Andraž. Kärnten, S Austria 46°46′N 14°49′E
Sankt Andrä *see* Szentendre
Sankt Anna *see* Sântana
108 K8 **Sankt Anton-am-Arlberg** Vorarlberg, W Austria 47°08′N 10°11′E
101 E16 **Sankt Augustin** Nordrhein-Westfalen, W Germany 50°46′N 07°10′E
Sankt-Bartholomäi *see* Palamuse
101 F24 **Sankt Blasien** Baden-Württemberg, SW Germany 47°43′N 08°09′E
109 R3 **Sankt Florian am Inn** Oberösterreich, N Austria 48°24′N 13°27′E
108 I7 **Sankt Gallen** *var.* St. Gallen, *Eng.* Saint Gall, *Fr.* St-Gall. Sankt Gallen, NE Switzerland 47°25′N 09°23′E
108 H8 **Sankt Gallen** *var.* St.Gallen, *Eng.* Saint Gall, *Fr.* St-Gall. ◈ *canton* NE Switzerland
108 J8 **Sankt Gallenkirch** Vorarlberg, W Austria 47°00′N 10°59′E
109 Q5 **Sankt Georgen** Salzburg, N Austria 47°59′N 12°57′E
Sankt Georgen *see* Đurđevac
Sankt-Georgen *see* Sfântu Gheorghe
109 R6 **Sankt Gilgen** Salzburg, NW Austria 47°46′N 13°21′E
Sankt Gotthard *see* Szentgotthárd
101 E20 **Sankt Ingbert** Saarland, SW Germany 49°17′N 07°07′E
Sankt-Jakobi *see* Viru-Jaagupi, Lääne-Virumaa, Estonia
Sankt-Jakobi *see* Pärnu-Jaagupi, Pärnumaa, Estonia
Sankt Johann *see* Sankt Johann in Tirol
109 T7 **Sankt Johann am Tauern** Steiermark, E Austria 47°20′N 14°27′E
109 Q7 **Sankt Johann im Pongau** Salzburg, NW Austria 47°22′N 13°13′E
109 P6 **Sankt Johann in Tirol** *var.* Sankt Johann. Tirol, W Austria 47°32′N 12°26′E
Sankt-Johannis *see* Järva-Jaani
108 L8 **Sankt Leonhard** Tirol, W Austria 47°05′N 10°53′E
Sankt Margarethen *see* Sankt Margarethen im Burgenland
109 Y5 **Sankt Margarethen im Burgenland** *var.* Sankt Margarethen. Burgenland, E Austria 47°49′N 16°38′E
Sankt Martin *see* Martin
109 X8 **Sankt Martin an der Raab** Burgenland, SE Austria 46°59′N 16°12′E
109 U7 **Sankt Michael in Obersteiermark** Steiermark, SE Austria 47°21′N 14°59′E
Sankt Michel *see* Mikkeli
Sankt Moritz *see* St. Moritz
108 E11 **Sankt Niklaus** Valais, S Switzerland 46°09′N 07°48′E

◆ Country ● Country Capital ◇ Dependent Territory ○ Dependent Territory Capital ◈ Administrative Regions ✈ International Airport ▲ Mountain ▲▲ Mountain Range Volcano ≈ River ◎ Lake ⊠ Reservoir

109 S7 **Sankt Nikolai** *var.* Sankt Nikolai im Sölktal. Steiermark, SE Austria 47°18′N 14°04′E
Sankt Nikolai im Sölktal *see* Sankt Nikolai
109 U9 **Sankt Paul** *var.* Sankt Paul im Lavanttal. Kärnten, S Austria 46°42′N 14°53′E
Sankt Paul im Lavanttal *see* Sankt Paul
Sankt Peter *see* Pivka
109 W9 **Sankt Peter am Ottersbach** Steiermark, SE Austria 46°49′N 15°48′E
124 J13 **Sankt-Peterburg** *prev.* Leningrad, Petrograd, *Eng.* Saint Petersburg, *Fin.* Pietari. Leningradskaya Oblast', NW Russian Federation 59°55′N 30°25′E
100 H8 **Sankt Peter-Ording** Schleswig-Holstein, N Germany 54°18′N 08°37′E
109 V4 **Sankt Pölten** Niederösterreich, N Austria 48°14′N 15°38′E
109 W7 **Sankt Ruprecht** *var.* Sankt Ruprecht an der Raab. Steiermark, SE Austria 47°10′N 15°41′E
Sankt Ruprecht an der Raab *see* Sankt Ruprecht
Sankt-Ulrich *see* Ortisei
109 T4 **Sankt Valentin** Niederösterreich, C Austria 48°11′N 14°33′E
Sankt Veit am Flaum *see* Rijeka
109 T9 **Sankt Veit an der Glan** *Slvn.* Št. Vid. Kärnten, S Austria 46°47′N 14°22′E
99 M21 **Sankt-Vith** *var.* Saint-Vith. Liège, E Belgium 50°17′N 06°07′E
101 E20 **Sankt Wendel** Saarland, SW Germany 49°28′N 07°10′E
109 R6 **Sankt Wolfgang** Salzburg, NW Austria 47°43′N 13°30′E
79 K21 **Sankuru** ≈ C Dem. Rep. Congo
40 D8 **San Lázaro, Cabo** *headland* NW Mexico 24°46′N 112°15′W
137 O16 **Şanlıurfa** *prev.* Sanli Urfa, Urfa; *anc.* Edessa. şanlıurfa, S Turkey 37°08′N 38°45′E
137 O16 **Şanlıurfa** *prev.* Urfa. ⬖ *province* SE Turkey
Sanli Urfa *see* Şanlıurfa
137 O16 **Şanlıurfa Yaylası** *plateau* SE Turkey
61 B18 **San Lorenzo** Santa Fe, C Argentina 32°45′S 60°45′W
57 M21 **San Lorenzo** Tarija, S Bolivia 21°25′S 64°45′W
56 C5 **San Lorenzo** Esmeraldas, N Ecuador 01°15′N 78°51′W
42 H8 **San Lorenzo** Valle, S Honduras 13°24′N 87°27′W
56 A6 **San Lorenzo, Cabo** *headland* W Ecuador 0°57′S 80°49′W
105 N8 **San Lorenzo de El Escorial** *var.* El Escorial. Madrid, C Spain 40°36′N 04°07′W
40 E5 **San Lorenzo, Isla** *island* NW Mexico
57 C14 **San Lorenzo, Isla** *island* W Peru
63 G20 **San Lorenzo, Monte** ▲ S Argentina 47°40′S 72°12′W
40 I9 **San Lorenzo, Río** ≈ C Mexico
104 J15 **Sanlúcar de Barrameda** Andalucía, S Spain 36°46′N 06°21′W
104 J14 **Sanlúcar la Mayor** Andalucía, S Spain 37°24′N 06°13′W
40 F11 **San Lucas** Baja California Sur, NW Mexico 22°50′N 109°52′W
40 E6 **San Lucas** *var.* Cabo San Lucas. Baja California Sur, NW Mexico 27°14′N 112°15′W
40 G11 **San Lucas, Cabo** *var.* San Lucas Cape. *headland* NW Mexico 22°52′N 109°53′W
San Lucas Cape *see* San Lucas, Cabo
62 J11 **San Luis** San Luis, C Argentina 33°18′S 66°18′W
42 E4 **San Luis** Petén, NE Guatemala 16°16′N 89°27′W
42 M7 **San Luis** Región Autónoma Atlántico Norte, NE Nicaragua 13°59′N 84°10′W
36 H15 **San Luis** Arizona, SW USA 32°27′N 114°45′W
37 T8 **San Luis** Colorado, C USA 37°09′N 105°24′W
54 J4 **San Luis** Falcón, N Venezuela 11°09′N 69°39′W
62 J11 **San Luis** *off.* Provincia de San Luis. ⬖ *province* C Argentina
41 N12 **San Luis de la Paz** Guanajuato, C Mexico 21°15′N 100°33′W
40 K8 **San Luis del Cordero** Durango, C Mexico 25°25′N 104°09′W
40 D4 **San Luis, Isla** *island* NW Mexico
42 E6 **San Luis Jilotepeque** Jalapa, SE Guatemala 14°40′N 89°42′W
57 M16 **San Luis, Laguna de** ◎ NW Bolivia
35 P13 **San Luis Obispo** California, W USA 35°17′N 120°40′W
37 R7 **San Luis Peak** ▲ Colorado, C USA 37°59′N 106°55′W
41 N11 **San Luis Potosí** San Luis Potosí, C Mexico 22°10′N 100°57′W
41 N11 **San Luis Potosí** ⬖ *state* C Mexico
San Luis, Provincia de *see* San Luis
35 O10 **San Luis Reservoir** ▦ California, W USA
40 D2 **San Luis Río Colorado** *var.* San Luis Río Colorado. Sonora, NW Mexico 32°26′N 114°48′W
San Luis Río Colorado *see* San Luis Río Colorado
37 S8 **San Luis Valley** *basin* Colorado, C USA
107 C19 **Sanluri** Sardegna, Italy, C Mediterranean Sea 39°34′N 08°54′E
61 D23 **San Manuel** Buenos Aires, E Argentina 37°47′S 58°50′W
36 M15 **San Manuel** Arizona, SW USA 32°36′N 110°37′W
106 F11 **San Marcello Pistoiese** Toscana, C Italy 44°03′N 10°46′E
107 N20 **San Marco Argentano** Calabria, SW Italy 39°31′N 16°07′E
54 E6 **San Marcos** Sucre, N Colombia 08°38′N 75°10′W
42 M14 **San Marcos** San José, C Costa Rica 09°39′N 84°00′W
42 B5 **San Marcos** San Marcos, W Guatemala 14°58′N 91°48′W
42 F6 **San Marcos** Ocotepeque, SW Honduras 14°23′N 88°57′W
41 O16 **San Marcos** Guerrero, S Mexico 16°45′N 99°22′W
25 S11 **San Marcos** Texas, SW USA 29°54′N 97°57′W
42 A5 **San Marcos** *off.* Departamento de San Marcos. ⬖ *department* W Guatemala
San Marcos de Arica *see* Arica
San Marcos, Departamento de *see* San Marcos
40 E6 **San Marcos, Isla** *island* NW Mexico
106 H11 **San Marino** ● (San Marino) C San Marino 43°54′N 12°27′E
106 I11 **San Marino** *off.* Republic of San Marino. ◆ *republic* S Europe
San Marino, Republic of *see* San Marino
62 I11 **San Martín** Mendoza, C Argentina 33°05′S 68°28′W
54 F11 **San Martín** Meta, C Colombia 03°43′N 73°42′W
56 D11 **San Martín** *off.* Departamento de San Martín. ⬖ *department* C Peru
194 I5 **San Martín** *Argentinian research station* Antarctica 68°18′S 67°03′W
63 H16 **San Martín de los Andes** Neuquén, W Argentina 40°11′S 71°22′W
San Martín, Departamento de *see* San Martín
104 M8 **San Martín de Valdeiglesias** Madrid, C Spain 40°21′N 04°24′W
63 G21 **San Martín, Lago** *var.* Lago O'Higgins. ◎ S Argentina
106 H6 **San Martino di Castrozza** Trentino-Alto Adige, N Italy 46°16′N 11°50′E
57 N16 **San Martín, Río** ≈ N Bolivia
San Martín Texmelucan *see* Texmelucan
35 N9 **San Mateo** California, W USA 37°33′N 122°19′W
55 O6 **San Mateo** Anzoátegui, NE Venezuela 09°48′N 64°36′W
42 B4 **San Mateo Ixtatán** Huehuetenango, W Guatemala 15°50′N 91°30′W
57 Q18 **San Matías** Santa Cruz, E Bolivia 16°20′S 58°24′W
63 K16 **San Matías, Golfo** *var.* Gulf of San Matías. *gulf* E Argentina
San Matías, Gulf of *see* San Matías, Golfo
15 O8 **Sanmaur** Québec, SE Canada 47°52′N 73°47′W
161 T10 **Sanmen Wan** *bay* E China
160 M6 **Sanmenxia** *var.* Shan Xian. Henan, C China 34°46′N 111°17′E
Sânmiclăuş Mare *see* Sânnicolau Mare
61 D14 **San Miguel** Corrientes, NE Argentina 28°02′S 57°41′W
57 L16 **San Miguel** El Beni, N Bolivia 16°43′S 61°06′W
42 G8 **San Miguel** San Miguel, SE El Salvador 13°27′N 88°11′W
40 L6 **San Miguel** Coahuila, N Mexico 29°10′N 101°28′W
40 J9 **San Miguel** *var.* San Miguel de Cruces. Durango, C Mexico 24°25′N 105°55′W
43 U16 **San Miguel** Panamá, SE Panama 08°27′N 78°51′W
35 P12 **San Miguel** California, W USA 35°45′N 120°42′W
42 B9 **San Miguel** ⬖ *department* E El Salvador
41 N13 **San Miguel de Allende** Guanajuato, C Mexico 20°56′N 100°48′W
San Miguel de Cruces *see* San Miguel
San Miguel de Ibarra *see* Ibarra
61 D21 **San Miguel del Monte** Buenos Aires, E Argentina 35°26′S 58°50′W
62 J7 **San Miguel de Tucumán** *var.* Tucumán. Tucumán, N Argentina 26°47′S 65°15′W
43 V16 **San Miguel, Golfo de** *gulf* S Panama
35 P15 **San Miguel Island** *island* California, W USA
42 L11 **San Miguelito** Río San Juan, S Nicaragua 11°22′N 84°54′W
43 T15 **San Miguelito** Panamá, C Panama 08°58′N 79°31′W
57 N18 **San Miguel, Río** ≈ E Bolivia
56 D6 **San Miguel, Río** ≈ Colombia/Ecuador
40 I7 **San Miguel, Río** ≈ N Mexico
42 G8 **San Miguel, Volcán de** ⛰ SE El Salvador 13°27′N 88°18′W
161 Q12 **Sanming** Fujian, SE China 26°11′N 117°37′E
106 F11 **San Miniato** Toscana, C Italy 43°40′N 10°53′E
San Murezzan *see* St. Moritz
Sannār *see* Sennar
107 M15 **Sannicandro Garganico** Puglia, SE Italy 41°50′N 15°32′E
40 H6 **San Nicolás** Sonora, NW Mexico 28°31′N 109°24′W
61 C19 **San Nicolás de los Arroyos** Buenos Aires, E Argentina 33°20′S 60°13′W
35 R16 **San Nicolas Island** *island* Channel Islands, California, W USA
Sânnicolaul-Mare *see* Sânnicolau Mare
116 E11 **Sânnicolau Mare** *var.* Sânnicolaul-Mare, *Hung.* Nagyszentmiklós; *prev.* Sânmiclăuş Mare, Sînnicolau Mare. Timiş, W Romania 46°05′N 20°38′E
123 Q6 **Sannikova, Proliv** *strait* NE Russian Federation
76 K16 **Sanniquellie** *var.* Saniquillie. NE Liberia 07°24′N 08°45′W
165 R7 **Sannohe** Aomori, Honshū, C Japan 40°23′N 141°16′E
Sanntaler Alpen *see* Kamniško-Savinjske Alpe
111 O17 **Sanok** Podkarpackie, SE Poland 49°31′N 22°14′E
54 E5 **San Onofre** Sucre, NW Colombia 09°45′N 75°33′W
57 K21 **San Pablo** Potosí, S Bolivia 21°43′S 66°38′W
171 O4 **San Pablo** *off.* San Pablo City. Luzon, N Philippines 14°04′N 121°16′E
San Pablo Balleza *see* Balleza
35 N8 **San Pablo Bay** *bay* California, W USA
San Pablo City *see* San Pablo
40 C6 **San Pablo, Punta** *headland* NW Mexico 27°12′N 114°30′W
43 R16 **San Pablo, Río** ≈ C Panama
171 P4 **San Pascual** Burias Island, C Philippines 13°06′N 122°59′E
121 Q16 **San Pawl il Baħar** *Eng.* Saint Paul's Bay. E Malta 35°57′N 14°24′E
61 C19 **San Pedro** Buenos Aires, E Argentina 33°43′S 59°45′W
62 K5 **San Pedro** Jujuy, N Argentina 24°12′S 64°55′W
60 G13 **San Pedro** Misiones, NE Argentina 26°38′S 54°12′W
42 H1 **San Pedro** Corozal, NE Belize 17°58′N 87°55′W
76 M17 **San-Pédro** S Ivory Coast 04°45′N 06°37′W
40 L8 **San Pedro** *var.* San Pedro de las Colonias. Coahuila, NE Mexico 25°47′N 102°57′W
62 O5 **San Pedro** San Pedro, SE Paraguay 24°08′S 57°08′W
62 O6 **San Pedro** *off.* Departamento de San Pedro. ⬖ *department* C Paraguay
44 G6 **San Pedro** ≈ C Cuba
77 N16 **San Pedro** ✈ (Yamoussoukro) C Ivory Coast 06°49′N 05°14′W
San Pedro *see* San Pedro del Pinatar
42 D5 **San Pedro Carchá** Alta Verapaz, C Guatemala 15°30′N 90°12′W
35 S16 **San Pedro Channel** *channel* California, W USA
62 I5 **San Pedro de Atacama** Antofagasta, N Chile 22°52′S 68°10′W
San Pedro de Durazno *see* Durazno
40 G5 **San Pedro de la Cueva** Sonora, NW Mexico 29°17′N 109°47′W
San Pedro de las Colonias *see* San Pedro
56 B11 **San Pedro de Lloc** La Libertad, NW Peru 07°26′S 79°31′W
105 S13 **San Pedro del Pinatar** *var.* San Pedro. Murcia, SE Spain 37°50′N 00°47′W
45 P9 **San Pedro de Macorís** SE Dominican Republic 18°30′N 69°18′W
San Pedro, Departamento de *see* San Pedro
40 C3 **San Pedro Mártir, Sierra** ▲▲ NW Mexico
San Pedro Pochutla *see* Pochutla
42 D2 **San Pedro, Río** ≈ Guatemala/Mexico
40 K10 **San Pedro, Río** ≈ C Mexico
104 J10 **San Pedro, Sierra de** ▲▲ W Spain
42 G5 **San Pedro Sula** Cortés, NW Honduras 15°26′N 88°01′W
San Pedro Tapanatepec *see* Tapanatepec
62 I4 **San Pedro, Volcán** ⛰ N Chile 21°46′S 68°13′W
106 E7 **San Pellegrino Terme** Lombardia, N Italy 45°53′N 09°42′E
25 T16 **San Perlita** Texas, SW USA 26°30′N 97°38′W
San Pietro *see* Supetar
San Pietro del Carso *see* Pivka
107 A20 **San Pietro, Isola di** *island* W Italy
32 K7 **Sanpoil River** ≈ Washington, NW USA
165 O9 **Sanpoku** *var.* Sampoku. Niigata, Honshū, C Japan 38°32′N 139°33′E
40 C3 **San Quintín** Baja California Norte, NW Mexico 30°28′N 115°58′W
40 B3 **San Quintín, Bahía de** *bay* NW Mexico
40 B3 **San Quintín, Cabo** *headland* NW Mexico 30°22′N 116°01′W
62 I12 **San Rafael** Mendoza, W Argentina 34°44′S 68°15′W
41 N9 **San Rafael** Nuevo León, NE Mexico 25°01′N 100°33′W
34 M8 **San Rafael** California, W USA 37°58′N 122°31′W
37 Q11 **San Rafael** New Mexico, SW USA 35°03′N 107°52′W
54 H4 **San Rafael** *var.* El Moján. Zulia, NW Venezuela 10°58′N 71°45′W
42 J8 **San Rafael del Norte** Jinotega, NW Nicaragua 13°12′N 86°06′W
42 J10 **San Rafael del Sur** Managua, SW Nicaragua 11°51′N 86°24′W
36 M5 **San Rafael Knob** ▲ Utah, W USA 38°46′N 110°45′W
35 Q14 **San Rafael Mountains** ▲▲ California, W USA
42 M13 **San Ramón** Alajuela, C Costa Rica 10°04′N 84°31′W
57 E14 **San Ramón** Junín, C Peru 11°08′S 75°18′W
61 F19 **San Ramón** Canelones, S Uruguay 34°18′S 55°55′W
62 K5 **San Ramón de la Nueva Orán** Salta, N Argentina 23°08′S 64°20′W
57 O16 **San Ramón, Río** ≈ E Bolivia
106 B11 **San Remo** Liguria, NW Italy 43°48′N 07°47′E
54 J3 **San Román, Cabo** *headland* NW Venezuela 12°10′N 70°01′W
61 C15 **San Roque** Corrientes, NE Argentina 28°35′S 58°45′W
188 I4 **San Roque** Saipan, S Northern Mariana Islands 15°15′S 145°47′E
104 K16 **San Roque** Andalucía, S Spain 36°13′N 05°23′W
25 R9 **San Saba** Texas, SW USA 31°13′N 98°44′W
25 Q9 **San Saba River** ≈ Texas, SW USA
61 D17 **San Salvador** Entre Ríos, E Argentina 31°38′S 58°30′W
42 F7 **San Salvador** ● (El Salvador) San Salvador, SW El Salvador 13°42′N 89°12′W
42 A10 **San Salvador** ⬖ *department* C El Salvador
44 K4 **San Salvador** *prev.* Watlings Island. *island* E Bahamas
42 F8 **San Salvador** ✈ La Paz, S El Salvador 13°27′N 89°04′W
62 J5 **San Salvador de Jujuy** *var.* Jujuy. Jujuy, N Argentina 24°10′S 65°20′W
42 F7 **San Salvador, Volcán de** ⛰ C El Salvador 13°58′N 89°14′W
77 Q14 **Sansanné-Mango** *var.* Mango. N Togo 10°21′N 00°28′E
45 S5 **San Sebastián** W Puerto Rico 18°21′N 67°00′W
63 J24 **San Sebastián, Bahía** *bay* S Argentina
Sansenhō *see* Sacheon
106 H12 **Sansepolcro** Toscana, C Italy 43°35′N 12°12′E
107 M16 **San Severo** Puglia, SE Italy 41°41′N 15°23′E
112 F11 **Sanski Most** ⬖ Federacija Bosna I Hercegovina, NW Bosnia and Herzegovina
171 W12 **Sansundi** Papua, E Indonesia 0°42′S 135°48′E
162 K9 **Sant** *var.* Mayhan. Övörhangay, C Mongolia 46°02′N 104°00′E
104 K11 **Santa Amalia** Extremadura, W Spain 39°00′N 06°01′W
60 F13 **Santa Ana** Misiones, NE Argentina 27°22′S 55°34′W
57 L16 **Santa Ana** El Beni, N Bolivia 13°43′S 65°37′W
42 E7 **Santa Ana** Santa Ana, NW El Salvador 13°59′N 89°34′W
40 F4 **Santa Ana** Sonora, NW Mexico 30°31′N 111°08′W
35 T16 **Santa Ana** California, W USA 33°45′N 117°52′W
55 N6 **Santa Ana** Nueva Esparta, NE Venezuela 09°15′N 64°39′W
42 A9 **Santa Ana** ⬖ *department* NW El Salvador
Santa Ana de Coro *see* Coro
35 U16 **Santa Ana Mountains** ▲▲ California, W USA
42 E7 **Santa Ana, Volcán de** *var.* La Matepec. ⛰ W El Salvador 13°49′N 89°36′W
42 G6 **Santa Bárbara** Santa Bárbara, W Honduras 14°56′N 88°11′W
40 J7 **Santa Barbara** Chihuahua, N Mexico 26°46′N 105°46′W
35 Q14 **Santa Barbara** California, W USA 34°24′N 119°40′W
54 L11 **Santa Bárbara** Amazonas, S Venezuela 03°55′N 67°06′W
54 I7 **Santa Bárbara** Barinas, W Venezuela 07°48′N 71°10′W
42 F5 **Santa Bárbara** ⬖ *department* NW Honduras
Santa Bárbara *see* Iscuandé
35 Q15 **Santa Barbara Channel** *channel* California, W USA
Santa Bárbara de Samaná *see* Samaná
35 R16 **Santa Barbara Island** *island* Channel Islands, California, W USA
54 E5 **Santa Catalina** Bolívar, N Colombia 10°36′N 75°17′W
43 R15 **Santa Catalina** Ngöbe Bugle, W Panama 08°46′N 81°18′W
104 G2 **Santa Cataliña de Armada** Galicia, NW Spain 43°02′N 08°49′W
35 T17 **Santa Catalina, Gulf of** *gulf* California, W USA
40 F8 **Santa Catalina, Isla** *island* NW Mexico
35 S16 **Santa Catalina Island** *island* Channel Islands, California, W USA
41 N8 **Santa Catarina** Nuevo León, NE Mexico 25°39′N 100°30′W
60 H13 **Santa Catarina** *off.* Estado de Santa Catarina. ⬖ *state* S Brazil
Santa Catarina de Tepehuanes *see* Tepehuanes
Santa Catarina, Estado de *see* Santa Catarina
60 L13 **Santa Catarina, Ilha de** *island* S Brazil
45 Q16 **Santa Catherina** Curaçao 12°07′N 68°46′W
44 E5 **Santa Clara** Villa Clara, C Cuba 22°25′N 78°01′W
35 N9 **Santa Clara** California, W USA 37°20′N 121°57′W
36 J8 **Santa Clara** Utah, W USA 37°07′N 113°39′W
Santa Clara *see* Santa Clara de Olimar
61 F18 **Santa Clara de Olimar** *var.* Santa Clara. Cerro Largo, NE Uruguay 32°50′S 54°54′W
61 A17 **Santa Clara de Saguier** Santa Fe, C Argentina 31°21′S 61°50′W
Santa Coloma *see* Santa Coloma de Gramenet
105 X5 **Santa Coloma de Farners** *var.* Santa Coloma de Farnés. Cataluña, NE Spain 41°52′N 02°39′E
Santa Coloma de Farnés *see* Santa Coloma de Farners
Santa Coloma de Gramanet *see* Santa Coloma de Gramenet
105 W6 **Santa Coloma de Gramenet** *var.* Santa Coloma; *prev.* Santa Coloma de Gramanet. Cataluña, NE Spain 41°28′N 02°14′E
Santa Comba *see* Uaco Cungo
104 H8 **Santa Comba Dão** Viseu, N Portugal 40°23′N 08°07′W
82 C10 **Santa Cruz** Uíge, NW Angola 06°56′S 16°25′E
57 N19 **Santa Cruz** *var.* Santa Cruz de la Sierra. Santa Cruz, C Bolivia 17°49′S 63°11′W
62 G12 **Santa Cruz** Libertador, C Chile 34°38′S 71°27′W
42 K13 **Santa Cruz** Guanacaste, W Costa Rica 10°15′N 85°35′W
44 I12 **Santa Cruz** W Jamaica 18°03′N 77°43′W
64 P6 **Santa Cruz** Madeira, Portugal, NE Atlantic Ocean 32°43′N 16°47′W
35 N10 **Santa Cruz** California, W USA 36°58′N 122°01′W
63 H20 **Santa Cruz** *off.* Provincia de Santa Cruz. ⬖ *province* S Argentina
57 O18 **Santa Cruz** ⬖ *department* E Bolivia
Santa Cruz *see* Puerto Santa Cruz
Santa Cruz *see* Viru-Viru
Santa Cruz Barillas *see* Barillas
59 O18 **Santa Cruz Cabrália** Bahia, E Brazil 16°17′S 39°03′W
Santa Cruz de El Seibo *see* El Seibo
64 N11 **Santa Cruz de la Palma** La Palma, Islas Canarias, Spain, NE Atlantic Ocean 28°41′N 17°46′W
Santa Cruz de la Sierra *see* Santa Cruz
105 O9 **Santa Cruz de la Zarza** Castilla-La Mancha, C Spain 39°59′N 03°10′W
42 C5 **Santa Cruz del Quiché** Quiché, W Guatemala 15°02′N 91°06′W
105 N8 **Santa Cruz del Retamar** Castilla-La Mancha, C Spain 40°08′N 04°14′W
Santa Cruz del Seibo *see* El Seibo
44 G7 **Santa Cruz del Sur** Camagüey, C Cuba 20°44′N 78°00′W
105 O11 **Santa Cruz de Mudela** Castilla-La Mancha, C Spain 38°37′N 03°27′W
64 Q11 **Santa Cruz de Tenerife** Tenerife, Islas Canarias, Spain, NE Atlantic Ocean 28°28′N 16°15′W
64 P11 **Santa Cruz de Tenerife** ⬖ *province* Islas Canarias, Spain, NE Atlantic Ocean
60 K9 **Santa Cruz do Rio Pardo** São Paulo, S Brazil 22°52′S 49°37′W
61 H15 **Santa Cruz do Sul** Rio Grande do Sul, S Brazil 29°42′S 52°25′W
57 C17 **Santa Cruz, Isla** *var.* Indefatigable Island, Isla Chávez. *island* Galapagos Islands, Ecuador, E Pacific Ocean
40 F8 **Santa Cruz, Isla** *island* NW Mexico
35 Q15 **Santa Cruz Island** *island* California, W USA
187 Q10 **Santa Cruz Islands** *island group* E Solomon Islands
Santa Cruz, Provincia de *see* Santa Cruz
63 I22 **Santa Cruz, Río** ≈ S Argentina
36 L15 **Santa Cruz River** ≈ Arizona, SW USA
61 C17 **Santa Elena** Entre Ríos, E Argentina 30°58′S 59°47′W
42 F2 **Santa Elena** Cayo, W Belize 17°08′N 89°04′W
25 R16 **Santa Elena** Texas, SW USA 26°43′N 98°30′W
56 A7 **Santa Elena, Bahía de** *bay* W Ecuador
55 R10 **Santa Elena de Uairén** Bolívar, E Venezuela 04°40′N 61°03′W
42 K12 **Santa Elena, Península** *peninsula* NW Costa Rica
56 A7 **Santa Elena, Punta** *headland* W Ecuador 02°11′S 81°00′W
104 L11 **Santa Eufemia** Andalucía, S Spain 38°36′N 04°54′W
107 N21 **Santa Eufemia, Golfo di** *gulf* S Italy
105 S4 **Santa Eulalia de Gállego** Aragón, NE Spain 42°16′N 00°46′W
105 V11 **Santa Eulalia del Río** Ibiza, Spain, W Mediterranean Sea 39°00′N 01°33′E
61 B17 **Santa Fe** Santa Fe, C Argentina 31°36′S 60°47′W
44 C6 **Santa Fé** *var.* La Fe. Isla de la Juventud, W Cuba 21°45′N 82°45′W
43 R16 **Santa Fé** Veraguas, C Panama 08°29′N 80°50′W
105 N14 **Santa Fe** Andalucía, S Spain 37°11′N 03°43′W
37 S10 **Santa Fe** *state capital* New Mexico, SW USA 35°41′N 105°56′W
61 B15 **Santa Fe** *off.* Provincia de Santa Fe. ⬖ *province* C Argentina
Santa Fe *see* Bogotá
Santa Fe de Bogotá *see* Bogotá
60 J7 **Santa Fé do Sul** São Paulo, S Brazil 20°13′S 50°56′W
57 B18 **Santa Fe, Isla** *var.* Barrington Island. *island* Galapagos Islands, Ecuador, E Pacific Ocean
Santa Fe, Provincia de *see* Santa Fe
23 V9 **Santa Fe River** ≈ Florida, SE USA
59 M15 **Santa Filomena** Piauí, E Brazil 09°06′S 45°52′W
40 G10 **Santa Genoveva** ▲ NW Mexico 23°07′N 109°56′W
153 S14 **Santahar** Rajshahi, NW Bangladesh 24°45′N 89°03′E
60 G11 **Santa Helena** Paraná, S Brazil 24°53′S 54°19′W
54 J5 **Santa Inés** Lara, N Venezuela 10°37′N 69°18′W
63 G24 **Santa Inés, Isla** *island* S Chile
62 J13 **Santa Isabel** La Pampa, C Argentina 36°11′S 66°59′W
43 U14 **Santa Isabel** Colón, N Panama 09°31′N 79°12′W
186 L8 **Santa Isabel** *var.* Bughotu. *island* N Solomon Islands
Santa Isabel *see* Malabo
58 D11 **Santa Isabel do Rio Negro** Amazonas, NW Brazil 0°40′S 64°56′W
61 C15 **Santa Lucia** Corrientes, NE Argentina 28°58′S 59°05′W
57 I17 **Santa Lucía** Puno, S Peru 15°45′S 70°34′W
61 F20 **Santa Lucía** *var.* Santa Lucia. Canelones, S Uruguay 34°26′S 56°25′W
42 B6 **Santa Lucía Cotzumalguapa** Escuintla, SW Guatemala 14°20′N 91°00′W
107 L23 **Santa Lucia del Mela** Sicilia, Italy, C Mediterranean Sea 38°08′N 15°17′E
35 O11 **Santa Lucia Range** ▲▲ California, W USA
40 D9 **Santa Margarita, Isla** *island* NW Mexico
62 J7 **Santa María** Catamarca, N Argentina 26°51′S 66°02′W
61 G15 **Santa Maria** Rio Grande do Sul, S Brazil 29°41′S 53°48′W
35 P13 **Santa Maria** California, W USA 34°56′N 120°25′W
64 Q4 **Santa Maria** ✈ Santa Maria, Azores, Portugal, NE Atlantic Ocean
64 P3 **Santa Maria** *island* Azores, Portugal, NE Atlantic Ocean
Santa Maria *see* Gaua
Santa María Asunción Tlaxiaco *see* Tlaxiaco
40 G9 **Santa María, Bahía** *bay* W Mexico
83 L21 **Santa Maria, Cabo de** *headland* S Mozambique 26°05′S 32°58′E
104 G15 **Santa Maria, Cabo de** *headland* S Portugal 36°57′N 07°55′W
44 J4 **Santa Maria, Cape** *headland* Long Island, C Bahamas 23°40′N 75°20′W
107 J17 **Santa Maria Capua Vetere** Campania, S Italy 41°05′N 14°15′E
104 G7 **Santa Maria da Feira** Aveiro, N Portugal 40°55′N 08°32′W
59 M17 **Santa Maria da Vitória** Bahia, E Brazil 13°26′S 44°09′W
55 N9 **Santa Maria de Erebato** Bolívar, SE Venezuela 05°09′N 64°50′W
55 N6 **Santa María de Ipire** Guárico, C Venezuela 08°51′N 65°21′W
Santa Maria del Buen Aire *see* Buenos Aires
40 J8 **Santa María del Oro** Durango, C Mexico 25°57′N 105°22′W
41 N12 **Santa María del Río** San Luis Potosí, C Mexico 21°48′N 100°42′W
Santa Maria di Castellabate *see* Castellabate
107 Q20 **Santa Maria di Leuca, Capo** *headland* SE Italy 39°48′N 18°21′E
108 K10 **Santa Maria-im-Munstertal** Graubünden, SE Switzerland 46°36′N 10°25′E
57 B18 **Santa María, Isla** *var.* Isla Floreana, Charles Island. *island* Galapagos Islands, Ecuador, E Pacific Ocean
40 J3 **Santa María, Laguna de** ◎ N Mexico
61 G16 **Santa Maria, Rio** ≈ S Brazil
43 R16 **Santa María, Río** ≈ C Panama
36 J12 **Santa Maria River** ≈ Arizona, SW USA
107 G15 **Santa Marinella** Lazio, C Italy 42°01′N 11°51′E
54 F4 **Santa Marta** Magdalena, N Colombia 11°14′N 74°13′W
104 J11 **Santa Marta** Extremadura, W Spain 38°37′N 06°39′W
54 F4 **Santa Marta, Sierra Nevada de** ▲▲ NE Colombia
Santa Maura *see* Lefkáda
35 S15 **Santa Monica** California, W USA 34°01′N 118°29′W
116 F10 **Sântana** *Ger.* Sankt Anna, *Hung.* Újszentanna; *prev.* Sîntana. Arad, W Romania 46°20′N 21°30′E
61 F16 **Santana, Coxilha de** *hill range* S Brazil
61 H16 **Santana da Boa Vista** Rio Grande do Sul, S Brazil 30°52′S 53°03′W
61 F16 **Santana do Livramento** *prev.* Livramento. Rio Grande do Sul, S Brazil 30°52′S 55°30′W
105 N2 **Santander** Cantabria, N Spain 43°28′N 03°48′W
54 F8 **Santander** *off.* Departamento de Santander. ⬖ *province* C Colombia
Santander, Departamento de *see* Santander
Santander Jiménez *see* Jiménez
Sant'Andrea *see* Svetac
107 B20 **Sant'Antioco** Sardegna, Italy, C Mediterranean Sea 39°03′N 08°28′E
105 V11 **Sant Antoni de Portmany** *Cas.* San Antonio Abad. Ibiza, Spain, W Mediterranean Sea 38°58′N 01°18′E
105 Y10 **Santanyí** Mallorca, Spain, W Mediterranean Sea 39°22′N 03°07′E
104 J13 **Santa Olalla del Cala** Andalucía, S Spain 37°54′N 06°13′W
35 R15 **Santa Paula** California, W USA 34°21′N 119°03′W
36 L4 **Santaquin** Utah, W USA 39°58′N 111°46′W
58 I12 **Santarém** Pará, N Brazil 02°26′S 54°41′W
104 G10 **Santarém** *anc.* Scalabis. Santarém, W Portugal 39°14′N 08°40′W
104 G10 **Santarém** ⬖ *district* C Portugal
44 F4 **Santaren Channel** *channel* W Bahamas
54 K10 **Santa Rita** Vichada, E Colombia 04°51′N 68°27′W
188 B16 **Santa Rita** SW Guam
42 H5 **Santa Rita** Cortés, NW Honduras 15°10′N 87°54′W
40 E9 **Santa Rita** Baja California Sur, NW Mexico 27°29′N 100°33′W
54 H5 **Santa Rita** Zulia, NW Venezuela 10°35′N 71°30′W
59 I19 **Santa Rita de Araguaia** Goiás, S Brazil 17°17′S 53°13′W
59 M16 **Santa Rita de Cassia** *var.* Cássia. Bahia, E Brazil 11°03′S 44°16′W
61 D14 **Santa Rosa** Corrientes, NE Argentina 28°18′S 58°04′W
62 K13 **Santa Rosa** La Pampa, C Argentina 36°38′S 64°15′W
61 G14 **Santa Rosa** Rio Grande do Sul, S Brazil 27°50′S 54°29′W
58 E10 **Santa Rosa** Roraima, N Brazil 03°41′N 62°29′W
56 B8 **Santa Rosa** El Oro, SW Ecuador 03°29′S 79°57′W
57 I16 **Santa Rosa** Puno, S Peru 14°38′S 70°45′W
34 M7 **Santa Rosa** California, W USA 38°27′N 122°42′W
37 U11 **Santa Rosa** New Mexico, SW USA 34°54′N 104°43′W
55 O6 **Santa Rosa** Anzoátegui, NE Venezuela 09°37′N 64°20′W
42 A3 **Santa Rosa** *off.* Departamento de Santa Rosa. ⬖ *department* SE Guatemala
Santa Rosa *see* Santa Rosa de Copán
63 J15 **Santa Rosa, Bajo de** *basin* E Argentina
42 F6 **Santa Rosa de Copán** *var.* Santa Rosa. Copán, W Honduras 14°48′N 88°43′W
54 E8 **Santa Rosa de Osos** Antioquia, C Colombia 06°40′N 75°27′W
Santa Rosa, Departamento de *see* Santa Rosa
35 Q15 **Santa Rosa Island** *island* California, W USA
23 O9 **Santa Rosa Island** *island* Florida, SE USA
40 E6 **Santa Rosalía** Baja California Sur, NW Mexico 27°20′N 112°20′W
54 K6 **Santa Rosalía** Portuguesa, NW Venezuela 09°02′N 69°01′W
188 C15 **Santa Rosa, Mount** ▲ NE Guam
35 V16 **Santa Rosa Mountains** ▲▲ California, W USA
35 T2 **Santa Rosa Range** ▲▲ Nevada, W USA
62 M8 **Santa Sylvina** Chaco, N Argentina 27°49′S 61°09′W
Santa Tecla *see* Nueva San Salvador
61 B19 **Santa Teresa** Santa Fe, C Argentina 33°30′S 60°45′W
59 O20 **Santa Teresa** Espírito Santo, SE Brazil 19°51′S 40°49′W
61 E21 **Santa Teresita** Buenos Aires, E Argentina 36°32′S 56°41′W
61 H19 **Santa Vitória do Palmar** Rio Grande do Sul, S Brazil 33°32′S 53°25′W
35 Q14 **Santa Ynez River** ≈ California, W USA
Sant Carles de la Rápida *see* Sant Carles de la Ràpita
105 U7 **Sant Carles de la Ràpita** *var.* Sant Carles de la Rápida. Cataluña, NE Spain 40°37′N 00°36′E
105 W5 **Sant Celoni** Cataluña, NE Spain 41°39′N 02°25′E
35 U17 **Santee** California, W USA 32°50′N 116°58′W
21 T13 **Santee River** ≈ South Carolina, SE USA
40 K15 **San Telmo, Punta** *headland* SW Mexico 18°19′N 103°30′W
107 O17 **Santeramo in Colle** Puglia, SE Italy 40°47′N 16°45′E
107 M23 **San Teresa di Riva** Sicilia, Italy, C Mediterranean Sea 38°00′N 15°25′E
105 X5 **Sant Feliu de Guíxols** *var.* San Feliú de Guixols. Cataluña, NE Spain 41°47′N 03°02′E
105 W6 **Sant Feliu de Llobregat** Cataluña, NE Spain 41°22′N 02°00′E
106 C7 **Santhià** Piemonte, NE Italy 45°21′N 08°11′E
61 F15 **Santiago** Rio Grande do Sul, S Brazil 29°11′S 54°52′W
62 H11 **Santiago** *var.* Gran Santiago. ● (Chile) Santiago, C Chile 33°30′S 70°40′W
45 N8 **Santiago** *var.* Santiago de los Caballeros. N Dominican Republic 19°27′N 70°42′W
40 G10 **Santiago** Baja California Sur, NW Mexico 23°32′N 109°47′W
41 O8 **Santiago** Nuevo León, NE Mexico 25°22′N 100°09′W
43 R16 **Santiago** Veraguas, S Panama 08°06′N 80°59′W
57 E16 **Santiago** Ica, SW Peru 14°14′S 75°44′W
62 H11 **Santiago** *off.* Región Metropolitana de Santiago, *var.* Metropolitan. ⬖ *region* C Chile
76 D10 **Santiago** *var.* São Tiago. *island* Ilhas de Sotavento, S Cape Verde
62 H11 **Santiago** ✈ Santiago, C Chile 33°27′S 70°40′W
104 G3 **Santiago** ✈ Galicia, NW Spain
Santiago *see* Santiago de Cuba, Cuba
Santiago *see* Grande de Santiago, Río, Mexico
Santiago *see* Santiago de Compostela
42 B6 **Santiago Atitlán** Sololá, SW Guatemala 14°39′N 91°12′W
43 Q16 **Santiago, Cerro** ▲ W Panama 08°27′N 81°42′W
104 G3 **Santiago de Compostela** *var.* Santiago, *Eng.* Compostella; *anc.* Campus Stellae. Galicia, NW Spain 42°52′N 08°33′W
44 I8 **Santiago de Cuba** *var.* Santiago. Santiago de Cuba, E Cuba 20°01′N 75°51′W
Santiago de Guayaquil *see* Guayaquil
62 K8 **Santiago del Estero** Santiago del Estero, C Argentina 27°51′S 64°16′W
61 A15 **Santiago del Estero** *off.* Provincia de Santiago del Estero. ⬖ *province* N Argentina
Santiago del Estero, Provincia de *see* Santiago del Estero
40 I8 **Santiago de los Caballeros** Sinaloa, W Mexico 25°33′N 107°22′W
Santiago de los Caballeros *see* Santiago, Dominican Republic
Santiago de los Caballeros *see* Ciudad de Guatemala, Guatemala
42 F8 **Santiago de María** Usulután, SE El Salvador 13°28′N 88°28′W
104 F12 **Santiago do Cacém** Setúbal, S Portugal 38°01′N 08°42′W
40 J12 **Santiago Ixcuintla** Nayarit, C Mexico 21°50′N 105°11′W
Santiago Jamiltepec *see* Jamiltepec
24 L11 **Santiago Mountains** ▲▲ Texas, SW USA
40 J9 **Santiago Papasquiaro** Durango, C Mexico 25°00′N 105°27′W
Santiago Pinotepa Nacional *see* Pinotepa Nacional

◆ Country
● Country Capital
◇ Dependent Territory
○ Dependent Territory Capital
⬖ Administrative Regions
✈ International Airport
▲ Mountain
▲▲ Mountain Range
⛰ Volcano
≈ River
◎ Lake
▦ Reservoir

Santiago, Región Metropolitana de *see* Santiago
56 C8 **Santiago, Río** ≈ N Peru
40 M10 **San Tiburcio** Zacatecas, C Mexico 24°08′N 101°29′W
105 N2 **Santillana** Cantabria, N Spain 43°24′N 04°06′W
54 I5 **San Timoteo** Zulia, NW Venezuela 09°50′N 71°05′W
Santi Quaranta *see* Sarandë
Santissima Trinidad *see* Jilong
105 O12 **Santisteban del Puerto** Andalucía, S Spain 38°15′N 03°11′W
105 S12 **Sant Joan d'Alacant** *Cast.* San Juan de Alicante. Valenciana, E Spain 38°26′N 00°27′W
105 U7 **Sant Jordi, Golf de** *gulf* NE Spain
105 U11 **Sant Josep de sa Talaia** *var.* San Jose. Ibiza, Spain, W Mediterranean Sea 38°55′N 1°18′E
162 G6 **Santmargats** *var.* Holboo. Dzavhan, W Mongolia 48°35′N 95°25′E
105 T8 **Sant Mateu** Valenciana, E Spain 40°28′N 00°10′E
25 S7 **Santo** Texas, SW USA 32°35′N 98°06′W
Santo *see* Espiritu Santo
60 M10 **Santo Amaro, Ilha de** *island* SE Brazil
61 G14 **Santo Ângelo** Rio Grande do Sul, S Brazil 28°17′S 54°15′W
76 C9 **Santo Antão** *island* Ilhas de Barlavento, N Cape Verde
60 J10 **Santo Antônio da Platina** Paraná, S Brazil 23°20′S 50°05′W
58 C13 **Santo Antônio do Içá** Amazonas, N Brazil 03°05′S 67°56′W
57 Q18 **Santo Corazón, Río** ≈ E Bolivia
44 E5 **Santo Domingo** Villa Clara, C Cuba 22°35′N 80°15′W
45 O9 **Santo Domingo** *prev.* Ciudad Trujillo. ● (Dominican Republic) SE Dominican Republic 18°30′N 69°57′W
40 E8 **Santo Domingo** Baja California Sur, NW Mexico 25°34′N 112°00′W
40 M10 **Santo Domingo** San Luis Potosí, C Mexico 23°18′N 101°42′W
42 L10 **Santo Domingo** Chontales, S Nicaragua 12°15′N 84°59′W
105 P4 **Santo Domingo de la Calzada** La Rioja, N Spain 42°26′N 02°57′W
56 B6 **Santo Domingo de los Colorados** Pichincha, NW Ecuador 0°13′S 79°09′W
Santo Domingo Tehuantepec *see* Tehuantepec
55 O6 **San Tomé** Anzoátegui, NE Venezuela 08°58′N 64°08′W
San Tomé de Guayana *see* Ciudad Guayana
105 R13 **Santomera** Murcia, SE Spain 38°03′N 01°05′W
105 O2 **Santoña** Cantabria, N Spain 43°27′N 03°28′W
Santorin *see* Santoríni
115 K22 **Santoríni** *var.* Santorin, *prev.* Thíra; *anc.* Thera. *island* Kykládes, Greece, Aegean Sea
60 M10 **Santos** São Paulo, S Brazil 23°56′S 46°22′W
65 J17 **Santos Plateau** *undersea feature* SW Atlantic Ocean 25°00′S 43°00′W
104 G6 **Santo Tirso** Porto, N Portugal 41°20′N 08°25′W
40 B2 **Santo Tomás** Baja California Norte, NW Mexico 31°32′N 116°26′W
42 L10 **Santo Tomás** Chontales, S Nicaragua 12°04′N 85°02′W
42 G5 **Santo Tomás de Castilla** Izabal, E Guatemala 15°40′N 88°36′W
40 B2 **Santo Tomás, Punta** *headland* NW Mexico 31°30′N 116°40′W
57 H16 **Santo Tomás, Río** ≈ C Peru
57 B18 **Santo Tomás, Volcán** 🌋 Galapagos Islands, Ecuador, E Pacific Ocean 0°46′S 91°01′W
61 F14 **Santo Tomé** Corrientes, NE Argentina 28°31′S 56°03′W
Santo Tomé de Guayana *see* Ciudad Guayana
98 H10 **Santpoort** Noord-Holland, W Netherlands 52°26′N 04°38′E
Santurce *see* Santurtzi
105 O2 **Santurtzi** *var.* Santurce, Santurzi. País Vasco, N Spain 43°20′N 03°03′W
Santurzi *see* Santurtzi
63 G20 **San Valentín, Cerro** ▲ S Chile 46°36′S 73°17′W
42 F8 **San Vicente** San Vicente, C El Salvador 13°38′N 88°42′W*
40 C2 **San Vicente** Baja California Norte, NW Mexico 31°20′N 116°15′W
188 H6 **San Vicente** Saipan, S Northern Mariana Islands
42 B9 **San Vicente** ◈ *department* E El Salvador
104 I10 **San Vicente de Alcántara** Extremadura, W Spain 39°21′N 07°07′W
105 N2 **San Vicente de Barakaldo** *var.* Baracaldo, *Basq.* San Bizenti-Barakaldo. País Vasco, N Spain 43°17′N 02°59′W
57 E15 **San Vicente de Cañete** *var.* Cañete. Lima, W Peru 13°06′S 76°23′W
104 M2 **San Vicente de la Barquera** Cantabria, N Spain 43°23′N 04°24′W
54 E12 **San Vicente del Caguán** Caquetá, S Colombia 02°07′N 74°47′W
42 F8 **San Vincente, Volcán de** 🌋 C El Salvador 13°34′N 88°50′W
43 O15 **San Vito** Puntarenas, SE Costa Rica 08°49′N 82°58′W
106 I7 **San Vito al Tagliamento** Friuli-Venezia Giulia, NE Italy 45°54′N 12°55′E
107 H23 **San Vito, Capo** *headland* Sicilia, Italy, C Mediterranean Sea 38°11′N 12°41′E
107 P18 **San Vito dei Normanni** Puglia, SE Italy 40°40′N 17°42′E
160 L17 **Sanya** *var.* Ya Xian. Hainan, S China 18°25′N 109°27′E
83 J16 **Sanyati** ≈ N Zimbabwe
25 Q16 **San Ygnacio** Texas, SW USA 27°04′N 99°26′W
160 L6 **Sanyuan** Shaanxi, C China 34°40′N 108°56′E
123 P11 **Sanyyakhtakh** Respublika Sakha (Yakutiya), NE Russian Federation 60°34′N 124°09′E
146 J15 **S. A.Nyýazow Adyndaky** *Rus.* Imeni S. A. Niyazova. Maryyskiy Velayat, S Turkmenistan 36°44′N 62°23′E
82 C10 **Sanza Pombo** Uíge, NW Angola 07°20′S 16°00′E
Sanzyô *see* Sanjō
104 G14 **São Bartolomeu de Messines** Faro, S Portugal 37°12′N 08°16′W
60 M10 **São Bernardo do Campo** São Paulo, S Brazil 23°45′S 46°34′W
61 F15 **São Borja** Rio Grande do Sul, S Brazil 28°35′S 56°01′W
104 H14 **São Brás de Alportel** Faro, S Portugal 37°09′N 07°55′W
60 M10 **São Caetano do Sul** São Paulo, S Brazil 23°37′S 46°34′W
60 L9 **São Carlos** São Paulo, S Brazil 22°02′S 47°53′W
59 P16 **São Cristóvão** Sergipe, E Brazil 10°59′S 37°10′W
61 F15 **São Fancisco de Assis** Rio Grande do Sul, S Brazil 29°32′S 55°07′W
58 K13 **São Félix** Pará, NE Brazil 06°43′S 51°56′W
São Félix *see* São Félix do Araguaia
59 J16 **São Félix do Araguaia** *var.* São Félix. Mato Grosso, W Brazil 11°36′S 50°40′W
59 J14 **São Félix do Xingu** Pará, NE Brazil 06°38′S 51°59′W
60 Q9 **São Fidélis** Rio de Janeiro, SE Brazil 21°37′S 41°40′W
76 D10 **São Filipe** Fogo, S Cape Verde 14°52′N 24°29′W
60 K12 **São Francisco do Sul** Santa Catarina, S Brazil 26°17′S 48°39′W
60 K12 **São Francisco, Ilha de** *island* S Brazil
59 P16 **São Francisco, Rio** ≈ E Brazil
61 G16 **São Gabriel** Rio Grande do Sul, S Brazil 30°17′S 54°17′W
60 P10 **São Gonçalo** Rio de Janeiro, SE Brazil 22°48′S 43°03′W
81 H23 **Sao Hill** Iringa, S Tanzania 08°19′S 35°11′E
60 R9 **São João da Barra** Rio de Janeiro, SE Brazil 21°39′S 41°04′W
104 G7 **São João da Madeira** Aveiro, N Portugal 40°52′N 08°28′W
58 M12 **São João de Cortes** Maranhão, E Brazil 02°30′S 44°27′W
59 M21 **São João del Rei** Minas Gerais, NE Brazil 21°08′S 44°15′W
59 N15 **São João do Piauí** Piauí, E Brazil 08°21′S 42°14′W
59 N14 **São João dos Patos** Maranhão, E Brazil 06°29′S 43°44′W
58 C11 **São Joaquim** Amazonas, NW Brazil 0°08′S 67°10′W
61 J14 **São Joaquim** Santa Catarina, S Brazil 28°20′S 49°55′W
60 L7 **São Joaquim da Barra** São Paulo, S Brazil 20°36′S 47°50′W
64 N2 **São Jorge** *island* Azores, Portugal, NE Atlantic Ocean
61 K14 **São José** Santa Catarina, S Brazil 27°34′S 48°39′W
60 M8 **São José do Rio Pardo** São Paulo, S Brazil 21°37′S 46°52′W
60 K8 **São José do Rio Preto** São Paulo, S Brazil 20°50′S 49°20′W
60 N10 **São Jose dos Campos** São Paulo, S Brazil 23°07′S 45°52′W
61 I17 **São Lourenço do Sul** Rio Grande do Sul, S Brazil 31°25′S 52°00′W
58 M12 **São Luís** *state capital* Maranhão, NE Brazil 02°34′S 44°16′W
58 F11 **São Luís** Roraima, N Brazil 01°11′N 60°15′W
58 M12 **São Luís, Ilha de** *island* NE Brazil
61 F14 **São Luiz Gonzaga** Rio Grande do Sul, S Brazil 28°24′S 54°58′W
São Mandol *see* São Manuel, Rio
47 U8 **Sao Manuel** ≈ C Brazil
59 H15 **São Manuel, Rio** *var.* São Mandol, Teles Pirés. ≈ C Brazil
58 C11 **São Marcelino** Amazonas, NW Brazil 0°53′N 67°16′W
58 N12 **São Marcos, Baía de** *bay* N Brazil
59 O20 **São Mateus** Espírito Santo, SE Brazil 18°44′S 39°53′W
60 J12 **São Mateus do Sul** Paraná, S Brazil 25°58′S 50°29′W
64 P3 **São Miguel** *island* Azores, Portugal, NE Atlantic Ocean
60 G13 **São Miguel d'Oeste** Santa Catarina, S Brazil 26°45′S 53°34′W
45 P9 **Saona, Isla** *island* SE Dominican Republic
172 H12 **Saondzou** ▲ Grande Comore, NW Comoros
103 R10 **Saône** ≈ E France
103 Q9 **Saône-et-Loire** ◈ *department* C France
76 D9 **São Nicolau** *Eng.* Saint Nicholas. *island* Ilhas de Barlavento, N Cape Verde
60 M10 **São Paulo** *state capital* São Paulo, S Brazil 23°33′S 46°39′W
60 K9 **São Paulo** *off.* Estado de São Paulo. ◈ *state* S Brazil
São Paulo de Loanda *see* Luanda
São Paulo, Estado de *see* São Paulo
São Pedro do Rio Grande do Sul *see* Rio Grande
104 H7 **São Pedro do Sul** Viseu, N Portugal 40°46′N 07°58′W
64 K13 **São Pedro e São Paulo** *undersea feature* C Atlantic Ocean 01°25′N 28°54′W
59 M14 **São Raimundo das Mangabeiras** Maranhão, E Brazil 07°00′S 45°30′W
59 Q14 **São Roque, Cabo de** *headland* E Brazil 05°29′S 35°16′W
São Salvador *see* Salvador, Brazil
São Salvador/São Salvador do Congo *see* M'Banza Congo, Angola
60 N10 **São Sebastião, Ilha de** *island* S Brazil
83 N19 **São Sebastião, Ponta** *headland* C Mozambique 22°09′S 35°33′E
104 F13 **São Teotónio** Beja, S Portugal 37°30′N 08°41′W
São Tiago *see* Santiago
79 B18 **São Tomé** ● (Sao Tome and Principe) São Tomé, S Sao Tome and Principe 0°22′N 06°41′E
79 B18 **São Tomé** ✈ São Tomé, S Sao Tome and Principe 0°24′N 06°39′E
79 B18 **São Tomé** *Eng.* Saint Thomas. *island* S Sao Tome and Principe
79 B17 **Sao Tome and Principe** *off.* Democratic Republic of Sao Tome and Principe. ◆ *republic* E Atlantic Ocean
Sao Tome and Principe, Democratic Republic of *see* Sao Tome and Principe
74 H9 **Saoura, Oued** ≈ NW Algeria
60 M10 **São Vicente** *Eng.* Saint Vincent. São Paulo, S Brazil 23°55′S 46°25′W
64 O5 **São Vicente** Madeira, Portugal, NE Atlantic Ocean 32°48′N 17°03′W
76 C9 **São Vicente** *Eng.* Saint Vincent. *island* Ilhas de Barlavento, N Cape Verde
104 F14 **São Vicente, Cabo de** *Eng.* Cape Saint Vincent, *Port.* Cabode São Vicente. *cape* S Portugal
São Vicente, Cabo de *see* São Vicente, Cabo de
Sápai *see* Sápes
Sapaleri, Cerro *see* Zapaleri, Cerro
Saparoea *see* Saparua
171 S13 **Saparua** *prev.* Saparoea. Pulau Saparau, C Indonesia 03°35′S 128°37′E
168 L11 **Sapat** Sumatera, W Indonesia 0°18′S 103°18′E
77 U17 **Sapele** Delta, S Nigeria 05°54′N 05°43′E
23 X7 **Sapelo Island** *island* Georgia, SE USA
23 X7 **Sapelo Sound** *sound* Georgia, SE USA
114 K13 **Sápes** *var.* Sápai. Anatolikí Makedonía kai Thráki, NE Greece 41°02′N 25°44′E
Sapiéntza *see* Sapiénza
115 D22 **Sapiénza** *var.* Sapiéntza. *island* S Greece
138 F12 **Sapir** *prev.* Sappir. Southern, S Israel 30°43′N 35°11′E
61 I15 **Sapiranga** Rio Grande do Sul, S Brazil 29°39′S 50°58′W
114 K13 **Sápka** ▲▲ NE Greece
105 X9 **Sa Pobla** Mallorca, Spain, W Mediterranean Sea 39°46′N 03°03′E
56 D11 **Saposoa** San Martín, N Peru 06°53′S 76°45′W
119 F16 **Sapotskin** *Pol.* Sopockinie, *Rus.* Sapotskino, Sopotskin. Hrodzyenskaya Voblasts', W Belarus 53°50′N 23°39′E
77 P13 **Sapoui** *var.* Sapouy. S Burkina 11°34′N 01°44′W
Sapouy *see* Sapoui
Sappir *see* Sapir
165 S4 **Sapporo** Hokkaidō, NE Japan 43°05′N 141°21′E
107 M19 **Sapri** Campania, S Italy 40°05′N 15°36′E
169 T16 **Sapudi, Pulau** *island* S Indonesia
27 P9 **Sapulpa** Oklahoma, C USA 36°00′N 96°06′W
142 J4 **Saqqez** *var.* Saghez, Sakiz, Saqqiz. Kordestān, NW Iran 36°31′N 46°16′E
Saqqiz *see* Saqqez
139 U8 **Sarābādī** Wāsiṭ, E Iraq 33°00′N 44°52′E
167 P10 **Sara Buri** *var.* Saraburi. Saraburi, C Thailand 14°32′N 100°53′E
Saraburi *see* Sara Buri
Sarafjagān *see* Salafchegān
24 K9 **Saragosa** Texas, SW USA 31°03′N 103°39′W
Saragossa *see* Zaragoza
Saragt *see* Sarahs
56 B8 **Saraguro** Loja, S Ecuador 03°42′S 79°18′W
146 I15 **Sarahs** *var.* Saragt, *Rus.* Serakhs. Ahal Welaýaty, S Turkmenistan 36°33′N 61°10′E
126 M6 **Sarai** Ryazanskaya Oblast', W Russian Federation 53°43′N 39°59′E
Sarāi *see* Sarāy
154 M12 **Saraipāli** Chhattīsgarh, C India 21°21′N 83°01′E
149 T9 **Sarāi Sidhu** Punjab, E Pakistan 30°35′N 72°02′E
93 M15 **Säräisniemi** Oulu, C Finland 64°25′N 26°50′E
113 I14 **Sarajevo** ● (Bosnia and Herzegovina) Federacija Bosna I Hercegovina, SE Bosnia and Herzegovina 43°53′N 18°24′E
112 I13 **Sarajevo** ✈ Federacija Bosna I Hercegovina, C Bosnia and Herzegovina 43°49′N 18°21′E
143 V4 **Sarakhs** Khorāsān-Razavī, NE Iran 36°50′N 61°00′E
115 H17 **Sarakíniko, Akrotírio** *headland* Évvoia, C Greece 38°46′N 23°43′E
115 I18 **Sarakinó** *island* Vóreies Sporádes, Greece, Aegean Sea
127 V7 **Saraktash** Orenburgskaya Oblast', W Russian Federation 51°46′N 56°23′E
30 L15 **Sara, Lake** ▣ Illinois, N USA
23 N8 **Saraland** Alabama, S USA 30°49′N 88°04′W
55 V9 **Saramacca** ◈ *district* N Suriname
55 V10 **Saramacca Rivier** ≈ C Suriname
166 M2 **Saramati** ▲ N Myanmar (Burma) 25°46′N 95°01′E
145 R10 **Saran'** *Kaz.* Saran. Karaganda, C Kazakhstan 49°47′N 73°02′E
18 K7 **Saranac Lake** New York, NE USA 44°18′N 74°06′W
18 K7 **Saranac River** ≈ New York, NE USA
Saranda *see* Sarandë
113 L23 **Sarandë** *var.* Saranda, *It.* Porto Edda; *prev.* Santi Quaranta. Vlorë, S Albania 39°53′N 20°E
61 H14 **Sarandi** Rio Grande do Sul, S Brazil 27°57′S 52°58′W
61 F19 **Sarandí del Yí** Durazno, C Uruguay 33°18′S 55°38′W
61 F19 **Sarandí Grande** Florida, S Uruguay 33°43′S 56°19′W
171 Q8 **Sarangani Islands** *island group* S Philippines
127 P5 **Saransk** Respublika Mordoviya, W Russian Federation 54°11′N 45°10′E
115 C14 **Sarantáporos** ≈ N Greece
114 H9 **Sarantsi** Sofiya, W Bulgaria 42°43′N 23°46′E
127 T3 **Sarapul** Udmurtskaya Respublika, NW Russian Federation 56°26′N 53°52′E
Sarâqeb *see* Sarāqib
138 I3 **Sarāqib** *Fr.* Sarâqeb. Idlib, N Syria 35°52′N 36°48′E
54 J5 **Sarare** Lara, N Venezuela 09°47′N 69°10′W
55 O10 **Sarariña** Amazonas, S Venezuela 04°10′N 64°31′W
143 S10 **Sar Ashk** Kermān, C Iran
23 V13 **Sarasota** Florida, SE USA 27°20′N 82°31′W
117 O11 **Sarata** Odes'ka Oblast', SW Ukraine 46°01′N 29°40′E
116 I10 **Sărăţel** *Hung.* Szeretfalva. Bistriţa-Năsăud, N Romania 47°02′N 24°24′E
25 X10 **Saratoga** Texas, SW USA 30°15′N 94°31′W
18 K10 **Saratoga Springs** New York, NE USA 43°04′N 73°47′W
127 P8 **Saratov** Saratovskaya Oblast', W Russian Federation 51°33′N 45°58′E
127 P8 **Saratovskaya Oblast'** ◈ *province* W Russian Federation
127 Q7 **Saratovskoye Vodokhranilishche** ▣ W Russian Federation
143 X13 **Sarāvān** Sīstān va Balūchestān, SE Iran 27°11′N 62°35′E
Saravan/Saravane *see* Salavan
169 S9 **Sarawak** ◈ *state* East Malaysia
Sarawak *see* Kuching
139 U6 **Sarāy** *var.* Sarāi. Diyālá, E Iraq 34°06′N 45°06′E
136 D10 **Saray** Tekirdağ, NW Turkey 41°27′N 27°56′E
76 J12 **Saraya** SE Senegal 12°50′N 11°45′W
143 W14 **Sarbāz** Sīstān va Balūchestān, SE Iran 26°38′N 61°13′E
143 U8 **Sarbīsheh** Khorāsān-e Janūbī, E Iran 32°35′N 59°50′E
111 J24 **Sárbogárd** Fejér, C Hungary 46°54′N 18°36′E
Şărcad *see* Sarkad
27 S7 **Sarcoxie** Missouri, C USA 37°04′N 94°07′W
152 L11 **Sārda** *Nep.* Kali. ≈ India/Nepal
152 G10 **Sardārshahr** Rājasthān, NW India 28°30′N 74°30′E
107 C18 **Sardegna** *Eng.* Sardinia. ◈ *region* Italy, C Mediterranean Sea
107 A18 **Sardegna** *Eng.* Sardinia. *island* Italy, C Mediterranean Sea
42 K13 **Sardinal** Guanacaste, NW Costa Rica 10°30′N 85°38′W
54 G7 **Sardinata** Norte de Santander, N Colombia 08°07′N 72°47′W
Sardinia *see* Sardegna
120 K8 **Sardinia-Corsica Trough** *undersea feature* Tyrrhenian Sea, C Mediterranean Sea
22 L2 **Sardis** Mississippi, S USA 34°25′N 89°55′W
22 L2 **Sardis Lake** ▣ Mississippi, S USA
27 P12 **Sardis Lake** ▣ Oklahoma, C USA
92 H12 **Sarek** ▲▲ N Sweden
92 H11 **Sarektjåhkkå** ▲ N Sweden 67°28′N 17°56′E
Sar-e Pol *see* Sar-e Pul
Sar-e Pol *see* Sar-e Pol-e Ẕahāb
142 J6 **Sar-e Pol-e Ẕahāb** *var.* Sar-e Pol, Sar-i Pul. Kermānshāhān, W Iran 34°28′N 45°52′E
149 N3 **Sar-e Pul** *var.* Sar-i-Pul; *prev.* Sar-e Pol. Sar-e Pul, N Afghanistan 36°16′N 65°55′E
149 O3 **Sar-e Pul** ◈ *province* N Afghanistan
Sarera, Teluk *see* Cenderawasih, Teluk
147 T13 **Sarez, Kŭli** *Rus.* Sarezskoye Ozero. ◎ SE Tajikistan
Sarezskoye Ozero *see* Sarez, Kŭli
64 G10 **Sargasso Sea** *sea* W Atlantic Ocean
149 U8 **Sargodha** Punjab, NE Pakistan 32°06′N 72°48′E
78 I13 **Sarh** *prev.* Fort-Archambault. Moyen-Chari, S Chad 09°08′N 18°22′E
143 P4 **Sārī** *var.* Sari, Sāri. Māzandarān, N Iran 36°37′N 53°05′E
115 N23 **Saría** *island* SE Greece
Sariasiya *see* Sariosiyo
40 F3 **Saric** Sonora, NW Mexico 31°08′N 111°22′W
188 K6 **Sarigan** *island* C Northern Mariana Islands
136 D14 **Sarıgöl** Manisa, SW Turkey 38°16′N 28°41′E
139 T6 **Sārihah** At Ta'mím, E Iraq 34°34′N 44°38′E
137 R12 **Sarıkamış** Kars, NE Turkey 40°18′N 42°36′E
169 R9 **Sarikei** Sarawak, East Malaysia 02°07′N 111°30′E
147 U12 **Sarikol Range** *Rus.* Sarykol'skiy Khrebet. ▲▲ China/Tajikistan
181 Y7 **Sarina** Queensland, NE Australia 21°34′S 149°12′E
Sarine *see* La Sarine
105 S5 **Sariñena** Aragón, NE Spain 41°47′N 00°10′W
147 O13 **Sariosiyo** *Rus.* Sariasiya. Surkhondaryo Viloyati, S Uzbekistan 38°25′N 67°51′E
Sar-i-Pul *see* Sar-e Pol, Afghanistan
Sar-i Pul *see* Sar-e Pol-e Ẕahāb, Iran
Sariqamish Kŭli *see* Sarygamyş Köli
149 V1 **Sarī Qūl** *Rus.* Ozero Zurkul', *Taj.* Zŭrkŭl. ◎ Afghanistan/Tajikistan *see also* Zŭrkŭl
Sarī Qūl *see* Zŭrkŭl
75 Q12 **Sarīr Tībistī** *var.* Serir Tibesti. *desert* S Libya
25 S15 **Sarita** Texas, SW USA 27°14′N 97°48′W
163 W14 **Sariwŏn** SW North Korea 38°30′N 125°52′E
114 P12 **Sarıyer** İstanbul, NW Turkey 41°11′N 29°03′E
97 L26 **Sark** *Fr.* Sercq. *island* Channel Islands
111 N24 **Sarkad** *Rom.* Şărcad. Békés, SE Hungary 46°44′N 21°25′E
145 W14 **Sarkand** *Kaz.* Sarqan. Almaty, SW Kazakhstan 45°24′N 79°55′E
152 D11 **Sarkāri Tala** Rājasthān, NW India 27°39′N 70°52′E
136 G15 **Şarkîkaraağaç** *var.* Şarki Karaağaç. Isparta, SW Turkey 38°04′N 31°22′E
Şarki Karaağaç *see* Şarkîkaraağaç
136 L13 **Şarkışla** Sivas, C Turkey 39°21′N 36°27′E
136 C11 **Şarköy** Tekirdağ, NW Turkey 40°37′N 27°07′E
Sárköz *see* Livada
Sarlat *see* Sarlat-la-Canéda
102 M13 **Sarlat-la-Canéda** *var.* Sarlat. Dordogne, SW France 44°54′N 01°12′E
109 S3 **Sarleinsbach** Oberösterreich, N Austria 48°33′N 13°55′E
Šarma *see* Ash Sharmah
171 Y12 **Sarmi** Papua, E Indonesia 01°51′S 138°45′E
63 I19 **Sarmiento** Chubut, S Argentina 45°38′S 69°07′W
63 H25 **Sarmiento, Monte** ▲ S Chile 54°28′S 70°49′W
94 J11 **Särna** Dalarna, C Sweden 61°40′N 13°10′E
108 F8 **Sarnen** Obwalden, C Switzerland 46°54′N 08°15′E
108 F9 **Sarner See** ◎ C Switzerland
14 D16 **Sarnia** Ontario, S Canada 42°58′N 82°23′W
116 L3 **Sarny** Rivnens'ka Oblast', NW Ukraine 51°20′N 26°35′E
171 O13 **Saroako** Sulawesi, C Indonesia 02°31′S 121°18′E
118 L13 **Sarochyna** *Rus.* Sorochino. Vitsyebskaya Voblasts', N Belarus 55°12′N 28°45′E
168 L12 **Sarolangun** Sumatera, W Indonesia 02°17′S 102°39′E
165 U3 **Saroma** Hokkaidō, NE Japan 44°01′N 143°43′E
165 V3 **Saroma-ko** ◎ Hokkaidō, NE Japan
Saronic Gulf *see* Saronikós Kólpos
115 H20 **Saronikós Kólpos** *Eng.* Saronic Gulf. *gulf* S Greece
106 D7 **Saronno** Lombardia, N Italy 45°38′N 09°02′E
136 B11 **Saros Körfezi** *gulf* NW Turkey
111 N20 **Sárospatak** Borsod-Abaúj-Zemplén, NE Hungary 48°18′N 21°30′E
127 O4 **Sarov** *prev.* Sarova. Respublika Mordoviya, SW Russian Federation 54°39′N 43°09′E
Sarova *see* Sarov
127 P12 **Sarpa** Respublika Kalmykiya, SW Russian Federation 47°00′N 45°42′E
127 P12 **Sarpa, Ozero** ◎ SW Russian Federation
Šar Planina *see* Mali i Sharrit
95 I16 **Sarpsborg** Østfold, S Norway 59°16′N 11°07′E
139 U5 **Sarqalā** At Ta'mím, N Iraq
Sarqan *see* Sarkand
103 U4 **Sarralbe** Moselle, NE France 49°02′N 07°01′E
Sarre *see* Saar, France/Germany
Sarre *see* Saarland, Germany
103 U5 **Sarrebourg** *Ger.* Saarburg. Moselle, NE France 48°43′N 07°03′E
Sarrebruck *see* Saarbrücken
103 U4 **Sarreguemines** *prev.* Saargemund. Moselle, NE France 49°06′N 07°04′E
104 I3 **Sarria** Galicia, NW Spain 42°47′N 07°25′W
105 S8 **Sarrión** Aragón, NE Spain 40°09′N 00°49′W
42 F4 **Sarstoon** *Sp.* Río Sarstún. ≈ Belize/Guatemala
Sarstún, Río *see* Sarstoon
123 Q9 **Sartang** ≈ NE Russian Federation
103 X16 **Sartène** Corse, France, C Mediterranean Sea 41°38′N 08°58′E
102 K7 **Sarthe** ◈ *department* NW France
102 K7 **Sarthe** ≈ N France
115 H15 **Sárti** Kentrikí Makedonía, N Greece 40°05′N 24°E
Sartu *see* Daqing
165 T1 **Sarufutsu** Hokkaidō, NE Japan 45°20′N 142°03′E
Saruhan *see* Manisa
152 G9 **Sarūpsar** Rājasthān, NW India 29°25′N 73°50′E
137 U13 **Şärur** *prev.* Il'ichevsk. SW Azerbaijan 39°30′N 44°59′E
Sarvani *see* Marneuli
111 G23 **Sárvár** Vas, W Hungary 47°15′N 16°59′E
143 P11 **Sarvestān** Fārs, S Iran 29°16′N 53°13′E
171 W12 **Sarwon** Papua, E Indonesia 0°58′S 136°08′E
145 P17 **Saryagash** *Kaz.* Saryaghash. Yuzhnyy Kazakhstan, S Kazakhstan 41°29′N 69°10′E
Saryaghash *see* Saryagash
145 R9 **Saryarka** *Eng.* Kazakh Uplands, Kirghiz Steppe. *uplands* C Kazakhstan
147 W8 **Sary-Bulak** Narynskaya Oblast', C Kyrgyzstan 41°56′N 75°44′E
147 U10 **Sary-Bulak** Oshskaya Oblast', SW Kyrgyzstan 40°49′N 73°44′E
117 S14 **Sarych, Mys** *headland* S Ukraine 44°23′N 33°44′E
147 Z7 **Sary-Dzhaz** *var.* Aksu He. ≈ China/Kyrgyzstan *see also* Aksu He
Sary-Dzhaz *see* Aksu He
146 F8 **Sarygamyş Köli** *Rus.* Sarykamyshkoye Ozero, *Uzb.* Sariqamish Kŭli. *salt lake* Kazakhstan/Uzbekistan
144 G13 **Sarykamys** *Kaz.* Saryqamys. Mangistau, SW Kazakhstan 45°58′N 53°30′E
Sarykamyshkoye Ozero *see* Sarygamyş Köli
145 N7 **Sarykol'** *prev.* Uritskiy. Kustanay, N Kazakhstan 53°19′N 65°34′E
Sarykol'skiy Khrebet *see* Sarikol Range
144 M10 **Sarykopa, Ozero** ◎ C Kazakhstan
145 V15 **Saryozek** *Kaz.* Saryözek. Almaty, SE Kazakhstan 44°22′N 77°57′E
144 E10 **Saryozen** *Kaz.* Kishiözen; *prev.* Malyy Uzen'. ≈ Kazakhstan/Russian Federation
Saryqamys *see* Sarykamys
145 S13 **Saryshagan** *Kaz.* Saryshaghan. Karaganda, SE Kazakhstan 46°05′N 73°38′E
Saryshaghan *see* Saryshagan
145 O13 **Sarysu** ≈ S Kazakhstan
147 T11 **Sary-Tash** Oshskaya Oblast', SW Kyrgyzstan 39°44′N 73°14′E
145 T12 **Saryterek** Karaganda, C Kazakhstan 47°46′N 74°06′E
Saryyazynskoye Vodokhranilishche *see* Saryýazy Suw Howdany
146 J15 **Saryýazy Suw Howdany** *Rus.* Saryyazynskoye Vodokhranilishche. ▣ S Turkmenistan
145 T14 **Saryyesik-Atyrau, Peski** *desert* E Kazakhstan
106 E10 **Sarzana** Liguria, NW Italy 44°07′N 09°59′E
188 B17 **Sasalaguan, Mount** ▲ S Guam
153 O14 **Sasarām** Bihār, N India 24°58′N 84°01′E
186 M8 **Sasari, Mount** ▲ Santa Isabel, N Solomon Islands 08°09′S 159°32′E
164 C13 **Sasebo** Nagasaki, Kyūshū, SW Japan 33°10′N 129°42′E
14 I9 **Saseginaga, Lac** ◎ Québec, SE Canada
Saseno *see* Sazan
11 R13 **Saskatchewan** ◈ *province* SW Canada
11 U14 **Saskatchewan** ≈ Manitoba/Saskatchewan, C Canada
11 T15 **Saskatoon** Saskatchewan, S Canada 52°10′N 106°40′W
11 T15 **Saskatoon** ✈ Saskatchewan, S Canada 52°15′N 107°05′W
123 N7 **Saskylakh** Respublika Sakha (Yakutiya), NE Russian Federation 71°56′N 114°07′E
42 L7 **Saslaya, Cerro** ▲ N Nicaragua 13°52′N 85°06′W
38 G17 **Sasmik, Cape** *headland* Tanaga Island, Alaska, USA 51°36′N 177°55′W
119 N19 **Sasnovy Bor** *Rus.* Sosnovyy Bor. Homyel'skaya Voblasts', SE Belarus 52°32′N 29°35′E
127 N5 **Sasovo** Ryazanskaya Oblast', W Russian Federation 54°19′N 41°54′E
25 S12 **Saspamco** Texas, SW USA 29°13′N 98°18′W
109 W9 **Sass** *var.* Sassbach. ≈ SE Austria
76 M17 **Sassandra** S Ivory Coast 04°58′N 06°08′W
76 M17 **Sassandra** *var.* Ibo, Sassandra Fleuve. ≈ S Ivory Coast
Sassandra Fleuve *see* Sassandra
107 B17 **Sassari** Sardegna, Italy, C Mediterranean Sea 40°44′N 08°33′E
Sassbach *see* Sass
98 H11 **Sassenheim** Zuid-Holland, W Netherlands 52°14′N 04°31′E
Sassmacken *see* Valdemārpils
100 O7 **Sassnitz** Mecklenburg-Vorpommern, NE Germany 54°32′N 13°39′E
99 E16 **Sas van Gent** Zeeland, SW Netherlands 51°13′N 03°48′E
145 W12 **Sasykkol', Ozero** ◎ E Kazakhstan
117 O12 **Sasyk, Ozero** *Rus.* Ozero Sasyk Kunduk, *var.* Ozero Kunduk. ◎ SW Ukraine
76 J12 **Satadougou** Kayes, SW Mali 12°40′N 11°25′W
164 C17 **Sata-misaki** Kyūshū, SW Japan
26 I7 **Satanta** Kansas, C USA 37°23′N 102°00′W
155 E15 **Sātāra** Mahārāshtra, W India 17°41′N 73°59′E
192 G15 **Sātaua** Savai'i, NW Samoa 13°26′S 172°40′W
188 M16 **Satawal** *island* Caroline Islands, C Micronesia
189 R17 **Satawan Atoll** *atoll* Mortlock Islands, C Micronesia
Sātbaev *see* Satpayev
23 Y12 **Satellite Beach** Florida, SE USA 28°10′N 80°35′W
95 M14 **Säter** Dalarna, C Sweden 60°21′N 15°45′E
Sathmar *see* Satu Mare
23 V7 **Satilla River** ≈ Georgia, SE USA
57 F14 **Satipo** *var.* San Francisco de Satipo. Junín, C Peru 11°19′S 74°37′W
122 F11 **Satka** Chelyabinskaya Oblast', C Russian Federation 55°08′N 58°54′E
153 T16 **Satkhira** Khulna, SW Bangladesh 22°43′N 89°06′E
146 J13 **Şatlyk** *Rus.* Shatlyk. Mary Welaýaty, C Turkmenistan 37°55′N 61°00′E
154 K9 **Satna** *prev.* Sutna. Madhya Pradesh, C India 24°33′N 80°50′E
103 R11 **Satolas** ✈ (Lyon) Rhône, E France 45°44′N 05°01′E
111 N20 **Sátoraljaújhely** Borsod-Abaúj-Zemplén, NE Hungary 48°24′N 21°39′E
145 O12 **Satpayev** *Kaz.* Sātbaev; *prev.* Nikol'skiy. Karaganda, C Kazakhstan 47°59′N 67°27′E
154 G11 **Sātpura Range** ▲▲ C India
165 Q10 **Satsuma-Sendai** Miyagi, Honshū, C Japan 38°16′N 140°52′E
Satsuma-Sendai *see* Sendai
167 P12 **Sattahip** *var.* Ban Sattahip, Ban Sattahipp. Chon Buri, S Thailand 12°36′N 100°56′E
92 L11 **Sattanen** Lappi, NE Finland 67°31′N 26°35′E
Satul *see* Satun
116 H9 **Satulung** *Hung.* Kővárhosszúfalu. Maramureş, N Romania 47°34′N 23°26′E
Satul-Vechi *see* Staro Selo
116 G8 **Satu Mare** *Ger.* Sathmar, *Hung.* Szatmárrnémeti. Satu Mare, NW Romania 47°46′N 22°55′E
116 G8 **Satu Mare** ◈ *county* NW Romania
167 N16 **Satun** *var.* Satul, Setul. Satun, SW Thailand 06°40′N 100°01′E
192 G16 **Satupa'iteau** Savai'i, W Samoa 13°46′S 172°26′W
Sau *see* Sava
14 F14 **Sauble** ≈ Ontario, S Canada
14 F13 **Sauble Beach** Ontario, S Canada 44°36′N 81°15′W
61 C16 **Sauce** Corrientes, NE Argentina 30°05′S 58°46′W
Sauce *see* Juan L. Lacaze
36 K15 **Sauceda Mountains** ▲▲ Arizona, SW USA
61 C17 **Sauce de Luna** Entre Ríos, E Argentina 31°15′S 59°09′W
63 L15 **Sauce Grande, Río** ≈ E Argentina
40 K6 **Saucillo** Chihuahua, N Mexico 28°01′N 105°17′W
95 D15 **Sauda** Rogaland, S Norway 59°38′N 06°23′E
145 Q16 **Saudakent** *Kaz.* Saūdakent; *prev.* Baykadam, *Kaz.* Bayqadam. Zhambyl, S Kazakhstan 43°49′N 69°56′E
92 J2 **Saudhárkrókur** Nordhurland Vestra, N Iceland 65°45′N 19°39′W
141 P9 **Saudi Arabia** *off.* Kingdom of Saudi Arabia, Al 'Arabīyah as Su'ūdīyah, *Ar.* Al Mamlakah al 'Arabīyah as Su'ūdīyah. ◆ *monarchy* SW Asia
Saudi Arabia, Kingdom of *see* Saudi Arabia
101 D19 **Sauer** *var.* Sûre. ≈ NW Europe *see also* Sûre
Sauer *see* Sûre
101 F15 **Sauerland** *forest* W Germany
14 F14 **Saugeen** ≈ Ontario, S Canada
18 K12 **Saugerties** New York, NE USA 42°04′N 73°55′W
Saugor *see* Sāgar
10 K15 **Saugstad, Mount** ▲ British Columbia, SW Canada 52°12′N 126°35′W
Sāūjbulāgh *see* Mahābād
102 J11 **Saujon** Charente-Maritime, W France 45°40′N 00°54′W
29 T7 **Sauk Centre** Minnesota, N USA 45°44′N 94°57′W
30 L8 **Sauk City** Wisconsin, N USA 43°16′N 89°43′W
29 U7 **Sauk Rapids** Minnesota, N USA 45°35′N 94°09′W
55 Y11 **Saül** C French Guiana 03°37′N 53°12′W
103 O7 **Sauldre** ≈ C France
101 I23 **Saulgau** Baden-Württemberg, SW Germany 48°03′N 09°28′E
103 Q8 **Saulieu** Côte d'Or, C France 47°15′N 04°15′E
118 G8 **Saulkrasti** C Latvia 57°14′N 24°25′E
15 S6 **Sault-aux-Cochons, Rivière du** ≈ Québec, SE Canada
31 Q4 **Sault Sainte Marie** Michigan, N USA 46°29′N 84°22′W
12 F14 **Sault Ste. Marie** Ontario, S Canada 46°30′N 84°17′W
145 P7 **Saumalkol'** *prev.* Volodarskoye. Severnyy Kazakhstan, N Kazakhstan 53°19′N 68°05′E
190 E13 **Sauma, Pointe** *headland* Île Alofi, W Wallis and Futuna 14°21′S 177°58′W
171 T16 **Saumlaki** *var.* Saumlakki. Pulau Yamdena, E Indonesia 07°53′S 131°18′E
Saumlakki *see* Saumlaki
15 R12 **Saumon, Rivière au** ≈ Québec, SE Canada
102 K8 **Saumur** Maine-et-Loire, NW France 47°16′N 00°04′W
185 F23 **Saunders, Cape** *headland* South Island, New Zealand 45°53′S 170°40′E
195 N13 **Saunders Coast** *physical region* Antarctica
65 B23 **Saunders Island** *island* NW Falkland Islands
65 C24 **Saunders Island Settlement** Saunders Island, NW Falkland Islands 51°22′S 60°05′W
82 F11 **Saurimo** *Port.* Henrique de Carvalho, Vila Henrique de Carvalho. Lunda Sul, NE Angola 09°39′S 20°24′E
55 S11 **Sauriwaunawa** S Guyana 03°10′N 59°51′W
82 D12 **Sautar** Malanje, NW Angola 11°10′S 18°26′E
45 S13 **Sauteurs** N Grenada 12°14′N 61°38′W
102 K13 **Sauveterre-de-Guyenne** Gironde, SW France 44°43′N 00°02′W
119 O14 **Sava** Mahilyowskaya Voblasts', E Belarus 54°22′N 30°49′E
42 J5 **Savá** Colón, N Honduras 15°30′N 86°16′W
84 H11 **Sava** *Eng.* Save, *Ger.* Sau, *Hung.* Száva. ≈ SE Europe
33 Y8 **Savage** Montana, NW USA 47°28′N 104°17′W
183 N16 **Savage River** Tasmania, SE Australia 41°34′S 145°15′E
77 R15 **Savalou** S Benin 07°59′N 01°58′E
30 K10 **Savanna** Illinois, N USA 42°05′N 90°09′W
23 X6 **Savannah** Georgia, SE USA 32°02′N 81°01′W
27 R2 **Savannah** Missouri, C USA 39°57′N 94°49′W
20 H10 **Savannah** Tennessee, S USA 35°12′N 88°15′W
21 O12 **Savannah River** ≈ Georgia/South Carolina, SE USA
167 S9 **Savannakhét** *var.* Khanthabouli. Savannakhét, S Laos 16°38′N 104°49′E
44 H12 **Savanna-La-Mar** W Jamaica 18°13′N 78°08′W
12 B10 **Savant Lake** ◎ Ontario, S Canada

◆ Country
● Country Capital
◇ Dependent Territory
○ Dependent Territory Capital
◈ Administrative Regions
✈ International Airport
▲ Mountain
▲▲ Mountain Range
🌋 Volcano
≈ River
◎ Lake
▣ Reservoir

155 F17 **Savanūr** Karnātaka, W India 14°58′N 75°19′E
93 J16 **Sävar** Västerbotten, N Sweden 63°52′N 20°33′E
Savaria see Szombathely
154 C11 **Sāvarkundla** var. Kundla. Gujarāt, W India 21°21′N 71°20′E
116 F11 **Săvârşin** Hung. Soborsin; prev. Săvirşin. Arad, W Romania 46°00′N 22°15′E
136 C13 **Savaştepe** Balıkesir, W Turkey 39°20′N 27°38′E
147 P11 **Savat** Rus. Savat. Sirdaryo Viloyati, E Uzbekistan 40°03′N 68°35′E
Savat see Savat
Sávdijári see Skaulo
77 R15 **Savè** SE Benin 08°04′N 02°29′E
83 N18 **Save** Inhambane, E Mozambique 21°07′S 34°35′E
102 L16 **Save** ≈ S France
83 L17 **Save** var. Sabi. ≈ Mozambique/Zimbabwe see also Sabi
Save see Sava
Save see Sabi
142 M6 **Sāveh** Markazī, W Iran 35°00′N 50°22′E
116 L8 **Săveni** Botoşani, NE Romania 47°57′N 26°52′E
103 N16 **Saverdun** Ariège, S France 43°15′N 01°34′E
103 U5 **Saverne** var. Zabern; anc. Tres Tabernae. Bas-Rhin, NE France 48°45′N 07°22′E
106 B9 **Savigliano** Piemonte, NW Italy 44°39′N 07°39′E
Savigsivik see Savissivik
109 U10 **Savinja** ≈ N Slovenia
106 H11 **Savio** ≈ C Italy
Săvirşin see Săvârşin
197 O11 **Savissivik** var. Savigsivik. ◈ Avannaarsua, N Greenland
93 N18 **Savitaipale** Etelä-Suomi, SE Finland 61°12′N 27°43′E
113 J15 **Šavnik** C Montenegro 42°57′N 19°04′E
108 I9 **Savognin** Graubünden, S Switzerland 46°34′N 09°35′E
103 T12 **Savoie** ◈ department E France
106 C10 **Savona** Liguria, NW Italy 44°18′N 08°29′E
93 N17 **Savonlinna** Swe. Nyslott. Itä-Suomi, E Finland 61°51′N 28°56′E
93 N17 **Savonranta** Itä-Suomi, E Finland 62°10′N 29°10′E
38 K10 **Savoonga** Saint Lawrence Island, Alaska, USA 63°40′N 170°29′W
30 M13 **Savoy** Illinois, N USA 40°03′N 88°15′W
117 O8 **Savran'** Odes'ka Oblast', SW Ukraine 48°07′N 30°00′E
137 R11 **Şavşat** Artvin, NE Turkey 41°15′N 42°30′E
95 L19 **Sävsjö** Jönköping, S Sweden 57°25′N 14°40′E
Savu, Kepulauan see Sawu, Kepulauan
92 M11 **Savukoski** Lappi, NE Finland 67°17′N 28°14′E
Savu, Pulau see Sawu, Pulau
187 Y14 **Savusavu** Vanua Levu, N Fiji 16°48′S 179°20′E
171 O17 **Savu Sea** Ind. Laut Sawu. sea S Indonesia
83 H17 **Savute** North-West, N Botswana 18°33′S 24°06′E
139 N7 **Şawāb Uqlat** well W Iraq
138 M7 **Sawāb, Wādī as** dry watercourse W Iraq
152 H13 **Sawāi Mādhopur** Rājasthān, N India 26°00′N 76°22′E
Sawakin see Suakin
167 R8 **Sawang Daen Din** Sakon Nakhon, E Thailand 17°28′N 103°27′E
167 O8 **Sawankhalok** var. Swankalok. Sukhothai, NW Thailand 17°19′N 99°50′E
165 P13 **Sawara** Chiba, Honshū, S Japan 35°52′N 140°31′E
37 R5 **Sawatch Range** ▲▲ Colorado, C USA
141 N12 **Sawdā', Jabal** ▲ SW Saudi Arabia 18°15′N 42°26′E
75 P9 **Sawdā', Jabal as** ▲▲ C Libya
Sawdirī see Sodiri
97 F14 **Sawel Mountain** ▲ C Northern Ireland, United Kingdom 54°49′N 07°04′W
75 X10 **Sawhāj** var. Sawhāj, var. Sohâg, Suliag. C Egypt 26°28′N 31°44′E
Sawhāj see Sawhāj
77 O15 **Sawla** N Ghana 09°14′N 02°26′W
141 X12 **Şawqirah** var. Suqrah. S Oman 18°16′N 56°34′E
141 X12 **Şawqirah, Dawḩat** var. Ghubbat Sawqirah, Sukra Bay, Suqrah Bay. bay S Oman
Sawqirah, Ghubbat see Şawqirah, Dawḩat
183 V5 **Sawtell** New South Wales, SE Australia 30°22′S 153°04′E
138 K7 **Şawt, Wādī aş** dry watercourse S Syria
171 O17 **Sawu, Kepulauan** var. Kepulauan Savu. island group S Indonesia
Sawu, Laut see Savu Sea
171 O17 **Sawu, Pulau** var. Pulau Sawu. island Kepulauan Sawu, S Indonesia
105 S12 **Sax** Valenciana, E Spain 38°33′N 00°49′W
Saxe see Sachsen
108 C11 **Saxon** Valais, SW Switzerland 46°07′N 07°09′E
Saxony see Sachsen
Saxony-Anhalt see Sachsen-Anhalt
77 R12 **Say** Niamey, SW Niger 13°08′N 02°20′E
15 V7 **Sayabec** Québec, SE Canada 48°33′N 67°42′W
Sayaboury see Xaignabouli
145 U12 **Sayak** Kaz. Sayaq. Karaganda, E Kazakhstan 46°54′N 77°17′E
57 D14 **Sayán** Lima, W Peru 11°10′S 77°08′W
129 T6 **Sayanskiy Khrebet** ▲▲ S Russian Federation
Sayaq see Sayak
146 K13 **Saýat** Rus. Sayat. Lebap Welaýaty, E Turkmenistan 38°44′N 63°51′E
42 D3 **Sayaxché** Petén, N Guatemala 16°34′N 90°14′W
Şaydā/Sayida see Saïda
162 J7 **Sayhan** var. Hüremt. Bulgan, C Mongolia 48°40′N 102°33′E
163 N10 **Sayhandulaan** var. Öldziyt. Dornogovĭ, SE Mongolia 44°42′N 109°10′E
162 K9 **Sayhan-Ovoo** var. Ongi. Dundgovĭ, C Mongolia 45°27′N 103°58′E
141 T15 **Sayḩūt** E Yemen 15°18′N 51°16′E
29 U14 **Saylorville Lake** ▣ Iowa, C USA
Saymenskiy Kanal see Saimaa Canal
163 N10 **Saynshand** Dornogovĭ, SE Mongolia 44°51′N 110°07′E
Saynshand see Sevrey
Sayn-Ust see Hohmorĭt
Say-Ötesh see Otes
138 J7 **Şayqal, Bahr** ◎ S Syria
Sayrab see Sayrob
158 H4 **Sayram Hu** ◎ NW China
26 K11 **Sayre** Oklahoma, C USA 35°18′N 99°38′W
18 H12 **Sayre** Pennsylvania, NE USA 41°57′N 76°30′W
18 K15 **Sayreville** New Jersey, NE USA 40°27′N 74°19′W
147 N13 **Sayrob** Rus. Sayrab. Surkhondaryo Viloyati, S Uzbekistan 38°03′N 66°54′E
40 L13 **Sayula** Jalisco, SW Mexico 19°52′N 103°36′W
141 R14 **Say'ūn** var. Saywūn. C Yemen 15°53′N 48°32′E
Say-Utës see Otes
10 K16 **Sayward** Vancouver Island, British Columbia, SW Canada 50°20′N 126°01′W
Saywūn see Say'ūn
Sayyāl see As Sayyāl
139 U8 **Sayyid 'Abīd** var. Saiyid Abid. Wāsiţ, E Iraq 32°51′N 45°07′E
113 J22 **Sazan** var. Ishulli i Sazanit, It. Saseno. island SW Albania
Sazanit, Ishulli i see Sazan
Sazau/Sazawa see Sázava
111 E17 **Sázava** var. Sazau, Ger. Sazawa. ≈ C Czech Republic
124 J14 **Sazonovo** Vologodskaya Oblast', NW Russian Federation 59°04′N 35°10′E
102 G6 **Scaër** Finistère, NW France 48°00′N 03°40′W
97 J15 **Scafell Pike** ▲ NW England, United Kingdom 54°26′N 03°10′W
Scalabis see Santarém
96 M2 **Scalloway** N Scotland, United Kingdom 60°10′N 01°17′W
38 M11 **Scammon Bay** Alaska, USA 61°50′N 165°34′W
Scammon Lagoon/Scammon, Laguna see Ojo de Liebre, Laguna
84 F7 **Scandinavia** geophysical region NW Europe
Scania see Skåne
96 K5 **Scapa Flow** sea basin N Scotland, United Kingdom
107 K26 **Scaramia, Capo** headland Sicilia, Italy, C Mediterranean Sea 36°46′N 14°29′E
14 H15 **Scarborough** Ontario, SE Canada 43°46′N 79°14′W
45 Z16 **Scarborough** prev. Port Louis. Tobago, Trinidad and Tobago 11°11′N 60°45′W
97 N16 **Scarborough** N England, United Kingdom 54°17′N 00°24′W
185 I17 **Scargill** Canterbury, South Island, New Zealand 42°57′S 172°57′E
96 E7 **Scarp** island NW Scotland, United Kingdom
Scarpanto see Kárpathos
Scarpanto Strait see Karpathou, Stenó
107 G25 **Scauri** Sicilia, Italy, C Mediterranean Sea 36°45′N 12°06′E
Scealg, Bá na see Ballinskelligs Bay
Scebeli see Shebeli
100 K10 **Schaale** ≈ N Germany
100 K9 **Schaalsee** ◎ N Germany
99 G18 **Schaerbeek** Brussels, C Belgium 50°52′N 04°21′E
108 G6 **Schaffhausen** Fr. Schaffhouse. Schaffhausen, N Switzerland 47°42′N 08°38′E
108 G6 **Schaffhausen** Fr. Schaffhouse. ◈ canton N Switzerland
Schaffhouse see Schaffhausen
98 I8 **Schagen** Noord-Holland, NW Netherlands 52°47′N 04°47′E
Schaken see Šakiai
98 M10 **Schalkhaar** Overijssel, E Netherlands 52°16′N 06°10′E
109 R3 **Schärding** Oberösterreich, N Austria 48°27′N 13°26′E
100 G9 **Scharhörn** island NW Germany
Schässburg see Sighişoara
Schaulen see Šiauliai
30 M10 **Schaumburg** Illinois, N USA 42°01′N 88°04′W
Schebschi Mountains see Shebshi Mountains
98 P6 **Scheemda** Groningen, NE Netherlands 53°10′N 06°58′E
100 I10 **Scheessel** Niedersachsen, NW Germany 53°11′N 09°33′E
13 N8 **Schefferville** Québec, E Canada 54°50′N 67°W
Schelde see Scheldt
99 D18 **Scheldt** Dut. Schelde, Fr. Escaut. ≈ W Europe
35 X5 **Schell Creek Range** ▲▲ Nevada, W USA
18 K10 **Schenectady** New York, NE USA 42°48′N 73°57′W
99 I17 **Scherpenheuvel** Fr. Montaigu. Vlaams Brabant, C Belgium 51°00′N 04°57′E
98 K11 **Scherpenzeel** Gelderland, C Netherlands 52°07′N 05°30′E
25 S12 **Schertz** Texas, SW USA 29°33′N 98°16′W
98 G11 **Scheveningen** Zuid-Holland, W Netherlands 52°07′N 04°18′E
98 G12 **Schiedam** Zuid-Holland, SW Netherlands 51°55′N 04°25′E
99 M24 **Schieren** Diekirch, NE Luxembourg 49°50′N 06°06′E
98 M4 **Schiermonnikoog** Fris. Skiermûntseach. Fryslân, N Netherlands 53°28′N 06°09′E
98 M4 **Schiermonnikoog** Fris. Skiermûntseach. island Waddeneilanden, N Netherlands
99 K14 **Schijndel** Noord-Brabant, S Netherlands 51°37′N 05°27′E
Schil see Jiu
99 H16 **Schilde** Antwerpen, N Belgium 51°14′N 04°35′E
Schillen see Zhilino
103 V5 **Schiltigheim** Bas-Rhin, NE France 48°38′N 07°47′E
106 G7 **Schio** Veneto, NE Italy 45°42′N 11°21′E
98 H10 **Schiphol** ✈ (Amsterdam) Noord-Holland, C Netherlands 52°18′N 04°48′E
Schippenbeil see Sępopol
Schiria see Şiria
Schivelbein see Świdwin
115 D22 **Schíza** island S Greece
175 U3 **Schjetman Reef** reef Antarctica
Schlackenwerth see Ostrov
109 R7 **Schladming** Steiermark, SE Austria 47°24′N 13°42′E
Schlan see Slaný
Schlanders see Silandro
100 I7 **Schlei** inlet N Germany
101 D17 **Schleiden** Nordrhein-Westfalen, W Germany 50°31′N 06°30′E
Schlelau see Szydłowiec
100 I7 **Schleswig** Schleswig-Holstein, N Germany 54°31′N 09°34′E
29 T13 **Schleswig** Iowa, C USA 42°10′N 95°27′W
100 H8 **Schleswig-Holstein** ◈ state N Germany
Schlettstadt see Sélestat
108 F7 **Schlieren** Zürich, N Switzerland 47°23′N 08°27′E
Schlochau see Człuchów
Schloppe see Człopa
101 I18 **Schlüchtern** Hessen, C Germany 50°19′N 09°27′E
101 J17 **Schmalkalden** Thüringen, C Germany 50°42′N 10°26′E
109 W2 **Schmida** ≈ NE Austria
65 P19 **Schmidt-Ott Seamount** var. Schmitt-Ott Seamount, Schmitt-Ott Tablemount. undersea feature SW Indian Ocean 39°37′S 13°00′E
Schmiegel see Šmigiel
Schmitt-Ott Seamount/Schmitt-Ott Tablemount see Schmidt-Ott Seamount
15 V3 **Schmon** ≈ Québec, SE Canada
101 M18 **Schneeberg** ▲ W Germany 50°03′N 11°51′E
Schneeberg see Veliki Snežnik
Schnee-Eifel see Schneifel
Schneekoppe see Sněžka
Schneidemühl see Piła
101 D18 **Schneifel** var. Schnee-Eifel. plateau W Germany
Schnelle Körös/Schnelle Kreisch see Crişul Repede
100 I11 **Schneverdingen** var. Schneverdingen (Wümme). Niedersachsen, NW Germany 53°07′N 09°48′E
Schneverdingen (Wümme) see Schneverdingen
Schoden see Skuodas
45 Q12 **Schœlcher** W Martinique 14°37′N 61°08′W
18 K10 **Schoharie** New York, NE USA 42°40′N 74°20′W
18 K11 **Schoharie Creek** ≈ New York, NE USA
115 J21 **Schoinoússa** island Kykládes, Greece, Aegean Sea
100 L13 **Schönebeck** Sachsen-Anhalt, C Germany 52°01′N 11°45′E
Schöneck see Skarszewy
100 O12 **Schönefeld** ✈ (Berlin) Berlin, NE Germany 52°23′N 13°29′E
101 K24 **Schongau** Bayern, S Germany 47°49′N 10°54′E
100 K13 **Schöningen** Niedersachsen, C Germany 52°07′N 10°58′E
Schönlanke see Trzcianka
Schönsee see Kowalewo Pomorskie
31 P10 **Schoolcraft** Michigan, N USA 42°05′N 85°39′W
98 O8 **Schoonebeek** Drenthe, NE Netherlands 52°39′N 06°57′E
98 I12 **Schoonhoven** Zuid-Holland, C Netherlands 51°57′N 04°51′E
98 H8 **Schoorl** Noord-Holland, NW Netherlands 52°42′N 04°40′E
Schooten see Schoten
101 F24 **Schopfheim** Baden-Württemberg, SW Germany 47°39′N 07°49′E
101 I21 **Schorndorf** Baden-Württemberg, S Germany 48°48′N 09°31′E
100 F10 **Schortens** Niedersachsen, NW Germany 53°31′N 07°57′E
99 H16 **Schoten** var. Schooten. Antwerpen, N Belgium 51°15′N 04°30′E
183 Q17 **Schouten Island** island Tasmania, SE Australia
186 C5 **Schouten Islands** island group NW Papua New Guinea
98 E13 **Schouwen** island SW Netherlands
Schreiberhau see Szklarska Poręba
109 U2 **Schrems** Niederösterreich, E Austria 48°48′N 15°05′E
101 L22 **Schrobenhausen** Bayern, SE Germany 48°33′N 11°14′E
18 L8 **Schroon Lake** ◎ New York, NE USA
108 J8 **Schruns** Vorarlberg, W Austria 47°04′N 09°54′E
Schubin see Szubin
25 U11 **Schulenburg** Texas, SW USA 29°40′N 96°54′W
Schuls see Scuol
108 E8 **Schüpfheim** Luzern, C Switzerland 47°02′N 07°23′E
35 S6 **Schurz** Nevada, W USA 38°55′N 118°48′W
101 I24 **Schussen** ≈ S Germany
Schüttenhofen see Sušice
29 R15 **Schuyler** Nebraska, C USA 41°25′N 97°04′W
18 L10 **Schuylerville** New York, NE USA 43°05′N 73°34′W
101 K20 **Schwabach** Bayern, SE Germany 49°20′N 11°02′E
Schwabenalb see Schwäbische Alb
101 I23 **Schwäbische Alb** var. Schwabenalb, Eng. Swabian Jura. ▲▲ S Germany
101 I22 **Schwäbisch Gmünd** var. Gmünd. Baden-Württemberg, SW Germany 48°49′N 09°48′E
101 I21 **Schwäbisch Hall** var. Hall. Baden-Württemberg, SW Germany 49°07′N 09°45′E
101 H16 **Schwalm** ≈ C Germany
109 V9 **Schwanberg** Steiermark, SE Austria 46°46′N 15°12′E
108 H8 **Schwanden** Glarus, E Switzerland 47°02′N 09°04′E
101 M20 **Schwandorf** Bayern, SE Germany 49°20′N 12°07′E
109 S5 **Schwanenstadt** Oberösterreich, NW Austria 48°03′N 13°47′E
169 S11 **Schwaner, Pegunungan** ▲▲ Borneo, N Indonesia
109 W5 **Schwarza** ≈ E Austria
109 P9 **Schwarzach** ≈ S Austria
101 M20 **Schwarzach** Cz. Černice. ≈ Czech Republic/Germany
Schwarzach see Schwarzach im Pongau
109 Q7 **Schwarzach im Pongau** var. Schwarzach. Salzburg, NW Austria 47°19′N 13°09′E
Schwarzawa see Svratka
101 N14 **Schwarze Elster** ≈ E Germany
Schwarze Körös see Crişul Negru
108 D9 **Schwarzenburg** Bern, W Switzerland 46°51′N 07°28′E
83 D21 **Schwarzrand** ▲▲ S Namibia
101 G23 **Schwarzwald** Eng. Black Forest. ▲▲ SW Germany
Schwarzwasser see Wda
39 P7 **Schwatka Mountains** ▲▲ Alaska, USA
109 N7 **Schwaz** Tirol, W Austria 47°21′N 11°44′E
109 Y4 **Schwechat** Niederösterreich, NE Austria 48°09′N 16°29′E
109 Y4 **Schwechat** ✈ (Wien) Wien, E Austria 48°04′N 16°31′E
100 P11 **Schwedt** Brandenburg, NE Germany 53°04′N 14°16′E
101 D19 **Schweich** Rheinland-Pfalz, SW Germany 49°49′N 06°44′E
Schweidnitz see Świdnica
101 J18 **Schweinfurt** Bayern, SE Germany 50°03′N 10°13′E
Schweiz see Switzerland
100 L9 **Schwerin** Mecklenburg-Vorpommern, N Germany 53°38′N 11°25′E
Schwerin see Skwierzyna
100 L9 **Schweriner See** ◎ N Germany
Schwertberg see Świecie
101 F15 **Schwerte** Nordrhein-Westfalen, W Germany 51°27′N 07°34′E
Schwiebus see Świebodzin
100 P13 **Schwielochsee** ◎ NE Germany
Schwihau see Švihov
Schwiz see Schwyz
108 G8 **Schwyz** var. Schwiz. Schwyz, C Switzerland 47°02′N 08°39′E
108 G8 **Schwyz** var. Schwiz. ◈ canton C Switzerland
14 J11 **Schyan** ≈ Québec, SE Canada
Schyl see Jiu
107 I24 **Sciacca** Sicilia, Italy, C Mediterranean Sea 37°31′N 13°05′E
Sciasciamana see Shashemenē
107 L26 **Scicli** Sicilia, Italy, C Mediterranean Sea 36°48′N 14°43′E
97 F25 **Scilly, Isles of** island group SW England, United Kingdom
111 H17 **Ścinawa** Ger. Steinau an der Elbe. Dolnośląskie, SW Poland 51°22′N 16°27′E
Scio see Chíos
31 S14 **Scioto River** ≈ Ohio, N USA
36 L5 **Scipio** Utah, W USA 39°15′N 112°06′W
33 X6 **Scobey** Montana, NW USA 48°47′N 105°25′W
183 T7 **Scone** New South Wales, SE Australia 32°02′S 150°51′E
Scoresby Sound/Scoresbysund see Ittoqqortoormiit
Scoresby Sund see Kangertittivaq
Scorno, Punta dello see Caprara, Punta
34 K3 **Scotia** California, W USA 40°34′N 124°07′W
47 Y14 **Scotia Plate** tectonic feature
47 V15 **Scotia Ridge** undersea feature S Atlantic Ocean
194 H2 **Scotia Sea** sea SW Atlantic Ocean
29 Q12 **Scotland** South Dakota, N USA 43°09′N 97°43′W
25 R5 **Scotland** Texas, SW USA 33°37′N 98°27′W
96 H11 **Scotland** ◈ national region Scotland, U K
21 W8 **Scotland Neck** North Carolina, SE USA 36°07′N 77°25′W
195 R13 **Scott Base** NZ research station Antarctica 77°52′S 167°18′E
10 J16 **Scott, Cape** headland Vancouver Island, British Columbia, SW Canada 50°43′N 128°24′W
26 I5 **Scott City** Kansas, C USA 38°28′N 100°55′W
27 Y7 **Scott City** Missouri, C USA 37°13′N 89°31′W
195 R14 **Scott Coast** physical region Antarctica
18 C15 **Scottdale** Pennsylvania, NE USA 40°05′N 79°35′W
195 Y11 **Scott Glacier** glacier Antarctica
195 Q17 **Scott Island** island Antarctica
26 L11 **Scott, Mount** ▲ Oklahoma, USA 34°52′N 98°34′W
32 G15 **Scott, Mount** ▲ Oregon, NW USA 42°53′N 122°06′W
34 M1 **Scott River** ≈ California, W USA
28 I13 **Scottsbluff** Nebraska, C USA 41°52′N 103°40′W
23 Q2 **Scottsboro** Alabama, S USA 34°40′N 86°01′W
31 P15 **Scottsburg** Indiana, N USA 38°42′N 85°47′W
183 P16 **Scottsdale** Tasmania, SE Australia 41°13′S 147°30′E
36 L13 **Scottsdale** Arizona, SW USA 33°31′N 111°54′W
45 O12 **Scotts Head Village** var. Cachacrou. S Dominica 15°12′N 61°22′W
192 L14 **Scott Shoal** undersea feature S Pacific Ocean
20 K7 **Scottsville** Kentucky, S USA 36°45′N 86°11′W
29 U14 **Scranton** Iowa, C USA 42°01′N 94°33′W
18 I13 **Scranton** Pennsylvania, NE USA 41°25′N 75°40′W
186 B6 **Screw** ≈ NW Papua New Guinea
29 R14 **Scribner** Nebraska, C USA 41°40′N 96°40′W
Scrobesbyrig' see Shrewsbury
14 I14 **Scugog** ≈ Ontario, SE Canada
14 I14 **Scugog, Lake** ◎ Ontario, SE Canada
97 N17 **Scunthorpe** E England, United Kingdom 53°35′N 00°39′W
108 K9 **Scuol** Ger. Schuls. Graubünden, E Switzerland 46°51′N 10°21′E
Scupi see Skopje
Scutari see Shkodër
113 K17 **Scutari, Lake** Alb. Liqeni i Shkodrës, SCr. Skadarsko Jezero. ◎ Albania/Montenegro
Scyros see Skýros
Scythopolis see Beit She'an
138 E11 **Sderot** prev. Sederot. Southern, S Israel 31°31′N 34°35′E
25 U13 **Seadrift** Texas, SW USA 28°25′N 96°42′W
21 Y4 **Seaford** var. Seaford City. Delaware, NE USA 38°39′N 75°35′W
Seaford City see Seaford
14 E15 **Seaforth** Ontario, S Canada 43°33′N 81°25′W
24 M6 **Seagraves** Texas, SW USA 32°56′N 102°33′W
11 X9 **Seal** ≈ Manitoba, C Canada
182 M10 **Sea Lake** Victoria, SE Australia 35°34′S 142°51′E
83 G26 **Seal, Cape** headland S South Africa 34°06′S 23°18′E
65 D26 **Sea Lion Islands** island group SE Falkland Islands
19 S8 **Seal Island** island Maine, NE USA
25 V11 **Sealy** Texas, SW USA 29°46′N 96°09′W
35 X12 **Searchlight** Nevada, W USA 35°27′N 114°54′W
27 V11 **Searcy** Arkansas, C USA 35°14′N 91°43′W
19 R7 **Searsport** Maine, NE USA 44°28′N 68°54′W
35 N10 **Seaside** California, W USA 36°36′N 121°51′W
32 F10 **Seaside** Oregon, NW USA 45°57′N 123°55′W
18 K16 **Seaside Heights** New Jersey, NE USA 39°56′N 74°03′W
32 H8 **Seattle** Washington, NW USA 47°35′N 122°20′W
32 H9 **Seattle-Tacoma** ✈ Washington, NW USA 47°04′N 122°27′W
185 J16 **Seaward Kaikoura Range** ▲▲ South Island, New Zealand
42 J9 **Sébaco** Matagalpa, W Nicaragua 12°51′N 86°08′W
19 P8 **Sebago Lake** ◎ Maine, NE USA
169 S13 **Sebangan, Teluk** bay Borneo, C Indonesia
Sebaste/Sebastia see Sivas
23 Y12 **Sebastian** Florida, SE USA 27°55′N 80°31′W
40 C5 **Sebastían Vizcaíno, Bahía** bay NW Mexico
19 R6 **Sebasticook Lake** ◎ Maine, NE USA
34 M7 **Sebastopol** California, W USA 38°22′N 122°50′W
Sebastopol see Sevastopol'
169 W8 **Sebatik, Pulau** island N Indonesia
19 R5 **Sebec Lake** ◎ Maine, NE USA
76 K12 **Sébékoro** Kayes, W Mali 13°00′N 09°03′W
Sebenico see Šibenik
40 G6 **Seberi, Cerro** ▲ NW Mexico 27°49′N 110°18′W
116 H11 **Sebeş** Ger. Mühlbach, Hung. Szászsebes; prev. Sebeşu Săsesc. Alba, W Romania 45°58′N 23°34′E
Sebes-Körös see Crişul Repede
Sebeşu Săsesc see Sebeş
31 R8 **Sebewaing** Michigan, N USA 43°43′N 83°27′W
124 F16 **Sebezh** Pskovskaya Oblast', W Russian Federation 56°19′N 28°31′E
137 N12 **Şebinkarahisar** Giresun, N Turkey 40°19′N 38°25′E
116 F11 **Sebiş** Hung. Borossebes. Arad, W Romania 46°21′N 22°09′E
Sebkra Azz el Matti see Azzel Matti, Sebkha
19 Q4 **Seboomook Lake** ◎ Maine, NE USA
74 G6 **Sebou** var. Sebu. ≈ N Morocco
20 I6 **Sebree** Kentucky, S USA 37°34′N 87°30′W
23 X13 **Sebring** Florida, SE USA 27°30′N 81°26′W
Sebta see Ceuta
Sebu see Sebou
169 U13 **Sebuku, Pulau** island N Indonesia
169 W8 **Sebuku, Teluk** bay Borneo, N Indonesia
106 F10 **Secchia** ≈ N Italy
10 L17 **Sechelt** British Columbia, SW Canada 49°25′N 123°37′W
56 C12 **Sechin, Río** ≈ W Peru
56 A10 **Sechura, Bahía de** bay NW Peru
185 A22 **Secretary Island** island SW New Zealand
155 I15 **Secunderābād** var. Sikandarabad. Andhra Pradesh, C India 17°30′N 78°33′E
57 L17 **Sécure, Río** ≈ C Bolivia
118 D10 **Seda** Telšiai, NW Lithuania 56°10′N 22°04′E
27 T5 **Sedalia** Missouri, C USA 38°42′N 93°15′W
103 R3 **Sedan** Ardennes, N France 49°42′N 04°56′E
27 P7 **Sedan** Kansas, C USA 37°07′N 96°11′W
105 N3 **Sedano** Castilla y León, N Spain 42°43′N 03°43′W
104 H10 **Seda, Ribeira de** stream C Portugal
185 K15 **Seddon** Marlborough, South Island, New Zealand 41°42′S 174°05′E
185 H15 **Seddonville** West Coast, South Island, New Zealand 41°35′S 171°59′E
143 U7 **Sedeh** Khorāsān-e Janūbī, E Iran 33°18′N 59°12′E
Sederot see Sderot
65 B23 **Sedge Island** island NW Falkland Islands
76 G12 **Sédhiou** SW Senegal 12°39′N 15°33′W
11 U16 **Sedley** Saskatchewan, S Canada 50°06′N 103°51′W
Sedlez see Siedlce
117 Q2 **Sedniv** Chernihivs'ka Oblast', N Ukraine 51°39′N 31°34′E
36 L11 **Sedona** Arizona, SW USA 34°52′N 111°45′W
Sedunum see Sion
118 F12 **Šeduva** Šiaulai, N Lithuania 55°45′N 23°46′E
141 Y8 **Seeb** var. Muscat Sīb Airport. ✈ (Masqaţ) NE Oman 23°36′N 58°27′E
Seeb see As Sīb
108 M7 **Seefeld-in-Tirol** Tirol, W Austria 47°19′N 11°16′E
83 E22 **Seeheim Noord** Karas, S Namibia 26°50′S 17°45′E
Seeland see Sjælland
195 N9 **Seelig, Mount** ▲ Antarctica 81°45′S 102°15′W
Seenu Atoll see Addu Atoll
Seeonee see Seoni
Seer see Dörgön
102 L5 **Sées** Orne, N France 48°36′N 00°11′E
101 J14 **Seesen** Niedersachsen, C Germany 51°54′N 10°11′E
Seesker Höhe see Szeska Góra
100 J10 **Seevetal** Niedersachsen, N Germany 53°24′N 10°01′E
109 V6 **Seewiesen** Steiermark, E Austria 47°37′N 15°16′E
136 J13 **Şefaatli** var. Kızılkoca. Yozgat, C Turkey 39°32′N 34°45′E
143 V9 **Sefīdābeh** Khorāsān-e Janūbī, E Iran 31°05′N 60°30′E
149 N3 **Sefid, Darya-ye** Pash. Āb-i-safed. ≈ N Afghanistan
148 K5 **Sefid Kūh, Selseleh-ye** Eng. Paropamisus Range. ▲ W Afghanistan 34°00′N 61°40′E
148 K5 **Sefid Kūh, Selseleh-ye** Eng. Paropamisus Range. ▲▲ W Afghanistan
142 M4 **Sefīd, Rūd-e** ≈ NW Iran
74 G6 **Sefrou** N Morocco 33°51′N 04°49′W
185 E19 **Sefton, Mount** ▲ South Island, New Zealand 43°43′S 169°58′E
171 S13 **Segaf, Kepulauan** island group E Indonesia
169 W7 **Segama, Sungai** ≈ East Malaysia
168 L9 **Segamat** Johor, Peninsular Malaysia 02°30′N 102°48′E
77 S13 **Ségbana** NE Benin 10°56′N 03°42′E
Segestica see Sisak
Segesvár see Sighişoara
171 T12 **Seget** Papua, E Indonesia 01°21′S 131°04′E
Segewold see Sigulda
124 J9 **Segezha** Respublika Kareliya, NW Russian Federation 63°39′N 34°24′E
Seghedin see Szeged
Segna see Senj
107 I16 **Segni** Lazio, C Italy 41°41′N 13°02′E
Segodunum see Rodez
105 S9 **Segorbe** Valenciana, E Spain 39°51′N 00°30′W
76 M12 **Ségou** var. Segu. Ségou, C Mali 13°26′N 06°12′W
76 M12 **Ségou** ◈ region SW Mali
54 E8 **Segovia** Antioquia, N Colombia 07°08′N 74°39′W
105 N7 **Segovia** Castilla y León, C Spain 40°57′N 04°07′W
104 M6 **Segovia** ◈ province Castilla y León, N Spain
Segoviao Wangkí see Coco, Río
124 J9 **Segozerskoye Vodokhranilishche** prev. Ozero Segozero. ◎ NW Russian Federation
102 J7 **Segré** Maine-et-Loire, NW France 47°41′N 00°51′W
105 U5 **Segre** ≈ NE Spain
Segu see Ségou
38 I17 **Seguam Island** island Aleutian Islands, Alaska, USA
38 I17 **Seguam Pass** strait Aleutian Islands, Alaska, USA
77 Y7 **Séguédine** Agadez, NE Niger 20°12′N 13°03′E
76 M15 **Séguéla** W Ivory Coast 07°58′N 06°44′W
25 S11 **Seguin** Texas, SW USA 29°34′N 97°58′W
38 E17 **Segula Island** island Aleutian Islands, Alaska, USA
62 K10 **Segundo, Río** ≈ C Argentina
105 Q12 **Segura** ≈ S Spain
105 P13 **Segura, Sierra de** ▲▲ S Spain
83 G18 **Sehithwa** North-West, N Botswana 20°28′S 22°43′E
154 H10 **Sehore** Madhya Pradesh, C India 23°12′N 77°08′E
186 G9 **Sehulea** Normanby Island, S Papua New Guinea 09°55′S 151°10′E
149 P15 **Sehwān** Sind, SE Pakistan 26°26′N 67°52′N
109 V8 **Seiersberg** Steiermark, SE Austria 47°01′N 15°22′E
26 L9 **Seiling** Oklahoma, C USA 36°09′N 98°55′W
103 S9 **Seille** ≈ E France
99 J20 **Seilles** Namur, SE Belgium 50°31′N 05°12′E
93 K17 **Seinäjoki** Swe. Östermyra. Länsi-Suomi, W Finland 62°45′N 22°55′E
12 B12 **Seine** ≈ Ontario, S Canada
102 M4 **Seine** ≈ N France
102 K4 **Seine, Baie de la** bay N France
Seine, Banc de la see Seine Seamount
103 O5 **Seine-et-Marne** ◈ department N France
102 L3 **Seine-Maritime** ◈ department N France
84 B14 **Seine Plain** undersea feature E Atlantic Ocean 34°00′N 12°15′W
84 B15 **Seine Seamount** var. Banc de la Seine. undersea feature E Atlantic Ocean 33°45′N 14°25′W
102 E6 **Sein, Île de** island NW France
171 Y14 **Seinma** Papua, E Indonesia 04°10′S 138°54′E
Seisbierrum see Sexbierum
109 U5 **Seitenstetten Markt** Niederösterreich, C Austria 48°03′N 14°41′E
Seiyo see Uwa
Seiyu see Chŏnju
95 H22 **Sejerø** island E Denmark
110 P7 **Sejny** Podlaskie, NE Poland 54°09′N 23°21′E
163 X15 **Sejong City** ● (South Korea) E South Korea 36°29′N 127°16′E
81 G20 **Seke** Shinyanga, N Tanzania 03°16′S 33°31′E
164 L13 **Seki** Gifu, Honshū, SW Japan 35°30′N 136°54′E
161 U12 **Sekibi-sho** island China/Japan/Taiwan
165 U3 **Sekihoku-tōge** pass Hokkaidō, NE Japan
Sekondi see Sekondi-Takoradi
77 P17 **Sekondi-Takoradi** var. Sekondi. S Ghana 04°55′N 01°45′W
80 J11 **Sek'ot'a** Āmara, N Ethiopia 12°41′N 39°05′E
Sekseüil see Saksaul'skoye
32 I9 **Selah** Washington, NW USA 46°39′N 120°31′W
168 J8 **Selangor** var. Negeri Selangor Darul Ehsan. ◈ state Peninsular Malaysia
Selânik see Thessaloníki
167 R10 **Selaphum** Roi Et, E Thailand 16°00′N 103°54′E
171 T16 **Selaru, Pulau** island Kepulauan Tanimbar, E Indonesia
171 U13 **Selassi** Papua, E Indonesia 03°16′S 132°50′E
168 J7 **Selatan, Selat** strait Peninsular Malaysia
168 K10 **Selatpanjang** Pulau Rantau, W Indonesia 01°00′N 102°44′E
39 N8 **Selawik** Alaska, USA 66°36′N 160°00′W
39 N8 **Selawik Lake** ◎ Alaska, USA
171 N14 **Selayar, Selat** strait Sulawesi, C Indonesia
95 C14 **Selbjørnsfjorden** fjord S Norway
94 H8 **Selbusjøen** ◎ S Norway
97 M17 **Selby** N England, United Kingdom 53°49′N 01°06′W
29 N8 **Selby** South Dakota, N USA 45°30′N 100°01′W
21 Z4 **Selbyville** Delaware, NE USA 38°28′N 75°12′W
136 B15 **Selçuk** var. Akıncılar. İzmir, SW Turkey 37°56′N 27°25′E
39 Q13 **Seldovia** Alaska, USA 59°26′N 151°42′W
107 M18 **Sele** anc. Silarius. ≈ S Italy
83 J19 **Selebi-Phikwe** Central, E Botswana 21°58′S 27°48′E
42 B5 **Selegua, Río** ≈ W Guatemala
129 X7 **Selemdzha** ≈ SE Russian Federation
129 U7 **Selenga** Mong. Selenge Mörön. ≈ Mongolia/Russian Federation
79 I19 **Selenge** Bandundu, W Dem. Rep. Congo 01°58′S 18°11′E
162 K6 **Selenge** var. Ingettolgoy. Bulgan, N Mongolia 49°27′N 103°59′E
162 L6 **Selenge** ◈ province N Mongolia
Selenge see Hyalganat, Bulgan, Mongolia
Selenge see Ih-Uul, Hövsgöl, Mongolia
Selenge Mörön see Selenga
123 N14 **Selenginsk** Respublika Buryatiya, S Russian Federation 52°00′N 106°40′E
Selenica see Selenicë
113 K22 **Selenicë** var. Selenica. Vlorë, SW Albania 40°32′N 19°38′E
123 Q8 **Selennyakh** ≈ NE Russian Federation
100 J8 **Selenter See** ◎ N Germany
Sele Sound see Soela Väin
103 U6 **Sélestat** Ger. Schlettstadt. Bas-Rhin, NE France 48°16′N 07°28′E
Seleucia see Silifke
92 I4 **Selfoss** Sudhurland, SW Iceland 63°56′N 20°59′W
28 M7 **Selfridge** North Dakota, N USA 46°01′N 100°52′W
76 I15 **Seli** ≈ N Sierra Leone
76 I11 **Sélibabi** var. Sélibaby. Guidimaka, S Mauritania 15°14′N 12°11′W
Sélibaby see Sélibabi
Selidovka/Selidovo see Selydove
124 I15 **Seliger, Ozero** ◎ W Russian Federation
36 J11 **Seligman** Arizona, SW USA 35°20′N 112°56′W
27 S8 **Seligman** Missouri, C USA 36°31′N 93°56′W
80 E6 **Selima Oasis** oasis N Sudan
76 L13 **Sélingué, Lac de** ▣ S Mali
Selinoús see Kréstena
18 G14 **Selinsgrove** Pennsylvania, NE USA 40°47′N 76°51′W
Selishche see Syelishcha
124 I16 **Selizharovo** Tverskaya Oblast', W Russian Federation 56°50′N 33°24′E
94 C10 **Selje** Sogn Og Fjordane, S Norway 62°02′N 05°22′E
11 X16 **Selkirk** Manitoba, S Canada 50°10′N 96°52′W
96 K13 **Selkirk** SE Scotland, United Kingdom 55°36′N 02°48′W
96 K13 **Selkirk** cultural region SE Scotland, United Kingdom
11 O16 **Selkirk Mountains** ▲▲ British Columbia, SW Canada
193 T11 **Selkirk Rise** undersea feature SE Pacific Ocean
115 F21 **Sellasía** Pelopónnisos, S Greece 37°14′N 22°24′E
44 M9 **Selle, Pic de la** var. La Selle. ▲ SE Haiti 18°18′N 71°55′W
102 M8 **Selles-sur-Cher** Loir-et-Cher, C France 47°16′N 01°31′E
36 K16 **Sells** Arizona, SW USA 31°54′N 111°52′W
Sellye see Sal'a
23 P5 **Selma** Alabama, S USA 32°24′N 87°01′W
35 Q11 **Selma** California, W USA 36°33′N 119°37′W
20 G10 **Selmer** Tennessee, S USA 35°10′N 88°34′W
173 N17 **Sel, Pointe au** headland W Réunion
Selselehye Kuhe Vākhān see Nicholas Range

◆ Country
● Country Capital
◇ Dependent Territory
○ Dependent Territory Capital
◈ Administrative Regions
✈ International Airport
▲ Mountain
▲▲ Mountain Range
Volcano
≈ River
◎ Lake
▣ Reservoir

127 S2 **Selty** Udmurtskaya Respublika, NW Russian Federation 57°19′N 52°09′E
Selukwe see Shurugwi
62 L9 **Selva** Santiago del Estero, N Argentina 29°46′S 62°02′W
11 T9 **Selwyn Lake** ◎ Northwest Territories/Saskatchewan, C Canada
10 K6 **Selwyn Mountains** ▲▲ Yukon Territory, NW Canada
181 T6 **Selwyn Range** ▲▲ Queensland, C Australia
117 W8 **Selydove** var. Selidovka, Rus. Selidovo. Donets'ka Oblast', SE Ukraine 48°06′N 37°16′E
Selzaete see Zelzate
Seman see Semanit, Lumi i
168 M15 **Semangka, Teluk** bay Sumatera, SW Indonesia
113 D22 **Semanit, Lumi i** var. Seman. ≈ W Albania
169 Q16 **Semarang** var. Samarang. Jawa, C Indonesia 06°58′S 110°29′E
169 Q10 **Sematan** Sarawak, East Malaysia 01°50′N 109°44′E
171 P17 **Semau, Pulau** island S Indonesia
169 V8 **Sembakung, Sungai** ≈ Borneo, N Indonesia
79 G17 **Sembé** Sangha, NW Congo 01°38′N 14°35′E
169 S13 **Sembulu, Danau** ◎ Borneo, N Indonesia
Semendria see Smederevo
117 R1 **Semenivka** Chernihivs'ka Oblast', N Ukraine 52°10′N 32°37′E
117 S6 **Semenivka** Rus. Semenovka. Poltavs'ka Oblast', NE Ukraine 49°36′N 33°10′E
127 O3 **Semenov** Nizhegorodskaya Oblast', W Russian Federation 56°47′N 44°27′E
Semenovka see Semenivka
169 S17 **Semeru, Gunung** var. Mahameru. ▲ Jawa, S Indonesia 08°01′S 112°53′E
145 V9 **Semey** prev. Semipalatinsk. Vostochnyy Kazakhstan, E Kazakhstan 50°26′N 80°16′E
Semezhevo see Syemyezhava
126 L7 **Semiluki** Voronezhskaya Oblast', W Russian Federation 51°46′N 39°00′E
33 W16 **Seminoe Reservoir** ⊠ Wyoming, C USA
27 O11 **Seminole** Oklahoma, C USA 35°13′N 96°40′W
24 M6 **Seminole** Texas, SW USA 32°43′N 102°39′W
23 S8 **Seminole, Lake** ⊠ Florida/Georgia, SE USA
Semiozernoye see Auliyekol'
Semipalatinsk see Semey
143 O9 **Semīrom** var. Samirum. Eşfahān, C Iran 31°20′N 51°50′E
38 F17 **Semisopochnoi Island** island Aleutian Islands, Alaska, USA
169 R11 **Semitau** Borneo, C Indonesia 0°30′N 111°59′E
81 E18 **Semliki** ≈ Uganda/Dem. Rep. Congo
143 P5 **Semnān** var. Samnān. Semnān, N Iran 35°37′N 53°21′E
143 Q5 **Semnān** off. Ostān-e Semnān. ◈ province N Iran
Semnān, Ostān-e see Semnān
99 K24 **Semois** ≈ SE Belgium
108 E8 **Sempacher See** ◎ C Switzerland
Sena see Vila de Sena
30 L12 **Senachwine Lake** ◎ Illinois, N USA
59 O14 **Senador Pompeu** Ceará, E Brazil 05°30′S 39°25′W
Sena Gallica see Senigallia
59 C15 **Sena Madureira** Acre, W Brazil 09°05′S 68°41′W
155 L25 **Senanayake Samudra** ◎ E Sri Lanka
83 G15 **Senanga** Western, SW Zambia 16°09′S 23°16′E
27 Y9 **Senath** Missouri, C USA 36°07′N 90°09′W
22 L2 **Senatobia** Mississippi, S USA 34°37′N 89°58′W
164 C16 **Sendai** var. Satsuma-Sendai. Kagoshima, Kyūshū, SW Japan 31°49′N 130°17′E
165 Q11 **Sendai-wan** bay E Japan
101 J23 **Senden** Bayern, S Germany 48°18′N 10°04′E
154 F11 **Sendhwa** Madhya Pradesh, C India 21°38′N 75°04′E
111 H21 **Senec** Ger. Wartberg, Hung. Szenc; prev. Szempcz. Bratislavský Kraj, W Slovakia 48°14′N 17°24′E
27 P3 **Seneca** Kansas, C USA 39°50′N 96°04′W
27 R8 **Seneca** Missouri, C USA 36°50′N 94°36′W
32 K13 **Seneca** Oregon, NW USA 44°06′N 118°57′W
21 O11 **Seneca** South Carolina, SE USA 34°41′N 82°57′W
18 G11 **Seneca Lake** ◎ New York, NE USA
31 U13 **Senecaville Lake** ⊠ Ohio, N USA
76 G11 **Senegal** off. Republic of Senegal, Fr. Sénégal. ◆ republic W Africa
76 H9 **Senegal** Fr. Sénégal. ≈ W Africa
Senegal, Republic of see Senegal
31 O4 **Seney Marsh** wetland Michigan, N USA
101 P14 **Senftenberg** Brandenburg, E Germany 51°31′N 14°01′E
82 L11 **Senga Hill** Northern, NE Zambia 09°26′S 31°12′E
158 G13 **Sênggê Zangbo** ≈ W China
171 Z13 **Senggi** Papua, E Indonesia 03°26′S 140°46′E
127 R5 **Sengiley** Ul'yanovskaya Oblast', W Russian Federation 53°54′N 48°51′E
63 I19 **Senguerr, Río** ≈ S Argentina
83 J16 **Sengwa** ≈ C Zimbabwe
Senia see Senj
111 H19 **Senica** Ger. Senitz, Hung. Szenice. Trnavský Kraj, W Slovakia 48°40′N 17°22′E
Seniça see Sjenica
106 J11 **Senigallia** anc. Sena Gallica. Marche, C Italy 43°43′N 13°13′E
136 F15 **Senirkent** Isparta, SW Turkey 38°07′N 30°34′E
Senitz see Senica
112 C10 **Senj** Ger. Zengg, It. Segna; anc. Senia. Lika-Senj, NW Croatia 44°58′N 14°55′E
Senj see Örgön
92 H9 **Senja** prev. Senjen. island N Norway
Senjen see Senja
161 U12 **Senkaku-shotō** island group SW Japan
137 R12 **Şenkaya** Erzurum, NE Turkey 40°33′N 42°17′E
83 I16 **Senkobo** Southern, S Zambia 17°38′S 25°58′E
103 O4 **Senlis** Oise, N France 49°13′N 02°33′E
Senmonorom see Sênmônoŭrôm
167 T12 **Sênmônoŭrôm** var. Senmonorom. Môndól Kiri, E Cambodia 12°27′N 107°12′E
80 G10 **Sennar** var. Sannār. Sinnar, C Sudan 13°31′N 33°38′E
Senno see Syanno
Senones see Sens
109 W11 **Senovo** E Slovenia 46°01′N 15°24′E
103 P6 **Sens** anc. Agendicum, Senones. Yonne, C France 48°12′N 03°17′E
Sensburg see Mrągowo
167 S11 **Sên, Stœng** ≈ C Cambodia
42 F7 **Sensuntepeque** Cabañas, NE El Salvador 13°52′N 88°38′W
112 L8 **Senta** Hung. Zenta. Vojvodina, N Serbia 45°57′N 20°04′E
Šent Andraž see Sankt Andrä
171 Y13 **Sentani, Danau** ◎ Papua, E Indonesia
28 J5 **Sentinel Butte** ▲ North Dakota, N USA 46°52′N 103°50′W
10 M13 **Sentinel Peak** ▲ British Columbia, W Canada 54°51′N 122°02′W
59 N16 **Sento Sé** Bahia, E Brazil 09°51′S 41°56′W
Šent Peter see Pivka
Št. Vid see Sankt Veit an der Glan
Seo de Urgel see La Seu d'Urgell
163 X17 **Seogwipo** prev. Sŏgwip'o. S South Korea 33°14′N 126°33′E
154 I7 **Seondha** Madhya Pradesh, C India 26°09′N 78°47′E
163 Y17 **Seongsan** prev. Sŏngsan. S South Korea
154 J11 **Seoni** prev. Seeonee. Madhya Pradesh, C India 22°06′N 79°36′E
163 X14 **Seoul** Jap. Keijō; prev. Kyŏngsŏng, Sŏul. ● (South Korea) NW South Korea 37°30′N 126°58′E
83 I17 **Sepako** Central, NE Botswana 19°50′S 26°29′E
184 I13 **Separation Point** headland South Island, New Zealand 40°46′S 172°58′E
169 V10 **Sepasu** Borneo, N Indonesia 0°44′N 117°38′E
186 B6 **Sepik** ≈ Indonesia/Papua New Guinea
Sepone see Muang Xépôn
110 M7 **Sępopol** Ger. Schippenbeil. Warmińsko-Mazurskie, N Poland 54°16′N 21°09′E
116 F10 **Şepreuş** Hung. Seprős. Arad, W Romania 46°34′N 21°44′E
Seprős see Şepreuş
Şepşi-Sângeorz/Sepsiszentgyörgy see Sfântu Gheorghe
15 W4 **Sept-Îles** Québec, SE Canada 50°11′N 66°19′W
105 N6 **Sepúlveda** Castilla y León, N Spain 41°18′N 03°45′W
104 K8 **Sequeros** Castilla y León, N Spain 40°31′N 06°04′W
104 L5 **Sequillo** ≈ NW Spain
32 G7 **Sequim** Washington, NW USA 48°04′N 123°06′W
35 S11 **Sequoia National Park** national park California, W USA
137 Q14 **Şerafettin Dağları** ▲▲ E Turkey
127 N10 **Serafimovich** Volgogradskaya Oblast', SW Russian Federation 49°34′N 42°43′E
171 Q10 **Serai** Sulawesi, N Indonesia 01°45′N 124°58′E
99 K19 **Seraing** Liège, E Belgium 50°37′N 05°31′E
Sêraitang see Baima
Serakhs see Sarahs
171 W13 **Serami** Papua, E Indonesia 02°11′S 136°46′E
171 R13 **Seram, Laut** Eng. Ceram Sea. sea E Indonesia
Serampore/Serampur see Shrīrāmpur
171 S13 **Seram, Pulau** var. Serang, Eng. Ceram. island Maluku, E Indonesia
169 N15 **Serang** Jawa, C Indonesia 06°07′S 106°09′E
Serang see Seram, Pulau
169 P9 **Serasan, Pulau** island Kepulauan Natuna, W Indonesia
169 P9 **Serasan, Selat** strait Indonesia/Malaysia
112 M13 **Serbia** off. Federal Republic of Serbia; prev. Yugoslavia, SCr. Jugoslavija. ◆ federal republic SE Europe
112 M12 **Serbia** Ger. Serbien, Serb. Srbija. ◈ republic Serbia
Serbia, Federal Republic of see Serbia
Serbien see Serbia
Sercq see Sark
146 D12 **Serdar** prev. Rus. Gyzyrlabat, Kizyl-Arvat. Balkan Welaýaty, W Turkmenistan 39°02′N 56°15′E
Serdica see Sofiya
Serdobol' see Sortavala
127 O7 **Serdobsk** Penzenskaya Oblast', W Russian Federation 52°30′N 44°16′E
145 X9 **Serebryansk** Vostochnyy Kazakhstan, E Kazakhstan 49°44′N 83°16′E
123 Q12 **Serebryanyy Bor** Respublika Sakha (Yakutiya), NE Russian Federation 56°40′N 124°46′E
111 H20 **Sered'** Hung. Szered. Trnavský Kraj, W Slovakia 48°19′N 17°45′E
117 S1 **Seredyna-Buda** Sums'ka Oblast', NE Ukraine 52°09′N 34°00′E
118 E13 **Seredžius** Tauragė, C Lithuania 55°04′N 23°24′E
136 I14 **Şereflikoçhisar** Ankara, C Turkey 38°56′N 33°31′E
106 D7 **Seregno** Lombardia, N Italy 45°39′N 09°12′E
103 P7 **Serein** ≈ C France
168 K9 **Seremban** Negeri Sembilan, Peninsular Malaysia 02°42′N 101°54′E
81 H20 **Serengeti Plain** plain N Tanzania
82 K13 **Serenje** Central, E Zambia 13°12′S 30°15′E
Seres see Sérres
116 J5 **Seret** ≈ W Ukraine
Seret/Sereth see Siret
115 I21 **Serfopoúla** island Kykládes, Greece, Aegean Sea
127 P4 **Sergach** Nizhegorodskaya Oblast', W Russian Federation 55°31′N 45°29′E
29 S13 **Sergeant Bluff** Iowa, C USA 42°24′N 96°19′W
163 P7 **Sergelen** Dornod, NE Mongolia 48°31′N 114°01′E
Sergelen see Tuvshinshiree
168 H8 **Sergeulangit, Pegunungan** ▲▲ Sumatera, NW Indonesia
122 L5 **Sergeya Kirova, Ostrova** island N Russian Federation
Sergeyevichi see Syarhyeyevichy
145 O7 **Sergeyevka** Severnyy Kazakhstan, N Kazakhstan 53°53′N 67°25′E
Sergiopol see Ayagoz
59 P16 **Sergipe** off. Estado de Sergipe. ◈ state E Brazil
Sergipe, Estado de see Sergipe
126 L3 **Sergiyev Posad** Moskovskaya Oblast', W Russian Federation 56°21′N 38°10′E
124 K5 **Sergozero, Ozero** ◎ NW Russian Federation
146 J17 **Serhetabat** prev. Rus. Gushgy, Kushka. Mary Welaýaty, S Turkmenistan 35°19′N 62°17′E
169 Q10 **Serian** Sarawak, East Malaysia 01°10′N 110°35′E
115 I21 **Sérifos** anc. Seriphos. island Kykládes, Greece, Aegean Sea
115 I21 **Sérifou, Stenó** strait SE Greece
136 F16 **Serik** Antalya, SW Turkey 36°55′N 31°06′E
106 E7 **Serio** ≈ N Italy
Seriphos see Sérifos
Serir Tibesti see Sarīr Tībistī
Sêrkog see Sêrtar
127 S5 **Sernovodsk** Samarskaya Oblast', W Russian Federation 53°56′N 51°16′E
127 R2 **Sernur** Respublika Mariy El, W Russian Federation 56°55′N 49°09′E
110 M11 **Serock** Mazowieckie, C Poland 52°30′N 21°03′E
61 B18 **Serodino** Santa Fe, C Argentina 32°33′S 60°52′W
Seroei see Serui
105 P14 **Serón** Andalucía, S Spain 37°20′N 02°28′W
99 E14 **Serooskerke** Zeeland, SW Netherlands 51°42′N 03°52′E
105 T6 **Seròs** Cataluña, NE Spain 41°27′N 00°24′E
122 G10 **Serov** Sverdlovskaya Oblast', C Russian Federation 59°42′N 60°32′E
83 I19 **Serowe** Central, SE Botswana 22°26′S 26°44′E
104 H13 **Serpa** Beja, S Portugal 37°56′N 07°36′W
Serpa Pinto see Menongue
182 A4 **Serpentine Lakes** salt lake South Australia
45 T15 **Serpent's Mouth, The** Sp. Boca de la Serpiente. strait Trinidad and Tobago/Venezuela
Serpiente, Boca de la see Serpent's Mouth, The
126 K4 **Serpukhov** Moskovskaya Oblast', W Russian Federation 54°54′N 37°26′E
104 I10 **Serra de São Mamede** ▲ C Portugal 39°18′N 07°19′W
60 K13 **Serra do Mar** ▲▲
Sérrai see Sérres
107 N22 **Serra San Bruno** Calabria, SW Italy 38°32′N 16°18′E
103 S14 **Serres** Hautes-Alpes, SE France 44°26′N 05°42′E
114 H13 **Sérres** var. Seres; prev. Sérrai. Kentrikí Makedonía, NE Greece 41°03′N 23°33′E
62 J9 **Serrezuela** Córdoba, C Argentina 30°38′S 65°26′W
59 O16 **Serrinha** Bahia, E Brazil 11°38′S 38°56′W
59 M19 **Serro** var. Sêrro. Minas Gerais, NE Brazil 18°38′S 43°22′W
Sêrro see Serro
Sert see Siirt
104 H9 **Sertã** var. Sertá. Castelo Branco, C Portugal 39°48′N 08°05′W
Sertá see Sertã
60 L8 **Sertãozinho** São Paulo, S Brazil 21°04′S 47°55′W
160 F7 **Sêrtar** var. Sêrkog. Sichuan, C China 32°18′N 100°18′E
124 G12 **Sertolovo** Leningradskaya Oblast', NW Russian Federation 60°08′N 30°06′E
171 W13 **Serui** prev. Seroei. Papua, E Indonesia 01°53′S 136°15′E
83 J19 **Serule** Central, E Botswana 21°58′S 27°20′E
169 S12 **Seruyan, Sungai** var. Sungai Pembuang. ≈ Borneo, N Indonesia
115 E14 **Sérvia** Dytikí Makedonía, N Greece 40°12′N 22°01′E
160 E7 **Sêrxü** var. Jugar. Sichuan, C China 32°54′N 98°06′E
123 R13 **Seryshevo** Amurskaya Oblast', SE Russian Federation 51°03′N 128°16′E
Sesana see Sežana
169 V8 **Sesayap, Sungai** ≈ Borneo, N Indonesia
Sesdlets see Siedlce
79 N17 **Sese** Orientale, N Dem. Rep. Congo 02°13′N 25°52′E
81 F18 **Sese Islands** island group S Uganda
83 H16 **Sesheke** var. Sesheko. Western, SE Zambia 17°28′S 24°20′E
Sesheko see Sesheke
106 C8 **Sesia** anc. Sessites. ≈ NW Italy
104 F11 **Sesimbra** Setúbal, S Portugal 38°26′N 09°06′W
115 N22 **Seskliό** island Dodekánisa, Greece, Aegean Sea
30 L16 **Sesser** Illinois, N USA 38°05′N 89°03′W
Sessites see Sesia
106 G11 **Sesto Fiorentino** Toscana, C Italy 43°50′N 11°12′E
106 E7 **Sesto San Giovanni** Lombardia, N Italy 45°32′N 09°14′E
106 A8 **Sestriere** Piemonte, NE Italy 45°00′N 06°54′E
106 D10 **Sestri Levante** Liguria, NW Italy 44°16′N 09°22′E
107 C20 **Sestu** Sardegna, Italy, C Mediterranean Sea 39°15′N 09°06′E
112 E8 **Sesvete** Zagreb, N Croatia 45°50′N 16°03′E
118 G12 **Šeta** Kaunas, C Lithuania 55°17′N 24°16′E
Setabis see Xàtiva
165 Q4 **Setana** Hokkaidō, NE Japan 42°27′N 139°52′E
103 Q16 **Sète** prev. Cette. Hérault, S France 43°24′N 03°42′E
58 J11 **Sete Ilhas** Amapá, NE Brazil 01°06′N 52°06′W
59 L20 **Sete Lagoas** Minas Gerais, NE Brazil 19°29′S 44°15′W
60 G10 **Sete Quedas, Ilha das** island S Brazil
92 I10 **Setermoen** Troms, N Norway 68°51′N 18°20′E
95 E17 **Setesdal** valley S Norway
43 W16 **Setetule, Cerro** ▲ SE Panama 07°51′N 77°37′W
21 Q5 **Seth** West Virginia, NE USA 38°06′N 81°40′W
Setia see Sezze
74 K5 **Sétif** var. Stif. N Algeria 36°11′N 05°24′E
164 L5 **Seto** Aichi, Honshū, SW Japan 35°14′N 137°06′E
164 G13 **Seto-naikai** Eng. Inland Sea. sea S Japan
165 V16 **Setouchi** var. Setoushi. Kagoshima, Amami-Ō-shima, SW Japan 44°19′N 142°58′E
Setoushi see Setouchi
74 F6 **Settat** W Morocco 33°03′N 07°37′W
79 D20 **Setté Cama** Ogooué-Maritime, SW Gabon 02°32′S 09°46′E
11 W13 **Setting Lake** ◎ Manitoba, C Canada
97 L16 **Settle** N England, United Kingdom 54°04′N 02°17′W
189 Y12 **Settlement** E Wake Island 19°17′N 166°38′E
104 F11 **Setúbal** Eng. Saint Ubes, Saint Yves. Setúbal, W Portugal 38°31′N 08°54′W
104 F11 **Setúbal** ◈ district S Portugal
104 F12 **Setúbal, Baía de** bay W Portugal
Setul see Satun
12 B10 **Seul, Lac** ◎ Ontario, S Canada
103 R8 **Seurre** Côte d'Or, C France 47°00′N 05°09′E
137 U11 **Sevan** C Armenia 40°32′N 44°56′E
137 V12 **Sevana Lich** Eng. Lake Sevan, Rus. Ozero Sevan. ◎ E Armenia
Sevan, Lake/Sevan, Ozero see Sevana Lich
77 N11 **Sévaré** Mopti, C Mali 14°32′N 04°06′W
117 S14 **Sevastopol'** Eng. Sebastopol. Avtonomna Respublika Krym, S Ukraine 44°36′N 33°33′E
25 R14 **Seven Sisters** Texas, SW USA 27°57′N 98°34′W
10 K13 **Seven Sisters Peaks** ▲ British Columbia, SW Canada 54°57′N 128°10′W
99 M15 **Sevenum** Limburg, SE Netherlands 51°25′N 06°01′E
103 P14 **Séverac-le-Château** Aveyron, S France 44°18′N 03°03′E
14 H13 **Severn** ≈ Ontario, S Canada
97 L21 **Severn** Wel. Hafren. ≈ England/Wales, United Kingdom
125 O11 **Severnaya Dvina** var. Northern Dvina. ≈ NW Russian Federation
127 N16 **Severnaya Osetiya-Alaniya, Respublika** Eng. North Ossetia; prev. Respublika Severnaya Osetiya, Severo-Osetinskaya SSR. ◈ autonomous republic SW Russian Federation
Severnaya Osetiya, Respublika see Severnaya Osetiya-Alaniya, Respublika
122 M5 **Severnaya Zemlya** var. Nicholas II Land. island group N Russian Federation
127 T5 **Severnoye** Orenburgskaya Oblast', W Russian Federation 54°03′N 52°31′E
35 S3 **Severn Troughs Range** ▲▲ Nevada, W USA
125 W3 **Severnyy** Respublika Komi, NW Russian Federation 67°38′N 64°13′E
144 I13 **Severnyy Chink Ustyurta** ▲▲ W Kazakhstan
125 Q13 **Severnyye Uvaly** var. Northern Ural Hills. hill range NW Russian Federation
145 O6 **Severnyy Kazakhstan** off. Severo-Kazakhstanskaya Oblast', var. North Kazakhstan, Kaz. Soltüstik Qazaqstan Oblysy. ◈ province N Kazakhstan
122 I6 **Severnyy, Ostrov** NW Russian Federation
125 V9 **Severnyy Ural** ▲▲ NW Russian Federation
Severo-Alichurskiy Khrebet see Alichuri Shimolí, Qatorkŭhi
123 N12 **Severobaykal'sk** Respublika Buryatiya, S Russian Federation 55°39′N 109°17′E
Severodonetsk see Syeverodonets'k
124 M8 **Severodvinsk** prev. Molotov, Sudostroy. Arkhangel'skaya Oblast', NW Russian Federation 64°32′N 39°50′E
Severo-Kazakhstanskaya Oblast' see Severnyy Kazakhstan
123 U11 **Severo-Kuril'sk** Sakhalinskaya Oblast', SE Russian Federation 50°38′N 155°57′E
124 J3 **Severomorsk** Murmanskaya Oblast', NW Russian Federation 69°00′N 33°16′E
Severo-Osetinskaya SSR see Severnaya Osetiya-Alaniya, Respublika
122 M7 **Severo-Sibirskaya Nizmennost'** var. North Siberian Plain, Eng. North Siberian Lowland. lowlands N Russian Federation
122 G10 **Severoural'sk** Sverdlovskaya Oblast', C Russian Federation 60°09′N 59°58′E
122 L11 **Severo-Yeniseyskiy** Krasnoyarskiy Kray, C Russian Federation 60°29′N 93°13′E
122 J12 **Seversk** Tomskaya Oblast', C Russian Federation 53°37′N 84°47′E
126 M11 **Severskiy Donets** Ukr. Sivers'kyy Donets'. ≈ Russian Federation/Ukraine see also Sivers'kyy Donets'
Severskiy Donets see Sivers'kyy Donets'
92 M9 **Sevettijärvi** Lappi, N Finland 69°31′N 28°40′E
36 M5 **Sevier Bridge Reservoir** ⊠ Utah, W USA
36 J4 **Sevier Desert** plain Utah, W USA
36 J5 **Sevier Lake** ◎ Utah, W USA
21 N9 **Sevierville** Tennessee, S USA 35°53′N 83°34′W
104 J14 **Sevilla** Eng. Seville; anc. Hispalis. Andalucía, SW Spain 37°24′N 05°59′W
104 J13 **Sevilla** ◈ province Andalucía, SW Spain
Sevilla de Niefang see Niefang
43 O16 **Sevilla, Isla** island SW Panama
Seville see Sevilla
114 J9 **Sevlievo** Gabrovo, N Bulgaria 43°01′N 25°06′E
Sevluš/Sevlyush see Vynohradiv
109 V11 **Sevnica** Ger. Lichtenwald. E Slovenia 46°00′N 15°20′E
162 J11 **Sevrey** var. Saynshand. Ömnögovĭ, S Mongolia 43°30′N 102°08′E
126 I7 **Sevsk** Bryanskaya Oblast', W Russian Federation 52°03′N 34°31′E
76 J15 **Sewa** ≈ E Sierra Leone
39 R12 **Seward** Alaska, USA 60°06′N 149°26′W
29 R15 **Seward** Nebraska, C USA 40°52′N 97°06′W
197 Q3 **Seward Peninsula** peninsula Alaska, USA
Seward's Folly see Alaska
62 H12 **Sewell** Libertador, C Chile 34°05′S 70°25′W
98 K5 **Sexbierum** Fris. Seisbierrum. Fryslân, N Netherlands 53°13′N 05°28′E
11 O13 **Sexsmith** Alberta, W Canada 55°18′N 118°45′W
41 W13 **Seybaplaya** Campeche, SE Mexico 19°39′N 90°36′W
173 N6 **Seychelles** off. Republic of Seychelles. ◆ republic W Indian Ocean
67 Z9 **Seychelles** island group NE Seychelles
173 N6 **Seychelles Bank** var. Le Banc des Seychelles. undersea feature W Indian Ocean 04°45′S 55°30′E
Seychelles, Le Banc des see Seychelles Bank
Seychelles, Republic of see Seychelles
172 H17 **Seychellois, Morne** ▲ Mahé, NE Seychelles
92 L2 **Seydhisfjördhur** Austurland, E Iceland 65°15′N 14°00′W
146 J12 **Seýdi** Rus. Seydi; prev. Neftezavodsk. Lebap Welaýaty, E Turkmenistan 39°31′N 62°53′E
136 G16 **Seydişehir** Konya, SW Turkey 37°25′N 31°51′E
136 J13 **Seyfe Gölü** ◎ C Turkey
Seyhan see Adana
136 K16 **Seyhan Barajı** ⊠ S Turkey
136 K17 **Seyhan Nehri** ≈ S Turkey
136 F13 **Seyitgazi** Eskişehir, W Turkey 39°27′N 30°42′E
126 J7 **Seym** ≈ W Russian Federation
117 S3 **Seym** ≈ N Ukraine
123 T9 **Seymchan** Magadanskaya Oblast', E Russian Federation 62°54′N 152°27′E
114 N12 **Seymen** Tekirdağ, NW Turkey 41°06′N 27°56′E
183 O11 **Seymour** Victoria, SE Australia 37°01′S 145°10′E
83 I25 **Seymour** Eastern Cape, S South Africa 32°33′S 26°46′E
29 W16 **Seymour** Iowa, C USA 40°40′N 93°07′W
27 U7 **Seymour** Missouri, C USA 37°09′N 92°46′W
25 Q5 **Seymour** Texas, SW USA 33°36′N 99°16′W
114 M12 **Şeytan Deresi** ≈ NW Turkey
109 S12 **Sežana** It. Sesana. SW Slovenia 45°42′N 13°52′E
103 P5 **Sézanne** Marne, N France 48°43′N 03°41′E
107 I16 **Sezze** anc. Setia. Lazio, C Italy 41°29′N 13°04′E
Sfákia see Chóra Sfakíon
115 D21 **Sfaktiría** island S Greece
116 J11 **Sfântu Gheorghe** Ger. Sankt-Georgen, Hung. Sepsiszentgyörgy; prev. Şepşi-Sângeorz, Sfîntu Gheorghe. Covasna, C Romania 45°52′N 25°49′E
117 N13 **Sfântu Gheorghe, Braţul** var. Gheorghe Braţul. ≈ E Romania
75 N6 **Sfax** Ar. Şafāqis. E Tunisia 34°45′N 10°45′E
75 N6 **Sfax** ✈ E Tunisia 34°43′N 10°37′E
Sfîntu Gheorghe see Sfântu Gheorghe
98 H13 **'s-Gravendeel** Zuid-Holland, SW Netherlands 51°48′N 04°36′E
98 F11 **'s-Gravenhage** var. Den Haag, Eng. The Hague, Fr. La Haye. ● (Netherlands-seat of government) Zuid-Holland, W Netherlands 52°07′N 04°17′E
98 G12 **'s-Gravenzande** Zuid-Holland, W Netherlands 52°00′N 04°10′E
Shaan/Shaanxi Sheng see Shaanxi
159 X11 **Shaanxi** var. Shaan, Shaanxi Sheng, Shan-hsi, Shenshi, Shensi. ◈ province C China
Shaartuz see Shahrtuz
Shaba see Katanga
Shabani see Zvishavane
81 N17 **Shabeellaha Dhexe** off. Gobolka Shabeellaha Dhexe. ◈ region E Somalia
Shabeellaha Dhexe, Gobolka see Shabeellaha Dhexe
81 L17 **Shabeellaha Hoose** off. Gobolka Shabeellaha Hoose. ◈ region S Somalia
Shabeellaha Hoose, Gobolka see Shabeellaha Hoose
Shabeelle, Webi see Shebeli
114 O7 **Shabla** Dobrich, NE Bulgaria 43°33′N 28°31′E
114 O7 **Shabla, Nos** headland NE Bulgaria 43°30′N 28°36′E
13 N9 **Shabogama Lake** ◎ Newfoundland and Labrador, E Canada
79 N20 **Shabunda** Sud-Kivu, E Dem. Rep. Congo 02°42′S 27°20′E
141 Q15 **Shabwah** C Yemen 15°09′N 46°46′E
158 F8 **Shache** var. Yarkant. Xinjiang Uygur Zizhiqu, NW China 38°27′N 77°16′E
Shacheng see Huailai
195 R12 **Shackleton Coast** physical region Antarctica
195 Z10 **Shackleton Ice Shelf** ice shelf Antarctica
Shaddādī see Ash Shadādah
28 K7 **Shadehill Reservoir** ⊠ South Dakota, N USA
122 G11 **Shadrinsk** Kurganskaya Oblast', C Russian Federation 56°08′N 63°18′E
31 O12 **Shafer, Lake** ⊠ Indiana, N USA
35 R13 **Shafter** California, W USA 35°27′N 119°15′W
24 J11 **Shafter** Texas, SW USA 29°49′N 104°18′W
97 L23 **Shaftesbury** S England, United Kingdom 51°01′N 02°12′W
185 F22 **Shag** ≈ South Island, New Zealand
145 V9 **Shagan** ≈ E Kazakhstan
39 O11 **Shageluk** Alaska, USA 62°40′N 159°33′W
122 K14 **Shagonar** Respublika Tyva, S Russian Federation 51°31′N 93°06′E
185 F22 **Shag Point** headland South Island, New Zealand 45°28′S 170°50′E
144 J12 **Shagyray, Plato** plain SW Kazakhstan
Shāhābād see Eslāmābād-e Gharb
168 K9 **Shah Alam** Selangor, Peninsular Malaysia 03°02′N 101°31′E
117 O12 **Shahany, Ozero** ◎ SW Ukraine
138 H9 **Shahbā'** anc. Philippopolis. As Suwaydā', S Syria 32°50′N 36°38′E
Shahbān see Ad Dayr
149 P17 **Shāh Bandar** Sind, SE Pakistan 23°59′N 67°54′E
149 P13 **Shahdād Kot** Sind, SW Pakistan 27°49′N 67°49′E
143 T10 **Shahdād, Namakzār-e** salt pan E Iran
149 Q15 **Shāhdādpur** Sind, SE Pakistan 25°56′N 68°40′E
154 K10 **Shahdol** Madhya Pradesh, C India 23°19′N 81°26′E
161 N7 **Sha He** ≈ C China
Shahe see Linze
Shahepu see Linze
153 N13 **Shāhganj** Uttar Pradesh, N India 26°03′N 82°41′E
152 C11 **Shāhgarh** Rājasthān, NW India 27°08′N 69°56′E
Sha Hi see Orūmīyeh, Daryācheh-ye
Shāhī see Qā'emshahr
Shahjahanabad see Delhi
152 L11 **Shāhjahānpur** Uttar Pradesh, N India 27°53′N 79°55′E
149 U7 **Shāhpur** Punjab, E Pakistan 32°15′N 72°32′E
Shāhpur see Shāhpur Chākar
152 G13 **Shāhpura** Rājasthān, N India 25°38′N 75°01′E
149 Q15 **Shāhpur Chākar** var. Shāhpur. Sind, SE Pakistan 26°11′N 68°44′E
148 M5 **Shahrak** Gōwr, C Afghanistan 34°09′N 64°16′E
143 Q11 **Shahr-e Bābak** Kermān, C Iran 30°08′N 55°04′E
143 N8 **Shahr-e Kord** var. Shahr Kord. Chahār MaḤall va Bakhtīārī, C Iran 32°20′N 50°52′E
143 O9 **Shahreẕā** var. Qomisheh, Qumisheh, Shahriza; prev. Qomsheh. Eşfahān, C Iran 32°01′N 51°51′E
147 S10 **Shahrikhon** Rus. Shakhrikhan. Andijon Viloyati, E Uzbekistan 40°42′N 72°03′E
147 P11 **Shahriston** Rus. Shakhristan. NW Tajikistan 39°45′N 68°47′E
Shahriza see Shahreẕā
Shahr-i-Zabul see Zābol
Shahr Kord see Shahr-e Kord
147 P14 **Shahrtuz** Rus. Shaartuz. SW Tajikistan 37°13′N 68°05′E
143 Q4 **Shāhrūd** prev. Emāmrūd, Emāmshahr. Semnān, N Iran 36°30′N 55°E
Shahsavār/Shahsawar see Tonekābon
Shaikh Ābid see Shaykh 'Ābid
Shaikh Fāris see Shaykh Fāris
Shaikh Najm see Shaykh Najm
138 K5 **Shā'ir, Jabal** ▲ C Syria 34°51′N 37°49′E
154 G10 **Shājāpur** Madhya Pradesh, C India 23°27′N 76°21′E
80 J8 **Shakal, Ras** headland NE Sudan 18°04′N 38°34′E
83 G17 **Shakawe** North West, NW Botswana 18°25′S 21°53′E
Shakhdarinskiy Khrebet see Shokhdara, Qatorkŭhi
Shakhrikhan see Shahrikhon
Shakhrisabz see Sharixon
Shakhristan see Shahriston
Shakhtërsk see Zuhres
145 R10 **Shakhtinsk** Karaganda, C Kazakhstan 49°40′N 72°37′E
126 L11 **Shakhty** Rostovskaya Oblast', SW Russian Federation 47°45′N 40°14′E
127 P2 **Shakhun'ya** Nizhegorodskaya Oblast', W Russian Federation 57°42′N 46°36′E
77 S15 **Shaki** Oyo, W Nigeria 08°37′N 03°25′E
81 J15 **Shakīso** Oromīya, C Ethiopia 05°33′N 38°48′E
29 V9 **Shakopee** Minnesota, N USA 44°48′N 93°31′W
165 R3 **Shakotan-misaki** headland Hokkaidō, NE Japan 43°22′N 140°28′E
39 N9 **Shaktoolik** Alaska, USA 64°19′N 161°05′W
81 J14 **Shala Hāyk'** ◎ C Ethiopia
124 M10 **Shalakusha** Arkhangel'skaya Oblast', NW Russian Federation 62°16′N 40°16′E
145 U8 **Shalday** Pavlodar, NE Kazakhstan 51°57′N 78°51′E
127 P16 **Shali** Chechenskaya Respublika, SW Russian Federation 43°03′N 45°55′E
141 W12 **Shalīm** var. Shelim. S Oman 18°07′N 55°39′E
Shaliuhe see Gangca
144 K12 **Shalkar** var. Chelkar. Aktyubinsk, W Kazakhstan 47°50′N 59°29′E
144 F9 **Shalkar, Ozero** prev. Chelkar Ozero. ◎ W Kazakhstan
21 V12 **Shallotte** North Carolina, SE USA 33°58′N 78°21′W
25 N5 **Shallowater** Texas, SW USA 33°41′N 102°00′W
124 K11 **Shal'skiy** Respublika Kareliya, NW Russian Federation 61°45′N 36°02′E
160 F9 **Shaluli Shan** ▲▲ C China
81 F22 **Shama** ≈ C Tanzania
11 Z11 **Shamattawa** Manitoba, C Canada 55°52′N 92°05′W
12 F8 **Shamattawa** ≈ Ontario, C Canada
Shām, Bādiyat ash see Syrian Desert
Shamiya see Ash Shāmīyah
141 X8 **Shām, Jabal ash** var. Jebel Sham. ▲ NW Oman 23°21′N 57°08′E
Sham, Jebel see Shām, Jabal ash
Shamkhor see Şämkir
18 G14 **Shamokin** Pennsylvania, NE USA 40°47′N 76°33′W
25 P2 **Shamrock** Texas, SW USA 35°12′N 100°15′W
Shana see Kuril'sk
Sha'nabī, Jabal ash see Chambi, Jebel
139 Y12 **Shanāwah** Al Başrah, E Iraq 30°57′N 47°25′E
Shancheng see Taining
159 T8 **Shandan** var. Qingyuan. Gansu, N China 38°50′N 101°08′E
Shandī see Shendi
161 Q5 **Shandong** var. Lu, Shandong Sheng, Shantung. ◈ province E China
161 R4 **Shandong Bandao** var. Shantung Peninsula. peninsula E China
Shandong Sheng see Shandong
139 U8 **Shandrūkh** Diyālá, E Iraq 33°20′N 45°19′E
83 J17 **Shangani** ≈ W Zimbabwe
161 O15 **Shangchuan Dao** island S China
Shangchuankou see Minhe
163 P12 **Shangdu** Nei Mongol Zizhiqu, N China 41°32′N 113°33′E
161 O11 **Shanggao** var. Aoyang. Jiangxi, S China 28°16′N 114°55′E
Shangguan see Daixian
161 S8 **Shanghai** var. Shang-hai. Shanghai Shi, E China 31°14′N 121°28′E
161 S8 **Shanghai Shi** var. Hu, Shanghai. ◈ municipality E China
161 P13 **Shanghang** var. Linjiang. Fujian, SE China 25°03′N 116°25′E
160 K14 **Shanglin** var. Dafeng. Guangxi Zhuangzu Zizhiqu, S China 23°26′N 108°32′E
160 L7 **Shangluo** prev. Shangxian, Shangzhou. Shaanxi, C China 33°51′N 109°55′E
83 G15 **Shangombo** Western, W Zambia 16/28′S 22°10′E
Shangpai/Shangpaihe see Feixi
161 O6 **Shangqiu** var. Zhuji. Henan, C China 34°24′N 115°37′E
161 Q10 **Shangrao** Jiangxi, S China 28°27′N 117°57′E
Shangxian see Shangluo
161 S9 **Shangyu** var. Baiguan. Zhejiang, SE China 30°03′N 120°52′E
163 X9 **Shangzhi** Heilongjiang, NE China 45°13′N 127°59′E
Shangzhou see Shangluo
Shanhe see Zhengning
163 W9 **Shanhetun** Heilongjiang, NE China 44°42′N 127°12′E
Shan-hsi see Shaanxi, China
Shan-hsi see Shanxi, China
159 O6 **Shankou** Xinjiang Uygur Zizhiqu, W China 42°02′N 94°08′E
184 M13 **Shannon** Manawatu-Wanganui, North Island, New Zealand 40°32′S 175°24′E
97 C17 **Shannon** Ir. An tSionainn. ≈ W Ireland
97 B19 **Shannon** ✈ W Ireland 52°42′N 08°57′W
167 N6 **Shan Plateau** plateau E Myanmar (Burma)
158 M6 **Shanshan** var. Piqan. Xinjiang Uygur Zizhiqu, NW China 42°53′N 90°18′E
Shansi see Shanxi
167 N5 **Shan State** ◈ state E Myanmar (Burma)
Shantar Islands see Shantarskiye Ostrova
123 S12 **Shantarskiye Ostrova** Eng. Shantar Islands. island group E Russian Federation

◆ Country ● Country Capital ◇ Dependent Territory ○ Dependent Territory Capital ◈ Administrative Regions ✈ International Airport ▲ Mountain ▲▲ Mountain Range Volcano ≈ River ◎ Lake ⊠ Reservoir

161 Q14 **Shantou** var. Shan-t'ou, Swatow. Guangdong, S China 23°23′N 116°39′E
Shan-t'ou see Shantou
Shantung see Shandong
Shantung Peninsula see Shandong Bandao
163 O14 **Shanxi** var. Jin, Shan-hsi, Shansi, Shanxi Sheng. ◆ province C China
161 P6 **Shanxian** var. Shan Xian. Shandong, E China 34°51′N 116°09′E
Shan Xian see Sanmenxia
Shan Xian see Shanxian
Shanxi Sheng see Shanxi
160 L7 **Shanyang** Shaanxi, C China 33°35′N 109°48′E
161 N13 **Shanyin** var. Daiyue. Shanxi, C China E Asia 39°30′N 112°56′E
161 O13 **Shaoguan** var. Shao-kuan, Cant. Kukong; prev. Ch'u-chiang. Guangdong, S China 24°57′N 113°38′E
Shao-kuan see Shaoguan
161 Q11 **Shaowu** Fujian, SE China 27°24′N 117°26′E
161 S9 **Shaoxing** Zhejiang, SE China 30°02′N 120°35′E
160 M12 **Shaoyang** var. Tangdukou. Hunan, S China 26°54′N 111°14′E
160 M11 **Shaoyang** var. Baoqing, Shao-yang; prev. Pao-king. Hunan, S China 27°13′N 111°31′E
Shao-yang see Shaoyang
96 K5 **Shapinsay** island NE Scotland, United Kingdom
125 S4 **Shapkina** ≈ NW Russian Federation
Shāpūr see Salmās
158 M4 **Shaqiuhe** Xinjiang Uygur Zizhiqu, W China 45°00′N 88°52′E
139 T2 **Shaqlāwa** var. Shaqlāwah. Arbīl, E Iraq 36°24′N 44°21′E
Shaqlāwah see Shaqlāwa
138 I8 **Shaqqā** As Suwaydā', S Syria 32°53′N 36°42′E
141 P7 **Shaqrā'** Ar Riyāḍ, C Saudi Arabia 25°11′N 45°08′E
Shaqrā see Shuqrah
145 W10 **Shar** var. Charsk. Vostochnyy Kazakhstan, E Kazakhstan 49°33′N 81°03′E
149 O6 **Sharan** Dāykundī, SE Afghanistan 33°28′N 66°19′E
149 Q7 **Sharan** var. Zareh Sharan. Paktīkā, E Afghanistan 33°08′N 68°47′E
Sharaqpur see Sharqpur
145 U8 **Sharbakty** Kaz. Sharbaqty; prev. Shcherbakty. Pavlodar, E Kazakhstan 52°28′N 78°00′E
Sharbaqty see Sharbakty
141 X12 **Sharbatāt** S Oman 17°57′N 56°14′E
Sharbatāt, Ra's see Sharbithāt, Ras
141 X12 **Sharbithāt, Ras** var. Ra's Sharbatāt. headland S Oman 17°55′N 56°30′E
14 K14 **Sharbot Lake** Ontario, SE Canada 44°45′N 76°46′W
145 P17 **Shardara** var. Chardara. Yuzhnyy Kazakhstan, S Kazakhstan 41°15′N 68°01′E
Shardara Dalasy see Step' Shardara
145 P17 **Shardarinskoye Vodokhranilishche** prev. Chardarinskoye Vodokhranilishche. ⊠ S Kazakhstan
162 F8 **Sharga** Govĭ-Altay, W Mongolia 46°16′N 95°32′E
Sharga see Tsagaan-Uul
116 M7 **Sharhorod** Vinnyts'ka Oblast', C Ukraine 48°46′N 28°05′E
Sharhulsan see Mandal-Ovoo
165 V3 **Shari** Hokkaidō, NE Japan 43°54′N 144°42′E
Shari see Chari
139 T6 **Shārī, Buḩayrat** ◎ C Iraq
147 N12 **Sharixon** Rus. Shakhrisabz. Qashqadaryo Viloyati, S Uzbekistan 39°01′N 66°45′E
Sharjah see Ash Shāriqah
118 K12 **Sharkawshchyna** var. Sharkowshchyna, Pol. Szarkowszczyzna, Rus. Sharkovshchina. Vitsyebskaya Voblasts', NW Belarus 55°27′N 27°28′E
180 G9 **Shark Bay** bay Western Australia
141 Y9 **Sharkh** E Oman 21°20′N 59°04′E
Sharkovshchina/ Sharkowshchyna see Sharkawshchyna
127 U6 **Sharlyk** Orenburgskaya Oblast', W Russian Federation 52°52′N 54°45′E
75 Y9 **Sharm ash Shaykh** var. Ofiral, Sharm el Sheikh. E Egypt 27°51′N 34°16′E
Sharm el Sheikh see Sharm ash Shaykh
18 B13 **Sharon** Pennsylvania, NE USA 41°12′N 80°28′W
26 H4 **Sharon Springs** Kansas, C USA 38°54′N 101°46′W
31 Q14 **Sharonville** Ohio, N USA 39°16′N 84°24′W
Sharourah see Sharūrah
29 O10 **Sharpe, Lake** ⊠ South Dakota, N USA
Sharqī, Al Jabal ash/Sharqi, Jebel esh see Anti-Lebanon
Sharqīyah, Al Minṭaqah ash see Ash Sharqīyah
138 I6 **Sharqīyat an Nabk, Jabal** ▲▲ W Syria
149 W8 **Sharqpur** var. Sharaqpur. Punjab, E Pakistan 31°29′N 74°08′E
141 Q13 **Sharūrah** var. Sharourah. Najrān, S Saudi Arabia 17°29′N 47°05′E
125 O14 **Shar'ya** Kostromskaya Oblast', NW Russian Federation 58°22′N 45°30′E
145 W15 **Sharyn** prev. Charyn. Almaty, SE Kazakhstan 43°48′N 79°22′E
145 V15 **Sharyn** var. Charyn. ≈ SE Kazakhstan
122 K13 **Sharypovo** Krasnoyarskiy Kray, C Russian Federation 55°33′N 89°12′E
83 J18 **Shashe** Central, NE Botswana 21°25′S 27°28′E
83 J18 **Shashe** var. Shashi. ≈ Botswana/Zimbabwe
81 J14 **Shashemenē** var. Shashemenne, Shashhamana, It. Sciasciamana. Oromīya, C Ethiopia 07°16′N 38°38′E
Shashemenne/ Shashhamana see Shashemenē
Shashi see Shashe
Shashi/Sha-shih/Shasi see Jingzhou, Hubei
35 N3 **Shasta Lake** ⊠ California, W USA
35 N2 **Shasta, Mount** ▲ California, W USA 41°24′N 122°11′W
127 O4 **Shatki** Nizhegorodskaya Oblast', W Russian Federation 55°09′N 44°04′E
Shatlyk see Şatlyk
Shatra see Ash Shaṭrah
119 K17 **Shatsk** Minskaya Voblasts', C Belarus 53°25′N 27°41′E
127 N5 **Shatsk** Ryazanskaya Oblast', W Russian Federation 54°02′N 41°38′E
26 J9 **Shattuck** Oklahoma, C USA 36°16′N 99°52′W
145 P16 **Shauil'dir** prev. Shaul'der. Yuzhnyy Kazakhstan, S Kazakhstan 42°45′N 68°21′E
Shaul'der see Shauil'dir
11 S17 **Shaunavon** Saskatchewan, S Canada 49°49′N 108°25′W
Shavat see Shovot
Shaviyani Atoll see North Miladhunmadulu Atoll
158 K4 **Shawan** var. Sandaohezi. Xinjiang Uygur Zizhiqu, NW China 44°21′N 85°37′E
14 G12 **Shawanaga** Ontario, S Canada 45°29′N 80°16′W
30 M6 **Shawano** Wisconsin, N USA 44°46′N 88°38′W
30 M6 **Shawano Lake** ◎ Wisconsin, N USA
15 P10 **Shawinigan** prev. Shawinigan Falls. Québec, SE Canada 46°33′N 72°45′W
Shawinigan Falls see Shawinigan
15 P10 **Shawinigan-Sud** Québec, SE Canada 46°30′N 72°43′W
138 J5 **Shawmarīyah, Jabal ash** ▲▲ C Syria
27 O11 **Shawnee** Oklahoma, C USA 35°20′N 96°55′W
14 K12 **Shawville** Québec, SE Canada 45°37′N 76°31′W
145 Q16 **Shayan** var. Chayan. Yuzhnyy Kazakhstan, S Kazakhstan 42°59′N 69°22′E
Shaykh see Ash Shakk
139 W9 **Shaykh 'Ābid** var. Shaikh Ābid. Wāsiţ, E Iraq 32°40′N 46°09′E
139 Y10 **Shaykh Fāris** var. Shaikh Fāris. Maysān, E Iraq 32°06′N 47°39′E
139 T7 **Shaykh Ḩātim** Baghdād, E Iraq 33°29′N 44°15′E
Shaykh, Jabal ash see Hermon, Mount
139 X10 **Shaykh Najm** var. Shaikh Najm. Maysān, E Iraq 32°04′N 46°54′E
139 W9 **Shaykh Sa'd** Maysān, E Iraq 32°35′N 46°16′E
147 T14 **Shazud** SE Tajikistan 37°45′N 72°22′E
119 N18 **Shchadryn** Rus. Shchedrin. Homyel'skaya Voblasts', SE Belarus 52°53′N 29°33′E
119 H18 **Shchara** ≈ SW Belarus
Shchedrin see Shchadryn
Shcheglovsk see Kemerovo
126 K5 **Shchëkino** Tul'skaya Oblast', W Russian Federation 53°57′N 37°33′E
125 S7 **Shchel'yayur** Respublika Komi, NW Russian Federation 65°19′N 53°27′E
Shcherbakty see Sharbakty
126 K7 **Shchigry** Kurskaya Oblast', W Russian Federation 51°53′N 36°49′E
Shchitkovichi see Shchytkavichy
117 Q2 **Shchors** Chernihivs'ka Oblast', N Ukraine 51°49′N 31°58′E
117 T8 **Shchors'k** Dnipropetrovs'ka Oblast', E Ukraine 48°20′N 34°07′E
Shchuchin see Shchuchyn
145 Q7 **Shchuchinsk** prev. Shchuchye. Akmola, N Kazakhstan 52°57′N 70°10′E
Shchuchye see Shchuchinsk
119 G16 **Shchuchyn** Pol. Szczuczyn Nowogródzki, Rus. Shchuchin. Hrodzyenskaya Voblasts', W Belarus 53°36′N 24°45′E
119 K17 **Shchytkavichy** Rus. Shchitkovichi. Minskaya Voblasts', C Belarus 53°13′N 27°59′E
122 J13 **Shebalino** Respublika Altay, S Russian Federation 51°16′N 85°41′E
126 J9 **Shebekino** Belgorodskaya Oblast', W Russian Federation 50°25′N 36°55′E
Shebelē Wenz, Wabē see Shebeli
81 L14 **Shebeli** Amh. Wabē Shebelē Wenz, It. Scebeli, Som. Webi Shabeelle. ≈ Ethiopia/ Somalia
113 M20 **Shebenikut, Maja e** ▲ E Albania 41°13′N 20°27′E
Sheberghān see Shibirghān
144 F14 **Shebir** Mangistau, SW Kazakhstan 44°52′N 52°01′E
31 N8 **Sheboygan** Wisconsin, N USA 43°46′N 87°44′W
77 X15 **Shebshi Mountains** var. Schebschi Mountains. ▲▲ E Nigeria
Shechem see Nablus
Shedadi see Ash Shadādah
13 P14 **Shediac** New Brunswick, SE Canada 46°13′N 64°35′W
126 L15 **Shedok** Krasnodarskiy Kray, SW Russian Federation 44°12′N 40°49′E
Sheekh see Shiikh
38 M11 **Sheenjek River** ≈ Alaska, USA
96 D13 **Sheep Haven** Ir. Cuan na gCaorach. inlet N Ireland
35 X10 **Sheep Range** ▲▲ Nevada, W USA
98 M13 **'s-Heerenberg** Gelderland, E Netherlands 51°52′N 06°15′E
97 P22 **Sheerness** SE England, United Kingdom 51°27′N 00°45′E
13 Q15 **Sheet Harbour** Nova Scotia, SE Canada 44°56′N 62°31′W
185 H18 **Sheffield** Canterbury, South Island, New Zealand 43°22′S 172°01′E
97 M18 **Sheffield** N England, United Kingdom 53°23′N 01°30′W
23 O2 **Sheffield** Alabama, S USA 34°46′N 87°42′W
29 V12 **Sheffield** Iowa, C USA 42°53′N 93°13′W
25 N10 **Sheffield** Texas, SW USA 30°42′N 101°49′W
63 H22 **Shehuen, Río** ≈ S Argentina
Shekhem see Nablus
149 V8 **Shekhūpura** Punjab, NE Pakistan 31°42′N 74°08′E
Sheki see Şäki
124 L14 **Sheksna** Vologodskaya Oblast', NW Russian Federation 59°11′N 38°32′E
123 T5 **Shelagskiy, Mys** headland NE Russian Federation 70°04′N 170°39′E
27 V3 **Shelbina** Missouri, C USA 39°41′N 92°02′W
13 P16 **Shelburne** Nova Scotia, SE Canada 43°47′N 65°20′W
14 G14 **Shelburne** Ontario, S Canada 44°04′N 80°12′W
33 R7 **Shelby** Montana, NW USA 48°30′N 111°52′W
21 Q10 **Shelby** North Carolina, SE USA 35°15′N 81°34′W
31 S12 **Shelby** Ohio, N USA 40°52′N 82°39′W
30 L14 **Shelbyville** Illinois, N USA 39°24′N 88°47′W
31 P14 **Shelbyville** Indiana, N USA 39°31′N 85°46′W
20 L5 **Shelbyville** Kentucky, S USA 38°13′N 85°12′W
27 V2 **Shelbyville** Missouri, C USA 39°48′N 92°01′W
20 J10 **Shelbyville** Tennessee, S USA 35°29′N 86°30′W
25 X8 **Shelbyville** Texas, SW USA 31°42′N 94°03′W
30 L14 **Shelbyville, Lake** ⊠ Illinois, N USA
29 S12 **Sheldon** Iowa, C USA 43°10′N 95°51′W
38 M11 **Sheldons Point** Alaska, USA 62°31′N 165°03′W
145 V15 **Shelek** prev. Chilik. Almaty, SE Kazakhstan 43°35′N 78°12′E
145 V15 **Shelek** prev. Chilik. ≈ SE Kazakhstan
Shelekhov Gulf see Shelikhova, Zaliv
123 U9 **Shelikhova, Zaliv** Eng. Shelekhov Gulf. gulf E Russian Federation
39 P14 **Shelikof Strait** strait Alaska, USA
Shelim see Shalīm
11 T14 **Shellbrook** Saskatchewan, S Canada 53°14′N 106°24′W
28 L3 **Shell Creek** ≈ North Dakota, N USA
Shellif see Chelif, Oued
22 I10 **Shell Keys** island group Louisiana, S USA
30 I4 **Shell Lake** Wisconsin, N USA 45°44′N 91°56′W
29 W12 **Shell Rock** Iowa, C USA 42°42′N 92°34′W
185 C26 **Shelter Point** headland Stewart Island, New Zealand 47°04′S 168°13′E
18 L13 **Shelton** Connecticut, NE USA 41°19′N 73°06′W
32 G8 **Shelton** Washington, NW USA 47°13′N 123°06′W
Shemakha see Şamaxı
145 W9 **Shemonaikha** Vostochnyy Kazakhstan, E Kazakhstan 50°38′N 81°55′E
127 Q4 **Shemursha** Chuvashskaya Respublika, W Russian Federation 54°57′N 47°27′E
38 D16 **Shemya Island** island Aleutian Islands, Alaska, USA
29 T16 **Shenandoah** Iowa, C USA 40°46′N 95°23′W
21 U4 **Shenandoah** Virginia, NE USA 38°26′N 78°34′W
21 U4 **Shenandoah Mountains** ridge West Virginia, NE USA
21 V3 **Shenandoah River** ≈ West Virginia, NE USA
77 W15 **Shendam** Plateau, C Nigeria 08°52′N 09°30′E
80 G8 **Shendi** var. Shandī. River Nile, NE Sudan 16°41′N 33°22′E
76 I15 **Shenge** SW Sierra Leone 07°54′N 12°54′W
146 L10 **Shengeldi** Rus. Chingildi. Navoiy Viloyati, N Uzbekistan 40°59′N 64°13′E
145 U15 **Shengel'dy** Almaty, SE Kazakhstan 44°04′N 77°31′E
113 K18 **Shëngjin** var. Shëngjini. Lezhë, NW Albania 41°49′N 19°34′E
Shëngjini see Shëngjin
Shengking see Liaoning
Sheng Xian/Shengxian see Shengzhou
161 S9 **Shengzhou** var. Shengxian, Sheng Xian. Zhejiang, SE China 29°36′N 120°42′E
Shenking see Liaoning
125 N11 **Shenkursk** Arkhangel'skaya Oblast', NW Russian Federation 62°10′N 42°58′E
160 L3 **Shenmu** Shaanxi, C China 38°49′N 110°27′E
113 L19 **Shën Noj i Madh** ▲ C Albania 41°23′N 20°07′E
160 L8 **Shennong Ding** ▲ C China 31°24′N 110°16′E
Shenshi/Shensi see Shaanxi
163 V12 **Shenyang** Chin. Shen-yang, Eng. Moukden, Mukden; prev. Fengtien. province capital Liaoning, NE China 41°50′N 123°26′E
Shen-yang see Shenyang
161 O15 **Shenzhen** Guangdong, S China 22°39′N 114°02′E
154 G8 **Sheopur** Madhya Pradesh, C India 25°41′N 76°42′E
116 L5 **Shepetivka** Rus. Shepetovka. Khmel'nyts'ka Oblast', NW Ukraine 50°12′N 27°01′E
Shepetovka see Shepetivka
25 W10 **Shepherd** Texas, SW USA 30°30′N 95°00′W
187 R14 **Shepherd Islands** island group C Vanuatu
20 K5 **Shepherdsville** Kentucky, S USA 38°00′N 85°42′W
183 O11 **Shepparton** Victoria, SE Australia 36°25′S 145°26′E
97 P22 **Sheppey, Isle of** island SE England, United Kingdom
Sherabad see Sherobod
9 O4 **Sherard, Cape** headland Nunavut, N Canada 74°36′N 80°10′W
97 L23 **Sherborne** S England, United Kingdom 50°58′N 02°30′W
76 H16 **Sherbro Island** island SW Sierra Leone
15 Q12 **Sherbrooke** Québec, SE Canada 45°23′N 71°55′W
29 T11 **Sherburn** Minnesota, N USA 43°39′N 94°43′W
78 H6 **Sherda** Borkou-Ennedi-Tibesti, N Chad 20°04′N 16°48′E
80 G7 **Shereik** River Nile, N Sudan 18°44′N 33°37′E
126 K3 **Sheremet'yevo** ✈ (Moskva) Moskovskaya Oblast', W Russian Federation 56°05′N 37°10′E
153 P14 **Sherghāti** Bihār, N India 24°35′N 84°51′E
27 U12 **Sheridan** Arkansas, C USA 34°18′N 92°22′W
33 W12 **Sheridan** Wyoming, C USA 44°47′N 106°59′W
182 G8 **Sheringa** South Australia 33°51′S 135°13′E
25 U5 **Sherman** Texas, SW USA 33°39′N 96°35′W
194 J10 **Sherman Island** island Antarctica
19 S4 **Sherman Mills** Maine, NE USA 45°51′N 68°23′W
29 O15 **Sherman Reservoir** ⊠ Nebraska, C USA
147 N14 **Sherobod** Rus. Sherabad. Surkhondaryo Viloyati, S Uzbekistan 37°43′N 66°59′E
147 O13 **Sherobod** Rus. Sherabad. ≈ S Uzbekistan
153 T14 **Sherpur** Dhaka, N Bangladesh 25°00′N 90°01′E
37 T4 **Sherrelwood** Colorado, C USA 39°49′N 105°00′W
99 J14 **'s-Hertogenbosch** Fr. Bois-le-Duc, Ger. Herzogenbusch. Noord-Brabant, S Netherlands 51°41′N 05°19′E
28 M2 **Sherwood** North Dakota, N USA 48°55′N 101°36′W
11 Q14 **Sherwood Park** Alberta, SW Canada 53°34′N 113°04′W
56 F13 **Sheshea, Río** ≈ E Peru
143 T5 **Sheshtamad** Khorāsān-Razavī, NE Iran 36°03′N 57°45′E
29 S10 **Shetek, Lake** ◎ Minnesota, N USA
96 M2 **Shetland Islands** island group NE Scotland, United Kingdom
144 F14 **Shetpe** Mangistau, SW Kazakhstan 44°06′N 52°03′E
154 C11 **Shetrunji** ≈ W India
Shevchenko see Aktau
117 W5 **Shevchenkove** Kharkivs'ka Oblast', E Ukraine 49°40′N 37°13′E
81 H14 **Shewa Gīmīra** Southern Nationalities, S Ethiopia 07°12′N 35°49′E
161 Q9 **Shexian** var. Huicheng, She Xian. Anhui, E China 29°53′N 118°27′E
She Xian see Shexian
161 R6 **Sheyang** prev. Hede. Jiangsu, E China 33°49′N 120°13′E
29 O4 **Sheyenne** North Dakota, N USA 47°49′N 99°08′W
29 P4 **Sheyenne River** ≈ North Dakota, N USA
96 G7 **Shiant Islands** island group NW Scotland, United Kingdom
123 U12 **Shiashkotan, Ostrov** island Kuril'skiye Ostrova, SE Russian Federation
31 R9 **Shiawassee River** ≈ Michigan, N USA
141 R14 **Shibām** C Yemen 15°49′N 48°24′E
Shibarghān see Shibirghān
165 O10 **Shibata** var. Sibata. Niigata, Honshū, C Japan 37°57′N 139°20′E
Shiberghan/Shiberghān see Shibirghān
Shibh Jazirat Sīnā' see Sinai
75 W8 **Shibīn al Kawm** var. Shibîn el Kôm. N Egypt 30°33′N 31°00′E
Shibîn el Kôm see Shibīn al Kawm
149 N2 **Shibirghān** var. Shibarghān, Shiberghan, Shiberghān; prev. Sheberghān. Jowzjān, N Afghanistan 36°41′N 65°45′E
143 O13 **Shīb, Kūh-e** ▲▲ S Iran
12 D8 **Shibogama Lake** ◎ Ontario, C Canada
Shibotsu-jima see Zelënyy, Ostrov
164 B16 **Shibushi** Kagoshima, Kyūshū, SW Japan 31°27′N 131°05′E
189 U13 **Shichiyo Islands** island group Chuuk, C Micronesia
Shickshock Mountains see Chic-Chocs, Monts
shiderti see Shiderty
Shiderti see Shiderty
145 S8 **Shiderty** prev. Shiderti. Pavlodar, NE Kazakhstan 51°40′N 74°50′E
145 S9 **Shiderty** prev. Shiderti. ≈ N Kazakhstan
96 G10 **Shiel, Loch** ◎ N Scotland, United Kingdom
164 J13 **Shiga** off. Shiga-ken, var. Siga. ◆ prefecture Honshū, SW Japan
Shiga-ken see Shiga
Shigatse see Xigazê
141 U13 **Shiḩan** oasis NE Yemen
Shih-chia-chuang/Shihmen see Shijiazhuang
158 K4 **Shihezi** Xinjiang Uygur Zizhiqu, NW China 44°21′N 85°59′E
Shiichi see Shyichy
80 N12 **Shiikh** prev. Sheekh. Togdheer, N Somalia 10°01′N 45°21′E
113 K19 **Shijak** var. Shijaku. Durrës, W Albania 41°21′N 19°34′E
Shijaku see Shijak
161 O4 **Shijiazhuang** var. Shih-chia-chuang; prev. Shihmen. province capital Hebei, E China 38°04′N 114°28′E
165 R5 **Shikabe** Hokkaidō, NE Japan 42°03′N 140°45′E
149 Q13 **Shikārpur** Sind, S Pakistan 27°59′N 68°39′E
127 Q7 **Shikhany** Saratovskaya Oblast', W Russian Federation 52°07′N 47°13′E
189 V12 **Shiki Islands** island group Chuuk, C Micronesia
164 G14 **Shikoku** var. Sikoku. island SW Japan
192 H5 **Shikoku Basin** var. Sikoku Basin. undersea feature N Philippine Sea 28°00′N 137°00′E
164 G14 **Shikoku-sanchi** ▲▲ Shikoku, SW Japan
165 X4 **Shikotan, Ostrov** Jap. Shikotan-tō. island NE Russian Federation
Shikotan-tō see Shikotan, Ostrov
165 R4 **Shikotsu-ko** var. Sikotu Ko. ◎ Hokkaidō, NE Japan
81 N15 **Shilabo** Sumalē, E Ethiopia 06°05′N 44°48′E
127 X7 **Shil'da** Orenburgskaya Oblast', W Russian Federation 51°46′N 59°48′E
139 V3 **Shilēr, Āw-e** ≈ E Iraq
153 S12 **Shiliguri** prev. Siliguri. West Bengal, NE India 26°46′N 88°24′E
Shiliu see Changjiang
129 V7 **Shilka** ≈ S Russian Federation
18 H15 **Shillington** Pennsylvania, NE USA 40°18′N 75°57′W
153 V13 **Shillong** state capital Meghālaya, NE India 25°37′N 91°54′E
126 M5 **Shilovo** Ryazanskaya Oblast', W Russian Federation 54°18′N 40°53′E
164 C14 **Shimabara** var. Simabara. Nagasaki, Kyūshū, SW Japan 32°48′N 130°20′E
164 C14 **Shimabara-wan** bay SW Japan
164 F12 **Shimane** off. Shimane-ken, var. Simane. ◆ prefecture Honshū, SW Japan
164 G11 **Shimane-hantō** peninsula Honshū, SW Japan
Shimane-ken see Shimane
123 Q13 **Shimanovsk** Amurskaya Oblast', SE Russian Federation 52°00′N 127°36′E
Shimanto see Nakamura
Shimbir Berris see Shimbiris
80 O12 **Shimbiris** var. Shimbir Berris. ▲ N Somalia 10°43′N 47°10′E
165 T4 **Shimizu** Hokkaidō, NE Japan 42°58′N 142°54′E
164 M14 **Shimizu** var. Simizu. Shizuoka, Honshū, S Japan 35°01′N 138°29′E
152 I8 **Shimla** prev. Simla. state capital Himāchal Pradesh, N India 31°07′N 77°09′E
165 N14 **Shimoda** var. Simoda. Shizuoka, Honshū, S Japan 34°40′N 138°55′E
165 O13 **Shimodate** var. Simodate. Ibaraki, Honshū, S Japan 36°20′N 140°00′E
155 F18 **Shimoga** Karnātaka, W India 13°56′N 75°31′E
164 C15 **Shimo-jima** island SW Japan
164 B15 **Shimo-Koshiki-jima** island SW Japan
81 J21 **Shimoni** Coast, S Kenya 04°40′S 39°22′E
164 D13 **Shimonoseki** var. Simonoseki, hist. Akamagaseki, Bakan. Yamaguchi, Honshū, SW Japan 33°57′N 130°54′E
124 G14 **Shimsk** Novgorodskaya Oblast', NW Russian Federation 58°12′N 30°43′E
141 W7 **Shināş** N Oman 24°45′N 56°24′E
148 J6 **Shīndand** prev. Shīndand. Herāt, W Afghanistan 33°19′N 62°09′E
Shīndand see Shīndand
Shinei see Xinying
162 H10 **Shinejinst** var. Dzalaa. Bayanhongor, C Mongolia 44°29′N 99°19′E
25 T12 **Shiner** Texas, SW USA 29°25′N 97°10′W
167 N1 **Shingbwiyang** Kachin State, N Myanmar (Burma) 26°40′N 96°14′E
Shingozha see Shynkozha
164 J15 **Shingū** var. Singû. Wakayama, Honshū, SW Japan 33°41′N 135°57′E
14 F8 **Shining Tree** Ontario, S Canada 47°36′N 81°12′W
165 P9 **Shinjō** var. Sinzyô. Yamagata, Honshū, C Japan 38°47′N 140°17′E
96 I7 **Shin, Loch** ◎ N Scotland, United Kingdom
21 S3 **Shinnston** West Virginia, NE USA 39°22′N 80°19′W
138 I6 **Shinshār** Fr. Chinnchâr. Ḩimş, W Syria 34°36′N 36°45′E
Shinshū see Jinju
165 T4 **Shintoku** Hokkaidō, NE Japan 43°03′N 142°50′E
81 G20 **Shinyanga** Shinyanga, NW Tanzania 03°40′S 33°25′E
81 G20 **Shinyanga** ◆ region N Tanzania
165 Q10 **Shiogama** var. Siogama. Miyagi, Honshū, C Japan 38°19′N 141°00′E
164 M12 **Shiojiri** var. Sioziri. Nagano, Honshū, S Japan 36°08′N 137°58′E
164 I15 **Shiono-misaki** headland Honshū, SW Japan 33°25′N 135°45′E
165 Q12 **Shioya-zaki** headland Honshū, C Japan 37°00′N 140°57′E
114 J9 **Shipchenski Prokhod** pass C Bulgaria
160 G14 **Shiping** Yunnan, SW China 23°45′N 102°23′E
13 P13 **Shippagan** var. Shippegan. New Brunswick, SE Canada 47°45′N 64°44′W
Shippegan see Shippagan
18 F15 **Shippensburg** Pennsylvania, NE USA 40°03′N 77°31′W
37 P9 **Shiprock** New Mexico, SW USA 36°47′N 108°41′W
37 O9 **Ship Rock** ▲ New Mexico, SW USA 36°41′N 108°50′W
15 R6 **Shipshaw** ≈ Québec, SE Canada
123 V10 **Shipunskiy, Mys** headland E Russian Federation 53°04′N 159°57′E
160 K7 **Shiquan** Shaanxi, C China 33°05′N 108°15′E
Shiquanhe see Gar
122 K13 **Shira** Respublika Khakasiya, S Russian Federation 54°35′N 89°58′E
Shirajganj Ghat see Sirajganj
165 P12 **Shirakawa** var. Sirakawa. Fukushima, Honshū, C Japan 37°07′N 140°11′E
164 M13 **Shirane-san** ▲ Honshū, S Japan 35°39′N 138°13′E
165 U14 **Shiranuka** Hokkaidō, NE Japan 42°57′N 144°01′E
195 N12 **Shirase Coast** physical region Antarctica
165 U3 **Shirataki** Hokkaidō, NE Japan 43°55′N 143°14′E
143 O11 **Shīrāz** var. Shīrāz. Fārs, S Iran 29°38′N 52°34′E
83 N15 **Shire** var. Chire. ≈ Malawi/ Mozambique
Shiree see Tsagaanhayrhan
Shireet see Bayandelger
165 W3 **Shiretoko-hantō** headland Hokkaidō, NE Japan 44°06′N 145°07′E
165 W3 **Shiretoko-misaki** headland Hokkaidō, NE Japan 44°20′N 145°19′E
127 N5 **Shiringushi** Respublika Mordoviya, W Russian Federation 53°50′N 42°49′E
148 M3 **Shīrīn Tagāb** Fāryāb, N Afghanistan 36°49′N 65°01′E
149 N2 **Shīrīn Tagāb** ≈ N Afghanistan
165 R6 **Shiriya-zaki** headland Honshū, C Japan 41°24′N 141°27′E
144 I12 **Shirkala, Gryada** plain W Kazakhstan
152 F11 **Shir Kolāyat** var. Kolāyat. Rājasthān, NW India 27°56′N 73°02′E
165 P10 **Shiroishi** var. Siroisi. Miyagi, Honshū, C Japan 38°00′N 140°38′E
Shirokoye see Shyroke
165 O10 **Shirone** var. Sirone. Niigata, Honshū, C Japan 37°46′N 139°00′E
164 L12 **Shirotori** Gifu, Honshū, SW Japan 35°53′N 136°52′E
197 T1 **Shirshov Ridge** undersea feature W Bering Sea
Shirshütür/Shirshyutyur, Peski see Şirşütür Gumy
143 T3 **Shīrvān** var. Shirwān. Khorāsān, NE Iran 37°25′N 57°55′E
Shirwa, Lake see Chilwa, Lake
Shirwān see Shīrvān
159 N5 **Shisanjianfang** Xinjiang Uygur Zizhiqu, W China 43°10′N 91°15′E
38 M16 **Shishaldin Volcano** ▲ Unimak Island, Alaska, USA 54°45′N 163°58′W
Shishchitsy see Shyshchytsy
83 G16 **Shishikola** North West, N Botswana 18°09′S 23°08′E
38 M8 **Shishmaref** Alaska, USA 66°15′N 166°04′W
Shisur see Ash Shişar
164 L13 **Shitara** Aichi, Honshū, SW Japan 35°06′N 137°33′E
152 D12 **Shiv** Rājasthān, NW India 26°11′N 71°14′E
Shivāji Sāgar see Konya Reservoir
154 H8 **Shivpuri** Madhya Pradesh, C India 25°28′N 77°41′E
36 J9 **Shivwits Plateau** plain Arizona, SW USA
Shiwalik Range see Siwalik Range
160 M8 **Shiyan** Hubei, C China 32°31′N 110°45′E
145 O15 **Shiyeli** prev. Chiili. Kzylorda, S Kazakhstan 44°13′N 66°46′E
Shizilu see Junan
160 H13 **Shizong** var. Danfeng. Yunnan, SW China 24°53′N 104°E
165 R10 **Shizugawa** Miyagi, Honshū, NE Japan 38°40′N 141°26′E
165 T5 **Shizunai** Hokkaidō, NE Japan 42°20′N 142°24′E
165 M14 **Shizuoka** var. Sizuoka. Shizuoka, Honshū, S Japan 34°59′N 138°20′E
164 M13 **Shizuoka** off. Shizuoka-ken, var. Sizuoka. ◆ prefecture Honshū, S Japan
Shizuoka-ken see Shizuoka
Shklov see Shklow
119 N15 **Shklow** Rus. Shklov. Mahilyowskaya Voblasts', E Belarus 54°13′N 30°18′E
113 K18 **Shkodër** var. Shkodra, It. Scutari, SCr. Skadar. Shkodër, NW Albania 42°03′N 19°31′E
113 K17 **Shkodër** ◆ district NW Albania
Shkodra see Shkodër
Shkodrës, Liqeni i see Scutari, Lake
113 L20 **Shkumbinit, Lumi i** var. Shkumbî, Shkumbin. ≈ C Albania
Shkumbî/Shkumbin see Shkumbinit, Lumi i
Shligigh, Cuan see Sligo Bay
122 L4 **Shmidta, Ostrov** island Severnaya Zemlya, N Russian Federation
183 S10 **Shoalhaven River** ≈ New South Wales, SE Australia
11 W16 **Shoal Lake** Manitoba, S Canada 50°28′N 100°36′W
31 O15 **Shoals** Indiana, N USA 38°40′N 86°47′W
164 I13 **Shōdo-shima** island SW Japan
Shōka see Zhanghua
122 M5 **Shokal'skogo, Proliv** strait N Russian Federation
147 T14 **Shokhdara, Qatorkŭhi** Rus. Shakhdarinskiy Khrebet. ▲▲ SE Tajikistan
145 T15 **Shokpar** Kaz. Shoqpar; prev. Chokpar. Zhambyl, S Kazakhstan 43°49′N 74°25′E
145 P15 **Sholakkorgan** var. Chulakkurgan. Yuzhnyy Kazakhstan, S Kazakhstan 43°45′N 69°10′E
145 N9 **Sholaksay** Kostanay, N Kazakhstan 51°45′N 64°45′E
Sholāpur see Solāpur
Sholdaneshty see Şoldăneşti
145 W15 **Shonzhy** prev. Chundzha. Almaty, SE Kazakhstan 43°32′N 79°28′E
Shoqpar see Shokpar
155 G21 **Shoranūr** Kerala, SW India 10°53′N 76°06′E
155 G16 **Shorāpur** Karnātaka, C India 16°34′N 76°48′E
147 O14 **Sho'rchi** Rus. Shurchi. Surkhondaryo Viloyati, S Uzbekistan 37°58′N 67°40′E
30 M11 **Shorewood** Illinois, N USA 41°31′N 88°12′W
Shorkazakhly, Solonchak see Kazakhlyshor, Solonchak
145 Q9 **Shortandy** Akmola, C Kazakhstan 51°45′N 71°01′E
149 O2 **Shōr Tappeh** var. Shortepa, Shor Tepe; prev. Shūr Tappeh. Balkh, N Afghanistan 37°22′N 66°49′E
Shortepa/Shor Tepe see Shōr Tappeh
186 J7 **Shortland Island** var. Alu. island Shortland Islands, NW Solomon Islands
Shosambetsu see Shosanbetsu
165 S2 **Shosanbetsu** var. Shosambetsu. Hokkaidō, NE Japan 44°31′N 141°47′E
33 O15 **Shoshone** Idaho, NW USA 42°56′N 114°24′W
35 T6 **Shoshone Mountains** ▲▲ Nevada, W USA
33 U12 **Shoshone River** ≈ Wyoming, C USA
83 I19 **Shoshong** Central, SE Botswana 23°02′S 26°31′E
33 V14 **Shoshoni** Wyoming, C USA 43°13′N 108°06′W
Shōshū see Sangju
117 S2 **Shostka** Sums'ka Oblast', NE Ukraine 51°52′N 33°30′E
185 C21 **Shotover** ≈ South Island, New Zealand
146 H9 **Shovot** Rus. Shavat. Xorazm Viloyati, W Uzbekistan 41°41′N 60°13′E
37 N12 **Show Low** Arizona, SW USA 34°15′N 110°01′W
Show Me State see Missouri
125 O4 **Shoyna** Nenetskiy Avtonomnyy Okrug, NW Russian Federation 67°50′N 44°09′E
124 M11 **Shozhma** Arkhangel'skaya Oblast', NW Russian Federation 61°57′N 40°10′E
117 Q7 **Shpola** Cherkas'ka Oblast', N Ukraine 49°00′N 31°27′E
Shqipëria/Shqipërisë, Republika e see Albania
22 G5 **Shreveport** Louisiana, S USA 32°32′N 93°45′W
97 K19 **Shrewsbury** hist. Scrobesbyrig'. W England, United Kingdom 52°43′N 02°45′W
152 D11 **Shri Mohangarh** prev. Sri Mohangorh. Rājasthān, NW India 27°17′N 71°18′E
153 S16 **Shrīrāmpur** prev. Serampore, Serampur. West Bengal, NE India 22°44′N 88°20′E
97 K19 **Shropshire** cultural region W England, United Kingdom
113 N17 **Shtime** Serb. Štimlje. C Kosovo 42°27′N 21°03′E
145 S16 **Shu** Kaz. Shū. Zhambyl, SE Kazakhstan 43°34′N 73°41′E
129 Q7 **Shu** Kaz. Shū; prev. Chu. ≈ Kazakhstan/Kyrgyzstan
160 G13 **Shuangbai** var. Tuodian. Yunnan, SW China 24°45′N 101°38′E
163 W9 **Shuangcheng** Heilongjiang, NE China 45°20′N 126°21′E
Shuangcheng see Zherong
160 E14 **Shuangjiang** var. Weiyuan. Yunnan, SW China 23°28′N 99°43′E
Shuangjiang see Jiangkou
Shuangjiang see Tongdao
163 U10 **Shuangliao** var. Zhengjiatun. Jilin, NE China 43°31′N 123°32′E
Shuang-liao see Liaoyuan
Shuangshipu see Fengxian
163 Y7 **Shuangyashan** var. Shuang-ya-shan. Heilongjiang, NE China 46°37′N 131°10′E
Shuang-ya-shan see Shuangyashan
Shu'aymiah see Shu'aymīyah
141 W12 **Shu'aymīyah** var. Shu'aymiah. S Oman 17°55′N 55°39′E
Shubarkuduk see Shubarkudyk
144 I10 **Shubarkudyk** prev. Shubarkuduk, Kaz. Shubarqudyq. Aktyubinsk, W Kazakhstan 49°09′N 56°31′E
Shubarqudyq see Shubarkudyk
145 N12 **Shubar-Tengiz, Ozero** ◎ C Kazakhstan
39 S5 **Shublik Mountains** ▲▲ Alaska, USA
Shubrā al Khaymah see Shubrâ el Kheima
121 U13 **Shubrâ el Kheima** var. Shubrā al Khaymah. N Egypt 30°06′N 31°15′E
158 E8 **Shufu** var. Tuokezhake. Xinjiang Uygur Zizhiqu, NW China 39°18′N 75°43′E
147 S14 **Shughnon, Qatorkŭhi** Rus. Shugnanskiy Khrebet. ▲▲ SE Tajikistan
Shugnanskiy Khrebet see Shughnon, Qatorkŭhi
161 Q6 **Shu He** ≈ E China
Shuicheng see Lupanshui
Shuiding see Huocheng
Shuidong see Dianbai
Shuiji see Laixi
Shū-Ile Taūlary see Gory Shu-Ile
Shuilocheng see Zhuanglang
Shuiluo see Zhuanglang
149 T10 **Shujāābād** Punjab, E Pakistan 29°53′N 71°23′E
Shū, Kazakhstan see Shu
Shū, Kazakhstan/ Kyrgyzstan see Shu
163 W9 **Shulan** Jilin, NE China 44°28′N 126°57′E
158 E8 **Shule** Xinjiang Uygur Zizhiqu, NW China 39°19′N 76°06′E
Shuleh see Shule He
159 Q8 **Shule He** var. Shuleh, Sulo. ≈ C China
30 K9 **Shullsburg** Wisconsin, N USA 42°37′N 90°12′W
Shulu see Xinji
39 N16 **Shumagin Islands** island group Alaska, USA
146 G7 **Shumanay** Qoraqalpog'iston Respublikasi, W Uzbekistan 42°42′N 58°56′E
114 M8 **Shumen** Shumen, NE Bulgaria 43°17′N 26°57′E
114 M8 **Shumen** ◆ province NE Bulgaria

◆ Country
● Country Capital
◇ Dependent Territory
○ Dependent Territory Capital
◆ Administrative Regions
✈ International Airport
▲ Mountain
▲▲ Mountain Range
Volcano
≈ River
◎ Lake
⊠ Reservoir

127 P4 **Shumerlya** Chuvashskaya Respublika, W Russian Federation 55°31′N 46°24′E
122 G11 **Shumikha** Kurganskaya Oblast', C Russian Federation 55°12′N 63°09′E
118 M12 **Shumilina** *Rus.* Shumilino. Vitsyebskaya Voblasts', NE Belarus 55°18′N 29°37′E
Shumilino *see* Shumilina
123 V11 **Shumshu, Ostrov** *island* SE Russian Federation
116 K5 **Shums'k** Ternopil's'ka Oblast', W Ukraine 50°06′N 26°04′E
Shūnan *see* Tokuyama
39 O7 **Shungnak** Alaska, USA 66°53′N 157°08′W
Shunsen *see* Chuncheon
Shuoxian *see* Shuozhou
161 N3 **Shuozhou** *var.* Shuoxian. Shanxi, C China 39°20′N 112°25′E
141 P16 **Shuqrah** *var.* Shaqrā. SW Yemen 13°26′N 45°44′E
Shurab *see* Shūrob
Shurchi *see* Sho'rchi
147 R11 **Shūrob** *Rus.* Shurab. NW Tajikistan 40°02′N 70°31′E
143 T10 **Shūr, Rūd-e** ~ E Iran
Shūr Tappeh *see* Shōr Tappeh
83 K17 **Shurugwi** *prev.* Selukwe. Midlands, C Zimbabwe 19°40′S 30°00′E
142 L8 **Shūsh** *anc.* Susa, *Bibl.* Shushan. Khūzestān, SW Iran 32°12′N 48°20′E
Shushan *see* Shūsh
142 L9 **Shūshtar** *var.* Shustar, Shushter. Khūzestān, SW Iran 32°03′N 48°51′E
Shushter/Shustar *see* Shūshtar
141 T9 **Shuṭfah, Qalamat** *well* E Saudi Arabia
139 V9 **Shuwayjah, Hawr ash** *var.* Hawr as Suwayqiyah. ◎ E Iraq
124 M16 **Shuya** Ivanovskaya Oblast', W Russian Federation 56°51′N 41°24′E
39 Q14 **Shuyak Island** *island* Alaska, USA
166 M4 **Shwebo** Sagaing, C Myanmar (Burma) 22°35′N 95°42′E
166 L7 **Shwedaung** Bago, Myanmar (Burma) 18°44′N 95°12′E
166 M7 **Shwegyin** Bago, Myanmar (Burma) 17°56′N 96°59′E
167 N4 **Shweli** *Chin.* Longchuan Jiang. ~ Myanmar (Burma)/China
166 M6 **Shwemyo** Mandalay, C Myanmar (Burma) 20°04′N 96°13′E
145 S14 **Shyganak** *var.* Čiganak, Chiganak, *Kaz.* Shyghanaq. Zhambyl, SE Kazakhstan 45°10′N 73°55′E
Shyghanaq *see* Shyganak
Shyghys Qazagastan Oblysy *see* Vostochnyy Kazakhstan
Shyghys Qongyrat *see* Shygys Konyrat
145 T12 **Shygys Konyrat**, *Kaz.* Shyghys Qongyrat. Karaganda, C Kazakhstan 47°01′N 75°05′E
119 M19 **Shyichy** *Rus.* Shiichi. Homyel'skaya Voblasts', SE Belarus 52°15′N 29°14′E
145 Q17 **Shymkent** *prev.* Chimkent. Yuzhnyy Kazakhstan, S Kazakhstan 42°19′N 69°36′E
144 H9 **Shyngghyrlau** *prev.* Chingirlau. Zapadnyy Kazakhstan, W Kazakhstan 51°10′N 53°44′E
144 G9 **Shyngyrlau** *prev.* Utva. ~ NW Kazakhstan
145 W11 **Shynkozha** *prev.* Shingozha. Vostochnyy Kazakhstan, E Kazakhstan 47°46′N 80°38′E
152 J5 **Shyok** Jammu and Kashmir, NW India 34°13′N 78°12′E
117 S9 **Shyroke** *Rus.* Shirokoye. Dnipropetrovs'ka Oblast', E Ukraine 47°41′N 33°16′E
117 O9 **Shyryayeve** Odes'ka Oblast', SW Ukraine 47°21′N 30°11′E
117 S5 **Shyshaky** Poltavs'ka Oblast', C Ukraine 49°54′N 34°00′E
119 K17 **Shyshchytsy** *Rus.* Shishchitsy. Minskaya Voblasts', C Belarus 53°13′N 27°33′E
149 Y3 **Siachen Muztāgh** ▲ NE Pakistan
Siadehan *see* Tākestān
148 M13 **Siāhān Range** ▲▲ W Pakistan
142 I1 **Siāh Chashmeh** *var.* Chālderān. Āzarbāyjān-e Gharbī, N Iran 39°02′N 44°22′E
149 W7 **Siālkot** Punjab, NE Pakistan 32°29′N 74°35′E
186 E7 **Sialum** Morobe, C Papua New Guinea 06°02′S 147°37′E
Siam *see* Thailand
Siam, Gulf of *see* Thailand, Gulf of
Sian *see* Xi'an
Siang *see* Brahmaputra
Siangtan *see* Xiangtan
169 N8 **Siantan, Pulau** *island* Kepulauan Anambas, W Indonesia
54 H11 **Siare, Río** ~ C Colombia
171 R6 **Siargao Island** *island* S Philippines
186 F72 **Siassi** Umboi Island, C Papua New Guinea 05°34′S 147°50′E
115 D14 **Siátista** Dytikí Makedonía, N Greece 40°16′N 21°34′E
166 K4 **Siatlai** Chin State, Myanmar (Burma) 22°05′N 93°36′E
171 P6 **Siaton** Negros, C Philippines 09°03′N 123°03′E
171 P6 **Siaton Point** *headland* Negros, C Philippines 09°03′N 123°00′E
118 F11 **Šiauliai** *Ger.* Schaulen. Siauliai, N Lithuania 55°55′N 23°21′E
118 E11 **Šiauliai** ◈ *province* N Lithuania
171 Q10 **Siau, Pulau** *island* N Indonesia
83 J15 **Siavonga** Southern, SE Zambia 16°33′S 28°42′E
Siazan' *see* Siyäzän
Sibah *see* As Sībah
107 N20 **Sibari** Calabria, S Italy 39°45′N 16°26′E
Sibata *see* Shibata
127 X6 **Sibay** Respublika Bashkortostan, W Russian Federation 52°40′N 58°39′E
93 M19 **Sibbo** *Fin.* Sipoo. Etelä-Suomi, S Finland 60°22′N 25°20′E
112 D13 **Šibenik** *It.* Sebenico. Šibenik-Knin, S Croatia 43°43′N 15°54′E
Sibenik *see* Šibenik-Knin
112 E13 **Šibenik-Knin** *off.* Šibenska Županija, *var.* Sibenik. ◈ *province* S Croatia
Šibenik-Knin *see* Drniš
Šibenska Županija *see* Šibenik-Knin
Siberia *see* Sibir'
Siberoet *see* Siberut, Pulau
168 H12 **Siberut, Pulau** *prev.* Siberoet. *island* Kepulauan Mentawai, W Indonesia
168 I12 **Siberut, Selat** *strait* W Indonesia
149 P11 **Sibi** Baluchistān, SW Pakistan 29°31′N 67°54′E
186 B9 **Sibidiri** Western, SW Papua New Guinea 08°58′S 142°14′E
123 N10 **Sibir'** *var.* Siberia. *physical region* NE Russian Federation
79 F20 **Sibiti** Lékoumou, S Congo 03°41′S 13°20′E
81 G21 **Sibiti** ~ C Tanzania
116 I12 **Sibiu** *Ger.* Hermannstadt, *Hung.* Nagyszeben. Sibiu, C Romania 45°48′N 24°09′E
116 I11 **Sibiu** ◈ *county* C Romania
29 S11 **Sibley** Iowa, C USA 43°24′N 95°45′W
169 R9 **Sibu** Sarawak, East Malaysia 02°18′N 111°49′E
42 G2 **Sibun** ~ E Belize
79 I15 **Sibut** *prev.* Fort-Sibut. Kémo, S Central African Republic 05°44′N 19°07′E
171 P4 **Sibuyan Island** *island* C Philippines
189 U1 **Sibylla Island** *island* N Marshall Islands
11 N16 **Sicamous** British Columbia, SW Canada 50°49′N 118°52′W
Sichelburger Gerbirge *see* Gorjanci
167 N14 **Sichon** *var.* Ban Sichon, Si Chon. Nakhon Si Thammarat, SW Thailand 09°03′N 99°51′E
Si Chon *see* Sichon
160 H9 **Sichuan** *var.* Chuan, Sichuan Sheng, Ssu-ch'uan, Szechuan, Szechwan. ◈ *province* C China
160 I9 **Sichuan Pendi** *basin* C China
Sichuan Sheng *see* Sichuan
103 S16 **Sicie, Cap** *headland* SE France 43°03′N 05°50′E
107 J24 **Sicilia** *Eng.* Sicily; *anc.* Trinacria. ◈ *region* Italy, C Mediterranean Sea
107 M24 **Sicilia** *Eng.* Sicily; *anc.* Trinacria. *island* Italy, C Mediterranean Sea
Sicilian Channel *see* Sicily, Strait of
107 H24 **Sicily, Strait of** *var.* Sicilian Channel. *strait* C Mediterranean Sea
42 K5 **Sico Tinto, Río** *var.* Río Negro. ~ NE Honduras
57 H16 **Sicuani** Cusco, S Peru 14°21′S 71°13′W
112 J10 **Šid** Vojvodina, NW Serbia 45°07′N 19°13′E
115 A15 **Sidári** Kérkyra, Iónia Nisiá, Greece, C Mediterranean Sea 39°47′N 19°43′E
169 Q11 **Sidas** Borneo, C Indonesia 0°24′N 109°46′E
98 O5 **Siddeburen** Groningen, NE Netherlands 53°15′N 06°52′E
154 D9 **Siddhapur** *prev.* Siddhpur, Sidhpur. Gujarāt, W India 23°57′N 72°28′E
Siddhpur *see* Siddhapur
155 I15 **Siddipet** Andhra Pradesh, C India 18°10′N 78°54′E
77 N14 **Sidéradougou** SW Burkina 10°39′N 04°16′W
107 N23 **Siderno** Calabria, SW Italy 38°18′N 16°19′E
Siders *see* Sierre
154 L9 **Sidhi** Madhya Pradesh, C India 24°24′N 81°54′E
Sidhirókastron *see* Sidirókastro
Sidhpur *see* Siddhapur
75 U7 **Sīdī Barrānī** NW Egypt 31°38′N 25°58′E
74 I6 **Sidi Bel Abbès** *var.* Sidi bel Abbès, Sidi-Bel-Abbès. NW Algeria 35°12′N 00°43′W
74 E7 **Sidi-Bennour** W Morocco 32°39′N 08°28′W
74 M6 **Sidi Bouzid** *var.* Gammouda, Sīdī Bu Zayd. C Tunisia 35°05′N 09°20′E
Sīdī Bu Zayd *see* Sidi Bouzid
74 D8 **Sidi-Ifni** SW Morocco 29°33′N 10°04′W
74 G6 **Sidi-Kacem** *prev.* Petitjean. N Morocco 34°21′N 05°46′W
114 G12 **Sidirókastro** *prev.* Sidhirókastron. Kentrikí Makedonía, NE Greece 41°14′N 23°23′E
194 L12 **Sidley, Mount** ▲ Antarctica 76°39′S 124°48′W
29 S16 **Sidney** Iowa, C USA 40°45′N 95°39′W
33 Y7 **Sidney** Montana, NW USA 47°42′N 104°10′W
28 J15 **Sidney** Nebraska, C USA 41°09′N 102°57′W
18 I11 **Sidney** New York, NE USA 42°18′N 75°21′W
31 R13 **Sidney** Ohio, N USA 40°16′N 84°09′W
23 T2 **Sidney Lanier, Lake** ⊠ Georgia, SE USA
122 J9 **Sidorovsk** Yamalo-Nenetskiy Avtonomnyy Okrug, N Russian Federation 66°34′N 82°12′E
Sidra *see* Surt
Sidra/Sidra, Gulf of *see* Surt, Khalīj, N Libya
Siebenbürgen *see* Transylvania
Sieben Dörfer *see* Săcele
110 O12 **Siedlce** *Ger.* Sedlez, *Rus.* Sesdlets. Mazowieckie, C Poland 52°10′N 22°18′E
101 E16 **Sieg** ~ W Germany
101 F16 **Siegen** Nordrhein-Westfalen, W Germany 50°53′N 08°02′E
109 X4 **Sieghartskirchen** Niederösterreich, E Austria 48°13′N 16°01′E
167 S12 **Siĕmbok** *prev.* Phumĭ Siĕmbok. Stœng Trêng, N Cambodia 13°28′N 105°59′E
110 O11 **Siemiatycze** Podlaskie, NE Poland 52°27′N 22°52′E
167 T11 **Siĕmpang** Stœng Trêng, NE Cambodia 14°07′N 106°24′E
167 R11 **Siĕmréab** *prev.* Siemreap. Siĕmréab, NW Cambodia 13°21′N 103°50′E
Siemreap *see* Siĕmréab
106 G12 **Siena** *Fr.* Sienne; *anc.* Saena Julia. Toscana, C Italy 43°20′N 11°20′E
Sienne *see* Siena
92 K12 **Sieppijärvi** Lappi, NW Finland 67°09′N 23°58′E
110 J13 **Sieradz** Sieradz, C Poland 51°36′N 18°42′E
110 K10 **Sierpc** Mazowieckie, C Poland 52°51′N 19°44′E
24 I9 **Sierra Blanca** Texas, SW USA 31°10′N 105°22′W
37 S14 **Sierra Blanca Peak** ▲ New Mexico, SW USA 33°22′N 105°48′W
35 P5 **Sierra City** California, W USA 39°34′N 120°35′W
63 I16 **Sierra Colorada** Río Negro, S Argentina 40°37′S 67°48′W
63 J16 **Sierra Grande** Río Negro, E Argentina 41°34′S 65°21′W
76 G15 **Sierra Leone** *off.* Republic of Sierra Leone. ◆ *republic* W Africa
64 M13 **Sierra Leone Basin** *undersea feature* E Atlantic Ocean 05°00′N 17°00′W
66 K8 **Sierra Leone Fracture Zone** *tectonic feature* E Atlantic Ocean
Sierra Leone, Republic of *see* Sierra Leone
Sierra Leone Ridge *see* Sierra Leone Rise
64 L13 **Sierra Leone Rise** *var.* Sierra Leone Ridge, Sierra Leone Schwelle. *undersea feature* E Atlantic Ocean 05°30′N 21°00′W
Sierra Leone Schwelle *see* Sierra Leone Rise
40 L7 **Sierra Mojada** Coahuila, NE Mexico 27°13′N 103°42′W
37 N16 **Sierra Vista** Arizona, SW USA 31°33′N 110°18′W
108 D10 **Sierre** *Ger.* Siders. Valais, SW Switzerland 46°18′N 07°33′E
36 L16 **Sierrita Mountains** ▲ Arizona, SW USA
Siete Moai *see* Ahu Akivi
76 M15 **Sifié** W Ivory Coast 07°59′N 06°55′W
115 I21 **Sífnos** *anc.* Siphnos. *island* Kykládes, Greece, Aegean Sea
115 I21 **Sífnou, Stenó** *strait* SE Greece
Siga *see* Shiga
103 P16 **Sigean** Aude, S France 43°02′N 02°58′E
Sighet *see* Sighetu Marmaţiei
Sighetul Marmaţiei *see* Sighetu Marmaţiei
116 I8 **Sighetu Marmaţiei** *var.* Sighet, Sighetul Marmaţiei, *Hung.* Máramarossziget. Maramureş, N Romania 47°56′N 23°53′E
116 I11 **Sighişoara** *Ger.* Schässburg, *Hung.* Segesvár. Mureş, C Romania 46°12′N 24°48′E
168 G7 **Sigli** Sumatera, W Indonesia 05°21′N 95°56′E
92 J1 **Siglufjördhur** Nordhurland Vestra, N Iceland 66°09′N 18°56′W
101 H23 **Sigmaringen** Baden-Württemberg, S Germany 48°04′N 09°12′E
101 N20 **Signalberg** ▲ SE Germany 49°30′N 12°34′E
36 I13 **Signal Peak** ▲ Arizona, SW USA 33°20′N 114°03′W
Signan *see* Xi'an
194 H1 **Signy** *UK research station* South Orkney Islands, Antarctica 60°27′S 45°35′W
29 X15 **Sigourney** Iowa, C USA 41°19′N 92°12′W
115 K17 **Sígri, Akrotírio** *headland* Lésvos, E Greece 39°12′N 25°49′E
Sigsbee Deep *see* Mexico Basin
47 N2 **Sigsbee Escarpment** *undersea feature* N Gulf of Mexico 26°00′N 92°30′W
56 C8 **Sigsig** Azuay, S Ecuador 03°04′S 78°50′W
95 O15 **Sigtuna** Stockholm, C Sweden 59°36′N 17°44′E
42 H6 **Siguatepeque** Comayagua, W Honduras 14°39′N 87°48′W
105 P7 **Sigüenza** Castilla-La Mancha, C Spain 41°04′N 02°38′W
105 R4 **Sigües** Aragón, NE Spain 42°39′N 01°00′W
76 K13 **Siguiri** NE Guinea 11°26′N 09°08′W
118 G8 **Sigulda** *Ger.* Segewold. C Latvia 57°08′N 24°51′E
167 Q14 **Sihanoukville** *var.* Kâmpóng Saôm; *prev.* Kompong Som. Kâmpóng Saôm, SW Cambodia 10°38′N 103°30′E
108 G8 **Sihlsee** ◎ NW Switzerland
93 K18 **Siikainen** Länsi-Suomi, SW Finland 61°52′N 21°49′E
93 M16 **Siilinjärvi** Itä-Suomi, C Finland 63°05′N 27°40′E
137 R15 **Siirt** *var.* Sert; *anc.* Tigranocerta. Siirt, SE Turkey 37°56′N 41°56′E
137 R15 **Siirt** *var.* Sert. ◈ *province* SE Turkey
187 N8 **Sikaiana** *var.* Stewart Islands. *island group* W Solomon Islands
Sikandarabad *see* Secunderābād
152 J11 **Sikandra Rao** Uttar Pradesh, N India 27°42′N 78°21′E
10 M11 **Sikanni Chief** British Columbia, W Canada 57°16′N 122°44′W
10 M11 **Sikanni Chief** ~ British Columbia, W Canada
152 H11 **Sīkar** Rājasthān, N India 27°33′N 75°12′E
76 M13 **Sikasso** Sikasso, S Mali 11°21′N 05°43′W
76 L13 **Sikasso** ◈ *region* SW Mali
167 N3 **Sikaw** Kachin State, Myanmar (Burma) 23°50′N 97°04′E
83 H14 **Sikelenge** Western, W Zambia 14°51′S 24°13′E
27 Y7 **Sikeston** Missouri, C USA 36°52′N 89°35′W
93 J14 **Sikfors** Norrbotten, N Sweden 65°29′N 21°17′E
123 T14 **Sikhote-Alin', Khrebet** ▲▲ SE Russian Federation
Siking *see* Xi'an
115 J22 **Síkinos** *island* Kykládes, Greece, Aegean Sea
153 S11 **Sikkim** *Tib.* Denjong. ◈ *state* N India
111 I26 **Siklós** Baranya, SW Hungary 45°51′N 18°18′E
Sikoku *see* Shikoku
Sikoku Basin *see* Shikoku Basin
83 G14 **Sikongo** Western, W Zambia 15°03′S 22°07′E
Sikotu Ko *see* Shikotsu-ko
Sikouri/Sikoúrion *see* Sykoúrio
123 P8 **Siktyakh** Respublika Sakha (Yakutiya), NE Russian Federation 69°45′N 124°42′E
118 D12 **Šilalė** Tauragė, W Lithuania 55°29′N 22°10′E
106 G5 **Silandro** *Ger.* Schlanders. Trentino-Alto Adige, N Italy 46°39′N 10°55′E
41 N12 **Silao** Guanajuato, C Mexico 20°56′N 101°28′W
Silarius *see* Sele
153 W14 **Silchar** Assam, NE India 24°49′N 92°48′E
108 G9 **Silenen** Uri, C Switzerland 46°49′N 08°39′E
21 T9 **Siler City** North Carolina, SE USA 35°43′N 79°27′W
33 U11 **Silesia** Montana, NW USA 45°32′N 108°52′W
110 F13 **Silesia** *physical region* SW Poland
74 K12 **Silet** S Algeria 22°45′N 04°51′E
Siletį *see* Silety
Siletitengiz *see* Siletyteniz, Ozero
145 R8 **Silety** *prev.* Sileti. ~ N Kazakhstan
145 R7 **Siletyteniz, Ozero** *Kaz.* Siletitengiz. ◎ N Kazakhstan
172 H16 **Silhouette** *island* Inner Islands, SE Seychelles
136 I17 **Silifke** *anc.* Seleucia. Içel, S Turkey 36°22′N 33°57′E
Siliguri *see* Shiliguri
156 J10 **Siling Co** ◎ W China
Silinhot *see* Xilinhot
192 G14 **Silisili, Mauga** ▲ Savai'i, C Samoa 13°37′S 172°26′W
114 M6 **Silistra** *var.* Silistria; *anc.* Durostorum. Silistra, NE Bulgaria 44°06′N 27°17′E
114 M7 **Silistra** ◈ *province* NE Bulgaria
Silistria *see* Silistra
136 D10 **Silivri** İstanbul, NW Turkey 41°05′N 28°15′E
94 L13 **Siljan** ◎ C Sweden
95 G22 **Silkeborg** Midtjylland, C Denmark 56°10′N 09°34′E
109 M8 **Sill** ~ W Austria
105 S10 **Silla** Valenciana, E Spain 39°22′N 00°25′W
62 H3 **Sillajguay, Cordillera** ▲ N Chile 19°45′S 68°39′W
118 K3 **Sillamäe** *Ger.* Sillamäggi. Ida-Virumaa, NE Estonia 59°23′N 27°45′E
Sillamäggi *see* Sillamäe
Sillein *see* Žilina
109 P9 **Sillian** Tirol, W Austria 46°45′N 12°25′E
112 B10 **Šilo** Primorje-Gorski Kotar, NW Croatia 45°09′N 14°39′E
27 R9 **Siloam Springs** Arkansas, C USA 36°11′N 94°32′W
25 X10 **Silsbee** Texas, SW USA 30°21′N 94°10′W
143 W15 **Sīlūp, Rūd-e** ~ SE Iran
118 C12 **Šilutė** *Ger.* Heydekrug. Klaipėda, W Lithuania 55°20′N 21°30′E
137 Q15 **Silvan** Diyarbakır, SE Turkey 38°08′N 41°E
108 J10 **Silvaplana** Graubünden, S Switzerland 46°27′N 09°45′E
Silva Porto *see* Kuito
58 M12 **Silva, Recife do** *reef* E Brazil
154 D12 **Silvassa** Dādra and Nagar Haveli, W India 20°13′N 73°03′E
29 X4 **Silver Bay** Minnesota, N USA 47°17′N 91°15′W
37 P15 **Silver City** New Mexico, SW USA 32°47′N 108°16′W
18 D10 **Silver Creek** New York, NE USA 42°32′N 79°10′W
37 N12 **Silver Creek** ~ Arizona, SW USA
27 P4 **Silver Lake** Kansas, C USA 39°06′N 95°51′W
32 I14 **Silver Lake** Oregon, NW USA 43°07′N 121°04′W
35 T9 **Silver Peak Range** ▲▲ Nevada, W USA
21 W3 **Silver Spring** Maryland, NE USA 39°00′N 77°01′W
Silver State *see* Colorado
Silver State *see* Nevada
37 Q7 **Silverton** Colorado, C USA 37°48′N 107°39′W
18 K16 **Silverton** New Jersey, NE USA 40°00′N 74°09′W
32 G11 **Silverton** Oregon, NW USA 45°00′N 122°46′W
25 N4 **Silverton** Texas, SW USA 34°28′N 101°18′W
104 G14 **Silves** Faro, S Portugal 37°11′N 08°26′W
54 D12 **Silvia** Cauca, SW Colombia 02°37′N 76°24′W
108 J9 **Silvrettagruppe** ▲ Austria/Switzerland
Sily-Vajdej *see* Vulcan
108 L7 **Silz** Tirol, W Austria 47°17′N 11°00′E
172 I13 **Sima** Anjouan, SE Comoros 12°11′S 44°18′E
Simabara *see* Shimabara
83 H15 **Simakando** Western, W Zambia 16°43′S 24°46′E
Simane *see* Shimane
119 L20 **Simanichy** *Rus.* Simonichi. Homyel'skaya Voblasts', SE Belarus 51°53′N 28°05′E
160 F14 **Simao** Yunnan, SW China 22°30′N 101°06′E
153 P12 **Simarā** Central, C Nepal 27°14′N 85°00′E
14 I8 **Simard, Lac** ◎ Québec, SE Canada
136 D13 **Simav** Kütahya, W Turkey 39°05′N 28°59′E
136 D13 **Simav Çayı** ~ NW Turkey
79 L18 **Simba** Orientale, N Dem. Rep. Congo 0°46′N 22°54′E
186 C7 **Simbai** Madang, N Papua New Guinea 05°12′S 144°33′E
Simbirsk *see* Ul'yanovsk
14 F17 **Simcoe** Ontario, S Canada 42°50′N 80°19′W
14 H14 **Simcoe, Lake** ◎ Ontario, S Canada
80 J11 **Simēn** ▲▲ N Ethiopia
114 K11 **Simeonovgrad** *prev.* Maritsa. Khaskovo, S Bulgaria 42°03′N 25°36′E
116 G11 **Simeria** *Ger.* Pischk, *Hung.* Piski. Hunedoara, W Romania 45°51′N 23°00′E
107 L24 **Simeto** ~ Sicilia, Italy, C Mediterranean Sea
168 G9 **Simeulue, Pulau** *island* NW Indonesia
117 T13 **Simferopol'** Avtonomna Respublika Krym, S Ukraine 44°55′N 33°06′E
117 T13 **Simferopol'** ✈ Avtonomna Respublika Krym, S Ukraine 44°55′N 34°04′E
Simi *see* Sými
152 M9 **Simikot** Far Western, NW Nepal 30°02′N 81°49′E
54 F7 **Simití** Bolívar, N Colombia 07°57′N 73°57′W
114 G11 **Simitli** Blagoevgrad, SW Bulgaria 41°57′N 23°06′E
35 S15 **Simi Valley** California, W USA 34°16′N 118°47′W
Simizu *see* Shimizu
Simla *see* Shimla
Şimlăul Silvaniei/Şimleul Silvaniei *see* Şimleu Silvaniei
116 G9 **Şimleu Silvaniei** *Hung.* Szilágysomlyó; *prev.* Şimlăul Silvaniei, Şimleul Silvaniei. Sălaj, NW Romania 47°12′N 22°49′E
Simmer *see* Simmerbach
101 E19 **Simmerbach** *var.* Simmer. ~ W Germany
101 F18 **Simmern** Rheinland-Pfalz, W Germany 50°00′N 07°30′E
22 I7 **Simmesport** Louisiana, S USA 30°58′N 91°48′W
119 F14 **Simnas** Alytus, S Lithuania 54°23′N 23°40′E
92 L13 **Simo** Lappi, NW Finland 65°40′N 25°04′E
Simoda *see* Shimoda
Simodate *see* Shimodate
92 M13 **Simojärvi** ◎ N Finland
92 L13 **Simojoki** ~ NW Finland
41 U15 **Simojovel** *var.* Simojovel de Allende. Chiapas, SE Mexico 17°14′N 92°40′W
Simojovel de Allende *see* Simojovel
56 B7 **Simon Bolívar** *var.* Guayaquil. ✈ (Quayaquil) Guayas, W Ecuador 02°16′S 79°54′W
54 L5 **Simon Bolívar** ✈ (Caracas) Vargas, N Venezuela 10°33′N 66°54′W
Simonichi *see* Simanichy
14 M12 **Simon, Lac** ◎ Québec, SE Canada
Simonoseki *see* Shimonoseki
Šimonovany *see* Partizánske
Simonstad *see* Simon's Town
83 E26 **Simon's Town** *var.* Simonstad. Western Cape, SW South Africa 34°12′S 18°26′E
Simony *see* Partizánske
Simpeln *see* Simplon
99 M18 **Simpelveld** Limburg, SE Netherlands 50°50′N 05°59′E
108 E11 **Simplon** *var.* Simpeln. Valais, SW Switzerland 46°13′N 08°01′E
108 E11 **Simplon Pass** *pass* S Switzerland
106 C6 **Simplon Tunnel** *tunnel* Italy/Switzerland
Simpson *see* Fort Simpson
182 G1 **Simpson Desert** *desert* Northern Territory/South Australia
10 J9 **Simpson Peak** ▲ British Columbia, W Canada 59°43′N 131°29′W
9 N7 **Simpson Peninsula** *peninsula* Nunavut, NE Canada
21 P11 **Simpsonville** South Carolina, SE USA 34°44′N 82°15′W
95 L23 **Simrishamn** Skåne, S Sweden 55°34′N 14°20′E
123 U13 **Simushir, Ostrov** *island* Kuril'skiye Ostrova, SE Russian Federation
168 G9 **Sinabang** Sumatera, W Indonesia 02°27′N 96°24′E
81 N15 **Sina Dhaqa** Galguduud, C Somalia 05°21′N 46°21′E
75 X8 **Sinai** *var.* Sinai Peninsula, *Ar.* Shibh Jazīrat Sīnā', Sīnā. *physical region* NE Egypt
116 J12 **Sinaia** Prahova, SE Romania 45°20′N 25°33′E
188 B16 **Sinajana** C Guam 13°28′N 144°45′E
40 H8 **Sinaloa** ◈ *state* C Mexico
54 H4 **Sinamaica** Zulia, NW Venezuela 11°06′N 71°52′W
163 X14 **Sinan-ni** SE North Korea 38°37′N 127°43′E
Sinā/Sinai Peninsula *see* Sinai
Sināwan *see* Sīnāwin
75 N8 **Sīnāwin** *var.* Sināwan. NW Libya 31°00′N 10°37′E
83 J16 **Sinazongwe** Southern, S Zambia 17°14′S 27°27′E
166 L6 **Sinbaungwe** Magway, W Myanmar (Burma) 19°44′N 95°10′E
166 L5 **Sinbyugyun** Magway, W Myanmar (Burma) 20°38′N 94°40′E
54 E6 **Since** Sucre, NW Colombia 09°14′N 75°08′W
54 E6 **Sincelejo** Sucre, NW Colombia 09°17′N 75°23′W
23 U4 **Sinclair, Lake** ⊠ Georgia, SE USA
10 M14 **Sinclair Mills** British Columbia, SW Canada 54°03′N 121°37′W
154 I8 **Sind** ~ N India
Sind *see* Sindh
95 H19 **Sindal** Nordjylland, N Denmark 57°29′N 10°13′E
171 P7 **Sindañgan** Mindanao, S Philippines 08°09′N 122°59′E
79 D19 **Sindara** Ngounié, W Gabon 01°07′S 10°41′E
152 E13 **Sindari** *prev.* Sindri. Rājasthān, N India 25°32′N 71°58′E
114 N8 **Sindel** Varna, E Bulgaria 43°07′N 27°35′E
101 H22 **Sindelfingen** Baden-Württemberg, SW Germany 48°43′N 09°E
155 G16 **Sindgi** Karnātaka, C India 17°01′N 76°22′E
149 Q14 **Sindh** *prev.* Sind. ◈ *province* SE Pakistan
118 G5 **Sindi** *Ger.* Zintenhof. Pärnumaa, SW Estonia 58°28′N 24°41′E
136 C13 **Sındırgı** Balıkesir, W Turkey 39°13′N 28°10′E
77 N14 **Sindou** SW Burkina 10°35′N 05°04′W
Sindri *see* Sindari
149 T9 **Sind Sāgar Doāb** *desert* E Pakistan
126 M11 **Sinegorskiy** Rostovskaya Oblast', SW Russian Federation 48°01′N 40°52′E
123 S9 **Sinegor'ye** Magadanskaya Oblast', E Russian Federation 62°04′N 150°33′E
114 O12 **Sinekli** İstanbul, NW Turkey 41°13′N 28°13′E
104 F12 **Sines** Setúbal, S Portugal 37°58′N 08°52′W
104 F12 **Sines, Cabo de** *headland* S Portugal 37°57′N 08°55′W
92 L12 **Sinettä** Lappi, NW Finland 66°39′N 25°25′E
186 H6 **Sinewit, Mount** ▲ New Britain, C Papua New Guinea 04°42′S 151°58′E
80 G11 **Singa** *var.* Sinja, Sinjah. Sinnar, E Sudan 13°11′N 33°55′E
78 J12 **Singako** Moyen-Chari, S Chad 09°52′N 19°31′E
Singan *see* Xi'an
168 K10 **Singapore** ● (Singapore) S Singapore 01°17′N 103°48′E
168 L10 **Singapore** *off.* Republic of Singapore. ◆ *republic* SE Asia
Singapore, Republic of *see* Singapore
169 U17 **Singaraja** Bali, C Indonesia 08°06′S 115°04′E
167 O10 **Sing Buri** *var.* Singhaburi. Sing Buri, C Thailand 14°56′N 100°21′E
101 H24 **Singen** Baden-Württemberg, S Germany 47°46′N 08°50′E
Sîngeorgiu de Pădure *see* Sângeorgiu de Pădure
Sîngeorz-Băi/Singeroz Băi *see* Sângeorz-Băi
116 M9 **Sîngerei** *var.* Sângerei; *prev.* Lazovsk. N Moldova 47°38′N 28°08′E
Singhaburi *see* Sing Buri
81 H21 **Singida** Singida, C Tanzania 04°45′S 34°48′E
81 G22 **Singida** ◈ *region* C Tanzania
Singidunum *see* Beograd
Singkaling Hkamti *see* Hkamti
171 N14 **Singkang** Sulawesi, C Indonesia 04°09′S 119°58′E
168 J11 **Singkarak, Danau** ◎ Sumatera, W Indonesia
169 N10 **Singkawang** Borneo, C Indonesia 0°57′N 108°57′E
168 M11 **Singkep, Pulau** *island* Kepulauan Lingga, W Indonesia
168 H9 **Singkilbaru** Sumatera, W Indonesia 02°18′N 97°47′E
183 T7 **Singleton** New South Wales, SE Australia 32°38′S 151°00′E
Singora *see* Songkhla
Singū *see* Shingū
Sining *see* Xining
107 D17 **Siniscola** Sardegna, Italy, C Mediterranean Sea 40°34′N 09°42′E
113 F14 **Sinj** Split-Dalmacija, SE Croatia 43°41′N 16°37′E
Sinjajevina *see* Sinjavina
139 P3 **Sinjār** Nīnawýa, NW Iraq 36°20′N 41°51′E
139 P2 **Sinjār, Jabal** ▲ N Iraq
Sinja/Sinjah *see* Singa
113 K15 **Sinjavina** *var.* Sinjajevina. ▲ C Montenegro
80 I7 **Sinkat** Red Sea, NE Sudan 18°52′N 36°51′E
Sinkiang/Sinkiang Uighur Autonomous Region *see* Xinjiang Uygur Zizhiqu
Sinmartin *see* Târnăveni
163 V13 **Sinmi-do** *island* NW North Korea
101 I18 **Sinn** ~ C Germany
Sinnamarie *see* Sinnamary
55 Y9 **Sinnamary** *var.* Sinnamarie. N French Guiana 05°23′N 53°00′W
80 G11 **Sinnar** ◈ *state* E Sudan
Sinneh *see* Sanandaj
18 E13 **Sinnemahoning Creek** ~ Pennsylvania, NE USA
Sînnicolau Mare *see* Sânnicolau Mare
Sinoe, Lacul *see* Sinoie, Lacul
Sinoia *see* Chinhoyi
117 N14 **Sinoie, Lacul** *prev.* Lacul Sinoe. *lagoon* SE Romania
59 H16 **Sinop** Mato Grosso, W Brazil 11°38′S 55°27′W
136 K10 **Sinop** *anc.* Sinope. Sinop, N Turkey 42°02′N 35°09′E
136 J10 **Sinop** ◈ *province* N Turkey
136 K10 **Sinop Burnu** *headland* N Turkey 42°02′N 35°12′E
Sinope *see* Sinop
Sino/Sinoe *see* Greenville
163 Y12 **Sinp'o** E North Korea 40°01′N 128°10′E
101 H20 **Sinsheim** Baden-Württemberg, SW Germany 49°15′N 08°53′E
Sintana *see* Sântana
169 R11 **Sintang** Borneo, C Indonesia 0°03′N 111°31′E
99 F14 **Sint Annaland** Zeeland, SW Netherlands 51°36′N 04°07′E
98 L5 **Sint Annaparochie** *Fris.* Sint Anne. Fryslân, N Netherlands 53°20′N 05°46′E
Sint Anne *see* Sint Annaparochie
45 V9 **Sint Eustatius** *Eng.* Saint Eustatius. *island* Sint Maarten
99 G19 **Sint-Genesius-Rode** *Fr.* Rhode-Saint-Genèse. Vlaams Brabant, C Belgium 50°45′N 04°21′E
99 F16 **Sint-Gillis-Waas** Oost-Vlaanderen, N Belgium 51°14′N 04°08′E
99 H17 **Sint-Katelijne-Waver** Antwerpen, C Belgium 51°05′N 04°31′E
99 E18 **Sint-Lievens-Houtem** Oost-Vlaanderen, NW Belgium 50°55′N 03°52′E
45 V9 **Sint Maarten** *Eng.* Saint Martin. ◇ *Dutch autonomous region* NE Caribbean Sea
99 F14 **Sint Maartensdijk** Zeeland, SW Netherlands 51°33′N 04°05′E
99 L19 **Sint-Martens-Voeren** *Fr.* Fouron-Saint-Martin. Limburg, NE Belgium 50°46′N 05°49′E
99 J14 **Sint-Michielsgestel** Noord-Brabant, S Netherlands 51°38′N 05°21′E
Sîn-Miclăuş *see* Gheorgheni
45 O16 **Sint Nicholaas** S Aruba 12°25′N 69°52′W
99 F16 **Sint-Niklaas** *Fr.* Saint-Nicolas. Oost-Vlaanderen, N Belgium 51°10′N 04°09′E
99 K14 **Sint-Oedenrode** Noord-Brabant, S Netherlands 51°34′N 05°28′E
25 T14 **Sinton** Texas, SW USA 28°02′N 97°33′W
99 G14 **Sint Philipsland** Zeeland, SW Netherlands 51°37′N 04°11′E
99 G19 **Sint-Pieters-Leeuw** Vlaams Brabant, C Belgium 50°47′N 04°16′E
104 E11 **Sintra** *prev.* Cintra. Lisboa, W Portugal 38°48′N 09°22′W
99 J18 **Sint-Truiden** *Fr.* Saint-Trond. Limburg, NE Belgium 50°48′N 05°13′E
99 H14 **Sint Willebrord** Noord-Brabant, S Netherlands 51°33′N 04°35′E
163 V13 **Sinŭiju** W North Korea 40°08′N 124°33′E
80 P13 **Sinujiif** Nugaal, NE Somalia 08°33′N 49°05′E
Sinus Aelaniticus *see* Aqaba, Gulf of
Sinus Gallicus *see* Lion, Golfe du
Sinyang *see* Xinyang
Sinyavka *see* Sinyawka
119 I18 **Sinyawka** *Rus.* Sinyavka. Minskaya Voblasts', SW Belarus 52°57′N 26°29′E
Sinying *see* Xinying
Sinyukha *see* Synyukha
Sinzyô *see* Shinjō
111 I24 **Sió** ~ W Hungary
171 O7 **Siocon** Mindanao, S Philippines 07°37′N 122°09′E
111 I24 **Siófok** Somogy, Hungary 46°54′N 18°03′E
Siogama *see* Shiogama
83 G15 **Sioma** Western, SW Zambia 16°39′S 23°36′E
108 D11 **Sion** *Ger.* Sitten; *anc.* Sedunum. Valais, SW Switzerland 46°15′N 07°23′E
103 O11 **Sioule** ~ C France
29 S12 **Sioux Center** Iowa, C USA 43°04′N 96°10′W
29 R13 **Sioux City** Iowa, C USA 42°30′N 96°24′W
29 R11 **Sioux Falls** South Dakota, N USA 43°33′N 96°45′W
12 B11 **Sioux Lookout** Ontario, S Canada 49°27′N 94°06′W
29 T12 **Sioux Rapids** Iowa, C USA 42°53′N 95°09′W
Sioux State *see* North Dakota
Sioziri *see* Shiojiri
171 P6 **Sipalay** Negros, C Philippines 09°46′N 122°25′E
55 V11 **Sipaliwini** ◈ *district* S Suriname
45 U15 **Siparia** Trinidad, Trinidad and Tobago 10°08′N 61°31′W
Siphnos *see* Sífnos
163 V11 **Siping** *var.* Ssu-p'ing, Szeping; *prev.* Ssu-p'ing-chieh. Jilin, NE China 43°09′N 124°22′E
11 X12 **Sipiwesk** Manitoba, C Canada 55°28′N 97°16′W
11 W13 **Sipiwesk Lake** ◎ Manitoba, C Canada
195 O11 **Siple Coast** *physical region* Antarctica
194 K12 **Siple Island** *island* Antarctica
194 K13 **Siple, Mount** ▲ Siple Island, Antarctica 73°25′S 126°24′W
Sipoo *see* Sibbo
112 G12 **Šipovo** Republika Srpska, W Bosnia and Herzegovina 44°16′N 17°05′E
23 O4 **Sipsey River** ~ Alabama, S USA
168 I13 **Sipura, Pulau** *island* W Indonesia
0 G16 **Siqueiros Fracture Zone** *tectonic feature* E Pacific Ocean
42 L10 **Siquia, Río** ~ SE Nicaragua
43 N13 **Siquirres** Limón, E Costa Rica 10°05′N 83°30′W
54 J5 **Siquisique** Lara, N Venezuela 10°36′N 69°45′W
155 G19 **Sīra** Karnātaka, W India 13°46′N 76°54′E
95 D16 **Sira** ~ S Norway
167 P12 **Si Racha** *var.* Ban Si Racha, Si Racha. Chon Buri, S Thailand 13°10′N 100°57′E
Si Racha *see* Si Racha
107 L25 **Siracusa** *Eng.* Syracuse. Sicilia, Italy, C Mediterranean Sea 37°04′N 15°17′E
153 T14 **Sirajganj** *var.* Shirajganj Ghat. Rajshahi, C Bangladesh 24°27′N 89°42′E
Sirakawa *see* Shirakawa
11 N14 **Sir Alexander, Mount** ▲ British Columbia, W Canada 54°00′N 120°33′W
137 O12 **Şiran** Gümüşhane, NE Turkey 40°12′N 39°07′E
77 Q12 **Sirba** ~ E Burkina
143 O17 **Şīr Banī Yās** *island* W United Arab Emirates
95 D17 **Sirdalsvatnet** ◎ S Norway
Sir Darya/Sirdaryo *see* Syr Darya
147 P10 **Sirdaryo** Sirdaryo Viloyati, E Uzbekistan 40°46′N 68°34′E
147 O11 **Sirdaryo Viloyati** *Rus.* Syrdar'inskaya Oblast'. ◈ *province* E Uzbekistan
Sir Donald Sangster International Airport *see* Sangster
181 S3 **Sir Edward Pellew Group** *island group* Northern Territory, NE Australia
116 K8 **Siret** *Ger.* Sereth, *Hung.* Szeret. Suceava, N Romania 47°55′N 26°05′E
116 K8 **Siret** *var.* Siretul, *Ger.* Sereth, *Rus.* Seret. ~ Romania/Ukraine
Siretul *see* Siret
140 K3 **Sirḥān, Wādī as** *dry watercourse* Jordan/Saudi Arabia
152 I8 **Sirhind** Punjab, N India 30°39′N 76°28′E

◆ Country ● Country Capital ◇ Dependent Territory ○ Dependent Territory Capital ◈ Administrative Regions ✈ International Airport ▲ Mountain ▲▲ Mountain Range Volcano ~ River ◎ Lake ⊠ Reservoir

116 F11 **Şiria** *Ger.* Schiria. Arad, W Romania 46°16′N 21°38′E
Sirya *see* Syria
143 S14 **Sīrīk** Hormozgān, SE Iran 26°32′N 57°07′E
167 P8 **Sirikit Reservoir** ◎ N Thailand
58 K12 **Sirituba, Ilha** *island* NE Brazil
143 R11 **Sīrjān** *prev.* Sa'īdābād. Kermān, S Iran 29°29′N 55°39′E
182 H9 **Sir Joseph Banks Group** *island group* South Australia
92 K11 **Sirkka** Lappi, N Finland 67°49′N 24°48′E
Sirna *see* Sýrna
137 R16 **Şırnak** Şırnak, SE Turkey 37°33′N 42°27′E
137 S16 **Şırnak** ◆ *province* SE Turkey
Siroisi *see* Shiroishi
155 J14 **Sironcha** Mahārāshtra, C India 18°51′N 80°03′E
Sirone *see* Shirone
Síros *see* Sýros
Sirotino *see* Sirotsina
118 M12 **Sirotsina** *Rus.* Sirotino. Vitsyebskaya Voblasts', N Belarus 55°23′N 29°37′E
152 H9 **Sirsa** Haryāna, NW India 29°32′N 75°04′E
173 Y17 **Sir Seewoosagur Ramgoolam** ✈ (port Louis) SE Mauritius
155 E18 **Sirsi** Karnātaka, W India 14°46′N 74°49′E
146 K12 **Sirşütür Gumy** *var.* Shirshütür, *Rus.* Peski Shirshyutyur. *desert* E Turkmenistan
Sirte *see* Surt
182 A2 **Sir Thomas, Mount** ▲ South Australia 27°09′S 129°49′E
Sirti, Gulf of *see* Surt, Khalīj
137 Y12 **Şirvan** *prev.* Āli-Bayramli. SE Azerbaijan 39°57′N 48°54′E
142 J5 **Sīrvān, Rūdkhāneh-ye** *var.* Nahr Diyālá, Sirwan. ⇝ Iran/Iraq *see also* Diyālá, Nahr
Sīrvān, Rudkhaneh-ye *see* Diyālá, Sirwan Nahr
118 H13 **Širvintos** Vilnius, SE Lithuania 55°01′N 24°58′E
Sīrwān *see* Diyālá, Nahr/Sīrvān, Rudkhaneh-ye
11 N15 **Sir Wilfrid Laurier, Mount** ▲ British Columbia, SW Canada 52°45′N 119°51′W
14 M10 **Sir-Wilfrid, Mont** ▲ Québec, SE Canada 46°57′N 75°33′W
Sisačko-Moslavačka Županija *see* Sisak-Moslavina
112 E9 **Sisak** *var.* Siscia, *Ger.* Sissek, *Hung.* Sziszek; *anc.* Segestica. Sisak-Moslavina, C Croatia 45°28′N 16°21′E
167 R10 **Si Sa Ket** *var.* Sisaket, Sri Saket. Si Sa Ket, E Thailand 15°08′N 104°18′E
Sisaket *see* Si Sa Ket
112 E9 **Sisak-Moslavina** *off.* Sisačko-Moslavačka Županija. ◆ *province* C Croatia
167 O8 **Si Satchanalai** Sukhothai, NW Thailand
Siscia *see* Sisak
83 G22 **Sishen** Northern Cape, NW South Africa 27°47′S 22°59′E
137 V13 **Sisian** SE Armenia 39°31′N 46°03′E
197 N13 **Sisimiut** *var.* Holsteinborg, Holsteinsborg, Holstenborg, Holstensborg. Kitaa, S Greenland 67°07′N 53°42′W
30 M1 **Siskiwit Bay** *lake bay* Michigan, N USA
34 L1 **Siskiyou Mountains** ▲▲ California/Oregon, W USA
Sisŏphŏn *see* Bânteay Méan Choay
108 E7 **Sissach** Basel Landschaft, NW Switzerland 47°28′N 07°48′E
186 B5 **Sissano** Sandaun, NW Papua New Guinea 03°02′S 142°01′E
Sissek *see* Sisak
29 R7 **Sisseton** South Dakota, N USA 45°39′N 97°03′W
143 W9 **Sīstān, Daryācheh-ye** *var.* Daryācheh-ye Hāmūn, Hāmūn-e Şāberī. ◎ Afghanistan/Iran *see also* Şāberī, Hāmūn-e
Sīstān, Daryācheh-ye *see* Şāberī, Hāmūn-e
143 V12 **Sīstān va Balūchestān** *off.* Ostān-e Sīstān va Balūchestān, *var.* Balūchestān va Sīstān. ◆ *province* SE Iran
Sīstān va Balūchestān, Ostān-e *see* Sīstān va Balūchestān
103 T14 **Sisteron** Alpes-de-Haute-Provence, SE France 44°12′N 05°55′E
32 H13 **Sisters** Oregon, NW USA 44°17′N 121°33′W
65 G15 **Sisters Peak** ▲ N Ascension Island 07°56′S 14°23′W
21 R3 **Sistersville** West Virginia, NE USA 39°33′N 81°00′W
Sistova *see* Svishtov
Sitakund *see* Sitakunda
153 V16 **Sitakunda** *var.* Sitakund. Chittagong, SE Bangladesh 22°35′N 91°40′E
153 P12 **Sītāmarhi** Bihār, N India 26°36′N 85°30′E
152 L11 **Sītāpur** Uttar Pradesh, N India 27°33′N 80°40′E
Sitaş Cristuru *see* Cristuru Secuiesc
115 L25 **Siteía** *var.* Sitía. Kríti, Greece, E Mediterranean Sea 35°13′N 26°06′E
105 V6 **Sitges** Cataluña, NE Spain 41°14′N 01°49′E
115 H15 **Sithoniá Atavyros** *peninsula* NE Greece
Sitía *see* Siteía
54 F4 **Sitionuevo** Magdalena, N Colombia 10°46′N 74°43′W
39 X13 **Sitka** Baranof Island, Alaska, USA 57°03′N 135°19′W
39 Q15 **Sitkinak Island** *island* Trinity Islands, Alaska, USA
Sittang *see* Sittoung
99 L17 **Sittard** Limburg, SE Netherlands 51°01′N 05°52′E
Sitten *see* Sion
108 H7 **Sitter** ⇝ NW Switzerland
109 U10 **Sittersdorf** Kärnten, S Austria 46°31′N 14°34′E
166 M7 **Sittoung** *var.* Sittang. ⇝ S Myanmar (Burma)
166 K6 **Sittwe** *var.* Akyab. Rakhine State, W Myanmar (Burma) 20°09′N 92°51′E
42 L8 **Siuna** Región Autónoma Atlántico Norte, NE Nicaragua 13°44′N 84°46′W
153 R15 **Siuri** West Bengal, NE India 23°54′N 87°32′E
Siut *see* Asyūţ
123 Q13 **Sivaki** Amurskaya Oblast', SE Russian Federation 52°39′N 126°43′E
136 M13 **Sivas** *anc.* Sebastia, Sebaste. Sivas, C Turkey 39°44′N 37°01′E
136 M13 **Sivas** ◆ *province* C Turkey
137 O15 **Siverek** Şanlıurfa, S Turkey 37°46′N 39°19′E
117 X6 **Sivers'k** Donets'ka Oblast', E Ukraine 48°52′N 38°07′E
124 G13 **Siverskiy** Leningradskaya Oblast', NW Russian Federation 59°21′N 30°01′E
117 X6 **Sivers'kyy Donets'** *Rus.* Severskiy Donets. ⇝ Russian Federation/Ukraine *see also* Severskiy Donets
Sivers'kyy Donets' *see* Severskiy Donets
125 W5 **Sivomaskinskiy** Respublika Komi, NW Russian Federation 66°42′N 62°33′E
136 G13 **Sivrihisar** Eskişehir, W Turkey 39°29′N 31°32′E
99 F22 **Sivry** Hainaut, S Belgium 50°10′N 04°11′E
123 V9 **Sivuchiy, Mys** *headland* E Russian Federation 56°45′N 163°13′E
Siwa *see* Sīwah
75 U9 **Sīwah** *var.* Siwa. NW Egypt 29°11′N 25°32′E
152 J9 **Siwalik Range** *var.* Shiwalik Range. ▲▲ India/Nepal
153 O13 **Siwān** Bihār, N India 26°14′N 84°21′E
43 O14 **Sixaola, Río** ⇝ Costa Rica/Panama
Six Counties, The *see* Northern Ireland
103 T16 **Six-Fours-les-Plages** Var, SE France 43°05′N 05°50′E
161 Q7 **Sixian** *var.* Si Xian. Anhui, E China 33°29′N 117°53′E
Si Xian *see* Sixian
22 J9 **Six Mile Lake** ◎ Louisiana, S USA
139 V3 **Siyāh Gūz** As Sulaymānīyah, E Iraq 35°49′N 45°45′E
155 L25 **Siyambalanduwa** Uva Province, SE Sri Lanka 06°54′N 81°32′E
137 Y10 **Siyäzän** *Rus.* Siazan'. NE Azerbaijan 41°05′N 49°05′E
Sizebolu *see* Sozopol
Sizuoka *see* Shizuoka
95 I24 **Sjælland** ◆ *region* SE Denmark
95 I24 **Sjælland** *Eng.* Zealand, *Ger.* Seeland. *island* E Denmark
Sjar *see* Sääre
113 L15 **Sjenica** *Turk.* Seniça. Serbia, SW Serbia 43°16′N 20°01′E
94 G11 **Sjoa** ⇝ S Norway
95 K23 **Sjöbo** Skåne, S Sweden 55°37′N 13°45′E
94 E9 **Sjøholt** Møre og Romsdal, S Norway 62°29′N 06°50′E
92 O1 **Sjuøyane** *island group* N Svalbard
Skadar *see* Shkodër
Skadarsko Jezero *see* Scutari, Lake
117 R11 **Skadovs'k** Khersons'ka Oblast', S Ukraine 46°07′N 32°53′E
95 I24 **Skælskør** Sjælland, E Denmark 55°16′N 11°18′E
92 I2 **Skagaströnd** *prev.* Höfdhakaupstadhur. Nordhurland Vestra, N Iceland 65°49′N 20°18′W
95 H19 **Skagen** Nordjylland, N Denmark 57°44′N 10°37′E
Skagerak *see* Skagerrak
95 L16 **Skagern** ◎ C Sweden
197 T17 **Skagerrak** *var.* Skagerak. *channel* N Europe
94 G12 **Skagge** ▲ S Norway 61°19′N 09°07′E
32 H7 **Skagit River** ⇝ Washington, NW USA
39 W12 **Skagway** Alaska, USA 59°27′N 135°18′W
92 K8 **Skaidi** Finnmark, N Norway 70°26′N 24°31′E
115 F21 **Skála** Pelopónnisos, S Greece 36°51′N 22°39′E
116 K6 **Skalat** *Pol.* Skałat. Ternopil's'ka Oblast', W Ukraine 49°27′N 25°59′E
95 J22 **Skälderviken** *inlet* Denmark/Sweden
92 I12 **Skalka** *Lapp.* Skalkká. ◎ N Sweden
Skalkká *see* Skalka
114 I12 **Skalotí** Anatolikí Makedonía kai Thráki, NE Greece 41°24′N 24°16′E
95 G22 **Skanderborg** Midtjylland, C Denmark 56°02′N 09°57′E
95 K22 **Skåne** *prev. Eng.* Scania. ◆ *county* S Sweden
75 N6 **Skanès** ✈ (Sousse) E Tunisia 35°36′N 10°56′E
95 C15 **Skånevik** Hordaland, S Norway 59°43′N 06°35′E
95 M18 **Skänninge** Östergötland, S Sweden 58°24′N 15°05′E
95 J23 **Skanör med Falsterbo** Skåne, S Sweden 55°24′N 12°48′E
115 H17 **Skantzoúra** *island* Vóreies Sporádes, Greece, Aegean Sea
95 K18 **Skara** Västra Götaland, S Sweden 58°23′N 13°25′E
95 M17 **Skärblacka** Östergötland, S Sweden 58°34′N 15°54′E
95 I18 **Skärhamn** Västra Götaland, S Sweden 57°59′N 11°33′E
95 I14 **Skarnes** Hedmark, S Norway 60°14′N 11°41′E
119 M21 **Skarodnaye** *Rus.* Skorodnoye. Homyel'skaya Voblasts', SE Belarus 51°38′N 28°50′E
110 I8 **Skarszewy** *Ger.* Schöneck. Pomorskie, NW Poland 54°04′N 18°25′E
111 M14 **Skarżysko-Kamienna** Świętokrzyskie, C Poland 51°07′N 20°52′E
95 K16 **Skattkärr** Värmland, C Sweden 59°25′N 13°42′E
118 D12 **Skaudvilė** Tauragė, SW Lithuania 55°25′N 22°33′E
92 J12 **Skaulo** *Lapp.* Sávdijári. Norrbotten, N Sweden 67°21′N 21°03′E
111 K17 **Skawina** Małopolskie, S Poland 49°59′N 19°49′E
10 K12 **Skeena** ⇝ British Columbia, SW Canada
10 J11 **Skeena Mountains** ▲▲ British Columbia, W Canada
97 O18 **Skegness** E England, United Kingdom 53°10′N 00°21′E
92 J4 **Skeidharársandur** *coast* S Iceland
93 J15 **Skellefteå** Västerbotten, N Sweden 64°45′N 20°58′E
93 I14 **Skellefteälven** ⇝ N Sweden
93 J15 **Skelleftehamn** Västerbotten, N Sweden 64°41′N 21°13′E
25 O2 **Skellytown** Texas, SW USA 35°34′N 101°10′W
95 J19 **Skene** Västra Götaland, S Sweden 57°30′N 12°34′E
97 G17 **Skerries** *Ir.* Na Sceirí. Dublin, E Ireland 53°35′N 06°07′W
95 H15 **Ski** Akershus, S Norway 59°43′N 10°50′E
115 G17 **Skíathos** Skíathos, Vóreies Sporádes, Greece, Aegean Sea 39°10′N 23°30′E
115 G17 **Skíathos** *island* Vóreies Sporádes, Greece, Aegean Sea
27 P9 **Skiatook** Oklahoma, C USA 36°22′N 96°00′W
27 P9 **Skiatook Lake** ⊠ Oklahoma, C USA
97 B22 **Skibbereen** *Ir.* An Sciobairín. Cork, SW Ireland 51°33′N 09°15′W
92 I9 **Skibotn** Troms, N Norway 69°22′N 20°18′E
119 F16 **Skidal'** *Rus.* Skidel'. Hrodzyenskaya Voblasts', W Belarus 53°35′N 24°15′E
97 K15 **Skiddaw** ▲ NW England, United Kingdom 54°37′N 03°07′W
Skidel' *see* Skidal'
25 T14 **Skidmore** Texas, SW USA 28°13′N 97°40′W
95 G16 **Skien** Telemark, S Norway 59°14′N 09°37′E
Skiermûntseach *see* Schiermonnikoog
110 L12 **Skierniewice** Łódzkie, C Poland 51°58′N 20°10′E
74 L5 **Skikda** *prev.* Philippeville. NE Algeria 36°51′N 07°E
30 M16 **Skillet Fork** ⇝ Illinois, N USA
95 L19 **Skillingaryd** Jönköping, S Sweden 57°27′N 14°05′E
115 B19 **Skinári, Akrotírio** *headland* Iónia Nisiá, Greece 37°55′N 20°57′E
95 M15 **Skinnskatteberg** Västmanland, C Sweden 59°50′N 15°41′E
182 M12 **Skipton** Victoria, SE Australia 37°44′S 143°21′E
97 L16 **Skipton** N England, United Kingdom 53°57′N 02°W
Skiropoula *see* Skyropoúla
Skíros *see* Skýros
95 F21 **Skive** Midtjylland, NW Denmark 56°34′N 09°02′E
94 F11 **Skjåk** Oppland, S Norway 61°52′N 08°21′E
95 F22 **Skjern** Midtjylland, W Denmark 55°57′N 08°30′E
95 F22 **Skjern Å** *var.* Skjern Aa. ⇝ W Denmark
Skjern Aa *see* Skjern Å
92 G12 **Skjerstad** Nordland, C Norway 67°14′N 15°00′E
92 J8 **Skjervøy** Troms, N Norway 70°03′N 20°56′E
92 I10 **Skjold** Troms, N Norway 69°03′N 19°18′E
111 I17 **Skoczów** Śląskie, S Poland 49°49′N 18°45′E
109 T11 **Škofja Loka** *Ger.* Bischoflack. NW Slovenia 46°12′N 14°16′E
94 N12 **Skog** Gävleborg, C Sweden 61°10′N 16°49′E
95 K16 **Skoghall** Värmland, C Sweden 59°20′N 13°30′E
31 N10 **Skokie** Illinois, N USA 42°01′N 87°43′W
116 H6 **Skole** L'vivs'ka Oblast', W Ukraine 49°04′N 23°29′E
115 D19 **Skóllis** ▲ S Greece 37°58′N 21°33′E
167 S13 **Skon** Kâmpóng Cham, C Cambodia 12°56′N 104°36′E
115 H17 **Skópelos** Skópelos, Vóreies Sporádes, Greece, Aegean Sea 39°07′N 23°43′E
115 H17 **Skópelos** *island* Vóreies Sporádes, Greece, Aegean Sea
126 L5 **Skopin** Ryazanskaya Oblast', W Russian Federation 53°46′N 39°37′E
113 N18 **Skopje** *var.* Üsküb, *Turk.* Üsküp, *prev.* Skoplje; *anc.* Scupi. ● (FYR Macedonia) N FYR Macedonia 42°N 21°28′E
113 O18 **Skopje** ✈ N FYR Macedonia 41°58′N 21°35′E
Skoplje *see* Skopje
110 I8 **Skórcz** *Ger.* Skurz. Pomorskie, N Poland 53°46′N 18°43′E
Skorodnoye *see* Skarodnaye
93 H16 **Skorped** Västernorrland, C Sweden 63°23′N 17°55′E
95 G21 **Skørping** Nordjylland, N Denmark 56°50′N 09°55′E
95 K18 **Skövde** Västra Götaland, S Sweden 58°24′N 13°52′E
123 Q13 **Skovorodino** Amurskaya Oblast', SE Russian Federation 54°03′N 123°47′E
19 Q6 **Skowhegan** Maine, NE USA 44°46′N 69°41′W
11 W15 **Skownan** Manitoba, S Canada 51°55′N 99°34′W
94 H13 **Skreia** Oppland, S Norway 60°37′N 11°00′E
Skripón *see* Orchómenos
118 H9 **Skrīveri** S Latvia 56°39′N 25°08′E
118 J11 **Skrudaliena** SE Latvia 55°50′N 26°42′E
118 D9 **Skrunda** W Latvia 56°39′N 22°01′E
95 C16 **Skudeneshavn** Rogaland, S Norway 59°10′N 05°16′E
95 C16 **Skudnesfjorden** S Norway
83 L20 **Skukuza** Mpumalanga, NE South Africa 25°01′S 31°35′E
97 B22 **Skull** *Ir.* An Scoil. SW Ireland 51°32′N 09°34′W
22 L3 **Skuna River** ⇝ Mississippi, S USA
29 X15 **Skunk River** ⇝ Iowa, C USA
Skuø *see* Skúvoy
118 C10 **Skuodas** *Ger.* Schoden, *Pol.* Szkudy. Klaipėda, NW Lithuania 56°16′N 21°30′E
95 K23 **Skurup** Skåne, S Sweden 55°28′N 13°30′E
Skurz *see* Skórcz
114 H8 **Skŭt** ⇝ NW Bulgaria
94 O13 **Skutskär** Uppsala, C Sweden 60°39′N 17°25′E
95 B19 **Skúvoy** *Dan.* Skuø. *island* C Faeroe Islands
Skvira *see* Skvyra
117 O5 **Skvyra** *Rus.* Skvira. Kyyivs'ka Oblast', N Ukraine 49°44′N 29°42′E
39 Q11 **Skwentna** Alaska, USA 61°56′N 151°03′W
110 E11 **Skwierzyna** *Ger.* Schwerin. Lubuskie, W Poland 52°37′N 15°27′E
96 G9 **Skye, Isle of** *island* NW Scotland, United Kingdom
36 K13 **Sky Harbor** ✈ (Phoenix) Arizona, SW USA 33°26′N 112°00′W
32 I8 **Skykomish** Washington, NW USA 47°40′N 121°20′W
Skylge *see* Terschelling
63 F19 **Skyring, Peninsula** *peninsula* S Chile
63 H24 **Skyring, Seno** *inlet* S Chile
115 H17 **Skyropoúla** *var.* Skiropoula. *island* Vóreies Sporádes, Greece, Aegean Sea
115 I17 **Skýros** *var.* Skíros. Skýros, Vóreies Sporádes, Greece, Aegean Sea 38°55′N 24°34′E
115 I17 **Skýros** *var.* Skíros; *anc.* Scyros. *island* Vóreies Sporádes, Greece, Aegean Sea
118 J12 **Slabodka** *Rus.* Slobodka. Vitsyebskaya Voblasts', NW Belarus 55°41′N 27°11′E
95 I23 **Slagelse** Sjælland, E Denmark 55°25′N 11°22′E
93 I14 **Slagnäs** Norrbotten, N Sweden 65°36′N 18°10′E
39 T10 **Slana** Alaska, USA 62°46′N 144°00′W
97 F20 **Slaney** *Ir.* An tSláine. ⇝ SE Ireland
116 J13 **Slănic** Prahova, SE Romania 45°14′N 25°58′E
116 K11 **Slănic Moldova** Bacău, E Romania 46°12′N 26°23′E
113 H16 **Slano** Dubrovnik-Neretva, SE Croatia 42°47′N 17°54′E
124 F13 **Slantsy** Leningradskaya Oblast', NW Russian Federation 59°06′N 28°00′E
111 C16 **Slaný** *Ger.* Schlan. Střední Čechy, NW Czech Republic 50°14′N 14°05′E
111 K16 **Śląskie** ◆ *province* S Poland
12 C10 **Slate Falls** Ontario, S Canada 51°11′N 91°32′W
27 T4 **Slater** Missouri, C USA 39°13′N 93°04′W
112 H9 **Slatina** *Hung.* Szlatina; *prev.* Podravska Slatina. Virovitica-Podravina, NE Croatia 45°40′N 17°46′E
116 I14 **Slatina** Olt, S Romania 45°27′N 24°21′E
25 N5 **Slaton** Texas, SW USA 33°26′N 101°38′W
95 H14 **Slattum** Akershus, S Norway 60°00′N 10°55′E
11 R10 **Slave** ⇝ Alberta/Northwest Territories, C Canada
68 E12 **Slave Coast** *coastal region* W Africa
11 P13 **Slave Lake** Alberta, SW Canada 55°17′N 114°46′W
122 I13 **Slavgorod** Altayskiy Kray, S Russian Federation 52°55′N 78°46′E
Slavgorod *see* Slawharad
Slavonia *see* Slavonija
112 G9 **Slavonija** *Eng.* Slavonia, *Ger.* Slawonien, *Hung.* Szlavonia, Szlavonország. *cultural region* NE Croatia
112 H10 **Slavonski Brod** *Ger.* Brod, *Hung.* Bród; *prev.* Brod, Brod na Savi. Brod-Posavina, NE Croatia 45°09′N 18°00′E
112 G10 **Slavonski Brod-Posavina** *off.* Brodsko-Posavska Županija, *var.* Brod-Posavina. ◆ *province* NE Croatia
116 L4 **Slavuta** Khmel'nyts'ka Oblast', NW Ukraine 50°18′N 26°52′E
117 P2 **Slavutych** Chernihivs'ka Oblast', N Ukraine 51°31′N 30°47′E
123 R15 **Slavyanka** Primorskiy Kray, SE Russian Federation 42°46′N 131°19′E
114 J8 **Slavyanovo** Pleven, N Bulgaria 43°28′N 24°52′E
Slavyansk *see* Slov"yans'k
126 K14 **Slavyansk-na-Kubani** Krasnodarskiy Kray, SW Russian Federation 45°16′N 38°09′E
119 N20 **Slavyechna** *Rus.* Slovechna. ⇝ Belarus/Ukraine
119 O16 **Slawharad** *Rus.* Slavgorod. Mahilyowskaya Voblasts', E Belarus 53°27′N 31°00′E
110 G7 **Sławno** Zachodnio-pomorskie, NW Poland 54°23′N 16°43′E
Slawonien *see* Slavonija
29 S10 **Slayton** Minnesota, N USA 43°59′N 95°45′W
97 N18 **Sleaford** E England, United Kingdom 52°59′N 00°28′W
97 A20 **Slea Head** *Ir.* Ceann Sléibhe. *headland* SW Ireland 52°05′N 10°25′W
96 G9 **Sleat, Sound of** *strait* NW Scotland, United Kingdom
Sledyuki *see* Slyedzyuki
12 I5 **Sleeper Islands** *island group* Nunavut, C Canada
31 O6 **Sleeping Bear Point** *headland* Michigan, N USA 44°54′N 86°02′W
29 T10 **Sleepy Eye** Minnesota, N USA 44°18′N 94°43′W
39 O11 **Sleetmute** Alaska, USA 61°42′N 157°10′W
Sléibhe, Ceann *see* Slea Head
Slēmānī *see* As Sulaymānīyah
195 O5 **Slessor Glacier** *glacier* Antarctica
22 L9 **Slidell** Louisiana, S USA 30°16′N 89°46′W
18 K12 **Slide Mountain** ▲ New York, NE USA 42°00′N 74°23′W
98 I13 **Sliedrecht** Zuid-Holland, C Netherlands 51°50′N 04°46′E
121 P16 **Sliema** N Malta 35°54′N 14°31′E
97 G16 **Slieve Donard** ▲ SE Northern Ireland, United Kingdom 54°10′N 05°57′W
Sligeach *see* Sligo
97 D16 **Sligo** *Ir.* Sligeach. Sligo, NW Ireland 54°17′N 08°28′W
97 C16 **Sligo** *Ir.* Sligeach. *cultural region* NW Ireland
97 C15 **Sligo Bay** *Ir.* Cuan Shligigh. *inlet* NW Ireland
18 B13 **Slippery Rock** Pennsylvania, NE USA 41°02′N 80°02′W
95 P19 **Slite** Gotland, SE Sweden 57°37′N 18°46′E
114 L9 **Sliven** *var.* Slivno. Sliven, C Bulgaria 42°42′N 26°21′E
114 L10 **Sliven** ◆ *province* C Bulgaria
114 G9 **Slivnitsa** Sofiya, W Bulgaria 42°51′N 23°01′E
Slivno *see* Sliven
114 L7 **Slivo Pole** Ruse, N Bulgaria 43°57′N 26°15′E
29 S13 **Sloan** Iowa, C USA 42°13′N 96°13′W
35 X12 **Sloan** Nevada, W USA 35°56′N 115°13′W
Slobodka *see* Slabodka
125 R14 **Slobodskoy** Kirovskaya Oblast', NW Russian Federation 58°43′N 50°12′E
Slobodzeya *see* Slobozia
117 O10 **Slobozia** *Rus.* Slobodzeya. E Moldova 46°45′N 29°42′E
116 L14 **Slobozia** Ialomiţa, SE Romania 44°34′N 27°23′E
98 O5 **Slochteren** Groningen, NE Netherlands 53°13′N 06°48′E
119 H17 **Slonim** *Pol.* Słonim. Hrodzyenskaya Voblasts', W Belarus 53°06′N 25°19′E
Słonim *see* Slonim
98 K7 **Sloten Meer** ◎ N Netherlands
Slot, The *see* New Georgia Sound
97 N22 **Slough** S England, United Kingdom 51°31′N 00°36′W
111 J20 **Slovakia** *off.* Slovenská Republika, *Ger.* Slowakei, *Hung.* Szlovákia, *Slvk.* Slovensko. ◆ *republic* C Europe
Slovak Ore Mountains *see* Slovenské rudohorie
Slovechna *see* Slavyechna
109 S12 **Slovenia** *off.* Republic of Slovenia, *Ger.* Slowenien, *Slvn.* Slovenija. ◆ *republic* SE Europe
Slovenia, Republic of *see* Slovenia
Slovenija *see* Slovenia
109 V10 **Slovenj Gradec** *Ger.* Windischgraz. N Slovenia 46°29′N 15°05′E
109 W10 **Slovenska Bistrica** *Ger.* Windischfeistritz. NE Slovenia 46°21′N 15°27′E
Slovenská Republika *see* Slovakia
109 W10 **Slovenske Konjice** E Slovenia 46°21′N 15°28′E
111 K20 **Slovenské rudohorie** *Eng.* Slovak Ore Mountains, *Ger.* Slowakisches Erzgebirge, Ungarisches Erzgebirge. ▲▲ C Slovakia
Slovensko *see* Slovakia
117 Y7 **Slov"yanoserbs'k** Luhans'ka Oblast', E Ukraine 48°41′N 39°00′E
117 W6 **Slov"yans'k** *Rus.* Slavyansk. Donets'ka Oblast', E Ukraine 48°51′N 37°38′E
Slowakei *see* Slovakia
Slowakisches Erzgebirge *see* Slovenské rudohorie
Slowenien *see* Slovenia
110 D11 **Słubice** *Ger.* Frankfurt. Lubuskie, W Poland 52°20′N 14°35′E
119 K19 **Sluch** *Rus.* Sluch'. ⇝ C Belarus
116 L4 **Sluch** ⇝ NW Ukraine
99 D16 **Sluis** Zeeland, SW Netherlands 51°18′N 03°22′E
112 D10 **Slunj** *Hung.* Szluin. Karlovac, C Croatia 45°06′N 15°35′E
110 I11 **Słupca** Wielkopolskie, C Poland 52°17′N 17°52′E
110 G6 **Słupia** *Ger.* Stolpe. ⇝ NW Poland
110 G6 **Słupsk** *Ger.* Stolp. Pomorskie, N Poland 54°28′N 17°01′E
119 K18 **Slutsk** Minskaya Voblasts', S Belarus 53°02′N 27°32′E
119 O16 **Slyedzyuki** *Rus.* Sledyuki. Mahilyowskaya Voblasts', E Belarus 53°35′N 30°22′E
97 A17 **Slyne Head** *Ir.* Ceann Léime. *headland* W Ireland 53°25′N 10°11′W
27 U14 **Smackover** Arkansas, C USA 33°21′N 92°43′W
95 L20 **Småland** *cultural region* S Sweden
95 K20 **Smålandsstenar** Jönköping, S Sweden 57°10′N 13°24′E
Small Malaita *see* Maramasike
13 O8 **Smallwood Reservoir** ◎ Newfoundland and Labrador, S Canada
119 N14 **Smalyany** *Rus.* Smolyany. Vitsyebskaya Voblasts', NE Belarus 54°36′N 30°04′E
119 L15 **Smalyavichy** *Rus.* Smolevichi. Minskaya Voblasts', C Belarus 54°02′N 28°05′E
74 C9 **Smara** *var.* Es Semara. N Western Sahara 26°45′N 11°44′W
119 I14 **Smarhon'** *Pol.* Smorgonie, *Rus.* Smorgon'. Hrodzyenskaya Voblasts', W Belarus 54°29′N 26°24′E
112 M11 **Smederevo** *Ger.* Semendria. Serbia, N Serbia 44°41′N 20°56′E
112 M12 **Smederevska Palanka** Serbia, C Serbia 44°24′N 20°56′E
95 M14 **Smedjebacken** Dalarna, C Sweden 60°08′N 15°25′E
116 L13 **Smeeni** Buzău, SE Romania 45°00′N 26°52′E
Smela *see* Smila
107 D16 **Smeralda, Costa** *cultural region* Sardegna, Italy, C Mediterranean Sea
111 J22 **Śmigiel** *Ger.* Schmiegel. Wielkopolskie, C Poland 52°02′N 16°33′E
117 Q6 **Smila** *Rus.* Smela. Cherkas'ka Oblast', C Ukraine 49°15′N 31°54′E
98 N7 **Smilde** Drenthe, NE Netherlands 52°57′N 06°28′E
11 S16 **Smiley** Saskatchewan, S Canada 51°40′N 109°24′W
25 T12 **Smiley** Texas, SW USA 29°16′N 97°38′W
Smilten *see* Smiltene
118 I8 **Smiltene** *Ger.* Smilten. N Latvia 57°25′N 25°53′E
123 T13 **Smirnykh** Ostrov Sakhalin, Sakhalinskaya Oblast', SE Russian Federation 49°43′N 142°48′E
11 Q13 **Smith** Alberta, W Canada 55°06′N 113°57′W
39 P4 **Smith Bay** *bay* Alaska, NW USA
12 I3 **Smith, Cape** *headland* Québec, NE Canada 60°50′N 78°06′W
26 L3 **Smith Center** Kansas, C USA 39°46′N 98°46′W
10 K13 **Smithers** British Columbia, SW Canada 54°45′N 127°10′W
21 V10 **Smithfield** North Carolina, SE USA 35°30′N 78°21′W
36 L1 **Smithfield** Utah, W USA 41°50′N 111°49′W
21 X7 **Smithfield** Virginia, NE USA 36°41′N 76°38′W
12 I3 **Smith Island** *island* Nunavut, C Canada
Smith Island *see* Sumisu-jima
20 H7 **Smithland** Kentucky, S USA 37°06′N 88°24′W
21 T7 **Smith Mountain Lake** *var.* Leesville Lake. ⊠ Virginia, NE USA
34 L1 **Smith River** California, W USA 41°54′N 124°09′W
33 R9 **Smith River** ⇝ Montana, NW USA
14 L13 **Smiths Falls** Ontario, SE Canada 44°54′N 76°01′W
33 N13 **Smiths Ferry** Idaho, NW USA 44°19′N 116°04′W
20 K7 **Smiths Grove** Kentucky, S USA 37°01′N 86°14′W
183 N15 **Smithton** Tasmania, SE Australia 40°54′S 145°06′E
18 L14 **Smithtown** Long Island, New York, NE USA 40°52′N 73°13′W
20 K9 **Smithville** Tennessee, S USA 35°59′N 85°49′W
25 T11 **Smithville** Texas, SW USA 30°04′N 97°32′W
Smohor *see* Hermagor
35 Q4 **Smoke Creek Desert** *desert* Nevada, W USA
11 O14 **Smoky** ⇝ Alberta, W Canada
182 E7 **Smoky Bay** South Australia 32°22′S 133°57′E
183 V6 **Smoky Cape** *headland* New South Wales, SE Australia 30°54′S 153°06′E
26 L4 **Smoky Hill River** ⇝ Kansas, C USA
26 L4 **Smoky Hills** *hill range* Kansas, C USA
11 Q14 **Smoky Lake** Alberta, SW Canada 54°08′N 112°26′W
94 E8 **Smøla** *island* W Norway
126 H4 **Smolensk** Smolenskaya Oblast', W Russian Federation 54°48′N 32°08′E
126 H4 **Smolenskaya Oblast'** ◆ *province* W Russian Federation
Smolensk-Moscow Upland *see* Smolensko-Moskovskaya Vozvyshennost'
126 J3 **Smolensko-Moskovskaya Vozvyshennost'** *var.* Smolensk-Moscow Upland. ▲▲ W Russian Federation
Smolevichi *see* Smalyavichy
115 C15 **Smólikas** *var.* Smólikas. ▲ W Greece 40°06′N 20°54′E
114 I12 **Smolyan** *prev.* Pashmakli. Smolyan, S Bulgaria 41°34′N 24°42′E
114 I12 **Smolyan** ◆ *province* S Bulgaria
Smolyany *see* Smalyany
33 S15 **Smoot** Wyoming, C USA 42°37′N 110°55′W
12 G12 **Smooth Rock Falls** Ontario, S Canada 49°17′N 81°37′W
Smorgon'/Smorgonie *see* Smarhon'
95 K23 **Smygehamn** Skåne, S Sweden 55°19′N 13°25′E
194 I7 **Smyley Island** *island* Antarctica
21 Y3 **Smyrna** Delaware, NE USA 39°18′N 75°36′W
23 S3 **Smyrna** Georgia, SE USA 33°52′N 84°30′W
20 J9 **Smyrna** Tennessee, S USA 36°00′N 86°30′W
Smyrna *see* İzmir
97 I16 **Snaefell** ▲ C Isle of Man 54°15′N 04°29′W
92 H3 **Snaefellsjökull** ▲ W Iceland 64°51′N 23°51′W
92 J3 **Snækollur** ▲ C Iceland 64°38′N 19°18′W
10 J4 **Snake** ⇝ Yukon Territory, NW Canada
29 O8 **Snake Creek** ⇝ South Dakota, N USA
183 P13 **Snake Island** *island* Victoria, SE Australia
35 Y6 **Snake Range** ▲▲ Nevada, W USA
32 K10 **Snake River** ⇝ NW USA
29 V6 **Snake River** ⇝ Minnesota, N USA
28 L12 **Snake River** ⇝ Nebraska, C USA
33 Q14 **Snake River Plain** *plain* Idaho, NW USA
93 F15 **Snåsa** Nord-Trøndelag, C Norway 64°16′N 12°25′E
21 O8 **Sneedville** Tennessee, S USA 36°31′N 83°13′W
98 K6 **Sneek** *Fris.* Snits. Fryslân, N Netherlands 53°02′N 05°40′E
Sneeuw-gebergte *see* Maoke, Pegunungan
95 F22 **Snejbjerg** Midtjylland, C Denmark 56°08′N 08°55′E
122 K9 **Snezhnogorsk** Krasnoyarskiy Kray, N Russian Federation 68°06′N 87°37′E
124 J3 **Snezhnogorsk** Murmanskaya Oblast', NW Russian Federation 69°12′N 33°20′E
Snezhnoye *see* Snizhne
111 G15 **Sněžka** *Ger.* Schneekoppe, *Pol.* Śnieżka. ▲ N Czech Republic/Poland 50°42′N 15°55′E
110 N8 **Śniardwy, Jezioro** *Ger.* Spirdingsee. ◎ NE Poland
Sniečkus *see* Visaginas
Śnieżka *see* Sněžka
117 R10 **Snihurivka** Mykolayivs'ka Oblast', S Ukraine 47°05′N 32°48′E
116 I5 **Snilov** ✈ (L'viv) L'vivs'ka Oblast', W Ukraine 49°45′N 23°59′E
111 O19 **Snina** *Hung.* Szinna. Prešovský Kraj, E Slovakia 49°N 22°10′E
Snits *see* Sneek
117 Y8 **Snizhne** *Rus.* Snezhnoye. Donets'ka Oblast', SE Ukraine 48°01′N 38°46′E
94 G10 **Snøhetta** *var.* Snohetta. ▲ S Norway 62°22′N 09°08′E
92 G12 **Snøtinden** ▲ C Norway 66°39′N 13°50′E
97 I18 **Snowdon** ▲ NW Wales, United Kingdom 53°04′N 04°04′W
97 I18 **Snowdonia** ▲▲ NW Wales, United Kingdom
Snowdrift *see* Łutselk'e
Snowdrift *see* Łutselk'e
37 N12 **Snowflake** Arizona, SW USA 34°30′N 110°04′W
21 Y5 **Snow Hill** Maryland, NE USA 38°11′N 75°23′W
21 W10 **Snow Hill** North Carolina, SE USA 35°26′N 77°39′W
194 H3 **Snowhill Island** *island* Antarctica
11 V13 **Snow Lake** Manitoba, C Canada 54°56′N 100°02′W
37 R5 **Snowmass Mountain** ▲ Colorado, C USA 39°07′N 107°04′W
18 M10 **Snow, Mount** ▲ Vermont, NE USA 42°56′N 72°52′W
34 M5 **Snow Mountain** ▲ California, W USA 39°44′N 123°01′W
Snow Mountains *see* Maoke, Pegunungan
33 N7 **Snowshoe Peak** ▲ Montana, NW USA 48°15′N 115°44′W
182 I8 **Snowtown** South Australia 33°49′S 138°13′E
36 K1 **Snowville** Utah, W USA 41°59′N 112°42′W
35 X3 **Snow Water Lake** ◎ Nevada, W USA
183 Q11 **Snowy Mountains** ▲▲ New South Wales/Victoria, SE Australia
183 Q12 **Snowy River** ⇝ New South Wales/Victoria, SE Australia
44 K5 **Snug Corner** Acklins Island, SE Bahamas 22°31′N 73°51′W
167 T13 **Snuŏl** Krâchéh, E Cambodia 12°04′N 106°26′E
116 J7 **Snyatyn** Ivano-Frankivs'ka Oblast', W Ukraine 48°30′N 25°50′E
26 L12 **Snyder** Oklahoma, C USA 34°37′N 98°56′W
25 O6 **Snyder** Texas, SW USA 32°43′N 100°54′W
172 H3 **Soalala** Mahajanga, W Madagascar 16°05′S 45°21′E
172 J4 **Soanierana-Ivongo** Toamasina, E Madagascar 16°53′S 49°35′E
171 R11 **Soasiu** *var.* Tidore. Pulau Tidore, E Indonesia 0°40′N 127°25′E
54 G8 **Soatá** Boyacá, C Colombia 06°23′N 72°40′W
172 I5 **Soavinandriana** Antananarivo, C Madagascar 19°09′S 46°43′E
77 V13 **Soba** Kaduna, C Nigeria 10°58′N 08°06′E
163 Y16 **Sobaek-sanmaek** ▲▲ South Korea
80 F13 **Sobat** ⇝ NE South Sudan
171 Z14 **Sobger, Sungai** ⇝ Papua, E Indonesia
171 V13 **Sobiei** Papua, E Indonesia 02°31′S 134°30′E
126 M3 **Sobinka** Vladimirskaya Oblast', W Russian Federation 56°00′N 39°55′E
127 S7 **Sobolevo** Orenburgskaya Oblast', W Russian Federation 51°57′N 51°42′E
Soborsin *see* Săvârşin
164 D15 **Sobo-san** ▲ Kyūshū, SW Japan 32°50′N 131°16′E
111 G14 **Sobótka** Dolnośląskie, SW Poland 50°53′N 16°48′E
59 O15 **Sobradinho** Bahia, E Brazil 09°33′S 40°56′W
Sobradinho, Barragem de *see* Sobradinho, Represa de
59 O16 **Sobradinho, Represa de** *var.* Barragem de Sobradinho. ⊠ E Brazil
58 O13 **Sobral** Ceará, E Brazil 03°45′S 40°20′W
105 T4 **Sobrarbe** *physical region* NE Spain
109 R10 **Soča** *It.* Isonzo. ⇝ Italy/Slovenia
110 L11 **Sochaczew** Mazowieckie, C Poland 52°15′N 20°15′E
126 L15 **Sochi** Krasnodarskiy Kray, SW Russian Federation 43°35′N 39°46′E
114 G13 **Sochós** *var.* Sohos, Sokhós. Kentrikí Makedonía, N Greece 40°49′N 23°23′E
191 R11 **Société, Archipel de la** *var.* Archipel de Tahiti, Îles de la Société, *Eng.* Society Islands. *island group* W French Polynesia
Société, Îles de la/Society Islands *see* Société, Archipel de la
21 T11 **Society Hill** South Carolina, SE USA 34°28′N 79°54′W
175 W9 **Society Ridge** *undersea feature* C Pacific Ocean
62 I5 **Socompa, Volcán** ⛰ N Chile 24°18′S 68°03′W
Soconusco, Sierra de *see* Madre, Sierra
54 G8 **Socorro** Santander, C Colombia 06°30′N 73°16′W
37 R13 **Socorro** New Mexico, SW USA 33°58′N 106°55′W
Socotra *see* Suquţrā
167 S14 **Soc Trăng** *var.* Khanh Hung. Soc Trăng, S Vietnam 09°36′N 105°58′E
105 P10 **Socuéllamos** Castilla-La Mancha, C Spain 39°18′N 02°48′W
35 W13 **Soda Lake** *salt flat* California, W USA

◆ Country
● Country Capital
◇ Dependent Territory
○ Dependent Territory Capital
◆ Administrative Regions
✈ International Airport
▲ Mountain
▲▲ Mountain Range
⛰ Volcano
⇝ River
◎ Lake
⊠ Reservoir

92 L11 **Sodankylä** Lappi, N Finland 67°26′N 26°35′E
Sodari *see* Sodiri
33 R15 **Soda Springs** Idaho, NW USA 42°39′N 111°36′W
Soddo/Soddu *see* Sodo
20 L10 **Soddy Daisy** Tennessee, S USA 35°14′N 85°11′W
95 N14 **Söderfors** Uppsala, C Sweden 60°23′N 17°14′E
94 N12 **Söderhamn** Gävleborg, C Sweden 61°19′N 17°10′E
95 N17 **Söderköping** Östergötland, S Sweden 58°28′N 16°20′E
95 N17 **Södermanland** ⬖ *county* C Sweden
95 O16 **Södertälje** Stockholm, C Sweden 59°11′N 17°39′E
80 D10 **Sodiri** *var.* Sawdirī, Sodari. Northern Kordofan, C Sudan 14°23′N 29°06′E
81 I14 **Sodo** *var.* Soddo, Soddu. Southern Nationalities, S Ethiopia 06°49′N 37°43′E
95 M19 **Södra Vi** Kalmar, S Sweden 57°45′N 15°45′E
18 G9 **Sodus Point** *headland* New York, NE USA 43°16′N 76°59′W
171 Q17 **Soe** *prev.* Soë. Timor, C Indonesia 09°51′S 124°29′E
Soebang *see* Subang
Soekaboemi *see* Sukabumi
169 N15 **Soekarno-Hatta** ✈ (Jakarta) Jawa, S Indonesia
Soëla-Sund *see* Soela Väin
118 E5 **Soela Väin** *prev. Eng.* Sele Sound, *Ger.* Dagden-Sund, Soëla-Sund. *strait* W Estonia
Soemba *see* Sumba, Pulau
Soembawa *see* Sumbawa
Soemenep *see* Sumenep
Soengaipenoeh *see* Sungaipenuh
Soerabaja *see* Surabaya
Soerakarta *see* Surakarta
101 G14 **Soest** Nordrhein-Westfalen, W Germany 51°34′N 08°06′E
98 J11 **Soest** Utrecht, C Netherlands 52°10′N 05°20′E
100 F11 **Soeste** ≈ NW Germany
98 J11 **Soesterberg** Utrecht, C Netherlands 52°07′N 05°17′E
115 E16 **Sofádes** *var.* Sofádhes. Thessalía, C Greece 39°20′N 22°06′E
Sofádhes *see* Sofádes
83 N18 **Sofala** Sofala, C Mozambique 20°04′S 34°43′E
83 N17 **Sofala** ⬖ *province* C Mozambique
83 N18 **Sofala, Baia de** *bay* C Mozambique
172 J3 **Sofia** *seasonal river* NW Madagascar
Sofia *see* Sofiya
115 G19 **Sofikó** Pelopónnisos, S Greece 37°46′N 23°04′E
Sofi-Kurgan *see* Sopu-Korgon
114 G10 **Sofiya** *var.* Sophia, *Eng.* Sofia, *Lat.* Serdica. ● (Bulgaria) Sofiya-Grad, W Bulgaria 42°42′N 23°20′E
114 H9 **Sofiya** ⬖ *province* W Bulgaria
114 G9 **Sofiya** ✈ Sofiya-Grad, W Bulgaria 42°42′N 23°26′E
114 G9 **Sofiya, Grad** ⬖ *municipality* W Bulgaria
Sofiyevka *see* Sofiyivka
117 S8 **Sofiyivka** *Rus.* Sofiyevka. Dnipropetrovs'ka Oblast', E Ukraine 48°04′N 33°55′E
123 R13 **Sofiysk** Khabarovskiy Kray, SE Russian Federation 52°20′N 133°37′E
123 R12 **Sofiysk** Khabarovskiy Kray, SE Russian Federation 51°32′N 139°46′E
124 I6 **Sofporog** Respublika Kareliya, NW Russian Federation 65°48′N 31°30′E
115 L23 **Sofraná** *prev.* Záfora. *island* Kykládes, Greece, Aegean Sea
165 Y14 **Sōfu-gan** *island* Izu-shotō, SE Japan
156 K10 **Sog** Xizang Zizhiqu, W China 31°52′N 93°40′E
54 G9 **Sogamoso** Boyacá, C Colombia 05°43′N 72°56′W
136 I11 **Soğanlı Çayı** ≈ N Turkey
94 E12 **Sogn** *physical region* S Norway
Sogndal *see* Sogndalsfjøra
94 E12 **Sogndalsfjøra** *var.* Sogndal. Sogn Og Fjordane, S Norway 61°13′N 07°05′E
95 E18 **Søgne** Vest-Agder, S Norway 58°05′N 07°49′E
94 D12 **Sognefjorden** *fjord* NE North Sea
94 C12 **Sogn Og Fjordane** ⬖ *county* S Norway
162 I11 **Sogo Nur** ◎ N China
159 T12 **Sogruma** Qinghai, W China 32°32′N 100°52′E
Sŏgwip'o *see* Seogwipo
Sohâg *see* Sawhāj
Sohar *see* Şuḩār
64 H9 **Sohm Plain** *undersea feature* NW Atlantic Ocean
100 H7 **Soholmer Au** ≈ N Germany
Sohos *see* Sochós
Sohrau *see* Żory
99 F20 **Soignies** Hainaut, SW Belgium 50°35′N 04°04′E
159 R15 **Soila** Xizang Zizhiqu, W China 30°40′N 97°07′E
103 P4 **Soissons** *anc.* Augusta Suessionum, Noviodunum. Aisne, N France 49°23′N 03°20′E
164 H13 **Sōja** Okayama, Honshū, SW Japan 34°40′N 133°42′E
152 F13 **Sojat** Rājasthān, N India 25°53′N 73°45′E
163 W13 **Sŏjosŏn-man** *inlet* W North Korea
116 I4 **Sokal'** *Rus.* Sokal. L'vivs'ka Oblast', NW Ukraine 50°29′N 24°17′E
163 Y14 **Sokcho** *prev.* Sokch'o. N South Korea 38°07′N 128°34′E
Sokch'o *see* Sokcho
136 B15 **Söke** Aydın, SW Turkey 37°46′N 27°24′E
189 N12 **Sokehs Island** *island* E Micronesia
79 M24 **Sokele** Katanga, SE Dem. Rep. Congo 09°54′S 24°38′E
147 R11 **Sokh** *Uzb.* Sŭkh. ≈ Kyrgyzstan/Uzbekistan
Sokh *see* So'x
Sokhós *see* Sochós
137 Q8 **Sokhumi** *Rus.* Sukhumi. NW Georgia 43°02′N 41°01′E
113 O14 **Sokobanja** Serbia, E Serbia 43°39′N 21°51′E
77 R15 **Sokodé** C Togo 08°58′N 01°10′E
123 T10 **Sokol** Magadanskaya Oblast', E Russian Federation 59°51′N 150°56′E
124 M13 **Sokol** Vologodskaya Oblast', NW Russian Federation 59°26′N 40°09′E
110 P9 **Sokółka** Podlaskie, NE Poland 53°24′N 23°31′E
76 M11 **Sokolo** Ségou, W Mali 14°43′N 06°02′W
111 A16 **Sokolov** *Ger.* Falkenau an der Eger; *prev.* Falknov nad Ohří. Karlovarský Kraj, W Czech Republic 50°10′N 12°38′E
111 O16 **Sokołów Małopolski** Podkarpackie, SE Poland 50°12′N 22°07′E
110 O11 **Sokołów Podlaski** Mazowieckie, C Poland 52°26′N 22°14′E
76 G11 **Sokone** W Senegal 13°53′N 16°22′W
77 T12 **Sokoto** Sokoto, NW Nigeria 13°05′N 05°16′E
77 T12 **Sokoto** ⬖ *state* NW Nigeria
77 S12 **Sokoto** ≈ NW Nigeria
Sokotra *see* Suquṭrā
147 U7 **Sokuluk** Chuyskaya Oblast', N Kyrgyzstan 42°53′N 74°19′E
116 L7 **Sokyryany** Chernivets'ka Oblast', W Ukraine 48°28′N 27°25′E
95 C16 **Sola** Rogaland, S Norway 58°53′N 05°36′E
187 R12 **Sola** Vanua Lava, N Vanuatu 13°51′S 167°34′E
95 C17 **Sola** ✈ (Stavanger) Rogaland, S Norway 58°54′N 05°36′E
81 H18 **Solai** Rift Valley, W Kenya 0°02′N 36°03′E
152 I8 **Solan** Himāchal Pradesh, N India 30°54′N 77°06′E
185 A25 **Solander Island** *island* SW New Zealand
Solano *see* Bahía Solano
155 F15 **Solāpur** *var.* Sholāpur. Mahārāshtra, W India 17°43′N 75°54′E
93 H16 **Solberg** Västernorrland, C Sweden 63°48′N 17°40′E
116 K9 **Solca** *Ger.* Solka. Suceava, N Romania 47°40′N 25°50′E
105 O16 **Sol, Costa del** *coastal region* S Spain
106 F5 **Solda** *Ger.* Sulden. Trentino-Alto Adige, N Italy 46°33′N 10°35′E
117 N9 **Şoldăneşti** *Rus.* Sholdaneshty. N Moldova 47°49′N 28°45′E
Soldau *see* Wkra
108 L8 **Sölden** Tirol, W Austria 46°58′N 11°01′E
27 P3 **Soldier Creek** ≈ Kansas, C USA
39 R12 **Soldotna** Alaska, USA 60°29′N 151°03′W
110 I10 **Solec Kujawski** Kujawsko-pomorskie, C Poland 53°04′N 18°09′E
61 B16 **Soledad** Santa Fe, C Argentina 30°38′S 60°52′W
55 E4 **Soledad** Atlántico, N Colombia 10°54′N 74°48′W
35 O11 **Soledad** California, W USA 36°25′N 121°19′W
55 O7 **Soledad** Anzoátegui, NE Venezuela 08°10′N 63°36′W
61 H15 **Soledade** Rio Grande do Sul, S Brazil 28°50′S 52°30′W
Isla Soledad *see* East Falkland
103 Y15 **Solenzara** Corse, France, C Mediterranean Sea 41°55′N 09°24′E
Soleure *see* Solothurn
94 C12 **Solheim** Hordaland, S Norway 60°54′N 05°30′E
125 N14 **Soligalich** Kostromskaya Oblast', NW Russian Federation 59°05′N 42°15′E
Soligorsk *see* Salihorsk
97 L20 **Solihull** C England, United Kingdom 52°25′N 01°45′W
125 U13 **Solikamsk** Permskiy Kray, NW Russian Federation 59°37′N 56°46′E
127 V8 **Sol'-Iletsk** Orenburgskaya Oblast', W Russian Federation 51°09′N 55°05′E
57 G17 **Solimana, Nevado** ▲ S Peru 15°24′S 72°49′W
58 E13 **Solimões, Rio** ≈ C Brazil
113 E14 **Solin** *It.* Salona; *anc.* Salonae. Split-Dalmacija, S Croatia 43°33′N 16°29′E
101 E15 **Solingen** Nordrhein-Westfalen, W Germany 51°10′N 07°05′E
Solka *see* Solca
93 H16 **Sollefteå** Västernorrland, C Sweden 63°09′N 17°15′E
95 O15 **Sollentuna** Stockholm, C Sweden 59°26′N 17°56′E
105 X9 **Sóller** Mallorca, Spain, W Mediterranean Sea 39°46′N 02°42′E
94 L13 **Sollerön** Dalarna, C Sweden 60°55′N 14°34′E
101 I14 **Solling** *hill range* C Germany
95 O16 **Solna** Stockholm, C Sweden 59°22′N 17°58′E
126 K3 **Solnechnogorsk** Moskovskaya Oblast', W Russian Federation 56°07′N 37°04′E
123 R10 **Solnechnyy** Khabarovskiy Kray, SE Russian Federation 50°41′N 136°42′E
123 S13 **Solnechnyy** Respublika Sakha (Yakutiya), NE Russian Federation 60°13′N 137°42′E
Solo *see* Surakarta
107 L17 **Solofra** Campania, S Italy 40°49′N 14°48′E
168 J11 **Solok** Sumatera, W Indonesia 0°45′S 100°42′E
42 C6 **Sololá** Sololá, W Guatemala 14°46′N 91°09′W
42 A2 **Sololá** *off.* Departamento de Sololá. ⬖ *department* SW Guatemala
Sololá, Departamento de *see* Sololá
81 J16 **Sololo** Eastern, N Kenya 03°31′N 38°39′E
42 C4 **Soloma** Huehuetenango, W Guatemala 15°38′N 91°25′W
38 M9 **Solomon** Alaska, USA 64°33′N 164°26′W
27 N4 **Solomon** Kansas, C USA 38°55′N 97°22′W
187 N9 **Solomon Islands** *prev.* British Solomon Islands Protectorate. ◆ *commonwealth republic* W Solomon Islands N Melanesia W Pacific Ocean
186 L7 **Solomon Islands** *island group* Papua New Guinea/Solomon Islands
26 M3 **Solomon River** ≈ Kansas, C USA
186 H8 **Solomon Sea** *sea* W Pacific Ocean
31 U11 **Solon** Ohio, N USA 41°23′N 81°26′W
117 T8 **Solone** Dnipropetrovs'ka Oblast', E Ukraine 48°12′N 34°49′E
171 P16 **Solor, Kepulauan** *island group* S Indonesia
126 M4 **Solotcha** Ryazanskaya Oblast', W Russian Federation 54°43′N 39°50′E
108 D7 **Solothurn** *Fr.* Soleure. Solothurn, NW Switzerland 47°13′N 07°32′E
108 D7 **Solothurn** *Fr.* Soleure. ⬖ *canton* NW Switzerland
124 J7 **Solovetskiye Ostrova** *island group* NW Russian Federation
105 V5 **Solsona** Cataluña, NE Spain 42°00′N 01°31′E
113 E14 **Šolta** *It.* Solta. *island* S Croatia
Solṭānābād *see* Kāshmar
142 L4 **Solṭānīyeh** Zanjān, NW Iran 36°24′N 48°50′E
100 I11 **Soltau** Niedersachsen, NW Germany 52°59′N 09°50′E
124 G14 **Sol'tsy** Novgorodskaya Oblast', W Russian Federation 58°09′N 30°23′E
Soltüstik Qazaqstan Oblysy *see* Severnyy Kazakhstan
Solun *see* Thessaloníki
113 O19 **Solunska Glava** ▲ C FYR Macedonia 41°43′N 21°24′E
95 L22 **Sölvesborg** Blekinge, S Sweden 56°04′N 14°35′E
97 J15 **Solway Firth** *inlet* England/Scotland, United Kingdom
82 I13 **Solwezi** North Western, NW Zambia 12°11′S 26°23′E
165 Q11 **Sōma** Fukushima, Honshū, C Japan 37°49′N 140°52′E
136 C13 **Soma** Manisa, W Turkey 39°10′N 27°36′E
Somali *see* Sumalē
81 O15 **Somalia** *off.* Somali Democratic Republic, *Som.* Jamuuriyada Demuqraadiga Soomaaliyeed, Soomaaliya; *prev.* Italian Somaliland, Somaliland Protectorate. ◆ *republic* E Africa
173 N6 **Somali Basin** *undersea feature* W Indian Ocean 0°00′N 52°00′E
Somali Democratic Republic *see* Somalia
80 N12 **Somaliland** ⬖ *disputed territory* N Somalia
Somaliland Protectorate *see* Somalia
67 Y8 **Somali Plain** *undersea feature* W Indian Ocean 01°00′N 51°30′E
112 J8 **Sombor** *Hung.* Zombor. Vojvodina, NW Serbia 45°46′N 19°07′E
99 H20 **Sombreffe** Namur, S Belgium 50°32′N 04°39′E
40 L10 **Sombrerete** Zacatecas, C Mexico 23°38′N 103°40′W
45 V8 **Sombrero** *island* N Anguilla
151 Q21 **Sombrero Channel** *channel* Nicobar Islands, India
116 H9 **Şomcuta Mare** *Hung.* Nagysomkút; *prev.* Somcuţa Mare. Maramureş, N Romania 47°29′N 23°30′E
Somcuţa Mare *see* Şomcuta Mare
167 R9 **Somdet** Kalasin, E Thailand 16°41′N 103°44′E
99 L15 **Someren** Noord-Brabant, SE Netherlands 51°23′N 05°42′E
93 L19 **Somero** Länsi-Suomi, SW Finland 60°37′N 23°30′E
33 P7 **Somers** Montana, NW USA 48°04′N 114°16′W
64 A12 **Somerset** *var.* Somerset Village. W Bermuda 32°18′N 64°53′W
37 Q5 **Somerset** Colorado, C USA 38°55′N 107°27′W
20 M7 **Somerset** Kentucky, S USA 37°05′N 84°36′W
19 O12 **Somerset** Massachusetts, NE USA 41°46′N 71°07′W
97 K23 **Somerset** *cultural region* SW England, United Kingdom
Somerset East *see* Somerset-Oos
64 A12 **Somerset Island** *island* W Bermuda
197 N9 **Somerset Island** *island* Queen Elizabeth Islands, Nunavut, NW Canada
Somerset Nile *see* Victoria Nile
83 I25 **Somerset-Oos** *var.* Somerset East. Eastern Cape, S South Africa 32°44′S 25°35′E
Somerset Village *see* Somerset
83 E26 **Somerset-Wes** *var.* Somerset West. Western Cape, SW South Africa 34°05′S 18°51′E
Somerset West *see* Somerset-Wes
Somers Islands *see* Bermuda
18 J17 **Somers Point** New Jersey, NE USA 39°18′N 74°34′W
19 P9 **Somersworth** New Hampshire, NE USA 43°15′N 70°52′W
36 H15 **Somerton** Arizona, SW USA 32°36′N 114°42′W
18 J14 **Somerville** New Jersey, NE USA 40°34′N 74°36′W
20 F10 **Somerville** Tennessee, S USA 35°14′N 89°24′W
25 U10 **Somerville** Texas, SW USA 30°21′N 96°31′W
25 T10 **Somerville Lake** ▦ Texas, SW USA
Someş/Somesch/Someşul *see* Szamos
103 N2 **Somme** ⬖ *department* N France
103 N2 **Somme** ≈ N France
95 L18 **Sommen** Jönköping, S Sweden 58°07′N 14°58′E
95 M18 **Sommen** ◎ S Sweden
101 K16 **Sömmerda** Thüringen, C Germany 51°10′N 11°07′E
Sommerein *see* Šamorín
Sommerfeld *see* Lubsko
55 Y11 **Sommet Tabulaire** *var.* Mont Itoupé. ▲▲ S French Guiana
111 H25 **Somogy** *off.* Somogy Megye. ⬖ *county* SW Hungary
Somogy Megye *see* Somogy
Somorja *see* Šamorín
105 N7 **Somosierra, Puerto de** *pass* N Spain
187 Y14 **Somosomo** Taveuni, N Fiji 16°46′S 179°57′W
42 I9 **Somotillo** Chinandega, NW Nicaragua 13°01′N 86°53′W
42 I8 **Somoto** Madriz, NW Nicaragua 13°29′N 86°36′W
110 I11 **Sompolno** Wielkopolskie, C Poland 52°24′N 18°30′E
102 J17 **Somport, Col du** *var.* Puerto de Somport, *Sp.* Somport; *anc.* Summus Portus. *pass* France/Spain *see also* Somport
99 K15 **Son** Noord-Brabant, S Netherlands 51°32′N 05°34′E
95 H15 **Son** Akershus, S Norway 59°32′N 10°42′E
154 L9 **Son** *var.* Sone. ≈ C India
43 R16 **Soná** Veraguas, W Panama 08°00′N 81°20′W
Sonag *see* Zêkog
Sonapur *see* Subarnapur
95 G24 **Sønderborg** *Ger.* Sonderburg. Syddanmark, SW Denmark 54°55′N 09°48′E
Sonderburg *see* Sønderborg
Sønderjyllands Amt *see* Syddanmark
101 K15 **Sondershausen** Thüringen, C Germany 51°22′N 10°52′E
Sondre Strømfjord *see* Kangerlussuaq
106 E6 **Sondrio** Lombardia, N Italy 46°11′N 09°52′E
Sone *see* Son
Sonepur *see* Subarnapur
57 K22 **Sonequera** ▲ S Bolivia 22°06′S 67°10′W
167 V12 **Sông Câu** Phu Yên, C Vietnam 13°26′N 109°12′E
167 R15 **Sông Đốc** Minh Hai, S Vietnam 09°03′N 104°51′E
81 H25 **Songea** Ruvuma, S Tanzania 10°42′S 35°39′E
163 X10 **Songhua Hu** ◎ NE China
163 Y7 **Songhua Jiang** *var.* Sungari. ≈ NE China
161 S8 **Songjiang** Shanghai Shi, E China 31°01′N 121°14′E
Sŏngjin *see* Kimch'aek
167 O16 **Songkhla** *var.* Songkla, *Mal.* Singora. Songkhla, SW Thailand 07°12′N 100°35′E
Songkla *see* Songkhla
163 T13 **Song Ling** ▲▲ NE China
129 U12 **Sông Ma** *Laos* Ma, Nam. ≈ Laos/Vietnam
163 W14 **Songnim** SW North Korea 38°43′N 125°40′E
82 B10 **Songo** Uíge, NW Angola 07°30′S 14°56′E
83 M15 **Songo** Tete, NW Mozambique 15°36′S 32°45′E
79 F21 **Songololo** Bas-Congo, SW Dem. Rep. Congo 05°40′S 14°05′E
160 H7 **Songpan** *var.* Jin'an, *Tib.* Sungpu. Sichuan, C China 32°49′N 103°39′E
Sŏngsan *see* Seongsan
161 R11 **Songxi** Fujian, SE China 27°33′N 118°46′E
160 M6 **Songxian** *var.* Song Xian. Henan, C China 34°11′N 112°04′E
Song Xian *see* Songxian
161 R10 **Songyang** *var.* Xiping; *prev.* Songyin. Zhejiang, SE China 28°29′N 119°27′E
Songyin *see* Songyang
163 V9 **Songyuan** *var.* Fu-yü, Petuna; *prev.* Fuyu. Jilin, NE China 45°10′N 124°52′E
Sonid Youqi *see* SaihanTal
Sonid Zuoqi *see* Mandalt
152 I10 **Sonīpat** Haryāna, N India 29°00′N 77°01′E
93 M15 **Sonkajärvi** Itä-Suomi, C Finland 63°40′N 27°30′E
167 R6 **Sơn La** Sơn La, N Vietnam 21°20′N 103°55′E
149 O16 **Sonmiāni** Baluchistān, S Pakistan 25°24′N 66°37′E
149 O16 **Sonmiāni Bay** *bay* S Pakistan
101 K18 **Sonneberg** Thüringen, C Germany 50°22′N 11°10′E
101 N24 **Sonntagshorn** ▲ Austria/Germany 47°40′N 12°42′E
Sonoita *see* Sonoyta
40 E3 **Sonoita, Rio** *var.* Río Sonoyta. ≈ Mexico/USA
35 N7 **Sonoma** California, W USA 38°16′N 122°28′W
35 T3 **Sonoma Peak** ▲ Nevada, W USA 40°50′N 117°34′W
35 P8 **Sonora** California, W USA 37°58′N 120°22′W
25 O10 **Sonora** Texas, SW USA 30°34′N 100°39′W
40 F5 **Sonora** ⬖ *state* NW Mexico
35 X17 **Sonoran Desert** *var.* Desierto de Altar. *desert* Mexico/USA *see also* Altar, Desierto de
40 G5 **Sonora, Río** ≈ NW Mexico
40 E2 **Sonoyta** *var.* Sonoita. Sonora, NW Mexico 31°49′N 112°50′W
Sonoyta, Río *see* Sonoita, Rio
142 K6 **Sonqor** *var.* Sunqur. Kermānshāhān, W Iran 34°45′N 47°39′E
105 N9 **Sonseca** *var.* Sonseca con Casalgordo. Castilla-La Mancha, C Spain 39°40′N 03°59′W
Sonseca con Casalgordo *see* Sonseca
54 E9 **Sonsón** Antioquia, W Colombia 05°45′N 75°18′W
42 E7 **Sonsonate** Sonsonate, W El Salvador 13°44′N 89°43′W
42 A9 **Sonsonate** ⬖ *department* SW El Salvador
188 A10 **Sonsorol Islands** *island group* S Palau
112 J9 **Sonta** *Hung.* Szond; *prev.* Szonta. Vojvodina, NW Serbia 45°34′N 19°06′E
167 S6 **Sơn Tây** *var.* Sontay. Ha Tây, N Vietnam 21°06′N 105°32′E
Sontay *see* Sơn Tây
101 J25 **Sonthofen** Bayern, S Germany 47°31′N 10°16′E
Soochow *see* Suzhou
80 O13 **Sool** *off.* Gobolka Sool. ⬖ *region* N Somalia
Soomaaliya/Soomaaliyeed, Jamuuriyada Demuqraadiga *see* Somalia
Soome Laht *see* Finland, Gulf of
23 V5 **Soperton** Georgia, SE USA 32°22′N 82°35′W
167 S6 **Sop Hao** Houaphan, N Laos 20°33′N 104°25′E
Sophia *see* Sofiya
171 S10 **Sopi** Pulau Morotai, E Indonesia 02°36′N 128°32′E
Sopianae *see* Pécs
171 U13 **Sopinusa** Papua, E Indonesia 03°31′S 132°55′E
81 B14 **Sopo** ≈ W South Sudan
Sopockinie/Sopotskin/Sopotskino *see* Sapotskin
114 I9 **Sopot** Plovdiv, C Bulgaria 42°39′N 24°43′E
110 I7 **Sopot** *Ger.* Zoppot. Pomorskie, N Poland 54°26′N 18°33′E
167 O8 **Sop Prap** *var.* Ban Sop Prap. Lampang, NW Thailand 17°55′N 99°20′E
111 G22 **Sopron** *Ger.* Ödenburg. Győr-Moson-Sopron, NW Hungary 47°40′N 16°35′E
147 U11 **Sopu-Korgon** *var.* Sofi-Kurgan. Oshskaya Oblast', SW Kyrgyzstan 40°03′N 73°30′E
152 H5 **Sopur** Jammu and Kashmir, NW India 34°19′N 74°30′E
107 J15 **Sora** Lazio, C Italy 41°43′N 13°37′E
154 N13 **Sorada** Orissa, E India 19°46′N 84°29′E
93 H17 **Söråker** Västernorrland, C Sweden 62°32′N 17°32′E
57 J17 **Sorata** La Paz, W Bolivia 15°47′S 68°38′W
Sorau/Sorau in der Niederlausitz *see* Żary
105 Q14 **Sorbas** Andalucía, S Spain 37°06′N 02°06′W
94 N11 **Sördellen** ◎ C Sweden
Sord/Sórd Choluim Chille *see* Swords
15 O11 **Sorel** Québec, SE Canada 46°03′N 73°06′W
183 P17 **Sorell** Tasmania, SE Australia 42°49′S 147°34′E
183 O17 **Sorell, Lake** ◎ Tasmania, SE Australia
106 E8 **Soresina** Lombardia, N Italy 45°17′N 09°51′E
95 D14 **Sørfjorden** *fjord* S Norway
94 N11 **Sörforsa** Gävleborg, C Sweden 61°45′N 17°00′E
103 R14 **Sorgues** Vaucluse, SE France 44°N 04°52′E
136 K13 **Sorgun** Yozgat, C Turkey 39°49′N 35°10′E
105 P5 **Soria** Castilla y León, N Spain 41°47′N 02°26′W
105 P6 **Soria** ⬖ *province* Castilla y León, N Spain
61 D19 **Soriano** Soriano, SW Uruguay 33°25′S 58°21′W
61 D19 **Soriano** ⬖ *department* SW Uruguay
92 O4 **Sørkapp** *headland* SW Svalbard 76°34′N 16°33′E
143 T5 **Sorkh, Kūh-e** ▲▲ NE Iran
95 I23 **Sorø** Sjælland, E Denmark 55°26′N 11°34′E
Soro *see* Ghazal, Bahr el
116 M8 **Soroca** *Rus.* Soroki. N Moldova 48°10′N 28°18′E
60 L10 **Sorocaba** São Paulo, S Brazil 23°29′S 47°27′W
Sorochino *see* Sarochyna
127 T7 **Sorochinsk** Orenburgskaya Oblast', W Russian Federation 52°26′N 53°10′E
Soroki *see* Soroca
188 H15 **Sorol** *atoll* Caroline Islands, W Micronesia
171 T12 **Sorong** Papua, E Indonesia 0°49′S 131°16′E
81 G17 **Soroti** C Uganda 01°42′N 33°37′E
Sørøy *see* Sørøya
92 J8 **Sørøya** *var.* Sørøy, *Lapp.* Sállan. *island* N Norway
104 G11 **Sorraia, Rio** ≈ C Portugal
92 I10 **Sørreisa** Troms, N Norway 69°08′N 18°09′E
107 K18 **Sorrento** *anc.* Surrentum. Campania, S Italy 40°37′N 14°23′E
104 H10 **Sor, Ribeira de** *stream* C Portugal
195 T3 **Sør Rondane** *Eng.* Sor Rondane Mountains. ▲▲ Antarctica
Sor Rondane Mountains *see* Sør Rondane
93 H14 **Sorsele** Västerbotten, N Sweden 65°31′N 17°34′E
107 B17 **Sorso** Sardegna, Italy, C Mediterranean Sea 40°46′N 08°33′E
171 P4 **Sorsogon** Luzon, N Philippines 12°57′N 124°04′E
105 U4 **Sort** Cataluña, NE Spain 42°25′N 01°07′E
124 H11 **Sortavala** *prev.* Serdobol'. Respublika Kareliya, NW Russian Federation 61°45′N 30°37′E
107 L25 **Sortino** Sicilia, Italy, C Mediterranean Sea 37°10′N 15°02′E
92 G10 **Sortland** Nordland, C Norway 68°44′N 15°25′E
94 G9 **Sør-Trøndelag** ⬖ *county* S Norway
95 I15 **Sørumsand** Akershus, S Norway 59°58′N 11°13′E
118 D6 **Sõrve Säär** *headland* SW Estonia 57°54′N 22°02′E
95 K22 **Sösdala** Skåne, S Sweden 56°00′N 13°36′E
105 R4 **Sos del Rey Católico** Aragón, NE Spain 42°30′N 01°13′W
93 F15 **Sösjöfjällen** ▲ C Sweden 63°51′N 13°15′E
126 K7 **Sosna** ≈ W Russian Federation
62 H12 **Sosneado, Cerro** ▲ W Argentina 34°44′S 69°52′W
125 S9 **Sosnogorsk** Respublika Komi, NW Russian Federation 63°33′N 53°55′E
124 J8 **Sosnovets** Respublika Kareliya, NW Russian Federation 64°25′N 34°23′E
Sosnovets *see* Sosnowiec
127 Q3 **Sosnovka** Chuvashskaya Respublika, W Russian Federation 56°18′N 47°14′E
125 S16 **Sosnovka** Kirovskaya Oblast', NW Russian Federation 56°15′N 51°20′E
124 M6 **Sosnovka** Murmanskaya Oblast', NW Russian Federation 66°28′N 40°31′E
126 M6 **Sosnovka** Tambovskaya Oblast', W Russian Federation 53°14′N 41°19′E
124 H12 **Sosnovo** *Fin.* Rautu. Leningradskaya Oblast', NW Russian Federation 60°30′N 30°13′E
127 V3 **Sosnovyy Bor** Respublika Bashkortostan, W Russian Federation 55°51′N 57°09′E
Sosnovyy Bor *see* Sasnovy Bor
111 J16 **Sosnowiec** *Ger.* Sosnowitz, *Rus.* Sosnovets. Śląskie, S Poland 50°16′N 19°07′E
Sosnowitz *see* Sosnowiec
117 R2 **Sosnytsya** Chernihivs'ka Oblast', N Ukraine 51°31′N 32°30′E
109 V10 **Šoštanj** N Slovenia 46°23′N 15°03′E
122 G10 **Sos'va** Sverdlovskaya Oblast', C Russian Federation 59°13′N 61°58′E
54 D12 **Sotará, Volcán** ⛰ S Colombia 02°04′N 76°40′W
76 D10 **Sotavento, Ilhas de** *var.* Leeward Islands. *island group* S Cape Verde
93 N15 **Sotkamo** Oulu, C Finland 64°06′N 28°30′E
109 W11 **Sotla** ≈ E Slovenia
41 P10 **Soto la Marina** Tamaulipas, C Mexico 23°44′N 98°10′W
41 P10 **Soto la Marina, Río** ≈ C Mexico
95 B14 **Sotra** *island* S Norway
41 X12 **Sotuta** Yucatán, SE Mexico 20°34′N 89°00′W
79 F17 **Souanké** Sangha, NW Congo 02°03′N 14°02′E
76 M17 **Soubré** S Ivory Coast 05°50′N 06°35′W
115 H24 **Soúda** *var.* Soúdha, *Eng.* Suda. Kríti, Greece, E Mediterranean Sea 35°29′N 24°04′E
Soúdha *see* Soúda
Soueida *see* As Suwaydā'
114 L12 **Souflí** *prev.* Souflíon. Anatolikí Makedonía kai Thráki, NE Greece 41°12′N 26°18′E
Souflíon *see* Souflí
45 S11 **Soufrière** W Saint Lucia 13°51′N 61°03′W
45 X6 **Soufrière** ⛰ Basse Terre, S Guadeloupe 16°03′N 61°39′W
102 M13 **Souillac** Lot, S France 44°53′N 01°29′E
173 Y17 **Souillac** S Mauritius 20°31′S 57°31′E
74 M5 **Souk Ahras** NE Algeria 36°14′N 08°00′E
Souk el Arba du Rharb/Souk-el-Arba-du-Rharb/Souk-el-Arba-el-Rhab *see* Souk-el-Arba-Rharb
74 E6 **Souk-el-Arba-Rharb** *var.* Souk el Arba du Rharb, Souk-el-Arba-du-Rharb, Souk-el-Arba-el-Rhab. NW Morocco 34°38′N 06°00′W
Soukhné *see* As Sukhnah
Sŏul *see* Seoul
102 J11 **Soulac-sur-Mer** Gironde, SW France 45°31′N 01°06′W
99 L19 **Soumagne** Liège, E Belgium 50°36′N 05°48′E
18 M14 **Sound Beach** Long Island, New York, NE USA 40°56′N 72°58′W
95 J22 **Sound, The** *Dan.* Øresund, *Swe.* Öresund. *strait* Denmark/Sweden
115 H20 **Soúnio, Akrotírio** *headland* C Greece 37°39′N 24°01′E
138 F8 **Soûr** *var.* Şūr; *anc.* Tyre. SW Lebanon 33°18′N 35°30′E
Sources, Mont-aux- *see* Phofung
104 G8 **Soure** Coimbra, N Portugal 40°04′N 08°38′W
11 W17 **Souris** Manitoba, S Canada 49°38′N 100°17′W
13 Q14 **Souris** Prince Edward Island, SE Canada 46°22′N 62°16′W
28 L2 **Souris River** *var.* Mouse River. ≈ Canada/USA
25 X10 **Sour Lake** Texas, SW USA 30°08′N 94°24′W
115 F17 **Soúrpi** Thessalía, C Greece 39°07′N 22°55′E
104 H11 **Sousel** Portalegre, C Portugal 38°57′N 07°40′W
75 N6 **Sousse** *var.* Sūsah. NE Tunisia 35°46′N 10°38′E
14 H11 **South** ≈ Ontario, S Canada
South *see* Sud
83 G23 **South Africa** *off.* Republic of South Africa, *Afr.* Suid-Afrika. ◆ *republic* S Africa
South Africa, Republic of *see* South Africa
46-47 **South America** *continent*
2 J17 **South American Plate** *tectonic feature*
97 M23 **Southampton** *hist.* Hamwih, *Lat.* Clausentum. S England, United Kingdom 50°54′N 01°23′W
19 N14 **Southampton** Long Island, New York, NE USA 40°52′N 72°22′W
9 P8 **Southampton Island** *island* Nunavut, NE Canada
151 P20 **South Andaman** *island* Andaman Islands, India, NE Indian Ocean
13 Q6 **South Aulatsivik Island** *island* Newfoundland and Labrador, E Canada
182 E4 **South Australia** ⬖ *state* S Australia
South Australian Abyssal Plain *see* South Australian Plain
192 G11 **South Australian Basin** *undersea feature* SW Indian Ocean 38°00′S 126°00′E
173 X12 **South Australian Plain** *var.* South Australian Abyssal Plain. *undersea feature* SE Indian Ocean
37 R13 **South Baldy** ▲ New Mexico, SW USA 33°59′N 107°11′W
23 Y14 **South Bay** Florida, SE USA 26°39′N 80°43′W
14 E12 **South Baymouth** Manitoulin Island, Ontario, S Canada 45°33′N 82°01′W
30 L10 **South Beloit** Illinois, N USA 42°29′N 89°02′W
31 O11 **South Bend** Indiana, N USA 41°40′N 86°15′W
25 R6 **South Bend** Texas, SW USA 32°58′N 98°39′W
32 F9 **South Bend** Washington, NW USA 46°38′N 123°48′W
South Beveland *see* Zuid-Beveland
South Borneo *see* Kalimantan Selatan
21 U7 **South Boston** Virginia, NE USA 36°42′N 78°58′W
182 F2 **South Branch Neales** *seasonal river* South Australia
21 U3 **South Branch Potomac River** ≈ West Virginia, NE USA
185 H19 **Southbridge** Canterbury, South Island, New Zealand 43°49′S 172°17′E
19 N12 **Southbridge** Massachusetts, NE USA 42°03′N 72°00′W
183 P17 **South Bruny Island** *island* Tasmania, SE Australia
18 L7 **South Burlington** Vermont, NE USA 44°27′N 73°08′W
44 M6 **South Caicos** *island* S Turks and Caicos Islands
South Cape *see* Ka Lae
23 V3 **South Carolina** *off.* State of South Carolina, *also known as* The Palmetto State. ⬖ *state* SE USA
South Carpathians *see* Carpaţii Meridionalii
South Celebes *see* Sulawesi Selatan
21 Q5 **South Charleston** West Virginia, NE USA 38°22′N 81°42′W
192 D7 **South China Basin** *undersea feature* SE South China Sea 15°00′N 115°00′E
169 R8 **South China Sea** *Chin.* Nan Hai, *Ind.* Laut Cina Selatan, *Vtn.* Biên Đông. *sea* SE Asia
33 Z10 **South Dakota** *off.* State of South Dakota, *also known as* The Coyote State, Sunshine State. ⬖ *state* N USA
23 X10 **South Daytona** Florida, SE USA 29°09′N 81°01′W
37 R10 **South Domingo Pueblo** New Mexico, SW USA 35°28′N 106°24′W
97 N23 **South Downs** *hill range* SE England, United Kingdom
83 I21 **South East** ⬖ *district* SE Botswana
65 H15 **South East Bay** *bay* Ascension Island, C Atlantic Ocean
183 O17 **South East Cape** *headland* Tasmania, SE Australia 43°36′S 146°52′E
38 K10 **Southeast Cape** *headland* Saint Lawrence Island, Alaska, USA 62°56′N 169°39′W
South-East Celebes *see* Sulawesi Tenggara
192 G12 **Southeast Indian Ridge** *undersea feature* Indian Ocean/Pacific Ocean 50°00′S 110°00′E
Southeast Island *see* Tagula Island
193 P13 **Southeast Pacific Basin** *var.* Belling Hausen Mulde. *undersea feature* SE Pacific Ocean 60°00′S 115°00′W
65 H15 **South East Point** *headland* SE Ascension Island
183 O14 **South East Point** *headland* Victoria, S Australia 39°10′S 146°21′E
44 L5 **Southeast Point** *headland* Mayaguana, SE Bahamas 22°15′N 72°44′W
191 Z3 **South East Point** *headland* Kiritimati, NE Kiribati 01°42′N 157°10′W
South-East Sulawesi *see* Sulawesi Tenggara
11 U12 **Southend** Saskatchewan, C Canada 56°20′N 103°14′W
97 P22 **Southend-on-Sea** E England, United Kingdom 51°33′N 00°43′E
83 H20 **Southern** *var.* Bangwaketse, Ngwaketze. ⬖ *district* SE Botswana
138 E13 **Southern** ⬖ *district* S Israel
83 N15 **Southern** ⬖ *region* S Malawi
155 J26 **Southern** ⬖ *province* S Sri Lanka
83 I15 **Southern** ⬖ *province* S Zambia
185 E19 **Southern Alps** ▲▲ South Island, New Zealand
190 K15 **Southern Cook Islands** *island group* S Cook Islands
180 K12 **Southern Cross** Western Australia 31°17′S 119°15′E
80 A12 **Southern Darfur** ⬖ *state* W Sudan
186 B7 **Southern Highlands** ⬖ *province* W Papua New Guinea
11 V11 **Southern Indian Lake** ◎ Manitoba, C Canada
80 E11 **Southern Kordofan** ⬖ *state* C Sudan
187 Z15 **Southern Lau Group** *island group* Lau Group, SE Fiji
81 I15 **Southern Nationalities** ⬖ *region* S Ethiopia
173 S13 **Southern Ocean** *ocean*
21 T10 **Southern Pines** North Carolina, SE USA 35°10′N 79°23′W
96 I13 **Southern Uplands** ▲▲ S Scotland, United Kingdom
Southern Urals *see* Yuzhnyy Ural
183 P16 **South Esk River** ≈ Tasmania, SE Australia
11 U16 **Southey** Saskatchewan, S Canada 50°53′N 104°27′W
27 V2 **South Fabius River** ≈ Missouri, C USA
31 S10 **Southfield** Michigan, N USA 42°28′N 83°12′W
192 K10 **South Fiji Basin** *undersea feature* S Pacific Ocean 26°00′S 175°00′E
97 Q22 **South Foreland** *headland* SE England, United Kingdom 51°08′N 01°22′E
35 P7 **South Fork American River** ≈ California, W USA
28 K7 **South Fork Grand River** ≈ South Dakota, N USA

◆ Country
● Country Capital
◇ Dependent Territory
○ Dependent Territory Capital
⬖ Administrative Regions
✈ International Airport
▲ Mountain
▲▲ Mountain Range
⛰ Volcano
≈ River
◎ Lake
▦ Reservoir

35 *T12* **South Fork Kern River** ≈ California, W USA
39 *Q7* **South Fork Koyukuk River** ≈ Alaska, USA
39 *Q11* **South Fork Kuskokwim River** ≈ Alaska, USA
26 *H2* **South Fork Republican River** ≈ C USA
26 *L3* **South Fork Solomon River** ≈ Kansas, C USA
31 *P5* **South Fox Island** *island* Michigan, N USA
20 *G8* **South Fulton** Tennessee, S USA *36°28′N 88°53′W*
195 *U10* **South Geomagnetic Pole** *pole* Antarctica
65 *J20* **South Georgia** *island* South Georgia and the South Sandwich Islands, SW Atlantic Ocean
65 *K21* **South Georgia and the South Sandwich Islands** ⬖ *UK Dependent Territory* SW Atlantic Ocean
47 *Y14* **South Georgia Ridge** ***var.*** North Scotia Ridge. *undersea feature* SW Atlantic Ocean *54°00′S 40°00′W*
181 *Q1* **South Goulburn Island** *island* Northern Territory, N Australia
153 *U16* **South Hatia Island** *island* SE Bangladesh
31 *O10* **South Haven** Michigan, N USA *42°24′N 86°16′W*
21 *V7* **South Hill** Virginia, NE USA *36°43′N 78°07′W*
South Holland ***see*** Zuid-Holland
21 *P8* **South Holston Lake** ⊠ Tennessee/Virginia, S USA
175 *N1* **South Honshu Ridge** *undersea feature* W Pacific Ocean
26 *M6* **South Hutchinson** Kansas, C USA *38°01′N 97°56′W*
151 *K21* **South Huvadhu Atoll** *atoll* S Maldives
173 *U14* **South Indian Basin** *undersea feature* Indian Ocean/Pacific Ocean *60°00′S 120°00′E*
11 *W11* **South Indian Lake** Manitoba, C Canada *56°48′N 98°56′W*
81 *I17* **South Island** *island* NW Kenya
185 *C20* **South Island** *island* S New Zealand
65 *B23* **South Jason** *island* Jason Islands, NW Falkland Islands
South Kalimantan ***see*** Kalimantan Selatan
South Kazakhstan ***see*** Yuzhnyy Kazakhstan
163 *X15* **South Korea** ***off.*** Republic of Korea, ***Kor.*** Taehan Min'guk. ◆ *republic* E Asia
35 *Q6* **South Lake Tahoe** California, W USA *38°56′N 119°57′W*
25 *N6* **Southland** Texas, SW USA *33°16′N 101°31′W*
185 *B23* **Southland** ***off.*** Southland Region. ⬖ *region* South Island, New Zealand
Southland Region ***see*** Southland
29 *N15* **South Loup River** ≈ Nebraska, C USA
151 *K19* **South Maalhosmadulu Atoll** *atoll* N Maldives
14 *E15* **South Maitland** ≈ Ontario, S Canada
192 *E8* **South Makassar Basin** *undersea feature* E Java Sea
31 *O6* **South Manitou Island** *island* Michigan, N USA
151 *K18* **South Miladhunmadulu Atoll** ***var.*** Noonu. *atoll* N Maldives
21 *X8* **South Mills** North Carolina, SE USA *36°28′N 76°18′W*
8 *H9* **South Nahanni** ≈ Northwest Territories, NW Canada
39 *P13* **South Naknek** Alaska, USA *58°39′N 157°01′W*
14 *M13* **South Nation** ≈ Ontario, SE Canada
44 *F9* **South Negril Point** *headland* W Jamaica *18°14′N 78°21′W*
151 *K20* **South Nilandhe Atoll** ***var.*** Dhaalu Atoll. *atoll* C Maldives
36 *L2* **South Ogden** Utah, W USA *41°09′N 111°58′W*
18 *M14* **Southold** Long Island, New York, NE USA *41°03′N 72°24′W*
194 *H1* **South Orkney Islands** *island group* Antarctica
137 *S9* **South Ossetia** *former autonomous region* SW Georgia
South Pacific Basin ***see*** Southwest Pacific Basin
19 *P7* **South Paris** Maine, NE USA *44°14′N 70°33′W*
189 *U13* **South Pass** *passage* Chuuk Islands, C Micronesia
33 *U15* **South Pass** *pass* Wyoming, C USA
20 *K10* **South Pittsburg** Tennessee, S USA *35°00′N 85°42′W*
28 *K15* **South Platte River** ≈ Colorado/Nebraska, C USA
31 *T16* **South Point** Ohio, N USA *38°25′N 82°35′W*
65 *G15* **South Point** *headland* S Ascension Island
31 *R6* **South Point** *headland* Michigan, N USA *44°51′N 83°17′W*
South Point ***see*** Ka Lae
195 *Q9* **South Pole** *pole* Antarctica
183 *P17* **Southport** Tasmania, SE Australia *43°26′S 146°57′E*
97 *K17* **Southport** NW England, United Kingdom *53°39′N 03°01′W*
21 *V12* **Southport** North Carolina, SE USA *33°55′N 78°00′W*
19 *P8* **South Portland** Maine, NE USA *43°38′N 70°14′W*
14 *H12* **South River** Ontario, S Canada *45°50′N 79°23′W*
21 *U11* **South River** ≈ North Carolina, SE USA
96 *K5* **South Ronaldsay** *island* NE Scotland, United Kingdom
36 *L2* **South Salt Lake** Utah, W USA *40°42′N 111°52′W*
65 *L21* **South Sandwich Islands** *island group* SW Atlantic Ocean
65 *K21* **South Sandwich Trench** *undersea feature* SW Atlantic Ocean *56°30′S 25°00′W*
11 *S16* **South Saskatchewan** ≈ Alberta/Saskatchewan, S Canada
65 *I21* **South Scotia Ridge** *undersea feature* S Scotia Sea
11 *V10* **South Seal** ≈ Manitoba, C Canada
194 *G4* **South Shetland Islands** *island group* Antarctica
65 *H22* **South Shetland Trough** *undersea feature* Atlantic Ocean/Pacific Ocean *61°00′S 59°30′W*
97 *M14* **South Shields** NE England, United Kingdom *55°N 01°25′W*
29 *R13* **South Sioux City** Nebraska, C USA *42°28′N 96°24′W*
192 *J9* **South Solomon Trench** *undersea feature* W Pacific Ocean
183 *V3* **South Stradbroke Island** *island* Queensland, E Australia
South Sulawesi ***see*** Sulawesi Selatan
South Sumatra ***see*** Sumatera Selatan
81 *E15* **South Sudan** ***off.*** Republic of South Sudan ◆ *republic* E Africa
184 *K11* **South Taranaki Bight** *bight* SE Tasman Sea
South Tasmania Plateau ***see*** Tasman Plateau
36 *M15* **South Tucson** Arizona, SW USA *32°11′N 110°56′W*
12 *H9* **South Twin Island** *island* Nunavut, C Canada
South Tyrol ***see*** Trentino-Alto Adige
96 *E9* **South Uist** *island* NW Scotland, United Kingdom
South-West ***see*** Sud-Ouest
South-West Africa/South West Africa ***see*** Namibia
65 *F15* **South West Bay** *bay* Ascension Island, C Atlantic Ocean
183 *N18* **South West Cape** *headland* Tasmania, SE Australia *43°34′S 146°01′E*
185 *B26* **South West Cape** *headland* Stewart Island, New Zealand *47°15′S 167°28′E*
38 *J10* **Southwest Cape** *headland* Saint Lawrence Island, Alaska, USA *63°19′N 171°27′W*
Southwest Indian Ocean Ridge ***see*** Southwest Indian Ridge
173 *N11* **Southwest Indian Ridge** ***var.*** Southwest Indian Ocean Ridge. *undersea feature* SW Indian Ocean *43°00′S 40°00′E*
192 *L10* **Southwest Pacific Basin** ***var.*** South Pacific Basin. *undersea feature* SE Pacific Ocean *40°00′S 150°00′W*
44 *H2* **Southwest Point** *headland* Great Abaco, N Bahamas *25°50′N 77°12′W*
191 *X3* **South West Point** *headland* Kiritimati, NE Kiribati *01°53′N 157°34′E*
65 *G25* **South West Point** *headland* SW Saint Helena *16°00′S 05°48′W*
25 *P5* **South Wichita River** ≈ Texas, SW USA
97 *Q20* **Southwold** E England, United Kingdom *52°15′N 01°36′E*
19 *Q12* **South Yarmouth** Massachusetts, NE USA *41°38′N 70°09′W*
116 *J10* **Sovata** ***Hung.*** Szováta. Mureş, C Romania *46°36′N 25°04′E*
107 *N22* **Soverato** Calabria, SW Italy *38°40′N 16°31′E*
121 *O4* **Sovereign Base Area** *uk military installation* S Cyprus
Sovetabad ***see*** Ghafurov
126 *C2* **Sovetsk** ***Ger.*** Tilsit. Kaliningradskaya Oblast', W Russian Federation *53°04′N 21°52′E*
125 *Q15* **Sovetsk** Kirovskaya Oblast', NW Russian Federation *57°37′N 49°02′E*
127 *N10* **Sovetskaya** Rostovskaya Oblast', SW Russian Federation *49°00′N 42°09′E*
Sovetskoye ***see*** Ketchenery
146 *I15* **Sovet"yab** ***prev.*** Sovet"yap. Ahal Welaýaty, S Turkmenistan *36°29′N 61°13′E*
Sovet"yap ***see*** Sovet"yab
117 *U12* **Sovyets'kyy** Avtonomna Respublika Krym, S Ukraine *45°20′N 34°54′E*
83 *I18* **Sowa** ***var.*** Sua. Central, NE Botswana *20°33′S 26°18′E*
83 *I18* **Sowa Pan** ***var.*** Sua Pan. *salt lake* NE Botswana
83 *J21* **Soweto** Gauteng, NE South Africa *26°08′S 27°54′E*
147 *R11* **So'x** ***Rus.*** Sokh. Farg'ona Viloyati, E Uzbekistan *39°56′N 71°10′E*
Sōya-kaikyō ***see*** La Pérouse Strait
165 *T1* **Sōya-misaki** *headland* Hokkaidō, NE Japan *45°31′N 141°55′E*
125 *N7* **Soyana** ≈ NW Russian Federation
146 *A8* **Soye, Mys** ***var.*** Mys Suz. *headland* NW Turkmenistan *41°47′N 52°27′E*
82 *A10* **Soyo** Dem. Rep. Congo, NW Angola *06°07′S 12°18′E*
80 *J10* **Soyra** ▲ C Eritrea *14°46′N 39°29′E*
145 *P15* **Sozak** ***Kaz.*** Sozaq; ***prev.*** Suzak. Yuzhnyy Kazakhstan, S Kazakhstan *44°09′N 68°28′E*
Sozaq ***see*** Sozak
119 *P16* **Sozh** ≈ NE Europe
114 *N10* **Sozopol** ***prev.*** Sizebolu; ***anc.*** Apollonia. Burgas, E Bulgaria *42°25′N 27°42′E*
99 *L20* **Spa** Liège, E Belgium *50°29′N 05°52′E*
194 *I7* **Spaatz Island** *island* Antarctica
144 *M14* **Space Launching Centre** *space station* Kzylorda, S Kazakhstan
105 *O7* **Spain** ***off.*** Kingdom of Spain, ***Sp.*** España; ***anc.*** Hispania, Iberia, ***Lat.*** Hispana. ◆ *monarchy* SW Europe
Spain, Kingdom of ***see*** Spain
Spalato ***see*** Split
97 *O19* **Spalding** E England, United Kingdom *52°49′N 00°06′W*
14 *D11* **Spanish** Ontario, S Canada *46°12′N 82°21′W*
36 *L3* **Spanish Fork** Utah, W USA *40°09′N 111°40′W*
64 *B12* **Spanish Point** *headland* C Bermuda *32°18′N 64°49′W*
14 *E9* **Spanish River** ≈ Ontario, S Canada
44 *K13* **Spanish Town** ***hist.*** St.Iago de la Vega. C Jamaica *18°N 76°57′W*
Spánta, Akrotírio ***see*** Spátha, Akrotírio
35 *Q5* **Sparks** Nevada, W USA *39°32′N 119°45′W*
Sparnacum ***see*** Épernay
95 *N16* **Sparreholm** Södermanland, C Sweden *59°04′N 16°51′E*
23 *U4* **Sparta** Georgia, SE USA *33°16′N 82°58′W*
30 *K16* **Sparta** Illinois, N USA *38°07′N 89°42′W*
31 *P9* **Sparta** Michigan, N USA *43°09′N 85°42′W*
21 *R8* **Sparta** North Carolina, SE USA *36°30′N 81°07′W*
20 *L9* **Sparta** Tennessee, S USA *35°55′N 85°30′W*
30 *I7* **Sparta** Wisconsin, N USA *43°57′N 90°50′W*
Sparta ***see*** Spárti
21 *Q11* **Spartanburg** South Carolina, SE USA *34°56′N 81°57′W*
115 *F21* **Spárti** ***Eng.*** Sparta. Pelopónnisos, S Greece *37°05′N 22°25′E*
107 *B21* **Spartivento, Capo** *headland* Sardegna, Italy, C Mediterranean Sea *38°52′N 08°50′E*
11 *P17* **Sparwood** British Columbia, SW Canada *49°45′N 114°45′W*
126 *I4* **Spas-Demensk** Kaluzhskaya Oblast', W Russian Federation *54°22′N 34°16′E*
126 *M4* **Spas-Klepiki** Ryazanskaya Oblast', W Russian Federation *55°08′N 40°15′E*
Spasovo ***see*** Kulen Vakuf
123 *R15* **Spassk-Dal'niy** Primorskiy Kray, SE Russian Federation *44°34′N 132°52′E*
126 *M5* **Spassk-Ryazanskiy** Ryazanskaya Oblast', W Russian Federation *54°25′N 40°21′E*
115 *H19* **Spáta** Attikí, C Greece *37°58′N 23°55′E*
121 *Q11* **Spátha, Akrotírio** ***var.*** Akrotírio Spánta. *headland* Kríti, Greece, E Mediterranean Sea *35°42′N 23°44′E*
Špatrjan ***see*** Paternion
28 *I9* **Spearfish** South Dakota, N USA *44°29′N 103°51′W*
25 *O1* **Spearman** Texas, SW USA *36°12′N 101°13′W*
65 *C25* **Speedwell Island** *island* S Falkland Islands
65 *C25* **Speedwell Island Settlement** S Falkland Islands *52°13′S 59°41′W*
65 *G25* **Speery Island** *island* S Saint Helena
45 *N14* **Speightstown** NW Barbados *13°15′N 59°39′W*
106 *I13* **Spello** Umbria, C Italy *43°00′N 12°41′E*
39 *R12* **Spenard** Alaska, USA *61°09′N 150°03′W*
Spence Bay ***see*** Taloyoak
31 *O14* **Spencer** Indiana, N USA *39°18′N 86°46′W*
29 *T12* **Spencer** Iowa, C USA *43°09′N 95°07′W*
29 *P12* **Spencer** Nebraska, C USA *42°52′N 98°42′W*
21 *S9* **Spencer** North Carolina, SE USA *35°41′N 80°26′W*
20 *L9* **Spencer** Tennessee, S USA *35°46′N 85°27′W*
21 *Q4* **Spencer** West Virginia, NE USA *38°48′N 81°22′W*
30 *K6* **Spencer** Wisconsin, N USA *44°46′N 90°17′W*
182 *G10* **Spencer, Cape** *headland* South Australia *35°17′S 136°52′E*
39 *V13* **Spencer, Cape** *headland* Alaska, USA *58°12′N 136°39′W*
182 *H9* **Spencer Gulf** *gulf* South Australia
18 *F9* **Spencerport** New York, NE USA *43°11′N 77°48′W*
31 *Q12* **Spencerville** Ohio, N USA *40°42′N 84°21′W*
115 *E17* **Spercheiáda** ***var.*** Sperhiada, Sperkhiás. Stereá Elláda, C Greece *38°54′N 22°07′E*
115 *E17* **Spercheiós** ≈ C Greece
Sperhiada ***see*** Spercheiáda
95 *G14* **Sperillen** ◎ S Norway
Sperkhiás ***see*** Spercheiáda
101 *I18* **Spessart** *hill range* C Germany
Spétsai ***see*** Spétses
115 *G21* **Spétses** ***prev.*** Spétsai. Spétses, S Greece *37°16′N 23°09′E*
115 *G21* **Spétses** *island* S Greece
96 *J8* **Spey** ≈ NE Scotland, United Kingdom
101 *G20* **Speyer** ***Eng.*** Spires; ***anc.*** Civitas Nemetum, Spira. Rheinland-Pfalz, SW Germany *49°18′N 08°26′E*
101 *G20* **Speyerbach** ≈ W Germany
107 *N20* **Spezzano Albanese** Calabria, SW Italy *39°40′N 16°17′E*
Spice Islands ***see*** Maluku
100 *F9* **Spiekeroog** *island* NW Germany
109 *W9* **Spielfeld** Steiermark, SE Austria *46°43′N 15°36′E*
65 *N21* **Spiess Seamount** *undersea feature* S Atlantic Ocean *53°00′S 02°00′W*
108 *E9* **Spiez** Bern, W Switzerland *46°42′N 07°41′E*
98 *G13* **Spijkenisse** Zuid-Holland, SW Netherlands *51°52′N 04°19′E*
39 *T6* **Spike Mountain** ▲ Alaska, USA *67°42′N 141°39′W*
115 *I25* **Spíli** Kríti, Greece, E Mediterranean Sea *35°12′N 24°33′E*
108 *D10* **Spillgerten** ▲ W Switzerland *46°34′N 07°25′E*
118 *F9* **Spilve** ✈ (Rīga) C Latvia *56°55′N 24°03′E*
107 *N17* **Spinazzola** Puglia, SE Italy *40°58′N 16°06′E*
149 *O9* **Spīn Bōldak** ***prev.*** Spīn Būldak. Kandahār, S Afghanistan *31°01′N 66°23′E*
Spīn Būldak ***see*** Spīn Bōldak
Spira ***see*** Speyer
Spirdingsee ***see*** Śniardwy, Jezioro
Spires ***see*** Speyer
29 *T11* **Spirit Lake** Iowa, C USA *43°25′N 95°06′W*
29 *T11* **Spirit Lake** ◎ Iowa, C USA
11 *N13* **Spirit River** Alberta, W Canada *55°46′N 118°51′W*
11 *S14* **Spiritwood** Saskatchewan, S Canada *53°18′N 107°33′W*
27 *R11* **Spiro** Oklahoma, C USA *35°14′N 94°37′W*
111 *L19* **Spišská Nová Ves** ***Ger.*** Neudorf, Zipser Neudorf, ***Hung.*** Igló. Košický Kraj, E Slovakia *48°58′N 20°35′E*
137 *T11* **Spitak** NW Armenia *40°51′N 44°17′E*
92 *O2* **Spitsbergen** *island* NW Svalbard
Spittal ***see*** Spittal an der Drau
109 *R9* **Spittal an der Drau** ***var.*** Spittal. Kärnten, S Austria *46°48′N 13°30′E*
109 *V3* **Spitz** Niederösterreich, NE Austria *48°24′N 15°22′E*
94 *D9* **Spjelkavik** Møre og Romsdal, S Norway *62°28′N 06°22′E*
25 *W10* **Splendora** Texas, SW USA *30°13′N 95°09′W*
113 *E14* **Split** ***It.*** Spalato. Split-Dalmacija, S Croatia *43°31′N 16°27′E*
113 *E14* **Split** ✈ Split-Dalmacija, S Croatia *43°33′N 16°19′E*
113 *E14* **Split-Dalmacija** ***off.*** Splitsko-Dalmatinska Županija. ⬖ *province* S Croatia
11 *X12* **Split Lake** ◎ Manitoba, C Canada
Splitsko-Dalmatinska Županija ***see*** Split-Dalmacija
108 *H10* **Splügen** Graubünden, S Switzerland *46°33′N 09°18′E*
Spodnji Dravograd ***see*** Dravograd
25 *P12* **Spofford** Texas, SW USA *29°10′N 100°24′W*
118 *J11* **Špoģi** SE Latvia *56°03′N 26°47′E*
32 *L8* **Spokane** Washington, NW USA *47°40′N 117°26′W*
32 *L8* **Spokane River** ≈ Washington, NW USA
106 *I13* **Spoleto** Umbria, C Italy *42°44′N 12°44′E*
30 *I4* **Spooner** Wisconsin, N USA *45°51′N 91°49′W*
30 *K12* **Spoon River** ≈ Illinois, N USA
21 *W5* **Spotsylvania** Virginia, NE USA *38°12′N 77°35′W*
32 *L8* **Sprague** Washington, NW USA *47°19′N 117°55′W*
170 *J5* **Spratly Island** *island* SW Spratly Islands
192 *E6* **Spratly Islands** ***Chin.*** Nansha Qundao. ◇ *disputed territory* SE Asia
32 *J12* **Spray** Oregon, NW USA *44°30′N 119°38′W*
112 *I11* **Spreča** ≈ N Bosnia and Herzegovina
100 *P13* **Spree** ≈ E Germany
100 *P13* **Spreewald** *wetland* NE Germany
101 *P14* **Spremberg** Brandenburg, E Germany *51°34′N 14°22′E*
25 *W11* **Spring** Texas, SW USA *30°03′N 95°24′W*
31 *Q10* **Spring Arbor** Michigan, N USA *42°12′N 84°33′W*
83 *E23* **Springbok** Northern Cape, W South Africa *29°44′S 17°56′E*
18 *I15* **Spring City** Pennsylvania, NE USA *40°10′N 75°33′W*
20 *L9* **Spring City** Tennessee, S USA *35°41′N 84°51′W*
36 *L4* **Spring City** Utah, W USA *39°28′N 111°30′W*
35 *W3* **Spring Creek** Nevada, W USA *40°45′N 115°40′W*
27 *S9* **Springdale** Arkansas, C USA *36°11′N 94°07′W*
31 *Q14* **Springdale** Ohio, N USA *39°17′N 84°29′W*
100 *I13* **Springe** Niedersachsen, N Germany *52°13′N 09°33′E*
37 *U9* **Springer** New Mexico, SW USA *36°21′N 104°35′W*
37 *W7* **Springfield** Colorado, C USA *37°24′N 102°36′W*
23 *W5* **Springfield** Georgia, SE USA *32°21′N 81°20′W*
30 *K14* **Springfield** *state capital* Illinois, N USA *39°48′N 89°39′W*
20 *L6* **Springfield** Kentucky, S USA *37°42′N 85°18′W*
18 *M12* **Springfield** Massachusetts, NE USA *42°06′N 72°32′W*
29 *T10* **Springfield** Minnesota, N USA *44°15′N 94°58′W*
27 *T7* **Springfield** Missouri, C USA *37°13′N 93°18′W*
31 *R13* **Springfield** Ohio, N USA *39°55′N 83°49′W*
32 *G13* **Springfield** Oregon, NW USA *44°03′N 123°01′W*
29 *Q12* **Springfield** South Dakota, N USA *42°51′N 97°54′W*
20 *J8* **Springfield** Tennessee, S USA *36°30′N 86°54′W*
18 *M9* **Springfield** Vermont, NE USA *43°18′N 72°27′W*
30 *K14* **Springfield, Lake** ⊠ Illinois, N USA
55 *T8* **Spring Garden** NE Guyana *06°58′N 58°34′W*
30 *K8* **Spring Green** Wisconsin, N USA *43°10′N 90°02′W*
29 *X11* **Spring Grove** Minnesota, N USA *43°33′N 91°38′W*
13 *P15* **Springhill** Nova Scotia, SE Canada *45°40′N 64°04′W*
23 *V12* **Spring Hill** Florida, SE USA *28°28′N 82°36′W*
27 *R4* **Spring Hill** Kansas, C USA *38°44′N 94°49′W*
22 *G4* **Springhill** Louisiana, S USA *33°01′N 93°27′W*
20 *I9* **Spring Hill** Tennessee, S USA *35°46′N 86°55′W*
21 *U10* **Spring Lake** North Carolina, SE USA *35°10′N 78°58′W*
24 *M4* **Springlake** Texas, SW USA *34°13′N 102°18′W*
35 *W11* **Spring Mountains** ▲▲ Nevada, W USA
65 *B24* **Spring Point** West Falkland, Falkland Islands *51°49′S 60°27′W*
27 *W9* **Spring River** ≈ Arkansas/Missouri, C USA
27 *S7* **Spring River** ≈ Missouri/Oklahoma, C USA
83 *J21* **Springs** Gauteng, NE South Africa *26°16′S 28°26′E*
185 *H16* **Springs Junction** West Coast, South Island, New Zealand *42°21′S 172°11′E*
181 *X8* **Springsure** Queensland, E Australia *24°09′S 148°06′E*
29 *W11* **Spring Valley** Minnesota, N USA *43°41′N 92°23′W*
18 *K13* **Spring Valley** New York, NE USA *41°10′N 73°58′W*
29 *N12* **Springview** Nebraska, C USA *42°49′N 99°45′W*
18 *D11* **Springville** New York, NE USA *42°27′N 78°52′W*
36 *L3* **Springville** Utah, W USA *40°10′N 111°36′W*
Sprottau ***see*** Szprotawa
15 *V4* **Sproule, Pointe** *headland* Québec, SE Canada *49°47′N 67°02′W*
11 *Q14* **Spruce Grove** Alberta, SW Canada *53°36′N 113°55′W*
21 *T4* **Spruce Knob** ▲ West Virginia, NE USA *38°40′N 79°37′W*
35 *X3* **Spruce Mountain** ▲ Nevada, W USA *40°33′N 114°46′W*
21 *P9* **Spruce Pine** North Carolina, SE USA *35°55′N 82°03′W*
98 *G13* **Spui** ≈ SW Netherlands
107 *O19* **Spulico, Capo** *headland* S Italy *39°57′N 16°38′E*
25 *O5* **Spur** Texas, SW USA *33°28′N 100°51′W*
97 *O17* **Spurn Head** *headland* E England, United Kingdom *53°34′N 00°06′E*
99 *H20* **Spy** Namur, S Belgium *50°29′N 04°43′E*
95 *I15* **Spydeberg** Østfold, S Norway *59°36′N 11°04′E*
185 *J17* **Spy Glass Point** *headland* South Island, New Zealand *42°33′S 173°31′E*
10 *L17* **Squamish** British Columbia, SW Canada *49°41′N 123°11′W*
19 *O8* **Squam Lake** ◎ New Hampshire, NE USA
19 *S2* **Squa Pan Mountain** ▲ Maine, NE USA *46°36′N 68°09′W*
39 *N16* **Squaw Harbor** Unga Island, Alaska, USA *55°12′N 160°41′W*
14 *E11* **Squaw Island** *island* Ontario, S Canada
107 *O22* **Squillace, Golfo di** *gulf* S Italy
107 *Q18* **Squinzano** Puglia, SE Italy *40°26′N 18°03′E*
Sráid na Cathrach ***see*** Milltown Malbay
167 *S11* **Srâlau** Stœng Trêng, N Cambodia *14°03′N 105°46′E*
Srath an Urláir ***see*** Stranorlar
112 *G10* **Srbac** ⬖ Republika Srpska, N Bosnia and Herzegovina
Srbija ***see*** Serbia
Srbinje ***see*** Foča
112 *K9* **Srbobran** ***var.*** Bácsszenttamás, ***Hung.*** Szenttamás. Vojvodina, N Serbia *45°33′N 19°46′E*
Srbobran ***see*** Donji Vakuf
167 *R13* **Srê Âmběl** Kaôh Kông, SW Cambodia *11°07′N 103°46′E*
112 *K13* **Srebrenica** Republika Srpska, E Bosnia and Herzegovina *44°04′N 19°18′E*
112 *I11* **Srebrenik** Federacija Bosna I Hercegovina, NE Bosnia and Herzegovina *44°42′N 18°30′E*
114 *K10* **Sredets** ***prev.*** Syulemeshlii. Stara Zagora, C Bulgaria *42°16′N 25°40′E*
114 *M10* **Sredets** ***prev.*** Grudovo. ⬖ Burgas, E Bulgaria
114 *M10* **Sredetska Reka** ≈ SE Bulgaria
123 *U9* **Sredinnyy Khrebet** ▲▲ E Russian Federation
114 *N7* **Sredishte** ***Rom.*** Beibunar; ***prev.*** Knyazhevo. Dobrich, NE Bulgaria *43°51′N 27°30′E*
114 *I10* **Sredna Gora** ▲▲ C Bulgaria
123 *R7* **Srednekolymsk** Respublika Sakha (Yakutiya), NE Russian Federation *67°28′N 153°52′E*
126 *K7* **Srednerusskaya Vozvyshennost'** ***Eng.*** Central Russian Upland. ▲▲ W Russian Federation
122 *L9* **Srednesibirskoye Ploskogor'ye** ***var.*** Central Siberian Uplands, ***Eng.*** Central Siberian Plateau. ▲▲ N Russian Federation
125 *V13* **Sredniy Ural** ▲▲ NW Russian Federation
167 *T12* **Srê Khtŭm** Môndól Kiri, E Cambodia *12°10′N 106°52′E*
110 *G12* **Śrem** Wielkopolskie, C Poland *52°07′N 17°00′E*
112 *K10* **Sremska Mitrovica** ***prev.*** Mitrovica, ***Ger.*** Mitrowitz. Vojvodina, NW Serbia *44°58′N 19°37′E*
167 *R11* **Srêng, Stœng** ≈ NW Cambodia
167 *R11* **Srê Noy** Siĕmréab, NW Cambodia *13°47′N 104°03′E*
Srepok, Sông ***see*** Srêpôk, Tônle
167 *T12* **Srêpôk, Tônle** ***var.*** Sông Srepok. ≈ Cambodia/Vietnam
123 *P13* **Sretensk** Zabaykal'skiy Kray, S Russian Federation *52°14′N 117°33′E*
169 *R10* **Sri Aman** Sarawak, East Malaysia *01°13′N 111°25′E*
117 *R4* **Sribne** Chernihivs'ka Oblast', N Ukraine *50°40′N 32°55′E*
Sri Jayawardanapura ***see*** Sri Jayewardenapura Kotte
155 *I25* **Sri Jayewardenapura Kotte** ***var.*** Sri Jayawardanapura. ● (Sri Lanka: legislative) Western Province, W Sri Lanka *06°54′N 79°58′E*
155 *M14* **Srīkākulam** Andhra Pradesh, E India *18°18′N 83°54′E*
155 *I25* **Sri Lanka** ***off.*** Democratic Socialist Republic of Sri Lanka; ***prev.*** Ceylon. ◆ *republic* S Asia
130 *F14* **Sri Lanka** *island* S Asia
Sri Lanka, Democratic Socialist Republic of ***see*** Sri Lanka
153 *V14* **Srimangal** Sylhet, E Bangladesh *24°19′N 91°40′E*
Sri Mohangorh ***see*** Shri Mohangarh
152 *H5* **Srīnagar** *state capital* Jammu and Kashmir, N India *34°07′N 74°50′E*
167 *N10* **Srinagarind Reservoir** ⊠ W Thailand
155 *F19* **Sringeri** Karnātaka, W India *13°26′N 75°13′E*
155 *K25* **Sri Pada** ***Eng.*** Adam's Peak. ▲ S Sri Lanka *06°49′N 80°25′E*
Sri Saket ***see*** Si Sa Ket
111 *G14* **Sroda Śląska** ***Ger.*** Neumarkt. Dolnośląskie, SW Poland *51°10′N 16°30′E*
110 *H12* **Środa Wielkopolska** Wielkopolskie, C Poland *52°13′N 17°17′E*
Srpska Kostajnica ***see*** Bosanska Kostajnica
113 *G14* **Srpska, Republika** ⬖ *republic* Bosnia and Herzegovina
Srpski Brod ***see*** Bosanski Brod
Ssu-ch'uan ***see*** Sichuan
Ssu-p'ing/Ssu-p'ing-chieh ***see*** Siping
Stablo ***see*** Stavelot
99 *G15* **Stabroek** Antwerpen, N Belgium *51°21′N 04°22′E*
Stackeln ***see*** Strenči
96 *I5* **Stack Skerry** *island* N Scotland, United Kingdom
100 *I9* **Stade** Niedersachsen, NW Germany *53°36′N 09°29′E*
94 *C10* **Stadlandet** *peninsula* S Norway
109 *R5* **Stadl-Paura** Oberösterreich, NW Austria *48°05′N 13°52′E*
119 *L20* **Stadolichy** ***Rus.*** Stodolichi. Homyel'skaya Voblasts', SE Belarus *51°44′N 28°30′E*
98 *P7* **Stadskanaal** Groningen, NE Netherlands *53°N 06°55′E*
101 *H16* **Stadtallendorf** Hessen, C Germany *50°49′N 09°01′E*
101 *K23* **Stadtbergen** Bayern, S Germany *48°21′N 10°50′E*
108 *G7* **Stäfa** Zürich, NE Switzerland *47°14′N 08°45′E*
95 *K23* **Staffanstorp** Skåne, S Sweden *55°38′N 13°13′E*
101 *K18* **Staffelstein** Bayern, C Germany *50°05′N 11°00′E*
97 *L19* **Stafford** C England, United Kingdom *52°48′N 02°07′W*
26 *L6* **Stafford** Kansas, C USA *37°57′N 98°36′W*
21 *W4* **Stafford** Virginia, NE USA *38°26′N 77°27′W*
97 *L19* **Staffordshire** *cultural region* C England, United Kingdom
19 *N12* **Stafford Springs** Connecticut, NE USA *41°57′N 72°18′W*
115 *H14* **Stágira** Kentrikí Makedonía, N Greece *40°31′N 23°46′E*
118 *G7* **Staicele** N Latvia *57°52′N 24°48′E*
Ştaierdorf-Anina ***see*** Anina
109 *V8* **Stainz** Steiermark, SE Austria *46°55′N 15°18′E*
Stájerlakanina ***see*** Anina
117 *Y7* **Stakhanov** Luhans'ka Oblast', E Ukraine *48°30′N 38°42′E*
108 *E11* **Stalden** Valais, SW Switzerland *46°12′N 07°55′E*
15 *S8* **St-Alexandre** Québec, SE Canada *47°39′N 69°36′W*
Stalin ***see*** Varna
Stalinabad ***see*** Dushanbe
Stalingrad ***see*** Volgograd
Staliniri ***see*** Tskhinvali
Stalino ***see*** Donets'k
Stalinobod ***see*** Dushanbe
Stalinov Štít ***see*** Gerlachovský štít
Stalinsk ***see*** Novokuznetsk
Stalins'kaya Oblast' ***see*** Donets'ka Oblast'
Stalinski Zaliv ***see*** Varnenski Zaliv
Stalin, Yazovir ***see*** Iskŭr, Yazovir
111 *N15* **Stalowa Wola** Podkarpackie, SE Poland *50°35′N 22°02′E*
114 *I11* **Stamboliyski** Plovdiv, C Bulgaria *42°09′N 24°32′E*
15 *Q7* **St-Ambroise** Québec, SE Canada *48°35′N 71°19′W*
97 *N19* **Stamford** E England, United Kingdom *52°39′N 00°32′W*
18 *L14* **Stamford** Connecticut, NE USA *41°03′N 73°32′W*
25 *P6* **Stamford** Texas, SW USA *32°55′N 99°49′W*
25 *Q6* **Stamford, Lake** ⊠ Texas, SW USA
108 *I10* **Stampa** Graubünden, SE Switzerland *46°21′N 09°35′E*
Stampalia ***see*** Astypálaia
27 *T14* **Stamps** Arkansas, C USA *33°22′N 93°30′W*
92 *G11* **Stamsund** Nordland, C Norway *68°07′N 13°50′E*
27 *R2* **Stanberry** Missouri, C USA *40°12′N 94°33′W*
195 *O3* **Stancomb-Wills Glacier** *glacier* Antarctica
83 *K21* **Standerton** Mpumalanga, E South Africa *26°57′S 29°14′E*
31 *R7* **Standish** Michigan, N USA *43°59′N 83°58′W*
20 *M6* **Stanford** Kentucky, S USA *37°30′N 84°40′W*
33 *S9* **Stanford** Montana, NW USA *47°08′N 110°15′W*
95 *P19* **Stånga** Gotland, SE Sweden *57°16′N 18°30′E*
94 *I13* **Stange** Hedmark, S Norway *60°40′N 11°05′E*
83 *L23* **Stanger** KwaZulu/Natal, E South Africa *29°20′S 31°18′E*
Stanimaka ***see*** Asenovgrad
Stanislau ***see*** Ivano-Frankivs'k
35 *P8* **Stanislaus River** ≈ California, W USA
Stanislav ***see*** Ivano-Frankivs'k
Stanislavskaya Oblast' ***see*** Ivano-Frankivs'ka Oblast'
Stanisławów ***see*** Ivano-Frankivs'k
Stanke Dimitrov ***see*** Dupnitsa
183 *O15* **Stanley** Tasmania, SE Australia *40°48′S 145°18′E*
65 *E24* **Stanley** ***var.*** Port Stanley, Puerto Argentino. ○ (Falkland Islands) East Falkland, Falkland Islands *51°45′S 57°56′W*
33 *O13* **Stanley** Idaho, NW USA *44°12′N 114°58′W*
28 *L3* **Stanley** North Dakota, N USA *48°19′N 102°23′W*
21 *U4* **Stanley** Virginia, NE USA *38°34′N 78°30′W*
30 *J6* **Stanley** Wisconsin, N USA *44°58′N 90°54′W*
79 *G21* **Stanley Pool** ***var.*** Pool Malebo. ◎ Congo/Dem. Rep. Congo
155 *H20* **Stanley Reservoir** ⊠ S India
Stanleyville ***see*** Kisangani
42 *G3* **Stann Creek** ⬖ *district* SE Belize
Stann Creek ***see*** Dangriga
123 *Q12* **Stanovoy Khrebet** ▲▲ SE Russian Federation
108 *F8* **Stans** Nidwalden, C Switzerland *46°57′N 08°23′E*
97 *O21* **Stansted** ✈ (London) Essex, E England, United Kingdom *51°53′N 00°16′E*
183 *U4* **Stanthorpe** Queensland, E Australia *28°35′S 151°52′E*
21 *N6* **Stanton** Kentucky, S USA *37°51′N 83°51′W*
31 *Q8* **Stanton** Michigan, N USA *43′19′N 85°04′W*
29 *Q14* **Stanton** Nebraska, C USA *41°57′N 97°13′W*
28 *L5* **Stanton** North Dakota, N USA *47°19′N 101°22′W*
25 *N7* **Stanton** Texas, SW USA *32°07′N 101°47′W*
32 *H7* **Stanwood** Washington, NW USA *48°14′N 122°22′W*
117 *Y7* **Stanychno-Luhans'ke** Luhans'ka Oblast', E Ukraine *48°39′N 39°30′E*
108 *K7* **Stanzach** Tirol, W Austria *47°24′N 10°36′E*
98 *M9* **Staphorst** Overijssel, E Netherlands *52°38′N 06°12′E*
14 *D18* **Staples** Ontario, S Canada *42°09′N 82°34′W*
29 *T6* **Staples** Minnesota, N USA *46°21′N 94°47′W*
28 *M14* **Stapleton** Nebraska, C USA *41°29′N 100°40′W*
25 *S8* **Star** Texas, SW USA *31°27′N 98°16′W*
111 *M14* **Starachowice** Świętokrzyskie, C Poland *51°04′N 21°02′E*
Stara Kanjiža ***see*** Kanjiža
111 *M18* **Stará L'ubovňa** ***Ger.*** Altlublau, ***Hung.*** Ólubló. Prešovský Kraj, E Slovakia *49°19′N 20°40′E*
112 *L10* **Stara Pazova** ***Ger.*** Altpasua, ***Hung.*** Ópazova. Vojvodina, N Serbia *44°59′N 20°10′E*
Stara Planina ***see*** Balkan Mountains
114 *L9* **Stara Reka** ≈ C Bulgaria
116 *M5* **Stara Synyava** Khmel'nyts'ka Oblast', W Ukraine *49°39′N 27°39′E*
116 *I2* **Stara Vyzhivka** Volyns'ka Oblast', NW Ukraine *51°27′N 24°25′E*
Staraya Belitsa ***see*** Staraya Byelitsa
119 *M14* **Staraya Byelitsa** ***Rus.*** Staraya Belitsa. Vitsyebskaya Voblasts', NE Belarus *54°42′N 29°38′E*
127 *R5* **Staraya Mayna** Ul'yanovskaya Oblast', W Russian Federation *54°36′N 48°57′E*
119 *O18* **Staraya Rudnya** Homyel'skaya Voblasts', SE Belarus *52°50′N 30°17′E*
124 *H14* **Staraya Russa** Novgorodskaya Oblast', W Russian Federation *57°59′N 31°18′E*
114 *K10* **Stara Zagora** ***Lat.*** Augusta Trajana. Stara Zagora, C Bulgaria *42°26′N 25°39′E*
114 *K10* **Stara Zagora** ⬖ *province* C Bulgaria
29 *S8* **Starbuck** Minnesota, N USA *45°36′N 95°31′W*
191 *W4* **Starbuck Island** ***prev.*** Volunteer Island. *island* E Kiribati
27 *V13* **Star City** Arkansas, C USA *33°56′N 91°52′W*
112 *F13* **Staretina** ▲▲ W Bosnia and Herzegovina
Stargard in Pommern ***see*** Stargard Szczeciński
110 *E9* **Stargard Szczeciński** ***Ger.*** Stargard in Pommern. Zachodnio-pomorskie, NW Poland *53°20′N 15°02′E*
187 *N10* **Star Harbour** *harbor* San Cristobal, SE Solomon Islands
Stari Bečej ***see*** Bečej
113 *F15* **Stari Grad** ***It.*** Cittavecchia. Split-Dalmacija, S Croatia *43°11′N 16°36′E*
124 *J16* **Staritsa** Tverskaya Oblast', W Russian Federation *56°28′N 34°51′E*
23 *V9* **Starke** Florida, SE USA *29°56′N 82°07′W*
22 *M4* **Starkville** Mississippi, S USA *33°27′N 88°49′W*
186 *B7* **Star Mountains** ***Ind.*** Pegunungan Sterren. ▲▲ Indonesia/Papua New Guinea
101 *L23* **Starnberg** Bayern, SE Germany *48°00′N 11°19′E*
101 *L24* **Starnberger See** ◎ SE Germany
Starobel'sk ***see*** Starobil's'k
117 *X8* **Starobesheve** Donets'ka Oblast', E Ukraine *47°45′N 38°01′E*
117 *Y6* **Starobil's'k** ***Rus.*** Starobel'sk. Luhans'ka Oblast', E Ukraine *49°16′N 38°56′E*
119 *K18* **Starobin** ***var.*** Starobyn. Minskaya Voblasts', S Belarus *52°44′N 27°28′E*
Starobyn ***see*** Starobin
126 *H6* **Starodub** Bryanskaya Oblast', W Russian Federation *52°30′N 32°56′E*
110 *I8* **Starogard Gdański** ***Ger.*** Preussisch-Stargard. Pomorskie, N Poland *53°57′N 18°29′E*
Staroikan ***see*** Ikan
Starokonstantinov ***see*** Starokostyantyniv
116 *L5* **Starokostyantyniv** ***Rus.*** Starokonstantinov. Khmel'nyts'ka Oblast', NW Ukraine *49°43′N 27°13′E*
126 *K12* **Starominskaya** Krasnodarskiy Kray, SW Russian Federation *46°31′N 39°03′E*
114 *L7* **Staro Selo** ***Rom.*** Satul-Vechi; ***prev.*** Star-Smil. Silistra, NE Bulgaria *43°58′N 26°32′E*
126 *K12* **Staroshcherbinovskaya** Krasnodarskiy Kray, SW Russian Federation *46°36′N 38°42′E*

◆ Country
● Country Capital
◇ Dependent Territory
○ Dependent Territory Capital
⬖ Administrative Regions
✈ International Airport
▲ Mountain
▲▲ Mountain Range
Volcano
≈ River
◎ Lake
⊠ Reservoir

127 V6 **Starosubkhangulovo** Respublika Bashkortostan, W Russian Federation 53°05′N 57°22′E
35 S4 **Star Peak** ▲ Nevada, W USA 40°31′N 118°09′W
15 T8 **St-Arsène** Québec, SE Canada 47°55′N 69°21′W
Star-Smil see Staro Selo
97 J25 **Start Point** headland SW England, United Kingdom 50°13′N 03°38′W
Startsy see Kirawsk
Starum see Stavoren
119 L18 **Staryya Darohi** Rus. Staryye Dorogi. Minskaya Voblasts', S Belarus 53°02′N 28°16′E
Staryye Dorogi see Staryya Darohi
127 T2 **Staryye Zyattsy** Udmurtskaya Respublika, NW Russian Federation 57°22′N 52°42′E
117 U13 **Staryy Krym** Avtonomna Respublika Krym, S Ukraine 45°03′N 35°06′E
126 K8 **Staryy Oskol** Belgorodskaya Oblast', W Russian Federation 51°21′N 37°52′E
116 H6 **Staryy Sambir** L'vivs'ka Oblast', W Ukraine 49°27′N 23°00′E
101 L14 **Stassfurt** var. Staßfurt. Sachsen-Anhalt, C Germany 51°51′N 11°35′E
Staßfurt see Stassfurt
111 M15 **Staszów** Świętokrzyskie, C Poland 50°33′N 21°07′E
29 W13 **State Center** Iowa, C USA 42°01′N 93°09′W
18 E14 **State College** Pennsylvania, NE USA 40°48′N 77°52′W
18 K15 **Staten Island** island New York, NE USA
Staten Island see Estados, Isla de los
23 U8 **Statenville** Georgia, SE USA 30°42′N 83°00′W
23 W5 **Statesboro** Georgia, SE USA 32°28′N 81°47′W
States, The see United States of America
21 R9 **Statesville** North Carolina, SE USA 35°46′N 80°54′W
95 G16 **Stathelle** Telemark, S Norway 59°01′N 09°40′E
30 K15 **Staunton** Illinois, N USA 39°00′N 89°47′W
21 T5 **Staunton** Virginia, NE USA 38°10′N 79°05′W
95 C16 **Stavanger** Rogaland, S Norway 58°58′N 05°43′E
99 L21 **Stavelot** Dut. Stablo. Liège, E Belgium 50°24′N 05°56′E
95 G16 **Stavern** Vestfold, S Norway 58°58′N 10°01′E
Stavers Island see Vostok Island
98 J7 **Stavoren** Fris. Starum. Fryslân, N Netherlands 52°52′N 05°22′E
115 K21 **Stavrí, Akrotírio** var. Akrotírio Stavrós. headland Naxos, Kykládes, Greece, Aegean Sea 37°12′N 25°32′E
126 M14 **Stavropol'** prev. Voroshilovsk. Stavropol'skiy Kray, SW Russian Federation 45°02′N 41°58′E
Stavropol' see Tol'yatti
126 M14 **Stavropol'skaya Vozvyshennost'** ▲▲ SW Russian Federation
126 M14 **Stavropol'skiy Kray** ◈ territory SW Russian Federation
115 H14 **Stavrós** Kentrikí Makedonía, N Greece 40°39′N 23°43′E
115 J24 **Stavrós, Akrotírio** headland Kríti, Greece, E Mediterranean Sea 35°25′N 24°57′E
Stavrós, Akrotírio see Stavrí, Akrotírio
114 I12 **Stavroúpoli** prev. Stavroúpolis. Anatolikí Makedonía kai Thráki, NE Greece 41°12′N 24°45′E
Stavroúpolis see Stavroúpoli
117 O6 **Stavyshche** Kyyivs'ka Oblast', N Ukraine 49°23′N 30°10′E
182 M11 **Stawell** Victoria, SE Australia 37°06′S 142°52′E
110 N9 **Stawiski** Podlaskie, NE Poland 53°22′N 22°08′E
14 G14 **Stayner** Ontario, S Canada 44°25′N 80°05′W
14 D17 **St. Clair** ≈ Canada/USA
37 R3 **Steamboat Springs** Colorado, C USA 40°28′N 106°51′W
15 U4 **Ste-Anne, Lac** ◎ Québec, SE Canada
20 M8 **Stearns** Kentucky, S USA 36°39′N 84°27′W
39 N10 **Stebbins** Alaska, USA 63°30′N 162°15′W
15 U7 **Ste-Blandine** Québec, SE Canada 48°22′N 68°27′W
108 K7 **Steeg** Tirol, W Austria 47°15′N 10°18′E
27 Y9 **Steele** Missouri, C USA 36°04′N 89°49′W
29 N5 **Steele** North Dakota, N USA 46°51′N 99°55′W
194 J5 **Steele Island** island Antarctica
30 K16 **Steeleville** Illinois, N USA 38°00′N 89°39′W
27 W6 **Steelville** Missouri, C USA 37°57′N 91°21′W
99 G14 **Steenbergen** Noord-Brabant, S Netherlands 51°35′N 04°19′E
Steenkool see Bintuni
11 O10 **Steen River** Alberta, W Canada 59°37′N 117°17′W
98 M8 **Steenwijk** Overijssel, N Netherlands 52°47′N 06°07′E
65 A23 **Steeple Jason** island Jason Islands, NW Falkland Islands
174 J8 **Steep Point** headland Western Australia 26°09′S 113°11′E
116 L9 **Ştefăneşti** Botoşani, NE Romania 47°44′N 27°15′E
Stefanie, Lake see Ch'ew Bahir
8 L5 **Stefansson Island** island Nunavut, N Canada
117 O10 **Ştefan Vodă** Rus. Suvorovo. SE Moldova 46°33′N 29°39′E
63 H18 **Steffen, Cerro** ▲ S Chile 44°27′S 71°42′W
108 D9 **Steffisburg** Bern, C Switzerland 46°47′N 07°38′E
95 J24 **Stege** Sjælland, SE Denmark 54°59′N 12°18′E
116 G10 **Ştei** Hung. Vaskohsziklás. Bihor, W Romania 46°34′N 22°28′E
Steier see Steyr
Steierdorf/Steierdorf-Anina see Anina
109 T7 **Steiermark** off. Land Steiermark, Eng. Styria. ◈ state C Austria
Steiermark, Land see Steiermark
101 J19 **Steigerwald** hill range C Germany
99 L17 **Stein** Limburg, SE Netherlands 50°58′N 05°45′E
Stein see Stein an der Donau
Stein see Kamnik, Slovenia
108 M8 **Steinach** Tirol, W Austria 47°07′N 11°30′E
Steinamanger see Szombathely
109 W3 **Stein an der Donau** var. Stein. Niederösterreich, NE Austria 48°25′N 15°35′E
Steinau an der Elbe see Ścinawa
11 Y16 **Steinbach** Manitoba, S Canada 49°32′N 96°40′W
Steiner Alpen see Kamniško-Savinjske Alpe
99 L24 **Steinfort** Luxembourg, W Luxembourg 49°39′N 05°55′E
100 H12 **Steinhuder Meer** ◎ NW Germany
93 E15 **Steinkjer** Nord-Trøndelag, C Norway 64°01′N 11°29′E
Stejarul see Karapelit
99 F16 **Stekene** Oost-Vlaanderen, NW Belgium 51°13′N 04°04′E
83 E26 **Stellenbosch** Western Cape, SW South Africa 33°56′S 18°51′E
98 F13 **Stellendam** Zuid-Holland, SW Netherlands 51°48′N 04°01′E
39 T12 **Steller, Mount** ▲ Alaska, USA 60°36′N 142°49′W
103 Y14 **Stello, Monte** ▲ Corse, France, C Mediterranean Sea 42°49′N 09°24′E
106 F5 **Stelvio, Passo dello** pass Italy/Switzerland
15 S7 **Ste-Maguerite Nord-Est** ≈ Québec, SE Canada
15 V4 **Ste-Marguerite, Pointe** headland Québec, SE Canada 50°01′N 66°43′W
12 J14 **Ste-Marie, Lac** ◎ Québec, S Canada
103 R3 **Stenay** Meuse, NE France 49°29′N 05°12′E
100 L12 **Stendal** Sachsen-Anhalt, C Germany 52°36′N 11°52′E
118 E8 **Stende** NW Latvia 57°09′N 22°33′E
182 H10 **Stenhouse Bay** South Australia 35°15′S 136°58′E
95 J23 **Stenløse** Hovedstaden, E Denmark 55°47′N 12°13′E
95 L19 **Stensjön** Jönköping, S Sweden 57°36′N 14°42′E
95 K18 **Stenstorp** Västra Götaland, S Sweden 58°15′N 13°45′E
95 I18 **Stenungsund** Västra Götaland, S Sweden 58°05′N 11°49′E
Stepanakert see Xankändi
137 T11 **Step'anavan** N Armenia 41°00′N 44°27′E
100 K9 **Stepenitz** ≈ N Germany
29 O10 **Stephan** South Dakota, N USA 44°12′N 99°25′W
29 R3 **Stephen** Minnesota, N USA 48°27′N 96°54′W
27 T14 **Stephens** Arkansas, C USA 33°25′N 93°04′W
184 J13 **Stephens, Cape** headland D'Urville Island, Marlborough, SW New Zealand 40°42′S 173°56′E
21 V3 **Stephens City** Virginia, NE USA 39°03′N 78°10′W
182 L6 **Stephens Creek** New South Wales, SE Australia 31°51′S 141°30′E
184 K13 **Stephens Island** island C New Zealand
31 N5 **Stephenson** Michigan, N USA 45°27′N 87°36′W
13 S12 **Stephenville** Newfoundland, Newfoundland and Labrador, SE Canada 48°33′N 58°34′W
25 S7 **Stephenville** Texas, SW USA 32°12′N 98°13′W
Step' Nardara see Step' Shardara
145 R8 **Stepnogorsk** Akmola, C Kazakhstan 52°04′N 72°18′E
127 O15 **Stepnoye** Stavropol'skiy Kray, SW Russian Federation 44°18′N 44°34′E
145 Q8 **Stepnyak** Akmola, N Kazakhstan 52°52′N 70°49′E
145 P17 **Step' Shardara** Kaz. Shardara Dalasy; prev. Step' Nardara. grassland S Kazakhstan
192 J17 **Steps Point** headland Tutuila, W American Samoa 14°23′S 170°46′W
115 F17 **Stereá Elláda** Eng. Greece Central var. Stereá Ellás. ◈ region C Greece
Stereá Ellás see Stereá Elláda
83 J24 **Sterkspruit** Eastern Cape, SE South Africa 30°31′S 27°22′E
127 U6 **Sterlibashevo** Respublika Bashkortostan, W Russian Federation 53°19′N 55°12′E
39 R12 **Sterling** Alaska, USA 60°32′N 150°51′W
37 V3 **Sterling** Colorado, C USA 40°37′N 103°12′W
30 K11 **Sterling** Illinois, N USA 41°47′N 89°42′W
26 M5 **Sterling** Kansas, C USA 38°12′N 98°12′W
25 O8 **Sterling City** Texas, SW USA 31°50′N 101°00′W
31 S9 **Sterling Heights** Michigan, N USA 42°34′N 83°01′W
21 W3 **Sterling Park** Virginia, NE USA 39°00′N 77°24′W
37 V2 **Sterling Reservoir** ▣ Colorado, C USA
22 I5 **Sterlington** Louisiana, S USA 32°42′N 92°05′W
127 U6 **Sterlitamak** Respublika Bashkortostan, W Russian Federation 53°39′N 56°00′E
Sternberg see Šternberk
111 H17 **Šternberk** Ger. Sternberg. Olomoucký Kraj, E Czech Republic 49°45′N 17°20′E
141 V17 **Stēroh** Suquṭrā, S Yemen 12°21′N 53°50′E
Sterren, Pegunungan see Star Mountains
110 G11 **Stęszew** Wielkopolskie, C Poland 52°16′N 16°41′E
Stettin see Szczecin
Stettiner Haff see Szczeciński, Zalew
11 Q15 **Stettler** Alberta, SW Canada 52°21′N 112°40′W
31 V13 **Steubenville** Ohio, N USA 40°21′N 80°37′W
97 O21 **Stevenage** E England, United Kingdom 51°55′N 00°14′W
23 Q1 **Stevenson** Alabama, S USA 34°52′N 85°50′W
32 H11 **Stevenson** Washington, NW USA 45°43′N 121°54′W
182 E1 **Stevenson Creek** seasonal river South Australia
39 Q13 **Stevenson Entrance** strait Alaska, USA
30 L6 **Stevens Point** Wisconsin, N USA 44°32′N 89°33′W
39 R8 **Stevens Village** Alaska, USA 66°01′N 149°02′W
33 P10 **Stevensville** Montana, NW USA 46°30′N 114°05′W
93 E25 **Stevns Klint** headland E Denmark 55°15′N 12°25′E
10 J12 **Stewart** British Columbia, W Canada 55°58′N 129°52′W
10 I6 **Stewart** ≈ Yukon Territory, NW Canada
10 I6 **Stewart Crossing** Yukon Territory, NW Canada 63°22′N 136°37′W
63 H25 **Stewart, Isla** island S Chile
185 B25 **Stewart Island** island S New Zealand
Stewart Islands see Sikaiana
181 W6 **Stewart, Mount** ▲ Queensland, E Australia 20°11′S 145°29′E
10 H6 **Stewart River** Yukon Territory, NW Canada 63°17′N 139°24′W
27 R3 **Stewartsville** Missouri, C USA 39°45′N 94°30′W
11 S16 **Stewart Valley** Saskatchewan, S Canada 50°34′N 107°47′W
29 W10 **Stewartville** Minnesota, N USA 43°51′N 92°29′W
Steyerlak-Anina see Anina
109 T5 **Steyr** var. Steier. Oberösterreich, N Austria 48°02′N 14°26′E
109 T5 **Steyr** ≈ NW Austria
15 T7 **St-Fabien** Québec, SE Canada 48°19′N 68°51′W
15 R11 **St-François, Lac** ◎ Québec, SE Canada
83 E25 **St. Helena Bay** bay SW South Africa
15 T8 **St-Hubert** Québec, SE Canada 47°46′N 69°15′W
29 P11 **Stickney** South Dakota, N USA 43°24′N 98°23′W
98 L5 **Stiens** Fryslân, N Netherlands 53°15′N 05°45′E
Stif see Sétif
27 Q11 **Stigler** Oklahoma, C USA 35°16′N 95°08′W
107 N18 **Stigliano** Basilicata, S Italy 40°24′N 16°13′E
95 N17 **Stigtomta** Södermanland, C Sweden 58°48′N 16°47′E
10 I11 **Stikine** ≈ British Columbia, W Canada
Stilida/Stilís see Stylída
95 G22 **Stilling** Midtjylland, C Denmark 56°04′N 10°00′E
29 W8 **Stillwater** Minnesota, N USA 45°04′N 92°48′W
27 O9 **Stillwater** Oklahoma, C USA 36°07′N 97°03′W
35 S5 **Stillwater Range** ▲▲ Nevada, W USA
18 I8 **Stillwater Reservoir** ▣ New York, NE USA
107 O22 **Stilo, Punta** headland S Italy 38°27′N 16°36′E
27 R10 **Stilwell** Oklahoma, C USA 35°48′N 94°37′W
Štimlje see Shtime
25 N1 **Stinnett** Texas, SW USA 35°49′N 101°27′W
113 P18 **Štip** E FYR Macedonia 41°45′N 22°10′E
Stira see Stýra
96 J12 **Stirling** C Scotland, United Kingdom 56°07′N 03°57′W
96 I12 **Stirling** cultural region C Scotland, United Kingdom
180 J14 **Stirling Range** ▲▲ Western Australia
15 R8 **St-Jean** ≈ Québec, SE Canada
93 E16 **Stjørdalshalsen** Nord-Trøndelag, C Norway 63°27′N 10°57′E
83 L22 **St. Lucia** KwaZulu/Natal, E South Africa 28°22′S 32°25′E
Stochód see Stokhid
101 H24 **Stockach** Baden-Württemberg, S Germany 47°51′N 09°01′E
25 S12 **Stockdale** Texas, SW USA 29°14′N 97°57′W
109 X3 **Stockerau** Niederösterreich, NE Austria 48°24′N 16°13′E
93 H20 **Stockholm** ● (Sweden) Stockholm, C Sweden 59°17′N 18°03′E
95 O15 **Stockholm** ◈ county C Sweden
Stockmannshof see Pļaviņas
97 L18 **Stockport** NW England, United Kingdom 53°25′N 02°10′W
65 K15 **Stocks Seamount** undersea feature C Atlantic Ocean 11°42′S 33°48′W
35 O8 **Stockton** California, W USA 37°56′N 121°19′W
26 L3 **Stockton** Kansas, C USA 39°27′N 99°17′W
27 S6 **Stockton** Missouri, C USA 37°43′N 93°49′W
30 J3 **Stockton Island** island Apostle Islands, Wisconsin, N USA
27 S7 **Stockton Lake** ▣ Missouri, C USA
97 M15 **Stockton-on-Tees** var. Stockton on Tees. N England, United Kingdom 54°34′N 01°19′W
Stockton on Tees see Stockton-on-Tees
24 M10 **Stockton Plateau** plain Texas, SW USA
28 M16 **Stockville** Nebraska, C USA 40°33′N 100°20′W
93 H17 **Stöde** Västernorrland, C Sweden 62°27′N 16°34′E
Stodolichi see Stadolichy
113 M19 **Stogovo Karaorman** ▲▲ W FYR Macedonia
Stoke see Stoke-on-Trent
97 L19 **Stoke-on-Trent** var. Stoke. C England, United Kingdom 53°N 02°10′W
182 M15 **Stokes Point** headland Tasmania, SE Australia 40°09′S 143°55′E
116 J2 **Stokhid** Pol. Stochód, Rus. Stokhod. ≈ NW Ukraine
Stokhod see Stokhid
92 I4 **Stokkseyri** Sudhurland, SW Iceland 63°49′N 21°00′W
92 G10 **Stokmarknes** Nordland, C Norway 68°34′N 14°55′E
Stol see Veliki Krš
113 H15 **Stolac** Federacija Bosna I Hercegovina, S Bosnia and Herzegovina 43°04′N 17°58′E
Stolbce see Stowbtsy
101 D16 **Stolberg** var. Stolberg im Rheinland. Nordrhein-Westfalen, W Germany 50°45′N 06°15′E
Stolberg im Rheinland see Stolberg
123 P6 **Stolbovoy, Ostrov** island NE Russian Federation
Stolbtsy see Stowbtsy
119 J20 **Stolin** Brestskaya Voblasts', SW Belarus 51°53′N 26°51′E
95 K14 **Stöllet** var. Norra Ny. Värmland, C Sweden 60°24′N 13°15′E
Stolp see Słupsk
Stolpe see Słupia
Stolpmünde see Ustka
115 F15 **Stómio** Thessalía, C Greece 39°51′N 22°45′E
14 J11 **Stonecliffe** Ontario, SE Canada 46°12′N 77°58′W
96 L10 **Stonehaven** NE Scotland, United Kingdom 56°59′N 02°14′W
97 M23 **Stonehenge** ancient monument Wiltshire, S England, United Kingdom
23 T3 **Stone Mountain** ▲ Georgia, SE USA 33°48′N 84°10′W
11 X16 **Stonewall** Manitoba, S Canada 50°08′N 97°20′W
21 S3 **Stonewood** West Virginia, NE USA 39°15′N 80°18′W
14 D17 **Stoney Point** Ontario, S Canada 42°18′N 82°32′W
92 H10 **Stonglandseidet** Troms, N Norway 69°03′N 17°06′E
65 N25 **Stonybeach Bay** bay Tristan da Cunha, SE Atlantic Ocean
35 N5 **Stony Creek** ≈ California, W USA
65 N25 **Stonyhill Point** headland S Tristan da Cunha
14 I14 **Stony Lake** ◎ Ontario, SE Canada
11 Q14 **Stony Plain** Alberta, SW Canada 53°31′N 114°04′W
21 R9 **Stony Point** North Carolina, SE USA 35°51′N 81°04′W
18 G8 **Stony Point** headland New York, NE USA 43°50′N 76°18′W
11 T10 **Stony Rapids** Saskatchewan, C Canada 59°14′N 105°48′W
39 P11 **Stony River** Alaska, USA 61°48′N 156°37′W
Stony Tunguska see Podkamennaya Tunguska
12 G10 **Stooping** ≈ Ontario, C Canada
100 I9 **Stör** ≈ N Germany
95 M15 **Storå** Örebro, S Sweden 59°44′N 15°10′E
95 J16 **Stora Gla** ◎ C Sweden
95 I16 **Stora Le** Nor. Store Le. ◎ Norway/Sweden
92 I12 **Stora Lulevatten** ◎ N Sweden
92 H13 **Storavan** ◎ N Sweden
93 I20 **Storby** Åland, SW Finland 60°12′N 19°33′E
94 E10 **Stordalen** Møre og Romsdal, S Norway 62°22′N 07°00′E
95 H23 **Storebælt** var. Store Bælt, Eng. Great Belt, Storebelt. channel Baltic Sea/Kattegat
Store Bælt see Storebælt
Storebelt see Storebælt
95 M19 **Storebro** Kalmar, S Sweden 57°36′N 15°30′E
95 J24 **Store Heddinge** Sjælland, SE Denmark 55°19′N 12°24′E
Store Le see Stora Le
93 E16 **Støren** Sør-Trøndelag, S Norway 63°02′N 10°16′E
92 O4 **Storfjorden** fjord S Norway
95 L15 **Storfors** Värmland, C Sweden 59°33′N 14°16′E
92 G13 **Storforshei** Nordland, C Norway 66°25′N 14°25′E
Storhammer see Hamar
93 F16 **Storlien** Jämtland, C Sweden 63°18′N 12°10′E
183 P17 **Storm Bay** inlet Tasmania, SE Australia
29 T12 **Storm Lake** Iowa, C USA 42°38′N 95°12′W
29 S13 **Storm Lake** ◎ Iowa, C USA
96 G7 **Stornoway** NW Scotland, United Kingdom 58°13′N 06°23′W
Storojineţ see Storozhynets'
92 P1 **Storøya** island NE Svalbard
125 S10 **Storozhevsk** Respublika Komi, NW Russian Federation 61°56′N 52°18′E
Storozhinets see Storozhynets'
116 K8 **Storozhynets'** Ger. Storozynetz, Rom. Storojineţ, Rus. Storozhinets. Chernivets'ka Oblast', W Ukraine 48°11′N 25°42′E
Storozynetz see Storozhynets'
92 H11 **Storriten** Lapp. Stuorrarijjda. ▲ C Norway 68°09′N 17°12′E
19 N12 **Storrs** Connecticut, NE USA 41°48′N 72°15′W
94 I11 **Storsjøen** ◎ S Norway
94 N13 **Storsjön** ◎ C Sweden
93 F16 **Storsjön** ◎ C Sweden
92 J9 **Storslett** Troms, N Norway 69°45′N 21°03′E
94 H11 **Storskrimtinden** ▲ S Norway 61°52′N 11°32′E
92 I9 **Storsteinnes** Troms, N Norway 69°13′N 19°14′E
Storstrøms Amt see Sjælland
93 J14 **Storsund** Norrbotten, N Sweden 65°36′N 20°40′E
94 J9 **Storsylen** Swe. Sylarna. ▲ Norway/Sweden 63°00′N 12°14′E
92 H11 **Stortoppen** ▲ N Sweden 67°33′N 17°27′E
93 H14 **Storuman** Västerbotten, N Sweden 65°05′N 17°10′E
93 H14 **Storuman** ◎ N Sweden
94 N13 **Storvik** Gävleborg, C Sweden 60°37′N 16°30′E
95 O14 **Storvreta** Uppsala, C Sweden 59°58′N 17°42′E
100 L10 **Störwasserstrasse** canal N Germany
29 V13 **Story City** Iowa, C USA 42°10′N 93°36′W
11 V17 **Stoughton** Saskatchewan, S Canada 49°40′N 103°01′W
19 O11 **Stoughton** Massachusetts, NE USA 42°07′N 71°06′W
30 L9 **Stoughton** Wisconsin, N USA 42°56′N 89°12′W
97 L23 **Stour** ≈ E England, United Kingdom
97 P21 **Stour** ≈ S England, United Kingdom
27 T5 **Stover** Missouri, C USA 38°26′N 92°59′W
95 G21 **Støvring** Nordjylland, N Denmark 56°53′N 09°52′E
119 J17 **Stowbtsy** Pol. Stolbce, Rus. Stolbtsy. Minskaya Voblasts', C Belarus 53°29′N 26°44′E
25 X11 **Stowell** Texas, SW USA 29°47′N 94°22′W
97 P20 **Stowmarket** E England, United Kingdom 52°05′N 00°54′E
114 N8 **Stozher** Dobrich, NE Bulgaria 43°27′N 27°49′E
97 E14 **Strabane** Ir. An Srath Bán. W Northern Ireland, United Kingdom 54°49′N 07°27′W
121 S11 **Strabo Trench** undersea feature C Mediterranean Sea
27 T7 **Strafford** Missouri, C USA 37°16′N 93°07′W
183 N17 **Strahan** Tasmania, SE Australia 42°10′S 145°18′E
111 C18 **Strakonice** Ger. Strakonitz. Jihočeský Kraj, S Czech Republic 49°14′N 13°55′E
Strakonitz see Strakonice
100 N8 **Stralsund** Mecklenburg-Vorpommern, NE Germany 54°18′N 13°06′E
99 L16 **Stramproy** Limburg, SE Netherlands 51°12′N 05°43′E
83 E26 **Strand** Western Cape, SW South Africa 34°06′S 18°50′E
94 E10 **Stranda** Møre og Romsdal, S Norway 62°18′N 06°56′E
97 G15 **Strangford Lough** Ir. Loch Cuan. inlet E Northern Ireland, United Kingdom
95 N16 **Strängnäs** Södermanland, C Sweden 59°22′N 17°02′E
97 E14 **Stranorlar** Ir. Srath an Urláir. NW Ireland 54°48′N 07°46′W
97 H14 **Stranraer** S Scotland, United Kingdom 54°54′N 05°02′W
11 U16 **Strasbourg** Saskatchewan, S Canada 51°05′N 104°58′W
103 V5 **Strasbourg** Ger. Strassburg; anc. Argentoratum. Bas-Rhin, NE France 48°35′N 07°45′E
109 T8 **Strassburg** Kärnten, S Austria 46°54′N 14°21′E
Strassburg see Strasbourg, France
Strassburg see Aiud, Romania
99 M25 **Strassen** Luxembourg, S Luxembourg 49°37′N 06°05′E
109 R5 **Strasswalchen** Salzburg, C Austria 47°59′N 13°19′E
14 F16 **Stratford** Ontario, S Canada 43°22′N 81°00′W
184 K10 **Stratford** Taranaki, North Island, New Zealand 39°20′S 174°16′E
35 Q11 **Stratford** California, W USA 36°10′N 119°47′W
29 V13 **Stratford** Iowa, C USA 42°16′N 93°55′W
27 O12 **Stratford** Oklahoma, C USA 34°48′N 96°57′W
25 N1 **Stratford** Texas, SW USA 36°21′N 102°05′W
30 K6 **Stratford** Wisconsin, N USA 44°53′N 90°13′W
Stratford see Stratford-upon-Avon
97 M20 **Stratford-upon-Avon** var. Stratford. C England, United Kingdom 52°12′N 01°41′W
183 O17 **Strathgordon** Tasmania, SE Australia 42°49′S 146°04′E
11 Q16 **Strathmore** Alberta, SW Canada 51°05′N 113°20′W
35 R11 **Strathmore** California, W USA 36°07′N 119°04′W
14 E16 **Strathroy** Ontario, S Canada 42°57′N 81°40′W
96 I6 **Strathy Point** headland N Scotland, United Kingdom 58°36′N 04°04′W
37 W4 **Stratton** Colorado, C USA 39°16′N 102°34′W
19 P6 **Stratton** Maine, NE USA 45°08′N 70°25′W
18 M10 **Stratton Mountain** ▲ Vermont, NE USA 43°05′N 72°55′W
101 N21 **Straubing** Bayern, SE Germany 48°53′N 12°35′E
100 O12 **Strausberg** Brandenburg, E Germany 52°34′N 13°52′E
32 K13 **Strawberry Mountain** ▲ Oregon, NW USA 44°18′N 118°43′W
29 X12 **Strawberry Point** Iowa, C USA 42°40′N 91°31′W
36 M3 **Strawberry Reservoir** ▣ Utah, W USA
36 M4 **Strawberry River** ≈ Utah, W USA
25 R7 **Strawn** Texas, SW USA 32°33′N 98°30′W
113 P17 **Straža** ▲ Bulgaria/FYR Macedonia 42°16′N 22°13′E
111 I19 **Strážov** Hung. Sztrazsó. ▲ NW Slovakia 48°59′N 18°29′E
182 F7 **Streaky Bay** South Australia 32°49′S 134°13′E
182 E7 **Streaky Bay** bay South Australia
30 L12 **Streator** Illinois, N USA 41°07′N 88°50′W
Streckenbach see Świdnik
Strednogorie see Pirdop
111 C17 **Středočeský Kraj** ◈ region C Czech Republic
29 O6 **Streeter** North Dakota, N USA 46°37′N 99°23′W
25 U8 **Streetman** Texas, SW USA 31°52′N 96°19′W
116 G13 **Strehaia** Mehedinţi, SW Romania 44°37′N 23°10′E
Strehlen see Strzelin
114 I10 **Strelcha** Pazardzhik, C Bulgaria 42°28′N 24°21′E
122 L12 **Strelka** Krasnoyarskiy Kray, C Russian Federation 58°05′N 92°54′E
124 L6 **Strel'na** ≈ NW Russian Federation
118 H7 **Strenči** Ger. Stackeln. N Latvia 57°38′N 25°42′E
15 V6 **St-René-de-Matane** Québec, SE Canada 48°42′N 67°22′W
108 K8 **Strengen** Tirol, W Austria 47°07′N 10°25′E
106 C6 **Stresa** Piemonte, NE Italy 45°52′N 08°32′E
Streshin see Streshyn
119 N18 **Streshyn** Rus. Streshin. Homyel'skaya Voblasts', SE Belarus 52°43′N 30°07′E
95 B18 **Streymoy** Dan. Strømø. island N Faeroe Islands
95 G23 **Strib** Syddtjylland, C Denmark 55°33′N 09°47′E
111 A17 **Stříbro** Ger. Mies. Plzeňský Kraj, W Czech Republic 49°44′N 12°55′E
186 B7 **Strickland** ≈ SW Papua New Guinea
Striegau see Strzegom
Strigonium see Esztergom
98 H13 **Strijen** Zuid-Holland, SW Netherlands 51°45′N 04°34′E
63 H21 **Strobel, Lago** ◎ S Argentina
61 B25 **Stroeder** Buenos Aires, E Argentina 40°11′S 62°35′W
115 C20 **Strofádes** island Iónia Nisiá, Greece, C Mediterranean Sea
Strofilia see Strofyliá
115 G17 **Strofyliá** var. Strofilia. Évvoia, C Greece 38°49′N 23°25′E
100 O10 **Strom** ≈ NE Germany
107 L22 **Stromboli** ⚶ Isola Stromboli, SW Italy 38°48′N 15°13′E
107 L22 **Stromboli, Isola** island Isole Eolie, S Italy
96 H9 **Stromeferry** N Scotland, United Kingdom 57°20′N 05°35′W
96 J5 **Stromness** N Scotland, United Kingdom 58°57′N 03°18′W
Strømø see Streymoy
94 N11 **Strömsbruk** Gävleborg, C Sweden 61°52′N 17°19′E
29 Q15 **Stromsburg** Nebraska, C USA 41°06′N 97°36′W
95 K21 **Strömsnäsbruk** Kronoberg, S Sweden 56°35′N 13°45′E
95 I17 **Strömstad** Västra Götaland, S Sweden 58°56′N 11°11′E
93 G16 **Strömsund** Jämtland, C Sweden 63°51′N 15°35′E
93 G15 **Ströms Vattudal** valley N Sweden
27 V14 **Strong** Arkansas, C USA 33°06′N 92°19′W
Strongilí see Strongylí
107 O21 **Strongoli** Calabria, SW Italy 39°17′N 17°03′E
31 T11 **Strongsville** Ohio, N USA 41°18′N 81°50′W
115 Q23 **Strongylí** var. Strongilí. island SE Greece
96 K5 **Stronsay** island NE Scotland, United Kingdom
97 L21 **Stroud** C England, United Kingdom 51°46′N 02°15′W
27 O10 **Stroud** Oklahoma, C USA 35°45′N 96°39′W
18 I14 **Stroudsburg** Pennsylvania, NE USA 40°59′N 75°12′W
95 F21 **Struer** Midtjylland, W Denmark 56°29′N 08°37′E
113 M20 **Struga** SW FYR Macedonia 41°11′N 20°40′E
Strugi-Kranyse see Strugi-Krasnyye
124 G14 **Strugi-Krasnyye** var. Strugi-Kranyse. Pskovskaya Oblast', W Russian Federation 58°19′N 29°09′E
114 G11 **Struma** Gk. Strymónas. ≈ Bulgaria/Greece see also Strymónas
Struma see Strymónas
97 G21 **Strumble Head** headland SW Wales, United Kingdom 52°01′N 05°05′W
Strumeshnitsa see Strumica
113 Q19 **Strumica** E FYR Macedonia 41°27′N 22°39′E
113 Q19 **Strumica** Bulg. Strumeshnitsa. ≈ Bulgaria/FYR Macedonia
114 G11 **Strumyani** Blagoevgrad, SW Bulgaria 41°41′N 23°13′E
31 V12 **Struthers** Ohio, N USA 41°03′N 80°36′W
114 I10 **Stryama** ≈ C Bulgaria
114 G13 **Strymónas** Bul. Struma. ≈ Bulgaria/Greece see also Struma
Strymónas see Struma
115 H14 **Strymonikós Kólpos** gulf N Greece
116 I6 **Stryy** L'vivs'ka Oblast', NW Ukraine 49°16′N 23°51′E
116 H6 **Stryy** ≈ W Ukraine
111 F14 **Strzegom** Ger. Striegau. Wałbrzych, SW Poland 50°59′N 16°20′E
110 E10 **Strzelce Krajeńskie** Ger. Friedeberg Neumark. Lubuskie, W Poland 52°52′N 15°30′E
111 I15 **Strzelce Opolskie** Ger. Gross Strehlitz. Opolskie, SW Poland 50°31′N 18°19′E
182 K3 **Strzelecki Creek** seasonal river South Australia
182 J3 **Strzelecki Desert** desert South Australia
111 G15 **Strzelin** Ger. Strehlen. Dolnośląskie, SW Poland 50°48′N 17°03′E
110 I11 **Strzelno** Kujawsko-pomorski, C Poland 52°38′N 18°11′E
111 N17 **Strzyżów** Podkarpackie, SE Poland 49°52′N 21°46′E
15 S8 **St-Siméon** Québec, SE Canada 47°50′N 69°55′W
Stua Laighean see Leinster, Mount
23 Y13 **Stuart** Florida, SE USA 27°12′N 80°15′W
29 U14 **Stuart** Iowa, C USA 41°30′N 94°19′W
29 O13 **Stuart** Nebraska, C USA 42°36′N 99°08′W
21 S8 **Stuart** Virginia, NE USA 36°38′N 80°19′W
10 L13 **Stuart** ≈ British Columbia, SW Canada
39 N10 **Stuart Island** island Alaska, USA
10 L13 **Stuart Lake** ◎ British Columbia, SW Canada
185 B22 **Stuart Mountains** ▲▲ South Island, New Zealand
182 F3 **Stuart Range** hill range South Australia
Stubaital see Neustift im Stubaital
95 I24 **Stubbekøbing** Sjælland, SE Denmark 54°53′N 12°04′E
45 P14 **Stubbs** Saint Vincent, Saint Vincent and the Grenadines 13°08′N 61°09′W
109 V6 **Stübming** ≈ E Austria
114 J11 **Studen Kladenets, Yazovir** ▣ S Bulgaria
185 G21 **Studholme** Canterbury, South Island, New Zealand 44°44′S 171°08′E
Stuhlweissenberg see Székesfehérvár
Stuhm see Sztum
12 C7 **Stull Lake** ◎ Ontario, C Canada
Stuorrarijjda see Storriten
126 L4 **Stupino** Moskovskaya Oblast', W Russian Federation 54°54′N 38°06′E
27 U4 **Sturgeon** Missouri, C USA 39°13′N 92°16′W
14 G10 **Sturgeon** ≈ Ontario, S Canada
31 N6 **Sturgeon Bay** Wisconsin, N USA 44°51′N 87°21′W
14 G11 **Sturgeon Falls** Ontario, S Canada 46°22′N 79°57′W
12 C11 **Sturgeon Lake** ◎ Ontario, S Canada
30 M3 **Sturgeon River** ≈ Michigan, N USA
20 H6 **Sturgis** Kentucky, S USA 37°33′N 87°58′W
31 P11 **Sturgis** Michigan, N USA 41°48′N 85°25′W
28 J9 **Sturgis** South Dakota, N USA 44°24′N 103°30′W
112 D10 **Šturlić** ◈ Federacija Bosna I Hercegovina, NW Bosnia and Herzegovina
111 J22 **Štúrovo** Hung. Párkány; prev. Parkan. Nitriansky Kraj, SW Slovakia 47°49′N 18°40′E
182 L4 **Sturt, Mount** hill New South Wales, SE Australia
181 P4 **Sturt Plain** plain Northern Territory, N Australia
181 T9 **Sturt Stony Desert** desert South Australia
83 J25 **Stutterheim** Eastern Cape, S South Africa 32°35′S 27°26′E
101 H21 **Stuttgart** Baden-Württemberg, SW Germany 48°47′N 09°12′E
27 W12 **Stuttgart** Arkansas, C USA 34°30′N 91°32′W
92 H2 **Stykkishólmur** Vesturland, W Iceland 65°04′N 22°43′W
115 F17 **Stylída** var. Stilida, Stilís. Stereá Elláda, C Greece 38°55′N 22°37′E
116 K2 **Styr** Rus. Styr'. ≈ Belarus/Ukraine
115 I19 **Stýra** var. Stira. Évvoia, C Greece 38°10′N 24°13′E
Styria see Steiermark
15 Y5 **St-Yvon** Québec, SE Canada 49°09′N 64°51′W
Su see Jiangsu
Sua see Sowa
171 Q17 **Suai** W East Timor 09°19′S 125°16′E
54 G9 **Suaita** Santander, C Colombia 06°07′N 73°30′W
80 I7 **Suakin** var. Sawakin. Red Sea, NE Sudan 19°06′N 37°17′E
161 T13 **Su'ao** Jap. Suō. N Taiwan 24°33′N 121°48′E
Suao see Suau
Sua Pan see Sowa Pan
40 G6 **Suaqui Grande** Sonora, NW Mexico 28°22′N 109°52′W
61 A16 **Suardi** Santa Fe, C Argentina 30°32′S 61°58′W
54 D11 **Suárez** Cauca, SW Colombia 02°55′N 76°41′W
186 G10 **Suau** var. Suao. Suaul Island, SE Papua New Guinea 10°39′S 150°03′E
118 G12 **Subačius** Panevėžys, NE Lithuania 55°46′N 24°45′E
168 K9 **Subang** prev. Soebang. Jawa, C Indonesia 06°32′S 107°45′E
169 O16 **Subang** ✈ (Kuala Lumpur) Pahang, Peninsular Malaysia
129 S10 **Subansiri** ≈ NE India
154 M12 **Subarnapur** prev. Sonepur. Sonepur. Orissa, E India 20°50′N 83°58′E
118 I11 **Subate** SE Latvia 56°00′N 25°54′E
139 N5 **Subaykhān** Dayr az Zawr, E Syria 34°52′N 40°35′E
Subei/Subei Mongolzu Zizhixian see Dangchengwan
169 P9 **Subi Besar, Pulau** island Kepulauan Natuna, W Indonesia
Subiyah see Aş Şubayḩīyah
26 I7 **Sublette** Kansas, C USA 37°28′N 100°52′W
112 K8 **Subotica** Ger. Maria-Theresiopel, Hung. Szabadka. Vojvodina, N Serbia 46°06′N 19°41′E
116 K9 **Suceava** Ger. Suczawa, Hung. Szucsava. Suceava, NE Romania 47°41′N 26°16′E
116 J9 **Suceava** ◈ county NE Romania
116 K9 **Suceava** Ger. Suczawa. ≈ N Romania
112 E12 **Sučevići** Zadar, SW Croatia 44°13′N 16°04′E
111 K17 **Sucha Beskidzka** Małopolskie, S Poland 49°44′N 19°36′E
111 M14 **Suchedniów** Świętokrzyskie, C Poland 51°01′N 20°49′E
42 A2 **Suchitepéquez** off. Departamento de Suchitepéquez. ◈ department SW Guatemala
Suchitepéquez, Departamento de see Suchitepéquez
Su-chou see Suzhou
Suchow see Xuzhou, Jiangsu, China
Suchow see Suzhou, Jiangsu, China
97 D17 **Suck** ≈ C Ireland

◆ Country
● Country Capital
◇ Dependent Territory
○ Dependent Territory Capital
◈ Administrative Regions
✈ International Airport
▲ Mountain
▲▲ Mountain Range
⚶ Volcano
≈ River
◎ Lake
▣ Reservoir

Sucker State see Illinois
186 F9 **Suckling, Mount** ▲ S Papua New Guinea 09°36′S 149°00′E
57 L19 **Sucre** hist. Chuquisaca, La Plata. ● (Bolivia-legal capital) Chuquisaca, S Bolivia 18°53′S 65°25′W
54 E6 **Sucre** Santander, N Colombia 08°50′N 74°22′W
56 A7 **Sucre** Manabí, W Ecuador 01°21′S 80°27′W
54 E6 **Sucre** off. Departamento de Sucre. ⬗ province N Colombia
55 O5 **Sucre** off. Estado Sucre. ⬗ state NE Venezuela
Sucre, Departamento de see Sucre
Sucre, Estado see Sucre
56 D6 **Sucumbíos** ⬗ province NE Ecuador
113 G15 **Sućuraj** Split-Dalmacija, S Croatia 43°07′N 17°10′E
58 K10 **Sucuriju** Amapá, NE Brazil 01°31′N 50°W
Suczawa see Suceava
79 E16 **Sud** Eng. South. ⬗ province S Cameroon
124 K13 **Suda** ≈ NW Russian Federation
Suda see Soúda
117 U13 **Sudak** Avtonomna Respublika Krym, S Ukraine 44°52′N 34°57′E
24 M4 **Sudan** Texas, SW USA 34°04′N 102°32′W
80 C10 **Sudan** off. Republic of Sudan, Ar. Jumhuriyat as-Sudan; prev. Anglo-Egyptian Sudan. ◆ republic N Africa
Sudanese Republic see Mali
Sudan, Jumhuriyat as- see Sudan
Sudan, Republic of see Sudan
14 F10 **Sudbury** Ontario, S Canada 46°29′N 81°W
97 P20 **Sudbury** E England, United Kingdom 52°04′N 00°43′E
Sud, Canal de see Gonâve, Canal de la
80 E13 **Sudd** swamp region C South Sudan
100 K10 **Sude** ≈ N Germany
Suderø see Sudhuroy
Sudest Island see Tagula Island
111 E15 **Sudeten** var. Sudetes, Sudetic Mountains, Cz./Pol. Sudety. ▲▲ Czech Republic/Poland
Sudetes/Sudetic Mountains/Sudety see Sudeten
92 G1 **Sudhureyri** Vestfirdhir, NW Iceland 66°08′N 23°31′W
92 J4 **Sudhurland** ⬗ region S Iceland
95 B19 **Sudhuroy** Dan. Suderø. island S Faeroe Islands
124 M15 **Sudislavl'** Kostromskaya Oblast', NW Russian Federation 57°55′N 41°45′E
Südkarpaten see Carpații Meridionalii
79 N20 **Sud-Kivu** off. Région Sud Kivu. ⬗ region E Dem. Rep. Congo
Sud Kivu, Région see Sud-Kivu
Südliche Morava see Južna Morava
100 E12 **Süd-Nord-Kanal** canal NW Germany
126 M3 **Sudogda** Vladimirskaya Oblast', W Russian Federation 55°58′N 40°57′E
Sudostroy see Severodvinsk
79 C15 **Sud-Ouest** Eng. South-West. ⬗ province W Cameroon
173 X17 **Sud Ouest, Pointe** headland SW Mauritius 20°27′S 57°18′E
187 P17 **Sud, Province** ⬗ province S New Caledonia
92 H4 **Sudurnes** ⬗ region SW Iceland
126 J8 **Sudzha** Kurskaya Oblast', W Russian Federation 51°12′N 35°19′E
81 D15 **Sue** ≈ W South Sudan
105 S10 **Sueca** Valenciana, E Spain 39°13′N 00°19′W
114 I10 **Sŭedinenie** Plovdiv, C Bulgaria 42°14′N 24°36′E
Suero see Alzira
75 X8 **Suez** Ar. As Suways, El Suweis. NE Egypt 29°59′N 32°33′E
75 W7 **Suez Canal** Ar. Qanāt as Suways. canal NE Egypt
Suez, Gulf of see Khalīj as Suways
11 R17 **Suffield** Alberta, SW Canada 50°15′N 111°05′W
21 X7 **Suffolk** Virginia, NE USA 36°44′N 76°37′W
97 P20 **Suffolk** cultural region E England, United Kingdom
142 J2 **Şūfiān** Āžarbāyjān-e Sharqī, N Iran 38°15′N 45°59′E
31 N12 **Sugar Creek** ≈ Illinois, N USA
30 L13 **Sugar Creek** ≈ Illinois, N USA
31 R3 **Sugar Island** island Michigan, N USA
25 V11 **Sugar Land** Texas, SW USA 29°37′N 95°37′W
19 P6 **Sugarloaf Mountain** ▲ Maine, NE USA 45°01′N 70°18′W
65 G24 **Sugar Loaf Point** headland N Saint Helena 15°54′S 05°43′W
136 G16 **Suğla Gölü** ◎ SW Turkey
123 T8 **Sugoy** ≈ E Russian Federation
158 F7 **Sugun** Xinjiang Uygur Zizhiqu, W China 39°46′N 76°45′E
147 U11 **Sugut, Gora** ▲ SW Kyrgyzstan 39°52′N 73°36′E
169 V6 **Sugut, Sungai** ≈ East Malaysia
159 O9 **Suhai Hu** ◎ C China
162 K14 **Suhait** Nei Mongol Zizhiqu, N China 39°29′N 105°11′E
141 X7 **Şuḩār** var. Sohar. N Oman 24°20′N 56°43′E
113 M17 **Suharekë** Serb. Suva Reka. S Kosovo 42°23′N 20°50′E
162 L6 **Sühbaatar** Selenge, N Mongolia 50°12′N 106°14′E
163 P8 **Sühbaatar** var. Haylaastay. Sühbaatar, E Mongolia 46°44′N 113°51′E
163 P9 **Sühbaatar** ⬗ province E Mongolia
101 K17 **Suhl** Thüringen, C Germany 50°37′N 10°43′E
108 F7 **Suhr** Aargau, N Switzerland 47°23′N 08°05′E
Sui'an see Zhangpu
Suicheng see Suixi
161 O12 **Suichuan** var. Quanjiang. Jiangxi, S China 26°26′N 114°34′E
Suid-Afrika see South Africa
160 L4 **Suide** var. Mingzhou. Shaanxi, C China 37°30′N 110°10′E
Suidwes-Afrika see Namibia
163 Y9 **Suifenhe** Heilongjiang, NE China 44°22′N 131°12′E
Suigen see Suwon
163 W8 **Suihua** Heilongjiang, NE China 46°40′N 127°00′E
Súilí, Loch see Swilly, Lough
161 Q6 **Suining** Jiangsu, E China 33°54′N 117°58′E
160 I9 **Suining** Sichuan, C China 30°31′N 105°33′E
103 Q4 **Suippes** Marne, N France 49°08′N 04°31′E
97 E20 **Suir** Ir. An tSiúir. ≈ S Ireland
165 J13 **Suita** Ōsaka, Honshū, SW Japan 34°39′N 135°27′E
160 L16 **Suixi** var. Suicheng. Guangdong, S China 21°23′N 110°14′E
Sui Xian see Suizhou
163 T13 **Suizhong** Liaoning, NE China 40°19′N 120°22′E
161 N8 **Suizhou** prev. Sui Xian. Hubei, C China 31°46′N 113°20′E
149 P17 **Sujāwal** Sind, SE Pakistan 24°36′N 68°06′E
169 O16 **Sukabumi** prev. Soekaboemi. Jawa, C Indonesia 06°55′S 106°56′E
169 Q12 **Sukadana, Teluk** bay Borneo, W Indonesia
165 P11 **Sukagawa** Fukushima, Honshū, C Japan 37°16′N 140°20′E
Sukarnapura see Jayapura
Sukarno, Puntjak see Jaya, Puncak
Sŭkh see Sokh
114 N8 **Sukha Reka** ≈ NE Bulgaria
114 J8 **Sukhindol** Veliko Turnovo, N Bulgaria 43°11′N 24°10′E
126 J5 **Sukhinichi** Kaluzhskaya Oblast', W Russian Federation 54°06′N 35°22′E
Sukhne see As Sukhnah
129 Q4 **Sukhona** var. Tot'ma. ≈ NW Russian Federation
167 O8 **Sukhothai** var. Sukotai. Sukhothai, W Thailand 17°00′N 99°51′E
Sukhumi see Sokhumi
Sukkertoppen see Maniitsoq
149 Q13 **Sukkur** Sind, SE Pakistan 27°45′N 68°46′E
Sukotai see Sukhothai
Sukra Bay see Şawqirah, Dawḩat
125 V15 **Suksun** Permskiy Kray, NW Russian Federation 57°10′N 57°27′E
165 F15 **Sukumo** Kōchi, Shikoku, SW Japan 32°55′N 132°42′E
94 B12 **Sula** island S Norway
125 Q5 **Sula** ≈ NW Russian Federation
117 R5 **Sula** ≈ N Ukraine
42 H6 **Sulaco, Río** ≈ NW Honduras
Sulaimaniya see As Sulaymānīyah
149 S10 **Sulaimān Range** ▲▲ C Pakistan
127 Q16 **Sulak** Respublika Dagestan, SW Russian Federation 43°19′N 47°28′E
127 Q16 **Sulak** ≈ SW Russian Federation
171 Q13 **Sula, Kepulauan** island group C Indonesia
136 I12 **Sulakyurt** var. Konur. Kırıkkale, N Turkey 40°10′N 33°42′E
171 P17 **Sulamu** Timor, S Indonesia 09°57′S 123°33′E
96 F5 **Sula Sgeir** island NW Scotland, United Kingdom
171 N13 **Sulawesi** Eng. Celebes. island C Indonesia
Sulawesi, Laut see Celebes Sea
171 N14 **Sulawesi Selatan** off. Propinsi Sulawesi Selatan, Eng. South Celebes, South Sulawesi. ⬗ province C Indonesia
Sulawesi Selatan, Propinsi see Sulawesi Selatan
171 P12 **Sulawesi Tengah** off. Propinsi Sulawesi Tengah, Eng. Central Celebes, Central Sulawesi. ⬗ province N Indonesia
Sulawesi Tengah, Propinsi see Sulawesi Tengah
171 O14 **Sulawesi Tenggara** off. Propinsi Sulawesi Tenggara, Eng. South-East Celebes, South-East Sulawesi. ⬗ province C Indonesia
Sulawesi Tenggara, Propinsi see Sulawesi Tenggara
171 P11 **Sulawesi Utara** off. Propinsi Sulawesi Utara, Eng. North Celebes, North Sulawesi. ⬗ province N Indonesia
Sulawesi Utara, Propinsi see Sulawesi Utara
139 T5 **Sulaymān Beg** At Ta'mím, N Iraq
95 D15 **Suldalsvatnet** ◎ S Norway
Sulden see Solda
110 E12 **Sulechów** Ger. Züllichau. Lubuskie, W Poland 52°05′N 15°37′E
110 E11 **Sulęcin** Lubuskie, W Poland 52°29′N 15°06′E
77 U14 **Suleja** Niger, C Nigeria 09°15′N 07°10′E
111 K14 **Sulejów** Łodzkie, S Poland 51°21′N 19°57′E
96 I5 **Sule Skerry** island N Scotland, United Kingdom
Suliag see Sawhāj
76 J16 **Sulima** S Sierra Leone 06°59′N 11°34′W
117 O13 **Sulina** Tulcea, SE Romania 45°07′N 29°40′E
117 N13 **Sulina, Braţul** ≈ SE Romania
100 H12 **Sulingen** Niedersachsen, NW Germany 52°40′N 08°48′E
Sulisjielmmá see Sulitjelma
92 H12 **Suliskongen** ▲ C Norway 67°10′N 16°16′E
92 H12 **Sulitjelma** Lapp. Sulisjielmmá. Nordland, C Norway 67°10′N 16°05′E
56 A9 **Sullana** Piura, NW Peru 04°54′S 80°42′W
23 N3 **Sulligent** Alabama, S USA 33°54′N 88°07′W
30 M14 **Sullivan** Illinois, N USA 39°36′N 88°36′W
31 N15 **Sullivan** Indiana, N USA 39°05′N 87°24′W
27 W5 **Sullivan** Missouri, C USA 38°12′N 91°09′W
Sullivan Island see Lanbi Kyun
96 M1 **Sullom Voe** NE Scotland, United Kingdom 60°24′N 01°09′W
103 O7 **Sully-sur-Loire** Loiret, C France 47°46′N 02°21′E
Sulmo see Sulmona
107 K15 **Sulmona** anc. Sulmo. Abruzzo, C Italy 42°03′N 13°56′E
Sulo see Shule He
114 M11 **Süloğlu** Edirne, NW Turkey 41°46′N 26°55′E
22 G9 **Sulphur** Louisiana, S USA 30°14′N 93°22′W
27 O12 **Sulphur** Oklahoma, C USA 34°31′N 96°58′W
28 K9 **Sulphur Creek** ≈ South Dakota, N USA
24 M5 **Sulphur Draw** ≈ Texas, SW USA
25 W5 **Sulphur River** ≈ Arkansas/Texas, SW USA
25 V6 **Sulphur Springs** Texas, SW USA 33°09′N 95°36′W
24 M6 **Sulphur Springs Draw** ≈ Texas, SW USA
14 D8 **Sultan** Ontario, S Canada 47°34′N 82°45′W
Sultānābād see Arāk
Sultan Alonto, Lake see Lanao, Lake
136 G15 **Sultan Dağları** ▲▲ C Turkey
114 N13 **Sultanköy** Tekirdağ, NW Turkey 41°01′N 27°58′E
171 Q7 **Sultan Kudarat** var. Nuling. Mindanao, S Philippines 07°20′N 124°16′E
152 M13 **Sultānpur** Uttar Pradesh, N India 26°15′N 82°04′E
171 O9 **Sulu Archipelago** island group SW Philippines
192 F7 **Sulu Basin** undersea feature SE South China Sea 08°00′N 121°30′E
Sülüktü see Sulyukta
Sulu, Laut see Sulu Sea
169 X6 **Sulu Sea** var. Laut Sulu. sea SW Philippines
145 O15 **Sulutobe** Kaz. Sulūtöbe. Kzylorda, S Kazakhstan 44°31′N 66°17′E
Sulūtöbe see Sulutobe
147 Q11 **Sulyukta** Kir. Sülüktü. Batkenskaya Oblast', SW Kyrgyzstan 39°57′N 69°31′E
Sulz see Sulz am Neckar
101 G22 **Sulz am Neckar** var. Sulz. Baden-Württemberg, SW Germany 48°22′N 08°37′E
101 L20 **Sulzbach-Rosenberg** Bayern, SE Germany 49°30′N 11°43′E
195 N13 **Sulzberger Bay** bay Antarctica
Sumail see Summēl
81 M14 **Sumalē** var. Somali. ⬗ E Ethiopia
113 F15 **Sumartin** Split-Dalmacija, S Croatia 43°17′N 16°52′E
32 H6 **Sumas** Washington, NW USA 49°00′N 122°15′W
168 J10 **Sumatera** Eng. Sumatra. island W Indonesia
168 J12 **Sumatera Barat** off. Propinsi Sumatera Barat, Eng. West Sumatra. ⬗ province W Indonesia
Sumatera Barat, Propinsi see Sumatera Barat
168 L13 **Sumatera Selatan** off. Propinsi Sumatera Selatan, Eng. South Sumatra. ⬗ province W Indonesia
Sumatera Selatan, Propinsi see Sumatera Selatan
168 H10 **Sumatera Utara** off. Propinsi Sumatera Utara, Eng. North Sumatra. ⬗ province W Indonesia
Sumatera Utara, Propinsi see Sumatera Utara
Sumatra see Sumatera
Šumava see Bohemian Forest
Sumayl see Summēl
139 U7 **Sumayr al Muḩammad** Diyālá, E Iraq 33°34′N 45°06′E
171 N17 **Sumba, Pulau** Eng. Sandalwood Island; prev. Soemba. island Nusa Tenggara, C Indonesia
146 D12 **Sumbar** ≈ W Turkmenistan
192 E9 **Sumbawa** prev. Soembawa. island Nusa Tenggara, C Indonesia
170 L16 **Sumbawabesar** Sumbawa, S Indonesia 08°30′S 117°25′E
81 F23 **Sumbawanga** Rukwa, W Tanzania 07°57′S 31°37′E
82 B12 **Sumbe** var. N'Gunza, Port. Novo Redondo. Cuanza Sul, W Angola 11°13′S 13°53′E
96 M3 **Sumburgh Head** headland NE Scotland, United Kingdom 59°51′N 01°16′W
111 H23 **Sümeg** Veszprém, W Hungary 47°01′N 17°13′E
80 C12 **Sumeih** Southern Darfur, S Sudan 09°50′N 27°39′E
169 T16 **Sumenep** prev. Soemenep. Pulau Madura, C Indonesia 07°01′S 113°51′E
Sumgait see Sumqayıt, Azerbaijan
Sumgait see Sumqayıtçay, Azerbaijan
165 Y14 **Sumisu-jima** Eng. Smith Island. island SE Japan
139 Q2 **Summēl** var. Sumail, Sumayl. Dahūk, N Iraq 36°52′N 42°51′E
31 O5 **Summer Island** island Michigan, N USA
32 H15 **Summer Lake** ◎ Oregon, NW USA
11 N17 **Summerland** British Columbia, SW Canada 49°35′N 119°45′W
13 P14 **Summerside** Prince Edward Island, SE Canada 46°24′N 63°46′W
21 R5 **Summersville** West Virginia, NE USA 38°17′N 80°52′W
21 R5 **Summersville Lake** ⊠ West Virginia, NE USA
21 S13 **Summerton** South Carolina, SE USA 33°36′N 80°21′W
23 R2 **Summerville** Georgia, SE USA 34°28′N 85°21′W
21 S14 **Summerville** South Carolina, SE USA 33°01′N 80°10′W
39 R10 **Summit** Alaska, USA 63°21′N 148°50′W
35 V6 **Summit Mountain** ▲ Nevada, W USA 39°23′N 116°25′W
37 R8 **Summit Peak** ▲ Colorado, C USA 37°21′N 106°42′W
Summus Portus see Somport, Col du
29 X12 **Sumner** Iowa, C USA 42°51′N 92°05′W
22 K3 **Sumner** Mississippi, S USA 33°58′N 90°22′W
185 H17 **Sumner, Lake** ◎ South Island, New Zealand
37 U12 **Sumner, Lake** ⊠ New Mexico, SW USA
111 G17 **Šumperk** Ger. Mährisch-Schönberg. Olomoucký Kraj, E Czech Republic 49°58′N 17°00′E
42 F7 **Sumpul, Río** ≈ El Salvador/Honduras
137 Z11 **Sumqayıt** Rus. Sumgait. E Azerbaijan 40°33′N 49°41′E
137 Y11 **Sumqayıtçay** Rus. Sumgait. ≈ E Azerbaijan
147 R9 **Sumsar** Dzhalal-Abadskaya Oblast', W Kyrgyzstan 41°12′N 71°16′E
117 S3 **Sums'ka Oblast'** var. Sumy, Rus. Sumskaya Oblast'. ⬗ province NE Ukraine
Sumskaya Oblast' see Sums'ka Oblast'
124 J8 **Sumskiy Posad** Respublika Kareliya, NW Russian Federation 64°12′N 35°22′E
21 S12 **Sumter** South Carolina, SE USA 33°54′N 80°22′W
117 T3 **Sumy** Sums'ka Oblast', NE Ukraine 50°54′N 34°49′E
Sumy see Sums'ka Oblast'
159 Q15 **Sumzom** Xizang Zizhiqu, W China 29°45′N 96°14′E
125 R15 **Suna** Kirovskaya Oblast', NW Russian Federation 57°53′N 50°04′E
124 I10 **Suna** ≈ NW Russian Federation
165 S3 **Sunagawa** Hokkaidō, NE Japan 43°30′N 141°55′E
153 V13 **Sunamganj** Sylhet, NE Bangladesh 25°04′N 91°24′E
163 W14 **Sunan** ✈ (P'yŏngyang) SW North Korea 39°12′N 125°40′E
Sunan/Sunan Yugurzu Zizhixian see Hongwansi
19 N9 **Sunapee Lake** ◎ New Hampshire, NE USA
139 P4 **Sunaysilah** salt marsh N Iraq
20 M8 **Sunbright** Tennessee, S USA 36°12′N 84°39′W
33 R6 **Sunburst** Montana, NW USA 48°51′N 111°54′W
183 N12 **Sunbury** Victoria, SE Australia 37°36′S 114°45′E
21 X8 **Sunbury** North Carolina, SE USA 36°27′N 76°34′W
18 G14 **Sunbury** Pennsylvania, NE USA 40°51′N 76°47′W
61 A17 **Sunchales** Santa Fe, C Argentina 30°58′S 61°35′W
163 Y16 **Suncheon** Jap. Junten, prev. Sunch'ŏn. S South Korea 34°56′N 127°29′E
Sunch'ŏn see Suncheon
36 K13 **Sun City** Arizona, SW USA 33°36′N 112°16′W
19 O9 **Suncook** New Hampshire, NE USA 43°07′N 71°25′W
161 P5 **Suncun** prev. Xinwen. Shandong, E China 35°49′N 117°36′E
Sunda Islands see Greater Sunda Islands
33 Z12 **Sundance** Wyoming, C USA 44°24′N 104°22′W
153 T17 **Sundarbans** wetland Bangladesh/India
154 M11 **Sundargarh** Orissa, E India 22°07′N 84°02′E
129 U15 **Sunda Shelf** undersea feature S South China Sea 05°00′N 107°00′E
Sunda Trench see Java Trench
129 U17 **Sunda Trough** undersea feature E Indian Ocean 08°50′S 109°30′E
95 O16 **Sundbyberg** Stockholm, C Sweden 59°22′N 17°58′E
97 M14 **Sunderland** var. Wearmouth. NE England, United Kingdom 54°55′N 01°23′W
101 F15 **Sundern** Nordrhein-Westfalen, W Germany 51°19′N 08°00′E
136 F12 **Sündiken Dağları** ▲▲ C Turkey
24 M5 **Sundown** Texas, SW USA 33°27′N 102°29′W
11 P16 **Sundre** Alberta, SW Canada 51°49′N 114°46′W
14 H12 **Sundridge** Ontario, S Canada 45°45′N 79°25′W
93 H17 **Sundsvall** Västernorrland, C Sweden 62°22′N 17°20′E
26 H4 **Sunflower, Mount** ▲ Kansas, C USA 39°01′N 102°02′W
Sunflower State see Kansas
169 N14 **Sungaibuntu** Sumatera, SW Indonesia 04°04′S 105°37′E
168 K12 **Sungaidareh** Sumatera, W Indonesia 0°58′S 101°30′E
167 P17 **Sungai Kolok** var. Sungai Ko-Lok. Narathiwat, SW Thailand 06°02′N 101°58′E
Sungai Ko-Lok see Sungai Kolok
168 K12 **Sungaipenuh** prev. Soengaipenoeh. Sumatera, W Indonesia 02°S 101°28′E
169 P11 **Sungaipinyuh** Borneo, C Indonesia 0°16′N 109°06′E
Sungari see Songhua Jiang
Sungaria see Dzungaria
Sungei Pahang see Pahang, Sungai
167 O8 **Sung Men** Phrae, NW Thailand 17°59′N 100°07′E
83 M15 **Sungo** Tete, NW Mozambique 16°31′S 33°58′E
Sungpu see Songpan
168 M13 **Sungsang** Sumatera, W Indonesia 02°22′S 104°50′E
114 M9 **Sungurlare** Burgas, E Bulgaria 42°47′N 26°46′E
136 J12 **Sungurlu** Çorum, N Turkey 40°10′N 34°23′E
112 F9 **Sunja** Sisak-Moslavina, C Croatia 45°21′N 16°33′E
153 Q12 **Sun Koshī** ≈ E Nepal
94 F9 **Sunndalen** valley S Norway
94 F9 **Sunndalsøra** Møre og Romsdal, S Norway 62°39′N 08°37′E
95 K15 **Sunne** Värmland, C Sweden 59°52′N 13°05′E
95 O15 **Sunnersta** Uppsala, C Sweden 59°46′N 17°40′E
94 C11 **Sunnfjord** physical region S Norway
95 C15 **Sunnhordland** physical region S Norway
94 D10 **Sunnmøre** physical region S Norway
37 N4 **Sunnyside** Utah, W USA 39°33′N 110°23′W
32 J10 **Sunnyside** Washington, NW USA 46°01′N 119°58′W
35 N9 **Sunnyvale** California, W USA 37°22′N 122°02′W
30 L8 **Sun Prairie** Wisconsin, N USA 43°12′N 89°12′W
Sunqur see Sonqor
25 N1 **Sunray** Texas, SW USA 36°01′N 101°49′W
22 I8 **Sunset** Louisiana, S USA 30°24′N 92°04′W
25 S5 **Sunset** Texas, SW USA 33°24′N 97°45′W
Sunset State see Oregon
181 Z10 **Sunshine Coast** cultural region Queensland, E Australia
Sunshine State see Florida
Sunshine State see New Mexico
Sunshine State see South Dakota
123 O10 **Suntar** Respublika Sakha (Yakutiya), NE Russian Federation 62°10′N 117°34′E
39 R10 **Suntrana** Alaska, USA 63°51′N 148°51′W
148 J15 **Suntsar** Baluchistān, SW Pakistan 25°30′N 62°03′E
163 W15 **Sunwi-do** island SW North Korea
163 W6 **Sunwu** Heilongjiang, NE China 49°29′N 127°15′E
77 O16 **Sunyani** W Ghana 07°22′N 02°18′W
Suō see Su'ao
93 M17 **Suolahti** Länsi-Suomi, C Finland 62°32′N 25°51′E
Suoločielgi see Saariselkä
Suomenlahti see Finland, Gulf of
Suomen Tasavalta/Suomi see Finland
93 N14 **Suomussalmi** Oulu, E Finland 64°54′N 29°05′E
165 E13 **Suō-nada** sea SW Japan
93 M17 **Suonenjoki** Itä-Suomi, C Finland 62°36′N 27°07′E
167 S13 **Suŏng** Kâmpóng Cham, C Cambodia 11°53′N 105°41′E
124 I10 **Suoyarvi** Respublika Kareliya, NW Russian Federation 62°02′N 32°24′E
Supanburi see Suphan Buri
57 D14 **Supe** Lima, W Peru 10°49′S 77°40′W
15 V7 **Supérieur, Lac** ◎ Québec, SE Canada
Supérieur, Lac see Superior, Lake
36 M14 **Superior** Arizona, SW USA 33°17′N 111°06′W
33 O9 **Superior** Montana, NW USA 47°11′N 114°53′W
29 P17 **Superior** Nebraska, C USA 40°01′N 98°04′W
30 I3 **Superior** Wisconsin, N USA 46°42′N 92°04′W
41 S17 **Superior, Laguna** lagoon S Mexico
31 N2 **Superior, Lake** Fr. Lac Supérieur. ◎ Canada/USA
36 L13 **Superstition Mountains** ▲▲ Arizona, SW USA
113 F14 **Supetar** It. San Pietro. Split-Dalmacija, S Croatia 43°22′N 16°34′E
167 O10 **Suphan Buri** var. Supanburi. Suphan Buri, W Thailand 14°29′N 100°10′E
171 V12 **Supiori, Pulau** island E Indonesia
188 K2 **Supply Reef** reef N Northern Mariana Islands
195 O7 **Support Force Glacier** glacier Antarctica
137 R10 **Supsa** prev. Sup'sa. ≈ W Georgia
Sup'sa see Supsa
Sūq 'Abs see 'Abs
139 W12 **Sūq ash Shuyūkh** Dhī Qār, SE Iraq 30°53′N 46°28′E
138 H4 **Şuqaylibīyah** Ḩamāh, W Syria 35°21′N 36°24′E
161 Q6 **Suqian** Jiangsu, E China 33°57′N 118°18′E
Suqrah see Şawqirah
Suqrah Bay see Şawqirah, Dawḩat
141 V16 **Suquţrā** var. Sokotra, Eng. Socotra. island SE Yemen
141 Z8 **Şūr** NE Oman 22°32′N 59°33′E
Şūr see Soûr
127 P5 **Sura** Penzenskaya Oblast', W Russian Federation 53°23′N 45°03′E
127 P4 **Sura** ≈ W Russian Federation
149 N12 **Sūrāb** Baluchistān, SW Pakistan 28°28′N 66°15′E
Surabaja see Surabaya
192 E8 **Surabaya** prev. Surabaja, Soerabaja. Jawa, C Indonesia 07°14′S 112°45′E
95 N15 **Surahammar** Västmanland, C Sweden 59°43′N 16°13′E
169 Q16 **Surakarta** Eng. Solo; prev. Soerakarta. Jawa, S Indonesia 07°32′S 110°50′E
Surakhany see Suraxanı
137 S10 **Surami** C Georgia 41°59′N 43°36′E
143 X13 **Sūrān** Sīstān va Balūchestān, SE Iran 27°18′N 61°58′E
111 I21 **Šurany** Hung. Nagysurány. Nitriansky Kraj, SW Slovakia 48°05′N 18°10′E
154 D12 **Sūrat** Gujarāt, W India 21°10′N 72°54′E
Suratdhani see Surat Thani
152 G9 **Sūratgarh** Rājasthān, NW India 29°20′N 73°59′E
167 N14 **Surat Thani** var. Suratdhani. Surat Thani, SW Thailand 09°09′N 99°20′E
119 Q16 **Suraw** Rus. Surov. ≈ E Belarus
137 Z11 **Suraxanı** Rus. Surakhany. E Azerbaijan 40°25′N 49°59′E
141 Y11 **Surayr** E Oman 19°56′N 57°47′E
138 K2 **Suraysāt** Ḩalab, N Syria 36°42′N 38°01′E
118 O12 **Surazh** Vitsyebskaya Voblasts', NE Belarus 55°25′N 30°44′E
126 H6 **Surazh** Bryanskaya Oblast', W Russian Federation 53°04′N 32°29′E
191 V17 **Sur, Cabo** headland Easter Island, Chile, E Pacific Ocean 27°11′S 109°26′W
112 L11 **Surčin** Serbia, N Serbia 44°48′N 20°19′E
116 H9 **Surduc** Hung. Szurduk. Sălaj, NW Romania 47°13′N 23°20′E
113 P16 **Surdulica** Serbia, SE Serbia 42°43′N 22°10′E
99 L24 **Sûre** var. Sauer. ≈ W Europe see also Sauer
Sûre see Sauer
154 C10 **Surendranagar** Gujarāt, W India 22°44′N 71°43′E
18 K16 **Surf City** New Jersey, NE USA 39°21′N 74°24′W
183 V3 **Surfers Paradise** Queensland, E Australia 27°54′S 153°18′E
21 U13 **Surfside Beach** South Carolina, SE USA 33°36′N 78°58′W
102 J10 **Surgères** Charente-Maritime, W France 46°07′N 00°44′W
122 H10 **Surgut** Khanty-Mansiyskiy Avtonomnyy Okrug-Yugra, C Russian Federation 61°13′N 73°28′E
122 K10 **Surgutikha** Krasnoyarskiy Kray, N Russian Federation 64°44′N 87°13′E
98 M6 **Surhuisterveen** Fris. Surhusterfean. Fryslân, N Netherlands 53°11′N 06°10′E
Surhusterfean see Surhuisterveen
105 V5 **Súria** Cataluña, NE Spain 41°50′N 01°45′E
143 P10 **Sūrīān** Fārs, S Iran
155 J15 **Suriāpet** Andhra Pradesh, C India 17°10′N 79°42′E
171 Q6 **Surigao** Mindanao, S Philippines 09°43′N 125°31′E
167 R10 **Surin** Surin, E Thailand 14°53′N 103°29′E
Surinam see Suriname
55 U11 **Suriname** off. Republic of Suriname, var. Surinam; prev. Dutch Guiana, Netherlands Guiana. ◆ republic N South America
Suriname, Republic of see Suriname
Sūrīya/Sūrīyah, Al-Jumhūrīyah al-'Arabīyah as- see Syria
Surkhab, Darya-i- see Kahmard, Daryā-ye
Surkhandar'inskaya Oblast' see Surxondaryo Viloyati
Surkhandar'ya see Surxondaryo
Surkhet see Birendranagar
147 R12 **Surkhob** ≈ C Tajikistan
137 P11 **Sürmene** Trabzon, NE Turkey 40°56′N 40°03′E
Surov see Suraw
127 N11 **Surovikino** Volgogradskaya Oblast', SW Russian Federation 48°39′N 42°46′E
35 N11 **Sur, Point** headland California, W USA 36°18′N 121°54′W
187 N15 **Surprise, Île** island N New Caledonia
61 E22 **Sur, Punta** headland E Argentina 50°59′S 69°10′W
Surrentum see Sorrento
28 M3 **Surrey** North Dakota, N USA 48°13′N 101°05′W
97 O22 **Surrey** cultural region SE England, United Kingdom
21 X7 **Surry** Virginia, NE USA 37°08′N 81°34′W
108 F8 **Sursee** Luzern, W Switzerland 47°11′N 08°07′E
127 P6 **Sursk** Penzenskaya Oblast', W Russian Federation 53°06′N 45°46′E
127 P5 **Surskoye** Ul'yanovskaya Oblast', W Russian Federation 54°28′N 46°47′E
75 P8 **Surt** var. Sidra, Sirte. N Libya 31°13′N 16°35′E
95 I19 **Surte** Västra Götaland, S Sweden 57°49′N 12°01′E
75 Q8 **Surt, Khalīj** Eng. Gulf of Sidra, Gulf of Sirti, Sidra. gulf N Libya
92 I5 **Surtsey** island S Iceland
137 N17 **Suruç** Şanlıurfa, S Turkey 36°58′N 38°24′E
168 L13 **Surulangun** Sumatera, W Indonesia 02°35′S 102°47′E
147 P13 **Surxondaryo** Rus. Surkhandar'ya. ≈ Tajikistan/Uzbekistan
147 N13 **Surxondaryo Viloyati** Rus. Surkhandar'inskaya Oblast'. ⬗ province S Uzbekistan
Süs see Susch
106 A8 **Susa** Piemonte, NE Italy 45°10′N 07°01′E
165 E12 **Susa** Yamaguchi, Honshū, SW Japan 34°35′N 131°34′E
Susa see Shūsh
113 E16 **Sušac** It. Cazza. island SW Croatia
Sūsah see Sousse
164 G14 **Susaki** Kōchi, Shikoku, SW Japan 33°22′N 133°13′E
165 I15 **Susami** Wakayama, Honshū, SW Japan 33°32′N 135°32′E
142 K9 **Sūsangerd** var. Susangird. Khūzestān, SW Iran 31°40′N 48°06′E
Susangird see Sūsangerd
35 P4 **Susanville** California, W USA 40°25′N 120°39′W
108 J9 **Susch** var. Süs. Graubünden, SE Switzerland 46°45′N 10°04′E
137 N12 **Suşehri** Sivas, N Turkey 40°11′N 38°06′E
Susiana see Khūzestān
111 B18 **Sušice** Ger. Schüttenhofen. Plzeňský Kraj, W Czech Republic 49°14′N 13°32′E
39 R11 **Susitna** Alaska, USA 61°32′N 150°30′W
39 R11 **Susitna River** ≈ Alaska, USA
127 Q3 **Suslonger** Respublika Mariy El, W Russian Federation 56°18′N 48°16′E
105 N14 **Suspiro del Moro, Puerto del** pass S Spain
18 H16 **Susquehanna River** ≈ New York/Pennsylvania, NE USA
13 O15 **Sussex** New Brunswick, SE Canada 45°43′N 65°32′W
18 J13 **Sussex** New Jersey, NE USA 41°12′N 74°34′W
21 W7 **Sussex** Virginia, NE USA 36°54′N 77°16′W
97 O23 **Sussex** cultural region S England, United Kingdom
183 S10 **Sussex Inlet** New South Wales, SE Australia 35°10′S 150°35′E
99 L17 **Susteren** Limburg, SE Netherlands 51°04′N 05°50′E
10 K12 **Sustut Peak** ▲ British Columbia, W Canada 56°25′N 126°34′W
123 S9 **Susuman** Magadanskaya Oblast', E Russian Federation 62°46′N 148°08′E
188 H6 **Susupe** ● (Northern Mariana Islands-judicial capital) Saipan, S Northern Mariana Islands
136 D12 **Susurluk** Balıkesir, NW Turkey 39°55′N 28°10′E
114 M13 **Susuzmüsellim** Tekirdağ, NW Turkey 41°04′N 27°03′E
136 F15 **Sütçüler** Isparta, SW Turkey 37°31′N 31°00′E
116 L13 **Şuţeşti** Brăila, SE Romania 45°13′N 27°27′E
83 F25 **Sutherland** Western Cape, SW South Africa 32°24′S 20°40′E
28 L15 **Sutherland** Nebraska, C USA 41°09′N 101°07′W
96 I7 **Sutherland** cultural region N Scotland, United Kingdom
185 B21 **Sutherland Falls** waterfall South Island, New Zealand
32 F14 **Sutherlin** Oregon, NW USA 43°23′N 123°18′W
149 V10 **Sutlej** ≈ India/Pakistan
Sutna see Satna
35 P7 **Sutter Creek** California, W USA 38°22′N 120°49′W
39 R11 **Sutton** Alaska, USA 61°42′N 148°53′W
29 Q16 **Sutton** Nebraska, C USA 40°36′N 97°52′W
21 R4 **Sutton** West Virginia, NE USA 38°41′N 80°43′W
12 F8 **Sutton** ≈ Ontario, C Canada
97 M19 **Sutton Coldfield** C England, United Kingdom 52°34′N 01°48′W
21 R4 **Sutton Lake** ⊠ West Virginia, NE USA
15 P13 **Sutton, Monts** hill range Québec, SE Canada
12 F8 **Sutton Ridges** ▲▲ Ontario, C Canada
165 Q4 **Suttsu** Hokkaidō, NE Japan 42°46′N 140°12′E
39 P15 **Sutwik Island** island Alaska, USA
Süüj see Dashinchilen
118 H5 **Suure-Jaani** Ger. Gross-Sankt-Johannis. Viljandimaa, S Estonia 58°34′N 25°28′E
118 J7 **Suur Munamägi** var. Munamägi, Ger. Eier-Berg. ▲ SE Estonia 57°42′N 27°03′E
118 F5 **Suur Väin** Ger. Grosser Sund. strait W Estonia
147 U8 **Suusamyr** Chuyskaya Oblast', C Kyrgyzstan 42°07′N 73°55′E
187 X14 **Suva** ● (Fiji) Viti Levu, W Fiji 18°08′S 178°27′E
187 X15 **Suva** ✈ Viti Levu, C Fiji 18°01′S 178°30′E
113 N18 **Suva Gora** ▲▲ W FYR Macedonia
118 H11 **Suvainiškis** Panevėžys, NE Lithuania 56°09′N 25°15′E
Suvalkai/Suvalki see Suwałki
113 P15 **Suva Planina** ▲▲ SE Serbia
Suva Reka see Suharekë
126 K5 **Suvorov** Tul'skaya Oblast', W Russian Federation 54°08′N 36°33′E
117 N12 **Suvorove** Odes'ka Oblast', SW Ukraine 45°35′N 28°58′E
114 M8 **Suvorovo** Varna, E Bulgaria 43°19′N 27°26′E
Suvorovo see Ştefan Vodă
Suwaik see As Suwayq
Suwaira see Aş Şuwayrah
110 O7 **Suwałki** Lith. Suvalkai, Rus. Suvalki. Podlaskie, NE Poland 54°06′N 22°56′E
167 R10 **Suwannaphum** Roi Et, E Thailand 15°36′N 103°46′E
23 V8 **Suwannee River** ≈ Florida/Georgia, SE USA
Şuwār see Aş Şuwār
190 K14 **Suwarrow** atoll N Cook Islands
143 R16 **Suwaydān** var. Sweiham. Abū Ẓaby, E United Arab Emirates 24°30′N 55°19′E
Suwaydá/Suwaydā', Muḩāfaẓat as see As Suwaydā'
Suwayqiyah, Hawr as see Shuwayjah, Hawr ash
Suways, Qanāt as see Suez Canal
Suweida see As Suwaydā'
Suweon see Suwon
163 X15 **Suwon** var. Suweon; prev. Suwŏn, Jap. Suigen. NW South Korea 37°17′N 127°03′E
Suwŏn see Suwon
Su Xian see Suzhou
143 R14 **Sūzā** Hormozgān, S Iran 26°50′N 56°05′E
Suzak see Sozak
165 K14 **Suzaka** Mie, Honshū, SW Japan 34°52′N 136°37′E
165 N12 **Suzaka** Nagano, Honshū, S Japan 36°38′N 138°20′E
126 M3 **Suzdal'** Vladimirskaya Oblast', W Russian Federation 56°27′N 40°29′E
161 P7 **Suzhou** var. Su Xian. Anhui, E China 33°38′N 117°02′E
161 R8 **Suzhou** var. Soochow, Su-chou, Suchow; prev. Wuhsien. Jiangsu, E China 31°23′N 120°34′E
Suzhou see Jiuquan
163 V12 **Suzi He** ≈ NE China
Suz, Mys see Soye, Mys
165 M10 **Suzu** Ishikawa, Honshū, SW Japan 37°24′N 137°12′E
165 M10 **Suzu-misaki** headland Honshū, SW Japan 37°31′N 137°19′E
Svågälv see Svågan
94 M10 **Svågan** var. Svågälv. ≈ C Sweden
Svalava/Svaljava see Svalyava

◆ Country
● Country Capital
◇ Dependent Territory
○ Dependent Territory Capital
⬗ Administrative Regions
✈ International Airport
▲ Mountain
▲▲ Mountain Range
Volcano
≈ River
◎ Lake
⊠ Reservoir

92 O2 **Svalbard** ◇ *Norwegian dependency* Arctic Ocean
92 J2 **Svalbardhseyri** Nordhurland Eystra, N Iceland 65°43′N 18°03′W
95 K22 **Svalöv** Skåne, S Sweden 55°55′N 13°06′E
116 H7 **Svalyava** *Cz.* Svalava, Svaljava, *Hung.* Szolyva. Zakarpats'ka Oblast', W Ukraine 48°33′N 23°00′E
92 O2 **Svanbergfjellet** ▲ C Svalbard 78°40′N 18°10′E
95 M24 **Svaneke** Bornholm, E Denmark 55°07′N 15°08′E
95 L22 **Svängsta** Blekinge, S Sweden 56°16′N 14°46′E
95 J16 **Svanskog** Värmland, C Sweden 59°10′N 12°34′E
95 L16 **Svartå** Örebro, C Sweden 59°13′N 14°07′E
95 L15 **Svartälven** ∿ C Sweden
92 G12 **Svartisen** *glacier* C Norway
117 X6 **Svatove** *Rus.* Svatovo. Luhans'ka Oblast', E Ukraine 49°24′N 38°11′E
Svatovo *see* Svatove
Sväty Kríž nad Hronom *see* Žiar nad Hronom
167 Q11 **Svay Chék, Stœng** ∿ Cambodia/Thailand
167 S13 **Svay Riĕng** Svay Riĕng, S Cambodia 11°05′N 105°48′E
92 O3 **Sveagruva** Spitsbergen, W Svalbard 77°53′N 16°42′E
95 K23 **Svedala** Skåne, S Sweden 55°30′N 13°15′E
118 H12 **Svėdesai** Utena, NE Lithuania 55°42′N 25°22′E
93 G18 **Sveg** Jämtland, C Sweden 62°02′N 14°20′E
118 C12 **Švėkšna** Klaipėda, W Lithuania 55°31′N 21°37′E
94 C11 **Svelgen** Sogn Og Fjordane, S Norway 61°47′N 05°18′E
95 H15 **Svelvik** Vestfold, S Norway 59°37′N 10°24′E
118 I13 **Švenčionėliai** *Pol.* Nowo-Święciany. Vilnius, SE Lithuania 55°10′N 26°00′E
118 I13 **Švenčionys** *Pol.* Swięciany. Vilnius, SE Lithuania 55°08′N 26°08′E
95 H24 **Svendborg** Syddtjylland, C Denmark 55°04′N 10°38′E
95 K19 **Svenljunga** Västra Götaland, S Sweden 57°30′N 13°05′E
92 P2 **Svenskøya** *island* E Svalbard
93 G17 **Svenstavik** Jämtland, C Sweden 62°40′N 14°24′E
95 G20 **Svenstrup** Nordjylland, N Denmark 56°58′N 09°52′E
118 H12 **Šventoji** ∿ C Lithuania
117 Z8 **Sverdlovs'k** *Rus.* Sverdlovsk; *prev.* Imeni Sverdlova Rudnik. Luhans'ka Oblast', E Ukraine 48°05′N 39°37′E
Sverdlovsk *see* Yekaterinburg
127 W2 **Sverdlovskaya Oblast'** ⬖ *province* C Russian Federation
122 K6 **Sverdrupa, Ostrov** *island* N Russian Federation
Sverige *see* Sweden
113 D15 **Svetac** *prev.* Sveti Andrea, *It.* Sant'Andrea. *island* SW Croatia
Sveti Andrea *see* Svetac
Sveti Nikola *see* Sveti Nikole
113 O18 **Sveti Nikole** *prev.* Sveti Nikola. C FYR Macedonia 41°54′N 21°55′E
Sveti Vrach *see* Sandanski
123 T14 **Svetlaya** Primorskiy Kray, SE Russian Federation 46°33′N 138°20′E
126 B2 **Svetlogorsk** Kaliningradskaya Oblast', W Russian Federation 54°56′N 20°09′E
122 K9 **Svetlogorsk** Krasnoyarskiy Kray, N Russian Federation 66°51′N 88°29′E
Svetlogorsk *see* Svyetlahorsk
127 N14 **Svetlograd** Stavropol'skiy Kray, SW Russian Federation 45°20′N 42°53′E
Svetlovodsk *see* Svitlovods'k
119 A14 **Svetlyy** *Ger.* Zimmerbude. Kaliningradskaya Oblast', W Russian Federation 54°42′N 20°07′E
127 Y8 **Svetlyy** Orenburgskaya Oblast', W Russian Federation 50°34′N 60°42′E
127 P7 **Svetlyy** Saratovskaya Oblast', W Russian Federation 51°42′N 45°40′E
124 G11 **Svetogorsk** *Fin.* Enso. Leningradskaya Oblast', NW Russian Federation 61°06′N 28°52′E
Svetozarevo *see* Jagodina
111 B18 **Švihov** *Ger.* Schwihau. Plzeňský Kraj, W Czech Republic 49°31′N 13°18′E
112 E13 **Svilaja** ▲▲ SE Croatia
112 N12 **Svilajnac** Serbia, C Serbia 44°15′N 21°12′E
114 L11 **Svilengrad** *prev.* Mustafa-Pasha. Khaskovo, S Bulgaria 41°45′N 26°14′E
Svinecea Mare, Munte *see* Svinecea Mare, Vârful
116 F13 **Svinecea Mare, Vârful** *var.* Munte Svinecea Mare. ▲ SW Romania 44°47′N 22°10′E
Svinø *see* Svínoy
95 B18 **Svínoy** *Dan.* Svinø. *island* NE Faeroe Islands
147 N14 **Svintsovyy Rudnik** *Turkm.* Swintsowyy Rudnik. Lebap Welaýaty, E Turkmenistan 37°54′N 66°25′E
118 I13 **Svir** *Rus.* Svir'. Minskaya Voblasts', NW Belarus 54°51′N 26°24′E
124 I12 **Svir'** *canal* NW Russian Federation
Svir', Ozero *see* Svir, Vozyera
119 I14 **Svir, Vozyera** *Rus.* Ozero Svir'. ◎ C Belarus
114 J7 **Svishtov** *prev.* Sistova. Veliko Tŭrnovo, N Bulgaria 43°37′N 25°20′E
119 F18 **Svislach** *Pol.* Świsłocz, *Rus.* Svisloch'. Hrodzyenskaya Voblasts', W Belarus 53°02′N 24°06′E
119 M17 **Svislach** *Rus.* Svisloch'. Mahilyowskaya Voblasts', E Belarus 53°26′N 28°59′E
119 L17 **Svislach** *Rus.* Svisloch'. ∿ E Belarus
Svisloch' *see* Svislach
111 F17 **Svitavy** *Ger.* Zwittau. Pardubický Kraj, C Czech Republic 49°45′N 16°27′E
117 S6 **Svitlovods'k** *Rus.* Svetlovodsk. Kirovohrads'ka Oblast', C Ukraine 49°05′N 33°15′E
Svizzera *see* Switzerland
123 Q13 **Svobodnyy** Amurskaya Oblast', SE Russian Federation 51°24′N 128°05′E
114 G9 **Svoge** Sofiya, W Bulgaria 42°58′N 23°20′E
92 G11 **Svolvær** Nordland, C Norway 68°15′N 14°40′E
111 F18 **Svratka** *Ger.* Schwarzawa. ∿ SE Czech Republic
113 P14 **Svrljig** Serbia, E Serbia 43°26′N 22°07′E
197 U10 **Svyataya Anna Trough** *var.* Saint Anna Trough. *undersea feature* N Kara Sea
124 M4 **Svyatoy Nos, Mys** *headland* NW Russian Federation 68°07′N 39°49′E
119 N18 **Svyetlahorsk** *Rus.* Svetlogorsk. Homyel'skaya Voblasts', SE Belarus 52°38′N 29°46′E
Swabian Jura *see* Schwäbische Alb
97 P19 **Swaffham** E England, United Kingdom 52°39′N 00°40′E
23 V5 **Swainsboro** Georgia, SE USA 32°36′N 82°19′W
83 C19 **Swakop** ∿ W Namibia
83 C19 **Swakopmund** Erongo, W Namibia 22°40′S 14°34′E
97 M15 **Swale** ∿ N England, United Kingdom
Swallow Island *see* Nendö
99 M16 **Swalmen** Limburg, SE Netherlands 51°13′N 06°02′E
12 G8 **Swan** ∿ Ontario, C Canada
97 L24 **Swanage** S England, United Kingdom 50°37′N 01°59′W
182 M10 **Swan Hill** Victoria, SE Australia 35°23′S 143°37′E
11 P13 **Swan Hills** Alberta, W Canada 54°41′N 116°20′W
65 D24 **Swan Island** *island* C Falkland Islands
Swankalok *see* Sawankhalok
29 U10 **Swan Lake** ◎ Minnesota, N USA
21 Y10 **Swanquarter** North Carolina, SE USA 35°24′N 76°20′W
182 J9 **Swan Reach** South Australia 34°39′S 139°35′E
11 V15 **Swan River** Manitoba, S Canada 52°06′N 101°17′W
183 P17 **Swansea** Tasmania, SE Australia 42°09′S 148°03′E
97 J22 **Swansea** *Wel.* Abertawe. S Wales, United Kingdom 51°38′N 03°57′W
21 R13 **Swansea** South Carolina, SE USA 33°47′N 81°06′W
19 S7 **Swans Island** *island* Maine, NE USA
28 L17 **Swanson Lake** ⊠ Nebraska, C USA
31 R11 **Swanton** Ohio, N USA 41°35′N 83°53′W
110 G11 **Swarzędz** Poznań, W Poland 52°24′N 17°05′E
Swatow *see* Shantou
83 L22 **Swaziland** *off.* Kingdom of Swaziland. ◆ *monarchy* S Africa
Swaziland, Kingdom of *see* Swaziland
93 G18 **Sweden** *off.* Kingdom of Sweden, *Swe.* Sverige. ◆ *monarchy* N Europe
Sweden, Kingdom of *see* Sweden
Swedru *see* Agona Swedru
25 V12 **Sweeny** Texas, SW USA 29°02′N 95°42′W
33 R6 **Sweetgrass** Montana, NW USA 48°58′N 111°58′W
32 G12 **Sweet Home** Oregon, NW USA 44°24′N 122°44′W
25 T12 **Sweet Home** Texas, SW USA 29°21′N 97°04′W
27 T4 **Sweet Springs** Missouri, C USA 38°57′N 93°24′W
20 M10 **Sweetwater** Tennessee, S USA 35°36′N 84°27′W
25 P7 **Sweetwater** Texas, SW USA 32°27′N 100°25′W
33 V15 **Sweetwater River** ∿ Wyoming, C USA
Sweiham *see* Suwaydān
83 F26 **Swellendam** Western Cape, SW South Africa 34°01′S 20°26′E
111 G15 **Świdnica** *Ger.* Schweidnitz. Wałbrzych, SW Poland 50°51′N 16°29′E
111 O14 **Świdnik** *Ger.* Streckenbach. Lubelskie, E Poland 51°14′N 22°41′E
110 F8 **Świdwin** *Ger.* Schivelbein. Zachodnio-pomorskie, NW Poland 53°47′N 15°44′E
111 F15 **Świebodzice** *Ger.* Freiburg in Schlesien, Swiebodzice. Walbrzych, SW Poland 50°54′N 16°23′E
110 E11 **Świebodzin** *Ger.* Schwiebus. Lubuskie, W Poland 52°15′N 15°31′E
Święciany *see* Švenčionys
110 I9 **Świecie** *Ger.* Schwertberg. Kujawsko-pomorskie, C Poland 53°24′N 18°24′E
111 L15 **Świętokrzyskie** ⬖ *province* S Poland
11 T16 **Swift Current** Saskatchewan, S Canada 50°17′N 107°49′W
98 K9 **Swifterbant** Flevoland, C Netherlands 52°36′N 05°33′E
183 Q12 **Swifts Creek** Victoria, SE Australia 37°17′S 147°41′E
96 E13 **Swilly, Lough** *Ir.* Loch Súilí. *inlet* N Ireland
97 M22 **Swindon** S England, United Kingdom 51°34′N 01°47′W
Swinemünde *see* Świnoujście
110 D8 **Świnoujście** *Ger.* Swinemünde. Zachodnio-pomorskie, NW Poland 53°54′N 14°13′E
Swintsowyy Rudnik *see* Svintsovyy Rudnik
Świsłocz *see* Svislach
Swiss Confederation *see* Switzerland
108 E9 **Switzerland** *off.* Swiss Confederation, *Fr.* La Suisse, *Ger.* Schweiz, *It.* Svizzera; *anc.* Helvetia. ◆ *federal republic* C Europe
97 F17 **Swords** *Ir.* Sord, Sórd Choluim Chille. Dublin, E Ireland 53°28′N 06°13′W
18 H13 **Swoyersville** Pennsylvania, NE USA 41°18′N 75°48′W
124 I10 **Syamozero, Ozero** ◎ NW Russian Federation
124 M13 **Syamzha** Vologodskaya Oblast', NW Russian Federation 60°02′N 41°09′E
118 N13 **Syanno** *Rus.* Senno. Vitsyebskaya Voblasts', NE Belarus 54°49′N 29°43′E
119 K16 **Syarhyeyevichy** *Rus.* Sergeyevichi. Minskaya Voblasts', C Belarus 53°30′N 27°45′E
124 I12 **Syas'stroy** Leningradskaya Oblast', NW Russian Federation 60°05′N 32°37′E
Sycaminum *see* Hefa
30 M10 **Sycamore** Illinois, N USA 41°59′N 88°41′W
126 J3 **Sychëvka** Smolenskaya Oblast', W Russian Federation 55°52′N 34°19′E
111 H14 **Syców** *Ger.* Gross Wartenberg. Dolnosląskie, SW Poland 51°18′N 17°42′E
95 F24 **Syddanmark** ⬖ *region* SW Denmark
14 E17 **Sydenham** ∿ Ontario, S Canada
Sydenham Island *see* Nonouti
183 T9 **Sydney** *state capital* New South Wales, SE Australia 33°55′S 151°10′E
13 R14 **Sydney** Cape Breton Island, Nova Scotia, SE Canada 46°10′N 60°10′W
Sydney Island *see* Manra
13 R14 **Sydney Mines** Cape Breton Island, Nova Scotia, SE Canada 46°14′N 60°19′W
Syedpur *see* Saidpur
119 K18 **Syelishcha** *Rus.* Selishche. Minskaya Voblasts', C Belarus 53°01′N 27°25′E
119 J18 **Syemyezhava** *Rus.* Semezhevo. Minskaya Voblasts', C Belarus 52°58′N 27°00′E
Syene *see* Aswān
117 X6 **Syeverodonets'k** *Rus.* Severodonetsk. Luhans'ka Oblast', E Ukraine 48°59′N 38°28′E
161 T6 **Syiao Shan** *island* SE China
100 H11 **Syke** Niedersachsen, NW Germany 52°55′N 08°49′E
94 D10 **Sykkylven** Møre og Romsdal, S Norway 62°23′N 06°35′E
Sykoúri *see* Sykoúrio
115 F15 **Sykoúrio** *var.* Sikouri, Sykoúri; *prev.* Sikoúrion. Thessalía, C Greece 39°46′N 22°35′E
125 R11 **Syktyvkar** *prev.* Ust'-Sysol'sk. Respublika Komi, NW Russian Federation 61°42′N 50°45′E
23 Q4 **Sylacauga** Alabama, S USA 33°10′N 86°15′W
Sylarna *see* Storsylen
153 V14 **Sylhet** Sylhet, NE Bangladesh 24°53′N 91°51′E
153 V13 **Sylhet** ⬖ *division* NE Bangladesh
100 G6 **Sylt** *island* NW Germany
21 O10 **Sylva** North Carolina, SE USA 35°23′N 83°13′W
125 V15 **Sylva** ∿ NW Russian Federation
23 W5 **Sylvania** Georgia, SE USA 32°45′N 81°38′W
31 R11 **Sylvania** Ohio, N USA 41°43′N 83°42′W
11 Q15 **Sylvan Lake** Alberta, SW Canada 52°18′N 114°02′W
33 T13 **Sylvan Pass** *pass* Wyoming, C USA
23 T7 **Sylvester** Georgia, SE USA 31°31′N 83°50′W
25 P6 **Sylvester** Texas, SW USA 32°42′N 100°15′W
10 L11 **Sylvia, Mount** ▲ British Columbia, W Canada 58°03′N 124°26′W
122 K11 **Sym** ∿ C Russian Federation
115 N22 **Sými** *var.* Simi. *island* Dodekánisa, Greece, Aegean Sea
117 U8 **Synel'nykove** Dnipropetrovs'ka Oblast', E Ukraine 48°19′N 35°32′E
125 U6 **Synya** Respublika Komi, NW Russian Federation 65°21′N 58°01′E
117 P7 **Synyukha** *Rus.* Sinyukha. ∿ S Ukraine
195 V2 **Syowa** *Japanese research station* Antarctica 68°58′S 40°07′E
26 H6 **Syracuse** Kansas, C USA 38°00′N 101°43′W
29 S16 **Syracuse** Nebraska, C USA 40°39′N 96°11′W
18 H10 **Syracuse** New York, NE USA 43°03′N 76°09′W
Syracuse *see* Siracusa
Syrdar'inskaya Oblast' *see* Sirdaryo Viloyati
Syrdariya *see* Syr Darya
144 L14 **Syr Darya** *var.* Sai Hun, Sir Darya, Syrdarya, *Kaz.* Syrdariya, *Rus.* Syrdar'ya, *Uzb.* Sirdaryo; *anc.* Jaxartes. ∿ C Asia
Syrdarya *see* Syr Darya
138 J6 **Syria** *off.* Syrian Arab Republic, *var.* Siria, Syrie, *Ar.* Al-Jumhūrīyah al-'Arabīyah as-Sūrīyah, Sūrīya. ◆ *republic* SW Asia
Syrian Arab Republic *see* Syria
138 L9 **Syrian Desert** *Ar.* Al Hamad, Bādiyat ash Shām. *desert* SW Asia
Syrie *see* Syria
115 L22 **Sýrna** *var.* Sirna. *island* Kykládes, Greece, Aegean Sea
115 I20 **Sýros** *var.* Síros. *island* Kykládes, Greece, Aegean Sea
93 M18 **Sysmä** Etelä-Suomi, S Finland 61°28′N 25°37′E
125 R12 **Sysola** ∿ NW Russian Federation
Syulemeshlii *see* Sredets
127 S2 **Syumsi** Udmurtskaya Respublika, NW Russian Federation 57°07′N 51°35′E
114 K10 **Syuyutliyka** ∿ C Bulgaria
Syvash, Zaliv *see* Syvash, Zatoka
117 U12 **Syvash, Zatoka** *Rus.* Zaliv Syvash. *inlet* S Ukraine
127 Q6 **Syzran'** Samarskaya Oblast', W Russian Federation 53°10′N 48°23′E
Szabadka *see* Subotica
111 N21 **Szabolcs-Szatmár-Bereg** *off.* Szabolcs-Szatmár-Bereg Megye. ⬖ *county* E Hungary
Szabolcs-Szatmár-Bereg Megye *see* Szabolcs-Szatmár-Bereg
110 G10 **Szamocin** *Ger.* Samotschin. Wielkopolskie, C Poland 53°02′N 17°04′E
116 H8 **Szamos** *var.* Someş, Someşul, *Ger.* Samosch, Somesch. ∿ Hungary/Romania
Szamosújvár *see* Gherla
110 G11 **Szamotuły** Poznań, W Poland 52°35′N 16°36′E
Szarkowszczyzna *see* Sharkawshchyna
111 M24 **Szarvas** Békés, SE Hungary 46°51′N 20°35′E
Szászmagyarós *see* Măieruş
Szászrégen *see* Reghin
Szászsebes *see* Sebeş
Szászváros *see* Orăştie
Szatmárnémeti *see* Satu Mare
Száva *see* Sava
111 P15 **Szczebrzeszyn** Lubelskie, E Poland 50°43′N 23°00′E
110 D9 **Szczecin** *Eng./Ger.* Stettin. Zachodnio-pomorskie, NW Poland 53°25′N 14°32′E
110 G8 **Szczecinek** *Ger.* Neustettin. Zachodnio-pomorskie, NW Poland 53°43′N 16°40′E
110 D8 **Szczeciński, Zalew** *var.* Stettiner Haff, *Ger.* Oderhaff. *bay* Germany/Poland
111 K15 **Szczekociny** Śląskie, S Poland 50°38′N 19°46′E
110 N8 **Szczuczyn** Podlaskie, NE Poland 53°34′N 22°17′E
Szczuczyn Nowogródzki *see* Shchuchyn
110 M8 **Szczytno** *Ger.* Ortelsburg. Warmińsko-Mazurskie, NE Poland 53°34′N 21°E
Szechuan/Szechwan *see* Sichuan
111 K21 **Szécsény** Nógrád, N Hungary 48°07′N 19°30′E
111 L25 **Szeged** *Ger.* Szegedin, *Rom.* Seghedin. Csongrád, SE Hungary 46°17′N 20°06′E
Szegedin *see* Szeged
111 N23 **Szeghalom** Békés, SE Hungary 47°01′N 21°09′E
Székelyhid *see* Săcueni
Székelykeresztúr *see* Cristuru Secuiesc
111 I23 **Székesfehérvár** *Ger.* Stuhlweissenberg; *anc.* Alba Regia. Fejér, W Hungary 47°13′N 18°24′E
Szeklerburg *see* Miercurea-Ciuc
Szekler Neumarkt *see* Târgu Secuiesc
111 J25 **Szekszárd** Tolna, S Hungary 46°21′N 18°41′E
Szempcz/Szenc *see* Senec
Szenice *see* Senica
Szentágota *see* Agnita
111 J22 **Szentendre** *Ger.* Sankt Andrä. Pest, N Hungary 47°40′N 19°02′E
111 L24 **Szentes** Csongrád, SE Hungary 46°40′N 20°17′E
111 F23 **Szentgotthárd** *Eng.* Saint Gotthard, *Ger.* Sankt Gotthard. Vas, W Hungary 46°57′N 16°18′E
Szentgyörgy *see* Đurđevac
Szenttamás *see* Srbobran
Széphely *see* Jebel
Szeping *see* Siping
Szered *see* Sered'
111 N21 **Szerencs** Borsod-Abaúj-Zemplén, NE Hungary 48°10′N 21°11′E
Szeret *see* Siret
Szeretfalva *see* Sărăţel
110 N7 **Szeska Góra** *var.* Szeskie Wygórza, *Ger.* Seesker Höhe. *hill* NE Poland
Szeskie Wygórza *see* Szeska Góra
111 H25 **Szigetvár** Baranya, SW Hungary 46°01′N 17°50′E
Szilágysomlyó *see* Şimleu Silvaniei
Szinna *see* Snina
Sziszek *see* Sisak
Szitás-Keresztúr *see* Cristuru Secuiesc
111 E15 **Szklarska Poręba** *Ger.* Schreiberhau. Dolnośląskie, SW Poland 50°50′N 15°30′E
Szkudy *see* Skuodas
Szlatina *see* Slatina
Szlavonia/Szlavonország *see* Slavonija
Szlovákia *see* Slovakia
Szluin *see* Slunj
111 L23 **Szolnok** Jász-Nagykun-Szolnok, C Hungary 47°11′N 20°12′E
Szolyva *see* Svalyava
111 G23 **Szombathely** *Ger.* Steinamanger; *anc.* Sabaria, Savaria. Vas, W Hungary 47°14′N 16°38′E
Szond/Szonta *see* Sonta
Szováta *see* Sovata
110 F13 **Szprotawa** *Ger.* Sprottau. Lubuskie, W Poland 51°33′N 15°32′E
Sztálinváros *see* Dunaújváros
Sztrazsó *see* Strážov
110 J8 **Sztum** *Ger.* Stuhm. Pomorskie, N Poland 53°54′N 19°01′E
110 H10 **Szubin** *Ger.* Schubin. Kujawsko-pomorskie, C Poland 53°04′N 17°49′E
Szucsava *see* Suceava
Szurduk *see* Surduc
111 M14 **Szydłowiec** *Ger.* Schlelau. Mazowieckie, C Poland 51°14′N 20°50′E

T

Taalintehdas *see* Dalsbruk
171 O4 **Taal, Lake** ◎ Luzon, NW Philippines
95 J23 **Taastrup** *var.* Tåstrup. Sjælland, E Denmark 55°39′N 12°19′E
111 I24 **Tab** Somogy, W Hungary 46°45′N 18°01′E
171 P4 **Tabaco** Luzon, N Philippines 13°22′N 123°42′E
186 G4 **Tabalo** Mussau Island, NE Papua New Guinea 01°22′S 149°37′E
104 K5 **Tábara** Castilla y León, N Spain 41°49′N 05°57′W
186 H5 **Tabar Islands** *island group* NE Papua New Guinea
Tabariya, Bahrat *see* Tiberias, Lake
143 S7 **Ţabas** *var.* Golshan. Yazd, C Iran 33°37′N 56°54′E
43 P15 **Tabasará, Serranía de** ▲▲ W Panama
41 U15 **Tabasco** ⬖ *state* SE Mexico
Tabasco *see* Grijalva, Río
127 Q2 **Tabashino** Respublika Mariy El, W Russian Federation 57°00′N 47°47′E
58 B13 **Tabatinga** Amazonas, N Brazil 04°14′S 69°44′W
74 G9 **Tabelbala** W Algeria 29°22′N 03°01′W
11 Q17 **Taber** Alberta, SW Canada 49°48′N 112°09′W
171 V15 **Taberfane** Pulau Trangan, E Indonesia 06°14′S 134°08′E
95 L19 **Taberg** Jönköping, S Sweden 57°42′N 14°05′E
191 O3 **Tabiteuea** *prev.* Drummond Island. *atoll* Tungaru, W Kiribati
171 O5 **Tablas Island** *island* C Philippines
184 Q10 **Table Cape** *headland* North Island, New Zealand 39°07′S 178°00′E
13 S13 **Table Mountain** ▲ Newfoundland, Newfoundland and Labrador, E Canada 47°39′N 59°15′W
173 P17 **Table, Pointe de la** *headland* SE Réunion 21°19′S 55°49′E
27 S8 **Table Rock Lake** ⊠ Arkansas/Missouri, C USA
36 K14 **Table Top** ▲ Arizona, SW USA 32°45′N 112°07′W
186 D8 **Tabletop, Mount** ▲ C Papua New Guinea 06°51′S 146°00′E
111 D18 **Tábor** Jihočeský Kraj, S Czech Republic 49°25′N 14°41′E
123 R7 **Tabor** Respublika Sakha (Yakutiya), NE Russian Federation 71°14′N 150°23′E
29 S15 **Tabor** Iowa, C USA 40°54′N 95°40′W
81 F21 **Tabora** Tabora, W Tanzania 05°04′S 32°49′E
81 F21 **Tabora** ⬖ *region* C Tanzania
21 U12 **Tabor City** North Carolina, SE USA 34°09′N 78°52′W
147 Q10 **Taboshar** NW Tajikistan 40°37′N 69°33′E
76 L18 **Tabou** *var.* Tabu. S Ivory Coast 04°28′N 07°20′W
142 J2 **Tabrīz** *var.* Tebriz; *anc.* Tauris. Āžarbāyjān-e Sharqi, NW Iran 38°05′N 46°18′E
Tabu *see* Tabou
191 W1 **Tabuaeran** *prev.* Fanning Island. *atoll* Line Islands, E Kiribati
171 O2 **Tabuk** Luzon, N Philippines 17°26′N 121°25′E
140 J4 **Tabūk** Tabūk, NW Saudi Arabia 28°25′N 36°34′E
140 J5 **Tabūk** *off.* Minţaqat Tabūk. ⬖ *province* NW Saudi Arabia
Tabūk, Minţaqat *see* Tabūk
187 Q13 **Tabwemasana, Mount** ▲ Espiritu Santo, W Vanuatu 15°22′S 166°44′E
95 O15 **Täby** Stockholm, C Sweden 59°29′N 18°04′E
41 N14 **Tacámbaro** Michoacán, SW Mexico 19°12′N 101°27′W
42 A5 **Tacaná, Volcán** ⛰ Guatemala/Mexico 15°07′N 92°06′W
43 X16 **Tacarcuna, Cerro** ▲ SE Panama 08°08′N 77°15′W
Tachau *see* Tachov
158 J3 **Tacheng** *var.* Qoqek. Xinjiang Uygur Zizhiqu, NW China 46°45′N 82°55′E
54 H7 **Táchira** *off.* Estado Táchira. ⬖ *state* W Venezuela
Táchira, Estado *see* Táchira
Tachoshui *see* Dazhuoshui
111 A17 **Tachov** *Ger.* Tachau. Plveňský Kraj, W Czech Republic 49°48′N 12°38′E
171 Q5 **Tacloban** *off.* Tacloban City. Leyte, C Philippines 11°15′N 125°E
Tacloban City *see* Tacloban
57 I19 **Tacna** Tacna, SE Peru 18°S 70°15′W
57 H18 **Tacna** *off.* Departamento de Tacna. ⬖ *department* S Peru
Tacna, Departamento de *see* Tacna
32 H8 **Tacoma** Washington, NW USA 47°15′N 122°27′W
18 L11 **Taconic Range** ▲▲ NE USA
62 L6 **Taco Pozo** Formosa, N Argentina 25°35′S 63°15′W
57 M20 **Tacsara, Cordillera de** ▲▲ S Bolivia
61 F17 **Tacuarembó** *prev.* San Fructuoso. Tacuarembó, C Uruguay 31°42′S 56°W
61 E18 **Tacuarembó** ⬖ *department* C Uruguay
61 F17 **Tacuarembó, Río** ∿ C Uruguay
83 I14 **Taculi** North Western, NW Zambia 14°17′S 26°51′E
171 Q8 **Tacurong** Mindanao, S Philippines 06°42′N 124°40′E
77 V8 **Tadek** ∿ NW Niger
74 J9 **Tademaït, Plateau du** *plateau* C Algeria
187 R17 **Tadine** Province des Îles Loyauté, E New Caledonia 21°33′S 167°54′E
80 M11 **Tadjoura, Golfe de** *Eng.* Gulf of Tajura. *inlet* E Djibouti
80 L11 **Tadjourah** E Djibouti 11°47′N 42°51′E
Tadmor/Tadmur *see* Tudmur
11 W10 **Tadoule Lake** ◎ Manitoba, C Canada
15 S8 **Tadoussac** Québec, SE Canada 48°09′N 69°43′W
155 H18 **Tādpatri** Andhra Pradesh, E India 14°55′N 77°59′E
Tadzhikabad *see* Tojikobod
Tadzhikistan *see* Tajikistan
163 Y14 **Taebaek-sanmaek** *prev.* T'aebaek-sanmaek. ▲▲ E South Korea
T'aebaek-sanmaek *see* Taebaek-sanmaek
Taechŏng-do *see* Daecheong-do
163 X13 **Taedong-gang** ∿ C North Korea
Taegu *see* Daegu
Taegu-gwangyŏksi *see* Daegu
Taehan-haehyŏp *see* Korea Strait
Taehan Min'guk *see* South Korea
Taejŏn *see* Daejeon
Taejŏn-gwangyŏksi *see* Daejeon
193 Z13 **Tafahi** *island* N Tonga
105 Q4 **Tafalla** Navarra, N Spain 42°32′N 01°41′W
77 W7 **Tafassâsset, Ténéré du** *desert* N Niger
75 M12 **Tafassâsset, Oued** ∿ SE Algeria
55 U11 **Tafelberg** ▲ S Suriname 03°55′N 56°09′W
97 J21 **Taff** ∿ SE Wales, United Kingdom
Tafila/Ţafīlah, Muḩāfaẓat aţ *see* Aţ Ţafīlah
77 N15 **Tafiré** N Ivory Coast 09°04′N 05°10′W
142 M6 **Tafresh** Markazī, W Iran 34°40′N 50°00′E
143 Q9 **Taft** Yazd, C Iran 31°45′N 54°14′E
35 R13 **Taft** California, W USA 35°08′N 119°27′W
25 T14 **Taft** Texas, SW USA 27°58′N 97°24′W
143 W12 **Taftān, Kūh-e** ▲ SE Iran 28°38′N 61°06′E
35 R13 **Taft Heights** California, W USA 35°06′N 119°29′W
189 Y14 **Tafunsak** Kosrae, E Micronesia 05°21′N 162°58′E
192 G16 **Tāga** Savai'i, SW Samoa 13°46′S 172°31′W
149 O6 **Tagāb** Dāikondī, E Afghanistan 33°53′N 66°23′E
39 O8 **Tagagawik River** ∿ Alaska, USA
165 Q10 **Tagajō** *var.* Tagazyô. Miyagi, Honshū, C Japan 38°18′N 140°58′E
126 K12 **Taganrog** Rostovskaya Oblast', SW Russian Federation 47°10′N 38°55′E
126 K12 **Taganrog, Gulf of** *Rus.* Taganrogskiy Zaliv, *Ukr.* Tahanroz'ka Zatoka. *gulf* Russian Federation/Ukraine
Taganrogskiy Zaliv *see* Taganrog, Gulf of
76 J8 **Tagant** ⬖ *region* C Mauritania
148 M14 **Tagas** Baluchistān, SW Pakistan 27°09′N 64°36′E
171 O4 **Tagaytay** Luzon, N Philippines 14°04′N 120°55′E
Tagazyô *see* Tagajō
171 P6 **Tagbilaran** *var.* Tagbilaran City. Bohol, C Philippines 09°41′N 123°54′E
Tagbilaran City *see* Tagbilaran
106 B10 **Taggia** Liguria, NW Italy 43°51′N 07°48′E
77 V9 **Taghouaji, Massif de** ▲ C Niger 17°13′N 08°37′E
107 J15 **Tagliacozzo** Lazio, C Italy 42°03′N 13°15′E
106 J7 **Tagliamento** ∿ NE Italy
149 N3 **Tagow Bāy** *var.* Bai. Sar-e Pul, N Afghanistan 35°41′N 66°01′E
146 H9 **Tagta** *var.* Tahta, *Rus.* Takhta. Daşoguz Welaýaty, N Turkmenistan 41°40′N 59°51′E
146 J16 **Tagtabazar** *var.* Takhtabazar. Mary Welaýaty, S Turkmenistan 35°57′N 62°49′E
59 L17 **Taguatinga** Tocantins, C Brazil 12°16′S 46°25′W
186 I10 **Tagula** Tagula Island, SE Papua New Guinea 11°21′S 153°11′E
186 I11 **Tagula Island** *prev.* Southeast Island, Sudest Island. *island* SE Papua New Guinea
171 Q7 **Tagum** Mindanao, S Philippines 07°22′N 125°51′E
54 C7 **Tagún, Cerro** *elevation* Colombia/Panama
105 P7 **Tagus** *Port.* Rio Tejo, *Sp.* Río Tajo. ∿ Portugal/Spain
64 M9 **Tagus Plain** *undersea feature* E Atlantic Ocean 37°30′N 12°00′W
191 S10 **Tahaa** *island* Îles Sous le Vent, W French Polynesia
191 U10 **Tahanea** *atoll* Îles Tuamotu, C French Polynesia
Tahanroz'ka Zatoka *see* Taganrog, Gulf of
74 K12 **Tahat** ▲ SE Algeria 23°15′N 05°34′E
163 U4 **Tahe** Heilongjiang, NE China 52°21′N 124°42′E
Tahilt *see* Tsogt
191 T10 **Tahiti** *island* Îles du Vent, W French Polynesia
Tahiti, Archipel de *see* Société, Archipel de la
118 E4 **Tahkuna Nina** *headland* W Estonia 59°06′N 22°35′E
148 K12 **Tāhlāb** ∿ W Pakistan
148 K12 **Tāhlāb, Dasht-i** *desert* SW Pakistan
27 R10 **Tahlequah** Oklahoma, C USA 35°57′N 94°58′W
35 Q6 **Tahoe City** California, W USA 39°09′N 120°09′W
35 P6 **Tahoe, Lake** ◎ California/Nevada, W USA
25 N6 **Tahoka** Texas, SW USA 33°10′N 101°47′W
32 F8 **Taholah** Washington, NW USA 47°19′N 124°17′W
77 T11 **Tahoua** Tahoua, W Niger 14°53′N 05°18′E
77 T11 **Tahoua** ⬖ *department* W Niger
31 P3 **Tahquamenon Falls** *waterfall* Michigan, N USA
31 P4 **Tahquamenon River** ∿ Michigan, N USA
139 V10 **Taḩrīr** Al Qādisīyah, S Iraq 31°58′N 45°34′E
10 K17 **Tahsis** Vancouver Island, British Columbia, SW Canada 49°42′N 126°31′W
75 W9 **Ţahţā** *var.* Ţaḩta. C Egypt 26°47′N 31°31′E
Tahta *see* Tagta
136 L15 **Tahtalı Dağları** ▲▲ C Turkey
57 I14 **Tahuamanu, Río** ∿ Bolivia/Peru
56 F13 **Tahuanía, Río** ∿ E Peru
191 X7 **Tahuata** *island* Îles Marquises, NE French Polynesia
76 L17 **Taï** SW Ivory Coast 05°52′N 07°28′W
161 P5 **Tai'an** Shandong, E China 36°13′N 117°12′E
191 R8 **Taiarapu, Presqu'île de** *peninsula* Tahiti, W French Polynesia
Taibad *see* Tāybād
160 K7 **Taibai Shan** ▲ C China 33°57′N 107°31′E
105 Q12 **Taibilla, Sierra de** ▲▲ S Spain
Taibus Qi *see* Baochang
Taichū *see* Taizhong
T'aichung *see* Taizhong
Taiden *see* Daejeon
161 T14 **Taidong** *Jap.* Taitō; *prev.* T'aitung. S Taiwan 22°43′N 121°10′E
185 E23 **Taieri** ∿ South Island, New Zealand
115 E21 **Taïgetos** ▲▲ S Greece
161 N4 **Taihang Shan** ▲▲ C China
184 M11 **Taihape** Manawatu-Wanganui, North Island, New Zealand 39°41′S 175°47′E
161 O7 **Taihe** Anhui, E China 33°14′N 115°35′E
161 O12 **Taihe** *var.* Chengjiang. Jiangxi, S China 26°47′N 114°52′E
Taihoku *see* T'aipei
161 P9 **Taihu** Anhui, E China 30°22′N 116°20′E
161 R8 **Tai Hu** ◎ E China
159 O9 **Taikang** *var.* Dorbod, Dorbod Mongolzu Zizhixian. Heilongjiang, NE China 46°50′N 124°25′E
161 O6 **Taikang** Henan, C China 34°01′N 114°59′E
165 T5 **Taiki** Hokkaidō, NE Japan 42°29′N 143°15′E
166 L8 **Taikkyi** Yangon, Myanmar (Burma) 17°16′N 95°55′E
Taikyū *see* Daegu
163 U8 **Tailai** Heilongjiang, NE China 46°25′N 123°25′E
168 I12 **Taileleo** Pulau Siberut, W Indonesia 01°45′S 99°06′E
182 J10 **Tailem Bend** South Australia 35°20′S 139°34′E
96 I8 **Tain** N Scotland, United Kingdom 57°49′N 04°04′W
161 S14 **Tainan** *prev.* Dainan, T'ainan. S Taiwan 23°01′N 120°05′E
115 E22 **Taínaro, Akrotírio** *cape* S Greece
161 Q11 **Taining** *var.* Shancheng. Fujian, SE China 26°55′N 117°13′E
191 W7 **Taiohae** *prev.* Madisonville. Nuku Hiva, NE French Polynesia 08°55′S 140°04′W
161 T13 **T'aipei** *Jap.* Taihoku; *prev.* Daihoku. ● (Taiwan) N Taiwan 25°02′N 121°28′E
168 J7 **Taiping** Perak, Peninsular Malaysia 04°54′N 100°42′E
Taiping *see* Chongzuo
163 S8 **Taiping Ling** ▲ NE China 47°27′N 120°27′E
165 Q4 **Taisei** Hokkaidō, NE Japan 42°13′N 139°52′E
165 G12 **Taisha** Shimane, Honshū, SW Japan 35°23′N 132°40′E
109 R4 **Taiskirchen** Oberösterreich, NW Austria 48°15′N 13°33′E
63 F20 **Taitao, Peninsula de** *peninsula* S Chile
Taitō *see* Taidong
T'aitung *see* Taidong
92 M13 **Taivalkoski** Oulu, E Finland 65°35′N 28°20′E
93 K19 **Taivassalo** Länsi-Suomi, SW Finland 60°35′N 21°36′E
161 T14 **Taiwan** *off.* Republic of China, *var.* Formosa, Formo'sa. ◆ *republic* E Asia
192 F5 **Taiwan** *var.* Formosa. *island* E Asia
Taiwan *see* Taizhong
T'aiwan Haihsia/Taiwan Haixia *see* Taiwan Strait
Taiwan Shan *see* Chungyang Shanmo
161 R13 **Taiwan Strait** *var.* Formosa Strait, *Chin.* T'aiwan Haihsia, Taiwan Haixia. *strait* China/Taiwan
161 N4 **Taiyuan** *var.* T'ai-yuan, T'ai-yüan; *prev.* Yangku. *province capital* Shanxi, C China 37°48′N 112°33′E
T'ai-yuan/T'ai-yüan *see* Taiyuan
161 S13 **Taizhong** *Jap.* Taichū; *prev.* T'aichung, Taiwan. C Taiwan 24°09′N 120°40′E
161 R7 **Taizhou** Jiangsu, E China 32°36′N 119°52′E
161 S10 **Taizhou** *var.* Jiaojiang; *prev.* Haimen. Zhejiang, SE China 28°36′N 121°19′E
Taizhou *see* Linhai
141 O16 **Ta'izz** SW Yemen 13°36′N 44°04′E
141 O16 **Ta'izz** ✈ SW Yemen 13°40′N 44°10′E
75 P12 **Tajarhī** SW Libya 24°21′N 14°28′E
147 P13 **Tajikistan** *off.* Republic of Tajikistan, *Rus.* Tadzhikistan, *Taj.* Jumhurii Tojikiston; *prev.* Tajik S.S.R. ◆ *republic* C Asia
Tajikistan, Republic of *see* Tajikistan
Tajik S.S.R *see* Tajikistan
165 O11 **Tajima** Fukushima, Honshū, C Japan 37°10′N 139°46′E
Tajoe *see* Tayu
Tajo, Río *see* Tagus
42 B5 **Tajumulco, Volcán** ▲ W Guatemala 15°04′N 91°50′W
105 P7 **Tajuña** ∿ C Spain
Tajura, Gulf of *see* Tadjoura, Golfe de
167 O9 **Tak** *var.* Rahaeng. Tak, W Thailand 16°51′N 99°08′E
189 U4 **Taka Atoll** *var.* Tōke. *atoll* Ratak Chain, N Marshall Islands
165 P12 **Takahagi** Ibaraki, Honshū, S Japan 36°42′N 140°42′E
165 H13 **Takahashi** *var.* Takahasi. Okayama, Honshū, SW Japan 34°48′N 133°38′E
Takahasi *see* Takahashi
189 P12 **Takaieu Island** *island* E Micronesia
184 I13 **Takaka** Tasman, South Island, New Zealand 40°52′S 172°49′E
170 M14 **Takalar** Sulawesi, C Indonesia 05°28′S 119°24′E
165 H13 **Takamatsu** *var.* Takamatu. Kagawa, Shikoku, SW Japan 34°19′N 133°59′E
Takamatu *see* Takamatsu

◆ Country
● Country Capital
◇ Dependent Territory
○ Dependent Territory Capital
⬖ Administrative Regions
✈ International Airport
▲ Mountain
▲▲ Mountain Range
⛰ Volcano
∿ River
◎ Lake
⊠ Reservoir

165 D14 **Takamori** Kumamoto, Kyūshū, SW Japan 32°50′N 131°08′E
165 D16 **Takanabe** Miyazaki, Kyūshū, SW Japan 32°13′N 131°31′E
170 M16 **Takan, Gunung** ▲ Pulau Sumba, S Indonesia 08°52′S 117°32′E
165 Q7 **Takanosu** *var.* Kita-Akita. Akita, Honshū, C Japan 40°13′N 140°23′E
Takao *see* Gaoxiong
165 L11 **Takaoka** Toyama, Honshū, SW Japan 36°44′N 137°02′E
184 N12 **Takapau** Hawke's Bay, North Island, New Zealand 40°01′S 176°21′E
191 U9 **Takapoto** *atoll* Îles Tuamotu, C French Polynesia
184 L5 **Takapuna** Auckland, North Island, New Zealand 36°48′S 174°46′E
165 J3 **Takarazuka** Hyōgo, Honshū, SW Japan 34°49′N 135°21′E
191 U9 **Takaroa** *atoll* Îles Tuamotu, C French Polynesia
165 N12 **Takasaki** Gunma, Honshū, S Japan 36°20′N 139°00′E
164 L12 **Takayama** Gifu, Honshū, SW Japan 36°09′N 137°16′E
164 K12 **Takefu** *var.* Echizen, Takehu. Fukui, Honshū, SW Japan 35°55′N 136°11′E
Takehu *see* Takefu
164 C14 **Takeo** Saga, Kyūshū, SW Japan 33°13′N 130°00′E
Takeo *see* Takêv
164 C17 **Take-shima** *island* Nansei-shotō, SW Japan
142 M5 **Tākestān** *var.* Takistan; *prev.* Siadehan. Qazvin, N Iran 36°02′N 49°40′E
164 D14 **Taketa** Ōita, Kyūshū, SW Japan 33°00′N 131°23′E
167 R13 **Takêv** *prev.* Takeo. Takêv, S Cambodia 10°59′N 104°47′E
167 O10 **Tak Fah** Nakhon Sawan, C Thailand
139 T13 **Takhādīd** *well* S Iraq
149 R3 **Takhār** ◈ *province* NE Afghanistan
Takhiatash *see* Taxiatosh
Ta Khmau *see* Kândal
Takhta *see* Tagta
Takhtabazar *see* Tagtabazar
145 O8 **Takhtabrod** Severnyy Kazakhstan, N Kazakhstan 52°35′N 67°37′E
Takhtakupyr *see* Taxtako'pir
142 M8 **Takht-e Shāh, Kūh-e** ▲▲ C Iran
77 V12 **Takiéta** Zinder, S Niger 13°43′N 08°33′E
8 J8 **Takijuq Lake** ◎ Nunavut, NW Canada
165 S3 **Takikawa** Hokkaidō, NE Japan 43°35′N 141°54′E
165 U3 **Takinoue** Hokkaidō, NE Japan 44°10′N 143°09′E
Takistan *see* Tākestān
185 B23 **Takitimu Mountains** ▲▲ South Island, New Zealand
Takkaze *see* Tekezē
165 R7 **Takko** Aomori, Honshū, C Japan 40°19′N 141°11′E
10 L13 **Takla Lake** ◎ British Columbia, SW Canada
Takla Makan Desert *see* Taklimakan Shamo
158 H9 **Taklimakan Shamo** *Eng.* Takla Makan Desert. *desert* NW China
167 T12 **Takôk** Môndól Kiri, E Cambodia 12°37′N 106°30′E
39 P10 **Takotna** Alaska, USA 62°59′N 156°03′W
Takow *see* Gaoxiong
123 O12 **Taksimo** Respublika Buryatiya, S Russian Federation 56°18′N 114°53′E
164 C13 **Taku** Saga, Kyūshū, SW Japan 33°19′N 130°06′E
10 I10 **Taku** 〰 British Columbia, W Canada
166 M15 **Takua Pa** *var.* Ban Takua Pa. Phangnga, SW Thailand 08°55′N 98°20′E
77 W16 **Takum** Taraba, E Nigeria 07°16′N 10°00′E
191 V10 **Takume** *atoll* Îles Tuamotu, C French Polynesia
190 L16 **Takutea** *island* S Cook Islands
186 K6 **Takuu Islands** *prev.* Mortlock Group. *island group* NE Papua New Guinea
119 L18 **Tal'** Minskaya Voblasts', S Belarus 52°52′N 27°58′E
40 L13 **Tala** Jalisco, C Mexico 20°39′N 103°45′W
61 F19 **Tala** Canelones, S Uruguay 34°24′S 55°45′W
Talabriga *see* Aveiro, Portugal
Talabriga *see* Talavera de la Reina, Spain
119 N14 **Talachyn** *Rus.* Tolochin. Vitsyebskaya Voblasts', NE Belarus 54°25′N 29°42′E
149 U7 **Talagang** Punjab, E Pakistan 32°55′N 72°29′E
105 V11 **Talaiassa** ▲ Ibiza, Spain, W Mediterranean Sea 38°55′N 1°17′E
155 J23 **Talaimannar** Northern Province, NW Sri Lanka 09°05′N 79°43′E
117 R3 **Talalayivka** Chernihivs'ka Oblast', N Ukraine 50°51′N 33°09′E
43 O15 **Talamanca, Cordillera de** ▲▲ S Costa Rica
56 A9 **Talara** Piura, NW Peru 04°31′S 81°17′W
104 L11 **Talarrubias** Extremadura, W Spain 39°03′N 05°14′W
147 S8 **Talas** Talasskaya Oblast', NW Kyrgyzstan 42°29′N 72°21′E
147 S8 **Talas** 〰 NW Kyrgyzstan
186 G7 **Talasea** New Britain, E Papua New Guinea 05°20′S 150°01′E
Talas Oblasty *see* Talasskaya Oblast'
147 S8 **Talasskaya Oblast'** *Kir.* Talas Oblasty. ◈ *province* NW Kyrgyzstan
147 S8 **Talasskiy Alatau, Khrebet** ▲▲ Kazakhstan/Kyrgyzstan
77 U12 **Talata Mafara** Zamfara, NW Nigeria 12°33′N 06°01′E
171 R9 **Talaud, Kepulauan** *island group* E Indonesia
104 M9 **Talavera de la Reina** *anc.* Caesarobriga, Talabriga. Castilla-La Mancha, C Spain 39°58′N 04°50′W
104 J11 **Talavera la Real** Extremadura, W Spain 38°53′N 06°46′W
186 F7 **Talawe, Mount** ▲ New Britain, C Papua New Guinea 05°30′S 148°24′E
23 S5 **Talbotton** Georgia, SE USA 32°40′N 84°32′W
183 R7 **Talbragar River** 〰 New South Wales, SE Australia
62 G13 **Talca** Maule, C Chile 35°28′S 71°42′W
62 F13 **Talcahuano** Bío Bío, C Chile 36°43′S 73°07′W
154 N12 **Tālcher** Orissa, E India 20°57′N 85°13′E
25 W5 **Talco** Texas, SW USA 33°21′N 95°06′W
145 V14 **Taldykorgan** *Kaz.* Taldyqorghan; *prev.* Taldy-Kurgan. Taldykorgan, SE Kazakhstan 45°N 78°23′E
Taldy-Kurgan/ Taldyqorghan *see* Taldykorgan
147 Y7 **Taldy-Suu** Issyk-Kul'skaya Oblast', E Kyrgyzstan 42°49′N 78°33′E
147 U10 **Taldy-Suu** Oshskaya Oblast', SW Kyrgyzstan 40°33′N 73°52′E
Tal-e Khosravī *see* Yāsūj
193 Y15 **Taleki Tonga** *island* Otu Tolu Group, C Tonga
193 Y15 **Taleki Vavu'u** *island* Otu Tolu Group, C Tonga
102 J13 **Talence** Gironde, SW France 44°49′N 00°35′W
145 U16 **Talgar** *Kaz.* Talghar. Almaty, SE Kazakhstan 43°17′N 77°15′E
Talghar *see* Talgar
171 Q12 **Taliabu, Pulau** *island* Kepulauan Sula, C Indonesia
115 L22 **Taliarós, Akrotírio** *headland* Astypálaia, Kykládes, Greece, Aegean Sea 36°31′N 26°18′E
Ta-lien *see* Dalian
27 Q12 **Talihina** Oklahoma, C USA 34°45′N 95°03′W
Talimardzhan *see* Tollimarjon
137 T12 **T'alin** *Rus.* Talin; *prev.* Verin T'alin. W Armenia 40°23′N 43°51′E
Talin *see* T'alin
81 E15 **Tali Post** Central Equatoria, S South Sudan 05°55′N 30°44′E
Taliq-an *see* Tāloqān
Taliş Dağları *see* Talish Mountains
142 L2 **Talish Mountains** *Az.* Taliş Dağları, *Per.* Kūhhā-ye Ţavālesh, *Rus.* Talyshskiye Gory. ▲▲ Azerbaijan/Iran
170 M16 **Taliwang** Sumbawa, C Indonesia 08°45′S 116°55′E
119 L17 **Tal'ka** Minskaya Voblasts', C Belarus 53°22′N 28°21′E
39 R11 **Talkeetna** Alaska, USA 62°19′N 150°06′W
39 R11 **Talkeetna Mountains** ▲▲ Alaska, USA
Talkhof *see* Puurmani
92 H2 **Tálknafjördhur** Vestfirdhir, W Iceland 65°38′N 23°51′W
139 Q3 **Tall 'Abţah** Nīnawá, N Iraq 35°52′N 42°40′E
138 M2 **Tall Abyaḑ** *var.* Tell Abiad. Ar Raqqah, N Syria 36°42′N 38°56′E
23 Q4 **Talladega** Alabama, S USA 33°26′N 86°06′W
139 Q2 **Tall 'Afar** Nīnawýa, N Iraq 36°22′N 42°27′E
23 S8 **Tallahassee** *prev.* Muskogean. *state capital* Florida, SE USA 30°26′N 84°17′W
22 L2 **Tallahatchie River** 〰 Mississippi, S USA
Tall al Abyaḑ *see* At Tall al Abyaḑ
139 W12 **Tall al Laḩm** Dhī Qār, S Iraq 30°46′N 46°22′E
183 P11 **Tallangatta** Victoria, SE Australia 36°15′S 147°13′E
23 R4 **Tallapoosa River** 〰 Alabama/Georgia, S USA
103 T13 **Tallard** Hautes-Alpes, SE France 44°30′N 06°04′E
139 Q3 **Tall ash Sha'īr** Nīnawá, N Iraq 36°11′N 42°26′E
23 Q5 **Tallassee** Alabama, S USA 32°32′N 85°53′W
139 R4 **Tall 'Azbah** Nīnawýa, NW Iraq 35°47′N 43°13′E
138 I5 **Tall Bīsah** Ḩimş, W Syria 34°50′N 36°44′E
139 R3 **Tall Ḩassūnah** Al Anbār, N Iraq 36°05′N 43°10′E
139 Q2 **Tall Ḩuqnah** *var.* Tell Huqnah. Nīnawá, N Iraq 36°33′N 42°34′E
Tallin *see* Tallinn
118 G3 **Tallinn** *Ger.* Reval, *Rus.* Tallin; *prev.* Revel. ● (Estonia) Harjumaa, NW Estonia 59°26′N 24°42′E
118 H3 **Tallinn** ✈ Harjumaa, NW Estonia 59°23′N 24°52′E
138 H5 **Tall Kalakh** *var.* Tell Kalakh. Ḩimş, C Syria 34°40′N 36°18′E
139 R2 **Tall Kayf** Nīnawýa, NW Iraq 36°30′N 43°08′E
Tall Kūchak *see* Tall Kūshik
139 P2 **Tall Kūshik** *var.* Tall Kūchak. Al Ḩasakah, E Syria 36°48′N 42°01′E
31 U12 **Tallmadge** Ohio, N USA 41°06′N 81°26′W
22 J5 **Tallulah** Louisiana, S USA 32°22′N 91°12′W
139 Q2 **Tall 'Uwaynāt** Nīnawýa, NW Iraq 36°43′N 42°18′E
139 Q2 **Tall Ẕāhir** Nīnawá, N Iraq 36°51′N 42°29′E
122 J13 **Tal'menka** Altayskiy Kray, S Russian Federation 53°55′N 83°26′E
122 K8 **Talnakh** Krasnoyarskiy Kray, N Russian Federation 69°26′N 88°27′E
117 P7 **Tal'ne** *Rus.* Tal'noye. Cherkas'ka Oblast', C Ukraine 48°55′N 30°40′E
Tal'noye *see* Tal'ne
80 E12 **Talodi** Southern Kordofan, C Sudan 10°40′N 30°25′E
188 B16 **Talofofo** SE Guam 13°21′N 144°45′E
188 B16 **Talofofo Bay** *bay* SE Guam
26 L9 **Taloga** Oklahoma, C USA 36°02′N 98°58′W
123 T10 **Talon** Magadanskaya Oblast', E Russian Federation 59°47′N 148°46′E
14 H11 **Talon, Lake** ◎ Ontario, S Canada
149 R2 **Tāloqān** *var.* Taliq-an. Takhār, NE Afghanistan 36°44′N 69°33′E
126 M8 **Talovaya** Voronezhskaya Oblast', W Russian Federation 51°07′N 40°46′E
9 N6 **Taloyoak** *prev.* Spence Bay. Nunavut, N Canada 69°30′N 93°25′W
25 Q8 **Talpa** Texas, SW USA 31°46′N 99°42′W
40 K13 **Talpa de Allende** Jalisco, C Mexico 20°22′N 104°51′W
23 S9 **Talquin, Lake** ⊠ Florida, SE USA
Talsen *see* Talsi
Talshand *see* Chandmanī
118 E8 **Talsi** *Ger.* Talsen. NW Latvia 57°14′N 22°35′E
143 V11 **Tal Sīāh** Sīstān va Balūchestān, SE Iran 28°19′N 57°43′E
62 G6 **Taltal** Antofagasta, N Chile 25°22′S 70°27′W
8 K10 **Taltson** 〰 Northwest Territories, NW Canada
168 K11 **Taluk** Sumatera, W Indonesia 0°32′S 101°35′E
92 J8 **Talvik** Finnmark, N Norway 70°02′N 22°59′E
182 M7 **Talyawalka Creek** 〰 New South Wales, SE Australia
Talyshskiye Gory *see* Talish Mountains
29 W14 **Tama** Iowa, C USA 41°58′N 92°34′W
Tama Abu, Banjaran *see* Penambo, Banjaran
169 U9 **Tamabo, Banjaran** ▲▲ East Malaysia
190 B16 **Tamakautoga** SW Niue 19°05′S 169°55′W
127 N7 **Tamala** Penzenskaya Oblast', W Russian Federation 52°32′N 43°18′E
77 P15 **Tamale** C Ghana 09°21′N 00°54′W
191 P3 **Tamana** *prev.* Rotcher Island. *atoll* Tungaru, W Kiribati
74 K12 **Tamanrasset** *var.* Tamenghest. S Algeria 22°49′N 05°32′E
74 J13 **Tamanrasset** *wadi* Algeria/Mali
166 M2 **Tamanthi** Sagaing, Myanmar (Burma) 25°17′N 95°18′E
97 I24 **Tamar** 〰 SW England, United Kingdom
Tamar *see* Tudmur
54 H9 **Támara** Casanare, C Colombia 05°51′N 72°09′W
54 F7 **Tamar, Alto de** ▲ C Colombia 07°25′N 74°28′W
173 X16 **Tamarin** E Mauritius 20°20′S 57°22′E
105 T5 **Tamarite de Litera** *var.* Tararite de Llitera. Aragón, NE Spain 41°52′N 00°25′E
111 I24 **Tamási** Tolna, S Hungary 46°39′N 18°17′E
Tamatave *see* Toamasina
41 O9 **Tamaulipas** ◈ *state* C Mexico
41 P10 **Tamaulipas, Sierra de** ▲▲ C Mexico
56 F12 **Tamaya, Río** 〰 E Peru
40 I9 **Tamazula** Durango, C Mexico 24°43′N 106°33′W
40 L14 **Tamazula** Jalisco, C Mexico 19°41′N 103°18′W
Tamazulápam *see* Tamazulapán
41 Q15 **Tamazulapán** *var.* Tamazulápam. Oaxaca, SE Mexico 17°41′N 97°33′W
41 P12 **Tamazunchale** San Luis Potosí, C Mexico 21°17′N 98°46′W
76 H11 **Tambacounda** SE Senegal 13°44′N 13°43′W
83 M16 **Tambara** Manica, C Mozambique 16°42′S 34°14′E
77 T13 **Tambawel** Sokoto, NW Nigeria 12°24′N 04°42′E
186 M9 **Tambea** Guadalcanal, C Solomon Islands 09°19′S 159°42′E
169 N10 **Tambelan, Kepulauan** *island group* W Indonesia
57 E15 **Tambo de Mora** Ica, W Peru 13°30′S 76°08′W
170 L16 **Tambora, Gunung** 🌋 Sumbawa, S Indonesia 08°16′S 117°59′E
61 E17 **Tambores** Paysandú, W Uruguay 31°50′S 56°17′W
57 F14 **Tambo, Río** 〰 C Peru
56 F7 **Tamboryacu, Río** 〰 N Peru
126 M7 **Tambov** Tambovskaya Oblast', W Russian Federation 52°43′N 41°28′E
126 L6 **Tambovskaya Oblast'** ◈ *province* W Russian Federation
104 H3 **Tambre** 〰 NW Spain
169 V7 **Tambunan** Sabah, East Malaysia 05°40′N 116°22′E
81 C15 **Tambura** Western Equatoria, SW South Sudan 05°38′N 27°30′E
Tamchaket *see* Tâmchekkeţ
76 J9 **Tâmchekkeţ** *var.* Tamchaket. Hodh el Gharbi, S Mauritania 17°23′N 10°37′W
167 T7 **Tam Điêp** Ninh Binh, N Vietnam 20°09′N 105°54′E
Tamdybulak *see* Tomdibuloq
54 H8 **Tame** Arauca, C Colombia 06°27′N 71°42′W
104 H6 **Tâmega, Rio** *Sp.* Río Támega. 〰 Portugal/Spain
Támega, Río *see* Tâmega, Rio
115 H20 **Tamélos, Akrotírio** *headland* Tziá, Kykládes, Greece, Aegean Sea 37°31′N 24°16′E
Tamenghest *see* Tamanrasset
77 V8 **Tamgak, Adrar** ▲ C Niger 19°10′N 08°39′E
76 I13 **Tamgue** ▲ NW Guinea 12°14′N 12°18′W
41 Q12 **Tamiahua** Veracruz-Llave, E Mexico 21°15′N 97°27′W
41 Q12 **Tamiahua, Laguna de** *lagoon* E Mexico
23 Y16 **Tamiami Canal** *canal* Florida, SE USA
188 F17 **Tamil Harbor** *harbor* Yap, W Micronesia
155 H21 **Tamil Nādu** *prev.* Madras. ◈ *state* SE India
99 H20 **Tamines** Namur, S Belgium 50°27′N 04°37′E
116 E12 **Tamiš** *Ger.* Temesch, *Hung.* Temes. 〰 Romania/Serbia
167 U10 **Tam Ky** Quang Nam-ƒa Năng, C Vietnam 15°32′N 108°30′E
Tammerfors *see* Tampere
Tammisaari *see* Ekenäs
95 N14 **Tämnaren** ◎ C Sweden
191 Q7 **Tamotoe, Passe** *passage* Tahiti, W French Polynesia
23 V12 **Tampa** Florida, SE USA 27°57′N 82°27′W
23 V12 **Tampa** ✈ Florida, SE USA 27°57′N 82°29′W
23 V13 **Tampa Bay** *bay* Florida, SE USA
93 L18 **Tampere** *Swe.* Tammerfors. Länsi-Suomi, W Finland 61°30′N 23°45′E
41 Q11 **Tampico** Tamaulipas, C Mexico 22°18′N 97°52′W
171 P14 **Tampo** Pulau Muna, C Indonesia 04°38′S 122°40′E
167 V11 **Tam Quan** Binh Đinh, C Vietnam 14°34′N 109°00′E
162 J13 **Tamsag Muchang** Nei Mongol Zizhiqu, N China 40°28′N 102°34′E
Tamsal *see* Tamsalu
118 I4 **Tamsalu** *Ger.* Tamsal. Lääne-Virumaa, NE Estonia 59°10′N 26°07′E
109 S8 **Tamsweg** Salzburg, SW Austria 47°08′N 13°49′E
188 C15 **Tamuning** NW Guam 13°29′N 144°47′E
183 T6 **Tamworth** New South Wales, SE Australia 31°07′S 150°54′E
97 M19 **Tamworth** C England, United Kingdom 52°39′N 01°40′W
81 K19 **Tana** *Finn.* Tenojoki, *Lapp.* Deatnu. 〰 SE Kenya *see also* Deatnu, Tenojoki
Tana *see* Deatnu/Tana
164 I15 **Tanabe** Wakayama, Honshū, SW Japan 33°43′N 135°22′E
92 L8 **Tana Bru** Finnmark, N Norway 70°11′N 28°06′E
39 T10 **Tanacross** Alaska, USA 63°30′N 143°21′W
92 L7 **Tanafjorden** *Lapp.* Deanuvuotna. *fjord* N Norway
38 G17 **Tanaga Island** *island* Aleutian Islands, Alaska, USA
38 G17 **Tanaga Volcano** ▲ Tanaga Island, Alaska, USA 51°53′N 178°08′W
107 M18 **Tanagro** 〰 S Italy
80 H11 **T'ana Hāyk'** *var.* Lake Tana. ◎ NW Ethiopia
168 H11 **Tanahbela, Pulau** *island* Kepulauan Batu, W Indonesia
171 H15 **Tanahjampea, Pulau** *island* W Indonesia
168 H11 **Tanahmasa, Pulau** *island* Kepulauan Batu, W Indonesia
Tanais *see* Don
152 L10 **Tanakpur** Uttarakhand, N India 29°04′N 80°06′E
Tana, Lake *see* T'ana Hāyk'
181 P5 **Tanami Desert** *desert* Northern Territory, N Australia
167 T14 **Tân An** Long An, S Vietnam 10°32′N 106°24′E
39 Q9 **Tanana** Alaska, USA 65°12′N 152°00′W
Tananarive *see* Antananarivo
39 Q9 **Tanana River** 〰 Alaska, USA
95 C16 **Tananger** Rogaland, S Norway 58°55′N 05°34′E
188 H5 **Tanapag** Saipan, S Northern Mariana Islands 15°14′S 145°45′E
188 H5 **Tanapag, Puetton** *bay* Saipan, S Northern Mariana Islands
106 C9 **Tanaro** 〰 N Italy
163 Y12 **Tanch'ŏn** E North Korea 40°22′N 128°49′E
40 M14 **Tancitaro, Cerro** 🌋 C Mexico 19°16′N 102°25′W
153 N12 **Tānda** Uttar Pradesh, N India 26°33′N 82°39′E
77 O15 **Tanda** E Ivory Coast 07°48′N 03°10′W
116 L14 **Ţăndărei** Ialomiţa, SE Romania 44°39′N 27°40′E
63 N14 **Tandil** Buenos Aires, E Argentina 37°18′S 59°10′W
78 H12 **Tandjilé** *off.* Préfecture du Tandjilé. ◈ *prefecture* SW Chad
Tandjilé, Préfecture du *see* Tandjilé
Tandjoeng *see* Tanjung
Tandjoengkarang *see* Bandar Lampung
Tandjoengpandan *see* Tanjungpandan
Tandjoengpinang *see* Tanjungpinang
Tandjoengredeb *see* Tanjungredeb
149 Q16 **Tando Allāhyār** Sind, SE Pakistan 25°28′N 68°44′E
149 Q17 **Tando Bāgo** Sind, SE Pakistan 24°48′N 68°59′E
149 Q16 **Tando Muhammad Khān** Sind, SE Pakistan 25°07′N 68°35′E
182 L7 **Tandou Lake** *seasonal lake* New South Wales, SE Australia
94 L11 **Tandsjöborg** Gävleborg, C Sweden 61°40′N 14°40′E
155 H15 **Tāndūr** Andhra Pradesh, C India 17°16′N 77°37′E
164 C17 **Tanega-shima** *island* Nansei-shotō, SW Japan
165 R7 **Taneichi** Iwate, Honshū, C Japan 40°23′N 141°42′E
Tanen Taunggyi *see* Tane Range
167 N8 **Tane Range** *Bur.* Tanen Taunggyi. ▲▲ W Thailand
111 P15 **Tanew** 〰 SE Poland
21 W2 **Taneytown** Maryland, NE USA 39°39′N 77°10′W
74 H12 **Tanezrouft** *desert* Algeria/Mali
138 L7 **Ţanf, Jabal aţ** ▲ SE Syria 33°32′N 38°43′E
81 J21 **Tanga** Tanga, E Tanzania 05°07′S 39°05′E
81 I22 **Tanga** ◈ *region* E Tanzania
153 T14 **Tangail** Dhaka, C Bangladesh 24°15′N 89°55′E
186 I5 **Tanga Islands** *island group* NE Papua New Guinea
155 K26 **Tangalla** Southern Province, S Sri Lanka 06°02′N 80°47′E
Tanganyika and Zanzibar *see* Tanzania
68 J13 **Tanganyika, Lake** ◎ E Africa
56 E7 **Tangarana, Río** 〰 N Peru
191 V16 **Tangaroa, Maunga** 🌋 Easter Island, Chile, E Pacific Ocean
Tangdukou *see* Shaoyang
74 G5 **Tanger** *var.* Tangiers, Tangier, *Fr./Ger.* Tangerk, *Sp.* Tánger; *anc.* Tingis. NW Morocco 35°49′N 05°49′W
169 N15 **Tangerang** Jawa, C Indonesia 06°14′S 106°36′E
Tangerk *see* Tanger
100 M12 **Tangermünde** Sachsen-Anhalt, C Germany 52°35′N 11°57′E
159 O12 **Tanggulashan** *var.* Togton Heyan, Tuotuoheyan. Qinghai, C China 34°13′N 92°25′E
156 K10 **Tanggula Shan** *var.* Dangla, Tangla Range. ▲▲ W China
159 N13 **Tanggula Shan** ▲ W China 33°18′N 91°10′E
156 K10 **Tanggula Shankou** *Tib.* Dang La. *pass* W China
161 N7 **Tanghe** Henan, C China 32°40′N 112°53′E
149 T5 **Tāngi** Khyber Pakhtunkhwa, NW Pakistan 34°18′N 71°42′E
Tangier *see* Tanger
21 Y5 **Tangier Island** *island* Virginia, NE USA
Tangiers *see* Tanger
22 K8 **Tangipahoa River** 〰 Louisiana, S USA
Tangla Range *see* Tanggula Shan
156 I10 **Tangra Yumco** *var.* Tangro Tso. ◎ W China
Tangro Tso *see* Tangra Yumco
157 T7 **Tangshan** *var.* T'ang-shan. Hebei, E China 39°39′N 118°15′E
T'ang-shan *see* Tangshan
77 R14 **Tanguiéta** NW Benin 10°35′N 01°19′E
163 X7 **Tangwang He** 〰 NE China
163 X7 **Tangyuan** Heilongjiang, NE China 46°45′N 129°52′E
167 S14 **Tân Hiêp** *var.* Phung Hiêp. Cân Thơ, S Vietnam 09°50′N 105°48′E
92 M11 **Tanhua** Lappi, N Finland 67°31′N 27°30′E
171 U16 **Tanimbar, Kepulauan** *island group* Maluku, E Indonesia
167 N12 **Tanintharyi** *var.* Tenasserim. Tanintharyi, S Myanmar (Burma) 12°05′N 99°00′E
167 N11 **Tanintharyi** *var.* Tenasserim. ◈ *division* S Myanmar (Burma)
139 U4 **Tānjarō** 〰 E Iraq
129 T15 **Tanjong Piai** *headland* Peninsular Malaysia
Tanjore *see* Thanjāvūr
169 U12 **Tanjung** *prev.* Tandjoeng. Borneo, C Indonesia 02°08′S 115°23′E
169 W9 **Tanjungbatu** Borneo, N Indonesia 02°19′N 118°03′E
Tanjungkarang/ Tanjungkarang-Telukbetung *see* Bandar Lampung
169 N13 **Tanjungpandan** *prev.* Tandjoengpandan. Pulau Belitung, W Indonesia 02°44′S 107°36′E
168 M10 **Tanjungpinang** *prev.* Tandjoengpinang. Pulau Bintan, W Indonesia 0°55′N 104°28′E
169 V9 **Tanjungredeb** *var.* Tanjungredep; *prev.* Tandjoengredeb. Borneo, C Indonesia 02°09′N 117°29′E
Tanjungredep *see* Tanjungredeb
149 S8 **Tānk** Khyber Pakhtunkhwa, NW Pakistan 32°14′N 70°29′E
187 S15 **Tanna** *island* S Vanuatu
93 F17 **Tännäs** Jämtland, C Sweden 62°27′N 12°40′E
Tannenhof *see* Krynica
108 K7 **Tannheim** Tirol, W Austria 47°30′N 10°32′E
Tannu-Tuva *see* Tyva, Respublika
171 Q12 **Tano** Pulau Taliabu, E Indonesia 01°51′S 124°55′E
77 O17 **Tano** 〰 S Ghana
152 D10 **Tanot** Rājasthān, NW India 27°44′N 70°17′E
77 V11 **Tanout** Zinder, C Niger 14°58′N 08°54′E
Tân Phu *see* Đinh Quan
41 P12 **Tanquián** San Luis Potosí, C Mexico 21°38′N 98°39′W
77 R13 **Tansarga** E Burkina 11°51′N 01°51′E
167 T13 **Tan Son Nhat** ✈ (Hô Chi Minh) Tây Ninh, S Vietnam 10°52′N 106°38′E
75 V8 **Ţanţā** *var.* Tanta, Tantā, Tantâ. N Egypt 30°42′N 31°00′E
74 D9 **Tan-Tan** SW Morocco 28°30′N 11°11′W
41 P12 **Tantoyuca** Veracruz-Llave, E Mexico 21°21′N 98°12′W
152 J12 **Tāntpur** Uttar Pradesh, N India 26°51′N 77°29′E
Tan-tung *see* Dandong
38 M12 **Tanunak** Alaska, USA 60°35′N 165°15′W
166 L5 **Ta-nyaung** Magway, W Myanmar (Burma) 20°49′N 94°40′E
167 S5 **Tân Yên** Tuyên Quang, N Vietnam 22°08′N 104°58′E
81 F22 **Tanzania** *off.* United Republic of Tanzania, *Swa.* Jamhuri ya Muungano wa Tanzania; *prev.* German East Africa, Tanganyika and Zanzibar. ◆ *republic* E Africa
Tanzania, Jamhuri ya Muungano wa *see* Tanzania
Tanzania, United Republic of *see* Tanzania
Tao'an *see* Taonan
163 T8 **Tao'er He** 〰 NE China
159 U11 **Tao He** 〰 C China
163 U9 **Taonan** *var.* Tao'an. Jilin, NE China 45°20′N 122°46′E
T'aon-an *see* Baicheng
Taongi *see* Bokaak Atoll
107 M23 **Taormina** *anc.* Tauromenium. Sicilia, Italy, C Mediterranean Sea 37°54′N 15°18′E
37 S9 **Taos** New Mexico, SW USA 36°24′N 105°35′W
Taoudenit *see* Taoudenni
77 O6 **Taoudenni** *var.* Taoudenit. Tombouctou, N Mali 22°46′N 03°54′W
74 G6 **Taounate** N Morocco 34°33′N 04°39′N
Taoyang *see* Lintao
161 S13 **Taoyuan** *Jap.* Tōen; *prev.* T'aoyüan. N Taiwan 25°00′N 121°15′E
118 I3 **Tapa** *Ger.* Taps. Lääne-Virumaa, NE Estonia 59°15′N 26°E
41 V17 **Tapachula** Chiapas, SE Mexico 14°53′N 92°18′W
Tapaiu *see* Gvardeysk
59 H14 **Tapajós, Rio** *var.* Tapajóz. 〰 NW Brazil
Tapajóz *see* Tapajós, Rio
61 C21 **Tapalqué** *var.* Tapalquén. Buenos Aires, E Argentina 36°21′S 60°01′W
Tapalquén *see* Tapalqué
Tapanahoni *see* Tapanahony Rivier
55 W11 **Tapanahony Rivier** *var.* Tapanahoni. 〰 E Suriname
41 T16 **Tapanatepec** *var.* San Pedro Tapanatepec. Oaxaca, SE Mexico 16°23′N 94°09′W
185 D23 **Tapanui** Otago, South Island, New Zealand 45°55′S 169°16′E
59 E14 **Tapauá** Amazonas, N Brazil 05°42′S 64°15′W
47 R7 **Tapauá, Rio** 〰 W Brazil
185 I14 **Tapawera** Tasman, South Island, New Zealand 41°24′S 172°50′E
61 I16 **Tapes** Rio Grande do Sul, S Brazil 30°40′S 51°25′W
76 K16 **Tapeta** C Liberia 06°36′N 08°52′W
154 H11 **Tāpi** *prev.* Tāpti. 〰 W India
104 J2 **Tapia de Casariego** Asturias, N Spain 43°34′N 06°56′W
56 F10 **Tapiche, Río** 〰 N Peru
167 N15 **Tapi, Mae Nam** *var.* Luang. 〰 SW Thailand
186 E8 **Tapini** Central, S Papua New Guinea 08°16′S 146°09′E
Tapirapecó, Serra *see* Tapirapecó, Sierra
55 N13 **Tapirapecó, Sierra** *Port.* Serra Tapirapecó. ▲▲ Brazil/Venezuela
77 R13 **Tapoa** 〰 Benin/Niger
188 H5 **Tapochau, Mount** ▲ Saipan, S Northern Mariana Islands
111 H24 **Tapolca** Veszprém, W Hungary 46°54′N 17°29′E
21 X5 **Tappahannock** Virginia, NE USA 37°55′N 76°54′W
31 U13 **Tappan Lake** ⊠ Ohio, N USA
165 Q6 **Tappi-zaki** *headland* Honshū, C Japan 41°15′N 140°19′E
Taps *see* Tapa
Tāpti *see* Tāpi
Tapuaemanu *see* Maiao
185 J16 **Tapuaenuku** ▲ South Island, New Zealand 42°00′S 173°39′E
171 N8 **Tapul Group** *island group* Sulu Archipelago, SW Philippines
58 E11 **Tapurmcuará** *var.* Tapuruquara. Amazonas, NW Brazil 0°17′S 65°00′W
Tapuruquara *see* Tapurmcuará
192 J17 **Taputapu, Cape** *headland* Tutuila, W American Samoa 14°20′S 170°51′W
141 W13 **Ţāqah** S Oman 17°02′N 54°23′E
139 T3 **Taqtaq** Arbīl, N Iraq 35°54′N 44°36′E
61 J15 **Taquara** Rio Grande do Sul, S Brazil 29°36′S 50°46′W
59 H19 **Taquari, Rio** 〰 C Brazil
60 L8 **Taquaritinga** São Paulo, S Brazil 21°22′S 48°29′W
122 I11 **Tara** Omskaya Oblast', C Russian Federation 56°54′N 74°17′E
83 I16 **Tara** Southern, S Zambia 16°56′S 26°50′E
113 J15 **Tara** 〰 Montenegro
112 K13 **Tara** ▲▲ W Serbia
77 W15 **Taraba** ◈ *state* E Nigeria
77 X15 **Taraba** 〰 E Nigeria
75 O7 **Ţarābulus** *var.* Ţarābulus al Gharb, *Eng.* Tripoli. ● (Libya) NW Libya 32°54′N 13°11′E
75 O7 **Tarābulus** ✈ NW Libya 32°37′N 13°07′E
Ţarābulus al Gharb *see* Ţarābulus
Tarābulus/Ţarābulus ash Shām *see* Tripoli
105 O7 **Taracena** Castilla-La Mancha, C Spain 40°39′N 03°08′W
117 N12 **Taraclia** *Rus.* Tarakilya. S Moldova 45°55′N 28°40′E
139 V10 **Tarād al Kahf** Dhī Qār, SE Iraq 31°58′N 45°58′E
183 R10 **Tarago** New South Wales, SE Australia 35°04′S 149°40′E
162 J8 **Taragt** *var.* Hüremt. Övörhangay, C Mongolia 46°18′N 102°27′E
169 V8 **Tarakan** Borneo, C Indonesia 03°20′N 117°38′E
169 V9 **Tarakan, Pulau** *island* N Indonesia
Tarakilya *see* Taraclia
165 P16 **Tarama-jima** *island* Sakishima-shotō, SW Japan
184 K10 **Taranaki** *off.* Taranaki Region. ◈ *region* North Island, New Zealand
184 K10 **Taranaki, Mount** *var.* Egmont. 🌋 North Island, New Zealand 39°16′S 174°04′E
Taranaki Region *see* Taranaki
105 O9 **Tarancón** Castilla-La Mancha, C Spain 40°01′N 03°01′W
188 M15 **Tarang Reef** *reef* C Micronesia
96 E7 **Taransay** *island* NW Scotland, United Kingdom
107 P18 **Taranto** *var.* Tarentum. Puglia, SE Italy 40°30′N 17°11′E
107 O19 **Taranto, Golfo di** *Eng.* Gulf of Taranto. *gulf* S Italy
Taranto, Gulf of *see* Taranto, Golfo di
62 G3 **Tarapacá** *off.* Región de Tarapacá. ◈ *region* N Chile
Tarapacá, Región de *see* Tarapacá
187 N9 **Tarapaina** Maramasike Island, N Solomon Islands 09°28′S 161°24′E
56 D10 **Tarapoto** San Martín, N Peru 06°31′S 76°23′W
138 M6 **Ţaraq an Na'jah** *hill range* E Syria
138 M6 **Ţaraq Sidāwī** *hill range* E Syria
103 Q11 **Tarare** Rhône, E France 45°54′N 04°26′E
Tararite de Llitera *see* Tamarite de Litera
184 M13 **Tararua Range** ▲▲ North Island, New Zealand
151 Q22 **Tarāsa Dwīp** *island* Nicobar Islands, India, NE Indian Ocean
103 Q15 **Tarascon** Bouches-du-Rhône, SE France 43°48′N 04°39′E
102 M17 **Tarascon-sur-Ariège** Ariège, S France 42°51′N 01°35′E
117 P6 **Tarashcha** Kyyivs'ka Oblast', N Ukraine 49°34′N 30°31′E
57 L18 **Tarata** Cochabamba, C Bolivia 17°35′S 66°04′W
57 I18 **Tarata** Tacna, SW Peru 17°30′S 70°00′W
190 H2 **Taratai** *atoll* Tungaru, W Kiribati
59 B15 **Tarauacá** Acre, W Brazil 08°06′S 70°45′W
59 B15 **Tarauacá, Rio** 〰 NW Brazil
191 Q8 **Taravao** Tahiti, W French Polynesia 17°44′S 149°19′W
191 R8 **Taravao, Baie de** *bay* Tahiti, W French Polynesia
191 Q8 **Taravao, Isthme de** *isthmus* Tahiti, W French Polynesia
103 X16 **Taravo** 〰 Corse, France, C Mediterranean Sea
190 J3 **Tarawa** ✈ Tarawa, W Kiribati 0°53′S 169°32′E
190 H2 **Tarawa** *atoll* Tungaru, W Kiribati
184 N10 **Tarawera** Hawke's Bay, North Island, New Zealand 39°03′S 176°34′E
184 N8 **Tarawera, Lake** ◎ North Island, New Zealand
184 N8 **Tarawera, Mount** ▲ North Island, New Zealand 38°13′S 176°29′E
105 S8 **Tarayuela** ▲ N Spain 40°28′N 00°22′W
145 R16 **Taraz** *prev.* Aulie Ata, Auliye-Ata, Dzhambul, Zhambyl. Zhambyl, S Kazakhstan 42°55′N 71°27′E
105 Q5 **Tarazona** Aragón, NE Spain 41°54′N 01°44′W
105 Q10 **Tarazona de la Mancha** Castilla-La Mancha, C Spain 39°16′N 01°55′W
145 X12 **Tarbagatay, Khrebet** ▲▲ China/Kazakhstan
96 J8 **Tarbat Ness** *headland* N Scotland, United Kingdom 57°51′N 03°48′W
149 U5 **Tarbela Reservoir** ⊠ N Pakistan
96 H12 **Tarbert** W Scotland, United Kingdom 55°52′N 05°26′W
96 F7 **Tarbert** NW Scotland, United Kingdom 57°54′N 06°48′W
102 K16 **Tarbes** *anc.* Bigorra. Hautes-Pyrénées, S France 43°14′N 00°04′E
21 W9 **Tarboro** North Carolina, SE USA 35°54′N 77°34′W
Tarca *see* Torysa
106 J6 **Tarcento** Friuli-Venezia Giulia, NE Italy 46°13′N 13°13′E
182 F5 **Tarcoola** South Australia 30°44′S 134°34′E
105 S5 **Tardienta** Aragón, NE Spain 41°58′N 00°31′W
102 L11 **Tardoire** 〰 W France
183 U7 **Taree** New South Wales, SE Australia 31°56′S 152°29′E
92 K12 **Tärendö** *Lapp.* Deargget. Norrbotten, N Sweden 67°10′N 22°40′E
Tarentum *see* Taranto
74 C9 **Tarfaya** SW Morocco 27°56′N 12°55′W
116 J13 **Târgovişte** *prev.* Tîrgovişte. Dâmboviţa, S Romania 44°54′N 25°29′E
Tărgovište *see* Tŭrgovishte
116 M12 **Târgu Bujor** *prev.* Tîrgu Bujor. Galaţi, E Romania 45°52′N 27°55′E
116 H13 **Târgu Cărbuneşti** *prev.* Tîrgu. Gorj, SW Romania 44°57′N 23°32′E
116 L9 **Târgu Frumos** *prev.* Tîrgu Frumos. Iaşi, NE Romania 47°12′N 27°00′E
116 H13 **Targu Jiu** *prev.* Tîrgu Jiu. Gorj, W Romania 45°03′N 23°20′E
116 H9 **Târgu Lăpuş** *prev.* Tîrgu Lăpuş. Maramureş, N Romania 47°28′N 23°54′E
Târgul-Neamţ *see* Târgu-Neamţ
Târgul-Săcuiesc *see* Târgu Secuiesc
116 I10 **Târgu Mureş** *prev.* Oşorhei, Tîrgu Mures, *Ger.* Neumarkt, *Hung.* Marosvásárhely. Mureş, C Romania 46°33′N 24°36′E
116 K9 **Târgu-Neamţ** *var.* Târgul-Neamţ; *prev.* Tîrgu-Neamţ. Neamţ, NE Romania 47°12′N 26°25′E
116 K11 **Târgu Ocna** *Hung.* Aknavásár; *prev.* Tîrgu Ocna. Bacău, E Romania 46°17′N 26°37′E
116 K11 **Târgu Secuiesc** *Ger.* Neumarkt, Szekler Neumarkt, *Hung.* Kezdivásárhely; *prev.* Chezdi-Oşorheiu, Târgul-Săcuiesc, Tîrgu Secuiesc. Covasna, E Romania 46°00′N 26°08′E
145 X10 **Targyn** Vostochnyy Kazakhstan, E Kazakhstan 49°32′N 82°47′E
Tar Heel State *see* North Carolina
186 C7 **Tari** Southern Highlands, W Papua New Guinea 05°52′S 142°58′E
162 J6 **Tarialan** *var.* Badrah. Hövsgöl, N Mongolia 49°33′N 101°58′E
162 I7 **Tariat** *var.* Horgo. Arhangay, C Mongolia 48°06′N 99°52′E
143 P17 **Ţarīf** Abū Ẓaby, C United Arab Emirates 24°02′N 53°47′E
104 K16 **Tarifa** Andalucía, S Spain 36°01′N 05°36′W
84 C14 **Tarifa, Punta de** *headland* SW Spain 36°01′N 05°39′W
57 M21 **Tarija** Tarija, S Bolivia 21°33′S 64°42′W
57 M21 **Tarija** ◈ *department* S Bolivia
141 R14 **Tarīm** C Yemen 16°N 48°50′E
Tarim Basin *see* Tarim Pendi

◆ Country
● Country Capital
◇ Dependent Territory
○ Dependent Territory Capital
◈ Administrative Regions
✈ International Airport
▲ Mountain
▲▲ Mountain Range
🌋 Volcano
〰 River
◎ Lake
⊠ Reservoir

81 G19 **Tarime** Mara, N Tanzania 01°20′S 34°24′E
129 S8 **Tarim He** ≈ NW China
159 H8 **Tarim Pendi** *Eng.* Tarim Basin. *basin* NW China
149 N7 **Tarīn Kōt** *var.* Terinkot; *prev.* Tarīn Kowt. Uruzgān, C Afghanistan 32°38′N 65°52′E
Tarīn Kowt *see* Tarīn Kōt
171 O12 **Taripa** Sulawesi, C Indonesia 01°51′S 120°46′E
117 Q12 **Tarkhankut, Mys** *headland* S Ukraine 45°20′N 32°32′E
27 Q1 **Tarkio** Missouri, C USA 40°25′N 95°24′W
122 J9 **Tarko-Sale** Yamalo-Nenetskiy Avtonomnyy Okrug, N Russian Federation 64°55′N 77°34′E
77 P17 **Tarkwa** S Ghana 05°16′N 01°59′W
171 O3 **Tarlac** Luzon, N Philippines 15°29′N 120°34′E
95 F22 **Tarm** Midtjylland, W Denmark 55°55′N 08°32′E
57 E14 **Tarma** Junín, C Peru 11°28′S 75°41′W
103 N15 **Tarn** ◆ *department* S France
102 M15 **Tarn** ≈ S France
111 L22 **Tarna** ≈ C Hungary
92 G13 **Tärnaby** Västerbotten, N Sweden 65°44′N 15°20′E
149 P8 **Tarnak Rūd** ≈ SE Afghanistan
116 J11 **Târnava Mare** *Ger.* Grosse Kokel, *Hung.* Nagy-Küküllő; *prev.* Tîrnava Mare. ≈ S Romania
116 I11 **Târnava Mică** *Ger.* Kleine Kokel, *Hung.* Kis-Küküllo; *prev.* Tîrnava Mică. ≈ C Romania
116 I11 **Târnăveni** *Ger.* Marteskirch, Martinskirch, *Hung.* Dicsőszentmárton; *prev.* Sînmartin, Tîrnăveni. Mureş, C Romania 46°20′N 24°17′E
102 L14 **Tarn-et-Garonne** ◆ *department* S France
111 P18 **Tarnica** ▲ SE Poland 49°05′N 22°43′E
111 N15 **Tarnobrzeg** Podkarpackie, SE Poland 50°35′N 21°40′E
125 N12 **Tarnogskiy Gorodok** Vologodskaya Oblast', NW Russian Federation 60°28′N 43°45′E
Tarnopol *see* Ternopil'
111 M16 **Tarnów** Małopolskie, S Poland 50°01′N 20°59′E
Tarnowice/Tarnowitz *see* Tarnowskie Góry
111 J16 **Tarnowskie Góry** *var.* Tarnowice, Tarnowskie Gory, *Ger.* Tarnowitz. Śląskie, S Poland 50°27′N 18°52′E
95 N14 **Tärnsjö** Västmanland, C Sweden 60°10′N 16°57′E
186 K7 **Taro** Choiseul, NW Solomon Islands 07°00′S 156°57′E
106 E9 **Taro** ≈ NW Italy
186 I6 **Taron** New Ireland, NE Papua New Guinea 04°22′S 153°04′E
74 E8 **Taroudannt** *var.* Taroudant. SW Morocco 30°31′N 08°50′W
Taroudant *see* Taroudannt
23 V12 **Tarpon, Lake** ◎ Florida, SE USA
23 V12 **Tarpon Springs** Florida, SE USA 28°09′N 82°45′W
107 G14 **Tarquinia** *anc.* Tarquinii, *hist.* Corneto. Lazio, C Italy 42°23′N 11°45′E
Tarquinii *see* Tarquinia
Tarraco *see* Tarragona
76 D10 **Tarrafal** Santiago, S Cape Verde 15°16′N 23°45′W
105 V6 **Tarragona** *anc.* Tarraco. Cataluña, E Spain 41°07′N 01°15′E
105 T7 **Tarragona** ◆ *province* Cataluña, NE Spain
183 O17 **Tarraleah** Tasmania, SE Australia 42°11′S 146°29′E
23 P3 **Tarrant City** Alabama, S USA 33°34′N 86°45′W
185 D21 **Tarras** Otago, South Island, New Zealand 44°48′S 169°25′E
Tarrasa *see* Terrassa
105 U5 **Tàrrega** *var.* Tarrega. Cataluña, NE Spain 41°39′N 01°09′E
21 W9 **Tar River** ≈ North Carolina, SE USA
Tarsatica *see* Rijeka
136 J17 **Tarsus** İçel, S Turkey 36°52′N 34°52′E
62 K4 **Tartagal** Salta, N Argentina 22°32′S 63°50′W
137 V12 **Tärtär** *Rus.* Terter. ≈ SW Azerbaijan
102 J15 **Tartas** Landes, SW France 43°52′N 00°45′W
Tartlau *see* Prejmer
Tartous/Tartouss *see* Ţarţūs
118 J5 **Tartu** *Ger.* Dorpat; *prev. Rus.* Yurev, Yury'ev. Tartumaa, SE Estonia 58°20′N 26°44′E
118 I5 **Tartumaa** *off.* Tartu Maakond. ◆ *province* E Estonia
Tartu Maakond *see* Tartumaa
138 H5 **Ţarţūs** *Fr.* Tartouss; *anc.* Tortosa. Ţarţūs, W Syria 34°55′N 35°52′E
138 H5 **Ţarţūs** *off.* Muḩāfaẓat Ţarţūs, *var.* Tartous, Tartus. ◆ *governorate* W Syria
Ţarţūs, Muḩāfaẓat *see* Ţarţūs
164 C16 **Tarumizu** Kagoshima, Kyūshū, SW Japan 31°30′N 130°40′E
126 K4 **Tarusa** Kaluzhskaya Oblast', W Russian Federation 54°45′N 37°10′E
117 N11 **Tarutyne** Odes'ka Oblast', SW Ukraine 46°11′N 29°09′E
162 I7 **Tarvagatyn Nuruu** ▲▲ N Mongolia
106 J6 **Tarvisio** Friuli-Venezia Giulia, NE Italy 46°31′N 13°33′E
Tarvisium *see* Treviso
57 O16 **Tarvo, Río** ≈ E Bolivia
14 G8 **Tarzwell** Ontario, S Canada 48°00′N 79°58′W
40 K5 **Tasajera, Sierra de la** ▲▲ N Mexico
145 S13 **Tasaral** Karaganda, C Kazakhstan 46°17′N 73°54′E
145 N15 **Tasboget** *Kaz.* Tasböget; *prev.* Tasbuget. Kzylorda, S Kazakhstan 44°46′N 65°38′E
Tasböget *see* Tasboget
Tasbuget *see* Tasboget
108 E11 **Tasch** Valais, SW Switzerland 46°04′N 07°43′E
Tasek Kenyir *see* Kenyir, Tasik
122 J14 **Tashanta** Respublika Altay, S Russian Federation 49°42′N 89°15′E
Tashauz *see* Daşoguz
Tashi Chho Dzong *see* Thimphu
153 U11 **Tashigang** E Bhutan 27°19′N 91°33′E
137 T11 **Tashir** *prev.* Kalinino. N Armenia 41°07′N 44°16′E
143 Q11 **Ţashk, Daryācheh-ye** ◎ C Iran
Tashkent *see* Toshkent
Tashkentskaya Oblast' *see* Toshkent Viloyati
Tashkepri *see* Daşköpri
Tash-Kömür *see* Tash-Kumyr
147 S9 **Tash-Kumyr** *Kir.* Tash-Kömür. Dzhalal-Abadskaya Oblast', W Kyrgyzstan 41°22′N 72°09′E
127 T7 **Tashla** Orenburgskaya Oblast', W Russian Federation 51°42′N 52°33′E
Tashqurghan *see* Khulm
122 J13 **Tashtagol** Kemerovskaya Oblast', S Russian Federation 52°49′N 88°00′E
95 H24 **Tåsinge** *island* C Denmark
12 M5 **Tasiujaq** Québec, E Canada 58°43′N 69°58′W
144 F8 **Taskala** *prev.* Kamenka. Zapadnyy Kazakhstan, NW Kazakhstan 51°06′N 51°16′E
77 W11 **Tasker** Zinder, C Niger 15°06′N 10°42′E
145 W12 **Taskesken** Vostochnyy Kazakhstan, E Kazakhstan 47°15′N 80°45′E
136 J10 **Taşköprü** Kastamonu, N Turkey 41°30′N 34°12′E
Taskuduk, Peski *see* Tosquduq Qumlari
186 G5 **Taskul** New Ireland, NE Papua New Guinea 02°34′S 150°25′E
137 S13 **Taşlıçay** Ağrı, E Turkey 39°37′N 43°23′E
185 H14 **Tasman** *off.* Tasman District. ◆ *unitary authority* South Island, New Zealand
192 J12 **Tasman Basin** *var.* East Australian Basin. *undersea feature* S Tasman Sea
185 I14 **Tasman Bay** *inlet* South Island, New Zealand
Tasman District *see* Tasman
192 I13 **Tasman Fracture Zone** *tectonic feature* S Indian Ocean
185 E19 **Tasman Glacier** *glacier* South Island, New Zealand
Tasman Group *see* Nukumanu Islands
183 N15 **Tasmania** *prev.* Van Diemen's Land. ◆ *state* SE Australia
183 Q16 **Tasmania** *island* SE Australia
185 H14 **Tasman Mountains** ▲▲ South Island, New Zealand
183 P17 **Tasman Peninsula** *peninsula* Tasmania, SE Australia
192 I11 **Tasman Plain** *undersea feature* W Tasman Sea
192 I12 **Tasman Plateau** *var.* South Tasmania Plateau. *undersea feature* SW Tasman Sea
192 I11 **Tasman Sea** *sea* SW Pacific Ocean
116 G9 **Tăşnad** *Ger.* Trestenberg, Trestendorf, *Hung.* Tasnád. Satu Mare, NW Romania 47°30′N 22°33′E
136 L11 **Taşova** Amasya, N Turkey 40°45′N 36°20′E
77 T10 **Tassara** Tahoua, W Niger 16°40′N 05°34′E
12 K4 **Tassialouc, Lac** ◎ Québec, C Canada
Tassili du Hoggar *see* Tassili Ta-n-Ahaggar
74 L11 **Tassili-n-Ajjer** *plateau* E Algeria
74 K14 **Tassili Ta-n-Ahaggar** *var.* Tassili du Hoggar, Tassili ta-n-Ahaggar. *plateau* S Algeria
Tassili ta-n-Ahaggar *see* Tassili Ta-n-Ahaggar
59 M15 **Tasso Fragoso** Maranhão, E Brazil 08°22′S 45°53′W
Tåstrup *see* Taastrup
145 O9 **Tasty-Taldy** Akmola, C Kazakhstan 50°47′N 66°31′E
143 W10 **Tāsūkī** Sīstān va Balūchestān, SE Iran
111 I22 **Tata** *Ger.* Totis. Komárom-Esztergom, NW Hungary 47°39′N 18°19′E
74 E8 **Tata** SW Morocco 29°38′N 08°04′W
Tataaihoa, Pointe *see* Vénus, Pointe
111 I22 **Tatabánya** Komárom-Esztergom, NW Hungary 47°33′N 18°23′E
191 X10 **Tatakoto** *atoll* Îles Tuamotu, E French Polynesia
75 N7 **Tataouine** *var.* Taṭāwīn. SE Tunisia 32°48′N 10°27′E
55 O5 **Tataracual, Cerro** ▲ NE Venezuela 10°13′N 64°20′W
117 O12 **Tatarbunary** Odes'ka Oblast', SW Ukraine 45°50′N 29°37′E
119 M17 **Tatarka** Mahilyowskaya Voblasts', E Belarus 53°15′N 28°50′E
Tatar Pazardzhik *see* Pazardzhik
122 I12 **Tatarsk** Novosibirskaya Oblast', C Russian Federation 55°08′N 75°58′E
Tatarskaya ASSR *see* Tatarstan, Respublika
123 T13 **Tatarskiy Proliv** *Eng.* Tatar Strait. *strait* SE Russian Federation
127 R4 **Tatarstan, Respublika** *prev.* Tatarskaya ASSR. ◆ *autonomous republic* W Russian Federation
Tatar Strait *see* Tatarskiy Proliv
Taṭāwīn *see* Tataouine
171 N12 **Tate** Sulawesi, N Indonesia 0°12′S 119°44′E
141 N11 **Tathlīth** 'Asīr, S Saudi Arabia 19°38′N 43°32′E
141 O11 **Tathlīth, Wādī** *dry watercourse* S Saudi Arabia
183 R11 **Tathra** New South Wales, SE Australia 36°46′S 149°58′E
127 P8 **Tatishchevo** Saratovskaya Oblast', W Russian Federation 51°43′N 45°35′E
39 S12 **Tatitlek** Alaska, USA 60°49′N 146°29′W
10 L15 **Tatla Lake** British Columbia, SW Canada 51°54′N 124°39′W
121 Q2 **Tatlısu** *Gk.* Akanthoú. N Cyprus 35°21′N 33°45′E
11 Z10 **Tatnam, Cape** *headland* Manitoba, C Canada 57°16′N 91°03′W
111 K18 **Tatra Mountains** *Ger.* Tatra, *Hung.* Tátra, *Pol./Slvk.* Tatry. ▲▲ Poland/Slovakia
Tatra/Tátra *see* Tatra Mountains
Tatry *see* Tatra Mountains
164 I13 **Tatsuno** *var.* Tatuno. Hyōgo, Honshū, SW Japan 34°54′N 134°30′E
Tatti *see* Tatty
145 S16 **Tatty** *prev.* Tatti. Zhambyl, S Kazakhstan 43°11′N 73°22′E
60 L10 **Tatuí** São Paulo, S Brazil 23°21′S 47°49′W
37 V14 **Tatum** New Mexico, SW USA 33°15′N 103°19′W
25 X7 **Tatum** Texas, SW USA 32°19′N 94°31′W
Ta-t'ung/Tatung *see* Datong
Tatuno *see* Tatsuno
137 R14 **Tatvan** Bitlis, SE Turkey 38°31′N 42°15′E
95 C16 **Tau** Rogaland, S Norway 59°04′N 05°55′E
192 L17 **Ta'ū** *var.* Tau. *island* Manua Islands, E American Samoa
193 W15 **Tau** *island* Tongatapu Group, N Tonga
59 O14 **Tauá** Ceará, E Brazil 06°04′S 40°26′W
60 N10 **Taubaté** São Paulo, S Brazil 23°S 45°36′W
101 I19 **Tauber** ≈ SW Germany
101 I19 **Tauberbiscofsheim** Baden-Württemberg, C Germany 49°37′N 09°39′E
Tauchik *see* Taushyk
191 W10 **Tauere** *atoll* Îles Tuamotu, C French Polynesia
101 H17 **Taufstein** ▲ C Germany 50°31′N 09°18′E
190 I17 **Taukoka** *island* SE Cook Islands
145 T15 **Taukum, Peski** *desert* SE Kazakhstan
184 L10 **Taumarunui** Manawatu-Wanganui, North Island, New Zealand 38°52′S 175°14′E
59 A15 **Taumaturgo** Acre, W Brazil 08°54′S 72°48′W
27 X6 **Taum Sauk Mountain** ▲ Missouri, C USA 37°34′N 90°43′W
83 H22 **Taung** North-West, N South Africa 27°32′S 24°48′E
166 L6 **Taungdwingyi** Magway, C Myanmar (Burma) 20°01′N 95°20′E
166 M6 **Taunggyi** Shan State, C Myanmar (Burma) 20°47′N 97°00′E
166 M7 **Taungoo** Bago, C Myanmar (Burma) 18°57′N 96°26′E
166 L5 **Taungtha** Mandalay, C Myanmar (Burma) 21°16′N 95°25′E
Taungup *see* Toungup
149 S9 **Taunsa** Punjab, E Pakistan 30°43′N 70°41′E
97 K23 **Taunton** SW England, United Kingdom 51°01′N 03°06′W
19 O12 **Taunton** Massachusetts, NE USA 41°54′N 71°03′W
101 F18 **Taunus** ▲▲ W Germany
101 G18 **Taunusstein** Hessen, W Germany 50°09′N 08°09′E
184 N9 **Taupo** Waikato, North Island, New Zealand 38°42′S 176°05′E
184 M9 **Taupo, Lake** ◎ North Island, New Zealand
109 R8 **Taurach** *var.* Taurachbach. ≈ E Austria
Taurachbach *see* Taurach
118 D12 **Tauragė** *Ger.* Tauroggen. Tauragė, SW Lithuania 55°16′N 22°17′E
118 D13 **Tauragė** ◆ *province* Lithuania
54 G10 **Tauramena** Casanare, C Colombia 05°02′N 72°43′W
184 N7 **Tauranga** Bay of Plenty, North Island, New Zealand 37°42′S 176°09′E
15 O10 **Taureau, Réservoir** ⊠ Québec, SE Canada
107 N22 **Taurianova** Calabria, SW Italy 38°22′N 16°01′E
Tauris *see* Tabrīz
184 I2 **Tauroa Point** *headland* North Island, New Zealand 35°09′S 173°02′E
Tauroggen *see* Tauragė
Tauromenium *see* Taormina
Taurus Mountains *see* Toros Dağları
Taus *see* Domažlice
144 E14 **Taushyk** *Kaz.* Taūshyq; *prev.* Tauchik. Mangistau, SW Kazakhstan 44°17′N 51°22′E
Taūshyq *see* Taushyk
105 R5 **Tauste** Aragón, NE Spain 41°55′N 01°15′W
191 V16 **Tautara, Motu** *island* Easter Island, Chile, E Pacific Ocean
191 R8 **Tautira** Tahiti, W French Polynesia 17°45′S 149°10′W
Tauz *see* Tovuz
Ţavālesh, Kūhhā-ye *see* Talish Mountains
136 D15 **Tavas** Denizli, SW Turkey 37°33′N 29°04′E
Tavastehus *see* Hämeenlinna
Tavau *see* Davos
122 G10 **Tavda** Sverdlovskaya Oblast', C Russian Federation 58°01′N 65°07′E
122 G10 **Tavda** ≈ C Russian Federation
105 T11 **Tavernes de la Valldigna** Valenciana, E Spain 39°03′N 00°13′W
81 I20 **Taveta** Coast, S Kenya 03°23′S 37°40′E
187 Y14 **Taveuni** *island* N Fiji
147 R13 **Tavildara** *Rus.* Tavil'dara, Tovil'-Dora. C Tajikistan 38°42′N 70°27′E
Tavin *see* Adaatsag
104 H14 **Tavira** Faro, S Portugal 37°07′N 07°39′W
97 I24 **Tavistock** SW England, United Kingdom 50°33′N 04°08′W
Tavoy *see* Dawei
Tavoy Island *see* Mali Kyun
115 E16 **Tavropoú, Techníti Límni** ⊠ C Greece
136 E13 **Tavşanlı** Kütahya, NW Turkey 39°34′N 29°28′E
187 X14 **Tavua** Viti Levu, W Fiji 17°27′S 177°51′E
97 J23 **Taw** ≈ SW England, United Kingdom
185 L14 **Tawa** Wellington, North Island, New Zealand 41°10′S 174°50′E
25 V6 **Tawakoni, Lake** ⊠ Texas, SW USA
153 V11 **Tawang** Arunāchal Pradesh, NE India 27°34′N 91°54′E
169 R17 **Tawang, Teluk** *bay* Jawa, S Indonesia
31 R7 **Tawas Bay** ◎ Michigan, N USA
31 R7 **Tawas City** Michigan, N USA 44°16′N 83°33′W
169 V8 **Tawau** Sabah, East Malaysia 04°16′N 117°54′E
141 U10 **Ţawīl, Qalamat aţ** *well* SE Saudi Arabia
171 N9 **Tawitawi** *island* Tawitawi Group, SW Philippines
Ţawkar *see* Tokar
Tāwūq *see* Dāqūq
Tawzar *see* Tozeur
41 O15 **Taxco** *var.* Taxco de Alarcón. Guerrero, S Mexico 18°32′N 99°37′W
Taxco de Alarcón *see* Taxco
146 H8 **Taxiatosh** *Rus.* Takhiatash. Qoraqalpog'iston Respublikasi, W Uzbekistan 42°27′N 59°27′E
158 D9 **Taxkorgan** *var.* Taxkorgan Tajik Zizhixian. Xinjiang Uygur Zizhiqu, NW China 37°43′N 75°13′E
Taxkorgan Tajik Zizhixian *see* Taxkorgan
146 H7 **Taxtako'pir** *Rus.* Takhtakupyr. Qoraqalpog'iston Respublikasi, NW Uzbekistan 43°04′N 60°23′E
96 J10 **Tay** ≈ C Scotland, United Kingdom
143 V6 **Tāybād** *var.* Taibad, Tāyybād, Tayyebāt. Khorāsān-Razavī, NE Iran 34°48′N 60°46′E
Taybert at Turkz *see* Ţayyibat at Turkī
124 J3 **Taybola** Murmanskaya Oblast', NW Russian Federation 68°30′N 33°18′E
81 M16 **Tayeeglow** Bakool, C Somalia 04°01′N 44°25′E
96 K11 **Tay, Firth of** *inlet* E Scotland, United Kingdom
122 J12 **Tayga** Kemerovskaya Oblast', S Russian Federation 56°02′N 85°26′E
Taygan *see* Delger
123 T9 **Taygonos, Mys** *headland* E Russian Federation 60°36′N 160°09′E
96 I11 **Tay, Loch** ◎ C Scotland, United Kingdom
11 N12 **Taylor** British Columbia, W Canada 56°09′N 120°43′W
29 O14 **Taylor** Nebraska, C USA 41°47′N 99°23′W
18 I13 **Taylor** Pennsylvania, NE USA 41°22′N 75°41′W
25 T10 **Taylor** Texas, SW USA 30°34′N 97°24′W
37 Q11 **Taylor, Mount** ▲ New Mexico, SW USA 35°14′N 107°36′W
37 R5 **Taylor Park Reservoir** ⊠ Colorado, C USA
37 R6 **Taylor River** ≈ Colorado, C USA
21 P11 **Taylors** South Carolina, SE USA 34°55′N 82°18′W
20 L5 **Taylorsville** Kentucky, S USA 38°01′N 85°21′W
21 R6 **Taylorsville** North Carolina, SE USA 35°56′N 81°10′W
30 L14 **Taylorville** Illinois, N USA 39°33′N 89°17′W
140 K5 **Taymā'** Tabūk, NW Saudi Arabia 27°39′N 38°32′E
122 M10 **Taymura** ≈ C Russian Federation
123 O7 **Taymylyr** Respublika Sakha (Yakutiya), NE Russian Federation 72°32′N 121°54′E
122 L7 **Taymyr, Ozero** ◎ N Russian Federation
122 M6 **Taymyr, Poluostrov** *peninsula* N Russian Federation
122 L8 **Taymyrskiy (Dolgano-Nenetskiy) Avtonomnyy Okrug** ◆ *autonomous district* Krasnoyarskiy Kray, N Russian Federation
167 S13 **Tây Ninh** Tây Ninh, S Vietnam 11°21′N 106°07′E
122 L12 **Tayshet** Irkutskaya Oblast', S Russian Federation 55°51′N 98°04′E
162 G8 **Tayshir** *var.* Tsagaan-Olom. Govĭ-Altay, C Mongolia 46°42′N 96°30′E
171 N5 **Taytay** Palawan, W Philippines 10°49′N 119°30′E
169 Q16 **Tayu** *prev.* Tajoe. Jawa, C Indonesia 06°32′S 111°02′E
Tāyybād/Tayyebāt *see* Tāybād
138 L5 **Ţayyibah** *var.* At Taybé. Ḩimş, C Syria 35°13′N 38°51′E
138 I4 **Ţayyibat at Turkī** *var.* Taybert at Turkz. Ḩamāh, W Syria 35°16′N 36°55′E
145 P7 **Tayynsha** *prev.* Krasnoarmeysk. Severnyy Kazakhstan, N Kazakhstan 53°52′N 69°51′E
122 J10 **Taz** ≈ N Russian Federation
74 G6 **Taza** NE Morocco 34°13′N 04°06′W
139 T4 **Tāza Khurmātū** At Ta'mím, E Iraq 35°18′N 44°22′E
165 Q8 **Tazawa-ko** ◎ Honshū, C Japan
21 N8 **Tazewell** Tennessee, S USA 36°27′N 83°34′W
21 Q7 **Tazewell** Virginia, NE USA 37°08′N 81°34′W
75 S11 **Tāzirbū** SE Libya 25°43′N 21°16′E
39 S11 **Tazlina Lake** ◎ Alaska, USA
122 J8 **Tazovskiy** Yamalo-Nenetskiy Avtonomnyy Okrug, N Russian Federation 67°33′N 78°21′E
137 U10 **Tbilisi** *Eng.* Tiflis. ● (Georgia) SE Georgia 41°41′N 44°55′E
137 T10 **Tbilisi** ✕ S Georgia 41°43′N 44°49′E
79 E14 **Tchabal Mbabo** ▲ NW Cameroon 07°12′N 12°16′E
Tchad *see* Chad
Tchad, Lac *see* Chad, Lake
77 S15 **Tchaourou** E Benin 08°58′N 02°40′E
79 E20 **Tchibanga** Nyanga, S Gabon 02°49′S 11°00′E
Tchien *see* Zwedru
77 Z6 **Tchigaï, Plateau du** ▲▲ NE Niger
77 V9 **Tchighozérine** Agadez, C Niger 17°15′N 07°48′E
77 T10 **Tchin-Tabaradene** Tahoua, W Niger 15°57′N 05°49′E
78 G13 **Tcholliré** Nord, NE Cameroon 08°48′N 14°00′E
Tchongking *see* Chongqing
22 K4 **Tchula** Mississippi, S USA 33°10′N 90°13′W
110 I7 **Tczew** *Ger.* Dirschau. Pomorskie, N Poland 54°05′N 18°46′E
116 I10 **Teaca** *Ger.* Tekendorf, *Hung.* Teke; *prev. Ger.* Teckendorf. Bistriţa-Năsăud, N Romania 46°55′N 24°30′E
40 J11 **Teacapán** Sinaloa, C Mexico 22°33′N 105°44′W
190 A10 **Teafuafou** *island* Funafuti Atoll, C Tuvalu
25 U8 **Teague** Texas, SW USA 31°37′N 96°16′W
191 R9 **Teahupoo** Tahiti, W French Polynesia 17°51′S 149°15′W
190 H15 **Te Aiti Point** *headland* Rarotonga, S Cook Islands 21°11′S 59°47′W
65 D24 **Teal Inlet** East Falkland, Falkland Islands 51°34′S 58°25′W
185 B22 **Te Anau** Southland, South Island, New Zealand 45°25′S 167°45′E
185 B22 **Te Anau, Lake** ◎ South Island, New Zealand
41 U15 **Teapa** Tabasco, SE Mexico 17°36′N 92°57′W
184 Q7 **Te Araroa** Gisborne, North Island, New Zealand 37°37′S 178°21′E
184 M7 **Te Aroha** Waikato, North Island, New Zealand 37°32′S 175°58′E
Teate *see* Chieti
190 A9 **Te Ava Fuagea** *channel* Funafuti Atoll, SE Tuvalu
190 B8 **Te Ava I Te Lape** *channel* Funafuti Atoll, SE Tuvalu
190 B9 **Te Ava Pua Pua** *channel* Funafuti Atoll, SE Tuvalu
184 M8 **Te Awamutu** Waikato, North Island, New Zealand 38°00′S 177°18′E
171 X12 **Teba** Papua, E Indonesia 01°27′S 137°54′E
104 L15 **Teba** Andalucía, S Spain 36°59′N 04°54′W
126 M15 **Teberda** Karachayevo-Cherkesskaya Respublika, SW Russian Federation 43°28′N 41°45′E
74 M6 **Tébessa** NE Algeria 35°21′N 08°06′E
62 O7 **Tebicuary, Río** ≈ S Paraguay
168 L13 **Tebingtinggi** Sumatera, W Indonesia 03°33′S 103°00′E
168 I8 **Tebingtinggi** Sumatera, N Indonesia 03°20′N 99°08′E
Tebingtinggi, Pulau *see* Rantau, Pulau
Tebriz *see* Tabrīz
137 U9 **T'ebulos Mta** *Rus.* Gora Tebulosmta; *prev.* Tebulos Mta. ▲ Georgia/Russian Federation 42°33′N 45°21′E
Tebulos Mta *see* T'ebulos Mta
Tebulosmta, Gora *see* T'ebulos Mta
41 Q14 **Tecamachalco** Puebla, S Mexico 18°52′N 97°44′W
40 B1 **Tecate** Baja California Norte, NW Mexico 32°33′N 116°38′W
136 M13 **Tecer Dağları** ▲▲ C Turkey
103 O17 **Tech** ≈ S France
77 P16 **Techiman** W Ghana 07°35′N 01°56′W
117 N15 **Techirghiol** Constanţa, SE Romania 44°03′N 28°37′E
74 A12 **Techla** *var.* Techlé. SW Western Sahara 21°39′N 14°57′W
Techlé *see* Techla
63 H18 **Tecka, Sierra de** ▲▲ SW Argentina
Teckendorf *see* Teaca
40 K13 **Tecolotlán** Jalisco, SW Mexico 20°10′N 104°07′W
40 K14 **Tecomán** Colima, SW Mexico 18°53′N 103°54′W
35 V12 **Tecopa** California, W USA 35°51′N 116°14′W
40 G5 **Tecoripa** Sonora, NW Mexico 28°38′N 109°58′W
41 N16 **Tecpan** *var.* Tecpan de Galeana. Guerrero, S Mexico 17°12′N 100°39′W
Tecpan de Galeana *see* Tecpan
40 J11 **Tecuala** Nayarit, C Mexico 22°24′N 105°30′W
116 L12 **Tecuci** Galaţi, E Romania 45°50′N 27°27′E
31 R10 **Tecumseh** Michigan, N USA 42°00′N 83°57′W
29 S16 **Tecumseh** Nebraska, C USA 40°22′N 96°12′W
27 O11 **Tecumseh** Oklahoma, C USA 35°15′N 96°56′W
Tedzhen *see* Harīrūd/Tejen
Tedzhen *see* Tejen
146 H15 **Tedzhenstroy** *Turkm.* Tejenstroy. Ahal Welaýaty, S Turkmenistan 36°57′N 60°49′E
Teel *see* Öndör-Ulaan
97 L15 **Tees** ≈ N England, United Kingdom
14 E15 **Teeswater** Ontario, S Canada 44°00′N 81°17′W
190 A10 **Tefala** *island* Funafuti Atoll, C Tuvalu
58 D13 **Tefé** Amazonas, N Brazil 03°24′S 64°45′W
74 K11 **Tefedest** ▲▲ S Algeria
136 E16 **Tefenni** Burdur, SW Turkey 37°19′N 29°45′E
58 D13 **Tefé, Rio** ≈ NW Brazil
169 P16 **Tegal** Jawa, C Indonesia 06°52′S 109°07′E
100 O12 **Tegel** ✕ (Berlin) Berlin, NE Germany 52°33′N 13°16′E
99 M15 **Tegelen** Limburg, SE Netherlands 51°20′N 06°09′E
101 L24 **Tegernsee** ◎ SE Germany
107 M18 **Teggiano** Campania, S Italy 40°25′N 15°28′E
77 U14 **Tegina** Niger, C Nigeria 10°06′N 06°10′E
Tegucigalpa *see* Central District
Tegucigalpa *see* Toncontín
Tegucigalpa *see* Francisco Morazán
77 U9 **Teguidda-n-Tessoumt** Agadez, C Niger 17°27′N 06°40′E
64 Q11 **Teguise** Lanzarote, Islas Canarias, Spain, NE Atlantic Ocean 29°04′N 13°38′W
122 K12 **Tegul'det** Tomskaya Oblast', C Russian Federation 57°16′N 87°58′E
35 S13 **Tehachapi** California, W USA 35°07′N 118°27′W
35 S13 **Tehachapi Mountains** ▲▲ California, W USA
Tehama *see* Tihāmah
Teheran *see* Tehrān
77 O14 **Téhini** NE Ivory Coast 09°36′N 03°40′W
143 N5 **Tehrān** *var.* Teheran. ● (Iran) Tehrān, N Iran 35°44′N 51°27′E
143 N6 **Tehrān** *off.* Ostān-e Tehrān, *var.* Tehran. ◆ *province* N Iran
Tehrān, Ostān-e *see* Tehrān
Tehri *see* Tīkamgarh
Tehri *see* New Tehri
41 Q15 **Tehuacán** Puebla, S Mexico 18°29′N 97°24′W
41 S17 **Tehuantepec** *var.* Santo Domingo Tehuantepec. Oaxaca, SE Mexico 16°18′N 95°14′W
41 S17 **Tehuantepec, Golfo de** *var.* Gulf of Tehuantepec. *gulf* S Mexico
Tehuantepec, Gulf of *see* Tehuantepec, Golfo de
Tehuantepec, Isthmus of *see* Tehuantepec, Istmo de
41 T16 **Tehuantepec, Istmo de** *var.* Isthmus of Tehuantepec. *isthmus* SE Mexico
0 I16 **Tehuantepec Ridge** *undersea feature* E Pacific Ocean 13°30′N 98°00′W
41 S16 **Tehuantepec, Río** ≈ SE Mexico
191 W10 **Tehuata** *atoll* Îles Tuamotu, C French Polynesia
64 O11 **Teide, Pico del** ▲ Gran Canaria, Islas Canarias, Spain, NE Atlantic Ocean 28°16′N 16°39′W
97 I21 **Teifi** ≈ SW Wales, United Kingdom
80 B9 **Teiga Plateau** *plateau* W Sudan
97 J24 **Teignmouth** SW England, United Kingdom 50°34′N 03°29′W
Teisen *see* Jecheon
116 H1 **Teiuş** *Ger.* Dreikirchen, *Hung.* Tövis. Alba, C Romania 46°12′N 23°40′E
169 U17 **Tejakula** Bali, C Indonesia 08°09′S 115°19′E
146 H14 **Tejen** *Rus.* Tedzhen. Ahal Welaýaty, S Turkmenistan 37°24′N 60°29′E
146 I15 **Tejen** *Per.* Harīrūd, *Rus.* Tedzhen. ≈ Afghanistan/Iran *see also* Harīrūd
Tejen *see* Harīrūd
Tejenstroy *see* Tedzhenstroy
35 S14 **Tejon Pass** *pass* California, W USA
Tejo, Rio *see* Tagus
41 O14 **Tejupilco** *var.* Tejupilco de Hidalgo. México, S Mexico 18°55′N 100°10′W
Tejupilco de Hidalgo *see* Tejupilco
184 P7 **Te Kaha** Bay of Plenty, North Island, New Zealand 37°45′S 177°42′E
29 S14 **Tekamah** Nebraska, C USA 41°46′N 96°13′W
184 I1 **Te Kao** Northland, North Island, New Zealand 34°40′S 172°57′E
185 F20 **Tekapo** ≈ South Island, New Zealand
185 F19 **Tekapo, Lake** ◎ South Island, New Zealand
184 P9 **Te Karaka** Gisborne, North Island, New Zealand 38°30′S 177°52′E
184 L7 **Te Kauwhata** Waikato, North Island, New Zealand 37°22′S 175°07′E
41 X12 **Tekax** *var.* Tekax de Álvaro Obregón. Yucatán, SE Mexico 20°07′N 89°10′W
Tekax de Álvaro Obregón *see* Tekax
136 A14 **Teke Burnu** *headland* W Turkey 38°06′N 26°35′E
114 M12 **Teke Deresi** ≈ NW Turkey
146 D10 **Tekedzhik, Gory** *hill range* NW Turkmenistan
145 V14 **Tekeli** Almaty, SE Kazakhstan 44°50′N 78°47′E
145 R7 **Teke, Ozero** ◎ N Kazakhstan
158 I5 **Tekes** Xinjiang Uygur Zizhiqu, NW China 43°15′N 81°43′E
145 W16 **Tekes** Almaty, SE Kazakhstan 42°40′N 80°01′E
Tekes *see* Tekes He
158 H5 **Tekes He** *Rus.* Tekes. ≈ China/Kazakhstan
Teke/Tekendorf *see* Teaca
80 I10 **Tekezē** *var.* Takkaze. ≈ Eritrea/Ethiopia
Tekhtin *see* Tsyakhtsin
136 C10 **Tekirdağ** *It.* Rodosto; *anc.* Bisanthe, Raidestos, Rhaedestus. Tekirdağ, NW Turkey 40°59′N 27°31′E
136 C10 **Tekirdağ** ◆ *province* NW Turkey
155 N14 **Tekkali** Andhra Pradesh, E India 18°37′N 84°15′E
115 K15 **Tekke Burnu** *Turk.* İlyasbaba Burnu. *headland* NW Turkey 40°03′N 26°12′E
137 Q13 **Tekman** Erzurum, NE Turkey 39°39′N 41°31′E
32 M9 **Tekoa** Washington, NW USA 47°13′N 117°05′W
190 H16 **Te Kou** ▲ Rarotonga, S Cook Islands 21°14′S 159°46′W
Tekrit *see* Tikrīt
171 P12 **Teku** Sulawesi, N Indonesia 0°46′S 123°25′E
184 L9 **Te Kuiti** Waikato, North Island, New Zealand 38°21′S 175°10′E
42 H4 **Tela** Atlántida, NW Honduras 15°46′N 87°25′W
138 F12 **Telalim** Southern, S Israel 30°58′N 34°47′E
Telanaipura *see* Jambi
137 U10 **Telavi** *prev.* T'elavi. E Georgia 41°55′N 45°29′E
T'elavi *see* Telavi
138 F10 **Tel Aviv** ◆ *district* W Israel
Tel Aviv-Jaffa *see* Tel Aviv-Yafo
138 F10 **Tel Aviv-Yafo** *var.* Tel Aviv-Jaffa. Tel Aviv, C Israel 32°05′N 34°46′E
111 E18 **Telč** *Ger.* Teltsch. Vysočina, C Czech Republic 49°10′N 15°28′E
186 B6 **Telefomin** Sandaun, NW Papua New Guinea 05°08′S 141°31′E
10 J10 **Telegraph Creek** British Columbia, W Canada 57°56′N 131°10′W
190 B10 **Telele** *island* Funafuti Atoll, C Tuvalu
60 J11 **Telêmaco Borba** Paraná, S Brazil 24°20′S 50°44′W
95 E15 **Telemark** ◆ *county* S Norway
62 J13 **Telén** La Pampa, C Argentina 36°20′S 65°31′W
Teleneshty *see* Teleneşti
116 M9 **Teleneşti** *Rus.* Teleneshty. C Moldova 47°35′N 28°20′E
104 J4 **Teleno, El** ▲ NW Spain 42°19′N 06°21′W
116 I15 **Teleorman** ◆ *county* S Romania
116 I14 **Teleorman** ≈ S Romania
25 V5 **Telephone** Texas, SW USA 33°48′N 96°00′W
35 U11 **Telescope Peak** ▲ California, W USA 36°09′N 117°03′W
Teles Pirés *see* São Manuel, Rio
97 L19 **Telford** W England, United Kingdom 52°42′N 02°28′W
108 L7 **Telfs** Tirol, W Austria 47°19′N 11°05′E
42 I9 **Telica** León, NW Nicaragua 12°30′N 86°52′W
42 J6 **Telica, Río** ≈ C Honduras
76 I13 **Télimélé** W Guinea 10°45′N 13°02′W
43 O14 **Telire, Río** ≈ Costa Rica/Panama
114 I8 **Telish** *prev.* Azizie. Pleven, N Bulgaria 43°20′N 24°15′E
41 R16 **Telixtlahuaca** *var.* San Francisco Telixtlahuaca. Oaxaca, SE Mexico 17°18′N 96°54′W
10 K13 **Telkwa** British Columbia, SW Canada 54°39′N 126°51′W
25 P4 **Tell** Texas, SW USA 34°18′N 100°20′W
Tell Abiad *see* Tall Abyaḑ
Tell Abiad/Tell Abyad *see* At Tall al Abyaḑ
31 O16 **Tell City** Indiana, N USA 37°56′N 86°47′W
38 M9 **Teller** Alaska, USA 65°15′N 166°21′W
Tell Huqnah *see* Tall Ḩuqnah
155 F20 **Tellicherry** *var.* Thalashsheri, Thalassery. Kerala, SW India 11°44′N 75°29′E *see also* Thalassery
20 M10 **Tellico Plains** Tennessee, S USA 35°19′N 84°18′W
Tell Kalakh *see* Tall Kalakh
Tell Mardīkh *see* Ebla
54 E11 **Tello** Huila, C Colombia 03°06′N 75°08′W
Tell Shedadi *see* Ash Shadādah
37 Q7 **Telluride** Colorado, C USA 37°56′N 107°48′W
117 X9 **Tel'manove** Donets'ka Oblast', E Ukraine 47°24′N 38°03′E
Tel'man/Tel'mansk *see* Gubadag
162 H6 **Telmen** *var.* Övögdiy. Dzavhan, C Mongolia 48°38′N 97°39′E
162 H6 **Telmen Nuur** ◎ NW Mongolia
Teloekbetoeng *see* Bandar Lampung
41 O15 **Teloloapán** Guerrero, S Mexico 18°21′N 99°52′W
Telo Martius *see* Toulon
Telposiz, Gora *see* Telpoziz, Gora
125 V8 **Telpoziz, Gora** *prev.* Gora Telposiz. ▲ NW Russian Federation 63°52′N 59°15′E
Telschen *see* Telšiai
63 J17 **Telsen** Chubut, S Argentina 42°27′S 66°59′W
118 D11 **Telšiai** *Ger.* Telschen. Telšiai, NW Lithuania 55°59′N 22°21′E
118 D11 **Telšiai** ◆ *province* NW Lithuania
Teltsch *see* Telč
Telukbetung *see* Bandar Lampung
168 H10 **Telukdalam** Pulau Nias, W Indonesia 0°34′N 97°47′E
14 H9 **Temagami** Ontario, S Canada 47°03′N 79°47′W
14 G9 **Temagami, Lake** ◎ Ontario, S Canada
190 H16 **Te Manga** ▲ Rarotonga, S Cook Islands 21°13′S 159°45′W
191 W12 **Tematagi** *prev.* Tematangi. *atoll* Îles Tuamotu, S French Polynesia
Tematangi *see* Tematagi
41 X11 **Temax** Yucatán, SE Mexico 21°10′N 88°53′W
171 E14 **Tembagapura** Papua, E Indonesia 04°10′S 137°19′E
129 U5 **Tembenchi** ≈ N Russian Federation
55 P6 **Temblador** Monagas, NE Venezuela 08°59′N 62°44′W
105 N9 **Tembleque** Castilla-La Mancha, C Spain 39°41′N 03°30′W
Temboni *see* Mitemele, Río
35 U16 **Temecula** California, W USA 33°29′N 117°09′W
168 K7 **Temengor, Tasik** ◎ Peninsular Malaysia
112 L9 **Temerin** Vojvodina, N Serbia 45°25′N 19°54′E
Temeschburg/Temeschwar *see* Timişoara
Temes-Kubin *see* Kovin
Temes/Temesch *see* Tamiš

◆ Country
● Country Capital
◇ Dependent Territory
○ Dependent Territory Capital
◆ Administrative Regions
✕ International Airport
▲ Mountain
▲▲ Mountain Range
Volcano
≈ River
◎ Lake
⊠ Reservoir

Temesvár/Temeswar see Timișoara
Teminaboean see Teminabuan
171 U12 Teminabuan prev. Teminaboean. Papua, E Indonesia 01°30′S 131°59′E
145 P17 Temirlan prev. Temirlanovka. Yuzhnyy Kazakhstan, S Kazakhstan 42°36′N 69°17′E
Temirlanovka see Temirlan
145 R10 Temirtau prev. Samarkandski, Samarkandskoye. Karaganda, C Kazakhstan 50°05′N 72°55′E
14 H10 Témiscaming Québec, SE Canada 46°40′N 79°04′W
Témiscamingue, Lac see Timiskaming, Lake
15 T8 Témiscouata, Lac ◎ Québec, SE Canada
127 N5 Temnikov Respublika Mordoviya, W Russian Federation 54°39′N 43°09′E
191 Y13 Temoe island Îles Gambier, E French Polynesia
183 Q9 Temora New South Wales, SE Australia 34°28′S 147°33′E
40 H7 Témoris Chihuahua, W Mexico 27°16′N 108°15′W
40 I5 Temósachic Chihuahua, N Mexico 28°55′N 107°42′W
187 Q10 Temotu var. Temotu Province. ◐ province E Solomon Islands
Temotu Province see Temotu
36 L14 Tempe Arizona, SW USA 33°24′N 111°54′W
Tempelburg see Czaplinek
107 C17 Tempio Pausania Sardegna, Italy, C Mediterranean Sea 40°55′N 09°07′E
42 K12 Tempisque, Río ≈ NW Costa Rica
25 T9 Temple Texas, SW USA 31°06′N 97°22′W
100 O12 Templehof ✈ (Berlin) Berlin, NE Germany 52°28′N 13°24′E
97 D19 Templemore Ir. An Teampall Mór. Tipperary, C Ireland 52°48′N 07°50′W
100 O11 Templin Brandenburg, NE Germany 53°07′N 13°31′E
41 P12 Tempoal var. Tempoal de Sánchez. Veracruz-Llave, E Mexico 21°32′N 98°23′W
Tempoal de Sánchez see Tempoal
41 P13 Tempoal, Río ≈ C Mexico
83 E14 Tempué Moxico, C Angola 13°36′S 18°56′E
126 J14 Temryuk Krasnodarskiy Kray, SW Russian Federation 45°15′N 37°26′E
99 G17 Temse Oost-Vlaanderen, N Belgium 51°08′N 04°13′E
63 F15 Temuco Araucanía, C Chile 38°45′S 72°37′W
185 G20 Temuka Canterbury, South Island, New Zealand 44°14′S 171°17′E
189 P13 Temwen Island island E Micronesia
56 C6 Tena Napo, C Ecuador 01°00′S 77°48′W
41 W13 Tenabo Campeche, E Mexico 20°02′N 90°12′W
Tenaghau see Aola
25 X7 Tenaha Texas, SW USA 31°56′N 94°14′W
39 X13 Tenake Chichagof Island, Alaska, USA 57°46′N 135°13′W
155 K16 Tenāli Andhra Pradesh, E India 16°13′N 80°36′E
Tenan see Cheonan
41 O14 Tenancingo var. Tenencingo de Degollado. México, S Mexico 18°57′N 99°39′W
191 X12 Tenararo island Groupe Actéon, SE French Polynesia
Tenasserim see Tanintharyi
Tenasserim see Tanintharyi
98 O5 Ten Boer Groningen, NE Netherlands 53°16′N 06°42′E
97 I21 Tenby SW Wales, United Kingdom 51°41′N 04°43′W
80 K11 Tendaho Āfar, NE Ethiopia 11°39′N 40°59′E
103 V14 Tende Alpes Maritimes, SE France 44°04′N 07°34′E
151 Q20 Ten Degree Channel strait Andaman and Nicobar Islands, India, E Indian Ocean
80 F11 Tendelti White Nile, E Sudan 13°01′N 31°55′E
76 G8 Te-n-Dghâmcha, Sebkhet var. Sebkha de Ndrhamcha, Sebkra de Ndaghamcha. salt lake W Mauritania
165 P10 Tendō Yamagata, Honshū, C Japan 38°22′N 140°22′E
74 H7 Tendrara NE Morocco 33°06′N 01°58′W
117 Q11 Tendrivs'ka Kosa spit S Ukraine
117 Q11 Tendrivs'ka Zatoka gulf S Ukraine
Tenencingo de Degollado see Tenancingo
77 N11 Ténenkou Mopti, C Mali 14°28′N 04°55′W
77 W9 Ténéré physical region C Niger
77 W9 Ténére, Erg du desert C Niger
64 O11 Tenerife island Islas Canarias, Spain, NE Atlantic Ocean
74 J5 Ténès NW Algeria 36°35′N 01°18′E
170 M15 Tengah, Kepulauan island group C Indonesia
Tengcheng see Tengxian
169 V11 Tenggarong Borneo, C Indonesia 0°23′S 117°00′E
162 J15 Tengger Shamo desert N China
168 L8 Tenggul, Pulau island Peninsular Malaysia
Tengiz Köl see Teniz, Ozero
76 M14 Tengréla var. Tingréla. N Ivory Coast 10°26′N 06°20′W
160 M14 Tengxian var. Tengcheng, Tengxian, Teng Xian. Guangxi Zhuangzu Zizhiqu, S China 23°24′N 110°49′E
Tengxian see Tengxian
Teng Xian see Tengxian
194 H2 Teniente Rodolfo Marsh Chilean research station South Shetland Islands, Antarctica 61°57′S 58°23′W
32 G9 Tenino Washington, NW USA 46°51′N 122°51′W
145 P9 Teniz, Ozero Kaz. Tengiz Köl. salt lake C Kazakhstan
112 I9 Tenja Osijek-Baranja, E Croatia 45°30′N 18°45′E
188 B16 Tenjo, Mount ▲ W Guam
155 H23 Tenkāsi Tamil Nādu, SE India 08°58′N 77°22′E
79 N24 Tenke Katanga, SE Dem. Rep. Congo 10°34′S 26°12′E
Tenke see Tinca
123 Q7 Tenkeli Respublika Sakha (Yakutiya), NE Russian Federation 70°09′N 140°39′E
27 R10 Tenkiller Ferry Lake ⊠ Oklahoma, C USA
77 Q13 Tenkodogo S Burkina 11°54′N 00°19′W
181 Q5 Tennant Creek Northern Territory, C Australia 19°40′S 134°16′E
20 G9 Tennessee off. State of Tennessee, also known as The Volunteer State. ◐ state SE USA
37 R5 Tennessee Pass pass Colorado, C USA
20 H10 Tennessee River ≈ S USA
23 N2 Tennessee Tombigbee Waterway canal Alabama/Mississippi, S USA
99 K22 Tenneville Luxembourg, SE Belgium 50°05′N 05°31′E
92 M11 Tenniöjoki ≈ NE Finland
92 L9 Tenojoki Lapp. Deatnu, Nor. Tana. ≈ Finland/Norway see also Deatnu, Tana
Tenojoki see Tana
169 U7 Tenom Sabah, East Malaysia 05°07′N 115°57′E
Tenos see Tínos
41 V15 Tenosique var. Tenosique de Pino Suárez. Tabasco, SE Mexico 17°30′N 91°24′W
Tenosique de Pino Suárez see Tenosique
22 I6 Tensas River ≈ Louisiana, S USA
23 O8 Tensaw River ≈ Alabama, S USA
74 E7 Tensift seasonal river W Morocco
171 O12 Tentena var. Tenteno. Sulawesi, C Indonesia 01°46′S 120°40′E
Tenteno see Tentena
183 U4 Tenterfield New South Wales, SE Australia 29°04′S 152°02′E
23 X16 Ten Thousand Islands island group Florida, SE USA
60 H9 Teodoro Sampaio São Paulo, S Brazil 22°30′S 52°13′W
59 N19 Teófilo Otoni var. Theophilo Ottoni. Minas Gerais, NE Brazil 17°52′S 41°31′W
116 K5 Teofipol' Khmel'nyts'ka Oblast', W Ukraine 50°00′N 26°22′E
Teohatu see Toahotu
41 P14 Teotihuacán ruins México, S Mexico
Teotilán see Teotitlán del Camino
41 Q15 Teotitlán del Camino var. Teotilán. Oaxaca, S Mexico 18°10′N 97°08′W
190 G12 Tepa Île Uvea, E Wallis and Futuna 13°19′S 176°09′W
191 P8 Tepaee, Récif reef Tahiti, W French Polynesia
40 L14 Tepalcatepec Michoacán, SW Mexico 19°11′N 102°50′W
190 A16 Tepa Point headland SW Niue 19°07′S 169°56′E
41 L13 Tepatitlán var. Tepatitlán de Morelos. Jalisco, SW Mexico 20°50′N 102°46′W
Tepatitlán de Morelos see Tepatitlán
40 J9 Tepehuanes var. Santa Catarina de Tepehuanes. Durango, C Mexico 25°22′N 105°42′W
Tepelena see Tepelenë
113 L22 Tepelenë var. Tepelena, It. Tepeleni. Gjirokastër, S Albania 40°18′N 20°00′E
Tepeleni see Tepelenë
40 K12 Tepic Nayarit, C Mexico 21°30′N 104°55′W
111 C15 Teplice Ger. Teplitz; prev. Teplice-Šanov, Teplitz-Schönau. Ústecký Kraj, NW Czech Republic 50°38′N 13°49′E
Teplice-Šanov/Teplitz/Teplitz-Schönau see Teplice
117 O7 Teplyk Vinnyts'ka Oblast', C Ukraine 48°40′N 29°46′E
123 R10 Teplyy Klyuch Respublika Sakha (Yakutiya), NE Russian Federation 62°46′N 137°01′E
40 E5 Tepoca, Cabo headland NW Mexico 29°19′N 112°24′W
191 W9 Tepoto island Îles du Désappointement, C French Polynesia
92 L11 Tepsa Lappi, N Finland 67°34′N 25°36′E
190 B8 Tepuka atoll Funafuti Atoll, C Tuvalu
184 N7 Te Puke Bay of Plenty, North Island, New Zealand 37°48′S 176°19′E
40 L13 Tequila Jalisco, SW Mexico 20°52′N 103°48′W
41 O13 Tequisquiapan Querétaro de Arteaga, C Mexico 20°34′N 99°52′W
77 Q12 Téra Tillabéri, W Niger 14°01′N 00°45′E
104 J5 Tera ≈ NW Spain
191 V1 Teraina prev. Washington Island. atoll Line Islands, E Kiribati
81 F15 Terakeka Central Equatoria, S South Sudan 05°26′N 31°45′E
107 J14 Teramo anc. Interamna. Abruzzi, C Italy 42°40′N 13°43′E
98 P7 Ter Apel Groningen, NE Netherlands 52°52′N 07°05′E
104 H11 Tera, Ribeira de ≈ S Portugal
185 K14 Terawhiti, Cape headland North Island, New Zealand 41°17′S 174°36′E
98 N12 Terborg Gelderland, E Netherlands 51°55′N 06°22′E
137 P13 Tercan Erzincan, NE Turkey 39°47′N 40°23′E
64 O2 Terceira ✈ Terceira, Azores, Portugal, NE Atlantic Ocean 38°43′N 27°13′W
64 O2 Terceira var. Ilha Terceira. island Azores, Portugal, NE Atlantic Ocean
Terceira, Ilha see Terceira
116 K6 Terebovlya Ternopil's'ka Oblast', W Ukraine 49°18′N 25°44′E
127 O15 Terek ≈ SW Russian Federation
Terekhovka see Tsyerakhowka
147 R9 Terek-Say Dzhalal-Abadskaya Oblast', W Kyrgyzstan 41°28′N 71°06′E
145 Z10 Terekty prev. Alekseevka, Alekseyevka. Vostochnyy Kazakhstan, E Kazakhstan 48°25′N 85°38′E
168 L7 Terengganu var. Trengganu. ◐ state Peninsular Malaysia
127 X7 Terensay Orenburgskaya Oblast', W Russian Federation 51°35′N 59°28′E
58 N13 Teresina var. Therezina. state capital Piauí, NE Brazil 05°09′S 42°46′W
60 P9 Teresópolis Rio de Janeiro, SE Brazil 22°25′S 42°59′W
110 P12 Terespol Lubelskie, E Poland 52°05′N 23°37′E
191 V16 Terevaka, Maunga ⛰ Easter Island, Chile, E Pacific Ocean 27°05′S 109°23′W
103 P3 Tergnier Aisne, N France 49°39′N 03°18′E
43 O14 Teribe, Río ≈ NW Panama
124 K3 Teriberka Murmanskaya Oblast', NW Russian Federation 69°10′N 35°18′E
Terinkot see Tarīn Kōt
Terisaqqan see Tersakkan
24 K12 Terlingua Texas, SW USA 29°18′N 103°36′W
24 K11 Terlingua Creek ≈ Texas, SW USA
62 K7 Termas de Río Hondo Santiago del Estero, N Argentina 27°29′S 64°52′W
136 M11 Terme Samsun, N Turkey 41°12′N 37°00′E
Termez see Termiz
Termia see Kýthnos
107 J23 Termini Imerese anc. Thermae Himerenses. Sicilia, Italy, C Mediterranean Sea 37°59′N 13°42′E
41 V14 Términos, Laguna de lagoon SE Mexico
77 X10 Termit-Kaoboul Zinder, C Niger 15°34′N 11°31′E
147 O14 Termiz Rus. Termez. Surkhondaryo Viloyati, S Uzbekistan 37°17′N 67°12′E
107 L15 Termoli Molise, C Italy 42°00′N 14°58′E
Termonde see Dendermonde
98 P5 Termunten Groningen, NE Netherlands 53°18′N 07°02′E
171 R11 Ternate Pulau Ternate, E Indonesia 0°48′N 127°23′E
109 T5 Ternberg Oberösterreich, N Austria 47°57′N 14°22′E
99 E15 Terneuzen var. Neuzen. Zeeland, SW Netherlands 51°20′N 03°50′E
123 T14 Terney Primorskiy Kray, SE Russian Federation 45°03′N 136°43′E
107 I14 Terni anc. Interamna Nahars. Umbria, C Italy 42°34′N 12°38′E
109 X6 Ternitz Niederösterreich, E Austria 47°43′N 16°02′E
117 V7 Ternivka Dnipropetrovs'ka Oblast', E Ukraine 48°30′N 36°05′E
116 K6 Ternopil' Pol. Tarnopol, Rus. Ternopol'. Ternopil's'ka Oblast', W Ukraine 49°32′N 25°38′E
Ternopil' see Ternopil's'ka Oblast'
116 I6 Ternopil's'ka Oblast' var. Ternopil', Rus. Ternopol'skaya Oblast'. ◐ province NW Ukraine
Ternopol' see Ternopil'
Ternopol'skaya Oblast' see Ternopil's'ka Oblast'
123 U13 Terpeniya, Mys headland Ostrov Sakhalin, SE Russian Federation 48°37′N 144°40′E
Térraba, Río see Grande de Térraba, Río
10 J13 Terrace British Columbia, W Canada 54°31′N 128°32′W
12 D12 Terrace Bay Ontario, S Canada 48°47′N 87°06′W
107 I16 Terracina Lazio, C Italy 41°18′N 13°13′E
93 F14 Terråk Troms, N Norway 65°03′N 12°22′E
26 M13 Terral Oklahoma, C USA 33°55′N 97°54′W
107 B19 Terralba Sardegna, Italy, C Mediterranean Sea 39°47′N 08°35′E
Terranova di Sicilia see Gela
Terranova Pausania see Olbia
105 W5 Terrassa Cast. Tarrasa. Cataluña, E Spain 41°34′N 02°01′E
15 O12 Terrebonne Québec, SE Canada 45°42′N 73°37′W
22 J11 Terrebonne Bay bay Louisiana, SE USA
31 N14 Terre Haute Indiana, N USA 39°27′N 87°24′W
25 U6 Terrell Texas, SW USA 32°44′N 96°16′W
Terre Neuve see Newfoundland and Labrador
33 Q14 Terreton Idaho, NW USA 43°49′N 112°25′W
103 T7 Territoire-de-Belfort ◐ department E France
33 X9 Terry Montana, NW USA 46°46′N 105°16′W
28 I9 Terry Peak ▲ South Dakota, N USA 44°19′N 103°49′W
136 H14 Tersakan Gölü ◎ C Turkey
145 O10 Tersakkan Kaz. Terisaqqan. ≈ C Kazakhstan
98 J4 Terschelling Fris. Skylge. island Waddeneilanden, N Netherlands
78 H10 Tersef Chari-Baguirmi, C Chad 12°55′N 16°49′E
147 X8 Terskey Ala-Too, Khrebet ▲▲ Kazakhstan/Kyrgyzstan
Terter see Tärtär
105 R8 Teruel anc. Turba. Aragón, E Spain 40°21′N 01°06′W
105 R7 Teruel ◐ province Aragón, E Spain
114 M7 Tervel prev. Kurtbunar, Rom. Curtbunar. Dobrich, NE Bulgaria 43°45′N 27°25′E
93 M16 Tervo Itä-Suomi, C Finland 62°57′N 26°48′E
92 L13 Tervola Lappi, NW Finland 66°04′N 24°49′E
Tervueren see Tervuren
99 H18 Tervuren var. Tervueren. Vlaams Brabant, C Belgium 50°48′N 04°28′E
162 G5 Tes var. Dzür. Dzavhan, W Mongolia 49°37′N 95°46′E
112 H11 Tešanj Federacija Bosna I Hercegovina, N Bosnia and Herzegovina 44°37′N 18°00′E
Teschen see Cieszyn
83 M19 Tesenane Inhambane, S Mozambique 22°48′S 34°02′E
80 I9 Teseney var. Tessenei. W Eritrea 15°05′N 36°42′E
39 P5 Teshekpuk Lake ◎ Alaska, USA
162 K6 Teshig Bulgan, N Mongolia 49°51′N 102°45′E
165 T2 Teshio Hokkaidō, NE Japan 44°49′N 141°46′E
165 T2 Teshio-sanchi ▲▲ Hokkaidō, NE Japan
14 L7 Tessier, Lac ◎ Québec, SE Canada
Těšín see Cieszyn
Tesiyn Gol see Tes-Khem
129 T7 Tes-Khem var. Tesiyn Gol. ≈ Mongolia/Russian Federation
112 H11 Teslić Republika Srpska, N Bosnia and Herzegovina 44°35′N 17°50′E
10 I9 Teslin Yukon Territory, W Canada 60°12′N 132°44′W
10 I8 Teslin ≈ British Columbia/Yukon Territory, W Canada
77 Q8 Tessalit Kidal, NE Mali 20°12′N 00°58′E
77 V12 Tessaoua Maradi, S Niger 13°46′N 07°55′E
99 J17 Tessenderlo Limburg, NE Belgium 51°05′N 05°04′E
Tessenei see Teseney
Tessin see Ticino
97 M23 Test ≈ S England, United Kingdom
Testama see Tõstamaa
55 P4 Testigos, Islas los island group N Venezuela
37 S10 Tesuque New Mexico, SW USA 35°45′N 105°55′W
103 O17 Têt var. Tet. ≈ S France
Tet see Têt
54 G5 Tetas, Cerro de las ▲ NW Venezuela 09°58′N 73°00′W
83 M15 Tete Tete, NW Mozambique 16°14′S 33°34′E
83 M15 Tete off. Província de Tete. ◐ province NW Mozambique
11 N15 Tête Jaune Cache British Columbia, SW Canada 52°52′N 119°22′W
184 O8 Te Teko Bay of Plenty, North Island, New Zealand 38°03′S 176°48′E
186 K9 Tetepare island New Georgia Islands, NW Solomon Islands
Tete, Província de see Tete
Teterev see Teteriv
116 M5 Teteriv Rus. Teterev. ≈ N Ukraine
100 M9 Teterow Mecklenburg-Vorpommern, NE Germany 53°47′N 12°34′E
114 I9 Teteven Lovech, N Bulgaria 42°54′N 24°18′E
191 T10 Tetiaroa atoll Îles du Vent, W French Polynesia
105 P14 Tetica de Bacares ▲ S Spain 37°15′N 02°24′W
Tetiyev see Tetiyiv
117 O6 Tetiyiv Rus. Tetiyev. Kyyivs'ka Oblast', N Ukraine 49°21′N 29°40′E
39 T10 Tetlin Alaska, USA 63°08′N 142°31′W
33 R8 Teton River ≈ Montana, NW USA
74 G5 Tétouan var. Tetouan, Tetuán. N Morocco 35°33′N 05°22′W
Tetova/Tetovë see Tetovo
114 L7 Tetovo Razgrad, N Bulgaria 43°49′N 26°21′E
113 N18 Tetovo Alb. Tetova, Tetovë, Turk. Kalkandelen. NW FYR Macedonia 42°01′N 20°58′E
115 E20 Tetrázio ▲ S Greece
Tetschen see Děčín
Tetuán see Tétouan
191 Q8 Tetufera, Mont ▲ Tahiti, W French Polynesia 17°40′S 149°26′W
127 R4 Tetyushi Respublika Tatarstan, W Russian Federation 54°55′N 48°46′E
108 I7 Teufen Ausser Rhoden, NE Switzerland 47°24′N 09°24′E
40 L12 Teul var. Teul de Gonzáles Ortega. Zacatecas, C Mexico 21°30′N 103°28′W
107 B21 Teulada Sardegna, Italy, C Mediterranean Sea 38°58′N 08°46′E
Teul de Gonzáles Ortega see Teul
11 X16 Teulon Manitoba, S Canada 50°20′N 97°14′W
42 I7 Teupasenti El Paraíso, S Honduras 14°13′N 86°42′W
165 S2 Teuri-tō island NE Japan
100 G13 Teutoburger Wald Eng. Teutoburg Forest. hill range NW Germany
Teutoburg Forest see Teutoburger Wald
93 K17 Teuva Swe. Östermark. Länsi-Suomi, W Finland 62°29′N 21°45′E
107 H15 Tevere Eng. Tiber. ≈ C Italy
Teverya see Tverya
96 K13 Teviot ≈ SE Scotland, United Kingdom
Tevli see Tewli
122 H11 Tevriz Omskaya Oblast', C Russian Federation 57°30′N 72°13′E
185 B24 Te Waewae Bay bay South Island, New Zealand
97 L21 Tewkesbury C England, United Kingdom 51°59′N 02°09′W
119 F19 Tewli Rus. Tevli. Brestskaya Voblasts', SW Belarus 52°20′N 24°15′E
159 U12 Têwo var. Dêngka; prev. Dêngkagoin. Gansu, C China 34°05′N 103°15′E
Tewulike see Hoxud
25 U12 Texana, Lake ◎ Texas, SW USA
27 S14 Texarkana Arkansas, C USA 33°26′N 94°02′W
25 X5 Texarkana Texas, SW USA 33°26′N 94°03′W
25 N9 Texas off. State of Texas, also known as Lone Star State. ◐ state S USA
25 W12 Texas City Texas, SW USA 29°23′N 94°55′W
41 P14 Texcoco México, C Mexico 19°32′N 98°52′W
98 I6 Texel island Waddeneilanden, NW Netherlands
26 H8 Texhoma Oklahoma, C USA 36°30′N 101°46′W
25 N1 Texhoma Texas, SW USA 36°30′N 101°46′W
37 W12 Texico New Mexico, SW USA 34°23′N 103°03′W
24 L1 Texline Texas, SW USA 36°22′N 103°01′W
41 P14 Texmelucan var. San Martín Texmelucan. Puebla, S Mexico 19°46′N 98°53′W
27 O13 Texoma, Lake ⊠ Oklahoma/Texas, C USA
25 N9 Texon Texas, SW USA 31°13′N 101°42′W
83 J23 Teyateyaneng NW Lesotho 29°04′S 27°51′E
124 M16 Teykovo Ivanovskaya Oblast', W Russian Federation 56°49′N 40°31′E
124 M16 Teza ≈ W Russian Federation
41 Q13 Teziutlán Puebla, S Mexico 19°49′N 97°22′W
153 W12 Tezpur Assam, NE India 26°39′N 92°47′E
Thaa Atoll see Kolhumadulu
9 N10 Tha-Anne ≈ Nunavut, NE Canada
83 K23 Thabana Ntlenyana var. Thabantshonyana, Mount Ntlenyana. ▲ E Lesotho 29°26′S 29°16′E
Thabantshonyana see Thabana Ntlenyana
83 J23 Thaba Putsoa ▲ C Lesotho 29°48′S 27°46′E
167 Q8 Tha Bo Nong Khai, E Thailand 17°52′N 102°34′E
103 T12 Thabor, Pic du ▲ E France 45°07′N 06°34′E
Tha Chin see Samut Sakhon
166 M7 Thagaya Bago, C Myanmar (Burma) 19°19′N 96°16′E
Thai, Ao see Thailand, Gulf of
167 T6 Thai Binh Thai Binh, N Vietnam 20°27′N 106°20′E
167 S7 Thai Hoa var. Nghia Dan. Nghê An, N Vietnam 19°21′N 105°26′E
167 P9 Thailand off. Kingdom of Thailand, Th. Prathet Thai; prev. Siam. ◆ monarchy SE Asia
167 P13 Thailand, Gulf of var. Gulf of Siam, Th. Ao Thai, Vtn. Vinh Thai Lan. gulf SE Asia
Thailand, Kingdom of see Thailand
Thai Lan, Vinh see Thailand, Gulf of
167 T6 Thai Nguyên Băc Thai, N Vietnam 21°36′N 105°50′E
167 S8 Thakhèk var. Muang Khammouan. Khammouan, C Laos 17°25′N 104°51′E
153 S13 Thakurgaon Rajshahi, NW Bangladesh 26°05′N 88°34′E
149 S6 Thal Khyber Pakhtunkhwa, NW Pakistan 33°24′N 70°32′E
167 S11 Thalabârivât prev. Phumĭ Thalabârĭvăt. Stœng Trêng, N Cambodia 13°34′N 105°57′E
166 M15 Thalang Phuket, SW Thailand 08°00′N 98°21′E
Thalashsheri see Tellicherry/Thalassery
167 Q10 Thalat Khae Nakhon Ratchasima, C Thailand 15°15′N 102°24′E
109 Q5 Thalgau Salzburg, NW Austria 47°49′N 13°19′E
108 G7 Thalwil Zürich, NW Switzerland 47°17′N 08°35′E
83 I20 Thamaga Kweneng, SE Botswana 24°41′S 25°31′E
Thamarīd see Thamarīt
141 V13 Thamarīt var. Thamarīd, Thumrayt. SW Oman 17°39′N 54°02′E
141 P16 Thamar, Jabal ▲ SW Yemen 13°46′N 45°32′E
184 M6 Thames Waikato, North Island, New Zealand 37°10′S 175°33′E
14 D17 Thames ≈ Ontario, S Canada
97 O22 Thames ≈ S England, United Kingdom
184 M6 Thames, Firth of gulf North Island, New Zealand
14 D17 Thamesville Ontario, S Canada 42°33′N 81°58′W
141 S13 Thamūd N Yemen 17°18′N 49°57′E
167 N9 Thanbyuzayat Mon State, S Myanmar (Burma) 15°58′N 97°44′E
166 K7 Thandwe var. Sandoway. Rakhine State, W Myanmar (Burma) 18°28′N 94°20′E
152 I9 Thānesar Haryāna, NW India 29°58′N 76°48′E
167 T7 Thanh Hoa Thanh Hoa, N Vietnam 19°49′N 105°48′E
Thanintari Taungdan see Bilauktaung Range
155 I21 Thanjāvūr prev. Tanjore. Tamil Nādu, SE India 10°46′N 79°09′E
Thanlwin see Salween
103 U7 Thann Haut-Rhin, NE France 47°51′N 07°04′E
167 O16 Tha Nong Phrom Phatthalung, SW Thailand 07°24′N 100°04′E
167 N13 Thap Sakae var. Thap Sakau. Prachuap Khiri Khan, SW Thailand 11°30′N 99°35′E
Thap Sakau see Thap Sakae
98 L10 't Harde Gelderland, E Netherlands 52°25′N 05°53′E
152 D11 Thar Desert var. Great Indian Desert, Indian Desert. desert India/Pakistan
181 V10 Thargomindah Queensland, C Australia 28°00′S 143°47′E
150 D11 Thar Pārkar desert SE Pakistan
139 S7 Tharthār al Furāt, Qanāt ath canal C Iraq
139 R7 Tharthār, Buḥayrat ath ◎ C Iraq
139 R5 Tharthār, Wādī ath dry watercourse N Iraq
167 N13 Tha Sae Chumphon, SW Thailand
167 N15 Tha Sala Nakhon Si Thammarat, SW Thailand 08°43′N 99°54′E
114 I13 Thásos Thásos, E Greece 40°47′N 24°43′E
115 I14 Thásos island E Greece
37 N14 Thatcher Arizona, SW USA 32°47′N 109°46′W
167 T5 Thât Khê var. Trâng Dinh. Lang Son, N Vietnam 22°15′N 106°26′E
166 M8 Thaton Mon State, Myanmar (Burma) 16°56′N 97°20′E
167 S9 That Phanom Nakhon Phanom, E Thailand 16°52′N 104°41′E
167 R10 Tha Tum Surin, E Thailand 15°18′N 103°39′E
103 P16 Thau, Bassin de var. Étang de Thau. ◎ S France
Thau, Étang de see Thau, Bassin de
166 L3 Thaungdut Sagaing, N Myanmar (Burma) 24°26′N 94°45′E
167 O8 Thaungyin Th. Mae Nam Moei. ≈ Myanmar (Burma)/Thailand
167 R8 Tha Uthen Nakhon Phanom, E Thailand 17°32′N 104°34′E
109 W2 Thaya var. Dyje. ≈ Austria/Czech Republic see also Dyje
Thaya see Dyje
27 V8 Thayer Missouri, C USA 36°31′N 91°34′W
166 L6 Thayetmyo Magway, C Myanmar (Burma) 19°20′N 95°10′E
33 S15 Thayne Wyoming, C USA 42°54′N 111°01′W
166 M5 Thazi Mandalay, C Myanmar (Burma) 20°50′N 96°04′E
Thebes see Thíva
44 L5 The Carlton var. Abraham Bay. Mayaguana, SE Bahamas 22°21′N 72°56′W
45 O14 The Crane var. Crane. S Barbados 13°06′N 59°27′W
32 I11 The Dalles Oregon, NW USA 45°36′N 121°10′W
28 M14 Thedford Nebraska, C USA 41°59′N 100°32′W
The Flatts Village see Flatts Village
The Hague see 's-Gravenhage
Theiss see Tisa/Tisza
8 M9 Thelon ≈ Northwest Territories, N Canada
11 V15 Theodore Saskatchewan, S Canada 51°25′N 103°01′W
23 N8 Theodore Alabama, S USA 30°33′N 88°10′W
36 L13 Theodore Roosevelt Lake ⊠ Arizona, SW USA
Theodosia see Feodosiya
Theophilo Ottoni see Teófilo Otoni
11 V13 The Pas Manitoba, C Canada 53°49′N 101°09′W
31 T14 The Plains Ohio, N USA 39°22′N 82°07′W
Thera see Santoríni
172 H17 Thérèse, Île island Inner Islands, NE Seychelles
Therezina see Teresina
115 L20 Thérma Ikaría, Dodekánisa, Greece, Aegean Sea 37°37′N 26°18′E
Thermae Himerenses see Termini Imerese
Thermae Pannonicae see Baden
Thermaic Gulf/Thermaicus Sinus see Thermaïkós Kólpos
121 Q8 Thermaïkós Kólpos Eng. Thermaic Gulf; anc. Thermaicus Sinus. gulf N Greece
Thermiá see Kýthnos
115 L17 Thermís Lésvos, E Greece 39°08′N 26°32′E
115 E18 Thérmo Dytikí Elláda, C Greece 38°32′N 21°42′E
33 V14 Thermopolis Wyoming, C USA 43°39′N 108°12′W
183 P10 The Rock New South Wales, SE Australia 35°18′S 147°07′E
195 O5 Theron Mountains ▲ Antarctica
The Sooner State see Oklahoma
115 G18 Thespiés Stereá Elláda, C Greece 38°18′N 23°08′E
115 E16 Thessalía Eng. Thessaly. ◐ region C Greece
14 C10 Thessalon Ontario, S Canada 46°15′N 83°34′W
115 G14 Thessaloníki Eng. Salonica, Salonika, SCr. Solun, Turk. Selânik. Kentrikí Makedonía, N Greece 40°38′N 22°58′E
115 G14 Thessaloníki ✈ Kentrikí Makedonía, N Greece 40°30′N 22°58′E
Thessaly see Thessalía
84 B12 Theta Gap undersea feature E Atlantic Ocean 12°40′W 43°30′N
97 P20 Thetford E England, United Kingdom 52°25′N 00°45′E
15 R11 Thetford-Mines Québec, SE Canada 46°07′N 71°16′W
113 K17 Theth var. Thethi. Shkodër, N Albania 42°25′N 19°45′E
Thethi see Theth
99 L20 Theux Liège, E Belgium 50°33′N 05°48′E
45 V9 The Valley ○ (Anguilla) E Anguilla 18°13′N 63°00′W
27 N10 The Village Oklahoma, C USA 35°33′N 97°33′W
The Volunteer State see Tennessee
25 W10 The Woodlands Texas, SW USA 30°09′N 95°27′E
Thiamis see Kalamás
Thian Shan see Tien Shan
Thibet see Xizang Zizhiqu
22 J9 Thibodaux Louisiana, S USA 29°48′N 90°49′W
29 S3 Thief Lake ◎ Minnesota, N USA
29 S3 Thief River ≈ Minnesota, C USA
29 S3 Thief River Falls Minnesota, N USA 48°07′N 96°10′W
Thièle see La Thielle
32 G14 Thielsen, Mount ▲ Oregon, NW USA 43°09′N 122°04′W
Thielt see Tielt
106 G7 Thiene Veneto, NE Italy 45°43′N 11°29′E
Thienen see Tienen
103 P11 Thiers Puy-de-Dôme, C France 45°51′N 03°33′E
76 F11 Thiès W Senegal 14°49′N 16°52′W
81 I19 Thika Central, S Kenya 01°03′S 37°05′E
Thikombia see Cikobia
151 K18 Thiladhunmathi Atoll var. Tiladummati Atoll. atoll N Maldives
Thimbu see Thimphu
153 T11 Thimphu var. Thimbu; prev. Tashi Chho Dzong. ● (Bhutan) W Bhutan 27°28′N 89°37′E
92 H2 Thingeyri Vestfirdhir, NW Iceland 65°52′N 23°28′W
92 I3 Thingvellir Sudhurland, SW Iceland 64°15′N 21°06′W
187 Q17 Thio Province Sud, C New Caledonia 21°37′S 166°13′E
103 T4 Thionville Ger. Diedenhofen. Moselle, NE France 49°22′N 06°11′E
77 O12 Thiou NW Burkina 13°42′N 02°34′W
115 K22 Thíra Santorini, Kykládes, Greece, Aegean Sea 36°25′N 25°26′E
Thíra see Santoríni
115 J22 Thirasía island Kykládes, Greece, Aegean Sea
97 M16 Thirsk N England, United Kingdom 54°07′N 01°17′W
14 F12 Thirty Thousand Islands island group Ontario, S Canada
95 F20 Thisted Midtjylland, NW Denmark 56°58′N 08°42′E
Thistil Fjord see Thistilfjördhur
92 L1 Thistilfjördhur var. Thistil Fjord. fjord NE Iceland
182 G9 Thistle Island island South Australia
Thithia see Cicia
Thiukhaoluang Phrahang see Luang Prabang Range
115 G18 Thíva Eng. Thebes; prev. Thívai. Stereá Elláda, C Greece 38°19′N 23°19′E
Thívai see Thíva
102 M12 Thiviers Dordogne, SW France 45°24′N 00°54′E
92 J4 Thjórsá ≈ C Iceland
9 N10 Thlewiaza ≈ Nunavut, NE Canada
8 L10 Thoa ≈ Northwest Territories, NW Canada
99 G14 Tholen Zeeland, SW Netherlands 51°31′N 04°13′E
99 F14 Tholen island SW Netherlands
26 L10 Thomas Oklahoma, C USA 35°44′N 98°45′W
21 T3 Thomas West Virginia, NE USA 39°09′N 79°28′W
27 U3 Thomas Hill Reservoir ⊠ Missouri, C USA
23 S5 Thomaston Georgia, SE USA 32°53′N 84°19′W
19 R7 Thomaston Maine, NE USA 44°06′N 69°10′W
25 T12 Thomaston Texas, SW USA 28°56′N 97°07′W
23 O6 Thomasville Alabama, S USA 31°54′N 87°42′W
23 T8 Thomasville Georgia, SE USA 30°49′N 83°57′W
21 S9 Thomasville North Carolina, SE USA 35°52′N 80°04′W
35 N5 Thomes Creek ≈ California, W USA
11 W12 Thompson Manitoba, C Canada 55°45′N 97°54′W
29 R4 Thompson North Dakota, N USA 47°45′N 97°07′W
0 F8 Thompson ≈ Alberta/British Columbia, SW Canada
33 O8 Thompson Falls Montana, NW USA 47°36′N 115°20′W
29 Q10 Thompson, Lake ◎ South Dakota, N USA
34 M3 Thompson Peak ▲ California, W USA 41°00′N 123°01′W
27 S2 Thompson River ≈ Missouri, C USA
185 A22 Thompson Sound sound South Island, New Zealand
8 J5 Thomsen ≈ Banks Island, Northwest Territories, NW Canada
23 V4 Thomson Georgia, SE USA 33°28′N 82°30′W
103 T10 Thonon-les-Bains Haute-Savoie, E France 46°22′N 06°30′E
103 O15 Thoré var. Thore. ≈ S France
Thore see Thoré
37 P11 Thoreau New Mexico, SW USA 35°24′N 108°13′W
Thorenburg see Turda
92 J3 Thórisvatn ◎ C Iceland
92 P4 Thor, Kapp headland S Svalbard 76°25′N 25°01′E
92 I4 Thorlákshöfn Sudhurland, SW Iceland 63°52′N 21°24′W
Thorn see Toruń
25 T10 Thorndale Texas, SW USA 30°36′N 97°12′W
14 H10 Thorne Ontario, S Canada 46°38′N 79°04′W
97 J14 Thornhill S Scotland, United Kingdom 55°13′N 03°46′W
25 U8 Thornton Texas, SW USA 31°24′N 96°34′W
Thornton Island see Millennium Island
14 H16 Thorold Ontario, S Canada 43°07′N 79°15′W
32 J9 Thorp Washington, NW USA 47°03′N 120°40′W
Thorshavn see Tórshavn
195 S3 Thorshavnheiane physical region Antarctica
92 L1 Thórshöfn Nordhurland Eystra, NE Iceland 66°09′N 15°18′W
Thospitis see Van Gölü
167 S14 Thôt Nôt Cân Thơ, S Vietnam 10°17′N 105°31′E
102 K8 Thouars Deux-Sèvres, W France 46°59′N 00°13′W
153 X14 Thoubal Manipur, NE India 24°40′N 94°00′E
102 K9 Thouet ≈ W France
Thoune see Thun
18 H7 Thousand Islands island Canada/USA
35 S15 Thousand Oaks California, W USA 34°10′N 118°50′W
114 L12 Thrace cultural region SE Europe
114 J13 Thracian Sea Gk. Thrakikó Pélagos; anc. Thracium Mare. sea Greece/Turkey
Thracium Mare/Thrakikó Pélagos see Thracian Sea

Thrá Lí, Bá *see* Tralee Bay
33 R11 **Three Forks** Montana, NW USA 45°53′N 111°34′W
162 M8 **Three Gorges Dam** *dam* Hubei, C China
160 L9 **Three Gorges Reservoir** ⊠ C China
11 Q16 **Three Hills** Alberta, SW Canada 51°43′N 113°15′W
183 N15 **Three Hummock Island** *island* Tasmania, SE Australia
184 H1 **Three Kings Islands** *island group* N New Zealand
175 P10 **Three Kings Rise** *undersea feature* W Pacific Ocean
77 O18 **Three Points, Cape** *headland* S Ghana 04°43′N 02°03′W
31 P10 **Three Rivers** Michigan, N USA 41°56′N 85°37′W
25 S13 **Three Rivers** Texas, SW USA 28°27′N 98°10′W
83 G24 **Three Sisters** Northern Cape, SW South Africa 31°51′S 23°04′E
32 H13 **Three Sisters** ▲ Oregon, NW USA 44°08′N 121°46′W
187 N10 **Three Sisters Islands** *island group* SE Solomon Islands
25 Q6 **Throckmorton** Texas, SW USA 33°11′N 99°12′W
180 M10 **Throssell, Lake** *salt lake* Western Australia
115 K25 **Thryptís** *var.* Thrýptis. ▲ Kriti, Greece, E Mediterranean Sea 35°06′N 25°51′E
167 U14 **Thuân Nam** *prev.* Ham Thuân Nam. Binh Thuân, S Vietnam 10°49′N 107°49′E
167 T13 **Thu Dâu Môt** *var.* Phu Cūong. Sông Be, S Vietnam 10°58′N 106°40′E
167 S6 **Thu Do** ✈ (Ha Nôi) Ha Nôi, N Vietnam 21°13′N 105°46′E
99 G21 **Thuin** Hainaut, S Belgium 50°21′N 04°18′E
149 Q12 **Thul** Sind, SE Pakistan 28°14′N 68°50′E
Thule *see* Qaanaaq
83 J18 **Thuli** *var.* Tuli. ≈ S Zimbabwe
Thumrayt *see* Thamarīt
108 D9 **Thun** *Fr.* Thoune. Bern, W Switzerland 46°46′N 07°38′E
12 C12 **Thunder Bay** Ontario, S Canada 48°27′N 89°12′W
30 M1 **Thunder Bay** *lake bay* S Canada
31 R6 **Thunder Bay** *lake bay* Michigan, N USA
31 R6 **Thunder Bay River** ≈ Michigan, N USA
27 N11 **Thunderbird, Lake** ⊠ Oklahoma, C USA
28 L8 **Thunder Butte Creek** ≈ South Dakota, N USA
108 E9 **Thuner See** ◎ C Switzerland
167 N15 **Thung Song** *var.* Cha Mai. Nakhon Si Thammarat, SW Thailand 08°10′N 99°41′E
108 H7 **Thur** ≈ N Switzerland
108 G6 **Thurgau** *Fr.* Thurgovie. ◈ *canton* NE Switzerland
Thurgovie *see* Thurgau
Thuringe *see* Thüringen
108 J7 **Thüringen** Vorarlberg, W Austria 47°12′N 09°48′E
101 J17 **Thüringen** *Eng.* Thuringia, *Fr.* Thuringe. ◈ *state* C Germany
101 J17 **Thüringer Wald** *Eng.* Thuringian Forest. ▲▲ C Germany
Thuringia *see* Thüringen
Thuringian Forest *see* Thüringer Wald
97 D19 **Thurles** *Ir.* Durlas. S Ireland 52°41′N 07°49′W
21 W2 **Thurmont** Maryland, NE USA 39°36′N 77°22′W
Thurø *see* Thurø By
95 H24 **Thurø By** *var.* Thurø. Syddtjylland, C Denmark 55°03′N 10°43′E
14 M12 **Thurso** Québec, SE Canada 45°36′N 75°13′W
96 J6 **Thurso** N Scotland, United Kingdom 58°35′N 03°32′W
194 I10 **Thurston Island** *island* Antarctica
108 I9 **Thusis** Graubünden, S Switzerland 46°40′N 09°27′E
Thýamis *see* Kalamás
95 E21 **Thyborøn** *var.* Tyborøn. Midtjylland, W Denmark 56°40′N 08°12′E
195 U3 **Thyer Glacier** *glacier* Antarctica
115 L20 **Thýmaina** *island* Dodekánisa, Greece, Aegean Sea
83 N15 **Thyolo** *var.* Cholo. Southern, S Malawi 16°03′S 35°11′E
183 U6 **Tia** New South Wales, SE Australia 31°14′S 151°51′E
54 H5 **Tía Juana** Zulia, NW Venezuela 10°18′N 71°24′W
Tiancheng *see* Chongyang
160 J14 **Tiandong** *var.* Pingma. Guangxi Zhuangzu Zizhiqu, S China 23°37′N 107°06′E
161 O3 **Tianjin** *var.* Tientsin. Tianjin Shi, E China 39°13′N 117°06′E
Tianjin *see* Tianjin Shi
161 P3 **Tianjin Shi** *var.* Jin, Tianjin, T'ien-ching, Tientsin. ◈ *municipality* E China
159 S10 **Tianjun** *var.* Xinyuan. Qinghai, C China 37°16′N 99°03′E
160 J13 **Tianlin** *var.* Leli. Guangxi Zhuangzu Zizhiqu, S China 24°27′N 106°03′E
Tian Shan *see* Tien Shan
159 W11 **Tianshui** Gansu, C China 34°33′N 105°51′E
150 I7 **Tianshuihai** Xinjiang Uygur Zizhiqu, W China 35°17′N 79°30′E
161 S10 **Tiantai** Zhejiang, SE China 29°11′N 121°01′E
160 J14 **Tianyang** *var.* Tianzhou. Guangxi Zhuangzu Zizhiqu, S China 23°50′N 106°52′E
Tianzhou *see* Tianyang
159 U9 **Tianzhu** *var.* Huazangsi, Tianzhu Zangzu Zizhixian. Gansu, C China 37°01′N 103°04′E
Tianzhu Zangzu Zizhixian *see* Tianzhu
191 Q7 **Tiarei** Tahiti, W French Polynesia 17°32′S 149°20′W
74 J6 **Tiaret** *var.* Tihert. NW Algeria 35°20′N 01°20′E
77 N17 **Tiassalé** S Ivory Coast 05°54′N 04°50′W
192 I16 **Ti'avea** Upolu, SE Samoa 13°58′S 171°30′W
Tiba *see* Chiba
60 J11 **Tibagi** *var.* Tibají. Paraná, S Brazil 24°29′S 50°29′W
60 J10 **Tibagi, Rio** *var.* Rio Tibají. ≈ S Brazil
Tibají *see* Tibagi
Tibají, Rio *see* Tibagi, Rio
139 Q9 **Tibal, Wādī** *dry watercourse* S Iraq
54 G9 **Tibaná** Boyacá, C Colombia 05°19′N 73°25′W
79 F14 **Tibati** Adamaoua, N Cameroon 06°25′N 12°33′E
76 K15 **Tibé, Pic de** ▲ SE Guinea 08°39′N 08°58′W
Tiber *see* Tevere, Italy
Tiber *see* Tivoli, Italy
Tiberias *see* Tverya
138 G8 **Tiberias, Lake** *var.* Chinnereth, Sea of Bahr Tabariya, Sea of Galilee, *Ar.* Bahrat Tabariya, *Heb.* Yam Kinneret. ◎ N Israel
67 Q5 **Tibesti** *var.* Tibesti Massif, *Ar.* Tibistī. ▲▲ N Africa
Tibesti Massif *see* Tibesti
Tibet *see* Xizang Zizhiqu
Tibetan Autonomous Region *see* Xizang Zizhiqu
Tibet, Plateau of *see* Qingzang Gaoyuan
Tibistī *see* Tibesti
14 K7 **Tiblemont, Lac** ◎ Québec, SE Canada
139 X9 **Ţīb, Nahr aţ** ≈ S Iraq
Tibnī *see* At Tibnī
182 L4 **Tibooburra** New South Wales, SE Australia 29°24′S 142°01′E
95 L18 **Tibro** Västra Götaland, S Sweden 58°25′N 14°11′E
40 E5 **Tiburón, Isla** *var.* Isla del Tiburón. *island* NW Mexico
Tiburón, Isla del *see* Tiburón, Isla
23 W14 **Tice** Florida, SE USA 26°40′N 81°49′W
Tichau *see* Tychy
114 L8 **Ticha, Yazovir** ⊠ NE Bulgaria
76 K9 **Tîchît** *var.* Tichitt. Tagant, C Mauritania 18°26′N 09°31′W
Tichitt *see* Tîchît
108 G11 **Ticino** *Fr./Ger.* Tessin. ◈ *canton* S Switzerland
106 D8 **Ticino** ≈ Italy/Switzerland
108 H11 **Ticino** *Ger.* Tessin. ≈ SW Switzerland
Ticinum *see* Pavia
41 X12 **Ticul** Yucatán, SE Mexico 20°22′N 89°30′W
95 K18 **Tidaholm** Västra Götaland, S Sweden 58°12′N 13°55′E
Tidjikdja *see* Tidjikja
76 J8 **Tidjikja** *var.* Tidjikdja; *prev.* Fort-Cappolani. Tagant, C Mauritania 18°31′N 11°24′W
Tidore *see* Soasiu
171 R11 **Tidore, Pulau** *island* E Indonesia
Tidra, Ile *see* Et Tîdra
77 N16 **Tiébissou** *var.* Tiebissou. C Ivory Coast 07°10′N 05°10′W
Tiebissou *see* Tiébissou
Tiefa *see* Diaobingshan
108 I9 **Tiefencastel** Graubünden, S Switzerland 46°40′N 09°33′E
Tiegenhof *see* Nowy Dwór Gdański
T'ieh-ling *see* Tieling
98 K13 **Tiel** Gelderland, C Netherlands 51°53′N 05°26′E
163 W7 **Tieli** Heilongjiang, NE China 46°57′N 128°01′E
163 V11 **Tieling** *var.* T'ieh-ling. Liaoning, NE China 42°19′N 123°52′E
152 L4 **Tielongtan** China/India 35°10′N 79°32′E
99 D17 **Tielt** *var.* Thielt. West-Vlaanderen, W Belgium 51°00′N 03°20′E
T'ien-ching *see* Tianjin Shi
99 I18 **Tienen** *var.* Thienen, *Fr.* Tirlemont. Vlaams Brabant, C Belgium 50°48′N 04°56′E
Tiên Giang, Sông *see* Mekong
147 X9 **Tien Shan** *Chin.* Thian Shan, Tian Shan, T'ien Shan, *Rus.* Tyan'-Shan'. ▲▲ C Asia
Tientsin *see* Tianjin
167 U6 **Tiên Yên** Quang Ninh, N Vietnam 21°19′N 107°24′E
95 O14 **Tierp** Uppsala, C Sweden 60°20′N 17°30′E
62 H7 **Tierra Amarilla** Atacama, N Chile 27°28′S 70°17′W
37 R9 **Tierra Amarilla** New Mexico, SW USA 36°42′N 106°31′W
41 R15 **Tierra Blanca** Veracruz-Llave, E Mexico 18°28′N 96°21′W
41 O16 **Tierra Colorada** Guerrero, S Mexico 17°10′N 99°30′W
63 J17 **Tierra Colorada, Bajo de la** *basin* SE Argentina
63 I25 **Tierra del Fuego** *off.* Provincia de la Tierra del Fuego. ◈ *province* S Argentina
63 J24 **Tierra del Fuego** *island* Argentina/Chile
Tierra del Fuego, Provincia de la *see* Tierra del Fuego
54 D7 **Tierralta** Córdoba, NW Colombia 08°10′N 76°04′W
104 K9 **Tiétar** ≈ W Spain
60 L10 **Tietê** São Paulo, S Brazil 23°04′S 47°41′W
60 J8 **Tietê, Rio** ≈ S Brazil
32 J9 **Tieton** Washington, NW USA 46°41′N 120°43′W
32 J6 **Tiffany Mountain** ▲ Washington, NW USA 48°40′N 119°55′W
31 S12 **Tiffin** Ohio, N USA 41°06′N 83°10′W
31 Q11 **Tiffin River** ≈ Ohio, N USA
Tiflis *see* Tbilisi
23 U7 **Tifton** Georgia, SE USA 31°27′N 83°31′W
171 R13 **Tifu** Pulau Buru, E Indonesia 03°46′S 126°36′E
38 L17 **Tigalda Island** *island* Aleutian Islands, Alaska, USA
115 I15 **Tigáni, Akrotírio** *headland* Límnos, E Greece 39°50′N 25°03′E
169 V6 **Tiga Tarok** Sabah, East Malaysia 06°57′N 117°07′E
117 O10 **Tighina** *Rus.* Bendery; *prev.* Bender. E Moldova 46°51′N 29°28′E
145 X9 **Tigiretskiy Khrebet** ▲▲ E Kazakhstan
79 F14 **Tignère** Adamaoua, N Cameroon 07°24′N 12°35′E
13 P14 **Tignish** Prince Edward Island, SE Canada 46°58′N 64°03′W
186 M10 **Tigoa** *var.* Tinggoa. Rennell, S Solomon Islands 11°39′S 160°13′E
Tigranocerta *see* Siirt
80 I11 **Tigray** ◈ *federal region* N Ethiopia
41 O11 **Tigre, Cerro del** ▲ C Mexico 23°06′N 99°13′W
56 F8 **Tigre, Río** ≈ N Peru
139 X10 **Tigris** *Ar.* Dijlah, *Turk.* Dicle. ≈ Iraq/Turkey
76 G9 **Tiguent** Trarza, SW Mauritania 17°15′N 16°00′W
74 M10 **Tiguentourine** E Algeria 27°59′N 09°16′E
77 V10 **Tiguidit, Falaise de** *ridge* C Niger
141 N13 **Tihāmah** *var.* Tehama. *plain* Saudi Arabia/Yemen
Tihert *see* Tiaret
Ti-hua/Tihwa *see* Ürümqi
41 Q13 **Tihuatlán** Veracruz-Llave, E Mexico 20°44′N 97°30′W
40 B1 **Tijuana** Baja California Norte, NW Mexico 32°32′N 117°01′W
42 E2 **Tikal** Petén, N Guatemala 17°11′N 89°36′W
154 I9 **Tīkamgarh** *prev.* Tehri. Madhya Pradesh, C India 24°44′N 78°50′E
158 L7 **Tikanlik** Xinjiang Uygur Zizhiqu, NW China 40°34′N 87°37′E
77 P12 **Tikaré** N Burkina 13°16′N 01°39′W
39 O12 **Tikchik Lakes** *lakes* Alaska, USA
191 T9 **Tikehau** *atoll* Îles Tuamotu, C French Polynesia
191 V9 **Tikei** *island* Îles Tuamotu, C French Polynesia
126 L13 **Tikhoretsk** Krasnodarskiy Kray, SW Russian Federation 45°51′N 40°07′E
124 I13 **Tikhvin** Leningradskaya Oblast', NW Russian Federation 59°37′N 33°30′E
193 P9 **Tiki Basin** *undersea feature* S Pacific Ocean
76 K13 **Tikinsso** ≈ NE Guinea
Tikirarjuaq *see* Whale Cove
184 Q8 **Tikitiki** Gisborne, North Island, New Zealand 37°49′S 178°23′E
79 D16 **Tiko** Sud-Ouest, SW Cameroon 04°02′N 09°19′E
139 S6 **Tikrīt** *var.* Tekrit. Şalāḩ ad Dīn, N Iraq 34°36′N 43°42′E
124 I8 **Tiksha** Respublika Kareliya, NW Russian Federation 64°07′N 32°31′E
124 I6 **Tikshozero, Ozero** ◎ NW Russian Federation
123 P7 **Tiksi** Respublika Sakha (Yakutiya), NE Russian Federation 71°40′N 128°47′E
Tiladummati Atoll *see* Thiladhunmathi Atoll
42 A6 **Tilapa** San Marcos, SW Guatemala 14°31′N 92°11′W
42 L13 **Tilarán** Guanacaste, NW Costa Rica 10°28′N 84°57′W
99 J14 **Tilburg** Noord-Brabant, S Netherlands 51°34′N 05°05′E
14 D17 **Tilbury** Ontario, S Canada 42°15′N 82°26′W
182 K4 **Tilcha** South Australia 29°37′S 140°52′E
Tilcha Creek *see* Callabonna Creek
29 Q14 **Tilden** Nebraska, C USA 42°03′N 97°49′W
25 R13 **Tilden** Texas, SW USA 28°27′N 98°43′W
14 H10 **Tilden Lake** Ontario, S Canada 46°35′N 79°36′W
116 G9 **Tileagd** *Hung.* Mezőtelegd. Bihor, W Romania 47°03′N 22°11′E
145 P9 **Tilekey** *prev.* Ladyzhenka. Akmola, C Kazakhstan 50°58′N 68°44′E
77 Q8 **Tilemsi, Vallée de** ≈ C Mali
123 V8 **Tilichiki** Krasnoyarskiy Kray, E Russian Federation 60°25′N 165°55′E
Tiligul *see* Tilihul
Tiligul'skiy Liman *see* Tilihul's'kyy Lyman
117 P9 **Tilihul** *Rus.* Tiligul. ≈ SW Ukraine
117 P10 **Tilihul's'kyy Lyman** *Rus.* Tiligul'skiy Liman. ◎ S Ukraine
Tilimsen *see* Tlemcen
Tilio Martius *see* Toulon
77 R11 **Tillabéri** *var.* Tillabéry. Tillabéri, W Niger 14°13′N 01°27′E
77 R11 **Tillabéri** ◈ *department* SW Niger
Tillabéry *see* Tillabéri
32 F11 **Tillamook** Oregon, NW USA 45°28′N 123°50′W
32 E11 **Tillamook Bay** *inlet* Oregon, NW USA
151 Q22 **Tillanchāng Dwīp** *island* Nicobar Islands, India, NE Indian Ocean
95 N15 **Tillberga** Västmanland, C Sweden 59°41′N 16°37′E
Tillenberg *see* Dyleń
21 S10 **Tillery, Lake** ⊠ North Carolina, SE USA
77 T10 **Tillia** Tahoua, W Niger 16°13′N 04°51′E
23 N8 **Tillmans Corner** Alabama, S USA 30°35′N 88°10′W
14 F17 **Tillsonburg** Ontario, S Canada 42°53′N 80°44′W
115 N22 **Tílos** *island* Dodekánisa, Greece, Aegean Sea
183 N5 **Tilpa** New South Wales, SE Australia 30°56′S 144°24′E
Tilsit *see* Sovetsk
31 N13 **Tilton** Illinois, N USA 40°06′N 87°39′W
126 K7 **Tim** Kurskaya Oblast', W Russian Federation 51°39′N 37°11′E
54 D12 **Timaná** Huila, S Colombia 01°58′N 75°55′W
Timan Ridge *see* Timanskiy Kryazh
125 Q6 **Timanskiy Kryazh** *Eng.* Timan Ridge. *ridge* NW Russian Federation
185 G20 **Timaru** Canterbury, South Island, New Zealand 44°23′S 171°15′E
127 S6 **Timashevo** Samarskaya Oblast', W Russian Federation 53°22′N 51°13′E
126 K13 **Timashevsk** Krasnodarskiy Kray, SW Russian Federation 45°37′N 38°57′E
Timbaki/Timbákion *see* Tympáki
22 K10 **Timbalier Bay** *bay* Louisiana, S USA
22 K11 **Timbalier Island** *island* Louisiana, S USA
76 L10 **Timbedgha** *var.* Timbédra. Hodh ech Chargui, SE Mauritania 16°17′N 08°14′W
Timbédra *see* Timbedgha
32 G10 **Timber** Oregon, NW USA 45°42′N 123°19′W
181 O3 **Timber Creek** Northern Territory, N Australia 15°35′S 130°21′E
28 M8 **Timber Lake** South Dakota, N USA 45°25′N 101°01′W
54 D12 **Timbío** Cauca, SW Colombia 02°20′N 76°40′W
54 C12 **Timbiquí** Cauca, SW Colombia 02°43′N 77°45′W
83 O17 **Timbue, Ponta** *headland* C Mozambique 18°49′S 36°22′E
Timbuktu *see* Tombouctou
169 W8 **Timbun Mata, Pulau** *island* E Malaysia
77 P8 **Timétrine** *var.* Ti-n-Kâr. *oasis* C Mali
Timfi *see* Týmfi
Timfristos *see* Tymfristós
77 V9 **Timia** Agadez, C Niger 18°07′N 08°49′E
171 X14 **Timika** Papua, E Indonesia 04°39′S 137°15′E
74 I9 **Timimoun** C Algeria 29°18′N 00°21′E
Timiris, Cap *see* Timirist, Râs
76 F8 **Timirist, Râs** *var.* Cap Timiris. *headland* NW Mauritania 19°18′N 16°28′W
145 O7 **Timiryazevo** Severnyy Kazakhstan, N Kazakhstan 53°45′N 66°33′E
116 E11 **Timiş** ◈ *county* SW Romania
14 H9 **Timiskaming, Lake** *Fr.* Lac Témiscamingue. ◎ Ontario/Québec, SE Canada
116 E11 **Timişoara** *Ger.* Temeschwar, Temeswar, *Hung.* Temesvár; *prev.* Temeschburg. Timiş, W Romania 45°46′N 21°17′E
116 E11 **Timisoara** ✈ Timiş, SW Romania 45°50′N 21°21′E
Timkovichi *see* Tsimkavichy
77 U8 **Ti-m-Meghsoï** ≈ NW Niger
100 K8 **Timmerdorfer Strand** Schleswig-Holstein, N Germany 53°59′N 10°50′E
14 F7 **Timmins** Ontario, S Canada 48°09′N 80°01′W
21 S12 **Timmonsville** South Carolina, SE USA 34°07′N 79°56′W
30 K5 **Timms Hill** ▲ Wisconsin, N USA 45°27′N 90°12′W
112 P12 **Timok** ≈ E Serbia
58 N13 **Timon** Maranhão, E Brazil 05°08′S 42°52′W
171 Q17 **Timor Sea** *sea* E Indian Ocean
Timor Timur *see* East Timor
Timor Trench *see* Timor Trough
192 G8 **Timor Trough** *var.* Timor Trench. *undersea feature* NE Timor Sea
61 A21 **Timote** Buenos Aires, E Argentina 35°22′S 62°13′W
54 I6 **Timotes** Mérida, NW Venezuela 08°57′N 70°46′W
25 X8 **Timpson** Texas, SW USA 31°54′N 94°24′W
123 Q11 **Timpton** ≈ NE Russian Federation
93 H17 **Timrå** Västernorrland, C Sweden 62°29′N 17°20′E
20 J10 **Tims Ford Lake** ⊠ Tennessee, S USA
168 L7 **Timur, Banjaran** ▲▲ Peninsular Malaysia
171 Q8 **Tinaca Point** *headland* Mindanao, S Philippines 05°35′N 125°18′E
54 K5 **Tinaco** Cojedes, N Venezuela 09°44′N 68°28′W
64 Q11 **Tinajo** Lanzarote, Islas Canarias, Spain, NE Atlantic Ocean 29°03′N 13°41′W
187 P10 **Tinakula** *island* Santa Cruz Islands, E Solomon Islands
54 K5 **Tinaquillo** Cojedes, N Venezuela 09°57′N 68°20′W
116 F10 **Tinca** *Hung.* Tenke. Bihor, W Romania 46°46′N 21°58′E
155 J20 **Tīndivanam** Tamil Nādu, SE India 12°15′N 79°41′E
74 E9 **Tindouf** W Algeria 27°43′N 08°09′W
74 E9 **Tindouf, Sebkha de** *salt lake* W Algeria
104 J2 **Tineo** Asturias, N Spain 43°20′N 06°25′W
77 R9 **Ti-n-Essako** Kidal, E Mali 18°30′N 02°27′E
Tinggoa *see* Tigoa
183 T5 **Tingha** New South Wales, SE Australia 29°56′S 151°13′E
Tingis *see* Tanger
Tinglett *see* Tinglev
95 F24 **Tinglev** *Ger.* Tinglett. Syddanmark, SW Denmark 54°57′N 09°15′E
56 E12 **Tingo María** Huánuco, C Peru 09°10′S 76°00′W
Tingréla *see* Tengréla
158 K16 **Tingri** *var.* Xêgar. Xizang Zizhiqu, W China 28°40′N 87°04′E
95 M21 **Tingsryd** Kronoberg, S Sweden 56°30′N 15°E
95 P19 **Tingstäde** Gotland, SE Sweden 57°45′N 18°36′E
62 H12 **Tinguiririca, Volcán** Ѫ C Chile 34°52′S 70°24′W
94 F9 **Tingvoll** Møre og Romsdal, S Norway 62°55′N 08°13′E
188 K8 **Tinian** *island* S Northern Mariana Islands
Ti-n-Kâr *see* Timétrine
Tinnevelly *see* Tirunelveli
95 G15 **Tinnoset** Telemark, S Norway 59°43′N 09°03′E
95 F15 **Tinnsjå** *prev.* Tinnsjø, *var.* Tinnsjö. ◎ S Norway *see also* Tinnsjø
Tinnsjø *see* Tinnsjå
Tinnsjö *see* Tinnsjå
Tino *see* Chino
115 J20 **Tínos** Tínos, Kykládes, Greece, Aegean Sea 37°33′N 25°08′E
115 J20 **Tínos** *anc.* Tenos. *island* Kykládes, Greece, Aegean Sea
153 R14 **Tinpahar** Jhārkhand, NE India 25°00′N 87°43′E
153 X11 **Tinsukia** Assam, NE India 27°28′N 95°20′E
76 K10 **Tîntâne** Hodh el Gharbi, S Mauritania 16°25′N 10°08′W
62 L7 **Tintina** Santiago del Estero, N Argentina 27°00′S 62°45′W
182 K10 **Tintinara** South Australia 35°54′S 140°04′E
104 I14 **Tinto** ≈ SW Spain
77 S8 **Ti-n-Zaouâtene** Kidal, NE Mali 19°56′N 02°45′E
Tiobraid Árann *see* Tipperary
28 K3 **Tioga** North Dakota, N USA 48°24′N 102°56′W
18 G12 **Tioga** Pennsylvania, NE USA 41°54′N 77°07′W
25 T5 **Tioga** Texas, SW USA 33°28′N 96°55′W
35 Q8 **Tioga Pass** *pass* California, W USA
18 G12 **Tioga River** ≈ New York/Pennsylvania, NE USA
Tioman Island *see* Tioman, Pulau
168 M9 **Tioman, Pulau** *var.* Tioman Island. *island* Peninsular Malaysia
18 C12 **Tionesta** Pennsylvania, NE USA 41°31′N 79°30′W
18 D12 **Tionesta Creek** ≈ Pennsylvania, NE USA
168 J13 **Tiop** Pulau Pagai Selatan, W Indonesia 03°12′S 100°21′E
18 H11 **Tioughnioga River** ≈ New York, NE USA
74 J5 **Tipasa** *var.* Tipaza. N Algeria 36°35′N 02°27′E
Tipaza *see* Tipasa
42 J10 **Tipitapa** Managua, W Nicaragua 12°08′N 86°04′W
31 R13 **Tipp City** Ohio, N USA 39°57′N 84°10′W
31 O12 **Tippecanoe River** ≈ Indiana, N USA
97 D20 **Tipperary** *Ir.* Tiobraid Árann. S Ireland 52°29′N 08°10′W
97 D19 **Tipperary** *Ir.* Tiobraid Árann. *cultural region* S Ireland
35 R12 **Tipton** California, W USA 36°02′N 119°19′W
31 P13 **Tipton** Indiana, N USA 40°19′N 86°00′W
29 Y14 **Tipton** Iowa, C USA 41°46′N 91°07′W
27 U5 **Tipton** Missouri, C USA 38°39′N 92°46′W
36 I10 **Tipton, Mount** ▲ Arizona, SW USA 35°32′N 114°11′W
20 F8 **Tiptonville** Tennessee, S USA 36°21′N 89°30′W
12 E12 **Tip Top Mountain** ▲ Ontario, S Canada 48°18′N 86°06′W
155 G19 **Tiptūr** Karnātaka, W India 13°17′N 76°31′E
Tiquisate *see* Pueblo Nuevo Tiquisate
58 L13 **Tiracambu, Serra do** ▲▲ E Brazil
Tirana *see* Tiranë
113 K19 **Tirana Rinas** ✈ Durrës, W Albania 41°25′N 19°41′E
113 L20 **Tiranë** *var.* Tirana. ● (Albania) Tiranë, C Albania 41°20′N 19°50′E
113 K20 **Tiranë** ◈ *district* W Albania
140 I5 **Tirān, Jazīrat** *island* Egypt/Saudi Arabia
106 F6 **Tirano** Lombardia, N Italy 46°13′N 10°10′E
182 I2 **Tirari Desert** *desert* South Australia
117 O10 **Tiraspol** *Rus.* Tiraspol'. E Moldova 46°50′N 29°35′E
Tiraspol' *see* Tiraspol
184 M8 **Tirau** Waikato, North Island, New Zealand 37°59′S 175°44′E
136 C14 **Tire** İzmir, SW Turkey 38°04′N 27°45′E
137 O11 **Tirebolu** Giresun, N Turkey 41°01′N 38°49′E
96 F11 **Tiree** *island* W Scotland, United Kingdom
Tîrgovişte *see* Târgovişte
Tîrgu *see* Târgu Cărbuneşti
Tîrgu Bujor *see* Târgu Bujor
Tîrgu Frumos *see* Târgu Frumos
Tîrgu Jiu *see* Targu Jiu
Tîrgu Lăpuş *see* Târgu Lăpuş
Tîrgu Mures *see* Târgu Mureş
Tîrgu-Neamţ *see* Târgu-Neamţ
Tîrgu Ocna *see* Târgu Ocna
Tîrgu Secuiesc *see* Târgu Secuiesc
149 T3 **Tirich Mīr** ▲ NW Pakistan 36°12′N 71°51′E
76 J5 **Tiris Zemmour** ◈ *region* N Mauritania
Tirlemont *see* Tienen
127 W5 **Tirlyanskiy** Respublika Bashkortostan, W Russian Federation 54°09′N 58°32′E
Tîrnava Mare *see* Târnava Mare
Tîrnava Mică *see* Târnava Mică
Tîrnăveni *see* Târnăveni
Tírnavos *see* Týrnavos
Tirnovo *see* Veliko Tŭrnovo
154 J11 **Tirodi** Madhya Pradesh, C India 21°40′N 79°44′E
108 K8 **Tirol** *off.* Land Tirol, *var.* Tyrol, *It.* Tirolo. ◈ *state* W Austria
Tirol, Land *see* Tirol
Tirolo *see* Tirol
Tirreno, Mare *see* Tyrrhenian Sea
107 B19 **Tirso** ≈ Sardegna, Italy, C Mediterranean Sea
95 H22 **Tirstrup** ✈ (Århus) Århus, C Denmark 56°17′N 10°36′E
155 I21 **Tiruchchirāppalli** *prev.* Trichinopoly. Tamil Nādu, SE India 10°50′N 78°43′E
155 H23 **Tirunelveli** *var.* Tinnevelly. Tamil Nādu, SE India 08°45′N 77°43′E
155 J19 **Tirupati** Andhra Pradesh, E India 13°39′N 79°25′E
155 I20 **Tiruppattūr** Tamil Nādu, SE India 12°28′N 78°31′E
155 H21 **Tiruppur** Tamil Nādu, SW India 11°05′N 77°20′E
Tiruvantapuram *see* Thiruvanathapuram/Trivandrum
155 I20 **Tiruvannāmalai** Tamil Nādu, SE India 12°13′N 79°07′E
112 L10 **Tisa** *Ger.* Theiss, *Hung.* Tisza, *Rus.* Tissa, *Ukr.* Tysa. ≈ SE Europe *see also* Tisza
Tisa *see* Tisza
Tischnowitz *see* Tišnov
11 U14 **Tisdale** Saskatchewan, S Canada 52°51′N 104°01′W
27 O13 **Tishomingo** Oklahoma, C USA 34°15′N 96°41′W
95 M17 **Tisnaren** ◎ S Sweden
111 F18 **Tišnov** *Ger.* Tischnowitz. Jihomoravský Kraj, SE Czech Republic 49°22′N 16°24′E
Tissa *see* Tisa/Tisza
74 J6 **Tissemsilt** N Algeria 35°37′N 01°48′E
153 S12 **Tista** ≈ NE India
112 L8 **Tisza** *Ger.* Theiss, *Rom./Slvn./SCr.* Tisa, *Rus.* Tissa, *Ukr.* Tysa. ≈ SE Europe *see also* Tisa
Tisza *see* Tisa
111 L23 **Tiszaföldvár** Jász-Nagykun-Szolnok, E Hungary 47°00′N 20°16′E
111 M22 **Tiszafüred** Jász-Nagykun-Szolnok, E Hungary 47°38′N 20°45′E
111 L23 **Tiszakécske** Bács-Kiskun, C Hungary 46°56′N 20°04′E
111 M21 **Tiszaújváros** *prev.* Leninváros. Borsod-Abaúj-Zemplén, NE Hungary 47°56′N 21°03′E
111 N21 **Tiszavasvári** Szabolcs-Szatmár-Bereg, NE Hungary 47°56′N 21°21′E
57 I17 **Titicaca, Lake** ◎ Bolivia/Peru
190 H17 **Titikaveka** Rarotonga, S Cook Islands 21°16′S 159°45′W
154 M13 **Titilāgarh** *var.* Titlagarh. Orissa, E India 20°18′N 83°09′E
168 K8 **Titiwangsa, Banjaran** ▲▲ Peninsular Malaysia
Titlagarh *see* Titilāgarh
Titograd *see* Podgorica
Titose *see* Chitose
Titova Mitrovica *see* Mitrovicë
Titovo Užice *see* Užice
113 M18 **Titov Vrv** ▲ NW FYR Macedonia 41°58′N 20°49′E
94 F7 **Titran** Sør-Trøndelag, S Norway 63°40′N 08°20′E
31 Q8 **Tittabawassee River** ≈ Michigan, N USA
116 J13 **Titu** Dâmboviţa, S Romania 44°40′N 25°32′E
79 M16 **Titule** Orientale, N Dem. Rep. Congo 03°20′N 25°23′E
23 X11 **Titusville** Florida, SE USA 28°37′N 80°50′W
18 C12 **Titusville** Pennsylvania, NE USA 41°36′N 79°39′W
76 G11 **Tivaouane** W Senegal 14°59′N 16°50′W
113 J17 **Tivat** SW Montenegro 42°25′N 18°43′E
14 E14 **Tiverton** Ontario, S Canada 44°15′N 81°31′W
97 J23 **Tiverton** SW England, United Kingdom 50°54′N 03°30′W
19 O12 **Tiverton** Rhode Island, NE USA 41°38′N 71°10′W
107 I15 **Tivoli** *anc.* Tiber. Lazio, C Italy 41°58′N 12°45′E
25 U13 **Tivoli** Texas, SW USA 28°26′N 96°54′W
141 Z8 **Ţīwī** NE Oman 22°43′N 59°20′E
41 Y11 **Tizimín** Yucatán, SE Mexico 21°10′N 88°09′W
74 K5 **Tizi Ouzou** *var.* Tizi-Ouzou. N Algeria 36°44′N 04°06′E
Tizi-Ouzou *see* Tizi Ouzou
74 D8 **Tiznit** SW Morocco 29°43′N 09°39′W
95 F23 **Tjæreborg** Syddtjylland, W Denmark 55°28′N 08°35′E
113 I14 **Tjentište** Republika Srpska, SE Bosnia and Herzegovina 43°23′N 18°42′E
98 L7 **Tjeukemeer** ◎ N Netherlands
Tjiamis *see* Ciamis
Tjiandjoer *see* Cianjur
Tjilatjap *see* Cilacap
Tjirebon *see* Cirebon
95 I18 **Tjörn** *island* S Sweden
92 O3 **Tjuvfjorden** *fjord* S Svalbard
Tkvarcheli *see* T'q'varcheli
40 L5 **Tlahualilo** Durango, N Mexico 26°06′N 103°25′W
41 P14 **Tlalnepantla** México, C Mexico 19°34′N 99°12′W
41 Q13 **Tlapacoyán** Veracruz-Llave, E Mexico 19°58′N 97°13′W
41 P16 **Tlapa de Comonfort** Guerrero, S Mexico 17°33′N 98°33′W
40 L13 **Tlaquepaque** Jalisco, C Mexico 20°36′N 103°19′W
Tlascala *see* Tlaxcala
41 P14 **Tlaxcala** *var.* Tlascala, Tlaxcala de Xicohténcatl. Tlaxcala, C Mexico 19°17′N 98°16′W
41 P14 **Tlaxcala** ◈ *state* S Mexico
Tlaxcala de Xicohténcatl *see* Tlaxcala
41 P14 **Tlaxco** *var.* Tlaxco de Morelos. Tlaxcala, S Mexico 19°38′N 98°06′W
Tlaxco de Morelos *see* Tlaxco
41 Q16 **Tlaxiaco** *var.* Santa María Asunción Tlaxiaco. Oaxaca, S Mexico 17°18′N 97°42′W
74 I6 **Tlemcen** *var.* Tilimsen, Tlemsen. NW Algeria 34°53′N 01°21′W
Tlemsen *see* Tlemcen
138 L4 **Tlété Ouâte Rharbi, Jebel** ▲ N Syria
116 J7 **Tlumach** Ivano-Frankivs'ka Oblast', W Ukraine 48°53′N 25°00′E
127 P17 **Tlyarata** Respublika Dagestan, SW Russian Federation 42°10′N 46°30′E
116 K10 **Toaca, Vârful** *prev.* Vîrful Toaca. ▲ NE Romania 46°58′N 25°55′E
Toaca, Vîrful *see* Toaca, Vârful
191 Q8 **Toahotu** *prev.* Teohatu. Tahiti, W French Polynesia
187 R13 **Toak** Ambrym, C Vanuatu 16°21′S 168°16′E
172 J4 **Toamasina** *prev./Fr.* Tamatave. Toamasina, E Madagascar 18°10′S 49°23′E
172 J4 **Toamasina** ◈ *province* E Madagascar
172 J4 **Toamasina** ✈ Toamasina, E Madagascar 18°10′S 49°23′E
21 X6 **Toano** Virginia, NE USA 37°22′N 76°46′W
191 U10 **Toau** *atoll* Îles Tuamotu, C French Polynesia
45 T6 **Toa Vaca, Embalse** ⊠ C Puerto Rico
62 K13 **Toay** La Pampa, C Argentina 36°43′S 64°22′W
159 R14 **Toba** Xizang Zizhiqu, W China 31°17′N 97°37′E
164 K14 **Toba** Mie, Honshū, SW Japan 34°29′N 136°51′E
168 I9 **Toba, Danau** ◎ Sumatera, W Indonesia
45 Y16 **Tobago** *island* NE Trinidad and Tobago
149 Q9 **Toba Kākar Range** ▲▲ NW Pakistan
105 Q12 **Tobarra** Castilla-La Mancha, C Spain 38°36′N 01°41′W
149 U9 **Toba Tek Singh** Punjab, E Pakistan 30°54′N 72°30′E
171 R11 **Tobelo** Pulau Halmahera, E Indonesia 01°45′N 127°59′E
14 E12 **Tobermory** Ontario, S Canada 45°15′N 81°39′W
96 G10 **Tobermory** W Scotland, United Kingdom 56°37′N 06°12′W
165 S4 **Tōbetsu** Hokkaidō, NE Japan 43°12′N 141°28′E
180 M6 **Tobin Lake** ◎ Western Australia
11 U14 **Tobin Lake** ◎ Saskatchewan, C Canada
35 T4 **Tobin, Mount** ▲ Nevada, W USA 40°25′N 117°28′W
165 O9 **Tobi-shima** *island* C Japan
169 N13 **Toboali** Pulau Bangka, W Indonesia 03°00′S 106°30′E
Tobol *see* Tobyl
122 H11 **Tobol'sk** Tyumenskaya Oblast', C Russian Federation 58°15′N 68°12′E
Tobruch/Tobruk *see* Ţubruq
125 R3 **Tobseda** Nenetskiy Avtonomnyy Okrug, NW Russian Federation 68°37′N 52°24′E
144 M8 **Tobyl** *prev.* Tobol. Kustanay, N Kazakhstan 52°42′N 62°36′E
144 L8 **Tobyl** *prev.* Tobol. ≈ Kazakhstan/Russian Federation
125 Q6 **Tobysh** ≈ NW Russian Federation
54 F10 **Tocaima** Cundinamarca, C Colombia 04°30′N 74°38′W
59 K16 **Tocantins** *off.* Estado do Tocantins. ◈ *state* C Brazil
Tocantins, Estado do *see* Tocantins
59 K15 **Tocantins, Rio** ≈ N Brazil
23 T2 **Toccoa** Georgia, SE USA 34°34′N 83°19′W
165 O12 **Tochigi** *off.* Tochigi-ken, *var.* Totigi. ◈ *prefecture* Honshū, S Japan
Tochigi-ken *see* Tochigi
165 O11 **Tochio** *var.* Totio. Niigata, Honshū, C Japan 37°27′N 139°00′E
95 J15 **Töcksfors** Värmland, C Sweden 59°30′N 11°49′E
42 J5 **Tocoa** Colón, N Honduras 15°40′N 86°01′W
62 H4 **Tocopilla** Antofagasta, N Chile 22°06′S 70°08′W
62 J4 **Tocorpuri, Cerro de** ▲ Bolivia/Chile 22°26′S 67°53′W
183 O10 **Tocumwal** New South Wales, SE Australia 35°53′S 145°35′E
54 K4 **Tocuyo de la Costa** Falcón, NW Venezuela 11°04′N 68°23′W
152 H13 **Toda Rāisingh** Rājasthān, N India 26°02′N 75°35′E
106 H13 **Todi** Umbria, C Italy 42°47′N 12°25′E
108 G9 **Tödi** ▲ NE Switzerland 46°52′N 08°53′E
171 T12 **Todlo** Papua, E Indonesia 0°46′S 130°50′E
165 S9 **Todoga-saki** *headland* Honshū, C Japan 39°33′N 142°02′E
59 P17 **Todos os Santos, Baía de** *bay* E Brazil
40 F10 **Todos Santos** Baja California Sur, NW Mexico 23°28′N 110°14′W
40 B2 **Todos Santos, Bahía de** *bay* NW Mexico
Toeban *see* Tuban
Toekang Besi Eilanden *see* Tukangbesi, Kepulauan
Toeloengagoeng *see* Tulungagung
Tōen *see* Taoyuan
185 D25 **Toetoes Bay** *bay* South Island, New Zealand
11 Q14 **Tofield** Alberta, SW Canada 53°22′N 112°39′W
10 K17 **Tofino** Vancouver Island, British Columbia, SW Canada 49°05′N 125°51′W
189 X17 **Tofol** Kosrae, E Micronesia
95 J20 **Tofta** Halland, S Sweden 57°10′N 12°19′E
95 H15 **Tofte** Buskerud, S Norway 59°31′N 10°33′E
95 F24 **Toftlund** Syddanmark, SW Denmark 55°12′N 09°04′E
193 X15 **Tofua** *island* Ha'apai Group, C Tonga
187 Q12 **Toga** *island* Torres Islands, N Vanuatu
80 N13 **Togdheer** *off.* Gobolka Togdheer. ◈ *region* NW Somalia
Togdheer, Gobolka *see* Togdheer
164 L11 **Togi** Ishikawa, Honshū, SW Japan 37°06′N 136°44′E
39 N13 **Togiak** Alaska, USA 59°03′N 160°31′W
171 O11 **Togian, Kepulauan** *island group* C Indonesia
77 Q15 **Togo** *off.* Togolese Republic; *prev.* French Togoland. ◆ *republic* W Africa
Togolese Republic *see* Togo

◆ Country
● Country Capital
◇ Dependent Territory
○ Dependent Territory Capital
◈ Administrative Regions
✈ International Airport
▲ Mountain
▲▲ Mountain Range
Ѫ Volcano
≈ River
◎ Lake
⊠ Reservoir

162 F8 **Tögrög** Govĭ-Altay, SW Mongolia *45°51'N 95°04'E*
162 F8 **Tögrög** *var.* Hoolt. Övörhangay, C Mongolia *45°31'N 103°06'E*
Tögrög *see* Manhan
159 N12 **Togton He** *var.* Tuotuo He. ≈ C China
Togton Heyan *see* Tanggulashan
Toguzak *see* Togyzak
144 L7 **Togyzak** *prev.* Toguzak. ≈ Kazakhstan/Russian Federation
37 P10 **Tohatchi** New Mexico, SW USA *35°51'N 108°45'W*
191 O7 **Tohiea, Mont** 🌋 Moorea, W French Polynesia *17°33'S 149°48'W*
137 N14 **Tohma Çayı** ≈ C Turkey
93 O17 **Tohmajärvi** Itä-Suomi, SE Finland *62°12'N 30°19'E*
93 L16 **Toholampi** Länsi-Suomi, W Finland *63°46'N 24°15'E*
Töhöm *see* Mandah
23 X12 **Tohopekaliga, Lake** ⊛ Florida, SE USA
164 M14 **Toi** Shizuoka, Honshū, S Japan *34°55'N 138°45'E*
190 B15 **Toi** N Niue *18°57'S 169°51'W*
93 L19 **Toijala** Länsi-Suomi, SW Finland *61°09'N 23°51'E*
171 P12 **Toima** Sulawesi, N Indonesia *0°48'S 122°21'E*
164 D17 **Toi-misaki** Kyūshū, SW Japan
171 Q17 **Toineke** Timor, S Indonesia *10°06'S 124°22'E*
Toirc, Inis *see* Inishturk
35 U6 **Toiyabe Range** ▲▲ Nevada, W USA
Tojikiston, Jumhurii *see* Tajikistan
147 R12 **Tojikobod** *Rus.* Tadzhikabad. C Tajikistan *39°08'N 70°54'E*
164 G12 **Tōjō** Hiroshima, Honshū, SW Japan *34°54'N 133°15'E*
39 T10 **Tok** Alaska, USA *63°20'N 142°59'W*
164 K13 **Tōkai** Aichi, Honshū, SW Japan *35°01'N 136°51'E*
111 N21 **Tokaj** Borsod-Abaúj-Zemplén, NE Hungary *48°08'N 21°25'E*
165 N11 **Tōkamachi** Niigata, Honshū, C Japan *37°08'N 138°44'E*
185 D25 **Tokanui** Southland, South Island, New Zealand *46°33'S 169°02'E*
80 I7 **Tokar** *var.* Ṭawkar. Red Sea, NE Sudan *18°27'N 37°41'E*
136 L12 **Tokat** Tokat, N Turkey *40°20'N 36°35'E*
136 L12 **Tokat** ◈ *province* N Turkey
Tŏkchŏk-kundo *see* Deokjeok-gundo
Tōke *see* Taka Atoll
190 J9 **Tokelau** ◇ *NZ overseas territory* W Polynesia
Tőketerebes *see* Trebišov
Tokhtamyshbek *see* Tŭkhtamish
24 M6 **Tokio** Texas, SW USA *33°09'N 102°31'W*
Tokio *see* Tōkyō
189 W11 **Toki Point** *point* NW Wake Island
Tokkuztara *see* Gongliu
117 V9 **Tokmak** *var.* Velykyy Tokmak. Zaporiz'ka Oblast', SE Ukraine *47°13'N 35°43'E*
Tokmak *see* Tomok
184 Q8 **Tokomaru Bay** Gisborne, North Island, New Zealand *38°10'S 178°18'E*
184 M8 **Tokoroa** Waikato, North Island, New Zealand *38°14'S 175°52'E*
76 K14 **Tokounou** C Guinea *09°43'N 09°46'W*
38 M12 **Toksook Bay** Alaska, USA *60°33'N 165°01'W*
Toksu *see* Xinhe
Toksum *see* Toksun
158 L6 **Toksun** *var.* Toksum. Xinjiang Uygur Zizhiqu, NW China *42°47'N 88°38'E*
147 T8 **Toktogul** Talasskaya Oblast', NW Kyrgyzstan *41°51'N 72°56'E*
147 T9 **Toktogul'skoye Vodokhranilishche** ⊠ W Kyrgyzstan
Toktomush *see* Tŭkhtamish
193 Y14 **Toku** *island* Vava'u Group, N Tonga
165 U16 **Tokunoshima** Kagoshima, Tokuno-shima, SW Japan
165 U16 **Tokuno-shima** *island* Nansei-shotō, SW Japan
164 I14 **Tokushima** *var.* Tokusima. Tokushima, Shikoku, SW Japan *34°04'N 134°28'E*
164 H14 **Tokushima** *off.* Tokushima-ken, *var.* Tokusima. ◈ *prefecture* Shikoku, SW Japan
Tokushima-ken *see* Tokushima
Tokusima *see* Tokushima
164 E13 **Tokuyama** *var.* Shūnan. Yamaguchi, Honshū, SW Japan *34°04'N 131°48'E*
165 N13 **Tōkyō** *var.* Tokio. ● (Japan) Tōkyō, Honshū, S Japan *35°40'N 139°45'E*
165 O13 **Tōkyō** *off.* Tōkyō-to. ◈ *capital district* Honshū, S Japan
Tōkyō-to *see* Tōkyō
145 T12 **Tokyrau** ≈ C Kazakhstan
149 O3 **Tokzār** *Pash.* Tukzār. Sar-e Pul, N Afghanistan *35°47'N 66°28'E*
145 W13 **Tokzhaylau** *prev.* Dzerzhinskoye. Almaty, SE Kazakhstan *45°49'N 81°04'E*
145 W13 **Tokzhaylau** *var.* Dzerzhinskoye. Taldykorgan, SE Kazakhstan *45°49'N 81°04'E*
189 U12 **Tol** *atoll* Chuuk Islands, C Micronesia
184 Q9 **Tolaga Bay** Gisborne, North Island, New Zealand *38°22'S 178°17'E*
172 I7 **Tôlañaro** *prev.* Faradofay, Fort-Dauphin. Toliara, SE Madagascar
162 D6 **Tolbo** Bayan-Ölgiy, W Mongolia *48°22'N 90°22'E*
Tolbukhin *see* Dobrich
60 G11 **Toledo** Paraná, S Brazil *24°45'S 53°41'W*
54 G8 **Toledo** Norte de Santander, N Colombia *07°16'N 72°28'W*
105 N9 **Toledo** *anc.* Toletum. Castilla-La Mancha, C Spain *39°52'N 04°02'W*
30 M14 **Toledo** Illinois, N USA *39°16'N 88°15'W*
29 W13 **Toledo** Iowa, C USA *42°00'N 92°34'W*
31 R11 **Toledo** Ohio, N USA *41°40'N 83°33'W*
32 F12 **Toledo** Oregon, NW USA *44°37'N 123°56'W*
32 G9 **Toledo** Washington, NW USA *46°27'N 122°49'W*
42 F3 **Toledo** ◈ *district* S Belize
104 M9 **Toledo** ◈ *province* Castilla-La Mancha, C Spain
25 Y7 **Toledo Bend Reservoir** ⊠ Louisiana/Texas, SW USA
104 M10 **Toledo, Montes de** ▲▲ C Spain
106 J12 **Tolentino** Marche, C Italy *43°08'N 13°17'E*
Toletum *see* Toledo
94 H10 **Tolga** Hedmark, S Norway *62°25'N 11°00'E*
158 J3 **Toli** Xinjiang Uygur Zizhiqu, NW China *45°55'N 83°33'E*
172 H7 **Toliara** *var.* Toliary; *prev.* Tuléar. Toliara, SW Madagascar *23°20'S 43°41'E*
172 H7 **Toliara** ◈ *province* SW Madagascar
Toliary *see* Toliara
118 H11 **Toliejai** *prev.* Kamajai. Panevėžys, NE Lithuania *55°16'N 25°30'E*
54 D11 **Tolima** *off.* Departamento del Tolima. ◈ *province* C Colombia
Tolima, Departamento del *see* Tolima
171 N11 **Tolitoli** Sulawesi, C Indonesia *01°05'N 120°50'E*
95 K22 **Tollarp** Skåne, S Sweden *55°55'N 14°00'E*
100 N9 **Tollense** ≈ NE Germany
100 N10 **Tollensesee** ⊛ NE Germany
36 K13 **Tolleson** Arizona, SW USA *33°25'N 112°15'W*
146 M13 **Tollimarjon** *Rus.* Talimardzhan. Qashqadaryo Viloyati, S Uzbekistan *38°22'N 65°31'E*
Tolmein *see* Tolmin
106 J6 **Tolmezzo** Friuli-Venezia Giulia, NE Italy *46°27'N 13°01'E*
109 S11 **Tolmin** *Ger.* Tolmein, *It.* Tolmino. W Slovenia *46°12'N 13°39'E*
Tolmino *see* Tolmin
111 J25 **Tolna** *Ger.* Tolnau. Tolna, S Hungary *46°26'N 18°47'E*
111 I24 **Tolna** *off.* Tolna Megye. ◈ *county* SW Hungary
Tolna Megye *see* Tolna
Tolnau *see* Tolna
79 I20 **Tolo** Bandundu, W Dem. Rep. Congo *02°57'S 18°35'E*
Tolochin *see* Talachyn
190 D12 **Toloke** Île Futuna, W Wallis and Futuna
30 M13 **Tolono** Illinois, N USA *39°59'N 88°16'W*
105 Q3 **Tolosa** País Vasco, N Spain *43°09'N 02°04'W*
Tolosa *see* Toulouse
171 O13 **Tolo, Teluk** *bay* Sulawesi, C Indonesia
39 R9 **Tolovana River** ≈ Alaska, USA
123 U10 **Tolstoy, Mys** *headland* E Russian Federation *59°12'N 155°04'E*
63 G15 **Toltén** Araucanía, C Chile *39°13'S 73°15'W*
63 G15 **Toltén, Río** ≈ S Chile
54 E6 **Tolú** Sucre, NW Colombia *09°32'N 75°34'W*
41 O14 **Toluca** *var.* Toluca de Lerdo. México, S Mexico *19°20'N 99°40'W*
Toluca de Lerdo *see* Toluca
41 O14 **Toluca, Nevado de** 🌋 C Mexico *19°05'N 99°45'W*
127 R6 **Tol'yatti** *prev.* Stavropol'. Samarskaya Oblast', W Russian Federation *53°32'N 49°27'E*
77 O12 **Toma** NW Burkina *12°46'N 02°51'W*
30 K7 **Tomah** Wisconsin, N USA *43°59'N 90°31'W*
30 L5 **Tomahawk** Wisconsin, N USA *45°27'N 89°40'W*
117 T8 **Tomakivka** Dnipropetrovs'ka Oblast', E Ukraine *47°47'N 34°45'E*
165 S4 **Tomakomai** Hokkaidō, NE Japan *42°38'N 141°32'E*
165 S2 **Tomamae** Hokkaidō, NE Japan *44°18'N 141°38'E*
104 G9 **Tomar** Santarém, W Portugal *39°36'N 08°25'W*
123 T13 **Tomari** Ostrov Sakhalin, Sakhalinskaya Oblast', SE Russian Federation *47°47'N 142°09'E*
115 C16 **Tómaros** ▲ W Greece *39°31'N 20°45'E*
Tomaschow *see* Tomaszów Mazowiecki
Tomaschow *see* Tomaszów Lubelski
61 E16 **Tomás Gomensoro** Artigas, N Uruguay *30°28'S 57°28'W*
117 N7 **Tomashpil'** Vinnyts'ka Oblast', C Ukraine *48°32'N 28°31'E*
Tomaszów *see* Tomaszów Mazowiecki
111 P15 **Tomaszów Lubelski** *Ger.* Tomaschow. Lubelskie, E Poland *50°29'N 23°23'E*
Tomaszów Mazowiecka *see* Tomaszów Mazowiecki
110 L13 **Tomaszów Mazowiecki** *var.* Tomaszów Mazowiecka; *prev.* Tomaszów, *Ger.* Tomaschow. Łódzkie, C Poland *51°33'N 20°E*
40 J13 **Tomatlán** Jalisco, C Mexico *19°53'N 105°18'W*
81 F15 **Tombe** Jonglei, E South Sudan *05°52'N 31°40'E*
23 N4 **Tombigbee River** ≈ Alabama/Mississippi, S USA
82 A10 **Tomboco** Dem. Rep. Congo, NW Angola *06°50'S 13°20'E*
77 O10 **Tombouctou** *Eng.* Timbuktu. Tombouctou, N Mali *16°47'N 03°03'W*
77 N9 **Tombouctou** ◈ *region* W Mali
37 N16 **Tombstone** Arizona, SW USA *31°42'N 110°04'W*
83 A15 **Tombua** *Port.* Porto Alexandre. Namibe, SW Angola *15°49'S 11°53'E*
83 J19 **Tom Burke** Limpopo, NE South Africa *23°07'S 28°01'E*
146 L9 **Tomdibuloq** *Rus.* Tamdybulak. Navoiy Viloyati, N Uzbekistan *41°48'N 64°33'E*
146 L9 **Tomditov-Tog'lari** ▲▲ N Uzbekistan
62 G13 **Tomé** Bío Bío, C Chile *36°38'S 72°57'W*
58 L12 **Tomé-Açu** Pará, NE Brazil *02°25'S 48°09'W*
95 L23 **Tomelilla** Skåne, S Sweden *55°33'N 14°00'E*
105 O10 **Tomelloso** Castilla-La Mancha, C Spain *39°09'N 03°01'W*
14 H10 **Tomiko Lake** ⊛ Ontario, S Canada
77 N12 **Tominian** Ségou, C Mali *13°18'N 04°39'W*
Tomini, Gulf of *see* Tomini, Teluk
171 N12 **Tomini, Teluk** *var.* Gulf of Tomini; *prev.* Teluk Gorontalo. *bay* Sulawesi, C Indonesia
165 Q11 **Tomioka** Fukushima, Honshū, C Japan *37°19'N 140°57'E*
113 G14 **Tomislavgrad** Federacija Bosna I Hercegovina, SW Bosnia and Herzegovina *43°43'N 17°15'E*
181 O9 **Tomkinson Ranges** ▲▲ South Australia/Western Australia
123 Q11 **Tommot** Respublika Sakha (Yakutiya), NE Russian Federation *58°57'N 126°24'E*
171 Q11 **Tomohon** Sulawesi, N Indonesia *01°19'N 124°49'E*
147 V7 **Tomok** *prev.* Tokmak. Chuyskaya Oblast', N Kyrgyzstan *42°50'N 75°18'E*
54 K9 **Tomo, Río** ≈ E Colombia
113 L21 **Tomorrit, Mali i** ▲ S Albania *40°43'N 20°12'E*
11 S17 **Tompkins** Saskatchewan, S Canada *50°03'N 108°49'W*
20 K8 **Tompkinsville** Kentucky, S USA *36°43'N 85°41'W*
171 N11 **Tompo** Sulawesi, N Indonesia *0°56'N 120°16'E*
180 I8 **Tom Price** Western Australia *22°48'S 117°49'E*
122 J12 **Tomsk** Tomskaya Oblast', C Russian Federation *56°30'N 85°05'E*
122 I11 **Tomskaya Oblast'** ◈ *province* C Russian Federation
18 K16 **Toms River** New Jersey, NE USA *39°56'N 74°09'W*
Tom Steed Lake *see* Tom Steed Reservoir
26 L12 **Tom Steed Reservoir** *var.* Tom Steed Lake. ⊠ Oklahoma, C USA
171 U13 **Tomu** Papua, E Indonesia *02°07'S 133°01'E*
158 H6 **Tomür Feng** *var.* Pobeda Peak, *Rus.* Pik Pobedy. ▲ China/Kyrgyzstan *42°02'N 80°07'E* *see also* Pobedy, Pik
Tomür Feng *see* Pobedy, Pik
189 N13 **Tomworoahlang** Pohnpei, E Micronesia
41 U17 **Tonalá** Chiapas, SE Mexico *16°08'N 93°41'W*
106 F6 **Tonale, Passo del** *pass* N Italy
164 I11 **Tonami** Toyama, Honshū, SW Japan *36°40'N 136°55'E*
58 C12 **Tonantins** Amazonas, W Brazil *02°58'S 67°30'W*
32 K6 **Tonasket** Washington, NW USA *48°41'N 119°27'W*
55 Y9 **Tonate** *var.* Macouria. N French Guiana *05°00'N 52°28'W*
18 D10 **Tonawanda** New York, NE USA *43°00'N 78°51'W*
42 I7 **Toncontín** *prev.* Tegucigalpa. ● (Honduras) Francisco Morazán, SW Honduras *14°04'N 87°11'W*
42 H7 **Toncontín** ✈ Central District, C Honduras *14°03'N 87°20'W*
171 Q11 **Tondano** Sulawesi, C Indonesia *01°19'N 124°56'E*
104 H7 **Tondela** Viseu, N Portugal *40°31'N 08°05'W*
95 F24 **Tønder** *Ger.* Tondern. Syddanmark, SW Denmark *54°57'N 08°53'E*
Tondern *see* Tønder
143 N4 **Tonekābon** *var.* Shahsawar, Tonkābon; *prev.* Shahsavār. Māzandarān, N Iran *36°40'N 51°25'E*
Tonezh *see* Tonyezh
193 Y14 **Tonga** *off.* Kingdom of Tonga, *var.* Friendly Islands. ◆ *monarchy* SW Pacific Ocean
175 R9 **Tonga** *island group* SW Pacific Ocean
Tongaat *see* oThongathi
Tonga, Kingdom of *see* Tonga
161 Q13 **Tong'an** *var.* Datong, Tong an. Fujian, SE China *24°43'N 118°07'E*
Tong an *see* Tong'an
27 Q4 **Tonganoxie** Kansas, C USA *39°06'N 95°05'W*
39 Y13 **Tongass National Forest** *reserve* Alaska, USA
193 Y16 **Tongatapu** ✈ Tongatapu, S Tonga *21°10'S 175°10'W*
193 Y16 **Tongatapu** *island* Tongatapu Group, S Tonga
193 Y16 **Tongatapu Group** *island group* S Tonga
175 S9 **Tonga Trench** *undersea feature* S Pacific Ocean
161 N8 **Tongbai Shan** ▲▲ C China
161 P8 **Tongcheng** Anhui, E China *31°16'N 117°00'E*
160 L6 **Tongchuan** Shaanxi, C China *35°10'N 109°03'E*
160 L12 **Tongdao** *var.* Tongdao Dongzu Zizhixian; *prev.* Shuangjiang. Hunan, S China *26°06'N 109°46'E*
Tongdao Dongzu Zizhixian *see* Tongdao
159 T11 **Tongde** *var.* Gabasumdo. Qinghai, C China *35°13'N 100°39'E*
99 K19 **Tongeren** *Fr.* Tongres. Limburg, NE Belgium *50°47'N 05°28'E*
Tonghae *see* Donghae
160 G13 **Tonghai** *var.* Xiushan. Yunnan, SW China *24°06'N 102°45'E*
163 X8 **Tonghe** Heilongjiang, NE China *46°00'N 128°45'E*
163 W11 **Tonghua** Jilin, NE China *41°45'N 125°50'E*
163 Z6 **Tongjiang** Heilongjiang, NE China *47°39'N 132°29'E*
163 Y13 **Tongjosŏn-man** *prev.* Broughton Bay. *bay* E North Korea
163 V7 **Tongken He** ≈ NE China
167 T7 **Tongking, Gulf of** *Chin.* Beibu Wan, *Vtn.* Vinh Băc Bô. *gulf* China/Vietnam
163 U10 **Tongliao** Nei Mongol Zizhiqu, N China *43°37'N 122°15'E*
161 Q9 **Tongling** Anhui, E China *30°55'N 117°50'E*
161 R9 **Tonglu** Zhejiang, SE China *29°50'N 119°38'E*
187 R14 **Tongoa** *island* Shepherd Islands, S Vanuatu
62 G9 **Tongoy** Coquimbo, C Chile *30°16'S 71°31'W*
160 L11 **Tongren** *var.* Rongwo. Guizhou, S China *27°44'N 109°10'E*
159 T11 **Tongren** *var.* Rongwo. Qinghai, C China *35°31'N 101°58'E*
Tongres *see* Tongeren
153 U11 **Tongsa** *var.* Tongsa Dzong. C Bhutan *27°33'N 90°30'E*
Tongsa Dzong *see* Tongsa
Tongshan *see* Fuding, Fujian, China
Tongshan *see* Xuzhou, Jiangsu, China
Tongshi *see* Wuzhishan
159 P12 **Tongtian He** *var.* Zhi Qu. ≈ C China
96 I6 **Tongue** N Scotland, United Kingdom *58°30'N 04°25'W*
44 H3 **Tongue of the Ocean** *strait* C Bahamas
33 X10 **Tongue River** ≈ Montana, NW USA
33 W11 **Tongue River Resevoir** ⊠ Montana, NW USA
159 V11 **Tongwei** *var.* Pingxiang. Gansu, C China *35°09'N 105°15'E*
159 W9 **Tongxin** Ningxia, N China *37°00'N 105°41'E*
163 U9 **Tongyu** *var.* Kaitong. Jilin, NE China *44°49'N 123°08'E*
160 J11 **Tongzi** *var.* Loushanguan. Guizhou, S China *28°08'N 106°49'E*
162 F8 **Tonhil** *var.* Dzüyl. Govĭ-Altay, SW Mongolia *46°09'N 93°55'E*
40 G5 **Tónichi** Sonora, NW Mexico *28°37'N 109°34'W*
81 D14 **Tonj** Warap, W South Sudan *07°18'N 28°41'E*
152 H13 **Tonk** Rājasthān, N India *26°10'N 75°50'E*
Tonkābon *see* Tonekābon
27 N8 **Tonkawa** Oklahoma, C USA *36°40'N 97°18'W*
167 Q12 **Tônlé Sap** *Eng.* Great Lake. ⊛ W Cambodia
102 L14 **Tonneins** Lot-et-Garonne, SW France *44°21'N 00°21'E*
103 Q7 **Tonnerre** Yonne, C France *47°50'N 04°00'E*
Tonoas *see* Dublon
35 U8 **Tonopah** Nevada, W USA *38°04'N 117°13'W*
164 H13 **Tonoshō** Okayama, Shōdo-shima, SW Japan *34°29'N 134°10'E*
43 S17 **Tonosí** Los Santos, S Panama *07°23'N 80°26'W*
95 H16 **Tønsberg** Vestfold, S Norway *59°16'N 10°25'E*
39 T11 **Tonsina** Alaska, USA *61°39'N 145°10'W*
95 D17 **Tonstad** Vest-Agder, S Norway *58°40'N 06°42'E*
193 X15 **Tonumea** *island* Nomuka Group, W Tonga
137 O11 **Tonya** Trabzon, NE Turkey *40°52'N 39°17'E*
119 K20 **Tonyezh** *Rus.* Tonezh. Homyel'skaya Voblasts', SE Belarus *51°50'N 27°48'E*
36 L3 **Tooele** Utah, W USA *40°32'N 112°18'W*
122 L13 **Toora-Khem** Respublika Tyva, S Russian Federation *52°25'N 96°01'E*
183 O5 **Toorale East** New South Wales, SE Australia *30°29'S 145°25'E*
83 H25 **Toorberg** ▲ S South Africa *32°02'S 24°02'E*
118 G5 **Tootsi** Pärnumaa, SW Estonia *58°34'N 24°43'E*
183 U3 **Toowoomba** Queensland, E Australia *27°35'S 151°54'E*
27 Q4 **Topeka** *state capital* Kansas, C USA *39°03'N 95°41'W*
122 J12 **Topki** Kemerovskaya Oblast', S Russian Federation *55°12'N 85°40'E*
111 M18 **Topľa** *Hung.* Toplya. ≈ NE Slovakia
Toplicza *see* Toplița
116 J10 **Toplița** *Ger.* Töplitz, *Hung.* Maroshevíz; *prev.* Toplița Română, *Hung.* Oláh-Toplicza, Toplicza. Harghita, C Romania *45°56'N 25°20'E*
Toplița Română/Töplitz *see* Toplița
Toplya *see* Topľa
111 I20 **Topoľčany** *Hung.* Nagytapolcsány. Nitriansky Kraj, W Slovakia *48°33'N 18°10'E*
40 G8 **Topolobampo** Sinaloa, C Mexico *25°36'N 109°04'W*
116 I13 **Topoloveni** Argeș, S Romania *44°49'N 25°02'E*
114 L11 **Topolovgrad** *prev.* Kavakli. Khaskovo, S Bulgaria *42°06'N 26°20'E*
Topolya *see* Bačka Topola
32 J10 **Toppenish** Washington, NW USA *46°22'N 120°18'W*
181 P4 **Top Springs Roadhouse** Northern Territory, N Australia *16°37'S 131°49'E*
189 U11 **Tora** *island* Chuuk, C Micronesia
Toraigh *see* Tory Island
189 U11 **Tora Island Pass** *passage* Chuuk Islands, C Micronesia
143 U5 **Torbat-e Ḩeydarīyeh** *var.* Turbat-i-Haidari. Khorāsān-Razavī, NE Iran *35°18'N 59°12'E*
143 V5 **Torbat-e Jām** *var.* Turbat-i-Jam. Khorāsān-Razavī, NE Iran *35°16'N 60°36'E*
39 Q11 **Torbert, Mount** ▲ Alaska, USA *61°30'N 152°15'W*
31 P6 **Torch Lake** ⊛ Michigan, N USA
Törcsvár *see* Bran
Torda *see* Turda
104 L6 **Tordesillas** Castilla y León, N Spain *41°30'N 05°00'W*
92 K13 **Töre** Norrbotten, N Sweden *65°55'N 22°40'E*
95 L17 **Töreboda** Västra Götaland, S Sweden *58°41'N 14°07'E*
95 J21 **Torekov** Skåne, S Sweden *56°25'N 12°39'E*
92 O3 **Torell Land** *physical region* SW Svalbard
105 U4 **Toretta de l'Orrí** *var.* Llorri; *prev.* Tossal de l'Orrí. ▲ NE Spain *42°24'N 01°15'E*
144 M14 **Toretum** Kyzylorda, S Kazakhstan *45°38'N 63°20'E*
117 Y8 **Torez** Donets'ka Oblast', SE Ukraine *48°00'N 38°38'E*
101 N14 **Torgau** Sachsen, E Germany *51°34'N 13°01'E*
145 R8 **Torgay** *Kaz.* Torghay; *prev.* Turgay. Akmola, W Kazakhstan *51°46'N 72°45'E*
145 N10 **Torgay** *prev.* Turgay. ≈ C Kazakhstan
Torgay Üstirti *see* Turgayskaya Stolovaya Strana
Torghay *see* Torgay
95 N22 **Torhamn** Blekinge, S Sweden *56°04'N 15°49'E*
99 C17 **Torhout** West-Vlaanderen, W Belgium *51°04'N 03°06'E*
106 B8 **Torino** *Eng.* Turin. Piemonte, NW Italy *45°03'N 07°39'E*
Tori-shima *see* Io-Tori-shima
81 F16 **Torit** Eastern Equatoria, S South Sudan *04°27'N 32°31'E*
186 H6 **Toriu** New Britain, E Papua New Guinea *04°39'S 151°42'E*
148 M4 **Torkestān, Selseleh-ye Band-e** *var.* Bandi-i Turkistan. ▲▲ NW Afghanistan
104 L7 **Tormes** ≈ W Spain
Tornacum *see* Tournai
Torneå *see* Tornio
92 K12 **Torneälven** *var.* Torniojoki, *Fin.* Tornionjoki. ≈ Finland/Sweden
92 I11 **Torneträsk** ⊛ N Sweden
13 O4 **Torngat Mountains** ▲▲ Newfoundland and Labrador, NE Canada
24 H8 **Tornillo** Texas, SW USA *31°26'N 106°06'W*
92 K13 **Tornio** *Swe.* Torneå. Lappi, NW Finland *65°50'N 24°18'E*
Torniojoki/Tornionjoki *see* Torneälven
61 B23 **Tornquist** Buenos Aires, E Argentina *38°08'S 62°15'W*
104 L6 **Toro** Castilla y León, N Spain *41°31'N 05°24'W*
62 H9 **Toro, Cerro del** ▲ N Chile *29°10'S 69°43'W*
77 R12 **Torodi** Tillabéri, SW Niger *13°05'N 01°46'E*
Törökbecse *see* Novi Bečej
186 J7 **Torokina** Bougainville Island, NE Papua New Guinea *06°12'S 155°04'E*
111 L23 **Törökszentmiklós** Jász-Nagykun-Szolnok, E Hungary *47°11'N 20°26'E*
42 G7 **Torola, Río** ≈ El Salvador/Honduras
Toronaíos, Kólpos *see* Kassándras, Kólpos
14 H15 **Toronto** *province capital* Ontario, S Canada *43°42'N 79°25'W*
31 V12 **Toronto** Ohio, N USA *40°27'N 80°36'W*
Toronto *see* Lester B. Pearson
27 P6 **Toronto Lake** ⊠ Kansas, C USA
35 V16 **Toro Peak** ▲ California, W USA *33°31'N 116°25'W*
124 H16 **Toropets** Tverskaya Oblast', W Russian Federation *56°29'N 31°37'E*
81 G18 **Tororo** E Uganda *0°42'N 34°12'E*
136 H16 **Toros Dağları** *Eng.* Taurus Mountains. ▲▲ S Turkey
183 N13 **Torquay** Victoria, SE Australia *38°21'S 144°18'E*
97 J24 **Torquay** SW England, United Kingdom *50°28'N 03°30'W*
104 M5 **Torquemada** Castilla y León, N Spain *42°02'N 04°17'W*
35 S16 **Torrance** California, W USA *33°50'N 118°20'W*
104 G12 **Torrão** Setúbal, S Portugal *38°18'N 08°13'W*
104 H8 **Torre, Alto da** ▲ C Portugal *40°21'N 07°31'W*
107 K18 **Torre Annunziata** Campania, S Italy *40°45'N 14°27'E*
105 T8 **Torreblanca** Valenciana, E Spain *40°14'N 00°12'E*
104 L15 **Torrecilla** ▲ S Spain *36°38'N 04°54'W*
105 P4 **Torrecilla en Cameros** La Rioja, N Spain *42°18'N 02°33'W*
105 N13 **Torredelcampo** Andalucía, S Spain *37°45'N 03°52'W*
107 K17 **Torre del Greco** Campania, S Italy *40°46'N 14°22'E*
104 I6 **Torre de Moncorvo** *var.* Moncorvo, Tôrre de Moncorvo. Bragança, N Portugal *41°10'N 07°03'W*
104 J9 **Torrejoncillo** Extremadura, W Spain *39°54'N 06°28'W*
105 O8 **Torrejón de Ardoz** Madrid, C Spain *40°27'N 03°29'W*
105 N7 **Torrelaguna** Madrid, C Spain *40°50'N 03°33'W*
105 N2 **Torrelavega** Cantabria, N Spain *43°21'N 04°03'W*
107 M16 **Torremaggiore** Puglia, SE Italy *41°42'N 15°17'E*
104 M15 **Torremolinos** Andalucía, S Spain *36°38'N 04°30'W*
182 I6 **Torrens, Lake** *salt lake* South Australia
105 S10 **Torrent** *Cas.* Torrente, *var.* Torrent de l'Horta. Valenciana, E Spain *39°27'N 00°28'W*
Torrent de l'Horta/Torrente *see* Torrent
40 L8 **Torreón** Coahuila, NE Mexico *25°47'N 103°21'W*
105 R13 **Torre-Pacheco** Murcia, SE Spain *37°43'N 00°57'W*
106 A8 **Torre Pellice** Piemonte, NE Italy *44°49'N 07°12'E*
105 O13 **Torreperogil** Andalucía, S Spain *38°02'N 03°17'W*
61 J15 **Torres** Rio Grande do Sul, S Brazil *29°20'S 49°43'W*
Torrès, Îles *see* Torres Islands
187 Q11 **Torres Islands** *Fr.* Îles Torrès. *island group* N Vanuatu
104 G9 **Torres Novas** Santarém, C Portugal *39°28'N 08°32'W*
181 V1 **Torres Strait** *strait* Australia/Papua New Guinea
104 F10 **Torres Vedras** Lisboa, C Portugal *39°05'N 09°15'W*
105 S13 **Torrevieja** Valenciana, E Spain *37°59'N 00°40'W*
186 B6 **Torricelli Mountains** ▲▲ NW Papua New Guinea
96 G8 **Torridon, Loch** *inlet* NW Scotland, United Kingdom
106 D9 **Torriglia** Liguria, NW Italy *44°31'N 09°08'E*
104 M9 **Torrijos** Castilla-La Mancha, C Spain *39°59'N 04°18'W*
18 L12 **Torrington** Connecticut, NE USA *41°48'N 73°07'W*
33 Z15 **Torrington** Wyoming, C USA *42°04'N 104°10'W*
Torröjen *see* Torrön
94 F16 **Torrön** *prev.* Torröjen. ⊛ C Sweden
105 N15 **Torrox** Andalucía, S Spain *36°45'N 03°58'W*
94 N13 **Torsåker** Gävleborg, C Sweden *60°31'N 16°30'E*
95 N21 **Torsås** Kalmar, S Sweden *56°24'N 16°00'E*
95 J14 **Torsby** Värmland, C Sweden *60°07'N 13°E*
95 N16 **Torshälla** Södermanland, C Sweden *59°25'N 16°28'E*
95 B19 **Tórshavn** *Dan.* Thorshavn. ○ Faeroe Islands *62°02'N 06°47'W*
Torshiz *see* Kāshmar
146 I9 **To'rtkok'l** *var.* Tŭrtkŭl, *Rus.* Turtkul'; *prev.* Petroaleksandrovsk. Qoraqalpog'iston Respublikasi, W Uzbekistan *41°35'N 61°E*
Tortoise Islands *see* Colón, Archipiélago de
45 T9 **Tortola** *island* C British Virgin Islands
106 D9 **Tortona** *anc.* Dertona. Piemonte, NW Italy *44°54'N 08°52'E*
107 L23 **Tortorici** Sicilia, Italy, C Mediterranean Sea *38°02'N 14°49'E*
105 U7 **Tortosa** *anc.* Dertosa. Cataluña, E Spain *40°49'N 00°31'E*
Tortosa *see* Ţarţūs
105 U7 **Tortosa, Cap** *cape* E Spain
44 L8 **Tortue, Île de la** *var.* Tortuga Island. *island* N Haiti
55 Y10 **Tortue, Montagne** ▲▲ C French Guiana
Tortuga, Isla *see* La Tortuga, Isla
Tortuga Island *see* Tortue, Île de la
54 C11 **Tortugas, Golfo** *gulf* W Colombia
45 T5 **Tortuguero, Laguna** *lagoon* N Puerto Rico
137 Q12 **Tortum** Erzurum, NE Turkey *40°20'N 41°36'E*
Torugart, Pereval *see* Turugart Shankou
137 O12 **Torul** Gümüşhane, NE Turkey *40°35'N 39°18'E*
110 J10 **Toruń** *Ger.* Thorn. Toruń, Kujawsko-pomorskie, C Poland *53°02'N 18°36'E*
95 K20 **Torup** Halland, S Sweden *56°57'N 13°04'E*
118 I6 **Tõrva** *Ger.* Törwa. Valgamaa, S Estonia *58°00'N 25°54'E*
Törwa *see* Tõrva
96 D13 **Tory Island** *Ir.* Toraigh. *island* NW Ireland
111 N19 **Torysa** *Hung.* Tarca. ≈ NE Slovakia
Törzburg *see* Bran
124 J16 **Torzhok** Tverskaya Oblast', W Russian Federation *57°04'N 34°55'E*
164 F15 **Tosa-Shimizu** *var.* Tosasimizu. Kōchi, Shikoku, SW Japan *32°47'N 132°58'E*
Tosasimizu *see* Tosa-Shimizu
164 G15 **Tosa-wan** *bay* SW Japan
83 H21 **Tosca** North-West, N South Africa *25°51'S 23°56'E*
106 F12 **Toscana** *Eng.* Tuscany. ◈ *region* C Italy
107 E14 **Toscano, Archipelago** *Eng.* Tuscan Archipelago. *island group* C Italy
106 G10 **Tosco-Emiliano, Appennino** *Eng.* Tuscan-Emilian Mountains. ▲▲ C Italy
Tōsei *see* Dongshi
165 N15 **To-shima** *island* Izu-shotō, SE Japan
147 Q9 **Toshkent** *Eng./Rus.* Tashkent. ● Toshkent Viloyati, E Uzbekistan *41°19'N 69°17'E*
147 Q9 **Toshkent** ✈ Toshkent Viloyati, E Uzbekistan *41°13'N 69°15'E*
147 P9 **Toshkent Viloyati** *Rus.* Tashkentskaya Oblast'. ◈ *province* E Uzbekistan
124 H13 **Tosno** Leningradskaya Oblast', NW Russian Federation *59°34'N 30°48'E*
159 Q10 **Toson Hu** ⊛ C China
162 H6 **Tosontsengel** Dzavhan, NW Mongolia *48°42'N 98°14'E*
162 J6 **Tosontsengel** *var.* Tsengel. Hövsgöl, N Mongolia *49°29'N 101°09'E*
146 I8 **Tosquduq Qumlari** *var.* Goshquduq Qum, Taskuduk, Peski. *desert* W Uzbekistan
Tossal de l'Orrí *see* Toretta de l'Orrí
61 A15 **Tostado** Santa Fe, C Argentina *29°15'S 61°45'W*
118 F6 **Tõstamaa** *Ger.* Testama. Pärnumaa, SW Estonia *58°20'N 23°59'E*
100 I10 **Tostedt** Niedersachsen, NW Germany *53°16'N 09°42'E*
136 J11 **Tosya** Kastamonu, N Turkey *41°02'N 34°02'E*
95 F15 **Totak** ⊛ S Norway
105 R13 **Totana** Murcia, SE Spain *37°45'N 01°30'W*
94 H13 **Toten** *physical region* S Norway
83 G18 **Toteng** North-West, C Botswana *20°25'S 23°00'E*
102 M3 **Tôtes** Seine-Maritime, N France *49°40'N 01°02'E*
Totigi *see* Tochigi
Totio *see* Tochio
Totis *see* Tata
189 U13 **Totiw** *island* Chuuk, C Micronesia
125 N13 **Tot'ma** *var.* Totma. Vologodskaya Oblast', NW Russian Federation *59°58'N 42°42'E*
Tot'ma *see* Sukhona
55 V9 **Totness** Coronie, N Suriname *05°53'N 56°19'W*
42 C5 **Totonicapán** Totonicapán, W Guatemala *14°58'N 91°12'W*
42 A2 **Totonicapán** *off.* Departamento de Totonicapán. ◈ *department* W Guatemala
Totonicapán, Departamento de *see* Totonicapán
61 B18 **Totoras** Santa Fe, C Argentina *32°35'S 61°11'W*
187 Y15 **Totoya** *island* S Fiji
183 Q7 **Tottenham** New South Wales, SE Australia *32°16'S 147°23'E*
164 I12 **Tottori** Tottori, Honshū, SW Japan *35°29'N 134°14'E*
164 H12 **Tottori** *off.* Tottori-ken. ◈ *prefecture* Honshū, SW Japan
Tottori-ken *see* Tottori
76 I6 **Touâjîl** Tiris Zemmour, N Mauritania *22°03'N 12°40'W*
76 L15 **Touba** W Ivory Coast *08°17'N 07°41'W*
76 G11 **Touba** W Senegal *14°55'N 15°53'W*
74 E7 **Toubkal, Jbel** ▲ W Morocco *31°00'N 07°50'W*
32 K10 **Touchet** Washington, NW USA *46°03'N 118°40'W*
103 P7 **Toucy** Yonne, C France *47°45'N 03°18'E*
77 O12 **Tougan** W Burkina *13°06'N 03°03'W*
74 L7 **Touggourt** NE Algeria *33°08'N 06°04'E*
77 Q12 **Tougouri** N Burkina *13°22'N 00°25'W*
76 J13 **Tougué** NW Guinea *11°29'N 11°48'W*
76 K12 **Toukoto** Kayes, W Mali *13°27'N 09°52'W*
103 S5 **Toul** Meurthe-et-Moselle, NE France *48°41'N 05°54'E*
76 L16 **Toulépleu** *var.* Toulobli. W Ivory Coast *06°37'N 08°27'W*
Touliu *see* Douliu
15 U3 **Toulnustouc** ≈ Québec, SE Canada
Toulobli *see* Toulépleu
103 T16 **Toulon** *anc.* Telo Martius, Tilio Martius. Var, SE France *43°07'N 05°56'E*
30 K12 **Toulon** Illinois, N USA *41°05'N 89°54'W*
102 M15 **Toulouse** *anc.* Tolosa. Haute-Garonne, S France *43°37'N 01°25'E*
102 M15 **Toulouse** ✈ Haute-Garonne, S France *43°38'N 01°19'E*
77 N16 **Toumodi** C Ivory Coast *06°34'N 05°01'W*
74 G9 **Tounassine, Hamada** *hill range* W Algeria
Toungoo *see* Taungoo
166 K7 **Toungup** *var.* Taungup. Rakhine State, W Myanmar (Burma) *18°50'N 94°14'E*
102 L8 **Touraine** *cultural region* C France
Tourane *see* Đa Năng
103 P1 **Tourcoing** Nord, N France *50°44'N 03°10'E*
104 F2 **Touriñán, Cabo** *headland* NW Spain *43°02'N 09°20'W*
76 J6 **Tourîne** Tiris Zemmour, N Mauritania *22°23'N 11°l50'W*
102 J3 **Tourlaville** Manche, N France *49°38'N 01°34'W*
99 D19 **Tournai** *var.* Tournay, *Dut.* Doornik; *anc.* Tornacum. Hainaut, SW Belgium *50°36'N 03°24'E*
102 L16 **Tournay** Hautes-Pyrénées, S France *43°10'N 00°16'E*
Tournay *see* Tournai
103 R12 **Tournon** Ardèche, E France *45°05'N 04°49'E*
103 R9 **Tournus** Saône-et-Loire, C France *46°33'N 04°53'E*
59 Q14 **Touros** Rio Grande do Norte, E Brazil *05°10'S 35°29'W*
102 L8 **Tours** *anc.* Caesarodunum, Turoni. Indre-et-Loire, C France *47°22'N 00°40'E*
183 Q17 **Tourville, Cape** *headland* Tasmania, SE Australia *42°09'S 148°20'E*
44 M9 **Toussaint Louverture** ✈ E Haiti *18°38'N 72°13'W*
162 L8 **Töv** ◈ *province* C Mongolia
54 H7 **Tovar** Mérida, NW Venezuela *08°22'N 71°50'W*
126 L5 **Tovarkovskiy** Tul'skaya Oblast', W Russian Federation *53°41'N 38°18'E*
Tovil'-Dora *see* Tavildara
Tövis *see* Teiuş
137 V11 **Tovuz** *Rus.* Tauz. W Azerbaijan *40°58'N 45°41'E*
165 R7 **Towada** Aomori, Honshū, C Japan *40°35'N 141°13'E*
184 K3 **Towai** Northland, North Island, New Zealand *35°29'S 174°06'E*
18 H12 **Towanda** Pennsylvania, NE USA *41°45'N 76°25'W*
29 W4 **Tower** Minnesota, N USA *47°48'N 92°16'W*
171 N12 **Towera** Sulawesi, N Indonesia *0°29'S 120°01'E*
Tower Island *see* Genovesa, Isla
180 M13 **Tower Peak** ▲ Western Australia *33°23'S 123°27'E*
35 U11 **Towne Pass** *pass* California, W USA
29 N3 **Towner** North Dakota, N USA *48°20'N 100°27'W*
33 R10 **Townsend** Montana, NW USA *46°19'N 111°31'W*
181 X6 **Townsville** Queensland, NE Australia *19°24'S 146°53'E*
Towoeti Meer *see* Towuti, Danau

◆ Country
● Country Capital
◇ Dependent Territory
○ Dependent Territory Capital
◈ Administrative Regions
✈ International Airport
▲ Mountain
▲▲ Mountain Range
🌋 Volcano
≈ River
⊛ Lake
⊠ Reservoir

148 K4 **Towraghoudī** Herāt, NW Afghanistan 35°13′N 62°19′E
21 X3 **Towson** Maryland, NE USA 39°25′N 76°36′W
171 O13 **Towuti, Danau** *Dut.* Towoeti Meer. ◎ Sulawesi, C Indonesia
Toxkan He *see* Ak-say
24 K9 **Toyah** Texas, SW USA 31°18′N 103°47′W
165 R4 **Tōya-ko** ◎ Hokkaidō, NE Japan
164 L11 **Toyama** Toyama, Honshū, SW Japan 36°41′N 137°13′E
164 L11 **Toyama** *off.* Toyama-ken. ◈ *prefecture* Honshū, SW Japan
Toyama-ken *see* Toyama
164 L11 **Toyama-wan** *bay* W Japan
164 H15 **Tōyo** Kōchi, Shikoku, SW Japan 33°22′N 134°18′E
Toyohara *see* Yuzhno-Sakhalinsk
164 L14 **Toyohashi** *var.* Toyohasi. Aichi, Honshū, SW Japan 34°46′N 137°22′E
Toyohasi *see* Toyohashi
164 L14 **Toyokawa** Aichi, Honshū, SW Japan 34°47′N 137°24′E
164 I14 **Toyooka** Hyōgo, Honshū, SW Japan 35°35′N 134°48′E
164 L13 **Toyota** Aichi, Honshū, SW Japan 35°04′N 137°09′E
165 T1 **Toyotomi** Hokkaidō, NE Japan 45°07′N 141°45′E
147 Q10 **To'ytepa** *Rus.* Toytepa. Toshkent Viloyati, E Uzbekistan 41°04′N 69°22′E
Toytepa *see* To'ytepa
74 M6 **Tozeur** *var.* Tawzar. W Tunisia 34°00′N 08°09′E
39 Q8 **Tozi, Mount** ▲ Alaska, USA 65°45′N 151°01′W
137 Q9 **T'q'varcheli** *Rus.* Tkvarcheli; *prev.* Tqvarch'eli. NW Georgia 42°51′N 41°42′E
Tqvarch'eli *see* T'q'varcheli
Trâblous *see* Tripoli
137 O11 **Trabzon** *Eng.* Trebizond; *anc.* Trapezus. Trabzon, NE Turkey 41°N 39°43′E
137 O11 **Trabzon** *Eng.* Trebizond. ◈ *province* NE Turkey
13 P13 **Tracadie** New Brunswick, SE Canada 47°32′N 64°57′W
Trachenberg *see* Żmigród
15 O11 **Tracy** Québec, SE Canada 45°59′N 73°07′W
35 O8 **Tracy** California, W USA 37°43′N 121°27′W
29 S10 **Tracy** Minnesota, N USA 44°14′N 95°37′W
20 K10 **Tracy City** Tennessee, S USA 35°15′N 85°44′W
106 D7 **Tradate** Lombardia, N Italy 45°43′N 08°57′E
84 F6 **Traena Bank** *undersea feature* E Norwegian Sea 66°15′N 09°45′E
29 W13 **Traer** Iowa, C USA 42°11′N 92°28′W
104 J16 **Trafalgar, Cabo de** *headland* SW Spain 36°10′N 06°03′W
Traiectum ad Mosam/ Traiectum Tungorum *see* Maastricht
Tráigh Mhór *see* Tramore
11 O17 **Trail** British Columbia, SW Canada 49°94′N 117°39′W
58 B11 **Traíra, Serra do** ▲▲ NW Brazil
109 V5 **Traisen** Niederösterreich, NE Austria 48°03′N 15°37′E
109 W4 **Traisen** ≈ NE Austria
109 X4 **Traiskirchen** Niederösterreich, NE Austria 48°01′N 16°18′E
Trajani Portus *see* Civitavecchia
Trajectum ad Rhenum *see* Utrecht
119 H14 **Trakai** *Ger.* Traken, *Pol.* Troki. Vilnius, SE Lithuania 54°39′N 24°58′E
Traken *see* Trakai
97 B20 **Tralee** *Ir.* Trá Lí. SW Ireland 52°16′N 09°42′W
97 A20 **Tralee Bay** *Ir.* Bá Thrá Lí. *bay* SW Ireland
Trá Lí *see* Tralee
Trälleborg *see* Trelleborg
Tralles Aydin *see* Aydın
61 J16 **Tramandaí** Rio Grande do Sul, S Brazil 30°01′S 50°11′W
108 C7 **Tramelan** Bern, W Switzerland 47°13′N 07°07′E
Trá Mhór *see* Tramore
97 E20 **Tramore** *Ir.* Tráigh Mhór, Trá Mhór. Waterford, S Ireland 52°10′N 07°10′W
95 L18 **Tranås** Jönköping, S Sweden 58°03′N 15°00′E
62 J7 **Trancas** Tucumán, N Argentina 26°11′S 65°20′W
104 I7 **Trancoso** Guarda, N Portugal 40°46′N 07°21′W
95 H22 **Tranebjerg** Midtjylland, C Denmark 55°51′N 10°36′E
95 K19 **Tranemo** Västra Götaland, S Sweden 57°30′N 13°20′E
167 N16 **Trang** Trang, S Thailand 07°33′N 99°36′E
171 V15 **Trangan, Pulau** *island* Kepulauan Aru, E Indonesia
Trâng Dinh *see* Thât Khê
183 Q7 **Trangie** New South Wales, SE Australia 32°01′S 147°58′E
94 K12 **Trängslet** Dalarna, C Sweden 61°22′N 13°43′E
107 N16 **Trani** Puglia, SE Italy 41°17′N 16°25′E
61 F17 **Tranqueras** Rivera, NE Uruguay 31°13′S 55°45′W
63 G17 **Tranqui, Isla** *island* S Chile
39 V6 **Trans-Alaska pipeline** *oil pipeline* Alaska, USA
195 Q10 **Transantarctic Mountains** ▲▲ Antarctica
Transcarpathian Oblast *see* Zakarpats'ka Oblast'
122 E9 **Trans-Siberian Railway** *railroad* Russian Federation
Transilvania *see* Transylvania
Transilvaniei, Alpi *see* Carpaţii Meridionalii
Transjordan *see* Jordan
172 L11 **Transkei Basin** *undersea feature* SW Indian Ocean 35°30′S 29°00′E
117 O10 **Transnistria** *cultural region* E Moldavia
Transsylvanische Alpen/ Transylvanian Alps *see* Carpaţii Meridionalii
94 K12 **Transtrand** Dalarna, C Sweden 61°06′N 13°19′E
116 G10 **Transylvania** *Eng.* Ardeal, Transilvania, *Ger.* Siebenbürgen, *Hung.* Erdély. *cultural region* NW Romania
167 S14 **Tra Ôn** Vinh Long, S Vietnam 09°58′N 105°58′E
107 H23 **Trapani** *anc.* Drepanum. Sicilia, Italy, C Mediterranean Sea 38°02′N 12°32′E
Trâpeăng Vêng *see* Kâmpóng Thum
Trapezus *see* Trabzon
114 L9 **Trapoklovo** Sliven, C Bulgaria 42°40′N 26°36′E
183 P13 **Traralgon** Victoria, SE Australia 38°15′S 146°36′E
76 H9 **Trarza** ◈ *region* SW Mauritania
Trasimenischersee *see* Trasimeno, Lago
106 H12 **Trasimeno, Lago** *Eng.* Lake of Perugia, *Ger.* Trasimenischersee. ◎ C Italy
95 J20 **Träslövsläge** Halland, S Sweden 57°02′N 12°18′E
Trás-os-Montes *see* Cucumbi
104 I6 **Trás-os-Montes e Alto Douro** *former province* N Portugal
167 Q12 **Trat** *var.* Bang Phra. Trat, S Thailand 12°16′N 102°30′E
Trá Tholl, Inis *see* Inishtrahull
Traù *see* Trogir
109 T4 **Traun** Oberösterreich, N Austria 48°14′N 14°15′E
109 S5 **Traun** ≈ N Austria
Traun, Lake *see* Traunsee
101 N23 **Traunreut** Bayern, SE Germany 47°58′N 12°36′E
109 S5 **Traunsee** *var.* Gmundner See, *Eng.* Lake Traun. ◎ N Austria
Trautenau *see* Trutnov
21 P11 **Travelers Rest** South Carolina, SE USA 34°58′N 82°26′W
182 L8 **Travellers Lake** *seasonal lake* New South Wales, SE Australia
31 P6 **Traverse City** Michigan, N USA 44°45′N 85°37′W
29 R7 **Traverse, Lake** ◎ Minnesota/South Dakota, N USA
185 I16 **Travers, Mount** ▲ South Island, New Zealand 42°01′S 172°46′E
11 P17 **Travers Reservoir** ⊠ Alberta, SW Canada
167 T14 **Tra Vinh** *var.* Phu Vinh. Tra Vinh, S Vietnam 09°57′N 106°20′E
25 S10 **Travis, Lake** ⊠ Texas, SW USA
112 H12 **Travnik** Federacija Bosna I Hercegovina, C Bosnia and Herzegovina 44°14′N 17°40′E
109 V11 **Trbovlje** *Ger.* Trifail. C Slovenia 46°10′N 15°03′E
23 V13 **Treasure Island** Florida, SE USA 27°46′N 82°46′W
Treasure State *see* Montana
186 I8 **Treasury Islands** *island group* NW Solomon Islands
106 D9 **Trebbia** *anc.* Trebia. ≈ NW Italy
100 N8 **Trebel** ≈ NE Germany
103 O16 **Trèbes** Aude, S France 43°12′N 02°26′E
Trebia *see* Trebbia
111 F18 **Třebíč** *Ger.* Trebitsch. Vysočina, C Czech Republic 49°13′N 15°52′E
113 I16 **Trebinje** Republika Srpska, S Bosnia and Herzegovina 42°42′N 18°19′E
Trebišnica *see* Trebišnjica
113 H16 **Trebišnjica** *var.* Trebišnica. ≈ S Bosnia and Herzegovina
111 N20 **Trebišov** *Hung.* Tőketerebes. Košický Kraj, E Slovakia 48°37′N 21°44′E
Trebitsch *see* Třebíč
Trebizond *see* Trabzon
Trebnitz *see* Trzebnica
109 V12 **Trebnje** SE Slovenia 45°54′N 15°01′E
111 D19 **Třeboň** *Ger.* Wittingau. Jihočeský Kraj, S Czech Republic 49°00′N 14°46′E
104 J15 **Trebujena** Andalucía, S Spain 36°52′N 06°11′W
100 I7 **Treene** ≈ N Germany
Tree Planters State *see* Nebraska
109 S9 **Treffen** Kärnten, S Austria 46°40′N 13°51′E
Trefynwy *see* Monmouth
102 G5 **Tréguier** Côtes d'Armor, NW France 48°50′N 03°12′W
61 G18 **Treinta y Tres** Treinta y Tres, E Uruguay 33°16′S 54°17′W
61 F18 **Treinta y Tres** ◈ *department* E Uruguay
122 F11 **Trëkhgornyy** Chelyabinskaya Oblast', C Russian Federation 54°42′N 58°25′E
114 F9 **Treklyanska Reka** ≈ W Bulgaria
102 K8 **Trélazé** Maine-et-Loire, NW France 47°27′N 00°28′W
63 K17 **Trelew** Chubut, SE Argentina 43°13′S 65°15′W
95 K23 **Trelleborg** *var.* Trälleborg. Skåne, S Sweden 55°22′N 13°10′E
113 P15 **Trem** ▲ SE Serbia 43°10′N 22°12′E
15 N11 **Tremblant, Mont** ▲ Québec, SE Canada 46°13′N 74°34′W
99 H17 **Tremelo** Vlaams Brabant, C Belgium 51°N 04°34′E
107 M15 **Tremiti, Isole** *island group* SE Italy
30 K12 **Tremont** Illinois, N USA 40°30′N 89°31′W
36 L1 **Tremonton** Utah, W USA 41°42′N 112°09′W
105 U4 **Tremp** Cataluña, NE Spain 42°09′N 00°53′E
30 J7 **Trempealeau** Wisconsin, N USA 44°00′N 91°25′W
15 P8 **Trenche** ≈ Québec, SE Canada
15 O7 **Trenche, Lac** ◎ Québec, SE Canada
111 I20 **Trenčiansky Kraj** ◈ *region* W Slovakia
111 I19 **Trenčín** *Ger.* Trentschin, *Hung.* Trencsén. Trenčiansky Kraj, W Slovakia 48°54′N 18°03′E
Trencsén *see* Trenčín
Trengganu *see* Terengganu
Trengganu, Kuala *see* Kuala Terengganu
61 A21 **Trenque Lauquen** Buenos Aires, E Argentina 36°01′S 62°47′W
14 J14 **Trent** ≈ Ontario, SE Canada
97 N18 **Trent** ≈ C England, United Kingdom
Trent *see* Trento
106 F5 **Trentino-Alto Adige** *Eng.* South Tyrol, *Ger.* Trentino-Südtirol; *prev.* Venezia Tridentina. ◈ *region* N Italy
Trentino-Südtirol *see* Trentino-Alto Adige
106 G6 **Trento** *Eng.* Trent, *Ger.* Trient; *anc.* Tridentum. Trentino-Alto Adige, N Italy 46°05′N 11°08′E
14 J15 **Trenton** Ontario, SE Canada 44°07′N 77°34′W
23 V10 **Trenton** Florida, SE USA 29°36′N 82°49′W
23 R1 **Trenton** Georgia, SE USA 34°52′N 85°27′W
31 S10 **Trenton** Michigan, N USA 42°08′N 83°10′W
27 S2 **Trenton** Missouri, C USA 40°04′N 93°37′W
28 M17 **Trenton** Nebraska, C USA 40°10′N 101°00′W
18 J15 **Trenton** *state capital* New Jersey, NE USA 40°13′N 74°45′W
21 W10 **Trenton** North Carolina, SE USA 35°03′N 77°20′W
20 G9 **Trenton** Tennessee, S USA 35°59′N 88°59′W
36 L1 **Trenton** Utah, W USA 41°53′N 111°57′W
Trentschin *see* Trenčín
Treptow an der Rega *see* Trzebiatów
61 C23 **Tres Arroyos** Buenos Aires, E Argentina 38°22′S 60°17′W
61 J15 **Três Cachoeiras** Rio Grande do Sul, S Brazil 29°21′S 49°48′W
106 E7 **Trescore Balneario** Lombardia, N Italy 45°43′N 09°52′E
41 V17 **Tres Cruces, Cerro** ▲ SE Mexico 15°28′N 92°27′W
57 K18 **Tres Cruces, Cordillera** ▲▲ W Bolivia
113 N18 **Treska** ≈ NW FYR Macedonia
113 I14 **Treskavica** ▲▲ SE Bosnia and Herzegovina
59 J20 **Três Lagoas** Mato Grosso do Sul, SW Brazil 20°46′S 51°43′W
40 H12 **Tres Marías, Islas** *island group* C Mexico
59 M19 **Três Marias, Represa** ⊠ SE Brazil
63 F20 **Tres Montes, Península** *headland* S Chile 46°49′S 75°29′W
105 O3 **Trespaderne** Castilla y León, N Spain 42°47′N 03°24′W
60 G13 **Três Passos** Rio Grande do Sul, S Brazil 27°33′S 53°55′W
61 A23 **Tres Picos, Cerro** ▲ E Argentina 38°10′S 61°54′W
63 G17 **Tres Picos, Cerro** ▲ SW Argentina 42°22′S 71°51′W
60 I12 **Três Pinheiros** Paraná, S Brazil 25°25′S 51°57′W
59 M21 **Três Pontas** Minas Gerais, SE Brazil 21°33′S 45°18′W
Tres Puntas, Cabo *see* Manabique, Punta
60 P9 **Três Rios** Rio de Janeiro, SE Brazil 22°06′S 43°15′W
Tres Tabernae *see* Saverne
Trestenberg/Trestendorf *see* Tăşnad
41 R15 **Tres Valles** Veracruz-Llave, SE Mexico 18°14′N 96°03′W
94 H12 **Tretten** Oppland, S Norway 61°19′N 10°19′E
Treuburg *see* Olecko
101 K21 **Treuchtlingen** Bayern, S Germany 48°57′N 10°55′E
100 N13 **Treuenbrietzen** Brandenburg, E Germany 52°06′N 12°52′E
63 H17 **Trevelín** Chubut, SW Argentina 43°02′S 71°27′W
Treves/Trèves *see* Trier
106 I13 **Trevi** Umbria, C Italy 42°52′N 12°46′E
106 E7 **Treviglio** Lombardia, N Italy 45°32′N 09°35′E
104 J4 **Trevinca, Peña** ▲ NW Spain 42°10′N 06°49′W
105 P3 **Treviño** Castilla y León, N Spain 42°45′N 02°41′W
106 I7 **Treviso** *anc.* Tarvisium. Veneto, NE Italy 45°40′N 12°15′E
97 G24 **Trevose Head** *headland* SW England, United Kingdom 50°33′N 05°03′W
Trg *see* Feldkirchen in Kärnten
183 P17 **Triabunna** Tasmania, SE Australia 42°33′S 147°55′E
21 W4 **Triangle** Virginia, NE USA 38°30′N 77°17′W
83 L18 **Triangle** Masvingo, SE Zimbabwe 20°58′S 31°28′E
115 L23 **Tría Nisía** *island* Kykládes, Greece, Aegean Sea
Triberg *see* Triberg im Schwarzwald
101 G23 **Triberg im Schwarzwald** *var.* Triberg. Baden-Württemberg, SW Germany 48°07′N 08°13′E
153 P11 **Tribhuvan** ✈ (Kathmandu) Central, C Nepal
54 C9 **Tribugá, Golfo de** *gulf* W Colombia
181 W4 **Tribulation, Cape** *headland* Queensland, NE Australia 16°14′S 145°48′E
108 M8 **Tribulaun** ▲ SW Austria 46°59′N 11°18′E
11 U17 **Tribune** Saskatchewan, S Canada 49°16′N 103°50′W
26 H5 **Tribune** Kansas, C USA 38°27′N 101°46′W
107 N18 **Tricarico** Basilicata, S Italy 40°37′N 16°09′E
107 Q19 **Tricase** Puglia, SE Italy 39°56′N 18°21′E
Trichinopoly *see* Tiruchchirāppalli
115 D18 **Trichonída, Límni** ◎ C Greece
155 G22 **Trichūr** *var.* Thrissur. Kerala, SW India 10°32′N 76°14′E *see also* Thrissur
Tricorno *see* Triglav
183 O8 **Trida** New South Wales, SE Australia 33°02′S 145°03′E
35 S1 **Trident Peak** ▲ Nevada, W USA 41°52′N 118°22′W
Tridentum/Trient *see* Trento
109 T6 **Trieben** Steiermark, SE Austria 47°29′N 14°30′E
101 D19 **Trier** *Eng.* Treves, *Fr.* Trèves; *anc.* Augusta Treverorum. Rheinland-Pfalz, SW Germany 49°45′N 06°39′E
106 K7 **Trieste** *Slvn.* Trst. Friuli-Venezia Giulia, NE Italy 45°39′N 13°45′E
Trieste, Golfo di/Triest, Golf von *see* Trieste, Gulf of
106 J8 **Trieste, Gulf of** *Cro.* Tršćanski Zaljev, *Ger.* Golf von Triest, *It.* Golfo di Trieste, *Slvn.* Tržaški Zaliv. *gulf* S Europe
109 W4 **Triesting** ≈ W Austria
Triêu Hai *see* Quang Tri
Trifail *see* Trbovlje
116 L9 **Trifeşti** Iaşi, NE Romania 47°30′N 27°31′E
109 S10 **Triglav** *It.* Tricorno. ▲ NW Slovenia 46°22′N 13°40′E
104 I14 **Trigueros** Andalucía, S Spain 37°24′N 06°50′W
115 E16 **Tríkala** *prev.* Trikkala. Thessalía, C Greece 39°33′N 21°46′E
115 E17 **Trikeriótis** ≈ C Greece
Trikkala *see* Tríkala
Trikomo/Tríkomon *see* İskele
97 F17 **Trim** *Ir.* Baile Átha Troim. Meath, E Ireland 53°34′N 06°47′W
108 E7 **Trimbach** Solothurn, NW Switzerland 47°22′N 07°53′E
109 Q5 **Trimmelkam** Oberösterreich, N Austria 48°02′N 12°55′E
29 U11 **Trimont** Minnesota, N USA 43°45′N 94°42′W
Trimontium *see* Plovdiv
Trinacria *see* Sicilia
155 K24 **Trincomalee** *var.* Trinkomali. Eastern Province, NE Sri Lanka 08°34′N 81°13′E
65 K16 **Trindade, Ilha da** *island* Brazil, W Atlantic Ocean
47 Y9 **Trindade Spur** *undersea feature* SW Atlantic Ocean 21°00′S 35°00′W
111 J17 **Třinec** *Ger.* Trzynietz. Moravskoslezský Kraj, E Czech Republic 49°41′N 18°39′E
57 M16 **Trinidad** El Beni, N Bolivia 14°52′S 64°54′W
54 H9 **Trinidad** Casanare, E Colombia 05°25′N 71°39′W
44 E6 **Trinidad** Sancti Spíritus, C Cuba 21°48′N 80°00′W
61 E19 **Trinidad** Flores, S Uruguay 33°35′S 56°54′W
37 U8 **Trinidad** Colorado, C USA 37°11′N 104°31′W
45 Y17 **Trinidad** *island* C Trinidad and Tobago
Trinidad *see* Jose Abad Santos
45 Y16 **Trinidad and Tobago** *off.* Republic of Trinidad and Tobago. ◆ *republic* SE West Indies
Trinidad and Tobago, Republic of *see* Trinidad and Tobago
63 F22 **Trinidad, Golfo** *gulf* S Chile
61 B24 **Trinidad, Isla** *island* E Argentina
107 N16 **Trinitapoli** Puglia, SE Italy 41°22′N 16°06′E
55 X10 **Trinité, Montagnes de la** ▲▲ C French Guiana
25 W9 **Trinity** Texas, SW USA 30°57′N 95°22′W
13 U12 **Trinity Bay** *inlet* Newfoundland, Newfoundland and Labrador, E Canada
39 P15 **Trinity Islands** *island group* Alaska, USA
35 N2 **Trinity Mountains** ▲▲ California, W USA
35 S4 **Trinity Peak** ▲ Nevada, W USA 40°13′N 118°43′W
35 S5 **Trinity Range** ▲▲ Nevada, W USA
35 N2 **Trinity River** ≈ California, W USA
25 V8 **Trinity River** ≈ Texas, SW USA
Trinkomali *see* Trincomalee
173 Y15 **Triolet** NW Mauritius 20°05′S 57°32′E
107 O20 **Trionto, Capo** *headland* S Italy 39°37′N 16°46′E
Tripití, Ákra *see* Trypití, Akrotírio
115 F20 **Trípoli** *prev.* Trípolis. Pelopónnisos, S Greece 37°31′N 22°22′E
138 G6 **Tripoli** *var.* Tarābulus, Ţarābulus ash Shām, Trâblous; *anc.* Tripolis. N Lebanon 34°30′N 35°42′E
29 X12 **Tripoli** Iowa, C USA 42°48′N 92°15′W
Tripoli *see* Ţarābulus
Trípolis *see* Trípoli, Greece
Tripolis *see* Tripoli, Lebanon
29 Q12 **Tripp** South Dakota, N USA 43°12′N 97°57′W
153 V15 **Tripura** *var.* Hill Tippera. ◈ *state* NE India
108 K8 **Trisanna** ≈ W Austria
100 H8 **Trischen** *island* NW Germany
65 M24 **Tristan da Cunha** ◇ *dependency of Saint Helena* SE Atlantic Ocean
67 P15 **Tristan da Cunha** *island* SE Atlantic Ocean
65 L18 **Tristan da Cunha Fracture Zone** *tectonic feature* S Atlantic Ocean
167 S14 **Tri Tôn** An Giang, S Vietnam 10°26′N 105°01′E
167 W10 **Triton Island** *island* S Paracel Islands
155 G24 **Trivandrum** *var.* Thiruvanathapuram, Tiruvantapuram. *state capital* Kerala, SW India 08°30′N 76°57′E
111 H20 **Trnava** *Ger.* Tyrnau, *Hung.* Nagyszombat. Trnavský Kraj, W Slovakia 48°22′N 17°36′E
111 H20 **Trnavský Kraj** ◈ *region* W Slovakia
Trnovo *see* Veliko Tŭrnovo
Trobriand Island *see* Kiriwina Island
Trobriand Islands *see* Kiriwina Islands
11 Q16 **Trochu** Alberta, SW Canada 51°48′N 113°12′W
109 U7 **Trofaiach** Steiermark, SE Austria 47°25′N 15°01′E
93 F14 **Trofors** Troms, N Norway 65°31′N 13°19′E
113 E14 **Trogir** *It.* Traù. Split-Dalmacija, S Croatia 43°32′N 16°13′E
112 F13 **Troglav** ▲ Bosnia and Herzegovina/Croatia 44°00′N 16°36′E
107 M16 **Troia** Puglia, SE Italy 41°21′N 15°19′E
107 K24 **Troina** Sicilia, Italy, C Mediterranean Sea 37°47′N 14°37′E
173 O16 **Trois-Bassins** W Réunion 21°05′S 55°18′E
101 E17 **Troisdorf** Nordrhein-Westfalen, W Germany 50°49′N 07°09′E
74 H5 **Trois Fourches, Cap des** *headland* NE Morocco 35°27′N 02°58′W
15 T8 **Trois-Pistoles** Québec, SE Canada 48°08′N 69°10′W
99 L21 **Trois-Ponts** Liège, E Belgium 50°22′N 05°52′E
15 P11 **Trois-Rivières** Québec, SE Canada 46°21′N 72°34′W
55 Y12 **Trois Sauts** S French Guiana 02°15′N 52°52′W
99 M22 **Troisvierges** Diekirch, N Luxembourg 50°07′N 06°00′E
122 F11 **Troitsk** Chelyabinskaya Oblast', S Russian Federation 54°04′N 61°31′E
125 T9 **Troitsko-Pechorsk** Respublika Komi, NW Russian Federation 62°39′N 56°06′E
127 V7 **Troitskoye** Orenburgskaya Oblast', W Russian Federation 52°23′N 56°24′E
Troki *see* Trakai
94 F9 **Trolla** ▲ S Norway 62°41′N 09°47′E
95 J18 **Trollhättan** Västra Götaland, S Sweden 58°17′N 12°20′E
94 G9 **Trollheimen** ▲▲ S Norway
94 E9 **Trolltindane** ▲ S Norway 62°30′N 07°43′E
58 H11 **Trombetas, Rio** ≈ NE Brazil
128 L16 **Tromelin, Île** *island* N Réunion
92 I9 **Troms** ◈ *county* N Norway
92 I9 **Tromsø** *Fin.* Tromssa. Troms, N Norway 69°39′N 19°01′E
84 F5 **Tromsøflaket** *undersea feature* W Barents Sea 18°30′E 71°30′N
Tromssa *see* Tromsø
94 H10 **Tron** ▲ S Norway 62°12′N 10°46′E
35 U12 **Trona** California, W USA 35°46′N 117°21′W
63 G16 **Tronador, Cerro** ▲ S Chile 41°12′S 71°51′W
94 H8 **Trondheim** *Ger.* Drontheim; *prev.* Nidaros, Trondhjem. Sør-Trøndelag, S Norway 63°25′N 10°24′E
94 H7 **Trondheimsfjorden** *fjord* S Norway
Trondhjem *see* Trondheim
107 J14 **Tronto** ≈ C Italy
121 P3 **Troódos** *var.* Troodos Mountains. ▲▲ C Cyprus
Troodos *see* Ólympos
Troodos Mountains *see* Troódos
96 I13 **Troon** W Scotland, United Kingdom 55°32′N 04°41′W
107 M22 **Tropea** Calabria, SW Italy 38°40′N 15°52′E
36 L7 **Tropic** Utah, W USA 37°37′N 112°04′W
64 L10 **Tropic Seamount** *var.* Banc du Tropique. *undersea feature* E Atlantic Ocean 23°50′N 20°40′W
Tropique, Banc du *see* Tropic Seamount
Tropoja *see* Tropojë
113 L17 **Tropojë** *var.* Tropoja. Kukës, N Albania 42°25′N 20°09′E
Troppau *see* Opava
95 O16 **Trosa** Södermanland, C Sweden 58°54′N 17°35′E
118 H12 **Troškūnai** Utena, E Lithuania 55°36′N 24°55′E
101 G23 **Trossingen** Baden-Württemberg, SW Germany 48°04′N 08°37′E
117 T4 **Trostyanets'** *Rus.* Trostyanets. Sums'ka Oblast', NE Ukraine 50°30′N 34°59′E
117 N7 **Trostyanets'** *Rus.* Trostyanets. Vinnyts'ka Oblast', C Ukraine 48°35′N 29°10′E
Trostyanets *see* Trostyanets'
116 L11 **Trotuş** ≈ E Romania
44 M8 **Trou-du-Nord** N Haiti 19°34′N 71°57′W
25 W7 **Troup** Texas, SW USA 32°08′N 95°07′W
8 I10 **Trout** ≈ Northwest Territories, NW Canada
33 N8 **Trout Creek** Montana, NW USA 47°51′N 115°40′W
32 H10 **Trout Lake** Washington, NW USA 45°59′N 121°33′W
12 B9 **Trout Lake** ◎ Ontario, S Canada
33 T12 **Trout Peak** ▲ Wyoming, C USA 44°36′N 109°33′W
102 L4 **Trouville** Calvados, N France 49°21′N 00°07′E
97 L22 **Trowbridge** S England, United Kingdom 51°20′N 02°13′W
23 Q6 **Troy** Alabama, S USA 31°48′N 85°58′W
27 Q3 **Troy** Kansas, C USA 39°45′N 95°06′W
27 W4 **Troy** Missouri, C USA 38°59′N 90°59′W
18 L10 **Troy** New York, NE USA 42°43′N 73°37′W
21 S10 **Troy** North Carolina, SE USA 35°23′N 79°54′W
31 R13 **Troy** Ohio, N USA 40°02′N 84°12′W
25 T9 **Troy** Texas, SW USA 31°12′N 97°18′W
114 I9 **Troyan** Lovech, N Bulgaria 42°52′N 24°42′E
114 I9 **Troyanski Prokhod** *pass* N Bulgaria
145 N6 **Troyebratskiy** Severnyy Kazakhstan, N Kazakhstan 54°25′N 66°03′E
103 Q6 **Troyes** *anc.* Augustobona Tricassium. Aube, N France 48°18′N 04°04′E
117 X5 **Troyits'ke** Luhans'ka Oblast', E Ukraine 49°55′N 38°18′E
35 W7 **Troy Peak** ▲ Nevada, W USA 38°18′N 115°27′W
113 G15 **Trpanj** Dubrovnik-Neretva, S Croatia 43°00′N 17°18′E
Tršćanski Zaljev *see* Trieste, Gulf of
Trst *see* Trieste
113 N14 **Trstenik** Serbia, C Serbia 43°38′N 21°01′E
126 I6 **Trubchevsk** Bryanskaya Oblast', W Russian Federation 52°33′N 33°45′E
Trubchular *see* Orlyak
37 S10 **Truchas Peak** ▲ New Mexico, SW USA 35°57′N 105°38′W
143 P16 **Trucial Coast** *physical region* C United Arab Emirates
Trucial States *see* United Arab Emirates
35 Q6 **Truckee** California, W USA 39°18′N 120°10′W
35 R5 **Truckee River** ≈ Nevada, W USA
127 Q13 **Trudfront** Astrakhanskaya Oblast', SW Russian Federation 45°56′N 47°42′E
14 I9 **Truite, Lac à la** ◎ Québec, SE Canada
42 K4 **Trujillo** Colón, NE Honduras 15°59′N 85°54′W
56 C12 **Trujillo** La Libertad, NW Peru 08°04′S 79°02′W
104 K10 **Trujillo** Extremadura, W Spain 39°28′N 05°53′W
54 I6 **Trujillo** Trujillo, NW Venezuela 09°20′N 70°38′W
54 I6 **Trujillo** *off.* Estado Trujillo. ◈ *state* W Venezuela
Trujillo, Estado *see* Trujillo
Truk *see* Chuuk
Truk Islands *see* Chuuk Islands
29 U10 **Truman** Minnesota, N USA 43°49′N 94°26′W
27 X10 **Trumann** Arkansas, C USA 35°40′N 90°30′W
36 J9 **Trumbull, Mount** ▲ Arizona, SW USA 36°22′N 113°09′W
114 F9 **Trŭn** Pernik, W Bulgaria 42°51′N 22°37′E
183 Q8 **Trundle** New South Wales, SE Australia 32°55′S 147°43′E
129 U13 **Trung Phân** *physical region* S Vietnam
Trupcilar *see* Orlyak
13 Q15 **Truro** Nova Scotia, SE Canada 45°24′N 63°18′W
97 H25 **Truro** SW England, United Kingdom 50°16′N 05°03′W
25 P5 **Truscott** Texas, SW USA 33°43′N 99°48′W
116 K9 **Truşeşti** Botoşani, NE Romania 47°45′N 27°01′E
116 H6 **Truskavets'** L'vivs'ka Oblast', W Ukraine 49°15′N 23°30′E
95 H22 **Trustrup** Midtjylland, C Denmark 56°20′N 10°46′E
10 M11 **Trutch** British Columbia, W Canada 57°42′N 123°00′W
37 Q14 **Truth Or Consequences** New Mexico, SW USA 33°07′N 107°15′W
111 F15 **Trutnov** *Ger.* Trautenau. Královéhradecký Kraj, N Czech Republic 50°34′N 15°55′E
103 P13 **Truyère** ≈ C France
114 K9 **Tryavna** Lovech, N Bulgaria 42°52′N 25°30′E
28 M14 **Tryon** Nebraska, C USA 41°33′N 100°57′W
115 J16 **Trypití, Akrotírio** *var.* Ákra Tripití. *headland* Ágios Efstrátios, E Greece 39°28′N 24°58′E
94 J12 **Trysil** Hedmark, S Norway 61°18′N 12°16′E
94 I11 **Trysilelva** ≈ S Norway
112 D10 **Tržac** Federacija Bosna I Hercegovina, NW Bosnia and Herzegovina 44°58′N 15°48′E
Tržaški Zaliv *see* Trieste, Gulf of
110 G10 **Trzcianka** *Ger.* Schönlanke. Pila, Wielkopolskie, C Poland 53°02′N 16°24′E
110 E7 **Trzebiatów** *Ger.* Treptow an der Rega. Zachodnio-pomorskie, NW Poland 54°04′N 15°14′E
111 G14 **Trzebnica** *Ger.* Trebnitz. Dolnośląskie, SW Poland 51°19′N 17°03′E
109 T10 **Tržič** *Ger.* Neumarktl. NW Slovenia 46°22′N 14°17′E
Trzynietz *see* Třinec
83 G21 **Tsabong** *var.* Tshabong. Kgalagadi, SW Botswana 26°03′S 22°27′E
162 G7 **Tsagaanchuluut** Dzavhan, C Mongolia 47°06′N 96°40′E
162 M8 **Tsagaandelger** *var.* Haraat. Dundgovĭ, C Mongolia 46°30′N 107°39′E
Tsagaanders *see* Bayantümen
162 G7 **Tsagaanhayrhan** *var.* Shiree. Dzavhan, W Mongolia 47°30′N 96°48′E
Tsagaannuur *see* Halhgol
Tsagaan-Olom *see* Tayshir
Tsagaan-Ovoo *see* Nariynteel
Tsagaantüngi *see* Altantsögts
162 H6 **Tsagaan-Uul** *var.* Sharga. Hövsgöl, N Mongolia 49°33′N 98°36′E
162 J5 **Tsagaan-Üür** *var.* Bulgan. Hövsgöl, N Mongolia 50°30′N 101°28′E
127 P12 **Tsagan Aman** Respublika Kalmykiya, SW Russian Federation 47°37′N 46°43′E
23 V11 **Tsala Apopka Lake** ◎ Florida, SE USA
Tsamkong *see* Zhanjiang
Tsangpo *see* Brahmaputra
Tsant *see* Deren
Tsao *see* Tsau
172 I4 **Tsaratanana** Mahajanga, C Madagascar 16°46′S 47°40′E
114 N10 **Tsarevo** *prev.* Michurin. Burgas, E Bulgaria 42°10′N 27°51′E
Tsarigrad *see* İstanbul
Tsaritsyn *see* Volgograd
114 K7 **Tsar Kaloyan** Ruse, N Bulgaria 43°36′N 26°14′E
Tsarskoye Selo *see* Pushkin
117 T7 **Tsarychanka** Dnipropetrovs'ka Oblast', E Ukraine 48°56′N 34°29′E
83 H21 **Tsatsu** Southern, S Botswana 25°21′S 24°45′E
83 G17 **Tsau** *var.* Tsao. North-West, NW Botswana 20°08′S 22°29′E
81 J20 **Tsavo** Coast, S Kenya 02°59′S 38°28′E
83 E21 **Tsawisis** Karas, S Namibia 26°18′S 18°09′E
Tschakathurn *see* Čakovec
Tschaslau *see* Čáslav
Tschenstochau *see* Częstochowa
Tschernembl *see* Črnomelj
28 K6 **Tschida, Lake** ⊠ North Dakota, N USA
Tschorna *see* Mustvee
162 G8 **Tseel** Govĭ-Altay, SW Mongolia 45°45′N 95°54′E
138 G8 **Tsefat** *var.* Safed, *Ar.* Safad; *prev.* Ẕefat. Northern, N Israel 32°57′N 35°27′E
126 M13 **Tselina** Rostovskaya Oblast', SW Russian Federation 46°31′N 41°01′E
Tselinograd *see* Astana
Tselinogradskaya Oblast *see* Akmola
Tsengel *see* Tosontsengel
162 J8 **Tsenher** *var.* Altan-Ovoo. Arhangay, C Mongolia 47°24′N 101°51′E
Tsenher *see* Mönhhayrhan
163 N8 **Tsenhermandal** *var.* Modot. Hentiy, C Mongolia 47°45′N 109°03′E
Tsentral'nyye Nizmennyye Garagumy *see* Merkezi Garagumy
83 E21 **Tses** Karas, S Namibia 25°58′S 18°08′E
Tseshevlya *see* Tsyeshawlya
162 E7 **Tsetseg** *var.* Tsetsegnuur. Hovd, W Mongolia 46°30′N 93°16′E
Tsetsegnuur *see* Tsetseg
Tsetsen Khan *see* Öndörhaan
162 J8 **Tsetserleg** Arhangay, C Mongolia 47°29′N 101°19′E
162 H6 **Tsetserleg** *var.* Halban. Hövsgöl, N Mongolia 49°30′N 97°33′E
162 J8 **Tsetserleg** *var.* Hujirt. Övörhangay, C Mongolia 46°50′N 102°38′E
77 R16 **Tsévié** S Togo 06°25′N 01°13′E
Tshabong *see* Tsabong
83 G20 **Tshane** Kgalagadi, SW Botswana 24°05′S 21°54′E
Tshangalele, Lac *see* Lufira, Lac de Retenue de la
83 H17 **Tshauxaba** Central, C Botswana 19°56′S 25°09′E
79 F21 **Tshela** Bas-Congo, W Dem. Rep. Congo 04°56′S 13°02′E
79 K22 **Tshibala** Kasai-Occidental, S Dem. Rep. Congo 06°53′S 22°01′E
79 J22 **Tshikapa** Kasai-Occidental, SW Dem. Rep. Congo 06°23′S 20°47′E
79 L22 **Tshilenge** Kasai Oriental , S Dem. Rep. Congo 06°17′S 23°48′E
79 L24 **Tshimbalanga** Katanga, S Dem. Rep. Congo 09°42′S 23°04′E
79 L22 **Tshimbulu** Kasai-Occidental, S Dem. Rep. Congo 06°27′S 22°54′E
Tshiumbe *see* Chiumbe
79 M21 **Tshofa** Kasai-Oriental, C Dem. Rep. Congo 05°13′S 25°13′E
79 K18 **Tshuapa** ≈ C Dem. Rep. Congo
83 J21 **Tshwane** *var.* Epitoli; *prev.* Pretoria. ● Gauteng, NE South Africa 25°41′S 28°12′E *see also* Pretoria
114 G7 **Tsibritsa** ≈ NW Bulgaria
Tsien Tang *see* Fuchun Jiang
114 I12 **Tsigansko Gradishte** ▲ Bulgaria/Greece 41°24′N 24°41′E
Tsihombe *see* Tsiombe
8 H7 **Tsiigehtchic** *prev.* Arctic Red River. Northwest Territories, NW Canada 67°24′N 133°40′W
125 Q7 **Tsil'ma** ≈ NW Russian Federation
119 J17 **Tsimkavichy** *Rus.* Timkovichi. Minskaya Voblasts', C Belarus 53°04′N 26°59′E
126 M11 **Tsimlyansk** Rostovskaya Oblast', SW Russian Federation 47°39′N 42°05′E
127 N11 **Tsimlyanskoye Vodokhranilishche** *var.* Tsimlyansk Vodoskhovshche, *Eng.* Tsimlyansk Reservoir. ⊠ SW Russian Federation
Tsimlyansk Reservoir *see* Tsimlyanskoye Vodokhranilishche
Tsimlyansk Vodoskhovshche *see* Tsimlyanskoye Vodokhranilishche
Tsinan *see* Jinan
Tsinghai *see* Qinghai, China
Tsing Hai *see* Qinghai Hu, China
Tsingtao/Tsingtau *see* Qingdao
Tsingyuan *see* Baoding
Tsinkiang *see* Quanzhou
Tsintao *see* Qingdao
83 D17 **Tsintsabis** Oshikoto, N Namibia 18°45′S 17°51′E
172 H8 **Tsiombe** *var.* Tsihombe. Toliara, S Madagascar
123 O13 **Tsipa** ≈ S Russian Federation
172 H5 **Tsiribihina** ≈ W Madagascar
172 I5 **Tsiroanomandidy** Antananarivo, C Madagascar 18°44′S 46°02′E
189 U13 **Tsis** *island* Chuuk, C Micronesia
Tsitsihar *see* Qiqihar
127 Q3 **Tsivil'sk** Chuvashskaya Respublika, W Russian Federation 55°51′N 47°30′E
137 T9 **Tskhinvali** *prev.* Staliniri, Ts'khinvali. C Georgia 42°12′N 43°58′E
119 J19 **Tsna** ≈ SW Belarus
124 I15 **Tsna** *var.* Zna. ≈ W Russian Federation

◆ Country
● Country Capital
◇ Dependent Territory
○ Dependent Territory Capital
◈ Administrative Regions
✈ International Airport
▲ Mountain
▲▲ Mountain Range
Volcano
≈ River
◎ Lake
⊠ Reservoir

162 G9 **Tsogt** var. Tahilt. Govĭ-Altay, W Mongolia 45°20′N 96°42′E
162 K10 **Tsogt-Ovoo** var. Doloon. Ömnögovĭ, S Mongolia 44°28′N 105°22′E
162 L10 **Tsogttsetsiy** var. Baruunsuu. Ömnögovĭ, S Mongolia 43°46′N 105°28′E
114 M9 **Tsonevo, Yazovir** prev. Yazovir Georgi Traykov. ⊠ NE Bulgaria
Tsoohor see Hürmen
164 K14 **Tsu** var. Tu. Mie, Honshū, SW Japan 34°41′N 136°30′E
165 O10 **Tsubame** var. Tubame. Niigata, Honshū, C Japan 37°40′N 138°56′E
165 V3 **Tsubetsu** Hokkaidō, NE Japan 43°43′N 144°01′E
165 O13 **Tsuchiura** var. Tutiura. Ibaraki, Honshū, S Japan 36°05′N 140°11′E
165 Q6 **Tsugaru-kaikyō** strait N Japan
164 E14 **Tsukumi** var. Tukumi. Ōita, Kyūshū, SW Japan 33°00′N 131°51′E
Tsul-Ulaan see Bayannuur
Tsul-Ulaan see Bayanuur
83 D17 **Tsumeb** Oshikoto, N Namibia 19°13′S 17°42′E
83 F17 **Tsumkwe** Otjozondjupa, NE Namibia 19°37′S 20°30′E
164 D15 **Tsuno** Miyazaki, Kyūshū, SW Japan 32°43′N 131°32′E
164 D12 **Tsuno-shima** island SW Japan
164 K12 **Tsuruga** var. Turuga. Fukui, Honshū, SW Japan 35°38′N 136°01′E
164 H12 **Tsurugi-san** ▲ Shikoku, SW Japan 33°50′N 134°04′E
165 P9 **Tsuruoka** var. Turuoka. Yamagata, Honshū, C Japan 38°44′N 139°48′E
164 C12 **Tsushima** prev. Izuhara. Nagasaki, Tsushima, SW Japan 34°11′N 129°16′E
164 C12 **Tsushima** var. Tsushima-tō, Tusima. island group SW Japan
Tsushima-tō see Tsushima
164 H12 **Tsuyama** var. Tuyama. Okayama, Honshū, SW Japan 35°04′N 134°01′E
83 G19 **Tswaane** Ghanzi, W Botswana 22°21′S 21°52′E
119 N16 **Tsyakhtsin** Rus. Tekhtin. Mahilyowskaya Voblasts', E Belarus 53°51′N 29°44′E
119 P19 **Tsyerakhowka** Rus. Terekhovka. Homyel'skaya Voblasts', SE Belarus 52°13′N 31°24′E
119 I17 **Tsyeshawlya** Rus. Cheshevlya, Tseshevlya. Brestskaya Voblasts', SW Belarus 53°14′N 25°49′E
Tsyurupinsk see Tsyurupyns'k
117 R10 **Tsyurupyns'k** Rus. Tsyurupinsk. Khersons'ka Oblast', S Ukraine 46°35′N 32°43′E
Tu see Tsu
186 C7 **Tua** ≈ C Papua New Guinea
Tuaim see Tuam
184 L6 **Tuakau** Waikato, North Island, New Zealand 37°16′S 174°56′E
97 C17 **Tuam** Ir. Tuaim. Galway, W Ireland 53°31′N 08°50′W
185 K14 **Tuamarina** Marlborough, South Island, New Zealand 41°27′S 174°00′E
Tuamotu, Archipel des see Tuamotu, Îles
193 Q9 **Tuamotu Fracture Zone** tectonic feature E Pacific Ocean
191 W9 **Tuamotu, Îles** var. Archipel des Tuamotu, Dangerous Archipelago, Tuamotu Islands. island group N French Polynesia
Tuamotu Islands see Tuamotu, Îles
175 X10 **Tuamotu Ridge** undersea feature C Pacific Ocean
167 R5 **Tuân Giao** Lai Châu, N Vietnam 21°34′N 103°24′E
171 O2 **Tuao** Luzon, N Philippines 17°42′N 121°25′E
190 B15 **Tuapa** NW Niue 18°57′S 169°59′W
43 N7 **Tuapi** Región Autónoma Atlántico Norte, NE Nicaragua 14°10′N 83°20′W
126 K15 **Tuapse** Krasnodarskiy Kray, SW Russian Federation 44°08′N 39°07′E
169 U6 **Tuaran** Sabah, East Malaysia 06°12′N 116°12′E
104 I6 **Tua, Rio** ≈ N Portugal
192 H15 **Tuasivi** Savai'i, C Samoa 13°38′S 172°08′W
185 B24 **Tuatapere** Southland, South Island, New Zealand 46°09′S 167°43′E
36 M9 **Tuba City** Arizona, SW USA 36°08′N 111°14′W
138 H11 **Ṭubah, Qaṣr aṭ** castle 'Ammān, C Jordan
Tubame see Tsubame
169 R16 **Tuban** prev. Toeban. Jawa, C Indonesia 06°55′S 112°01′E
141 O16 **Tuban, Wādī** dry watercourse SW Yemen
61 K14 **Tubarão** Santa Catarina, S Brazil 28°29′S 49°00′W
98 O10 **Tubbergen** Overijssel, E Netherlands 52°25′N 06°46′E
Tubeke see Tubize
101 H22 **Tübingen** var. Tuebingen. Baden-Württemberg, SW Germany 48°32′N 09°04′E
127 W6 **Tubinskiy** Respublika Bashkortostan, W Russian Federation 52°48′N 58°18′E
99 G19 **Tubize** Dut. Tubeke. Walloon Brabant, C Belgium 50°43′N 04°14′E
76 J16 **Tubmanburg** NW Liberia 06°50′N 10°53′W
75 T7 **Ṭubruq** Eng. Tobruk, It. Tobruch. NE Libya 32°05′N 23°59′E
191 T13 **Tubuai** island Îles Australes, SW French Polynesia
Tubuai, Îles/Tubuai Islands see Australes, Îles
Tubuai-Manu see Maiao
40 F3 **Tubutama** Sonora, NW Mexico 30°51′N 111°31′W
54 K4 **Tucacas** Falcón, N Venezuela 10°50′N 68°22′W
59 P16 **Tucano** Bahia, E Brazil 10°52′S 38°48′W
57 P19 **Tucavaca, Río** ≈ E Bolivia
110 H8 **Tuchola** Kujawsko-pomorskie, C Poland 53°36′N 17°50′E
111 M17 **Tuchów** Małopolskie, S Poland 49°53′N 21°04′E
23 S3 **Tucker** Georgia, SE USA 33°53′N 84°10′W
27 W10 **Tuckerman** Arkansas, C USA 35°43′N 91°12′W
64 B12 **Tucker's Town** E Bermuda 32°20′N 64°42′W
Tuckum see Tukums
36 M15 **Tucson** Arizona, SW USA 32°14′N 111°01′W
62 J7 **Tucumán** off. Provincia de Tucumán. ◈ province N Argentina
Tucumán see San Miguel de Tucumán
Tucumán, Provincia de see Tucumán
37 V11 **Tucumcari** New Mexico, SW USA 35°10′N 103°43′W
58 H13 **Tucunaré** Pará, N Brazil 05°15′S 55°49′W
55 Q6 **Tucupita** Delta Amacuro, NE Venezuela 09°02′N 62°04′W
58 K13 **Tucuruí, Represa de** ⊠ NE Brazil
110 F9 **Tuczno** Zachodnio-pomorskie, NW Poland 53°12′N 16°08′E
Tuddo see Tudu
105 Q5 **Tudela** Basq. Tutera; anc. Tutela. Navarra, N Spain 42°04′N 01°37′W
104 M6 **Tudela de Duero** Castilla y León, N Spain 41°35′N 04°34′W
162 G6 **Tüdevtey** var. Oygon. Dzavhan, N Mongolia 48°57′N 96°33′E
138 K6 **Tudmur** var. Tadmur, Tamar, Gk. Palmyra, Bibl. Tadmor. Ḥimṣ, C Syria 34°36′N 38°15′E
118 J4 **Tudu** Ger. Tuddo. Lääne-Virumaa, NE Estonia 59°12′N 26°52′E
Tuebingen see Tübingen
122 J14 **Tuekta** Respublika Altay, S Russian Federation 50°51′N 85°52′E
104 I5 **Tuela, Rio** ≈ N Portugal
153 X12 **Tuensang** Nāgāland, NE India 26°16′N 94°45′E
136 L15 **Tufanbeyli** Adana, C Turkey 38°15′N 36°13′E
Tüffer see Laško
186 F9 **Tufi** Northern, S Papua New Guinea 09°08′S 149°20′S
193 O3 **Tufts Plain** undersea feature N Pacific Ocean
Tugalan see Kolkhozobod
67 V14 **Tugela** ≈ SE South Africa
21 P6 **Tug Fork** ≈ S USA
39 P15 **Tugidak Island** island Trinity Islands, Alaska, USA
171 O2 **Tuguegarao** Luzon, N Philippines 17°37′N 121°48′E
123 S12 **Tugur** Khabarovskiy Kray, SE Russian Federation 53°43′N 137°00′E
161 P4 **Tuhai He** ≈ E China
104 G4 **Tui** Galicia, NW Spain 42°02′N 08°37′W
77 O13 **Tui** var. Grand Balé. ≈ W Burkina
57 J16 **Tuichi, Río** ≈ W Bolivia
64 Q11 **Tuineje** Fuerteventura, Islas Canarias, Spain, NE Atlantic Ocean 28°18′N 14°03′W
43 X16 **Tuira, Río** ≈ SE Panama
Tuisarkan see Tūysarkān
Tujiabu see Yongxiu
127 W5 **Tukan** Respublika Bashkortostan, W Russian Federation 53°58′N 57°29′E
171 P14 **Tukangbesi, Kepulauan** Dut. Toekang Besi Eilanden. island group C Indonesia
147 V13 **Tükhtamish** Rus. Toktomush; prev. Tokhtamyshbek. SE Tajikistan 37°51′N 74°41′E
184 O12 **Tukituki** ≈ North Island, New Zealand
Tu-k'ou see Panzhihua
121 P12 **Tükrah** NE Libya 32°32′N 20°35′E
8 H6 **Tuktoyaktuk** Northwest Territories, NW Canada 69°27′N 133°W
168 I9 **Tuktuk** Pulau Samosir, W Indonesia 02°32′N 98°43′E
Tukumi see Tsukumi
118 E9 **Tukums** Ger. Tuckum. W Latvia 56°58′N 23°12′E
81 G24 **Tukuyu** prev. Neu-Langenburg. Mbeya, S Tanzania 09°14′S 33°39′E
Tukzār see Tokzār
41 O13 **Tula** var. Tula de Allende. Hidalgo, C Mexico 20°01′N 99°21′W
41 O11 **Tula** Tamaulipas, C Mexico 22°59′N 99°43′W
126 K5 **Tula** Tul'skaya Oblast', W Russian Federation 54°11′N 37°39′E
Tulach Mhór see Tullamore
Tula de Allende see Tula
186 M9 **Tulaghi** var. Tulagi. Florida Islands, C Solomon Islands 09°04′S 160°09′E
Tulagi see Tulaghi
159 N10 **Tulagt Ar Gol** ≈ W China
41 P13 **Tulancingo** Hidalgo, C Mexico 20°34′N 98°25′W
35 R11 **Tulare** California, W USA 36°12′N 119°21′W
29 P9 **Tulare** South Dakota, N USA 44°43′N 98°29′W
35 Q12 **Tulare Lake Bed** salt flat California, W USA
37 S14 **Tularosa** New Mexico, SW USA 33°04′N 106°01′W
37 P13 **Tularosa Mountains** ▲▲ New Mexico, SW USA
37 S15 **Tularosa Valley** basin New Mexico, SW USA
83 E25 **Tulbagh** Western Cape, SW South Africa 33°17′S 19°09′E
56 C5 **Tulcán** Carchi, N Ecuador 0°44′N 77°43′W
117 N13 **Tulcea** Tulcea, E Romania 45°11′N 28°49′E
117 N13 **Tulcea** ◈ county SE Romania
Tul'chin see Tul'chyn
117 N7 **Tul'chyn** Rus. Tul'chin. Vinnyts'ka Oblast', C Ukraine 48°40′N 28°49′E
Tuléar see Toliara
35 O1 **Tulelake** California, W USA 41°57′N 121°30′W
116 J10 **Tulgheş** Hung. Gyergyótölgyes. Harghita, C Romania 46°57′N 25°46′E
Tuli see Thuli
25 N4 **Tulia** Texas, SW USA 34°32′N 101°46′W
8 I9 **Tulita** prev. Fort Norman, Norman. Northwest Territories, NW Canada 64°55′N 125°25′W
20 J10 **Tullahoma** Tennessee, S USA 35°21′N 86°12′W
183 N12 **Tullamarine** ✈ (Melbourne) Victoria, SE Australia 37°40′S 144°46′E
183 Q7 **Tullamore** New South Wales, SE Australia 32°39′S 147°35′E
97 E18 **Tullamore** Ir. Tulach Mhór. Offaly, C Ireland 53°16′N 07°30′W
103 N12 **Tulle** anc. Tutela. Corrèze, C France 45°16′N 01°46′E
109 X3 **Tulln** var. Oberhollabrunn. Niederösterreich, NE Austria 48°20′N 16°02′E
109 W4 **Tulln** ≈ NE Austria
22 H6 **Tullos** Louisiana, S USA 31°48′N 92°19′W
97 F19 **Tullow** Ir. An Tullach. Carlow, SE Ireland 52°48′N 06°44′W
181 W5 **Tully** Queensland, NE Australia 18°03′S 145°56′E
124 J3 **Tuloma** ≈ NW Russian Federation
27 P9 **Tulsa** Oklahoma, C USA 36°09′N 96°W
153 N11 **Tulsipur** Mid Western, W Nepal 28°01′N 82°22′E
126 K6 **Tul'skaya Oblast'** ◈ province W Russian Federation
126 L14 **Tul'skiy** Respublika Adygeya, SW Russian Federation 44°26′N 40°12′E
186 E5 **Tulu** Manus Island, N Papua New Guinea 01°58′S 146°50′E
54 D10 **Tuluá** Valle del Cauca, W Colombia 04°01′N 76°16′W
116 M12 **Tulucești** Galați, E Romania 45°35′N 28°01′E
39 N12 **Tuluksak** Alaska, USA 61°06′N 160°57′W
41 Z12 **Tulum, Ruinas de** ruins Quintana Roo, SE Mexico
169 R17 **Tulungagung** prev. Toeloengagoeng. Jawa, C Indonesia 08°03′S 111°54′E
186 J6 **Tulun Islands** var. Kilinailau Islands; prev. Carteret Islands. island group NE Papua New Guinea
126 M4 **Tuma** Ryazanskaya Oblast', W Russian Federation 55°09′N 40°27′E
54 B12 **Tumaco** Nariño, SW Colombia 01°51′N 78°46′W
54 B12 **Tumaco, Bahía de** bay SW Colombia
Tuman-gang see Tumen
42 L8 **Tuma, Río** ≈ N Nicaragua
95 O16 **Tumba** Stockholm, C Sweden 59°12′N 17°49′E
Tumba, Lac see Ntomba, Lac
169 S12 **Tumbangsenamang** Borneo, C Indonesia 01°17′S 112°21′E
183 Q10 **Tumbarumba** New South Wales, SE Australia 35°47′S 148°03′E
56 A8 **Tumbes** Tumbes, NW Peru 03°33′S 80°27′W
56 A9 **Tumbes** off. Departamento de Tumbes. ◈ department NW Peru
Tumbes, Departamento de see Tumbes
19 P5 **Tumbledown Mountain** ▲ Maine, NE USA 45°27′N 70°28′W
11 N13 **Tumbler Ridge** British Columbia, W Canada 55°06′N 120°51′W
95 N16 **Tumbo** prev. Rekarne. Västmanland, C Sweden 59°25′N 16°04′E
167 Q12 **Tumbŏt, Phnum** ▲ W Cambodia 12°23′N 102°57′E
182 G9 **Tumby Bay** South Australia 34°22′S 136°05′E
163 Y10 **Tumen** Jilin, NE China 42°56′N 129°47′E
163 Y11 **Tumen** Chin. Tumen Jiang, Kor. Tuman-gang, Rus. Tumyn'tszyan. ≈ E Asia
Tumen Jiang see Tumen
55 Q8 **Tumeremo** Bolívar, E Venezuela 07°17′N 61°30′W
155 G19 **Tumkūr** Karnātaka, W India 13°20′N 77°06′E
96 I10 **Tummel** ≈ C Scotland, United Kingdom
188 B15 **Tumon Bay** bay W Guam
77 P14 **Tumu** NW Ghana 10°55′N 01°59′W
58 I10 **Tumuc-Humac Mountains** var. Serra Tumucumaque. ▲▲ South America
Tumucumaque, Serra see Tumuc-Humac Mountains
183 Q10 **Tumut** New South Wales, SE Australia 35°20′S 148°14′E
158 F7 **Tumxuk** var. Urad Qianqi. Xinjiang Uygur Zizhiqu, NW China 78°40′N 39°54′E
Tumyn'tszyan see Tumen
Tün see Ferdows
45 U14 **Tunapuna** Trinidad, Trinidad and Tobago 10°38′N 61°23′W
60 K11 **Tunas** Paraná, S Brazil 24°57′S 49°05′W
Tunbridge Wells see Royal Tunbridge Wells
114 L11 **Tunca Nehri** Bul. Tundzha. ≈ Bulgaria/Turkey see also Tundzha
Tunca Nehri see Tundzha
137 O14 **Tunceli** var. Kalan. Tunceli, E Turkey 39°07′N 39°34′E
137 O14 **Tunceli** ◈ province C Turkey
152 J12 **Tūndla** Uttar Pradesh, N India 27°13′N 78°14′E
81 I25 **Tunduru** Ruvuma, S Tanzania 11°08′S 37°21′E
114 L10 **Tundzha** Turk. Tunca Nehri. ≈ Bulgaria/Turkey see also Tunca Nehri
Tundzha see Tunca Nehri
162 I6 **Tünel** var. Bulag. Hövsgöl, N Mongolia 49°51′N 100°41′E
155 H17 **Tungabhadra** ≈ S India
155 F17 **Tungabhadra Reservoir** ◎ S India
191 P2 **Tungaru** prev. Gilbert Islands. island group W Kiribati
171 P7 **Tungawan** Mindanao, S Philippines 07°33′N 122°22′E
Tungdor see Mainling
T'ung-shan see Xuzhou
161 Q16 **Tungsha Tao** Chin. Dongsha Qundao, Eng. Pratas Island. island S Taiwan
Tungshih see Dongshi
8 H9 **Tungsten** Northwest Territories, W Canada 62°N 128°09′W
Tung-t'ing Hu see Dongting Hu
56 A13 **Tungurahua** ◈ province C Ecuador
95 F14 **Tunhovdfjorden** ◎ S Norway
22 K2 **Tunica** Mississippi, S USA 34°40′N 90°22′W
75 N5 **Tunis** var. Tūnis. ● (Tunisia) NE Tunisia 36°53′N 10°10′E
75 N5 **Tunis, Golfe de** Ar. Khalīj Tūnis. gulf NE Tunisia
75 N6 **Tunisia** off. Tunisian Republic, Ar. Al Jumhūrīyah at Tūnisīyah, Fr. République Tunisienne. ◆ republic N Africa
Tunisian Republic see Tunisia
Tunisienne, République see Tunisia
Tūnisīyah, Al Jumhūrīyah at see Tunisia
Tūnis, Khalīj see Tunis, Golfe de
54 G9 **Tunja** Boyacá, C Colombia 05°33′N 73°23′W
93 F14 **Tunnsjøen** Lapp. Dåtnejaevrie. ◎ C Norway
39 N12 **Tuntutuliak** Alaska, USA 60°21′N 162°40′W
197 P14 **Tunu** ◈ province E Greenland
147 U8 **Tunuk** Chuyskaya Oblast', C Kyrgyzstan 42°11′N 73°55′E
13 Q6 **Tunungayualok Island** island Newfoundland and Labrador, E Canada
62 H11 **Tunuyán** Mendoza, W Argentina 33°35′S 69°00′W
62 I11 **Tunuyán, Río** ≈ W Argentina
Tunxi see Huangshan
Tuodian see Shuangbai
Tuoji see Zhongba
Tuokezhake see Shufu
35 P9 **Tuolumne River** ≈ California, W USA
Tuong Buong see Tương Đương
167 R7 **Tương Đương** var. Tuong Buong. Nghệ An, N Vietnam 19°15′N 104°30′E
160 I13 **Tuoniang Jiang** ≈ S China
Tuotiereke see Jeminay
Tuotuo He see Togton He
Tuotuoheyan see Tanggulashan
Tüp see Tyup
60 J9 **Tupã** São Paulo, S Brazil 21°57′S 50°28′W
191 S10 **Tupai** var. Motu Iti. atoll Îles Sous le Vent, W French Polynesia
61 G15 **Tupanciretã** Rio Grande do Sul, S Brazil 29°06′S 53°48′W
22 M2 **Tupelo** Mississippi, S USA 34°15′N 88°42′W
59 K18 **Tupiraçaba** Goiás, S Brazil 14°33′S 48°40′W
57 L21 **Tupiza** Potosí, S Bolivia 21°27′S 65°45′W
144 D14 **Tupkaragan, Mys** prev. Mys Tyub-Karagan. headland SW Kazakhstan 44°40′N 50°19′E
11 N13 **Tupper** British Columbia, W Canada 55°30′N 119°59′W
18 J8 **Tupper Lake** ◎ New York, NE USA
146 J10 **Tuproqqal'a** Khorazm Viloyati, W Uzbekistan 40°52′N 62°00′E
146 J10 **Tuproqqal'a** Rus. Turpakkla. Xorazm Viloyati, W Uzbekistan 40°52′N 62°00′E
62 H11 **Tupungato, Volcán** ⛰ W Argentina 33°27′S 69°42′W
163 T9 **Tuquan** Nei Mongol Zizhiqu, N China 45°21′N 121°36′E
54 C13 **Túquerres** Nariño, SW Colombia 01°06′N 77°37′W
153 U13 **Tura** Meghālaya, NE India 25°33′N 90°14′E
122 M10 **Tura** Krasnoyarskiy Kray, N Russian Federation 64°20′N 100°17′E
122 G10 **Tura** ≈ C Russian Federation
140 M10 **Turabah** Makkah, W Saudi Arabia 22°00′N 42°00′E
55 O8 **Turagua, Cerro** ▲ C Venezuela 06°59′N 64°34′W
184 L12 **Turakina** Manawatu-Wanganui, North Island, New Zealand 40°03′S 175°13′E
185 K15 **Turakirae Head** headland North Island, New Zealand 41°26′S 174°54′E
186 B8 **Turama** ≈ S Papua New Guinea
122 K13 **Turan** Respublika Tyva, S Russian Federation 52°11′N 93°40′E
184 M10 **Turangi** Waikato, North Island, New Zealand 39°01′S 175°47′E
146 F11 **Turan Lowland** var. Turan Plain, Kaz. Turan Oypaty, Rus. Turanskaya Nizmennost', Turk. Turan Pesligi, Uzb. Turon Pasttekisligi. plain C Asia
Turan Oypaty/Turan Pesligi/Turan Plain/Turanskaya Nizmennost' see Turan Lowland
Turan Pasttekisligi see Turan Lowland
138 K7 **Ṭurāq al 'Ilab** hill range S Syria
119 K20 **Turaw** Rus. Turov. Homyel'skaya Voblasts', SE Belarus 52°04′N 27°44′E
140 L2 **Ṭurayf** Al Ḥudūd ash Shamālīyah, NW Saudi Arabia 31°43′N 38°40′E
Turba see Teruel
54 E5 **Turbaco** Bolívar, N Colombia 10°20′N 75°25′W
148 K15 **Turbat** Baluchistān, SW Pakistan 26°02′N 62°56′E
Turbat-i-Haidari see Torbat-e Ḥeydarīyeh
Turbat-i-Jam see Torbat-e Jām
54 D7 **Turbo** Antioquia, NW Colombia 08°06′N 76°44′W
Turčianský Svätý Martin see Martin
116 H10 **Turda** Ger. Thorenburg, Hung. Torda. Cluj, NW Romania 46°35′N 23°50′E
142 M7 **Ţūreh** Markazī, W Iran 34°02′N 49°09′E
191 X12 **Tureia** atoll Îles Tuamotu, SE French Polynesia
110 I12 **Turek** Wielkopolskie, C Poland 52°01′N 18°30′E
93 L19 **Turenki** Etelä-Suomi, SW Finland 60°55′N 24°38′E
Turfan see Turpan
Turgay see Torgay
Turgay see Torgay
144 M8 **Turgayskaya Stolovaya Strana** Kaz. Torgay Üstirti. plateau Kazakhstan/Russian Federation
Turgel see Türi
114 L8 **Türgovishte** prev. Eski Dzhumaya, Tărgovište. Türgovishte, N Bulgaria 43°15′N 26°34′E
114 L8 **Türgovishte** ◈ province N Bulgaria
136 C14 **Turgutlu** Manisa, W Turkey 38°30′N 27°43′E
136 L12 **Turhal** Tokat, N Turkey 40°23′N 36°05′E
118 H4 **Türi** Ger. Turgel. Järvamaa, N Estonia 58°48′N 25°28′E
105 S9 **Turia** ≈ E Spain
58 M12 **Turiaçu** Maranhão, E Brazil 01°40′S 45°22′W
Turin see Torino
116 J2 **Turiya** Pol. Turja, Rus. Tur'ya; prev. Tur"ya. ≈ NW Ukraine
116 I3 **Turiys'k** Volyns'ka Oblast', NW Ukraine 51°05′N 24°31′E
Turja see Turiya
116 H6 **Turka** L'vivs'ka Oblast', W Ukraine 49°07′N 23°01′E
81 H16 **Turkana, Lake** var. Lake Rudolf. ◎ N Kenya
Turkestan see Turkistan
147 Q12 **Turkestan Range** Rus. Turkestanskiy Khrebet. ▲▲ C Asia
Turkestanskiy Khrebet see Turkestan Range
111 M23 **Túrkeve** Jász-Nagykun-Szolnok, E Hungary 47°06′N 20°42′E
25 O4 **Turkey** Texas, SW USA 34°23′N 100°54′W
136 H14 **Turkey** off. Republic of Turkey, Turk. Türkiye Cumhuriyeti. ◆ republic SW Asia
181 N4 **Turkey Creek** Western Australia 16°54′S 128°12′E
26 M9 **Turkey Creek** ≈ Oklahoma, C USA
37 T9 **Turkey Mountains** ▲▲ New Mexico, SW USA
Turkey, Republic of see Turkey
29 X11 **Turkey River** ≈ Iowa, C USA
127 N7 **Turki** Saratovskaya Oblast', W Russian Federation 52°00′N 43°16′E
121 O1 **Turkish Republic of Northern Cyprus** ◇ disputed territory Cyprus
145 P16 **Turkistan** prev. Turkestan. Yuzhnyy Kazakhstan, S Kazakhstan 43°18′N 68°18′E
Turkistan, Bandi-i see Torkestān, Selseleh-ye Band-e
Türkiye Cumhuriyeti see Turkey
146 K12 **Türkmenabat** prev. Rus. Chardzhev, Chardzhou, Chardzhui, Lenin-Turkmenski, Turkm. Chärjew. Lebap Welaýaty, E Turkmenistan 39°07′N 63°30′E
146 A11 **Türkmen Aylagy** Rus. Turkmenskiy Zaliv. lake gulf W Turkmenistan
Turkmenbashi see Türkmenbaşy
146 A10 **Türkmenbaşy** Rus. Turkmenbashi; prev. Krasnovodsk. Balkan Welaýaty, W Turkmenistan 40°N 53°04′E
146 A10 **Türkmenbasy Aylagy** prev. Rus. Krasnovodskiy Zaliv, Turkm. Krasnowodsk Aylagy. lake Gulf W Turkmenistan
146 J14 **Türkmengala** Rus. Turkmen-kala; prev. Turkmen-Kala. Mary Welaýaty, S Turkmenistan 37°25′N 62°19′E
146 G13 **Turkmenistan**; prev. Turkmenskaya Soviet Socialist Republic. ◆ republic C Asia
Turkmen-kala/Turkmen-Kala see Türkmengala
Turkmenskaya Soviet Socialist Republic see Turkmenistan
Turkmenskiy Zaliv see Türkmen Aylagy
136 L16 **Türkoğlu** Kahramanmaraş, S Turkey 37°24′N 36°49′E
44 L6 **Turks and Caicos Islands** ◇ UK dependent territory N West Indies
64 G10 **Turks and Caicos Islands** UK dependant territory N West Indies
45 N6 **Turks Islands** island group SE Turks and Caicos Islands
93 K19 **Turku** Swe. Åbo. Länsi-Suomi, SW Finland 60°27′N 22°17′E
81 H17 **Turkwel** seasonal river NW Kenya
27 P9 **Turley** Oklahoma, C USA 36°14′N 95°58′W
35 P9 **Turlock** California, W USA 37°29′N 120°52′W
118 I12 **Turmantas** Utena, NE Lithuania 55°41′N 26°27′E
Turmberg see Wieżyca
54 L5 **Turmero** Aragua, N Venezuela 10°14′N 66°40′W
184 N13 **Turnagain, Cape** headland North Island, New Zealand 40°30′S 176°36′E
Turnau see Turnov
42 H2 **Turneffe Islands** island group E Belize
18 M11 **Turners Falls** Massachusetts, NE USA 42°36′N 72°31′W
11 P16 **Turner Valley** Alberta, SW Canada 50°43′N 114°19′W
99 I16 **Turnhout** Antwerpen, N Belgium 51°19′N 04°57′E
109 V5 **Türnitz** Niederösterreich, E Austria 47°56′N 15°26′E
11 S12 **Turnor Lake** ◎ Saskatchewan, C Canada
111 E15 **Turnov** Ger. Turnau. Liberecký Kraj, N Czech Republic 50°36′N 15°10′E
Tŭrnovo see Veliko Tŭrnovo
116 I15 **Turnu Măgurele** var. Turnu-Măgurele. Teleorman, S Romania 43°44′N 24°53′E
Turnu Severin see Drobeta-Turnu Severin
Turócszentmárton see Martin
Turoni see Tours
Turov see Turaw
Turpakkla see Tuproqqal'a
158 M6 **Turpan** var. Turfan. Xinjiang Uygur Zizhiqu, NW China 42°55′N 89°06′E
Turpan Depression see Turpan Pendi
158 M6 **Turpan Pendi** Eng. Turpan Depression. depression NW China
158 M5 **Turpan Zhan** Xinjiang Uygur Zizhiqu, W China 43°10′N 89°06′E
Turpentine State see North Carolina
44 H8 **Turquino, Pico** ▲ E Cuba 19°54′N 76°55′W
27 Y10 **Turrell** Arkansas, C USA 35°22′N 90°13′W
43 N14 **Turrialba** Cartago, E Costa Rica 09°56′N 83°40′W
96 K8 **Turriff** NE Scotland, United Kingdom 57°32′N 02°28′W
139 V7 **Tursāq** Diyālá, E Iraq 33°27′N 45°47′E
Turshiz see Kāshmar
Tursunzade see Tursunzoda
147 P13 **Tursunzoda** Rus. Tursunzade; prev. Regar. W Tajikistan 38°30′N 68°10′E
Turt see Hanh
Türtkül/Turtkul' see To'rtko'l
29 O9 **Turtle Creek** ≈ South Dakota, N USA
30 K4 **Turtle Flambeau Flowage** ⊠ Wisconsin, N USA
11 S14 **Turtleford** Saskatchewan, S Canada 53°21′N 108°48′W
28 M4 **Turtle Lake** North Dakota, N USA 47°31′N 100°53′W
92 K12 **Turtola** Lappi, NW Finland 66°39′N 23°55′E
122 M10 **Turu** ≈ N Russian Federation
Turuga see Tsuruga
147 V10 **Turugart Pass** pass China/Kyrgyzstan
158 E7 **Turugart Shankou** var. Pereval Torugart. pass China/Kyrgyzstan
122 K9 **Turukhan** ≈ N Russian Federation
122 K9 **Turukhansk** Krasnoyarskiy Kray, N Russian Federation 65°50′N 87°48′E
139 N3 **Ţurumbah** well NE Syria
Turuoka see Tsuruoka
Turush see Turysh
60 K7 **Turvo, Rio** ≈ S Brazil
Tur"ya see Turiya
144 H14 **Turysh** prev. Turush. Mangistau, SW Kazakhstan 45°24′N 56°02′E
23 O4 **Tuscaloosa** Alabama, S USA 33°13′N 87°34′W
23 O4 **Tuscaloosa, Lake** ◎ Alabama, S USA
Tuscan Archipelago see Toscano, Archipelago
Tuscan-Emilian Mountains see Tosco-Emiliano, Appennino
Tuscany see Toscana
35 V2 **Tuscarora** Nevada, W USA 41°16′N 116°13′W
18 F15 **Tuscarora Mountain** ridge Pennsylvania, NE USA
30 M14 **Tuscola** Illinois, N USA 39°46′N 88°19′W
25 P7 **Tuscola** Texas, SW USA 32°12′N 99°48′W
23 O2 **Tuscumbia** Alabama, S USA 34°43′N 87°42′W
92 O4 **Tusenøyane** island group S Svalbard
144 K13 **Tushchybas, Zaliv** prev. Zaliv Paskevicha. lake gulf SW Kazakhstan
Tusima see Tsushima
171 Y15 **Tusirah** Papua, E Indonesia 06°46′S 140°19′E
23 Q5 **Tuskegee** Alabama, S USA 32°25′N 85°41′W
94 E8 **Tustna** island S Norway
39 R12 **Tustumena Lake** ◎ Alaska, USA
110 K13 **Tuszyn** Łódzkie, C Poland 51°36′N 19°31′E
137 S13 **Tutak** Ağrı, E Turkey 39°34′N 42°48′E
185 C20 **Tutamoe Range** ▲▲ North Island, New Zealand
Tutasev see Tutayev
124 L15 **Tutayev** var. Tutasev. Yaroslavskaya Oblast', W Russian Federation 57°51′N 39°29′E
Tutela see Tulle, France
Tutela see Tudela, Spain
Tutera see Tudela
155 H23 **Tuticorin** Tamil Nādu, SE India 08°48′N 78°10′E
113 L15 **Tutin** Serbia, S Serbia 43°00′N 20°20′E
184 O10 **Tutira** Hawke's Bay, North Island, New Zealand 39°14′S 176°53′E
Tutiura see Tsuchiura
122 K10 **Tutonchny** Krasnoyarskiy Kray, N Russian Federation 64°12′N 93°52′E
114 L6 **Tutrakan** Silistra, NE Bulgaria 44°03′N 26°38′E
29 N5 **Tuttle** North Dakota, N USA 47°07′N 99°58′W
26 M11 **Tuttle** Oklahoma, C USA 35°17′N 97°48′W
27 O3 **Tuttle Creek Lake** ⊠ Kansas, C USA
101 H23 **Tuttlingen** Baden-Württemberg, S Germany 47°59′N 08°49′E
171 R16 **Tutuala** East Timor 08°23′S 127°12′E
192 K17 **Tutuila** island W American Samoa
83 I18 **Tutume** Central, E Botswana 20°26′S 27°02′E
39 N7 **Tututalak Mountain** ▲ Alaska, USA 67°51′N 161°27′W
22 K3 **Tutwiler** Mississippi, S USA 34°00′N 90°25′W
162 L8 **Tuul Gol** ≈ N Mongolia
93 O16 **Tuupovaara** Itä-Suomi, E Finland 62°30′N 30°40′E
Tuva see Tyva, Respublika
190 E7 **Tuvalu** prev. Ellice Islands. ◆ commonwealth republic SW Pacific Ocean
Tuvinskaya ASSR see Tyva, Respublika
163 O9 **Tuvshinshiree** var. Sergelen. Sühbaatar, E Mongolia 46°12′N 111°48′E
141 P9 **Ţuwayq, Jabal** ▲ C Saudi Arabia
138 H13 **Ţuwayyil ash Shihāq** desert S Jordan
11 U16 **Tuxford** Saskatchewan, S Canada 50°33′N 105°32′W
167 U12 **Tu Xoay** Đăc Lăc, S Vietnam 12°18′N 107°33′E
40 L14 **Tuxpan** Jalisco, C Mexico 19°33′N 103°21′W
40 J12 **Tuxpan** Nayarit, C Mexico 21°57′N 105°12′W
41 Q12 **Tuxpán** var. Tuxpán de Rodríguez Cano. Veracruz-Llave, E Mexico 20°58′N 97°23′W
Tuxpán de Rodríguez Cano see Tuxpán
41 R15 **Tuxtepec** var. San Juan Bautista Tuxtepec. Oaxaca, S Mexico 18°02′N 96°05′W
41 U16 **Tuxtla** var. Tuxtla Gutiérrez. Chiapas, SE Mexico 16°44′N 93°03′W
Tuxtla see San Andrés Tuxtla
Tuxtla Gutiérrez see Tuxtla
Tuyama see Tsuyama
167 T5 **Tuyên Quang** Tuyên Quang, N Vietnam 21°48′N 105°18′E
167 U13 **Tuy Hoa** Binh Thuân, S Vietnam 11°03′N 108°12′E
167 V12 **Tuy Hoa** Phu Yên, S Vietnam 13°02′N 109°15′E
127 U5 **Tuymazy** Respublika Bashkortostan, W Russian Federation 54°36′N 53°40′E
Tuy Phong see Liên Hương
142 L6 **Tūysarkān** var. Tuisarkan, Tuyserkān. Hamadān, W Iran 34°31′N 48°30′E
Tuyserkān see Tūysarkān
Tuyuk see Tuyyk
145 W16 **Tuyyk** Kaz. Tuyyq; prev. Tuyuk. Taldykorgan, SE Kazakhstan 43°07′N 79°24′E
Tuyyq see Tuyyk
136 I14 **Tuz Gölü** ◎ C Turkey
125 Q15 **Tuzha** Kirovskaya Oblast', NW Russian Federation 57°37′N 48°02′E
113 K17 **Tuzi** S Montenegro 42°22′N 19°21′E
139 T5 **Tūz Khurmātū** At Ta'mím, N Iraq 34°56′N 44°38′E
112 I11 **Tuzla** Federacija Bosna I Hercegovina, NE Bosnia and Herzegovina 44°33′N 18°40′E
117 N15 **Tuzla** Constanța, SE Romania 43°58′N 28°38′E
137 T12 **Tuzluca** Iğdır, E Turkey 40°02′N 43°39′E
95 J20 **Tvååker** Halland, S Sweden 57°04′N 12°25′E
95 F17 **Tvedestrand** Aust-Agder, S Norway 58°36′N 08°55′E
124 J16 **Tver'** prev. Kalinin. Tverskaya Oblast', W Russian Federation 56°53′N 35°52′E
126 I15 **Tverskaya Oblast'** ◈ province W Russian Federation
124 I15 **Tvertsa** ≈ W Russian Federation
138 G9 **Tverya** var. Tiberias; prev. Teverya. Northern, N Israel 32°48′N 35°32′E
95 F16 **Tvietsund** Telemark, S Norway 59°00′N 08°34′E
110 H13 **Twardogóra** Ger. Festenberg. Dolnośląskie, SW Poland 51°21′N 17°27′E
14 J14 **Tweed** Ontario, SE Canada 44°29′N 77°19′W
96 K13 **Tweed** ≈ England/Scotland, United Kingdom
98 O7 **Tweede-Exloërmond** Drenthe, NE Netherlands 52°55′N 06°55′E
183 V3 **Tweed Heads** New South Wales, SE Australia 28°10′S 153°32′E
98 M11 **Twello** Gelderland, E Netherlands 52°14′N 06°07′E
35 W15 **Twentynine Palms** California, W USA 34°08′N 116°03′W
25 P9 **Twin Buttes Reservoir** ⊠ Texas, SW USA
33 O15 **Twin Falls** Idaho, NW USA 42°34′N 114°28′W
39 N13 **Twin Hills** Alaska, USA 59°06′N 160°21′W
11 O11 **Twin Lakes** Alberta, W Canada 57°47′N 117°30′W
33 O12 **Twin Peaks** ▲ Idaho, NW USA 44°37′N 114°24′W
185 I14 **Twins, The** ▲ South Island, New Zealand 41°14′S 172°38′E
29 S5 **Twin Valley** Minnesota, N USA 47°15′N 96°15′W
100 G11 **Twistringen** Niedersachsen, NW Germany 52°48′N 08°39′E
185 E20 **Twizel** Canterbury, South Island, New Zealand 44°04′S 171°12′E
29 X5 **Two Harbors** Minnesota, N USA 47°01′N 91°40′W
11 R14 **Two Hills** Alberta, SW Canada 53°40′N 111°43′W
31 N7 **Two Rivers** Wisconsin, N USA 44°10′N 87°33′W
116 H8 **Tyachiv** Zakarpats'ka Oblast', W Ukraine 48°02′N 23°35′E
Tyan'-Shan' see Tien Shan
166 L3 **Tyao** ≈ Myanmar (Burma)/India
117 R6 **Tyasmin** ≈ N Ukraine
23 X6 **Tybee Island** Georgia, SE USA 32°00′N 80°51′W
Tyborøen see Thyborøn
111 J16 **Tychy** Ger. Tichau. Śląskie, S Poland 50°12′N 19°01′E
111 O16 **Tyczyn** Podkarpackie, SE Poland 49°58′N 22°03′E
94 I8 **Tydal** Sør-Trøndelag, S Norway 63°01′N 11°36′E
115 H24 **Tyflós** ≈ Kríti, Greece, E Mediterranean Sea
21 S3 **Tygart Lake** ⊠ West Virginia, NE USA
123 Q13 **Tygda** Amurskaya Oblast', SE Russian Federation 53°07′N 126°12′E
21 Q11 **Tyger River** ≈ South Carolina, SE USA
32 I11 **Tygh Valley** Oregon, NW USA 45°15′N 121°12′W
94 F12 **Tyin** ◎ S Norway

◆ Country
● Country Capital
◇ Dependent Territory
○ Dependent Territory Capital
◈ Administrative Regions
✈ International Airport
▲ Mountain
▲▲ Mountain Range
⛰ Volcano
≈ River
◎ Lake
⊠ Reservoir

29 S10 Tyler Minnesota, N USA 44°16′N 96°07′W
25 W7 Tyler Texas, SW USA 32°21′N 95°18′W
25 W7 Tyler, Lake ⊠ Texas, SW USA
22 K7 Tylertown Mississippi, S USA 31°07′N 90°08′W
117 P10 Tylihuls'kyy Lyman ◎ SW Ukraine
Tylos see Bahrain
115 C15 Týmfi var. Timfi. ▲ W Greece 39°58′N 20°51′E
115 E17 Tymfristós var. Timfristos. ▲ C Greece 38°57′N 21°49′E
115 J25 Tympáki var. Timbaki; prev. Timbákion. Kríti, Greece, E Mediterranean Sea 35°04′N 24°47′E
123 Q12 Tynda Amurskaya Oblast', SE Russian Federation 55°09′N 124°44′E
29 Q12 Tyndall South Dakota, N USA 42°57′N 97°52′W
97 L14 Tyne ↝ N England, United Kingdom
97 M14 Tynemouth NE England, United Kingdom 55°01′N 01°24′W
97 L14 Tyneside cultural region NE England, United Kingdom
94 H10 Tynset Hedmark, S Norway 61°45′N 10°49′E
39 Q12 Tyonek Alaska, USA 61°04′N 151°08′W
Tyôsi see Chôshi
Tyras see Dniester
Tyras see Bilhorod-Dnistrovs'kyy
Tyre see Soûr
95 G14 Tyrifjorden ◎ S Norway
95 K22 Tyringe Skåne, S Sweden 56°09′N 13°35′E
123 R13 Tyrma Khabarovskiy Kray, SE Russian Federation 50°00′N 132°04′E
Tyrnau see Trnava
115 F15 Týrnavos var. Tírnavos. Thessalía, C Greece 39°45′N 22°18′E
127 N16 Tyrnyauz Kabardino-Balkarskaya Respublika, SW Russian Federation 43°19′N 42°55′E
Tyrol see Tirol
18 E14 Tyrone Pennsylvania, NE USA 40°41′N 78°12′W
97 E15 Tyrone cultural region W Northern Ireland, United Kingdom
Tyros see Bahrain
182 M10 Tyrrell, Lake salt lake Victoria, SE Australia
84 H14 Tyrrhenian Basin undersea feature Tyrrhenian Sea, C Mediterranean Sea 39°30′N 13°00′E
120 L8 Tyrrhenian Sea It. Mare Tirreno. sea N Mediterranean Sea
94 J12 Tyrsil ↝ Hedmark, S Norway
Tysa see Tisa/Tisza
116 J7 Tysmenytsya Ivano-Frankivs'ka Oblast', W Ukraine 48°54′N 24°50′E
95 C14 Tysnesøya island S Norway
95 C14 Tysse Hordaland, S Norway 60°23′N 05°46′E
95 D14 Tyssedal Hordaland, S Norway 60°07′N 06°36′E
95 O17 Tystberga Södermanland, C Sweden 58°51′N 17°15′E
118 E12 Tytuvėnai Šiaulai, C Lithuania 55°36′N 23°14′E
Tyub-Karagan, Mys see Tupkaragan, Mys
147 V8 Tyugel'-Say Narynskaya Oblast', C Kyrgyzstan 41°57′N 74°40′E
122 H11 Tyukalinsk Omskaya Oblast', C Russian Federation 55°56′N 72°02′E
127 V7 Tyul'gan Orenburgskaya Oblast', W Russian Federation 52°27′N 56°08′E
122 G11 Tyumen' Tyumenskaya Oblast', C Russian Federation 57°11′N 65°29′E
122 H11 Tyumenskaya Oblast' ◆ province C Russian Federation
147 Y7 Tyup Kir. Tüp. Issyk-Kul'skaya Oblast', NE Kyrgyzstan 42°44′N 78°18′E
122 L14 Tyva, Respublika prev. Tannu-Tuva, Tuva, Tuvinskaya ASSR. ◆ autonomous republic C Russian Federation
117 N7 Tyvriv Vinnyts'ka Oblast', C Ukraine 49°01′N 28°28′E
97 J21 Tywi ↝ S Wales, United Kingdom
97 I19 Tywyn W Wales, United Kingdom 52°35′N 04°06′W
83 K20 Tzaneen Limpopo, NE South Africa 23°50′S 30°09′E
Tzekung see Zigong
115 I20 Tziá prev. Kéa, Kéos; anc. Ceos. island Kykládes, Greece, Aegean Sea
41 X12 Tzucacab Yucatán, SE Mexico 20°04′N 89°03′W

U

82 B12 Uaco Cungo var. Waku Kungo, Port. Santa Comba. Cuanza Sul, C Angola 11°21′S 15°04′E
UAE see United Arab Emirates
191 X7 Ua Huka island Îles Marquises, NE French Polynesia
58 E10 Uaiacás Roraima, N Brazil 03°28′N 63°13′W
Uamba see Wamba
Uanle Uen see Wanlaweyn
191 W7 Ua Pu island Îles Marquises, NE French Polynesia
81 L17 Uar Garas spring/well SW Somalia 01°19′N 41°22′E
58 G12 Uatumã, Rio ↝ C Brazil
Ua Uíbh Fhailí see Offaly
58 C11 Uaupés, Rio var. Rio Vaupés. ↝ Brazil/Colombia see also Vaupés, Río
Uaupés, Rio see Vaupés, Río
Uba see Oba
145 N6 Ubagan Kaz. Obagan. ↝ Kazakhstan/Russian Federation
186 G7 Ubai New Britain, E Papua New Guinea 05°38′S 150°45′E
79 J15 Ubangi Fr. Oubangui. ↝ C Africa
Ubangi-Shari see Central African Republic
116 M3 Ubarts' Ukr. Ubort'. ↝ Belarus/Ukraine see also Ubort'
Ubarts' see Ubort'
54 F9 Ubaté Cundinamarca, C Colombia 05°20′N 73°50′W
60 N10 Ubatuba São Paulo, S Brazil 23°26′S 45°04′W
149 R12 Ubauro Sind, SE Pakistan 28°08′N 69°43′E
171 Q6 Ubay Bohol, C Philippines 10°02′N 124°29′E
103 U14 Ubaye ↝ SE France
Ubayid, Wadi al see Ubayyiḍ, Wādī al
139 N8 Ubaylah Al Anbār, W Iraq 33°06′N 40°13′E
139 O10 Ubayyiḍ, Wādī al var. Wadi al Ubayid. dry watercourse SW Iraq
98 L13 Ubbergen Gelderland, E Netherlands 51°49′N 05°54′E
164 E13 Ube Yamaguchi, Honshū, SW Japan 33°57′N 131°15′E
105 O13 Úbeda Andalucía, S Spain 38°01′N 03°22′W
109 V7 Übelbach var. Markt-Übelbach. Steiermark, SE Austria 47°13′N 15°15′E
59 L20 Uberaba Minas Gerais, SE Brazil 19°47′S 47°57′W
57 Q19 Uberaba, Laguna ◎ E Bolivia
59 K19 Uberlândia Minas Gerais, SE Brazil 18°17′S 48°17′W
101 H24 Überlingen Baden-Württemberg, S Germany 47°46′N 09°10′E
77 U16 Ubiaja Edo, S Nigeria 06°39′N 06°23′E
104 K3 Ubiña, Peña ▲ NW Spain 43°01′N 05°58′W
57 H17 Ubinas, Volcán ⛰ S Peru 16°16′S 70°49′W
Ubol Rajadhani/Ubol Ratchathani see Ubon Ratchathani
167 P9 Ubolratna Reservoir ⊠ C Thailand
167 S10 Ubon Ratchathani var. Muang Ubon, Ubol Rajadhani, Ubol Ratchathani, Udon Ratchathani. Ubon Ratchathani, E Thailand 15°15′N 104°50′E
119 L20 Ubort' Bel. Ubarts'. ↝ Belarus/Ukraine see also Ubarts'
Ubort' see Ubarts'
104 K15 Ubrique Andalucía, S Spain 36°42′N 05°27′W
Ubsu-Nur, Ozero see Uvs Nuur
79 M18 Ubundu Orientale, C Dem. Rep. Congo 0°24′S 25°30′E
146 J13 Üçajy var. Uchajy, Rus. Uch-Adzhi. Mary Welaýaty, C Turkmenistan 38°06′N 62°44′E
137 X11 Ucar Rus. Udzhary. C Azerbaijan 40°31′N 47°40′E
56 G13 Ucayali off. Departamento de Ucayali. ◆ department E Peru
Ucayali, Departamento de see Ucayali
56 F10 Ucayali, Río ↝ C Peru
Uccle see Ukkel
Uch-Adzhi/Üchajy see Üçajy
127 X4 Uchaly Respublika Bashkortostan, W Russian Federation 54°19′N 59°33′E
Ucharal see Usharal
164 C17 Uchinoura Kagoshima, Kyūshū, SW Japan 31°16′N 131°04′E
165 R5 Uchiura-wan bay NW Pacific Ocean
Uchkuduk see Uchquduq
147 S9 Uchqo'rg'on Rus. Uchkurghan. Namangan Viloyati, E Uzbekistan 41°06′N 72°04′E
146 K8 Uchquduq Rus. Uchkuduk. Navoiy Viloyati, N Uzbekistan 42°12′N 63°27′E
Uchsay see Uchsoy
146 G6 Uchsoy Rus. Uchsay. Qoraqalpogʻiston Respublikasi, NW Uzbekistan 43°51′N 58°51′E
Uchtagan Gumy/Uchtagan, Peski see Uçtagan Gumy
123 R11 Uchur ↝ E Russian Federation
100 O10 Uckermark cultural region E Germany
10 K17 Ucluelet Vancouver Island, British Columbia, SW Canada 48°55′N 125°34′W
146 D10 Uçtagan Gumy var. Uchtagan Gumy, Rus. Peski Uchtagan. desert NW Turkmenistan
122 M13 Uda ↝ S Russian Federation
123 R12 Uda ↝ E Russian Federation
123 N6 Udachnyy Respublika Sakha (Yakutiya), NE Russian Federation 66°27′N 112°18′E
155 G21 Udagamandalam var. Ooty, Udhagamandalam; prev. Ootacamund. Tamil Nādu, SW India 11°28′N 76°42′E
152 F14 Udaipur prev. Oodeypore. Rājasthān, N India 24°35′N 73°41′E
Udayadhani see Uthai Thani
143 N16 'Udayd, Khawr al var. Khor al Udeid. inlet Qatar/Saudi Arabia
112 D11 Udbina Lika-Senj, W Croatia 44°33′N 15°46′E
95 I18 Uddevalla Västra Götaland, S Sweden 58°20′N 11°56′E
Uddjaur see Uddjaure
92 H13 Uddjaure var. Uddjaur. ◎ N Sweden
Udeid, Khor al see 'Udayd, Khawr al
99 K14 Uden Noord-Brabant, SE Netherlands 51°40′N 05°37′E
Uden see Udenhout
99 J14 Udenhout var. Uden. Noord-Brabant, S Netherlands 51°37′N 05°09′E
155 H14 Udgīr Mahārāshtra, C India 18°23′N 77°06′E
Udhagamandalam see Udagamandalam
152 H6 Udhampur Jammu and Kashmir, NW India 32°55′N 75°07′E
139 X14 'Udhaybah, 'Uqlat al well S Iraq
106 J7 Udine anc. Utina. Friuli-Venezia Giulia, NE Italy 46°05′N 13°10′E
175 T14 Udintsev Fracture Zone tectonic feature S Pacific Ocean
Udipi see Udupi
Udmurtia see Udmurtskaya Respublika
127 S2 Udmurtskaya Respublika Eng. Udmurtia. ◆ autonomous republic NW Russian Federation
124 J15 Udomlya Tverskaya Oblast', W Russian Federation 57°53′N 34°59′E
Udon Ratchathani see Ubon Ratchathani
167 Q8 Udon Thani var. Ban Mak Khaeng, Udorndhani. Udon Thani, N Thailand 17°25′N 102°45′E
Udorndhani see Udon Thani
189 U12 Udot atoll Chuuk Islands, C Micronesia
123 S12 Udskaya Guba bay E Russian Federation
123 R12 Udskoye Khabarovskiy Kray, SE Russian Federation 54°32′N 134°26′E
155 E19 Udupi var. Udipi. Karnātaka, SW India 13°18′N 74°46′E
Udzhary see Ucar
100 O9 Uecker ↝ NE Germany
100 P9 Ueckermünde Mecklenburg-Vorpommern, NE Germany 53°43′N 14°03′E
164 M12 Ueda var. Uyeda. Nagano, Honshū, S Japan 36°27′N 138°13′E
79 L16 Uele var. Welle. ↝ NE Dem. Rep. Congo
123 W5 Uelen Chukotskiy Avtonomnyy Okrug, NE Russian Federation 66°01′N 169°52′W
Uele (upper course) see Kibali, Dem. Rep. Congo
Uele (upper course) see Uolo, Río, Equatorial Guinea/Gabon
100 J11 Uelzen Niedersachsen, N Germany 52°58′N 10°34′E
164 J14 Ueno Mie, Honshū, SW Japan 34°45′N 136°08′E
127 V4 Ufa Respublika Bashkortostan, W Russian Federation 54°46′N 56°02′E
127 V4 Ufa ↝ W Russian Federation
Ufra see Kenar
83 C18 Ugab ↝ C Namibia
118 D8 Ugāle NW Latvia 57°16′N 21°58′E
81 F17 Uganda off. Republic of Uganda. ◆ republic E Africa
Uganda, Republic of see Uganda
138 G4 Ugarit Ar. Ra's Shamrah. site of ancient city Al Lādhiqīyah, NW Syria
39 O14 Ugashik Alaska, USA 57°30′N 157°24′W
107 Q19 Ugento Puglia, SE Italy 39°53′N 18°09′E
105 O15 Ugíjar Andalucía, S Spain 36°58′N 03°03′W
103 T11 Ugine Savoie, E France 45°45′N 06°25′E
123 R13 Uglegorsk Amurskaya Oblast', S Russian Federation 51°40′N 128°05′E
Ugleural'sk see Ugleural'skiy
125 V13 Ugleural'skiy prev. Polovinka, Ugleural'sk. Permskiy Kray, NW Russian Federation 58°57′N 57°37′E
124 L15 Uglich Yaroslavskaya Oblast', W Russian Federation 57°33′N 38°23′E
126 I4 Ugra ↝ W Russian Federation
147 V9 Ugyut Narynskaya Oblast', C Kyrgyzstan 41°22′N 74°49′E
111 H19 Uherské Hradiště Ger. Ungarisch-Hradisch. Zlínský Kraj, E Czech Republic 49°05′N 17°26′E
111 H19 Uherský Brod Ger. Ungarisch-Brod. Zlínský Kraj, E Czech Republic 49°01′N 17°40′E
111 B17 Úhlava Ger. Angel. ↝ W Czech Republic
Uhorshchyna see Hungary
31 T13 Uhrichsville Ohio, N USA 40°23′N 81°21′W
Uhuru Peak see Kilimanjaro
96 G8 Uig N Scotland, United Kingdom 57°35′N 06°22′W
82 B10 Uíge Port. Carmona, Vila Marechal Carmona. Uíge, NW Angola 07°37′S 15°02′E
82 B10 Uíge ◆ province N Angola
193 Y15 Uiha island Ha'apai Group, C Tonga
189 U13 Uijec island Chuuk, C Micronesia
163 X14 Uijeongbu Jap. Giseifu; prev. Ŭijŏngbu. NW South Korea 37°42′N 127°02′E
Ŭijŏngbu see Uijeongbu
Uil see Oyyl
36 M3 Uinta Mountains ▲ Utah, W USA
83 C18 Uis Erongo, NW Namibia 21°08′S 14°49′E
83 I25 Uitenhage Eastern Cape, S South Africa 33°44′S 25°27′E
98 H9 Uitgeest Noord-Holland, W Netherlands 52°32′N 04°43′E
98 I11 Uithoorn Noord-Holland, C Netherlands 52°14′N 04°50′E
98 O4 Uithuizen Groningen, NE Netherlands 53°24′N 06°40′E
98 O4 Uithuizermeeden Groningen, NE Netherlands 53°25′N 06°43′E
189 R6 Ujae Atoll var. Wūjae. atoll Ralik Chain, W Marshall Islands
Ujain see Ujjain
111 I16 Ujazd Opolskie, S Poland 50°22′N 18°20′E
Új-Becse see Novi Bečej
Ujda see Oujda
189 N5 Ujelang Atoll var. Wujlān. atoll Ralik Chain, W Marshall Islands
111 N21 Újfehértó Szabolcs-Szatmár-Bereg, E Hungary 47°48′N 21°40′E
Újgradiska see Nova Gradiška
164 J13 Uji var. Uzi. Kyōto, Honshū, SW Japan 34°54′N 135°48′E
81 E21 Ujiji Kigoma, W Tanzania 04°55′S 29°39′E
154 G10 Ujjain prev. Ujain. Madhya Pradesh, C India 23°11′N 75°50′E
Újlak see Ilok
'Ujmān see 'Ajmān
Újmoldova see Moldova Nouă
Újszentanna see Sântana
Ujungpandang see Makassar
Ujung Salang see Phuket
Újvidék see Novi Sad
UK see United Kingdom
154 E11 Ukāi Reservoir ⊠ W India
81 G19 Ukara Island island N Tanzania
'Ukash, Wādī see 'Akāsh, Wādī
81 F19 Ukerewe Island island N Tanzania
139 S9 Ukhayḍir Al Anbār, C Iraq 32°28′N 43°36′E
153 X13 Ukhrul Manipur, NE India 25°08′N 94°24′E
125 S9 Ukhta Respublika Komi, NW Russian Federation 63°31′N 53°48′E
34 L6 Ukiah California, W USA 39°07′N 123°14′W
32 K12 Ukiah Oregon, NW USA 45°06′N 118°57′W
99 G18 Ukkel Fr. Uccle. Brussels, C Belgium 50°47′N 04°19′E
118 G13 Ukmergė Pol. Wiłkomierz. Vilnius, C Lithuania 55°16′N 24°46′E
Ukraina see Ukraine
116 L6 Ukraine off. Ukraine, Rus. Ukraina, Ukr. Ukrayina; prev. Ukrainian Soviet Socialist Republic, Ukrainskay S.S.R. ◆ republic SE Europe
Ukraine see Ukraine
Ukrainian Soviet Socialist Republic see Ukraine
Ukrainskay S.S.R/ Ukrayina see Ukraine
82 B13 Uku Cuanza Sul, NW Angola 11°25′S 14°18′E
164 B13 Uku-jima island Gotō-rettō, SW Japan
83 F20 Ukwi Kgalagadi, SW Botswana 23°41′S 20°26′E
118 M13 Ula Rus. Ulla. Vitsyebskaya Voblasts', N Belarus 55°14′N 29°15′E
136 C16 Ula Muğla, SW Turkey 37°08′N 28°25′E
118 M13 Ula Rus. Ulla. ↝ N Belarus
162 L7 Ulaanbaatar Eng. Ulan Bator; prev. Urga. ● (Mongolia) Töv, C Mongolia 47°55′N 106°57′E
Ulaan-Ereg see Bayanmönh
162 E5 Ulaangom Uvs, NW Mongolia 49°56′N 92°06′E
162 D5 Ulaanhus var. Bilüü. Bayan-Ölgiy, W Mongolia 48°54′N 89°40′E
Ulaantolgoy see Möst
Ulaan-Uul see Öldziyt, Bayanhongor, Mongolia
Ulaan-Uul see Erdene, Dornogovĭ, Mongolia
162 M14 Ulan var. Otog Qi. Nei Mongol Zizhiqu, N China 39°05′N 107°58′E
159 R10 Ulan var. Xireg; prev. Xiligou. Qinghai, C China 36°59′N 98°21′E
Ulan Bator see Ulaanbaatar
162 L13 Ulan Buh Shamo desert N China
Ulanhad see Chifeng
163 T8 Ulanhot Nei Mongol Zizhiqu, N China 46°02′N 122°E
127 Q14 Ulan Khol Respublika Kalmykiya, SW Russian Federation 45°27′N 46°48′E
163 P13 Ulan Qab var. Jining. Nei Mongol Zizhiqu, N China 40°59′N 113°08′E
162 M13 Ulansuhai Nur ◎ N China
123 N14 Ulan-Ude prev. Verkhneudinsk. Respublika Buryatiya, S Russian Federation 51°55′N 107°40′E
159 N12 Ulan Ul Hu ◎ C China
187 N9 Ulawa Island island SE Solomon Islands
138 J7 'Ulayyānīyah, Bi'r al var. Al Hilbeh. well S Syria
123 S12 Ul'banskiy Zaliv strait E Russian Federation
Ulbo see Olib
113 J18 Ulcinj S Montenegro 41°56′N 19°14′E
Uldz see Norovlin
Uleåborg see Oulu
Uleälv see Oulujoki
95 G16 Ulefoss Telemark, S Norway 59°17′N 09°15′E
Uleträsk see Oulujärvi
113 L19 Ulëz var. Ulëza. Dibër, C Albania 41°42′N 19°52′E
Ulëza see Ulëz
95 F22 Ulfborg Midtjylland, W Denmark 56°16′N 08°21′E
98 N13 Ulft Gelderland, E Netherlands 51°53′N 06°23′E
162 G7 Uliastay prev. Jibhalanta. Dzavhan, W Mongolia 47°47′N 96°53′E
188 F8 Ulimang Babeldaob, N Palau
67 T10 Ulindi ↝ W Dem. Rep. Congo
188 H14 Ulithi Atoll atoll Caroline Islands, W Micronesia
112 N10 Uljma Vojvodina, NE Serbia 45°04′N 21°08′E
Ul'kayak see Ol'keyyek
145 Q7 Ul'ken-Karoy, Ozero prev. Ul'ken-Karoy, Ozero. ◎ N Kazakhstan
Ul'ken-Karoy, Ozero see Ul'ken-Karoy, Ozero
Ülkenözen see Karaozen
Ülkenqobda see Kobda
104 G3 Ulla ↝ NW Spain
Ulla see Ula
183 S10 Ulladulla New South Wales, SE Australia 35°21′S 150°25′E
153 T14 Ullapara Rajshahi, W Bangladesh 24°20′N 89°34′E
96 H7 Ullapool N Scotland, United Kingdom 57°54′N 05°10′W
95 J20 Ullared Halland, S Sweden 57°07′N 12°45′E
105 T7 Ulldecona Cataluña, NE Spain 40°36′N 00°27′E
92 I9 Ullsfjorden fjord N Norway
97 K15 Ullswater ◎ NW England, United Kingdom
101 I22 Ulm Baden-Württemberg, S Germany 48°24′N 09°59′E
33 R8 Ulm Montana, NW USA 47°27′N 111°32′W
183 V5 Ulmarra New South Wales, SE Australia 29°37′S 153°06′E
116 K13 Ulmeni Buzău, C Romania 45°08′N 26°43′E
116 K14 Ulmeni Călărași, S Romania 44°08′N 26°43′E
42 L7 Ulmukhuás Región Autónoma Atlántico Norte, NE Nicaragua 14°20′N 84°30′W
188 C8 Ulong var. Aulong. island Palau Islands, N Palau
83 N14 Ulongué var. Ulongwé. Tete, NW Mozambique 14°34′S 34°21′E
Ulongwé see Ulongué
95 K19 Ulricehamn Västra Götaland, S Sweden 57°47′N 13°25′E
98 N5 Ulrum Groningen, NE Netherlands 53°24′N 06°20′E
163 Z16 Ulsan Jap. Urusan. SE South Korea 35°33′N 129°19′E
94 D10 Ulsteinvik Møre og Romsdal, S Norway 62°21′N 05°53′E
97 D15 Ulster ◆ province Northern Ireland, United Kingdom/Ireland
171 Q10 Ulu Pulau Siau, N Indonesia 02°46′N 125°22′E
123 Q11 Ulu Respublika Sakha (Yakutiya), NE Russian Federation 60°18′N 127°27′E
42 H5 Ulúa, Río ↝ NW Honduras
136 D12 Ulubat Gölü ◎ NW Turkey
136 E12 Uludağ ▲ NW Turkey 40°08′N 29°13′E
158 D7 Ulugqat Xinjiang Uygur Zizhiqu, W China 39°45′N 74°10′E
136 J16 Ulukışla Niğde, S Turkey 37°33′N 34°29′E
189 O15 Ulul island Caroline Islands, C Micronesia
83 L22 Ulundi KwaZulu/Natal, E South Africa 28°18′S 31°26′E
158 M3 Ulungur He ↝ NW China
158 K2 Ulungur Hu ◎ NW China
181 P8 Uluṟu var. Ayers Rock. monolith Northern Territory, C Australia
97 K16 Ulverston NW England, United Kingdom 54°13′N 03°08′W
183 O16 Ulverstone Tasmania, SE Australia 41°09′S 146°10′E
94 D13 Ulvik Hordaland, S Norway 60°34′N 06°53′E
93 J18 Ulvila Länsi-Suomi, W Finland 61°26′N 21°55′E
117 O8 Ul'yanovka Kirovohrads'ka Oblast', C Ukraine 48°18′N 30°15′E
127 Q5 Ul'yanovsk prev. Simbirsk. Ul'yanovskaya Oblast', W Russian Federation 54°17′N 48°21′E
127 Q5 Ul'yanovskaya Oblast' ◆ province W Russian Federation
Ul'yanovskiy see Botakara
Ul'yanovskiy Kanal see Ul'yanow Kanali
146 M13 Ul'yanow Kanali Rus. Ul'yanovskiy Kanal. canal Turkmenistan/Uzbekistan
Ulyshylanshyq see Uly-Zhylanshyk
26 H6 Ulysses Kansas, C USA 37°36′N 101°23′W
145 O12 Ulytau, Gory ▲ C Kazakhstan
145 N11 Uly-Zhylanshyk Kaz. Ulyshylanshyq. ↝ C Kazakhstan
112 A9 Umag It. Umago. Istra, NW Croatia 45°25′N 13°32′E
Umago see Umag
41 W12 Umán Yucatán, SE Mexico 20°51′N 89°43′W
117 O7 Uman' Rus. Uman. Cherkas'ka Oblast', C Ukraine 48°45′N 30°10′E
189 V13 Uman atoll Chuuk Islands, C Micronesia
Uman see Uman'
Umanak/Umanaq see Uummannaq
'Umān, Khalīj see Oman, Gulf of
'Umān, Salṭanat see Oman
154 K10 Umaria Madhya Pradesh, C India 23°34′N 80°49′E
149 R16 Umarkot Sind, SE Pakistan 25°22′N 69°48′E
188 B17 Umatac SW Guam 13°17′N 144°40′E
188 A17 Umatac Bay bay SW Guam
139 S6 Umayqah Ṣalāḥ ad Dīn, C Iraq 34°32′N 43°45′E
124 J5 Umba Murmanskaya Oblast', NW Russian Federation 66°39′N 34°24′E
138 I8 Umbāshī, Khirbat al ruins As Suwaydā', S Syria
80 A12 Umbelasha ↝ W South Sudan
106 H12 Umbertide Umbria, C Italy 43°16′N 12°21′E
61 B17 Umberto var. Humberto. Santa Fe, C Argentina 30°52′S 61°19′W
186 E7 Umboi Island var. Rooke Island. island C Papua New Guinea
124 J4 Umbozero, Ozero ◎ NW Russian Federation
106 H13 Umbria ◆ region C Italy
Umbrian-Machigian Mountains see Umbro-Marchigiano, Appennino
106 I12 Umbro-Marchigiano, Appennino Eng. Umbrian-Machigian Mountains. ▲ C Italy
93 J16 Umeå Västerbotten, N Sweden 63°50′N 20°15′E
93 H14 Umeälven ↝ N Sweden
39 Q5 Umiat Alaska, USA 69°22′N 152°09′W
83 K23 Umlazi KwaZulu/Natal, E South Africa 29°58′S 30°50′E
139 X10 Umm al Baqar, Hawr var. Birkat ad Dawaymah. spring S Iraq
139 Q5 Umm al Faṭūr var. Umm al Tūz. Ṣalāḥ ad Dīn, C Iraq 34°53′N 42°42′E
141 U12 Umm al Ḥayt, Wādī var. Wādī amilhayt. seasonal river SW Oman
Umm al Qaiwain see Umm al Qaywayn
143 R15 Umm al Qaywayn var. Umm al Qaiwain. Umm al Qaywayn, NE United Arab Emirates 25°43′N 55°55′E
Umm al Tūz see Umm al Faṭūr
138 J3 Umm 'Āmūd Ḥalab, N Syria 35°57′N 37°39′E
141 Y10 Umm ar Ruṣāṣ var. Umm Ruṣayṣ. W Oman 20°26′N 58°48′E
141 X9 Umm as Samīn salt flat C Oman
141 V9 Umm az Zumūl oasis E Saudi Arabia
80 A9 Umm Buru Western Darfur, W Sudan 15°01′N 23°36′E
80 A12 Umm Dafag Southern Darfur, W Sudan 10°28′N 23°20′E
Umm Durmān see Omdurman
138 F9 Umm el Fahm Haifa, N Israel 32°30′N 35°06′E
80 F9 Umm Inderab Northern Kordofan, C Sudan 15°12′N 31°54′E
80 C10 Umm Keddada Northern Darfur, W Sudan 13°36′N 26°42′E
140 J7 Umm Lajj Tabūk, W Saudi Arabia 25°02′N 37°19′E
138 L10 Umm Maḥfur ↝ N Jordan
139 Y13 Umm Qaṣr Al Baṣrah, SE Iraq 30°02′N 47°55′E
Umm Ruṣayṣ see Umm ar Ruṣāṣ
80 F11 Umm Ruwaba var. Umm Ruwābah, Um Ruwāba. Northern Kordofan, C Sudan 12°54′N 31°13′E
Umm Ruwābah see Umm Ruwaba
143 N16 Umm Sa'īd var. Musay'īd. S Qatar 24°57′N 51°32′E
139 Y10 Umm Sawān, Hawr ◎ S Iraq
138 K10 Umm Ṭuways, Wādī dry watercourse N Jordan
38 J17 Umnak Island island Aleutian Islands, Alaska, USA
32 F13 Umpqua River ↝ Oregon, NW USA
82 D13 Umpulo Bié, C Angola 12°43′S 17°42′E
154 I12 Umred Mahārāshtra, C India 20°54′N 79°19′E
Um Ruwāba see Umm Ruwaba
Umtali see Mutare
Umtata see Mthatha
77 V17 Umuahia Abia, SW Nigeria 05°30′N 07°33′E
60 H10 Umuarama Paraná, S Brazil 23°45′S 53°20′W
Umvuma see Mvuma
83 K18 Umzingwani ↝ S Zimbabwe
112 D11 Una ↝ Bosnia and Herzegovina/Croatia
112 E12 Unac ↝ W Bosnia and Herzegovina
23 T6 Unadilla Georgia, SE USA 32°15′N 83°44′W
18 I10 Unadilla River ↝ New York, NE USA
59 L18 Unaí Minas Gerais, SE Brazil 16°24′S 46°49′W
39 N10 Unalakleet Alaska, USA 63°52′N 160°47′W
38 K17 Unalaska Island island Aleutian Islands, Alaska, USA
185 I16 Una, Mount ▲ South Island, New Zealand 42°12′S 172°34′E
82 N13 Unango Niassa, N Mozambique 12°45′S 35°28′E
Unao see Unnāo
92 L12 Unari Lappi, N Finland 67°07′N 25°37′E
141 O6 'Unayzah var. Anaiza. Al Qaṣīm, C Saudi Arabia 26°03′N 44°00′E
138 L10 'Unayzah, Jabal ▲ Jordan/Saudi Arabia 32°09′N 39°11′E
Unci see Almería
57 K19 Uncía Potosí, C Bolivia 18°30′S 66°29′W
37 Q7 Uncompahgre Peak ▲ Colorado, C USA 38°04′N 107°27′W
37 P6 Uncompahgre Plateau plain Colorado, C USA
95 L17 Unden ◎ S Sweden
28 M4 Underwood North Dakota, N USA 47°25′N 101°09′W
171 T13 Undur Pulau Seram, E Indonesia 03°41′S 130°38′E
Undur Khan see Öndörhaan
126 H6 Unecha Bryanskaya Oblast', W Russian Federation 52°51′N 32°38′E
39 N16 Unga Unga Island, Alaska, USA 55°14′N 160°34′W
Ungaria see Hungary
183 P8 Ungarie New South Wales, SE Australia 33°39′S 146°54′E
Ungarisch-Brod see Uherský Brod
Ungarisches Erzgebirge see Slovenské rudohorie
Ungarisch-Hradisch see Uherské Hradiště
Ungarn see Hungary
12 M4 Ungava Bay bay Québec, E Canada
12 J2 Ungava, Péninsule d' peninsula Québec, SE Canada
Ungeny see Ungheni
116 M9 Ungheni Rus. Ungeny. W Moldova 47°13′N 27°48′E
Unguja see Zanzibar
146 G10 Üngüz Angyrsyndaky Garagum Rus. Zaunguzskiye Garagumy. desert N Turkmenistan
146 H11 Unguz, Solonchakovyye Vpadiny salt marsh C Turkmenistan
Ungvár see Uzhhorod
60 I12 União da Vitória Paraná, S Brazil 26°13′S 51°05′W
111 G17 Uničov Ger. Mährisch-Neustadt. Olomoucký Kraj, E Czech Republic 49°48′N 17°05′E
110 J12 Uniejów Łódzkie, C Poland 51°58′N 18°46′E
112 A11 Unije island W Croatia
38 L16 Unimak Island island Aleutian Islands, Alaska, USA
38 L16 Unimak Pass strait Aleutian Islands, Alaska, USA
62 J12 Unión San Luis, C Argentina 35°09′S 65°55′W
27 W5 Union Missouri, C USA 38°27′N 91°01′W
32 L12 Union Oregon, NW USA 45°12′N 117°51′W
21 Q11 Union South Carolina, SE USA 34°42′N 81°37′W
21 R6 Union West Virginia, NE USA 37°36′N 80°34′W
61 B25 Unión, Bahía bay E Argentina
31 Q13 Union City Indiana, N USA 40°12′N 84°50′W
31 Q10 Union City Michigan, N USA 42°03′N 85°06′W
18 C12 Union City Pennsylvania, NE USA 41°54′N 79°51′W
20 G8 Union City Tennessee, S USA 36°26′N 89°03′W
32 G14 Union Creek Oregon, NW USA 42°54′N 122°26′W
83 G25 Uniondale Western Cape, SW South Africa 33°40′S 23°07′E
40 K13 Unión de Tula Jalisco, SW Mexico 19°58′N 104°16′W
30 M9 Union Grove Wisconsin, N USA 42°39′N 88°03′W
45 Y15 Union Island island S Saint Vincent and the Grenadines
Union of Myanmar see Burma
46 K5 Union Reefs reef SW Mexico
0 D7 Union Seamount undersea feature NE Pacific Ocean 49°35′N 132°45′W
23 Q6 Union Springs Alabama, S USA 32°08′N 85°43′W
20 H6 Uniontown Kentucky, S USA 37°46′N 87°55′W
18 C16 Uniontown Pennsylvania, NE USA 39°54′N 79°44′W
27 T1 Unionville Missouri, C USA 40°28′N 93°00′W
141 V8 United Arab Emirates Ar. Al Imārāt al 'Arabīyah al Muttaḥidah, abbrev. UAE; prev. Trucial States. ◆ federation SW Asia
United Arab Republic see Egypt
97 H14 United Kingdom off. United Kingdom of Great Britain and Northern Ireland, abbrev. UK. ◆ monarchy NW Europe
United Kingdom of Great Britain and Northern Ireland see United Kingdom
United Mexican States see Mexico
United Provinces see Uttar Pradesh
16 L10 United States of America off. United States of America, var. America, The States, abbrev. U.S., USA. ◆ federal republic North America
United States of America see United States of America
124 J10 Unitsa Respublika Kareliya, NW Russian Federation 62°31′N 34°31′E
11 S15 Unity Saskatchewan, S Canada 52°27′N 109°10′W
Unity State see Wahda
105 Q8 Universales, Montes ▲ C Spain
27 X4 University City Missouri, C USA 38°40′N 90°19′W
187 Q13 Unmet Malekula, C Vanuatu 16°09′S 167°16′E
101 F15 Unna Nordrhein-Westfalen, W Germany 51°32′N 07°41′E
Unnan see Kisuki
152 L12 Unnāo prev. Unao. Uttar Pradesh, N India 26°32′N 80°30′E
187 R15 Unpongkor Erromango, S Vanuatu 18°48′S 169°01′E
Unruhstadt see Kargowa
96 M1 Unst island NE Scotland, United Kingdom
101 K16 Unstrut ↝ C Germany
Unterdrauburg see Dravograd
Unterlimbach see Lendava
101 L23 Unterschleissheim Bayern, SE Germany 48°16′N 11°34′E
101 H24 Untersee ◎ Germany/Switzerland
100 O10 Unterueckersee ◎ NE Germany
Unterwalden former canton see Nidwalden, Obwalden
55 N12 Unturán, Sierra de ▲ Brazil/Venezuela
159 N11 Unuli Horog Qinghai, W China 35°10′N 91°50′E
136 M11 Ünye Ordu, W Turkey 41°08′N 37°14′E
Unza see Unzha
125 O14 Unzha var. Unza. ↝ NW Russian Federation
79 E17 Uolo, Río var. Eyo (lower course), Mbini, Uele (upper course), Woleu; prev. Benito. ↝ Equatorial Guinea/Gabon
55 Q10 Uonán Bolívar, SE Venezuela 04°33′N 62°10′W
161 T12 Uotsuri-shima island China/Japan/Taiwan
165 M11 Uozu Toyama, Honshū, SW Japan 36°50′N 137°25′E
42 L12 Upala Alajuela, NW Costa Rica 10°52′N 85°W
55 P7 Upata Bolívar, E Venezuela 08°02′N 62°25′W
79 M23 Upemba, Lac ◎ SE Dem. Rep. Congo
145 R11 Upenskoye prev. Uspenskiy. Karaganda, C Kazakhstan 48°45′N 72°46′E
197 O12 Upernavik var. Upernivik. Kitaa, C Greenland 73°06′N 55°42′W
Upernivik see Upernavik
83 F22 Upington Northern Cape, W South Africa 28°28′S 21°14′E
Uplands see Ottawa
192 I16 'Upolu island SE Samoa
38 G11 'Upolu Point var. Upolu Point. headland Hawai'i, USA, C Pacific Ocean 20°15′N 155°51′W
Upper Austria see Oberösterreich
Upper Bann see Bann
14 M13 Upper Canada Village tourist site Ontario, SE Canada
18 I16 Upper Darby Pennsylvania, NE USA 39°57′N 75°15′W
28 L2 Upper Des Lacs Lake ⊠ North Dakota, N USA
185 L14 Upper Hutt Wellington, North Island, New Zealand 41°06′S 175°06′E
29 X11 Upper Iowa River ↝ Iowa, C USA
32 H15 Upper Klamath Lake ◎ Oregon, NW USA
34 M6 Upper Lake California, W USA 39°07′N 122°53′W
35 Q1 Upper Lake ◎ California, W USA
10 K9 Upper Liard Yukon Territory, W Canada 60°01′N 128°59′W
97 E16 Upper Lough Erne ◎ SW Northern Ireland, United Kingdom
80 F12 Upper Nile ◆ state NE South Sudan

◆ Country
● Country Capital
◇ Dependent Territory
○ Dependent Territory Capital
◆ Administrative Regions
✈ International Airport
▲ Mountain
▲ Mountain Range
⛰ Volcano
↝ River
◎ Lake
⊠ Reservoir

29 T3 **Upper Red Lake** ⊛ Minnesota, N USA
31 S12 **Upper Sandusky** Ohio, N USA *40°49′N 83°16′W*
Upper Volta *see* Burkina
95 O15 **Upplands Väsby** *var.* Upplandsväsby. Stockholm, C Sweden *59°29′N 18°04′E*
Upplandsväsby *see* Upplands Väsby
95 O15 **Uppsala** Uppsala, C Sweden *59°52′N 17°38′E*
95 O14 **Uppsala** ◈ *county* C Sweden
38 J12 **Upright Cape** *headland* Saint Matthew Island, Alaska, USA *60°19′N 172°15′W*
20 K6 **Upton** Kentucky, S USA *37°25′N 85°53′W*
33 Y13 **Upton** Wyoming, C USA *44°06′N 104°37′W*
141 N7 **'Uqlat aş Şuqūr** Al Qaşīm, W Saudi Arabia *25°51′N 42°13′E*
Uqsuqtuuq *see* Gjoa Haven
Uqturpan *see* Wushi
54 C7 **Urabá, Golfo de** *gulf* NW Colombia
Uracas *see* Farallon de Pajaros
uradqianqi *see* Wulashan, N China
Uradar'ya *see* O'radaryo
Urad Qianqi *see* Xishanzui, N China
165 U5 **Urahoro** Hokkaidō, NE Japan *42°47′N 143°41′E*
165 T5 **Urakawa** Hokkaidō, NE Japan *42°11′N 142°42′E*
Ural *see* Zhayyk
183 T6 **Uralla** New South Wales, SE Australia *30°39′S 151°30′E*
Ural Mountains *see* Ural'skiye Gory
144 F8 **Ural'sk** *Kaz.* Oral. Zapadnyy Kazakhstan, NW Kazakhstan *51°12′N 51°17′E*
Ural'skaya Oblast' *see* Zapadnyy Kazakhstan
127 W5 **Ural'skiye Gory** *var.* Ural'skiy Khrebet, *Eng.* Ural Mountains. ▲▲ Kazakhstan/ Russian Federation
Ural'skiy Khrebet *see* Ural'skiye Gory
138 I3 **Urām aş Şughrá** Ḩalab, N Syria *36°10′N 36°55′E*
183 P10 **Urana** New South Wales, SE Australia *35°22′S 146°16′E*
11 S10 **Uranium City** Saskatchewan, C Canada *59°30′N 108°46′W*
58 F10 **Uraricoera** Roraima, N Brazil *03°26′N 60°54′W*
47 S5 **Uraricoera, Rio** ≋ N Brazil
Ura-Tyube *see* Üroteppa
165 O13 **Urawa** *var.* Saitama. Saitama, Honshū, S Japan *35°52′N 139°40′E*
122 H10 **Uray** Khanty-Mansiyskiy Avtonomnyy Okrug-Yugra, C Russian Federation *60°07′N 64°38′E*
141 R7 **'Uray'irah** Ash Sharqīyah, E Saudi Arabia *25°59′N 48°52′E*
30 M13 **Urbana** Illinois, N USA *40°06′N 88°12′W*
31 R13 **Urbana** Ohio, N USA *40°04′N 83°46′W*
29 V14 **Urbandale** Iowa, C USA *41°37′N 93°42′W*
106 I11 **Urbania** Marche, C Italy *43°40′N 12°33′E*
106 I11 **Urbino** Marche, C Italy *43°45′N 12°38′E*
57 H16 **Urcos** Cusco, S Peru *13°40′S 71°38′W*
105 N10 **Urda** Castilla-La Mancha, C Spain *39°25′N 03°43′W*
Urda *see* Khan Ordasy
Urdgol *see* Chandmanĭ
105 O3 **Urduña** *var.* Orduña. País Vasco, N Spain *43°00′N 03°00′W*
Urdunn *see* Jordan
Urdzhar *see* Urzhar
97 L16 **Ure** ≋ N England, United Kingdom
119 K18 **Urechcha** *Rus.* Urech'ye. Minskaya Voblasts', S Belarus *52°57′N 27°54′E*
Urech'ye *see* Urechcha
127 P2 **Uren'** Nizhegorodskaya Oblast', W Russian Federation *57°30′N 45°48′E*
122 J9 **Urengoy** Yamalo-Nenetskiy Avtonomnyy Okrug, N Russian Federation *65°52′N 78°42′E*
184 K10 **Urenui** Taranaki, North Island, New Zealand *38°59′S 174°25′E*
187 Q12 **Ureparapara** *island* Banks Islands, N Vanuatu
40 G5 **Ures** Sonora, NW Mexico *29°26′N 110°24′W*
Urfa *see* Şanlıurfa
Urga *see* Ulaanbaatar
162 F6 **Urgamal** *var.* Hungiy. Dzavhan, W Mongolia *48°31′N 94°15′E*
146 H9 **Urganch** *Rus.* Urgench; *prev.* Novo-Urgench. Xorazm Viloyati, W Uzbekistan *41°40′N 60°32′E*
Urgench *see* Urganch
136 J14 **Ürgüp** Nevşehir, C Turkey *38°39′N 34°55′E*
147 O12 **Urgut** Samarqand Viloyati, C Uzbekistan *39°26′N 67°15′E*
158 K3 **Urho** Xinjiang Uygur Zizhiqu, W China *46°05′N 84°51′E*
152 G5 **Uri** Jammu and Kashmir, NW India *34°05′N 74°03′E*
108 G9 **Uri** ◈ *canton* C Switzerland
54 F11 **Uribe** Meta, C Colombia *03°01′N 74°33′W*
54 H4 **Uribia** La Guajira, N Colombia *11°45′N 72°19′W*
116 G12 **Uricani** *Hung.* Hobicaurikány. Hunedoara, SW Romania *45°18′N 23°03′E*
57 M21 **Uriondo** Tarija, S Bolivia *21°43′S 64°40′W*
40 I7 **Urique** Chihuahua, N Mexico *27°16′N 107°51′W*
40 I7 **Urique, Río** ≋ N Mexico
56 E9 **Urituyacu, Río** ≋ N Peru
Uritskiy *see* Sarykol'
98 K8 **Urk** Flevoland, N Netherlands *52°40′N 05°35′E*
136 B14 **Urla** İzmir, W Turkey *38°19′N 26°47′E*
116 K13 **Urlaţi** Prahova, SE Romania *44°59′N 26°15′E*
127 V4 **Urman** Respublika Bashkortostan, W Russian Federation *54°53′N 56°52′E*
147 P12 **Urmetan** W Tajikistan *39°27′N 68°13′E*
Urmia *see* Orūmīyeh
Urmia, Lake *see* Orūmīyeh, Daryācheh-ye
Urmiyeh *see* Orūmīyeh
Uroševac *see* Ferizaj
147 P11 **Üroteppa** *Rus.* Ura-Tyube. NW Tajikistan *39°55′N 68°57′E*
54 D8 **Urrao** Antioquia, W Colombia *06°16′N 76°10′W*
Ursat'yevskaya *see* Xovos
Urt *see* Gurvantes
127 X7 **Urtazym** Orenburgskaya Oblast', W Russian Federation *52°12′N 58°48′E*
59 K18 **Uruaçu** Goiás, C Brazil *14°38′S 49°06′W*
40 M14 **Uruapan** *var.* Uruapan del Progreso. Michoacán, SW Mexico *19°26′N 102°04′W*
Uruapan del Progreso *see* Uruapan
57 G15 **Urubamba, Cordillera** ▲▲ C Peru
57 G14 **Urubamba, Río** ≋ C Peru
58 G12 **Urucará** Amazonas, N Brazil *02°30′S 57°45′W*
61 E16 **Uruguaiana** Rio Grande do Sul, S Brazil *29°45′S 57°05′W*
Uruguai, Rio *see* Uruguay
61 E18 **Uruguay** *off.* Oriental Republic of Uruguay; *prev.* La Banda Oriental. ◆ *republic* E South America
61 E15 **Uruguay** *var.* Rio Uruguai, Río Uruguay. ≋ E South America
Uruguay, Oriental Republic of *see* Uruguay
Uruguay, Río *see* Uruguay
Urukthapel *see* Ngeruktabel
Urumchi *see* Ürümqi
Urumi Yeh *see* Orūmīyeh, Daryācheh-ye
158 L5 **Ürümqi** *var.* Tihwa, Urumchi, Urumqi, Urumtsi, Wu-lu-k'o-mu-shi, Wu-lu-mu-ch'i; *prev.* Ti-hua. Xinjiang Uygur Zizhiqu, NW China *43°52′N 87°31′E*
Urumtsi *see* Ürümqi
Urundi *see* Burundi
183 V6 **Urunga** New South Wales, SE Australia *30°33′S 152°58′E*
188 C15 **Uruno Point** *headland* NW Guam *13°37′N 144°50′E*
123 U13 **Urup, Ostrov** *island* Kuril'skiye Ostrova, SE Russian Federation
141 P11 **'Uruq al Mawārid** *desert* S Saudi Arabia
Urusan *see* Ulsan
127 T5 **Urussu** Respublika Tatarstan, W Russian Federation *54°34′N 53°23′E*
184 K10 **Uruti** Taranaki, North Island, New Zealand *38°57′S 174°32′E*
57 K19 **Uru Uru, Lago** ⊛ W Bolivia
55 P9 **Uruyén** Bolívar, SE Venezuela *05°40′N 62°26′W*
149 O7 **Uruzgān** ; *prev.* Orūzgān. Uruzgān, C Afghanistan *32°58′N 66°39′E*
149 N6 **Uruzgān** *prev.* Orūzgān. ◈ *province* C Afghanistan
165 T3 **Uryū-gawa** ≋ Hokkaidō, NE Japan
165 T2 **Uryū-ko** ⊛ Hokkaidō, NE Japan
127 N8 **Uryupinsk** Volgogradskaya Oblast', SW Russian Federation *50°51′N 41°59′E*
145 X12 **Urzhar** *prev.* Urdzhar. Vostochnyy Kazakhstan, E Kazakhstan *47°06′N 81°33′E*
125 R16 **Urzhum** Kirovskaya Oblast', NW Russian Federation *57°09′N 49°56′E*
116 K13 **Urziceni** Ialomiţa, SE Romania *44°43′N 26°39′E*
164 E14 **Usa** Ōita, Kyūshū, SW Japan *33°31′N 131°22′E*
125 T6 **Usa** ≋ NW Russian Federation
136 E14 **Uşak** *prev.* Ushak. Uşak, W Turkey *38°42′N 29°25′E*
136 D14 **Uşak** *var.* Ushak. ◈ *province* W Turkey
83 C19 **Usakos** Erongo, W Namibia *22°01′S 15°32′E*
81 J21 **Usambara Mountains** ▲▲ NE Tanzania
81 G23 **Usangu Flats** *wetland* SW Tanzania
65 D24 **Usborne, Mount** ▲ East Falkland, Falkland Islands *51°35′S 58°57′W*
100 O8 **Usedom** *island* NE Germany
99 M24 **Useldange** Diekirch, C Luxembourg *49°47′N 05°59′E*
119 L16 **Usha** ≋ C Belarus
Ushachi *see* Ushachy
118 L13 **Ushachy** *Rus.* Ushachi. Vitsyebskaya Voblasts', N Belarus *55°11′N 28°37′E*
Ushak *see* Uşak
122 L4 **Ushakova, Ostrov** *island* Severnaya Zemlya, N Russian Federation
Ushant *see* Ouessant, Île d'
145 W13 **Usharal** *prev.* Ucharal. Almaty, E Kazakhstan *46°08′N 80°55′E*
164 B15 **Ushibuka** *var.* Usibuka. Kumamoto, Shimo-jima, SW Japan *32°12′N 130°00′E*
Ushi Point *see* Sabaneta, Puntan
145 V14 **Ushtobe** *Kaz.* Üshtöbe. Almaty, SE Kazakhstan *45°15′N 77°59′E*
Üshtöbe *see* Ushtobe
63 I25 **Ushuaia** Tierra del Fuego, S Argentina *54°48′S 68°19′W*
39 R10 **Usibelli** Alaska, USA *63°54′N 148°41′W*
Usibuka *see* Ushibuka
186 D7 **Usino** Madang, N Papua New Guinea *05°40′S 145°31′E*
125 U6 **Usinsk** Respublika Komi, NW Russian Federation *66°01′N 57°37′E*
97 K22 **Usk** *Wel.* Wysg. ≋ SE Wales, United Kingdom
Uskočke Planine/ Uskokengebirge *see* Gorjanci
Uskoplje *see* Gornji Vakuf
Üsküb/Üsküp *see* Skopje
114 M11 **Üsküpdere** Kırklareli, NW Turkey *41°41′N 27°21′E*
126 L7 **Usman'** Lipetskaya Oblast', W Russian Federation *52°04′N 39°41′E*
118 D8 **Usmas Ezers** ⊛ NW Latvia
125 U13 **Usol'ye** Permskiy Kray, NW Russian Federation *59°27′N 56°33′E*
41 T16 **Uspanapa, Río** ≋ SE Mexico
Uspenskiy *see* Upenskoye
103 O11 **Ussel** Corrèze, C France *45°33′N 02°18′E*
163 Z6 **Ussuri** *var.* Usuri, Wusuri, *Chin.* Wusuli Jiang. ≋ China/Russian Federation
123 S15 **Ussuriysk** *prev.* Nikol'sk, Nikol'sk-Ussuriyskiy, Voroshilov. Primorskiy Kray, SE Russian Federation *43°48′N 131°59′E*
136 J10 **Usta Burnu** *headland* N Turkey *41°58′N 34°30′E*
149 P13 **Usta Muhammad** Baluchistān, SW Pakistan *28°07′N 68°00′E*
123 V11 **Ust'-Bol'sheretsk** Kamchatskiy Kray, E Russian Federation *52°48′N 156°12′E*
127 N9 **Ust'-Buzulukskaya** Volgogradskaya Oblast', SW Russian Federation *50°12′N 42°06′E*
111 C16 **Ustecký Kraj** ◈ *region* NW Czech Republic
108 G7 **Uster** Zürich, NE Switzerland *47°21′N 08°49′E*
107 I22 **Ustica, Isola d'** *island* S Italy
122 M11 **Ust'-Ilimsk** Irkutskaya Oblast', C Russian Federation *57°57′N 102°30′E*
111 C15 **Ústí nad Labem** *Ger.* Aussig. Ústecký Kraj, NW Czech Republic *50°41′N 14°04′E*
111 F17 **Ústí nad Orlicí** *Ger.* Wildenschwert. Pardubický Kraj, C Czech Republic *49°58′N 16°24′E*
Ustinov *see* Izhevsk
113 J14 **Ustiprača** ◈ Republika Srpska, SE Bosnia and Herzegovina
122 H11 **Ust'-Ishim** Omskaya Oblast', C Russian Federation *57°42′N 70°58′E*
110 G6 **Ustka** *Ger.* Stolpmünde. Pomorskie, N Poland *54°35′N 16°50′E*
123 V9 **Ust'-Kamchatsk** Kamchatskiy Kray, E Russian Federation *56°14′N 162°28′E*
145 X9 **Ust'-Kamenogorsk** *Kaz.* Öskemen. Vostochnyy Kazakhstan, E Kazakhstan *49°58′N 82°36′E*
123 T10 **Ust'-Khayryuzovo** Krasnoyarskiy Kray, E Russian Federation *57°07′N 156°37′E*
122 I14 **Ust'-Koksa** Respublika Altay, S Russian Federation *50°15′N 85°45′E*
125 S11 **Ust'-Kulom** Respublika Komi, NW Russian Federation *61°42′N 53°42′E*
123 Q8 **Ust'-Kuyga** Respublika Sakha (Yakutiya), NE Russian Federation *69°59′N 135°27′E*
126 L14 **Ust'-Labinsk** Krasnodarskiy Kray, SW Russian Federation *44°40′N 40°46′E*
123 R10 **Ust'-Maya** Respublika Sakha (Yakutiya), NE Russian Federation *60°27′N 134°28′E*
123 R9 **Ust'-Nera** Respublika Sakha (Yakutiya), NE Russian Federation *64°28′N 143°01′E*
123 P12 **Ust'-Nyukzha** Amurskaya Oblast', S Russian Federation *56°30′N 121°32′E*
123 O7 **Ust'-Olenëk** Respublika Sakha (Yakutiya), NE Russian Federation *73°03′N 119°34′E*
123 T9 **Ust'-Omchug** Magadanskaya Oblast', E Russian Federation *61°07′N 149°17′E*
122 M13 **Ust'-Ordynskiy** Irkutskaya Oblast', S Russian Federation *52°50′N 104°42′E*
125 N8 **Ust'-Pinega** Arkhangel'skaya Oblast', NW Russian Federation *64°09′N 41°55′E*
122 K8 **Ust'-Port** Krasnoyarskiy Kray, N Russian Federation *69°42′N 84°25′E*
114 L11 **Ustrem** *prev.* Vakav. Yambol, E Bulgaria *42°01′N 26°28′E*
111 O18 **Ustrzyki Dolne** Podkarpackie, SE Poland *49°26′N 22°36′E*
Ust'-Sysol'sk *see* Syktyvkar
125 R7 **Ust'-Tsil'ma** Respublika Komi, NW Russian Federation *65°25′N 52°09′E*
Ust Urt *see* Ustyurt Plateau
125 O11 **Ust'ya** ≋ NW Russian Federation
124 K6 **Ust'ye Varzugi** Murmanskaya Oblast', NW Russian Federation *66°16′N 36°47′E*
123 V10 **Ust'yevoye** *prev.* Kirovskiy. Kamchatskiy Kray, E Russian Federation *54°06′N 155°48′E*
117 R8 **Ustynivka** Kirovohrads'ka Oblast', C Ukraine *47°58′N 32°32′E*
144 H15 **Ustyurt Plateau** *var.* Ust Urt, *Uzb.* Ustyurt Platosi. *plateau* Kazakhstan/ Uzbekistan
Ustyurt Platosi *see* Ustyurt Plateau
124 K14 **Ustyuzhna** Vologodskaya Oblast', NW Russian Federation *58°50′N 36°25′E*
158 J4 **Usu** Xinjiang Uygur Zizhiqu, NW China *44°27′N 84°37′E*
171 O13 **Usu** Sulawesi, C Indonesia *02°34′S 120°58′E*
164 E14 **Usuki** Ōita, Kyūshū, SW Japan *33°07′N 131°48′E*
42 G8 **Usulután** Usulután, SE El Salvador *13°20′N 88°26′W*
42 B9 **Usulután** ◈ *department* SE El Salvador
41 W16 **Usumacinta, Río** ≋ Guatemala/Mexico
Usumbura *see* Bujumbura
Usuri *see* Ussuri
U.S./USA *see* United States of America
171 W14 **Uta** Papua, E Indonesia *04°28′S 136°03′E*
36 K5 **Utah** *off.* State of Utah, *also known as* Beehive State, Mormon State. ◈ *state* W USA
36 L3 **Utah Lake** ⊛ Utah, W USA
Utaidhani *see* Uthai Thani
93 M14 **Utajärvi** Oulu, C Finland *64°45′N 26°25′E*
Utamboni *see* Mitemele, Río
Utaradit *see* Uttaradit
165 T3 **Utashinai** *var.* Utasinai. Hokkaidō, NE Japan *43°32′N 142°03′E*
Utasinai *see* Utashinai
193 Y14 **'Uta Vava'u** *island* Vava'u Group, N Tonga
37 V9 **Ute Creek** ≋ New Mexico, SW USA
118 H12 **Utena** Utena, E Lithuania *55°30′N 25°34′E*
118 H12 **Utena** ◈ *province* Lithuania
37 V10 **Ute Reservoir** ⊠ New Mexico, SW USA
167 O10 **Uthai Thani** *var.* Muang Uthai Thani, Udayadhani, Utaidhani. Uthai Thani, W Thailand *15°22′N 100°03′E*
149 O15 **Uthal** Baluchistān, SW Pakistan *25°53′N 66°37′E*
uThongathi *see* oThongathi
18 I10 **Utica** New York, NE USA *43°06′N 75°15′W*
105 R10 **Utiel** Valenciana, E Spain *39°33′N 01°13′W*
11 O13 **Utikuma Lake** ⊛ Alberta, W Canada
42 I4 **Utila, Isla de** *island* Islas de la Bahía, N Honduras
Utina *see* Udine
59 O17 **Utinga** Bahia, E Brazil *12°05′S 41°07′W*
Utirik *see* Utrik Atoll
95 M22 **Utlängan** *island* S Sweden
117 U11 **Utlyuts'kyy Lyman** *bay* S Ukraine
95 P16 **Utö** Stockholm, C Sweden *58°55′N 18°19′E*
25 Q12 **Utopia** Texas, SW USA *29°30′N 99°31′W*
98 J11 **Utrecht** *Lat.* Trajectum ad Rhenum. Utrecht, C Netherlands *52°06′N 05°07′E*
83 K22 **Utrecht** KwaZulu/Natal, E South Africa *27°40′S 30°20′E*
98 I11 **Utrecht** ◈ *province* C Netherlands
104 K14 **Utrera** Andalucía, S Spain *37°10′N 05°47′W*
189 V4 **Utrik Atoll** *var.* Utirik, Utrōk, Utrōnk. *atoll* Ratak Chain, N Marshall Islands
Utrōk/Utrōnk *see* Utrik Atoll
95 B16 **Utsira** *island* SW Norway
92 L8 **Utsjoki** *var.* Ohcejohka. Lappi, N Finland *69°54′N 27°01′E*
165 O12 **Utsunomiya** *var.* Utunomiya. Tochigi, Honshū, S Japan *36°36′N 139°53′E*
127 P13 **Utta** Respublika Kalmykiya, SW Russian Federation *46°22′N 46°03′E*
167 O8 **Uttaradit** *var.* Utaradit. Uttaradit, N Thailand *17°38′N 100°05′E*
152 J9 **Uttarakhand** ◈ *state* N India
152 J8 **Uttarkāshi** Uttarakhand, N India *30°45′N 78°19′E*
152 K11 **Uttar Pradesh** *prev.* United Provinces, United Provinces of Agra and Oudh. ◈ *state* N India
45 T5 **Utuado** C Puerto Rico *18°17′N 66°41′W*
158 K3 **Utubulak** Xinjiang Uygur Zizhiqu, W China *46°50′N 86°15′E*
39 N5 **Utukok River** ≋ Alaska, USA
Utunomiya *see* Utsunomiya
187 P10 **Utupua** *island* Santa Cruz Islands, E Solomon Islands
Utva *see* Shyngyrlau
189 Y15 **Utwe** Kosrae, E Micronesia
189 X15 **Utwe Harbor** *harbor* Kosrae, E Micronesia
Uubulan *see* Hayrhan
163 O8 **Uulbayan** *var.* Dzüünbulag. Sühbaatar, E Mongolia *46°30′N 112°22′E*
118 G6 **Uulu** Pärnumaa, SW Estonia *58°15′N 24°32′E*
197 N13 **Uummannaq** *var.* Umanak, Umanaq. ◈ Kitaa, C Greenland
Uummannarsuaq *see* Nunap Isua
162 E4 **Üüreg Nuur** ⊛ NW Mongolia
Uusikaarlepyy *see* Nykarleby
93 J19 **Uusikaupunki** *Swe.* Nystad. Länsi-Suomi, SW Finland *60°48′N 21°25′E*
127 S2 **Uva** Udmurtskaya Respublika, NW Russian Federation *56°41′N 52°15′E*
155 K25 **Uva** ◈ *province* SE Sri Lanka
113 L14 **Uvac** ≋ W Serbia
25 Q12 **Uvalde** Texas, SW USA *29°14′N 99°49′W*
119 O18 **Uvaravichy** *Rus.* Uvarovichi. Homyel'skaya Voblasts', SE Belarus *52°36′N 30°44′E*
54 J11 **Uvá, Río** ≋ E Colombia
Uvarovichi *see* Uvaravichy
127 N7 **Uvarovo** Tambovskaya Oblast', W Russian Federation *51°58′N 42°13′E*
122 H10 **Uvat** Tyumenskaya Oblast', C Russian Federation *59°11′N 68°37′E*
190 G12 **Uvea, Île** *island* N Wallis and Futuna
81 E21 **Uvinza** Kigoma, W Tanzania *05°08′S 30°23′E*
79 O20 **Uvira** Sud-Kivu, E Dem. Rep. Congo *03°24′S 29°05′E*
162 E5 **Uvs** ◈ *province* NW Mongolia
162 F5 **Uvs Nuur** *var.* Ozero Ubsu-Nur. ⊛ Mongolia/Russian Federation
164 F14 **Uwa** *var.* Seiyo. Ehime, Shikoku, SW Japan *33°22′N 132°29′E*
164 F14 **Uwajima** *var.* Uwazima. Ehime, Shikoku, SW Japan *33°13′N 132°32′E*
80 B5 **'Uwaynāt, Jabal al** *var.* Jebel Uweinat. ▲ Libya/Sudan *21°51′N 25°01′E*
Uwazima *see* Uwajima
Uweinat, Jebel *see* 'Uwaynāt, Jabal al
14 H14 **Uxbridge** Ontario, S Canada *44°07′N 79°07′W*
Uxellodunum *see* Issoudun
Uxin Qi *see* Dabqig, N China
41 X12 **Uxmal, Ruinas** *ruins* Yucatán, SE Mexico
129 Q5 **Uy** ≋ Kazakhstan/Russian Federation
144 K15 **Uyaly** Kzylorda, S Kazakhstan *44°22′N 61°16′E*
123 R8 **Uyandina** ≋ NE Russian Federation
162 J8 **Uyanga** *var.* Ongi. Övörhangay, C Mongolia *46°30′N 102°18′E*
Üydzen *see* Manlay
Uyeda *see* Ueda
122 K5 **Uyedineniya, Ostrov** *island* N Russian Federation
77 V17 **Uyo** Akwa Ibom, S Nigeria *05°00′N 07°57′E*
162 D8 **Üyönch** Hovd, W Mongolia *46°04′N 92°05′E*
Uyuk *see* Oyyk
141 V13 **'Uyūn** SW Oman *17°19′N 53°50′E*
57 K20 **Uyuni** Potosí, W Bolivia *20°27′S 66°48′W*
57 J20 **Uyuni, Salar de** *wetland* SW Bolivia
146 I9 **Uzbekistan** *off.* Republic of Uzbekistan. ◆ *republic* C Asia
Uzbekistan, Republic of *see* Uzbekistan
158 D8 **Uzbel Shankou** *Rus.* Pereval Kyzyl-Dzhiik. *pass* China/ Tajikistan
146 B11 **Uzboý** *prev. Rus.* Imeni 26 Bakinskikh Komissarov, *Turkm.* 26 Baku Komissarlary Adyndaky. Balkan Welaýaty, W Turkmenistan *39°24′N 54°04′E*
119 J17 **Uzda** Minskaya Voblasts', C Belarus *53°29′N 27°10′E*
103 N12 **Uzerche** Corrèze, C France *45°24′N 01°35′E*
103 R14 **Uzès** Gard, S France *44°00′N 04°25′E*
147 T10 **Uzgen** *Kir.* Özgön. Oshskaya Oblast', SW Kyrgyzstan *40°42′N 73°17′E*
117 O3 **Uzh** ≋ N Ukraine
Uzhgorod *see* Uzhhorod
116 G7 **Uzhhorod** *Rus.* Uzhgorod; *prev.* Ungvár. Zakarpats'ka Oblast', W Ukraine *48°36′N 22°19′E*
Uzi *see* Uji
112 K13 **Užice** *prev.* Titovo Užice. Serbia, W Serbia *43°52′N 19°51′E*
Uzin *see* Uzyn
126 L5 **Uzlovaya** Tul'skaya Oblast', W Russian Federation *54°01′N 38°15′E*
108 H7 **Uznach** Sankt Gallen, NE Switzerland *47°12′N 09°00′E*
Uzunagach *see* Uzynagash
136 B10 **Uzunköprü** Edirne, NW Turkey *41°18′N 26°40′E*
118 D11 **Užventis** Šiaulai, C Lithuania *55°49′N 22°38′E*
117 P5 **Uzyn** *Rus.* Uzin. Kyyivs'ka Oblast', N Ukraine *49°52′N 30°27′E*
145 U16 **Uzynagash** *prev.* Uzunagach. Almaty, SE Kazakhstan *43°08′N 76°20′E*
145 N7 **Uzynkol'** *prev.* Lenīn, Leninskoye. Kustanay, N Kazakhstan *54°05′N 65°23′E*

V

Vääksy *see* Asikkala
83 H23 **Vaal** ≋ C South Africa
93 M14 **Vaala** Oulu, C Finland *64°34′N 26°49′E*
93 N19 **Vaalimaa** Etelä-Suomi, SE Finland *60°34′N 27°49′E*
99 M19 **Vaals** Limburg, SE Netherlands *50°46′N 06°01′E*
93 J16 **Vaasa** *Swe.* Vasa; *prev.* Nikolainkaupunki. Länsi-Suomi, W Finland *63°07′N 21°39′E*
98 L10 **Vaassen** Gelderland, E Netherlands *52°18′N 05°59′E*
118 G11 **Vabalninkas** Panevėžys, NE Lithuania *55°59′N 24°45′E*
Vabkent *see* Vobkent
111 J22 **Vác** *Ger.* Waitzen. Pest, N Hungary *47°46′N 19°08′E*
61 I14 **Vacaria** Rio Grande do Sul, S Brazil *28°31′S 50°52′W*
35 N7 **Vacaville** California, W USA *38°21′N 121°59′W*
103 R15 **Vaccarès, Étang de** ⊛ SE France
44 L10 **Vache, Île à** *island* SW Haiti
173 Y16 **Vacoas** W Mauritius *20°18′S 57°29′E*
32 G10 **Vader** Washington, NW USA *46°23′N 122°58′W*
94 D12 **Vadheim** Sogn Og Fjordane, S Norway *61°12′N 05°48′E*
154 D11 **Vadodara** *prev.* Baroda. Gujarāt, W India *22°19′N 73°14′E*
92 M8 **Vadsø** *Fin.* Vesisaari. Finnmark, N Norway *70°07′N 29°47′E*
95 L17 **Vadstena** Östergötland, S Sweden *58°26′N 14°55′E*
108 I8 **Vaduz** ● (Liechtenstein) W Liechtenstein *47°08′N 09°32′E*
Vág *see* Váh
125 N12 **Vaga** ≋ NW Russian Federation
94 G11 **Vågåmo** Oppland, S Norway *61°52′N 09°06′E*
112 D12 **Vaganski Vrh** ▲ W Croatia *44°24′N 15°32′E*
95 A19 **Vágar** *Dan.* Vågø. *island* W Faeroe Islands
Vágbeszterce *see* Považská Bystrica
95 L19 **Vaggeryd** Jönköping, S Sweden *57°30′N 14°10′E*
137 T12 **Vagharshapat** *var.* Ejmiadzin, Ejmiatsin, Etchmiadzin, *Rus.* Echmiadzin. W Armenia *40°10′N 44°17′E*
95 O16 **Vagnhärad** Södermanland, C Sweden *58°57′N 17°32′E*
Vågø *see* Vágar
104 G7 **Vagos** Aveiro, N Portugal *40°33′N 08°42′W*
Vágsellye *see* Sal'a
92 H10 **Vågsfjorden** *fjord* N Norway
94 C10 **Vågsøy** *island* S Norway
Vágújhely *see* Nové Mesto nad Váhom
111 I21 **Váh** *Ger.* Waag, *Hung.* Vág. ≋ W Slovakia
93 K16 **Vähäkyrö** Länsi-Suomi, W Finland *63°04′N 22°05′E*
191 X11 **Vahitahi** *atoll* Îles Tuamotu, E French Polynesia
Váhtjer *see* Gällivare
Vaidei *see* Vulcan
22 L4 **Vaiden** Mississippi, S USA *33°19′N 89°42′W*
155 I23 **Vaigai** ≋ SE India
191 V16 **Vaihu** Easter Island, Chile, E Pacific Ocean *27°10′S 109°22′W*
118 I6 **Väike Emajõgi** ≋ S Estonia
118 I4 **Väike-Maarja** *Ger.* Klein-Marien. Lääne-Virumaa, NE Estonia *59°07′N 26°16′E*
Väike-Salatsi *see* Mazsalaca
37 R4 **Vail** Colorado, C USA *39°36′N 106°20′W*
193 V15 **Vaina** Tongatapu, S Tonga *21°12′S 175°10′W*
118 E5 **Väinameri** *prev.* Muhu Väin, *Ger.* Moon-Sund. *sea* E Baltic Sea
93 N18 **Vainikkala** Etelä-Suomi, SE Finland *60°54′N 28°18′E*
118 D10 **Vaiņode** SW Latvia *56°25′N 21°52′E*
155 H23 **Vaippār** ≋ SE India
191 W11 **Vairaatea** *atoll* Îles Tuamotu, C French Polynesia
191 R8 **Vairao** Tahiti, W French Polynesia *17°48′S 149°17′W*
103 R14 **Vaison-la-Romaine** Vaucluse, SE France *44°15′N 05°04′E*
190 G11 **Vaitupu** Île Uvea, E Wallis and Futuna *13°14′S 176°09′W*
190 F7 **Vaitupu** *atoll* C Tuvalu
Vajdahunyad *see* Hunedoara
Vajdej *see* Vulcan
78 K12 **Vakaga** ◈ *prefecture* NE Central African Republic
114 H10 **Vakarel** Sofiya, W Bulgaria *42°35′N 23°40′E*
Vakav *see* Ustrem
137 O11 **Vakfıkebir** Trabzon, NE Turkey *41°03′N 39°19′E*
122 J10 **Vakh** ≋ C Russian Federation
Vakhon, Qatorkŭhi *see* Nicholas Range
147 P14 **Vakhsh** SW Tajikistan *37°46′N 68°48′E*
147 Q12 **Vakhsh** ≋ SW Tajikistan
127 P1 **Vakhtan** Nizhegorodskaya Oblast', W Russian Federation *58°00′N 46°43′E*
94 C13 **Vaksdal** Hordaland, S Norway *60°29′N 05°45′E*
Valachia *see* Wallachia
108 D11 **Valais** *Ger.* Wallis. ◈ *canton* SW Switzerland
113 M21 **Valamarës, Mali i** ▲ SE Albania *40°48′N 20°31′E*
127 S2 **Valamaz** Udmurtskaya Respublika, NW Russian Federation *57°36′N 52°07′E*
113 Q19 **Valandovo** SE FYR Macedonia *41°20′N 22°33′E*
111 I18 **Valašské Meziříčí** *Ger.* Wallachisch-Meseritsch, *Pol.* Wałeckie Międzyrzecze. Zlínský Kraj, E Czech Republic *49°29′N 17°57′E*
115 I17 **Valáxa** *island* Vóreies Sporádes, Greece, Aegean Sea
95 K16 **Vålberg** Värmland, C Sweden *59°24′N 13°12′E*
116 H12 **Vâlcea** *prev.* Vîlcea. ◈ *county* SW Romania
63 J16 **Valcheta** Río Negro, E Argentina *40°42′S 66°08′W*
15 P12 **Valcourt** Québec, SE Canada *45°28′N 72°18′W*
Valdai Hills *see* Valdayskaya Vozvyshennost'
104 M3 **Valdavia** ≋ N Spain
124 I15 **Valday** Novgorodskaya Oblast', W Russian Federation *57°57′N 33°20′E*
124 I15 **Valdayskaya Vozvyshennost'** *var.* Valdai Hills. *hill range* W Russian Federation
104 L9 **Valdecañas, Embalse de** ⊠ W Spain
118 E8 **Valdemārpils** *Ger.* Sassmacken. NW Latvia *57°23′N 22°36′E*
95 N18 **Valdemarsvik** Östergötland, S Sweden *58°13′N 16°35′E*
105 N8 **Valdemoro** Madrid, C Spain *40°12′N 03°40′W*
105 O11 **Valdepeñas** Castilla-La Mancha, C Spain *38°46′N 03°24′W*
104 L5 **Valderaduey** ≋ NE Spain
104 L5 **Valderas** Castilla y León, N Spain *42°05′N 05°27′W*
105 T7 **Valderrobres** *var.* Vall-de-roures. Aragón, NE Spain *40°53′N 00°08′E*
63 K17 **Valdés, Península** *peninsula* SE Argentina
56 C5 **Valdéz** *var.* Limones. Esmeraldas, NW Ecuador *01°13′N 79°00′W*
39 S11 **Valdez** Alaska, USA *61°08′N 146°21′W*
Valdia *see* Weldiya
103 U11 **Val d'Isère** Savoie, E France *45°23′N 07°03′E*
63 G15 **Valdivia** Los Ríos, C Chile *39°50′S 73°13′W*
Valdivia Bank *see* Valdivia Seamount
65 P17 **Valdivia Seamount** *var.* Valdivia Bank. *undersea feature* E Atlantic Ocean *26°15′S 06°25′E*
103 N4 **Val-d'Oise** ◈ *department* N France
14 J8 **Val-d'Or** Québec, SE Canada *48°06′N 77°42′W*
23 U8 **Valdosta** Georgia, SE USA *30°49′N 83°16′W*
94 G13 **Valdres** *physical region* S Norway
32 L13 **Vale** Oregon, NW USA *43°59′N 117°15′W*
116 F9 **Valea lui Mihai** *Hung.* Érmihályfalva. Bihor, NW Romania *47°31′N 22°08′E*
11 N15 **Valemount** British Columbia, SW Canada *52°46′N 119°17′W*
59 O17 **Valença** Bahia, E Brazil *13°22′S 39°06′W*
104 F4 **Valença do Minho** Viana do Castelo, N Portugal *42°02′N 08°38′W*
59 N14 **Valença do Piauí** Piauí, E Brazil *06°26′S 41°46′W*
103 N8 **Valençay** Indre, C France *47°10′N 01°31′E*
103 R13 **Valence** *anc.* Valentia, Valentia Julia, Ventia. Drôme, E France *44°56′N 04°54′E*
105 S10 **Valencia** Valenciana, E Spain *39°29′N 00°24′W*
54 K5 **Valencia** Carabobo, N Venezuela *10°12′N 68°02′W*
105 R10 **Valencia** *Cat.* València. ◈ *province* Valenciana, E Spain
105 S10 **Valencia** ✈ Valencia, E Spain
104 I10 **Valencia de Alcántara** Extremadura, W Spain *39°25′N 07°14′W*
104 L4 **Valencia de Don Juan** Castilla y León, N Spain *42°17′N 05°31′W*
105 U9 **Valencia, Golfo de** *var.* Gulf of Valencia. *gulf* E Spain
Valencia, Gulf of *see* Valencia, Golfo de
97 A21 **Valencia Island** *Ir.* Dairbhre. *island* SW Ireland
105 R10 **Valenciana** *var.* Valencia, *Cat.* València; *anc.* Valentia. ◈ *autonomous community* NE Spain
Valencia/València *see* Valenciana
103 P2 **Valenciennes** Nord, N France *50°21′N 03°32′E*
116 K13 **Vălenii de Munte** Prahova, SE Romania *45°11′N 26°02′E*
Valentia *see* Valence, France
Valentia *see* Valenciana
Valentia Julia *see* Valence
103 T8 **Valentigney** Doubs, E France *47°27′N 06°49′E*
28 M12 **Valentine** Nebraska, C USA *42°53′N 100°31′W*
24 J10 **Valentine** Texas, SW USA *30°35′N 104°30′W*
Valentine State *see* Oregon
106 C8 **Valenza** Piemonte, NW Italy *45°01′N 08°37′E*
94 I13 **Våler** Hedmark, S Norway *60°39′N 11°52′E*
54 I6 **Valera** Trujillo, NW Venezuela *09°21′N 70°38′W*
192 M11 **Valerie Guyot** S Pacific Ocean *33°00′S 164°00′W*
Valetta *see* Valletta
118 I7 **Valga** *Ger.* Walk, *Latv.* Valka. Valgamaa, S Estonia *57°48′N 26°04′E*
118 I7 **Valgamaa** *var.* Valga Maakond. ◈ *province* S Estonia
Valga Maakond *see* Valgamaa
43 Q15 **Valiente, Península** *peninsula* NW Panama
103 X16 **Valinco, Golfe de** *gulf* Corse, France, C Mediterranean Sea
112 L12 **Valjevo** Serbia, W Serbia *44°17′N 19°54′E*
Valjok *see* Válljohka
118 I7 **Valka** *Ger.* Walk. N Latvia *57°48′N 26°01′E*
Valka *see* Valga
93 L18 **Valkeakoski** Länsi-Suomi, W Finland *61°17′N 24°05′E*
93 M19 **Valkeala** Etelä-Suomi, S Finland *60°55′N 26°49′E*
99 L18 **Valkenburg** Limburg, SE Netherlands *50°52′N 05°50′E*
99 K15 **Valkenswaard** Noord-Brabant, S Netherlands *51°21′N 05°29′E*
119 G15 **Valkininkai** Alytus, S Lithuania *54°22′N 24°51′E*
117 U5 **Valky** Kharkivs'ka Oblast', E Ukraine *49°51′N 35°40′E*
41 Y12 **Valladolid** Yucatán, SE Mexico *20°39′N 88°13′W*
104 M5 **Valladolid** Castilla y León, NW Spain *41°39′N 04°45′W*
104 L5 **Valladolid** ◈ *province* Castilla y León, N Spain
103 U15 **Vallauris** Alpes-Maritimes, SE France *43°34′N 07°03′E*
Vall-de-roures *see* Valderrobres
Vall D'Uxó *see* La Vall d'Uixó
95 E16 **Valle** Aust-Agder, S Norway *59°13′N 07°33′E*
105 N2 **Valle** Cantabria, N Spain *43°14′N 04°16′W*
42 H8 **Valle** ◈ *department* S Honduras
105 N8 **Vallecas** Madrid, C Spain *40°23′N 03°37′W*
37 Q8 **Vallecito Reservoir** ⊠ Colorado, C USA
106 A7 **Valle d'Aosta** *Fr.* Vallée d'Aoste. ◈ *region* NW Italy
41 O14 **Valle de Bravo** México, S Mexico *19°19′N 100°08′W*
55 N5 **Valle de Guanape** Anzoátegui, N Venezuela *09°54′N 65°41′W*
54 M6 **Valle de La Pascua** Guárico, N Venezuela *09°15′N 66°00′W*
54 B11 **Valle del Cauca** *off.* Departamento del Valle del Cauca. ◈ *province* W Colombia
Valle del Cauca, Departamento del *see* Valle del Cauca
41 N13 **Valle de Santiago** Guanajuato, C Mexico *20°25′N 101°15′W*
40 J7 **Valle de Zaragoza** Chihuahua, N Mexico *27°25′N 105°50′W*
54 G5 **Valledupar** Cesar, N Colombia *10°31′N 73°16′W*
Vallée d'Aoste *see* Valle d'Aosta
76 G10 **Vallée de Ferlo** ≋ NW Senegal
57 M19 **Vallegrande** Santa Cruz, C Bolivia *18°30′S 64°06′W*
41 P8 **Valle Hermoso** Tamaulipas, C Mexico *25°39′N 97°49′W*
35 N8 **Vallejo** California, W USA *38°08′N 122°16′W*
62 G8 **Vallenar** Atacama, N Chile *28°35′S 70°44′W*
95 O15 **Vallentuna** Stockholm, C Sweden *59°32′N 18°05′E*
121 P16 **Valletta** *prev.* Valetta. ● (Malta) E Malta *35°54′N 14°31′E*
27 N6 **Valley Center** Kansas, C USA *37°49′N 97°22′W*
29 Q5 **Valley City** North Dakota, N USA *46°57′N 97°58′W*
32 I15 **Valley Falls** Oregon, NW USA *42°28′N 120°16′W*
Valleyfield *see* Salaberry-de-Valleyfield
21 S4 **Valley Head** West Virginia, NE USA *38°33′N 80°01′W*
25 T8 **Valley Mills** Texas, SW USA *31°36′N 97°27′W*
75 W10 **Valley of the Kings** *ancient monument* E Egypt
29 R11 **Valley Springs** South Dakota, N USA *43°34′N 96°28′W*
20 K5 **Valley Station** Kentucky, S USA *38°06′N 85°52′W*
11 O13 **Valleyview** Alberta, W Canada *55°02′N 117°17′W*
25 T5 **Valley View** Texas, SW USA *33°27′N 97°08′W*
61 C21 **Vallimanca, Arroyo** ≋ E Argentina

◆ Country
● Country Capital
◇ Dependent Territory
○ Dependent Territory Capital
◈ Administrative Regions
✈ International Airport
▲ Mountain
▲▲ Mountain Range
Volcano
≋ River
⊛ Lake
⊠ Reservoir

92 L9 **Válljohka** var. Valjok. Finnmark, N Norway 69°40′N 25°52′E
107 M19 **Vallo della Lucania** Campania, S Italy 40°13′N 15°15′E
108 B9 **Vallorbe** Vaud, W Switzerland 46°43′N 06°21′E
105 V6 **Valls** Cataluña, NE Spain 41°18′N 01°15′E
94 N11 **Vallsta** Gävleborg, C Sweden 61°30′N 16°25′E
94 N12 **Vallvik** Gävleborg, C Sweden 61°10′N 17°15′E
11 T17 **Val Marie** Saskatchewan, S Canada 49°15′N 107°44′W
118 H7 **Valmiera** Est. Volmari, Ger. Wolmar. N Latvia 57°34′N 25°26′E
105 N3 **Valnera** ▲ N Spain 43°08′N 03°39′W
102 J3 **Valognes** Manche, N France 49°31′N 01°28′W
Valona see Vlorë
Valona Bay see Vlorës, Gjiri i
104 G6 **Valongo** var. Valongo de Gaia. Porto, N Portugal 41°11′N 08°30′W
Valongo de Gaia see Valongo
104 M5 **Valoria la Buena** Castilla y León, N Spain 41°48′N 04°33′W
119 J15 **Valozhyn** Pol. Wołożyn, Rus. Volozhin. Minskaya Voblasts', C Belarus 54°05′N 26°32′E
104 I5 **Valpaços** Vila Real, N Portugal 41°36′N 07°17′W
62 G11 **Valparaíso** Valparaíso, C Chile 33°05′S 71°18′W
40 L11 **Valparaíso** Zacatecas, C Mexico 22°49′N 103°28′W
23 P8 **Valparaiso** Florida, SE USA 30°30′N 86°28′W
31 N11 **Valparaiso** Indiana, N USA 41°28′N 87°04′W
62 G11 **Valparaíso** off. Región de Valparaíso. ◈ region C Chile
Valparaíso, Región de see Valparaíso
Valpo see Valpovo
112 I9 **Valpovo** Hung. Valpó. Osijek-Baranja, E Croatia 45°40′N 18°25′E
103 R14 **Valréas** Vaucluse, SE France 44°22′N 05°00′E
Vals see Vals-Platz
154 D12 **Valsād** prev. Bulsar. Gujarāt, W India 20°40′N 72°55′E
Valsbaai see False Bay
171 T12 **Valse Pisang, Kepulauan** island group E Indonesia
108 H9 **Vals-Platz** var. Vals. Graubünden, S Switzerland 46°39′N 09°09′E
171 X16 **Vals, Tanjung** headland Papua, SE Indonesia 08°26′S 137°35′E
93 N15 **Valtimo** Itä-Suomi, E Finland 63°39′N 28°49′E
115 D17 **Váltou** ▲▲ C Greece
127 O12 **Valuyevka** Rostovskaya Oblast', SW Russian Federation 46°48′N 43°49′E
126 K9 **Valuyki** Belgorodskaya Oblast', W Russian Federation 50°11′N 38°07′E
36 L2 **Val Verda** Utah, W USA 40°51′N 111°53′W
64 N12 **Valverde** Hierro, Islas Canarias, Spain, NE Atlantic Ocean 27°48′N 17°55′W
104 I13 **Valverde del Camino** Andalucía, S Spain 37°35′N 06°45′W
95 G23 **Vamdrup** Syddanmark, C Denmark 55°26′N 09°18′E
94 L12 **Våmhus** Dalarna, C Sweden 61°07′N 14°30′E
93 K18 **Vammala** Länsi-Suomi, SW Finland 61°20′N 22°55′E
Vámosudvarhely see Odorheiu Secuiesc
137 S14 **Van** Van, E Turkey 38°30′N 43°23′E
25 V7 **Van** Texas, SW USA 32°31′N 95°38′W
137 T14 **Van** ◈ province E Turkey
137 T11 **Vanadzor** prev. Kirovakan. N Armenia 40°49′N 44°29′E
25 U5 **Van Alstyne** Texas, SW USA 33°25′N 96°34′W
33 W10 **Vananda** Montana, NW USA 46°22′N 106°58′W
116 I11 **Vânători** Hung. Héjjasfalva; prev. Vînători. Mureş, C Romania 46°14′N 24°56′E
191 W12 **Vanavana** atoll Îles Tuamotu, SE French Polynesia
Vana-Vāndra see Vāndra
122 M11 **Vanavara** Krasnoyarskiy Kray, C Russian Federation 60°19′N 102°19′E
15 Q8 **Van Bruyssel** Québec, SE Canada 47°56′N 72°08′W
27 R10 **Van Buren** Arkansas, C USA 35°28′N 94°25′W
19 S1 **Van Buren** Maine, NE USA 47°07′N 67°57′W
27 W7 **Van Buren** Missouri, C USA 37°00′N 91°00′W
19 T5 **Vanceboro** Maine, NE USA 45°31′N 67°25′W
21 W10 **Vanceboro** North Carolina, SE USA 35°16′N 77°06′W
21 O4 **Vanceburg** Kentucky, S USA 38°36′N 84°40′W
45 W10 **Vance W. Amory** ✈ Nevis, Saint Kitts and Nevis 17°08′N 62°36′W
Vanch see Vanj
10 L17 **Vancouver** British Columbia, SW Canada 49°13′N 123°06′W
32 G11 **Vancouver** Washington, NW USA 45°38′N 122°39′W
10 L17 **Vancouver** ✈ British Columbia, SW Canada 49°03′N 123°00′W
10 K16 **Vancouver Island** island British Columbia, SW Canada
Vanda see Vantaa
171 X13 **Van Daalen** ≈ Papua, E Indonesia
30 L15 **Vandalia** Illinois, N USA 38°57′N 89°05′W
27 V3 **Vandalia** Missouri, C USA 39°18′N 91°29′W
31 R13 **Vandalia** Ohio, N USA 39°53′N 84°12′W
25 U13 **Vanderbilt** Texas, SW USA 28°45′N 96°37′W
31 Q10 **Vandercook Lake** Michigan, N USA 42°11′N 84°23′W
10 L14 **Vanderhoof** British Columbia, SW Canada 53°54′N 124°00′W
18 K8 **Vanderwhacker Mountain** ▲ New York, NE USA 43°54′N 74°06′W
181 P1 **Van Diemen Gulf** gulf Northern Territory, N Australia
Van Diemen's Land see Tasmania
118 H5 **Vändra** Ger. Fennern; prev. Vana-Vändra. Pärnumaa, SW Estonia 58°39′N 25°00′E
Vandsburg see Więcbork
34 L4 **Van Duzen River** ≈ California, W USA
118 F13 **Vandžiogala** Kaunas, C Lithuania 55°07′N 23°55′E
41 N10 **Vanegas** San Luis Potosí, C Mexico 23°53′N 100°55′W
Vaner, Lake see Vänern
95 K17 **Vänern** Eng. Lake Vaner; prev. Lake Vener. ◎ S Sweden
95 J18 **Vänersborg** Västra Götaland, S Sweden 58°16′N 12°22′E
94 F12 **Vang** Oppland, S Norway 61°07′N 08°34′E
172 I7 **Vangaindrano** Fianarantsoa, SE Madagascar 23°21′S 47°35′E
137 S14 **Van Gölü** Eng. Lake Van; anc. Thospitis. salt lake E Turkey
186 L9 **Vangunu** island New Georgia Islands, NW Solomon Islands
24 J9 **Van Horn** Texas, SW USA 31°03′N 104°51′W
187 Q11 **Vanikolo** var. Vanikoro. island Santa Cruz Islands, E Solomon Islands
Vanikoro see Vanikolo
186 A5 **Vanimo** Sandaun, NW Papua New Guinea 02°40′S 141°17′E
123 T13 **Vanino** Khabarovskiy Kray, SE Russian Federation 49°10′N 140°18′E
155 G19 **Vānīvilāsa Sāgara** ⊠ SW India
147 S13 **Vanj** Rus. Vanch. S Tajikistan 38°22′N 71°27′E
116 G14 **Vânju Mare** prev. Vînju Mare. Mehedinţi, SW Romania 44°25′N 22°52′E
15 N12 **Vankleek Hill** Ontario, SE Canada 45°32′N 74°39′W
Van, Lake see Van Gölü
93 I16 **Vännäs** Västerbotten, N Sweden 63°54′N 19°43′E
93 J15 **Vännäsby** Västerbotten, N Sweden 63°55′N 19°53′E
102 H7 **Vannes** anc. Dariorigum. Morbihan, NW France 47°40′N 02°45′W
92 I8 **Vannøya** island N Norway
103 T12 **Vanoise, Massif de la** ▲▲ E France
83 E24 **Vanrhynsdorp** Western Cape, SW South Africa 31°36′S 18°45′E
21 P7 **Vansant** Virginia, NE USA 37°13′N 82°03′W
94 L13 **Vansbro** Dalarna, C Sweden 60°32′N 14°15′E
95 D18 **Vanse** Vest-Agder, S Norway 58°04′N 06°40′E
9 P7 **Vansittart Island** island Nunavut, NE Canada
93 M20 **Vantaa** Swe. Vanda. Etelä-Suomi, S Finland 60°18′N 25°01′E
93 L19 **Vantaa** ✈ (Helsinki) Etelä-Suomi, S Finland 60°18′N 25°01′E
32 J9 **Vantage** Washington, NW USA 46°55′N 119°55′W
187 Z14 **Vanua Balavu** prev. Vanua Mbalavu. island Lau Group, E Fiji
187 R12 **Vanua Lava** island Banks Islands, N Vanuatu
187 Y13 **Vanua Levu** island N Fiji
Vanua Mbalavu see Vanua Balavu
187 R12 **Vanuatu** off. Republic of Vanuatu; prev. New Hebrides. ◆ republic SW Pacific Ocean
175 P8 **Vanuatu** island group SW Pacific Ocean
Vanuatu, Republic of see Vanuatu
31 Q12 **Van Wert** Ohio, N USA 40°52′N 84°34′W
187 Q17 **Vao** Province Sud, S New Caledonia 22°40′S 167°29′E
Vapincum see Gap
117 N7 **Vapnyarka** Vinnyts'ka Oblast', C Ukraine 48°31′N 28°44′E
103 T15 **Var** ◈ department SE France
103 U14 **Var** ≈ SE France
95 J18 **Vara** Västra Götaland, S Sweden 58°16′N 12°57′E
Varadinska Županija see Varaždin
118 J10 **Varakļāni** C Latvia 56°36′N 26°40′E
106 C7 **Varallo** Piemonte, NE Italy 45°51′N 08°16′E
143 O5 **Varāmīn** var. Veramin. Tehrān, N Iran 35°19′N 51°40′E
153 N14 **Vārānasi** prev. Banaras, Benares, hist. Kasi. Uttar Pradesh, N India 25°20′N 83°E
125 T3 **Varandey** Nenetskiy Avtonomnyy Okrug, NW Russian Federation 68°48′N 57°54′E
92 M8 **Varangerbotn** Lapp. Vuonnabahta. Finnmark, N Norway 70°09′N 28°28′E
92 M8 **Varangerfjorden** Lapp. Várjjatvuotna. fjord N Norway
92 M8 **Varangerhalvøya** Lapp. Várnjárga. peninsula N Norway
Varannó see Vranov nad Topľou
107 M15 **Varano, Lago di** ◎ SE Italy
118 J13 **Varapayeva** Rus. Voropayevo. Vitsyebskaya Voblasts', NW Belarus 55°09′N 27°13′E
Varasd see Varaždin
112 E7 **Varaždin** Ger. Warasdin, Hung. Varasd. Varaždin, N Croatia 46°18′N 16°21′E
112 E7 **Varaždin** off. Varadinska Županija. ◈ province N Croatia
106 C10 **Varazze** Liguria, NW Italy 44°21′N 08°35′E
95 J20 **Varberg** Halland, S Sweden 57°06′N 12°15′E
113 Q19 **Vardar** Gk. Axiós. ≈ FYR Macedonia/Greece see also Axiós
Vardar see Axiós
95 F23 **Varde** Syddtjylland, W Denmark 55°38′N 08°31′E
137 V12 **Vardenis** E Armenia 40°11′N 45°43′E
92 N8 **Vardø** Fin. Vuoreija. Finnmark, N Norway 70°22′N 31°06′E
115 E18 **Vardoúsia** ▲▲ C Greece
Vareia see Logroño
100 G10 **Varel** Niedersachsen, NW Germany 53°24′N 08°07′E
119 G15 **Varėna** Pol. Orany. Alytus, S Lithuania 54°13′N 24°35′E
15 O12 **Varennes** Québec, SE Canada 45°42′N 73°25′W
103 P10 **Varennes-sur-Allier** Allier, C France 46°17′N 03°24′E
112 I12 **Vareš** Federacija Bosna I Hercegovina, E Bosnia and Herzegovina 44°12′N 18°19′E
106 D7 **Varese** Lombardia, N Italy 45°49′N 08°50′E
116 J12 **Vârful Moldoveanu** var. Moldoveanul; prev. Vîrful Moldoveanu. ▲ C Romania 45°35′N 24°48′E
Varganzi see Warganza
95 J18 **Vårgårda** Västra Götaland, S Sweden 58°00′N 12°49′E
54 L4 **Vargas** off. Estado Vargas. ◈ state N Venezuela
95 J18 **Vargön** Västra Götaland, S Sweden 58°21′N 12°22′E
95 C17 **Varhaug** Rogaland, S Norway 58°37′N 05°39′E
Várjjatvuotna see Varangerfjorden
93 N17 **Varkaus** Itä-Suomi, C Finland 62°20′N 27°50′E
92 J2 **Varmahlidh** Nordhurland Vestra, N Iceland 65°32′N 19°33′W
95 J15 **Värmland** ◈ county C Sweden
95 K16 **Värmlandsnäs** peninsula S Sweden
114 N8 **Varna** prev. Stalin; anc. Odessus. Varna, E Bulgaria 43°14′N 27°56′E
114 N8 **Varna** ◈ province E Bulgaria
114 N8 **Varna** ✈ Varna, E Bulgaria 43°16′N 27°52′E
95 L20 **Värnamo** Jönköping, S Sweden 57°11′N 14°03′E
114 N8 **Varnenski Zaliv** prev. Stalinski Zaliv. bay E Bulgaria
114 N8 **Varnensko Ezero** estuary E Bulgaria
118 D11 **Varniai** Telšiai, W Lithuania 55°45′N 22°22′E
Várnjárga see Varangerhalvøya
Varnoús see Baba
111 D14 **Varnsdorf** Ger. Warnsdorf. Ústecký Kraj, NW Czech Republic 50°57′N 14°35′E
111 I23 **Várpalota** Veszprém, W Hungary 47°12′N 18°08′E
Varshava see Warszawa
118 K6 **Värska** Põlvamaa, SE Estonia 57°58′N 27°37′E
98 N12 **Varsseveld** Gelderland, E Netherlands 51°55′N 06°28′E
115 D19 **Vartholomió** prev. Vartholomión. Dytikí Elláda, S Greece 37°52′N 21°12′E
Vartholomión see Vartholomió
137 Q14 **Varto** Muş, E Turkey 39°10′N 41°28′E
95 K18 **Vartofta** Västra Götaland, S Sweden 58°06′N 13°40′E
93 O17 **Värtsilä** Itä-Suomi, E Finland 62°10′N 30°35′E
Värtsilä see Vyartsilya
117 R4 **Varva** Chernihivs'ka Oblast', NE Ukraine 50°31′N 32°43′E
59 H18 **Várzea Grande** Mato Grosso, SW Brazil 15°39′S 56°08′W
106 D9 **Varzi** Lombardia, N Italy 44°51′N 09°13′E
Varzimanor Ayni see Ayní
124 K5 **Varzuga** ≈ NW Russian Federation
103 P8 **Varzy** Nièvre, C France 47°22′N 03°22′E
111 G23 **Vas** off. Vas Megye. ◈ county W Hungary
Vasa see Vaasa
190 A9 **Vasafua** island Funafuti Atoll, C Tuvalu
111 O21 **Vásárosnamény** Szabolcs-Szatmár-Bereg, E Hungary 48°10′N 22°18′E
104 H13 **Vascão, Ribeira de** ≈ S Portugal
116 G10 **Vaşcău** Hung. Vaskoh. Bihor, NE Romania 46°28′N 22°30′E
Vascongadas, Provincias see País Vasco
Vashess Bay see Vaskess Bay
125 O8 **Vashka** ≈ NW Russian Federation
Väsht see Khāsh
Vasilevichi see Vasilyevichy
115 G14 **Vasiliká** Kentrikí Makedonía, NE Greece 40°28′N 23°08′E
115 C18 **Vasilikí** Lefkáda, Iónia Nisiá, Greece, C Mediterranean Sea 38°36′N 20°37′E
115 K25 **Vasilikí** Kríti, Greece, E Mediterranean Sea 35°04′N 25°49′E
119 G16 **Vasilishki** Pol. Wasiliszki. Hrodzyenskaya Voblasts', W Belarus 53°47′N 24°51′E
Vasil Kolarov see Pamporovo
Vasil'kov see Vasyl'kiv
119 N19 **Vasilyevichy** Rus. Vasilevichi. Homyel'skaya Voblasts', SE Belarus 52°15′N 29°50′E
191 Y3 **Vaskess Bay** var. Vashess Bay. bay Kiritimati, E Kiribati
Vaskoh see Vaşcău
Vaskohsziklás see Ştei
116 M10 **Vaslui** Vaslui, C Romania 46°38′N 27°44′E
116 L11 **Vaslui** ◈ county NE Romania
Vas Megye see Vas
31 R8 **Vassar** Michigan, N USA 43°22′N 83°34′W
95 E15 **Vassdalsegga** ▲ S Norway 59°47′N 07°07′E
60 P9 **Vassouras** Rio de Janeiro, SE Brazil 22°24′S 43°38′W
95 N15 **Västerås** Västmanland, C Sweden 59°37′N 16°33′E
93 G15 **Västerbotten** ◈ county N Sweden
94 K12 **Västerdalälven** ≈ C Sweden
95 O16 **Västerhaninge** Stockholm, C Sweden 59°07′N 18°06′E
94 M10 **Västernorrland** ◈ county C Sweden
95 N19 **Västervik** Kalmar, S Sweden 57°44′N 16°40′E
95 M15 **Västmanland** ◈ county C Sweden
107 L15 **Vasto** anc. Histonium. Abruzzo, C Italy 42°07′N 14°43′E
95 J19 **Västra Götaland** ◈ county S Sweden
95 J16 **Västra Silen** ◎ S Sweden
111 G23 **Vasvár** Ger. Eisenburg. Vas, W Hungary 47°03′N 16°48′E
117 U9 **Vasylivka** Zaporiz'ka Oblast', SE Ukraine 47°26′N 35°18′E
117 O5 **Vasyl'kiv** var. Vasil'kov. Kyyivs'ka Oblast', N Ukraine 50°12′N 30°18′E
117 V8 **Vasyl'kivka** Dnipropetrovs'ka Oblast', E Ukraine 48°12′N 36°00′E
122 I11 **Vasyugan** ≈ C Russian Federation
103 N8 **Vatan** Indre, C France 47°06′N 01°49′E
Vaté see Efate
115 C18 **Vathy** prev. Itháki. Itháki, Iónia Nisiá, Greece, C Mediterranean Sea 38°22′N 20°43′E
107 G15 **Vatican City** off. Vatican City. ◆ papal state S Europe
Vatican City see Vatican City
107 M22 **Vaticano, Capo** headland S Italy 38°37′N 15°49′E
92 K3 **Vatnajökull** glacier SE Iceland
95 P15 **Vätö** Stockholm, C Sweden 59°48′N 18°55′E
187 Z16 **Vatoa** island Lau Group, SE Fiji
172 J5 **Vatomandry** Toamasina, E Madagascar 19°20′S 48°58′E
116 J9 **Vatra Dornei** Ger. Dorna Watra. Suceava, NE Romania 47°20′N 25°21′E
116 J9 **Vatra Moldoviţei** Suceava, NE Romania 47°37′N 25°36′E
Vätter, Lake see Vättern
95 L18 **Vättern** Eng. Lake Vatter; prev. Lake Vetter. ◎ S Sweden
187 X5 **Vatulele** island SW Fiji
117 P7 **Vatutine** Cherkas'ka Oblast', C Ukraine 49°01′N 31°04′E
187 W15 **Vatu Vara** island Lau Group, E Fiji
103 R14 **Vaucluse** ◈ department SE France
103 S5 **Vaucouleurs** Meuse, NE France 48°37′N 05°38′E
108 B9 **Vaud** Ger. Waadt. ◈ canton SW Switzerland
15 N12 **Vaudreuil** Québec, SE Canada 45°24′N 74°01′W
37 T12 **Vaughn** New Mexico, SW USA 34°36′N 105°12′W
54 I14 **Vaupés** off. Comisaría del Vaupés. ◈ province SE Colombia
Vaupés, Comisaría del see Vaupés
54 J13 **Vaupés, Río** var. Rio Uaupés. ≈ Brazil/Colombia see also Uaupés, Rio
Vaupés, Río see Uaupés, Rio
103 Q15 **Vauvert** Gard, S France 43°42′N 04°16′E
11 R17 **Vauxhall** Alberta, SW Canada 50°05′N 112°09′W
99 K23 **Vaux-sur-Sûre** Luxembourg, SE Belgium 49°55′N 05°34′E
172 J4 **Vavatenina** Toamasina, E Madagascar 17°25′S 49°11′E
193 Y14 **Vava'u Group** island group N Tonga
76 M16 **Vavoua** W Ivory Coast 07°23′N 06°29′W
127 S2 **Vavozh** Udmurtskaya Respublika, NW Russian Federation 56°48′N 51°53′E
155 K23 **Vavuniya** Northern Province, N Sri Lanka 08°45′N 80°30′E
119 G17 **Vawkavysk** Pol. Wołkowysk, Rus. Volkovysk. Hrodzyenskaya Voblasts', W Belarus 53°10′N 24°28′E
119 F17 **Vawkavyskaye Wzvyshsha** Rus. Volkovyskiye Vysoty. hill range W Belarus
95 P15 **Vaxholm** Stockholm, C Sweden 59°25′N 18°21′E
95 L21 **Växjö** var. Vexiö. Kronoberg, S Sweden 56°52′N 14°50′E
125 T1 **Vaygach, Ostrov** island NW Russian Federation
137 V13 **Vayk'** prev. Azizbekov. SE Armenia 39°41′N 45°28′E
Vazáš see Vittangi
125 P8 **Vazhgort** prev. Chasovo. Respublika Komi, NW Russian Federation 64°06′N 46°44′E
45 V10 **V. C. Bird** ✈ (St. John's) Antigua, Antigua and Barbuda 17°07′N 61°49′W
167 R13 **Veal Renh** prev. Phumī Veal Renh. Kâmpôt, SW Cambodia 10°43′N 103°49′E
29 Q7 **Veblen** South Dakota, N USA 45°50′N 97°17′W
98 N9 **Vecht** Ger. Vechte. ≈ Germany/Netherlands see also Vechte
Vecht see Vechte
100 G12 **Vechta** Niedersachsen, NW Germany 52°44′N 08°16′E
100 E12 **Vechte** Dut. Vecht. ≈ Germany/Netherlands see also Vecht
Vechte see Vecht
118 I8 **Vecpiebalga** C Latvia 57°03′N 25°47′E
118 G9 **Vecumnieki** C Latvia 56°36′N 24°30′E
95 C16 **Vedavågen** Rogaland, S Norway 59°18′N 05°13′E
Vedāvati see Hagari
95 J20 **Veddige** Halland, S Sweden 57°16′N 12°19′E
116 J15 **Vedea** ≈ S Romania
127 P16 **Vedeno** Chechenskaya Respublika, SW Russian Federation 42°57′N 46°02′E
95 C16 **Vedvågen** Rogaland, S Norway 59°18′N 05°13′E
98 O6 **Veendam** Groningen, NE Netherlands 53°05′N 06°53′E
98 K12 **Veenendaal** Utrecht, C Netherlands 52°03′N 05°33′E
99 E14 **Veere** Zeeland, SW Netherlands 51°33′N 03°40′E
24 M2 **Vega** Texas, SW USA 35°14′N 102°26′W
92 E13 **Vega** island C Norway
45 T5 **Vega Baja** C Puerto Rico 18°27′N 66°23′W
38 D17 **Vega Point** headland Kiska Island, Alaska, USA 51°49′N 177°19′E
95 F17 **Vegår** ◎ S Norway
99 K14 **Veghel** Noord-Brabant, S Netherlands 51°37′N 05°33′E
Veglia see Krk
114 E13 **Vegorítida, Límni** var. Límni Vegorítis. ◎ N Greece
Vegorítis, Límni see Vegorítida, Límni
11 Q14 **Vegreville** Alberta, SW Canada 53°30′N 112°02′W
95 K21 **Veinge** Halland, S Sweden 56°33′N 13°04′E
61 B21 **Veinticinco de Mayo** var. 25 de Mayo. Buenos Aires, E Argentina 35°27′S 60°11′W
63 I14 **Veinticinco de Mayo** La Pampa, C Argentina 37°45′S 67°40′W
119 F15 **Veisiejai** Alytus, S Lithuania 54°06′N 23°42′E
95 F23 **Vejen** Syddtjylland, W Denmark 55°29′N 09°13′E
104 K16 **Vejer de la Frontera** Andalucía, S Spain 36°15′N 05°58′W
95 G23 **Vejle** Syddanmark, C Denmark 55°43′N 09°33′E
Vejle Amt see Syddanmark
114 M7 **Vekilski** Shumen, NE Bulgaria 43°33′N 27°19′E
54 G3 **Vela, Cabo de la** headland NE Colombia 12°14′N 72°13′W
Vela Goa see Goa
113 F15 **Vela Luka** Dubrovnik-Neretva, S Croatia 42°57′N 16°43′E
61 G19 **Velázquez** Rocha, E Uruguay 34°05′S 54°16′W
101 E15 **Velbert** Nordrhein-Westfalen, W Germany 51°22′N 07°03′E
109 S9 **Velden** Kärnten, S Austria 46°37′N 13°59′E
Veldes see Bled
99 K15 **Veldhoven** Noord-Brabant, S Netherlands 51°24′N 05°24′E
112 C11 **Velebit** ▲▲ C Croatia
114 N11 **Veleka** ≈ SE Bulgaria
109 V10 **Velenje** Ger. Wöllan. N Slovenia 46°22′N 15°07′E
190 E12 **Vele, Pointe** headland Île Futuna, S Wallis and Futuna
113 O18 **Veles** Turk. Köprülü. C FYR Macedonia 41°43′N 21°49′E
113 M20 **Velešta** SW FYR Macedonia 41°16′N 20°37′E
115 F16 **Velestíno** prev. Velestínon. Thessalía, C Greece 39°23′N 22°45′E
Velestínon see Velestíno
Velevshchina see Vyelyewshchyna
54 F9 **Vélez** Santander, C Colombia 06°02′N 73°43′W
105 Q13 **Vélez Blanco** Andalucía, S Spain 37°43′N 02°07′W
104 M17 **Vélez de la Gomera, Peñon de** island group S Spain
105 N15 **Vélez-Málaga** Andalucía, S Spain 36°47′N 04°06′W
105 Q13 **Vélez Rubio** Andalucía, S Spain 37°39′N 02°04′W
Velha Goa see Goa
Velho see Porto Velho
112 E8 **Velika Gorica** Zagreb, N Croatia 45°43′N 16°03′E
112 C9 **Velika Kapela** ▲▲ NW Croatia
Velika Kikinda see Kikinda
112 D10 **Velika Kladuša** Federacija Bosna I Hercegovina, NW Bosnia and Herzegovina 45°10′N 15°48′E
112 N11 **Velika Morava** var. Glavn'a Morava, Morava, Ger. Grosse Morava. ≈ C Serbia
112 N12 **Velika Plana** Serbia, C Serbia 44°20′N 21°01′E
109 U10 **Velika Raduha** ▲ N Slovenia 46°24′N 14°46′E
123 V7 **Velikaya** ≈ NE Russian Federation
124 F15 **Velikaya** ≈ W Russian Federation
Velikaya Berestovitsa see Vyalikaya Byerastavitsa
Velikaya Lepetikha see Velyka Lepetykha
Veliki Bečkerek see Zrenjanin
112 P12 **Veliki Krš** var. Stol. ▲ E Serbia 44°10′N 22°09′E
114 L8 **Veliki Preslav** prev. Preslav. Shumen, NE Bulgaria 43°09′N 26°50′E
112 B9 **Veliki Risnjak** ▲ NW Croatia 45°30′N 14°31′E
109 T13 **Veliki Snežnik** Ger. Schneeberg, It. Monte Nevoso. ▲ SW Slovenia 45°36′N 14°25′E
112 J13 **Veliki Stolac** ▲ E Bosnia and Herzegovina 43°55′N 19°15′E
Velikiy Bor see Vyaliki Bor
124 G16 **Velikiye Luki** Pskovskaya Oblast', W Russian Federation 56°20′N 30°27′E
124 H14 **Velikiy Novgorod** prev. Novgorod. Novgorodskaya Oblast', W Russian Federation 58°32′N 31°15′E
125 P12 **Velikiy Ustyug** Vologodskaya Oblast', NW Russian Federation 60°46′N 46°18′E
112 N11 **Veliko Gradište** Serbia, NE Serbia 44°46′N 21°28′E
155 I18 **Velikonda Range** ▲▲ SE India
114 K9 **Veliko Tŭrnovo** prev. Tirnovo, Trnovo, Tŭrnovo. Veliko Tŭrnovo, N Bulgaria 43°05′N 25°40′E
114 K8 **Veliko Tŭrnovo** ◈ province N Bulgaria
Velikovec see Völkermarkt
125 R5 **Velikovisochnoye** Nenetskiy Avtonomnyy Okrug, NW Russian Federation 67°13′N 52°00′E
76 H12 **Vélingara** C Senegal 15°00′N 14°39′W
76 H11 **Vélingara** S Senegal 13°12′N 14°05′W
114 H11 **Velingrad** Pazardzhik, C Bulgaria 42°01′N 23°59′E
126 H3 **Velizh** Smolenskaya Oblast', W Russian Federation 55°30′N 31°06′E
111 F16 **Velká Deštná** var. Deštná, Grosskoppe, Ger. Deschnaer Koppe. ▲ NE Czech Republic 50°18′N 16°25′E
111 F18 **Velké Meziříčí** Ger. Grossmeseritsch. Vysočina, C Czech Republic 49°22′N 16°02′E
92 N1 **Velkomstpynten** headland NW Svalbard 79°51′N 11°37′E
111 K21 **Veľký Krtíš** Banskobystrický Kraj, C Slovakia 48°13′N 19°21′E
186 J8 **Vella Lavella** var. Mbilua. island New Georgia Islands, NW Solomon Islands
107 I15 **Velletri** Lazio, C Italy 41°41′N 12°47′E
95 K23 **Vellinge** Skåne, S Sweden 55°29′N 13°00′E
155 I19 **Vellore** Tamil Nādu, SE India 12°56′N 79°09′E
Velobriga see Viana do Castelo
115 G21 **Velopoúla** island S Greece
98 M12 **Velp** Gelderland, SE Netherlands 52°00′N 05°59′E
Velsen see Velsen-Noord
98 H9 **Velsen-Noord** var. Velsen. Noord-Holland, W Netherlands 52°27′N 04°40′E
125 N12 **Vel'sk** var. Velsk. Arkhangel'skaya Oblast', NW Russian Federation 61°03′N 42°01′E
Velsuna see Orvieto
98 K10 **Veluwemeer** lake channel C Netherlands
28 M3 **Velva** North Dakota, N USA 48°03′N 100°55′W
Velvendos/Velvendós see Velventós
115 E14 **Velventós** var. Velvendos, Velvendós. Dytikí Makedonía, N Greece 40°15′N 22°04′E
117 S5 **Velyka Bahachka** Poltavs'ka Oblast', C Ukraine 49°46′N 33°44′E
117 S9 **Velyka Lepetykha** Rus. Velikaya Lepetikha. Khersons'ka Oblast', S Ukraine 47°09′N 33°59′E
117 O10 **Velyka Mykhaylivka** Odes'ka Oblast', SW Ukraine 47°07′N 29°49′E
117 W8 **Velyka Novosilka** Donets'ka Oblast', E Ukraine 47°49′N 36°49′E
117 S9 **Velyka Oleksandrivka** Khersons'ka Oblast', S Ukraine 47°17′N 33°16′E
117 T4 **Velyka Pysarivka** Sums'ka Oblast', NE Ukraine 50°25′N 35°28′E
116 G6 **Velykyy Bereznyy** Zakarpats'ka Oblast', W Ukraine 48°54′N 22°27′E
117 W4 **Velykyy Burluk** Kharkivs'ka Oblast', E Ukraine 50°04′N 37°25′E
Velykyy Tokmak see Tokmak
173 P7 **Vema Fracture Zone** tectonic feature W Indian Ocean
65 P18 **Vema Seamount** undersea feature SW Indian Ocean 31°38′S 08°19′E
93 F17 **Vemdalen** Jämtland, C Sweden 62°26′N 13°50′E
95 N19 **Vena** Kalmar, S Sweden 57°31′N 16°00′E
41 N11 **Venado** San Luis Potosí, C Mexico 22°56′N 101°05′W
62 L11 **Venado Tuerto** Entre Ríos, E Argentina 33°45′S 61°56′W
61 A19 **Venado Tuerto** Santa Fe, C Argentina 33°46′S 61°57′W
107 K16 **Venafro** Molise, C Italy 41°28′N 14°03′E
55 Q9 **Venamo, Cerro** ▲ E Venezuela 05°56′N 61°25′W
106 B8 **Venaria** Piemonte, NW Italy 45°09′N 07°40′E
103 U15 **Vence** Alpes-Maritimes, SE France 43°45′N 07°07′E
104 H5 **Venda Nova** Vila Real, N Portugal 41°40′N 07°58′W
104 G11 **Vendas Novas** Évora, S Portugal 38°41′N 08°27′W
102 J9 **Vendée** ◈ department NW France
103 Q6 **Vendeuvre-sur-Barse** Aube, NE France 48°08′N 04°17′E
102 M7 **Vendôme** Loir-et-Cher, C France 47°48′N 01°04′E
Venedig see Venezia
Vener, Lake see Vänern
106 I8 **Veneta, Laguna** lagoon NE Italy
Venetia see Venezia
39 S7 **Venetie** Alaska, USA 67°00′N 146°25′W
106 H8 **Veneto** var. Venezia Euganea. ◈ region NE Italy
114 M7 **Venets** Shumen, NE Bulgaria 43°33′N 26°56′E
126 L5 **Venev** Tul'skaya Oblast', W Russian Federation 54°18′N 38°16′E
106 I8 **Venezia** Eng. Venice, Fr. Venise, Ger. Venedig; anc. Venetia. Veneto, NE Italy 45°26′N 12°20′E
Venezia Euganea see Veneto
Venezia, Golfo di see Venice, Gulf of
Venezia Tridentina see Trentino-Alto Adige
54 K8 **Venezuela** off. Republic of Venezuela; prev. Estados Unidos de Venezuela, United States of Venezuela. ◆ republic N South America
Venezuela, Cordillera de see Costa, Cordillera de la
Venezuela, Estados Unidos de see Venezuela
54 I4 **Venezuela, Golfo de** Eng. Gulf of Maracaibo, Gulf of Venezuela. gulf NW Venezuela
Venezuela, Gulf of see Venezuela, Golfo de
64 F11 **Venezuelan Basin** undersea feature E Caribbean Sea
Venezuela, Republic of see Venezuela
Venezuela, United States of see Venezuela
155 D16 **Vengurla** Mahārāshtra, W India 15°55′N 73°39′E
39 O15 **Veniaminof, Mount** ▲ Alaska, USA 56°12′N 159°24′W
23 V14 **Venice** Florida, SE USA 27°06′N 82°27′W
22 L10 **Venice** Louisiana, S USA 29°15′N 89°20′W
Venice see Venezia
106 J8 **Venice, Gulf of** It. Golfo di Venezia, Slvn. Beneški Zaliv. gulf N Adriatic Sea
Venise see Venezia
94 K13 **Venjan** Dalarna, C Sweden 60°58′N 13°55′E
94 K13 **Venjansjön** ◎ C Sweden
155 J18 **Venkatagiri** Andhra Pradesh, E India 14°00′N 79°39′E
99 M15 **Venlo** prev. Venloo. Limburg, SE Netherlands 51°22′N 06°11′E
Venloo see Venlo
95 E18 **Vennesla** Vest-Agder, S Norway 58°15′N 08°00′E
107 M17 **Venosa** anc. Venusia. Basilicata, S Italy 40°57′N 15°49′E
Venoste, Alpi see Ötztaler Alpen
Venraij see Venray
99 M14 **Venray** var. Venraij. Limburg, SE Netherlands 51°32′N 05°59′E
118 C8 **Venta** Ger. Windau. ≈ Latvia/Lithuania
Venta Belgarum see Winchester
40 G9 **Ventana, Punta Arena de la** var. Punta de la Ventana. headland NW Mexico 24°03′N 109°49′W
Ventana, Punta de la see Ventana, Punta Arena de la
61 B23 **Ventana, Sierra de la** hill range E Argentina
Ventia see Valence
191 S11 **Vent, Îles du** var. Windward Islands. island group Archipel de la Société, W French Polynesia
191 R10 **Vent, Îles Sous le** var. Leeward Islands. island group Archipel de la Société, W French Polynesia
106 B11 **Ventimiglia** Liguria, NW Italy 43°47′N 07°37′E
97 M24 **Ventnor** S England, United Kingdom 50°36′N 01°11′W
18 J17 **Ventnor City** New Jersey, NE USA 39°19′N 74°27′W
103 S14 **Ventoux, Mont** ▲ SE France 44°12′N 05°21′E
118 C8 **Ventspils** Ger. Windau. NW Latvia 57°22′N 21°34′E
54 M10 **Ventuari, Río** ≈ S Venezuela
35 R15 **Ventura** California, W USA 34°15′N 119°18′W
182 F8 **Venus Bay** South Australia 33°15′S 134°42′E
Venusia see Venosa
191 P7 **Vénus, Pointe** var. Pointe Tataaihoa. headland Tahiti, W French Polynesia 17°28′S 149°29′W
41 V16 **Venustiano Carranza** Chiapas, SE Mexico 16°21′N 92°33′W
41 N7 **Venustiano Carranza, Presa** ⊠ NE Mexico
61 B15 **Vera** Santa Fe, C Argentina 29°28′S 60°10′W
105 Q14 **Vera** Andalucía, S Spain 37°15′N 01°51′W
63 K18 **Vera, Bahía** bay E Argentina
41 R14 **Veracruz** var. Veracruz Llave. Veracruz-Llave, E Mexico 19°10′N 96°09′W
Veracruz see Veracruz-Llave
41 Q13 **Veracruz-Llave** var. Veracruz. ◈ state E Mexico
Veracruz Llave see Veracruz
43 Q16 **Veraguas** off. Provincia de Veraguas. ◈ province W Panama
Veraguas, Provincia de see Veraguas
Veramin see Varāmīn
154 B12 **Verāval** Gujarāt, W India 20°54′N 70°22′E
106 C6 **Verbania** Piemonte, NW Italy 45°56′N 08°34′E
107 N20 **Verbicaro** Calabria, SW Italy 39°44′N 15°51′E
108 D11 **Verbier** Valais, SW Switzerland 46°06′N 07°14′E
Vercellae see Vercelli
106 C8 **Vercelli** anc. Vercellae. Piemonte, NW Italy 45°19′N 08°25′E
103 S13 **Vercors** physical region E France
Verdal see Verdalsøra
93 E16 **Verdalsøra** var. Verdal. Nord-Trøndelag, C Norway 63°47′N 11°27′E
Verde, Cabo see Cape Verde
44 J5 **Verde, Cape** headland Long Island, C Bahamas 22°51′N 75°50′W
104 M2 **Verde, Costa** coastal region N Spain
Verde Grande, Río/Verde Grande y de Belem, Río see Verde, Río
100 H11 **Verden** Niedersachsen, NW Germany 52°55′N 09°14′E
57 P16 **Verde, Río** ≈ Bolivia/Brazil
59 J19 **Verde, Rio** ≈ SE Brazil
40 M12 **Verde, Río** var. Río Verde Grande, Río Verde Grande y de Belem. ≈ C Mexico
41 Q16 **Verde, Río** ≈ SE Mexico
36 L13 **Verde River** ≈ Arizona, SW USA
Verdhikoúsa/Verdhikoússa see Verdikoússa
27 Q8 **Verdigris River** ≈ Kansas/Oklahoma, C USA
115 E15 **Verdikoússa** var. Verdhikoúsa, Verdhikoússa. Thessalía, C Greece 39°47′N 21°59′E
103 S15 **Verdon** ≈ SE France
15 O12 **Verdun** Québec, SE Canada 45°27′N 73°36′W
103 S4 **Verdun** var. Verdun-sur-Meuse; anc. Verodunum. Meuse, NE France 49°09′N 05°25′E
Verdun-sur-Meuse see Verdun
83 J21 **Vereeniging** Gauteng, NE South Africa 26°41′S 27°56′E
Veremeyki see Vyeramyeyki

◆ Country ● Country Capital ◇ Dependent Territory ○ Dependent Territory Capital ◈ Administrative Regions ✈ International Airport ▲ Mountain ▲▲ Mountain Range Volcano ≈ River ◎ Lake ⊠ Reservoir

125 *T14* **Vereshchagino** Permskiy Kray, NW Russian Federation *58°06′N 54°38′E*
76 *G14* **Verga, Cap** *headland* W Guinea *10°12′N 14°27′W*
61 *G18* **Vergara** Treinta y Tres, E Uruguay *32°58′S 53°54′W*
108 *G11* **Vergeletto** Ticino, S Switzerland *46°13′N 08°34′E*
18 *L8* **Vergennes** Vermont, NE USA *44°09′N 73°13′W*
Veria *see* Véroia
104 *I5* **Verín** Galicia, NW Spain *41°55′N 07°26′W*
Verin T'alin *see* T'alin
118 *K6* **Veriora** Põlvamaa, SE Estonia *57°57′N 27°23′E*
117 *T7* **Verkhivtseve** Dnipropetrovs'ka Oblast', E Ukraine *48°27′N 34°15′E*
Verkhnedvinsk *see* Vyerkhnyadzvinsk
122 *K10* **Verkhneimbatsk** Krasnoyarskiy Kray, N Russian Federation *63°06′N 88°03′E*
124 *I3* **Verkhnetulomskiy** Murmanskaya Oblast', NW Russian Federation *68°37′N 31°46′E*
124 *I3* **Verkhnetulomskoye Vodokhranilishche** ⊠ NW Russian Federation
Verkhneudinsk *see* Ulan-Ude
123 *P10* **Verkhnevilyuysk** Respublika Sakha (Yakutiya), NE Russian Federation *63°44′N 119°59′E*
127 *W5* **Verkhniy Avzyan** Respublika Bashkortostan, W Russian Federation *53°31′N 57°26′E*
127 *Q11* **Verkhniy Baskunchak** Astrakhanskaya Oblast', SW Russian Federation *48°14′N 46°43′E*
127 *W3* **Verkhniye Kigi** Respublika Bashkortostan, W Russian Federation *55°25′N 58°40′E*
117 *T9* **Verkhniy Rohachyk** Khersons'ka Oblast', S Ukraine *47°16′N 34°16′E*
123 *Q11* **Verkhnyaya Amga** Respublika Sakha (Yakutiya), NE Russian Federation *59°34′N 127°07′E*
125 *V6* **Verkhnyaya Inta** Respublika Komi, NW Russian Federation *65°55′N 60°07′E*
125 *O10* **Verkhnyaya Toyma** Arkhangel'skaya Oblast', NW Russian Federation *62°12′N 44°57′E*
126 *K6* **Verkhov'ye** Orlovskaya Oblast', W Russian Federation *52°49′N 37°20′E*
116 *I8* **Verkhovyna** Ivano-Frankivs'ka Oblast', W Ukraine *48°09′N 24°48′E*
123 *P8* **Verkhoyanskiy Khrebet** ▲▲ NE Russian Federation
117 *T7* **Verkn'odniprovs'k** Dnipropetrovs'ka Oblast', E Ukraine *48°40′N 34°17′E*
101 *G14* **Verl** Nordrhein-Westfalen, NW Germany *51°52′N 08°30′E*
92 *N1* **Verlegenhuken** *headland* N Svalbard *80°03′N 16°15′E*
82 *A9* **Vermelha, Ponta** *headland* NW Angola *05°40′S 12°09′E*
103 *P7* **Vermenton** Yonne, C France *47°40′N 03°43′E*
11 *R14* **Vermilion** Alberta, SW Canada *53°21′N 110°52′W*
31 *T11* **Vermilion** Ohio, N USA *41°25′N 82°21′W*
22 *I10* **Vermilion Bay** *bay* Louisiana, S USA
29 *V4* **Vermilion Lake** ◎ Minnesota, N USA
14 *F9* **Vermilion River** ∽ Ontario, S Canada
30 *L12* **Vermilion River** ∽ Illinois, N USA
29 *R12* **Vermillion** South Dakota, N USA *42°46′N 96°55′W*
29 *R12* **Vermillion River** ∽ South Dakota, N USA
15 *O9* **Vermillon, Rivière** ∽ Québec, SE Canada
115 *E14* **Vérmio** ▲▲ N Greece
18 *L8* **Vermont** *off.* State of Vermont, ***also known as*** Green Mountain State. ◈ *state* NE USA
113 *K16* **Vermosh** *var.* Vermoshi. Shkodër, N Albania *42°37′N 19°42′E*
Vermoshi *see* Vermosh
37 *O3* **Vernal** Utah, W USA *40°27′N 109°31′W*
14 *G11* **Verner** Ontario, S Canada *46°24′N 80°04′W*
102 *M5* **Verneuil-sur-Avre** Eure, N France *48°44′N 00°55′E*
114 *D13* **Vérno** ▲▲ N Greece
11 *N17* **Vernon** British Columbia, SW Canada *50°17′N 119°19′W*
102 *M4* **Vernon** Eure, N France *49°04′N 01°28′E*
23 *N3* **Vernon** Alabama, S USA *33°45′N 88°06′W*
31 *P15* **Vernon** Indiana, N USA *38°59′N 85°39′W*
25 *Q4* **Vernon** Texas, SW USA *34°11′N 99°17′W*
32 *G10* **Vernonia** Oregon, NW USA *45°51′N 123°11′W*
14 *G12* **Vernon, Lake** ◎ Ontario, S Canada
22 *G7* **Vernon Lake** ⊠ Louisiana, S USA
23 *Y13* **Vero Beach** Florida, SE USA *27°38′N 80°24′W*
Verőcze *see* Virovitica
Verodunum *see* Verdun
115 *E14* **Véroia** *var.* Veria, Vérroia, ***Turk.*** Karaferiye. Kentrikí Makedonía, N Greece *40°32′N 22°11′E*
106 *E8* **Verolanuova** Lombardia, N Italy *45°20′N 10°06′E*
14 *K14* **Verona** Ontario, SE Canada *44°30′N 76°42′W*
106 *G8* **Verona** Veneto, NE Italy *45°27′N 11°E*
29 *P6* **Verona** North Dakota, N USA *46°19′N 98°03′W*
30 *L9* **Verona** Wisconsin, N USA *42°59′N 89°33′W*
61 *E20* **Verónica** Buenos Aires, E Argentina *35°25′S 57°16′W*
22 *J9* **Verret, Lake** ◎ Louisiana, S USA
Vérroia *see* Véroia
103 *N5* **Versailles** Yvelines, N France *48°48′N 02°08′E*
31 *P15* **Versailles** Indiana, N USA *39°04′N 85°16′W*
20 *M5* **Versailles** Kentucky, S USA *38°02′N 84°45′W*
27 *U5* **Versailles** Missouri, C USA *38°25′N 92°51′W*
31 *Q13* **Versailles** Ohio, N USA *40°13′N 84°28′W*
Versecz *see* Vršac
108 *A10* **Versoix** Genève, SW Switzerland *46°17′N 06°10′E*
15 *Z6* **Verte, Pointe** *headland* Québec, SE Canada *48°36′N 64°10′W*
111 *I22* **Vértes** ▲▲ NW Hungary
44 *G6* **Vertientes** Camagüey, C Cuba *21°18′N 78°11′W*
114 *G13* **Vertískos** ▲▲ N Greece
102 *I8* **Vertou** Loire-Atlantique, NW France *47°10′N 01°28′W*
Verulamium *see* St Albans
99 *L19* **Verviers** Liège, E Belgium *50°36′N 05°52′E*
103 *Y14* **Vescovato** Corse, France, C Mediterranean Sea *42°30′N 09°27′E*
99 *L20* **Vesdre** ∽ E Belgium
117 *U10* **Vesele** *Rus.* Veseloye. Zaporiz'ka Oblast', S Ukraine *47°00′N 34°52′E*
111 *D18* **Veselí nad Lužnicí** *var.* Weseli an der Lainsitz, ***Ger.*** Frohenbruck. Jihočeský Kraj, S Czech Republic *49°11′N 14°40′E*
114 *M9* **Veselinovo** Shumen, NE Bulgaria *43°01′N 27°02′E*
126 *L12* **Veselovskoye Vodokhranilishche** ⊠ SW Russian Federation
Veseloye *see* Vesele
117 *Q9* **Veselynove** Mykolayivs'ka Oblast', S Ukraine *47°21′N 31°15′E*
Veseya *see* Vyasyeya
126 *M10* **Veshenskaya** Rostovskaya Oblast', SW Russian Federation *49°37′N 41°43′E*
127 *Q5* **Veshkayma** Ul'yanovskaya Oblast', W Russian Federation *54°04′N 47°06′E*
Vesisaari *see* Vadsø
Vesontio *see* Besançon
103 *T7* **Vesoul** *anc.* Vesulium, Vesulum. Haute-Saône, E France *47°37′N 06°09′E*
95 *J20* **Vessigebro** Halland, S Sweden *56°58′N 12°40′E*
95 *D17* **Vest-Agder** ◈ *county* S Norway
23 *P4* **Vestavia Hills** Alabama, S USA *33°27′N 86°47′W*
84 *F6* **Vesterålen** *island* NW Norway
92 *G10* **Vesterålen** *island group* N Norway
87 *V3* **Vestervig** Midtjylland, NW Denmark *56°46′N 08°20′E*
92 *H2* **Vestfirdhir** ◈ *region* NW Iceland
92 *G11* **Vestfjorden** *fjord* C Norway
95 *G16* **Vestfold** ◈ *county* S Norway
Vestmanhavn *see* Vestmanna
95 *B18* **Vestmanna** *Dan.* Vestmanhavn. Streymoy, N Faeroe Islands *62°09′N 07°11′W*
92 *I4* **Vestmannaeyjar** Sudhurland, S Iceland *63°26′N 20°14′W*
94 *E9* **Vestnes** Møre og Romsdal, S Norway *62°39′N 07°00′E*
92 *H3* **Vesturland** ◈ *region* W Iceland
92 *G11* **Vestvågøya** *island* C Norway
Vesulium/Vesulum *see* Vesoul
Vesuna *see* Périgueux
107 *K17* **Vesuvio** *Eng.* Vesuvius. ⛰ S Italy *40°48′N 14°29′E*
Vesuvius *see* Vesuvio
124 *K14* **Ves'yegonsk** Tverskaya Oblast', W Russian Federation *58°40′N 37°13′E*
111 *I23* **Veszprém** *Ger.* Veszprim. Veszprém, W Hungary *47°06′N 17°54′E*
111 *H23* **Veszprém** *off.* Veszprém Megye. ◈ *county* W Hungary
Veszprém Megye *see* Veszprém
Veszprim *see* Veszprém
Vetka *see* Vyetka
95 *M19* **Vetlanda** Jönköping, S Sweden *57°26′N 15°05′E*
127 *P1* **Vetluga** Nizhegorodskaya Oblast', W Russian Federation *57°51′N 45°45′E*
125 *P14* **Vetluga** ∽ NW Russian Federation
125 *O14* **Vetluzhskiy** Kostromskaya Oblast', NW Russian Federation *58°21′N 45°25′E*
127 *P2* **Vetluzhskiy** Nizhegorodskaya Oblast', W Russian Federation *57°10′N 45°07′E*
114 *K7* **Vetovo** Ruse, N Bulgaria *43°42′N 26°16′E*
107 *H14* **Vetralla** Lazio, C Italy *42°18′N 12°03′E*
Vetrino *see* Vyetryna
122 *L7* **Vetrovaya, Gora** ▲ N Russian Federation *73°54′N 95°00′E*
Vetter, Lake *see* Vättern
106 *J13* **Vettore, Monte** ▲ C Italy *42°49′N 13°15′E*
99 *A17* **Veurne** *var.* Furnes. West-Vlaanderen, W Belgium *51°04′N 02°40′E*
31 *Q15* **Vevay** Indiana, N USA *38°45′N 85°08′W*
108 *C10* **Vevey** *Ger.* Vivis; ***anc.*** Vibiscum. Vaud, SW Switzerland *46°28′N 06°51′E*
Vexiö *see* Växjö
103 *S13* **Veynes** Hautes-Alpes, SE France *44°33′N 05°51′E*
103 *N11* **Vézère** ∽ W France
114 *I9* **Vezhen** ▲ C Bulgaria *42°45′N 24°22′E*
136 *K11* **Vezirköprü** Samsun, N Turkey *41°09′N 35°27′E*
57 *J18* **Viacha** La Paz, W Bolivia *16°40′S 68°17′W*
27 *R10* **Vian** Oklahoma, C USA *35°30′N 94°56′W*
Viana de Castelo *see* Viana do Castelo
104 *H12* **Viana do Alentejo** Évora, S Portugal *38°20′N 08°00′W*
104 *I4* **Viana do Bolo** Galicia, NW Spain *42°10′N 07°06′W*
104 *G5* **Viana do Castelo** *var.* Viana de Castelo; ***anc.*** Velobriga. Viana do Castelo, NW Portugal *41°41′N 08°50′W*
104 *G5* **Viana do Castelo** *var.* Viana de Castelo. ◈ *district* N Portugal
98 *J12* **Vianen** Utrecht, C Netherlands *52°N 05°06′E*
167 *Q8* **Viangchan** *Eng./Fr.* Vientiane. ● (Laos) C Laos *17°58′N 102°38′E*
167 *P6* **Viangphoukha** *var.* Vieng Pou Kha. Louang Namtha, N Laos *20°41′N 101°03′E*
104 *K13* **Viar** ∽ SW Spain
106 *E11* **Viareggio** Toscana, C Italy *43°52′N 10°15′E*
103 *O14* **Viaur** ∽ S France
Vibiscum *see* Vevey
95 *G21* **Viborg** Midtjylland, NW Denmark *56°28′N 09°25′E*
29 *R12* **Viborg** South Dakota, N USA *43°10′N 97°04′W*
Viborg Amt *see* Midtjylland
107 *N22* **Vibo Valentia** *prev.* Monteleone di Calabria; ***anc.*** Hipponium. Calabria, SW Italy *38°40′N 16°06′E*
105 *W5* **Vic** *var.* Vich; ***anc.*** Ausa, Vicus Ausonensis. Cataluña, NE Spain *41°56′N 02°16′E*
102 *K16* **Vic-en-Bigorre** Hautes-Pyrénées, S France *43°23′N 00°04′E*
40 *K10* **Vicente Guerrero** Durango, C Mexico *23°30′N 104°24′W*
41 *P10* **Vicente Guerrero, Presa** *var.* Presa de las Adjuntas. ⊠ NE Mexico
Vicentia *see* Vicenza
106 *G8* **Vicenza** *anc.* Vicentia. Veneto, NE Italy *45°32′N 11°31′E*
Vich *see* Vic
54 *J10* **Vichada** *off.* Comisaría del Vichada. ◈ *province* E Colombia
Vichada, Comisaría del *see* Vichada
54 *K10* **Vichada, Río** ∽ E Colombia
61 *G17* **Vichadero** Rivera, NE Uruguay *31°45′S 54°41′W*
Vichegda *see* Vychegda
124 *M16* **Vichuga** Ivanovskaya Oblast', W Russian Federation *57°13′N 41°51′E*
103 *P10* **Vichy** Allier, C France *46°08′N 03°26′E*
26 *K9* **Vici** Oklahoma, C USA *36°09′N 99°18′W*
95 *I19* **Vickan** Halland, S Sweden *57°25′N 12°00′E*
31 *P10* **Vicksburg** Michigan, N USA *42°07′N 85°31′W*
22 *J5* **Vicksburg** Mississippi, S USA *32°21′N 90°52′W*
103 *O12* **Vic-sur-Cère** Cantal, C France *45°00′N 02°36′E*
59 *I21* **Víctor** Mato Grosso do Sul, SW Brazil *21°39′S 53°21′W*
29 *X14* **Victor** Iowa, C USA *41°45′N 92°18′W*
182 *I10* **Victor Harbor** South Australia *35°33′S 138°37′E*
61 *C18* **Victoria** Entre Ríos, E Argentina *32°40′S 60°10′W*
10 *L17* **Victoria** *province capital* Vancouver Island, British Columbia, SW Canada *48°25′N 123°22′W*
45 *R14* **Victoria** NW Grenada *12°12′N 61°42′W*
42 *H6* **Victoria** Yoro, NW Honduras *15°01′N 87°28′W*
121 *O15* **Victoria** *var.* Rabat. Gozo, NW Malta *36°02′N 14°14′E*
116 *I12* **Victoria** *Ger.* Viktoriastadt. Braşov, C Romania *45°44′N 24°41′E*
172 *H17* **Victoria** ● (Seychelles) Mahé, SW Seychelles *04°38′S 28°28′E*
25 *U13* **Victoria** Texas, SW USA *28°47′N 96°59′W*
183 *N12* **Victoria** ◈ *state* SE Australia
174 *K7* **Victoria** ∽ Western Australia
Victoria *see* Labuan, East Malaysia
Victoria *see* Masvingo, Zimbabwe
Victoria Bank *see* Vitória Seamount
11 *Y15* **Victoria Beach** Manitoba, S Canada *50°40′N 96°30′W*
Victoria de Durango *see* Durango
Victoria de las Tunas *see* Las Tunas
83 *I16* **Victoria Falls** Matabeleland North, W Zimbabwe *17°55′S 25°51′E*
83 *I16* **Victoria Falls** *waterfall* Zambia/Zimbabwe
83 *I16* **Victoria Falls** ✈ Matabeleland North, W Zimbabwe *18°03′S 25°48′E*
Victoria Falls *see* Iguaçu, Salto do
63 *F19* **Victoria, Isla** *island* Archipiélago de los Chonos, S Chile
8 *K6* **Victoria Island** *island* Northwest Territories/Nunavut, NW Canada
182 *L8* **Victoria, Lake** ◎ New South Wales, SE Australia
68 *I12* **Victoria, Lake** *var.* Victoria Nyanza. ◎ E Africa
195 *S13* **Victoria Land** *physical region* Antarctica
187 *X14* **Victoria, Mount** ▲ Viti Levu, W Fiji *17°37′S 178°00′E*
166 *L5* **Victoria, Mount** ▲ W Myanmar (Burma) *21°13′N 93°53′E*
186 *E9* **Victoria, Mount** ▲ S Papua New Guinea *08°51′S 147°36′E*
81 *F17* **Victoria Nile** *var.* Somerset Nile. ∽ C Uganda
Victoria Nyanza *see* Victoria, Lake
42 *G3* **Victoria Peak** ▲ SE Belize *16°50′N 88°38′W*
185 *H16* **Victoria Range** ▲▲ South Island, New Zealand
181 *O3* **Victoria River** ∽ Northern Territory, N Australia
181 *P3* **Victoria River Roadhouse** Northern Territory, N Australia *15°37′S 131°07′E*
15 *Q11* **Victoriaville** Québec, SE Canada *46°04′N 71°57′W*
Victoria-Wes *see* Victoria West
83 *G24* **Victoria West** *Afr.* Victoria-Wes. Northern Cape, W South Africa *31°25′S 23°08′E*
62 *J13* **Victorica** La Pampa, C Argentina *36°15′S 65°25′W*
Victor, Mount *see* Dronning Fabiolafjella
35 *U14* **Victorville** California, W USA *34°32′N 117°17′W*
62 *G9* **Vicuña** Coquimbo, N Chile *30°00′S 70°44′W*
62 *K11* **Vicuña Mackenna** Córdoba, C Argentina *33°53′S 64°25′W*
Vicus Ausonensis *see* Vic
Vicus Elbii *see* Viterbo
33 *X7* **Vida** Montana, NW USA *47°52′N 105°30′W*
23 *V6* **Vidalia** Georgia, SE USA *32°13′N 82°24′W*
22 *J7* **Vidalia** Louisiana, S USA *31°34′N 91°25′W*
95 *F22* **Videbæk** Midtjylland, C Denmark *56°08′N 08°38′E*
60 *I13* **Videira** Santa Catarina, S Brazil *27°00′S 51°08′W*
116 *J14* **Videle** Teleorman, S Romania *44°15′N 25°27′E*
Videm-Krško *see* Krško
Vídeň *see* Wien
104 *H12* **Vidigueira** Beja, S Portugal *38°12′N 07°48′W*
114 *J9* **Vidima** ∽ N Bulgaria
114 *G7* **Vidin** *anc.* Bononia. Vidin, NW Bulgaria *44°00′N 22°52′E*
114 *F8* **Vidin** ◈ *province* NW Bulgaria
154 *H10* **Vidisha** Madhya Pradesh, C India *23°30′N 77°50′E*
25 *Y10* **Vidor** Texas, SW USA *30°07′N 94°01′W*
95 *L20* **Vidöstern** ◎ S Sweden
92 *J13* **Vidsel** Norrbotten, N Sweden *65°49′N 20°31′E*
118 *H9* **Vidzemes Augstiene** ▲▲ C Latvia
118 *J12* **Vidzy** Vitsyebskaya Voblasts', NW Belarus *55°24′N 26°38′E*
63 *L16* **Viedma** Río Negro, E Argentina *40°50′S 62°58′W*
63 *H22* **Viedma, Lago** ◎ S Argentina
45 *O11* **Vieille Case** *var.* Itassi. N Dominica *15°36′N 61°24′W*
104 *M2* **Vieja, Peña** ▲ N Spain *43°09′N 04°47′W*
24 *J10* **Vieja, Sierra** ▲▲ Texas, SW USA
40 *E4* **Viejo, Cerro** ▲ NW Mexico *30°16′N 112°18′W*
56 *B9* **Viejo, Cerro** ▲ N Peru *04°54′S 79°24′W*
118 *E10* **Viekšniai** Telšiai, NW Lithuania *56°14′N 22°33′E*
105 *U3* **Vielha** *var.* Viella. Cataluña, NE Spain *42°41′N 00°47′E*
Viella *see* Vielha
99 *L21* **Vielsalm** Luxembourg, E Belgium *50°17′N 05°55′E*
Vieng Pou Kha *see* Viangphoukha
23 *T6* **Vienna** Georgia, SE USA *32°05′N 83°48′W*
30 *L17* **Vienna** Illinois, N USA *37°24′N 88°55′W*
27 *V5* **Vienna** Missouri, C USA *38°12′N 91°59′W*
21 *Q3* **Vienna** West Virginia, NE USA *39°19′N 81°33′W*
Vienna *see* Wien, Austria
Vienna *see* Vienne, France
103 *R11* **Vienne** *anc.* Vienna. Isère, E France *45°32′N 04°53′E*
102 *L10* **Vienne** ◈ *department* W France
102 *L9* **Vienne** ∽ W France
Vientiane *see* Viangchan
Vientos, Paso de los *see* Windward Passage
45 *V6* **Vieques** *var.* Isabel Segunda. E Puerto Rico *18°08′N 65°25′W*
45 *V6* **Vieques, Isla de** *island* E Puerto Rico
45 *V6* **Vieques, Pasaje de** *passage* E Puerto Rico
45 *V5* **Vieques, Sonda de** *sound* E Puerto Rico
Vierdörfer *see* Săcele
93 *M15* **Vieremä** Itä-Suomi, C Finland *63°42′N 27°02′E*
99 *M14* **Vierlingsbeek** Noord-Brabant, SE Netherlands *51°36′N 06°01′E*
101 *G20* **Viernheim** Hessen, W Germany *49°32′N 08°35′E*
101 *D15* **Viersen** Nordrhein-Westfalen, W Germany *51°16′N 06°24′E*
108 *G8* **Vierwaldstätter See** ***Eng.*** Lake of Lucerne. ◎ C Switzerland
103 *N8* **Vierzon** Cher, C France *47°13′N 02°04′E*
40 *L8* **Viesca** Coahuila, NE Mexico *25°25′N 102°45′W*
118 *H10* **Viesīte** *Ger.* Eckengraf. S Latvia *56°21′N 25°30′E*
107 *N15* **Vieste** Puglia, SE Italy *41°52′N 16°11′E*
167 *T8* **Vietnam** *off.* Socialist Republic of Vietnam, ***Vtn.*** Công Hoa Xa Hôi Chu Nghia Viêt Nam. ◆ *republic* SE Asia
Vietnam, Socialist Republic of *see* Vietnam
167 *S5* **Viêt Quang** Ha Giang, N Vietnam *22°24′N 104°48′E*
Vietri *see* Viêt Tri
167 *S6* **Viêt Tri** *var.* Vietri. Vinh Phu, N Vietnam *21°20′N 105°26′E*
30 *L4* **Vieux Desert, Lac** ◎ Michigan/Wisconsin, N USA
45 *Y13* **Vieux Fort** S Saint Lucia *13°43′N 60°57′W*
45 *X6* **Vieux-Habitants** Basse Terre, SW Guadeloupe *16°04′N 61°45′W*
119 *G14* **Vievis** Vilnius, S Lithuania *54°46′N 24°51′E*
171 *N2* **Vigan** Luzon, N Philippines *17°34′N 102°21′E*
106 *D8* **Vigevano** Lombardia, N Italy *45°19′N 08°51′E*
107 *N18* **Viggiano** Basilicata, S Italy *40°21′N 15°54′E*
58 *L12* **Vigia** Pará, NE Brazil *0°50′S 48°07′W*
41 *Y12* **Vigía Chico** Quintana Roo, SE Mexico *19°49′N 87°31′W*
45 *T11* **Vigie** *prev.* George F L Charles. ✈ (Castries) NE Saint Lucia *14°01′N 60°59′W*
102 *K17* **Vignemale** *var.* Pic de Vignemale. ▲ France/Spain *42°48′N 00°06′W*
Vignemale, Pic de *see* Vignemale
106 *G10* **Vignola** Emilia-Romagna, C Italy *44°28′N 11°00′E*
104 *G4* **Vigo** Galicia, NW Spain *42°15′N 08°44′W*
104 *G4* **Vigo, Ría de** *estuary* NW Spain
94 *D9* **Vigra** *island* S Norway
95 *C17* **Vigrestad** Rogaland, S Norway *58°34′N 05°42′E*
93 *L15* **Vihanti** Oulu, C Finland *64°29′N 25°E*
149 *U10* **Vihāri** Punjab, E Pakistan *30°03′N 72°32′E*
102 *K8* **Vihiers** Maine-et-Loire, NW France *47°09′N 00°37′W*
111 *O19* **Vihorlat** ▲ E Slovakia *48°54′N 22°09′E*
93 *L19* **Vihti** Etelä-Suomi, S Finland *60°25′N 24°16′E*
Viipuri *see* Vyborg
93 *M16* **Viitasaari** Länsi-Suomi, C Finland *63°05′N 25°52′E*
118 *K3* **Viivikonna** Ida-Virumaa, NE Estonia *59°19′N 27°41′E*
155 *K16* **Vijayawāda** *prev.* Bezwada. Andhra Pradesh, SE India *16°34′N 80°40′E*
Vijosa/Vijosë *see* Aóos, Albania/Greece
Vijosa/Vijosë *see* Vjosës, Lumi i, Albania/Greece
92 *J4* **Vík** Sudhurland, S Iceland *63°25′N 18°58′W*
Vik *see* Vikøyri
94 *L13* **Vika** Dalarna, C Sweden *60°55′N 14°30′E*
92 *L12* **Vikajärvi** Lappi, N Finland *66°37′N 26°10′E*
94 *L13* **Vikarbyn** Dalarna, C Sweden *60°57′N 15°00′E*
95 *J22* **Viken** Skåne, S Sweden *56°09′N 12°36′E*
95 *L17* **Viken** ◎ C Sweden
95 *G15* **Vikersund** Buskerud, S Norway *59°58′N 09°59′E*
114 *G11* **Vikhren** ▲ SW Bulgaria *41°45′N 23°24′E*
11 *R15* **Viking** Alberta, SW Canada *53°07′N 111°50′W*
84 *E7* **Viking Bank** *undersea feature* N North Sea *60°35′N 02°35′E*
95 *M14* **Vikmanshyttan** Dalarna, C Sweden *60°19′N 15°55′E*
94 *D12* **Vikøyri** *var.* Vik. Sogn Og Fjordane, S Norway *61°04′N 06°34′E*
93 *H17* **Viksjö** Västernorrland, C Sweden *62°45′N 17°30′E*
Viktoriastadt *see* Victoria
Vila *see* Port-Vila
Vila Arriaga *see* Bibala
Vila Artur de Paiva *see* Cubango
Vila Baleira *see* Porto Santo
Vila Bela da Santissima Trindade *see* Mato Grosso
58 *B12* **Vila Bittencourt** Amazonas, NW Brazil *01°25′S 69°24′W*
Vila da Ponte *see* Cubango
64 *O2* **Vila da Praia da Vitória** Terceira, Azores, Portugal, NE Atlantic Ocean *38°44′N 27°04′W*
Vila de Aljustrel *see* Cangamba
Vila de Almoster *see* Chiange
Vila de João Belo *see* Xai-Xai
Vila de Macia *see* Macia
Vila de Manhiça *see* Manhiça
Vila de Manica *see* Manica
Vila de Mocímboa da Praia *see* Mocímboa da Praia
83 *N16* **Vila de Sena** *var.* Sena. Sofala, C Mozambique *17°25′S 34°59′E*
104 *F14* **Vila do Bispo** Faro, S Portugal *37°05′N 08°53′W*
104 *G6* **Vila do Conde** Porto, NW Portugal *41°21′N 08°45′W*
Vila do Maio *see* Maio
64 *P3* **Vila do Porto** Santa Maria, Azores, Portugal, NE Atlantic Ocean *36°57′N 25°10′W*
83 *K15* **Vila do Zumbo** *prev.* Vila do Zumbu, Zumbo. Tete, NW Mozambique *15°36′S 30°30′E*
Vila do Zumbu *see* Vila do Zumbo
105 *T8* **Vilafamés** *prev.* Villafamés. Valenciana, E Spain *40°07′N 00°03′W*
104 *I6* **Vila Flor** *var.* Vila Flôr. Bragança, N Portugal *41°18′N 07°09′W*
105 *V6* **Vilafranca del Penedès** *var.* Villafranca del Panadés. Cataluña, NE Spain *41°21′N 01°42′E*
104 *F10* **Vila Franca de Xira** *var.* Vilafranca de Xira. Lisboa, C Portugal *38°57′N 08°59′W*
Vila Gago Coutinho *see* Lumbala N'Guimbo
104 *G3* **Vilagarcía** *var.* Villagarcía de Arosa. Galicia, NW Spain *42°35′N 08°45′W*
Vila General Machado *see* Camacupa
Vila Henrique de Carvalho *see* Saurimo
102 *I7* **Vilaine** ∽ NW France
Vila João de Almeida *see* Chibia
118 *K8* **Viļaka** *Ger.* Marienhausen. NE Latvia *57°12′N 27°43′E*
104 *I2* **Vilalba** Galicia, NW Spain *43°17′N 07°41′W*
Vila Marechal Carmona *see* Uíge
Vila Mariano Machado *see* Ganda
172 *G3* **Vilanandro, Tanjona** ***prev./Fr.*** Cap Saint-André. *headland* W Madagascar *16°10′S 44°27′E*
Vilanculos *see* Vilankulo
118 *J10* **Viļāni** E Latvia *56°33′N 26°55′E*
83 *N19* **Vilankulo** *var.* Vilanculos. Inhambane, E Mozambique *22°01′S 35°19′E*
Vila Norton de Matos *see* Balombo
104 *G6* **Vila Nova de Famalicão** *var.* Vila Nova de Famalicao. Braga, N Portugal *41°24′N 08°31′W*
104 *I6* **Vila Nova de Foz Côa** *var.* Vila Nova de Fozcôa. Guarda, N Portugal *41°05′N 07°09′W*
Vila Nova de Fozcôa *see* Vila Nova de Foz Côa
104 *F6* **Vila Nova de Gaia** Porto, NW Portugal *41°08′N 08°37′W*
Vila Nova de Portimão *see* Portimão
105 *V6* **Vilanova i La Geltru** Cataluña, NE Spain *41°15′N 01°42′E*
Vila Pereira de Eça *see* N'Giva
104 *H6* **Vila Pouca de Aguiar** Vila Real, N Portugal *41°30′N 07°38′W*
104 *H6* **Vila Real** *var.* Vila Rial. Vila Real, N Portugal *41°17′N 07°45′W*
105 *T9* **Vila-real** *var.* Vila-real de los Infantes; ***prev.*** Villarreal. Valenciana, E Spain *39°56′N 00°08′W*
104 *H6* **Vila Real** ◈ *district* N Portugal
Vila-real de los Infantes *see* Vila-real
104 *H14* **Vila Real de Santo António** Faro, S Portugal *37°12′N 07°25′W*
104 *J7* **Vilar Formoso** Guarda, N Portugal *40°37′N 06°50′W*
Vila Rial *see* Vila Real
59 *J15* **Vila Rica** Mato Grosso, W Brazil *09°52′S 50°44′W*
Vila Robert Williams *see* Caála
Vila Salazar *see* N'Dalatando
Vila Serpa Pinto *see* Menongue
Vila Teixeira da Silva *see* Bailundo
Vila Teixeira de Sousa *see* Luau
104 *H9* **Vila Velha de Ródão** Castelo Branco, C Portugal *39°39′N 07°40′W*
104 *G5* **Vila Verde** Braga, N Portugal *41°39′N 08°27′W*
104 *H11* **Vila Viçosa** Évora, S Portugal *38°46′N 07°25′W*
57 *G15* **Vilcabamba, Cordillera de** ▲▲ C Peru
Vîlcea *see* Vâlcea
122 *J4* **Vil'cheka, Zemlya** *Eng.* Wilczek Land. *island* Zemlya Frantsa-Iosifa, NW Russian Federation
95 *F22* **Vildbjerg** Midtjylland, C Denmark *56°12′N 08°47′E*
Vileyka *see* Vilyeyka
93 *H15* **Vilhelmina** Västerbotten, N Sweden *64°38′N 16°40′E*
59 *F17* **Vilhena** Rondônia, W Brazil *12°40′S 60°08′W*
115 *G19* **Vília** Attikí, C Greece *38°09′N 23°21′E*
119 *I14* **Viliya** *Lith.* Neris. ∽ W Belarus
Viliya *see* Neris
118 *H5* **Viljandi** *Ger.* Fellin. Viljandimaa, S Estonia *58°22′N 25°30′E*
118 *H5* **Viljandimaa** *var.* Viljandi Maakond. ◈ *province* SW Estonia
Viljandi Maakond *see* Viljandimaa
119 *E14* **Vilkaviškis** *Pol.* Wyłkowyszki. Marijampolė, SW Lithuania *54°39′N 23°03′E*
118 *F13* **Vilkija** Kaunas, C Lithuania *55°02′N 23°36′E*
197 *V9* **Vil'kitskogo, Proliv** *strait* N Russian Federation
Vilkovo *see* Vylkove
57 *L21* **Villa Abecia** Chuquisaca, S Bolivia *21°00′S 65°18′W*
41 *N5* **Villa Acuña** *var.* Ciudad Acuña. Coahuila, NE Mexico *29°18′N 100°58′W*
40 *J4* **Villa Ahumada** Chihuahua, N Mexico *30°38′N 106°30′W*
45 *O9* **Villa Altagracia** C Dominican Republic *18°43′N 70°13′W*
56 *L13* **Villa Bella** El Beni, N Bolivia *10°21′S 65°25′W*
104 *J3* **Villablino** Castilla y León, N Spain *42°55′N 06°21′W*
54 *K6* **Villa Bruzual** Portuguesa, N Venezuela *09°20′N 69°06′W*
105 *O9* **Villacañas** Castilla-La Mancha, C Spain *39°38′N 03°20′W*
105 *O12* **Villacarrillo** Andalucía, S Spain *38°07′N 03°05′W*
104 *M7* **Villacastín** Castilla y León, N Spain *40°46′N 04°25′W*
Villa Cecilia *see* Ciudad Madero
109 *S9* **Villach** *Slvn.* Beljak. Kärnten, S Austria *46°36′N 13°49′E*
107 *B20* **Villacidro** Sardegna, Italy, C Mediterranean Sea *39°28′N 08°43′E*
Villa Concepción *see* Concepción
104 *L4* **Villada** Castilla y León, N Spain *42°15′N 04°59′W*
40 *M10* **Villa de Cos** Zacatecas, C Mexico *23°20′N 102°20′W*
54 *L5* **Villa de Cura** *var.* Cura. Aragua, N Venezuela *10°00′N 67°30′W*
Villa del Nevoso *see* Ilirska Bistrica
Villa del Pilar *see* Pilar
104 *M13* **Villa del Río** Andalucía, S Spain *37°59′N 04°17′W*
Villa de Méndez *see* Méndez
42 *H6* **Villa de San Antonio** Comayagua, W Honduras *14°24′N 87°37′W*
105 *N4* **Villadiego** Castilla y León, N Spain *42°31′N 04°01′W*
Villafamés *see* Vilafamés
41 *U16* **Villa Flores** Chiapas, SE Mexico *16°12′N 93°16′W*
104 *J3* **Villafranca del Bierzo** Castilla y León, N Spain *42°36′N 06°49′W*
105 *S8* **Villafranca del Cid** Valenciana, E Spain *40°25′N 00°15′W*
104 *J11* **Villafranca de los Barros** Extremadura, W Spain *38°34′N 06°20′W*
105 *N10* **Villafranca de los Caballeros** Castilla-La Mancha, C Spain *39°26′N 03°21′W*
Villafranca del Panadés *see* Vilafranca del Penedès
106 *F8* **Villafranca di Verona** Veneto, NE Italy *45°22′N 10°51′E*
107 *J23* **Villafrati** Sicilia, Italy, C Mediterranean Sea *37°53′N 13°30′E*
Villagarcía de Arosa *see* Vilagarcía
41 *O9* **Villagrán** Tamaulipas, C Mexico *24°29′N 99°30′W*
61 *C17* **Villaguay** Entre Ríos, E Argentina *31°55′S 59°01′W*
62 *O6* **Villa Hayes** Presidente Hayes, S Paraguay *25°05′S 57°25′W*
41 *U15* **Villahermosa** *prev.* San Juan Bautista. Tabasco, SE Mexico *17°56′N 92°50′W*
105 *O11* **Villahermosa** Castilla-La Mancha, C Spain *38°46′N 02°52′W*
64 *O11* **Villahermoso** Gomera, Islas Canarias, Spain, NE Atlantic Ocean *38°46′N 02°52′W*
Villa Hidalgo *see* Hidalgo
105 *T12* **Villajoyosa** *Cat.* La Vila Joíosa. Valenciana, E Spain *38°31′N 00°14′W*
Villa Juárez *see* Juárez
Villalba *see* Collado Villalba
41 *N8* **Villaldama** Nuevo León, NE Mexico *26°29′N 100°27′W*
104 *L5* **Villalón de Campos** Castilla y León, N Spain *42°05′N 05°03′W*
61 *A25* **Villalonga** Buenos Aires, E Argentina *39°55′S 62°35′W*
104 *L5* **Villalpando** Castilla y León, N Spain *41°51′N 05°25′W*
40 *K9* **Villa Madero** *var.* Francisco l. Madero. Durango, C Mexico *24°28′N 104°20′W*
41 *O9* **Villa Mainero** Tamaulipas, C Mexico *24°32′N 99°39′W*
Villamaña *see* Villamañán
104 *L4* **Villamañán** *var.* Villamaña. Castilla y León, N Spain *42°19′N 05°35′W*
62 *L10* **Villa María** Córdoba, C Argentina *32°23′S 63°15′W*
61 *C17* **Villa María Grande** Entre Ríos, E Argentina *31°39′S 59°54′W*
57 *K21* **Villa Martín** Potosí, SW Bolivia *20°46′S 67°45′W*
104 *K15* **Villamartin** Andalucía, S Spain *36°52′N 05°38′W*
62 *J8* **Villa Mazán** La Rioja, NW Argentina *28°43′S 66°25′W*
62 *J11* **Villa Mercedes** *var.* Mercedes. San Luis, C Argentina *33°40′S 65°25′W*
Villamil *see* Puerto Villamil
Villa Nador *see* Nador
54 *G5* **Villanueva** La Guajira, N Colombia *10°37′N 72°58′W*
42 *H5* **Villanueva** Cortés, NW Honduras *15°14′N 88°00′W*
40 *L11* **Villanueva** Zacatecas, C Mexico *22°24′N 102°53′W*
42 *I9* **Villa Nueva** Chinandega, NW Nicaragua *12°58′N 86°46′W*
37 *T11* **Villanueva** New Mexico, SW USA *35°18′N 105°20′W*
104 *M12* **Villanueva de Córdoba** Andalucía, S Spain *38°20′N 04°38′W*
105 *O12* **Villanueva del Arzobispo** Andalucía, S Spain *38°10′N 03°00′W*
104 *K11* **Villanueva de la Serena** Extremadura, W Spain *38°58′N 05°48′W*
104 *L5* **Villanueva del Campo** Castilla y León, N Spain *41°59′N 05°25′W*
105 *O11* **Villanueva de los Infantes** Castilla-La Mancha, C Spain *38°45′N 03°01′W*
61 *C14* **Villa Ocampo** Santa Fe, C Argentina *28°28′S 59°22′W*
40 *J8* **Villa Ocampo** Durango, C Mexico *26°29′N 105°30′W*
40 *J7* **Villa Orestes Pereyra** Durango, C Mexico *26°30′N 105°38′W*
105 *N3* **Villarcayo** Castilla y León, N Spain *42°56′N 03°34′W*
104 *L5* **Villardefrades** Castilla y León, N Spain *41°43′N 05°15′W*
105 *S9* **Villar del Arzobispo** Valenciana, E Spain *39°44′N 00°50′W*
105 *Q6* **Villaroya de la Sierra** Aragón, NE Spain *41°28′N 01°46′W*
Villarreal *see* Vila-real
62 *P6* **Villarrica** Guairá, SE Paraguay *25°45′S 56°28′W*
63 *G15* **Villarrica, Volcán** ⛰ S Chile *39°28′S 71°57′W*
105 *P10* **Villarrobledo** Castilla-La Mancha, C Spain *39°16′N 02°36′W*
105 *N10* **Villarrubia de los Ojos** Castilla-La Mancha, C Spain *39°14′N 03°36′W*
18 *J17* **Villas** New Jersey, NE USA *39°01′N 74°54′W*
105 *O3* **Villasana de Mena** Castilla y León, N Spain *43°05′N 03°16′W*
107 *M23* **Villa San Giovanni** Calabria, S Italy *38°12′N 15°39′E*
61 *D18* **Villa San José** Entre Ríos, E Argentina *32°01′S 58°20′W*
Villa Sanjurjo *see* Al-Hoceïma
105 *P6* **Villasayas** Castilla y León, N Spain *41°19′N 02°36′W*
107 *C20* **Villasimius** Sardegna, Italy, C Mediterranean Sea *39°10′N 09°30′E*
41 *N6* **Villa Unión** Coahuila, NE Mexico *28°18′N 100°43′W*
40 *K10* **Villa Unión** Durango, C Mexico *23°59′N 104°01′W*
40 *J10* **Villa Unión** Sinaloa, C Mexico *23°10′N 106°12′W*
62 *K12* **Villa Valeria** Córdoba, C Argentina *34°21′S 64°56′W*
105 *N8* **Villaverde** Madrid, C Spain *40°21′N 03°43′W*
54 *F10* **Villavicencio** Meta, C Colombia *04°09′N 73°38′W*
104 *L2* **Villaviciosa** Asturias, N Spain *43°29′N 05°26′W*
104 *L12* **Villaviciosa de Córdoba** Andalucía, S Spain *38°04′N 05°00′W*
57 *L22* **Villazón** Potosí, S Bolivia *22°05′S 65°35′W*
14 *J8* **Villebon, Lac** ◎ Québec, SE Canada
Ville de Kinshasa *see* Kinshasa
102 *J5* **Villedieu-les-Poêles** Manche, N France *48°51′N 01°12′W*
Villefranche *see* Villefranche-sur-Saône
103 *N16* **Villefranche-de-Lauragais** Haute-Garonne, S France *43°24′N 01°42′E*
103 *N14* **Villefranche-de-Rouergue** Aveyron, S France *44°21′N 02°02′E*

◆ Country
● Country Capital
◇ Dependent Territory
○ Dependent Territory Capital
◈ Administrative Regions
✈ International Airport
▲ Mountain
▲▲ Mountain Range
⛰ Volcano
∽ River
◎ Lake
⊠ Reservoir

103 R10 **Villefranche-sur-Saône** *var.* Villefranche. Rhône, E France 46°00′N 04°40′E
14 H9 **Ville-Marie** Québec, SE Canada 47°21′N 79°26′W
102 M15 **Villemur-sur-Tarn** Haute-Garonne, S France 43°50′N 01°32′E
105 S11 **Villena** Valenciana, E Spain 38°39′N 00°52′W
Villeneuve-d'Agen *see* Villeneuve-sur-Lot
102 L13 **Villeneuve-sur-Lot** *var.* Villeneuve-d'Agen, *hist.* Gajac. Lot-et-Garonne, SW France 44°24′N 00°43′E
103 P6 **Villeneuve-sur-Yonne** Yonne, C France 48°04′N 03°21′E
22 H8 **Ville Platte** Louisiana, S USA 30°41′N 92°16′W
103 R11 **Villeurbanne** Rhône, E France 45°46′N 04°54′E
101 G23 **Villingen-Schwenningen** Baden-Württemberg, S Germany 48°04′N 08°27′E
29 T15 **Villisca** Iowa, C USA 40°55′N 94°58′W
Villmanstrand *see* Lappeenranta
Vilna *see* Vilnius
119 H14 **Vilnius** *Pol.* Wilno, *Ger.* Wilna; *prev. Rus.* Vilna. ● (Lithuania) Vilnius, SE Lithuania 54°41′N 25°20′E
119 H14 **Vilnius** ✈ Vilnius, SE Lithuania 54°33′N 25°17′E
117 S7 **Vil'nohirs'k** Dnipropetrovs'ka Oblast', E Ukraine 48°31′N 34°01′E
117 U8 **Vil'nyans'k** Zaporiz'ka Oblast', SE Ukraine 47°56′N 35°22′E
93 L17 **Vilppula** Länsi-Suomi, W Finland 62°02′N 24°30′E
101 M20 **Vils** ≈ SE Germany
118 C5 **Vilsandi** *island* W Estonia
117 P8 **Vil'shanka** *Rus.* Olshanka. Kirovohrads'ka Oblast', C Ukraine 48°12′N 30°54′E
101 O22 **Vilshofen** Bayern, SE Germany 48°36′N 13°10′E
155 J20 **Viluppuram** Tamil Nādu, SE India 12°54′N 79°40′E
113 I16 **Vilusi** W Montenegro 42°44′N 18°34′E
99 G18 **Vilvoorde** *Fr.* Vilvorde. Vlaams Brabant, C Belgium 50°56′N 04°25′E
Vilvorde *see* Vilvoorde
119 J14 **Vilyeyka** *Pol.* Wilejka, *Rus.* Vileyka. Minskaya Voblasts', NW Belarus 54°30′N 26°55′E
122 V11 **Vilyuchinsk** Kamchatskiy Kray, E Russian Federation 52°55′N 158°28′E
123 P10 **Vilyuy** ≈ NE Russian Federation
123 P10 **Vilyuysk** Respublika Sakha (Yakutiya), NE Russian Federation 63°42′N 121°20′E
123 N10 **Vilyuyskoye Vodokhranilishche** ▦ NE Russian Federation
104 G2 **Vimianzo** Galicia, NW Spain 43°06′N 09°03′W
95 M19 **Vimmerby** Kalmar, S Sweden 57°40′N 15°50′E
102 L5 **Vimoutiers** Orne, N France 48°56′N 00°10′E
93 L16 **Vimpeli** Länsi-Suomi, W Finland 63°10′N 23°50′E
79 G14 **Vina** ≈ Cameroon/Chad
62 G11 **Viña del Mar** Valparaíso, C Chile 33°02′S 71°35′W
19 R8 **Vinalhaven Island** *island* Maine, NE USA
105 T8 **Vinaròs** Valenciana, E Spain 40°29′N 00°28′E
Vînători *see* Vânători
31 N15 **Vincennes** Indiana, N USA 38°42′N 87°30′W
195 Y12 **Vincennes Bay** *bay* Antarctica
25 O7 **Vincent** Texas, SW USA 32°30′N 101°10′W
95 H24 **Vindeby** Syddtjylland, C Denmark 54°55′N 11°09′E
93 I15 **Vindeln** Västerbotten, N Sweden 64°11′N 19°45′E
95 F21 **Vinderup** Midtjylland, C Denmark 56°29′N 08°48′E
Vindhya Mountains *see* Vindhya Range
153 N14 **Vindhya Range** *var.* Vindhya Mountains. ▲▲ N India
Vindobona *see* Wien
20 K6 **Vine Grove** Kentucky, S USA 37°48′N 85°58′W
18 J17 **Vineland** New Jersey, NE USA 39°29′N 75°02′W
116 E11 **Vinga** Arad, W Romania 46°00′N 21°14′E
95 M16 **Vingåker** Södermanland, C Sweden 59°02′N 15°52′E
167 S8 **Vinh** Nghê An, N Vietnam 18°42′N 105°41′E
104 I5 **Vinhais** Bragança, N Portugal 41°50′N 07°00′W
Vinh Linh *see* Hô Xa
Vinh Loi *see* Bac Liêu
167 S14 **Vinh Long** *var.* Vinhlong. Vinh Long, S Vietnam 10°15′N 105°59′E
Vinhlong *see* Vinh Long
113 Q18 **Vinica** NE FYR Macedonia 41°53′N 22°30′E
109 V13 **Vinica** SE Slovenia 45°28′N 15°12′E
114 G8 **Vinishte** Montana, NW Bulgaria 43°30′N 23°04′E
27 Q8 **Vinita** Oklahoma, C USA 36°38′N 95°09′W
Vînju Mare *see* Vânju Mare
98 I11 **Vinkeveen** Utrecht, C Netherlands 52°13′N 04°55′E
116 L6 **Vin'kivtsi** Khmel'nyts'ka Oblast', W Ukraine 49°02′N 27°13′E
112 I10 **Vinkovci** *Ger.* Winkowitz, *Hung.* Vinkovcze. Vukovar-Srijem, E Croatia 45°18′N 18°45′E
Vinkovcze *see* Vinkovci
Vinnitsa *see* Vinnytsya
Vinnitskaya Oblast'/Vinnytsya *see* Vinnyts'ka Oblast'
116 M7 **Vinnyts'ka Oblast'** *var.* Vinnytsya, *Rus.* Vinnitskaya Oblast'. ◈ *province* C Ukraine
117 N6 **Vinnytsya** *Rus.* Vinnitsa. Vinnyts'ka Oblast', C Ukraine 49°14′N 28°30′E
117 N6 **Vinnytsya** ✈ Vinnyts'ka Oblast', N Ukraine 49°13′N 28°40′E
Vinogradov *see* Vynohradiv
194 L8 **Vinson Massif** ▲ Antarctica 78°45′S 85°19′W
94 G11 **Vinstra** Oppland, S Norway 61°36′N 09°45′E
116 K12 **Vintilă Vodă** Buzău, SE Romania 45°28′N 26°43′E
29 X13 **Vinton** Iowa, C USA 42°10′N 92°01′W
22 F9 **Vinton** Louisiana, S USA 30°10′N 93°37′W
155 J17 **Vinukonda** Andhra Pradesh, E India 16°03′N 79°41′E
Vioara *see* Ocnele Mari
83 E23 **Vioolsdrif** Northern Cape, SW South Africa 28°50′S 17°38′E
82 M13 **Viphya Mountains** ▲▲ C Malawi
171 Q4 **Virac** Catanduanes Island, N Philippines 13°39′N 124°17′E
124 K8 **Virandozero** Respublika Kareliya, NW Russian Federation 63°59′N 36°00′E
137 P16 **Viranşehir** Şanlıurfa, SE Turkey 37°13′N 39°32′E
154 D13 **Virār** Mahārāshtra, W India 19°30′N 72°48′E
11 W16 **Virden** Manitoba, S Canada 49°50′N 100°57′W
30 K14 **Virden** Illinois, N USA 39°30′N 89°46′W
Virdois *see* Virrat
102 J5 **Vire** Calvados, N France 48°50′N 00°53′W
102 J4 **Vire** ≈ N France
83 A15 **Virei** Namibe, SW Angola 15°43′S 12°54′E
Vîrful Moldoveanu *see* Vârful Moldoveanu
35 R5 **Virgina Peak** ▲ Nevada, W USA 39°46′N 119°26′W
45 U9 **Virgin Gorda** *island* C British Virgin Islands
83 I22 **Virginia** Free State, C South Africa 28°06′S 26°53′E
30 K13 **Virginia** Illinois, N USA 39°57′N 90°12′W
29 W4 **Virginia** Minnesota, N USA 47°31′N 92°32′W
21 T6 **Virginia** *off.* Commonwealth of Virginia, *also known as* Mother of Presidents, Mother of States, Old Dominion. ◈ *state* NE USA
21 Y7 **Virginia Beach** Virginia, NE USA 36°51′N 75°59′W
33 R11 **Virginia City** Montana, NW USA 45°17′N 111°54′W
35 Q6 **Virginia City** Nevada, W USA 39°19′N 119°39′W
14 H8 **Virginiatown** Ontario, S Canada 48°09′N 79°35′W
Virgin Islands *see* British Virgin Islands
45 T9 **Virgin Islands (US)** *var.* Virgin Islands of the United States; *prev.* Danish West Indies. ◇ *US unincorporated territory* E West Indies
Virgin Islands of the United States *see* Virgin Islands (US)
45 T9 **Virgin Passage** *passage* Puerto Rico/Virgin Islands (US)
35 Y10 **Virgin River** ≈ Nevada/Utah, W USA
Virihaur *see* Virihaure
92 H12 **Virihaure** *Lapp.* Virihávrre, *var.* Virihaur. ◎ N Sweden
Virihávrre *see* Virihaure
167 T11 **Virôchey** Rôtânôkiri, NE Cambodia 13°59′N 106°49′E
93 N19 **Virolahti** Etelä-Suomi, S Finland 60°33′N 27°37′E
30 J8 **Viroqua** Wisconsin, N USA 43°33′N 90°54′W
112 G8 **Virovitica** *Ger.* Virovititz, *Hung.* Verőcze; *prev. Ger.* Werowitz. Virovitica-Podravina, NE Croatia 45°49′N 17°25′E
112 G8 **Virovitica-Podravina** *off.* Virovitičko-Podravska Županija. ◈ *province* NE Croatia
Virovitičko-Podravska Županija *see* Virovitica-Podravina
Virovititz *see* Virovitica
113 J17 **Virpazar** S Montenegro 42°15′N 19°06′E
93 L17 **Virrat** *Swe.* Virdois. Länsi-Suomi, W Finland 62°14′N 23°50′E
95 M20 **Virserum** Kalmar, S Sweden 57°17′N 15°18′E
99 K25 **Virton** Luxembourg, SE Belgium 49°34′N 05°32′E
118 F5 **Virtsu** *Ger.* Werder. Läänemaa, W Estonia 58°35′N 23°33′E
56 C12 **Virú** La Libertad, C Peru 08°24′S 78°40′W
Virudhunagar *see* Virudunagar
155 H23 **Virudunagar** *var.* Virudhunagar; *prev.* Virudupatti. Tamil Nādu, SE India 09°35′N 77°57′E
Virudupatti *see* Virudunagar
118 I3 **Viru-Jaagupi** *Ger.* Sankt-Jakobi. Lääne-Virumaa, NE Estonia 59°14′N 26°29′E
57 N19 **Viru-Viru** *var.* Santa Cruz. ✈ (Santa Cruz) Santa Cruz, C Bolivia 17°49′S 63°12′W
113 E15 **Vis** *It.* Lissa; *anc.* Issa. *island* S Croatia
Vis *see* Fish
118 I12 **Visaginas** *prev.* Sniečkus. Utena, E Lithuania 55°36′N 26°22′E
155 M15 **Visākhapatnam** *var.* Vishakhapatnam. Andhra Pradesh, SE India 17°45′N 83°19′E
35 R11 **Visalia** California, W USA 36°19′N 119°19′W
Vişău *see* Vişeu
95 P19 **Visby** *Ger.* Wisby. Gotland, SE Sweden 57°37′N 18°20′E
197 N9 **Viscount Melville Sound** *prev.* Melville Sound. *sound* Northwest Territories, N Canada
99 L19 **Visé** Liège, E Belgium 50°44′N 05°42′E
112 K13 **Višegrad** Republika Srpska, SE Bosnia and Herzegovina 43°46′N 19°18′E
58 L12 **Viseu** Pará, NE Brazil 01°10′S 46°09′W
104 H7 **Viseu** *prev.* Vizeu. Viseu, N Portugal 40°40′N 07°55′W
104 H7 **Viseu** *var.* Vizeu. ◈ *district* N Portugal
116 I8 **Vişeu** *Hung.* Visó; *prev.* Vişău. ≈ NW Romania
116 I8 **Vişeu de Sus** *var.* Vişeul de Sus, *Ger.* Oberwischau, *Hung.* Felsővisó. Maramureş, N Romania 47°43′N 23°24′E
Vişeul de Sus *see* Vişeu de Sus
Vishakhapatnam *see* Visākhapatnam
125 R10 **Vishera** ≈ NW Russian Federation
95 J19 **Viskafors** Västra Götaland, S Sweden 57°37′N 12°50′E
95 J20 **Viskan** ≈ S Sweden
95 L21 **Vislanda** Kronoberg, S Sweden 56°46′N 14°30′E
Vislinskiy Zaliv *see* Vistula Lagoon
Visó *see* Vişeu
112 H13 **Visoko** ◈ Federacija Bosna I Hercegovina, C Bosnia and Herzegovina
106 A9 **Viso, Monte** ▲ NW Italy 44°42′N 07°04′E
108 E10 **Visp** Valais, SW Switzerland 46°18′N 07°53′E
108 E10 **Vispa** ≈ S Switzerland
95 M21 **Vissefjärda** Kalmar, S Sweden 56°31′N 15°34′E
100 I11 **Visselhövede** Niedersachsen, NW Germany 52°58′N 09°36′E
95 G23 **Vissenbjerg** Syddtjylland, C Denmark 55°23′N 10°08′E
35 U17 **Vista** California, W USA 33°12′N 117°14′W
58 C11 **Vista Alegre** Amazonas, NW Brazil 01°23′N 68°13′W
114 J13 **Vistonída, Límni** ◎ NE Greece
Vistula *see* Wisła
119 A14 **Vistula Lagoon** *Ger.* Frisches Haff, *Pol.* Zalew Wiślany, *Rus.* Vislinskiy Zaliv. *lagoon* Poland/Russian Federation
114 I8 **Vit** ≈ NW Bulgaria
Vitebsk *see* Vitsyebsk
Vitebskaya Oblast' *see* Vitsyebskaya Voblasts'
107 H14 **Viterbo** *anc.* Vicus Elbii. Lazio, C Italy 42°25′N 12°08′E
112 H12 **Vitez** Federacija Bosna I Hercegovina, C Bosnia and Herzegovina 44°08′N 17°47′E
167 S14 **Vi Thanh** Cân Thơ, S Vietnam 09°45′N 105°28′E
Viti *see* Fiji
186 E7 **Vitiaz Strait** *strait* NE Papua New Guinea
104 J7 **Vitigudino** Castilla y León, N Spain 41°00′N 06°26′W
175 Q9 **Viti Levu** *island* W Fiji
187 W15 **Viti Levu** *island* W Fiji
123 O11 **Vitim** ≈ C Russian Federation
123 O12 **Vitimskiy** Irkutskaya Oblast', C Russian Federation 58°12′N 113°10′E
109 V2 **Vitis** Niederösterreich, N Austria 48°45′N 15°09′E
59 O20 **Vitória** *state capital* Espírito Santo, SE Brazil 20°19′S 40°21′W
Vitoria *see* Vitoria-Gasteiz
Vitoria Bank *see* Vitória Seamount
59 N18 **Vitória da Conquista** Bahia, E Brazil 14°53′S 40°52′W
105 P3 **Vitoria-Gasteiz** *var.* Vitoria, *Eng.* Vittoria. País Vasco, N Spain 42°51′N 02°40′W
65 J16 **Vitória Seamount** *var.* Victoria Bank, Vitoria Bank. *undersea feature* C Atlantic Ocean 18°48′S 37°24′W
112 F13 **Vitorog** ▲ SW Bosnia and Herzegovina 44°06′N 17°03′E
102 J6 **Vitré** Ille-et-Vilaine, NW France 48°07′N 01°12′W
103 R5 **Vitry-le-François** Marne, N France 48°43′N 04°36′E
114 D13 **Vítsi** *var.* Vítsoi. ▲ N Greece 40°39′N 21°23′E
Vítsoi *see* Vítsi
118 N13 **Vitsyebsk** *Rus.* Vitebsk. Vitsyebskaya Voblasts', NE Belarus 55°11′N 30°10′E
118 K13 **Vitsyebskaya Voblasts'** *prev. Rus.* Vitebskaya Oblast'. ◈ *province* N Belarus
92 J11 **Vittangi** *Lapp.* Vazáš. Norrbotten, N Sweden 67°40′N 21°39′E
103 R8 **Vitteaux** Côte d'Or, C France 47°24′N 04°31′E
103 S6 **Vittel** Vosges, NE France 48°13′N 05°57′E
95 N15 **Vittinge** Västmanland, C Sweden 59°52′N 17°04′E
107 K25 **Vittoria** Sicilia, Italy, C Mediterranean Sea 36°56′N 14°30′E
Vittoria *see* Vitoria-Gasteiz
106 I7 **Vittorio Veneto** Veneto, NE Italy 45°59′N 12°18′E
175 Q7 **Vityaz Trench** *undersea feature* W Pacific Ocean
108 G8 **Vitznau** Luzern, W Switzerland 47°01′N 08°28′E
104 I1 **Viveiro** Galicia, NW Spain 43°39′N 07°35′W
105 S9 **Viver** Valenciana, E Spain 39°55′N 00°36′W
103 Q13 **Viverais, Monts du** ▲▲ C France
122 L9 **Vivi** ≈ N Russian Federation
22 F4 **Vivian** Louisiana, S USA 32°52′N 93°59′W
29 N10 **Vivian** South Dakota, N USA 43°53′N 100°16′W
103 R13 **Viviers** Ardèche, E France 44°31′N 04°40′E
Vivis *see* Vevey
83 K19 **Vivo** Limpopo, NE South Africa 22°58′S 29°13′E
102 L10 **Vivonne** Vienne, W France 46°25′N 00°15′E
Vizakna *see* Ocna Sibiului
105 O2 **Vizcaya** *Basq.* Bizkaia. ◈ *province* País Vasco, N Spain
Vizcaya, Golfo de *see* Biscay, Bay of
136 C10 **Vize** Kırklareli, NW Turkey 41°34′N 27°45′E
122 K4 **Vize, Ostrov** *island* Severnaya Zemlya, N Russian Federation
Vizeu *see* Viseu
155 M15 **Vizianagaram** *var.* Vizianagram. Andhra Pradesh, E India 18°07′N 83°25′E
Vizianagram *see* Vizianagaram
103 S12 **Vizille** Isère, E France 45°05′N 05°46′E
125 R11 **Vizinga** Respublika Komi, NW Russian Federation 61°06′N 50°09′E
116 M13 **Viziru** Brăila, SE Romania 45°00′N 27°43′E
113 K21 **Vjosës, Lumi i** *var.* Vijosa, Vijosë, *Gk.* Aóos. ≈ Albania/Greece *see also* Aóos
Vjosës, Lumi i *see* Aóos
99 H18 **Vlaams Brabant** ◈ *province* C Belgium
99 G18 **Vlaanderen** *Eng.* Flanders, *Fr.* Flandre. *cultural region* Belgium/France
98 G12 **Vlaardingen** Zuid-Holland, SW Netherlands 51°55′N 04°21′E
116 F10 **Vlădeasa, Vârful** *prev.* Vîrful Vlădeasa. ▲ NW Romania 46°45′N 22°46′E
Vlădeasa, Vîrful *see* Vlădeasa, Vârful
113 P16 **Vladičin Han** Serbia, SE Serbia 42°44′N 22°04′E
127 O16 **Vladikavkaz** *prev.* Dzaudzhikau, Ordzhonikidze. Respublika Severnaya Osetiya, SW Russian Federation 42°58′N 44°41′E
126 M3 **Vladimir** Vladimirskaya Oblast', W Russian Federation 56°09′N 40°21′E
Vladimirets *see* Voldymyerets'
144 M7 **Vladimirovka** Kostanay, N Kazakhstan 53°30′N 64°02′E
Vladimirovka *see* Yuzhno-Sakhalinsk
126 L3 **Vladimirskaya Oblast'** ◈ *province* W Russian Federation
126 I3 **Vladimirskiy Tupik** Smolenskaya Oblast', W Russian Federation 55°45′N 33°25′E
Vladimir-Volynskiy *see* Volodymyr-Volyns'kyy
123 Q7 **Vladivostok** Primorskiy Kray, SE Russian Federation 43°09′N 131°53′E
117 U13 **Vladyslavivka** Avtonomna Respublika Krym, S Ukraine 45°09′N 35°25′E
98 P6 **Vlagtwedde** Groningen, NE Netherlands 53°02′N 07°07′E
Vlajna *see* Kukavica
112 J12 **Vlasenica** ◈ Republika Srpska, E Bosnia and Herzegovina
112 G12 **Vlašić** ▲ C Bosnia and Herzegovina 44°18′N 17°40′E
111 D17 **Vlašim** *Ger.* Wlaschim. Středočesky Kraj, C Czech Republic 49°42′N 14°54′E
113 P15 **Vlasotince** Serbia, SE Serbia 42°58′N 22°07′E
123 Q7 **Vlasovo** Respublika Sakha (Yakutiya), NE Russian Federation 70°41′N 134°49′E
98 I11 **Vleuten** Utrecht, C Netherlands 52°07′N 05°01′E
98 I5 **Vlieland** *Fris.* Flylân. *island* Waddeneilanden, N Netherlands
98 I5 **Vliestroom** *strait* NW Netherlands
99 J14 **Vlijmen** Noord-Brabant, S Netherlands 51°42′N 05°14′E
99 E15 **Vlissingen** *Eng.* Flushing, *Fr.* Flessingue. Zeeland, SW Netherlands 51°26′N 03°34′E
Vlodava *see* Włodawa
Vlonë/Vlora *see* Vlorë
113 K22 **Vlorë** *prev.* Vlonë, *It.* Valona, Vlora. Vlorë, SW Albania 40°28′N 19°31′E
113 K22 **Vlorë** ◈ *district* SW Albania
113 K22 **Vlorës, Gjiri i** *var.* Valona Bay. *bay* SW Albania
Vlotslavsk *see* Włocławek
111 C16 **Vltava** *Ger.* Moldau. ≈ W Czech Republic
126 K3 **Vnukovo** ✈ (Moskva) Gorod Moskva, W Russian Federation 55°30′N 36°52′E
146 L11 **Vobkent** *Rus.* Vabkent. Buxoro Viloyati, C Uzbekistan 40°01′N 64°25′E
25 Q9 **Voca** Texas, SW USA 30°58′N 99°09′W
109 R5 **Vöcklabruck** Oberösterreich, NW Austria 48°01′N 13°38′E
112 D13 **Vodice** Šibenik-Knin, S Croatia 43°46′N 15°46′E
124 K10 **Vodlozero, Ozero** ◎ NW Russian Federation
112 A10 **Vodnjan** *It.* Dignano d'Istria. Istra, NW Croatia 44°57′N 13°51′E
125 S9 **Vodnyy** Respublika Komi, NW Russian Federation 63°31′N 53°21′E
145 V15 **Vodokhranilishche Kapshagay** *Kaz.* Qapshagay Böyeni; *prev.* Kapchagayskoye Vodokhranilishche. ▦ SE Kazakhstan
124 I6 **Vodokhranilishche, Kumskoye** ◎ NW Russian Federation
95 G20 **Vodskov** Nordjylland, N Denmark 57°07′N 10°02′E
92 H4 **Vogar** Sudurnes, SW Iceland 63°58′N 22°20′W
Vogelkop *see* Doberai, Jazirah
77 X15 **Vogel Peak** *prev.* Dimlang. ▲ E Nigeria 08°16′N 11°44′E
101 H17 **Vogelsberg** ▲▲ C Germany
106 D8 **Voghera** Lombardia, N Italy 44°59′N 09°01′E
112 I13 **Vogošća** Federacija Bosna I Hercegovina, SE Bosnia and Herzegovina 43°55′N 18°20′E
101 M17 **Vogtland** *historical region* E Germany
125 V12 **Vogul'skiy Kamen', Gora** ▲ NW Russian Federation 60°10′N 58°41′E
187 P16 **Voh** Province Nord, C New Caledonia 20°57′S 164°41′E
Vohémar *see* Iharaña
172 H8 **Vohimena, Tanjona** *Fr.* Cap Sainte Marie. *headland* S Madagascar 25°20′S 45°06′E
172 J6 **Vohipeno** Fianarantsoa, SE Madagascar 22°21′S 47°51′E
118 H5 **Võhma** *Ger.* Wöchma. Viljandimaa, S Estonia 58°37′N 25°34′E
81 J20 **Voi** Coast, S Kenya 03°23′S 38°35′E
76 K15 **Voinjama** N Liberia 08°25′N 09°42′W
103 S12 **Voiron** Isère, E France 45°22′N 05°35′E
109 V8 **Voitsberg** Steiermark, SE Austria 47°04′N 15°09′E
95 F24 **Vojens** *Ger.* Woyens. Syddanmark, SW Denmark 55°15′N 09°19′E
112 K9 **Vojvodina** *Ger.* Wojwodina. Vojvodina, N Serbia
15 S6 **Volant** ≈ Québec, SE Canada
Volaterrae *see* Volterra
43 P15 **Volcán** *var.* Hato del Volcán. Chiriquí, W Panama 08°45′N 82°38′W
Volcano Islands *see* Kazan-rettō
Volchansk *see* Vovchans'k
Volchya *see* Vovcha
94 D10 **Volda** Møre og Romsdal, S Norway 62°07′N 06°04′E
116 K3 **Voldymyerets'** *Russ.* Vladimirets. Rivnens'ka Oblast', NW Ukraine 51°24′N 25°52′E
98 J9 **Volendam** Noord-Holland, C Netherlands 52°30′N 05°04′E
124 L15 **Volga** Yaroslavskaya Oblast', W Russian Federation 57°56′N 38°23′E
29 R10 **Volga** South Dakota, N USA 44°19′N 96°55′W
122 C11 **Volga** ≈ NW Russian Federation
Volga-Baltic Waterway *see* Volgo-Baltiyskiy Kanal
Volga Uplands *see* Privolzhskaya Vozvyshennost'
124 L13 **Volgo-Baltiyskiy Kanal** *var.* Volga-Baltic Waterway. *canal* NW Russian Federation
126 M12 **Volgodonsk** Rostovskaya Oblast', SW Russian Federation 47°35′N 42°03′E
127 O10 **Volgograd** *prev.* Stalingrad, Tsaritsyn. Volgogradskaya Oblast', SW Russian Federation 48°42′N 44°29′E
127 N9 **Volgogradskaya Oblast'** ◈ *province* SW Russian Federation
127 P10 **Volgogradskoye Vodokhranilishche** ▦ SW Russian Federation
101 J19 **Volkach** Bayern, C Germany 49°51′N 10°15′E
109 U9 **Völkermarkt** *Slvn.* Velikovec. Kärnten, S Austria 46°40′N 14°38′E
124 I12 **Volkhov** Leningradskaya Oblast', NW Russian Federation 59°56′N 32°19′E
101 D20 **Völklingen** Saarland, SW Germany 49°15′N 06°51′E
Volkovysk *see* Vawkavysk
Volkovyskiye Vysoty *see* Vawkavyskaye Wzvyshsha
83 K22 **Volksrust** Mpumalanga, E South Africa 27°22′S 29°54′E
98 L8 **Vollenhove** Overijssel, N Netherlands 52°40′N 05°58′E
119 L16 **Volma** ≈ C Belarus
Volmari *see* Valmiera
117 W9 **Volnovakha** Donets'ka Oblast', SE Ukraine 47°36′N 37°32′E
116 K6 **Volochys'k** Khmel'nyts'ka Oblast', W Ukraine 49°32′N 26°14′E
117 O6 **Volodarka** Kyyivs'ka Oblast', N Ukraine 49°31′N 29°55′E
117 W9 **Volodars'ke** Donets'ka Oblast', E Ukraine 47°11′N 37°19′E
127 R13 **Volodarskiy** Astrakhanskaya Oblast', SW Russian Federation 46°23′N 48°39′E
Volodarskoye *see* Saumalkol'
117 N8 **Volodars'k-Volyns'kyy** Zhytomyrs'ka Oblast', N Ukraine 50°37′N 28°28′E
116 I3 **Volodymyr-Volyns'kyy** *Pol.* Włodzimierz, *Rus.* Vladimir-Volynskiy. Volyns'ka Oblast', NW Ukraine 50°51′N 24°19′E
124 L14 **Vologda** Vologodskaya Oblast', W Russian Federation 59°10′N 39°55′E
124 L12 **Vologodskaya Oblast'** ◈ *province* NW Russian Federation
126 K3 **Volokolamsk** Moskovskaya Oblast', W Russian Federation 56°03′N 35°57′E
126 K9 **Volokonovka** Belgorodskaya Oblast', W Russian Federation 50°30′N 37°54′E
115 G16 **Vólos** Thessalía, C Greece 39°21′N 22°58′E
124 M11 **Voloshka** Arkhangel'skaya Oblast', NW Russian Federation 61°19′N 40°06′E
Vološinovo *see* Novi Bečej
116 H7 **Volovets'** Zakarpats'ka Oblast', W Ukraine 48°42′N 23°12′E
Volozhin *see* Valozhyn
127 Q7 **Vol'sk** Saratovskaya Oblast', W Russian Federation 52°04′N 47°20′E
77 Q17 **Volta** ≈ SE Ghana
Volta Blanche *see* White Volta
77 P16 **Volta, Lake** ▦ SE Ghana
Volta Noire *see* Black Volta
60 O9 **Volta Redonda** Rio de Janeiro, SE Brazil 22°31′S 44°05′W
Volta Rouge *see* Red Volta
106 F12 **Volterra** *anc.* Volaterrae. Toscana, C Italy 43°23′N 10°52′E
107 K17 **Volturno** ≈ S Italy
113 I15 **Volujak** ▲▲ NW Montenegro
Volunteer Island *see* Starbuck Island
65 F24 **Volunteer Point** *headland* East Falkland, Falkland Islands 51°32′S 57°44′W
114 H13 **Vólvi, Límni** ◎ N Greece
Volyn *see* Volyns'ka Oblast'
116 I3 **Volyns'ka Oblast'** *var.* Volyn, *Rus.* Volynskaya Oblast'. ◈ *province* NW Ukraine
Volynskaya Oblast' *see* Volyns'ka Oblast'
127 Q3 **Volzhsk** Respublika Mariy El, W Russian Federation 55°53′N 48°21′E
127 O10 **Volzhskiy** Volgogradskaya Oblast', SW Russian Federation 48°49′N 44°40′E
172 I7 **Vondrozo** Fianarantsoa, SE Madagascar 22°50′S 47°20′E
39 P10 **Von Frank Mountain** ▲ Alaska, USA 63°36′N 154°29′W
115 C17 **Vónitsa** Dytikí Elláda, W Greece 38°55′N 20°53′E
118 J6 **Võnnu** *Ger.* Wendau. Tartumaa, SE Estonia 58°17′N 27°06′E
98 G12 **Voorburg** Zuid-Holland, W Netherlands 52°04′N 04°22′E
98 H11 **Voorschoten** Zuid-Holland, W Netherlands 52°08′N 04°26′E
98 M11 **Voorst** Gelderland, E Netherlands 52°10′N 06°10′E
98 K11 **Voorthuizen** Gelderland, C Netherlands 52°12′N 05°36′E
92 L2 **Vopnafjördhur** Austurland, E Iceland 65°45′N 14°51′W
92 L2 **Vopnafjördhur** *bay* E Iceland
Vora *see* Vorë
119 H15 **Voranava** *Pol.* Werenów, *Rus.* Voronovo. Hrodzyenskaya Voblasts', W Belarus 54°09′N 25°19′E
108 I8 **Vorarlberg** *off.* Land Vorarlberg. ◈ *state* W Austria
Vorarlberg, Land *see* Vorarlberg
109 X7 **Vorau** Steiermark, E Austria 47°22′N 15°55′E
98 N11 **Vorden** Gelderland, E Netherlands 52°07′N 06°18′E
108 H9 **Vorderrhein** ≈ SE Switzerland
92 J2 **Vordhufell** ▲ N Iceland 65°42′N 18°45′W
95 I24 **Vordingborg** Sjælland, SE Denmark 55°01′N 11°55′E
113 K19 **Vorë** *var.* Vora. Tiranë, W Albania 41°23′N 19°37′E
115 H17 **Vóreies Sporádes** *var.* Vóreioi Sporádes, Vórioi Sporádhes, *Eng.* Northern Sporades. *island group* E Greece
Vóreioi Sporádes *see* Vóreies Sporádes
115 J17 **Vóreion Aigaíon** *Eng.* Aegean North. ◈ *region* SE Greece
115 G18 **Vóreios Evvoïkós Kólpos** *var.* Voreiós Evvoïkós Kólpos. *gulf* E Greece
197 S16 **Voring Plateau** *undersea feature* N Norwegian Sea 67°00′N 04°00′E
Vórioi Sporádhes *see* Vóreies Sporádes
125 W4 **Vorkuta** Respublika Komi, NW Russian Federation 67°27′N 64°E
95 I14 **Vorma** ≈ S Norway
118 E4 **Vormsi** *var.* Vormsi Saar, *Ger.* Worms, *Swed.* Ormsö. *island* W Estonia
Vormsi Saar *see* Vormsi
127 N7 **Vorona** ≈ W Russian Federation
126 L7 **Voronezh** Voronezhskaya Oblast', W Russian Federation 51°40′N 39°13′E
126 L7 **Voronezh** ≈ W Russian Federation
126 K8 **Voronezhskaya Oblast'** ◈ *province* W Russian Federation
Voronovitsya *see* Voronovytsya
Voronovo *see* Voranava
117 N6 **Voronovytsya** *Rus.* Voronovitsya. Vinnyts'ka Oblast', C Ukraine 49°06′N 28°49′E
122 K7 **Vorontsovo** Krasnoyarskiy Kray, N Russian Federation 71°45′N 83°31′E
124 K3 **Voron'ya** ≈ NW Russian Federation
Voropayevo *see* Varapayeva
Voroshilov *see* Ussuriysk
Voroshilovgrad *see* Luhans'ka Oblast', Ukraine
Voroshilovgrad *see* Luhans'k, Ukraine
Voroshilovgradskaya Oblast' *see* Luhans'ka Oblast'
Voroshilovsk *see* Stavropol', Russian Federation
Voroshilovsk *see* Alchevs'k
137 V13 **Vorotan** *Az.* Bärguşad. ≈ Armenia/Azerbaijan
127 P3 **Vorotynets** Nizhegorodskaya Oblast', W Russian Federation 56°06′N 46°06′E
117 S3 **Vorozhba** Sums'ka Oblast', NE Ukraine 51°10′N 34°15′E
117 T5 **Vorskla** ≈ Russian Federation/Ukraine
99 I17 **Vorst** Antwerpen, N Belgium 51°06′N 05°01′E
83 G21 **Vorstershoop** North-West, N South Africa 25°46′S 22°57′E
118 H6 **Võrtsjärv** *Ger.* Wirz-See. ◎ SE Estonia
118 J7 **Võru** *Ger.* Werro. Võrumaa, SE Estonia 57°51′N 27°01′E
147 R11 **Vorukh** N Tajikistan 39°51′N 70°34′E
118 I7 **Võrumaa** *off.* Võru Maakond. ◈ *province* SE Estonia
Võru Maakond *see* Võrumaa
83 G24 **Vosburg** Northern Cape, W South Africa 30°35′S 22°52′E
147 Q14 **Vose'** *Rus.* Vose; *prev.* Aral. SW Tajikistan 37°51′N 69°31′E
103 S6 **Vosges** ◈ *department* NE France
103 U6 **Vosges** ▲▲ NE France
124 K13 **Voskresenkoye** Vologodskaya Oblast', NW Russian Federation 59°25′N 37°56′E
126 L4 **Voskresensk** Moskovskaya Oblast', W Russian Federation 55°19′N 38°42′E
127 P2 **Voskresenskoye** Nizhegorodskaya Oblast', W Russian Federation 57°00′N 45°33′E
127 V6 **Voskresenskoye** Respublika Bashkortostan, W Russian Federation 53°07′N 56°07′E
94 D13 **Voss** Hordaland, S Norway 60°38′N 06°25′E
94 D13 **Voss** *physical region* S Norway
99 I16 **Vosselaar** Antwerpen, N Belgium 51°19′N 04°55′E
94 D13 **Vosso** ≈ S Norway
Vostochno-Kazakhstanskaya Oblast' *see* Vostochnyy Kazakhstan
123 S5 **Vostochno-Sibirskoye More** *Eng.* East Siberian Sea. *sea* Arctic Ocean
145 X10 **Vostochnyy Kazakhstan** *off.* Vostochno-Kazakhstanskaya Oblast', *var.* East Kazakhstan, *Kaz.* Shyghys Qazagastan Oblysy. ◈ *province* E Kazakhstan
122 L13 **Vostochnyy Sayan** *Eng.* Eastern Sayans, *Mong.* Dzüün Soyonï Nuruu. ▲▲ Mongolia/Russian Federation
Vostock Island *see* Vostok Island
195 U10 **Vostok** *Russian research station* Antarctica 77°18′S 105°32′E
191 X5 **Vostok Island** *var.* Vostock Island; *prev.* Stavers Island. *island* Line Islands, SE Kiribati
127 T2 **Votkinsk** Udmurtskaya Respublika, NW Russian Federation 57°04′N 54°00′E
125 U15 **Votkinskoye Vodokhranilishche** *var.* Votkinsk Reservoir. ▦ NW Russian Federation
Votkinsk Reservoir *see* Votkinskoye Vodokhranilishche
60 J7 **Votuporanga** São Paulo, S Brazil 20°26′S 49°53′W
104 H7 **Vouga, Rio** ≈ N Portugal
115 E14 **Voúrinos** ▲▲ N Greece
115 G24 **Voúxa, Akrotírio** *headland* Kríti, Greece, E Mediterranean Sea 35°37′N 23°34′E
103 R4 **Vouziers** Ardennes, N France 49°24′N 04°42′E
117 V7 **Vovcha** *Rus.* Volchya. ≈ E Ukraine
117 V4 **Vovchans'k** *Rus.* Volchansk. Kharkivs'ka Oblast', E Ukraine 50°19′N 36°55′E
103 N6 **Voves** Eure-et-Loir, C France 48°18′N 01°39′E
79 M14 **Vovodo** ≈ S Central African Republic
94 M12 **Voxna** Gävleborg, C Sweden 61°21′N 15°35′E
94 L11 **Voxnan** ≈ C Sweden
114 F7 **Voynishka Reka** ≈ NW Bulgaria
125 T9 **Voyvozh** Respublika Komi, NW Russian Federation 62°54′N 54°52′E
124 M12 **Vozhega** Vologodskaya Oblast', NW Russian Federation 60°27′N 40°11′E
124 L12 **Vozhe, Ozero** ◎ NW Russian Federation
117 Q9 **Voznesens'k** *Rus.* Voznesensk. Mykolayivs'ka Oblast', S Ukraine 47°34′N 31°21′E
124 J12 **Voznesen'ye** Leningradskaya Oblast', NW Russian Federation 61°00′N 35°24′E
144 J14 **Vozrozhdeniya, Ostrov** *Uzb.* Wozrojdeniye Oroli. *island* Kazakhstan/Uzbekistan
95 G20 **Vrå** *var.* Vraa. Nordjylland, N Denmark 57°21′N 09°57′E
Vraa *see* Vrå
114 H9 **Vrachesh** Sofiya, W Bulgaria 42°52′N 23°45′E
115 C19 **Vrachíonas** ▲ Zákynthos, Iónia Nisiá, Greece, C Mediterranean Sea 37°49′N 20°43′E
117 P8 **Vradiyivka** Mykolayivs'ka Oblast', S Ukraine 47°51′N 30°37′E
113 G14 **Vran** ▲ SW Bosnia and Herzegovina 43°35′N 17°30′E
116 K12 **Vrancea** ◈ *county* E Romania
147 T14 **Vrang** SE Tajikistan 37°03′N 72°26′E
123 T4 **Vrangelya, Ostrov** *Eng.* Wrangel Island. *island* NE Russian Federation
112 H13 **Vranica** ▲ C Bosnia and Herzegovina 43°57′N 17°43′E
113 O16 **Vranje** Serbia, SE Serbia 42°33′N 21°55′E
Vranov *see* Vranov nad Topl'ou
111 N19 **Vranov nad Topl'ou** *var.* Vranov, *Hung.* Varannó. Prešovský Kraj, E Slovakia 48°54′N 21°41′E
114 H8 **Vratsa** Vratsa, NW Bulgaria 43°13′N 23°34′E
114 H8 **Vratsa** ◈ *province* NW Bulgaria
114 F10 **Vrattsa** *prev.* Mirovo. Kyustendil, W Bulgaria 42°15′N 22°33′E
112 G11 **Vrbanja** ≈ NW Bosnia and Herzegovina
112 K9 **Vrbas** Vojvodina, NW Serbia 45°34′N 19°39′E
112 G13 **Vrbas** ≈ N Bosnia and Herzegovina
112 E8 **Vrbovec** Zagreb, N Croatia 45°53′N 16°24′E
112 C9 **Vrbovsko** Primorje-Gorski Kotar, NW Croatia 45°22′N 15°06′E
111 E15 **Vrchlabí** *Ger.* Hohenelbe. Královéhradecký Kraj, N Czech Republic 50°38′N 15°35′E
83 J22 **Vrede** Free State, E South Africa 27°25′S 29°10′E
100 E13 **Vreden** Nordrhein-Westfalen, NW Germany 52°01′N 06°50′E
83 E25 **Vredenburg** Western Cape, SW South Africa 32°55′S 18°00′E
99 I23 **Vresse-sur-Semois** Namur, SE Belgium 49°52′N 04°56′E
95 L16 **Vretstorp** Örebro, C Sweden 59°03′N 14°51′E
113 G15 **Vrgorac** *prev.* Vrhgorac. Split-Dalmacija, SE Croatia 43°10′N 17°24′E
Vrhgorac *see* Vrgorac
109 T12 **Vrhnika** *Ger.* Oberlaibach. W Slovenia 45°57′N 14°18′E
155 I21 **Vriddhāchalam** Tamil Nādu, SE India 11°33′N 79°18′E
98 N6 **Vries** Drenthe, NE Netherlands 53°04′N 06°34′E
98 O10 **Vriezenveen** Overijssel, E Netherlands 52°25′N 06°37′E
95 L20 **Vrigstad** Jönköping, S Sweden 57°19′N 14°30′E
108 H9 **Vrin** Graubünden, S Switzerland 46°40′N 09°06′E
112 E13 **Vrlika** Split-Dalmacija, S Croatia 43°54′N 16°24′E
113 M14 **Vrnjačka Banja** Serbia, C Serbia 43°36′N 20°55′E
Vrondádhes/Vrondados *see* Vrontádos

◆ Country
● Country Capital
◇ Dependent Territory
○ Dependent Territory Capital
◈ Administrative Regions
✈ International Airport
▲ Mountain
▲▲ Mountain Range
🌋 Volcano
≈ River
◎ Lake
▦ Reservoir

115 *L18* **Vrontádos** *var.* Vrondados; *prev.* Vrondádhes. Chíos, E Greece *38°25′N 26°08′E*
98 *N9* **Vroomshoop** Overijssel, E Netherlands *52°28′N 06°35′E*
112 *N10* **Vršac** *Ger.* Werschetz, *Hung.* Versecz. Vojvodina, NE Serbia *45°08′N 21°18′E*
112 *M10* **Vršački Kanal** *canal* N Serbia
83 *H21* **Vryburg** North-West, N South Africa *26°57′S 24°44′E*
83 *K22* **Vryheid** KwaZulu/Natal, E South Africa *27°45′S 30°48′E*
111 *I18* **Vsetín** *Ger.* Wsetin. Zlínský Kraj, E Czech Republic *49°21′N 17°57′E*
111 *J20* **Vtáčnik** *Hung.* Madaras, Ptacsnik; *prev.* Ptačnik. ▲ W Slovakia *48°38′N 18°38′E*
Vuadil' *see* Wodil
114 *I11* **Vŭcha** ≈ SW Bulgaria
Vučitrn *see* Vushtrri
99 *J14* **Vught** Noord-Brabant, S Netherlands *51°37′N 05°19′E*
117 *W8* **Vuhledar** Donets'ka Oblast', E Ukraine *47°48′N 37°11′E*
112 *I9* **Vuka** ≈ E Croatia
113 *K17* **Vukël** *var.* Vukli. Shkodër, N Albania *42°29′N 19°39′E*
Vukli *see* Vukël
112 *J9* **Vukovar** *Hung.* Vukovár. Vukovar-Srijem, E Croatia *45°18′N 18°45′E*
Vukovarsko-Srijemska Županija *see* Vukovar-Srijem
112 *I10* **Vukovar-Srijem** *off.* Vukovarsko-Srijemska Županija. ◈ *province* E Croatia
125 *U8* **Vuktyl** Respublika Komi, NW Russian Federation *63°49′N 57°07′E*
11 *Q17* **Vulcan** Alberta, SW Canada *50°27′N 113°12′W*
116 *G12* **Vulcan** *Ger.* Wulkan, *Hung.* Zsilyvajdevulkán; *prev.* Crivadia Vulcanului, Vaidei, *Hung.* Sily-Vajdej, Vajdej. Hunedoara, W Romania *45°22′N 23°16′E*
116 *M12* **Vulcăneşti** *Rus.* Vulkaneshty. S Moldova *45°41′N 28°25′E*
107 *L22* **Vulcano, Isola** *island* Isole Eolie, S Italy
114 *G7* **Vŭlchedrŭm** Montana, NW Bulgaria *43°42′N 23°25′E*
114 *N8* **Vŭlchidol** *prev.* Kurt-Dere. Varna, E Bulgaria *43°25′N 27°33′E*
Vulkaneshty *see* Vulcăneşti
123 *V11* **Vulkannyy** Kamchatskiy Kray, E Russian Federation *53°01′N 158°26′E*
36 *J13* **Vulture Mountains** ▲▲ Arizona, SW USA
167 *T14* **Vung Tau** *prev. Fr.* Cape Saint Jacques, Cap Saint-Jacques. Ba Ria-Vung Tau, S Vietnam *10°21′N 107°04′E*
187 *X15* **Vunisea** Kadavu, SE Fiji *19°04′S 178°10′E*
Vuohčču *see* Vuotso
93 *N15* **Vuokatti** Oulu, C Finland *64°08′N 28°16′E*
93 *M15* **Vuolijoki** Oulu, C Finland *64°09′N 27°00′E*
Vuolleriebme *see* Vuollerim
92 *J13* **Vuollerim** *Lapp.* Vuolleriebme. Norrbotten, N Sweden *66°24′N 20°36′E*
Vuonnabahta *see* Varangerbotn
Vuoreija *see* Vardø
92 *L10* **Vuotso** *Lapp.* Vuohčču. Lappi, N Finland *68°04′N 27°05′E*
114 *J11* **Vŭrbitsa** *prev.* Filevo. Khaskovo, S Bulgaria *42°02′N 25°25′E*
114 *J12* **Vŭrbitsa** ≈ S Bulgaria
127 *Q4* **Vurnary** Chuvashskaya Respublika, W Russian Federation *55°30′N 46°59′E*
114 *G8* **Vŭrshets** Montana, NW Bulgaria *43°14′N 23°20′E*
Vusan *see* Busan
113 *N16* **Vushtrri** *Serb.* Vučitrn. N Kosovo *42°49′N 21°00′E*
119 *F17* **Vyalikaya Byerastavitsa** *Pol.* Brzostowica Wielka, *Rus.* Bol'shaya Berëstovitsa; *prev.* Velikaya Berestovitsa. Hrodzyenskaya Voblasts', SW Belarus *53°12′N 24°03′E*
119 *N20* **Vyaliki Bor** *Rus.* Velikiy Bor. Homyel'skaya Voblasts', SE Belarus *52°02′N 29°56′E*
119 *J18* **Vyaliki Rozhan** *Rus.* Bol'shoy Rozhan. Minskaya Voblasts', S Belarus *52°46′N 27°07′E*
124 *H10* **Vyartsilya** *Fin.* Värtsilä. Respublika Kareliya, NW Russian Federation *62°07′N 30°43′E*
119 *K17* **Vyasyeya** *Rus.* Veseya. Minskaya Voblasts', C Belarus *53°04′N 27°41′E*
125 *R15* **Vyatka** ≈ NW Russian Federation
Vyatka *see* Kirov
125 *S16* **Vyatskiye Polyany** Kirovskaya Oblast', NW Russian Federation *56°15′N 51°06′E*
123 *S14* **Vyazemskiy** Khabarovskiy Kray, SE Russian Federation *47°28′N 134°39′E*
126 *I4* **Vyaz'ma** Smolenskaya Oblast', W Russian Federation *55°09′N 34°20′E*
127 *N3* **Vyazniki** Vladimirskaya Oblast', W Russian Federation *56°15′N 42°06′E*
127 *O8* **Vyazovka** Volgogradskaya Oblast', SW Russian Federation *50°57′N 43°57′E*
119 *J14* **Vyazyn'** Minskaya Voblasts', NW Belarus *54°25′N 27°10′E*
124 *G11* **Vyborg** *Fin.* Viipuri. Leningradskaya Oblast', NW Russian Federation *60°44′N 28°47′E*
125 *P11* **Vychegda** *var.* Vichegda. ≈ NW Russian Federation
119 *L14* **Vyelyewshchyna** *Rus.* Velevshchina. Vitsyebskaya Voblasts', N Belarus *54°44′N 28°35′E*
119 *P16* **Vyeramyeyki** *Rus.* Veremeyki. Mahilyowskaya Voblasts', E Belarus *53°46′N 31°17′E*
118 *K11* **Vyerkhnyadzvinsk** *Rus.* Verkhnedvinsk. Vitsyebskaya Voblasts', N Belarus *55°47′N 27°56′E*
119 *P18* **Vyetka** *Rus.* Vetka. Homyel'skaya Voblasts', SE Belarus *52°33′N 31°10′E*
118 *L12* **Vyetryna** *Rus.* Vetrino. Vitsyebskaya Voblasts', N Belarus *55°25′N 28°28′E*
Vygonovskoye, Ozero *see* Vyhanashchanskaye, Vozyera
124 *J9* **Vygozero, Ozero** ◎ NW Russian Federation
119 *I18* **Vyhanashchanskaye, Vozyera** *prev.* Vozyera Vyhanawskaye, *Rus.* Ozero Vygonovskoye. ◎ SW Belarus
Vyhanawskaye, Vozyera *see* Vyhanashchanskaye, Vozyera
127 *N4* **Vyksa** Nizhegorodskaya Oblast', W Russian Federation *55°21′N 42°10′E*
117 *O12* **Vylkove** *Rus.* Vilkovo. Odes'ka Oblast', SW Ukraine *45°24′N 29°37′E*
125 *R9* **Vym'** ≈ NW Russian Federation
116 *H8* **Vynohradiv** *Cz.* Sevluš, *Hung.* Nagyszöllös, *Rus.* Vinogradov; *prev.* Sevlyush. Zakarpats'ka Oblast', W Ukraine *48°09′N 23°01′E*
124 *G13* **Vyritsa** Leningradskaya Oblast', NW Russian Federation *59°25′N 30°20′E*
97 *J19* **Vyrnwy** *Wel.* Afon Efyrnwy. ≈ E Wales, United Kingdom
145 *X9* **Vyshe Ivanovskiy Belak, Gora** ▲ E Kazakhstan *50°16′N 83°46′E*
117 *P4* **Vyshhorod** Kyyivs'ka Oblast', N Ukraine *50°36′N 30°28′E*
124 *I15* **Vyshniy Volochek** Tverskaya Oblast', W Russian Federation *57°37′N 34°33′E*
111 *G18* **Vyškov** *Ger.* Wischau. Jihomoravský Kraj, SE Czech Republic *49°17′N 17°01′E*
111 *E18* **Vysočina** *prev.* Jihlavský Kraj. ◈ *region* N Czech Republic
119 *E19* **Vysokaye** *Rus.* Vysokoye. Brestskaya Voblasts', SW Belarus *52°20′N 23°18′E*
111 *F17* **Vysoké Mýto** *Ger.* Hohenmauth. Pardubický Kraj, C Czech Republic *49°57′N 16°10′E*
117 *S9* **Vysokopillya** Khersons'ka Oblast', S Ukraine *47°28′N 33°30′E*
126 *K3* **Vysokovsk** Moskovskaya Oblast', W Russian Federation *56°12′N 36°42′E*
Vysokoye *see* Vysokaye
124 *K12* **Vytegra** Vologodskaya Oblast', NW Russian Federation *60°59′N 36°27′E*
116 *J8* **Vyzhnytsya** Chernivets'ka Oblast', W Ukraine *48°14′N 25°10′E*

W

77 *O14* **Wa** NW Ghana *10°07′N 02°28′W*
Waadt *see* Vaud
Waag *see* Váh
Waagbistritz *see* Považská Bystrica
Waagneustadtl *see* Nové Mesto nad Váhom
81 *M16* **Waajid** Gedo, SW Somalia *03°37′N 43°19′E*
98 *L13* **Waal** ≈ S Netherlands
187 *O16* **Waala** Province Nord, W New Caledonia *19°46′S 163°41′E*
99 *I14* **Waalwijk** Noord-Brabant, S Netherlands *51°42′N 05°04′E*
99 *E16* **Waarschoot** Oost-Vlaanderen, NW Belgium *51°09′N 03°35′E*
186 *C7* **Wabag** Enga, W Papua New Guinea *05°28′S 143°40′E*
15 *N7* **Wabano** ≈ Québec, SE Canada
11 *P11* **Wabasca** ≈ Alberta, SW Canada
31 *P12* **Wabash** Indiana, N USA *40°47′N 85°48′W*
29 *X9* **Wabasha** Minnesota, N USA *44°22′N 92°01′W*
31 *N13* **Wabash River** ≈ N USA
14 *C7* **Wabatongushi Lake** ◎ Ontario, S Canada
81 *L15* **Wabē Gestro Wenz** ≈ SE Ethiopia
14 *B9* **Wabos** Ontario, S Canada *46°48′N 84°06′W*
11 *W13* **Wabowden** Manitoba, C Canada *54°57′N 98°38′W*
110 *J9* **Wąbrzeźno** Kujawsko-pomorskie, C Poland *53°18′N 18°55′E*
21 *U12* **Waccamaw River** ≈ South Carolina, SE USA
23 *U11* **Waccasassa Bay** *bay* Florida, SE USA
99 *F16* **Wachtebeke** Oost-Vlaanderen, NW Belgium *51°10′N 03°52′E*
25 *T8* **Waco** Texas, SW USA *31°33′N 97°10′W*
26 *M3* **Waconda Lake** *var.* Great Elder Reservoir. ⊞ Kansas, C USA
Wadai *see* Ouaddaï
Wad Al-Hajarah *see* Guadalajara
164 *I12* **Wadayama** Hyōgo, Honshū, SW Japan *35°19′N 134°51′E*
80 *D10* **Wad Banda** Southern Kordofan, C Sudan *13°08′N 27°56′E*
75 *P9* **Waddān** NW Libya *29°10′N 16°08′E*
98 *J4* **Waddeneilanden** *Eng.* West Frisian Islands. *island group* N Netherlands
98 *J6* **Waddenzee** *var.* Wadden Zee. *sea* SE North Sea
Wadden Zee *see* Waddenzee
10 *L16* **Waddington, Mount** ▲ British Columbia, SW Canada *51°17′N 125°16′W*
98 *H12* **Waddinxveen** Zuid-Holland, C Netherlands *52°03′N 04°38′E*
11 *U15* **Wadena** Saskatchewan, S Canada *51°57′N 103°48′W*
29 *T6* **Wadena** Minnesota, N USA *46°27′N 95°07′W*
108 *G7* **Wädenswil** Zürich, N Switzerland *47°14′N 08°41′E*
21 *S11* **Wadesboro** North Carolina, SE USA *34°59′N 80°03′W*
155 *G16* **Wādi** Karnātaka, C India *17°00′N 76°58′E*
138 *G10* **Wādī as Sīr** *var.* Wadi es Sir. 'Ammān, NW Jordan *31°57′N 35°49′E*
Wadi es Sir *see* Wādī as Sīr
80 *F5* **Wadi Halfa** *var.* Wādī Ḥalfā'. Northern, N Sudan *21°46′N 31°17′E*
138 *G13* **Wādī Mūsā** *var.* Petra. Ma'ān, S Jordan *30°19′N 35°29′E*
23 *V4* **Wadley** Georgia, SE USA *32°52′N 82°24′W*
Wad Madanī *see* Wad Medani
80 *G10* **Wad Medani** *var.* Wad Madanī. Gezira, C Sudan *14°24′N 33°30′E*
80 *F10* **Wad Nimr** White Nile, C Sudan *14°32′N 32°10′E*
165 *U16* **Wadomari** Kagoshima, Okinoerabu-jima, SW Japan *27°25′N 128°40′E*
111 *K17* **Wadowice** Małopolskie, S Poland *49°54′N 19°29′E*
35 *R5* **Wadsworth** Nevada, W USA *39°39′N 119°16′W*
31 *T12* **Wadsworth** Ohio, N USA *41°01′N 81°43′W*
25 *T11* **Waelder** Texas, SW USA *29°42′N 97°16′W*
Waereghem *see* Waregem
163 *U13* **Wafangdian** *var.* Fuxian, Fu Xian. Liaoning, NE China *39°36′N 122°00′E*
171 *R13* **Waflia** Pulau Buru, E Indonesia *03°10′S 126°05′E*
Wagadugu *see* Ouagadougou
98 *K12* **Wageningen** Gelderland, SE Netherlands *51°58′N 05°40′E*
55 *V9* **Wageningen** Nickerie, NW Suriname *05°44′N 56°45′W*
9 *O8* **Wager Bay** *inlet* Nunavut, N Canada
183 *P10* **Wagga Wagga** New South Wales, SE Australia *35°11′S 147°22′E*
180 *J13* **Wagin** Western Australia *33°16′S 117°26′E*
108 *H8* **Wägitaler See** ◎ SW Switzerland
29 *P12* **Wagner** South Dakota, N USA *43°04′N 98°17′W*
27 *Q9* **Wagoner** Oklahoma, C USA *35°58′N 92°23′W*
37 *U10* **Wagon Mound** New Mexico, SW USA *36°00′N 104°42′W*
32 *J14* **Wagontire** Oregon, NW USA *43°15′N 119°51′W*
110 *H10* **Wągrowiec** Wielkopolskie, C Poland *52°49′N 17°11′E*
149 *U6* **Wāh** Punjab, NE Pakistan *33°50′N 72°44′E*
171 *S13* **Wahai** Pulau Seram, E Indonesia *02°48′S 129°29′E*
169 *V10* **Wahau, Sungai** ≈ Borneo, C Indonesia
Wahaybah, Ramlat Al *see* Wahībah, Ramlat Āl
80 *D13* **Wahda** *var.* Unity State. ◈ *state* N South Sudan
38 *D9* **Wahiawā** *var.* Wahiawa. O'ahu, Hawaii, USA, C Pacific Ocean *21°30′N 158°01′W*
Wahībah, Ramlat Ahl *see* Wahībah, Ramlat Āl
141 *Y9* **Wahībah, Ramlat Āl** *var.* Ramlat Ahl Wahībah, Ramlat Al Wahaybah, *Eng.* Wahībah Sands. *desert* N Oman
Wahībah Sands *see* Wahībah, Ramlat Āl
101 *E16* **Wahn** ✈ (Köln) Nordrhein-Westfalen, W Germany *50°51′N 07°09′E*
29 *R15* **Wahoo** Nebraska, C USA *41°12′N 96°37′W*
29 *R6* **Wahpeton** North Dakota, N USA *46°16′N 96°36′W*
Wahran *see* Oran
36 *J6* **Wah Wah Mountains** ▲▲ Utah, W USA
38 *D9* **Waialua** O'ahu, Hawaii, USA, C Pacific Ocean *21°34′N 158°07′W*
38 *D9* **Wai'anae** *var.* Waianae. O'ahu, Hawaii, USA, C Pacific Ocean *21°26′N 158°11′W*
184 *Q8* **Waiapu** ≈ North Island, New Zealand
185 *I17* **Waiau** Canterbury, South Island, New Zealand *42°39′S 173°03′E*
185 *I17* **Waiau** ≈ South Island, New Zealand
185 *B23* **Waiau** ≈ South Island, New Zealand
101 *H21* **Waiblingen** Baden-Württemberg, S Germany *48°49′N 09°19′E*
Waidhofen *see* Waidhofen an der Ybbs, Niederösterreich, Austria
Waidhofen *see* Waidhofen an der Thaya, Niederösterreich, Austria
109 *V2* **Waidhofen an der Thaya** *var.* Waidhofen. Niederösterreich, NE Austria *48°49′N 15°17′E*
109 *U5* **Waidhofen an der Ybbs** *var.* Waidhofen. Niederösterreich, E Austria *47°58′N 14°47′E*
171 *T11* **Waigeo, Pulau** *island* Maluku, E Indonesia
184 *L5* **Waiheke Island** *island* N New Zealand
184 *M7* **Waihi** Waikato, North Island, New Zealand *37°22′S 175°51′E*
185 *C20* **Waihou** ≈ North Island, New Zealand
Waikaboebak *see* Waikabubak
171 *N17* **Waikabubak** *prev.* Waikaboebak. Pulau Sumba, C Indonesia *09°40′S 119°25′E*
185 *D23* **Waikaia** ≈ South Island, New Zealand
185 *D23* **Waikaka** Southland, South Island, New Zealand *45°55′S 168°59′E*
184 *L13* **Waikanae** Wellington, North Island, New Zealand *40°52′S 175°03′E*
184 *M7* **Waikare, Lake** ◎ North Island, New Zealand
184 *O9* **Waikaremoana, Lake** ◎ North Island, New Zealand
185 *I17* **Waikari** Canterbury, South Island, New Zealand *42°50′S 172°41′E*
184 *L8* **Waikato** *off.* Waikato Region. ◈ *region* North Island, New Zealand
184 *M8* **Waikato** ≈ North Island, New Zealand
Waikato Region *see* Waikato
182 *J9* **Waikerie** South Australia *34°12′S 139°57′E*
185 *F23* **Waikouaiti** Otago, South Island, New Zealand *45°36′S 170°39′E*
38 *H11* **Wailea** Hawaii, USA, C Pacific Ocean *19°53′N 155°07′W*
38 *F10* **Wailuku** Maui, Hawaii, USA, C Pacific Ocean *20°53′N 156°30′W*
185 *H18* **Waimakariri** ≈ South Island, New Zealand
38 *D9* **Waimānalo Beach** *var.* Waimanalo Beach. O'ahu, Hawaii, USA, C Pacific Ocean *21°20′N 157°42′W*
185 *G15* **Waimangaroa** West Coast, South Island, New Zealand *41°41′S 171°49′E*
185 *G21* **Waimate** Canterbury, South Island, New Zealand *44°44′S 171°03′E*
38 *G11* **Waimea** *var.* Kamuela. Hawaii, USA, C Pacific Ocean *20°02′N 155°20′W*
38 *D9* **Waimea** *var.* Maunawai. O'ahu, Hawaii, USA, C Pacific Ocean *21°39′N 158°04′W*
38 *B8* **Waimea** Kaua'i, Hawaii, USA, C Pacific Ocean *21°57′N 159°40′W*
99 *M20* **Waimes** Liège, E Belgium *50°25′N 06°10′E*
154 *J11* **Wainganga** *var.* Wain River. ≈ C India
Waingapoe *see* Waingapu
171 *N17* **Waingapu** *prev.* Waingapoe. Pulau Sumba, C Indonesia *09°40′S 120°16′E*
55 *S7* **Waini** ≈ N Guyana
55 *S7* **Waini Point** *headland* NW Guyana *08°24′N 59°48′W*
Wain River *see* Wainganga
11 *R15* **Wainwright** Alberta, SW Canada *52°50′N 110°51′W*
39 *O5* **Wainwright** Alaska, USA *70°38′N 160°02′W*
184 *K4* **Waiotira** Northland, North Island, New Zealand *35°56′S 174°11′E*
184 *M11* **Waiouru** Manawatu-Wanganui, North Island, New Zealand *39°28′S 175°41′E*
171 *W14* **Waipa** Papua, E Indonesia *03°47′S 136°16′E*
184 *L8* **Waipa** ≈ North Island, New Zealand
184 *P9* **Waipaoa** ≈ North Island, New Zealand
185 *D25* **Waipapa Point** *headland* South Island, New Zealand *46°39′S 168°51′E*
185 *I18* **Waipara** Canterbury, South Island, New Zealand *43°04′S 172°45′E*
184 *N12* **Waipawa** Hawke's Bay, North Island, New Zealand *39°57′S 176°36′E*
184 *K4* **Waipu** Northland, North Island, New Zealand *35°58′S 174°25′E*
184 *N12* **Waipukurau** Hawke's Bay, North Island, New Zealand *40°01′S 176°34′E*
171 *U14* **Wair** Pulau Kai Besar, E Indonesia *05°16′S 133°09′E*
Wairakai *see* Wairakei
184 *N9* **Wairakei** *var.* Wairakai. Waikato, North Island, New Zealand *38°37′S 176°05′E*
185 *M14* **Wairarapa, Lake** ◎ North Island, New Zealand
185 *J15* **Wairau** ≈ South Island, New Zealand
184 *P10* **Wairoa** Hawke's Bay, North Island, New Zealand *39°03′S 177°26′E*
184 *P10* **Wairoa** ≈ North Island, New Zealand
184 *J4* **Wairoa** ≈ North Island, New Zealand
184 *N9* **Waitahanui** Waikato, North Island, New Zealand *38°48′S 176°04′E*
184 *M6* **Waitakaruru** Waikato, North Island, New Zealand *37°14′S 175°22′E*
185 *F21* **Waitaki** ≈ South Island, New Zealand
184 *K10* **Waitara** Taranaki, North Island, New Zealand *39°01′S 174°14′E*
184 *M7* **Waitoa** Waikato, North Island, New Zealand *37°36′S 175°37′E*
184 *L8* **Waitomo Caves** Waikato, North Island, New Zealand *38°17′S 175°06′E*
184 *L11* **Waitotara** Taranaki, North Island, New Zealand *39°49′S 174°43′E*
184 *L11* **Waitotara** ≈ North Island, New Zealand
32 *L10* **Waitsburg** Washington, NW USA *46°16′N 118°09′W*
Waitzen *see* Vác
184 *L6* **Waiuku** Auckland, North Island, New Zealand *37°15′S 174°45′E*
164 *L10* **Wajima** *var.* Wazima. Ishikawa, Honshū, SW Japan *37°23′N 136°53′E*
81 *K17* **Wajir** North Eastern, NE Kenya *01°46′N 40°05′E*
79 *J17* **Waka** Equateur, NW Dem. Rep. Congo *01°04′N 20°11′E*
81 *I14* **Waka** Southern Nationalities, S Ethiopia *07°12′N 37°19′E*
14 *D9* **Wakami Lake** ◎ Ontario, S Canada
164 *I12* **Wakasa** Tottori, Honshū, SW Japan *35°18′N 134°25′E*
164 *J12* **Wakasa-wan** *bay* C Japan
185 *C22* **Wakatipu, Lake** ◎ South Island, New Zealand
11 *T15* **Wakaw** Saskatchewan, S Canada *52°40′N 105°45′W*
164 *I14* **Wakayama** Wakayama, Honshū, SW Japan *34°12′N 135°09′E*
164 *I15* **Wakayama** *off.* Wakayama-ken. ◈ *prefecture* Honshū, SW Japan
Wakayama-ken *see* Wakayama
26 *K4* **Wa Keeney** Kansas, C USA *39°02′N 99°53′W*
185 *I14* **Wakefield** Tasman, South Island, New Zealand *41°24′S 173°03′E*
97 *M17* **Wakefield** N England, United Kingdom *53°42′N 01°29′W*
27 *O4* **Wakefield** Kansas, C USA *39°12′N 97°00′W*
30 *L4* **Wakefield** Michigan, N USA *46°27′N 89°55′W*
21 *U9* **Wake Forest** North Carolina, SE USA *35°58′N 78°30′W*
Wakeham Bay *see* Kangiqsujuaq
189 *Y11* **Wake Island** ◇ *US unincorporated territory* NW Pacific Ocean
189 *Y12* **Wake Island** ✈ NW Pacific Ocean
189 *Y12* **Wake Island** *atoll* NW Pacific Ocean
189 *X12* **Wake Lagoon** *lagoon* Wake Island, NW Pacific Ocean
166 *L8* **Wakema** Ayeyarwady, SW Myanmar (Burma) *16°36′N 95°11′E*
Wakhan *see* Khandūd
164 *H14* **Waki** Tokushima, Shikoku, SW Japan *34°04′N 134°10′E*
165 *T1* **Wakkanai** Hokkaidō, NE Japan *45°25′N 141°39′E*
83 *K22* **Wakkerstroom** Mpumalanga, E South Africa *27°21′S 30°10′E*
14 *C10* **Wakomata Lake** ◎ Ontario, S Canada
183 *N10* **Wakool** New South Wales, SE Australia *35°30′S 144°22′E*
Wakra *see* Al Wakrah
Waku Kungo *see* Uaco Cungo
186 *J7* **Wakunai** Bougainville Island, NE Papua New Guinea *05°52′S 155°10′E*
Walachei/Walachia *see* Wallachia
155 *K26* **Walawe Ganga** ≈ S Sri Lanka
111 *F15* **Wałbrzych** *Ger.* Waldenburg, Waldenburg in Schlesien. Dolnośląskie, SW Poland *50°45′N 16°20′E*
183 *T6* **Walcha** New South Wales, SE Australia *31°01′S 151°38′E*
101 *K24* **Walchensee** ◎ SE Germany
99 *D14* **Walcheren** *island* SW Netherlands
29 *Z14* **Walcott** Iowa, C USA *41°34′N 90°46′W*
33 *W16* **Walcott** Wyoming, C USA *41°46′N 106°46′W*
99 *G21* **Walcourt** Namur, S Belgium *50°16′N 04°26′E*
110 *G9* **Wałcz** *Ger.* Deutsch Krone. Zachodnio-pomorskie, NW Poland *53°17′N 16°29′E*
108 *H7* **Wald** Zürich, N Switzerland *47°17′N 08°56′E*
109 *U3* **Waldaist** ≈ N Austria
180 *I9* **Waldburg Range** ▲▲ Western Australia
37 *R3* **Walden** Colorado, C USA *40°43′N 106°16′W*
18 *K13* **Walden** New York, NE USA *41°35′N 74°09′W*
Waldenburg/Waldenburg in Schlesien *see* Wałbrzych
11 *T15* **Waldheim** Saskatchewan, S Canada *52°38′N 106°35′W*
Waldia *see* Weldiya
101 *M23* **Waldkraiburg** Bayern, SE Germany *48°10′N 12°23′E*
27 *T14* **Waldo** Arkansas, C USA *33°21′N 93°18′W*
23 *V9* **Waldo** Florida, SE USA *29°47′N 82°07′W*
19 *R7* **Waldoboro** Maine, NE USA *44°06′N 69°22′W*
21 *W4* **Waldorf** Maryland, NE USA *38°36′N 76°54′W*
32 *F12* **Waldport** Oregon, NW USA *44°25′N 124°04′W*
27 *S11* **Waldron** Arkansas, C USA *34°54′N 94°09′W*
195 *Y13* **Waldron, Cape** *headland* Antarctica *66°08′S 116°00′E*
101 *F24* **Waldshut-Tiengen** Baden-Württemberg, S Germany *47°37′N 08°13′E*
171 *P12* **Walea, Selat** *strait* Sulawesi, C Indonesia
Wałeckie Międzyrzecze *see* Valašské Meziříčí
108 *H8* **Walensee** ◎ NW Switzerland
38 *L8* **Wales** Alaska, USA *65°36′N 168°03′W*
97 *J20* **Wales** *Wel.* Cymru. ◈ *national region* Wales, United Kingdom
9 *O7* **Wales Island** *island* Nunavut, NE Canada
77 *P14* **Walewale** N Ghana *10°21′N 00°48′W*
99 *M24* **Walferdange** Luxembourg, C Luxembourg *49°39′N 06°08′E*
183 *Q5* **Walgett** New South Wales, SE Australia *30°02′S 148°14′E*
194 *K10* **Walgreen Coast** *physical region* Antarctica
29 *Q2* **Walhalla** North Dakota, N USA *48°55′N 97°55′W*
21 *O11* **Walhalla** South Carolina, SE USA *34°46′N 83°05′W*
79 *O19* **Walikale** Nord-Kivu, E Dem. Rep. Congo *01°29′S 28°05′E*
Walk *see* Valga, Estonia
Walk *see* Valka, Latvia
29 *U5* **Walker** Minnesota, N USA *47°06′N 94°35′W*
15 *V4* **Walker, Lac** ◎ Québec, SE Canada
35 *S7* **Walker Lake** ◎ Nevada, W USA
35 *R6* **Walker River** ≈ Nevada, W USA
28 *K10* **Wall** South Dakota, N USA *43°58′N 102°12′W*
173 *U9* **Wallaby Plateau** *undersea feature* E Indian Ocean
33 *N8* **Wallace** Idaho, NW USA *47°28′N 115°55′W*
21 *V11* **Wallace** North Carolina, SE USA *34°42′N 77°59′W*
14 *D17* **Wallaceburg** Ontario, S Canada *42°34′N 82°22′W*
22 *F5* **Wallace Lake** ⊞ Louisiana, S USA
11 *P13* **Wallace Mountain** ▲ Alberta, W Canada *54°50′N 115°57′W*
116 *J14* **Wallachia** *var.* Walachia, *Ger.* Walachei, *Rom.* Valachia. *cultural region* S Romania
Wallachisch-Meseritsch *see* Valašské Meziříčí
183 *U4* **Wallangarra** New South Wales, SE Australia *28°56′S 151°57′E*
182 *I8* **Wallaroo** South Australia *33°56′S 137°38′E*
32 *L10* **Walla Walla** Washington, NW USA *46°03′N 118°20′W*
101 *H19* **Walldürn** Baden-Württemberg, SW Germany *49°34′N 09°22′E*
100 *F12* **Wallenhorst** Niedersachsen, NW Germany *52°21′N 08°01′E*
Wallenthal *see* Haţeg
109 *S4* **Wallern** Oberösterreich, N Austria *48°13′N 13°58′E*
Wallern *see* Wallern im Burgenland
109 *Z5* **Wallern im Burgenland** *var.* Wallern. Burgenland, E Austria *47°44′N 16°57′E*
18 *M9* **Wallingford** Vermont, NE USA *43°27′N 72°56′W*
25 *V11* **Wallis** Texas, SW USA *29°38′N 96°05′W*
Wallis *see* Valais
192 *K9* **Wallis and Futuna** *Fr.* Territoire de Wallis et Futuna. ◇ *French overseas territory* C Pacific Ocean
108 *G7* **Wallisellen** Zürich, N Switzerland *47°25′N 08°36′E*
Wallis et Futuna, Territoire de *see* Wallis and Futuna
190 *H11* **Wallis, Îles** *island group* N Wallis and Futuna
99 *G20* **Wallonia** *cultural region* SW Belgium
31 *Q5* **Walloon Lake** ◎ Michigan, N USA
32 *K10* **Wallula** Washington, NW USA *46°03′N 118°54′W*
32 *K10* **Wallula, Lake** ◎ Washington, NW USA
21 *S8* **Walnut Cove** North Carolina, SE USA *36°18′N 80°08′W*
35 *N8* **Walnut Creek** California, W USA *37°52′N 122°04′W*
26 *K5* **Walnut Creek** ≈ Kansas, C USA
27 *W9* **Walnut Ridge** Arkansas, C USA *36°06′N 90°56′W*
25 *S7* **Walnut Springs** Texas, SW USA *32°05′N 97°42′W*
182 *L10* **Walpeup** Victoria, SE Australia *35°09′S 142°01′E*
187 *R17* **Walpole, Île** *island* SE New Caledonia
39 *N13* **Walrus Islands** *island group* Alaska, USA
97 *L19* **Walsall** C England, United Kingdom *52°35′N 01°58′W*
37 *T7* **Walsenburg** Colorado, C USA *37°37′N 104°46′W*
11 *S17* **Walsh** Alberta, SW Canada *49°58′N 110°03′W*
37 *W7* **Walsh** Colorado, C USA *37°20′N 102°17′W*
100 *I11* **Walsrode** Niedersachsen, NW Germany *52°52′N 09°36′E*
Waltenberg *see* Zalău
21 *R14* **Walterboro** South Carolina, SE USA *32°54′N 80°21′W*
Walter F.George Lake *see* Walter F. George Reservoir
23 *R6* **Walter F. George Reservoir** *var.* Walter F.George Lake. ⊞ Alabama/Georgia, SE USA
26 *M12* **Walters** Oklahoma, C USA *34°22′N 98°18′W*
101 *J16* **Waltershausen** Thüringen, C Germany *50°53′N 10°33′E*
173 *N10* **Walters Shoal** *var.* Walters Shoals. *reef* S Madagascar
Walters Shoals *see* Walters Shoal
22 *M3* **Walthall** Mississippi, S USA *33°36′N 89°16′W*
20 *M4* **Walton** Kentucky, S USA *38°52′N 84°36′W*
18 *J11* **Walton** New York, NE USA *42°10′N 75°07′W*
79 *O20* **Walungu** Sud-Kivu, E Dem. Rep. Congo *02°40′S 28°37′E*
Walvisbaai *see* Walvis Bay
83 *C19* **Walvis Bay** *Afr.* Walvisbaai. Erongo, NW Namibia *22°59′S 14°34′E*
83 *B19* **Walvis Bay** *bay* NW Namibia
Walvish Ridge *see* Walvis Ridge
65 *O17* **Walvis Ridge** *var.* Walvish Ridge. *undersea feature* E Atlantic Ocean *28°00′S 03°00′E*
171 *X16* **Wamal** Papua, E Indonesia *08°00′S 139°06′E*
171 *U15* **Wamar, Pulau** *island* Kepulauan Aru, E Indonesia
79 *O17* **Wamba** Orientale, NE Dem. Rep. Congo *02°10′N 27°59′E*
77 *V15* **Wamba** Nassarawa, C Nigeria *08°57′N 08°35′E*
79 *H22* **Wamba** *var.* Uamba. ≈ Angola/Dem. Rep. Congo
27 *P4* **Wamego** Kansas, C USA *39°12′N 96°18′W*
18 *I10* **Wampsville** New York, NE USA *43°03′N 75°40′W*
42 *K6* **Wampú, Río** ≈ E Honduras
171 *X16* **Wan** Papua, E Indonesia *08°15′S 138°00′E*
Wan *see* Anhui
183 *N4* **Wanaaring** New South Wales, SE Australia *29°42′S 144°07′E*
185 *D21* **Wanaka** Otago, South Island, New Zealand *44°42′S 169°09′E*
185 *D20* **Wanaka, Lake** ◎ South Island, New Zealand
171 *W14* **Wanapiri** Papua, E Indonesia *04°21′S 135°52′E*
14 *F9* **Wanapitei** ≈ Ontario, S Canada
14 *F10* **Wanapitei Lake** ◎ Ontario, S Canada
18 *K14* **Wanaque** New Jersey, NE USA *41°02′N 74°17′W*
171 *U12* **Wanau** Papua, E Indonesia *01°20′S 132°40′E*
185 *F22* **Wanbrow, Cape** *headland* South Island, New Zealand *45°07′S 170°59′E*
Wancheng *see* Wanning
Wanchuan *see* Zhangjiakou
171 *W13* **Wandai** *var.* Komeyo. Papua, E Indonesia *03°35′S 136°15′E*
163 *Z8* **Wanda Shan** ▲▲ NE China
197 *R11* **Wandel Sea** *sea* Arctic Ocean
160 *D13* **Wanding** *var.* Wandingzhen. Yunnan, SW China *24°01′N 98°00′E*
Wandingzhen *see* Wanding
99 *H20* **Wanfercée-Baulet** Hainaut, S Belgium *50°27′N 04°37′E*
184 *L12* **Wanganui** Manawatu-Wanganui, North Island, New Zealand *39°56′S 175°02′E*
184 *L11* **Wanganui** ≈ North Island, New Zealand
183 *P11* **Wangaratta** Victoria, SE Australia *36°22′S 146°17′E*
160 *J8* **Wangcang** *var.* Donghe; *prev.* Fengjiaba, Hongjiang. Sichuan, C China *32°15′N 106°16′E*
Wangda *see* Zogang
101 *I24* **Wangen im Allgäu** Baden-Württemberg, S Germany *47°40′N 09°49′E*
Wangerin *see* Węgorzyno
100 *F9* **Wangerooge** *island* NW Germany
171 *W13* **Wanggar** Papua, E Indonesia *03°22′S 135°15′E*
160 *J13* **Wangmo** *var.* Fuxing. Guizhou, S China *25°08′N 106°08′E*
Wangolodougou *see* Ouangolodougou
161 *S9* **Wangpan Yang** *sea* E China
163 *Y10* **Wangqing** Jilin, NE China *43°19′N 129°42′E*
167 *P8* **Wang Saphung** Loei, C Thailand *17°18′N 101°45′E*
167 *O6* **Wan Hsa-la** Shan State, E Myanmar (Burma) *20°27′N 98°39′E*
55 *W9* **Wanica** ◈ *district* Suriname
79 *M18* **Wanie-Rukula** Orientale, C Dem. Rep. Congo *0°13′N 25°34′E*
Wankie *see* Hwange
Wanki, Río *see* Coco, Río
81 *N17* **Wanlaweyn** *var.* Wanle Weyn, *It.* Uanle Uen. Shabeellaha Hoose, SW Somalia *02°36′N 44°47′E*
Wanle Weyn *see* Wanlaweyn
180 *I12* **Wanneroo** Western Australia *31°40′S 115°35′E*
160 *L17* **Wanning** *var.* Wancheng. Hainan, S China *18°55′N 110°27′E*
167 *Q8* **Wanon Niwat** Sakon Nakhon, E Thailand *17°39′N 103°45′E*
155 *H16* **Wanparti** Andhra Pradesh, C India *16°19′N 78°06′E*
Wansen *see* Wiązów
160 *L11* **Wanshan** Guizhou, S China *27°45′N 109°12′E*
99 *M14* **Wanssum** Limburg, SE Netherlands *51°31′N 06°04′E*
184 *N12* **Wanstead** Hawke's Bay, North Island, New Zealand *40°09′S 176°31′E*
Wanxian *see* Wanzhou
188 *F16* **Wanyaan** Yap, Micronesia
160 *K8* **Wanyuan** Sichuan, C China *32°05′N 108°08′E*
161 *O11* **Wanzai** *var.* Kangle. Jiangxi, S China *28°06′N 114°27′E*
99 *J20* **Wanze** Liège, E Belgium *50°32′N 05°16′E*
160 *K9* **Wanzhou** *var.* Wanxian. Chongqing Shi, C China *30°48′N 108°21′E*
31 *R12* **Wapakoneta** Ohio, N USA *40°34′N 84°11′W*
12 *D7* **Wapaseese** ≈ Ontario, C Canada
32 *I10* **Wapato** Washington, NW USA *46°27′N 120°25′W*
29 *Y15* **Wapello** Iowa, C USA *41°10′N 91°13′W*
11 *N13* **Wapiti** ≈ Alberta/British Columbia, SW Canada
27 *X7* **Wappapello Lake** ⊞ Missouri, C USA
18 *K13* **Wappingers Falls** New York, NE USA *41°36′N 73°54′W*
29 *X13* **Wapsipinicon River** ≈ Iowa, C USA
14 *L9* **Wapus** ≈ Québec, SE Canada
160 *H7* **Waqên** Sichuan, C China *33°05′N 102°34′E*
21 *Q7* **War** West Virginia, NE USA *37°18′N 81°39′W*
155 *J15* **Warangal** Andhra Pradesh, C India *18°N 79°35′E*
Warasdin *see* Varaždin
183 *O16* **Waratah** Tasmania, SE Australia *41°28′S 145°34′E*
183 *O14* **Waratah Bay** *bay* Victoria, SE Australia
101 *H15* **Warburg** Nordrhein-Westfalen, W Germany *51°30′N 09°11′E*
182 *I1* **Warburton Creek** *seasonal river* South Australia
180 *M9* **Warbuton** Western Australia *26°17′S 126°18′E*
99 *M20* **Warche** ≈ E Belgium
Wardag/Wardak *see* Wardak
149 *P5* **Wardak** *prev.* Vardak, *Pash.* Wardag. ◈ *province* E Afghanistan
32 *K9* **Warden** Washington, NW USA *46°58′N 119°02′W*
154 *I12* **Wardha** Mahārāshtra, W India *20°41′N 78°40′E*
Wardija Point *see* Wardija, Ras il-
121 *N15* **Wardija, Ras il-** *var.* Ras il- Wardija, Wardija Point. *headland* Gozo, NW Malta *36°03′N 14°11′E*
Wardija, Ras il- *see* Wardija, Ras il-
139 *P3* **Wardīyah** Nīnawá, N Iraq *36°18′N 41°45′E*
185 *E19* **Ward, Mount** ▲ South Island, New Zealand *43°49′S 169°54′E*
10 *L11* **Ware** British Columbia, W Canada *57°26′N 125°41′W*
99 *D18* **Waregem** *var.* Waereghem. West-Vlaanderen, W Belgium *50°53′N 03°26′E*
99 *J19* **Waremme** Liège, E Belgium *50°41′N 05°15′E*

◆ Country
● Country Capital
◇ Dependent Territory
○ Dependent Territory Capital
◈ Administrative Regions
✈ International Airport
▲ Mountain
▲▲ Mountain Range
Ѫ Volcano
≈ River
◎ Lake
⊞ Reservoir

100 N10 Waren Mecklenburg-Vorpommern, NE Germany 53°32′N 12°42′E
171 W13 Waren Papua, E Indonesia 02°13′S 136°21′E
101 F14 Warendorf Nordrhein-Westfalen, W Germany 51°57′N 08°00′E
21 P12 Ware Shoals South Carolina, SE USA 34°24′N 82°15′W
98 N4 Warffum Groningen, NE Netherlands 53°22′N 06°34′E
81 O15 Wargalo Mudug, E Somalia 06°06′N 47°40′E
146 M12 Warganza Rus. Varganzi. Qashqadaryo Viloyati, S Uzbekistan 39°18′N 66°00′E
Wargla see Ouargla
183 T4 Warialda New South Wales, SE Australia 29°34′S 150°35′E
154 F13 Wāri Godri Mahārāshtra, C India 19°28′N 75°43′E
167 R10 Warin Chamrap Ubon Ratchathani, E Thailand 15°11′N 104°51′E
25 R11 Waring Texas, SW USA 29°56′N 98°48′W
39 O8 Waring Mountains ▲▲ Alaska, USA
110 M12 Warka Mazowieckie, E Poland 51°45′N 21°12′E
184 L5 Warkworth Auckland, North Island, New Zealand 36°23′S 174°42′E
171 U12 Warmandi Papua, E Indonesia 0°21′S 132°38′E
83 E22 Warmbad Karas, S Namibia 28°29′S 18°41′E
98 H8 Warmenhuizen Noord-Holland, NW Netherlands 52°43′N 04°45′E
110 M8 Warmińsko-Mazurskie ◈ province C Poland
97 L22 Warminster S England, United Kingdom 51°13′N 02°12′W
18 I15 Warminster Pennsylvania, NE USA 40°11′N 75°04′W
35 V8 Warm Springs Nevada, W USA 38°10′N 116°21′W
32 H12 Warm Springs Oregon, NW USA 44°51′N 121°24′W
21 S5 Warm Springs Virginia, NE USA 38°03′N 79°48′W
100 M8 Warnemünde Mecklenburg-Vorpommern, NE Germany 54°10′N 12°03′E
27 Q10 Warner Oklahoma, C USA 35°29′N 95°18′W
35 Q2 Warner Mountains ▲▲ California, W USA
23 T5 Warner Robins Georgia, SE USA 32°38′N 83°38′W
57 N18 Warnes Santa Cruz, C Bolivia 17°30′S 63°11′W
100 M9 Warnow ≈ NE Germany
Warnsdorf see Varnsdorf
98 M11 Warnsveld Gelderland, E Netherlands 52°08′N 06°14′E
154 I13 Warora Mahārāshtra, C India 20°12′N 79°01′E
182 L11 Warracknabeal Victoria, SE Australia 36°17′S 142°26′E
183 O13 Warragul Victoria, SE Australia 38°11′S 145°55′E
80 D13 Warrap Warrap, W South Sudan 08°08′N 28°37′E
81 D14 Warrap ◈ state W South Sudan
183 O4 Warrego River seasonal river New South Wales/Queensland, E Australia
183 Q6 Warren New South Wales, SE Australia 31°41′S 147°51′E
11 X16 Warren Manitoba, S Canada 50°05′N 97°33′W
27 V14 Warren Arkansas, C USA 33°38′N 92°05′W
31 S10 Warren Michigan, N USA 42°29′N 83°02′W
29 R3 Warren Minnesota, N USA 48°12′N 96°46′W
31 U11 Warren Ohio, N USA 41°14′N 80°49′W
18 D12 Warren Pennsylvania, NE USA 41°52′N 79°09′W
25 X10 Warren Texas, SW USA 30°33′N 94°24′W
97 G16 Warrenpoint Ir. An Pointe. SE Northern Ireland, United Kingdom 54°07′N 06°16′W
27 S4 Warrensburg Missouri, C USA 38°46′N 93°44′W
83 H22 Warrenton Northern Cape, N South Africa 28°07′S 24°51′E
23 U4 Warrenton Georgia, SE USA 33°24′N 82°39′W
27 W4 Warrenton Missouri, C USA 38°48′N 91°08′W
21 V8 Warrenton North Carolina, SE USA 36°24′N 78°11′W
21 V4 Warrenton Virginia, NE USA 38°43′N 77°48′W
77 U17 Warri Delta, S Nigeria 05°26′N 05°34′E
97 L18 Warrington C England, United Kingdom 53°24′N 02°37′W
23 O9 Warrington Florida, SE USA 30°22′N 87°16′W
23 P3 Warrior Alabama, S USA 33°49′N 86°49′W
182 L13 Warrnambool Victoria, SE Australia 38°23′S 142°30′E
29 T2 Warroad Minnesota, N USA 48°55′N 95°18′W
183 S6 Warrumbungle Range ▲▲ New South Wales, SE Australia
154 J12 Wārsa Mahārāshtra, C India 20°42′N 79°58′E
31 P11 Warsaw Indiana, N USA 41°13′N 85°52′W
20 L4 Warsaw Kentucky, S USA 38°47′N 84°55′W
27 T5 Warsaw Missouri, C USA 38°14′N 93°23′W
18 E10 Warsaw New York, NE USA 42°44′N 78°06′W
21 V10 Warsaw North Carolina, SE USA 35°00′N 78°05′W
21 X5 Warsaw Virginia, NE USA 37°57′N 76°46′W
Warsaw/Warschau see Warszawa
81 N17 Warshiikh Shabeellaha Dhexe, C Somalia 02°22′N 45°52′E
101 G15 Warstein Nordrhein-Westfalen, W Germany 51°27′N 08°21′E
110 M11 Warszawa Eng. Warsaw, Ger. Warschau, Rus. Varshava. ● (Poland) Mazowieckie, C Poland 52°15′N 21°E
110 J13 Warta Sieradz, C Poland 51°43′N 18°37′E
110 D11 Warta Ger. Warthe. ≈ W Poland
Wartberg see Senec
20 M9 Wartburg Tennessee, S USA 36°08′N 84°37′W
108 J7 Warth Vorarlberg, NW Austria 47°16′N 10°11′E
Warthe see Warta
169 U12 Waru Borneo, C Indonesia 01°24′S 116°37′E
171 T13 Waru Pulau Seram, E Indonesia 03°24′S 130°38′E
139 N6 Wa'r, Wādī al dry watercourse E Syria
183 U3 Warwick Queensland, E Australia 28°12′S 152°E
15 Q11 Warwick Québec, SE Canada 45°55′N 72°00′W
97 M20 Warwick C England, United Kingdom 52°17′N 01°34′W
18 K13 Warwick New York, NE USA 41°15′N 74°21′W
29 P4 Warwick North Dakota, N USA 47°49′N 98°42′W
19 O12 Warwick Rhode Island, NE USA 41°40′N 71°21′W
97 L20 Warwickshire cultural region C England, United Kingdom
14 G14 Wasaga Beach Ontario, S Canada 44°30′N 80°00′W
77 U13 Wasagu Kebbi, NW Nigeria 11°25′N 05°48′E
36 M2 Wasatch Range ▲▲ W USA
35 R12 Wasco California, W USA 35°34′N 119°20′W
29 V10 Waseca Minnesota, N USA 44°04′N 93°30′W
14 H13 Washago Ontario, S Canada 44°46′N 79°48′W
19 S2 Washburn Maine, NE USA 46°46′N 68°08′W
28 M5 Washburn North Dakota, N USA 47°15′N 101°02′W
30 K3 Washburn Wisconsin, N USA 46°41′N 90°53′W
31 S14 Washburn Hill hill Ohio, N USA
154 H13 Wāshīm Mahārāshtra, C India 20°06′N 77°08′E
97 M14 Washington NE England, United Kingdom 54°54′N 01°31′W
23 U3 Washington Georgia, SE USA 33°44′N 82°44′W
30 L12 Washington Illinois, N USA 40°42′N 89°24′W
31 N15 Washington Indiana, N USA 38°40′N 87°10′W
29 X15 Washington Iowa, C USA 41°18′N 91°41′W
27 O3 Washington Kansas, C USA 39°49′N 97°03′W
27 W5 Washington Missouri, C USA 38°31′N 91°01′W
21 X9 Washington North Carolina, SE USA 35°33′N 77°04′W
18 B15 Washington Pennsylvania, NE USA 40°11′N 80°16′W
25 V10 Washington Texas, SW USA 30°18′N 96°08′W
36 J8 Washington Utah, W USA 37°07′N 113°30′W
21 V4 Washington Virginia, NE USA 38°43′N 78°11′W
32 I9 Washington off. State of Washington, also known as Chinook State, Evergreen State. ◈ state NW USA
Washington see Washington Court House
31 S14 Washington Court House var. Washington. Ohio, NE USA 39°32′N 83°29′W
21 W4 Washington DC ● (USA) District of Columbia, NE USA 38°54′N 77°02′W
31 O5 Washington Island island Wisconsin, N USA
Washington Island see Teraina
19 O7 Washington, Mount ▲ New Hampshire, NE USA 44°16′N 71°18′W
26 M11 Washita River ≈ Oklahoma/Texas, C USA
97 O18 Wash, The inlet E England, United Kingdom
32 L9 Washtucna Washington, NW USA 46°44′N 118°19′W
Wasiliszki see Vasilishki
110 P9 Wasilków Podlaskie, NE Poland 53°12′N 23°15′E
39 R11 Wasilla Alaska, USA 61°34′N 149°26′W
55 U9 Wasjabo Sipaliwini, NW Suriname 05°09′N 57°09′W
12 I10 Waskaganish prev. Fort Rupert, Rupert House. Québec, SE Canada 51°30′N 79°45′W
11 X11 Waskaiowaka Lake ◎ Manitoba, C Canada
11 T14 Waskesiu Lake Saskatchewan, C Canada 53°56′N 106°05′W
25 X7 Waskom Texas, SW USA 32°28′N 94°03′W
110 G13 Wąsosz Dolnośląskie, SW Poland 51°36′N 16°30′E
42 M6 Waspam var. Waspán. Región Autónoma Atlántico Norte, NE Nicaragua 14°41′N 84°04′W
Waspán see Waspam
165 T3 Wassamu Hokkaidō, NE Japan 44°01′N 142°25′E
108 G9 Wassen Uri, C Switzerland 46°42′N 08°34′E
98 G11 Wassenaar Zuid-Holland, W Netherlands 52°09′N 04°23′E
99 N24 Wasserbillig Grevenmacher, E Luxembourg 49°43′N 06°30′E
Wasserburg see Wasserburg am Inn
101 M23 Wasserburg am Inn var. Wasserburg. Bayern, SE Germany 48°02′N 12°12′E
101 I17 Wasserkuppe ▲ C Germany 50°30′N 09°55′E
103 R5 Wassy Haute-Marne, N France 48°32′N 04°54′E
171 N14 Watampone var. Bone. Sulawesi, C Indonesia 04°33′S 120°20′E
171 R13 Watawa Pulau Buru, E Indonesia 03°36′S 127°13′E
Watenstedt-Salzgitter see Salzgitter
18 M13 Waterbury Connecticut, NE USA 41°33′N 73°01′W
21 R11 Wateree Lake ⊠ South Carolina, SE USA
21 R12 Wateree River ≈ South Carolina, SE USA
97 E20 Waterford Ir. Port Láirge. Waterford, S Ireland 52°15′N 07°08′W
31 S9 Waterford Michigan, N USA 42°42′N 83°24′W
97 E20 Waterford Ir. Port Láirge. cultural region S Ireland
97 E21 Waterford Harbour Ir. Cuan Phort Láirge. inlet S Ireland
98 G12 Wateringen Zuid-Holland, W Netherlands 52°02′N 04°16′E
99 G19 Waterloo Walloon Brabant, C Belgium 50°43′N 04°24′E
14 F16 Waterloo Ontario, S Canada 43°28′N 80°32′W
15 P12 Waterloo Québec, SE Canada 45°20′N 72°28′W
30 K16 Waterloo Illinois, N USA 38°20′N 90°09′W
29 X13 Waterloo Iowa, C USA 42°31′N 92°16′W
18 G10 Waterloo New York, NE USA 42°54′N 76°51′W
30 L4 Watersmeet Michigan, N USA 46°16′N 89°10′W
23 V9 Watertown Florida, SE USA 30°11′N 82°36′W
18 I8 Watertown New York, NE USA 43°37′N 75°56′W
29 R9 Watertown South Dakota, N USA 44°54′N 97°07′W
30 M8 Watertown Wisconsin, N USA 43°12′N 88°44′W
22 L3 Water Valley Mississippi, S USA 34°09′N 89°37′W
27 O3 Waterville Kansas, C USA 39°41′N 96°45′W
17 V6 Waterville Maine, NE USA 44°34′N 69°41′W
29 V10 Waterville Minnesota, N USA 44°13′N 93°34′W
18 I10 Waterville New York, NE USA 42°55′N 75°18′W
14 E16 Watford Ontario, S Canada 42°57′N 81°51′W
97 N21 Watford E England, United Kingdom 51°39′N 00°24′W
28 K4 Watford City North Dakota, N USA 47°48′N 103°16′W
141 X12 Wāṭif S Oman 18°34′N 56°31′E
18 G11 Watkins Glen New York, NE USA 42°23′N 76°53′W
Watlings Island see San Salvador
171 U15 Watnil Pulau Kai Kecil, E Indonesia 05°45′S 132°39′E
26 M10 Watonga Oklahoma, C USA 35°52′N 98°26′W
11 T16 Watrous Saskatchewan, S Canada 51°40′N 105°29′W
37 T10 Watrous New Mexico, SW USA 35°48′N 104°58′W
79 P16 Watsa Orientale, NE Dem. Rep. Congo 03°00′N 29°31′E
31 N12 Watseka Illinois, N USA 40°46′N 87°44′W
79 J19 Watsikengo Equateur, C Dem. Rep. Congo 0°49′S 20°34′E
182 C5 Watson South Australia 30°32′S 131°29′E
11 U15 Watson Saskatchewan, S Canada 52°13′N 104°30′W
195 O10 Watson Escarpment ▲▲ Antarctica
10 K9 Watson Lake Yukon Territory, W Canada 60°05′N 128°47′W
35 N10 Watsonville California, W USA 36°53′N 121°43′W
167 Q8 Wattay ✈ (Viangchan) Viangchan, C Laos 18°03′N 102°36′E
109 N7 Wattens Tirol, W Austria 47°18′N 11°37′E
20 M9 Watts Bar Lake ⊠ Tennessee, S USA
108 H7 Wattwil Sankt Gallen, NE Switzerland 47°18′N 09°06′E
171 T14 Watubela, Kepulauan island group E Indonesia
101 N24 Watzmann ▲ SE Germany 47°32′N 12°56′E
186 E8 Wau Morobe, C Papua New Guinea 07°22′S 146°40′E
81 D14 Wau var. Wāw. Western Bahr el Ghazal, W South Sudan 07°43′N 28°01′E
29 Q8 Waubay South Dakota, N USA 45°19′N 97°18′W
29 Q8 Waubay Lake ◎ South Dakota, N USA
183 U7 Wauchope New South Wales, SE Australia 31°30′S 152°46′E
23 W13 Wauchula Florida, SE USA 27°33′N 81°48′W
30 M10 Wauconda Illinois, N USA 42°15′N 88°08′W
182 J7 Waukaringa South Australia 32°19′S 139°27′E
31 N10 Waukegan Illinois, N USA 42°21′N 87°50′W
30 M9 Waukesha Wisconsin, N USA 43°01′N 88°14′W
29 X11 Waukon Iowa, C USA 43°16′N 91°28′W
30 L8 Waunakee Wisconsin, N USA 43°13′N 89°28′W
30 L7 Waupaca Wisconsin, N USA 44°23′N 89°04′W
30 M8 Waupun Wisconsin, N USA 43°40′N 88°43′W
26 M13 Waurika Oklahoma, C USA 34°10′N 98°00′W
26 M12 Waurika Lake ⊠ Oklahoma, C USA
30 L6 Wausau Wisconsin, N USA 44°58′N 89°40′W
31 R11 Wauseon Ohio, N USA 41°33′N 84°08′W
30 L7 Wautoma Wisconsin, N USA 44°05′N 89°17′W
30 M9 Wauwatosa Wisconsin, N USA 43°03′N 88°03′W
22 L9 Waveland Mississippi, S USA 30°17′N 89°22′W
97 Q20 Waveney ≈ E England, United Kingdom
184 L11 Waverley Taranaki, North Island, New Zealand 39°45′S 174°35′E
29 W12 Waverly Iowa, C USA 42°43′N 92°28′W
27 T4 Waverly Missouri, C USA 39°12′N 93°31′W
29 R15 Waverly Nebraska, C USA 40°56′N 96°27′W
18 G12 Waverly New York, NE USA 42°00′N 76°33′W
20 H8 Waverly Tennessee, S USA 36°04′N 87°49′W
21 W7 Waverly Virginia, NE USA 37°02′N 77°06′W
99 H19 Wavre Walloon Brabant, C Belgium 50°43′N 04°37′E
166 M8 Waw Bago, SW Myanmar (Burma) 17°26′N 96°40′E
Wāw see Wau
14 B7 Wawa Ontario, S Canada 47°59′N 84°43′W
77 T14 Wawa Niger, W Nigeria 09°52′N 04°33′E
75 Q11 Wāw al Kabīr S Libya 25°21′N 16°41′E
43 N7 Wawa, Río var. Rio Huahua. ≈ NE Nicaragua
186 B8 Wawoi ≈ SW Papua New Guinea
25 T7 Waxahachie Texas, SW USA 32°23′N 96°52′W
158 L9 Waxxari Xinjiang Uygur Zizhiqu, NW China 38°43′N 87°11′E
Wayaobu see Zichang
23 V7 Waycross Georgia, SE USA 31°13′N 82°21′W
180 K10 Way, Lake ◎ Western Australia
31 P9 Wayland Michigan, N USA 42°40′N 85°38′W
29 R13 Wayne Nebraska, C USA 42°13′N 97°01′W
18 K14 Wayne New Jersey, NE USA 40°57′N 74°16′W
21 P5 Wayne West Virginia, NE USA 38°14′N 82°27′W
23 V4 Waynesboro Georgia, SE USA 33°04′N 82°01′W
22 M7 Waynesboro Mississippi, S USA 31°40′N 88°39′W
20 H10 Waynesboro Tennessee, S USA 35°20′N 87°49′W
21 U5 Waynesboro Virginia, NE USA 38°04′N 78°54′W
18 B16 Waynesburg Pennsylvania, NE USA 39°51′N 80°10′W
27 U6 Waynesville Missouri, C USA 37°48′N 92°11′W
21 O10 Waynesville North Carolina, SE USA 35°29′N 82°59′W
26 L8 Waynoka Oklahoma, C USA 36°36′N 98°53′W
Wazan see Ouazzane
Wazima see Wajima
149 V7 Wazīrābād Punjab, NE Pakistan 32°28′N 74°04′E
Wazzan see Ouazzane
110 I8 Wda var. Czarna Woda, Ger. Schwarzwasser. ≈ N Poland
187 Q16 Wé Province des Îles Loyauté, E New Caledonia 20°55′S 167°15′E
97 O23 Weald, The lowlands SE England, United Kingdom
186 A9 Weam Western, SW Papua New Guinea 08°33′S 141°10′E
97 L15 Wear ≈ N England, United Kingdom
Wearmouth see Sunderland
26 L10 Weatherford Oklahoma, C USA 35°31′N 98°42′W
25 S6 Weatherford Texas, SW USA 32°47′N 97°48′W
34 M3 Weaverville California, W USA 40°42′N 122°57′W
27 R7 Webb City Missouri, C USA 37°07′N 94°28′W
192 G8 Weber Basin undersea feature S Ceram Sea
Webfoot State see Oregon
18 F9 Webster New York, NE USA 43°12′N 77°25′W
29 Q8 Webster South Dakota, N USA 45°19′N 97°31′W
29 V13 Webster City Iowa, C USA 42°28′N 93°49′W
27 X5 Webster Groves Missouri, C USA 38°32′N 90°20′W
21 S4 Webster Springs var. Addison. West Virginia, NE USA 38°29′N 80°52′W
171 S11 Weda, Teluk bay Pulau Halmahera, E Indonesia
65 B25 Weddell Island var. Isla de San Jorge. island W Falkland Islands
65 K22 Weddell Plain undersea feature SW Atlantic Ocean 65°00′S 40°00′W
65 K23 Weddell Sea sea SW Atlantic Ocean
65 B25 Weddell Settlement Weddell Island, W Falkland Islands 52°53′S 60°54′W
182 M11 Wedderburn Victoria, SE Australia 36°26′S 143°37′E
100 I9 Wedel Schleswig-Holstein, N Germany 53°35′N 09°42′E
92 N3 Wedel Jarlsberg Land physical region SW Svalbard
100 I12 Wedemark Niedersachsen, NW Germany 52°33′N 09°43′E
10 M17 Wedge Mountain ▲ British Columbia, SW Canada 50°10′N 122°43′W
23 R4 Wedowee Alabama, S USA 33°16′N 85°28′W
171 U15 Weduar Pulau Kai Besar, E Indonesia 05°55′S 132°51′E
35 N2 Weed California, W USA 41°26′N 122°24′W
15 Q12 Weedon Centre Québec, SE Canada 45°40′N 71°28′W
18 E13 Weedville Pennsylvania, NE USA 41°15′N 78°28′W
100 F10 Weener Niedersachsen, NW Germany 53°09′N 07°19′E
29 S16 Weeping Water Nebraska, C USA 40°52′N 96°08′W
99 L16 Weert Limburg, SE Netherlands 51°15′N 05°43′E
98 I10 Weesp Noord-Holland, C Netherlands 52°18′N 05°03′E
183 S5 Wee Waa New South Wales, SE Australia 30°16′S 149°27′E
110 N7 Węgorzewo Ger. Angerburg. Warmińsko-Mazurskie, NE Poland 54°12′N 21°49′E
110 E9 Węgorzyno Ger. Wangerin. Zachodnio-pomorskie, NW Poland 53°34′N 15°35′E
110 N11 Węgrów Ger. Bingerau. Mazowieckie, C Poland 52°22′N 22°00′E
98 N5 Wehe-Den Hoorn Groningen, NE Netherlands 53°20′N 06°29′E
98 M12 Wehl Gelderland, E Netherlands 51°58′N 06°13′E
Wehlau see Znamensk
168 F7 Weh, Pulau island NW Indonesia
Wei see Weifang
161 P1 Weichang prev. Zhuizishan. Hebei, E China 41°55′N 117°45′E
Weichang see Weishan
Weichsel see Wisła
101 M16 Weida Thüringen, C Germany 50°46′N 12°05′E
Weiden see Weiden in der Oberpfalz
101 M19 Weiden in der Oberpfalz var. Weiden. Bayern, SE Germany 49°40′N 12°10′E
161 Q4 Weifang var. Wei, Wei-fang; prev. Weihsien. Shandong, E China 36°44′N 119°10′E
161 S4 Weihai Shandong, E China 37°30′N 122°04′E
160 K6 Wei He ≈ C China
Weihsien see Weifang
101 G17 Weilburg Hessen, W Germany 50°31′N 08°18′E
101 K24 Weilheim in Oberbayern Bayern, SE Germany 47°50′N 11°09′E
183 P4 Weilmoringle New South Wales, SE Australia 29°13′S 146°51′E
101 L16 Weimar Thüringen, C Germany 50°59′N 11°20′E
25 U11 Weimar Texas, SW USA 29°42′N 96°46′W
160 L6 Weinan Shaanxi, C China 34°30′N 109°30′E
108 H6 Weinfelden Thurgau, NE Switzerland 47°33′N 09°09′E
101 I24 Weingarten Baden-Württemberg, S Germany 47°49′N 09°37′E
101 G20 Weinheim Baden-Württemberg, SW Germany 49°33′N 08°40′E
160 H11 Weining var. Caohai, Weining Yizu Huizu Miaozu Zizhixian. Guizhou, S China 26°51′N 104°16′E
Weining Yizu Huizu Miaozu Zizhixian see Weining
181 V2 Weipa Queensland, NE Australia 12°43′S 142°01′E
11 Y11 Weir River Manitoba, C Canada 56°44′N 94°06′W
21 R1 Weirton West Virginia, NE USA 40°24′N 80°37′W
32 M13 Weiser Idaho, NW USA 44°15′N 116°58′W
160 F12 Weishan var. Weichang. Yunnan, SW China 25°22′N 100°19′E
161 P6 Weishan Hu ◎ E China
101 M15 Weisse Elster Eng. White Elster. ≈ Czech Republic/Germany
Weisse Körös/Weisse Kreisch see Crişul Alb
108 L7 Weissenbach am Lech Tirol, W Austria 47°27′N 10°39′E
Weissenburg see Wissembourg, France
Weissenburg see Alba Iulia, Romania
101 K21 Weissenburg in Bayern Bayern, SE Germany 49°02′N 10°59′E
101 M15 Weissenfels var. Weißenfels. Sachsen-Anhalt, C Germany 51°12′N 11°58′E
109 R9 Weissensee ◎ S Austria
Weissenstein see Paide
108 E11 Weisshorn var. Flüela Wisshorn. ▲ SW Switzerland 46°06′N 07°43′E
Weisskirchen see Bela Crkva
23 R3 Weiss Lake ⊠ Alabama, S USA
101 Q14 Weisswasser Lus. Běla Woda. Sachsen, E Germany 51°30′N 14°37′E
99 M22 Weiswampach Diekirch, N Luxembourg 50°08′N 06°05′E
109 U2 Weitra Niederösterreich, N Austria 48°41′N 14°54′E
161 O4 Weixian var. Wei Xian. Hebei, E China 36°59′N 115°15′E
Wei Xian see Weixian
159 V11 Weiyuan var. Qingyuan. Gansu, C China 35°07′N 104°12′E
Weiyuan see Shuangjiang
160 F14 Weiyuan Jiang ≈ SW China
109 W7 Weiz Steiermark, SE Austria 47°13′N 15°38′E
Weizhou see Wenchuan
160 K16 Weizhou Dao island S China
110 I6 Wejherowo Pomorskie, NW Poland 54°36′N 18°12′E
27 Q8 Welch Oklahoma, C USA 36°52′N 95°06′W
24 M6 Welch Texas, SW USA 32°52′N 102°06′W
21 Q6 Welch West Virginia, NE USA 37°26′N 81°36′W
45 O14 Welchman Hall C Barbados 13°10′N 59°34′W
80 J11 Weldiya var. Waldia, It. Valdia. Āmara, N Ethiopia 11°45′N 39°39′E
21 W8 Weldon North Carolina, SE USA 36°25′N 77°36′W
25 V9 Weldon Texas, SW USA 31°00′N 95°33′W
99 M19 Welkenraedt Liège, E Belgium 50°40′N 05°58′E
193 O2 Welker Seamount undersea feature N Pacific Ocean 55°07′N 140°18′W
83 I22 Welkom Free State, C South Africa 27°59′S 26°44′E
14 H16 Welland Ontario, S Canada 42°59′N 79°14′W
14 G16 Welland ≈ Ontario, S Canada
97 O19 Welland ≈ C England, United Kingdom
14 H17 Welland Canal canal Ontario, S Canada
155 K25 Wellawaya Uva Province, SE Sri Lanka 06°44′N 81°07′E
Welle see Uele
181 T4 Wellesley Islands island group Queensland, N Australia
99 J22 Wellin Luxembourg, SE Belgium 50°06′N 05°05′E
97 N20 Wellingborough C England, United Kingdom 52°19′N 00°42′W
183 R7 Wellington New South Wales, SE Australia 32°33′S 148°59′E
14 J15 Wellington Ontario, SE Canada 43°59′N 77°21′W
185 L14 Wellington ● Wellington, North Island, New Zealand 41°17′S 174°47′E
83 E26 Wellington Western Cape, SW South Africa 33°39′S 19°00′E
37 T2 Wellington Colorado, C USA 40°42′N 105°00′W
27 N7 Wellington Kansas, C USA 37°17′N 97°25′W
35 R7 Wellington Nevada, W USA 38°45′N 119°22′W
31 T11 Wellington Ohio, N USA 41°10′N 82°13′W
25 P3 Wellington Texas, SW USA 34°52′N 100°13′W
36 M4 Wellington Utah, W USA 39°31′N 110°45′W
185 M14 Wellington off. Wellington Region. ◈ region (New Zealand) North Island, New Zealand
185 L14 Wellington ✈ Wellington, North Island, New Zealand 41°19′S 174°48′E
Wellington see Wellington, Isla
63 F22 Wellington, Isla var. Wellington. island S Chile
183 P12 Wellington, Lake ◎ Victoria, SE Australia
Wellington Region see Wellington
29 X14 Wellman Iowa, C USA 41°27′N 91°50′W
24 M6 Wellman Texas, SW USA 33°03′N 102°25′W
97 K22 Wells SW England, United Kingdom 51°13′N 02°39′W
29 V11 Wells Minnesota, N USA 43°45′N 93°43′W
35 X2 Wells Nevada, W USA 41°07′N 114°58′W
25 W8 Wells Texas, SW USA 31°28′N 94°54′W
18 F12 Wellsboro Pennsylvania, NE USA 41°43′N 77°39′W
21 R1 Wellsburg West Virginia, NE USA 40°15′N 80°37′W
184 K4 Wellsford Auckland, North Island, New Zealand 36°17′S 174°30′E
180 L9 Wells, Lake ◎ Western Australia
181 N4 Wells, Mount ▲ Western Australia 17°39′S 127°08′E
97 P18 Wells-next-the-Sea E England, United Kingdom 52°58′N 00°48′E
31 T15 Wellston Ohio, N USA 39°07′N 82°31′W
27 O10 Wellston Oklahoma, C USA 35°41′N 97°03′W
18 E11 Wellsville New York, NE USA 42°06′N 77°55′W
31 V12 Wellsville Ohio, N USA 40°36′N 80°39′W
36 L1 Wellsville Utah, W USA 41°38′N 111°55′W
36 I14 Wellton Arizona, SW USA 32°40′N 114°09′W
109 S4 Wels anc. Ovilava. Oberösterreich, N Austria 48°10′N 14°02′E
99 K15 Welschap ✈ (Eindhoven) Noord-Brabant, S Netherlands 51°27′N 05°22′E
100 P10 Welse ≈ NE Germany
22 H9 Welsh Louisiana, S USA 30°12′N 92°49′W
97 K19 Welshpool Wel. Y Trallwng. E Wales, United Kingdom 52°38′N 03°06′W
97 O21 Welwyn Garden City E England, United Kingdom 51°48′N 00°13′W
79 K18 Wema Equateur, NW Dem. Rep. Congo 0°25′S 21°33′E
81 G21 Wembere ≈ C Tanzania
11 N13 Wembley Alberta, W Canada 55°07′N 119°12′W
12 I9 Wemindji prev. Nouveau-Comptoir, Paint Hills. Québec, C Canada 53°00′N 78°42′W
99 G18 Wemmel Vlaams Brabant, C Belgium 50°54′N 04°18′E
32 J8 Wenatchee Washington, NW USA 47°50′N 120°48′W
160 M17 Wenchang Hainan, S China 19°34′N 110°46′E
161 R11 Wencheng var. Daxue. Zhejiang, SE China 27°48′N 120°01′E
77 P16 Wenchi W Ghana 07°45′N 02°02′W
Wen-chou/Wenchow see Wenzhou
160 H8 Wenchuan var. Weizhou. Sichuan, C China 31°29′N 103°39′E
Wendau see Võnnu
Wenden see Cēsis
161 S4 Wendeng Shandong, E China 37°10′N 122°00′E
81 J14 Wendo Southern Nationalities, S Ethiopia 06°34′N 38°28′E
36 J2 Wendover Utah, W USA 40°41′N 114°00′W
14 D9 Wenebegon ≈ Ontario, S Canada
14 D8 Wenebegon Lake ◎ Ontario, S Canada
108 E9 Wengen Bern, W Switzerland 46°38′N 07°57′E
161 O13 Wengyuan var. Longxian. Guangdong, S China 24°22′N 114°06′E
189 P15 Weno prev. Moen. Chuuk, C Micronesia
189 V12 Weno prev. Moen. atoll Chuuk Islands, C Micronesia
158 N13 Wenquan Qinghai, C China 33°16′N 91°44′E
159 H4 Wenquan var. Arixang, Bogeda'er. Xinjiang Uygur Zizhiqu, NW China 45°00′N 81°02′E
Wenquan see Yingshan
160 H14 Wenshan var. Kaihua. Yunnan, SW China 23°22′N 104°21′E
158 H6 Wensu Xinjiang Uygur Zizhiqu, W China 41°15′N 80°11′E
182 L8 Wentworth New South Wales, SE Australia 34°04′S 141°53′E
27 W4 Wentzville Missouri, C USA 38°48′N 90°51′W
159 V12 Wenxian var. Wen Xian. Gansu, C China 32°57′N 104°42′E
Wen Xian see Wenxian
161 S10 Wenzhou var. Wen-chou, Wenchow. Zhejiang, SE China 28°02′N 120°36′E
34 L4 Weott California, W USA 40°19′N 123°57′W
99 I20 Wépion Namur, SE Belgium 50°24′N 04°53′E
100 O11 Werbellinsee ◎ NE Germany
99 L21 Werbomont Liège, E Belgium 50°22′N 05°43′E
83 G20 Werda Kgalagadi, S Botswana 25°13′S 23°16′E
81 N14 Werdēr Sumalē, E Ethiopia 06°59′N 45°20′E
Werder see Virtsu
Werenów see Voranava
171 U13 Weri Papua, E Indonesia 03°10′S 132°39′E
98 I13 Werkendam Noord-Brabant, S Netherlands 51°48′N 04°54′E
101 M20 Wernberg-Köblitz Bayern, SE Germany 49°31′N 12°10′E
101 J18 Werneck Bayern, C Germany 50°00′N 10°06′E
101 K14 Wernigerode Sachsen-Anhalt, C Germany 51°51′N 10°48′E
Werowitz see Virovitica
101 J16 Werra ≈ C Germany
183 N12 Werribee Victoria, SE Australia 37°55′S 144°39′E
183 T6 Werris Creek New South Wales, SE Australia 31°22′S 150°40′E
Werro see Võru
Werschetz see Vršac
101 K23 Wertach ≈ S Germany
101 I19 Wertheim Baden-Württemberg, SW Germany 49°45′N 09°31′E
98 J8 Wervershoof Noord-Holland, NW Netherlands 52°43′N 05°09′E
Wervicq see Wervik
99 C18 Wervik var. Wervicq, Werwick. West-Vlaanderen, W Belgium 50°47′N 03°03′E
Werwick see Wervik
101 D14 Wesel Nordrhein-Westfalen, W Germany 51°39′N 06°37′E
Weseli an der Lainsitz see Veselí nad Lužnicí
Wesenberg see Rakvere
100 H12 Weser ≈ NW Germany
Wes-Kaap see Western Cape
25 S17 Weslaco Texas, SW USA 26°09′N 97°59′W
14 J13 Weslemkoon Lake ◎ Ontario, SE Canada
181 R1 Wessel Islands island group Northern Territory, N Australia
29 P9 Wessington South Dakota, N USA 44°27′N 98°40′W
29 P10 Wessington Springs South Dakota, N USA 44°02′N 98°33′W
25 T8 West Texas, SW USA 31°48′N 97°05′W
West see Ouest
30 M9 West Allis Wisconsin, N USA 43°01′N 88°00′W
182 E8 Westall, Point headland South Australia 32°54′S 134°04′E
194 M10 West Antarctica prev. Lesser Antarctica. physical region Antarctica
14 G11 West Arm Ontario, S Canada 46°16′N 80°25′W
West Australian Basin see Wharton Basin
West Azerbaijan see Āžarbāyjān-e Gharbī
11 N17 Westbank British Columbia, SW Canada 49°50′N 119°37′W
138 F10 West Bank disputed region SW Asia
14 E11 West Bay Manitoulin Island, Ontario, S Canada 45°48′N 82°09′W
22 L11 West Bay bay Louisiana, S USA
30 M8 West Bend Wisconsin, N USA 43°26′N 88°13′W
153 R16 West Bengal ◈ state NE India
West Borneo see Kalimantan Barat
29 Y14 West Branch Iowa, C USA 41°40′N 91°21′W
31 R7 West Branch Michigan, N USA 44°16′N 84°14′W
18 F13 West Branch Susquehanna River ≈ Pennsylvania, NE USA
97 L20 West Bromwich C England, United Kingdom 52°29′N 01°59′W
19 P8 Westbrook Maine, NE USA 43°42′N 70°21′W
29 T10 Westbrook Minnesota, N USA 44°02′N 95°26′W
29 Y15 West Burlington Iowa, C USA 40°49′N 91°09′W
96 L2 West Burra island NE Scotland, United Kingdom
30 J8 Westby Wisconsin, N USA 43°40′N 90°52′W
44 L6 West Caicos island W Turks and Caicos Islands
185 A24 West Cape headland South Island, New Zealand 45°51′S 166°26′E
174 L4 West Caroline Basin undersea feature SW Pacific Ocean 04°00′N 138°00′E
18 I16 West Chester Pennsylvania, NE USA 39°56′N 75°35′W
185 E18 West Coast off. West Coast Region. ◈ region South Island, New Zealand
West Coast Region see West Coast
25 V12 West Columbia Texas, SW USA 29°08′N 95°39′W
29 W10 West Concord Minnesota, N USA 44°09′N 92°54′W

◆ Country
● Country Capital
◇ Dependent Territory
○ Dependent Territory Capital
◈ Administrative Regions
✈ International Airport
▲ Mountain
▲▲ Mountain Range
⛰ Volcano
≈ River
◎ Lake
⊠ Reservoir

29 V14 **West Des Moines** Iowa, C USA 41°33´N 93°42´W
37 Q6 **West Elk Peak** ▲ Colorado, C USA 38°43´N 107°12´W
44 F1 **West End** Grand Bahama Island, N Bahamas 26°36´N 78°55´W
44 F1 **West End Point** *headland* Grand Bahama Island, N Bahamas 26°40´N 78°58´W
98 O7 **Westerbork** Drenthe, NE Netherlands 52°49´N 06°36´E
98 N3 **Westereems** *strait* Germany/Netherlands
98 O9 **Westerhaar-Vriezenveensewijk** Overijssel, E Netherlands 52°28´N 06°38´E
100 G6 **Westerland** Schleswig-Holstein, N Germany 54°54´N 08°19´E
99 I17 **Westerlo** Antwerpen, N Belgium 51°05´N 04°55´E
19 N13 **Westerly** Rhode Island, NE USA 41°22´N 71°45´W
81 G18 **Western** ❖ *province* W Kenya
153 N11 **Western** ❖ *zone* C Nepal
186 A8 **Western** ❖ *province* SW Papua New Guinea
186 K9 **Western** ❖ *province* S Solomon Islands
186 J8 **Western** *off.* Western Province. ❖ *province* NW Solomon Islands
155 J26 **Western** ❖ *province* SW Sri Lanka
83 G15 **Western** ❖ *province* SW Zambia
180 K8 **Western Australia** ❖ *state* W Australia
80 A13 **Western Bahr el Ghazal** ❖ *state* W South Sudan
Western Bug *see* Bug
83 F25 **Western Cape** *off.* Western Cape Province, *Afr.* Wes-Kaap. ❖ *province* SW South Africa
Western Cape Province *see* Western Cape
80 A11 **Western Darfur** ❖ *state* W Sudan
Western Desert *see* Şaḩrā' al Gharbīyah
118 G9 **Western Dvina** *Bel.* Dzvina, *Ger.* Düna, *Latv.* Daugava, *Rus.* Zapadnaya Dvina. ≈ W Europe
81 D15 **Western Equatoria** ❖ *state* SW South Sudan
155 E16 **Western Ghats** ▲▲ SW India
186 C7 **Western Highlands** ❖ *province* C Papua New Guinea
Western Isles *see* Outer Hebrides
21 T3 **Westernport** Maryland, NE USA 39°29´N 79°03´W
Western Province *see* Western
Western Punjab *see* Punjab
74 B10 **Western Sahara** ◇ *disputed territory* N Africa
Western Samoa *see* Samoa
Western Sayans *see* Zapadnyy Sayan
Western Scheldt *see* Westerschelde
Western Sierra Madre *see* Madre Occidental, Sierra
99 E15 **Westerschelde** *Eng.* Western Scheldt; *prev.* Honte. *inlet* S North Sea
31 S13 **Westerville** Ohio, N USA 40°07´N 82°55´W
101 F17 **Westerwald** ▲▲ W Germany
65 C25 **West Falkland** *var.* Gran Malvina, Isla Gran Malvina. *island* W Falkland Islands
29 R5 **West Fargo** North Dakota, N USA 46°49´N 96°51´W
188 M15 **West Fayu Atoll** *atoll* Caroline Islands, C Micronesia
18 C11 **Westfield** New York, NE USA 42°18´N 79°34´W
30 L7 **Westfield** Wisconsin, N USA 43°56´N 89°31´W
West Flanders *see* West-Vlaanderen
27 S10 **West Fork** Arkansas, C USA 35°55´N 94°11´W
29 P16 **West Fork Big Blue River** ≈ Nebraska, C USA
29 U12 **West Fork Des Moines River** ≈ Iowa/Minnesota, C USA
25 S5 **West Fork Trinity River** ≈ Texas, SW USA
30 L16 **West Frankfort** Illinois, N USA 37°54´N 88°55´W
98 I8 **West-Friesland** *physical region* NW Netherlands
West Frisian Islands *see* Waddeneilanden
19 T5 **West Grand Lake** ◎ Maine, NE USA
18 M12 **West Hartford** Connecticut, NE USA 41°44´N 72°45´W
18 M13 **West Haven** Connecticut, NE USA 41°16´N 72°57´W
27 X12 **West Helena** Arkansas, C USA 34°33´N 90°38´W
28 M2 **Westhope** North Dakota, N USA 48°54´N 101°01´W
195 Y8 **West Ice Shelf** *ice shelf* Antarctica
47 R2 **West Indies** *island group* SE North America
West Irian *see* Papua
West Irian Jaya *see* Papua Barat
West Java *see* Jawa Barat
36 L3 **West Jordan** Utah, W USA 40°37´N 111°55´W
West Kalimantan *see* Kalimantan Barat
99 D14 **Westkapelle** Zeeland, SW Netherlands 51°32´N 03°26´E
West Kazakhstan *see* Zapadnyy Kazakhstan
31 O13 **West Lafayette** Indiana, N USA 40°24´N 86°54´W
31 T13 **West Lafayette** Ohio, N USA 40°16´N 81°45´W
West Lake *see* Kagera
29 Y14 **West Liberty** Iowa, C USA 41°34´N 91°15´W
21 O5 **West Liberty** Kentucky, S USA 37°56´N 83°16´W
Westliche Morava *see* Zapadna Morava
10 J13 **Westlock** Alberta, SW Canada 54°12´N 113°50´W
14 E17 **West Lorne** Ontario, S Canada 42°36´N 81°35´W
96 J12 **West Lothian** *cultural region* S Scotland, United Kingdom
99 H16 **Westmalle** Antwerpen, N Belgium 51°18´N 04°40´E
192 G6 **West Mariana Basin** *var.* Perece Vela Basin. *undersea feature* W Pacific Ocean 15°00´N 137°00´E
97 E17 **Westmeath** *Ir.* An Iarmhí, Na H-Iarmhidhe. *cultural region* C Ireland
27 Y11 **West Memphis** Arkansas, C USA 35°09´N 90°11´W
21 W2 **Westminster** Maryland, NE USA 39°34´N 77°00´W
21 O11 **Westminster** South Carolina, SE USA 34°39´N 83°06´W
22 I5 **West Monroe** Louisiana, S USA 32°31´N 92°09´W
18 D15 **Westmont** Pennsylvania, NE USA 40°16´N 78°55´W
27 O3 **Westmoreland** Kansas, C USA 39°23´N 96°30´W
35 W17 **Westmorland** California, W USA 33°02´N 115°37´W
186 E6 **West New Britain** ❖ *province* E Papua New Guinea
West New Guinea *see* Papua
83 K18 **West Nicholson** Matabeleland South, S Zimbabwe 21°06´S 29°25´E
29 T14 **West Nishnabotna River** ≈ Iowa, C USA
175 P11 **West Norfolk Ridge** *undersea feature* W Pacific Ocean
25 P12 **West Nueces River** ≈ Texas, SW USA
West Nusa Tenggara *see* Nusa Tenggara Barat
29 T11 **West Okoboji Lake** ◎ Iowa, C USA
33 R16 **Weston** Idaho, NW USA 42°01´N 119°29´W
21 R4 **Weston** West Virginia, NE USA 39°03´N 80°28´W
97 J22 **Weston-super-Mare** SW England, United Kingdom 51°21´N 02°59´W
23 Z14 **West Palm Beach** Florida, SE USA 26°43´N 80°03´W
West Papua *see* Papua
188 E9 **West Passage** *passage* Babeldaob, N Palau
23 O9 **West Pensacola** Florida, SE USA 30°25´N 87°16´W
27 V8 **West Plains** Missouri, C USA 36°44´N 91°51´W
35 P7 **West Point** California, W USA 38°21´N 120°33´W
23 R5 **West Point** Georgia, SE USA 32°52´N 85°10´W
22 M3 **West Point** Mississippi, S USA 33°36´N 88°39´W
29 R14 **West Point** Nebraska, C USA 41°50´N 96°42´W
21 X6 **West Point** Virginia, NE USA 37°31´N 76°48´W
182 G10 **West Point** *headland* South Australia 35°01´S 135°58´E
65 B24 **Westpoint Island Settlement** Westpoint Island, NW Falkland Islands 51°21´S 60°41´W
23 R4 **West Point Lake** ⊠ Alabama/Georgia, SE USA
97 B16 **Westport** *Ir.* Cathair na Mart. Mayo, W Ireland 53°48´N 09°32´W
185 G15 **Westport** West Coast, South Island, New Zealand 41°46´S 171°37´E
32 F10 **Westport** Oregon, NW USA 46°07´N 123°22´W
32 F9 **Westport** Washington, NW USA 46°53´N 124°06´W
31 S15 **West Portsmouth** Ohio, N USA 38°45´N 83°01´W
West Punjab *see* Punjab
11 V14 **Westray** Manitoba, C Canada 53°30´N 101°19´W
96 J4 **Westray** *island* NE Scotland, United Kingdom
14 F9 **Westree** Ontario, S Canada 47°25´N 81°32´W
97 L16 **West Riding** *cultural region* N England, United Kingdom
West River *see* Xi Jiang
30 J7 **West Salem** Wisconsin, N USA 43°54´N 91°04´W
65 H21 **West Scotia Ridge** *undersea feature* W Scotia Sea
West Sepik *see* Sandaun
173 N4 **West Sheba Ridge** *undersea feature* W Indian Ocean 12°45´N 48°15´E
West Siberian Plain *see* Zapadno-Sibirskaya Ravnina
31 S11 **West Sister Island** *island* Ohio, N USA
West-Skylge *see* West-Terschelling
West Sumatra *see* Sumatera Barat
98 J5 **West-Terschelling** *Fris.* West-Skylge. Fryslân, N Netherlands 53°23´N 05°15´E
64 J7 **West Thulean Rise** *undersea feature* N Atlantic Ocean
29 X12 **West Union** Iowa, C USA 42°57´N 91°48´W
31 R15 **West Union** Ohio, N USA 38°47´N 83°33´W
21 R3 **West Union** West Virginia, NE USA 39°18´N 80°47´W
31 N13 **Westville** Illinois, N USA 40°02´N 87°38´W
21 R3 **West Virginia** *off.* State of West Virginia, *also known as* Mountain State. ❖ *state* NE USA
99 A17 **West-Vlaanderen** *Eng.* West Flanders. ❖ *province* W Belgium
35 R7 **West Walker River** ≈ California/Nevada, W USA
35 P4 **Westwood** California, W USA 40°18´N 121°02´W
183 P9 **West Wyalong** New South Wales, SE Australia 33°56´S 147°10´E
171 Q16 **Wetar, Pulau** *island* Kepulauan Damar, E Indonesia
Wetar, Selat *see* Wetar Strait
171 R16 **Wetar Strait** *var.* SelatWetar. *strait* Nusa Tenggara, S Indonesia
11 Q15 **Wetaskiwin** Alberta, SW Canada 52°57´N 113°20´W
81 K21 **Wete** Pemba, E Tanzania 05°03´S 39°41´E
166 M4 **Wetlet** Sagaing, C Myanmar (Burma) 22°43´N 95°22´E
37 T6 **Wet Mountains** ▲▲ Colorado, C USA
101 E15 **Wetter** Nordrhein-Westfalen, W Germany 51°22´N 07°24´E
101 H17 **Wetter** ≈ W Germany
99 F17 **Wetteren** Oost-Vlaanderen, NW Belgium 51°06´N 03°59´E
108 F7 **Wettingen** Aargau, N Switzerland 47°28´N 08°20´E
27 P11 **Wetumka** Oklahoma, C USA 35°14´N 96°14´W
23 Q5 **Wetumpka** Alabama, S USA 32°32´N 86°12´W
108 G7 **Wetzikon** Zürich, N Switzerland 47°19´N 08°48´E
101 G17 **Wetzlar** Hessen, W Germany 50°33´N 08°30´E
99 C18 **Wevelgem** West-Vlaanderen, W Belgium 50°48´N 03°12´E
38 M6 **Wevok** *var.* Wewuk. Alaska, USA 68°52´N 166°05´W
23 R9 **Wewahitchka** Florida, SE USA 30°06´N 85°12´W
186 C6 **Wewak** East Sepik, NW Papua New Guinea 03°35´S 143°35´E
27 O11 **Wewoka** Oklahoma, C USA 35°09´N 96°30´W
Wewuk *see* Wevok
97 F20 **Wexford** *Ir.* Loch Garman. SE Ireland 52°21´N 06°31´W
97 F20 **Wexford** *Ir.* Loch Garman. *cultural region* SE Ireland
30 L7 **Weyauwega** Wisconsin, N USA 44°16´N 88°54´W
11 U17 **Weyburn** Saskatchewan, S Canada 49°39´N 103°51´W
Weyer *see* Weyer Markt
109 U5 **Weyer Markt** *var.* Weyer. Oberösterreich, N Austria 47°52´N 14°39´E
100 H11 **Weyhe** Niedersachsen, NW Germany 53°00´N 08°52´E
97 L24 **Weymouth** S England, United Kingdom 50°36´N 02°28´W
19 P11 **Weymouth** Massachusetts, NE USA 42°13´N 70°56´W
99 H18 **Wezembeek-Oppem** Vlaams Brabant, C Belgium 50°51´N 04°28´E
98 M9 **Wezep** Gelderland, E Netherlands 52°28´N 06°E
184 M9 **Whakamaru** Waikato, North Island, New Zealand 38°27´S 175°48´E
184 O8 **Whakatane** Bay of Plenty, North Island, New Zealand 37°58´S 177°E
184 O8 **Whakatane** ≈ North Island, New Zealand
9 O9 **Whale Cove** *var.* Tikirarjuaq. Nunavut, C Canada 62°14´N 92°10´W
96 M2 **Whalsay** *island* NE Scotland, United Kingdom
184 L11 **Whangaehu** ≈ North Island, New Zealand
184 M6 **Whangamata** Waikato, North Island, New Zealand 37°13´S 175°54´E
184 Q9 **Whangara** Gisborne, North Island, New Zealand 38°34´S 178°12´E
184 K3 **Whangarei** Northland, North Island, New Zealand 35°44´S 174°18´E
184 K3 **Whangaruru Harbour** *inlet* North Island, New Zealand
25 V12 **Wharton** Texas, SW USA 29°19´N 96°08´W
173 U8 **Wharton Basin** *var.* West Australian Basin. *undersea feature* E Indian Ocean
185 E18 **Whataroa** West Coast, South Island, New Zealand 43°17´S 170°20´E
8 K10 **Wha Ti** *prev.* Lac la Martre. Northwest Territories, W Canada 63°10´N 117°12´W
8 J9 **Wha Ti** Northwest Territories, W Canada 63°10´N 117°12´W
184 K6 **Whatipu** Auckland, North Island, New Zealand 37°17´S 174°44´E
33 Y16 **Wheatland** Wyoming, C USA 42°03´N 104°57´W
14 D18 **Wheatley** Ontario, S Canada 42°06´N 82°27´W
30 M10 **Wheaton** Illinois, N USA 41°52´N 88°06´W
29 R7 **Wheaton** Minnesota, N USA 45°48´N 96°30´W
37 T4 **Wheat Ridge** Colorado, C USA 39°44´N 105°06´W
25 P2 **Wheeler** Texas, SW USA 35°26´N 100°17´W
23 O2 **Wheeler Lake** ⊠ Alabama, S USA
35 Y6 **Wheeler Peak** ▲ Nevada, W USA 39°00´N 114°17´W
37 T9 **Wheeler Peak** ▲ New Mexico, SW USA 36°34´N 105°25´W
31 S15 **Wheelersburg** Ohio, N USA 38°43´N 82°51´W
21 R2 **Wheeling** West Virginia, NE USA 40°05´N 80°43´W
97 L16 **Whernside** ▲ N England, United Kingdom 54°13´N 02°27´W
182 F9 **Whidbey, Point** *headland* South Australia 34°36´S 135°08´E
180 I7 **Whim Creek** Western Australia 20°51´S 117°54´E
10 L17 **Whistler** British Columbia, SW Canada 50°07´N 122°57´W
21 W8 **Whitakers** North Carolina, SE USA 36°06´N 77°43´W
14 H15 **Whitby** Ontario, S Canada 43°52´N 78°56´W
97 N15 **Whitby** N England, United Kingdom 54°29´N 00°37´W
10 G6 **White** ≈ Yukon Territory, W Canada
13 T11 **White Bay** *bay* Newfoundland, Newfoundland and Labrador, E Canada
20 I8 **White Bluff** Tennessee, S USA 36°06´N 87°13´W
28 J6 **White Butte** ▲ North Dakota, N USA 46°23´N 103°18´W
19 R5 **White Cap Mountain** ▲ Maine, NE USA 45°33´N 69°15´W
22 J9 **White Castle** Louisiana, S USA 30°10´N 91°09´W
182 M5 **White Cliffs** New South Wales, SE Australia 30°52´S 143°04´E
31 P8 **White Cloud** Michigan, N USA 43°34´N 85°47´W
11 P14 **Whitecourt** Alberta, SW Canada 54°10´N 115°38´W
25 O2 **White Deer** Texas, SW USA 35°26´N 101°10´W
White Elster *see* Weisse Elster
24 M5 **Whiteface** Texas, SW USA 33°36´N 102°36´W
18 K7 **Whiteface Mountain** ▲ New York, NE USA 44°22´N 73°54´W
29 W5 **Whiteface Reservoir** ⊠ Minnesota, N USA
33 O7 **Whitefish** Montana, NW USA 48°24´N 114°20´W
31 N9 **Whitefish Bay** Wisconsin, N USA 43°09´N 87°54´W
31 Q3 **Whitefish Bay** *lake bay* Canada/USA
14 E11 **Whitefish Falls** Ontario, S Canada 46°06´N 81°42´W
14 B7 **Whitefish Lake** ◎ Ontario, S Canada
29 U6 **Whitefish Lake** ◎ Minnesota, C USA
31 Q3 **Whitefish Point** *headland* Michigan, N USA 46°46´N 84°57´W
31 O4 **Whitefish River** ≈ Michigan, N USA
25 O4 **Whiteflat** Texas, SW USA 34°06´N 100°55´W
27 V12 **White Hall** Arkansas, C USA 34°18´N 92°05´W
30 K14 **White Hall** Illinois, N USA 39°26´N 90°24´W
31 O8 **Whitehall** Michigan, N USA 43°24´N 86°21´W
18 L9 **Whitehall** New York, NE USA 43°33´N 73°24´W
31 S13 **Whitehall** Ohio, N USA 39°58´N 82°53´W
30 J7 **Whitehall** Wisconsin, N USA 44°22´N 91°20´W
97 J15 **Whitehaven** NW England, United Kingdom 54°33´N 03°35´W
10 I8 **Whitehorse** *territory capital* Yukon Territory, W Canada 60°41´N 135°08´W
184 O7 **White Island** *island* NE New Zealand
14 K13 **White Lake** ◎ Ontario, SE Canada
22 H10 **White Lake** ◎ Louisiana, S USA
186 G7 **Whiteman Range** ▲▲ New Britain, E Papua New Guinea
183 Q15 **Whitemark** Tasmania, SE Australia 40°10´S 148°01´E
35 S9 **White Mountains** ▲▲ California/Nevada, W USA
19 N7 **White Mountains** ▲▲ Maine/New Hampshire, NE USA
80 F11 **White Nile** ❖ *state* C Sudan
81 E14 **White Nile** *Ar.* Al Baḩr al Abyaḑ, An Nīl al Abyaḑ, Bahr el Jebel. ≈ NE South Sudan
67 U7 **White Nile** *var.* Bahr el Jebel. ≈ S Sudan
25 W5 **White Oak Creek** ≈ Texas, SW USA
10 H9 **White Pass** *pass* Canada/USA
32 I9 **White Pass** *pass* Washington, NW USA
21 O9 **White Pine** Tennessee, S USA 36°06´N 83°17´W
18 K14 **White Plains** New York, NE USA 41°01´N 73°45´W
37 N13 **Whiteriver** Arizona, SW USA 33°50´N 109°57´W
28 M11 **White River** South Dakota, N USA 43°34´N 100°45´W
27 W12 **White River** ≈ Arkansas, SE USA
37 P3 **White River** ≈ Colorado/Utah, C USA
31 N15 **White River** ≈ Indiana, N USA
31 O8 **White River** ≈ Michigan, N USA
28 K11 **White River** ≈ South Dakota, N USA
25 O5 **White River** ≈ Texas, SW USA
18 M8 **White River** ≈ Vermont, NE USA
25 O5 **White River Lake** ⊠ Texas, SW USA
32 H11 **White Salmon** Washington, NW USA 45°43´N 121°29´W
18 I10 **Whitesboro** New York, NE USA 43°07´N 75°17´W
25 T5 **Whitesboro** Texas, SW USA 33°39´N 96°54´W
21 O7 **Whitesburg** Kentucky, S USA 37°07´N 82°52´W
White Sea *see* Beloye More
White Sea-Baltic Canal/White Sea Canal *see* Belomorsko-Baltiyskiy Kanal
63 I25 **Whiteside, Canal** *channel* S Chile
33 S10 **White Sulphur Springs** Montana, NW USA 46°33´N 110°54´W
21 R6 **White Sulphur Springs** West Virginia, NE USA 37°48´N 80°18´W
20 J6 **Whitesville** Kentucky, S USA 37°40´N 86°48´W
32 I10 **White Swan** Washington, NW USA 46°22´N 120°46´W
21 U12 **Whiteville** North Carolina, SE USA 34°20´N 78°42´W
20 F10 **Whiteville** Tennessee, S USA 35°19´N 89°09´W
77 Q13 **White Volta** *var.* Nakambé, *Fr.* Volta Blanche. ≈ Burkina/Ghana
30 M9 **Whitewater** Wisconsin, N USA 42°51´N 88°43´W
37 P14 **Whitewater Baldy** ▲ New Mexico, SW USA 33°19´N 108°38´W
23 X17 **Whitewater Bay** *bay* Florida, SE USA
31 Q14 **Whitewater River** ≈ Indiana/Ohio, N USA
11 V16 **Whitewood** Saskatchewan, S Canada 50°19´N 102°16´W
28 J9 **Whitewood** South Dakota, N USA 44°27´N 103°38´W
25 U5 **Whitewright** Texas, SW USA 33°30´N 96°23´W
97 I15 **Whithorn** S Scotland, United Kingdom 54°44´N 04°26´W
184 M6 **Whitianga** Waikato, North Island, New Zealand 36°50´S 175°42´E
19 N11 **Whitinsville** Massachusetts, NE USA 42°06´N 71°40´W
20 M8 **Whitley City** Kentucky, S USA 36°45´N 84°29´W
21 Q11 **Whitmire** South Carolina, SE USA 34°30´N 81°36´W
31 R10 **Whitmore Lake** Michigan, N USA 42°26´N 83°44´W
195 N9 **Whitmore Mountains** ▲▲ Antarctica
14 I12 **Whitney** Ontario, SE Canada 45°29´N 78°11´W
25 T8 **Whitney** Texas, SW USA 31°56´N 97°20´W
25 S8 **Whitney, Lake** ⊠ Texas, SW USA
35 S11 **Whitney, Mount** ▲ California, W USA 37°45´N 119°55´W
181 Y6 **Whitsunday Group** *island group* Queensland, E Australia
25 S6 **Whitt** Texas, SW USA 32°55´N 98°01´W
29 U12 **Whittemore** Iowa, C USA 43°03´N 94°25´W
39 R12 **Whittier** Alaska, USA 60°46´N 148°40´W
35 T15 **Whittier** California, W USA 33°58´N 118°01´W
83 I25 **Whittlesea** Eastern Cape, S South Africa 32°08´S 26°51´E
20 K10 **Whitwell** Tennessee, S USA 35°12´N 85°31´W
8 L10 **Wholdaia Lake** ◎ Northwest Territories, NW Canada
182 H7 **Whyalla** South Australia 33°04´S 137°34´E
Whydah *see* Ouidah
14 F13 **Wiarton** Ontario, S Canada 44°44´N 81°10´W
171 O13 **Wiau** Sulawesi, C Indonesia 03°08´S 121°22´E
111 H15 **Wiązów** *Ger.* Wansen. Dolnośląskie, SW Poland 50°49´N 17°13´E
33 Y8 **Wibaux** Montana, NW USA 46°57´N 104°11´W
27 N6 **Wichita** Kansas, C USA 37°42´N 97°20´W
25 R5 **Wichita Falls** Texas, SW USA 33°55´N 98°30´W
26 L11 **Wichita Mountains** ▲▲ Oklahoma, C USA
25 R5 **Wichita River** ≈ Texas, SW USA
96 K6 **Wick** N Scotland, United Kingdom 58°26´N 03°06´W
36 K13 **Wickenburg** Arizona, SW USA 33°57´N 112°41´W
24 L8 **Wickett** Texas, SW USA 31°34´N 103°00´W
180 I7 **Wickham** Western Australia 20°40´S 117°11´E
182 M14 **Wickham, Cape** *headland* Tasmania, SE Australia 39°36´S 143°55´E
20 G7 **Wickliffe** Kentucky, S USA 36°58´N 89°04´W
97 G19 **Wicklow** *Ir.* Cill Mhantáin. E Ireland 52°59´N 06°03´W
97 F19 **Wicklow** *Ir.* Cill Mhantáin. *cultural region* E Ireland
97 G19 **Wicklow Head** *Ir.* Ceann Chill Mhantáin. *headland* E Ireland 52°57´N 06°00´W
97 F18 **Wicklow Mountains** *Ir.* Sléibhte Chill Mhantáin. ▲▲ E Ireland
14 H10 **Wicksteed Lake** ◎ Ontario, S Canada
Wida *see* Ouidah
65 G15 **Wideawake Airfield** ✈ (Georgetown) SW Ascension Island
97 K18 **Widnes** NW England, United Kingdom 53°22´N 02°44´W
110 H9 **Więcbork** *Ger.* Vandsburg. Kujawsko-pomorskie, C Poland 53°21´N 17°31´E
101 E17 **Wied** ≈ W Germany
101 F16 **Wiehl** Nordrhein-Westfalen, W Germany 50°57´N 07°33´E
111 L17 **Wieliczka** Małopolskie, S Poland 50°N 20°02´E
110 H12 **Wielkopolskie** ❖ *province* SW Poland
111 J14 **Wieluń** Sieradz, C Poland 51°14´N 18°33´E
109 X4 **Wien** *Eng.* Vienna, *Hung.* Bécs, *Slvk.* Vídeň, *Slvn.* Dunaj; *anc.* Vindobona. ● (Austria) Wien, NE Austria 48°13´N 16°22´E
109 X4 **Wien** *off.* Land Wien, *Eng.* Vienna. ❖ *state* NE Austria
109 X5 **Wiener Neustadt** Niederösterreich, E Austria 47°49´N 16°08´E
Wien, Land *see* Wien
110 G7 **Wieprza** *Ger.* Wipper. ≈ NW Poland
98 O10 **Wierden** Overijssel, E Netherlands 52°22´N 06°35´E
98 I7 **Wieringerwerf** Noord-Holland, NW Netherlands 52°51´N 05°01´E
Wieruschow *see* Wieruszów
111 I14 **Wieruszów** *Ger.* Wieruschow. Łódzkie, C Poland 51°18´N 18°09´E
109 V9 **Wies** Steiermark, SE Austria 46°40´N 15°16´E
Wiesbachhorn *see* Grosses Wiesbachhorn
101 G18 **Wiesbaden** Hessen, W Germany 50°06´N 08°14´E
Wieselburg and Ungarisch-Altenburg/Wieselburg-Ungarisch-Altenburg *see* Mosonmagyaróvár
Wiesenhof *see* Ostrołęka
101 G20 **Wiesloch** Baden-Württemberg, SW Germany 49°18´N 08°42´E
100 F10 **Wiesmoor** Niedersachsen, NW Germany 53°22´N 07°46´E
110 I7 **Wieżyca** *Ger.* Turmberg. *hill* Pomorskie, N Poland
97 L17 **Wigan** NW England, United Kingdom 53°33´N 02°38´W
37 U3 **Wiggins** Colorado, C USA 40°11´N 104°03´W
22 M8 **Wiggins** Mississippi, S USA 30°50´N 89°09´W
Wigorna Ceaster *see* Worcester
97 I14 **Wigtown** S Scotland, United Kingdom 54°53´N 04°27´W
97 H14 **Wigtown** *cultural region* SW Scotland, United Kingdom
97 I15 **Wigtown Bay** *bay* SW Scotland, United Kingdom
98 L13 **Wijchen** Gelderland, SE Netherlands 51°48´N 05°44´E
92 N1 **Wijdefjorden** *fjord* NW Svalbard
98 M10 **Wijhe** Overijssel, E Netherlands 52°22´N 06°07´E
98 J12 **Wijk bij Duurstede** Utrecht, C Netherlands 51°58´N 05°21´E
98 J13 **Wijk en Aalburg** Noord-Brabant, S Netherlands 51°45´N 05°06´E
99 H16 **Wijnegem** Antwerpen, N Belgium 51°13´N 04°32´E
14 E11 **Wikwemikong** Manitoulin Island, Ontario, S Canada 45°46´N 81°43´W
108 H7 **Wil** Sankt Gallen, NE Switzerland 47°28´N 09°03´E
29 R16 **Wilber** Nebraska, C USA 40°28´N 96°57´W
32 K8 **Wilbur** Washington, NW USA 47°45´N 118°42´W
27 Q11 **Wilburton** Oklahoma, C USA 34°57´N 95°20´W
182 M6 **Wilcannia** New South Wales, SE Australia 31°34´S 143°23´E
18 D12 **Wilcox** Pennsylvania, NE USA 41°34´N 78°40´W
Wilczek Land *see* Vil'cheka, Zemlya
109 U6 **Wildalpen** Steiermark, E Austria 47°40´N 14°54´E
31 O13 **Wildcat Creek** ≈ Indiana, N USA
108 L9 **Wilde Kreuzspitze** *It.* Picco di Croce. ▲ Austria/Italy 46°53´N 10°51´E
Wildenschwert *see* Ústí nad Orlicí
98 O6 **Wildervank** Groningen, NE Netherlands 53°04´N 06°52´E
100 G11 **Wildeshausen** Niedersachsen, NW Germany 52°54´N 08°26´E
108 D10 **Wildhorn** ▲ SW Switzerland 46°21´N 07°22´E
11 R17 **Wild Horse** Alberta, SW Canada 49°00´N 110°19´W
27 N12 **Wildhorse Creek** ≈ Oklahoma, C USA
28 L14 **Wild Horse Hill** ▲ Nebraska, C USA 41°52´N 101°56´W
109 W8 **Wildon** Steiermark, SE Austria 46°53´N 15°29´E
24 M2 **Wildorado** Texas, SW USA 35°12´N 102°10´W
29 R6 **Wild Rice River** ≈ Minnesota/North Dakota, N USA
Wilejka *see* Vilyeyka
195 Y9 **Wilhelm II Coast** *physical region* Antarctica
195 X9 **Wilhelm II Land** *physical region* Antarctica
55 U11 **Wilhelmina Gebergte** ▲▲ C Suriname
18 B13 **Wilhelm, Lake** ⊠ Pennsylvania, NE USA
92 O2 **Wilhelmøya** *island* C Svalbard
Wilhelm-Pieck-Stadt *see* Guben
109 W4 **Wilhelmsburg** Niederösterreich, E Austria 48°07´N 15°37´E
100 G10 **Wilhelmshaven** Niedersachsen, NW Germany 53°31´N 08°07´E
Wilia/Wilja *see* Neris
18 H13 **Wilkes Barre** Pennsylvania, NE USA 41°15´N 75°50´W
21 R9 **Wilkesboro** North Carolina, SE USA 36°08´N 81°09´W
195 W15 **Wilkes Coast** *physical region* Antarctica
189 W12 **Wilkes Island** *island* N Wake Island
195 X12 **Wilkes Land** *physical region* Antarctica
11 S15 **Wilkie** Saskatchewan, S Canada 52°27´N 108°42´W
194 I6 **Wilkins Ice Shelf** *ice shelf* Antarctica
182 D4 **Wilkinsons Lakes** *salt lake* South Australia
Wiłkomierz *see* Ukmergė
182 K11 **Willalooka** South Australia 36°24´S 140°20´E
32 G11 **Willamette River** ≈ Oregon, NW USA
183 O8 **Willandra Billabong Creek** *seasonal river* New South Wales, SE Australia
32 F9 **Willapa Bay** *inlet* Washington, NW USA
27 T7 **Willard** Missouri, C USA 37°18´N 93°25´W
37 S12 **Willard** New Mexico, SW USA 34°36´N 106°01´W
31 S12 **Willard** Ohio, N USA 41°03´N 82°43´W
36 L1 **Willard** Utah, W USA 41°23´N 112°01´W
186 G6 **Willaumez Peninsula** *headland* New Britain, E Papua New Guinea 05°03´S 150°04´E
37 N15 **Willcox** Arizona, SW USA 32°13´N 109°49´W
37 N16 **Willcox Playa** *salt flat* Arizona, SW USA
99 G17 **Willebroek** Antwerpen, C Belgium 51°04´N 04°22´E
45 P16 **Willemstad** ○ Curaçao 12°07´N 68°54´W
99 G14 **Willemstad** Noord-Brabant, S Netherlands 51°40´N 04°27´E
11 S11 **William** ≈ Saskatchewan, C Canada
23 O6 **William "Bill" Dannelly Reservoir** ⊠ Alabama, S USA
182 G3 **William Creek** South Australia 28°55´S 136°23´E
181 T15 **William, Mount** ▲ South Australia
36 K11 **Williams** Arizona, SW USA 35°15´N 112°11´W
29 X14 **Williamsburg** Iowa, C USA 41°39´N 92°00´W
20 M8 **Williamsburg** Kentucky, S USA 36°44´N 84°10´W
31 R15 **Williamsburg** Ohio, N USA 39°00´N 84°02´W
21 X6 **Williamsburg** Virginia, NE USA 37°17´N 76°43´W
10 M15 **Williams Lake** British Columbia, SW Canada 52°08´N 122°09´W
21 P6 **Williamson** West Virginia, NE USA 37°42´N 82°16´W
31 N13 **Williamsport** Indiana, N USA 40°18´N 87°18´W
18 G13 **Williamsport** Pennsylvania, NE USA 41°16´N 77°03´W
21 W9 **Williamston** North Carolina, SE USA 35°53´N 77°05´W
21 P11 **Williamston** South Carolina, SE USA 34°37´N 82°28´W
20 M4 **Williamstown** Kentucky, S USA 38°39´N 84°32´W
18 L10 **Williamstown** Massachusetts, NE USA 42°41´N 73°11´W
18 J16 **Willingboro** New Jersey, NE USA 40°01´N 74°52´W
11 Q14 **Willingdon** Alberta, SW Canada 53°49´N 112°08´W
25 W10 **Willis** Texas, SW USA 30°25´N 95°28´W
108 F8 **Willisau** Luzern, W Switzerland 47°07´N 08°00´E
83 F24 **Williston** Northern Cape, W South Africa 31°20´S 20°52´E
23 V10 **Williston** Florida, SE USA 29°23´N 82°27´W
28 J3 **Williston** North Dakota, N USA 48°07´N 103°37´W
21 Q13 **Williston** South Carolina, SE USA 33°24´N 81°25´W
10 L12 **Williston Lake** ⊠ British Columbia, W Canada
34 L5 **Willits** California, W USA 39°24´N 123°22´W
29 T8 **Willmar** Minnesota, N USA 45°07´N 95°02´W
10 K11 **Will, Mount** ▲ British Columbia, W Canada 57°31´N 128°48´W
31 T11 **Willoughby** Ohio, N USA 41°38´N 81°24´W
11 U17 **Willow Bunch** Saskatchewan, S Canada 49°30´N 105°41´W
32 J11 **Willow Creek** ≈ Oregon, NW USA
39 R11 **Willow Lake** Alaska, USA 61°44´N 150°02´W
8 I9 **Willowlake** ≈ Northwest Territories, NW Canada
83 H25 **Willowmore** Eastern Cape, S South Africa 33°18´S 23°30´E
30 L5 **Willow Reservoir** ⊠ Wisconsin, N USA
35 N5 **Willows** California, W USA 39°28´N 122°12´W
27 V7 **Willow Springs** Missouri, C USA 36°59´N 91°58´W
182 I7 **Wilmington** South Australia 32°42´S 138°08´E
21 Y2 **Wilmington** Delaware, NE USA 39°45´N 75°33´W
21 V12 **Wilmington** North Carolina, SE USA 34°14´N 77°55´W
31 R14 **Wilmington** Ohio, N USA 39°27´N 83°49´W
20 M6 **Wilmore** Kentucky, S USA 37°51´N 84°39´W
29 R8 **Wilmot** South Dakota, N USA 45°24´N 96°51´W
Wilna/Wilno *see* Vilnius
101 G16 **Wilnsdorf** Nordrhein-Westfalen, W Germany 50°49´N 08°06´E
99 G16 **Wilrijk** Antwerpen, N Belgium 51°11´N 04°25´E
100 I10 **Wilseder Berg** *hill* NW Germany
67 Z12 **Wilshaw Ridge** *undersea feature* W Indian Ocean 17°30´S 56°30´E
21 V9 **Wilson** North Carolina, SE USA 35°43´N 77°56´W
25 N5 **Wilson** Texas, SW USA 33°21´N 101°44´W
182 A7 **Wilson Bluff** *headland* South Australia/Western Australia 31°41´S 129°01´E
35 Y7 **Wilson Creek Range** ▲▲ Nevada, W USA
23 O1 **Wilson Lake** ⊠ Alabama, S USA
26 M4 **Wilson Lake** ⊠ Kansas, SE USA
37 P7 **Wilson, Mount** ▲ Colorado, C USA 37°50´N 107°59´W
183 P13 **Wilsons Promontory** *peninsula* Victoria, SE Australia
29 Y14 **Wilton** Iowa, C USA 41°35´N 91°01´W
19 P7 **Wilton** Maine, NE USA 44°35´N 70°15´W
28 M5 **Wilton** North Dakota, N USA 47°09´N 100°46´W
97 L22 **Wiltshire** *cultural region* S England, United Kingdom
99 M23 **Wiltz** Diekirch, NW Luxembourg 49°58´N 05°56´E
180 K9 **Wiluna** Western Australia 26°34´S 120°14´E
99 M23 **Wilwerwiltz** Diekirch, NE Luxembourg 49°59´N 06°00´E
29 P5 **Wimbledon** North Dakota, N USA 47°08´N 98°25´W
42 K7 **Wina** *var.* Güina. Jinotega, N Nicaragua 14°00´N 85°14´W
31 O12 **Winamac** Indiana, N USA 41°03´N 86°37´W
81 G19 **Winam Gulf** *var.* Kavirondo Gulf. *gulf* SW Kenya
83 I22 **Winburg** Free State, C South Africa 28°31´S 27°01´E
19 N10 **Winchendon** Massachusetts, NE USA 42°41´N 72°01´W
14 M13 **Winchester** Ontario, SE Canada 45°07´N 75°19´W
97 M23 **Winchester** *hist.* Wintanceaster, *Lat.* Venta Belgarum. S England, United Kingdom 51°04´N 01°19´W
32 M10 **Winchester** Idaho, NW USA 46°13´N 116°35´W
30 J14 **Winchester** Illinois, N USA 39°38´N 90°28´W
31 Q13 **Winchester** Indiana, N USA 40°11´N 84°57´W
20 M5 **Winchester** Kentucky, S USA 38°00´N 84°10´W
18 M10 **Winchester** New Hampshire, NE USA 42°46´N 72°21´W
20 K10 **Winchester** Tennessee, S USA 35°11´N 86°06´W
21 V3 **Winchester** Virginia, NE USA 39°11´N 78°12´W
99 L22 **Wincrange** Diekirch, NW Luxembourg 50°03´N 05°55´E
10 I5 **Wind** ≈ Yukon Territory, NW Canada

◆ Country
● Country Capital
◇ Dependent Territory
○ Dependent Territory Capital
❖ Administrative Regions
✈ International Airport
▲ Mountain
▲▲ Mountain Range
Volcano
≈ River
◎ Lake
⊠ Reservoir

183 S8 **Windamere, Lake** ◎ New South Wales, SE Australia
Windau *see* Ventspils, Latvia
Windau *see* Venta, Latvia/Lithuania
18 D15 **Windber** Pennsylvania, NE USA 40°12′N 78°47′W
23 T3 **Winder** Georgia, SE USA 33°59′N 83°43′W
97 K15 **Windermere** NW England, United Kingdom 54°24′N 02°54′W
14 C7 **Windermere Lake** ◎ Ontario, S Canada
31 U11 **Windham** Ohio, N USA 41°14′N 81°03′W
83 D19 **Windhoek** *Ger.* Windhuk. ● (Namibia) Khomas, C Namibia 22°34′S 17°06′E
83 D20 **Windhoek** ✕ Khomas, C Namibia 22°31′S 17°04′E
Windhuk *see* Windhoek
15 O8 **Windigo** Québec, SE Canada 47°45′N 73°19′W
15 O8 **Windigo** ≈ Québec, SE Canada
Windischfeistritz *see* Slovenska Bistrica
109 T6 **Windischgarsten** Oberösterreich, W Austria 47°42′N 14°21′E
Windischgraz *see* Slovenj Gradec
37 T16 **Wind Mountain** ▲ New Mexico, SW USA 32°01′N 105°35′W
29 T10 **Windom** Minnesota, N USA 43°52′N 95°07′W
37 Q7 **Windom Peak** ▲ Colorado, C USA 37°37′N 107°35′W
181 U9 **Windorah** Queensland, C Australia 25°25′S 142°41′E
37 O10 **Window Rock** Arizona, SW USA 35°40′N 109°03′W
31 N9 **Wind Point** *headland* Wisconsin, N USA 42°46′N 87°46′W
33 U14 **Wind River** ≈ Wyoming, C USA
13 P15 **Windsor** Nova Scotia, SE Canada 45°00′N 64°09′W
14 C17 **Windsor** Ontario, S Canada 42°18′N 83°W
15 Q12 **Windsor** Québec, SE Canada 45°34′N 72°00′W
97 N22 **Windsor** S England, United Kingdom 51°29′N 00°39′W
37 T3 **Windsor** Colorado, C USA 40°28′N 104°54′W
18 M12 **Windsor** Connecticut, NE USA 41°51′N 72°38′W
27 T5 **Windsor** Missouri, C USA 38°31′N 93°31′W
21 X9 **Windsor** North Carolina, SE USA 36°00′N 76°57′W
18 M12 **Windsor Locks** Connecticut, NE USA 41°55′N 72°37′W
25 R5 **Windthorst** Texas, SW USA 33°34′N 98°26′W
45 Z14 **Windward Islands** *island group* E West Indies
Windward Islands *see* Barlavento, Ilhas de, Cape Verde
Windward Islands *see* Vent, Îles du, Archipel de la Société, French Polynesia
44 K8 **Windward Passage** *Sp.* Paso de los Vientos. *channel* Cuba/Haiti
55 T9 **Wineperu** C Guyana 06°10′N 58°34′W
23 O3 **Winfield** Alabama, S USA 33°55′N 87°49′W
29 Y15 **Winfield** Iowa, C USA 41°07′N 91°26′W
27 O7 **Winfield** Kansas, C USA 37°14′N 97°00′W
25 W6 **Winfield** Texas, SW USA 33°10′N 95°06′W
21 Q4 **Winfield** West Virginia, NE USA 38°30′N 81°54′W
29 N5 **Wing** North Dakota, N USA 47°06′N 100°16′W
183 U7 **Wingham** New South Wales, SE Australia 31°52′S 152°24′E
12 G16 **Wingham** Ontario, S Canada 43°54′N 81°19′W
33 T8 **Winifred** Montana, NW USA 47°33′N 109°26′W
12 E9 **Winisk Lake** ◎ Ontario, C Canada
24 L8 **Wink** Texas, SW USA 31°45′N 103°09′W
36 M14 **Winkelman** Arizona, SW USA 32°59′N 110°46′W
11 X17 **Winkler** Manitoba, S Canada 49°12′N 97°55′W
109 Q9 **Winklern** Tirol, W Austria 46°54′N 12°54′E
Winkowitz *see* Vinkovci
32 G9 **Winlock** Washington, NW USA 46°29′N 122°56′W
77 P17 **Winneba** SE Ghana 05°22′N 00°38′W
29 U11 **Winnebago** Minnesota, N USA 43°46′N 94°10′W
29 R13 **Winnebago** Nebraska, C USA 42°14′N 96°28′W
30 M7 **Winnebago, Lake** ◎ Wisconsin, N USA
30 M7 **Winneconne** Wisconsin, N USA 44°07′N 88°44′W
35 T3 **Winnemucca** Nevada, W USA 40°59′N 117°44′W
35 R4 **Winnemucca Lake** ◎ Nevada, W USA
101 H21 **Winnenden** Baden-Württemberg, SW Germany 48°52′N 09°22′E
29 N11 **Winner** South Dakota, N USA 43°22′N 99°51′W
33 U9 **Winnett** Montana, NW USA 47°00′N 108°18′W
14 I9 **Winneway** Québec, SE Canada 47°35′N 78°33′W
22 H6 **Winnfield** Louisiana, S USA 31°55′N 92°38′W
29 U4 **Winnibigoshish, Lake** ◎ Minnesota, N USA
25 X11 **Winnie** Texas, SW USA 29°49′N 94°22′W
11 Y16 **Winnipeg** *province capital* Manitoba, S Canada 49°53′N 97°10′W
11 X16 **Winnipeg** ✕ Manitoba, S Canada 49°56′N 97°16′W
0 J8 **Winnipeg** ≈ Manitoba, S Canada
11 X16 **Winnipeg Beach** Manitoba, S Canada 50°25′N 96°59′W
11 W14 **Winnipeg, Lake** ◎ Manitoba, C Canada
11 W15 **Winnipegosis** Manitoba, S Canada 51°36′N 99°59′W
11 W15 **Winnipegosis, Lake** ◎ Manitoba, C Canada
19 O8 **Winnipesaukee, Lake** ◎ New Hampshire, NE USA
22 I6 **Winnsboro** Louisiana, S USA 32°09′N 91°43′W
21 R12 **Winnsboro** South Carolina, SE USA 34°22′N 81°05′W
25 W6 **Winnsboro** Texas, SW USA 33°01′N 95°16′W
29 X10 **Winona** Minnesota, N USA 44°03′N 91°37′W
22 L4 **Winona** Mississippi, S USA 33°30′N 89°42′W
27 W7 **Winona** Missouri, C USA 37°00′N 91°19′W
25 W7 **Winona** Texas, SW USA 32°29′N 95°10′W
18 M7 **Winooski River** ≈ Vermont, NE USA
98 P6 **Winschoten** Groningen, NE Netherlands 53°09′N 07°03′E
100 J10 **Winsen** Niedersachsen, N Germany 53°22′N 10°13′E
36 M11 **Winslow** Arizona, SW USA 35°01′N 110°42′W
19 Q7 **Winslow** Maine, NE USA 44°33′N 69°35′W
18 M12 **Winsted** Connecticut, NE USA 41°55′N 73°03′W
32 F14 **Winston** Oregon, NW USA 43°07′N 123°24′W
21 S9 **Winston Salem** North Carolina, SE USA 36°06′N 80°15′W
98 N5 **Winsum** Groningen, NE Netherlands 53°20′N 06°31′E
Wintanceaster *see* Winchester
23 W11 **Winter Garden** Florida, SE USA 28°34′N 81°35′W
10 J16 **Winter Harbour** Vancouver Island, British Columbia, SW Canada 50°28′N 128°03′W
23 W12 **Winter Haven** Florida, SE USA 28°01′N 81°43′W
23 X11 **Winter Park** Florida, SE USA 28°36′N 81°20′W
25 P8 **Winters** Texas, SW USA 31°57′N 99°57′W
29 U15 **Winterset** Iowa, C USA 41°19′N 94°00′W
98 O12 **Winterswijk** Gelderland, E Netherlands 51°58′N 06°44′E
108 G6 **Winterthur** Zürich, NE Switzerland 47°30′N 08°43′E
29 U9 **Winthrop** Minnesota, N USA 44°32′N 94°22′W
32 J7 **Winthrop** Washington, NW USA 48°28′N 120°13′W
181 V7 **Winton** Queensland, E Australia 22°22′S 143°04′E
185 C24 **Winton** Southland, South Island, New Zealand 46°08′S 168°20′E
21 X8 **Winton** North Carolina, SE USA 36°24′N 76°57′W
101 K15 **Wipper** ≈ C Germany
101 K14 **Wipper** ≈ C Germany
Wipper *see* Wieprza
182 G6 **Wirraminna** South Australia 31°10′S 136°13′E
182 F4 **Wirrida** South Australia 29°34′S 134°33′E
182 F7 **Wirrulla** South Australia 32°27′S 134°33′E
Wirsitz *see* Wyrzysk
Wirz-See *see* Võrtsjärv
97 O19 **Wisbech** E England, United Kingdom 52°39′N 00°08′E
Wisby *see* Visby
19 Q8 **Wiscasset** Maine, NE USA 44°01′N 69°41′W
Wischau *see* Vyškov
30 J5 **Wisconsin** *off.* State of Wisconsin, *also known as* Badger State. ◆ *state* N USA
30 L8 **Wisconsin Dells** Wisconsin, N USA 43°37′N 89°43′W
30 L8 **Wisconsin, Lake** ⊠ Wisconsin, N USA
30 L7 **Wisconsin Rapids** Wisconsin, N USA 44°24′N 89°50′W
30 L7 **Wisconsin River** ≈ Wisconsin, N USA
33 P11 **Wisdom** Montana, NW USA 45°36′N 113°27′W
21 P7 **Wise** Virginia, NE USA 37°00′N 82°36′W
39 Q7 **Wiseman** Alaska, USA 67°24′N 150°06′W
96 J12 **Wishaw** W Scotland, United Kingdom 55°47′N 03°56′W
29 O6 **Wishek** North Dakota, N USA 46°12′N 99°33′W
32 I11 **Wishram** Washington, NW USA 45°40′N 120°53′W
111 J17 **Wisła** Śląskie, S Poland 49°39′N 18°50′E
110 K11 **Wisła** *Eng.* Vistula, *Ger.* Weichsel. ≈ C Poland
Wiślany, Zalew *see* Vistula Lagoon
111 M16 **Wisłoka** ≈ SE Poland
100 L9 **Wismar** Mecklenburg-Vorpommern, N Germany 53°54′N 11°28′E
29 R14 **Wisner** Nebraska, C USA 41°59′N 96°54′W
103 V4 **Wissembourg** *var.* Weissenburg. Bas-Rhin, NE France 49°03′N 07°57′E
30 J6 **Wissota, Lake** ⊠ Wisconsin, N USA
97 O18 **Witham** ≈ E England, United Kingdom
97 O17 **Withernsea** E England, United Kingdom 53°46′N 00°01′W
37 Q13 **Withington, Mount** ▲ New Mexico, SW USA 33°52′N 107°29′W
23 U8 **Withlacoochee River** ≈ Florida/Georgia, SE USA
110 H11 **Witkowo** Wielkopolskie, C Poland 52°27′N 17°49′E
97 M21 **Witney** S England, United Kingdom 51°47′N 01°30′W
101 E15 **Witten** Nordrhein-Westfalen, W Germany 51°25′N 07°19′E
101 N14 **Wittenberg** Sachsen-Anhalt, E Germany 51°53′N 12°39′E
30 L6 **Wittenberg** Wisconsin, N USA 44°53′N 89°20′W
100 L11 **Wittenberge** Brandenburg, N Germany 52°59′N 11°45′E
103 U7 **Wittenheim** Haut-Rhin, NE France 47°49′N 07°19′E
180 I7 **Wittenoom** Western Australia 22°17′S 118°22′E
Wittingau *see* Třeboň
100 K12 **Wittingen** Niedersachsen, C Germany 52°42′N 10°43′E
101 E18 **Wittlich** Rheinland-Pfalz, SW Germany 49°59′N 06°54′E
100 F9 **Wittmund** Niedersachsen, NW Germany 53°34′N 07°46′E
100 M10 **Wittstock** Brandenburg, NE Germany 53°10′N 12°29′E
186 F6 **Witu Islands** *island group* E Papua New Guinea
110 O7 **Wiżajny** Podlaskie, NE Poland 54°22′N 22°51′E
55 W10 **W. J. van Blommesteinmeer** ⊠ E Suriname
110 L11 **Wkra** *Ger.* Soldau. ≈ C Poland
110 I6 **Władysławowo** Pomorskie, N Poland 54°48′N 18°25′E
Wlaschim *see* Vlašim
111 E14 **Wleń** *Ger.* Lähn. Dolnośląskie, SW Poland 51°00′N 15°39′E
110 J11 **Włocławek** *Ger./Rus.* Vlotslavsk. Kujawsko-pomorskie, C Poland 52°39′N 19°03′E
110 P13 **Włodawa** *Rus.* Vlodava. Lubelskie, SE Poland 51°33′N 23°31′E
Włodzimierz *see* Volodymyr-Volyns'kyy
111 K15 **Włoszczowa** Świętokrzyskie, C Poland 50°51′N 19°58′E
83 C19 **Wlotzkasbaken** Erongo, W Namibia 22°26′S 14°30′E
15 R12 **Woburn** Québec, SE Canada 45°22′N 70°52′W
19 O11 **Woburn** Massachusetts, NE USA 42°28′N 71°09′W
Wocheiner Feistritz *see* Bohinjska Bistrica
Wöchma *see* Võhma
147 S11 **Wodil** *var.* Vuadil'. Farg'ona Viloyati, E Uzbekistan 40°10′N 71°43′E
181 V14 **Wodonga** Victoria, SE Australia 36°11′S 146°55′E
111 I17 **Wodzisław Śląski** *Ger.* Loslau. Śląskie, S Poland 49°59′N 18°27′E
98 I11 **Woerden** Zuid-Holland, C Netherlands 52°06′N 04°54′E
98 I8 **Wognum** Noord-Holland, NW Netherlands 52°40′N 05°01′E
Wohlau *see* Wołów
108 F7 **Wohlen** Aargau, NW Switzerland 47°21′N 08°17′E
195 R2 **Wohlthat Massivet** *Eng.* Wohlthat Mountains. ▲▲ Antarctica
Wohlthat Mountains *see* Wohlthat Massivet
Wojerecy *see* Hoyerswerda
Wōjjā *see* Wotje Atoll
Wojwodina *see* Vojvodina
171 V15 **Wokam, Pulau** *island* Kepulauan Aru, E Indonesia
97 N22 **Woking** SE England, United Kingdom 51°20′N 00°34′W
Woldenberg Neumark *see* Dobiegniew
188 K15 **Woleai Atoll** *atoll* Caroline Islands, W Micronesia
Woleu *see* Uolo, Río
79 E17 **Woleu-Ntem** *off.* Province du Woleu-Ntem, *var.* Le Woleu-Ntem. ◆ *province* W Gabon
Woleu-Ntem, Province du *see* Woleu-Ntem
32 F15 **Wolf Creek** Oregon, NW USA 42°40′N 123°22′W
26 K9 **Wolf Creek** ≈ Oklahoma/Texas, SW USA
37 R7 **Wolf Creek Pass** *pass* Colorado, C USA
19 O9 **Wolfeboro** New Hampshire, NE USA 43°34′N 71°10′W
25 U5 **Wolfe City** Texas, SW USA 33°22′N 96°04′W
14 L15 **Wolfe Island** *island* Ontario, SE Canada
101 M14 **Wolfen** Sachsen-Anhalt, E Germany 51°40′N 12°16′E
100 J13 **Wolfenbüttel** Niedersachsen, C Germany 52°10′N 10°33′E
109 T4 **Wolfern** Oberösterreich, N Austria 48°06′N 14°16′E
109 Q6 **Wolfgangsee** *var.* Abersee, St Wolfgangsee. ◎ N Austria
39 P9 **Wolf Mountain** ▲ Alaska, USA 65°20′N 154°08′W
33 X7 **Wolf Point** Montana, NW USA 48°05′N 105°40′W
22 L8 **Wolf River** ≈ Mississippi, S USA
30 M7 **Wolf River** ≈ Wisconsin, N USA
109 U9 **Wolfsberg** Kärnten, SE Austria 46°50′N 14°50′E
100 K12 **Wolfsburg** Niedersachsen, N Germany 52°25′N 10°47′E
57 B17 **Wolf, Volcán** ✶ Galapagos Islands, Ecuador, E Pacific Ocean 0°01′N 91°22′W
100 O8 **Wolgast** Mecklenburg-Vorpommern, NE Germany 54°04′N 13°47′E
108 F8 **Wolhusen** Luzern, W Switzerland 47°04′N 08°06′E
110 D8 **Wolin** *Ger.* Wollin. Zachodnio-pomorskie, NW Poland 53°52′N 14°35′E
109 Y3 **Wolkersdorf** Niederösterreich, NE Austria 48°24′N 16°31′E
Wołkowysk *see* Vawkavysk
Wöllan *see* Velenje
8 J6 **Wollaston, Cape** *headland* Victoria Island, Northwest Territories, NW Canada 71°00′N 118°21′W
63 J25 **Wollaston, Isla** *island* S Chile
11 U11 **Wollaston Lake** Saskatchewan, C Canada 58°05′N 103°38′W
11 T10 **Wollaston Lake** ◎ Saskatchewan, C Canada
8 J6 **Wollaston Peninsula** *peninsula* Victoria Island, Northwest Territories/Nunavut NW Canada
Wollin *see* Wolin
183 S9 **Wollongong** New South Wales, SE Australia 34°25′S 150°52′E
Wolmar *see* Valmiera
100 L13 **Wolmirstedt** Sachsen-Anhalt, C Germany 52°15′N 11°37′E
110 M11 **Wołomin** Mazowieckie, C Poland 52°20′N 21°11′E
110 G13 **Wołów** *Ger.* Wohlau. Dolnośląskie, SW Poland 51°21′N 16°40′E
Wołożyn *see* Valozhyn
14 G11 **Wolseley Bay** Ontario, S Canada 46°05′N 80°16′W
29 P10 **Wolsey** South Dakota, N USA 44°22′N 98°28′W
110 F12 **Wolsztyn** Wielkopolskie, C Poland 52°07′N 16°07′E
98 M7 **Wolvega** *Fris.* Wolvegea. Fryslân, N Netherlands 52°53′N 06°E
Wolvegea *see* Wolvega
97 K19 **Wolverhampton** C England, United Kingdom 52°36′N 02°08′W
Wolverine State *see* Michigan
99 G18 **Wolvertem** Vlaams Brabant, C Belgium 50°55′N 04°19′E
99 H16 **Wommelgem** Antwerpen, N Belgium 51°12′N 04°32′E
186 D7 **Wonenara** *var.* Wonerara. Eastern Highlands, C Papua New Guinea 06°46′S 145°54′E
Wonerara *see* Wonenara
Wongalara Lake *see* Wongalarroo Lake
183 N6 **Wongalarroo Lake** *var.* Wongalara Lake. *seasonal lake* New South Wales, SE Australia
163 Y15 **Wonju** *Jap.* Genshū; *prev.* Wŏnju. N South Korea 37°21′N 127°57′E
Wŏnju *see* Wonju
10 M12 **Wonowon** British Columbia, W Canada 56°46′N 121°54′W
163 X13 **Wŏnsan** SE North Korea 39°11′N 127°21′E
183 O13 **Wonthaggi** Victoria, SE Australia 38°38′S 145°37′E
23 N2 **Woodall Mountain** ▲ Mississippi, S USA 34°47′N 88°14′W
23 W7 **Woodbine** Georgia, SE USA 30°58′N 81°43′W
29 S14 **Woodbine** Iowa, C USA 41°44′N 95°42′W
18 J17 **Woodbine** New Jersey, NE USA 39°12′N 74°47′W
21 W4 **Woodbridge** Virginia, NE USA 38°40′N 77°17′W
183 V4 **Woodburn** New South Wales, SE Australia 29°07′S 153°23′E
32 G11 **Woodburn** Oregon, NW USA 45°08′N 122°51′W
20 K9 **Woodbury** Tennessee, S USA 35°49′N 86°06′W
183 V5 **Wooded Bluff** *headland* New South Wales, SE Australia 29°24′S 153°22′E
183 V3 **Woodenbong** New South Wales, SE Australia 28°24′S 152°39′E
35 R11 **Woodlake** California, W USA 36°24′N 119°06′W
35 N7 **Woodland** California, W USA 38°41′N 121°46′W
19 T5 **Woodland** Maine, NE USA 45°10′N 67°25′W
32 G10 **Woodland** Washington, NW USA 45°54′N 122°44′W
37 T5 **Woodland Park** Colorado, C USA 38°59′N 105°03′W
186 I9 **Woodlark Island** *var.* Murua Island. *island* SE Papua New Guinea
Woodle Island *see* Kuria
11 T17 **Wood Mountain** ▲▲ Saskatchewan, S Canada
30 K15 **Wood River** Illinois, N USA 38°51′N 90°06′W
29 P16 **Wood River** Nebraska, C USA 40°48′N 98°33′W
39 R9 **Wood River** ≈ Alaska, USA
39 O13 **Wood River Lakes** *lakes* Alaska, USA
182 C1 **Woodroffe, Mount** ▲ South Australia 26°19′S 131°42′E
21 P11 **Woodruff** South Carolina, SE USA 34°44′N 82°02′W
30 K4 **Woodruff** Wisconsin, N USA 45°55′N 89°41′W
25 T14 **Woodsboro** Texas, SW USA 28°14′N 97°19′W
31 U13 **Woodsfield** Ohio, N USA 39°45′N 81°07′W
181 P4 **Woods, Lake** ◎ Northern Territory, N Australia
11 Z16 **Woods, Lake of the** *Fr.* Lac des Bois. ◎ Canada/USA
25 Q6 **Woodson** Texas, SW USA 33°00′N 99°01′W
13 N14 **Woodstock** New Brunswick, SE Canada 46°10′N 67°38′W
14 F16 **Woodstock** Ontario, S Canada 43°07′N 80°46′W
30 M10 **Woodstock** Illinois, N USA 42°18′N 88°27′W
18 M9 **Woodstock** Vermont, NE USA 43°37′N 72°33′W
21 U4 **Woodstock** Virginia, NE USA 38°55′N 78°31′W
19 N8 **Woodsville** New Hampshire, NE USA 44°08′N 72°02′W
184 M12 **Woodville** Manawatu-Wanganui, North Island, New Zealand 40°22′S 175°59′E
22 J7 **Woodville** Mississippi, S USA 31°06′N 91°18′W
25 X9 **Woodville** Texas, SW USA 30°47′N 94°26′W
26 K9 **Woodward** Oklahoma, C USA 36°26′N 99°25′W
29 O5 **Woodworth** North Dakota, N USA 47°06′N 99°19′W
171 W12 **Wool** Papua, E Indonesia 01°38′S 135°34′E
183 V5 **Woolgoolga** New South Wales, E Australia 30°04′S 153°09′E
182 H6 **Woomera** South Australia 31°12′S 136°52′E
19 O12 **Woonsocket** Rhode Island, NE USA 41°58′N 71°27′W
29 P10 **Woonsocket** South Dakota, N USA 44°03′N 98°16′W
31 T12 **Wooster** Ohio, N USA 40°48′N 81°56′W
80 L12 **Woqooyi Galbeed** *off.* Gobolka Woqooyi Galbeed. ◆ *region* NW Somalia
Woqooyi Galbeed, Gobolka *see* Woqooyi Galbeed
108 E8 **Worb** Bern, C Switzerland 46°54′N 07°36′E
83 F26 **Worcester** Western Cape, SW South Africa 33°41′S 19°22′E
97 L20 **Worcester** *hist.* Wigorna Ceaster. W England, United Kingdom 52°11′N 02°13′W
19 N11 **Worcester** Massachusetts, NE USA 42°17′N 71°48′W
97 L20 **Worcestershire** *cultural region* C England, United Kingdom
32 H16 **Worden** Oregon, NW USA 42°04′N 121°50′W
109 O6 **Wörgl** Tirol, W Austria 47°29′N 12°04′E
171 V15 **Workai, Pulau** *island* Kepulauan Aru, E Indonesia
97 J15 **Workington** NW England, United Kingdom 54°39′N 03°33′W
98 K7 **Workum** Fryslân, N Netherlands 52°58′N 05°25′E
33 V13 **Worland** Wyoming, C USA 44°01′N 107°57′W
see São João de Cortes
Wormatia *see* Worms
99 N25 **Wormeldange** Grevenmacher, E Luxembourg 49°37′N 06°25′E
98 I9 **Wormer** Noord-Holland, C Netherlands 52°30′N 04°50′E
101 G19 **Worms** *anc.* Augusta Vangionum, Borbetomagus, Wormatia. Rheinland-Pfalz, SW Germany 49°38′N 08°22′E
Worms *see* Vormsi
101 K21 **Wörnitz** ≈ S Germany
25 U8 **Wortham** Texas, SW USA 31°47′N 96°27′W
101 G21 **Wörth am Rhein** Rheinland-Pfalz, SW Germany 49°04′N 08°16′E
109 S9 **Wörther See** ◎ S Austria
97 O23 **Worthing** SE England, United Kingdom 50°48′N 00°23′W
29 S11 **Worthington** Minnesota, N USA 43°37′N 95°37′W
31 S13 **Worthington** Ohio, N USA 40°05′N 83°01′W
35 W8 **Worthington Peak** ▲ Nevada, W USA 37°57′N 115°32′W
171 Y13 **Wosi** Papua, E Indonesia 03°55′S 138°54′E
171 V13 **Wosimi** Papua, E Indonesia 02°44′S 134°34′E
189 R5 **Wotho Atoll** *var.* Wōtto. *atoll* Ralik Chain, W Marshall Islands
189 V5 **Wotje Atoll** *var.* Wōjjā. *atoll* Ratak Chain, E Marshall Islands
Wotoe *see* Wotu
Wottawa *see* Otava
Wōtto *see* Wotho Atoll
171 O13 **Wotu** *prev.* Wotoe. Sulawesi, C Indonesia 02°34′S 120°46′E
98 K11 **Woudenberg** Utrecht, C Netherlands 52°05′N 05°25′E
98 I13 **Woudrichem** Noord-Brabant, S Netherlands 51°49′N 05°E
43 N8 **Wounta** *var.* Huaunta. Región Autónoma Atlántico Norte, NE Nicaragua 13°30′N 83°32′W
171 P14 **Wowoni, Pulau** *island* C Indonesia
81 J17 **Woyamdero Plain** *plain* E Kenya
Woyens *see* Vojens
Wozrojdeniye Oroli *see* Vozrozhdeniya, Ostrov
Wrangel Island *see* Vrangelya, Ostrov
39 Y13 **Wrangell** Wrangell Island, Alaska, USA 56°28′N 132°22′W
38 C15 **Wrangell, Cape** *headland* Attu Island, Alaska, USA 52°55′N 172°28′E
39 S11 **Wrangell, Mount** ▲ Alaska, USA 62°00′N 144°01′W
39 T11 **Wrangell Mountains** ▲▲ Alaska, USA
197 S7 **Wrangel Plain** *undersea feature* Arctic Ocean
96 H6 **Wrath, Cape** *headland* N Scotland, United Kingdom 58°37′N 05°01′W
37 W3 **Wray** Colorado, C USA 40°01′N 102°12′W
44 K13 **Wreck Point** *headland* C Jamaica 17°50′N 76°55′W
83 C23 **Wreck Point** *headland* W South Africa 28°52′S 16°17′E
23 V4 **Wrens** Georgia, SE USA 33°12′N 82°23′W
97 K18 **Wrexham** NE Wales, United Kingdom 53°03′N 03°W
27 R13 **Wright City** Oklahoma, C USA 34°03′N 95°00′W
194 J12 **Wright Island** *island* Antarctica
13 N9 **Wright, Mont** ▲ Québec, E Canada 52°36′N 67°40′W
25 X5 **Wright Patman Lake** ⊠ Texas, SW USA
36 M16 **Wrightson, Mount** ▲ Arizona, SW USA 31°42′N 110°51′W
23 U5 **Wrightsville** Georgia, SE USA 32°43′N 82°43′W
21 W12 **Wrightsville Beach** North Carolina, SE USA 34°12′N 77°48′W
35 T15 **Wrightwood** California, W USA 34°21′N 117°37′W
8 H9 **Wrigley** Northwest Territories, W Canada 63°16′N 123°39′W
111 G14 **Wrocław** *Eng./Ger.* Breslau. Dolnośląskie, SW Poland 51°07′N 17°01′E
110 F10 **Wronki** *Ger.* Fronicken. Wielkopolskie, C Poland 52°42′N 16°22′E
110 H11 **Września** Wielkopolskie, C Poland 52°19′N 17°34′E
110 F12 **Wschowa** Lubuskie, W Poland 51°49′N 16°15′E
Wsetin *see* Vsetín
161 O5 **Wu'an** Hebei, E China 36°45′N 114°12′E
180 I12 **Wubin** Western Australia 30°05′S 116°43′E
163 W9 **Wuchang** Heilongjiang, NE China 44°55′N 127°13′E
Wuchang *see* Wuhan
Wu-chou/Wuchow *see* Wuzhou
160 M16 **Wuchuan** *var.* Meilu. Guangdong, S China 21°28′N 110°49′E
160 K10 **Wuchuan** *var.* Duru, Gelaozu Miaozu Zhizhixian. Guizhou, S China 28°40′N 108°04′E
163 O13 **Wuchuan** Nei Mongol Zizhiqu, N China 41°04′N 111°28′E
163 V6 **Wudalianchi** *var.* Qingshan; *prev.* Dedu. Heilongjiang, NE China 48°40′N 126°06′E
159 O11 **Wudaoliang** Qinghai, C China 35°16′N 93°03′E
141 Q13 **Wuday'ah** *spring/well* S Saudi Arabia 17°03′N 47°06′E
77 V13 **Wudil** Kano, N Nigeria 11°46′N 08°49′E
160 G12 **Wuding** *var.* Jincheng. Yunnan, SW China 25°30′N 102°21′E
182 G8 **Wudinna** South Australia 33°06′S 135°30′E
Wudu *see* Longnan
160 L9 **Wufeng** Hubei, C China 30°09′N 110°31′E
161 O11 **Wugong Shan** ▲▲ S China
157 P7 **Wuhai** *var.* Haibowan. Nei Mongol Zizhiqu, N China 39°40′N 106°48′E
161 O9 **Wuhan** *var.* Han-kou, Han-k'ou, Hanyang, Wuchang, Wu-han; *prev.* Hankow. *province capital* Hubei, C China 30°35′N 114°19′E
Wu-han *see* Wuhan
161 Q7 **Wuhe** Anhui, E China 33°05′N 117°55′E
Wuhsien *see* Suzhou
Wuhsi/Wu-his *see* Wuxi
161 Q8 **Wuhu** *var.* Wu-na-mu. Anhui, E China 31°23′N 118°25′E
Wūjae *see* Ujae Atoll
160 K11 **Wu Jiang** ≈ C China
158 L5 **Wujiaqu** Xinjiang Uygur Zizhiqu, NW China 44°11′N 87°30′E
Wujlān *see* Ujelang Atoll
77 W15 **Wukari** Taraba, E Nigeria 07°51′N 09°49′E
Wulan *see* Jingyuan
152 H4 **Wular Lake** ◎ NE India
162 M13 **Wulashan** Nei Mongol Zizhiqu, N China 40°43′N 108°45′E
160 H11 **Wulian Feng** ▲▲ SW China
160 F13 **Wuliang Shan** ▲▲ SW China
160 K11 **Wuling Shan** ▲▲ S China
109 Y5 **Wulka** ≈ E Austria
Wulkan *see* Vulcan
109 T3 **Wullowitz** Oberösterreich, N Austria 48°37′N 14°27′E
Wu-lu-k'o-mu-shi/Wu-lu-mu-ch'i *see* Ürümqi
79 D14 **Wum** Nord-Ouest, NE Cameroon 06°24′N 10°04′E
160 H12 **Wumeng Shan** ▲▲ SW China
160 K14 **Wuming** Guangxi Zhuangzu Zizhiqu, S China 23°12′N 108°11′E
100 I10 **Wümme** ≈ NW Germany
Wu-na-mu *see* Wuhu
171 X13 **Wunen** Papua, E Indonesia 03°40′S 138°31′E
12 D9 **Wunnummin Lake** ◎ Ontario, C Canada
80 D13 **Wun Rog** Warap, W South Sudan 09°00′N 28°20′E
101 M18 **Wunsiedel** Bayern, E Germany 50°02′N 12°00′E
100 I12 **Wunstorf** Niedersachsen, NW Germany 52°25′N 09°25′E
166 M3 **Wuntho** Sagaing, Myanmar (Burma) 23°52′N 95°43′E
101 F15 **Wupper** ≈ W Germany
101 E15 **Wuppertal** *prev.* Barmen-Elberfeld. Nordrhein-Westfalen, W Germany 51°16′N 07°12′E
160 K5 **Wuqi** Shaanxi, C China 36°57′N 108°15′E
158 E7 **Wuqia** Xinjiang Uygur Zizhiqu, NW China 39°50′N 75°19′E
161 P4 **Wuqiao** *var.* Sangyuan. Hebei, E China 37°40′N 116°21′E
101 L23 **Würm** ≈ SE Germany
77 T12 **Wurno** Sokoto, NW Nigeria 13°15′N 05°24′E
101 I19 **Würzburg** Bayern, SW Germany 49°48′N 09°56′E
101 N15 **Wurzen** Sachsen, E Germany 51°21′N 12°48′E
160 L9 **Wu Shan** ▲ C China
158 G7 **Wushi** *var.* Uqturpan. Xinjiang Uygur Zizhiqu, NW China 41°07′N 79°09′E
Wusih *see* Wuxi
65 N18 **Wüst Seamount** *undersea feature* S Atlantic Ocean 32°00′S 00°06′E
Wusuli Jiang/Wusuri *see* Ussuri
161 N3 **Wutai Shan** *var.* Beitai Ding. ▲ C China 39°00′N 114°00′E
160 H10 **Wutongqiao** Sichuan, C China 29°21′N 103°48′E
159 P6 **Wutongwozi Quan** *spring* NW China
99 H15 **Wuustwezel** Antwerpen, N Belgium 51°24′N 04°34′E
186 B4 **Wuvulu Island** *island* NW Papua New Guinea
159 U9 **Wuwei** *var.* Liangzhou. Gansu, C China 37°58′N 102°40′E
161 R8 **Wuxi** *var.* Wuhsi, Wu-hsi, Wusih. Jiangsu, E China 31°35′N 120°19′E
Wuxing *see* Huzhou
160 L14 **Wuxuan** Guangxi Zhuangzu Zizhiqu, S China 23°40′N 109°41′E
Wuyang *see* Zhenyuan
160 K11 **Wuyang He** ≈ S China
163 X6 **Wuyiling** Heilongjiang, NE China 48°36′N 129°24′E
161 Q11 **Wuyishan** *prev.* Chong'an. Fujian, SE China 27°48′N 118°03′E
157 T12 **Wuyi Shan** ▲▲ SE China
162 M13 **Wuyuan** Nei Mongol Zizhiqu, N China 41°05′N 108°15′E
160 L17 **Wuzhishan** *prev.* Tongshi. Hainan, S China 18°37′N 109°34′E
160 L17 **Wuzhi Shan** ▲ S China 18°52′N 109°36′E
159 W8 **Wuzhong** Ningxia, N China 37°58′N 106°09′E
160 M14 **Wuzhou** *var.* Wu-chou, Wuchow. Guangxi Zhuangzu Zizhiqu, S China 23°30′N 111°21′E
18 H12 **Wyalusing** Pennsylvania, NE USA 41°40′N 76°13′W
182 M10 **Wycheproof** Victoria, SE Australia 36°06′S 143°13′E
97 K21 **Wye** *Wel.* Gwy. ≈ England/Wales, United Kingdom
Wyłkowyszki *see* Vilkaviškis
97 P19 **Wymondham** E England, United Kingdom 52°29′N 01°10′E
29 R17 **Wymore** Nebraska, C USA 40°07′N 96°39′W
182 E5 **Wynbring** South Australia 30°34′S 133°27′E
181 N3 **Wyndham** Western Australia 15°28′S 128°08′E
29 R6 **Wyndmere** North Dakota, N USA 46°16′N 97°07′W
27 X11 **Wynne** Arkansas, C USA 35°14′N 90°48′W
27 N12 **Wynnewood** Oklahoma, C USA 34°39′N 97°09′W
183 O15 **Wynyard** Tasmania, SE Australia 40°57′S 145°33′E
11 U15 **Wynyard** Saskatchewan, S Canada 51°46′N 104°10′W
33 V11 **Wyola** Montana, NW USA 45°07′N 107°23′W
182 A4 **Wyola Lake** *salt lake* South Australia
31 P9 **Wyoming** Michigan, N USA 42°54′N 85°42′W
33 V14 **Wyoming** *off.* State of Wyoming, *also known as* Equality State. ◆ *state* C USA
33 S15 **Wyoming Range** ▲▲ Wyoming, C USA
183 T8 **Wyong** New South Wales, SE Australia 33°18′S 151°27′E
110 G9 **Wyrzysk** *Ger.* Wirsitz. Wielkopolskie, C Poland 53°09′N 17°15′E
Wysg *see* Usk
110 O10 **Wysokie Mazowieckie** Łomża, E Poland 52°54′N 22°34′E
110 M11 **Wyszków** *Ger.* Probstberg. Mazowieckie, NE Poland 52°36′N 21°28′E
110 L11 **Wyszogród** Mazowieckie, C Poland 52°24′N 20°14′E
21 R7 **Wytheville** Virginia, NE USA 36°57′N 81°07′W
111 L15 **Wyżyna Małopolska** *plateau*

X

80 Q12 **Xaafuun** *It.* Hafun. Bari, NE Somalia 10°25′N 51°17′E
80 Q12 **Xaafuun, Raas** *var.* Ras Hafun. *cape* NE Somalia
Xabia *see* Jávea
42 C4 **Xaclbal, Río** *var.* Xalbal. ≈ Guatemala/Mexico
137 Y10 **Xaçmaz** *Rus.* Khachmas. N Azerbaijan 41°26′N 48°47′E
80 O12 **Xadeed** *var.* Haded. *physical region* N Somalia
159 O14 **Xagquka** Xizang Zizhiqu, W China 31°47′N 92°46′E
Xai *see* Oudômxai
158 F10 **Xaidulla** Xinjiang Uygur Zizhiqu, W China 36°27′N 77°46′E
167 Q7 **Xaignabouli** *prev.* Muang Xaignabouri, *Fr.* Sayaboury. Xaignabouli, N Laos 19°16′N 101°43′E
167 R7 **Xai Lai Leng, Phou** ▲ Laos/Vietnam 19°13′N 104°09′E
158 L15 **Xainza** Xizang Zizhiqu, W China 30°54′N 88°36′E
158 L16 **Xaitongmoin** Xizang Zizhiqu, W China 29°27′N 88°13′E
83 F17 **Xaixai** *var.* Caecae. North-West, NW Botswana 19°52′S 21°04′E
83 M20 **Xai-Xai** *prev.* João Belo, Vila de João Belo. Gaza, S Mozambique 25°01′S 33°37′E
Xalbal *see* Xaclbal, Río
80 P13 **Xalin** Sool, N Somalia 09°16′N 49°00′E
146 H7 **Xalqobod** *Rus.* Khalkabad. Qoraqalpog'iston Respublikasi, W Uzbekistan 42°42′N 59°46′E
160 F11 **Xamgyi'nyilha** *var.* Jiantang; *prev.* Zhongdian. Yunnan, SW China 27°48′N 99°41′E
167 R6 **Xam Nua** *var.* Sam Neua. Houaphan, N Laos 20°24′N 104°03′E
82 D11 **Xá-Muteba** *Port.* Cinco de Outubro. Lunda Norte, NE Angola 09°34′S 17°50′E
Xangda *see* Nangqên
83 C16 **Xangongo** *Port.* Rocadas. Cunene, SW Angola 16°43′S 15°01′E
137 W12 **Xankändi** *Rus.* Khankendi; *prev.* Stepanakert. SW Azerbaijan 39°50′N 46°44′E
114 J13 **Xánthi** Anatolikí Makedonía kai Thráki, NE Greece 41°09′N 24°54′E
60 H13 **Xanxerê** Santa Catarina, S Brazil 26°52′S 52°25′W
81 O15 **Xarardheere** Mudug, E Somalia 04°45′N 47°54′E
137 Z11 **Xärä Zirä Adasi** *Rus.* Ostrov Bulla. *island* E Azerbaijan
162 K13 **Xar Burd** *prev.* Bayan Nuru. Nei Mongol Zizhiqu, N China 40°09′N 104°48′E
163 T11 **Xar Moron** ≈ NE China
163 T11 **Xar Moron** ≈ N China
Xarra *see* Xarrë
113 L23 **Xarrë** *var.* Xarra. Vlorë, S Albania 39°45′N 20°01′E
82 D12 **Xassengue** Lunda Sul, NW Angola 10°28′S 18°32′E
105 S11 **Xàtiva** *Cas.* Xátiva, *var.* Jativa; *anc.* Setabis. Valenciana, E Spain 39°00′N 00°32′W
Xauen *see* Chefchaouen
60 K10 **Xavantes, Represa de** *var.* Represa de Chavantes. ⊠ S Brazil
158 I7 **Xayar** Xinjiang Uygur Zizhiqu, W China 41°16′N 82°52′E

◆ Country
● Country Capital
◇ Dependent Territory
○ Dependent Territory Capital
✦ Administrative Regions
✕ International Airport
▲ Mountain
▲▲ Mountain Range
✶ Volcano
≈ River
◎ Lake
⊠ Reservoir

Xäzär Dänizi *see* Caspian Sea
167 *S8* **Xé Bangfai** C Laos
167 *T9* **Xé Banghiang** *var.* Bang Hieng. S Laos
Xêgar *see* Tingri
167 *T10* **Xékong** *vaar.* Lamam. Xékong, S Laos *15°22′N 106°40′E*
31 *R14* **Xenia** Ohio, N USA *39°40′N 83°55′W*
Xeres *see* Jerez de la Frontera
115 *E15* **Xeriás** C Greece
115 *G17* **Xeró** ▲ Évvoia, C Greece *38°52′N 23°18′E*
Xhumo *see* Cum
161 *N15* **Xiachuan Dao** *island* S China
Xiacun *see* Rushan
Xiaguan *see* Dali
159 *U11* **Xiahe** *var.* Labrang. Gansu, C China *35°12′N 102°28′E*
161 *Q13* **Xiamen** *var.* Hsia-men; *prev.* Amoy. Fujian, SE China *24°28′N 118°05′E*
160 *L6* **Xi'an** *var.* Changan, Sian, Signan, Siking, Singan, Xian. *province capital* Shaanxi, C China *34°16′N 108°54′E*
160 *L10* **Xianfeng** *var.* Gaoleshan. Hubei, C China *29°45′N 109°10′E*
Xiang *see* Hunan
161 *N7* **Xiangcheng** Henan, C China *33°51′N′N 113°27′E*
160 *F10* **Xiangcheng** *var.* Sampê, *Tib.* Qagchêng. Sichuan, C China *28°52′N 99°45′E*
160 *M8* **Xiangfan** *var.* Xiangyang. Hubei, C China *32°07′N 112°00′E*
Xianggang *see* Hong Kong
161 *N10* **Xiang Jiang** S China
Xiangkhoang *see* Phônsaven
167 *Q7* **Xiangkhoang, Plateau de** *var.* Plain of Jars. *plateau* N Laos
161 *N11* **Xiangtan** *var.* Hsiang-t'an, Siangtan. Hunan, S China *27°53′N 112°55′E*
161 *N11* **Xiangxiang** Hunan, S China *27°50′N 112°31′E*
Xiangyang *see* Xiangfan
161 *S10* **Xianju** Zhejiang, SE China *28°53′N 120°41′E*
Xianshui *see* Dawu
160 *F8* **Xianshui He** C China
161 *N9* **Xiantao** *var.* Mianyang. Hubei, C China *30°20′N 113°31′E*
161 *R10* **Xianxia Ling** ▲▲ SE China
160 *K6* **Xianyang** Shaanxi, C China *34°26′N 118°40′E*
158 *L5* **Xiaocaohu** Xinjiang Uygur Zizhiqu, W China *45°44′N 90°07′E*
161 *O9* **Xiaogan** Hubei, C China *30°55′N 113°54′E*
Xiaogang *see* Dongxiang
163 *W6* **Xiao Hinggan Ling** *Eng.* Lesser Khingan Range. ▲▲ NE China
160 *M6* **Xiao Shan** ▲▲ C China
160 *M12* **Xiao Shui** S China
Xiaoxi *see* Pinghe
161 *P6* **Xiaoxian** *var.* Longcheng, Xiao Xian. Anhui, E China *34°11′N 116°56′E*
Xiao Xian *see* Xiaoxian
160 *G11* **Xichang** Sichuan, C China *27°52′N 102°16′E*
41 *P11* **Xicoténcatl** Tamaulipas, C Mexico *22°59′N 98°54′W*
Xieng Khouang *see* Phônsaven
Xieng Ngeun *see* Muong Xiang Ngeun
160 *J11* **Xifeng** *var.* Yongjing. Guizhou, S China *27°15′N 106°44′E*
Xifeng *see* Qingcheng
Xigang *see* Helan
158 *L16* **Xigazê** *var.* Jih-k'a-tse, Shigatse, Xigaze. Xizang Zizhiqu, W China *29°18′N 88°50′E*
159 *W11* **Xihe** *var.* Hanyuan. Gansu, C China *34°00′N 105°24′E*
160 *I8* **Xi He** C China
Xihuachi *see* Heshui
159 *W10* **Xiji** Ningxia, N China *36°02′N 105°33′E*
160 *M14* **Xi Jiang** *var.* Hsi Chiang, *Eng.* West River. S China
159 *Q7* **Xijian Quan** *spring* NW China
160 *K15* **Xijin Shuiku** S China
Xilaganí *see* Xylaganí
Xiligou *see* Ulan
160 *I13* **Xilin** *var.* Bada. Guangxi Zhuangzu Zizhiqu, S China *24°30′N 105°00′E*
163 *Q10* **Xilinhot** *var.* Silinhot. Nei Mongol Zizhiqu, N China *43°58′N 116°07′E*
Xilinji *see* Mohe
Xilokastro *see* Xylókastro
Xin *see* Xinjiang Uygur Zizhiqu
Xin'an *see* Anlong
Xin'anjiang Shuiku *see* Qiandao Hu
Xin'anzhen *see* Xinyi
Xin Barag Youqi *see* Altan Emel
Xin Barag Zuoqi *see* Amgalang
163 *W12* **Xinbin** *var.* Xinbin Manzu Zizhixian. Liaoning, NE China *41°44′N 125°02′E*
Xinbin Manzu Zizhixian *see* Xinbin
161 *O7* **Xincai** Henan, C China *32°47′N 114°58′E*
Xincheng *see* Zhaojue
Xindu *see* Luhuo
161 *O13* **Xinfeng** *var.* Jiading. Jiangxi, S China *25°23′N 114°48′E*
161 *O14* **Xinfengjiang Shuiku** S China
Xing'an *see* Ankang
Xingba *see* Lhünzê
163 *T13* **Xingcheng** Liaoning, NE China *40°38′N 120°47′E*
Xingcheng *see* Xingning
82 *E11* **Xinge** Lunda Norte, NE Angola *09°44′S 19°10′E*
161 *P12* **Xingguo** *var.* Lianjiang. Jiangxi, S China *26°25′N 115°22′E*
159 *S11* **Xinghai** *var.* Ziketan. Qinghai, C China *35°12′N 102°28′E*
161 *R7* **Xinghua** Jiangsu, E China *32°54′N 119°48′E*
Xingkai Hu *see* Khanka, Lake
161 *P13* **Xingning** *prev.* Xingcheng. Guangdong, S China *24°05′N 115°47′E*
160 *I13* **Xingren** Guizhou, S China *25°26′N 105°08′E*
161 *O4* **Xingtai** Hebei, E China *37°08′N 114°29′E*
59 *J14* **Xingu, Rio** C Brazil
159 *P6* **Xingxingxia** Xinjiang Uygur Zizhiqu, NW China *41°48′N 95°01′E*
160 *I13* **Xingyi** Guizhou, S China *25°04′N 104°51′E*
158 *I6* **Xinhe** *var.* Toksu. Xinjiang Uygur Zizhiqu, NW China *41°32′N 82°39′E*
163 *Q10* **Xin Hot** Nei Mongol Zizhiqu, N China *43°58′N 114°59′E*
Xinhua *see* Funing
163 *T12* **Xinhui** *var.* Aohan Qi. Nei Mongol Zizhiqu, N China *42°12′N 119°57′E*
159 *T10* **Xining** *var.* Hsining, Hsi-ning, Sining. *province capital* Qinghai, C China *36°37′N 101°46′E*
161 *O4* **Xinji** *prev.* Shulu. Hebei, E China *37°55′N 115°14′E*
161 *P10* **Xinjian** Jiangxi, S China *28°37′N 115°46′E*
Xinjiang *see* Xinjiang Uygur Zizhiqu
162 *D8* **Xinjiang Uygur Zizhiqu** *var.* Sinkiang, Sinkiang Ughur Autonomous Region, Xin, Xinjiang. ◆ *autonomous region* NW China
160 *H9* **Xinjin** *var.* Meixing, *Tib.* Zainlha. Sichuan, C China *30°27′N 103°46′E*
Xinjin *see* Pulandian
Xinjing *see* Jingxi
163 *U12* **Xinmin** Liaoning, NE China *41°58′N 122°51′E*
160 *M12* **Xinning** *var.* Jinshi. Hunan, S China *26°34′N 110°57′E*
Xinning *see* Ningxian
Xinning *see* Fusui
Xinpu *see* Lianyungang
Xinshan *see* Anyuan
161 *P5* **Xintai** Shandong, E China *35°54′N 117°44′E*
Xinwen *see* Suncun
Xin Xian *see* Xinzhou
161 *N6* **Xinxiang** Henan, C China *35°13′N 113°48′E*
161 *O8* **Xinyang** *var.* Hsin-yang, Sinyang. Henan, C China *32°09′N 114°04′E*
161 *Q6* **Xinyi** *var.* Xin'anzhen. Jiangsu, E China *34°17′N 118°14′E*
161 *Q6* **Xinyi He** E China
161 *S14* **Xinying** *var.* Sinying, *Jap.* Shinei; *prev.* Hsinying. C Taiwan *23°12′N 120°15′E*
161 *O11* **Xinyu** Jiangxi, S China *27°51′N 115°00′E*
158 *I5* **Xinyuan** *var.* Künes. Xinjiang Uygur Zizhiqu, NW China *43°25′N 83°12′E*
Xinyuan *see* Tianjun
162 *M13* **Xinzhao Shan** ▲ N China *39°37′N 107°51′E*
161 *N3* **Xinzhou** *var.* Xin Xian. Shanxi, C China *38°24′N 112°43′E*
Xinzhou *see* Longlin
161 *S13* **Xinzhu** *var.* Hsinchu. N Taiwan *24°48′N 120°59′E*
104 *H4* **Xinzo de Limia** Galicia, NW Spain *42°05′N 07°45′W*
Xions *see* Książ Wielkopolski
161 *O7* **Xiping** Henan, C China *33°22′N 114°00′E*
Xiping *see* Songyang
159 *T11* **Xiqing Shan** ▲▲ C China
59 *N16* **Xique-Xique** Bahia, E Brazil *10°47′S 42°44′W*
Xireg *see* Ulan
115 *E14* **Xirovoúni** ▲ N Greece *40°31′N 21°58′E*
162 *M13* **Xishanzui** *prev.* Urad Qianqi. Nei Mongol Zizhiqu, N China *40°43′N 108°41′E*
160 *J11* **Xishui** *var.* Donghuang. Guizhou, S China *28°24′N 106°09′E*
Xi Ujimqin Qi *see* Bayan Ul
160 *K11* **Xiushan** *var.* Zhonghe. Chongqing Shi, C China *28°23′N 108°52′E*
Xiushan *see* Tonghai
161 *O10* **Xiu Shui** S China
Xiuyan *see* Qingjian
146 *H9* **Xiva** *Rus.* Khiva, Khiwa. Xorazm Viloyati, W Uzbekistan *41°22′N 60°22′E*
158 *J16* **Xixabangma Feng** ▲ W China *28°25′N 85°47′E*
160 *M7* **Xixia** Henan, C China *33°30′N 111°25′E*
Xixón *see* Gijón
Xixona *see* Jijona
Xizang *see* Xizang Zizhiqu
Xizang Gaoyuan *see* Qingzang Gaoyuan
160 *E9* **Xizang Zizhiqu** *var.* Thibet, Tibetan Autonomous Region, Xizang, *Eng.* Tibet. ◆ *autonomous region* W China
163 *U14* **Xizhong Dao** *island* N China
Xoi *see* Qüxü
146 *H8* **Xo'jayli** *Rus.* Khodzheyli. Qoraqalpog'iston Respublikasi, W Uzbekistan *42°23′N 59°27′E*
Xolotlán *see* Managua, Lago de
147 *I9* **Xonqa** *var.* Khonqa, *Rus.* Khanka. Xorazm Viloyati, W Uzbekistan *41°31′N 60°39′E*
146 *H9* **Xorazm Viloyati** *Rus.* Khorezmskaya Oblast'. ◆ *province* W Uzbekistan
159 *N9* **Xorkol** Xinjiang Uygur Zizhiqu, NW China *38°45′N 91°07′E*
147 *P11* **Xovos** *var.* Ursat'yevskaya, *Rus.* Khavast. Sirdaryo Viloyati, E Uzbekistan *40°14′N 68°46′E*
41 *X14* **Xpujil** Quintana Roo, E Mexico *18°30′N 89°24′W*
161 *Q8* **Xuancheng** *var.* Xuanzhou. Anhui, E China *30°57′N 118°53′E*
167 *T9* **Xuân Đuc** Quang Binh, C Vietnam *17°19′N 106°38′E*
160 *L9* **Xuan'en** *var.* Zhushan. Hubei, C China *30°03′N 109°26′E*
160 *K8* **Xuanhan** Sichuan, C China *31°25′N 107°41′E*
161 *O2* **Xuanhua** Hebei, E China *40°36′N 115°01′E*
161 *P4* **Xuanhui He** E China
167 *T8* **Xuân Sơn** Quang Binh, C Vietnam *17°42′N 105°58′E*
H12 **Xuanwei** Yunnan, China *26°08′N 104°04′E*
Xuanzhou *see* Xuancheng
161 *N7* **Xuchang** Henan, C China *34°03′N 113°48′E*
Xucheng *see* Xuwen
137 *X10* **Xudat** *Rus.* Khudat. NE Azerbaijan *41°37′N 48°39′E*
81 *M16* **Xuddur** *var.* Hudur, *It.* Oddur. Bakool, SW Somalia *04°07′N 43°47′E*
80 *O13* **Xudun** Sool, N Somalia *09°12′N 47°34′E*
160 *L11* **Xuefeng Shan** ▲▲ S China
161 *S13* **Xue Shan** *prev.* Hsüeh Shan. ▲ N Taiwan
147 *O13* **Xufar** Surkhondaryo Viloyati, S Uzbekistan *38°31′N 67°45′E*
Xulun Hobot Qagan *see* Qagan Nur
42 *F2* **Xunantunich** *ruins* Cayo, W Belize
163 *W6* **Xun He** NE China
160 *L7* **Xun He** C China
160 *L14* **Xun Jiang** S China
163 *W5* **Xunke** *var.* Bianjiang; *prev.* Qike. Heilongjiang, NE China *49°35′N 128°27′E*
161 *P13* **Xunwu** *var.* Changning. Jiangxi, S China *24°59′N 115°33′E*
161 *O3* **Xushui** Hebei, E China *39°01′N 115°38′E*
160 *L16* **Xuwen** *var.* Xucheng. Guangdong, S China *20°21′N 110°09′E*
160 *I11* **Xuyong** *var.* Yongning. Sichuan, C China *28°17′N 105°21′E*
161 *P6* **Xuzhou** *var.* Hsu-chou, Suchow, Tongshan; *prev.* T'ung-shan. Jiangsu, E China *34°17′N 117°09′E*
114 *K13* **Xylaganí** *var.* Xilaganí. Anatolikí Makedonía kai Thráki, NE Greece *40°58′N 25°27′E*
115 *F19* **Xylókastro** *var.* Xilokastro. Pelopónnisos, S Greece *38°04′N 22°36′E*

Y

160 *H9* **Ya'an** *var.* Yaan. Sichuan, C China *30°N 102°57′E*
182 *L10* **Yaapeet** Victoria, SE Australia *35°48′S 142°03′E*
79 *D15* **Yabassi** Littoral, W Cameroon *04°30′N 09°59′E*
81 *J15* **Yabēlo** Oromīya, C Ethiopia *04°53′N 38°01′E*
114 *H9* **Yablanitsa** Lovech, N Bulgaria *43°01′N 24°06′E*
43 *N7* **Yablis** Región Autónoma Atlántico Norte, NE Nicaragua *14°08′N 83°44′W*
123 *O14* **Yablonovyy Khrebet** ▲▲ S Russian Federation
162 *J14* **Yabrai Shan** ▲▲ NE China
45 *U6* **Yabucoa** E Puerto Rico *18°02′N 65°53′W*
160 *J11* **Yachi He** S China
32 *H10* **Yacolt** Washington, NW USA *45°49′N 122°22′W*
54 *M10* **Yacuaray** Amazonas, S Venezuela *04°12′N 66°30′W*
57 *M22* **Yacuiba** Tarija, S Bolivia *22°00′S 63°43′W*
57 *K16* **Yacuma, Río** C Bolivia
155 *H16* **Yādgīr** Karnātaka, C India *16°46′N 77°09′E*
21 *R8* **Yadkin River** North Carolina, SE USA
21 *R9* **Yadkinville** North Carolina, SE USA *36°07′N 80°40′W*
127 *P3* **Yadrin** Chuvashskaya Respublika, W Russian Federation *55°55′N 46°10′E*
Yaegama-shotō *see* Yaeyama-shotō
Yaeme-saki *see* Paimi-saki
165 *O16* **Yaeyama-shotō** *var.* Yaegama-shotō. *island group* SW Japan
75 *O8* **Yafran** NW Libya *32°04′N 12°31′E*
165 *S2* **Yagashiri-tō** *island* NE Japan
65 *H21* **Yaghan Basin** *undersea feature* SE Pacific Ocean
123 *S9* **Yagodnoye** Magadanskaya Oblast', E Russian Federation *62°37′N 149°18′E*
Yagotin *see* Yahotyn
78 *G12* **Yagoua** Extrême-Nord, NE Cameroon *10°23′N 15°13′E*
159 *Q11* **Yagradagzê Shan** ▲ C China *35°06′N 95°41′E*
Yaguachi *see* Yaguachi Nuevo
56 *B7* **Yaguachi Nuevo** *var.* Yaguachi. Guayas, W Ecuador *02°06′S 79°43′W*
Yaguarón, Río *see* Jaguarão, Rio
117 *Q11* **Yahorlyts'kyy Lyman** *bay* S Ukraine
117 *Q5* **Yahotyn** *Rus.* Yagotin. Kyyivs'ka Oblast', N Ukraine *50°15′N 31°48′E*
40 *L12* **Yahualica** Jalisco, SW Mexico *21°11′N 102°29′W*
79 *L17* **Yahuma** Orientale, N Dem. Rep. Congo *01°12′N 23°00′E*
136 *K15* **Yahyalı** Kayseri, C Turkey *38°08′N 35°23′E*
167 *N15* **Yai, Khao** ▲ SW Thailand *08°45′N 99°32′E*
164 *M14* **Yaizu** Shizuoka, Honshū, S Japan *34°52′N 138°20′E*
160 *G9* **Yajiang** *var.* Hekou, *Tib.* Nyagquka. Sichuan, C China *30°05′N 100°57′E*
119 *O14* **Yakawlyevichi** *Rus.* Yakovlevichi. Vitsyebskaya Voblasts', NE Belarus *54°20′N 30°31′E*
163 *S6* **Yakeshi** Nei Mongol Zizhiqu, N China *49°16′N 120°42′E*
32 *I9* **Yakima** Washington, NW USA *46°36′N 120°30′W*
32 *J10* **Yakima River** Washington, NW USA
Yakkabag *see* Yakkabog'
147 *N12* **Yakkabog'** *Rus.* Yakkabag. Qashqadaryo Viloyati, S Uzbekistan *38°57′N 66°35′E*
148 *L12* **Yakmach** Baluchistān, SW Pakistan *28°48′N 63°48′E*
77 *O12* **Yako** W Burkina *12°59′N 02°15′W*
39 *W13* **Yakobi Island** *island* Alexander Archipelago, Alaska, USA
79 *K16* **Yakoma** Equateur, N Dem. Rep. Congo *04°04′N 22°23′E*
114 *H11* **Yakoruda** Blagoevgrad, SW Bulgaria *42°01′N 23°40′E*
Yakovlevichi *see* Yakawlyevichi
127 *T2* **Yakshur-Bod'ya** Udmurtskaya Respublika, NW Russian Federation *57°10′N 53°10′E*
165 *Q5* **Yakumo** Hokkaidō, NE Japan *42°18′N 140°15′E*
164 *B17* **Yaku-shima** *island* Nansei-shotō, SW Japan
39 *V12* **Yakutat** Alaska, USA *59°33′N 139°44′W*
39 *U12* **Yakutat Bay** *inlet* Alaska, USA
Yakutia/Yakutiya/Yakutiya, Respublika *see* Sakha (Yakutiya), Respublika
123 *Q10* **Yakutsk** Respublika Sakha (Yakutiya), NE Russian Federation *62°10′N 129°50′E*
167 *O17* **Yala** Yala, SW Thailand *06°32′N 101°19′E*
182 *D6* **Yalata** South Australia *31°30′S 131°53′E*
31 *S9* **Yale** Michigan, N USA *43°07′N 82°45′W*
180 *I11* **Yalgoo** Western Australia *28°23′S 116°43′E*
114 *O12* **Yalıköy** İstanbul, NW Turkey *41°29′N 28°19′E*
79 *L14* **Yalinga** Haute-Kotto, C Central African Republic *06°47′N 23°09′E*
119 *M17* **Yalizava** *Rus.* Yelizovo. Mahilyowskaya Voblasts', E Belarus *53°24′N 29°01′E*
44 *L13* **Yallahs Hill** ▲ E Jamaica *17°53′N 76°31′W*
22 *L3* **Yalobusha River** Mississippi, S USA
79 *H15* **Yaloké** Ombella-Mpoko, W Central African Republic *05°15′N 17°12′E*
160 *E7* **Yalong Jiang** C China
136 *E11* **Yalova** Yalova, NW Turkey *40°40′N 29°17′E*
136 *E11* **Yalova** ◆ *province* NW Turkey
Yaloveny *see* Ialoveni
Yalpug *see* Ialpug
Yalpug, Ozero *see* Yalpuh, Ozero
117 *N12* **Yalpuh, Ozero** *Rus.* Ozero Yalpug. SW Ukraine
117 *T14* **Yalta** Avtonomna Respublika Krym, S Ukraine *44°30′N 34°09′E*
163 *W12* **Yalu** *Chin.* Yalu Jiang, *Jap.* Oryokko, *Kor.* Amnok-kang. China/North Korea
Yalu Jiang *see* Yalu
136 *F14* **Yalvaç** Isparta, SW Turkey *38°16′N 31°09′E*
165 *R9* **Yamada** Iwate, Honshū, C Japan *39°27′N 141°56′E*
165 *D14* **Yamaga** Kumamoto, Kyūshū, SW Japan *33°02′N 130°41′E*
165 *P10* **Yamagata** Yamagata, Honshū, C Japan *38°15′N 140°19′E*
165 *P9* **Yamagata** *off.* Yamagata-ken. ◆ *prefecture* Honshū, C Japan
Yamagata-ken *see* Yamagata
164 *C16* **Yamagawa** Kagoshima, Kyūshū, SW Japan *31°12′N 130°37′E*
164 *E13* **Yamaguchi** *var.* Yamaguti. Yamaguchi, Honshū, SW Japan *34°11′N 131°26′E*
164 *E13* **Yamaguchi** *off.* Yamaguchi-ken, *var.* Yamaguti. ◆ *prefecture* Honshū, SW Japan
Yamaguchi-ken *see* Yamaguchi
Yamaguti *see* Yamaguchi
125 *X5* **Yamalo-Nenetskiy Avtonomnyy Okrug** ◆ *autonomous district* N Russian Federation
122 *J7* **Yamal, Poluostrov** *peninsula* N Russian Federation
165 *N13* **Yamanashi** *off.* Yamanashi-ken, *var.* Yamanasi. ◆ *prefecture* Honshū, S Japan
Yamanashi-ken *see* Yamanashi
Yamanasi *see* Yamanashi
Yamanīyah, Al Jumhūrīyah al *see* Yemen
127 *W5* **Yamantau** ▲ W Russian Federation *53°11′N 57°30′E*
Yamasaki *see* Yamazaki
15 *P12* **Yamaska** Québec, SE Canada
192 *G4* **Yamato Ridge** *undersea feature* S Sea of Japan *39°20′N 135°00′E*
164 *I13* **Yamazaki** *var.* Yamasaki. Hyōgo, Honshū, SW Japan *35°00′N 134°31′E*
183 *V5* **Yamba** New South Wales, SE Australia *29°28′S 153°22′E*
81 *D16* **Yambio** *var.* Yambiyo. Western Equatoria, S South Sudan *04°34′N 28°21′E*
Yambiyo *see* Yambio
114 *L10* **Yambol** *Turk.* Yanboli. Yambol, E Bulgaria *42°29′N 26°30′E*
114 *M11* **Yambol** ◆ *province* E Bulgaria
79 *M17* **Yambuya** Orientale, N Dem. Rep. Congo *01°22′N 24°21′E*
171 *T15* **Yamdena, Pulau** *prev.* Jamdena. *island* Kepulauan Tanimbar, E Indonesia
165 *O14* **Yame** Fukuoka, Kyūshū, SW Japan *33°14′N 130°32′E*
166 *M6* **Yamethin** Mandalay, C Myanmar (Burma) *20°24′N 96°08′E*
186 *C6* **Yaminbot** East Sepik, NW Papua New Guinea *04°34′S 143°56′E*
181 *U9* **Yamma Yamma, Lake** Queensland, C Australia
76 *M16* **Yamoussoukro** ● (Ivory Coast) C Ivory Coast *06°51′N 05°21′W*
37 *P3* **Yampa River** Colorado, C USA
117 *S2* **Yampil'** Sums'ka Oblast', NE Ukraine *51°57′N 33°49′E*
116 *M8* **Yampil'** Vinnyts'ka Oblast', C Ukraine *48°15′N 28°18′E*
123 *T9* **Yamsk** Magadanskaya Oblast', E Russian Federation *59°33′N 154°04′E*
152 *J8* **Yamuna** *prev.* Jumna. N India
152 *I9* **Yamunānagar** Haryāna, N India *30°07′N 77°17′E*
Yamundá *see* Nhamundá, Rio
145 *U8* **Yamyshevo** Pavlodar, NE Kazakhstan *51°49′N 77°28′E*
159 *N16* **Yamzho Yumco** W China
123 *Q8* **Yana** NE Russian Federation
186 *H9* **Yanaba Island** *island* SE Papua New Guinea
155 *L16* **Yanam** *var.* Yanaon. Pondicherry, E India *16°45′N 82°16′E*
160 *L5* **Yan'an** *var.* Yanan. Shaanxi, C China *36°35′N 109°27′E*
Yanaon *see* Yanam
127 *U3* **Yanaul** ▲ Respublika Bashkortostan, W Russian Federation *56°15′N 54°57′E*
118 *O12* **Yanavichy** *Rus.* Yanovichi. Vitsyebskaya Voblasts', NE Belarus *55°17′N 30°42′E*
Yanboli *see* Yambol
140 *K8* **Yanbu' al Baḥr** Al Madīnah, W Saudi Arabia *24°07′N 38°03′E*
21 *T8* **Yanceyville** North Carolina, SE USA *36°25′N 79°22′W*
161 *R7* **Yancheng** Jiangsu, E China *33°28′N 120°10′E*
159 *W8* **Yanchi** Ningxia, N China *37°49′N 107°24′E*
160 *L5* **Yanchuan** Shaanxi, C China *36°54′N 110°04′E*
183 *O10* **Yanco Creek** *seasonal river* New South Wales, SE Australia
183 *O6* **Yanda Creek** *seasonal river* New South Wales, SE Australia
182 *K4* **Yandama Creek** *seasonal river* New South Wales/South Australia
161 *S11* **Yandang Shan** ▲▲ SE China
159 *O6* **Yandun** Xinjiang Uygur Zizhiqu, W China *42°24′N 94°08′E*
76 *L13* **Yanfolila** Sikasso, SW Mali *11°08′N 08°12′W*
79 *M18* **Yangambi** Orientale, N Dem. Rep. Congo *0°46′N 24°24′E*
158 *M15* **Yangbajain** Xizang Zizhiqu, W China *30°05′N 90°35′E*
Yangcheng *see* Yangshan, Guangdong, S China
Yangchow *see* Yangzhou
160 *M15* **Yangchun** *var.* Chuncheng. Guangdong, S China *22°16′N 111°49′E*
161 *N2* **Yanggao** *var.* Longquàn. Shanxi, C China *40°24′N 113°51′E*
Yanggeta *see* Yaqeta
Yangiabad *see* Yangiobod
Yangibazar *see* Dzhany-Bazar, Kyrgyzstan
Yangi-Bazar *see* Kofarnihon, Tajikistan
Yangiklshak *see* Yangiqishloq
146 *M13* **Yangi-Nishon** *Rus.* Yang-Nishan. Qashqadaryo Viloyati, S Uzbekistan *38°37′N 65°39′E*
147 *Q9* **Yangiobod** *Rus.* Yangiabad. Toshkent Viloyati, E Uzbekistan *41°10′N 70°10′E*
147 *O10* **Yangiqishloq** *Rus.* Yangiklshak. Jizzax Viloyati, C Uzbekistan *40°27′N 67°06′E*
147 *P11* **Yangiyer** Sirdaryo Viloyati, E Uzbekistan *40°19′N 68°48′E*
147 *P9* **Yangiyoʻl** *Rus.* Yangiyul'. Toshkent Viloyati, E Uzbekistan *41°12′N 69°05′E*
Yangiyul' *see* Yangiyoʻl
160 *M15* **Yangjiang** Guangdong, S China *21°50′N 112°02′E*
Yangku *see* Taiyuan
Yang-Nishan *see* Yangi-Nishon
166 *L8* **Yangon** *Eng.* Rangoon. Yangon, S Myanmar (Burma) *16°50′N 96°11′E*
166 *M8* **Yangon** *Eng.* Rangoon. ◆ *division* SW Myanmar (Burma)
161 *N4* **Yangquan** Shanxi, C China *37°52′N 113°29′E*
161 *N13* **Yangshan** *var.* Yangcheng. Guangdong, S China *24°32′N 112°36′E*
167 *U12* **Yang Sin, Chu** ▲ S Vietnam *12°23′N 108°25′E*
Yangtze *see* Chang Jiang/Jinsha Jiang
Yangtze *see* Chang Jiang
Yangtze Kiang *see* Chang Jiang
161 *R7* **Yangzhou** *var.* Yangchow. Jiangsu, E China *32°22′N 119°22′E*
160 *L5* **Yan He** C China
163 *Y10* **Yanji** Jilin, NE China *42°54′N 129°31′E*
Yanji *see* Longjing
Yanjing *see* Yanyuan
29 *Q12* **Yankton** South Dakota, N USA *42°52′N 97°24′W*
161 *O12* **Yanling** *prev.* Lingxian, Ling Xian. Hunan, S China *26°32′N 113°48′E*
Yannina *see* Ioánnina
123 *Q7* **Yano-Indigirskaya Nizmennost'** *plain* NE Russian Federation
Yanovichi *see* Yanavichy
155 *K24* **Yan Oya** N Sri Lanka
158 *K6* **Yanqi** *var.* Yanqi Huizu Zizhixian. Xinjiang Uygur Zizhiqu, NW China *42°04′N 86°32′E*
Yanqi Huizu Zizhixian *see* Yanqi
161 *Q10* **Yanshan** *var.* Hekou. Jiangxi, S China *28°18′N 117°43′E*
160 *H14* **Yanshan** *var.* Jiangna. Yunnan, SW China *23°36′N 104°20′E*
161 *P2* **Yan Shan** ▲▲ E China
163 *X8* **Yanshou** Heilongjiang, NE China *45°27′N 128°19′E*
123 *Q7* **Yanskiy Zaliv** *bay* N Russian Federation
183 *O4* **Yantabulla** New South Wales, SE Australia *29°22′S 145°00′E*
161 *R4* **Yantai** *var.* Yan-t'ai; *prev.* Chefoo, Chih-fu. Shandong, E China *37°30′N 121°22′E*
118 *A13* **Yantarnyy** *Ger.* Palmnicken. Kaliningradskaya Oblast', W Russian Federation *54°53′N 19°59′E*
114 *J9* **Yantra** Gabrovo, N Bulgaria *42°58′N 25°19′E*
114 *K9* **Yantra** N Bulgaria
160 *G11* **Yanyuan** *var.* Yanjing. Sichuan, C China *27°30′N 101°22′E*
161 *P5* **Yanzhou** Shandong, E China *35°35′N 116°53′E*
79 *E16* **Yaoundé** *var.* Yaunde. ● (Cameroon) Centre, S Cameroon *03°51′N 11°31′E*
188 *I14* **Yap** ◆ *state* W Micronesia
188 *F16* **Yap** *island* Caroline Islands, W Micronesia
57 *M18* **Yapacani, Rio** C Bolivia
171 *W14* **Yapa Kopra** Papua, E Indonesia *04°18′S 135°05′E*
Yapan *see* Yapen, Selat
Yapanskoye More *see* East Sea/Japan, Sea of
77 *P15* **Yapei** N Ghana *09°10′N 01°08′W*
12 *M10* **Yapeitso, Mont** ▲ Québec, E Canada *52°18′N 70°24′W*
171 *W12* **Yapen, Pulau** *prev.* Japen. *island* E Indonesia
171 *W12* **Yapen, Selat** *var.* Yapan. *strait* Papua, E Indonesia
61 *E15* **Yapeyú** Corrientes, NE Argentina *29°28′S 56°50′W*
136 *I11* **Yapraklı** Çankırı, N Turkey *40°45′N 33°46′E*
174 *M3* **Yap Trench** *var.* Yap Trough. *undersea feature* SE Philippine Sea *08°30′N 138°00′E*
Yap Trough *see* Yap Trench
Yapurá *see* Caquetá, Río, Brazil/Colombia
Yapurá *see* Japurá, Rio, Brazil/Colombia
197 *I12* **Yaqaga** *island* N Fiji
197 *H12* **Yaqeta** *prev.* Yanggeta. *island* Yasawa Group, NW Fiji
40 *G6* **Yaqui** Sonora, NW Mexico *27°21′N 109°59′W*
32 *E12* **Yaquina Bay** *bay* Oregon, NW USA
40 *G6* **Yaqui, Río** NW Mexico
54 *K5* **Yaracuy** *off.* Estado Yaracuy. ◆ *state* NW Venezuela
Yaracuy, Estado *see* Yaracuy
146 *E13* **Yarajy** *Rus.* Yaradzhi. Ahal Welaýaty, C Turkmenistan *38°12′N 57°40′E*
Yaradzhi *see* Yarajy
125 *Q15* **Yaransk** Kirovskaya Oblast', NW Russian Federation *57°18′N 47°52′E*
136 *F17* **Yardımcı Burnu** *headland* SW Turkey *36°10′N 30°25′E*
97 *Q19* **Yare** E England, United Kingdom
125 *S9* **Yarega** Respublika Komi, NW Russian Federation *63°27′N 53°28′E*
116 *I7* **Yaremcha** Ivano-Frankivs'ka Oblast', W Ukraine *48°27′N 24°34′E*
189 *Q9* **Yaren (district)** ● (Nauru) SW Nauru *0°33′S 166°54′E*
125 *Q10* **Yarensk** Arkhangel'skaya Oblast', NW Russian Federation *62°09′N 49°03′E*
155 *F16* **Yargatti** Karnātaka, W India *16°07′N 75°11′E*
164 *M12* **Yariga-take** ▲ Honshū, S Japan *36°20′N 137°38′E*
141 *O15* **Yarīm** W Yemen *14°15′N 44°23′E*
54 *F14* **Yarí, Río** SW Colombia
54 *K5* **Yaritagua** Yaracuy, N Venezuela *10°05′N 69°07′W*
Yarkand *see* Yarkant He
Yarkant *see* Shache
158 *E9* **Yarkant He** *var.* Yarkand. NW China
149 *U3* **Yarkhūn** NW Pakistan
Yarlung Zangbo Jiang *see* Brahmaputra
116 *L6* **Yarmolyntsi** Khmel'nyts'ka Oblast', W Ukraine *49°13′N 26°53′E*
13 *O16* **Yarmouth** Nova Scotia, SE Canada *43°53′N 66°09′W*
Yarmouth *see* Great Yarmouth
Yaroslav *see* Jarosław
124 *L15* **Yaroslavl'** Yaroslavskaya Oblast', W Russian Federation *57°38′N 39°53′E*
124 *K14* **Yaroslavskaya Oblast'** ◆ *province* W Russian Federation
123 *N11* **Yaroslavskiy** Respublika Sakha (Yakutiya), NE Russian Federation *60°10′N 114°12′E*
183 *P13* **Yarram** Victoria, SE Australia *38°36′S 146°40′E*
183 *O11* **Yarrawonga** Victoria, SE Australia *36°04′S 145°58′E*
182 *L4* **Yarriarraburra Swamp** *wetland* New South Wales, SE Australia
122 *I8* **Yar-Sale** Yamalo-Nenetskiy Avtonomnyy Okrug, N Russian Federation *66°52′N 70°42′E*
122 *K11* **Yartsevo** Krasnoyarskiy Kray, C Russian Federation *60°15′N 90°09′E*
126 *I4* **Yartsevo** Smolenskaya Oblast', W Russian Federation *55°03′N 32°46′E*
54 *E8* **Yarumal** Antioquia, NW Colombia *06°59′N 75°25′W*
187 *W14* **Yasawa Group** *island group* NW Fiji
77 *V12* **Yashi** Katsina, N Nigeria *12°21′N 07°56′E*
77 *S14* **Yashikera** Kwara, W Nigeria *09°40′N 03°19′E*
147 *T14* **Yashilkŭl** *Rus.* Ozero Yashil'kul'. SE Tajikistan
Yashil'kul', Ozero *see* Yashilkŭl
165 *P9* **Yashima** Akita, Honshū, C Japan *39°10′N 140°10′E*
127 *P13* **Yashkul'** Respublika Kalmykiya, SW Russian Federation *46°09′N 45°22′E*
146 *F13* **Yashlyk** Ahal Welaýaty, C Turkmenistan *37°46′N 58°51′E*
Yasinovataya *see* Yasynuvata
114 *N10* **Yasna Polyana** Burgas, E Bulgaria *42°18′N 27°35′E*
167 *R10* **Yasothon** Yasothon, E Thailand *15°46′N 104°12′E*
183 *R10* **Yass** New South Wales, SE Australia *34°52′S 148°55′E*
Yassy *see* Iaşi
164 *H12* **Yasugi** Shimane, Honshū, SW Japan *35°25′N 133°12′E*
143 *N10* **Yāsūj** *var.* Yesuj; *prev.* Tal-e Khosravī. Kohkīlūyeh va Būyer AḤmad, C Iran *30°40′N 51°34′E*
136 *M11* **Yasun Burnu** *headland* N Turkey *41°07′N 37°40′E*
117 *X8* **Yasynuvata** *Rus.* Yasinovataya. Donets'ka Oblast', SE Ukraine *48°05′N 37°57′E*
136 *C15* **Yatağan** Muğla, SW Turkey *37°22′N 28°08′E*
165 *Q7* **Yatate-tōge** *pass* Honshū, C Japan
187 *Q17* **Yaté** Province Sud, S New Caledonia *22°10′S 166°56′E*
27 *P6* **Yates Center** Kansas, C USA *37°54′N 95°44′W*
185 *B21* **Yates Point** *headland* South Island, New Zealand *44°30′S 167°49′E*
9 *N9* **Yathkyed Lake** Nunavut, NE Canada
171 *T16* **Yatoke** Pulau Babar, E Indonesia *07°51′S 129°49′E*
79 *M18* **Yatolema** Orientale, N Dem. Rep. Congo *0°25′N 24°35′E*
164 *C15* **Yatsushiro** *var.* Yatusiro. Kumamoto, Kyūshū, SW Japan *32°30′N 130°34′E*
164 *C15* **Yatsushiro-kai** *bay* SW Japan
138 *F11* **Yatta** *var.* Yuta. S West Bank *31°29′N 35°10′E*
81 *J20* **Yatta Plateau** *plateau* SE Kenya
Yatusiro *see* Yatsushiro
57 *F17* **Yauca, Río** SW Peru
45 *S6* **Yauco** W Puerto Rico *18°02′N 66°51′W*
Yaunde *see* Yaoundé
Yavan *see* Yovon
Yavarí *see* Javari, Rio
56 *G9* **Yavari Mirim, Río** NE Peru
40 *G7* **Yavaros** Sonora, NW Mexico *26°40′N 109°32′W*
154 *I13* **Yavatmāl** Mahārāshtra, C India *20°22′N 78°11′E*
54 *M9* **Yaví, Cerro** ▲ C Venezuela *05°43′N 65°51′W*
43 *W16* **Yaviza** Darién, SE Panama *08°09′N 77°41′W*
138 *F10* **Yavne** Central, W Israel *31°52′N 34°45′E*
116 *H5* **Yavoriv** *Pol.* Jaworów, *Rus.* Yavorov. L'vivs'ka Oblast', NW Ukraine *49°57′N 23°22′E*
Yavorov *see* Yavoriv
164 *F14* **Yawatahama** Ehime, Shikoku, SW Japan *33°27′N 132°24′E*
Ya Xian *see* Sanya
136 *L17* **Yayladaği** Hatay, S Turkey *35°55′N 36°00′E*
125 *V13* **Yayva** Permskiy Kray, NW Russian Federation *59°19′N 57°15′E*
125 *V12* **Yayva** NW Russian Federation
143 *Q9* **Yazd** *var.* Yezd. Yazd, C Iran *31°55′N 54°22′E*
143 *Q8* **Yazd** *off.* Ostān-e Yazd, *var.* Yezd. ◆ *province* C Iran
Yazd, Ostān-e *see* Yazd
Yazgulemskiy Khrebet *see* Yazgulom, Qatorkŭhi
147 *S13* **Yazgulom, Qatorkŭhi** *Rus.* Yazgulemskiy Khrebet. ▲▲ S Tajikistan
22 *K5* **Yazoo City** Mississippi, S USA *32°51′N 90°24′W*
22 *K5* **Yazoo River** Mississippi, S USA
Yazovir Georgi Traykov *see* Tsonevo, Yazovir
127 *Q5* **Yazykovka** Ul'yanovskaya Oblast', W Russian Federation *54°19′N 47°22′E*
109 *U4* **Ybbs** Niederösterreich, NE Austria *48°10′N 15°03′E*
109 *U4* **Ybbs** C Austria
95 *G22* **Yding Skovhøj** *hill* C Denmark
115 *G20* **Ýdra** *var.* Ídhra, Idra. Ýdra, S Greece *37°20′N 23°28′E*
115 *G21* **Ýdra** *var.* Ídhra. *island* Ýdra, S Greece
115 *G20* **Ýdras, Kólpos** *strait* S Greece
167 *N10* **Ye** Mon State, S Myanmar (Burma) *15°15′N 97°50′E*
183 *O12* **Yea** Victoria, SE Australia *37°15′S 145°27′E*
167 *P13* **Yeay Sên** *prev.* Phumĭ Yeay Sên. Kaôh Kông, SW Cambodia *11°09′N 103°09′E*
Yebaishou *see* Jianping
78 *I5* **Yebbi-Bou** Borkou-Ennedi-Tibesti, N Chad *21°12′N 17°55′E*
158 *F9* **Yecheng** *var.* Kargilik. Xinjiang Uygur Zizhiqu, NW China *37°54′N 77°26′E*
105 *R11* **Yecla** Murcia, SE Spain *38°36′N 01°07′W*
40 *H6* **Yécora** Sonora, NW Mexico *28°23′N 108°56′W*
Yedintsy *see* Edineţ
124 *J13* **Yefimovskiy** Leningradskaya Oblast', NW Russian Federation *59°32′N 34°34′E*
126 *K6* **Yefremov** Tul'skaya Oblast', W Russian Federation *53°10′N 38°02′E*
159 *T11* **Yêgainnyin** *var.* Henan Mongolzu Zizhixian. Qinghai, C China *34°42′N 101°36′E*
137 *U12* **Yegbhegis** *Rus.* Yekhegis. C Armenia

◆ Country
● Country Capital
◇ Dependent Territory
○ Dependent Territory Capital
◆ Administrative Regions
✈ International Airport
▲ Mountain
▲▲ Mountain Range
Volcano
River
Lake
Reservoir

137 U12 **Yeghegnadzor** C Armenia 39°45′N 45°20′E
145 T10 **Yegindybulak** *Kaz.* Egindibulaq. Karaganda, C Kazakhstan 49°45′N 75°45′E
126 L4 **Yegor'yevsk** Moskovskaya Oblast', W Russian Federation 55°29′N 39°03′E
Yehuda, Haré *see* Judaean Hills
81 E15 **Yei** ≈ S South Sudan
161 P8 **Yeji** *var.* Yejiaji. Anhui, E China 31°52′N 115°58′E
Yejiaji *see* Yeji
122 G10 **Yekaterinburg** *prev.* Sverdlovsk. Sverdlovskaya Oblast', C Russian Federation 56°52′N 60°35′E
Yekaterinodar *see* Krasnodar
Yekaterinoslav *see* Dnipropetrovs'k
123 R13 **Yekaterinoslavka** Amurskaya Oblast', SE Russian Federation 50°23′N 129°03′E
127 O7 **Yekaterinovka** Saratovskaya Oblast', W Russian Federation 52°01′N 44°11′E
76 K16 **Yekepa** NE Liberia 07°35′N 08°32′W
Yekhegis *see* Yeghegis
145 T8 **Yekibastuz** *prev.* Ekibastuz. Pavlodar, NE Kazakhstan 51°42′N 75°22′E
127 T3 **Yelabuga** Respublika Tatarstan, W Russian Federation 55°46′N 52°07′E
Yela Island *see* Rossel Island
127 O8 **Yelan'** Volgogradskaya Oblast', SW Russian Federation 51°00′N 43°40′E
117 Q9 **Yelanets'** *Rus.* Yelanets. Mykolayivs'ka Oblast', S Ukraine 47°40′N 31°51′E
144 I9 **Yelek** *Kaz.* Elek; *prev.* Ilek. ≈ Kazakhstan/Russian Federation
126 L7 **Yelets** Lipetskaya Oblast', W Russian Federation 52°37′N 38°29′E
125 W4 **Yeletskiy** Respublika Komi, NW Russian Federation 67°03′N 64°05′E
76 J11 **Yélimané** Kayes, W Mali 15°06′N 10°43′W
Yelisavetpol *see* Gäncä
Yelizavetgrad *see* Kirovohrad
123 T12 **Yelizavety, Mys** *headland* SE Russian Federation 54°20′N 142°39′E
Yelizovo *see* Yalizava
127 S5 **Yelkhovka** Samarskaya Oblast', W Russian Federation 53°51′N 50°16′E
96 M1 **Yell** *island* NE Scotland, United Kingdom
155 E17 **Yellāpur** Karnātaka, W India 15°06′N 74°50′E
11 U17 **Yellow Grass** Saskatchewan, S Canada 49°51′N 104°09′W
Yellowhammer State *see* Alabama
11 O15 **Yellowhead Pass** *pass* Alberta/British Columbia, SW Canada
8 K10 **Yellowknife** *territory capital* Northwest Territories, W Canada 62°30′N 114°29′W
8 K9 **Yellowknife** ≈ Northwest Territories, NW Canada
23 P8 **Yellow River** ≈ Alabama/Florida, S USA
30 K7 **Yellow River** ≈ Wisconsin, N USA
30 J6 **Yellow River** ≈ Wisconsin, N USA
30 I4 **Yellow River** ≈ Wisconsin, N USA
Yellow River *see* Huang He
157 V8 **Yellow Sea** *Chin.* Huang Hai, *Kor.* Hwang-Hae. *sea* E Asia
33 S13 **Yellowstone Lake** ◎ Wyoming, C USA
33 T13 **Yellowstone National Park** *national park* Wyoming, NW USA
33 Y8 **Yellowstone River** ≈ Montana/Wyoming, NW USA
96 L1 **Yell Sound** *strait* N Scotland, United Kingdom
27 U9 **Yellville** Arkansas, C USA 36°12′N 92°41′W
122 K10 **Yeloguy** ≈ C Russian Federation
Yëloten *see* Ýolöten
119 M20 **Yel'sk** Homyel'skaya Voblasts', SE Belarus 51°48′N 29°09′E
77 T13 **Yelwa** Kebbi, W Nigeria 10°52′N 04°46′E
21 R15 **Yemassee** South Carolina, SE USA 32°41′N 80°51′W
141 O15 **Yemen** *off.* Republic of Yemen, *Ar.* Al Jumhuriyah al Yamaniyah, Al Yaman. ♦ *republic* SW Asia
Yemen, Republic of *see* Yemen
116 M4 **Yemil'chyne** Zhytomyrs'ka Oblast', N Ukraine 50°51′N 27°49′E
124 M10 **Yemtsa** Arkhangel'skaya Oblast', NW Russian Federation 63°04′N 40°18′E
124 M10 **Yemtsa** ≈ NW Russian Federation
125 R10 **Yemva** *prev.* Zheleznodorozhnyy. Respublika Komi, NW Russian Federation 62°38′N 50°59′E
77 U17 **Yenagoa** Bayelsa, S Nigeria 4°58′N 6°16′E
117 X7 **Yenakiyeve** *Rus.* Yenakiyevo; *prev.* Ordzhonikidze, Rykovo. Donets'ka Oblast', E Ukraine 48°13′N 38°13′E
Yenakiyevo *see* Yenakiyeve
166 L6 **Yenangyaung** Magway, W Myanmar (Burma) 20°28′N 94°54′E
167 S5 **Yên Bai** Yên Bai, N Vietnam 21°43′N 104°54′E
183 P9 **Yenda** New South Wales, SE Australia 34°16′S 146°15′E
77 Q14 **Yendi** NE Ghana 09°30′N 00°01′W
Yëndum *see* Zhag'yab
158 E8 **Yengisar** Xinjiang Uygur Zizhiqu, NW China 38°50′N 76°11′E
136 H11 **Yenice Çayı** *var.* Filyos Çayı. ≈ N Turkey
121 R1 **Yenierenköy** *var.* Yialousa, *Gk.* Agialoúsa. NE Cyprus 35°33′N 34°13′E
Yenipazar *see* Novi Pazar
136 E12 **Yenişehir** Bursa, NW Turkey 40°17′N 29°38′E
Yenisei Bay *see* Yeniseyskiy Zaliv
122 K12 **Yeniseysk** Krasnoyarskiy Kray, C Russian Federation 58°23′N 92°06′E
197 W10 **Yeniseyskiy Zaliv** *var.* Yenisei Bay. *bay* N Russian Federation
127 Q12 **Yenotayevka** Astrakhanskaya Oblast', SW Russian Federation 47°16′N 47°01′E
124 L4 **Yenozero, Ozero** ◎ NW Russian Federation
Yenping *see* Nanping
39 Q11 **Yentna River** ≈ Alaska, USA
180 M10 **Yeo, Lake** *salt lake* Western Australia
163 Z15 **Yeongcheon** *Jap.* Eisen; *prev.* Yŏngch'ŏn. SE South Korea 35°56′N 128°55′E
163 Y15 **Yeongju** *Jap.* Eishū; *prev.* Yŏngju. C South Korea 36°48′N 128°37′E
163 Y17 **Yeosu** *Jap.* Reisui; *prev.* Yŏsu. S South Korea 34°45′N 127°41′E
183 R7 **Yeoval** New South Wales, SE Australia 32°45′S 148°39′E
97 K23 **Yeovil** SW England, United Kingdom 50°57′N 02°39′W
40 H6 **Yepachic** Chihuahua, N Mexico 28°27′N 108°25′W
181 Y8 **Yeppoon** Queensland, E Australia 23°05′S 150°42′E
126 M5 **Yeraktur** Ryazanskaya Oblast', W Russian Federation 54°45′N 41°09′E
Yeraliyev *see* Kuryk
146 F12 **Yerbent** Ahal Welaýaty, C Turkmenistan 39°19′N 58°34′E
123 N11 **Yerbogachën** Irkutskaya Oblast', C Russian Federation 61°07′N 108°03′E
137 T12 **Yerevan** *Eng.* Erivan. ● (Armenia) C Armenia 40°12′N 44°31′E
137 U12 **Yerevan** ✕ C Armenia 40°07′N 44°34′E
145 R9 **Yereymentau** *var.* Jermentau, *Kaz.* Ereymentaū. Akmola, C Kazakhstan 51°38′N 73°10′E
145 R9 **Yereymentau, Gory** *prev.* Gory Yermentau. ▲ C Kazakhstan
127 O12 **Yergeni** *hill range* SW Russian Federation
Yeriho *see* Jericho
35 R6 **Yerington** Nevada, W USA 38°58′N 119°10′W
136 J13 **Yerköy** Yozgat, C Turkey 39°39′N 34°28′E
114 L13 **Yerlisu** Edirne, NW Turkey 40°45′N 26°38′E
Yermak *see* Aksu
Yermentau, Gory *see* Yereymentau, Gory
125 R5 **Yërmitsa** Respublika Komi, NW Russian Federation 66°57′N 52°15′E
35 V14 **Yermo** California, W USA 34°54′N 116°49′W
123 P13 **Yerofey Pavlovich** Amurskaya Oblast', SE Russian Federation 53°58′N 121°49′E
99 F15 **Yerseke** Zeeland, SW Netherlands 51°30′N 04°03′E
127 Q8 **Yershov** Saratovskaya Oblast', W Russian Federation 51°18′N 48°16′E
145 S7 **Yertis** *Kaz.* Ertis; *prev.* Irtyshsk. Pavlodar, NE Kazakhstan 53°21′N 75°27′E
129 R5 **Yertis** *var.* Irtish, *Kaz.* Ertis; *prev.* Irtysh. ≈ C Asia
125 P9 **Yërtom** Respublika Komi, NW Russian Federation 63°27′N 47°52′E
56 D13 **Yerupaja, Nevado** ▲ C Peru 10°23′S 76°58′W
Yerushalayim *see* Jerusalem
105 R4 **Yesa, Embalse de** ⊠ NE Spain
144 F11 **Yesbol** *prev.* Kulagino. Atyrau, W Kazakhstan 48°30′N 51°33′E
144 F9 **Yesensay** Zapadnyy Kazakhstan, NW Kazakhstan 49°59′N 51°19′E
144 F9 **Yesensay** Zapadnyy Kazakhstan, NW Kazakhstan 49°58′N 51°19′E
145 V15 **Yesik** *Kaz.* Esik; *prev.* Issyk. Almaty, SE Kazakhstan 42°23′N 77°25′E
145 O8 **Yesil'** *Kaz.* Esil. Akmola, C Kazakhstan 51°58′N 66°24′E
129 R6 **Yesil'** *Kaz.* Esil. ≈ Kazakhstan/Russian Federation
136 K15 **Yeşilhisar** Kayseri, C Turkey 38°22′N 35°08′E
136 L11 **Yeşilırmak** *var.* Iris. ≈ N Turkey
37 U12 **Yeso** New Mexico, SW USA 34°25′N 104°36′W
Yeso *see* Hokkaidō
127 N15 **Yessentuki** Stavropol'skiy Kray, SW Russian Federation 44°06′N 42°51′E
122 M9 **Yessey** Krasnoyarskiy Kray, N Russian Federation 68°18′N 101°49′E
105 P12 **Yeste** Castilla-La Mancha, C Spain 38°21′N 02°18′W
Yesuj *see* Yāsūj
183 T4 **Yetman** New South Wales, SE Australia 28°56′S 150°47′E
76 L4 **Yetti** *physical region* N Mauritania
166 M4 **Ye-u** Sagaing, C Myanmar (Burma) 22°49′N 95°26′E
102 H9 **Yeu, Île d'** *island* NW France
Yevlakh *see* Yevlax
137 W11 **Yevlax** *Rus.* Yevlakh. C Azerbaijan 40°36′N 47°10′E
117 S13 **Yevpatoriya** Avtonomna Respublika Krym, S Ukraine 45°12′N 33°23′E
Ye Xian *see* Laizhou
126 K12 **Yeya** ≈ SW Russian Federation
158 I10 **Yeyik** Xinjiang Uygur Zizhiqu, W China 36°44′N 83°14′E
126 K12 **Yeysk** Krasnodarskiy Kray, SW Russian Federation 46°41′N 38°15′E
Yezd *see* Yazd
Yezerishche *see* Yezyaryshcha
Yezhou *see* Jianshi
Yezo *see* Hokkaidō
118 N11 **Yezyaryshcha** *Rus.* Yezerishche. Vitsyebskaya Voblasts', NE Belarus 55°50′N 29°59′E
Yialí *see* Gyalí
Yialousa *see* Yenierenköy
163 V7 **Yi'an** Heilongjiang, NE China 47°52′N 125°13′E
Yiannitsá *see* Giannitsá
160 I10 **Yibin** Sichuan, C China 28°50′N 104°35′E
158 K13 **Yibug Caka** ◎ W China
160 M9 **Yichang** Hubei, C China 30°37′N 111°02′E
160 L5 **Yichuan** *var.* Danzhou. Shaanxi, C China 36°05′N 110°02′E
157 W3 **Yichun** Heilongjiang, NE China 47°41′N 129°10′E
161 O11 **Yichun** Jiangxi, S China 27°45′N 114°22′E
160 M9 **Yidu** *prev.* Zhicheng. Hubei, C China 30°21′N 111°27′E
Yidu *see* Qingzhou
188 C15 **Yigo** NE Guam 13°33′N 144°53′E
161 Q5 **Yi He** ≈ E China
163 X8 **Yilan** Heilongjiang, NE China 46°18′N 129°36′E
136 C9 **Yıldız Dağları** ▲▲ NW Turkey
136 L13 **Yıldızeli** Sivas, N Turkey 39°52′N 36°37′E
163 U4 **Yilehuli Shan** ▲▲ NE China
163 S7 **Yimin He** ≈ NE China
159 W8 **Yinchuan** *var.* Yinch'uan, Yin-ch'uan, Yinchwan. *province capital* Ningxia, N China 38°30′N 106°19′E
Yinchwan *see* Yinchuan
Yindu He *see* Indus
Yingcheng *see* Yingde
161 N14 **Yingde** *var.* Yingcheng. Guangdong, S China 24°08′N 113°21′E
163 U13 **Yingkou** *var.* Ying-k'ou, Yingkow; *prev.* Newchwang, Niuchwang. Liaoning, NE China 40°40′N 122°17′E
Yingkow *see* Yingkou
161 P9 **Yingshan** *var.* Wenquan. Hubei, C China 30°45′N 115°41′E
161 Q10 **Yingtan** Jiangxi, S China 28°17′N 117°03′E
Yin-hsien *see* Ningbo
158 H5 **Yining** *var.* I-ning, *Uigh.* Gulja, Kuldja. Xinjiang Uygur Zizhiqu, NW China 43°53′N 81°18′E
160 K11 **Yinjiang** *var.* Yinjiang Tujiazu Miaozu Zizhixian. Guizhou, S China 28°22′N 108°07′E
Yinjiang Tujiazu Miaozu Zizhixian *see* Yinjiang
166 L4 **Yinmabin** Sagaing, C Myanmar (Burma) 22°05′N 94°57′E
163 N13 **Yin Shan** ▲▲ N China
Yinshan *see* Guangshui
Yin-tu Ho *see* Indus
159 P15 **Yi'ong Zangbo** ≈ W China
Yioúra *see* Gyáros
81 J14 **Yirga 'Alem** *It.* Irgalem. Southern Nationalities, S Ethiopia 06°43′N 38°24′E
61 E19 **Yí, Río** ≈ C Uruguay
81 E14 **Yirol** El Buhayrat, C South Sudan 06°34′N 30°33′E
163 S8 **Yirshi** *var.* Yirxie. Nei Mongol Zizhiqu, N China 47°16′N 119°51′E
Yirxie *see* Yirshi
Yishan *see* Guanyun
Yishi *see* Linyi
161 Q5 **Yishui** Shandong, E China 35°50′N 118°39′E
Yisrael/Yisra'el *see* Israel
Yíthion *see* Gýtheio
Yitiaoshan *see* Jingtai
163 W10 **Yitong** *var.* Yitong Manzu Zizhixian. Jilin, NE China 43°23′N 125°19′E
Yitong Manzu Zizhixian *see* Yitong
159 P5 **Yiwu** *var.* Aratürük. Xinjiang Uygur Zizhiqu, NW China 43°16′N 94°38′E
163 U12 **Yiwulü Shan** ▲▲ N China
163 T12 **Yixian** *var.* Yizhou. Liaoning, NE China 41°29′N 121°21′E
159 R15 **Yixing** Jiangsu, China 31°14′N 119°18′E
161 N10 **Yiyang** Hunan, S China 28°39′N 112°10′E
161 Q10 **Yiyang** Jiangxi, S China 28°21′N 117°23′E
161 N13 **Yizhang** Hunan, S China 25°24′N 112°51′E
Yizhou *see* Yixian
93 K19 **Yläne** Länsi-Suomi, SW Finland 60°51′N 22°26′E
93 L14 **Yli-Ii** Oulu, C Finland 65°21′N 25°55′E
93 L14 **Ylikiiminki** Oulu, C Finland 65°00′N 26°10′E
92 N13 **Yli-Kitka** ◎ NE Finland
93 K17 **Ylistaro** Länsi-Suomi, W Finland 62°58′N 22°30′E
92 K13 **Ylitornio** Lappi, NW Finland 66°19′N 23°40′E
93 L15 **Ylivieska** Oulu, W Finland 64°05′N 24°30′E
93 L18 **Ylöjärvi** Länsi-Suomi, W Finland 61°31′N 23°37′E
95 N17 **Yngaren** ◎ C Sweden
25 T12 **Yoakum** Texas, SW USA 29°17′N 97°09′W
77 X13 **Yobe** ◆ *state* NE Nigeria
165 R3 **Yobetsu-dake** Ѫ Hokkaidō, NE Japan 43°15′N 140°27′E
80 L11 **Yoboki** C Djibouti 11°30′N 42°04′E
22 M4 **Yockanookany River** ≈ Mississippi, S USA
22 L2 **Yocona River** ≈ Mississippi, S USA
171 Y15 **Yodom** Papua, E Indonesia 07°12′S 139°24′E
169 Q16 **Yogyakarta** *prev.* Djokjakarta, Jogjakarta, Jokyakarta. Jawa, C Indonesia 07°48′S 110°24′E
169 P17 **Yogyakarta** *off.* Daerah Istimewa Yogyakarta, *var.* Djokjakarta, Jogjakarta, Jokyakarta. ◆ *autonomous district* S Indonesia
Yogyakarta, Daerah Istimewa *see* Yogyakarta
165 Q3 **Yoichi** Hokkaidō, NE Japan 43°11′N 140°45′E
42 G6 **Yojoa, Lago de** ◎ NW Honduras
79 G16 **Yokadouma** Est, SE Cameroon 03°26′N 15°06′E
164 K13 **Yokkaichi** *var.* Yokkaiti. Mie, Honshū, SW Japan 34°58′N 136°38′E
Yokkaiti *see* Yokkaichi
79 E15 **Yoko** Centre, C Cameroon 05°29′N 12°19′E
165 V15 **Yokoate-jima** *island* Nansei-shotō, SW Japan
165 R6 **Yokohama** Aomori, Honshū, C Japan 41°04′N 141°14′E
165 O14 **Yokosuka** Kanagawa, Honshū, S Japan 35°18′N 139°39′E
164 G12 **Yokota** Shimane, Honshū, SW Japan 35°10′N 133°03′E
165 Q9 **Yokote** Akita, Honshū, C Japan 39°20′N 140°33′E
77 Y14 **Yola** Adamawa, E Nigeria 09°08′N 12°24′E
79 L19 **Yolombo** Equateur, C Dem. Rep. Congo 01°36′S 23°13′E
146 J14 **Ýolöten** *Rus.* Yëloten; *prev.* Iolotan'. Mary Welaýaty, S Turkmenistan 37°15′N 62°18′E
165 Y15 **Yome-jima** *island* Ogasawara-shotō, SE Japan
76 K16 **Yomou** SE Guinea 07°30′N 09°13′W
171 Y15 **Yomuka** Papua, E Indonesia 07°25′S 138°36′E
188 C16 **Yona** E Guam 13°24′N 144°46′E
164 H12 **Yonago** Tottori, Honshū, SW Japan 35°30′N 134°15′E
165 N16 **Yonaguni** Okinawa, SW Japan 24°29′N 123°00′E
165 N16 **Yonaguni-jima** *island* Nansei-shotō, SW Japan
165 T16 **Yonaha-dake** ▲ Okinawa, SW Japan 26°43′N 128°13′E
163 X14 **Yŏnan** SW North Korea 37°50′N 126°15′E
165 P10 **Yonezawa** Yamagata, Honshū, C Japan 37°56′N 140°06′E
161 Q12 **Yong'an** *var.* Yongan. Fujian, SE China 25°58′N 117°26′E
Yong'an *see* Fengjie
159 T9 **Yongchang** Gansu, N China 38°15′N 101°56′E
161 P7 **Yongcheng** Henan, C China 33°56′N 116°21′E
Yŏngch'ŏn *see* Yeongcheon
160 J10 **Yongchuan** Chongqing Shi, C China 29°27′N 105°56′E
159 U10 **Yongdeng** Gansu, C China 35°58′N 103°27′E
Yongding *see* Yongren
129 W9 **Yongding He** ≈ E China
161 P11 **Yongfeng** *var.* Enjiang. Jiangxi, S China 27°19′N 115°23′E
158 L5 **Yongfeng** *var.* Yongfengqu. Xinjiang Uygur Zizhiqu, W China 43°28′N 87°09′E
Yongfengqu *see* Yongfeng
160 L13 **Yongfu** Guangxi Zhuangzu Zizhiqu, S China 24°57′N 109°59′E
163 X13 **Yŏnghŭng** E North Korea 39°31′N 127°14′E
159 U10 **Yongjing** *var.* Liujiaxia. Gansu, C China 36°00′N 103°30′E
Yŏngju *see* Yeongju
Yongning *see* Xuyong
160 E12 **Yongping** Yunnan, SW China 25°30′N 99°28′E
160 G12 **Yongren** *var.* Yongding. Yunnan, SW China 26°09′N 101°40′E
160 L10 **Yongshun** *var.* Lingxi. Hunan, S China 29°02′N 109°46′E
161 P10 **Yongxiu** *var.* Tujiabu. Jiangxi, S China 29°09′N 115°47′E
Yongzhou *see* Lingling
Yongzhou *see* Zhishan
18 K14 **Yonkers** New York, NE USA 40°56′N 73°51′W
103 Q7 **Yonne** ◆ *department* C France
103 P6 **Yonne** ≈ C France
54 H9 **Yopal** *var.* El Yopal. Casanare, C Colombia 05°20′N 72°19′W
158 E8 **Yopurga** *var.* Yukuriawat. Xinjiang Uygur Zizhiqu, NW China 39°13′N 76°44′E
147 S11 **Yordon** *var.* Iordan, *Rus.* Jardan. Farg'ona Viloyati, E Uzbekistan 39°59′N 71°44′E
180 J12 **York** Western Australia 31°55′S 116°52′E
97 M16 **York** *anc.* Eboracum, Eburacum. N England, United Kingdom 53°58′N 01°05′W
23 N5 **York** Alabama, S USA 32°29′N 88°18′W
29 Q15 **York** Nebraska, C USA 40°52′N 97°35′W
18 G16 **York** Pennsylvania, NE USA 39°57′N 76°44′W
21 R11 **York** South Carolina, SE USA 34°59′N 81°14′W
14 J13 **York** ≈ Ontario, SE Canada
15 X6 **York** ≈ Québec, SE Canada
181 V1 **York, Cape** *headland* Queensland, NE Australia 10°40′S 142°36′E
182 I9 **Yorke Peninsula** *peninsula* South Australia
182 I9 **Yorketown** South Australia 35°01′S 137°38′E
19 P9 **York Harbor** Maine, NE USA 43°10′N 70°37′W
York, Kap *see* Innaanganeq
21 X6 **York River** ≈ Virginia, NE USA
97 M16 **Yorkshire** *cultural region* N England, United Kingdom
97 L16 **Yorkshire Dales** *physical region* N England, United Kingdom
11 V16 **Yorkton** Saskatchewan, S Canada 51°12′N 102°29′W
25 T12 **Yorktown** Texas, SW USA 28°58′N 97°30′W
21 X6 **Yorktown** Virginia, NE USA 37°14′N 76°32′W
30 M11 **Yorkville** Illinois, N USA 41°38′N 88°27′W
42 I5 **Yoro** Yoro, C Honduras 15°08′N 87°10′W
42 H5 **Yoro** ◆ *department* N Honduras
165 T16 **Yoron-jima** *island* Nansei-shotō, SW Japan
77 N13 **Yorosso** Sikasso, S Mali 12°21′N 04°47′W
35 R8 **Yosemite National Park** *national park* California, W USA
127 Q3 **Yoshkar-Ola** Respublika Mariy El, W Russian Federation 56°38′N 47°54′E
Yösönbulag *see* Altay
162 K8 **Yösöndzüyl** *var.* Mönhbulag. Övörhangay, C Mongolia 46°48′N 103°25′E
171 Y16 **Yos Sudarso, Pulau** *var.* Pulau Dolak, Pulau Kolepom; *prev.* Jos Sudarso. *island* E Indonesia
Yŏsu *see* Yeosu
165 R4 **Yōtei-zan** ▲ Hokkaidō, NE Japan 42°50′N 140°46′E
97 D21 **Youghal** *Ir.* Eochaill. Cork, S Ireland 51°57′N 07°50′W
97 D21 **Youghal Bay** *Ir.* Cuan Eochaille. *inlet* S Ireland
18 C15 **Youghiogheny River** ≈ Pennsylvania, NE USA
160 K14 **You Jiang** ≈ S China
183 Q9 **Young** New South Wales, SE Australia 34°19′S 148°20′E
11 T15 **Young** Saskatchewan, S Canada 51°44′N 105°44′W
61 E18 **Young** Río Negro, W Uruguay 32°44′S 57°36′W
182 G5 **Younghusband, Lake** *salt lake* South Australia
182 J10 **Younghusband Peninsula** *peninsula* South Australia
184 Q10 **Young Nicks Head** *headland* North Island, New Zealand 39°38′S 177°03′E
185 D20 **Young Range** ▲▲ South Island, New Zealand
191 Q15 **Young's Rock** *island* Pitcairn Island, Pitcairn Islands
11 R16 **Youngstown** Alberta, SW Canada 51°32′N 111°12′W
31 V12 **Youngstown** Ohio, N USA 41°06′N 80°39′W
159 N9 **Youshashan** Qinghai, C China 38°12′N 90°58′E
Youth, Isle of *see* Juventud, Isla de la
77 N11 **Youvarou** Mopti, C Mali 15°19′N 04°15′W
160 K10 **Youyang** *var.* Zhongduo. Chongqing Shi, C China 28°48′N 108°48′E
163 Y7 **Youyi** Heilongjiang, NE China 46°51′N 131°54′E
147 P13 **Yovon** *Rus.* Yavan. SW Tajikistan 38°19′N 69°02′E
136 J13 **Yozgat** Yozgat, C Turkey 39°49′N 34°48′E
136 K13 **Yozgat** ◆ *province* C Turkey
62 O6 **Ypacaraí** *var.* Ypacaray. Central, S Paraguay 25°23′S 57°16′W
Ypacaray *see* Ypacaraí
62 P5 **Ypané, Río** ≈ C Paraguay
Ypres *see* Ieper
114 I13 **Ypsário** *var.* Ipsario. ▲ Thásos, E Greece 40°43′N 24°39′E
31 R10 **Ypsilanti** Michigan, N USA 42°12′N 83°36′W
34 M1 **Yreka** California, W USA 41°43′N 122°39′W
Yrendagüé *see* General Eugenio A. Garay
144 L11 **Yrghyz** *prev.* Irgiz. Aktyubinsk, C Kazakhstan 48°36′N 61°14′E
186 G5 **Ysabel Channel** *channel* N Papua New Guinea
14 K8 **Yser, Lac** ◎ Québec, SE Canada
147 Y8 **Yshtyk** Issyk-Kul'skaya Oblast', E Kyrgyzstan 41°34′N 78°21′E
Yssel *see* IJssel
103 Q12 **Yssingeaux** Haute-Loire, C France 45°09′N 04°07′E
95 K23 **Ystad** Skåne, S Sweden 55°25′N 13°51′E
Ysyk-Köl *see* Issyk-Kul', Ozero
Ysyk-Köl *see* Balykchy
Ysyk-Köl Oblasty *see* Issyk-Kul'skaya Oblast'
96 L8 **Ythan** ≈ NE Scotland, United Kingdom
Y Trallwng *see* Welshpool
94 C13 **Ytre Arna** Hordaland, S Norway 60°28′N 05°25′E
94 B12 **Ytre Sula** *island* S Norway
93 G17 **Ytterhogdal** Jämtland, C Sweden 62°10′N 14°55′E
Yu *see* Henan
Yuan *see* Red River
Yuancheng *see* Heyuan, Guangdong, S China
Yuan Jiang *see* Red River
161 S13 **Yuanlin** *Jap.* Inrin; *prev.* Yüanlin. C Taiwan 23°57′N 120°33′E
161 N3 **Yuanping** Shanxi, C China 38°26′N 112°42′E
Yuanquan *see* Anxi
Yuanshan *see* Lianping
161 O11 **Yuan Shui** ≈ S China
35 O6 **Yuba City** California, W USA 39°07′N 121°40′W
35 O6 **Yuba River** ≈ California, W USA
80 H13 **Yubdo** Oromīya, C Ethiopia 09°05′N 35°28′E
41 X12 **Yucatán** ◆ *state* SE Mexico
47 O3 **Yucatan Basin** *var.* Yucatan Deep. *undersea feature* N Caribbean Sea 20°00′N 84°00′W
Yucatán, Canal de *see* Yucatan Channel
41 Y10 **Yucatan Channel** *Sp.* Canal de Yucatán. *channel* Cuba/Mexico
Yucatan Deep *see* Yucatan Basin
Yucatan Peninsula *see* Yucatán, Península de
41 X13 **Yucatán, Península de** *Eng.* Yucatan Peninsula. *peninsula* Guatemala/Mexico
36 I11 **Yucca** Arizona, SW USA 34°49′N 114°06′W
35 V15 **Yucca Valley** California, W USA 34°06′N 116°30′W
161 P4 **Yucheng** Shandong, E China 37°01′N 116°37′E
Yuci *see* Jinzhong
129 X5 **Yudoma** ≈ E Russian Federation
161 P12 **Yudu** *var.* Gongjiang. Jiangxi, C China 26°02′N 115°24′E
Yue *see* Guangdong
Yuecheng *see* Yuexi
160 M12 **Yuecheng Ling** ▲▲ S China
Yuegai *see* Qumarlêb
Yuegaitan *see* Qumarlêb
181 P7 **Yuendumu** Northern Territory, N Australia 22°19′S 131°51′E
Yue Shan, Tai *see* Lantau Island
160 H10 **Yuexi** *var.* Yuecheng. Sichuan, C China 28°50′N 102°36′E
161 N10 **Yueyang** Hunan, S China 29°24′N 113°08′E
125 U14 **Yug** Permskiy Kray, NW Russian Federation 57°49′N 56°08′E
125 P13 **Yug** ≈ NW Russian Federation
123 R10 **Yugorënok** Respublika Sakha (Yakutiya), NE Russian Federation 59°46′N 137°36′E
122 H9 **Yugorsk** Khanty-Mansiyskiy Avtonomnyy Okrug-Yugra, C Russian Federation 61°17′N 63°25′E
122 H7 **Yugorskiy Poluostrov** *peninsula* NW Russian Federation
Yugoslavia *see* Serbia
146 K14 **Yugo-Vostochnyye Garagumy** *prev.* Yugo-Vostochnyye Karakumy. *desert* E Turkmenistan
Yugo-Vostochnyye Karakumy *see* Yugo-Vostochnyye Garagumy
Yuhu *see* Eryuan
161 S10 **Yuhuan Dao** *island* SE China
160 L14 **Yu Jiang** ≈ S China
Yujin *see* Qianwei
159 P9 **Yuka** Qinghai, W China 38°03′N 94°45′E
123 S7 **Yukagirskoye Ploskogor'ye** *plateau* NE Russian Federation
159 P9 **Yuke He** ≈ C China
118 L11 **Yukhavichy** *Rus.* Yukhovichi. Vitsyebskaya Voblasts', N Belarus 56°02′N 28°39′E
126 J4 **Yukhnov** Kaluzhskaya Oblast', W Russian Federation 54°43′N 35°15′E
Yukhovichi *see* Yukhavichy
79 J20 **Yuki** *var.* Yuki Kengunda. Bandundu, W Dem. Rep. Congo 03°57′S 19°30′E
Yuki Kengunda *see* Yuki
26 M10 **Yukon** Oklahoma, C USA 35°30′N 97°45′W
0 F4 **Yukon** ≈ Canada/USA
Yukon *see* Yukon Territory
39 S7 **Yukon Flats** *salt flat* Alaska, USA
Yukon, Territoire du *see* Yukon Territory
10 I5 **Yukon Territory** *var.* Yukon, *Fr.* Territoire du Yukon. ◆ *territory* NW Canada
137 T16 **Yüksekova** Hakkâri, SE Turkey 37°35′N 44°17′E
123 N10 **Yukta** Krasnoyarskiy Kray, C Russian Federation 63°16′N 106°04′E
165 O13 **Yukuhashi** *var.* Yukuhasi. Fukuoka, Kyūshū, SW Japan 33°41′N 131°00′E
Yukuhasi *see* Yukuhashi
Yukuriawat *see* Yopurga
125 O9 **Yula** ≈ NW Russian Federation
181 P8 **Yulara** Northern Territory, N Australia 25°15′S 130°57′E
127 W6 **Yuldybayevo** Respublika Bashkortostan, W Russian Federation 52°22′N 57°55′E
23 W8 **Yulee** Florida, SE USA 30°37′N 81°36′W
158 K7 **Yuli** *var.* Lopnur. Xinjiang Uygur Zizhiqu, NW China 41°24′N 86°12′E
161 T14 **Yuli** *prev.* Yüli. C Taiwan 23°23′N 121°18′E
160 L15 **Yulin** Guangxi Zhuangzu Zizhiqu, S China 22°37′N 110°08′E
160 L4 **Yulin** Shaanxi, C China 38°14′N 109°48′E
161 T14 **Yuli Shan** *prev.* Yüli Shan. ▲ E Taiwan 23°23′N 121°14′E
160 F11 **Yulong Xueshan** ▲ SW China 27°09′N 100°10′E
36 H14 **Yuma** Arizona, SW USA 32°40′N 114°38′W
37 W3 **Yuma** Colorado, C USA 40°07′N 102°43′W
54 K5 **Yumare** Yaracuy, N Venezuela 10°37′N 68°41′W
63 G14 **Yumbel** Bío Bío, C Chile 37°05′S 72°40′W
79 N19 **Yumbi** Maniema, E Dem. Rep. Congo 01°14′S 26°14′E
159 Q7 **Yumendong** *prev.* Yumenzhen. Gansu, N China 40°19′N 97°12′E
159 R8 **Yumendong** *prev.* Laojunmiao. Gansu, N China 39°49′N 97°47′E
Yumenzhen *see* Yumendong
158 J3 **Yumin** *var.* Karabura. Xinjiang Uygur Zizhiqu, NW China 46°14′N 82°52′E
Yun *see* Yunnan
136 G14 **Yunak** Konya, W Turkey 38°50′N 31°42′E
45 O8 **Yuna, Río** ≈ E Dominican Republic
38 I17 **Yunaska Island** *island* Aleutian Islands, Alaska, USA
160 M6 **Yuncheng** Shanxi, C China 35°07′N 110°45′E
Yuncheng *see* Yunfu
161 N14 **Yunfu** *var.* Yuncheng. Guangdong, S China 22°56′N 112°02′E
57 L18 **Yungas** *physical region* E Bolivia
Yungki *see* Jilin
Yung-ning *see* Nanning
160 I12 **Yungui Gaoyuan** *plateau* SW China
Yunjinghong *see* Jinghong
160 M15 **Yunkai Dashan** ▲▲ S China
Yunki *see* Jilin
160 E11 **Yun Ling** ▲▲ SW China
Yunling *see* Yunxiao
161 N9 **Yunmeng** Hubei, C China 31°04′N 113°45′E
157 N14 **Yunnan** *var.* Yun, Yunnan Sheng, Yünnan, Yun-nan. ◆ *province* SW China
Yunnan *see* Kunming
Yunnan Sheng *see* Yunnan
Yünnan/Yun-nan *see* Yunnan
165 P15 **Yunomae** Kumamoto, Kyūshū, SW Japan 32°16′N 131°00′E
161 N8 **Yun Shui** ≈ C China
182 J7 **Yunta** South Australia 32°37′S 139°33′E
161 Q14 **Yunxiao** *var.* Yunling. Fujian, SE China 23°56′N 117°16′E
160 K9 **Yunyang** Sichuan, C China 31°03′N 109°43′E
Yunzhong *see* Huairen
193 S9 **Yupanqui Basin** *undersea feature* E Pacific Ocean
Yuping *see* Libo, Guizhou, China
Yuping *see* Pingbian, Yunnan, China
Yuratishki *see* Yuratsishki
119 I15 **Yuratsishki** *Pol.* Juraciszki, *Rus.* Yuratishki. Hrodzyenskaya Voblasts', W Belarus 54°02′N 25°56′E
Yurev *see* Tartu
122 J12 **Yurga** Kemerovskaya Oblast', S Russian Federation 55°42′N 84°59′E
Yurihonjō *see* Honjō
56 E10 **Yurimaguas** Loreto, N Peru 05°54′S 76°07′W
127 P3 **Yurino** Respublika Mariy El, W Russian Federation 56°19′N 46°15′E
41 N13 **Yuriria** Guanajuato, C Mexico 20°12′N 101°09′W
125 T13 **Yurla** Komi-Permyatskiy Okrug, NW Russian Federation 59°18′N 54°19′E
Yuruá, Río *see* Juruá, Rio
114 M13 **Yürük** Tekirdağ, NW Turkey 40°58′N 27°09′E
158 G10 **Yurungkax He** ≈ W China
125 Q14 **Yur'ya** *var.* Jarja. Kirovskaya Oblast', NW Russian Federation 59°01′N 49°22′E
Yur'yev *see* Tartu
125 N16 **Yur'yevets** Ivanovskaya Oblast', W Russian Federation 57°19′N 43°01′E
126 M3 **Yur'yev-Pol'skiy** Vladimirskaya Oblast', W Russian Federation 56°28′N 39°39′E
117 V7 **Yur"yivka** Dnipropetrovs'ka Oblast', E Ukraine 48°45′N 36°01′E
42 I7 **Yuscarán** El Paraíso, S Honduras 13°55′N 86°51′W
161 P12 **Yu Shan** ▲ S China
124 I7 **Yushkozero** Respublika Kareliya, NW Russian Federation 64°46′N 32°13′E
124 I7 **Yushkozerskoye Vodokhranilishche** *var.* Ozero Kujto. ◎ NW Russian Federation
169 W9 **Yushu** Jilin, China E Asia 44°48′N 126°55′E
159 R13 **Yushu** *var.* Gyêgu. Qinghai, C China 33°04′N 97°E
127 P12 **Yusta** Respublika Kalmykiya, SW Russian Federation 47°06′N 46°16′E
124 I10 **Yustozero** Respublika Kareliya, NW Russian Federation 62°44′N 33°31′E
137 Q11 **Yusufeli** Artvin, NE Turkey 40°50′N 41°31′E
164 F14 **Yusuhara** Kōchi, Shikoku, SW Japan 33°22′N 132°52′E
125 T14 **Yus'va** Permskiy Kray, NW Russian Federation 58°48′N 54°59′E
Yuta *see* Yatta
161 P2 **Yutian** Hebei, E China 39°52′N 117°44′E
158 H10 **Yutian** *var.* Keriya, Mugalla. Xinjiang Uygur Zizhiqu, NW China 36°49′N 81°31′E
62 K5 **Yuto** Jujuy, NW Argentina 23°35′S 64°28′W
62 P7 **Yuty** Caazapá, S Paraguay 26°31′S 56°20′W
160 G13 **Yuxi** Yunnan, SW China 24°22′N 102°28′E
161 O2 **Yuxian** *prev.* Yu Xian. Hebei, E China 39°50′N 114°33′E
Yu Xian *see* Yuxian
165 Q9 **Yuzawa** Akita, Honshū, C Japan 39°11′N 140°29′E
125 N16 **Yuzha** Ivanovskaya Oblast', W Russian Federation 56°34′N 42°00′E
Yuzhno-Alichurskiy Khrebet *see* Alichuri Janubí, Qatorkŭhi
Yuzhno-Kazakhstanskaya Oblast' *see* Yuzhnyy Kazakhstan
123 T13 **Yuzhno-Sakhalinsk** *Jap.* Toyohara; *prev.* Vladimirovka. Ostrov Sakhalin, Sakhalinskaya Oblast', SE Russian Federation 46°58′N 142°45′E
127 P14 **Yuzhno-Sukhokumsk** Respublika Dagestan, SW Russian Federation 44°43′N 45°32′E
145 Z10 **Yuzhnyy Altay, Khrebet** ▲▲ E Kazakhstan
Yuzhnyy Bug *see* Pivdennyy Buh
145 O15 **Yuzhnyy Kazakhstan** *off.* Yuzhno-Kazakhstanskaya Oblast', *Eng.* South Kazakhstan, *Kaz.* Ongtüstik Qazaqstan Oblysy; *prev.* Chimkentskaya Oblast'. ◆ *province* S Kazakhstan

♦ Country
● Country Capital
◇ Dependent Territory
○ Dependent Territory Capital
◆ Administrative Regions
✕ International Airport
▲ Mountain
▲▲ Mountain Range
Ѫ Volcano
≈ River
◎ Lake
⊠ Reservoir

123 U10 **Yuzhnyy, Mys** *headland* E Russian Federation 57°44′N 156°49′E
122 H6 **Yuzhnyy, Ostrov** *island* NW Russian Federation
127 W6 **Yuzhnyy Ural** *var.* Southern Urals. ▲▲ W Russian Federation
159 V10 **Yuzhong** Gansu, C China 35°52′N 104°09′E
Yuzhou *see* Chongqing
103 N5 **Yvelines** ◈ *department* N France
108 B9 **Yverdon** *var.* Yverdon-les-Bains, *Ger.* Iferten; *anc.* Eborodunum. Vaud, W Switzerland 46°47′N 06°38′E
Yverdon-les-Bains *see* Yverdon
102 M3 **Yvetot** Seine-Maritime, N France 49°37′N 00°48′E
Ýylanly *see* Gurbansoltan Eje

Z

147 T12 **Zaalayskiy Khrebet** *Taj.* Qatorkŭhi Pasi Oloy. ▲▲ Kyrgyzstan/Tajikistan
Zaamin *see* Zomin
Zaandam *see* Zaanstad
98 I10 **Zaanstad** *prev.* Zaandam. Noord-Holland, C Netherlands 52°27′N 04°49′E
Zabadani *see* Az Zabdānī
Zabalatstsye *see* Zabalotstsye
112 L9 **Žabalj** *Ger.* Josefsdorf, *Hung.* Zsablya; *prev.* Józseffalva. Vojvodina, N Serbia 45°22′N 20°01′E
119 L18 **Zabalotstsye** *prev.* Zabalatstsye, *Rus.* Zabolot'ye. Homyel'skaya Voblasts', SE Belarus 52°40′N 28°34′E
Zāb aş Şaghīr, Nahraz *see* Little Zab
123 P14 **Zabaykal'sk** Zabaykal'skiy Kray, S Russian Federation 49°37′N 117°20′E
123 O12 **Zabaykal'skiy Kray** ◈ *province* S Russian Federation
Zāb-e Kūchek, Rūdkhāneh-ye *see* Little Zab
Zabeln *see* Sabile
Zabéré *see* Zabré
Zabern *see* Saverne
141 N16 **Zabīd** W Yemen 14°N 43°E
141 O16 **Zabīd, Wādī** *dry watercourse* SW Yemen
Żabinka *see* Zhabinka
Ząbkowice *see* Ząbkowice Śląskie
111 G15 **Ząbkowice Śląskie** *var.* Ząbkowice, *Ger.* Frankenstein, Frankenstein in Schlesien. Dolnośląskie, SW Poland 50°35′N 16°48′E
110 P10 **Zabłudów** Podlaskie, NE Poland 53°00′N 23°21′E
112 D8 **Zabok** Krapina-Zagorje, N Croatia 46°00′N 15°48′E
143 W9 **Zābol** *var.* Shahr-i-Zabul, Zabul; *prev.* Nasratabad. Sīstān va Balūchestān, E Iran 31°N 61°32′E
Zābol *see* Zābul
143 W13 **Zābolī** Sīstān va Balūchestān, SE Iran 27°09′N 61°32′E
Zabolot'ye *see* Zabalotstsye
77 Q13 **Zabré** *var.* Zabéré. S Burkina 11°13′N 00°34′W
111 G17 **Zábřeh** *Ger.* Hohenstadt. Olomoucký Kraj, E Czech Republic 49°52′N 16°53′E
111 J16 **Zabrze** *Ger.* Hindenburg, Hindenburg in Oberschlesien. Śląskie, S Poland 50°18′N 18°47′E
149 O7 **Zābul** *prev.* Zābol. ◈ *province* SE Afghanistan
Zabul/Zābul *see* Zābol
42 E6 **Zacapa** Zacapa, E Guatemala 14°59′N 89°33′W
42 A3 **Zacapa** *off.* Departamento de Zacapa. ◈ *department* E Guatemala
Zacapa, Departamento de *see* Zacapa
40 M14 **Zacapú** Michoacán, SW Mexico 19°49′N 101°48′W
41 V14 **Zacatal** Campeche, SE Mexico 18°40′N 91°52′W
40 M11 **Zacatecas** Zacatecas, C Mexico 22°46′N 102°33′W
40 L10 **Zacatecas** ◈ *state* C Mexico
42 F8 **Zacatecoluca** La Paz, S El Salvador 13°29′N 88°51′W
41 P15 **Zacatepec** Morelos, S Mexico 18°40′N 99°11′W
41 Q13 **Zacatlán** Puebla, S Mexico 19°56′N 97°58′W
144 F8 **Zachagansk** *Kaz.* Zashaghan. Zapadnyy Kazakhstan, NW Kazakhstan 51°04′N 51°13′E
115 D20 **Zacháro** *var.* Zaharo, Zakháro. Dytikí Elláda, S Greece 37°29′N 21°40′E
22 J8 **Zachary** Louisiana, S USA 30°39′N 91°09′W
117 U6 **Zachepylivka** Kharkivs'ka Oblast', E Ukraine 49°13′N 35°15′E
Zachist'ye *see* Zachystsye
110 E9 **Zachodnio-pomorskie** ◈ *province* NW Poland
119 L14 **Zachystsye** *Rus.* Zachist'ye. Minskaya Voblasts', NW Belarus 54°24′N 28°45′E
40 L13 **Zacoalco** *var.* Zacoalco de Torres. Jalisco, SW Mexico 20°14′N 103°33′W
Zacoalco de Torres *see* Zacoalco
41 P13 **Zacualtipán** Hidalgo, C Mexico 20°39′N 98°42′W
112 C12 **Zadar** *It.* Zara; *anc.* Iader. Zadar, SW Croatia 44°07′N 15°15′E
112 C12 **Zadar** *off.* Zadarsko-Kninska Županija, Zadar-Knin. ◈ *province* SW Croatia
Zadar-Knin *see* Zadar
Zadarsko-Kninska Županija *see* Zadar
166 M14 **Zadetkyi Kyun** *var.* St.Matthew's Island. *island* Mergui Archipelago, S Myanmar (Burma)
67 Q9 **Zadié** *var.* Djadié. ≈ NE Gabon
159 Q13 **Zadoi** *var.* Qapugtang. Qinghai, C China 32°56′N 95°21′E
126 L7 **Zadonsk** Lipetskaya Oblast', W Russian Federation 52°25′N 38°55′E
Za'farâna *see* Za'farānah
75 X8 **Za'farānah** *var.* Za'farâna. E Egypt 29°06′N 32°34′E
149 W7 **Zafarwāl** Punjab, E Pakistan 32°20′N 74°53′E
121 Q1 **Zafer Burnu** *var.* Cape Andreas, Cape Apostolas Andreas, *Gk.* Akrotíri Apostólou Andréa. *cape* NE Cyprus
107 J23 **Zafferano, Capo** *headland* Sicilia, Italy, C Mediterranean Sea 38°06′N 13°31′E
114 M7 **Zafirovo** Silistra, NE Bulgaria 44°00′N 26°51′E
Záfora *see* Sofraná
104 J12 **Zafra** Extremadura, W Spain 38°25′N 06°27′W
110 E13 **Żagań** *var.* Zagań, Żegań, *Ger.* Sagan. Lubuskie, W Poland 51°37′N 15°20′E
118 F10 **Žagarė** *Pol.* Żagory. Šiaulai, N Lithuania 56°22′N 23°16′E
Zagazig *see* Az Zaqāzīq
74 M5 **Zaghouan** *var.* Zaghwān. NE Tunisia 36°26′N 10°05′E
Zaghwān *see* Zaghouan
115 G16 **Zagorá** Thessalía, C Greece 39°27′N 23°06′E
Zagorod'ye *see* Zaharoddzye
Żagory *see* Žagarė
Zágráb *see* Zagreb
112 E8 **Zagreb** *Ger.* Agram, *Hung.* Zágráb. ● (Croatia) Zagreb, N Croatia 45°48′N 15°58′E
112 E8 **Zagreb** *prev.* Grad Zagreb. ◈ *province* N Croatia
142 L7 **Zāgros, Kūhhā-ye** *Eng.* Zagros Mountains. ▲▲ W Iran
Zagros Mountains *see* Zāgros, Kūhhā-ye
112 O12 **Žagubica** Serbia, E Serbia 44°13′N 21°47′E
Zagunao *see* Lixian
111 L22 **Zagyva** ≈ N Hungary
Zaharo *see* Zacháro
119 G19 **Zaharoddzye** *Rus.* Zagorod'ye. *physical region* SW Belarus
143 W11 **Zāhedān** *var.* Zahidan; *prev.* Duzdab. Sīstān va Balūchestān, SE Iran 29°31′N 60°51′E
Zahidan *see* Zāhedān
Zahlah *see* Zahlé
138 H7 **Zahlé** *var.* Zahlah. C Lebanon 33°51′N 35°54′E
146 J14 **Zähmet** *Rus.* Zakhmet. Mary Welaýaty, C Turkmenistan 37°48′N 62°33′E
111 O20 **Záhony** Szabolcs-Szatmár-Bereg, NE Hungary 48°26′N 22°11′E
141 N13 **Zahrān** 'Asīr, S Saudi Arabia 17°48′N 43°28′E
139 R12 **Zahrat al Baṭn** *hill range* S Iraq
120 H11 **Zahrez Chergui** *var.* Zahrez Chergui. *marsh* N Algeria
Zainlha *see* Xinjin
127 S4 **Zainsk** Respublika Tatarstan, W Russian Federation 55°12′N 52°01′E
82 A10 **Zaire** *prev.* Congo. ◈ *province* NW Angola
Zaire *see* Congo (river)
Zaire *see* Congo (Democratic Republic of)
112 P13 **Zaječar** Serbia, E Serbia 43°54′N 22°16′E
83 L18 **Zaka** Masvingo, E Zimbabwe 20°20′S 31°29′E
122 M14 **Zakamensk** Respublika Buryatiya, S Russian Federation 50°18′N 102°57′E
116 G7 **Zakarpats'ka Oblast'** *Eng.* Transcarpathian Oblast, *Rus.* Zakarpatskaya Oblast'. ◈ *province* W Ukraine
Zakarpatskaya Oblast' *see* Zakarpats'ka Oblast'
Zakataly *see* Zaqatala
Zakháro *see* Zacháro
Zakhidnyy Buh/Zakhodni Buh *see* Bug
Zakhmet *see* Zähmet
139 Q1 **Zākhō** *var.* Zākhū. Dahūk, N Iraq 37°09′N 42°40′E
Zākhū *see* Zākhō
Zákinthos *see* Zákynthos
111 L18 **Zakopane** Małopolskie, S Poland 49°17′N 19°57′E
78 J12 **Zakouma** Salamat, S Chad 10°47′N 19°51′E
115 L25 **Zákros** Kríti, Greece, E Mediterranean Sea 35°06′N 26°12′E
115 C19 **Zákynthos** *var.* Zákinthos. Zákynthos, W Greece 37°47′N 20°54′E
115 C20 **Zákynthos** *var.* Zákinthos, *It.* Zante. *island* Iónia Nisoí, Greece, C Mediterranean Sea
115 C19 **Zakýnthou, Porthmós** *strait* SW Greece
111 G24 **Zala** *off.* Zala Megye. ◈ *county* W Hungary
111 G24 **Zala** ≈ W Hungary
138 M4 **Zalābiyah** Dayr az Zawr, C Syria 35°39′N 39°51′E
111 G24 **Zalaegerszeg** Zala, W Hungary 46°51′N 16°49′E
104 K11 **Zalamea de la Serena** Extremadura, W Spain 38°38′N 05°37′W
104 J13 **Zalamea la Real** Andalucía, S Spain 37°41′N 06°40′W
Zala Megye *see* Zala
163 U7 **Zalantun** *var.* Butha Qi. Nei Mongol Zizhiqu, N China 47°58′N 122°44′E
111 G23 **Zalaszentgrót** Zala, SW Hungary 46°57′N 17°05′E
Zalatna *see* Zlatna
116 G9 **Zalău** *Ger.* Waltenberg, *Hung.* Zilah; *prev. Ger.* Zillenmarkt. Sălaj, NW Romania 47°11′N 23°03′E
109 V10 **Žalec** *Ger.* Sachsenfeld. C Slovenia 46°15′N 15°08′E
110 K8 **Zalewo** *Ger.* Saalfeld. Warmińsko-Mazurskie, NE Poland 53°54′N 19°39′E
141 N9 **Zalim** Makkah, W Saudi Arabia 22°46′N 42°12′E
80 A11 **Zalingei** *var.* Zalinje. Western Darfur, W Sudan 12°51′N 23°29′E
Zalinje *see* Zalingei
116 K7 **Zalishchyky** Ternopil's'ka Oblast', W Ukraine 48°40′N 25°43′E
Zallah *see* Zillah
98 J13 **Zaltbommel** Gelderland, C Netherlands 51°49′N 05°15′E
124 H15 **Zaluch'ye** Novgorodskaya Oblast', NW Russian Federation 57°40′N 31°45′E
Zamak *see* Zamakh
141 Q14 **Zamakh** *var.* Zamak. N Yemen 16°26′N 47°35′E
136 K15 **Zamantı Irmağı** ≈ C Turkey
Zambesi/Zambeze *see* Zambezi
83 G14 **Zambezi** North Western, W Zambia 13°34′S 23°08′E
83 K15 **Zambezi** *var.* Zambesi, *Port.* Zambeze. ≈ S Africa
83 O15 **Zambézia** *off.* Província da Zambézia. ◈ *province* C Mozambique
Zambézia, Província da *see* Zambézia
83 I14 **Zambia** *off.* Republic of Zambia; *prev.* Northern Rhodesia. ◆ *republic* S Africa
Zambia, Republic of *see* Zambia
171 O8 **Zamboanga** *off.* Zamboanga City. Mindanao, S Philippines 06°56′N 122°03′E
Zamboanga City *see* Zamboanga
54 E5 **Zambrano** Bolívar, N Colombia 09°45′N 74°50′W
110 N10 **Zambrów** Łomża, E Poland 52°59′N 22°14′E
83 L14 **Zâmbuè** Tete, NW Mozambique 15°03′S 30°49′E
77 T13 **Zamfara** ≈ NW Nigeria
Zamkog *see* Zamtang
56 C9 **Zamora** Zamora Chinchipe, S Ecuador 04°04′S 78°52′W
104 K6 **Zamora** Castilla y León, NW Spain 41°30′N 05°45′W
104 K5 **Zamora** ◈ *province* Castilla y León, NW Spain
Zamora *see* Barinas
56 A13 **Zamora Chinchipe** ◈ *province* S Ecuador
40 M13 **Zamora de Hidalgo** Michoacán, SW Mexico 20°N 102°18′W
111 P15 **Zamość** *Rus.* Zamoste. Lubelskie, E Poland 50°44′N 23°16′E
Zamoste *see* Zamość
160 G7 **Zamtang** *var.* Zamkog; *prev.* Gamba. Sichuan, C China 32°19′N 100°55′E
75 O8 **Zamzam, Wādī** *dry watercourse* NW Libya
79 F20 **Zanaga** Lékoumou, S Congo 02°50′S 13°53′E
41 T16 **Zanatepec** Oaxaca, SE Mexico 16°28′N 94°24′W
105 P9 **Záncara** ≈ C Spain
Zancle *see* Messina
158 G14 **Zanda** Xizang Zizhiqu, W China 31°29′N 79°50′E
98 H10 **Zandvoort** Noord-Holland, W Netherlands 52°22′N 04°31′E
39 P8 **Zane Hills** *hill range* Alaska, USA
31 T13 **Zanesville** Ohio, N USA 39°55′N 82°02′W
Zanga *see* Hrazdan
Zangoza *see* Sangüesa
142 L4 **Zanjān** *var.* Zenjan, Zinjan. Zanjān, NW Iran 36°40′N 48°30′E
142 L4 **Zanjān** *off.* Ostān-e Zanjān, *var.* Zenjan, Zinjan. ◈ *province* NW Iran
Zanjān, Ostān-e *see* Zanjān
Zante *see* Zákynthos
81 J22 **Zanzibar** Zanzibar, E Tanzania 06°10′S 39°12′E
81 J22 **Zanzibar** ◈ *region* E Tanzania
81 J22 **Zanzibar** *Swa.* Unguja. *island* E Tanzania
81 J22 **Zanzibar Channel** *channel* E Tanzania
161 N8 **Zaoyang** Hubei, C China 32°10′N 112°45′E
165 P10 **Zaō-zan** ▲ Honshū, C Japan 38°06′N 140°27′E
124 J2 **Zaozërsk** Murmanskaya Oblast', NW Russian Federation 69°25′N 32°25′E
161 Q6 **Zaozhuang** Shandong, E China 34°53′N 117°38′E
28 L4 **Zap** North Dakota, N USA 47°18′N 101°55′W
112 L13 **Zapadna Morava** *Ger.* Westliche Morava. ≈ C Serbia
124 H16 **Zapadnaya Dvina** Tverskaya Oblast', W Russian Federation 56°17′N 32°03′E
Zapadnaya Dvina *see* Western Dvina
Zapadno-Kazakhstanskaya Oblast' *see* Zapadnyy Kazakhstan
122 I9 **Zapadno-Sibirskaya Ravnina** *Eng.* West Siberian Plain. *plain* C Russian Federation
Zapadnyy Bug *see* Bug
144 E9 **Zapadnyy Kazakhstan** *off.* Zapadno-Kazakhstanskaya Oblast', *Eng.* West Kazakhstan, *Kaz.* Batys Qazaqstan Oblysy; *prev.* Ural'skaya Oblast'. ◈ *province* NW Kazakhstan
122 K13 **Zapadnyy Sayan** *Eng.* Western Sayans. ▲▲ S Russian Federation
63 H15 **Zapala** Neuquén, W Argentina 38°54′S 70°06′W
62 I4 **Zapaleri, Cerro** *var.* Cerro Sapaleri. ▲ N Chile 22°51′S 67°10′W
25 Q16 **Zapata** Texas, SW USA 26°57′N 99°17′W
44 D5 **Zapata, Península de** *peninsula* W Cuba
61 G19 **Zapicán** Lavalleja, S Uruguay 33°31′S 54°55′W
65 J19 **Zapiola Ridge** *undersea feature* SW Atlantic Ocean
65 L19 **Zapiola Seamount** *undersea feature* S Atlantic Ocean 38°15′S 26°15′W
124 I2 **Zapolyarnyy** Murmanskaya Oblast', NW Russian Federation 69°24′N 30°53′E
117 U8 **Zaporizhzhya** *Rus.* Zaporozh'ye; *prev.* Aleksandrovsk. Zaporiz'ka Oblast', SE Ukraine 47°47′N 35°12′E
Zaporizhzhya *see* Zaporiz'ka Oblast'
117 U9 **Zaporiz'ka Oblast'** *var.* Zaporizhzhya, *Rus.* Zaporozhskaya Oblast'. ◈ *province* SE Ukraine
Zaporozhskaya Oblast' *see* Zaporiz'ka Oblast'
Zaporozh'ye *see* Zaporizhzhya
40 L14 **Zapotiltic** Jalisco, SW Mexico 19°40′N 103°29′W
158 G13 **Zapug** Xizang Zizhiqu, W China
137 V10 **Zaqatala** *Rus.* Zakataly. NW Azerbaijan 41°38′N 46°38′E
159 P13 **Zaqên** Qinghai, W China 33°23′N 94°31′E
159 Q13 **Za Qu** ≈ C China
136 M13 **Zara** Sivas, C Turkey 39°55′N 37°44′E
Zara *see* Zadar
Zarafshan *see* Zarafshon
147 P12 **Zarafshon** *Rus.* Zeravshan. W Tajikistan 39°12′N 68°36′E
146 L9 **Zarafshon** *Rus.* Zarafshan. Navoiy Viloyati, N Uzbekistan 41°33′N 64°09′E
Zarafshon *see* Zeravshan
147 O12 **Zarafshon, Qatorkŭhi** *Rus.* Zeravshanskiy Khrebet, *Uzb.* Zarafshon Tizmasi. ▲▲ Tajikistan/Uzbekistan
Zarafshon Tizmasi *see* Zarafshon, Qatorkŭhi
54 E7 **Zaragoza** Antioquia, N Colombia 07°30′N 74°52′W
40 I5 **Zaragoza** Chihuahua, N Mexico 29°36′N 107°41′W
41 N6 **Zaragoza** Coahuila, NE Mexico 28°31′N 100°54′W
41 O10 **Zaragoza** Nuevo León, NE Mexico 23°59′N 99°49′W
105 R5 **Zaragoza** *Eng.* Saragossa; *anc.* Caesaraugusta, Salduba. Aragón, NE Spain 41°39′N 00°54′W
105 R6 **Zaragoza** ◈ *province* Aragón, NE Spain
105 R5 **Zaragoza** ✈ Aragón, NE Spain 41°38′N 00°53′W
143 S10 **Zarand** Kermān, C Iran 30°50′N 56°35′E
148 J9 **Zaranj** Nīmrōz, SW Afghanistan 30°59′N 61°54′E
118 I11 **Zarasai** Utena, E Lithuania 55°44′N 26°17′E
62 N12 **Zárate** *prev.* General José F.Uriburu. Buenos Aires, E Argentina 34°06′S 59°03′W
105 Q2 **Zarautz** *var.* Zarauz. País Vasco, N Spain 43°17′N 02°10′W
Zarauz *see* Zarautz
Zaravecchia *see* Biograd na Moru
Zarāyīn *see* Zarēn
126 L4 **Zaraysk** Moskovskaya Oblast', W Russian Federation 54°48′N 38°54′E
55 N6 **Zaraza** Guárico, N Venezuela 09°23′N 65°20′W
Zarbdar *see* Zarbdor
147 P11 **Zarbdor** *Rus.* Zarbdar. Jizzax Viloyati, C Uzbekistan 40°04′N 68°10′E
142 M8 **Zard Kūh** ▲ SW Iran 32°19′N 50°03′E
124 I5 **Zarechensk** Murmanskaya Oblast', NW Russian Federation 66°39′N 31°27′E
127 P6 **Zarechnyy** Penzenskaya Oblast', W Russian Federation 53°12′N 45°12′E
Zareh Sharan *see* Sharan
39 Y14 **Zarembo Island** *island* Alexander Archipelago, Alaska, USA
139 V4 **Zarēn** *var.* Zarāyīn. As Sulaymānīyah, E Iraq 35°16′N 45°43′E
149 Q7 **Zarghūn Shahr** *var.* Katawaz. Paktīkā, SE Afghanistan 32°40′N 68°20′E
77 V13 **Zaria** Kaduna, C Nigeria 11°06′N 07°42′E
116 K2 **Zarichne** Rivnens'ka Oblast', NW Ukraine 51°49′N 26°09′E
122 J13 **Zarinsk** Altayskiy Kray, S Russian Federation 53°34′N 85°22′E
116 J12 **Zărneşti** *Hung.* Zernest. Braşov, C Romania 45°34′N 25°18′E
115 J25 **Zarós** Kríti, Greece, E Mediterranean Sea 35°08′N 24°54′E
100 O9 **Zarow** ≈ NE Germany
Zarqa *see* Az Zarqā'
Zarqa/Muḩāfaẓat az Zarqā' *see* Az Zarqā'
111 G20 **Záruby** ▲ W Slovakia 48°30′N 17°24′E
56 B8 **Zaruma** El Oro, SW Ecuador 03°46′S 79°38′W
110 E13 **Żary** *Ger.* Sorau, Sorau in der Niederlausitz. Lubuskie, W Poland 51°44′N 15°09′E
54 D10 **Zarzal** Valle del Cauca, W Colombia 04°24′N 76°01′W
42 I7 **Zarzalar, Cerro** ▲ S Honduras 14°15′N 86°49′W
Zashaghan *see* Zachagansk
152 I5 **Zāskār** ≈ NE India
152 I5 **Zāskār Range** ▲▲ NE India
119 K15 **Zaslawye** Minskaya Voblasts', C Belarus 54°01′N 27°16′E
116 K7 **Zastavna** Chernivets'ka Oblast', W Ukraine 48°30′N 25°51′E
111 B16 **Žatec** *Ger.* Saaz. Ústecký Kraj, NW Czech Republic 50°20′N 13°35′E
Zaumgarten *see* Chrzanów
Zaunguzskiye Garagumy *see* Üngüz Angyrsyndaky Garagum
25 X9 **Zavalla** Texas, SW USA 31°09′N 94°25′W
99 H18 **Zaventem** Vlaams Brabant, C Belgium 50°53′N 04°28′E
99 H18 **Zaventem** ✈ (Brussel/Bruxelles) Vlaams Brabant, C Belgium 50°55′N 04°28′E
Zavertse *see* Zawiercie
114 L7 **Zavet** Razgrad, NE Bulgaria 43°46′N 26°40′E
127 O12 **Zavetnoye** Rostovskaya Oblast', SW Russian Federation 47°10′N 43°54′E
156 M3 **Zavhan Gol** ≈ W Mongolia
112 H12 **Zavidovići** Federacija Bosna I Hercegovina, N Bosnia and Herzegovina 44°26′N 18°07′E
123 R13 **Zavitinsk** Amurskaya Oblast', SE Russian Federation 50°23′N 128°57′E
Zawia *see* Az Zāwiyah
111 K15 **Zawiercie** *Rus.* Zavertse. Śląskie, S Poland 50°29′N 19°24′E
75 P11 **Zawīlah** *var.* Zuwaylah, *It.* Zueila. C Libya 26°10′N 15°07′E
138 I4 **Zāwīyah, Jabal az** ▲ NW Syria
109 Y3 **Zaya** ≈ NE Austria
166 M8 **Zayatkyi** Bago, C Myanmar (Burma) 17°48′N 96°27′E
145 Y11 **Zaysan** Vostochnyy Kazakhstan, E Kazakhstan 47°30′N 84°55′E
Zaysan Köl *see* Zaysan, Ozero
145 Y11 **Zaysan, Ozero** *Kaz.* Zaysan Köl. ◎ E Kazakhstan
159 R16 **Zayü** *var.* Gyigang. Xizang Zizhiqu, W China 28°36′N 97°25′E
Zayyq *see* Zhayyk
44 F6 **Zaza** ≈ C Cuba
116 K5 **Zbarazh** Ternopil's'ka Oblast', W Ukraine 49°40′N 25°47′E
116 J5 **Zboriv** Ternopil's'ka Oblast', W Ukraine 49°40′N 25°09′E
111 F18 **Zbraslav** Jihomoravský Kraj, SE Czech Republic 49°13′N 16°19′E
116 K6 **Zbruch** ≈ W Ukraine
Žďár *see* Žďár nad Sázavou
111 F17 **Žďár nad Sázavou** *Ger.* Saar in Mähren; *prev.* Žďár. Vysočina, C Czech Republic 49°34′N 16°00′E
116 K4 **Zdolbuniv** *Pol.* Zdolbunów, *Rus.* Zdolbunov. Rivnens'ka Oblast', NW Ukraine 50°33′N 26°15′E
Zdolbunov/Zdolbunów *see* Zdolbuniv
110 J13 **Zduńska Wola** Sieradz, C Poland 51°37′N 18°57′E
117 O4 **Zdvizh** ≈ N Ukraine
Zdzięciół *see* Dzyatlava
111 I16 **Zdzieszowice** *Ger.* Odertal. Opolskie, SW Poland 50°24′N 18°06′E
Zealand *see* Sjælland
188 K6 **Zealandia Bank** *undersea feature* C Pacific Ocean
63 H20 **Zeballos, Monte** ▲ S Argentina 47°04′S 71°32′W
83 K20 **Zebediela** Limpopo, NE South Africa 24°16′S 29°21′E
113 L18 **Zebës, Mali i** *var.* Mali i Zebës. ▲ NE Albania 41°57′N 20°16′E
Zebës, Mali i *see* Zebës, Mali
21 V9 **Zebulon** North Carolina, SE USA 35°49′N 78°19′W
112 K8 **Žednik** *Hung.* Bácsjózseffalva. Vojvodina, N Serbia 45°58′N 19°40′E
99 C15 **Zeebrugge** West-Vlaanderen, NW Belgium 51°20′N 03°13′E
183 N16 **Zeehan** Tasmania, SE Australia 41°54′S 145°19′E
99 L14 **Zeeland** Noord-Brabant, SE Netherlands 51°42′N 05°40′E
29 N7 **Zeeland** North Dakota, N USA 45°57′N 99°49′W
99 E14 **Zeeland** ◈ *province* SW Netherlands
83 I21 **Zeerust** North-West, N South Africa 25°33′S 26°06′E
98 K10 **Zeewolde** Flevoland, C Netherlands 52°20′N 05°32′E
Zefat *see* Tsefat
Żegań *see* Żagań
Zehden *see* Cedynia
100 O11 **Zehdenick** Brandenburg, NE Germany 52°58′N 13°19′E
Zē-i Bādīnān *see* Great Zab
Zeiden *see* Codlea
146 M14 **Zeidskoye Vodokhranilishche** ⊠ E Turkmenistan
Zē-i Kōya *see* Little Zab
181 P7 **Zeil, Mount** ▲ Northern Territory, C Australia 23°31′S 132°41′E
98 J12 **Zeist** Utrecht, C Netherlands 52°05′N 05°15′E
101 M16 **Zeitz** Sachsen-Anhalt, E Germany 51°03′N 12°08′E
159 T11 **Zêkog** *var.* Zequ; *prev.* Sonag. Qinghai, C China 35°03′N 101°30′E
Zelaya Norte *see* Atlántico Norte, Región Autónoma
Zelaya Sur *see* Atlántico Sur, Región Autónoma
99 F17 **Zele** Oost-Vlaanderen, NW Belgium 51°04′N 04°02′E
110 N12 **Żelechów** Lubelskie, E Poland 51°49′N 21°57′E
113 H14 **Zelena Glava** ▲ SE Bosnia and Herzegovina 43°32′N 17°55′E
113 P20 **Zelen Breg** ▲ S Macedonia 41°10′N 22°14′E
113 I14 **Zelengora** ▲ S Bosnia and Herzegovina
124 I5 **Zelenoborskiy** Murmanskaya Oblast', NW Russian Federation 66°52′N 32°25′E
127 R3 **Zelenodol'sk** Respublika Tatarstan, W Russian Federation 55°52′N 48°49′E
117 S9 **Zelenodol's'k** Dnipropetrovs'ka Oblast', E Ukraine 47°38′N 33°41′E
122 J12 **Zelenogorsk** Krasnoyarskiy Kray, C Russian Federation 56°08′N 94°29′E
126 K3 **Zelenograd** Moskovskaya Oblast', W Russian Federation 56°02′N 37°08′E
118 B13 **Zelenogradsk** *Ger.* Cranz, Kranz. Kaliningradskaya Oblast', W Russian Federation 54°58′N 20°30′E
127 O15 **Zelenokumsk** Stavropol'skiy Kray, SW Russian Federation 44°22′N 43°48′E
165 X4 **Zelënyy, Ostrov** *var.* Shibotsu-jima. *island* NE Russian Federation
Železna Kapela *see* Eisenkappel
Železna Vrata *see* Demir Kapija
112 L11 **Železniki** Serbia, N Serbia 44°45′N 20°23′E
98 N12 **Zelhem** Gelderland, E Netherlands 52°00′N 06°21′E
113 N18 **Želino** NW FYR Macedonia 42°00′N 21°06′E
113 M14 **Željin** ▲ C Serbia
101 K17 **Zella-Mehlis** Thüringen, C Germany 50°40′N 10°40′E
109 P7 **Zell am See** *var.* Zell-am-See. Salzburg, S Austria 47°19′N 12°47′E
Zell-am-See *see* Zell am See
109 N7 **Zell am Ziller** Tirol, W Austria 47°13′N 11°52′E
Zelle *see* Celle
109 W2 **Zellerndorf** Niederösterreich, NE Austria 48°40′N 15°57′E
109 U7 **Zeltweg** Steiermark, S Austria 47°12′N 14°46′E
119 G17 **Zel'va** *Pol.* Zelwa. Hrodzyenskaya Voblasts', W Belarus 53°09′N 24°49′E
118 H13 **Želva** Vilnius, C Lithuania 55°13′N 25°07′E
Zelwa *see* Zel'va
99 E16 **Zelzate** *var.* Selzaete. Oost-Vlaanderen, NW Belgium 51°12′N 03°49′E
118 E11 **Žemaičių Aukštumas** *physical region* W Lithuania
118 C12 **Žemaičių Naumiestis** Klaipėda, SW Lithuania 55°22′N 21°39′E
119 L14 **Zembin** *var.* Zyembin. Minskaya Voblasts', C Belarus 54°22′N 28°13′E
127 N6 **Zemetchino** Penzenskaya Oblast', W Russian Federation 53°31′N 42°35′E
79 M15 **Zémio** Haut-Mbomou, E Central African Republic 05°04′N 25°07′E
41 R16 **Zempoaltepec, Cerro** ▲ SE Mexico 17°04′N 95°54′W
99 G17 **Zemst** Vlaams Brabant, C Belgium 50°59′N 04°28′E
112 L11 **Zemun** Serbia, N Serbia 44°52′N 20°25′E
Zendajan *see* Zindah Jān
Zendeh Jān *see* Zindah Jān
Zengg *see* Senj
112 H12 **Zenica** Federacija Bosna I Hercegovina, C Bosnia and Herzegovina 44°12′N 17°53′E
Zenjan *see* Zanjān
Zen'kov *see* Zin'kiv
Zenshū *see* Jeonju
Zenta *see* Senta
82 B11 **Zenza do Itombe** Cuanza Norte, NW Angola 09°22′S 14°10′E
112 H12 **Žepče** Federacija Bosna I Hercegovina, N Bosnia and Herzegovina 44°26′N 18°00′E
23 W12 **Zephyrhills** Florida, SE USA 28°13′N 82°10′W
158 F9 **Zepu** *var.* Poskam. Xinjiang Uygur Zizhiqu, NW China 38°10′N 77°18′E
Zequ *see* Zêkog
147 Q12 **Zeravshan** *Taj./Uzb.* Zarafshon. ≈ Tajikistan/Uzbekistan
Zeravshan *see* Zarafshon
Zeravshanskiy Khrebet *see* Zarafshon, Qatorkŭhi
101 M14 **Zerbst** Sachsen-Anhalt, E Germany 51°57′N 12°05′E
Zerenda *see* Zerendy
145 P8 **Zerendy** *prev.* Zerenda. Akmola, N Kazakhstan 52°56′N 69°09′E
110 H12 **Żerków** Wielkopolskie, C Poland 52°03′N 17°33′E
108 E11 **Zermatt** Valais, SW Switzerland 46°00′N 07°45′E
Zernest *see* Zărneşti
108 J9 **Zernez** Graubünden, SE Switzerland 46°42′N 10°06′E
126 L12 **Zernograd** Rostovskaya Oblast', SW Russian Federation 46°52′N 40°13′E
Zestafoni *see* Zest'aponi
137 S9 **Zest'aponi** *Rus.* Zestafoni; *prev.* Zestap'oni. C Georgia 42°09′N 43°00′E
Zestap'oni *see* Zest'aponi
98 H12 **Zestienhoven** ✈ (Rotterdam) Zuid-Holland, SW Netherlands 51°57′N 04°30′E
113 J16 **Zeta** ≈ C Montenegro
8 L6 **Zeta Lake** ◎ Victoria Island, Northwest Territories, N Canada
98 L12 **Zetten** Gelderland, SE Netherlands 51°55′N 05°43′E
101 M17 **Zeulenroda** Thüringen, C Germany 50°40′N 11°58′E
100 H10 **Zeven** Niedersachsen, NW Germany 53°17′N 09°16′E
98 M12 **Zevenaar** Gelderland, SE Netherlands 51°55′N 06°05′E
99 H14 **Zevenbergen** Noord-Brabant, S Netherlands 51°39′N 04°36′E
129 X6 **Zeya** ≈ SE Russian Federation
Zeya Reservoir *see* Zeyskoye Vodokhranilishche
143 T11 **Zeynalābād** Kermān, C Iran 29°56′N 57°29′E
123 R12 **Zeyskoye Vodokhranilishche** *Eng.* Zeya Reservoir. ⊠ SE Russian Federation
104 H8 **Zêzere, Rio** ≈ C Portugal
Zgerzh *see* Zgierz
138 H6 **Zgharta** N Lebanon 34°24′N 35°54′E
110 K12 **Zgierz** *Ger.* Neuhof, *Rus.* Zgerzh. Łódź, C Poland 51°55′N 19°20′E
111 E14 **Zgorzelec** *Ger.* Görlitz. Dolnośląskie, SW Poland 51°10′N 15°E
119 F19 **Zhabinka** *Pol.* Żabinka. Brestskaya Voblasts', SW Belarus 52°12′N 24°01′E
Zhaggo *see* Luhuo
159 R15 **Zhag'yab** *var.* Yêndum. Xizang Zizhiqu, W China 30°42′N 97°33′E
Zhailma *see* Zhayylma
145 N14 **Zhalagash** *prev.* Dzhalagash. Kzylorda, S Kazakhstan 45°06′N 64°40′E
145 V16 **Zhalanash** Almaty, SE Kazakhstan 43°04′N 78°08′E
145 S7 **Zhalauly, Ozero** ◎ NE Kazakhstan
145 W10 **Zhalgyztobe** *prev.* Zhangiztobe. Vostochnyy Kazakhstan, E Kazakhstan 49°15′N 81°16′E
144 E9 **Zhalpaktal** *Kaz.* Zhalpaqtal; *prev.* Furmanovo. Zapadnyy Kazakhstan, W Kazakhstan 49°43′N 49°28′E
Zhalpaqtal *see* Zhalpaktal
119 G16 **Zhaludok** *Rus.* Zheludok. Hrodzyenskaya Voblasts', W Belarus 53°36′N 24°59′E
Zhaman-Akkol', Ozero *see* Akkol', Ozero
145 Q14 **Zhambyl** *off.* Zhambylskaya Oblast', *Kaz.* Zhambyl Oblysy; *prev.* Dzhambulskaya Oblast'. ◈ *province* S Kazakhstan
Zhambyl *see* Taraz
Zhambyl Oblysy/Zhambylskaya Oblast' *see* Zhambyl
Zhamo *see* Bomi
145 S12 **Zhamshy** ≈ C Kazakhstan
144 M15 **Zhanadariya** *prev.* Zhanadar'ya. Kzylorda, S Kazakhstan 44°41′N 64°39′E
Zhanadar'ya *see* Zhanadariya
144 E10 **Zhanakazan** *prev.* Novaya Kazanka. Zapadnyy Kazakhstan, W Kazakhstan 48°57′N 49°34′E
145 O15 **Zhanakorgan** *Kaz.* Zhangaqorghan. Kzylorda, S Kazakhstan 43°57′N 67°14′E
159 N16 **Zhanang** *var.* Chatang. Xizang Zizhiqu, W China 29°15′N 91°20′E
145 T12 **Zhanaortalyk** Karaganda, C Kazakhstan 47°31′N 75°42′E
144 F15 **Zhanaozen** *Kaz.* Zhangaözen; *prev.* Novyy Uzen'. Mangistau, W Kazakhstan 43°22′N 52°50′E
145 Q16 **Zhanatas** Zhambyl, S Kazakhstan 43°36′N 69°43′E
Zhangaözen *see* Zhanaozen
Zhangaqazaly *see* Ayteke Bi
Zhangaqorghan *see* Zhanakorgan
161 O2 **Zhangbei** Hebei, E China 41°13′N 114°43′E
Zhang-chia-k'ou *see* Zhangjiakou
Zhangdian *see* Zibo
Zhanggu *see* Danba
163 X9 **Zhangguangcai Ling** ▲▲ NE China
161 S13 **Zhanghua** *Jap.* Shōka; *prev.* Changhua. C Taiwan 24°06′N 120°31′E
Zhangiztobe *see* Zhalgyztobe
159 W11 **Zhangjiachuan** Gansu, N China 34°55′N 106°26′E
160 L10 **Zhangjiajie** *var.* Dayong. Hunan, S China 29°10′N 110°22′E
161 O2 **Zhangjiakou** *var.* Changkiakow, Zhang-chia-k'ou, *Eng.* Kalgan; *prev.* Wanchuan. Hebei, E China 40°48′N 114°51′E
161 Q13 **Zhangping** Fujian, SE China 25°21′N 117°29′E
161 Q13 **Zhangpu** *var.* Sui'an. Fujian, SE China 24°08′N 117°36′E
163 U11 **Zhangwu** Liaoning, NE China 42°21′N 122°32′E
159 S8 **Zhangye** *var.* Ganzhou. Gansu, N China 38°58′N 100°30′E
161 Q13 **Zhangzhou** Fujian, SE China 24°31′N 117°40′E
163 W6 **Zhan He** ≈ NE China
Zhänibek *see* Dzhanibek
160 L16 **Zhanjiang** *var.* Chanchiang, Chan-chiang, *Cant.* Tsamkong, *Fr.* Fort-Bayard. Guangdong, S China 21°10′N 110°20′E
145 V14 **Zhansugirov** *prev.* Dzhansugurov. Almaty, SE Kazakhstan 45°23′N 79°29′E
163 V8 **Zhaodong** Heilongjiang, NE China 46°03′N 125°58′E
Zhaoge *see* Qixian
160 H11 **Zhaojue** *var.* Xincheng. Sichuan, C China 28°03′N 102°50′E
161 N14 **Zhaoqing** Guangdong, S China 23°08′N 112°26′E
Zhaoren *see* Changwu
158 H5 **Zhaosu** *var.* Mongolküre. Xinjiang Uygur Zizhiqu, NW China 43°09′N 81°07′E
160 H11 **Zhaotong** Yunnan, SW China 27°20′N 103°29′E
163 V9 **Zhaoyuan** Heilongjiang, NE China 45°30′N 125°05′E
163 V9 **Zhaozhou** Heilongjiang, NE China 45°42′N 125°11′E
145 X13 **Zharbulak** Vostochnyy Kazakhstan, E Kazakhstan 46°04′N 82°05′E
158 J15 **Zhari Namco** ◎ W China
144 H12 **Zharkamys** *Kaz.* Zharqamys. Aktyubinsk, W Kazakhstan 47°58′N 56°33′E
145 W15 **Zharkent** *prev.* Panfilov. Taldykorgan, SE Kazakhstan 44°10′N 80°01′E
124 H17 **Zharkovskiy** Tverskaya Oblast', W Russian Federation 55°51′N 32°19′E
145 W11 **Zharma** Vostochnyy Kazakhstan, E Kazakhstan 48°48′N 80°55′E
144 F14 **Zharmysh** Mangistau, SW Kazakhstan 44°12′N 52°27′E
Zharqamys *see* Zharkamys
118 L13 **Zhary** Vitsyebskaya Voblasts', N Belarus 55°05′N 28°40′E

◆ Country
● Country Capital
◇ Dependent Territory
○ Dependent Territory Capital
◈ Administrative Regions
✈ International Airport
▲ Mountain
▲▲ Mountain Range
🌋 Volcano
≈ River
◎ Lake
⊠ Reservoir

Zhaslyk *see* Jasliq
158 *J14* **Zhaxi Co** ◎ W China
127 *X6* **Zhayyk** *Kaz.* Zayyq, *var.* Ural. ≈ Kazakhstan/Russian Federation
144 *L9* **Zhayylma** *prev.* Zhailma. Kostanay, N Kazakhstan *51°34′N 61°39′E*
Zhdanov *see* Beyläqan
Zhdanov *see* Mariupol'
Zhe *see* Zhejiang
161 *R10* **Zhejiang** *var.* Che-chiang, Chekiang, Zhe, Zhejiang Sheng. ◈ *province* SE China
Zhejiang Sheng *see* Zhejiang
145 *S7* **Zhelezinka** Pavlodar, N Kazakhstan *53°35′N 75°16′E*
119 *C14* **Zheleznodorozhnyy** *Ger.* Gerdauen. Kaliningradskaya Oblast', W Russian Federation *54°21′N 21°17′E*
Zheleznodorozhnyy *see* Yemva
122 *K12* **Zheleznogorsk** Krasnoyarskiy, C Russian Federation *56°20′N 93°36′E*
126 *J7* **Zheleznogorsk** Kurskaya Oblast', W Russian Federation *52°22′N 35°21′E*
127 *N15* **Zheleznovodsk** Stavropol'skiy Kray, SW Russian Federation *44°12′N 43°01′E*
Zhëltyye Vody *see* Zhovti Vody
Zheludok *see* Zhaludok
144 *H12* **Zhem** *prev.* Emba. ≈ W Kazakhstan
160 *K7* **Zhenba** Shaanxi, C China *32°42′N 107°55′E*
160 *I13* **Zhenfeng** *var.* Mingu. Guizhou, S China *25°27′N 105°38′E*
Zhengjiatun *see* Shuangliao
159 *X10* **Zhengning** *var.* Shanhe. Gansu, N China *35°29′N 108°21′E*
Zhengxiangbai Qi *see* Qagan Nur
161 *N6* **Zhengzhou** *var.* Ch'eng-chou, Chengchow; *prev.* Chenghsien. *province capital* Henan, C China *34°45′N 113°38′E*
161 *R8* **Zhenjiang** *var.* Chenkiang. Jiangsu, E China *32°08′N 119°30′E*
163 *U9* **Zhenlai** Jilin, NE China *45°52′N 123°11′E*
160 *I11* **Zhenxiong** Yunnan, SW China *27°31′N 104°52′E*
160 *K11* **Zhenyuan** *var.* Wuyang. Guizhou, S China *27°07′N 108°33′E*
161 *R11* **Zherong** *var.* Shuangcheng. Fujian, SE China *27°16′N 119°54′E*
145 *U15* **Zhetigen** *prev.* Nikolayevka. Almaty, SE Kazakhstan *43°39′N 77°10′E*
Zhetiqara *see* Zhitikara
144 *F15* **Zhetybay** Mangistau, SW Kazakhstan *43°35′N 52°05′E*
145 *P17* **Zhetysay** *var.* Dzhetysay. Yuzhnyy Kazakhstan *40°45′N 68°18′E*
145 *W14* **Zhetysuskiy Alatau** *prev.* Dzhungarskiy Alatau. ▲▲ China/Kazakhstan
160 *M11* **Zhexi Shuiku** ⊠ C China
145 *O12* **Zhezdy** Karaganda, C Kazakhstan *48°06′N 67°01′E*
145 *O12* **Zhezkazgan** *Kaz.* Zhezqazghan; *prev.* Dzhezkazgan. Karaganda, C Kazakhstan *47°49′N 67°44′E*
Zhezqazghan *see* Zhezkazgan
Zhicheng *see* Yidu
Zhidachov *see* Zhydachiv
159 *Q12* **Zhidoi** *var.* Gyaijêpozhanggê. Qinghai, C China *33°55′N 95°39′E*
122 *M13* **Zhigalovo** Irkutskaya Oblast', S Russian Federation *54°47′N 105°00′E*
127 *R6* **Zhigulevsk** Samarskaya Oblast', W Russian Federation *53°24′N 49°30′E*
118 *D13* **Zhilino** *Ger.* Schillen. Kaliningradskaya Oblast', W Russian Federation *54°55′N 21°54′E*
Zhiloy, Ostrov *see* Çilov Adası
127 *O8* **Zhirnovsk** Volgogradskaya Oblast', SW Russian Federation *51°01′N 44°49′E*
160 *M12* **Zhishan** *prev.* Yongzhou. Hunan, S China *26°12′N 111°36′E*
Zhishan *see* Lingling
144 *L8* **Zhitikara** *Kaz.* Zhetiqara; *prev.* Džetygara. Kostanay, NW Kazakhstan *52°14′N 61°12′E*
Zhitkovichi *see* Zhytkavichy
Zhitomir *see* Zhytomyr
Zhitomirskaya Oblast' *see* Zhytomyrs'ka Oblast'
126 *J5* **Zhizdra** Kaluzhskaya Oblast', W Russian Federation *53°38′N 34°39′E*
119 *N18* **Zhlobin** Homyel'skaya Voblasts', SE Belarus *52°53′N 30°01′E*
Zhmerinka *see* Zhmerynka
116 *M7* **Zhmerynka** *Rus.* Zhmerinka. Vinnyts'ka Oblast', C Ukraine *49°00′N 28°02′E*
149 *R9* **Zhob** *var.* Fort Sandeman. Baluchistān, SW Pakistan *31°21′N 69°31′E*
149 *R8* **Zhob** ≈ C Pakistan
Zhodino *see* Zhodzina
119 *L15* **Zhodzina** *Rus.* Zhodino. Minskaya Voblasts', C Belarus *54°06′N 28°21′E*
123 *Q5* **Zhokhova, Ostrov** *island* Novosibirskiye Ostrova, NE Russian Federation
Zholkev/Zholkva *see* Zhovkva
Zhondor *see* Jondor
158 *I15* **Zhongba** *var.* Tuoji. Xizang Zizhiqu, W China *29°37′N 84°11′E*
Zhongba *see* Jiangyou
Zhongdian *see* Xamgyi'nyilha
Zhongduo *see* Youyang
Zhonghe *see* Xiushan
Zhonghua Renmin Gongheguo *see* China
159 *V9* **Zhongning** Ningxia, N China *37°26′N 105°40′E*
Zhongping *see* Huize
161 *N15* **Zhongshan** Guangdong, S China *22°30′N 113°20′E*
195 *X7* **Zhongshan** *Chinese research station* Antarctica *69°23′S 76°34′E*
160 *M6* **Zhongtiao Shan** ▲▲ C China
159 *V9* **Zhongwei** Ningxia, N China *37°31′N 105°10′E*
160 *K9* **Zhongxian** *var.* Zhongzhou. Chongqing Shi, C China *30°16′N 108°03′E*
161 *N9* **Zhongxiang** Hubei, C China *31°12′N 112°35′E*
Zhongzhou *see* Zhongxian
144 *M14* **Zhosaly** *prev.* Dzhusaly. Kzylorda, SW Kazakhstan *45°29′N 64°04′E*
161 *O7* **Zhoukou** *var.* Zhoukouzhen. Henan, C China *33°32′N 114°40′E*
Zhoukouzhen *see* Zhoukou
161 *S9* **Zhoushan** Zhejiang, S China
Zhoushan Islands *see* Zhoushan Qundao
161 *S9* **Zhoushan Qundao** *Eng.* Zhoushan Islands. *island group* SE China
116 *I5* **Zhovkva** *Pol.* Żółkiew, *Rus.* Zholkev, Zholkva; *prev.* Nesterov. L'vivs'ka Oblast', NW Ukraine *50°04′N 24°E*
117 *S7* **Zhovti Vody** *Rus.* Zhëltyye Vody. Dnipropetrovs'ka Oblast', E Ukraine *48°24′N 33°30′E*
117 *Q10* **Zhovtneve** *Rus.* Zhovtnevoye. Mykolayivs'ka Oblast', S Ukraine *46°50′N 32°00′E*
Zhovtnevoye *see* Zhovtneve
Zhi Qu *see* Tongtian He
114 *K9* **Zhrebchevo, Yazovir** ⊠ C Bulgaria
163 *V13* **Zhuanghe** Liaoning, NE China *39°42′N 123°00′E*
159 *W11* **Zhuanglang** *var.* Shuiluo; *prev.* Shuilocheng. Gansu, C China *35°06′N 106°21′E*
145 *P15* **Zhuantobe** *Kaz.* Zhūantöbe. Yuzhnyy Kazakhstan, S Kazakhstan *44°45′N 68°50′E*
161 *Q5* **Zhucheng** Shandong, E China *35°58′N 119°24′E*
159 *V12* **Zhugqu** Gansu, C China *33°51′N 104°14′E*
161 *N15* **Zhuhai** Guangdong, S China *22°16′N 113°30′E*
Zhuizishan *see* Weichang
Zhuji *see* Shangqiu
126 *I5* **Zhukovka** Bryanskaya Oblast', W Russian Federation *53°33′N 33°48′E*
161 *N7* **Zhumadian** Henan, C China *32°58′N 114°03′E*
161 *S13* **Zhunan** *prev.* Chunan. N Taiwan *24°44′N 120°51′E*
Zhuo Xian *see* Zhuozhou
161 *O3* **Zhuozhou** *prev.* Zhuo Xian. Hebei, E China *39°22′N 115°40′E*
162 *L14* **Zhuozi Shan** ▲ N China *39°28′N 106°58′E*
113 *M17* **Zhur** *Serb.* Žur. S Kosovo *42°10′N 20°37′E*
Zhuravichi *see* Zhuravichy
119 *O17* **Zhuravichy** *Rus.* Zhuravichi. Homyel'skaya Voblasts', SE Belarus *53°15′N 30°33′E*
145 *Q8* **Zhuravlevka** Akmola, N Kazakhstan *52°00′N 69°59′E*
117 *Q4* **Zhurivka** Kyyivs'ka Oblast', N Ukraine *50°28′N 31°48′E*
144 *J11* **Zhuryn** Aktyubinsk, W Kazakhstan *49°13′N 57°36′E*
145 *T15* **Zhusandala, Step'** *grassland* SE Kazakhstan
160 *L8* **Zhushan** Hubei, C China *32°11′N 110°05′E*
Zhushan *see* Xuan'en
Zhuyang *see* Dazhu
161 *N11* **Zhuzhou** Hunan, S China *27°52′N 112°52′E*
116 *I6* **Zhydachiv** *Pol.* Żydaczów, *Rus.* Zhidachov. L'vivs'ka Oblast', NW Ukraine *49°20′N 24°08′E*
144 *G9* **Zhympity** *Kaz.* Zhympīty; *prev.* Dzhambeyty. Zapadnyy, W Kazakhstan *50°16′N 52°34′E*
119 *K19* **Zhytkavichy** *Rus.* Zhitkovichi. Homyel'skaya Voblasts', SE Belarus *52°14′N 27°52′E*
117 *N4* **Zhytomyr** *Rus.* Zhitomir. Zhytomyrs'ka Oblast', NW Ukraine *50°17′N 28°40′E*
Zhytomyr *see* Zhytomyrs'ka Oblast'
116 *M4* **Zhytomyrs'ka Oblast'** *var.* Zhytomyr, *Rus.* Zhitomirskaya Oblast'. ◈ *province* N Ukraine
153 *U15* **Zia** ✈ (Dhaka) Dhaka, C Bangladesh
111 *J20* **Žiar nad Hronom** *var.* Sväty Kríž nad Hronom, *Ger.* Heiligenkreuz, *Hung.* Garamszentkereszt. Banskobystrický Kraj, C Slovakia *48°36′N 18°52′E*
161 *Q4* **Zibo** *var.* Zhangdian. Shandong, E China *36°51′N 118°01′E*
160 *L4* **Zichang** *prev.* Wayaobu. Shaanxi, C China *37°08′N 109°40′E*
Zichenau *see* Ciechanów
111 *G15* **Ziębice** *Ger.* Münsterberg in Schlesien. Dolnośląskie, SW Poland *50°37′N 17°01′E*
Ziebingen *see* Cybinka
Ziegenhais *see* Głuchołazy
110 *E12* **Zielona Góra** *Ger.* Grünberg, Grünberg in Schlesien, Grüneberg. Lubuskie, W Poland *51°56′N 15°31′E*
99 *F14* **Zierikzee** Zeeland, SW Netherlands *51°39′N 03°55′E*
160 *I10* **Zigong** *var.* Tzekung. Sichuan, C China *29°20′N 104°48′E*
76 *G12* **Ziguinchor** SW Senegal *12°34′N 16°20′W*
41 *N16* **Zihuatanejo** Guerrero, S Mexico *17°39′N 101°33′W*
Ziketan *see* Xinghai
Zilah *see* Zalău
127 *W7* **Zilair** Respublika Bashkortostan, W Russian Federation *52°12′N 57°15′E*
136 *L12* **Zile** Tokat, N Turkey *40°18′N 35°52′E*
111 *J18* **Žilina** *Ger.* Sillein, *Hung.* Zsolna. Zlínský Kraj, N Slovakia *49°13′N 18°44′E*
111 *J19* **Žilinský Kraj** ◈ *region* N Slovakia
75 *Q9* **Zillah** *var.* Zallah. C Libya *28°30′N 17°33′E*
Zillenmarkt *see* Zalău
109 *N7* **Ziller** ≈ W Austria
Zillertal Alps *see* Zillertaler Alpen
109 *N8* **Zillertaler Alpen** *Eng.* Zillertal Alps, *It.* Alpi Aurine. ▲▲ Austria/Italy
118 *K10* **Zilupe** *Ger.* Rosenhof. E Latvia *56°10′N 28°06′E*
41 *O13* **Zimapán** Hidalgo, C Mexico *20°45′N 99°21′W*
83 *I16* **Zimba** Southern, S Zambia *17°20′S 26°11′E*
83 *J17* **Zimbabwe** *off.* Republic of Zimbabwe; *prev.* Rhodesia. ◆ *republic* S Africa
Zimbabwe, Republic of *see* Zimbabwe
116 *H10* **Zimbor** *Hung.* Magyarzsombor. Sălaj, NW Romania *47°00′N 23°16′E*
Zimmerbude *see* Svetlyy
116 *J15* **Zimnicea** Teleorman, S Romania *43°39′N 25°21′E*
114 *L9* **Zimnitsa** Yambol, E Bulgaria *42°34′N 26°37′E*
127 *N12* **Zimovniki** Rostovskaya Oblast', SW Russian Federation *47°07′N 42°29′E*
148 *J5* **Zindah Jān** *var.* Zendajan, Zindajān; *prev.* Zendeh Jān. Herāt, NW Afghanistan *34°55′N 61°53′E*
Zindajān *see* Zindah Jān
77 *V12* **Zinder** Zinder, S Niger *13°47′N 09°02′E*
77 *W11* **Zinder** ◈ *department* S Niger
77 *P12* **Ziniaré** C Burkina *12°35′N 01°18′W*
Zinjan *see* Zanjān
141 *P16* **Zinjibār** SW Yemen *13°08′N 45°23′E*
117 *T4* **Zin'kiv** *var.* Zen'kov. Poltavs'ka Oblast', NE Ukraine *50°11′N 34°22′E*
Zinov'yevsk *see* Kirovohrad
Zintenhof *see* Sindi
31 *N10* **Zion** Illinois, N USA *42°27′N 87°49′W*
54 *F10* **Zipaquirá** Cundinamarca, C Colombia *05°03′N 74°01′W*
Zipser Neudorf *see* Spišská Nová Ves
111 *H23* **Zirc** Veszprém, W Hungary *47°16′N 17°52′E*
113 *D14* **Žirje** *It.* Zuri. *island* S Croatia
Zirknitz *see* Cerknica
108 *M7* **Zirl** Tirol, W Austria *47°17′N 11°16′E*
101 *K20* **Zirndorf** Bayern, SE Germany *49°27′N 10°57′E*
160 *M11* **Zi Shui** ≈ C China
109 *Y3* **Zistersdorf** Niederösterreich, NE Austria *48°32′N 16°45′E*
41 *O14* **Zitácuaro** Michoacán, SW Mexico *19°28′N 100°21′W*
Zito *see* Lhorong
101 *Q16* **Zittau** Sachsen, E Germany *50°53′N 14°48′E*
112 *I12* **Živinice** Federacija Bosna I Hercegovina, E Bosnia and Herzegovina *44°26′N 18°39′E*
Ziwa Magharibi *see* Kagera
81 *J14* **Ziway Hāyk'** ◎ C Ethiopia
161 *N12* **Zixing** Hunan, S China *26°01′N 113°25′E*
127 *W7* **Ziyanchurino** Orenburgskaya Oblast', W Russian Federation *51°36′N 56°58′E*
160 *K8* **Ziyang** Shaanxi, C China *32°33′N 108°27′E*
111 *I20* **Zlaté Moravce** *Hung.* Aranyosmarót. Nitriansky Kraj, SW Slovakia *48°24′N 18°20′E*
112 *K13* **Zlatibor** ▲▲ W Serbia
114 *L9* **Zlati Voyvoda** Sliven, C Bulgaria *42°36′N 26°13′E*
116 *G11* **Zlatna** *Ger.* Kleinschlatten, *Hung.* Zalatna; *prev. Ger.* Goldmarkt. Alba, C Romania *46°08′N 23°11′E*
114 *I8* **Zlatna Panega** Lovech, N Bulgaria *43°07′N 24°09′E*
114 *N8* **Zlatni Pyasŭtsi** Dobrich, NE Bulgaria *43°19′N 28°03′E*
122 *F11* **Zlatoust** Chelyabinskaya Oblast', C Russian Federation *55°12′N 59°33′E*
111 *M19* **Zlatý Stôl** *Ger.* Goldener Tisch, *Hung.* Aranyosasztal. ▲ C Slovakia *48°45′N 20°39′E*
113 *P18* **Zletovo** NE FYR Macedonia *42°00′N 22°14′E*
111 *H18* **Zlín** *prev.* Gottwaldov. Zlínský Kraj, E Czech Republic *49°14′N 17°40′E*
111 *H19* **Zlínský Kraj** ◈ *region* E Czech Republic
75 *O7* **Zlīṭan** W Libya *32°28′N 14°34′E*
110 *F9* **Złocieniec** *Ger.* Falkenburg in Pommern. Zachodnio-pomorskie, NW Poland *53°31′N 16°01′E*
110 *J13* **Złoczew** Sieradz, S Poland *51°24′N 18°36′E*
Złoczów *see* Zolochiv
111 *F14* **Złotoryja** *Ger.* Goldberg. Dolnośląskie, W Poland *51°08′N 15°57′E*
110 *G9* **Złotów** Wielkopolskie, C Poland *53°22′N 17°02′E*
110 *G13* **Żmigród** *Ger.* Trachenberg. Dolnośląskie, SW Poland *51°31′N 16°55′E*
126 *J6* **Zmiyevka** Orlovskaya Oblast', W Russian Federation *52°39′N 36°20′E*
117 *V5* **Zmiyiv** Kharkivs'ka Oblast', E Ukraine *49°40′N 36°22′E*
Zna *see* Tsna
Znaim *see* Znojmo
126 *M7* **Znamenka** Tambovskaya Oblast', W Russian Federation *52°24′N 42°28′E*
Znamenka *see* Znam"yanka
119 *C14* **Znamens** Astrakhanskaya Oblast', W Russian Federation *54°37′N 21°13′E*
127 *P10* **Znamensk** *Ger.* Wehlau. Kaliningradskaya Oblast', W Russian Federation *48°33′N 46°18′E*
117 *R7* **Znam"yanka** *Rus.* Znamenka. Kirovohrads'ka Oblast', C Ukraine *48°41′N 32°40′E*
110 *H10* **Żnin** Kujawsko-pomorskie, C Poland *52°50′N 17°41′E*
111 *F19* **Znojmo** *Ger.* Znaim. Jihomoravský Kraj, SE Czech Republic *48°52′N 16°04′E*
79 *N16* **Zobia** Orientale, N Dem. Rep. Congo *02°57′N 25°55′E*
83 *N15* **Zóbuè** Tete, NW Mozambique *15°36′S 34°26′E*
98 *G12* **Zoetermeer** Zuid-Holland, W Netherlands *52°04′N 04°30′E*
108 *E7* **Zofingen** Aargau, N Switzerland *47°18′N 07°57′E*
159 *R15* **Zogang** *var.* Wangda. Xizang Zizhiqu, W China *29°41′N 97°54′E*
106 *E7* **Zogno** Lombardia, N Italy *45°49′N 09°42′E*
142 *M10* **Zohreh, Rūd-e** ≈ SW Iran
160 *H7* **Zoigê** *var.* Dagcagoin. Sichuan, C China *33°44′N 102°57′E*
Żółkiew *see* Zhovkva
108 *D8* **Zollikofen** Bern, W Switzerland *47°00′N 07°24′E*
Zolochev *see* Zolochiv
117 *U4* **Zolochiv** *Rus.* Zolochev. Kharkivs'ka Oblast', E Ukraine *50°16′N 35°58′E*
116 *J5* **Zolochiv** *Pol.* Złoczów, *var.* Zolochev. L'vivs'ka Oblast', W Ukraine *49°48′N 24°51′E*
117 *X7* **Zolote** *Rus.* Zolotoye. Luhans'ka Oblast', E Ukraine *48°42′N 38°33′E*
117 *Q6* **Zolotonosha** Cherkas'ka Oblast', C Ukraine *49°39′N 32°05′E*
Zolotoye *see* Zolote
Zólyom *see* Zvolen
83 *N15* **Zomba** Southern, S Malawi *15°22′S 35°23′E*
Zombor *see* Sombor
99 *D17* **Zomergem** Oost-Vlaanderen, NW Belgium *51°07′N 03°31′E*
147 *P11* **Zomin** *Rus.* Zaamin. Jizzax Viloyati, C Uzbekistan *39°56′N 68°16′E*
79 *I15* **Zongo** Equateur, N Dem. Rep. Congo *04°18′N 18°42′E*
136 *G10* **Zonguldak** Zonguldak, NW Turkey *41°26′N 31°47′E*
136 *H10* **Zonguldak** ◈ *province* NW Turkey
99 *K17* **Zonhoven** Limburg, NE Belgium *50°59′N 05°22′E*
142 *J2* **Zonūz** Āžarbāyjān-e Khāvarī, NW Iran *38°32′N 45°54′E*
103 *Y16* **Zonza** Corse, France, C Mediterranean Sea *41°49′N 09°13′E*
Zoppot *see* Sopot
Zorgho *see* Zorgo
77 *Q13* **Zorgo** *var.* Zorgho. C Burkina *12°15′N 00°37′W*
104 *K10* **Zorita** Extremadura, W Spain *39°18′N 05°42′W*
147 *U14* **Zorkŭl** *Rus.* Ozero Zorkul'. ◎ SE Tajikistan
Zorkul', Ozero *see* Zorkŭl
56 *A8* **Zorritos** Tumbes, N Peru *03°43′S 80°42′W*
111 *J16* **Żory** *var.* Zory, *Ger.* Sohrau. Śląskie, S Poland *50°04′N 18°42′E*
76 *K15* **Zorzor** N Liberia *07°46′N 09°28′W*
99 *E18* **Zottegem** Oost-Vlaanderen, NW Belgium *50°52′N 03°49′E*
77 *R15* **Zou** ≈ S Benin
78 *H6* **Zouar** Borkou-Ennedi-Tibesti, N Chad *20°25′N 16°28′E*
76 *J6* **Zouérat** *var.* Zouérate, Zouîrât. Tiris Zemmour, N Mauritania *22°44′N 12°29′W*
Zouérate *see* Zouérat
Zoug *see* Zug
Zouîrât *see* Zouérat
76 *M16* **Zoukougbeu** C Ivory Coast *09°47′N 06°50′W*
98 *M5* **Zoutkamp** Groningen, NE Netherlands *53°22′N 06°17′E*
99 *J18* **Zoutleeuw** *Fr.* Leau. Vlaams Brabant, C Belgium *50°49′N 05°06′E*
112 *L9* **Zrenjanin** *prev.* Petrovgrad, Veliki Bečkerek, *Ger.* Grossbetschkerek, *Hung.* Nagybecskerek. Vojvodina, N Serbia *45°23′N 20°24′E*
112 *E10* **Zrinska Gora** ▲▲ C Croatia
Zsablya *see* Žabalj
101 *N16* **Zschopau** ≈ E Germany
Zsebely *see* Jebel
Zsibó *see* Jibou
Zsilyvajdevulkán *see* Vulcan
Zsil/Zsily *see* Jiu
Zsolna *see* Žilina
Zsombolya *see* Jimbolia
Zsupanya *see* Županja
55 *N7* **Zuata** Anzoátegui, NE Venezuela *08°24′N 65°13′W*
105 *N14* **Zubia** Andalucía, S Spain *37°10′N 03°36′W*
65 *P16* **Zubov Seamount** *undersea feature* E Atlantic Ocean *20°45′S 08°45′E*
124 *I16* **Zubtsov** Tverskaya Oblast', W Russian Federation *56°10′N 34°34′E*
108 *M8* **Zuckerhütl** ▲ SW Austria *46°57′N 11°07′E*
Zueila *see* Zawīlah
76 *M16* **Zuénoula** C Ivory Coast *07°26′N 06°03′W*
105 *S5* **Zuera** Aragón, NE Spain *41°52′N 00°47′W*
141 *V13* **Ẓufār** *Eng.* Dhofar. *physical region* SW Oman
108 *G8* **Zug** *Fr.* Zoug. Zug, C Switzerland *47°11′N 08°31′E*
108 *G8* **Zug** *Fr.* Zoug. ◈ *canton* C Switzerland
137 *R9* **Zugdidi** W Georgia *42°30′N 41°52′E*
108 *G8* **Zuger See** ◎ NW Switzerland
101 *K25* **Zugspitze** ▲ S Germany *47°25′N 10°58′E*
117 *X8* **Zuhres** *Rus.* Shakhtërsk. Donets'ka Oblast', SE Ukraine *48°01′N 38°16′E*
99 *E15* **Zuid-Beveland** *var.* South Beveland. *island* SW Netherlands
98 *K10* **Zuidelijk-Flevoland** *polder* C Netherlands
Zuider Zee *see* IJsselmeer
98 *G12* **Zuid-Holland** *Eng.* South Holland. ◈ *province* W Netherlands
98 *N5* **Zuidhorn** Groningen, NE Netherlands *53°15′N 06°25′E*
98 *O6* **Zuidlaardermeer** ◎ NE Netherlands
98 *O6* **Zuidlaren** Drenthe, NE Netherlands *53°06′N 06°41′E*
99 *K14* **Zuid-Willemsvaart Kanaal** *canal* S Netherlands
98 *N8* **Zuidwolde** Drenthe, NE Netherlands *52°40′N 06°25′E*
Zuitai/Zuitaizi *see* Kangxian
105 *O14* **Zújar** Andalucía, S Spain *37°33′N 02°52′W*
104 *L11* **Zújar** ≈ W Spain
104 *L11* **Zújar, Embalse del** ⊠ W Spain
80 *J9* **Zula** E Eritrea *15°19′N 39°40′E*
54 *G6* **Zulia** *off.* Estado Zulia. ◈ *state* NW Venezuela
Zulia, Estado *see* Zulia
Zullapara *see* Maungdaw
Züllichau *see* Sulechów
105 *P3* **Zumárraga** País Vasco, N Spain *43°05′N 02°19′W*
112 *D8* **Žumberačko Gorje** *var.* Gorjanči, Uskocke Planine, Žumberak, *Ger.* Uskokengebirge; *prev.* Sichelburger Gerbirge. ▲ Croatia/Slovenia *see also* Gorjanci
Žumberak *see* Gorjanci/Žumberačko Gorje
194 *K7* **Zumberge Coast** *coastal feature* Antarctica
Zumbo *see* Vila do Zumbo
29 *W10* **Zumbro Falls** Minnesota, N USA *44°15′N 92°25′W*
29 *W10* **Zumbro River** ≈ Minnesota, N USA
29 *W10* **Zumbrota** Minnesota, N USA *44°18′N 92°37′W*
99 *H15* **Zundert** Noord-Brabant, S Netherlands *51°28′N 04°40′E*
Zungaria *see* Dzungaria
77 *U14* **Zungeru** Niger, C Nigeria *09°49′N 06°10′E*
161 *P2* **Zunhua** Hebei, E China *40°10′N 117°58′E*
37 *O11* **Zuni** New Mexico, SW USA *35°03′N 108°52′W*
37 *P11* **Zuni Mountains** ▲▲ New Mexico, SW USA
160 *J11* **Zunyi** Guizhou, S China *27°40′N 106°56′E*
160 *J15* **Zuo Jiang** ≈ China/Vietnam
Zuoqi *see* Gegan Gol
108 *J9* **Zuoz** Graubünden, SE Switzerland *46°37′N 09°58′E*
112 *I10* **Županja** *Hung.* Zsupanya. Vukovar-Srijem, E Croatia *45°03′N 18°42′E*
Žur *see* Zhur
127 *T2* **Zura** Udmurtskaya Respublika, NW Russian Federation *57°36′N 53°19′E*
139 *V8* **Zurbāṭīyah** Wāsiṭ, E Iraq *33°13′N 46°07′E*
Zuri *see* Žirje
108 *F7* **Zürich** *Eng./Fr.* Zurich, *It.* Zurigo. Zürich, N Switzerland *47°23′N 08°33′E*
108 *G6* **Zürich** *Eng./Fr.* Zurich. ◈ *canton* N Switzerland
Zurich, Lake *see* Zürichsee
108 *G7* **Zürichsee** *Eng.* Lake Zurich. ◎ NE Switzerland
Zurigo *see* Zürich
149 *V1* **Zŭrkŭl** *Pash.* Sarī Qūl, *Rus.* Ozero Zurkul'. ◎ Afghanistan/Tajikistan *see also* Sarī Qūl
Zŭrkŭl *see* Sarī Qūl
Zurkul', Ozero *see* Sarī Qūl/Zŭrkŭl
110 *K10* **Żuromin** Mazowieckie, C Poland *53°00′N 19°54′E*
108 *J8* **Zürs** Vorarlberg, W Austria *47°11′N 10°11′E*
77 *T13* **Zuru** Kebbi, W Nigeria *11°28′N 05°13′E*
108 *F6* **Zurzach** Aargau, N Switzerland *47°33′N 08°21′E*
101 *J22* **Zusam** ≈ S Germany
98 *M11* **Zutphen** Gelderland, E Netherlands *52°09′N 06°12′E*
75 *N7* **Zuwārah** NW Libya *32°56′N 12°06′E*
Zuwaylah *see* Zawīlah
125 *R14* **Zuyevka** Kirovskaya Oblast', NW Russian Federation *58°24′N 51°08′E*
161 *N10* **Zuzhou** Hunan, S China *27°52′N 113°00′E*
Zvenigorodka *see* Zvenyhorodka
117 *P6* **Zvenyhorodka** *Rus.* Zvenigorodka. Cherkas'ka Oblast', C Ukraine *49°05′N 30°58′E*
123 *N12* **Zvezdnyy** Irkutskaya Oblast', C Russian Federation *56°43′N 106°22′E*
125 *U14* **Zvëzdnyy** Permskiy Kray, NW Russian Federation *57°45′N 56°20′E*
83 *K18* **Zvishavane** *prev.* Shabani. Matabeleland South, S Zimbabwe *20°20′S 30°02′E*
111 *J20* **Zvolen** *Ger.* Altsohl, *Hung.* Zólyom. Banskobystrický Kraj, C Slovakia *48°35′N 19°06′E*
112 *J12* **Zvornik** E Bosnia and Herzegovina *44°24′N 19°07′E*
98 *M5* **Zwaagwesteinde** *Fris.* De Westerein. Fryslân, N Netherlands *53°16′N 06°08′E*
98 *H10* **Zwanenburg** Noord-Holland, C Netherlands *52°22′N 04°44′E*
98 *L8* **Zwarte Meer** ◎ N Netherlands
98 *M9* **Zwarte Water** ≈ N Netherlands
98 *M8* **Zwartsluis** Overijssel, E Netherlands *52°39′N 06°04′E*
76 *L17* **Zwedru** *var.* Tchien. E Liberia *06°04′N 08°07′W*
98 *O8* **Zweeloo** Drenthe, NE Netherlands *52°48′N 06°45′E*
101 *E20* **Zweibrücken** *Fr.* Deux-Ponts, *Lat.* Bipontium. Rheinland-Pfalz, SW Germany *49°15′N 07°22′E*
108 *D9* **Zweisimmen** Fribourg, W Switzerland *46°33′N 07°22′E*
101 *M15* **Zwenkau** Sachsen, E Germany *51°11′N 12°19′E*
109 *V3* **Zwettl** Wien, NE Austria *48°28′N 14°17′E*
109 *T3* **Zwettl an der Rodl** Oberösterreich, N Austria *48°28′N 14°17′E*
99 *D18* **Zwevegem** West-Vlaanderen, W Belgium *50°48′N 03°20′E*
101 *M17* **Zwickau** Sachsen, E Germany *50°43′N 12°31′E*
101 *N16* **Zwickauer Mulde** ≈ E Germany
101 *O21* **Zwiesel** Bayern, SE Germany *49°02′N 13°14′E*
98 *H13* **Zwijndrecht** Zuid-Holland, SW Netherlands *51°49′N 04°39′E*
Zwischenwässern *see* Medvode
Zwittau *see* Svitavy
110 *N13* **Zwoleń** Mazowieckie, SE Poland *51°21′N 21°37′E*
98 *M9* **Zwolle** Overijssel, E Netherlands *52°31′N 06°06′E*
22 *G6* **Zwolle** Louisiana, S USA *31°37′N 93°38′W*
110 *K12* **Żychlin** Łódzkie, C Poland *52°15′N 19°38′E*
Żydaczów *see* Zhydachiv
Zyembin *see* Zembin
Zyôetu *see* Jōetsu
110 *L12* **Żyrardów** Mazowieckie, C Poland *52°02′N 20°28′E*
123 *S8* **Zyryanka** Respublika Sakha (Yakutiya), NE Russian Federation *65°45′N 150°43′E*
145 *Y9* **Zyryanovsk** Vostochnyy Kazakhstan, E Kazakhstan *49°45′N 84°16′E*

◆ Country
● Country Capital
◇ Dependent Territory
○ Dependent Territory Capital
◈ Administrative Regions
✈ International Airport
▲ Mountain
▲▲ Mountain Range
Volcano
≈ River
◎ Lake
⊠ Reservoir

Picture Credits

Dorling Kindersley would like to express their thanks to the following individuals, companies, and institutions for their help in preparing this atlas.

Earth Resource Mapping Ltd., Egham, Surrey
Brian Groombridge, World Conservation Monitoring Centre, Cambridge
The British Library, London
British Library of Political and Economic Science, London
The British Museum, London
The City Business Library, London
King's College, London
National Meteorological Library and Archive, Bracknell
The Printed Word, London
The Royal Geographical Society, London
University of London Library
Paul Beardmore
Philip Boyes
Hayley Crockford
Alistair Dougal
Reg Grant
Louise Keane
Zoe Livesley
Laura Porter
Jeff Eidenshink
Chris Hornby
Rachelle Smith
Ray Pinchard
Robert Meisner
Fiona Strawbridge

Every effort has been made to trace the copyright holders and we apologize in advance for any unintentional omissions. We would be pleased to insert the appropriate acknowledgment in any subsequent edition of this publication.

Adams Picture Library: 86CLA; **G Andrews:** 186CR; **Ardea London Ltd:** K Ghana 150C; M Iljima 132TC; R Waller 148TR; Art Directors **Aspect Picture Library:** P Carmichael 160TR; 131CR(below); G Tompkinson 190TRB; **Axiom:** C Bradley 148CA, 158CA; J Holmes xivCRA, xxivBCR, xxviiCRB, 150TCR, 166TL, J Morris 75TL, 77CRB, J Spaull 134BL; **Bridgeman Art Library, London / New York:** Collection of the Earl of Pembroke, Wilton House xxBC; **The J. Allan Cash Photolibrary:** xlBR, xliiCLA, xlivCL, 10BC, 60CL, 69CLB, 70CL, 72CLB, 75BR, 76BC, 87BL, 109BR, 138BCL, 141TL, 154CR, 178BR, 181TR; **Bruce Coleman Ltd:** 86BC, 98CL, 100TC; S Alden 192BC(below); Atlantide xxviTCR, 138BR; E Bjurstrom 141BR; S Bond 96CRB; T Buchholz xvCL, 92TR, 123TCL; J Burton xxiiiC; J Cancalosi 181TRB; B J Coates xxvBL, 192CL; B Coleman 63TL; B & C Colhoun 2TR, 36CB; A Compost xxiiiCBR; Dr S Coyne 45TL; G Cubitt xviTCL, 169BR, 178TR, 184TR; P Davey xxviiCLB, 121TL(below); N Devore 189CBL; S J Doylee xxiiCRR; H Flygare xviiCRA; M P L Fogden 17C(above) ; Jeff Foott Productions xxiiiCRB, 11CRA; M Freeman 91BRA; P van Gaalen 86TR; G Gualco 140C; B Henderson 194CR; Dr C Henneghien 69C; HPH Photography, H Van den Berg 69CR; C Hughes 69BCL; C James xxxixTC; J Johnson 39CR, 197TR; J Jurka 91CA; S C Kaufman 28C; S J Krasemann 33TR; H Lange 10TRB, 68CA; C Lockwood 32BC; L C Marigo xxiiBC, xxviiCLA, 49CRA, 59BR; M McCoy 187TR; D Meredith 3CR; J Murray xvCR, 179BR; Orion Press 165CR(above); Orion Services & Trading Co. Inc. 164CR; C Ott 17BL; Dr E Pott 9TR, 40CL, 87C, 93TL, 194CLB; F Prenzel 186BC, 193BC; M Read 42BR, 43CRB; H Reinhard xxiiCR, xxviiTR, 194BR; L Lee Rue III 151BCL; J Shaw xixTL; K N Swenson 194BC; P Terry 115CR; N Tomalin 54BCL; P Ward 78TC; S Widstrand 57TR; K Wothe 91C, 173TCL; J T Wright 127BR; **Colorific:** Black Star / L Mulvehil 156CL; Black Star / R Rogers 57BR; Black Star / J Rupp 161BCR; Camera Tres / C. Meyer 59BRA; R Caputo / Matrix 78CL; J. Hill 117CLB; M Koene 55TR; G Satterley xliiCLAR; M Yamashita 156BL, 167CR(above); **Comstock:** 108CRB; Corbis UK Ltd: 170TR, 170BL; **D Cousens:** 147 CRA; **Corbis:** Bob Daemmrich 6BL; Bryan Denton xxxCBL; Julie Dermansky / Julie Dermansky xxviiiTC; Everett Kennedy Brown / Epa 165CB; Kimimasa Mayama / Reuters 168CL(above); mosaaberizing / Demotix xxxCBR; Ocean 60BL; Ocean 135CL; Sucheta DAS / Reuters xxviBCR; Rob Widdis / epa 30CA; **Sue Cunningham Photographic:** 51CR; S Alden 192BC(below) **James Davis Travel Photography:** xxxviTCB, xxxviTR, xxxviCL, 13CA, 19BC, 49TLB, 56BCR, 57CLA, 61BCL, 93BC, 94TC, 102TR, 120CB, 158BC, 179CRA, 191BR; **Dorling Kindersley:** Paul Harris xxiiTR; Nigel Hicks xxiiBM; Jamie Marshall 181TR; Bharath Ramamrutham 155BR; Colin Sinclair 133BMR; George Dunnet: 124CA; **Environmental Picture Library:** Chris Westwood 126C; **Eye Ubiquitous:** xlCA; L. Fordyce 12CLA; L Johnstone 6CRA, 28BLA, 30CB; S. Miller xxiCA; M Southern 73BLA; **Chris Fairclough Colour Library:** xliBR; **Ffotograff:** N. Tapsell 158CL; **FLPA -Images of nature:** 123TR; **Geoscience Features:** xviBCR, xviBR, 102CL, 108BC, 122BR; Solar Film 64TC; **Getty Images:** Kim Steele 161BCL; **gettyone stone**: 131BC, 133BR, 164CR(above); G Johnson 130BL; R Passmore 120TR; D Austen 187CL; G Allison 186CL; L Ulrich 17TL; M Vines 17BL; R Wells 193BL; **Robert Harding Picture Library:** xviiTC, xxivCR, xxxC, xxxvTC, 2TLB, 3CA, 15CRB, 15CR, 37BC, 38CRA, 50BL, 95BR, 99CR, 114CR, 122BL, 131CLA, 142CB, 143TL, 147TR, 168TR, 168CA, 166BR; P G. Adam 13TCB; D Atchison-Jones 70BLA; J Bayne 72BCL; B Schuster 80CR; C Bowman 50BR, 53CA, 62CL, 70CRL; C Campbell xxiBC; G Corrigan 159CRB, 161CRB; P Craven xxxvBL; R Cundy 69BR; Delu 79BC; A Durand 111BR; Financial Times 142BR; R Frerck 51BL; T Gervis 3BCL, 7CR; I Griffiths xxxCL, 77TL; T Hall 166CRA; D Harney 142CA; S Harris xliiiBCL; G Hellier xvCRB, 135BL; F Jackson 137BCR; Jacobs xxxviiTL; P Koch 139TR; F Joseph Land 122TR; Y Marcoux 9BR; S Massif xvBC; A Mills 88CLB; L Murray 114TR; R Rainford xlivBL; G Renner 74CB, 194C; C Rennie 48CL, 116BR; R Richardson 118CL; P Van Riel 48BR; E Rooney 124TR; Sassoon xxivCL, 148CLB; Jochen Schlenker 193CL; P Scholey 176TR; M Short 137TL; E Simanor xxviiCR; V Southwell 139CR; J Strachan 42TR, 111BL, 132BCR; C Tokeley 131CLA; A C Waltham 161C; T Waltham xviiBL, xxiiCLLL, 138CRB; Westlight 37CR; N Wheeler 139BL; A Williams xxxviiiBR, xlTR; A Woolfitt 95BRA; Paul Harris: 168TC; **Hutchison Library:** 131CR (above) 6BL; P. Collomb 137CR; C. Dodwell 130TR; S Errington 70BCL; P. Hellyer 142BC; J. Horner xxxiTC; R. Ian Lloyd 134CRA; J.Nowell 135CLB, 143TC; A Zvoznikov xxiiCL; **Image Bank:** 87BR; J Banagan 190BCA; A Becker xxivBCL; M Khansa 121CR, M Isy-Schwart 193CR(above), 191CL; Khansa K Forest 163TR; Lomeo xxivTCR; T Madison 170TL(below); C Molyneux xxiiCRRR; C Navajas xviiiTR; Ocean Images Inc. 192CLB; J van Os xviiTCR; S Proehl 6CL; T Rakke xixTC, 64CL; M Reitz 196CA; M Romanelli 166CL(below); G A Rossi 151BCR, 176BLA; B Roussel 109TL; S Satushek xviiBCR; Stock Photos / J M Spielman xxivTRL; **Images Colour Library:** xxiiCLL, xxxixTR, xliCR, xliiiBL, 3BR, 19BR, 37TL, 44TL, 62TC, 91BR, 102CLB, 103CR, 150CL, 180CA; 164BC, 165TL; **Impact Photos:** J & G Andrews 186BL; C. Bluntzer 156BR; Cosmos / G. Buthaud 65BC; S Franklin 126BL; A. le Garsmeur 131C; C Jones xxxiCB, 70BL; V. Nemirousky 137BR; J Nicholl 76TCR; C. Penn 187C(below); G Sweeney xviiBR, 196CB, 196TR, J & G Andrews 186TR; **JVZ Picture Library:** T Nilson 135TC; **Frank Lane Picture Agency:** xxiTCR, xxiiiBL, 93TR; A Christiansen 58CRA; J Holmes xivBL; S. McCutcheon 3C; Silvestris 173TCR; D Smith xxiiBCL; W Wisniewsli 195BR; **Leeds Castle Foundation:** xxxviiBC; **Magnum:** Abbas 83CR, 136CA; S Franklin 134CRB; D Hurn 4BCL; P. Jones-Griffiths 191BL; H Kubota xviBCL, 156CLB; F Maver xviBL; S McCurry 73CL, 133BCR; G. Rodger 74TR; C Steele Perkins 72BL; **Mountain Camera / John Cleare:** 153TR; C Monteath 153CR; **Nature Photographers:** E.A. Janes 112CL; **Natural Science Photos:** M Andera 110C; **Network Photographers Ltd.:** C Sappa / Rapho 119BL; **N.H.P.A.:** N. J. Dennis xxiiiCL; D Heuchlin xxiiiCLA; S Krasemann 15BL, 25BR, 38TC; K Schafer 49CB; R Tidman 160CLB; D Tomlinson 145CR; M Wendler 48TR; **Nottingham Trent University:** T Waltham xivCL, xvBR; **Novosti:** 144BLA; **Oxford Scientific Films:** D Allan xxiiTR; H R Bardarson xviiiBC; D Bown xxiiiCBLL; M Brown 140BL; M Colbeck 147CAR; W Faidley 3TL; L Gould xxiiiTRB; D Guravich xxiiiTR; P Hammerschmidy / Okapia 87CLA; M Hill 57TL, 195TR; C Menteath ; J Netherton 2CRB; S Osolinski 82CA; R Packwood 72CA; M Pitts 179TC; N Rosing xxiiiCBL, 9TR, 197BR; D Simonson 57C; Survival Anglia / C Catton 137TR; R Toms xxiiiBR; K Wothe xxiBL, xviiCLA; **Panos Pictures:** B Aris 133C; P Barker xxivBR; T Bolstao 153BR; N Cooper 82CB, 153TC; J-L Dugast 166C(below), 167BR; J Hartley 73CA, 90CL; J Holmes 149BC; J Morris 76CLB; M Rose 146TR; D Sansoni 155CL; C Stowers 163TL; **Edward Parker:** 49TL, 49CLB; **Pictor International:** xivBR, xvBRA, xixTCL, xxCL, 3CLA, 17BR, 20TR, 20CRB, 23BCA, 23CL, 26CB, 27BC, 33TRB, 34BC, 34BR, 34CR, 38CB, 38CL, 43CL, 63BR, 65TC, 82CL, 83CLB, 99BR, 107CLA, 166TR, 171CL(above), 180CLB, 185TL; **Pictures Colour Library:** xxiBCL, xxiiBR, xxviBCL, 6BR, 15TR, 8TR, 16CL(above), 19TL, 20BL, 24C, 24CLA, 27TR, 32TRB, 36BC, 41CA, 43CRA, 68BL, 90TCB, 94BL, 99BL, 106CA, 107CLB, 107CR, 107BR, 117BL, 164BC, 192BL, K Forest 165TL(below); **Planet Earth Pictures:** 193CR(below); D Barrett 148CB, 184CA; R Coomber 16BL; G Douwma 172BR; E Edmonds 173BR; J Lythgoe 196BL; A Mounter 172CR; M Potts 6CA; P Scoones xxTR; J Walencik 110TR; J Waters 53BCL; **Popperfoto:** Reuters / J Drake xxxiiCLA; **Rex Features:** 165CR; Antelope xxxiiCLB; M Friedel xxiCR; J Shelley xxxCR; Sipa Press xxxCR; Sipa Press / Chamussy 176BL; **Robert Harding Picture Library:** C. Tokeley 131TL; J Strachan 132BL; Franz Joseph Land 122TR; Franz Joseph Land 364/7088 123BL, 169C(above), 170C(above), Tony Waltham 186CR(below), Y Marcoux 9BR; **Russia & Republics Photolibrary:** M Wadlow 118CR, 119CL, 124BC, 124CL, 125TL, 125BR, 126TCR; **Science Photo Library:** Earth Satellite Corporation xixTRB, xxxiCR, 49BCL; F Gohier xiCR; J Heseltine xviTCB; K Kent xvBLA; P Menzell xvBL; N.A.S.A. xBC; D Parker xivBC; University of Cambridge Collection Air Pictures 87CLB; RJ Wainscoat / P Arnold, Inc. xiBC; D Weintraub xiBL; **South American Pictures:** 57BL, 62TR; R Francis 52BL; Guyana Space Centre 50TR; T Morrison 49CRB, 49BL, 50CR, 52TR, 54TR, 61C; **Southampton Oceanography:** xviiiBL; **Sovofoto / Eastfoto:** xxxiiCBR; **Spectrum Colour Library:** 50BC, 160BC; J King 145BR; **Frank Spooner Pictures:** Gamma-Liason/Vogel 131CL(above); 26CRB; E. Baitel xxxiiBC; Bernstein xxxiCL; Contrast 112CR; Diard / Photo News 113CL; Liaison / C. Hires xxxiiTCB; Liaison / Nickelsberg xxxiiTR; Marleen 113TL; Novosti 116CA; P. Piel xxxCA; H Stucke 188CLB, 190CA; Torrengo / Figaro 78BR; A Zamur 113BL; **Still Pictures:** C Caldicott 77TC; A Crump 189CL; M & C Denis-Huot xxiiBL, 78CR, 81BL; M Edwards xxiCRL, 53BL, 64CR, 69BLA, 155BR; J Frebet 53CLB; H Giradet 53TC; E Parker 52CL; M Gunther 121BC; **Tony Stone Images:** xxviTR, 4CA, 7BL, 7CL, 13CRB, 39BR, 58C, 97BC, 101BR, 106TR, 109CL, 109CRB, 164CLB, 165C,180CB, 181BR, 188BC, 192TR; G Allison 18TR, 31CRB, 187CRB; D Armand 14TCB; D Austen 180TR, 186CL, 187CL; J Beatty 74CL; O Benn xxviBR; K Biggs xxiTL; R Bradbury 44BR; R A Butcher xxviTL; J Callahan xxviiCRA; P Chesley 185BCL, 188C; W Clay 30BL, 31CRA; J Cornish 96BL, 107TL; C Condina 41CB; T Craddock xxivTR; P Degginger 36CLB; Demetrio 5BR; N DeVore xxivBC; A Diesendruck 60BR; S Egan 87CRA, 96BR; R Elliot xxiiBCR; S Elmore 19C; J Garrett 73CR; S Grandadam 14BR; R Grosskopf 28BL; D Hanson 104BC; C Harvey 69TL; G Hellier 110BL, 165CR; S Huber 103CRB; D Hughs xxxiBR; A Husmo 91TR; G Irvine 31BC; J Jangoux 58CL; D Johnston xviiTR; A Kehr 113C; R Koskas xviTR; J Lamb 96CRA; J Lawrence 75CRA; L Lefkowitz 7CA; M Lewis 45CLA; S Mayman 55BR; Murray & Associates 45CR; G Norways 104CA; N Parfitt xxviiCL, 68TCR, 81TL; R Passmore 121TR; N Press xviBCA; E Pritchard 88CA, 90CLR; T Raymond 21BL, 29TR; L Resnick 74BR; M Rogers 80BR; A Sacks 28TCB; C Saule 90CR; S Schulhof xxivTC; P Seaward 34CL; M Segal 32BL; V Shenai 152CL; R Sherman 26CL; H Sitton 136CR; R Smith xxvBLA, 56C; S Studd 108CLA; H Strand 49BR, 63TR; P Tweedie 177CR; L Ulrich 17BL; M Vines 17TC; A B Wadham 60CR; J Warden 63CLB; R Wells 23CRA, 193BL; G Yeowell 34BL; **Telegraph Colour Library:** 61CRB, 61TCR, 157TL; R Antrobus xxxixBR; J Sims 26BR; **Topham Picturepoint:** xxxiCBL, 162BR, 168TR, 168BC; **Travel Ink:** A Cowin 88TR; **Trip:** 140BR, 144CA, 155CRA; B Ashe 159TR; D Cole 190BCL, 190CR; D Davis 89BL; I Deineko xxxiTR; J Dennis 22BL; Dinodia 154CL; Eye Ubiquitous / L Fordyce 2CLB; A Gasson 149CR; W Jacobs 43TL, 54BL, 177BC, 178CLA, 185BCR, 186BL; P Kingsbury 112C; K Knight 177BR; V Kolpakov 147BL; T Noorits 87TL, 119BR, 146CL; R Power 41TR; N Ray 166BL, 168TC; C Rennie 116CLB; V Sidoropolev 145TR; E Smith 183BC, 183TL; **Woodfin Camp & Associates:** 92BLR; **World Pictures:** xvCRA, xviiCRA, 9CRB, 22CL, 23BC, 24BL, 35BL, 40TR, 51TR, 71BR, 80TCR, 82TR, 83BL, 86BCR, 96TC, 98BL, 100CR, 101CR, 103BC, 105TC, 157BL, 161BCL, 162CLB, 172CLB, 172BC, 179BL, 182CB, 183C, 184CL, 185CR; 121BR, 121TT; **Zefa Picture Library:** xviBLR, xviiBCL, xviiiCL, 3CL, 8BC, 8CT, 9CR, 13BC, 14TC, 16TR, 21TL, 22CRB, 25BL, 32TCR, 36BCR, 59BCL, 65TCL, 69CLA, 79TL, 81BR, 87CRB, 92C, 98C, 99TL, 100BL, 107TR, 118CRB, 120BL; 122C(below), 124CLA, 164BR, 183TR; Anatol 113BR; Barone 114BL; Brandenburg 5C; A J Brown 44TR; H J Clauss 55CLB; Damm 71BC; Evert 92BL; W Felger 3BL; J Fields 189CRA; R Frerck 4BL; G Heil 56BR; K Heibig 115BR; Heilman 28BC; Hunter 8C; Kitchen 10TR, 8CL, 8BL, 9TR; Dr H Kramarz 7BLA, 123CR(below); Mehlio 155BL; J F Raga 24TR; Rossenbach 105BR; Streichan 89TL; T Stewart 13TR, 19CR; Sunak 54BR, 162TR; D H Teuffen 95TL; B Zaunders 40BC.
Additional Photography: Geoff Dann; Rob Reichenfeld; H Taylor; Jerry Young.

Map Credits

World Population Density map, page xxiv:

Source:LandScanTM Global Population Database. Oak Ridge, TN; Oak Ridge National Laboratory.
Available at http://www.ornl.gov/landscan/.

NORTH AMERICA

CANADA
Pages 8–15

UNITED STATES OF AMERICA
Pages 16–39

MEXICO
Pages 40–41

BELIZE
Pages 42–43

COSTA RICA
Pages 42–43

EL SALVADOR
Pages 42–43

GUATEMALA
Pages 42–43

HONDURAS
Pages 42–43

GRENADA
Pages 44–45

HAITI
Pages 44–45

JAMAICA
Pages 44–45

ST KITTS & NEVIS
Pages 44–45

ST LUCIA
Pages 44–45

ST VINCENT & THE GRENADINES
Pages 44–45

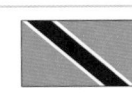

TRINIDAD & TOBAGO
Pages 44–45

SOUTH AMERICA

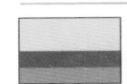

COLOMBIA
Pages 54–55

URUGUAY
Pages 60–61

CHILE
Pages 62–63

PARAGUAY
Pages 62–63

AFRICA

ALGERIA
Pages 74–75

EGYPT
Pages 74–75

LIBYA
Pages 74–75

MOROCCO
Pages 74–75

TUNISIA
Pages 74–75

LIBERIA
Pages 76–77

MALI
Pages 76–77

MAURITANIA
Pages 76–77

NIGER
Pages 76–77

NIGERIA
Pages 76–77

SENEGAL
Pages 76–77

SIERRA LEONE
Pages 76–77

TOGO
Pages 76–77

BURUNDI
Pages 80–81

DJIBOUTI
Pages 80–81

ERITREA
Pages 80–81

ETHIOPIA
Pages 80–81

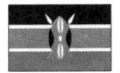

KENYA
Pages 80–81

RWANDA
Pages 80–81

SOMALIA
Pages 80–81

SUDAN
Pages 80–81

NAMIBIA
Pages 82–83

SOUTH AFRICA
Pages 82–83

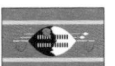

SWAZILAND
Pages 82–83

ZAMBIA
Pages 82–83

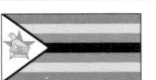

ZIMBABWE
Pages 82–83

COMOROS
Pages 172–173

MADAGASCAR
Pages 172–173

MAURITIUS
Pages 172–173

LUXEMBOURG
Pages 98–99

NETHERLANDS
Pages 98–99

GERMANY
Pages 100–101

FRANCE
Pages 102–103

MONACO
Pages 102–103

ANDORRA
Pages 104–105

PORTUGAL
Pages 104–105

SPAIN
Pages 104–105

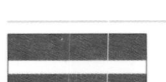

POLAND
Pages 110–111

SLOVAKIA
Pages 110–111

ALBANIA
Pages 112–113

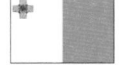

BOSNIA & HERZEGOVINA
Pages 112–113

CROATIA
Pages 112–113

KOSOVO (disputed)
Pages 112–113

MACEDONIA
Pages 112–113

MONTENEGRO
Pages 112–113

LATVIA
Pages 118–119

LITHUANIA
Pages 118–119

CYPRUS
Pages 120–121

MALTA
Pages 120–121

RUSSIAN FEDERATION
Pages 122–127

ASIA

ARMENIA
Pages 136–137

AZERBAIJAN
Pages 136–137

GEORGIA
Pages 136–137

TURKEY
Pages 136–137/114–115

QATAR
Pages 140–143

SAUDI ARABIA
Pages 140–141

UNITED ARAB EMIRATES
Pages 140–143

YEMEN
Pages 140–141

IRAN
Pages 142–143

KAZAKHSTAN
Pages 144–145

KYRGYZSTAN
Pages 146–147

TAJIKISTAN
Pages 146–147

CHINA
Pages 158–163

MONGOLIA
Pages 156–157/162–163

NORTH KOREA
Pages 156–157/162–163

SOUTH KOREA
Pages 156–157/162–163

TAIWAN
Pages 160–161

JAPAN
Pages 164–165

MYANMAR
Pages 166–167

CAMBODIA
Pages 166–167

SINGAPORE
Pages 168–169

MALDIVES
Pages 172–173

AUSTRALASIA & OCEANIA

AUSTRALIA
Pages 180–183

NEW ZEALAND
Pages 184–185

PAPUA NEW GUINEA
Pages 186–187

FIJI
Pages 186–187

SOLOMON ISLANDS
Pages 186–187

VANUATU
Pages 186–18